ç *ch* in German *ich*: a (j) sound as in *yes*, said without voice; similar to the first sound in *huge*.

β *b* in Spanish *Habana*: a voiced fricative sound similar to (v), but made by the two lips.

ʎ *ll* in Spanish *llamar*, *gl* in Italian *consiglio*: similar to the (lj) sequence in *million*, but with the tongue tip lowered and the sounds said simultaneously.

ɥ *u* in French *lui*: a short (y).

ɲ *gn* in French *vigne*, Italian *gnocchi*, *ñ* in Spanish *España*: similar to the (nj) sequence in *onion*, but with the tongue tip lowered and the two sounds said simultaneously.

ɣ *g* in Spanish *luego*: a weak (g) made with voiced friction.

Length

The symbol ː denotes length and is shown together with certain vowel symbols when the vowels are typically long.

Stress

Three grades of stress are shown in the transcriptions by the presence or absence of marks placed immediately *before* the affected syllable. Primary or strong stress is shown by ˈ, while secondary or weak stress is shown by ˌ. Unstressed syllables are not marked. In *photographic* (ˌfəʊtəˈgræfɪk), for example, the first syllable carries secondary stress and the third primary stress, while the second and fourth are unstressed.

List of Abbreviations used in the Dictionary

adj	adjective
adv	adverb(ial)
Amerind	American Indian
Anthropol.	Anthropology
Archaeol	Archaeology
Architect	Architecture
Austral	Australian
Bibliog	Bibliography
Biochem	Biochemistry
Brit	British
C	century (e.g. C14 = 14th century)
°C	degrees Celsius
Chem	Chemistry
E	east(ern)
e.g.	for example
Embryol	Embryology
Entomol	Entomology
esp	especially
est.	estimate
ft.	foot *or* feet
i.e.	that is
in.	inch(es)
Inf	Informal
interj	interjection
intr	intransitive
km	kilometre(s)
m	metre(s)
Maths	Mathematics
Med	Medicine
Myth	Mythology
n	noun
N	north(ern)
NE	northeast(ern)
no.	number
NW	northwest(ern)
NZ	New Zealand
Ornithol	Ornithology
Pathol	Pathology
Pharmacol	Pharmacology
Photog	Photography
Physiol	Physiology
pop.	population
Psychol	Psychology
pt.	point
R.C.	Roman Catholic
S	south(ern)
Scot	Scottish, Scots
SE	Southeast(ern)
SW	southwest(ern)
Telecom	Telecommunications
Theol	Theology
tr	transitive
US	United States
vb	verb
Vet	Veterinary Science
W	west(ern)
wt.	weight

Collins

ENGLISH DICTIONARY

BANK *of* ENGLISH

This dictionary has been compiled with constant reference to the Bank of English, a unique database containing over 524 million words of written and spoken English, enabling Collins lexicographers to analyse how the language is actually used and how it is changing. The Bank of English was set up as a joint initiative by HarperCollins Publishers and the University of Birmingham to be a resource for language research and lexicography. It contains a very wide range of material from books, newspapers, radio, TV, magazines, letters and talks reflecting the whole spectrum of English today. Its size and range make it an unequalled resource, and the purpose-built software for its analysis is unique to Collins Dictionaries.

This ensures that Collins Dictionaries accurately reflect English as it is used today in a way that is most helpful to the dictionary or thesaurus user.

Collins

ENGLISH DICTIONARY

COMPLETE AND UNABRIDGED

Collins

An Imprint of HarperCollins*Publishers*

sixth edition 2003

HarperCollins Publishers
Westerhill Road, Bishopbriggs, Glasgow G64 2QT
Great Britain

www.collinsdictionaries.com

ISBN 0-00-710982-2
with thumb index 0-00-710983-0

Acknowledgements
We would like to thank those authors and publishers who kindly gave permission for copyright material to be used in the Bank of English. We would also like to thank Times Newspapers Ltd for providing valuable data.

Note
Entered words that we have reason to believe constitute trademarks have been designated as such. However, neither the presence nor absence of such designation should be regarded as affecting the legal status of any trademark.

A catalogue record for this book is available from the British Library

This edition prepared in conjunction with Market House Books Ltd, Aylesbury, England
Typeset by Market House Books Ltd, Aylesbury, England

Computing support by Mark Taylor

Printed in Italy by Legoprint S.P.A.

Contents

Foreword

English is a world language, is indeed the major world language in many fields of endeavour, and as such is subject to enormous and rapid change. In this, the Sixth Edition of Collins English Dictionary, we at Collins Dictionaries continue our tradition of providing the most up-to-date and reliable information on the English language the world over. Thousands of new words from general language have been added. At the same time, the technical and scientific coverage for which the dictionary is renowned has been further expanded, updated and refined by leading experts in their respective fields. In addition, the design of the text has undergone a complete overhaul. We feel sure that the enhanced clarity and accessibility of layout thereby achieved will help those consulting the dictionary to find in the shortest possible time precisely the information, both old and new, that they seek.

For this edition we have worked with our extensive network of consultants to update our coverage of Australian, New Zealand, Canadian, South African and United States English, so as accurately to reflect the continuing evolution of these varieties of World English in their different corners of the globe. As regards English in the British Isles we have paid particular attention to the continuing vitality of regional usage and expanded our coverage, with the help of many local contributors who took part with great enthusiasm.

In the areas of scientific and specialist vocabulary we have focussed in particular on fields where language change is particularly rapid and significant, such as Astronomy, Biology, Business, Chemistry, Computer Science, Earth Sciences, Economics, Engineering, Film and Broadcasting, Law, Marketing, Mathematics, Medicine, Military terms, Pharmacology, Physics, Veterinary Science and Zoology.

It is noticeable how rapidly traditional strictures on formerly taboo words have been relaxed over the last few years. This trend is reflected in changes to the "warning labels" given to some of the earthier words in our language, as well as in some new usage notes on certain of these words.

In order to keep abreast of all these rapid changes to the English language Collins Dictionaries are able to draw on the unique resources of The Bank of English®. This is a vast collection of post-1990 electronically held texts, both written and spoken, currently containing 524 million words of World Englishes. In addition, Collins is able to draw on the largest corpus of Australian English available. The Bank of English® makes use, among other sources, of data drawn daily from websites and thereby gives editors access to the very latest information on words which are either entirely new to English or which are changing their meaning. By means of sophisticated computer programs, lists of possible new words can now be extracted automatically from incoming data, to be then sifted and analysed by editors. The work of the Bank of English® is supplemented by the more traditional method of asking readers and consultants to make suggestions, whose value can then be measured against the objective data in the Bank of English®.

Finally, the changes to the typography of the book have been designed to improve readability and look-up, and to make crucial information within entries stand out more clearly.

We all create and change language, and Collins Dictionaries actively involve members of the public in the process of recording these changes. If you wish to contact us to suggest a new usage, word or phrase, you can do so by emailing us at language.networks@harpercollins.co.uk.

Jeremy Butterfield
Editor

Editorial Staff

Editors
Jeremy Butterfield

Elspeth Summers | Andrew Holmes | John Daintith

Alan Isaacs | Jonathan Law | Elizabeth Martin

Publishing Management
Elaine Higgleton

Publishing Co-ordination
Paige Weber

Series Editor
Lorna Sinclair Knight

Contributors
Sandra Anderson, Jennifer Baird, George Davidson, Lorna Gilmour, Elizabeth Gordon, Alice Grandison, Penny Hands, Geoffrey Hughes, Bill Krebs, Mike Munro, Anne Stibbs, Fraser Sutherland

---

The publishers would like to thank the following contributors to previous editions of this dictionary:

General Consultant
J M Sinclair

Editor
Patrick Hanks

Managing Editor
Thomas Hill Long

Editorial Director
Laurence Urdang

and other contributors to previous editions:

A J Aitken, M V Aldridge, S R R Allsopp, James Arthurs, R K Bansal, James Barnes, Stuart Bathgate, T de Bhaldraithe, Ephraim Borowski, David Bourke, Professor Angela M Bowey, Angus Boyd, Professor Thomas Carbery, Laurence Chizlett, Professor M Christopher, Sandra Clarke, R Cutler, Brian Russell Davis, P Donaldson, Andrew Doswell, Colonel Andrew Duncan, Patrick Drysdale, Major S R Elliot, Richard Fryer, A C Gimson, Ian A Gordon, Dr W Gratzer, R J Gregg, Rev Canon D W Gundry, Steve Higgs, Sandra Holmes, Lloyd Humberstone, Cmdr I Johnston RN, J Kalema, David Kilby, The Rev D Lancashire, L W Lanham, Richard Latham, Patrick Leggatt, William T McLeod, Marian Makins, Bob Marsden, Bruce Martin, Harold Orton, Jenny Oswald, C H Parsons, Helen Peck, Catherine Playford, Alexander Purdie, J P Quayle, W S Ramson, Gerry Riach, Miranda Robertson, Christopher Sion, N J Small, Peter J Smith, Sister Isabel Smyth, J Spencer, Professor Stuart Sutherland, Dr Eric Taylor, John Todd, Loreto Todd, Ingrid von Essen, M J Walker, J W Warren, Stanley White, G A Wilkes, Professor Yorick Wilks, T C Wooldridge, U Yong-ee, Catherine M Young

The publishers would also like to thank everyone who contributed to the Regional Dialects Campaign, especially the following contributors:

Don Alexander, Clifford Dunkley, John Germon and the Ashburton Devon Dialect Club, Chris Kilkenny and The Northumbrian Association, Listeners of BBC Radio Derby, Neil Pettitt, Readers of *The Dalesman*, *The Hull Daily Mail*, and the *Yorkshire Post*, Charlotte Robertson, Derek Stanton and the Lancashire Dialect Society.

Specialist Contributors
For the Sixth Edition

Astronomy
Dr Graham Woan
Department of Physics and Astronomy,
University of Glasgow

Biology
Professor John R Coggins
Institute of Biomedical and Life Sciences,
University of Glasgow

Botany
Dr Andrew Lack
School of Molecular and Biological Science,
Oxford Brookes University

Business
Dr John Pallister
Business School,
Cardiff University

Chemistry
Alice Brewer
David Mountford
Department of Chemistry,
Imperial College, London

Chemical Engineering
Professor R L Reuben
Department of Mechanical and Chemical Engineering,
Heriot-Watt University, Edinburgh

Civil Engineering
Ian Stewart
Department of Civil Engineering,
University of Strathclyde, Glasgow

Computer Science
Ian Sinclair
Author, *Collins Dictionary of Computers and IT*

Electronic and Electrical Engineering
Professor D Geoffrey Smith
Department of Electronic and Electrical Engineering,
University of Strathclyde, Glasgow

Environmental Science
Professor Roger Gurney
Environmental Systems Science Centre,
University of Reading

Film and Broadcasting
Shelly Townsend
Headquarters, Los Angeles

General Engineering
Dr Alexander J Bell
Heriot-Watt University, Edinburgh

Genetics
Professor Jeffrey Thorne
Bioinformatics Research Center,
North Carolina State University

Geology
Dr Philip Janney
The Field Museum of Natural History
Chicago

Law
Aviva Golden
Author, *Everyday Law*

Professor Alan Wilson
School of Law,
University of East London

Mathematics
Dr Gregory Sankaran
Department of Mathematical Sciences,
University of Bath

Medicine
Dr J K Aronson
Radcliffe Infirmary, Oxford

Professor Roger D Sturrock
Department of Medicine,
University of Glasgow

Military
Will Fowler
TD, MA, Dp J, AI Exp E

Palaeontology
Dr Wendy Taylor
University of Chicago

Pharmacology
Dr J K Aronson
Radcliffe Infirmary, Oxford

Physics
Professor Hugh Summers
Department of Physics and Applied Physics,
University of Strathclyde, Glasgow

Statistics
Dr James Akira Doi
Department of Statistics,
North Carolina State University

Veterinary Science
Dr Mike Davies
Provet Limited

Zoology
Dr Nick Downs
University of Aberdeen

Guide to the Use of the Dictionary

Collins English Dictionary is designed to be easy to use so that you can go straight to the word you want. The Guide that follows sets out the main principles on which the Dictionary is arranged and enables you to make full use of the Dictionary by showing the whole range of information that it contains.

1 HEADWORD

All main entries, including place names, biographies, abbreviations, prefixes, and suffixes, are printed in large boldface type and are listed in strict alphabetical order. This applies even if the headword consists of more than one word.

1.1 Order of entries

Words that have the same spelling but are derived from different sources (homographs) are entered separately with superscript numbers after the headwords.

saw[1] (sɔː) NOUN 1 any of various hand tools...
saw[2] (sɔː) VERB the past tense of **see.**
saw[3] (sɔː) NOUN a wise saying, maxim, or proverb...

A word with a capital initial letter, if entered separately, follows the lower-case form. For example, **Arras** follows **arras**.

1.2 Place names

If a place has more than one name, its main entry is given at the name most often used in modern English, with a cross-reference at other names. Thus, the main entry for the capital of Bavaria is at **Munich**, with a cross-reference at **München**. If a place name has no current anglicized form, its main entry is at the form of the name used in the official language of the area. Thus, the main entry is at **Brno**, with a cross-reference at **Brünn**. Historical names of importance are also given, with dates where these can be ascertained.

Paris (ˈpærɪs; *French* pari) NOUN...Ancient name: **Lutetia.**
Volgograd (*Russian* vəlgaˈgrat; *English* ˈvɒlgəˌgræd) NOUN...Former names: **Tsaritsyn** (until 1925), **Stalingrad** (1925–61).

Statistical information about places has been obtained from the most up-to-date and reliable sources available. Population figures have been compiled from the most recent census available at the time of going to press. The date of the census is always given. Where no census figure is available, the most reliable recent estimate has been given, with a date.

1.3 Abbreviations, acronyms, and symbols

Abbreviations, acronyms, and symbols are entered as headwords in the main alphabetical list. In line with modern practice, full stops are not used with symbols (**Ga**), nor for most abbreviations that are either strings of initials (**MA**, **mph**) or contractions (**St**, **Mr**). However, stops are used for an abbreviation of a word that is not a contraction (**Brig.**) and for strings of lower-case initials that could form a word (**c.o.d.**). Alternative forms with stops are only shown for certain standard abbreviations (**e.g.** or **eg**) but it can be assumed that nearly all abbreviations are equally acceptable with or without stops.

Alphanumeric representations of words such as those now commonly used in electronic communication – **GR8** (great), **B4** (before), etc. – are ordered such that the numeral is not regarded as representing a letter or a word. Instead, such entries are ordered like other alphanumeric abbreviations, for example **G8** (Group of Eight) and **K2** (the mountain).

gr
GR
Gr.
GR8
Graafian follicle

This rule, however, do not apply to the small number of alphanumeric representations of words that start with a numeral. In such cases the numeral is spelled out as the letter or series of letters that it represents.

foretriangle
4EVA
forever

tonight
2NITE
tonk[1]

1.4 **Prefixes, suffixes, and combining forms**

Prefixes (e.g. **in-**, **pre-**, **sub-**), suffixes (e.g. **-able**, **-ation**, **-ity**), and combining forms (e.g. **psycho-**, **-iatry**) have been entered as headwords if they are still used freely to produce new words in English.

1.5 **Plural headwords**

Words that have a standard use or uses in the plural may be entered as separate headwords at both singular and plural forms, with a cross-reference to the plural form at the singular entry if other headwords intervene.

affair (əˈfɛə) NOUN 1 a thing to be done or attended to...◆ See also **affairs.**

affairs (əˈfɛəz) PLURAL NOUN 1 personal or business interests...

1.6 **Variant spellings**

Common acceptable variant spellings of English words are given as alternative forms of the headword.

capitalize *or* **capitalise** (ˈkæpɪtəˌlaɪz) VERB...

2 **PRONUNCIATION**

Pronunciations of words in this Dictionary represent those that are common in educated speech. They are transcribed in the International Phonetic Alphabet (IPA). A Key to the Pronunciation Symbols is printed on the front endpapers. The pronunciation is normally given in brackets immediately after the headword.

abase (əˈbeɪs) VERB (*tr*) 1 to humble...

The stress pattern is marked by the symbols ˈ for primary stress and ˌ for secondary stress. The stress mark precedes the syllable to which it applies.

2.1 **Variant pronunciations**

When a headword has an acceptable variant pronunciation or stress pattern, the variant is given by repeating only the syllable or syllables that change.

economic (ˌiːkəˈnɒmɪk, ˌɛkə-) ADJECTIVE 1 of or relating to...

2.2 **Pronunciations with different parts of speech**

When two or more parts of speech of a word have different pronunciations, the pronunciations are shown in brackets before the relevant group of senses.

record NOUN (ˈrɛkɔːd) 1 an account in permanent form...◆ VERB (rɪˈkɔːd) (*mainly tr*) 19 to set down in some permanent form...

2.3 **Pronunciation of individual senses**

If one sense of a headword has a different pronunciation from that of the rest, the pronunciation is given in brackets after the sense number.

conjure (ˈkʌndʒə) VERB 1 (*intr*) to practise conjuring or be a conjuror. 2 (*intr*) to call upon supposed supernatural forces by spells and incantations. 3 (kənˈdʒʊə) (*tr*) to appeal earnestly or strongly to: *I conjure you to help me...*

2.4 **Foreign words and phrases**

Foreign words or phrases are printed in boldface italic type and are given foreign-language pronunciations only unless they are regarded as having become accepted in English.

haut monde *French* (o mɔ̃d) NOUN...

3 **INFLECTED FORMS**

Inflected forms of nouns, verbs, and adjectives are shown immediately after the part-of-speech label if they are irregular or, in certain cases, if they are regular but might cause confusion.

3.1 **Regular inflections**

Where inflections are not shown, it may be assumed that they are formed as follows:

nouns. Regular plurals are formed by the addition of -s (e.g. pencils, monkeys) or, in the case of nouns ending in -s, -x, -z, -ch, or -sh, by the addition of -es (e.g. losses).

verbs. In regularly inflected verbs: the third person singular of the present tense is formed by the addition of -s to the infinitive (e.g. plays) or, for verbs ending in -s, -x, -z, -ch, or -sh, by the addition of -es (e.g. passes, reaches) the past tense and past participle are formed by the addition of -ed to the infinitive (e.g. played) the present participle is formed by the addition of -ing to the infinitive (e.g. playing). Verbs that end in a consonant plus -e (e.g. locate, snare) regularly lose the final -e before the addition of -ed and -ing.

adjectives. The regular comparatives and superlatives of adjectives are formed by adding -er and -est to the base (e.g. short, shorter, shortest). Adjectives that end in a consonant plus -e regularly lose the -e before -er and -est (e.g. fine, finer, finest).

3.2 **Irregular and unfamiliar inflections**

Inflected forms are shown for the following:
Nouns and verbs whose inflections involve a change in internal spelling.

goose[1] (guːs) NOUN, *plural* **geese**...

drive (draɪv) VERB **drives, driving, drove** (drəʊv), **driven**...

Nouns, verbs, and adjectives that end in a consonant plus y, where y is changed to i before inflectional endings.

augury ('ɔ:gjʊrɪ) NOUN, *plural* **-ries**...

Nouns having identical singular and plural forms.

sheep (ʃi:p) NOUN, *plural* **sheep**...

Nouns that closely resemble others but form their plurals differently.

mongoose ('mɒŋˌgu:s) NOUN, *plural* **-gooses**...

Nouns that end in -ful, -o, and -us.

handful ('hændfʊl) NOUN, *plural* **-fuls**...
tomato (tə'mɑ:təʊ) NOUN, *plural* **-toes**...
prospectus (prə'spɛktəs) NOUN, *plural* **-tuses**...

Nouns whose plurals are not regular English inflections.

basis ('beɪsɪs) NOUN, *plural* **-ses** (-si:z)...

Plural nouns whose singulars are not regular English forms.

bacteria (bæk'tɪərɪə) PLURAL NOUN, *singular* **-rium** (-rɪəm)...

Nouns whose plurals have regular spellings but involve a change in pronunciation.

house NOUN (haʊs), *plural* **houses** ('haʊzɪz)...

Multiword nouns when it is not obvious which word takes a plural inflection.

attorney-at-law NOUN, *plural* **attorneys-at-law**...

Adjectives that change their roots to form comparatives and superlatives.

good (gʊd) ADJECTIVE **better, best**...

Adjectives and verbs that double their final consonant before adding endings.

fat (fæt)...◆ ADJECTIVE **fatter, fattest**...
control (kən'trəʊl) VERB **-trols, -trolling, -trolled**...

Verbs that are regular and do not (as might be expected) double their final consonant before adding endings.

gallop ('gæləp) VERB **-lops, -loping, -loped**...

Verbs and adjectives that end in a vowel plus -e.

canoe (kə'nu:)...◆ VERB **-noes, -noeing, -noed**...
free (fri:) ADJECTIVE **freer, freest**...◆ VERB **frees, freeing, freed**...

PARTS OF SPEECH

A part-of-speech label in small capital letters precedes the sense or senses relating to that part of speech.

4.1 Standard parts of speech

The standard parts of speech used are as follows:

ADJECTIVE, ADVERB, CONJUNCTION, INTERJECTION, NOUN, PREPOSITION, PRONOUN, and VERB.

4.2 Less traditional parts of speech

Certain other less traditional parts of speech have been used in this Dictionary. They are as follows:

determiners. Such words as *that, this, my, his*, etc., which used to be classed as demonstrative and possessive adjectives and/or pronouns, have been classified in this Dictionary as determiners. The label *determiner* also replaces the traditional classification for words like *the, a, some, any*, as well as the numerals, and possessives such as *my* and *your*. Many determiners can have a pronoun function without change of meaning, and this is indicated as in the following example:

some (sʌm; *unstressed* səm) DETERMINER...2 **a** an unknown or unspecified quantity or amount of: *there's some rice on the table; he owns some horses.* **b** (*as pronoun; functioning as singular or plural*): *we'll buy some*...

sentence connectors. This description replaces the traditional classification of certain words, such as *therefore* and *however*, as adverbs or conjunctions. These words link sentences together rather in the manner of conjunctions; however, they are not confined to the first position in a clause as conjunctions are.

sentence substitutes. Sentence substitutes are words such as *yes, no, perhaps, definitely*, and *maybe*. They can stand as meaningful utterances by themselves. They are distinguished in this Dictionary from interjections such as *ouch, ah, damn*, etc., which are expressions of emotional reaction rather than meaningful utterances.

4.3 Words used as more than one part of speech

If a word can be used as more than one part of speech, the senses of one part of speech are separated from the others by a lozenge (◆).

> **lure** (lʊə) VERB (*tr*)...[2] *Falconry* to entice (a hawk or falcon) from the air to the falconer by a lure. ◆ NOUN [3] a person or thing that lures...

GRAMMATICAL INFORMATION

Grammatical information is provided in brackets and typically in italics to distinguish it from other types of information.

5.1 Adjectives and determiners

Some adjectives and determiners are restricted by usage to a particular position relative to the nouns they qualify. This is indicated by the following labels:

postpositive (used predicatively or after the noun, but not before the noun):

> **ablaze** (əˈbleɪz) ADJECTIVE (*postpositive*), ADVERB [1] on fire; burning....

immediately postpositive (always used immediately following the noun qualified and never used predicatively):

> **galore** (gəˈlɔː) DETERMINER (*immediately postpositive*) in great numbers or quantity: *there were daffodils galore in the park...*

prenominal (used before the noun, and never used predicatively):

> **chief** (tʃiːf)...◆ ADJECTIVE [5] (*prenominal*) **a** most important; principal. **b** highest in rank or authority...

5.2 Intensifiers

Adjectives and adverbs that perform an exclusively intensifying function, with no addition of meaning, are described as (intensifier) without further explanation.

> **blooming** (ˈbluːmɪŋ) ADVERB, ADJECTIVE *Brit informal* (intensifier): *a blooming genius; blooming painful...*

5.3 Conjunctions

Conjunctions are divided into two classes, marked by the following labels placed in brackets:

coordinating. Coordinating conjunctions connect words, phrases, or clauses that perform an identical function and are not dependent on each other. They include and, but, and or.

subordinating. Subordinating conjunctions introduce clauses that are dependent on a main clause in a complex sentence. They include where, until, and or.

Some conjunctions, such as while and whereas, can function as either coordinating or subordinating conjunctions.

5.4 Singular and plural labelling of nouns

Headwords and senses that are apparently plural in form but that take a singular verb, etc., are marked '*functioning as singular*'.

> **physics** (ˈfɪzɪks) NOUN (*functioning as singular*) [1] the branch of science...

Headwords and senses that appear to be singular, such as collective nouns, but that take a plural verb, etc., are marked '*functioning as plural*'.

> **cattle** (ˈkætᵊl) NOUN (*functioning as plural*) [1] bovid mammals of the tribe *Bovini...*

Headwords and senses that may take either a singular or plural verb, etc., are marked '*functioning as singular or plural*'.

> **bellows** (ˈbɛləʊz) NOUN (*functioning as singular or plural*) [1] Also called: **pair of bellows.** an instrument consisting of an air chamber...

5.5 Modifiers

A noun that is commonly used as if it were an adjective is labelled *modifier*. If the sense of the modifier can be understood from the sense of the noun, the modifier is shown without further explanation, with an example to illustrate its use.

> **denim** (ˈdɛnɪm) NOUN *Textiles* [1] **a** a hard-wearing twill-weave cotton fabric used for trousers, work clothes, etc. **b** (*as modifier*): *a denim jacket...*

If the sense of the modifier cannot be understood from the sense of the noun, or if it is related to more than one of the noun senses, its meaning and/or usage is explained separately.

> **key**[1] (kiː) NOUN...[24] (*modifier*) of great importance: *a key issue...*

5.6 Verbs

The principal parts given are: 3rd person singular of the present tense; present participle; past tense; past participle if different from the past tense.

5.7 Intransitive and transitive verbs

When a sense of a verb is restricted to transitive use, it is labelled (*tr*); if it is intransitive only, it is labelled (*intr*). If all the senses of a verb are transitive or all are intransitive, the appropriate label appears before the first numbered sense and is not repeated.

Absence of a label is significant: it indicates that the sense may be used both transitively and intransitively.

If nearly all the senses of a verb are transitive, the label (*mainly tr*) appears immediately before the first numbered sense. An individual sense may then be labelled (*also intr*) to show that it is both transitive and intransitive, or it may be labelled (*intr*) to show that it is intransitive only.

> **carry** ('kærɪ) VERB **-ries, -rying, -ried.** (*mainly tr*) [1] (*also intr*) to take or bear (something) from one place to another: *to carry a baby in one's arms.* [2] to transfer for consideration; take: *he carried his complaints to her superior*...[27] (*intr*) (of a ball, projectile, etc.) to travel through the air or reach a specified point: *his first drive carried to the green.*

Similarly, all the senses of a verb may be labelled (*mainly intr*) and the labels (*also tr*) and (*tr*) introduced before individual senses as required.

When a sense of a verb may be transitive or intransitive, a direct object that would typically follow its transitive use is sometimes shown in brackets. The brackets should be ignored in order to obtain the intransitive use.

> **act** (ækt)...◆ VERB...[11] to perform (a part or role) in a play...

When the object of the transitive use of a verb constitutes the subject of the intransitive use, this is shown as follows:

> **fire** (faɪə)...◆ VERB [25] to discharge (a firearm or projectile) or (of a firearm, etc.) to be discharged...

When the intransitive use of a verb functions with a preposition but the transitive use does not, an equivalent preposition is given in brackets.

> **differentiate** (ˌdɪfəˈrɛnʃɪˌeɪt) VERB...[2] (when *intr*, often foll by *between*) to perceive, show, or make a difference (in or between); discriminate

5.8 Copulas

A verb that takes a complement is labelled *copula.*

> **seem** (siːm) VERB (may take an infinitive) [1] (*copula*) to appear to the mind or eye; look: *this seems nice; the car seems to be running well*

5.9 Phrasal verbs

Verbal constructions consisting of a verb and a prepositional or an adverbial particle are given headword status if the meaning of the phrasal verb cannot be deduced from the separate meanings of the verb and the particle.

Phrasal verbs are labelled to show four possible distinctions:

a transitive verb with an adverbial particle (*tr, adverb*); a transitive verb with a prepositional particle (*tr, preposition*); an intransitive verb with an adverbial particle (*intr, adverb*); an intransitive verb with a prepositional particle (*intr, preposition*):

> **turn on**...[4] (*tr, adverb*) *Informal* to produce (charm, tears, etc.) suddenly or automatically...
>
> **take for** VERB (*tr, preposition*) *Informal* to consider or suppose to be, esp mistakenly: *the fake coins were taken for genuine; who do you take me for?*
>
> **break off**...[3] (*intr, adverb*) to stop abruptly; halt: *he broke off in the middle of his speech*
>
> **turn on**...[2] (*intr, preposition*) to depend or hinge on: *the success of the party turns on you...*

As with the labelling of other verbs, the absence of a label is significant. If there is no label (*tr*) or (*intr*), the verb may be used either transitively or intransitively. If there is no label (*adverb*) or (*preposition*), the particle may be either adverbial or prepositional.

Any noun, adjective, or modifier formed from a phrasal verb is entered under the phrasal-verb headword. In some cases, where the noun or adjective is more common than the verb, the phrasal verb is entered after the noun or adjective form:

> **breakaway** ('breɪkəˌweɪ) NOUN [1] **a** loss or withdrawal of a group of members from an association, club, etc. **b** (*as modifier*): *a breakaway faction*...◆ VERB **break away.** (*intr, adverb*) [4] (often foll by *from*) to leave hastily or escape...

A cross-reference is given at the main verb when related phrasal verbs are entered as headwords but are separated from it by more than five intervening entries.

> **fit**[1] (fɪt) VERB...◆ See also **fit in, fit out, fit up...**

6 RESTRICTIVE LABELS

If a particular sense is restricted as to appropriateness, connotation, subject field, etc., an italic label is placed immediately before the relevant definition.

> **hang on** VERB (*intr*...[5] (*adverb*) *Informal* to wait or remain: *hang on for a few minutes.*

If a label applies to all senses of one part of speech, it is placed immediately after the part-of-speech label.

> **assured** (əˈʃʊəd) ADJECTIVE...◆ NOUN [4] *Chiefly Brit* **a** the beneficiary under a life assurance policy. **b** the person whose life is insured....

If a label applies to all senses of a headword, it is placed immediately after the pronunciation (or inflections).

con[1] (kɒn) *Informal* ◆ NOUN 1 **a** short for **confidence trick. b** (*as modifier*): *con man*. ◆ VERB **cons, conning, conned**. 2 (*tr*) to swindle or defraud

6.1 Usage labels

Slang. This refers to words or senses that are racy or extremely informal. The appropriate contexts in which slang is used are restricted, for example, to members of a particular social group or those engaged in a particular activity. Slang words are inappropriate in formal speech or writing.

Informal. This label applies to words or senses that may be widely used, especially in conversation, letter-writing, etc., but that are not common in formal writing. Such words are subject to fewer contextual restrictions than slang words.

Taboo. This label applies to words that are not acceptable in polite use. The reader is advised to avoid the use of such words if he or she wishes to be sure of avoiding social disapproval.

Offensive. This label indicates that a word might be regarded as offensive by the person described or referred to, even if the speaker uses the word without any malicious intention.

Derogatory. This implies that the connotations of a word are unpleasant with intent on the part of the speaker or writer.

Not standard. This label is given to words or senses that are frequently encountered but widely regarded as incorrect and therefore avoided by careful speakers and writers.

Archaic. This label denotes a word or sense that is no longer in common use but that may be found in literary works or used to impart a historical colour to contemporary writing.

Obsolete. This label denotes a word or sense that is no longer in use. In specialist or technical fields the label often implies that the term has been superseded.

The word ‘formerly’ is placed in brackets before a sense or set of senses when the practice, concept, etc., being described, rather than the word itself, is obsolete or out of date.
A number of other usage labels, such as *Ironic*, *Facetious*, and *Euphemistic*, are used where appropriate.

More extended help on usage is provided in usage notes after certain entries. See section 13 of the *Guide to the Use of the Dictionary.*

6.2 Subject-field labels

A number of italic labels are used to indicate that a word or sense is used in a particular specialist or technical field. Subject-field labels are given either in full (e.g. *Astronomy*, *Philosophy*) or only slightly abbreviated, so that the full label may be easily understood.

6.3 National and regional labels

Words or senses restricted to or associated with a particular country or region are labelled regional labels accordingly. The following labels are the ones most frequently used: *Austral* (Australian), *Brit* (British), *Canadian*, *Caribbean*, *Irish*, *NZ* (New Zealand), *S African*, *Scot* (Scottish), *US* (United States).

The label *Brit* is used mainly to distinguish a particular word or sense from its North American equivalent or to identify a term or concept that does not exist in North American English. The North American equivalent may be given in boldface type after the appropriate numbered sense.

Regional dialects (*Scot and northern English dialect*, *Midland dialect*, etc.) have been specified as precisely as possible, even at the risk of overrestriction, in order to give the reader an indication of the appropriate regional flavour.

7 MEANING

The meaning of each headword in this Dictionary is explained in one or more definitions, together with information about context, typical use, and other relevant facts.

Where a headword has more than one sense, each sense is given separately and numbered in order to avoid confusion.

Example sentences and phrases illustrating the use of a sense are given at the end of many definitions.

7.1 Order of senses

As a general rule, where a headword has more than one sense, the first sense given is the one most common in current usage.

complexion (kəmˈplɛkʃən) NOUN 1 the colour and general appearance of a person's skin, esp of the face. 2 aspect, character, or nature: *the general complexion of a nation's finances*. 3 *Obsolete* **a** the temperament of a person...

Where the editors consider that a current sense is the 'core meaning' in that it illuminates the meaning of other senses, the core meaning may be placed first.

> **competition** (ˌkɒmpɪˈtɪʃən) NOUN 1 the act of competing; rivalry. 2 a contest in which a winner is selected from among two or more entrants. 3 a series of games, sports events, etc. 4 the opposition offered by a competitor or competitors...

Subsequent senses are arranged so as to give a coherent account of the meaning of a headword. If a word is used as more than one part of speech, all the senses of each part of speech are grouped together in a single block. Within a part-of-speech block, closely related senses are grouped together; technical senses usually follow general senses; archaic and obsolete senses follow technical senses; idioms and fixed phrases are usually placed last.

7.2 Scientific and technical definitions

Units, physical quantities, formulas, etc. In accordance with the recommendations of the International Standards Organization, all scientific measurements are expressed in SI units (*Système International d'Unités*). Measurements and quantities in more traditional units are often given as well as SI units. The entries for chemical compounds give the systematic names as well as the more familiar popular names.

Plants and animals. When the scientific (Latin) names of phyla, divisions, classes, orders, families, genera, and species are used in definitions, they are printed in italic type and all except the specific name have an initial capital letter. Taxonomic information is always given.

> **moss** (mɒs) NOUN 1 any bryophyte of the phylum *Bryophyta*, typically growing in dense mats on trees...
>
> **capybara** (ˌkæpɪˈbɑːrə) NOUN the largest rodent: a pig-sized amphibious hystricomorph, *Hydrochoerus hydrochaeris*...

CROSS-REFERENCES

The main entry is always given at the most common spelling or form of the word. Cross-reference entries refer to this main entry. Thus the entry for **deoxyribonucleic acid** cross-cross-refers to **DNA**, where the full explanation is given.

8.1 Comparisons

Cross-references introduced by the words 'See also' or 'Compare' refer the reader to additional information elsewhere in the Dictionary. If the cross-reference is preceded by a lozenge (◆), it applies to all senses of the headword that have gone before it, unless otherwise stated. If there is no lozenge, the cross-reference applies only to the sense immediately preceding it.

8.2 Variant spellings

Variant spellings (e.g. **foetus**...a variant spelling of **fetus**) are generally entered as cross-references if their place in the alphabetical list is more than ten entries distant from the main entry.

8.3 Alternative names

Alternative names or terms are printed in boldface type and introduced by the words 'Also' or 'Also called'. If the alternative name or term is preceded by a lozenge, it applies to the entire entry.

9 RELATED ADJECTIVES

Certain nouns, especially of Germanic origin, have related adjectives that are derived from Latin or French. For example, *mural* (from Latin) is an adjective related in meaning to *wall*. Such adjectives are shown in a number of cases after the sense (or part-of-speech block) to which they are related.

> **wall** (wɔːl) NOUN 1 **a** a vertical construction made of stone, brick, wood, etc...Related adjective: **mural**...

10 IDIOMS

Fixed noun phrases, such as **dark horse**, and certain other idioms are given full headword status. Other idioms are placed under the key word of the idiom, as a separate sense, generally at the end of the appropriate part-of-speech block.

> **ground**[1] (graʊnd) NOUN... 21 **break new ground.** to do something that has not been done before...

11 ETYMOLOGIES

Etymologies are placed after the definition, and preceded by ▷HISTORY. They are given for all headwords except those that are derivative forms (consisting of a base word and a suffix or prefix), compound words, inflected forms, and proper names. Thus, the headword manage has been given an etymology but the related headwords **manageable** (equivalent to *manage* plus the suffix *-able*), **management** (*manage* plus *-ment*), manager (*manage* plus *-er*), **manageress** (*manager* plus *-ess*), etc., do not have etymologies.

Inflected forms such as **saw** (the past tense of *see*) and obvious compounds such as **mothball** are not given an etymology. Many headwords, such as **enlighten** and **prepossess**, consist of a prefix and a base word and are not accompanied by etymologies since the essential etymological information is shown for the component parts, all of which are entered in the

Dictionary as headwords in their own right (in this instance, **en-**, **light**, **-en** and **pre-**, **possess**).

The purpose of the etymologies is to trace briefly the history of the word back from the present day, through its first recorded appearance in English, to its origin, often in some source language other than English. The etymologies show the history of the word both in English (wherever there has been significant change in form or sense) and in its pre-English source languages. Since records of both Latin and Ancient Greek exist, it is usually possible to show the actual Latin or Greek form of the source of an English word. In the case of English words of Germanic origin, cognate forms in one or more Germanic languages are shown. These cognate forms are words from the same (lost) Germanic originals, and the chief cognate languages cited are Old Norse, Swedish, Danish, German, Dutch, and Old Saxon.

All the languages and linguistic terminology used in the etymologies are entries in their own right in the Dictionary. Words printed in SMALL CAPITALS refer the reader to other headwords where relevant or additional information, either in the definition text or in the etymology, may be found.

11.1 Dating

The etymology records the first known occurrence (a written citation) of a word in English. Words first appearing in the language during the Middle English period or later are dated by century, abbreviated C.

> **mantis** (ˈmæntɪs) NOUN, *plural* **-tises** *or* **-tes** (-ti:z)...
> ▷**HISTORY** C17: New Latin, from Greek: prophet, alluding to its praying posture

This indicates that there is a written citation for **mantis** in the seventeenth century, when the word was in use as a New Latin term in the scientific vocabulary of the time. The absence of a New Latin or Greek form in the etymology means that the form of the word was the same in those languages as in English.

11.2 Old English

Native words from Old English are not dated, written records of Old English being comparatively scarce, but are simply identified as being of Old Engish origin.

> **mar** (mɑː) VERB **mars, marring, marred**...
> ▷**HISTORY** Old English *merran;* compare Old Saxon *merrian* to hinder, Old Norse *merja* to bruise

12 DERIVED WORDS

Words derived from a base word by the addition of suffixes such as *-ly*, *-ness*, etc., are entered in boldface type immediately after the etymology or after the last definition if there is no etymology. The meanings of such words may be deduced from the meanings of the suffix and the headword.

13 LANGUAGE NOTES

A brief note contained in a Language Note box has been added after a number of entries in order to comment on matters of usage. These comments reflect current English usage, based on the evidence provided by the Bank of English, as well as detailing historical practice.

> **ago** (əˈgəʊ) ADVERB in the past: *five years ago; long ago.*
> ▷**HISTORY** C14 *ago,* from Old English *āgān* to pass away

> **Language note** The use of *ago* with *since* (*it's ten years ago since he wrote the novel*) is redundant and should be avoided: *it is ten years since he wrote the novel.*

Aa

a *or* **A** (eɪ) NOUN, *plural* **a's, A's** *or* **As.** [1] the first letter and first vowel of the modern English alphabet. [2] any of several speech sounds represented by this letter, in English as in *take, bag, calm, shortage,* or *cobra.* [3] Also called: **alpha.** the first in a series, esp the highest grade or mark, as in an examination. [4] **from A to Z.** from start to finish, thoroughly and in detail.

a^{1} (ə; *stressed or emphatic* eɪ) DETERMINER (*indefinite article;* used before an initial consonant. Compare **an**^{1}) [1] used preceding a singular countable noun, if the noun is not previously specified or known: *a dog; a terrible disappointment.* [2] used preceding a proper noun to indicate that a person or thing has some of the qualities of the one named: *a Romeo; a Shylock.* [3] used preceding a noun or determiner of quantity: *a cupful; a dozen eggs; a great many; to read a lot.* [4] used preceding a noun indicating a concrete or abstract thing capable of being divided: *half a loaf; a quarter of a minute.* [5] (preceded by *once, twice, several times,* etc.) each or every; per: *once a day; fifty pence a pound.* [6] a certain; one: *to change policy at a stroke; a Mr Jones called.* [7] (preceded by *not*) any at all: *not a hope.* ◆ Compare **the**^{1}.

a^{2} (ə) VERB an informal or dialect word for **have**: *they'd a said if they'd known.*

a^{3} (ə) PREPOSITION (usually linked to the preceding noun) an informal form of **of**: *sorta sad; a kinda waste.*

a^{4} SYMBOL FOR: [1] acceleration. [2] are(s) (metric measure of land). [3] atto-. [4] *Chess* See **algebraic notation.**

A SYMBOL FOR: [1] *Music* **a** a note having a frequency of 440 hertz (**A above middle C**) or this value multiplied or divided by any power of 2; the sixth note of the scale of C major. **b** a key, string, or pipe producing this note. **c** the major or minor key having this note as its tonic. [2] a human blood type of the ABO group, containing the A antigen. [3] (in Britain) a major arterial road: *the A3 runs from London to Portsmouth.* [4] (formerly, in Britain) **a** a film certified for viewing by anyone, but which contains material that some parents may not wish their children to see. **b** (*as modifier*): *an A film.* [5] mass number. [6] the number 10 in hexadecimal notation. [7] *Cards* ace. [8] argon (now superseded by **Ar**). [9] ampere(s). [10] Also: **at.** ampere-turn. [11] absolute (temperature). [12] (in circuit diagrams) ammeter. [13] area. [14] (*in combination*) atomic: *an A-bomb; an A-plant.* [15] *Chem* affinity. [16] *Biochem* adenine. [17] *Logic* a universal affirmative categorical proposition, such as *all men are mortal:* often symbolized as **SaP**. Compare **E, I**^{2}**, O**^{1}. [from Latin *a(ffirmo)* I affirm] [18] **a** a person whose job is in top management, or who holds a senior administrative or professional position. **b** (*as modifier*): *an A worker.* ◆ See also **occupation groupings.** ◆ [19] INTERNATIONAL CAR REGISTRATION FOR Austria.

Å SYMBOL FOR angstrom unit.

A. ABBREVIATION FOR: [1] acre(s) or acreage. [2] America(n). [3] answer.

a', aa, *or* **aw** (ɔː) DETERMINER *Scot* variants of **all.**

a-^{1} *or before a vowel* **an-** PREFIX not; without; opposite to: *atonal; asocial.*
▷**HISTORY** from Greek *a-, an-* not, without

a-^{2} PREFIX [1] on; in; towards: *afoot; abed; aground; aback.* [2] *Literary or archaic* (*used before a present participle*) in the act or process of: *come a-running; go a-hunting.* [3] in the condition or state of: *afloat; alive; asleep.*

A1, A-1, *or* **A-one** (ˈeɪˈwʌn) ADJECTIVE [1] in good health; physically fit. [2] *Informal* first class; excellent. [3] (of a vessel) with hull and equipment in first-class condition.

A3^{1} NOUN **a** a standard paper size, 297 × 420 mm. **b** (*as adjective*): *an A3 book.* ◆ See also **A sizes.**

A3^{2} *Text messaging* ABBREVIATION FOR anytime, anywhere, anyplace.

A4 NOUN **a** a standard paper size, 210 × 297 mm. **b** (*as adjective*): *an A4 book.* ◆ See also **A sizes.**

A5 NOUN **a** a standard paper size (half A4), 148 × 210 mm. **b** (*as adjective*): *A5 notepaper.* ◆ See also **A sizes.**

aa^{1} (ˈɑːɑː) NOUN a volcanic rock consisting of angular blocks of lava with a very rough surface.
▷**HISTORY** Hawaiian

aa^{2} ABBREVIATION FOR **ana**^{1}.

AA ABBREVIATION FOR: [1] **Alcoholics Anonymous.** [2] anti-aircraft. [3] Architectural Association. [4] (in Britain) Automobile Association. [5] (in Britain) Advertising Association. ◆ SYMBOL FOR: [6] (in Britain, formerly) a film that may not be shown publicly to a child under fourteen.

AAA ABBREVIATION FOR: [1] *Brit* Amateur Athletic Association. [2] anti-aircraft artillery. See also **triple A.** [3] *US* Automobile Association of America. [4] Automobile Association of Australia.

Aachen (ˈɑːkən; *German* ˈaːxən) NOUN a city and spa in W Germany, in North Rhine-Westphalia: the northern capital of Charlemagne's empire. Pop.: 243 600 (1999 est.). French name: **Aix-la-Chapelle.**

Aalborg *or* **Ålborg** (*Danish* ˈɔlbɔr) NOUN a city and port in Denmark, in N Jutland. Pop.: 161 161 (2000 est.).

Aalesund (*Norwegian* ˈoːləsun) NOUN a variant spelling of **Ålesund.**

aalii (ɑːˈliːiː) NOUN a bushy sapindaceous shrub, *Dodonaea viscosa,* of Australia, Hawaii, Africa, and tropical America, having small greenish flowers and sticky foliage.
▷**HISTORY** Hawaiian

Aalst (aːlst) NOUN the Flemish name for **Alost.**

AAM ABBREVIATION FOR: [1] air-to-air missile. [2] *Text messaging* as a matter of fact.

A & E ABBREVIATION FOR Accident and Emergency (department in hospitals).

A & M ABBREVIATION FOR: [1] Agricultural and Mechanical. [2] Ancient and Modern (hymn book).

A & P (in New Zealand) ABBREVIATION FOR Agricultural and Pastoral (Association, Show, etc.).

A & R ABBREVIATION FOR artists and repertoire.

AAP ABBREVIATION FOR: [1] Australian Associated Press. [2] (in the US) affirmative action program.

Aarau (*German* ˈaːrau) NOUN a town in N Switzerland, capital of Aargau canton: capital of the Helvetic Republic from 1798 to 1803. Pop.: 15 881 (1990).

aardvark (ˈɑːdˌvɑːk) NOUN a nocturnal mammal, *Orycteropus afer,* the sole member of its family (*Orycteropodidae*) and order (*Tubulidentata*). It inhabits the grasslands of Africa, has long ears and snout, and feeds on termites. Also called: **ant bear.**
▷**HISTORY** C19: from obsolete Afrikaans, from *aarde* earth + *varken* pig

aardwolf (ˈɑːdˌwʊlf) NOUN, *plural* **-wolves.** a nocturnal mammal, *Proteles cristatus,* that inhabits the plains of southern Africa and feeds on termites and insect larvae: family *Hyaenidae* (hyenas), order *Carnivora* (carnivores).
▷**HISTORY** C19: from Afrikaans, from *aarde* earth + *wolf* wolf

Aargau (*German* ˈaːrgau) NOUN a canton in N Switzerland. Capital: Aarau. Pop.: 540 600 (2000 est.). Area: 1404 sq. km (542 sq. miles). French name: **Argovie.**

Aarhus *or* **Århus** (*Danish* ˈɔrhuːs) NOUN a city and port in Denmark, in E Jutland. Pop.: 284 846 (2000 est.).

AARNet ABBREVIATION FOR Australian Academic Research Network.

Aaron (ˈɛərən) NOUN *Old Testament* the first high priest of the Israelites, brother of Moses (Exodus 4:14).

Aaronic (ɛəˈrɒnɪk) ADJECTIVE [1] of or relating to Aaron, his family, or the priestly dynasty initiated by him. [2] of or relating to the Israelite high priesthood. [3] of or relating to the priesthood in general. [4] *Mormon Church* denoting or relating to the second order of the Mormon priesthood.

Aaron's beard NOUN another name for **rose of Sharon** (sense 1).

Aaron's rod NOUN [1] the rod used by Aaron in performing a variety of miracles in Egypt. It later blossomed and produced almonds (Numbers 17). [2] a widespread Eurasian scrophulariaceous plant, *Verbascum thapsus,* having woolly leaves and tall erect spikes of yellow flowers.

A'asia ABBREVIATION FOR Australasia.

Ab (æb) NOUN a variant of **Av.**

AB ABBREVIATION FOR: [1] Also: **a.b.** able-bodied seaman. [2] (in the US) Bachelor of Arts. [3] (esp in postal addresses) Alberta (Canada). ◆ SYMBOL FOR: [4] a human blood type of the ABO group, containing both the A antigen and the B antigen.

ab-^{1} PREFIX away from; off; outside of; opposite to: *abnormal; abaxial; aboral.*
▷**HISTORY** from Latin *ab* away from

ab-^{2} PREFIX denoting a cgs unit of measurement in the electromagnetic system: *abvolt.*
▷**HISTORY** abstracted from ABSOLUTE

aba (ˈæbə) NOUN [1] a type of cloth from Syria, made of goat hair or camel hair. [2] a sleeveless outer garment of such cloth.
▷**HISTORY** from Arabic

ABA ABBREVIATION FOR: [1] (in Britain) Amateur Boxing Association. [2] American Booksellers Association.

abac (ˈeɪbæk) NOUN another name for **nomogram.**
▷**HISTORY** C20: from French, from Latin ABACUS

abaca (ˈæbəkə) NOUN [1] a Philippine plant, *Musa textilis,* related to the banana: family *Musaceae.* Its leafstalks are the source of Manila hemp. [2] another name for **Manila hemp.**
▷**HISTORY** via Spanish from Tagalog *abaká*

aback (əˈbæk) ADVERB [1] **taken aback. a** startled or disconcerted. **b** *Nautical* (of a vessel or sail) having the wind against the forward side so as to prevent forward motion. [2] *Rare* towards the back; backwards.
▷**HISTORY** Old English *on bæc* to the back

abactinal (æbˈæktɪnᵊl) ADJECTIVE *Zoology* (of organisms showing radial symmetry) situated away from or opposite to the mouth; aboral.
▸**abˈactinally** ADVERB

abacus (ˈæbəkəs) NOUN, *plural* **-ci** (-ˌsaɪ) *or* **-cuses.** [1] a counting device that consists of a frame holding rods on which a specific number of beads are free to move. Each rod designates a given denomination, such as units, tens, hundreds, etc., in the decimal system, and each bead represents a digit or a specific number of digits. [2] *Architect* the flat upper part of the capital of a column.
▷**HISTORY** C16: from Latin, from Greek *abax* board covered with sand for tracing calculations, from Hebrew *ābhāq* dust

Abadan (ˌæbəˈdɑːn) NOUN a port in SW Iran, on an island in the Shatt-al-Arab delta. Pop.: 206 073 (1996).

Abaddon (əˈbædᵊn) NOUN [1] the Devil (Revelation 9:11). [2] (in rabbinical literature) a part of Gehenna; Hell.
▷**HISTORY** Hebrew: literally, destruction

abaft (əˈbɑːft) *Nautical* ◆ ADVERB, ADJECTIVE (*postpositive*) [1] closer to the stern than to another place on a vessel: *with the wind abaft.* ◆ PREPOSITION [2] behind; aft of: *abaft the mast.*
▷**HISTORY** C13 *on baft; baft* from Old English *beæftan,* from *be* by + *æftan* behind

Abakan (*Russian* abaˈkan) NOUN a city in S central Russia, capital of the Khakass Republic, at the confluence of the Yenisei and Abakan Rivers. Pop.: 169 000 (1999 est.).

abalone (ˌæbəˈləʊnɪ) NOUN any of various edible

marine gastropod molluscs of the genus *Haliotis,* having an ear-shaped shell that is perforated with a row of respiratory holes. The shells are used for ornament or decoration. Also called: **ear shell.** See also **ormer.**
▷HISTORY C19: from American Spanish *abulón;* origin unknown

abampere (æb'æmpɛə) NOUN the cgs unit of current in the electromagnetic system; the constant current that, when flowing through two parallel straight infinitely long conductors 1 centimetre apart, will produce a force between them of 2 dynes per centimetre: equivalent to 10 amperes. Abbreviation: **abamp.**

abandon (ə'bændən) VERB (*tr*) [1] to forsake completely; desert; leave behind: *to abandon a baby; drivers had to abandon their cars.* [2] **abandon ship.** the order given to the crew of a ship that is about to sink to take to the lifeboats. [3] to give up completely: *to abandon a habit; to abandon hope.* [4] to yield control of or concern in; relinquish: *to abandon office.* [5] to give up (something begun) before completion: *to abandon a job; the game was abandoned.* [6] to surrender (oneself) to emotion without restraint. [7] to give (insured property that has suffered partial loss or damage) to the insurers in order that a claim for a total loss may be made. ◆ NOUN [8] freedom from inhibitions, restraint, concern, or worry: *she danced with abandon.*
▷HISTORY C14 *abandounen* (vb), from Old French, from *a bandon* under one's control, in one's power, from *a* at, to + *bandon* control, power
▸**a'bandonment** NOUN

abandoned (ə'bændənd) ADJECTIVE [1] deserted: *an abandoned windmill.* [2] forsaken: *an abandoned child.* [3] unrestrained; uninhibited: *wild, abandoned dancing.* [4] depraved; profligate.

abandonee (ə,bændə'ni:) NOUN *Law* a person to whom something is formally relinquished, esp an insurer having the right to salvage a wreck.

abapical (æb'eɪpɪkᵊl) ADJECTIVE *Biology* away from or opposite the apex.

à bas *French* (a bɑ) INTERJECTION down with!

abase (ə'beɪs) VERB (*tr*) [1] to humble or belittle (oneself, etc.). [2] to lower or reduce, as in rank or estimation.
▷HISTORY C15 *abessen,* from Old French *abaissier* to make low. See BASE[2]
▸**a'basement** NOUN

abash (ə'bæʃ) VERB (*tr; usually passive*) to cause to feel ill at ease, embarrassed, or confused; make ashamed.
▷HISTORY C14: via Norman French from Old French *esbair* to be astonished, from *es-* out + *bair* to gape, yawn
▸**abashedly** (ə'bæʃɪdlɪ) ADVERB ▸**a'bashment** NOUN

abate (ə'beɪt) VERB [1] to make or become less in amount, intensity, degree, etc.: *the storm has abated.* [2] (*tr*) *Law* **a** to remove, suppress, or terminate (a nuisance). **b** to suspend or extinguish (a claim or action). **c** to annul (a writ). [3] (*intr*) *Law* (of a writ, legal action, etc.) to become null and void. [4] (*tr*) to subtract or deduct, as part of a price.
▷HISTORY C14: from Old French *abatre* to beat down, fell

abatement (ə'beɪtmənt) NOUN [1] diminution or alleviation; decrease. [2] suppression or termination: *the abatement of a nuisance.* [3] the amount by which something is reduced, such as the cost of an article. [4] *Property law* a decrease in the payment to creditors or legatees when the assets of the debtor or estate are insufficient to meet all payments in full. [5] *Property law* (formerly) a wrongful entry on land by a stranger who takes possession after the death of the owner and before the heir has entered into possession.

abatis *or* **abattis** ('æbətɪs, 'æbəti:) NOUN *Fortifications* [1] a rampart of felled trees bound together placed with their branches outwards. [2] a barbed-wire entanglement before a position.
▷HISTORY C18: from French, from *abattre* to fell

abator (ə'beɪtə) NOUN *Law* a person who effects an abatement.

abattoir ('æbə,twɑ:) NOUN another name for **slaughterhouse.**
▷HISTORY C19: French, from *abattre* to fell

abaxial (æb'æksɪəl) ADJECTIVE facing away from the axis, as the surface of a leaf. Compare **adaxial.**

Abba ('æbə) NOUN [1] *New Testament* father (used of God). [2] a title given to bishops and patriarchs in the Syrian, Coptic, and Ethiopian Churches.
▷HISTORY from Aramaic

abbacy ('æbəsɪ) NOUN, *plural* **-cies.** the office, term of office, or jurisdiction of an abbot or abbess.
▷HISTORY C15: from Church Latin *abbātia,* from *abbāt-* ABBOT

abbatial (ə'beɪʃəl) ADJECTIVE of or relating to an abbot, abbess, or abbey.
▷HISTORY C17: from Church Latin *abbātiālis,* from *abbāt-* ABBOT; see -AL[1]

abbé ('æbeɪ; *French* abe) NOUN [1] a French abbot. [2] a title used in addressing any other French cleric, such as a priest.

Abbe condenser ('æbɪ; *German* 'a:bə) NOUN a microscope condenser invented by Ernst Abbe (1840-1905), German physicist.

abbed (æbd) ADJECTIVE *Informal* displaying well-developed abdominal muscles.

abbess ('æbɪs) NOUN the female superior of a convent.
▷HISTORY C13: from Old French, from Church Latin *abbātissa*

Abbeville (*French* abəvil) NOUN a town in N France: brewing, sugar-refining, and carpet industries. Pop.: 24 590 (1990).

Abbevillian (æb'vɪlɪən, -jən) *Archaeol* ◆ NOUN [1] the period represented by Lower Palaeolithic European sites containing the earliest hand axes, dating from the Mindel glaciation. See also **Acheulian.** ◆ ADJECTIVE [2] of or relating to this period.
▷HISTORY C20: after ABBEVILLE, where the stone tools were discovered

abbey ('æbɪ) NOUN [1] a building inhabited by a community of monks or nuns governed by an abbot or abbess. [2] a church built in conjunction with such a building. [3] such a community of monks or nuns.
▷HISTORY C13: via Old French *abeie* from Church Latin *abbātia* ABBACY

Abbey Theatre NOUN an influential theatre in Dublin (opened 1904): associated with it were Synge, Yeats, Lady Gregory, and O'Casey. It was destroyed by fire in 1951 but was rebuilt; it reopened in 1966.

abbot ('æbət) NOUN the superior of an abbey of monks. Related adjective: **abbatial.**
▷HISTORY Old English *abbod,* from Church Latin *abbāt-* (stem of *abbas*), ultimately from Aramaic *abbā* ABBA
▸**'abbot,ship** *or* **'abbotcy** NOUN

abbrev. *or* **abbr.** ABBREVIATION FOR abbreviation.

abbreviate (ə'bri:vɪ,eɪt) VERB (*tr*) [1] to shorten (a word or phrase) by contraction or omission of some letters or words. [2] to shorten (a speech or piece of writing) by omitting sections, paraphrasing, etc. [3] to cut short.
▷HISTORY C15: from the past participle of Late Latin *abbreviāre,* from Latin *brevis* brief
▸**ab'brevi,ator** NOUN

abbreviation (ə,bri:vɪ'eɪʃən) NOUN [1] a shortened or contracted form of a word or phrase used in place of the whole. [2] the process or result of abbreviating.

ABC[1] NOUN [1] (*plural in US*) the rudiments of a subject. [2] an alphabetical guide to a subject. [3] (*often plural in US*) the alphabet.

ABC[2] ABBREVIATION FOR: [1] (formerly, of weapons or warfare) atomic, biological, and chemical. [2] Australian Broadcasting Corporation. [3] American Broadcasting Company. [4] **Audit Bureau of Circulation.** [5] *Austral* Australian-born Chinese: a person with Chinese parents, born and raised in Australia. [6] *US* American-born Chinese: a person with Chinese parents, born and raised in the US.

abcoulomb (æb'ku:lɒm) NOUN the cgs unit of electric charge in the electromagnetic system; the charge per second passing any cross section of a conductor through which a steady current of 1 abampere is flowing: equivalent to 10 coulombs.

Abdias (æb'daɪəs) NOUN *Bible* the Douay form of **Obadiah.**

abdicate ('æbdɪ,keɪt) VERB to renounce (a throne, power, responsibility, rights, etc.), esp formally.
▷HISTORY C16: from the past participle of Latin *abdicāre* to proclaim away, disclaim
▸**abdicable** ('æbdɪkəbᵊl) ADJECTIVE ▸**,abdi'cation** NOUN
▸**abdicative** (æb'dɪkətɪv) ADJECTIVE ▸**'abdi,cator** NOUN

abdomen ('æbdəmən, æb'dəʊ-) NOUN [1] the region of the body of a vertebrate that contains the viscera other than the heart and lungs. In mammals it is separated from the thorax by the diaphragm. [2] the front or surface of this region; belly. Related adjective: **coeliac.** [3] (in arthropods) the posterior part of the body behind the thorax, consisting of up to ten similar segments.
▷HISTORY C16: from Latin; origin obscure
▸**abdominal** (æb'dɒmɪnᵊl) ADJECTIVE ▸**ab'dominally** ADVERB

abdominal crunch NOUN another term for **sit-up.**

abdominal thrust NOUN another name for **Heimlich manoeuvre.**

abducens nerve (æb'dju:sənz) NOUN either of the sixth pair of cranial nerves, which supply the lateral rectus muscle of the eye.
▷HISTORY see ABDUCENT

abducent (æb'dju:sᵊnt) ADJECTIVE (of a muscle) abducting.
▷HISTORY C18: from Latin *abdūcent-, abdūcens* leading away, from *abdūcere,* from *ab-* away + *dūcere* to lead, carry

abduct (æb'dʌkt) VERB (*tr*) [1] to remove (a person) by force or cunning; kidnap. [2] (of certain muscles) to pull (a leg, arm, etc.) away from the median axis of the body. Compare **adduct.**
▷HISTORY C19: from the past participle of Latin *abdūcere* to lead away
▸**ab'ductor** NOUN

abduction (æb'dʌkʃən) NOUN [1] the act of taking someone away by force or cunning; kidnapping. [2] the action of certain muscles in pulling a leg, arm, etc. away from the median axis of the body.

abeam (ə'bi:m) ADVERB, ADJECTIVE (*postpositive*) at right angles to the length and directly opposite the centre of a vessel or aircraft.
▷HISTORY C19: A-[2] + BEAM

abecedarian (,eɪbi:si:'dɛərɪən) NOUN [1] a person who is learning the alphabet or the rudiments of a subject. ◆ ADJECTIVE [2] alphabetically arranged.
▷HISTORY C17: from Late Latin *abecedarius,* from the letters *a, b, c, d*

abed (ə'bɛd) ADVERB *Archaic* in bed.

Abednego (ə'bɛdnɪ,gəʊ) NOUN *Old Testament* one of Daniel's three companions who, together with Shadrach and Meshach, was miraculously saved from destruction in Nebuchadnezzar's fiery furnace (Daniel 3:12–30).

Abel ('eɪbᵊl) NOUN *Old Testament* the second son of Adam and Eve, a shepherd, murdered by his brother Cain (Genesis 4:1–8).

abele (ə'bi:l, 'eɪbᵊl) NOUN another name for **white poplar.**
▷HISTORY C16: from Dutch *abeel,* ultimately related to Latin *albus* white

Abelian group (ə'bi:lɪən) NOUN a group the defined binary operation of which is commutative: if *a* and *b* are members of an Abelian group then *ab* = *ba*.
▷HISTORY C19: named after Niels Henrik *Abel* (1802–29), Norwegian mathematician

abelmosk ('eɪbᵊl,mɒsk) NOUN a tropical bushy malvaceous plant, *Hibiscus abelmoschus,* cultivated for its yellow-and-crimson flowers and for its musk-scented seeds, which yield an oil used in perfumery. Also called: **musk mallow.**
▷HISTORY New Latin, from Arabic *abu'l misk* father of musk

Abeokuta (,æbɪəʊ'ku:tə) NOUN a town in W Nigeria, capital of Ogun state. Pop.: 427 400 (1996 est.).

Aberdare (,æbə'dɛə) NOUN a town in South Wales, in Rhondda, Cynon, Taff county borough. Pop.: 29 040 (1991).

Aberdeen (,æbə'di:n) NOUN [1] a city in NE Scotland, on the North Sea: centre for processing North Sea oil and gas; university (1494). Pop.: 217 260 (1996 est.). [2] **City of.** a council area in NE Scotland, established in 1996. Pop.: 212 125 (2001). Area: 186 sq. km (72 sq. miles).

Aberdeen Angus NOUN a black hornless breed of beef cattle originating in Scotland.

Aberdeenshire (,æbə'di:n,ʃɪə, -ʃə) NOUN a council

area and historical county of N Scotland, on the North Sea: became part of Grampian Region in 1975 but reinstated as an independent unitary authority (with adjusted borders) in 1996: rises to the Grampian and Cairngorm Mountains in the SW: chiefly agricultural (esp sheep and stock raising). Administrative centre: Aberdeen. Pop.: 226 871 (2001). Area 6319 sq. km (2439 sq. miles).

Aberdeen terrier NOUN a former name for **Scottish terrier.**

aberdevine (ˌæbədɪ'viːn) NOUN a former name for the **siskin** (sense 1), as a cagebird
▷HISTORY C18: of unknown origin

Aberdonian (ˌæbə'dəʊnɪən) NOUN **1** a native or inhabitant of Aberdeen. ◆ ADJECTIVE **2** of or relating to Aberdeen or its inhabitants.

Aberfan (ˌæbə'væn) NOUN a coal-mining village in S Wales, in Merthyr Tydfil county borough: scene of a disaster in 1966 when a slag heap collapsed onto part of the village killing 144 people (including 116 children).

abernethy (ˌæbə'nɛθɪ) NOUN a crisp unleavened biscuit.
▷HISTORY C19: perhaps named after Dr. John *Abernethy* (1764–1831), English surgeon interested in diet

aberrant (æ'bɛrənt) ADJECTIVE **1** deviating from the normal or usual type, as certain animals from the group in which they are classified. **2** behaving in an abnormal or untypical way. **3** deviating from truth, morality, etc.
▷HISTORY rare before C19: from the present participle of Latin *aberrāre* to wander away
▸**ab'errance** *or* **ab'errancy** NOUN

aberration (ˌæbə'reɪʃən) NOUN **1** deviation from what is normal, expected, or usual. **2** departure from truth, morality, etc. **3** a lapse in control of one's mental faculties. **4** *Optics* a defect in a lens or mirror that causes the formation of either a distorted image (see **spherical aberration**) or one with coloured fringes (see **chromatic aberration**). **5** *Astronomy* the apparent displacement of a celestial body due to the finite speed of light and the motion of the observer with the earth.

Aberystwyth (ˌæbə'rɪstwɪθ) NOUN a resort and university town in Wales, in Ceredigion on Cardigan Bay. Pop.: 11 154 (1991).

abet (ə'bɛt) VERB **abets, abetting, abetted.** (*tr*) to assist or encourage, esp in crime or wrongdoing.
▷HISTORY C14: from Old French *abeter* to lure on, entice, from *beter* to bait
▸**a'betment** *or* **a'bettal** NOUN ▸**a'better** *or* (*esp law*) **a'bettor** NOUN

abeyance (ə'beɪəns) NOUN **1** (usually preceded by *in* or *into*) a state of being suspended or put aside temporarily. **2** (usually preceded by *in*) *Law* an indeterminate state of ownership, as when the person entitled to an estate has not been ascertained.
▷HISTORY C16–17: from Anglo-French, from Old French *abeance* expectation, literally a gaping after, a reaching towards
▸**a'beyant** ADJECTIVE

abfarad (æb'færæd, -əd) NOUN the cgs unit of capacitance in the electromagnetic system; the capacitance of a capacitor having a charge of 1 abcoulomb and a potential difference of 1 abvolt between its conductors: equivalent to 10^9 farads.

ABH ABBREVIATION FOR **actual bodily harm.**

abhenry (æb'hɛnrɪ) NOUN, *plural* **-ries.** the cgs unit of inductance in the electromagnetic system; the inductance that results when a rate of change of current of 1 abampere per second generates an induced emf of 1 abvolt: equivalent to 10^{-9} henry.

abhor (əb'hɔː) VERB **-hors, -horring, -horred.** (*tr*) to detest vehemently; find repugnant; reject.
▷HISTORY C15: from Latin *abhorrēre* to shudder at, shrink from, from *ab-* away from + *horrēre* to bristle, shudder
▸**ab'horrer** NOUN

abhorrence (əb'hɒrəns) NOUN **1** a feeling of extreme loathing or aversion. **2** a person or thing that is loathsome.

abhorrent (əb'hɒrənt) ADJECTIVE **1** repugnant; loathsome. **2** (when *postpositive,* foll by *of*) feeling extreme aversion or loathing (for): *abhorrent of vulgarity.* **3** (usually *postpositive* and foll by *to*) conflicting (with): *abhorrent to common sense.*
▸**ab'horrently** ADVERB

Abia (æb'iːa) NOUN a state of SE Nigeria. Capital: Umuahia. Pop.: 2 569 362 (1995 est). Area (including Imo state): 11 850 sq. km (4575 sq. miles).

Abib (*Hebrew* ɑ'biːb) NOUN *Judaism* an older name for the month of **Nisan** (Exodus 13:4).
▷HISTORY Hebrew *ābhībh* ear of grain, hence the month when grain was fresh

abide (ə'baɪd) VERB **abides, abiding, abode** *or* **abided. 1** (*tr*) to tolerate; put up with. **2** (*tr*) to accept or submit to; suffer: *to abide the court's decision.* **3** (*intr;* foll by *by*) **a** to comply (with): *to abide by the decision.* **b** to remain faithful (to): *to abide by your promise.* **4** (*intr*) to remain or continue. **5** (*intr*) *Archaic* to dwell. **6** (*tr*) *Archaic* to await in expectation. **7** (*tr*) *Archaic* to withstand or sustain; endure: *to abide the onslaught.*
▷HISTORY Old English *ābīdan,* from *a-* (intensive) + *bīdan* to wait, bide
▸**a'bidance** NOUN ▸**a'bider** NOUN

abiding (ə'baɪdɪŋ) ADJECTIVE permanent; enduring: *an abiding belief.*
▸**a'bidingly** ADVERB

Abidjan (ˌæbɪ'dʒɑːn; *French* abidʒɑ̃) NOUN a port in the Côte d'Ivoire, on the Gulf of Guinea: the legislative capital (Yamoussoukro became the administrative capital in 1983). Pop.: 2 797 000 (1995 est.).

abietic acid (ˌæbɪ'ɛtɪk) NOUN a yellowish powder occurring naturally as a constituent of rosin and used in lacquers, varnishes, and soap. Formula: $C_{19}H_{29}COOH$; melting pt.: 173°C.
▷HISTORY C19 *abietic,* from Latin *abiēt-,* from *abiēs* silver fir (the acid originally being extracted from the resin)

Abigail ('æbɪˌgeɪl) NOUN *Old Testament* the woman who brought provisions to David and his followers and subsequently became his wife (I Samuel 25:1–42).

Abilene ('æbɪˌliːn) NOUN a city in central Texas. Pop.: 115 930 (2000).

ability (ə'bɪlɪtɪ) NOUN, *plural* **-ties. 1** possession of the qualities required to do something; necessary skill, competence, or power: *the ability to cope with a problem.* **2** considerable proficiency; natural capability: *a man of ability.* **3** (*plural*) special talents.
▷HISTORY C14: from Old French from Latin *habilitās* aptitude, handiness, from *habilis* ABLE

Abingdon ('æbɪŋdən) NOUN a market town in S England, in Oxfordshire. Pop.: 35 234 (1991).

ab initio *Latin* (æb ɪ'nɪʃɪˌəʊ) from the start.

abiogenesis (ˌeɪbaɪəʊ'dʒɛnɪsɪs) NOUN **1** Also called: **autogenesis.** the hypothetical process by which living organisms first arose on earth from nonliving matter. **2** another name for **spontaneous generation.** Compare **biogenesis.**
▷HISTORY C19: New Latin, from A-[1] + BIO- + GENESIS
▸ˌ**abioge'netic** ADJECTIVE ▸**abiogenist** (ˌeɪbaɪ'ɒdʒɪnɪst) NOUN

abiosis (ˌeɪbaɪ'əʊsɪs) NOUN absence of life.
▷HISTORY C20: from A-[1] + Greek *biōsis* a way of living
▸**abiotic** (ˌeɪbaɪ'ɒtɪk) ADJECTIVE

abirritant (æb'ɪrɪtənt) ADJECTIVE **1** relieving irritation. ◆ NOUN **2** any drug or agent that relieves irritation.

abirritate (æb'ɪrɪˌteɪt) VERB (*tr*) *Med, obsolete* to soothe or make less irritable.

abject ('æbdʒɛkt) ADJECTIVE **1** utterly wretched or hopeless. **2** miserable; forlorn; dejected. **3** indicating humiliation; submissive: *an abject apology.* **4** contemptible; despicable; servile: *an abject liar.*
▷HISTORY C14 (in the sense: rejected, cast out): from Latin *abjectus* thrown or cast away, from *abjicere,* from *ab-* away + *jacere* to throw
▸**ab'jection** NOUN ▸**'abjectly** ADVERB ▸**'abjectness** NOUN

abjure (əb'dʒʊə) VERB (*tr*) **1** to renounce or retract, esp formally, solemnly, or under oath. **2** to abstain from or reject.
▷HISTORY C15: from Old French *abjurer* or Latin *abjurāre* to deny on oath
▸ˌ**abju'ration** NOUN ▸**ab'jurer** NOUN

Abkhaz (æb'kɑːz) NOUN **1** (*plural* **-khaz**) Also called: **Abkhazi, Abkhazian.** a member of a Georgian people living east of the Black Sea. **2** the language of this people, belonging to the North-West Caucasian family.

Abkhazia (æb'kɑːzɪə) NOUN an administrative division of NW Georgia, between the Black Sea and the Caucasus Mountains: a subtropical region, with mountains rising over 3900 m (13 000 ft.); Abkhazian separatists seized control of the region in 1993. Capital: Sukhumi. Pop.: 516 600 (1993 est.). Area: 8600 sq. km (3320 sq. miles). Also called: **Abkhaz Autonomous Republic.**

abl. ABBREVIATION FOR ablative.

ablactation (ˌæblæk'teɪʃən) NOUN **1** the weaning of an infant. **2** the cessation of milk secretion in the breasts.

ablate (æb'leɪt) VERB (*tr*) to remove by ablation.
▷HISTORY C20: back formation from ABLATION

ablation (æb'leɪʃən) NOUN **1** the surgical removal of an organ, structure, or part. **2** the melting or wearing away of an expendable part, such as the heat shield of a space re-entry vehicle on passing through the earth's atmosphere. **3** the wearing away of a rock or glacier.
▷HISTORY C15: from Late Latin *ablātiōn-,* from Latin *auferre* to carry away, remove

ablative ('æblətɪv) *Grammar* ◆ ADJECTIVE **1** (in certain inflected languages such as Latin) denoting a case of nouns, pronouns, and adjectives indicating the agent in passive sentences or the instrument, manner, or place of the action described by the verb. ◆ NOUN **2** **a** the ablative case. **b** a word or speech element in the ablative case.

ablative absolute NOUN an absolute construction in Latin grammar in which a governor noun and a modifier in the ablative case function as a sentence modifier; for example, *hostibus victis,* "the enemy having been beaten".

ablator (æb'leɪtə) NOUN the heat shield of a space vehicle, which melts or wears away during re-entry into the earth's atmosphere.
▷HISTORY C20: from ABLATION

ablaut ('æblaʊt; *German* 'aplaut) NOUN *Linguistics* vowel gradation, esp in Indo-European languages. See **gradation** (sense 5).
▷HISTORY German, coined 1819 by Jakob Grimm from *ab* off + *Laut* sound

ablaze (ə'bleɪz) ADJECTIVE (*postpositive*), ADVERB **1** on fire; burning. **2** brightly illuminated. **3** emotionally aroused.

able ('eɪbᵊl) ADJECTIVE **1** (*postpositive*) having the necessary power, resources, skill, time, opportunity, etc., to do something: *able to swim.* **2** capable; competent; talented: *an able teacher.* **3** *Law* qualified, competent, or authorized to do some specific act.
▷HISTORY C14: ultimately from Latin *habilis* easy to hold, manageable, apt, from *habēre* to have, hold + *-ilis* -ILE

-able SUFFIX FORMING ADJECTIVES **1** capable of, suitable for, or deserving of (being acted upon as indicated): *enjoyable; pitiable; readable; separable; washable.* **2** inclined to; given to; able to; causing: *comfortable; reasonable; variable.*
▷HISTORY via Old French from Latin *-ābilis, -ībilis,* forms of *-bilis,* adjectival suffix
▸**-ably** SUFFIX FORMING ADVERBS ▸**-ability** SUFFIX FORMING NOUNS

able-bodied ADJECTIVE physically strong and healthy; robust.

able-bodied seaman NOUN an ordinary seaman, esp one in the merchant navy, who has been trained in certain skills. Also: **able seaman.** Abbreviations: **AB, a.b.**

abled ('eɪbᵊld) ADJECTIVE having a range of physical powers as specified (esp in the phrases **less abled, differently abled**).

ableism ('eɪbᵊlˌɪzəm) NOUN discrimination against disabled or handicapped people.

able rating NOUN (esp in the Royal Navy) a rating who is qualified to perform certain duties of seamanship.

abloom (ə'bluːm) ADJECTIVE (*postpositive*) in flower; blooming.

ablution (ə'bluːʃən) NOUN **1** the ritual washing of a priest's hands or of sacred vessels. **2** (*often plural*) the act of washing (esp in the phrase **perform one's**

ablutions). [3] (*plural*) *Military, informal* a washing place.
▷HISTORY C14: ultimately from Latin *ablūere* to wash away
▸**ab'lutionary** ADJECTIVE

ably ('eɪblɪ) ADVERB in a competent or skilful manner.

ABM ABBREVIATION FOR **antiballistic missile.**

Abnaki (æb'nɑ:kɪ) NOUN [1] (*plural* **-ki** *or* **-kis**) a member of a North American Indian people formerly living in Maine and Quebec. [2] the language of this people, belonging to the Algonquian family.

abnegate ('æbnɪˌgeɪt) VERB (*tr*) to deny to oneself; renounce (privileges, pleasure, etc.).
▷HISTORY C17: from Latin *abnegāre* to deny
▸ˌ**abne'gation** NOUN ▸'**abneˌgator** NOUN

Abney level ('æbnɪ) NOUN a surveying instrument consisting of a spirit level and a sighting tube, used to measure the angle of inclination of a line from the observer to another point.
▷HISTORY C20: named after Sir William *Abney* (1843–1920), British chemist and physicist

abnormal (æb'nɔ:məl) ADJECTIVE [1] not normal; deviating from the usual or typical; extraordinary. [2] *Informal* odd in behaviour or appearance; strange.
▷HISTORY C19: AB-¹ + NORMAL, replacing earlier *anormal* from Medieval Latin *anormalus,* a blend of Late Latin *anōmalus* ANOMALOUS + Latin *abnormis* departing from a rule
▸**ab'normally** ADVERB

abnormality (ˌæbnɔ:'mælɪtɪ) NOUN, *plural* **-ties.** [1] an abnormal feature, event, etc. [2] a physical malformation; deformity. [3] deviation from the typical or usual; irregularity.

abnormal psychology NOUN the study of behaviour patterns that diverge widely from generally accepted norms, esp those of a pathological nature.

Abo ('æbəʊ) NOUN, *plural* **Abos.** (*sometimes not capital*) *Austral informal, offensive* **a** short for **Aborigine. b** (*as modifier*): *an Abo reserve.*

Åbo ('o:bu:) NOUN the Swedish name for **Turku.**

aboard (ə'bɔ:d) ADVERB, ADJECTIVE (*postpositive*), PREPOSITION [1] on, in, onto, or into (a ship, train, aircraft, etc.). [2] *Nautical* alongside (a vessel). [3] **all aboard!** a warning to passengers to board a vehicle, ship, etc.

abode¹ (ə'bəʊd) NOUN a place in which one lives; one's home.
▷HISTORY C17: n formed from ABIDE

abode² (ə'bəʊd) VERB a past tense and past participle of **abide.**

abohm (æb'əʊm, 'æbˌəʊm) NOUN the cgs unit of resistance in the electromagnetic system: equivalent to 10^{-9} ohm.

aboideau ('æbəˌdəʊ) *or* **aboiteau** ('æbəˌtəʊ) NOUN, *plural* **-deaus, -deaux** (-ˌdəʊz) *or* **-teaus, -teaux** (-ˌtəʊz). (in the Canadian Maritimes) [1] a dyke with a sluicegate that allows flood water to drain but keeps the sea water out. [2] a sluicegate in a dyke.
▷HISTORY Canadian French

abolish (ə'bɒlɪʃ) VERB (*tr*) to do away with (laws, regulations, customs, etc.); put an end to.
▷HISTORY C15: from Old French *aboliss-* (lengthened stem of *abolir*), ultimately from Latin *abolēre* to destroy
▸**a'bolishable** ADJECTIVE ▸**a'bolisher** NOUN ▸**a'bolishment** NOUN

abolition (ˌæbə'lɪʃən) NOUN [1] the act of abolishing or the state of being abolished; annulment. [2] (*often capital*) (in British territories) the ending of the slave trade (1807) or the ending of slavery (1833): accomplished after a long campaign led by William Wilberforce. [3] (*often capital*) (in the US) the emancipation of the slaves, accomplished by the Emancipation Proclamation issued in 1863 and ratified in 1865.
▷HISTORY C16: from Latin *abolitio,* from *abolēre* to destroy
▸ˌ**abo'litionary** ADJECTIVE ▸ˌ**abo'litionism** NOUN
▸ˌ**abo'litionist** NOUN, ADJECTIVE

abomasum (ˌæbə'meɪsəm) NOUN the fourth and last compartment of the stomach of ruminants, which receives and digests food from the psalterium and passes it on to the small intestine.
▷HISTORY C18: New Latin, from AB-¹ + *omāsum* bullock's tripe

A-bomb NOUN short for **atomic bomb.**

abominable (ə'bɒmɪnəbᵊl) ADJECTIVE [1] offensive; loathsome; detestable. [2] *Informal* very bad, unpleasant, or inferior: *abominable weather; abominable workmanship.*
▷HISTORY C14: from Latin *abōminābilis,* from *abōminārī* to ABOMINATE
▸**a'bominably** ADVERB

abominable snowman NOUN a large legendary manlike or apelike creature, alleged to inhabit the Himalayan Mountains. Also called: **yeti.**
▷HISTORY a translation of Tibetan *metohkangmi,* from *metoh* foul + *kangmi* snowman

abominate (ə'bɒmɪˌneɪt) VERB (*tr*) to dislike intensely; loathe; detest.
▷HISTORY C17: from the past participle of Latin *abōminārī* to regard as an ill omen, from *ab-* away from + *ōmin-,* from OMEN
▸**a'bomiˌnator** NOUN

abomination (əˌbɒmɪ'neɪʃən) NOUN [1] a person or thing that is disgusting. [2] an action that is vicious, vile, etc. [3] intense loathing.

abondance (*French* abɔ̃dɑ̃s) NOUN *Cards* a variant spelling of **abundance** (sense 6).

à bon marché *French* (a bɔ̃ marʃe) ADVERB at a bargain price.

aboral (æb'ɔ:rəl) ADJECTIVE *Zoology* away from or opposite the mouth.

aboriginal (ˌæbə'rɪdʒɪnᵊl) ADJECTIVE existing in a place from the earliest known period; indigenous; autochthonous.
▸ˌ**abo'riginally** ADVERB

Aboriginal (ˌæbə'rɪdʒɪnᵊl) ADJECTIVE [1] of, relating to, or characteristic of the native peoples of Australia. ◆ NOUN [2] another word for an Australian **Aborigine.**

Aboriginality (ˌæbəˌrɪdʒɪ'nælɪtɪ) NOUN the state of being Aboriginal, esp with regard to having a common Aboriginal culture.

aborigine (ˌæbə'rɪdʒɪnɪ) NOUN an original inhabitant of a country or region who has been there from the earliest known times.
▷HISTORY C16: back formation from *aborigines,* from Latin: inhabitants of Latium in pre-Roman times, probably representing some tribal name but associated in folk etymology with *ab origine* from the beginning

Aborigine (ˌæbə'rɪdʒɪnɪ) NOUN [1] Also called: **native Australian, Aboriginal,** (Austral) **native,** (Austral) **Black.** a member of a dark-skinned hunting and gathering people who were living in Australia when European settlers arrived. [2] any of the languages of this people. See also **Australian** (sense 3).

aborning (ə'bɔ:nɪŋ) ADVERB *US* while being born, developed, or realized (esp in the phrase **die aborning**).
▷HISTORY C20: from A-² + *borning,* from BORN

abort (ə'bɔ:t) VERB [1] to undergo or cause (a woman) to undergo the termination of pregnancy before the fetus is viable. [2] (*tr*) to cause (a fetus) to be expelled from the womb before it is viable. [3] (*intr*) to fail to come to completion; go wrong. [4] (*tr*) to stop the development of; cause to be abandoned. [5] (*intr*) to give birth to a dead or nonviable fetus. [6] (of a space flight, military operation, etc.) to fail or terminate prematurely. [7] (*intr*) (of an organism or part of an organism) to fail to develop into the mature form. ◆ NOUN [8] the premature termination or failure of (a space flight, military operation, etc.).
▷HISTORY C16: from Latin *abortāre,* from the past participle of *aborīrī* to miscarry, from *ab-* wrongly, badly + *orīrī* to appear, arise, be born

abortifacient (əˌbɔ:tɪ'feɪʃənt) ADJECTIVE [1] causing abortion. ◆ NOUN [2] a drug or agent that causes abortion.

abortion (ə'bɔ:ʃən) NOUN [1] an operation or other procedure to terminate pregnancy before the fetus is viable. [2] the premature termination of pregnancy by spontaneous or induced expulsion of a nonviable fetus from the uterus. [3] the products of abortion; an aborted fetus. [4] the arrest of development of an organ. [5] a failure to develop to completion or maturity: *the project proved an abortion.* [6] a person or thing that is deformed.
▸**a'bortional** ADJECTIVE

abortionist (ə'bɔ:ʃənɪst) NOUN [1] a person who performs abortions, esp illegally. [2] a person who is in favour of abortion on demand.

abortion pill NOUN a drug, such as mifepristone, used to terminate a pregnancy in its earliest stage.

abortive (ə'bɔ:tɪv) ADJECTIVE [1] failing to achieve a purpose; fruitless. [2] (of organisms) imperfectly developed; rudimentary. [3] causing abortion; abortifacient.

ABO system NOUN a system for classifying human blood on the basis of the presence or absence of two antigens on the red cell membrane: there are four such blood types (A, B, AB, and O).

Aboukir Bay *or* **Abukir Bay** (ˌæbu:'kɪə) NOUN a bay on the N coast of Egypt, where the Nile enters the Mediterranean: site of the Battle of the Nile (1798), in which Nelson defeated the French fleet. Arabic name: **Abu Qîr** (abu'ki:r).

aboulia (ə'bu:lɪə, -'bju:-) NOUN a variant spelling of **abulia.**

abound (ə'baʊnd) VERB (*intr*) [1] to exist or occur in abundance; be plentiful: *a swamp in which snakes abound.* [2] (foll by *with* or *in*) to be plentifully supplied (with); teem (with): *the gardens abound with flowers; the fields abound in corn.*
▷HISTORY C14: via Old French from Latin *abundāre* to overflow, from *undāre* to flow, from *unda* wave

about (ə'baʊt) PREPOSITION [1] relating to; concerning; on the subject of. [2] near or close to (in space or time). [3] carried on: *I haven't any money about me.* [4] on every side of; all the way around. [5] active in or engaged in: *she is about her business.* [6] **about to. a** on the point of; intending to: *she was about to jump.* **b** (*with a negative*) determined not to: *nobody is about to miss it.* ◆ ADVERB [7] approximately; near in number, time, degree, etc.: *about 50 years old.* [8] nearby. [9] here and there; from place to place; in no particular direction: *walk about to keep warm.* [10] all around; on every side. [11] in or to the opposite direction: *he turned about and came back.* [12] in rotation or revolution: *turn and turn about.* [13] used in informal phrases to indicate understatement: *I've had just about enough of your insults; it's about time you stopped.* [14] *Archaic* in circumference; around. ◆ ADJECTIVE [15] (*predicative*) active; astir after sleep: *up and about.* [16] (*predicative*) in existence, current, or in circulation: *there aren't many about nowadays.*
▷HISTORY Old English *abūtan, onbūtan* on the outside of, around, from ON + *būtan* outside

about-ship VERB **-ships, -shipping, -shipped.** (*intr*) *Nautical* to manoeuvre a vessel onto a new tack.

about turn *or US* **about face** INTERJECTION [1] a military command to a formation of men to reverse the direction in which they are facing. ◆ NOUN **about-turn,** *or US* **about-face.** [2] a complete change or reversal, as of opinion, attitude, direction, etc. ◆ VERB **about-turn,** *or US* **about-face.** [3] (*intr*) to perform an about-turn.

above (ə'bʌv) PREPOSITION [1] on top of or higher than; over: *the sky above the earth.* [2] greater than in quantity or degree: *above average in weight.* [3] superior to or prior to: *to place honour above wealth.* [4] too honourable or high-minded for: *above petty gossiping.* [5] too respected for; beyond: *above suspicion; above reproach.* [6] too difficult to be understood by: *the talk was above me.* [7] louder or higher than (other noise): *I heard her call above the radio.* [8] in preference to: *I love you above all others.* [9] north of: *which town lies just above London?* [10] upstream from. [11] **above all.** most of all; especially. [12] **above and beyond.** in addition to. [13] **above oneself.** presumptuous or conceited. ◆ ADVERB [14] in or to a higher place: *the sky above.* [15] **a** in a previous place (in something written). **b** (*in combination*): *the above-mentioned clause.* [16] higher in rank or position. [17] in or concerned with heaven: *seek the things that are above.* ◆ NOUN [18] **the above.** something that is above or previously mentioned. ◆ ADJECTIVE [19] mentioned or appearing in a previous place (in something written).
▷HISTORY Old English *abufan,* from *a-* on + *bufan* above

above board ADJECTIVE (**aboveboard** *when*

prenominal), ADVERB in the open; without dishonesty, concealment, or fraud.

above-the-line ADJECTIVE [1] denoting entries printed above the horizontal line on a company's profit-and-loss account separating the entries that show how the profit (or loss) was made from the entries showing how the profit is to be distributed. [2] (of an advertising campaign) employing an advertising agency to use the press, television, radio, cinema, and posters. [3] (in national accounts) denoting transactions concerned with revenue shown above a horizontal line that separates them from capital transactions. Compare **below-the-line.**

ab ovo *Latin* (æb 'əʊvəʊ) from the beginning.
▷HISTORY literally: from the egg

Abp *or* **abp** ABBREVIATION FOR archbishop.

abracadabra (ˌæbrəkə'dæbrə) INTERJECTION [1] a spoken formula, used esp by conjurors. ◆ NOUN [2] a word used in incantations, etc., considered to possess magic powers. [3] gibberish; nonsense.
▷HISTORY C17: from Latin: magical word used in certain Gnostic writings, perhaps related to Greek *Abraxas;* see ABRAXAS

abrade (ə'breɪd) VERB (*tr*) to scrape away or wear down by friction; erode.
▷HISTORY C17: from Latin *abrādere* to scrape away, from AB-^{1} + *rādere* to scrape
▸**a'bradant** NOUN ▸**a'brader** NOUN

Abraham ('eɪbrəˌhæm, -həm) NOUN [1] *Old Testament* the first of the patriarchs, the father of Isaac and the founder of the Hebrew people (Genesis 11–25). [2] **Abraham's bosom.** the place where the just repose after death (Luke 16:22).

abranchiate (ə'bræŋkɪɪt, -ˌeɪt) *or* **abranchial** ADJECTIVE *Zoology* having no gills.
▷HISTORY C19: A-^{1} + BRANCHIATE

abrasion (ə'breɪʒən) NOUN [1] the process of scraping or wearing down by friction. [2] a scraped area or spot; graze. [3] *Geography* the effect of mechanical erosion of rock, esp a river bed, by rock fragments scratching and scraping it; wearing down. Compare **attrition** (sense 4f), **corrasion.**
▷HISTORY C17: from Medieval Latin *abrāsiōn-*, from the past participle of Latin *abrādere* to ABRADE

abrasive (ə'breɪsɪv) NOUN [1] a substance or material such as sandpaper, pumice, or emery, used for cleaning, grinding, smoothing, or polishing. ◆ ADJECTIVE [2] causing abrasion; grating; rough. [3] irritating in manner or personality; causing tension or annoyance.
▸**a'brasiveness** NOUN

abraxas (ə'bræksəs) *or* **abrasax** (ə'bræsəks) NOUN an ancient charm composed of Greek letters: originally believed to have magical powers and inscribed on amulets, etc., but from the second century A.D. personified by Gnostics as a deity, the source of divine emanations.
▷HISTORY from Greek: invented word

abreact (ˌæbrɪ'ækt) VERB (*tr*) *Psychoanal* to alleviate (emotional tension) through abreaction.

abreaction (ˌæbrɪ'ækʃən) NOUN *Psychoanal* the release and expression of emotional tension associated with repressed ideas by bringing those ideas into consciousness.

abreast (ə'brɛst) ADJECTIVE (*postpositive*) [1] alongside each other and facing in the same direction. [2] (foll by *of* or *with*) up to date (with); fully conversant (with).

abri (æ'briː) NOUN a shelter or place of refuge, esp in wartime.
▷HISTORY French, from Latin *apricum* an open place

abridge (ə'brɪdʒ) VERB (*tr*) [1] to reduce the length of (a written work) by condensing or rewriting. [2] to curtail; diminish. [3] *Archaic* to deprive of (privileges, rights, etc.).
▷HISTORY C14: via Old French *abregier* from Late Latin *abbreviāre* to shorten
▸**a'bridgable** *or* **a'bridgeable** ADJECTIVE ▸**a'bridger** NOUN

abridgment *or* **abridgement** (ə'brɪdʒmənt) NOUN [1] a shortened version of a written work. [2] the act of abridging or state of being abridged.

abroach (ə'brəʊtʃ) ADJECTIVE (*postpositive*) (of a cask, barrel, etc.) tapped; broached.
▷HISTORY C14: from Old French *abrochier* from *a-* to + *brochier* to BROACH^{1}

abroad (ə'brɔːd) ADVERB [1] to or in a foreign country or countries. ◆ ADJECTIVE (*postpositive*) [2] (of news, rumours, etc.) in general circulation; current. [3] out in the open. [4] over a wide area. [5] *Archaic* in error.
▷HISTORY C13: from A-^{2} + BROAD

abrogate ('æbrəʊˌgeɪt) VERB (*tr*) to cancel or revoke formally or officially; repeal; annul.
▷HISTORY C16: from Latin *abrogātus* repealed, from AB-^{1} + *rogāre* to propose (a law)
▸ˌ**abro'gation** NOUN ▸'**abroˌgator** NOUN

abrupt (ə'brʌpt) ADJECTIVE [1] sudden; unexpected. [2] brusque or brief in speech, manner, etc.; curt. [3] (of a style of writing or speaking) making sharp transitions from one subject to another; disconnected. [4] precipitous; steep. [5] *Botany* shaped as though a part has been cut off; truncate. [6] *Geology* (of strata) cropping out suddenly.
▷HISTORY C16: from Latin *abruptus* broken off, from AB-^{1} + *rumpere* to break
▸**ab'ruptly** ADVERB ▸**ab'ruptness** NOUN

abruption (ə'brʌpʃən) NOUN a breaking off of a part or parts from a mass.
▷HISTORY C17: from Latin *abruptio;* see ABRUPT

Abruzzi (*Italian* a'bruttsi) *or* **Abruzzo** (*Italian* a'bruttso) NOUN a region of S central Italy, between the Apennines and the Adriatic: separated from the former administrative region **Abruzzi e Molise** in 1965. Capital: Aquila. Pop.: 1 279 016 (2000 est.). Area: 10 794 sq. km (4210 sq. miles).

abs (æbz) PLURAL NOUN *Informal* abdominal muscles.

ABS ABBREVIATION FOR acrylonitrile-butadiene-styrene: any of a range of tough copolymers used esp for making moulded articles.

Absalom ('æbsələm) NOUN *Old Testament* the third son of David, who rebelled against his father and was eventually killed by Joab (II Samuel 15–18).

ABS brake NOUN another name for **antilock brake.**
▷HISTORY from German *Antiblockiersystem*

abscess ('æbsɛs, -sɪs) NOUN [1] a localized collection of pus formed as the product of inflammation and usually caused by bacteria. ◆ VERB [2] (*intr*) to form such a collection of pus.
▷HISTORY C16: from Latin *abscessus* a going away, a throwing off of bad humours, hence an abscess, from *abscēdere* to go away
▸'**abscessed** ADJECTIVE

abscise (æb'saɪz) VERB to separate or be separated by abscission.
▷HISTORY C17: from Latin *abscīsus*, from *abscīdere* to cut off

abscissa (æb'sɪsə) NOUN, *plural* **-scissas** *or* **-scissae** (-'sɪsiː). the horizontal or *x*-coordinate of a point in a two-dimensional system of Cartesian coordinates. It is the distance from the *y*-axis measured parallel to the *x*-axis. Compare **ordinate.**
▷HISTORY C17: New Latin, originally *linea abscissa* a cut-off line

abscission (æb'sɪʒən, -'sɪʃ-) NOUN [1] the separation of leaves, branches, flowers, and bark from plants by the formation of an abscission layer. [2] the act of cutting off.
▷HISTORY C17: from Latin *abscissiōn-*, from AB-^{1} + *scissiō* a cleaving

abscission layer NOUN a layer of parenchyma cells that is formed at the bases of fruits, flowers, and leaves before abscission. As the parenchyma disintegrates, the organ becomes separated from the plant.

abscond (əb'skɒnd) VERB (*intr*) to run away secretly, esp from an open institution or to avoid prosecution or punishment.
▷HISTORY C16: from Latin *abscondere* to hide, put away, from *abs-* AB-^{1} + *condere* to stow
▸**ab'sconder** NOUN

abseil ('æbsaɪl) VERB (*intr*) [1] *Mountaineering* to descend a steep slope or vertical drop by a rope secured from above and coiled around one's body or through karabiners attached to one's body in order to control the speed of descent. [2] to descend by rope from a helicopter. ◆ NOUN [3] an instance or the technique of abseiling. ◆ Also called: **rappel.**
▷HISTORY C20: from German *abseilen* to descend by a rope, from *ab-* down + *Seil* rope

absence ('æbsəns) NOUN [1] the state of being away. [2] the time during which a person or thing is away. [3] the fact of being without something; lack.
▷HISTORY C14: via Old French from Latin *absentia*, from *absēns* a being away

absent ADJECTIVE ('æbsənt) [1] away or not present. [2] lacking; missing. [3] inattentive; absent-minded. ◆ VERB (æb'sɛnt) [4] (*tr*) to remove (oneself) or keep away.
▷HISTORY C14: from Latin *absent-*, stem of *absēns*, present participle of *abesse* to be away
▸**ab'senter** NOUN

absentee (ˌæbsən'tiː) NOUN **a** a person who is absent. **b** (*as modifier*): *an absentee voter.*

absenteeism (ˌæbsən'tiːɪzəm) NOUN persistent absence from work, school, etc.

absentee landlord NOUN a landlord who does not live in or near a property from which he draws an income.

absente reo (æb'sɛntɪ 'riːəʊ) *Law* in the absence of the defendant.
▷HISTORY Latin, literally: the defendant being absent

absently ('æbsəntlɪ) ADVERB in an absent-minded or preoccupied manner; inattentively.

absent-minded ADJECTIVE preoccupied; forgetful; inattentive.
▸ˌ**absent-'mindedly** ADVERB ▸ˌ**absent-'mindedness** NOUN

absent without leave *Military* the full form of **AWOL.**

absinthe *or* **absinth** ('æbsɪnθ) NOUN [1] a potent green alcoholic drink, technically a gin, originally having high wormwood content. [2] another name for **wormwood** (the plant).
▷HISTORY C15: via French and Latin from Greek *apsinthion* wormwood

absinthism ('æbsɪnˌθɪzəm) NOUN *Pathol* a diseased condition resulting from excessive drinking of absinthe.

absit omen *Latin* ('æbsɪt 'əʊmɛn) may the presentiment not become real or take place.
▷HISTORY literally: may the (evil) omen be absent

absolute ('æbsəˌluːt) ADJECTIVE [1] complete; perfect. [2] free from limitations, restrictions, or exceptions; unqualified: *an absolute choice.* [3] having unlimited authority; despotic: *an absolute ruler.* [4] undoubted; certain: *the absolute truth.* [5] not dependent on, conditioned by, or relative to anything else; independent: *an absolute term in logic; the absolute value of a quantity in physics.* [6] pure; unmixed: *absolute alcohol.* [7] (of a grammatical construction) syntactically independent of the main clause, as for example the construction *Joking apart* in the sentence *Joking apart, we'd better leave now.* [8] *Grammar* (of a transitive verb) used without a direct object, as the verb *intimidate* in the sentence *His intentions are good, but his rough manner tends to intimidate.* [9] *Grammar* (of an adjective) used as a noun, as for instance *young* and *aged* in the sentence *The young care little for the aged.* [10] *Physics* **a** (*postpositive*) (of a pressure measurement) not relative to atmospheric pressure: *the pressure was 5 bar absolute.* Compare **gauge** (sense 18). **b** denoting absolute or thermodynamic temperature. [11] *Maths* **a** (of a constant) never changing in value. **b** (of an inequality) unconditional. **c** (of a term) not containing a variable. [12] *Law* (of a court order or decree) coming into effect immediately and not liable to be modified; final. See **decree absolute.** [13] *Law* (of a title to property, etc.) not subject to any encumbrance or condition. ◆ NOUN [14] something that is absolute.
▷HISTORY C14: from Latin *absolūtus* unconditional, freed from, from *absolvere.* See ABSOLVE

Absolute ('æbsəˌluːt) NOUN (*sometimes not capital*) [1] *Philosophy* **a** the ultimate basis of reality. **b** that which is totally unconditioned, unrestricted, pure, perfect, or complete. [2] (in the philosophy of Hegel) that towards which all things evolve dialectically.

absolute alcohol NOUN a liquid containing at least 99 per cent of pure ethanol by weight.

absolute ceiling NOUN the maximum height above sea level, usually measured in feet or metres, at which an aircraft can maintain horizontal flight. Compare **service ceiling.**

absolute configuration NOUN *Chem* the spatial arrangement of atoms or groups in a chemical compound about an asymmetric atom. Also called: **absolute stereochemistry.** See **chirality.**

absolute humidity NOUN the humidity of the atmosphere, usually expressed as the number of grams of water contained in 1 cubic metre of air. Compare **relative humidity.**

absolute judgment NOUN *Psychol* any judgment about a single stimulus, e.g. about the value of one of its properties or about whether it is present or absent. Compare **comparative judgment.**

absolutely (ˌæbsəˈluːtlɪ) ADVERB [1] in an absolute manner, esp completely or perfectly. ◆ SENTENCE SUBSTITUTE [2] yes; certainly; unquestionably.

absolute magnitude NOUN the apparent magnitude a given star would have if it were situated at a distance of 10 parsecs (32.6 light years) from the earth.

absolute majority NOUN a number of votes totalling over 50 per cent, such as the total number of votes or seats obtained by a party that beats the combined opposition. Compare **relative majority.**

absolute monarchy NOUN a monarchy without constitutional limits. Compare **constitutional monarchy.**

absolute music NOUN music that is not designed to depict or evoke any scene or event. Compare **programme music.**

absolute pitch NOUN [1] Also called (not in technical usage): **perfect pitch.** the ability to identify exactly the pitch of a note without comparing it to another. [2] the exact pitch of a note determined by its number of vibrations per second.

absolute temperature NOUN another name for **thermodynamic temperature, Kelvin temperature.**

absolute threshold NOUN *Psychol* the minimum intensity of a stimulus at which it can just be perceived. Compare **difference threshold.**

absolute unit NOUN [1] a unit of measurement forming part of the electromagnetic cgs system, such as an abampere or abcoulomb. [2] a unit of measurement forming part of a system of units that includes a unit of force defined so that it is independent of the acceleration of free fall.

absolute value NOUN *Maths* [1] the positive real number equal to a given real but disregarding its sign. Written $|x|$. Where r is positive, $|r| = r = |-r|$. [2] Also called: **modulus.** a measure of the magnitude of a complex number, represented by the length of a line in the Argand diagram: $|x + iy| = \sqrt{(x^2 + y^2)}$, so $|4 + 3i| = 5$.

absolute viscosity NOUN a full name for **viscosity**, used to distinguish it from kinematic viscosity and specific viscosity

absolute zero NOUN the lowest temperature theoretically attainable, at which the particles constituting matter would be in the lowest energy states available; the zero of thermodynamic temperature; zero on the International Practical Scale of Temperature: equivalent to –273.15°C or –459.67°F.

absolution (ˌæbsəˈluːʃən) NOUN [1] the act of absolving or the state of being absolved; release from guilt, obligation, or punishment. [2] *Christianity* **a** a formal remission of sin pronounced by a priest in the sacrament of penance. **b** the prescribed form of words granting such a remission.
▷HISTORY C12: from Latin *absolūtiōn-* acquittal, forgiveness of sins, from *absolvere* to ABSOLVE
▸**absolutory** (æbˈsɒljʊtərɪ, -trɪ) ADJECTIVE

absolutism (ˈæbsəluːˌtɪzəm) NOUN [1] the principle or practice of a political system in which unrestricted power is vested in a monarch, dictator, etc.; despotism. [2] *Philosophy* **a** any theory which holds that truth or moral or aesthetic value is absolute and universal and not relative to individual or social differences. Compare **relativism. b** the doctrine that reality is unitary and unchanging and that change and diversity are mere illusion. See also **monism** (sense 2). [3] *Christianity* an uncompromising form of the doctrine of predestination.
▸**ˈabsoˌlutist** NOUN, ADJECTIVE

absolve (əbˈzɒlv) VERB (*tr*) [1] (usually foll by *from*) to release from blame, sin, punishment, obligation, or responsibility. [2] to pronounce not guilty; acquit; pardon.
▷HISTORY C15: from Latin *absolvere* to free from, from AB-[1] + *solvere* to make loose
▸**abˈsolvable** ADJECTIVE ▸**abˈsolver** NOUN

absorb (əbˈsɔːb, -ˈzɔːb) VERB (*tr*) [1] to soak or suck up (liquids). [2] to engage or occupy (the interest, attention, or time) of (someone); engross. [3] to receive or take in (the energy of an impact). [4] *Physics* to take in (all or part of incident radiated energy) and retain the part that is not reflected or transmitted. [5] to take in or assimilate; incorporate. [6] to accept and find a market for (goods, etc.). [7] to pay for as part of a commercial transaction: *the distributor absorbed the cost of transport.* [8] *Chem* to cause to undergo a process in which one substance, usually a liquid or gas, permeates into or is dissolved by a liquid or solid: *porous solids absorb water; hydrochloric acid absorbs carbon dioxide.* Compare **adsorb.**
▷HISTORY C15: via Old French from Latin *absorbēre* to suck, swallow, from AB-[1] + *sorbēre* to suck
▸**abˌsorbaˈbility** NOUN ▸**abˈsorbable** ADJECTIVE

absorbance (əbˈsɔːbəns, -ˈzɔː-) NOUN *Physics* a measure of the light-absorbing ability of an object, expressed as the logarithm to base 10 of the reciprocal of the internal transmittance. See **transmittance.**

absorbed (əbˈsɔːbd, -ˈzɔːbd) ADJECTIVE engrossed; deeply interested.
▸**absorbedly** (əbˈsɔːbɪdlɪ, -ˈzɔː-) ADVERB

absorbed dose NOUN the amount of energy transferred by nuclear or ionizing radiation to a unit mass of absorbing material.

absorbefacient (əbˌsɔːbɪˈfeɪʃənt, -ˌzɔː-) *Med* ◆ NOUN [1] a medicine or other agent that promotes absorption. ◆ ADJECTIVE [2] causing or promoting absorption.

absorbent (əbˈsɔːbənt, -ˈzɔː-) ADJECTIVE [1] able to absorb. ◆ NOUN [2] a substance that absorbs.
▸**abˈsorbency** NOUN

absorbent cotton NOUN a US term for **cotton wool** (sense 1).

absorber (əbˈsɔːbə, -ˈzɔː-) NOUN [1] a person or thing that absorbs. [2] *Physics* a material that absorbs radiation or causes it to lose energy.

absorbing (əbˈsɔːbɪŋ, -ˈzɔːb-) ADJECTIVE occupying one's interest or attention; engrossing; gripping.
▸**abˈsorbingly** ADVERB

absorptance (əbˈsɔːptəns, -ˈzɔːp-) *or* **absorption factor** NOUN *Physics* a measure of the ability of an object to absorb radiation, equal to the ratio of the absorbed radiant flux to the incident flux. For a layer of material the ratio of the flux absorbed between the entry and exit surfaces of the layer to the flux leaving the entry surface is the **internal absorptance.** Symbol: α. Compare **reflectance, transmittance.**
▷HISTORY C20: ABSORPTION + -ANCE

absorption (əbˈsɔːpʃən, -ˈzɔːp-) NOUN [1] the process of absorbing or the state of being absorbed. [2] *Physiol* **a** normal assimilation by the tissues of the products of digestion. **b** the passage of a gas, fluid, drug, etc., through the mucous membranes or skin. [3] *Physics* a reduction of the intensity of any form of radiated energy as a result of energy conversion in a medium, such as the conversion of sound energy into heat. [4] *Immunol* the process of removing superfluous antibodies or antigens from a mixture using a reagent.
▷HISTORY C16: from Latin *absorptiōn-*, from *absorbēre* to ABSORB
▸**abˈsorptive** ADJECTIVE

absorption costing NOUN a method of cost accounting in which overheads are apportioned to cost centres, where they are absorbed using predetermined rates. Compare **marginal costing.**

absorption spectrum NOUN the characteristic pattern of dark lines or bands that occurs when electromagnetic radiation is passed through an absorbing medium into a spectroscope. An equivalent pattern occurs as coloured lines or bands in the emission spectrum of that medium.

absorptivity (ˌæbsɔːpˈtɪvɪtɪ, -zɔːp-) NOUN *Physics* a measure of the ability of a material to absorb radiation, equal to the internal absorptance of a homogeneous layer of the material under conditions in which the path of the radiation has unit length and the boundaries of the layer have no influence.

absquatulate (æbˈskwɒtjʊˌleɪt) VERB (*intr*) to leave; decamp.
▷HISTORY C19: humorous formation as if from Latin

abstain (əbˈsteɪn) VERB (*intr;* usually foll by *from*) [1] to choose to refrain: *he abstained from alcohol.* [2] to refrain from voting, esp in a committee, legislature, etc.
▷HISTORY C14: via Old French from Latin *abstinēre*, from *abs-* AB-[1] + *tenēre* to hold, keep
▸**abˈstainer** NOUN

abstemious (əbˈstiːmɪəs) ADJECTIVE moderate or sparing, esp in the consumption of alcohol or food; temperate.
▷HISTORY C17: from Latin *abstēmius*, from *abs-* AB-[1] + *tēm-*, from *tēmētum* intoxicating drink
▸**abˈstemiously** ADVERB ▸**abˈstemiousness** NOUN

abstention (əbˈstɛnʃən) NOUN [1] a voluntary decision not to act; the act of refraining or abstaining. [2] the act of withholding one's vote.
▷HISTORY C16: from Late Latin *abstentiōn-*, from Latin *abstinēre.* See ABSTAIN
▸**abˈstentious** ADJECTIVE

abstergent (əbˈstɜːdʒənt) ADJECTIVE cleansing or scouring.
▷HISTORY C17: from Latin *abstergent-, abstergens* wiping off, from *abs-* away, off + *tergēre* to wipe

abstinence (ˈæbstɪnəns) NOUN [1] the act or practice of refraining from some action or from the use of something, esp alcohol. [2] *Chiefly RC Church* the practice of refraining from specific kinds of food or drink, esp from meat, as an act of penance.
▷HISTORY C13: via Old French from Latin *abstinentia*, from *abstinēre* to ABSTAIN
▸**ˈabstinent** ADJECTIVE

abstract ADJECTIVE (ˈæbstrækt) [1] having no reference to material objects or specific examples; not concrete. [2] not applied or practical; theoretical. [3] hard to understand; recondite; abstruse. [4] denoting art characterized by geometric, formalized, or otherwise nonrepresentational qualities. [5] defined in terms of its formal properties: *an abstract machine.* [6] *Philosophy* (of an idea) functioning for some empiricists as the meaning of a general term: *the word "man" does not name all men but the abstract idea of manhood.* ◆ NOUN (ˈæbstrækt) [7] a condensed version of a piece of writing, speech, etc.; summary. [8] an abstract term or idea. [9] an abstract painting, sculpture, etc. [10] **in the abstract.** without reference to specific circumstances or practical experience. ◆ VERB (æbˈstrækt) (*tr*) [11] to think of (a quality or concept) generally without reference to a specific example; regard theoretically. [12] to form (a general idea) by abstraction. [13] (ˈæbstrækt) (*also intr*) to summarize or epitomize. [14] to remove or extract. [15] *Euphemistic* to steal.
▷HISTORY C14 (in the sense: extracted): from Latin *abstractus* drawn off, removed from (something specific), from *abs-* AB-[1] + *trahere* to draw

abstracted (æbˈstræktɪd) ADJECTIVE [1] lost in thought; preoccupied. [2] taken out or separated; extracted.
▸**abˈstractedly** ADVERB ▸**abˈstractedness** NOUN

abstract expressionism NOUN a school of painting in New York in the 1940s that combined the spontaneity of expressionism with abstract forms in unpremeditated, apparently random, compositions. See also **action painting, tachisme.**

abstraction (æbˈstrækʃən) NOUN [1] absence of mind; preoccupation. [2] the process of formulating generalized ideas or concepts by extracting common qualities from specific examples. [3] an idea or concept formulated in this way: *good and evil are abstractions.* [4] *Logic* an operator that forms a class name or predicate from any given expression. See also **lambda-calculus.** [5] an abstract painting, sculpture, etc. [6] the act of withdrawing or removing.
▸**abˈstractive** ADJECTIVE ▸**abˈstractively** ADVERB

abstractionism (æbˈstrækʃəˌnɪzəm) NOUN the theory and practice of the abstract, esp of abstract art.
▸**abˈstractionist** NOUN

abstract noun NOUN a noun that refers to an abstract concept, as for example *kindness.* Compare **concrete noun.**

abstract of title NOUN *Property law* a summary of the ownership of land, showing the original grant, conveyances, and any incumbrances.

abstriction (æb'strɪkʃən) NOUN the separation and release of a mature spore from a sporophore by the formation of a septum. This process occurs in some fungi.
▷HISTORY C17: from Latin AB-[1] + *strictio* a binding, from *stringere* to bind

abstruse (əb'struːs) ADJECTIVE not easy to understand; recondite; esoteric.
▷HISTORY C16: from Latin *abstrūsus* thrust away, concealed, from *abs-* AB-[1] + *trūdere* to thrust
▸**ab'strusely** ADVERB ▸**ab'struseness** NOUN

absurd (əb'sɜːd) ADJECTIVE [1] at variance with reason; manifestly false. [2] ludicrous; ridiculous. ◆ NOUN [3] *Philosophy* (*sometimes capital;* often preceded by *the*) the conception of the world, esp in Existentialist thought, as neither designed nor predictable but irrational and meaningless. ◆ See also **theatre of the absurd.**
▷HISTORY C16: via French from Latin *absurdus* dissonant, senseless, from AB-[1] (intensive) + *surdus* dull-sounding, indistinct
▸**ab'surdity** *or* **ab'surdness** NOUN ▸**ab'surdly** ADVERB

ABTA ('æbtə) NOUN ACRONYM FOR Association of British Travel Agents.

Abu Dhabi ('æbuː 'dɑːbɪ) NOUN a sheikdom (emirate) of SE Arabia, on the S coast of the Persian Gulf: the chief sheikdom and capital of the United Arab Emirates, consisting principally of the port of Abu Dhabi and a desert hinterland; contains major oilfields. Pop.: 1 186 000 (2001 est.). Area: 67 350 sq. km (25 998 sq. miles).

Abuja (ə'buːdʒə) NOUN the federal capital of Nigeria, in the centre of the country. Pop.: 350 100 (1996 est.).

Abukir Bay (ˌæbuː'kɪə) NOUN a variant spelling of **Aboukir Bay.**

abulia *or* **aboulia** (ə'buːlɪə, -'bjuː-) NOUN *Psychiatry* a pathological inability to take decisions.
▷HISTORY C19: New Latin, from Greek *aboulia* lack of resolution, from A-[1] + *boulē* will
▸**a'bulic** ADJECTIVE

abundance (ə'bʌndəns) NOUN [1] a copious supply; great amount. [2] fullness or benevolence: *from the abundance of my heart.* [3] degree of plentifulness. [4] *Chem* the extent to which an element or ion occurs in the earth's crust or some other specified environment: often expressed in parts per million or as a percentage. [5] *Physics* the ratio of the number of atoms of a specific isotope in a mixture of isotopes of an element to the total number of atoms present: often expressed as a percentage: *the abundance of neon-22 in natural neon is 8.82 per cent.* [6] Also called: **abondance.** a call in solo whist undertaking to make nine tricks. [7] affluence.
▷HISTORY C14: via Old French from Latin *abundantia,* from *abundāre* to ABOUND

abundant (ə'bʌndənt) ADJECTIVE [1] existing in plentiful supply. [2] (*postpositive;* foll by *in*) having a plentiful supply (of). [3] (of a chemical element or mineral) occurring to an extent specified in relation to other elements or minerals in the earth's crust or some other specified environment. [4] (of an isotope) occurring to an extent specified in relation to other isotopes in a mixture of isotopes.
▷HISTORY C14: from Latin *abundant-,* present participle of *abundāre* to ABOUND

abundantly (ə'bʌndəntlɪ) ADVERB [1] very: *he made his disagreement with her abundantly clear.* [2] plentifully; in abundance.

ab urbe condita *Latin* (æb 'ɜːbɪ 'kɒndɪtə) the full form of **AUC** (sense **a**).
▷HISTORY literally: from the founding of the city

A bursary NOUN *NZ* the higher of two bursaries available for students entering university, polytechnic, etc. Compare **B bursary.**

abuse VERB (ə'bjuːz) (*tr*) [1] to use incorrectly or improperly; misuse. [2] to maltreat, esp physically or sexually. [3] to speak insultingly or cruelly to; revile. [4] (*reflexive*) to masturbate. ◆ NOUN (ə'bjuːs) [5] improper, incorrect, or excessive use; misuse. [6] maltreatment of a person; injury. [7] insulting, contemptuous, or coarse speech. [8] an evil, unjust, or corrupt practice. [9] See **child abuse.** [10] *Archaic* a deception.
▷HISTORY C14 (vb): via Old French from Latin *abūsus,* past participle of *abūtī* to misuse, from AB-[1] + *ūtī* to USE
▸**a'buser** NOUN

Abu Simbel (ˌæbuː 'sɪmbəl) NOUN a former village in S Egypt: site of two temples of Rameses II, which were moved to higher ground (1966–67) before the area behind the Aswan High Dam was flooded. Also called: **Ipsambul.**

abusive (ə'bjuːsɪv) ADJECTIVE [1] characterized by insulting or coarse language. [2] characterized by maltreatment. [3] incorrectly used; corrupt.
▸**a'busively** ADVERB ▸**a'busiveness** NOUN

abut (ə'bʌt) VERB **abuts, abutting, abutted.** (usually foll by *on, upon,* or *against*) to adjoin, touch, or border on (something) at one end.
▷HISTORY C15: from Old French *abouter* to join at the ends, border on; influenced by *abuter* to touch at an end, buttress

abutilon (ə'bjuːtɪlən) NOUN any shrub or herbaceous plant of the malvaceous genus *Abutilon,* such as the flowering maple, that have showy white, yellow, or red flowers.
▷HISTORY C18: New Latin from Arabic

abutment (ə'bʌtmənt) *or* **abuttal** NOUN [1] the state or process of abutting. [2] **a** something that abuts. **b** the thing on which something abuts. **c** the point of junction between them. [3] *Architect, civil engineering* a construction that takes the thrust of an arch or vault or supports the end of a bridge.

abuttals (ə'bʌtəlz) PLURAL NOUN *Property law* the boundaries of a plot of land where it abuts against other property.

abutter (ə'bʌtə) NOUN *Property law* the owner of adjoining property.

abuzz (ə'bʌz) ADJECTIVE (*postpositive*) humming, as with conversation, activity, etc.; buzzing.

ABV ABBREVIATION FOR alcohol by volume: the number of ml of ethyl alcohol present in each 100 ml of an alcoholic beverage when measured at 20°C; displayed on the packaging of alcoholic drinks in EU countries and used to calculate the amount of tax payable.

abvolt ('æbˌvəʊlt) NOUN the cgs unit of potential difference in the electromagnetic system; the potential difference between two points when work of 1 erg must be done to transfer 1 abcoulomb of charge from one point to the other: equivalent to 10^{-8} volt.

abwatt ('æbˌwɒt) NOUN the cgs unit of power in the electromagnetic system, equal to the power dissipated when a current of 1 abampere flows across a potential difference of 1 abvolt: equivalent to 10^{-7} watt.

aby *or* **abye** (ə'baɪ) VERB **abys** *or* **abyes, abying, abought.** (*tr*) *Archaic* to pay the penalty for; redeem.
▷HISTORY Old English *ābycgan* to pay for, atone for, from *bycgan* to buy

Abydos (ə'baɪdəs) NOUN [1] an ancient town in central Egypt: site of many temples and tombs. [2] an ancient Greek colony on the Asiatic side of the Dardanelles (Hellespont): scene of the legend of Hero and Leander.

abysm (ə'bɪzəm) NOUN an archaic word for **abyss.**
▷HISTORY C13: via Old French from Medieval Latin *abysmus* ABYSS

abysmal (ə'bɪzməl) ADJECTIVE [1] immeasurable; very great: *abysmal stupidity.* [2] *Informal* extremely bad: *an abysmal film.*
▸**a'bysmally** ADVERB

abyss (ə'bɪs) NOUN [1] a very deep or unfathomable gorge or chasm. [2] anything that appears to be endless or immeasurably deep, such as time, despair, or shame. [3] hell or the infernal regions conceived of as a bottomless pit.
▷HISTORY C16: via Late Latin from Greek *abussos* bottomless (as in the phrase *abussos limnē* bottomless lake), from A-[1] + *bussos* depth

abyssal (ə'bɪsəl) ADJECTIVE [1] of or belonging to the ocean depths, esp below 2000 metres (6500 feet): *abyssal zone.* [2] *Geology* another word for **plutonic.**

Abyssinia (ˌæbɪ'sɪnɪə) NOUN a former name for **Ethiopia.**

Abyssinian (ˌæbɪ'sɪnɪən) NOUN [1] a native or inhabitant of Abyssinia. ◆ ADJECTIVE [2] of or relating to Abyssinia or its inhabitants.

Abyssinian cat NOUN a variety of cat with a long body and a short brown coat with black or dark brown markings.

Abyssinian guinea pig NOUN a breed of short-haired guinea pig with rosettes all over its body.

abyssopelagic (əˌbɪsəʊpɛ'lædʒɪk) ADJECTIVE referring to or occurring in the region of deep water above the floor of the ocean.

ac THE INTERNET DOMAIN NAME FOR Ascension Island.

Ac THE CHEMICAL SYMBOL FOR actinium.

AC ABBREVIATION FOR: [1] **alternating current.** Compare **DC.** [2] ante Christum. [Latin: before Christ] [3] Air Corps. [4] athletic club. [5] Companion of the Order of Australia. [6] appellation d'origine contrôlée: the highest French wine classification; indicates that the wine meets strict requirements concerning area of production, strength, etc. Compare ***VDQS, vin de pays,*** or ***vin de table.*** [7] Aelodau'r Cynulliad: Member of the Assembly (that is, the National Assembly of Wales).

a.c. *Obsolete* ABBREVIATION FOR (in prescriptions) ante cibum.
▷HISTORY Latin: before meals

a/c *Book-keeping* ABBREVIATION FOR: [1] account. [2] account current.

A/C (in Canada) ABBREVIATION FOR Air Commodore.

ACA ABBREVIATION FOR Associate of the Institute of Chartered Accountants.

acacia (ə'keɪʃə) NOUN [1] any shrub or tree of the tropical and subtropical leguminous genus *Acacia,* having compound or reduced leaves and small yellow or white flowers in dense inflorescences. See also **wattle** (sense 4). [2] **false acacia.** another name for **locust** (senses 2, 3). [3] **gum acacia.** another name for **gum arabic.**
▷HISTORY C16: from Latin, from Greek *akakia,* perhaps related to *akē* point

academe ('ækəˌdiːm) NOUN *Literary* [1] any place of learning, such as a college or university. [2] **the grove(s) of Academe.** the academic world.
▷HISTORY C16: first used by Shakespeare in *Love's Labour's Lost* (1594); see ACADEMY

academia (ˌækə'diːmɪə) NOUN the academic world.

academic (ˌækə'dɛmɪk) ADJECTIVE [1] belonging or relating to a place of learning, esp a college, university, or academy. [2] of purely theoretical or speculative interest: *an academic argument.* [3] excessively concerned with intellectual matters and lacking experience of practical affairs. [4] (esp of a schoolchild) having an aptitude for study. [5] conforming to set rules and traditions; conventional: *an academic painter.* [6] relating to studies such as languages, philosophy, and pure science, rather than applied, technical, or professional studies. ◆ NOUN [7] a member of a college or university.
▸**ˌaca'demically** ADVERB

academicals (ˌækə'dɛmɪkəlz) PLURAL NOUN another term for **academic dress.**

academic dress NOUN formal dress, usually comprising cap, gown, and hood, worn by university staff and students.

academician (əˌkædə'mɪʃən, ˌækədə-) NOUN a member of an academy (sense 1).

academicism (ˌækə'dɛmɪˌsɪzəm) *or* **academism** (ə'kædəˌmɪzəm) NOUN adherence to rules and traditions in art, literature, etc.; conventionalism.

academy (ə'kædəmɪ) NOUN, *plural* **-mies.** [1] an institution or society for the advancement of literature, art, or science. [2] a school for training in a particular skill or profession: *a military academy.* [3] a secondary school: now used only as part of a name, and often denoting a private school.
▷HISTORY C16: via Latin from Greek *akadēmeia* name of the grove where Plato taught, named after the legendary hero *Akadēmos*

Academy (ə'kædəmɪ) NOUN **the.** [1] **a** the grove or garden near Athens where Plato taught in the late 4th century B.C. **b** the school of philosophy founded by Plato. **c** the members of this school and their successors. [2] short for the **French Academy, Royal Academy,** etc.

Academy Award NOUN the official name for an **Oscar.**

Acadia (ə'keɪdɪə) NOUN [1] **a** the Atlantic Provinces of Canada. **b** the French-speaking areas of these provinces. [2] (formerly) a French colony in the present-day Atlantic Provinces: ceded to Britain in 1713. ◆ French name: **Acadie** (akadi).

Acadian (əˈkeɪdɪən) ADJECTIVE 1 denoting or relating to Acadia or its inhabitants. ◆ NOUN 2 any of the early French settlers in Nova Scotia, many of whom were deported to Louisiana in the 18th century. See also **Cajun**.

acajou (ˈækəˌʒuː) NOUN 1 a type of mahogany used by cabinet-makers in France. 2 a less common name for **cashew**.
▷HISTORY C18: via French from Portuguese *acajú,* from Tupi

acalculia (ˌækælˈkjuːlɪə) NOUN *Psychol* an inability to make simple mathematical calculations.
▷HISTORY C20: from A-[1] + Latin *calculāre* to calculate

acaleph (ˈækəˌlɛf) NOUN *Obsolete* any of the coelenterates of the former taxonomic group *Acalephae,* which included the jellyfishes.
▷HISTORY C18: from New Latin, from Greek *akalēphē* a sting

acanthaceous (ˌækənˈθeɪʃəs) ADJECTIVE 1 of or relating to the *Acanthaceae,* a mainly tropical and subtropical family of flowering plants that includes the acanthus. 2 having spiny or prickly outgrowths.

acanthine (əˈkænθaɪn, -θiːn) ADJECTIVE 1 of or resembling an acanthus. 2 decorated with acanthus leaves.

acantho- *or before a vowel* **acanth-** COMBINING FORM indicating a spine or thorn: *acanthocephalan.*
▷HISTORY New Latin from Greek *akanthos* thorn plant, from *akantha* thorn

acanthocephalan (əˌkænθəʊˈsɛfələn) NOUN 1 any of the parasitic wormlike invertebrates of the phylum *Acanthocephala,* the adults of which have a spiny proboscis and live in the intestines of vertebrates. ◆ ADJECTIVE 2 of, relating to, or belonging to the *Acanthocephala.*

acanthoid (əˈkænθɔɪd) ADJECTIVE resembling a spine; spiny.

acanthopterygian (ˌækənˌθɒptəˈrɪdʒɪən) ADJECTIVE 1 of, relating to, or belonging to the *Acanthopterygii,* a large group of teleost fishes having spiny fin rays. The group includes most saltwater bony fishes. ◆ NOUN 2 any fish belonging to the *Acanthopterygii.* ◆ Compare **malacopterygian.**
▷HISTORY C19: from New Latin *Acanthopterygii,* from ACANTHO- + Greek *pterúgion* fin

acanthous (əˈkænθəs) ADJECTIVE another term for **spinous.**

acanthus (əˈkænθəs) NOUN, *plural* **-thuses** *or* **-thi** (-θaɪ). 1 any shrub or herbaceous plant of the genus *Acanthus,* native to the Mediterranean region but widely cultivated as ornamental plants, having large spiny leaves and spikes of white or purplish flowers: family *Acanthaceae.* See also **bear's-breech.** 2 a carved ornament based on the leaves of the acanthus plant, esp as used on the capital of a Corinthian column.
▷HISTORY C17: New Latin, from Greek *akanthos,* from *akantha* thorn, spine

a cappella (ɑː kəˈpɛlə) ADJECTIVE, ADVERB *Music* without instrumental accompaniment.
▷HISTORY Italian: literally, according to (the style of the) chapel

Acapulco (ˌækəˈpʊlkəʊ; *Spanish* akaˈpulko) NOUN a port and resort in SW Mexico, in Guerrero state. Pop.: 619 253 (2000 est.). Official name: **Acapulco de Juárez** (*Spanish* de ˈxwares).

acariasis (ˌækəˈraɪəsɪs) NOUN infestation of the hair follicles and skin with acarids, esp mites.
▷HISTORY C19: New Latin. See ACARUS, -IASIS

acaricide (əˈkærɪˌsaɪd) NOUN any drug or formulation for killing acarids.

acarid (ˈækərɪd) *or* **acaridan** (əˈkærɪdᵊn) NOUN 1 any of the small arachnids of the order *Acarina* (or *Acari*), which includes the ticks and mites. ◆ ADJECTIVE 2 of or relating to the order *Acarina.*
▷HISTORY C19: from ACARUS

acaroid (ˈækəˌrɔɪd) ADJECTIVE resembling a mite or tick.
▷HISTORY C19: see ACARUS, -OID

acaroid gum *or* **resin** NOUN a red alcohol-soluble resin that exudes from various species of grass tree, esp *Xanthorrhoea hastilis,* and is used in varnishes, for coating paper, etc. Also called: **gum acaroides, acaroid resin.**

▷HISTORY C19 *acaroid,* of uncertain origin (apparently not related to ACARUS)

acarology (ˌækəˈrɒlədʒɪ) NOUN the study of mites and ticks.

acarpellous *or US* **acarpelous** (eɪˈkɑːpələs) ADJECTIVE (of flowers) having no carpels.

acarpous (eɪˈkɑːpəs) ADJECTIVE (of plants) producing no fruit.
▷HISTORY from Greek *akarpos,* from A-[1] + *karpos* fruit

acarus (ˈækərəs) NOUN, *plural* **-ri** (-ˌraɪ). any of the free-living mites of the widely distributed genus *Acarus,* several of which, esp *A. siro,* are serious pests of stored flour, grain, etc.
▷HISTORY C17: New Latin, from Greek *akari* a small thing, a mite

ACAS *or* **Acas** (ˈeɪkæs) NOUN (in Britain) ACRONYM FOR Advisory Conciliation and Arbitration Service.

acatalectic (æˌkætəˈlɛktɪk) *Prosody* ◆ ADJECTIVE 1 having the necessary number of feet or syllables, esp having a complete final foot. ◆ NOUN 2 a verse having the full number of syllables.
▷HISTORY C16: via Late Latin from Greek *akatalēktikos.* See A-[1], CATALECTIC

acaudal (eɪˈkɔːdᵊl) *or* **acaudate** ADJECTIVE *Zoology* having no tail.

acaulescent (ˌækɔːˈlɛsᵊnt) ADJECTIVE having no visible stem or a very short one.

acauline (ˈækɔːˌlaɪn) *or* **acaulose** ADJECTIVE *Biology* having no stem.

ACC (in New Zealand) ABBREVIATION FOR Accident Compensation Corporation.

acc. ABBREVIATION FOR: 1 *Book-keeping* account. 2 *Grammar* accusative.

acca *or* **acker** (ˈækə) NOUN *Austral informal* an academic.
▷HISTORY C20: shortened form of ACADEMIC

ACCA ABBREVIATION FOR Associate of the Chartered Association of Certified Accountants.

Accad (ˈækæd) NOUN a variant spelling of **Akkad.**

Accademia (*Italian* akkaˈdɛmja) NOUN an art gallery in Venice housing a collection of paintings by Venetian masters from the 13th to 18th centuries. Full name: **Galleria dell' Accademia** (*Italian* galleˈria dell akkaˈdɛmja).

ACCC ABBREVIATION FOR Australian Competition and Consumer Commission.

accede (ækˈsiːd) VERB (*intr;* usually foll by *to*) 1 to assent or give one's consent; agree. 2 to enter upon or attain (to an office, right, etc.): *the prince acceded to the throne.* 3 *International law* to become a party (to an agreement between nations, etc.), as by signing a treaty.
▷HISTORY C15: from Latin *accēdere* to approach, agree, from *ad-* to + *cēdere* to go, yield
▸**ac'cedence** NOUN ▸**ac'ceder** NOUN

accel. ABBREVIATION FOR accelerando.

accelerando (ækˌsɛləˈrændəʊ) *Music* ◆ ADJECTIVE, ADVERB 1 (to be performed) with increasing speed. ◆ NOUN, *plural* **-dos.** 2 an increase in speed.
▷HISTORY Italian

accelerant (ækˈsɛlərənt) NOUN *Chem* another name for **accelerator** (sense 3).
▷HISTORY C20: from Latin from *accelerāns,* present participle of *accelerāre* to go faster

accelerate (ækˈsɛləˌreɪt) VERB 1 to go, occur, or cause to go or occur more quickly; speed up. 2 (*tr*) to cause to happen sooner than expected. 3 (*tr*) to increase the velocity of (a body, reaction, etc.); cause acceleration.
▷HISTORY C16: from Latin *accelerātus,* from *accelerāre* to go faster, from *ad-* (intensive) + *celerāre* to hasten, from *celer* swift
▸**ac'celerable** ADJECTIVE ▸**ac'celerative** *or* **ac'celeratory** ADJECTIVE

acceleration (ækˌsɛləˈreɪʃən) NOUN 1 the act of accelerating or the state of being accelerated. 2 the rate of increase of speed or the rate of change of velocity. Symbol: *a.*

acceleration of free fall NOUN the acceleration of a body falling freely in a vacuum near the surface of the earth in the earth's gravitational field: the standard value is 9.806 65 metres per second per second or 32.174 feet per second per second. Symbol: *g.* Also called: **acceleration due to gravity, acceleration of gravity.**

accelerator (ækˈsɛləˌreɪtə) NOUN 1 a device for increasing speed, esp a pedal for controlling the fuel intake in a motor vehicle; throttle. 2 Also called (not in technical usage): **atom smasher.** *Physics* a machine for increasing the kinetic energy of subatomic particles or atomic nuclei and focusing them on a target. 3 *Chem* a substance that increases the speed of a chemical reaction, esp one that increases the rate of vulcanization of rubber, the rate of development in photography, the rate of setting of synthetic resins, or the rate of setting of concrete; catalyst. 4 *Economics* (in an economy) the relationship between the rate of change in output or sales and the consequent change in the level of investment. 5 *Anatomy* a muscle or nerve that increases the rate of a function.

accelerometer (ækˌsɛləˈrɒmɪtə) NOUN an instrument for measuring acceleration, esp of an aircraft or rocket.

accent NOUN (ˈæksənt) 1 the characteristic mode of pronunciation of a person or group, esp one that betrays social or geographical origin. 2 the relative prominence of a spoken or sung syllable, esp with regard to stress or pitch. Compare **pitch**[1] (sense 28), **stress** (sense 3). 3 a mark (such as ˈ, ˌ, ˊ or ˋ) used in writing to indicate the stress or prominence of a syllable. Such a mark may also be used to indicate that a written syllable is to be pronounced, esp when such pronunciation is not usual, as in *turnèd.* 4 any of various marks or symbols conventionally used in writing certain languages to indicate the quality of a vowel, or for some other purpose, such as differentiation of homographs. See **acute** (sense 10), **grave**[2] (sense 5), **circumflex.** 5 (in some languages, such as Chinese) any of the tones that have phonemic value in distinguishing one word from another. Compare **tone** (sense 7). 6 rhythmic stress in verse or prose. 7 *Music* **a** stress placed on certain notes in a piece of music, indicated by a symbol printed over the note concerned. **b** the rhythmic pulse of a piece or passage, usually represented as the stress on the first beat of each bar. See also **syncopation.** 8 *Maths* either of two superscript symbols indicating a specific unit, such as feet (′), inches (″), minutes of arc (′), or seconds of arc (″). 9 a distinctive characteristic of anything, such as taste, pattern, style, etc. 10 particular attention or emphasis: *an accent on learning.* 11 a strongly contrasting detail: *a blue rug with red accents.* ◆ VERB (ækˈsɛnt) (*tr*) 12 to mark with an accent in writing, speech, music, etc. 13 to lay particular emphasis or stress on.
▷HISTORY C14: via Old French from Latin *accentus,* from *ad-* to + *cantus* chant, song. The Latin is a rendering of Greek *prosōidia* a song sung to music, the tone of a syllable

accentor (ækˈsɛntə) NOUN any small sparrow-like songbird of the genus *Prunella,* family *Prunellidae,* which inhabit mainly mountainous regions of Europe and Asia. See also **hedge sparrow.**

accentual (ækˈsɛntʃʊəl) ADJECTIVE 1 of, relating to, or having accents; rhythmic. 2 *Prosody* of or relating to verse based on the number of stresses in a line rather than on the number of syllables. Compare **quantitative.**
▸**ac'centually** ADVERB

accentuate (ækˈsɛntʃʊˌeɪt) VERB (*tr*) to stress or emphasize.
▸**acˌcentu'ation** NOUN

accept (əkˈsɛpt) VERB (*mainly tr*) 1 to take or receive (something offered). 2 to give an affirmative reply to: *to accept an invitation.* 3 to take on the responsibilities, duties, etc., of: *he accepted office.* 4 to tolerate or accommodate oneself to. 5 to consider as true or believe in (a philosophy, theory, etc.): *I cannot accept your argument.* 6 (*may take a clause as object*) to be willing to grant or believe: *you must accept that he lied.* 7 to receive with approval or admit, as into a community, group, etc. 8 *Commerce* to agree to pay (a bill, draft, shipping document, etc.), esp by signing. 9 to receive as adequate, satisfactory, or valid. 10 to receive, take, or hold (something applied, inserted, etc.). 11 (*intr;* sometimes foll by *of*) *Archaic* to take or receive an offer, invitation, etc.
▷HISTORY C14: from Latin *acceptāre,* from *ad-* to + *capere* to take
▸**ac'cepter** NOUN

acceptable (əkˈsɛptəbᵊl) ADJECTIVE [1] satisfactory; adequate. [2] pleasing; welcome. [3] tolerable. ▸**acˌceptaˈbility** *or* **acˈceptableness** NOUN ▸**acˈceptably** ADVERB

acceptance (əkˈsɛptəns) NOUN [1] the act of accepting or the state of being accepted or acceptable. [2] favourable reception; approval. [3] (often foll by *of*) belief (in) or assent (to). [4] *Commerce* **a** a formal agreement by a debtor to pay a draft, bill, etc. **b** the document so accepted. Compare **bank acceptance.** [5] (*plural*) *Austral and NZ* a list of horses accepted as starters in a race. [6] *Contract law* words or conduct by which a person signifies his assent to the terms and conditions of an offer or agreement.

acceptant (əkˈsɛptənt) ADJECTIVE receiving willingly; receptive.

acceptation (ˌæksɛpˈteɪʃən) NOUN the accepted meaning, as of a word, phrase, etc.

accepted (əkˈsɛptɪd) ADJECTIVE commonly approved or recognized; customary; established. ▸**acˈceptedly** ADVERB

accepting house NOUN a financial institution that guarantees a bill of exchange, as a result of which it can be discounted on more favourable terms.

acceptor (əkˈsɛptə) NOUN [1] *Commerce* the person or organization on which a draft or bill of exchange is drawn after liability has been accepted, usually by signature. [2] Also called: **acceptor impurity.** *Electronics* an impurity, such as gallium, added to a semiconductor material to increase its p-type conductivity by increasing the number of holes in the semiconductor. Compare **donor** (sense 5). [3] *Electronics* a circuit tuned to accept a particular frequency. [4] *Chem* the atom or group that accepts electrons in a coordinate bond.

access (ˈæksɛs) NOUN [1] the act of approaching or entering. [2] the condition of allowing entry, esp (of a building or room) allowing entry by wheelchairs, prams, etc. [3] the right or privilege to approach, reach, enter, or make use of something. [4] a way or means of approach or entry. [5] the opportunity or right to see or approach someone: *she fights for divorce and free access to her children.* [6] (*modifier*) designating programmes made by the general public as distinguished from those made by professional broadcasters: *access television.* [7] a sudden outburst or attack, as of rage or disease. ◆ VERB [8] to gain access to; make accessible or available. [9] (*tr*) *Computing* **a** to obtain or retrieve (information) from a storage device. **b** to place (information) in a storage device. See also **direct access, sequential access.**
▹**HISTORY** C14: from Old French or from Latin *accessus* an approach, from *accēdere* to ACCEDE

accessary (əkˈsɛsərɪ) NOUN, *plural* **-ries**, ADJECTIVE *Law* a less common spelling of **accessory.** ▸**acˈcessarily** ADVERB ▸**acˈcessariness** NOUN

access course NOUN (in Britain) an intensive course of study for people without academic qualifications that enables them to apply for higher education.

accessible (əkˈsɛsəbᵊl) ADJECTIVE [1] easy to approach, enter, or use. [2] **accessible to.** likely to be affected by; open to; susceptible to. [3] obtainable; available. [4] *Logic* (of a possible world) surveyable from some other world so that the truth value of statements about it can be known. A statement *possibly p* is true in a world W if and only if *p* is true in some worlds accessible to W. ▸**acˌcessiˈbility** NOUN ▸**acˈcessibly** ADVERB

accession (əkˈsɛʃən) NOUN [1] the act of entering upon or attaining to an office, right, condition, etc. [2] an increase due to an addition. [3] an addition, as to a collection. [4] *Property law* **a** an addition to land or property by natural increase or improvement. **b** the owner's right to the increased value of such land. [5] *International law* the formal acceptance of a convention or treaty. [6] agreement; consent. [7] a less common word for **access** (sense 1). ◆ VERB [8] (*tr*) to make a record of (additions to a collection). ▸**acˈcessional** ADJECTIVE

accession number NOUN *Library science* the number given to record a new addition to a collection.

accessorius (ˌæksɛsˈɔːrɪəs) NOUN *Anatomy* a muscle or nerve that has an augmenting action.

accessorize *or* **accessorise** (əkˈsɛsəˌraɪz) VERB (*tr*) to add accessories to: *accessorize a plain jacket with feminine jewellery.*

accessory (əkˈsɛsərɪ) NOUN, *plural* **-ries.** [1] a supplementary part or object, as of a car, appliance, etc. [2] (*often plural*) a small accompanying item of dress, esp of women's dress. [3] a person who incites someone to commit a crime or assists the perpetrator of a crime, either before or during its commission. ◆ ADJECTIVE [4] supplementary; additional; subordinate. [5] assisting in or having knowledge of an act, esp a crime.
▹**HISTORY** C17: from Late Latin *accessōrius:* see ACCESS
▸**accessorial** (ˌæksɛˈsɔːrɪəl) ADJECTIVE ▸**acˈcessorily** ADVERB ▸**acˈcessoriness** NOUN

accessory fruit NOUN another name for **pseudocarp.**

accessory nerve NOUN either one of the eleventh pair of cranial nerves, which supply the muscles of the head, shoulders, larynx, and pharynx and the viscera of the abdomen and thorax.

accessory shoe NOUN *Photog* a bracket on top of a camera to which a flash unit or other accessory may be fitted.

access road NOUN a road providing a means of entry into a region or of approach to another road, esp a motorway.

access time NOUN *Computing* the time required to retrieve a piece of stored information.

acciaccatura (ɑːˌtʃɑːkɑːˈtʊərə) NOUN, *plural* **-ras** *or* **-re** (-reɪ, -riː). [1] a small grace note melodically adjacent to a principal note and played simultaneously with or immediately before it. [2] (in modern music) a very short appoggiatura.
▹**HISTORY** C18: Italian: literally, a crushing sound

accidence (ˈæksɪdəns) NOUN inflectional morphology; the part of grammar concerned with changes in the form of words by internal modification or by affixation, for the expression of tense, person, case, number, etc.
▹**HISTORY** C15: from Latin *accidentia* accidental matters, hence inflections of words, from *accidere* to happen. See ACCIDENT

accident (ˈæksɪdənt) NOUN [1] an unforeseen event or one without an apparent cause. [2] anything that occurs unintentionally or by chance; chance; fortune: *I met him by accident.* [3] a misfortune or mishap, esp one causing injury or death. [4] Also called: **adjunct.** *Logic, philosophy* a nonessential attribute or characteristic of something (as opposed to substance). [5] *Metaphysics* a property as contrasted with the substance in which it inheres. [6] *Geology* a surface irregularity in a natural formation, esp in a rock formation or a river system.
▹**HISTORY** C14: via Old French from Latin *accident-* chance, happening, from the present participle of *accidere* to befall, happen, from *ad-* to + *cadere* to fall

accidental (ˌæksɪˈdɛntᵊl) ADJECTIVE [1] occurring by chance, unexpectedly, or unintentionally. [2] nonessential; incidental. [3] *Music* denoting sharps, flats, or naturals that are not in the key signature of a piece. [4] *Logic* (of a property) not essential; contingent. ◆ NOUN [5] an incidental, nonessential, or supplementary circumstance, factor, or attribute. [6] *Music* a symbol denoting a sharp, flat, or natural that is not a part of the key signature. ▸ˌ**acciˈdentally** ADVERB

accident insurance NOUN insurance providing compensation for accidental injury or death.

accidentology (ˌæksɪdənˈtɒlədʒɪ) NOUN the study of the prevention of accidents.

accident-prone ADJECTIVE more liable than most people to be involved in accidents.

accident proneness NOUN the unconscious tendency, thought to exist in some people, to involve themselves in a large number of accidents.

accidie (ˈæksɪdɪ) *or* **acedia** NOUN spiritual sloth; apathy; indifference.
▹**HISTORY** in use C13 to C16 and revived C19: via Late Latin from Greek *akēdia,* from A-[1] + *kēdos* care

accipiter (ækˈsɪpɪtə) NOUN any hawk of the genus *Accipiter,* typically having short rounded wings and a long tail.
▹**HISTORY** C19: New Latin, from Latin: hawk

accipitrine (ækˈsɪpɪˌtraɪn, -trɪn) ADJECTIVE [1] Also: **accipitral** (ækˈsɪpɪtrəl). of, relating to, or resembling a hawk; rapacious. [2] of, relating to, or belonging to the subfamily *Accipitrinae,* which includes the hawks.

acclaim (əˈkleɪm) VERB [1] (*tr*) to acknowledge publicly the excellence of (a person, act, etc.). [2] to salute with cheering, clapping, etc.; applaud. [3] (*tr*) to acknowledge publicly that (a person) has (some position, quality, etc.): *they acclaimed him king.* ◆ NOUN [4] an enthusiastic approval, expression of enthusiasm, etc.
▹**HISTORY** C17: from Latin *acclāmāre* to shout at, shout applause, from *ad-* to + *clamāre* to shout
▸**acˈclaimer** NOUN

acclamation (ˌækləˈmeɪʃən) NOUN [1] an enthusiastic reception or exhibition of welcome, approval, etc. [2] an expression of approval by a meeting or gathering through shouts or applause. [3] *Canadian* an instance of electing or being elected without opposition: *there were two acclamations in the 1985 election.* [4] **by acclamation. a** by an overwhelming majority without a ballot. **b** *Canadian* (of an election or electoral victory) without opposition: *he won by acclamation.*
▸**acclamatory** (əˈklæmətərɪ, -trɪ) ADJECTIVE

acclimatize, acclimatise (əˈklaɪməˌtaɪz), *or* **acclimate** (əˈklaɪmeɪt, ˈæklɪˌmeɪt) VERB to adapt or become accustomed to a new climate or environment.
▸**acˈclimaˌtizable** *or* **acˈclimaˌtisable** *or* **acˈclimatable** ADJECTIVE ▸**acˌclimatiˈzation** *or* **acˌclimatiˈsation** *or* ˌ**accliˈmation** NOUN ▸**acˈclimaˌtizer** *or* **acˈclimaˌtiser** NOUN

acclivity (əˈklɪvɪtɪ) NOUN, *plural* **-ties.** an upward slope, esp of the ground. Compare **declivity.**
▹**HISTORY** C17: from Latin *acclīvitās,* from *acclīvis* sloping up, steep
▸**acˈclivitous** *or* **acclivous** (əˈklaɪvəs) ADJECTIVE

accolade (ˈækəˌleɪd, ˌækəˈleɪd) NOUN [1] strong praise or approval; acclaim. [2] an award or honour. [3] the ceremonial gesture used to confer knighthood, originally an embrace, now a touch on the shoulder with a sword. [4] a rare word for **brace** (sense 7). [5] *Architect* a curved ornamental moulding, esp one having the shape of an ogee arch.
▹**HISTORY** C17: via French and Italian from Vulgar Latin *accollāre* (unattested) to hug; related to Latin *collum* neck

accommodate (əˈkɒməˌdeɪt) VERB [1] (*tr*) to supply or provide, esp with lodging or board and lodging. [2] (*tr*) to oblige or do a favour for. [3] to adjust or become adjusted; adapt. [4] (*tr*) to bring into harmony; reconcile. [5] (*tr*) to allow room for; contain. [6] (*tr*) to lend money to, esp on a temporary basis until a formal loan has been arranged.
▹**HISTORY** C16: from Latin *accommodāre* to make fit, from *ad-* to + *commodus* having the proper measure
▸**acˈcommoˌdative** ADJECTIVE

accommodating (əˈkɒməˌdeɪtɪŋ) ADJECTIVE willing to help; kind; obliging.
▸**acˈcommoˌdatingly** ADVERB

accommodation (əˌkɒməˈdeɪʃən) NOUN [1] lodging or board and lodging. [2] adjustment, as of differences or to new circumstances; adaptation, settlement, or reconciliation. [3] something fulfilling a need, want, etc.; convenience or facility. [4] *Physiol* the automatic or voluntary adjustment of the shape of the lens of the eye for far or near vision. [5] willingness to help or oblige. [6] *Commerce* a loan, usually made as an act of favour by a bank before formal credit arrangements are agreed.

accommodation address NOUN an address on letters, etc., to a person or business that does not wish or is not able to receive post at a permanent or actual address.

accommodation bill NOUN *Commerce* a bill of exchange cosigned by a guarantor: designed to strengthen the acceptor's credit. Also called: **windbill, windmill.**

accommodation ladder NOUN *Nautical* a flight of stairs or a ladder for lowering over the side of a ship for access to and from a small boat, pier, etc.

accommodation platform *or* **rig** NOUN a platform or semisubmersible rig specially built or adapted to act as living accommodation for offshore personnel in the oil industry.

accompaniment (əˈkʌmpənɪmənt, əˈkʌmpnɪ-) NOUN 1 something that accompanies or is served or used with something else. 2 something inessential or subsidiary that is added, as for ornament or symmetry. 3 *Music* a subordinate part for an instrument, voices, or an orchestra.

accompanist (əˈkʌmpənɪst, əˈkʌmpnɪst) *or sometimes US* **accompanyist** (əˈkʌmpəniːɪst) NOUN a person who plays a musical accompaniment for another performer, esp a pianist accompanying a singer.

accompany (əˈkʌmpənɪ, əˈkʌmpnɪ) VERB **-nies, -nying, -nied.** 1 (*tr*) to go along with, so as to be in company with or escort. 2 (*tr; foll by with*) to supplement: *the food is accompanied with a very hot mango pickle.* 3 (*tr*) to occur, coexist, or be associated with. 4 to provide a musical accompaniment for (a performer).
▷HISTORY C15: from Old French *accompaignier,* from *compaing* COMPANION[1]
▸**acˈcompanier** NOUN

accomplice (əˈkɒmplɪs, əˈkʌm-) NOUN a person who helps another in committing a crime.
▷HISTORY C15: from *a complice,* interpreted as one word. See COMPLICE

accomplish (əˈkɒmplɪʃ, əˈkʌm-) VERB (*tr*) 1 to manage to do; achieve. 2 to conclude successfully; complete.
▷HISTORY C14: from Old French *acomplir* to complete, ultimately from Latin *complēre* to fill up. See COMPLETE
▸**acˈcomplishable** ADJECTIVE ▸**acˈcomplisher** NOUN

accomplished (əˈkɒmplɪʃt, əˈkʌm-) ADJECTIVE 1 successfully completed; achieved. 2 expert; proficient.

accomplishment (əˈkɒmplɪʃmənt, əˈkʌm-) NOUN 1 the act of carrying out or achieving. 2 something achieved or successfully completed. 3 (*often plural*) skill or talent. 4 (*often plural*) social grace, style, and poise.

accord (əˈkɔːd) NOUN 1 agreement; conformity; accordance (esp in the phrase **in accord with**). 2 consent or concurrence of opinion. 3 **with one accord.** unanimously. 4 pleasing relationship between sounds, colours, etc.; harmony. 5 a settlement of differences, as between nations; compromise. 6 **of one's own accord.** voluntarily. ◆ VERB 7 to be or cause to be in harmony or agreement. 8 (*tr*) to grant; bestow.
▷HISTORY C12: via Old French from Latin *ad-* to + *cord-,* stem of *cor* heart
▸**acˈcordable** ADJECTIVE ▸**acˈcorder** NOUN

accordance (əˈkɔːdəns) NOUN 1 conformity; agreement; accord (esp in the phrase **in accordance with**). 2 the act of granting; bestowal: *accordance of rights.*

accordant (əˈkɔːdᵊnt) ADJECTIVE (*usually postpositive* and foll by *with*) in conformity or harmony.
▸**acˈcordantly** ADVERB

according (əˈkɔːdɪŋ) ADJECTIVE 1 (foll by *to*) in proportion; in relation: *salary will be according to age and experience.* 2 (foll by *to*) on the report (of); as stated (by). 3 (foll by *to*) in conformity (with); in accordance (with): *everything went according to plan.* 4 (foll by *as*) depending (on whether). 5 *Not standard* dependent on: *it's all according where you want to go.*

accordingly (əˈkɔːdɪŋlɪ) ADVERB 1 in an appropriate manner; suitably. ◆ SENTENCE CONNECTOR 2 consequently.

accordion (əˈkɔːdɪən) NOUN 1 a portable box-shaped instrument of the reed organ family, consisting of metallic reeds that are made to vibrate by air from a set of bellows controlled by the player's hands. Notes are produced by means of studlike keys. 2 short for **piano accordion.**
▷HISTORY C19: from German *Akkordion,*from *Akkord* harmony, chord
▸**acˈcordionist** NOUN

accordion pleats PLURAL NOUN tiny knife pleats.

accost (əˈkɒst) VERB 1 (*tr*) to approach, stop, and speak to (a person), as to ask a question, accuse of a crime, solicit sexually, etc. ◆ NOUN 2 *Rare* a greeting.
▷HISTORY C16: from Late Latin *accostāre* to place side by side, from Latin *costa* side, rib
▸**acˈcostable** ADJECTIVE

accouchement *French* (akuʃmɑ̃; *English* əˈkuːʃmənt) NOUN childbirth or the period of confinement.
▷HISTORY C19: from *accoucher* to put to bed, to give birth. See COUCH

accoucheur *French* (akuʃœr) NOUN a male obstetrician or midwife.
▷HISTORY literally: one who is present at the bedside

accoucheuse *French* (akuʃøz) NOUN a female obstetrician or midwife.
▷HISTORY literally: one who is present at the bedside

account (əˈkaʊnt) NOUN 1 a verbal or written report, description, or narration of some occurrence, event, etc. 2 an explanation of conduct, esp one made to someone in authority. 3 ground; basis; consideration (often in the phrases **on this (that, every, no,** etc.) **account, on account of**). 4 importance, consequence, or value: *of little account.* 5 assessment; judgment. 6 profit or advantage: *to turn an idea to account.* 7 part or behalf (only in the phrase **on one's** *or* **someone's account**). 8 *Finance* **a** a business relationship between a bank, department store, stockbroker, etc., and a depositor, customer, or client permitting the latter certain banking or credit services. **b** the sum of money deposited at a bank. **c** the amount of credit available to the holder of an account. **d** a record of these. 9 a statement of monetary transactions with the resulting balance. 10 (on the London Stock Exchange) the period, ordinarily of a fortnight's duration, in which transactions formerly took place and at the end of which settlements were made. 11 *Book-keeping* a chronological list of debits and credits relating to a specified asset, liability, expense, or income of a business and forming part of the ledger. 12 **a** a regular client or customer, esp a firm that purchases commodities on credit. **b** an area of business assigned to another: *they transferred their publicity account to a new agent.* 13 **call** (*or* **bring**) **to account. a** to insist on explanation. **b** to rebuke; reprimand. **c** to hold responsible. 14 **give a good** (**bad,** etc.) **account of oneself.** to perform well (badly, etc.): *he gave a poor account of himself in the examination.* 15 **on account. a** on credit. **b** Also: **to account.** as partial payment. 16 **on account of.** (*preposition*) because of; by reason of. 17 **take account of** *or* **take into account.** to take into consideration; allow for. 18 **settle** *or* **square accounts with. a** to pay or receive a balance due. **b** to get revenge on (someone). 19 See **bank account** or **credit account.** ◆ VERB 20 (*tr*) to consider or reckon: *he accounts himself poor.*
▷HISTORY C13: from Old French *acont,* from *conter, compter* to COUNT[1]

accountable (əˈkaʊntəbᵊl) ADJECTIVE 1 responsible to someone or for some action; answerable. 2 able to be explained.
▸**ac͵countaˈbility** NOUN ▸**acˈcountably** ADVERB

accountancy (əˈkaʊntənsɪ) NOUN the profession or business of an accountant.

accountant (əˈkaʊntənt) NOUN a person concerned with the maintenance and audit of business accounts and the preparation of consultant reports in tax and finance.

account day NOUN (on the London Stock Exchange) the day on which deliveries and payments relating to transactions made during the preceding account are made.

account executive NOUN an executive in an advertising agency or public relations firm who manages a client's account.

account for VERB (*intr, preposition*) 1 to give reasons for (an event, act, etc.). 2 to make or provide a reckoning of (expenditure, payments, etc.). 3 to be responsible for destroying, killing, or putting (people, aircraft, etc.) out of action.

accounting (əˈkaʊntɪŋ) NOUN **a** the skill or practice of maintaining and auditing accounts and preparing reports on the assets, liabilities, etc., of a business. **b** (*as modifier*): *an accounting period; accounting entity.*

account payable NOUN *Accounting, US* a current liability account showing amounts payable by a firm to suppliers for purchases of materials, stocks, or services on credit.

account receivable NOUN *Accounting, US* a current asset account showing amounts payable to a firm by customers who have made purchases of goods and services on credit.

accouplement (əˈkʌpᵊlmənt) NOUN a timber joist or beam that serves as a tie or support.
▷HISTORY C15: French, from *accoupler,* from Latin *copulāre* to COUPLE

accoutre *or US* **accouter** (əˈkuːtə) VERB (*tr; usually passive*) to provide with equipment or dress, esp military.
▷HISTORY C16: from Old French *accoustrer* to equip with clothing, ultimately related to Latin *consuere* to sew together

accoutrement (əˈkuːtrəmənt, əˈkuːtə-) *or US* **accouterment** (əˈkuːtərmənt) NOUN 1 equipment worn by soldiers in addition to their clothing and weapons. 2 (*usually plural*) clothing, equipment, etc.; trappings: *the correct accoutrements for any form of sport.*

Accra (əˈkrɑː) NOUN the capital of Ghana, a port on the Gulf of Guinea: built on the site of three 17th-century trading fortresses founded by the English, Dutch, and Danish. Pop.: 1 446 000 (1998 est.).

accredit (əˈkrɛdɪt) VERB (*tr*) 1 to ascribe or attribute. 2 to give official recognition to; sanction; authorize. 3 to certify or guarantee as meeting required standards. 4 (often foll by *at* or *to*) **a** to furnish or send (an envoy, etc.) with official credentials. **b** to appoint (someone) as an envoy, etc. 5 *NZ* to pass (a candidate) for university entrance on school recommendation without external examination: *there are six accrediting schools in the area.*
▷HISTORY C17: from French *accréditer,* from the phrase *mettre à crédit* to put to CREDIT
▸**ac͵crediˈtation** NOUN

accrescent (æˈkrɛsᵊnt) ADJECTIVE *Botany* (of a calyx or other part) continuing to grow after flowering.
▷HISTORY C18: from Latin *accrēscere* to continue to grow, from *crēscere* to grow

accrete (əˈkriːt) VERB 1 to grow or cause to grow together; be or become fused. 2 to make or become bigger, as by addition.
▷HISTORY C18: back formation from ACCRETION

accretion (əˈkriːʃən) NOUN 1 any gradual increase in size, as through growth or external addition. 2 something added, esp extraneously, to cause growth or an increase in size. 3 the growing together of normally separate plant or animal parts. 4 *Pathol* **a** abnormal union or growing together of parts; adhesion. **b** a mass of foreign matter collected in a cavity. 5 *Law* an increase in the share of a beneficiary in an estate, as when a co-beneficiary fails to take his share. 6 *Astronomy* the process in which matter under the influence of gravity is attracted to and increases the mass of a celestial body. The matter usually forms an **accretion disc** around the accreting object. 7 *Geology* the process in which a continent is enlarged by the tectonic movement and deformation of the earth's crust.
▷HISTORY C17: from Latin *accretiō* increase, from *accrēscere.* See ACCRUE
▸**acˈcretive** *or* **acˈcretionary** ADJECTIVE

accretionary wedge *or* **prism** NOUN *Geology* a body of deformed sediments, wedge-shaped in two dimensions or prism-shaped in three dimensions, that has been scraped off the surface of the oceanic lithosphere as it moves downwards beneath a continent or island arc. The sediments are added to the continental edge.

Accrington (ˈækrɪŋtən) NOUN a town in NW England, in SE Lancashire. Pop.: 36 466 (1991).

accrual (əˈkruːəl) NOUN 1 the act of accruing. 2 something that has accrued. 3 *Accounting* a charge incurred in one accounting period that has not been paid by the end of it.

accrue (əˈkruː) VERB **-crues, -cruing, -crued.** (*intr*) 1 to increase by growth or addition, esp (of capital) to increase by periodic addition of interest. 2 (often foll by *to*) to fall naturally (to); come into the possession (of); result (for). 3 *Law* (of a right or demand) to become capable of being enforced.
▷HISTORY C15: from Old French *accreue* growth,

ultimately from Latin *accrēscere* to increase, from *ad-* to, in addition + *crēscere* to grow

acculturate (əˈkʌltʃəˌreɪt) VERB (of a cultural or social group) to assimilate the cultural traits of another group.
▷HISTORY C20: from AD- + CULTURE + -ATE[1]
▸**acˌculturˈation** NOUN

accumbent (əˈkʌmbənt) ADJECTIVE 1 *Botany* (of plant parts and plants) lying against some other part or thing. 2 a rare word for **recumbent.**
▷HISTORY C18: from Latin *accumbere* to recline
▸**acˈcumbency** NOUN

accumulate (əˈkjuːmjʊˌleɪt) VERB to gather or become gathered together in an increasing quantity; amass; collect.
▷HISTORY C16: from Latin *accumulātus,* past participle of *accumulāre* to heap up, from *cumulus* a heap
▸**acˈcumulable** ADJECTIVE ▸**acˈcumulative** ADJECTIVE ▸**acˈcumulatively** ADVERB ▸**acˈcumulativeness** NOUN

accumulation (əˌkjuːmjʊˈleɪʃən) NOUN 1 the act or process of collecting together or becoming collected. 2 something that has been collected, gathered, heaped, etc. 3 *Finance* **a** the continuous growth of capital by retention of interest or earnings. **b** (in computing the yield on a bond purchased at a discount) the amount that is added to each yield to bring the cost of the bond into equality with its par value over its life. Compare **amortization** (sense 2). 4 the taking of a first and an advanced university degree simultaneously.

accumulation point NOUN *Maths* another name for **limit point.**

accumulator (əˈkjuːmjʊˌleɪtə) NOUN 1 Also called: **battery, storage battery.** a rechargeable device for storing electrical energy in the form of chemical energy, consisting of one or more separate secondary cells. 2 *Horse racing, Brit* a collective bet, esp on four or more races, in which the stake and winnings on each successive race are carried forward to become the stake on the next, so that both stakes and winnings accumulate progressively so long as the bet continues to be a winning one. 3 **a** a register in a computer or calculator used for holding the results of a computation or data transfer. **b** a location in a computer store in which arithmetical results are produced.

accuracy (ˈækjʊrəsɪ) NOUN, *plural* **-cies.** 1 faithful measurement or representation of the truth; correctness; precision. 2 *Physics, chem* the degree of agreement between a measured or computed value of a physical quantity and the standard or accepted value for that quantity.

accurate (ˈækjərɪt) ADJECTIVE 1 faithfully representing or describing the truth. 2 showing a negligible or permissible deviation from a standard: *an accurate ruler.* 3 without error; precise; meticulous. 4 *Maths* **a** (to *n* significant digits) representing the first *n* digits of the given number starting with the first nonzero digit, but approximating to the nearest digit in the final position: *since* $\pi = 3.14159...$, *the approximation 3.1416 is accurate to 5 significant digits.* **b** (to *n* decimal places) giving the first *n* digits after the decimal point without further approximation: $\pi = 3.1415$ *is in this sense accurate to 4 decimal places.*
▷HISTORY C16: from Latin *accūrātus,* past participle of *accūrāre* to perform with care, from *cūra* care
▸**ˈaccurately** ADVERB ▸**ˈaccurateness** NOUN

accursed (əˈkɜːsɪd, əˈkɜːst) *or* **accurst** (əˈkɜːst) ADJECTIVE 1 under or subject to a curse; doomed. 2 (*prenominal*) hateful; detestable; execrable.
▷HISTORY Old English *ācursod,* past participle of *ācursian* to put under a CURSE
▸**accursedly** (əˈkɜːsɪdlɪ) ADVERB ▸**acˈcursedness** NOUN

accusal (əˈkjuːzᵊl) NOUN another word for **accusation.**

accusation (ˌækjuˈzeɪʃən) NOUN 1 an allegation that a person is guilty of some fault, offence, or crime; imputation. 2 a formal charge brought against a person stating the crime that he is alleged to have committed.

accusative (əˈkjuːzətɪv) ADJECTIVE 1 *Grammar* denoting a case of nouns, pronouns, and adjectives in inflected languages that is used to identify the direct object of a finite verb, of certain prepositions, and for certain other purposes. See also **objective** (sense 5). 2 another word for **accusatorial.** ◆ NOUN 3 *Grammar* **a** the accusative case. **b** a word or speech element in the accusative case.
▷HISTORY C15: from Latin; in grammar, from the phrase *cāsus accūsātīvus* accusative case, a mistaken translation of Greek *ptōsis aitiatikē* the case indicating causation. See ACCUSE
▸**accusatival** (əˌkjuːzəˈtaɪvᵊl) ADJECTIVE ▸**acˈcusatively** ADVERB

accusatorial (əˌkjuːzəˈtɔːrɪəl) *or* **accusatory** (əˈkjuːzətərɪ, -trɪ, ˌækjʊˈzeɪtərɪ) ADJECTIVE 1 containing or implying blame or strong criticism. 2 *Law* denoting criminal procedure in which the prosecutor is distinct from the judge and the trial is conducted in public. Compare **inquisitorial** (sense 3).

accuse (əˈkjuːz) VERB to charge (a person or persons) with some fault, offence, crime, etc.; impute guilt or blame.
▷HISTORY C13: via Old French from Latin *accūsāre* to call to account, from *ad-* to + *causa* lawsuit
▸**acˈcuser** NOUN ▸**acˈcusing** ADJECTIVE ▸**acˈcusingly** ADVERB

accused (əˈkjuːzd) NOUN (preceded by *the*) *Law* the defendant or defendants appearing on a criminal charge.

accustom (əˈkʌstəm) VERB (*tr;* usually foll by *to*) to make (oneself) familiar (with) or used (to), as by practice, habit, or experience.
▷HISTORY C15: from Old French *acostumer,* from *costume* CUSTOM

accustomed (əˈkʌstəmd) ADJECTIVE 1 usual; customary. 2 (*postpositive;* foll by *to*) used or inured (to). 3 (*postpositive;* foll by *to*) in the habit (of): *accustomed to walking after meals.*

Accutron (ˈækjuːˌtrɒn) NOUN *Trademark* a type of watch in which the balance wheel and hairspring are replaced by a tuning fork kept in vibration by a tiny internal battery.

AC/DC ADJECTIVE *Informal* (of a person) bisexual.
▷HISTORY C20: humorous reference to electrical apparatus that is adaptable for ALTERNATING CURRENT and DIRECT CURRENT

ace (eɪs) NOUN 1 any die, domino, or any of four playing cards with one spot. 2 a single spot or pip on a playing card, die, etc. 3 *Tennis* a winning serve that the opponent fails to reach. 4 *Golf, chiefly US* a hole in one. 5 a fighter pilot accredited with destroying several enemy aircraft. 6 *Informal* an expert or highly skilled person: *an ace at driving.* 7 **an ace up one's sleeve** *or* **an ace in the hole.** a hidden and powerful advantage. 8 **hold all the aces.** to have all the advantages or power. 9 **play one's ace.** to use one's best weapon or resource. 10 **within an ace of.** almost to the point of: *he came within an ace of winning.* ◆ ADJECTIVE 11 *Informal* superb; excellent. ◆ VERB (*tr*) 12 *Tennis* to serve an ace against. 13 *Golf, chiefly US* to play (a hole) in one stroke. 14 *US and Canadian* to perform extremely well or score very highly in (an examination, etc.).
▷HISTORY C13: via Old French from Latin *as* a unit, perhaps from a Greek variant of *heis* one

ACE (eɪs) NOUN ACRONYM FOR: 1 (in Britain) Advisory Centre for Education; a private organization offering advice on schools to parents. 2 Allied Command Europe. 3 angiotensin-converting enzyme. See **ACE inhibitor.**

-acea SUFFIX FORMING PLURAL PROPER NOUNS denoting animals belonging to a class or order: *Crustacea* (class); *Cetacea* (order).
▷HISTORY New Latin, from Latin, neuter plural of *-āceus* -ACEOUS

-aceae SUFFIX FORMING PLURAL PROPER NOUNS denoting plants belonging to a family: *Liliaceae; Ranunculaceae.*
▷HISTORY New Latin, from Latin, feminine plural of *-āceus* -ACEOUS

acedia (əˈsiːdɪə) NOUN another word for **accidie.**

ACE inhibitor NOUN any one of a class of drugs, including captopril, enalapril, and ramipril, that cause the arteries to widen by preventing the synthesis of angiotensin: used to treat high blood pressure and heart failure.
▷HISTORY C20: from *a(ngiotensin-)c(onverting) e(nzyme) inhibitor*

Aceldama (əˈsɛldəmə) NOUN *New Testament* the place near Jerusalem that was bought with the 30 pieces of silver paid to Judas for betraying Jesus (Matthew 27:8; Acts 1:19).
▷HISTORY C14: from Aramaic *haqēl demā* field of blood

acellular (eɪˈsɛljʊlə) ADJECTIVE *Biology* not made up of or containing cells.

acentric (eɪˈsɛntrɪk) ADJECTIVE 1 without a centre. 2 not on centre; eccentric. 3 *Genetics* (of a chromosome or chromosome fragment) lacking a centromere. ◆ NOUN 4 an acentric chromosome or fragment.

-aceous SUFFIX FORMING ADJECTIVES relating to, belonging to, having the nature of, or resembling: *herbaceous; larvaceous.*
▷HISTORY New Latin, from Latin *-āceus* of a certain kind; related to *-āc, -āx,* adjectival suffix

acephalous (əˈsɛfələs) ADJECTIVE 1 having no head or one that is reduced and indistinct, as certain insect larvae. 2 having or recognizing no ruler or leader.
▷HISTORY C18: via Medieval Latin from Greek *akephalos.* See A-[1], -CEPHALIC

acer (ˈeɪsə) NOUN any tree or shrub of the genus *Acer,* often cultivated for their brightly coloured foliage. See also **maple.**

ACER ABBREVIATION FOR Australian Council for Educational Research.

acerate (ˈæsəˌreɪt, -rɪt) ADJECTIVE another word for **acerose.**
▷HISTORY C19: from Latin *ācer* sharp + -ATE[1]

acerbate (ˈæsəˌbeɪt) VERB (*tr*) 1 to embitter or exasperate. 2 to make sour or bitter.
▷HISTORY C18: from Latin *acerbātus,* past participle of *acerbāre* to make sour

acerbic (əˈsɜːbɪk) ADJECTIVE harsh, bitter, or astringent; sour.
▷HISTORY C17: from Latin *acerbus* sour, bitter

acerbity (əˈsɜːbɪtɪ) NOUN, *plural* **-ties.** 1 vitriolic or embittered speech, temper, etc. 2 sourness or bitterness of taste.

acerose (ˈæsəˌrəʊs, -ˌrəʊz) *or* **acerous** ADJECTIVE shaped like a needle, as pine leaves.
▷HISTORY C18: from Latin *acerōsus* full of chaff (erroneously used by Linnaeus as if derived from *ācer* sharp)

acervate (əˈsɜːvɪt, -ˌveɪt) ADJECTIVE growing in heaps or clusters.
▷HISTORY C19: from Latin *acervātus,* from *acervāre* to heap up, from *acervus* a heap
▸**aˈcervately** ADVERB

acescent (əˈsɛsᵊnt) ADJECTIVE slightly sour or turning sour.
▷HISTORY C18: from Latin *acēscent-,* from *acēscere* to become sour, from *ācer* sharp
▸**aˈcescence** *or* **aˈcescency** NOUN

acetabulum (ˌæsɪˈtæbjʊləm) NOUN, *plural* **-la** (-lə). 1 the deep cuplike cavity on the side of the hipbone that receives the head of the thighbone. 2 a round muscular sucker in flatworms, leeches, and cephalopod molluscs. 3 the aperture in the thorax of an insect that holds the leg.
▷HISTORY Latin: vinegar cup, hence a cuplike cavity, from *acētum* vinegar + *-abulum,* suffix denoting a container

acetal (ˈæsɪˌtæl) NOUN 1 1,1-diethoxyethane; a colourless volatile liquid used as a solvent and in perfumes. Formula: $CH_3CH(OC_2H_5)_2$. 2 any organic compound containing the group $-CH(OR_1)OR_2$, where R_1 and R_2 are other organic groups.
▷HISTORY C19: from German *Azetal,* from ACETO- + ALCOHOL

acetaldehyde (ˌæsɪˈtældɪˌhaɪd) NOUN a colourless volatile pungent liquid, miscible with water, used in the manufacture of organic compounds and as a solvent and reducing agent. Formula: CH_3CHO. Systematic name: **ethanal.**

acetamide (ˌæsɪˈtæmaɪd, əˈsɛtɪˌmaɪd) *or* **acetamid** (ˌæsɪˈtæmɪd, əˈsɛtɪmɪd) NOUN a white or colourless soluble deliquescent crystalline compound, used in the manufacture of organic chemicals. Formula: CH_3CONH_2.
▷HISTORY C19: from German *Azetamid,* from ACETO- + AMIDE

acetanilide (ˌæsɪˈtænɪˌlaɪd) *or* **acetanilid** (ˌæsɪˈtænɪlɪd) NOUN a white crystalline powder used in the manufacture of dyes and rubber, as an analgesic in medicine, and as a precursor in penicillin manufacture. Formula: $C_6H_5NHCOCH_3$.

▷HISTORY C19: from ACETO- + ANILINE + -IDE

acetate ('æsɪˌteɪt) NOUN [1] any salt or ester of acetic acid, containing the monovalent ion CH_3COO^- or the group CH_3COO-. Systematic name: **ethanoate.** [2] (*modifier*) consisting of, containing, or concerned with the group CH_3COO-: *acetate group or radical.* [3] short for **acetate rayon** or **cellulose acetate.** [4] a sound recording disc composed of an acetate lacquer coating on an aluminium or plastic base: used for demonstration or other short-term purposes.
▷HISTORY C19: from ACETIC + -ATE[1]
▸'aceˌtated ADJECTIVE

acetate rayon NOUN a synthetic textile fibre made from cellulose acetate. Also called: **acetate.**

acetic (ə'siːtɪk, ə'sɛt-) ADJECTIVE of, containing, producing, or derived from acetic acid or vinegar.
▷HISTORY C19: from Latin *acētum* vinegar

acetic acid NOUN a colourless pungent liquid, miscible with water, widely used in the manufacture of acetic anhydride, vinyl acetate, plastics, pharmaceuticals, dyes, etc. Formula: CH_3COOH. Systematic name: **ethanoic acid.** See also **glacial acetic acid, vinegar.**

acetic anhydride NOUN a colourless pungent liquid used in the manufacture of cellulose and vinyl acetates for synthetic fabrics. Formula: $(CH_3CO)_2O$.

acetify (ə'sɛtɪˌfaɪ) VERB **-fies, -fying, -fied.** to become or cause to become acetic acid or vinegar.
▸**aˌcetifi'cation** NOUN ▸**a'cetiˌfier** NOUN

aceto- *or before a vowel* **acet-** COMBINING FORM containing an acetyl group or derived from acetic acid: *acetone.*
▷HISTORY from Latin *acētum* vinegar

acetometer (ˌæsɪ'tɒmɪtə) NOUN a device for measuring the concentration of acetic acid in a solution, esp in vinegar.

acetonaemia *or US* **acetonemia** (ˌəsiːtəʊ'niːmɪə, əˌsiːtə-) NOUN another name for **ketosis.**

acetone ('æsɪˌtəʊn) NOUN a colourless volatile flammable pungent liquid, miscible with water, used in the manufacture of chemicals and as a solvent and thinner for paints, varnishes, and lacquers. Formula: CH_3COCH_3. Systematic name: **propanone.**
▷HISTORY C19: from German *Azeton,* from ACETO- + -ONE
▸**acetonic** (ˌæsɪ'tɒnɪk) ADJECTIVE

acetone body NOUN another name for **ketone body.**

acetonuria (ˌəsiːtəʊ'njʊərɪə, əˌsiːtə-) NOUN another name for **ketonuria.**

acetophenetidin (əˌsiːtəʊfə'nɛtɪdɪn) NOUN another name for **phenacetin.**

acetous ('æsɪtəs, ə'siː-) *or* **acetose** ('æsɪˌtəʊs, -ˌtəʊz) ADJECTIVE [1] containing, producing, or resembling acetic acid or vinegar. [2] tasting like vinegar.
▷HISTORY C18: from Late Latin *acētōsus* vinegary, from *acētum* vinegar

acetum (ə'siːtəm) NOUN [1] another name for **vinegar.** [2] a solution that has dilute acetic acid as solvent.
▷HISTORY Latin

acetyl ('æsɪˌtaɪl, ə'siːtaɪl) NOUN (*modifier*) of, consisting of, or containing the monovalent group CH_3CO-: *acetyl group or radical.*
▷HISTORY C19: from ACET(IC) + -YL
▸**acetylic** (ˌæsɪ'tɪlɪk) ADJECTIVE

acetylate (ə'sɛtɪˌleɪt) VERB [1] (*tr*) to introduce an acetyl group into (a chemical compound). [2] (*intr*) (of a chemical compound) to gain or suffer substitution of an acetyl group.
▸**aˌcety'lation** NOUN

acetyl chloride NOUN a colourless pungent liquid used as an acetylating agent. Formula: CH_3COCl. Also called: **ethanoyl chloride.**

acetylcholine (ˌæsɪtaɪl'kəʊliːn, -lɪn) NOUN a chemical substance secreted at the ends of many nerve fibres, esp in the autonomic nervous system, and responsible for the transmission of nervous impulses. Formula: $CH_3CO_2(CH_2)_2N\ (CH_3)_3^+$.

acetylcholinesterase (əˈsiːtaɪlˌkəʊliːn'ɛstəˌreɪz, 'æsɪtaɪl-) NOUN an enzyme in nerve cells that is responsible for the destruction of acetylcholine and thus for switching off excitation of the nerve.

acetylene (ə'sɛtɪˌliːn) NOUN [1] a colourless flammable gas used in the manufacture of organic chemicals and in cutting and welding metals. Formula: C_2H_2. Systematic name: **ethyne.** [2] **a** another name for **alkyne. b** (*as modifier*): *acetylene series.*
▸**acetylenic** (əˌsɛtɪ'lɛnɪk) ADJECTIVE

acetylide (ə'sɛtɪˌlaɪd) NOUN any of a class of carbides in which the carbon is present as a diatomic divalent ion (C_2^{2-}). They are formally derivatives of acetylene.

acetylsalicylic acid (ˌæsɪtaɪlˌsælɪ'sɪlɪk, ə'siːtaɪl-) NOUN the chemical name for **aspirin.**

acey-deucy ('eɪsɪ'djuːsɪ) NOUN a form of backgammon.

ACGI ABBREVIATION FOR Associate of the City and Guilds Institute.

ach (ɑːx) INTERJECTION *Scot* an expression of surprise, impatience, disgust, etc. Also: **och.**

Achaea (ə'kiːə) *or* **Achaia** (ə'kaɪə) NOUN [1] a department of Greece, in the N Peloponnese. Capital: Patras. Pop.: 300 078 (1991). Area: 3209 sq. km (1239 sq. miles). Modern Greek name: **Akhaïa.** [2] a province of ancient Greece, in the N Peloponnese on the Gulf of Corinth: enlarged as a Roman province in 27 B.C.

Achaean (ə'kiːən) *or* **Achaian** (ə'kaɪən) NOUN [1] a member of a principal Greek tribe in the Mycenaean era. [2] a native or inhabitant of the later Greek province of Achaea. ◆ ADJECTIVE [3] of or relating to Achaea or the Achaeans.

Achaean League NOUN a confederation of Achaean cities formed in the early third century B.C., which became a political and military force in Greece, directed particularly against Macedonian domination of the Peloponnesus.

Achaemenid (ə'kiːmənɪd, ə'kɛm-) NOUN, *plural* **Achaemenids, Achaemenidae** (ˌækɪ'mɛnɪˌdiː) *or* **Achaemenides** (ˌækɪ'mɛnɪˌdiːz). any member of a Persian dynasty of kings, including Cyrus the Great, that ruled from about 550 to 331 B.C., when Darius III was overthrown by Alexander the Great.
▷HISTORY from Greek, after *Akhaimenēs,* name of the founder

achalasia (ˌækə'leɪzɪə) NOUN *Pathol* failure of the cardiac sphincter of the oesophagus to relax, resulting in difficulty in swallowing.
▷HISTORY New Latin, from A-[1] + Greek *chalasis* relaxation

acharya (a'tʃærɪə) NOUN *Hinduism* a prominent religious teacher and spiritual guide.
▷HISTORY from Sanskrit, literally: teacher

Achates (ə'keɪtiːz) NOUN [1] *Classical myth* Aeneas' faithful companion in Virgil's *Aeneid.* [2] a loyal friend.

ache (eɪk) VERB (*intr*) [1] to feel, suffer, or be the source of a continuous dull pain. [2] to suffer mental anguish. ◆ NOUN [3] a continuous dull pain.
▷HISTORY Old English *ācan* (vb), *æce* (n), Middle English *aken* (vb), *ache* (n). Compare BAKE, BATCH
▸ **'aching** ADJECTIVE ▸ **'achingly** ADVERB

Achelous (ˌækɪ'ləʊəs) NOUN *Classical myth* a river god who changed into a snake and a bull while fighting Hercules but was defeated when Hercules broke off one of his horns.

achene *or* **akene** (ə'kiːn) NOUN a dry one-seeded indehiscent fruit with the seed distinct from the fruit wall. It may be smooth, as in the buttercup, or feathery, as in clematis.
▷HISTORY C19: from New Latin *achaenium* that which does not yawn or open, from A-[1] + Greek *khainein* to yawn
▸**a'chenial** *or* **a'kenial** ADJECTIVE

Achernar ('eɪkəˌnɑː) NOUN the brightest star in the constellation Eridanus, visible only in the S hemisphere. Visual magnitude: 0.5; spectral type: B3V; distance: 144 light years.
▷HISTORY from Arabic *ākhīr al-nahr,* literally: end of the river, alluding to the star's location in the constellation

Acheron ('ækəˌrɒn) NOUN *Greek myth* [1] one of the rivers in Hades over which the souls of the dead were ferried by Charon. Compare **Styx.** [2] the underworld or Hades.

Acheulian *or* **Acheulean** (ə'ʃuːlɪən, -jən) *Archaeol* ◆ NOUN [1] (in Europe) the period in the Lower Palaeolithic following the Abbevillian, represented by the use of soft hammerstones in hand axe production made of chipped stone, bone, antler, or wood. The Acheulian dates from the Riss glaciation. [2] (in Africa) the period represented by every stage of hand axe development. ◆ ADJECTIVE [3] of or relating to this period.
▷HISTORY C20: after *St. Acheul,* town in northern France

à cheval *French* (a ʃəval) ADVERB (of a bet, esp in roulette) made on two adjacent numbers, cards, etc.
▷HISTORY literally: on horseback

achieve (ə'tʃiːv) VERB (*tr*) [1] to bring to a successful conclusion; accomplish; attain. [2] to gain as by hard work or effort: *to achieve success.*
▷HISTORY C14: from Old French *achever* to bring to an end, from the phrase *a chef* to a head, to a conclusion
▸**a'chievable** ADJECTIVE ▸**a'chiever** NOUN

achievement (ə'tʃiːvmənt) NOUN [1] something that has been accomplished, esp by hard work, ability, or heroism. [2] successful completion; accomplishment. [3] *Heraldry* a less common word for **hatchment.**

achievement age NOUN *Psychol* the age at which a child should be able to perform a standardized test successfully. Compare **mental age.**

achievement quotient NOUN *Psychol* a measure of ability derived by dividing an individual's achievement age by his actual age. Abbreviation: **AQ.**

achievement test NOUN *Psychol* a test designed to measure the effects that learning and teaching have on individuals.

achillea (ˌækɪ'liːə) NOUN any plant of the N temperate genus *Achillea,* with white, yellow, or purple flowers, some species of which are widely grown as garden plants: family *Asteraceae* (composites). See also **sneezewort, yarrow.**
▷HISTORY from ACHILLES, who was credited with discovering medicinal properties in the plant

Achilles (ə'kɪliːz) NOUN *Greek myth* Greek hero, the son of Peleus and the sea goddess Thetis: in the *Iliad* the foremost of the Greek warriors at the siege of Troy. While he was a baby his mother plunged him into the river Styx making his body invulnerable except for the heel by which she held him. After slaying Hector, he was killed by Paris who wounded him in the heel.
▸**Achillean** (ˌækɪ'liːən) ADJECTIVE

Achilles heel NOUN a small but fatal weakness.

Achilles tendon NOUN the fibrous cord that connects the muscles of the calf to the heelbone.

Achill Island ('ækɪl) NOUN an island in the Republic of Ireland, off the W coast of Co. Mayo. Area: 148 sq. km (57 sq. miles). Pop.: 2853 (1991).

achimenes (ˌækɪ'miːniːz) NOUN any plant of the tropical S American tuberous-rooted perennial genus *Achimenes,* with showy red, blue, or white tubular flowers, some of which are grown as greenhouse plants: family *Gesneriaceae.*
▷HISTORY from Latin *achaemenis,* from Greek *achaimenis,* a species of euphorbia

Achitophel (ə'kɪtəˌfɛl) NOUN *Bible* the Douay spelling of **Ahithophel.**

achlamydeous (ˌæklə'mɪdɪəs) ADJECTIVE (of flowers such as the willow) having neither petals nor sepals.
▷HISTORY C19: from Greek *a-* not, without + *chlamys* cloak

ach-laut ('æklaut, 'æx-) NOUN (*sometimes capital*) *Phonetics* the voiceless velar fricative sound that is written as *ch* in Scottish *loch* or in German *ach,* often allophonic with the ich-laut. See also **ich-laut.**
▷HISTORY from German, from *ach* ah + *Laut* sound

achlorhydria (ˌeɪklɔː'haɪdrɪə) NOUN the absence of free hydrochloric acid in the gastric juice.
▷HISTORY C20: New Latin; see A-[1], CHLORO-, HYDRO-

achondrite (eɪ'kɒndraɪt) NOUN a rare stony meteorite that consists mainly of silicate minerals and has the texture of igneous rock but contains no chondrules. Compare **chondrite.**
▸**achondritic** (ˌeɪkɒn'drɪtɪk) ADJECTIVE

achondroplasia (eɪˌkɒndrəʊ'pleɪzɪə) NOUN a skeletal disorder, characterized by failure of normal

conversion of cartilage into bone, that begins during fetal life and results in dwarfism.
▷HISTORY C20: New Latin; see A-[1], CHONDRO-, -PLASIA
▸**achondroplastic** (eɪˌkɒndrəʊˈplæstɪk) ADJECTIVE

achromat (ˈækrəˌmæt) NOUN 1 Also called: **achromatic lens.** a lens designed to bring light of two chosen wavelengths to the same focal point, thus reducing chromatic aberration. Compare **apochromat.** 2 a person who has no colour vision at all and can distinguish only black, white, and grey. The condition is very rare.

achromatic (ˌækrəˈmætɪk) ADJECTIVE 1 without colour. 2 capable of reflecting or refracting light without chromatic aberration. 3 *Cytology* **a** not staining with standard dyes. **b** of or relating to achromatin. 4 *Music* **a** involving no sharps or flats. **b** another word for **diatonic.** 5 denoting a person who is an achromat.
▸**ˌachroˈmatically** ADVERB ▸**achromatism** (əˈkrəʊməˌtɪzəm) *or* **achromaticity** (əˌkrəʊməˈtɪsɪtɪ) NOUN

achromatic colour NOUN *Physics* colour, such as white, black, and grey, that is devoid of hue. See **colour** (sense 2).

achromatin (əˈkrəʊmətɪn) NOUN the material of the nucleus of a cell that does not stain with basic dyes. Compare **chromatin.**

achromatize *or* **achromatise** (əˈkrəʊməˌtaɪz) VERB (*tr*) to make achromatic; to remove colour from.
▸**aˌchromatiˈzation** *or* **aˌchromatiˈsation** NOUN

achromatous (əˈkrəʊmətəs) ADJECTIVE having little or no colour or less than is normal.

achromic (əˈkrəʊmɪk) *or* **achromous** ADJECTIVE colourless.

achy (ˈeɪkɪ) ADJECTIVE **achier, achiest.** affected by a continuous dull pain; aching.

ach-y-fi (ˌaxəˈviː, ˌʌx-) INTERJECTION *Welsh dialect* an expression of disgust or abhorrence.
▷HISTORY Welsh, probably from *ach, achy* general exclamation of disgust + *fi* I, me

acicula (əˈsɪkjʊlə) NOUN, *plural* **-lae** (-ˌliː). a needle-shaped part, such as a spine, prickle, or crystal.
▷HISTORY C19: New Latin, diminutive of *acus* needle
▸**aˈcicular** ADJECTIVE

aciculate (əˈsɪkjʊlɪt, -ˌleɪt) *or* **aciculated** ADJECTIVE 1 having aciculae. 2 marked with or as if with needle scratches.

aciculum (əˈsɪkjʊləm) NOUN, *plural* **-lums** *or* **-la** (-lə). a needle-like bristle that provides internal support for the appendages (chaetae) of some polychaete worms.
▷HISTORY C19: New Latin; see ACICULA

acid (ˈæsɪd) NOUN 1 any substance that dissociates in water to yield a sour corrosive solution containing hydrogen ions, having a pH of less than 7, and turning litmus red. See also **Lewis acid.** 2 a sour-tasting substance. 3 a slang name for **LSD.** ◆ ADJECTIVE 4 *Chem* **a** of, derived from, or containing acid: *an acid radical.* **b** being or having the properties of an acid: *sodium bicarbonate is an acid salt.* 5 sharp or sour in taste. 6 cutting, sharp, or hurtful in speech, manner, etc.; vitriolic; caustic. 7 (of rain, snow, etc.) containing pollutant acids in solution. 8 (of igneous rocks) having a silica content of more than 60% of the total and containing at least one tenth quartz. 9 *Metallurgy* of or made by a process in which the furnace or converter is lined with an acid material: *acid steel.*
▷HISTORY C17 (first used by Francis Bacon): from French *acide* or Latin *acidus,* from *acēre* to be sour or sharp
▸**ˈacidly** ADVERB ▸**ˈacidness** NOUN ▸**ˈacidy** ADJECTIVE

acid anhydride NOUN another name for **anhydride** (sense 3).

acidanthera (ˌæsɪˈdænθərə) NOUN any plant of the African cormous genus *Acidanthera,* cultivated for its graceful tubular white and red or white and purple flowers, often scented: family *Iridaceae.*
▷HISTORY from Greek *akis* point + New Latin *anthera* anther, from the shape of the anthers

acid drop NOUN a boiled sweet with a sharp taste.

acid dye NOUN a dye in which the chromophore is part of a negative ion usually applied from an acidic solution.

acid-fast ADJECTIVE (of bacteria and tissues) resistant to decolorization by mineral acids after staining.

acid-forming ADJECTIVE 1 (of an oxide or element) yielding an acid when dissolved in water or having an oxide that forms an acid in water; acidic. 2 (of foods) producing an acid residue following digestion.

acid halide NOUN another name for **acyl halide.**

acidhead (ˈæsɪdˌhɛd) NOUN *Slang* a person who uses LSD.

Acid House *or* **Acid** NOUN a type of funk-based electronically edited disco music of the late 1980s, which has hypnotic sound effects and is associated with hippy culture and the use of the drug ecstasy.
▷HISTORY C20: perhaps from ACID (LSD) + HOUSE (MUSIC)

acidic (əˈsɪdɪk) ADJECTIVE 1 another word for **acid.** 2 (of an oxide) yielding an acid in aqueous solution.

acidify (əˈsɪdɪˌfaɪ) VERB **-fies, -fying, -fied.** to convert into or become acid.
▸**aˈcidiˌfiable** ADJECTIVE ▸**aˌcidifiˈcation** NOUN
▸**aˈcidiˌfier** NOUN

acidimeter (ˌæsɪˈdɪmɪtə) NOUN 1 any instrument or standard solution for determining the amount of acid in a sample solution. 2 another name for **acidometer.**

acidimetry (ˌæsɪˈdɪmɪtrɪ) NOUN the determination of the amount of acid present in a solution, measured by an acidimeter or by volumetric analysis.
▸**acidimetric** (ˌæsɪdɪˈmɛtrɪk) *or* **ˌacidiˈmetrical** ADJECTIVE
▸**ˌacidiˈmetrically** ADVERB

acidity (əˈsɪdɪtɪ) NOUN, *plural* **-ties.** 1 the quality or state of being acid. 2 the amount of acid present in a solution, often expressed in terms of pH. 3 another name for **hyperacidity.**

acidometer (ˌæsɪˈdɒmɪtə) NOUN a type of hydrometer for measuring the relative density of an acid solution, esp the acid in a battery. Also called: **acidimeter.**

acidophil (ˈæsɪdəʊˌfɪl, əˈsɪdə-) *or* **acidophile** (ˈæsɪdəʊˌfaɪl, əˈsɪdə-) ADJECTIVE *also* **acidophilic** (ˌæsɪdəʊˈfɪlɪk, əˌsɪdə-), **acidophilous** (ˌæsɪˈdɒfɪləs). 1 (of cells or cell contents) easily stained by acid dyes. 2 (of microorganisms) growing well in an acid environment. ◆ NOUN 3 an acidophil organism.
▷HISTORY C20: see ACID, -PHILE

acidophilus milk (ˌæsɪˈdɒfɪləs) NOUN *Med* milk fermented by bacteria of the species *Lactobacillus acidophilus,* used in treating disorders of the gastrointestinal tract.

acidosis (ˌæsɪˈdəʊsɪs) NOUN a condition characterized by an abnormal increase in the acidity of the blood and extracellular fluids.
▸**acidotic** (ˌæsɪˈdɒtɪk) ADJECTIVE

acid rain NOUN rain that contains a high concentration of pollutants, chiefly sulphur dioxide and nitrogen oxide, released into the atmosphere by the burning of fossil fuels such as coal or oil.

acid rock NOUN a type of rock music characterized by electronically amplified bizarre instrumental effects.
▷HISTORY C20: from ACID (sense 3), alluding to its supposed inspiration by drug-induced states of consciousness

acid salt NOUN *Chem* a salt formed by partial replacement of the acidic hydrogen atoms of the parent acid.

acid soil NOUN a soil that gives a pH reaction of below about 6, found especially in cool moist areas where soluble bases are leached away.

acid test NOUN a rigorous and conclusive test to establish worth or value: *the play passed the critic's acid test.*
▷HISTORY C19: from the testing of gold with nitric acid

acidulate (əˈsɪdjʊˌleɪt) VERB (*tr*) to make slightly acid or sour.
▷HISTORY C18: ACIDULOUS + -ATE[1]
▸**aˌciduˈlation** NOUN

acidulous (əˈsɪdjʊləs) *or* **acidulent** ADJECTIVE 1 rather sour. 2 sharp or sour in speech, manner, etc.; acid.
▷HISTORY C18: from Latin *acidulus* sourish, diminutive of *acidus* sour

acid value NOUN the number of milligrams of potassium hydroxide required to neutralize the free fatty acid in one gram of a fat, oil, resin, etc.

acierate (ˈæsɪəˌreɪt) VERB (*tr*) to change (iron) into steel.
▷HISTORY C19: from French *acier* steel, from Latin *aciēs* sharpness
▸**ˌacierˈation** NOUN

ACII ABBREVIATION FOR Associate of the Chartered Insurance Institute.

acinaciform (ˌæsɪˈnæsɪˌfɔːm) ADJECTIVE (of leaves) shaped like a scimitar; curved.
▷HISTORY C19: via Latin *acīnacēs,* from Greek *akinakēs* short sword, ultimately from Iranian + -FORM

aciniform (əˈsɪnɪˌfɔːm) ADJECTIVE shaped like a bunch of grapes.
▷HISTORY C19: from New Latin *aciniformis;* see ACINUS

acinus (ˈæsɪnəs) NOUN, *plural* **-ni** (-ˌnaɪ). 1 *Anatomy* any of the terminal saclike portions of a compound gland. 2 *Botany* any of the small drupes that make up the fruit of the blackberry, raspberry, etc. 3 *Botany, obsolete* a collection of berries, such as a bunch of grapes.
▷HISTORY C18: New Latin, from Latin: grape, berry
▸**acinic** (əˈsɪnɪk) *or* **ˈacinous** *or* **ˈacinose** ADJECTIVE

Acis (ˈeɪsɪs) NOUN *Greek myth* a Sicilian shepherd and the lover of the nymph Galatea. In jealousy, Polyphemus crushed him with a huge rock, and his blood was turned by Galatea into a river.

ack-ack (ˈækˌæk) NOUN *Military* 1 **a** anti-aircraft fire. **b** (*as modifier*): *ack-ack guns.* 2 anti-aircraft arms.
▷HISTORY C20: British army World War I phonetic alphabet for AA, abbreviation of *anti-aircraft*

ackee *or* **akee** (ˈækiː) NOUN 1 **a** a sapindaceous tree, *Blighia sapida,* native to tropical Africa and cultivated in the Caribbean for its fruit, edible when cooked. **b** the red pear-shaped fruit of this tree. 2 a sapindaceous tree, *Melicoccus bijugatus,* that grows on some Caribbean islands and is valued for its timber and edible fruit. 3 the green tough-skinned berry of this tree.
▷HISTORY C18: of African origin

ack-emma (ˈækˈɛmə) ADVERB *Old-fashioned* in the morning; a.m.
▷HISTORY World War I phonetic alphabet for A, M

acker (ˈækə) NOUN 1 *Austral informal* a variant spelling of **acca.** 2 *Austral slang* a pimple.
▷HISTORY for sense 2, a shortened form of ACNE

acknowledge (əkˈnɒlɪdʒ) VERB (*tr*) 1 (*may take a clause as object*) to recognize or admit the existence, truth, or reality of. 2 to indicate recognition or awareness of, as by a greeting, glance, etc. 3 to express appreciation or thanks for: *to acknowledge a gift.* 4 to make the receipt of known to the sender: *to acknowledge a letter.* 5 to recognize, esp in legal form, the authority, rights, or claims of.
▷HISTORY C15: probably from earlier *knowledge,* on the model of Old English *oncnāwan,* Middle English *aknowen* to confess, recognize
▸**acˈknowledgeable** ADJECTIVE ▸**acˈknowledger** NOUN

acknowledgment *or* **acknowledgement** (əkˈnɒlɪdʒmənt) NOUN 1 the act of acknowledging or state of being acknowledged. 2 something done or given as an expression of thanks, as a reply to a message, etc. 3 (*plural*) an author's statement acknowledging his use of the works of other authors, usually printed at the front of a book.

aclinic line (əˈklɪnɪk) NOUN another name for **magnetic equator.**
▷HISTORY C19: *aclinic,* from Greek *aklinēs* not bending, from A-[1] + *klinein* to bend, lean

ACLU ABBREVIATION FOR American Civil Liberties Union.

ACM ABBREVIATION FOR Air Chief Marshal.

acme (ˈækmɪ) NOUN the culminating point, as of achievement or excellence; summit; peak.
▷HISTORY C16: from Greek *akmē*

acme screw thread NOUN a type of screw thread having inclined flat flanks and a flat top and bottom: used in machine tools.

acne (ˈæknɪ) NOUN a chronic skin disease common in adolescence, involving inflammation of the

sebaceous glands and characterized by pustules on the face, neck, and upper trunk. Also called: **acne vulgaris.** ◆ See also **rosacea.**
▷HISTORY C19: New Latin, from a misreading of Greek *akmē* eruption on the face. See ACME

acnode (ˈækˌnəʊd) NOUN a point whose coordinates satisfy the equation of a curve although it does not lie on the curve; an isolated point. The origin is an acnode of the curve $y^2 + x^2 = x^3$.
▷HISTORY C19: from Latin *acus* a needle + NODE
▸**acˈnodal** ADJECTIVE

Acol (ˈækᵊl) NOUN *Bridge* a popular British bidding system favouring light opening bids and a flexible approach.
▷HISTORY C20: named after a club in Acol Road, London

acolyte (ˈækəˌlaɪt) NOUN [1] a follower or attendant. [2] *Christianity* an officer who attends or assists a priest.
▷HISTORY C16: via Old French and Medieval Latin from Greek *akolouthos* a follower

Aconcagua (*Spanish* akonˈkaɣwa) NOUN a mountain in W Argentina: the highest peak in the Andes and in the W Hemisphere. Height: 6960 m (22 835 ft.).

aconite (ˈækəˌnaɪt) *or* **aconitum** (ˌækəˈnaɪtəm) NOUN [1] any of various N temperate plants of the ranunculaceous genus *Aconitum,* such as monkshood and wolfsbane, many of which are poisonous. Compare **winter aconite.** [2] the dried poisonous root of many of these plants, sometimes used as an antipyretic.
▷HISTORY C16: via Old French or Latin from Greek *akoniton* aconite, monkshood
▸**aconitic** (ˌækəˈnɪtɪk) ADJECTIVE

Açôres (əˈsorəʃ) NOUN the Portuguese name for (the) **Azores.**

acorn (ˈeɪkɔːn) NOUN the fruit of an oak tree, consisting of a smooth thick-walled nut in a woody scaly cuplike base.
▷HISTORY C16: a variant (through influence of *corn*) of Old English *æcern* the fruit of a tree, acorn; related to Gothic *akran* fruit, yield

acorn barnacle *or* **shell** NOUN any of various barnacles, such as *Balanus balanoides,* that live attached to rocks and have a volcano-shaped shell from the top of which protrude feathery food-catching appendages (cirri).

acorn valve *or US* **tube** NOUN a small electronic valve, approximately acorn-shaped with small closely-spaced electrodes, used in ultrahigh-frequency applications.

acorn worm NOUN any of various small burrowing marine animals of the genus *Balanoglossus* and related genera, having an elongated wormlike body with an acorn-shaped eversible proboscis at the head end: subphylum *Hemichordata* (hemichordates).

acotyledon (əˌkɒtɪˈliːdᵊn) NOUN any plant, such as a fern or moss, that does not possess cotyledons.
▸**aˌcotyˈledonous** ADJECTIVE

acouchi *or* **acouchy** (əˈkuːʃɪ) NOUN, *plural* **-chis** *or* **-chies.** any of several South American rodents of the genus *Myoprocta,* closely related to the agoutis but much smaller, with a white-tipped tail: family *Dasyproctidae.*
▷HISTORY C19: via French from a native name in Guiana

acoustic (əˈkuːstɪk) *or* **acoustical** ADJECTIVE [1] of or related to sound, the sense of hearing, or acoustics. [2] designed to respond to, absorb, or control sound: *an acoustic tile.* [3] (of a musical instrument or recording) without electronic amplification: *an acoustic bass; an acoustic guitar.*
▷HISTORY C17: from Greek *akoustikos,* from *akouein* to hear
▸**aˈcoustically** ADVERB

acoustic coupler NOUN *Computing* a device converting computer-data signals into acoustic form for transmission down a telephone line, through the handset microphone. See also **modem.**

acoustic feature NOUN *Phonetics* any of the acoustic components or elements present in a speech sound and capable of being experimentally observed, recorded, and reproduced.

acoustic guitar NOUN an ordinary guitar, which produces its normal sound through the sounding board and is not amplified in any way. Compare **electric guitar.**

acoustician (ˌækʊˈstɪʃən) NOUN an expert in acoustics.

acoustic nerve NOUN the former name for **vestibulocochlear nerve.**

acoustic phonetics NOUN (*functioning as singular*) the branch of phonetics concerned with the acoustic properties of human speech. Compare **auditory phonetics, articulatory phonetics.**

acoustics (əˈkuːstɪks) NOUN [1] (*functioning as singular*) the scientific study of sound and sound waves. [2] (*functioning as plural*) the characteristics of a room, auditorium, etc., that determine the fidelity with which sound can be heard within it.

acoustic shock NOUN a condition characterized by dizziness and partial hearing loss suffered by some people exposed to sudden loud noises over telephone or radio headsets; associated esp with workers in call centres.

acoustoelectronic (əˌkuːstəʊˌɪlɛkˈtrɒnɪk) ADJECTIVE denoting a device in which electronic signals are converted into acoustic waves, esp in delay lines, etc. Also: **electroacoustic.**
▸**aˌcoustoˌelecˈtronics** NOUN

acquaint (əˈkweɪnt) VERB (*tr*) [1] (foll by *with* or *of*) to make (a person) familiar or conversant (with); inform (of). [2] (foll by *with*) *Chiefly US* to introduce (to); bring into contact (with).
▷HISTORY C13: via Old French and Medieval Latin from Latin *accognitus,* from *accognōscere* to know perfectly, from *ad-* (intensive) + *cognōscere* to know

acquaintance (əˈkweɪntəns) NOUN [1] a person with whom one has been in contact but who is not a close friend. [2] knowledge of a person or thing, esp when slight. [3] **make the acquaintance of.** to come into social contact with. [4] those persons collectively whom one knows. [5] *Philosophy* the relation between a knower and the object of his knowledge, as contrasted with knowledge by description (esp in the phrase **knowledge by acquaintance**).
▸**acˈquaintanceˌship** NOUN

acquaintance violence NOUN impulsive aggressive behaviour towards someone with whom the attacker has been in contact.

acquainted (əˈkweɪntɪd) ADJECTIVE (*postpositive*) [1] (sometimes foll by *with*) on terms of familiarity but not intimacy. [2] (foll by *with*) having knowledge or experience (of); familiar (with).

acquiesce (ˌækwɪˈɛs) VERB (*intr;* often foll by *in* or *to*) to comply (with); assent (to) without protest.
▷HISTORY C17: from Latin *acquiēscere* to remain at rest, agree without protest, from *ad-* at + *quiēscere* to rest, from *quiēs* QUIET
▸**ˌacquiˈescence** NOUN ▸**ˌacquiˈescent** ADJECTIVE
▸**ˌacquiˈescently** ADVERB

> **Language note** The use of *to* after *acquiesce* was formerly regarded as incorrect, but is now acceptable.

acquire (əˈkwaɪə) VERB (*tr*) to get or gain (something, such as an object, trait, or ability), esp more or less permanently.
▷HISTORY C15: via Old French from Latin *acquīrere,* from *ad-* in addition + *quaerere* to get, seek
▸**acˈquirable** ADJECTIVE ▸**acˈquirement** NOUN ▸**acˈquirer** NOUN

acquired behaviour NOUN *Psychol* the behaviour of an organism resulting from the effects of the environment.

acquired characteristic NOUN a characteristic of an organism that results from increased use or disuse of an organ or the effects of the environment and cannot be inherited. See also **Lamarckism.**

acquired drive NOUN *Psychol* a drive, like the desire for money, that has not been inherited but is learned, presumably because it leads to the satisfaction of innate drives.

acquired immune deficiency syndrome *or* **acquired immunodeficiency syndrome** NOUN the full name for **AIDS.**

acquired immunity NOUN the immunity produced by exposure of an organism to antigens, which stimulates the production of antibodies.

acquired taste NOUN [1] a liking for something that is at first considered unpleasant. [2] the thing so liked.

acquisition (ˌækwɪˈzɪʃən) NOUN [1] the act of acquiring or gaining possession. [2] something acquired. [3] a person or thing of special merit added to a group. [4] *Astronautics* the process of locating a spacecraft, satellite, etc., esp by radar, in order to gather tracking and telemetric information.
▷HISTORY C14: from Latin *acquīsītiōn-,* from *acquīrere* to ACQUIRE

acquisition accounting NOUN an accounting procedure in which the assets of a company that has recently been taken over are changed from the book value to the fair market value.

acquisitive (əˈkwɪzɪtɪv) ADJECTIVE inclined or eager to acquire things, esp material possessions.
▸**acˈquisitively** ADVERB ▸**acˈquisitiveness** NOUN

acquit (əˈkwɪt) VERB **-quits, -quitting, -quitted.** (*tr*) [1] (foll by *of*) **a** to free or release (from a charge of crime). **b** to pronounce not guilty. [2] (foll by *of*) to free or relieve (from an obligation, duty, responsibility, etc.). [3] to repay or settle (something, such as a debt or obligation). [4] to perform (one's part); conduct (oneself).
▷HISTORY C13: from Old French *aquiter,* from *quiter* to release, free from, QUIT
▸**acˈquitter** NOUN

acquittal (əˈkwɪtᵊl) NOUN [1] *Criminal law* the deliverance and release of a person appearing before a court on a charge of crime, as by a finding of not guilty. [2] a discharge or release from an obligation, duty, debt, etc.

acquittance (əˈkwɪtəns) NOUN [1] a release from or settlement of a debt, etc. [2] a record of this, such as a receipt.

acre (ˈeɪkə) NOUN [1] a unit of area used in certain English-speaking countries, equal to 4840 square yards or 4046.86 square metres. [2] (*plural*) **a** land, esp a large area. **b** *Informal* a large amount: *he has acres of space in his room.* [3] **farm the long acre.** *NZ* to graze cows on the verge of a road.
▷HISTORY Old English *æcer* field, acre; related to Old Norse *akr,* German *Acker,* Latin *ager* field, Sanskrit *ajra* field

Acre NOUN [1] (ˈɑːkrə) a state of W Brazil: mostly unexplored tropical forests; acquired from Bolivia in 1903. Capital: Rio Branco. Pop.: 557 337 (2000 est.). Area: 152 589 sq. km (58 899 sq. miles). [2] (ˈeɪkə, ˈɑːkə) a city and port in N Israel, strategically situated on the **Bay of Acre** in the E Mediterranean: taken and retaken during the Crusades (1104, 1187, 1191, 1291), taken by the Turks (1517), by Egypt (1832), and by the Turks again (1839). Pop.: 40 500 (1989 est.). Old Testament name: **Accho** (ɑːˈkəʊ). Arabic name: **ʿAkka** (ɑːˈkɑː). Hebrew name: **ʿAkko** (ɑːˈkəʊ).

acreage (ˈeɪkərɪdʒ) NOUN [1] land area in acres. ◆ ADJECTIVE [2] *Austral* of or relating to a large allotment of land, esp in a rural area.

acred (ˈeɪkəd) ADJECTIVE (*usually in combination*) having acres of land: *a many-acred farm; a well-acred nobleman.*

acre-foot NOUN, *plural* **-feet.** the volume of water that would cover an area of 1 acre to a depth of 1 foot: equivalent to 43 560 cubic feet or 1233.5 cubic metres.

acre-inch NOUN the volume of water that would cover an area of 1 acre to a depth of 1 inch; one twelfth of an acre-foot: equivalent to 3630 cubic feet or 102.8 cubic metres.

acrid (ˈækrɪd) ADJECTIVE [1] unpleasantly pungent or sharp to the smell or taste. [2] sharp or caustic, esp in speech or nature.
▷HISTORY C18: from Latin *ācer* sharp, sour; probably formed on the model of ACID
▸**acridity** (əˈkrɪdɪtɪ) *or* **ˈacridness** NOUN ▸**ˈacridly** ADVERB

acridine (ˈækrɪˌdiːn) NOUN a colourless crystalline solid used in the manufacture of dyes. Formula: $C_{13}H_9N$.

acriflavine (ˌækrɪˈfleɪvɪn, -viːn) NOUN a brownish or orange-red powder used in medicine as an antiseptic and disinfectant. Formula: $C_{14}H_{14}N_3Cl$.
▷HISTORY C20: from ACRIDINE + FLAVIN

acriflavine hydrochloride NOUN a red crystalline water-soluble solid substance obtained from acriflavine and used as an antiseptic. Also called: **flavine.**

Acrilan ('ækrɪˌlæn) NOUN *Trademark* an acrylic fibre or fabric, characterized by strength, softness, and crease-resistance and used for clothing, upholstery, carpets, etc.

acrimonious (ˌækrɪ'məʊnɪəs) ADJECTIVE characterized by bitterness or sharpness of manner, speech, temper, etc.
▸ ˌ**acri'moniously** ADVERB ▸ ˌ**acri'moniousness** NOUN

acrimony ('ækrɪmənɪ) NOUN, *plural* **-nies.** bitterness or sharpness of manner, speech, temper, etc.
▷ HISTORY C16: from Latin *ācrimōnia,* from *ācer* sharp, sour

acro- COMBINING FORM 1 denoting something at a height, summit, top, tip, beginning, or end: *acropolis; acrogen.* 2 denoting an extremity of the human body: *acromegaly.*
▷ HISTORY from Greek *akros* extreme, topmost

acrobat ('ækrəˌbæt) NOUN 1 an entertainer who performs acts that require skill, agility, and coordination, such as tumbling, swinging from a trapeze, or walking a tightrope. 2 a person noted for his frequent and rapid changes of position or allegiances: *a political acrobat.*
▷ HISTORY C19: via French from Greek *akrobatēs* acrobat, one who walks on tiptoe, from ACRO- + *bat-,* from *bainein* to walk
▸ ˌ**acro'batic** ADJECTIVE ▸ ˌ**acro'batically** ADVERB

acrobatics (ˌækrə'bætɪks) NOUN 1 (*functioning as plural*) the skills or feats of an acrobat. 2 (*functioning as singular*) the art of an acrobat. 3 (*functioning as plural*) any activity requiring agility and skill: *mental acrobatics.*

acrocarpous (ˌækrəʊ'kɑːpəs) ADJECTIVE (of mosses) having clustered upright stems and the reproductive parts borne at the tip of a stem. ◆ Compare **pleurocarpous.**
▷ HISTORY C19: from New Latin, from Greek *akrokarpos*

acrocentric (ˌækrəʊ'sɛntrɪk) ADJECTIVE 1 (of a chromosome) having the centromere at one end. ◆ NOUN 2 an acrocentric chromosome.

acrocyanosis (ˌækrəʊˌsaɪə'nəʊsɪs) NOUN cyanosis of the hands and feet due to poor circulation of the blood.

acrodont ('ækrəˌdɒnt) ADJECTIVE 1 (of the teeth of some reptiles) having no roots and being fused at the base to the margin of the jawbones. See also **pleurodont** (sense 1). 2 having acrodont teeth.
▷ HISTORY C19: from ACRO- + -ODONT

acrodrome ('ækrəˌdrəʊm) ADJECTIVE (of the veins of a leaf) running parallel to the edges of the leaf and fusing at the tip. Also: **acrodromous** (ə'krɒdrəməs).
▷ HISTORY from ACRO- + -DROMOUS

acrogen ('ækrədʒən) NOUN any flowerless plant, such as a fern or moss, in which growth occurs from the tip of the main stem.
▷ HISTORY C19: from ACRO- + Greek *genēs* born; see -GEN
▸ **acrogenic** (ˌækrə'dʒɛnɪk) *or* **acrogenous** (ə'krɒdʒɪnəs) ADJECTIVE ▸ **a'crogenously** ADVERB

acrolein (ə'krəʊlɪɪn) NOUN a colourless or yellowish flammable poisonous pungent liquid used in the manufacture of resins and pharmaceuticals. Formula: CH_2:CHCHO.
▷ HISTORY C19: from Latin *ācer* sharp + *olēre* to smell + -IN

acrolith ('ækrəlɪθ) NOUN (esp in ancient Greek sculpture) a wooden, often draped figure with only the head, hands, and feet in stone.
▷ HISTORY C19: via Latin *acrolithus* from Greek *akrolithos* having stone extremities
▸ ˌ**acro'lithic** ADJECTIVE

acromegaly (ˌækrəʊ'mɛgəlɪ) NOUN a chronic disease characterized by enlargement of the bones of the head, hands, and feet, and swelling and enlargement of soft tissue, esp the tongue. It is caused by excessive secretion of growth hormone by the pituitary gland. Compare **gigantism.**
▷ HISTORY C19: from French *acromégalie,* from ACRO- + Greek *megal-,* stem of *megas* big
▸ **acromegalic** (ˌækrəʊmɪ'gælɪk) ADJECTIVE, NOUN

acromion (ə'krəʊmɪən) NOUN, *plural* **-mia** (-mɪə). the outermost edge of the spine of the shoulder blade.
▷ HISTORY C17: New Latin, from Greek *akrōmion* the point of the shoulder, from ACRO- + *ōmion,* diminutive of *ōmos* shoulder

acronychal, acronycal, *or US* **acronical** (ə'krɒnɪkᵊl) ADJECTIVE occurring at sunset: *the star has an acronychal rising.*
▷ HISTORY C16: from Greek *akronychos* at sunset, from ACRO- + *nykh-, nyx* night
▸ **a'cronychally** *or* **a'cronycally** *or US* **a'cronically** ADVERB

acronym ('ækrənɪm) NOUN a pronounceable name made up of a series of initial letters or parts of words; for example, *UNESCO* for the *United Nations Educational, Scientific, and Cultural Organization.*
▷ HISTORY C20: from ACRO- + -ONYM
▸ ˌ**acro'nymic** *or* **acronymous** (ə'krɒnɪməs) ADJECTIVE

acroparaesthesia (ˌækrəʊˌpæres'θiːzɪə) *or US* **acroparesthesia** NOUN *Pathol* a persistent sensation of numbness and tingling in the hands and feet.

acropetal (ə'krɒpɪtᵊl) ADJECTIVE (of leaves and flowers) produced in order from the base upwards so that the youngest are at the apex. Compare **basipetal.**

acrophobia (ˌækrə'fəʊbɪə) NOUN abnormal fear or dread of being at a great height.
▷ HISTORY C19: from ACRO- + -PHOBIA
▸ ˌ**acro'phobic** ADJECTIVE

acropolis (ə'krɒpəlɪs) NOUN the citadel of an ancient Greek city.
▷ HISTORY C17: from Greek, from ACRO- + *polis* city

Acropolis (ə'krɒpəlɪs) NOUN the citadel of Athens on which the Parthenon and the Erechtheum stand.

acrospire ('ækrəˌspaɪə) NOUN the first shoot developing from the plumule of a germinating grain seed.
▷ HISTORY C17: from obsolete *akerspire,* from *aker* EAR[2] + *spire* sprout, SPIRE[1]; the modern form is influenced by ACRO-

across (ə'krɒs) PREPOSITION 1 from one side to the other side of. 2 on or at the other side of. 3 so as to transcend boundaries or barriers: *people united across borders by religion and history; the study of linguistics across cultures.* ◆ ADVERB 4 from one side to the other. 5 on or to the other side.
▷ HISTORY C13 *on croice, acros,* from Old French *a croix* crosswise

across-the-board ADJECTIVE 1 (of salary increases, taxation cuts, etc.) affecting all levels or classes equally. 2 *Horse racing* the US term for **each way.**

acrostic (ə'krɒstɪk) NOUN **a** a number of lines of writing, such as a poem, certain letters of which form a word, proverb, etc. A **single acrostic** is formed by the initial letters of the lines, a **double acrostic** by the initial and final letters, and a **triple acrostic** by the initial, middle, and final letters. **b** the word, proverb, etc., so formed. **c** (*as modifier*): *an acrostic sonnet.*
▷ HISTORY C16: via French from Greek *akrostikhis,* from ACRO- + *stikhos* line of verse, STICH
▸ **a'crostically** ADVERB

acroter (ə'krəʊtə, 'ækrətə) NOUN *Architect* a plinth bearing a statue, etc., at either end or at the apex of a pediment.
▷ HISTORY C18: from French, from Latin *acroterium,* from Greek *akrōtērion* summit, from *akros* extreme

acrylic (ə'krɪlɪk) ADJECTIVE 1 of, derived from, or concerned with acrylic acid. ◆ NOUN 2 short for **acrylic fibre, acrylic resin.** 3 a paint or colour containing acrylic resin.
▷ HISTORY C20: from ACROLEIN + -YL + -IC

acrylic acid NOUN a colourless corrosive pungent liquid, miscible with water, used in the manufacture of acrylic resins. Formula: CH_2:CHCOOH. Systematic name: **propenoic acid.**

acrylic fibre NOUN a textile fibre, such as Orlon or Acrilan, produced from acrylonitrile.

acrylic resin NOUN any of a group of polymers or copolymers of acrylic acid, its esters, or amides, used as synthetic rubbers, textiles, paints, adhesives, and as plastics such as Perspex.

acrylonitrile (ˌækrɪləʊ'naɪtraɪl) NOUN a colourless liquid that is miscible with water and has toxic fumes: used in the manufacture of acrylic fibres and resins, rubber, and thermoplastics. Formula: CH_2:CHCN. Also called: **vinylcyanide.**
▷ HISTORY C20: from ACRYLIC + NITRILE

acrylyl ('ækrɪlɪl) NOUN (*modifier*) of, consisting of, or containing the monovalent group CH_2:CHCO-: *acrylyl group or radical.*

act (ækt) NOUN 1 something done or performed; a deed. 2 the performance of some physical or mental process; action. 3 (*capital when part of a name*) the formally codified result of deliberation by a legislative body; a law, edict, decree, statute, etc. 4 (*often plural*) a formal written record of transactions, proceedings, etc., as of a society, committee, or legislative body. 5 a major division of a dramatic work. 6 **a** a short performance of skill, a comic sketch, dance, etc., esp one that is part of a programme of light entertainment. **b** those giving such a performance. 7 an assumed attitude or pose, esp one intended to impress. 8 *Philosophy* an occurrence effected by the volition of a human agent, usually opposed at least as regards its explanation to one which is causally determined. Compare **event** (sense 4). ◆ VERB 9 (*intr*) to do something; carry out an action. 10 (*intr*) to function in a specified way; operate; react: *his mind acted quickly.* 11 to perform (a part or role) in a play, etc. 12 (*tr*) to present (a play, etc.) on stage. 13 (*intr;* usually foll by *for* or *as*) to be a substitute (for); function in place (of). 14 (*intr;* foll by *as*) to serve the function or purpose (of): *the glass acted as protection.* 15 (*intr*) to conduct oneself or behave (as if one were): *she usually acts like a lady.* 16 (*intr*) to behave in an unnatural or affected way. 17 (*copula*) to pose as; play the part of: *to act the fool.* 18 (*copula*) to behave in a manner appropriate to (esp in the phrase **act one's age**). 19 (*copula*) *Not standard* to seem or pretend to be: *to act tired.* 20 **clean up one's act.** to start to behave in a responsible manner. 21 **get in on the act.** *Informal* to become involved in a profitable undertaking or advantageous situation in order to share in the benefits. 22 **get one's act together.** *Informal* to become organized or prepared. ◆ See also **act on, act out, act up.**
▷ HISTORY C14: from Latin *actus* a doing, performance, and *actum* a thing done, from the past participle of *agere* to do
▸ **'actable** ADJECTIVE ▸ ˌ**acta'bility** NOUN

ACT[1] ABBREVIATION FOR: 1 Australian Capital Territory. 2 (formerly in Britain) advance corporation tax.

ACT[2] (ækt) NOUN (in New Zealand) ACRONYM FOR Association of Consumers and Taxpayers: a small political party of the right.

Actaeon (æk'tiːən, 'æktɪən) NOUN *Greek myth* a hunter of Boeotia who, having accidentally seen Artemis bathing, was turned into a stag and torn apart by his own hounds.

actant ('æktənt) NOUN *Linguistics* (in valency grammar) a noun phrase functioning as the agent of the main verb of a sentence.

actg ABBREVIATION FOR acting.

ACTH NOUN adrenocorticotrophic hormone; a polypeptide hormone, secreted by the anterior lobe of the pituitary gland, that stimulates growth of the adrenal gland and the synthesis and secretion of corticosteroids. It is used in treating rheumatoid arthritis, allergic and skin diseases, and many other disorders. Also called: **corticotrophin.**

actin ('æktɪn) NOUN a protein that participates in many kinds of cell movement, including muscle contraction, during which it interacts with filaments of a second protein, myosin.
▷ HISTORY C20: from ACT + -IN

actinal ('æktɪnᵊl, æk'taɪnᵊl) ADJECTIVE 1 of or denoting the oral part of a radiate animal, such as a jellyfish, sea anemone, or sponge, from which the rays, tentacles, or arms grow. 2 possessing rays or tentacles, as a jellyfish.
▷ HISTORY C19: see ACTINO-, -AL[1]
▸ **'actinally** ADVERB

acting ('æktɪŋ) ADJECTIVE (*prenominal*) 1 taking on duties temporarily, esp as a substitute for another: *the acting president.* 2 operating or functioning: *an acting order.* 3 intended for stage performance; provided with directions for actors: *an acting version of "Hedda Gabler".* ◆ NOUN 4 the art or profession of an actor.

actinia (æk'tɪnɪə) NOUN, *plural* **-tiniae** (-'tɪnɪˌiː) *or* **-tinias**. any sea anemone of the genus *Actinia,* which are common in rock pools.
▷HISTORY C18: New Latin, literally: things having a radial structure. See ACTINO-, -IA

actinic (æk'tɪnɪk) ADJECTIVE (of radiation) producing a photochemical effect.
▷HISTORY C19: from ACTINO- + -IC
▸**ac'tinically** ADVERB ▸**'actinˌism** NOUN

actinide ('æktɪˌnaɪd) NOUN a member of the actinide series. Also called: **actinon.**
▷HISTORY C19: from ACTINO- + -IDE

actinide series NOUN a series of 15 radioactive elements with increasing atomic numbers from actinium to lawrencium.

actiniform (æk'tɪnɪˌfɔːm) ADJECTIVE another word for **actinoid.**
▷HISTORY C20: from ACTINO- + -FORM

actinium (æk'tɪnɪəm) NOUN a radioactive element of the actinide series, occurring as a decay product of uranium. It is used as an alpha-particle source and in neutron production. Symbol: Ac; atomic no.: 89; half-life of most stable isotope, ^{227}Ac: 21.6 years; relative density: 10.07; melting pt.: 1051°C; boiling pt.: 3200 ± 300°C.
▷HISTORY C19: New Latin, from ACTINO- + -IUM

actinium series NOUN a radioactive decay series that starts with uranium-235 and ends with lead-207.

actino- *or before a vowel* **actin-** COMBINING FORM [1] indicating a radial structure: *actinomorphic.* [2] indicating radioactivity or radiation: *actinometer.*
▷HISTORY from Greek *aktino-,* from *aktis* beam, ray

actinobacillosis (æktiːnəʊˌbæsɪl'əʊsɪs) NOUN *Vet science* a disease of cattle and sheep, caused by infection with an *Actinobacillus lignieresii* and characterized by soft tissue lesions, esp of the tongue. Also called: **wooden tongue, woody tongue, cruels.**

actinochemistry (ækˌtɪnəʊ'kɛmɪstrɪ) NOUN another name for **photochemistry.**

actinodermatitis (ˌæktɪnəʊˌdɜːmə'taɪtɪs) NOUN dermatitis from exposure to radiation, esp ultraviolet light or X-rays.

actinoid ('æktɪˌnɔɪd) ADJECTIVE having a radiate form, as a sea anemone or starfish.

actinolite (æk'tɪnəˌlaɪt) NOUN a green mineral of the amphibole group consisting of calcium magnesium iron silicate. Formula: $Ca_2(Mg,Fe)_5Si_8O_{22}(OH)_2$.
▷HISTORY C19: from ACTINO- (from the radiating crystals in some forms) + -LITE

actinomere ('æktɪnəʊˌmɪə) NOUN another name for **antimere.**

actinometer (ˌæktɪ'nɒmɪtə) NOUN an instrument for measuring the intensity of radiation, esp of the sun's rays.
▸**actinometric** (ˌæktɪnəʊ'mɛtrɪk) *or* **ˌactino'metrical** ADJECTIVE ▸**ˌacti'nometry** NOUN

actinomorphic (ˌæktɪnəʊ'mɔːfɪk) *or* **actinomorphous** ADJECTIVE *Botany* (esp of a flower) having radial symmetry, as buttercups. See also **zygomorphic.**
▸**'actinoˌmorphy** NOUN

actinomycete (ˌæktɪnəʊmaɪ'siːt) NOUN any bacterium of the group *Actinomycetes,* usually filamentous in form.
▷HISTORY C20: from ACTINO- + -MYCETE

actinomycin (ˌæktɪnəʊ'maɪsɪn) NOUN any of several toxic antibiotics obtained from bacteria of the genus *Streptomyces,* used in treating some cancers; the most commonly used is dactinomycin (actinomycin D).

actinomycosis (ˌæktɪnəʊmaɪ'kəʊsɪs) NOUN a fungal disease of cattle and of cats and dogs, sometimes transmitted to humans esp by bites, characterized by a swelling of the affected part, most often the jaw or lungs. Nontechnical name: **lumpy jaw.**
▸**actinomycotic** (ˌæktɪnəʊmaɪ'kɒtɪk) ADJECTIVE

actinon ('æktɪˌnɒn) NOUN [1] a radioisotope of radon that is a decay product of radium. Symbol: An or ^{219}Rn; atomic no.: 86; half-life: 3.92s. [2] another name for **actinide.**
▷HISTORY C20: New Latin, from ACTINIUM + -ON

actinopod (æk'tɪnəˌpɒd) NOUN any protozoan of the phylum *Actinopoda,* such as a radiolarian or a heliozoan, having stiff radiating cytoplasmic projections.

actinotherapy (ˌæktɪnəʊ'θɛrəpɪ) NOUN a former name for **radiotherapy.**

actinouranium (ˌæktɪnəʊjʊ'reɪnɪəm) NOUN the isotope of uranium that has a mass number of 235.

actinozoan (ˌæktɪnəʊ'zəʊən) NOUN, ADJECTIVE another word for **anthozoan.**

action ('ækʃən) NOUN [1] the state or process of doing something or being active; operation. [2] something done, such as an act or deed. [3] movement or posture during some physical activity. [4] activity, force, or energy: *a man of action.* [5] (*usually plural*) conduct or behaviour. [6] *Law* **a** a legal proceeding brought by one party against another, seeking redress of a wrong or recovery of what is due; lawsuit. **b** the right to bring such a proceeding. [7] the operating mechanism, esp in a piano, gun, watch, etc. [8] (of a guitar) the distance between the strings and the fingerboard. [9] (of keyboard instruments) the sensitivity of the keys to touch. [10] the force applied to a body: *the reaction is equal and opposite to the action.* [11] the way in which something operates or works. [12] *Physics* **a** a property of a system expressed as twice the mean kinetic energy of the system over a given time interval multiplied by the time interval. **b** the product of work or energy and time, usually expressed in joule seconds: *Planck's constant of action.* [13] the events that form the plot of a story, film, play, or other composition. [14] *Military* **a** a minor engagement. **b** fighting at sea or on land: *he saw action in the war.* [15] *Philosophy* behaviour which is voluntary and explicable in terms of the agent's reasons, as contrasted with that which is coerced or determined causally. [16] *Brit* short for **industrial action.** [17] *Informal* the profits of an enterprise or transaction (esp in the phrase **a piece of the action**). [18] *Slang* the main activity, esp social activity. ◆ VERB (*tr*) [19] to put into effect; take action concerning: *matters decided at the meeting cannot be actioned until the following week.* ◆ INTERJECTION [20] a command given by a film director to indicate that filming is to begin. See also **cue**[1] (senses 1, 8).
▷HISTORY C14 *accioun,* ultimately from Latin *āctiōn-,* stem of *āctiō,* from *agere* to do, act

actionable ('ækʃənəbᵊl) ADJECTIVE *Law* affording grounds for legal action.
▸**'actionably** ADVERB

action at a distance NOUN *Physics* the supposed interaction of two separated bodies without any intervening medium. In modern theories all interactions are assumed to require a field of force.

actioner ('ækʃənə) NOUN *Informal* a film with a fast-moving plot, usually containing scenes of violence.

action figure NOUN a small figure of a character from a film, television programme, comic book etc., designed as a toy and often collected by enthusiasts.

action painting ◆ NOUN a development of abstract expressionism evolved in the 1940s, characterized by broad vigorous brush strokes and accidental effects of thrown, smeared, dripped, or spattered paint. Also called: **tachisme.** See also **abstract expressionism.**

action potential NOUN a localized change in electrical potential, from about –70 mV to +30 mV and back again, that occurs across a nerve fibre during transmission of a nerve impulse.

action replay NOUN the rerunning of a small section of a television film or tape of a match or other sporting contest, often in slow motion. US and Canadian name: **instant replay.**

action stations PLURAL NOUN [1] *Military* the positions taken up by individuals in preparation for or during a battle. ◆ INTERJECTION [2] *Military* a command to take up such positions. [3] *Informal* a warning to get ready for something.

Actium ('æktɪəm) NOUN a town of ancient Greece that overlooked the naval battle in 31 B.C. at which Octavian's fleet under Agrippa defeated that of Mark Antony and Cleopatra.

activate ('æktɪˌveɪt) VERB (*tr*) [1] to make active or capable of action. [2] *Physics* to make radioactive. [3] *Chem* **a** to increase the rate of (a reaction). **b** so as to treat (a substance, such as carbon or alumina) so as to increase powers of adsorption. [4] *Physiol* to prepare by arousal (the body or one of its organs (e.g. the brain)) for action. [5] to purify (sewage) by aeration. [6] *US military* to create, mobilize, or organize (a unit).
▸**ˌacti'vation** NOUN ▸**'actiˌvator** NOUN

activated alumina NOUN a granular highly porous and adsorptive form of aluminium oxide, used for drying gases and as an oil-filtering material and catalyst.

activated carbon NOUN a porous highly adsorptive form of carbon used to remove colour or impurities from liquids and gases, in the separation and extraction of chemical compounds, and in the recovery of solvents. Also called: **activated charcoal, active carbon.**

activated sludge NOUN a mass of aerated precipitated sewage added to untreated sewage to bring about purification by hastening decomposition by microorganisms.

active ('æktɪv) ADJECTIVE [1] in a state of action; moving, working, or doing something. [2] busy or involved: *an active life.* [3] physically energetic. [4] exerting influence; effective: *an active ingredient.* [5] *Grammar* **a** denoting a voice of verbs used to indicate that the subject of a sentence is performing the action or causing the event or process described by the verb, as *kicked* in *The boy kicked the football.* Compare **passive** (sense 5). **b** another word for **nonstative.** [6] being fully engaged in military service (esp in the phrase **on active service**). [7] (of a volcano) erupting periodically; not extinct. Compare **dormant** (sense 3), **extinct** (sense 3). [8] *Astronomy* (of the sun) exhibiting a large number of sunspots, solar flares, etc., and a marked variation in intensity and frequency of radio emission. Compare **quiet** (sense 8). [9] *Commerce* **a** producing or being used to produce profit, esp in the form of interest: *active balances.* **b** of or denoting stocks or shares that have been actively bought and sold as recorded in the Official List of the London Stock Exchange. [10] *Electronics* **a** containing a source of power: *an active network.* **b** capable of amplifying a signal or controlling some function: *an active component; an active communication satellite.* ◆ NOUN [11] *Grammar* **a** the active voice. **b** an active verb. [12] *Chiefly US* a member of an organization who participates in its activities.
▷HISTORY C14: from Latin *āctīvus.* See ACT, -IVE
▸**'actively** ADVERB ▸**'activeness** NOUN

active centre NOUN *Biochem* the region in an enzyme molecule in which the reactive groups that participate in its action are juxtaposed. Also called: **active site.**

active galaxy NOUN a galaxy that emits usually large amounts of energy from a very compact central source, such as Seyfert galaxies, radio galaxies, and quasars. Also called: **active galactic nucleus.**

active list NOUN *Military* a list of officers available for full duty.

active matrix NOUN *Computing* **a** a liquid crystal display in which each pixel is individually controlled to provide a sharp image at a wide viewing angle; it is used in laptop and notebook computers. **b** (*as modifier*): *an active-matrix screen.*

active optics NOUN (*functioning as singular*) a system to compensate for any deformation caused by gravity in the surface accuracy and alignment of the mirrors of an astronomical telescope by means of actuators that control the movable mirror supports.

active safety NOUN the practice of taking measures to avoid accidents, as opposed to merely reducing their consequences. Compare **passive safety.**

active service *or esp US* **active duty** NOUN military duty in an operational area.

active transport NOUN *Biochem, physiol* a process by which molecules are enabled to pass across a membrane from a region in which they are in a low concentration to one of high concentration; this requires the expenditure of energy in metabolism and is assisted by carrier proteins, commonly referred to as pumps.

active vocabulary NOUN the total number of words a person uses in his own speech and writing. Compare **passive vocabulary.**

activism ('æktɪˌvɪzəm) NOUN a policy of taking

direct and often militant action to achieve an end, esp a political or social one.
▸ **'activist** NOUN

activity (æk'tɪvɪtɪ) NOUN, *plural* **-ties.** 1 the state or quality of being active. 2 lively action or movement. 3 any specific deed, action, pursuit, etc.: *recreational activities.* 4 the number of disintegrations of a radioactive substance in a given unit of time, usually expressed in curies or disintegrations per second. 5 **a** the capacity of a substance to undergo chemical change. **b** the effective concentration of a substance in a chemical system. The **absolute activity** of a substance B, λ_B, is defined as exp ($\mu_B RT$) where μ_B is the chemical potential.

act of contrition NOUN *Christianity* a short prayer of penitence.

act of faith NOUN *Christianity* an act that demonstrates or tests a person's religious beliefs.

act of God NOUN *Law* a sudden and inevitable occurrence caused by natural forces and not by the agency of man, such as a flood, earthquake, or a similar catastrophe.

act of war NOUN an aggressive act, usually employing military force, which constitutes an immediate threat to peace.

actomyosin (ˌæktəʊ'maɪəsɪn) NOUN a complex protein in skeletal muscle that is formed by actin and myosin and which, when stimulated, shortens to cause muscle contraction.

acton ('æktən) NOUN (in medieval Europe) 1 a jacket or jerkin, originally of quilted cotton, worn under a coat of mail. 2 a leather jacket padded with mail.
▷ HISTORY C14: from Old French *auqueton,* probably ultimately from Arabic *alqutun* the cotton

Acton ('æktən) NOUN a district of the London borough of Ealing.

act on *or* **upon** VERB (*intr, preposition*) 1 to regulate one's behaviour in accordance with (advice, information, etc.). 2 to have an effect on (illness, a part of the body, etc.).

actor ('æktə) NOUN 1 a person who acts in a play, film, broadcast, etc. 2 *Informal* a person who puts on a false manner in order to deceive others (often in the phrase **bad actor**).

> **Language note** To avoid referring to people by their gender, *actor* is often used as a general term for women and men who act.

act out VERB (*adverb*) 1 (*tr*) to reproduce (an idea, former event, etc.) in actions, often by mime. 2 *Psychiatry* to express unconsciously (a repressed impulse or experience) in overt behaviour.

ACTRA ('æktrə) NOUN ACRONYM FOR Alliance of Canadian Cinema, Television, and Radio Artists.

actress ('æktrɪs) NOUN 1 a woman who acts in a play, film, broadcast, etc. 2 *Informal* a woman who puts on a false manner in order to deceive others.

actressy ('æktrɪsɪ) ADJECTIVE exaggerated and affected in manner; theatrical.

Acts of the Apostles NOUN the fifth book of the New Testament, describing the development of the early Church from Christ's ascension into heaven to Paul's sojourn at Rome. Often shortened to: **Acts.**

ACTT ABBREVIATION FOR Association of Cinematograph and Television Technicians.

ACTU ABBREVIATION FOR Australian Council of Trade Unions.

actual ('æktʃʊəl) ADJECTIVE 1 existing in reality or as a matter of fact. 2 real or genuine. 3 existing at the present time; current. 4 (usually preceded by *your*) *Brit informal, often facetious* (intensifier): *that music's by your actual Mozart, isn't it?* ◆ See also **actuals.**
▷ HISTORY C14 *actuel* existing, from Late Latin *āctuālis* relating to acts, practical, from Latin *āctus* ACT

> **Language note** The excessive use of *actual* and *actually* should be avoided. They are unnecessary in sentences such as *in actual fact, he is forty-two,* and *he did actually go to the play but did not enjoy it.*

actual bodily harm NOUN *Criminal law* injury caused by one person to another that interferes with the health or comfort of the victim. Abbreviation: **ABH.**

actualité (ˌæktʃʊ'ælɪteɪ; *French* aktɥalite) NOUN *Humorous* the truth: *economic with the actualité.*
▷ HISTORY C20: French: literally, truth

actuality (ˌæktʃʊ'ælɪtɪ) NOUN, *plural* **-ties.** 1 true existence; reality. 2 (*sometimes plural*) a fact or condition that is real.

actualize *or* **actualise** ('æktʃʊəˌlaɪz) VERB (*tr*) 1 to make actual or real. 2 to represent realistically.
▸ **ˌactuali'zation** *or* **ˌactuali'sation** NOUN

actually ('æktʃʊəlɪ) ADVERB 1 **a** as an actual fact; really. **b** (*as sentence modifier*): *actually, I haven't seen him.* 2 at present. 3 *Informal* a parenthetic filler used to add slight emphasis: *I don't know, actually.*

actuals ('æktʃʊəlz) PLURAL NOUN See **physicals.**

actual sin NOUN *Christianity* any sin that a person commits of his own free will and for which he is personally responsible. Compare **original sin.**

actuary ('æktʃʊərɪ) NOUN, *plural* **-aries.** a person qualified to calculate commercial risks and probabilities involving uncertain future events, esp in such contexts as life assurance.
▷ HISTORY C16 (meaning: registrar): from Latin *āctuārius* one who keeps accounts, from *actum* public business, and *acta* documents, deeds. See ACT, -ARY
▸ **actuarial** (ˌæktʃʊ'ɛərɪəl) ADJECTIVE

actuate ('æktʃʊˌeɪt) VERB (*tr*) 1 to put into action or mechanical motion. 2 to motivate or incite into action: *actuated by unworthy desires.*
▷ HISTORY C16: from Medieval Latin *actuātus,* from *actuāre* to incite to action, from Latin *āctus* ACT
▸ **ˌactu'ation** NOUN ▸ **'actuˌator** NOUN

act up VERB (*intr, adverb*) *Informal* to behave in a troublesome way: *the engine began to act up.*

acuity (ə'kjuːɪtɪ) NOUN 1 keenness or acuteness, esp in vision or thought. 2 the capacity of the eye to see fine detail, measured by determining the finest detail that can just be detected.
▷ HISTORY C15: from Old French, from Latin *acūtus* ACUTE

aculeate (ə'kjuːlɪɪt, -ˌeɪt) *or* **aculeated** ADJECTIVE 1 cutting; pointed. 2 having prickles or spines, as a rose. 3 having a sting, as bees, wasps, and ants.
▷ HISTORY C17: from Latin *acūleātus;* see ACULEUS

aculeus (ə'kjuːlɪəs) NOUN 1 a prickle or spine, such as the thorn of a rose. 2 a sting or ovipositor.
▷ HISTORY C19: from Latin, diminutive of *acus* needle

acumen ('ækjʊˌmɛn, ə'kjuːmən) NOUN the ability to judge well; keen discernment; insight.
▷ HISTORY C16: from Latin: sharpness, from *acuere* to sharpen, from *acus* needle
▸ **a'cuminous** ADJECTIVE

acuminate ADJECTIVE (ə'kjuːmɪnɪt, -ˌneɪt) 1 narrowing to a sharp point, as some types of leaf. ◆ VERB (ə'kjuːmɪˌneɪt) 2 (*tr*) to make pointed or sharp.
▷ HISTORY C17: from Latin *acūmināre* to sharpen; see ACUMEN
▸ **aˌcumi'nation** NOUN

acupoint ('ækjʊˌpɔɪnt) NOUN any of the specific points on the body where a needle is inserted in acupuncture or pressure is applied in acupressure.
▷ HISTORY C19: from ACU(PUNCTURE) + POINT

acupressure ('ækjʊˌprɛʃə) NOUN another name for **shiatsu.**
▷ HISTORY C19: from ACU(PUNCTURE) + PRESSURE

acupuncture ('ækjʊˌpʌŋktʃə) NOUN the insertion of the tips of needles into the skin at specific points for the purpose of treating various disorders by stimulating nerve impulses. Originally Chinese, this method of treatment is practised in many parts of the world. Also called: **stylostixis.**
▷ HISTORY C17: from Latin *acus* needle + PUNCTURE
▸ **'acuˌpunctural** ADJECTIVE ▸ **'acuˌpuncturist** NOUN

acutance (ə'kjuːtᵊns) NOUN a physical rather than subjective measure of the sharpness of a photographic image.

acute (ə'kjuːt) ADJECTIVE 1 penetrating in perception or insight. 2 sensitive to details; keen. 3 of extreme importance; crucial. 4 sharp or severe; intense: *acute pain; an acute drought.* 5 having a sharp end or point. 6 *Maths* **a** (of an angle) less than 90°. **b** (of a triangle) having all its interior angles less than 90°. 7 (of a disease) **a** arising suddenly and manifesting intense severity. **b** of relatively short duration. Compare **chronic** (sense 2). 8 *Phonetics* **a** (of a vowel or syllable in some languages with a pitch accent, such as ancient Greek) spoken or sung on a higher musical pitch relative to neighbouring syllables or vowels. **b** of or relating to an accent (´) placed over vowels, denoting that the vowel is pronounced with higher musical pitch (as in ancient Greek), with a certain special quality (as in French), etc. Compare (for senses 8a, 8b) **grave**[2] (sense 5), **circumflex.** 9 (of a hospital, hospital bed, or ward) intended to accommodate short-term patients with acute illnesses. ◆ NOUN 10 an acute accent.
▷ HISTORY C14: from Latin *acūtus,* past participle of *acuere* to sharpen, from *acus* needle
▸ **a'cutely** ADVERB ▸ **a'cuteness** NOUN

acute accent NOUN the diacritical mark (´), used in the writing system of some languages to indicate that the vowel over which it is placed has a special quality (as in French *été*) or that it receives the strongest stress in the word (as in Spanish *hablé*).

acute arch NOUN another name for **lancet arch.**

acute dose NOUN a total dose of radiation administered over such a short period that biological recovery is impossible.

ACW ABBREVIATION FOR aircraftwoman.

acyclic (eɪ'saɪklɪk, eɪ'sɪklɪk) ADJECTIVE 1 *Chem* not cyclic; having an open chain structure. 2 *Botany* having flower parts arranged in a spiral rather than a whorl.

acyl ('eɪsaɪl) NOUN 1 (*modifier*) of, denoting, or containing the monovalent group of atoms RCO-, where R is an organic group: *acyl group or radical; acyl substitution.* 2 an organometallic compound in which a metal atom is directly bound to an acyl group.
▷ HISTORY C20: from ACID + -YL

acyl anhydride NOUN another name for **anhydride** (sense 3).

acylation (ˌeɪsaɪ'leɪʃən) NOUN the introduction into a chemical compound of an acyl group.

acyl halide NOUN any derivative of carboxylic acid in which the hydroxyl group has been replaced by a halogen atom. Also called: **acid halide.**

ad[1] (æd) NOUN short for **advertisement.**

ad[2] (æd) NOUN *Tennis, US and Canadian* short for **advantage.** Brit equivalent: **van.**

ad[3] THE INTERNET DOMAIN NAME FOR Andorra.

AD ABBREVIATION FOR: 1 same as **A.D.** 2 *Military* active duty. 3 *Military* air defence. 4 Dame of the Order of Australia.

A.D. *or* **AD** (indicating years numbered from the supposed year of the birth of Christ) ABBREVIATION FOR anno Domini: *70* A.D. Compare **B.C.**
▷ HISTORY Latin: in the year of the Lord

> **Language note** In strict usage, A.D. is only employed with specific years: *he died in 1621* A.D., but *he died in the 17th century* (and not *the 17th century* A.D.). Formerly the practice was to write A.D. preceding the date (A.D. *1621*), and it is also strictly correct to omit *in* when A.D. is used, since this is already contained in the meaning of the Latin *anno Domini* (in the year of Our Lord), but this is no longer general practice. B.C. is used with both specific dates and indications of the period: *Heraclitus was born about 540* B.C.; *the battle took place in the 4th century* B.C.

ad- PREFIX 1 to; towards: *adsorb; adverb.* 2 near; next to: *adrenal.*
▷ HISTORY from Latin: to, towards. As a prefix in words of Latin origin, *ad-* became *ac-, af-, ag-, al-, an-, acq-, ar-, as-,* and *at-* before *c, f, g, l, n, q, r, s,* and *t,* and became *a-* before *gn, sc, sp, st*

-ad[1] SUFFIX FORMING NOUNS 1 a group or unit (having so many parts or members): *triad.* 2 an epic poem concerning (the subject indicated by the stem): *Dunciad.*
▷ HISTORY via Latin from Greek *-ad-* (plural *-ades*), originally forming adjectives; names of epic poems are all formed on the model of the *Iliad*

-ad[2] SUFFIX FORMING ADVERBS denoting direction towards a specified part in anatomical descriptions: *cephalad.*

▷HISTORY from Latin *ad* to, towards

Ada ('eɪdə) NOUN a high-level computer programming language designed for dealing with real-time processing problems: used for military and other systems.
▷HISTORY C20: named after *Ada,* Lady Lovelace, the English mathematician, daughter of Lord Byron (1815–52), who worked with Charles Babbage (1792–1871) and whose description of his computing machines preserved them for posterity

adactylous (eɪ'dæktɪləs) ADJECTIVE possessing no fingers or toes.
▷HISTORY C19: from A-[1] + DACTYL + -OUS

adage ('ædɪdʒ) NOUN a traditional saying that is accepted by many as true or partially true; proverb.
▷HISTORY C16: via Old French from Latin *adagium;* related to *āio* I say

adagio (ə'dɑːdʒɪˌəʊ; *Italian* a'dadʒo) *Music* ◆ ADJECTIVE, ADVERB [1] (to be performed) slowly. ◆ NOUN, *plural* **-gios.** [2] a movement or piece to be performed slowly. [3] *Ballet* a slow section of a pas de deux.
▷HISTORY C18: Italian, from *ad* at + *agio* ease

Adam[1] ('ædəm) NOUN [1] *Old Testament* the first man, created by God: the progenitor of the human race (Genesis 2–3). [2] **not know (someone) from Adam.** to have no knowledge of or acquaintance with (someone). [3] **the old Adam.** the evil supposedly inherent in human nature.

Adam[2] NOUN MODIFIER in the neoclassical style made popular by Robert Adam (1728–92), Scottish architect and furniture designer.

adamant ('ædəmənt) ADJECTIVE [1] unshakable in purpose, determination, or opinion; unyielding. [2] a less common word for **adamantine** (sense 1). ◆ NOUN [3] any extremely hard or apparently unbreakable substance. [4] a legendary stone said to be impenetrable, often identified with the diamond or loadstone.
▷HISTORY Old English: from Latin *adamant-,* stem of *adamas,* from Greek; literal meaning perhaps: unconquerable, from A-[1] + *daman* to tame, conquer
▸'**adamantly** ADVERB

adamantine (ˌædə'mæntaɪn) ADJECTIVE [1] very hard; unbreakable or unyielding. [2] having the lustre of a diamond.

Adamawa (ˌædə'mɑːwə) NOUN a small group of languages of W Africa, spoken chiefly in E Nigeria, N Cameroon, the Central African Republic, and N Democratic Republic of Congo (formerly Zaïre), forming a branch of the Niger-Congo family.

Adamite ('ædəˌmaɪt) NOUN [1] a human being. [2] a nudist, esp a member of an early Christian sect who sought to imitate Adam.
▸**Adamitic** (ˌædə'mɪtɪk) ADJECTIVE

Adams ('ædəmz) NOUN a mountain in SW Washington, in the Cascade Range. Height: 3751 m (12 307 ft.).

Adam's ale *or* **wine** NOUN *Old-fashioned jocular* water.
▷HISTORY C17: from the name of the first man to appear in the Old Testament

Adam's apple NOUN the visible projection of the thyroid cartilage of the larynx at the front of the neck.

adamsite ('ædəmˌzaɪt) NOUN a yellow poisonous crystalline solid that readily sublimes; diphenylaminechlorarsine. It is used in chemical warfare as a vomiting agent. Formula: $C_6H_4AsClNHC_6H_4$; relative density: 1.65; melting pt.: 195°C; boiling pt.: 410°C. Also called: **phenarsazine chloride.**
▷HISTORY C20: named after Roger *Adams* (1899–1971), American chemist

Adam's-needle NOUN a North American liliaceous plant, *Yucca filamentosa,* that has a tall woody stem, stiff pointed leaves, and large clusters of white flowers arranged in spikes. It is cultivated as an ornamental plant. See also **Spanish bayonet.**

Adams-Stokes syndrome (-'stəʊks) NOUN another term for **heart block.**
▷HISTORY C19: named after R. *Adams* (1791–1875) and W. *Stokes* (1804–78), Irish physicians

Adana ('ædənə) NOUN a city in S Turkey, capital of Adana province. Pop.: 1 066 544 (1995 est.). Also called: **Seyhan.**

adapt (ə'dæpt) VERB [1] (often foll by *to*) to adjust (someone or something, esp oneself) to different conditions, a new environment, etc. [2] (*tr*) to fit, change, or modify to suit a new or different purpose: *to adapt a play for use in schools.*
▷HISTORY C17: from Latin *adaptāre,* from *ad-* to + *aptāre* to fit, from *aptus* APT
▸**a'daptable** ADJECTIVE ▸**aˌdapta'bility** *or* **a'daptableness** NOUN ▸**a'daptive** ADJECTIVE

adaptation (ˌædəp'teɪʃən, ˌædæp-) NOUN [1] the act or process of adapting or the state of being adapted; adjustment. [2] something that is produced by adapting something else. [3] something that is changed or modified to suit new conditions or needs. [4] *Biology* an inherited or acquired modification in organisms that makes them better suited to survive and reproduce in a particular environment. [5] *Physiol* the decreased response of a sense organ to a repeated or sustained stimulus. [6] *Psychol* (in learning theory) the weakening of a response to a stimulus with repeated presentation of the stimulus without reinforcement; applied mainly to innate responses. [7] *Social welfare* alteration to a dwelling to make it suitable for a disabled person, as by replacing steps with ramps.

adaption (ə'dæpʃən) NOUN another word for **adaptation.**

adaptive optics NOUN (*functioning as singular*) a technique used to increase the resolution of a ground-based astronomical telescope by counteracting the effects of the atmosphere on the image. A deforming mirror in the light path of the telescope maintains a pointlike image of the celestial body using either a real star or a laser beam as a reference.

adaptive radiation NOUN evolution of a number of divergent species from a common ancestor, each species becoming adapted to occupy a different environment. This type of evolution occurred in the Tertiary manuals and the Mesozoic reptiles.

adaptor *or* **adapter** (ə'dæptə) NOUN [1] a person or thing that adapts. [2] any device for connecting two parts, esp ones that are of different sizes or have different mating fitments. [3] **a** a plug used to connect an electrical device to a mains supply when they have different types of terminals. **b** a device used to connect several electrical appliances to a single mains socket.

Adar (a'dar) NOUN (in the Jewish calendar) the twelfth month of the year according to biblical reckoning and the sixth month of the civil year, usually falling within February and March. In a leap year, an additional month **Adar Rishon** (first Adar) is intercalated between Shevat and Adar, and the latter is known as **Adar Sheni** (second Adar).
▷HISTORY from Hebrew

adaxial (æd'æksɪəl) ADJECTIVE facing towards the axis, as the surface of a leaf that faces the stem. Compare **abaxial.**

ADC ABBREVIATION FOR: [1] **aide-de-camp.** [2] **analogue-digital converter.**

add (æd) VERB [1] to combine (two or more numbers or quantities) by addition. [2] (*tr;* foll by *to*) to increase (a number or quantity) by another number or quantity using addition. [3] (*tr;* often foll by *to*) to join (something) to something else in order to increase the size, quantity, effect, or scope; unite (with): *to add insult to injury.* [4] (*intr;* foll by *to*) to have an extra and increased effect (on): *her illness added to his worries.* [5] (*tr*) to say or write further. [6] (*tr;* foll by *in*) to include. ◆ See also **add up.**
▷HISTORY C14: from Latin *addere,* literally: to put to, from *ad-* to + *-dere* to put

ADD ABBREVIATION FOR **attention deficit disorder.**

addax ('ædæks) NOUN a large light-coloured antelope, *Addax nasomaculatus,* having ribbed loosely spiralled horns and inhabiting desert regions in N Africa: family *Bovidae,* order *Artiodactyla.*
▷HISTORY C17: Latin, from an unidentified ancient N African language

added sixth NOUN a chord much used esp in jazz, consisting of a triad with an added sixth above the root. Also called: **added sixth chord.** Compare **sixth chord.**

addend ('ædɛnd, ə'dɛnd) NOUN any of a set of numbers that is to be added. Compare **sum** (sense 1).
▷HISTORY C20: short for ADDENDUM

addendum (ə'dɛndəm) NOUN, *plural* **-da** (-də). [1] something added; an addition. [2] a supplement or appendix to a book, magazine, etc. [3] the radial distance between the major and pitch cylinders of an external screw thread. [4] the radial distance between the pitch circle and tip of a gear tooth.
▷HISTORY C18: from Latin, literally: a thing to be added, neuter gerundive of *addere* to ADD

adder[1] ('ædə) NOUN [1] Also called: **viper.** a common viper, *Vipera berus,* that is widely distributed in Europe, including Britain, and Asia and is typically dark greyish in colour with a black zigzag pattern along the back. [2] any of various similar venomous or nonvenomous snakes. ◆ See also **death adder, puff adder.**
▷HISTORY Old English *nǣdre* snake; in Middle English *a naddre* was mistaken for *an addre;* related to Old Norse *nathr,* Gothic *nadrs*

adder[2] ('ædə) NOUN a person or thing that adds, esp a single element of an electronic computer, the function of which is to add a single digit of each of two inputs.

adder's-meat NOUN another name for the **greater stitchwort** (see **stitchwort**).

adder's-mouth NOUN any of various orchids of the genus *Malaxis* that occur in all parts of the world except Australia and New Zealand and have small usually greenish flowers. See also **bog orchid.**

adder's-tongue NOUN [1] any of several terrestrial ferns of the genus *Ophioglossum,* esp *O. vulgatum,* that grow in the N hemisphere and have a spore-bearing body that sticks out like a spike from the leaf: family *Ophioglossaceae.* [2] another name for **dogtooth violet.**

addict VERB (ə'dɪkt) [1] (*tr; usually passive;* often foll by *to*) to cause (someone or oneself) to become dependent (on something, esp a narcotic drug). ◆ NOUN ('ædɪkt) [2] a person who is addicted, esp to narcotic drugs. [3] *Informal* a person who is devoted to something: *a jazz addict.*
▷HISTORY C16 (as adjective and as verb; noun use C20): from Latin *addictus* given over, from *addīcere* to give one's assent to, from *ad-* to + *dīcere* to say

addiction (ə'dɪkʃən) NOUN the condition of being abnormally dependent on some habit, esp compulsive dependency on narcotic drugs.

addictive (ə'dɪktɪv) ADJECTIVE of, relating to, or causing addiction.

adding ('ædɪŋ) NOUN [1] an act or instance of addition. ◆ ADJECTIVE [2] of, for, or relating to addition. [3] (in systemic grammar) denoting a bound clause that qualifies the meaning of an antecedent noun rather than of the sentence as a whole. Compare **contingency** (sense 4).

adding machine NOUN a mechanical device, operated manually or electrically, for adding and often subtracting, multiplying, and dividing.

Addis Ababa ('ædɪs 'æbəbə) NOUN the capital of Ethiopia, on a central plateau 2400 m (8000 ft.) above sea level: founded in 1887; became capital in 1896. Pop.: 2 316 400 (1994 est.).

Addison's disease ('ædɪsᵊnz) NOUN a disease characterized by deep bronzing of the skin, anaemia, and extreme weakness, caused by underactivity of the adrenal glands. Also called: **adrenal insufficiency.**
▷HISTORY C19: named after Thomas *Addison* (1793–1860), British physician who identified it

addition (ə'dɪʃən) NOUN [1] the act, process, or result of adding. [2] a person or thing that is added or acquired. [3] a mathematical operation in which the sum of two numbers or quantities is calculated. Usually indicated by the symbol **+**. [4] *Chiefly US and Canadian* a part added to a building or piece of land; annexe. [5] *Obsolete* a title following a person's name. [6] **in addition.** (*adverb*) also; as well; besides. [7] **in addition to.** (*preposition*) besides; as well as.
▷HISTORY C15: from Latin *additiōn-,* from *addere* to ADD

additional (ə'dɪʃənᵊl) ADJECTIVE added or supplementary.
▸**ad'ditionally** ADVERB

additionality (əˌdɪʃə'nælɪtɪ) NOUN [1] (in Britain) the principle that money raised by the National

Lottery should only be spent on projects that would not otherwise be funded by government spending. 2 (in the European Union) the principle that the EU contributes to the funding of a project in a member country provided that the member country also contributes.

Additional Member System NOUN a system of voting in which people vote separately for the candidate and the party of their choice. Parties are allocated extra seats if the number of constituencies they win does not reflect their overall share of the vote. See also **proportional representation.**

additive ('ædɪtɪv) ADJECTIVE 1 characterized or produced by addition; cumulative. ◆ NOUN 2 any substance added to something to improve it, prevent deterioration, etc. 3 short for **food additive.**
▷HISTORY C17: from Late Latin *additīvus,* from *addere* to ADD

additive process NOUN a photographic process in which the desired colours are produced by adding together appropriate proportions of three primary colours. Compare **subtractive process.**

addle[1] ('æd°l) VERB 1 to make or become confused or muddled. 2 to make or become rotten. ◆ ADJECTIVE 3 (*in combination*) indicating a confused or muddled state: *addle-brained; addle-pated.*
▷HISTORY C18 (verb), back formation from *addled,* from C13 *addle* rotten, from Old English *adela* filth; related to dialect German *Addel* liquid manure

addle[2] ('æd°l) VERB *Northern English dialect* to earn (money or one's living).
▷HISTORY C13 *addlen,* from Old Norse *öthlask* to gain possession of property, from *ōthal* property

add-on NOUN a feature that can be added to a standard model or package to give increased benefits.

address (ə'drɛs) NOUN 1 the conventional form by which the location of a building is described. 2 the written form of this, as on a letter or parcel, preceded by the name of the person or organization for whom it is intended. 3 the place at which someone lives. 4 a speech or written communication, esp one of a formal nature. 5 skilfulness or tact. 6 *Archaic* manner or style of speaking or conversation. 7 *Computing* a number giving the location of a piece of stored information. See also **direct access.** 8 *Brit government* a statement of the opinions or wishes of either or both Houses of Parliament that is sent to the sovereign. 9 the alignment or position of a part, component, etc., that permits correct assembly or fitting. 10 (*usually plural*) expressions of affection made by a man in courting a woman. ◆ VERB **-dresses, -dressing; -dressed** *or obsolete or poetic* **-drest.** (*tr*) 11 to mark (a letter, parcel, etc.) with an address. 12 to speak to, refer to in speaking, or deliver a speech to. 13 (used reflexively; foll by *to*) **a** to speak or write to: *he addressed himself to the chairman.* **b** to apply oneself to: *he addressed himself to the task.* 14 to direct (a message, warning, etc.) to the attention of. 15 to consign or entrust (a ship or a ship's cargo) to a factor, merchant, etc. 16 to adopt a position facing (the ball in golf, a partner in a dance, the target in archery, etc.). 17 to treat of; deal with: *chapter 10 addresses the problem of transitivity.* 18 an archaic word for **woo.**
▷HISTORY C14 (in the sense: to make right, adorn) and C15 (in the modern sense: to direct words): via Old French from Vulgar Latin *addrictiāre* (unattested) to make straight, direct oneself towards, from Latin *ad-* to + *dīrectus* DIRECT
▸**ad'dresser** *or* **ad'dressor** NOUN

addressable (ə'drɛsəb°l) ADJECTIVE *Computing* possessing or capable of being reached by an address.
▸**ad͵dressa'bility** NOUN

addressee (͵ædrɛ'si:) NOUN 1 a person or organization to whom a letter, parcel, etc., is addressed. 2 a person who is addressed in conversation, a speech, a poem, etc.

Addressograph (ə'drɛsəʊ͵grɑ:f, -͵græf) NOUN *Trademark* a machine for addressing envelopes, etc.

adduce (ə'dju:s) VERB (*tr*) to cite (reasons, examples, etc.) as evidence or proof.
▷HISTORY C15: from Latin *addūcere* to lead or bring to
▸**ad'ducent** ADJECTIVE ▸**ad'ducible** *or* **ad'duceable** ADJECTIVE ▸**adduction** (ə'dʌkʃən) NOUN

adduct (ə'dʌkt) VERB (*tr*) 1 (of a muscle) to draw or pull (a leg, arm, etc.) towards the median axis of the body. Compare **abduct** (sense 2). ◆ NOUN 2 *Chem* a compound formed by direct combination of two or more different compounds or elements.
▷HISTORY C19: from Latin *addūcere;* see ADDUCE
▸**ad'duction** NOUN

adductor (ə'dʌktə) NOUN a muscle that adducts.

add up VERB (*adverb*) 1 to find the sum (of). 2 (*intr*) to result in a correct total. 3 (*intr*) *Informal* to make sense. 4 (*intr; foll by to*) to amount to.

addy ('ædɪ) NOUN, *plural* **addies.** *Informal* an e-mail address.

-ade SUFFIX FORMING NOUNS a sweetened drink made of various fruits: *lemonade; limeade.*
▷HISTORY from French, from Latin *-āta* made of, feminine past participle of verbs ending in *-āre*

Adelaide ('ædɪ͵leɪd) NOUN the capital of South Australia: **Port Adelaide,** 11 km (7 miles) away on St. Vincent Gulf, handles the bulk of exports. Pop.: 1 081 000 (1995 est.).

Adélie Land ('ædɪlɪ; *French* adeli) NOUN a part of Antarctica, between Wilkes Land and George V Land: under French sovereignty. Also called: **Adélie Coast.** French name: **Terre Adélie.**

ademption (ə'dɛmpʃən) NOUN *Property law* the failure of a specific legacy, as by a testator disposing of the subject matter in his lifetime.
▷HISTORY C16: from Latin *ademptiōn-* a taking away, from *adimere* to take away, take to (oneself), from *ad-* to + *emere* to buy, take

Aden ('eɪd°n) NOUN 1 the main port and commercial capital of Yemen, on the N coast of the **Gulf of Aden,** an arm of the Indian Ocean at the entrance to the Red Sea: capital of South Yemen until 1990: formerly an important port of call on shipping routes to the East. Pop.: 562 000 (1995 est.). 2 a former British colony and protectorate on the S coast of the Arabian Peninsula: became part of South Yemen in 1967, now part of Yemen. Area: 195 sq. km (75 sq. miles).

adenectomy (͵ædə'nɛktəmɪ) NOUN, *plural* **-mies.** 1 surgical removal of a gland. 2 another name for **adenoidectomy.**
▷HISTORY C19: from ADENO- + -ECTOMY

adenine ('ædənɪn, -͵ni:n, -͵naɪn) NOUN a purine base present in tissues of all living organisms as a constituent of the nucleic acids DNA and RNA and of certain coenzymes; 6-aminopurine. Formula: $C_5H_5N_5$; melting pt.: 360–365°C.

adenitis (͵ædə'naɪtɪs) NOUN inflammation of a gland or lymph node.
▷HISTORY C19: New Latin, from ADENO- + -ITIS

adeno- *or before a vowel* **aden-** COMBINING FORM gland or glandular: *adenoid; adenology.*
▷HISTORY New Latin, from Greek *adēn* gland

adenocarcinoma (͵ædɪnəʊ͵kɑ:sɪ'nəʊmə) NOUN, *plural* **-mas** *or* **-mata** (-mətə). 1 a malignant tumour originating in glandular tissue. 2 a malignant tumour with a glandlike structure.

adenohypophysis (͵ædɪnəʊhaɪ'pɒfɪsɪs) NOUN the anterior lobe of the pituitary gland. Compare **neurohypophysis.**

adenoid ('ædɪ͵nɔɪd) ADJECTIVE 1 of or resembling a gland. 2 of or relating to lymphoid tissue, as that found in the lymph nodes, spleen, tonsils, etc. 3 of or relating to the adenoids.
▷HISTORY C19: from Greek *adenoeidēs.* See ADENO-, -OID

adenoidal (͵ædɪ'nɔɪd°l) ADJECTIVE 1 having the nasal tones or impaired breathing of one with enlarged adenoids. 2 another word for **adenoid** (for all senses).

adenoidectomy (͵ædɪnɔɪ'dɛktəmɪ) NOUN, *plural* **-mies.** surgical removal of the adenoids.

adenoids ('ædɪ͵nɔɪdz) PLURAL NOUN a mass of lymphoid tissue at the back of the throat behind the uvula: when enlarged it often restricts nasal breathing, esp in young children. Technical name: **pharyngeal tonsil.**

adenoma (͵ædɪ'nəʊmə) NOUN, *plural* **-mas** *or* **-mata** (-mətə). 1 a tumour, usually benign, occurring in glandular tissue. 2 a tumour having a glandlike structure.

adenopathy (͵ædɪ'nɒpəθɪ) NOUN *Pathol* 1 enlargement of the lymph nodes. 2 enlargement of a gland.

adenosine (æ'dɛnə͵si:n, ͵ædɪ'nəʊsi:n) NOUN *Biochem* a nucleoside formed by the condensation of adenine and ribose. It is present in all living cells in a combined form, as in ribonucleic acids. Formula: $C_{10}H_{13}N_5O_4$.
▷HISTORY C20: a blend of ADENINE + RIBOSE

adenosine diphosphate NOUN the full name of **ADP.**

adenosine monophosphate (͵mɒnəʊ'fɒsfeɪt) NOUN another term for **adenylic acid.** Abbreviation: **AMP.**

adenosine triphosphate NOUN the full name of **ATP.**

adenovirus (͵ædɪnəʊ'vaɪrəs) NOUN any of a group of viruses that can cause upper respiratory diseases in man. Compare **enterovirus, myxovirus.**

adenylic acid (͵ædə'nɪlɪk) NOUN a nucleotide consisting of adenine, ribose or deoxyribose, and a phosphate group. It is a constituent of DNA or RNA. Also called: **adenosine monophosphate.**

adept ADJECTIVE (ə'dɛpt) 1 very proficient in something requiring skill or manual dexterity. 2 skilful; expert. ◆ NOUN ('ædɛpt) 3 a person who is skilled or proficient in something.
▷HISTORY C17: from Medieval Latin *adeptus,* from Latin *adipiscī* to attain, from *ad-* to + *apiscī* to attain
▸**a'deptly** ADVERB ▸**a'deptness** NOUN

adequate ('ædɪkwɪt) ADJECTIVE able to fulfil a need or requirement without being abundant, outstanding, etc.
▷HISTORY C17: from Latin *adaequāre* to equalize, from *ad-* to + *aequus* EQUAL
▸**adequacy** ('ædɪkwəsɪ) NOUN ▸**'adequately** ADVERB

à deux *French* (a dø) ADJECTIVE, ADVERB of or for two persons.

ADFA ABBREVIATION FOR Australian Defence Force Academy.

ADH ABBREVIATION FOR antidiuretic hormone. See **vasopressin.**

adhan (͵a'ðɑ:n) NOUN *Islam* a call to prayer.
▷HISTORY changed from Arabic *adhān,* literally: announcement

ADHD ABBREVIATION FOR attention deficit hyperactivity disorder.

adhere (əd'hɪə) VERB (*intr*) 1 (usually foll by *to*) to stick or hold fast. 2 (foll by *to*) to be devoted (to a political party, cause, religion, etc.); be a follower (of). 3 (foll by *to*) to follow closely or exactly: *adhere to the rules.*
▷HISTORY C16: via Medieval Latin *adhērēre* from Latin *adhaerēre* to stick to
▸**ad'herence** NOUN

> **Language note** See at **adhesion.**

adherent (əd'hɪərənt) NOUN 1 (usually foll by *of*) a supporter or follower. ◆ ADJECTIVE 2 sticking, holding fast, or attached.

adhesion (əd'hi:ʒən) NOUN 1 the quality or condition of sticking together or holding fast. 2 ability to make firm contact without skidding or slipping. 3 attachment or fidelity, as to a political party, cause, etc. 4 an attraction or repulsion between the molecules of unlike substances in contact: distinguished from *cohesion.* 5 *Pathol* abnormal union of structures or parts.
▷HISTORY C17: from Latin *adhaesiōn-* a sticking. See ADHERE

> **Language note** *Adhesion* is the preferred term when talking about sticking or holding fast in a physical sense. *Adherence* is preferred when talking about attachment to a political party, cause, etc.

adhesive (əd'hi:sɪv) ADJECTIVE 1 able or designed to adhere; sticky: *adhesive tape.* 2 tenacious or clinging. ◆ NOUN 3 a substance used for sticking objects together, such as glue, cement, or paste.
▸**ad'hesively** ADVERB ▸**ad'hesiveness** NOUN

adhesive binding NOUN *Bookbinding* a style of binding used mainly for paperback books, where the backs of the gathered sections are trimmed and inserted into a cover along with adhesive to hold the pages and cover together. Also called: **perfect binding.**

ad hoc (æd 'hɒk) ADJECTIVE, ADVERB for a particular purpose only; lacking generality or justification: *an ad hoc decision; an ad hoc committee.*
▷HISTORY Latin, literally: to this

adhocracy (æd'hɒkrəsɪ) NOUN management that responds to urgent problems rather than planning to avoid them.

ad hominem *Latin* (æd 'hɒmɪˌnɛm) ADJECTIVE, ADVERB [1] directed against a person rather than against his arguments. [2] based on or appealing to emotion rather than reason. ◆ Compare **ad rem.** See also **argumentum ad hominem.**
▷HISTORY literally: to the man

adiabatic (ˌædɪə'bætɪk, ˌeɪ-) ADJECTIVE [1] (of a thermodynamic process) taking place without loss or gain of heat. ◆ NOUN [2] a curve or surface on a graph representing the changes in two or more characteristics (such as pressure and volume) of a system undergoing an adiabatic process.
▷HISTORY C19: from Greek *adiabatos* not to be crossed, impassable (to heat), from A-[1] + *diabatos* passable, from *dia-* across + *bainein* to go

adiactinic (ˌædɪæk'tɪnɪk) ADJECTIVE *Physics* denoting a substance that does not transmit radiation affecting photochemically sensitive materials, such as a safelight in a photographic darkroom.

adiaphorism (ˌædɪ'æfəˌrɪzəm) NOUN a Christian Protestant theological theory that certain rites and actions are matters of indifference in religion since not forbidden by the Scriptures.
▷HISTORY C19: see ADIAPHOROUS
▸**ˌadi'aphorist** NOUN ▸**ˌadiˌapho'ristic** ADJECTIVE

adiaphorous (ˌædɪ'æfərəs) ADJECTIVE *Med* having no effect for good or ill, as a drug or placebo.
▷HISTORY C17: from Greek *adiaphoros* indifferent, from A-[1] + *diaphoros* different

adiathermancy (ˌædɪə'θɜːmənsɪ) NOUN another name for **athermancy.**
▸**ˌadia'thermanous** ADJECTIVE

adieu (ə'djuː; *French* adjø) SENTENCE SUBSTITUTE, NOUN, *plural* **adieus** *or* **adieux** (ə'djuːz; *French* adjø). goodbye; farewell.
▷HISTORY C14: from Old French, from *a* to + *dieu* God

Adige (*Italian* 'aːdidʒe) NOUN a river in N Italy, flowing southeast to the Adriatic. Length: 354 km (220 miles).

Adi Granth (ˌaːdɪ 'grʌnt) NOUN another name for **Guru Granth.**
▷HISTORY from Punjabi: first book

ad infinitum (æd ˌɪnfɪ'naɪtəm) ADVERB without end; endlessly; to infinity. Abbreviation: **ad inf.**
▷HISTORY Latin

ad interim (æd 'ɪntərɪm) ADJECTIVE, ADVERB for the meantime; for the present: *ad interim measures.* Abbreviation: **ad int.**
▷HISTORY Latin

adios (ˌædɪ'ɒs; *Spanish* a'ðjos) SENTENCE SUBSTITUTE goodbye; farewell.
▷HISTORY literally: to God

adipic acid (ə'dɪpɪk) NOUN a colourless crystalline solid used in the preparation of nylon. Formula: $HOOC(CH_2)_4COOH$.
▷HISTORY C19: from New Latin *adiposus* fat + -IC

adipocere (ˌædɪpəʊ'sɪə, 'ædɪpəʊˌsɪə) NOUN a waxlike fatty substance formed during the decomposition of corpses. Nontechnical name: **grave-wax.**
▷HISTORY C19: via French from New Latin *adiposus* fat (see ADIPOSE) + French *cire* wax
▸**adipocerous** (ˌædɪ'pɒsərəs) ADJECTIVE

adipocyte ('ædɪpəʊˌsaɪt) NOUN a fat cell that accumulates and stores fats.

adipose ('ædɪˌpəʊs, -ˌpəʊz) ADJECTIVE [1] of, resembling, or containing fat; fatty. ◆ NOUN [2] animal fat.
▷HISTORY C18: from New Latin *adiposus,* from Latin *adeps* fat

adipose fin NOUN a posterior dorsal fin occurring in some fish, such as those of the salmon and catfish families.

Adiprene ('ædɪpriːn) NOUN *Trademark* a polyurethane elastomer with exceptional abrasion resistance and strength.

adipsia (eɪ'dɪpsɪə) NOUN [1] complete lack of thirst. [2] abnormal abstinence from drinking.
▷HISTORY C20: from A-[1] + Greek *dipsa* thirst

Adirondack Mountains (ˌædɪ'rɒndæk) *or* **Adirondacks** PLURAL NOUN a mountain range in NE New York State. Highest peak: Mount Marcy, 1629 m (5344 ft.).

adit ('ædɪt) NOUN an almost horizontal shaft into a mine, for access or drainage.
▷HISTORY C17: from Latin *aditus* an approach, from *adīre,* from *ad-* towards + *īre* to go

Adivasi ('ɑːdɪˌvɑːsɪ) NOUN a member of any of the aboriginal peoples of India.
▷HISTORY Sanskrit, from *adi* beginning + *vasi* dweller

adj. ABBREVIATION FOR: [1] adjective. [2] Also: **adjt.** adjutant.

adjacent (ə'dʒeɪsənt) ADJECTIVE [1] being near or close, esp having a common boundary; adjoining; contiguous. [2] *Maths* **a** (of a pair of vertices in a graph) joined by a common edge. **b** (of a pair of edges in a graph) meeting at a common vertex. ◆ NOUN [3] *Geometry* the side lying between a specified angle and a right angle in a right-angled triangle.
▷HISTORY C15: from Latin *adjacēre* to lie next to, from *ad-* near + *jacēre* to lie
▸**ad'jacency** NOUN ▸**ad'jacently** ADVERB

adjacent angles PLURAL NOUN two angles that have the same vertex and a side in common.

adjective ('ædʒɪktɪv) NOUN [1] **a** a word imputing a characteristic to a noun or pronoun. **b** (*as modifier*): *an adjective phrase.* Abbreviation: **adj.** ◆ ADJECTIVE [2] additional or dependent. [3] (of law) relating to court practice and procedure, as opposed to the principles of law dealt with by the courts. Compare **substantive** (sense 7).
▷HISTORY C14: from Late Latin *adjectīvus* attributive, from *adjicere* to throw to, add, from *ad-* to + *jacere* to throw; in grammatical sense, from the Latin phrase *nōmen adjectīvum* attributive noun
▸**adjectival** (ˌædʒɪk'taɪvəl) ADJECTIVE

adjigo ('ædʒɪˌgəʊ) NOUN a yam plant, *Dioscorea hastifolia,* native to SW Australia that has edible tubers.
▷HISTORY C19: from a native Australian language

adjoin (ə'dʒɔɪn) VERB [1] to be next to (an area of land, etc.). [2] (*tr; foll by to*) to join; affix or attach.
▷HISTORY C14: via Old French from Latin *adjungere,* from *ad-* to + *jungere* to join

adjoining (ə'dʒɔɪnɪŋ) ADJECTIVE being in contact; connected or neighbouring.

adjoint ('ædˌdʒɔɪnt) NOUN *Maths* **a** another name for **Hermitian conjugate. b** a generalization in category theory of this notion.

adjourn (ə'dʒɜːn) VERB [1] (*intr*) (of a court, etc.) to close at the end of a session. [2] to postpone or be postponed, esp temporarily or to another place. [3] (*tr*) to put off (a problem, discussion, etc.) for later consideration; defer. [4] (*intr*) *Informal* **a** to move elsewhere: *let's adjourn to the kitchen.* **b** to stop work.
▷HISTORY C14: from Old French *ajourner* to defer to an arranged day, from *a-* to + *jour* day, from Late Latin *diurnum,* from Latin *diurnus* daily, from *diēs* day
▸**ad'journment** NOUN

adjudge (ə'dʒʌdʒ) VERB (*tr; usually passive*) [1] to pronounce formally; declare: *he was adjudged the winner.* [2] **a** to determine judicially; judge. **b** to order or pronounce by law; decree: *he was adjudged bankrupt.* **c** to award (costs, damages, etc.). [3] *Archaic* to sentence or condemn.
▷HISTORY C14: via Old French from Latin *adjūdicāre.* See ADJUDICATE

adjudicate (ə'dʒuːdɪˌkeɪt) VERB [1] (when *intr,* usually foll by *upon*) to give a decision (on), esp a formal or binding one. [2] (*intr*) to act as an adjudicator. [3] (*tr*) *Chess* to determine the likely result of (a game) by counting relative value of pieces, positional strength, etc. [4] (*intr*) to serve as a judge or arbiter, as in a competition.
▷HISTORY C18: from Latin *adjūdicāre* to award something to someone, from *ad-* to + *jūdicāre* to act as a judge, from *jūdex* judge
▸**adˌjudi'cation** NOUN ▸**adjudicative** (ə'dʒuːdɪkətɪv) ADJECTIVE

adjudicator (ə'dʒuːdɪˌkeɪtə) NOUN [1] a judge, esp in a competition. [2] an arbitrator, esp in a dispute.

adjunct ('ædʒʌŋkt) NOUN [1] something incidental or not essential that is added to something else. [2] a person who is subordinate to another. [3] *Grammar* **a** part of a sentence other than the subject or the predicate. **b** (in systemic grammar) part of a sentence other than the subject, predicator, object, or complement; usually a prepositional or adverbial group. **c** part of a sentence that may be omitted without making the sentence ungrammatical; a modifier. [4] *Logic* another name for **accident** (sense 4). ◆ ADJECTIVE [5] added or connected in a secondary or subordinate position; auxiliary.
▷HISTORY C16: from Latin *adjunctus,* past participle of *adjungere* to ADJOIN
▸**adjunctive** (ə'dʒʌŋktɪv) ADJECTIVE ▸**'adjunctly** ADVERB

adjunction (ə'dʒʌŋkʃən) NOUN (in phrase-structure grammar) the relationship between a branch of a tree representing a sentence to other branches to its left or right that descend from the same node immediately above.

adjure (ə'dʒʊə) VERB (*tr*) [1] to command, often by exacting an oath; charge. [2] to appeal earnestly to.
▷HISTORY C14: from Latin *adjūrāre* to swear to, from *ad-* to + *jūrāre* to swear, from *jūs* oath
▸**adjuration** (ˌædʒʊə'reɪʃən) NOUN ▸**ad'juratory** ADJECTIVE
▸**ad'jurer** *or* **ad'juror** NOUN

adjust (ə'dʒʌst) VERB [1] (*tr*) to alter slightly, esp to achieve accuracy; regulate: *to adjust the television.* [2] to adapt, as to a new environment, etc. [3] (*tr*) to put into order. [4] (*tr*) *Insurance* to determine the amount payable in settlement of (a claim).
▷HISTORY C17: from Old French *adjuster,* from *ad-* to + *juste* right, JUST
▸**ad'justable** ADJECTIVE ▸**ad'justably** ADVERB ▸**ad'juster** NOUN

adjustment (ə'dʒʌstmənt) NOUN [1] the act of adjusting or state of being adjusted. [2] a control for regulating: *the adjustment for volume is beside the speaker.*

adjutant ('ædʒətənt) NOUN [1] an officer who acts as administrative assistant to a superior officer. Abbreviations: **adjt, adj.** [2] short for **adjutant bird.**
▷HISTORY C17: from Latin *adjūtāre* to AID
▸**'adjutancy** NOUN

adjutant bird *or* **stork** NOUN either of two large carrion-eating storks, *Leptoptilos dubius* or *L. javanicus,* which are closely related and similar to the marabou and occur in S and SE Asia.
▷HISTORY so called for its supposedly military gait

adjutant general NOUN, *plural* **adjutants general.** [1] *Brit army* **a** a member of the Army Board responsible for personnel and administrative functions. **b** a general's executive officer. [2] *US army* the adjutant of a military unit with general staff.

adjuvant ('ædʒəvənt) ADJECTIVE [1] aiding or assisting. ◆ NOUN [2] something that aids or assists; auxiliary. [3] *Med* a drug or other substance that enhances the activity of another. [4] *Immunol* a substance that enhances the immune response stimulated by an antigen when injected with the antigen.
▷HISTORY C17: from Latin *adjuvāns,* present participle of *adjuvāre,* from *juvāre* to help

adland ('ædˌlænd) NOUN *Informal* the advertising industry and the people who work in it.
▷HISTORY C20: from AD(VERTISING) + LAND

Adlerian (æd'lɪərɪən) ADJECTIVE of or relating to the Austrian psychiatrist Alfred Adler (1870–1937) or his ideas.

ad-lib (æd'lɪb) VERB **-libs, -libbing, -libbed.** [1] to improvise and deliver without preparation (a speech, musical performance, etc.). ◆ ADJECTIVE (**ad lib** *when predicative*) [2] improvised; impromptu. ◆ ADVERB **ad lib.** [3] without restraint; freely. [4] *Music* short for **ad libitum.** ◆ NOUN [5] an improvised performance, often humorous.
▷HISTORY C18: short for Latin *ad libitum,* literally: according to pleasure
▸**ad-'libber** NOUN

ad libitum ('lɪbɪtʊm, -təm) ADJECTIVE, ADVERB *Music* (to be performed) at the performer's discretion. Often shortened to: **ad lib.**
▷HISTORY see AD-LIB

ad litem *Latin* (æd 'laɪtɛm) ADJECTIVE (formerly, esp of a guardian) appointed for a lawsuit.

Adm. ABBREVIATION FOR Admiral.

adman ('ædˌmæn, -mən) NOUN, *plural* **-men.** *Informal* a person who works in advertising.

admeasure (æd'mɛʒə) VERB [1] to measure out

(land, etc.) as a share; apportion. 2 (*tr*) to determine the dimensions, capacity, weight, and other details of (a vessel), as for an official registration, documentation, or yacht handicap rating.
▷HISTORY C14 *amesuren,* from Old French *amesurer,* from *mesurer* to MEASURE; the modern form derives from AD- + MEASURE
▸**ad'measurement** NOUN

Admetus (æd'mi:təs) NOUN *Greek myth* a king of Thessaly, one of the Argonauts, who was married to Alcestis.

admin ('ædmɪn) NOUN *Informal* short for **administration.**

adminicle (æd'mɪnɪkᵊl) NOUN *Law* something contributing to prove a point without itself being complete proof.
▷HISTORY C16: from Latin *adminiculum* support

administer (əd'mɪnɪstə) VERB (*mainly tr*) 1 (*also intr*) to direct or control (the affairs of a business, government, etc.). 2 to put into execution; dispense: *administer justice.* 3 (when *intr,* foll by *to*) to give or apply (medicine, assistance, etc.) as a remedy or relief. 4 to apply formally; perform: *to administer extreme unction.* 5 to supervise or impose the taking of (an oath, etc.). 6 to manage or distribute (an estate, property, etc.).
▷HISTORY C14 *amynistre,* via Old French from Latin *administrare,* from *ad-* to + *ministrāre* to MINISTER

administrate (əd'mɪnɪˌstreɪt) VERB to manage or direct (the affairs of a business, institution, etc.).

administration (ədˌmɪnɪ'streɪʃən) NOUN 1 management of the affairs of an organization, such as a business or institution. 2 the duties of an administrator. 3 the body of people who administer an organization. 4 the conduct of the affairs of government. 5 term of office: often used of presidents, governments, etc. 6 the executive branch of government along with the public service; the government as a whole. 7 (*often capital*) *Chiefly US* the political executive, esp of the US; the government. 8 *Chiefly US* a government board, agency, authority, etc. 9 *Property law* **a** the conduct or disposal of the estate of a deceased person. **b** the management by a trustee of an estate subject to a trust. 10 **a** the administering of something, such as a sacrament, oath, or medical treatment. **b** the thing that is administered.
▸**ad'ministrative** ADJECTIVE ▸**ad'ministratively** ADVERB

administration order NOUN *Law* 1 an order by a court appointing a person to manage a company that is in financial difficulty, in an attempt to ensure the survival of the company or achieve the best realization of its assets. 2 an order by a court for the administration of the estate of a debtor who has been ordered by the court to pay money that he owes.

administrator (əd'mɪnɪˌstreɪtə) NOUN 1 a person who administers the affairs of an organization, official body, etc. 2 *Property law* a person authorized to manage an estate, esp when the owner has died intestate or without having appointed executors.
▸**adˌminis'tratrix** FEMININE NOUN

admirable ('ædmərəbᵊl) ADJECTIVE deserving or inspiring admiration; excellent.
▸**'admirably** ADVERB

admiral ('ædmərəl) NOUN 1 the supreme commander of a fleet or navy. 2 Also called: **admiral of the fleet, fleet admiral.** a naval officer of the highest rank, equivalent to general of the army or field marshal. 3 a senior naval officer entitled to fly his own flag. See also **rear admiral, vice admiral.** 4 *Chiefly Brit* the master of a fishing fleet. 5 any of various nymphalid butterflies, esp the red admiral or white admiral.
▷HISTORY C13 *amyral,* from Old French *amiral* emir, and from Medieval Latin *admīrālis* (the spelling with *d* probably influenced by *admīrābilis* admirable); both from Arabic *amīr* emir, commander, esp in the phrase *amīr-al* commander of, as in *amīr-al-bahr* commander of the sea
▸**'admiralˌship** NOUN

admiralty ('ædmərəltɪ) NOUN, *plural* **-ties.** 1 the office or jurisdiction of an admiral. 2 **a** jurisdiction over naval affairs. **b** (*as modifier*): *admiralty law.*

Admiralty Board NOUN **the.** (formerly) a department of the British Ministry of Defence, responsible for the administration and planning of the Royal Navy.

Admiralty House NOUN the official residence of the Governor General of Australia, in Sydney.

Admiralty Islands PLURAL NOUN a group of about 40 volcanic and coral islands in the SW Pacific, part of Papua New Guinea, in the Bismarck Archipelago: main island: Manus. Pop.: 35 200 (1995). Area: about 2000 sq. km (800 sq. miles). Also called: **Admiralties.**

Admiralty mile NOUN another name for **nautical mile.**

Admiralty Range NOUN a mountain range in Antarctica, on the coast of Victoria Land, northwest of the Ross Sea.

admiration (ˌædmə'reɪʃən) NOUN 1 pleasurable contemplation or surprise. 2 a person or thing that is admired: *she was the admiration of the court.* 3 *Archaic* wonder.

admire (əd'maɪə) VERB (*tr*) 1 to regard with esteem, respect, approval, or pleased surprise. 2 *Archaic* to wonder at.
▷HISTORY C16: from Latin *admīrāri* to wonder at, from *ad-* to, at + *mīrāri* to wonder, from *mīrus* wonderful
▸**ad'mirer** NOUN ▸**ad'miring** ADJECTIVE ▸**ad'miringly** ADVERB

admissible (əd'mɪsəbᵊl) ADJECTIVE 1 able or deserving to be considered or allowed. 2 deserving to be admitted or allowed to enter. 3 *Law* (esp of evidence) capable of being or bound to be admitted in a court of law.
▸**adˌmissi'bility** *or* **ad'missibleness** NOUN

admission (əd'mɪʃən) NOUN 1 permission to enter or the right, authority, etc., to enter. 2 the price charged for entrance. 3 acceptance for a position, office, etc. 4 a confession, as of a crime, mistake, etc. 5 an acknowledgment of the truth or validity of something.
▷HISTORY C15: from Latin *admissiōn-,* from *admittere* to ADMIT
▸**ad'missive** ADJECTIVE

admit (əd'mɪt) VERB **-mits, -mitting, -mitted.** (*mainly tr*) 1 (*may take a clause as object*) to confess or acknowledge (a crime, mistake, etc.). 2 (*may take a clause as object*) to concede (the truth or validity of something). 3 to allow to enter; let in. 4 (foll by *to*) to allow participation (in) or the right to be part (of): *to admit to the profession.* 5 (when *intr,* foll by *of*) to allow (of); leave room (for). 6 (*intr*) to give access: *the door admits onto the lawn.*
▷HISTORY C14: from Latin *admittere* to let come or go to, from *ad-* to + *mittere* to send

admittance (əd'mɪtᵊns) NOUN 1 the right or authority to enter. 2 the act of giving entrance. 3 *Electrical engineering* the reciprocal of impedance, usually measured in siemens. It can be expressed as a complex quantity, the real part of which is the conductance and the imaginary part the susceptance. Symbol *y*.

admittedly (əd'mɪtɪdlɪ) ADVERB (*sentence modifier*) willingly conceded: *admittedly I am afraid.*

admix (əd'mɪks) VERB (*tr*) *Rare* to mix or blend.
▷HISTORY C16: back formation from obsolete *admixt,* from Latin *admīscēre* to mix with

admixture (əd'mɪkstʃə) NOUN 1 a less common word for **mixture.** 2 anything added in mixing; ingredient.

admonish (əd'mɒnɪʃ) VERB (*tr*) 1 to reprove firmly but not harshly. 2 to advise to do or against doing something; warn; caution.
▷HISTORY C14: via Old French from Vulgar Latin *admonestāre* (unattested), from Latin *admonēre* to put one in mind of, from *monēre* to advise
▸**ad'monisher** *or* **ad'monitor** NOUN ▸**admonition** (ˌædmə'nɪʃən) NOUN ▸**ad'monitory** ADJECTIVE

ADN INTERNATIONAL CAR REGISTRATION FOR Yemen (from Aden).

adnate ('ædneɪt) ADJECTIVE *Botany* growing closely attached to an adjacent part or organ.
▷HISTORY C17: from Latin *adnātus,* a variant form of *agnātus* AGNATE

ad nauseam (æd 'nɔ:zɪˌæm, -sɪ-) ADVERB to a disgusting extent.
▷HISTORY Latin: to (the point of) nausea

adnexa (æd'nɛksə) PLURAL NOUN *Anatomy* adjoining organs, esp of the uterus.
▷HISTORY C19: New Latin: appendages
▸**ad'nexal** ADJECTIVE

adnominal (əd'nɒmɪnᵊl) *Grammar* ◆ NOUN 1 a word modifying a noun. ◆ ADJECTIVE 2 of or relating to an adnoun.

adnoun ('ædnaʊn) NOUN an adjective used as a noun; absolute adjective.
▷HISTORY C18: from Latin *ad* to + NOUN, formed on the model of ADVERB

ado (ə'du:) NOUN bustling activity; fuss; bother; delay (esp in the phrases **without more ado, with much ado**).
▷HISTORY C14: from the phrase *at do* a to-do, from Old Norse *at* to (marking the infinitive) + DO[1]

ADO *Austral* ABBREVIATION FOR accumulated day off.

adobe (ə'dəʊbɪ) NOUN 1 **a** a sun-dried brick used for building. **b** (*as modifier*): *an adobe house.* 2 a building constructed of such bricks. 3 the clayey material from which such bricks are made.
▷HISTORY C19: from Spanish

adobe flat NOUN *Chiefly US* a gently sloping clayey plain formed by a short-lived stream or flood water.

adolescence (ˌædə'lɛsəns) NOUN the period in human development that occurs between the beginning of puberty and adulthood.
▷HISTORY C15: via Old French from Latin *adolēscentia,* from *adolēscere* to grow up, from *alēscere* to grow, from *alēre* to feed, nourish

adolescent (ˌædə'lɛsᵊnt) ADJECTIVE 1 of or relating to adolescence. 2 *Informal* behaving in an immature way; puerile. ◆ NOUN 3 an adolescent person.

Adonai (ˌædɒ'naɪ, -'neɪaɪ) NOUN *Judaism* a name for God.
▷HISTORY C15: from Hebrew: lord; compare ADONIS

Adonic (ə'dəʊnɪk) ADJECTIVE 1 (in classical prosody) of or relating to a verse line consisting of a dactyl (–⏑⏑) followed by a spondee (– –) or by a trochee (–⏑), thought to have been first used in laments for Adonis. 2 of or relating to Adonis. ◆ NOUN 3 an Adonic line or verse.

Adonis (ə'dəʊnɪs) NOUN 1 *Greek myth* a handsome youth loved by Aphrodite. Killed by a wild boar, he was believed to spend part of the year in the underworld and part on earth, symbolizing the vegetative cycle. 2 a handsome young man.
▷HISTORY C16: from Latin, via Greek *Adōnis* from Phoenician *adōni* my lord, a title of the god Tammuz; related to Hebrew ADONAI

adopt (ə'dɒpt) VERB (*tr*) 1 *Law* to bring (a person) into a specific relationship, esp to take (another's child) as one's own child. 2 to choose and follow (a plan, technique, etc.). 3 to take over (an idea, etc.) as if it were one's own. 4 to take on; assume: *to adopt a title.* 5 to accept (a report, etc.).
▷HISTORY C16: from Latin *adoptāre* to choose for oneself, from *optāre* to choose
▸**ˌadop'tee** NOUN ▸**a'doption** NOUN

adopted (ə'dɒptɪd) ADJECTIVE having been adopted: *an adopted child.* Compare **adoptive.**

adoption panel NOUN *Social welfare* (in Britain) a committee appointed by an adoption agency, such as a local authority, to make recommendations concerning the suitability of prospective adoption cases.

adoptive (ə'dɒptɪv) ADJECTIVE 1 acquired or related by adoption: *an adoptive father.* 2 of or relating to adoption. Compare **adopted.**

adorable (ə'dɔ:rəbᵊl) ADJECTIVE 1 very attractive; charming; lovable. 2 *Becoming rare* deserving or eliciting adoration.
▸**a'dorably** ADVERB

adoration (ˌædə'reɪʃən) NOUN 1 deep love or esteem. 2 the act of worshipping.

adore (ə'dɔ:) VERB 1 (*tr*) to love intensely or deeply. 2 to worship (a god) with religious rites. 3 (*tr*) *Informal* to like very much: *I adore chocolate.*
▷HISTORY C15: via French from Latin *adōrāre,* from *ad-* to + *ōrāre* to pray
▸**a'dorer** NOUN ▸**a'doring** ADJECTIVE ▸**a'doringly** ADVERB

adorn (ə'dɔ:n) VERB (*tr*) 1 to decorate: *she adorned her hair with flowers.* 2 to increase the beauty, distinction, etc., of.

▷**HISTORY** C14: via Old French from Latin *adōrnāre*, from *ōrnāre* to furnish, prepare
▸**a'dornment** NOUN

Adowa ('ɑːduˌwɑː) NOUN a variant spelling of **Aduwa.**

ADP NOUN *Biochem* adenosine diphosphate; a nucleotide derived from ATP with the liberation of energy that is then used in the performance of muscular work.

Adrastea (ə'dræstɪə) NOUN a small satellite of Jupiter, discovered in 1979.

Adrastus (ə'dræstəs) NOUN *Greek myth* a king of Argos and leader of the Seven against Thebes of whom he was the sole survivor.

ad referendum ADVERB, ADJECTIVE subject to agreement by others and finalization of details: *an ad referendum contract.*
▷**HISTORY** Latin

ad rem *Latin* (æd 'rɛm) ADJECTIVE, ADVERB to the point; without digression: *to reply ad rem; an ad rem discussion.* Compare **ad hominem.**

adrenal (ə'driːnᵊl) ADJECTIVE 1 on or near the kidneys. 2 of or relating to the adrenal glands or their secretions. ◆ NOUN 3 an adrenal gland.
▷**HISTORY** C19: from AD- (near) + RENAL

adrenal gland NOUN an endocrine gland at the anterior end of each kidney. Its medulla secretes adrenaline and noradrenaline and its cortex secretes several steroid hormones. Also called: **suprarenal gland.**

Adrenalin (ə'drɛnəlɪn) NOUN *Trademark* a brand of **adrenaline.**

adrenaline *or* **adrenalin** (ə'drɛnəlɪn) NOUN a hormone that is secreted by the adrenal medulla in response to stress and increases heart rate, pulse rate, and blood pressure, and raises the blood levels of glucose and lipids. It is extracted from animals or synthesized for such medical uses as the treatment of asthma. Chemical name: aminohydroxyphenylpropionic acid; formula: $C_9H_{13}NO_3$. US name: **epinephrine.**

adrenal insufficiency NOUN another name for **Addison's disease.**

adrenalized *or* **adrenalised** (ə'driːnəlaɪzd) ADJECTIVE tense or highly charged: *adrenalized with excitement.*

adrenergic (ˌædrə'nɜːdʒɪk) ADJECTIVE releasing or activated by adrenaline or an adrenaline-like substance.
▷**HISTORY** C20: ADRENALINE + Greek *ergon* work

adrenocorticotrophic (əˌdriːnəʊˌkɔːtəkəʊ'trɒfɪk) *or* **adrenocorticotropic** (əˌdriːnəʊˌkɔːtəkəʊ'trɒpɪk) ADJECTIVE stimulating the adrenal cortex.

adrenocorticotrophic hormone NOUN the full name of **ACTH.**

Adrianople (ˌeɪdrɪə'nəʊpᵊl) *or* **Adrianopolis** (ˌeɪdrɪə'nɒpəlɪs) NOUN former names of **Edirne.**

Adrian Quist (ˌeɪdrɪən 'kwɪst) ADJECTIVE *Austral slang* intoxicated; drunk.
▷**HISTORY** rhyming slang for PISSED

Adriatic (ˌeɪdrɪ'ætɪk) ADJECTIVE 1 of or relating to the Adriatic Sea, or to the inhabitants of its coast or islands. ◆ NOUN 2 **the.** short for the **Adriatic Sea.**

Adriatic Sea NOUN an arm of the Mediterranean between Italy and the Balkan Peninsula.

adrift (ə'drɪft) ADJECTIVE (*postpositive*), ADVERB 1 floating without steering or mooring; drifting. 2 without purpose; aimless. 3 *Informal* off course or amiss: *the project went adrift.*

adroit (ə'drɔɪt) ADJECTIVE 1 skilful or dexterous. 2 quick in thought or reaction.
▷**HISTORY** C17: from French *à droit* according to right, rightly
▸**a'droitly** ADVERB ▸**a'droitness** NOUN

adscititious (ˌædsɪ'tɪʃəs) ADJECTIVE added or supplemental; additional.
▷**HISTORY** C17: from Latin *adscītus* admitted (from outside), from *adscīscere* to admit, from *scīscere* to seek to know, from *scīre* to know
▸ˌ**adsci'titiously** ADVERB

adscription (əd'skrɪpʃən) NOUN a less common word for **ascription.**

adsorb (əd'sɔːb, -'zɔːb) VERB to undergo or cause to undergo a process in which a substance, usually a gas, accumulates on the surface of a solid forming a thin film, often only one molecule thick: *to adsorb hydrogen on nickel; oxygen adsorbs on tungsten.* Compare **absorb** (sense 8).
▷**HISTORY** C19: AD- + *-sorb* as in ABSORB
▸**ad'sorbable** ADJECTIVE ▸**adˌsorba'bility** NOUN
▸**ad'sorption** NOUN

adsorbate (əd'sɔːbeɪt, -bɪt, -'zɔː-) NOUN a substance that has been or is to be adsorbed on a surface.

adsorbent (əd'sɔːbənt, -'zɔː-) ADJECTIVE 1 capable of adsorption. ◆ NOUN 2 a material, such as activated charcoal, on which adsorption can occur.

adsuki bean (æd'zuːkɪ) NOUN a variant spelling of **adzuki bean.**

adsum ('ædˌsʊm) SENTENCE SUBSTITUTE I am present.
▷**HISTORY** Latin

aduki (æ'duːkɪ) NOUN a variant of **adzuki.**

adularescent (əˌdjʊlə'rɛsənt) ADJECTIVE (of minerals, such as moonstone) having or emitting a milky or bluish iridescence.
▷**HISTORY** C19: from ADULAR(IA) + -ESCENT
▸**aˌdula'rescence** NOUN

adularia (ˌædjʊ'lɛərɪə) NOUN a white or colourless glassy variety of orthoclase in the form of prismatic crystals. It occurs in metamorphic rocks and is a minor gemstone. Formula: $KAlSi_3O_8$.
▷**HISTORY** C18: via Italian from French *adulaire,* after *Adula,* a group of mountains in Switzerland

adulate ('ædjʊˌleɪt) VERB (*tr*) to flatter or praise obsequiously.
▷**HISTORY** C17: back formation from C15 *adulation,* from Latin *adūlāri* to flatter
▸'**aduˌlator** NOUN

adulation (ˌædjʊ'leɪʃən) NOUN obsequious flattery or praise; extreme admiration.

adulatory (ˌædjʊ'leɪtərɪ, 'ædjʊˌleɪtərɪ) ADJECTIVE expressing praise, esp obsequiously; flattering.

Adullamite (ə'dʌləˌmaɪt) NOUN a person who has withdrawn from a political group and joined with a few others to form a dissident group.
▷**HISTORY** C19: originally applied to members of the British House of Commons who withdrew from the Liberal party (1866); alluding to the cave of *Adullam* in the Bible, to which David and others fled (1 Samuel 22: 1–2)

adult ('ædʌlt, ə'dʌlt) ADJECTIVE 1 having reached maturity; fully developed. 2 of or intended for mature people: *adult education.* 3 regarded as suitable only for adults, because of being pornographic: *adult films.* ◆ NOUN 4 a person who has attained maturity; a grownup. 5 a mature fully grown animal or plant. 6 *Law* a person who has attained the age of legal majority (18 years for most purposes). Compare **infant.**
▷**HISTORY** C16: from Latin *adultus,* from *adolēscere* to grow up, from *alēscere* to grow, from *alēre* to feed, nourish
▸'**adulthood** NOUN

adulterant (ə'dʌltərənt) NOUN 1 a substance or ingredient that adulterates. ◆ ADJECTIVE 2 adulterating.

adulterate VERB (ə'dʌltəˌreɪt) 1 (*tr*) to debase by adding inferior material: *to adulterate milk with water.* ◆ ADJECTIVE (ə'dʌltərɪt, -ˌreɪt) 2 adulterated; debased or impure. 3 a less common word for **adulterous.**
▷**HISTORY** C16: from Latin *adulterāre* to corrupt, commit adultery, probably from *alter* another, hence to approach another, commit adultery
▸**aˌdulter'ation** NOUN ▸**a'dulterˌator** NOUN

adulterer (ə'dʌltərə) NOUN a person who has committed adultery.
▷**HISTORY** C16: originally also *adulter,* from Latin *adulter,* back formation from *adulterāre* to ADULTERATE

adulteress (ə'dʌltərəs) NOUN a woman who has committed adultery.

adulterine (ə'dʌltərɪn, -ˌriːn, -ˌraɪn) ADJECTIVE 1 of or made by adulteration; fake. 2 conceived in adultery: *an adulterine child.*

adulterous (ə'dʌltərəs) ADJECTIVE 1 of, characterized by, or inclined to adultery. 2 an obsolete word for **adulterate** (sense 2).
▸**a'dulterously** ADVERB

adultery (ə'dʌltərɪ) NOUN, *plural* **-teries.** voluntary sexual intercourse between a married man or woman and a partner other than the legal spouse.
▷**HISTORY** C15 *adulterie,* altered (as if directly from Latin *adulterium*) from C14 *avoutrie,* via Old French from Latin *adulterium,* from *adulter,* back formation from *adulterāre.* See ADULTERATE

adultese (ˌædʌl'tiːz) NOUN vocabulary, idiom, etc., that is typical of adult speakers.
▷**HISTORY** C20: from ADULT + -ESE

Adult Training Centre NOUN *Social welfare* a day centre, run by a local authority, for mentally handicapped people to gain work experience.

adumbral (æd'ʌmbrəl) ADJECTIVE *Usually poetic* shadowy.
▷**HISTORY** C19: from AD- (in the sense: in) + Latin *umbra* shadow

adumbrate ('ædʌmˌbreɪt) VERB (*tr*) 1 to outline; give a faint indication of. 2 to foreshadow. 3 to overshadow; obscure.
▷**HISTORY** C16: from Latin *adumbrātus* represented only in outline, from *adumbrāre* to cast a shadow on, from *umbra* shadow
▸ˌ**adum'bration** NOUN ▸**adumbrative** (æd'ʌmbrətɪv) ADJECTIVE ▸**ad'umbratively** ADVERB

adust (ə'dʌst) ADJECTIVE *Archaic* 1 dried up or darkened by heat; burnt or scorched. 2 gloomy or melancholy.
▷**HISTORY** C14 (in the sense: gloomy): from Latin *adūstus,* from *adūrere* to set fire to, from *ūrere* to burn

Aduwa *or* **Adowa** ('ɑːduˌwɑː) NOUN a town in N Ethiopia: Emperor Menelik II defeated the Italians here in 1896. Pop.: 17 476 (1989 est.). Italian name: **Adua** (a'dua).

adv. ABBREVIATION FOR: 1 adverb. 2 adverbial.

ad val. ABBREVIATION FOR ad valorem.

ad valorem (æd və'lɔːrəm) ADJECTIVE, ADVERB (of taxes) in proportion to the estimated value of the goods taxed. Abbreviations: **ad val, a.v, A/V.**
▷**HISTORY** from Latin

advance (əd'vɑːns) VERB 1 to go or bring forward in position. 2 (foll by *on*) to move (towards) in a threatening manner. 3 (*tr*) to present for consideration; suggest. 4 to bring or be brought to a further stage of development; improve; further. 5 (*tr*) to cause (an event) to occur earlier. 6 (*tr*) to supply (money, goods, etc.) beforehand, either for a loan or as an initial payment. 7 to increase (a price, value, rate of occurrence, etc.) or (of a price, etc.) to be increased. 8 (*intr*) to improve one's position; be promoted: *he advanced rapidly in his job.* 9 (*tr*) *Archaic* to promote in rank, status, or position. ◆ NOUN 10 forward movement; progress in time or space. 11 improvement; progress in development. 12 *Commerce* **a** the supplying of commodities or funds before receipt of an agreed consideration. **b** the commodities or funds supplied in this manner. **c** (*as modifier*): *an advance supply.* 13 Also called: **advance payment.** a money payment made before it is legally due: *this is an advance on your salary.* 14 a loan of money. 15 an increase in price, value, rate of occurrence, etc. 16 a less common word for **advancement** (sense 1). 17 **in advance. a** beforehand: *payment in advance.* **b** (foll by *of*) ahead in time or development: *ideas in advance of the time.* 18 (*modifier*) forward in position or time: *advance booking; an advance warning.* ◆ See also **advances.**
▷**HISTORY** C15 *advauncen,* altered (on the model of words beginning with Latin *ad-*) from C13 *avauncen,* via Old French from Latin *abante* from before, from *ab-* away from + *ante* before
▸**ad'vancer** NOUN ▸**ad'vancingly** ADVERB

advance corporation tax NOUN a former UK tax in which a company paying a dividend had to deduct the basic rate of income tax from the grossed-up value of the dividend and pay it to the Inland Revenue. Abbreviation: **ACT.**

advanced (əd'vɑːnst) ADJECTIVE 1 being ahead in development, knowledge, progress, etc.: *advanced studies.* 2 having reached a comparatively late stage: *a man of advanced age.* 3 ahead of the times: *advanced views on religion.*

advanced gas-cooled reactor NOUN a nuclear reactor using carbon dioxide as the coolant, graphite as the moderator, and ceramic uranium dioxide cased in stainless steel as the fuel. Abbreviation: **AGR.**

Advanced Higher NOUN (in Scotland) 1 **a** the highest level of qualification offered within the school system, replacing the former Certificate of Sixth Year Studies. **b** (*as modifier*): *Advanced Higher*

Maths. 2 a pass in a particular subject at Advanced Higher level.

advance directive NOUN another name for **living will**.

Advanced level NOUN (in Britain) the formal name for **A level**.

advanced skills teacher NOUN *Brit education* a teacher who has achieved high standards of classroom practice and success and who, after passing a national assessment, is paid to share his or her skills and experience with other teachers. Abbreviation: **AST**.

advance guard NOUN 1 a military unit sent ahead of a main body to find gaps in enemy defences, clear away minor opposition, and prevent unexpected contact. 2 a temporary military detachment sent ahead of a force to prepare for a landing or other operation, esp by making reconnaissance.

advance man NOUN *US* an agent of a political candidate or other public figure who travels in advance of the candidate to organize publicity, arrange meetings, and make security checks.

advancement (əd'vɑːnsmənt) NOUN 1 promotion in rank, status, etc.; preferment. 2 a less common word for **advance** (senses 10, 11). 3 *Property law* the use during a testator's lifetime of money or property for the benefit of a child or other person who is a prospective beneficiary in the testator's will.

advance notice NOUN See **notice** (sense 6).

advance poll NOUN *Canadian* (in an election) a poll held prior to election day to permit voters who expect to be absent then to cast their ballots.

advance ratio NOUN *Aeronautics* 1 the ratio of wind speed along the axis of a rotor or propeller to the speed of the blade tip. 2 the ratio of forward flight speed to the speed of the rotor tip of a helicopter.

advances (əd'vɑːnsɪz) PLURAL NOUN (*sometimes singular;* often foll by *to* or *towards*) personal overtures made in an attempt to become friendly, gain a favour, etc.

advantage (əd'vɑːntɪdʒ) NOUN 1 (often foll by *over* or *of*) superior or more favourable position or power: *he had an advantage over me because of his experience*. 2 benefit or profit (esp in the phrase **to one's advantage**). 3 *Tennis* **a** the point scored after deuce. **b** the resulting state of the score. 4 **take advantage of. a** to make good use of. **b** to impose upon the weakness, good nature, etc., of; abuse. **c** to seduce. 5 **to advantage.** to good effect: *he used his height to advantage at the game*. 6 **you have the advantage of me.** you know me but I do not know you.
▷HISTORY C14 *avantage* (later altered to *advantage* on the model of words beginning with Latin *ad-*), from Old French *avant* before, from Latin *abante* from before, away. See ADVANCE

advantaged (əd'vɑːntɪdʒd) ADJECTIVE in a superior social or economic position.

advantageous (ˌædvən'teɪdʒəs) ADJECTIVE producing advantage.
▸ˌ**advan'tageously** ADVERB ▸ˌ**advan'tageousness** NOUN

advection (əd'vɛkʃən) NOUN the transference of heat energy in a horizontal stream of gas, esp of air.
▷HISTORY C20: from Latin *advectiō* conveyance, from *advehere*, from *ad-* to + *vehere* to carry

advent ('ædvɛnt, -vənt) NOUN an arrival or coming, esp one which is awaited.
▷HISTORY C12: from Latin *adventus*, from *advenīre*, from *ad-* to + *venīre* to come

Advent ('ædvɛnt, -vənt) NOUN *Christianity* the season including the four Sundays preceding Christmas or (in Eastern Orthodox churches) the forty days preceding Christmas.

Advent calendar NOUN *Brit* a large card with a brightly coloured sometimes tinselled design on it that contains small numbered doors for children to open on each of the days of Advent, revealing pictures beneath them.

Adventist ('ædvɛntɪst, 'ædvən-) NOUN a member of any of the Christian groups, such as the **Seventh-Day Adventists** that hold that the Second Coming of Christ is imminent.

adventitia (ˌædvɛn'tɪʃɪə, -'tɪʃə) NOUN the outermost covering of an organ or part, esp the outer coat of a blood vessel.
▷HISTORY C19: New Latin, from the neuter plural of Latin *adventīcius;* see ADVENTITIOUS

adventitious (ˌædvɛn'tɪʃəs) ADJECTIVE 1 added or appearing accidentally or unexpectedly. 2 (of a plant or animal part) developing in an abnormal position, as a root that grows from a stem.
▷HISTORY C17: from Latin *adventīcius* coming from outside, from *adventus* a coming
▸ˌ**adven'titiously** ADVERB

adventive (əd'vɛntɪv) *Biology* ◆ ADJECTIVE 1 (of a species) introduced to a new area and not yet established there; exotic. ◆ NOUN 2 such a plant or animal. ◆ Also called: **casual**.

Advent Sunday NOUN the first of the four Sundays of Advent, and the one that falls nearest to November 30.

adventure (əd'vɛntʃə) NOUN 1 a risky undertaking of unknown outcome. 2 an exciting or unexpected event or course of events. 3 a hazardous financial operation; commercial speculation. 4 *Obsolete* **a** danger or misadventure. **b** chance. ◆ VERB 5 to take a risk or put at risk. 6 (*intr;* foll by *into, on, upon*) to dare to go or enter (into a place, dangerous activity, etc.). 7 to dare to say (something): *he adventured his opinion*.
▷HISTORY C13 *aventure* (later altered to *adventure* after the Latin spelling), via Old French ultimately from Latin *advenīre* to happen to (someone), arrive
▸**ad'ventureful** ADJECTIVE

adventure playground NOUN *Brit* a playground for children that contains building materials, discarded industrial parts, etc., used by the children to build with, hide in, climb on, etc.

adventurer (əd'vɛntʃərə) NOUN 1 a person who seeks adventure, esp one who seeks success or money through daring exploits. 2 a person who seeks money or power by unscrupulous means. 3 a speculator.

adventuress (əd'vɛntʃərɪs) NOUN 1 a woman who seeks adventure, esp one who seeks success or money through daring exploits. 2 a woman who seeks money or power by unscrupulous means. 3 a speculator.

adventure tourism NOUN *Austral and NZ* tourism involving activities that are physically challenging.

adventurism (əd'vɛntʃəˌrɪzəm) NOUN recklessness, esp in politics and finance.
▸**ad'venturist** NOUN

adventurous (əd'vɛntʃərəs) ADJECTIVE 1 Also: **adventuresome.** daring or enterprising. 2 dangerous; involving risk.
▸**ad'venturously** ADVERB

adverb ('ædˌvɜːb) NOUN **a** a word or group of words that serves to modify a whole sentence, a verb, another adverb, or an adjective; for example, *probably, easily, very,* and *happily* respectively in the sentence *They could probably easily envy the very happily married couple*. **b** (*as modifier*): *an adverb marker*. Abbreviation: **adv.**
▷HISTORY C15–C16: from Latin *adverbium* adverb, literally: added word, a translation of Greek *epirrhēma* a word spoken afterwards

adverbial (æd'vɜːbɪəl) NOUN 1 a word or group of words playing the grammatical role of an adverb, such as *in the rain* in the sentence *I'm singing in the rain*. ◆ ADJECTIVE 2 of or relating to an adverb or adverbial.
▸**ad'verbially** ADVERB

adversarial (ˌædvɜː'sɛərɪəl) ADJECTIVE 1 pertaining to or characterized by antagonism and conflict. 2 *Brit* having or involving opposing parties or interests in a legal contest. US term: **adversary**.

adversary ('ædvəsərɪ) NOUN, *plural* **-saries.** 1 a person or group that is hostile to someone; enemy. 2 an opposing contestant in a game or sport. ◆ ADJECTIVE 3 the US term for **adversarial** (sense 2).
▷HISTORY C14: from Latin *adversārius*, from *adversus* against. See ADVERSE

adversative (əd'vɜːsətɪv) *Grammar* ◆ ADJECTIVE 1 (of a word, phrase, or clause) implying opposition or contrast. *But* and *although* are adversative conjunctions introducing adversative clauses. ◆ NOUN 2 an adversative word or speech element.

adverse ('ædvɜːs, æd'vɜːs) ADJECTIVE 1 antagonistic or inimical; hostile: *adverse criticism*. 2 unfavourable to one's interests: *adverse circumstances*. 3 contrary or opposite in direction or position: *adverse winds*. 4 (of leaves, flowers, etc.) facing the main stem. Compare **averse** (sense 2).
▷HISTORY C14: from Latin *adversus* opposed to, hostile, from *advertere* to turn towards, from *ad-* to, towards + *vertere* to turn
▸**ad'versely** ADVERB ▸**ad'verseness** NOUN

adverse possession NOUN *Property law* the occupation or possession of land by a person not legally entitled to it. If continued unopposed for a period specifed by law, such occupation extinguishes the title of the rightful owner.

adverse pressure gradient NOUN *Aerodynamics* an increase of pressure in the direction of flow.

adversity (əd'vɜːsɪtɪ) NOUN, *plural* **-ties.** 1 distress; affliction; hardship. 2 an unfortunate event or incident.

advert[1] (əd'vɜːt) VERB (*intr;* foll by *to*) to draw attention (to); refer (to).
▷HISTORY C15: from Latin *advertere* to turn one's attention to. See ADVERSE

advert[2] ('ædvɜːt) NOUN *Brit informal* short for **advertisement**.

advertence (əd'vɜːtəns) *or* **advertency** NOUN heedfulness or attentiveness.
▸**ad'vertent** ADJECTIVE ▸**ad'vertently** ADVERB

advertise *or sometimes US* **advertize** ('ædvəˌtaɪz) VERB 1 to present or praise (goods, a service, etc.) to the public, esp in order to encourage sales. 2 to make (something, such as a vacancy, article for sale, etc.) publicly known, as to possible applicants, buyers, etc.: *to advertise a job*. 3 (*intr;* foll by *for*) to make a public request (for), esp in a newspaper, etc.: *she advertised for a cook*. 4 *Obsolete* to warn; caution.
▷HISTORY C15: from a lengthened stem of Old French *avertir,* ultimately from Latin *advertere* to turn one's attention to. See ADVERSE
▸'**adverˌtiser** *or* (*sometimes US*) '**adverˌtizer** NOUN

advertisement *or sometimes US* **advertizement** (əd'vɜːtɪsmənt, -tɪz-) NOUN any public notice, as a printed display in a newspaper, short film on television, announcement on radio, etc., designed to sell goods, publicize an event, etc. Shortened forms: **ad, advert**.

advertising *or sometimes US* **advertizing** ('ædvəˌtaɪzɪŋ) NOUN 1 the promotion of goods or services for sale through impersonal media, such as radio or television. 2 the business that specializes in creating such publicity. 3 advertisements collectively; publicity.

advertising agency NOUN an organization that creates advertising material, contracts for publication space, and sometimes undertakes market research on behalf of its clients.

Advertising Standards Authority NOUN an independent UK body set up by the advertising industry to ensure that all advertisements comply with the British Code of Advertising Practice. Abbreviation: **ASA**.

advertorial (ˌædvɜː'tɔːrɪəl) NOUN advertising material presented under the guise of editorial material.
▷HISTORY C20: from ADVERT[2] + (EDIT)ORIAL

advice (əd'vaɪs) NOUN 1 recommendation as to appropriate choice of action; counsel. 2 (*sometimes plural*) formal notification of facts, esp when communicated from a distance.
▷HISTORY C13 *avis* (later *advise*), via Old French from a Vulgar Latin phrase based on Latin *ad* to, according to + *vīsum* view (hence: according to one's view, opinion)

advice note NOUN a document sent by a supplier to a customer to inform him that goods he ordered have been dispatched. It usually gives details such as the quantity of goods and how they have been sent.

advisable (əd'vaɪzəbᵊl) ADJECTIVE worthy of recommendation; prudent; sensible.
▸**ad'visably** ADVERB ▸**adˌvisa'bility** *or* **ad'visableness** NOUN

advise (əd'vaɪz) VERB (*when tr, may take a clause as*

object or an infinitive) [1] to offer advice (to a person or persons); counsel: *he advised the king; to advise caution; he advised her to leave.* [2] *(tr; sometimes foll by of) Formal* to inform or notify. [3] *(intr; foll by with) Chiefly US, obsolete in Brit* to consult or discuss.
▷HISTORY C14: via Old French from Vulgar Latin *advīsāre* (unattested) to consider, from Latin *ad-* to + *vīsāre* (unattested), from *vīsere* to view, from *vidēre* to see

advised (əd'vaɪzd) ADJECTIVE resulting from deliberation. See also **ill-advised, well-advised.**
▸**advisedly** (əd'vaɪzɪdlɪ) ADVERB

advisement (əd'vaɪzmənt) NOUN *Chiefly US, archaic in Britain* consultation; deliberation.

adviser *or* **advisor** (əd'vaɪzə) NOUN [1] a person who advises. [2] *Education* a person responsible for advising students on academic matters, career guidance, etc. [3] *Brit education* a subject specialist who advises heads of schools on current teaching methods and facilities.

advisory (əd'vaɪzərɪ) ADJECTIVE [1] giving advice; empowered to make recommendations: *an advisory body.* ◆ NOUN, *plural* **-ries.** [2] a statement issued to give advice, recommendations, or a warning: *a travel advisory.* [3] a person or organization with an advisory function: *the Prime Minister's media advisory.*

advisory teacher NOUN *Brit* a teacher who visits schools to advise teachers on curriculum developments within a particular subject area.

advocaat ('ædvəʊˌkɑː, -ˌkɑːt, 'ædvə-) NOUN a liqueur having a raw egg base.
▷HISTORY C20: Dutch, from *advocatenborrel,* from *advocaat* ADVOCATE (noun) + *borrel* drink

advocacy ('ædvəkəsɪ) NOUN, *plural* **-cies.** active support, esp of a cause.

advocate VERB ('ædvəˌkeɪt) [1] *(tr; may take a clause as object)* to support or recommend publicly; plead for or speak in favour of. ◆ NOUN ('ædvəkɪt, -ˌkeɪt) [2] a person who upholds or defends a cause; supporter. [3] a person who intercedes on behalf of another. [4] a person who pleads his client's cause in a court of law. See also **barrister, solicitor, counsellor.** [5] *Scots Law* the usual word for **barrister.**
▷HISTORY C14: via Old French from Latin *advocātus* legal witness, advocate, from *advocāre* to call as witness, from *vocāre* to call
▸ˌ**advo'catory** ADJECTIVE

Advocate Depute NOUN a Scottish law officer with the functions of public prosecutor.

advocation (ˌædvə'keɪʃən) NOUN *Scots Law, papal law* the transfer to itself by a superior court of an action pending in a lower court.

advocatus diaboli *Latin* (ˌædvə'kɑːtəs daɪ'æbəˌlaɪ) NOUN another name for the **devil's advocate.**

advowson (əd'vaʊzᵊn) NOUN *English ecclesiastical law* the right of presentation to a vacant benefice.
▷HISTORY C13: via Anglo-French and Old French from Latin *advocātiōn-* the act of summoning, from *advocāre* to summon

advt ABBREVIATION FOR advertisement.

Adygei *or* **Adyghe** ('ɑːdɪˌgeɪ, ˌɑːdɪ'geɪ, ˌɑːdɪ'ge) NOUN [1] *(plural* **-gei, -geis** *or* **-ghe, -ghes)** a member of a Circassian people of the Northwest Caucasus. [2] the Circassian language, esp its Western dialect. Compare **Kabardian.**

Adygei Republic *or* **Adygea** (ˌɑːdɪ'geɪə; *Russian* adɪ'geja) NOUN a constituent republic of SW Russia, bordering on the Caucasus Mountains: chiefly agricultural but with some mineral resources. Capital: Maikop. Pop.: 449 000 (2000 est.). Area: 7600 sq. km (2934 sq. miles).

adynamia (ˌædɪ'neɪmɪə) NOUN *Obsolete* loss of vital power or strength, esp as the result of illness; weakness or debility.
▷HISTORY C19: New Latin, from A-[1] + *-dynamia,* from Greek *dunamis* strength, force
▸**adynamic** (ˌædɪ'næmɪk) ADJECTIVE

adytum ('ædɪtəm) NOUN, *plural* **-ta** (-tə). the most sacred place of worship in an ancient temple from which the laity was prohibited.
▷HISTORY C17: Latin, from Greek *aduton* a place not to be entered, from A-[1] + *duein* to enter

adze *or US* **adz** (ædz) NOUN a heavy hand tool with a steel cutting blade attached at right angles to a wooden handle, used for dressing timber.
▷HISTORY Old English *adesa*

Adzhar Autonomous Republic (ə'dʒɑː) *or* **Adzharia** (ə'dʒɑːrɪə) NOUN an administrative division of SW Georgia, on the Black Sea: part of Turkey from the 17th century until 1878; mostly mountainous, reaching 2805 m (9350 ft.), with a subtropical coastal strip. Capital: Batumi. Pop.: 386 700 (1993 est.). Area: 3000 sq. km (1160 sq. miles).

adzuki (æd'zuːkɪ), **aduki** (ə'duːkɪ), *or* **adsuki** NOUN [1] a leguminous plant, *Phaseolus angularis,* that has yellow flowers and pods containing edible brown seeds and is widely cultivated as a food crop in China and Japan. [2] the seed of this plant. Also: **adzuki bean.**
▷HISTORY *adzuki,* from Japanese: red bean

æ *or* **Æ** [1] a digraph in Latin representing either a native diphthong, as in *æquus,* or a Greek αι *(ai)* in Latinized spellings, as in *æschylus*: now usually written *ae,* or *e* in some words, such as *demon.* [2] a ligature used in Old and early Middle English to represent the vowel sound of *a* in *cat.* [3] a ligature used in modern phonetic transcription also representing the vowel sound *a* in *cat.*

ae[1] (e) *or* **yae** DETERMINER *Scot* one; a single.
▷HISTORY from Old English *ān*

ae[2] THE INTERNET DOMAIN NAME FOR United Arab Emirates.

ae. ABBREVIATION FOR aetatis.
▷HISTORY Latin: at the age of; aged

AEA (in Britain) ABBREVIATION FOR **Atomic Energy Authority.**

AE & P ABBREVIATION FOR Ambassador Extraordinary and Plenipotentiary.

AEC (in the US) ABBREVIATION FOR **Atomic Energy Commission.**

aeciospore ('iːsɪəˌspɔː) NOUN any of the spores produced in an aecium of the rust fungi, which spread to and infect the primary host. Also called: **aecidospore.**
▷HISTORY C20: from AECIUM + SPORE

aecium ('iːsɪəm) *or* **aecidium** (iː'sɪdɪəm) NOUN, *plural* **-cia** (-sɪə) *or* **-cidia** (-'sɪdɪə). a globular or cup-shaped structure in some rust fungi in which aeciospores are produced.
▷HISTORY C19: New Latin, from Greek *aikia* injury (so called because of the damage the fungi cause)

AECL ABBREVIATION FOR Atomic Energy of Canada Limited.

aedes (eɪ'iːdiːz) NOUN any mosquito of the genus *Aedes* (formerly *Stegomyia*) of tropical and subtropical regions, esp *A. aegypti,* which transmits yellow fever and dengue.
▷HISTORY C20: New Latin, from Greek *aēdēs* unpleasant, from A-[1] + *ēdos* pleasant

aedicule ('ɛdɪˌkjuːl) NOUN an opening such as a door or a window, framed by columns on either side, and a pediment above.
▷HISTORY C19: from Latin *aediculum* small house, from *aedēs* building

aedile *or sometimes US* **edile** ('iːdaɪl) NOUN a magistrate of ancient Rome in charge of public works, games, buildings, and roads.
▷HISTORY C16: from Latin *aedīlis* concerned with buildings, from *aedēs* a building

Aeëtes (iː'iːtiːz) NOUN *Greek myth* a king of Colchis, father of Medea and keeper of the Golden Fleece.

Aegean (iː'dʒiːən) ADJECTIVE [1] of or relating to the Aegean Sea or Islands. [2] of or relating to the Bronze Age civilization of Greece, Asia Minor, and the Aegean Islands.

Aegean Islands PLURAL NOUN the islands of the Aegean Sea, including the Cyclades, Dodecanese, Euboea, and Sporades. The majority are under Greek administration.

Aegean Sea NOUN an arm of the Mediterranean between Greece and Turkey.

Aegeus (iː'dʒiːuːs, 'iːdʒɪəs) NOUN *Greek myth* an Athenian king and father of Theseus.

Aegina (iː'dʒaɪnə) NOUN [1] an island in the Aegean Sea, in the Saronic Gulf. Area: 85 sq. km (33 sq. miles). [2] a town on the coast of this island: a city-state of ancient Greece. [3] **Gulf of.** another name for the **Saronic Gulf.** Greek name: **Aiyina.**

Aegir ('iːdʒɪə) NOUN *Norse myth* the god of the sea.

aegis *or sometimes US* **egis** ('iːdʒɪs) NOUN [1] sponsorship or protection; auspices (esp in the phrase **under the aegis of**). [2] *Greek myth* the shield of Zeus, often represented in art as a goatskin.
▷HISTORY C18: from Latin, from Greek *aigis* shield of Zeus, perhaps related to *aig-,* stem of *aix* goat

Aegisthus (iː'dʒɪsθəs) NOUN *Greek myth* a cousin to and the murderer of Agamemnon, whose wife Clytemnestra he had seduced. He usurped the kingship of Mycenae until Orestes, Agamemnon's son, returned home and killed him.

Aegospotami (ˌiːgəs'pɒtəˌmaɪ) NOUN a river of ancient Thrace that flowed into the Hellespont. At its mouth the Spartan fleet under Lysander defeated the Athenians in 405 B.C., ending the Peloponnesian War.

aegrotat ('aɪgrəʊˌtæt, 'iː-, iː'grəʊtæt) NOUN [1] (in British and certain other universities, and, sometimes, schools) a certificate allowing a candidate to pass an examination although he has missed all or part of it through illness. [2] a degree or other qualification obtained in such circumstances.
▷HISTORY C19: Latin, literally: he is ill

Aegyptus (iː'dʒɪptəs) NOUN *Greek myth* a king of Egypt and twin brother of Danaüs.

-aemia, -haemia *or US* **-emia, -hemia** NOUN COMBINING FORM denoting blood, esp a specified condition of the blood in names of diseases: *leukaemia.*
▷HISTORY New Latin, from Greek *-aimia,* from *haima* blood

Aeneas (ɪ'niːəs) NOUN *Classical myth* a Trojan prince, the son of Anchises and Aphrodite, who escaped the sack of Troy and sailed to Italy via Carthage and Sicily. After seven years, he and his followers established themselves near the site of the future Rome.

Aeneid (ɪ'niːɪd) NOUN an epic poem in Latin by Virgil relating the experiences of Aeneas after the fall of Troy, written chiefly to provide an illustrious historical background for Rome.

aeolian (iː'əʊlɪən) ADJECTIVE of or relating to the wind; produced or carried by the wind.
▷HISTORY C18: from AEOLUS, god of the winds

Aeolian *or* **Eolian** (iː'əʊlɪən) NOUN [1] a member of a Hellenic people who settled in Thessaly and Boeotia and colonized Lesbos and parts of the Aegean coast of Asia Minor. ◆ ADJECTIVE [2] of or relating to this people or their dialect of Ancient Greek; Aeolic. [3] of or relating to Aeolus. [4] denoting or relating to an authentic mode represented by the ascending natural diatonic scale from A to A: the basis of the modern minor key. See also **Hypo-.**

aeolian deposits PLURAL NOUN *Geology* sediments, such as loess, made up of windblown grains of sand or dust.

aeolian harp NOUN a stringed instrument that produces a musical sound when a current of air or wind passes over the strings. Also called: **wind harp.**

Aeolian Islands PLURAL NOUN another name for the **Lipari Islands.**

aeolian tone NOUN the musical tone produced by the passage of a current of air over a stretched string, etc., as in an aeolian harp.

Aeolic *or* **Eolic** (iː'ɒlɪk, iː'əʊlɪk) ADJECTIVE [1] of or relating to the Aeolians or their dialect. ◆ NOUN [2] one of four chief dialects of Ancient Greek, spoken chiefly in Thessaly, Boeotia, and Aeolis. ◆ Compare **Arcadic, Doric, Ionic.** See also **Attic** (sense 3).

aeolipile (iː'ɒlɪˌpaɪl) NOUN a device illustrating the reactive forces of a gas jet: usually a spherical vessel mounted so as to rotate and equipped with angled exit pipes from which steam within it escapes.
▷HISTORY C17: from Latin *aeolīpilae* balls of AEOLUS or *aeolīpylae* gates of AEOLUS

Aeolis ('iːəlɪs) *or* **Aeolia** (iː'əʊlɪə) NOUN the ancient name for the coastal region of NW Asia Minor, including the island of Lesbos, settled by the Aeolian Greeks (about 1000 B.C.).

aeolotropic (ˌiːələʊ'trɒpɪk) ADJECTIVE a less common word for **anisotropic.**
▷HISTORY C19: from Greek *aiolos* fickle + -TROPIC

Aeolus ('iːələs, iː'əʊləs) NOUN *Greek myth* [1] the god of the winds. [2] the founding king of the Aeolians in Thessaly.

aeon *or esp US* **eon** ('iːən, 'iːɒn) NOUN [1] an immeasurably long period of time; age. [2] a period

of one thousand million years. [3] (*often capital*) *Gnosticism* one of the powers emanating from the supreme being and culminating in the demiurge.
▷HISTORY C17: from Greek *aiōn* an infinitely long time

aeonian *or* **eonian** (iːˈəʊnɪən) ADJECTIVE *Literary* everlasting.

aepyornis (ˌiːpɪˈɔːnɪs) NOUN any of the large extinct flightless birds of the genus *Aepyornis*, remains of which have been found in Madagascar.
▷HISTORY C19: New Latin, from Greek *aipus* high + *ornis* bird

aer- COMBINING FORM a variant of **aero-** before a vowel.

aerate (ˈɛəreɪt) VERB (*tr*) [1] to charge (a liquid) with a gas, esp carbon dioxide, as in the manufacture of effervescent drink. [2] to expose to the action or circulation of the air, so as to purify.
▸**aerˈation** NOUN ▸**ˈaerator** NOUN

aerenchyma (ɛəˈrɛŋkɪmə) NOUN plant tissue with large air-filled spaces, which is typical of aquatic plants and allows air to reach waterlogged parts.
▷HISTORY C19: from AER(O)- + Greek *enkhuma* infusion

aeri- COMBINING FORM a variant of **aero-**.

aerial (ˈɛərɪəl) ADJECTIVE [1] of, relating to, or resembling air. [2] existing, occurring, moving, or operating in the air: *aerial cable car; aerial roots of a plant.* [3] ethereal; light and delicate. [4] imaginary; visionary. [5] extending high into the air; lofty. [6] of or relating to aircraft: *aerial combat.* ◆ NOUN [7] Also called: **antenna.** the part of a radio or television system having any of various shapes, such as a dipole, Yagi, long-wire, or vertical aerial, by means of which radio waves are transmitted or received.
▷HISTORY C17: via Latin from Greek *aērios*, from *aēr* air

aerialist (ˈɛərɪəlɪst) NOUN *Chiefly US* a trapeze artist or tightrope walker.

aerial ladder NOUN the US and Canadian term for **turntable ladder.**

aerial perspective NOUN a means of indicating relative distance in terms of a gradation of clarity, tone, and colour, esp blue. Also called: **atmospheric perspective.**

aerial pingpong NOUN *Austral slang* Australian Rules football.

aerial top dressing NOUN the process of spreading lime, fertilizer, etc. over farmland from an aeroplane.

aerie (ˈɛərɪ, ˈɪərɪ) NOUN a variant spelling (esp US) of **eyrie.**

aeriform (ˈɛərɪˌfɔːm) ADJECTIVE [1] having the form of air; gaseous. [2] unsubstantial.

aerify (ˈɛərɪˌfaɪ) VERB **-fies, -fying, -fied.** [1] to change or cause to change into a gas. [2] to mix or combine with air.
▸**ˌaerifiˈcation** NOUN

aero¹ (ˈɛərəʊ) NOUN (*modifier*) of or relating to aircraft or aeronautics: *an aero engine.*

aero² AN INTERNET DOMAIN NAME FOR an organization in the air-transport industry.

aero-, aeri-, *or before a vowel* **aer-** COMBINING FORM [1] denoting air, atmosphere, or gas: *aerodynamics.* [2] denoting aircraft: *aeronautics.*
▷HISTORY ultimately from Greek *aēr* air

aeroacoustics (ˌɛərəʊəˈkuːstɪks) NOUN (*functioning as singular*) the study of the generation and transmittance of sound by fluid flow.

aeroballistics (ˌɛərəʊbəˈlɪstɪks) NOUN (*functioning as singular*) the ballistics of projectiles dropped, launched, or fired from aircraft.

aerobatics (ˌɛərəʊˈbætɪks) NOUN (*functioning as singular or plural*) spectacular or dangerous manoeuvres, such as loops or rolls, performed in an aircraft or glider; stunt flying.
▷HISTORY C20: from AERO- + (ACRO)BATICS
▸**ˌaeroˈbatic** ADJECTIVE

aerobe (ˈɛərəʊb) *or* **aerobium** (ɛəˈrəʊbɪəm) NOUN, *plural* **-obes** *or* **-obia** (-ˈəʊbɪə). an organism that requires oxygen for respiration. Compare **anaerobe.**
▷HISTORY C19: from AERO- + Greek *bios* life. Compare MICROBE

aerobic (ɛəˈrəʊbɪk) ADJECTIVE [1] (of an organism or process) depending on oxygen. [2] of or relating to aerobes. [3] designed for or relating to aerobics: *aerobic shoes; aerobic dances.* ◆ Compare **anaerobic.**

aerobics (ɛəˈrəʊbɪks) NOUN (*functioning as singular*) any system of sustained exercises designed to increase the amount of oxygen in the blood and strengthen the heart and lungs.
▸**aerˈobicist** NOUN

aerobiology (ˌɛərəʊbaɪˈɒlədʒɪ) NOUN the study of airborne organisms, spores, etc.
▸**aerobiological** (ˌɛərəʊˌbaɪəˈlɒdʒɪkᵊl) ADJECTIVE
▸**ˌaerobioˈlogically** ADVERB ▸**ˌaerobiˈologist** NOUN

aerobiosis (ˌɛərəʊbaɪˈəʊsɪs) NOUN life in the presence of oxygen.
▸**aerobiotic** (ˌɛərəʊbaɪˈɒtɪk) ADJECTIVE

aerobraking (ˈɛərəʊˌbreɪkɪŋ) NOUN the use of aerodynamic braking in extremely low-density atmospheres in space at hypersonic Mach numbers.

aerodonetics (ˌɛərəʊdəˈnɛtɪks) NOUN (*functioning as singular*) the study of soaring or gliding flight, esp the study of gliders.
▷HISTORY C20: from Greek *aerodonetos* tossed in the air, from AERO- + *donētos*, past participle of *donein* to toss

aerodrome (ˈɛərəˌdrəʊm) *or US* **airdrome** (ˈɛəˌdrəʊm) NOUN *Obsolete* a landing area, esp for private aircraft, that is usually smaller than an airport.

aerodynamic braking NOUN [1] the use of aerodynamic drag to slow spacecraft re-entering the atmosphere. [2] the use of airbrakes to retard flying vehicles or objects. [3] the use of a parachute or reversed thrust to decelerate an aircraft before landing.

aerodynamics (ˌɛərəʊdaɪˈnæmɪks) NOUN (*functioning as singular*) the study of the dynamics of gases, esp of the forces acting on a body passing through air. Compare **aerostatics** (sense 1).
▸**ˌaerodyˈnamic** ADJECTIVE ▸**ˌaerodyˈnamically** ADVERB
▸**ˌaerodyˈnamicist** NOUN

aerodyne (ˈɛərəʊˌdaɪn) NOUN any heavier-than-air machine, such as an aircraft, that derives the greater part of its lift from aerodynamic forces.
▷HISTORY C20: back formation from AERODYNAMIC; see DYNE

aeroembolism (ˌɛərəʊˈɛmbəˌlɪzəm) NOUN a former name for **air embolism.**

aero engine NOUN an engine for powering an aircraft.

aerofoil (ˈɛərəʊˌfɔɪl) *or US and Canadian* **airfoil** (ˈɛəˌfɔɪl) NOUN a cross section of an aileron, wing, tailplane, or rotor blade.

aerogel (ˈɛərəˌdʒɛl) NOUN a colloid that has a continuous solid phase containing dispersed gas.

aerogram *or* **aerogramme** (ˈɛərəˌgræm) NOUN [1] Also called: **air letter.** an airmail letter written on a single sheet of lightweight paper that folds and is sealed to form an envelope. [2] another name for **radiotelegram.**

aerography (ɛəˈrɒgrəfɪ) NOUN *Archaic* the description of the character of the upper atmosphere.

aerolite (ˈɛərəˌlaɪt) NOUN a stony meteorite consisting of silicate minerals.
▸**aerolitic** (ˌɛərəˈlɪtɪk) ADJECTIVE

aerology (ɛəˈrɒlədʒɪ) NOUN the study of the atmosphere, particularly its upper layers.
▸**aerologic** (ˌɛərəˈlɒdʒɪk) *or* **ˌaeroˈlogical** ADJECTIVE
▸**aerˈologist** NOUN

aeromechanic (ˌɛərəʊmɪˈkænɪk) NOUN [1] an aircraft mechanic. ◆ ADJECTIVE [2] of or relating to aeromechanics.

aeromechanics (ˌɛərəʊmɪˈkænɪks) NOUN (*functioning as singular*) the mechanics of gases, esp air.
▸**ˌaeromeˈchanical** ADJECTIVE

aerometeorograph (ˌɛərəʊˈmiːtɪərəˌgrɑːf, -ˌgræf) NOUN *Chiefly US* an aircraft instrument that records temperature, humidity, and atmospheric pressure.

aerometer (ɛəˈrɒmɪtə) NOUN an instrument for determining the mass or density of a gas, esp air.
▸**aerometric** (ˌɛərəˈmɛtrɪk) ADJECTIVE

aerometry (ɛəˈrɒmɪtrɪ) NOUN another name for **pneumatics.**

aeron. ABBREVIATION FOR: [1] aeronautics. [2] aeronautical.

aeronaut (ˈɛərəˌnɔːt) NOUN a person who flies in a lighter-than-air craft, esp the pilot or navigator.

aeronautical (ˌɛərəˈnɔːtɪkᵊl) ADJECTIVE of or relating to aeronauts or aeronautics.
▸**ˌaeroˈnautically** ADVERB

aeronautical engineering NOUN the branch of engineering concerned with the design, production, and maintenance of aircraft.
▸**aeronautical engineer** NOUN

aeronautics (ˌɛərəˈnɔːtɪks) NOUN (*functioning as singular*) the study or practice of all aspects of flight through the air.

aeroneurosis (ˌɛərəʊnjʊˈrəʊsɪs) NOUN a functional disorder of aeroplane pilots characterized by anxiety and various psychosomatic disturbances, caused by insufficient oxygen at high altitudes and the emotional tension of flying.

aeronomy (ɛəˈrɒnəmɪ) NOUN the science of the earth's upper atmosphere.

aero-optics (ˌɛərəʊˈɒptɪks) NOUN (*functioning as singular*) the study of the effect of aircraft-induced and atmospheric disturbances on the efficiency of laser weapons.

aeropause (ˈɛərəˌpɔːz) NOUN the region of the upper atmosphere above which aircraft cannot fly.

aerophagia (ˌɛərəˈfeɪdʒɪə, -dʒə) *or* **aerophagy** (ɛəˈrɒfədʒɪ) NOUN spasmodic swallowing of air, a habit that can lead to belching and stomach pain.

aerophobia (ˌɛərəˈfəʊbɪə) NOUN a pathological fear of draughts of air.
▸**ˌaeroˈphobic** ADJECTIVE

aerophyte (ˈɛərəˌfaɪt) NOUN another name for **epiphyte.**

aeroplane (ˈɛərəˌpleɪn) *or US and Canadian* **airplane** (ˈɛəˌpleɪn) NOUN a heavier-than-air powered flying vehicle with fixed wings.
▷HISTORY C19: from French *aéroplane*, from AERO- + Greek *-planos* wandering, related to PLANET

aeroplane cloth *or* **fabric** NOUN [1] a strong fabric made from cotton, linen, and nylon yarns, used for some light aircraft fuselages and wings. [2] a similar lightweight fabric used for clothing. ◆ Also called: **aircraft fabric.**

aeroplane spin NOUN a wrestling attack in which a wrestler lifts his opponent onto his shoulders and spins around, leaving the opponent dizzy.

aerosol (ˈɛərəˌsɒl) NOUN [1] a colloidal dispersion of solid or liquid particles in a gas; smoke or fog. [2] a substance, such as a paint, polish, or insecticide, dispensed from a small metal container by a propellant under pressure. [3] Also called: **air spray.** such a substance together with its container.
▷HISTORY C20: from AERO- + SOL(UTION)

aerospace (ˈɛərəˌspeɪs) NOUN [1] the atmosphere and space beyond. [2] (*modifier*) of or relating to rockets, missiles, space vehicles, etc., that fly or operate in aerospace: *the aerospace industry.*

aerosphere (ˈɛərəˌsfɪə) NOUN *Archaic* the entire atmosphere surrounding the earth.

aerostat (ˈɛərəˌstæt) NOUN a lighter-than-air craft, such as a balloon.
▷HISTORY C18: from French *aérostat*, from AERO- + Greek *-statos* standing
▸**ˌaeroˈstatic** *or* **ˌaeroˈstatical** ADJECTIVE

aerostatics (ˌɛərəˈstætɪks) NOUN (*functioning as singular*) [1] the study of gases in equilibrium and bodies held in equilibrium in gases. Compare **aerodynamics.** [2] the study of lighter-than-air craft, such as balloons.

aerostation (ˈɛərəˌsteɪʃən) NOUN the science of operating lighter-than-air craft.

aerostructure (ˈɛərəʊˌstrʌktʃə) NOUN any separately manufactured unit, component, or section of an aircraft or other vehicle capable of flight.

aerothermodynamics (ˌɛərəʊˌθɜːməʊdaɪˈnæmɪks) NOUN (*functioning as singular*) the study of the exchange of heat between solids and gases, esp of the heating effect on aircraft flying through the air at very high speeds.
▸**ˌaeroˌthermodyˈnamic** ADJECTIVE

aerugo (ɪˈruːgəʊ) NOUN (esp of old bronze) another name for **verdigris.**
▷HISTORY C18: from Latin, from *aes* copper, bronze
▸**aeruginous** (ɪˈruːdʒɪnəs) ADJECTIVE

aery[1] ('ɛərɪ, 'eɪərɪ) ADJECTIVE *Poetic* [1] a variant spelling of **airy**. [2] lofty, insubstantial, or visionary.
▷HISTORY C16: via Latin from Greek *aērios,* from *aēr* AIR

aery[2] ('ɛərɪ, 'ɪərɪ) NOUN, *plural* **aeries.** a variant spelling of **eyrie.**

Aesculapian (ˌiːskjʊ'leɪpɪən) ADJECTIVE of or relating to Aesculapius or to the art of medicine.

Aesculapius (ˌiːskjʊ'leɪpɪəs) NOUN the Roman god of medicine or healing. Greek counterpart: **Asclepius.**

Aesir ('eɪsɪə) PLURAL NOUN the chief gods of Norse mythology dwelling in Asgard.
▷HISTORY Old Norse, literally: gods

aesthesia *or US* **esthesia** (iːs'θiːzɪə) NOUN the normal ability to experience sensation, perception, or sensitivity.
▷HISTORY C20: back formation from ANAESTHESIA

aesthete *or US* **esthete** ('iːsθiːt) NOUN a person who has or who affects a highly developed appreciation of beauty, esp in poetry and the visual arts.
▷HISTORY C19: back formation from AESTHETICS

aesthetic (iːs'θɛtɪk, ɪs-) *or sometimes US* **esthetic** ADJECTIVE *also* **aesthetical,** *or sometimes US* **esthetical.** [1] connected with aesthetics or its principles. [2] **a** relating to pure beauty rather than to other considerations. **b** artistic or relating to good taste: *an aesthetic consideration.* ◆ NOUN [3] a principle of taste or style adopted by a particular person, group, or culture: *the Bauhaus aesthetic of functional modernity.*
▸**aes'thetically** *or* (*sometimes US*) **es'thetically** ADVERB

aesthetician *or sometimes US* **esthetician** (ˌiːsθɪ'tɪʃən, ˌɛs-) NOUN [1] a student of aesthetics. [2] another name for **beauty therapist.**

aestheticism *or sometimes US* **estheticism** (iːs'θɛtɪˌsɪzəm, ɪs-) NOUN [1] the doctrine that aesthetic principles are of supreme importance and that works of art should be judged accordingly. [2] sensitivity to beauty, esp in art, music, literature, etc.

aesthetic labour NOUN workers employed by a company for their appearance or accent, with the aim of promoting the company's image.

aesthetics *or sometimes US* **esthetics** (iːs'θɛtɪks, ɪs-) NOUN (*functioning as singular*) [1] the branch of philosophy concerned with the study of such concepts as beauty, taste, etc. [2] the study of the rules and principles of art.
▷HISTORY C18: from Greek *aisthētikos* perceptible by the senses, from *aisthesthai* to perceive

aestival *or US* **estival** (iː'staɪv^{ə}l, 'ɛstɪ-) ADJECTIVE *Rare* of or occurring in summer.
▷HISTORY C14: from French, from Late Latin *aestīvālis,* from Latin *aestās* summer

aestivate *or US* **estivate** ('iːstɪˌveɪt, 'ɛs-) VERB (*intr*) [1] to pass the summer. [2] (of animals such as the lungfish) to pass the summer or dry season in a dormant condition. Compare **hibernate.**
▷HISTORY C17: from Latin *aestīvātus,* from *aestīvāre* to stay during the summer, from *aestās* summer
▸**'aestiˌvator** *or* (*US*) **'estiˌvator** NOUN

aestivation *or US* **estivation** (ˌiːstɪ'veɪʃən, ˌɛs-) NOUN [1] the act or condition of aestivating. [2] the arrangement of the parts of a flower bud, esp the sepals and petals.

aet. *or* **aetat.** ABBREVIATION FOR aetatis.
▷HISTORY Latin: at the age of

aether ('iːθə) NOUN a variant spelling of **ether** (senses 3–5).

aethereal (ɪ'θɪərɪəl) ADJECTIVE a variant spelling of **ethereal** (senses 1, 2, 3).
▸**aethereality** (ɪˌθɪərɪ'ælɪtɪ) NOUN ▸**ae'thereally** ADVERB

aetiological *or* **etiological** (ˌiːtɪə'lɒdʒɪk^{ə}l) ADJECTIVE [1] of or relating to aetiology. [2] *Philosophy* (of an explanation) in terms of causal precedents, as opposed, for instance, to the intentions of an agent.
▸**ˌaetio'logically** *or* **ˌetio'logically** ADVERB

aetiology *or* **etiology** (ˌiːtɪ'ɒlədʒɪ) NOUN, *plural* **-gies.** [1] the philosophy or study of causation. [2] the study of the causes of diseases. [3] the cause of a disease.
▷HISTORY C16: from Late Latin *aetologia,* from Greek *aitiologia,* from *aitia* cause
▸**ˌaeti'ologist** *or* **ˌeti'ologist** NOUN

Aetna ('ɛtnə) NOUN the Latin name for Mount **Etna.**

Aetolia (iː'təʊlɪə) NOUN a mountainous region forming (with the region of Acarnania) a department of W central Greece, north of the Gulf of Patras: a powerful federal state in the 3rd century B.C. Chief city: Missolonghi. Pop. (with Acarnania): 228 180 (1991). Area: 5461 sq. km (2108 sq. miles).

AEW ABBREVIATION FOR airborne early warning (aircraft).

af THE INTERNET DOMAIN NAME FOR Afghanistan.

AF ABBREVIATION FOR: [1] Anglo-French. [2] **automatic focus.** [3] **audio frequency.** [4] (in Canada) Air Force.

a.f. ABBREVIATION FOR audio frequency.

A/F (in auction catalogues, etc.) ABBREVIATION FOR as found.

AFAIK *Text messaging* ABBREVIATION FOR as far as I know.

afar (ə'fɑː) ADVERB [1] at, from, or to a great distance. ◆ NOUN [2] a great distance (esp in the phrase **from afar**).
▷HISTORY C14 *a fer,* altered from earlier *on fer* and *of fer;* see A-[2], FAR

Afars and the Issas ('ɑːfɑːz, 'iːsɑːs) NOUN **Territory of the.** a former name (1967–77) of **Djibouti.**

AFB ABBREVIATION FOR (US) Air Force Base.

AFC ABBREVIATION FOR: [1] Air Force Cross. [2] Association Football Club. [3] automatic flight control. [4] **automatic frequency control.**

afeard *or* **afeared** (ə'fɪəd) ADJECTIVE (*postpositive*) an archaic or dialect word for **afraid.**
▷HISTORY Old English *āfǣred,* from *afǣran* to frighten, from *fǣran* to FEAR

afebrile (æ'fiːbraɪl, eɪ-) ADJECTIVE without fever.

aff (æf) *Scot* ◆ ADVERB [1] off. ◆ PREPOSITION [2] off. [3] from; out of.
▷HISTORY Old English *of;* Old Norse *af*

affable ('æfəb^{ə}l) ADJECTIVE [1] showing warmth and friendliness; kindly; mild; benign. [2] easy to converse with; approachable; amicable.
▷HISTORY C16: from Latin *affābilis* easy to talk to, from *affārī* to talk to, from *ad-* to + *fārī* to speak; compare FABLE, FATE
▸**ˌaffa'bility** NOUN ▸**'affably** ADVERB

affair (ə'fɛə) NOUN [1] a thing to be done or attended to; matter; business: *this affair must be cleared up.* [2] an event or happening: *a strange affair.* [3] (*qualified by an adjective or descriptive phrase*) something previously specified, esp a man-made object; thing: *our house is a tumbledown affair.* [4] a sexual relationship between two people who are not married to each other. ◆ See also **affairs.**
▷HISTORY C13: from Old French, from *à faire* to do

affaire *French* (afɛr) NOUN a love affair.

affaire d'amour *French* (afɛr damur) NOUN, *plural* ***affaires d'amour*** (afɛr damur). a love affair.

affaire de coeur *French* (afɛr də kœr) NOUN, *plural* ***affaires de coeur*** (afɛr də kœr). an affair of the heart; love affair.

affaire d'honneur *French* (afɛr dɔnœr) NOUN, *plural* ***affaires d'honneur*** (afɛr dɔnœr). a duel.

affairs (ə'fɛəz) PLURAL NOUN [1] personal or business interests: *his affairs were in disorder.* [2] matters of public interest: *current affairs.*

affect[1] VERB (ə'fɛkt) (*tr*) [1] to act upon or influence, esp in an adverse way: *damp affected the sparking plugs.* [2] to move or disturb emotionally or mentally: *her death affected him greatly.* [3] (of pain, disease, etc.) to attack. ◆ NOUN ('æfɛkt, ə'fɛkt) [4] *Psychol* the emotion associated with an idea or set of ideas. See also **affection.**
▷HISTORY C17: from Latin *affectus,* past participle of *afficere* to act upon, from *ad-* to + *facere* to do

affect[2] (ə'fɛkt) VERB (*mainly tr*) [1] to put on an appearance or show of; make a pretence of: *to affect ignorance.* [2] to imitate or assume, esp pretentiously: *to affect an accent.* [3] to have or use by preference: *she always affects funereal clothing.* [4] to adopt the character, manner, etc., of: *he was always affecting the politician.* [5] (of plants or animals) to live or grow in: *penguins affect an arctic climate.* [6] to incline naturally or habitually towards: *falling drops of liquid affect roundness.*
▷HISTORY C15: from Latin *affectāre* to strive after, pretend to have; related to *afficere* to AFFECT[1]

affectation (ˌæfɛk'teɪʃən) NOUN [1] an assumed manner of speech, dress, or behaviour, esp one that is intended to impress others. [2] (often foll by *of*) deliberate pretence or false display: *affectation of nobility.*
▷HISTORY C16: from Latin *affectātiōn-* an aiming at, striving after, from *affectāre;* see AFFECT[2]

affected[1] (ə'fɛktɪd) ADJECTIVE (*usually postpositive*) [1] deeply moved, esp by sorrow or grief: *he was greatly affected by her departure.* [2] changed, esp detrimentally.
▷HISTORY C17: from AFFECT[1] + -ED[2]

affected[2] (ə'fɛktɪd) ADJECTIVE [1] behaving, speaking, etc., in an artificial or assumed way, esp in order to impress others. [2] feigned: *affected indifference.* [3] *Archaic* inclined; disposed.
▷HISTORY C16: from AFFECT[2] + -ED[2]
▸**af'fectedly** ADVERB ▸**af'fectedness** NOUN

affecting (ə'fɛktɪŋ) ADJECTIVE evoking feelings of pity, sympathy, or pathos; moving.
▸**af'fectingly** ADVERB

affection (ə'fɛkʃən) NOUN [1] a feeling of fondness or tenderness for a person or thing; attachment. [2] (*often plural*) emotion, feeling, or sentiment: *to play on a person's affections.* [3] *Pathol* any disease or pathological condition. [4] *Psychol* any form of mental functioning that involves emotion. See also **affect** (sense 1). [5] the act of affecting or the state of being affected. [6] *Archaic* inclination or disposition.
▷HISTORY C13: from Latin *affectiōn-* disposition, from *afficere* to AFFECT[1]
▸**af'fectional** ADJECTIVE

affectionate (ə'fɛkʃənɪt) ADJECTIVE having or displaying tender feelings, affection, or warmth: *an affectionate mother; an affectionate letter.*
▸**af'fectionately** ADVERB

affective (ə'fɛktɪv) ADJECTIVE [1] *Psychol* relating to affects. [2] concerned with or arousing the emotions or affection.
▸**affectivity** (ˌæfɛk'tɪvɪtɪ) *or* **af'fectiveness** NOUN

affective disorder NOUN any mental disorder, such as depression or mania, that is characterized by abnormal disturbances of mood.

affective psychosis NOUN a severe mental disorder characterized by extreme moods of either depression or mania.

affectless (ə'fɛktlɪs) ADJECTIVE **a** showing no emotion or concern for others. **b** not giving rise to any emotion or feeling: *an affectless novel.*
▷HISTORY C20: from AFFECT[1] (sense 4) + -LESS

affenpinscher ('æfənˌpɪnʃə) NOUN a small wire-haired breed of dog of European origin, having tufts of hair on the muzzle.
▷HISTORY German, literally: monkey-terrier, so called because its face resembles a monkey's

afferent ('æfərənt) ADJECTIVE bringing or directing inwards to a part or an organ of the body, esp towards the brain or spinal cord. Compare **efferent.**
▷HISTORY C19: from Latin *afferre* to carry to, from *ad-* to + *ferre* to carry

affettuoso (æˌfɛtjuː'əʊsəʊ) ADJECTIVE, ADVERB *Music* with feeling.
▷HISTORY C18: from Italian

affiance (ə'faɪəns) VERB [1] (*tr*) to bind (a person or oneself) in a promise of marriage; betroth. ◆ NOUN [2] *Archaic* a solemn pledge, esp a marriage contract.
▷HISTORY C14: via Old French from Medieval Latin *affīdāre* to trust (oneself) to, from *fīdāre* to trust, from *fīdus* faithful

affiant (ə'faɪənt) NOUN *US law* a person who makes an affidavit.
▷HISTORY C19: Old French, from *affier* to trust to, from Medieval Latin *affīdāre;* see AFFIANCE

affiche *French* (afiʃ) NOUN a poster or advertisement, esp one drawn by an artist, as for the opening of an exhibition.
▷HISTORY C18: from *afficher* to post

affidavit (ˌæfɪ'deɪvɪt) NOUN *Law* a declaration in writing made upon oath before a person authorized to administer oaths, esp for use as evidence in court.
▷HISTORY C17: from Medieval Latin, literally: he declares on oath, from *affīdare* to trust (oneself) to; see AFFIANCE

affiliate VERB (ə'fɪlɪˌeɪt) [1] (*tr;* foll by *to* or *with*) to receive into close connection or association (with a larger body, group, organization, etc.); adopt as a member, branch, etc. [2] (foll by *with*) to associate (oneself) or be associated, esp as a subordinate or

subsidiary; bring or come into close connection: *he affiliated himself with the Union.* ◆ NOUN (əˈfɪlɪɪt, -ˌeɪt) 3 **a** a person or organization that is affiliated with another. **b** (*as modifier*): *an affiliate member.*
▷HISTORY C18: from Medieval Latin *affīliātus* adopted as a son, from *affīlīare,* from Latin *filius* son
▸**af͵fili'ation** NOUN

affiliation order NOUN *Law* (formerly) an order made by a magistrates' court that a man adjudged to be the father of an illegitimate child shall contribute a specified periodic sum towards the child's maintenance.

affiliation proceedings PLURAL NOUN (formerly) legal proceedings, usually initiated by an unmarried mother, claiming legal recognition that a particular man is the father of her child, often associated with a claim for financial support.

affine (ˈæfaɪn) ADJECTIVE *Maths* of, characterizing, or involving transformations which preserve collinearity, esp in classical geometry, those of translation, rotation and reflection in an axis.
▷HISTORY C16: via French from Latin *affīnis* bordering on, related

affined (əˈfaɪnd) ADJECTIVE closely related; connected.

affinity (əˈfɪnɪtɪ) NOUN, *plural* **-ties.** 1 (foll by *with* or *for*) a natural liking, taste, or inclination towards a person or thing. 2 the person or thing so liked. 3 a close similarity in appearance or quality; inherent likeness. 4 relationship by marriage or by ties other than of blood, as by adoption. Compare **consanguinity.** 5 similarity in structure, form, etc., between different animals, plants, or languages. 6 *Chem* **a** the tendency for two substances to combine; chemical attraction. **b** a measure of the tendency of a chemical reaction to take place expressed in terms of the free energy change. Symbol: *A.* 7 *Biology* a measure of the degree of interaction between two molecules, such as an antigen and antibody or a hormone and its receptor.
▷HISTORY C14: via Old French from Latin *affīnitāt-* connected by marriage, from *affīnis* bordering on, related
▸**af'finitive** ADJECTIVE

affinity card NOUN 1 *Brit* a credit card issued by a bank or credit-card company, which donates a small percentage of the money spent using the card to a specified charity. 2 *US* a card entitling members of an affinity group (e.g. club, college) to a discount when used for purchases.

affirm (əˈfɜːm) VERB (*mainly tr*) 1 (*may take a clause as object*) to declare to be true; assert positively. 2 to uphold, confirm, or ratify. 3 (*intr*) *Law* to make an affirmation.
▷HISTORY C14: via Old French from Latin *affirmāre* to present (something) as firm or fixed, assert, from *ad-* to + *firmāre* to make FIRM[1]
▸**af'firmer** *or* **af'firmant** NOUN

affirmation (ˌæfəˈmeɪʃən) NOUN 1 the act of affirming or the state of being affirmed. 2 a statement of the existence or truth of something; assertion. 3 *Law* a solemn declaration permitted on grounds of conscientious objection to taking an oath.

affirmative (əˈfɜːmətɪv) ADJECTIVE 1 confirming or asserting something as true or valid: *an affirmative statement.* 2 indicating agreement or assent: *an affirmative answer.* 3 *Logic* **a** (of a categorial proposition) affirming the satisfaction by the subject of the predicate, as in *all birds have feathers; some men are married.* **b** not containing negation. Compare **negative** (sense 12). ◆ NOUN 4 a positive assertion. 5 a word or phrase stating agreement or assent, such as *yes* (esp in the phrase **answer in the affirmative**). 6 *Logic* an affirmative proposition. 7 **the affirmative.** *Chiefly US and Canadian* the side in a debate that supports the proposition. ◆ SENTENCE SUBSTITUTE 8 *Military* a signal codeword used to express assent or confirmation.
▸**af'firmatively** ADVERB

affirmative action NOUN *US* a policy or programme designed to counter discrimination against minority groups and women in areas such as employment and education. Brit equivalent: **positive discrimination.**

affix VERB (əˈfɪks) (*tr;* usually foll by *to* or *on*) 1 to attach, fasten, join, or stick: *to affix a poster to the wall.* 2 to add or append: *to affix a signature to a document.* 3 to attach or attribute (guilt, blame, etc.). ◆ NOUN (ˈæfɪks) 4 a linguistic element added to a word or root to produce a derived or inflected form: *-ment* in *establishment* is a derivational affix; *-s* in *drowns* is an inflectional affix. See also **prefix, suffix, infix.** 5 something fastened or attached; appendage.
▷HISTORY C15: from Medieval Latin *affixāre,* from *ad-* to + *fixāre* to FIX
▸**affixation** (ˌæfɪkˈseɪʃən) *or* **affixture** (əˈfɪkstʃə) NOUN

afflatus (əˈfleɪtəs) NOUN an impulse of creative power or inspiration, esp in poetry, considered to be of divine origin (esp in the phrase **divine afflatus**).
▷HISTORY C17: Latin, from *afflātus,* from *afflāre* to breathe or blow on, from *flāre* to blow

afflict (əˈflɪkt) VERB (*tr*) to cause suffering or unhappiness to; distress greatly.
▷HISTORY C14: from Latin *afflictus,* past participle of *afflīgere* to knock against, from *flīgere* to knock, to strike
▸**af'flictive** ADJECTIVE

afflicting (əˈflɪktɪŋ) ADJECTIVE deeply distressing; painful.

affliction (əˈflɪkʃən) NOUN 1 a condition of great distress, pain, or suffering. 2 something responsible for physical or mental suffering, such as a disease, grief, etc.

affluence (ˈæflʊəns) NOUN 1 an abundant supply of money, goods, or property; wealth. 2 *Rare* abundance or profusion.

affluent (ˈæflʊənt) ADJECTIVE 1 rich; wealthy. 2 abundant; copious. 3 flowing freely. ◆ NOUN 4 *Archaic* a tributary stream.
▷HISTORY C15: from Latin *affluent-,* present participle of *affluere* to flow towards, from *fluere* to flow

affluential (ˌæflʊˈɛnʃəl) NOUN an affluent person who does not display his or her wealth in the form of material possessions.

affluent society NOUN a society in which the material benefits of prosperity are widely available.

affluenza (ˌæflʊˈɛnzə) NOUN the guilt or lack of motivation experienced by people who have made or inherited large amounts of money. Also called: **sudden-wealth syndrome.**
▷HISTORY C20: from AFF(LUENT) + (IN)FLUENZA

afflux (ˈæflʌks) NOUN a flowing towards a point: *an afflux of blood to the head.*
▷HISTORY C17: from Latin *affluxus,* from *fluxus* FLUX

afford (əˈfɔːd) VERB 1 (preceded by *can, could,* etc.) to be able to do or spare something, esp without incurring financial difficulties or without risk of undesirable consequences: *we can afford to buy a small house; I can afford to give you one of my chess sets; we can't afford to miss this play.* 2 to give, yield, or supply: *the meeting afforded much useful information.*
▷HISTORY Old English *geforthian* to further, promote, from *forth* FORTH; the Old English prefix *ge-* was later reduced to *a-,* and the modern spelling (C16) is influenced by words beginning *aff-*
▸**af'fordable** ADJECTIVE ▸**af͵forda'bility** NOUN

afforest (əˈfɒrɪst) VERB (*tr*) to plant trees on; convert into forested land.
▷HISTORY C15: from Medieval Latin *afforestāre,* from *forestis* FOREST
▸**af͵forest'ation** NOUN

affranchise (əˈfræntʃaɪz) VERB (*tr*) to release from servitude or an obligation.
▷HISTORY C15: from Old French *afranchiss-,* a stem of *afranchir,* from *franchir* to free; see FRANK
▸**af'franchisement** NOUN

affray (əˈfreɪ) NOUN 1 *Law* a fight, noisy quarrel, or disturbance between two or more persons in a public place. ◆ VERB 2 (*tr*) *Archaic* to frighten.
▷HISTORY C14: via Old French from Vulgar Latin *exfridāre* (unattested) to break the peace; compare German *Friede* peace

affreightment (əˈfreɪtmənt) NOUN a contract hiring a ship to carry goods.
▷HISTORY C19: from French *affréter* to charter a ship, from *fret* FREIGHT

affricate (ˈæfrɪkɪt) NOUN a composite speech sound consisting of a stop and a fricative articulated at the same point, such as the sound written *ch,* as in *chair.*
▷HISTORY C19: from Latin *affricāre* to rub against, from *fricāre* to rub; compare FRICTION

affricative (əˈfrɪkətɪv, ˈæfrəˌkeɪ-) NOUN 1 another word for **affricate.** ◆ ADJECTIVE 2 of, relating to, or denoting an affricate.

affright (əˈfraɪt) *Archaic or poetic* ◆ VERB 1 (*tr*) to frighten. ◆ NOUN 2 a sudden terror.
▷HISTORY Old English *āfyrhtan,* from *a-,* a prefix indicating the beginning or end of an action + *fyrhtan* to FRIGHT

affront (əˈfrʌnt) NOUN 1 a deliberate insult. ◆ VERB (*tr*) 2 to insult, esp openly. 3 to offend the pride or dignity of. 4 *Obsolete* to confront defiantly.
▷HISTORY C14: from Old French *afronter* to strike in the face, from Vulgar Latin *affrontāre* (unattested), from the Latin phrase *ad frontem* to the face

affusion (əˈfjuːʒən) NOUN the baptizing of a person by pouring water onto his head. Compare **aspersion** (sense 3), **immersion.**
▷HISTORY C17: from Late Latin *affūsiōn-* a pouring upon, from *affundere,* from *fundere* to pour

AFG INTERNATIONAL CAR REGISTRATION FOR Afghanistan.

Afg. *or* **Afgh.** ABBREVIATION FOR Afghanistan.

afghan (ˈæfgæn, -gən) NOUN 1 a knitted or crocheted wool blanket or shawl, esp one with a geometric pattern. 2 a sheepskin coat, often embroidered and having long fur trimming around the edges.

Afghan (ˈæfgæn, -gən) *or* **Afghani** (æfˈgænɪ, -ˈgɑː-) NOUN 1 a native, citizen, or inhabitant of Afghanistan. 2 another name for **Pashto** (the language). 3 *History* an Indian camel driver employed in the outback of Australia. ◆ ADJECTIVE 4 denoting or relating to Afghanistan, its people, or their language.

Afghan hound NOUN a tall graceful breed of hound with a long silky coat.

afghani (æfˈgɑːnɪ) NOUN the standard monetary unit of Afghanistan, divided into 100 puli.

Afghanistan (æfˈgænɪˌstɑːn, -ˌstæn) NOUN a republic in central Asia: became independent in 1919; occupied by Soviet troops, 1979–89; controlled by mujaheddin forces from 1992 until 1996 when Taliban forces seized power; in the US-led 'war against terrorism' (2001) the Taliban were overthrown and replaced by an interim administration; generally arid and mountainous, with the Hindu Kush range rising over 7500 m (25 000 ft.) and fertile valleys of the Amu Darya, Helmand, and Kabul Rivers. Official languages: Pashto and Dari (Persian), Tajik also widely spoken. Religion: Muslim. Currency: afghani. Capital: Kabul. Pop.: 26 813 000 (2001 est). Area: 657 500 sq. km (250 000 sq. miles).

aficionado (əˌfɪʃjəˈnɑːdəʊ; *Spanish* afiθjoˈnaðo) NOUN, *plural* **-dos** (-dəʊz; *Spanish* -ðos). 1 an ardent supporter or devotee: *a jazz aficionado.* 2 a devotee of bullfighting.
▷HISTORY Spanish, from *aficionar* to arouse affection, from *afición* AFFECTION

afield (əˈfiːld) ADVERB, ADJECTIVE (*postpositive*) 1 away from one's usual surroundings or home (esp in the phrase **far afield**). 2 off the subject; away from the point (esp in the phrase **far afield**). 3 in or to the field, esp the battlefield.

afire (əˈfaɪə) ADVERB, ADJECTIVE (*postpositive*) 1 on fire; ablaze. 2 intensely interested or passionate: *he was afire with enthusiasm for the new plan.*

AFIS NOUN Automated Fingerprint Identification System: a computer system that scans fingerprints from crime scenes and compares them with millions of others around the world.

AFK *Text messaging* ABBREVIATION FOR away from keyboard.

AFL ABBREVIATION FOR Australian Football League: the national body for Australian Rules football.

aflame (əˈfleɪm) ADVERB, ADJECTIVE (*postpositive*) 1 in flames; ablaze. 2 deeply aroused, as with passion: *he was aflame with desire.* 3 (of the face) red or inflamed.

aflatoxin (ˌæfləˈtɒksɪn) NOUN a toxin produced by the fungus *Aspergillus flavus* growing on peanuts, maize, etc., causing liver disease (esp cancer) in man.
▷HISTORY C20: from *A(spergillus) fla(vus)* + TOXIN

AFL-CIO ABBREVIATION FOR American Federation of Labor and Congress of Industrial Organizations: a federation of independent American trade unions formed by the union of these two groups in 1955.

afloat (əˈfləʊt) ADJECTIVE (*postpositive*), ADVERB 1 floating. 2 aboard ship; at sea. 3 covered with water; flooded. 4 aimlessly drifting: *afloat in a sea of indecision.* 5 in circulation; afoot: *nasty rumours were afloat.* 6 free of debt; solvent.

aflutter (əˈflʌtə) ADJECTIVE (*postpositive*), ADVERB in or into a nervous or excited state.

AFM ABBREVIATION FOR Air Force Medal.

AFN (in Canada) ABBREVIATION FOR Assembly of First Nations.

AFNOR ABBREVIATION FOR Association Française de Normalisation: the standards organization of France.

afoot (əˈfʊt) ADJECTIVE (*postpositive*), ADVERB 1 in circulation or operation; astir: *mischief was afoot.* 2 on or by foot.

afore (əˈfɔː) ADVERB, PREPOSITION, CONJUNCTION an archaic or dialect word for **before**.

aforementioned (əˈfɔːˌmɛnʃənd) ADJECTIVE (*usually prenominal*) (chiefly in legal documents) stated or mentioned before or already.

aforesaid (əˈfɔːˌsɛd) ADJECTIVE (*usually prenominal*) (chiefly in legal documents) spoken of or referred to previously.

aforethought (əˈfɔːˌθɔːt) ADJECTIVE (*immediately postpositive*) premeditated (esp in the phrase **malice aforethought**).

aforetime (əˈfɔːˌtaɪm) ADVERB *Archaic* formerly.

a fortiori (eɪ ˌfɔːtɪˈɔːraɪ, -rɪ, ɑː) ADVERB for similar but more convincing reasons: *if Britain cannot afford a space programme, then, a fortiori, neither can India.*
▷HISTORY Latin

afoul (əˈfaʊl) ADVERB, ADJECTIVE (*postpositive*) 1 (usually foll by *of*) in or into a state of difficulty, confusion, or conflict (with). 2 (often foll by *of*) in or into an entanglement or collision (with) (often in the phrase **run afoul of**): *a yacht with its sails afoul; the boat ran afoul of a steamer.*

afp ABBREVIATION FOR alpha-fetoprotein.

AFRAeS (in Britain) ABBREVIATION FOR Associate Fellow of the Royal Aeronautical Society.

afraid (əˈfreɪd) ADJECTIVE (*postpositive*) 1 (often foll by *of*) feeling fear or apprehension; frightened: *he was afraid of cats.* 2 reluctant (to do something), as through fear or timidity: *he was afraid to let himself go.* 3 (often foll by *that*; used to lessen the effect of an unpleasant statement) regretful: *I'm afraid that I shall have to tell you to go.*
▷HISTORY C14 *affraied,* past participle of AFFRAY (to frighten)

A-frame ADJECTIVE (of a house) constructed with an A-shaped elevation.

afreet *or* **afrit** (ˈæfriːt, əˈfriːt) NOUN *Arabian myth* a powerful evil demon or giant monster.
▷HISTORY C19: from Arabic *ʿifrīt*

afresh (əˈfrɛʃ) ADVERB once more; once again; anew.

Africa (ˈæfrɪkə) NOUN the second largest of the continents, on the Mediterranean in the north, the Atlantic in the west, and the Red Sea, Gulf of Aden, and Indian Ocean in the east. The Sahara desert divides the continent unequally into North Africa (an early centre of civilization, in close contact with Europe and W Asia, now inhabited chiefly by Arabs) and Africa south of the Sahara (relatively isolated from the rest of the world until the 19th century and inhabited chiefly by Negroid peoples). It was colonized mainly in the 18th and 19th centuries by Europeans and now comprises independent nations. The largest lake is Lake Victoria and the chief rivers are the Nile, Niger, Congo, and Zambezi. Pop.: 755 919 000 (1998 est.). Area: about 30 300 000 sq. km (11 700 000 sq. miles).

African (ˈæfrɪkən) ADJECTIVE 1 denoting or relating to Africa or any of its peoples, languages, nations, etc. ◆ NOUN 2 a native, inhabitant, or citizen of any of the countries of Africa. 3 a member or descendant of any of the peoples of Africa, esp a Black.

Africana (ˌæfrɪˈkɑːnə) PLURAL NOUN objects of cultural or historical interest of southern African origin.

African-American NOUN 1 an American of African descent. ◆ ADJECTIVE 2 of or relating to Americans of African descent.

African-Canadian NOUN 1 a Canadian of African descent. ◆ ADJECTIVE 2 of or relating to Canadians of African descent.

African horse sickness NOUN *Vet science* a fatal infectious disease of horses, mules, and donkeys, which is transmitted by insect vectors. It is caused by an arbovirus and is characterized by pulmonary or cardiac signs.

Africanism (ˈæfrɪkəˌnɪzəm) NOUN something characteristic of Africa or Africans, esp a characteristic feature of an African language when introduced into a non-African language.

Africanist (ˈæfrɪkənɪst) NOUN a person specializing in the study of African affairs or culture.

Africanize *or* **Africanise** (ˈæfrɪkəˌnaɪz) VERB (*tr*) to make African, esp to give control of (policy, government, etc.) to Africans.
▸ **ˌAfricaniˈzation** *or* **ˌAfricaniˈsation** NOUN

African lily NOUN another name for **agapanthus**.

African mahogany NOUN 1 any of several African trees of the meliaceous genus *Khaya,* esp *K. ivorensis,* that have wood similar to that of true mahogany. 2 the wood of any of these trees, used for furniture, etc. 3 any of various other African woods that resemble true mahogany.

African National Congress NOUN (in South Africa) a political party, founded in 1912 as an African nationalist movement and banned there from 1960 to 1990 because of its active opposition to apartheid: in 1994 won South Africa's first multiracial elections. Abbreviation: **ANC**.

African swine fever NOUN *Vet science* a highly contagious fatal disease of pigs caused by a myxovirus. The disease is characterized by fever, blotches on the skin, depression, and lack of coordination.

African time NOUN *South African slang* unpunctuality.

African Union NOUN an organization of African states established in 2002 as successor to the OAU; it aims to encourage economic development and political stability through increased cooperation between its members. Abbreviation: **AU**.

African violet NOUN any of several tropical African plants of the genus *Saintpaulia,* esp *S. ionantha,* cultivated as house plants, with violet, white, or pink flowers and hairy leaves: family *Gesneriaceae*.

Afrikaans (ˌæfrɪˈkɑːns, -ˈkɑːnz) NOUN one of the official languages of the Republic of South Africa, closely related to Dutch. Sometimes called: **South African Dutch**.
▷HISTORY C20: from Dutch: African

Afrikander *or* **Africander** (afriˈkandə, ˌæfrɪˈkændə) NOUN 1 a breed of humpbacked beef cattle originally raised in southern Africa. 2 a southern African breed of fat-tailed sheep. 3 a former name for an **Afrikaner**.
▷HISTORY C19: from South African Dutch, formed on the model of *Hollander*

Afrikaner (afriˈkaːnə, ˌæfrɪˈkɑːnə) NOUN a White native of the Republic of South Africa whose mother tongue is Afrikaans. See also **Boer**.

Afrikanerdom (afriˈkaːnədəm, ˌæfrɪˈkɑːnədəm) NOUN (in South Africa) Afrikaner nationalism based on pride in the Afrikaans language and culture, conservative Calvinism, and a sense of heritage as pioneers.

afrit (ˈæfriːt, əˈfriːt) NOUN a variant spelling of **afreet**.

Afro (ˈæfrəʊ) NOUN, *plural* **-ros**. a hairstyle in which the hair is shaped into a wide frizzy bush.
▷HISTORY C20: independent use of AFRO-

Afro- COMBINING FORM indicating Africa or African: *Afro-Asiatic.*

Afro-American NOUN, ADJECTIVE another word for **African-American**.

Afro-Asian ADJECTIVE of or relating to both Africa and Asia, esp as part of the Third World.

Afro-Asiatic NOUN 1 Also called: **Semito-Hamitic**. a family of languages of SW Asia and N Africa, consisting of the Semitic, ancient Egyptian, Berber, Cushitic, and Chadic subfamilies. ◆ ADJECTIVE 2 denoting, belonging to, or relating to this family of languages.

Afro-Caribbean ADJECTIVE 1 denoting or relating to Caribbean people of African descent or their culture. ◆ NOUN 2 a Caribbean of African descent.

Afro-chain NOUN (in the Caribbean) a large chain necklace with a central pendant: usually worn with a dashiki by men.

Afro-comb NOUN a comb with a handle and long teeth used esp on curly hair.

Afro-Cuban ADJECTIVE of or relating to a type of jazz influenced by Cuban variants of African rhythms. Compare **Cu-bop**.

Afro-pessimism NOUN the belief that the provision of aid to African countries is futile.

afrormosia (ˌæfrɔːˈməʊzɪə) NOUN a hard teaklike wood obtained from tropical African trees of the leguminous genus *Pericopsis*.
▷HISTORY C20: from AFRO- + *Ormosia* (genus name)

AFSLAET ABBREVIATION FOR Associate Fellow of the Society of Licensed Aircraft Engineers and Technologists.

aft (ɑːft) ADVERB, ADJECTIVE *Chiefly nautical* towards or at the stern or rear: *the aft deck; aft of the engines.*
▷HISTORY C17: perhaps a shortened form of earlier ABAFT

after (ˈɑːftə) PREPOSITION 1 following in time; in succession to: *after dinner; time after time.* 2 following; behind: *they entered one after another.* 3 in pursuit or search of: *chasing after a thief; he's only after money.* 4 concerning: *to inquire after his health.* 5 considering: *after what you have done, you shouldn't complain.* 6 next in excellence or importance to: *he ranked Jonson after Shakespeare.* 7 in imitation of; in the manner of: *a statue after classical models.* 8 in accordance with or in conformity to: *a man after her own heart.* 9 with a name derived from: *Mary was named after her grandmother.* 10 *US* past (the hour of): *twenty after three.* 11 **after all**. **a** in spite of everything: *it's only a game, after all.* **b** in spite of expectations, efforts, etc.: *he won the race after all!* 12 **after you**. please go, enter, etc., before me. ◆ ADVERB 13 at a later time; afterwards. 14 coming afterwards; in pursuit. 15 *Nautical* further aft; sternwards. ◆ CONJUNCTION 16 (*subordinating*) at a time later than that at which: *he came after I had left.* ◆ ADJECTIVE 17 *Nautical* further aft: *the after cabin.*
▷HISTORY Old English *æfter;* related to Old Norse *aptr* back, *eptir* after, Old High German *aftar*

afterbirth (ˈɑːftəˌbɜːθ) NOUN the placenta and fetal membranes expelled from the uterus after the birth of the offspring.

afterbody (ˈɑːftəˌbɒdɪ) NOUN, *plural* **-bodies**. any discarded part that continues to trail a satellite, rocket, etc., in orbit.

afterbrain (ˈɑːftəˌbreɪn) NOUN a nontechnical name for **myelencephalon**.

afterburner (ˈɑːftəˌbɜːnə) NOUN 1 a device in the exhaust system of an internal-combustion engine for removing or rendering harmless potentially dangerous components in the exhaust gases. 2 a system of fuel injection and combustion located behind the turbine of an aircraft jet engine to produce additional thrust.

afterburning (ˈɑːftəˌbɜːnɪŋ) NOUN 1 Also called: **reheat**. a process in which additional fuel is ignited in the exhaust gases of a jet engine to produce additional thrust. 2 irregular burning of fuel in a rocket motor after the main burning has ceased. 3 persistence of combustion in an internal-combustion engine, either in an incorrect part of the cycle or after the ignition has been switched off.

aftercare (ˈɑːftəˌkɛə) NOUN 1 support services by a welfare agency for a person discharged from an institution, such as hospital, hostel, or prison. 2 *Med* the care before and after discharge from hospital of a patient recovering from an illness or operation. 3 any system of maintenance or upkeep of an appliance or product: *contact lens aftercare.*

afterdamp (ˈɑːftəˌdæmp) NOUN a poisonous mixture of gases containing carbon dioxide, carbon monoxide, and nitrogen formed after the explosion of firedamp in coal mines. See also **whitedamp.**

afterdeck ('ɑːftəˌdɛk) NOUN *Nautical* the unprotected deck behind the bridge of a ship.

aftereffect ('ɑːftərɪˌfɛkt) NOUN [1] any result occurring some time after its cause. [2] *Med* any delayed response to a stimulus or agent. Compare **side effect.** [3] *Psychol* any illusory sensation caused by a stimulus that has ceased.

afterglow ('ɑːftəˌgləʊ) NOUN [1] the glow left after a light has disappeared, such as that sometimes seen after sunset. [2] the glow of an incandescent metal after the source of heat has been removed. [3] *Physics* luminescence persisting on the screen of a cathode-ray tube or in a gas-discharge tube after the power supply has been disconnected. [4] a trace, impression, etc., of past emotion, brilliance, etc.

afterheat ('ɑːftəˌhiːt) NOUN the heat generated in a nuclear reactor after it has been shut down, produced by residual radioactivity in the fuel elements.

afterimage ('ɑːftərˌɪmɪdʒ) NOUN a sustained or renewed sensation, esp visual, after the original stimulus has ceased. Also called: **aftersensation, photogene.**

afterlife ('ɑːftəˌlaɪf) NOUN life after death or at a later time in a person's lifetime.

aftermath ('ɑːftəˌmɑːθ, -ˌmæθ) NOUN [1] signs or results of an event or occurrence considered collectively, esp of a catastrophe or disaster: *the aftermath of war.* [2] *Agriculture* a second mowing or crop of grass from land that has already yielded one crop earlier in the same year.
▷HISTORY C16: AFTER + *math* a mowing, from Old English *mæth*

aftermost ('ɑːftəˌməʊst) ADJECTIVE closer or closest to the rear or (in a vessel) the stern; last.

afternoon (ˌɑːftə'nuːn) NOUN [1] **a** the period of the day between noon and evening. **b** (*as modifier*): *afternoon tea.* [2] a middle or later part: *the afternoon of life.*

afternoons (ˌɑːftə'nuːnz) ADVERB *Informal* during the afternoon, esp regularly.

afterpains ('ɑːftəˌpeɪnz) PLURAL NOUN cramplike pains caused by contraction of the uterus after childbirth.

afterpeak ('ɑːftəˌpiːk) NOUN *Nautical* the space behind the aftermost bulkhead, often used for storage.

afterpiece ('ɑːftəˌpiːs) NOUN a brief usually comic dramatic piece presented after a play.

after-ripening NOUN *Botany* the period of internal change that is necessary in some apparently mature seeds before germination can occur.

afters ('ɑːftəz) NOUN (*functioning as singular or plural*) *Brit* [1] *Informal* dessert; sweet. [2] *Slang* a confrontation or physical violence between football players immediately after they have been involved in a challenge for the ball.

aftersensation ('ɑːftəsɛnˌseɪʃən) NOUN another word for **afterimage.**

aftershaft ('ɑːftəˌʃɑːft) NOUN *Ornithol* a secondary feather arising near the base of a contour feather.

aftershave lotion ('ɑːftəˌʃeɪv) NOUN a lotion, usually styptic and perfumed, for application to the face after shaving. Often shortened to: **aftershave.**

aftershock ('ɑːftəˌʃɒk) NOUN one of a series of minor tremors occurring after the main shock of an earthquake. Compare **foreshock.**

aftershow ('ɑːftəˌʃəʊ) NOUN **a** a party held after a public performance of a play or film. **b** (*as modifier*): *an aftershow bash.*

aftersun ('ɑːftəˌsʌn) NOUN **a** a moisturizing lotion applied to the skin to soothe sunburn and avoid peeling. **b** (*as modifier*): *aftersun lotion.*

aftertaste ('ɑːftəˌteɪst) NOUN [1] a taste that lingers on after eating or drinking. [2] a lingering impression or sensation.

afterthought ('ɑːftəˌθɔːt) NOUN [1] a comment, reply, etc., that occurs to one after the opportunity to deliver it has passed. [2] an addition to something already completed.

afterwards ('ɑːftəwədz) *or* **afterward** ADVERB after an earlier event or time; subsequently.
▷HISTORY Old English *æfterweard, æfteweard,* from AFT + WARD

afterword ('ɑːftəˌwɜːd) NOUN an epilogue or postscript in a book, etc.

afterworld ('ɑːftəˌwɜːld) NOUN a world inhabited after death.

AFTN ABBREVIATION FOR Aeronautical Fixed Telecommunications Network: a worldwide system of radio and cable links for transmitting and recording messages.

AFV ABBREVIATION FOR armoured fighting vehicle.

ag THE INTERNET DOMAIN NAME FOR Antigua and Barbuda.

Ag THE CHEMICAL SYMBOL FOR silver.
▷HISTORY from Latin *argentum*

AG ABBREVIATION FOR: [1] Adjutant General. [2] **Attorney General.** [3] Aktiengesellschaft.
▷HISTORY (for sense 3) German: joint-stock company

aga *or* **agha** ('ɑːgə) NOUN (in the Ottoman Empire) [1] a title of respect, often used with the title of a senior position. [2] a military commander.
▷HISTORY C17: Turkish, literally: lord

Aga ('ɑːgə) NOUN *Trademark, Brit* a cooking range and heating system powered by solid fuel, electricity, or gas.
▷HISTORY C20: from (*Svenskaa*) *A*(*ktiebolaget*) *Ga*(*sackumulator*), the original Swedish manufacturer

Agadir (ˌægə'dɪə) NOUN a port in SW Morocco, which became the centre of an international crisis (1911), when a gunboat arrived to protect German interests. Britain issued a strong warning to Germany but the French negotiated and war was averted. In 1960 the town was virtually destroyed by an earthquake, about 10 000 people being killed. Pop.: 155 244 (1994).

again (ə'gɛn, ə'geɪn) ADVERB [1] another or second time; once more; anew: *he had to start again.* [2] once more in a previously experienced or encountered place, state, or condition: *he is ill again; he came back again.* [3] in addition to the original amount, quantity, etc. (esp in the phrases **as much again; half as much again**). [4] (*sentence modifier*) on the other hand: *he might come and then again he might not.* [5] besides; also: *she is beautiful and, again, intelligent.* [6] *Archaic* in reply; back: *he answered again to the questioning voice.* [7] **again and again.** continuously; repeatedly. [8] (*used with a negative*) *Caribbean* any more; any longer: *I don't eat pumpkin again.* ◆ SENTENCE CONNECTOR [9] moreover; furthermore: *again, it could be said that he is not dead.*
▷HISTORY Old English *ongegn* opposite to, from A-² + *gegn* straight

against (ə'gɛnst, ə'geɪnst) PREPOSITION [1] opposed to; in conflict or disagreement with: *they fought against the legislation.* [2] standing or leaning beside or in front of: *a ladder against the wall.* [3] coming in contact with: *the branches of a tree brushed against the bus.* [4] in contrast to: *silhouettes are outlines against a light background.* [5] having an adverse or unfavourable effect on: *the economic system works against small independent companies.* [6] as a protection from or means of defence from the adverse effects of: *a safeguard against contaminated water.* [7] in exchange for or in return for. [8] *Now rare* in preparation for: *he gave them warm clothing against their journey through the night.* [9] **as against.** as opposed to or as compared with: *he had two shots at him this time as against only one last time.*
▷HISTORY C12 *ageines,* from *again, ageyn,* etc., AGAIN + *-es* genitive ending; the spelling with *-t* (C16) was probably due to confusion with superlatives ending in *-st*

Aga Khan ('ɑːgə 'kɑːn) NOUN the hereditary title of the head of the Ismaili sect of Muslims.

agalactia (ˌægə'læktɪə) NOUN *Pathol, obsolete* absence or failure of secretion of milk.
▷HISTORY C19: New Latin, from A-¹ + Greek *galaktos* milk

agalloch (ə'gæləк) NOUN another name for **eaglewood.**
▷HISTORY C17: from Greek *agallokhon*

agama ('ægəmə, ə'gæmə) NOUN [1] any small terrestrial lizard of the genus *Agama,* which inhabit warm regions of the Old World: family *Agamidae.* [2] Also called: **agamid** ('ægəmɪd, ə'gæmɪd). any other lizard of the family *Agamidae,* which occur in the Old World and Australia and show a wide range of habits and diversity of structure.
▷HISTORY C19: Carib

Agamemnon (ˌægə'mɛmnɒn) NOUN *Greek myth* a king of Mycenae who led the Greeks at the siege of Troy. On his return home he was murdered by his wife Clytemnestra and her lover Aegisthus. See also **Menelaus.**

agamete (ə'gæmiːt) NOUN a reproductive cell, such as the merozoite of some protozoans, that develops into a new form without fertilization.
▷HISTORY C19: from Greek *agametos* unmarried; see A-¹, GAMETE

agamic (ə'gæmɪk) ADJECTIVE asexual; occurring or reproducing without fertilization.
▷HISTORY C19: from Greek *agamos* unmarried, from A-¹ + *gamos* marriage
▸**a'gamically** ADVERB

agamogenesis (ˌægəməʊ'dʒɛnɪsɪs) NOUN asexual reproduction, such as fission or parthenogenesis.
▷HISTORY C19: AGAMIC + GENESIS
▸**agamogenetic** (ˌægəməʊdʒə'nɛtɪk) ADJECTIVE
▸**ˌagamoge'netically** ADVERB

agamogony (ˌægə'mɒgənɪ) NOUN another name for **schizogony.**

agamont ('ægəmɒnt) NOUN another name for **schizont.**

agamospermy ('ægəməʊˌspɜːmɪ) NOUN *Botany* formation of seeds in the absence of fertilization; a form of apomixis.
▷HISTORY C19: AGAMIC + Greek *sperma* seed

Agaña (ə'gɑːnjə) NOUN the capital of the Pacific island of Guam, on its W coast. Pop.: 2000 (1995 est.).

agapanthus (ˌægə'pænθəs) NOUN a liliaceous plant, *Agapanthus africanus,* of southern Africa, having rounded clusters of blue or white funnel-shaped flowers. Also called: **African lily.**
▷HISTORY C19: New Latin, from Greek *agapē* love + *anthos* flower

agape (ə'geɪp) ADJECTIVE (*postpositive*) [1] (esp of the mouth) wide open. [2] very surprised, expectant, or eager, esp as indicated by a wide open mouth.
▷HISTORY C17: A-² + GAPE

Agape ('ægəpɪ) NOUN *Christianity* [1] Christian love, esp as contrasted with erotic love; charity. [2] a communal meal in the early Church taken in commemoration of the Last Supper; love feast.
▷HISTORY C17: Greek *agapē* love

agar ('eɪgə) NOUN a complex gelatinous carbohydrate obtained from seaweeds, esp those of the genus *Gelidium,* used as a culture medium for bacteria, a laxative, in food such as ice cream as a thickening agent (**E406**), etc. Also called: **agar-agar.**
▷HISTORY C19: Malay

agaric ('ægərɪk, ə'gærɪk) NOUN [1] any saprotrophic basidiomycetous fungus of the family *Agaricaceae,* having gills on the underside of the cap. The group includes the edible mushrooms and poisonous forms such as the fly agaric. [2] the dried spore-producing bodies of certain fungi, esp *Polyphorus officinalis* (or *Boletus laricis*), formerly used in medicine.
▷HISTORY C16: via Latin *agaricum,* from Greek *agarikon,* perhaps named after *Agaria,* a town in Sarmatia
▸**agaricaceous** (əˌgærɪ'keɪʃəs) ADJECTIVE

Agartala ('ʌgətəˌlɑː) NOUN a city in NE India, capital of the state of Tripura. Pop.: 157 636 (1991).

Aga saga NOUN *Brit* a novel or drama depicting the lives and concerns of the English middle classes.
▷HISTORY C20: allusion to the popularity of AGA cookers among the English middle classes

agate¹ ('ægɪt) NOUN [1] an impure microcrystalline form of quartz consisting of a variegated, usually banded chalcedony, used as a gemstone and in making pestles and mortars, burnishers, and polishers. Formula: SiO_2. [2] a playing marble of this quartz or resembling it. [3] *Printing* the US and Canadian name for **ruby** (sense 5).
▷HISTORY C16: via French from Latin *achātēs,* from Greek *akhatēs*

agate² (ə'geɪt) ADVERB *Northern English dialect* on the way.
▷HISTORY C16: A-² + GATE³

agateware (ˈægɪtˌwɛə) NOUN ceramic ware made to resemble agate or marble.

agave (əˈgeɪvɪ, ˈægeɪv) NOUN any plant of the genus *Agave*, native to tropical America, with tall flower stalks rising from a massive, often armed, rosette of thick fleshy leaves: family *Agavaceae*. Some species are the source of fibres such as sisal or of alcoholic beverages such as pulque and tequila. See also **century plant**.
▷HISTORY C18: New Latin, from Greek *agauē*, feminine of *agauos* illustrious, probably alluding to the height of the plant

AGC ABBREVIATION FOR **automatic gain control**.

age (eɪdʒ) NOUN [1] the period of time that a person, animal, or plant has lived or is expected to live: *the age of a tree; what age was he when he died?; the age of a horse is up to thirty years.* [2] the period of existence of an object, material, group, etc.: *the age of this table is 200 years.* [3] **a** a period or state of human life: *he should know better at his age; she had got beyond the giggly age.* **b** (*as modifier*): *age group.* [4] the latter part of life. [5] **a** a period of history marked by some feature or characteristic; era. **b** (*capital when part of a name*): *the Middle Ages; the Space Age.* [6] generation: *the Edwardian age.* [7] *Geology, palaeontol* **a** a period of the earth's history distinguished by special characteristics: *the age of reptiles.* **b** the period during which a stage of rock strata is formed; a subdivision of an epoch. [8] *Myth* any of the successive periods in the legendary history of man, which were, according to Hesiod, the golden, silver, bronze, heroic, and iron ages. [9] (*often plural*) *Informal* a relatively long time: *she was an age washing her hair; I've been waiting ages.* [10] *Psychol* the level in years that a person has reached in any area of development, such as mental or emotional, compared with the normal level for his chronological age. See also **achievement age, mental age.** [11] **age before beauty.** (often said humorously when yielding precedence) older people take precedence over younger people. [12] **of age.** adult and legally responsible for one's actions (usually at 18 or, formerly, 21 years). ◆ VERB **ages, ageing** *or* **aging, aged.** [13] to grow or make old or apparently old; become or cause to become old or aged. [14] to begin to seem older: *to have aged a lot in the past year.* [15] *Brewing* to mature or cause to mature.
▷HISTORY C13: via Old French from Vulgar Latin *aetātīcum* (unattested), from Latin *aetās*, ultimately from *aevum* lifetime; compare AEON

-age SUFFIX FORMING NOUNS [1] indicating a collection, set, or group: *acreage; baggage.* [2] indicating a process or action or the result of an action: *haulage; passage; breakage.* [3] indicating a state, condition, or relationship: *bondage; parentage.* [4] indicating a house or place: *orphanage.* [5] indicating a charge or fee: *postage.* [6] indicating a rate: *dosage; mileage.*
▷HISTORY from Old French, from Late Latin *-āticum*, noun suffix, neuter of *-āticus*, adjectival suffix, from *-ātus* -ATE[1] + *-icus* -IC

age allowance NOUN an income tax allowance given to taxpayers aged 65 or over.

aged (ˈeɪdʒɪd) ADJECTIVE [1] **a** advanced in years; old. **b** (*as collective noun; preceded by the*): *the aged.* [2] of, connected with, or characteristic of old age. [3] (eɪdʒd) (*postpositive*) having the age of: *a woman aged twenty.* [4] *Geography* (*not in technical use*) having reached an advanced stage of erosion.

agee *or* **ajee** (əˈdʒiː) *Scot and English dialect* ◆ ADJECTIVE [1] awry, crooked, or ajar. ◆ ADVERB [2] awry; at an angle.
▷HISTORY C19: A-[2] + GEE[1]

age hardening NOUN the hardening of metals by spontaneous structural changes over a period of time. See also **precipitation hardening.**

ageing *or* **aging** (ˈeɪdʒɪŋ) NOUN [1] the process of growing old or developing the appearance and characteristics of old age. [2] the change of properties that occurs in some metals after heat treatment or cold working. ◆ ADJECTIVE [3] becoming or appearing older or elderly: *an ageing car.* [4] giving or creating the appearance of age or elderliness: *that dress is really ageing on her.*

ageism *or* **agism** (ˈeɪdʒɪzəm) NOUN discrimination against people on the grounds of age; specifically, discrimination against the elderly.
▸ˈ**ageist** *or* ˈ**agist** ADJECTIVE

ageless (ˈeɪdʒlɪs) ADJECTIVE [1] apparently never growing old. [2] timeless; eternal: *an ageless quality.*
▸ˈ**agelessness** NOUN

Agen (*French* aʒɑ̃) NOUN a market town in SW France, on the Garonne river. Pop.: 32 220 (1990).

agency (ˈeɪdʒənsɪ) NOUN, *plural* **-cies.** [1] a business or other organization providing a specific service: *an employment agency.* [2] the place where an agent conducts business. [3] the business, duties, or functions of an agent. [4] action, power, or operation: *the agency of fate.* [5] intercession or mediation. [6] one of the administrative organizations of a government.
▷HISTORY C17: from Medieval Latin *agentia*, from Latin *agere* to do

agenda (əˈdʒɛndə) NOUN [1] (*functioning as singular*) Also called: **agendum.** a schedule or list of items to be attended to. [2] (*functioning as plural*) Also called: **agendas, agendums.** matters to be attended to, as at a meeting of a committee.
▷HISTORY C17: Latin, literally: things to be done, from *agere* to do

agenesis (eɪˈdʒɛnɪsɪs) NOUN [1] (of an animal or plant) imperfect development. [2] impotence or sterility.
▸**agenetic** (ˌeɪdʒəˈnɛtɪk) ADJECTIVE

agent (ˈeɪdʒənt) NOUN [1] a person who acts on behalf of another person, group, business, government, etc.; representative. [2] a person or thing that acts or has the power to act. [3] a phenomenon, substance, or organism that exerts some force or effect: *a chemical agent.* [4] the means by which something occurs or is achieved; instrument: *wind is an agent of plant pollination.* [5] a person representing a business concern, esp a travelling salesman. [6] *Brit* short for **estate agent.** [7] short for **secret agent.**
▷HISTORY C15: from Latin *agent-*, noun use of the present participle of *agere* to do
▸**agential** (eɪˈdʒɛnʃəl) ADJECTIVE

agent-general NOUN, *plural* **agents-general.** a representative in London of a Canadian province or an Australian state.

agentive (ˈeɪdʒəntɪv) *or* **agential** (eɪˈdʒɛnʃəl) *Grammar* ◆ ADJECTIVE [1] (in some inflected languages) denoting a case of nouns, etc., indicating the agent described by the verb. [2] (of a speech element) indicating agency: *"-er" in "worker" is an agentive suffix.* ◆ NOUN [3] **a** the agentive case. **b** a word or element in the agentive case.

agent of production NOUN another name for **factor of production.**

Agent Orange NOUN a highly poisonous herbicide used as a spray for defoliation and crop destruction, esp by US forces during the Vietnam War.
▷HISTORY C20: named after the identifying colour stripe on its container

agent provocateur *French* (aʒɑ̃ prɔvɔkatœr) NOUN, *plural* ***agents provocateurs*** (aʒɑ̃ prɔvɔkatœr). a secret agent employed to provoke suspected persons to commit illegal acts and so be discredited or liable to punishment.

age of consent NOUN [1] the age at which a person is considered legally competent to consent to sexual intercourse. [2] the age at which a person can enter into a legally binding contract.

Age of Reason NOUN (usually preceded by *the*) the 18th century in W Europe. See also **Enlightenment.**

age-old *or* **age-long** ADJECTIVE very old or of long duration; ancient.

age-proof ADJECTIVE [1] not adversely affected by a person's age: *an age-proof career.* ◆ VERB [2] (*tr*) to make (something) age-proof.

ageratum (ˌædʒəˈreɪtəm) NOUN any tropical American plant of the genus *Ageratum*, such as *A. houstonianum* and *A. conyzoides*, which have thick clusters of purplish-blue flowers.
▷HISTORY C16: New Latin, via Latin from Greek *agēraton* that which does not age, from A-[1] + *gērat-*, stem of *gēras* old age; the flowers of the plant remain vivid for a long time

ageusia (eɪˈgjuːsɪə) NOUN *Pathol* lack of the sense of taste.
▷HISTORY C20: from A-[1] + Greek *geusis* taste

Aggadah (əgəˈda) NOUN, *plural* **Aggadoth** (-ˈdɔːt, -ˈdəʊt). *Judaism* [1] **a** a homiletic passage of the Talmud. **b** collectively, the homiletic part of traditional Jewish literature, as contrasted with Halacha, consisting of elaborations on the biblical narratives or tales from the lives of the ancient Rabbis. [2] any traditional homiletic interpretation of scripture. ◆ Also called: **Aggadatah** (əˈgadəta), **Haggadah.**
▷HISTORY from Hebrew

agger (ˈædʒə) NOUN an earthwork or mound forming a rampart, esp in a Roman military camp.
▷HISTORY C14: from Latin *agger* a heap, from *ad-* to + *gerere* to carry, bring

aggers (ˈægəz) ADJECTIVE *Austral slang* aggressive.

aggiornamento *Italian* (addʒornaˈmento) NOUN, *plural* ***-ti*** (-ti). *RC Church* the process of bringing up to date methods, ideas, etc.

agglomerate VERB (əˈglɒməˌreɪt) [1] to form or be formed into a mass or cluster; collect. ◆ NOUN (əˈglɒmərɪt, -ˌreɪt) [2] a confused mass. [3] a rock consisting of angular fragments of volcanic lava. Compare **conglomerate** (sense 2). ◆ ADJECTIVE (əˈglɒmərɪt, -ˌreɪt) [4] formed into a mass.
▷HISTORY C17: from Latin *agglomerāre*, from *glomerāre* to wind into a ball, from *glomus* ball, mass
▸**agˌglomerˈation** NOUN ▸**agˈglomerative** ADJECTIVE

agglutinate VERB (əˈgluːtɪˌneɪt) [1] to adhere or cause to adhere, as with glue. [2] *Linguistics* to combine or be combined by agglutination. [3] (*tr*) to cause (bacteria, red blood cells, etc.) to clump together. ◆ ADJECTIVE (əˈgluːtɪnɪt, -ˌneɪt) [4] united or stuck, as by glue.
▷HISTORY C16: from Latin *agglūtināre* to glue to, from *gluten* glue
▸**agˌglutinaˈbility** NOUN ▸**agˈglutinable** ADJECTIVE
▸**agˈglutinant** ADJECTIVE

agglutination (əˌgluːtɪˈneɪʃən) NOUN [1] the act or process of agglutinating. [2] the condition of being agglutinated; adhesion. [3] a united mass or group of parts. [4] *Chem* the formation of clumps of particles in a suspension. [5] *Biochem* proteinaceous particles, such as blood cells and bacteria, that form clumps in antibody–antigen reactions. [6] *Immunol* the formation of a mass of particles, such as erythrocytes, by the action of antibodies. [7] *Linguistics* the building up of words from component morphemes in such a way that these undergo little or no change of form or meaning in the process of combination.

agglutinative (əˈgluːtɪnətɪv) ADJECTIVE [1] tending to join or capable of joining. [2] Also: **agglomerative.** *Linguistics* denoting languages, such as Hungarian, whose morphology is characterized by agglutination. Compare **analytic** (sense 3), **synthetic** (sense 3), **polysynthetic.**

agglutinin (əˈgluːtɪnɪn) NOUN a substance, such as an antibody or a lectin, that causes agglutination of cells or bacteria.
▷HISTORY C19: AGGLUTINATE + -IN

agglutinogen (ˌægluˈtɪnədʒən) NOUN an antigen that reacts with or stimulates the formation of a specific agglutinin.
▷HISTORY C20: from AGGLUTINATE + -GEN

aggrade (əˈgreɪd) VERB (*tr*) to build up the level of (any land surface) by the deposition of sediment. Compare **degrade** (sense 4).
▸**aggradation** (ˌægrəˈdeɪʃən) NOUN

aggrandize *or* **aggrandise** (ˈægrənˌdaɪz, əˈgrænˌdaɪz) VERB (*tr*) [1] to increase the power, wealth, prestige, scope, etc., of. [2] to cause (something) to seem greater; magnify; exaggerate.
▷HISTORY C17: from Old French *aggrandiss-*, long stem of *aggrandir* to make bigger, from Latin *grandis* GRAND; the ending *-ize* is due to the influence of verbs ending in *-ise, -ize*
▸**aggrandizement** *or* **aggrandisement** (əˈgrændɪzmənt) NOUN ▸ˈ**aggranˌdizer** *or* ˈ**aggranˌdiser** NOUN

aggravate (ˈægrəˌveɪt) VERB (*tr*) [1] to make (a disease, situation, problem, etc.) worse or more severe. [2] *Informal* to annoy; exasperate, esp by deliberate and persistent goading.
▷HISTORY C16: from Latin *aggravāre* to make heavier, from *gravis* heavy
▸ˈ**aggraˌvating** ADJECTIVE ▸ˌ**aggraˈvation** NOUN

aggravated (ˈægrəˌveɪtɪd) ADJECTIVE *Law* (of a criminal offence) made more serious by its circumstances.

aggravated trespass NOUN *Law* an offence in

which a trespasser in the open air attempts to interfere with a lawful activity, such as hunting.

aggregate ADJECTIVE ('ægrɪgɪt, -ˌgeɪt) [1] formed of separate units collected into a whole; collective; corporate. [2] (of fruits and flowers) composed of a dense cluster of carpels or florets. ◆ NOUN ('ægrɪgɪt, -ˌgeɪt) [3] a sum or assemblage of many separate units; sum total. [4] *Geology* a rock, such as granite, consisting of a mixture of minerals. [5] the sand and stone mixed with cement and water to make concrete. [6] a group of closely related biotypes produced by apomixis, such as brambles, which are the *Rubus fruticosus* aggregate. [7] **in the aggregate.** taken as a whole. ◆ VERB ('ægrɪˌgeɪt) [8] to combine or be combined into a body, etc. [9] (*tr*) to amount to (a number).
▷HISTORY C16: from Latin *aggregāre* to add to a flock or herd, attach (oneself) to, from *grex* flock
▸**'aggregately** ADVERB ▸**aggregative** ('ægrɪˌgeɪtɪv) ADJECTIVE

aggregation (ˌægrɪ'geɪʃən) NOUN [1] the act or process of aggregating. [2] *Ecology* dispersion in which the individuals of a species are closer together than if they were randomly dispersed.

aggregator ('ægrɪˌgeɪtə) NOUN [1] a business organization that collates the details of an individual's financial affairs so that the information can be presented on a single website. [2] a firm that brings together a large group of consumers on whose behalf it negotiates reduced rates for good or services, esp in the energy sector.

aggress (ə'grɛs) VERB (*intr*) to attack first or begin a quarrel.
▷HISTORY C16: from Medieval Latin *aggressāre* to attack, from Latin *aggredī* to attack, approach

aggression (ə'grɛʃən) NOUN [1] an attack or harmful action, esp an unprovoked attack by one country against another. [2] any offensive activity, practice, etc.: *an aggression against personal liberty.* [3] *Psychol* a hostile or destructive mental attitude or behaviour.
▷HISTORY C17: from Latin *aggression-*, from *aggrēdi* to attack
▸**aggressor** (ə'grɛsə) NOUN

aggressive (ə'grɛsɪv) ADJECTIVE [1] quarrelsome or belligerent: *an aggressive remark.* [2] assertive; vigorous: *an aggressive business executive.*
▸**ag'gressively** ADVERB ▸**ag'gressiveness** NOUN

aggressive accountancy NOUN *Euphemistic* dishonest or deliberately misleading accounting practices.

aggrieve (ə'gri:v) VERB (*tr*) [1] (*often impersonal or passive*) to grieve; distress; afflict: *it aggrieved her much that she could not go.* [2] to injure unjustly, esp by infringing a person's legal rights.
▷HISTORY C14 *agreven*, via Old French from Latin *aggravāre* to AGGRAVATE

aggrieved (ə'gri:vd) ADJECTIVE feeling resentment at having been treated unjustly.
▸**aggrievedly** (ə'gri:vɪdlɪ) ADVERB

aggro ('ægrəʊ) NOUN *Brit slang* aggressive behaviour, esp by youths in a gang.
▷HISTORY C20: from AGGRAVATION

agha ('ɑ:gə) NOUN a variant spelling of **aga.**

aghast (ə'gɑ:st) ADJECTIVE (*postpositive*) overcome with amazement or horror.
▷HISTORY C13 *agast*, from Old English *gæstan* to frighten. The spelling with *gh* is on the model of GHASTLY

agile ('ædʒaɪl) ADJECTIVE [1] quick in movement; nimble. [2] mentally quick or acute.
▷HISTORY C15: from Latin *agilis*, from *agere* to do, act
▸**'agilely** ADVERB ▸**agility** (ə'dʒɪlɪtɪ) NOUN

agin (ə'gɪn) PREPOSITION an informal, facetious, or dialect word for **against.**
▷HISTORY C19: from obsolete *again* AGAINST

Agincourt ('ædʒɪnˌkɔ:t; *French* aʒɛ̃kur) NOUN a battle fought in 1415 near the village of Azincourt, N France: a decisive victory for English longbowmen under Henry V over French forces vastly superior in number.

agio ('ædʒɪəʊ) NOUN, *plural* **-ios.** [1] **a** the difference between the nominal and actual values of a currency. **b** the charge payable for conversion of the less valuable currency. [2] a percentage payable for the exchange of one currency into another. [3] an allowance granted to compensate for differences in currency values, as on foreign bills of exchange. [4] an informal word for **agiotage.**
▷HISTORY C17: from Italian, literally: ease

agiotage ('ædʒətɪdʒ) NOUN [1] the business of exchanging currencies. [2] speculative dealing in stock exchange securities or foreign exchange.
▷HISTORY C19: French, from AGIO

agist (ə'dʒɪst) VERB (*tr*) *Law* [1] to care for and feed (cattle or horses) for payment. [2] to assess and charge (land or its owner) with a public burden, such as a tax.
▷HISTORY C14: from Old French *agister*, from *gister* to lodge, ultimately from Latin *jacēre* to lie down

agitate ('ædʒɪˌteɪt) VERB [1] (*tr*) to excite, disturb, or trouble (a person, the mind, or feelings); worry. [2] (*tr*) to cause to move vigorously; shake, stir, or disturb. [3] (*intr; often foll by for or against*) to attempt to stir up public opinion for or against something. [4] (*tr*) to discuss or debate in order to draw attention to or gain support for (a cause, etc.): *to agitate a political cause.*
▷HISTORY C16: from Latin *agitātus*, from *agitāre* to move to and fro, set into motion, from *agere* to act, do
▸**'agiˌtated** ADJECTIVE ▸**'agiˌtatedly** ADVERB

agitated depression NOUN severe depression accompanied by extreme anxiety and agitation. Also called: **agitated melancholia.**

agitation (ˌædʒɪ'teɪʃən) NOUN [1] a state of excitement, disturbance, or worry. [2] the act of moving something vigorously; the shaking or stirring of something. [3] the act of attempting to stir up public opinion for or against something.
▸**ˌagi'tational** ADJECTIVE

agitato (ˌædʒɪ'tɑ:təʊ) ADJECTIVE, ADVERB *Music* (to be performed) in an agitated manner.

agitator ('ædʒɪˌteɪtə) NOUN [1] a person who agitates for or against a cause, etc. [2] a device, machine, or part used for mixing, shaking, or vibrating a material, usually a fluid.

agitpop ('ædʒɪtˌpɒp) NOUN the use of pop music to promote political propaganda.

agitprop ('ædʒɪtˌprɒp) NOUN [1] (*often capital*) (formerly) a bureau of the Central Committee of the Communist Party of the Soviet Union, in charge of agitation and propaganda on behalf of Communism. [2] **a** any promotion, as in the arts, of political propaganda, esp of a Communist nature. **b** (*as modifier*): *agitprop theatre.*
▷HISTORY C20: short for Russian *Agitpropbyuro*, from *agit(atsiya)* agitation + *prop(aganda)* propaganda

Aglaia (ə'glaɪə) NOUN *Greek myth* one of the three Graces.
▷HISTORY Greek: splendour, from *aglaos* splendid

agleam (ə'gli:m) ADJECTIVE (*postpositive*) glowing; gleaming.

aglet ('æglɪt) *or* **aiglet** NOUN [1] a metal sheath or tag at the end of a shoelace, ribbon, etc. [2] a variant spelling of **aiguillette.** [3] any ornamental pendant.
▷HISTORY C15: from Old French *aiguillette* a small needle

agley (ə'gleɪ, ə'glaɪ, ə'gli:) *or* **aglee** (ə'gli:) ADVERB, ADJECTIVE *Scot* awry; askew.
▷HISTORY from *gley* squint

aglimmer (ə'glɪmə) ADJECTIVE (*postpositive*) glimmering.

aglitter (ə'glɪtə) ADJECTIVE (*postpositive*) sparkling; glittering.

aglossia (ə'glɒsɪə) NOUN *Pathol* congenital absence of the tongue.
▷HISTORY C19: from A-[1] + GLOSSA + -IA
▸**a'glossal** ADJECTIVE ▸**a'glossate** ADJECTIVE

aglow (ə'gləʊ) ADJECTIVE (*postpositive*) glowing.

aglu *or* **agloo** ('æglu:) NOUN *Canadian* a breathing hole made in ice by a seal.
▷HISTORY C19: from Eskimo

AGM ABBREVIATION FOR **annual general meeting.**

agma ('ægmə) NOUN *Phonetics* the symbol (ŋ), used to represent a velar nasal consonant, as in *long* (lɒŋ) or *tank* (tæŋk).

agminate ('ægmɪnɪt, -ˌneɪt) ADJECTIVE gathered or clustered together.
▷HISTORY C19: from Latin *agmen* a moving throng

AGN ABBREVIATION FOR active galactic nucleus. See **active galaxy.**

agnail ('ægˌneɪl) NOUN another name for **hangnail.**

agnate ('ægneɪt) ADJECTIVE [1] related by descent from a common male ancestor. [2] related in any way; cognate. ◆ NOUN [3] a male or female descendant by male links from a common male ancestor.
▷HISTORY C16: from Latin *agnātus* born in addition, added by birth, from *agnāsci*, from *ad-* in addition + *gnāsci* to be born
▸**agnatic** (æg'nætɪk) ADJECTIVE ▸**ag'nation** NOUN

agnathan (æg'neɪθən) NOUN [1] any jawless eel-like aquatic vertebrate of the superclass *Agnatha*, which includes the lampreys and hagfishes. ◆ ADJECTIVE [2] of, relating to, or belonging to the superclass *Agnatha*. See also **cyclostome.**
▷HISTORY C19: from New Latin *agnatha*, from A-[1] + Greek *gnathos* jaw

agnathous (æg'neɪθəs) ADJECTIVE *Zoology* (esp of lampreys and hagfishes) lacking jaws.

Agni ('ʌgnɪ) NOUN *Hinduism* the god of fire, one of the three chief deities of the Vedas.
▷HISTORY Sanskrit: fire

agnoiology (ˌægnɔɪ'ɒlədʒɪ) NOUN *Philosophy* the theory of ignorance.
▷HISTORY C19: from Greek *a-* without + *gnōsis* knowledge

agnomen (æg'nəʊmɛn) NOUN, *plural* **-nomina** (-'nɒmɪnə). [1] the fourth name or second cognomen occasionally acquired by an ancient Roman. See also **cognomen, nomen, praenomen.** [2] another word for **nickname.**
▷HISTORY C18: from Late Latin, from *ad-* in addition to + *nōmen* name
▸**agnominal** (æg'nɒmɪnᵊl) ADJECTIVE

agnosia (æg'nəʊzɪə) NOUN *Psychol* loss or diminution of the power to recognize familiar objects or people, usually as a result of brain damage.
▷HISTORY C20: New Latin, from Greek *agnōsia*, from *a-* without + *gnōsis* knowledge
▸**ag'nosic** ADJECTIVE

agnostic (æg'nɒstɪk) NOUN [1] a person who holds that knowledge of a Supreme Being, ultimate cause, etc., is impossible. Compare **atheist, theist.** [2] a person who claims, with respect to any particular question, that the answer cannot be known with certainty. ◆ ADJECTIVE [3] of or relating to agnostics.
▷HISTORY C19: coined 1869 by T. H. Huxley from A-[1] + GNOSTIC
▸**ag'nosticism** NOUN

Agnus Dei ('ægnʊs 'deɪɪ) NOUN *Christianity* [1] the figure of a lamb bearing a cross or banner, emblematic of Christ. [2] a chant beginning with these words or a translation of them, forming part of the Roman Catholic Mass or sung as an anthem in the Anglican liturgy. [3] a wax medallion stamped with a lamb as emblem of Christ and blessed by the pope.
▷HISTORY Latin: Lamb of God

ago (ə'gəʊ) ADVERB in the past: *five years ago; long ago.*
▷HISTORY C14 *ago*, from Old English *āgān* to pass away

> **Language note** The use of *ago* with *since* (*it's ten years ago since he wrote the novel*) is redundant and should be avoided: *it is ten years since he wrote the novel.*

agog (ə'gɒg) ADJECTIVE (*postpositive*) highly impatient, eager, or curious.
▷HISTORY C15: perhaps from Old French *en gogues* in merriments, origin unknown

à gogo (ə 'gəʊˌgəʊ) ADJECTIVE, ADVERB *Informal* as much as one likes; galore: *champagne à gogo.*
▷HISTORY C20: from French

-agogue *or esp US* **-agog** NOUN COMBINING FORM [1] indicating a person or thing that leads or incites to action: *pedagogue; demagogue.* [2] denoting a substance that stimulates the secretion of something: *galactagogue.*
▷HISTORY via Late Latin from Greek *agōgos* leading, from *agein* to lead
▸**-agogic** ADJECTIVE COMBINING FORM ▸**-agogy** NOUN COMBINING FORM

agon ('ægəʊn, -gɒn) NOUN, *plural* **agones** (ə'gəʊni:z). (in ancient Greece) a festival at which competitors contended for prizes. Among the best known were the Olympic, Pythian, Nemean, and Isthmian Games.
▷HISTORY C17: Greek: contest, from *agein* to lead

agone (ə'gɒn) ADVERB an archaic word for **ago.**

agonic (ə'gɒnɪk, eɪ'gɒnɪk) ADJECTIVE forming no angle.
▷HISTORY C19: from Greek *agōnos,* from A-[1] + *gōnia* angle

agonic line NOUN an imaginary line on the surface of the earth connecting points of zero magnetic declination.

agonist ('ægənɪst) NOUN [1] any muscle that is opposed in action by another muscle. Compare **antagonist** (sense 2). [2] a competitor, as in an agon.
▷HISTORY C17: from Greek *agōn* AGON

agonistic (ˌægə'nɪstɪk) ADJECTIVE [1] striving for effect; strained. [2] eager to win in discussion or argument; competitive.
▷HISTORY C17: via Late Latin from Greek *agōnistikos,* from *agōn* contest

agonize *or* **agonise** ('ægəˌnaɪz) VERB [1] to suffer or cause to suffer agony. [2] (*intr*) to make a desperate effort; struggle; strive.
▷HISTORY C16: via Medieval Latin from Greek *agōnizesthai* to contend for a prize, from *agōn* AGON
▸**'agoˌnizingly** *or* **'agoˌnisingly** ADVERB

agony ('ægənɪ) NOUN, *plural* **-nies.** [1] acute physical or mental pain; anguish. [2] the suffering or struggle preceding death. [3] **pile, put,** *or* **turn on the agony.** *Brit informal* to exaggerate one's distress for sympathy or greater effect. [4] (*modifier*) relating to or advising on personal problems about which people have written to the media: *agony column; agony writer.*
▷HISTORY C14: via Late Latin from Greek *agōnia* struggle, from *agōn* contest

agony aunt NOUN (*sometimes capital*) a person who writes the replies to readers' letters in an **agony column** (sense 1).

agony column NOUN [1] a magazine or newspaper feature in which advice is offered to readers who have sent in letters about their personal problems. [2] a part of a newspaper containing advertisements for lost relatives, personal messages, etc.

agora[1] ('ægərə) NOUN, *plural* **-rae** (-ri:, -raɪ). (*often capital*) **a** the marketplace in Athens, used for popular meetings, or any similar place of assembly in ancient Greece. **b** the meeting itself.
▷HISTORY from Greek, from *agorein* to gather

agora[2] (ˌægə'rɑ:) NOUN, *plural* **-rot** (-'rɒt). an Israeli monetary unit worth one hundredth of a shekel.
▷HISTORY Hebrew, from *āgōr* to collect

agoraphobia (ˌægərə'fəʊbɪə) NOUN a pathological fear of being in public places, often resulting in the sufferer becoming housebound.
▸**ˌagora'phobic** ADJECTIVE, NOUN

agouti (ə'gu:tɪ) NOUN, *plural* **-tis** *or* **-ties.** [1] any hystricomorph rodent of the genus *Dasyprocta,* of Central and South America and the Caribbean: family *Dasyproctidae.* Agoutis are agile and long-legged, with hooflike claws, and are valued for their meat. [2] a pattern of fur in certain rodents, characterized by irregular stripes.
▷HISTORY C18: via French and Spanish from Guarani

AGR ABBREVIATION FOR **advanced gas-cooled reactor.**

agr. *or* **agric.** ABBREVIATION FOR: [1] agricultural. [2] agriculture.

Agra ('ɑ:grə) NOUN a city in N India, in W Uttar Pradesh on the Jumna River: a capital of the Mogul empire until 1658; famous for its Mogul architecture, esp the Taj Mahal. Pop.: 899 195 (1991).

agraffe *or sometimes US* **agrafe** (ə'græf) NOUN [1] a fastening consisting of a loop and hook, formerly used in armour and clothing. [2] a metal cramp used to connect stones.
▷HISTORY C18: from French, from *grafe* a hook

Agram ('a:gram) NOUN the German name for **Zagreb.**

agranulocytosis (əˌgrænjʊləʊsaɪ'təʊsɪs) NOUN a serious and sometimes fatal illness characterized by a marked reduction of leucocytes, usually caused by hypersensitivity to certain drugs.
▷HISTORY C20: New Latin; see A-[1], GRANULE, -CYTE, -OSIS

agrapha ('ægrəfə) PLURAL NOUN *Christianity* sayings of Jesus not recorded in the canonical Gospels.
▷HISTORY Greek: things not written, from A-[1] + *graphein* to write

agraphia (ə'græfɪə) NOUN loss of the ability to write, resulting from a brain lesion.
▷HISTORY C19: New Latin, from A-[1] + Greek *graphein* to write

agrarian (ə'grɛərɪən) ADJECTIVE [1] of or relating to land or its cultivation or to systems of dividing landed property. [2] of or relating to rural or agricultural matters. ◆ NOUN [3] a person who favours the redistribution of landed property.
▷HISTORY C16: from Latin *agrārius,* from *ager* field, land
▸**a'grarianism** NOUN

agree (ə'gri:) VERB **agrees, agreeing, agreed.** (*mainly intr*) [1] (often foll by *with*) to be of the same opinion; concur. [2] (*also tr;* when *intr,* often foll by *to;* when *tr, takes a clause as object or an infinitive*) to give assent; consent: *she agreed to go home; I'll agree to that.* [3] (*also tr;* when *intr,* foll by *on* or *about;* when *tr, may take a clause as object*) to come to terms (about); arrive at a settlement (on): *they agreed a price; they agreed on the main points.* [4] (foll by *with*) to be similar or consistent; harmonize; correspond. [5] (foll by *with*) to be agreeable or suitable (to one's health, temperament, etc.). [6] (*tr; takes a clause as object*) to concede or grant; admit: *they agreed that the price they were asking was too high.* [7] (*tr*) to make consistent with: *to agree the balance sheet with the records by making adjustments, writing off, etc.* [8] *Grammar* to undergo agreement.
▷HISTORY C14: from Old French *agreer,* from the phrase *a gre* at will or pleasure

agreeable (ə'grɪəbᵊl) ADJECTIVE [1] pleasing; pleasant. [2] prepared to consent. [3] (foll by *to* or *with*) in keeping; consistent: *salaries agreeable with current trends.* [4] (foll by *to*) to one's liking: *the terms were not agreeable to him.*
▸**a'greeableness** NOUN ▸**a'greeably** ADVERB

agreed (ə'gri:d) ADJECTIVE [1] determined by common consent: *the agreed price.* ◆ INTERJECTION [2] an expression of agreement or consent.

agreement (ə'gri:mənt) NOUN [1] the act of agreeing. [2] a settlement, esp one that is legally enforceable; covenant; treaty. [3] a contract or document containing such a settlement. [4] the state of being of the same opinion; concord; harmony. [5] the state of being similar or consistent; correspondence; conformity. [6] *Grammar* the determination of the inflectional form of one word by some grammatical feature, such as number or gender, of another word, esp one in the same sentence. Also called: **concord.** [7] See **collective agreement, national agreement.**
▷HISTORY C14: from Old French

agrestal (ə'grɛstəl) ADJECTIVE (of uncultivated plants such as weeds) growing on cultivated land.

agrestic (ə'grɛstɪk) ADJECTIVE [1] rural; rustic. [2] unpolished; uncouth.
▷HISTORY C17: from Latin *agrestis,* from *ager* field

agribusiness ('ægrɪˌbɪznɪs) NOUN the various businesses collectively that process, distribute, and support farm products.
▷HISTORY C20: from AGRI(CULTURE) + BUSINESS

agric. *or* **agr.** ABBREVIATION FOR: [1] agricultural. [2] agriculture.

agriculture ('ægrɪˌkʌltʃə) NOUN the science or occupation of cultivating land and rearing crops and livestock; farming; husbandry. Related adjective: **geoponic.**
▷HISTORY C17: from Latin *agricultūra,* from *ager* field, land + *cultūra* CULTURE
▸**ˌagri'cultural** ADJECTIVE ▸**ˌagri'culturally** ADVERB
▸**ˌagri'culturist** *or* **ˌagri'culturalist** NOUN

Agrigento (*Italian* agri'dʒɛnto) NOUN a town in Italy, in SW Sicily: site of six Greek temples. Pop.: 56 372 (1990). Former name (until 1927): **Girgenti** (gɜ:'gɛntɪ).

agrimony ('ægrɪmənɪ) NOUN [1] any of various N temperate rosaceous plants of the genus *Agrimonia,* which have compound leaves, long spikes of small yellow flowers, and bristly burlike fruits. [2] any of several other plants, such as hemp agrimony.
▷HISTORY C15: altered from *egrimonie* (C14), via Old French from Latin *agrimōnia,* variant of *argemōnia* from Greek *argemōnē* poppy

agro- COMBINING FORM denoting fields, soil, or agriculture: *agronomy.*
▷HISTORY from Greek *agros* field

agrobiology (ˌægrəʊbaɪ'ɒlədʒɪ) NOUN the science of plant growth and nutrition in relation to agriculture.
▸**agrobiological** (ˌægrəʊˌbaɪə'lɒdʒɪkᵊl) ADJECTIVE
▸**ˌagrobi'ologist** NOUN

agrochemical (ˌægrəʊ'kɛmɪkᵊl) NOUN a chemical, such as a pesticide, used for agricultural purposes.

agroforestry (ˌægrəʊ'fɒrɪstrɪ) NOUN a method of farming integrating herbaceous and tree crops.

agrology (ə'grɒlədʒɪ) NOUN the scientific study of soils and their potential productivity.
▸**agrological** (ˌægrə'lɒdʒɪkᵊl) ADJECTIVE

agronomics (ˌægrə'nɒmɪks) NOUN (*functioning as singular*) the branch of economics dealing with the distribution, management, and productivity of land.
▸**ˌagro'nomic** *or* **ˌagro'nomical** ADJECTIVE

agronomy (ə'grɒnəmɪ) NOUN the science of cultivation of land, soil management, and crop production.
▸**a'gronomist** NOUN

agrostemma (ˌægrəʊ'stɛmə) NOUN [1] See **corncockle.** [2] See **silene.**
▷HISTORY New Latin, from Greek *agros* a field + *stemma* a garland

agrostology (ˌægrə'stɒlədʒɪ) NOUN the branch of botany concerned with the study of grasses.
▷HISTORY C19: from Greek *agrōstis* a type of grass + -LOGY

agroterrorism (ˌægrəʊ'tɛrərɪzəm) NOUN the use of biological agents as weapons against agricultural and food-supply industries.
▷HISTORY C20: from AGRO- + TERRORISM

aground (ə'graʊnd) ADVERB, ADJECTIVE (*postpositive*) on or onto the ground or bottom, as in shallow water.

agrypnotic (ˌægrɪp'nɒtɪk) ADJECTIVE [1] *Obsolete* inducing, relating to, or characterized by insomnia. ◆ NOUN [2] *Obsolete* a drug or agent that induces insomnia.
▷HISTORY C20: from Greek *agrupnos* wakeful, from *agrein* to pursue + *hupnos* sleep

agt ABBREVIATION FOR: [1] agent. [2] agreement.

agterskot ('axtəˌskɒt) NOUN *South African* the final payment to a farmer for crops. Compare **voorskot.**
▷HISTORY C20: Afrikaans *agter* after + *skot* shot, payment

aguardiente *Spanish* (aɣwar'ðjente) NOUN any inferior brandy or similar spirit, esp from Spain, Portugal, or South America.
▷HISTORY C19: Spanish: burning water

Aguascalientes (*Spanish* aɣwaska'ljentes) NOUN [1] a state in central Mexico. Pop.: 943 506 (2000). Area: 5471 sq. km (2112 sq. miles). [2] a city in central Mexico, capital of Aguascalientes state, about 1900 m (6200 ft.) above sea level, with hot springs. Pop.: 594 056 (2000 est.).

ague ('eɪgju:) NOUN [1] a fever with successive stages of fever and chills esp when caused by malaria. [2] a fit of shivering.
▷HISTORY C14: from Old French (*fievre*) *ague* acute fever; see ACUTE
▸**'aguish** ADJECTIVE

agueweed ('eɪgju:ˌwi:d) NOUN [1] a North American gentianaceous plant, *Gentiana quinquefolia,* that has clusters of pale blue-violet or white flowers. [2] another name for **boneset.**

Agulhas (ə'gʌləs) NOUN **Cape.** a headland in South Africa, the southernmost point of the African continent.

ah (ɑ:) INTERJECTION an exclamation expressing pleasure, pain, sympathy, etc., according to the intonation of the speaker.

AH (indicating years in the Muslim system of dating, numbered from the Hegira (622 A.D.)) ABBREVIATION FOR anno Hegirae.
▷HISTORY Latin

aha (ɑ:'hɑ:) INTERJECTION an exclamation expressing

triumph, surprise, etc., according to the intonation of the speaker.

Ahab ('eɪhæb) NOUN *Old Testament* the king of Israel from approximately 869 to 850 B.C. and husband of Jezebel: rebuked by Elijah (I Kings 16:29–22:40).

aha moment NOUN an instant at which the solution to a problem becomes clear.

Ahasuerus (əˌhæzju:'ɪərəs) NOUN *Old Testament* a king of ancient Persia and husband of Esther, generally identified with Xerxes.

ahead (ə'hɛd) ADJECTIVE [1] (*postpositive*) in front; in advance. ◆ ADVERB [2] at or in the front; in advance; before. [3] onwards; forwards: *go straight ahead.* [4] **ahead of. a** in front of; at a further advanced position than. **b** *Stock Exchange* in anticipation of: *the share price rose ahead of the annual figures.* [5] **be ahead.** *Informal* to have an advantage; be winning: *to be ahead on points.* [6] **get ahead.** to advance or attain success.

ahem (ə'hɛm) INTERJECTION a clearing of the throat, used to attract attention, express doubt, etc.

ahemeral (æ'hɛmərᵊl, eɪ-) ADJECTIVE not constituting a full 24-hour day.
▷**HISTORY** C20: from Greek *a-* not + *hēmera* a day

AHHA ('ɑ:hɑ:) NOUN ACRONYM FOR after hours home avoider: a young person who prefers to spend the time after work socializing, rather than return to an empty home.

ahimsa (ɑ:'hɪmsɑ:) NOUN (in Hindu, Buddhist, and Jainist philosophy) the law of reverence for, and nonviolence to, every form of life.
▷**HISTORY** Sanskrit, from A-¹ + *himsā* injury

ahistorical (ˌeɪhɪs'tɒrɪkəl) *or* **ahistoric** ADJECTIVE not related to history; not historical.

Ahithophel (ə'hɪθəˌfɛl) *or* **Achitophel** NOUN *Old Testament* a member of David's council, who became one of Absalom's advisers in his rebellion and hanged himself when his advice was overruled (II Samuel 15:12–17:23).

Ahmadiyyah (ˌamə'di:jə) *or* **Ahmadiyah** NOUN [1] a messianic Islamic sect founded in Qadian, India, in 1889 by Mirza Ghulam Ahmad; it split into two branches in 1914. [2] any of various Sufi sects.

Ahmedabad *or* **Ahmadabad** ('ɑ:mədəˌbɑ:d) NOUN a city in W India, in Gujarat: famous for its mosque. Pop.: 2 872 865 (1991).

Ahmednagar *or* **Ahmadnagar** (ˌɑ:məd'nʌgə) NOUN a city in W India, in Maharashtra: formerly one of the kingdoms of Deccan. Pop.: 181 015 (1991).

A horizon NOUN the top layer of a soil profile, usually dark-coloured and containing humus and from which soluble salts may have been leached. See **B horizon, C horizon.**

ahoy (ə'hɔɪ) INTERJECTION *Nautical* a hail used to call a ship or to attract attention.

AHQ ABBREVIATION FOR Army Headquarters.

Ahriman ('ɑ:rɪmən) NOUN *Zoroastrianism* the supreme evil spirit and diabolical opponent of Ormazd.

Ahura Mazda (ə'hʊərə 'mæzdə) NOUN *Zoroastrianism* another name for **Ormazd.**

Ahvenanmaa ('ɑhvɛnɑmmɑ:) NOUN the Finnish name for the **Åland Islands.**

Ahwaz (ɑ:'wɑ:z) *or* **Ahvaz** (ɑ:'vɑ:z) NOUN a town in SW Iran, on the Karun River. Pop.: 804 980 (1996).

ai¹ ('ɑ:ɪ) NOUN, *plural* **ais.** another name for **three-toed sloth** (see **sloth** (sense 1)).
▷**HISTORY** C17: from Portuguese, from Tupi

ai² THE INTERNET DOMAIN NAME FOR Anguilla.

AI ABBREVIATION FOR: [1] **artificial insemination.** [2] **artificial intelligence.**

AIA ABBREVIATION FOR Associate of the Institute of Actuaries.

AICC ABBREVIATION FOR All India Congress Committee: the national assembly of the Indian National Congress.

aid (eɪd) VERB [1] to give support to (someone to do something); help or assist. [2] (*tr*) to assist financially. ◆ NOUN [3] assistance; help; support. [4] a person, device, etc., that helps or assists: *a teaching aid.* [5] Also: **artificial aid.** *Mountaineering* any of various devices such as piton or nut when used as a direct help in the ascent. [6] (in medieval Europe; in England after 1066) a feudal payment made to the king or any lord by his vassals, usually on certain occasions such as the marriage of a daughter or the knighting of an eldest son. [7] **in aid of.** *Brit informal* in support of; for the purpose of.
▷**HISTORY** C15: via Old French *aidier* from Latin *adjūtāre* to help, from *juvāre* to help
▸'**aider** NOUN

Aid *or* **-aid** NOUN COMBINING FORM denoting a charitable organization or function that raises money for a cause: *Band Aid; Ferryaid.*

AID ABBREVIATION FOR: [1] acute infectious disease. [2] artificial insemination (by) donor: former name for Donor Insemination (DI).

aid climbing NOUN *Mountaineering* climbing that employs mechanical devices (aids) to accomplish difficult manoeuvres (artificial moves). Also called: **peg climbing, pegging, artificial climbing.**

aide (eɪd) NOUN [1] an assistant. [2] *Social welfare* an unqualified assistant to a professional welfare worker. [3] short for **aide-de-camp.**

aide-de-camp *or* **aid-de-camp** ('eɪd də 'kɒŋ) NOUN, *plural* **aides-de-camp** *or* **aids-de-camp.** a military officer serving as personal assistant to a senior. Abbreviation: **ADC.**
▷**HISTORY** C17: from French: camp assistant

aide-mémoire *French* (ɛdmemwar; *English* 'eɪd mɛm'wɑ:) NOUN, *plural* ***aides-mémoire*** (ɛdmemwar; *English* 'eɪdz mɛm'wɑ:). a memorandum or summary of the items of an agreement, etc.
▷**HISTORY** from *aider* to help + *mémoire* memory

Aidin ('aɪdɪn) NOUN a variant spelling of **Aydin.**

AIDS *or* **Aids** (eɪdz) NOUN ACRONYM FOR acquired immune (or immuno-)deficiency syndrome: a condition, caused by a virus, in which certain white blood cells (lymphocytes) are destroyed, resulting in loss of the body's ability to protect itself against disease. AIDS is transmitted by sexual intercourse, through infected blood and blood products, and through the placenta.

AIDS-related complex NOUN See **ARC.**

AIF *History* ABBREVIATION FOR Australian Imperial Force.

aiglet ('eɪglɪt) NOUN a variant of **aglet.**

aigrette *or* **aigret** ('eɪgrɛt, eɪ'grɛt) NOUN [1] a long plume worn on hats or as a headdress, esp one of long egret feathers. [2] an ornament or piece of jewellery in imitation of a plume of feathers.
▷**HISTORY** C19: French

aiguille (eɪ'gwi:l, 'eɪgwi:l) NOUN [1] a rock mass or mountain peak shaped like a needle. [2] an instrument for boring holes in rocks or masonry.
▷**HISTORY** C19: French, literally: needle

aiguillette (ˌeɪgwɪ'lɛt) NOUN [1] an ornamentation worn by certain military officers, consisting of cords with metal tips. [2] a variant of **aglet.**

AIH ABBREVIATION FOR artificial insemination (by) husband.

aikido ('aɪkɪdəʊ) NOUN a Japanese system of self-defence employing similar principles to judo, but including blows from the hands and feet.
▷**HISTORY** from Japanese, from *ai* to join, receive + *ki* spirit, force + *do* way

aikona ('aɪkɔ:nə) INTERJECTION *South African* an informal word expressing strong negation.
▷**HISTORY** from Nguni

ail (eɪl) VERB [1] (*tr*) to trouble; afflict. [2] (*intr*) to feel unwell.
▷**HISTORY** Old English *eglan* to trouble, from *egle* troublesome, painful, related to Gothic *agls* shameful

ailanthus (eɪ'lænθəs) NOUN, *plural* **-thuses.** an E Asian simaroubaceous deciduous tree, *Ailanthus altissima,* planted in Europe and North America, having pinnate leaves, small greenish flowers, and winged fruits. Also called: **tree of heaven.**
▷**HISTORY** C19: New Latin, from native name (in Amboina) *ai lanto* tree (of) the gods

aileron ('eɪlərɒn) NOUN a flap hinged to the trailing edge of an aircraft wing to provide lateral control, as in a bank or roll.
▷**HISTORY** C20: from French, diminutive of *aile* wing

ailing ('eɪlɪŋ) ADJECTIVE unwell or unsuccessful.

ailment ('eɪlmənt) NOUN a slight but often persistent illness.

ailurophile (aɪ'lʊərəˌfaɪl) NOUN a person who likes cats.
▷**HISTORY** C20: facetious coinage from Greek *ailuros* cat + -PHILE
▸**ailurophilia** (aɪˌlʊərə'fɪlɪə) NOUN

ailurophobe (aɪ'lʊərəˌfəʊb) NOUN a person who dislikes or is afraid of cats.
▷**HISTORY** C20: from Greek *ailuros* cat + -PHOBE

aim (eɪm) VERB [1] to point (a weapon, missile, etc.) or direct (a blow) at a particular person or object; level. [2] (*tr*) to direct (satire, criticism, etc.) at a person, object, etc. [3] (*intr;* foll by *at* or an infinitive) to propose or intend: *we aim to leave early.* [4] (*intr;* often foll by *at* or *for*) to direct one's efforts or strive (towards): *to aim at better communications; to aim high.* ◆ NOUN [5] the action of directing something at an object. [6] the direction in which something is pointed; line of sighting (esp in the phrase **to take aim**). [7] the object at which something is aimed; target. [8] intention; purpose.
▷**HISTORY** C14: via Old French *aesmer* from Latin *aestimāre* to ESTIMATE

AIM ABBREVIATION FOR **Alternative Investment Market.**

aimless ('eɪmlɪs) ADJECTIVE having no goal, purpose, or direction.
▸'**aimlessly** ADVERB ▸'**aimlessness** NOUN

ain¹ (eɪn) DETERMINER a Scot word for **own.**

ain² ('ɑ:jɪn) NOUN a variant of **ayin.**

Ain (*French* ɛ̃) NOUN [1] a department in E central France, in Rhône-Alpes region. Capital: Bourg. Pop.: 515 270 (1999). Area: 5785 sq. km (2256 sq. miles). [2] a river in E France, rising in the Jura Mountains and flowing south to the Rhône. Length: 190 km (118 miles).

ain't (eɪnt) *Not standard* CONTRACTION OF am not, is not, are not, have not, *or* has not: *I ain't seen it.*

Aintab (aɪn'tɑ:b) NOUN the former name (until 1921) of **Gaziantep.**

A into G *NZ slang* ABBREVIATION FOR arse into gear (esp in the phrase **get your A into G**).

Aintree ('eɪntrɪ) NOUN a suburb of Liverpool, in Merseyside: site of the racecourse over which the Grand National steeplechase has been run since 1839.

Ainu ('aɪnu:) NOUN [1] (*plural* **-nus, -nu**) a member of the aboriginal people of Japan, now mostly intermixed with Mongoloid immigrants whose skin colour is more yellowish. [2] the language of this people, sometimes tentatively associated with Altaic, still spoken in parts of Hokkaido and elsewhere.
▷**HISTORY** Ainu: man

aïoli (aɪ'əʊlɪ, eɪ-) NOUN garlic mayonnaise.
▷**HISTORY** from French *ail* garlic

air (ɛə) NOUN [1] the mixture of gases that forms the earth's atmosphere. At sea level dry air has a density of 1.226 kilograms per cubic metre and consists of 78.08 per cent nitrogen, 20.95 per cent oxygen, 0.93 per cent argon, 0.03 per cent carbon dioxide, with smaller quantities of ozone and inert gases; water vapour varies between 0 and 4 per cent and in industrial areas sulphur gases may be present as pollutants. [2] the space above and around the earth; sky. Related adjective: **aerial.** [3] breeze; slight wind. [4] public expression; utterance: *to give air to one's complaints.* [5] a distinctive quality: *an air of mystery.* [6] a person's distinctive appearance, manner, or bearing. [7] *Music* **a** a simple tune for either vocal or instrumental performance. **b** another word for **aria.** [8] transportation in aircraft (esp in the phrase **by air**). [9] an archaic word for **breath** (senses 1–3). [10] *Austral informal* the height gained when getting airborne in surfing, snowboarding, etc. [11] **clear the air.** to rid a situation of tension or discord by settling misunderstandings, etc. [12] **give (someone) the air.** *Slang* to reject or dismiss (someone). [13] **in the air. a** in circulation; current. **b** in the process of being decided; unsettled. [14] **into thin air.** leaving no trace behind. [15] **on** (*or* **off**) **the air.** (not) in the act of broadcasting or (not) being broadcast on radio or television. [16] **out of** *or* **from thin air.** suddenly and unexpectedly. [17] **take the air.** to go out of doors, as for a short walk or ride. [18] **up in the air. a** uncertain. **b** *Informal* agitated or excited. [19] **walk on air.** to feel elated or exhilarated. [20] (*modifier*) *Astrology* of or

relating to a group of three signs of the zodiac, Gemini, Libra, and Aquarius. Compare **earth** (sense 10), **fire** (sense 24), **water** (sense 12). ◆ VERB [21] to expose or be exposed to the air so as to cool or freshen; ventilate: *to air a room.* [22] to expose or be exposed to warm or heated air so as to dry: *to air linen.* [23] (*tr*) to make known publicly; display; publicize: *to air one's opinions.* [24] (*intr*) (of a television or radio programme) to be broadcast. ◆ See also **airs**.
▷HISTORY C13: via Old French and Latin from Greek *aēr* the lower atmosphere

Aïr ('ɑːɪə) NOUN a mountainous region of N central Niger, in the Sahara, rising to 1500 m (5000 ft.): a former native kingdom. Area: about 77 700 sq. km (30 000 sq. miles). Also called: **Asben, Azbine.**

AIR ABBREVIATION FOR All India Radio.

air alert NOUN *Military* [1] the condition in which combat aircraft are airborne and ready for an operation. [2] a signal to prepare for this.

air bag NOUN a safety device in a car, consisting of a bag that inflates automatically in an accident and prevents the passengers from being thrown forwards.

air base NOUN a centre from which military aircraft operate. Also called: **air station.**

air bed NOUN an inflatable mattress.

air bladder NOUN [1] *Ichthyol* an air-filled sac, lying above the alimentary canal in bony fishes, that regulates buoyancy at different depths by a variation in the pressure of the air. Also called: **swim bladder.** [2] any air-filled sac, such as one of the bladders of seaweeds.

airboat ('ɛəˌbəʊt) NOUN another name for **swamp boat.**

airborne ('ɛəˌbɔːn) ADJECTIVE [1] conveyed by or through the air. [2] (of aircraft) flying; in the air.

air brake NOUN [1] a brake operated by compressed air, esp in heavy vehicles and trains. [2] Also called: **dive brake.** an articulated flap or small parachute for reducing the speed of an aircraft. [3] a rotary fan or propeller connected to a shaft to reduce its speed.

airbrick ('ɛəˌbrɪk) NOUN *Chiefly Brit* a brick with holes in it, put into the wall of a building for ventilation.

air bridge NOUN *Brit* a link by air transport between two places, esp two places separated by a stretch of sea.

airbrush ('ɛəˌbrʌʃ) NOUN [1] an atomizer for spraying paint or varnish by means of compressed air. ◆ VERB (*tr*) [2] to paint or varnish (something) by using an airbrush. [3] to improve the image of (a person or thing) by concealing defects beneath a bland exterior: *an airbrushed version of the government's record.*

airburst ('ɛəˌbɜːst) NOUN the explosion of a bomb, shell, etc., in the air.

Airbus ('ɛəˌbʌs) NOUN *Trademark* a commercial aircraft manufactured and marketed by an international consortium of aerospace companies.

air chief marshal NOUN a senior officer of the Royal Air Force and certain other air forces, of equivalent rank to admiral in the Royal Navy. Abbreviation: **ACM.**

air cleaner NOUN a filter that prevents dust and other particles from entering the air-intake of an internal-combustion engine. Also called: **air filter.**

Air Command NOUN *Canadian* the Canadian air force.

air commodore NOUN a senior officer of the Royal Air Force and certain other air forces, of equivalent rank to brigadier in the Army.

air-con ('ɛəˌkɒn) NOUN *Informal* air conditioning.

air-condition VERB (*tr*) to apply air conditioning to.

air conditioning NOUN a system or process for controlling the temperature and sometimes the humidity and purity of the air in a house, etc.
▸**air conditioner** NOUN

air-cool VERB (*tr*) to cool (an engine) by a flow of air. Compare **water-cool.**

air corridor NOUN an air route along which aircraft are allowed to fly.

air cover NOUN **a** the use of aircraft to provide aerial protection for ground forces against enemy air attack. **b** the aircraft used in this. ◆ Also called: **air support.**

aircraft ('ɛəˌkrɑːft) NOUN, *plural* **-craft**. any machine capable of flying by means of buoyancy or aerodynamic forces, such as a glider, helicopter, or aeroplane.

aircraft carrier NOUN a warship built with an extensive flat deck space for the launch and recovery of aircraft.

aircraft cloth *or* **fabric** NOUN variants of **aeroplane cloth.**

aircraftman ('ɛəˌkrɑːftmən) NOUN, *plural* **-men**. a serviceman of the most junior rank in the RAF. Also (not in official use): **aircraftsman.**
▸'**aircraftˌwoman** *or* (*not in official use*) '**aircraftsˌwoman** FEMININE NOUN

aircrew ('ɛəˌkruː) NOUN (*sometimes functioning as plural*) the crew of an aircraft.

air curtain NOUN an air stream across a doorway to exclude draughts, etc.

air cushion NOUN [1] an inflatable cushion, usually made of rubber or plastic. [2] the pocket of air that supports a hovercraft. [3] a form of pneumatic suspension consisting of a constricted volume of air. See also **air spring.**

air cylinder NOUN a cylinder containing air, esp one fitted with a piston and used for damping purposes.

air dam NOUN any device, such as a spoiler, that reduces air resistance and increases the stability of a car, aircraft, etc.

Airdrie ('ɛədrɪ; *Scot* 'erdrɪ) NOUN a town in W central Scotland, in North Lanarkshire, E of Glasgow: manufacturing and pharmaceutical industries. Pop.: 36 998 (1991).

airdrome ('ɛəˌdrəʊm) NOUN the US name for **aerodrome.**

airdrop ('ɛəˌdrɒp) NOUN [1] a delivery of supplies, troops, etc., from an aircraft by parachute. ◆ VERB **-drops, -dropping, -dropped.** [2] (*tr*) to deliver (supplies, etc.) by an airdrop.

air-dry VERB **-dries, -drying, -dried.** (*tr*) to dry by exposure to the air.

Aire (ɛə) NOUN a river in N England rising in the Pennines and flowing southeast to the Ouse. Length: 112 km (70 miles).

Airedale ('ɛəˌdeɪl) NOUN a large rough-haired tan-coloured breed of terrier characterized by a black saddle-shaped patch covering most of the back. Also called: **Airedale terrier.**
▷HISTORY C19: name of a district in Yorkshire

air embolism *or* **aeroembolism** NOUN the presence in the tissues and blood of a gas, such as air or nitrogen bubbles, caused by an injection of air or, in the case of nitrogen, by an abrupt and substantial reduction in the ambient pressure. See **decompression sickness.**

air engine NOUN [1] an engine that uses the expansion of heated air to drive a piston. [2] a small engine that uses compressed air to drive a piston.

air-entrained concrete NOUN a low-density type of concrete throughout which small air bubbles are dispersed in order to increase its frost resistance: used for making roads. With 1 per cent of air, the loss of strength is approximately 5 per cent.

airfield ('ɛəˌfiːld) NOUN a landing and taking-off area for aircraft, usually with permanent buildings.

air filter NOUN another name for **air cleaner.**

airflow ('ɛəˌfləʊ) NOUN the flow of air in a wind tunnel or past a moving aircraft, car, train, etc.; airstream.

airfoil ('ɛəˌfɔɪl) NOUN the US and Canadian name for **aerofoil.**

air force NOUN [1] **a** the branch of a nation's armed services primarily responsible for air warfare. **b** (*as modifier*): *an air-force base.* [2] a formation in the US and certain other air forces larger than an air division but smaller than an air command.

airframe ('ɛəˌfreɪm) NOUN the body of an aircraft, excluding its engines.

air freight NOUN [1] freight transported by aircraft. ◆ VERB **air-freight.** [2] (*tr*) to send (goods) to their destination by aircraft.

air frost NOUN the deposition of ice condensed from water vapour in the atmosphere on the surface when the air temperature is below 0°C.

air gas NOUN another name for **producer gas.**

airglow ('ɛəˌgləʊ) NOUN the faint light from the upper atmosphere in the night sky, esp in low latitudes.

air guitar NOUN an imaginary guitar played while miming to rock music.

air gun NOUN a gun discharged by means of compressed air.

air hardening NOUN a process of hardening high-alloy steels by heating and cooling in a current of air. Compare **oil hardening.**

airhead[1] ('ɛəˌhɛd) NOUN *Military* an area secured in hostile territory, used as a base for the supply and evacuation of troops and equipment by air.
▷HISTORY C20: modelled on BEACHHEAD

airhead[2] ('ɛəˌhɛd) NOUN *Slang* a stupid or simple-minded person; idiot.
▷HISTORY C20: from AIR + HEAD

air hole NOUN [1] a hole that allows the passage of air, esp for ventilation. [2] a section of open water in a frozen surface. [3] a less common name for **air pocket** (sense 1).

air hostess NOUN a stewardess on an airliner.

airily ('ɛərɪlɪ) ADVERB [1] in a jaunty or high-spirited manner. [2] in a light or delicate manner.

airiness ('ɛərɪnɪs) NOUN [1] the quality or condition of being fresh, light, or breezy. [2] lightness of heart; gaiety.

airing ('ɛərɪŋ) NOUN [1] **a** exposure to air or warmth, as for drying or ventilation. **b** (*as modifier*): *airing cupboard.* [2] an excursion in the open air. [3] exposure to public debate.

air-intake NOUN [1] **a** an opening in an aircraft through which air is drawn, esp for the engines. **b** the amount of air drawn in. [2] the part of a carburettor or similar device through which air enters an internal-combustion engine. [3] any opening, etc., through which air enters, esp for combustion or cooling purposes.

air jacket NOUN [1] an air-filled envelope or compartment surrounding a machine or part to reduce the rate at which heat is transferred to or from it. Compare **water jacket.** [2] a less common name for **life jacket.**

airless ('ɛəlɪs) ADJECTIVE [1] lacking fresh air; stuffy or sultry. [2] devoid of air.
▸'**airlessness** NOUN

air letter NOUN another name for **aerogram** (sense 1).

airlift ('ɛəˌlɪft) NOUN [1] the transportation by air of passengers, troops, cargo, etc., esp when other routes are blocked. ◆ VERB [2] (*tr*) to transport by an airlift.

air-lift pump NOUN a pump that pumps liquid by injecting air into the lower end of an open pipe immersed in the liquid: often used in boreholes.

airline ('ɛəˌlaɪn) NOUN [1] **a** a system or organization that provides scheduled flights for passengers or cargo. **b** (*as modifier*): *an airline pilot.* [2] a hose or tube carrying air under pressure. [3] *Chiefly US* a beeline.

airliner ('ɛəˌlaɪnə) NOUN a large passenger aircraft.

airlock ('ɛəˌlɒk) NOUN [1] a bubble in a pipe causing an obstruction or stoppage to the flow. [2] an airtight chamber with regulated air pressure used to gain access to a space that has air under pressure.

airmail ('ɛəˌmeɪl) NOUN [1] the system of conveying mail by aircraft. [2] mail conveyed by aircraft. ◆ ADJECTIVE [3] of, used for, or concerned with airmail. ◆ VERB [4] (*tr*) to send by airmail.

airman ('ɛəmən) NOUN, *plural* **-men**. an aviator, esp a man who serves in his country's air force.
▸'**airˌwoman** FEMININE NOUN

air marshal NOUN [1] a senior Royal Air Force officer of equivalent rank to a vice admiral in the Royal Navy. [2] a Royal Australian Air Force officer of the highest rank. [3] a Royal New Zealand Air Force officer of the highest rank when chief of defence forces. [4] a person employed to travel as an armed guard on commercial flights to protect against hijacking.

air mass NOUN a large body of air having characteristics of temperature, moisture, and pressure that are approximately uniform horizontally.

air mile NOUN another name for **nautical mile** (sense 1).

Air Miles PLURAL NOUN points awarded by certain companies to purchasers of flight tickets and some other products that may be used to pay for other flights.

air-minded ADJECTIVE interested in or promoting aviation or aircraft.
▸ **ˈair-ˌmindedness** NOUN

air miss NOUN a situation in which two aircraft pass very close to one another in the air; near miss.

Air Officer NOUN a term used to denote the appointment of any officer in the Royal Air Force above the rank of Air Commodore to a position of command.

airplane (ˈɛəˌpleɪn) NOUN the US and Canadian name for **aeroplane.**

air plant NOUN an epiphyte, esp an orchid of the large Old World tropical genus *Aerides,* grown for its white scented flowers spotted with red, purple, or rose, or a bromeliad, esp of the genus *Tillandsia.*

airplay (ˈɛəˌpleɪ) NOUN (of recorded music) radio exposure.

air pocket NOUN 1 a localized region of low air density or a descending air current, causing an aircraft to suffer an abrupt decrease in height. 2 any pocket of air that prevents the flow of a liquid or gas, as in a pipe.

airport (ˈɛəˌpɔːt) NOUN a landing and taking-off area for civil aircraft, usually with surfaced runways and aircraft maintenance and passenger facilities.

air power NOUN the strength of a nation's air force.

air pump NOUN a device for pumping air in or out of something.

air rage NOUN aggressive behaviour by an airline passenger that endangers the safety of the crew or other passengers.

air raid NOUN **a** an attack by hostile aircraft. **b** (*as modifier*): *an air-raid shelter.*

air-raid warden NOUN a member of a civil defence organization responsible for enforcing regulations, etc., during an air attack.

air rifle NOUN a rifle discharged by compressed air.

airs (ɛəz) PLURAL NOUN affected manners intended to impress others (esp in the phrases **give oneself airs, put on airs**).

air sac NOUN 1 any of the membranous air-filled extensions of the lungs of birds, which increase the efficiency of gaseous exchange in the lungs. 2 any of the thin-walled extensions of the tracheae of insects having a similar function.

air scoop NOUN a device fitted to the surface of an aircraft to provide air pressure or ventilation from the airflow.

Air Scout NOUN a scout belonging to a scout troop that specializes in flying, gliding, etc. See **Scout.**

airscrew (ˈɛəˌskruː) NOUN *Brit* an aircraft propeller.

air-sea rescue NOUN an air rescue at sea.

air shaft NOUN a shaft for ventilation, esp in a mine or tunnel.

airship (ˈɛəˌʃɪp) NOUN a lighter-than-air self-propelled craft. Also called: **dirigible, zeppelin.**

air shot NOUN *Golf* a shot that misses the ball completely but counts as a stroke.

airshow (ˈɛəˌʃəʊ) NOUN an occasion when an air base is open to the public and a flying display and, usually, static exhibitions are held.

airsick (ˈɛəˌsɪk) ADJECTIVE sick or nauseated from travelling in an aircraft.
▸ **ˈairˌsickness** NOUN

airside (ˈɛəˌsaɪd) NOUN the part of an airport nearest the aircraft, the boundary of which is the security check, customs, passport control, etc. Compare **landside** (sense 1).

air sock NOUN another name for **windsock.**

airspace (ˈɛəˌspeɪs) NOUN the atmosphere above the earth or part of the earth, esp the atmosphere above a country deemed to be under its jurisdiction.

airspeed (ˈɛəˌspiːd) NOUN the speed of an aircraft relative to the air in which it moves. Compare **groundspeed.**

air spray NOUN another name for **aerosol** (sense 3).

air spring NOUN *Mechanical engineering* an enclosed pocket of air used to absorb shock or sudden fluctuations of load.

air station NOUN an airfield, usually smaller than an airport but having facilities for the maintenance of aircraft.

airstream (ˈɛəˌstriːm) NOUN 1 a wind, esp at a high altitude. 2 a current of moving air.

airstrip (ˈɛəˌstrɪp) NOUN a cleared area for the landing and taking off of aircraft; runway. Also called: **landing strip.**

airt (ɛət; *Scot* ert) *or* **airth** (ɛəθ; *Scot* erθ) NOUN *Scot* a direction or point of the compass, esp the direction of the wind; quarter; region.
▹**HISTORY** C14: from Scots Gaelic *aird* point of the compass, height

air terminal NOUN 1 *Brit* a building in a city from which air passengers are taken by road or rail to an airport or the terminal building of an airport. 2 a building at an airport from which air passengers depart or at which they arrive.

airtight (ˈɛəˌtaɪt) ADJECTIVE 1 not permitting the passage of air either in or out. 2 having no weak points; rigid or unassailable: *this categorization is hardly airtight.*

airtime (ˈɛəˌtaɪm) NOUN 1 the time allocated to a particular programme, item, topic, or type of material on radio or television. 2 the time of the start of a radio or television broadcast.

air-to-air ADJECTIVE operating between aircraft in flight.

air traffic NOUN 1 the organized movement of aircraft within a given space. 2 the passengers, cargo, or mail carried by aircraft.

air-traffic control NOUN an organization that determines the altitude, speed, and direction at which planes fly in a given area, giving instructions to pilots by radio.
▸ **air-traffic controller** NOUN

airtsy-mairtsy (ˈɛətsɪˈmɛətsɪ) ADJECTIVE *Midlands English dialect* affected; effeminate.

air turbine NOUN a small turbine driven by compressed air, esp one used as a starter for engines.

air valve NOUN 1 a device for controlling the flow of air in a pipe. 2 a valve for exhausting air from a fluid system, esp from a central-heating installation. See also **bleed valve.**

air vesicle *or* **cavity** NOUN 1 a large air-filled intercellular space in some aquatic plants. 2 a large intercellular space in a leaf into which a stoma opens.

air vice-marshal NOUN 1 a senior Royal Air Force officer of equivalent rank to a rear admiral in the Royal Navy. 2 a Royal Australian Air Force officer of the second highest rank. 3 a Royal New Zealand Air Force officer of the highest rank. Abbreviation: **AVM.**

airwaves (ˈɛəˌweɪvz) PLURAL NOUN *Informal* radio waves used in radio and television broadcasting.

airway (ˈɛəˌweɪ) NOUN 1 an air route, esp one that is fully equipped with emergency landing fields, navigational aids, etc. 2 a passage for ventilation, esp in a mine. 3 a passage down which air travels from the nose or mouth to the lungs. 4 *Med* a tubelike device inserted via the throat to keep open the airway of an unconscious patient.

air waybill NOUN a document made out by the consignor of goods by air freight giving details of the goods and the name of the consignee.

airworthy (ˈɛəˌwɜːðɪ) ADJECTIVE (of an aircraft) safe to fly.
▸ **ˈairˌworthiness** NOUN

airy (ˈɛərɪ) ADJECTIVE **airier, airiest.** 1 abounding in fresh air. 2 spacious or uncluttered. 3 nonchalant; superficial. 4 visionary; fanciful: *airy promises; airy plans.* 5 of or relating to air. 6 weightless and insubstantial: *an airy gossamer.* 7 light and graceful in movement. 8 having no material substance: *airy spirits.* 9 high up in the air; lofty. 10 performed in the air; aerial.

airy-fairy (ˈɛərɪˈfɛərɪ) ADJECTIVE 1 *Informal* fanciful and unrealistic: *an airy-fairy scheme.* 2 delicate to the point of being insubstantial; light.
▹**HISTORY** C19: from Tennyson's poem *Lillian* (1830), where the central figure is described as "Airy, fairy Lillian"

AIS ABBREVIATION FOR Australian Institute of Sport.

aisle (aɪl) NOUN 1 a passageway separating seating areas in a theatre, church, etc.; gangway. 2 a lateral division in a church flanking the nave or chancel. 3 **(rolling) in the aisles.** *Informal* (of an audience) overcome with laughter.
▹**HISTORY** C14 *ele* (later *aile, aisle,* through confusion with *isle* (island)), via Old French from Latin *āla* wing
▸ **aisled** ADJECTIVE ▸ **ˈaisleless** ADJECTIVE

Aisne (eɪn; *French* ɛn) NOUN 1 a department of NE France, in Picardy region. Capital: Laon. Pop.: 535 842 (1999). Area: 7428 sq. km (2897 sq. miles). 2 a river in N France, rising in the Argonne Forest and flowing northwest and west to the River Oise: scene of a major Allied offensive in 1918 which turned the tide finally against Germany in World War I. Length: 282 km (175 miles).

ait (eɪt) *or* **eyot** NOUN *Dialect* an islet, esp in a river.
▹**HISTORY** Old English *ȳgett* small island, from *ieg* ISLAND

aitch (eɪtʃ) NOUN the letter *h* or the sound represented by it: *he drops his aitches.*
▹**HISTORY** C16: a phonetic spelling

aitchbone (ˈeɪtʃˌbəʊn) NOUN 1 the rump bone or floor of the pelvis in cattle. 2 a cut of beef from or including the rump bone.
▹**HISTORY** C15 hach-boon, altered from earlier *nache-bone, nage-bone* (*a nache* mistaken for *an ache, an aitch;* compare ADDER[1]); *nache* buttock, via Old French from Late Latin *natica,* from Latin *natis* buttock

Aix-en-Provence (*French* ɛksɑ̃prɔvɑ̃s) NOUN a city and spa in SE France: the medieval capital of Provence. Pop.: 134 222 (1999). Also called: **Aix.**

Aix-la-Chapelle (*French* ɛkslaʃapɛl) NOUN the French name for **Aachen.**

Aix-les-Bains (*French* ɛkslebɛ̃) NOUN a town in E France: a resort with sulphurous springs. Pop.: 24 830 (1990).

Aíyina (ˈɛjina) NOUN transliteration of the Modern Greek name for **Aegina.**

AJA ABBREVIATION FOR Australian Journalists' Association.

Ajaccio (əˈdʒætsɪˌəʊ, -ˈdʒeɪ-) NOUN the capital of Corsica, a port on the W coast. Pop.: 55 279 (1990 est.).

ajar[1] (əˈdʒɑː) ADJECTIVE (*postpositive*), ADVERB (esp of a door or window) slightly open.
▹**HISTORY** C18: altered form of obsolete *on char,* literally: on the turn; *char,* from Old English *cierran* to turn

ajar[2] (əˈdʒɑː) ADJECTIVE (*postpositive*) not in harmony.
▹**HISTORY** C19: altered form of *at jar* at discord. See JAR[2]

Ajax (ˈeɪdʒæks) NOUN *Greek myth* 1 the son of Telamon; a Greek hero of the Trojan War who killed himself in vexation when Achilles' armour was given to Odysseus. 2 called *Ajax the Lesser,* a Locrian king, a swift-footed Greek hero of the Trojan War.

AJC ABBREVIATION FOR Australian Jockey Club.

Ajmer (ʌdʒˈmɪə) NOUN a city in NW India, in Rajasthan: textile centre. Pop.: 402 700 (1991).

AK ABBREVIATION FOR: 1 Alaska. 2 Knight of the Order of Australia.

AK-47 NOUN a type of Kalashnikov assault rifle.
▹**HISTORY** C20: from *A(utomat) K(alashnikov)*

a.k.a. *or* **AKA** ABBREVIATION FOR also known as.

Akademi (əˈkɑːdəmɪ) NOUN (in India) a learned society.

Akan (ˈɑːkɑːn) NOUN 1 (*plural* **-kan** *or* **-kans**) a member of a people of Ghana and the E Ivory Coast. 2 the language of this people, having two chief dialects, Fanti and Twi, and belonging to the Kwa branch of the Niger-Congo family.

akaryote (eɪˈkærɪəʊt) NOUN *Biology* a cell without a nucleus.
▹**HISTORY** from A-[1] + KARYO- + *-ote* as in *zygote*
▸ **aˌkaryˈotic** ADJECTIVE

Akela (ɑːˈkeɪlə) NOUN *Brit* the adult leader of a pack of Cub Scouts. US equivalent: **Den Mother.**
▷HISTORY C20: after a character in Kipling's *The Jungle Book* (1894–95), who is the leader of a wolfpack

akene (əˈkiːn) NOUN a variant spelling of **achene.**

Akhaïa (aˈxaːja) NOUN transliteration of the modern Greek name for **Achaea.**

akhara (əˈkɑːrɑː) NOUN (in India) a gymnasium.

akimbo (əˈkɪmbəʊ) ADJECTIVE, ADVERB **(with) arms akimbo.** with hands on hips and elbows projecting outwards.
▷HISTORY C15 *in kenebowe,* literally: in keen bow, that is, in a sharp curve

akin (əˈkɪn) ADJECTIVE (*postpositive*) **1** related by blood; of the same kin. **2** (often foll by *to*) having similar characteristics, properties, etc.

akita (əˈkiːtə) NOUN a large powerfully-built dog of a Japanese breed with erect ears, a typically white coat, and a large full tail carried curled over its back.
▷HISTORY C20: named after a district in N Japan

Akkad *or* **Accad** (ˈækæd) NOUN **1** a city on the Euphrates in N Babylonia, the centre of a major empire and civilization (2360–2180 B.C.). Ancient name: **Agade** (əˈgɑːdɪ, əˈgeɪdɪ). **2** an ancient region lying north of Babylon, from which the Akkadian language and culture is named.

Akkadian *or* **Accadian** (əˈkædɪən, əˈkeɪ-) NOUN **1** a member of an ancient Semitic people who lived in central Mesopotamia in the third millennium B.C. **2** the extinct language of this people, belonging to the E Semitic subfamily of the Afro-Asiatic family. ◆ ADJECTIVE **3** of or relating to this people or their language.

Akkerman (*Russian* akɪrˈman) NOUN the former name (until 1946) of **Byelgorod-Dnestrovski.**

Akmola *or* **Aqmola** (ækˈməʊlə; *Kazakh* ɑkmɔˈlɑ) NOUN the former name (1994–98) of **Astana.**

Akmolinsk (*Russian* akˈmɔlinsk) NOUN the former name (until 1961) of **Akmola.**

akrasia (əˈkreɪzɪə) NOUN *Philosophy* weakness of will; acting in a way contrary to one's sincerely held moral values.
▷HISTORY C20: from A-[2] + Greek *kratos* power
▸**aˈkratic** ADJECTIVE

Akron (ˈækrən) NOUN a city in NE Ohio. Pop.: 217 074 (2000).

Aksum *or* **Axum** (ˈɑːksʊm) NOUN an ancient town in N Ethiopia, in the Tigré region: capital of the Aksumite Empire (1st to 6th centuries A.D.). According to tradition, the Ark of the Covenant was brought here from Jerusalem.

Aktyubinsk (*Russian* akˈtjubinsk) NOUN the former name (until 1991) of **Aqtöbe.**

Akubra (əˈkuːbrə) NOUN *Trademark* a brand of Australian hat.

Akure (əˈkuːre) NOUN a city in SW Nigeria, capital of Ondo state: agricultural trade centre. Pop.: 162 300 (1996 est.).

akvavit (ˈɑːkvɑːˌviːt) NOUN a variant spelling of **aquavit.**

al THE INTERNET DOMAIN NAME FOR Albania.

Al THE CHEMICAL SYMBOL FOR aluminium.

AL ABBREVIATION FOR: **1** Alabama. **2** Anglo-Latin. **3** (in the US and Canada) American League (of baseball teams). ◆ **4** INTERNATIONAL CAR REGISTRATION FOR Albania.

-al[1] SUFFIX FORMING ADJECTIVES of; related to; connected with: *functional; sectional; tonal.*
▷HISTORY from Latin *-ālis*

-al[2] SUFFIX FORMING NOUNS the act or process of doing what is indicated by the verb stem: *rebuttal; recital; renewal.*
▷HISTORY via Old French *-aille, -ail,* from Latin *-ālia,* neuter plural used as substantive, from *-ālis* -AL[1]

-al[3] SUFFIX FORMING NOUNS **1** indicating an aldehyde: *ethanal.* **2** indicating a pharmaceutical product: *phenobarbital.*
▷HISTORY shortened from ALDEHYDE

ala (ˈeɪlə) NOUN, *plural* **alae** (ˈeɪliː). **1** *Zoology* a wing or flat winglike process or structure, such as a part of some bones and cartilages. **2** *Botany* a winglike part, such as one of the wings of a sycamore seed or one of the flat petals of a sweet pea flower.
▷HISTORY C18: from Latin *āla* a wing

à la (ɑː lɑː, æ lə; *French* a la) PREPOSITION **1** in the manner or style of. **2** as prepared in (a particular place) or by or for (a particular person).
▷HISTORY C17: from French, short for *à la mode de* in the style of

Ala. ABBREVIATION FOR Alabama.

Alabama (ˌæləˈbæmə) NOUN **1** a state of the southeastern US, on the Gulf of Mexico: consists of coastal and W lowlands crossed by the Tombigbee, Black Warrior, and Alabama Rivers, with parts of the Tennessee Valley and Cumberland Plateau in the north; noted for producing cotton and white marble. Capital: Montgomery. Pop.: 4 447 100 (2000). Area: 131 333 sq. km (50 708 sq. miles). Abbreviations: **Ala,** (with zip code) **AL. 2** a river in Alabama, flowing southwest to the Mobile and Tensaw Rivers. Length: 507 km (315 miles).

Alabamian (ˌæləˈbæmɪən) ADJECTIVE **1** of or relating to Alabama or its inhabitants. ◆ NOUN **2** a native or inhabitant of Alabama.

alabaster (ˈæləˌbɑːstə, -ˌbæstə) NOUN **1** a fine-grained usually white, opaque, or translucent variety of gypsum used for statues, vases, etc. **2** a variety of hard semitranslucent calcite, often banded like marble. ◆ ADJECTIVE **3** of or resembling alabaster.
▷HISTORY C14: from Old French *alabastre,* from Latin *alabaster,* from Greek *alabastros*
▸**ˌalaˈbastrine** ADJECTIVE

à la carte (ɑː lɑː ˈkɑːt, æ lə; *French* a la kart) ADJECTIVE, ADVERB **1** (of a menu or a section of a menu) having dishes listed separately and individually priced. Compare **table d'hôte. 2** (of a dish) offered on such a menu; not part of a set meal.
▷HISTORY C19: from French, literally: according to the card

alack (əˈlæk) *or* **alackaday** (əˈlækəˌdeɪ) INTERJECTION an archaic or poetic word for **alas.**
▷HISTORY C15: from *a* ah! + *lack* loss, LACK

alacrity (əˈlækrɪtɪ) NOUN liveliness or briskness.
▷HISTORY C15: from Latin *alacritās,* from *alacer* lively
▸**aˈlacritous** ADJECTIVE

Ala Dağ *or* **Ala Dagh** (*Turkish* ɑˈlɑ dɑː) NOUN **1** the E part of the Taurus Mountains, in SE Turkey, rising over 3600 m (12 000 ft.). **2** a mountain range in E Turkey, rising over 3300 m (11 000 ft.). **3** a mountain range in NE Turkey, rising over 3000 m (10 000 ft.).

Aladdin (əˈlædɪn) NOUN (in *The Arabian Nights' Entertainments*) a poor youth who obtains a magic lamp and ring, with which he summons genies who grant his wishes.

Aladdin's cave NOUN **1** a place containing fabulous riches. **2** a place where something is abundant: *an Aladdin's cave of presents for children.*

Alagez *or* **Alagöz** (ɑlɑˈgœz) NOUN the Turkish name for (Mount) **Aragats.**

Alagoas (*Portuguese* alaˈgoːaʃ) NOUN a state in NE Brazil, on the Atlantic coast. Capital: Maceió. Pop.: 2 817 903 (2000). Area: 30 776 sq. km (11 031 sq. miles).

Alai (ɑːˈlaɪ) NOUN a mountain range in central Asia, in SW Kyrgyzstan, running from the Tian Shan range in China into Tajikistan. Average height: 4800 m (16 000 ft.), rising over 5850 m (19 500 ft.).

à la king (ɑː lɑː ˈkɪŋ, æ lə) ADJECTIVE (*usually postpositive*) cooked in a cream sauce with mushrooms and green peppers.

alalia (æˈleɪlɪə) NOUN a complete inability to speak; mutism.
▷HISTORY A-[1] + -LALIA

alameda (ˌæləˈmeɪdə) NOUN *Chiefly southwestern US* a public walk or promenade lined with trees, often poplars.

Alamein (ˈæləˌmeɪn) NOUN See **El Alamein.**

Alamo (ˈæləˌməʊ) NOUN **the.** a mission in San Antonio, Texas, the site of a siege and massacre in 1836 by Mexican forces under Santa Anna of a handful of American rebels fighting for Texan independence from Mexico.

à la mode (ɑː lɑː ˈməʊd, æ lə; *French* a la mɔd) ADJECTIVE **1** fashionable in style, design, etc. **2** (of meats) braised with vegetables in wine. **3** *Chiefly US and Canadian* (of desserts) served with ice cream.
▷HISTORY C17: from French: according to the fashion

alamode (ˈæləˌməʊd) NOUN a soft light silk used for shawls and dresses, esp in the 19th century. See also **surah.**
▷HISTORY C17: from À LA MODE

Åland Islands (ˈɑːlənd, ˈɔːlənd; *Swedish* ˈoːland) PLURAL NOUN a group of over 6000 islands under Finnish administration, in the Gulf of Bothnia. Capital: Mariehamn. Pop.: 24 847 (1992). Finnish name: **Ahvenanmaa.**

Alania (əˈlænɪə) NOUN another name for **North Ossetian Republic.**

alanine (ˈæləˌniːn, -ˌnaɪn) NOUN a nonessential aliphatic amino acid that occurs in many proteins.
▷HISTORY C19: from German *Alanin,* from AL(DEHYDE) + *-an-* (euphonic infix) + *-in* -INE[2]

alannah (əˈlænə) INTERJECTION *Irish* my child: used as a term of address or endearment.
▷HISTORY from Irish Gaelic *a leanbh*

Al-Anon (ˈæləˌnɒn) NOUN an association for the families and friends of alcoholics to give mutual support.

Alaouite *or* **Alawite** (ˈæləˌwiːt) NOUN **1** a member of a Shiite sect of Syrian Muslims. ◆ ADJECTIVE **2** of or relating to this sect.
▷HISTORY via French from Arabic, from *ʼalaoui* upper, celestial, from *ʼala* (vb) to excel, surpass

alap (əˈlɑːp) NOUN Indian vocal music without words.

al-Aqsa (æl ˈæksə) NOUN See **Dome of the Rock.**

alar (ˈeɪlə) ADJECTIVE **1** relating to, resembling, or having wings or alae. **2** denoting the cells at the base of a moss leaf, to the sides, that sometimes differ in structure from cells in the rest of the leaf.
▷HISTORY C19: from Latin *āla* a wing

Alar (ˈeɪlɑː) NOUN a chemical sprayed on cultivated apple trees in certain countries, to increase fruit set. Also called: **daminozide.**

alarm (əˈlɑːm) VERB (*tr*) **1** to fill with apprehension, anxiety, or fear. **2** to warn about danger; alert. **3** to fit or activate a burglar alarm on a house, car, etc. ◆ NOUN **4** fear or terror aroused by awareness of danger; fright. **5** apprehension or uneasiness: *the idea of failing filled him with alarm.* **6** a noise, signal, etc., warning of danger. **7** any device that transmits such a warning: *a burglar alarm.* **8 a** the device in an alarm clock that triggers off the bell or buzzer. **b** short for **alarm clock. 9** *Archaic* a call to arms. **10** *Fencing* a warning or challenge made by stamping the front foot.
▷HISTORY C14: from Old French *alarme,* from Old Italian *all'arme* to arms; see ARM[2]
▸**aˈlarming** ADJECTIVE ▸**aˈlarmingly** ADVERB

alarm clock NOUN a clock with a mechanism that sounds at a set time: used esp for waking a person up.

alarmist (əˈlɑːmɪst) NOUN **1** a person who alarms or attempts to alarm others needlessly or without due grounds. **2** a person who is easily alarmed. ◆ ADJECTIVE **3** characteristic of an alarmist.
▸**aˈlarmism** NOUN

alarum (əˈlærəm, -ˈlɑːr-, -ˈlɛər-) NOUN **1** *Archaic* an alarm, esp a call to arms. **2** (used as a stage direction, esp in Elizabethan drama) a loud disturbance or conflict (esp in the phrase **alarums and excursions**).
▷HISTORY C15: variant of ALARM

alary (ˈeɪlərɪ, ˈæ-) ADJECTIVE of, relating to, or shaped like wings.
▷HISTORY C17: from Latin *ālārius,* from *āla* wing

alas (əˈlæs) INTERJECTION an exclamation of grief, compassion, or alarm.
▷HISTORY C13: from Old French *ha las!* oh wretched!; *las* from Latin *lassus* weary

Alas. ABBREVIATION FOR Alaska.

Alaska (əˈlæskə) NOUN **1** the largest state of the US, in the extreme northwest of North America: the aboriginal inhabitants are Eskimos; the earliest White settlements were made by the Russians; it was purchased by the US from Russia in 1867. It is mostly mountainous and volcanic, rising over 6000 m (20 000 ft.), with the Yukon basin in the central region; large areas are covered by tundra; it has important mineral resources (chiefly coal, oil, and natural gas). Capital: Juneau. Pop.: 626 932 (2000). Area: 1 530 694 sq. km (591 004 sq. miles).

Abbreviations: **Alas,** (with zip code) **AK.** [2] **Gulf of.** the N part of the Pacific, between the Alaska Peninsula and the Alexander Archipelago.

Alaska Highway NOUN a road extending from Dawson Creek, British Columbia, to Fairbanks, Alaska: built by the US Army (1942). Length: 2452 km (1523 miles). Originally called: **Alcan Highway.**

Alaskan (ə'læskən) ADJECTIVE [1] of or relating to Alaska or its inhabitants. ◆ NOUN [2] a native or inhabitant of Alaska.

Alaska Peninsula NOUN an extension of the mainland of SW Alaska between the Pacific and the Bering Sea, ending in the Aleutian Islands. Length: about 644 km (400 miles).

Alaska Range NOUN a mountain range in S central Alaska. Highest peak: Mount McKinley, 6194 m (20 320 ft.).

alate ('eɪleɪt) ADJECTIVE having wings or winglike extensions.
▷HISTORY C17: from Latin *ālātus,* from *āla* wing

alb (ælb) NOUN *Christianity* a long white linen vestment with sleeves worn by priests and others.
▷HISTORY Old English *albe,* from Medieval Latin *alba* (*vestis*) white (clothing)

Alb. ABBREVIATION FOR Albania(n).

Albacete (*Spanish* alβa'θete) NOUN a city in SE Spain: metal goods manufacturing. Pop.: 145 454 (1998 est.).

albacore ('ælbəˌkɔː) NOUN a tunny, *Thunnus alalunga,* occurring mainly in warm regions of the Atlantic and Pacific. It has very long pectoral fins and is a valued food fish. Also called: **long-fin tunny.**
▷HISTORY C16: from Portuguese *albacor,* from Arabic *al-bakrah,* from *al* the + *bakr* young camel

Alba Longa ('ælbə 'lɒŋgə) NOUN a city of ancient Latium, southeast of modern Rome: the legendary birthplace of Romulus and Remus.

Albania (æl'beɪnɪə) NOUN a republic in SE Europe, on the Balkan Peninsula: became independent in 1912 after more than four centuries of Turkish rule; established as a republic (1946) under Communist rule; multiparty constitution adopted in 1991. It is generally mountainous, rising over 2700 m (9000 ft.), with extensive forests. Language: Albanian. Religion: Muslim majority. Currency: lek. Capital: Tirana. Pop.: 3 091 000 (2001 est.). Area: 28 749 sq. km (11 100 sq. miles).

Albanian (æl'beɪnɪən) NOUN [1] the official language of Albania: of uncertain relationship within the Indo-European family, but thought to be related to ancient Illyrian. [2] **a** a native, citizen, or inhabitant of Albania. **b** a native speaker of Albanian. ◆ ADJECTIVE [3] of or relating to Albania, its people, or their language.

Albany ('ɔːlbənɪ) NOUN [1] a city in E New York State, on the Hudson River: the state capital. Pop.: 195 658 (2000). [2] a river in central Canada, flowing east and northeast to James Bay. Length: 982 km (610 miles).

albata (æl'beɪtə) NOUN a variety of German silver consisting of nickel, copper, and zinc.
▷HISTORY C19: from Latin, literally: clothed in white, from *albus* white

albatross ('ælbəˌtrɒs) NOUN [1] any large oceanic bird of the genera *Diomedea* and *Phoebetria,* family *Diomedeidae,* of cool southern oceans: order *Procellariiformes* (petrels). They have long narrow wings and are noted for a powerful gliding flight. See also **wandering albatross.** [2] a constant and inescapable burden or handicap: *an albatross of debt.* [3] *Golf* a score of three strokes under par for a hole.
▷HISTORY C17: from Portuguese *alcatraz* pelican, from Arabic *al-ghattās,* from *al* the + *ghattās* white-tailed sea eagle; influenced by Latin *albus* white: C20 in sense 2, from *The Rime of the Ancient Mariner* (1798) by English poet Samuel Taylor Coleridge (1772–1834)

albedo (æl'biːdəʊ) NOUN [1] the ratio of the intensity of light reflected from an object, such as a planet, to that of the light it receives from the sun. [2] *Physics* the probability that a neutron passing through a surface will return through that surface.
▷HISTORY C19: from Church Latin: whiteness, from Latin *albus* white

albeit (ɔːl'biːɪt) CONJUNCTION even though.
▷HISTORY C14 *al be it,* that is, although it be (that)

Albemarle Sound ('ælbəˌmɑːl) NOUN an inlet of the Atlantic in NE North Carolina. Length: about 96 km (60 miles).

Alberich (*German* 'albərɪç) NOUN (in medieval German legend) the king of the dwarfs and guardian of the treasures of the Nibelungs.

albert ('ælbət) NOUN [1] a kind of watch chain usually attached to a waistcoat. [2] *Brit* a standard size of notepaper, 6 × 3⅞ inches.
▷HISTORY C19: named after Prince *Albert* (1819–61), Prince Consort of Queen Victoria of Great Britain and Ireland

Albert ('ælbət) NOUN **Lake.** a lake in E Africa, between the Democratic Republic of Congo (formerly Zaïre) and Uganda in the great Rift Valley, 660 m (2200 ft.) above sea level: a source of the Nile, fed by the Victoria Nile, which leaves as the Albert Nile. Area: 5345 sq.km (2064 sq. miles). Former name: **Lake Mobutu.**

Alberta (æl'bɜːtə) NOUN a province of W Canada: mostly prairie, with the Rocky Mountains in the southwest. Capital: Edmonton. Pop.: 3 064 200 (2001 est.). Area: 661 188 sq. km (255 285 sq. miles). Abbreviations: **Alta, AB.**

Alberta clipper NOUN *Meteorol* (in Canada) an area of low pressure that forms in winter near the Rocky Mountains.

Albertan (æl'bɜːtən) ADJECTIVE [1] of or relating to Alberta or its inhabitants. ◆ NOUN [2] a native or inhabitant of Alberta.

Albert Edward NOUN a mountain in SE New Guinea, in the Owen Stanley Range. Height: 3993 m (13 100 ft.).

albertite ('ælbəˌtaɪt) NOUN a black solid variety of bitumen that has a conchoidal fracture and occurs in veins in oil-bearing strata.
▷HISTORY C19: named after *Albert* county, New Brunswick, Canada, where it is mined

albescent (æl'bɛsᵊnt) ADJECTIVE shading into, growing, or becoming white.
▷HISTORY C19: from Latin *albēscere* to grow white, from *albus* white
▸**al'bescence** NOUN

Albi (*French* albi) NOUN a town in S France: connected with the Albigensian heresy and the crusade against it. Pop.: 48 700 (1990).

Albigenses (ˌælbɪ'dʒɛnsiːz) PLURAL NOUN members of a Manichean sect that flourished in S France from the 11th to the 13th century.
▷HISTORY from Medieval Latin: inhabitants of Albi, from *Albiga* ALBI
▸**ˌAlbi'gensian** ADJECTIVE ▸**ˌAlbi'gensianism** NOUN

albino (æl'biːnəʊ) NOUN, *plural* **-nos.** [1] a person with congenital absence of pigmentation in the skin, eyes, and hair. [2] any animal or plant that is deficient in pigment.
▷HISTORY C18: via Portuguese from Spanish, from *albo* white, from Latin *albus*
▸**albinic** (æl'bɪnɪk) *or* **ˌalbin'istic** ADJECTIVE ▸**albinism** ('ælbɪˌnɪzəm) NOUN ▸**albinotic** (ˌælbɪ'nɒtɪk) ADJECTIVE

Albion ('ælbɪən) NOUN *Archaic or poetic* Britain or England.
▷HISTORY C13: from Latin, of Celtic origin

albite ('ælbaɪt) NOUN a colourless, milky-white, yellow, pink, green, or black mineral of the feldspar group and plagioclase series, found in igneous sedimentary and metamorphic rocks. It is used in the manufacture of glass and ceramics. Composition: sodium aluminium silicate. Formula: $NaALSi_3O_8$. Crystal structure: triclinic.
▷HISTORY C19: from Latin *albus* white
▸**albitic** (æl'bɪtɪk) ADJECTIVE

Ålborg (*Danish* 'ɔlbɔr) NOUN a variant spelling of **Aalborg.**

album ('ælbəm) NOUN [1] a book or binder consisting of blank pages, pockets, or envelopes for keeping photographs, stamps, autographs, drawings, poems, etc. [2] one or more CDs, cassettes, or long-playing records released as a single item. [3] a booklike holder containing sleeves for gramophone records. [4] *Chiefly Brit* an anthology, usually large and illustrated.
▷HISTORY C17: from Latin: blank tablet, from *albus* white

albumblatt ('ælbəmˌblæt) NOUN *Music* a short occasional instrumental composition, usually light in character.
▷HISTORY C19: German: album-leaf

albumen ('ælbjʊmɪn, -mɛn) NOUN [1] the white of an egg; the nutritive and protective gelatinous substance, mostly an albumin, that surrounds the yolk. [2] a rare name for **endosperm.** [3] a variant spelling of **albumin.**
▷HISTORY C16: from Latin: white of an egg, from *albus* white

albumenize *or* **albumenise** (æl'bjuːmɪˌnaɪz) VERB (*tr*) to coat with a solution containing albumen or albumin.

albumin *or* **albumen** ('ælbjʊmɪn) NOUN any of a group of simple water-soluble proteins that are coagulated by heat and are found in blood plasma, egg white, etc.
▷HISTORY C19: from ALBUMEN + -IN

albuminate (æl'bjuːmɪˌneɪt) NOUN *Now rare* any of several substances formed from albumin by the action of acid or alkali.

albuminoid (æl'bjuːmɪˌnɔɪd) ADJECTIVE [1] resembling albumin. ◆ NOUN [2] another name for **scleroprotein.**

albuminous (æl'bjuːmɪnəs) ADJECTIVE of or containing albumin.

albuminuria (ælˌbjuːmɪ'njʊərɪə) NOUN *Pathol* the presence of albumin in the urine. Also called: **proteinuria.**

albumose ('ælbjʊˌməʊs, -ˌməʊz) NOUN the US name for **proteose.**
▷HISTORY C19: from ALBUMIN + -OSE²

Albuquerque ('ælbəˌkɜːkɪ) NOUN a city in central New Mexico, on the Rio Grande. Pop.: 448 607 (2000).

alburnum (æl'bɜːnəm) NOUN a former name for **sapwood.**
▷HISTORY C17: from Latin: sapwood, from *albus* white

Albury-Wodonga ('ɔːbərɪ, -brɪ wə'dɒŋgə) NOUN an urban growth centre in SE Australia, in S central New South Wales, on the Murray River: commercial centre of an agricultural region. Pop.: 63 610 (1991).

alcahest ('ælkəˌhɛst) NOUN a variant spelling of **alkahest.**

Alcaic (æl'keɪɪk) ADJECTIVE [1] of or relating to a metre used by the 7th-century B.C. Greek lyric poet Alcaeus, consisting of a strophe of four lines each with four feet. ◆ NOUN [2] (*usually plural*) verse written in the Alcaic form.
▷HISTORY C17: from Late Latin *Alcaicus* of Alcaeus

alcaide (æl'keɪd; *Spanish* al'kaiðe) NOUN (in Spain and Spanish America) [1] the commander of a fortress or castle. [2] the governor of a prison.
▷HISTORY C16: from Spanish, from Arabic *al-qā'id* the captain, commander, from *qād* to give orders

alcalde (æl'kældɪ; *Spanish* al'kalde) *or* **alcade** (æl'keɪd) NOUN (in Spain and Spanish America) the mayor or chief magistrate in a town.
▷HISTORY C17: from Spanish, from Arabic *al-qādī* the judge, from *qadā* to judge

Alcan Highway ('ælkæn) NOUN original name of the **Alaska Highway.**

Alcántara (æl'kæntɑːrə) NOUN a town in W Spain: a Roman bridge spans the River Tagus. Pop.: 2317 (1981).

Alcatraz ('ælkəˌtræz) NOUN an island in W California, in San Francisco Bay: a federal prison until 1963.

alcazar (ˌælkə'zɑː; *Spanish* al'kaθar) NOUN any of various palaces or fortresses built in Spain by the Moors.
▷HISTORY C17: from Spanish, from Arabic *al-qasr* the castle

Alcazar de San Juan ('ælkəˌzɑː; *Spanish* al'kaθar) NOUN a town in S central Spain: associated with Cervantes and Don Quixote. Pop.: 25 679 (1991).

Alcestis (æl'sɛstɪs) NOUN *Greek myth* the wife of king Admetus of Thessaly. To save his life, she died in his place, but was rescued from Hades by Hercules.

alchemist ('ælkəmɪst) NOUN a person who practises alchemy.

alchemize *or* **alchemise** ('ælkəˌmaɪz) VERB (*tr*) to alter (an element, metal, etc.) by alchemy; transmute.

alchemy ('ælkəmɪ) NOUN, *plural* **-mies.** [1] the

pseudoscientific predecessor of chemistry that sought a method of transmuting base metals into gold, an elixir to prolong life indefinitely, a panacea or universal remedy, and an alkahest or universal solvent. 2 a power like that of alchemy: *her beauty had a potent alchemy.*
▷HISTORY C14 *alkamye,* via Old French from Medieval Latin *alchimia,* from Arabic *al-kīmiyā',* from *al* the + *kīmiyā'* transmutation, from Late Greek *khēmeia* the art of transmutation
▸**alchemic** (æl'kɛmɪk) *or* **al'chemical** *or* **ˌalchem'istic** ADJECTIVE

alcheringa (ˌæltʃə'rɪŋgə) NOUN another name for **Dreamtime.**
▷HISTORY from a native Australian language, literally: dream time

Alchevsk (æl'tʃɛvsk) NOUN a city in the E Ukraine. Pop.: 120 900 (1998 est.). Former name (until 1992): **Kommunarsk.**

Alcides (æl'saɪdiːz) NOUN another name for **Hercules**[1] (sense 1).

alcidine ('ælsɪˌdaɪn) ADJECTIVE of, relating to, or belonging to the *Alcidae,* a family of sea birds including the auks, guillemots, puffins, and related forms.
▷HISTORY C20: from New Latin *Alcidae,* from *Alca* type genus

Alcinoüs (æl'sɪnəʊəs) NOUN (in Homer's *Odyssey*) a Phaeacian king at whose court the shipwrecked Odysseus told of his wanderings. See also **Nausicaä.**

ALCM ABBREVIATION FOR air-launched cruise missile: a type of cruise missile that can be launched from an aircraft.

Alcmene (ælk'miːnɪ) NOUN *Greek myth* the mother of Hercules by Zeus who visited her in the guise of her husband, Amphitryon.

alcohol ('ælkəˌhɒl) NOUN 1 a colourless flammable liquid, the active principle of intoxicating drinks, produced by the fermentation of sugars, esp glucose, and used as a solvent and in the manufacture of organic chemicals. Formula: C_2H_5OH. Also called: **ethanol, ethyl alcohol.** 2 a drink or drinks containing this substance. 3 *Chem* any one of a class of organic compounds that contain one or more hydroxyl groups bound to carbon atoms. The simplest alcohols have the formula ROH, where R is an alkyl group. Compare **phenol** (sense 2). See also **diol, triol.**
▷HISTORY C16: via New Latin from Medieval Latin, from Arabic *al-kuhl* powdered antimony; see KOHL

alcohol-free ADJECTIVE 1 (of beer or wine) containing only a trace of alcohol. Compare **low-alcohol.** 2 (of a period of time) during which no alcoholic drink is consumed: *there should be one or two alcohol-free days a week.*

alcoholic (ˌælkə'hɒlɪk) NOUN 1 a person affected by alcoholism. ♦ ADJECTIVE 2 of, relating to, containing, or resulting from alcohol.

alcoholicity (ˌælkəhɒ'lɪsɪtɪ) NOUN the strength of an alcoholic liquor.

Alcoholics Anonymous NOUN an association of alcoholics who try, esp by mutual assistance, to overcome alcoholism.

alcoholism ('ælkəhɒˌlɪzəm) NOUN a condition in which dependence on alcohol harms a person's health, social functioning, or family life.

alcoholize *or* **alcoholise** ('ælkəhɒˌlaɪz) VERB (*tr*) to turn into alcoholic drink, as by fermenting or mixing with alcohol.
▸**ˌalcoˌholi'zation** *or* **ˌalcoˌholi'sation** NOUN

alcoholometer (ˌælkəhɒ'lɒmɪtə) NOUN an instrument, such as a specially calibrated hydrometer, for determining the percentage of alcohol in a liquid.

alcool ('ælkuːl) NOUN a form of pure grain spirit distilled in Quebec.
▷HISTORY from French: alcohol

alcopop ('ælkəʊˌpɒp) NOUN *Informal* an alcoholic drink that tastes like a soft drink.
▷HISTORY C20: from ALCO(HOL) + POP[1] (sense 11)

Alcoran *or* **Alkoran** (ˌælkɒ'rɑːn) NOUN another name for the **Koran.**
▸**ˌAlco'ranic** *or* **ˌAlko'ranic** ADJECTIVE

alcove ('ælkəʊv) NOUN 1 a recess or niche in the wall of a room, as for a bed, books, etc. 2 any recessed usually vaulted area, as in a garden wall. 3 any covered or secluded spot, such as a summerhouse.
▷HISTORY C17: from French *alcôve,* from Spanish *alcoba,* from Arabic *al-qubbah* the vault, arch

Alcyone[1] (æl'saɪənɪ) NOUN *Greek myth* Also called: **Halcyone.** the daughter of Aeolus and wife of Ceyx, who drowned herself in grief for her husband's death. She was transformed into a kingfisher. See also **Ceyx.**

Alcyone[2] (æl'saɪənɪ) NOUN the brightest star system in the Pleiades, located in the constellation Taurus.

Ald. *or* **Aldm.** ABBREVIATION FOR Alderman.

Aldabra (æl'dæbrə) NOUN an island group in the Indian Ocean: part of the British Indian Ocean Territory (1965–76); now administratively part of the Seychelles.

Aldan (*Russian* al'dan) NOUN a river in E Russia in the SE Sakha Republic, rising in the **Aldan Mountains** and flowing north and west to the Lena River. Length: about 2700 km (1700 miles).

Aldebaran (æl'dɛbərən) NOUN a binary star, one component of which is a red giant, the brightest star in the constellation Taurus. It appears in the sky close to the star cluster Hyades. Visual magnitude: 0.85; spectral type: K5III; distance: 65 light years.
▷HISTORY C14: via Medieval Latin from Arabic *al-dabarān* the follower (of the Pleiades)

Aldeburgh ('ɔːlbərə) NOUN a small resort in SE England, in Suffolk: site of an annual music festival established in 1948 by Benjamin Britten. Pop.: 2654 (1991).

aldehyde ('ældɪˌhaɪd) NOUN 1 any organic compound containing the group -CHO. Aldehydes are oxidized to carboxylic acids and take part in many addition reactions. 2 (*modifier*) consisting of, containing, or concerned with the group -CHO: *aldehyde group or radical.*
▷HISTORY C19: from New Latin *al(cohol) dehyd(rogenātum)* dehydrogenated alcohol
▸**aldehydic** (ˌældə'hɪdɪk) ADJECTIVE

al dente *Italian* (al 'dɛnte) ADJECTIVE (of a pasta dish) cooked so as to be firm when eaten.
▷HISTORY literally: to the tooth

alder ('ɔːldə) NOUN 1 any N temperate betulaceous shrub or tree of the genus *Alnus,* having toothed leaves and conelike fruits. The bark is used in dyeing and tanning and the wood for bridges, etc. because it resists underwater rot. 2 any of several similar trees or shrubs.
▷HISTORY Old English *alor;* related to Old High German *elira,* Latin *alnus*

alder buckthorn NOUN a Eurasian rhamnaceous shrub, *Frangula alnus,* with small greenish flowers and black berry-like fruits.

alder fly NOUN any of various neuropterous insects of the widely distributed group *Sialoidea,* such as *Sialis lutaria,* that have large broad-based hind wings, produce aquatic larvae, and occur near water.

alderman ('ɔːldəmən) NOUN, *plural* **-men.** 1 (in England and Wales until 1974) one of the senior members of a local council, elected by other councillors. 2 (in the US, Canada, Australia, etc.) a member of the governing body of a municipality. 3 *History* a variant spelling of **ealdorman.** ♦ Abbreviations (for senses 1, 2): **Ald, Aldm.**
▷HISTORY Old English *aldormann,* from *ealdor* chief (comparative of *eald* OLD) + *mann* MAN
▸**aldermanic** (ˌɔːldə'mænɪk) ADJECTIVE ▸**'aldermanry** NOUN ▸**'aldermanˌship** NOUN

Aldermaston ('ɔːldəˌmɑːstən) NOUN a village in S England, in West Berkshire unitary authority, Berkshire, SW of Reading: site of the Atomic Weapons Research Establishment and starting point of the Aldermaston marches (1958–63), organized by the Campaign for Nuclear Disarmament. Pop.: 2157 (1987 est.).

Alderney ('ɔːldənɪ) NOUN 1 one of the Channel Islands, in the English Channel: separated from the French coast by a dangerous tidal channel (the **Race of Alderney**). Pop.: 2147 (1996). Area: 8 sq. km (3 sq. miles). French name: **Aurigny.** 2 an early, but now extinct, breed of dairy cattle originating from the island of Alderney.

Aldershot ('ɔːldəˌʃɒt) NOUN a town in S England, in Hampshire: site of a large military camp. Pop.: 51 356 (1991).

Aldis lamp ('ɔːldɪs) NOUN a portable lamp used to transmit Morse code.
▷HISTORY C20: originally a trademark, after A. C. W. *Aldis,* its inventor

aldohexose (ˌældəʊ'hɛksəʊs, -əʊz) NOUN any aldose containing six carbon atoms, such as glucose or mannose.

aldol ('ældɒl) NOUN 1 a colourless or yellowish oily liquid, miscible with water, used in the manufacture of rubber accelerators, as an organic solvent, in perfume, and as a hypnotic and sedative. Formula: $CH_3CHOHCH_2CHO$. Systematic name: **3-hydroxybutanal.** 2 any organic compound containing the functional group $-CHOHCH_2CHO$. 3 (*modifier*) consisting of, containing, or concerned with the group $-CHOHCH_2CHO$: *aldol group or radical; aldol reaction.*
▷HISTORY C19: from ALD(EHYDE) + -OL[1]

aldose ('ældəʊs, -dəʊz) NOUN a sugar that contains the aldehyde group or is a hemiacetal.
▷HISTORY C20: from ALD(EHYDE) + -OSE[2]

aldosterone (æl'dɒstəˌrəʊn) NOUN the principal mineralocorticoid secreted by the adrenal cortex. A synthesized form is used in the treatment of Addison's disease. Formula: $C_{21}H_{27}O_5$.
▷HISTORY C20: from ALD(EHYDE) + -O- + STER(OL) + -ONE

aldoxime (æl'dɒksiːm) NOUN an oxime formed by reaction between hydroxylamine and an aldehyde.

Aldridge-Brownhills ('ɔːldrɪdʒ'braʊnˌhɪlz) NOUN a town in central England, in Walsall unitary authority, West Midlands: formed by the amalgamation of neighbouring towns in 1966. Pop.: 37 444 (1991).

aldrin ('ɔːldrɪn) NOUN a brown to white poisonous crystalline solid, more than 95 per cent of which consists of the compound $C_{12}H_8Cl_6$, which is used as an insecticide. Melting pt.: 105°C.
▷HISTORY C20: named after K. *Alder* (1902–58) German chemist

ale (eɪl) NOUN 1 a beer fermented in an open vessel using yeasts that rise to the top of the brew. Compare **beer, lager**[1]. 2 (formerly) an alcoholic drink made by fermenting a cereal, esp barley, but differing from beer by being unflavoured by hops. 3 *Chiefly Brit* another word for **beer.**
▷HISTORY Old English *alu, ealu;* related to Old Norse *öl,* Old Saxon *alofat*

aleatory ('eɪlɪətərɪ, -trɪ) *or* **aleatoric** (ˌeɪlɪə'tɒrɪk) ADJECTIVE 1 dependent on chance. 2 (esp of a musical composition) involving elements chosen at random by the performer.
▷HISTORY C17: from Latin *āleātōrius,* from *āleātor* gambler, from *ālea* game of chance, dice, of uncertain origin

alecithal (eɪ'lɛsɪθəl) ADJECTIVE *Zoology* (of an ovum) having little or no yolk.
▷HISTORY from A-[1] + Greek *lekithos* egg yolk

ale conner NOUN *English history* a local official appointed to examine the measure and quality of ale, beer, and bread.
▷HISTORY C14: from ALE + *conner,* from Old English *cunnere* one who tests

alecost ('eɪlˌkɒst) NOUN another name for **costmary.**

Alecto (ə'lɛktəʊ) NOUN *Greek myth* one of the three Furies; the others are Megaera and Tisiphone.

alee (ə'liː) ADVERB, ADJECTIVE (*postpositive*) *Nautical* on or towards the lee: *with the helm alee.* Compare **aweather.**

alegar ('eɪlɪgə, 'æ-) NOUN malt vinegar.
▷HISTORY C14: from ALE + VINEGAR

alehouse ('eɪlˌhaʊs) NOUN 1 *Archaic* a place where ale was sold; tavern. 2 *Informal* another name for **pub.**

Aleksandropol (*Russian* alɪksan'drɔpəlj) NOUN the former name (from 1837 until after the Revolution) of **Leninakan.**

Aleksandrovsk (*Russian* alɪk'sandrəfsk) NOUN the former name (until 1921) of **Zaporozhye.**

Alemanni (ˌælə'mɑːnɪ) NOUN a West Germanic people who settled in the 4th century A.D. between the Rhine, the Main, and the Danube.
▷HISTORY C18: from Latin, of Germanic origin; related to Gothic *alamans* a totality of people

Alemannic (ˌæləˈmænɪk) NOUN 1 **a** the group of High German dialects spoken in Alsace, Switzerland, and SW Germany. **b** the language of the ancient Alemanni, from which these modern dialects have developed. See also **Old High German.** ◆ ADJECTIVE 2 of or relating to the Alemanni, their speech, or the High German dialects descended from it.
▷HISTORY C18: from Late Latin *Alamannicus,* of Germanic origin

alembic (əˈlɛmbɪk) NOUN 1 an obsolete type of retort used for distillation. 2 anything that distils or purifies.
▷HISTORY C14: from Medieval Latin *alembicum,* from Arabic *al-anbīq* the still, from Greek *ambix* cup

alembicated (əˈlɛmbɪˌkeɪtɪd) ADJECTIVE (of a literary style) excessively refined; precious.
▸**aˌlembiˈcation** NOUN

Alençon (*French* alɑ̃sɔ̃) NOUN a town in NW France: early lace-manufacturing centre. Pop.: 31 140 (1990).

Alençon lace NOUN an elaborate lace worked on a hexagonal mesh and used as a border, or a machine-made copy of this.

aleph (ˈɑːlɪf; *Hebrew* ˈaːlɛf) NOUN the first letter in the Hebrew alphabet (א) articulated as a glottal stop and transliterated with a superior comma (ʼ).
▷HISTORY Hebrew: ox

aleph-bet (ˈɑlefˈbet) *or* **aleph-beis** (ˈɑlefˈbeis) NOUN the Hebrew alphabet.
▷HISTORY from the first two letters

aleph-null *or* **aleph-zero** NOUN the smallest infinite cardinal number; the cardinal number of the set of positive integers. Symbol: $\aleph_0$.

Aleppo (əˈlɛpəʊ) NOUN an ancient city in NW Syria: industrial and commercial centre. Pop.: 1 582 930 (1994). French name: **Alep** (alɛp). Arabic name: **Haleb** (ˈhalɛp).

Aleppo gall NOUN a type of nutgall occurring in oaks in W Asia and E Europe.

alerce (əˈlɜːs, æˈlɜːsɪ) NOUN 1 the wood of the sandarac tree. 2 a cupressus-like Chilean pine, *Fitzroya cupressoides,* cut for timber.
▷HISTORY Spanish: larch, from Latin *larix,* influenced by Arabic *al-arz*

alert (əˈlɜːt) ADJECTIVE (*usually postpositive*) 1 vigilantly attentive: *alert to the problems.* 2 brisk, nimble, or lively. ◆ NOUN 3 an alarm or warning, esp a siren warning of an air raid. 4 the period during which such a warning remains in effect. 5 **on the alert. a** on guard against danger, attack, etc. **b** watchful; ready: *on the alert for any errors.* ◆ VERB (*tr*) 6 to warn or signal (troops, police, etc.) to prepare for action. 7 to warn of danger, an attack, etc.
▷HISTORY C17: from Italian *all'erta* on the watch, from *erta* lookout post, from *ergere* to build up, from Latin *ērigere;* see ERECT
▸**aˈlertly** ADVERB ▸**aˈlertness** NOUN

-ales SUFFIX FORMING PLURAL PROPER NOUNS denoting plants belonging to an order: *Rosales; Filicales.*
▷HISTORY New Latin, from Latin, plural of *-ālis* -AL[1]

Alessandria (*Italian* alesˈsandrja) NOUN a town in NW Italy, in Piedmont. Pop.: 93 866 (1990).

Ålesund *or* **Aalesund** (*Norwegian* ˈoːləsun) NOUN a port and market town in W Norway, on an island between Bergen and Trondheim: fishing and sealing fleets. Pop.: 35 862 (1990).

alethic (əˈliːθɪk) ADJECTIVE *Logic* **a** of or relating to such philosophical concepts as truth, necessity, possibility, contingency, etc. **b** designating the branch of modal logic that deals with the formalization of these concepts.
▷HISTORY C20: from Greek *alētheia* truth

aleurone layer (əˈlʊərən, -rəʊn) *or* **aleuron** (əˈlʊərɒn, -rən) NOUN the outer protein-rich layer of certain seeds, esp of cereal grains.
▷HISTORY C19: from Greek *aleuron* flour

Aleut (æˈluːt, ˈæliːˌʊt) NOUN 1 a member of a people inhabiting the Aleutian Islands and SW Alaska, related to the Eskimos. 2 the language of this people, related to Eskimo.
▷HISTORY from Russian *aleút,* probably of Chukchi origin

Aleutian (əˈluːʃən) ADJECTIVE 1 of, denoting, or relating to the Aleutian Islands, the Aleuts, or their language. ◆ NOUN 2 another word for **Aleut.**

Aleutian Islands PLURAL NOUN a chain of over 150 volcanic islands, extending southwestwards from the Alaska Peninsula between the N Pacific and the Bering Sea.

A level NOUN (in Britain) 1 **a** a public examination in a subject taken for the General Certificate of Education (**GCE**), usually at the age of 17–18. **b** the course leading to this examination. **c** (*as modifier*): *A-level maths.* 2 a pass in a particular subject at A level: *she has three A levels.*

A2 level NOUN *Brit education* **a** the second part of an A-level course, taken after the AS level examination. **b** the examination at the end of this.

alevin (ˈælɪvɪn) NOUN a young fish, esp a young salmon or trout.
▷HISTORY C19: from French, from Old French *alever* to rear (young), from Latin *levāre* to raise

alewife (ˈeɪlˌwaɪf) NOUN, *plural* **-wives.** a North American fish, *Pomolobus pseudoharengus,* similar to the herring *Clupea harengus:* family *Clupeidae* (herrings).
▷HISTORY C19: perhaps an alteration (through influence of *alewife,* that is, a large rotund woman, alluding to the fish's shape) of French *alose* shad

Alexander Archipelago (ˌælɪgˈzɑːndə) NOUN a group of over 1000 islands along the coast of SE Alaska.

Alexander I Island NOUN an island of Antarctica, west of Palmer Land, in the Bellingshausen Sea. Length: about 378 km (235 miles).

alexanders (ˌælɪgˈzɑːndəz) NOUN 1 a biennial umbelliferous plant, *Smyrnium olusatrum,* native to S Europe, with dense umbels of yellow-green flowers and black fruits. 2 **golden alexanders.** an umbelliferous plant, *Zizia aurea,* of North America, having yellow flowers in compound umbels.
▷HISTORY Old English, from Medieval Latin *alexandrum,* probably (through association in folk etymology with *Alexander* the Great) changed from Latin *holus atrum* black vegetable

Alexander technique NOUN a technique for developing awareness of one's posture and movement in order to improve it.
▷HISTORY C20: named after Frederick Matthias *Alexander* (died 1955), Australian actor who originated it

Alexandria (ˌælɪgˈzændrɪə, -ˈzɑːn-) NOUN the chief port of Egypt, on the Nile Delta: cultural centre of ancient times, founded by Alexander the Great (332 B.C.). Pop.: 3 328 196 (1996). Arabic name: **El Iskandariyah.**

Alexandrian (ˌælɪgˈzændrɪən, -ˈzɑːn-) ADJECTIVE 1 of or relating to Alexander the Great (356–323 B.C.), king of Macedon, who conquered Greece (336), Egypt (331), and the Persian Empire (328). 2 of or relating to Alexandria in Egypt. 3 relating to the Hellenistic philosophical, literary, and scientific ideas that flourished in Alexandria in the last three centuries B.C. 4 (of writers, literary works, etc.) erudite and imitative rather than original or creative. ◆ NOUN 5 a native or inhabitant of Alexandria.

Alexandrine (ˌælɪgˈzændraɪn, -drɪn, -ˈzɑːn-) *Prosody* ◆ NOUN 1 a line of verse having six iambic feet, usually with a caesura after the third foot. ◆ ADJECTIVE 2 of, characterized by, or written in Alexandrines.
▷HISTORY C16: from French *alexandrin,* from *Alexandre,* title of 15th-century poem written in this metre

alexandrite (ˌælɪgˈzændraɪt) NOUN a green variety of chrysoberyl used as a gemstone.
▷HISTORY C19: named after *Alexander* I (1777–1825), tsar of Russia (1801–25); see -ITE[1]

Alexandroúpolis (*Greek* alɛksanˈðrupɔlis) NOUN a port in NE Greece, in W Thrace. Pop.: 39 283 (1991 est.). Former name (until the end of World War I): **Dedéagach.**

alexia (əˈlɛksɪə) NOUN a disorder of the central nervous system characterized by impaired ability to read. Nontechnical name: **word blindness.** Compare **aphasia.**
▷HISTORY C19: from New Latin, from A-[1] + Greek *lexis* speech; influenced in meaning by Latin *legere* to read

alexin (əˈlɛksɪn) NOUN *Immunol* a former word for **complement** (sense 9).
▷HISTORY C19: from German, from Greek *alexein* to ward off
▸**alexinic** (ˌælɪkˈsɪnɪk) ADJECTIVE

alexipharmic (əˌlɛksɪˈfɑːmɪk) *Med* ◆ ADJECTIVE 1 acting as an antidote. ◆ NOUN 2 an antidote.
▷HISTORY C17: from Greek *alexipharmakon* antidote, from *alexein* to avert + *pharmakon* drug

alf (ælf) NOUN *Austral slang* an uncultivated Australian.
▷HISTORY from shortening of the name *Alfred*

ALF (in Britain) ABBREVIATION FOR **Animal Liberation Front.**

Alfa (ˈælfə) NOUN a variant spelling of **Alpha** (sense 2).

alfalfa (ælˈfælfə) NOUN a leguminous plant, *Medicago sativa,* of Europe and Asia, having compound leaves with three leaflets and clusters of small purplish flowers. It is widely cultivated for forage and as a nitrogen fixer and used as a commercial source of chlorophyll. Also called: **lucerne.**
▷HISTORY C19: from Spanish, from Arabic *al-fasfasah,* from *al* the + *fasfasah* the best sort of fodder

Al Fatah (æl ˈfætə) NOUN See **Fatah.**

alfilaria *or* **alfileria** (ˌælfɪˈlɛərɪə) NOUN a geraniaceous plant, *Erodium cicutarium,* native to Europe, with finely divided leaves and small pink or purplish flowers. It is widely naturalized in North America and is used as fodder. Also called: **pin clover.**
▷HISTORY via American Spanish from Spanish *alfilerillo,* from *alfiler* pin, from Arabic *al-khilāl* the thorn

alforja (ælˈfɔːdʒə) NOUN *Southwestern US* a saddlebag made of leather or canvas.
▷HISTORY C17: from Spanish, from Arabic *al-khurj* the saddlebag

alfresco (ælˈfrɛskəʊ) ADJECTIVE, ADVERB in the open air.
▷HISTORY C18: from Italian: in the cool

Alfvén wave (æˈvɛn) NOUN a generally transverse magnetohydrodynamic wave that is propagated in a plasma.
▷HISTORY C20: after Hannes Olaf Gosta *Alfvén* (1908–95), Swedish physicist

Alg. ABBREVIATION FOR Algeria(n).

algae (ˈældʒiː) PLURAL NOUN, *singular* **alga** (ˈælgə). unicellular or multicellular organisms formerly classified as plants, occurring in fresh or salt water or moist ground, that have chlorophyll and other pigments but lack true stems, roots, and leaves. Algae, which are now regarded as protoctists, include the seaweeds, diatoms, and spirogyra.
▷HISTORY C16: from Latin, plural of *alga* seaweed, of uncertain origin
▸**algal** (ˈælgəl) ADJECTIVE

algarroba *or* **algaroba** (ˌælgəˈrəʊbə) NOUN 1 another name for **mesquite** or **carob.** 2 the edible pod of these trees.
▷HISTORY C19: from Spanish, from Arabic *al* the + *kharrūbah* CAROB

Algarve (ælˈgɑːv) NOUN **the.** an area in the south of Portugal, on the Atlantic; it approximately corresponds to the administrative district of Faro: fishing and tourism important.

algebra (ˈældʒɪbrə) NOUN 1 a branch of mathematics in which arithmetical operations and relationships are generalized by using alphabetic symbols to represent unknown numbers or members of specified sets of numbers. 2 the branch of mathematics dealing with more abstract formal structures, such as sets, groups, fields, etc.
▷HISTORY C14: from Medieval Latin, from Arabic *al-jabr* the bone-setting, reunification, mathematical reduction
▸**algebraist** (ˌældʒɪˈbreɪɪst) NOUN

algebraic (ˌældʒɪˈbreɪɪk) *or* **algebraical** ADJECTIVE 1 of or relating to algebra: *an algebraic expression.* 2 using or relating to finite numbers, operations, or relationships.
▸**ˌalgeˈbraically** ADVERB

algebraic function NOUN *Maths* any function which can be constructed in a finite number of steps from the elementary operations and the inverses of any function already constructed. Compare **transcendental function.**

algebraic notation NOUN *Chess* the standard method of denoting the squares on the chessboard, by allotting a letter, a, b, c, up to h, to each of the files running up the board from White's side, starting from the left, and a number to each of the ranks across the board, starting with White's first rank.

algebraic number NOUN any number that is a root of a polynomial equation having rational coefficients such as √2 but not π. Compare **transcendental number.**

Algeciras (ˌældʒɪˈsɪrəs; *Spanish* alxeˈθiras) NOUN a port and resort in SW Spain, on the Strait of Gibraltar: scene of a conference of the Great Powers in 1906. Pop.: 101 972 (1998 est.).

Algeria (ælˈdʒɪərɪə) NOUN a republic in NW Africa, on the Mediterranean: became independent in 1962, after more than a century of French rule; one-party constitution adopted in 1976; religious extremists led a campaign of violence from 1988 until 2000; consists chiefly of the N Sahara, with the Atlas Mountains in the north, and contains rich deposits of oil and natural gas. Official language: Arabic; French also widely spoken, and Berber. Religion: Muslim. Currency: dinar. Capital: Algiers. Pop.: 30 821 000 (2001 est.). Area: about 2 382 800 sq. km (920 000 sq. miles). French name: **Algérie** (alʒeri).

Algerian (ælˈdʒɪərɪən) ADJECTIVE 1 of or relating to Algeria or its inhabitants. ◆ NOUN 2 a native or inhabitant of Algeria.

algerine (ˌældʒəˈriːn) NOUN a soft striped woollen cloth.
▷HISTORY C19: from French, from *algérien* Algerian: because the cloth was originally made in Algeria

Algerine (ˌældʒəˈriːn) ADJECTIVE 1 of or relating to Algeria or its inhabitants. ◆ NOUN 2 a native or inhabitant of Algeria.

algesia (ælˈdʒiːzɪə, -sɪə) NOUN *Physiol* the capacity to feel pain.
▷HISTORY New Latin from Greek *algēsis* sense of pain
▸**alˈgesic** *or* **alˈgetic** ADJECTIVE

-algia NOUN COMBINING FORM denoting pain or a painful condition of the part specified: *neuralgia; odontalgia.*
▷HISTORY from Greek *algos* pain
▸**-algic** ADJECTIVE COMBINING FORM

algicide (ˈældʒɪˌsaɪd) NOUN any substance that kills algae.

algid (ˈældʒɪd) ADJECTIVE *Med* chilly or cold.
▷HISTORY C17: from Latin *algidus,* from *algēre* to be cold
▸**alˈgidity** NOUN

Algiers (ælˈdʒɪəz) NOUN the capital of Algeria, an ancient port on the Mediterranean; until 1830 a centre of piracy. Pop.: 1 519 570 (1998). Arabic name: **Al-Jezair** (ˌældʒɛˈzɑːɪə). French name: **Alger** (alʒe).

algin (ˈældʒɪn) NOUN alginic acid or one of its esters or salts, esp the gelatinous solution obtained as a by-product in the extraction of iodine from seaweed, used in mucilages and for thickening jellies.

alginate (ˈældʒɪˌneɪt) NOUN a salt or ester of alginic acid.

alginic acid (ælˈdʒɪnɪk) NOUN a white or yellowish powdery polysaccharide having marked hydrophilic properties. Extracted from kelp, it is used mainly in the food and textile industries and in cosmetics and pharmaceuticals. Formula: $(C_6H_8O_6)_n$; molecular wt.: 32 000–250 000.

algo- COMBINING FORM denoting pain: *algometer; algophobia.*
▷HISTORY from Greek *algos* pain

algoid (ˈælgɔɪd) ADJECTIVE resembling or relating to algae.

Algol[1] (ˈælgɒl) NOUN the second brightest star in Perseus, the first known eclipsing binary. Visual magnitude: 2.2–3.5; period: 68.8 hours; spectral type (brighter component): B8V.
▷HISTORY C14: from Arabic *al ghūl* the GHOUL

Algol[2] (ˈælgɒl) NOUN a computer programming language designed for mathematical and scientific purposes; a high-level language.
▷HISTORY C20 *alg(orithmic) o(riented) l(anguage)*

algolagnia (ˌælgəˈlægnɪə) NOUN a perversion in which sexual pleasure is gained from the experience or infliction of pain. See also **sadism, masochism.**
▸ˌ**algoˈlagnic** ADJECTIVE ▸ˌ**algoˈlagnist** NOUN

algology (ælˈgɒlədʒɪ) NOUN the branch of biology concerned with the study of algae.
▸**algological** (ˌælgəˈlɒdʒɪkᵊl) ADJECTIVE ▸ˌ**algoˈlogically** ADVERB ▸**alˈgologist** NOUN

algometer (ælˈgɒmɪtə) NOUN an instrument for measuring sensitivity to pressure (**pressure algometer**) or to pain.
▸**alˈgometry** NOUN

Algonkian (ælˈgɒŋkɪən) NOUN, ADJECTIVE 1 an obsolete term for **Proterozoic.** 2 a variant of **Algonquian.**

Algonquian (ælˈgɒŋkɪən, -kwɪ-) *or* **Algonkian** NOUN 1 a family of North American Indian languages whose speakers ranged over an area stretching from the Atlantic between Newfoundland and Delaware to the Rocky Mountains, including Micmac, Mahican, Ojibwa, Fox, Blackfoot, Cheyenne, and Shawnee. Some linguists relate it to Muskogean in a Macro-Algonquian phylum. 2 (*plural* **-ans** *or* **-an**) a member of any of the North American Indian peoples that speak one of these languages. ◆ ADJECTIVE 3 denoting, belonging to, or relating to this linguistic family or its speakers.

Algonquin (ælˈgɒŋkɪn, -kwɪn) *or* **Algonkin** (ælˈgɒŋkɪn) NOUN 1 (*plural* **-quins, -quin** *or* **-kins, -kin**) a member of a North American Indian people formerly living along the St Lawrence and Ottawa Rivers in Canada. 2 the language of this people, a dialect of Ojibwa. ◆ NOUN, ADJECTIVE 3 a variant of **Algonquian.**
▷HISTORY C17: from Canadian French, earlier written as *Algoumequin;* perhaps related to Micmac *algoomaking* at the fish-spearing place

Algonquin Park NOUN a provincial park in S Canada, in E Ontario, containing over 1200 lakes. Area: 7100 sq. km (2741 sq. miles).

algophobia (ˌælgəˈfəʊbɪə) NOUN *Psychiatry* an acute fear of experiencing or witnessing bodily pain.

algor (ˈælgɔː) NOUN *Med, obsolete* chill.
▷HISTORY C15: from Latin

algorism (ˈælgəˌrɪzəm) NOUN 1 the Arabic or decimal system of counting. 2 the skill of computation using any system of numerals. 3 another name for **algorithm.**
▷HISTORY C13: from Old French *algorisme,* from Medieval Latin *algorismus,* from Arabic *al-khuwārizmi,* from the name of abu-Ja'far Mohammed ibn-Mūsa *al-Khuwārizmi,* ninth-century Persian mathematician
▸ˌ**algoˈrismic** ADJECTIVE

algorithm (ˈælgəˌrɪðəm) NOUN 1 a logical arithmetical or computational procedure that if correctly applied ensures the solution of a problem. Compare **heuristic.** 2 *Logic, maths* a recursive procedure whereby an infinite sequence of terms can be generated. ◆ Also called: **algorism.**
▷HISTORY C17: changed from ALGORISM, through influence of Greek *arithmos* number
▸ˌ**algoˈrithmic** ADJECTIVE ▸ˌ**algoˈrithmically** ADVERB

Alhambra (ælˈhæmbrə) NOUN a citadel and palace in Granada, Spain, built for the Moorish kings during the 13th and 14th centuries: noted for its rich ornamentation.
▸**Alhambresque** (ˌælhæmˈbrɛsk) ADJECTIVE

Al Hijrah *or* **Al Hijra** (æl ˈhɪdʒrə) NOUN an annual Muslim festival marking the beginning of the Muslim year. It commemorates Mohammed's move from Mecca to Medina and involves the exchange of gifts and the telling of stories about Mohammed. See also **Hegira.**
▷HISTORY from Arabic, *hijrah* emigration or flight

Al Hufuf *or* **Al Hofuf** (æl huˈfuːf) NOUN a town in E Saudi Arabia: a trading centre with nearby oilfields and oases. Pop.: 225 847 (1992).

alias (ˈeɪlɪəs) ADVERB 1 at another time or place known as or named: *Dylan, alias Zimmerman.* ◆ NOUN, *plural* **-ases.** 2 an assumed name.
▷HISTORY C16: from Latin *aliās* (adverb) otherwise, at another time, from *alius* other

aliasing (ˈeɪlɪəsɪŋ) NOUN *Radio, television* the error in a vision or sound signal arising from limitations in the system that generates or processes the signal.

Ali Baba (ˈælɪ ˈbɑːbə) NOUN (in *The Arabian Nights' Entertainments*) a poor woodcutter who discovers that the magic words "open sesame" will open the doors of the cave containing the treasure of the Forty Thieves.

alibi (ˈælɪˌbaɪ) NOUN, *plural* **-bis.** 1 *Law* **a** a defence by an accused person that he was elsewhere at the time the crime in question was committed. **b** the evidence given to prove this. 2 *Informal* an excuse. ◆ VERB 3 (*tr*) to provide with an alibi.
▷HISTORY C18: from Latin *alibī* elsewhere, from *alius* other + *-bī* as in *ubī* where

Alicante (ˌælɪˈkæntɪ) NOUN a port in SE Spain: commercial centre. Pop.: 272 432 (1998 est.).

Alice (ˈælɪs) *or* **the Alice** NOUN *Austral slang* short for **Alice Springs.**

Alice band NOUN an ornamental band worn across the front of the hair to hold it back from the face.

Alice-in-Wonderland ADJECTIVE fantastic; irrational.
▷HISTORY C20: alluding to the absurdities of Wonderland in Lewis Carroll's book

Alice Springs NOUN a town in central Australia, in the Northern Territory, in the Macdonnell Ranges. Pop.: 24 852 (1994). Former name (until 1931): **Stuart.**

alicyclic (ˌælɪˈsaɪklɪk, -ˈsɪk-) ADJECTIVE (of an organic compound) having aliphatic properties, in spite of the presence of a ring of carbon atoms.
▷HISTORY C19: from German *alicyclisch,* from ALI(PHATIC) + CYCLIC

alidade (ˈælɪˌdeɪd) *or* **alidad** (ˈælɪˌdæd) NOUN 1 a surveying instrument used in plane-tabling for drawing lines of sight on a distant object and taking angular measurements. 2 the upper rotatable part of a theodolite, including the telescope and its attachments.
▷HISTORY C15: from French, from Medieval Latin *allidada,* from Arabic *al-'idāda* the revolving radius of a circle

alien (ˈeɪljən, ˈeɪlɪən) NOUN 1 a person owing allegiance to a country other than that in which he lives; foreigner. 2 any being or thing foreign to the environment in which it now exists. 3 (in science fiction) a being from another world, sometimes specifically an extraterrestrial. ◆ ADJECTIVE 4 unnaturalized; foreign. 5 having foreign allegiance: *alien territory.* 6 unfamiliar; strange: *an alien quality in a work of art.* 7 (*postpositive* and foll by *to*) repugnant or opposed (to): *war is alien to his philosophy.* 8 (in science fiction) of or from another world. ◆ VERB 9 (*tr*) *Rare* to transfer (property, etc.) to another.
▷HISTORY C14: from Latin *aliēnus* foreign, from *alius* other
▸**alienage** (ˈeɪljənɪdʒ, ˈeɪlɪə-) NOUN

alienable (ˈeɪljənəbᵊl, ˈeɪlɪə-) ADJECTIVE *Law* (of property) transferable to another owner.
▸ˌ**alienaˈbility** NOUN

alienate (ˈeɪljəˌneɪt, ˈeɪlɪə-) VERB (*tr*) 1 to cause (a friend, sympathizer, etc.) to become indifferent, unfriendly, or hostile; estrange. 2 to turn away; divert: *to alienate the affections of a person.* 3 *Law* to transfer the ownership of (property, title, etc.) to another person.
▸ˈ**alienˌator** NOUN

alienation (ˌeɪljəˈneɪʃən, ˌeɪlɪə-) NOUN 1 a turning away; estrangement. 2 the state of being an outsider or the feeling of being isolated, as from society. 3 *Psychiatry* a state in which a person's feelings are inhibited so that eventually both the self and the external world seem unreal. 4 *Law* **a** the transfer of property, as by conveyance or will, into the ownership of another. **b** the right of an owner to dispose of his property.

alienee (ˌeɪljəˈniː, ˌeɪlɪə-) NOUN *Law* a person to whom a transfer of property is made.

alienism (ˈeɪljəˌnɪzəm, ˈeɪlɪə-) NOUN *Obsolete* the study and treatment of mental illness.

alienist (ˈeɪljənɪst, ˈeɪlɪə-) NOUN 1 *US* a psychiatrist who specializes in the legal aspects of mental illness. 2 *Obsolete* a person who practises alienism.

alienor ('eɪljənə, 'eɪlɪə-) NOUN *Law* a person who transfers property to another.

aliform ('ælɪˌfɔːm, 'eɪlɪ-) ADJECTIVE wing-shaped; alar.
▷HISTORY C19: from New Latin *āliformis*, from Latin *āla* a wing

Aligarh (ˌɑːlɪ'gɜː, ˌælɪ-) NOUN a city in N India, in W Uttar Pradesh, with a famous Muslim university (1920). Pop.: 480 520 (1991).

alight[1] (ə'laɪt) VERB **alights, alighting, alighted** *or* **alit.** (*intr*) [1] (usually foll by *from*) to step out (of) or get down (from): *to alight from a taxi.* [2] to come to rest; settle; land: *a thrush alighted on the wall.*
▷HISTORY Old English *ālīhtan*, from A-[2] + *līhtan* to make less heavy, from *līht* LIGHT[2]

alight[2] (ə'laɪt) ADJECTIVE (*postpositive*), ADVERB [1] burning; on fire. [2] illuminated; lit up.
▷HISTORY Old English *ālīht* lit up, from *ālīhtan* to light up; see LIGHT[1]

alighting gear NOUN another name for **undercarriage** (sense 1).

align (ə'laɪn) VERB [1] to place or become placed in a line. [2] to bring (components or parts, such as the wheels of a car) into proper or desirable coordination or relation. [3] (*tr*; usually foll by *with*) to bring (a person, country, etc.) into agreement or cooperation with the policy, etc. of another person or group. [4] (*tr*) *Psychol* to integrate or harmonize the aims, practices, etc. of a group. [5] (usually followed by *with*) *Psychol* to identify with or match the behaviour, thoughts, etc. of another person.
▷HISTORY C17: from Old French *aligner*, from *à ligne* into line

alignment (ə'laɪnmənt) NOUN [1] arrangement in a straight line. [2] the line or lines formed in this manner. [3] alliance or union with a party, cause, etc. [4] proper or desirable coordination or relation of components. [5] a ground plan of a railway, motor road, etc. [6] *Archaeol* an arrangement of one or more ancient rows of standing stones, of uncertain significance. [7] *Psychol* integration or harmonization of aims, practices, etc. within a group. [8] *Psychol* identification with or matching of the behaviour, thoughts, etc. of another person.

alike (ə'laɪk) ADJECTIVE (*postpositive*) [1] possessing the same or similar characteristics: *they all look alike to me.* ◆ ADVERB [2] in the same or a similar manner, way, or degree: *they walk alike.*
▷HISTORY Old English *gelīc*; see LIKE[1]

aliment NOUN ('ælɪmənt) [1] something that nourishes or sustains the body or mind. [2] *Scots Law* another term for **alimony.** ◆ VERB ('ælɪˌmɛnt) [3] (*tr*) *Obsolete* to support or sustain.
▷HISTORY C15: from Latin *alimentum* food, from *alere* to nourish
▸ˌ**ali'mental** ADJECTIVE

alimentary (ˌælɪ'mɛntərɪ, -trɪ) ADJECTIVE [1] of or relating to nutrition. [2] providing sustenance or nourishment. [3] *Scots Law* free from the claims of creditors: *an alimentary trust.*

alimentary canal *or* **tract** NOUN the tubular passage extending from the mouth to the anus, through which food is passed and digested.

alimentation (ˌælɪmɛn'teɪʃən) NOUN [1] nourishment. [2] sustenance; support.
▸ˌ**ali'mentative** ADJECTIVE

alimony ('ælɪmənɪ) NOUN *Law* (formerly) an allowance paid under a court order by one spouse to another when they are separated but not divorced. See also **maintenance.**
▷HISTORY C17: from Latin *alimōnia* sustenance, from *alere* to nourish

aline (ə'laɪn) VERB a rare spelling of **align.**
▸**a'linement** NOUN ▸**a'liner** NOUN

A-line ADJECTIVE (of a garment, esp a skirt or dress) flaring slightly from the waist or shoulders.

aliped ('ælɪˌpɛd) ADJECTIVE [1] (of bats and similar animals) having the digits connected by a winglike membrane. ◆ NOUN [2] an aliped animal.
▷HISTORY C19: from Latin *ālipēs* having winged feet, from *āla* wing + -PED

aliphatic (ˌælɪ'fætɪk) ADJECTIVE (of an organic compound) not aromatic, esp having an open chain structure, such as alkanes, alkenes, and alkynes.
▷HISTORY C19: from Greek *aleiphat-*, *aleiphar* oil

aliquant ('ælɪkwənt) ADJECTIVE *Maths* of, signifying, or relating to a quantity or number that is not an exact divisor of a given quantity or number: *5 is an aliquant part of 12.* Compare **aliquot** (sense 1).
▷HISTORY C17: from New Latin, from Latin *aliquantus* somewhat, a certain quantity of

aliquot ('ælɪˌkwɒt) ADJECTIVE [1] *Maths* of, signifying, or relating to an exact divisor of a quantity or number: *3 is an aliquot part of 12.* Compare **aliquant.** [2] consisting of equal quantities: *the sample was divided into five aliquot parts.* ◆ NOUN [3] an aliquot part.
▷HISTORY C16: from Latin: several, a few

alison ('ælɪsᵊn) NOUN [1] **sweet alison.** another name for **sweet alyssum.** [2] **small alison.** a rare compact annual, *Alyssum alyssoides,* having small yellow flowers: family *Brassicaceae* (crucifers).
▷HISTORY altered from ALYSSUM

A list NOUN **a** the most socially desirable category. **b** (*as modifier*): *an A-list event.* ◆ Compare **B list.**

alit (ə'lɪt) VERB a rare past tense and past participle of **alight[1]**.

aliterate (eɪ'lɪtərɪt) NOUN [1] a person who is able to read but disinclined to do so. ◆ ADJECTIVE [2] of or relating to aliterates.

aliunde (ˌeɪlɪ'ʌndɪ) ADVERB, ADJECTIVE from a source extrinsic to the matter, document, or instrument under consideration: *evidence aliunde.*
▷HISTORY Latin: from elsewhere

alive (ə'laɪv) ADJECTIVE (*postpositive*) [1] (of people, animals, plants, etc.) living; having life. [2] in existence; active: *they kept hope alive; the tradition was still alive.* [3] (*immediately postpositive and usually used with a superlative*) of those living; now living: *the happiest woman alive.* [4] full of life; lively: *she was wonderfully alive for her age.* [5] (usually foll by *with*) animated: *a face alive with emotion.* [6] (foll by *to*) aware (of); sensitive (to). [7] (foll by *with*) teeming (with): *the mattress was alive with fleas.* [8] *Electronics* another word for **live[2]** (sense 11). [9] **alive and kicking.** (of a person) active and in good health. [10] **look alive!** hurry up! get busy!
▷HISTORY Old English *on līfe* in LIFE
▸**a'liveness** NOUN

aliyah NOUN *Judaism* [1] (ali'ja) (*plural* **-yoth** (-'jɒt)) immigration to the Holy Land. [2] (ə'liːə) the honour of being called to read from the Torah.
▷HISTORY from Hebrew, literally: act of going up, ascent

alizarin (ə'lɪzərɪn) NOUN a brownish-yellow powder or orange-red crystalline solid used as a dye and in the manufacture of other dyes. Formula: $C_6H_4(CO)_2C_6H_2(OH)_2$.
▷HISTORY C19: probably from French *alizarine,* probably from Arabic *al-'asārah* the juice, from *'asara* to squeeze

alk. ABBREVIATION FOR alkali.

alkahest *or* **alcahest** ('ælkəˌhɛst) NOUN the hypothetical universal solvent sought by alchemists.
▷HISTORY C17: apparently coined by Paracelsus on the model of Arabic words

alkali ('ælkəˌlaɪ) NOUN, *plural* **-lis** *or* **-lies.** [1] *Chem* a soluble base or a solution of a base. [2] a soluble mineral salt that occurs in arid soils and some natural waters.
▷HISTORY C14: from Medieval Latin, from Arabic *al-qili* the ashes (of the plant saltwort)

alkalic (æl'kælɪk) ADJECTIVE [1] (of igneous rocks) containing large amounts of alkalis, esp sodium and potassium. [2] another word for **alkaline.**

alkali flat NOUN an arid plain encrusted with alkaline salts derived from the streams draining into it.

alkalify ('ælkəlɪˌfaɪ, æl'kæl-) VERB **-fies, -fying, -fied.** to make or become alkaline.

alkali metal NOUN any of the monovalent metals lithium, sodium, potassium, rubidium, caesium, and francium, belonging to group 1A of the periodic table. They are all very reactive and electropositive.

alkalimeter (ˌælkə'lɪmɪtə) NOUN [1] an apparatus for determining the concentration of alkalis in solution. [2] an apparatus for determining the quantity of carbon dioxide in carbonates.
▸**alkalimetric** (ˌælkəlɪ'mɛtrɪk) ADJECTIVE

alkalimetry (ˌælkə'lɪmɪtrɪ) NOUN determination of the amount of alkali or base in a solution, measured by an alkalimeter or by volumetric analysis.

alkaline ('ælkəˌlaɪn) ADJECTIVE having the properties of or containing an alkali.

alkaline earth NOUN [1] Also called: **alkaline earth metal** *or* **alkaline earth element.** any of the divalent electropositive metals beryllium, magnesium, calcium, strontium, barium, and radium, belonging to group 2A of the periodic table. [2] an oxide of one of the alkaline earth metals.

alkaline soil NOUN a soil that gives a pH reaction of 8.5 or above, found esp in dry areas where the soluble salts, esp of sodium, have not been leached away but have accumulated in the B horizon of the soil profile.

alkalinity (ˌælkə'lɪnɪtɪ) NOUN [1] the quality or state of being alkaline. [2] the amount of alkali or base in a solution, often expressed in terms of pH.

alkali soil NOUN a soil that gives a pH reaction of 8.5 or above, found esp in dry areas where the soluble salts, esp of sodium, have not been leached away but have accumulated in the B horizon of the soil profile.

alkalize *or* **alkalise** ('ælkəˌlaɪz) VERB (*tr*) to make alkaline.
▸'**alkaˌlizable** *or* '**alkaˌlisable** ADJECTIVE

alkaloid ('ælkəˌlɔɪd) NOUN any of a group of nitrogenous basic compounds found in plants, typically insoluble in water and physiologically active. Common examples are morphine, strychnine, quinine, nicotine, and caffeine.

alkalosis (ˌælkə'ləʊsɪs) NOUN an abnormal increase in the alkalinity of the blood and extracellular fluids.

alkane ('ælkeɪn) NOUN **a** any saturated aliphatic hydrocarbon with the general formula C_nH_{2n+2}. **b** (*as modifier*): *alkane series.* ◆ Also called: **paraffin.**

alkanet ('ælkəˌnɛt) NOUN [1] a European boraginaceous plant, *Alkanna tinctoria,* the roots of which yield a red dye. [2] Also called: **anchusin, alkannin.** the dye obtained from this plant. [3] any of certain hairy blue-flowered Old World plants of the boraginaceous genus *Anchusa* (or *Pentaglottis*), such as *A. sempervirens* of Europe. See also **bugloss.** [4] another name for **puccoon** (sense 1).
▷HISTORY C14: from Spanish *alcaneta,* diminutive of *alcana* henna, from Medieval Latin *alchanna,* from Arabic *al* the + *hinnā'* henna

alkene ('ælkiːn) NOUN **a** any unsaturated aliphatic hydrocarbon with the general formula C_nH_{2n}. Also called: **olefine, olefin. b** (*as modifier*): *alkene series.* ◆ Also called: **olefine.**

Alkmaar (*Dutch* 'ɑlkmaːr) NOUN a city in the W Netherlands, in North Holland. Pop.: 92 962 (1994).

alko *or* **alco** ('ælkəʊ) NOUN, *plural* **alkos, alcos.** *Austral slang* a heavy drinker or alcoholic.

Alkoran *or* **Alcoran** (ˌælkɒ'rɑːn) NOUN a less common name for the **Koran.**

alky *or* **alkie** ('ælkɪ) NOUN, *plural* **-kies.** *Slang* a heavy drinker or alcoholic.

alkyd resin ('ælkɪd) NOUN any synthetic resin made from a dicarboxylic acid, such as phthalic acid, and diols or triols: used in paints and adhesives.

alkyl ('ælkɪl) NOUN [1] (*modifier*) of, consisting of, or containing the monovalent group C_nH_{2n+1}: *alkyl group or radical.* [2] an organometallic compound, such as tetraethyl lead, containing an alkyl group bound to a metal atom.
▷HISTORY C19: from German, from *Alk*(*ohol*) ALCOHOL + -YL

alkylating agent ('ælkɪˌleɪtɪŋ) NOUN any cytotoxic drug containing alkyl groups, such as chlorambucil, that acts by damaging DNA; widely used in chemotherapy.

alkylation (ˌælkɪ'leɪʃən) NOUN [1] the attachment of an alkyl group to an organic compound, usually by the addition or substitution of a hydrogen atom or halide group. [2] the addition of an alkane hydrocarbon to an alkene in producing high-octane fuels.

alkyne ('ælkaɪn) NOUN **a** any unsaturated aliphatic hydrocarbon that has a formula of the type C_nH_{2n-2}. **b** (*as modifier*): *alkyne series.* ◆ Also called: **acetylene.**

all (ɔːl) DETERMINER [1] **a** the whole quantity or amount of; totality of; every one of a class: *all the rice; all men are mortal.* **b** (*as pronoun; functioning as singular or plural*): *all of it is nice; all are welcome.* **c** (*in combination with a noun used as a modifier*): *an all-ticket match; an all-amateur tournament; an all-night sitting.* [2] the greatest possible: *in all earnestness.* [3] any whatever: *to lose all hope of recovery; beyond all doubt.* [4] **above all.** most of all; especially. [5] **after all.** See **after** (sense 11). [6] **all along.** all the time. [7] **all but.** almost; nearly: *all but dead.* [8] **all of.** no less or smaller than: *she's all of thirteen years.* [9] **all over.** **a** finished; at an end: *the affair is all over between us.* **b** over the whole area (of something); everywhere (in, on, etc.): *all over England.* **c** Also (Irish): **all out.** typically; representatively (in the phrase **that's me (you, him, us, them,** *etc.*) **all over**). **d** unduly effusive towards. **e** *Sport* in a dominant position over. [10] See **all in.** [11] **all in all.** **a** everything considered: *all in all, it was a great success.* **b** the object of one's attention or interest: *you are my all in all.* [12] **all that.** Also: **that.** (*usually used with a negative*) *Informal* (intensifier): *she's not all that intelligent.* [13] **all the.** (foll by a comparative adjective or adverb) so much (more or less) than otherwise: *we must work all the faster now.* [14] **all too.** definitely but regrettably: *it's all too true.* [15] **and all.** *Brit informal* as well; too: *and you can take that smile off your face and all.* [16] **and all that.** *Informal* **a** and similar or associated things; et cetera: *coffee, tea, and all that will be served in the garden.* **b** used as a filler or to make what precedes more vague: in this sense, it often occurs with concessive force: *she was sweet and pretty and all that, but I still didn't like her.* **c** See **that** (sense 4). [17] **as all that.** as one might expect or hope: *she's not as pretty as all that, but she has personality.* [18] **at all.** **a** (*used with a negative or in a question*) in any way whatsoever or to any extent or degree: *I didn't know that at all.* **b** even so; anyway: *I'm surprised you came at all.* [19] **be all for.** *Informal* to be strongly in favour of. [20] **be all that.** *Informal, chiefly US* to be exceptionally good, talented, or attractive. [21] **for all.** **a** in so far as; to the extent that: *for all anyone knows, he was a baron.* **b** notwithstanding: *for all my pushing, I still couldn't move it.* [22] **for all that.** in spite of that: *he was a nice man for all that.* [23] **in all.** altogether: *there were five of them in all.* ◆ ADVERB [24] (in scores of games) apiece; each: *the score at half time was three all.* ◆ NOUN [25] (preceded by *my, your, his,* etc.) (one's) complete effort or interest: *to give your all; you are my all.* [26] totality or whole. ◆ Related prefixes **pan-, panto-.**
▷HISTORY Old English *eall;* related to Old High German *al,* Old Norse *allr,* Gothic *alls* all

all- COMBINING FORM a variant of **allo-** before a vowel.

alla breve ('ælə 'breɪvɪ; *Italian* 'alla 'breːve) NOUN [1] a musical time signature indicating two or four minims to a bar. ◆ ADJECTIVE, ADVERB [2] twice as fast as normal. Musical symbol: ¢.
▷HISTORY C19: Italian, literally: (according) to the breve

Allah ('ælə) NOUN *Islam* the Muslim name for God; the one Supreme Being.
▷HISTORY C16: from Arabic, from *al* the + *Ilāh* god; compare Hebrew *elōah*

Allahabad (ˌæləhə'bæd, -'bɑːd) NOUN a city in N India, in SE Uttar Pradesh at the confluence of the Ganges and Jumna Rivers: Hindu pilgrimage centre. Pop.: 792 858 (1991).

Allahu Akbar ('ælaˌhu 'akˌbaː) INTERJECTION *Islam* an exclamation used in the call to prayer and also used as a call to the defence of Muslims, an expression of approval, and a funeral litany.
▷HISTORY from Arabic, literally: God is most great

all-American ADJECTIVE *US* [1] representative of the whole of the United States. [2] composed exclusively of American members. [3] (of a person) typically American: *the company looks for all-American clean-cut college students.*

Allan-a-Dale (ˌælənə'deɪl) NOUN (in English balladry) a member of Robin Hood's band who saved his sweetheart from an enforced marriage and married her himself.

allanite ('æləˌnaɪt) NOUN a rare black or brown mineral consisting of the hydrated silicate of calcium, aluminium, iron, cerium, lanthanum, and other rare earth minerals. It occurs in granites and other igneous rocks. Formula: $(Ca,Ce,La,Y)_2(Al,Fe,Be,Mn,Mg)_3(SiO_4)_3(OH)$.
▷HISTORY C19: named after T. *Allan* (1777–1833), English mineralogist

allantoid (ə'læntɔɪd) ADJECTIVE [1] relating to or resembling the allantois. [2] *Botany* shaped like a sausage. ◆ NOUN [3] another name for **allantois.**
▷HISTORY C17: from Greek *allantoeidēs* sausage-shaped, from *allas* sausage + -OID
▸**allantoidal** (ˌælən'tɔɪdᵊl) ADJECTIVE

allantois (ˌælən'təʊɪs, ə'læntɔɪs) NOUN a membranous sac growing out of the ventral surface of the hind gut of embryonic reptiles, birds, and mammals. It combines with the chorion to form the mammalian placenta.
▷HISTORY C17: New Latin, irregularly from Greek *allantoeidēs* sausage-shaped, ALLANTOID
▸**allantoic** (ˌælən'təʊɪk) ADJECTIVE

alla prima ('ɑːlɑː 'priːmə) ADJECTIVE (of a painting) painted with a single layer of paint, in contrast to paintings built up layer by layer.
▷HISTORY C19: from Italian: at once

allargando (ˌɑːlɑː'gændəʊ) ADJECTIVE, ADVERB *Music* (to be performed) with increasing slowness.
▷HISTORY Italian, from *allargare* to make slow or broad

all-around ADJECTIVE (*prenominal*) the US equivalent of **all-round.**

allay (ə'leɪ) VERB [1] to relieve (pain, grief, etc.) or be relieved. [2] (*tr*) to reduce (fear, anger, etc.).
▷HISTORY Old English *ālecgan* to put down, from *lecgan* to LAY[1]

All Blacks PLURAL NOUN **the.** the international Rugby Union football team of New Zealand.
▷HISTORY so named because of the players' black playing strip

all clear NOUN [1] a signal, usually a siren, indicating that some danger, such as an air raid, is over. [2] an indication that obstacles are no longer present; permission to proceed: *he received the all clear on the plan.*

all-dayer (ˌɔːl'deɪə) NOUN an entertainment, such as a pop concert or film screening, that lasts all day.

all-dressed ADJECTIVE *Canadian* (of a hot dog, hamburger, etc.) served with all available garnishes.

allegation (ˌælɪ'geɪʃən) NOUN [1] the act of alleging. [2] an unproved statement or assertion, esp one in an accusation.

allege (ə'lɛdʒ) VERB (*tr; may take a clause as object*) [1] to declare in or as if in a court of law; state without or before proof: *he alleged malpractice.* [2] to put forward (an argument or plea) for or against an accusation, claim, etc. [3] *Archaic* to cite or quote, as to confirm.
▷HISTORY C14 *aleggen,* ultimately from Latin *allēgāre* to dispatch on a mission, from *lēx* law

alleged (ə'lɛdʒd) ADJECTIVE (*prenominal*) [1] stated or described to be such; presumed: *the alleged murderer.* [2] dubious: *an alleged miracle.*

allegedly (ə'lɛdʒɪdlɪ) ADVERB [1] reportedly; supposedly: *payments allegedly made to a former colleague.* [2] (*sentence modifier*) it is alleged that. ◆ INTERJECTION [3] an exclamation expressing disbelief or scepticism.

> **Language note** In recent years it has become common for speakers to include *allegedly* in statements that are controversial or possibly even defamatory. The implication is that, by saying *allegedly,* the speaker is distancing himself or herself from the controversy and even protecting himself or herself from possible prosecution. However, the effect created may be deliberate. The use of *allegedly* can be a signal that, although the statement may seem outrageous, it is in fact true: *He was drunk at work. Allegedly.* Conversely, it is also possible to use *allegedly* as an expression of ironic scepticism: *He's a hard worker. Allegedly.*

Allegheny Mountains (ˌælɪ'geɪnɪ) *or* **Alleghenies** PLURAL NOUN a mountain range in Pennsylvania, Maryland, Virginia, and West Virginia: part of the Appalachian system; rising from 600 m (2000 ft.) to over 1440 m (4800 ft.).

allegiance (ə'liːdʒəns) NOUN [1] loyalty, as of a subject to his sovereign or of a citizen to his country. [2] (in feudal society) the obligations of a vassal to his liege lord. See also **fealty, homage** (sense 2).
▷HISTORY C14: from Old French *ligeance,* from *lige* LIEGE

allegorical (ˌælɪ'gɒrɪkᵊl) *or* **allegoric** ADJECTIVE used in, containing, or characteristic of allegory.
▸**ˌalle'gorically** ADVERB

allegorize *or* **allegorise** ('ælɪgəˌraɪz) VERB [1] to transform (a story, narrative, fable, etc.) into or compose in the form of allegory. [2] (*tr*) to interpret allegorically.
▸**ˌallegori'zation** *or* **ˌallegori'sation** NOUN

allegory ('ælɪgərɪ) NOUN, *plural* **-ries.** [1] a poem, play, picture, etc., in which the apparent meaning of the characters and events is used to symbolize a deeper moral or spiritual meaning. [2] the technique or genre that this represents. [3] use of such symbolism to illustrate truth or a moral. [4] anything used as a symbol or emblem.
▷HISTORY C14: from Old French *allegorie,* from Latin *allēgoria,* from Greek, from *allēgorein* to speak figuratively, from *allos* other + *agoreuein* to make a speech in public, from *agora* a public gathering
▸**'allegorist** NOUN

allegretto (ˌælɪ'grɛtəʊ) *Music* ◆ ADJECTIVE, ADVERB [1] (to be performed) fairly quickly or briskly. ◆ NOUN, *plural* **-tos.** [2] a piece or passage to be performed in this manner.
▷HISTORY C19: diminutive of ALLEGRO

allegro (ə'leɪgrəʊ, -'lɛg-) *Music* ◆ ADJECTIVE, ADVERB [1] (to be performed) quickly, in a brisk lively manner. ◆ NOUN, *plural* **-gros.** [2] a piece or passage to be performed in this manner.
▷HISTORY C17: from Italian: cheerful, from Latin *alacer* brisk, lively

allele (ə'liːl) NOUN any of two or more variants of a gene that have the same relative position on homologous chromosomes and are responsible for alternative characteristics, such as smooth or wrinkled seeds in peas. Also called: **allelomorph** (ə'liːləˌmɔːf). See also **multiple alleles.**
▷HISTORY C20: from German *Allel,* shortened from *allelomorph,* from Greek *allēl-* one another + *morphē* form
▸**al'lelic** ADJECTIVE ▸**al'lelism** NOUN

allelopathy (ˌælɪ'lɒpəθɪ) NOUN the inhibitory effect of one living plant upon another by the release of toxic substances.
▷HISTORY from French *allélopathie,* from Greek *allēl-* one another + *pathos* suffering

alleluia (ˌælɪ'luːjə) INTERJECTION [1] praise the Lord! Used more commonly in liturgical contexts in place of *hallelujah.* ◆ NOUN [2] a song of praise to God.
▷HISTORY C14: via Medieval Latin from Hebrew *hallelūyāh*

allemande ('ælɪmænd; *French* almɑ̃d) NOUN [1] the first movement of the classical suite, composed in a moderate tempo in a time signature of four-four. [2] any of several German dances. [3] a figure in country dancing or square dancing by means of which couples change position in the set.
▷HISTORY C17: from French *danse allemande* German dance

Allen ('ælən) NOUN [1] **Bog of.** a region of peat bogs in central Ireland, west of Dublin. Area: over 10 sq. km (3.75 sq. miles). [2] **Lough.** a lake in Ireland, in county Leitrim.

Allen key NOUN an L-shaped tool consisting of a rod having a hexagonal cross section, used to turn a screw (**Allen screw**) with a hexagonal recess in the head. A different size of key is required for each size of screw.

Allentown ('ælənˌtaʊn) NOUN a city in E Pennsylvania, on the Lehigh River. Pop.: 106 632 (2000).

Alleppey ('ʌləpɪ) NOUN a port in S India, in Kerala on the Malabar Coast. Pop.: 174 666 (1991).

allergen ('æləˌdʒɛn) NOUN any substance capable of inducing an allergy.
▸**ˌaller'genic** ADJECTIVE

allergic (ə'lɜːdʒɪk) ADJECTIVE [1] of, relating to, having, or caused by an allergy. [2] (*postpositive;* foll by *to*) *Informal* having an aversion (to): *he's allergic to work.*

allergic rhinitis NOUN *Pathol* a technical name for **hay fever.**

allergist ('ælədʒɪst) NOUN a physician skilled in the diagnosis and treatment of diseases or conditions caused by allergy.

allergy ('ælədʒɪ) NOUN, *plural* **-gies.** 1 a hypersensitivity to a substance that causes the body to react to any contact with that substance. Hay fever is an allergic reaction to pollen. 2 *Informal* aversion: *he has an allergy to studying.*
▷**HISTORY** C20: from German *Allergie* (indicating a changed reaction), from Greek *allos* other + *ergon* activity

allethrin (æ'leθrɪn) NOUN a clear viscous amber-coloured liquid used as an insecticide and synergist. Formula: $C_{19}H_{26}O_3$; relative density: 1.005.
▷**HISTORY** C20: from ALL(YL) + (PYR)ETHRIN

alleviate (ə'li:vɪˌeɪt) VERB (*tr*) to make (pain, sorrow, etc.) easier to bear; lessen; relieve.
▷**HISTORY** C15: from Late Latin *alleviāre* to mitigate, from Latin *levis* light
▸**alˌleviˈation** NOUN ▸**alˈleviative** ADJECTIVE ▸**alˈleviˌator** NOUN

Language note See at **ameliorate.**

alley[1] ('ælɪ) NOUN 1 a narrow lane or passage, esp one between or behind buildings. 2 See **bowling alley.** 3 *Tennis, chiefly US* the space between the singles and doubles sidelines. 4 a walk in a park or garden, esp one lined with trees or bushes. 5 **up** (*or* **down**) **one's alley.** a variant of **up one's street** (see **street** (sense 8)).
▷**HISTORY** C14: from Old French *alee,* from *aler* to go, ultimately from Latin *ambulāre* to walk

alley[2] ('ælɪ) NOUN a large playing marble.
▷**HISTORY** C18: shortened and changed from ALABASTER

alley cat NOUN a homeless cat that roams in back streets.

alley gate NOUN a metal spiked gate erected behind a terrace of houses to deter burglars.

alleyway ('ælɪˌweɪ) NOUN a narrow passage; alley.

all-fired *Slang, chiefly US* ◆ ADJECTIVE 1 (*prenominal*) excessive; extreme. ◆ ADVERB 2 (intensifier): *don't be so all-fired sure of yourself!*
▷**HISTORY** altered from *hell-fired*

all-flying tail NOUN a type of aircraft tailplane in which the whole of the tailplane is moved for control purposes.

All Fools' Day NOUN another name for **April Fools' Day** (see **April fool**).

all fours NOUN 1 both the arms and legs of a person or all the legs of a quadruped (esp in the phrase **on all fours**). 2 another name for **seven-up.**

all hail INTERJECTION an archaic greeting or salutation.
▷**HISTORY** C14, literally: all health (to someone)

Allhallows (ˌɔ:l'hæləuz) NOUN 1 a less common term for **All Saints' Day.** 2 **Allhallows Eve.** a less common name for **Halloween.**

Allhallowtide (ˌɔ:l'hæləuˌtaɪd) NOUN the season of All Saints' Day (Allhallows).

allheal ('ɔ:lˌhi:l) NOUN any of several plants reputed to have healing powers, such as selfheal and valerian.

alliaceous (ˌælɪ'eɪʃəs) ADJECTIVE 1 of or relating to *Allium,* a genus of plants that have a strong onion or garlic smell and often have bulbs: family *Alliaceae.* The genus occurs in the N hemisphere and includes onion, garlic, leek, chive, and shallot. 2 tasting or smelling like garlic or onions. 3 of, relating to, or belonging to the *Alliaceae,* a family of flowering plants that includes the genus *Allium.*
▷**HISTORY** C18: from Latin *allium* garlic; see -ACEOUS

alliance (ə'laɪəns) NOUN 1 the act of allying or state of being allied; union; confederation. 2 a formal agreement or pact, esp a military one, between two or more countries to achieve a particular aim. 3 the countries involved in such an agreement. 4 a union between families through marriage. 5 affinity or correspondence in qualities or characteristics. 6 *Botany* a taxonomic category consisting of a group of related families; subclass.
▷**HISTORY** C13: from Old French *aliance,* from *alier* to ALLY

Alliance (ə'laɪəns) NOUN (in Britain) **a the.** the Social Democratic Party and the Liberal Party acting or regarded as a political entity from 1981 to 1988. **b** (*as modifier*): *an Alliance candidate.*

allied (ə'laɪd, 'ælaɪd) ADJECTIVE 1 joined, as by treaty, agreement, or marriage; united. 2 of the same type or class; related.

Allied ('ælaɪd) ADJECTIVE of or relating to the Allies.

Allier (*French* alje) NOUN 1 a department of central France, in Auvergne region. Capital: Moulins. Pop.: 344 721 (1999). Area: 7382 sq. km (2879 sq. miles). 2 a river in S central France, rising in the Cévennes and flowing north to the Loire. Length: over 403 km (250 miles).

allies ('ælaɪz) NOUN the plural of **ally.**

Allies ('ælaɪz) PLURAL NOUN 1 (in World War I) the powers of the Triple Entente (France, Russia, and Britain) together with the nations allied with them. 2 (in World War II) the countries that fought against the Axis. The main Allied powers were Britain and the Commonwealth countries, the US, the Soviet Union, France, China, and Poland. See also **Axis.**

alligator ('ælɪˌgeɪtə) NOUN 1 a large crocodilian, *Alligator mississipiensis,* of the southern US, having powerful jaws and sharp teeth and differing from the crocodiles in having a shorter and broader snout: family *Alligatoridae* (alligators and caymans). 2 a similar but smaller species, *A. sinensis,* occurring in China near the Yangtse River. 3 any crocodilian belonging to the family *Alligatoridae.* 4 any of various tools or machines having adjustable toothed jaws, used for gripping, crushing, or compacting.
▷**HISTORY** C17: from Spanish *el lagarto* the lizard, from Latin *lacerta*

alligator pear NOUN another name for **avocado.**

alligator pepper NOUN *Chiefly W African* 1 a tropical African zingiberaceous plant, *Amomum melegueta,* having red or orange spicy seed capsules. 2 the capsules or seeds of this plant, used as a spice.

all-important ADJECTIVE crucial; vital.

all in ADJECTIVE 1 (*postpositive*) *Informal* completely exhausted; tired out. ◆ ADVERB, ADJECTIVE (**all-in** *when prenominal*) 2 **a** with all expenses or costs included in the price: *the flat is one hundred pounds a week all in.* **b** (*prenominal*): *the all-in price is thirty pounds.*

all-inclusive ADJECTIVE including everything; comprehensive.

all-in wrestling NOUN another name for **freestyle** (sense 2b).

alliterate (ə'lɪtəˌreɪt) VERB 1 to contain or cause to contain alliteration. 2 (*intr*) to speak or write using alliteration.

alliteration (əˌlɪtə'reɪʃən) NOUN the use of the same consonant (**consonantal alliteration**) or of a vowel, not necessarily the same vowel (**vocalic alliteration**), at the beginning of each word or each stressed syllable in a line of verse, as in *around the rock the ragged rascal ran.*
▷**HISTORY** C17: from Medieval Latin *alliterātiō* (from Latin *al-* (see AD-) + *litera* letter), on the model of *obliterātiō* OBLITERATION
▸**alˈliterative** ADJECTIVE

allium ('ælɪəm) NOUN any plant of the genus *Allium,* such as the onion, garlic, shallot, leek, or chive: family *Alliaceae.*
▷**HISTORY** C19: from Latin: garlic

all-nighter (ˌɔ:l'naɪtə) NOUN an entertainment, such as a pop concert or film screening, that lasts all night.

allo- *or before a vowel* **all-** COMBINING FORM indicating difference, variation, or opposition: *allopathy; allomorph; allophone; allonym.*
▷**HISTORY** from Greek *allos* other, different

Alloa ('æləuə) NOUN a town in E central Scotland, the administrative centre of Clackmannanshire. Pop.: 18 842 (1991).

allocate ('æləˌkeɪt) VERB (*tr*) 1 to assign or allot for a particular purpose. 2 a less common word for **locate** (sense 2).
▷**HISTORY** C17: from Medieval Latin *allocāre,* from Latin *locāre* to place, from *locus* a place
▸**ˈalloˌcatable** ADJECTIVE

allocation (ˌælə'keɪʃən) NOUN 1 the act of allocating or the state of being allocated. 2 a part that is allocated; share. 3 *Accounting, Brit* a system of dividing overhead expenses between the various departments of a business. 4 *Social welfare* (in a Social Services Department) the process of assigning **referrals** to individual workers, thus changing their status to **cases.**

allochthonous (ə'lɒkθənəs) ADJECTIVE (of rocks, deposits, etc.) found in a place other than where they or their constituents were formed. Compare **autochthonous** (sense 1).
▷**HISTORY** C20: from Greek *allokhthon,* from ALLO- + *khthōn* (genitive *khthonos*) earth

allocution (ˌælə'kju:ʃən) NOUN *Rhetoric* a formal or authoritative speech or address, esp one that advises, informs, or exhorts.
▷**HISTORY** C17: from Late Latin *allocūtiō,* from Latin *alloquī* to address, from *loquī* to speak

allodial (ə'ləudɪəl) ADJECTIVE 1 (of land) held as an allodium. 2 (of tenure) characterized by or relating to the system of holding land in absolute ownership: *the allodial system.* 3 (of people) holding an allodium.

allodium (ə'ləudɪəm) *or* **allod** ('ælɒd) NOUN, *plural* **-lodia** (-'ləudɪə) *or* **-lods.** *History* lands held in absolute ownership, free from such obligations as rent or services due to an overlord. Also: **alodium.**
▷**HISTORY** C17: from Medieval Latin, from Old German *allōd* (unattested) entire property, from *al-* ALL + *-ōd* property; compare Old High German *ōt,* Old English *ēad* property

allogamy (ə'lɒgəmɪ) NOUN cross-fertilization in flowering plants.
▸**alˈlogamous** ADJECTIVE

allograft ('æləuˌgrɑ:ft) NOUN a tissue graft from a donor genetically unrelated to the recipient.

allograph ('æləˌgrɑ:f) NOUN 1 a document written by a person who is not a party to it. 2 a signature made by one person on behalf of another. Compare **autograph.** 3 *Linguistics* any of the written symbols that constitute a single grapheme: m *and* M *are allographs in the Roman alphabet.*
▸**allographic** (ˌælə'græfɪk) ADJECTIVE

allomerism (ə'lɒməˌrɪzəm) NOUN similarity of crystalline structure in substances of different chemical composition.
▸**allomeric** (ˌælə'merɪk) *or* **alˈlomerous** ADJECTIVE

allometry (ə'lɒmɪtrɪ) NOUN 1 the study of the growth of part of an organism in relation to the growth of the entire organism. 2 a change in proportion of any of the parts of an organism that occurs during growth.
▸**allometric** (ˌælə'metrɪk) ADJECTIVE

allomone ('æləˌməun) NOUN a chemical substance secreted externally by certain animals, such as insects, affecting the behaviour or physiology of another species detrimentally. Compare **pheromone.**

allomorph ('æləˌmɔ:f) NOUN 1 *Linguistics* any of the phonological representations of a single morpheme. For example, the final (s) and (z) sounds of *bets* and *beds* are allomorphs of the English noun-plural morpheme. 2 any of two or more different crystalline forms of a chemical compound, such as a mineral.
▸**ˌalloˈmorphic** ADJECTIVE

allomorphism (ˌælə'mɔ:fɪzəm) NOUN variation in the crystalline form of a chemical compound.

allonym ('ælənɪm) NOUN a name, often one of historical significance or that of another person, assumed by a person, esp an author.

allopath ('æləˌpæθ) *or* **allopathist** (ə'lɒpəθɪst) NOUN a person who practises or is skilled in allopathy.

allopathic (ˌælə'pæθɪk) ADJECTIVE of, relating to, or used in allopathy.
▸**ˌalloˈpathically** ADVERB

allopathy (ə'lɒpəθɪ) NOUN the orthodox medical method of treating disease, by inducing a condition different from or opposed to the cause of the disease. Compare **homeopathy.**
▸**allopathic** (ˌælə'pæθɪk) ADJECTIVE ▸**ˌalloˈpathically** ADVERB

allopatric (ˌælə'pætrɪk) ADJECTIVE (of biological speciation or species) taking place or existing in areas that are geographically separated from one another. Compare **sympatric.**
▷**HISTORY** C20: from ALLO- + *-patric,* from Greek *patris* native land
▸**ˌalloˈpatrically** ADVERB

allophane ('æləˌfeɪn) NOUN a variously coloured amorphous mineral consisting of hydrated

aluminium silicate and occurring in cracks in some sedimentary rocks.
▷**HISTORY** C19: from Greek *allophanēs* appearing differently, from ALLO- + *phainesthai* to appear

allophone ('ælə,fəʊn) NOUN 1 any of several speech sounds that are regarded as contextual or environmental variants of the same phoneme. In English the aspirated initial (p) in *pot* and the unaspirated (p) in *spot* are allophones of the phoneme /p/. 2 *Canadian* a Canadian whose native language is neither French nor English.
▸**allophonic** (,ælə'fɒnɪk) ADJECTIVE

allopolyploid (,ælə'pɒlɪ,plɔɪd) ADJECTIVE 1 (of cells, organisms, etc.) having more than two sets of haploid chromosomes inherited from different species. ◆ NOUN 2 an interspecific hybrid of this type that is therefore fertile. ◆ See also **autopolyploid, polyploid.**
▸**,allo'poly,ploidy** NOUN

allopurinol (,æləʊ'pjʊərɪ,nɒl) NOUN a synthetic drug that reduces blood concentrations of uric acid and is administered orally in the treatment of gout. Formula: $C_5H_4N_4O$.
▷**HISTORY** C20: from ALLO- + PURINE + -OL[1]

All-Ordinaries Index NOUN an index of share prices on the Australian Stock Exchange giving a weighted arithmetic average of 245 ordinary shares.

allosaur ('ælə,sɔː) *or* **allosaurus** (,ælə'sɔːrəs) NOUN any large carnivorous bipedal dinosaur of the genus *Antrodemus* (formerly *Allosaurus*), common in North America in late Jurassic times: suborder *Theropoda* (theropods).
▷**HISTORY** C19: from ALLO- + -SAUR

allosteric (,æləʊ'stɪərɪk) ADJECTIVE *Biochem* of, relating to, or designating a function of an enzyme in which the structure and activity of the enzyme are modified by the binding of a metabolic molecule.

allot (ə'lɒt) VERB **-lots, -lotting, -lotted.** (*tr*) 1 to assign or distribute (shares, etc.). 2 to designate for a particular purpose: *money was allotted to cover expenses.* 3 (foll by *to*) apportion: *we allotted two hours to the case.*
▷**HISTORY** C16: from Old French *aloter,* from *lot* portion, LOT

allotment (ə'lɒtmənt) NOUN 1 the act of allotting; apportionment. 2 a portion or amount allotted. 3 *Brit* a small piece of usually public land rented by an individual for cultivation.

allotrope ('ælə,trəʊp) NOUN any of two or more physical forms in which an element can exist: *diamond and graphite are allotropes of carbon.*

allotropous (ə'lɒtrəpəs) ADJECTIVE (of flowers) having the nectar accessible to any species of insect.

allotropy (ə'lɒtrəpɪ) *or* **allotropism** NOUN the existence of an element in two or more physical forms. The most common elements having this property are carbon, sulphur, and phosphorus.
▸**allotropic** (,ælə'trɒpɪk) ADJECTIVE ▸**,allo'tropically** ADVERB

all'ottava (ælə'tɑːvə) ADJECTIVE, ADVERB *Music* to be played an octave higher or lower than written. Symbol: 8va.
▷**HISTORY** Italian: at the octave

allottee (əlɒt'iː) NOUN a person to whom something is allotted.

allotype ('ælə,taɪp) NOUN 1 *Biology* an additional type specimen selected because of differences from the original type specimen, such as opposite sex or morphological details. 2 *Immunol* any of the variant forms of a particular immunoglobulin found among members of the same species.

all-out *Informal* ◆ ADJECTIVE 1 using one's maximum powers: *an all-out effort.* ◆ ADVERB **all out.** 2 to one's maximum effort or capacity: *he went all out on the home stretch.*

all-over ADJECTIVE covering the entire surface.

allow (ə'laʊ) VERB 1 (*tr*) to permit (to do something); let. 2 (*tr*) to set aside: *five hours were allowed to do the job.* 3 (*tr*) to let enter or stay: *they don't allow dogs.* 4 (*tr*) to acknowledge or concede (a point, claim, etc.). 5 (*tr*) to let have; grant: *he was allowed few visitors.* 6 (*intr;* foll by *for*) to take into account: *allow for delays.* 7 (*intr;* often foll by *of*) to permit; admit: *a question that allows of only one reply.* 8 (*tr; may take a clause as object*) *US dialect* to assert; maintain. 9 (*tr*) *Archaic* to approve; accept.
▷**HISTORY** C14: from Old French *alouer,* from Late Latin *allaudāre* to extol, influenced by Medieval Latin *allocāre* to assign, ALLOCATE

allowable (ə'laʊəb°l) ADJECTIVE permissible; admissible.
▸**al'lowably** ADVERB

allowance (ə'laʊəns) NOUN 1 an amount of something, esp money or food, given or allotted usually at regular intervals. 2 a discount, as in consideration for something given in part exchange or to increase business; rebate. 3 (in Britain) an amount of a person's income that is not subject to a particular tax and is therefore deducted before his or her liability to taxation is assessed. 4 a portion set aside to compensate for something or to cover special expenses. 5 *Brit education* a salary supplement given to a teacher who is appointed to undertake extra duties and responsibilities. 6 admission; concession. 7 the act of allowing; sanction; toleration. 8 something allowed. 9 **make allowances** (*or* **allowance**). (usually foll by *for*) **a** to take mitigating circumstances into account in consideration (of). **b** to allow (for). ◆ VERB 10 (*tr*) to supply (something) in limited amounts.

Alloway ('ælə,weɪ) NOUN a village in Scotland, in South Ayrshire, S of Ayr: birthplace of Robert Burns.

allowedly (ə'laʊɪdlɪ) ADVERB (*sentence modifier*) by general admission or agreement; admittedly.

alloy NOUN ('ælɔɪ, ə'lɔɪ) 1 a metallic material, such as steel, brass, or bronze, consisting of a mixture of two or more metals or of metallic elements with nonmetallic elements. Alloys often have physical properties markedly different from those of the pure metals. 2 something that impairs the quality or reduces the value of the thing to which it is added. ◆ VERB (ə'lɔɪ) (*tr*) 3 to add (one metal or element to another metal or element) to obtain a substance with a desired property. 4 to debase (a pure substance) by mixing with an inferior element. 5 to diminish or impair.
▷**HISTORY** C16: from Old French *aloi* a mixture, from *aloier* to combine, from Latin *alligāre,* from *ligāre* to bind

alloyed junction NOUN a semiconductor junction used in some junction transistors and formed by alloying metal contacts, functioning as emitter and collector regions, to a wafer of semiconductor that acts as the base region. Compare **diffused junction.**

allozyme ('æləʊ,zaɪm) NOUN any one of a number of different structural forms of the same enzyme coded for by a different allele.
▷**HISTORY** C20: from ALLO- + (EN)ZYME

all-powerful ADJECTIVE possessing supreme power; omnipotent.

all right ADJECTIVE (*postpositive except in slang use*), ADVERB 1 adequate; satisfactory. 2 unharmed; safe. 3 **all-right.** *US slang* **a** acceptable: *an all-right book.* **b** reliable: *an all-right guy.* ◆ SENTENCE SUBSTITUTE 4 very well: used to express assent. ◆ ADVERB 5 satisfactorily; adequately: *the car goes all right.* 6 without doubt: *he's a bad one, all right.* ◆ Also: **alright.**

> **Language note** See at **alright.**

all-round ADJECTIVE 1 efficient in all respects, esp in sport; versatile: *an all-round player.* 2 comprehensive; many-sided; not narrow: *an all-round education.*

all-rounder NOUN a versatile person, esp in a sport.

All Saints' Day NOUN a Christian festival celebrated on Nov. 1 to honour all the saints.

allseed ('ɔːl,siːd) NOUN any of several plants that produce many seeds, such as knotgrass.

all-sorts PLURAL NOUN a mixture, esp a mixture of liquorice sweets.

All Souls' Day NOUN *RC Church* a day of prayer (Nov. 2) for the dead in purgatory.

allspice ('ɔːl,spaɪs) NOUN 1 a tropical American myrtaceous tree, *Pimenta officinalis,* having small white flowers and aromatic berries. 2 the whole or powdered seeds of this berry used as a spice, having a flavour said to resemble a mixture of cinnamon, cloves, and nutmeg. ◆ Also called: **pimento, Jamaica pepper.**

all square ADJECTIVE (*postpositive*) 1 mutually clear of all debts or obligations. 2 (of contestants or teams in sports) having equal scores.

all-star ADJECTIVE (*prenominal*) consisting of star performers.

all-time ADJECTIVE (*prenominal*) *Informal* unsurpassed in some respect at a particular time: *an all-time record.*

all told ADVERB (*sentence modifier*) taking every one into account; in all: *we were seven all told.*

allude (ə'luːd) VERB (*intr;* foll by *to*) 1 to refer indirectly, briefly, or implicitly. 2 (loosely) to mention.
▷**HISTORY** C16: from Latin *allūdere,* from *lūdere* to sport, from *lūdus* a game

> **Language note** Avoid confusion with **elude.**

allure (ə'ljʊə, ə'lʊə) VERB 1 (*tr*) to entice or tempt (someone) to a person or place or to a course of action; attract. ◆ NOUN 2 attractiveness; appeal: *the cottage's allure was its isolation.*
▷**HISTORY** C15: from Old French *alurer,* from *lure* bait, LURE
▸**al'lurement** NOUN ▸**al'lurer** NOUN

alluring (ə'ljʊərɪŋ, ə'lʊə-) ADJECTIVE enticing; fascinating; attractive.
▸**al'luringly** ADVERB

allusion (ə'luːʒən) NOUN 1 the act of alluding. 2 a passing reference; oblique or obscure mention.
▷**HISTORY** C16: from Late Latin *allūsiō,* from Latin *allūdere* to sport with, ALLUDE

allusive (ə'luːsɪv) ADJECTIVE containing or full of allusions.
▸**al'lusively** ADVERB ▸**al'lusiveness** NOUN

alluvial (ə'luːvɪəl) ADJECTIVE 1 of or relating to alluvium. ◆ NOUN 2 another name for **alluvium.** 3 *Austral and NZ* alluvium containing any heavy mineral, esp gold.

alluvial fan *or* **cone** NOUN a fan-shaped accumulation of silt, sand, gravel, and boulders deposited by fast-flowing mountain rivers when they reach flatter land.

alluvial mining NOUN a method of extracting minerals by dredging alluvial deposits.

alluvion (ə'luːvɪən) NOUN 1 **a** the wash of the sea or of a river. **b** an overflow or flood. **c** matter deposited as sediment; alluvium. 2 *Law* the gradual formation of new land, as by the recession of the sea or deposit of sediment on a riverbed.
▷**HISTORY** C16: from Latin *alluviō* an overflowing, from *luere* to wash

alluvium (ə'luːvɪəm) NOUN, *plural* **-viums** *or* **-via** (-vɪə). a fine-grained fertile soil consisting of mud, silt, and sand deposited by flowing water on flood plains, in river beds, and in estuaries.
▷**HISTORY** C17: from Latin; see ALLUVION

All Whites PLURAL NOUN **the.** the former name for the international soccer team of New Zealand.
▷**HISTORY** so named because of the players' white strip and also an allusion to ALL BLACKS

ally VERB (ə'laɪ) **-lies, -lying, -lied.** (usually foll by *to* or *with*) 1 to unite or be united, esp formally, as by treaty, confederation, or marriage. 2 (*tr; usually passive*) to connect or be related, as through being similar or compatible. ◆ NOUN ('ælaɪ, ə'laɪ), *plural* **-lies.** 3 a country, person, or group allied with another. 4 a plant, animal, substance, etc., closely related to another in characteristics or form.
▷**HISTORY** C14: from Old French *alier* to join, from Latin *alligāre* to bind to, from *ligāre* to bind

allyl ('ælaɪl, 'ælɪl) NOUN (*modifier*) of, consisting of, or containing the monovalent group $CH_2{:}CHCH_2^-$: *allyl group or radical; allyl resin.*
▷**HISTORY** C19: from Latin *allium* garlic + -YL; first distinguished in a compound isolated from garlic

allyl alcohol NOUN a colourless pungent poisonous liquid used in the manufacture of resins, plasticizers, and other organic chemicals. Formula: $CH_2{:}CHCH_2OH$; relative density: 0.85; melting pt.: –129°C; boiling pt.: 96.9°C.

allyl resin NOUN any of several thermosetting synthetic resins made by polymerizing esters of allyl alcohol with a dibasic acid. They are used as adhesives.

allyl sulphide NOUN a colourless liquid that smells like garlic and is used as a flavouring. Formula: $(CH_2{:}CHCH_2)_2S$; relative density: 0.888; boiling pt.: 139°C.

allyou ('ɔːlˌjuː, 'ɔːˌjʊ) PRONOUN *(used in addressing more than one person) Caribbean informal* all of you.

Alma-Ata *(Russian* ɑl'maa'ta) NOUN the former name of **Almaty.**

Almada *(Portuguese* ɑl'maːdə) NOUN a town in S central Portugal, on the S bank of the Tagus estuary opposite Lisbon: statue of Christ 110 m (360 ft.) high, erected 1959. Pop.: 153 189 (1991).

Almadén *(Spanish* alma'θen) NOUN a town in S Spain: rich cinnabar mines, worked since Roman times. Pop.: 7723 (1991).

Al Madinah (ˌæl mæ'diːnə) NOUN the Arabic name for **Medina.**

Almagest ('ælməˌdʒest) NOUN [1] a work on astronomy compiled by Ptolemy in the 2nd century A.D containing a description of the geocentric system of the universe and a star catalogue. [2] *(sometimes not capital)* any of various similar medieval treatises on astrology, astronomy, or alchemy.
▷**HISTORY** C14: from Old French, from Arabic *al-majisti,* from *al* the + *majisti,* from Greek *megistē* greatest (treatise)

alma mater ('ælmə 'mɑːtə, 'meɪtə) NOUN *(often capitals)* one's school, college, or university.
▷**HISTORY** C17: from Latin: bountiful mother

almanac ('ɔːlməˌnæk) NOUN a yearly calendar giving statistical information on events and phenomena, such as the phases of the moon, times of sunrise and sunset, tides, anniversaries, etc. Also (archaic): **almanack.**
▷**HISTORY** C14: from Medieval Latin *almanachus,* perhaps from Late Greek *almenikhiaka*

almandine ('ælməndɪn, -ˌdaɪn) NOUN a deep violet-red garnet that consists of iron aluminium silicate and is used as a gemstone. Formula: $Fe_3Al_2(SiO_4)_3$.
▷**HISTORY** C17: from French, from Medieval Latin *alabandīna,* from *Alabanda,* ancient city of Asia Minor where these stones were cut

Al Mansûrah (ˌæl mæn'sʊərə) NOUN a variant of **El Mansûra.**

Al Marj (æl 'mɑːdʒ) NOUN an ancient town in N Libya: founded in about 550 B.C. Pop.: 25 166 (latest est.). Italian name: **Barce.**

Almaty (æl'mɑːtɪ) NOUN a city in SE Kazakhstan; capital of Kazakhstan (1991–97): an important trading centre. Pop.: 1 129 400 (1999). Former name (until 1927): **Verny.** Also called: **Alma-Ata.**

Almelo *(Dutch* 'ɑlməloː) NOUN a city in the E Netherlands, in Overijssel province. Pop.: 64 589 (1994).

almemar (æl'miːmɑː) NOUN *Judaism* (in Ashkenazic usage) the raised platform in a synagogue on which the reading desk stands. Also called: **bema, bimah, bima.**
▷**HISTORY** from Hebrew, from Arabic *al-minbar* the pulpit, platform

Almería *(Spanish* alme'ria) NOUN a port in S Spain. Pop.: 168 025 (1998 est.).

almighty (ɔːl'maɪtɪ) ADJECTIVE [1] all-powerful; omnipotent. [2] *Informal* (intensifier): *an almighty row.* ♦ ADVERB [3] *Informal* (intensifier): *an almighty loud bang.*
▸**al'mightily** ADVERB ▸**al'mightiness** NOUN

Almighty (ɔːl'maɪtɪ) NOUN **the.** another name for **God.**

Almohade ('ælməˌheɪd, -ˌheɪdiː) *or* **Almohad** ('ælməˌhæd) NOUN, *plural* **-hades** *or* **-hads.** a member of a group of puritanical Muslims, originally Berbers, who arose in S Morocco in the 12th century as a reaction against the corrupt Almoravides and who ruled Spain and all Maghrib from about 1147 to after 1213.
▷**HISTORY** from Arabic *al-muwahhid*

almond ('ɑːmənd) NOUN [1] a small widely cultivated rosaceous tree, *Prunus amygdalus,* that is native to W Asia and has pink flowers and a green fruit containing an edible nutlike seed. [2] the oval-shaped nutlike edible seed of this plant, which has a yellowish-brown shell. [3] *(modifier)* made of or containing almonds: *almond cake.* Related adjectives: **amygdaline, amygdaloid.** [4] **a** a pale yellowish-brown colour. **b** *(as adjective)*: *almond wallpaper.* [5] Also called: **almond green. a** yellowish-green colour. **b** *(as adjective)*: *an almond skirt.* [6] anything shaped like an almond nut.
▷**HISTORY** C13: from Old French *almande,* from Medieval Latin *amandula,* from Latin *amygdala,* from Greek *amugdalē*

almond-eyed ADJECTIVE having narrow oval eyes.

almoner ('ɑːmənə) NOUN [1] *Brit obsolete* a trained hospital social worker responsible for the welfare of patients. [2] (formerly) a person who distributes alms or charity on behalf of a household or institution.
▷**HISTORY** C13: from Old French *almosnier,* from *almosne* alms, from Vulgar Latin *alemosina* (unattested), from Late Latin *eleēmosyna;* see ALMS

almonry ('ɑːmənrɪ) NOUN, *plural* **-ries.** *History* the house of an almoner, usually the place where alms were given.
▷**HISTORY** C15: from Old French *almosnerie;* see ALMONER, ALMS

Almoravide (æl'mɔːrəˌvaɪd) *or* **Almoravid** (æl'mɔːrəvɪd) NOUN a member of a fanatical people of Berber origin and Islamic faith, who founded an empire in N Africa that spread over much of Spain in the 11th century A.D.
▷**HISTORY** from Arabic *al-murābitūn* the holy ones

almost ('ɔːlməʊst) ADVERB little short of being; very nearly.

alms (ɑːmz) PLURAL NOUN charitable donations of money or goods to the poor or needy.
▷**HISTORY** Old English *ælmysse,* from Late Latin *eleēmosyna,* from Greek *eleēmosunē* pity; see ELEEMOSYNARY

almshouse ('ɑːmzˌhaʊs) NOUN [1] *Brit history* a privately supported house offering accommodation to the aged or needy. [2] *Chiefly Brit* another name for **poorhouse.**

almsman ('ɑːmzmən) NOUN, *plural* **-men.** *Archaic* a person who gives or receives alms.

almswoman ('ɑːmzwʊmən) NOUN, *plural* **-women.** *Archaic* a woman who gives or receives alms.

almucantar *or* **almacantar** (ˌælmə'kæntə) NOUN [1] a circle on the celestial sphere parallel to the horizontal plane. [2] an instrument for measuring altitudes.
▷**HISTORY** C14: from French, from Arabic *almukantarāt* sundial

almuce ('ælmjuːs) NOUN a fur-lined hood or cape formerly worn by members of certain religious orders, more recently by canons of France.
▷**HISTORY** C15: from Old French *aumusse,* from Medieval Latin *almucia,* of unknown origin

Alnico ('ælnɪˌkəʊ) NOUN *Trademark* an alloy of aluminium, nickel, cobalt, iron, and copper, used to make permanent magnets.

alodium (ə'ləʊdɪəm) NOUN, *plural* **-dia** (-dɪə). a variant spelling of **allodium.**
▸**a'lodial** ADJECTIVE

aloe ('æləʊ) NOUN, *plural* **-oes.** [1] any plant of the liliaceous genus *Aloe,* chiefly native to southern Africa, with fleshy spiny-toothed leaves and red or yellow flowers. [2] **American aloe.** another name for **century plant.**
▷**HISTORY** C14: from Latin *aloē,* from Greek
▸**aloetic** (ˌæləʊ'etɪk) ADJECTIVE

aloes ('æləʊz) NOUN *(functioning as singular)* [1] Also called: **aloes wood.** another name for **eaglewood.** [2] **bitter aloes.** a bitter purgative drug made from the leaves of several species of aloe.

aloe vera ('æləʊ 'vɪərə) NOUN a juice obtained from the leaves of a liliaceous plant, *Aloe vera,* used as an emollient in skin and hair preparations.

aloft (ə'lɒft) ADVERB, ADJECTIVE *(postpositive)* [1] in or into a high or higher place; up above. [2] *Nautical* in or into the rigging of a vessel.
▷**HISTORY** C12: from Old Norse *ā lopt* in the air; see LIFT[1], LOFT

aloha (ə'ləʊə, ɑː'ləʊhɑː) NOUN, SENTENCE SUBSTITUTE a Hawaiian word for **hello** or **goodbye.**

aloin ('æləʊɪn) NOUN a bitter crystalline compound derived from various species of aloe: used as a laxative and flavouring agent.
▷**HISTORY** C19: from ALOE + -IN

alone (ə'ləʊn) ADJECTIVE *(postpositive),* ADVERB [1] apart from another or others; solitary. [2] without anyone or anything else: *one man alone could lift it.* [3] without equal; unique: *he stands alone in the field of microbiology.* [4] to the exclusion of others; only: *she alone believed him.* [5] **leave** *or* **let alone** *or* **be.** to refrain from annoying or interfering with. [6] **leave** *or* **let well (enough) alone.** to refrain from interfering with something that is satisfactory. [7] **let alone.** much less; not to mention: *he can't afford beer, let alone whisky.*
▷**HISTORY** Old English *al one,* literally: all (entirely) one

along (ə'lɒŋ) PREPOSITION [1] over or for the length of, esp in a more or less horizontal plane: *along the road.* ♦ ADVERB [2] continuing over the length of some specified thing. [3] in accompaniment; together with some specified person or people: *he says he'd like to come along.* [4] forward: *the horse trotted along at a steady pace.* [5] to a more advanced state: *he got the work moving along.* [6] **along with.** accompanying; together with: *consider the advantages along with the disadvantages.*
▷**HISTORY** Old English *andlang,* from *and-* against + *lang* LONG[1]; compare Old Frisian *andlinga,* Old Saxon *antlang*

> **Language note** See at **plus.**

alongshore (əˌlɒŋ'ʃɔː) ADVERB, ADJECTIVE *(postpositive)* close to, by, or along a shore.

alongside (ə'lɒŋˌsaɪd) PREPOSITION [1] (often foll by *of*) along the side of; along beside: *alongside the quay.* ♦ ADVERB [2] along the side of some specified thing: *come alongside.*

aloof (ə'luːf) ADJECTIVE distant, unsympathetic, or supercilious in manner, attitude, or feeling.
▷**HISTORY** C16: from A-[1] + *loof,* a variant of LUFF
▸**a'loofly** ADVERB ▸**a'loofness** NOUN

alopecia (ˌælə'piːʃɪə) NOUN loss of hair, esp on the head; baldness.
▷**HISTORY** C14: from Latin, from Greek *alōpekia,* originally: mange in foxes, from *alōpēx* fox

Alost *(French* alɔst) NOUN a town in central Belgium, in East Flanders province. Pop.: 76 256 (1995 est.). Flemish name: **Aalst.**

aloud (ə'laʊd) ADVERB, ADJECTIVE *(postpositive)* [1] in a normal voice; not in a whisper. [2] in a spoken voice; not silently. [3] *Archaic* in a loud voice.

alow (ə'ləʊ) ADVERB, ADJECTIVE *(postpositive) Nautical* in or into the lower rigging of a vessel, near the deck.

alp (ælp) NOUN [1] (in the European Alps) an area of pasture above the valley bottom but below the mountain peaks. [2] a high mountain. ♦ See also **Alps, Australian Alps.**
▷**HISTORY** C14: back formation from *Alps,* from French *Alpes* (pl), from Latin *Alpēs,* from Greek *Alpeis*

ALP ABBREVIATION FOR Australian Labor Party.

alpaca[1] (æl'pækə) NOUN [1] a domesticated cud-chewing artiodactyl mammal, *Lama pacos,* closely related to the llama and native to South America: family *Camelidae.* Its dark shaggy hair is a source of wool. [2] the cloth made from the wool of this animal. [3] a glossy fabric simulating this, used for linings, etc.
▷**HISTORY** C18: via Spanish from Aymara *allpaca*

alpaca[2] *or sometimes* **alpacca** (æl'pækə) NOUN a type of nickel silver used in jewellery.
▷**HISTORY** of uncertain origin

alpenglow ('ælpənˌgləʊ) NOUN a reddish light on the summits of snow-covered mountain peaks at sunset or sunrise.
▷**HISTORY** partial translation of German *Alpenglühen,* from *Alpen* ALPS + *glühen* to GLOW

alpenhorn ('ælpənˌhɔːn) NOUN another name for **alphorn.**

alpenstock ('ælpənˌstɒk) NOUN an early form of ice axe, consisting of a stout stick with an iron tip and sometimes having a pick and adze at the head, formerly used by mountain climbers.
▷**HISTORY** C19: from German, from *Alpen* ALPS + *Stock* STICK[1]

Alpes-de-Haute-Provence *(French* alpdəotprɔvɑ̃s) NOUN a department of SE France in Provence-Alpes-Côte-d'Azur region. Capital: Digne.

Pop.: 139 561 (1999). Area: 6988 sq. km (2725 sq. miles). Former name: **Basses-Alpes.**

Alpes Maritimes (*French* alp maritim) NOUN a department of the SE corner of France in Provence-Alpes-Côte-d'Azur region. Capital: Nice. Pop.: 1 011 326 (1999). Area: 4298 sq. km (1676 sq. miles).

alpestrine (æl'pestrɪn) ADJECTIVE (of plants) growing at high altitudes; subalpine.
▷HISTORY C19: from Medieval Latin *alpestris,* from Latin *Alpēs* the Alps

alpha ('ælfə) NOUN 1 the first letter in the Greek alphabet (Α, α), a vowel transliterated as *a.* 2 *Brit* the highest grade or mark, as in an examination. 3 (*modifier*) **a** involving or relating to helium-4 nuclei: *an alpha particle.* **b** relating to one of two or more allotropes or crystal structures of a solid: *alpha iron.* **c** relating to one of two or more isomeric forms of a chemical compound, esp one in which a group is attached to the carbon atom to which the principal group is attached. 4 (*modifier*) denoting the dominant person or animal in a group: *the alpha male.*
▷HISTORY via Latin from Greek, of Phoenician origin; related to Hebrew *āleph,* literally: ox

Alpha ('ælfə) NOUN 1 (*foll by the genitive case of a specified constellation*) usually the brightest star in a constellation: *Alpha Centauri.* 2 *Communications* a code word for the letter *a.*

alpha and omega NOUN 1 the first and last, a phrase used in Revelation 1:8 to signify God's eternity. 2 the basic reason or meaning; most important part.

alphabet ('ælfəˌbɛt) NOUN 1 a set of letters or other signs used in a writing system, usually arranged in a fixed order, each letter or sign being used to represent one or sometimes more than one phoneme in the language being transcribed. 2 any set of symbols or characters, esp one representing sounds of speech. 3 basic principles or rudiments, as of a subject.
▷HISTORY C15: from Late Latin *alphabētum,* from Greek *alphabētos,* from the first two letters of the Greek alphabet; see ALPHA, BETA

alphabetical (ˌælfə'bɛtɪkᵊl) *or* **alphabetic** ADJECTIVE 1 in the conventional order of the letters or symbols of an alphabet. 2 of, characterized by, or expressed by an alphabet.
▸ **ˌalpha'betically** ADVERB

alphabetize *or* **alphabetise** ('ælfəbəˌtaɪz) VERB (*tr*) 1 to arrange in conventional alphabetical order. 2 to express by an alphabet.
▸ **ˌalphabeti'zation** *or* **ˌalphabeti'sation** NOUN
▸ **'alphabetˌizer** *or* **'alphabetˌiser** NOUN

alpha-blocker NOUN any of a class of drugs that prevent the stimulation of alpha adrenoceptors, a type of receptor in the sympathetic nervous system, by adrenaline and noradrenaline and that therefore cause widening of blood vessels: used in the treatment of high blood pressure and prostatic hyperplasia.

Alpha Centauri system (sɛn'tɔːrɪ) NOUN a star system comprising the binary star **Alpha Centauri A** and **B** and Proxima Centauri (also called **Alpha Centauri C**), which is 0.1 light years closer to the sun. Visual magnitude: 0.01 (A), 1.33 (B); spectral type: G2V (A); distance from earth: 4.3 light years. Also called: **Rigil Kent.** See also **Proxima.**

alpha decay NOUN the radioactive decay process resulting in emission of alpha particles.

alpha emitter NOUN a radioactive isotope that emits alpha particles.

alpha-fetoprotein (ˌælfəˌfiːtəʊ'prəʊtiːn) NOUN a protein that forms in the liver of the human fetus. Excessive quantities in the amniotic fluid and maternal blood may indicate spina bifida in the fetus; low levels may point to Down's syndrome. Abbreviation: **afp.**

alpha helix NOUN *Biochem* a helical conformation of a polypeptide chain, found abundantly in the structure of proteins.

alpha-hydroxy acid NOUN a type of organic acid, commonly used in skin-care preparations, that has a hydroxyl group attached to the carbon atom next to the carbon atom carrying the carboxyl group.

alpha iron NOUN a magnetic allotrope of iron that is stable below 910°C; ferrite.

alpha-linolenic acid NOUN another name for **lenolenic acid.**

alphanumeric (ˌælfənjuː'mɛrɪk) *or* **alphameric** (ˌælfə'mɛrɪk) ADJECTIVE (of a character set, code, or file of data) consisting of alphabetical and numerical symbols.
▸ **ˌalphanu'merically** *or* **ˌalpha'merically** ADVERB

alpha particle NOUN a helium-4 nucleus, containing two neutrons and two protons, emitted during some radioactive transformations.

alpha privative NOUN (in Greek grammar) the letter alpha (or *an-* before vowels) used as a negative or privative prefix. It appears in English words derived from Greek, as in *atheist, anaesthetic.*

alpha radiation NOUN alpha particles emitted from a radioactive isotope.

alpha ray NOUN ionizing radiation consisting of a stream of alpha particles.

alpha rhythm *or* **wave** NOUN *Physiol* the normal bursts of electrical activity from the cerebral cortex of a drowsy or inactive person, occurring at a frequency of 8 to 12 hertz and detectable with an electroencephalograph. See also **brain wave.**

alpha stock NOUN any of the most active securities on the Stock Exchange of which there are between 100 and 200; at least ten market makers must continuously display the prices of an alpha stock and all transactions in them must be published immediately.

alpha-test NOUN 1 an in-house test of a new or modified piece of computer software. ◆ VERB (*tr*) 2 to test (software) in this way. Compare **beta-test.**

Alpheus (æl'fiːəs) NOUN *Greek myth* a river god, lover of the nymph Arethusa. She changed into a spring to evade him, but he changed into a river and mingled with her.

Alphonsus (æl'fɒnsəs) NOUN a crater in the SE quadrant of the moon, about 112 km in diameter, in which volcanic activity may have occurred.

alphorn ('ælpˌhɔːn) *or* **alpenhorn** NOUN *Music* a wind instrument used in the Swiss Alps, consisting of a very long tube of wood or bark with a cornet-like mouthpiece.
▷HISTORY C19: from German *Alpenhorn* Alps horn

alphosis (æl'fəʊsɪs) NOUN *Pathol* absence of skin pigmentation, as in albinism.
▷HISTORY C19: from New Latin, from Greek *alphos* leprosy

alpine ('ælpaɪn) ADJECTIVE 1 of or relating to high mountains. 2 (of plants) growing on mountains, esp above the limit for tree growth. 3 connected with or used in mountaineering in medium-sized glaciated mountain areas such as the Alps. 4 *Skiing* of or relating to racing events on steep prepared slopes, such as the slalom and downhill. Compare **nordic.** ◆ NOUN 5 a plant that is native or suited to alpine conditions.

Alpine ('ælpaɪn) ADJECTIVE 1 of or relating to the Alps or their inhabitants. 2 *Geology* **a** of or relating to an episode of mountain building in the Tertiary period during which the Alps were formed. **b** of or relating to a high mountainous environment heavily modified by glacial erosion.

alpine-style ADJECTIVE, ADVERB *Mountaineering* of or in an ascent (esp in high mountains like the Himalayas) in which the climbers carry all their equipment with them in a single ascent from base to summit.

alpinist ('ælpɪnɪst) NOUN a mountaineer who climbs in medium-sized glaciated mountain areas such as the Alps.
▸ **'alpinism** NOUN

Alps (ælps) PLURAL NOUN 1 a mountain range in S central Europe, extending over 1000 km (650 miles) from the Mediterranean coast of France and NW Italy through Switzerland, N Italy, and Austria to Slovenia. Highest peak: Mont Blanc, 4807 m (15 771 ft.). 2 a range of mountains in the NW quadrant of the moon, which is cut in two by a straight fracture, the **Alpine Valley.**

al-Qaeda *or* **al-Qaida** (æl'kaɪdə, ælkɑː'iːdə) NOUN a loosely-knit militant Islamic organization led and funded by Osama bin Laden, by whom it was established in the late 1980s from Arab volunteers who had fought the Soviet troops previously based in Afghanistan; known or believed to be behind a number of operations against Western, especially US, interests, including bomb attacks on two US embassies in Africa in 1998 and the destruction of the World Trade Center in New York in 2001.
▷HISTORY C20: from Arabic *al-qa'ida* the base

already (ɔːl'rɛdɪ) ADVERB 1 by or before a stated or implied time: *he is already here.* 2 at a time earlier than expected: *is it ten o'clock already?*

alright (ɔːl'raɪt) ADVERB, SENTENCE SUBSTITUTE, ADJECTIVE a variant spelling of **all right.**

> **Language note** The form *alright,* though very common, is still considered by many people to be wrong or less acceptable than *all right.*

ALS ABBREVIATION FOR autograph letter signed.

Alsace (æl'sæs; *French* alzas) NOUN a region and former province of NE France, between the Vosges mountains and the Rhine: famous for its wines. Area: 8280 sq. km (3196 sq. miles). Ancient name: **Alsatia.** German name: **Elsass.**

Alsace-Lorraine NOUN an area of NE France, comprising the modern regions of Alsace and Lorraine: under German rule 1871–1919 and 1940–44. Area: 14 522 sq. km (5607 sq. miles). German name: **Elsass-Lothringen.**

Alsatia (æl'seɪʃə) NOUN 1 the ancient name for **Alsace.** 2 an area around Whitefriars, London, in the 17th century, which was a sanctuary for criminals and debtors.

Alsatian (æl'seɪʃən) NOUN 1 a large wolflike breed of dog often used as a guard or guide dog and by the police. Also called: **German shepherd, German shepherd dog.** 2 a native or inhabitant of Alsace. 3 (in the 17th century) a criminal or debtor who took refuge in the Whitefriars area of London. ◆ ADJECTIVE 4 of or relating to Alsace or its inhabitants.

alsike ('ælsaɪk, -sɪk, 'ɔːl-) NOUN a clover, *Trifolium hybridum,* native to Europe and Asia but widely cultivated as a forage crop. It has trifoliate leaves and pink or whitish flowers. Also called: **alsike clover.**
▷HISTORY C19: named after *Alsike,* Sweden

Al Sirat (ˌæl sɪ'ræt) NOUN *Islam* 1 the correct path of religion. 2 the razor-edged bridge by which all who enter paradise must pass.
▷HISTORY from Arabic: the road, from Latin *via strāta* paved way

also ('ɔːlsəʊ) ADVERB 1 (*sentence modifier*) in addition; as well; too. ◆ SENTENCE CONNECTOR 2 besides; moreover.
▷HISTORY Old English *alswā;* related to Old High German *alsō,* Old Frisian *alsa;* see ALL, SO[1]

also-ran NOUN 1 a contestant, horse, etc., failing to finish among the first three in a race. 2 an unsuccessful person; loser or nonentity.

alstroemeria (ˌælstrə'miːrɪə) NOUN any plant of the tuberous perennial liliaceous genus *Alstroemeria,* originally S American, grown for their brightly coloured orchid-like flowers. Also called: **Peruvian lily.**
▷HISTORY named by Linnaeus for his friend Baron Klas von *Alstroemer*

alt (ælt) *Music* ◆ ADJECTIVE 1 (esp of vocal music) high in pitch. 2 of or relating to the octave commencing with the G above the top line of the treble staff. ◆ NOUN 3 **in alt.** in the octave directly above the treble staff.
▷HISTORY C16: from Provençal, from Latin *altus* high, deep

Alta. ABBREVIATION FOR Alberta.

Altaic (æl'teɪɪk) NOUN 1 a postulated family of languages of Asia and SE Europe, consisting of the Turkic, Mongolic, and Tungusic branches, and perhaps also Japanese, Korean, and Ainu. See also **Ural-Altaic.** ◆ ADJECTIVE 2 denoting, belonging to, or relating to this linguistic family or its speakers.

Altai Mountains (ɑː'taɪ) PLURAL NOUN a mountain system of central Asia, in W Mongolia, W China, and S Russia. Highest peak: Belukha, 4506 m (14 783 ft.).

Altair ('æltɛə) NOUN the brightest star in the constellation Aquila. Visual magnitude: 0.77; spectral type: A7V; distance: 16.8 light years.

▷HISTORY Arabic, from *al* the + *tā'ir* bird

Altai Republic NOUN another name for **Gorno-Altai Republic.**

Altamira (*Spanish* alta'mira) NOUN a cave in N Spain, SW of Santander, noted for Old Stone Age wall drawings.

altar ('ɔːltə) NOUN 1 a raised place or structure where sacrifices are offered and religious rites performed. 2 (in Christian churches) the communion table. 3 a step in the wall of a dry dock upon which structures supporting a vessel can stand. 4 **lead to the altar.** *Informal* to marry.
▷HISTORY Old English, from Latin *altāria* (plural) altar, from *altus* high

altar boy NOUN *RC Church, Church of England* a boy serving as an acolyte.

altar cloth NOUN *Christianity* the cloth used for covering an altar: often applied also to the frontal.

altarpiece ('ɔːltə,piːs) NOUN a work of art set above and behind an altar; a reredos.

altazimuth (æl'tæzɪməθ) NOUN an instrument for measuring the altitude and azimuth of a celestial body by the horizontal and vertical rotation of a telescope.
▷HISTORY C19: from ALT(ITUDE) + AZIMUTH

altazimuth mounting NOUN a telescope mounting that allows motion of the telescope about a vertical axis (in azimuth) and a horizontal axis (in altitude).

alt.country (ɔːlt) NOUN a genre of country music originating in the 1990s and influenced by both early country music and contemporary rock music.
▷HISTORY C20: from ALT(ERNATIVE) + COUNTRY

Altdorf (*German* 'altdɔrf) NOUN a town in central Switzerland, capital of Uri canton: setting of the William Tell legend. Pop.: 8150 (1990).

Alte Pinakothek (*German* 'altə pinako'teːk) NOUN a museum in Munich housing a collection of paintings dating from the Middle Ages to the late 18th century.

alter ('ɔːltə) VERB 1 to make or become different in some respect; change. 2 (*tr*) *Informal, chiefly US* a euphemistic word for **castrate** or **spay.**
▷HISTORY C14: from Old French *alterer,* from Medieval Latin *alterāre* to change, from Latin *alter* other
▸**'alterable** ADJECTIVE ▸**'alterably** ADVERB ▸**,altera'bility** NOUN

alteration (,ɔːltə'reɪʃən) NOUN 1 an adjustment, change, or modification. 2 the act of altering or state of being altered.

alterative ('ɔːltərətɪv) ADJECTIVE 1 likely or able to produce alteration. 2 *Obsolete* (of a drug) able to restore normal health. ◆ NOUN 3 *Obsolete* a drug that restores normal health.

altercate ('ɔːltə,keɪt) VERB (*intr*) to argue, esp heatedly; dispute.
▷HISTORY C16: from Latin *altercārī* to quarrel with another, from *alter* other

altercation (,ɔːltə'keɪʃən) NOUN an angry or heated discussion or quarrel; argument.

altered chord NOUN *Music* a chord in which one or more notes are chromatically changed by the introduction of accidentals.

alter ego ('æltər 'iːgəʊ, 'ɛgəʊ) NOUN 1 a second self. 2 a very close and intimate friend.
▷HISTORY Latin: other self

alternant (ɔːl'tɜːnənt) ADJECTIVE alternating.
▷HISTORY C17: from French, from Latin *alternāre* to ALTERNATE

alternate VERB ('ɔːltə,neɪt) 1 (often foll by *with*) to occur or cause to occur successively or by turns: *day and night alternate.* 2 (*intr;* often foll by *between*) to swing repeatedly from one condition, action, etc., to another: *he alternates between success and failure.* 3 (*tr*) to interchange regularly or in succession. 4 (*intr*) (of an electric current, voltage, etc.) to reverse direction or sign at regular intervals, usually sinusoidally, the instantaneous value varying continuously. 5 (*intr;* often foll by *for*) *Theatre* to understudy another actor or actress. ◆ ADJECTIVE (ɔːl'tɜːnɪt) 6 occurring by turns: *alternate feelings of love and hate.* 7 every other or second one of a series: *he came to work on alternate days.* 8 being a second or further choice; alternative: *alternate director.* 9 *Botany* **a** (of leaves, flowers, etc.) arranged singly at different heights on either side of the stem. **b** (of parts of a flower) arranged opposite the spaces between other parts. Compare **opposite** (sense 4). ◆ NOUN ('ɔːltənɪt, ɔːl'tɜːnɪt) 10 *US and Canadian* a person who substitutes for another in his absence; stand-in.
▷HISTORY C16: from Latin *alternāre* to do one thing and then another, from *alternus* one after the other, from *alter* other

alternate angles PLURAL NOUN two angles at opposite ends and on opposite sides of a transversal cutting two lines.

alternately (ɔːl'tɜːnɪtlɪ) ADVERB in an alternating sequence or position.

alternating current NOUN a continuous electric current that periodically reverses direction, usually sinusoidally. Abbreviation: **AC.** Compare **direct current.**

alternating-gradient focusing NOUN *Physics* a method of focusing beams of charged particles in high-energy accelerators, in which a series of magnetic or electrostatic lenses alternately converge and diverge the beam, producing a net focusing effect and thus preventing the beam from spreading.

alternation (,ɔːltə'neɪʃən) NOUN 1 successive change from one condition or action to another and back again repeatedly. 2 *Logic* another name for **disjunction** (sense 3).

alternation of generations NOUN the production within the life cycle of an organism of alternating asexual and sexual reproductive forms. It occurs in many plants and lower animals. Also called: **metagenesis, heterogenesis, digenesis, xenogenesis.**

alternative (ɔːl'tɜːnətɪv) NOUN 1 a possibility of choice, esp between two things, courses of action, etc. 2 either of such choices: *we took the alternative of walking.* ◆ ADJECTIVE 3 presenting a choice, esp between two possibilities only. 4 (of two things) mutually exclusive. 5 denoting a lifestyle, culture, art form, etc., regarded by its adherents as preferable to that of contemporary society because it is less conventional, materialistic, or institutionalized, and, often, more in harmony with nature. 6 *Logic* another word for **disjunctive** (sense 3).
▸**al'ternatively** ADVERB ▸**al'ternativeness** NOUN

alternative curriculum NOUN *Brit, education* any course of study offered as an alternative to the National Curriculum.

alternative energy NOUN a form of energy derived from a natural source, such as the sun, wind, tides, or waves. Also called: **renewable energy.**

alternative hypothesis NOUN *Statistics* the hypothesis that given data do not conform with a given null hypothesis. The null hypothesis is accepted only if its probability exceeds a predetermined significance level. See **hypothesis testing.** Compare **null hypothesis.**

Alternative Investment Market NOUN a market on the London Stock Exchange enabling small companies to raise capital and have their shares traded in a market without the expenses of a main-market listing. Abbreviation: **AIM.**

alternative medicine NOUN another name for **complementary medicine.** See also **holism** (sense 2).

Alternative Vote NOUN (*modifier*) of or relating to a system of voting in which voters list the candidates in order of preference. If no candidate obtains more than 50% of first-preference votes, the votes for the bottom candidate are redistributed according to the voters' next preference. See **proportional representation.**

alternator ('ɔːltə,neɪtə) NOUN an electrical machine that generates an alternating current.

althaea *or US* **althea** (æl'θiːə) NOUN 1 any Eurasian plant of the malvaceous genus *Althaea,* such as the hollyhock, having tall spikes of showy white, yellow, or red flowers. 2 another name for **rose of Sharon** (sense 2).
▷HISTORY C17: from Latin *althaea,* from Greek *althaia* marsh mallow (literally: healing plant), from Greek *althein* to heal

Althing ('ælθɪŋ) NOUN the bicameral parliament of Iceland.

althorn ('ælt,hɔːn) NOUN a valved brass musical instrument belonging to the saxhorn or flügelhorn families.

Althorp House ('ɔːlθɔːp, -θrʌp) NOUN a mansion in Northamptonshire: seat of the Earls Spencer since 1508; originally a medieval house; altered (1787) to its present neoclassical style by Henry Holland. Diana, Princess of Wales is buried on Round Oval Island in the centre of the ornamental lake in Althorp Park.

although (ɔːl'ðəʊ) CONJUNCTION (*subordinating*) despite the fact that; even though: *although she was ill, she worked hard.*

alti- COMBINING FORM indicating height or altitude: *altimeter.*
▷HISTORY from Latin *altus* high

altimeter (æl'tɪmɪtə, 'æltɪ,miːtə) NOUN an instrument that indicates height above sea level, esp one based on an aneroid barometer and fitted to an aircraft.

altimetry (æl'tɪmɪtrɪ) NOUN the science of measuring altitudes, as with an altimeter.
▸**altimetrical** (,æltɪ'metrɪkᵊl) ADJECTIVE ▸**,alti'metrically** ADVERB

Altiplano (*Spanish* alti'plano) NOUN a plateau of the Andes, covering two thirds of Bolivia and extending into S Peru: contains Lake Titicaca. Height: 3000 m (10 000 ft.) to 3900 m (13 000 ft.).

altissimo (æl'tɪsɪ,məʊ) ADJECTIVE 1 (of music) very high in pitch. 2 of or relating to the octave commencing on the G lying an octave above the treble clef. ◆ NOUN 3 **in altissimo.** in the octave commencing an octave above the treble clef.
▷HISTORY Italian, literally: highest

altitude ('æltɪ,tjuːd) NOUN 1 the vertical height of an object above some chosen level, esp above sea level; elevation. 2 *Geometry* the perpendicular distance from the vertex to the base of a geometrical figure or solid. 3 Also called: **elevation.** *Astronomy, navigation* the angular distance of a celestial body from the horizon measured along the vertical circle passing through the body. Compare **azimuth** (sense 1). 4 *Surveying* the angle of elevation of a point above the horizontal plane of the observer. 5 (*often plural*) a high place or region.
▷HISTORY C14: from Latin *altitūdō,* from *altus* high, deep
▸**,alti'tudinal** ADJECTIVE

altitude sickness NOUN another name for **mountain sickness.**

alto ('æltəʊ) NOUN, *plural* **-tos.** 1 the highest adult male voice; countertenor. 2 (in choral singing) a shortened form of **contralto.** 3 a singer with such a voice. 4 another name for **viola**[1] (sense 1). 5 a flute, saxophone, etc., that is the third or fourth highest instrument in its group. ◆ ADJECTIVE 6 denoting a flute, saxophone, etc., that is the third or fourth highest instrument in its group.
▷HISTORY C18: from Italian: high, from Latin *altus*

alto- COMBINING FORM high: *altocumulus; altostratus.*
▷HISTORY from Latin *altus* high

alto clef NOUN the clef that establishes middle C as being on the third line of the staff. Also called: **viola clef.** See also **C clef.**

altocumulus (,æltəʊ'kjuːmjʊləs) NOUN, *plural* **-li** (-laɪ). a globular cloud at an intermediate height of about 2400 to 6000 metres (8000 to 20 000 feet).

altogether (,ɔːltə'gɛðə, 'ɔːltə,gɛðə) ADVERB 1 with everything included: *altogether he owed me sixty pounds.* 2 completely; utterly; totally: *he was altogether mad.* 3 on the whole: *altogether it was a very good party.* ◆ NOUN 4 **in the altogether.** *Informal* naked.

alto horn NOUN another term for **althorn.**

altoist ('æltəʊɪst) NOUN a person who plays the alto saxophone.

Alton Towers ('ɒltən) NOUN a 19th-century Gothic Revival mansion with extensive gardens in NW central England, in Staffordshire: site of a large amusement park.

alto-relievo *or* **alto-rilievo** (,æltəʊrɪ'liːvəʊ) NOUN, *plural* **-vos.** another name for **high relief.**
▷HISTORY C18: from Italian

altostratus (,æltəʊ'streɪtəs, -'strɑː-) NOUN, *plural* **-ti** (-taɪ). a layer cloud at an intermediate height of about 2400 to 6000 metres (8000 to 20 000 feet).

altrices ('æltrɪsiːz) PLURAL NOUN altricial birds.

altricial (æl'trɪʃəl) ADJECTIVE [1] (of the young of some species of birds after hatching) naked, blind, and dependent on the parents for food. ◆ NOUN [2] an altricial bird, such as a pigeon. ◆ Compare **precocial**.
▷HISTORY C19: from New Latin *altriciālis,* from Latin *altrix* a nurse, from *alere* to nourish

Altrincham ('ɔːltrɪŋəm) NOUN a residential town in NW England, in Trafford unitary authority, Greater Manchester. Pop.: 40 042 (1991).

alt.rock (ɔːlt) NOUN a genre of rock music regarded by its practitioners and fans as being outside the mainstream.
▷HISTORY C20: from ALT(ERNATIVE) + ROCK

altruism ('æltruːˌɪzəm) NOUN [1] the principle or practice of unselfish concern for the welfare of others. [2] the philosophical doctrine that right action is that which produces the greatest benefit to others. ◆ Compare **egoism**. See also **utilitarianism**.
▷HISTORY C19: from French *altruisme,* from Italian *altrui* others, from Latin *alterī,* plural of *alter* other
▸**'altruist** NOUN ▸**ˌaltru'istic** ADJECTIVE ▸**ˌaltru'istically** ADVERB

ALU *Computing* ABBREVIATION FOR arithmetic and logic unit.

aludel ('æljuˌdɛl) NOUN *Chem* a pear-shaped vessel, open at both ends, formerly used with similar vessels for collecting condensates, esp of subliming mercury.
▷HISTORY C16: via Old French from Spanish, from Arabic *al-uthāl* the vessel

alula ('æljʊlə) NOUN, *plural* **-lae** (-liː). another name for **bastard wing**.
▷HISTORY C18: New Latin: a little wing, from Latin *āla* a wing
▸**'alular** ADJECTIVE

alum ('æləm) NOUN [1] Also called: **potash alum**. a colourless soluble hydrated double sulphate of aluminium and potassium used in the manufacture of mordants and pigments, in dressing leather and sizing paper, and in medicine as a styptic and astringent. Formula: $K_2SO_4.Al_2(SO_4)_3.24H_2O$. [2] any of a group of isomorphic double sulphates of a monovalent metal or group and a trivalent metal. Formula: $X_2SO_4.Y_2(SO_4)_3.24H_2O$, where X is monovalent and Y is trivalent.
▷HISTORY C14: from Old French, from Latin *alūmen*

alumina (ə'luːmɪnə) NOUN another name for **aluminium oxide**.
▷HISTORY C18: from New Latin, plural of Latin *alūmen* ALUM

aluminate (ə'luːmɪneɪt) NOUN a salt of the ortho or meta acid forms of aluminium hydroxide containing the ions AlO_2^- or AlO_3^{3-}.

aluminiferous (əˌluːmɪ'nɪfərəs) ADJECTIVE containing or yielding aluminium or alumina.

aluminium (ˌælju'mɪnɪəm) *or US and Canadian* **aluminum** (ə'luːmɪnəm) NOUN a light malleable ductile silvery-white metallic element that resists corrosion; the third most abundant element in the earth's crust (8.1 per cent), occurring only as a compound, principally in bauxite. It is used, esp in the form of its alloys, in aircraft parts, kitchen utensils, etc. Symbol: Al; atomic no.: 13; atomic wt.: 26.9815; valency: 3; relative density: 2.699; melting pt.: 660.45°C; boiling pt.: 2520°C.

aluminium bronze NOUN any of a range of copper alloys that contain between 5 and 10 per cent aluminium.

aluminium hydroxide NOUN a white crystalline powder derived from bauxite and used in the manufacture of glass and ceramics, aluminium and its salts, and in dyeing. Formula: $Al(OH)_3$ or $Al_2O_3.3H_2O$.

aluminium oxide NOUN a white or colourless insoluble powder occurring naturally as corundum and used in the production of aluminium and its compounds, abrasives, glass, and ceramics. Formula: Al_2O_3. Also called: **alumina**. See also **activated alumina**.

aluminium sulphate NOUN a white crystalline salt used in the paper, textile, and dyeing industries and in the purification of water. Formula: $Al_2(SO_4)_3$.

aluminize *or* **aluminise** (ə'luːmɪˌnaɪz) VERB (*tr*) to cover with aluminium or aluminium paint.

aluminosilicate (əˌluːmɪnəʊ'sɪlɪkɪt) NOUN a silicate in which some of the silicon in the tetrahedral unit SiO_4 has been replaced by aluminium.

aluminothermy (ə'luːmɪnəʊˌθɜːmɪ) NOUN a process for reducing metallic oxides using finely divided aluminium powder. The mixture of aluminium and the oxide is ignited, causing the aluminium to be oxidized and the metal oxide to be reduced to the metal. Also called: **thermite process**.

aluminous (ə'luːmɪnəs) ADJECTIVE [1] resembling aluminium. [2] another word for **aluminiferous**.
▸**aluminosity** (əˌluːmɪ'nɒsɪtɪ) NOUN

aluminous cement NOUN another term for **Ciment Fondu**.

alumna (ə'lʌmnə) NOUN, *plural* **-nae** (-niː). *Chiefly US and Canadian* a female graduate of a school, college, etc.
▷HISTORY C19: feminine of ALUMNUS

alumnus (ə'lʌmnəs) NOUN, *plural* **-ni** (-naɪ). *Chiefly US and Canadian* a graduate of a school, college, etc.
▷HISTORY C17: from Latin: nursling, pupil, foster son, from *alere* to nourish

alumroot ('æləmˌruːt) NOUN [1] any of several North American plants of the saxifragaceous genus *Heuchera,* having small white, reddish, or green bell-shaped flowers and astringent roots. [2] the root of such a plant.

Alundum (ə'lʌndəm) NOUN *Trademark* a hard material composed of fused alumina, used as an abrasive and a refractory.

alunite ('æljuˌnaɪt) NOUN a white, grey, or reddish mineral consisting of hydrated aluminium sulphate. It occurs in volcanic igneous rocks and is a source of potassium and aluminium compounds. Formula: $KAl_3(SO_4)_2(OH)_6$.
▷HISTORY C19: from French *alun* alum (from Latin *alūmen*) + -ITE[1]

alveolar (æl'vɪələ, ˌælvɪ'əʊlə) ADJECTIVE [1] *Anatomy* of, relating to, or resembling an alveolus. [2] denoting the part of the jawbone containing the roots of the teeth. [3] (of a consonant) articulated with the tongue in contact with the projecting part of the jawbone immediately behind the upper teeth. ◆ NOUN [4] an alveolar consonant, such as the speech sounds written *t, d,* and *s* in English.

alveolate (æl'vɪəlɪt, -ˌleɪt) ADJECTIVE [1] having many alveoli. [2] resembling the deep pits of a honeycomb.
▷HISTORY C19: from Late Latin *alveolātus* forming a channel, hollowed, from Latin: ALVEOLUS
▸**ˌalveo'lation** NOUN

alveolus (æl'vɪələs) NOUN, *plural* **-li** (-ˌlaɪ). [1] any small pit, cavity, or saclike dilation, such as a honeycomb cell. [2] any of the sockets in which the roots of the teeth are embedded. [3] any of the tiny air sacs in the lungs at the end of the bronchioles, through which oxygen is taken into the blood.
▷HISTORY C18: from Latin: a little hollow, diminutive of *alveus*

alvine ('ælvɪn, -vaɪn) ADJECTIVE *Obsolete* of or relating to the intestines or belly.
▷HISTORY C18: from Latin *alvus* belly

always ('ɔːlweɪz, -wɪz) ADVERB [1] without exception; on every occasion; every time: *he always arrives on time.* [2] continually; repeatedly. [3] in any case: *you could always take a day off work.* [4] *Informal* for ever; without end: *our marriage is for always.* ◆ Also (archaic): **alway**.
▷HISTORY C13 *alles weiss,* from Old English *ealne weg,* literally: all the way; see ALL, WAY

alyssum ('ælɪsəm) NOUN any widely cultivated herbaceous garden plant of the genus *Alyssum,* having clusters of small yellow or white flowers: family *Brassicaceae* (crucifers). See also **sweet alyssum, alison**.
▷HISTORY C16: from New Latin, from Greek *alusson,* from *alussos* (adj) curing rabies, referring to the ancient belief in the plant's healing properties

Alzheimer's disease ('æltsˌhaɪməz) NOUN a disorder of the brain resulting in a progressive decline in intellectual and physical abilities and eventual dementia. Often shortened to: **Alzheimer's**.
▷HISTORY C20: named after A. *Alzheimer* (1864–1915), German physician who first identified it

am[1] (æm; *unstressed* əm) VERB (used with *I*) a form of the present tense (indicative mood) of **be**.
▷HISTORY Old English *eam;* related to Old Norse *em,* Gothic *im,* Old High German *bim,* Latin *sum,* Greek *eimi,* Sanskrit *asmi*

am[2] [1] See **AM** (sense 5). [2] See **a.m.**

am[3] THE INTERNET DOMAIN NAME FOR Armenia.

Am THE CHEMICAL SYMBOL FOR americium.

AM ABBREVIATION FOR: [1] associate member. [2] Assembly Member (of the National Assembly of Wales). [3] Albert Medal. [4] *US* Master of Arts. [5] Also: **am. amplitude modulation**. [6] See **a.m.** [7] Member of the Order of Australia.

A/M (in Canada) ABBREVIATION FOR Air Marshal.

Am. ABBREVIATION FOR America(n).

a.m., A.M., am, *or* **AM** (indicating the time period from midnight to midday) ABBREVIATION FOR ante meridiem. Compare **p.m.**
▷HISTORY Latin: before noon

AMA ABBREVIATION FOR: [1] American Medical Association. [2] Australian Medical Association.

amabokoboko (ama'bɒkɒbɒkɒ) PLURAL NOUN *South African* an African name for the **Springbok** rugby team.
▷HISTORY C20: from Nguni *ama,* a plural prefix + *bokoboko,* from *bok* a diminutive of SPRINGBOK

amadavat (ˌæmədə'væt) NOUN another name for **avadavat**.

amadoda (ama'dəʊda) PLURAL NOUN *South African* grown men.
▷HISTORY from Nguni *ama,* a plural prefix + *doda* men

amadou ('æməˌduː) NOUN a spongy substance made from certain fungi, such as *Polyporus* (or *Fomes*) *fomentarius* and related species, used as tinder to light fires, in medicine to stop bleeding, and, esp formerly, by anglers to dry off dry flies between casts.
▷HISTORY C18: from French, from Provençal: lover, from Latin *amātor,* from *amāre* to love; so called because it readily ignites

Amagasaki (əˌmɑːgə'sɑːkɪ) NOUN an industrial city in Japan, in W Honshu, on Osaka Bay. Pop.: 488 574 (1995).

amah ('ɑːmə, 'æmə) NOUN (in the East, esp formerly) a nurse or maidservant, esp one of Chinese origin. Compare **ayah**.
▷HISTORY C19: from Portuguese *ama* nurse, wet nurse

amain (ə'meɪn) ADVERB *Archaic or poetic* with great strength, speed, or haste.
▷HISTORY C16: from A-[2] + MAIN[1]

amakwerekwere (ˌama'kwerɪ'kwerɪ) PLURAL NOUN *South African informal* a term used by Blacks to refer to foreign Africans.
▷HISTORY C20: of uncertain origin

Amalekite (ə'mæləˌkaɪt) NOUN *Old Testament* a member of a nomadic tribe descended from Esau (Genesis 36:12), dwelling in the desert between Sinai and Canaan and hostile to the Israelites: they were defeated by Saul and destroyed by David (I Samuel 15–30).

Amalfi (ə'mælfɪ) NOUN a town in Italy: a major Mediterranean port from the 10th to the 18th century, now a resort.

amalgam (ə'mælgəm) NOUN [1] an alloy of mercury with another metal, esp with silver: *dental amalgam.* [2] a rare white metallic mineral that consists of silver and mercury and occurs in deposits of silver and cinnabar. [3] a blend or combination.
▷HISTORY C15: from Medieval Latin *amalgama,* of obscure origin

amalgamate (ə'mælgəˌmeɪt) VERB [1] to combine or cause to combine; unite. [2] to alloy (a metal) with mercury.

amalgamation (əˌmælgə'meɪʃən) NOUN [1] the action or process of amalgamating. [2] the state of being amalgamated. [3] a method of extracting precious metals from their ores by treatment with mercury to form an amalgam. [4] *Commerce* another word for **merger** (sense 1).

Amalthea[1] (ˌæmæl'θiːə) NOUN *Greek myth* **a** a nymph who brought up the infant Zeus on goat's milk. **b** the goat itself. ◆ Also: **Amaltheia**.

Amalthea[2] (ˌæmæl'θiːə) NOUN an inner satellite of Jupiter.

amandla (a'mɑːndla) NOUN *South African* a

political slogan calling for power to the Black population.
▷HISTORY C20: Nguni, literally: power

amanita (ˌæməˈnaɪtə) NOUN any of various saprotrophic agaricaceous fungi constituting the genus *Amanita,* having white gills and a broken membranous ring (volva) around the stalk. The genus includes several highly poisonous species, such as death cap, destroying angel, and fly agaric.
▷HISTORY C19: from Greek *amanitai* (plural) a variety of fungus

amanuensis (əˌmænjuˈɛnsɪs) NOUN, *plural* **-ses** (-siːz). a person employed to take dictation or to copy manuscripts.
▷HISTORY C17: from Latin *āmanuensis,* from the phrase *servus ā manū* slave at hand (that is, handwriting)

Amapá (*Portuguese* ˌaməˈpɑː) NOUN a state of N Brazil, on the Amazon delta. Capital: Macapá. Pop.: 475 843 (2000). Area: 143 716 sq. km (55 489 sq. miles).

amaranth (ˈæməˌrænθ) NOUN 1 *Poetic* an imaginary flower that never fades. 2 any of numerous tropical and temperate plants of the genus *Amaranthus,* having tassel-like heads of small green, red, or purple flowers: family *Amaranthaceae.* See also **love-lies-bleeding, tumbleweed, pigweed** (sense 1). 3 a synthetic red food colouring (**E123**), used in packet soups, cake mixes, etc.
▷HISTORY C17: from Latin *amarantus,* from Greek *amarantos* unfading, from A-[1] + *marainein* to fade

amaranthaceous (ˌæmərænˈθeɪʃəs) ADJECTIVE of, relating to, or belonging to the *Amaranthaceae* (or *Amarantaceae*), a family of tropical and temperate herbaceous or shrubby flowering plants that includes the amaranths and cockscomb.

amaranthine (ˌæməˈrænθaɪn) ADJECTIVE 1 of a dark reddish-purple colour. 2 of or resembling the amaranth.

amarelle (ˈæməˌrel) NOUN a variety of sour cherry that has pale red fruit and colourless juice. Compare **morello.**
▷HISTORY C20: from German, from Medieval Latin *amārellum,* from Latin *amārus* bitter; compare MORELLO

amaretto (æməˈretəʊ) NOUN an Italian liqueur with a flavour of almonds.
▷HISTORY C20: from Italian *amaro* bitter

Amarillo (ˌæməˈrɪləʊ) NOUN an industrial city in NW Texas. Pop.: 173 627 (2000).

amaryllidaceous (ˌæməˌrɪlɪˈdeɪʃəs) ADJECTIVE of, relating to, or belonging to the *Amaryllidaceae,* a family of widely cultivated flowering plants having bulbs and including the amaryllis, snowdrop, narcissus, and daffodil.

amaryllis (ˌæməˈrɪlɪs) NOUN 1 Also called: **belladonna lily.** an amaryllidaceous plant, *Amaryllis belladonna,* native to southern Africa and having large lily-like reddish or white flowers. 2 any of several related plants, esp hippeastrum.
▷HISTORY C18: from New Latin, from Latin: named after AMARYLLIS

Amaryllis (ˌæməˈrɪlɪs) NOUN (in pastoral poetry) a name for a shepherdess or country girl.

amass (əˈmæs) VERB 1 (*tr*) to accumulate or collect (esp riches, etc.). 2 to gather in a heap; bring together.
▷HISTORY C15: from Old French *amasser,* from *masse* MASS
▸**aˈmasser** NOUN

amateur (ˈæmətə, -tʃə, -ˌtjʊə, ˌæməˈtɜː) NOUN 1 a person who engages in an activity, esp a sport, as a pastime rather than professionally or for gain. 2 an athlete or sportsman. 3 a person unskilled in or having only a superficial knowledge of a subject or activity. 4 a person who is fond of or admires something. 5 (*modifier*) consisting of or for amateurs: *an amateur event.* ◆ ADJECTIVE 6 amateurish; not professional or expert: *an amateur approach.*
▷HISTORY C18: from French, from Latin *amātor* lover, from *amāre* to love
▸**ˈamateurism** NOUN

amateurish (ˈæmətərɪʃ, -tʃər-, -ˌtʃʊər-, ˌæməˈtɜːrɪʃ) ADJECTIVE lacking professional skill or expertise.
▸**ˈamateurishly** ADVERB ▸**ˈamateurishness** NOUN

Amati (əˈmɑːtɪ) NOUN, *plural* **Amatis.** a violin or other stringed instrument made by any member of the Amati family of Italian violin makers (active in Cremona in the 16th and 17th centuries).

amative (ˈæmətɪv) ADJECTIVE a rare word for **amorous.**
▷HISTORY C17: from Medieval Latin *amātīvus,* from Latin *amāre* to love
▸**ˈamatively** ADVERB ▸**ˈamativeness** NOUN

amatol (ˈæməˌtɒl) NOUN an explosive mixture of ammonium nitrate and TNT, used in shells and bombs.
▷HISTORY C20: from AM(MONIUM) + (TRINITRO)TOL(UENE)

amatory (ˈæmətərɪ) *or* **amatorial** (ˌæməˈtɔːrɪəl) ADJECTIVE of, relating to, or inciting sexual love or desire.
▷HISTORY C16: from Latin *amātōrius,* from *amāre* to love

amaurosis (ˌæmɔːˈrəʊsɪs) NOUN *Pathol* blindness, esp when occurring without observable damage to the eye.
▷HISTORY C17: via New Latin from Greek: darkening, from *amauroun* to dim, darken
▸**amaurotic** (ˌæmɔːˈrɒtɪk) ADJECTIVE

amaut *or* **amowt** (əˈmaʊt) NOUN *Canadian* a hood on an Eskimo woman's parka for carrying a child.
▷HISTORY from Eskimo

amaze (əˈmeɪz) VERB (*tr*) 1 to fill with incredulity or surprise; astonish. 2 an obsolete word for **bewilder.** ◆ NOUN 3 an archaic word for **amazement.**
▷HISTORY Old English *āmasian*

amazement (əˈmeɪzmənt) NOUN 1 incredulity or great astonishment; complete wonder or surprise. 2 *Obsolete* bewilderment or consternation.

amazing (əˈmeɪzɪŋ) ADJECTIVE causing wonder or astonishment: *amazing feats.*
▸**aˈmazingly** ADVERB

amazon (ˈæməzᵊn) NOUN any of various tropical American parrots of the genus *Amazona,* such as *A. farinosa* (green amazon), having a short tail and mainly green plumage.

Amazon[1] (ˈæməzᵊn) NOUN 1 *Greek myth* one of a race of women warriors of Scythia near the Black Sea. 2 one of a legendary tribe of female warriors of South America. 3 (*often not capital*) any tall, strong, or aggressive woman.
▷HISTORY C14: via Latin from Greek *Amazōn,* of uncertain origin
▸**Amazonian** (ˌæməˈzəʊnɪən) ADJECTIVE

Amazon[2] (ˈæməzᵊn) NOUN a river in South America, rising in the Peruvian Andes and flowing east through N Brazil to the Atlantic: in volume, the largest river in the world; navigable for 3700 km (2300 miles). Length: over 6440 km (4000 miles). Area of basin: over 5 827 500 sq. km (2 250 000 sq. miles).

amazon ant NOUN any of several small reddish ants of the genus *Polyergus,* esp *P. rufescens,* that enslave the young of other ant species.

Amazonas (ˌæməˈzəʊnəs) NOUN a state of W Brazil, consisting of the central Amazon basin: vast areas of unexplored tropical rainforest. Capital: Manaus. Pop.: 2 840 889 (2000). Area: 1 542 277 sq. km (595 474 sq. miles).

Amazonia (æməˈzəʊnɪə) NOUN the land around the Amazon river.

Amazonian (æməˈzəʊnɪən) ADJECTIVE of or relating to the Amazon river, the land around it, or the inhabitants of this land.

amazonite (ˈæməzəˌnaɪt) NOUN a green variety of microcline used as a gemstone. Formula: $KAlSi_3O_8$. Also called: **Amazon stone.**

Ambala (əmˈbɑːlə) NOUN a city in N India, in Haryana: site of archaeological remains of a prehistoric Indian civilization: grain, cotton, food processing. Pop.: 119 338 (1991).

ambary *or* **ambari** (æmˈbɑːrɪ) NOUN, *plural* **-ries** *or* **-ris.** 1 a tropical Asian malvaceous plant, *Hibiscus cannabinus,* that yields a fibre similar to jute. 2 the fibre derived from this plant. ◆ Also called: **kenaf.**
▷HISTORY C20: from Hindi *ambārī*

ambassador (æmˈbæsədə) NOUN 1 short for **ambassador extraordinary and plenipotentiary;** a diplomatic minister of the highest rank, accredited as permanent representative to another country or sovereign. 2 **ambassador extraordinary.** a diplomatic minister of the highest rank sent on a special mission. 3 **ambassador plenipotentiary.** a diplomatic minister of the first rank with treaty-signing powers. 4 **ambassador-at-large.** *US* an ambassador with special duties who may be sent to more than one government. 5 an authorized representative or messenger.
▷HISTORY C14: from Old French *ambassadeur,* from Italian *ambasciator,* from Old Provençal *ambaisador,* from *ambaisa* (unattested) mission, errand; see EMBASSY
▸**amˈbassadress** FEMININE NOUN ▸**ambassadorial** (æmˌbæsəˈdɔːrɪəl) ADJECTIVE ▸**amˈbassadorˌship** NOUN

ambatch *or* **ambach** (ˈæmˌbætʃ) NOUN a tree or shrub of the Nile Valley, *Aeschynomene elaphroxylon,* valued for its light-coloured pithlike wood.
▷HISTORY C19: probably from the Ethiopian name

amber (ˈæmbə) NOUN 1 **a** a yellow or yellowish-brown hard translucent fossil resin derived from extinct coniferous trees that occurs in Tertiary deposits and often contains trapped insects. It is used for jewellery, ornaments, etc. **b** (*as modifier*): *an amber necklace.* Related adjective: **succinic.** 2 **fly in amber.** a strange relic or reminder of the past. 3 **a** a medium to dark brownish-yellow colour, often somewhat orange, similar to that of the resin. **b** (*as adjective*): *an amber dress.* 4 an amber traffic light used as a warning between red and green.
▷HISTORY C14: from Medieval Latin *ambar,* from Arabic *ʿanbar* ambergris

amber fluid NOUN *Austral slang* beer.

amber gambler NOUN *Brit informal* a driver who races through traffic lights when they are at amber.

ambergris (ˈæmbəˌgriːs, -ˌgrɪs) NOUN a waxy substance consisting mainly of cholesterol secreted by the intestinal tract of the sperm whale and often found floating in the sea: used in the manufacture of perfumes.
▷HISTORY C15: from Old French *ambre gris* grey amber

amberjack (ˈæmbəˌdʒæk) NOUN any of several large carangid fishes of the genus *Seriola,* esp *S. dumerili,* with golden markings when young, occurring in tropical and subtropical Atlantic waters.
▷HISTORY C19: from AMBER + JACK[1]

amberoid (ˈæmbəˌrɔɪd) *or* **ambroid** NOUN a synthetic amber made by compressing pieces of amber and other resins together at a high temperature.

ambi- COMBINING FORM indicating both: *ambidextrous; ambivalence; ambiversion.*
▷HISTORY from Latin: round, on both sides, both, from *ambo* both; compare AMPHI-

ambidentate (ˌæmbɪˈdɛnteɪt) ADJECTIVE *Chem* another word for **amphidentate.**

ambidextrous (ˌæmbɪˈdɛkstrəs) ADJECTIVE 1 equally expert with each hand. 2 *Informal* highly skilled or adept. 3 underhanded; deceitful.
▸**ambidexterity** (ˌæmbɪdɛkˈstɛrɪtɪ) *or* ˌ**ambiˈdextrousness** NOUN ▸ˌ**ambiˈdextrously** ADVERB

ambience *or* **ambiance** (ˈæmbɪəns; *French* ɑ̃bjɑ̃s) NOUN the atmosphere of a place.
▷HISTORY C19: from French *ambiance,* from *ambiant* surrounding; see AMBIENT

ambient (ˈæmbɪənt) ADJECTIVE 1 of or relating to the immediate surroundings: *the ambient temperature was 15°C.* 2 creating a relaxing atmosphere: *ambient music.* ◆ NOUN 3 *Informal* ambient music.
▷HISTORY C16: from Latin *ambiēns* going round, from *ambīre,* from AMBI- + *īre* to go

ambient noise NOUN the level of the total noise in an area.

ambiguity (ˌæmbɪˈgjuːɪtɪ) NOUN, *plural* **-ties.** 1 the possibility of interpreting an expression in two or more distinct ways. 2 an instance of this, as in the sentence *they are cooking apples.* 3 vagueness or uncertainty of meaning: *there are several ambiguities in the situation.*

ambiguous (æmˈbɪgjʊəs) ADJECTIVE 1 having more than one possible interpretation or meaning. 2 difficult to understand or classify; obscure.
▷HISTORY C16: from Latin *ambiguus* going here and there, uncertain, from *ambigere* to go around, from AMBI- + *agere* to lead, act
▸**amˈbiguously** ADVERB ▸**amˈbiguousness** NOUN

ambiophony (ˌæmbɪˈɒfənɪ) NOUN the

reproduction of sound to create an illusion to a listener of being in a spacious room, such as a concert hall.

ambipolar (ˌæmbɪˈpəʊlə) ADJECTIVE *Electronics* (of plasmas and semiconductors) involving both positive and negative charge carriers.

ambisexual (ˌæmbɪˈsɛksjʊəl) ADJECTIVE 1 *Biology* relating to or affecting both the male and female sexes. 2 Also: **ambosexual.** bisexual.

ambisonics (ˌæmbɪˈsɒnɪks) NOUN (*functioning as singular*) the technique of reproducing and transmitting surround sound. See **surround sound.**

ambit (ˈæmbɪt) NOUN 1 scope or extent. 2 limits, boundary, or circumference.
▷HISTORY C16: from Latin *ambitus* a going round, from *ambīre* to go round, from AMBI- + *īre* to go

ambition (æmˈbɪʃən) NOUN 1 strong desire for success, achievement, or distinction. 2 something so desired; goal; aim.
▷HISTORY C14: from Old French, from Latin *ambitiō* a going round (of candidates), a striving to please, from *ambīre* to go round; see AMBIT

ambitious (æmˈbɪʃəs) ADJECTIVE 1 having a strong desire for success or achievement; wanting power, money, etc. 2 necessitating extraordinary effort or ability: *an ambitious project.* 3 (often foll by *of*) having a great desire (for something or to do something).
▸**amˈbitiously** ADVERB ▸**amˈbitiousness** NOUN

ambivalence (æmˈbɪvələns) *or* **ambivalency** NOUN the simultaneous existence of two opposed and conflicting attitudes, emotions, etc.
▸**amˈbivalent** ADJECTIVE

ambivert (ˈæmbɪˌvɜːt) NOUN *Psychol* a person who is intermediate between an extrovert and an introvert.
▸**ambiversion** (ˌæmbɪˈvɜːʃən) NOUN

amble (ˈæmbəl) VERB (*intr*) 1 to walk at a leisurely relaxed pace. 2 (of a horse) to move slowly, lifting both legs on one side together. 3 to ride a horse at an amble or leisurely pace. ◆ NOUN 4 a leisurely motion in walking. 5 a leisurely walk. 6 the ambling gait of a horse.
▷HISTORY C14: from Old French *ambler,* from Latin *ambulāre* to walk
▸ˈ**ambler** NOUN

Ambleside (ˈæmbəlˌsaɪd) NOUN a town in NW England, in Cumbria: a tourist centre for the Lake District. Pop.: 2905 (1991).

amblygonite (æmˈblɪɡəˌnaɪt) NOUN a white or greyish mineral consisting of lithium aluminium fluorophosphate in triclinic crystalline form. It is a source of lithium. Formula: $(Li,Na)Al(PO_4)(F,OH)$.
▷HISTORY C16: from Greek *amblugōnios,* from *amblus* blunt + *gōnia* angle; referring to the obtuse angles in its crystals

amblyopia (ˌæmblɪˈəʊpɪə) NOUN impaired vision with no discernible damage to the eye or optic nerve.
▷HISTORY C18: New Latin, from Greek *ambluōpia,* from *amblus* dull, dim + *ōps* eye
▸**amblyopic** (ˌæmblɪˈɒpɪk) ADJECTIVE

ambo[1] (ˈæmbəʊ) NOUN, *plural* **ambos** *or* **ambones** (æmˈbəʊniːz). either of two raised pulpits from which the gospels and epistles were read in early Christian churches.
▷HISTORY C17: from Medieval Latin, from Greek *ambōn* raised rim, pulpit

ambo[2] (ˈæmbəʊ) NOUN, *plural* **ambos.** *Austral informal* 1 an ambulance driver. 2 an ambulance.

amboceptor (ˈæmbəʊˌsɛptə) NOUN an immune body formed in the blood during infection or immunization that serves to link the complement to the antigen.
▷HISTORY C20: from Latin *ambō* both (see AMBI-) + (RE)CEPTOR

Amboina (æmˈbɔɪnə) NOUN 1 an island in Indonesia, in the Moluccas. Capital: Amboina. Area: 1000 sq. km (386 sq. miles). 2 Also called: **Ambon** (ˈɑːmbɔːn). a port in the Moluccas, the capital of Amboina island.

Amboise (*French* ɑ̃bwaz) NOUN a town in NW central France, on the River Loire: famous castle, a former royal residence. Pop.: 11 415 (latest est.).

ambosexual (ˌæmbəʊˈsɛksjʊəl) ADJECTIVE a variant of **ambisexual.**

amboyna *or* **amboina** (æmˈbɔɪnə) NOUN the mottled curly-grained wood of an Indonesian leguminous tree, *Pterocarpus indicus,* used in making furniture.
▷HISTORY C19: from the island of AMBOINA

ambroid (ˈæmbrɔɪd) NOUN a variant of **amberoid.**

ambrosia (æmˈbrəʊzɪə) NOUN 1 *Classical myth* the food of the gods, said to bestow immortality. Compare **nectar** (sense 2). 2 anything particularly delightful to taste or smell. 3 another name for **beebread.** 4 any of various herbaceous plants constituting the genus *Ambrosia,* mostly native to America but widely naturalized: family *Asteraceae* (composites). The genus includes the ragweeds.
▷HISTORY C16: via Latin from Greek: immortality, from *ambrotos,* from A-[1] + *brotos* mortal
▸**amˈbrosial** *or* **amˈbrosian** ADJECTIVE ▸**amˈbrosially** ADVERB

ambrosia beetle NOUN any of various small beetles of the genera *Anisandrus, Xyleborus,* etc., that bore tunnels into solid wood, feeding on fungi growing in the tunnels: family *Scolytidae* (bark beetles).

ambrotype (ˈæmbrəʊˌtaɪp) NOUN *Photog* an early type of glass negative that could be made to appear as a positive by backing it with black varnish or paper.
▷HISTORY C19: from Greek *ambrotos* immortal + -TYPE; see AMBROSIA

ambry (ˈæmbrɪ) *or* **aumbry** (ˈɔːmbrɪ) NOUN, *plural* **-bries.** 1 a recessed cupboard in the wall of a church near the altar, used to store sacred vessels, etc. 2 *Obsolete* a small cupboard or other storage space.
▷HISTORY C14: from Old French *almarie,* from Medieval Latin *almārium,* from Latin *armārium* chest for storage, from *arma* arms

ambsace *or* **amesace** (ˈeɪmzˌeɪs, ˈæmz-) NOUN 1 double ace, the lowest throw at dice. 2 bad luck.
▷HISTORY C13: from Old French *ambes as,* both aces; *as* from Latin: unit

ambulacrum (ˌæmbjʊˈleɪkrəm) NOUN, *plural* **-ra** (-rə). any of five radial bands on the ventral surface of echinoderms, such as the starfish and sea urchin, on which the tube feet are situated.
▷HISTORY C19: from Latin: avenue, from *ambulāre* to walk
▸ˌ**ambuˈlacral** ADJECTIVE

ambulance (ˈæmbjʊləns) NOUN a motor vehicle designed to carry sick or injured people.
▷HISTORY C19: from French, based on (*hôpital*) *ambulant* mobile or field (hospital), from Latin *ambulāre* to walk

ambulance chaser NOUN *US slang* a lawyer who seeks to encourage and profit from the lawsuits of accident victims.
▸**ambulance chasing** NOUN

ambulance stocks PLURAL NOUN high performance stocks and shares recommended by a broker to a dissatisfied client to improve their relationship.

ambulant (ˈæmbjʊlənt) ADJECTIVE 1 moving about from place to place. 2 *Med* another word for **ambulatory** (sense 3).

ambulate (ˈæmbjʊˌleɪt) VERB (*intr*) to wander about or move from one place to another.
▷HISTORY C17: from Latin *ambulāre* to walk, AMBLE
▸ˌ**ambuˈlation** NOUN

ambulatory (ˈæmbjʊlətərɪ) ADJECTIVE 1 of, relating to, or designed for walking. 2 changing position; not fixed. 3 Also: **ambulant.** able to walk. 4 *Law* (esp of a will) capable of being altered or revoked. ◆ NOUN, *plural* **-ries.** 5 *Architect* **a** an aisle running around the east end of a church, esp one that passes behind the sanctuary. **b** a place for walking, such as an aisle or a cloister.

ambuscade (ˌæmbəˈskeɪd) NOUN 1 an ambush. ◆ VERB 2 to ambush or lie in ambush.
▷HISTORY C16: from French *embuscade,* from Old Italian *imboscata,* probably of Germanic origin; compare AMBUSH

ambush (ˈæmbʊʃ) NOUN 1 the act of waiting in a concealed position in order to launch a surprise attack. 2 a surprise attack from such a position. 3 the concealed position from which such an attack is launched. 4 the person or persons waiting to launch such an attack. ◆ VERB 5 to lie in wait (for). 6 (*tr*) to attack suddenly from a concealed position.
▷HISTORY C14: from Old French *embuschier* to position in ambush, from *em-* IM- + *-buschier,* from *busche* piece of firewood, probably of Germanic origin; see BUSH[1]

AMDG ABBREVIATION FOR ad majorem Dei gloriam (the Jesuit motto).
▷HISTORY Latin: to the greater glory of God

am-dram *Brit informal* ABBREVIATION FOR amateur dramatics.

ameba (əˈmiːbə) NOUN, *plural* **-bae** (-biː) *or* **-bas.** the usual US spelling of **amoeba.**
▸**aˈmebic** ADJECTIVE

ameer (əˈmɪə) NOUN 1 a variant spelling of **emir.** 2 (formerly) the ruler of Afghanistan; amir.

ameiosis (ˌeɪmaɪˈəʊsɪs) NOUN *Biology* the absence of pairing of chromosomes during meiosis.

amelia (əˈmiːlɪə) NOUN *Pathol* the congenital absence of arms or legs.
▷HISTORY from A-[1] + Greek *melos* limb + -IA

ameliorate (əˈmiːljəˌreɪt) VERB to make or become better; improve.
▷HISTORY C18: from MELIORATE, influenced by French *améliorer* to improve, from Old French *ameillorer* to make better, from *meillor* better, from Latin *melior*
▸**ameliorable** (əˈmiːljərəbəl) ADJECTIVE ▸**aˈmeliorant** NOUN ▸**aˈmeliorative** ADJECTIVE ▸**aˈmelioˌrator** NOUN

> **Language note** *Ameliorate* is often wrongly used where *alleviate* is meant. *Ameliorate* is properly used to mean 'improve', not 'make easier to bear', so one should talk about *alleviating* pain or hardship, not *ameliorating* it.

amelioration (əˌmiːljəˈreɪʃən) NOUN 1 the act or an instance of ameliorating or the state of being ameliorated. 2 something that ameliorates; an improvement. 3 Also called: **elevation.** *Linguistics* (of the meaning of a word) a change from pejorative to neutral or positively pleasant. The word *nice* has achieved its modern meaning by amelioration from the earlier sense *foolish, silly.*

ameloblast (əˈmiːləʊblæst, -blɑːst) NOUN a type of cell involved in forming dental enamel.
▷HISTORY C19: from (EN)AMEL + -O- + -BLAST

amelogenesis (əˌmiːləʊˈdʒɛnɪsɪs) NOUN the production of enamel by ameloblasts.

amen (ˌeɪˈmɛn, ˌɑːˈmɛn) INTERJECTION 1 so be it!: a term used at the end of a prayer or religious statement. ◆ NOUN 2 the use of the word *amen,* as at the end of a prayer. 3 **say amen to.** to express strong approval of or support for (an assertion, hope, etc.).
▷HISTORY C13: via Late Latin via Greek from Hebrew *āmēn* certainly

Amen, Amon, *or* **Amūn** (ˈɑːmən) NOUN *Egyptian myth* a local Theban god, having a ram's head and symbolizing life and fertility, identified by the Egyptians with the national deity Amen-Ra.

amenable (əˈmiːnəbəl) ADJECTIVE 1 open or susceptible to suggestion; likely to listen, cooperate, etc. 2 accountable for behaviour to some authority; answerable. 3 capable of being or liable to be tested, judged, etc.
▷HISTORY C16: from Anglo-French, from Old French *amener* to lead up, from Latin *mināre* to drive (cattle), from *minārī* to threaten
▸**aˌmenaˈbility** *or* **aˈmenableness** NOUN ▸**aˈmenably** ADVERB

amen corner NOUN **the.** *US* the part of a church, usually to one side of the pulpit, occupied by people who lead the responsive amens during the service.

amend (əˈmɛnd) VERB (*tr*) 1 to improve; change for the better. 2 to remove faults from; correct. 3 to alter or revise (legislation, a constitution, etc.) by formal procedure.
▷HISTORY C13: from Old French *amender,* from Latin *ēmendāre* to EMEND
▸**aˈmendable** ADJECTIVE ▸**aˈmender** NOUN

amendatory (əˈmɛndətərɪ, -trɪ) ADJECTIVE *US* serving to amend; corrective.

amende honorable *French* (amɑ̃d ɔnɔrablə) NOUN, *plural* ***amendes honorables*** (amɑ̃dz ɔnɔrablə). a public apology and reparation made to satisfy the

honour of the person wronged. Sometimes shortened to ***amende.***
▷HISTORY C18: literally: honourable compensation

amendment (ə'mɛndmənt) NOUN 1 the act of amending; correction. 2 an addition, alteration, or improvement to a motion, document, etc.

amends (ə'mɛndz) NOUN *(functioning as singular)* recompense or compensation given or gained for some injury, insult, etc.: *to make amends.*
▷HISTORY C13: from Old French *amendes* fines, from *amende* compensation, from *amender* to EMEND

amenity (ə'mi:nɪtɪ) NOUN, *plural* **-ties.** 1 *(often plural)* a useful or pleasant facility or service: *a swimming pool was just one of the amenities.* 2 the fact or condition of being pleasant or agreeable. 3 *(usually plural)* a social courtesy or pleasantry.
▷HISTORY C14: from Latin *amoenitās* pleasantness, from *amoenus* agreeable

amenity bed NOUN (in Britain) a hospital bed whose occupant receives free treatment but pays for nonmedical advantages, such as privacy. Also called (informal): **pay bed.**

amenorrhoea *or esp US* **amenorrhea** (æˌmɛnə'rɪə, eɪ-) NOUN abnormal absence of menstruation.
▷HISTORY C19: from A-[1] + MENO- + -RRHOEA

Amen-Ra (ˌɑ:mən'rɑ:) NOUN *Egyptian myth* the sun-god; the principal deity during the period of Theban hegemony.

a mensa et thoro (eɪ 'mɛnsə ɛt 'θɔ:rəʊ) ADJECTIVE *Law* denoting or relating to a form of divorce in which the parties remain married but do not cohabit: abolished in England in 1857.
▷HISTORY Latin: from table and bed

ament[1] ('æmənt, 'eɪmənt) NOUN another name for **catkin.** Also called: **amentum** (ə'mɛntəm).
▷HISTORY C18: from Latin *āmentum* strap, thong
▸ˌ**amen'taceous** ADJECTIVE ▸ˌ**amen'tiferous** ADJECTIVE

ament[2] (æ'mɛnt, 'eɪmənt) NOUN *Psychiatry* a mentally deficient person.
▷HISTORY C19: from Latin *āment-, āmens* without mind; see AMENTIA

amentia (ə'mɛnʃə) NOUN severe mental deficiency, usually congenital. Compare **dementia.**
▷HISTORY C14: from Latin: insanity, from *āmēns* mad, from *mēns* mind

Amer. ABBREVIATION FOR America(n).

amerce (ə'mɜ:s) VERB *(tr) Obsolete* 1 *Law* to punish by a fine. 2 to punish with any arbitrary penalty.
▷HISTORY C14: from Anglo-French *amercier,* from Old French *à merci* at the mercy (because the fine was arbitrarily fixed); see MERCY
▸**a'merceable** ADJECTIVE ▸**a'mercement** NOUN ▸**a'mercer** NOUN

America (ə'mɛrɪkə) NOUN 1 short for the **United States of America.** 2 Also called: **the Americas.** the American continent, including North, South, and Central America.
▷HISTORY C16: from *Americus,* Latin form of *Amerigo;* after Amerigo Vespucci (?1454–1512), Florentine navigator in the New World

American (ə'mɛrɪkən) ADJECTIVE 1 of or relating to the United States of America, its inhabitants, or their form of English. 2 of or relating to the American continent. ◆ NOUN 3 a native or citizen of the US. 4 a native or inhabitant of any country of North, Central, or South America. 5 the English language as spoken or written in the United States.

Americana (əˌmɛrɪ'kɑ:nə) PLURAL NOUN objects, such as books, documents, relics, etc., relating to America, esp in the form of a collection.

American aloe NOUN another name for **century plant.**

American chameleon NOUN another name for **anole.**

American cheese NOUN a type of smooth hard white or yellow cheese similar to a mild Cheddar.

American cloth NOUN a glazed or waterproofed cotton cloth.

American Curl NOUN a breed of slender cat with curled-back ears and a plumed tail.

American Dream NOUN **the.** the notion that the American social, economic, and political system makes success possible for every individual.

American eagle NOUN another name for **bald eagle,** esp when depicted as the national emblem of the US.

American Expeditionary Forces PLURAL NOUN the troops sent to Europe by the US during World War I.

American Federation of Labor NOUN the first permanent national labour movement in America, founded in 1886. It amalgamated with the Congress of Industrial Organizations in 1955. See also **AFL-CIO.**

American football NOUN 1 a team game similar to rugby, with 11 players on each side. Forward passing is allowed and planned strategies and formations for play are decided during the course of the game. 2 the oval-shaped inflated ball used in this game.

American Indian NOUN 1 Also called: **Indian, Red Indian, Amerindian, Native American.** a member of any of the indigenous peoples of North, Central, or South America, having Mongoloid affinities, notably straight black hair and a yellow to brown skin. ◆ ADJECTIVE 2 Also: **Amerindian.** of or relating to any of these peoples, their languages, or their cultures.

American Indian Movement NOUN a militant movement or grouping of American Indians, organized in 1968 to combat discrimination, injustice, etc.

Americanism (ə'mɛrɪkəˌnɪzəm) NOUN 1 a custom, linguistic usage, or other feature peculiar to or characteristic of the United States, its people, or their culture. 2 loyalty to the United States, its people, customs, etc.

Americanist (ə'mɛrɪkənɪst) NOUN a person who studies some aspect of America, such as its history or languages.

Americanize *or* **Americanise** (ə'mɛrɪkəˌnaɪz) VERB to make or become American in outlook, attitudes, etc.
▸**Aˌmericani'zation** *or* **Aˌmericani'sation** NOUN
▸**A'mericanˌizer** *or* **A'mericanˌiser** NOUN

American pit bull terrier NOUN another name for **pit bull terrier.**

American plan NOUN *US* a hotel rate in which the charge includes meals. Compare **European plan.**

American Revolution NOUN the usual US term for **War of American Independence.**

American Samoa NOUN the part of Samoa administered by the US. Capital: Pago Pago. Pop.: 58 000 (2001 est.). Area: 197 sq. km (76 sq. miles).

American sign language NOUN See **Ameslan.**

American Standard Version NOUN a revised version of the Authorized (King James) Version of the Bible, published by a committee of American scholars in 1901.

American trypanosomiasis NOUN *Pathol* another name for **Chagas' disease.**

American Wake NOUN *Irish* an all-night farewell party for a person about to emigrate to America.

American wirehair ('waɪəˌhɛə) NOUN a breed of medium-large cat with a coarse wiry coat.

America's Cup NOUN an international yachting trophy, first won by the schooner *America* in 1851 and held as a challenge trophy by the New York Yacht Club until 1983.

americium (ˌæmə'rɪsɪəm) NOUN a white metallic transuranic element artificially produced from plutonium. It is used as an alpha-particle source. Symbol: Am; atomic no.: 95; half-life of most stable isotope, ^{243}Am: 7.4×10^3 years; valency: 2,3,4,5, or 6; relative density: 13.67; melting pt.: 1176°C; boiling pt.: 2607°C (est.).
▷HISTORY C20: from AMERICA (because it was discovered at Berkeley, California) + -IUM

Amerindian (ˌæmə'rɪndɪən) NOUN *also* **Amerind** ('æmərɪnd), ADJECTIVE another word for **American Indian.**
▸ˌ**Amer'indic** ADJECTIVE

Amersfoort (*Dutch* 'a:mərsfo:rt) NOUN a town in the central Netherlands, in E Utrecht province. Pop.: 123 367 (1999 est.).

amesace ('eɪmzˌeɪs, 'æmz-) NOUN a variant spelling of **ambsace.**

Ameslan ('æməsˌlæn) NOUN American sign language: a language in which meaning is conveyed by hand gestures and their position in relation to the upper part of the body. Abbreviation: **ASL.**
▷HISTORY C20: from *Ame(rican) s(ign) lan(guage)*

Ames test (eɪmz) NOUN a method of preliminary screening for carcinogens, based on their ability to cause mutations in bacteria.
▷HISTORY named after Bruce *Ames* (born 1928), US biochemist who invented the test

ametabolic (əˌmɛtə'bɒlɪk) ADJECTIVE (of certain insects) having no obvious metamorphosis.

amethyst ('æmɪθɪst) NOUN 1 a purple or violet transparent variety of quartz used as a gemstone. Formula: SiO_2. 2 a purple variety of sapphire; oriental amethyst. 3 the purple colour of amethyst.
▷HISTORY C13: from Old French *amatiste,* from Latin *amethystus,* from Greek *amethustos,* literally: not drunken, from A-[1] + *methuein* to make drunk; referring to the belief that the stone could prevent intoxication
▸**amethystine** (ˌæmɪ'θɪstaɪn) ADJECTIVE

ametropia (ˌæmɪ'trəʊpɪə) NOUN loss of ability to focus images on the retina, caused by an imperfection in the refractive function of the eye.
▷HISTORY C19: New Latin, from Greek *ametros* unmeasured (from A-[1] + *metron* measure) + *ōps* eye

Amex ('æmɛks) NOUN ACRONYM FOR: 1 *Trademark* American Express. 2 American Stock Exchange.

AMF ABBREVIATION FOR Australian Military Forces.

Amfortas (æm'fɔ:təs) NOUN (in medieval legend) the leader of the knights of the Holy Grail.

Amhara (æm'hɑ:rə) NOUN 1 a region of NW Ethiopia: formerly a kingdom. 2 an inhabitant of the former kingdom of Amhara.

Amharic (æm'hærɪk) NOUN 1 the official language of Ethiopia, belonging to the SE Semitic subfamily of the Afro-Asiatic family. ◆ ADJECTIVE 2 denoting or relating to this language.

ami *French* (ami) NOUN a male friend.

amiable ('eɪmɪəbᵊl) ADJECTIVE having or displaying a pleasant or agreeable nature; friendly.
▷HISTORY C14: from Old French, from Late Latin *amīcābilis* AMICABLE
▸ˌ**amia'bility** *or* **'amiableness** NOUN ▸**'amiably** ADVERB

amianthus (ˌæmɪ'ænθəs) NOUN any of the fine silky varieties of asbestos.
▷HISTORY C17: from Latin *amiantus,* from Greek *amiantos* unsullied, from A-[1] + *miainein* to pollute
▸ˌ**ami'anthine** *or* ˌ**ami'anthoid** *or* ˌ**amian'thoidal** ADJECTIVE

amicable ('æmɪkəbᵊl) ADJECTIVE characterized by friendliness: *an amicable agreement.*
▷HISTORY C15: from Late Latin *amīcābilis,* from Latin *amīcus* friend; related to *amāre* to love
▸ˌ**amica'bility** *or* **'amicableness** NOUN ▸**'amicably** ADVERB

amice[1] ('æmɪs) NOUN *Christianity* a rectangular piece of white linen worn by priests around the neck and shoulders under the alb or, formerly, on the head.
▷HISTORY C15: from Old French *amis,* plural of *amit,* or from Medieval Latin *amicia,* both from Latin *amictus* cloak, from *amicīre* to clothe, from *am-* AMBI- + *iacere* to throw

amice[2] ('æmɪs) NOUN another word for **almuce.**

AMICE ABBREVIATION FOR Associate Member of the Institution of Civil Engineers.

AMIChemE ABBREVIATION FOR Associate Member of the Institution of Chemical Engineers.

amicus curiae (æ'mi:kʊs 'kjʊərɪˌi:) NOUN, *plural* **amici curiae** (æ'mi:kaɪ). *Law* a person not directly engaged in a case who advises the court.
▷HISTORY Latin, literally: friend of the court

amid (ə'mɪd) *or* **amidst** PREPOSITION in the middle of; among.
▷HISTORY Old English *on middan* in the middle; see MID[1]

Amida (amidə) NOUN the Japanese name for **Amitabha.**

Amidah (ami'da:, a'midə) NOUN *Judaism* the central prayer in each of the daily services, recited silently and standing. Also called: **Shemona Esrei.**

amide ('æmaɪd) NOUN 1 any organic compound containing the functional group $-CONH_2$. 2 *(modifier)* consisting of, containing, or concerned with the group $-CONH_2$: *amide group or radical.* 3 an inorganic compound having the general formula $M(NH_2)_x$, where M is a metal atom.

▷HISTORY C19: from AM(MONIA) + -IDE
▸**amidic** (əˈmɪdɪk) ADJECTIVE

amido- COMBINING FORM (in chemistry) indicating the presence of an amide group.
▷HISTORY from AMIDE

Amidol (ˈæmɪdɒl) NOUN *Trademark* a grey to colourless soluble crystalline solid that is used as a photographic developer; 2,4-diaminophenol dihydrochloride. Formula: $C_6H_3(NH_2)_2(OH).2HCl$.

amidships (əˈmɪdʃɪps) ADVERB, ADJECTIVE (*postpositive*) *Nautical* at, near, or towards the centre of a vessel.

amie *French* (ami) NOUN a female friend.

AMIEE (in Britain) ABBREVIATION FOR Associate Member of the Institution of Electrical Engineers.

Amiens (ˈæmɪənz; *French* amjɛ̃) NOUN a city in N France: its Gothic cathedral is the largest church in France. Pop.: 135 501 (1999).

amigo (æˈmiːgəʊ, ə-) NOUN, *plural* **-gos**. a friend; comrade.
▷HISTORY Spanish, from Latin *amicus*

AMIMechE (in Britain) ABBREVIATION FOR Associate Member of the Institution of Mechanical Engineers.

Amin (æˈmiːn, ɑː-) NOUN **Lake**. a former official name for (Lake) **Edward**.

amine (əˈmiːn, ˈæmɪn) NOUN an organic base formed by replacing one or more of the hydrogen atoms of ammonia by organic groups.
▷HISTORY C19: from AM(MONIUM) + -INE[2]

-amine NOUN COMBINING FORM indicating an amine: *histamine; methylamine*.

amino (əˈmaɪnəʊ, -ˈmiː-) NOUN (*modifier*) of, consisting of, or containing the group of atoms $-NH_2$: *amino group or radical; amino acid*.

amino- COMBINING FORM indicating the presence of an amino group: *aminobenzoic acid*.
▷HISTORY from AMINE

amino acid NOUN any of a group of organic compounds containing one or more amino groups, $-NH_2$, and one or more carboxyl groups, -COOH. The alpha-amino acids $RCH(NH_2)COOH$ (where R is either hydrogen or an organic group) are the component molecules of proteins; some can be synthesized in the body (**nonessential amino acids**) and others cannot and are thus essential components of the diet (**essential amino acids**).

amino acid sequence NOUN the unique sequence of amino acids that characterizes a given protein.

aminobenzoic acid (əˌmaɪnəʊbɛnˈzəʊɪk, -ˌmiː-) NOUN a derivative of benzoic acid existing in three isomeric forms, the *para-* form being used in the manufacture of dyes and sunburn preventatives. Formula: $NH_2C_6H_4COOH$.

aminophenazone (əˌmaɪnəʊˈfiːnəˌzəʊn, -ˌmiː-) NOUN a crystalline compound used to reduce pain and fever. Formula: $C_{13}H_{17}N_3O$. Also called: **aminopyrine**.

aminophenol (əˌmaɪnəʊˈfiːnɒl, -ˌmiː-) NOUN *Chem* any of three isomeric forms that are soluble crystalline solids, used as a dye intermediate (meta- and ortho-), in dyeing hair, fur, and textiles (ortho- and para-), and as a photographic developer (para-). Formula: $C_6H_4NH_2OH$.

aminophylline (æmɪˈnɒfɪliːn) NOUN a derivative of theophylline that relaxes smooth muscle and is used mainly to dilate the airways in the treatment of asthma and emphysema.
▷HISTORY C20: from AMINO- + PHYLLO- + -INE[2]

aminopyrine (əˌmaɪnəʊˈpaɪriːn, -ˌmiː-) NOUN another name for **aminophenazone**.

amino resin NOUN any thermosetting synthetic resin formed by copolymerization of amines or amides with aldehydes. Amino resins are used as adhesives and as coatings for paper and textiles. See also **urea-formaldehyde resin, melamine**.

amir (əˈmɪə) NOUN 1 a variant spelling of **emir**. 2 (formerly) the ruler of Afghanistan; ameer.
▷HISTORY C19: from Arabic, variant of EMIR
▸**aˈmirate** NOUN

Amish (ˈɑːmɪʃ, ˈæ-) ADJECTIVE 1 of or relating to a US and Canadian Mennonite sect that traces its origin to Jakob Amman. ◆ NOUN 2 **the**. the Amish people.
▷HISTORY C19: from German *Amisch*, after Jakob *Amman*, 17th-century Swiss Mennonite bishop

amiss (əˈmɪs) ADVERB 1 in an incorrect, inappropriate, or defective manner. 2 **take (something) amiss**. to be annoyed or offended by (something). ◆ ADJECTIVE 3 (*postpositive*) wrong, incorrect, or faulty.
▷HISTORY C13 *a mis*, from *mis* wrong; see MISS[1]

Amitabha (ˌamiˈtɑbə) NOUN *Buddhism* (in Pure Land sects) a Bodhisattva who presides over a Pure Land in the west of the universe. Japanese name: **Amida**.
▷HISTORY Sanskrit, literally: immeasurable light, from *amita* infinite + *ābhā* light

amitosis (ˌæmɪˈtəʊsɪs) NOUN an unusual form of cell division in which the nucleus and cytoplasm divide by constriction without the formation of chromosomes; direct cell division.
▷HISTORY C19: A-[1] + MITOSIS
▸**amitotic** (ˌæmɪˈtɒtɪk) ADJECTIVE ▸ˌ**amiˈtotically** ADVERB

amitriptyline (ˌæmɪˈtrɪptɪˌliːn, -lɪn) NOUN a tricyclic antidepressant drug. Formula: $C_{20}H_{23}N$.
▷HISTORY C20: from AMINO + TRYPTAMINE + METHYL + -INE[2]

amity (ˈæmɪtɪ) NOUN, *plural* **-ties**. friendship; cordiality.
▷HISTORY C15: from Old French *amité*, from Medieval Latin *amīcitās* friendship, from Latin *amīcus* friend

AMM ABBREVIATION FOR antimissile (missile).

Amman (əˈmɑːn) NOUN the capital of Jordan, northeast of the Dead Sea: ancient capital of the Ammonites, rebuilt by Ptolemy in the 3rd century B.C. Pop.: 969 598 (1994). Ancient names: **Rabbath Ammon, Philadelphia**.

ammeter (ˈæmˌmiːtə) NOUN an instrument for measuring an electric current in amperes.
▷HISTORY C19: AM(PERE) + -METER

ammine (ˈæmiːn, əˈmiːn) NOUN a compound that has molecules containing one or more ammonia molecules bound to another molecule, group, or atom by coordinate bonds. Also called: **ammoniate, ammonate**.
▷HISTORY C19: from AMM(ONIA) + -INE[2]

ammo (ˈæməʊ) NOUN *Informal* short for **ammunition**.

ammocoete (ˈæməˌsiːt) NOUN the larva of primitive jawless vertebrates, such as the lamprey, that lives buried in mud and feeds on microorganisms.
▷HISTORY C19: from New Latin *ammocoetēs*, literally: that lie in sand, from Greek *ammos* sand + *koitē* bed, from *keisthai* to lie

Ammon[1] (ˈæmən) NOUN *Old Testament* the ancestor of the Ammonites.

Ammon[2] (ˈæmən) NOUN *Myth* the classical name of the Egyptian god Amen, identified by the Greeks with Zeus and by the Romans with Jupiter.

ammonal (ˈæmənᵊl) NOUN an explosive made by mixing TNT, ammonium nitrate, and aluminium powder.
▷HISTORY C20: from AMMON(IUM) + AL(UMINIUM)

ammonate (ˈæməˌneɪt) NOUN another name for **ammine**.

ammonia (əˈməʊnɪə, -njə) NOUN 1 a colourless pungent highly soluble gas mainly used in the manufacture of fertilizers, nitric acid, and other nitrogenous compounds, and as a refrigerant and solvent. Formula: NH_3. 2 a solution of ammonia in water, containing the compound ammonium hydroxide.
▷HISTORY C18: from New Latin, from Latin (*sal*) *ammōniacus* (sal) AMMONIAC[1]

ammoniac[1] (əˈməʊnɪˌæk) ADJECTIVE a variant of **ammoniacal**.

ammoniac[2] (əˈməʊnɪˌæk) NOUN a strong-smelling gum resin obtained from the stems of the N Asian umbelliferous plant *Dorema ammoniacum* and formerly used as an expectorant, stimulant, perfume, and in porcelain cement. Also called: **gum ammoniac**.
▷HISTORY C14: from Latin *ammōniacum*, from Greek *ammōniakos* belonging to Ammon (apparently the gum resin was extracted from plants found in Libya near the temple of Ammon)

ammoniacal (ˌæməˈnaɪəkᵊl) ADJECTIVE of, containing, using, or resembling ammonia. Also: **ammoniac**.

ammonia clock NOUN an atomic clock based on the frequency of inversion of the ammonia molecule.

ammoniate (əˈməʊnɪˌeɪt) VERB 1 to unite or treat with ammonia. ◆ NOUN 2 another name for **ammine**.
▸**amˌmoniˈation** NOUN

ammonic (əˈmɒnɪk, əˈməʊnɪk) ADJECTIVE of or concerned with ammonia or ammonium compounds.
▸**amˈmonical** ADJECTIVE

ammonify (əˈmɒnɪˌfaɪ, əˈməʊnɪ-) VERB **-fies, -fying, -fied**. to treat or impregnate with ammonia or a compound of ammonia.
▸**amˌmonifiˈcation** NOUN

ammonite[1] (ˈæməˌnaɪt) NOUN 1 any extinct marine cephalopod mollusc of the order *Ammonoidea*, which were common in Mesozoic times and generally had a coiled partitioned shell. Their closest modern relative is the pearly nautilus. 2 the shell of any of these animals, commonly occurring as a fossil.
▷HISTORY C18: from New Latin *Ammōnītēs*, from Medieval Latin *cornū Ammōnis*, literally: horn of Ammon
▸**ammonitic** (ˌæməˈnɪtɪk) ADJECTIVE

ammonite[2] (ˈæməˌnaɪt) NOUN 1 an explosive consisting mainly of ammonium nitrate with smaller amounts of other substances, such as TNT. 2 a nitrogenous fertilizer made from animal wastes.
▷HISTORY C20: from AMMO(NIUM) + NI(TRA)TE

Ammonites (ˈæməˌnaɪts) PLURAL NOUN *Old Testament* a nomadic tribe living east of the Jordan: a persistent enemy of the Israelites.

ammonium (əˈməʊnɪəm, -njəm) NOUN (*modifier*) of, consisting of, or containing the monovalent group NH_4– or the ion NH_4^+: *ammonium compounds*.

ammonium carbamate NOUN a white soluble crystalline compound produced by reaction between dry ammonia and carbon dioxide and used as a nitrogen fertilizer. Formula: $(NH_4)CO_2NH_2$.

ammonium carbonate NOUN 1 an unstable pungent soluble white powder that is a double salt of ammonium bicarbonate and ammonium carbamate: used in the manufacture of baking powder, smelling salts, and ammonium compounds. Formula: $(NH_4)HCO_3.(NH_4)CO_2NH_2$. 2 an unstable substance that is produced by treating this compound with ammonia. Formula: $(NH_4)_2CO_3$.

ammonium chloride NOUN a white soluble crystalline solid used chiefly as an electrolyte in dry batteries and as a mordant and soldering flux. Formula: NH_4Cl. Also called: **sal ammoniac**.

ammonium hydroxide NOUN a compound existing only in aqueous solution, formed when ammonia dissolves in water to form ammonium ions and hydroxide ions. Formula: NH_4OH.

ammonium ion NOUN the ion NH_4^+, formed from ammonia and present in aqueous solutions of ammonia and in many salts.

ammonium nitrate NOUN a colourless highly soluble crystalline solid used mainly as a fertilizer and in explosives and pyrotechnics. Formula: NH_4NO_3.

ammonium sulphate NOUN a white soluble crystalline solid used mainly as a fertilizer and in water purification. Formula: $(NH_4)_2SO_4$.

ammonolysis (ˌæməˈnɒlɪsɪs) NOUN *Chem* solvolysis in liquid ammonia.

ammunition (ˌæmjʊˈnɪʃən) NOUN 1 any projectiles, such as bullets, rockets, etc., that can be discharged from a weapon. 2 bombs, missiles, chemicals, biological agents, nuclear materials, etc., capable of use as weapons. 3 any means of defence or attack, as in an argument.
▷HISTORY C17: from obsolete French *amunition*, by mistaken division from earlier *la munition*; see MUNITION

amnesia (æmˈniːzjə, -ʒjə, -zɪə) NOUN a defect in memory, esp one resulting from pathological cause, such as brain damage or hysteria.
▷HISTORY C19: via New Latin from Greek: forgetfulness, probably from *amnēstia* oblivion; see AMNESTY

▸**amnesiac** (æm'ni:zɪˌæk) *or* **amnesic** (æm'ni:sɪk, -zɪk) ADJECTIVE, NOUN

amnesty ('æmnɪstɪ) NOUN, *plural* **-ties.** [1] a general pardon, esp for offences against a government. [2] a period during which a law is suspended to allow offenders to admit their crime without fear of prosecution. [3] *Law* a pardon granted by the Crown or Executive and effected by statute. ◆ VERB **-ties, -tying, -tied.** [4] (*tr*) to overlook or forget (an offence).
▹HISTORY C16: from Latin *amnēstia,* from Greek: oblivion, from *amnēstos* forgetting, from A-[1] + *-mnēstos,* from *mnasthai* to remember

Amnesty International NOUN an international organization founded in Britain in 1961 that works to secure the release of people imprisoned for their beliefs, to ban the use of torture, and to abolish the death penalty. Abbreviation: **AI.**

amniocentesis (ˌæmnɪəʊsɛn'ti:sɪs) NOUN, *plural* **-ses** (-si:z). removal of some amniotic fluid by the insertion into the womb of a hollow needle, for therapeutic or diagnostic purposes.
▹HISTORY C20: from AMNION + *centesis,* from Greek *kentēsis* a puncture, from *kentein* to prick

amnion ('æmnɪən) NOUN, *plural* **-nions** *or* **-nia** (-nɪə). the innermost of two membranes (see also **chorion**) enclosing an embryonic reptile, bird, or mammal.
▹HISTORY C17: via New Latin from Greek: a little lamb, from *amnos* a lamb

amniote ('æmnɪəʊt) NOUN any vertebrate animal, such as a reptile, bird, or mammal, that possesses an amnion, chorion, and allantois during embryonic development. Compare **anamniote.**

amniotic (ˌæmnɪ'ɒtɪk) ADJECTIVE of or relating to the amnion.

amniotic fluid NOUN the fluid surrounding the fetus in the womb.

amoeba *or US* **ameba** (ə'mi:bə) NOUN, *plural* **-bae** (-bi:) *or* **-bas.** any protozoan of the phylum *Rhizopoda,* esp any of the genus *Amoeba,* able to change shape because of the movements of cell processes (pseudopodia). They live in fresh water or soil or as parasites in man and animals.
▹HISTORY C19: from New Latin, from Greek *amoibē* change, from *ameibein* to change, exchange
▸**a'moebic** *or US* **a'mebic** ADJECTIVE

amoebaean *or* **amoebean** (ˌæmɪ'bi:ən) ADJECTIVE *Prosody* of or relating to lines of verse dialogue that answer each other alternately.

amoebiasis (ˌæmɪ'baɪəsɪs) NOUN, *plural* **-ses** (-ˌsi:z). infection, esp of the intestines, caused by the parasitic amoeba *Endamoeba histolytica.*

amoebic dysentery NOUN inflammation of the intestines caused by the parasitic amoeba *Endamoeba histolytica.*

amoebocyte *or US* **amebocyte** (ə'mi:bəˌsaɪt) NOUN any cell having properties similar to an amoeba, such as shape, mobility, and ability to engulf particles.

amoeboid *or US* **ameboid** (ə'mi:bɔɪd) ADJECTIVE of, related to, or resembling amoebae.

amok (ə'mʌk, ə'mɒk) *or* **amuck** (ə'mʌk) NOUN [1] a state of murderous frenzy, originally observed among Malays. ◆ ADVERB [2] **run amok.** to run about with or as if with a frenzied desire to kill.
▹HISTORY C17: from Malay *amoq* furious assault

Amon ('ɑ:mən) NOUN *Egyptian myth* a variant spelling of **Amen.**

among (ə'mʌŋ) *or* **amongst** PREPOSITION [1] in the midst of: *he lived among the Indians.* [2] to each of: *divide the reward among yourselves.* [3] in the group, class, or number of: *ranked among the greatest writers.* [4] taken out of (a group): *he is only one among many.* [5] with one another within a group; by the joint action of: *a lot of gossip among the women employees; decide it among yourselves.*
▹HISTORY Old English *amang,* contracted from *on gemang* in the group of, from ON + *gemang* crowd; see MINGLE, MONGREL

> **Language note** See at **between.**

amontillado (əˌmɒntɪ'lɑ:dəʊ) NOUN a medium dry Spanish sherry, not as pale in colour as a fino.
▹HISTORY C19: from Spanish *vino amontillado* wine of *Montilla,* town in Spain

amoral (eɪ'mɒrəl) ADJECTIVE [1] having no moral quality; nonmoral. [2] without moral standards or principles.
▸**amorality** (ˌeɪmɒ'rælɪtɪ) NOUN ▸**a'morally** ADVERB

> **Language note** *Amoral* is often wrongly used where *immoral* is meant. *Immoral* is properly used to talk about the breaking of moral rules, *amoral* about people who have no moral code or about places or situations where moral considerations do not apply.

amoretto (ˌæmə'rɛtəʊ) *or* **amorino** (ˌæmɔ:'ri:nəʊ) NOUN, *plural* **-retti** (-'rɛtɪ) *or* **-rini** (-'ri:nɪ). (esp in painting) a small chubby naked boy representing a cupid. Also called: **putto.**
▹HISTORY C16: from Italian, diminutive of *Amore* Cupid, from Latin *Amor* Love

amorist ('æmərɪst) NOUN a lover or a writer about love.

amoroso (ˌæmə'rəʊsəʊ) ADJECTIVE, ADVERB [1] *Music* (to be played) lovingly. ◆ NOUN [2] a rich sweetened sherry of a dark colour.
▹HISTORY from Italian and Spanish: AMOROUS

amorous ('æmərəs) ADJECTIVE [1] inclined towards or displaying love or desire. [2] in love. [3] of or relating to love.
▹HISTORY C14: from Old French, from Medieval Latin *amōrōsus,* from Latin *amor* love
▸**'amorously** ADVERB ▸**'amorousness** NOUN

amor patriae *Latin* ('æmɔ: 'pætrɪˌi:) NOUN love of one's country; patriotism.

amorphous (ə'mɔ:fəs) ADJECTIVE [1] lacking a definite shape; formless. [2] of no recognizable character or type. [3] (of chemicals, rocks, etc.) not having a crystalline structure.
▹HISTORY C18: from New Latin, from Greek *amorphos* shapeless, from A-[1] + *morphē* shape
▸**a'morphism** NOUN ▸**a'morphously** ADVERB
▸**a'morphousness** NOUN

amortization *or* **amortisation** (əˌmɔ:taɪ'zeɪʃən) NOUN [1] **a** the process of amortizing a debt. **b** the money devoted to amortizing a debt. [2] (in computing the redemption yield on a bond purchased at a premium) the amount that is subtracted from the annual yield. Compare **accumulation** (sense 3b).
▸**amortizement** *or* **amortisement** (ə'mɔ:tɪzmənt) NOUN

amortize *or* **amortise** (ə'mɔ:taɪz) VERB (*tr*) [1] *Finance* to liquidate (a debt, mortgage, etc.) by instalment payments or by periodic transfers to a sinking fund. [2] to write off (a wasting asset) by annual transfers to a sinking fund. [3] *Property law* (formerly) to transfer (lands, etc.) in mortmain.
▹HISTORY C14: from Medieval Latin *admortizāre,* from Old French *amortir* to reduce to the point of death, ultimately from Latin *ad* to + *mors* death
▸**a'mortizable** *or* **a'mortisable** ADJECTIVE

Amos ('eɪmɒs) NOUN *Old Testament* [1] a Hebrew prophet of the 8th century B.C. [2] the book containing his oracles.

amount (ə'maʊnt) NOUN [1] extent; quantity; supply. [2] the total of two or more quantities; sum. [3] the full value, effect, or significance of something. [4] a principal sum plus the interest on it, as in a loan. ◆ VERB [5] (*intr;* usually foll by *to*) to be equal or add up in effect, meaning, or quantity.
▹HISTORY C13: from Old French *amonter* to go up, from *amont* upwards, from *a* to + *mont* mountain (from Latin *mōns*)

> **Language note** The use of a plural noun after *amount of* (*an amount of bananas; the amount of refugees*) should be avoided: *a quantity of bananas; the number of refugees.*

amount of substance NOUN a measure of the number of entities (atoms, molecules, ions, electrons, etc.) present in a substance, expressed in moles.

amour *French* (amur) NOUN a love affair, esp a secret or illicit one.
▹HISTORY C13: from Old French, from Latin *amor* love

amour-propre *French* (amurprɔprə) NOUN self-respect.

amowt (ə'maʊt) NOUN a variant spelling of **amaut.**

Amoy (ə'mɔɪ) NOUN [1] a port in SE China, in Fujian province on **Amoy Island,** at the mouth of the Jiu-long River opposite Taiwan: one of the first treaty ports opened to European trade (1842). Pop.: 368 786 (1990 est.). Modern Chinese name: **Xiamen.** [2] the dialect of Chinese spoken in Amoy, Taiwan, and elsewhere: a Min dialect.

amp (æmp) NOUN [1] an ampere. [2] *Informal* an amplifier. ◆ VERB [3] *Austral informal* to excite or become excited. ◆ See also **amp up.**

AMP ABBREVIATION FOR: [1] **adenosine monophosphate.** [2] Australian Mutual Provident Society.

amp. ampere.

ampelopsis (ˌæmpɪ'lɒpsɪs) NOUN any woody vine of the vitaceous genus *Ampelopsis,* of tropical and subtropical Asia and America.
▹HISTORY C19: from New Latin, from Greek *ampelos* grapevine

amperage ('æmpərɪdʒ) NOUN the magnitude of an electric current measured in amperes, esp the rated current of an electrical component or device.

ampere ('æmpɛə) NOUN [1] the basic SI unit of electric current; the constant current that, when maintained in two parallel conductors of infinite length and negligible cross section placed 1 metre apart in free space, produces a force of 2×10^{-7} newton per metre between them. 1 ampere is equivalent to 1 coulomb per second. [2] a former unit of electric current (**international ampere**); the current that, when passed through a solution of silver nitrate, deposits silver at the rate of 0.001118 gram per second. 1 international ampere equals 0.999835 ampere. ◆ Abbreviation: **amp.** Symbol: A.
▹HISTORY C19: named after André Marie *Ampère* (1775–1836), French physicist and mathematician

ampere-hour NOUN a practical unit of quantity of electricity; the quantity that flows in one hour through a conductor carrying a current of 1 ampere. 1 ampere-hour is equivalent to 3600 coulombs. Abbreviation: **a.h.**

ampere-turn NOUN a unit of magnetomotive force; the magnetomotive force produced by a current of 1 ampere passing through one complete turn of a coil. 1 ampere-turn is equivalent to $4\pi/10$ or 1.257 gilberts. Abbreviations: **At, A.**

ampersand ('æmpəˌsænd) NOUN the character (&), meaning *and: John Brown & Co.*
▹HISTORY C19: shortened from *and per se and,* that is, the symbol & by itself (represents) *and*

amphetamine (æm'fɛtəˌmi:n, -mɪn) NOUN a synthetic colourless volatile liquid used medicinally as the white crystalline sulphate, mainly for its stimulant action on the central nervous system, although it also stimulates the sympathetic nervous system. It can have unpleasant or dangerous side effects and drug dependence can occur; 1-phenyl-2-aminopropane. Formula: $C_6H_5CH_2CH(NH_2)CH_3$.
▹HISTORY C20: from A(LPHA) + M(ETHYL) + PH(ENYL) + ET(HYL) + -AMINE

amphi- PREFIX [1] on both sides; at both ends; of both kinds: *amphipod; amphitrichous; amphibious.* [2] around: *amphibole.*
▹HISTORY from Greek

amphiarthrosis (ˌæmfɪɑ:'θrəʊsɪs) NOUN, *plural* **-ses** (-si:z). *Anatomy* a type of articulation permitting only slight movement, as between the vertebrae of the backbone.
▹HISTORY C19: from AMPHI- + Greek *arthrōsis* articulation, from *arthron* a joint

amphibian (æm'fɪbɪən) NOUN [1] any cold-blooded vertebrate of the class *Amphibia,* typically living on land but breeding in water. Their aquatic larvae (tadpoles) undergo metamorphosis into the adult form. The class includes the newts and salamanders, frogs and toads, and caecilians. [2] a type of aircraft able to land and take off from both water and land. [3] any vehicle able to travel on both water and land. ◆ ADJECTIVE [4] another word for **amphibious.** [5] of, relating to, or belonging to the class *Amphibia.*

amphibiotic (ˌæmfɪbaɪ'ɒtɪk) ADJECTIVE having an aquatic larval form and a terrestrial adult form, as amphibians.

amphibious (æm'fɪbɪəs) ADJECTIVE [1] able to live both on land and in the water, as frogs, toads, etc. [2] designed for operation on or from both water and land. [3] relating to military forces and

equipment organized for operations launched from the sea against an enemy shore. [4] having a dual or mixed nature.
▷HISTORY C17: from Greek *amphibios*, literally: having a double life, from AMPHI- + *bios* life
▸**am'phibiously** ADVERB ▸**am'phibiousness** NOUN

amphiblastic (ˌæmfɪˈblæstɪk) ADJECTIVE (of animal ova) showing complete but unequal cleavage after fertilization.

amphiblastula (ˌæmfɪˈblæstjʊlə) NOUN the free-swimming larva of certain sponges, which consists of a hollow spherical mass of cells some of which have flagella.

amphibole (ˈæmfɪˌbəʊl) NOUN any of a large group of minerals consisting of the silicates of calcium, iron, magnesium, sodium, and aluminium, usually in the form of long slender dark-coloured crystals. Members of the group, including hornblende, actinolite, and tremolite, are common constituents of igneous rocks.
▷HISTORY C17: from French, from Greek *amphibolos* uncertain; so called from the large number of varieties in the group

amphibolite (æmˈfɪbəˌlaɪt) NOUN a metamorphic rock consisting mainly of amphibole and plagioclase.

amphibology (ˌæmfɪˈbɒlədʒɪ) *or* **amphiboly** (æmˈfɪbəlɪ) NOUN, *plural* **-gies** *or* **-lies**. ambiguity of expression, esp when due to a grammatical construction, as in *save rags and waste paper*.
▷HISTORY C14: from Late Latin *amphibologia*, ultimately from Greek *amphibolos* ambiguous; see AMPHIBOLE, -LOGY
▸ˌ**amphi'bolic** *or* **amphibolous** (æmˈfɪbələs) ADJECTIVE
▸**amphibological** (æmˌfɪbəˈlɒdʒɪkᵊl) ADJECTIVE
▸**amˌphibo'logically** ADVERB

amphibrach (ˈæmfɪˌbræk) NOUN *Prosody* a metrical foot consisting of a long syllable between two short syllables (⏑–⏑). Compare **cretic**.
▷HISTORY C16: from Latin, from Greek *amphibrakhus*, literally: both ends being short, from AMPHI- + *brakhus* short
▸ˌ**amphi'brachic** ADJECTIVE

amphichroic (ˌæmfɪˈkrəʊɪk) *or* **amphichromatic** (ˌæmfɪkrəʊˈmætɪk) ADJECTIVE producing two colours, one on reacting with an acid, the other on reacting with a base.

amphicoelous (ˌæmfɪˈsiːləs) ADJECTIVE (of the vertebrae of most fishes and some amphibians) concave at the anterior and posterior ends.
▷HISTORY C19: from AMPHI- + Greek *koilos* hollow

amphictyon (æmˈfɪktɪən) NOUN a delegate to an amphictyonic council.
▷HISTORY C16: back formation from *amphictyons*, from Greek *amphiktiones* neighbours, from AMPHI- + *ktizein* to found

amphictyony (æmˈfɪktɪənɪ) NOUN, *plural* **-nies**. (in ancient Greece) a religious association of states for the maintenance of temples and the cults connected with them.
▸**amphictyonic** (æmˌfɪktɪˈɒnɪk) ADJECTIVE

amphidentate (ˌæmfɪˈdɛnteɪt) ADJECTIVE (of a ligand) able to coordinate through either of two different atoms, as in CN^-. Also: **ambidentate**.

amphidiploid (ˌæmfɪˈdɪplɔɪd) NOUN a plant originating from hybridization between two species in which the chromosome number is the sum of the chromosome numbers of both parental species. It behaves as an independent species.

amphigory (ˈæmfɪgərɪ) *or* **amphigouri** (ˈæmfɪˌgʊərɪ) NOUN, *plural* **-ries** *or* **-ris**. a piece of nonsensical writing in verse or, less commonly, prose.
▷HISTORY C19: from French *amphigouri*, of unknown origin
▸**amphigoric** (ˌæmfɪˈgɒrɪk) ADJECTIVE

amphimacer (æmˈfɪməsə) NOUN *Prosody* another word for **cretic**.
▷HISTORY C16: from Latin *amphimacrus*, from Greek *amphimakros* both ends being long, from AMPHI- + *makros* long

amphimixis (ˌæmfɪˈmɪksɪs) NOUN, *plural* **-mixes** (-ˈmɪksiːz). true sexual reproduction by the fusion of gametes from two organisms. Compare **apomixis**.
▷HISTORY C19: from AMPHI- + Greek *mixis* a blending, from *mignunai* to mingle
▸ˌ**amphi'mictic** ADJECTIVE

amphioxus (ˌæmfɪˈɒksəs) NOUN, *plural* **-oxi** (-ˈɒksaɪ) *or* **-oxuses**. another name for the **lancelet**.
▷HISTORY C19: from New Latin: both ends being sharp, from AMPHI- + Greek *oxus* sharp

amphipathic (ˌæmfɪˈpæθɪk) *or* **amphipath** (ˈæmfɪˌpæθ) ADJECTIVE *Chem, biochem* of or relating to a molecule that possesses both hydrophobic and hydrophilic elements, such as are found in detergents, or phospholipids of biological membranes.

amphipod (ˈæmfɪˌpɒd) NOUN [1] any marine or freshwater crustacean of the order *Amphipoda*, such as the sand hoppers, in which the body is laterally compressed: subclass *Malacostraca*. ◆ ADJECTIVE [2] of, relating to, or belonging to the *Amphipoda*.

amphipodous (æmˈfɪpədəs) ADJECTIVE (of certain invertebrates, such as sand hoppers) having both swimming and jumping appendages.

amphiprostyle (æmˈfɪprəˌstaɪl, ˌæmfɪˈprəʊstaɪl) ADJECTIVE [1] (esp of a classical temple) having a set of columns at both ends but not at the sides. ◆ NOUN [2] a temple of this kind.
▸**amˌphipro'stylar** ADJECTIVE

amphiprotic (ˌæmfɪˈprəʊtɪk) ADJECTIVE another word for **amphoteric**.

amphisbaena (ˌæmfɪsˈbiːnə) NOUN, *plural* **-nae** (-niː) *or* **-nas**. [1] any worm lizard of the genus *Amphisbaena*. [2] *Classical myth* a poisonous serpent having a head at each end and able to move forwards or backwards.
▷HISTORY C16: via Latin from Greek *amphisbaina*, from *amphis* both ways + *bainein* to go
▸ˌ**amphis'baenic** ADJECTIVE

amphistomatal (ˌæmfɪˈstəʊmətᵊl) *or* **amphistomatic** (ˌæmfɪstəˈmætɪk) ADJECTIVE (of a leaf) having stomata on both surfaces.

amphistomous (ˌæmfɪˈstəʊməs) ADJECTIVE (of certain animals, such as leeches) having a sucker at either end of the body.

amphistylar (ˌæmfɪˈstaɪlə) ADJECTIVE [1] (esp of a classical temple) having a set of columns at both ends or at both sides. ◆ NOUN [2] a temple of this kind.

amphitheatre *or US* **amphitheater** (ˈæmfɪˌθɪətə) NOUN [1] a building, usually circular or oval, in which tiers of seats rise from a central open arena, as in those of ancient Rome. [2] a place where contests are held; arena. [3] any level circular area of ground surrounded by higher ground. [4] **a** the first tier of seats in the gallery of a theatre. **b** any similarly designated seating area in a theatre. [5] a lecture room in which seats are tiered away from a central area.
▸**amphitheatric** (ˌæmfɪθɪˈætrɪk) *or* ˌ**amphithe'atrical** ADJECTIVE ▸ˌ**amphithe'atrically** ADVERB

amphithecium (ˌæmfɪˈθiːsɪəm) NOUN, *plural* **-cia** (-sɪə). the outer layer of cells of the sporophyte of mosses and liverworts that develops into the outer parts of the spore-bearing capsule.
▷HISTORY C19: from New Latin, from AMPHI- + Greek *thēkion* a little case, from *thēkē* case

amphitricha (æmˈfɪtrɪkə) PLURAL NOUN bacteria that have flagella at both ends.
▷HISTORY C20: from AMPHI- + *-tricha*, from Greek *thrix* hair
▸**am'phitrichous** ADJECTIVE

Amphitrite (ˌæmfɪˈtraɪtɪ) NOUN *Greek myth* a sea goddess, wife of Poseidon and mother of Triton.

amphitropous (æmˈfɪtrəpəs) ADJECTIVE (of a plant ovule) partially inverted so that the base and the micropyle at the apex are the same distance from the funicle.

Amphitryon (æmˈfɪtrɪən) NOUN *Greek myth* the grandson of Perseus and husband of Alcmene.

amphora (ˈæmfərə) NOUN, *plural* **-phorae** (-fəˌriː) *or* **-phoras**. an ancient Greek or Roman two-handled narrow-necked jar for oil, wine, etc.
▷HISTORY C17: from Latin, from Greek *amphoreus*, from AMPHI- + *phoreus* bearer, from *pherein* to bear

amphoric (æmˈfɒrɪk) ADJECTIVE resembling the sound produced by blowing into a bottle. Amphoric breath sounds are heard through a stethoscope placed over a cavity in the lung.

amphoteric (ˌæmfəˈtɛrɪk) ADJECTIVE *Chem* able to function as either a base or an acid. Also: **amphiprotic**.
▷HISTORY C19: from Greek *amphoteros* each of two (from *amphō* both) + -IC

ampicillin (ˌæmpɪˈsɪlɪn) NOUN a semisynthetic penicillin used to treat various infections.

ample (ˈæmpᵊl) ADJECTIVE [1] more than sufficient; abundant: *an ample helping*. [2] large in size, extent, or amount: *of ample proportions*.
▷HISTORY C15: from Old French, from Latin *amplus* spacious
▸'**ampleness** NOUN

amplexicaul (æmˈplɛksɪˌkɔːl) ADJECTIVE (of some sessile leaves, stipules, etc.) having an enlarged base that encircles the stem.
▷HISTORY C18: from New Latin *amplexicaulis*, from Latin *amplectī* to embrace + *caulis* stalk

amplification (ˌæmplɪfɪˈkeɪʃən) NOUN [1] the act or result of amplifying. [2] material added to a statement, story, etc., in order to expand or clarify it. [3] a statement, story, etc., with such additional material. [4] *Electronics* **a** the increase in strength of an electrical signal by means of an amplifier. **b** another word for **gain**[1] (sense 13). [5] *Genetics* Also called: **gene amplification**. the production of multiple copies of a particular gene or DNA sequence. It can occur naturally or artificially, by genetic engineering techniques.

amplifier (ˈæmplɪˌfaɪə) NOUN [1] an electronic device used to increase the strength of the signal fed into it. [2] such a device used for the amplification of audio frequency signals in a radio, etc. [3] *Photog* an additional lens for altering the focal length of a camera lens. [4] a person or thing that amplifies.

amplify (ˈæmplɪˌfaɪ) VERB **-fies, -fying, -fied.** [1] (*tr*) to increase in size, extent, effect, etc., as by the addition of extra material; augment; enlarge; expand. [2] *Electronics* to produce amplification of (electrical signals); increase the amplitude of (signals). [3] (*tr*) *US* to exaggerate. [4] (*intr*) to expand or enlarge a speech, narrative, etc.
▷HISTORY C15: from Old French *amplifier*, ultimately from Latin *amplificāre* to enlarge, from *amplus* spacious + *facere* to make
▸'**ampliˌfiable** ADJECTIVE

amplitude (ˈæmplɪˌtjuːd) NOUN [1] greatness of extent; magnitude. [2] abundance or copiousness. [3] breadth or scope, as of the mind. [4] *Astronomy* the angular distance along the horizon measured from true east or west to the point of intersection of the vertical circle passing through a celestial body. [5] Also called: **argument**. *Maths* (of a complex number) the angle that the vector representing the complex number makes with the positive real axis. If the point (x, y) has polar coordinates (r, θ), the amplitude of $x + iy$ is θ, that is, arctan y/x. Compare **modulus** (sense 2). See also **Argand diagram**. [6] *Physics* the maximum variation from the zero or mean value of a periodically varying quantity.
▷HISTORY C16: from Latin *amplitūdō* breadth, from *amplus* spacious

amplitude modulation NOUN [1] one of the principal methods of transmitting audio, visual, or other types of information using radio waves, the relevant signal being superimposed onto a radio-frequency carrier wave. The frequency of the carrier wave remains unchanged but its amplitude is varied in accordance with the amplitude of the input signal. Abbreviations: **AM, am.** Compare **frequency modulation**. [2] a wave that has undergone this process.

amply (ˈæmplɪ) ADVERB more than sufficiently; fully; generously: *he was amply rewarded*.

ampoule (ˈæmpuːl, -pjuːl) *or esp US* **ampule** NOUN *Med* a small glass vessel in which liquids for injection are hermetically sealed.

ampulla (æmˈpʊlə) NOUN, *plural* **-pullae** (-ˈpʊliː). [1] *Anatomy* the dilated end part of certain ducts or canals, such as the end of a uterine tube. [2] *Christianity* **a** a vessel for containing the wine and water used at the Eucharist. **b** a small flask for containing consecrated oil. [3] a Roman two-handled bottle for oil, wine, or perfume.
▷HISTORY C16: from Latin, diminutive of AMPHORA
▸**ampullaceous** (ˌæmpʊˈleɪʃəs) *or* ˌ**ampul'laceal** ADJECTIVE ▸**ampullar** (æmˈpʊlə) *or* **ampullary** (æmˈpʊlərɪ) ADJECTIVE

amp up VERB (*tr, adverb*) *Informal* [1] to increase. [2] to increase the power or force of (something). [3] to excite, arouse, or work up (a person, emotions, etc.).

amputate ('æmpjʊˌteɪt) VERB *Surgery* to remove (all or part of a limb, esp an arm or leg).
▷**HISTORY** C17: from Latin *amputāre*, from *am-* around + *putāre* to trim, prune
▸ˌ**ampu'tation** NOUN ▸'**ampuˌtator** NOUN

amputee (ˌæmpjʊ'tiː) NOUN a person who has had a limb amputated.

Amravati (æm'rɑːvətɪ) NOUN a town in central India, in NE Maharashtra: cotton centre. Pop.: 421 576 (1991). Former name: **Amraoti** ('æmˌrɑːətɪ, 'ʌm-).

amrit ('æmrit) NOUN *Sikhism* a sanctified solution of sugar and water used in the Amrit Ceremony.
▷**HISTORY** from Punjabi: nectar

amrita *or* **amreeta** (æm'riːtə) NOUN *Hindu myth* 1 the ambrosia of the gods that bestows immortality. 2 the immortality it confers.
▷**HISTORY** from Sanskrit *amrta* immortal, from *a-* without + *mrta* death

Amrit Ceremony NOUN *Sikhism* the ceremony of initiation into the Khalsa, at which amrit is drunk by and sprinkled on the heads of candidates for initiation.

Amritsar (æm'rɪtsə) NOUN a city in India, in NW Punjab: centre of the Sikh religion; site of a massacre in 1919 of unarmed supporters of Indian self-government by British troops; in 1984 the Golden Temple, fortified by Sikhs, was attacked by Indian troops with the loss of many Sikh lives. Pop.: 708 835 (1991).

Amsterdam (ˌæmstə'dæm; *Dutch* ɑmstər'dɑm) NOUN the commercial capital of the Netherlands, a major industrial centre and port on the IJsselmeer, connected with the North Sea by canal: built on about 100 islands within a network of canals. Pop.: 727 053 (1999 est.).

amt ABBREVIATION FOR amount.

amu ABBREVIATION FOR atomic mass unit.

AMU (in Britain) ABBREVIATION FOR Associated Metalworkers Union.

amuck (ə'mʌk) NOUN, ADVERB a variant of **amok**.

Amu Darya (*Russian* a'mu darj'ja) NOUN a river in central Asia, rising in the Pamirs and flowing northwest through the Hindu Kush and across Turkmenistan and Uzbekistan to its delta in the Aral Sea: forms much of the N border of Afghanistan and is important for irrigation. Length: 2400 km (1500 miles). Ancient name: **Oxus**.

amulet ('æmjʊlɪt) NOUN a trinket or piece of jewellery worn as a protection against evil; charm.
▷**HISTORY** C17: from Latin *amulētum*, of unknown origin

Amūn ('ɑːmən) NOUN *Egyptian myth* a variant spelling of **Amen**.

Amundsen Sea ('ɑːmʊndsən) NOUN a part of the South Pacific Ocean, in Antarctica off Byrd Land.

Amur (ə'mʊə) NOUN a river in NE Asia, rising in N Mongolia as the Argun and flowing southeast, then northeast to the Sea of Okhotsk: forms the boundary between Manchuria and Russia. Length: about 4350 km (2700 miles). Modern Chinese name: **Heilong Jiang**.

amusable *or* **amuseable** (ə'mjuːzəbᵊl) ADJECTIVE capable of being amused.

amuse (ə'mjuːz) VERB (*tr*) 1 to keep pleasantly occupied; entertain; divert. 2 to cause to laugh or smile.
▷**HISTORY** C15: from Old French *amuser* to cause to be idle, from *muser* to MUSE[1]

amuse-bouche *French* (amyzbuʃ) NOUN an appetizer before a meal.
▷**HISTORY** from French *amuser* amuse, gratify + *bouche* mouth

amusement (ə'mjuːzmənt) NOUN 1 something that amuses, such as a game or other pastime. 2 a mechanical device used for entertainment, as at a fair. 3 the act of amusing or the state or quality of being amused.

amusement arcade NOUN *Brit* a covered area having coin-operated game machines.

amusement park NOUN an open-air entertainment area consisting of stalls, side shows, etc.

amusing (ə'mjuːzɪŋ) ADJECTIVE mildly entertaining; pleasantly diverting; causing a smile or laugh.
▸**a'musingly** ADVERB

amygdala (ə'mɪgdələ) NOUN, *plural* **-lae** (-ˌliː). *Anatomy* an almond-shaped part, such as a tonsil or a lobe of the cerebellum.
▷**HISTORY** C16: from Medieval Latin: ALMOND

amygdalate (ə'mɪgdəlɪt, -ˌleɪt) ADJECTIVE relating to, having, or bearing almonds.

amygdale (ə'mɪgdeɪl) NOUN a vesicle in a volcanic rock, formed from a bubble of escaping gas, that has become filled with light-coloured minerals, such as quartz and calcite. Also called: **amygdule** (ə'mɪgdjuːl).
▷**HISTORY** C19: from Greek: ALMOND

amygdalin (ə'mɪgdəlɪn) NOUN a white soluble bitter-tasting crystalline glycoside extracted from bitter almonds and stone fruits such as peaches and apricots. Formula: $C_6H_5CHCNOC_{12}H_{21}O_{10}$.

amygdaline (ə'mɪgdəlɪn, -ˌlaɪn) ADJECTIVE 1 *Anatomy* of or relating to a tonsil. 2 of or resembling almonds.

amygdaloid (ə'mɪgdəˌlɔɪd) NOUN 1 a volcanic igneous rock containing amygdales. ◆ ADJECTIVE 2 having the shape of an almond. 3 a less common form of **amygdaloidal** (sense 1).

amygdaloidal (əˌmɪgdə'lɔɪdᵊl) ADJECTIVE 1 (of a volcanic rock) containing amygdales. 2 a less common form of **amygdaloid** (sense 2).

amyl ('æmɪl) NOUN (*modifier, no longer in technical usage*) of, consisting of, or containing any of eight isomeric forms of the monovalent group C_5H_{11}-: *amyl group or radical*. See also **pentyl**.
▷**HISTORY** C19: from Latin: AMYLUM

amylaceous (ˌæmɪ'leɪʃəs) ADJECTIVE of or resembling starch.

amyl acetate NOUN another name (no longer in technical usage) for **pentyl acetate**.

amyl alcohol NOUN a colourless flammable liquid existing in eight isomeric forms that is used as a solvent and in the manufacture of organic compounds and pharmaceuticals. Formula: $C_5H_{11}OH$.

amylase ('æmɪˌleɪz) NOUN any of several enzymes that hydrolyse starch and glycogen to simple sugars, such as glucose. They are present in saliva.

amylene ('æmɪˌliːn) NOUN another name (no longer in technical usage) for **pentene**.

amyl nitrite NOUN a yellowish unstable volatile fragrant liquid used in medicine as a vasodilator and in perfumes. Formula: $(CH_3)_2CHCH_2CH_2NO_2$.

amylo- *or before a vowel* **amyl-** COMBINING FORM indicating starch: *amylolysis*; *amylase*.
▷**HISTORY** from Latin: AMYLUM

amyloid ('æmɪˌlɔɪd) NOUN 1 *Pathol* a complex protein resembling starch, deposited in tissues in some degenerative diseases. 2 any substance resembling starch. ◆ ADJECTIVE 3 starchlike.

amyloidosis (ˌæmɪlɔɪ'dəʊsɪs) NOUN *Pathol* the deposition of amyloid in various tissues of the body, as occurs in certain chronic infections.

amylolysis (ˌæmɪ'lɒlɪsɪs) NOUN the conversion of starch into sugar.
▸**amylolytic** (əˌmaɪləʊ'lɪtɪk) ADJECTIVE

amylopectin (ˌæmɪləʊ'pɛktɪn) NOUN the major component of starch (about 80 per cent), consisting of branched chains of glucose units. It is insoluble and gives a red-brown colour with iodine. Compare **amylose**.

amylopsin (ˌæmɪ'lɒpsɪn) NOUN an enzyme of the pancreatic juice that converts starch into sugar; pancreatic amylase.
▷**HISTORY** C19: from AMYLO(LYSIS) + (PE)PSIN

amylose ('æmɪˌləʊz, -ləʊs) NOUN the minor component (about 20 per cent) of starch, consisting of long unbranched chains of glucose units. It is soluble in water and gives an intense blue colour with iodine. Compare **amylopectin**.

amylum ('æmɪləm) NOUN another name for **starch** (sense 2).
▷**HISTORY** Latin, from Greek *amulon* fine meal, starch, from *amulos* not ground at the mill, from A-[1] + *mulē* mill

amyotonia (ˌeɪmaɪə'təʊnɪə) NOUN another name for **myotonia**.

amyotrophic lateral sclerosis (ˌæmɪəʊ'trəʊfɪk) NOUN a form of motor neurone disease in which degeneration of motor tracts in the spinal cord causes progressive muscular paralysis starting in the limbs. Also called: **Lou Gehrig's disease**.

amyotrophy (ˌæmɪ'ɒtrəfɪ) NOUN *Pathol* wasting of muscles, caused by disease of the nerves supplying them.

Amytal ('æmɪˌtæl) NOUN *Trademark* a barbiturate, a brand of amobarbital, used as a sedative and hypnotic.

an[1] (æn; *unstressed* ən) DETERMINER (*indefinite article*) a form of **a**[1] used before an initial vowel sound: *an old car; an elf; an honour*.
▷**HISTORY** Old English *ān* ONE

> **Language note** *An* was formerly often used before words that begin with *h* and are unstressed on the first syllable: *an hotel*; *an historic meeting*. Sometimes the initial *h* was not pronounced. This usage is now becoming obsolete.

an[2] *or* **an'** (æn; *unstressed* ən) CONJUNCTION (*subordinating*) an obsolete or dialect word for **if**. See **and** (sense 9).

an[3] THE INTERNET DOMAIN NAME FOR Netherlands Antilles.

An[1] (ɑːn) NOUN *Myth* the Sumerian sky god. Babylonian counterpart: **Anu**.

An[2] THE CHEMICAL SYMBOL FOR actinon.

AN ABBREVIATION FOR Anglo-Norman.

an- *or before a consonant* **a-** PREFIX not; without: *anaphrodisiac*.
▷**HISTORY** from Greek

-an, -ean, *or* **-ian** SUFFIX 1 (*forming adjectives and nouns*) belonging to or relating to; a person belonging to or coming from: *European*. 2 (*forming adjectives and nouns*) typical of or resembling; a person typical of: *Elizabethan*. 3 (*forming adjectives and nouns*) adhering to or following; an adherent of: *Christian*. 4 (*forming nouns*) a person who specializes or is expert in: *dietitian*; *phonetician*.
▷**HISTORY** from Latin *-ānus*, suffix of adjectives

ana[1] ('eɪnə, 'ɑːnə) ADVERB *Pharmacol, obsolete* (of ingredients in a prescription) in equal quantities. Abbreviation: **aa**.
▷**HISTORY** C16: via Medieval Latin from Greek: of every one similarly

ana[2] ('ɑːnə) NOUN 1 a collection of reminiscences, sketches, etc., of or about a person or place. 2 an item of or for such a collection.
▷**HISTORY** C18: independent use of -ANA

ANA *Commerce* ABBREVIATION FOR Article Number Association: (in Britain) an organization of manufacturers, retailers, and wholesalers that provides a system (**article numbering**) by which a product is identified by a unique machine-readable number (see **bar code**) compatible with article-numbering systems used in other countries.

ana- *or before a vowel* **an-** PREFIX 1 up; upwards: *anadromous*. 2 again: *anagram*. 3 back; backwards: *anatropous*.
▷**HISTORY** from Greek *ana*

-ana *or* **-iana** SUFFIX FORMING NOUNS denoting a collection of objects or information relating to a particular individual, subject, or place: *Shakespeareana*; *Victoriana*; *Americana*.
▷**HISTORY** New Latin, from Latin *-āna*, literally: matters relating to, neuter plural of *-ānus*; see -AN

anabaena (ˌænə'biːnə) NOUN, *plural* **-nas**. any freshwater alga of the genus *Anabaena*, sometimes occurring in drinking water, giving it a fishy taste and smell.
▷**HISTORY** New Latin, from Greek *anabainein* to shoot up, go up, from ANA- + *bainein* to go; so called because they rise to the surface at intervals

anabantid (ˌænə'bæntɪd) NOUN 1 any of various spiny-finned fishes constituting the family *Anabantidae* and including the fighting fish, climbing perch, and gourami. See also **labyrinth fish**. ◆ ADJECTIVE 2 of, relating to, or belonging to the family *Anabantidae*.

Anabaptist (ˌænə'bæptɪst) NOUN 1 a member of any of various 16th-century Protestant movements that rejected infant baptism, insisted that adults be rebaptized, and sought to establish Christian

communism. [2] a member of a later Protestant sect holding the same doctrines, esp with regard to baptism. ◆ ADJECTIVE [3] of or relating to these movements or sects or their doctrines.
▷**HISTORY** C16: from Ecclesiastical Latin *anabaptista,* from *anabaptīzāre* to baptize again, from Late Greek *anabaptizein;* see ANA-, BAPTIZE
▸ **ˌAnaˈbaptism** NOUN

anabas (ˈænəˌbæs) NOUN any of several labyrinth fishes of the genus Anabas, esp the **climbing fish**.
▷**HISTORY** C19: from New Latin, from Greek *anabainein* to go up; see ANABAENA

anabasis (əˈnæbəsɪs) NOUN, *plural* **-ses** (-ˌsiːz). [1] the march of Cyrus the Younger and his Greek mercenaries from Sardis to Cunaxa in Babylonia in 401 B.C., described by Xenophon in his *Anabasis*. Compare **katabasis.** [2] any military expedition, esp one from the coast to the interior.
▷**HISTORY** C18: from Greek: a going up, ascent, from *anabainein* to go up; see ANABAENA

anabatic (ˌænəˈbætɪk) ADJECTIVE *Meteorol* (of air currents) rising upwards, esp up slopes. Compare **katabatic.**
▷**HISTORY** C19: from Greek *anabatikos* relating to ascents, from *anabainein* to go up; see ANABASIS

anabiosis (ˌænəbaɪˈəʊsɪs) NOUN the ability to return to life after apparent death; suspended animation.
▷**HISTORY** C19: via New Latin from Greek, from *anabioein* to come back to life, from ANA- + *bios* life
▸**anabiotic** (ˌænəbaɪˈɒtɪk) ADJECTIVE

anableps (ˈænəˌblɛps) NOUN, *plural* **-bleps.** any of various cyprinodont fishes constituting the genus *Anableps,* which includes the four-eyed fishes.
▷**HISTORY** New Latin, literally: one who looks up, from Greek, from *anablepein* to look up

anabolic (ˌænəˈbɒlɪk) ADJECTIVE of or relating to anabolism.

anabolic steroid NOUN any of a group of synthetic steroid hormones (androgens) used to stimulate muscle and bone growth for therapeutic or athletic purposes.

anabolism (əˈnæbəˌlɪzəm) NOUN a metabolic process in which complex molecules are synthesized from simpler ones with the storage of energy; constructive metabolism. Compare **catabolism.**
▷**HISTORY** C19: from ANA- + (META)BOLISM

anabolite (əˈnæbəˌlaɪt) NOUN a product of anabolism.
▸**anabolitic** (əˌnæbəˈlɪtɪk) ADJECTIVE

anabranch (ˈɑːnəˌbrɑːntʃ) NOUN a stream that leaves a river and enters it again further downstream.
▷**HISTORY** C19: from *ana(stomosing) branch*

anacardiaceous (ˌænəˌkɑːdɪˈeɪʃəs) ADJECTIVE of, relating to, or belonging to the *Anacardiaceae,* a chiefly tropical family of trees and shrubs many of which have edible drupes. The family includes the cashew, mango, pistachio, and sumach.
▷**HISTORY** C19: from New Latin *Anacardiāceae,* from ANA- + Greek *kardia* heart; so called from the shape of the top of the fruit stem

anachorism (əˈnækəˌrɪzəm) NOUN a geographical misplacement; something located in an incongruous position. Compare **anachronism.**
▷**HISTORY** C19: from ANA- + *khōros* place

anachronic (ˌænəˈkrɒnɪk) *or* **anachronical** ADJECTIVE out of chronological order or out of date.
▷**HISTORY** C19: see ANACHRONISM
▸ **ˌanaˈchronically** ADVERB

anachronism (əˈnækrəˌnɪzəm) NOUN [1] the representation of an event, person, or thing in a historical context in which it could not have occurred or existed. [2] a person or thing that belongs or seems to belong to another time.
▷**HISTORY** C17: from Latin *anachronismus,* from Greek *anakhronismos* a mistake in chronology, from *anakhronizein* to err in a time reference, from ANA- + *khronos* time
▸ **aˌnachroˈnistic** ADJECTIVE ▸ **aˌnachroˈnistically** ADVERB

anaclinal (ˌænəˈklaɪnᵊl) ADJECTIVE (of valleys and similar formations) progressing in a direction opposite to the dip of the surrounding rock strata.
▷**HISTORY** C19: see ANA-, -CLINE

anaclitic (ˌænəˈklɪtɪk) ADJECTIVE *Psychoanal* of or relating to relationships that are characterized by the strong dependence of one person on others or another.
▷**HISTORY** C20: from Greek *anaklitos* for leaning upon; see ANA-, -CLINE
▸**anaclisis** (ˌænəˈklaɪsɪs) NOUN

anacoluthia (ˌænəkəˈluːθɪə) NOUN *Rhetoric* lack of grammatical sequence, esp within a single sentence.
▸ **ˌanacoˈluthic** ADJECTIVE

anacoluthon (ˌænəkəˈluːθɒn) NOUN, *plural* **-tha** (-θə). *Rhetoric* a construction that involves the change from one grammatical sequence to another within a single sentence; an example of anacoluthia.
▷**HISTORY** C18: from Late Latin, from Greek *anakolouthon,* from *anakolouthos* not consistent, from AN- + *akolouthos* following

anaconda (ˌænəˈkɒndə) NOUN a very large nonvenomous arboreal and semiaquatic snake, *Eunectes murinus,* of tropical South America, which kills its prey by constriction: family *Boidae* (boas).
▷**HISTORY** C18: probably changed from Sinhalese *henakandayā* whip snake, from *hena* lightning + *kanda* stem; originally referring to a snake of Sri Lanka

anacoustic (ˌænəˈkuːstɪk) ADJECTIVE unable to support the propagation of sound; soundless.

Anacreontic (əˌnækrɪˈɒntɪk) (*sometimes not capital*) ADJECTIVE [1] in the manner of the Greek lyric poet Anacreon (?572–?488 B.C.), noted for his short songs celebrating love and wine. ◆ [2] NOUN (of verse) in praise of love or wine; amatory or convivial. [3] an Anacreontic poem.
▸ **Aˌnacreˈontically** ADVERB

anacrusis (ˌænəˈkruːsɪs) NOUN, *plural* **-ses** (-siːz). [1] *Prosody* one or more unstressed syllables at the beginning of a line of verse. [2] *Music* **a** an unstressed note or group of notes immediately preceding the strong first beat of the first bar. **b** another word for **upbeat.**
▷**HISTORY** C19: from Greek *anakrousis* prelude, from *anakrouein* to strike up, from ANA- + *krouein* to strike
▸**anacrustic** (ˌænəˈkrʌstɪk) ADJECTIVE

anadem (ˈænəˌdɛm) NOUN *Poetic* a garland for the head.
▷**HISTORY** C17: from Latin *anadēma* wreath, from Greek *anadēma,* from *anadein* to wreathe, from ANA- + *dein* to bind

anadiplosis (ˌænədɪˈpləʊsɪs) NOUN *Rhetoric* repetition of the words or phrase at the end of one sentence, line, or clause at the beginning of the next.
▷**HISTORY** C16: via Latin from Greek: repetition, from *anadiploun* to double back, from ANA- + *diploun* to double

anadromous (əˈnædrəməs) ADJECTIVE (of fishes such as the salmon) migrating up rivers from the sea in order to breed. Compare **catadromous.**
▷**HISTORY** C18: from Greek *anadromos* running upwards, from ANA- + *dromos* a running

Anadyr (*Russian* aˈnadɨrj) NOUN [1] a town in Russia, in NE Siberia at the mouth of the Anadyr River. Pop.: 6586 (1993 est.). [2] a mountain range in Russia, in NE Siberia, rising over 1500 m (5000 ft.). [3] a river in Russia, rising in mountains on the Arctic Circle, south of the Anadyr Range, and flowing east to the Gulf of Anadyr. Length: 725 km (450 miles). [4] **Gulf of.** an inlet of the Bering Sea, off the coast of NE Russia.

anaemia *or US* **anemia** (əˈniːmɪə) NOUN [1] a deficiency in the number of red blood cells or in their haemoglobin content, resulting in pallor, shortness of breath, and lack of energy. [2] lack of vitality or vigour. [3] pallid complexion.
▷**HISTORY** C19: from New Latin, from Greek *anaimia* lack of blood, from AN- + *haima* blood

anaemic *or US* **anemic** (əˈniːmɪk) ADJECTIVE [1] relating to or suffering from anaemia. [2] pale and sickly looking; lacking vitality.

anaerobe (æˈnɛərəʊb, ˈænərəʊb) *or* **anaerobium** (ˌænɛəˈrəʊbɪəm) NOUN, *plural* **-obes** *or* **-obia** (-ˈəʊbɪə). an organism that does not require oxygen for respiration. Compare **aerobe.**

anaerobic (ˌænɛəˈrəʊbɪk) ADJECTIVE [1] (of an organism or process) requiring the absence of or not dependent on the presence of oxygen. [2] of or relating to anaerobes. ◆ Compare **aerobic.**
▸ **ˌanaerˈobically** ADVERB

anaerobiosis (ˌænɛərəʊbaɪˈəʊsɪs) NOUN life in the absence of oxygen.

anaesthesia *or US* **anesthesia** (ˌænɪsˈθiːzɪə) NOUN [1] local or general loss of bodily sensation, esp of touch, as the result of nerve damage or other abnormality. [2] loss of sensation, esp of pain, induced by drugs: called **general anaesthesia** when consciousness is lost and **local anaesthesia** when only a specific area of the body is involved. [3] a general dullness or lack of feeling.
▷**HISTORY** C19: from New Latin, from Greek *anaisthēsia* absence of sensation, from AN- + *aisthēsis* feeling

anaesthesiology *or US* **anesthesiology** (ˌænɪsˌθiːzɪˈɒlədʒɪ) NOUN the US name for **anaesthetics.**

anaesthetic *or US* **anesthetic** (ˌænɪsˈθɛtɪk) NOUN [1] a substance that causes anaesthesia. ◆ ADJECTIVE [2] causing or characterized by anaesthesia.

anaesthetics (ˌænɪsˈθɛtɪks) NOUN (*functioning as singular*) the science, study, and practice of anaesthesia and its application. US name: **anesthesiology.**

anaesthetist (əˈniːsθətɪst) NOUN [1] *Brit* a qualified doctor specializing in the administration of anaesthetics. US name: **anesthesiologist.** [2] *US* a person qualified to administer anaesthesia, often a nurse or someone other than a physician. Compare **anesthesiologist.**

anaesthetize, anaesthetise, *or US* **anesthetize** (əˈniːsθəˌtaɪz) VERB (*tr*) to render insensible to pain by administering an anaesthetic.
▸ **aˌnaesthetiˈzation** *or* **aˌnaesthetiˈsation** *or US* **aˌnesthetiˈzation** NOUN

anaglyph (ˈænəˌglɪf) NOUN [1] *Photog* a stereoscopic picture consisting of two images of the same object, taken from slightly different angles, in two complementary colours, usually red and cyan (green-blue). When viewed through spectacles having one red and one cyan lens, the images merge to produce a stereoscopic sensation. [2] anything cut to stand in low relief, such as a cameo.
▷**HISTORY** C17: from Greek *anagluphē* carved in low relief, from ANA- + *gluphē* carving, from *gluphein* to carve
▸ **ˌanaˈglyphic** *or* **ˌanaˈglyphical** *or* **anaglyptic** (ˌænəˈglɪptɪk) *or* **ˌanaˈglyptical** ADJECTIVE ▸**anaglyphy** (əˈnægləfɪ, ˈænəˌglɪfɪ) NOUN

Anaglypta (ˌænəˈglɪptə) NOUN *Trademark* a type of thick embossed wallpaper.
▷**HISTORY** C19: from Greek *anagluptos;* see ANAGLYPH

anagnorisis (ˌænægˈnɒrɪsɪs) NOUN, *plural* **-ses** (-ˌsiːz). (in Greek tragedy) the recognition or discovery by the protagonist of the identity of some character or the nature of his own predicament, which leads to the resolution of the plot; denouement.
▷**HISTORY** from Greek: recognition

anagoge *or* **anagogy** (ˈænəˌgɒdʒɪ) NOUN [1] allegorical or spiritual interpretation, esp of sacred works such as the Bible. [2] *Christianity* allegorical interpretation of the Old Testament as typifying or foreshadowing subjects in the New Testament.
▷**HISTORY** C18: via Late Latin from Greek *anagōgē* a lifting up, from *anagein,* from ANA- + *agein* to lead
▸**anagogic** (ˌænəˈgɒdʒɪk) *or* **ˌanaˈgogical** ADJECTIVE
▸ **ˌanaˈgogically** ADVERB

anagram (ˈænəˌgræm) NOUN a word or phrase the letters of which can be rearranged into another word or phrase.
▷**HISTORY** C16: from New Latin *anagramma,* shortened from Greek *anagrammatismos,* from *anagrammatizein* to transpose letters, from ANA- + *gramma* a letter
▸**anagrammatic** (ˌænəgrəˈmætɪk) *or* **ˌanagramˈmatical** ADJECTIVE ▸ **ˌanagramˈmatically** ADVERB

anagrammatize *or* **anagrammatise** (ˌænəˈgræməˌtaɪz) VERB to arrange into an anagram.
▸ **ˌanaˈgrammaˌtism** NOUN ▸ **ˌanaˈgrammatist** NOUN

anagrammer (ˈænəˌgræmə) NOUN a person who enjoys solving anagrams.

Anaheim (ˈænəˌhaɪm) NOUN a city in SW California: site of Disneyland. Pop.: 328 014 (2000).

anal (ˈeɪnᵊl) ADJECTIVE [1] of, relating to, or near the anus. [2] *Psychoanal* **a** relating to a stage of psychosexual development during which the child's interest is concentrated on the anal region

and excremental functions. **b** designating personality traits in the adult, such as orderliness, meanness, stubbornness, etc., due to fixation at the anal stage of development. Compare **genital** (sense 2), **oral** (sense 7), **phallic** (sense 2).
▷HISTORY C18: from New Latin *ānālis;* see ANUS
▸ **'anally** ADVERB

anal canal NOUN the terminal part of the rectum forming the passage to the anus.

analcite (æ'nælsaɪt, 'æn^əl,saɪt, -sɪt) *or* **analcime** (æ'nælsɪm, -saɪm, -siːm) NOUN a white, grey, or colourless zeolite mineral consisting of hydrated sodium aluminium silicate in cubic crystalline form. Formula: $NaAlSi_2O_6.H_2O$.
▷HISTORY C19: from Greek *analkimos* weak (from AN- + *alkimos* strong, from *alkē* strength) + -ITE[1]

analects ('ænə,lɛkts) *or* **analecta** (,ænə'lɛktə) PLURAL NOUN selected literary passages from one or more works.
▷HISTORY C17: via Latin from Greek *analekta,* from *analegein* to collect up, from *legein* to gather
▸ **,ana'lectic** ADJECTIVE

analemma (,ænə'lɛmə) NOUN, *plural* **-mas** *or* **-mata** (-mətə). a graduated scale shaped like a figure eight that indicates the daily declination of the sun.
▷HISTORY C17: from Latin: sundial, pedestal of sundial, from Greek *analēmma* pedestal, from *analambanein* to support
▸ **analemmatic** (,ænəlɛ'mætɪk) ADJECTIVE

analeptic (,æn^ə'lɛptɪk) ADJECTIVE [1] (of a drug, etc.) stimulating the central nervous system. ◆ NOUN [2] any drug, such as doxapram, that stimulates the central nervous system. [3] (formerly) a restorative remedy or drug.
▷HISTORY C17: from New Latin *analēpticus,* from Greek *analēptikos* stimulating, from *analambanein* to take up; see ANALEMMA

anal erotic NOUN a person with anal personality traits.

anal fin NOUN a median ventral unpaired fin, situated between the anus and the tail fin in fishes, that helps to maintain stable equilibrium.

analgesia (,æn^əl'dʒiːzɪə, -sɪə) *or* **analgia** (æn'ældʒɪə) NOUN [1] inability to feel pain. [2] the relief of pain.
▷HISTORY C18: via New Latin from Greek: insensibility, from AN- + *algēsis* sense of pain

analgesic (,æn^əl'dʒiːzɪk, -sɪk) ADJECTIVE [1] of or causing analgesia. ◆ NOUN [2] a substance that produces analgesia.

anal intercourse NOUN a form of sexual intercourse in which the penis is inserted into the anus.

analog ('ænə,lɒg) NOUN a variant spelling of **analogue.**

> **Language note** The spelling *analog* is a US variant of *analogue* in all its senses, and is also the generally preferred spelling in the computer industry.

analog computer NOUN a mechanical, electrical, or electronic computer that performs arithmetical operations by using some variable physical quantity, such as mechanical movement or voltage, to represent numbers.

analogize *or* **analogise** (ə'nælə,dʒaɪz) VERB [1] (*intr*) to make use of analogy, as in argument; draw comparisons. [2] (*tr*) to make analogous or reveal analogy in.

analogous (ə'næləgəs) ADJECTIVE [1] similar or corresponding in some respect. [2] *Biology* (of organs and parts) having the same function but different evolutionary origin: *the paddle of a whale and the fin of a fish are analogous.* Compare **homologous** (sense 4). [3] *Linguistics* formed by analogy: *an analogous plural.*
▷HISTORY C17: from Latin *analogus,* from Greek *analogos* proportionate, from ANA- + *logos* speech, ratio
▸ **a'nalogously** ADVERB ▸ **a'nalogousness** NOUN

> **Language note** The use of *with* after *analogous* should be avoided: *swimming has no event that is analogous to* (not *with*) *the 100 metres in athletics.*

analogue *or sometimes US* **analog** ('ænə,lɒg) NOUN [1] **a** a physical object or quantity, such as a pointer on a dial or a voltage, used to measure or represent another quantity. **b** (*as modifier*): *analogue watch; analogue recording.* [2] something analogous to something else. [3] *Biology* an analogous part or organ. [4] *Chem* **a** an organic chemical compound related to another by substitution of hydrogen atoms with alkyl groups: *toluene is an analogue of benzene.* **b** an organic compound that is similar in structure to another organic compound: *thiols are sulphur analogues of alcohols.*

> **Language note** See at **analog.**

analogue clock *or* **watch** NOUN a clock or watch in which the hours, minutes, and sometimes seconds are indicated by hands on a dial. Compare **digital clock.**

analogue-digital converter NOUN a device converting an analogue electrical signal into a digital representation so that it can be processed by a digital system. Abbreviation: **ADC.**

analogue recording NOUN a sound recording process in which an audio input is converted into an analogous electrical waveform.

analogy (ə'nælədʒɪ) NOUN, *plural* **-gies.** [1] agreement or similarity, esp in a certain limited number of features or details. [2] a comparison made to show such a similarity: *to draw an analogy between an atom and the solar system.* [3] *Biology* the relationship between analogous organs or parts. [4] *Logic, maths* a form of reasoning in which a similarity between two or more things is inferred from a known similarity between them in other respects. [5] *Linguistics* imitation of existing models or regular patterns in the formation of words, inflections, etc.: *a child may use "sheeps" as the plural of "sheep" by analogy with "dog", "dogs", "cat", "cats", etc.*
▷HISTORY C16: from Greek *analogia* ratio, correspondence, from *analogos* ANALOGOUS
▸ **analogical** (,ænə'lɒdʒɪk^əl) *or* **,ana'logic** ADJECTIVE
▸ **,ana'logically** ADVERB ▸ **a'nalogist** NOUN

analphabetic (,ænælfə'bɛtɪk, æn,æl-) ADJECTIVE [1] not in alphabetical order. ◆ NOUN, ADJECTIVE [2] a less common word for **illiterate.**
▷HISTORY C20: from Greek *analphabētos;* see AN-, ALPHABET
▸ **,analpha'betically** ADVERB

anal retentive *Psychoanal* ◆ NOUN [1] a person who exhibits anal personality traits. ◆ ADJECTIVE **anal-retentive.** [2] exhibiting anal personality traits.

analysand (ə'nælɪ,sænd) NOUN any person who is undergoing psychoanalysis.
▷HISTORY C20: from ANALYSE + *-and,* on the model of *multiplicand*

analyse *or US* **analyze** ('æn^ə,laɪz) VERB (*tr*) [1] to examine in detail in order to discover meaning, essential features, etc. [2] to break down into components or essential features: *to analyse a financial structure.* [3] to make a mathematical, chemical, grammatical, etc., analysis of. [4] another word for **psychoanalyse.**
▷HISTORY C17: back formation from ANALYSIS
▸ **,ana'lysable** *or US* **,ana'lyzable** ADJECTIVE ▸ **,analy'sation** *or US* **,analy'zation** NOUN ▸ **'ana,lyser** *or US* **'ana,lyzer** NOUN

analysis (ə'nælɪsɪs) NOUN, *plural* **-ses** (-,siːz). [1] the division of a physical or abstract whole into its constituent parts to examine or determine their relationship or value. Compare **synthesis** (sense 1). [2] a statement of the results of this. [3] short for **psychoanalysis.** [4] *Chem* **a** the decomposition of a substance into its elements, radicals, or other constituents in order to determine the kinds of constituents present (**qualitative analysis**) or the amount of each constituent (**quantitative analysis**). **b** the result obtained by such a determination. [5] *Linguistics* the use of word order together with word function to express syntactic relations in a language, as opposed to the use of inflections. Compare **synthesis** (sense 4). [6] *Maths* the branch of mathematics principally concerned with the properties of functions, largely arising out of calculus. [7] *Philosophy* (in the writings of Kant) the separation of a concept from another that contains it. Compare **synthesis** (sense 6a). [8] **in the last, final,** *or* **ultimate analysis.** after everything has been given due consideration.
▷HISTORY C16: from New Latin, from Greek *analusis,* literally: a dissolving, from *analuein,* from ANA- + *luein* to loosen

analysis of variance NOUN *Statistics* any of a number of techniques for resolving the observed variance between sets of data into components, esp to determine whether the difference between two samples is explicable as random sampling variation with the same underlying population. Abbreviation: **ANOVA.**

analysis situs NOUN a former name for **topology** (sense 2).

analyst ('ænəlɪst) NOUN [1] a person who analyses or is skilled in analysis. [2] short for **psychoanalyst.**

analytic (,ænə'lɪtɪk) *or* **analytical** (,ænə'lɪtɪk^əl) ADJECTIVE [1] relating to analysis. [2] capable of or given to analysing: *an analytic mind.* [3] Also: **isolating.** *Linguistics* denoting languages, such as Chinese, whose morphology is characterized by analysis. Compare **synthetic** (sense 3), **agglutinative** (sense 2), **polysynthetic.** [4] *Logic* (of a proposition) **a** true by virtue of the meanings of the words alone without reference to the facts, as *all spinsters are unmarried.* **b** true or false by virtue of meaning alone; so *all spinsters are married* is analytically false. ◆ Compare **synthetic** (sense 4), **a priori.** [5] Also: **regular, holomorphic.** *Maths* (of a function of a complex variable) having a derivative at each point of its domain.
▷HISTORY C16: via Late Latin from Greek *analutikos* from *analuein* to dissolve, break down; see ANALYSIS
▸ **,ana'lytically** ADVERB

analytical geometry NOUN the branch of geometry that uses algebraic notation and analysis to locate a geometric point in terms of a coordinate system; coordinate geometry.

analytical philosophy NOUN a school of philosophy which flourished in the first half of the 20th century and which sought to resolve philosophical problems by analysing the language in which they are expressed, esp in terms of formal logic as in Russell's theory of descriptions. Compare **linguistic philosophy.**

analytical psychology NOUN a school of psychoanalysis founded by Jung as a result of disagreements with Freud. See also **archetype, collective unconscious.**

analytical reagent NOUN a chemical compound of a known high standard of purity.

Anam (æ'næm, 'ænæm) NOUN a variant spelling of **Annam.**

Anambra (ə'næmbrə) NOUN a state of S Nigeria, formed in 1976 from part of East-Central State. Capital: Enugu. Pop.: 3 094 783 (1995 est.). Area: 4844 sq. km (1870 sq. miles).

anamnesis (,ænæm'niːsɪs) NOUN, *plural* **-ses** (-siːz). [1] the ability to recall past events; recollection. [2] the case history of a patient.
▷HISTORY C17: via New Latin from Greek, from *anamimnēskein* to recall, from *mimnēskein* to call to mind

anamnestic (,ænæm'nɛstɪk) ADJECTIVE [1] of or relating to anamnesis. [2] *Immunol* denoting a response to antigenic stimulation characterized by the production of large amounts of antibody specific to a different antigen from that which elicited the response.
▸ **,anam'nestically** ADVERB

anamniote (æn'æmnɪəʊt) NOUN any vertebrate animal, such as a fish or amphibian, that lacks an amnion, chorion, and allantois during embryonic development. Compare **amniote.**
▸ **anamniotic** (æn,æmnɪ'ɒtɪk) ADJECTIVE

anamorphic (,ænə'mɔːfɪk) ADJECTIVE of, relating to, or caused by anamorphosis or anamorphism.

anamorphic lens NOUN a component in the optical system of a film projector for converting standard 35mm film images into wide-screen format.

anamorphism (,ænə'mɔː,fɪzəm) NOUN intense metamorphism of a rock in which high-density complex minerals are formed from simpler minerals of lower density.

anamorphoscope (,ænə'mɔːfə,skəʊp) NOUN an optical device, such as a cylindrical lens, for correcting an image that has been distorted by anamorphosis.

anamorphosis (ˌænəˈmɔːfəsɪs, -mɔːˈfəʊsɪs) NOUN, *plural* **-ses** (-ˌsiːz). [1] *Optics* **a** an image or drawing distorted in such a way that it becomes recognizable only when viewed in a specified manner or through a special device. **b** the process by which such images or drawings are produced. [2] the evolution of one type of organism from another by a series of gradual changes.
▷HISTORY C18: from Greek, from *anamorphoun* to transform, from *morphē* form, shape

ananas (əˈnænəs) NOUN another name for the **pineapple**, or for a related tropical American bromeliaceous plant, the pinguin, that has an edible plum-shaped fruit.
▷HISTORY C17: from the native name in Peru

Anancy *or* **Anansi** (əˈnænsɪ) NOUN a character in Caribbean folklore, a cunning trickster generally depicted as a spider with a human head; the subject of many **Anancy stories**, the character has its origins among the Ashanti of W Africa.

anandrous (ænˈændrəs) ADJECTIVE (of flowers) having no stamens.
▷HISTORY C19: from Greek *anandros* lacking males, from AN- + *anēr* man

Ananias (ˌænəˈnaɪəs) NOUN [1] *New Testament* a Jewish Christian of Jerusalem who was struck dead for lying (Acts 5). [2] a liar.

Ananke (əˈnæŋkɪ) NOUN a small outer satellite of Jupiter.

ananthous (ænˈænθəs) ADJECTIVE (of higher plants) having no flowers.
▷HISTORY C19: from Greek *ananthēs*, from AN- + *anthos* flower

anapaest *or* **anapest** (ˈænəpest, -piːst) NOUN *Prosody* a metrical foot of three syllables, the first two short, the last long (⏑⏑–).
▷HISTORY C17: via Latin from Greek *anapaistos* reversed (that is, a dactyl reversed), from *anapaiein*, from *ana-* back + *paiein* to strike
▸ˌ**anaˈpaestic** *or* ˌ**anaˈpestic** ADJECTIVE

anaphase (ˈænəˌfeɪz) NOUN [1] the third stage of mitosis, during which the chromatids separate and migrate towards opposite ends of the spindle. See also **prophase, metaphase, telophase.** [2] the corresponding stage of the first division of meiosis.
▷HISTORY C19: from ANA- + PHASE

anaphora (əˈnæfərə) NOUN [1] *Grammar* the use of a word such as a pronoun that has the same reference as a word previously used in the same discourse. In the sentence *John wrote the essay in the library but Peter did it at home*, both *did* and *it* are examples of anaphora. Compare **cataphora, exophoric.** [2] *Rhetoric* the repetition of a word or phrase at the beginning of successive clauses.
▷HISTORY C16: via Latin from Greek: repetition, from *anapherein*, from ANA- + *pherein* to bear

anaphoresis (ˌænəfəˈriːsɪs) NOUN *Chem* the movement of suspended charged particles towards the anode in an electric field.

anaphoric (ˌænəˈfɒrɪk) ADJECTIVE of or relating to anaphorism.
▸ˌ**anaˈphorically** ADVERB

anaphrodisiac (ˌænæfrəˈdɪzɪˌæk) ADJECTIVE [1] tending to lessen sexual desire. ◆ NOUN [2] an anaphrodisiac drug.
▸ˌ**anaphroˈdisia** NOUN

anaphylactic shock NOUN a severe, sometimes fatal, reaction to a substance to which a person has an extreme sensitivity, often involving respiratory difficulty and circulation failure.

anaphylaxis (ˌænəfɪˈlæksɪs) NOUN extreme sensitivity to an injected antigen, esp a protein, following a previous injection.
▷HISTORY C20: from ANA- + (PRO)PHYLAXIS
▸ˌ**anaphyˈlactic** *or* ˌ**anaphyˈlactoid** ADJECTIVE
▸ˌ**anaphyˈlactically** ADVERB

anaplasia (ˌænəˈpleɪsɪə) NOUN reversion of plant or animal cells to a simpler less differentiated form.

anaplasmosis (ˌænəplæzˈməʊsɪs) NOUN another name for **gallsickness.**

anaplastic (ˌænəˈplæstɪk) ADJECTIVE [1] of or relating to anaplasia. [2] relating to plastic surgery.

anaplasty (ˈænəˌplæstɪ) NOUN *Surgery* another name for **plastic surgery.**

anaptyxis (ˌænæpˈtɪksɪs) NOUN, *plural* **-tyxes** (-ˈtɪksiːz). the insertion of a short vowel between consonants in order to make a word more easily pronounceable.
▷HISTORY C19: via New Latin from Greek *anaptuxis*, from *anaptussein* to unfold, from ANA- + *ptussein* to fold
▸**anaptyctic** (ˌænæpˈtɪktɪk) *or* ˌ**anapˈtyctical** ADJECTIVE

Anapurna (ˌænəˈpʊənə) NOUN a variant spelling of **Annapurna.**

anarch (ˈænɑːk) NOUN *Archaic* an instigator or personification of anarchy.

anarchism (ˈænəˌkɪzəm) NOUN [1] *Political theory* a doctrine advocating the abolition of government. [2] the principles or practice of anarchists.

anarchist (ˈænəkɪst) NOUN [1] a person who advocates the abolition of government and a social system based on voluntary cooperation. [2] a person who causes disorder or upheaval.
▸ˌ**anarˈchistic** ADJECTIVE

anarchy (ˈænəkɪ) NOUN [1] general lawlessness and disorder, esp when thought to result from an absence or failure of government. [2] the absence or lack of government. [3] the absence of any guiding or uniting principle; disorder; chaos. [4] the theory or practice of political anarchism.
▷HISTORY C16: from Medieval Latin *anarchia*, from Greek *anarkhia*, from *anarkhos* without a ruler, from AN- + *arkh-* leader, from *arkhein* to rule
▸**anarchic** (ænˈɑːkɪk) *or* **anˈarchical** ADJECTIVE
▸**anˈarchically** ADVERB

anarthria (ænˈɑːθrɪə) NOUN *Pathol* loss of the ability to speak coherently.
▷HISTORY C19: New Latin, from Greek *anarthros* lacking vigour, from AN- + *arthros* joint

anarthrous (ænˈɑːθrəs) ADJECTIVE [1] (of a noun) used without an article. [2] having no joints or articulated limbs.
▷HISTORY C19: from Greek *anarthros*, from AN- + *arthros* joint, definite article
▸**anˈarthrously** ADVERB ▸**anˈarthrousness** NOUN

anasarca (ˌænəˈsɑːkə) NOUN *Pathol* a generalized accumulation of serous fluid within the subcutaneous connective tissue, resulting in oedema.
▷HISTORY C14: from New Latin, from ANA- (puffed up) + Greek *sarx* flesh
▸ˌ**anaˈsarcous** ADJECTIVE

anastigmat (æˈnæstɪgˌmæt, ˌænəˈstɪgmæt) NOUN a lens or system of lenses designed to be free of astigmatism.

anastigmatic (ˌænəstɪgˈmætɪk) ADJECTIVE (of a lens or optical device) not astigmatic. Also: **stigmatic.**

anastomose (əˈnæstəˌməʊz) VERB to join (two parts of a blood vessel, etc.) by anastomosis.

anastomosis (əˌnæstəˈməʊsɪs) NOUN, *plural* **-ses** (-siːz). [1] a natural connection between two tubular structures, such as blood vessels. [2] the surgical union of two hollow organs or parts that are normally separate. [3] the separation and rejoining in a reticulate pattern of the veins of a leaf or of branches.
▷HISTORY C16: via New Latin from Greek: opening, from *anastomoun* to equip with a mouth, from *stoma* mouth
▸**anastomotic** (əˌnæstəˈmɒtɪk) ADJECTIVE

anastrophe (əˈnæstrəfɪ) NOUN *Rhetoric* another term for **inversion** (sense 3).
▷HISTORY C16: from Greek, from *anastrephein* to invert

anat. ABBREVIATION FOR: [1] anatomical. [2] anatomy.

anata (ˈænətə) NOUN (in Theravada Buddhism) the belief that since all things are constantly changing, there can be no such thing as a permanent, unchanging self: one of the three basic characteristics of existence. Sanskrit word: **anatman.** Compare **anicca, dukkha.**
▷HISTORY Pali, literally: no self

anatase (ˈænəˌteɪz) NOUN a rare blue or black mineral that consists of titanium oxide in tetragonal crystalline form and occurs in veins in igneous rocks. Formula: TiO_2. Also called: **octahedrite.**
▷HISTORY C19: from French, from Greek *anatasis* an extending (referring to the length of the crystals), from *anateinein* to stretch out

anathema (əˈnæθəmə) NOUN, *plural* **-mas.** [1] a detested person or thing: *he is anathema to me.* [2] a formal ecclesiastical curse of excommunication or a formal denunciation of a doctrine. [3] the person or thing so cursed. [4] a strong curse; imprecation.
▷HISTORY C16: via Church Latin from Greek: something accursed, dedicated (to evil), from *anatithenai* to dedicate, from ANA- + *tithenai* to set

anathematize *or* **anathematise** (əˈnæθɪməˌtaɪz) VERB to pronounce an anathema (upon a person, etc.); curse.
▸**aˌnathematiˈzation** *or* **aˌnathematiˈsation** NOUN

Anatolia (ˌænəˈtəʊlɪə) NOUN the Asian part of Turkey, occupying the peninsula between the Black Sea, the Mediterranean, and the Aegean: consists of a plateau, largely mountainous, with salt lakes in the interior. Historical name: **Asia Minor.**

Anatolian (ˌænəˈtəʊlɪən) ADJECTIVE [1] of or relating to Anatolia or its inhabitants. [2] denoting, belonging to, or relating to an ancient family of languages related to the Indo-European family and including Hittite. ◆ NOUN [3] this family of languages, sometimes regarded as a branch of Indo-European. [4] a native or inhabitant of Anatolia.

Anatolian shepherd dog NOUN a large powerfully-built dog of a breed with a large head and a short dense cream or fawn coat, originally used for guarding sheep.

anatomical (ˌænəˈtɒmɪkᵊl) ADJECTIVE of or relating to anatomy.
▸ˌ**anaˈtomically** ADVERB

anatomical snuffbox NOUN the triangular depression on the back of the hand between the thumb and the index finger.

anatomist (əˈnætəmɪst) NOUN an expert in anatomy.

anatomize *or* **anatomise** (əˈnætəˌmaɪz) VERB (*tr*) [1] to dissect (an animal or plant). [2] to examine in minute detail.
▸**aˌnatomiˈzation** *or* **aˌnatomiˈsation** NOUN ▸**aˈnatoˌmizer** *or* **aˈnatoˌmiser** NOUN

anatomy (əˈnætəmɪ) NOUN, *plural* **-mies.** [1] the science concerned with the physical structure of animals and plants. [2] the physical structure of an animal or plant or any of its parts. [3] a book or treatise on this subject. [4] dissection of an animal or plant. [5] any detailed analysis: *the anatomy of a crime.* [6] *Informal* the human body.
▷HISTORY C14: from Latin *anatomia*, from Greek *anatomē*, from *anatemnein* to cut up, from ANA- + *temnein* to cut

anatropous (əˈnætrəpəs) ADJECTIVE (of a plant ovule) inverted during development by a bending of the stalk (funicle) attaching it to the carpel wall. Compare **orthotropous.**
▷HISTORY C19: from ANA- (inverted) + -TROPOUS

anatto (əˈnætəʊ) NOUN, *plural* **-tos.** a variant spelling of **annatto.**

anaxial (ænˈæksɪəl) ADJECTIVE *Biology* asymmetrical.

anbury (ˈænbərɪ) NOUN, *plural* **-buries.** [1] a soft spongy tumour occurring in horses and oxen. [2] *Brit dialect* another name for **club root.**
▷HISTORY C16: of uncertain origin

ANC ABBREVIATION FOR **African National Congress.**

-ance *or* **-ancy** SUFFIX FORMING NOUNS indicating an action, state or condition, or quality: *hindrance; tenancy; resemblance.* Compare **-ence.**
▷HISTORY via Old French from Latin *-antia;* see -ANCY

ancestor (ˈænsestə) NOUN [1] (*often plural*) a person from whom another is directly descended, esp someone more distant than a grandparent; forefather. [2] an early type of animal or plant from which a later, usually dissimilar, type has evolved. [3] a person or thing regarded as a forerunner of a later person or thing: *the ancestor of the modern camera.*
▷HISTORY C13: from Old French *ancestre*, from Late Latin *antecēssor* one who goes before, from Latin *antecēdere;* see ANTECEDE
▸ˈ**ancestress** FEMININE NOUN

ancestral (ænˈsestrəl) ADJECTIVE [1] of, inherited from, or derived from ancestors: *his ancestral home.* ◆ NOUN [2] *Logic* a relation that holds between *x* and *y* if there is a chain of instances of a given relation leading from *x* to *y.* Thus the ancestral of *parent of* is *ancestor of,* since *x* is the ancestor of *y* if

and only if *x* is a parent of...a parent of...a parent of *y*.
▸**an'cestrally** ADVERB

ancestry ('ænsɛstrɪ) NOUN, *plural* **-tries.** [1] lineage or descent, esp when ancient, noble, or distinguished. [2] ancestors collectively.

Anchises (æn'kaɪsiːz) NOUN *Classical myth* a Trojan prince and father of Aeneas. In the *Aeneid,* he is rescued by his son at the fall of Troy and dies in Sicily.

anchor ('æŋkə) NOUN [1] any of several devices, usually of steel, attached to a vessel by a cable and dropped overboard so as to grip the bottom and restrict the vessel's movement. [2] an object used to hold something else firmly in place: *the rock provided an anchor for the rope.* [3] a source of stability or security: *religion was his anchor.* [4] **a** a metal cramp, bolt, or similar fitting, esp one used to make a connection to masonry. **b** (*as modifier*): *anchor bolt; anchor plate.* [5] **a** the rear person in a tug-of-war team. **b** short for **anchorman** or **anchorwoman.** [6] **at anchor.** (of a vessel) anchored. [7] **cast, come to,** *or* **drop anchor.** to anchor a vessel. [8] **drag anchor.** See **drag** (sense 13). [9] **ride at anchor.** to be anchored. [10] **weigh anchor.** to raise a vessel's anchor or (of a vessel) to have its anchor raised in preparation for departure. ◆ VERB [11] to use an anchor to hold (a vessel) in one place. [12] to fasten or be fastened securely; fix or become fixed firmly. [13] (*tr*) *Radio, television* to act as an anchorman on. ◆ See also **anchors.**
▷**HISTORY** Old English *ancor,* from Latin *ancora,* from Greek *ankura;* related to Greek *ankos* bend; compare Latin *uncus* bent, hooked

anchorage¹ ('æŋkərɪdʒ) NOUN [1] the act of anchoring. [2] any place where a vessel is anchored. [3] a place designated for vessels to anchor. [4] a fee imposed for anchoring. [5] anything used as an anchor. [6] a source of security or strength. [7] something that supplies a secure hold for something else.

anchorage² ('æŋkərɪdʒ) NOUN the cell or retreat of an anchorite.

Anchorage ('æŋkərɪdʒ) NOUN the largest city in Alaska, a port in the south, at the head of Cook Inlet. Pop.: 260 283 (2000).

anchorette (ˌæŋkə'rɛt) NOUN *Informal* (in broadcasting) a young and inexperienced anchorwoman.
▷**HISTORY** C20: from ANCHOR (sense 5b) + ETTE (sense 2)

anchor ice NOUN *Canadian* ice that forms at the bottom of a lake or river.

anchorite ('æŋkəˌraɪt) NOUN a person who lives in seclusion, esp a religious recluse; hermit.
▷**HISTORY** C15: from Medieval Latin *anchorīta,* from Late Latin *anachōrēta,* from Greek *anakhōrētēs,* from *anakhōrein* to retire, withdraw, from *khōra* a space
▸**'anchoress** FEMININE NOUN

anchorman ('æŋkəmæn) NOUN, *plural* **-men.** [1] *Sport* the last person in a team to compete, esp in a relay race. [2] (in broadcasting) a person in a central studio who links up and maintains contact with various outside camera units, reporters, etc.

anchor ring NOUN a ring made from an iron bar of circular cross-section.

anchors ('æŋkəz) PLURAL NOUN *Slang* the brakes of a motor vehicle: *he rammed on the anchors.*

anchorwoman ('æŋkəˌwʊmən) NOUN, *plural* **-women.** [1] *Sport* the last woman in a team to compete, esp in a relay race. [2] (in broadcasting) a woman in a central studio who links up and maintains contact with various outside camera units, reporters, etc.

anchoveta (ˌæntʃə'vɛtə) NOUN a small anchovy, *Cetengraulis mysticetus,* of the American Pacific, used as bait by tuna fishermen.
▷**HISTORY** C20: Spanish, diminutive of *anchova* ANCHOVY

anchovy ('æntʃəvɪ) NOUN, *plural* **-vies** *or* **-vy.** any of various small marine food fishes of the genus *Engraulis* and related genera, esp *E. encrasicolus* of S Europe: family *Clupeidae* (herrings). They have a salty taste and are often tinned or made into a paste or essence.
▷**HISTORY** C16: from Spanish *anchova,* perhaps ultimately from Greek *aphuē* small fish

anchovy pear NOUN a Jamaican tree, *Grias cauliflora,* bearing edible fruits that taste like the mango: family *Lecythidaceae.*
▷**HISTORY** C18: so called from the use of the fruit as an hors d'oeuvre

anchusa (æŋ'kjuːsə) NOUN any Eurasian plant of the boraginaceous genus *Anchusa,* having rough hairy stems and leaves and blue flowers. See also **alkanet** (sense 3), **bugloss.**
▷**HISTORY** C18: from Latin

anchusin (æŋ'kjuːsɪn) NOUN another name for **alkanet** (sense 2).

anchylose ('æŋkɪˌləʊz) VERB a former spelling of **ankylose.**
▸ˌ**anchy'losis** NOUN ▸**anchylotic** (ˌæŋkɪ'lɒtɪk) ADJECTIVE

anchylostomiasis (ˌæŋkɪˌlɒstə'maɪəsɪs) NOUN a variant of **ancylostomiasis.**

ancien régime *French* (ɑ̃sjɛ̃ reʒim) NOUN, *plural* ***anciens régimes*** (ɑ̃sjɛ̃ reʒim). [1] the political and social system of France before the Revolution of 1789. [2] a former or outdated regime.
▷**HISTORY** literally: old regime

ancient¹ ('eɪnʃənt) ADJECTIVE [1] dating from very long ago: *ancient ruins.* [2] very old; aged. [3] of the far past, esp before the collapse of the Western Roman Empire (476 A.D.). Compare **medieval, modern.** [4] *Law* having existed since before the time of legal memory. ◆ NOUN [5] (*often plural*) a member of a civilized nation in the ancient world, esp a Greek, Roman, or Hebrew. [6] (*often plural*) one of the classical authors of Greek or Roman antiquity. [7] *Archaic* an old man.
▷**HISTORY** C14: from Old French *ancien,* from Vulgar Latin *anteanus* (unattested), from Latin *ante* before
▸**'ancientness** NOUN

ancient² ('eɪnʃənt) NOUN *Archaic* [1] a flag or other banner; standard. [2] a standard-bearer; ensign.
▷**HISTORY** C16: changed from ENSIGN through the influence of ANCIENT¹

Ancient Greek NOUN the Greek language from the earliest records to about 300 B.C., the chief dialect areas of which were Aeolic, Arcadic, Doric, and Ionic (including Attic). Compare **Koine, Late Greek, Medieval Greek.**

ancient history NOUN [1] the history of the **ancient world** from the earliest known civilizations to the collapse of the Western Roman Empire in 476 A.D. [2] *Informal* a recent event or fact sufficiently familiar to have lost its pertinence.

ancient lights NOUN (*usually functioning as singular*) the legal right to receive, by a particular window or windows, adequate and unobstructed daylight.

anciently ('eɪnʃəntlɪ) ADVERB in ancient times.

ancient monument NOUN *Brit* a historical building or the remains of one, usually dating from no later than the medieval period, that has been designated as worthy of preservation and is often in the care of a government department.

Ancient of Days NOUN a name for God, originating in the Authorized Version of the Old Testament (Daniel 7:9).

ancient wisdom NOUN pre-Christian knowledge, philosophy, and beliefs.

ancillary (æn'sɪlərɪ) ADJECTIVE [1] subsidiary. [2] auxiliary; supplementary: *ancillary services.* ◆ NOUN, *plural* **-laries.** [3] a subsidiary or auxiliary thing or person: *the company has an ancillary abroad.*
▷**HISTORY** C17: from Latin *ancillāris* concerning maidservants, from *ancilla,* diminutive of *ancūla* female servant

ancipital (æn'sɪpɪtᵊl) *or* **ancipitous** (æn'sɪpɪtəs) ADJECTIVE *Biology* flattened and having two edges: *ancipital stems.*
▷**HISTORY** C18: from Latin *anceps* two-headed

Ancohuma (ˌæŋkəʊ'uːmə) NOUN one of the two peaks of Mount **Sorata.**

ancon ('æŋkɒn) *or* **ancone** ('æŋkəʊn) NOUN, *plural* **ancones** (æŋ'kəʊniːz). [1] *Architect* a projecting bracket or console supporting a cornice. [2] a former technical name for **elbow.**
▷**HISTORY** C18: from Greek *ankōn* a bend
▸**anconal** (æŋ'kəʊnᵊl) *or* **anconeal** (æŋ'kəʊnɪəl) ADJECTIVE

Ancona (*Italian* aŋ'koːna) NOUN a port in central Italy, on the Adriatic, capital of the Marches: founded by Greeks from Syracuse in about 390 B.C. Pop.: 100 597 (1994 est.).

-ancy SUFFIX FORMING NOUNS a variant of **-ance,** indicating condition or quality *expectancy; poignancy.*

ancylostomiasis (ˌænsɪˌlɒstə'maɪəsɪs), **ankylostomiasis,** *or* **anchylostomiasis** NOUN infestation of the human intestine with blood-sucking hookworms, causing progressive anaemia. Also called: **hookworm disease.**
▷**HISTORY** from New Latin, from *Ancylostoma* genus of hookworms, from Greek *ankulos* hooked, crooked + *stoma* mouth

and (ænd; *unstressed* ənd, ən) CONJUNCTION (*coordinating*) [1] along with; in addition to: *boys and girls.* [2] as a consequence: *he fell down and cut his knee.* [3] afterwards: *we pay the man and go through that door.* [4] (preceded by *good* or *nice*) (intensifier): *the sauce is good and thick.* [5] plus: *two and two equals four.* [6] used to join identical words or phrases to give emphasis or indicate repetition or continuity: *better and better; we ran and ran; it rained and rained.* [7] used to join two identical words or phrases to express a contrast between instances of what is named: *there are jobs and jobs.* [8] *Informal* used in place of *to* in infinitives after verbs such as *try, go,* and *come*: *try and see it my way.* [9] an obsolete word for **if**: *and it please you.* Informal spellings: **an, an', 'n.** ◆ NOUN [10] (*usually plural*) an additional matter or problem: *ifs, ands, or buts.*
▷**HISTORY** Old English *and;* related to Old Frisian *anda,* Old Saxon *ande,* Old High German *anti,* Sanskrit *atha*

Language note See at **to.**

AND INTERNATIONAL CAR REGISTRATION FOR Andorra.

-and *or* **-end** SUFFIX FORMING NOUNS indicating a person or thing that is to be dealt with in a specified way: *analysand; dividend; multiplicand.*
▷**HISTORY** from Latin gerundives ending in *-andus, -endus*

Andalusia (ˌændə'luːzɪə) NOUN a region of S Spain, on the Mediterranean and the Atlantic, with the Sierra Morena in the north, the Sierra Nevada in the southeast, and the Guadalquivir River flowing over fertile lands between them; a centre of Moorish civilization; it became an autonomous region in 1981. Area: about 87 280 sq. km (33 700 sq. miles). Spanish name: **Andalucía** (andalu'θia).

andalusite (ˌændə'luːsaɪt) NOUN a grey, pink, or brown hard mineral consisting of aluminium silicate in orthorhombic crystalline form. It occurs in metamorphic rocks and is used as a refractory and as a gemstone. Formula: Al_2SiO_5.

Andaman and Nicobar Islands ('ændəmən, 'nɪkəʊˌbɑː) PLURAL NOUN a territory of India, in the E Bay of Bengal, consisting of two groups of over 200 islands. Capital: Port Blair. Pop.: 356 265 (2001). Area: 8140 sq. km (3143 sq. miles).

Andaman Islands PLURAL NOUN a group of islands in the E Bay of Bengal, part of the Indian territory of the Andaman and Nicobar Islands. Area: 6408 sq. km (2474 sq. miles). Pop.: 240 089 (1991 est.).

Andaman Sea NOUN part of the Bay of Bengal, between the Andaman and Nicobar Islands and the Malay Peninsula.

andante (æn'dæntɪ) *Music* ◆ ADJECTIVE, ADVERB [1] (to be performed) at a moderately slow tempo. ◆ NOUN [2] a passage or piece to be performed in this manner.
▷**HISTORY** C18: Italian: going, from *andare* to go, from Latin *ambulāre* to walk

andantino (ˌændæn'tiːnəʊ) *Music* ◆ ADJECTIVE, ADVERB [1] (to be performed) slightly faster, or slightly more slowly, than andante. ◆ NOUN, *plural* **-nos.** [2] a passage or piece to be performed in this manner.
▷**HISTORY** C19: diminutive of ANDANTE

AND circuit *or* **gate** (ænd) NOUN *Computing* a logic circuit having two or more input wires and one output wire that has a high-voltage output signal if and only if all input signals are at a high voltage simultaneously: used extensively as a basic circuit in computers. Compare **NAND circuit, NOR circuit, OR circuit.**

▷HISTORY C20: so named because the action performed on electrical signals is similar to the operation of the conjunction *and* in logical constructions

Andean (æn'diːən, 'ændɪən) ADJECTIVE of, relating to, or resembling the Andes.

Anderlecht (*Flemish* 'ɑndərlɛxt) NOUN a town in central Belgium, a suburb of Brussels. Pop.: 87 880 (1991).

Anderson ('ændəsᵊn) NOUN a river in N Canada, in the Northwest Territories, rising in lakes north of Great Bear Lake and flowing west and north to the Beaufort Sea. Length: about 580 km (360 miles).

Anderson shelter NOUN *Brit* a small prefabricated air-raid shelter of World War II consisting of an arch of corrugated metal and designed to be partly buried in people's gardens and covered with earth for protection.
▷HISTORY C20: so named because its use was adopted while Sir John *Anderson* was Home Secretary (1939–40)

Andes ('ændiːz) PLURAL NOUN a major mountain system of South America, extending for about 7250 km (4500 miles) along the entire W coast, with several parallel ranges or cordilleras and many volcanic peaks: rich in minerals, including gold, silver, copper, iron ore, and nitrates. Average height: 3900 m (13 000 ft.). Highest peak: Aconcagua, 6960 m (22 835 ft.).

andesine ('ændɪˌziːn, -zɪn) NOUN a feldspar mineral of the plagioclase series consisting of an aluminium silicate of sodium and calcium. Formula: $NaAlSi_3O_8.CaAl_2Si_2O_8$.
▷HISTORY C19: from the ANDES (where it is found) + -INE[1]

andesite ('ændɪˌzaɪt) NOUN a fine-grained tan or grey volcanic rock consisting of plagioclase feldspar, esp andesine, amphibole, and pyroxene.
▷HISTORY C19: from ANDES + -ITE[1]

Andhra Pradesh ('ændrə prɑː'dɛʃ) NOUN a state of SE India, on the Bay of Bengal: formed in 1953 from parts of Madras and Hyderabad states. Capital: Hyderabad. Pop.: 75 727 541 (2001). Area: about 275 068 sq. km (106 204 sq. miles).

andiron ('ændˌaɪən) NOUN another name for **firedog.**
▷HISTORY C14: from Old French *andier,* of unknown origin; influenced by IRON

Andizhan (*Russian* andi'ʒan) NOUN a city in E Uzbekistan. Pop.: 288 000 (1998 est.).

Andong ('æn'dʊŋ) NOUN a port in E China, in Liaoning province at the mouth of the Yalu River. Pop.: 188 452 (1995). Also called: **Tan-tung.**

and/or CONJUNCTION (*coordinating*) used to join terms when either one or the other or both is indicated: *passports and/or other means of identification.*

> **Language note** Many people think that *and/or* is only acceptable in legal and commercial contexts. In other contexts, it is better to use *or both: some alcoholics lose their jobs or their driving licences or both* (not *their jobs and/or their driving licences*).

Andorra (æn'dɔːrə) NOUN a mountainous principality in SW Europe, between France and Spain: according to tradition, given independence by Charlemagne in the 9th century for helping to fight the Moors; placed under the joint sovereignty of the Comte de Foix and the Spanish bishop of Urgel in 1278; under the joint overlordship of the French head of state and the bishop of Urgel from the 16th century; adopted a constitution reducing the powers of the overlords in 1993. Languages: Catalan (official), French, and Spanish. Religion: Roman Catholic. Currency: euro. Capital: Andorra la Vella. Pop.: 66 900 (2001 est). Area: 464 sq. km (179 sq. miles). Official name: **Principat d'Andorra.**

Andorra la Vella (*Spanish* an'dɔrra la 'beʎa) NOUN the capital of Andorra, situated in the west of the principality. Pop.: 21 189 (2000 est.). French name: **Andorre la Vieille** (ɑ̃dɔr la vjej).

Andorran (æn'dɔːrən) ADJECTIVE 1 of or relating to Andorra or its inhabitants. ◆ NOUN 2 a native or inhabitant of Andorra.

andouille *French* (ɑ̃duj) NOUN a spicy smoked pork sausage with a blackish skin.

andradite ('ændrəˌdaɪt) NOUN a yellow, green, or brownish-black garnet that consists of calcium iron silicate and is used as a gemstone. Formula: $Ca_3Fe_2(SiO_4)_3$.
▷HISTORY C19: named after J. B. d'*Andrada* e Silva (1763–1838), Brazilian mineralogist; see -ITE[1]

Andreanof Islands (ˌændrɪ'ɑːnɒf) PLURAL NOUN a group of islands in the central Aleutian Islands, Alaska. Area: 3710 sq. km (1432 sq. miles).

Andrew ('ændruː) NOUN *New Testament* **Saint.** one of the twelve apostles of Jesus; the brother of Peter; patron saint of Scotland. Feast day: Nov. 30.

andro- *or before a vowel* **andr-** COMBINING FORM 1 male; masculine: *androsterone.* 2 (in botany) stamen or anther: *androecium.*
▷HISTORY from Greek *anēr* (genitive *andros*) man

androcentric (ˌændrəʊ'sentrɪk) ADJECTIVE having or regarding man or the male sex as central or primary.
▸ˌ**andro'centrism** NOUN

Androcles ('ændrəˌkliːz) *or* **Androclus** ('ændrəkləs) NOUN (in Roman legend) a slave whose life was spared in the arena by a lion from whose paw he had once extracted a thorn.

androclinium (ˌændrə'klɪnɪəm) NOUN, *plural* **-clinia** (-'klɪnɪə). another name for **clinandrium.**
▷HISTORY C19: New Latin, from ANDRO- + *-clinium,* from Greek *klinē* slope; see CLINO-

androdioecious (ˌændrəʊdaɪ'iːʃəs) ADJECTIVE (of a plant species) having hermaphrodite and male flowers on separate plants.

androecium (æn'driːsɪəm) NOUN, *plural* **-cia** (-sɪə). the stamens of a flowering plant collectively.
▷HISTORY C19: from New Latin, from ANDRO- + Greek *oikion* a little house
▸**an'droecial** ADJECTIVE

androgen ('ændrədʒən) NOUN any of several steroids, produced as hormones by the testes or made synthetically, that promote development of male sexual organs and male secondary sexual characteristics.
▸**androgenic** (ˌændrə'dʒɛnɪk) ADJECTIVE

androgenous (æn'drɒdʒɪnəs) ADJECTIVE *Biology* producing only male offspring.

androgyne ('ændrəˌdʒaɪn) NOUN another word for **hermaphrodite.**
▷HISTORY C17: from Old French, via Latin from Greek *androgunos,* from *anēr* man + *gunē* woman

androgynophore (ˌændrəʊ'gaɪnəʊfɔː) NOUN another name for **androphore.**

androgynous (æn'drɒdʒɪnəs) ADJECTIVE 1 *Botany* having male and female flowers in the same inflorescence, as cuckoo pint. 2 having male and female characteristics; hermaphrodite.
▸**an'drogyny** NOUN

android ('ændrɔɪd) NOUN 1 (in science fiction) a robot resembling a human being. ◆ ADJECTIVE 2 resembling a human being.
▷HISTORY C18: from Late Greek *androeidēs* manlike; see ANDRO-, -OID

andrology (æn'drɒlədʒɪ) NOUN the branch of medicine concerned with diseases in men, esp of the reproductive organs.
▷HISTORY C20: from ANDRO- + -LOGY
▸**an'drologist** NOUN

Andromache (æn'drɒməkɪ) NOUN *Greek myth* the wife of Hector.

Andromeda[1] (æn'drɒmɪdə) NOUN *Greek myth* the daughter of Cassiopeia and wife of Perseus, who saved her from a sea monster.

Andromeda[2] (æn'drɒmɪdə) NOUN, *Latin genitive* **Andromedae** (æn'drɒmɪˌdiː). a constellation in the N hemisphere lying between Cassiopeia and Pegasus, the three brightest stars being of the second magnitude. It contains the **Andromeda Galaxy** a spiral galaxy 2.2 million light years away.

andromonoecious (ˌændrəʊmɒ'niːʃəs) ADJECTIVE (of a plant species) having hermaphrodite and male flowers on the same plant.

andropause ('ændrəʊˌpɔːz) NOUN the period, usually occurring between the ages of 45 and 55, during which a man's testosterone levels may fall, leading to a reduction in vigour and sexual drive. Also called: **male menopause.**
▷HISTORY C20: from ANDRO- + (MENO)PAUSE

androphore ('ændrəʊfɔː) NOUN *Botany* an extension of the receptacle carrying the androecium and the gynoecium, typical of the caper family (*Capparidaceae*). Also called: **androgynophore.**

Andropov (æn'drɒpɒv; *Russian* ən'drɔːpəf) NOUN a former name (1984–91) for **Rybinsk.**

Andros ('ændrəs) NOUN 1 an island in the Aegean Sea, the northernmost of the Cyclades: long famous for wine. Capital: Andros. Pop.: 8155 (1990). Area: about 311 sq. km (120 sq. miles). 2 an island in the N Caribbean, the largest of the Bahamas. Pop.: 8177 (1990). Area: 4144 sq. km (1600 sq. miles).

androsphinx ('ændrəˌsfɪŋks) NOUN, *plural* **-sphinxes** *or* **-sphinges** (-ˌsfɪndʒiːz). a sphinx having the head of a man.

androsterone (æn'drɒstəˌrəʊn) NOUN an androgenic steroid hormone produced in the testes. Formula: $C_{19}H_{30}O_2$.

-androus ADJECTIVE COMBINING FORM (in botany) indicating number or type of stamens: *diandrous.*
▷HISTORY from New Latin *-andrus,* from Greek *-andros,* from *anēr* man

-andry NOUN COMBINING FORM indicating number of husbands: *polyandry.*
▷HISTORY from Greek *-andria,* from *anēr* man

Andvari (æn'dwɑːrɪ) NOUN *Norse myth* a dwarf who possessed a treasure hoard, which was robbed by Loki.

ane (eɪn) DETERMINER, PRONOUN, NOUN a Scot word for **one.**

-ane SUFFIX FORMING NOUNS indicating an alkane hydrocarbon: *hexane.*
▷HISTORY coined to replace *-ene, -ine,* and *-one*

anear (ə'nɪə) *Archaic* ◆ PREPOSITION 1 near. ◆ ADVERB 2 nearly.

anecdotage ('ænɪkˌdəʊtɪdʒ) NOUN 1 anecdotes collectively. 2 *Humorous* talkative or garrulous old age.

anecdotal (ˌænɛk'dəʊtᵊl) ADJECTIVE containing or consisting exclusively of anecdotes rather than connected discourse or research conducted under controlled conditions.

anecdote ('ænɪkˌdəʊt) NOUN a short usually amusing account of an incident, esp a personal or biographical one.
▷HISTORY C17: from Medieval Latin *anecdota* unpublished items, from Greek *anekdotos* unpublished, from AN- + *ekdotos* published, from *ekdidonai,* from *ek-* out + *didonai* to give
▸ˌ**anec'dotic** ADJECTIVE ▸ˌ**anec'dotalist** *or* '**anecˌdotist** NOUN

anecdysis (ˌænɛk'daɪsɪs) NOUN the period between moults in arthropods.
▷HISTORY C20: New Latin, from Greek; see AN-, ECDYSIS

anechoic (ˌænɪ'kəʊɪk) ADJECTIVE having a low degree of reverberation of sound: *an anechoic recording studio.*

anelace ('ænəˌleɪs) NOUN a variant spelling of **anlace.**

anele (ə'niːl) VERB (*tr*) *Archaic* to anoint, esp to give extreme unction to.
▷HISTORY C14 *anelen,* from *an-* (from Old English *an-* ON) + *elen* to anoint (from *ele* oil, from Latin *oleum*)

anemia (ə'niːmɪə) NOUN the usual US spelling of **anaemia.**
▷HISTORY C19: from New Latin, from Greek *anaimia* lack of blood

anemic (ə'niːmɪk) ADJECTIVE the usual US spelling of **anaemic.**

anemo- COMBINING FORM indicating wind: *anemometer; anemophilous.*
▷HISTORY from Greek *anemos* wind

anemochore (ə'niːməʊˌkɔː) NOUN a plant in which the fruits or seeds are dispersed by wind.
▸**aˌnemo'chorous** ADJECTIVE

anemograph (ə'nɛməʊˌgrɑːf) NOUN a self-recording anemometer.
▸**anemographic** (əˌnɛməʊ'græfɪk) ADJECTIVE
▸**aˌnemo'graphically** ADVERB

anemography (ˌænɪ'mɒgrəfɪ) NOUN *Meteorol* the technique of recording wind measurements.

anemology (ˌænɪˈmɒlədʒɪ) NOUN *Archaic* the study of winds.

anemometer (ˌænɪˈmɒmɪtə) NOUN [1] Also called: **wind gauge.** an instrument for recording the speed and often the direction of winds. [2] any instrument that measures the rate of movement of a fluid.
▸**anemometric** (ˌænɪməʊˈmɛtrɪk) *or* ˌ**anemoˈmetrical** ADJECTIVE

anemometry (ˌænɪˈmɒmɪtrɪ) NOUN *Meteorol* the technique of measuring wind speed and direction.

anemone (əˈnɛmənɪ) NOUN any ranunculaceous woodland plant of the genus *Anemone* of N temperate regions, such as the white-flowered *A. nemorosa* (**wood anemone** or **windflower**). Some cultivated anemones have lilac, pale blue, pink, purple, or red flowers. See also **pasqueflower**. Compare **sea anemone** (an animal).
▹HISTORY C16: via Latin from Greek: windflower, from *anemos* wind

anemone fish NOUN any of various damselfishes of the genus *Amphiprion,* such as *A. percula* (clown anemone fish), that usually live closely associated with sea anemones.

anemophilous (ˌænɪˈmɒfɪləs) ADJECTIVE (of flowering plants such as grasses) pollinated by the wind. Compare **entomophilous.**
▸ˌ**aneˈmophily** NOUN

anemoscope (əˈnɛməˌskəʊp) NOUN *Meteorol* any device that shows the presence and direction of a wind.

anencephalic (ˌænɛnsəˈfælɪk) ADJECTIVE born with no or only a partial brain.
▹HISTORY AN- + ENCEPHALIC
▸**anencephaly** (ˌænɛnˈsɛfəlɪ) NOUN

anent (əˈnɛnt) PREPOSITION *Scot* [1] lying against; alongside. [2] concerning; about.
▹HISTORY Old English *on efen,* literally: on even (ground)

anergy (ˈænədʒɪ) NOUN [1] lack of energy. [2] *Immunol* diminution or lack of immunity to an antigen.
▹HISTORY from New Latin *anergia,* from AN- + Greek *ergon* work
▸**anergic** (æˈnɜːdʒɪk) ADJECTIVE

aneroid (ˈænəˌrɔɪd) ADJECTIVE not containing a liquid.
▹HISTORY C19: from French, from AN- + Greek *nēros* wet + -OID

aneroid barometer NOUN a device for measuring atmospheric pressure without the use of fluids. It consists of a partially evacuated metal chamber, the thin corrugated lid of which is displaced by variations in the external air pressure. This displacement is magnified by levers and made to operate a pointer.

anesthesia (ˌænɪsˈθiːzɪə) NOUN the usual US spelling of **anaesthesia.**

anesthesiologist *or* **anaesthesiologist** (ˌænɪsˌθiːzɪˈɒlədʒɪst) NOUN the US name for an **anaesthetist**; in the US, a qualified doctor specializing in the administration of anaesthesia. Compare **anesthetist.**

anesthetic (ˌænɪsˈθɛtɪk) NOUN, ADJECTIVE the usual US spelling of **anaesthetic.**

anesthetist (əˈnɛsθətɪst) NOUN (in the US) a person qualified to administer anaesthesia, often a nurse or someone other than a physician. Compare **anesthesiologist.**

anestrus (ænˈiːstrəs) NOUN a variant spelling (esp US) of **anoestrus.**
▸**anˈestrous** ADJECTIVE

anethole (ˈænɪˌθəʊl) NOUN a white water-soluble crystalline substance with a liquorice-like odour, used as a flavouring and a sensitizer in the processing of colour photographs. Formula: $CH_3CH{:}CHC_6H_4OCH_3$.
▹HISTORY C19: from Latin *anēthum* dill, anise, from Greek *anēthon*

Aneto (*Spanish* aˈneto) NOUN **Pico de** (ˈpiko de). a mountain in N Spain, near the French border: the highest in the Pyrenees. Height: 3404 m (11 168 ft.).

aneuploid (ˈænjʊˌplɔɪd) ADJECTIVE [1] (of polyploid cells or organisms) having a chromosome number that is not an exact multiple of the haploid number, caused by one chromosome set being incomplete. ◆ NOUN [2] a cell or individual of this type. ◆ Compare **euploid.**
▸ˈ**aneuˌploidy** NOUN

aneurin (əˈnjʊərɪn) NOUN a less common name for **thiamine.**
▹HISTORY C20: from A(NTI-) + (POLY)NEUR(ITIS) + (VITAM)IN

aneurysm *or* **aneurism** (ˈænjəˌrɪzəm) NOUN a sac formed by abnormal dilation of the weakened wall of a blood vessel.
▹HISTORY C15: from Greek *aneurusma,* from *aneurunein* to dilate, from *eurunein* to widen
▸ˌ**aneuˈrysmal** *or* ˌ**aneuˈrismal** *or* ˌ**aneurysˈmatic** *or* ˌ**aneurisˈmatic** ADJECTIVE ▸ˌ**aneuˈrysmally** *or* ˌ**aneuˈrismally** *or* ˌ**aneurysˈmatically** *or* ˌ**aneurisˈmatically** ADVERB

anew (əˈnjuː) ADVERB [1] over again; once more. [2] in a different way; afresh.
▹HISTORY Old English *of nīwe;* see OF, NEW

anfractuosity (ˌænfræktʃʊˈɒsɪtɪ) NOUN [1] the condition or quality of being anfractuous. [2] a winding, circuitous, or intricate passage, surface, process, etc.

anfractuous (ænˈfræktʃʊəs) ADJECTIVE characterized by twists and turns; convoluted.
▹HISTORY C17: from Late Latin *anfractuōsus,* from Latin *anfractus* a digression, literally: a bending

Angara (*Russian* angaˈra) NOUN a river in S Russia, in Siberia, flowing from Lake Baikal north and west to the Yenisei River: important for hydroelectric power. Length: 1840 km (1150 miles).

Angarsk (*Russian* anˈgarsk) NOUN an industrial city in SE central Russia, northwest of Irkutsk. Pop.: 266 600 (1999 est.).

angary (ˈæŋgərɪ) NOUN *International law* the right of a belligerent state to use the property of a neutral state or to destroy it if necessary, subject to payment of full compensation to the owners.
▹HISTORY C19: from French *angarie,* from Late Latin *angaria* enforced service, from Greek *angareia* office of a courier, from *angaros* courier, of Persian origin

angashore (ˈæŋɪʃɔːr) NOUN *Irish* a miserable person given to complaining.
▹HISTORY from Irish Gaelic *ainniseoir*

angel (ˈeɪndʒəl) NOUN [1] *Theol* one of a class of spiritual beings attendant upon God. In medieval angelology they are divided by rank into nine orders: seraphim, cherubim, thrones, dominations (or dominions), virtues, powers, principalities (or princedoms), archangels, and angels. [2] a divine messenger from God. [3] a guardian spirit. [4] a conventional representation of any of these beings, depicted in human form with wings. [5] *Informal* a person, esp a woman, who is kind, pure, or beautiful. [6] *Informal* an investor in a venture, esp a backer of a theatrical production. [7] Also called: **angel-noble.** a former English gold coin with a representation of the archangel Michael on it, first minted in Edward IV's reign. [8] *Informal* an unexplained signal on a radar screen.
▹HISTORY Old English, from Late Latin *angelus,* from Greek *angelos* messenger

angel cake *or esp US* **angel food cake** NOUN a very light sponge cake made without egg yolks.

angel dust NOUN a slang name for **PCP.**

Angeleno (ˌændʒəˈliːnəʊ) NOUN, *plural* **-nos.** a native or inhabitant of Los Angeles.

Angel Falls NOUN a waterfall in SE Venezuela, on the Caroní River. Height (probably the highest in the world): 979 m (3211 ft.).

angelfish (ˈeɪndʒəlˌfɪʃ) NOUN, *plural* **-fish** *or* **-fishes.** [1] any of various small tropical marine percoid fishes of the genus *Pomacanthus* and related genera, which have a deep flattened brightly coloured body and brushlike teeth: family *Chaetodontidae.* See also **butterfly fish.** [2] Also called: **scalare.** a South American cichlid, *Pterophyllum scalare,* of the Amazon region, having a compressed body and large dorsal and anal fins: a popular aquarium fish. [3] another name for **angel shark.**

angel gear NOUN *Austral informal* the neutral gear in a motor vehicle, esp when used to coast downhill.

angelic (ænˈdʒɛlɪk) ADJECTIVE [1] of or relating to angels. [2] Also: **angelical.** resembling an angel in beauty, purity, etc.
▸**anˈgelically** ADVERB

angelica (ænˈdʒɛlɪkə) NOUN [1] Also called: **archangel.** any tall umbelliferous plant of the genus *Angelica,* having compound leaves and clusters of small white or greenish flowers, esp *A. archangelica,* the aromatic seeds, leaves, and stems of which are used in medicine and cookery. [2] the candied stems of this plant, used for decorating and flavouring sweet dishes.
▹HISTORY C16: from Medieval Latin *(herba) angelica* angelic (herb)

angelology (ˌeɪndʒəˈlɒlədʒɪ) NOUN a doctrine or theory treating of angels.

angel shark *or* **angelfish** NOUN any of several sharks constituting the family *Squatinidae,* such as *Squatina squatina,* that have very large flattened pectoral fins and occur in the Atlantic and Pacific Oceans. Also called: **monkfish.**

angels-on-horseback NOUN *Brit* a savoury of oysters wrapped in bacon slices and served on toast.

angel's tears NOUN *(functioning as singular)* another name for **moonflower** (sense 2).

Angelus (ˈændʒɪləs) NOUN *RC Church* [1] a series of prayers recited in the morning, at midday, and in the evening, commemorating the Annunciation and Incarnation. [2] the bell (**Angelus bell**) signalling these prayers.
▹HISTORY C17: Latin, from the phrase *Angelus domini nuntiavit Mariae* the angel of the Lord brought tidings to Mary

anger (ˈæŋgə) NOUN [1] a feeling of great annoyance or antagonism as the result of some real or supposed grievance; rage; wrath. ◆ VERB [2] *(tr)* to make angry; enrage.
▹HISTORY C12: from Old Norse *angr* grief; related to Old English *enge,* Old High German *engi* narrow, Latin *angere* to strangle

Angers (*French* ɑ̃ʒe) NOUN a city in W France, on the River Maine. Pop.: 151 279 (1999).

Angevin (ˈændʒɪvɪn) NOUN [1] a native or inhabitant of Anjou. [2] *History* a member of the Plantagenet royal line descended from Geoffrey, Count of Anjou, esp one of the kings of England from Henry II to John (1154–1216). ◆ ADJECTIVE [3] of or relating to Anjou or its inhabitants. [4] of or relating to the Plantagenet kings of England between 1154 and 1216.
▹HISTORY from French, from medieval Latin *Andegavinus,* from *Andegavum,* ANGERS capital of ANJOU

angina (ænˈdʒaɪnə) NOUN [1] any disease marked by painful attacks of spasmodic choking, such as Vincent's angina and quinsy. [2] Also called: **angina pectoris** (ˈpɛktərɪs). a sudden intense pain in the chest, often accompanied by feelings of suffocation, caused by momentary lack of adequate blood supply to the heart muscle.
▹HISTORY C16: from Latin: quinsy, from Greek *ankhonē* a strangling
▸**anˈginal** ADJECTIVE ▸**anginose** (ænˈdʒaɪnəʊs, -nəʊz) *or* **anˈginous** ADJECTIVE

angio- *or before a vowel* **angi-** COMBINING FORM indicating a blood or lymph vessel; seed vessel: *angiology; angiosperm; angioma.*
▹HISTORY from Greek *angeion* vessel

angiogenesis (ˌændʒɪəˈgɛnɪsɪs) NOUN the induction of blood-vessel growth, often in association with a particular organ or tissue, or with a tumour.

angiogram (ˈændʒɪəʊˌgræm) NOUN an X-ray picture obtained by angiography.

angiography (ˌændʒɪˈɒgrəfɪ) NOUN a method of obtaining an X-ray of blood vessels by injecting into them a substance, such as one containing iodine, that shows up as opaque on an X-ray picture.

angiology (ˌændʒɪˈɒlədʒɪ) NOUN the branch of medical science concerned with the blood vessels and the lymphatic system.

angioma (ˌændʒɪˈəʊmə) NOUN, *plural* **-mas** *or* **-mata** (-mətə). a tumour consisting of a mass of blood vessels (**haemangioma**) or a mass of lymphatic vessels (**lymphangioma**).
▸ˌ**angiˈomatous** ADJECTIVE

angioplasty (ˈændʒɪəˌplæstɪ) NOUN a surgical technique for restoring normal blood flow through an artery narrowed or blocked by atherosclerosis, either by inserting a balloon into the narrowed section and inflating it or by using a laser beam.

angiosperm ('ændʒɪəˌspɜːm) NOUN any seed-bearing plant of the phylum *Angiospermophyta* (division *Angiospermae* in traditional systems), in which the ovules are enclosed in an ovary, which develops into the fruit after fertilization; any flowering plant. Compare **gymnosperm.**
► ˌangio'spermous ADJECTIVE

angiotensin (ˌændʒɪə'tɛnsɪn) NOUN a peptide of physiological importance that is capable of causing constriction of blood vessels, which raises blood pressure.
▷HISTORY from ANGIO- + TENSE[1] + -IN

Angkor ('æŋkɔː) NOUN a large area of ruins in NW Cambodia, containing **Angkor Thom** (tɔːm), the capital of the former Khmer Empire, and **Angkor Wat** (wɒt), a three-storey temple, which were overgrown with dense jungle from the 14th to 19th centuries.

angle[1] ('æŋgᵊl) NOUN 1 the space between two straight lines that diverge from a common point or between two planes that extend from a common line. 2 the shape formed by two such lines or planes. 3 the extent to which one such line or plane diverges from another, measured in degrees or radians. 4 an angular projection or recess; corner. 5 standpoint; point of view: *look at the question from another angle; the angle of a newspaper article.* 6 *Informal* a selfish or devious motive or purpose. 7 See **angle iron.** ◆ VERB 8 to move in or bend into angles or an angle. 9 (*tr*) to produce (an article, statement, etc.) with a particular point of view. 10 (*tr*) to present, direct, or place at an angle. 11 (*intr*) to turn or bend in a different direction: *the path angled sharply to the left.*
▷HISTORY C14: from French, from Old Latin *angulus* corner

angle[2] ('æŋgᵊl) VERB (*intr*) 1 to fish with a hook and line. 2 (often foll by *for*) to attempt to get: *he angled for a compliment.* ◆ NOUN 3 *Obsolete* any piece of fishing tackle, esp a hook.
▷HISTORY Old English *angul* fish-hook; related to Old High German *ango,* Latin *uncus,* Greek *onkos*

Angle ('æŋgᵊl) NOUN a member of a West Germanic people from N Germany who invaded and settled large parts of E and N England in the 5th and 6th centuries A.D.
▷HISTORY from Latin *Anglus,* from Germanic (compare ENGLISH), an inhabitant of *Angul,* a district in Schleswig (now *Angeln*), a name identical with Old English *angul* hook, ANGLE[2], referring to its shape

angle bracket NOUN either of a pair of brackets having the shapes < and >.

angledug ('æŋgᵊlˌdʌg) NOUN *Southwestern English dialect* an earthworm. Also: **angletwitch.**

angle iron NOUN 1 Also called: **angle, angle bar.** an iron or a steel structural bar that has an L-shaped cross section. 2 any piece of iron or steel forming an angle, esp a right angle.

angle of advance NOUN *Engineering* 1 the angle in excess of 90° that a steam-engine valve gear is in advance of the crank. 2 the angle between the point of ignition and bottom dead-centre in a spark-ignition engine.

angle of attack NOUN the acute angle between the chord line of an aerofoil and the undisturbed relative airflow. Also called: **angle of incidence.**

angle of bank NOUN the angle between the lateral axis of an aircraft in flight and the horizontal.

angle of deviation NOUN the angle between the direction of the refracted ray and the direction of the incident ray when a ray of light passes from one medium to another.

angle of dip NOUN the full name for **dip** (sense 27).

angle of friction NOUN *Physics* the angle of a plane to the horizontal when a body placed on the plane will just start to slide. The tangent of the angle of friction is the **coefficient of static friction.**

angle of incidence NOUN 1 the angle that a line or beam of radiation makes with the normal to the surface at the point of incidence. 2 another name for **angle of attack.** 3 Also called: **rigging angle of incidence.** the angle between the chord line of an aircraft wing or tailplane and the aircraft's longitudinal axis.

angle of reflection NOUN the angle that a beam of reflected radiation makes with the normal to a surface at the point of reflection.

angle of refraction NOUN the angle that a refracted beam of radiation makes with the normal to the surface between two media at the point of refraction.

angle of repose NOUN the maximum angle to the horizontal at which rocks, soil, etc., will remain without sliding.

angle plate NOUN a steel structural plate, esp one in the shape of a right-angled triangle, used to connect structural members and stiffen frameworks.

angler ('æŋglə) NOUN 1 a person who fishes with a rod and line. 2 *Informal* a person who schemes or uses devious methods to secure an advantage. 3 Also called: **angler fish.** any spiny-finned fish of the order *Pediculati* (or *Lophiiformes*). They live at the bottom of the sea and typically have a long spiny movable dorsal fin with which they lure their prey.

Anglesey ('æŋgᵊlsɪ) NOUN an island and county of N Wales, formerly part of Gwynedd (1974–96), separated from the mainland by the Menai Strait. Administrative centre: Llangefni. Pop.: 66 828 (2001). Area: 720 sq. km (278 sq. miles). Welsh name: **Ynys Môn.**

anglesite ('æŋgᵊlˌsaɪt) NOUN a white or grey secondary mineral consisting of lead sulphate in orthorhombic crystalline form. It occurs in lead-ore deposits and is a source of lead. Formula: $PbSO_4$.
▷HISTORY C19: from ANGLESEY, where it was first found

angletwitch ('æŋgᵊlˌtwɪtʃ) NOUN another word for **angledug.**

angleworm ('æŋgᵊlˌwɜːm) NOUN an earthworm used as bait by anglers.

Anglia ('æŋglɪə) NOUN a Latin name for **England.**

Anglian ('æŋglɪən) ADJECTIVE 1 of or relating to the Angles or to the Anglian dialects of Old English. ◆ NOUN 2 the group of Old and Middle English dialects spoken in the Midlands and the north of England, divided into Mercian and Northumbrian. See also **Kentish, West Saxon.** ◆ See also **East Anglia.**

Anglican ('æŋglɪkən) ADJECTIVE 1 denoting or relating to the Anglican communion. ◆ NOUN 2 a member of the Church of England or one of the Churches in full communion with it.
▷HISTORY C17: from Medieval Latin *Anglicānus,* from *Anglicus* English, from Latin *Anglī* the Angles

Anglican Church NOUN any Church of the Anglican Communion or the Anglican Communion itself.

Anglican Communion NOUN a group of Christian Churches including the Church of England, the Church of Ireland, the Episcopal Church in Scotland, the Church in Wales, and the Episcopal Church in the US, all of which are in full communion with each other.

Anglicanism ('æŋglɪkəˌnɪzəm) NOUN the doctrine and practice of the Church of England and other Anglican Churches.

Anglice ('æŋglɪsɪ) ADVERB in English: *Roma, Anglice Rome.*
▷HISTORY from Medieval Latin

Anglicism ('æŋglɪˌsɪzəm) NOUN 1 a word, phrase, or idiom peculiar to the English language, esp as spoken in England. 2 an English attitude, custom, etc. 3 the fact or quality of being English.

Anglicist ('æŋglɪsɪst) *or* **Anglist** NOUN *Rare* an expert in or student of English literature or language.

anglicize, anglicise ('æŋglɪˌsaɪz), *or* **anglify** ('æŋglɪˌfaɪ) VERB **-cizes, -cizing, -cized, -cises, -cising, -cised** *or* **-fies, -fying, -fied.** (*sometimes capital*) to make or become English in outlook, attitude, form, etc.
► ˌanglici'zation *or* ˌanglici'sation NOUN

angling ('æŋglɪŋ) NOUN **a** the art or sport of catching fish with a rod and line and a baited hook or other lure, such as a fly; fishing. **b** (*as modifier*): *an angling contest.*

Anglo ('æŋgləʊ) NOUN, *plural* **-glos.** 1 *US* a White inhabitant of the United States who is not of Latin extraction. 2 *Austral derogatory* an Australian of Anglo-Celtic descent.

Anglo- ('æŋgləʊ-) COMBINING FORM denoting English or England: *Anglo-Saxon.*
▷HISTORY from Medieval Latin *Anglī*

Anglo-American ADJECTIVE 1 of or relating to relations between England and the United States or their peoples. ◆ NOUN 2 *Chiefly US* an inhabitant or citizen of the United States who was or whose ancestors were born in England.

Anglo-Catholic ADJECTIVE 1 of or relating to a group within the Church of England or the Anglican Communion that emphasizes the Catholic elements in its teaching and practice. ◆ NOUN 2 a member of this group.
► ˌAnglo-Ca'tholiˌcism NOUN

Anglo-Celtic NOUN, ADJECTIVE *Austral* of or relating to an inhabitant of Australia who was or whose ancestors were born in the British Isles.

Anglo-Egyptian Sudan NOUN the former name (1899–1956) of the **Sudan.**

Anglo-French ADJECTIVE 1 of or relating to England and France. 2 of or relating to Anglo-French. ◆ NOUN 3 the Norman-French language of medieval England.

Anglo-Indian ADJECTIVE 1 of or relating to England and India. 2 denoting or relating to Anglo-Indians. 3 (of a word) introduced into English from an Indian language. ◆ NOUN 4 a person of mixed English and Indian descent. 5 an English person who lives or has lived for a long time in India.

Anglo-Irish NOUN 1 (preceded by *the; functioning as plural*) the inhabitants of Ireland of English birth or descent. 2 the English language as spoken in Ireland. ◆ ADJECTIVE 3 of or relating to the Anglo-Irish. 4 of or relating to English and Irish. 5 of or relating to the English language as spoken in Ireland.

Anglomania (ˌæŋgləʊ'meɪnɪə) NOUN excessive respect for English customs, etc.
► ˌAnglo'maniˌac NOUN

Anglo-Norman *History* ◆ ADJECTIVE 1 relating to the Norman conquerors of England, their society, or their language. ◆ NOUN 2 a Norman inhabitant of England after 1066. 3 the Anglo-French language.

Anglophile ('æŋgləʊfɪl, -ˌfaɪl) *or* **Anglophil** NOUN 1 a person having admiration for England or the English. ◆ ADJECTIVE 2 marked by or possessing such admiration.
► **Anglophilia** (ˌæŋgləʊ'fɪlɪə) NOUN ► **Anglophiliac** (ˌæŋgləʊ'fɪlɪˌæk) *or* **Anglophilic** (ˌæŋgləʊ'fɪlɪk) ADJECTIVE

Anglophobe ('æŋgləʊˌfəʊb) NOUN 1 a person who hates or fears England or its people. 2 *Canadian* a person who hates or fears Canadian Anglophones.
► ˌAnglo'phobia NOUN

Anglophone ('æŋgləˌfəʊn) (*often not capital*) NOUN 1 a person who speaks English, esp a native speaker. ◆ ADJECTIVE 2 speaking English.

Anglo-Saxon NOUN 1 a member of any of the West Germanic tribes (Angles, Saxons, and Jutes) that settled in Britain from the 5th century A.D. and were dominant until the Norman conquest. 2 the language of these tribes. See **Old English.** 3 any White person whose native language is English and whose cultural affiliations are those common to Britain and the US. 4 *Informal* plain blunt English, esp English containing taboo words. ◆ ADJECTIVE 5 forming part of the Germanic element in Modern English: *"forget" is an Anglo-Saxon word.* 6 of or relating to the Anglo-Saxons or the Old English language. 7 of or relating to the White Protestant culture of Britain, Australia, and the US. 8 *Informal* (of English speech or writing) plain and blunt. 9 of or relating to Britain and the US, esp their common legal, political, and commercial cultures, as compared to continental Europe.

Angola (æŋ'gəʊlə) NOUN a republic in SW Africa, on the Atlantic: includes the enclave of Cabinda, north of the River Congo; a Portuguese possession from 1575 until its independence in 1975; multiparty constitution adopted in 1991; factional violence. It consists of a narrow coastal plain with a large fertile plateau in the east. Currency: kwanza. Religion: Christian majority. Capital: Luanda. Pop.: 10 366 000 (2001 est.). Area: 1 246 693 sq. km (481 351 sq. miles).

Angolan (æŋ'gəʊlən) ADJECTIVE 1 of or relating to Angola or its inhabitants. ◆ NOUN 2 a native or inhabitant of Angola.

angophora (æŋ'gɒfərə) NOUN any tree of the genus *Angophora*, related to the eucalyptus and native to E Australia.
▷HISTORY New Latin, from Greek *angeion* vessel + *phoreus* bearer

angora (æŋ'gɔːrə) NOUN (*sometimes capital*) **a** the long soft hair of the outer coat of the Angora goat or the fur of the Angora rabbit. **b** yarn, cloth, or clothing made from this hair. **c** a material made to resemble this yarn or cloth. **d** (*as modifier*): *an angora sweater*. See also **mohair.**

Angora NOUN [1] (æŋ'gɔːrə, 'æŋgərə) the former name (until 1930) of **Ankara.** [2] (æŋ'gɔːrə) short for **Angora cat, Angora goat** or **Angora rabbit.**

Angora cat NOUN [1] a long-haired variety of cat, originating in Britain from crosses between Abyssinian and Siamese breeds in the 1960s. [2] a former Turkish breed of cats popular in the 19th century.

Angora goat NOUN a breed of domestic goat with long soft hair.

Angora rabbit NOUN a breed of rabbit with long usually white silky hair.

Angostura (*Spanish* aŋgɔs'tura) NOUN the former name (1764–1846) for **Ciudad Bolívar.**

angostura bark (ˌæŋgə'stjʊərə) NOUN the bitter aromatic bark of certain South American rutaceous trees of the genus *Cusparia* or *Galipea,* formerly used medicinally to reduce fever.

Angostura bitters PLURAL NOUN *Trademark* a bitter aromatic tonic made from gentian and various spices and vegetable colourings, used as a flavouring in alcoholic drinks.

Angra do Heroísmo (*Portuguese* 'ɐ̃ŋgrə duː iru'iʃmu) NOUN a port in the Azores, on Terceira Island. Pop.: 11 670 (1991).

angry ('æŋgrɪ) ADJECTIVE **-grier, -griest.** [1] feeling or expressing annoyance, animosity, or resentment; enraged. [2] suggestive of anger: *angry clouds.* [3] severely inflamed: *an angry sore.*
▸ **'angrily** ADVERB

> **Language note** It was formerly considered incorrect to talk about being *angry at* a person, but this use is now acceptable.

angry young man NOUN [1] (*often capitals*) one of several British novelists and playwrights of the 1950s who shared a hostility towards the established traditions and ruling elements of their country. [2] any similarly rebellious person.

angst (æŋst; *German* aŋst) NOUN [1] an acute but nonspecific sense of anxiety or remorse. [2] (in Existentialist philosophy) the dread caused by man's awareness that his future is not determined but must be freely chosen.
▷HISTORY German

angstrom ('æŋstrʌm, -strəm) NOUN a unit of length equal to 10^{-10} metre, used principally to express the wavelengths of electromagnetic radiations. It is equivalent to 0.1 nanometre. Symbol: Å *or* A. Also called: **angstrom unit.**
▷HISTORY C20: named after Anders J. *Ångström* (1814–74), Swedish physicist

angsty ('æŋstɪ) ADJECTIVE **angstier, angstiest.** *Informal* displaying or feeling angst, esp in a self-conscious manner: *two angsty teenagers.*

Anguilla (æŋ'gwɪlə) NOUN an island in the Caribbean, in the Leeward Islands: part of the British associated state of St Kitts-Nevis-Anguilla from 1967 until 1980, when it reverted to the status of a British dependency and is now a UK Overseas Territory. Pop.: 8960 (1992). Area: 90 sq. km (35 sq. miles).

anguilliform (æŋ'gwɪlɪˌfɔːm) ADJECTIVE having the shape or form of an eel.
▷HISTORY C17: from Latin *anguilla* eel, diminutive of *anguis* snake

anguine ('æŋgwɪn) ADJECTIVE of, relating to, or similar to a snake.
▷HISTORY C17: from Latin *anguīnus,* from *anguis* snake

anguish ('æŋgwɪʃ) NOUN [1] extreme pain or misery; mental or physical torture; agony. ◆ VERB [2] to afflict or be afflicted with anguish.
▷HISTORY C13: from Old French *angoisse* a strangling, from Latin *angustia* narrowness, from *angustus* narrow

anguished ('æŋgwɪʃt) ADJECTIVE feeling or expressing anguish.

angular ('æŋgjʊlə) ADJECTIVE [1] lean or bony. [2] awkward or stiff in manner or movement. [3] having an angle or angles. [4] placed at an angle. [5] measured by an angle or by the rate at which an angle changes.
▷HISTORY C15: from Latin *angulāris,* from *angulus* ANGLE[1]
▸ **'angularly** ADVERB ▸ **'angularness** NOUN

angular acceleration NOUN [1] the rate of change of angular velocity. [2] *Astronautics* the acceleration of a space vehicle around an axis.

angular displacement NOUN *Physics* the angle through which a point, line, or body is rotated about a specific axis in a given direction.

angular frequency NOUN *Physics* the frequency of a periodic process, wave system, etc., expressed in radians per second.

angularity (ˌæŋgjʊ'lærɪtɪ) NOUN, *plural* **-ties.** [1] the condition of being angular. [2] an angular form or shape.

angular magnification NOUN *Physics* the ratio of the angle subtended at the eye by an image formed by an optical instrument to the angle subtended at the unaided eye by the object.

angular momentum NOUN a property of a mass or system of masses turning about some fixed point; it is conserved in the absence of the action of external forces.

angular velocity NOUN the velocity of a body rotating about a specified axis measured as the rate of change of the angle subtended at that axis by the path of the body. Symbol: ω.

angulate ADJECTIVE ('æŋgjʊlɪt, -ˌleɪt) [1] having angles or an angular shape. ◆ VERB ('æŋgjʊˌleɪt) [2] to make or become angular.
▷HISTORY C18: from Late Latin *angulāre* to make angled, from Latin *angulus* ANGLE[1]
▸ **'anguˌlated** ADJECTIVE

angulation (ˌæŋgjʊ'leɪʃən) NOUN [1] an angular formation. [2] the precise measurement of angles.

Angus ('æŋgəs) NOUN a council area of E Scotland on the North Sea: the historical county of Angus became part of Tayside region in 1975; reinstated as a unitary authority (excluding City of Dundee) in 1996. Administrative centre: Forfar. Pop.: 108 400 (2001). Area: 2181 sq. km (842 sq. miles).

Angus Og (əʊg) NOUN *Irish myth* the god of love and beauty.

angwantibo (æŋ'gwæntɪˌbəʊ) NOUN, *plural* **-bos.** a rare gold-coloured prosimian primate of tropical Africa, *Arctocebus calabarensis,* having digits that are specialized as a pair of pincers for climbing: family *Lorisidae* (lorises). Also called: **golden potto.**
▷HISTORY C19: from Efik

Anhalt (*German* 'anhalt) NOUN a former duchy and state of central E Germany, now part of the state of Saxony-Anhalt: part of East Germany until 1990.

anharmonic (ˌænhɑː'mɒnɪk) ADJECTIVE *Physics* of or concerned with an oscillation whose frequency is not an integral factor or multiple of the base frequency.

anhedral (æn'hiːdrəl) NOUN the downward inclination of an aircraft wing in relation to the lateral axis. Compare **dihedral** (sense 4).

anhidrosis (ˌænhɪ'drəʊsɪs) *or* **anidrosis** NOUN *Pathol* the absence of sweating.
▷HISTORY from AN- + Greek *hidrōs* sweat + -OSIS

anhidrotic (ˌænhɪ'drɒtɪk) *Med* ◆ ADJECTIVE [1] curbing the secretion of sweat. ◆ NOUN [2] a substance that suppresses sweating.

anhinga (æn'hɪŋgə) NOUN another name for **darter** (the bird).
▷HISTORY C18: via Portuguese from Tupi

Anhui *or* **Anhwei** ('æn'weɪ) NOUN a province of E China, crossed by the Yangtze River. Capital: Hefei. Pop.: 59 860 000 (2000). Area: 139 860 sq. km (54 000 sq. miles).

anhydride (æn'haɪdraɪd, -drɪd) NOUN [1] a compound that has been formed from another compound by dehydration. [2] a compound that forms an acid or base when added to water. [3] Also called: **acid anhydride** *or* **acyl anhydride.** any organic compound containing the group -CO.O.CO- formed by removal of one water molecule from two carboxyl groups.
▷HISTORY C19: from ANHYDR(OUS) + -IDE

anhydrite (æn'haɪdraɪt) NOUN a colourless or greyish-white mineral, found in sedimentary rocks. It is used in the manufacture of cement, fertilizers, and chemicals. Composition: anhydrous calcium sulphate. Formula: $CaSO_4$. Crystal structure: orthorhombic.
▷HISTORY C19: from ANHYDR(OUS) + -ITE[1]

anhydrous (æn'haɪdrəs) ADJECTIVE containing no water, esp no water of crystallization.
▷HISTORY C19: from Greek *anudros;* see AN-, HYDRO-

ani ('ɑːnɪ) NOUN, *plural* **anis.** any of several gregarious tropical American birds of the genus *Crotophaga:* family *Cuculidae* (cuckoos). They have a black plumage, long square-tipped tail, and heavily hooked bill.
▷HISTORY Spanish *aní,* from Tupi

Aniakchak (ˌænɪ'æktʃæk) NOUN an active volcanic crater in SW Alaska, on the Alaska Peninsula: the largest explosion crater in the world. Height: 1347 m (4420 ft.). Diameter: 9 km (6 miles).

anicca ('ænɪkə) NOUN (in Theravada Buddhism) the belief that all things, including the self, are impermanent and constantly changing: the first of the three basic characteristics of existence. Compare **anatta, dukkha.**
▷HISTORY Pali, literally: impermanence

aniconic (ˌænaɪ'kɒnɪk) ADJECTIVE (of images of deities, symbols, etc.) not portrayed in a human or animal form.
▷HISTORY C19: from AN- + ICONIC

anil ('ænɪl) NOUN a leguminous West Indian shrub, *Indigofera suffruticosa:* a source of indigo. Also called: **indigo.**
▷HISTORY C16: from Portuguese, from Arabic *an-nīl,* the indigo, from Sanskrit *nīla* dark blue

anile ('ænaɪl, 'eɪnaɪl) ADJECTIVE of or like a feeble old woman.
▷HISTORY C17: from Latin *anīlis,* from *anus* old woman
▸ **anility** (ə'nɪlɪtɪ) NOUN

aniline ('ænɪlɪn, -ˌliːn) NOUN a colourless oily pungent poisonous liquid used in the manufacture of dyes, plastics, pharmaceuticals, and explosives. Formula: $C_6H_5NH_2$. Also called: **phenylamine.**

aniline dye NOUN any synthetic dye originally made from raw materials, such as aniline, obtained from coal tar.

anilingus (ˌeɪnɪ'lɪŋgəs) NOUN sexual stimulation involving oral contact with the anus.
▷HISTORY C20: from *ani-* ANUS + *-lingus,* as in CUNNILINGUS

anim. ABBREVIATION FOR animato.

anima ('ænɪmə) NOUN (in Jungian psychology) **a** the feminine principle as present in the male unconscious. **b** the inner personality, which is in communication with the unconscious. See also **animus.**
▷HISTORY Latin: air, breath, spirit, feminine of ANIMUS

animadversion (ˌænɪmæd'vɜːʃən) NOUN [1] criticism or censure. [2] a carefully considered observation.

animadvert (ˌænɪmæd'vɜːt) VERB (*intr*) [1] (usually foll by *on* or *upon*) to comment with strong criticism (upon); make censorious remarks (about). [2] to make an observation or comment.
▷HISTORY C16: from Latin *animadvertere* to notice, pay attention, from *animus* mind + *advertere* to turn to, from *vertere* to turn

animal ('ænɪməl) NOUN [1] *Zoology* any living organism characterized by voluntary movement, the possession of cells with noncellulose cell walls and specialized sense organs enabling rapid response to stimuli, and the ingestion of complex organic substances such as plants and other animals. Related prefix: **zoo-.** [2] any mammal, esp any mammal except man. [3] a brutish person. [4] *Facetious* a person or thing (esp in the phrase **no such animal**). [5] *Austral informal* a very dirty car. ◆ ADJECTIVE [6] of, relating to, or derived from animals: *animal products; an animal characteristic.* [7] of or

relating to the physical needs or desires; carnal; sensual.
▷HISTORY C14: from Latin *animal* (n), from *animālis* (adj) living, breathing; see ANIMA

animalcule (ˌænɪˈmælkjuːl) *or* **animalculum** (ˌænɪˈmælkjʊləm) NOUN, *plural* **-cules** *or* **-cula** (-kjʊlə). a microscopic animal such as an amoeba or rotifer.
▷HISTORY C16: from New Latin *animalculum* a small ANIMAL
▸ˌaniˈmalcular ADJECTIVE

animal husbandry NOUN the science of breeding, rearing, and caring for farm animals.

animalier (ˈænɪməˌlɪə, ˌænɪˈmælɪeɪ) NOUN **a** a painter or sculptor of animal subjects, esp a member of a group of early 19th-century French sculptors who specialized in realistic figures of animals, usually in bronze. **b** (*as modifier*): *an animalier bronze.*
▷HISTORY from French

animalism (ˈænɪməˌlɪzəm) NOUN [1] satisfaction of or preoccupation with physical matters; sensuality. [2] the doctrine or belief that man lacks a spiritual nature. [3] a trait or mode of behaviour typical of animals.
▸ˈanimalist NOUN

animality (ˌænɪˈmælɪtɪ) NOUN [1] the animal side of man, as opposed to the intellectual or spiritual. [2] the fact of being or having the characteristics of an animal.

animalize *or* **animalise** (ˈænɪməˌlaɪz) VERB (*tr*) to rouse to brutality or sensuality or make brutal or sensual.
▸ˌanimaliˈzation *or* ˌanimaliˈsation NOUN

animal kingdom NOUN a category of living organisms comprising all animals. Compare **plant kingdom, mineral kingdom.**

Animal Liberation Front NOUN (in Britain) an animal-rights movement often using direct action. Abbreviation: **ALF.**

animal magnetism NOUN [1] *Sometimes facetious* the quality of being attractive, esp to members of the opposite sex. [2] *Obsolete* hypnotism.

animal rights PLURAL NOUN **a** the rights of animals to be protected from exploitation and abuse by humans. **b** (*as modifier*): *the animal-rights lobby.*

animal spirits PLURAL NOUN cheerful and exuberant boisterousness.
▷HISTORY originally, referring to a vital force believed to be dispatched throughout the body by the brain

animal starch NOUN a less common name for **glycogen.**

animate VERB (ˈænɪˌmeɪt) (*tr*) [1] to give life to or cause to come alive. [2] to make lively; enliven. [3] to encourage or inspire. [4] to impart motion to; move to action or work. [5] to record on film or video tape so as to give movement to: *an animated cartoon.* ◆ ADJECTIVE (ˈænɪmɪt) [6] being alive or having life. [7] gay, spirited, or lively.
▷HISTORY C16: from Latin *animāre* to fill with breath, make alive, from *anima* breath, spirit

animated (ˈænɪˌmeɪtɪd) ADJECTIVE [1] full of vivacity and spirit; lively. [2] characterized by movement and activity: *an animated scene met her eye.* [3] possessing life; animate. [4] moving or appearing to move as if alive: *an animated display.* [5] pertaining to cinematographic animation.
▸ˈaniˌmatedly ADVERB

animated cartoon NOUN a film produced by photographing a series of gradually changing drawings, etc., which give the illusion of movement when the series is projected rapidly.

animation (ˌænɪˈmeɪʃən) NOUN [1] liveliness; vivacity. [2] the condition of being alive. [3] **a** the techniques used in the production of animated cartoons. **b** a variant of **animated cartoon.**

animatism (ˈænɪməˌtɪzəm) NOUN the belief that inanimate objects have consciousness.

animato (ˌænɪˈmɑːtəʊ) ADJECTIVE, ADVERB *Music* (to be performed) in a lively manner.
▷HISTORY Italian

animator *or* **animater** (ˈænɪˌmeɪtə) NOUN [1] an artist who produces animated cartoons. [2] *Canadian* a person who coordinates or facilitates something, esp a television or radio presenter.

animatronic (ˌænɪməˈtrɒnɪk) ADJECTIVE of, concerned with, or operated by animatronics: *animatronic dinosaurs.*

animatronics (ˌænɪməˈtrɒnɪks) NOUN (*functioning as singular*) a branch of film and theatre technology that combines traditional puppetry techniques with electronics to create lifelike animated effects.
▷HISTORY C20: from ANIMA(TION) + (ELEC)TRONICS

anime (ˈænɪˌmeɪ) NOUN a type of Japanese animated film with themes and styles similar to manga comics.
▷HISTORY C20: from Japanese

animé[1] (ˈænɪˌmeɪ, -mɪ) NOUN any of various resins, esp that obtained from the tropical American leguminous tree *Hymenaea courbaril.*
▷HISTORY French: of uncertain origin

animé[2] (ˈænɪˌmeɪ) ADJECTIVE, ADVERB *Music* the French word for **animato.**

animism (ˈænɪˌmɪzəm) NOUN [1] the belief that natural objects, phenomena, and the universe itself have desires and intentions. [2] (in the philosophies of the Greek philosophers Plato (?427–?347 B.C.) and Pythagoras (?580–?500 B.C.)) the hypothesis that there is an immaterial force that animates the universe.
▷HISTORY C19: from Latin *anima* vital breath, spirit
▸ˈanimist NOUN ▸animistic (ˌænɪˈmɪstɪk) ADJECTIVE

animosity (ˌænɪˈmɒsɪtɪ) NOUN, *plural* **-ties.** a powerful and active dislike or hostility; enmity.
▷HISTORY C15: from Late Latin *animōsitās,* from Latin *animōsus* spirited, from ANIMUS

animus (ˈænɪməs) NOUN [1] intense dislike; hatred; animosity. [2] motive, intention, or purpose. [3] (in Jungian psychology) the masculine principle present in the female unconscious. See also **anima.**
▷HISTORY C19: from Latin: mind, spirit

anion (ˈænˌaɪən) NOUN a negatively charged ion; an ion that is attracted to the anode during electrolysis. Compare **cation.**
▷HISTORY C19: from ANA- + ION
▸anionic (ˌænaɪˈɒnɪk) ADJECTIVE

anise (ˈænɪs) NOUN a Mediterranean umbelliferous plant, *Pimpinella anisum,* having clusters of small yellowish-white flowers and liquorice-flavoured seeds (see **aniseed**).
▷HISTORY C13: from Old French *anis,* via Latin from Greek *anison*

aniseed (ˈænɪˌsiːd) NOUN the liquorice-flavoured aromatic seeds of the anise plant, used medicinally for expelling intestinal gas and in cookery as a flavouring, esp in cakes and confections. Also called: **anise.**

aniseikonia (ˌænaɪsaɪˈkəʊnɪə) NOUN a condition caused by a defect in the lens of the eye in which the images produced in the two eyes differ in size or shape.
▷HISTORY C20: New Latin, from ANISO- + Greek *eikon* image
▸ˌaniseiˈkonic ADJECTIVE

anisette (ˌænɪˈzɛt, -ˈsɛt) NOUN a liquorice-flavoured liqueur made from aniseed.
▷HISTORY C19: from French; see ANISE, -ETTE

aniso- *or before a vowel* **anis-** COMBINING FORM not equal: *anisogamy.*
▷HISTORY New Latin, from Greek *anisos;* see AN-, ISO-

anisocercal (ænˌaɪsəʊˈsɜːkᵊl) ADJECTIVE (of fish) having unequal tail-fin lobes.
▷HISTORY C19: from ANISO- + Greek *kerkos* tail

anisodactyl (ænˌaɪsəʊˈdæktɪl, ˌænaɪ-) ADJECTIVE *also* **anisodactylous.** [1] (of the feet of passerine birds) having the first toe directed backwards and the other three toes directed forwards. ◆ NOUN [2] a bird having this type of feet.

anisogamy (ˌænaɪˈsɒgəmɪ) NOUN a type of sexual reproduction in which the gametes are dissimilar, either in size alone or in size and form.
▸ˌaniˈsogamous ADJECTIVE

anisole (ˈænɪˌsəʊl) NOUN a colourless pleasant-smelling liquid used as a solvent and vermicide and in perfume and flavouring. Formula: $C_6H_5OCH_3$; relative density: 0.996; melting pt.: –37.5°C; boiling pt.: 155°C. Also called: **methoxybenzene.**
▷HISTORY C19: from ANISE + -OLE[1]

anisomeric (ænˌaɪsəʊˈmɛrɪk) ADJECTIVE (of a chemical compound) lacking isomers.

anisomerous (ˌænɪˈsɒmərəs) ADJECTIVE (of flowers) having floral whorls that differ in the number of their parts. Compare **isomerous** (sense 2).

anisometric (ænˌaɪsəʊˈmɛtrɪk) ADJECTIVE [1] not isometric; having unsymmetrical parts or unequal measurements. [2] (of a crystal) having unequal axes.

anisometropia (ænˌaɪsəʊməˈtrəʊpɪə, ˌænaɪ-) NOUN an imbalance in the power of the two eyes to refract light.

anisomorphic (ænˌaɪsəʊˈmɔːfɪk) ADJECTIVE *Linguistics* differing in the semantic scope of terms referring to the real world: for instance, English and Russian are anisomorphic with regard to colour terms, English treating light blue and navy blue as shades of one colour but Russian treating these two shades as unrelated.

anisophyllous (æˌnaɪsəʊˈfɪləs) ADJECTIVE another word for **heterophyllous.**
▸anˈisoˌphylly NOUN

anisotropic (ænˌaɪsəʊˈtrɒpɪk, ˌænaɪ-) ADJECTIVE [1] not isotropic; having different physical properties in different directions: *anisotropic crystals.* [2] (of a plant) responding unequally to an external stimulus in different parts of the plant.
▸anˌisoˈtropically ADVERB ▸anisotropy (ˌænaɪˈsɒtrəpɪ) NOUN

Anjou (*French* ɑ̃ʒu) NOUN a former province of W France, in the Loire valley: a medieval countship from the 10th century, belonging to the English crown from 1154 until 1204; annexed by France in 1480. Related adjective: **Angevin.**

Ankara (ˈæŋkərə) NOUN the capital of Turkey: an ancient city in the Anatolian highlands: first a capital in the 3rd century B.C., in the Celtic kingdom of Galatia. Pop.: 2 984 099 (1997). Ancient name: **Ancyra.** Former name (until 1930): **Angora.**

ankerite (ˈæŋkəˌraɪt) NOUN a greyish to brown mineral that resembles dolomite and consists of a carbonate of calcium, magnesium, and iron. Formula: $(Ca,Mg,Fe)CO_3$.
▷HISTORY C19: named after M. J. *Anker* (died 1843), Austrian mineralogist

ankh (æŋk) NOUN a tau cross with a loop on the top, symbolizing eternal life: often appearing in Egyptian personal names, such as Tutankhamen. Also called: **ansate cross, crux ansata.**
▷HISTORY from Egyptian *ʿnh* life, soul

Anking (ˈɑːnˈkɪŋ) NOUN a variant transliteration of the Chinese name for **Anqing.**

ankle (ˈæŋkᵊl) NOUN [1] the joint connecting the leg and the foot. See **talus**[1]. [2] the part of the leg just above the foot.
▷HISTORY C14: from Old Norse; related to German, Dutch *enkel,* Latin *angulus* ANGLE[1]

ankle biter NOUN *Austral slang* a child.

anklebone (ˈæŋkᵊlˌbəʊn) NOUN the nontechnical name for **talus**[1].

ankle sock NOUN (*often plural*) *Brit* a short sock coming up to the ankle. US term: **anklet.**

anklet (ˈæŋklɪt) NOUN [1] an ornamental chain worn around the ankle. [2] the US word for **ankle sock.**

ankus (ˈæŋkəs) NOUN, *plural* **-kus** *or* **-kuses.** a stick used, esp in India, for goading elephants.
▷HISTORY from Hindi

ankylosaur (ˈæŋkɪləʊˌsɔː) NOUN any of various quadrupedal herbivorous ornithischian dinosaurs constituting the suborder *Ankylosauria,* which were most abundant in upper Cretaceous times and had a very heavily armoured tanklike body.
▷HISTORY C20: from New Latin, from Greek *ankulos* crooked + -SAUR

ankylose *or* **anchylose** (ˈæŋkɪˌləʊs, -ˌləʊz) VERB (of bones in a joint, etc.) to fuse or stiffen by ankylosis.

ankylosis *or* **anchylosis** (ˌæŋkɪˈləʊsɪs) NOUN abnormal adhesion or immobility of the bones in a joint, as by a direct joining of the bones, a fibrous growth of tissues within the joint, or surgery.
▷HISTORY C18: from New Latin, from Greek *ankuloun* to crook
▸ankylotic *or* anchylotic (ˌæŋkɪˈlɒtɪk) ADJECTIVE

ankylostomiasis (ˌæŋkɪˌlɒstəˈmaɪəsɪs) NOUN a variant of **ancylostomiasis.**

anlace ('ænlɪs) *or* **anelace** NOUN a medieval short dagger with a broad tapering blade.
▷HISTORY C13: of unknown origin

anlage ('ænˌlɑːgə) NOUN, *plural* **-gen** (-gən) *or* **-ges.** another word for **primordium.**
▷HISTORY German: predisposition, layout

anna ('ænə) NOUN a former Indian copper coin, worth one sixteenth of a rupee.
▷HISTORY C18: from Hindi *ānā*

Annaba ('ænəbə) NOUN a port in NE Algeria: site of the Roman city of Hippo Regius. Pop.: 348 554 (1998). Former name: **Bône.**

annabergite ('ænəˌbɜːgaɪt) NOUN a rare green secondary mineral consisting of hydrated nickel arsenate in monoclinic crystalline form. Formula: $Ni_3(AsO_4)_2.8H_2O$. Also called: **nickel bloom.**
▷HISTORY C19: named after *Annaberg* in Saxony, where it was discovered; see -ITE[1]

annal ('ænᵊl) NOUN the recorded events of one year. See also **annals.**

annals ('ænᵊlz) PLURAL NOUN [1] yearly records of events, generally in chronological order. [2] history or records of history in general. [3] regular reports of the work of a society, learned body, etc.
▷HISTORY C16: from Latin *(librī) annālēs* yearly (books), from *annus* year
▸**'annalist** NOUN ▸**ˌannal'istic** ADJECTIVE

Annam *or* **Anam** (æ'næm, 'ænæm) NOUN a former kingdom (3rd century–1428), empire (1428–1884), and French protectorate (1884–1945) of E Indochina: now part of Vietnam.

Annamese (ˌænə'miːz) ADJECTIVE [1] of or relating to Annam. ◆ ADJECTIVE, NOUN [2] a former word for **Vietnamese.**

Annapolis (ə'næpəlɪs) NOUN the capital of Maryland, near the mouth of the Severn River on Chesapeake Bay: site of the US Naval Academy. Pop.: 33 187 (1990).

Annapolis Royal NOUN a town in SE Canada in W Nova Scotia on an arm of the Bay of Fundy: the first settlement in Canada (1605). Pop.: 633 (1991). Former name (until 1710): **Port Royal.**

Annapurna *or* **Anapurna** (ˌænə'pʊənə) NOUN a massif of the Himalayas, in Nepal. Highest peak: 8078 m (26 502 ft.).

Ann Arbor (æn 'ɑːbə) NOUN a city in SE Michigan: seat of the University of Michigan. Pop.: 114 024 (2000).

annates ('æneɪts, -əts) PLURAL NOUN *RC Church* the first year's revenue of a see, an abbacy, or a minor benefice, paid to the pope.
▷HISTORY C16: plural of French *annate,* from Medieval Latin *annāta,* from Latin *annus* year

annatto *or* **anatto** (ə'nætəʊ) NOUN, *plural* **-tos.** [1] a small tropical American tree, *Bixa orellana,* having red or pinkish flowers and pulpy seeds that yield a dye: family *Bixaceae.* [2] the yellowish-red dye obtained from the pulpy outer layer of the coat of the seeds of this tree, used for colouring fabrics, butter, varnish, etc.
▷HISTORY from Carib

anneal (ə'niːl) VERB [1] to temper or toughen (something) by heat treatment. [2] to subject to or undergo some physical treatment, esp heating, that removes internal stress, crystal defects, and dislocations. [3] *(tr)* to toughen or strengthen (the will, determination, etc.). [4] (often foll by *out*) *Physics* to disappear or cause to disappear by a rearrangement of atoms: *defects anneal out at different temperatures.* ◆ NOUN [5] an act of annealing.
▷HISTORY Old English *onǣlan,* from ON + *ǣlan* to burn, from *āl* fire
▸**an'nealer** NOUN

Annecy (*French* ansi) NOUN [1] a city and resort in E France, on Lake Annecy. Pop.: 51 143 (1990). [2] **Lake.** a lake in E France, in the Alps.

annelid ('ænəlɪd) NOUN [1] any worms of the phylum *Annelida,* in which the body is divided into segments both externally and internally. The group includes the earthworms, lugworm, ragworm, and leeches. ◆ ADJECTIVE [2] of, relating to, or belonging to the *Annelida.*
▷HISTORY C19: from New Latin *Annelida,* from French *annelés,* literally: the ringed ones, from Old French *annel* ring, from Latin *ānellus,* from *ānulus* ring
▸**annelidan** (ə'nɛlɪdən) NOUN, ADJECTIVE

annex VERB (æ'nɛks) *(tr)* [1] to join or add, esp to something larger; attach. [2] to add (territory) by conquest or occupation. [3] to add or append as a condition, warranty, etc. [4] to appropriate without permission. ◆ NOUN ('ænɛks) [5] a variant spelling (esp US) of **annexe.**
▷HISTORY C14: from Medieval Latin *annexāre,* from Latin *annectere* to attach to, from *nectere* to join
▸**an'nexable** ADJECTIVE

annexation (ˌænɪk'seɪʃən, -ɛk-) NOUN [1] the act of annexing, esp territory, or the condition of being annexed. [2] something annexed.
▸**ˌannex'ational** ADJECTIVE ▸**ˌannex'ationism** NOUN ▸**ˌannex'ationist** NOUN

annexe *or esp US* **annex** ('ænɛks) NOUN [1] **a** an extension to a main building. **b** a building used as an addition to a main building nearby. [2] something added or annexed, esp a supplement to a document.

annihilate (ə'naɪəˌleɪt) VERB [1] *(tr)* to destroy completely; extinguish. [2] *(tr) Informal* to defeat totally, as in debate or argument. [3] *(intr) Physics* to undergo annihilation.
▷HISTORY C16: from Late Latin *annihilāre* to bring to nothing, from Latin *nihil* nothing
▸**annihilable** (ə'naɪələbᵊl) ADJECTIVE ▸**an'nihilative** ADJECTIVE ▸**an'nihiˌlator** NOUN

annihilation (əˌnaɪə'leɪʃən) NOUN [1] total destruction. [2] the act of annihilating. [3] *Physics* the destruction of a particle and its antiparticle when they collide. The annihilation of an electron with a positron generates two or, very rarely, three photons of **annihilation radiation.** The annihilation of a nucleon with its antiparticle generates several pions.

anniversary (ˌænɪ'vɜːsərɪ) NOUN, *plural* **-ries.** [1] the date on which an event occurred in some previous year: *a wedding anniversary.* [2] the celebration of this. ◆ ADJECTIVE [3] of or relating to an anniversary. [4] recurring every year, esp on the same date.
▷HISTORY C13: from Latin *anniversārius* returning every year, from *annus* year + *vertere* to turn

anniversary day NOUN *NZ* a day for celebrating the foundation date of one of the former Provinces.

anno Domini ('ænəʊ 'dɒmɪˌnaɪ, -ˌniː) ADVERB [1] the full form of **A.D.** or **AD.** ◆ NOUN [2] *Informal* advancing old age.
▷HISTORY Latin: in the year of our Lord

anno regni *Latin* ('ænəʊ 'rɛgnaɪ) in the year of the reign.

annotate ('ænəʊˌteɪt, 'ænə-) VERB to supply (a written work, such as an ancient text) with critical or explanatory notes.
▷HISTORY C18: from Latin *annotāre,* from *nota* mark
▸**'annoˌtatable** ADJECTIVE ▸**'annoˌtative** ADJECTIVE
▸**'annoˌtator** NOUN

annotation (ˌænəʊ'teɪʃən, ˌænə-) NOUN [1] the act of annotating. [2] a note added in explanation, etc., esp of some literary work.

announce (ə'naʊns) VERB [1] *(tr; may take a clause as object)* to make known publicly; proclaim. [2] *(tr)* to declare the arrival of: *to announce a guest.* [3] *(tr; may take a clause as object)* to reveal to the mind or senses; presage: *the dark clouds announced rain.* [4] *(intr)* to work as an announcer, as on radio or television. [5] *US* to make known (one's intention to run as a candidate): *to announce for the presidency.*
▷HISTORY C15: from Old French *anoncer,* from Latin *annuntiāre,* from *nuntius* messenger

announcement (ə'naʊnsmənt) NOUN [1] a public statement. [2] a brief item or advertisement, as in a newspaper. [3] a formal printed or written invitation. [4] the act of announcing.

announcer (ə'naʊnsə) NOUN a person who announces, esp one who reads the news, introduces programmes, etc., on radio or television.

anno urbis conditae *Latin* ('ænəʊ 'ɜːbɪs 'kɒndɪˌtiː) the full form of **AUC** (sense b).
▷HISTORY literally: in the year of the founding of the city

annoy (ə'nɔɪ) VERB [1] to irritate or displease. [2] to harass with repeated attacks.
▷HISTORY C13: from Old French *anoier,* from Late Latin *inodiāre* to make hateful, from Latin *in odiō (esse)* (to be) hated, from *odium* hatred
▸**an'noyer** NOUN

annoyance (ə'nɔɪəns) NOUN [1] the feeling of being annoyed. [2] the act of annoying. [3] a person or thing that annoys.

annoying (ə'nɔɪɪŋ) ADJECTIVE causing irritation or displeasure.
▸**an'noyingly** ADVERB

annual ('ænjʊəl) ADJECTIVE [1] occurring, done, etc., once a year or every year; yearly: *an annual income.* [2] lasting for a year: *an annual subscription.* ◆ NOUN [3] a plant that completes its life cycle in less than one year. Compare **perennial** (sense 3), **biennial** (sense 3). [4] a book, magazine, etc., published once every year.
▷HISTORY C14: from Late Latin *annuālis,* from Latin *annuus* yearly, from *annus* year
▸**'annually** ADVERB

annual general meeting NOUN *Brit* the statutory meeting of the directors and shareholders of a company or of the members of a society, held once every financial year, at which the annual report is presented. Abbreviation: **AGM.**

annualize *or* **annualise** ('ænjʊəˌlaɪz) VERB *(tr)* to convert (a rate of interest) to an annual rate when it is quoted for a period of less than a year: *credit card companies are obliged to quote an annualized percentage rate to borrowers.*

annual parallax NOUN See **parallax** (sense 2).

annual percentage rate NOUN the annual equivalent of a rate of interest when the rate is quoted more frequently than annually, usually monthly. Abbreviation: **APR.**

annual report NOUN a report presented by the directors of a company to its shareholders each year, containing the profit-and-loss account, the balance sheet, and details of the past year's activity.

annual ring NOUN a ring of wood indicating one year's growth, seen in the transverse section of stems and roots of woody plants growing in temperate climates. Also called: **tree ring.**

annuitant (ə'njuːɪtənt) NOUN a person in receipt of or entitled to an annuity.

annuity (ə'njuːɪtɪ) NOUN, *plural* **-ties.** [1] a fixed sum payable at specified intervals, esp annually, over a period, such as the recipient's life, or in perpetuity, in return for a premium paid either in instalments or in a single payment. [2] the right to receive or the duty to pay such a sum.
▷HISTORY C15: from French *annuité,* from Medieval Latin *annuitās,* from Latin *annuus* ANNUAL

annul (ə'nʌl) VERB **-nuls, -nulling, -nulled.** *(tr)* to make (something, esp a law or marriage) void; cancel the validity of; abolish.
▷HISTORY C14: from Old French *annuller,* from Late Latin *annullāre* to bring to nothing, from Latin *nullus* not any; see NULL
▸**an'nullable** ADJECTIVE

annular ('ænjʊlə) ADJECTIVE ring-shaped; of or forming a ring.
▷HISTORY C16: from Latin *annulāris,* from *annulus, ānulus* ring
▸**annularity** (ˌænjʊ'lærɪtɪ) NOUN ▸**'annularly** ADVERB

annular eclipse NOUN an eclipse of the sun in which the moon does not cover the entire disc of the sun, so that a ring of sunlight surrounds the shadow of the moon. Compare **total eclipse, partial eclipse.**

annular ligament NOUN *Anatomy* any of various ligaments that encircle a part, such as the wrist, ankle, or trachea.

annulate ('ænjʊlɪt, -ˌleɪt) ADJECTIVE having, composed of, or marked with rings.
▷HISTORY C19: from Latin *ānulātus,* from *ānulus* a ring
▸**'annuˌlated** ADJECTIVE

annulation (ˌænjʊ'leɪʃən) NOUN [1] the formation of rings. [2] a ringlike formation or part.

annulet ('ænjʊlɪt) NOUN [1] *Architect* a moulding in the form of a ring, as at the top of a column adjoining the capital. [2] *Heraldry* a ring-shaped device on a shield; hollow roundel. [3] a little ring.
▷HISTORY C16: from Latin *ānulus* ring + -ET

annulment (ə'nʌlmənt) NOUN [1] a formal invalidation, as of a marriage, judicial proceeding, etc. [2] the act of annulling.

annulose ('ænjʊˌləʊs, -ˌləʊz) ADJECTIVE (of earthworms, crustaceans, and similar animals)

having a body formed of a series of rings; segmented.
▷HISTORY C19: from New Latin *annulōsus;* see ANNULUS

annulus (ˈænjʊləs) NOUN, *plural* **-li** (-ˌlaɪ) *or* **-luses.** [1] the area between two concentric circles. [2] a ring-shaped part, figure, or space.
▷HISTORY C16: from Latin, variant of *ānulus* ring

annunciate (əˈnʌnsɪˌeɪt, -ʃɪ-) VERB (*tr*) a less common word for **announce.**
▷HISTORY C16: from *annunciātus,* Medieval Latin misspelling of *annuntiātus,* past participle of Latin *annuntiāre;* see ANNOUNCE
▸**anˌnunciˈation** NOUN ▸**annunciative** (əˈnʌnsɪətɪv, -ʃətɪv) *or* **annunciatory** (əˈnʌnsɪətərɪ, -ʃə-) ADJECTIVE

Annunciation (əˌnʌnsɪˈeɪʃən) NOUN [1] **the.** *New Testament* the announcement of the Incarnation by the angel Gabriel to the Virgin Mary (Luke 1:26–38). [2] Also called: **Annunciation Day.** the festival commemorating this, held on March 25 (Lady Day).

annunciator (əˈnʌnsɪˌeɪtə) NOUN [1] a device that gives a visual indication as to which of a number of electric circuits has operated, such as an indicator in a hotel showing in which room a bell has been rung. [2] a device giving an audible signal indicating the position of a train. [3] a less common word for **announcer.**

annus horribilis (ˈænʊs hɒˈriːbɪlɪs) NOUN a terrible year.
▷HISTORY C20: from Latin, modelled on ANNUS MIRABILIS, first used by Elizabeth II of the year 1992

annus mirabilis *Latin* (ˈænʊs mɪˈræbɪlɪs) NOUN, *plural* ***anni mirabiles*** (ˈænaɪ mɪˈræbɪliːz). a year of wonders, catastrophes, or other notable events.

anoa (əˈnəʊə) NOUN the smallest of the cattle tribe *Anoa depressicornis,* having small straight horns and inhabiting the island of Celebes in Indonesia. Compare **tamarau.**
▷HISTORY from a native name in Celebes

anobiid (əˈnəʊbɪɪd) NOUN any coleopterous beetle of the family *Anobiidae,* in which the pronotum characteristically forms a hood that more or less covers the head. The family includes such notorious pests as the **furniture beetle** (*Anobium punctatum*) and the **deathwatch beetle**, the larvae of which attack furniture and beams. See also **deathwatch.**

anode (ˈænəʊd) NOUN [1] the positive electrode in an electrolytic cell. [2] Also called (esp US): **plate.** the positively charged electrode in an electronic valve. [3] the negative terminal of a primary cell. Compare **cathode.**
▷HISTORY C19: from Greek *anodos* a way up, from *hodos* a way; alluding to the movement of the current to or from the positive pole
▸**anodal** (eɪˈnəʊdᵊl) *or* **anodic** (əˈnɒdɪk) ADJECTIVE

anodize *or* **anodise** (ˈænəˌdaɪz) VERB to coat (a metal, such as aluminium or magnesium) with a protective oxide film by electrolysis.

anodontia (ˌænəʊˈdɒnʃɪə) NOUN the congenital absence of teeth.
▷HISTORY from AN- + Greek *odōn* tooth + -IA

anodyne (ˈænəˌdaɪn) NOUN [1] a drug that relieves pain; analgesic. [2] anything that alleviates mental distress. ◆ ADJECTIVE [3] capable of relieving pain or distress.
▷HISTORY C16: from Latin *anōdynus,* from Greek *anōdunos* painless, from AN- + *odunē* pain

anoestrus *or US* **anestrus** (ænˈiːstrəs) NOUN a period of sexual inactivity between two periods of oestrus in many mammals.
▷HISTORY C20: New Latin; see AN-, OESTRUS
▸**anˈoestrous** *or US* **anˈestrous** ADJECTIVE

anoint (əˈnɔɪnt) VERB (*tr*) [1] to smear or rub over with oil or an oily liquid. [2] to apply oil to as a sign of consecration or sanctification in a sacred rite.
▷HISTORY C14: from Old French *enoint,* from *enoindre,* from Latin *inunguere,* from IN-^{2} + *unguere* to smear with oil
▸**aˈnointer** NOUN ▸**aˈnointment** NOUN

anointing of the sick NOUN *RC Church* a sacrament in which a person who is seriously ill or dying is anointed by a priest with consecrated oil. Former name: **extreme unction.**

anole (əˈnəʊl) NOUN any small arboreal tropical American insectivorous lizards of the genus *Anolis,* such as *A. carolinensis* (**green anole**): family *Iguanidae* (iguanas). They are able to change the colour of their skin. Also called: **American chameleon.**
▷HISTORY C18 *annolis,* from French *anolis,* from Carib *anoli*

anomalistic month NOUN the interval between two successive passages of the moon through perigee; 27.55455 days.

anomalistic year NOUN the interval between two successive passages of the earth through perihelion; 365.25964 mean solar days.

anomalous (əˈnɒmələs) ADJECTIVE deviating from the normal or usual order, type, etc.; irregular, abnormal, or incongruous.
▷HISTORY C17: from Late Latin *anōmalus,* from Greek *anōmalos* uneven, inconsistent, from AN- + *homalos* even, from *homos* one and the same
▸**aˈnomalously** ADVERB ▸**aˈnomalousness** NOUN

anomalous monism NOUN the philosophical doctrine that although all mental states consist merely in states of the brain, there exist no regular correspondences between classes of mental and physical states, and so no psychophysical laws. See also **identity theory.**

anomaly (əˈnɒməlɪ) NOUN, *plural* **-lies.** [1] something anomalous. [2] deviation from the normal or usual order, type, etc.; irregularity. [3] *Astronomy* **a** Also called: **true anomaly.** the angle between a planet, the sun, and the previous perihelion of the planet. **b** Also called: **eccentric anomaly.** the angle between the periapsis of a particular point on a circle round the orbit as seen from the centre of the orbit. This point is obtained by producing a perpendicular to the major axis of the ellipse through the orbiting body until it reaches the circumference of the circle. **c** Also called: **mean anomaly.** the angle between the periapsis of an orbit and the position of an imaginary body orbiting at a constant angular speed and in the same period as the real orbiting body. [4] *Geology* **a** Also called: **gravity anomaly.** a deviation from the normal value of gravity at the earth's surface, caused by density differences at depth, for example those caused by a buried mineral body. **b** Also called: **magnetic anomaly.** a magnetic field, for example one produced by a buried mineral body, that deviates from an expected or standard value, usually that of the earth's magnetic field.
▸**aˌnomaˈlistic** ADJECTIVE ▸**aˌnomaˈlistically** ADVERB

anomie *or* **anomy** (ˈænəʊmɪ) NOUN *Sociol* lack of social or moral standards in an individual or society.
▷HISTORY from Greek *anomia* lawlessness, from A-^{1} + *nomos* law
▸**anomic** (əˈnɒmɪk) ADJECTIVE

anon (əˈnɒn) ADVERB *Archaic or literary* [1] in a short time; soon. [2] **ever and anon.** now and then.
▷HISTORY Old English *on āne,* literally: in one, that is, immediately

anon. ABBREVIATION FOR anonymous.

anonym (ˈænənɪm) NOUN [1] a less common word for **pseudonym.** [2] an anonymous person or publication.

anonymize *or* **anonymise** (əˈnɒnɪˌmaɪz) VERB (*tr*) to carry out or organize in such a way as to preserve anonymity: *anonymized AIDS screening.*

anonymous (əˈnɒnɪməs) ADJECTIVE [1] from or by a person, author, etc., whose name is unknown or withheld: *an anonymous letter.* [2] having no known name. [3] lacking individual characteristics; unexceptional. [4] (*often capital*) denoting an organization which provides help to applicants who remain anonymous: *Alcoholics Anonymous.*
▷HISTORY C17: via Late Latin from Greek *anōnumos,* from AN- + *onoma* name
▸**anonymity** (ˌænəˈnɪmɪtɪ) NOUN ▸**aˈnonymously** ADVERB ▸**aˈnonymousness** NOUN

anopheles (əˈnɒfɪˌliːz) NOUN, *plural* **-les.** any of various mosquitoes constituting the genus *Anopheles,* some species of which transmit the malaria parasite to man.
▷HISTORY C19: via New Latin from Greek *anōphelēs* useless, from AN- + *ōphelein* to help, from *ophelos* help

anorak (ˈænəˌræk) NOUN [1] a warm waterproof hip-length jacket usually with a hood, originally worn in polar regions, but now worn for any outdoor activity. [2] *Informal* a socially inept person with a hobby considered by most people to be boring.
▷HISTORY from Eskimo *ánorâq*

anorexia (ˌænɒˈrɛksɪə) NOUN [1] loss of appetite. [2] Also called: **anorexia nervosa** (nɜːˈvəʊsə). a disorder characterized by fear of becoming fat and refusal of food, leading to debility and even death.
▷HISTORY C17: via New Latin from Greek, from AN- + *orexis* appetite
▸ˌ**anoˈrectic** *or* ˌ**anoˈrexic** ADJECTIVE, NOUN

anorthic (ænˈɔːθɪk) ADJECTIVE another word for **triclinic.**
▷HISTORY C19: from AN- + ORTHO- + -IC

anorthite (ænˈɔːθaɪt) NOUN a white to greyish-white or reddish-white mineral of the feldspar group and plagioclase series, found chiefly in igneous rocks and more rarely in metamorphic rocks. It is used in the manufacture of glass and ceramics. Composition: calcium aluminium silicate. Formula: $CaAl_2Si_2O_8$. Crystal structure: triclinic.
▷HISTORY C19: from AN- + ORTHO- + -ITE^1
▸**anorthitic** (ˌænɔːˈθɪtɪk) ADJECTIVE

anorthosite (ænˈɔːθəˌsaɪt) NOUN a coarse-grained plutonic igneous rock consisting almost entirely of plagioclase feldspar.
▷HISTORY C19: from French *anorthose* (see AN-, ORTHO-) + -ITE^1

anosmia (ænˈɒzmɪə, -ˈɒs-) NOUN *Pathol* loss of the sense of smell, usually as the result of a lesion of the olfactory nerve, disease in another organ or part, or obstruction of the nasal passages.
▷HISTORY C19: from New Latin, from AN- + Greek *osmē* smell, from *ozein* to smell
▸**anosmatic** (ˌænɒzˈmætɪk) *or* **anˈosmic** ADJECTIVE

another (əˈnʌðə) DETERMINER [1] **a** one more; an added: *another chance.* **b** (*as pronoun*): *help yourself to another.* [2] **a** a different; alternative: *another era from ours.* **b** (*as pronoun*): *to try one path, then another.* [3] **a** a different example of the same sort: *another Beethoven.* **b** (*as pronoun*): *we got rid of one loafer, but I think this new man's another.* [4] **another place.** the other House of Parliament (used in the House of Commons to refer to the House of Lords and vice versa).
▷HISTORY C14: originally *an other*

A.N. Other NOUN *Brit* an unnamed person: used in team lists, etc., to indicate a place that remains to be filled.

ANOVA (ˈænəʊvə) NOUN ACRONYM FOR **analysis of variance.**

anoxaemia *or US* **anoxemia** (ˌænɒkˈsiːmɪə) NOUN a deficiency in the amount of oxygen in the arterial blood.
▷HISTORY C19: from New Latin, from AN- + OX(YGEN) + -AEMIA
▸ˌ**anoxˈaemic** *or US* ˌ**anoxˈemic** ADJECTIVE

anoxia (ænˈɒksɪə) NOUN [1] lack or absence of oxygen. [2] a deficiency of oxygen in tissues and organs. Compare **hypoxia.**
▷HISTORY C20: from AN- + OX(YGEN) + -IA
▸**anˈoxic** ADJECTIVE

Anqing (ˈɑːnˈtʃɪŋ) *or* **Anking** NOUN a city in E China, in SW Anhui province on the Yangtze River: famous seven-storeyed pagoda. Pop.: 356 920 (1999 est.).

ansate (ˈænseɪt) ADJECTIVE having a handle or handle-like part.
▷HISTORY C19: from Latin *ansātus,* from *ansa* handle

Anschluss (ˈænʃlʊs) NOUN a political or economic union, esp the annexation of Austria by Nazi Germany (1938).
▷HISTORY German: from *anschliessen* to join

anserine (ˈænsəˌraɪn, -rɪn) *or* **anserous** (ˈænsərəs) ADJECTIVE [1] of or resembling a goose. [2] of, relating to, or belonging to the subfamily *Anserinae,* which includes geese, swans, and certain ducks: family *Anatidae,* order *Anseriformes.* [3] silly; foolish.
▷HISTORY C19: from Latin *anserīnus,* from *anser* goose

Anshan (ˌænˈʃæn) NOUN [1] a city in NE China, in Liaoning province. Pop.: 1 285 849 (1999 est.). [2] an ancient city and region in Persia, associated with Elam.

ANSI ABBREVIATION FOR American National Standards Institution.

answer (ˈɑːnsə) NOUN [1] a reply, either spoken or written, as to a question, request, letter, or article. [2] a reaction or response in the form of an action: *drunkenness was his answer to disappointment.* [3] a solution, esp of a mathematical problem. [4] *Law* **a** a party's written reply to his opponent's interrogatories. **b** (in divorce law) the respondent's written reply to the petition. [5] a musical phrase that follows the subject of a fugue, reproducing it a fifth higher or a fourth lower. ◆ VERB [6] (when *tr, may take a clause as object*) to reply or respond (to) by word or act: *to answer a question; he answered; to answer the door; he answered that he would come.* [7] (*tr*) to reply correctly to; solve or attempt to solve: *I could answer only three questions.* [8] (*intr;* usually foll by *to*) to respond or react (to a stimulus, command, etc.): *the steering answers to the slightest touch.* [9] (*tr*) to pay off (a debt, obligation, etc.); discharge. [10] (when *intr,* often foll by *for*) to meet the requirements (of); be satisfactory (for); serve the purpose (of): *this will answer his needs; this will answer for a chisel.* [11] (when *intr,* foll by *to*) to match or correspond (esp in the phrase **answer** (or **answer to**) **the description**). [12] (*tr*) to give a defence or refutation of (a charge) or in (an argument).
▷HISTORY Old English *andswaru* an answer; related to Old Frisian *ondser,* Old Norse *andsvar;* see SWEAR

answerable (ˈɑːnsərəbᵊl) ADJECTIVE [1] (*postpositive;* foll by *for* or *to*) responsible or accountable: *answerable for someone's safety; answerable to one's boss.* [2] able to be answered.
▸ **ˌanswera'bility** *or* **'answerableness** NOUN ▸ **'answerably** ADVERB

answer back VERB (*adverb*) to reply rudely to (a person, esp someone in authority) when one is expected to remain silent.

answer for VERB (*intr, preposition*) [1] to be liable or responsible for (a person's actions, behaviour, etc.). [2] to vouch for or speak on behalf of (a person). [3] to suffer or atone for (one's wrongdoing).

answering machine NOUN a device by means of which a telephone call is answered automatically and the caller enabled to leave a recorded message. In full: **telephone answering machine.** Also called: **answerphone.**

ant (ænt) NOUN [1] any small social insect of the widely distributed hymenopterous family *Formicidae,* typically living in highly organized colonies of winged males, wingless sterile females (workers), and fertile females (queens), which are winged until after mating. See also **army ant, fire ant, slave ant, wood ant.** Related adjective: **formic.** [2] **white ant.** another name for a **termite.** [3] **have ants in one's pants.** *Slang* to be restless or impatient.
▷HISTORY Old English *ǣmette;* related to Old High German *āmeiza,* Old Norse *meita;* see EMMET

an't *Chiefly Brit* [1] (ɑːnt) a rare variant spelling of **aren't.** [2] (eɪnt) *Dialect* a variant spelling of **ain't.**

ant- PREFIX a variant of **anti-**: *antacid.*

-ant SUFFIX FORMING ADJECTIVES AND NOUNS causing or performing an action or existing in a certain condition; the agent that performs an action: *pleasant; claimant; deodorant; protestant; servant.*
▷HISTORY from Latin *-ant-,* ending of present participles of the first conjugation

anta (ˈæntə) NOUN, *plural* **antae** (ˈæntiː). *Architect* a pilaster attached to the end of a side wall or sometimes to the side of a doorway.

Antabuse (ˈæntəˌbjuːs) NOUN *Trademark* a drug, a brand of disulfiram, used in the treatment of alcoholism, that acts by inducing nausea and other unpleasant symptoms following ingestion of alcohol; tetraethylthiuram disulphide.

antacid (æntˈæsɪd) NOUN [1] a substance used to neutralize acidity, esp in the stomach. ◆ ADJECTIVE [2] having the properties of this substance.

Antaeus (ænˈtiːəs) NOUN *Greek myth* an African giant who was invincible as long as he touched the ground, but was lifted into the air by Hercules and crushed to death.

antagonism (ænˈtægəˌnɪzəm) NOUN [1] openly expressed and usually mutual opposition. [2] the inhibiting or nullifying action of one substance or organism on another. [3] *Physiol* the normal opposition between certain muscles. [4] *Biology* the inhibition or interference of growth of one kind of organism by another.

antagonist (ænˈtægənɪst) NOUN [1] an opponent or adversary, as in a contest, drama, sporting event, etc. [2] any muscle that opposes the action of another. Compare **agonist** (sense 1). [3] a drug that counteracts the effects of another drug. Compare **synergist** (sense 1).

antagonistic (ænˌtægəˈnɪstɪk) ADJECTIVE [1] in active opposition. [2] mutually opposed.
▸ **anˌtago'nistically** ADVERB

antagonize *or* **antagonise** (ænˈtægəˌnaɪz) VERB (*tr*) [1] to make hostile; annoy or irritate. [2] to act in opposition to or counteract.
▷HISTORY C17: from Greek *antagōnizesthai,* from ANTI- + *agōnizesthai* to strive, from *agōn* contest
▸ **an'tagoˌnizable** *or* **an'tagoˌnisable** ADJECTIVE
▸ **anˌtagoni'zation** *or* **anˌtagoni'sation** NOUN

Antakiya (ˌæntɑːˈkiːjə) NOUN the Arabic name for **Antioch.**

Antakya (ɑnˈtɑkjɑ) NOUN the Turkish name for **Antioch.**

antalkali (æntˈælkəˌlaɪ) NOUN, *plural* **-lis** *or* **-lies.** a substance that neutralizes alkalis, esp one used to treat alkalosis.
▸ **antalkaline** (æntˈælkəˌlaɪn, -lɪn) ADJECTIVE, NOUN

Antalya (*Turkish* ɑnˈtɑljɑ) NOUN a port in SW Turkey, on the **Gulf of Antalya.** Pop.: 512 086 (1997).

Antananarivo (ˌæntəˌnænəˈriːvəʊ) NOUN the capital of Madagascar, on the central plateau: founded in the 17th century by a Hova chief; university (1961). Pop.: 1 052 835 (1993). Former name: **Tananarive.**

Antarctic (æntˈɑːktɪk) NOUN [1] **the.** Also called: **Antarctic Zone.** Antarctica and the surrounding waters. ◆ ADJECTIVE [2] of or relating to the south polar regions.
▷HISTORY C14: via Latin from Greek *antarktikos;* see ANTI-, ARCTIC

Antarctica (æntˈɑːktɪkə) NOUN a continent around the South Pole: consists of an ice-covered plateau, 1800–3000 m (6000 ft. to 10 000 ft.) above sea level, and mountain ranges rising to 4500 m (15 000 ft.) with some volcanic peaks; average temperatures all below freezing and human settlement is confined to research stations.

Antarctic Archipelago NOUN the former name of the **Palmer Archipelago.**

Antarctic beech NOUN any tree of the genus *Nothofagus,* related to the beech and native to temperate Australasia and South America, esp *Nothofagus cunninghamii* of SE Australia or *Nothofagus moorei* of NE Australia

Antarctic Circle NOUN the imaginary circle around the earth, parallel to the equator, at latitude 66° 32′ S; it marks the southernmost point at which the sun appears above the level of the horizon at the winter solstice.

Antarctic Ocean NOUN the sea surrounding Antarctica, consisting of the most southerly parts of the Pacific, Atlantic, and Indian Oceans. Also called: **Southern Ocean.**

Antarctic Peninsula NOUN the largest peninsula of Antarctica, between the Weddell Sea and the Pacific: consists of Graham Land in the north and the Palmer Peninsula in the south. Former name (until 1964): **Palmer Peninsula.**

Antarctic prion NOUN another name for **dove prion.**

Antares (ænˈtɛəriːz) NOUN the brightest star in the constellation Scorpius. It is a variable binary star whose main component, a red supergiant, is associated with a fainter green component. Visual magnitude: 1.2 (red), 6.8 (green); spectral type: M1.5Ib (red); distance: 600 light years.
▷HISTORY from Greek *Antarēs,* literally: simulating Mars (in colour), from ANTI- + *Arēs* Mars

ant bear NOUN another name for **aardvark.**

ant bird NOUN any of various dull-coloured South American passerine birds of the family *Formicariidae,* such as *Hylophylax naevioides* (spotted ant bird), that typically feed on ants. Also called: **bush shrike, ant thrush.**

ant cow NOUN an insect, esp an aphid, that excretes a sweet honey-like substance that is collected and eaten by ants.

ante (ˈæntɪ) NOUN [1] the gaming stake put up before the deal in poker by the players. [2] *Informal* a sum of money representing a person's share, as in a syndicate. [3] **up the ante.** *Informal* to increase the costs, risks, or considerations involved in taking an action or reaching a conclusion: *whenever they reached their goal, they upped the ante by setting more complex challenges for themselves.* ◆ VERB **-tes, -teing; -ted** *or* **-teed.** [4] to place (one's stake) in poker. [5] (usually foll by *up*) *Informal, chiefly US* to pay.

ante- PREFIX before in time or position; previous to; in front of: *antedate; antechamber.*
▷HISTORY from Latin

anteater (ˈæntˌiːtə) NOUN [1] any toothless edentate mammal of the family *Myrmecophagidae* of Central and South America, esp *Myrmecophaga tridactyla* (or *jubata*) (**giant anteater**), having a long tubular snout used for eating termites. See also **tamandua.** [2] **scaly anteater.** another name for **pangolin.** [3] **spiny anteater.** another name for **echidna.** [4] **banded anteater.** another name for **numbat.**

antebellum (ˌæntɪˈbɛləm) ADJECTIVE of or during the period before a war, esp the American Civil War: *the antebellum South.*
▷HISTORY Latin *ante bellum,* literally: before the war

antecede (ˌæntɪˈsiːd) VERB (*tr*) to go before, as in time, order, etc.; precede.
▷HISTORY C17: from Latin *antecēdere,* from *cēdere* to go

antecedence (ˌæntɪˈsiːdᵊns) NOUN [1] precedence; priority. [2] *Astronomy* retrograde motion.

antecedent (ˌæntɪˈsiːdᵊnt) NOUN [1] an event, circumstance, etc., that happens before another. [2] *Grammar* a word or phrase to which a pronoun refers. In the sentence "People who live in glass houses shouldn't throw stones," *people* is the antecedent of *who.* [3] *Logic* the hypothetical clause, usually introduced by "if", in a conditional statement: that which implies the other. [4] *Maths* an obsolescent name for **numerator** (sense 1). [5] **denying the antecedent.** *Logic* the fallacy of inferring the falsehood of the consequent of a conditional statement, given the truth of the conditional and the falsehood of its antecedent, as *if there are five of them, there are more than four: there are not five, so there are not more than four.* ◆ ADJECTIVE [6] preceding in time or order; prior. ◆ See also **antecedents.**

antecedents (ˌæntɪˈsiːdᵊnts) PLURAL NOUN [1] ancestry. [2] a person's past history.

antechamber (ˈæntɪˌtʃeɪmbə) NOUN another name for **anteroom.**
▷HISTORY C17: from Old French, from Italian *anticamera;* see ANTE-, CHAMBER

antechoir (ˈæntɪˌkwaɪə) NOUN the part of a church in front of the choir, usually enclosed by screens, tombs, etc.

antedate VERB (ˈæntɪˌdeɪt, ˌæntɪˈdeɪt) (*tr*) [1] to be or occur at an earlier date than. [2] to affix a date to (a document, etc.) that is earlier than the actual date. [3] to assign a date to (an event, etc.) that is earlier than its previously assigned date. [4] to cause to occur sooner. ◆ NOUN (ˈæntɪˌdeɪt) [5] an earlier date.

antediluvian (ˌæntɪdɪˈluːvɪən, -daɪ-) ADJECTIVE [1] belonging to the ages before the biblical Flood (Genesis 7, 8). [2] old-fashioned or antiquated. ◆ NOUN [3] an antediluvian person or thing.
▷HISTORY C17: from ANTE- + Latin *dīluvium* flood

antefix (ˈæntɪˌfɪks) NOUN, *plural* **-fixes** *or* **-fixa** (-ˌfɪksə). a carved ornament at the eaves of a roof to hide the joint between the tiles.
▷HISTORY C19: from Latin *antefixa* (things) fastened in front, from *fīgere* to FIX
▸ **antefixal** (ˌæntɪˈfɪksəl) ADJECTIVE

antelope (ˈæntɪˌləʊp) NOUN, *plural* **-lopes** *or* **-lope.** [1] any bovid mammal of the subfamily *Antilopinae,* of Africa and Asia. They are typically graceful, having long legs and horns, and include the gazelles, springbok, impala, gerenuk, blackbuck, and dik-diks. [2] any of various similar bovids of Africa and Asia. [3] **American antelope.** another name for **pronghorn.**
▷HISTORY C15: from Old French *antelop,* from Medieval Latin *antalopus,* from Late Greek *antholops* a legendary beast

antemeridian (ˌæntɪməˈrɪdɪən) ADJECTIVE before noon; in the morning.
▷HISTORY C17: from Latin *antemerīdiānus;* see ANTE-, MERIDIAN

ante meridiem (ˈæntɪ məˈrɪdɪəm) the full form of **a.m.**

▷**HISTORY** Latin, from ANTE- + *merīdiēs* midday

ante-mortem ADJECTIVE, ADVERB (esp in legal or medical contexts) before death.
▷**HISTORY** Latin

antenatal (ˌæntɪˈneɪtᵊl) ADJECTIVE [1] occurring or present before birth; during pregnancy. ◆ NOUN [2] Also called: **prenatal.** *Informal* an examination during pregnancy.
▸ˌ**ante'natally** ADVERB

antenna (ænˈtɛnə) NOUN [1] (*plural* **-nae** (-niː)) one of a pair of mobile appendages on the heads of insects, crustaceans, etc., that are often whiplike and respond to touch and taste but may be specialized for swimming or attachment. [2] (*plural* **-nas**) another name for **aerial** (sense 7).
▷**HISTORY** C17: from Latin: sail yard, of obscure origin
▸**an'tennal** *or* **an'tennary** ADJECTIVE

antennule (ænˈtɛnjuːl) NOUN one of a pair of small mobile appendages on the heads of crustaceans in front of the antennae, usually having a sensory function.
▷**HISTORY** C19: from French, diminutive of ANTENNA

antenuptial marriage contract (ˌæntɪˈnʌpʃəl, -tʃəl) NOUN a contract made between a man and a woman before they marry, agreeing on the distribution of their assets in the event of divorce. Sometimes shortened to **antenuptial.**

antependium (ˌæntɪˈpɛndɪəm) NOUN, *plural* **-dia** (-dɪə). a covering hung over the front of an altar.
▷**HISTORY** C17: from Medieval Latin, from Latin ANTE- + *pendēre* to hang

antepenult (ˌæntɪpɪˈnʌlt) NOUN the third last syllable in a word.
▷**HISTORY** C16: shortened from Latin (*syllaba*) *antepaenultima;* see ANTE-, PENULT

antepenultimate (ˌæntɪpɪˈnʌltɪmɪt) ADJECTIVE [1] third from last. ◆ NOUN [2] anything that is third from last.

anteposition (ˈæntɪpəˌzɪʃən) NOUN *Botany* the position opposite a given part of a plant.

ante-post ADJECTIVE *Brit* (of a bet) placed before the runners in a race are confirmed.

anterior (ænˈtɪərɪə) ADJECTIVE [1] situated at or towards the front. [2] earlier in time. [3] *Zoology* of or near the head end. [4] *Botany* (of part of a flower or leaf) situated farthest away from the main stem. ◆ Compare **posterior.**
▷**HISTORY** C17: from Latin, comparative of *ante* before
▸**anteriority** (ænˌtɪərɪˈɒrɪtɪ) NOUN

anterograde amnesia (ˈæntərəʊˌɡreɪd) NOUN amnesia caused by brain damage in which the memory loss relates to events occurring after the damage. Compare **retrograde amnesia.**
▷**HISTORY** from Latin *anterior* previous and -GRADE

anteroom (ˈæntɪˌruːm, -ˌrʊm) NOUN a room giving entrance to a larger room, often used as a waiting room.

antetype (ˈæntɪˌtaɪp) NOUN an earlier form; prototype.

anteversion (ˌæntɪˈvɜːʃən) NOUN abnormal forward tilting of a bodily organ, esp the uterus.

antevert (ˌæntɪˈvɜːt) VERB (*tr*) to displace (an organ or part) by tilting it forward.
▷**HISTORY** C17: from Latin *antevertere* to go in front, from *vertere* to turn

anthelion (æntˈhiːlɪən, ænˈθiː-) NOUN, *plural* **-lia** (-lɪə). [1] a faint halo sometimes seen in polar or high altitude regions around the shadow of an object cast onto a thick cloud bank or fog. [2] a white spot occasionally appearing on the parhelic circle at the same height as and opposite to the sun.
▷**HISTORY** C17: from Late Greek, from *anthēlios* opposite the sun, from ANTE- + *hēlios* sun

anthelix (æntˈhiːlɪks, ænˈθiː-) *or* **antihelix** NOUN, *plural* **-helices** (-ˈhiːlɪsiːz) *or* **-helixes.** *Anatomy* a prominent curved fold of cartilage just inside the outer rim of the external ear.

anthelmintic (ˌænθɛlˈmɪntɪk), **anthelminthic** (ˌænθɛlˈmɪnθɪk), *or* **antihelminthic** (ˌæntɪhɛlˈmɪnθɪk) NOUN *Med* another name for **vermifuge.**

anthem (ˈænθəm) NOUN [1] a song of loyalty or devotion, as to a nation or college: *a national anthem.* [2] a musical composition for a choir, usually set to words from the Bible, sung as part of a church service. [3] a religious chant sung antiphonally. [4] a popular rock or pop song.
▷**HISTORY** Old English *antemne,* from Late Latin *antiphōna* ANTIPHON
▸**anthemic** (ænˈθɛmɪk) ADJECTIVE

anthemion (ænˈθiːmɪən) NOUN, *plural* **-mia** (-mɪə). a floral design, used esp in ancient Greek and Roman architecture and decoration, usually consisting of honeysuckle, lotus, or palmette leaf motifs.
▷**HISTORY** from Greek: a little flower, from *anthos* flower

anther (ˈænθə) NOUN the terminal part of a stamen consisting usually of two lobes each containing two sacs in which the pollen matures.
▷**HISTORY** C18: from New Latin *anthēra,* from Latin: a remedy prepared from flowers, from Greek, from *anthēros* flowery, from *anthos* flower
▸ˈ**antheral** ADJECTIVE

antheridium (ˌænθəˈrɪdɪəm) NOUN, *plural* **-ia** (-ɪə). the male sex organ of algae, fungi, bryophytes, and spore-bearing vascular plants, such as ferns, which produces antherozoids.
▷**HISTORY** C19: from New Latin, diminutive of *anthēra* ANTHER
▸ˌ**anther'idial** ADJECTIVE

antherozoid (ˌænθərəˈzəʊɪd, -ˈzɔɪd) NOUN one of many small male gametes produced in an antheridium.
▷**HISTORY** C19: see ANTHER, ZO(O)ID

anthesis (ænˈθiːsɪs) NOUN the time when a flower becomes sexually functional.
▷**HISTORY** C19: via New Latin from Greek: full bloom, from *anthein* to bloom, from *anthos* flower

ant hill NOUN [1] a mound of soil, leaves, etc., near the entrance of an ants' nest, carried and deposited there by the ants while constructing the nest. [2] a mound of earth, usually about 2 metres high, built up by termites in forming a nest.

antho- COMBINING FORM denoting a flower: *anthophore; anthotaxy; anthozoan.*
▷**HISTORY** from Greek *anthos*

anthocyanin (ˌænθəʊˈsaɪənɪn) *or* **anthocyan** (ˌænθəʊˈsaɪən) NOUN any of a class of water-soluble glycosidic pigments, esp those responsible for the red and blue colours in flowers. They are closely related to vitamins E and P.
▷**HISTORY** C19: from ANTHO- + *-cyanin,* from Greek *kuanos* dark blue

anthodium (ænˈθəʊdɪəm) NOUN, *plural* **-dia** (-dɪə). *Botany* another name for **capitulum** (sense 1).
▷**HISTORY** C19: from New Latin, from Greek *anthōdēs* flower-like, from *anthos* flower + *-ōdēs* -OID

anthologize *or* **anthologise** (ænˈθɒləˌdʒaɪz) VERB to compile or put into an anthology.

anthology (ænˈθɒlədʒɪ) NOUN, *plural* **-gies.** [1] a collection of literary passages or works, esp poems, by various authors. [2] any printed collection of literary pieces, songs, works of art, etc.
▷**HISTORY** C17: from Medieval Latin *anthologia,* from Greek, literally: a flower gathering, from *anthos* flower + *legein* to collect
▸**anthological** (ˌænθəˈlɒdʒɪkᵊl) ADJECTIVE ▸**an'thologist** NOUN

anthophilous (ænˈθɒfɪləs) ADJECTIVE [1] (esp of insects) frequenting flowers. [2] feeding on flowers.

anthophore (ˈænθəʊˌfɔː, -θə-) NOUN an elongation of the receptacle of a flower between the calyx and corolla.

anthotaxy (ˈænθəˌtæksɪ) NOUN the arrangement of flowers on a stem or parts on a flower.

anthozoan (ˌænθəˈzəʊən) NOUN [1] any of the solitary or colonial sessile marine coelenterates of the class *Anthozoa,* including the corals, sea anemones, and sea pens, in which the body is in the form of a polyp. ◆ ADJECTIVE [2] Also: **actinozoan.** of or relating to the class *Anthozoa.*

anthracene (ˈænθrəˌsiːn) NOUN a colourless tricyclic crystalline solid having a slight blue fluorescence, used in the manufacture of chemicals, esp diphenylamine and alizarin, and as crystals in scintillation counters. Formula: $C_6H_4(CH)_2C_6H_4$.
▷**HISTORY** C19: from ANTHRAX + -ENE

anthracite (ˈænθrəˌsaɪt) NOUN a hard jet-black coal that burns slowly with a nonluminous flame giving out intense heat. Fixed carbon content: 86–98 per cent; calorific value: 3.14×10^7–3.63×10^7 J/kg. Also called: **hard coal.**
▷**HISTORY** C19: from Latin *anthracītes* type of bloodstone, from Greek *anthrakitēs* coal-like, from *anthrax* coal, ANTHRAX
▸**anthracitic** (ˌænθrəˈsɪtɪk) ADJECTIVE

anthracnose (ænˈθræknəʊs) NOUN any of several fungus diseases of plants and trees, such as vines and beans, characterized by oval dark depressed spots on the fruit and elsewhere.
▷**HISTORY** C19: from French, from Greek *anthrax* coal, carbuncle + *nosos* disease

anthracoid (ˈænθrəˌkɔɪd) ADJECTIVE [1] resembling anthrax. [2] resembling carbon, coal, or charcoal.

anthracosis (ˌænθrəˈkəʊsɪs) NOUN a lung disease due to inhalation of coal dust. Informal name: **coal miner's lung.**

anthraquinone (ˌænθrəkwɪˈnəʊn, -ˈkwɪnəʊn) NOUN a yellow crystalline solid used in the manufacture of dyes, esp **anthraquinone dyes**, which have excellent colour properties. Formula: $C_6H_4(CO)_2C_6H_4$.
▷**HISTORY** C19: ANTHRA(CENE) + QUINONE

anthrax (ˈænθræks) NOUN, *plural* **-thraces** (-θrəˌsiːz). [1] a highly infectious and often fatal disease of herbivores, esp cattle and sheep, characterized by fever, enlarged spleen, and swelling of the throat. Carnivores are relatively resistant. It is caused by the spore-forming bacterium *Bacillus anthracis* and can be transmitted to man. [2] a pustule or other lesion caused by this disease.
▷**HISTORY** C19: from Late Latin, from Greek: carbuncle

anthrop. ABBREVIATION FOR: [1] anthropological. [2] anthropology.

anthropic (ænˈθrɒpɪk) ADJECTIVE of or relating to human beings.

anthropic principle NOUN *Astronomy* the cosmological theory that the presence of life in the universe limits the ways in which the very early universe could have evolved.

anthropo- COMBINING FORM indicating man or human: *anthropology; anthropomorphism.*
▷**HISTORY** from Greek *anthrōpos*

anthropocentric (ˌænθrəpəʊˈsɛntrɪk) ADJECTIVE regarding man as the most important and central factor in the universe.
▸ˌ**anthropo'centrism** NOUN

anthropogenesis (ˌænθrəpəʊˈdʒɛnɪsɪs) *or* **anthropogeny** (ˌænθrəˈpɒdʒɪnɪ) NOUN the study of the origins of man.
▸**anthropogenetic** (ˌænθrəpəʊdʒɪˈnɛtɪk) ADJECTIVE

anthropogenic (ˌænθrəpəʊˈdʒɛnɪk) ADJECTIVE [1] relating to anthropogenesis. [2] created by people or caused by human activity: *anthropogenic pollution.*

anthropoid (ˈænθrəˌpɔɪd) ADJECTIVE [1] resembling man. [2] resembling an ape; apelike. [3] of or relating to the suborder *Anthropoidea.* ◆ NOUN [4] any primate of the suborder *Anthropoidea,* including monkeys, apes, and man. Compare **prosimian.**
▸ˌ**anthro'poidal** ADJECTIVE

anthropoid ape NOUN any primate of the family *Pongidae,* having no tail, elongated arms, and a highly developed brain. The group includes gibbons, orang-utans, chimpanzees, and gorillas.

anthropology (ˌænθrəˈpɒlədʒɪ) NOUN the study of humans, their origins, physical characteristics, institutions, religious beliefs, social relationships, etc. See also **cultural anthropology, ethnology, physical anthropology, social anthropology.**
▸**anthropological** (ˌænθrəpəˈlɒdʒɪkᵊl) ADJECTIVE
▸ˌ**anthropo'logically** ADVERB ▸ˌ**anthro'pologist** NOUN

anthropometry (ˌænθrəˈpɒmɪtrɪ) NOUN the comparative study of sizes and proportions of the human body.
▸**anthropometric** (ˌænθrəpəˈmɛtrɪk) *or* ˌ**anthropo'metrical** ADJECTIVE ▸ˌ**anthropo'metrically** ADVERB
▸ˌ**anthro'pometrist** NOUN

anthropomorphic (ˌænθrəpəˈmɔːfɪk) ADJECTIVE [1] of or relating to anthropomorphism. [2] resembling the human form.
▸ˈ**anthropoˌmorph** NOUN ▸ˌ**anthropo'morphically** ADVERB

anthropomorphism (ˌænθrəpəˈmɔːfɪzəm) NOUN the attribution of human form or behaviour to a deity, animal, etc.
▸ˌ**anthropo'morphist** NOUN

anthropomorphize *or* **anthropomorphise**

(ˌænθrəpəˈmɔːfaɪz) VERB to attribute or ascribe human form or behaviour to (a god, animal, object, etc.).

anthropomorphosis (ˌænθrəpəˈmɔːfəsɪs) NOUN transformation into human form.

anthropomorphous (ˌænθrəpəˈmɔːfəs) ADJECTIVE [1] shaped like a human being. [2] another word for **anthropomorphic.**
▸ˌ**anthropoˈmorphously** ADVERB

anthropopathy (ˌænθrəˈpɒpəθɪ) *or* **anthropopathism** NOUN the attribution of human passions, etc., to a deity, object, etc.
▸**anthropopathic** (ˌænθrəpəˈpæθɪk) ADJECTIVE

anthropophagi (ˌænθrəˈpɒfəˌgaɪ) PLURAL NOUN, *singular* **-gus** (-gəs). cannibals.
▷HISTORY C16: from Latin, from Greek *anthrōpophagos;* see ANTHROPO-, -PHAGY

anthropophagite (ˌænθrəˈpɒfəˌgaɪt) NOUN a rare word for **cannibal.**
▸**anthropophagy** (ˌænθrəˈpɒfədʒɪ) NOUN
▸**anthropophagic** (ˌænθrəpəˈfædʒɪk) ADJECTIVE
▸ˌ**anthroˈpophagous** ADJECTIVE

anthropophyte (ænˈθrɒpəˌfaɪt) NOUN a plant species accidentally introduced during the cultivation of another.

anthroposophy (ˌænθrəˈpɒsəfɪ) NOUN the spiritual and mystical teachings of Rudolph Steiner, based on the belief that creative activities such as myth making, which formed a part of life in earlier times, are psychologically valuable, esp for educational and therapeutic purposes.
▸**anthroposophic** (ˌænθrəpəʊˈsɒfɪk) ADJECTIVE
▸ˌ**anthroˈposophist** NOUN

anthurium (ænˈθjʊərɪəm) NOUN any of various tropical American aroid plants constituting the genus *Anthurium,* many of which are cultivated as house plants for their showy foliage and their flowers, which are borne in a long-stalked spike surrounded by a flaring heart-shaped white or red bract.
▷HISTORY C19: New Latin, from ANTHO- + Greek *oura* a tail

anti (ˈæntɪ) *Informal* ◆ ADJECTIVE [1] opposed to a party, policy, attitude, etc.: *he won't join because he is rather anti.* ◆ NOUN [2] an opponent of a party, policy, etc.

anti- PREFIX [1] against; opposing: *anticlerical; antisocial.* [2] opposite to: *anticlimax; antimere.* [3] rival; false: *antipope.* [4] counteracting, inhibiting, or neutralizing: *antifreeze; antihistamine.*
▷HISTORY from Greek *anti*

anti-abortion ADJECTIVE opposed to abortion: *anti-abortion activists.*
▸ˌ**anti-aˈbortionist** NOUN, ADJECTIVE

anti-ageing ADJECTIVE of or relating to any product or procedure claiming to reverse or slow down the effects of ageing.

anti-aircraft (ˌæntɪˈɛəkrɑːft) NOUN (*modifier*) of or relating to defence against aircraft attack: *anti-aircraft batteries.*

anti-alias VERB (*tr*) to process (a digital graphic image) so that it has a smooth, rather than a jagged, edge.

anti-American ADJECTIVE opposed to anything of or relating to the United States of America.

anti-androgen (ˌæntɪˈændrədʒən) NOUN any of a class of drugs that oppose the action of androgens; used in the treatment of prostate cancer and various male sexual disorders.

anti-apartheid ADJECTIVE opposed to apartheid: *the anti-apartheid movement.*

antiar (ˈæntɪˌɑː) NOUN another name for **upas** (senses 1, 2).
▷HISTORY from Javanese

anti-atom NOUN an atom composed of antiparticles, in which the nucleus contains antiprotons with orbiting positrons.

antibacterial (ˌæntɪbækˈtɪərɪəl) ADJECTIVE effective against bacteria.

antiballistic (ˌæntɪbəˈlɪstɪk) ADJECTIVE of or relating to defence against ballistic weapons.

antiballistic missile NOUN a missile designed to destroy an incoming ballistic missile before it reaches its target. Abbreviation: **ABM.**

antibaryon (ˌæntɪˈbærɪən) NOUN *Physics* the antiparticle of any of the baryons.

Antibes (*French* ɑ̃tib) NOUN a port and resort in SE France, on the Mediterranean: an important Roman town. Pop.: 60 000 (latest est.).

antibiosis (ˌæntɪbaɪˈəʊsɪs) NOUN an association between two organisms, esp microorganisms, that is harmful to one of them.

antibiotic (ˌæntɪbaɪˈɒtɪk) NOUN [1] any of various chemical substances, such as penicillin, streptomycin, chloramphenicol, and tetracycline, produced by various microorganisms, esp fungi, or made synthetically and capable of destroying or inhibiting the growth of microorganisms, esp bacteria. ◆ ADJECTIVE [2] of or relating to antibiotics.

antibody (ˈæntɪˌbɒdɪ) NOUN, *plural* **-bodies.** any of various proteins produced in the blood in response to the presence of an antigen. By becoming attached to antigens on infectious organisms antibodies can render them harmless or cause them to be destroyed. See also **immunoglobulin.**

anti-Bolshevik NOUN [1] a person who is opposed to Bolshevism. ◆ ADJECTIVE [2] opposed to Bolshevism: *anti-Bolshevik propaganda.*

anti-British ADJECTIVE opposed to anything characteristic of or relating to Britain.

antic (ˈæntɪk) NOUN [1] *Archaic* an actor in a ludicrous or grotesque part; clown; buffoon. ◆ ADJECTIVE [2] *Archaic* fantastic; grotesque. ◆ See also **antics.**
▷HISTORY C16: from Italian *antico* something ancient, or grotesque (from its application to fantastic carvings found in ruins of ancient Rome); see ANTIQUE

antical (ˈæntɪkᵊl) ADJECTIVE (of the position of plant parts) in front of or above another part; anterior.
▷HISTORY from ANTE- + -ICAL

anticapitalist (ˌæntɪˈkæpɪtəlɪst) ADJECTIVE [1] opposed to or against the principles or practice of capitalism: *anticapitalist riots.* ◆ NOUN [2] someone opposed to or against capitalism: *a group of anticapitalists.*

anticatalyst (ˌæntɪˈkætəlɪst) NOUN [1] a substance that destroys or diminishes the activity of a catalyst. [2] another name for **inhibitor** (sense 2).

anticathode (ˌæntɪˈkæθəʊd) NOUN the target electrode for the stream of electrons in a vacuum tube, esp an X-ray tube.

anti-Catholic ADJECTIVE [1] opposed to the beliefs, practices, and adherents of the Roman Catholic Church. ◆ NOUN [2] someone opposed to the Roman Catholic Church and its adherents: *he called him an anti-Catholic.*
▸ˌ**anti-CaˈtholiˌcismNOUN**

anticensorship (ˌæntɪˈsɛnsəʃɪp) ADJECTIVE opposed to a policy or programme of censoring.

antichlor (ˈæntɪˌklɔː) NOUN a substance used to remove chlorine from a material after bleaching or to neutralize the chlorine present.
▷HISTORY C19: from ANTI- + CHLOR(INE)
▸ˌ**antichloˈristic** ADJECTIVE

anticholinergic (ˌæntɪˌkɒlɪˈnɜːdʒɪk) ADJECTIVE [1] *Physiol* blocking nerve impulses through the parasympathetic nerves. ◆ NOUN [2] *Med* a drug or agent that blocks these nerve impulses, used to control intestinal spasm, increase the heart rate, dilate the pupils for examination of the eyes, dry secretions in anaesthesia, and in some forms to treat Alzheimer's disease.

anticholinesterase (ˌæntɪˌkɒləˈnɛstəˌreɪz) NOUN any of a group of substances that inhibit the action of cholinesterase.

Antichrist (ˈæntɪˌkraɪst) NOUN [1] *New Testament* the antagonist of Christ, expected by early Christians to appear and reign over the world until overthrown at Christ's Second Coming. [2] (*sometimes not capital*) an enemy of Christ or Christianity.
▸ˌ**Antiˈchristian** ADJECTIVE

anticipant (ænˈtɪsɪpənt) ADJECTIVE [1] operating in advance; expectant. ◆ NOUN [2] a person who anticipates.

anticipate (ænˈtɪsɪˌpeɪt) VERB (*mainly tr*) [1] (*may take a clause as object*) to foresee and act in advance of: *he anticipated the fall in value by selling early.* [2] to thwart by acting in advance of; forestall: *I anticipated his punch by moving out of reach.* [3] (*also intr*) to mention (something) before its proper time: *don't anticipate the climax of the story.* [4] (*may take a clause as object*) to regard as likely; expect; foresee: *he anticipated that it would happen.* [5] to make use of in advance of possession: *he anticipated his salary in buying a house.* [6] to pay (a bill, etc.) before it falls due. [7] to cause to happen sooner: *the spread of nationalism anticipated the decline of the Empire.*
▷HISTORY C16: from Latin *anticipāre* to take before, realize beforehand, from *anti-* ANTE- + *capere* to take
▸**anˈticiˌpator** NOUN ▸**anˈticipatory** *or* **anˈticipative** ADJECTIVE ▸**anˈticipatorily** *or* **anˈticipatively** ADVERB

> **Language note** The use of *anticipate* to mean *expect* should be avoided.

anticipation (ænˌtɪsɪˈpeɪʃən) NOUN [1] the act of anticipating; expectation, premonition, or foresight. [2] the act of taking or dealing with funds before they are legally available or due. [3] *Music* an unstressed, usually short note introduced before a downbeat and harmonically related to the chord immediately following it. Compare **suspension** (sense 11).

anticlastic (ˌæntɪˈklæstɪk) ADJECTIVE *Maths* (of a surface) having a curvature, at a given point and in a particular direction, that is of the opposite sign to the curvature at that point in a perpendicular direction. Compare **synclastic.**

anticlerical (ˌæntɪˈklɛrɪkᵊl) ADJECTIVE [1] opposed to the power and influence of the clergy, esp in politics. ◆ NOUN [2] a supporter of an anticlerical party.
▸ˌ**antiˈclericalism** NOUN

anticlimax (ˌæntɪˈklaɪmæks) NOUN [1] a disappointing or ineffective conclusion to a series of events, etc. [2] a sudden change from a serious subject to one that is disappointing or ludicrous. [3] *Rhetoric* a descent in discourse from the significant or important to the trivial, inconsequential, etc.
▸**anticlimactic** (ˌæntɪklaɪˈmæktɪk) ADJECTIVE
▸ˌ**anticliˈmactically** ADVERB

anticlinal (ˌæntɪˈklaɪnᵊl) ADJECTIVE [1] of, relating to, or resembling an anticline. [2] *Botany* of or relating to the plane at right angles to the surface of an organ.

anticline (ˈæntɪˌklaɪn) NOUN a formation of stratified rock raised up, by folding, into a broad arch so that the strata slope down on both sides from a common crest. Compare **syncline.**

anticlinorium (ˌæntɪklaɪˈnɔːrɪəm) NOUN, *plural* **-noria** (-ˈnɔːrɪə). a vast elongated anticline with its strata further folded into anticlines and synclines.

anticlockwise (ˌæntɪˈklɒkˌwaɪz) ADVERB, ADJECTIVE in the opposite direction to the rotation of the hands of a clock. US equivalent: **counterclockwise.**

anticoagulant (ˌæntɪkəʊˈægjʊlənt) ADJECTIVE [1] acting to prevent or impair coagulation, esp of blood. ◆ NOUN [2] an agent that prevents or impairs coagulation.

anticoincidence (ˌæntɪkəʊˈɪnsɪdəns) NOUN (*modifier*) of or relating to an electronic circuit that produces an output pulse if one but not both of its input terminals receives a pulse within a specified interval of time. Compare **coincidence** (sense 3).

anti-Communist NOUN [1] a person who is opposed to Communism: *a staunch anti-Communist.* ◆ ADJECTIVE [2] opposed to Communism: *a big anti-Communist demonstration.*

anticonvulsant (ˌæntɪkənˈvʌlsənt) NOUN [1] any of a class of drugs used to prevent or abolish convulsions. ◆ ADJECTIVE [2] of or relating to this class of drugs.

Anti-Corn Law League NOUN an organization founded in 1839 by Richard Cobden and John Bright to oppose the Corn Laws, which were repealed in 1846.

Anticosti (ˌæntɪˈkɒstɪ) NOUN an island of E Canada, in the Gulf of St Lawrence; part of Quebec. Area: 7881 sq. km (3043 sq. miles).

antics (ˈæntɪks) PLURAL NOUN absurd or grotesque acts or postures.

anticyclone (ˌæntɪˈsaɪkləʊn) NOUN *Meteorol* a body of moving air of higher pressure than the surrounding air, in which the pressure decreases away from the centre. Winds circulate around the centre in a clockwise direction in the N hemisphere

and anticlockwise in the S hemisphere. Also called: **high.**
▸**anticyclonic** (ˌæntɪsaɪˈklɒnɪk) ADJECTIVE

antidazzle mirror (ˈæntɪˌdæzᵊl) NOUN a rear-view mirror for road vehicles that only partially reflects headlights behind.

antidemocratic (ˌæntɪˌdɛməˈkrætɪk) ADJECTIVE opposed to the principles or practice of democracy: *anti-democratic forces.*

antidepressant (ˌæntɪdɪˈprɛsᵊnt) NOUN 1 any of a class of drugs used to alleviate depression. ♦ ADJECTIVE 2 of or relating to this class of drugs.

antidiuretic (ˌæntɪˌdaɪjʊˈrɛtɪk) ADJECTIVE (of a hormone, treatment, etc.) acting on the kidneys to control water excretion.

antidiuretic hormone NOUN another name for **vasopressin.** Abbreviation: **ADH.**

antidote (ˈæntɪˌdəʊt) NOUN 1 *Med* a drug or agent that counteracts or neutralizes the effects of a poison. 2 anything that counteracts or relieves a harmful or unwanted condition; remedy.
▹HISTORY C15: from Latin *antidotum,* from Greek *antidoton* something given as a countermeasure, from ANTI- + *didonai* to give
▸ˌ**antiˈdotal** ADJECTIVE

antidromic (ˌæntɪˈdrɒmɪk) ADJECTIVE (of nerve fibres) conducting nerve impulses in a direction opposite to normal.
▹HISTORY from ANTI- + Greek *dromos* course

antidune (ˈæntɪˌdjuːn) NOUN a sand hill or inclined bedding plane that forms a steep slope against the direction of a fast-flowing current.

antiemetic (ˌæntɪɪˈmɛtɪk) ADJECTIVE 1 preventing vomiting. ♦ NOUN 2 any antiemetic drug, such as promethazine or metoclopramide.

anti-Establishment ADJECTIVE opposed to established authority.

Antietam (ænˈtiːtəm) NOUN a creek in NW Maryland, flowing into the Potomac: scene of a Civil War battle (1862), in which the Confederate forces of General Robert E. Lee were defeated.

anti-European ADJECTIVE 1 opposed to the European Union or to political union of the countries of Europe. ♦ NOUN 2 a person who is opposed to the European Union or to political union of the countries of Europe.
▸**anti-Europeanism** NOUN

antifascist (ˌæntɪˈfæʃɪst) ADJECTIVE opposed to fascism: *an antifascist demonstration.*

antifebrile (ˌæntɪˈfiːbraɪl) ADJECTIVE 1 reducing fever; antipyretic. ♦ NOUN 2 *Obsolete* an antifebrile agent or drug.

Antifederalist (ˌæntɪˈfɛdərəlɪst, -ˈfɛdrə-) NOUN 1 *US history* a person who opposed the ratification of the Constitution in 1789 and thereafter allied with Thomas Jefferson's Antifederal Party, which opposed extension of the powers of the federal Government. 2 (*often not capital*) any person who opposes federalism.

antiferromagnetism (ˌæntɪˌfɛrəʊˈmægnɪˌtɪzəm) NOUN *Physics* the phenomenon exhibited by substances that resemble paramagnetic substances in the value of their relative permeability but that behave like ferromagnetic substances when their temperature is varied. See also **ferrimagnetism.**

antifouling (ˌæntɪˈfaʊlɪŋ) ADJECTIVE 1 (of a paint or other coating) inhibiting the growth of barnacles and other marine organisms on a ship's bottom. ♦ NOUN 2 an antifouling paint or other coating.

antifreeze (ˈæntɪˌfriːz) NOUN a liquid, usually ethylene glycol (ethanediol), added to cooling water to lower its freezing point, esp for use in an internal-combustion engine.

antifriction metal (ˌæntɪˈfrɪkʃən) NOUN another name for **white metal.**

antifungal (ˌæntɪˈfʌŋgᵊl) ADJECTIVE 1 inhibiting the growth of fungi. 2 (of a drug) possessing antifungal properties and therefore used to treat fungal infections. Also: **antimycotic.**

antigen (ˈæntɪdʒən, -ˌdʒɛn) NOUN a substance that stimulates the production of antibodies.
▹HISTORY C20: from ANTI(BODY) + -GEN
▸ˌ**antiˈgenic** ADJECTIVE ▸ˌ**antiˈgenically** ADVERB

antigenic determinant NOUN the specific part of an antigen molecule to which an antibody becomes attached.

anti-globalizer *or* **anti-globaliser** NOUN a political activist who challenges the concept of globalization and promotes practices that do not cause environmental damage.

antiglobulin (ˌæntɪˈglɒbjʊlɪn) NOUN a serum containing an antibody specific to an immunoglobulin.

Antigone (ænˈtɪgənɪ) NOUN *Greek myth* daughter of Oedipus and Jocasta, who was condemned to death for cremating the body of her brother Polynices in defiance of an edict of her uncle, King Creon of Thebes.

anti-G suit NOUN another name for **G-suit.**

Antigua (ænˈtiːgə) NOUN an island in the Caribbean, one of the Leeward Islands: a British colony, with its dependency Barbuda, until 1967, when it became a British associated state; it became independent in 1981 as part of the state of Antigua and Barbuda. Area: 279 sq. km (108 sq. miles).

Antigua and Barbuda NOUN a state in the Caribbean, comprising the islands of Antigua, Barbuda, and Redonda: gained independence in 1981: a member of the Commonwealth. Official language: English. Religion: Christian majority. Currency: East Caribbean dollar. Capital: St John's. Pop.: 71 500 (2001 est.). Area: 442 sq. km (171 sq. miles).

Antiguan (ænˈtiːgən) ADJECTIVE 1 of or relating to Antigua or its inhabitants. ♦ NOUN 2 a native or inhabitant of Antigua.

antihalation (ˌantɪhəˈleɪʃən) NOUN *Photog* **a** a process by which light, passing through the emulsion on a film or plate, is not reflected back into it but is absorbed by a layer of dye or pigment, usually on the back of the film, thus preventing halation. **b** (*as modifier*): *antihalation backing.*

antihelix (ˌæntɪˈhiːlɪks) NOUN, *plural* **-helices** (-ˈhiːlɪsiːz) *or* **-helixes.** a variant spelling of **anthelix.**

antihero (ˈæntɪˌhɪərəʊ) NOUN, *plural* **-roes.** a central character in a novel, play, etc., who lacks the traditional heroic virtues.

antihistamine (ˌæntɪˈhɪstəˌmiːn, -mɪn) NOUN any drug that neutralizes the effects of histamine, used esp in the treatment of allergies.

antihydrogen (ˈæntɪˌhaɪdrədʒən) NOUN hydrogen in which the nucleus is an antiproton with an orbiting positron.

anti-icer NOUN a device fitted to an aircraft to prevent the formation of ice. Compare **de-icer.**

anti-imperialist ADJECTIVE 1 opposed to imperialism: *anti-imperialist movements.* ♦ NOUN 2 a person who is opposed to imperialism.
▸ˌ**anti-imˈperialism** NOUN

anti-inflammatory ADJECTIVE 1 reducing inflammation. ♦ NOUN 2 any anti-inflammatory drug, such as cortisone, aspirin, or ibuprofen.

anti-inflationary ADJECTIVE of or relating to measures to counteract or combat inflation.

antiknock (ˌæntɪˈnɒk) NOUN a compound, such as lead tetraethyl, added to petrol to reduce knocking in the engine.

Anti-Lebanon NOUN a mountain range running north and south between Syria and Lebanon, east of the Lebanon Mountains. Highest peak: Mount Hermon, 2814 m (9232 ft.).

antilepton (ˌæntɪˈlɛptən) NOUN *Physics* the antiparticle of any of the leptons.

Antilles (ænˈtɪliːz) PLURAL NOUN **the.** a group of islands in the Caribbean consisting of the **Greater Antilles** and the **Lesser Antilles.**

antilock brake (ˈæntɪˌlɒk) NOUN a brake fitted to some road vehicles that prevents skidding and improves control by sensing and compensating for overbraking. Also called: **ABS brake.**

antilog (ˈæntɪˌlɒg) NOUN short for **antilogarithm.**

antilogarithm (ˌæntɪˈlɒgəˌrɪðəm) NOUN a number whose logarithm to a given base is a given number: *100 is the antilogarithm of 2 to base 10.* Often shortened to: **antilog.**
▸ˌ**antiˌlogaˈrithmic** ADJECTIVE

antilogy (ænˈtɪlədʒɪ) NOUN, *plural* **-gies.** a contradiction in terms.
▹HISTORY C17: from Greek *antilogia*

antimacassar (ˌæntɪməˈkæsə) NOUN a cloth covering the back and arms of chairs, etc., to prevent soiling or as decoration.
▹HISTORY C19: from ANTI- + MACASSAR (OIL)

antimagnetic (ˌæntɪmægˈnɛtɪk) ADJECTIVE of or constructed of a material that does not acquire permanent magnetism when exposed to a magnetic field: *an antimagnetic watch.*

antimalarial (ˌæntɪməˈlɛərɪəl) ADJECTIVE 1 effective in the treatment of malaria. ♦ NOUN 2 an antimalarial drug or agent.

antimasque (ˈæntɪˌmɑːsk) NOUN a comic or grotesque dance, presented between the acts of a masque.

antimatter (ˈæntɪˌmætə) NOUN a form of matter composed of antiparticles, such as antihydrogen, consisting of antiprotons and positrons.

antimere (ˈæntɪˌmɪə) NOUN a part or organ of a bilaterally or radially symmetrical organism that corresponds to a similar structure on the other side of the axis, such as the right or left limb of a four-legged animal. Also called: **actinomere.**
▸**antimeric** (ˌæntɪˈmɛrɪk) ADJECTIVE ▸**antimerism** (ænˈtɪməˌrɪzəm) NOUN

antimetabolite (ˌæntɪmɪˈtæbəˌlaɪt) NOUN any drug that acts by disrupting the normal growth of a cell. Sulfonamide drugs are antimetabolites and some antimetabolites are used in cancer treatment.

antimicrobial (ˈæntɪmaɪˈkrəʊbrᵊl) ADJECTIVE capable of destroying or inhibiting the growth of disease-causing microbes.

antimissile (ˌæntɪˈmɪsaɪl) ADJECTIVE 1 relating to defensive measures against missile attack: *an antimissile system.* ♦ NOUN 2 Also called: **antimissile missile.** a defensive missile used to intercept and destroy attacking missiles. Abbreviation: **AMM.**

antimonarchist (ˌæntɪˈmɒnəkɪst) ADJECTIVE 1 opposed to a monarchy. ♦ NOUN 2 a person who is opposed to a monarchy.

antimonial (ˌæntɪˈməʊnɪəl) ADJECTIVE 1 of or containing antimony. ♦ NOUN 2 a drug or agent containing antimony.

antimonic (ˌæntɪˈmɒnɪk) ADJECTIVE of or containing antimony in the pentavalent state.

antimonous (ˈæntɪmənəs) ADJECTIVE of or containing antimony in the trivalent state.

antimony (ˈæntɪmənɪ) NOUN a toxic metallic element that exists in two allotropic forms and occurs principally in stibnite. The stable form is a brittle silvery-white crystalline metal that is added to alloys to increase their strength and hardness and is used in semiconductors. Symbol: Sb; atomic no.: 51; atomic wt.: 121.757; valency: 0, –3, +3, or +5; relative density: 6.691; melting pt.: 630.76°C; boiling pt.: 1587°C.
▹HISTORY C15: from Medieval Latin *antimōnium,* of uncertain origin

antimonyl (ˈæntɪmənɪl, ænˈtɪm-) NOUN (*modifier*) of, consisting of, or containing the monovalent group SbO-: *an antimonyl group or radical.*

antimony potassium tartrate NOUN a colourless odourless poisonous crystalline salt used as a mordant for textiles and leather, as an insecticide, and as an anthelmintic. Formula: $K(SbO)C_4H_4O_6$. Also called: **tartar emetic.**

antimuon (ˌæntɪˈmjuːɒn) NOUN the antiparticle of a muon.

antimutagen (ˌæntɪˈmjuːtədʒən) NOUN any substance that acts against a mutagen.

antimycotic (ˌæntɪmaɪˈkɒtɪk) ADJECTIVE another word for **antifungal.**

antinationalist (ˌæntɪˈnæʃənəlɪst) NOUN 1 a person who is opposed to nationalism. ♦ ADJECTIVE 2 opposed to nationalism.

anti-Nazi ADJECTIVE 1 opposing any individual or group that espouses Nazi ideologies. ♦ NOUN 2 a person who is opposed to Nazism.

antineutrino (ˌæntɪnjuːˈtriːnəʊ) NOUN, *plural* **-nos.** the antiparticle of a neutrino; a particle having oppositely directed spin to a neutrino, that is, spin in the direction of its momentum.

antineutron (ˌæntɪˈnjuːtrɒn) NOUN the antiparticle of a neutron; a particle having the same mass as the neutron but a magnetic moment of opposite sign.

anting (ˈæntɪŋ) NOUN the placing or rubbing of ants by birds on their feathers. The body fluids of the ants are thought to repel parasites.

antinode (ˈæntɪˌnəʊd) NOUN *Physics* a point at

which the amplitude of one of the two kinds of displacement in a standing wave has maximum value. Generally the other kind of displacement has its minimum value at this point. See also **standing wave.** Compare **node.**
▸ **ˌantiˈnodal** ADJECTIVE

antinoise (ˈæntɪˌnɔɪz) NOUN sound generated so that it is out of phase with a noise, such as that made by an engine, in order to reduce the noise level by interference.

antinomian (ˌæntɪˈnəʊmɪən) ADJECTIVE [1] relating to the doctrine that by faith and the dispensation of grace a Christian is released from the obligation of adhering to any moral law. ◆ NOUN [2] a member of a Christian sect holding such a doctrine.
▸ **ˌantiˈnomianism** NOUN

antinomy (ænˈtɪnəmɪ) NOUN, *plural* **-mies.** [1] opposition of one law, principle, or rule to another; contradiction within a law. [2] *Philosophy* contradiction existing between two apparently indubitable propositions; paradox.
▷ HISTORY C16: from Latin *antinomia,* from Greek: conflict between laws, from ANTI- + *nomos* law
▸ **antinomic** (ˌæntɪˈnɒmɪk) ADJECTIVE ▸ **ˌantiˈnomically** ADVERB

antinovel (ˈæntɪˌnɒvᵊl) NOUN a type of prose fiction in which conventional or traditional novelistic elements are rejected. Also called: **anti-roman, nouveau roman.**

antinuclear (ˌæntɪˈnjuːklɪə) ADJECTIVE opposed to nuclear weapons.
▸ **ˌantiˈnuclearist** NOUN

antinucleon (ˌæntɪˈnjuːklɪˌɒn) NOUN an antiproton or an antineutron.

Antioch (ˈæntɪˌɒk) NOUN a city in S Turkey, on the Orantes River: ancient commercial centre and capital of Syria (300–64 B.C.); early centre of Christianity. Pop.: 137 200 (1994 est.). Arabic name: **Antakiya.** Turkish name: **Antakya.**

antioxidant (ˌæntɪˈɒksɪdənt) NOUN [1] any substance that retards deterioration by oxidation, esp of fats, oils, foods, petroleum products, or rubber. [2] *Biology* a substance, such as vitamin C, vitamin E, or beta carotene, that counteracts the damaging effects of oxidation in a living organism.

antiparallel (ˌæntɪˈpærəˌlɛl) ADJECTIVE [1] *Physics* parallel but pointing in the opposite direction. [2] *Maths* (of vectors) parallel but having opposite directions.

antiparticle (ˈæntɪˌpɑːtɪkᵊl) NOUN any of a group of elementary particles that have the same mass and spin as their corresponding particle but have opposite values for all other nonzero quantum numbers. When a particle collides with its antiparticle, mutual annihilation occurs.

antipasto (ˌæntɪˈpɑːstəʊ, -ˈpæs-) NOUN, *plural* **-tos.** a course of hors d'oeuvres in an Italian meal.
▷ HISTORY Italian: before food

antipathetic (ænˌtɪpəˈθɛtɪk, ˌæntɪpə-) *or* **antipathetical** ADJECTIVE (often foll by *to*) having or arousing a strong aversion.
▸ **ˌantipaˈthetically** ADVERB

antipathy (ænˈtɪpəθɪ) NOUN, *plural* **-thies.** [1] a feeling of intense aversion, dislike, or hostility. [2] the object of such a feeling.
▷ HISTORY C17: from Latin *antipathia,* from Greek *antipatheia,* from ANTI- + *patheia* feeling

antiperiodic (ˌæntɪˌpɪərɪˈɒdɪk) *Med* ◆ ADJECTIVE [1] *Obsolete* efficacious against recurring attacks of a disease. ◆ NOUN [2] *Obsolete* an antiperiodic drug or agent.

antiperistalsis (ˌæntɪˌpɛrɪˈstælsɪs) NOUN *Physiol* contractions of the intestine that force the contents in the opposite direction to the normal.
▸ **ˌantiˌperiˈstaltic** ADJECTIVE

antipersonnel (ˌæntɪˌpɜːsəˈnɛl) ADJECTIVE (of weapons, etc.) designed to cause casualties to personnel rather than to destroy equipment or defences. Abbreviation: **AP.**

antiperspirant (ˌæntɪˈpɜːspərənt) NOUN [1] an astringent substance applied to the skin to reduce or prevent perspiration. ◆ ADJECTIVE [2] reducing or preventing perspiration.

antiphlogistic (ˌæntɪfləˈdʒɪstɪk) ADJECTIVE [1] *Obsolete* of or relating to the prevention or alleviation of inflammation. ◆ NOUN [2] an antiphlogistic agent or drug.

antiphon (ˈæntɪfən) NOUN [1] a short passage, usually from the Bible, recited or sung as a response after certain parts of a liturgical service. [2] a psalm, hymn, etc., chanted or sung in alternate parts. [3] any response or answer.
▷ HISTORY C15: from Late Latin *antiphōna* sung responses, from Late Greek, plural of *antiphōnon* (something) responsive, from *antiphōnos,* from ANTI- + *phōnē* sound

antiphonal (ænˈtɪfənəl) ADJECTIVE [1] sung or recited in alternation. ◆ NOUN [2] another word for **antiphonary.**
▸ **anˈtiphonally** ADVERB

antiphonary (ænˈtɪfənərɪ) NOUN, *plural* **-naries.** [1] a bound collection of antiphons, esp for use in the divine office. ◆ ADJECTIVE [2] of or relating to such a book.

antiphony (ænˈtɪfənɪ) NOUN, *plural* **-nies.** [1] the antiphonal singing of a musical composition by two choirs. [2] any musical or other sound effect that answers or echoes another.

antiphrasis (ænˈtɪfrəsɪs) NOUN *Rhetoric* the use of a word in a sense opposite to its normal one, esp for ironic effect.
▷ HISTORY C16: via Late Latin from Greek, from ANTI- + *phrasis,* from *phrazein* to speak

anti-pill ADJECTIVE denoting a material that does not form pills or that resists pilling.

antipodal (ænˈtɪpədᵊl) ADJECTIVE [1] of or relating to diametrically opposite points on the earth's surface. [2] exactly or diametrically opposite.

antipode (ˈæntɪpəʊd) NOUN the exact or direct opposite.

antipodes (ænˈtɪpəˌdiːz) PLURAL NOUN [1] either or both of two points, places, or regions that are situated diametrically opposite to one another on the earth's surface, esp the country or region opposite one's own. [2] the people who live there. [3] *(often capital)* **the.** Australia and New Zealand. [4] *(sometimes functioning as singular)* the exact or direct opposite.
▷ HISTORY C16: via Late Latin from Greek, plural of *antipous* having the feet opposite, from ANTI- + *pous* foot
▸ **antipodean** (ænˌtɪpəˈdiːən) ADJECTIVE

Antipodes Islands PLURAL NOUN **the.** a group of small uninhabited islands in the South Pacific, southeast of and belonging to New Zealand. Area: 62 sq. km (24 sq. miles).

antipollution (ˌæntɪpəˈluːʃən) ADJECTIVE [1] (of measures, policies, etc.) designed to combat pollution and its causes. [2] opposed to pollution and its causes: *antipollution banners.*

antipope (ˈæntɪˌpəʊp) NOUN a rival pope elected in opposition to one who has been canonically chosen.

antiproton (ˈæntɪˌprəʊtɒn) NOUN the antiparticle of the proton; a particle having the same mass as the proton but an equal and opposite charge.

antipsychiatry (ˌæntɪsaɪˈkaɪətrɪ) NOUN an approach to mental disorders that makes use of concepts derived from existentialism, psychoanalysis, and sociological theory.

antipsychotic (ˌæntɪsaɪˈkɒtɪk) ADJECTIVE [1] preventing or treating psychosis. ◆ NOUN [2] any antipsychotic drug, such as chlorpromazine: used to treat such conditions as schizophrenia.

antipyretic (ˌæntɪpaɪˈrɛtɪk) ADJECTIVE [1] preventing or alleviating fever. ◆ NOUN [2] an antipyretic remedy or drug.
▸ **antipyresis** (ˌæntɪpaɪˈriːsɪs) NOUN

antipyrine (ˌæntɪˈpaɪrɪn, -riːn) NOUN a drug formerly used to reduce pain and fever. Formula: $C_{11}H_{12}N_2O$. Also called: **phenazine.**

antiquarian (ˌæntɪˈkwɛərɪən) ADJECTIVE [1] concerned with the study of antiquities or antiques. ◆ NOUN [2] the largest size of handmade drawing paper, 53 × 31 inches. [3] a less common name for **antiquary.**
▸ **ˌantiˈquarianism** NOUN

antiquark (ˈæntɪkwɑːk) NOUN the antiparticle of a quark.

antiquary (ˈæntɪkwərɪ) NOUN, *plural* **-quaries.** a person who collects, deals in, or studies antiques, ancient works of art, or ancient times. Also called: **antiquarian.**

antiquate (ˈæntɪˌkweɪt) VERB *(tr)* [1] to make obsolete or old-fashioned. [2] to give an old or antique appearance to.
▷ HISTORY C15: from Latin *antīquāre* to make old, from *antīquus* ancient

antiquated (ˈæntɪˌkweɪtɪd) ADJECTIVE [1] outmoded; obsolete. [2] aged; ancient.
▸ **ˈantiˌquatedness** NOUN

antique (ænˈtiːk) NOUN [1] **a** a decorative object, piece of furniture, or other work of art created in an earlier period, that is collected and valued for its beauty, workmanship, and age. **b** (*as modifier*): *an antique shop.* [2] any object made in an earlier period. [3] **the.** the style of ancient art, esp Greek or Roman art, or an example of it. ◆ ADJECTIVE [4] made in or in the style of an earlier period. [5] of or belonging to the distant past, esp of or in the style of ancient Greece or Rome. [6] *Informal* old-fashioned; out-of-date. [7] *Archaic* aged or venerable. [8] (of paper) not calendered or coated; having a rough surface. ◆ VERB [9] *(tr)* to give an antique appearance to.
▷ HISTORY C16: from Latin *antīquus* ancient, from *ante* before

antiquey (ænˈtiːkɪ) ADJECTIVE *Informal* having the appearance of an antique.

antiquities (ænˈtɪkwɪtɪz) PLURAL NOUN remains or relics, such as statues, buildings, or coins, that date from ancient times.

antiquity (ænˈtɪkwɪtɪ) NOUN, *plural* **-ties.** [1] the quality of being ancient or very old: *a vase of great antiquity.* [2] the far distant past, esp the time preceding the Middle Ages in Europe. [3] the people of ancient times collectively; the ancients.

antirachitic (ˌæntɪrəˈkɪtɪk) ADJECTIVE [1] preventing or curing rickets. ◆ NOUN [2] an antirachitic remedy or agent.

antiracism (ˌæntɪˈreɪsɪzəm) NOUN the policy of challenging racism and promoting racial tolerance.
▸ **ˌantiˈracist** NOUN, ADJECTIVE

antireligious (ˌæntɪrɪˈlɪdʒəs) ADJECTIVE opposed to religious ideas, beliefs, and organizations: *antireligious propaganda.*

Antiremonstrant (ˌæntɪrɪˈmɒnstrənt) NOUN *Dutch Reformed Church* the party that opposed the Remonstrants.

antirepublican (ˌæntɪrɪˈpʌblɪkən) ADJECTIVE [1] opposed to the principles or practice of republicanism. ◆ NOUN [2] a person who is opposed to the principles or practice of republicanism.

antiriot (ˌæntɪˈraɪət) ADJECTIVE (of police officers, equipment, measures, etc.) designed for or engaged in the control of crowds.

anti-roll bar NOUN a crosswise rubber-mounted bar in the suspension of a motor vehicle, which counteracts the movement downward on one side when cornering.

anti-roman *French* (ɑ̃tirɔmɑ̃) NOUN, *plural* **anti-romans** (ɑ̃tirɔmɑ̃). another term for **antinovel.**
▷ HISTORY literally: anti-novel

antirrhinum (ˌæntɪˈraɪnəm) NOUN any scrophulariaceous plant of the genus *Antirrhinum,* esp the snapdragon, which have two-lipped flowers of various colours.
▷ HISTORY C16: via Latin from Greek *antirrhinon,* from ANTI- (imitating) + *rhis* nose; so called from a fancied likeness to an animal's snout

antirust (ˌæntɪˈrʌst) ADJECTIVE (of a product or procedure) effective against rust.

Antisana (*Spanish* antiˈsana) NOUN a volcano in N central Ecuador, in the Andes. Height: 5756 m (18 885 ft.).

antiscientific (ˌæntɪˌsaɪənˈtɪfɪk) ADJECTIVE opposed to the principles, methods, or aims of science.

antiscorbutic (ˌæntɪskɔːˈbjuːtɪk) ADJECTIVE [1] preventing or curing scurvy. ◆ NOUN [2] an antiscorbutic remedy or agent.

anti-Semite NOUN a person who persecutes or discriminates against Jews.
▸ **ˌanti-ˈSemitism** NOUN

anti-Semitic ADJECTIVE prejudiced against or hostile to Jews.
▸ **ˌanti-Seˈmitically** ADVERB

antisepsis (ˌæntɪˈsɛpsɪs) NOUN [1] destruction of undesirable microorganisms, such as those that cause disease or putrefaction. Compare **asepsis.** [2]

the state or condition of being free from such microorganisms.

antiseptic (ˌæntɪˈsɛptɪk) ADJECTIVE [1] of, relating to, or effecting antisepsis. [2] entirely free from contamination. [3] *Informal* lacking spirit or excitement; clinical. ♦ NOUN [4] an antiseptic agent or substance.
▸ **ˌantiˈseptically** ADVERB

antiserum (ˌæntɪˈsɪərəm) NOUN, *plural* **-rums** *or* **-ra** (-rə). blood serum containing antibodies against a specific antigen, used to treat or provide immunity to a disease.

anti-site NOUN a website through which people can express their contempt for a particular person, organization, pop group, etc.

antislavery (ˌæntɪˈsleɪvərɪ) ADJECTIVE opposed to slavery, esp slavery of Blacks.

antisocial (ˌæntɪˈsəʊʃəl) ADJECTIVE [1] avoiding the company of other people; unsociable. [2] contrary or injurious to the interests of society in general.
▸ **ˌantiˈsocially** ADVERB

anti-Soviet ADJECTIVE [1] opposed to anything characteristic of or relating to the former Soviet Union and its government: *anti-Soviet propaganda.* [2] opposed to the government and policies of the former Soviet Union: *they are not pro-Nazi but anti-Soviet.*

antispasmodic (ˌæntɪspæzˈmɒdɪk) ADJECTIVE [1] preventing or arresting spasms, esp in smooth muscle. ♦ NOUN [2] an antispasmodic drug.

antistatic (ˌæntɪˈstætɪk) ADJECTIVE (of a substance, textile, etc.) retaining sufficient moisture to provide a conducting path, thus avoiding the effects of static electricity.

antistrophe (ænˈtɪstrəfɪ) NOUN [1] (in ancient Greek drama) **a** the second of two movements made by a chorus during the performance of a choral ode. **b** the second part of a choral ode sung during this movement. [2] (in classical prosody) the second of two metrical systems used alternately within a poem. ♦ See also **strophe.**
▷ HISTORY C17: via Late Latin from Greek *antistrophē* an answering turn, from ANTI- + *strophē* a turning
▸ **antistrophic** (ˌæntɪˈstrɒfɪk) ADJECTIVE
▸ **ˌantiˈstrophically** ADVERB

antisubmarine (ˌæntɪˌsʌbməˈriːn) ADJECTIVE [1] (of weapons, missiles, etc.) designed to combat or destroy submarines. [2] (of warfare, tactics, etc.) against submarines.

antisymmetric (ˌæntɪsɪˈmɛtrɪk) ADJECTIVE *Logic* (of a relation) never holding between a pair of arguments *x* and *y* when it holds between *y* and *x* except when *x* = *y*, as *"…is no younger than…"*. Compare **asymmetric, symmetric** (sense 1), **nonsymmetric.** [2] *Maths* symmetric except for a change of sign.

antitank (ˌæntɪˈtæŋk) ADJECTIVE designed to immobilize or destroy armoured vehicles: *antitank weapons.* Abbreviation: **ATK.**

antiterrorist (ˌæntɪˈtɛrərɪst) ADJECTIVE relating to measures, policies, or organizations designed to combat terrorist activity.

antitheft (ˌæntɪˈθɛft) ADJECTIVE (of a device, campaign, system, etc.) designed to prevent theft.

antithesis (ænˈtɪθɪsɪs) NOUN, *plural* **-ses** (-ˌsiːz). [1] the exact opposite. [2] contrast or opposition. [3] *Rhetoric* the juxtaposition of contrasting ideas, phrases, or words so as to produce an effect of balance, such as *my words fly up, my thoughts remain below.* [4] *Philosophy* the second stage in the **Hegelian dialectic** contradicting the **thesis** before resolution by the **synthesis.**
▷ HISTORY C15: via Latin from Greek: a setting against, from ANTI- + *tithenai* to place

antithetical (ˌæntɪˈθɛtɪkəl) *or* **antithetic** ADJECTIVE [1] of the nature of antithesis. [2] directly contrasted.

antitoxin (ˌæntɪˈtɒksɪn) NOUN [1] an antibody that neutralizes a toxin. [2] blood serum that contains a specific antibody.
▸ **ˌantiˈtoxic** ADJECTIVE

antitrades (ˈæntɪˌtreɪdz) PLURAL NOUN winds in the upper atmosphere blowing in the opposite direction from and above the trade winds.

antitragus (ænˈtɪtrəgəs) NOUN, *plural* **-gi** (-ˌdʒaɪ). a cartilaginous projection of the external ear opposite the tragus.
▷ HISTORY C19: from New Latin, from Greek *antitragos;* see ANTI-, TRAGUS

antitranspirant (ˌæntɪˈtrænspɪrənt) NOUN any substance that decreases transpiration and, usually, photosynthesis.

antitrust (ˌæntɪˈtrʌst) NOUN (*modifier*) *Chiefly US* regulating or opposing trusts, monopolies, cartels, or similar organizations, esp in order to prevent unfair competition.

antitussive (ˌæntɪˈtʌsɪv) ADJECTIVE [1] alleviating or suppressing coughing. ♦ NOUN [2] an antitussive drug.
▷ HISTORY from ANTI- + Latin *tussis* a cough

antitype (ˈæntɪˌtaɪp) NOUN [1] a person or thing that is foreshadowed or represented by a type or symbol, esp a character or event in the New Testament prefigured in the Old Testament. [2] an opposite type.
▸ **antitypic** (ˌæntɪˈtɪpɪk) *or* **ˌantiˈtypical** ADJECTIVE
▸ **ˌantiˈtypically** ADVERB

antivenin (ˌæntɪˈvɛnɪn) *or* **antivenene** (ˌæntɪvɪˈniːn) NOUN an antitoxin that counteracts a specific venom, esp snake venom.
▷ HISTORY C19: from ANTI- + VEN(OM) + -IN

antiviral (ˌæntɪˈvaɪrəl) ADJECTIVE [1] inhibiting the growth of viruses. ♦ NOUN [2] any antiviral drug: used to treat diseases caused by viruses, such as herpes infections and AIDS.

antivivisection (ˌæntɪˌvɪvɪˈsɛkʃən) ADJECTIVE opposed to the act or practice or performing experiments on living animals, involving cutting into or dissecting the body.

antiwar (ˌæntɪˈwɔː) ADJECTIVE opposed to war: *the antiwar movement.*

antiworld (ˈæntɪˌwɜːld) NOUN a hypothetical or supposed world or universe composed of antimatter.

anti-Zionist NOUN [1] a person who is opposed to Zionism. ♦ ADJECTIVE [2] opposed to Zionism: *he was anti-Zionist and not anti-Semitic.*

antler (ˈæntlə) NOUN one of a pair of bony outgrowths on the heads of male deer and some related species of either sex. The antlers are shed each year and those of some species grow more branches as the animal ages.
▷ HISTORY C14: from Old French *antoillier,* from Vulgar Latin *anteoculare* (unattested) (something) in front of the eye

antler moth NOUN a European noctuid moth, *Cerapteryx* (or *Charaeas*) *graminis,* that has white antler-like markings on the forewings and produces larvae that periodically cause great damage to pastures and grasslands.

Antlia (ˈæntlɪə) NOUN, *Latin genitive* **Antliae** (ˈæntlɪˌiː). a faint constellation in the S hemisphere close to Hydra and Vela.
▷ HISTORY C19: from Latin, from Greek: bucket

antlike (ˈæntˌlaɪk) ADJECTIVE [1] of or like an ant or ants. [2] characterized by scurrying activity or teeming restlessness.

antlion (ˈæntˌlaɪən) NOUN [1] Also called: **antlion fly.** any of various neuropterous insects of the family *Myrmeleontidae,* which typically resemble dragonflies and are most common in tropical regions. [2] Also called (US): **doodlebug.** the larva of this insect, which has very large jaws and buries itself in the sand to await its prey.

Antofagasta (ˌæntəfəˈgæstə; *Spanish* antofaˈɣasta) NOUN a port in N Chile. Pop.: 243 048 (1999 est.).

Antonine Wall (ˈæntənaɪn) NOUN a Roman frontier defence work across S Scotland, extending between the River Clyde and the Firth of Forth. It was built in 142 A.D. on the orders of Antoninus Pius (86–161 A.D.), emperor of Rome (138–161).

antonomasia (ˌæntənəˈmeɪzɪə) NOUN *Rhetoric* [1] the substitution of a title or epithet for a proper name, such as *his highness.* [2] the use of a proper name for an idea: *he is a Daniel come to judgment.*
▷ HISTORY C16: via Latin from Greek, from *antonomazein* to name differently, from *onoma* name
▸ **antonomastic** (ˌæntənəˈmæstɪk) ADJECTIVE
▸ **ˌantonoˈmastically** ADVERB

Anton Piller order (ˈæntɒn ˈpɪlə) NOUN *Law* the former name for **search order.**
▷ HISTORY C20: named after the plaintiff in a case (1976) in which such an order was made

antonym (ˈæntənɪm) NOUN a word that means the opposite of another word: *"empty" is an antonym of "full".*
▷ HISTORY C19: from Greek *antōnumia,* from ANTI- + *onoma* name
▸ **antonymous** (ænˈtɒnɪməs) ADJECTIVE

antre (ˈæntə) NOUN *Archaic* a cavern or cave.
▷ HISTORY C17: from French, from Latin *antrum,* from Greek *antron*

Antrim (ˈæntrɪm) NOUN [1] a historical county of NE Northern Ireland, famous for the Giant's Causeway on the N coast: in 1973 it was replaced for administrative purposes by the districts of Antrim, Ballymena, Ballymoney, Carrickfergus, Larne, Moyle, Newtownabbey, and parts of Belfast and Lisburn. Area: 3100 sq. km (1200 sq. miles). [2] a district of Northern Ireland, in Co. Antrim. Pop.: 48 366 (2001). Area: 415 sq. km (160 sq. miles).

antrorse (ænˈtrɔːs) ADJECTIVE *Biology* directed or pointing upwards or forwards.
▷ HISTORY C19: from New Latin *antrorsus,* from *antero-* front + *-orsus,* as in Latin *introrsus;* see INTRORSE
▸ **anˈtrorsely** ADVERB

antrum (ˈæntrəm) NOUN, *plural* **-tra** (-trə). *Anatomy* a natural cavity, hollow, or sinus, esp in a bone.
▷ HISTORY C14: from Latin: cave, from Greek *antron*
▸ **ˈantral** ADJECTIVE

Antseranana (ˌæntsɪˈrænənə) NOUN a port in N Madagascar: former French naval base. Pop.: 54 418 (1990). Former name: **Diégo-Suarez.**

antsy (ˈæntsɪ) ADJECTIVE **antsier, antsiest.** *Informal* restless, nervous, and impatient.

Antung (ˈænˈtʊŋ) NOUN a variant transliteration of the Chinese name for **Andong.**

antwackie (ˈæntwækɪ) ADJECTIVE *Northern English dialect* old-fashioned.

Antwerp (ˈæntwɜːp) NOUN [1] a province of N Belgium. Pop.: 1 643 972 (2000 est.). Area: 2859 sq. km (1104 sq. miles). [2] a port in N Belgium, capital of Antwerp province, on the River Scheldt: a major European port. Pop.: 446 525 (2000 est.). Flemish name: **Antwerpen** (ˈɑntwɛrpə). French name: **Anvers.**

Anu (ˈɑːnuː) NOUN *Babylonian myth* the sky god.

ANU ABBREVIATION FOR Australian National University.

Anubis (əˈnjuːbɪs) NOUN *Egyptian myth* a deity, a son of Osiris, who conducted the dead to judgment. He is represented as having a jackal's head and was identified by the Greeks with Hermes.

Anuradhapura (əˈnʊərədəˌpʊərə, ˌʌnʊˈrɑːdə-) NOUN a town in Sri Lanka: ancient capital of Ceylon; site of the sacred bo tree and place of pilgrimage for Buddhists. Pop.: 42 600 (1995 est.).

anuran (əˈnjʊərən) NOUN [1] any of the vertebrates of the order *Anura* (or *Salientia*), characterized by absence of a tail and very long hind legs specialized for hopping: class *Amphibia* (amphibians). The group includes the frogs and toads. ♦ ADJECTIVE [2] of, relating to, or belonging to the order *Anura.* ♦ Also: **salientian.**
▷ HISTORY C20: from New Latin *Anura,* from AN- + Greek *oura* tail

anuresis (ˌænjʊˈriːsɪs) NOUN *Pathol* inability to urinate even though urine is formed by the kidneys and retained in the urinary bladder. Compare **anuria.**
▷ HISTORY C20: New Latin, from AN- + Greek *ouresis* urination, from *ouron* urine

anuria (əˈnjʊərɪə) NOUN *Pathol* complete suppression of urine formation, often as the result of a kidney disorder. Compare **anuresis, oliguria.**
▷ HISTORY C19: from New Latin, from AN- + Greek *ouron* urine

anurous (æˈnjʊərəs) ADJECTIVE *Zoology* lacking a tail; tailless; acaudate.
▷ HISTORY C19: from AN- + Greek *oura* tail

anus (ˈeɪnəs) NOUN the excretory opening at the end of the alimentary canal. Related adjective: **anal.**
▷ HISTORY C16: from Latin

Anvers (ɑ̃vɛr) NOUN the French name for **Antwerp.**

anvil (ˈænvɪl) NOUN [1] a heavy iron or steel block on which metals are hammered during forging. [2] any part having a similar shape or function, such as the lower part of a telegraph key. [3] the fixed jaw of a measurement device against which the piece to

be measured is held. [4] *Anatomy* the nontechnical name for **incus.**
▷**HISTORY** Old English *anfealt;* related to Old High German *anafalz,* Middle Dutch *anvilte;* see ON, FELT[2]

anxiety (æŋˈzaɪɪtɪ) NOUN, *plural* **-ties.** [1] a state of uneasiness or tension caused by apprehension of possible future misfortune, danger, etc.; worry. [2] intense desire; eagerness. [3] *Psychol* a state of intense apprehension or worry often accompanied by physical symptoms such as shaking, intense feelings in the gut, etc., common in mental illness or after a very distressing experience. See also **angst.**
▷**HISTORY** C16: from Latin *anxietas;* see ANXIOUS

anxiety disorder NOUN any of various mental disorders characterized by extreme anxiety and including panic disorder, post-traumatic stress disorder, and **generalized anxiety disorder.**

anxiety neurosis NOUN a relatively mild form of mental illness characterized by extreme distress and agitation, often occurring without any obvious cause.

anxiolytic (ˌæŋksɪəʊˈlɪtɪk) NOUN [1] any of a class of drugs that reduce anxiety. ◆ ADJECTIVE [2] of or relating to this class of drugs.

anxious (ˈæŋkʃəs, ˈæŋʃəs) ADJECTIVE [1] worried and tense because of possible misfortune, danger, etc.; uneasy. [2] fraught with or causing anxiety; worrying; distressing: *an anxious time.* [3] intensely desirous; eager: *anxious for promotion.*
▷**HISTORY** C17: from Latin *anxius;* related to Latin *angere* to torment; see ANGER, ANGUISH
▸ˈ**anxiously** ADVERB ▸ˈ**anxiousness** NOUN

any (ˈɛnɪ) DETERMINER [1] **a** one, some, or several, as specified, no matter how much or many, what kind or quality, etc.: *any cheese in the cupboard is yours; you may take any clothes you like.* **b** (*as pronoun; functioning as singular or plural*): *take any you like.* [2] (*usually used with a negative*) **a** even the smallest amount or even one: *I can't stand any noise.* **b** (*as pronoun; functioning as singular or plural*): *don't give her any.* [3] whatever or whichever; no matter what or which: *any dictionary will do; any time of day.* [4] an indefinite or unlimited amount or number (esp in the phrases **any amount** or **number**): *any number of friends.* ◆ ADVERB [5] (*usually used with a negative*) **a** (foll by a comparative adjective) to even the smallest extent: *it isn't any worse now.* **b** *Not standard* at all: *he doesn't care any.*
▷**HISTORY** Old English *ǣnig;* related to Old Frisian *ēnig,* Old High German *einag,* Old Norse *einigr* anyone, Latin *ūnicus* unique; see AN[1], ONE

Anyang (ˈɑːnˈjɑːŋ) NOUN a town in E China, in Henan province: archaeological site and capital of the Shang dynasty. Pop.: 527 982 (1999 est.).

anybody (ˈɛnɪˌbɒdɪ, -bədɪ) PRONOUN [1] any person; anyone. [2] (*usually used with a negative or a question*) a person of any importance: *he isn't anybody in this town.* ◆ NOUN, *plural* **-bodies.** [3] (often preceded by *just*) any person at random; no matter who.

anyhow (ˈɛnɪˌhaʊ) ADVERB [1] in any case; at any rate. [2] in any manner or by any means whatever. [3] in a haphazard manner; carelessly.

any more *or esp US* **anymore** (ˌɛnɪˈmɔː) ADVERB any longer; still; now or from now on; nowadays: *he does not work here any more.*

anyone (ˈɛnɪˌwʌn, -wən) PRONOUN [1] any person; anybody. [2] (*used with a negative or a question*) a person of any importance: *is he anyone in this town?* [3] (often preceded by *just*) any person at random; no matter who.

anyplace (ˈɛnɪˌpleɪs) ADVERB *US and Canadian informal* in, at, or to any unspecified place.

anyroad (ˈɛnɪˌrəʊd) ADVERB a northern English dialect word for **anyway.**

anything (ˈɛnɪˌθɪŋ) PRONOUN [1] any object, event, action, etc., whatever: *anything might happen.* ◆ NOUN [2] a thing of any kind: *have you anything to declare?* ◆ ADVERB [3] in any way: *he wasn't anything like his father.* [4] **anything but.** by no means; not in the least: *she was anything but happy.* [5] **like anything.** (intensifier; usually euphemistic): *he ran like anything.*

anyway (ˈɛnɪˌweɪ) ADVERB [1] in any case; at any rate; nevertheless; anyhow. [2] in a careless or haphazard manner. [3] Usually **any way.** in any manner; by any means.

anyways (ˈɛnɪˌweɪz) ADVERB *US and Canadian* a nonstandard word for **anyway.**

anywhere (ˈɛnɪˌwɛə) ADVERB [1] in, at, or to any place. [2] **get anywhere.** to be successful: *it took three years before he got anywhere.* [3] **anywhere from.** any quantity, time, degree, etc., above a specified limit: *he could be anywhere from 40 to 50 years old.*

anywheres (ˈɛnɪˌwɛəz) ADVERB *US* a nonstandard word for **anywhere.**

anywise (ˈɛnɪˌwaɪz) ADVERB *Chiefly US* in any way or manner; at all.

ANZ ABBREVIATION FOR Australian and New Zealand Banking Group.

ANZAAS (ˈænzəs, -zæs) NOUN ACRONYM FOR Australian and New Zealand Association for the Advancement of Science.

Anzac (ˈænzæk) NOUN [1] (in World War I) a soldier serving with the Australian and New Zealand Army Corps. [2] (now) any Australian or New Zealand soldier. [3] the Anzac landing at Gallipoli in 1915.

Anzac Day NOUN 25 April, a public holiday in Australia and New Zealand commemorating the Anzac landing at Gallipoli in 1915.

Anzio (ˈænzɪˌəʊ; *Italian* ˈantsjo) NOUN a port and resort on the W coast of Italy: site of Allied landings in World War II. Pop.: 32 383 (1991 est.).

ANZUS (ˈænzəs) NOUN ACRONYM FOR Australia, New Zealand, and the United States, with reference to the security alliance between them.

ao THE INTERNET DOMAIN NAME FOR Angola.

AO ABBREVIATION FOR Officer of the Order of Australia.

A/O *or* **a/o** *Accounting, banking* ABBREVIATION FOR account of.

AOB *or* **a.o.b.** ABBREVIATION FOR any other business.

AOC ABBREVIATION FOR appellation d'origine contrôlée. See **AC** (sense 6).

AOCB ABBREVIATION FOR any other competent business.

AOH ABBREVIATION FOR Ancient Order of Hibernians: an Irish Catholic nationalist association founded in the 19th century; an important political force up to the founding of the Irish Free State (1922).

A-OK *or* **A-okay** ADJECTIVE *Informal, chiefly US* in perfect working order; excellent.
▷**HISTORY** C20: from *a(ll systems) OK*

AONB (in England, Wales, and Northern Ireland) ABBREVIATION FOR Area of Outstanding Natural Beauty: an area designated by the appropriate government bodies as requiring protection to conserve and enhance its natural beauty.

AOR *Music* ◆ ABBREVIATION FOR: [1] album-oriented rock. [2] adult-oriented rock. [3] *US* album-oriented radio.

Aorangi-Mount Cook (ˌeɪəʊˈræŋɪ) NOUN the official name for Mount **Cook.**

aorist (ˈeɪərɪst, ˈɛərɪst) NOUN *Grammar* a tense of the verb in classical Greek and in certain other inflected languages, indicating past action without reference to whether the action involved was momentary or continuous. Compare **perfect** (sense 8), **imperfect** (sense 4).
▷**HISTORY** C16: from Greek *aoristos* not limited, from A-[1] + *horistos* restricted, from *horizein* to define
▸ˌ**aoˈristic** ADJECTIVE ▸ˌ**aoˈristically** ADVERB

aorta (eɪˈɔːtə) NOUN, *plural* **-tas** *or* **-tae** (-tiː). the main vessel in the arterial network, which conveys oxygen-rich blood from the heart to all parts of the body except the lungs.
▷**HISTORY** C16: from New Latin, from Greek *aortē,* literally: something lifted, from *aeirein* to raise
▸**aˈortic** *or* **aˈortal** ADJECTIVE

aortitis (ˌeɪɔːˈtaɪtɪs) NOUN inflammation of the aorta.

Aosta (*Italian* aˈɔsta) NOUN a town in NW Italy, capital of Valle d'Aosta region: Roman remains. Pop.: 36 339 (1990).

Aotearoa (ˈæɒˌtɪəˌroːə) NOUN the Maori name for **New Zealand.**
▷**HISTORY** from Maori *ao tea roa* Land of the Long White Cloud

aoudad (ˈɑːʊˌdæd) NOUN a wild mountain sheep, *Ammotragus lervia,* of N Africa, having horns curved in a semicircle and long hair covering the neck and forelegs. Also called: **Barbary sheep.**
▷**HISTORY** from French, from Berber *audad*

ap (æp) son of: occurring as part of some surnames of Welsh origin: *ap Thomas.*
▷**HISTORY** from Welsh *mab* son

AP ABBREVIATION FOR: [1] Air Police. [2] Associated Press.

a.p. *Obsolete* (in prescriptions, etc.) ante prandium.
▷**HISTORY** Latin: before a meal

ap- PREFIX a variant of **apo-**: *aphelion.*

apace (əˈpeɪs) ADVERB quickly; rapidly.
▷**HISTORY** C14: probably from Old French *à pas,* at a (good) pace

apache (əˈpɑːʃ, -ˈpæʃ; *French* apaʃ) NOUN a Parisian gangster or ruffian.
▷**HISTORY** from French: APACHE

Apache (əˈpætʃɪ) NOUN [1] (*plural* **Apaches** *or* **Apache**) a member of a North American Indian people, formerly nomadic and warlike, inhabiting the southwestern US and N Mexico. [2] the language of this people, belonging to the Athapascan group of the Na-Dene phylum.
▷**HISTORY** from Mexican Spanish, probably from Zuñi *Apachu,* literally: enemy

apache dance NOUN a fast violent dance in French vaudeville, supposedly between a Parisian gangster and his girl.

apanage (ˈæpənɪdʒ) NOUN a variant spelling of **appanage.**

aparejo *Spanish* (apaˈrexo) NOUN, *plural* ***-jos*** (-xos). *Southwestern US* a kind of packsaddle made of stuffed leather cushions.
▷**HISTORY** American Spanish: equipment, from *aparejar* to make ready; see APPAREL

apart (əˈpɑːt) ADJECTIVE (*postpositive*), ADVERB [1] to pieces or in pieces: *he had the television apart on the floor.* [2] placed or kept separately or to one side for a particular purpose, reason, etc.; aside (esp in the phrases **set** *or* **put apart**). [3] separate in time, place, or position; at a distance: *he stood apart from the group; two points three feet apart.* [4] not being taken into account; aside: *these difficulties apart, the project ran smoothly.* [5] individual; distinct; separate: *a race apart.* [6] separately or independently in use, thought, or function: *considered apart, his reasoning was faulty.* [7] **apart from.** (*preposition*) besides; other than. ◆ See also **take apart, tell apart.**
▷**HISTORY** C14: from Old French *a part* at (the) side

apartheid (əˈpɑːthaɪt, -heɪt) NOUN (in South Africa) the official government policy of racial segregation; officially renounced in 1992.
▷**HISTORY** C20: Afrikaans, from *apart* APART + *-heid* -HOOD

apartment (əˈpɑːtmənt) NOUN [1] (*often plural*) any room in a building, usually one of several forming a suite, esp one that is spacious and well furnished and used as living accommodation, offices, etc. [2] **a** another name (esp US and Canadian) for **flat**[2] (sense 1). **b** (*as modifier*): *apartment building; apartment house.*
▷**HISTORY** C17: from French *appartement,* from Italian *appartamento,* from *appartare* to set on one side, separate

apatetic (ˌæpəˈtɛtɪk) ADJECTIVE of or relating to coloration that disguises and protects an animal.
▷**HISTORY** C19: from Greek *apatētikos* deceitful, from *apateuein* to deceive

apathetic (ˌæpəˈθɛtɪk) ADJECTIVE having or showing little or no emotion; indifferent.
▷**HISTORY** C18: from APATHY + PATHETIC
▸ˌ**apaˈthetically** ADVERB

apathy (ˈæpəθɪ) NOUN [1] absence of interest in or enthusiasm for things generally considered interesting or moving. [2] absence of emotion.
▷**HISTORY** C17: from Latin, from Greek *apatheia,* from *apathēs* without feeling, from A-[1] + *pathos* feeling

apatite (ˈæpəˌtaɪt) NOUN a pale green to purple mineral, found in igneous rocks and metamorphosed limestones. It is used in the manufacture of phosphorus, phosphates, and fertilizers. Composition: calcium fluorophosphate or calcium chlorophosphate. General formula: $Ca_5(PO_4,CO_3)_3(F,OH,Cl)$. Crystal structure: hexagonal.
▷**HISTORY** C19: from German *Apatit,* from Greek

apatē deceit; from its misleading similarity to other minerals

APB (in the US and Canada) ABBREVIATION FOR all-points bulletin.

APC NOUN [1] acetylsalicylic acid, phenacetin, and caffeine; the mixture formerly used in headache and cold tablets. [2] *Austral slang* a quick wash.
▷HISTORY for sense 2: abbreviation for *armpits and crotch*

ape (eɪp) NOUN [1] any of various primates, esp those of the family *Pongidae* (see **anthropoid ape**), in which the tail is very short or absent. See also **great ape.** [2] (*not in technical use*) any monkey. [3] an imitator; mimic. [4] *US informal* a coarse, clumsy, or rude person. ◆ VERB [5] (*tr*) to imitate.
▷HISTORY Old English *apa;* related to Old Saxon *ape,* Old Norse *api,* Old High German *affo*
▸**'ape,like** ADJECTIVE

apeak (ə'piːk) ADVERB, ADJECTIVE *Nautical* in a vertical or almost vertical position: *with the oars apeak.*

APEC ('eɪpɛk) NOUN ACRONYM FOR Asia-Pacific Economic Cooperation.

Apeldoorn ('æpᵊl,dɔːn; *Dutch* 'aːpəldoːrn) NOUN a town in the Netherlands, in central Gelderland province: nearby is the summer residence of the Dutch royal family. Pop.: 152 860 (1999 est.).

apeman ('eɪp,mæn) NOUN, *plural* **-men.** any of various extinct apelike primates thought to have been the forerunners, or closely related to the forerunners, of modern man.

Apennines ('æpə,naɪnz) PLURAL NOUN [1] a mountain range in Italy, extending over 1250 km (800 miles) from the northwest to the southernmost tip of the peninsula. Highest peak: Monte Corno, 2912 m (9554 ft.). [2] a mountain range lying in the N quadrants of the moon, extending over 950 km along the SE border of the Mare Imbrium and rising to 6200 m.

aperçu *French* (apɛrsy) NOUN [1] an outline; summary. [2] an insight.
▷HISTORY from *apercevoir* to PERCEIVE

aperient (ə'pɪərɪənt) *Med* ◆ ADJECTIVE [1] laxative. ◆ NOUN [2] a mild laxative.
▷HISTORY C17: from Latin *aperīre* to open

aperiodic (,eɪpɪərɪ'ɒdɪk) ADJECTIVE [1] not periodic; not occurring at regular intervals. [2] *Physics* **a** (of a system or instrument) being damped sufficiently to reach equilibrium without oscillation. **b** (of an oscillation or vibration) not having a regular period. **c** (of an electrical circuit) not having a measurable resonant frequency.
▸**,aperi'odically** ADVERB ▸**aperiodicity** (,eɪpɪərɪə'dɪsɪtɪ) NOUN

apéritif (ɑː,pɛrɪ'tiːf, ə,pɛr-) NOUN an alcoholic drink, esp a wine, drunk before a meal to whet the appetite.
▷HISTORY C19: from French, from Medieval Latin *aperitīvus,* from Latin *aperīre* to open

aperture ('æpətʃə) NOUN [1] a hole, gap, crack, slit, or other opening. [2] *Physics* **a** a usually circular and often variable opening in an optical instrument or device that controls the quantity of radiation entering or leaving it. **b** the diameter of such an opening. See also **relative aperture.**
▷HISTORY C15: from Late Latin *apertūra* opening, from Latin *aperīre* to open

aperture priority NOUN *Photog* an automatic exposure system in which the photographer selects the aperture and the camera then automatically sets the correct shutter speed. Compare **shutter priority.**

aperture synthesis NOUN an array of radio telescopes used in radio astronomy to simulate a single large-aperture telescope. Some such instruments use movable dishes while others use fixed dishes.

apery ('eɪpərɪ) NOUN, *plural* **-eries.** imitative behaviour; mimicry.

apetalous (eɪ'pɛtələs) ADJECTIVE (of flowering plants) having no petals.
▷HISTORY C18: from New Latin *apetalus,* see A-[1], PETAL
▸**a'petaly** NOUN

apex ('eɪpɛks) NOUN, *plural* **apexes** *or* **apices** ('æpɪ,siːz, 'eɪ-). [1] the highest point; vertex. [2] the pointed end or tip of something. [3] a pinnacle or high point, as of a career, etc. [4] Also called: **solar apex.** *Astronomy* the point on the celestial sphere, lying in the constellation Hercules, towards which the sun appears to move at a velocity of 20 kilometres per second relative to the nearest stars.
▷HISTORY C17: from Latin: point

APEX ('eɪpɛks) NOUN ACRONYM FOR: [1] Advance Purchase Excursion: a reduced airline or long-distance rail fare that must be paid a specified number of days in advance. [2] (in Britain) Association of Professional, Executive, Clerical, and Computer Staff.

Apex Club NOUN (in Australia) an association of business and professional men founded to promote community welfare.
▸**Apexian** (eɪ'pɛksɪən) ADJECTIVE, NOUN

apgar score *or* **rating** ('æpgɑː) NOUN a system for determining the condition of an infant at birth by allotting a maximum of 2 points to each of the following: heart rate, breathing effort, muscle tone, response to stimulation, and colour.
▷HISTORY C20: named after V. *Apgar* (1909–74), US anaesthetist

aphaeresis *or* **apheresis** (ə'fɪərɪsɪs) NOUN the omission of a letter or syllable at the beginning of a word.
▷HISTORY C17: via Late Latin from Greek, from *aphairein* to remove
▸**aphaeretic** *or* **apheretic** (,æfə'rɛtɪk) ADJECTIVE

aphagia (ə'feɪdʒɪə) NOUN *Pathol* refusal or inability to swallow.
▷HISTORY C20: from A-[1] + Greek *aphagein* to consume

aphakia (ə'feɪkɪə) NOUN absence of the lens of an eye, congenital or otherwise.
▷HISTORY from A-[1] + Greek *phakos* lentil + -IA

aphanite ('æfə,naɪt) NOUN any fine-grained rock, such as a basalt, containing minerals that cannot be distinguished with the naked eye.
▷HISTORY C19: from Greek *aphanēs* invisible

aphasia (ə'feɪzɪə) NOUN a disorder of the central nervous system characterized by partial or total loss of the ability to communicate, esp in speech or writing. Compare **alexia.**
▷HISTORY C19: via New Latin from Greek, from A-[1] + *-phasia,* from *phanai* to speak
▸**a'phasi,ac** *or* **a'phasic** ADJECTIVE, NOUN

aphelandra (,æfə'lændrə) NOUN any shrub of the evergreen genus *Aphelandra,* originally from tropical America, widely grown as a house plant for its variegated shiny leaves and brightly coloured flowers: family *Acanthaceae.*
▷HISTORY from Greek *aphelēs* simple + *andros,* genitive of *anēr* man, male, because the anthers are single celled

aphelion (æp'hiːlɪən, ə'fiː-) NOUN, *plural* **-lia** (-lɪə). the point in its orbit when a planet or comet is at its greatest distance from the sun. Compare **perihelion.**
▷HISTORY C17: from New Latin *aphēlium* (with pseudo-Greek ending *-ion*) from AP- + Greek *hēlios* sun
▸**ap'helian** ADJECTIVE

apheliotropic (æp,hiːlɪə'trɒpɪk, ə,fiː-) ADJECTIVE *Biology* growing in a direction away from the sunlight.
▷HISTORY C19: see APO-, HELIOTROPIC
▸**apheliotropism** (æp,hiːlɪ'ɒtrə,pɪzəm, ə,fiː-) NOUN

aphesis ('æfɪsɪs) NOUN the gradual disappearance of an unstressed vowel at the beginning of a word, as in *squire* from *esquire.*
▷HISTORY C19: from Greek, from *aphienai* to set free, send away
▸**aphetic** (ə'fɛtɪk) ADJECTIVE ▸**a'phetically** ADVERB

aphid ('eɪfɪd) NOUN any of the small homopterous insects of the family *Aphididae,* which feed by sucking the juices from plants. Also called: **plant louse.** See also **greenfly, blackfly.**
▷HISTORY C19: back formation from *aphides,* plural of APHIS
▸**aphidian** (ə'fɪdɪən) ADJECTIVE, NOUN ▸**a'phidious** ADJECTIVE

aphis ('eɪfɪs) NOUN, *plural* **aphides** ('eɪfɪ,diːz). [1] any of various aphids constituting the genus *Aphis,* such as the blackfly. [2] any other aphid.
▷HISTORY C18: from New Latin (coined by Linnaeus for obscure reasons)

aphonia (ə'fəʊnɪə) *or* **aphony** ('æfənɪ) NOUN loss of the voice caused by damage to the vocal tract.
▷HISTORY C18: via New Latin from Greek, from A-[1] + *phōnē* sound, voice

aphonic (ə'fɒnɪk) ADJECTIVE [1] affected with aphonia. [2] *Phonetics* **a** not representing a spoken sound, as *k* in *know.* **b** voiceless or devoiced.

aphorism ('æfə,rɪzəm) NOUN a short pithy saying expressing a general truth; maxim.
▷HISTORY C16: from Late Latin *aphorismus,* from Greek *aphorismos* definition, from *aphorizein* to define, set limits to, from *horos* boundary
▸**'aphorist** NOUN

aphoristic (,æfə'rɪstɪk) ADJECTIVE [1] of, relating to, or resembling an aphorism. [2] tending to write or speak in aphorisms.

aphorize *or* **aphorise** ('æfə,raɪz) VERB (*intr*) to write or speak in aphorisms.

aphotic (ə'fɒtɪk) ADJECTIVE [1] characterized by or growing in the absence of light: *an aphotic plant.* [2] of or relating to the zone of an ocean below that to which sunlight can penetrate, usually about 90m (300 ft.). This is the lowest level at which photosynthesis can take place.
▷HISTORY C20: from A-[1] + *-photic,* from Greek *phōs* light

aphrodisiac (,æfrə'dɪzɪæk) NOUN [1] a drug, food, etc., that excites sexual desire. ◆ ADJECTIVE [2] exciting or heightening sexual desire.
▷HISTORY C18: from Greek *aphrodisiakos,* from *aphrodisios* belonging to APHRODITE

Aphrodite (,æfrə'daɪtɪ) NOUN *Greek myth* the goddess of love and beauty, daughter of Zeus. Roman counterpart: **Venus.** Also called: **Cytherea.**

aphtha ('æfθə) NOUN, *plural* **-thae** (-θiː). [1] a small ulceration on a mucous membrane, as in thrush, caused by a fungal infection. [2] *Vet science* another name for **foot and mouth disease.**
▷HISTORY C17: via Latin from Greek: mouth-sore, thrush
▸**'aphthous** ADJECTIVE

aphyllous (ə'fɪləs) ADJECTIVE (of plants) having no leaves.
▷HISTORY C19: from New Latin *aphyllus,* from Greek *aphullos,* from A-[1] + *phullon* leaf
▸**a'phylly** NOUN

Apia (æ'pɪə, 'æpɪə) NOUN the capital of (Western) Samoa: a port on the N coast of Upolu. Pop.: 38 000 (1999 est.).

apian ('eɪpɪən) ADJECTIVE of, relating to, or resembling bees.
▷HISTORY C19: from Latin *apiānus,* from *apis* bee

apiarian (,eɪpɪ'ɛərɪən) ADJECTIVE of or relating to the breeding and care of bees.

apiarist ('eɪpɪərɪst) NOUN a person who studies or keeps bees.

apiary ('eɪpɪərɪ) NOUN, *plural* **-aries.** a place where bees are kept, usually in beehives.
▷HISTORY C17: from Latin *apiārium* from *apis* bee

apical ('æpɪkᵊl, 'eɪ-) ADJECTIVE [1] of, at, or being the apex. [2] of or denoting a consonant articulated with the tip of the tongue, such as (t) or (d).
▷HISTORY C19: from New Latin *apicālis,* from Latin: APEX
▸**'apically** ADVERB

apices ('æpɪ,siːz, 'eɪ-) NOUN a plural of **apex.**

apiculate (ə'pɪkjʊlɪt, -,leɪt) ADJECTIVE (of leaves) ending in a short sharp point.
▷HISTORY C19: from New Latin *apiculātus,* from *apiculus* a short point, from APEX

apiculture ('eɪpɪ,kʌltʃə) NOUN the breeding and care of bees.
▷HISTORY C19: from Latin *apis* bee + CULTURE
▸**,api'cultural** ADJECTIVE ▸**,api'culturist** NOUN

apiece (ə'piːs) ADVERB (*postpositive*) for, to, or from each one: *they were given two apples apiece.*

à pied *French* (a pje) ADVERB, ADJECTIVE (*postpositive*) on foot.

Apiezon (,æpɪ'eɪzɒn) ADJECTIVE *Trademark* designating any of a number of hydrocarbon oils, greases, or waxes, characterized by a low vapour pressure and used in vacuum equipment.

API gravity scale NOUN the American Petroleum Institute gravity scale: a universally accepted scale of the relative density of fluids that is used in fuel technology and is measured in degrees API. One degree API is equal to (141.5/*d*)–131.5, where *d* = relative density at 288.7K. See also **Baumé scale.**

Apis ('ɑːpɪs) NOUN (in ancient Egypt) a sacred bull worshipped at Memphis.

apish ('eɪpɪʃ) ADJECTIVE 1 stupid; foolish. 2 resembling an ape. 3 slavishly imitative.
▸**'apishly** ADVERB ▸**'apishness** NOUN

apivorous (eɪ'pɪvərəs) ADJECTIVE eating bees: *apivorous birds.*
▷HISTORY C19: from Latin *apis* bee + -VOROUS

aplacental (ˌeɪplə'sentᵊl, ˌæplə-) ADJECTIVE (of monotremes and marsupials) having no placenta.

aplanatic (ˌæplə'nætɪk) ADJECTIVE (of a lens or mirror) free from spherical aberration.
▷HISTORY C18: from Greek *aplanētos* prevented from wandering, from A-[1] + *planētos,* from *planaein* to wander
▸**ˌapla'natically** ADVERB

aplanetic (ˌæplə'nɛtɪk) ADJECTIVE (esp of some algal and fungal spores) nonmotile or lacking a motile stage.
▷HISTORY variant of APLANATIC

aplanospore (ə'pleɪnəʊˌspɔː) NOUN a nonmotile asexual spore produced by certain algae and fungi.
▷HISTORY C20: from A-[1] + Greek *planos* wandering + SPORE

aplasia (ə'pleɪzɪə) NOUN *Pathol* congenital absence or abnormal development of an organ or part.
▷HISTORY C19: New Latin, from A-[1] + *-plasia,* from Greek *plassein* to form

aplastic (eɪ'plæstɪk) ADJECTIVE 1 relating to or characterized by aplasia. 2 failing to develop into new tissue; defective in the regeneration of tissue, as of blood cells: *aplastic anaemia.*

aplenty (ə'plɛntɪ) ADJECTIVE (*postpositive*), ADVERB in plenty.

aplite ('æplaɪt) *or* **haplite** NOUN a light-coloured fine-grained acid igneous rock with a sugary texture, consisting of quartz and feldspars.
▷HISTORY C19: from German *Aplit,* from Greek *haploos* simple + -ITE[1]
▸**aplitic** (æp'lɪtɪk) *or* **hap'litic** ADJECTIVE

aplomb (ə'plɒm) NOUN equanimity, self-confidence, or self-possession.
▷HISTORY C18: from French: rectitude, uprightness, from *à plomb* according to the plumb line, vertically

apneusis (æp'nuːsɪs) NOUN *Pathol* protracted gasping inhalation followed by short inefficient exhalation, which can cause asphyxia.
▷HISTORY from A-[1] + Greek *pnein* to breathe

apneustic (æp'nuːstɪk) ADJECTIVE 1 of or relating to apneusis. 2 (of certain animals) having no specialized organs for respiration.

apnoea *or US* **apnea** (æp'nɪə) NOUN a temporary inability to breathe.
▷HISTORY C18: from New Latin, from Greek *apnoia,* from A-[1] + *pnein* to breathe

Apo ('ɑːpəʊ) NOUN the highest mountain in the Philippines, on SE Mindanao: active volcano with three peaks. Height: 2954 m (9690 ft.).

apo- *or* **ap-** PREFIX 1 away from; off: *apogee.* 2 indicating separation of: *apocarpous.* 3 indicating a lack or absence of: *apogamy.* 4 indicating derivation from or relationship to: *apomorphine.*
▷HISTORY from Greek *apo* away, off

Apoc. ABBREVIATION FOR: 1 Apocalypse. 2 Apocrypha or Apocryphal.

apocalypse (ə'pɒkəlɪps) NOUN 1 a prophetic disclosure or revelation. 2 an event of great importance, violence, etc., like the events described in the Apocalypse.
▷HISTORY C13: from Late Latin *apocalypsis,* from Greek *apokalupsis,* from *apokaluptein* to disclose, from APO- + *kaluptein* to hide

Apocalypse (ə'pɒkəlɪps) NOUN *Bible* (in the Vulgate and Douay versions of the Bible) the Book of Revelation.

apocalyptic (əˌpɒkə'lɪptɪk) ADJECTIVE 1 outstanding in revelation, prophecy, or significance. 2 of or like an apocalypse.
▸**aˌpoca'lyptically** ADVERB

apocarp ('æpəˌkɑːp) NOUN an apocarpous gynoecium or fruit.

apocarpous (ˌæpə'kɑːpəs) ADJECTIVE (of the ovaries of flowering plants such as the buttercup) consisting of separate carpels. Compare **syncarpous.**

apochromat (ˌæpə'krəʊmæt) *or* **apochromatic lens** NOUN a lens, consisting of three or more elements of different types of glass, that is designed to bring light of three colours to the same focal point, thus reducing its chromatic aberration. Compare **achromat.**

apochromatic (ˌæpəkrə'mætɪk) ADJECTIVE (of a lens) almost free from spherical and chromatic aberration.
▸**apochromatism** (ˌæpə'krəʊməˌtɪzəm) NOUN

apocopate (ə'pɒkəˌpeɪt) VERB (*tr*) to omit the final sound or sounds of (a word).
▸**aˌpoco'pation** NOUN

apocope (ə'pɒkəpɪ) NOUN omission of the final sound or sounds of a word.
▷HISTORY C16: via Late Latin from Greek *apokopē,* from *apokoptein* to cut off

apocrine ('æpəkraɪn, -krɪn) ADJECTIVE denoting a type of glandular secretion in which part of the secreting cell is lost with the secretion, as in mammary glands. Compare **merocrine, holocrine.**
▷HISTORY C20: from APO- + *-crine,* from Greek *krinein* to separate

Apocrypha (ə'pɒkrɪfə) NOUN **the.** (*functioning as singular or plural*) 1 the 14 books included as an appendix to the Old Testament in the Septuagint and the Vulgate but not included in the Hebrew canon. They are not printed in Protestant versions of the Bible. 2 *RC Church* another name for the **Pseudepigrapha.**
▷HISTORY C14: via Late Latin *apocrypha* (*scripta*) hidden (writings), from Greek, from *apokruptein* to hide away

apocryphal (ə'pɒkrɪfəl) ADJECTIVE 1 of questionable authenticity. 2 (*sometimes capital*) of or like the Apocrypha. 3 untrue; counterfeit.
▸**a'pocryphally** ADVERB

Apocryphal Gospels PLURAL NOUN accounts of Christ's life that are not recognized as part of the New Testament.

apocynaceous (əˌpɒsɪ'neɪʃəs) ADJECTIVE of, relating to, or belonging to the *Apocynaceae,* a family of mostly tropical flowering plants with latex in their stems, including the dogbane, periwinkle, oleander, and some lianas.
▷HISTORY C19: from New Latin *Apocynum* type genus, from Latin: dogbane, from Greek *apokunon,* from *kuōn* dog

apocynthion (ˌæpə'sɪnθɪən) NOUN the point at which a spacecraft in lunar orbit is farthest from the moon. Compare **apolune, pericynthion.**
▷HISTORY C20: from APO- (away) + *cynthion,* from Latin *Cynthia* goddess of the moon

apodal ('æpədᵊl) *or* **apodous** ADJECTIVE (of snakes, eels, etc.) without feet; having no obvious hind limbs or pelvic fins.
▷HISTORY C18: from Greek *apous* from A-[1] + *pous* foot

apodeictic (ˌæpə'daɪktɪk) *or* **apodictic** (ˌæpə'dɪktɪk) ADJECTIVE 1 unquestionably true by virtue of demonstration. 2 *Logic, archaic* **a** necessarily true. **b** asserting that a property holds necessarily. ◆ Compare **problematic** (sense 2), **assertoric.**
▷HISTORY C17: from Latin *apodīcticus,* from Greek *apodeiktikos* clearly demonstrating, from *apodeiknunai* to demonstrate
▸**ˌapo'deictically** *or* **ˌapo'dictically** ADVERB

apodosis (ə'pɒdəsɪs) NOUN, *plural* **-ses** (-ˌsiːz). *Logic, grammar* the consequent of a conditional statement, as *the game will be cancelled* in *if it rains the game will be cancelled.* Compare **protasis.**
▷HISTORY C17: via Late Latin from Greek: a returning or answering (clause), from *apodidonai* to give back

apoenzyme (ˌæpəʊ'ɛnzaɪm) NOUN a protein component that together with a coenzyme forms an enzyme.

apogamy (ə'pɒgəmɪ) NOUN 1 a type of reproduction, occurring in some ferns, in which the sporophyte develops from the gametophyte without fusion of gametes. 2 the development of a diploid cell in the embryo sac of flowering plants into an embryo without being fertilized.
▸**apogamic** (ˌæpə'gæmɪk) ADJECTIVE ▸**a'pogamous** ADJECTIVE

apogee ('æpəˌdʒiː) NOUN 1 the point in its orbit around the earth when the moon or an artificial satellite is at its greatest distance from the earth. Compare **perigee.** 2 the highest point.
▷HISTORY C17: from New Latin *apogaeum* (influenced by French *apogée*), from Greek *apogaion,* from *apogaios* away from the earth, from APO- + *gaia* earth
▸**ˌapo'gean** ADJECTIVE

apogeotropism (ˌæpədʒɪ'ɒtrəˌpɪzəm) NOUN negative geotropism, as shown by plant stems.
▷HISTORY C19: from Greek *apogaios* away from the earth + *tropos* a turn
▸**apogeotropic** (ˌæpəˌdʒɪə'trɒpɪk) ADJECTIVE

apolitical (ˌeɪpə'lɪtɪkᵊl) ADJECTIVE politically neutral; without political attitudes, content, or bias.

Apollinaris (əˌpɒlɪ'nɛərɪs) NOUN an effervescent mineral water.
▷HISTORY C19: named after *Apollinarisburg,* near Bonn, Germany

apollo[1] (ə'pɒləʊ) NOUN, *plural* **-los.** a strikingly handsome youth.

apollo[2] (ə'pɒləʊ) NOUN, *plural* **-los.** a handsome Eurasian mountain butterfly, *Parnassius apollo,* with palish wings and prominent red ocelli.

Apollo[1] (ə'pɒləʊ) NOUN *Classical myth* the god of light, poetry, music, healing, and prophecy: son of Zeus and Leto.

Apollo[2] (ə'pɒləʊ) NOUN any of a series of manned US spacecraft designed to explore the moon and surrounding space. **Apollo 11** made the first moon landing in July 1969.

Apollonian (ˌæpə'ləʊnɪən) ADJECTIVE 1 of or relating to Apollo or the cult of Apollo. 2 (*sometimes not capital*) (in the philosophy of Nietzsche) denoting or relating to the set of static qualities that encompass form, reason, harmony, sobriety, etc. 3 (*often not capital*) harmonious; serene; ordered. ◆ Compare **Dionysian.**

Apollyon (ə'pɒljən) NOUN *New Testament* the destroyer, a name given to the Devil (Revelation 9:11).
▷HISTORY C14: via Late Latin from Greek, from *apollunai* to destroy totally

apologetic (əˌpɒlə'dʒɛtɪk) ADJECTIVE 1 expressing or anxious to make apology; contrite. 2 protecting or defending in speech or writing.
▸**aˌpolo'getically** ADVERB

apologetics (əˌpɒlə'dʒɛtɪks) NOUN (*functioning as singular*) 1 the branch of theology concerned with the defence and rational justification of Christianity. 2 a defensive method of argument.

apologia (ˌæpə'ləʊdʒɪə) NOUN a formal written defence of a cause or one's beliefs or conduct.

apologist (ə'pɒlədʒɪst) NOUN a person who offers a defence by argument.

apologize *or* **apologise** (ə'pɒləˌdʒaɪz) VERB (*intr*) 1 to express or make an apology; acknowledge failings or faults. 2 to make a formal defence in speech or writing.
▸**a'poloˌgizer** *or* **a'poloˌgiser** NOUN

apologue ('æpəˌlɒg) NOUN an allegory or moral fable.
▷HISTORY C17: from Latin, from Greek *apologos*

apology (ə'pɒlədʒɪ) NOUN, *plural* **-gies.** 1 a verbal or written expression of regret or contrition for a fault or failing. 2 a poor substitute or offering. 3 another word for **apologia.**
▷HISTORY C16: from Old French *apologie,* from Late Latin *apologia,* from Greek: a verbal defence, from APO- + *logos* speech

apolune ('æpəˌluːn) NOUN the point in a lunar orbit when a spacecraft is at its greatest distance from the moon. Compare **apocynthion, perilune.**
▷HISTORY C20: from APO- + *-lune,* from Latin *lūna* moon

apomict ('æpəˌmɪkt) NOUN an organism, esp a plant, produced by apomixis.

apomixis (ˌæpə'mɪksɪs) NOUN, *plural* **-mixes** (-'mɪksiːz). (esp in plants) any of several types of asexual reproduction, such as parthenogenesis and apogamy, in which fertilization does not take place. Compare **amphimixis.**
▷HISTORY C20: New Latin, from Greek APO- + *mixis* a mixing
▸**ˌapo'mictic** ADJECTIVE

apomorphine (ˌæpə'mɔːfiːn, -fɪn) NOUN a white

crystalline alkaloid, derived from morphine, that is used medicinally as an emetic, as an expectorant, and in Parkinson's disease. Formula: $C_{17}H_{17}NO_2$.

aponeurosis (ˌæpənjʊəˈrəʊsɪs) NOUN, *plural* **-ses** (-siːz). *Anatomy* a white fibrous sheet of tissue by which certain muscles are attached to bones.
▷HISTORY C17: via New Latin from Greek, from *aponeurousthai* to change into a tendon, from *neuron* tendon
▸**aponeurotic** (ˌæpənjʊəˈrɒtɪk) ADJECTIVE

apophasis (əˈpɒfəsɪs) NOUN *Rhetoric* the device of mentioning a subject by stating that it will not be mentioned: *I shall not discuss his cowardice or his treachery.*
▷HISTORY C17: via Latin from Greek: denial, from APO- + *phanai* to say

apophthegm *or* **apothegm** (ˈæpəˌθɛm) NOUN a short cryptic remark containing some general or generally accepted truth; maxim.
▷HISTORY C16: from Greek *apophthegma,* from *apophthengesthai* to speak one's opinion frankly, from *phthengesthai* to speak
▸**apophthegmatic** *or* **apothegmatic** (ˌæpəθɛgˈmætɪk) ADJECTIVE

apophyge (əˈpɒfɪdʒɪ) NOUN *Architect* the outward curve at each end of the shaft of a column, adjoining the base or capital. Also called: **hypophyge.**
▷HISTORY C16: from Greek *apophugē,* literally: escape, from *apopheugein* to escape from

apophyllite (əˈpɒfɪˌlaɪt, ˌæpəˈfɪlaɪt) NOUN a white, colourless, pink, or green mineral consisting of a hydrated silicate of calcium, potassium, and fluorine in tetragonal crystalline form. It occurs in cracks in volcanic rocks. Formula: $KCa_4(Si_4O_{10})_2(OH_1F).8H_2O$.
▷HISTORY C19: from French, from APO- + Greek *phullon* leaf + -ITE[1]; referring to its tendency to exfoliate

apophysis (əˈpɒfɪsɪs) NOUN, *plural* **-ses** (-ˌsiːz). 1 a process, outgrowth, or swelling from part of an animal or plant. 2 *Geology* a tapering offshoot from a larger igneous intrusive mass.
▷HISTORY C17: via New Latin from Greek *apophusis* a sideshoot, from APO- + *phusis* growth
▸**apophysate** (əˈpɒfɪsɪt, -seɪt) ADJECTIVE ▸**apophysial** (ˌæpəˈfɪzɪəl) ADJECTIVE

apoplast (ˈæpəˌplæst) NOUN *Botany* the nonprotoplasmic component of a plant, including the cell walls and intercellular material.

apoplectic (ˌæpəˈplɛktɪk) ADJECTIVE 1 of or relating to apoplexy. 2 *Informal* furious. ◆ NOUN 3 a person having apoplexy.
▸ˌ**apoˈplectically** ADVERB

apoplexy (ˈæpəˌplɛksɪ) NOUN sudden loss of consciousness, often followed by paralysis, caused by rupture or occlusion of a blood vessel in the brain.
▷HISTORY C14: from Old French *apoplexie,* from Late Latin *apoplēxia,* from Greek: from *apoplēssein* to cripple by a stroke, from *plēssein* to strike

apoprotein (ˈæpəˌprəʊtiːn) NOUN *Biochem* any conjugated protein from which the prosthetic group has been removed, such as apohaemoglobin (the protein of haemoglobin without its haem group).

apoptosis (ˌæpəpˈtəʊsɪs) NOUN *Biology* the programmed death of some of an organism's cells as part of its natural growth and development. Also called: **programmed cell death.**
▷HISTORY C20: from Greek: a falling away, from APO- + *ptōsis* a falling

aporia (əˈpɔːrɪə) NOUN 1 *Rhetoric* a doubt, real or professed, about what to do or say. 2 *Philosophy* puzzlement occasioned by the raising of philosophical objections without any proffered solutions, esp in the works of Socrates.
▷HISTORY C16: from Greek, literally: a state of being at a loss
▸**aporetic** (ˌæpəˈrɛtɪk) ADJECTIVE

aport (əˈpɔːt) ADVERB, ADJECTIVE (*postpositive*) *Nautical* on or towards the port side: *with the helm aport.*

aposematic (ˌæpəsɪˈmætɪk) ADJECTIVE (of the coloration of certain distasteful or poisonous animals) characterized by bright conspicuous markings, which predators recognize and learn to avoid; warning.
▷HISTORY C19: from APO- + Greek *sēma* sign

aposiopesis (ˌæpəʊˌsaɪəˈpiːsɪs) NOUN, *plural* **-ses** (-siːz). *Rhetoric* the device of suddenly breaking off in the middle of a sentence as if unwilling to continue.
▷HISTORY C16: via Late Latin from Greek, from *aposiōpaein* to be totally silent, from *siōpaein* to be silent
▸**aposiopetic** (ˌæpəʊˌsaɪəˈpɛtɪk) ADJECTIVE

apospory (ˈæpəˌspɔːrɪ) NOUN 1 *Botany* development of the gametophyte from the sporophyte without the formation of spores. 2 the development of an embryo of a flowering plant outside the embryo sac, from a cell of the nucellus or chalaza.
▷HISTORY C19: from APO- + SPORE + -Y[1]

apostasy (əˈpɒstəsɪ) NOUN, *plural* **-sies.** abandonment of one's religious faith, party, a cause, etc.
▷HISTORY C14: from Church Latin *apostasia,* from Greek *apostasis* desertion, from *apostanai* to stand apart from, desert

apostate (əˈpɒsteɪt, -tɪt) NOUN 1 a person who abandons his religion, party, cause, etc. ◆ ADJECTIVE 2 guilty of apostasy.
▸**apostatical** (ˌæpəˈstætɪkᵊl) ADJECTIVE

apostatize *or* **apostatise** (əˈpɒstəˌtaɪz) VERB (*intr*) to forsake or abandon one's belief, faith, or allegiance.

a posteriori (eɪ pɒsˌtɛrɪˈɔːraɪ, -rɪ, ɑː) ADJECTIVE *Logic* 1 relating to or involving inductive reasoning from particular facts or effects to a general principle. 2 derived from or requiring evidence for its validation or support; empirical; open to revision. 3 *Statistics* See **posterior probability.** ◆ Compare **a priori, synthetic** (sense 4).
▷HISTORY C18: from Latin, literally: from the latter (that is, from effect to cause)

apostil (əˈpɒstɪl) NOUN a marginal note.
▷HISTORY C16: from French *apostille,* from Old French *apostiller* to make marginal notes, from Medieval Latin *postilla,* probably from Latin *post illa* (*verba*) after those (words)

apostle (əˈpɒsᵊl) NOUN 1 (*often capital*) one of the 12 disciples chosen by Christ to preach his gospel. 2 any prominent Christian missionary, esp one who first converts a nation or people. 3 an ardent early supporter of a cause, reform movement, etc. 4 *Mormon Church* a member of a council of twelve officials appointed to administer and preside over the Church.
▷HISTORY Old English *apostol,* from Church Latin *apostolus,* from Greek *apostolos* a messenger, from *apostellein* to send forth

apostle bird NOUN a gregarious grey-and-brown Australian nest-building bird, *Struthidea cinerea.*
▷HISTORY C20: so called for its apparent habit of congregating in groups of twelve

Apostles' Creed NOUN a concise statement of Christian beliefs dating from about 500 A.D., traditionally ascribed to the Apostles.

apostle spoon NOUN a silver spoon with a figure of one of the Apostles on the handle.

apostolate (əˈpɒstəlɪt, -ˌleɪt) NOUN the office, authority, or mission of an apostle.

apostolic (ˌæpəˈstɒlɪk) ADJECTIVE 1 of, relating to, deriving from, or contemporary with the Apostles. 2 of or relating to the teachings or practice of the Apostles. 3 of or relating to the pope regarded as chief successor of the Apostles.
▸ˌ**aposˈtolical** ADJECTIVE ▸ˌ**aposˈtolically** ADVERB

apostolic delegate NOUN *RC Church* a representative of the pope sent to countries that do not have full or regular diplomatic relations with the Holy See.

Apostolic Fathers PLURAL NOUN the Fathers of the early Church who immediately followed the Apostles.

Apostolic See NOUN 1 *RC Church* the see of the pope regarded as the successor to Saint Peter. 2 (*often not capitals*) a see established by one of the Apostles.

Apostolic succession NOUN the doctrine that the authority of Christian bishops derives from the Apostles through an unbroken line of consecration.

apostrophe[1] (əˈpɒstrəfɪ) NOUN the punctuation mark ' used to indicate the omission of a letter or number, such as *he's* for *he has* or *he is,* also used in English to form the possessive, as in *John's father* and *twenty pounds' worth.*
▷HISTORY C17: from Late Latin, from Greek *apostrophos* mark of elision, from *apostrephein* to turn away

apostrophe[2] (əˈpɒstrəfɪ) NOUN *Rhetoric* a digression from a discourse, esp an address to an imaginary or absent person or a personification.
▷HISTORY C16: from Latin *apostrophē,* from Greek: a turning away, digression
▸**apostrophic** (ˌæpəˈstrɒfɪk) ADJECTIVE

apostrophize *or* **apostrophise** (əˈpɒstrəˌfaɪz) VERB (*tr*) *Rhetoric* to address an apostrophe to.

apothecaries' measure NOUN a system of liquid volume measure used in pharmacy in which 60 minims equal 1 fluid drachm, 8 fluid drachms equal 1 fluid ounce, and 20 fluid ounces equal 1 pint.

apothecaries' weight NOUN a system of weights, formerly used in pharmacy, based on the Troy ounce, which contains 480 grains. 1 grain is equal to 0.065 gram.

apothecary (əˈpɒθɪkərɪ) NOUN, *plural* **-caries.** 1 an archaic word for **pharmacist.** 2 *Law* a chemist licensed by the Society of Apothecaries of London to prescribe, prepare, and sell drugs.
▷HISTORY C14: from Old French *apotecaire,* from Late Latin *apothēcārius* warehouseman, from *apothēca,* from Greek *apothēkē* storehouse

apothecium (ˌæpəˈθiːsɪəm) NOUN, *plural* **-cia** (-sɪə). *Botany* a cup-shaped structure that contains the asci, esp in lichens; a type of ascocarp.
▷HISTORY C19: from New Latin, from APO- + Greek *thēkion* a little case
▸**apothecial** (ˌæpəˈθiːsɪəl) ADJECTIVE

apothegm (ˈæpəˌθɛm) NOUN a variant spelling of **apophthegm.**

apothem (ˈæpəˌθɛm) NOUN the perpendicular line or distance from the centre of a regular polygon to any of its sides.
▷HISTORY C20: from APO- + Greek *thema,* from *tithenai* to place

apotheosis (əˌpɒθɪˈəʊsɪs) NOUN, *plural* **-ses** (-siːz). 1 the elevation of a person to the rank of a god; deification. 2 glorification of a person or thing. 3 a glorified ideal.
▷HISTORY C17: via Late Latin from Greek: deification, from *theos* god

apotheosize *or* **apotheosise** (əˈpɒθɪəˌsaɪz) VERB (*tr*) 1 to deify. 2 to glorify or idealize.

apotropaic (ˌæpəʊtrəˈpeɪɪk) ADJECTIVE preventing or intended to prevent evil.
▷HISTORY C19: from Greek *apotropaios* turning away (evil), from *apotrepein;* see APO-, TROPE

app (æp) NOUN *Computing, informal* short for **application program.**

appal *or US* **appall** (əˈpɔːl) VERB **-pals, -palling, -palled** *or US* **-palls, -palling, -palled.** (*tr*) to fill with horror; shock or dismay.
▷HISTORY C14: from Old French *appalir* to turn pale

Appalachia (ˌæpəˈleɪtʃɪə) NOUN a highland region of the eastern US, containing the Appalachian Mountains, extending from Pennsylvania to Alabama.

Appalachian (ˌæpəˈleɪtʃɪən) ADJECTIVE 1 of, from, or relating to the Appalachian Mountains. 2 *Geology* of or relating to an episode of mountain building in the late Palaeozoic era during which the Appalachian Mountains were formed.

Appalachian Mountains *or* **Appalachians** PLURAL NOUN a mountain system of E North America, extending from Quebec province in Canada to central Alabama in the US: contains rich deposits of anthracite, bitumen, and iron ore. Highest peak: Mount Mitchell, 2038 m (6684 ft.).

appalling (əˈpɔːlɪŋ) ADJECTIVE causing extreme dismay, horror, or revulsion.
▸**apˈpallingly** ADVERB

Appaloosa (ˌæpəˈluːsə) NOUN a breed of horse, originally from America, typically having a spotted rump.
▷HISTORY C19: perhaps from *Palouse,* river in Idaho

appanage *or* **apanage** (ˈæpənɪdʒ) NOUN 1 land or other provision granted by a king for the support of a member of the royal family, esp a younger son. 2 a natural or customary accompaniment or perquisite, as to a job or position.

▷HISTORY C17: from Old French, from Medieval Latin *appānāgium*, from *appānāre* to provide for, from Latin *pānis* bread

apparat (ˌæpəˈrɑːt) NOUN the Communist Party organization in the former Soviet Union and other states.
▷HISTORY Russian, literally: APPARATUS

apparatchik (ˌæpəˈrɑːtʃɪk) NOUN 1 a member of a Communist apparat. 2 an official or bureaucrat in any organization.

apparatus (ˌæpəˈreɪtəs, -ˈrɑːtəs, ˈæpəˌreɪtəs) NOUN, *plural* **-ratus** *or* **-ratuses.** 1 a collection of instruments, machines, tools, parts, or other equipment used for a particular purpose. 2 a machine having a specific function: *breathing apparatus.* 3 the means by which something operates; organization: *the apparatus of government.* 4 *Anatomy* any group of organs having a specific function.
▷HISTORY C17: from Latin, from *apparāre* to make ready

apparatus criticus (ˈkrɪtɪkəs) NOUN textual notes, list of variant readings, etc., relating to a document, esp in a scholarly edition of a text.
▷HISTORY Latin: critical apparatus

apparel (əˈpærəl) NOUN 1 something that covers or adorns, esp outer garments or clothing. 2 *Nautical* a vessel's gear and equipment. ◆ VERB **-els, -elling, -elled** *or US* **-els, -eling, -eled.** 3 *Archaic (tr)* to clothe, adorn, etc.
▷HISTORY C13: from Old French *apareillier* to make ready, from Vulgar Latin *appariculāre* (unattested), from Latin *apparāre,* from *parāre* to prepare

apparent (əˈpærənt, əˈpɛər-) ADJECTIVE 1 readily seen or understood; evident; obvious. 2 *(usually prenominal)* seeming, as opposed to real: *his apparent innocence belied his complicity in the crime.* 3 *Physics* as observed but ignoring such factors as the motion of the observer, changes in the environment, etc. Compare **true** (sense 9).
▷HISTORY C14: from Latin *appārēns,* from *appārēre* to APPEAR
▸**apˈparentness** NOUN

apparently (əˈpærəntlɪ, əˈpɛər-) ADVERB *(sentence modifier)* it appears that; as far as one knows; seemingly.

apparent magnitude NOUN another name for **magnitude** (sense 4).

apparent movement NOUN *Psychol* the sensation of seeing movement when nothing actually moves in the environment, as when two neighbouring lights are switched on and off in rapid succession.

apparition (ˌæpəˈrɪʃən) NOUN 1 an appearance, esp of a ghost or ghostlike figure. 2 the figure so appearing; phantom; spectre. 3 the act of appearing or being visible.
▷HISTORY C15: from Late Latin *appāritiō,* from Latin: attendance, from *appārēre* to APPEAR

apparitor (əˈpærɪtə) NOUN an officer who summons witnesses and executes the orders of an ecclesiastical and (formerly) a civil court.
▷HISTORY C15: from Latin: public servant, from *appārēre* to APPEAR

appassionato (əˌpæsjəˈnɑːtəʊ) ADJECTIVE, ADVERB *Music* (to be performed) in an impassioned manner.

appeal (əˈpiːl) NOUN 1 a request for relief, aid, etc. 2 the power to attract, please, stimulate, or interest: *a dress with appeal.* 3 an application or resort to another person or authority, esp a higher one, as for a decision or confirmation of a decision. 4 *Law* **a** the judicial review by a superior court of the decision of a lower tribunal. **b** a request for such review. **c** the right to such review. 5 *Cricket* a verbal request to the umpire from one or more members of the fielding side to declare a batsman out. 6 *English law* (formerly) a formal charge or accusation: *appeal of felony.* ◆ VERB 7 *(intr)* to make an earnest request for relief, support, etc. 8 *(intr)* to attract, please, stimulate, or interest. 9 *Law* to apply to a superior court to review (a case or particular issue decided by a lower tribunal). 10 *(intr)* to resort (to), as for a decision or confirmation of a decision. 11 *(intr) Cricket* to ask the umpire to declare a batsman out. 12 *(intr)* to challenge the umpire's or referee's decision.
▷HISTORY C14: from Old French *appeler,* from Latin *appellāre* to entreat (literally: to approach), from *pellere* to push, drive
▸**apˈpealable** ADJECTIVE ▸**apˈpealer** NOUN

appealing (əˈpiːlɪŋ) ADJECTIVE attractive or pleasing.
▸**apˈpealingly** ADVERB

appear (əˈpɪə) VERB *(intr)* 1 to come into sight or view. 2 *(copula; may take an infinitive)* to seem or look: *the evidence appears to support you.* 3 to be plain or clear, as after further evidence, etc.: *it appears you were correct after all.* 4 to develop or come into being; occur: *faults appeared during testing.* 5 to become publicly available; be published: *his biography appeared last month.* 6 to perform or act: *he has appeared in many London productions.* 7 to be present in court before a magistrate or judge: *he appeared on two charges of theft.*
▷HISTORY C13: from Old French *aparoir,* from Latin *appārēre* to become visible, attend upon, from *pārēre* to appear

appearance (əˈpɪərəns) NOUN 1 the act or an instance of appearing, as to the eye, before the public, etc. 2 the outward or visible aspect of a person or thing: *her appearance was stunning; it has the appearance of powdered graphite.* 3 an outward show; pretence: *he gave an appearance of working hard.* 4 *(often plural)* one of the outward signs or indications by which a person or thing is assessed: *first appearances are deceptive.* 5 *Law* **a** the formal attendance in court of a party in an action. **b** formal notice that a party or his legal representative intends to maintain or contest the issue: *to enter an appearance.* 6 *Philosophy* **a** the outward or phenomenal manifestation of things. **b** the world as revealed by the senses, as opposed to its real nature. Compare **reality** (sense 4). 7 **keep up appearances.** to maintain the public impression of wellbeing or normality. 8 **put in** *or* **make an appearance.** to come or attend briefly, as out of politeness. 9 **to all appearances.** to the extent that can easily be judged; apparently.

appearance money NOUN money paid by a promoter of an event to a particular celebrity in order to ensure that the celebrity takes part in the event.

appease (əˈpiːz) VERB *(tr)* 1 to calm, pacify, or soothe, esp by acceding to the demands of. 2 to satisfy or quell (an appetite or thirst, etc.).
▷HISTORY C16: from Old French *apaisier,* from *pais* peace, from Latin *pax*
▸**apˈpeasable** ADJECTIVE ▸**apˈpeaser** NOUN

appeasement (əˈpiːzmənt) NOUN 1 the policy of acceding to the demands of a potentially hostile nation in the hope of maintaining peace. 2 the act of appeasing.

appel (əˈpɛl; *French* apɛl) NOUN *Fencing* 1 a stamp of the foot, used to warn of one's intent to attack. 2 a sharp blow with the blade made to procure an opening.
▷HISTORY from French: challenge

appellant (əˈpɛlənt) NOUN 1 a person who appeals. 2 *Law* the party who appeals to a higher court from the decision of a lower tribunal. ◆ ADJECTIVE 3 *Law* another word for **appellate.**
▷HISTORY C14: from Old French; see APPEAL

appellate (əˈpɛlɪt) ADJECTIVE *Law* 1 of or relating to appeals. 2 (of a tribunal) having jurisdiction to review cases on appeal and to reverse decisions of inferior courts.
▷HISTORY C18: from Latin *appellātus* summoned, from *appellāre* to APPEAL

appellation (ˌæpɪˈleɪʃən) NOUN 1 an identifying name or title. 2 the act of naming or giving a title to.

appellative (əˈpɛlətɪv) NOUN 1 an identifying name or title; appellation. 2 *Grammar* another word for **common noun.** ◆ ADJECTIVE 3 of or relating to a name or title. 4 (of a proper noun) used as a common noun.
▸**apˈpellatively** ADVERB

appellee (ˌæpɛˈliː) NOUN *Law* a person who is accused or appealed against.
▷HISTORY C16: from Old French *apele* summoned; see APPEAL

append (əˈpɛnd) VERB *(tr)* 1 to add as a supplement: *to append a footnote.* 2 to attach; hang on.
▷HISTORY C15: from Late Latin *appendere* to hang (something) from, from Latin *pendere* to hang

appendage (əˈpɛndɪdʒ) NOUN 1 an ancillary or secondary part attached to a main part; adjunct. 2 *Zoology* any organ that projects from the trunk of animals such as arthropods. 3 *Botany* any subsidiary part of a plant, such as a branch or leaf.

appendant (əˈpɛndənt) ADJECTIVE 1 attached, affixed, or added. 2 attendant or associated as an accompaniment or result. 3 a less common word for **pendent.** 4 *Law* relating to another right. ◆ NOUN 5 a person or thing attached or added. 6 *Property law* a subordinate right or interest, esp in or over land, attached to a greater interest and automatically passing with the sale of the latter.

appendicectomy (əˌpɛndɪˈsɛktəmɪ) *or esp US and Canadian* **appendectomy** (ˌæpənˈdɛktəmɪ) NOUN, *plural* **-mies.** surgical removal of any appendage, esp the vermiform appendix.

appendicitis (əˌpɛndɪˈsaɪtɪs) NOUN inflammation of the vermiform appendix.

appendicle (əˈpɛndɪkᵊl) NOUN a small appendage.
▷HISTORY C17: from Latin *appendicula;* see APPENDIX

appendicular (ˌæpənˈdɪkjʊlə) ADJECTIVE 1 relating to an appendage or appendicle. 2 *Anatomy* of or relating to the vermiform appendix.

appendix (əˈpɛndɪks) NOUN, *plural* **-dices** (-dɪˌsiːz) *or* **-dixes.** 1 a body of separate additional material at the end of a book, magazine, etc., esp one that is documentary or explanatory. 2 any part that is dependent or supplementary in nature or function; appendage. 3 *Anatomy* See **vermiform appendix.**
▷HISTORY C16: from Latin: an appendage, from *appendere* to APPEND

Appenzell (*German* apənˈtsɛl, ˈapəntsɛl) NOUN 1 a canton of NE Switzerland, divided in 1597 into the Protestant demicanton of **Appenzell Outer Rhodes** and the Catholic demicanton of **Appenzell Inner Rhodes.** Capitals: Herisau and Appenzell. Pop.: 54 104 and 14 750 (1996 est.) respectively. Areas: 243 sq. km (94 sq. miles) and 171 sq. km (66 sq. miles) respectively. 2 a town in NE Switzerland, capital of Appenzell Inner Rhodes demicanton. Pop.: 5157 (1990).

apperceive (ˌæpəˈsiːv) VERB *(tr)* 1 to be aware of perceiving. 2 *Psychol* to comprehend by assimilating (a perception) to ideas already in the mind.
▷HISTORY C19: from Old French *aperceveir,* from Latin *percipere* to PERCEIVE

apperception (ˌæpəˈsɛpʃən) NOUN *Psychol* 1 the attainment of full awareness of a sensation or idea. 2 the act or process of apperceiving.
▸ˌ**apperˈceptive** ADJECTIVE

appertain (ˌæpəˈteɪn) VERB *(intr; usually foll by to)* to belong (to) as a part, function, right, etc.; relate (to) or be connected (with).
▷HISTORY C14: from Old French *apertenir* to belong, from Late Latin *appertinēre,* from Latin AD- + *pertinēre* to PERTAIN

appestat (ˈæpɪstæt) NOUN a neural control centre within the hypothalamus of the brain that regulates the sense of hunger and satiety.
▷HISTORY C20: from APPE(TITE) + -STAT

appetence (ˈæpɪtəns) *or* **appetency** NOUN, *plural* **-tences** *or* **-tencies.** 1 a natural craving or desire. 2 a natural or instinctive inclination. 3 an attraction or affinity.
▷HISTORY C17: from Latin *appetentia,* from *appetere* to crave

appetite (ˈæpɪˌtaɪt) NOUN 1 a desire for food or drink. 2 a desire to satisfy a bodily craving, as for sexual pleasure. 3 (usually foll by *for*) a desire, liking, or willingness: *a great appetite for work.*
▷HISTORY C14: from Old French *apetit,* from Latin *appetītus* a craving, from *appetere* to desire ardently
▸**appetitive** (əˈpɛtɪtɪv, ˈæpɪˌtaɪtɪv) ADJECTIVE

appetizer *or* **appetiser** (ˈæpɪˌtaɪzə) NOUN 1 a small amount of food or drink taken to stimulate the appetite. 2 any stimulating foretaste.

appetizing *or* **appetising** (ˈæpɪˌtaɪzɪŋ) ADJECTIVE pleasing or stimulating to the appetite; delicious; tasty.

Appian Way (ˈæpɪən) NOUN a Roman road in Italy, extending from Rome to Brindisi: begun in 312 B.C. by Appius Claudius Caecus. Length: about 560 km (350 miles).

applaud (ə'plɔ:d) VERB 1 to indicate approval of (a person, performance, etc.) by clapping the hands. 2 (*usually tr*) to offer or express approval or praise of (an action, person, or thing): *I applaud your decision.*
▷HISTORY C15: from Latin *applaudere* to clap, from *plaudere* to beat, applaud
▸**ap'plauder** NOUN ▸**ap'plauding** ADJECTIVE ▸**ap'plaudingly** ADVERB

applause (ə'plɔ:z) NOUN appreciation or praise, esp as shown by clapping the hands.

apple ('æpᵊl) NOUN 1 a rosaceous tree, *Malus sieversii*, native to Central Asia but widely cultivated in temperate regions in many varieties, having pink or white fragrant flowers and firm rounded edible fruits. ◆ See also **crab apple.** 2 the fruit of this tree, having red, yellow, or green skin and crisp whitish flesh. 3 the wood of this tree. 4 any of several unrelated trees that have fruits similar to the apple, such as the custard apple, sugar apple, and May apple. See also **love apple, oak apple, thorn apple.** 5 **apple of one's eye.** a person or thing that is very precious or much loved. 6 **bad** *or* **rotten apple.** a person with a corrupting influence. ◆ See also **apples.**
▷HISTORY Old English *æppel;* related to Old Saxon *appel,* Old Norse *apall,* Old High German *apful*

apple blight NOUN an aphid, *Eriosoma lanigera,* that is covered with a powdery waxy secretion and infests apple trees. Also called: **American blight.**

apple box NOUN an ornamental Australian tree, *Eucalyptus bridgesiana,* having heart-shaped juvenile leaves, large lanceolate adult leaves, and conical fruits. Also called: **apple gum.**

apple butter NOUN a jam made from stewed spiced apples.

Appleby ('æpᵊlbɪ) NOUN a town in NW England, in Cumbria: famous for its annual horse fair. Pop.: 2570 (1991).

applecart ('æpᵊl,kɑ:t) NOUN 1 a cart or barrow from which apples and other fruit are sold in the street. 2 **upset the applecart.** to spoil plans or arrangements.

appledrain ('æpᵊl,dreɪn) NOUN *Southwestern English dialect* a wasp.

apple green NOUN **a** a bright light green or moderate yellowish-green. **b** (*as adjective*): *an apple-green carpet.*

Apple Islander NOUN *Austral informal* a native or inhabitant of Tasmania.

Apple Isle NOUN **the.** *Austral informal* Tasmania.

applejack ('æpᵊl,dʒæk) NOUN a brandy made from apples; distilled cider. Also called: **applejack brandy, apple brandy.**

apple maggot NOUN a fruit fly, *Rhagoletis pomonella,* the larvae of which bore into and feed on the fruit of apple trees: family *Trypetidae.*

apple of discord NOUN *Greek myth* a golden apple inscribed "For the fairest." It was claimed by Hera, Athena, and Aphrodite, to whom Paris awarded it, thus beginning a chain of events that led to the Trojan War.

apple-pie bed NOUN *Brit* a way of making a bed so as to prevent the person from entering it.

apple-pie order NOUN *Informal* perfect order or condition.

apple polisher NOUN *Informal* a sycophant; toady.

apples ('æpᵊlz) PLURAL NOUN 1 See **apples and pears.** 2 **she's apples.** *Austral and NZ informal* all is going well.

apples and pears PLURAL NOUN *Cockney rhyming slang* stairs. Often shortened to: **apples.**

apple sauce NOUN 1 a purée of stewed apples often served with pork. 2 *US and Canadian slang* nonsense; rubbish.

applet ('æplɪt) NOUN *Computing* a computer program that runs within a page on the World Wide Web.
▷HISTORY C20: from APP(LICATION PROGRAM) + -LET

Appleton layer NOUN another name for **F region** (of the ionosphere).
▷HISTORY C20: named after Sir Edward *Appleton* (1892–1965), English physicist

appley ('æplɪ) ADJECTIVE resembling or tasting like an apple: *an excellent, appley wine.*

appliance (ə'plaɪəns) NOUN 1 a machine or device, esp an electrical one used domestically. 2 any piece of equipment having a specific function. 3 a device fitted to a machine or tool to adapt it for a specific purpose. 4 another name for a **fire engine.**

applicable ('æplɪkəbᵊl, ə'plɪkə-) ADJECTIVE being appropriate or relevant; able to be applied; fitting.
▸**,applica'bility** *or* **'applicableness** NOUN ▸**'applicably** ADVERB

applicant ('æplɪkənt) NOUN a person who applies, as for a job, grant, support, etc.; candidate.
▷HISTORY C15: from Latin *applicāns,* from *applicāre* to APPLY

application (,æplɪ'keɪʃən) NOUN 1 the act of applying to a particular purpose or use. 2 relevance or value: *the practical applications of space technology.* 3 the act of asking for something: *an application for leave.* 4 a verbal or written request, as for a job, etc.: *he filed his application.* 5 diligent effort or concentration: *a job requiring application.* 6 something, such as a healing agent or lotion, that is applied, esp to the skin. 7 *Logic, maths* the process of determining the value of a function for a given argument. 8 short for **application program** or **applications package.**

application program NOUN a computer program that is written and designed for a specific need or purpose.

applications package NOUN *Computing* a specialized program or set of specialized programs and associated documentation designed to carry out a particular task.

applicative (ə'plɪkətɪv) ADJECTIVE relevant or applicable.
▸**ap'plicatively** ADVERB

applicator ('æplɪ,keɪtə) NOUN a device, such as a spatula or rod, for applying a medicine, glue, etc.

applicatory ('æplɪkətərɪ) ADJECTIVE suitable for application.

applied (ə'plaɪd) ADJECTIVE related to or put to practical use: *applied mathematics.* Compare **pure** (sense 5).

appliqué (æ'pli:keɪ) NOUN 1 a decoration or trimming of one material sewn or otherwise fixed onto another. 2 the practice of decorating in this way. ◆ VERB **-qués, -quéing, -quéd.** 3 (*tr*) to sew or fix (a decoration) on as an appliqué.
▷HISTORY C18: from French, literally: applied

apply (ə'plaɪ) VERB **-plies, -plying, -plied.** 1 (*tr*) to put to practical use; utilize; employ. 2 (*intr*) to be relevant, useful, or appropriate. 3 (*tr*) to cause to come into contact with; put onto. 4 (*intr;* often foll by *for*) to put in an application or request. 5 (*tr;* often foll by *to*) to devote (oneself, one's efforts) with diligence. 6 (*tr*) to bring into operation or use: *the police only applied the law to aliens.* 7 (*tr*) to refer (a word, epithet, etc.) to a person or thing.
▷HISTORY C14: from Old French *aplier,* from Latin *applicāre* to attach to
▸**ap'plier** NOUN

appoggiatura (ə,pɒdʒə'tʊərə) NOUN, *plural* **-ras** *or* **-re** (-reɪ). *Music* an ornament consisting of a nonharmonic note (short or long) preceding a harmonic one either before or on the stress. See also **acciaccatura** (sense 2).
▷HISTORY C18: from Italian, literally: a propping, from *appoggiare* to prop, support

appoint (ə'pɔɪnt) VERB (*mainly tr*) 1 (*also intr*) to assign officially, as for a position, responsibility, etc.: *he was appointed manager.* 2 to establish by agreement or decree; fix: *a time was appointed for the duel.* 3 to prescribe or ordain: *laws appointed by tribunal.* 4 *Property law* to nominate (a person), under a power granted in a deed or will, to take an interest in property. 5 to equip with necessary or usual features; furnish: *a well-appointed hotel.*
▷HISTORY C14: from Old French *apointer* to put into a good state, from *a point* in good condition, literally: to a POINT
▸**ap'pointer** NOUN

appointee (əpɔɪn'ti:, ,æp-) NOUN 1 a person who is appointed. 2 *Property law* a person to whom property is granted under a power of appointment.

appointive (ə'pɔɪntɪv) ADJECTIVE *Chiefly US* relating to or filled by appointment: *an appointive position.*

appointment (ə'pɔɪntmənt) NOUN 1 an arrangement to meet a person or be at a place at a certain time. 2 the act of placing in a job or position. 3 the person who receives such a job or position. 4 the job or position to which such a person is appointed. 5 (*usually plural*) a fixture or fitting. 6 *Property law* nomination to an interest in property under a deed or will.

appointment television NOUN televison programmes that people set aside time to watch.

appointment viewing NOUN the practice of setting time aside to watch particular television programmes.

appointor (ə'pɔɪntə, əpɔɪn'tɔ:) NOUN *Property law* a person to whom a power to nominate persons to take property is given by deed or will. See also **power of appointment.**

Appomattox (,æpə'mætəks) NOUN a village in central Virginia where the Confederate army under Robert E. Lee surrendered to Ulysses S. Grant's Union forces on April 9, 1865, effectively ending the American Civil War.

apport (ə'pɔ:t) NOUN 1 **a** the production of objects by apparently supernatural means at a spiritualists' seance. **b** the objects produced. 2 *Obsolete* bearing; demeanour. 3 (*plural*) *Obsolete* things brought as offerings; revenues.
▷HISTORY C15: from Old French *aport,* from *aporter* (vb), from Latin AD- + *portāre* to carry

apportion (ə'pɔ:ʃən) VERB (*tr*) to divide, distribute, or assign appropriate shares of; allot proportionally: *to apportion the blame.*
▸**ap'portionable** ADJECTIVE ▸**ap'portioner** NOUN

apportionment (ə'pɔ:ʃənmənt) NOUN 1 the act of apportioning. 2 *US government* the proportional distribution of the seats in a legislative body, esp the House of Representatives, on the basis of population.

apposable (ə'pəʊzəbᵊl) ADJECTIVE 1 capable of being apposed or brought into apposition. 2 *Anatomy* another word for **opposable** (sense 2).

appose (ə'pəʊz) VERB (*tr*) 1 to place side by side or near to each other. 2 (usually foll by *to*) to place (something) near or against another thing.
▷HISTORY C16: from Old French *apposer,* from *poser* to put, from Latin *pōnere*

apposite ('æpəzɪt) ADJECTIVE well suited for the purpose; appropriate; apt.
▷HISTORY C17: from Latin *appositus* placed near, from *appōnere,* from *pōnere* to put, place
▸**'appositely** ADVERB ▸**'appositeness** NOUN

apposition (,æpə'zɪʃən) NOUN 1 a putting into juxtaposition. 2 a grammatical construction in which a word, esp a noun phrase, is placed after another to modify its meaning. 3 *Biology* growth in the thickness of a cell wall by the deposition of successive layers of material. Compare **intussusception** (sense 2).
▸**,appo'sitional** ADJECTIVE

appositive (ə'pɒzɪtɪv) ADJECTIVE 1 *Grammar* **a** standing in apposition. **b** another word for **nonrestrictive.** 2 of or relating to apposition. ◆ NOUN 3 an appositive word or phrase.
▸**ap'positively** ADVERB

appraisal (ə'preɪzᵊl) *or* **appraisement** NOUN 1 an assessment or estimation of the worth, value, or quality of a person or thing. See also **performance appraisal.** 2 a valuation of property or goods.

appraisal drilling NOUN (in the oil industry) drilling carried out once oil or gas has been discovered in order to assess the extent of the field, the reserves, the possible rate of production, and the properties of the oil or gas.

appraise (ə'preɪz) VERB (*tr*) 1 to assess the worth, value, or quality of. 2 to make a valuation of, as for taxation purposes.
▷HISTORY C15: from Old French *aprisier,* from *prisier* to PRIZE[2]
▸**ap'praisable** ADJECTIVE ▸**ap'praiser** NOUN ▸**ap'praisingly** ADVERB ▸**ap'praisive** ADJECTIVE ▸**ap'praisively** ADVERB

> **Language note** *Appraise* is sometimes wrongly used where *apprise* is meant: *they had been apprised (not appraised) of my arrival.*

appreciable (ə'pri:ʃɪəbᵊl, -ʃəbᵊl) ADJECTIVE sufficient to be easily seen, measured, or noticed.
▸**ap'preciably** ADVERB

appreciate (ə'pri:ʃɪˌeɪt, -sɪ-) VERB *(mainly tr)* 1 to feel thankful or grateful for: *to appreciate a favour.* 2 *(may take a clause as object)* to take full or sufficient account of: *to appreciate a problem.* 3 to value highly: *to appreciate Shakespeare.* 4 *(usually intr)* to raise or increase in value.
▷HISTORY C17: from Medieval Latin *appretiāre* to value, prize, from Latin *pretium* PRICE
▸**ap'preciˌator** NOUN

appreciation (əˌpri:ʃɪ'eɪʃən, -sɪ-) NOUN 1 thanks or gratitude. 2 assessment of the true worth or value of persons or things. 3 perceptive recognition of qualities, as in art. 4 an increase in value, as of goods or property. 5 a written review of a book, etc., esp when favourable.

appreciative (ə'pri:ʃɪətɪv, -ʃə-) *or* **appreciatory** ADJECTIVE feeling, expressing, or capable of appreciation.
▸**ap'preciatively** *or* **ap'preciatorily** ADVERB
▸**ap'preciativeness** NOUN

apprehend (ˌæprɪ'hɛnd) VERB 1 *(tr)* to arrest and escort into custody; seize. 2 to perceive or grasp mentally; understand. 3 *(tr)* to await with fear or anxiety; dread.
▷HISTORY C14: from Latin *apprehendere* to lay hold of

apprehensible (ˌæprɪ'hɛnsɪbᵊl) ADJECTIVE capable of being comprehended or grasped mentally.
▸**ˌappreˌhensi'bility** NOUN ▸**ˌappre'hensibly** ADVERB

apprehension (ˌæprɪ'hɛnʃən) NOUN 1 fear or anxiety over what may happen. 2 the act of capturing or arresting. 3 the faculty of comprehending; understanding. 4 a notion or conception.

apprehensive (ˌæprɪ'hɛnsɪv) ADJECTIVE fearful or anxious.
▸**ˌappre'hensively** ADVERB ▸**ˌappre'hensiveness** NOUN

apprentice (ə'prɛntɪs) NOUN 1 someone who works for a skilled or qualified person in order to learn a trade or profession, esp for a recognized period. 2 any beginner or novice. ◆ VERB 3 *(tr)* to take, place, or bind as an apprentice.
▷HISTORY C14: from Old French *aprentis,* from Old French *aprendre* to learn, from Latin *apprehendere* to APPREHEND
▸**ap'prenticeˌship** NOUN

appressed (ə'prɛst) ADJECTIVE pressed closely against, but not joined to, a surface: *leaves appressed to a stem.*
▷HISTORY C18: from Latin *appressus,* from *apprimere,* from *premere* to press

appressorium (ˌæprɛ'sɔ:rɪəm) NOUN, *plural* **-ria** (-rɪə). *Botany* a flattened hypha of a parasitic fungus that penetrates the host tissues.
▷HISTORY from New Latin, from Latin *appressus;* see APPRESSED

apprise *or* **apprize** (ə'praɪz) VERB *(tr; often foll by of)* to make aware; inform.
▷HISTORY C17: from French *appris,* from *apprendre* to teach; learn; see APPREHEND

Language note See at **appraise**.

appro ('æprəʊ) NOUN an informal shortening of **approval**: *on appro.*

approach (ə'prəʊtʃ) VERB 1 to come nearer in position, time, quality, character, etc., to (someone or something). 2 *(tr)* to make advances to, as with a proposal, suggestion, etc. 3 *(tr)* to begin to deal with: *to approach a problem.* 4 *(tr) Rare* to cause to come near. ◆ NOUN 5 the act of coming towards or drawing close or closer. 6 a close approximation. 7 the way or means of entering or leaving; access. 8 *(often plural)* an advance or overture to a person. 9 a means adopted in tackling a problem, job of work, etc. 10 Also called: **approach path.** the course followed by an aircraft preparing for landing.
▷HISTORY C14: from Old French *aprochier,* from Late Latin *appropiāre* to draw near, from Latin *prope* near

approachable (ə'prəʊtʃəbᵊl) ADJECTIVE 1 capable of being approached; accessible. 2 (of a person) friendly.
▸**apˌproacha'bility** *or* **ap'proachableness** NOUN

approach shot NOUN 1 *Golf* Also called: **approach.** a shot made to or towards the green after a tee shot. 2 *Tennis* a deep drive, usually hit with slice to keep the ball low, designed to enable the player to make an approach to the net.

approbate ('æprəˌbeɪt) VERB *(tr)* 1 *Scots Law* to accept as valid. 2 **approbate and reprobate.** *Scots Law* to accept part of a document and reject those parts unfavourable to one's interests. 3 *Chiefly US* to sanction officially.
▷HISTORY C15: from Latin *approbāre* to approve, from *probāre* to test

approbation (ˌæprə'beɪʃən) NOUN 1 commendation; praise. 2 official recognition or approval. 3 an obsolete word for **proof.**
▸**'approˌbative** *or* **'approˌbatory** ADJECTIVE

appropriacy (ə'prəʊprɪəsɪ) NOUN the condition of delicate and precise fittingness of a word or expression to its context, even when it is chosen from a number of close synonyms.

appropriate ADJECTIVE (ə'prəʊprɪɪt) 1 right or suitable; fitting. 2 *Rare* particular; own: *they had their appropriate methods.* ◆ VERB (ə'prəʊprɪˌeɪt) *(tr)* 3 to take for one's own use, esp illegally or without permission. 4 to put aside (funds, etc.) for a particular purpose or person.
▷HISTORY C15: from Late Latin *appropriāre* to make one's own, from Latin *proprius* one's own; see PROPER
▸**ap'propriable** ADJECTIVE ▸**ap'propriately** ADVERB
▸**ap'propriateness** NOUN ▸**ap'propriative** ADJECTIVE
▸**ap'propriˌator** NOUN

appropriation (əˌprəʊprɪ'eɪʃən) NOUN 1 the act of setting apart or taking for one's own use. 2 a sum of money set apart for a specific purpose, esp by a legislature.

approval (ə'pru:vᵊl) NOUN 1 the act of approving. 2 formal agreement; sanction. 3 a favourable opinion; commendation. 4 **on approval.** (of articles for sale) for examination with an option to buy or return.

approve¹ (ə'pru:v) VERB 1 (when *intr,* often foll by *of*) to consider fair, good, or right; commend (a person or thing). 2 *(tr)* to authorize or sanction. 3 *(tr) Obsolete* to demonstrate or prove by trial.
▷HISTORY C14: from Old French *aprover,* from Latin *approbāre* to approve, from *probāre* to test, PROVE
▸**ap'provingly** ADVERB

approve² (ə'pru:v) VERB *(tr) Law* to improve or increase the value of (waste or common land), as by enclosure.
▷HISTORY C15: from Old French *approuer* to turn to advantage, from *prou* advantage

approved school NOUN (in Britain) a former name for **community home.**

approved social worker NOUN *Social welfare* (in England) a qualified social worker specially trained in mental-health work, who is approved by his employing local authority to apply for a mentally disordered person to be admitted to hospital and detained there, or to apply for the person to be received into the guardianship of the local authority.

approx. ABBREVIATION FOR approximate(ly).

approximal (ə'prɒksɪməl) ADJECTIVE *Anatomy* situated side by side; close together: *approximal teeth or fillings.*

approximate ADJECTIVE (ə'prɒksɪmɪt) 1 almost accurate or exact. 2 inexact; rough; loose: *only an approximate fit.* 3 much alike; almost the same. 4 near; close together. ◆ VERB (ə'prɒksɪˌmeɪt) 5 (usually foll by *to*) to come or bring near or close; be almost the same (as). 6 *Maths* to find an expression for (some quantity) accurate to a specified degree. See **accurate** (sense 4).
▷HISTORY C15: from Late Latin *approximāre,* from Latin *proximus* nearest, from *prope* near
▸**ap'proximative** ADJECTIVE

approximately (ə'prɒksɪmɪtlɪ) ADVERB close to; around; roughly or in the region of.

approximation (əˌprɒksɪ'meɪʃən) NOUN 1 the process or result of making a rough calculation, estimate, or guess: *he based his conclusion on his own approximation of the fuel consumption.* 2 an imprecise or unreliable record or version: *an approximation of what really happened.* 3 *Maths* an inexact number, relationship, or theory that is sufficiently accurate for a specific purpose. 4 *Maths* **a** an estimate of the value of some quantity to a desired degree of accuracy. **b** an expression in simpler terms than a given expression which approximates to it.

appulse (ə'pʌls) NOUN a very close approach of two celestial bodies so that they are in conjunction but no eclipse or occultation occurs.
▷HISTORY C17: from Latin *appulsus* brought near, from *appellere* to drive towards, from *pellere* to drive
▸**ap'pulsive** ADJECTIVE ▸**ap'pulsively** ADVERB

appurtenance (ə'pɜ:tɪnəns) NOUN 1 a secondary or less significant thing or part. 2 *(plural)* accessories or equipment. 3 *Property law* a minor right, interest, or privilege which passes when the title to the principal property is transferred.
▷HISTORY C14: from Anglo-French *apurtenance,* from Old French *apartenance,* from *apartenir* to APPERTAIN

appurtenant (ə'pɜ:tɪnənt) ADJECTIVE 1 relating, belonging, or accessory. ◆ NOUN 2 another word for **appurtenance.**

APR ABBREVIATION FOR **annual percentage rate.**

Apr. ABBREVIATION FOR April.

APRA ABBREVIATION FOR Australian Performing Right Association.

apraxia (ə'præksɪə) NOUN a disorder of the central nervous system caused by brain damage and characterized by impaired ability to carry out purposeful muscular movements.
▷HISTORY C19: via New Latin from Greek: inactivity, from A-¹ + *praxis* action
▸**a'praxic** *or* **a'practic** ADJECTIVE

après-ski (ˌæpreɪ'ski:) NOUN **a** a social activity following a day's skiing. **b** *(as modifier)*: *an après-ski outfit.*
▷HISTORY French, literally: after ski

apricot ('eɪprɪˌkɒt) NOUN 1 a rosaceous tree, *Prunus armeniaca,* native to Africa and W Asia, but widely cultivated for its edible fruit. 2 the downy yellow juicy edible fruit of this tree, which resembles a small peach.
▷HISTORY C16: earlier *apricock,* from Portuguese *(albricoque)* or Spanish, from Arabic *al-birqūq* the apricot, from Late Greek *praikokion,* from Latin *praecox* early-ripening; see PRECOCIOUS

April ('eɪprəl) NOUN the fourth month of the year, consisting of 30 days.
▷HISTORY C14: from Latin *Aprīlis,* probably of Etruscan origin

April fool NOUN an unsuspecting victim of a practical joke or trick traditionally performed on the first of April (**April Fools' Day** *or* **All Fools' Day**).

a priori (eɪ praɪ'ɔ:raɪ, ɑ: prɪ'ɔ:rɪ) ADJECTIVE 1 *Logic* relating to or involving deductive reasoning from a general principle to the expected facts or effects. 2 *Logic* known to be true independently of or in advance of experience of the subject matter; requiring no evidence for its validation or support. 3 *Statistics* See **prior probability, mathematical probability.** ◆ Compare **a posteriori, analytic** (sense 4).
▷HISTORY C18: from Latin, literally: from the previous (that is, from cause to effect)
▸**apriority** (ˌeɪpraɪ'ɒrɪtɪ) NOUN

apriorism (eɪ'praɪəˌrɪzəm) NOUN the philosophical doctrine that there may be genuine knowledge independent of experience. Compare **rationalism** (sense 2), **sensationalism** (sense 3).

apron ('eɪprən) NOUN 1 a protective or sometimes decorative or ceremonial garment worn over the front of the body and tied around the waist. 2 the part of a stage extending in front of the curtain line; forestage. 3 a hard-surfaced area in front of or around an aircraft hangar, terminal building, etc., upon which aircraft can stand. 4 a continuous conveyor belt composed usually of slats linked together. 5 a protective plate screening the operator of a machine, artillery piece, etc. 6 a ground covering of concrete or other material used to protect the underlying earth from water erosion. 7 a panel or board between a window and a skirting in a room. 8 *Geology* a sheet of sand, gravel, etc., deposited at the front of a moraine. 9 *Golf* the part of the fairway leading onto the green. 10 *Machinery* the housing for the lead screw gears of a lathe. 11 another name for **skirt** (sense 3). 12 **tied to someone's apron strings.** dependent on or dominated by someone, esp a mother or wife. ◆ VERB 13 *(tr)* to protect or provide with an apron.
▷HISTORY C16: mistaken division (as if *an apron*) of earlier *a napron,* from Old French *naperon* a little cloth, from *nape* cloth, from Latin *mappa* napkin

apron stage NOUN a stage that projects into the

auditorium so that the audience sit on three sides of it.

apropos (ˌæprəˈpəʊ) ADJECTIVE 1 appropriate; pertinent. ◆ ADVERB 2 appropriately or pertinently. 3 by the way; incidentally. 4 **apropos of.** (*preposition*) with regard to; in respect of.
▷HISTORY C17: from French *à propos* to the purpose

aprotic (eɪˈprəʊtɪk) ADJECTIVE *Chem* (of solvents) neither accepting nor donating hydrogen ions.

apse (æps) NOUN 1 Also called: **apsis.** a domed or vaulted semicircular or polygonal recess, esp at the east end of a church. 2 *Astronomy* another name for **apsis** (sense 1).
▷HISTORY C19: from Latin *apsis,* from Greek: a fitting together, arch, from *haptein* to fasten
▸**apsidal** (æpˈsaɪdᵊl, ˈæpsɪdᵊl) ADJECTIVE

apsis (ˈæpsɪs) NOUN, *plural* **apsides** (æpˈsaɪdiːz, ˈæpsɪˌdiːz). 1 Also called: **apse.** either of two points lying at the extremities of an eccentric orbit of a planet, satellite, etc., such as the aphelion and perihelion of a planet or the apogee and perigee of the moon. The **line of apsides** connects two such points and is the principal axis of the orbit. 2 another name for **apse** (sense 1).
▷HISTORY C17: via Latin from Greek; see APSE
▸**apsidal** (æpˈsaɪdᵊl, ˈæpsɪdᵊl) ADJECTIVE

apt (æpt) ADJECTIVE 1 suitable for the circumstance or purpose; appropriate. 2 (*postpositive; foll by an infinitive*) having a tendency (to behave as specified). 3 having the ability to learn and understand easily; clever (esp in the phrase **an apt pupil**).
▷HISTORY C14: from Latin *aptus* fitting, suitable, from *apere* to fasten
▸**ˈaptly** ADVERB ▸**ˈaptness** NOUN

APT ABBREVIATION FOR Advanced Passenger Train.

apt. *plural* **apts.** ABBREVIATION FOR apartment.

apteral (ˈæptərəl) ADJECTIVE 1 (esp of a classical temple) not having columns at the sides. 2 (of a church) having no aisles.
▷HISTORY C19: from Greek *apteros* wingless; see APTEROUS

apterous (ˈæptərəs) ADJECTIVE 1 (of insects) without wings, as silverfish and springtails. 2 without winglike expansions, as some plant stems, seeds, and fruits.
▷HISTORY C18: from Greek *apteros* wingless, from A-[1] + *pteron* wing
▸**ˈapterˌism** NOUN

apterygial (ˌæptəˈrɪdʒɪəl) ADJECTIVE (of eels, certain insects, etc.) lacking such paired limbs as wings or fins.
▷HISTORY C20: from New Latin *apteryx* wingless creature; see APTEROUS

apteryx (ˈæptərɪks) NOUN another name for **kiwi** (the bird).
▷HISTORY C19: from New Latin: wingless creature; see APTEROUS

aptitude (ˈæptɪˌtjuːd) NOUN 1 inherent or acquired ability. 2 ease in learning or understanding; intelligence. 3 the condition or quality of being apt.
▷HISTORY C15: via Old French from Late Latin *aptitūdō,* from Latin *aptus* APT

aptitude test NOUN a test designed to assess a person's ability to do a particular type of work.

Apulia (əˈpjuːljə) NOUN a region of SE Italy, on the Adriatic. Capital: Bari. Pop.: 4 085 239 (2000 est.). Area: 19 223 sq. km (7422 sq. miles). Italian name: **Puglia.**

Apure (*Spanish* aˈpure) NOUN a river in W Venezuela, rising in the Andes and flowing east to the Orinoco. Length: about 676 km (420 miles).

Apurimac (ˌæpuːˈriːmæk) NOUN a river in S Peru, rising in the Andes and flowing northwest into the Urubamba River. Length: about 885 km (550 miles).

Apus (ˈeɪpəs) NOUN, *Latin genitive* **Apodis** (ˈæpədɪs). a constellation in the S hemisphere situated near Musca and Octans.
▷HISTORY New Latin, from Greek *apous,*literally: footless, from A-[1] + *pous* foot

apyrexia (ˌæpaɪˈrɛksɪə) NOUN absence of fever.
▷HISTORY C19: from A-[1] + Greek *puretos* fever
▸**ˌapyˈretic** ADJECTIVE

aq THE INTERNET DOMAIN NAME FOR Antarctica.

AQ ABBREVIATION FOR **achievement quotient.**

aq. *or* **Aq.** ABBREVIATION FOR: 1 aqua. [Latin: water] 2 aqueous.

Aqaba *or* **Akaba** (ˈækəbə) NOUN the only port in Jordan, in the southwest, on the **Gulf of Aqaba**. Pop.: 46 090 (1990 est.).

Aqmola (ækˈməʊlə; *Kazakh* ɑkmɔˈlɑ) NOUN a variant spelling of **Akmola.**

Aqtöbe (ækˈtjuːbɪ; *Kazakh* aktøˈbe) NOUN an industrial city in W Kazakhstan. Pop.: 258 900 (1995 est.). Former name (until 1991): **Aktyubinsk.**

aqua (ˈækwə) NOUN, *plural* **aquae** (ˈækwiː) *or* **aquas.** 1 water: used in compound names of certain liquid substances (as in **aqua regia**) or solutions of substances in water (as in **aqua ammoniae**), esp in the names of pharmacological solutions. ◆ ADJECTIVE 2 short for **aquamarine** (sense 2).
▷HISTORY Latin: water

aquaculture (ˈækwəˌkʌltʃə) *or* **aquiculture** NOUN the cultivation of freshwater and marine resources, both plant and animal, for human consumption or use.

aquaerobics *or* **aquarobics** (ˌækwəˈrəʊbɪks) NOUN (*functioning as singular*) the practice of exercising to music in a swimming pool.
▷HISTORY C20: from Latin *aqua* water + AEROBICS

aqua fortis (ˈfɔːtɪs) NOUN an obsolete name for **nitric acid.**
▷HISTORY C17: from Latin, literally: strong water

aqualung (ˈækwəˌlʌŋ) NOUN breathing apparatus used by divers, etc., consisting of a mouthpiece attached to air cylinders strapped to the back.

aquamarine (ˌækwəməˈriːn) NOUN 1 a pale greenish-blue transparent variety of beryl used as a gemstone. 2 **a** a pale blue to greenish-blue colour. **b** (*as adjective*): *an aquamarine dress.*
▷HISTORY C19: from New Latin *aqua marīna,* from Latin: sea water (referring to the gem's colour)

aquanaut (ˈækwənɔːt) NOUN 1 a person who lives and works underwater. 2 a person who swims or dives underwater.
▷HISTORY C20: from AQUA + *-naut,* as in ASTRONAUT

aquaphobia (ˌækwəˈfəʊbɪə) NOUN an abnormal fear of water, esp because of the possibility of drowning. Compare **hydrophobia** (sense 2).

aquaplane (ˈækwəˌpleɪn) NOUN 1 a single board on which a person stands and is towed by a motorboat at high speed, as in water skiing. ◆ VERB (*intr*) 2 to ride on an aquaplane. 3 (of a motor vehicle travelling at high speeds in wet road conditions) to rise up onto a thin film of water between the tyres and road surface so that actual contact with the road is lost.

aquaporin (ˌækwəˈpɔːrɪn) NOUN any one of a group of proteins in cell membranes that allow the passage of water across the membrane.

aqua regia (ˈriːdʒɪə) NOUN a yellow fuming corrosive mixture of one part nitric acid and three to four parts hydrochloric acid, used in metallurgy for dissolving metals, including gold. Also called: **nitrohydrochloric acid.**
▷HISTORY C17: from New Latin: royal water; referring to its use in dissolving gold, the royal metal

aquarelle (ˌækwəˈrɛl) NOUN 1 a method of watercolour painting in transparent washes. 2 a painting done in this way.
▷HISTORY C19: from French
▸**ˌaquaˈrellist** NOUN

aquarist (ˈækwərɪst) NOUN 1 the curator of an aquarium. 2 a person who studies aquatic life.

aquarium (əˈkwɛərɪəm) NOUN, *plural* **-riums** *or* **-ria** (-rɪə). 1 a tank, bowl, or pool in which aquatic animals and plants are kept for pleasure, study, or exhibition. 2 a building housing a collection of aquatic life, as for exhibition.
▷HISTORY C19: from Latin *aquārius* relating to water, on the model of VIVARIUM

Aquarius (əˈkwɛərɪəs) NOUN, *Latin genitive* **Aquarii** (əˈkwɛərɪˌaɪ). 1 *Astronomy* a zodiacal constellation in the S hemisphere lying between Pisces and Capricorn on the ecliptic. 2 *Astrology* **a** Also called: **the Water Carrier.** the eleventh sign of the zodiac, symbol ♒, having a fixed air classification and ruled by the planets Saturn and Uranus. The sun is in this sign between about Jan. 20 and Feb. 18. **b** a person born during a period when the sun is in this sign. ◆ ADJECTIVE 3 *Astrology* born under or characteristic of Aquarius. ◆ Also (for senses 2b, 3): **Aquarian** (əˈkwɛərɪən).
▷HISTORY Latin

aquashow (ˈækwəˌʃəʊ) *or US* **aquacade** (ˈækwəˌkeɪd) NOUN an exhibition of swimming and diving, often accompanied by music.

aquatic (əˈkwætɪk, əˈkwɒt-) ADJECTIVE 1 growing, living, or found in water. 2 *Sport* performed in or on water. ◆ NOUN 3 a marine or freshwater animal or plant.
▷HISTORY C15: from Latin *aquāticus,* from *aqua* water

aquatics (əˈkwætɪks, əˈkwɒt-) PLURAL NOUN sports or pastimes performed in or on the water.

aquatint (ˈækwəˌtɪnt) NOUN 1 a technique of etching copper with acid to produce an effect resembling the flat tones of wash or watercolour. The tone or tint is obtained by acid (aqua) biting through the pores of a ground that only partially protects the copper. 2 an etching made in this way. ◆ VERB 3 (*tr*) to etch (a block, etc.) in aquatint.
▷HISTORY C18: from Italian *acqua tinta:* dyed water

aquavit (ˈækwəˌvɪt) NOUN a grain- or potato-based spirit from the Scandinavian countries, flavoured with aromatic seeds and spices, esp caraway. Also called: **akvavit.**
▷HISTORY from Scandinavian; see AQUA VITAE

aqua vitae (ˈviːtaɪ, ˈvaɪtiː) NOUN an archaic name for **brandy.**
▷HISTORY Medieval Latin: water of life

aqueduct (ˈækwɪˌdʌkt) NOUN 1 a conduit used to convey water over a long distance, either by a tunnel or more usually by a bridge. 2 a structure, usually a bridge, that carries such a conduit or a canal across a valley or river. 3 a channel in an organ or part of the body, esp one that conveys a natural body fluid.
▷HISTORY C16: from Latin *aquaeductus,* from *aqua* water + *dūcere* to convey

aqueous (ˈeɪkwɪəs, ˈækwɪ-) ADJECTIVE 1 of, like, or containing water. 2 dissolved in water: *aqueous ammonia.* 3 (of rocks, deposits, etc.) formed from material laid down in water.
▷HISTORY C17: from Medieval Latin *aqueus,* from Latin *aqua* water

aqueous humour NOUN *Physiol* the watery fluid within the eyeball between the cornea and the lens.

aquiculture (ˈeɪkwɪˌkʌltʃə, ˈækwɪ-) NOUN 1 another name for **hydroponics.** 2 a variant of **aquaculture.**
▸**ˈaquiˌcultural** ADJECTIVE ▸**ˈaquiˌculturist** NOUN

aquifer (ˈækwɪfə) NOUN a porous deposit of rock, such as a sandstone, containing water that can be used to supply wells.

Aquila[1] (ˈækwɪlə, əˈkwɪlə) NOUN, *Latin genitive* **Aquilae** (ˈækwɪˌliː). a constellation lying in the Milky Way close to Cygnus and situated on the celestial equator. The brightest star is Altair.
▷HISTORY from Latin: eagle

Aquila[2] (ˈækwɪlə; *Italian* ˈaːkwila) *or* **l'Aquila** NOUN a city in central Italy, capital of Abruzzi region. Pop.: 67 820 (1990). Official name: **Aquila degli Abruzzi** (ˈdeʎʎi aˈbruttsi).

aquilegia (ˌækwɪˈliːdʒɪə) NOUN another name for **columbine[1]**.
▷HISTORY C19: from Medieval Latin, of uncertain origin

Aquileia (ˌækwɪˈliːə) NOUN a town in NE Italy, at the head of the Adriatic: important Roman centre, founded in 181 B.C. Pop.: 3451 (1990 est.).

aquiline (ˈækwɪˌlaɪn) ADJECTIVE 1 (of a nose) having the curved or hooked shape of an eagle's beak. 2 of or resembling an eagle.
▷HISTORY C17: from Latin *aquilīnus,* from *aquila* eagle

Aquitaine (ˌækwɪˈteɪn; *French* akitɛn) NOUN a region of SW France, on the Bay of Biscay: a former Roman province and medieval duchy. It is generally flat in the west, rising to the slopes of the Massif Central in the northeast and the Pyrenees in the south; mainly agricultural. Ancient name: **Aquitania** (ˌækwɪˈteɪnɪə).

ar THE INTERNET DOMAIN NAME FOR Argentina.

Ar THE CHEMICAL SYMBOL FOR argon.

AR ABBREVIATION FOR: 1 Arkansas. 2 Autonomous Region. 3 Also: **A/R.** (in the US and Canada) accounts receivable.

Ar. ABBREVIATION FOR: [1] Arabia(n). [2] Also: **Ar.** Arabic.

a.r. ABBREVIATION FOR anno regni.
▷HISTORY Latin: in the year of the reign

-ar SUFFIX FORMING ADJECTIVES of; belonging to; like: *linear; polar; minuscular.*
▷HISTORY via Old French *-er* from Latin *-āris,* replacing *-ālis* (-AL[1]) after stems ending in *l*

Ara ('ɑːrə) NOUN, *Latin genitive* **Arae** ('ɑːriː). a constellation in the S hemisphere near Scorpius.
▷HISTORY from Latin: altar

ARA ABBREVIATION FOR (in Britain) Associate of the Royal Academy.

Arab ('ærəb) NOUN [1] a member of a Semitic people originally inhabiting Arabia, who spread throughout the Middle East, N Africa, and Spain during the seventh and eighth centuries A.D. [2] a lively intelligent breed of horse, mainly used for riding. [3] (*modifier*) of or relating to the Arabs: *the Arab nations.*
▷HISTORY C14: from Latin *Arabs,* from Greek *Araps,* from Arabic *'Arab*

arabesque (ˌærəˈbɛsk) NOUN [1] *Ballet* a classical position in which the dancer has one leg raised behind and both arms stretched out in one of several conventional poses. [2] *Music* a piece or movement with a highly ornamented or decorated melody. [3] *Arts* **a** a type of curvilinear decoration in painting, metalwork, etc., with intricate intertwining leaf, flower, animal, or geometrical designs. **b** a design of flowing lines. ◆ ADJECTIVE [4] designating, of, or decorated in this style.
▷HISTORY C18: from French, from Italian *arabesco* in the Arabic style

Arabia (əˈreɪbɪə) NOUN a great peninsula of SW Asia, between the Red Sea and the Persian Gulf: consists chiefly of a desert plateau, with mountains rising over 3000 m (10 000 ft.) in the west and scattered oases; includes the present-day countries of Saudi Arabia, Yemen, Oman, Bahrain, Qatar, Kuwait, and the United Arab Emirates. Area: about 2 600 000 sq. km (1 000 000 sq. miles).

Arabian (əˈreɪbɪən) ADJECTIVE [1] of or relating to Arabia or the Arabs. ◆ NOUN [2] another word for **Arab.**

Arabian camel NOUN a domesticated camel, *Camelus dromedarius,* having one hump on its back and used as a beast of burden in the hot deserts of N Africa and SW Asia. See also **dromedary.** Compare **Bactrian camel.**

Arabian Desert NOUN [1] a desert in E Egypt, between the Nile, the Gulf of Suez, and the Red Sea: mountainous parts rise over 1800 m (6000 ft.). Area: about 220 000 sq. km (85 000 sq. miles). [2] a desert, mainly in Saudi Arabia, forming the desert area of the Arabian Peninsula, esp in the north. Area: about 2 330 000 sq. km (900 000 sq. miles).

Arabian Nights' Entertainments NOUN **The.** a collection of oriental folk tales dating from the tenth century. Often shortened to: **the Arabian Nights.** Also called: **the Thousand and One Nights.**

Arabian Sea NOUN the NW part of the Indian Ocean, between Arabia and India.

Arabic ('ærəbɪk) NOUN [1] the language of the Arabs, spoken in a variety of dialects; the official language of Algeria, Egypt, Iraq, Jordan, the Lebanon, Libya, Morocco, Saudi Arabia, the Sudan, Syria, Tunisia, and Yemen. It is estimated to be the native language of some 75 million people throughout the world. It belongs to the Semitic subfamily of the Afro-Asiatic family of languages and has its own alphabet, which has been borrowed by certain other languages such as Urdu. ◆ ADJECTIVE [2] denoting or relating to this language, any of the peoples that speak it, or the countries in which it is spoken.

arabica bean (əˈræbɪkə) NOUN a high-quality coffee bean, obtained from the tree *Coffea arabica.*

Arabic numeral NOUN one of the symbols 0,1,2,3,4,5,6,7,8,9 (opposed to *Roman numerals*).

arabinose (əˈræbɪˌnəʊz, -ˌnəʊs) NOUN a pentose sugar in plant gums, esp of cedars and pines. It is used as a culture medium in bacteriology. Formula: $C_5H_{10}O_5$.
▷HISTORY C19: from *arabin* (from (GUM) ARAB(IC) + -IN) + -OSE[2]

arabis ('ærəbɪs) NOUN any plant of the annual or perennial genus *Arabis,* some of which form low-growing mats with downy grey foliage and white flowers: family *Brassicaceae* (crucifers). Also called: **rock cress.**
▷HISTORY New Latin, from Greek *arabis* (fem) of Arabia

Arabist ('ærəbɪst) NOUN a student or expert in Arabic culture, language, history, etc.

arable ('ærəbᵊl) ADJECTIVE [1] (of land) being or capable of being tilled for the production of crops. [2] of, relating to, or using such land: *arable farming.* ◆ NOUN [3] arable land or farming.
▷HISTORY C15: from Latin *arābilis* that can be ploughed, from *arāre* to plough

Arab League NOUN the league of independent Arab states formed in 1945 to further cultural, economic, military, political, and social cooperation.

Araby ('ærəbɪ) NOUN an archaic or poetic name for **Arabia.**

Aracajú (*Portuguese* arəkəˈʒu) NOUN a port in E Brazil, capital of Sergipe state. Pop.: 460 898 (2000).

araceous (əˈreɪʃəs) ADJECTIVE another word for **aroid** (sense 1).
▷HISTORY C19: from New Latin *Arāceae;* see ARUM

arachidonic acid (ˌærəkəˈdɒnɪk) NOUN a fatty acid occurring in animal cells: the metabolic precursor of several groups of biologically active substances, including prostaglandins.

Arachne (əˈræknɪ) NOUN *Greek myth* a maiden changed into a spider for having presumptuously challenged Athena to a weaving contest.
▷HISTORY from Greek *arakhnē* spider

arachnid (əˈræknɪd) NOUN any terrestrial chelicerate arthropod of the class *Arachnida,* characterized by simple eyes and four pairs of legs. The group includes the spiders, scorpions, ticks, mites, and harvestmen.
▷HISTORY C19: from New Latin *Arachnida,* from Greek *arakhnē* spider
▸**aˈrachnidan** ADJECTIVE, NOUN

arachnoid (əˈræknɔɪd) NOUN [1] the middle of the three membranes (see **meninges**) that cover the brain and spinal cord. [2] another name for **arachnid.** ◆ ADJECTIVE [3] of or relating to the middle of the three meninges. [4] *Botany* consisting of or covered with soft fine hairs or fibres. [5] of or relating to the arachnids.

arachnology (ˌærækˈnɒlədʒɪ) NOUN the study of arachnids.
▸**ˌarachˈnologist** NOUN

arachnophobia (əˌræknəˈfəʊbɪə) NOUN an abnormal fear of spiders.
▷HISTORY C20: from Greek *arakhnē* spider + -PHOBIA

Arad ('æræd) NOUN a city in W Romania, on the Mures River: became part of Romania after World War I, after belonging successively to Turkey, Austria, and Hungary. Pop.: 184 619 (1997 est.).

Arafat ('ærəfæt) NOUN a hill in W Saudi Arabia, near Mecca: a sacred site of Islam, visited by pilgrims performing the **hajj.** Also called: **Jabal ar Rahm.**

Arafura Sea (ˌærəˈfʊərə) NOUN a part of the W Pacific Ocean, between N Australia and SW New Guinea.

Aragats (*Russian* ˌaraˈgats) NOUN **Mount.** a volcanic mountain in NW Armenia. Height: 4090 m (13 419 ft.). Turkish name: **Alagez.**

Aragon ('ærəgən) NOUN an autonomous region of NE Spain: independent kingdom from the 11th century until 1479, when it was united with Castile to form modern Spain. Pop.: 1 189 909 (2000 est.). Area: 47 609 sq. km (18 382 sq. miles).

Aragonese (ˌærəgəˈniːz) NOUN, *plural* **-nese.** [1] a native or inhabitant of Aragon. ◆ ADJECTIVE [2] of or relating to Aragon or its inhabitants.

aragonite (əˈrægəˌnaɪt) NOUN a generally white or grey mineral, found in sedimentary rocks and as deposits from hot springs. Composition: calcium carbonate. Formula: $CaCO_3$. Crystal structure: orthorhombic.
▷HISTORY C19: from ARAGON + -ITE[1]

Araguaia *or* **Araguaya** (ˌɑːrəˈgwaɪə) NOUN a river in central Brazil, rising in S central Mato Grosso state and flowing north to the Tocantins River. Length: over 1771 km (1100 miles).

arak ('ærək) NOUN a variant spelling of **arrack.**

Arakan Yoma (ˌɑːrɑːˈkɑːn ˈjəʊmɑː) NOUN a mountain range in Myanmar, between the Irrawaddy River and the W coast: forms a barrier between Myanmar and India; teak forests.

Araks (aˈraks) NOUN the Russian name for the **Aras.**

Araldite ('ærəlˌdaɪt) NOUN *Trademark* a strong epoxy resin best known as a glue.

aralia (əˈreɪlɪə) NOUN any plant of the genus *Aralia* of trees, shrubs, and herbaceous plants. The greenhouse and house plant generally known as aralia is *Schefflera elegantissima* of a related genus, grown for its decorative evergreen foliage: family *Araliaceae.*
▷HISTORY New Latin, of uncertain origin

araliaceous (əˌreɪlɪˈeɪʃəs) ADJECTIVE of, relating to, or belonging to the *Araliaceae,* a chiefly tropical family of trees, shrubs, or woody climbers having small clusters of whitish or greenish flowers. The family includes the ivy and ginseng.

Aral Sea ('ærəl) NOUN a lake in Kazakhstan and Uzbekistan, east of the Caspian Sea, formerly the fourth largest lake in the world: shallow and saline, now badly polluted; use of its source waters for irrigation led to a loss of over 50% of its area between 1967 and 1997. Area (including salt flats): about 64 750 sq. km (25 000 sq. miles). Also called: **Lake Aral.**

Aram ('ɛəræm, -rəm) NOUN the biblical name for ancient Syria.

Aramaean *or* **Aramean** (ˌærəˈmiːən) ADJECTIVE [1] of or relating to Aram (the biblical name for ancient Syria). ◆ NOUN [2] a native or inhabitant of Aram.

Aramaic (ˌærəˈmeɪɪk) NOUN [1] an ancient language of the Middle East, still spoken in parts of Syria and the Lebanon, belonging to the NW Semitic subfamily of the Afro-Asiatic family. Originally the speech of Aram, in the 5th century B.C. it spread to become the lingua franca of the Persian empire. See also **Biblical Aramaic.** ◆ ADJECTIVE [2] of, relating to, or using this language.

Aran ('ærən) ADJECTIVE [1] of or relating to the Aran Islands. [2] made of thick undyed wool with its natural oils retained: *an Aran sweater.*

Aranda ('ærəndə) NOUN [1] an Aboriginal people of S central Australia. [2] the language of this people.

araneid (əˈreɪnɪɪd) NOUN any of numerous arachnids constituting the order *Araneae* (or *Araneida*), which comprises the spiders.
▷HISTORY C19: from New Latin *Araneida,* from Latin *arānea* spider

Aran Islands PLURAL NOUN a group of three islands in the Atlantic, off the W coast of the Republic of Ireland: Aranmore or Inishmore (the largest), Inishmaan, and Inisheer. Pop.: 1000 (latest est.). Area: 46 sq. km (18 sq. miles).

Arapaho (əˈræpəˌhəʊ) NOUN [1] (*plural* **-hos** *or* **-ho**) a member of a North American Indian people of the Plains, now living chiefly in Oklahoma and Wyoming. [2] the language of this people, belonging to the Algonquian family.

arapaima (ˌærəˈpaɪmə) NOUN a very large primitive freshwater teleost fish, *Arapaima gigas,* that occurs in tropical South America and can attain a length of 4.5 m (15 ft.) and a weight of 200 kg (440 lbs): family *Osteoglossidae.*
▷HISTORY via Portuguese from Tupi

Ararat ('ærəˌræt) NOUN an extinct volcanic mountain massif in E Turkey: two main peaks; **Great Ararat** 5155 m (16 916 ft.), said to be the resting place of Noah's Ark after the Flood (Genesis 8:4), and **Little Ararat** 3914 m (12 843 ft.).

araroba (ˌærəˈrəʊbə) NOUN [1] a Brazilian leguminous tree, *Andira araroba.* [2] Also called: **Goa powder.** a bitter yellow powder obtained from cavities in the wood of this tree, formerly used in medicine to treat skin ailments. See also **chrysarobin.**
▷HISTORY from Portuguese, probably from Tupi, from *arara* parrot + *yba* tree

Aras (æˈræs) NOUN a river rising in mountains in Turkish Armenia and flowing east to the Caspian Sea: forms part of the E border of Turkey and the N border of Iran. Length: about 1100 km (660 miles). Ancient name: **Araxes.** Russian name: **Araks.**

Araucania (ˌærɔːˈkeɪnɪə; *Spanish* arauˈkanja) NOUN

a region of central Chile, inhabited by Araucanian Indians.

Araucanian (ˌærɔːˈkeɪnɪən) NOUN [1] a South American Indian language; thought to be an isolated branch of the Penutian phylum, spoken in Chile and W Argentina. [2] a member of the people who speak this language. ◆ ADJECTIVE [3] of or relating to this people or their language.

araucaria (ˌærɔːˈkɛərɪə) NOUN any tree of the coniferous genus *Araucaria* of South America, Australia, and Polynesia, such as the monkey puzzle and bunya-bunya.
▷HISTORY C19: from New Latin *(arbor) Araucaria* (tree) from *Arauco,* a province in Chile

Arawakan (ˌærəˈwækən) NOUN [1] a family of American Indian languages found throughout NE South America. ◆ ADJECTIVE [2] of or relating to the peoples speaking these languages.

Araxes (əˈræksiːz) NOUN the ancient name for the **Aras.**

arbalest *or* **arbalist** (ˈɑːbəlɪst) NOUN a large medieval crossbow, usually cocked by mechanical means.
▷HISTORY C11: from Old French *arbaleste,* from Late Latin *arcuballista,* from Latin *arcus* bow + BALLISTA

Arbela (ɑːˈbiːlə) NOUN an ancient city in Assyria, near which the **Battle of Arbela** took place (331 B.C.), in which Alexander the Great defeated the Persians. Modern name: **Erbil.**

Arbil (ˈɑːbɪl) NOUN a variant spelling of **Erbil.**

arbiter (ˈɑːbɪtə) NOUN [1] a person empowered to judge in a dispute; referee; arbitrator. [2] a person having complete control of something.
▷HISTORY C15: from Latin, of obscure origin

arbitrage (ˈɑːbɪˌtrɑːʒ, ˈɑːbɪtrɪdʒ) NOUN *Finance* **a** the purchase of currencies, securities, or commodities in one market for immediate resale in others in order to profit from unequal prices. **b** *(as modifier): arbitrage operations.*
▷HISTORY C15: from French, from *arbitrer* to ARBITRATE
▸**arbitrageur** (ˌɑːbɪtræˈʒɜː) NOUN

arbitral (ˈɑːbɪtrəl) ADJECTIVE of or relating to arbitration.

arbitrament (ɑːˈbɪtrəmənt) NOUN [1] the decision or award made by an arbitrator upon a disputed matter. [2] the power or authority to pronounce such a decision. [3] another word for **arbitration.**

arbitrary (ˈɑːbɪtrərɪ) ADJECTIVE [1] founded on or subject to personal whims, prejudices, etc.; capricious. [2] having only relative application or relevance; not absolute. [3] (of a government, ruler, etc.) despotic or dictatorial. [4] *Maths* not representing any specific value: *an arbitrary constant.* [5] *Law* (esp of a penalty or punishment) not laid down by statute; within the court's discretion.
▷HISTORY C15: from Latin *arbitrārius* arranged through arbitration, uncertain
▸ˈ**arbitrarily** ADVERB ▸ˈ**arbitrariness** NOUN

arbitrate (ˈɑːbɪˌtreɪt) VERB [1] to settle or decide (a dispute); achieve a settlement between parties. [2] to submit to or settle by arbitration.
▷HISTORY C16: from Latin *arbitrārī* to give judgment; see ARBITER
▸ˈ**arbitrable** ADJECTIVE ▸ˈ**arbiˌtrator** NOUN

arbitration (ˌɑːbɪˈtreɪʃən) NOUN [1] *Law* the hearing and determination of a dispute, esp an industrial dispute, by an impartial referee selected or agreed upon by the parties concerned. [2] *International law* the procedure laid down for the settlement of international disputes.

arbitress (ˈɑːbɪtrɪs) NOUN a female arbitrator.

arbor^{1} (ˈɑːbə) NOUN the US spelling of **arbour.**

arbor^{2} (ˈɑːbə) NOUN [1] a rotating shaft in a machine or power tool on which a milling cutter or grinding wheel is fitted. [2] a rotating shaft or mandrel on which a workpiece is fitted for machining. [3] *Metallurgy* a part, piece, or structure used to reinforce the core of a mould.
▷HISTORY C17: from Latin: tree, mast

arboraceous (ˌɑːbəˈreɪʃəs) ADJECTIVE *Literary* [1] resembling a tree. [2] wooded.

arboreal (ɑːˈbɔːrɪəl) ADJECTIVE [1] of, relating to, or resembling a tree. [2] living in or among trees: *arboreal monkeys.*

arboreous (ɑːˈbɔːrɪəs) ADJECTIVE [1] thickly wooded; having many trees. [2] another word for **arborescent.**

arborescent (ˌɑːbəˈrɛsᵊnt) ADJECTIVE having the shape or characteristics of a tree.
▸ˌ**arboˈrescence** NOUN

arboretum (ˌɑːbəˈriːtəm) NOUN, *plural* **-ta** (-tə) *or* **-tums.** a place where trees or shrubs are cultivated for their scientific or educational interest.
▷HISTORY C19: from Latin, from *arbor* tree

arboriculture (ˈɑːbərɪˌkʌltʃə) NOUN the cultivation of trees or shrubs, esp for the production of timber.
▸ˌ**arboriˈcultural** ADJECTIVE ▸ˌ**arboriˈculturist** NOUN

arborio rice (ɑːˈbɔːrɪəʊ) NOUN a variety of round-grain rice used for making risotto.
▷HISTORY C20: after *Arborio,* a town in N Italy

arborist (ˈɑːbərɪst) NOUN a specialist in the cultivation of trees.

arborization *or* **arborisation** (ˌɑːbəraɪˈzeɪʃən) NOUN a branching treelike appearance in certain fossils and minerals.

arbor vitae (ˈɑːbɔː ˈviːtaɪ, ˈvaɪtiː) NOUN any of several Asian and North American evergreen coniferous trees of the genera *Thuja* and *Thujopsis,* esp *Thuja occidentalis,* having tiny scalelike leaves and egglike cones. See also **red cedar.**
▷HISTORY C17: from New Latin, literally: tree of life

arbour (ˈɑːbə) NOUN [1] a leafy glade or bower shaded by trees, vines, shrubs, etc., esp when trained about a trellis. [2] *Obsolete* an orchard, garden, or lawn.
▷HISTORY C14 *erber,* from Old French *herbier,* from Latin *herba* grass

arbovirus (ˈɑːbəʊˌvaɪrəs) NOUN any one of a group of viruses that cause such diseases as encephalitis and dengue and are transmitted to humans by arthropods, esp insects and ticks.
▷HISTORY C20: from *ar(thropod-)bo(rne) virus*

Arbroath (ɑːˈbrəʊθ) NOUN a port and resort in E Scotland, in Angus: scene of the barons of Scotland's declaration of independence to Pope John XXII in 1320. Pop.: 23 474 (1991).

arbuscular mycorrhiza (ɑːˈbʌskjʊlə) NOUN another name for **endotrophic mycorrhiza.**

arbutus (ɑːˈbjuːtəs) NOUN, *plural* **-tuses.** [1] any of several temperate ericaceous shrubs of the genus *Arbutus,* esp the strawberry tree of S Europe. They have clusters of white or pinkish flowers, broad evergreen leaves, and strawberry-like berries. [2] See **trailing arbutus.**
▷HISTORY C16: from Latin; related to *arbor* tree

arc (ɑːk) NOUN [1] something curved in shape. [2] part of an unbroken curved line. [3] a luminous discharge that occurs when an electric current flows between two electrodes or any other two surfaces separated by a small gap and a high potential difference. [4] *Astronomy* a circular section of the apparent path of a celestial body. [5] *Maths* a section of a curve, graph, or geometric figure. ◆ VERB **arcs, arcing, arced** *or* **arcs, arcking, arcked.** [6] *(intr)* to form an arc. ◆ PREFIX [7] *Maths* specifying an inverse trigonometric function: usually written **arcsin, arctan, arcsec,** etc., or sometimes $\mathbf{sin^{-1}}$, $\mathbf{tan^{-1}}$, $\mathbf{sec^{-1}}$, etc.
▷HISTORY C14: from Old French, from Latin *arcus* bow, arch

ARC ABBREVIATION FOR AIDS-related complex: an early condition in which a person infected with the AIDS virus may suffer from such mild symptoms as loss of weight, fever, etc.

arcade (ɑːˈkeɪd) NOUN [1] a set of arches and their supporting columns. [2] a covered and sometimes arched passageway, usually with shops on one or both sides. [3] a building, or part of a building, with an arched roof.
▷HISTORY C18: from French, from Italian *arcata,* from *arco,* from Latin *arcus* bow, arch

Arcadia (ɑːˈkeɪdɪə) NOUN [1] a department of Greece, in the central Peloponnese. Capital: Tripolis. Pop.: 105 309 (1991). Area: 4367 sq. km (1686 sq. miles). [2] Also called (poetic): **Arcady** (ˈɑːkədɪ). the traditional idealized rural setting of Greek and Roman bucolic poetry and later in the literature of the Renaissance.

Arcadian (ɑːˈkeɪdɪən) ADJECTIVE [1] of or relating to Arcadia or its inhabitants, esp the idealized Arcadia of pastoral poetry. [2] rustic or bucolic: *a life of Arcadian simplicity.* ◆ NOUN [3] an inhabitant of Arcadia. [4] a person who leads or prefers a quiet simple rural life.
▸**Arˈcadianism** NOUN

Arcadic (ɑːˈkeɪdɪk) ADJECTIVE [1] of or relating to the Arcadians or to their dialect of Ancient Greek. ◆ NOUN [2] one of four chief dialects of Ancient Greek; the dialect spoken by the Arcadians. See also **Attic** (sense 3). ◆ Compare **Aeolic, Doric, Ionic.**

arcana (ɑːˈkeɪnə, -ˈkɑː-) NOUN either of the two divisions (the **minor arcana** and the **major arcana**) of a pack of tarot cards.

arcane (ɑːˈkeɪn) ADJECTIVE requiring secret knowledge to be understood; mysterious; esoteric.
▷HISTORY C16: from Latin *arcānus* secret, hidden, from *arcēre* to shut up, keep safe
▸**arˈcanely** ADVERB ▸**arˈcaneness** NOUN

arcanum (ɑːˈkeɪnəm) NOUN, *plural* **-na** (-nə). [1] *(sometimes plural)* a profound secret or mystery known only to initiates. [2] a secret of nature sought by alchemists.
▷HISTORY C16: from Latin; see ARCANE

arcature (ˈɑːkətʃə) NOUN [1] a small-scale arcade. [2] a set of blind arches attached to the wall of a building as decoration.

arc-boutant *French* (arkbutɑ̃) NOUN, *plural* ***arcs-boutants*** (arkbutɑ̃). another name for **flying buttress.**

arccos (ˈɑːˌkɒs) *Maths* ABBREVIATION FOR arc-cosine: the function the value of which for a given argument between –1 and 1 is the angle in radians (between 0 and π), the cosine of which is that argument: the inverse of the cosine function.

Arc de Triomphe (ˈɑːk də ˈtriːəʊmf; *French* ark də trijɔ̃f) NOUN the triumphal arch in Paris begun by Napoleon I to commemorate his victories of 1805–6 and completed in 1836.

arc furnace NOUN a furnace in which the charge is heated by an electric arc.

arch^{1} (ɑːtʃ) NOUN [1] a curved structure, normally in the vertical plane, that spans an opening. [2] Also called: **archway.** a structure in the form of an arch that serves as a gateway. [3] something curved like an arch. [4] **a** any of various parts or structures of the body having a curved or archlike outline, such as the transverse portion of the aorta (**arch of the aorta**) or the raised bony vault formed by the tarsal and metatarsal bones (**arch of the foot**). **b** one of the basic patterns of the human fingerprint, formed by several curved ridges one above the other. Compare **loop**^{1} (sense 10a), **whorl** (sense 3). ◆ VERB [5] *(tr)* to span (an opening) with an arch. [6] to form or cause to form an arch or a curve resembling that of an arch: *the cat arched its back.* [7] *(tr)* to span or extend over: *the bridge arched the flooded stream.*
▷HISTORY C14: from Old French *arche,* from Vulgar Latin *arca* (unattested), from Latin *arcus* bow, ARC

arch^{2} (ɑːtʃ) ADJECTIVE [1] *(prenominal)* chief; principal; leading: *his arch rival.* [2] *(prenominal)* very experienced; expert: *an arch criminal.* [3] knowing or superior. [4] playfully or affectedly roguish or mischievous.
▷HISTORY C16: independent use of ARCH-
▸ˈ**archly** ADVERB ▸ˈ**archness** NOUN

arch. ABBREVIATION FOR: [1] archaic. [2] archaism.

arch- *or* **archi-** COMBINING FORM [1] chief; principal; of highest rank: *archangel; archbishop; archduke.* [2] eminent above all others of the same kind; extreme: *archenemy; archfiend; archfool.*
▷HISTORY ultimately from Greek *arkhi-,* from *arkhein* to rule

-arch NOUN COMBINING FORM leader; ruler; chief: *patriarch; monarch; heresiarch.*
▷HISTORY from Greek *-arkhēs,* from *arkhein* to rule; compare ARCH-

archaean (ɑːˈkiən) NOUN any member of the *Archaea,* a domain of prokaryotic microorganisms, distinguished from bacteria on molecular phylogenetic grounds and often found in hostile environments, such as volcanic vents and hot springs.

Archaean *or esp US* **Archean** (ɑːˈkiːən) ADJECTIVE [1] of or relating to the highly metamorphosed rocks formed in the early Precambrian era. [2] the earlier of two divisions of the Precambrian era, during which the earliest forms of life are assumed to have appeared.

archaebacteria (ˌɑːkɪbækˈtɪərɪə), PLURAL NOUN (formerly) a group of microorganisms now regarded as members of the *Archaea*. ◆ See **archaean.**
▷**HISTORY** from ARCHAEO- + BACTERIA

archaeo- *or* **archeo-** COMBINING FORM [1] indicating ancient or primitive time or condition: *archaeology; archaeopteryx.* [2] of, involving, or denoting the study of remains from archaeological sites: *archaeozoology.*
▷**HISTORY** from Greek *arkhaio-,* from *arkhaios,* from *arkhein* to begin

archaeoastronomy *or* **archeoastronomy** (ˌɑːkɪəʊəˈstrɒnəmɪ) NOUN the scientific study of the beliefs and practices concerning astronomy that existed in ancient and prehistoric civilizations.
▸ **ˌarchaeoasˈtronomer** *or* **ˌarcheoasˈtronomer** NOUN

archaeobotany *or* **archeobotany** (ˌɑːkɪəʊˈbɒtənɪ) NOUN the analysis and interpretation of plant remains found at archaeological sites.
▸ **ˌarchaeoˈbotanist** *or* **ˌarcheoˈbotanist** NOUN

archaeol. ABBREVIATION FOR archaeology.

archaeology *or* **archeology** (ˌɑːkɪˈɒlədʒɪ) NOUN the study of man's past by scientific analysis of the material remains of his cultures. See also **prehistory, protohistory.**
▷**HISTORY** C17: from Late Latin *archaeologia,* from Greek *arkhaiologia* study of what is ancient, from *arkhaios* ancient (from *arkhē* beginning)
▸ **archaeological** *or* **archeological** (ˌɑːkɪəˈlɒdʒɪkᵊl) ADJECTIVE ▸ **ˌarchaeoˈlogically** *or* **ˌarcheoˈlogically** ADVERB
▸ **ˌarchaeˈologist** *or* **ˌarcheˈologist** NOUN

archaeomagnetism *or* **archeomagnetism** (ˌɑːkɪəʊˈmægnɪˌtɪzəm) NOUN an archaeological technique for dating certain clay objects by measuring the extent to which they have been magnetized by the earth's magnetic field.

archaeopteryx (ˌɑːkɪˈɒptərɪks) NOUN any of several extinct primitive birds constituting the genus *Archaeopteryx,* esp *A. lithographica,* which occurred in Jurassic times and had teeth, a long tail, well-developed wings, and a body covering of feathers.
▷**HISTORY** C19: from ARCHAEO- + Greek *pterux* winged creature

archaeornis (ˌɑːkɪˈɔːnɪs) NOUN an extinct primitive Jurassic bird, formerly placed in the genus *Archaeornis* but now thought to be a species of archaeopteryx.
▷**HISTORY** C19: New Latin, from ARCHAEO- + Greek *ornis* bird

Archaeozoic *or esp US* **Archeozoic** (ˌɑːkɪəˈzəʊɪk) ADJECTIVE a former word for **Archaean.**

archaeozoology *or* **archeozoology** (ˌɑːkɪəʊzəʊˈɒlədʒɪ, -zuː-) NOUN the analysis and interpretation of animal remains found at archaeological sites.
▸ **ˌarchaeozoˈologist** *or* **ˌarcheozoˈologist** NOUN

archaic (ɑːˈkeɪɪk) ADJECTIVE [1] belonging to or characteristic of a much earlier period; ancient. [2] out of date; antiquated: *an archaic prison system.* [3] (of idiom, vocabulary, etc.) characteristic of an earlier period of a language and not in ordinary use.
▷**HISTORY** C19: from French *archaïque,* from Greek *arkhaïkos,* from *arkhaios* ancient, from *arkhē* beginning, from *arkhein* to begin
▸ **arˈchaically** ADVERB

archaism (ˈɑːkɪˌɪzəm, -keɪ-) NOUN [1] the adoption or imitation of something archaic, such as a word or an artistic or literary style. [2] an archaic word, expression, style, etc.
▷**HISTORY** C17: from New Latin *archaismus,* from Greek *arkhaïsmos,* from *arkhaizein* to model one's style upon that of ancient writers; see ARCHAIC
▸ **ˈarchaist** NOUN ▸ **ˌarchaˈistic** ADJECTIVE

archaize *or* **archaise** (ˈɑːkɪˌaɪz, -keɪ-) VERB *(tr)* to give an archaic appearance or character to, as by the use of archaisms.
▸ **ˈarchaˌizer** *or* **ˈarchaˌiser** NOUN

archangel (ˈɑːkˌeɪndʒəl) NOUN [1] a principal angel, a member of the order ranking immediately above the angels in medieval angelology. [2] another name for **angelica** (sense 1). [3] **yellow archangel.** a Eurasian herbaceous plant (*Lamiastrum luteum*) that has yellow helmet-shaped flowers: family *Lamiaceae* (labiates). [4] a bronze-coloured breed of domestic pigeon with black markings.
▸ **archangelic** (ˌɑːkænˈdʒɛlɪk) ADJECTIVE

Archangel (ˈɑːkˌeɪndʒəl) NOUN a port in NW Russia, on the Dvina River: major centre for the timber trade and White Sea fisheries. Pop.: 366 200 (1999 est.). Russian name: **Arkhangelsk.**

archbishop (ˈɑːtʃˈbɪʃəp) NOUN a bishop of the highest rank. Abbreviations: **abp, Abp, Arch, Archbp.**

archbishopric (ˈɑːtʃˈbɪʃəprɪk) NOUN [1] the rank, office, or jurisdiction of an archbishop. [2] the area governed by an archbishop.

Archbp ABBREVIATION FOR archbishop.

Archd. ABBREVIATION FOR: [1] archdeacon. [2] archduke.

arch dam NOUN a dam that is curved in the horizontal plane and usually built of concrete, in which the horizontal thrust is taken by abutments in the sides of a valley. Arch dams must be built on solid rock, as a yielding material would cause a failure.

archdeacon (ˈɑːtʃˈdiːkən) NOUN [1] an Anglican clergyman ranking just below a bishop and having supervisory duties under the bishop. [2] a clergyman of similar rank in other Churches.

archdeaconry (ˈɑːtʃˈdiːkənrɪ) NOUN, *plural* **-ries.** [1] the office, rank, or duties of an archdeacon. [2] the residence of an archdeacon.

archdiocese (ˌɑːtʃˈdaɪəˌsiːs, -sɪs) NOUN the diocese of an archbishop.
▸ **archdiocesan** (ˌɑːtʃdaɪˈɒsɪsᵊn) ADJECTIVE

archducal (ˈɑːtʃˈdjuːkᵊl) ADJECTIVE of or relating to an archduke, archduchess, or archduchy.

archduchess (ˈɑːtʃˈdʌtʃɪs) NOUN [1] the wife or widow of an archduke. [2] (since 1453) a princess of the Austrian imperial family, esp a daughter of the Austrian emperor.

archduchy (ˈɑːtʃˈdʌtʃɪ) NOUN, *plural* **-duchies.** the territory ruled by an archduke or archduchess.

archduke (ˈɑːtʃˈdjuːk) NOUN a chief duke, esp (since 1453) a prince of the Austrian imperial dynasty.

Archean (ɑːˈkiːən) ADJECTIVE a variant spelling (esp US) of **Archaean.**

arched (ɑːtʃt) ADJECTIVE [1] provided with or spanned by an arch or arches. [2] shaped like an arch; curved.

archegonium (ˌɑːkɪˈgəʊnɪəm) NOUN, *plural* **-nia** (-nɪə). a female sex organ, occurring in mosses, spore-bearing vascular plants, and gymnosperms, that produces a single egg cell in its swollen base.
▷**HISTORY** C19: from New Latin, from Greek *arkhegonos* original parent, from *arkhe-* chief, first + *gonos* seed, race
▸ **ˌarcheˈgoniate** ADJECTIVE

archenemy (ˈɑːtʃˈɛnɪmɪ) NOUN, *plural* **-mies.** [1] a chief enemy. [2] *(often capital; preceded by the)* the devil.

archenteron (ɑːˈkɛntəˌrɒn) NOUN the cavity within an embryo at the gastrula stage of development that eventually becomes the digestive cavity.
▷**HISTORY** C19: from Greek *arkhē* beginning + *enteron* intestine
▸ **archenteric** (ˌɑːkənˈtɛrɪk) ADJECTIVE

archeology (ˌɑːkɪˈɒlədʒɪ) NOUN a variant spelling of **archaeology.**

Archeozoic (ˌɑːkɪəˈzəʊɪk) ADJECTIVE a variant spelling (esp US) of **Archaeozoic.**

archer (ˈɑːtʃə) NOUN a person skilled in the use of a bow and arrow.
▷**HISTORY** C13: from Old French *archier,* from Late Latin *arcārius,* from Latin *arcus* bow

Archer (ˈɑːtʃə) NOUN **the.** the constellation Sagittarius, the ninth sign of the zodiac.

archerfish (ˈɑːtʃəˌfɪʃ) NOUN, *plural* **-fish** *or* **-fishes.** any freshwater percoid fish of the family *Toxotidae* of S and SE Asia and Australia, esp *Toxotes jaculatrix,* that catch insects by spitting water at them.

archery (ˈɑːtʃərɪ) NOUN [1] the art or sport of shooting with bows and arrows. [2] archers or their weapons collectively.

Arches (ˈɑːtʃɪz) PLURAL NOUN **Court of Arches.** *Church of England* the court of appeal of the Province of Canterbury, formerly held under the arches of Bow Church.

archespore (ˈɑːkɪˌspɔː) *or* **archesporium** (ˌɑːkɪˈspɔːrɪəm) NOUN, *plural* **-spores** *or* **-sporia** (-ˈspɔːrɪə). *Botany* the cell or group of cells in a sporangium that gives rise to spores.
▸ **ˌarcheˈsporial** ADJECTIVE

archetypal (ˌɑːkɪˈtaɪpəl) *or* **archetypical** (ˌɑːkɪˈtɪpɪkᵊl) ADJECTIVE [1] perfect or typical as a specimen of something. [2] being an original model or pattern or a prototype. [3] *Psychoanal* of or relating to Jungian archetypes. [4] constantly recurring as a symbol or motif in literature, painting, etc.
▸ **ˌarcheˈtypally** *or* **ˌarcheˈtypically** ADVERB

archetype (ˈɑːkɪˌtaɪp) NOUN [1] a perfect or typical specimen. [2] an original model or pattern; prototype. [3] *Psychoanal* one of the inherited mental images postulated by Jung as the content of the collective unconscious. [4] a constantly recurring symbol or motif in literature, painting, etc.
▷**HISTORY** C17: from Latin *archetypum* an original, from Greek *arkhetupon,* from *arkhetupos* first-moulded; see ARCH-, TYPE

archfiend (ˌɑːtʃˈfiːnd) NOUN *(often capital)* **the.** the chief of fiends or devils; Satan.

archi- COMBINING FORM a variant of **arch-.**

Archibald prize (ˈɑːtʃɪbɔːld) NOUN *Austral* an annual prize awarded by the Trustees of the Art Gallery of New South Wales since 1921, for outstanding contributions to art, letters, science, and politics.
▷**HISTORY** named after Jules François *Archibald* (1856–1919), Australian journalist

archicarp (ˈɑːkɪˌkɑːp) NOUN a female reproductive structure in ascomycetous fungi that consists of a cell or hypha and develops into the ascogonium.

archidiaconal (ˌɑːkɪdaɪˈækənᵊl) ADJECTIVE of or relating to an archdeacon or his office.

archidiaconate (ˌɑːkɪdaɪˈækənɪt) NOUN the office, term of office, or area of jurisdiction of an archdeacon.

archiepiscopal (ˌɑːkɪɪˈpɪskəpᵊl) ADJECTIVE of or associated with an archbishop.

archiepiscopate (ˌɑːkɪɪˈpɪskəpɪt, -ˌpeɪt) *or* **archiepiscopacy** (ˌɑːkɪɪˈpɪskəpəsɪ) NOUN the rank, office, or term of office of an archbishop.

archil (ˈɑːtʃɪl) NOUN a variant spelling of **orchil.**

Archilochian (ˌɑːkɪˈləʊkɪən) ADJECTIVE denoting or relating to the 7th century B.C. Greek poet Archilochus or his verse, esp the iambic trimeters or trochaic tetrameters used by him.

archimage (ˈɑːkɪˌmeɪdʒ) NOUN a great magician or wizard.
▷**HISTORY** C16: from ARCHI- + *mage,* from Latin *magus* magician

archimandrite (ˌɑːkɪˈmændraɪt) NOUN *Greek Orthodox Church* the head of a monastery or a group of monasteries.
▷**HISTORY** C16: from Late Latin *archimandrīta,* from Late Greek *arkhimandritēs,* from ARCHI- + *mandra* monastery

Archimedean (ˌɑːkɪˈmiːdɪən, -mɪˈdiːən) ADJECTIVE of or relating to Archimedes, the Greek mathematician and physicist (?287–212 B.C.).

Archimedes (ˌɑːkɪˈmiːdiːz) NOUN a walled plain in the NE quadrant of the moon, about 80 km in diameter.

Archimedes' principle NOUN a law of physics stating that the apparent upward force (buoyancy) of a body immersed in a fluid is equal to the weight of the displaced fluid.

Archimedes' screw *or* **Archimedean screw** (ˌɑːkɪˈmiːdɪən, -mɪˈdiːən) NOUN an ancient type of water-lifting device making use of a spiral passage in an inclined cylinder. The water is raised when the spiral is rotated.

archine (ɑːˈʃiːn) NOUN a Russian unit of length equal to about 71 cm.
▷**HISTORY** from Russian *arshin,* of Turkic origin

archipelago (ˌɑːkɪˈpɛlɪˌgəʊ) NOUN, *plural* **-gos** *or* **-goes.** [1] a group of islands. [2] a sea studded with islands.
▷**HISTORY** C16 (meaning: the Aegean Sea): from Italian *arcipelago,* literally: the chief sea (perhaps originally a mistranslation of Greek *Aigaion pelagos* the Aegean Sea), from ARCHI- + *pelago* sea, from Latin *pelagus,* from Greek *pelagos*
▸ **archipelagic** (ˌɑːkɪpəˈlædʒɪk) *or* **archipelagian** (ˌɑːkɪpəˈleɪdʒɪən) ADJECTIVE

archiphoneme (ˈɑːkɪˌfəʊniːm, ˌɑːkɪˈfəʊniːm)

NOUN *Phonetics* an abstract linguistic unit representing two or more phonemes when the distinction between these has been neutralized: conventionally shown by a capital letter within slashes, as /T/ for /t/ and /d/ in German *Rat* and *Rad*.

archit. ABBREVIATION FOR architecture.

architect (ˈɑːkɪˌtɛkt) NOUN 1 a person qualified to design buildings and to superintend their erection. 2 a person similarly qualified in another form of construction: *a naval architect.* 3 any planner or creator: *the architect of the expedition.*
▷HISTORY C16: from French *architecte,* from Latin *architectus,* from Greek *arkhitektōn* director of works, from ARCHI- + *tektōn* workman; related to *tekhnē* art, skill

architectonic (ˌɑːkɪtɛkˈtɒnɪk) ADJECTIVE 1 denoting, relating to, or having architectural qualities. 2 *Metaphysics* of or relating to the systematic classification of knowledge.
▷HISTORY C16: from Late Latin *architectonicus* concerning architecture; see ARCHITECT
▸ˌ**architecˈtonically** ADVERB

architectonics (ˌɑːkɪtɛkˈtɒnɪks) NOUN (*functioning as singular*) 1 the science of architecture. 2 *Metaphysics* the scientific classification of knowledge.

architecture (ˈɑːkɪˌtɛktʃə) NOUN 1 the art and science of designing and superintending the erection of buildings and similar structures. 2 a style of building or structure: *Gothic architecture.* 3 buildings or structures collectively. 4 the structure or design of anything: *the architecture of the universe.* 5 the internal organization of a computer's components with particular reference to the way in which data is transmitted. 6 the arrangement of the various devices in a complete computer system or network.
▸ˌ**archiˈtectural** ADJECTIVE ▸ˌ**archiˈtecturally** ADVERB

architrave (ˈɑːkɪˌtreɪv) NOUN *Architect* 1 the lowest part of an entablature that bears on the columns. 2 a moulding around a doorway, window opening, etc.
▷HISTORY C16: via French from Italian, from ARCHI- + *trave* beam, from Latin *trabs*

archival storage NOUN a method of retaining information outside of the internal memory of a computer.

archive (ˈɑːkaɪv) NOUN (*often plural*) 1 a collection of records of or about an institution, family, etc. 2 a place where such records are kept. 3 *Computing* data transferred to a tape or disk for long-term storage rather than frequent use. ◆ VERB (*tr*) 4 to store (documents, data, etc.) in an archive or other repository.
▷HISTORY C17: from Late Latin *archīvum,* from Greek *arkheion* repository of official records, from *arkhē* government
▸**arˈchival** ADJECTIVE

archivist (ˈɑːkɪvɪst) NOUN a person in charge of archives, their collection, and cataloguing.

archivolt (ˈɑːkɪˌvəʊlt) NOUN *Architect* 1 a moulding around an arch, sometimes decorated. 2 the under surface of an arch.
▷HISTORY C18: from Italian *archivolto;* see ARC, VAULT[1]

archon (ˈɑːkɒn, -kən) NOUN (in ancient Athens) one of the nine chief magistrates.
▷HISTORY C17: from Greek *arkhōn* ruler, from *arkhein* to rule
▸ˈ**archonˌship** NOUN

archpriest (ˈɑːtʃˈpriːst) NOUN *Christianity* 1 (formerly) a chief assistant to a bishop, performing many of his sacerdotal functions during his absence. 2 a senior priest.
▸ˈ**archˈpriestˌhood** *or* ˈ**archˈpriestˌship** NOUN

archway (ˈɑːtʃˌweɪ) NOUN a passageway or entrance under an arch or arches.

-archy NOUN COMBINING FORM government; rule: *anarchy; monarchy.*
▷HISTORY from Greek *-arkhia;* see -ARCH
▸**-archic** ADJECTIVE COMBINING FORM ▸**-archist** NOUN COMBINING FORM

arc light NOUN a light source in which an arc between two electrodes, usually carbon, produces intense white illumination. Also called: **arc lamp.**

ARCM ABBREVIATION FOR Associate of the Royal College of Music.

arcograph (ˈɑːkəˌgrɑːf, -ˌgræf) NOUN *Geometry* an instrument used for drawing arcs without using a central point. Also called: **cyclograph.**

ARCS ABBREVIATION FOR Associate of the Royal College of Science.

arcsin (ˈɑːkˌsaɪn) *Maths* ABBREVIATION FOR arcsine: the function the value of which for a given argument between –1 and 1 is the angle in radians (between –π/2 and π/2), the sine of which is that argument: the inverse of the sine function.

arctan (ˈɑːkˌtæn) *Maths* ABBREVIATION FOR arctangent: the function the value of which for a given argument is the angle in radians (between –π/2 and π/2) the tangent of which is that argument: the inverse of the tangent function.

arctic (ˈɑːktɪk) ADJECTIVE 1 of or relating to the Arctic: *arctic temperatures.* 2 *Informal* cold; freezing: *the weather at Christmas was arctic.* ◆ NOUN 3 *US* a high waterproof overshoe with buckles. 4 (*modifier*) designed or suitable for conditions of extreme cold: *arctic clothing.*
▷HISTORY C14: from Latin *arcticus,* from Greek *arktikos* northern, literally: pertaining to (the constellation of) the Bear, from *arktos* bear

Arctic (ˈɑːktɪk) NOUN 1 **the.** Also called: **Arctic Zone.** the regions north of the Arctic Circle. ◆ ADJECTIVE 2 of or relating to the regions north of the Arctic Circle.

arctic char NOUN a char, *Salvelinus alpinus,* that occurs in northern and arctic seas.

Arctic Circle NOUN the imaginary circle round the earth, parallel to the equator, at latitude 66° 32′ N; it marks the northernmost point at which the sun appears above the level of the horizon on the winter solstice.

arctic fox NOUN a fox, *Alopex lagopus,* of arctic regions, whose fur is dark grey in the summer and white in the winter. See also **blue fox.**

arctic hare NOUN a large hare, *Lepus arcticus,* of the Canadian Arctic whose fur is white in winter.

Arctic Ocean NOUN the ocean surrounding the North Pole, north of the Arctic Circle. Area: about 14 100 000 sq. km (5 440 000 sq. miles).

arctic tern NOUN a black-capped tern, *Sterna paradisea,* that breeds in the Arctic and then migrates as far south as the Antarctic.

arctic willow NOUN a low-growing shrub, *Salix arctica,* of the tundra.

arctiid (ˈɑːktɪɪd) NOUN any moth of the family *Arctiidae,* which includes the footman, ermine, and tiger moths.

Arctogaea (ˌɑːktəˈdʒiːə) NOUN a zoogeographical area comprising the Palaearctic, Nearctic, Oriental, and Ethiopian regions. Compare **Neogaea, Notogaea.**

Arctogaean (ˌɑːktəˈdʒiːən) ADJECTIVE of or relating to Arctogaea.

arctophile (ˈɑːktəʊˌfaɪl) NOUN a person who collects teddy bears or is fond of them.
▷HISTORY C20: from Greek *arktos* bear + -PHILE

Arcturus (ɑːkˈtjʊərəs) NOUN the brightest star in the constellation Boötes: a red giant. Visual magnitude: –0.4; spectral type: K2III; distance: 37 light years.
▷HISTORY C14: from Latin, from Greek *Arktouros,* from *arktos* bear + *ouros* guard, keeper
▸**Arcˈturian** ADJECTIVE

arcuate (ˈɑːkjuːɪt, -ˌeɪt) ADJECTIVE shaped or bent like an arc or bow: *arcuate leaves; arcuate fibres of the cerebrum.* Also: **arcuated.**
▷HISTORY C17: from Latin *arcuāre,* from *arcus* ARC
▸ˈ**arcuately** ADVERB

arcuation (ˌɑːkjʊˈeɪʃən) NOUN 1 the use of arches or vaults in buildings. 2 an arrangement of arches.
▷HISTORY C17: from Late Latin *arcuātiō* arch, from Latin *arcuāre* to curve

arcus senilis (ˈɑːkəs sɪˈnaɪlɪs) NOUN an opaque circle around the cornea of the eye, often seen in elderly people.
▷HISTORY Latin: senile bow

arc welding NOUN a technique in which metal is welded by heat generated by an electric arc struck between two electrodes or between one electrode and the metal workpiece.
▸**arc welder** NOUN

-ard *or* **-art** SUFFIX FORMING NOUNS indicating a person who does something, esp to excess, or is characterized by a certain quality: *braggart; drunkard; dullard.*
▷HISTORY via Old French from Germanic *-hard* (literally: hardy, bold), the final element in many Germanic masculine names, such as *Bernhard* Bernard, *Gerhart* Gerard, etc.

ardeb (ˈɑːdɛb) NOUN a unit of dry measure used in Egypt and other Middle Eastern countries. In Egypt it is approximately equal to 0.195 cubic metres.
▷HISTORY C19: from Arabic *ardabb,* from Greek *artabē* a Persian measure

Ardèche (*French* ardɛʃ) NOUN a department of S France, in Rhône-Alpes region. Capital: Privas. Pop.: 286 023 (1999). Area: 5556 sq. km (2167 sq. miles).

Arden (ˈɑːdᵊn) NOUN **Forest of.** a region of N Warwickshire, part of a former forest: scene of Shakespeare's *As You Like It.*

Ardennes (ɑːˈdɛn; *French* ardɛn) NOUN 1 a department of NE France, in Champagne-Ardenne region. Capital: Mézières. Pop.: 290 130 (1999). Area: 5253 sq. km (2049 sq. miles). 2 **the.** a wooded plateau in SE Belgium, Luxembourg, and NE France: scene of heavy fighting in both World Wars.

ardent (ˈɑːdᵊnt) ADJECTIVE 1 expressive of or characterized by intense desire or emotion; passionate: *ardent love.* 2 intensely enthusiastic; eager: *an ardent longing.* 3 glowing, flashing, or shining: *ardent eyes.* 4 *Rare* burning: *an ardent fever.*
▷HISTORY C14: from Latin *ārdēre* to burn
▸ˈ**ardency** NOUN ▸ˈ**ardently** ADVERB

ardent spirits PLURAL NOUN spirits, such as rum, whisky, etc.

ardour *or US* **ardor** (ˈɑːdə) NOUN 1 feelings of great intensity and warmth; fervour. 2 eagerness; zeal.
▷HISTORY C14: from Old French *ardour,* from Latin *ārdor,* from *ārdēre* to burn

Ards (ɑːdz) NOUN a district of Northern Ireland, in Co. Down. Pop.: 73 244 (2001). Area: 368 sq. km (142 sq. miles).

arduous (ˈɑːdjʊəs) ADJECTIVE 1 requiring great physical or mental effort; difficult to accomplish; strenuous. 2 hard to endure; harsh: *arduous conditions.* 3 hard to overcome or surmount; steep or difficult: *an arduous track.*
▷HISTORY C16: from Latin *arduus* steep, difficult
▸ˈ**arduously** ADVERB ▸ˈ**arduousness** NOUN

are[1] (ɑː; *unstressed* ə) VERB the plural form of the present tense (indicative mood) of **be** and the singular form used with *you.*
▷HISTORY Old English *aron,* second person plural of *bēon* to BE

are[2] (ɑː) NOUN a unit of area equal to 100 sq. metres or 119.599 sq. yards; one hundredth of a hectare. Symbol: a.
▷HISTORY C19: from French, from Latin *ārea* piece of ground; see AREA

area (ˈɛərɪə) NOUN 1 any flat, curved, or irregular expanse of a surface. 2 **a** the extent of a two-dimensional surface enclosed within a specified boundary or geometric figure: *the area of Ireland; the area of a triangle.* **b** the two-dimensional extent of the surface of a solid, or of some part thereof, esp one bounded by a closed curve: *the area of a sphere.* 3 a section, portion, or part: *an area of the body; an area of the sky.* 4 region; district; locality: *a mountainous area.* 5 **a** a geographical division of administrative responsibility. **b** (*as modifier*): *area manager.* 6 a part or section, as of a building, town, etc., having some specified function or characteristic: *reception area; commercial area; slum area.* 7 Also called: **areaway.** a sunken area, usually enclosed, giving light, air, and sometimes access to a cellar or basement. 8 the range, extent, or scope of anything. 9 a subject field or field of study. 10 any unoccupied or unused flat open piece of ground. 11 the ground on which a building stands, or the ground surrounding a building. 12 *Anatomy* any of the various regions of the cerebral cortex. 13 *Computing* any part of a computer memory assigned to store data of a specified type.
▷HISTORY C16: from Latin: level ground, open space, threshing-floor; related to *ārēre* to be dry
▸ˈ**areal** ADJECTIVE

area code NOUN a number prefixed to an

individual telephone number: used in making long-distance calls.

Area of Outstanding Natural Beauty NOUN See **AONB**.

areaway ('ɛərɪəˌweɪ) NOUN 1 a passageway between parts of a building or between different buildings. 2 See **area** (sense 7).

areca ('ærɪkə, ə'ri:kə) NOUN any of various tall palms of the genus *Areca,* which are native to SE Asia and have white flowers and orange or red egg-shaped nuts.
▷HISTORY C16: from Portuguese, from Malayalam *adekka*

Arecibo Observatory (*Spanish* are'θiβo) NOUN an observatory in Puerto Rico at which the world's largest dish radio telescope (diameter 305 m) is situated. It is operated by the National Astronomy and Ionosphere Center.

areg (ə'rɛg) NOUN a plural of **erg**².

arena (ə'ri:nə) NOUN 1 **a** an enclosure or platform, usually surrounded by seats on all sides, in which sports events, contests, entertainments, etc., take place: *a boxing arena.* **b** (*as modifier*): *arena stage.* 2 the central area of an ancient Roman amphitheatre, in which gladiatorial contests and other spectacles were held. 3 a sphere or scene of conflict or intense activity: *the political arena.*
▷HISTORY C17: from Latin *harēna* sand, place where sand was strewn for the combats

arenaceous (ˌærɪ'neɪʃəs) ADJECTIVE 1 (of sedimentary rocks and deposits) composed of sand or sandstone. Compare **argillaceous** and **rudaceous**. 2 (of plants) growing best in a sandy soil.
▷HISTORY C17: from Latin *harēnāceus* sandy, from *harēna* sand

arena theatre NOUN another term for **theatre-in-the-round**.

arene ('æri:n) NOUN an aromatic hydrocarbon.
▷HISTORY C20: from AR(OMATIC) + -ENE

arenicolous (ˌærɪ'nɪkələs) ADJECTIVE growing or living in sand or sandy places: *arenicolous plants.*
▷HISTORY C19: from Latin *harēna* sand + *colere* to inhabit

arenite ('ærəˌnaɪt, ə'ri:-) NOUN any arenaceous rock; a sandstone.
▷HISTORY C20: from Latin *harēna* sand + -ITE¹
▸**arenitic** (ˌærə'nɪtɪk) ADJECTIVE

aren't (ɑ:nt) 1 CONTRACTION OF are not. 2 *Informal, chiefly Brit* (used in interrogative sentences) CONTRACTION OF am not.

areography (ˌɛərɪ'ɒgrəfɪ) NOUN the description of the physical features, such as the surface, atmosphere, etc., of the planet Mars.
▷HISTORY C19: from Greek *Areos* Mars + -GRAPHY

areola (ə'rɪələ) NOUN, *plural* **-lae** (-ˌli:) *or* **-las**. *Anatomy* any small circular area, such as the pigmented ring around the human nipple or the inflamed area surrounding a pimple.
▷HISTORY C17: from Latin: diminutive of AREA
▸**a'reolar** *or* **areolate** (ə'rɪəlɪt, -ˌleɪt) ADJECTIVE
▸**areolation** (əˌrɪə'leɪʃən) NOUN

areole ('ærɪəʊl) NOUN 1 *Biology* a space outlined on a surface, such as an area between veins on a leaf or on an insect's wing. 2 a sunken area on a cactus from which spines, hairs, etc., arise.
▸**'areoˌlate** ADJECTIVE

Areopagite (ˌærɪ'ɒpədʒaɪt) NOUN a member of the Areopagus, a judicial council of ancient Athens that met on the hill of that name.

Areopagus (ˌærɪ'ɒpəgəs) NOUN 1 **a** the hill to the northwest of the Acropolis in Athens. **b** (in ancient Athens) the judicial council whose members (Areopagites) met on this hill. 2 *Literary* any high court.
▷HISTORY via Latin from Greek *Areiopagus,* contracted from *Areios pagos,* hill of Ares

Arequipa (ˌærɪ'ki:pə; *Spanish* are'kipa) NOUN a city in S Peru, at an altitude of 2250 m (7500 ft.): founded in 1540 on the site of an Inca city. Pop.: 710 103 (1998 est.).

Ares ('ɛəri:z) NOUN *Greek myth* the god of war, born of Zeus and Hera. Roman counterpart: **Mars**.

arête (ə'reɪt, ə'rɛt) NOUN a sharp ridge separating two cirques or glacial valleys in mountainous regions.
▷HISTORY C19: from French: fishbone, backbone (of a fish), ridge, sharp edge, from Latin *arista* ear of corn, fishbone

arethusa (ˌærɪ'θju:zə) NOUN a North American orchid, *Arethusa bulbosa,* having one long narrow leaf and one rose-purple flower fringed with yellow.

Arethusa (ˌærɪ'θju:zə) NOUN *Greek myth* a nymph who was changed into a spring on the island of Ortygia to escape the amorous advances of the river god Alpheus.

Arezzo (ə'rɛtsəʊ; *Italian* a'rettso) NOUN a city in central Italy, in E Tuscany. Pop.: 91 527 (1990). Ancient Latin name: **Arretium**.

Arg. ABBREVIATION FOR Argentina.

argal ('ɑ:gəl) NOUN another name for **argol**.

argali ('ɑ:gəlɪ) *or* **argal** NOUN, *plural* **-gali** *or* **-gals**. a wild sheep, *Ovis ammon,* inhabiting semidesert regions in central Asia: family *Bovidae,* order *Artiodactyla.* It is the largest of the sheep, having massive horns in the male, which may almost form a circle.
▷HISTORY C18: from Mongolian

Argand diagram ('ɑ:gænd) NOUN *Maths* a diagram in which complex numbers are represented by the points in the plane the coordinates of which are respectively the real and imaginary parts of the number, so that the number $x + iy$ is represented by the point (x, y), or by the corresponding vector $\langle x, y\rangle$. If the polar coordinates of (x, y) are (r, θ), r is the modulus and θ the argument of $x + iy$.
▷HISTORY C19: named after Jean-Robert *Argand* (1768–1822), French mathematician

argent ('ɑ:dʒənt) NOUN **a** an archaic or poetic word for **silver**. **b** (*as adjective; often postpositive, esp in heraldry*): *a bend argent.*
▷HISTORY C15: from Old French, from Latin

Argenteuil (*French* arʒɑ̃tœj) NOUN a suburb of Paris, France, with a convent (656) that became famous when Héloïse was abbess (12th century). Pop.: 93 096 (1990).

argentic (ɑ:'dʒɛntɪk) ADJECTIVE *Chem* of or containing silver in the divalent or trivalent state.

argentiferous (ˌɑ:dʒən'tɪfərəs) ADJECTIVE containing or bearing silver.

Argentina (ˌɑ:dʒən'ti:nə) NOUN a republic in southern South America: colonized by the Spanish from 1516 onwards; gained independence in 1816 and became a republic in 1852; ruled by military dictatorships for much of the 20th century; civilian rule restored in 1983; consists chiefly of subtropical plains and forests (the Chaco) in the north, temperate plains (the pampas) in the central parts, the Andes in the west, and an infertile plain extending to Tierra del Fuego in the south (Patagonia); an important meat producer. Language: Spanish. Religion: Roman Catholic. Currency: peso. Capital: Buenos Aires. Pop.: 37 487 000 (2001 est.). Area: 2 776 653 sq. km (1 072 067 sq. miles). Also called: **the Argentine**.

argentine ('ɑ:dʒənˌtaɪn) ADJECTIVE 1 of, relating to, or resembling silver. ◆ NOUN 2 any of various small marine salmonoid fishes, such as *Argentina sphyraena,* that constitute the family *Argentinidae* and are characterized by a long silvery body.

Argentine ('ɑ:dʒənˌti:n, -ˌtaɪn) NOUN 1 **the**. another name for **Argentina**. 2 a native or inhabitant of Argentina. ◆ ADJECTIVE 3 of or relating to Argentina. ◆ Also (for senses 2, 3): **Argentinian** (ˌɑ:dʒən'tɪnɪən).

argentite ('ɑ:dʒənˌtaɪt) NOUN a dark grey mineral that consists of silver sulphide, usually in cubic crystalline forms, and occurs in veins, often with native silver. It is found esp in Mexico, Nevada, and Saxony and is an important source of silver. Formula: Ag_2S.

argentous (ɑ:'dʒɛntəs) ADJECTIVE *Chem* of or containing silver in the monovalent state.

argentum (ɑ:'dʒɛntəm) NOUN an obsolete name for **silver**.
▷HISTORY Latin

argie-bargie ('ɑ:dʒɪ'bɑ:dʒɪ) NOUN a variant spelling of **argy-bargy**.

argil ('ɑ:dʒɪl) NOUN clay, esp potters' clay.
▷HISTORY C16: from Latin *argilla* white clay, from Greek *argillos*

argillaceous (ˌɑ:dʒɪ'leɪʃəs) ADJECTIVE (of sedimentary rocks and deposits) composed of very fine-grained material, such as clay, shale, etc. Compare **arenaceous** (sense 1) and **rudaceous**.

argilliferous (ˌɑ:dʒɪ'lɪfərəs) ADJECTIVE containing or yielding clay: *argilliferous rocks.*

argillite ('ɑ:dʒɪˌlaɪt) NOUN any argillaceous rock, esp a hardened mudstone.
▷HISTORY C18: from Latin *argilla* clay (from Greek *argillos*) + -ITE¹
▸**argillitic** (ˌɑ:dʒɪ'lɪtɪk) ADJECTIVE

arginine ('ɑ:dʒɪˌnaɪn) NOUN an essential amino acid of plant and animal proteins, necessary for nutrition and for the production of excretory urea.
▷HISTORY C19: from German *Arginin,* of uncertain origin

Argive ('ɑ:dʒaɪv, -gaɪv) ADJECTIVE 1 (in Homer, Virgil, etc.) of or relating to the Greeks besieging Troy, esp those from Argos. 2 of or relating to Argos or Argolis. 3 a literary word for **Greek**. ◆ NOUN 4 an ancient Greek, esp one from Argos or Argolis.

argle-bargle (ˌɑ:gᵊl'bɑ:gᵊl) NOUN another word for **argy-bargy**.

Argo¹ ('ɑ:gəʊ) NOUN *Greek myth* the ship in which Jason sailed in search of the Golden Fleece.

Argo² ('ɑ:gəʊ) NOUN, *Latin genitive* **Argus** ('ɑ:gəs). an extensive constellation in the S hemisphere now subdivided into the smaller constellations of **Puppis**, **Vela**, **Carina**, and **Pyxis**. Also called: **Argo Navis** ('neɪvɪs).

argol ('ɑ:gɒl) *or* **argal** NOUN crude potassium hydrogentartrate, deposited as a crust on the sides of wine vats.
▷HISTORY C14: from Anglo-French *argoil,* of unknown origin

Argolis ('ɑ:gəlɪs) NOUN 1 a department and ancient region of Greece, in the NE Peloponnese. Capital: Nauplion. Pop.: 97 636 (1991). Area: 2261 sq. km (873 sq. miles). 2 **Gulf of.** an inlet of the Aegean Sea, in the E Peloponnese.

argon ('ɑ:gɒn) NOUN an extremely unreactive colourless odourless element of the rare gas series that forms almost 1 per cent (by volume) of the atmosphere. It is used in electric lights. Symbol: Ar; atomic no.: 18; atomic wt.: 39.948; density: 1.7837 kg/m³; freezing pt.: –189.3°C; boiling pt.: –185.9°C.
▷HISTORY C19: from Greek, from *argos* idle, inactive, from A-¹ + *ergon* work

Argonaut ('ɑ:gəˌnɔ:t) NOUN 1 *Greek myth* one of the heroes who sailed with Jason in quest of the Golden Fleece. 2 a person who took part in the Californian gold rush of 1849. 3 another name for the **paper nautilus**.
▷HISTORY C16: from Greek *Argonautēs,* from *Argō* the name of Jason's ship + *nautēs* sailor
▸ˌ**Argo'nautic** ADJECTIVE

Argonne ('ɑ:gɒn; *French* argɔn) NOUN **the.** a wooded region of NE France: scene of major battles in both World Wars.

argonon ('ɑ:gəˌnɒn) NOUN another name for **inert gas** (sense 1).
▷HISTORY C20: from ARGON + -ON (indicating an inert gas)

Argos ('ɑ:gɒs, -gəs) NOUN an ancient city in SE Greece, in the NE Peloponnese: one of the oldest Greek cities, it dominated the Peloponnese in the 7th century B.C. Pop.: 22 000 (1995 est.).

argosy ('ɑ:gəsɪ) NOUN, *plural* **-sies**. *Archaic or poetic* a large abundantly laden merchant ship, or a fleet of such ships.
▷HISTORY C16: from Italian *Ragusea* (*nave*) (ship) of Ragusa

argot ('ɑ:gəʊ) NOUN slang or jargon peculiar to a particular group, esp (formerly) a group of thieves.
▷HISTORY C19: from French, of unknown origin
▸**argotic** (ɑ:'gɒtɪk) ADJECTIVE

Argovie (argɔvi) NOUN the French name for **Aargau**.

arguable ('ɑ:gjʊəbᵊl) ADJECTIVE 1 capable of being disputed; doubtful. 2 capable of being supported by argument; plausible.

arguably ('ɑ:gjʊəblɪ) ADVERB (*sentence modifier*) it can be argued that.

argue ('ɑ:gju:) VERB **-gues, -guing, -gued.** 1 (*intr*) to quarrel; wrangle: *they were always arguing until I arrived.* 2 (*intr;* often foll by *for* or *against*) to present supporting or opposing reasons or cases in a dispute; reason. 3 (*tr; may take a clause as object*) to try to prove by presenting reasons; maintain. 4

(*tr; often passive*) to debate or discuss: *the case was fully argued before agreement was reached.* 5 (*tr*) to persuade: *he argued me into going.* 6 (*tr*) to give evidence of; suggest: *her looks argue despair.*
▷HISTORY C14: from Old French *arguer* to assert, charge with, from Latin *arguere* to make clear, accuse; related to Latin *argūtus* clear, *argentum* silver
▸'**arguer** NOUN

argufy ('ɑːgjʊˌfaɪ) VERB **-fies, -fying, -fied.** *Facetious or dialect* to argue or quarrel, esp over something trivial.

argument ('ɑːgjʊmənt) NOUN 1 a quarrel; altercation. 2 a discussion in which reasons are put forward in support of and against a proposition, proposal, or case; debate: *the argument on birth control will never be concluded.* 3 (*sometimes plural*) a point or series of reasons presented to support or oppose a proposition. 4 a summary of the plot or subject of a book, etc. 5 *Logic* **a** a process of deductive or inductive reasoning that purports to show its conclusion to be true. **b** formally, a sequence of statements one of which is the conclusion and the remainder the premises. 6 *Logic* an obsolete name for the middle term of a syllogism. 7 *Maths* **a** an element to which an operation, function, predicate, etc., applies, esp the independent variable of a function. **b** another name for **amplitude** (sense 5) of a complex number.

argumentation (ˌɑːgjʊmɛnˈteɪʃən) NOUN 1 the process of reasoning methodically. 2 a less common word for **argument** (senses 2, 3).

argumentative (ˌɑːgjʊˈmɛntətɪv) ADJECTIVE 1 given to arguing; contentious. 2 characterized by argument; controversial.
▸ˌ**arguˈmentatively** ADVERB ▸ˌ**arguˈmentativeness** NOUN

argument from design NOUN another name for **teleological argument.**

argumentum ad hominem *Latin* (ˌɑːgjʊˈmɛntʊm æd ˈhɒmɪˌnɛm) NOUN *Logic* 1 fallacious argument that attacks not an opponent's beliefs but his motives or character. 2 argument that shows an opponent's statement to be inconsistent with his other beliefs. 3 an instance of either of these.
▷HISTORY literally: argument to the person

argus ('ɑːgəs) NOUN any of various brown butterflies, esp the **Scotch argus** (*Erebia aethiops*) found on moorland and in forests up to a height of 2000 m.

Argus ('ɑːgəs) NOUN 1 *Greek myth* a giant with a hundred eyes who was made guardian of the heifer Io. After he was killed by Hermes his eyes were transferred to the peacock's tail. 2 a vigilant person; guardian.

Argus-eyed ADJECTIVE keen-sighted; observant; vigilant.

argus pheasant NOUN either of two pheasants, *Argusianus argus* (great argus) or *Rheinardia ocellata* (crested argus), occurring in SE Asia and Indonesia. The males have very long tails marked with eyelike spots.

argy-bargy *or* **argie-bargie** ('ɑːdʒɪˈbɑːdʒɪ) NOUN, *plural* **-bargies.** *Brit informal* a wrangling argument or verbal dispute. Also called: **argle-bargle.**
▷HISTORY C19: from Scottish, compound based on dialect *argle*, probably from ARGUE

argyle (ɑːˈgaɪl) ADJECTIVE 1 made of knitted or woven material with a diamond-shaped pattern of two or more colours. ◆ NOUN 2 (*often plural*) a sock made of this.
▷HISTORY C20: after Campbell of *Argyle* (Argyll), the pattern being an adaptation of the tartan of this clan

Argyll and Bute (ɑːˈgaɪl) NOUN a council area in W Scotland on the Atlantic Ocean: in 1975 the historical counties of Argyllshire and Bute became part of Strathclyde region; in 1996 they were reinstated as a single unitary authority. Argyll and Bute is mountainous and includes the islands of Bute, Mull, Islay, and Jura. Administrative centre: Lochgilphead. Pop.: 91 306 (2001). Area: 6930 sq. km (2676 sq. miles).

Argyllshire (ɑːˈgaɪlˌʃɪə, -ʃə) NOUN (until 1975) a county of W Scotland, part of Strathclyde region (1975–96), now part of Argyll and Bute.

Argyrol ('ɑːdʒɪˌrɒl, ɑːˈdʒɪərɒl) NOUN *Trademark* a dark brown compound of silver and a protein, used medicinally as a local antiseptic.

arhat ('ɑːhət) NOUN a Buddhist, esp a monk who has achieved enlightenment and at death passes to nirvana. Compare **Bodhisattva.**
▷HISTORY from Sanskrit: worthy of respect, from *arhati* he deserves

Århus (*Danish* 'ɔrhuːs) NOUN a variant spelling of **Aarhus.**

aria ('ɑːrɪə) NOUN an elaborate accompanied song for solo voice from a cantata, opera, or oratorio. See also **da capo.**
▷HISTORY C18: from Italian: tune, AIR

Ariadne (ˌærɪˈædnɪ) NOUN *Greek myth* daughter of Minos and Pasiphaë: she gave Theseus the thread with which he found his way out of the Minotaur's labyrinth.

-arian SUFFIX FORMING NOUNS indicating a person or thing that advocates, believes, or is associated with something: *vegetarian; millenarian; librarian.*
▷HISTORY from Latin *-ārius* -ARY + -AN

Arianism ('ɛərɪəˌnɪzəm) NOUN the doctrine of the Greek Christian theologian Arius (?250–336 A.D.), pronounced heretical at the Council of Nicaea, which asserted that Christ was not of one substance with the Father, but a creature raised by the Father to the dignity of Son of God.

Arica (əˈriːkə; *Spanish* aˈrika) NOUN a port in extreme N Chile: awarded to Chile in 1929 after the lengthy Tacna-Arica dispute with Peru; outlet for Bolivian and Peruvian trade. Pop.: 178 547 (1999 est.). See also **Tacna-Arica.**

arid ('ærɪd) ADJECTIVE 1 having little or no rain; dry; parched with heat. 2 devoid of interest.
▷HISTORY C17: from Latin *āridus*, from *ārēre* to be dry
▸**aridity** (əˈrɪdɪtɪ) *or* '**aridness** NOUN ▸'**aridly** ADVERB

arid zone NOUN either of the zones of latitude 15–30° N and S characterized by very low rainfall and desert or semidesert terrain.

Ariège (*French* arjɛʒ) NOUN a department of SW France, in Midi-Pyrénées region. Capital: Foix. Pop.: 137 205 (1999). Area: 4903 sq. km (1912 sq. miles).

ariel ('ɛərɪəl) NOUN an Arabian gazelle, *Gazella arabica* (or *dama*).
▷HISTORY C19: from Arabic *aryal*

Ariel ('ɛərɪəl) NOUN the smallest of the four large satellites of Uranus.

Aries ('ɛəriːz) NOUN, *Latin genitive* **Arietis** (əˈraɪɪtɪs). 1 *Astronomy* a small zodiacal constellation in the N hemisphere lying between Taurus and Pisces on the ecliptic and having a second-magnitude star. 2 *Astrology* **a** Also called: **the Ram.** the first sign of the zodiac, symbol ♈, having a cardinal fire classification, ruled by the planet Mars. The sun is in this sign between about March 21 and April 19. **b** a person born during the period when the sun is in this sign. ◆ ADJECTIVE 3 *Astrology* born under or characteristic of Aries. ◆ Also (for senses 2b, 3): **Arien** ('ɛərɪən).
▷HISTORY C14: from Latin: ram

arietta (ˌærɪˈɛtə; *Italian* ariˈetta) *or* **ariette** (ˌærɪˈɛt) NOUN, *plural* **-ettas, -ette** (-ˈette) *or* **-ettes.** a short relatively uncomplicated aria.
▷HISTORY C18: from Italian, diminutive of ARIA

aright (əˈraɪt) ADVERB correctly; rightly; properly.

ariki ('ɑːrɪkɪ) NOUN, *plural* **ariki.** *NZ* the first-born male or female in a notable family; chief.
▷HISTORY Maori

aril ('ærɪl) NOUN an appendage on certain seeds, such as those of the yew and nutmeg, developed from or near the funicle of the ovule and often brightly coloured and fleshy.
▷HISTORY C18: from New Latin *arillus*, from Medieval Latin *arilli* raisins, pips of grapes
▸'**arilˌlate** ADJECTIVE

arillode ('ærɪˌləʊd) NOUN a structure in certain seeds that resembles an aril but is developed from the micropyle of the ovule.
▷HISTORY C19: from ARIL + -ODE[1]

Arimathea *or* **Arimathaea** (ˌærɪməˈθiːə) NOUN a town in ancient Palestine: location unknown.

Ariminum (əˈrɪmɪnəm) NOUN the ancient name of **Rimini.**

arioso (ˌɑːrɪˈəʊzəʊ, ˌæ-) NOUN, *plural* **-sos** *or* **-si** (-siː). *Music* a recitative with the lyrical quality of an aria.
▷HISTORY C18: from Italian, from ARIA

arise (əˈraɪz) VERB **arises, arising, arose, arisen.** (*intr*) 1 to come into being; originate. 2 (foll by *from*) to spring or proceed as a consequence; result. 3 to get or stand up, as from a sitting, kneeling, or lying position. 4 to come into notice. 5 to move upwards; ascend.
▷HISTORY Old English *ārīsan*; related to Old Saxon *arīsan*, Old High German *irrīsan*; see RISE

arista (əˈrɪstə) NOUN, *plural* **-tae** (-tiː). 1 a stiff bristle such as the awn of some grasses and cereals. 2 a bristle-like appendage on the antennae of some insects.
▷HISTORY C17: from Latin: ear of corn, fishbone
▸**aˈristate** ADJECTIVE

Aristaeus (ˌærɪˈstiːəs) NOUN *Greek myth* a son of Apollo and Cyrene: protector of herds and fields.

Aristarchus (ˌærɪˈstɑːkəs) NOUN a crater in the NE quadrant of the moon, having a diameter of about 37 kilometres, which is the brightest formation on the moon.

aristo ('ærɪstəʊ, əˈrɪstəʊ) NOUN, *plural* **-tos.** *Informal* short for **aristocrat.**

aristocracy (ˌærɪˈstɒkrəsɪ) NOUN, *plural* **-cies.** 1 a privileged class of people usually of high birth; the nobility. 2 such a class as the ruling body of a state. 3 government by such a class. 4 a state governed by such a class. 5 a class of people considered to be outstanding in a sphere of activity.
▷HISTORY C16: from Late Latin *aristocratia*, from Greek *aristokratia* rule by the best-born, from *aristos* best; see -CRACY

aristocrat ('ærɪstəˌkræt) NOUN 1 a member of the aristocracy; a noble. 2 a person who has the manners or qualities of a member of a privileged or superior class. 3 a person who advocates aristocracy as a form of government.

aristocratic (ˌærɪstəˈkrætɪk) ADJECTIVE 1 relating to or characteristic of aristocracy or an aristocrat. 2 elegant or stylish in appearance and behaviour.
▸ˌ**aristoˈcratically** ADVERB

Aristotelian (ˌærɪstəˈtiːlɪən) ADJECTIVE 1 of or relating to Aristotle (384–322 B.C.), the Greek philosopher or his philosophy. 2 (of a philosophical position) derived from that of Aristotle, or incorporating such of his major doctrines as the distinctions between matter and form, and substance and accident, or the primacy of individuals over universals. ◆ NOUN 3 a follower of Aristotle.

Aristotelian logic (ˌærɪstəˈtiːlɪən) NOUN the logical theories of Aristotle as developed in the Middle Ages, concerned mainly with syllogistic reasoning: traditional as opposed to modern or symbolic logic.

aristotle ('ærɪˌstɒtᵊl) NOUN *Austral slang* 1 a bottle. 2 the buttocks or anus.
▷HISTORY rhyming slang; in sense 2, shortened from *bottle and glass* arse

Aristotle ('ærɪˌstɒtᵊl) NOUN a prominent crater in the NW quadrant of the moon about 83 kilometres in diameter.

arithmetic (əˈrɪθmətɪk) NOUN 1 the branch of mathematics concerned with numerical calculations, such as addition, subtraction, multiplication, and division. 2 one or more calculations involving numerical operations. 3 knowledge of or skill in using arithmetic: *his arithmetic is good.* ◆ ADJECTIVE (ˌærɪθˈmɛtɪk) *also* ˌ**arithˈmetical.** 4 of, relating to, or using arithmetic.
▷HISTORY C13: from Latin *arithmētica*, from Greek *arithmētikē*, from *arithmein* to count, from *arithmos* number
▸ˌ**arithˈmetically** ADVERB ▸**aˌrithmeˈtician** NOUN

arithmetic mean NOUN an average value of a set of integers, terms, or quantities, expressed as their sum divided by their number: *the arithmetic mean of 3, 4, and 8 is 5.* Often shortened to: **mean.** Also called: **average.** Compare **geometric mean.**

arithmetic progression NOUN a sequence of numbers or quantities, each term of which differs from the succeeding term by a constant amount, such as 3,6,9,12. Compare **geometric progression.**

-arium SUFFIX FORMING NOUNS indicating a place for or associated with something: *aquarium; planetarium; solarium.*
▷HISTORY from Latin *-ārium*, neuter of *-ārius* -ARY

Ariz. ABBREVIATION FOR Arizona.

Arizona (ˌærɪˈzəʊnə) NOUN a state of the

southwestern US: consists of the Colorado plateau in the northeast, including the Grand Canyon, divided from desert in the southwest by mountains rising over 3750 m (12 500 ft.). Capital: Phoenix. Pop.: 5 130 632 (2000). Area: 293 750 sq. km (113 417 sq. miles). Abbreviations: **Ariz**, (with zip code) **AZ**.

Arjuna (ˈɑːdʒʊnə) NOUN *Hindu myth* the most important of the five princes in the *Mahabharata*. Krishna served as his charioteer in the battle with the Kauravas.

ark (ɑːk) NOUN [1] the vessel that Noah built and in which he saved himself, his family, and a number of animals and birds during the Flood (Genesis 6–9). [2] **out of the ark**. *Informal* very old; out of date. [3] a place or thing offering shelter or protection. [4] *Dialect* a chest, box, or coffer.
▷HISTORY Old English *arc*, from Latin *arca* box, chest

Ark (ɑːk) NOUN *Judaism* [1] Also called: **Holy Ark**. the cupboard at the front of a synagogue, usually in the eastern wall, in which the Torah scrolls are kept. [2] Also called: **Ark of the Covenant**. the most sacred symbol of God's presence among the Hebrew people, carried in their journey from Sinai to the Promised Land (Canaan) and eventually enshrined in the holy of holies of the Temple in Jerusalem.

Ark. ABBREVIATION FOR Arkansas.

Arkansan (ɑːˈkænzən) NOUN [1] a native or inhabitant of Arkansas. ◆ ADJECTIVE [2] of or relating to Arkansas.

Arkansas NOUN [1] (ˈɑːkənˌsɔː) a state of the southern US: mountainous in the north and west, with the alluvial plain of the Mississippi in the east; has the only diamond mine in the US; the chief US producer of bauxite. Capital: Little Rock. Pop.: 2 673 400 (2000). Area: 134 537 sq. km (51 945 sq. miles). Abbreviations: **Ark**, (with zip code) **AR**. [2] (ɑːˈkænzəs) a river in the S central US, rising in central Colorado and flowing east and southeast to join the Mississippi in Arkansas. Length: 2335 km (1450 miles).

Arkhangelsk (arˈxangɪljsk) NOUN the Russian name for **Archangel**.

arkose (ˈɑːkəʊs) NOUN a sandstone consisting of grains of feldspar and quartz cemented by a mixture of quartz and clay minerals.
▷HISTORY C19: from French

Arlberg (*German* ˈarlˌbɛrk) NOUN a mountain pass in W Austria: a winter sports region. Height: 1802 m (5910 ft.).

Arles (ɑːlz; *French* arl) NOUN [1] a city in SE France, on the Rhône: Roman amphitheatre. Pop.: 52 590 (1990). [2] **Kingdom of**. a kingdom in SE France which had dissolved by 1378: known as the Kingdom of Burgundy until about 1200.

Arlington (ˈɑːlɪŋtən) NOUN a county of N Virginia: site of **Arlington National Cemetery**.

Arlon (*French* arlɔ̃) NOUN a town in SE Belgium, capital of Luxembourg province. Pop.: 17 000 (1991 est.).

arm[1] (ɑːm) NOUN [1] (in man) either of the upper limbs from the shoulder to the wrist. Related adjective: **brachial**. [2] the part of either of the upper limbs from the elbow to the wrist; forearm. [3] **a** the corresponding limb of any other vertebrate. **b** an armlike appendage of some invertebrates. [4] an object that covers or supports the human arm, esp the sleeve of a garment or the side of a chair, sofa, etc. [5] anything considered to resemble an arm in appearance, position, or function, esp something that branches out from a central support or larger mass: *an arm of the sea; the arm of a record player*. [6] an administrative subdivision of an organization: *an arm of the government*. [7] power; authority: *the arm of the law*. [8] any of the specialist combatant sections of a military force, such as cavalry, infantry, etc. [9] *Nautical* See **yardarm**. [10] *Sport, esp ball games* ability to throw or pitch: *he has a good arm*. [11] **an arm and a leg**. *Informal* a large amount of money. [12] **arm in arm**. with arms linked. [13] **at arm's length**. at a distance; away from familiarity with or subjection to another. [14] **give one's right arm**. *Informal* to be prepared to make any sacrifice. [15] **in the arms of Morpheus**. sleeping. [16] **with open arms**. with great warmth and hospitality: *to welcome someone with open arms*. ◆ VERB [17] (*tr*) *Archaic* to walk arm in arm with.
▷HISTORY Old English; related to German *Arm*, Old Norse *armr* arm, Latin *armus* shoulder, Greek *harmos* joint
▸ˈ**armless** ADJECTIVE ▸ˈ**armˌlike** ADJECTIVE

arm[2] (ɑːm) VERB (*tr*) [1] to equip with weapons as a preparation for war. [2] to provide (a person or thing) with something that strengthens, protects, or increases efficiency: *he armed himself against the cold*. [3] **a** to activate (a fuse) so that it will explode at the required time. **b** to prepare (an explosive device) for use by introducing a fuse or detonator. [4] *Nautical* to pack arming into (a sounding lead). ◆ NOUN [5] (*usually plural*) a weapon, esp a firearm. ◆ See also **arms**.
▷HISTORY C14: (n) back formation from *arms*, from Old French *armes*, from Latin *arma*; (vb) from Old French *armer* to equip with arms, from Latin *armāre*, from *arma* arms, equipment

Arm. ABBREVIATION FOR Armenia(n).

ARM ABBREVIATION FOR: [1] adjustable rate mortgage. ◆ INTERNATIONAL CAR REGISTRATION FOR: [2] Armenia.

armada (ɑːˈmɑːdə) NOUN a large number of ships or aircraft.
▷HISTORY C16: from Spanish, from Medieval Latin *armāta* fleet, armed forces, from Latin *armāre* to provide with arms

Armada (ɑːˈmɑːdə) NOUN (usually preceded by *the*) See **Spanish Armada**.

armadillo (ˌɑːməˈdɪləʊ) NOUN, *plural* **-los**. [1] any edentate mammal of the family *Dasypodidae* of Central and South America and S North America, such as *Priodontes giganteus* (**giant armadillo**). They are burrowing animals, with peglike rootless teeth and a covering of strong horny plates over most of the body. [2] **fairy armadillo**. another name for **pichiciego**.
▷HISTORY C16: from Spanish, diminutive of *armado* armed (man), from Latin *armātus* armed; compare ARMADA

Armageddon (ˌɑːməˈgɛdᵊn) NOUN [1] *New Testament* the final battle at the end of the world between the forces of good and evil, God against the kings of the earth (Revelation 16:16). [2] a catastrophic and extremely destructive conflict, esp World War I viewed as this.
▷HISTORY C19: from Late Latin *Armagedōn*, from Greek, from Hebrew *har megiddōn*, mountain district of *Megiddo*, in N Palestine, site of various battles in the Old Testament

Armagh (ɑːˈmɑː) NOUN [1] a historical county of S Northern Ireland: in 1973 it was replaced for administrative purposes by the districts of Armagh and Craigavon. Area: 1326 sq. km (512 sq. miles). [2] a district in Northern Ireland, in Co. Armagh. Pop.: 54 263 (2001). Area: 667 sq. km (258 sq. miles). [3] a town in S Northern Ireland, in Armagh district, Co. Armagh: seat of Roman Catholic and Protestant archbishops. Pop.: 14 640 (1991).

Armagnac (ˈɑːmənˌjæk) NOUN a dry brown brandy distilled in the French district of Gers.
▷HISTORY from *Armagnac*, the former name of this region

Armalite (ˈɑːməlaɪt) NOUN *Trademark* a lightweight high-velocity rifle of various calibres, capable of automatic and semiautomatic operation.
▷HISTORY C20: from *Armalite* Division, Fairchild Engine and Airplane Company, manufacturers

armament (ˈɑːməmənt) NOUN [1] (*often plural*) the weapon equipment of a military vehicle, ship, or aircraft. [2] a military force raised and armed ready for war. [3] preparation for war involving the production of equipment and arms.
▷HISTORY C17: from Latin *armāmenta* utensils, from *armāre* to equip

armamentarium (ˌɑːməmɛnˈtɛərɪəm) NOUN, *plural* **-iums** *or* **-ia** (-ɪə). the items that comprise the material and equipment used by a physician in his professional practice.

armature (ˈɑːmətjʊə) NOUN [1] a revolving structure in an electric motor or generator, wound with the coils that carry the current. [2] any part of an electric machine or device that moves under the influence of a magnetic field or within which an electromotive force is induced. [3] Also called: **keeper**. a soft iron or steel bar placed across the poles of a permanent magnet to close the magnetic circuit. [4] such a bar placed across the poles of an electromagnet to transmit mechanical force. [5] *Sculpture* a framework to support the clay or other material used in modelling. [6] the protective outer covering of an animal or plant. [7] *Archaic* armour.
▷HISTORY C15: from Latin *armātūra* armour, equipment, from *armāre* to furnish with equipment; see ARM[2]

armband (ˈɑːmˌbænd) NOUN [1] a band of material worn round the arm, such as one bearing an identifying mark, etc., or a black one indicating mourning. [2] an inflatable buoyancy aid, worn on the upper arm of a person learning to swim. [3] an elasticated band worn round the upper arm to keep the shirtsleeve in place.

armchair (ˈɑːmˌtʃɛə) NOUN [1] a chair, esp an upholstered one, that has side supports for the arms or elbows. [2] (*modifier*) taking no active part; lacking practical experience; theoretical: *an armchair strategist*. [3] (*modifier*) participated in away from the place of action or in the home: *armchair theatre*.

Armco (ˈɑːmkəʊ) NOUN *Trademark* a metal safety barrier erected at the side of motor-racing circuits, esp on corners.

armed[1] (ɑːmd) ADJECTIVE [1] equipped with or supported by arms, armour, etc. [2] prepared for conflict or any difficulty. [3] (of an explosive device) prepared for use; having a fuse or detonator installed. [4] (of plants) having the protection of thorns, spines, etc.

armed[2] (ɑːmd) ADJECTIVE **a** having an arm or arms. **b** (*in combination*): *long-armed; one-armed*.

armed forces PLURAL NOUN the military forces of a nation or nations, including the army, navy, air force, marines, etc.

armed response vehicle NOUN a police vehicle carrying armed officers who are trained to respond to incidents involving firearms.

Armenia (ɑːˈmiːnɪə) NOUN [1] a republic in NW Asia: originally part of the historic Armenian kingdom; acquired by Russia in 1828; became the Armenian Soviet Socialist Republic in 1936; gained independence in 1991. It is mountainous, rising over 4000 m (13 000 ft.). Language: Armenian. Religion: Christian (Armenian Apostolic) majority. Currency: dram. Capital: Yerevan. Pop.: 3 807 000 (2001 est.). Area: 29 800 sq. km (11 490 sq. miles). [2] a former kingdom in W Asia, between the Black Sea and the Caspian Sea, south of Georgia. [3] a town in central Colombia: centre of a coffee-growing district. Pop.: 283 842 (1997 est.).

Armenian (ɑːˈmiːnɪən) NOUN [1] a native or inhabitant of Armenia or an Armenian-speaking person elsewhere. [2] the language of the Armenians: an Indo-European language probably belonging to the Thraco-Phrygian branch, but containing many non-Indo-European elements. [3] an adherent of the Armenian Church or its doctrines. ◆ ADJECTIVE [4] of or relating to Armenia, its inhabitants, their language, or the Armenian Church.

Armenian Church NOUN the national Church of Armenia, founded in the early fourth century A.D., the dogmas and liturgy of which are similar to those of the Orthodox Church.

Armentières (ˈɑːmənˌtɪəz; *French* armɑ̃tjɛr) NOUN a town in N France: site of battles in both World Wars. Pop.: 26 240 (1990).

armeria (ɑːˈmiːrɪə) NOUN the generic name for **thrift** (sense 2).
▷HISTORY New Latin, from *flos armeriae*, a species of dianthus

armes parlantes (*French* arm parlɑ̃t) PLURAL NOUN *Heraldry* arms using devices to illustrate the name of the bearers, such as a rose and a wall to illustrate the name *Rosewall*.
▷HISTORY literally: speaking arms

armet (ˈɑːmɛt) NOUN a close-fitting medieval visored helmet with a neck guard.
▷HISTORY C16: from Old French, from Old Spanish *almete*, from Old French HELMET

armful (ˈɑːmfʊl) NOUN, *plural* **-fuls**. the amount that can be held by one or both arms.

armhole (ˈɑːmˌhəʊl) NOUN the opening in an article of clothing through which the arm passes and to which a sleeve is often fitted.

Armidale (ˈɑːmɪˌdeɪl) NOUN a town in Australia, in NE New South Wales: a centre for tourism. Pop.: 21 606 (1991 est.).

armiger (ˈɑːmɪdʒə) NOUN [1] a person entitled to

bear heraldic arms, such as a sovereign or nobleman. [2] a squire carrying the armour of a medieval knight.
▷HISTORY C16: from Medieval Latin: squire, from Latin: armour-bearer, from *arma* arms + *gerere* to carry, bear
▸**armigerous** (ɑːˈmɪdʒərəs) ADJECTIVE

armillary (ˈɑːmɪlərɪ, ɑːˈmɪlərɪ) ADJECTIVE of or relating to bracelets.
▷HISTORY C17: from New Latin *armillaris*, from Latin *armilla* bracelet

armillary sphere NOUN a model of the celestial sphere consisting of rings representing the relative positions of the celestial equator, ecliptic, etc., used by early astronomers for determining the positions of stars.

arming (ˈɑːmɪŋ) NOUN [1] the act of taking arms or providing with arms. [2] *Nautical* a greasy substance, such as tallow, packed into the recess at the bottom of a sounding lead to pick up samples of sand, gravel, etc., from the bottom.

Arminian (ɑːˈmɪnɪən) ADJECTIVE [1] denoting, relating to, or believing in the Christian Protestant doctrines of Jacobus Arminius (real name *Jacob Harmensen*.; 1560–1609), the Dutch theologian, published in 1610, which rejected absolute predestination and insisted that the sovereignty of God is compatible with free will in man. These doctrines deeply influenced Wesleyan and Methodist theology. ◆ NOUN [2] a follower of such doctrines.
▸**Arˈminianˌism** NOUN

armipotent (ɑːˈmɪpətənt) ADJECTIVE *Literary* strong in arms or war.
▷HISTORY C14: from Latin *armipotēns*, from *arma* arms + *potēns* powerful, from *posse* to be able
▸**arˈmipotence** NOUN

armistice (ˈɑːmɪstɪs) NOUN an agreement between opposing armies to suspend hostilities in order to discuss peace terms; truce.
▷HISTORY C18: from New Latin *armistitium*, from Latin *arma* arms + *sistere* to stop, stand still

Armistice Day NOUN the anniversary of the signing of the armistice that ended World War I, on Nov. 11, 1918, now kept on Remembrance Sunday. See also **Remembrance Sunday**. US name: **Veterans Day**.

armlet (ˈɑːmlɪt) NOUN [1] a small arm, as of a lake, the sea, etc. [2] a band or bracelet worn round the arm for ornament, identification, etc. [3] a very short sleeve on a garment.

armoire (ɑːmˈwɑː) NOUN a large cabinet, originally used for storing weapons.
▷HISTORY C16: from French, from Old French *armaire*, from Latin *armārium* chest, closet; see AMBRY

armor (ˈɑːmə) NOUN the US spelling of **armour**.

armorial (ɑːˈmɔːrɪəl) ADJECTIVE [1] of or relating to heraldry or heraldic arms. ◆ NOUN [2] a book of coats of arms.

Armorica (ɑːˈmɒrɪkə) NOUN an ancient name for Brittany.

Armorican (ɑːˈmɒrɪkən) NOUN [1] a native or inhabitant of Armorica (an ancient name for Brittany). ◆ ADJECTIVE [2] of or relating to Armorica.

armory (ˈɑːmərɪ) NOUN, *plural* **-mories**. the usual US spelling of **armoury**.

armour *or US* **armor** (ˈɑːmə) NOUN [1] any defensive covering, esp that of metal, chain mail, etc., worn by medieval warriors to prevent injury to the body in battle. [2] the protective metal plates on a tank, warship, etc. [3] *Military* armoured fighting vehicles in general; military units equipped with these. [4] any protective covering, such as the shell of certain animals. [5] *Nautical* the watertight suit of a diver. [6] *Engineering* permanent protection for an underwater structure. [7] heraldic insignia; arms. ◆ VERB [8] (*tr*) to equip or cover with armour.
▷HISTORY C13: from Old French *armure*, from Latin *armātūra* armour, equipment

armour-bearer NOUN *History* a retainer who carried the arms or armour of a warrior.

armoured *or US* **armored** (ˈɑːməd) ADJECTIVE [1] having a protective covering, such as armour or bone. [2] comprising units making use of armoured vehicles: *an armoured brigade*. [3] (of glass) toughened.

armoured car NOUN [1] *Military* a fast lightly armed and armoured vehicle, mainly used for reconnaissance. [2] any vehicle strengthened by armoured plate, esp a security van for transporting cash and valuables.

armourer *or US* **armorer** (ˈɑːmərə) NOUN [1] a person who makes or mends arms and armour. [2] a person employed in the maintenance of small arms and weapons in a military unit.

armour plate NOUN a tough heavy steel, usually containing chromium, nickel, and molybdenum and often hardened on the surface, used for protecting warships, tanks, etc.

armoury *or US* **armory** (ˈɑːmərɪ) NOUN, *plural* **-mouries** *or* **-mories**. [1] a secure place for the storage of weapons. [2] armour generally. [3] **a** *US* a National Guard base. **b** *US* a building in which training in the use of arms and drill takes place; drill hall. **c** (*plural*) *Canadian* such a building used for training and as headquarters by a reserve unit of the armed forces. [4] resources, as of arguments or objections, on which to draw: *they thought they had proved him wrong, but he still had a few weapons in his armoury*. [5] *US* a place where arms are made.

armpit (ˈɑːmˌpɪt) NOUN [1] the small depression beneath the arm where it joins the shoulder. Technical name: **axilla**. Related adjective: **axillary**. [2] *Slang* an extremely unpleasant place: *the armpit of the Mediterranean*.

armrest (ˈɑːmˌrest) NOUN the part of a chair, sofa, etc., that supports the arm. Sometimes shortened to: **arm**.

arms (ɑːmz) PLURAL NOUN [1] weapons collectively. See also **small arms**. [2] military exploits: *prowess in arms*. [3] the official heraldic symbols of a family, state, etc., including a shield with distinctive devices, and often supports, a crest, or other insignia. [4] **bear arms. a** to carry weapons. **b** to serve in the armed forces. **c** to have a coat of arms. [5] **in** *or* **under arms.** armed and prepared for war. [6] **lay down one's arms.** to stop fighting; surrender. [7] **present arms.** *Military* **a** a position of salute in which the rifle is brought up to a position vertically in line with the body, muzzle uppermost and trigger guard to the fore. **b** the command for this drill. [8] **take (up) arms.** to prepare to fight. [9] **to arms!** arm yourselves! [10] **up in arms.** indignant; prepared to protest strongly.
▷HISTORY C13: from Old French *armes*, from Latin *arma*; see ARM²

arm's-length ADJECTIVE [1] lacking intimacy or friendliness, esp when possessing some special connection, such as previous closeness: *we now have an arm's-length relationship*. [2] (of commercial transactions) in accordance with market values, disregarding any connection such as common ownership of the companies involved.

arms race NOUN the continuing competitive attempt by two or more nations each to have available to it more and more powerful weapons than the other(s).

armure (ˈɑːmjʊə) NOUN a silk or wool fabric with a small cobbled pattern.
▷HISTORY C19: from French: ARMOUR

arm wrestling NOUN a contest in which two people sit facing each other each with one elbow resting on a table, clasp hands, and each tries to force the other's arm flat onto the table while keeping his own elbow touching the table.

army (ˈɑːmɪ) NOUN, *plural* **-mies**. [1] the military land forces of a nation. [2] a military unit usually consisting of two or more corps with supporting arms and services. [3] (*modifier*) of, relating to, or characteristic of an army: *army rations*. [4] any large body of people united for some specific purpose. [5] a large number of people, animals, etc.; multitude.
▷HISTORY C14: from Old French *armee*, from Medieval Latin *armāta* armed forces; see ARMADA

army ant NOUN any of various mainly tropical American predatory ants of the subfamily *Dorylinae*, which live in temporary nests and travel in vast hordes preying on other animals. Also called: **legionary ant**. See also **driver ant**.

Army List NOUN *Brit* an official list of all serving commissioned officers of the army and reserve officers liable for recall.

army worm NOUN [1] the caterpillar of a widely distributed noctuid moth, *Leucania unipuncta*, which travels in vast hordes and is a serious pest of cereal crops in North America. [2] any of various similar caterpillars.

Arnhem (ˈɑːnəm) NOUN a city in the E Netherlands, capital of Gelderland province, on the Rhine: site of a World War II battle. Pop.: 137 222 (1999 est.).

Arnhem Land NOUN a region of N Australia in the N Northern Territory, large areas of which are reserved for native Australians.

arnica (ˈɑːnɪkə) NOUN [1] any N temperate or arctic plant of the genus *Arnica*, typically having yellow flowers: family *Asteraceae* (composites). [2] the tincture of the dried flower heads of any of these plants, esp *A. montana*, used in treating bruises.
▷HISTORY C18: from New Latin, of unknown origin

Arno (ˈɑːnəʊ) NOUN a river in central Italy, rising in the Apennines and flowing through Florence to the Ligurian Sea. Length: about 240 km (150 miles).

Arnold (ˈɑːnᵊld) NOUN a town in N central England, in S Nottinghamshire. Pop.: 37 646 (1991).

aroha (ˈɑːrɒhə) NOUN *NZ* love, compassion, or affectionate regard.
▷HISTORY Maori

aroid (ˈærɔɪd, ˈɛər-) ADJECTIVE [1] Also: **araceous**. of, relating to, or belonging to the *Araceae*, a family of plants having small flowers massed on a spadix surrounded by a large petaloid spathe. The family includes arum, calla, and anthurium. ◆ NOUN [2] any plant of the *Araceae*.
▷HISTORY C19: from New Latin *Arum* type genus + -OID; see ARUM

aroint thee *or* **ye** (əˈrɔɪnt) SENTENCE SUBSTITUTE *Archaic* away! begone!
▷HISTORY C17: of unknown origin

aroma (əˈrəʊmə) NOUN [1] a distinctive usually pleasant smell, esp of spices, wines, and plants. [2] a subtle pervasive quality or atmosphere.
▷HISTORY C18: via Latin from Greek: spice

aromatherapy (əˌrəʊməˈθɛrəpɪ) NOUN the use of fragrant essential oils extracted from plants as a treatment in complementary medicine to relieve tension and cure certain minor ailments.
▸**aˌromaˈtherapist** NOUN

aromatic (ˌærəˈmætɪk) ADJECTIVE [1] having a distinctive, usually fragrant smell. [2] (of an organic compound) having an unsaturated ring containing alternating double and single bonds, esp containing a benzene ring; exhibiting aromaticity. Compare **aliphatic**. ◆ NOUN [3] something, such as a plant or drug, giving off a fragrant smell.
▸ˌ**aroˈmatically** ADVERB

aromaticity (əˌrəʊməˈtɪsɪtɪ) NOUN [1] the property of certain planar cyclic conjugated molecules, esp benzene, of behaving like unsaturated molecules and undergoing substitution reactions rather than addition as a result of delocalization of electrons in the ring. [2] the quality or state of having an aroma.

aromatize *or* **aromatise** (əˈrəʊməˌtaɪz) VERB [1] (*tr*) to make aromatic. [2] to convert (an aliphatic compound) to an aromatic compound.
▸**aˌromatiˈzation** *or* **aˌromatiˈsation** NOUN

arose (əˈrəʊz) VERB the past tense of **arise**.

around (əˈraʊnd) PREPOSITION [1] situated at various points in: *a lot of shelves around the house*. [2] from place to place in: *driving around Ireland*. [3] somewhere in or near: *to stay around the house*. [4] approximately in: *it happened around 1957, I think*. ◆ ADVERB [5] in all directions from a point of reference: *he owns the land for ten miles around*. [6] in the vicinity, esp restlessly but idly: *to wait around; stand around*. [7] here and there; in no particular place or direction: *dotted around*. [8] *Informal* (of people) active and prominent in a particular area or profession: *some pop stars are around for only a few years*. [9] *Informal* present in some place (the exact location being inexact): *he's around here somewhere*. [10] *Informal* in circulation; available: *that type of phone has been around for some years now*. [11] *Informal* to many places, so as to have gained considerable experience, often of a worldly or social nature: *he gets around; I've been around*.

▷HISTORY C17 (rare earlier): from A-[2] + ROUND

> **Language note** In American English, *around* is usually used instead of *round* in adverbial and prepositional senses, except in a few fixed phrases such as *all year round*. The use of *around* in adverbial senses is less common in British English.

arouse (əˈraʊz) VERB 1 (*tr*) to evoke or elicit (a reaction, emotion, or response); stimulate. 2 to awaken from sleep.
▸**aˈrousal** NOUN ▸**aˈrouser** NOUN

arpa (ˈɑːpə) AN INTERNET DOMAIN NAME FOR a site concerned with Internet infrastructure.
▷HISTORY C20: acronym of *A(ddress) (and) R(outing) P(arameter) A(rea)*

arpeggio (ɑːˈpɛdʒɪəʊ) NOUN, *plural* **-gios.** 1 a chord whose notes are played in rapid succession rather than simultaneously. 2 an ascending and descending figuration used in practising the piano, voice, etc.
▷HISTORY C18: from Italian, from *arpeggiare* to perform on the harp, from *arpa* HARP

arpent (ˈɑːpənt; *French* arpɑ̃) NOUN 1 a former French unit of length equal to 190 feet (approximately 58 metres). 2 an old French unit of land area equal to about one acre: still used in Quebec and Louisiana.
▷HISTORY C16: from Old French, probably from Late Latin *arepennis* half an acre, of Gaulish origin; related to Middle Irish *airchenn* unit of land measure

arquebus (ˈɑːkwɪbəs) *or* **harquebus** NOUN a portable long-barrelled gun dating from the 15th century: fired by a wheel-lock or matchlock. Also called: **hackbut, hagbut.**
▷HISTORY C16: via Old French *harquebuse* from Middle Dutch *hakebusse,* literally: hook gun, from the shape of the butt, from *hake* hook + *busse* box, gun, from Late Latin *busis* box

arr. ABBREVIATION FOR: 1 arranged (by). 2 arrival.

arrack *or* **arak** (ˈærək) NOUN a coarse spirit distilled in various Eastern countries from grain, rice, sugar cane, etc.
▷HISTORY C17: from Arabic *ʻaraq* sweat, sweet juice, liquor

arraign (əˈreɪn) VERB (*tr*) 1 to bring (a prisoner) before a court to answer an indictment. 2 to call to account; complain about; accuse.
▷HISTORY C14: from Old French *araisnier* to speak, accuse, from A-[2] + *raisnier,* from Vulgar Latin *ratiōnāre* (unattested) to talk, argue, from Latin *ratiō* a reasoning
▸**arˈraigner** NOUN ▸**arˈraignment** NOUN

Arran (ˈærən) NOUN an island off the SW coast of Scotland, in the Firth of Clyde. Pop.: 4000 (latest est.). Area: 427 sq. km (165 sq. miles).

arrange (əˈreɪndʒ) VERB 1 (*tr*) to put into a proper, systematic, or decorative order. 2 (*tr; may take a clause as object or an infinitive*) to arrive at an agreement or understanding about; settle. 3 (when *intr*, often foll by *for;* when *tr, may take a clause as object or an infinitive*) to make plans or preparations in advance (for something): *we arranged for her to be met.* 4 (*tr*) to adapt (a musical composition) for performance in a different way, esp on different instruments. 5 (*tr*) to adapt (a play, etc.) for broadcasting. 6 (*intr;* often foll by *with*) to come to an agreement.
▷HISTORY C14: from Old French *arangier,* from A-[2] + *rangier* to put in a row, RANGE
▸**arˈrangeable** ADJECTIVE ▸**arˈranger** NOUN

arrangement (əˈreɪndʒmənt) NOUN 1 the act of arranging or being arranged. 2 the form in which things are arranged: *he altered the arrangement of furniture in the room.* 3 a thing composed of various ordered parts; the result of arranging: *a flower arrangement.* 4 (*often plural*) a preparatory measure taken or plan made; preparation. 5 an agreement or settlement; understanding. 6 an adaptation of a piece of music for performance in a different way, esp on different instruments from those for which it was originally composed. 7 an adaptation (of a play, etc.) for broadcasting.

arrant (ˈærənt) ADJECTIVE utter; out-and-out: *an arrant fool.*
▷HISTORY C14: a variant of ERRANT (wandering, vagabond); sense developed from its frequent use in phrases like *arrant thief* (hence: notorious)
▸**ˈarrantly** ADVERB

arras (ˈærəs) NOUN a wall hanging, esp of tapestry.

Arras (ˈærəs; *French* arɑs) NOUN a town in N France: formerly famous for tapestry; severely damaged in both World Wars. Pop.: 42 715 (1990).

array (əˈreɪ) NOUN 1 an impressive display or collection. 2 an orderly or regular arrangement, esp of troops in battle order. 3 *Poetic* rich clothing; apparel. 4 *Maths* a sequence of numbers or symbols in a specified order. 5 *Maths* a set of numbers or symbols arranged in rows and columns, as in a determinant or matrix. 6 *Electronics* an arrangement of aerials spaced to give desired directional characteristics, used esp in radar. 7 *Law* a panel of jurors. 8 the arming of military forces. 9 *Computing* a regular data structure in which individual elements may be located by reference to one or more integer index variables, the number of such indices being the number of dimensions in the array. ◆ VERB (*tr*) 10 to dress in rich attire; adorn. 11 to arrange in order (esp troops for battle); marshal. 12 *Law* to draw up (a panel of jurors).
▷HISTORY C13: from Old French *aroi* arrangement, from *arayer* to arrange, of Germanic origin; compare Old English *arǣdan* to make ready
▸**arˈrayal** NOUN

arrears (əˈrɪəz) NOUN 1 (*sometimes singular*) Also called: **arrearage** (əˈrɪərɪdʒ). something outstanding or owed. 2 **in arrears** *or* **arrear.** late in paying a debt or meeting an obligation.
▷HISTORY C18: from obsolete *arrear* (adv) behindhand, from Old French *arere,* from Medieval Latin *adretrō,* from Latin *ad* to + *retrō* backwards

arrest (əˈrɛst) VERB (*tr*) 1 to deprive (a person) of liberty by taking him into custody, esp under lawful authority. 2 to seize (a ship) under lawful authority. 3 to slow or stop the development or progress of (a disease, growth, etc.). 4 to catch and hold (one's attention, sight, etc.). 5 **arrest judgment.** *Law* to stay proceedings after a verdict, on the grounds of error or possible error. 6 **can't get arrested.** *Informal* (of a performer) is unrecognized and unsuccessful: *he can't get arrested here but is a megastar in the States.* ◆ NOUN 7 the act of taking a person into custody, esp under lawful authority. 8 the act of seizing and holding a ship under lawful authority. 9 the state of being held, esp under lawful authority: *under arrest.* 10 Also called: **arrestation** (ˌærɛsˈteɪʃən). the slowing or stopping of the development or progress of something. 11 the stopping or sudden cessation of motion of something: *a cardiac arrest.*
▷HISTORY C14: from Old French *arester,* from Vulgar Latin *arrestāre* (unattested), from Latin *ad* at, to + *restāre* to stand firm, stop

arrestable (əˈrɛstəbᵊl) ADJECTIVE 1 liable to be arrested. 2 (of an offence) such that an offender may be arrested without a warrant.

arrester (əˈrɛstə) NOUN 1 a person who arrests. 2 a thing that stops or checks motion, esp a mechanism of wires for slowing aeroplanes as they land on an aircraft carrier.

arresting (əˈrɛstɪŋ) ADJECTIVE attracting attention; striking.
▸**arˈrestingly** ADVERB

arrestment (əˈrɛstmənt) NOUN *Scots Law* the seizure of money or property to prevent a debtor paying one creditor in advance of another.

arrest of judgment NOUN *Law* a stay of proceedings after a verdict, on the grounds of error or possible error.

Arretine (ˈærɪˌtaɪn) ADJECTIVE of or relating to Arretium (the ancient Latin name of Arezzo, a city in central Italy).

Arretine ware NOUN another term for **Samian ware** (sense 2).

Arretium (æˈriːtɪəm, -ˈrɛt-) NOUN the ancient Latin name of **Arezzo.**
▸**Arretine** (ˈærɪˌtaɪn) ADJECTIVE

arrhythmia (əˈrɪðmɪə) NOUN any variation from the normal rhythm in the heartbeat.
▷HISTORY C19: New Latin, from Greek *arrhuthmia,* from A-[1] + *rhuthmos* RHYTHM

arrière-ban *French* (arjɛrbɑ̃) NOUN 1 (in medieval France) a summons to the king's vassals to do military service. 2 the vassals so assembled for military service.
▷HISTORY C16: changed from Old French *herban* call to arms, of Germanic origin; compare Old High German *heriban,* from *heri* army + *ban* summons, BAN[2]

arrière-pensée *French* (arjɛrpɑ̃se) NOUN an unrevealed thought or intention.
▷HISTORY C19: literally: behind thought

Ar Rimal (ɑːr rɪˈmɑːl) NOUN another name for **Rubʻ al Khali.**

arris (ˈærɪs) NOUN, *plural* **-ris** *or* **-rises.** a sharp edge at the meeting of two surfaces at an angle with one another, as at two adjacent sides of a stone block.
▷HISTORY C17: apparently from Old French *areste* beard of grain, sharp ridge; see ARÊTE

arrish (ˈærɪʃ) NOUN *Southwest English dialect* corn stubble.
▷HISTORY Old English *ersc*

arrival (əˈraɪvᵊl) NOUN 1 the act or time of arriving. 2 a person or thing that arrives or has arrived. 3 the reaching of a condition or objective.

arrive (əˈraɪv) VERB (*intr*) 1 to come to a certain place during or after a journey; reach a destination. 2 (foll by *at*) to agree upon; reach: *to arrive at a decision.* 3 to occur eventually: *the moment arrived when pretence was useless.* 4 *Informal* (of a baby) to be born. 5 *Informal* to attain success or gain recognition.
▷HISTORY C13: from Old French *ariver,* from Vulgar Latin *arrīpāre* (unattested) to land, reach the bank, from Latin *ad* to + *rīpa* river bank
▸**arˈriver** NOUN

arrivederci *Italian* (arriveˈdertʃi) SENTENCE SUBSTITUTE goodbye.

arrivisme (ˌæriːˈviːzmə; *French* arivism) NOUN unscrupulous ambition.

arriviste (ˌæriːˈviːst; *French* arivist) NOUN a person who is unscrupulously ambitious.
▷HISTORY French: see ARRIVE, -IST

arroba (əˈrəʊbə) NOUN, *plural* **-bas.** 1 a unit of weight, approximately equal to 11 kilograms, used in some Spanish-speaking countries. 2 a unit of weight, approximately equal to 15 kilograms, used in some Portuguese-speaking countries. 3 a liquid measure used in some Spanish-speaking countries with different values, but in Spain used as a wine-measure, approximately equal to 16 litres.
▷HISTORY C16: from Spanish, from Arabic *ar-rubʻ* the quarter (of a quintal)

arrogant (ˈærəgənt) ADJECTIVE having or showing an exaggerated opinion of one's own importance, merit, ability, etc.; conceited; overbearingly proud: *an arrogant teacher; an arrogant assumption.*
▷HISTORY C14: from Latin *arrogāre* to claim as one's own; see ARROGATE
▸**ˈarrogance** NOUN ▸**ˈarrogantly** ADVERB

arrogate (ˈærəˌgeɪt) VERB 1 (*tr*) to claim or appropriate for oneself presumptuously or without justification. 2 (*tr*) to attribute or assign to another without justification.
▷HISTORY C16: from Latin *arrogāre,* from *rogāre* to ask
▸**ˌarroˈgation** NOUN ▸**arrogative** (əˈrɒgətɪv) ADJECTIVE
▸**ˈarroˌgator** NOUN

arrondissement (*French* arɔ̃dismɑ̃) NOUN (in France) 1 the largest administrative subdivision of a department. 2 a municipal district of certain cities, esp Paris.
▷HISTORY C19: from *arrondir* to make round, from AB-[1] + *-rondir* from *rond* ROUND

arrow (ˈærəʊ) NOUN 1 a long slender pointed weapon, usually having feathers fastened at the end as a balance, that is shot from a bow. Related adjective: **sagittal.** 2 any of various things that resemble an arrow in shape, function, or speed, such as a sign indicating direction or position. ◆ See also **arrows.**
▷HISTORY Old English *arwe;* related to Old Norse *ör,* Gothic *arhvazna,* Latin *arcus* bow, ARCH[1]

arrowgrass (ˈærəʊˌgrɑːs) NOUN either of two species, **sea arrowgrass** (*Triglochin maritima*) or **marsh arrowgrass** (*T. palustris*), of monocotyledonous perennials having long thin fleshy leaves and spikes of inconspicuous flowers.
▷HISTORY C18: named from the shape of the fruits when open

arrowhead ('ærəʊˌhɛd) NOUN [1] the pointed tip of an arrow, often removable from the shaft. [2] something that resembles the head of an arrow in shape, such as a triangular decoration on garments used to reinforce joins. [3] any aquatic herbaceous plant of the genus *Sagittaria*, esp *S. sagittifolia*, having arrow-shaped aerial leaves and linear submerged leaves: family *Alismataceae*.

arrowroot ('ærəʊˌruːt) NOUN [1] a white-flowered West Indian plant, *Maranta arundinacea*, whose rhizomes yield an easily digestible starch: family *Marantaceae*. [2] the starch obtained from this plant. [3] any of several other plants whose rhizomes or roots yield starch.

arrows ('ærəʊz) NOUN (*functioning as singular*) *Brit* an informal name for **darts**.

arrowwood ('ærəʊˌwʊd) NOUN any of various trees or shrubs, esp certain viburnums, having long straight tough stems formerly used by North American Indians to make arrows.

arrowworm ('ærəʊˌwɜːm) NOUN any small marine invertebrate of the genus *Sagitta*, having an elongated transparent body with fins and prehensile oral bristles: phylum *Chaetognatha* (chaetognaths).

arroyo (ə'rɔɪəʊ) NOUN, *plural* **-os**. *Chiefly southwestern US* a steep-sided stream bed that is usually dry except after heavy rain.
▷HISTORY C19: from Spanish

Arru Islands ('ɑːruː) PLURAL NOUN a variant spelling of **Aru Islands**.

arse (ɑːs) *or US and Canadian* **ass** NOUN *Slang* [1] the buttocks. [2] the anus. [3] a stupid person; fool. [4] sexual intercourse. [5] *Austral* effrontery; cheek. [6] **get one's arse into gear**. to start to do something seriously and quickly. ◆ Also called (for senses 2, 3): **arsehole** ('ɑːsˌhəʊl), (US and Canadian) **asshole**.

> **Language note** Dating back at least a thousand years, and taboo till around the middle of the 20th century, this venerable "Anglo-Saxon" word now seems unlikely to cause offence in all but the most formal contexts. Its acceptability has possibly been helped by such useful verb formations as "to arse about" and "I can't be arsed".

arse *or US and Canadian* **ass about** or **around** VERB (*intr, adverb*) *Slang* to play the fool; act stupidly, esp in an irritating manner.

arse *or US and Canadian* **ass licker** NOUN *Slang* a person who curries favour.
▸**'arse-ˌlicking** *or* (*US and Canadian*) **'ass-ˌlicking** ADJECTIVE, NOUN

arsed (ɑːst) ADJECTIVE **be arsed**. *Slang* to be willing, inclined, or prepared (esp in the phrase **can't be arsed**).

arsenal ('ɑːsənᵊl) NOUN [1] a store for arms, ammunition, and other military items. [2] a workshop or factory that produces munitions. [3] a store of anything regarded as weapons: *an arsenal of destructive arguments*.
▷HISTORY C16: from Italian *arsenale* dockyard, from the original Venetian *arsenal* dockyard and naval store, from Arabic *dār sinā'ah*, from *dār* house + *sinā'ah* manufacture

arsenate ('ɑːsəˌneɪt, -nɪt) NOUN a salt or ester of arsenic acid, esp a salt containing the ion $A_5O_4^{3-}$.

arsenic NOUN ('ɑːsnɪk) [1] a toxic metalloid element, existing in several allotropic forms, that occurs principally in realgar and orpiment and as the free element. It is used in transistors, lead-based alloys, and high-temperature brasses. Symbol: As; atomic no.: 33; atomic wt.: 74.92159; valency: –3, 0, +3, or +5; relative density: 5.73 (grey); melting pt.: 817°C at a pressure of $3MN/m^2$ (grey); sublimes at 613°C (grey). [2] a nontechnical name for **arsenic trioxide**. ◆ ADJECTIVE (ɑː'sɛnɪk) [3] of or containing arsenic, esp in the pentavalent state.
▷HISTORY C14: from Latin *arsenicum*, from Greek *arsenikon* yellow orpiment, from Syriac *zarnīg* (influenced in form by Greek *arsenikos* virile)

arsenic acid NOUN a white poisonous soluble crystalline solid used in the manufacture of arsenates and insecticides. Formula: H_3AsO_4.

arsenical (ɑː'sɛnɪkᵊl) ADJECTIVE [1] of or containing arsenic. ◆ NOUN [2] a drug or insecticide containing arsenic.

arsenic trioxide NOUN a white poisonous powder used in the manufacture of glass and as an insecticide, rat poison, and weedkiller. Formula: As_2O_3. Also called: **arsenic**.

arsenide ('ɑːsəˌnaɪd) NOUN a compound in which arsenic is the most electronegative element.

arsenious (ɑː'siːnɪəs) *or* **arsenous** ('ɑːsɪnəs) ADJECTIVE of or containing arsenic in the trivalent state.

arsenite ('ɑːsɪˌnaɪt) NOUN a salt or ester of arsenous acid, esp a salt containing the ion $A_5O_3^{3-}$.

arsenopyrite (ˌɑːsɪnəʊ'paɪraɪt, ɑːˌsɛnə-) NOUN a white or grey metallic mineral consisting of a sulphide of iron and arsenic that forms monoclinic crystals with an orthorhombic shape: an ore of arsenic. Formula: FeAsS. Also called: **mispickel**.

arsey ('ɑːsɪ) ADJECTIVE **arsier, arsiest**. *Slang* aggressive, irritable, or argumentative.

arsine ('ɑːsiːn) NOUN a colourless poisonous gas used in the manufacture of organic compounds, to dope transistors, and as a military poisonous gas. Formula: AsH_3.

arsis ('ɑːsɪs) NOUN, *plural* **-ses** (-siːz). (in classical prosody) the long syllable or part on which the ictus falls in a metrical foot. Compare **thesis** (sense 6).
▷HISTORY C18: via Late Latin from Greek, from *airein* to raise

ARSM (in Britain) ABBREVIATION FOR Associate of the Royal School of Mines.

ars nova ('ɑːz 'nəʊvə) NOUN a style of music of the 14th century, characterized by great freedom and variety of rhythm and melody contrasted with the strictness of the music of the 13th century.
▷HISTORY Latin, literally: new art

arson ('ɑːsᵊn) NOUN *Criminal law* the act of intentionally or recklessly setting fire to another's property or to one's own property for some improper reason.
▷HISTORY C17: from Old French, from Medieval Latin *ārsiō*, from Latin *ārdēre* to burn; see ARDENT
▸**'arsonist** NOUN

arsphenamine (ɑːs'fɛnəmɪn, -ˌmiːn) NOUN a drug containing arsenic, formerly used in the treatment of syphilis and related infections.

ars poetica ('ɑːz pəʊ'ɛtɪkə) NOUN the art of poetry.

arsy-versy ('ɑːsɪ'vɜːsɪ) ADVERB *Slang* [1] backwards or upside down. [2] in reverse.
▷HISTORY C16: from ARSE + Latin *versus* turned, modelled on compounds like *hurly-burly*

art[1] (ɑːt) NOUN [1] **a** the creation of works of beauty or other special significance. **b** (*as modifier*): *an art movement*. [2] the exercise of human skill (as distinguished from *nature*). [3] imaginative skill as applied to representations of the natural world or figments of the imagination. [4] **a** the products of man's creative activities; works of art collectively, esp of the visual arts, sometimes also music, drama, dance, and literature. **b** (*as modifier*): *an art gallery*. See also **arts, fine art**. [5] excellence or aesthetic merit of conception or execution as exemplified by such works. [6] any branch of the visual arts, esp painting. [7] (*modifier*) intended to be artistic or decorative: *art needlework*. [8] **a** any field using the techniques of art to display artistic qualities: *advertising art*. **b** (*as modifier*): *an art film*. [9] *Journalism* photographs or other illustrations in a newspaper, etc. [10] method, facility, or knack: *the art of threading a needle; the art of writing letters*. [11] the system of rules or principles governing a particular human activity: *the art of government*. [12] artfulness; cunning. [13] **get something down to a fine art**. to become highly proficient at something through practice. ◆ See also **arts**.
▷HISTORY C13: from Old French, from Latin *ars* craftsmanship

art[2] (ɑːt) VERB *Archaic* (used with the pronoun *thou*) a singular form of the present tense (indicative mood) of **be**.
▷HISTORY Old English *eart*, part of *bēon* to BE

ART ABBREVIATION FOR assisted reproductive technology.

-art SUFFIX FORMING NOUNS a variant of **-ard**.

artal ('ɑːtɑːl) NOUN a plural of **rotl**.

Art Deco ('dɛkəʊ) NOUN **a** a style of interior decoration, jewellery, architecture, etc., at its height in the 1930s and characterized by geometrical shapes, stylized natural forms, and symmetrical utilitarian designs adapted to mass production. **b** (*as modifier*): *an Art-Deco carpet*.
▷HISTORY C20: shortened from *art décoratif*, after the *Exposition des arts décoratifs* held in Paris in 1925

art director NOUN a person responsible for the sets and costumes in a film.

artefact *or* **artifact** ('ɑːtɪˌfækt) NOUN [1] something made or given shape by man, such as a tool or a work of art, esp an object of archaeological interest. [2] anything man-made, such as a spurious experimental result. [3] *Cytology* a structure seen in tissue after death, fixation, staining, etc., that is not normally present in the living tissue.
▷HISTORY C19: from Latin phrase *arte factum*, from *ars* skill + *facere* to make

artel (ɑː'tɛl) NOUN [1] (in the former Soviet Union) a cooperative union or organization, esp of producers, such as peasants. [2] (in prerevolutionary Russia) a quasi-cooperative association of people engaged in the same activity.
▷HISTORY from Russian *artel'*, from Italian *artieri* artisans, from *arte* work, from Latin *ars* ART[1]

Artemis ('ɑːtɪmɪs) NOUN *Greek myth* the virgin goddess of the hunt and the moon: the twin sister of Apollo. Roman counterpart: **Diana**. Also called: **Cynthia**.

artemisia (ˌɑːtɪ'miːzɪə) NOUN any herbaceous perennial plant of the genus *Artemisia*, of the N hemisphere, such as mugwort, sagebrush, and wormwood: family *Asteraceae* (composites).
▷HISTORY C14: via Latin from Greek, probably from ARTEMIS

Arte Povera (*Italian* ˌarte po'vera) NOUN a style of minimal art originating in Italy in the late 1960s, making use of cheap and commonly available materials such as stones, newspapers etc.
▷HISTORY C20: Italian, literally: poor art

arterial (ɑː'tɪərɪəl) ADJECTIVE [1] of, relating to, or affecting an artery or arteries: *arterial disease*. [2] denoting or relating to the usually bright red reoxygenated blood returning from the lungs or gills that circulates in the arteries. [3] being a major route, esp one with many minor branches: *an arterial road*.
▸**ar'terially** ADVERB

arterialize *or* **arterialise** (ɑː'tɪərɪəˌlaɪz) VERB (*tr*) [1] to change (venous blood) into arterial blood by replenishing the depleted oxygen. [2] to vascularize (tissues). [3] to provide with arteries.
▸**arˌteriali'zation** *or* **arˌteriali'sation** NOUN

arterio- COMBINING FORM artery or arteries: *arteriosclerosis*.
▷HISTORY from Greek; see ARTERY

arteriography (ɑːˌtɪərɪ'ɒgrəfɪ) NOUN the X-ray examination of an artery or arterial system after injection of a contrast medium into the bloodstream.

arteriole (ɑː'tɪərɪˌəʊl) NOUN *Anatomy* any of the small subdivisions of an artery that form thin-walled vessels ending in capillaries.
▷HISTORY C19: from New Latin *arteriola*, from Latin *artēria* ARTERY

arteriosclerosis (ɑːˌtɪərɪəʊsklɪə'rəʊsɪs) NOUN, *plural* **-ses** (-siːz). a pathological condition of the circulatory system characterized by thickening and loss of elasticity of the arterial walls. Nontechnical name: **hardening of the arteries**.
▸**arteriosclerotic** (ɑːˌtɪərɪəʊsklɪə'rɒtɪk) ADJECTIVE

arteriovenous (ɑːˌtɪərɪəʊ'viːnəs) ADJECTIVE of, relating to, or affecting an artery and a vein.

arteritis (ˌɑːtə'raɪtɪs) NOUN *Pathol* inflammation of an artery.

artery ('ɑːtərɪ) NOUN, *plural* **-teries**. [1] any of the tubular thick-walled muscular vessels that convey oxygenated blood from the heart to various parts of the body. Compare **pulmonary artery, vein**. [2] a major road or means of communication in any complex system.
▷HISTORY C14: from Latin *artēria*, related to Greek *aortē* the great artery, AORTA

artesian well (ɑː'tiːzɪən, -ʒən) NOUN a well sunk through impermeable strata into strata receiving water from an area at a higher altitude than that of

the well, so that there is sufficient pressure to force water to flow upwards.
▷HISTORY C19: from French *artésien,* from Old French *Arteis* Artois, old province, where such wells were common

Artex (ˈɑːtɛks) NOUN *Trademark* a brand of coating for walls and ceilings that gives a textured finish.

art form NOUN [1] a conventionally established form of artistic composition, such as the symphony or the sonnet. [2] a genre or activity viewed or treated as an art form.

artful (ˈɑːtfʊl) ADJECTIVE [1] cunning or tricky. [2] skilful in achieving a desired end. [3] *Archaic* characterized by skill or art. [4] *Archaic* artificial.
▸**ˈartfully** ADVERB ▸**ˈartfulness** NOUN

art house NOUN [1] a cinema which specializes in showing films which are not part of the commercial mainstream. ◆ ADJECTIVE [2] **a** of or relating to such films or a cinema which specializes in showing them. **b** *(as modifier): the surprise art-house hit of the season.*

arthralgia (ɑːˈθrældʒə) NOUN *Pathol* pain in a joint.
▸**arˈthralgic** ADJECTIVE

arthrectomy (ɑːˈθrɛktəmɪ) NOUN, *plural* **-mies**. surgical excision of a joint.

arthritis (ɑːˈθraɪtɪs) NOUN inflammation of a joint or joints characterized by pain and stiffness of the affected parts, caused by gout, rheumatic fever, etc. See also **rheumatoid arthritis.**
▷HISTORY C16: via Latin from Greek: see ARTHRO-, -ITIS
▸**arthritic** (ɑːˈθrɪtɪk) ADJECTIVE, NOUN

arthro- *or before a vowel* **arthr-** COMBINING FORM indicating a joint: *arthritis; arthropod.*
▷HISTORY from Greek *arthron*

arthrodia (ɑːˈθrəʊdɪə) NOUN *Anatomy, zoology* a joint.
▸**arˈthrodial** ADJECTIVE

arthrography (ɑːˈθrɒɡrəfɪ) NOUN the X-ray examination of a joint after injection of a contrast medium into the joint space.

arthromere (ˈɑːθrəˌmɪə) NOUN any of the segments of the body of an arthropod.
▸**arthromeric** (ˌɑːθrəˈmɛrɪk) ADJECTIVE

arthroplasty (ˈɑːθrəˌplæstɪ) NOUN surgical repair of a diseased joint.

arthropod (ˈɑːθrəˌpɒd) NOUN any invertebrate of the phylum *Arthropoda,* having jointed limbs, a segmented body, and an exoskeleton made of chitin. The group includes the crustaceans, insects, arachnids, and centipedes.
▸**arthropodous** (ɑːˈθrɒpədəs) *or* **arˈthropodal** ADJECTIVE

arthroscope (ˈɑːθrəˌskəʊp) NOUN a tubular instrument that is inserted into the capsule of a joint to examine the joint, extract tissue, etc.
▸**ˌarthroˈscopic** ADJECTIVE ▸**arthroscopy** (ɑːˈθrɒskəpɪ) NOUN

arthrospore (ˈɑːθrəˌspɔː) NOUN [1] a sporelike cell of ascomycetous fungi and some algae produced by a breaking of the hyphae. [2] a resting sporelike cell produced by some bacteria.
▸**ˌarthroˈsporic** *or* **ˌarthroˈsporous** ADJECTIVE

Arthur (ˈɑːθə) NOUN [1] a legendary king of the Britons in the sixth century A.D., who led Celtic resistance against the Saxons: possibly based on a historical figure; represented as leader of the Knights of the Round Table at Camelot. [2] **not know whether one is Arthur or Martha.** *Austral and NZ informal* to be in a state of confusion.

Arthurian (ɑːˈθjʊərɪən) ADJECTIVE of or relating to King Arthur and his Knights of the Round Table.

arti (ˈʌrtɪ) NOUN *Hinduism* a ritual performed in homes and temples in which incense and light is offered to a deity.
▷HISTORY Hindi

artic (ɑːˈtɪk) NOUN *Informal* short for **articulated lorry.**

artichoke (ˈɑːtɪˌtʃəʊk) NOUN [1] Also called: **globe artichoke.** a thistle-like Eurasian plant, *Cynara scolymus,* cultivated for its large edible flower head containing many fleshy scalelike bracts: family *Asteraceae* (composites). [2] the unopened flower head of this plant, which can be cooked and eaten. [3] See **Jerusalem artichoke.**
▷HISTORY C16: from Italian *articiocco,* from Old Spanish *alcarchofa,* from Arabic *al-kharshūf*

article (ˈɑːtɪkəl) NOUN [1] one of a class of objects; item: *an article of clothing.* [2] an unspecified or previously named thing, esp a small object: *he put the article on the table.* [3] a distinct part of a subject or action. [4] a written composition on a subject, often being one of several found in a magazine, newspaper, etc. [5] *Grammar* a kind of determiner, occurring in many languages including English, that lacks independent meaning but may serve to indicate the specificity of reference of the noun phrase with which it occurs. See also **definite article, indefinite article.** [6] a clause or section in a written document such as a treaty, contract, statute, etc. [7] **in articles.** formerly, undergoing training, according to the terms of a written contract, in the legal profession. [8] *(often capital) Christianity* See **article of faith, Thirty-nine Articles.** [9] *Archaic* a topic or subject. ◆ VERB *(tr)* [10] *Archaic* to accuse.
▷HISTORY C13: from Old French, from Latin *articulus* small joint, from *artus* joint

articled (ˈɑːtɪkəld) ADJECTIVE bound by a written contract, such as one that governs a period of training: *an articled clerk.*

article numbering NOUN *Commerce* See **ANA.**

article of faith NOUN [1] *Christianity* any of the clauses or propositions into which a creed or other statement of doctrine is divided. [2] a deeply held belief.

articles of association PLURAL NOUN [1] the constitution and regulations of a registered company as required by the British Companies Acts. [2] the document containing these.

Articles of Confederation PLURAL NOUN the agreement made by the original 13 states in 1777 establishing a confederacy to be known as the United States of America; replaced by the Constitution of 1788.

Articles of War PLURAL NOUN [1] the disciplinary and legal procedures by which the naval and military forces of Great Britain were bound before the 19th century. [2] the regulations of the US army, navy, and air force until the Uniform Code of Military Justice replaced them in 1951.

articular (ɑːˈtɪkjʊlə) ADJECTIVE of or relating to joints or to the structural components in a joint.
▷HISTORY C15: from Latin *articulāris* concerning the joints, from *articulus* small joint; see ARTICLE

articulate ADJECTIVE (ɑːˈtɪkjʊlɪt) [1] able to express oneself fluently and coherently: *an articulate lecturer.* [2] having the power of speech. [3] distinct, clear, or definite; well-constructed: *an articulate voice; an articulate document.* [4] *Zoology* (of arthropods and higher vertebrates) possessing joints or jointed segments. ◆ VERB (ɑːˈtɪkjʊˌleɪt) [5] to speak or enunciate (words, syllables, etc.) clearly and distinctly. [6] *(tr)* to express coherently in words. [7] *(intr) Zoology* to be jointed or form a joint. [8] *(tr)* to separate into jointed segments.
▷HISTORY C16: from Latin *articulāre* to divide into joints; see ARTICLE
▸**arˈticulately** ADVERB ▸**arˈticulateness** *or* **arˈticulacy** NOUN

articulated vehicle NOUN a large vehicle (esp a lorry) made in two separate sections, a tractor and a trailer, connected by a pivoted bar.

articulation (ɑːˌtɪkjʊˈleɪʃən) NOUN [1] the act or process of speaking or expressing in words. [2] **a** the process of articulating a speech sound. **b** the sound so produced, esp a consonant. [3] the act or the state of being jointed together. [4] the form or manner in which something is jointed. [5] *Zoology* **a** a joint such as that between bones or arthropod segments. **b** the way in which jointed parts are connected. [6] *Botany* the part of a plant at which natural separation occurs, such as the joint between leaf and stem. [7] a joint or jointing.
▸**arˈticulatory** ADJECTIVE

articulator (ɑːˈtɪkjʊˌleɪtə) NOUN [1] a person or thing that articulates. [2] *Phonetics* any vocal organ that takes part in the production of a speech sound. Such organs are of two types: those that can move, such as the tongue, lips, etc. (**active articulators**), and those that remain fixed, such as the teeth, the hard palate, etc. (**passive articulators**).

articulatory loop NOUN *Psychol* a short-term memory system that enables a person to remember short strings of words by rehearsing them repeatedly in his head.

articulatory phonetics NOUN *(functioning as singular)* the branch of phonetics concerned with the production of speech sounds. Compare **acoustic phonetics, auditory phonetics.**

artifact (ˈɑːtɪˌfækt) NOUN a variant spelling of **artefact.**

artifice (ˈɑːtɪfɪs) NOUN [1] a clever expedient; ingenious stratagem. [2] crafty or subtle deception. [3] skill; cleverness. [4] a skilfully contrived device. [5] *Obsolete* craftsmanship.
▷HISTORY C16: from Old French, from Latin *artificium* skill, from *artifex* one possessed of a specific skill, from *ars* skill + *-fex,* from *facere* to make

artificer (ɑːˈtɪfɪsə) NOUN [1] a skilled craftsman. [2] a clever or inventive designer. [3] a serviceman trained in mechanics.

artificial (ˌɑːtɪˈfɪʃəl) ADJECTIVE [1] produced by man; not occurring naturally: *artificial materials of great strength.* [2] made in imitation of a natural product, esp as a substitute; not genuine: *artificial cream.* [3] pretended; assumed; insincere: *an artificial manner.* [4] lacking in spontaneity; affected: *an artificial laugh.* [5] *Biology* relating to superficial characteristics not based on the interrelationships of organisms: *an artificial classification.*
▷HISTORY C14: from Latin *artificiālis* belonging to art, from *artificium* skill, ARTIFICE
▸**artificiality** (ˌɑːtɪˌfɪʃɪˈælɪtɪ) NOUN ▸**ˌartiˈficially** ADVERB

artificial aid NOUN *Mountaineering* another name for **aid** (sense 5).

artificial climbing NOUN another name for **aid climbing.**

artificial daylight NOUN *Physics* artificial light having approximately the same spectral characteristics as natural daylight.

artificial disintegration NOUN *Physics* radioactive transformation of a substance by bombardment with high-energy particles, such as alpha particles or neutrons.

artificial feel NOUN a system, used in aircraft that have fully powered control surfaces, providing the pilot with simulated aerodynamic forces on the controls.

artificial horizon NOUN [1] Also called: **gyro horizon.** an aircraft instrument, using a gyroscope, that indicates the aircraft's attitude in relation to the horizontal. [2] *Astronomy* a level reflecting surface, such as one of mercury, that measures the altitude of a celestial body as half the angle between the body and its reflection.

artificial insemination NOUN introduction of spermatozoa into the vagina or uterus by means other than sexual union. See **AI, AIH, DI.**

artificial intelligence NOUN the study of the modelling of human mental functions by computer programs. Abbreviation: **AI.**

artificialize *or* **artificialise** (ˌɑːtɪˈfɪʃəˌlaɪz) VERB *(tr)* to render artificial.

artificial kidney NOUN *Med* a mechanical apparatus for performing haemodialysis.

artificial language NOUN an invented language, esp one intended as an international medium of communication or for use with computers. Compare **natural language.**

artificial respiration NOUN [1] any of various methods of restarting breathing after it has stopped, by manual rhythmic pressure on the chest, mouth-to-mouth breathing, etc. [2] any method of maintaining respiration artificially, as by use of an iron lung.

artillery (ɑːˈtɪlərɪ) NOUN [1] guns, cannon, howitzers, mortars, etc., of calibre greater than 20 mm. [2] troops or military units specializing in using such guns. [3] the science dealing with the use of guns. [4] devices for discharging heavy missiles, such as catapults or slings.
▷HISTORY C14: from Old French *artillerie,* from *artillier* to equip with weapons, of uncertain origin

artilleryman (ɑːˈtɪlərɪmən) NOUN, *plural* **-men.** a serviceman who serves in an artillery unit.

artillery plant NOUN any of various tropical urticaceous plants of the genus *Pilea,* such as *P. microphylla,* all having stamens that discharge their pollen explosively.

artiodactyl (ˌɑːtɪəʊˈdæktɪl) NOUN [1] any placental mammal of the order *Artiodactyla,* having hooves with an even number of toes; an even-toed

ungulate. The order includes pigs, hippopotamuses, camels, deer, cattle, and antelopes. ◆ ADJECTIVE 2 of, relating to, or belonging to the order *Artiodactyla*.
▷HISTORY C19: from New Latin *artiodactylus*, from Greek *ártios* even + *daktulos* digit
▸ˌ**artio'dactylous** ADJECTIVE

artisan (ˈɑːtɪˌzæn, ˌɑːtɪˈzæn) NOUN 1 a skilled workman; craftsman. 2 *Obsolete* an artist.
▷HISTORY C16: from French, from Old Italian *artigiano*, from *arte* ART[1]
▸**artisanal** (ɑːˈtɪzənəl, ˈɑːtɪzənəl) ADJECTIVE

artist (ˈɑːtɪst) NOUN 1 a person who practises or is skilled in an art, esp painting, drawing, or sculpture. 2 a person who displays in his work qualities required in art, such as sensibility and imagination. 3 a person whose profession requires artistic expertise, esp a designer: *a commercial artist*. 4 a person skilled in some task or occupation: *an artist at bricklaying*. 5 *Obsolete* an artisan. 6 *Slang* a person devoted to or proficient in something: *a booze artist; a con artist*.

artiste (ɑːˈtiːst; *French* artist) NOUN 1 an entertainer, such as a singer or dancer. 2 a person who is highly skilled in some occupation: *a hair artiste*.

artistic (ɑːˈtɪstɪk) ADJECTIVE 1 of or characteristic of art or artists. 2 performed, made, or arranged decoratively and tastefully; aesthetically pleasing. 3 appreciative of and sensitive to beauty in art. 4 naturally gifted with creative skill.
▸**ar'tistically** ADVERB

artistry (ˈɑːtɪstrɪ) NOUN 1 artistic workmanship, ability, or quality. 2 artistic pursuits. 3 great skill.

artless (ˈɑːtlɪs) ADJECTIVE 1 free from deceit, guile, or artfulness; ingenuous: *an artless remark*. 2 natural, without artifice; unpretentious: *artless elegance*. 3 without art or skill.
▸ˈ**artlessly** ADVERB ▸ˈ**artlessness** NOUN

art music NOUN music written by a composer rather than passed on by oral tradition. Compare **folk music**.

Art Nouveau (ɑː nuːˈvəʊ; *French* ar nuvo) NOUN **a** a style of art and architecture of the 1890s, characterized by swelling sinuous outlines and stylized natural forms, such as flowers and leaves. **b** (*as modifier*): *an Art-Nouveau mirror*.
▷HISTORY French, literally: new art

Artois (*French* artwa) NOUN a former province of N France.

art paper NOUN a high-quality type of paper having a smooth coating of china clay or similar substance on it.

arts (ɑːts) PLURAL NOUN 1 **a the.** imaginative, creative, and nonscientific branches of knowledge considered collectively, esp as studied academically. **b** (*as modifier*): *an arts degree*. 2 See **fine art.** 3 cunning or crafty actions or plots; schemes.

Arts and Crafts PLURAL NOUN decorative handicraft and design, esp that of the **Arts and Crafts movement**, in late nineteenth-century Britain, which sought to revive medieval craftsmanship.

art union NOUN *Austral and NZ* a lottery, often with prizes other than cash.

artwork (ˈɑːtˌwɜːk) NOUN all the original nontextual matter in a publication, esp the illustrations.

arty (ˈɑːtɪ) ADJECTIVE **artier, artiest.** *Informal* having an ostentatious or affected interest in or desire to imitate artists or artistic standards.
▸ˈ**artiness** NOUN

arty-crafty ADJECTIVE *Informal* affectedly artistic, esp in a homespun or rural style.

arty-farty ADJECTIVE *Informal* artistic in a pretentious way.

Aruba (əˈruːbə; *Dutch* ɑˈryːbaː) NOUN an island in the Caribbean, off the NW coast of Venezuela, a dependency of the Netherlands with special status; part of the Netherlands Antilles until 1986. Chief town: Oranjestad. Pop.: 97 200 (2001 est.). Area: about 181 sq. km (70 sq. miles).

arugula (əˈruːgjʊlə) NOUN another name for **rocket**[2] (sense 1).
▷HISTORY C20: from N Italian dialect

Aru Islands *or* **Arru Islands** (ˈɑːruː) PLURAL NOUN a group of islands in Indonesia, in the SW Moluccas. Area: about 8500 sq. km (3300 sq. miles).

arum (ˈɛərəm) NOUN 1 any plant of the aroid genus *Arum*, of Europe and the Mediterranean region, having arrow-shaped leaves and a typically white spathe. See also **cuckoopint.** 2 **arum lily.** another name for **calla** (sense 1).
▷HISTORY C16: from Latin, a variant of *aros* wake-robin, from Greek *aron*

Arunachal Pradesh (ˌɑːrəˈnɑːkəl prəˈdɛʃ) NOUN a state in NE India, formed in 1986 from the former Union Territory. Capital: Itanagar. Pop.: 1 091 117 (2001). Area: 83 743 sq. km (32 648 sq. miles). Former name (until 1972): **North East Frontier Agency.**

Arundel (ˈærəndəl) NOUN a town in S England, in West Sussex: 11th-century castle. Pop.: 3033 (1991).

arundinaceous (əˌrʌndɪˈneɪʃəs) ADJECTIVE *Botany* resembling a reed.
▷HISTORY C17: from Latin *harundinãceus*, from *harundō* a reed

aruspex (əˈrʌspɛks) NOUN, *plural* **-pices** (-pɪˌsiːz). a variant spelling of **haruspex.**

Aruwimi (ˌɑːruːˈwiːmɪ) NOUN a river in NE Democratic Republic of Congo (formerly Zaïre), rising near Lake Albert as the Ituri and flowing west into the River Congo. Length: about 1288 km (800 miles).

ARV ABBREVIATION FOR armed response vehicle.

arvo (ˈɑːvəʊ) NOUN *Austral informal* afternoon.

-ary SUFFIX 1 (*forming adjectives*) of; related to; belonging to: *cautionary; rudimentary*. 2 (*forming nouns*) **a** a person connected with or engaged in: *missionary*. **b** a thing relating to; a place for: *commentary; aviary*.
▷HISTORY from Latin *-ārius, -āria, -ārium*

Aryan *or* **Arian** (ˈɛərɪən) NOUN 1 (in Nazi ideology) a Caucasian of non-Jewish descent, esp of the Nordic type. 2 a member of any of the peoples supposedly descended from the Indo-Europeans, esp a speaker of an Iranian or Indic language in ancient times. ◆ ADJECTIVE 3 of, relating to, or characteristic of an Aryan or Aryans. ◆ ADJECTIVE, NOUN 4 *Archaic* Indo-European.
▷HISTORY C19: from Sanskrit *ārya* of noble birth

Aryanize *or* **Aryanise** (ˈɛərɪəˌnaɪz) VERB (*tr*) (in Nazi ideology) to purge (politics and society) of all non-Aryan elements or people; make characteristically Aryan.

aryl (ˈærɪl) NOUN 1 (*modifier*) *Chem* of, consisting of, or containing an aromatic group: *aryl group or radical*. 2 an organometallic compound in which a metal atom is bound to an aryl group.
▷HISTORY C20: from AR(OMATIC) + -YL

arytenoid *or* **arytaenoid** (ˌærɪˈtiːnɔɪd) ADJECTIVE *also* **arytenoidal.** 1 denoting either of two small cartilages of the larynx that are attached to the vocal cords. 2 denoting any of three small muscles of the larynx that narrow the space between the vocal cords. ◆ NOUN 3 an arytenoid cartilage or muscle.
▷HISTORY C18: from New Latin *arytaenoīdes*, from Greek *arutainoeidēs* shaped like a ladle, from *arutaina* ladle

as[1] (æz; *unstressed* əz) CONJUNCTION (*subordinating*) 1 (often preceded by *just*) while; when; at the time that: *he caught me as I was leaving*. 2 in the way that: *dancing as only she can*. 3 that which; what: *I did as I was told*. 4 (of) which fact, event, etc. (referring to the previous statement): *to become wise, as we all know, is not easy*. 5 **as it were.** in a way; so to speak; as if it were really so. 6 **as you were. a** a military command to withdraw an order, return to the previous position, etc. **b** a statement to withdraw something just said. 7 since; seeing that: *as you're in charge here, you'd better tell me where to wait*. 8 in the same way that: *he died of cancer, as his father had done*. 9 in spite of the extent to which: *intelligent as you are, I suspect you will fail*. 10 for instance: *capital cities, as London*. ◆ ADVERB, CONJUNCTION 11 **a** used correlatively before an adjective or adverb and before a noun phrase or a clause to indicate identity of extent, amount, etc.: *she is as heavy as her sister; she is as heavy now as she used to be*. **b** used with this sense after a noun phrase introduced by *the same*: *the same height as her sister*. ◆ PREPOSITION 12 in the role of; being: *as his friend, I am probably biased*. 13 **as for** *or* **to.** with reference to: *as for my past, I'm not telling you anything*. 14 **as from** *or* **of.** *Formal* (in expressions of time) from: *fares will rise as from January 11*. 15 **as if** *or* **though.** as it would be if: *he talked as if he knew all about it*. 16 **as (it) is.** in the existing state of affairs: *as it is, I shall have difficulty finishing all this work, without any more*. 17 **as per.** See **per** (sense 3). 18 **as regards.** See **regard** (sense 6). 19 **as such.** See **such** (sense 3). 20 **such as.** See **such** (sense 5). 21 **as was.** in a previous state. 22 **as well.** See **well**[1] (sense 13). 23 **as yet.** up to now; so far.
▷HISTORY Old English *alswā* likewise; see ALSO

Language note See at **like.**

as[2] (æs) NOUN 1 an ancient Roman unit of weight approximately equal to 1 pound troy (373 grams). 2 the standard monetary unit and copper coin of ancient Rome.
▷HISTORY C17: from Latin *ās* unity, probably of Etruscan origin

as[3] THE INTERNET DOMAIN NAME FOR American Samoa.

As SYMBOL FOR: 1 *Chem* arsenic. 2 altostratus.

AS ABBREVIATION FOR: 1 Also: **A.S.** Anglo-Saxon. 2 antisubmarine. 3 Australian Standards.

ASA ABBREVIATION FOR: 1 (in Britain) Amateur Swimming Association. 2 (in Britain) **Advertising Standards Authority.** 3 (in the US) American Standards Association.

ASA/BS ABBREV an obsolete expression of the speed of a photographic film, replaced by the ISO rating.
▷HISTORY C20: from *American Standards Association/British Standard*

asafoetida *or* **asafetida** (ˌæsəˈfɛtɪdə) NOUN a bitter resin with an unpleasant onion-like smell, obtained from the roots of some umbelliferous plants of the genus *Ferula*: formerly used as a carminative, antispasmodic, and expectorant.
▷HISTORY C14: from Medieval Latin, from *asa* gum (compare Persian *azā* mastic) + Latin *foetidus* evil-smelling, FETID

asana (ˈɑːsənə) NOUN any of various postures in yoga. See also **hatha yoga.**
▷HISTORY Sanskrit

a.s.a.p. ABBREVIATION FOR as soon as possible.

asarabacca (ˌæsərəˈbækə) NOUN a perennial evergreen Eurasian plant, *Asarum europaeum*, having kidney-shaped leaves and a single brownish flower: family *Aristolochiaceae*.

asarum (ˈæsərəm) NOUN the dried strong-scented root of the wild ginger plant: a flavouring agent and source of an aromatic oil used in perfumery, formerly used in medicine.
▷HISTORY C19: via New Latin from Latin: hazelwort, from Greek *asaron*

ASB ABBREVIATION FOR: 1 (in Britain) Accounting Standards Board. 2 Alternative Service Book (of the Church of England).

Asben (æsˈbɛn) NOUN another name for **Aïr** (region of the Sahara).

asbestos (æsˈbɛstɒs, -təs) NOUN **a** any of the fibrous amphibole and serpentine minerals, esp chrysotile and tremolite, that are incombustible and resistant to chemicals. It was formerly widely used in the form of fabric or board as a heat-resistant structural material. **b** (*as modifier*): *asbestos matting*.
▷HISTORY C14 (originally applied to a mythical stone the heat of which could not be extinguished): via Latin from Greek: from *asbestos* inextinguishable, from A-[1] + *sbennunai* to extinguish
▸**as'bestine** ADJECTIVE

asbestosis (ˌæsbɛsˈtəʊsɪs) NOUN inflammation of the lungs resulting from chronic inhalation of asbestos particles.

Ascanius (æˈskeɪnɪəs) NOUN *Roman myth* the son of Aeneas and Creusa; founder of Alba Longa, mother city of Rome. Also called: **Iulus.**

ASCAP (ˈæskæp) NOUN ACRONYM FOR American Society of Composers, Authors, and Publishers.

ascariasis (ˌæskəˈraɪəsɪs) NOUN infestation of the intestines with the roundworm *Ascaris lumbricoides*, causing abdominal pain, nausea and vomiting, weight loss, etc.

ascarid (ˈæskərɪd) NOUN any parasitic nematode worm of the family *Ascaridae*, such as the common roundworm of man and pigs.

▷**HISTORY** C14: from New Latin *ascaridae,* from Greek *askarides,* plural of *askaris*

ascend (ə'sɛnd) VERB [1] to go or move up (a ladder, hill, slope, etc.); mount; climb. [2] (*intr*) to slope or incline upwards. [3] (*intr*) to rise to a higher point, level, degree, etc. [4] to follow (a river) upstream towards its source. [5] to trace (a genealogy, etc.) back in time. [6] to sing or play (a scale, arpeggio, etc.) from the lower to higher notes. [7] **ascend the throne.** to become king or queen.
▷**HISTORY** C14: from Latin *ascendere,* from *scandere*

ascendancy, ascendency (ə'sɛndənsɪ), **ascendance,** *or* **ascendence** NOUN the condition of being dominant, esp through superior economic or political power.

ascendant *or* **ascendent** (ə'sɛndənt) ADJECTIVE [1] proceeding upwards; rising. [2] dominant, superior, or influential. [3] *Botany* another term for **ascending.** ◆ NOUN [4] *Rare* an ancestor. [5] a position or condition of dominance, superiority or control. [6] *Astrology* (*sometimes capital*) **a** a point on the ecliptic that rises on the eastern horizon at a particular moment and changes as the earth rotates on its axis. **b** the sign of the zodiac containing this point. [7] **in the ascendant.** increasing in influence, prosperity, etc.

ascender (ə'sɛndə) NOUN [1] *Printing* **a** the part of certain lower-case letters, such as *b* or *h,* that extends above the body of the letter. **b** any letter having such a part. [2] a person or thing that ascends. [3] another word for **ascendeur.**

ascendeur (*French* asɑ̃dœr) NOUN *Mountaineering* a metal grip that is threaded on a rope and can be alternately tightened and slackened as an aid to climbing the rope: used attached to slings for the feet and waist. Also called: **ascender.**
▷**HISTORY** C20

ascending (ə'sɛndɪŋ) ADJECTIVE [1] moving upwards; rising. [2] *Botany* sloping or curving upwards: *the ascending stem of a vine.*

ascension (ə'sɛnʃən) NOUN [1] the act of ascending. [2] *Astronomy* the rising of a star above the horizon.
▸**as'censional** ADJECTIVE

Ascension[1] (ə'sɛnʃən) NOUN *New Testament* the passing of Jesus Christ from earth into heaven (Acts 1:9).

Ascension[2] (ə'sɛnʃən) NOUN an island in the S Atlantic, northwest of St Helena: uninhabited until claimed by Britain in 1815. Pop.: 1117 (1993). Area: 88 sq. km (34 sq. miles).

Ascension Day NOUN *Christianity* the 40th day after Easter, when the Ascension of Christ into heaven is celebrated.

ascensionist (ə'sɛnʃənɪst) NOUN *Mountaineering* a person who has completed a mountain ascent, esp a notable one.

Ascensiontide (ə'sɛnʃən,taɪd) NOUN the ten days from Ascension Day to the day before Whit Sunday.

ascent (ə'sɛnt) NOUN [1] the act of ascending; climb or upward movement: *the ascent of hot gases.* [2] an upward slope; incline or gradient. [3] movement back through time, as in tracing of earlier generations (esp in the phrase **line of ascent**).

ascertain (,æsə'teɪn) VERB (*tr*) [1] to determine or discover definitely. [2] *Archaic* to make certain.
▷**HISTORY** C15: from Old French *acertener* to make certain
▸**,ascer'tainable** ADJECTIVE ▸**,ascer'tainably** ADVERB
▸**,ascer'tainment** NOUN

ascesis (ə'siːsɪs) NOUN, *plural* **-ses** (-siːz). the exercise of self-discipline.
▷**HISTORY** C19: from Greek, from *askein* to exercise

ascetic (ə'sɛtɪk) NOUN [1] a person who practises great self-denial and austerities and abstains from worldly comforts and pleasures, esp for religious reasons. [2] (in the early Christian Church) a monk. ◆ ADJECTIVE *also* **as'cetical.** [3] rigidly abstinent or abstemious; austere. [4] of or relating to ascetics or asceticism. [5] intensely rigorous in religious austerities.
▷**HISTORY** C17: from Greek *askētikos,* from *askētēs,* from *askein* to exercise
▸**as'cetically** ADVERB

asceticism (ə'sɛtɪ,sɪzəm) NOUN [1] the behaviour, discipline, or outlook of an ascetic, esp of a religious ascetic. [2] the principles of ascetic practices, esp in the early Christian Church. [3] the theory and system of ascetic practices.

Aschaffenburg (*German* a'ʃafənburk) NOUN a city in Germany, on the River Main in Bavaria: seat of the Imperial Diet (1447); ceded to Bavaria in 1814. Pop.: 62 050 (latest est.).

asci ('æsaɪ, 'æskaɪ) NOUN the plural of **ascus.**

ascidian (ə'sɪdɪən) NOUN [1] any minute marine invertebrate animal of the class *Ascidiacea,* such as the sea squirt, the adults of which are degenerate and sedentary: subphylum *Tunicata* (tunicates). [2] **ascidian tadpole.** the free-swimming larva of an ascidian, having a tadpole-like tail containing the notochord and nerve cord. ◆ ADJECTIVE [3] of, relating to, or belonging to the *Ascidiacea.*

ascidium (ə'sɪdɪəm) NOUN, *plural* **-cidia** (-'sɪdɪə). part of a plant that is shaped like a pitcher, such as the modified leaf of the pitcher plant.
▷**HISTORY** C18: from New Latin, from Greek *askidion* a little bag, from *askos* bag

ASCII ('æskiː) NOUN ACRONYM FOR American standard code for information interchange: a computer code for representing alphanumeric characters.

ascites (ə'saɪtiːz) NOUN, *plural* **ascites.** accumulation of serous fluid in the peritoneal cavity.
▷**HISTORY** C14: from Latin: a kind of dropsy, from Greek *askitēs,* from *askos* wineskin
▸**ascitic** (ə'sɪtɪk) ADJECTIVE

asclepiadaceous (æ,skliːpɪə'deɪʃəs) ADJECTIVE of, relating to, or belonging to the *Asclepiadaceae,* a family of mostly tropical and subtropical flowering plants, including the milkweed and swallowwort, having pollen in the form of a waxy mass (pollinium): now usually regarded as a subfamily of the *Apocynaceae.*
▷**HISTORY** C19: from New Latin *Asclēpias* genus name, from Latin, from Greek *asklēpias,* named after ASCLEPIUS

Asclepiadean (æ,skliːpɪə'diːən) *Prosody* ◆ ADJECTIVE [1] of or relating to a type of classical verse line consisting of a spondee, two or three choriambs, and an iamb. ◆ NOUN [2] Also called: **Asclepiad.** an Asclepiadean verse.
▷**HISTORY** C17: via Latin from Greek *Asklēpiadēs* (about 270 B.C.), who invented the verse form

asclepias (ə'skliːpɪəs) NOUN any plant of the perennial mostly tuberous genus *Asclepias;* some are grown as garden or greenhouse plants for their showy orange-scarlet or purple flowers: family *Asclepiadaceae.* Sometimes called: **milkweed.**
▷**HISTORY** Greek *asklēpias* swallowwort

Asclepius (ə'skliːpɪəs) NOUN *Greek myth* a god of healing; son of Apollo. Roman counterpart: **Aesculapius** (,iːskjʊ'leɪpɪəs).

asco- COMBINING FORM indicating a bladder or ascus: *ascomycete.*
▷**HISTORY** from Greek *askos* bladder

ascocarp ('æskə,kɑːp) NOUN (in some ascomycetous fungi) a globular structure containing the asci. See **apothecium, perithecium.**

ascogonium (,æskə'gəʊnɪəm) NOUN, *plural* **-nia** (-nɪə). a female reproductive body in some ascomycetous fungi in which, after fertilization, the asci develop.

Ascoli Piceno (*Italian* 'askoli pi'tʃeːno) NOUN a town in E central Italy, in the Marches: capital of the Roman province of Picenum; site of the massacre of all its Roman citizens in the Social War in 90 B.C. Pop.: 52 667 (1990). Latin name: **Asculum Picenum** ('æskjʊləm paɪ'siːnəm).

ascomycete (,æskəmaɪ'siːt) NOUN any fungus of the phylum *Ascomycota* (formerly class *Ascomycetes*) in which the spores (ascospores) are formed inside a club-shaped cell (ascus). The group includes yeast, penicillium, aspergillus, truffles, and certain mildews.
▸**,ascomy'cetous** ADJECTIVE

ascorbic acid (ə'skɔːbɪk) NOUN a white crystalline vitamin present in plants, esp citrus fruits, tomatoes, and green vegetables. A deficiency in the diet of man leads to scurvy. Formula: $C_6H_8O_6$. Also called: **vitamin C.**
▷**HISTORY** C20 *ascorbic* from A-[1] + SCORB(UT)IC

ascospore ('æskə,spɔː) NOUN one of the spores (usually eight in number) that are produced in an ascus.

ascot ('æskət) NOUN a cravat with wide square ends, usually secured with an ornamental stud.
▷**HISTORY** C20: named after ASCOT, where it was probably first worn

Ascot ('æskət) NOUN a town in S England, in Bracknell Forest unitary authority, Berkshire: noted for its horse-race meetings, esp **Royal Ascot,** a four-day meeting held in June. Pop.: 13 500 (latest est.).

ascribe (ə'skraɪb) VERB (*tr*) [1] to credit or assign, as to a particular origin or period: *to ascribe parts of a play to Shakespeare.* [2] to attribute as a quality; consider as belonging to: *to ascribe beauty to youth.*
▷**HISTORY** C15: from Latin *ascrībere* to enrol, from *ad* in addition + *scrībere* to write
▸**as'cribable** ADJECTIVE

> **Language note** *Ascribe* is sometimes wrongly used where *subscribe* is meant: *I do not subscribe* (not *ascribe*) *to this view.*

ascription (ə'skrɪpʃən) *or* **adscription** (əd'skrɪpʃən) NOUN [1] the act of ascribing. [2] a statement ascribing something to someone, esp praise to God.
▷**HISTORY** C16: from Latin *ascrīptiō,* from *ascrībere* to ASCRIBE

ascus ('æskəs) NOUN, *plural* **asci** ('æsaɪ, 'æskaɪ). a saclike structure that produces (usually) eight ascospores during sexual reproduction in ascomycetous fungi such as yeasts and mildews.
▷**HISTORY** C19: from New Latin, from Greek *askos* bag

ASDE ABBREVIATION FOR Airport Surface Detection Equipment: a radar system that is used by aircraft controllers to assist in the safe manoeuvring of aircraft on the ground.

asdic ('æzdɪk) NOUN an early form of **sonar.**
▷**HISTORY** C20: from *A(nti-)S(ubmarine) D(etection) I(nvestigation) C(ommittee)*

-ase SUFFIX FORMING NOUNS indicating an enzyme: *oxidase.*
▷**HISTORY** abstracted from DIASTASE

ASEAN ('æsɪ,æn) NOUN ACRONYM FOR Association of Southeast Asian Nations.

aseismic (eɪ'saɪzmɪk) ADJECTIVE [1] denoting a region free of earthquakes. [2] (*not in technical use*) denoting a region free of all but a few small earthquakes. [3] (of buildings, etc.) designed to withstand earthquakes.

aseity (eɪ'siːɪtɪ) NOUN *Philosophy* existence derived from itself, having no other source.
▷**HISTORY** C17: from Medieval Latin *aseitas,* from Latin *ā* from + *sē* oneself

asepalous (æ'sɛpələs) ADJECTIVE (of a plant or flower) having no sepals.

asepsis (ə'sɛpsɪs, eɪ-) NOUN [1] the state of being free from living pathogenic organisms. [2] the methods of achieving a germ-free condition.

aseptate (eɪ'sɛpteɪt) ADJECTIVE *Biology* not divided into cells or sections by septa.

aseptic (ə'sɛptɪk, eɪ-) ADJECTIVE [1] free from living pathogenic organisms; sterile. [2] aiming to achieve a germ-free condition.

asexual (eɪ'sɛksjʊəl, æ-) ADJECTIVE [1] having no apparent sex or sex organs. [2] (of reproduction) not involving the fusion of male and female gametes, as in vegetative reproduction, fission, or budding.
▸**asexuality** (eɪ,sɛksjʊ'ælɪtɪ, æ-) NOUN ▸**a'sexually** ADVERB

Asgard ('æsgɑːd) *or* **Asgarth** ('æsgɑːθ) NOUN *Norse myth* the dwelling place of the principal gods, the Aesir.

ash[1] (æʃ) NOUN [1] the nonvolatile products and residue formed when matter is burnt. [2] any of certain compounds formed by burning. See **soda ash.** [3] fine particles of lava thrown out by an erupting volcano. [4] a light silvery grey colour, often with a brownish tinge. ◆ See also **ashes.** Related adjective: **cinereous.**
▷**HISTORY** Old English *æsce;* related to Old Norse, Old High German *aska,* Gothic *azgō,* Latin *aridus* dry

ash[2] (æʃ) NOUN [1] any oleaceous tree of the genus

Fraxinus, esp *F. excelsior* of Europe and Asia, having compound leaves, clusters of small greenish flowers, and winged seeds. [2] the close-grained durable wood of any of these trees, used for tool handles, etc. [3] any of several trees resembling the ash, such as the mountain ash. [4] *Austral* any of several Australian trees resembling the ash, esp of the eucalyptus genus.
▷HISTORY Old English *æsc;* related to Old Norse *askr,* Old Saxon, Old High German *ask,* Lithuanian *uosis*

ash³ (æʃ) NOUN the digraph æ, as in Old English, representing a front vowel approximately like that of the *a* in Modern English *hat.* The character is also used to represent this sound in the International Phonetic Alphabet.

ASH (æʃ) NOUN (in Britain) ACRONYM FOR Action on Smoking and Health.

ashamed (əˈʃeɪmd) ADJECTIVE (*usually postpositive*) [1] overcome with shame, guilt, or remorse. [2] (foll by *of*) suffering from feelings of inferiority or shame in relation to (a person, thing, or deed). [3] (foll by *to*) unwilling through fear of humiliation, shame, etc.
▷HISTORY Old English *āscamod,* past participle of *āscamian* to shame, from *scamu* SHAME
▸**ashamedly** (əˈʃeɪmɪdlɪ) ADVERB

Ashanti (əˈʃæntɪ) NOUN [1] an administrative region of central Ghana: former native kingdom, suppressed by the British in 1900 after four wars. Capital: Kumasi. Pop.: 2 485 766 (1991 est.). Area: 24 390 sq. km (9417 sq. miles). [2] (*plural* **-ti** *or* **-tis**) a native or inhabitant of Ashanti.

A shares PLURAL NOUN *Brit* those ordinary shares in a company which carry restricted voting rights or other restrictions.

ash blond NOUN [1] **a** a very light blond colour. **b** (*as adjective*): *ash-blond hair.* [2] a person whose hair is this colour. ♦ Also: **ash blonde.** FEMININE

Ashby-de-la-Zouch (ˌæʃbɪˌdələˈzuːʃ) NOUN a town in central England, in Leicestershire: Mary, Queen of Scots, was imprisoned (1569) in the castle. Pop.: 10 595 (1991).

ash can NOUN a US word for **dustbin.** Also called: **garbage can, ash bin, trash can.**

Ash Can School NOUN a group of US painters including Robert Henri and later George Bellows, founded in 1907, noted for their depiction of the sordid aspects of city life.

Ashdod (ˈæʃdɒd) NOUN a town in central Israel, on the Mediterranean coast: an important city in the Philistine Empire, with its artificial harbour (1961) it is now a major port. Pop.: 155 800 (1999 est.).

ashen¹ (ˈæʃən) ADJECTIVE [1] drained of colour; pallid. [2] consisting of or resembling ashes. [3] of a pale greyish colour.

ashen² (ˈæʃən) ADJECTIVE of, relating to, or made from the ash tree or its timber.

Asher (ˈæʃə) NOUN the son of Jacob and ancestor of one of the 12 tribes of Israel.

ashes (ˈæʃɪz) PLURAL NOUN [1] ruins or remains, as after destruction or burning: *the city was left in ashes.* [2] the remains of a human body after cremation.

Ashes (ˈæʃɪz) PLURAL NOUN **the.** a cremated cricket stump in a pottery urn now preserved at Lord's. Victory or defeat in test matches between England and Australia is referred to as winning, losing, or retaining the Ashes.
▷HISTORY from the mock obituary of English cricket in *The Times* in 1882 after a great Australian victory at the Oval, in which it was said that the body would be cremated and the ashes taken to Australia

ashet (ˈæʃɪt) NOUN *Scot and northern English dialect* a shallow oval dish or large plate.
▷HISTORY C16: from French *assiette*

Ashford (ˈæʃfəd) NOUN a market town in SE England, in central Kent. Pop.: 52 002 (1991).

Ashkenazi (ˌæʃkəˈnɑːzɪ) NOUN, *plural* **-zim** (-zɪm). [1] (*modifier*) of or relating to the Jews of Germany and E Europe. [2] a Jew of German or E European descent. [3] the pronunciation of Hebrew used by these Jews. ♦ Compare **Sephardi.**
▷HISTORY C19: Late Hebrew, from Hebrew *Ashkenaz,* the son of Gomer (Genesis 10:3; I Chronicles 1:6), a descendant of Noah through Japheth, and hence taken to be identified with the ancient Ascanians of Phrygia and, in the medieval period, the Germans

ashkey (ˈæʃkiː) NOUN the winged fruit of the ash.

Ashkhabad (*Russian* aʃxaˈbat) *or* **Ashgabat** (ˈɑːʃgəbæt; *Turkmen* ɑʃgɑˈbɑt) NOUN the capital of Turkmenistan. Pop.: 605 000 (1999 est.).

ashlar *or* **ashler** (ˈæʃlə) NOUN [1] a block of hewn stone with straight edges for use in building. [2] Also called: **ashlar veneer.** a thin dressed stone with straight edges, used to face a wall. [3] masonry made of ashlar.
▷HISTORY C14: from Old French *aisselier* crossbeam, from *ais* board, from Latin *axis* axletree; see AXIS¹

ashlaring (ˈæʃlərɪŋ) NOUN [1] ashlars collectively. [2] a number of short upright boards forming the wall of a garret, cutting off the acute angle between the rafters and the floor.

Ashmolean Museum (æʃˈməʊlɪən, ˌæʃməˈlɪən) NOUN a museum, attached to Oxford University and founded in 1683, noted for its paintings and archaeological collections.
▷HISTORY C19: named after Elias *Ashmole* (1617–92), English antiquary who donated the first collection

ashore (əˈʃɔː) ADVERB [1] towards or onto land from the water: *we swam ashore.* ♦ ADJECTIVE (*postpositive*), ADVERB [2] on land, having come from the water: *a day ashore before sailing.*

ashplant (ˈæʃˌplɑːnt) NOUN a walking stick made from an ash sapling.

ashram (ˈæʃrəm, ˈɑːʃ-) NOUN [1] a religious retreat or community where a Hindu holy man lives. [2] a house that provides accommodation for destitute people.
▷HISTORY from Sanskrit *āśrama,* from *ā-* near + *śrama* religious exertion

Ashton-under-Lyne (laɪn) NOUN a town in NW England, in Tameside unitary authority, Greater Manchester. Pop.: 43 906 (1991).

Ashtoreth (ˈæʃtəˌrɛθ) NOUN *Old Testament* an ancient Semitic fertility goddess, identified with Astarte and Ishtar.

ashtray (ˈæʃˌtreɪ) NOUN a receptacle for tobacco ash, cigarette butts, etc.

Ashur (ˈæʃʊə) NOUN a variant spelling of **Assur.**

Ash Wednesday NOUN the first day of Lent, named from the practice of Christians of placing ashes on their heads as a sign of penitence.

ashy (ˈæʃɪ) ADJECTIVE **ashier, ashiest.** [1] of a pale greyish colour; ashen. [2] consisting of, covered with, or resembling ash.

'Asi (ˈæsɪ) NOUN the Arabic name for the **Orontes.**

Asia (ˈeɪʃə, ˈeɪʒə) NOUN the largest of the continents, bordering on the Arctic Ocean, the Pacific Ocean, the Indian Ocean, and the Mediterranean and Red Seas in the west. It includes the large peninsulas of Asia Minor, India, Arabia, and Indochina and the island groups of Japan, Indonesia, the Philippines, and Ceylon (Sri Lanka); contains the mountain ranges of the Hindu Kush, Himalayas, Pamirs, Tian Shan, Urals, and Caucasus, the great plateaus of India, Iran, and Tibet, vast plains and deserts, and the valleys of many large rivers including the Mekong, Irrawaddy, Indus, Ganges, Tigris, and Euphrates. Pop.: 3 589 233 000 (1998 est.). Area: 44 391 162 sq. km (17 139 445 sq. miles).

asiago (ˌæzɪˈɑːgəʊ) NOUN either of two varieties (ripened or fresh) of a cow's-milk cheese produced in NE Italy.
▷HISTORY Italian

Asia Minor NOUN the historical name for **Anatolia.**

Asian (ˈeɪʃən, ˈeɪʒən) ADJECTIVE [1] of or relating to Asia or to any of its peoples or languages. ♦ NOUN [2] a native or inhabitant of Asia or a descendant of one.

> **Language note** The use of *Asian* or *Asiatic* as a noun can be offensive and should be avoided.

Asian flu NOUN a type of influenza recurring in worldwide epidemics, caused by a virus (A2 strain or subsequent antigenic variants), which apparently originated in China in 1957.

Asian pear NOUN [1] a tropical pear tree, esp any of several varieties of Japanese pear *Pyrus serotina.* [2] Also called: **nashi.** the fruit of the Japanese pear, which resembles a large yellow apple, has crisp juicy flesh, and is cultivated in Japan, Korea, the US, and New Zealand.

Asian semi-longhair (-ˈlɒŋˌhɛə) NOUN another name for **Tiffanie.**

Asian shorthair (ˈʃɔːtˌhɛə) NOUN a generic term for a group of breeds of short-haired cat of Burmese type, including the Bombay.

Asiatic (ˌeɪʃɪˈætɪk, -zɪ-) NOUN, ADJECTIVE another word for **Asian.**

> **Language note** See at **Asian.**

Asiatic beetle NOUN a Japanese scarabaeid beetle, *Anomala orientalis,* introduced into Hawaii and the northeastern US: a serious pest of sugar cane and cereal crops because it destroys the roots.

Asiatic cholera NOUN another name for **cholera.**

aside (əˈsaɪd) ADVERB [1] on or to one side: *they stood aside to let him pass.* [2] out of hearing; in or into seclusion: *he took her aside to tell her of his plan.* [3] away from oneself: *he threw the book aside.* [4] out of mind or consideration: *he put aside all fears.* [5] in or into reserve: *to put aside money for old age.* [6] **aside from.** (*preposition*) *Chiefly US and Canadian* **a** besides: *he has money aside from his possessions.* **b** except for: *he has nothing aside from the clothes he stands in.* Compare **apart** (sense 7). ♦ NOUN [7] something spoken by an actor, intended to be heard by the audience, but not by the others on stage. [8] any confidential statement spoken in undertones. [9] a digression.

A-side NOUN the side of a gramophone record regarded as the more important one.

asinine (ˈæsɪˌnaɪn) ADJECTIVE [1] obstinate or stupid. [2] resembling an ass.
▷HISTORY C16: from Latin *asinīnus,* from *asinus* ASS¹
▸ˈ**asiˌninely** ADVERB ▸**asininity** (ˌæsɪˈnɪnɪtɪ) NOUN

ASIO ABBREVIATION FOR Australian Security Intelligence Organization.

Asir (æˈsɪə) NOUN a region of SW Saudi Arabia, in the Southern Province on the Red Sea: under Turkish rule until 1933. Area: 81 000 sq. km (31 000 sq. miles).

-asis SUFFIX FORMING NOUNS a variant of **-iasis.**

A sizes *or* **A series** NOUN a series of paper sizes approved by the International Standards Organization, running from 2AO to A7, each size (defined in mm) being half as large as the one preceding it, as follows: **2AO,** 1189 × 1682; **AO,** 841 × 1189; **A1,** 594 × 841; **A2,** 420 × 594; **A3,** 297 × 420; **A4,** 210 × 297; **A5,** 148 × 210; **A6,** 105 × 148; **A7,** 74 × 105.

ask (ɑːsk) VERB [1] (often foll by *about*) to put a question (to); request an answer (from): *she asked (him) about God.* [2] (*tr*) to inquire about: *she asked him the time of the train; she asked the way.* [3] (*tr*) to direct or put (a question). [4] (*may take a clause as object or an infinitive;* often foll by *for*) to make a request or demand: *she asked (him) for information; they asked for a deposit.* [5] (*tr*) to demand or expect (esp in the phrases **ask a lot of, ask too much of**). [6] (*tr*) Also: **ask out, ask over.** to request (a person) politely to come or go to a place; invite: *he asked her to the party.* [7] (*tr*) to need; require: *the job asks both time and patience.* [8] (*tr*) *Archaic* to proclaim (marriage banns). ♦ NOUN [9] **a big** *or* **tough ask.** *Austral and NZ informal* a task which is difficult to fulfil. ♦ See also **ask after, ask for.**
▷HISTORY Old English *āscian;* related to Old Frisian *āskia,* Old Saxon *ēscon,* Old High German *eiscōn*
▸ˈ**asker** NOUN

Ask (ɑːsk) NOUN *Norse myth* the first man, created by the gods from an ash tree.

ask after *or Scot* **ask for** VERB (*preposition*) to make inquiries about the health of (someone): *he asked after her mother.*

askance (əˈskæns) *or* **askant** (əˈskænt) ADVERB [1] with an oblique glance. [2] with doubt or mistrust.
▷HISTORY C16: of unknown origin

askari (asˈkaːri) NOUN (in East Africa) a soldier or policeman.
▷HISTORY C19: from Arabic: soldier

askew (əˈskjuː) ADVERB, ADJECTIVE at an oblique angle; towards one side; awry.

ask for VERB (*preposition*) [1] to try to obtain by requesting: *he asked for help.* [2] (*intr*) *Informal* to behave in a provocative manner that is regarded as inviting (trouble): *she's asking for trouble; you're asking for it.* [3] *Scot* to ask after.

asking price NOUN the price suggested by a seller but usually considered to be subject to bargaining.

Askja ('ɑːskjə) NOUN a volcano in E central Iceland: active in 1961; largest crater in Iceland. Height: 1510 m (4954 ft.). Area of crater: 88 sq. km (34 sq. miles).

asl ABBREVIATION FOR: [1] above sea level. [2] age, sex, and location.

ASL ABBREVIATION FOR American Sign Language. See **Ameslan.**

aslant (ə'slɑːnt) ADVERB [1] at a slant. ◆ PREPOSITION [2] at a slant across or athwart.

asleep (ə'sliːp) ADJECTIVE (*postpositive*) [1] in or into a state of sleep. [2] in or into a dormant or inactive state. [3] (of limbs, esp when the blood supply to them has been restricted) numb; lacking sensation. [4] *Euphemistic* dead.

ASLEF ('æzlɛf) NOUN (in Britain) ◆ ACRONYM FOR Associated Society of Locomotive Engineers and Firemen.

AS level NOUN *Brit* [1] **a** a public examination taken for the General Certificate of Education, with a smaller course content than an A level: since 2000 taken either as the first part of a full A level or as a qualification in its own right. **b** the course leading to this examination. **c** (*as modifier*): *AS-level English.* [2] a pass in a subject at AS level: *I've got three AS levels.*

ASLIB ('æzlɪb) NOUN ACRONYM FOR Association for Information Management.

aslope (ə'sləʊp) ADVERB, ADJECTIVE (*postpositive*) sloping.

ASM ABBREVIATION FOR: [1] air-to-surface missile. [2] *Theatre* assistant stage manager.

Asmara (æs'mɑːrə) NOUN the capital of Eritrea; cathedral (1922); Grand Mosque (1937); university (1958). Pop.: 431 000 (1995 est.).

Asmodeus (æs'məʊdɪəs, ˌæsməʊ'diːəs) NOUN (in Jewish demonology) prince of the demons.
▷**HISTORY** via Latin *Asmodaeus*, from Avestan *Aēsma-daēva*, spirit of anger

Asnières (*French* anjɛr) NOUN a suburb of Paris, France, on the Seine. Pop.: 72 250 (1990).

Aso ('ɑːsəʊ) NOUN a group of five volcanic cones in Japan on central Kyushu, one of which, Naka-dake, has the largest crater in the world, between 16 km (10 miles) and 24 km (15 miles) in diameter. Highest cone: 1592 m (5223 ft.). Also called: **Asosan** (ˌɑːsəʊ'sɑːn).

asocial (eɪ'səʊʃəl) ADJECTIVE [1] avoiding contact; not gregarious. [2] unconcerned about the welfare of others. [3] hostile to society or social practices.

asp¹ (æsp) NOUN [1] the venomous snake, probably *Naja haje* (Egyptian cobra), that caused the death of Cleopatra and was formerly used by the Pharaohs as a symbol of their power over life and death. See also **uraeus.** [2] Also called: **asp viper.** a viper, *Vipera aspis*, that occurs in S Europe and is very similar to but smaller than the adder. [3] **horned asp.** another name for **horned viper.**
▷**HISTORY** C15: from Latin *aspis*, from Greek

asp² (æsp) NOUN an archaic name for the **aspen.**
▷**HISTORY** Old English *æspe*; related to Old Norse *ösp*, Old High German *aspa*

asparagine (ə'spærəˌdʒiːn, -dʒɪn) NOUN a nonessential amino acid, a component of proteins.
▷**HISTORY** C19: from French, from Latin *asparagus* ASPARAGUS + -INE²

asparagus (ə'spærəgəs) NOUN [1] any Eurasian liliaceous plant of the genus *Asparagus*, esp the widely cultivated *A. officinalis*, having small scaly or needle-like leaves. [2] the succulent young shoots of *A. officinalis*, which may be cooked and eaten. [3] **asparagus fern.** a fernlike species of asparagus, *A. plumosus*, native to southern Africa.
▷**HISTORY** C15: from Latin, from Greek *asparagos*, of obscure origin

aspartame (ə'spɑːˌteɪm) NOUN an artificial sweetener produced from aspartic acid. Formula: $C_{14}H_{18}N_2O_5$.
▷**HISTORY** C20: from ASPART(IC ACID) + (*phenyl*)*a*(*lanine*) *m*(*ethyl*) *e*(*ster*)

aspartic acid (ə'spɑːtɪk) NOUN a nonessential amino acid that is a component of proteins and acts as a neurotransmitter.
▷**HISTORY** C19: from ASPAR(AGUS) + -IC

aspect ('æspɛkt) NOUN [1] appearance to the eye; visual effect: *the physical aspect of the landscape.* [2] a distinct feature or element in a problem, situation, etc.; facet: *to consider every aspect of a problem.* [3] the way in which a problem, idea, etc., may be considered: *to consider a problem from every aspect.* [4] a facial expression; manner of appearing: *a severe aspect.* [5] a position facing a particular direction; outlook: *the southern aspect of a house.* [6] a view in a certain direction: *a good aspect of the village from the tower.* [7] a surface that faces in a given direction: *the ventral aspect of a fish.* [8] *Astrology* any of several specific angular distances between two planets or a planet and the Ascendant or Midheaven measured, from the earth, in degrees along the ecliptic. [9] *Grammar* a category of verbs or verbal inflections that expresses such features as the continuity, repetition, or completedness of the action described. Compare **perfective** (sense 2), **progressive** (senses 8, 10). [10] *Botany* **a** the compass direction to which a plant habitat is exposed, or the degree of exposure. **b** the effect of the seasons on the appearance of plants. [11] *Archaic* glance or gaze.
▷**HISTORY** C14: from Latin *aspectus* a sight, from *aspicere*, from *ad-* to, at + *specere* to look

aspect ratio NOUN [1] the ratio of width to height of the picture on a television or cinema screen. [2] *Aeronautics* the ratio of the span of a wing to its mean chord.

aspectual (æ'spɛktjʊəl) ADJECTIVE of or relating to grammatical aspect.

aspen ('æspən) NOUN [1] any of several trees of the salicaceous genus *Populus*, such as *P. tremula* of Europe, in which the leaves are attached to the stem by long flattened stalks so that they quiver in the wind. Archaic name: **asp.** ◆ ADJECTIVE [2] *Archaic, chiefly literary* trembling.
▷**HISTORY** Old English *æspe*; see ASP²

aspendicitis (əˌspɛndɪ'saɪtɪs) NOUN *Jocular* an inability to control the amount one spends.
▷**HISTORY** C20: from a blend of SPEND and APPENDICITIS

asper ('æspə) NOUN a former Turkish monetary unit, a silver coin, worth 1/120 of a piastre.
▷**HISTORY** from Turkish, ultimately from Latin: rough, harsh

asperate ('æspəˌreɪt) *or* **asperous** ('æspərəs) ADJECTIVE (of plant parts) having a rough surface due to a covering of short stiff hairs.

Asperger's syndrome ('æspɜːgəz) NOUN a form of autism in which the sufferer has limited but obsessive interests, and has difficulty relating to other people.
▷**HISTORY** C20: named after Hans *Asperger* (20th century), Austrian physician who first described it

Asperges (æ'spɜːdʒiːz) NOUN *RC Church* [1] a short rite preceding Mass, in which the celebrant sprinkles those present with holy water to the accompaniment of the chant *Asperges me, Domine.* [2] the chant opening with these words.
▷**HISTORY** C16: from Latin *Asperges* (*me hyssopo*) Thou shalt purge (me with hyssop)

aspergillosis (æˌspɜːdʒɪ'ləʊsɪs) NOUN, *plural* **-ses** (-siːz). a rare fungal infection, esp of the mucous membranes or lungs, caused by various species of *Aspergillus.*
▷**HISTORY** C19: from New Latin, from ASPERGILLUS

aspergillum (ˌæspə'dʒɪləm) *or* **aspergill** ('æspədʒɪl) NOUN, *plural* **-gilla** (-'dʒɪlə), **-gillums** *or* **-gills**. another term for **aspersorium** (sense 2).
▷**HISTORY** C17: from New Latin *aspergillum*, from Latin *aspergere*, from *spargere* to sprinkle

aspergillus (ˌæspə'dʒɪləs) NOUN, *plural* **-gilli** (-'dʒɪlaɪ). any ascomycetous fungus of the genus *Aspergillus*, having chains of conidia attached like bristles to a club-shaped stalk: family *Aspergillaceae.*
▷**HISTORY** C19: from New Latin *aspergillum* (from its similar appearance)

asperity (æ'spɛrɪtɪ) NOUN, *plural* **-ties.** [1] roughness or sharpness of temper. [2] roughness or harshness of a surface, sound, taste, etc. [3] a condition hard to endure; affliction. [4] *Physics* the elastically compressed region of contact between two surfaces caused by the normal force.
▷**HISTORY** C16: from Latin *asperitās*, from *asper* rough

aspermia (ə'spɜːmɪə) NOUN *Pathol* the failure to form or emit semen.

asperse (ə'spɜːs) VERB (*tr*) [1] to spread false rumours about; defame. [2] *Rare* to sprinkle, as with water in baptism.
▷**HISTORY** C15: from Latin *aspersus*, from *aspergere* to sprinkle
▸**as'perser** NOUN ▸**as'persive** ADJECTIVE ▸**as'persively** ADVERB

aspersion (ə'spɜːʃən) NOUN [1] a disparaging or malicious remark; slanderous accusation (esp in the phrase **cast aspersions** (**on**)). [2] the act of defaming. [3] *Rare* the act of sprinkling, esp of water in baptism.

aspersorium (ˌæspə'sɔːrɪəm) NOUN, *plural* **-ria** (-rɪə) *or* **-riums.** *RC Church* [1] a basin containing holy water with which worshippers sprinkle themselves. [2] Also called: **aspergillum.** a perforated instrument used to sprinkle holy water.

asphalt ('æsfælt, 'æʃ-, -fɔːlt) NOUN [1] any of several black semisolid substances composed of bitumen and inert mineral matter. They occur naturally in parts of America and as a residue from petroleum distillation: used as a waterproofing material and in paints, dielectrics, and fungicides. [2] a mixture of this substance with gravel, used in road-surfacing and roofing materials. [3] (*modifier*) containing or surfaced with asphalt. ◆ VERB [4] (*tr*) to cover with asphalt.
▷**HISTORY** C14: from Late Latin *aspaltus*, from Greek *asphaltos*, probably from A-¹ + *sphallein* to cause to fall; referring to its use as a binding agent
▸**as'phaltic** ADJECTIVE

asphaltite (æs'fæltaɪt) NOUN any of various naturally occurring hydrocarbons that resemble asphalt but have a higher melting point.

aspherical surface NOUN *Photog* a lens or mirror surface that does not form part of a sphere and is used to reduce aberrations.

asphodel ('æsfəˌdel) NOUN [1] any of various S European liliaceous plants of the genera *Asphodelus* and *Asphodeline*, having clusters of white or yellow flowers. Compare **bog asphodel.** [2] any of various other plants, such as the daffodil. [3] an unidentified flower of Greek legend, probably a narcissus, said to cover the Elysian fields.
▷**HISTORY** C16: from Latin *asphodelus*, from Greek *asphodelos*, of obscure origin

asphyxia (æs'fɪksɪə) NOUN lack of oxygen in the blood due to restricted respiration; suffocation. If severe enough and prolonged, it causes death.
▷**HISTORY** C18: from New Latin, from Greek *asphuxia* a stopping of the pulse, from A-¹ + *sphuxis* pulse, from *sphuzein* to throb
▸**as'phyxial** ADJECTIVE

asphyxiant (æs'fɪksɪənt) ADJECTIVE [1] causing asphyxia. ◆ NOUN [2] anything that causes asphyxia: *carbon monoxide is an asphyxiant.*

asphyxiate (æs'fɪksɪˌeɪt) VERB to cause asphyxia in or undergo asphyxia; smother; suffocate.
▸**asˌphyxi'ation** NOUN ▸**as'phyxiˌator** NOUN

aspic¹ ('æspɪk) NOUN a savoury jelly based on meat or fish stock, used as a relish or a mould for meat, vegetables, etc.
▷**HISTORY** C18: from French: aspic (jelly), ASP¹; variously explained as referring to its colour or coldness as compared to that of the snake

aspic² ('æspɪk) NOUN an archaic word for **asp¹**.
▷**HISTORY** C17: from French, from Old Provençal *espic* spike, from Latin *spīca*, head (of flower); compare SPIKENARD

aspic³ ('æspɪk) NOUN either of two species of lavender, *Lavandula spica* or *L. latifolia*, that yield an oil used in perfumery: family *Lamiaceae* (labiates).
▷**HISTORY** C16: from Old French, a variant of *aspe* ASP²

aspidistra (ˌæspɪ'dɪstrə) NOUN any Asian plant of the liliaceous genus *Aspidistra*, esp *A. lurida*, a popular house plant with long tough evergreen leaves and purplish flowers borne on the ground.
▷**HISTORY** C19: from New Latin, from Greek *aspis* shield, on the model of *Tupistra* genus of liliaceous plants

Aspinwall ('æspɪnˌwɔːl) NOUN the former name of **Colón**.

aspirant ('æspɪrənt, ə'spaɪərənt) NOUN [1] a person who aspires, as to a high position. ◆ ADJECTIVE [2] aspiring or striving.

aspirate VERB ('æspɪˌreɪt) (*tr*) [1] *Phonetics* **a** to articulate (a stop) with some force, so that breath escapes with audible friction as the stop is released. **b** to pronounce (a word or syllable) with an initial *h*. [2] to draw in or remove by inhalation or suction, esp to suck (air or fluid) from a body cavity or to inhale (fluid) into the lungs after vomiting. [3] to supply air to (an internal-combustion engine). ◆ NOUN ('æspɪrɪt) [4] *Phonetics* **a** a stop pronounced with an audible release of breath. **b** the glottal fricative represented in English and several other languages as *h*. ◆ ADJECTIVE ('æspɪrɪt) [5] *Phonetics* (of a stop) pronounced with a forceful and audible expulsion of breath.

aspiration (ˌæspɪ'reɪʃən) NOUN [1] strong desire to achieve something, such as success. [2] the aim of such desire. [3] **a** the act of breathing. **b** a breath. [4] *Phonetics* **a** the pronunciation of a stop with an audible and forceful release of breath. **b** the friction of the released breath. **c** an aspirated consonant. [5] removal of air or fluid from a body cavity by suction. [6] *Med* **a** the sucking of fluid or foreign matter into the air passages of the body. **b** the removal of air or fluid from the body by suction.
▸**aspiratory** (ə'spaɪrətərɪ, -trɪ, 'æspɪrətərɪ, -trɪ) ADJECTIVE

aspirator ('æspɪˌreɪtə) NOUN a device employing suction, such as a jet pump or one for removing fluids from a body cavity.

aspire (ə'spaɪə) VERB (*intr*) [1] (usually foll by *to* or *after*) to yearn (for) or have a powerful or ambitious plan, desire, or hope (to do or be something): *to aspire to be a great leader*. [2] to rise to a great height.
▷**HISTORY** C15: from Latin *aspīrāre* to breathe upon, from *spīrāre* to breathe
▸**as'pirer** NOUN ▸**as'piring** ADJECTIVE

aspirin ('æsprɪn) NOUN, *plural* **-rin** *or* **-rins.** [1] a white crystalline compound widely used in the form of tablets to relieve pain and fever, to reduce inflammation, and to prevent strokes. Formula: $CH_3COOC_6H_4COOH$. Chemical name: **acetylsalicylic acid.** [2] a tablet of aspirin.
▷**HISTORY** C19: from German, from *A(cetyl)* + *Spir(säure)* spiraeic acid (modern salicylic acid) + -IN; see also SPIRAEA

asplanchnic (eɪ'splæŋknɪk) ADJECTIVE *Zoology* having no gut.

asplenium (æ'spliːnɪəm) NOUN any fern of the very large genus *Asplenium*, of worldwide distribution. Some, esp the bird's nest fern (*A. nidus*), are grown as greenhouse or house plants for their decorative evergreen fronds: family *Polypodiaceae*. See also **spleenwort.**
▷**HISTORY** New Latin, from Latin *asplēnum*, from Greek *asplēnon* spleenwort, from *a-* not + *splēn* spleen (from its reputed medicinal properties)

aspro ('æsprəʊ) NOUN, *plural* **-pros.** *Austral informal* an associate professor at an academic institution.
▷**HISTORY** C20: from AS(SOCIATE) + PRO(FESSOR)

asquint (ə'skwɪnt) ADVERB, ADJECTIVE (*postpositive*) with a glance from the corner of the eye, esp a furtive one.
▷**HISTORY** C13: perhaps from Dutch *schuinte* slant, of obscure origin

ass[1] (æs) NOUN [1] either of two perissodactyl mammals of the horse family (*Equidae*), *Equus asinus* (**African wild ass**) or *E. hemionus* (**Asiatic wild ass**). They are hardy and sure-footed, having longer ears than the horse. Related adjective: **asinine.** [2] (*not in technical use*) the domesticated variety of the African wild ass; donkey. [3] a foolish or ridiculously pompous person. [4] **not within an ass's roar of.** *Irish informal* not close to obtaining, winning, etc.: *she wasn't within an ass's roar of it*.
▷**HISTORY** Old English *assa*, probably from Old Irish *asan*, from Latin *asinus;* related to Greek *onos* ass

ass[2] (æs) NOUN [1] the usual US and Canadian word for **arse.** [2] *US and Canadian offensive slang* sexual intercourse or a woman considered sexually (esp in the phrase **piece of ass**). [3] **cover one's ass.** *Slang, chiefly US and Canadian* to take such action as one considers necessary to avoid censure, ridicule, etc. at a later time.
▷**HISTORY** Old English *ærs;* see ARSE

assagai ('æsəˌgaɪ) NOUN, *plural* **-gais.** a variant spelling of **assegai.**

assai[1] (æ'saɪ) ADVERB *Music* (usually preceded by a musical direction) very: *allegro assai*.
▷**HISTORY** Italian: enough

assai[2] (æ'saɪ) NOUN [1] any of several Brazilian palm trees of the genus *Euterpe*, esp *E. edulis*, that have small dark purple fleshy edible fruit. [2] a beverage made from the fruit of this tree.
▷**HISTORY** via Brazilian Portuguese from Tupi

assail (ə'seɪl) VERB (*tr*) [1] to attack violently; assault. [2] to criticize or ridicule vehemently, as in argument. [3] to beset or disturb: *his mind was assailed by doubts*. [4] to encounter with the intention of mastering: *to assail a problem; to assail a difficult mountain ridge*.
▷**HISTORY** C13: from Old French *asalir*, from Vulgar Latin *assalīre* (unattested) to leap upon, from Latin *assilīre*, from *salīre* to leap
▸**as'sailable** ADJECTIVE ▸**as'sailer** NOUN ▸**as'sailment** NOUN

assailant (ə'seɪlənt) NOUN a person who attacks another, either physically or verbally.

assam ('æsæm; *Malay* 'asam) NOUN (in Malaysia) tamarind as used in cooking. **Assam ikan** is a dish of fish cooked with tamarind.
▷**HISTORY** from Malay *asam* sour

Assam (æ'sæm) NOUN [1] a state of NE India, situated in the central Brahmaputra valley: tropical forest, with the heaviest rainfall in the world; produces large quantities of tea. Capital: Dispur. Pop.: 26 638 407 (2001 est.). Area: 78 438 sq. km (30 673 sq. miles). [2] a high-quality black tea grown in the state of Assam.

Assamese (ˌæsə'miːz) NOUN [1] the state language of Assam, belonging to the Indic branch of the Indo-European family and closely related to Bengali. [2] (*plural* **-mese**) a native or inhabitant of Assam. ◆ ADJECTIVE [3] of or relating to Assam, its people, or their language.

assassin (ə'sæsɪn) NOUN a murderer, esp one who kills a prominent political figure.
▷**HISTORY** C16: from Medieval Latin *assassīnus*, from Arabic *hashshāshīn*, plural of *hashshāsh* one who eats HASHISH

Assassin (ə'sæsɪn) NOUN a member of a secret sect of Muslim fanatics operating in Persia and Syria from about 1090 to 1256, murdering their victims, usually Crusaders.

assassinate (ə'sæsɪˌneɪt) VERB (*tr*) [1] to murder (a person, esp a public or political figure), usually by a surprise attack. [2] to ruin or harm (a person's reputation, etc.) by slander.
▸**asˌsassi'nation** NOUN

assassin bug NOUN any long-legged predatory, often blood-sucking, insect of the heteropterous family *Reduviidae*.

assassin fly NOUN another name for **robber fly.**

assault (ə'sɔːlt) NOUN [1] a violent attack, either physical or verbal. [2] *Law* an intentional or reckless act that causes another person to expect to be subjected to immediate and unlawful violence. Compare **battery** (sense 4), **assault and battery.** [3] **a** the culmination of a military attack, in which fighting takes place at close quarters. **b** (*as modifier*): *assault troops*. [4] rape or attempted rape. ◆ VERB (*tr*) [5] to make an assault upon. [6] to rape or attempt to rape.
▷**HISTORY** C13: from Old French *asaut*, from Vulgar Latin *assaltus* (unattested), from *assalīre* (unattested) to leap upon; see ASSAIL
▸**as'saulter** NOUN ▸**as'saultive** ADJECTIVE

assault and battery NOUN *Criminal law* a threat of attack to another person followed by actual attack, which need amount only to touching with hostile intent.

assault course NOUN an obstacle course designed to give soldiers practice in negotiating hazards in making an assault.

assay VERB (ə'seɪ) [1] to subject (a substance, such as silver or gold) to chemical analysis, as in the determination of the amount of impurity. [2] (*tr*) to attempt (something or to do something). [3] (*tr; may take a clause as object*) to test, analyse, or evaluate: *to assay the significance of early childhood experience*. ◆ NOUN (ə'seɪ, 'æseɪ) [4] **a** an analysis, esp a determination of the amount of metal in an ore or the amounts of impurities in a precious metal. **b** (*as modifier*): *an assay office*. [5] a substance undergoing an analysis. [6] a written report on the results of an analysis. [7] a test. [8] *Archaic* an attempt.
▷**HISTORY** C14: from Old Northern French *assai;* see ESSAY
▸**as'sayable** ADJECTIVE ▸**as'sayer** NOUN

assegai *or* **assagai** ('æsəˌgaɪ) NOUN, *plural* **-gais.** [1] a southern African cornaceous tree, *Curtisia faginea*, the wood of which is used for making spears. [2] a sharp light spear, esp one made of this wood.
▷**HISTORY** C17: from Portuguese *azagaia*, from Arabic *az zaghāyah*, from *al* the + *zaghāyah* assegai, from Berber

assemblage (ə'semblɪdʒ) NOUN [1] a number of things or persons assembled together; collection; assembly. [2] a list of dishes served at a meal or the dishes themselves. [3] the act or process of assembling or the state of being assembled. [4] (ˌæsəm'blɑːʒ) a three-dimensional work of art that combines various objects into an integrated whole.

assemble (ə'semb[ə]l) VERB [1] to come or bring together; collect or congregate. [2] to fit or join together (the parts of something, such as a machine): *to assemble the parts of a kit*. [3] to run (a computer program) that converts a set of symbolic data, usually in the form of specific single-step instructions, into machine language.
▷**HISTORY** C13: from Old French *assembler*, from Vulgar Latin *assimulāre* (unattested) to bring together, from Latin *simul* together

assemblé *French* (asɑ̃ble) NOUN *Ballet* a sideways leap in which the feet come together in the air in preparation for landing.
▷**HISTORY** literally: brought together

assembler (ə'semblə) NOUN [1] a type of computer program that converts a program written in assembly language into machine code. Compare **compiler** (sense 2). [2] another name for **assembly language.**

assembly (ə'semblɪ) NOUN, *plural* **-blies.** [1] a number of people gathered together, esp for a formal meeting held at regular intervals. [2] the act of assembling or the state of being assembled. [3] the process of putting together a number of parts to make a machine or other product. [4] *Machinery* a group of mating components before or after fitting together. [5] *Military* **a** a signal for personnel to assemble, as by drum, bugle, etc. **b** (*as modifier*): *an assembly area*.

Assembly (ə'semblɪ) NOUN, *plural* **-blies.** [1] the lower chamber in various American state legislatures. See also **House of Assembly, legislative assembly, National Assembly.** [2] *NZ* short for **General Assembly.**

assembly language NOUN *Computing* a low-level programming language that allows a programmer complete control of the machine code to be generated.

assembly line NOUN a sequence of machines, tools, operations, workers, etc., in a factory, arranged so that at each stage a further process is carried out.

assemblyman (ə'semblɪmən) NOUN, *plural* **-men.** (*sometimes capital*) a member of an assembly, esp a legislature.

Assembly of First Nations NOUN the national organization which represents the First Nations in Canada. Abbreviation: **AFN.**

Assen (*Dutch* 'ɑsə) NOUN a city in the N Netherlands, capital of Drenthe province. Pop.: 52 268 (1994).

assent (ə'sent) NOUN [1] agreement, as to a statement, proposal, etc.; acceptance. [2] hesitant agreement; compliance. [3] sanction. ◆ VERB [4] (*intr;* usually foll by *to*) to agree or express agreement.
▷**HISTORY** C13: from Old French *assenter*, from Latin *assentīrī*, from *sentīre* to think

assentation (ˌæsen'teɪʃən) NOUN servile or hypocritical agreement.

assentient (ə'senʃɪənt) ADJECTIVE [1] approving or agreeing. ◆ NOUN [2] a person who assents.

assentor (ə'sentə) NOUN *Brit government* any of the eight voters legally required to endorse the nomination of a candidate in a parliamentary or local election in addition to the nominator and seconder.

assert (əˈsɜːt) VERB (*tr*) [1] to insist upon (rights, claims, etc.). [2] (*may take a clause as object*) to state to be true; declare categorically. [3] to put (oneself) forward in an insistent manner.
▷HISTORY C17: from Latin *asserere* to join to oneself, from *serere* to join
▸**asˈserter** *or* **asˈsertor** NOUN ▸**asˈsertible** ADJECTIVE

assertion (əˈsɜːʃən) NOUN [1] a positive statement, usually made without an attempt at furnishing evidence. [2] the act of asserting.

assertive (əˈsɜːtɪv) ADJECTIVE [1] confident and direct in claiming one's rights or putting forward one's views. [2] given to making assertions or bold demands; dogmatic or aggressive.
▸**asˈsertively** ADVERB ▸**asˈsertiveness** NOUN

assertoric (ˌæsɜːˈtɒrɪk) ADJECTIVE *Logic* [1] (of a statement) stating a fact, as opposed to expressing an evaluative judgment. [2] *Obsolete* judging what is rather than what may or must be. ◆ Compare **apodeictic** (sense 2), **problematic** (sense 2).

assess (əˈsɛs) VERB (*tr*) [1] to judge the worth, importance, etc., of; evaluate. [2] (foll by *at*) to estimate the value of (income, property, etc.) for taxation purposes: *the estate was assessed at three thousand pounds.* [3] to determine the amount of (a fine, tax, damages, etc.). [4] to impose a tax, fine, etc., on (a person or property).
▷HISTORY C15: from Old French *assesser*, from Latin *assidēre* to sit beside, from *sedēre* to sit
▸**asˈsessable** ADJECTIVE

assessment (əˈsɛsmənt) NOUN [1] the act of assessing, esp (in Britain) the evaluation of a student's achievement on a course. [2] an amount determined as payable. [3] a valuation set on taxable property, income, etc. [4] evaluation; estimation.

assessment arrangements PLURAL NOUN *Brit education* nationally standardized plans for pupil assessment in different subjects based on attainment targets at the end of each key stage in the National Curriculum.

assessor (əˈsɛsə) NOUN [1] a person who evaluates the merits, importance, etc., of something, esp (in Britain) work prepared as part of a course of study. [2] a person who values property for taxation. [3] a person who estimates the value of damage to property for insurance purposes. [4] a person with technical expertise called in to advise a court on specialist matters. [5] a person who shares another's position or rank, esp in an advisory capacity.
▸**assessorial** (ˌæsɛˈsɔːrɪəl) ADJECTIVE

asset (ˈæsɛt) NOUN anything valuable or useful: *experience is their main asset.* See also **assets.**
▷HISTORY C19: back formation from ASSETS

asset-backed fund NOUN a fund in which the money is invested in property, shares, etc., rather than being deposited with a bank or building society.

assets (ˈæsɛts) PLURAL NOUN [1] *Accounting* the property and claims against debtors that a business enterprise may apply to discharge its liabilities. Assets may be fixed, current, liquid, or intangible and are shown balanced against liabilities. Compare **liabilities.** [2] *Law* the property available to an executor or administrator for settlement of the debts and payment of legacies of the estate of a deceased or insolvent person. [3] any property owned by a person or firm.
▷HISTORY C16 (in the sense: enough to discharge one's liabilities): via Anglo-French from Old French *asez* enough, from Vulgar Latin *ad satis* (unattested), from Latin *ad* up to + *satis* enough

asset-stripping NOUN *Commerce* the practice of taking over a failing company at a low price and then selling the assets piecemeal.
▸ˈ**asset-ˌstripper** NOUN

asset value NOUN the value of a share in a company calculated by dividing the difference between the total of its assets and its liabilities by the number of ordinary shares issued.

asseverate (əˈsɛvəˌreɪt) VERB (*tr*) to assert or declare emphatically or solemnly.
▷HISTORY C18: from Latin *assevērāre* to do (something) earnestly, from *sevērus* SEVERE
▸**asˌseverˈation** NOUN

assez (ˈæseɪ) ADVERB *Music* (as part of a musical direction) fairly; rather.
▷HISTORY C19: French: enough

asshole (ˈæsˌhəʊl) NOUN *Slang, derogatory* the usual US and Canadian word for **arsehole** (see **arse**).

Asshur (ˈæʃʊə) NOUN a variant spelling of **Assur.**

assibilate (əˈsɪbɪˌleɪt) VERB *Phonetics* [1] (*intr*) (of a speech sound) to be changed into a sibilant. [2] (*tr*) to pronounce (a speech sound) with or as a sibilant.
▷HISTORY C19: from Late Latin *assībilāre* to hiss at, from *sībilāre* to hiss; see SIBILANT
▸**asˌsibiˈlation** NOUN

assiduity (ˌæsɪˈdjuːɪtɪ) NOUN, *plural* **-ties.** [1] constant and close application. [2] (*often plural*) devoted attention.

assiduous (əˈsɪdjʊəs) ADJECTIVE [1] hard-working; persevering: *an assiduous researcher.* [2] undertaken with perseverance and care: *assiduous editing.*
▷HISTORY C16: from Latin *assiduus* sitting down to (something), from *assidēre* to sit beside, from *sedēre* to sit
▸**asˈsiduously** ADVERB ▸**asˈsiduousness** NOUN

assign (əˈsaɪn) VERB (*mainly tr*) [1] to select for and appoint to a post, etc.: *to assign an expert to the job.* [2] to give out or allot (a task, problem, etc.): *to assign advertising to an expert.* [3] to set apart (a place, person, time, etc.) for a particular function or event: *to assign a day for the meeting.* [4] to attribute to a specified cause, origin, or source; ascribe: *to assign a stone cross to the Vikings.* [5] to transfer (one's right, interest, or title to property) to someone else. [6] (*also intr*) *Law* (formerly) to transfer (property) to trustees so that it may be used for the benefit of creditors. [7] *Military* to allocate (men or materials) on a permanent basis. Compare **attach** (sense 6). [8] *Computing* to place (a value corresponding to a variable) in a memory location. ◆ NOUN [9] *Law* a person to whom property is assigned; assignee.
▷HISTORY C14: from Old French *assigner*, from Latin *assignāre*, from *signāre* to mark out
▸**asˈsignable** ADJECTIVE ▸**asˌsignaˈbility** NOUN ▸**asˈsignably** ADVERB ▸**asˈsigner** NOUN

assignat (ˈæsɪɡˌnæt, ˌæsɪˈnjɑː; *French* asiɲa) NOUN *French history* the paper money issued by the Constituent Assembly in 1789, backed by the confiscated land of the Church and the émigrés.
▷HISTORY C18: from French, from Latin *assignātum* something appointed; see ASSIGN

assignation (ˌæsɪɡˈneɪʃən) NOUN [1] a secret or forbidden arrangement to meet, esp one between lovers. [2] the act of assigning; assignment. [3] *Law chiefly Scot* another word for **assignment.**
▷HISTORY C14: from Old French, from Latin *assignātiō* a marking out; see ASSIGN

assignee (ˌæsaɪˈniː) NOUN [1] *Law* a person to whom some right, interest, or property is transferred. [2] *Austral history* a convict who had undergone assignment.

assignment (əˈsaɪnmənt) NOUN [1] something that has been assigned, such as a mission or task. [2] a position or post to which a person is assigned. [3] the act of assigning or state of being assigned. [4] *Law* **a** the transfer to another of a right, interest, or title to property, esp personal property: *assignment of a lease.* **b** the document effecting such a transfer. **c** the right, interest, or property transferred. [5] *Law* (formerly) the transfer, esp by an insolvent debtor, of property in trust for the benefit of his creditors. [6] *Logic* a function that associates specific values with each variable in a formal expression. [7] *Austral history* a system (1789–1841) whereby a convict could become the unpaid servant of a freeman.

assignor (ˌæsɪˈnɔː) NOUN *Law* a person who transfers or assigns property.

assimilate (əˈsɪmɪˌleɪt) VERB [1] (*tr*) to learn (information, a procedure, etc.) and understand it thoroughly. [2] (*tr*) to absorb (food) and incorporate it into the body tissues. [3] (*intr*) to become absorbed, incorporated, or learned and understood. [4] (usually foll by *into* or *with*) to bring or come into harmony; adjust or become adjusted: *the new immigrants assimilated easily.* [5] (usually foll by *to* or *with*) to become or cause to become similar. [6] (usually foll by *to*) *Phonetics* to change (a consonant) or (of a consonant) to be changed into another under the influence of one adjacent to it: *(n) often assimilates to (ŋ) before (k), as in "include".*
▷HISTORY C15: from Latin *assimilāre* to make one thing like another, from *similis* like, SIMILAR
▸**asˈsimilable** ADJECTIVE ▸**asˈsimilably** ADVERB ▸**asˌsimiˈlation** NOUN ▸**asˈsimilative** *or* **asˈsimilatory** ADJECTIVE ▸**asˈsimiˌlator** NOUN ▸**asˈsimilatively** ADVERB

Assiniboine[1] (əˈsɪnɪˌbɔɪn) NOUN a river in W Canada, rising in E Saskatchewan and flowing southeast and east to the Red River at Winnipeg. Length: over 860 km (500 miles).

Assiniboine[2] (əˈsɪnəˌbɔɪn) NOUN [1] (*plural* **-boine** *or* **-boines**) a member of a North American Indian people living in Alberta, Saskatchewan, and Montana; one of the Sioux peoples. [2] the language of this people, belonging to the Siouan family.

Assisi (*Italian* asˈsiːzi) NOUN a town in central Italy, in Umbria: birthplace of St Francis, who founded the Franciscan religious order here in 1208. Pop.: 24 790 (1990).

assist (əˈsɪst) VERB [1] to give help or support to (a person, cause, etc.); aid. [2] to work or act as an assistant or subordinate to (another). [3] *Ice hockey* to help (a team-mate) to score, as by passing the puck. [4] (*intr;* foll by *at*) *Archaic* to be present; attend. ◆ NOUN [5] *US and Canadian* the act of helping; aid; assistance. [6] *Baseball* the act of a player who throws or deflects a batted ball in such a way that a team is enabled to put out an opponent. [7] *Sport* **a** a pass or other action by a player which enables another player to score a goal. **b** a credit given for such an action.
▷HISTORY C15: from French *assister* to be present, from Latin *assistere* to stand by, from *sistere* to cause to stand, from *stāre* to stand
▸**asˈsister** NOUN

assistance (əˈsɪstəns) NOUN [1] help; support. [2] the act of assisting. [3] *Brit informal* See **national assistance.**

assistant (əˈsɪstənt) NOUN [1] **a** a person who assists, esp in a subordinate position. **b** (*as modifier*): *assistant manager.* [2] See **shop assistant.** ◆ ADJECTIVE [3] *Archaic* helpful or useful as an aid.

assistant professor NOUN *US and Canadian* a university teacher lower in rank than an associate professor.

assistant referee NOUN *Soccer* the official name for **linesman** (sense 1).

assisted living (əˈsɪstɪd) NOUN **a** a living environment for elderly people, in which personal and medical care are supplied. **b** (*as modifier*): *private assisted-living apartments.*

assistive (əˈsɪstɪv) ADJECTIVE providing a means of reducing a physical impairment: *an assistive device such as a hearing aid.*

Assiut (æˈsjuːt) NOUN a variant spelling of **Asyut.**

assize (əˈsaɪz) NOUN [1] (in the US) **a** a sitting of a legislative assembly or administrative body. **b** an enactment or order of such an assembly. [2] *English history* a trial or judicial inquest, the writ instituting such inquest, or the verdict. [3] *Scots Law* **a** trial by jury. **b** another name for **jury**[1].
▷HISTORY C13: from Old French *assise* session, from *asseoir* to seat, from Latin *assidēre* to sit beside; see ASSESS

assizes (əˈsaɪzɪz) PLURAL NOUN (formerly in England and Wales) the sessions, usually held four times a year, of the principal court in each county, exercising civil and criminal jurisdiction, attended by itinerant judges: replaced in 1971 by crown courts.

assn ABBREVIATION FOR association.

assoc. ABBREVIATION FOR: [1] associate(d). [2] association.

associate VERB (əˈsəʊʃɪˌeɪt, -sɪ-) (usually foll by *with*) [1] (*tr*) to link or connect in the mind or imagination: *to associate Christmas with fun.* [2] (*intr*) to keep company; mix socially: *to associate with writers.* [3] (*intr*) to form or join an association, group, etc. [4] (*tr; usually passive*) to consider in conjunction; connect: *rainfall is associated with humidity.* [5] (*tr*) to bring (a person, esp oneself) into friendship, partnership, etc. [6] (*tr; often passive*) to express agreement or allow oneself to be connected (with): *Bertrand Russell was associated with the peace movement.* ◆ NOUN (əˈsəʊʃɪɪt, -ˌeɪt, -sɪ-) [7] a person joined with another or others in an enterprise, business, etc.; partner; colleague. [8] a companion or friend. [9] something that usually accompanies

another thing; concomitant: *hope is an associate to happiness.* [10] a person having a subordinate position in or admitted to only partial membership of an institution, association, etc. ◆ ADJECTIVE (əˈsəʊʃɪɪt, -ˌeɪt, -sɪ-) (*prenominal*) [11] joined with another or others in an enterprise, business, etc.; having equal or nearly equal status: *an associate director.* [12] having partial rights and privileges or subordinate status: *an associate member.* [13] accompanying; concomitant.
▷HISTORY C14: from Latin *associāre* to ally with, from *sociāre* to join, from *socius* an ally
▸**asˈsociable** ADJECTIVE ▸**asˈsociˌator** NOUN ▸**asˈsociatory** ADJECTIVE ▸**asˈsociateˌship** NOUN

associated statehood NOUN the semi-independent political status of various former British colonies in the Caribbean from 1967 until each became an independent state in the British Commonwealth, by which Britain retained responsibility for defence and some aspects of foreign affairs. The **associated states** were Anguilla, Antigua, Dominica, Grenada, St Kitts-Nevis, St Lucia, and St Vincent and the Grenadines.

associate professor NOUN [1] (in the US and Canada) a university teacher lower in rank than a full professor but higher than an assistant professor. [2] (in New Zealand) a senior lecturer holding the rank below professor.

association (əˌsəʊsɪˈeɪʃən, -ʃɪ-) NOUN [1] a group of people having a common purpose or interest; a society or club. [2] the act of associating or the state of being associated. [3] friendship or companionship: *their association will not last.* [4] a mental connection of ideas, feelings, or sensations: *association of revolution with bloodshed.* [5] *Psychol* the mental process of linking ideas so that the recurrence of one idea automatically recalls the other. See also **free association.** [6] *Chem* the formation of groups of molecules and ions, esp in liquids, held together by weak chemical bonds. [7] *Ecology* a group of similar plants that grow in a uniform environment and contain one or more dominant species.

association football NOUN a more formal name for **soccer.**

associationism (əˌsəʊsɪˈeɪʃəˌnɪzəm) NOUN *Psychol* a theory that all mental activity is based on connections between basic mental events, such as sensations and feelings.

association law NOUN *Psychol* any law governing the association of ideas.

associative (əˈsəʊʃɪətɪv) ADJECTIVE [1] of, relating to, or causing association or union. [2] *Maths, logic* **a** being independent of the grouping of numbers, symbols, or terms within a given set, as in conjunction or in an expression such as (2 × 3) × 4 = 2 × (3 × 4). **b** referring to this property: *the associative laws of arithmetic.*

associative cortex NOUN *Anatomy* the part of the cortex that does not have direct connections to the senses or motor system and is thought to be involved in higher mental processes.

associative storage NOUN *Computing* a storage device in which the information is identified by content rather than by an address. Also called: **content-addressable storage.**

assoil (əˈsɔɪl) VERB (*tr*) *Archaic* [1] to absolve; set free. [2] to atone for.
▷HISTORY C13: from Old French *assoldre,* from Latin *absolvere* to ABSOLVE

assonance (ˈæsənəns) NOUN [1] the use of the same vowel sound with different consonants or the same consonant with different vowels in successive words or stressed syllables, as in a line of verse. Examples are *time* and *light* or *mystery* and *mastery.* [2] partial correspondence; rough similarity.
▷HISTORY C18: from French, from Latin *assonāre* to sound, from *sonāre* to sound
▸**ˈassonant** ADJECTIVE, NOUN ▸**assonantal** (ˌæsəˈnæntᵊl) ADJECTIVE

assort (əˈsɔːt) VERB [1] (*tr*) to arrange or distribute into groups of the same type; classify. [2] (*intr;* usually foll by *with*) to fit or fall into a class or group; match. [3] (*tr*) to supply with an assortment of merchandise. [4] (*tr*) to put in the same category as others; group. [5] (*intr;* usually foll by *with*) *Rare* to keep company; consort.
▷HISTORY C15: from Old French *assorter,* from *sorte* SORT
▸**asˈsortative** *or* **asˈsortive** ADJECTIVE ▸**asˈsortatively** ADVERB ▸**asˈsorter** NOUN

assorted (əˈsɔːtɪd) ADJECTIVE [1] consisting of various kinds mixed together; miscellaneous: *assorted sweets.* [2] arranged in sorts; classified: *assorted categories.* [3] matched; suited (esp in the combinations **well-assorted, ill-assorted**).

assortment (əˈsɔːtmənt) NOUN [1] a collection or group of various things or sorts. [2] the act of assorting.

ASSR ABBREVIATION FOR (formerly) Autonomous Soviet Socialist Republic.

asst ABBREVIATION FOR assistant.

assuage (əˈsweɪdʒ) VERB (*tr*) [1] to soothe, moderate, or relieve (grief, pain, etc.). [2] to give relief to (thirst, appetite, etc.); satisfy. [3] to pacify; calm.
▷HISTORY C14: from Old French *assouagier,* from Vulgar Latin *assuāviāre* (unattested) to sweeten, from Latin *suāvis* pleasant; see SUAVE
▸**asˈsuagement** NOUN ▸**asˈsuager** NOUN ▸**assuasive** (əˈsweɪsɪv) ADJECTIVE

Assuan *or* **Assouan** (ɑːsˈwɑːn) NOUN variant spellings of **Aswan.**

assume (əˈsjuːm) VERB (*tr*) [1] (*may take a clause as object*) to take for granted; accept without proof; suppose: *to assume that someone is sane.* [2] to take upon oneself; undertake or take on or over (a position, responsibility, etc.): *to assume office.* [3] to pretend to; feign: *he assumed indifference, although the news affected him deeply.* [4] to take or put on; adopt: *the problem assumed gigantic proportions.* [5] to appropriate or usurp (power, control, etc.); arrogate: *the revolutionaries assumed control of the city.* [6] *Christianity* (of God) to take up (the soul of a believer) into heaven.
▷HISTORY C15: from Latin *assūmere* to take up, from *sūmere* to take up, from SUB- + *emere* to take
▸**asˈsumable** ADJECTIVE ▸**asˈsumer** NOUN

assumed (əˈsjuːmd) ADJECTIVE [1] false; fictitious: *an assumed name.* [2] taken for granted: *an assumed result.* [3] usurped; arrogated: *an assumed authority.*

assuming (əˈsjuːmɪŋ) ADJECTIVE [1] expecting too much; presumptuous; arrogant. ◆ CONJUNCTION [2] (often foll by *that*) if it is assumed or taken for granted (that): *even assuming he understands the problem, he will never take any action.*

assumpsit (əˈsʌmpsɪt) NOUN *Law* (before 1875) an action to recover damages for breach of an express or implied contract or agreement that was not under seal.
▷HISTORY C17: from Latin, literally: he has undertaken, from *assūmere* to ASSUME

assumption (əˈsʌmpʃən) NOUN [1] the act of taking something for granted or something that is taken for granted. [2] an assuming of power or possession of something. [3] arrogance; presumption. [4] *Logic* a statement that is used as the premise of a particular argument but may not be otherwise accepted. Compare **axiom** (sense 4).
▷HISTORY C13: from Latin *assūmptiō* a taking up, from *assūmere* to ASSUME
▸**asˈsumptive** ADJECTIVE ▸**asˈsumptively** ADVERB

Assumption (əˈsʌmpʃən) NOUN *Christianity* [1] the taking up of the Virgin Mary (body and soul) into heaven when her earthly life was ended. [2] the feast commemorating this, celebrated by Roman Catholics on Aug. 15.

Assur, Asur (ˈæsə), **Asshur,** *or* **Ashur** (ˈæʃʊə) NOUN [1] the supreme national god of the ancient Assyrians, chiefly a war god, whose symbol was an archer within a winged disc. [2] one of the chief cities of ancient Assyria, on the River Tigris about 100 km (60 miles) downstream from the present-day city of Mosul.

assurance (əˈʃʊərəns) NOUN [1] a statement, assertion, etc., intended to inspire confidence or give encouragement: *she was helped by his assurance that she would cope.* [2] a promise or pledge of support: *he gave an assurance of help when needed.* [3] freedom from doubt; certainty: *his assurance about his own superiority infuriated her.* [4] forwardness; impudence. [5] *Chiefly Brit* insurance providing for certainties such as death as contrasted with fire or theft.

assure (əˈʃʊə) VERB (*tr; may take a clause as object*) [1] to cause to feel sure or certain; convince: *to assure a person of one's love.* [2] to promise; guarantee: *he assured us that he would come.* [3] to state positively or with assurance. [4] to make (an event) certain; ensure. [5] *Chiefly Brit* to insure against loss, esp of life. [6] *Property law* another word for **convey.**
▷HISTORY C14: from Old French *aseürer* to assure, from Medieval Latin *assēcūrāre* to secure or make sure, from *sēcūrus* SECURE
▸**asˈsurable** ADJECTIVE ▸**asˈsurer** NOUN

assured (əˈʃʊəd) ADJECTIVE [1] made certain; sure; guaranteed. [2] self-assured. [3] *Chiefly Brit* insured, esp by a life assurance policy. ◆ NOUN [4] *Chiefly Brit* **a** the beneficiary under a life assurance policy. **b** the person whose life is insured.
▸**assuredly** (əˈʃʊərɪdlɪ) ADVERB ▸**asˈsuredness** NOUN

assured tenancy NOUN *Brit* an agreement between a government-approved body such as a housing association and a tenant for occupation of a newly-built house or flat at an agreed market rent, under which the tenant has security of tenure. Compare **regulated tenancy.**

assurgent (əˈsɜːdʒənt) ADJECTIVE (of leaves, stems, etc.) curving or growing upwards; rising.
▷HISTORY C16: from Latin *assurgere* to rise up, from *surgere* to rise
▸**asˈsurgency** NOUN

Assyria (əˈsɪrɪə) NOUN an ancient kingdom of N Mesopotamia: it established an empire that stretched from Egypt to the Persian Gulf, reaching its greatest extent between 721 and 633 B.C. Its chief cities were Assur and Nineveh.

Assyrian (əˈsɪrɪən) NOUN [1] an inhabitant of ancient Assyria. [2] **a** the extinct language of the ancient Assyrians, belonging to the E Semitic subfamily of the Afro-Asiatic family and regarded as a dialect of Akkadian. **b** a dialect of Aramaic, spoken by modern Assyrians. ◆ ADJECTIVE [3] of, relating to, or characteristic of the ancient or modern Assyrians, their language, or culture.

Assyriology (əˌsɪrɪˈɒlədʒɪ) NOUN the study of the culture, history, and archaeological remains of ancient Assyria.
▸**Asˌsyriˈologist** NOUN

AST ABBREVIATION FOR: [1] **Atlantic Standard Time.** [2] automated screen trading (in securities). [3] *Brit education* advanced skills teacher.

astable (eɪˈsteɪbᵊl) ADJECTIVE [1] not stable. [2] *Electronics* capable of oscillating between two states.

Astana (æˈstænə) NOUN the capital of Kazakhstan, in the N of the country; replaced Almaty as a capital in 1997; an important railway junction. Pop: 313 000 (1999 est.). Former names: **Akmolinsk** (until 1961), **Tselinograd** (1961–94), **Akmola** (1994–98).

Astanga yoga *or* **Ashtanga** (æˈʃtæŋgə) NOUN a revived ancient form of yoga that involves a fast and powerful series of movements.

Astarte (æˈstɑːtɪ) NOUN a fertility goddess worshipped by the Phoenicians: identified with Ashtoreth of the Hebrews and Ishtar of the Babylonians and Assyrians.

astatic (æˈstætɪk, eɪ-) ADJECTIVE [1] not static; unstable. [2] *Physics* **a** having no tendency to assume any particular position or orientation. **b** (of a galvanometer) having two mutually compensating magnets arranged so that the instrument is independent of the earth's magnetic field.
▷HISTORY C19: from Greek *astatos* unsteady; see A-[1], STATIC
▸**aˈstatically** ADVERB ▸**aˈstatiˌcism** NOUN

astatide (ˈæstəˌtaɪd) NOUN *Chem* a binary compound of astatine with a more electropositive element.

astatine (ˈæstəˌtiːn, -tɪn) NOUN a radioactive element of the halogen series: a decay product of uranium and thorium that occurs naturally in minute amounts and is artificially produced by bombarding bismuth with alpha particles. Symbol: At; atomic no.: 85; half-life of most stable isotope, ^{210}At: 8.1 hours; probable valency: 1,3,5, or 7; melting pt.: 302°C; boiling pt.: 337°C (est.).
▷HISTORY C20: from Greek *astatos* unstable (see ASTATIC) + -INE[2]

aster (ˈæstə) NOUN [1] any plant of the genus *Aster,* having white, blue, purple, or pink daisy-like flowers: family *Asteraceae* (composites). Compare

golden aster. 2 **China aster.** a related Chinese plant, *Callistephus chinensis,* widely cultivated for its showy brightly coloured flowers. 3 *Cytology* a group of radiating microtubules that surrounds the centrosome before and during mitosis.
▷**HISTORY** C18: from New Latin, from Latin *aster* star, from Greek

-aster SUFFIX FORMING NOUNS a person or thing that is inferior or bears only a poor resemblance to what is specified: *poetaster.*
▷**HISTORY** from Latin: suffix indicating imperfect resemblance

astereognosis (əˌstɛrɪəʊ'gnəʊsɪs) NOUN inability to recognize objects by touch.
▷**HISTORY** A-[1] + STEREO- + -GNOSIS

asteriated (æ'stɪərɪˌeɪtɪd) ADJECTIVE (of a crystal, esp a gemstone) exhibiting a star-shaped figure in transmitted or reflected light.

asterisk ('æstərɪsk) NOUN 1 a star-shaped character (*) used in printing or writing to indicate a cross-reference to a footnote, an omission, etc. 2 **a** (in historical linguistics) this sign used to indicate an unattested reconstructed form. **b** (in descriptive linguistics) this sign used to indicate that an expression is ungrammatical or in some other way unacceptable. ◆ VERB 3 (*tr*) to mark with an asterisk.
▷**HISTORY** C17: from Late Latin *asteriscus* a small star, from Greek *asteriskos,* from *astēr* star

asterism ('æstəˌrɪzəm) NOUN 1 three asterisks arranged in a triangle (∴ or ∵), to draw attention to the text that follows. 2 a starlike effect seen in some minerals and gemstones when viewed by reflected or transmitted light. 3 a cluster of stars, which may be a subset or a superset of a constellation.
▷**HISTORY** C16: from Greek *asterismos* arrangement of constellations, from *astēr* star

astern (ə'stɜːn) ADVERB, ADJECTIVE (*postpositive*) *Nautical* 1 at or towards the stern. 2 with the stern first: *full speed astern!* 3 aft of the stern of a vessel.

asternal (æ'stɜːn(ə)l, eɪ-) ADJECTIVE *Anatomy* 1 not connected or joined to the sternum. 2 lacking a sternum.

asteroid ('æstəˌrɔɪd) NOUN 1 Also called: **minor planet, planetoid.** any of numerous small celestial bodies that move around the sun mainly between the orbits of Mars and Jupiter. Their diameters range from 930 kilometres (Ceres) to less than one kilometre. 2 Also called: **asteroidean** (ˌæstə'rɔɪdɪən). any echinoderm of the class *Asteroidea;* a starfish. ◆ ADJECTIVE *also* **asteroidal** (ˌæstə'rɔɪd(ə)l). 3 of, relating to, or belonging to the class *Asteroidea.* 4 shaped like a star.
▷**HISTORY** C19: from Greek *asteroeidēs* starlike, from *astēr* a star

asthenia (æs'θiːnɪə) *or* **astheny** ('æsθənɪ) NOUN *Pathol* an abnormal loss of strength; debility.
▷**HISTORY** C19: via New Latin from Greek *astheneia* weakness, from A-[1] + *sthenos* strength

asthenic (æs'θɛnɪk) ADJECTIVE 1 of, relating to, or having asthenia; weak. 2 (in constitutional psychology) referring to a physique characterized by long limbs and a small trunk: claimed to be associated with a schizoid personality. See also **somatotype.** ◆ NOUN 3 a person having long limbs and a small trunk.

asthenopia (ˌæsθɪ'nəʊpɪə) NOUN a technical name for **eyestrain.**
▷**HISTORY** C19: from New Latin, from Greek *asthenēs* weak (from A-[1] + *sthenos* strength) + *ōps* eye
▸**asthenopic** (ˌæsθɪ'nɒpɪk) ADJECTIVE

asthenosphere (əs'θiːnəˌsfɪə, -'θɛn-) NOUN a thin semifluid layer of the earth (100–200 km thick), below the outer rigid lithosphere, forming part of the mantle and thought to be able to flow vertically and horizontally, enabling sections of lithosphere to subside, rise, and undergo lateral movement. See also **isostasy.**
▷**HISTORY** C20: from *astheno-,* from Greek *asthenēs* weak + SPHERE

asthma ('æsmə) NOUN a respiratory disorder, often of allergic origin, characterized by difficulty in breathing, wheezing, and a sense of constriction in the chest.
▷**HISTORY** C14: from Greek: laborious breathing, from *azein* to breathe hard

asthmatic (æs'mætɪk) ADJECTIVE 1 of, relating to, or having asthma. ◆ NOUN 2 a person who has asthma.
▸**asth'matically** ADVERB

Asti ('æstɪ) NOUN a town in NW Italy: famous for its sparkling wine (**Asti spumante** (spuː'mæntɪ)). Pop.: 74 649 (1990).

astigmatic (ˌæstɪg'mætɪk) ADJECTIVE 1 relating to or affected with astigmatism. ◆ NOUN 2 a person who has astigmatism.
▷**HISTORY** C19: from A-[1] + Greek *stigmat-, stigma* spot, focus; see STIGMA
▸**ˌastig'matically** ADVERB

astigmatism (ə'stɪgməˌtɪzəm) *or* **astigmia** (ə'stɪgmɪə) NOUN 1 a defect of a lens resulting in the formation of distorted images; caused by the curvature of the lens being different in different planes. 2 faulty vision resulting from defective curvature of the cornea or lens of the eye.

astilbe (ə'stɪlbɪ) NOUN any perennial saxifragaceous plant of the genus *Astilbe* of E Asia and North America: cultivated for their ornamental spikes or panicles of pink or white flowers.
▷**HISTORY** C19: New Latin, from Greek: not glittering, from A-[1] + *stilbē,* from *stilbein* to glitter; referring to its inconspicuous individual flowers

astir (ə'stɜː) ADJECTIVE (*postpositive*) 1 awake and out of bed. 2 in motion; on the move.

ASTM ABBREVIATION FOR American Society for Testing and Materials.

Astolat ('æstəʊˌlæt) NOUN a town in Arthurian legend: location unknown.

astomatous (æ'stɒmətəs, -'stəʊ-) ADJECTIVE 1 (of animals) having no mouth. 2 (of plants) having no stomata.

astonied (ə'stɒnɪd) ADJECTIVE *Archaic* stunned; dazed.
▷**HISTORY** C14: from *astonyen* to ASTONISH

astonish (ə'stɒnɪʃ) VERB (*tr*) to fill with amazement; surprise greatly.
▷**HISTORY** C15: from earlier *astonyen* (see ASTONIED), from Old French *estoner,* from Vulgar Latin *extonāre* (unattested) to strike with thunder, from Latin *tonāre* to thunder

astonishing (ə'stɒnɪʃɪŋ) ADJECTIVE causing great surprise or amazement; astounding.
▸**a'stonishingly** ADVERB

astonishment (ə'stɒnɪʃmənt) NOUN 1 extreme surprise; amazement. 2 a cause of amazement.

Astoria (ə'stɔːrɪə) NOUN a port in NW Oregon, near the mouth of the Columbia River: founded as a fur-trading post in 1811 by John Jacob Astor. Pop.: 10 069 (1990).

astound (ə'staʊnd) VERB (*tr*) to overwhelm with amazement and wonder; bewilder.
▷**HISTORY** C17: from *astoned* amazed, from Old French *estoné,* from *estoner* to ASTONISH

astounding (ə'staʊndɪŋ) ADJECTIVE causing amazement and wonder; bewildering.
▸**a'stoundingly** ADVERB

astr. *or* **astron.** ABBREVIATION FOR 1 astronomical. 2 astronomy.

astraddle (ə'stræd(ə)l) ADJECTIVE 1 (*postpositive*) with a leg on either side of something. ◆ PREPOSITION 2 astride.

astragal ('æstrəg(ə)l) NOUN 1 *Architect* **a** Also called: **bead.** a small convex moulding, usually with a semicircular cross section. **b** a moulding having the form of a string of beads. 2 *Furniture* a glazing bar, esp in a bookcase. 3 *Anatomy* the ankle or anklebone.
▷**HISTORY** C17: from Latin *astragalus,* from Greek *astragalos* anklebone, hence, small round moulding

astragalus (æ'strægələs) NOUN, *plural* **-li** (-ˌlaɪ). *Anatomy* another name for **talus**[1].
▷**HISTORY** C16: via New Latin from Latin: ASTRAGAL

astrakhan (ˌæstrə'kæn, -'kɑːn) NOUN 1 a fur, usually black or grey, made of the closely curled wool of lambs from Astrakhan. 2 a cloth with curled pile resembling this. 3 (*modifier*) made of such fur or cloth: *an astrakhan collar.*

Astrakhan (ˌæstrə'kæn, -'kɑːn; *Russian* 'astrəxənj) NOUN a city in SE Russia, on the delta of the Volga River, 21 m (70 ft.) below sea level. Pop.: 488 000 (1999 est.).

astral ('æstrəl) ADJECTIVE 1 relating to, proceeding from, consisting of, or resembling the stars: *an astral body.* 2 *Biology* of or relating to the aster occurring in dividing cells. 3 *Theosophy* denoting or relating to a supposed supersensible substance believed to form the material of a second body for each person, taking the form of an aura discernible to certain gifted individuals.
▷**HISTORY** C17: from Late Latin *astrālis,* from Latin *astrum* star, from Greek *astron*
▸**'astrally** ADVERB

astraphobia *or* **astrophobia** (ˌæstrə'fəʊbɪə) NOUN a fear of thunder and lightning.
▷**HISTORY** C20: see ASTRO-, -PHOBIA
▸**ˌastra'phobic** *or* **ˌastro'phobic** ADJECTIVE

astray (ə'streɪ) ADJECTIVE (*postpositive*), ADVERB 1 out of the correct path or direction. 2 out of the right, good, or expected way; into error.
▷**HISTORY** C13: from Old French *estraie* roaming, from *estraier* to STRAY

astrict (ə'strɪkt) VERB (*tr*) *Archaic* to bind, confine, or constrict.
▷**HISTORY** C16: from Latin *astrictus* drawn closely together, from *astringere* to tighten, from *stringere* to bind
▸**as'triction** NOUN ▸**as'trictive** ADJECTIVE ▸**as'trictively** ADVERB

astride (ə'straɪd) ADJECTIVE (*postpositive*) 1 with a leg on either side. 2 with the legs far apart. ◆ PREPOSITION 3 with a leg on either side of. 4 with a part on both sides of.

astringent (ə'strɪndʒənt) ADJECTIVE 1 severe; harsh. 2 sharp or invigorating. 3 causing contraction of body tissues, checking blood flow, or restricting secretions of fluids; styptic. ◆ NOUN 4 an astringent drug or lotion.
▷**HISTORY** C16: from Latin *astringēns* drawing together; see ASTRICT
▸**as'tringency** *or* **as'tringence** NOUN ▸**as'tringently** ADVERB

astro- COMBINING FORM 1 indicating a heavenly body, star, or star-shaped structure: *astrology; astrocyte.* 2 indicating outer space: *astronautics.*
▷**HISTORY** from Greek, from *astron* star

astrobiology (ˌæstrəʊbaɪ'ɒlədʒɪ) NOUN the branch of biology that investigates the possibility of life elsewhere in the universe.

astrobleme ('æstrəˌbliːm) NOUN a mark on the earth's surface, usually circular, formed by a large ancient meteorite impact.
▷**HISTORY** C20: from ASTRO- + Greek *blēma* shot, wound

astrobotany (ˌæstrəʊ'bɒtənɪ) NOUN the branch of botany that investigates the possibility that plants grow on other planets.

astrochemistry (ˌæstrəʊ'kɛmɪstrɪ) NOUN the study of the chemistry of celestial bodies and space, esp by means of spectroscopy.

astrocompass (ˌæstrəʊ'kʌmpəs) NOUN a navigational instrument for giving directional bearings from the centre of the earth to a particular star. It is carried in long-range aircraft, ships, spacecraft, etc.

astrocyte ('æstrəʊˌsaɪt) NOUN any of the star-shaped cells in the tissue supporting the brain and spinal cord (neuroglia).

astrodome ('æstrəˌdəʊm) NOUN 1 Also called: **astrohatch.** a transparent dome on the top of an aircraft, through which observations can be made, esp of the stars. 2 a large domed sports stadium.

astrodynamics (ˌæstrəʊdaɪ'næmɪks) NOUN (*functioning as singular*) the study of the motion of natural and artificial bodies in space.

astrogeology (ˌæstrəʊdʒɪ'ɒlədʒɪ) NOUN the study of the structure, composition, and history of other planets and other bodies in the solar system.

astroid ('æstrɔɪd) NOUN *Maths* a hypocycloid having four cusps.
▷**HISTORY** C19: from ASTRO- + -OID

astrol. ABBREVIATION FOR 1 astrological. 2 astrology.

astrolabe ('æstrəˌleɪb) NOUN an instrument used by early astronomers to measure the altitude of stars and planets and also as a navigational aid. It consists of a graduated circular disc with a movable sighting device. Compare **sextant.**
▷**HISTORY** C13: via Old French and Medieval Latin from Greek, from *astrolabos* (adj), literally: star-taking, from *astron* star + *lambanein* to take

astrology (əˈstrɒlədʒɪ) NOUN [1] the study of the motions and relative positions of the planets, sun, and moon, interpreted in terms of human characteristics and activities. [2] the primitive study of celestial bodies, which formed the basis of astronomy.
▷HISTORY C14: from Old French *astrologie*, from Latin *astrologia*, from Greek, from *astrologos* (originally: astronomer); see ASTRO-, -LOGY
▸**asˈtrologer** *or* **asˈtrologist** NOUN ▸**astrological** (ˌæstrəˈlɒdʒɪkəl) ADJECTIVE ▸**ˌastroˈlogically** ADVERB

astrometry (əˈstrɒmɪtrɪ) NOUN the branch of astronomy concerned with the measurement of the position and motion of celestial bodies.
▸**astrometric** (ˌæstrəˈmɛtrɪk) *or* **ˌastroˈmetrical** ADJECTIVE

astronaut (ˈæstrəˌnɔːt) NOUN a person trained for travelling in space. See also **cosmonaut.**
▷HISTORY C20: from ASTRO- + *-naut* from Greek *nautēs* sailor, on the model of *aeronaut*

astronautics (ˌæstrəˈnɔːtɪks) NOUN (*functioning as singular*) the science and technology of space flight.
▸**ˌastroˈnautic** *or* **ˌastroˈnautical** ADJECTIVE
▸**ˌastroˈnautically** ADVERB

astronavigation (ˌæstrəʊˌnævɪˈgeɪʃən) NOUN another term for **celestial navigation.**
▸**ˌastroˈnaviˌgator** NOUN

astronomer (əˈstrɒnəmə) NOUN a scientist who studies astronomy.

Astronomer Royal NOUN an honorary title awarded to an eminent British astronomer: until 1972, the Astronomer Royal was also director of the Royal Greenwich Observatory.

astronomical (ˌæstrəˈnɒmɪkəl) *or* **astronomic** ADJECTIVE [1] enormously large; immense. [2] of or relating to astronomy.
▸**ˌastroˈnomically** ADVERB

astronomical clock NOUN [1] a complex clock showing astronomical phenomena, such as the phases of the moon. [2] any clock showing sidereal time used in observatories.

astronomical telescope NOUN any telescope designed and mounted for use in astronomy. Such telescopes usually form inverted images. See **Cassegrain telescope, Newtonian telescope, equatorial mounting.**

astronomical unit NOUN a unit of distance used in astronomy equal to the mean distance between the earth and the sun. 1 astronomical unit is equivalent to 1.495×10^{11} metres or about 9.3×10^{7} miles.

astronomical year NOUN another name for **year.** See **year** (sense 4).

astronomy (əˈstrɒnəmɪ) NOUN the scientific study of the individual celestial bodies (excluding the earth) and of the universe as a whole. Its various branches include astrometry, astrodynamics, cosmology, and astrophysics.
▷HISTORY C13: from Old French *astronomie*, from Latin *astronomia*, from Greek; see ASTRO-, -NOMY

astrophotography (ˌæstrəʊfəˈtɒgrəfɪ) NOUN the photography of celestial bodies used in astronomy.
▸**astrophotographic** (ˌæstrəʊˌfəʊtəˈgræfɪk) ADJECTIVE

astrophysics (ˌæstrəʊˈfɪzɪks) NOUN (*functioning as singular*) the branch of physics concerned with the physical and chemical properties, origin, and evolution of the celestial bodies.
▸**ˌastroˈphysical** ADJECTIVE ▸**ˌastroˈphysicist** NOUN

astrotourist (ˈæstrəʊˌtʊərɪst) NOUN a person who pays to travels into space as a form of recreation.
▸**ˌastroˈtourism** NOUN

Asturias (æˈstʊərɪˌæs) NOUN a region and former kingdom of NW Spain, consisting of a coastal plain and the Cantabrian Mountains: a Christian stronghold against the Moors (8th to 13th centuries); rich mineral resources.

astute (əˈstjuːt) ADJECTIVE having insight or acumen; perceptive; shrewd.
▷HISTORY C17: from Latin *astūtus* cunning, from *astus* (n) cleverness
▸**asˈtutely** ADVERB ▸**asˈtuteness** NOUN

Astyanax (æˈstaɪəˌnæks) NOUN *Greek myth* the young son of Hector and Andromache, who was hurled from the walls of Troy by the Greeks.

astylar (æˈstaɪlə, eɪ-) ADJECTIVE *Architect* without columns or pilasters.
▷HISTORY C19: from A-[1] + Greek *stulos* pillar

Asunción (*Spanish* asunˈsjon) NOUN the capital and chief port of Paraguay, on the Paraguay River, 1530 km (950 miles) from the Atlantic. Pop.: 502 426 (1992).

asunder (əˈsʌndə) ADVERB, ADJECTIVE (*postpositive*) in or into parts or pieces; apart: *to tear asunder.*
▷HISTORY Old English *on sundran* apart; see SUNDER

Asur (ˈæsə) NOUN a variant spelling of **Assur.**

ASW ABBREVIATION FOR antisubmarine warfare.

Aswan, Assuan, *or* **Assouan** (ɑːsˈwɑːn) NOUN an ancient town in SE Egypt, on the Nile, just below the First Cataract. Pop.: 219 017 (1996 est.). Ancient name: **Syene.**

Aswan High Dam NOUN a dam on the Nile forming a reservoir (Lake Nasser) extending 480 km (300 miles) from the First to the Third Cataracts: opened in 1971, it was built 6 km (4 miles) upstream from the old **Aswan Dam** (built in 1902 and twice raised). Height of dam: 109 m (365 ft.).

aswarm (əˈswɔːm) ADJECTIVE (*postpositive*) filled, esp with moving things; swarming: *flower beds aswarm with bees.*

asyllabic (ˌæsɪˈlæbɪk, ˌeɪ-) ADJECTIVE not functioning in the manner of a syllable.

asylum (əˈsaɪləm) NOUN [1] a safe or inviolable place of refuge, esp as formerly offered by the Christian Church to criminals, outlaws, etc.; sanctuary (often in the phrase **give asylum to**). [2] shelter; refuge. [3] *International law* refuge afforded to a person whose extradition is sought by a foreign government: *political asylum.* [4] *Obsolescent* an institution for the shelter, treatment, or confinement of individuals, esp a mental hospital (formerly termed **lunatic asylum**).
▷HISTORY C15: via Latin from Greek *asulon* refuge, from *asulos* that may not be seized, from A-[1] + *sulon* right of seizure

asylum seeker NOUN a person who, from fear of persecution for reasons of race, religion, social group, or political opinion, has crossed an international frontier into a country in which he or she hopes to be granted refugee status.

asylum shopper NOUN a migrant who passes through several countries before applying for asylum in a country that appears to be the most accommodating.

asymmetric (ˌæsɪˈmɛtrɪk, ˌeɪ-) *or* **asymmetrical** ADJECTIVE [1] not symmetrical; lacking symmetry; misproportioned. [2] *Chem* **a** (of a molecule) having its atoms and radicals arranged unsymmetrically. **b** (of a carbon atom) attached to four different atoms or radicals so that stereoisomerism results. **c** involving chiral molecules: *asymmetric synthesis.* [3] *Electrical engineering* (of conductors) having different conductivities depending on the direction of current flow, as of diodes. [4] *Aeronautics* having unequal thrust, as caused by an inoperative engine in a twin-engined aircraft. [5] *Logic, maths* (of a relation) never holding between a pair of values *x* and *y* when it holds between *y* and *x*, as "*…is the father of…*". Compare **symmetric** (sense 1), **antisymmetric, nonsymmetric.**
▸**ˌasymˈmetrically** ADVERB

asymmetric bars ADVERB, PLURAL NOUN *Gymnastics* **a** (*functioning as plural*) a pair of wooden or fibreglass bars placed parallel to each other but set at different heights, for various exercises. **b** (*functioning as singular*) an event in a gymnastic competition in which competitors exercise on such bars.

asymmetric time NOUN musical time consisting of an odd number of beats in each bar divided into uneven combinations, such as 3 + 2, 4 + 3, 2 + 3 + 2, etc.

asymmetry (æˈsɪmɪtrɪ, eɪ-) NOUN lack or absence of symmetry in spatial arrangements or in mathematical or logical relations.

asymptomatic (æˌsɪmptəˈmætɪk, eɪ-) ADJECTIVE (of a disease or suspected disease) without symptoms; providing no subjective evidence of existence.
▸**aˌsymptoˈmatically** ADVERB

asymptote (ˈæsɪmˌtəʊt) NOUN a straight line that is closely approached by a plane curve so that the perpendicular distance between them decreases to zero as the distance from the origin increases to infinity.
▷HISTORY C17: from Greek *asumptōtos* not falling together, from A-[1] + SYN- + *ptōtos* inclined to fall, from *piptein* to fall

asymptotic (ˌæsɪmˈtɒtɪk) *or* **asymptotical** ADJECTIVE [1] of or referring to an asymptote. [2] (of a function, series, formula, etc.) approaching a given value or condition, as a variable or an expression containing a variable approaches a limit, usually infinity.
▸**ˌasympˈtotically** ADVERB

asynapsis (ˌeɪsɪˈnæpsɪs) NOUN *Biology* failure of pairing of chromosomes at meiosis.

asynchronism (æˈsɪŋkrəˌnɪzəm, eɪ-) NOUN a lack of synchronism; occurrence at different times.
▸**aˈsynchronous** ADJECTIVE ▸**aˈsynchronously** ADVERB

asyndetic (ˌæsɪnˈdɛtɪk) ADJECTIVE [1] (of a catalogue or index) without cross references. [2] (of a linguistic construction) having no conjunction, as in *I came, I saw, I conquered.*
▸**ˌasynˈdetically** ADVERB

asyndeton (æˈsɪndɪtən) NOUN, *plural* **-deta** (-dɪtə). [1] the omission of a conjunction between the parts of a sentence. [2] an asyndetic construction. Compare **syndeton.**
▷HISTORY C16: from New Latin, from Greek *asundeton*, from *asundetos* unconnected, from A-[1] + *sundein* to bind together

asynergia (ˌæsɪˈnɜːdʒɪə) *or* **asynergy** (əˌsɪnədʒɪ) NOUN *Pathol* lack of coordination between muscles or parts, as occurs in cerebellar disease.

asystole (əˈsɪstəlɪ) NOUN *Pathol* the absence of heartbeat; cardiac arrest.
▸**asystolic** (ˌæsɪsˈtɒlɪk) ADJECTIVE

Asyut *or* **Assiut** (æˈsjuːt) NOUN an ancient city in central Egypt, on the Nile. Pop.: 321 000 (1992 est.). Ancient Greek name: **Lycopolis.**

at[1] (æt) PREPOSITION [1] used to indicate location or position: *are they at the table?; staying at a small hotel.* [2] towards; in the direction of: *looking at television; throwing stones at windows.* [3] used to indicate position in time: *come at three o'clock.* [4] engaged in; in a state of (being): *children at play; stand at ease; he is at his most charming today.* [5] (in expressions concerned with habitual activity) during the passing of (esp in the phrase **at night**): *he used to work at night.* [6] for; in exchange for: *it's selling at four pounds.* [7] used to indicate the object of an emotion: *angry at the driver; shocked at his behaviour.* [8] **where it's at.** *Slang* the real place of action.
▷HISTORY Old English *æt*; related to Old Norse *at* to, Latin *ad* to

at[2] (ɑːt, æt) NOUN, *plural* **at.** a Laotian monetary unit worth one hundredth of a kip.
▷HISTORY from Thai

at[3] THE INTERNET DOMAIN NAME FOR Austria.

At [1] THE CHEMICAL SYMBOL FOR astatine. [2] Also: **A.** SYMBOL FOR ampere-turn.

AT ABBREVIATION FOR **attainment target.**

at. ABBREVIATION FOR: [1] Also: **atm.** atmosphere (unit of pressure). [2] atomic.

Atabrine (ˈætəˌbriːn, -brɪn) NOUN See **Atebrin.**

Atacama Desert (*Spanish* ataˈkama) NOUN a desert region along the W coast of South America, mainly in N Chile: a major source of nitrates. Area: about 80 000 sq. km (31 000 sq. miles).

atactic (eɪˈtæktɪk) ADJECTIVE [1] *Chem* (of a polymer) having random sequence of the stereochemical arrangement of groups on carbon atoms in the chain; not stereospecific. [2] *Pathol* relating to or displaying ataxia.

ataghan (ˈætəˌgæn) NOUN a variant of **yataghan.**

Atalanta (ˌætəˈlæntə) NOUN *Greek myth* a maiden who agreed to marry any man who could defeat her in a running race. She lost to Hippomenes when she paused to pick up three golden apples that he had deliberately dropped.

ataman (ˈætəmən) NOUN, *plural* **-mans.** an elected leader of the Cossacks; hetman.
▷HISTORY from Russian, from Polish *hetman*, from German *Hauptmann* (literally: head man)

ataractic (ˌætəˈræktɪk) *or* **ataraxic** (ˌætəˈræksɪk) ADJECTIVE [1] able to calm or tranquillize. ◆ NOUN [2] *Obsolete* an ataractic drug.

ataraxia (ˌætəˈræksɪə) *or* **ataraxy** (ˈætəˌræksɪ) NOUN calmness or peace of mind; emotional tranquillity.

▷**HISTORY** C17: from Greek: serenity, from *ataraktos* undisturbed, from A-[1] + *tarassein* to trouble

atavism ('ætəˌvɪzəm) NOUN [1] the recurrence in a plant or animal of certain primitive characteristics that were present in an ancestor but have not occurred in intermediate generations. [2] reversion to a former or more primitive type.
▷**HISTORY** C19: from French *atavisme,* from Latin *atavus* strictly: great-grandfather's grandfather, probably from *atta* daddy + *avus* grandfather
▸**'atavist** NOUN ▸**atavic** (ə'tævɪk) ADJECTIVE

atavistic (ˌætə'vɪstɪk) ADJECTIVE of or relating to reversion to a former or more primitive type.
▸**ˌata'vistically** ADVERB

ataxia (ə'tæksɪə) *or* **ataxy** (ə'tæksɪ) NOUN *Pathol* lack of muscular coordination.
▷**HISTORY** C17: via New Latin from Greek: lack of coordination, from A-[1] + *-taxia,* from *tassein* to put in order
▸**a'taxic** *or* **a'tactic** ADJECTIVE

ATB *Text messaging* ABBREVIATION FOR all the best.

Atbara ('ætbərə, æt'bɑː-) NOUN [1] a town in NE Sudan. Pop.: 73 000 (latest est.). [2] a river in NE Africa, rising in N Ethiopia and flowing through E Sudan to the Nile at Atbara. Length: over 800 km (500 miles).

ATC ABBREVIATION FOR: [1] air-traffic control. [2] (in Britain) Air Training Corps.

at-desk ADJECTIVE carried out at a person's desk at his or her place of work: *an at-desk massage.*

ate (ɛt, eɪt) VERB the past tense of **eat.**

Ate ('eɪtɪ, 'ɑːtɪ) NOUN *Greek myth* a goddess who makes men blind so that they will blunder into guilty acts.
▷**HISTORY** C16: via Latin from Greek *atē* a rash impulse

-ate[1] SUFFIX [1] *(forming adjectives)* possessing; having the appearance or characteristics of: *fortunate; palmate; Latinate.* [2] *(forming nouns)* a chemical compound, esp a salt or ester of an acid: *carbonate; stearate.* [3] *(forming nouns)* the product of a process: *condensate.* [4] forming verbs from nouns and adjectives: *hyphenate; rusticate.*
▷**HISTORY** from Latin *-ātus,* past participial ending of verbs ending in *-āre*

-ate[2] SUFFIX FORMING NOUNS denoting office, rank, or a group having a certain function: *episcopate; electorate.*
▷**HISTORY** from Latin *-ātus,* suffix (fourth declension) of collective nouns

atelectasis (ˌætə'lɛktəsɪs) NOUN [1] failure of the lungs to expand fully at birth. [2] collapse of the lung or a part of the lung, usually caused by bronchial obstruction.
▷**HISTORY** C19: New Latin, from Greek *atelēs* imperfect + *ektasis* extension

atelier ('ætəlˌjeɪ; *French* atəlje) NOUN an artist's studio or workshop.
▷**HISTORY** C17: from Old French *astelier* workshop, from *astele* chip of wood, from Latin *astula* splinter, from *assis* board

a tempo (ɑː 'tɛmpəʊ) *Music* ◆ ADJECTIVE, ADVERB [1] to the original tempo. ◆ NOUN [2] a passage thus marked. ◆ Also: **tempo primo.**
▷**HISTORY** Italian: in (the original) time

Aten *or* **Aton** ('ɑːtᵊn) NOUN (in ancient Egypt) the solar disc worshipped as the sole god in the reign of Akhenaten.

Athabaska *or* **Athabasca** (ˌæθə'bæskə) NOUN [1] **Lake.** a lake in W Canada, in NW Saskatchewan and NE Alberta. Area: about 7770 sq. km (3000 sq. miles). [2] a river in W Canada, rising in the Rocky Mountains and flowing northeast to Lake Athabaska. Length: 1230 km (765 miles).

Athamas ('æθəˌmæs) NOUN *Greek myth* a king of Orchomenus in Boeotia; the father of Phrixus and Helle by his first wife Nephele, whom he deserted for Ino.

athame ('ɑːθæmeɪ) NOUN (in Wicca) a witch's ceremonial knife, usually with a black handle, used in rituals rather than for cutting or carving.

Athanasian (ˌæθə'neɪʃən) ADJECTIVE of or relating to Saint Athanasius, the patriarch of Alexandria (?296–373 A.D.).

Athanasian Creed (ˌæθə'neɪʃən) NOUN *Christianity* a profession of faith widely used in the Western Church which, though formerly attributed to Athanasius, probably originated in Gaul between 381 and 428 A.D.

Athapascan, Athapaskan (ˌæθə'pæskən), **Athabascan,** *or* **Athabaskan** (ˌæθə'bæskən) NOUN [1] a group of North American Indian languages belonging to the Na-Dene phylum, including Apache and Navaho. [2] a speaker of one of these languages.
▷**HISTORY** from Cree *athapaskaaw* scattered grass or reeds

Atharva-Veda (ə'tɑːvə'veɪdə) NOUN *Hinduism* the fourth and latest Veda, largely consisting of priestly spells and incantations.

atheism ('eɪθɪˌɪzəm) NOUN rejection of belief in God or gods.
▷**HISTORY** C16: from French *athéisme,* from Greek *atheos* godless, from A-[1] + *theos* god
▸**'atheist** NOUN, ADJECTIVE ▸**ˌathe'istic** *or* **ˌathe'istical** ADJECTIVE ▸**ˌathe'istically** ADVERB

atheling ('æθəlɪŋ) NOUN (in Anglo-Saxon England) a prince of any of the royal dynasties.
▷**HISTORY** Old English *ætheling,* from *æthelu* noble family + -ING[3]; related to Old High German *adaling,* Old Norse *öthlingr*

athematic (ˌæθɪ'mætɪk) ADJECTIVE [1] *Music* not based on themes. [2] *Linguistics* (of verbs) having a suffix attached immediately to the stem, without an intervening vowel.

Athena (ə'θiːnə) *or* **Athene** (ə'θiːnɪ) NOUN *Greek myth* a virgin goddess of wisdom, practical skills, and prudent warfare. She was born, fully armed, from the head of Zeus. Also called: **Pallas Athena, Pallas.** Roman counterpart: **Minerva.**

athenaeum *or US* **atheneum** (ˌæθɪ'niːəm) NOUN [1] an institution for the promotion of learning. [2] a building containing a reading room or library, esp one used by such an institution.
▷**HISTORY** C18: from Late Latin, from Greek *Athēnaion* temple of Athene, frequented by poets and teachers

Athenaeum *or sometimes US* **Atheneum** (ˌæθɪ'niːəm) NOUN [1] (in ancient Greece) a building sacred to the goddess Athena, esp the Athenian temple that served as a gathering place for the learned. [2] (in imperial Rome) the academy of learning established near the Forum in about 135 A.D. by Hadrian.

Athenian (ə'θiːnɪən) NOUN [1] a native or inhabitant of Athens. ◆ ADJECTIVE [2] of or relating to Athens.

Athens ('æθɪnz) NOUN the capital of Greece, in the southeast near the Saronic Gulf: became capital after independence in 1834; ancient city-state, most powerful in the 5th century B.C.; contains the hill citadel of the Acropolis. Pop.: 772 072 (1991). Greek name: **Athinai** (a'θinɛ).

athermancy (æ'θɜːmənsɪ) NOUN an inability to transmit radiant heat or infrared radiation. Also called: **adiathermancy.**
▷**HISTORY** C19: from Greek *athermantos* not heated, from A-[1] + *thermainein* to heat, from *thermē* heat; compare DIATHERMANCY

athermanous (æ'θɜːmənəs) ADJECTIVE capable of stopping radiant heat or infrared radiation.

atherogenic (ˌæθərəʊ'dʒɛnɪk) ADJECTIVE causing atheroma.
▸**ˌathero'genesis** NOUN

atheroma (ˌæθə'rəʊmə) NOUN, *plural* **-mas** *or* **-mata** (-mətə). *Pathol* a fatty deposit on or within the inner lining of an artery, often causing an obstruction to the blood flow.
▷**HISTORY** C18: via Latin from Greek *athērōma* tumour full of matter resembling gruel, from *athēra* gruel
▸**atheromatous** (ˌæθə'rɒmətəs, -'rəʊ-) ADJECTIVE

atherosclerosis (ˌæθərəʊsklɪə'rəʊsɪs) NOUN, *plural* **-ses** (-siːz). a degenerative disease of the arteries characterized by patchy thickening of the inner lining of the arterial walls, caused by deposits of fatty material; a form of arteriosclerosis. See **atheroma.**
▷**HISTORY** C20: from New Latin, from Greek *athēra* gruel (see ATHEROMA) + SCLEROSIS
▸**atherosclerotic** (ˌæθərəʊsklɪə'rɒtɪk) ADJECTIVE

athetosis (ˌæθə'təʊsɪs) NOUN *Pathol* a condition characterized by uncontrolled rhythmic writhing movement, esp of fingers, hands, head, and tongue, caused by cerebral lesion.
▷**HISTORY** C19: from Greek *athetos* not in place, from A-[1] + *tithenai* to place
▸**'atheˌtoid** ADJECTIVE

athirst (ə'θɜːst) ADJECTIVE *(postpositive)* [1] (often foll by *for*) having an eager desire; longing. [2] *Archaic* thirsty.

athlete ('æθliːt) NOUN [1] a person trained to compete in sports or exercises involving physical strength, speed, or endurance. [2] a person who has a natural aptitude for physical activities. [3] *Chiefly Brit* a competitor in track and field events.
▷**HISTORY** C18: from Latin via Greek *athlētēs,* from *athlein* to compete for a prize, from *athlos* a contest

athlete's foot NOUN a fungal infection of the skin of the foot, esp between the toes and on the soles. Technical name: **tinea pedis.**

athletic (æθ'lɛtɪk) ADJECTIVE [1] physically fit or strong; muscular or active. [2] of, relating to, or suitable for an athlete or for athletics. [3] of or relating to a person with a muscular and well-proportioned body. See also **somatotype.**
▸**ath'letically** ADVERB ▸**ath'leticism** NOUN

athletics (æθ'lɛtɪks) NOUN *(functioning as plural or singular)* [1] **a** track and field events. **b** *(as modifier)*: *an athletics meeting.* [2] sports or exercises engaged in by athletes. [3] the theory or practice of athletic activities and training.

athletic support NOUN a more formal term for **jockstrap.**

athodyd ('æθəʊˌdaɪd) NOUN another name for **ramjet.**
▷**HISTORY** C20: from *a(ero)-th(erm)ody(namic) d(uct)*

Atholl brose ('æθəl) NOUN *Scot* a mixture of whisky and honey left to ferment before consumption.
▷**HISTORY** C19: after *Atholl,* a district of central Scotland

at-home NOUN [1] another name for **open day.** [2] a social gathering in a person's home.

Athos ('æθɒs, 'eɪ-) NOUN **Mount.** a mountain in NE Greece, in Macedonia Central region: site of the Monastic Republic of Mount Athos, autonomous since 1927 and inhabited by Greek Orthodox Basilian monks in 20 monasteries founded in the 10th century. Pop.: 1557 (1991).

athwart (ə'θwɔːt) ADVERB [1] transversely; from one side to another. ◆ PREPOSITION [2] across the path or line of (esp a ship). [3] in opposition to; against.
▷**HISTORY** C15: from A-[2] + THWART

athwartships (ə'θwɔːtˌʃɪps) ADVERB *Nautical* from one side to the other of a vessel at right angles to the keel.

-atic SUFFIX FORMING ADJECTIVES of the nature of the thing specified: *problematic.*
▷**HISTORY** from French *-atique,* from Greek *-atikos*

atigi ('ætəgɪ, ə'tiːgɪ) NOUN a type of parka worn by the Inuit in Canada.

atilt (ə'tɪlt) ADVERB, ADJECTIVE *(postpositive)* [1] in a tilted or inclined position. [2] *Archaic* in or as if in a joust.

-ation SUFFIX FORMING NOUNS indicating an action, process, state, condition, or result: *arbitration; cogitation; hibernation; moderation.* Compare **-ion, -tion.**
▷**HISTORY** from Latin *-ātiōn-,* suffix of abstract nouns, from *-ātus* -ATE[1] + *-iōn* -ION

atishoo (ə'tɪʃuː) INTERJECTION a representation of the sound of a sneeze.
▷**HISTORY** C19: of imitative origin

-ative SUFFIX FORMING ADJECTIVES of, relating to, or tending to: *authoritative; decorative; informative.*
▷**HISTORY** from Latin *-ātīvus,* from *ātus* -ATE[1] + *īvus* -IVE

ATK ABBREVIATION FOR: [1] antitank. [2] *Text messaging, email, etc.* at the keyboard.

Atlanta (ət'læntə) NOUN a city in N Georgia: the state capital. Pop.: 416 474 (2000).

Atlantean (ˌætlæn'tiːən, ət'læntɪən) ADJECTIVE [1] *Literary* of, relating to, or like Atlas; extremely strong. [2] of or connected with Atlantis.

atlantes (ət'læntiːz) NOUN the plural of **atlas** (sense 4).

Atlantic (ət'læntɪk) NOUN [1] **the** short for the **Atlantic Ocean.** ◆ ADJECTIVE [2] of or relating to or bordering the Atlantic Ocean. [3] of or relating to Atlas or the Atlas Mountains.

▷HISTORY C15: from Latin *Atlanticus,* from Greek (*pelagos*) *Atlantikos* (the sea) of Atlas (so called because it lay beyond the Atlas Mountains)

Atlantic Charter NOUN the joint declaration issued by F. D. Roosevelt and Winston Churchill on Aug. 14, 1941, consisting of eight principles to guide a postwar settlement.

Atlantic City NOUN a resort in SE New Jersey on Absecon Beach, an island on the Atlantic coast. Pop.: 37 986 (1990).

Atlantic Intracoastal Waterway NOUN a system of inland and coastal waterways along the Atlantic coast of the US from Cape Cod to Florida Bay. Length: 2495 km (1550 miles).

Atlanticism (ət'læntɪ,sɪzəm) NOUN advocacy of close cooperation in military, political, and economic matters between Western Europe, esp the UK, and the US.

▸**At'lanticist** NOUN

Atlantic Ocean NOUN the world's second largest ocean, bounded in the north by the Arctic, in the south by the Antarctic, in the west by North and South America, and in the east by Europe and Africa. Greatest depth: 9220 m (30 246 ft.). Area: about 81 585 000 sq. km (31 500 000 sq. miles).

Atlantic Provinces PLURAL NOUN **the.** certain of the Canadian provinces with coasts facing the Gulf of St Lawrence or the Atlantic: New Brunswick, Nova Scotia, Prince Edward Island, and Newfoundland.

Atlantic Standard Time NOUN the local time used in eastern Canada, four hours behind Greenwich Mean Time. Abbreviation: **AST.**

Atlantis (ət'læntɪs) NOUN (in ancient legend) a continent said to have sunk beneath the Atlantic Ocean west of the Straits of Gibraltar.

atlas ('ætləs) NOUN [1] a collection of maps, usually in book form. [2] a book of charts, graphs, etc., illustrating aspects of a subject: *an anatomical atlas.* [3] *Anatomy* the first cervical vertebra, attached to and supporting the skull in man. Compare **axis**[1] (sense 3). [4] (*plural* **atlantes**) *Architect* another name for **telamon.** [5] a standard size of drawing paper, 26 × 17 inches.

▷HISTORY C16: via Latin from Greek; first applied to maps, from depictions of Atlas supporting the heavens in 16th-century collections of maps

Atlas ('ætləs) NOUN [1] *Greek myth* a Titan compelled to support the sky on his shoulders as punishment for rebelling against Zeus. [2] a US intercontinental ballistic missile, also used in launching spacecraft. [3] *Astronomy* a small satellite of Saturn, discovered in 1980.

Atlas Mountains PLURAL NOUN a mountain system of N Africa, between the Mediterranean and the Sahara. Highest peak: Mount Toubkal, 4165 m (13 664 ft.).

Atli ('ɑːtlɪ) NOUN *Norse myth* a king of the Huns who married Gudrun for her inheritance and was slain by her after he killed her brothers.

ATM ABBREVIATION FOR: [1] **automated teller machine.** [2] asynchronous transfer mode: used in digital communications, etc. [3] *Text messaging* at the moment.

atm. ABBREVIATION FOR atmosphere (unit of pressure). Also: **at.**

atman ('ɑːtmən) NOUN *Hinduism* [1] the personal soul or self; the thinking principle as manifested in consciousness. [2] Brahman considered as the Universal Soul, the great Self or Person that dwells in the entire created order.

▷HISTORY from Sanskrit *ātman* breath; compare Old High German *ātum* breath

atmo- COMBINING FORM air or vapour: *atmometer; atmosphere.*

▷HISTORY via New Latin from Greek *atmos* vapour

atmolysis (æt'mɒlɪsɪs) NOUN, *plural* **-ses** (-,siːz). a method of separating gases that depends on their differential rates of diffusion through a porous substance.

atmometer (æt'mɒmɪtə) NOUN an instrument for measuring the rate of evaporation of water into the atmosphere. Also called: **evaporimeter, evaporometer.**

▸**at'mometry** NOUN

atmosphere ('ætməs,fɪə) NOUN [1] the gaseous envelope surrounding the earth or any other celestial body. See also **troposphere, stratosphere, mesosphere, ionosphere.** [2] the air or climate in a particular place: *the atmosphere was thick with smoke.* [3] a general pervasive feeling or mood: *an atmosphere of elation.* [4] the prevailing tone or mood of a novel, symphony, painting, or other work of art. [5] a special mood or character associated with a place. [6] any local gaseous environment or medium: *an inert atmosphere.* [7] Abbreviations: **at, atm.** a unit of pressure; the pressure that will support a column of mercury 760 mm high at 0°C at sea level. 1 atmosphere is equivalent to 101 325 newtons per square metre or 14.72 pounds per square inch.

▸**,atmos'pheric** *or* **,atmos'pherical** ADJECTIVE

▸**,atmos'pherically** ADVERB

atmospheric perspective NOUN another term for **aerial perspective.**

atmospheric pressure NOUN the pressure exerted by the atmosphere at the earth's surface. It has an average value of 1 atmosphere.

atmospherics (,ætməs'fɛrɪks) PLURAL NOUN [1] electrical disturbances produced in the atmosphere by natural causes such as lightning. [2] radio interference, heard as crackling or hissing in receivers, caused by electrical disturbance.

atmospheric window NOUN wavelengths of the electromagnetic spectrum that can be transmitted through the earth's atmosphere. Atmospheric windows occur in the visible, infrared, and radio regions of the spectrum.

ATN ABBREVIATION FOR: [1] arc tangent. [2] **augmented transition network.**

at. no. ABBREVIATION FOR atomic number.

A to J (in New Zealand) ABBREVIATION FOR Appendices to Journals (of the House of Representatives or Parliament).

atoll ('ætɒl, ə'tɒl) NOUN a circular coral reef or string of coral islands surrounding a lagoon.

▷HISTORY C17: from *atollon,* native name in the Maldive Islands

atom ('ætəm) NOUN [1] **a** the smallest quantity of an element that can take part in a chemical reaction. **b** this entity as a source of nuclear energy: *the power of the atom.* See also **atomic structure.** [2] any entity regarded as the indivisible building block of a theory. [3] the hypothetical indivisible particle of matter postulated by certain ancient philosophers as the fundamental constituent of matter. See also **atomism.** [4] a very small amount or quantity; minute fragment: *to smash something to atoms; there is not an atom of truth in his allegations.*

▷HISTORY C16: via Old French and Latin, from Greek *atomos* (n), from *atomos* (adj) that cannot be divided, from A-[1] + *temnein* to cut

atomic (ə'tɒmɪk) ADJECTIVE [1] of, using, or characterized by atomic bombs or atomic energy: *atomic warfare.* [2] of, related to, or comprising atoms: *atomic hydrogen.* [3] extremely small; minute. [4] *Logic* (of a sentence, formula, etc.) having no internal structure at the appropriate level of analysis. In predicate calculus, *Fa* is an **atomic sentence** and *Fx* an **atomic predicate.**

▸**a'tomically** ADVERB

atomic age NOUN **the.** the current historical period, initiated by the development of the first atomic bomb towards the end of World War II and now marked by a balance of power between nations possessing the hydrogen bomb and the use of nuclear power as a source of energy.

atomic bomb *or* **atom bomb** NOUN a type of bomb in which the energy is provided by nuclear fission. Uranium-235 and plutonium-239 are the isotopes most commonly used in atomic bombs. Also called: **A-bomb, fission bomb.** Compare **fusion bomb.**

atomic clock NOUN an extremely accurate clock in which an electrical oscillator is controlled by the natural vibrations of an atomic or molecular system such as caesium or ammonia.

atomic cocktail NOUN an aqueous solution of radioactive substance administered orally as part of the treatment for cancer.

atomic energy NOUN another name for **nuclear energy.**

Atomic Energy Authority NOUN (in Britain) a government body established in 1954 to control research and development in atomic energy. Abbreviation: **AEA.**

Atomic Energy Commission NOUN (in the US) a federal board established in 1946 to administer and develop domestic atomic energy programmes. Abbreviation: **AEC.**

atomic heat NOUN the product of an element's atomic weight and its specific heat (capacity).

atomicity (,ætə'mɪsɪtɪ) NOUN [1] the state of being made up of atoms. [2] the number of atoms in the molecules of an element. [3] a less common name for **valency.**

atomic mass NOUN *Chem* [1] the mass of an isotope of an element in atomic mass units. [2] short for **relative atomic mass;** see **atomic weight.**

atomic mass unit NOUN a unit of mass used to express atomic and molecular weights that is equal to one twelfth of the mass of an atom of carbon-12. It is equivalent to 1.66×10^{-27} kg. Abbreviation: **amu.** Also called: **unified atomic mass unit, dalton.**

atomic number NOUN the number of protons in the nucleus of an atom of an element. Abbreviation: **at. no.** Symbol: *Z.* Also called: **proton number.**

atomic pile NOUN the original name for a **nuclear reactor.**

atomic power NOUN another name for **nuclear power.**

atomic structure NOUN the concept of an atom as a central positively charged nucleus consisting of protons and neutrons surrounded by a number of electrons. The number of electrons is equal to the number of protons: the whole entity is thus electrically neutral.

atomic theory NOUN [1] any theory in which matter is regarded as consisting of atoms, esp that proposed by John Dalton postulating that elements are composed of atoms that can combine in definite proportions to form compounds. [2] the current concept of the atom as an entity with a definite structure. See **atomic structure.**

atomic volume NOUN the atomic weight (relative atomic mass) of an element divided by its density.

atomic weight NOUN the former name for **relative atomic mass.** Abbreviation: **at. wt.**

atomism ('ætə,mɪzəm) NOUN [1] an ancient philosophical theory, developed by Democritus, the Greek philosopher (?460–?370 B.C.) and Lucretius, the Roman poet and philosopher (?96–55 B.C.), that the ultimate constituents of the universe are atoms: see **atom** (sense 3). [2] **a** any of a number of theories that hold that some objects or phenomena can be explained as constructed out of a small number of distinct types of simple indivisible entities. **b** any theory that holds that an understanding of the parts is logically prior to an understanding of the whole. Compare **holism** (sense 3). [3] *Psychol* the theory that experiences and mental states are composed of elementary units.

▸**'atomist** NOUN, ADJECTIVE ▸**,atom'istic** *or* **,atom'istical** ADJECTIVE ▸**,atom'istically** ADVERB

atomize *or* **atomise** ('ætə,maɪz) VERB [1] to separate or be separated into free atoms. [2] to reduce (a liquid or solid) to fine particles or spray or (of a liquid or solid) to be reduced in this way. [3] (*tr*) to destroy by weapons, esp nuclear weapons.

▸**,atomi'zation** *or* **,atomi'sation** NOUN

atomizer *or* **atomiser** ('ætə,maɪzə) NOUN a device for reducing a liquid to a fine spray, such as the nozzle used to feed oil into a furnace or an enclosed bottle with a fine outlet used to spray perfumes or medicines.

atom smasher NOUN *Physics* the nontechnical name for **accelerator** (sense 2).

atomy[1] ('ætəmɪ) NOUN, *plural* **-mies.** *Archaic* [1] an atom or minute particle. [2] a minute creature.

▷HISTORY C16: from Latin *atomī* atoms, but used as if singular; see ATOM

atomy[2] ('ætəmɪ) NOUN, *plural* **-mies.** an obsolete word for **skeleton.**

▷HISTORY C16: from mistaken division of ANATOMY (as if *an atomy*)

Aton ('ɑːtᵊn) NOUN a variant spelling of **Aten.**

atonal (eɪ'təʊnᵊl, æ-) ADJECTIVE *Music* having no established key. Compare **tonal** (sense 2).

▸**a'tonalism** NOUN ▸**a'tonally** ADVERB

atonality (ˌeɪtəʊ'nælɪtɪ, ˌæ-) NOUN [1] absence of or disregard for an established musical key in a composition. [2] the principles of composition embodying this and providing a radical alternative to the diatonic system. ◆ Compare **tonality.**

atone (ə'təʊn) VERB [1] *(intr; foll by for)* to make amends or reparation (for a crime, sin, etc.). [2] *(tr)* to expiate: *to atone a guilt with repentance.* [3] *Obsolete* to be in or bring into agreement.
▷HISTORY C16: back formation from ATONEMENT
▸**a'tonable** *or* **a'toneable** ADJECTIVE ▸**a'toner** NOUN

atonement (ə'təʊnmənt) NOUN [1] satisfaction, reparation, or expiation given for an injury or wrong. [2] *(often capital) Christian theol* **a** the reconciliation of man with God through the life, sufferings, and sacrificial death of Christ. **b** the sufferings and death of Christ. [3] *Christian Science* the state in which the attributes of God are exemplified in man. [4] *Obsolete* reconciliation or agreement.
▷HISTORY C16: from Middle English phrase *at onement* in harmony

atonic (eɪ'tɒnɪk, æ-) ADJECTIVE [1] (of a syllable, word, etc.) carrying no stress; unaccented. [2] *Pathol* relating to or characterized by atony. ◆ NOUN [3] an unaccented or unstressed syllable, word, etc., such as *for* in *food for thought.*
▷HISTORY C18: from Latin *atonicus,* from Greek *atonos* lacking tone; see ATONY
▸**atonicity** (ˌætə'nɪsɪtɪ, ˌeɪtəʊ-) NOUN

atony ('ætənɪ) NOUN [1] *Pathol* lack of normal tone or tension, as in muscles; abnormal relaxation of a muscle. [2] *Phonetics* lack of stress or accent on a syllable or word.
▷HISTORY C17: from Latin *atonia,* from Greek: tonelessness, from *atonos* slack, from A-[1] + *tonos* TONE

atop (ə'tɒp) ADVERB [1] on top; at the top. ◆ PREPOSITION [2] on top of; at the top of.

atopic (ə'tɒpɪk) ADJECTIVE *Immunol* of or relating to hereditary hypersensitivity to certain allergens.

atopy ('ætəʊpɪ) NOUN *Immunol* a hereditary tendency to be hypersensitive to certain allergens.

-ator SUFFIX FORMING NOUNS a person or thing that performs a certain action: *agitator; escalator; radiator.*
▷HISTORY from Latin *-ātor;* see -ATE[1] -OR[1]

-atory SUFFIX FORMING ADJECTIVES of, relating to, characterized by, or serving to: *circulatory; exploratory; migratory; explanatory.*
▷HISTORY from Latin *-ātōrius;* see -ATE[1], -ORY[2]

ATP[1] NOUN adenosine triphosphate; a nucleotide found in the mitochondria of all plant and animal cells. It is the major source of energy for cellular reactions, this energy being released during its conversion to ADP. Formula: $C_{10}H_{16}N_5O_{13}P_3$.

ATP[2] ABBREVIATION FOR: [1] advanced turboprop. [2] Association of Tennis Professionals. [3] automatic train protection: a safety system which automatically prevents a train from passing through a stop signal.

ATPase (ˌeɪtiː'piːˌeɪz) NOUN adenosine triphosphatase; an enzyme that converts ATP to ADP.

atrabilious (ˌætrə'bɪljəs) *or* **atrabiliar** ADJECTIVE *Rare* irritable.
▷HISTORY C17: from Latin *ātra bīlis* black bile, from *āter* black + *bīlis* BILE[1]
▸ˌ**atra'biliousness** NOUN

atrazine ('ætrəziːn) NOUN a white crystalline compound widely used as a weedkiller. Formula: $C_8H_{14}N_5Cl$.
▷HISTORY C20: from A(MINO) TR(I)AZINE

atresia (ə'triːʒɪə, -ʒə) NOUN absence of or unnatural narrowing of a body channel.
▷HISTORY C19: New Latin, from Greek *atrētos* not perforated

Atreus ('eɪtrɪˌuːs, 'eɪtrɪəs) NOUN *Greek myth* a king of Mycenae, son of Pelops, father of Agamemnon and Menelaus, and member of the family known as the **Atreids** ('eɪtrɪɪdz).

atrioventricular (ˌeɪtrɪəʊvɛn'trɪkjʊlə) ADJECTIVE *Anatomy* of, relating to, or affecting both the atria and the ventricles of the heart: *atrioventricular disease.*
▷HISTORY C19: from *atrio-,* from New Latin *atrium* heart chamber (see ATRIUM) + VENTRICULAR

atrip (ə'trɪp) ADJECTIVE *(postpositive) Nautical* (of an anchor) no longer caught on the bottom; tripped; aweigh.

atrium ('eɪtrɪəm, 'ɑː-) NOUN, *plural* **atria** ('eɪtrɪə, 'ɑː-). [1] the open main court of a Roman house. [2] a central often glass-roofed hall that extends through several storeys in a building, such as a shopping centre or hotel. [3] a court in front of an early Christian or medieval church, esp one flanked by colonnades. [4] *Anatomy* a cavity or chamber in the body, esp the upper chamber of each half of the heart.
▷HISTORY C17: from Latin; related to *āter* black, perhaps originally referring to the part of the house that was blackened by smoke from the hearth
▸'**atrial** ADJECTIVE

atrocious (ə'trəʊʃəs) ADJECTIVE [1] extremely cruel or wicked; ruthless: *atrocious deeds.* [2] horrifying or shocking: *an atrocious road accident.* [3] *Informal* very bad; detestable: *atrocious writing.*
▷HISTORY C17: from Latin *ātrōx* dreadful, from *āter* black
▸**a'trociously** ADVERB ▸**a'trociousness** NOUN

atrocity (ə'trɒsɪtɪ) NOUN, *plural* **-ties.** [1] behaviour or an action that is wicked or ruthless. [2] the fact or quality of being atrocious. [3] *(usually plural)* acts of extreme cruelty, esp against prisoners or civilians in wartime.

atrophic rhinitis NOUN another name for **bull nose.**

atrophy ('ætrəfɪ) NOUN, *plural* **-phies.** [1] a wasting away of an organ or part, or a failure to grow to normal size as the result of disease, faulty nutrition, etc. [2] any degeneration or diminution, esp through lack of use. ◆ VERB **-phies, -phying, -phied.** [3] to waste away or cause to waste away.
▷HISTORY C17: from Late Latin *atrophia,* from Greek, from *atrophos* ill-fed, from A-[1] + *-trophos* from *trephein* to feed
▸**atrophic** (ə'trɒfɪk) ADJECTIVE

atropine ('ætrəˌpiːn, -pɪn) *or* **atropin** ('ætrəpɪn) NOUN a poisonous alkaloid obtained from deadly nightshade, having an inhibitory action on the autonomic nervous system. It is used medicinally in pre-anaesthetic medication, to speed a slow heart rate, and as an emergency first-aid counter to exposure to chemical warfare nerve agents. Formula: $C_{17}H_{23}NO_3$.
▷HISTORY C19: from New Latin *atropa* deadly nightshade, from Greek *atropos* unchangeable, inflexible; see ATROPOS

Atropos ('ætrəˌpɒs) NOUN *Greek myth* the one of the three Fates who severs the thread of life.
▷HISTORY Greek, from *atropos* that may not be turned, from A-[1] + *-tropos* from *trepein* to turn

attaboy ('ætəˌbɔɪ) SENTENCE SUBSTITUTE *Slang, chiefly US* an expression of approval or exhortation.

attach (ə'tætʃ) VERB *(mainly tr)* [1] to join, fasten, or connect. [2] *(reflexive or passive)* to become associated with or join, as in a business or other venture: *he attached himself to the expedition.* [3] *(intr; foll by to)* to be inherent (in) or connected (with): *responsibility attaches to the job.* [4] to attribute or ascribe: *to attach importance to an event.* [5] to include or append, esp as a condition: *a proviso is attached to the contract.* [6] *(usually passive) Military* to place on temporary duty with another unit. [7] *(usually passive)* to put (a member of an organization) to work in a different unit or agency, either with an expectation of reverting to, or while retaining some part of, the original working arrangement. [8] to appoint officially. [9] *Law* to arrest or take (a person, property, etc.) with lawful authority. [10] *Obsolete* to seize.
▷HISTORY C14: from Old French *atachier* to fasten, changed from *estachier* to fasten with a stake, from *estache* STAKE[1]
▸**at'tachable** ADJECTIVE ▸**at'tacher** NOUN

attaché (ə'tæʃeɪ; *French* ataʃe) NOUN [1] a specialist attached to a diplomatic mission: *military attaché.* [2] *Brit* a junior member of the staff of an embassy or legation.
▷HISTORY C19: from French: someone attached (to a mission), from *attacher* to ATTACH

attaché case NOUN a small flat rectangular briefcase used for carrying documents, papers, etc.

attached (ə'tætʃt) ADJECTIVE [1] (foll by *to*) fond (of); full of regard (for): *he was very attached to the old lady.* [2] married, engaged, or associated in an exclusive sexual relationship: *it's no good dancing with her, she's already attached.*

attachment (ə'tætʃmənt) NOUN [1] a means of securing; a fastening. [2] (often foll by *to*) affection or regard (for); devotion (to): *attachment to a person or to a cause.* [3] an object to be attached, esp a supplementary part: *an attachment for an electric drill.* [4] the act of attaching or the state of being attached. [5] **a** the arrest of a person for disobedience to a court order. **b** the lawful seizure of property and placing of it under control of a court. **c** a writ authorizing such arrest or seizure. [6] *Law* the binding of a debt in the hands of a garnishee until its disposition has been decided by the court.

attachment of earnings NOUN (in Britain) a court order requiring an employer to deduct amounts from an employee's wages to pay debts or honour financial obligations.

attack (ə'tæk) VERB [1] to launch a physical assault (against) with or without weapons; begin hostilities (with). [2] *(intr)* to take the initiative in a game, sport, etc.: *after a few minutes, the team began to attack.* [3] *(tr)* to direct hostile words or writings at; criticize or abuse vehemently. [4] *(tr)* to turn one's mind or energies vigorously to (a job, problem, etc.). [5] *(tr)* to begin to injure or affect adversely; corrode, corrupt, or infect: *rust attacked the metal.* [6] *(tr)* to attempt to rape. ◆ NOUN [7] the act or an instance of attacking. [8] strong criticism or abuse: *an unjustified attack on someone's reputation.* [9] an offensive move in a game, sport, etc. [10] commencement of a task, etc. [11] any sudden and usually severe manifestation of a disease or disorder: *a heart attack; an attack of indigestion.* [12] **the attack.** *Ball games* the players in a team whose main role is to attack the opponents' goal or territory. [13] *Music* decisiveness in beginning a passage, movement, or piece. [14] *Music* the speed with which a note reaches its maximum volume. [15] an attempted rape.
▷HISTORY C16: from French *attaquer,* from Old Italian *attaccare* to attack, attach, from *estaccare* to attach, from *stacca* STAKE[1]; compare ATTACH
▸**at'tackable** ADJECTIVE ▸**at'tacker** NOUN

attack ad NOUN a public notice, such as a printed display or a short film on television, in which a political party criticizes or abuses an opponent.

attain (ə'teɪn) VERB [1] *(tr)* to achieve or accomplish (a task, goal, aim, etc.). [2] *(tr)* to reach or arrive at in space or time: *to attain old age.* [3] *(intr;* often foll by *to)* to arrive (at) with effort or exertion: *to attain to glory.*
▷HISTORY C14: from Old French *ateindre,* from Latin *attingere* to reach, from *tangere* to touch
▸**at'tainable** ADJECTIVE ▸**atˌtaina'bility** *or* **at'tainableness** NOUN

attainder (ə'teɪndə) NOUN [1] (formerly) the extinction of a person's civil rights resulting from a sentence of death or outlawry on conviction for treason or felony. See also **bill of attainder.** [2] *Obsolete* dishonour. ◆ Archaic equivalent: **attainture** (ə'teɪntʃə).
▷HISTORY C15: from Anglo-French *attaindre* to convict, from Old French *ateindre* to ATTAIN

attainment (ə'teɪnmənt) NOUN an achievement or the act of achieving; accomplishment.

attainment target NOUN *Brit education* a general defined level of ability that a pupil is expected to achieve in every subject at each key stage in the National Curriculum. Abbreviation: **AT.**

attaint (ə'teɪnt) VERB *(tr) Archaic* [1] to pass judgment of death or outlawry upon (a person); condemn by bill of attainder. [2] to dishonour or disgrace. [3] to accuse or prove to be guilty. [4] (of sickness) to affect or strike (somebody). ◆ NOUN [5] a less common word for **attainder.** [6] a dishonour; taint.
▷HISTORY C14: from Old French *ateint* convicted, from *ateindre* to ATTAIN

attar ('ætə), **otto** ('ɒtəʊ), *or* **ottar** ('ɒtə) NOUN an essential oil from flowers, esp the damask rose, used pure or as a base for perfume: *attar of roses.*
▷HISTORY C18: from Persian *'atir* perfumed, from *'itr* perfume, from Arabic

attemper (ə'tɛmpə) VERB *(tr) Archaic* [1] to modify by blending; temper. [2] to moderate or soothe. [3] to accommodate or bring into harmony.
▸**at'temperment** NOUN

attempt (ə'tɛmpt) VERB (*tr*) 1 to make an effort (to do something) or to achieve (something); try. 2 to try to surmount (an obstacle). 3 to try to climb: *they will attempt the north wall of the Eiger.* 4 *Archaic* to attack. 5 *Archaic* to tempt. ◆ NOUN 6 an endeavour to achieve something; effort. 7 a result of an attempt or endeavour. 8 an attack, esp with the intention to kill: *an attempt on his life.*
▷**HISTORY** C14: from Old French *attempter,* from Latin *attemptāre* to strive after, from *tentāre* to try
▸**at'temptable** ADJECTIVE ▸**at'tempter** NOUN

> **Language note** *Attempt* should not be used in the passive when followed by an infinitive: *attempts were made to find a solution* (not *a solution was attempted to be found*).

attend (ə'tɛnd) VERB 1 to be present at (an event, meeting, etc.). 2 (when *intr,* foll by *to*) to give care; minister. 3 (when *intr,* foll by *to*) to pay attention; listen. 4 (*tr; often passive*) to accompany or follow: *a high temperature attended by a severe cough.* 5 (*intr;* foll by *on* or *upon*) to follow as a consequence (of). 6 (*intr;* foll by *to*) to devote one's time; apply oneself: *to attend to the garden.* 7 (*tr*) to escort or accompany. 8 (*intr;* foll by *on* or *upon*) to wait (on); serve; provide for the needs (of): *to attend on a guest.* 9 (*tr*) *Archaic* to wait for; expect. 10 (*intr*) *Obsolete* to delay.
▷**HISTORY** C13: from Old French *atendre,* from Latin *attendere* to stretch towards, from *tendere* to extend
▸**at'tender** NOUN

attendance (ə'tɛndəns) NOUN 1 the act or state of attending. 2 the number of persons present: *an attendance of 5000 at the festival.* 3 *Obsolete* attendants collectively; retinue.

attendance allowance NOUN (in Britain) a tax-free noncontributory welfare benefit for people over 65 years old who are so severely disabled that they need frequent attention or continual supervision for a period of six months or more.

attendance centre NOUN (in Britain) a place at which young offenders are required to attend regularly instead of going to prison.

attendant (ə'tɛndənt) NOUN 1 a person who accompanies or waits upon another. 2 a person employed to assist, guide, or provide a service for others, esp for the general public: *a lavatory attendant.* 3 a person who is present. 4 a logical consequence or natural accompaniment: *hatred is often an attendant of jealousy.* ◆ ADJECTIVE 5 being in attendance. 6 associated; accompanying; related: *attendant problems.*

attendee (əˌtɛn'diː) NOUN a person who is present at a specified event.

attention (ə'tɛnʃən) NOUN 1 concentrated direction of the mind, esp to a problem or task. 2 consideration, notice, or observation: *a new matter has come to our attention.* 3 detailed care or special treatment: *to pay attention to one's appearance.* 4 (*usually plural*) an act of consideration, courtesy, or gallantry indicating affection or love: *attentions given to a lover.* 5 the motionless position of formal military alertness, esp in drill when an upright position is assumed with legs and heels together, arms to the sides, head and eyes facing to the front. 6 *Psychol* the act of concentrating on any one of a set of objects or thoughts. See also **selective attention.** ◆ SENTENCE SUBSTITUTE 7 the order to be alert or to adopt a position of formal military alertness.
▷**HISTORY** C14: from Latin *attentiō,* from *attendere* to apply the mind to; see ATTEND

attention deficit disorder NOUN a disorder, particularly of children, characterized by excessive activity and inability to concentrate on one task for any length of time. Abbreviation: **ADD**.

attention deficit hyperactivity disorder NOUN a form of attention deficit disorder in which hyperactivity is a prominent symptom. Abbreviation: **ADHD**.

attentive (ə'tɛntɪv) ADJECTIVE 1 paying attention; listening carefully; observant. 2 (*postpositive;* often foll by *to*) careful to fulfil the needs or wants (of); considerate (about): *she was always attentive to his needs.*
▸**at'tentively** ADVERB ▸**at'tentiveness** NOUN

attenuant (ə'tɛnjʊənt) ADJECTIVE 1 causing dilution or thinness, esp of the blood. ◆ NOUN 2 *Obsolete* an attenuant drug or agent.

attenuate VERB (ə'tɛnjʊˌeɪt) 1 to weaken or become weak; reduce in size, strength, density, or value. 2 to make or become thin or fine; extend. 3 (*tr*) to make (a pathogenic bacterium, virus, etc.) less virulent, as by culture in special media or exposure to heat. ◆ ADJECTIVE (ə'tɛnjʊɪt, -ˌeɪt) 4 diluted, weakened, slender, or reduced. 5 *Botany* tapering gradually to a point.
▷**HISTORY** C16: from Latin *attenuāre* to weaken, from *tenuis* thin

attenuation (əˌtɛnjʊ'eɪʃən) NOUN 1 the act of attenuating or the state of being attenuated. 2 the loss of energy suffered by radiation as it passes through matter, esp as a result of absorption or scattering.

attenuator (ə'tɛnjʊˌeɪtə) NOUN 1 *Physics* any device designed to reduce the power of a wave or electrical signal without distorting it. 2 a person or thing that attenuates.

attercop ('ætəkɒp) NOUN *Archaic or dialect* 1 a spider. 2 an ill-natured person.
▷**HISTORY** Old English *attorcoppa,* from *ātor* poison and possibly *cop* head

attest (ə'tɛst) VERB 1 (*tr*) to affirm the correctness or truth of. 2 (when *intr,* usually foll by *to*) to witness (an act, event, etc.) or bear witness to (an act, event, etc.) as by signature or oath. 3 (*tr*) to make evident; demonstrate: *his life of luxury attests his wealth.* 4 (*tr*) to provide evidence for: *the marks in the ground attested the presence of a fossil.*
▷**HISTORY** C16: from Latin *attestārī* to prove, from *testārī* to bear witness, from *testis* a witness
▸**at'testable** ADJECTIVE ▸**at'testant** *or* **at'tester** *or* (*esp in legal usage*) **at'testor** *or* **at'testator** NOUN ▸**attestation** (ˌætɛ'steɪʃən) NOUN

attested (ə'tɛstɪd) ADJECTIVE *Brit* (of cattle, etc.) certified to be free from a disease, esp from tuberculosis.

Att. Gen. *or* **Atty. Gen.** ABBREVIATION FOR Attorney General.

attic ('ætɪk) NOUN 1 a space or room within the roof of a house. 2 *Architect* a storey or low wall above the cornice of a classical façade.
▷**HISTORY** C18: special use of ATTIC from the use of Attic-style pilasters to adorn the façade of the top storey

Attic ('ætɪk) ADJECTIVE 1 of or relating to Attica, its inhabitants, or the dialect of Greek spoken there, esp in classical times. 2 (*often not capital*) classically elegant, simple, or pure: *an Attic style.* ◆ NOUN 3 the dialect of Ancient Greek spoken and written in Athens: the chief literary dialect of classical Greek. See also **Aeolic, Arcadic, Doric, Ionic.**

Attica ('ætɪkə) NOUN a region and department of E central Greece: in ancient times the territory of Athens. Capital: Athens. Pop.: 3 764 348 (2001). Area: 14 157 sq. km (5466 sq. miles).

Atticism ('ætɪˌsɪzəm) NOUN 1 the idiom or character of the Attic dialect of Ancient Greek, esp in the Hellenistic period. 2 an elegant, simple, and clear expression.
▸**'Atticist** NOUN

Attic order NOUN a low pilaster of any order set into the cornice of a building.

Attic salt *or* **wit** NOUN refined incisive wit.

attire (ə'taɪə) VERB 1 (*tr*) to dress, esp in fine elegant clothes; array. ◆ NOUN 2 clothes or garments, esp if fine or decorative. 3 the antlers of a mature male deer.
▷**HISTORY** C13: from Old French *atirier* to put in order, from *tire* row; see TIER[1]

Attis ('ætɪs) NOUN *Classical myth* a youth of Phrygia, loved by the goddess Cybele. In a jealous passion she caused him to go mad, whereupon he castrated himself and died.

attitude ('ætɪˌtjuːd) NOUN 1 the way a person views something or tends to behave towards it, often in an evaluative way. 2 a theatrical pose created for effect (esp in the phrase **strike an attitude**). 3 a position of the body indicating mood or emotion. 4 *Informal* a hostile manner: *don't give me attitude, my girl.* 5 the orientation of an aircraft's axes in relation to some plane, esp the horizontal. See also **axis**[1] (sense 1). 6 the orientation of a spacecraft in relation to its direction of motion. 7 *Ballet* a classical position in which the body is upright and one leg raised and bent behind.
▷**HISTORY** C17: from French, from Italian *attitudine* disposition, from Late Latin *aptitūdō* fitness, from Latin *aptus* APT
▸ˌ**atti'tudinal** ADJECTIVE

attitudinize *or* **attitudinise** (ˌætɪ'tjuːdɪˌnaɪz) VERB (*intr*) to adopt a pose or opinion for effect; strike an attitude.
▸ˌ**atti'tudiˌnizer** *or* ˌ**atti'tudiˌniser** NOUN

attn ABBREVIATION FOR attention.

atto- PREFIX denoting 10^{-18}: *attotesla*. Symbol: a.
▷**HISTORY** from Norwegian, Danish *atten* eighteen

attolaser ('ætəʊˌleɪzə) NOUN a high-power laser capable of producing pulses with a duration measured in attoseconds.

attophysics ('ætəʊˌfɪzɪks) NOUN the physics of structures and artefacts with dimensions in the attometre range or of devices, such as lasers, capable of productng pulses with a duration measured in attoseconds.

attorn (ə'tɜːn) VERB (*intr*) 1 *Law* to acknowledge a new owner of land as one's landlord. 2 *Feudal history* to transfer allegiance or do homage to a new lord.
▷**HISTORY** C15: from Old French *atourner* to direct to, from *tourner* to TURN
▸**at'tornment** NOUN

attorney (ə'tɜːnɪ) NOUN 1 a person legally appointed or empowered to act for another. 2 *US* a lawyer qualified to represent clients in legal proceedings. 3 *South African* a solicitor.
▷**HISTORY** C14: from Old French *atourné,* from *atourner* to direct to; see ATTORN
▸**at'torneyˌship** NOUN

attorney-at-law NOUN, *plural* **attorneys-at-law**. *Law* 1 *Now chiefly US* a lawyer qualified to represent in court a party to a legal action. 2 *Brit obsolete* a solicitor.

attorney general NOUN, *plural* **attorneys general** *or* **attorney generals.** 1 a country's chief law officer and senior legal adviser to its government. 2 (in the US) the chief law officer and legal adviser of a state government. 3 (in some states of the US) a public prosecutor.

Attorney General NOUN 1 (in the United Kingdom except Scotland) the senior law officer and chief legal counsel of the Crown: a member of the government and of the House of Commons. 2 (in the US) the chief law officer and legal adviser to the Administration: head of the Department of Justice and member of the cabinet. 3 (in Australia and New Zealand) the chief government law officer: a member of Parliament and usually a cabinet minister.

attract (ə'trækt) VERB (*mainly tr*) 1 to draw (notice, a crowd of observers, etc.) to oneself by conspicuous behaviour or appearance (esp in the phrase **attract attention**). 2 (*also intr*) to exert a force on (a body) that tends to cause an approach or oppose a separation: *the gravitational pull of the earth attracts objects to it.* 3 to possess some property that pulls or draws (something) towards itself: *jam attracts wasps.* 4 (*also intr*) to exert a pleasing, alluring, or fascinating influence (upon); be attractive (to).
▷**HISTORY** C15: from Latin *attrahere* to draw towards, from *trahere* to pull
▸**at'tractable** ADJECTIVE ▸**at'tractor** *or* **at'tracter** NOUN

attractant (ə'træktənt) NOUN a substance that attracts, esp a chemical (**sex attractant**) produced by an insect and attracting insects of the same species. See also **pheromone.**

attraction (ə'trækʃən) NOUN 1 the act, power, or quality of attracting. 2 a person or thing that attracts or is intended to attract. 3 a force by which one object attracts another, such as the gravitational or electrostatic force. 4 a change in the form of one linguistic element caused by the proximity of another element.

attractive (ə'træktɪv) ADJECTIVE 1 appealing to the senses or mind through beauty, form, character, etc. 2 arousing interest: *an attractive opportunity.* 3 possessing the ability to draw or pull: *an attractive force.*
▸**at'tractively** ADVERB ▸**at'tractiveness** NOUN

attrib. ABBREVIATION FOR: 1 attribute. 2 attributive.

attribute VERB (ə'trıbju:t) [1] (*tr; usually foll by to*) to regard as belonging (to), produced (by), or resulting (from); ascribe (to): *to attribute a painting to Picasso.* ◆ NOUN ('ætrı,bju:t) [2] a property, quality, or feature belonging to or representative of a person or thing. [3] an object accepted as belonging to a particular office or position. [4] *Grammar* **a** an adjective or adjectival phrase. **b** an attributive adjective. [5] *Logic* the property, quality, or feature that is affirmed or denied concerning the subject of a proposition.
▷HISTORY C15: from Latin *attribuere* to associate with, from *tribuere* to give
▸**at'tributable** ADJECTIVE ▸**at'tributer** *or* **at'tributor** NOUN
▸**attribution** (,ætrı'bju:ʃən) NOUN

attribution theory NOUN *Psychol* the theory that tries to explain how people link actions and emotions to particular causes, both internal and external.

attributive (ə'trıbjutıv) ADJECTIVE [1] relating to an attribute. [2] *Grammar* (of an adjective or adjectival phrase) modifying a noun and constituting part of the same noun phrase, in English normally preceding the noun, as *black* in *Fido is a black dog* (as opposed to *Fido is black*). Compare **predicative.** [3] *Philosophy* relative to an understood domain, as *small* in *that elephant is small.* ◆ NOUN [4] an attributive adjective.
▸**at'tributively** ADVERB ▸**at'tributiveness** NOUN

attrit (ə'trıt) VERB **-trits, -tritting, -tritted.** *US slang* (*tr*) [1] to wear down or dispose of gradually. [2] to kill.
▷HISTORY C18: back formation from ATTRITION

attrition (ə'trıʃən) NOUN [1] the act of wearing away or the state of being worn away, as by friction. [2] constant wearing down to weaken or destroy (often in the phrase **war of attrition**). [3] Also called: **natural wastage.** a decrease in the size of the workforce of an organization achieved by not replacing employees who retire or resign. [4] *Geography* the grinding down of rock particles by friction during transportation by water, wind, or ice. Compare **abrasion** (sense 3), **corrasion.** [5] *Theol* sorrow for sin arising from fear of damnation, esp as contrasted with contrition, which arises purely from love of God.
▷HISTORY C14: from Late Latin *attrītiō* a rubbing against something, from Latin *atterere* to weaken, from *terere* to rub
▸**at'tritional** ADJECTIVE ▸**attritive** (ə'traıtıv) ADJECTIVE

Attu ('ætu:) NOUN the westernmost of the Aleutian Islands, off the coast of SW Alaska: largest of the Near Islands.

attune (ə'tju:n) VERB (*tr*) [1] to adjust or accustom (a person or thing); acclimatize. [2] to tune (a musical instrument).

atty ABBREVIATION FOR attorney.

atua ('ɑ:tu:ə) NOUN *NZ* a spirit or demon.
▷HISTORY Maori

ATV ABBREVIATION FOR all-terrain vehicle: a vehicle with treads or wheels designed to travel on rough uneven ground.

atween (ə'twi:n) PREPOSITION an archaic or Scot word for **between.**

at. wt. ABBREVIATION FOR atomic weight.

atypical (eı'tıpık^{ə}l) ADJECTIVE not typical; deviating from or not conforming to type.
▸**a'typically** ADVERB

au THE INTERNET DOMAIN NAME FOR Australia.

Au THE CHEMICAL SYMBOL FOR gold.
▷HISTORY from New Latin *aurum*

AU ABBREVIATION FOR: [1] **African Union.** [2] Also: **a.u.** angstrom unit. [3] Also: **a.u. astronomical unit.**

aubade (*French* obad) NOUN [1] a song or poem appropriate to or greeting the dawn. [2] a romantic or idyllic prelude or overture. ◆ Compare **serenade.**
▷HISTORY C19: from French, from Old Provençal *aubada* (unattested), from *auba* dawn, ultimately from Latin *albus* white

Aube (*French* ob) NOUN [1] a department of N central France, in Champagne-Ardenne region. Capital: Troyes. Pop.: 292 131 (1999). Area: 6026 sq. km (2350 sq. miles). [2] a river in N central France, flowing northwest to the Seine. Length: about 225 km (140 miles).

auberge (*French* obɛrʒ) NOUN an inn or tavern.
▷HISTORY C17: from French, from Old Provençal *alberga,* of Germanic origin; compare Old Saxon *heriberga* army shelter

aubergine ('əubə,ʒi:n) NOUN [1] a tropical Old World solanaceous plant, *Solanum melongena,* widely cultivated for its egg-shaped typically dark purple fruit. US, Canadian, and Australian name: **eggplant.** [2] the fruit of this plant, which is cooked and eaten as a vegetable. [3] **a** a dark purple colour. **b** (*as adjective*): *an aubergine dress.*
▷HISTORY C18: from French, from Catalan *albergínia,* from Arabic *al-bādindjān,* ultimately from Sanskrit *vatin-ganah,* of obscure origin

Aubervilliers (*French* obɛrvilje) NOUN an industrial suburb of Paris, on the Seine. Pop.: 67 840 (1990). Former name: **Notre-Dame-des-Vertus** (*French* nɔtrədamdevɛrty).

aubrietia, aubrieta, *or* **aubretia** (ɔ:'bri:ʃə) NOUN any trailing purple-flowered plant of the genus *Aubrietia,* native to European mountains but widely planted in rock gardens: family *Brassicaceae* (crucifers).
▷HISTORY C19: from New Latin, named after Claude *Aubriet,* 18th-century French painter of flowers and animals

auburn ('ɔ:b^{ə}n) NOUN **a** a moderate reddish-brown colour. **b** (*as adjective*): *auburn hair.*
▷HISTORY C15 (originally meaning: blond): from Old French *alborne* blond, from Medieval Latin *alburnus* whitish, from Latin *albus* white

Aubusson (*French* obysɔ̃) NOUN [1] a town in central France, in the Creuse department: a centre for flat-woven carpets and for tapestries since the 16th century. Pop.: 5000 (latest est.). ◆ ADJECTIVE [2] denoting or relating to these carpets or tapestries.

AUC ABBREVIATION FOR (indicating years numbered from the founding of Rome, taken as 753 B.C.) **a** ab urbe condita. **b** anno urbis conditae.

Auckland ('ɔ:klənd) NOUN the chief port of New Zealand, in the northern part of North Island: former capital of New Zealand (1840–65). Pop. (urban area): 381 800 (1999 est.).

Auckland Islands PLURAL NOUN a group of six uninhabited islands, south of New Zealand. Area: 611 sq. km (234 sq. miles).

au contraire *French* (o kɔ̃trɛr) ADVERB on the contrary.

au courant *French* (o kurɑ̃) ADJECTIVE up-to-date, esp in knowledge of current affairs.
▷HISTORY literally: in the current

auction ('ɔ:kʃən) NOUN [1] a public sale of goods or property, esp one in which prospective purchasers bid against each other until the highest price is reached. Compare **Dutch auction.** [2] the competitive calls made in bridge and other games before play begins, undertaking to win a given number of tricks if a certain suit is trumps. [3] See **auction bridge.** ◆ VERB [4] (*tr; often foll by off*) to sell by auction.
▷HISTORY C16: from Latin *auctiō* an increasing, from *augēre* to increase

auction bridge NOUN a variety of bridge, now generally superseded by contract bridge, in which all the tricks made score towards game.

auctioneer (,ɔ:kʃə'nıə) NOUN [1] a person who conducts an auction by announcing the lots and controlling the bidding. ◆ VERB [2] (*tr*) to sell by auction.

auctorial (ɔ:k'tɔ:rıəl) ADJECTIVE of or relating to an author.
▷HISTORY C19: from Latin *auctor* AUTHOR

audacious (ɔ:'deıʃəs) ADJECTIVE [1] recklessly bold or daring; fearless. [2] impudent or presumptuous.
▷HISTORY C16: from Latin *audāx* bold, from *audēre* to dare
▸**au'daciously** ADVERB ▸**au'daciousness** *or* **audacity** (ɔ:'dæsıtı) NOUN

Aude (*French* od) NOUN a department of S France on the Gulf of Lions, in Languedoc-Roussillon region. Capital: Carcassonne. Pop.: 309 770 (1999). Area: 6342 sq. km (2473 sq. miles).

audible ('ɔ:dıb^{ə}l) ADJECTIVE [1] perceptible to the hearing; loud enough to be heard. ◆ NOUN [2] *American football* a change of playing tactics called by the quarterback when the offense is lined up at the line of scrimmage.
▷HISTORY C16: from Late Latin *audībilis,* from Latin *audīre* to hear
▸**,audi'bility** *or* **'audibleness** NOUN ▸**'audibly** ADVERB

audience ('ɔ:dıəns) NOUN [1] a group of spectators or listeners, esp at a public event such as a concert or play. [2] the people reached by a book, film, or radio or television programme. [3] the devotees or followers of a public entertainer, lecturer, etc.; regular public. [4] an opportunity to put one's point of view, such as a formal interview with a monarch or head of state.
▷HISTORY C14: from Old French, from Latin *audientia* a hearing, from *audīre* to hear

audile ('ɔ:dıl, 'ɔ:daıl) *Psychol* ◆ NOUN [1] a person who possesses a faculty for auditory imagery that is more distinct than his visual or other imagery. ◆ ADJECTIVE [2] of or relating to such a person.
▷HISTORY C19: from AUD(ITORY) + -ILE

audio ('ɔ:dı,əu) NOUN (*modifier*) [1] of or relating to sound or hearing: *audio frequency.* [2] relating to or employed in the transmission, reception, or reproduction of sound. [3] of, concerned with, or operating at audio frequencies. ◆ Compare **video.**
▷HISTORY C20: independent use of AUDIO-

audio- COMBINING FORM indicating hearing or sound: *audiometer; audiovisual.*
▷HISTORY from Latin *audīre* to hear

audio book NOUN a reading of a book recorded on tape.

audio conference NOUN a meeting that is conducted by the use of audio telecommunications.

audio description NOUN a facility provided for visually impaired people in which a film, television programme, or play is described through audio technology.

audio frequency NOUN a frequency in the range 20 hertz to 20 000 hertz. A sound wave of this frequency would be audible to the human ear.

audiogenic (,ɔ:dıəu'dʒɛnık) ADJECTIVE caused or produced by sound or an audio frequency: *an audiogenic epileptic fit.*

audiogram ('ɔ:dıəu,græm) NOUN a graphic record of the acuity of hearing of a person obtained by means of an audiometer.

audiology (,ɔ:dı'ɒlədʒı) NOUN the scientific study of hearing, often including the treatment of persons with hearing defects.
▸**audiological** (,ɔ:dıə'lɒdʒık^{ə}l) ADJECTIVE
▸**,audio'logically** ADVERB ▸**,audi'ologist** NOUN

audiometer (,ɔ:dı'ɒmıtə) NOUN an instrument for testing the intensity and frequency range of sound that is capable of detection by the human ear.
▸**audiometric** (,ɔ:dıəu'mɛtrık) ADJECTIVE
▸**,audio'metrically** ADVERB ▸**,audi'ometrist** NOUN
▸**,audi'ometry** NOUN

audiophile ('ɔ:dıəu,faıl) NOUN a person who has a great interest in high-fidelity sound reproduction.

audio response NOUN a computer response that is audible rather than textual or graphical.

audiotypist ('ɔ:dıəu,taıpıst) NOUN a typist trained to type from a dictating machine.
▸**'audio,typing** NOUN

audiovisual (,ɔ:dıəu'vızjuəl, -ʒuəl) ADJECTIVE (esp of teaching aids) involving or directed at both hearing and sight: *the language class had new audiovisual equipment.*
▸**,audio'visually** ADVERB

audiphone ('ɔ:dı,fəun) NOUN a type of hearing aid consisting of a diaphragm that, when placed against the upper teeth, conveys sound vibrations to the inner ear.

audit ('ɔ:dıt) NOUN [1] **a** an inspection, correction, and verification of business accounts, conducted by an independent qualified accountant. **b** (*as modifier*): *audit report.* [2] *US* an audited account. [3] any thoroughgoing check or examination. [4] *Archaic* a hearing. ◆ VERB [5] to inspect, correct, and certify (accounts, etc.). [6] *US and Canadian* to attend (classes, etc.) as an auditor.
▷HISTORY C15: from Latin *audītus* a hearing, from *audīre* to hear

Audit Bureau of Circulation NOUN an organization that collects, audits, and publishes monthly circulation figures for newspapers and magazines. Abbreviation: **ABC.**

audition (ɔ:'dıʃən) NOUN [1] a test at which a performer or musician is asked to demonstrate his ability for a particular role, etc. [2] the act, sense, or power of hearing. ◆ VERB [3] to judge by means of or be tested in an audition.

▷HISTORY C16: from Latin *audītiō* a hearing, from *audīre* to hear

auditioner (ɔːˈdɪʃənə) NOUN a person who attends an audition.

auditor (ˈɔːdɪtə) NOUN 1 a person qualified to audit accounts. 2 a person who hears or listens. 3 *Austral, US and Canadian* a registered student who attends a class that is not an official part of his course of study, without actively participating it.
▷HISTORY C14: from Old French *auditeur,* from Latin *audītor* a hearer
▸ ˌaudiˈtorial ADJECTIVE

Auditor General NOUN (in Canada) a federal official responsible for auditing government departments and making an annual report.

auditorium (ˌɔːdɪˈtɔːrɪəm) NOUN, *plural* **-toriums** *or* **-toria** (-ˈtɔːrɪə). 1 the area of a concert hall, theatre, school, etc., in which the audience sits. 2 *US and Canadian* a building for public gatherings or meetings.
▷HISTORY C17: from Latin: a judicial examination, from *audītōrius* concerning a hearing; see AUDITORY

auditory (ˈɔːdɪtərɪ, -trɪ) ADJECTIVE *also* **auditive** (ˈɔːdɪtɪv). 1 of or relating to hearing, the sense of hearing, or the organs of hearing. ◆ NOUN 2 an archaic word for **audience** or **auditorium.**
▷HISTORY C14: from Latin *audītōrius* relating to hearing, from *audīre* to hear

auditory phonetics NOUN (*functioning as singular*) the branch of phonetics concerned with the perception of speech sounds by humans. Compare **acoustic phonetics, articulatory phonetics.**

audit trail NOUN a record of all the transactions or data entries that a person or firm has carried out over a specific period.

AUEW (in Britain) ABBREVIATION FOR Amalgamated Union of Engineering Workers.

au fait *French* (o fɛ; *English* əʊ ˈfeɪ) ADJECTIVE fully informed; in touch or expert.
▷HISTORY C18: literally: to the point

Aufklärung *German* (ˈaufklɛːruŋ) NOUN the Enlightenment, esp in Germany.

au fond *French* (o fɔ̃) ADVERB fundamentally; essentially.
▷HISTORY literally: at the bottom

auf Wiedersehen *German* (auf ˈviːdərzeːən) SENTENCE SUBSTITUTE goodbye, until we see each other again.

Aug. ABBREVIATION FOR August.

Augean (ɔːˈdʒiːən) ADJECTIVE extremely dirty or corrupt.
▷HISTORY C16: after *Augeas;* see AUGEAN STABLES

Augean stables PLURAL NOUN *Greek myth* the stables, not cleaned for 30 years, where King Augeas kept 3000 oxen. Hercules diverted the River Alpheus through them and cleaned them in a day.

augend (ˈɔːdʒɛnd, ɔːˈdʒɛnd) NOUN a number to which another number, the addend, is added.
▷HISTORY from Latin *augendum* that is to be increased, from *augēre* to increase

auger (ˈɔːgə) NOUN 1 a hand tool with a bit shaped like a corkscrew, for boring holes in wood. 2 a larger tool of the same kind for boring holes in the ground.
▷HISTORY C15 *an augur,* resulting from mistaken division of earlier *a nauger,* from Old English *nafugār* nave (of a wheel) spear (that is, tool for boring hubs of wheels), from *nafu* NAVE[2] + *gār* spear; see GORE[2]

Auger effect (ˈaugə) NOUN the spontaneous emission of an electron instead of a photon by an excited ion as a result of a vacancy being filled in an inner electron shell.
▷HISTORY C20: named after Pierre *Auger* (1899–1993), French physicist

aught[1] *or* **ought** (ɔːt) (*used with a negative or in conditional or interrogative sentences or clauses*) *Archaic or literary* ◆ PRONOUN 1 anything at all; anything whatever (esp in the phrase **for aught I know**). ◆ ADVERB 2 *Dialect* in any least part; to any degree.
▷HISTORY Old English *āwiht,* from *ā* ever, AY[1] + *wiht* thing; see WIGHT[1]

aught[2] *or* **ought** (ɔːt) NOUN a less common word for **nought** (zero).

augite (ˈɔːgaɪt) NOUN a black or greenish-black mineral of the pyroxene group, found in igneous rocks. Composition: calcium magnesium iron aluminium silicate. General formula: $(Ca,Mg,Fe,Al)(Si,Al)_2O_6$. Crystal structure: monoclinic.
▷HISTORY C19: from Latin *augītēs,* from Greek, from *augē* brightness
▸ **augitic** (ɔːˈgɪtɪk) ADJECTIVE

augment VERB (ɔːgˈmɛnt) 1 to make or become greater in number, amount, strength, etc.; increase. 2 (*tr*) *Music* to increase (a major or perfect interval) by a semitone. Compare **diminish** (sense 3). 3 (*tr*) (in Greek and Sanskrit grammar) to prefix a vowel or diphthong to (a verb) to form a past tense. ◆ NOUN (ˈɔːgment) 4 (in Greek and Sanskrit grammar) a vowel or diphthong prefixed to a verb to form a past tense.
▷HISTORY C15: from Late Latin *augmentāre* to increase, from *augmentum* growth, from Latin *augēre* to increase
▸ **augˈmentable** ADJECTIVE ▸ **augˈmentor** *or* **augˈmenter** NOUN

augmentation (ˌɔːgmɛnˈteɪʃən) NOUN 1 the act of augmenting or the state of being augmented. 2 the amount by which something is increased. 3 *Music* the presentation of a subject of a fugue, in which the note values are uniformly increased. Compare **diminution** (sense 2).

augmentative (ɔːgˈmɛntətɪv) ADJECTIVE 1 tending or able to augment. 2 *Grammar* **a** denoting an affix that may be added to a word to convey the meaning *large* or *great;* for example, the suffix *-ote* in Spanish, where *hombre* means man and *hombrote* big man. **b** denoting a word formed by the addition of an augmentative affix. ◆ NOUN 3 *Grammar* an augmentative word or affix. ◆ Compare (for senses 2, 3) **diminutive.**
▸ **augˈmentatively** ADVERB

augmented (ɔːgˈmɛntɪd) ADJECTIVE 1 *Music* (of an interval) increased or expanded from the state of being perfect or major by the raising of the higher note or the dropping of the lower note by one semitone: *C to G is a perfect fifth, but C to G sharp is an augmented fifth.* Compare **diminished** (sense 2). 2 *Music* **a** denoting a chord based upon an augmented triad: *an augmented seventh chord.* **b** denoting a triad consisting of the root plus a major third and an augmented fifth. **c** (*postpositive*) (esp in jazz) denoting a chord having as its root the note specified: *D augmented.* 3 having been increased, esp in number: *an augmented orchestra.*

augmented transition network NOUN (in certain schools of linguistics) a formalism, usually expressed as a diagram, having the power of a Turing machine, used as the basis of processes transforming sentences into their syntactic representations. Abbreviation: **ATN.**

au gratin (*French* o gratɛ̃) ADJECTIVE covered and cooked with browned breadcrumbs and sometimes cheese.
▷HISTORY French, literally: with the grating

Augsburg (*German* ˈauksbʊrk) NOUN a city in S Germany, in Bavaria: founded by the Romans in 14 B.C.; site of the diet that produced the **Peace of Augsburg** (1555), which ended the struggles between Lutherans and Catholics in the Holy Roman Empire and established the principle that each ruler should determine the form of worship in his lands. Pop.: 254 400 (1999 est.). Roman name: **Augusta Vindelicorum** (auˈguːstə vɪnˈdɛlɪˌkəʊrəm).

augur (ˈɔːgə) NOUN 1 Also called: **auspex.** (in ancient Rome) a religious official who observed and interpreted omens and signs to help guide the making of public decisions. 2 any prophet or soothsayer. ◆ VERB 3 to predict (some future event), as from signs or omens. 4 (*tr; may take a clause as object*) to be an omen (of); presage. 5 (*intr*) to foreshadow future events to be as specified; bode: *this augurs well for us.*
▷HISTORY C14: from Latin: a diviner, perhaps from *augēre* to increase
▸ **augural** (ˈɔːgjʊrəl) ADJECTIVE ▸ **ˈaugurship** NOUN

augury (ˈɔːgjʊrɪ) NOUN, *plural* **-ries.** 1 the art of or a rite conducted by an augur. 2 a sign or portent; omen.

august (ɔːˈgʌst) ADJECTIVE 1 dignified or imposing: *an august presence.* 2 of noble birth or high rank: *an august lineage.*
▷HISTORY C17: from Latin *augustus;* related to *augēre* to increase
▸ **auˈgustly** ADVERB ▸ **auˈgustness** NOUN

August (ˈɔːgəst) NOUN the eighth month of the year, consisting of 31 days.
▷HISTORY Old English, from Latin, named after Augustus (63 B.C.–14 A.D.), Roman emperor

Augusta (ɔːˈgʌstə) NOUN 1 a town in the US, in Georgia. Pop.: 44 639 (1990). 2 a port in S Italy, in E Sicily. Pop.: 38 900 (latest est.). 3 a city in the US, in Maine: the state capital; founded (1628) as a trading post; timber industry. Pop.: 21 325 (1990).

auguste *or* **august** (auˈguːst, ˈauˌgʊst) NOUN (*often capital*) a type of circus clown who usually wears battered ordinary clothes and is habitually maladroit or unlucky.
▷HISTORY C20: French, from German

Augustine (ɔːˈgʌstɪn) NOUN a member of an Augustinian order.

Augustinian (ˌɔːgəˈstɪnɪən) ADJECTIVE 1 of or relating to Saint Augustine of Hippo (354–430 A.D.), one of the Fathers of the Christian Church, or to his doctrines, or any of the Christian religious orders that were founded on his doctrines. ◆ NOUN 2 a member of any of several religious orders, such as the **Augustinian Canons, Augustinian Hermits,** and **Austin Friars** which are governed by the rule of Saint Augustine. 3 a person who follows the doctrines of Saint Augustine.

au jus *French* (o ʒy) ADJECTIVE (of meat) served in its own gravy.
▷HISTORY literally: with the juice

auk (ɔːk) NOUN 1 any of various diving birds of the family *Alcidae* of northern oceans having a heavy body, short tail, narrow wings, and a black-and-white plumage: order *Charadriiformes.* See also **great auk, razorbill.** 2 **little auk.** Also called: **dovekie.** a small short-billed auk, *Plautus alle,* abundant in Arctic regions.
▷HISTORY C17: from Old Norse *ālka;* related to Swedish *alka,* Danish *alke*

auklet (ˈɔːklɪt) NOUN any of various small auks of the genera *Aethia* and *Ptychoramphus.*

au lait (əʊ ˈleɪ; *French* o lɛ) ADJECTIVE prepared or served with milk.
▷HISTORY French, literally: with milk

auld (ɔːld) ADJECTIVE a Scot word for **old.**
▷HISTORY Old English *āld*

auld lang syne (ˈɔːld læŋ ˈsəɪn, ˈsaɪn, ˈzaɪn) NOUN old times; times past, esp those remembered with affection or nostalgia.
▷HISTORY Scottish, literally: old long since

Auld Reekie (ˈriːkɪ) NOUN *Scot* a nickname for **Edinburgh.**
▷HISTORY literally: Old Smoky

aulic (ˈɔːlɪk) ADJECTIVE *Rare* relating to a royal court.
▷HISTORY C18: from Latin *aulicus,* from Greek *aulikos* belonging to a prince's court, from *aulē* court

Aulic Council NOUN a council, founded in 1498, of the Holy Roman Emperor. It functioned mainly as a judicial body.

Aulis (ˈɔːlɪs) NOUN an ancient town in E central Greece, in Boeotia: traditionally the harbour from which the Greeks sailed at the beginning of the Trojan war.

Auliye-Ata (ˈaʊlijə ˈætə) NOUN a city in S Kazakhstan: chemical manufacturing. Pop.: 330 100 (1999). Former name (1938–91): **Dzhambul.**

aumbry (ˈɔːmbrɪ) NOUN, *plural* **-bries.** a variant of **ambry.**

Aum Shinrikyo (ˈaʊm ˌʃɪnrɪˈkjəʊ) NOUN a syncretistic Japanese cult combining elements of Buddhism, Hinduism, and Christianity, founded by Shoko Asahara in 1986; responsible for a number of murders and in particular a nerve-gas attack on the Tokyo underground in 1995. Also called: **Supreme Truth Cult.**
▷HISTORY C20: from Sanskrit *aum* OM + Japanese *shinri kyo* supreme truth

au naturel *French* (o natyrɛl) ADJECTIVE, ADVERB 1 naked; nude. 2 uncooked or plainly cooked.
▷HISTORY literally: in (a) natural (condition)

aunt (ɑːnt) NOUN (*often capital, esp as a term of address*) 1 a sister of one's father or mother. 2 the wife of one's uncle. 3 a term of address used by children for any woman, esp for a friend of the parents. 4 **my (sainted) aunt!** an exclamation of surprise or amazement.

▷**HISTORY** C13: from Old French *ante,* from Latin *amita* a father's sister

auntie *or* **aunty** ('ɑːntɪ) NOUN, *plural* **-ies.** 1 a familiar or diminutive word for **aunt.** 2 *Austral slang* a male homosexual.

Auntie ('ɑːntɪ) NOUN *Brit* an informal name for the **BBC.**

auntie man NOUN *Caribbean informal* an effeminate or homosexual male.

Aunt Sally ('sælɪ) NOUN, *plural* **-lies.** *Brit* 1 a figure of an old woman's head, typically with a clay pipe, used in fairgrounds and fêtes as a target for balls or other objects. 2 any person who is a target for insults or criticism. 3 something set up as a target for disagreement or attack.

Aunty ('ɑːntɪ) NOUN *Austral* an informal name for the **Australian Broadcasting Association.**

au pair (əʊ 'pɛə; *French* o pɛr) NOUN 1 **a** a young foreigner, usually a girl, who undertakes housework in exchange for board and lodging, esp in order to learn the language. **b** (*as modifier*): *an au pair girl.* 2 a young person who lives temporarily with a family abroad in exchange for a reciprocal arrangement with his or her own family. ◆ VERB 3 (*intr*) to work as an au pair. ◆ ADVERB 4 as an au pair: *she worked au pair in Greece.*
▷**HISTORY** C20: from French: on an equal footing

aura ('ɔːrə) NOUN, *plural* **auras** *or* **aurae** ('ɔːriː). 1 a distinctive air or quality considered to be characteristic of a person or thing. 2 any invisible emanation, such as a scent or odour. 3 *Pathol* strange sensations, such as noises in the ears or flashes of light, that immediately precede an attack, esp of epilepsy. 4 (in parapsychology) an invisible emanation produced by and surrounding a person or object: alleged to be discernible by individuals of supernormal sensibility.
▷**HISTORY** C18: via Latin from Greek: breeze

aural¹ ('ɔːrəl) ADJECTIVE of or relating to the sense or organs of hearing; auricular.
▷**HISTORY** C19: from Latin *auris* ear
▸**'aurally** ADVERB

aural² ('ɔːrəl) ADJECTIVE of or relating to an aura.

aurar ('ɔːrɑː) NOUN the plural of **eyrir.**

aureate ('ɔːrɪɪt, -ˌeɪt) ADJECTIVE 1 covered with gold; gilded. 2 of a golden colour. 3 (of a style of writing or speaking) excessively elaborate or ornate; florid.
▷**HISTORY** C15: from Late Latin *aureātus* gilded, from Latin *aureus* golden, from *aurum* gold
▸**'aureately** ADVERB ▸**'aureateness** NOUN

aureole ('ɔːrɪˌəʊl) *or* **aureola** (ɔː'riːələ) NOUN 1 (esp in paintings of Christian saints and the deity) a border of light or radiance enveloping the head or sometimes the whole of a figure represented as holy. 2 a less common word for **halo.** 3 another name for **corona** (sense 2).
▷**HISTORY** C13: from Old French *auréole,* from Medieval Latin (*corōna*) *aureola* golden (crown), from Latin *aureolus* golden, from *aurum* gold

Aureomycin (ˌɔːrɪəʊ'maɪsɪn) NOUN *Trademark* a brand of **chlortetracycline.**

aureus ('ɔːrɪəs) NOUN, *plural* **aurei** ('ɔːrɪˌaɪ). a gold coin of the Roman Empire.
▷**HISTORY** Latin: golden; see AUREATE

au revoir *French* (o rəvwar) SENTENCE SUBSTITUTE goodbye.
▷**HISTORY** literally: to the seeing again

auric ('ɔːrɪk) ADJECTIVE of or containing gold in the trivalent state.
▷**HISTORY** C19: from Latin *aurum* gold

auricle ('ɔːrɪkəl) NOUN 1 **a** the upper chamber of the heart; atrium. **b** a small sac in the atrium of the heart. 2 Also called: **pinna.** *Anatomy* the external part of the ear. 3 Also called: **auricula.** *Biology* an ear-shaped part or appendage, such as that occurring at the join of the leaf blade and the leaf sheath in some grasses.
▷**HISTORY** C17: from Latin *auricula* the external ear, from *auris* ear
▸**'auricled** ADJECTIVE

auricula (ɔː'rɪkjʊlə) NOUN, *plural* **-lae** (-ˌliː) *or* **-las.** 1 Also called: **bear's-ear.** a widely cultivated alpine primrose, *Primula auricula,* with leaves shaped like a bear's ear. 2 another word for **auricle** (sense 3).
▷**HISTORY** C17: from New Latin, from Latin: external ear; see AURICLE

auricular (ɔː'rɪkjʊlə) ADJECTIVE 1 of, relating to, or received by the sense or organs of hearing; aural. 2 shaped like an ear. 3 of or relating to an auricle of the heart. 4 (of feathers) occurring in tufts surrounding the ears of owls and similar birds. ◆ NOUN 5 (*usually plural*) an auricular feather.
▸**au'ricularly** ADVERB

auriculate (ɔː'rɪkjʊlɪt, -ˌleɪt) *or* **auriculated** ADJECTIVE 1 having ears. 2 *Botany* having ear-shaped parts or appendages. 3 Also: **auriform** ('ɔːrɪˌfɔːm). shaped like an ear; auricular.
▸**au'riculately** ADVERB

auriferous (ɔː'rɪfərəs) ADJECTIVE (of rock) containing gold; gold-bearing.
▷**HISTORY** C18: from Latin *aurifer* gold-bearing, from *aurum* gold + *ferre* to bear

Auriga (ɔː'raɪgə) NOUN, *Latin genitive* **Aurigae** (ɔː'raɪdʒiː). a conspicuous constellation in the N hemisphere between the Great Bear and Orion, at the edge of the Milky Way. It contains the first magnitude star Capella and the supergiant eclipsing binary star **Epsilon Aurigae.**
▷**HISTORY** Latin: charioteer

Aurignacian (ˌɔːrɪg'neɪʃən) ADJECTIVE of, relating to, or produced during a flint culture of the Upper Palaeolithic type characterized by the use of bone and antler tools, pins, awls, etc., and also by cave art and evidence of the beginnings of religion.
▷**HISTORY** C20: from French *Aurignacien,* after *Aurignac,* France, in the Pyrenees, near which is the cave where remains were discovered

auriscope ('ɔːrɪˌskəʊp) NOUN a medical instrument for examinig the external ear. Also called: **otoscope.**
▸**auriscopic** (ˌɔːrɪ'skɒpɪk) ADJECTIVE

aurist ('ɔːrɪst) NOUN a former name for: **audiologist.**

aurochs ('ɔːrɒks) NOUN, *plural* **-rochs.** a recently extinct member of the cattle tribe, *Bos primigenius,* that inhabited forests in N Africa, Europe, and SW Asia. It had long horns and is thought to be one of the ancestors of modern cattle. Also called: **urus.**
▷**HISTORY** C18: from German, from Old High German *ūrohso,* from *ūro* bison + *ohso* OX

aurora (ɔː'rɔːrə) NOUN, *plural* **-ras** *or* **-rae** (-riː). 1 an atmospheric phenomenon consisting of bands, curtains, or streamers of light, usually green, red, or yellow, that move across the sky in polar regions. It is caused by collisions between air molecules and charged particles from the sun that are trapped in the earth's magnetic field. 2 *Poetic* the dawn.
▷**HISTORY** C14: from Latin: dawn; see EAST
▸**au'roral** ADJECTIVE ▸**au'rorally** ADVERB

Aurora¹ (ɔː'rɔːrə) NOUN 1 the Roman goddess of the dawn. Greek counterpart: **Eos.** 2 the dawn or rise of something.

Aurora² (ɔː'rɔːrə) NOUN another name for **Maewo.**

aurora australis (ɒ'streɪlɪs) NOUN (*sometimes capital*) the aurora seen around the South Pole. Also called: **southern lights.**
▷**HISTORY** New Latin: southern aurora

aurora borealis (ˌbɔːrɪ'eɪlɪs) NOUN (*sometimes capital*) the aurora seen around the North Pole. Also called: **northern lights.**
▷**HISTORY** C17: New Latin: northern aurora

aurous ('ɔːrəs) ADJECTIVE of or containing gold, esp in the monovalent state.
▷**HISTORY** C19: apparently from French *aureux,* from Late Latin *aurōsus* gold-coloured, from Latin *aurum* gold

aurum ('ɔːrəm) NOUN *Obsolete* gold.
▷**HISTORY** C16: Latin

AUS 1 INTERNATIONAL CAR REGISTRATION FOR Australia. ◆ 2 ABBREVIATION FOR Australian Union of Students.

Aus. ABBREVIATION FOR: 1 Australia(n). 2 Austria(n).

Auschwitz (*German* 'aʊʃvɪts) NOUN an industrial town in S Poland; site of a Nazi concentration camp during World War II. Pop.: 45 400 (latest est.). Polish name: **Oświęcim.**

auscultate ('ɔːskəlˌteɪt) VERB to examine (a patient) by means of auscultation.
▸**'auscul,tator** NOUN

auscultation (ˌɔːskəl'teɪʃən) NOUN 1 the diagnostic technique in medicine of listening to the various internal sounds made by the body, usually with the aid of a stethoscope. 2 the act of listening.
▷**HISTORY** C19: from Latin *auscultātiō* a listening, from *auscultāre* to listen attentively; related to Latin *auris* ear
▸**auscultatory** (ɔː'skʌltətərɪ) *or* **auscultative** (ɔː'skʌltətɪv, 'ɔːskəlˌteɪtɪv) ADJECTIVE

ausforming ('ausˌfɔːmɪŋ) NOUN a treatment to strengthen hard steels, prior to quenching, in which the specimen is plastically deformed while it is in the austenite temperature range.
▷**HISTORY** C20: from AUS(TENITIC) + (DE)FORM

Ausgleich *German* ('ausglaiç) NOUN the agreement (1867) that established the Dual Monarchy of Austria-Hungary.
▷**HISTORY** German: levelling out, from *aus* OUT + *gleichen* to be similar

Auslese ('ausˌleɪsə) NOUN a white wine, usually sweet, produced in Germany from individually selected bunches of very ripe grapes.
▷**HISTORY** C20: from German, literally: selection

auspex ('ɔːspɛks) NOUN, *plural* **auspices** ('ɔːspɪˌsiːz). *Roman history* another word for **augur** (sense 1).
▷**HISTORY** C16: from Latin: observer of birds, from *avis* bird + *specere* to look

auspice ('ɔːspɪs) NOUN, *plural* **-pices** (-pɪsɪz). 1 (*usually plural*) patronage or guidance (esp in the phrase **under the auspices of**). 2 (*often plural*) a sign or omen, esp one that is favourable.
▷**HISTORY** C16: from Latin *auspicium* augury from birds; see AUSPEX

auspicious (ɔː'spɪʃəs) ADJECTIVE 1 favourable or propitious. 2 *Archaic* prosperous or fortunate.
▸**aus'piciously** ADVERB ▸**aus'piciousness** NOUN

> **Language note** The use of *auspicious* to mean 'very special' (as in *this auspicious occasion*) should be avoided.

Aussat ('ɒsæt, 'ɒzæt) NOUN the Australian-owned communications satellite launched in 1985.

Aussie ('ɒzɪ) ADJECTIVE, NOUN an informal word for **Australian** or (rare) **Australia.**

Aussie battler NOUN *Austral slang* an Australian working-class person. Also called: **little Aussie battler.**

Aust. ABBREVIATION FOR: 1 Australia(n). 2 Austria(n).

austenite ('ɔːstəˌnaɪt) NOUN 1 a solid solution of carbon in face-centred-cubic gamma iron, usually existing above 723°C. 2 the gamma phase of iron, stabilized at low temperatures by the addition of such elements as nickel.
▷**HISTORY** C20: named after Sir William C. Roberts-*Austen* (1843–1902), English metallurgist
▸**austenitic** (ˌɔːstə'nɪtɪk) ADJECTIVE

austenitic stainless steel NOUN an alloy of iron, usually containing at least 8 per cent of nickel and 18 per cent of chromium, used where corrosion resistance, heat resistance, creep resistance, or nonmagnetic properties are required.

Auster ('ɔːstə) NOUN *Poetic* the south wind.
▷**HISTORY** C14: Latin

austere (ɒ'stɪə) ADJECTIVE 1 stern or severe in attitude or manner: *an austere schoolmaster.* 2 grave, sober, or serious: *an austere expression.* 3 self-disciplined, abstemious, or ascetic: *an austere life.* 4 severely simple or plain: *an austere design.*
▷**HISTORY** C14: from Old French *austère,* from Latin *austērus* sour, from Greek *austēros* astringent; related to Greek *hauein* to dry
▸**aus'terely** ADVERB ▸**aus'tereness** NOUN

austerity (ɒ'stɛrɪtɪ) NOUN, *plural* **-ties.** 1 the state or quality of being austere. 2 (*often plural*) an austere habit, practice, or act. 3 **a** reduced availability of luxuries and consumer goods, esp when brought about by government policy. **b** (*as modifier*): *an austerity budget.*

Austerlitz ('ɔːstəlɪts) NOUN a town in the Czech Republic, in Moravia: site of Napoleon's victory over the Russian and Austrian armies in 1805. Pop.: 4747 (latest est.). Czech name: **Slavkov.**

Austin¹ ('ɒstɪn) NOUN a city in central Texas, on the Colorado River: state capital since 1845. Pop.: 656 462 (2000).

Austin² ('ɒstɪn) ADJECTIVE, NOUN another word for **Augustinian.**

▷HISTORY C14: shortened form of Augustine (354–430 A.D.), saint and one of the Fathers of the Christian Church

austral[1] ('ɔːstrəl) ADJECTIVE of or coming from the south: *austral winds*.
▷HISTORY C14: from Latin *austrālis*, from *auster* the south wind

austral[2] (aʊ'strɑːl) NOUN, *plural* **-trales**. a former monetary unit of Argentina equal to 100 centavos, replaced by the peso.
▷HISTORY from Spanish; see AUSTRAL[1]

Austral. ABBREVIATION FOR: [1] Australasia. [2] Australia(n).

Australasia (ˌɒstrə'leɪzɪə) NOUN [1] Australia, New Zealand, and neighbouring islands in the S Pacific Ocean. [2] (loosely) the whole of Oceania.

Australasian (ˌɒstrə'leɪzɪən) NOUN [1] a native or inhabitant of Australasia. ◆ ADJECTIVE [2] of or relating to Australia, New Zealand, and the neighbouring islands. [3] (of organizations) having members in Australia and New Zealand.

Australia (ɒ'streɪlɪə) NOUN a country and the smallest continent, situated between the Indian Ocean and the Pacific: a former British colony, now an independent member of the Commonwealth, constitutional links with Britain formally abolished in 1986; consists chiefly of a low plateau, mostly arid in the west, with the basin of the Murray River and the Great Dividing Range in the east and the Great Barrier Reef off the NE coast. Official language: English. Religion: Christian majority. Currency: dollar. Capital: Canberra. Pop.: 19 358 000 (2001 est.). Area: 7 682 300 sq. km (2 966 150 sq. miles).

Australia Day NOUN a public holiday in Australia, commemorating the landing of the British in 1788: observed on the first Monday after January 26.

Australian (ɒ'streɪlɪən) NOUN [1] a native or inhabitant of Australia. [2] the form of English spoken in Australia. [3] a linguistic phylum consisting of the languages spoken by the native Australians. ◆ ADJECTIVE [4] of, relating to, or characteristic of Australia, the Australians, or their form of English. [5] of, relating to, or belonging to the phylum of languages spoken by the native Australians. [6] of or denoting a zoogeographical region consisting of Australia, New Zealand, Polynesia, New Guinea, and the Moluccas.

Australiana (ɒˌstreɪlɪ'ɑːnə) PLURAL NOUN objects or documents relating to Australia and its history or culture esp in the form of a collection.

Australian Alps PLURAL NOUN a mountain range in SE Australia, in E Victoria and SE New South Wales. Highest peak: Mount Kosciusko, 2195 m (7316 ft.).

Australian Antarctic Territory NOUN the area of Antarctica, other than Adélie Land, that is administered by Australia, lying south of latitude 60°S and between longitudes 45°E and 160°E.

Australian Capital Territory NOUN a territory of SE Australia, within New South Wales: consists of two exclaves, one containing Canberra, the capital of Australia, and one at Jervis Bay. Pop.: 310 170 (1999 est.). Area: 2432 sq. km (939 sq. miles). Former name: **Federal Capital Territory.**

Australian cattle dog NOUN a compact strongly-built dog of a breed with pricked ears and a smooth bluish-grey coat, often used for controlling and moving cattle.

Australianism (ɒ'streɪlɪəˌnɪzəm) NOUN [1] the Australian national character or spirit. [2] loyalty to Australia, its political independence, culture, etc. [3] a linguistic usage, custom, or other feature peculiar to or characteristic of Australia, its people, or their culture.

Australianize *or* **Australianise** (ɒ'streɪlɪəˌnaɪz) VERB (esp of a new immigrant) to adopt or cause to adopt Australian habits and attitudes; integrate into Australian society.

Australian Mist NOUN a breed of medium-sized cat with a short spotted or marbled coat. Former name **Spotted Mist.**

Australian Rules NOUN (*functioning as singular*) a game resembling rugby football, played in Australia between teams of 18 men each on an oval pitch, with a ball resembling a large rugby ball. Players attempt to kick the ball between posts (without crossbars) at either end of the pitch, scoring six points for a goal (between the two main posts) and one point for a behind (between either of two outer posts and the main posts). They may punch or kick the ball and run with it provided that they bounce it every ten yards. Also called: **national code.**

Australian salmon NOUN another name for **kahawai.**

Australian salute NOUN *Austral informal* a movement of the hand and arm made to brush flies away from one's face.

Australian silky terrier NOUN a small compact variety of terrier with pricked ears and a long straight silky coat.

Australian terrier NOUN a small wire-haired breed of terrier similar to the cairn.

Australian Tiffanie NOUN another name for **Tiffanie.**

Austral Islands ('ɔːstrəl) PLURAL NOUN another name for the **Tubuai Islands.**

Australoid ('ɒstrəˌlɔɪd) ADJECTIVE [1] denoting, relating to, or belonging to a racial group that includes the native Australians and certain other peoples of southern Asia and the Pacific islands, characterized by dark skin, flat retreating forehead, and medium stature. ◆ NOUN [2] any member of this racial group.

australopithecine (ˌɒstrələʊ'pɪθɪˌsiːn) NOUN [1] any of various extinct apelike primates of the genus *Australopithecus* and related genera, remains of which have been discovered in southern and E Africa. Some species are estimated to be over 4.5 million years old. See also **zinjanthropus.** ◆ ADJECTIVE [2] of or relating to any of these primates.
▷HISTORY C20: from New Latin *Australopithecus*, from Latin *austrālis* southern, AUSTRAL[1] + Greek *pithēkos* ape

Australorp ('ɒstrəˌlɔːp) NOUN a heavy black breed of domestic fowl.
▷HISTORY shortened from *Austral(ian Black) Orp(ington)*

Austrasia (ɒ'streɪʒə, -ʃə) NOUN the eastern region of the kingdom of the Merovingian Franks that had its capital at Metz and lasted from 511 A.D. until 814 A.D. It covered the area now comprising NE France, Belgium, and western Germany.

Austria ('ɒstrɪə) NOUN a republic in central Europe: ruled by the Hapsburgs from 1282 to 1918; formed a dual monarchy with Hungary in 1867 and became a republic in 1919; a member of the European Union; contains part of the Alps, the Danube basin in the east, and extensive forests. Official language: German. Religion: Roman Catholic majority. Currency: euro. Capital: Vienna. Pop.: 8 069 000 (2001 est). Area: 83 849 sq. km (32 374 sq. miles). German name: **Österreich.**

Austria-Hungary NOUN the Dual Monarchy established in 1867, consisting of what are now Austria, Hungary, the Czech Republic, Slovakia, Slovenia, Croatia, and Bosnia-Herzegovina, and parts of Poland, Romania, Ukraine, and Italy. The empire was broken up after World War I.

Austrian ('ɒstrɪən) ADJECTIVE [1] of or relating to Austria or its inhabitants. ◆ NOUN [2] a native or inhabitant of Austria.

Austrian blind NOUN a window blind consisting of rows of vertically gathered fabric that may be drawn up to form a series of ruches.

Austro-[1] ('ɒstrəʊ-) COMBINING FORM southern: *Austro-Asiatic.*
▷HISTORY from Latin *auster* the south wind

Austro-[2] ('ɒstrəʊ-) COMBINING FORM Austrian: *Austro-Hungarian.*

Austro-Asiatic NOUN a hypothetical phylum or superfamily of languages consisting of Mon-Khmer and certain other languages of India and South-East Asia. Links with Malayo-Polynesian have also been suggested.

Austro-Hungarian ADJECTIVE of or relating to the Dual Monarchy of Austria-Hungary (1867-1918).

Austronesia (ˌɒstrəʊ'niːʒə, -ʃə) NOUN the islands of the central and S Pacific, including Indonesia, Melanesia, Micronesia, and Polynesia.

Austronesian (ˌɒstrəʊ'niːʒən, -ʃən) ADJECTIVE [1] of or relating to Austronesia, its peoples, or their languages. ◆ NOUN [2] another name for **Malayo-Polynesian.**

AUT ABBREVIATION FOR Association of University Teachers.

aut- COMBINING FORM a variant of **auto-** before a vowel.

autacoid ('ɔːtəˌkɔɪd) NOUN *Physiol* any natural internal secretion, esp one that exerts an effect similar to a drug.
▷HISTORY C20: from AUTO- + Greek *akos* cure + -OID

autarchy[1] ('ɔːtɑːkɪ) NOUN, *plural* **-chies.** [1] unlimited rule; autocracy. [2] self-government; self-rule.
▷HISTORY C17: from Greek *autarkhia*, from *autarkhos* autocratic; see AUTO-, -ARCHY
▸**au'tarchic** *or* **au'tarchical** ADJECTIVE

autarchy[2] ('ɔːtɑːkɪ) NOUN, *plural* **-chies.** a variant spelling (now rare) of **autarky.**

autarky ('ɔːtɑːkɪ) NOUN, *plural* **-kies.** [1] (esp of a political unit) a system or policy of economic self-sufficiency aimed at removing the need for imports. [2] an economically self-sufficient country.
▷HISTORY C17: from Greek *autarkeia*, from *autarkēs* self-sufficient, from AUTO- + *arkein* to suffice
▸**au'tarkic** ADJECTIVE ▸**'autarkist** NOUN

autecious (ɔː'tiːʃəs) ADJECTIVE a variant spelling of **autoecious.**

autecology (ˌɔːtɪ'kɒlədʒɪ) NOUN the ecological study of an individual organism or species. Compare **synecology.**
▸**ˌauteco'logical** ADJECTIVE

auteur (ɔː'tɜː) NOUN a director whose creative influence on a film is so great as to be considered its author.
▷HISTORY French: author
▸**au'teurism** NOUN ▸**au'teurist** ADJECTIVE

authentic (ɔː'θɛntɪk) ADJECTIVE [1] of undisputed origin or authorship; genuine: *an authentic signature.* [2] accurate in representation of the facts; trustworthy; reliable: *an authentic account.* [3] (of a deed or other document) duly executed, any necessary legal formalities having been complied with. [4] *Music* **a** using period instruments and historically researched scores and playing techniques in an attempt to perform a piece as it would have been played at the time it was written. **b** (*in combination*): *an authentic-instrument performance.* [5] *Music* **a** (of a mode as used in Gregorian chant) commencing on the final and ending an octave higher. **b** (of a cadence) progressing from a dominant to a tonic chord. Compare **plagal.**
▷HISTORY C14: from Late Latin *authenticus* coming from the author, from Greek *authentikos*, from *authentēs* one who acts independently, from AUTO- + *hentēs* a doer
▸**au'thentically** ADVERB ▸**authenticity** (ˌɔːθɛn'tɪsɪtɪ) NOUN

authenticate (ɔː'θɛntɪˌkeɪt) VERB (*tr*) [1] to establish as genuine or valid. [2] to give authority or legal validity to.
▸**auˌthenti'cation** NOUN ▸**au'thentiˌcator** NOUN

authigenic (ˌɔːθɪ'dʒɛnɪk) ADJECTIVE (of minerals) having crystallized in a sediment during or after deposition.
▷HISTORY C19: from German *authigene* from Greek *authigenēs* native + -IC

author ('ɔːθə) NOUN [1] a person who composes a book, article, or other written work. Related adjective: **auctorial.** [2] a person who writes books as a profession; writer. [3] the writings of such a person: *reviewing a postwar author.* [4] an originator or creator: *the author of this plan.* ◆ VERB (*tr*) [5] to write or originate.
▷HISTORY C14: from Old French *autor*, from Latin *auctor* author, from *augēre* to increase
▸**authorial** (ɔː'θɔːrɪəl) ADJECTIVE

authoress ('ɔːθəˌrɛs) NOUN *Now usually disparaging* a female author.

authoring ('ɔːθərɪŋ) NOUN *Computing* **a** the creation of documents, esp multimedia documents. **b** (*as modifier*): *an authoring tool.*

authoritarian (ɔːˌθɒrɪ'tɛərɪən) ADJECTIVE [1] favouring, denoting, or characterized by strict obedience to authority. [2] favouring, denoting, or relating to government by a small elite with wide powers. [3] despotic; dictatorial; domineering. ◆

NOUN [4] a person who favours or practises authoritarian policies.
▸ **au,thori'tarianism** NOUN

authoritative (ɔː'θɒrɪtətɪv) ADJECTIVE [1] recognized or accepted as being true or reliable: *an authoritative article on drugs.* [2] exercising or asserting authority; commanding: *an authoritative manner.* [3] possessing or supported by authority; official: *an authoritative communiqué.*
▸ **au'thoritatively** ADVERB ▸ **au'thoritativeness** NOUN

authority (ɔː'θɒrɪtɪ) NOUN, *plural* **-ties.** [1] the power or right to control, judge, or prohibit the actions of others. [2] (*often plural*) a person or group of people having this power, such as a government, police force, etc. [3] a position that commands such a power or right (often in the phrase **in authority**). [4] such a power or right delegated, esp from one person to another; authorization: *she has his authority.* [5] the ability to influence or control others: *a man of authority.* [6] an expert or an authoritative written work in a particular field: *he is an authority on Ming china.* [7] evidence or testimony: *we have it on his authority that she is dead.* [8] confidence resulting from great expertise: *the violinist lacked authority in his cadenza.* [9] (*capital when part of a name*) a public board or corporation exercising governmental authority in administering some enterprise: *Independent Broadcasting Authority.* [10] *Law* **a** a judicial decision, statute, or rule of law that establishes a principle; precedent. **b** legal permission granted to a person to perform a specified act.
▷**HISTORY** C14: from French *autorité,* from Latin *auctōritas,* from *auctor* AUTHOR

authorize *or* **authorise** ('ɔːθə,raɪz) VERB (*tr*) [1] to confer authority upon (someone to do something); empower. [2] to permit (someone to do or be something) with official sanction: *a dealer authorized by a manufacturer to retail his products.*
▸ **,authori'zation** *or* **,authori'sation** NOUN ▸ **'author,izer** *or* **'author,iser** NOUN

Authorized Version NOUN **the.** an English translation of the Bible published in 1611 under James I. Also called: **King James Version, King James Bible.**

authorship ('ɔːθə,ʃɪp) NOUN [1] the origin or originator of a written work, plan, etc.: *a book of unknown authorship.* [2] the profession of writing books.

Auth. Ver. ABBREVIATION FOR Authorized Version (of the Bible).

autism ('ɔːtɪzəm) NOUN *Psychiatry* abnormal self-absorption, usually affecting children, characterized by lack of response to people and actions and limited ability to communicate: children suffering from autism often do not learn to speak.
▷**HISTORY** C20: from Greek *autos* self + -ISM
▸ **au'tistic** ADJECTIVE, NOUN

auto ('ɔːtəʊ) NOUN, *plural* **-tos.** *US and Canadian informal* **a** short for **automobile. b** (*as modifier*): *auto parts.*

auto- *or sometimes before a vowel* **aut-** COMBINING FORM [1] self; same; of or by the same one: *autobiography.* [2] acting from or occurring within; self-caused: *autohypnosis.* [3] self-propelling; automatic: *automobile.*
▷**HISTORY** from Greek *autos* self

autoallogamy (,ɔːtəʊə'lɒgəmɪ) NOUN the ability of some plants of a species to cross-pollinate and others to self-pollinate.

autoantibody (,ɔːtəʊ'æntɪ,bɒdɪ) NOUN, *plural* **-bodies.** an antibody reacting with an antigen that is a part of the organism in which the antibody is formed.

autobahn ('ɔːtə,bɑːn) NOUN a motorway in German-speaking countries.
▷**HISTORY** from German, from *Auto* car + *Bahn* road

autobiographical (,ɔːtə,baɪə'græfɪkᵊl) ADJECTIVE [1] of or concerned with one's own life. [2] of or relating to an autobiography.
▸ **,auto,bio'graphically** ADVERB

autobiography (,ɔːtəʊbaɪ'ɒgrəfɪ, ,ɔːtəbaɪ-) NOUN, *plural* **-phies.** an account of a person's life written or otherwise recorded by that person.
▸ **,autobi'ographer** NOUN

autocade ('ɔːtəʊ,keɪd) NOUN *US* another name for **motorcade.**

autocatalysis (,ɔːtəʊkə'tælɪsɪs) NOUN, *plural* **-ses** (-,siːz). the catalysis of a reaction in which the catalyst is one of the products of the reaction.

autocephalous (,ɔːtəʊ'sɛfələs) ADJECTIVE [1] (of an Eastern Christian Church) governed by its own national synods and appointing its own patriarchs or prelates. [2] (of a bishop) independent of any higher governing body.
▸ **autocephalic** (,ɔːtəʊsɪ'fælɪk) ADJECTIVE ▸ **,auto'cephaly** NOUN

autochanger ('ɔːtəʊ,tʃeɪndʒə) NOUN [1] a device in a record player that enables a small stack of records to be dropped automatically onto the turntable one at a time and played separately. [2] a record player with such a device.

autochthon (ɔː'tɒkθən, -θɒn) NOUN, *plural* **-thons** *or* **-thones** (-θə,niːz). [1] (*often plural*) one of the earliest known inhabitants of any country; aboriginal. [2] an animal or plant that is native to a particular region.
▷**HISTORY** C17: from Greek *autokhthōn* from the earth itself, from AUTO- + *khthōn* the earth

autochthonous (ɔː'tɒkθənəs), **autochthonic** (,ɔːtɒk'θɒnɪk), *or* **autochthonal** ADJECTIVE [1] (of rocks, deposits, etc.) found where they and their constituents were formed. Compare **allochthonous.** [2] inhabiting a place or region from earliest known times; aboriginal. [3] *Physiol* (of some functions, such as heartbeat) originating within an organ rather than from external stimulation.
▸ **au'tochthonism** *or* **au'tochthony** NOUN ▸ **au'tochthonously** ADVERB

autocidal (,ɔːtəʊ'saɪdᵊl) ADJECTIVE (of insect pest control) effected by the introduction of sterile or genetically altered individuals into the wild population.

autoclave ('ɔːtə,kleɪv) NOUN [1] a strong sealed vessel used for chemical reactions at high pressure. [2] an apparatus for sterilizing objects (esp surgical instruments) or for cooking by means of steam under pressure. [3] *Civil engineering* a vessel in which freshly cast concrete or sand-lime bricks are cured very rapidly in high-pressure steam. ◆ VERB [4] (*tr*) to put in or subject to the action of an autoclave.
▷**HISTORY** C19: from French AUTO- + *-clave,* from Latin *clāvis* key

autocorrelation (,ɔːtəʊ,kɒrɪ'leɪʃən) NOUN *Statistics* the condition occurring when successive items in a series are correlated so that their covariance is not zero and they are not independent. Also called: **serial correlation.**

autocracy (ɔː'tɒkrəsɪ) NOUN, *plural* **-cies.** [1] government by an individual with unrestricted authority. [2] the unrestricted authority of such an individual. [3] a country, society, etc., ruled by an autocrat.

autocrat ('ɔːtə,kræt) NOUN [1] a ruler who possesses absolute and unrestricted authority. [2] a domineering or dictatorial person.

autocratic (,ɔːtə'krætɪk) ADJECTIVE [1] of or relating to an absolute and unrestricted ruler. [2] domineering or dictatorial.
▸ **,auto'cratically** ADVERB

autocross ('ɔːtəʊ,krɒs) NOUN a form of motor sport in which cars race over a half-mile circuit of rough grass. See also **motocross, rallycross.**

Autocue ('ɔːtəʊ,kjuː) NOUN *Trademark* an electronic television prompting device whereby a prepared script, unseen by the audience, is enlarged line by line for the speaker. US and Canadian name (trademark): **Teleprompter.**

autocutie ('ɔːtəʊ,kjuːtɪ) NOUN *Informal* a young and attractive but inexperienced female television presenter.
▷**HISTORY** C20: from AUTOCUE + CUTIE

autocycle ('ɔːtəʊ,saɪkᵊl) NOUN *Obsolete* a bicycle powered or assisted by a small engine.

auto-da-fé (,ɔːtəʊdə'feɪ) NOUN, *plural* **autos-da-fé.** [1] *History* a ceremony of the Spanish Inquisition including the pronouncement and execution of sentences passed on sinners or heretics. [2] the burning to death of people condemned as heretics by the Inquisition.
▷**HISTORY** C18: from Portuguese, literally: act of the faith

autodestruct (,ɔːtəʊdɪ'strʌkt) ADJECTIVE *also* **autodestructive.** [1] likely to or possessing the power to destroy or obliterate itself or its possessor: *autodestruct mechanism.* ◆ VERB (*intr*) [2] (of a missile, machine, etc.) to destroy itself.

autodidact ('ɔːtəʊ,daɪdækt) NOUN a person who is self-taught.
▷**HISTORY** C16: from Greek *autodidaktos* self-taught, from *autos* self + *didaskein* to teach
▸ **,autodi'dactic** ADJECTIVE

autodyne ('ɔːtəʊ,daɪn) ADJECTIVE *Electronics* denoting or relating to an electrical circuit in which the same elements and valves are used as oscillator and detector.

autoecious *or sometimes US* **autecious** (ɔː'tiːʃəs) ADJECTIVE [1] (of parasites, esp the rust fungi) completing the entire life cycle on a single species of host. Compare **heteroecious.** [2] (of plants, esp mosses) having male and female reproductive organs on the same plant.
▷**HISTORY** C19: from AUTO- + *-oecious,* from Greek *oikia* house
▸ **au'toecism** *or* (*sometimes US*) **au'tecism** NOUN

autoeroticism (,ɔːtəʊɪ'rɒtɪ,sɪzəm) *or* **autoerotism** (,ɔːtəʊ'ɛrə,tɪzəm) NOUN *Psychol* the arousal and use of one's own body as a sexual object, as through masturbation.
▸ **,autoe'rotic** ADJECTIVE

autoexposure (,ɔːtəɪk'spəʊʒə) NOUN another name for **automatic exposure.**

autofocus ('ɔːtəʊ,fəʊkəs) NOUN another name for **automatic focus.**

autogamy (ɔː'tɒgəmɪ) NOUN [1] self-fertilization in flowering plants. [2] a type of sexual reproduction, occurring in some protozoans, in which the uniting gametes are derived from the same cell.
▸ **au'togamous** *or* **autogamic** (,ɔːtə'gæmɪk) ADJECTIVE

autogenesis (,ɔːtəʊ'dʒɛnɪsɪs) *or* **autogeny** (ɔː'tɒdʒɪnɪ) NOUN another word for **abiogenesis** (sense 1).
▸ **autogenetic** (,ɔːtəʊdʒɪ'nɛtɪk) ADJECTIVE

autogenic training (,ɔːtəʊ'dʒɛnɪk) NOUN a technique for reducing stress through mental exercises to produce physical relaxation. Also called: **autogenics.**

autogenous (ɔː'tɒdʒɪnəs) ADJECTIVE [1] **a** originating within the body. Compare **heterogenous. b** denoting a vaccine made from bacteria obtained from the patient's own body. [2] self-generated; self-produced. [3] denoting a weld in which the filler metal and the parent metal are of similar composition.
▸ **au'togenously** ADVERB

autogiro *or* **autogyro** (,ɔːtəʊ'dʒaɪrəʊ) NOUN, *plural* **-ros.** a self-propelled aircraft supported in flight mainly by unpowered rotating horizontal blades. Also called: **gyroplane.** Compare **helicopter.**
▷**HISTORY** C20: originally a trademark

autograft ('ɔːtə,grɑːft) NOUN *Surgery* a tissue graft obtained from one part of a patient's body for use on another part.

autograph ('ɔːtə,grɑːf, -,græf) NOUN [1] **a** a handwritten signature, esp that of a famous person. **b** (*as modifier*): *an autograph album.* [2] a person's handwriting. [3] **a** a book, document, etc., handwritten by its author; original manuscript; holograph. **b** (*as modifier*): *an autograph letter.* ◆ VERB (*tr*) [4] to write one's signature on or in; sign. [5] to write with one's own hand.
▷**HISTORY** C17: from Late Latin, from Greek *autographos,* from *autos* self + *graphein* to write
▸ **autographic** (,ɔːtə'græfɪk) *or* **,auto'graphical** ADJECTIVE
▸ **,auto'graphically** ADVERB

autography (ɔː'tɒgrəfɪ) NOUN [1] the writing of something in one's own handwriting; something handwritten. [2] the precise reproduction of an illustration or of writing.

Autoharp ('ɔːtəʊ,hɑːp) NOUN *Trademark* a zither-like musical instrument used in country-and-western music, equipped with button-controlled dampers that can prevent selected strings from sounding, thus allowing chords to be played. It is plucked with the fingers or a plectrum.

autohypnosis (,ɔːtəʊhɪp'nəʊsɪs) NOUN *Psychol* the process or result of self-induced hypnosis.
▸ **autohypnotic** (,ɔːtəʊhɪp'nɒtɪk) ADJECTIVE
▸ **,autohyp'notically** ADVERB

autoicous (ɔː'tɔɪkəs) ADJECTIVE (of plants, esp

mosses) having male and female reproductive organs on the same plant.
▷HISTORY C19: from AUTO- + Greek *oikos* dwelling

autoimmune (ˌɔːtəʊɪˈmjuːn) ADJECTIVE (of a disease) caused by the action of antibodies produced against substances normally present in the body.
▸ˌautoimˈmunity NOUN

autoinfection (ˌɔːtəʊɪnˈfɛkʃən) NOUN infection by a pathogenic agent already within the body or infection transferred from one part of the body to another.

autoinoculation (ˌɔːtəʊɪˌnɒkjʊˈleɪʃən) NOUN the inoculation of microorganisms (esp viruses) from one part of the body into another, usually in the form of a vaccine.

autointoxication (ˌɔːtəʊɪnˌtɒksɪˈkeɪʃən) NOUN self-poisoning caused by absorption of toxic products originating within the body. Also called: **autotoxaemia.**

autoionization *or* **autoionisation** (ˌɔːtəʊˌaɪənaɪˈzeɪʃən) NOUN *Physics* the process in which spontaneous decay of excited atoms or molecules results in emission of electrons, rather than photons.

autojumble (ˈɔːtəʊˌdʒʌmbᵊl) NOUN a sale of second-hand car parts, esp for car enthusiasts.

autokinetic (ˌɔːtəʊkɪˈnɛtɪk, -kaɪ-) ADJECTIVE automatically self-moving.

autokinetic phenomenon NOUN *Psychol* the apparent movement of a fixed point of light when observed in a darkened room. The effect is produced by small eye movements for which the brain is unable to compensate, having no other reference points.

autoloading (ˈɔːtəʊˌləʊdɪŋ) ADJECTIVE self-loading.

autologous (ɔːˈtɒləgəs) ADJECTIVE (of a tissue graft, blood transfusion, etc.) originating from the recipient rather than from a donor.

Autolycus[1] (ɔːˈtɒlɪkəs) NOUN a crater in the NW quadrant of the moon about 38 km in diameter and 3000 m deep.

Autolycus[2] (ɔːˈtɒlɪkəs) NOUN *Greek myth* a thief who stole cattle from his neighbour Sisyphus and prevented him from recognizing them by making them invisible.

autolyse *or US* **autolyze** (ˈɔːtəˌlaɪz) VERB *Biochem* to undergo or cause to undergo autolysis.

autolysin (ˌɔːtəˈlaɪsɪn, ɔːˈtɒlɪ-) NOUN any agent that produces autolysis.

autolysis (ɔːˈtɒlɪsɪs) NOUN the destruction of cells and tissues of an organism by enzymes produced by the cells themselves.
▷HISTORY C20: via German from Greek *autos* self + *lusis* loosening, release
▸**autolytic** (ˌɔːtəˈlɪtɪk) ADJECTIVE

automat (ˈɔːtəˌmæt) NOUN 1 Also called: **vending machine.** a machine that automatically dispenses goods, such as cigarettes, when money is inserted. 2 *Chiefly US* an area or room, sometimes having restaurant facilities, where food and other goods are supplied from vending machines.

automata (ɔːˈtɒmətə) NOUN a plural of **automaton.**

automata theory NOUN the formal study of the power of computation of abstract machines.

automate (ˈɔːtəˌmeɪt) VERB to make (a manufacturing process, factory, etc.) automatic, or (of a manufacturing process, etc.) to be made automatic.

automated teller machine NOUN a computerized cash dispenser. Abbreviation: **ATM.**

automatic (ˌɔːtəˈmætɪk) ADJECTIVE 1 performed from force of habit or without conscious thought; lacking spontaneity; mechanical: *an automatic smile.* 2 **a** (of a device, mechanism, etc.) able to activate, move, or regulate itself. **b** (of an act or process) performed by such automatic equipment. 3 (of the action of a muscle, gland, etc.) involuntary or reflex. 4 occurring as a necessary consequence: *promotion is automatic after a year.* 5 (of a firearm) **a** utilizing some of the force of or gas from each explosion to eject the empty shell case, replace it with a new one, and fire continuously until release of the trigger. Compare **semiautomatic** (sense 2). **b** short for **semiautomatic** (sense 2). ◆ See also **machine** (sense 5). ◆ NOUN 6 an automatic firearm. 7 a motor vehicle having automatic transmission. 8 a machine that operates automatically.
▷HISTORY C18: from Greek *automatos* acting independently
▸ˌautoˈmatically ADVERB ▸**automaticity** (ˌɔːtəʊməˈtɪsɪtɪ) NOUN

automatic camera NOUN a camera in which the lens aperture or the shutter speed or both are automatically adjusted to the prevailing conditions.

automatic door NOUN a self-opening door.

automatic exposure NOUN the automatic adjustment of the lens aperture and shutter speed of a camera by a control mechanism. Also called: **autoexposure.**

automatic focus NOUN **a** a system in a camera which automatically adjusts the lens so that the object being photographed is in focus, often one using infrared light to estimate the distance of the object from the camera. **b** (*as modifier*): *automatic-focus lens.* Abbreviation: **AF.** Also called: **autofocus.**

automatic frequency control NOUN a system in a radio or television receiver by which the tuning of an incoming signal is accurately maintained. Abbreviation: **AFC.**

automatic gain control NOUN control of a radio receiver in which the gain varies inversely with the magnitude of the input, thus maintaining the output at an approximately constant level. Abbreviation: **AGC.**

automatic pilot NOUN 1 Also called: **autopilot.** a device that automatically maintains an aircraft on a preset course. 2 **on automatic pilot.** *Informal* acting without conscious thought because of tiredness, shock, or familiarity with the task being performed.

automatic repeat NOUN a key on the keyboard of a typewriter, computer, etc., which, when depressed continuously, produces the character repeatedly until the key is released.

automatic transmission NOUN a transmission system in a motor vehicle, usually incorporating a fluid clutch, in which the gears change automatically.

automatic vending NOUN selling goods by vending machines.

automation (ˌɔːtəˈmeɪʃən) NOUN 1 the use of methods for controlling industrial processes automatically, esp by electronically controlled systems, often reducing manpower. 2 the extent to which a process is so controlled.

automatism (ɔːˈtɒməˌtɪzəm) NOUN 1 the state or quality of being automatic; mechanical or involuntary action. 2 *Law, philosophy* the explanation of an action, or of action in general, as determined by the physiological states of the individual, admissible in law as a defence when the physiological state is involuntary, as in sleepwalking. 3 *Psychol* the performance of actions, such as sleepwalking, without conscious knowledge or control. 4 the suspension of consciousness sought or achieved by certain artists and writers to allow free flow of uncensored thoughts.
▸auˈtomatist NOUN

automatize *or* **automatise** (ɔːˈtɒməˌtaɪz) VERB to make (a process, etc.) automatic or (of a process, etc.) to be made automatic.
▸auˌtomatiˈzation *or* auˌtomatiˈsation NOUN

automaton (ɔːˈtɒməˌtɒn, -tᵊn) NOUN, *plural* **-tons** *or* **-ta** (-tə). 1 a mechanical device operating under its own hidden power; robot. 2 a person who acts mechanically or leads a routine monotonous life.
▷HISTORY C17: from Latin, from Greek, from *automatos* spontaneous, self-moving
▸auˈtomatous ADJECTIVE

autometer (ˈɔːtəʊˌmiːtə) NOUN a small device inserted in a photocopier to enable the process of copying to begin and to record the number of copies made.

automobile (ˈɔːtəməˌbiːl) NOUN another word (esp US) for **car** (sense 1).
▸**automobilist** (ˌɔːtəməˈbiːlɪst, -ˈməʊbɪlɪst) NOUN

automobilia (ˌɔːtəməˈbiːlɪə) PLURAL NOUN items connected with cars and motoring of interest to the collector.

automotive (ˌɔːtəˈməʊtɪv) ADJECTIVE 1 relating to motor vehicles. 2 self-propelling.

autonomic (ˌɔːtəˈnɒmɪk) ADJECTIVE 1 occurring involuntarily or spontaneously. 2 of or relating to the autonomic nervous system. 3 Also: **autonomous.** (of plant movements) occurring as a result of internal stimuli.
▸ˌautoˈnomically ADVERB

autonomic nervous system NOUN the section of the nervous system of vertebrates that controls the involuntary actions of the smooth muscles, heart, and glands. It has two divisions: the sympathetic and the parasympathetic. Compare **somatic nervous system.**

autonomics (ˌɔːtəˈnɒmɪks) NOUN (*functioning as singular*) *Electronics* the study of self-regulating systems for process control.

autonomous (ɔːˈtɒnəməs) ADJECTIVE 1 (of a community, country, etc.) possessing a large degree of self-government. 2 of or relating to an autonomous community. 3 independent of others. 4 *Philosophy* **a** acting or able to act in accordance with rules and principles of one's own choosing. **b** (in the moral philosophy of Kant, of an individual's will) directed to duty rather than to some other end. Compare **heteronomous** (sense 3). See also **categorical imperative.** 5 *Biology* existing as an organism independent of other organisms or parts. 6 a variant spelling of **autonomic** (sense 3).
▷HISTORY C19: from Greek *autonomos* living under one's own laws, from AUTO- + *nomos* law
▸auˈtonomously ADVERB

autonomy (ɔːˈtɒnəmɪ) NOUN, *plural* **-mies.** 1 the right or state of self-government, esp when limited. 2 a state, community, or individual possessing autonomy. 3 freedom to determine one's own actions, behaviour, etc. 4 *Philosophy* **a** the doctrine that the individual human will is or ought to be governed only by its own principles and laws. See also **categorical imperative. b** the state in which one's actions are autonomous.
▷HISTORY C17: from Greek *autonomia* freedom to live by one's own laws; see AUTONOMOUS
▸auˈtonomist NOUN

autophyte (ˈɔːtəˌfaɪt) NOUN an autotrophic plant, such as any green plant.
▸**autophytic** (ˌɔːtəˈfɪtɪk) ADJECTIVE ▸ˌautoˈphytically ADVERB

autopilot (ˌɔːtəˈpaɪlət, -təʊ-) NOUN short for **automatic pilot.**

autopista (ˌɔːtəˈpiːstə) NOUN a Spanish motorway.
▷HISTORY from Spanish: auto(mobile) track

autoplasty (ˈɔːtəˌplæstɪ) NOUN surgical repair of defects by grafting or transplanting tissue from the patient's own body.
▸ˌautoˈplastic ADJECTIVE

autopolyploid (ˌɔːtəʊˈpɒlɪˌplɔɪd) ADJECTIVE 1 (of cells, organisms, etc.) having more than two sets of haploid chromosomes inherited from a single species. ◆ NOUN 2 an organism or cell of this type. ◆ See also **allopolyploid, polyploid.**
▸ˌautoˈpolyˌploidy NOUN

autopsy (ˈɔːtəpsɪ, ɔːˈtɒp-) NOUN, *plural* **-sies.** 1 Also called: **necropsy, postmortem examination.** dissection and examination of a dead body to determine the cause of death. 2 an eyewitness observation. 3 any critical analysis.
▷HISTORY C17: from New Latin *autopsia*, from Greek: seeing with one's own eyes, from AUTO- + *opsis* sight

autoput (ˈɔːtəʊˌpʊt) NOUN a motorway in the former Yugoslavia.
▷HISTORY from Serbo-Croat: auto(mobile) road

autoradiograph (ˌɔːtəʊˈreɪdɪəˌgrɑːf, -ˌgræf) NOUN a photograph showing the distribution of a radioactive substance in a specimen. The photographic plate is exposed by radiation from the specimen. Also called: **radioautograph.**
▸**autoradiographic** (ˌɔːtəʊˌreɪdɪəˈgræfɪk) ADJECTIVE
▸**autoradiography** (ˌɔːtəʊˌreɪdɪˈɒgrəfɪ) NOUN

autorickshaw (ˈɔːtəʊˈrɪkʃɔː) NOUN (in India) a light three-wheeled vehicle driven by a motorcycle engine.

autorotation (ˌɔːtəʊrəʊˈteɪʃən) NOUN the continuous rotation of a body in an airflow, such as that of the rotor blades of a helicopter in an unpowered descent.

autoroute (ˈɔːtəʊˌruːt) NOUN a French motorway.
▷HISTORY from French, from *auto* car + *route* road

autosome ('ɔːtəˌsəʊm) NOUN any chromosome that is not a sex chromosome.
▸ **ˌauto'somal** ADJECTIVE

autospore ('ɔːtəʊˌspɔː) NOUN a nonmotile algal spore that develops adult characteristics before being released.

autostability (ˌɔːtəʊstə'bɪlɪtɪ) NOUN the property of being stable either as a result of inherent characteristics or of built-in devices.

autostrada ('ɔːtəʊˌstrɑːdə) NOUN an Italian motorway.
▷ HISTORY from Italian, from *auto* car + *strada* road

autosuggestion (ˌɔːtəʊsə'dʒɛstʃən) NOUN a process of suggestion in which the person unconsciously supplies or consciously attempts to supply the means of influencing his own behaviour or beliefs.
▸ **ˌautosug'gestive** ADJECTIVE

autotimer ('ɔːtəʊˌtaɪmə) NOUN a device for turning a system on and off automatically at times predetermined by advance setting.

autotomize *or* **autotomise** (ɔː'tɒtəˌmaɪz) VERB to cause (a part of the body) to undergo autotomy.

autotomy (ɔː'tɒtəmɪ) NOUN, *plural* **-mies.** the casting off by an animal of a part of its body, to facilitate escape when attacked.
▸ **autotomic** (ˌɔːtə'tɒmɪk) ADJECTIVE

autotoxaemia *or US* **autotoxemia** (ˌɔːtəʊtɒk'siːmɪə) NOUN another name for **autointoxication.**

autotoxin (ˌɔːtə'tɒksɪn) NOUN any poison or toxin formed in the organism upon which it acts. See **autointoxication.**
▸ **ˌauto'toxic** ADJECTIVE

autotransformer (ˌɔːtəʊtræns'fɔːmə) NOUN a transformer in which part of the winding is common to both primary and secondary circuits.

autotrophic (ˌɔːtə'trɒfɪk) ADJECTIVE (of organisms such as green plants) capable of manufacturing complex organic nutritive compounds from simple inorganic sources such as carbon dioxide, water, and nitrates, using energy from the sun. Compare **heterotrophic.**
▸ **autotroph** ('ɔːtətrəʊf) NOUN

autotype ('ɔːtəˌtaɪp) NOUN [1] a photographic process for producing prints in black and white, using a carbon pigment. [2] an exact copy of a manuscript, etc.; facsimile.
▸ **autotypic** (ˌɔːtə'tɪpɪk) ADJECTIVE ▸ **'autoˌtypy** NOUN

autowinder ('ɔːtəʊˌwaɪndə) NOUN *Photog* a battery-operated device for advancing the film in a camera automatically after each exposure. Compare **motor drive.**

autoxidation (ɔːˌtɒksɪ'deɪʃən) NOUN *Chem* **a** oxidation by exposure to atmospheric oxygen. **b** oxidation that will only occur when another oxidation reaction is taking place in the same system.

autumn ('ɔːtəm) NOUN [1] (*sometimes capital*) **a** Also called (esp US): **fall.** the season of the year between summer and winter, astronomically from the September equinox to the December solstice in the N hemisphere and from the March equinox to the June solstice in the S hemisphere. **b** (*as modifier*): *autumn leaves.* [2] a period of late maturity, esp one followed by a decline.
▷ HISTORY C14: from Latin *autumnus,* perhaps of Etruscan origin

autumnal (ɔː'tʌmnᵊl) ADJECTIVE of, occurring in, or characteristic of autumn.
▸ **au'tumnally** ADVERB

autumnal equinox NOUN [1] the time at which the sun crosses the plane of the equator away from the relevant hemisphere, making day and night of equal length. It occurs about Sept. 23 in the N hemisphere (March 21 in the S hemisphere). [2] *Astronomy* **a** the point, lying in the constellation Virgo, at which the sun's ecliptic intersects the celestial equator. **b** the time at which this occurs as the sun travels north to south (23 September).

autumn crocus NOUN a liliaceous plant, *Colchicum autumnale,* of Europe and N Africa having pink or purplish autumn flowers. Also called: **meadow saffron.** Compare **saffron.**

autunite ('ɔːtəˌnaɪt) NOUN a yellowish fluorescent radioactive mineral consisting of a hydrated calcium uranium phosphate in tetragonal crystalline form. It is found in uranium ores. Formula: $Ca(UO_2)_2(PO_4)_2.10–12H_2O$.
▷ HISTORY C19: named after *Autun* in France, one of the places where it was found, + -ITE[1]

Auvergne (əʊ'vɛən, əʊ'vɜːn; *French* ovɛrɲ) NOUN a region of S central France: largely mountainous, rising over 1800 m (6000 ft.).

auxanometer (ˌɔːksə'nɒmɪtə) NOUN an instrument that measures the linear growth of plant shoots.
▷ HISTORY C19: from Greek *auxanein* to increase + -METER

Aux Cayes (əʊ 'keɪ; *French* o kaj) NOUN the former name of **Les Cayes.**

Auxerre (*French* ozɛr) NOUN a town in central France, capital of the Yonne department; Gothic cathedral. Pop.: 40 600 (1990).

auxesis (ɔːg'ziːsɪs, ɔːk'siː-) NOUN growth in animal or plant tissues resulting from an increase in cell size without cell division.
▷ HISTORY C16: via Latin from Greek: increase, from *auxein* to increase, grow

auxiliaries (ɔːg'zɪljərɪz, -'zɪlə-) PLURAL NOUN foreign or allied troops serving another nation; mercenaries.

auxiliary (ɔːg'zɪljərɪ, -'zɪlə-) ADJECTIVE [1] secondary or supplementary. [2] supporting. [3] *Nautical* (of a sailing vessel) having an engine: *an auxiliary sloop.* ◆ NOUN, *plural* **-ries.** [4] a person or thing that supports or supplements; subordinate or assistant. [5] *Nautical* **a** a sailing vessel with an engine. **b** the engine of such a vessel. [6] *Navy* a vessel such as a tug, hospital ship, etc., not used for combat.
▷ HISTORY C17: from Latin *auxiliārius* bringing aid, from *auxilium* help, from *augēre* to increase, enlarge, strengthen

auxiliary note NOUN *Music* a nonharmonic note occurring between two harmonic notes.

auxiliary power unit NOUN an additional engine fitted to an aircraft to operate when the main engines are not in use.

auxiliary rotor NOUN the tail rotor of a helicopter, used for directional and rotary control.

auxiliary verb NOUN a verb used to indicate the tense, voice, mood, etc., of another verb where this is not indicated by inflection, such as English *will* in *he will go, was* in *he was eating* and *he was eaten, do* in *I do like you,* etc.

auxin ('ɔːksɪn) NOUN any of various plant hormones, such as indoleacetic acid, that promote growth and control fruit and flower development. Synthetic auxins are widely used in agriculture and horticulture.
▷ HISTORY C20: from Greek *auxein* to grow

auxochrome ('ɔːksəˌkrəʊm) NOUN a group of atoms that can be attached to a chromogen to convert it into a dye.

auxocyte ('ɔːksəˌsaɪt) NOUN any cell undergoing meiosis, esp an oocyte or spermatocyte.

auxospore ('ɔːksəˌspɔː) NOUN a diatom cell before its silicaceous cell wall is formed.

auxotonic (ˌɔːksə'tɒnɪk) ADJECTIVE (of muscle contraction) occurring against increasing force.

auxotroph ('ɔːksətrəʊf) NOUN a mutant strain of microorganism having nutritional requirements additional to those of the normal organism.
▸ **ˌauxo'trophic** ADJECTIVE

Av (æv) *or* **Ab** NOUN (in the Jewish calendar) the fifth month of the year according to biblical reckoning and the eleventh month in the civil year, usually falling within July and August.
▷ HISTORY from Hebrew

AV ABBREVIATION FOR Authorized Version (of the Bible).

av. ABBREVIATION FOR average.

Av. *or* **av.** ABBREVIATION FOR avenue.

a.v. *or* **A/V** ABBREVIATION FOR ad valorem.

a-v, A-V, *or* **AV** ABBREVIATION FOR audiovisual.

ava (ə'vɔː) ADVERB *Scot* at all.
▷ HISTORY Scot form of *of all*

avadavat (ˌævədə'væt) *or* **amadavat** (ˌæmədə'væt) NOUN either of two Asian weaverbirds of the genus *Estrilda,* esp *E. amandava,* having a red plumage: often kept as cagebirds.
▷ HISTORY C18: from *Ahmadabad,* Indian city from which these birds were brought to Europe

avail (ə'veɪl) VERB [1] to be of use, advantage, profit, or assistance (to). [2] **avail oneself of.** to make use of to one's advantage. ◆ NOUN [3] use or advantage (esp in the phrases **of no avail, to little avail**).
▷ HISTORY C13 *availen,* from *vailen,* from Old French *valoir,* from Latin *valēre* to be strong, prevail
▸ **a'vailingly** ADVERB

available (ə'veɪləbᵊl) ADJECTIVE [1] obtainable or accessible; capable of being made use of; at hand. [2] *US politics derogatory* suitable for public office, usually as a result of having an inoffensive character: *Smith was a particularly available candidate.*
▸ **aˌvaila'bility** *or* **a'vailableness** NOUN ▸ **a'vailably** ADVERB

avalanche ('ævəˌlɑːntʃ) NOUN [1] **a** a fall of large masses of snow and ice down a mountain. **b** a fall of rocks, sand, etc. [2] a sudden or overwhelming appearance of a large quantity of things: *an avalanche of letters.* [3] *Physics* a group of ions or electrons produced by a single ion or electron as a result of a collision with some other form of matter. ◆ VERB [4] to come down overwhelmingly (upon).
▷ HISTORY C18: from French, by mistaken division from *la valanche,* from *valanche,* from (northwestern Alps) dialect *lavantse;* related to Old Provençal *lavanca,* of obscure origin

Avalon ('ævəˌlɒn) NOUN *Celtic myth* an island paradise in the western seas: in Arthurian legend it is where King Arthur was taken after he was mortally wounded.
▷ HISTORY from Medieval Latin *insula avallonis* island of Avalon, from Old Welsh *aballon* apple

Avalon Peninsula NOUN a large peninsula of Newfoundland, between Trinity and Placentia Bays. Area: about 10 000 sq. km (4000 sq. miles).

avant- PREFIX of or belonging to the avant-garde of a specified field.

avant-garde (ˌævɒŋ'gɑːd; *French* avɑ̃gard) NOUN [1] those artists, writers, musicians, etc., whose techniques and ideas are markedly experimental or in advance of those generally accepted. ◆ ADJECTIVE [2] of such artists, etc., their ideas, or techniques. [3] radical; daring.
▷ HISTORY from French: VANGUARD
▸ **ˌavant-'gardism** NOUN ▸ **ˌavant-'gardist** NOUN

avantist (æ'vɒntɪst) NOUN short for **avant-gardist.**

Avar ('eɪvɑː, 'ævɑː) NOUN [1] a member of a people of unknown origin in E Europe from the 6th to the early 9th century A.D.: crushed by Charlemagne around 800. [2] a member of a people of the Caucasas. [3] the language of this people, belonging to the North-East Caucasian family.

avarice ('ævərɪs) NOUN extreme greed for riches; cupidity.
▷ HISTORY C13: from Old French, from Latin *avaritia,* from *avārus* covetous, from *avēre* to crave
▸ **ˌava'ricious** ADJECTIVE ▸ **ˌava'riciously** ADVERB
▸ **ˌava'riciousness** NOUN

avascular (ə'væskjʊlə) ADJECTIVE (of certain tissues, such as cartilage) lacking blood vessels.

avast (ə'vɑːst) SENTENCE SUBSTITUTE *Nautical* stop! cease!
▷ HISTORY C17: perhaps from Dutch *hou'vast* hold fast

avatar ('ævəˌtɑː) NOUN [1] *Hinduism* the manifestation of a deity, notably Vishnu, in human, superhuman, or animal form. [2] a visible manifestation or embodiment of an abstract concept; archetype. [3] a movable image that represents a person in a virtual reality environment or in cyberspace.
▷ HISTORY C18: from Sanskrit *avatāra* a going down, from *avatarati* he descends, from *ava* down + *tarati* he passes over

avaunt (ə'vɔːnt) SENTENCE SUBSTITUTE *Archaic* go away! depart!
▷ HISTORY C15: from Old French *avant!* forward!, from Late Latin *ab ante* forward, from Latin *ab* from + *ante* before

AVC ABBREVIATION FOR additional voluntary contribution: one of a series of supplementary payments made to a pension fund.

avdp. ABBREVIATION FOR avoirdupois.

ave ('ɑːvɪ, 'ɑːveɪ) SENTENCE SUBSTITUTE welcome or farewell.
▷ HISTORY Latin

Ave[1] ('ɑːvɪ) NOUN *RC Church* [1] short for **Ave Maria:**

see **Hail Mary**. [2] the time for the Angelus to be recited, so called because of the threefold repetition of the Ave Maria in this devotion. [3] the beads of the rosary used to count the number of Ave Marias said.
▷HISTORY C13: from Latin: hail!

Ave² *or* **ave** ABBREVIATION FOR avenue.

Avebury (ˈeɪvbərɪ) NOUN a village in Wiltshire, site of an extensive neolithic stone circle.

Aveiro (*Portuguese* əˈveːiru) NOUN a port in N central Portugal, on the **Aveiro lagoon**: ancient Roman town; linked by canal with the Atlantic Ocean. Pop.: 35 250 (1991). Ancient name: **Talabriga** (ˌtæləˈbriːgə).

avel (ˈavɛl) NOUN *Judaism* a variant of **ovel**.

Avellaneda (*Spanish* aβeʎaˈneða) NOUN a city in E Argentina, an industrial suburb of Buenos Aires. Pop.: 342 193 (1999 est.).

Ave Maria (məˈriːə) NOUN another name for **Hail Mary**.
▷HISTORY C14: from Medieval Latin: hail, Mary!

avenge (əˈvɛndʒ) VERB (*usually tr*) to inflict a punishment in retaliation for (harm, injury, etc.) done to (a person or persons); take revenge for or on behalf of: *to avenge a crime; to avenge a murdered friend*.
▷HISTORY C14: from Old French *avengier*, from *vengier*, from Latin *vindicāre*; see VENGEANCE, VINDICATE
▸**aˈvenger** NOUN

> **Language note** The use of *avenge* with a reflexive pronoun was formerly considered incorrect, but is now acceptable: *she avenged herself on the man who killed her daughter.*

avens (ˈævɪnz) NOUN, *plural* **-ens**. (*functioning as singular*) [1] any of several temperate or arctic rosaceous plants of the genus *Geum*, such as *G. rivale* (**water avens**), which has a purple calyx and orange-pink flowers. See also **herb bennet**. [2] **mountain avens**. either of two trailing evergreen white-flowered rosaceous shrubs of the genus *Dryas* that grow on mountains in N temperate regions and in the Arctic.
▷HISTORY C15: from Old French *avence*, from Medieval Latin *avencia* variety of clover

Aventine (ˈævɪnˌtaɪn, -tɪn) NOUN one of the seven hills on which Rome was built.

aventurine, aventurin (əˈvɛntjʊrɪn), *or* **avanturine** (əˈvæntjʊrɪn) NOUN [1] a dark-coloured glass, usually green or brown, spangled with fine particles of gold, copper, or some other metal. [2] Also called: **sunstone**. a light-coloured translucent variety of orthoclase feldspar containing reddish-gold particles of iron compounds. [3] a variety of quartz containing red or greenish particles of iron oxide or mica: a gemstone.
▷HISTORY C19: from French, from Italian *avventurina*, from *avventura* chance; so named because usually found by accident; see ADVENTURE

avenue (ˈævɪˌnjuː) NOUN [1] **a** a broad street, often lined with trees. **b** (*capital as part of a street name*) a road, esp in a built-up area: *Shaftesbury Avenue*. [2] a main approach road, as to a country house. [3] a way bordered by two rows of trees: *an avenue of oaks*. [4] a line of approach: *explore every avenue*.
▷HISTORY C17: from French, from *avenir* to come to, from Latin *advenīre*, from *venīre* to come

aver (əˈvɜː) VERB **avers, averring, averred**. (*tr*) [1] to state positively; assert. [2] *Law* to allege as a fact or prove to be true.
▷HISTORY C14: from Old French *averer*, from Medieval Latin *adverāre*, from Latin *vērus* true
▸**aˈverment** NOUN

average (ˈævərɪdʒ, ˈævrɪdʒ) NOUN [1] the typical or normal amount, quality, degree, etc.: *above average in intelligence*. [2] Also called: **arithmetic mean**. the result obtained by adding the numbers or quantities in a set and dividing the total by the number of members in the set: *the average of 3, 4, and 8 is 5*. [3] (of a continuously variable ratio, such as speed) the quotient of the differences between the initial and final values of the two quantities that make up the ratio: *his average over the journey was 30 miles per hour*. [4] *Maritime law* **a** a loss incurred or damage suffered by a ship or its cargo at sea. **b** the equitable apportionment of such loss among the interested parties. [5] (*often plural*) *Stock Exchange* a simple or weighted average of the prices of a selected group of securities computed in order to facilitate market comparisons. [6] **on** (**the** *or* **an**) **average**. usually; typically: *on average, he goes twice a week*. ◆ ADJECTIVE [7] usual or typical. [8] mediocre or inferior: *his performance was only average*. [9] constituting a numerical average: *the average age; an average speed*. [10] approximately typical of a range of values: *the average contents of a matchbox*. ◆ VERB [11] (*tr*) to obtain or estimate a numerical average of. [12] (*tr*) to assess the general quality of. [13] (*tr*) to perform or receive a typical number of: *to average eight hours' work a day*. [14] (*tr*) to divide up proportionately: *they averaged the profits among the staff*. [15] (*tr*) to amount to or be on average: *the children averaged 15 years of age*. [16] (*intr*) *Stock Exchange* to purchase additional securities in a holding whose price has fallen (**average down**) or risen (**average up**) in anticipation of a speculative profit after further increases in price.
▷HISTORY C15 *averay* loss arising from damage to ships or cargoes (shared equitably among all concerned, hence the modern sense), from Old Italian *avaria*, ultimately from Arabic *awār* damage, blemish
▸**ˈaveragely** ADVERB

average adjuster NOUN a person who calculates average claims, esp for marine insurance. See **average** (sense 4).

average deviation NOUN *Statistics* another name for **mean deviation**.

Averno (*Italian* aˈvɛrno) NOUN a crater lake in Italy, near Naples: in ancient times regarded as an entrance to hell. Latin name: **Avernus** (əˈvɜːnəs).
▷HISTORY from Latin, from Greek *aornos* without birds, from A-[1] + *ornis* bird; referring to the legend that the lake's sulphurous exhalations killed birds

Averroism (ˌævəˈrəʊɪzəm, əˈvɛrəʊ-) NOUN the teachings of Averroës (Arabic name *ibn-Rushd*; 1126–88), the Arab philosopher and physician in Spain.
▸**ˌAverˈroist** NOUN ▸**ˌAverroˈistic** ADJECTIVE

averse (əˈvɜːs) ADJECTIVE [1] (*postpositive*; usually foll by *to*) opposed, disinclined, or loath. [2] (of leaves, flowers, etc.) turned away from the main stem. Compare **adverse** (sense 4).
▷HISTORY C16: from Latin *āversus*, from *āvertere* to turn from, from *vertere* to turn
▸**aˈversely** ADVERB ▸**aˈverseness** NOUN

aversion (əˈvɜːʃən) NOUN [1] (usually foll by *to* or *for*) extreme dislike or disinclination; repugnance. [2] a person or thing that arouses this: *he is my pet aversion*.

aversion therapy NOUN *Psychiatry* a method of suppressing an undesirable habit, such as excessive smoking, by causing the subject to associate an unpleasant effect, such as an electric shock or nausea, with the habit.

aversive (əˈvɜːsɪv) ADJECTIVE tending to dissuade or repel.
▸**aˈversively** ADVERB

avert (əˈvɜːt) VERB (*tr*) [1] to turn away or aside: *to avert one's gaze*. [2] to ward off; prevent from occurring: *to avert danger*.
▷HISTORY C15: from Old French *avertir*, from Latin *āvertere*; see AVERSE
▸**aˈvertible** *or* **aˈvertable** ADJECTIVE

Aves (ˈeɪviːz) PLURAL NOUN the class of vertebrates comprising the birds. See **bird** (sense 1).
▷HISTORY pl of Latin *avis* bird

Avesta (əˈvɛstə) NOUN a collection of sacred writings of Zoroastrianism, including the Songs of Zoroaster.

Avestan (əˈvɛstən) *or* **Avestic** (əˈvɛstɪk) NOUN [1] the oldest recorded language of the Iranian branch of the Indo-European family; the language of the Avesta. Formerly called: **Zend**. ◆ ADJECTIVE [2] of or relating to the Avesta or its language.

Aveyron (*French* avɛrɔ̃) NOUN a department of S France in Midi-Pyrénées region. Capital: Rodez. Pop.: 263 808 (1999). Area: 8771 sq. km (3421 sq. miles).

avgolemono (ˌævgəˈlɛmənəʊ) NOUN a Greek soup made with eggs, lemon juice, and rice.
▷HISTORY C20: from Modern Greek

avian (ˈeɪvɪən) ADJECTIVE of, relating to, or resembling a bird.
▷HISTORY C19: from Latin *avis* bird

aviarist (ˈeɪvjərɪst) NOUN a person who keeps an aviary.

aviary (ˈeɪvjərɪ) NOUN, *plural* **aviaries**. a large enclosure in which birds are kept.
▷HISTORY C16: from Latin *aviārium*, from *aviārius* concerning birds, from *avis* bird

aviate (ˈeɪvɪˌeɪt) VERB to pilot or fly in an aircraft.

aviation (ˌeɪvɪˈeɪʃən) NOUN [1] **a** the art or science of flying aircraft. **b** the design, production, and maintenance of aircraft. [2] *US* military aircraft collectively.
▷HISTORY C19: from French, from Latin *avis* bird

aviation medicine NOUN the branch of medicine concerned with the effects on man of flight in the earth's atmosphere. Compare **space medicine**.

aviator (ˈeɪvɪˌeɪtə) NOUN *Old-fashioned* the pilot of an aeroplane or airship; flyer.
▸**ˈaviˌatrix** *or* **ˈaviˌatress** FEMININE NOUN

aviculture (ˈeɪvɪˌkʌltʃə) NOUN the keeping and rearing of birds.
▸**ˌaviˈculturist** NOUN

avid (ˈævɪd) ADJECTIVE [1] very keen; enthusiastic: *an avid reader*. [2] (*postpositive*; often foll by *for* or *of*) eager (for); desirous (of); greedy (for): *avid for revenge*.
▷HISTORY C18: from Latin *avidus*, from *avēre* to long for
▸**ˈavidly** ADVERB

avidin (ˈævɪdɪn, əˈvɪdɪn) NOUN a protein, found in egg-white, that combines with biotin to form a stable compound that cannot be absorbed, leading to a biotin deficiency in the consumer.
▷HISTORY C20: from AVID + (BIO)IN; from its characteristic avidity for biotin

avidity (əˈvɪdɪtɪ) NOUN [1] the quality or state of being avid. [2] **a** eagerness. **b** greed; avarice. [3] *Chem* **a** the strength of an acid or base in proportion to its degree of dissociation. **b** another term for **affinity** (sense 6b). [4] *Immunol* a measure of antigen-to-antibody binding, based on the rate of formation of the complex.

Aviemore (ˌævɪˈmɔː) NOUN a winter sports resort in Scotland, in Moray between the Monadhliath and Cairngorm Mountains. Pop.: 2214 (1991).

avifauna (ˌeɪvɪˈfɔːnə) NOUN all the birds in a particular region.
▸**ˌaviˈfaunal** ADJECTIVE

Avignon (*French* aviɲɔ̃) NOUN a city in SE France, on the Rhône: seat of the papacy (1309–77); famous 12th-century bridge, now partly destroyed. Pop.: 181 136 (1990).

Ávila (*Spanish* ˈaβila) NOUN a city in central Spain: 11th-century granite walls and Romanesque cathedral. Pop.: 45 092 (1988 est.).

avionics (ˌeɪvɪˈɒnɪks) NOUN [1] (*functioning as singular*) the science and technology of electronics applied to aeronautics and astronautics. [2] (*functioning as plural*) the electronic circuits and devices of an aerospace vehicle.
▷HISTORY C20: from *avi(ation electr)onics*
▸**ˌaviˈonic** ADJECTIVE

avirulent (æˈvɪrʊlənt) ADJECTIVE (esp of bacteria) not virulent.

avitaminosis (æˌvɪtəmɪnˈəʊsɪs, ˌævɪˌtæmɪˈnəʊsɪs) NOUN, *plural* **-ses** (-siːz). any disease caused by a vitamin deficiency in the diet.

avizandum (ˌævɪˈzændəm) NOUN *Scots Law* **a** a judge's or court's decision to consider a case privately before giving judgment. **b** a judge's or court's private consideration of a case before giving judgment. **c** the period during which judgment is delayed in these circumstances. A judge or court makes avizandum when time is needed to consider arguments or submissions made. ◆ Compare **CAV**.
▷HISTORY from Medieval Latin, from *avizare* to consider; see ADVISE

Avlona (ævˈləʊnə) NOUN the ancient name for **Vlorë**.

AVM (in Britain) ABBREVIATION FOR Air Vice-Marshal.

avn ABBREVIATION FOR aviation.

avocado (ˌævəˈkɑːdəʊ) NOUN, *plural* **-dos**. [1] a pear-shaped fruit having a leathery green or

blackish skin, a large stony seed, and a greenish-yellow edible pulp. 2 the tropical American lauraceous tree, *Persea americana,* that bears this fruit. 3 a dull greenish colour resembling that of the fruit. ◆ Also called (for senses 1, 2): **avocado pear, alligator pear.**
▷**HISTORY** C17: from Spanish *aguacate,* from Nahuatl *ahuacatl* testicle, alluding to the shape of the fruit

avocation (ˌævəˈkeɪʃən) NOUN 1 *Formal* a minor occupation undertaken as a diversion. 2 *Not standard* a person's regular job or vocation.
▷**HISTORY** C17: from Latin *āvocātiō* a calling away, diversion from, from *āvocāre* to distract, from *vocāre* to call

avocet (ˈævəˌsɛt) NOUN any of several long-legged shore birds of the genus *Recurvirostra,* such as the European *R. avosetta,* having black-and-white plumage and a long upward-curving bill: family *Recurvirostridae,* order *Charadriiformes.*
▷**HISTORY** C18: from French *avocette,* from Italian *avocetta,* of uncertain origin

Avogadro's constant *or* **number** NOUN the number of atoms or molecules in a mole of a substance, equal to $6.022\,52 \times 10^{23}$. Symbol: L or N_A.
▷**HISTORY** named after Amedeo *Avogadro* (1776–1856), Italian physicist

Avogadro's law *or* **hypothesis** NOUN the principle that equal volumes of all gases contain the same number of molecules at the same temperature and pressure.

avoid (əˈvɔɪd) VERB (*tr*) 1 to keep out of the way of. 2 to refrain from doing. 3 to prevent from happening: *to avoid damage to machinery.* 4 *Law* to make (a plea, contract, etc.) void; invalidate; quash. 5 *Obsolete* to expel. 6 *Obsolete* to depart from.
▷**HISTORY** C14: from Anglo-French *avoider,* from Old French *esvuidier,* from *vuidier* to empty, VOID
▸**aˈvoidable** ADJECTIVE ▸**aˈvoidably** ADVERB ▸**aˈvoider** NOUN

avoidance (əˈvɔɪdəns) NOUN 1 the act of keeping away from or preventing from happening. 2 *Law* **a** the act of annulling or making void. **b** the countering of an opponent's plea with fresh evidence. 3 *Ecclesiastical law* the state of a benefice having no incumbent.

avoidant (əˈvɔɪdənt) ADJECTIVE (of behaviour) demonstrating a tendency to avoid intimacy or interaction with others.

avoirdupois *or* **avoirdupois weight** (ˌævədəˈpɔɪz, ˌævwɑːdjuːˈpwɑː) NOUN a system of weights used in many English-speaking countries. It is based on the pound, which contains 16 ounces or 7000 grains. 100 pounds (US) or 112 pounds (Brit.) is equal to 1 hundredweight and 20 hundredweights equals 1 ton. Abbreviations: **avdp, avoir.**
▷**HISTORY** C14: from Old French *aver de peis* goods of weight

Avon (ˈeɪvᵊn) NOUN 1 a former county of SW England, created in 1974 from areas of N Somerset and S Gloucestershire: replaced in 1996 by the unitary authorities of Bath and North East Somerset (Somerset), North Somerset (Somerset), South Gloucestershire (Gloucestershire), and Bristol. 2 a river in central England, rising in Northamptonshire and flowing southwest through Stratford-on-Avon to the River Severn at Tewkesbury. Length: 154 km (96 miles). 3 a river in SW England, rising in Gloucestershire and flowing south and west through Bristol to the Severn estuary at **Avonmouth**. Length: 120 km (75 miles). 4 a river in S England, rising in Wiltshire and flowing south to the English Channel. Length: about 96 km (60 miles).

avouch (əˈvaʊtʃ) VERB (*tr*) *Archaic* 1 to vouch for; guarantee. 2 to acknowledge. 3 to assert.
▷**HISTORY** C16: from Old French *avochier* to summon, call on, from Latin *advocāre;* see ADVOCATE
▸**aˈvouchment** NOUN

avow (əˈvaʊ) VERB (*tr*) 1 to state or affirm. 2 to admit openly. 3 *Law, rare* to justify or maintain (some action taken).
▷**HISTORY** C13: from Old French *avouer* to confess, from Latin *advocāre* to appeal to, call upon; see AVOUCH, ADVOCATE
▸**aˈvowable** ADJECTIVE ▸**aˈvowal** NOUN ▸**avowed** (əˈvaʊd) ADJECTIVE ▸**avowedly** (əˈvaʊɪdlɪ) ADVERB ▸**aˈvower** NOUN

avruga (əˈvruːɡə) NOUN herring roe with a smoky flavour, sometimes used as a less expensive alternative to caviar.
▷**HISTORY** Spanish

avulsion (əˈvʌlʃən) NOUN 1 a forcible tearing away or separation of a bodily structure or part, either as the result of injury or as an intentional surgical procedure. 2 *Law* the sudden removal of soil from one person's land to that of another, as by flooding.
▷**HISTORY** C17: from Latin *āvulsiō,* from *āvellere* to pluck away, from *vellere* to pull, pluck

avuncular (əˈvʌŋkjʊlə) ADJECTIVE 1 of or concerned with an uncle. 2 resembling an uncle; friendly; helpful.
▷**HISTORY** C19: from Latin *avunculus* (maternal) uncle, diminutive of *avus* grandfather

avunculate (əˈvʌŋkjʊlɪt) NOUN 1 the custom in some societies of assigning rights and duties to a maternal uncle concerning his sister's son. ◆ ADJECTIVE 2 of, relating to, or governed by this custom.

aw[1] (ɔː) DETERMINER *Scot* a variant spelling of **a'** (all).

aw[2] (ɔː) INTERJECTION *Informal, chiefly US* an expression of disapproval, commiseration, or appeal.

aw[3] THE INTERNET DOMAIN NAME FOR Aruba.

AWA ABBREVIATION FOR Amalgamated Wireless (Australasia) Ltd.

awa' (əˈwɔː) ADVERB *Scot* away; departed; onward.

AWACS *or* **Awacs** (ˈeɪwæks) NOUN ACRONYM FOR airborne warning and control system.

await (əˈweɪt) VERB 1 (*tr*) to wait for; expect. 2 (*tr*) to be in store for. 3 (*intr*) to wait, esp with expectation. 4 (*tr*) *Obsolete* to wait for in order to ambush.

awake (əˈweɪk) VERB **awakes, awaking; awoke** *or* **awaked; awoken** *or* **awaked.** 1 to emerge or rouse from sleep; wake. 2 to become or cause to become alert. 3 (usually foll by *to*) to become or make aware (of): *to awake to reality.* 4 Also: **awaken.** (*tr*) to arouse (feelings, etc.) or cause to remember (memories, etc.). ◆ ADJECTIVE (*postpositive*) 5 not sleeping. 6 (sometimes foll by *to*) lively or alert.
▷**HISTORY** Old English *awacian, awacan;* see WAKE[1]

Language note See at **wake**[1].

awakening (əˈweɪkənɪŋ, əˈweɪknɪŋ) NOUN the start of a feeling or awareness in a person: *a picture of an emotional awakening.*

award (əˈwɔːd) VERB (*tr*) 1 to give (something due), esp as a reward for merit: *to award prizes.* 2 *Law* to declare to be entitled, as by decision of a court of law or an arbitrator. ◆ NOUN 3 something awarded, such as a prize or medal: *an award for bravery.* 4 (in Australia and New Zealand) the amount of an award wage (esp in the phrase **above award**). 5 *Law* **a** the decision of an arbitrator. **b** a grant made by a court of law, esp of damages in a civil action.
▷**HISTORY** C14: from Anglo-Norman *awarder,* from Old Northern French *eswarder* to decide after investigation, from *es-* EX-[1] + *warder* to observe; see WARD
▸**aˈwardable** ADJECTIVE ▸**aˌwardˈee** NOUN ▸**aˈwarder** NOUN

award wage NOUN (in Australia and New Zealand) statutory minimum pay for a particular group of workers. Sometimes shortened to: **award.**

aware (əˈwɛə) ADJECTIVE 1 (*postpositive;* foll by *of*) having knowledge; cognizant: *aware of his error.* 2 informed of current developments: *politically aware.*
▷**HISTORY** Old English *gewær;* related to Old Saxon, Old High German *giwar* Latin *verērī* to be fearful; see BEWARE, WARY
▸**aˈwareness** NOUN

awash (əˈwɒʃ) ADVERB, ADJECTIVE (*postpositive*) *Nautical* 1 at a level even with the surface of the sea. 2 washed over by the waves.

away (əˈweɪ) ADVERB 1 from a particular place; off: *to swim away.* 2 in or to another, usual, or proper place: *to put toys away.* 3 apart; at a distance: *to keep away from strangers.* 4 out of existence: *the music faded away.* 5 indicating motion, displacement, transfer, etc., from a normal or proper place, from a person's own possession, etc.: *to turn one's head away; to give away money.* 6 indicating activity that is wasteful or designed to get rid of something: *to sleep away the hours.* 7 continuously: *laughing away; fire away.* 8 **away with.** a command for a person to go or be removed: *away with you; away with him to prison!* 9 **far and away.** by a very great margin: *far and away the biggest meal he'd ever eaten.* 10 **from away.** *Canadian* from a part of Canada other than Newfoundland. ◆ ADJECTIVE (*usually postpositive*) 11 not present: *away from school.* 12 distant: *he is a good way away.* 13 having started; released: *he was away before sunrise; bombs away!* 14 (*also prenominal*) *Sport* played on an opponent's ground: *an away game.* 15 *Golf* (of a ball or player) farthest from the hole. 16 *Baseball* (of a player) having been put out. 17 *Horse racing* relating to the outward portion or first half of a race. ◆ NOUN 18 *Sport* a game played or won at an opponent's ground. ◆ INTERJECTION 19 an expression of dismissal.
▷**HISTORY** Old English *on weg* on way

awayday (əˈweɪˌdeɪ) NOUN a trip taken for pleasure, relaxation, etc.; day excursion.
▷**HISTORY** C20: from *awayday ticket,* name applied to some special-rate railway day returns

awe (ɔː) NOUN 1 overwhelming wonder, admiration, respect, or dread. 2 *Archaic* power to inspire fear or reverence. ◆ VERB 3 (*tr*) to inspire with reverence or dread.
▷**HISTORY** C13: from Old Norse *agi;* related to Gothic *agis* fear, Greek *akhesthai* to be grieved
▸**ˈaweless** *or US* **ˈawless** ADJECTIVE

aweather (əˈwɛðə) ADVERB, ADJECTIVE (*postpositive*) *Nautical* towards the weather: *with the helm aweather.* Compare **alee.**

aweigh (əˈweɪ) ADJECTIVE (*postpositive*) *Nautical* (of an anchor) no longer hooked into the bottom; hanging by its rode.

awe-inspiring ADJECTIVE causing or worthy of admiration or respect; amazing or magnificent.

awesome (ˈɔːsəm) ADJECTIVE 1 inspiring or displaying awe. 2 *Slang* excellent or outstanding.
▸**ˈawesomely** ADVERB ▸**ˈawesomeness** NOUN

awestruck (ˈɔːˌstrʌk) *or* **awe-stricken** ADJECTIVE overcome or filled with awe.

awful (ˈɔːfʊl) ADJECTIVE 1 nasty or ugly. 2 *Archaic* inspiring reverence or dread. 3 *Archaic* overcome with awe; reverential. ◆ ADVERB 4 *Not standard* (intensifier): *an awful cold day.*
▷**HISTORY** C13: see AWE, -FUL
▸**ˈawfulness** NOUN

awfully (ˈɔːfəlɪ, ˈɔːflɪ) ADVERB 1 in an unpleasant, bad, or reprehensible manner. 2 *Informal* (intensifier): *I'm awfully keen to come.* 3 *Archaic* so as to express or inspire awe.

awheel (əˈwiːl) ADVERB on wheels.

awhile (əˈwaɪl) ADVERB for a brief period.

awkward (ˈɔːkwəd) ADJECTIVE 1 lacking dexterity, proficiency, or skill; clumsy; inept: *the new recruits were awkward in their exercises.* 2 ungainly or inelegant in movements or posture: *despite a great deal of practice she remained an awkward dancer.* 3 unwieldy; difficult to use: *an awkward implement.* 4 embarrassing: *an awkward moment.* 5 embarrassed: *he felt awkward about leaving.* 6 difficult to deal with; requiring tact: *an awkward situation; an awkward customer.* 7 deliberately uncooperative or unhelpful: *he could help but he is being awkward.* 8 dangerous or difficult: *an awkward ascent of the ridge.* 9 *Obsolete* perverse.
▷**HISTORY** C14 *awk,* from Old Norse *öfugr* turned the wrong way round + -WARD
▸**ˈawkwardly** ADVERB ▸**ˈawkwardness** NOUN

awl (ɔːl) NOUN a pointed hand tool with a fluted blade used for piercing wood, leather, etc. See also **bradawl.**
▷**HISTORY** Old English *æl;* related to Old Norse *alr,* Old High German *āla,* Dutch *aal,* Sanskrit *ārā*

awlwort (ˈɔːlˌwɜːt) NOUN a small stemless aquatic plant, *Subularia aquatica,* of the N hemisphere, having slender sharp-pointed leaves and minute, often submerged, white flowers: family *Brassicaceae* (crucifers).

awn (ɔːn) NOUN any of the bristles growing from the spikelets of certain grasses, including cereals.
▷**HISTORY** Old English *agen* ear of grain; related to

Old Norse *ǫgn* chaff, Gothic *ahana,* Old High German *agana,* Greek *akōn* javelin
▸**awned** ADJECTIVE ▸**'awnless** ADJECTIVE

awning ('ɔ:nɪŋ) NOUN a roof of canvas or other material supported by a frame to provide protection from the weather, esp one placed over a doorway or part of a deck of a ship.
▷HISTORY C17: of uncertain origin

awoke (ə'wəʊk) VERB a past tense or (now rare or dialectal) past participle of **awake.**

AWOL ('eɪwɒl) *or* **A.W.O.L.** ADJECTIVE *Military* absent without leave; absent from one's post or duty without official permission but without intending to desert.

AWRE ABBREVIATION FOR Atomic Weapons Research Establishment.

awry (ə'raɪ) ADVERB, ADJECTIVE *(postpositive)* 1 with a slant or twist to one side; askew. 2 away from the appropriate or right course; amiss.
▷HISTORY C14 *on wry;* see A-[2], WRY

AWS ABBREVIATION FOR automatic warning system: a train safety system which gives audible warnings about the signals being passed, and can apply the brakes automatically if necessary.

aw-shucks (,ɔ:'ʃʌks) ADJECTIVE *(prenominal)* seeming to be modest, self-deprecating, or shy: *don't be fooled by his aw-shucks attitude.*
▷HISTORY C20: from the US interjection *aw shucks,* an expression of modesty or diffidence

AWU ABBREVIATION FOR Australian Workers' Union.

axe *or US* **ax** (æks) NOUN, *plural* **axes.** 1 a hand tool with one side of its head forged and sharpened to a cutting edge, used for felling trees, splitting timber, etc. See also **hatchet.** 2 **an axe to grind. a** an ulterior motive. **b** a grievance. **c** a pet subject. 3 **the axe.** *Informal* **a** dismissal, esp from employment; the sack (esp in the phrase **get the axe**). **b** *Brit* severe cutting down of expenditure, esp the removal of unprofitable sections of a public service. 4 *US slang* any musical instrument, esp a guitar or horn. ◆ VERB *(tr)* 5 to chop or trim with an axe. 6 *Informal* to dismiss (employees), restrict (expenditure or services), or terminate (a project).
▷HISTORY Old English *æx;* related to Old Frisian *axa,* Old High German *acchus,* Old Norse *öx,* Latin *ascia,* Greek *axinē*

axebird ('æksbɜ:d) NOUN *Austral* a nightjar of northern Queensland and New Guinea with a cry that sounds like a chopping axe.

axe-breaker NOUN *Austral* an Australian oleaceous tree, *Notelaea longifolia,* yielding very hard timber.

axel ('æksəl) NOUN *Skating* a jump in which the skater takes off from the forward outside edge of one skate, makes one and a half, two and a half, or three and a half turns in the air, and lands on the backward outside edge of the other skate.
▷HISTORY C20: named after *Axel* Paulsen (died 1938), Norwegian skater

axeman *or US* **axman** ('æksmən) NOUN, *plural* **-men.** 1 a man who wields an axe, esp to cut down trees. 2 a person who makes cuts in expenditure or services, esp on behalf of another: *the chancellor's axeman.* 3 *US slang* a man who plays a musical instrument, esp a guitar.

axenic (eɪ'zi:nɪk) ADJECTIVE (of a biological culture or culture medium) free from other microorganisms; uncontaminated.
▷HISTORY C20: see A-[1], XENO-, -IC

axes[1] ('æksi:z) NOUN the plural of **axis**[1].

axes[2] ('æksɪz) NOUN the plural of **axe.**

axial ('æksɪəl) ADJECTIVE 1 relating to, forming, or characteristic of an axis. 2 situated in, on, or along an axis.
▸**,axi'ality** NOUN ▸**'axially** ADVERB

axial-flow compressor NOUN a device for compressing a gas by accelerating it tangentially by means of bladed rotors, to increase its kinetic energy, and then diffusing it through static vanes (stators), to increase its pressure.

axial skeleton NOUN the bones that together comprise the skull and the vertebral column.

axial vector NOUN another name for **pseudovector.**

axil ('æksɪl) NOUN the angle between the upper surface of a branch or leafstalk and the stem from which it grows.
▷HISTORY C18: from Latin *axilla* armpit

axile ('æksɪl, -saɪl) ADJECTIVE *Botany* of, relating to, or attached to the axis.

axilemma (,æksɪ'lɛmə) NOUN a variant spelling of **axolemma.**

axilla (æk'sɪlə) NOUN, *plural* **-lae** (-li:). 1 the technical name for the **armpit.** 2 the area on the undersurface of a bird's wing corresponding to the armpit.
▷HISTORY C17: from Latin: armpit

axillary (æk'sɪlərɪ) ADJECTIVE 1 of, relating to, or near the armpit. 2 *Botany* growing in or related to the axil: *an axillary bud.* ◆ NOUN, *plural* **-laries.** 3 *(usually plural)* Also called: **axillar** (æk'sɪlə, 'æksɪlə). one of the feathers growing from the axilla of a bird's wing.

axiology (,æksɪ'ɒlədʒɪ) NOUN *Philosophy* the theory of values, moral or aesthetic.
▷HISTORY C20: from Greek *axios* worthy
▸**axiological** (,æksɪə'lɒdʒɪkəl) ADJECTIVE ▸**,axio'logically** ADVERB ▸**,axi'ologist** NOUN

axiom ('æksɪəm) NOUN 1 a generally accepted proposition or principle, sanctioned by experience; maxim. 2 a universally established principle or law that is not a necessary truth: *the axioms of politics.* 3 a self-evident statement. 4 *Logic, maths* a statement or formula that is stipulated to be true for the purpose of a chain of reasoning: the foundation of a formal deductive system. Compare **assumption** (sense 4).
▷HISTORY C15: from Latin *axiōma* a principle, from Greek, from *axioun* to consider worthy, from *axios* worthy

axiomatic (,æksɪə'mætɪk) *or* **axiomatical** ADJECTIVE 1 relating to or resembling an axiom; self-evident. 2 containing maxims; aphoristic. 3 (of a logical system) consisting of a set of axioms from which theorems are derived by **transformation rules.** Compare **natural deduction.**
▸**,axio'matically** ADVERB

axion ('æksɪ,ɒn) NOUN *Physics* a hypothetical neutral elementary particle postulated to account for certain conservation laws in the strong interaction.
▷HISTORY C20: from AXI(OM) + -ON

axis[1] ('æksɪs) NOUN, *plural* **axes** ('æksi:z). 1 a real or imaginary line about which a body, such as an aircraft, can rotate or about which an object, form, composition, or geometrical construction is symmetrical. 2 one of two or three reference lines used in coordinate geometry to locate a point in a plane or in space. 3 *Anatomy* the second cervical vertebra. Compare **atlas** (sense 3). 4 *Botany* the main central part of a plant, typically consisting of the stem and root, from which secondary branches and other parts develop. 5 an alliance between a number of states to coordinate their foreign policy. 6 Also called: **principal axis.** *Optics* the line of symmetry of an optical system, such as the line passing through the centre of a lens. 7 *Geology* an imaginary line along the crest of an anticline or the trough of a syncline. 8 *Crystallog* one of three lines passing through the centre of a crystal and used to characterize its symmetry.
▷HISTORY C14: from Latin: axletree, earth's axis; related to Greek *axōn* axis

axis[2] ('æksɪs) NOUN, *plural* **axises.** any of several S Asian deer of the genus *Axis,* esp *A. axis.* They typically have a reddish-brown white-spotted coat and slender antlers.
▷HISTORY C18: from Latin: Indian wild animal, of uncertain identity

Axis ('æksɪs) NOUN **a the.** the alliance of Nazi Germany, Fascist Italy, and Japan, established in 1936 and lasting until their defeat in World War II. **b** *(as modifier)*: *the Axis powers.*

axis of evil NOUN North Korea, Iraq, and Iran when considered together as a perceived threat to world stability.
▷HISTORY C21: coined by George W Bush, 43rd US President

axle ('æksəl) NOUN a bar or shaft on which a wheel, pair of wheels, or other rotating member revolves.
▷HISTORY C17: from Old Norse *öxull;* related to German *Achse;* see AXIS[1]

axletree ('æksəl,tri:) NOUN a bar fixed across the underpart of a wagon or carriage that has rounded ends on which the wheels revolve.

Axminster carpet ('æks,mɪnstə) NOUN a type of patterned carpet with a cut pile. Often shortened to: **Axminster.**
▷HISTORY after *Axminster,* in Devon, where such carpets are made

axolemma (,æksə'lɛmə) *or* **axilemma** NOUN the membrane that encloses the axon of a nerve cell.

axolotl ('æksə,lɒtəl) NOUN 1 any of several aquatic salamanders of the North American genus *Ambystoma,* esp *A. mexicanum* (**Mexican axolotl**), in which the larval form (including external gills) is retained throughout life under natural conditions (see **neoteny**): family *Ambystomidae.* 2 any of various other North American salamanders in which neoteny occurs or is induced.
▷HISTORY C18: from Nahuatl, from *atl* water + *xolotl* servant, doll

axon ('æksɒn) *or* **axone** ('æksəʊn) NOUN the long threadlike extension of a nerve cell that conducts nerve impulses from the cell body. Compare **dendrite.**
▷HISTORY C19: via New Latin from Greek: axis, axle, vertebra
▸**'axonal** ADJECTIVE

axonometric projection (,æksənə'mɛtrɪk) NOUN a geometric drawing of an object, such as a building, in three dimensions showing the verticals and horizontals projected to scale but with diagonals and curves distorted, so that the whole appears inclined.

axonometry (,æksə'nɒmɪtrɪ) NOUN the branch of crystallography concerned with measurement of the axes of crystals.

axseed ('æks,si:d) NOUN another name for **crown vetch.**

Axum ('ɑ:ksum) NOUN a variant spelling of **Aksum.**

ay[1] (eɪ) ADVERB *Archaic, poetic* ever; always.
▷HISTORY C12 *ai,* from Old Norse *ei;* related to Old English *ā* always, Latin *aevum* an age, Greek *aiōn*

ay[2] *or* **aye** (eɪ) INTERJECTION *Archaic, poetic* an expression of misery or surprise.
▷HISTORY C14 *ey:* from an involuntary cry of surprise

ay[3] (aɪ) SENTENCE SUBSTITUTE, NOUN a variant spelling of **aye**[1].

Ayacucho (*Spanish* aja'kutʃo) NOUN a city in SE Peru: nearby is the site of the battle (1824) that won independence for Peru. Pop.: 118 960 (1998 est.).

ayah ('aɪə) NOUN (in the East, Africa, and other parts of the former British Empire) a maidservant, nursemaid, or governess, esp one of Indian or Malay origin. Compare **amah.**
▷HISTORY C18: from Hindi *āyā,* from Portuguese *aia,* from Latin *avia* grandmother

ayahuasca (,aɪə'wɑ:skə) NOUN a Brazilian plant, *Banisteriopsis caapi,* that has winged fruits and yields a powerful hallucinogenic alkaloid sometimes used to treat certain disorders of the central nervous system: family *Malpighiaceae.*
▷HISTORY C20: from Quechua

ayatollah (,aɪə'tɒlə) NOUN one of a class of Iranian Shiite religious leaders.
▷HISTORY via Persian from Arabic, from *aya* sign + *Allah* god

Aycliffe ('eɪklɪf) NOUN a town in Co. Durham: founded as a new town in 1947. Pop.: 40 000 (latest est.).

Aydin *or* **Aidin** ('aɪdɪn) NOUN a town in SW Turkey: an ancient city of Lydia. Pop.: 133 757 (1997). Ancient name: **Tralles.**

aye[1] *or* **ay** (aɪ) SENTENCE SUBSTITUTE 1 yes: archaic or dialectal except in voting by voice. 2 **aye aye. a** an expression of compliance, esp used by seamen. **b** *Brit* an expression of amused surprise, esp at encountering something that confirms one's suspicions, expectations, etc. ◆ NOUN 3 **a** a person who votes in the affirmative. **b** an affirmative vote. ◆ Compare **nay.**
▷HISTORY C16: probably from pronoun *I,* expressing assent

aye[2] (əɪ) ADVERB *Scot* always; still.
▷HISTORY Old Norse *ei* ever; Old English *ā;* compare Latin *aevum* an age, Greek *aion* aeon, *aiei* ever, always

aye-aye ('aɪ,aɪ) NOUN a rare nocturnal arboreal prosimian primate of Madagascar, *Daubentonia*

madagascariensis, related to the lemurs: family *Daubentoniidae*. It has long bony fingers and rodent-like incisor teeth adapted for feeding on insect larvae and bamboo pith.
▷HISTORY C18: from French, from Malagasy *aiay*, probably of imitative origin

Ayers Rock (ɛəz) NOUN the former name of **Uluru**.

ayin (ˈɑːjɪn; *Hebrew* ˈaji:n) NOUN the 16th letter in the Hebrew alphabet (ע), originally a pharyngeal fricative, that is now silent and transliterated by a raised inverted comma (ʽ).
▷HISTORY Hebrew

Aylesbury (ˈeɪlzbərɪ, -brɪ) NOUN a town in SE central England, administrative centre of Buckinghamshire. Pop.: 58 058 (1991).

Aymara (ˌaɪməˈrɑː) NOUN 1 (*plural* **-ras** *or* **-ra**) a member of a South American Indian people of Bolivia and Peru. 2 the language of this people, probably related to Quechua.
▷HISTORY from Spanish *aimará*, of American Indian origin
▸ˌ**Aymaˈran** ADJECTIVE

Ayodha (ɑːɪˈjəʊdjɑː) NOUN an ancient town in N India, in Uttar Pradesh state: as the birthplace of Rama it is sacred to Hindus; also a Buddhist centre. Also called: **Awadh** (əˈwɒd), **Oudh** (aʊd).

ayont (əˈjɒnt) ADVERB, PREPOSITION *Scot* beyond.
▷HISTORY *a*, from Old English *an* on + *yont* YON

Ayr (ɛə) NOUN a port in SW Scotland, in South Ayrshire. Pop.: 47 962 (1991).

Ayrshire (ˈɛəʃɪə, -ʃə) NOUN 1 a historical county of SW Scotland, formerly part of Strathclyde region (1975–96), now divided into the council areas of North Ayrshire, South Ayrshire, and East Ayrshire. 2 any one of a hardy breed of brown-and-white dairy cattle.

Ayurveda (ˈɑːjʊˌveɪdə, -ˌviːdə) NOUN *Hinduism* an ancient medical treatise on the art of healing and prolonging life, sometimes regarded as a fifth Veda.
▷HISTORY from Sanskrit, from *āyur* life + *veda* knowledge
▸ˌ**Ayurˈvedic** ADJECTIVE

Ayutthaya (ɑːˈjuːtəjə) NOUN a city in S Thailand, on the Chao Phraya River: capital of the country until 1767; noted for its canals and ruins. Pop.: 61 185 (1990). Also called: **Ayudhya** (ɑːˈjuːdjə), **Ayuthia** (ɑːˈjuːθɪə).

az THE INTERNET DOMAIN NAME FOR Azerbaijan.

AZ 1 ABBREVIATION FOR Arizona. ◆ 2 INTERNATIONAL CAR REGISTRATION FOR Azerbaijan.

az. ABBREVIATION FOR azimuth.

aza- *or before a vowel* **az-** COMBINING FORM denoting the presence of nitrogen, esp a nitrogen atom in place of a -CH group or an -NH group in place of a -CH_2 group: *azathioprine*.
▷HISTORY C20: from AZ(O)- + *-a-*

azalea (əˈzeɪljə) NOUN any ericaceous plant of the group *Azalea*, formerly a separate genus but now included in the genus *Rhododendron*: cultivated for their showy pink or purple flowers.
▷HISTORY C18: via New Latin from Greek, from *azaleos* dry; from its supposed preference for a dry situation

azan (ɑːˈzɑːn) NOUN *Islam* the call to prayer five times a day, usually by a muezzin from a minaret.
▷HISTORY from Arabic *adhān*, from *adhina* to proclaim, invite; see MUEZZIN

Azania (əˈzɑːnɪə, əˈzɑːnjə) NOUN another name (used esp by many Black political activists) for **South Africa**.
▷HISTORY perhaps from Arabic *Adzan* East Africa

Azanian (əˈzɑːnɪən, əˈzɑːnjən) NOUN 1 a native or inhabitant of Azania (another name used esp by many Black political activists for South Africa). ◆ ADJECTIVE 2 of or relating to Azania.

AZAPO (aˈzapəʊ) NOUN ACRONYM FOR Azanian People's Organization.

azathioprine (ˌæzəˈθaɪəˌpriːn) NOUN a synthetic drug that suppresses the normal immune responses of the body and is administered orally during and after organ transplantation and also in certain types of autoimmune disease. Formula: $C_9H_7N_7O_2S$.
▷HISTORY C20: from AZA- + THIO- + P(U)RINE

Azazel (əˈzeɪzᵊl, ˈæzəˌzɛl) NOUN 1 *Old Testament* a desert demon to whom the scapegoat bearing the sins of Israel was sent out once a year on the Day of Atonement (Leviticus 16:1–28). 2 (in later Jewish and Gnostic writings and in Muslim tradition) a prince of demons.

Azbine (æzˈbiːn) NOUN another name for **Aïr**.

azedarach (əˈzɛdəˌræk) NOUN 1 the astringent bark of the chinaberry tree, formerly used as an emetic and cathartic. 2 another name for **chinaberry** (sense 1).
▷HISTORY C18: from French *azédarac*, from Persian *āzād dirakht*, from *āzād* free, noble + *dirakht* tree

azeotrope (əˈziːəˌtrəʊp) NOUN a mixture of liquids that boils at a constant temperature, at a given pressure, without change of composition.
▷HISTORY C20: from A-[1] + *zeo-*, from Greek *zein* to boil + -TROPE
▸**azeotropic** (ˌeɪzɪəˈtrɒpɪk) ADJECTIVE

Azerbaijan (ˌæzəbaɪˈdʒɑːn) NOUN 1 a republic in NW Asia: the region was acquired by Russia from Persia in the early 19th century; became the Azerbaijan Soviet Socialist Republic in 1936 and gained independence in 1991; consists of dry subtropical steppes around the Aras and Kura rivers, surrounded by the Caucasus; contains the extensive Baku oilfields. Language: Azerbaijani. Religion: Shiite Muslim. Currency: manat. Capital: Baku. Pop.: 8 105 000 (2001 est). Area: 86 600 sq. km (33 430 sq. miles). 2 a mountainous region of NW Iran, separated from the republic of Azerbaijan by the Aras River: divided administratively into **Eastern Azerbaijan** and **Western Azerbaijan**. Capitals: Tabriz and Rezaiyeh. Pop.: 5 562 926 (1991).

Azerbaijani (ˌæzəbaɪˈdʒɑːnɪ) NOUN 1 (*plural* **-ni** *or* **-nis**) a native or inhabitant of Azerbaijan. Sometimes shortened to: **Azeri**. 2 the language of this people, belonging to the Turkic branch of the Altaic family.

Azeri (əˈzɛərɪ) NOUN short for **Azerbaijani** (sense 1).

azerty *or* **AZERTY keyboard** (əˈzɜːtɪ) NOUN a common European version of typewriter keyboard layout with the characters a, z, e, r, t, and y positioned on the top row of alphabetic characters at the left side of the keyboard.

azide (ˈeɪzaɪd) NOUN 1 any compound containing the monovalent group $-N_3$ or the monovalent ion N_3^-. 2 (*modifier*) consisting of, containing, or concerned with the group $-N_3$ or the ion N_3^-: *azide group or radical*.

Azilian (əˈzɪlɪən) NOUN 1 a Palaeolithic culture of Spain and SW France that can be dated to the 10th millennium B.C., characterized by flat bone harpoons and schematically painted pebbles. ◆ ADJECTIVE 2 of or relating to this culture.
▷HISTORY C19: named after Mas d'Azil, France, where artefacts were found

azimuth (ˈæzɪməθ) NOUN 1 *Astronomy, navigation* the angular distance usually measured clockwise from the north point of the horizon to the intersection with the horizon of the vertical circle passing through a celestial body. Compare **altitude** (sense 3). 2 *Surveying* the horizontal angle of a bearing clockwise from a standard direction, such as north.
▷HISTORY C14: from Old French *azimut*, from Arabic *as-sumūt*, plural of *as-samt* the path, from Latin *semita* path
▸**azimuthal** (ˌæzɪˈmʌθəl) ADJECTIVE ▸ˌ**aziˈmuthally** ADVERB

azimuthal projection NOUN another term for **zenithal projection**.

azine (ˈeɪziːn, -zɪn) NOUN any organic compound having a six-membered ring containing at least one nitrogen atom. See also **diazine, triazine**.

azo (ˈeɪzəʊ, ˈæ-) ADJECTIVE of, consisting of, or containing the divalent group -N:N-: *an azo group or radical*. See also **diazo**.
▷HISTORY independent use of AZO-

azo- *or before a vowel* **az-** COMBINING FORM indicating the presence of an azo group: *azobenzene*.
▷HISTORY from French *azote* nitrogen, from Greek *azōos* lifeless, from A-[1] + *zōē* life

azobenzene (ˌeɪzəʊˈbɛnziːn, -bɛnˈziːn) NOUN 1 a yellow or orange crystalline solid used mainly in the manufacture of dyes. Formula: $C_6H_5N{:}NC_6H_5$. 2 any organic compound that is a substituted derivative of azobenzene.

azo dye NOUN any of a class of artificial dyes that contain the azo group. They are usually red, brown, or yellow and are obtained from aromatic amines.

azoic (əˈzəʊɪk, eɪ-) ADJECTIVE without life; characteristic of the ages that have left no evidence of life in the form of organic remains.
▷HISTORY C19: from Greek *azōos* lifeless; see AZO-

azole (ˈeɪzəʊl, əˈzəʊl) NOUN 1 an organic five-membered ring compound containing one or more atoms in the ring, the number usually being specified by a prefix: *diazole*; *triazole*. 2 a less common name for **pyrrole**.
▷HISTORY from AZO- + -OLE[1], on the model of *diazole*

azonal soil (eɪˈzəʊnᵊl) NOUN soil that has a profile determined predominantly by factors other than local climate and vegetation. Azonal soils include some mountain, alluvial, marine, glacial, windblown, and volcanic soils. Compare **intrazonal soil, zonal soil**.

azoospermia (eɪˌzəʊəˈspɜːmɪə) NOUN *Pathol* absence of spermatozoa in the semen.
▸**aˌzooˈspermic** ADJECTIVE

Azores (əˈzɔːz) PLURAL NOUN **the.** three groups of volcanic islands in the N Atlantic, since 1976 an autonomous region of Portugal. Capital: Ponta Delgada (on São Miguel). Pop.: 242 073 (2001). Area: 2335 sq. km (901 sq. miles). Portuguese name: **Açôres**.

azotaemia *or esp US* **azotemia** (ˌæzəˈtiːmɪə) NOUN *Pathol* a less common name for **uraemia**.
▷HISTORY C20: see AZOTE, -AEMIA
▸**azotaemic** *or* (*esp US*) **azotemic** (ˌæzəˈtiːmɪk) ADJECTIVE

azote (ˈeɪzəʊt, əˈzəʊt) NOUN an obsolete name for **nitrogen**.
▷HISTORY C18: from French, from Greek *azōtos* ungirded, intended for Greek *azōos* lifeless

azoth (ˈæzɒθ) NOUN 1 the alchemical name for **mercury**, regarded as the first principle of all metals 2 the panacea postulated by Paracelsus.
▷HISTORY from Arabic *az-zā'ūq* the mercury

azotic (eɪˈzɒtɪk) ADJECTIVE of, containing, or concerned with nitrogen.

azotize *or* **azotise** (ˈeɪzəˌtaɪz) VERB a less common word for **nitrogenize**.

azotobacter (əˈzəʊtəʊˌbæktə) NOUN any bacterium of the family *Azotobacteriaceae*, important in nitrogen fixation in the soil.
▷HISTORY New Latin; see AZOTE, BACTERIA

Azov (ˈɑːzɒv) NOUN **Sea of.** a shallow arm of the Black Sea, to which it is connected by the Kerch Strait: almost entirely landlocked; fed chiefly by the River Don. Area: about 37 500 sq. km (14 500 sq. miles).

Azrael (ˈæzreɪl, -rɪəl) NOUN (in Jewish and Islamic angelology) the angel who separates the soul from the body at death.

AZT ABBREVIATION FOR azidothymidine. Also called: **zidovudine**.

Aztec (ˈæztɛk) NOUN 1 a member of a Mexican Indian people who established a great empire, centred on the valley of Mexico, that was overthrown by Cortés and his followers in the early 16th century. 2 the language of the Aztecs. See also **Nahuatl**. ◆ ADJECTIVE *also* **Aztecan**. 3 of, relating to, or characteristic of the Aztecs, their civilization, or their language.
▷HISTORY C18: from Spanish *Azteca*, from Nahuatl *Aztecatl*, from *Aztlan*, their traditional place of origin, literally: near the cranes, from *azta* cranes + *tlan* near

azure (ˈæʒə, -ʒʊə, ˈeɪ-) NOUN 1 a deep blue, occasionally somewhat purple, similar to the colour of a clear blue sky. 2 *Poetic* a clear blue sky. ◆ ADJECTIVE 3 of the colour azure; serene. 4 (*usually postpositive*) *Heraldry* of the colour blue.
▷HISTORY C14: from Old French *azur*, from Old Spanish, from Arabic *lāzaward* lapis lazuli, from Persian *lāzhuward*

azurite (ˈæʒʊˌraɪt) NOUN an azure-blue mineral associated with copper deposits. It is a source of copper. Composition: copper carbonate. Formula: $Cu_3(CO_3)_2(OH)_2$. Crystal structure: monoclinic.

azygospore (əˈzaɪgəʊˌspɔː) NOUN a thick-walled spore produced by parthenogenesis in certain algae and fungi. Also called: **parthenospore**.

azygous (ˈæzɪgəs) ADJECTIVE *Biology* developing or occurring singly.
▷HISTORY C17: via New Latin from Greek *azugos*, from A-[1] + *zugon* YOKE

Bb

b *or* **B** (biː) NOUN, *plural* **b's, B's** *or* **Bs.** [1] the second letter and first consonant of the modern English alphabet. [2] a speech sound represented by this letter, usually a voiced bilabial stop, as in *bell.* [3] Also: **beta.** the second in a series, esp the second highest grade in an examination.

b *Chess* See **algebraic notation.**

B SYMBOL FOR: [1] *Music* **a** a note having a frequency of 493.88 hertz (**B above middle C**) or this value multiplied or divided by any power of 2; the seventh note of the scale of C major. **b** a key, string, or pipe producing this note. **c** the major or minor key having this note as its tonic. [2] the supporting or less important of two things: *the B side of a record.* [3] a human blood type of the ABO group, containing the B antigen. [4] (in Britain) a secondary road. [5] the number 11 in hexadecimal notation. [6] *Chem* boron. [7] magnetic flux density. [8] *Chess* bishop. [9] (on Brit. pencils, signifying degree of softness of lead) black: *B; 2B; 3B.* Compare **H** (sense 5). [10] Also: **b.** *Physics* bel. [11] *Physics* baryon number. [12] balboa. [13] belga. [14] bolivar. [15] *Photog* B-setting. [16] **a** a person whose job is in middle management, or who holds an intermediate administrative or professional position. **b** (*as modifier*): *a B worker.* ◆ See also **occupation groupings.** ◆ [17] INTERNATIONAL CAR REGISTRATION FOR Belgium.

B4 *Text messaging* ABBREVIATION FOR before.

b. ABBREVIATION FOR: [1] born. [2] *Cricket* bowled.

B. ABBREVIATION FOR: [1] (on maps, etc.) bay. [2] British.

B- (of US military aircraft) ABBREVIATION FOR bomber: *B-52.*

ba THE INTERNET DOMAIN NAME FOR Bosnia and Herzegovina.

Ba^{1} (bɑː) NOUN *Egyptian myth* the soul, represented as a bird with a human head.

Ba^{2} THE CHEMICAL SYMBOL FOR barium.

BA ABBREVIATION FOR: [1] Bachelor of Arts. [2] British Academy. [3] British Airways. [4] British Association (for the Advancement of Science). [5] **British Association screw thread.**

ba' *or* **Ba'** (bɔː, bɑː) NOUN *Scot* [1] (usually preceded by *the*) a game somewhat like rugby played in Orkney at Christmas and New Year between two very large teams of players. [2] (usually preceded by *the*) Also called: **handba'.** a similar game played at Jedburgh in the Scottish Borders in mid February. [3] the stuffed leather ball used in these games.
▷HISTORY Scots form of BALL

baa (bɑː) VERB **baas, baaing, baaed.** [1] (*intr*) to make the cry of a sheep; bleat. ◆ NOUN [2] the cry made by sheep.

BAA NOUN the main airports operator in the United Kingdom; until privatization in 1987, an abbreviation for British Airports Authority.

Baader-Meinhof Gang (*German* 'baːdər 'mainhoːf) NOUN **the.** a group of West German terrorists, active in the 1970s, who were dedicated to the violent overthrow of capitalist society. Also called: **Red Army Faction.**
▷HISTORY C20: named after its leading members, Andreas *Baader* (1943–77) and Ulrike *Meinhof* (1934-76)

Baal (bɑːl) NOUN [1] any of several ancient Semitic fertility gods. [2] *Phoenician myth* the sun god and supreme national deity. [3] (*sometimes not capital*) any false god or idol.
▷HISTORY from Hebrew *bá'al* lord, master

Baalbek ('bɑːlbɛk) NOUN a town in E Lebanon: an important city in Phoenician and Roman times; extensive ruins. Pop.: 15 600 (1995 est.). Ancient name: **Heliopolis.**

baalebos *Yiddish* ('baləbɔs) NOUN, *plural* ***baalebatim*** (balə'batəm). [1] the master of the house. [2] the proprietor of a business, etc. [3] *Slang* an officious person.

▷HISTORY from Hebrew *ba'al La-bayis* master of the house

baas (bɑːs) NOUN a South African word for **boss**^{1}: used by Africans and Coloureds in addressing European managers or overseers.
▷HISTORY C17: from Afrikaans, from Middle Dutch *baes* master; see BOSS^{1}

baaskap *or* **baasskap** ('bɑːsˌkap) NOUN (*sometimes capital*) (in South Africa) control by Whites of non-Whites.
▷HISTORY from Afrikaans, from BAAS + *-skap* -SHIP

Ba'ath (bɑː'ɑːθ) NOUN a variant of **Ba'th.**

baba ('bɑːbɑː; *French* baba) NOUN a small cake of leavened dough, sometimes mixed with currants and usually soaked in rum (**rum baba**).
▷HISTORY C19: from French, from Polish, literally: old woman

babaco ('bæbəˌkəʊ, bə'bɑːkəʊ) NOUN, *plural* **-cos.** [1] a subtropical parthenocarpic tree, *Carica pentagona,* originating in South America, cultivated for its fruit: family *Caricaceae.* [2] the greenish-yellow egg-shaped fruit of this tree, having a delicate fragrance and no pips.

baba ghanoush *or* **baba gannoujh** (baba ga'nuːʃ) NOUN a thick purée of aubergines, tahini, olive oil, lemon juice and garlic, originating in North Africa and the Mediterranean.
▷HISTORY from Arabic

babalas ('babalas) ADJECTIVE *South African* drunk; hungover.
▷HISTORY C20: Afrikaans, from Zulu *I-babalazi* drunk

babassu (ˌbɑːbə'suː) NOUN a Brazilian palm tree, *Orbignya martiana* (or *O. speciosa*), having hard edible nuts that yield an oil used in making soap, margarine, etc.
▷HISTORY from Portuguese *babaçú,* from a native Amerindian word

babbitt ('bæbɪt) VERB (*tr*) to line (a bearing) or face (a surface) with Babbitt metal or a similar soft alloy.

Babbitt ('bæbɪt) NOUN *US derogatory* a narrow-minded and complacent member of the middle class.
▷HISTORY C20: after George *Babbitt,* central character in the novel *Babbitt* (1922) by Sinclair Lewis
▸ **'Babbittry** NOUN

Babbitt metal NOUN any of a number of alloys originally based on tin, antimony, and copper but now often including lead: used esp in bearings. Sometimes shortened to: **Babbitt.**
▷HISTORY C19: named after Isaac *Babbitt* (1799–1862), American inventor

babble ('bæb^{ə}l) VERB [1] to utter (words, sounds, etc.) in an incoherent or indistinct jumble. [2] (*intr*) to talk foolishly, incessantly, or irrelevantly. [3] (*tr*) to disclose (secrets, confidences, etc.) carelessly or impulsively. [4] (*intr*) (of streams, birds, etc.) to make a low murmuring or bubbling sound. ◆ NOUN [5] incoherent or foolish speech; chatter. [6] a murmuring or bubbling sound.
▷HISTORY C13: compare Dutch *babbelen,* Swedish *babbla,* French *babiller* to prattle, Latin *babulus* fool; probably all of imitative origin
▸ **'babblement** NOUN ▸ **'babbling** NOUN, ADJECTIVE

babbler ('bæblə) NOUN [1] a person who babbles. [2] any of various insect-eating birds of the Old World tropics and subtropics that have a loud incessant song: family *Muscicapidae* (warblers, thrushes, etc.).

babbling brook NOUN *Austral slang* a cook.
▷HISTORY rhyming slang

babe (beɪb) NOUN [1] a baby. [2] *Informal* a naive, gullible, or unsuspecting person (often in the phrase **a babe in arms**). [3] *Slang* a girl or young woman, esp an attractive one.

babe-in-a-cradle NOUN a tall orchid, *Epiblema grandiflorum,* of SW Australia with lilac to mauve flowers.
▷HISTORY named from a fancied resemblance of its column to a baby in a cradle

Babel ('beɪb^{ə}l) NOUN [1] *Old Testament* **a** Also called: **Tower of Babel.** a tower presumptuously intended to reach from earth to heaven, the building of which was frustrated when Jehovah confused the language of the builders (Genesis 11:1–10). **b** the city, probably Babylon, in which this tower was supposedly built. [2] (*often not capital*) **a** a confusion of noises or voices. **b** a scene of noise and confusion.
▷HISTORY from Hebrew *Bābhél,* from Akkadian *Bāb-ilu,* literally: gate of God

Bab el Mandeb ('bæb ɛl 'mændɛb) NOUN a strait between SW Arabia and E Africa, connecting the Red Sea with the Gulf of Aden.

babesiosis (bəˌbiːˈzɪˈəʊsɪs) NOUN *Vet science* a tick-borne disease of domesticated and wild mammals as well as humans, caused by a protozoan of the genera *Babesia* and characterized by fever, anaemia, jaundice, and in severe cases death.

Babi ('bɑːbɪ) NOUN [1] a disciple of the Bab, a Persian religious leader (1819–50), who was executed as a heretic of Islam. [2] another word for **Babism.**

babiche (bɑː'biːʃ) NOUN *Canadian* thongs or lacings of rawhide.
▷HISTORY C19: from Canadian French, of Algonquian origin

babies'-breath NOUN a variant of **baby's-breath.**

Babinski effect *or* **reflex** (bə'bɪnskɪ) NOUN *Physiol* the reflex curling upwards of the toes (instead of inwards) when the sole of the foot is stroked, normal in infants below the age of two but a pathological condition in adults.
▷HISTORY after Joseph *Babinski* (1857–1932), French neuropathologist

babirusa (ˌbɑːbɪ'ruːsə) NOUN a wild pig, *Babyrousa babyrussa,* inhabiting marshy forests in Indonesia. It has an almost hairless wrinkled skin and enormous curved canine teeth.
▷HISTORY C17: from Malay, from *bābī* hog + *rūsa* deer

Babism ('bɑːbɪzəm) NOUN a pantheistic Persian religious sect, founded in 1844 by the Bab, a Persian religious leader (1819–50), who was executed as a heretic of Islam. It forbids polygamy, concubinage, begging, trading in slaves, and indulgence in alcohol and drugs. Compare **Baha'ism.**

baboon (bə'buːn) NOUN any of several medium-sized omnivorous Old World monkeys of the genus *Papio* (or *Chaeropithecus*) and related genera, inhabiting open rocky ground or wooded regions of Africa. They have an elongated muzzle, large teeth, and a fairly long tail. See also **hamadryas, gelada.**
▷HISTORY C14 *babewyn* gargoyle, later, baboon, from Old French *babouin,* from *baboue* grimace; related to Old French *babine* a thick lip

Babo's law ('bæbəʊz) NOUN *Chem* the law stating that the vapour pressure of a solution is reduced in proportion to the amount of solute added.
▷HISTORY C19: named after Lambert von *Babo* (1818–99), German chemist who formulated it

babu ('bɑːbuː) NOUN (in India) a title or form of address more or less equivalent to *Mr,* placed before a person's full name or after his first name.
▷HISTORY Hindi, literally: father

babul (bɑː'buːl, 'bɑːbuːl) NOUN any of several leguminous trees of the genus *Acacia,* esp *A. arabica* of N Africa and India, which bear small yellow flowers and are a source of gum arabic, tannin, and hardwood.

▷HISTORY from Persian *babūl*; related to Sanskrit *babbūla*

babushka (bəˈbuːʃkə) NOUN [1] a headscarf tied under the chin, worn by Russian peasant women. [2] (in Russia) an old woman.
▷HISTORY Russian: grandmother, from *baba* old woman

baby (ˈbeɪbɪ) NOUN, *plural* **-bies.** [1] **a** a newborn or recently born child; infant. **b** (*as modifier*): *baby food.* [2] the youngest or smallest of a family or group. [3] **a** a newborn or recently born animal. **b** (*as modifier*): *baby rabbits.* [4] *Usually derogatory* an immature person. [5] *Slang* a young woman or sweetheart: often used as a term of address expressing affection. [6] a project of personal concern. [7] **be left holding the baby.** to be left with the responsibility. [8] **throw the baby out with the bath water.** to lose the essential element by indiscriminate rejection. ◆ ADJECTIVE [9] (*prenomial*) comparatively small of its type: *a baby car.* ◆ VERB **-bies, -bying, -bied.** (*tr*) [10] to treat with love and attention. [11] to treat (someone) like a baby; pamper or overprotect.
▷HISTORY C14: probably childish reduplication; compare MAMA, PAPA
▸ˈ**babyhood** NOUN ▸ˈ**babyish** ADJECTIVE

baby bond NOUN *Brit* a sum of money invested shortly after the birth of a child, the returns of which may not be collected until the child reaches adulthood.

baby bonus NOUN *Canadian informal* family allowance.

baby boom NOUN a sharp increase in the birth rate of a population, esp the one that occurred after World War II. Also called (esp Brit): **the bulge.**

baby-boomer NOUN a person born during a baby boom, esp (in Britain and the US) one born during the years 1945–55.

Baby-bouncer NOUN *Trademark* a seat on springs suspended from a door frame, etc., in which a baby may be placed for exercise.

baby broker NOUN an adoption service, esp on the Internet.

Baby Buggy NOUN [1] *Trademark Brit* a kind of child's light pushchair. [2] *US and Canadian informal* a small pram.

baby carriage NOUN Also: **baby buggy.** the US and Canadian name for **pram**[1].

baby-face NOUN [1] a smooth round face like a baby's. [2] a person with such a face.

baby grand NOUN a small grand piano, approximately 5 feet long. Compare **boudoir grand, concert grand.**

Babylon (ˈbæbɪlən) NOUN [1] the chief city of ancient Mesopotamia: first settled around 3000 B.C. See also **Hanging Gardens of Babylon.** [2] *Derogatory* (in Protestant polemic) the Roman Catholic Church, regarded as the seat of luxury and corruption. [3] *Derogatory* any society or group in a society considered as corrupt or as a place of exile by another society or group, esp White Britain as viewed by some West Indians.
▷HISTORY via Latin and Greek from Hebrew *Bābhel*; see BABEL

Babylonia (ˌbæbɪˈləʊnɪə) NOUN the southern kingdom of ancient Mesopotamia: a great empire from about 2200–538 B.C., when it was conquered by the Persians.

Babylonian (ˌbæbɪˈləʊnɪən) NOUN [1] an inhabitant of ancient Babylon or Babylonia. [2] the extinct language of Babylonia, belonging to the E Semitic subfamily of the Afro-Asiatic family: a dialect of Akkadian. ◆ ADJECTIVE [3] of, relating to, or characteristic of ancient Babylon or Babylonia, its people, or their language. [4] decadent or depraved.

Babylonian captivity NOUN [1] the exile of the Jews in Babylonia from about 586 to about 538 B.C. [2] the exile of the seven popes in Avignon (1309–77).

baby-minder NOUN a person who is paid to look after other people's babies or very young children.
▸ˈ**baby-ˌminding** NOUN

baby-mother NOUN a young mother who has been abandoned by the baby's father just before or after the birth.

baby pig disease NOUN *Vet science* a metabolic disorder of neonatal piglets characterized by low blood glucose concentrations as a result of inadequate nutrition.

baby's-breath *or* **babies'-breath** NOUN [1] a tall Eurasian caryophyllaceous plant, *Gypsophila paniculata*, bearing small white or pink fragrant flowers. [2] any of several other plants, such as the grape hyacinth and certain bedstraws, that have small scented flowers.

baby-sit VERB **-sits, -sitting, -sat.** (*intr*) to act or work as a baby-sitter.
▸ˈ**baby-ˌsitting** NOUN, ADJECTIVE

baby-sitter NOUN a person who takes care of a child or children while the parents are out.

baby snatcher NOUN *Informal* [1] a person who steals a baby from its pram. [2] another name for **cradle snatcher.**

baby talk NOUN [1] the speech of very young children learning to talk. [2] an adult's imitation of this.

baby tooth NOUN another term for **milk tooth.**

baby-walker NOUN a light frame on casters or wheels to help a baby learn to walk. US equivalent: **go-cart.**

baby wipe NOUN a disposable moistened medicated paper towel, usually supplied in a plastic drum or packet, used for cleaning babies.

Bacău (ˈbækaʊ) NOUN a city in E Romania on the River Bistrila: oil refining, textiles, paper. Pop.: 209 689 (1997 est.).

Baccalauréat (ˌbækəˈlɔːrɪˌɑː) NOUN (esp in France) a school-leaving examination that qualifies the successful candidates for entrance to university.
▷HISTORY C20: from French, from Medieval Latin *baccalaureus* bachelor

baccalaureate (ˌbækəˈlɔːrɪɪt) NOUN [1] the university degree of Bachelor or Arts, Bachelor of Science, etc. [2] an internationally recognized programme of study, comprising different subjects, offered as an alternative to a course of A levels in Britain. [3] *US* a farewell sermon delivered at the commencement ceremonies in many colleges and universities.
▷HISTORY C17: from Medieval Latin *baccalaureātus*, from *baccalaureus* advanced student, alteration of *baccalārius* BACHELOR; influenced in folk etymology by Latin *bāca* berry + *laureus* laurel

baccarat (ˈbækəˌrɑː, ˌbækəˈrɑː; *French* bakara) NOUN a card game in which two or more punters gamble against the banker.
▷HISTORY C19: from French *baccara*, of unknown origin

baccate (ˈbækeɪt) ADJECTIVE *Botany* [1] like a berry in form, texture, etc. [2] bearing berries.
▷HISTORY C19: from Latin *bāca* berry

Bacchae (ˈbækiː) PLURAL NOUN the priestesses or female devotees of Bacchus.
▷HISTORY Latin, from Greek *Bakkhai*, plural of *Bakkhē* priestess of BACCHUS

bacchanal (ˈbækənᵊl) NOUN [1] a follower of Bacchus. [2] a drunken and riotous celebration. [3] a participant in such a celebration; reveller. ◆ ADJECTIVE [4] of or relating to Bacchus.
▷HISTORY C16: from Latin *Bacchānālis*; see BACCHUS

bacchanalia (ˌbækəˈneɪlɪə) PLURAL NOUN [1] (*often capital*) orgiastic rites associated with Bacchus. [2] any drunken revelry.

bacchanalian (ˌbækəˈneɪlɪən) ADJECTIVE [1] characterized by or involving drunken revelry. [2] (*often capital*) of or relating to the orgiastic rites associated with Bacchus.

bacchant (ˈbækənt) NOUN, *plural* **bacchants, bacchantes** (bəˈkæntɪz). [1] a priest or votary of Bacchus. [2] a drunken reveller.
▷HISTORY C17: from Latin *bacchāns*, from *bacchārī* to celebrate the BACCHANALIA

bacchante (bəˈkæntɪ) NOUN, *plural* **bacchantes** (bəˈkæntɪz). [1] a priestess or female votary of Bacchus. [2] a drunken female reveller.

Bacchic (ˈbækɪk) ADJECTIVE [1] of or relating to Bacchus. [2] (*often not capital*) riotously drunk.

bacchius (bæˈkaɪəs) NOUN, *plural* **-chii** (-ˈkaɪaɪ). *Prosody* a metrical foot of one short syllable followed by two long ones (⏑––). Compare **dactyl.**
▷HISTORY C16: from Latin, from Greek *Bakkheios* (*pous*) a Bacchic (foot)

Bacchus (ˈbækəs) NOUN (in ancient Greece and Rome) a god of wine and giver of ecstasy, identified with Dionysus.
▷HISTORY C15: from Latin, from Greek *Bakkhos*; related to Latin *bāca* small round fruit, berry

bacciferous (bækˈsɪfərəs) ADJECTIVE bearing berries.
▷HISTORY C17: from Latin *bācifer*, from *bāca* berry + *ferre* to bear

bacciform (ˈbæksɪˌfɔːm) ADJECTIVE *Botany* shaped like a berry.

baccivorous (bækˈsɪvərəs) ADJECTIVE feeding on berries.

baccy (ˈbækɪ) NOUN *Brit* an informal name for **tobacco.**

bach[1] (bax, bɑːk) NOUN *Welsh* a term of friendly address: used esp after a person's name.
▷HISTORY Welsh, literally: little one

bach[2] (bætʃ) *Austral and NZ* ◆ VERB [1] a variant spelling of **batch**[2]. ◆ NOUN [2] a simple cottage, esp at the seaside.

bachelor (ˈbætʃələ, ˈbætʃlə) NOUN [1] **a** an unmarried man. **b** (*as modifier*): *a bachelor flat.* [2] **a** a person who holds the degree of Bachelor of Arts, Bachelor of Education, Bachelor of Science, etc. **b** the degree itself. [3] Also called: **bachelor-at-arms.** (in the Middle Ages) a young knight serving a great noble. [4] **bachelor seal.** a young male seal, esp a fur seal, that has not yet mated.
▷HISTORY C13: from Old French *bacheler* youth, squire, from Vulgar Latin *baccalāris* (unattested) farm worker, of Celtic origin; compare Irish Gaelic *bachlach* peasant
▸ˈ**bachelorhood** NOUN

bachelor apartment NOUN *Canadian* a flat consisting of one room that is used as a sitting room and bedroom, as well as a kitchenette and a bathroom.

bachelorette (ˌbætʃələˈrɛt) NOUN *Jocular* a young unmarried professional woman.
▷HISTORY C20: BACHELOR + -ETTE (sense 2)

bachelor girl NOUN a young unmarried woman, esp one who is self-supporting.

Bachelor of Arts NOUN [1] a degree conferred on a person who has successfully completed his undergraduate studies, usually in a branch of the liberal arts or humanities. [2] a person who holds this degree.

Bachelor of Science NOUN [1] a degree conferred on a person who has successfully completed his undergraduate studies in a branch of the sciences. [2] a person who holds this degree.

bachelor's-buttons NOUN (*functioning as singular or plural*) any of various plants of the daisy family with button-like flower heads.

Bach flower remedy NOUN *Trademark* an alternative medicine consisting of a distillation from various flowers, designed to counteract negative states of mind and restore emotional balance.
▷HISTORY C20: after Dr E. *Bach* (1886–1936), homeopath who developed this system

Bach trumpet (bɑːx) NOUN a modern small three-valved trumpet for playing clarino passages in Bach's music.

bacillaemia *or US* **bacillemia** (ˌbæsɪˈliːmɪə) NOUN *Pathol* the presence of bacilli in the blood.

bacillary (bəˈsɪlərɪ) *or* **bacillar** (bəˈsɪlə) ADJECTIVE [1] of, relating to, or caused by bacilli. [2] Also: **bacilliform** (bəˈsɪlɪˌfɔːm). shaped like a short rod.

bacilluria (ˌbæsɪˈljʊərɪə) NOUN *Pathol* the presence of bacilli in the urine.

bacillus (bəˈsɪləs) NOUN, *plural* **-cilli** (-ˈsɪlaɪ). [1] any rod-shaped bacterium, such as a clostridium bacterium. Compare **coccus** (sense 1), **spirillum** (sense 1). [2] any of various rodlike spore-producing bacteria constituting the family *Bacillaceae*, esp of the genus *Bacillus*.
▷HISTORY C19: from Latin: a small staff, from *baculum* walking stick

bacitracin (ˌbæsɪˈtreɪsɪn) NOUN an antibiotic used mainly in treating bacterial skin infections: obtained from the bacterium *Bacillus subtilis*.
▷HISTORY C20: BACI(LLUS) + *-trac-* from Margaret *Tracy* (born 1936), American girl in whose blood *Bacillus subtilis* was found; see -IN

back[1] (bæk) NOUN [1] the posterior part of the

human body, extending from the neck to the pelvis. Related adjective: **dorsal.** 2 the corresponding or upper part of an animal. 3 the spinal column. 4 the part or side of an object opposite the front. 5 the part or side of anything less often seen or used: *the back of a carpet; the back of a knife.* 6 the part or side of anything that is furthest from the front or from a spectator: *the back of the stage.* 7 the convex part of something: *the back of a hill; the back of a ship.* 8 something that supports, covers, or strengthens the rear of an object. 9 *Ball games* **a** a mainly defensive player behind a forward. **b** the position of such a player. 10 the part of a book to which the pages are glued or that joins the covers. 11 *Mining* **a** the side of a passage or layer nearest the surface. **b** the earth between that level and the next. 12 the upper surface of a joist, rafter, slate, tile, etc., when in position. Compare **bed** (sense 13). 13 **at one's back.** behind, esp. in support or pursuit. 14 **at the back of one's mind.** not in one's conscious thoughts. 15 **behind one's back.** without one's knowledge; secretly or deceitfully. 16 **break one's back.** to overwork or work very hard. 17 **break the back of.** to complete the greatest or hardest part of (a task). 18 **(flat) on one's back.** incapacitated, esp. through illness. 19 **get off someone's back.** *Informal* to stop criticizing or pestering someone. 20 **have on one's back.** to be burdened with. 21 **on someone's back.** *Informal* criticizing or pestering someone. 22 **put one's back into.** to devote all one's strength to (a task). 23 **put (*or* get) someone's back up.** to annoy someone. 24 **see the back of.** to be rid of. 25 **back of beyond. a the.** a very remote place. **b** *Austral* in such a place (esp. in the phrase **out back of beyond**). 26 **turn one's back on. a** to turn away from in anger or contempt. **b** to refuse to help; abandon. 27 **with one's back to the wall.** in a difficult or desperate situation. ◆ VERB (*mainly tr*) 28 (*also intr*) to move or cause to move backwards. 29 to provide support, money, or encouragement for (a person, enterprise, etc.). 30 to bet on the success of: *to back a horse.* 31 to provide with a back, backing, or lining. 32 to provide with a music accompaniment: *a soloist backed by an orchestra.* 33 to provide a background for; be at the back of: *mountains back the town.* 34 to countersign or endorse. 35 *Archaic* to mount the back of. 36 (*intr; foll by on or onto*) to have the back facing (towards): *the house backs onto a river.* 37 (*intr*) (of the wind) to change direction in an anticlockwise direction. Compare **veer**[1] (sense 3a). 38 *Nautical* to position (a sail) so that the wind presses on its opposite side. 39 **back and fill. a** *Nautical* to manoeuvre the sails by alternately filling and emptying them of wind to navigate in a narrow place. **b** to vacillate in one's opinion. ◆ ADJECTIVE (*prenominal*) 40 situated behind: *a back lane.* 41 of the past: *back issues of a magazine.* 42 owing from an earlier date: *back rent.* 43 *Chiefly US, Austral, and NZ* remote: *back country.* 44 (of a road) not direct. 45 moving in a backward direction: *back current.* 46 *Phonetics* of, relating to, or denoting a vowel articulated with the tongue retracted towards the soft palate, as for the vowels in English *hard, fall, hot, full, fool.* ◆ ADVERB 47 at, to, or towards the rear; away from something considered to be the front; backwards; behind. 48 in, to, or towards the original starting point, place, or condition: *to go back home; put the book back; my headache has come back.* 49 in or into the past: *to look back on one's childhood.* 50 in reply, repayment, or retaliation: *to hit someone back; pay back a debt; to answer back.* 51 in check: *the dam holds back the water.* 52 in concealment; in reserve: *to keep something back; to hold back information.* 53 **back and forth.** to and fro. 54 **back to front. a** in reverse. **b** in disorder. ◆ See also **back down, back off, back out, back up.**
▷**HISTORY** Old English *bæc*; related to Old Norse *bak*, Old Frisian *bek*, Old High German *bah*

back[2] (bæk) NOUN a large tub or vat, esp one used by brewers.
▷**HISTORY** C17: from Dutch *bak* tub, cistern, from Old French *bac*, from Vulgar Latin *bacca* (unattested) vessel for liquids

backache ('bæk,eɪk) NOUN an ache or pain in one's back.

back bacon NOUN lean bacon from the back of a pig's loin.

backbeat ('bæk,biːt) NOUN the second and fourth beats in music written in even time or, in more complex time signatures, the last beat of the bar. Compare **downbeat** (sense 1).

backbencher ('bæk'bɛntʃə) NOUN *Brit, Austral, NZ* a Member of Parliament who does not hold office in the government or opposition.

backbend ('bæk,bɛnd) NOUN a gymnastic exercise in which the trunk is bent backwards until the hands touch the floor.

backbite ('bæk,baɪt) VERB **-bites, -biting, -bit; -bitten** *or* **-bit.** to talk spitefully about (an absent person). ▸ **'back,biter** NOUN

backblocks ('bæk,blɒks) PLURAL NOUN *Austral and NZ* bush or remote farming area far distant from city amenities.
▸ **'back,block** ADJECTIVE ▸ **'back,blocker** NOUN

backboard ('bæk,bɔːd) NOUN 1 a board that is placed behind something to form or support its back. 2 a board worn to straighten or support the back, as after surgery. 3 (in basketball) a flat upright surface supported on a high frame, under which the basket is attached.

back boiler NOUN a tank or series of pipes at the back of a fireplace for heating water. US name: **water back.**

backbone ('bæk,bəʊn) NOUN 1 a nontechnical name for **spinal column.** 2 something that resembles the spinal column in function, position, or appearance. 3 strength of character; courage. 4 the main or central mountain range of a country or region. 5 *Nautical* the main longitudinal members of a vessel, giving structural strength. 6 *Computing* (in computer networks) a large-capacity, high-speed central section by which other network segments are connected.

backbreaker ('bæk,breɪkə) NOUN 1 a wrestling hold in which a wrestler uses his knee or shoulder as a fulcrum to bend his opponent's body backwards. 2 *Informal* an extremely arduous task.

backbreaking ('bæk,breɪkɪŋ) ADJECTIVE demanding great effort; exhausting.

backburn ('bæk,bɜːn) *Austral and NZ* ◆ VERB (*tr*) 1 to clear (an area of scrub, bush, etc.) by creating a new fire that burns in the opposite direction to the line of advancing fire. ◆ NOUN 2 the act or result of backburning.

back burner NOUN **on the back burner.** put aside for the time being, as a subject that is not of immediate concern but that may be activated later; postponed.

backchat ('bæk,tʃæt) NOUN *Informal* the act of answering back, esp impudently.

backcloth ('bæk,klɒθ) NOUN a large painted curtain hanging at the back of a stage set. Also called: **backdrop.**

backcomb ('bæk,kəʊm) VERB to comb the under layers of (the hair) towards the roots to give more bulk to a hairstyle. Also: **tease.**

back country NOUN *Austral and NZ* land remote from a town or settled area.

backcourt ('bæk,kɔːt) NOUN 1 *Tennis chiefly US* the part of the court between the service line and the baseline. 2 (in various court games) the area nearest the back boundary line.

backcross ('bæk,krɒs) VERB 1 to mate (a hybrid of the first generation) with one of its parents. ◆ NOUN 2 the offspring so produced. 3 the act or process of backcrossing.

backdate (,bæk'deɪt) VERB (*tr*) to make effective from an earlier date: *the pay rise was backdated to August.*

back door NOUN 1 a door at the rear or side of a building. 2 a means of entry to a job, position, etc., that is secret, underhand, or obtained through influence.

back down VERB 1 (*intr, adverb*) to withdraw an earlier claim. 2 (*tr*) *Rowing* to cause (a boat) to move backwards by pushing rather than pulling on the oars. ◆ NOUN **backdown.** 3 abandonment of an earlier claim.

backdrop ('bæk,drɒp) NOUN 1 another name for **backcloth.** 2 the background to any scene or situation.

backed (bækt) ADJECTIVE **a** having a back or backing. **b** (*in combination*): *high-backed; black-backed.*

back emf NOUN *Electrical engineering* an electromagnetic force appearing in an inductive circuit in such a direction as to oppose any change of current in the circuit.

back emission NOUN *Electronics* the secondary emission of electrons from an anode.

back end 1 NOUN *Northern English dialect* autumn. ◆ ADJECTIVE **back-end.** 2 (of money, costs, etc.) required or incurred after a project has been completed.
▷**HISTORY** from the phrase *the back end of the year*

back-end load NOUN the final charges of commission and expenses made by an investment trust, insurance policy, etc., when the investor is paid out.
▸ **back-end loading** NOUN

backer ('bækə) NOUN 1 a person who gives financial or other support. 2 a person who bets on a competitor or contestant.

backfield ('bæk,fiːld) NOUN *American football* 1 (usually preceded by *the*) the quarterback and running backs in a team. 2 the area behind the line of scrimmage from which the backfield begin each play.

backfile ('bæk,faɪl) NOUN the archives of a newspaper or magazine.

backfill ('bæk,fɪl) VERB 1 (*tr*) to refill an excavated trench, esp (in archaeology) at the end of an investigation. ◆ NOUN 2 the soil used to do this.

backfire (,bæk'faɪə) VERB (*intr*) 1 (of an internal-combustion engine) to emit a loud noise as a result of an explosion in the inlet manifold or exhaust system. 2 to fail to have the desired or expected effect: *his plans backfired on him.* 3 to start a controlled fire in order to halt an advancing forest or prairie fire by creating a barren area. ◆ NOUN 4 (in an internal-combustion engine) **a** an explosion of unburnt gases in the exhaust system. **b** a premature explosion in a cylinder or inlet manifold. 5 a controlled fire started to create a barren area that will halt an advancing forest or prairie fire.

back foot NOUN **on the back foot.** at a disadvantage; outmanoeuvred or outclassed by an opponent: *they were on the back foot directly from the kick-off.*

back formation NOUN 1 the invention of a new word on the assumption that a familiar word is derived from it. The verbs *edit* and *burgle* in English were so created from *editor* and *burglar.* 2 a word formed by this process.

back four NOUN *Soccer* the defensive players in many modern team formations: usually two fullbacks and two centre backs.

backgammon ('bæk,gæmən, bæk'gæmən) NOUN 1 a game for two people played on a board with pieces moved according to throws of the dice. 2 the most complete form of win in this game.
▷**HISTORY** C17: BACK[1] + *gammon*, variant of GAME[1]

back green NOUN *Central Scot urban dialect* grass or a garden at the back of a house, esp a tenement.

background ('bæk,graʊnd) NOUN 1 the part of a scene or view furthest from the viewer. 2 **a** an inconspicuous or unobtrusive position (esp in the phrase **in the background**). **b** (*as modifier*): *a background influence.* 3 *Art* **a** the plane or ground in a picture upon which all other planes or forms appear superimposed. **b** the parts of a picture that appear most distant. Compare **foreground, middle-distance.** 4 a person's social class, education, training, or experience. 5 **a** the social, historical, or technical circumstances that lead up to or help to explain something: *the background to the French Revolution.* **b** (*as modifier*): *background information.* 6 **a** a low level of sound, lighting, etc., whose purpose is to be an unobtrusive or appropriate accompaniment to something else, such as a social activity, conversation, or the action of a film. **b** (*as modifier*): *background music.* 7 Also called: **background radiation.** *Physics* low-intensity radiation as, for example, from small amounts of radioisotopes in soil, air, building materials, etc. 8 *Electronics* **a** unwanted effects, such as noise, occurring in a measuring instrument, electronic device, etc. **b** (*as modifier*): *background interference.*

background processing NOUN *Computing* the ability of a system to perform a low-priority task while, at the same time, dealing with a main application.

backhand ('bæk,hænd) NOUN 1 *Sport* **a** a stroke

made across the body with the back of the hand facing the direction of the stroke. **b** (*as modifier*): *a backhand return.* 2 the side on which backhand strokes are made. 3 handwriting slanting to the left. ◆ ADVERB 4 with a backhand stroke. ◆ VERB (*tr*) 5 *Sport* to play (a shot) backhand.

backhanded (ˌbækˈhændɪd) ADJECTIVE 1 (of a blow, shot, stroke, etc.) performed with the arm moving across the body. 2 double-edged; equivocal: *a backhanded compliment.* 3 (of handwriting) slanting to the left. 4 (of a rope) twisted in the opposite way from the normal right-handed direction. ◆ ADVERB 5 in a backhanded manner.
▸ **ˌbackˈhandedly** ADVERB ▸ **ˌbackˈhandedness** NOUN

backhander (ˈbækˌhændə) NOUN 1 a backhanded stroke or blow. 2 *Informal* an indirect attack. 3 *Slang* a bribe.

backie (ˈbækɪ) NOUN *Brit informal* a ride on the back of someone's bicycle.

backing (ˈbækɪŋ) NOUN 1 support given to a person, cause, or enterprise. 2 a body of supporters. 3 something that forms, protects, supports, or strengthens the back of something. 4 *Theatre* a scenic cloth or flat placed behind a window, door, etc., in a set to mask the offstage space. 5 musical accompaniment, esp for a pop singer. 6 the support in gold or precious metals for a country's issue of money in notes. 7 *Meteorol* an anticlockwise change in wind direction. 8 *Northern English* a passageway running behind a row of terraced houses.

backing dog NOUN *NZ and Australia* a dog that moves a flock of sheep by jumping on their backs.

backing store NOUN a computer storage device, usually a disk, that provides additional storage space for information so that it can be accessed and referred to when required and may be copied into the processor if needed.

backlash (ˈbækˌlæʃ) NOUN 1 a reaction or recoil between interacting worn or badly fitting parts in a mechanism. 2 the play between parts. 3 a sudden and adverse reaction, esp to a political or social development: *a public backlash against the government.*

backless (ˈbæklɪs) ADJECTIVE (of a dress) low-cut at the back.

back light NOUN light falling on a photographic or television subject from the rear.

backlist (ˈbækˌlɪst) NOUN a publisher's previously published books that are still available. See also **frontlist, mid-list.**

backlit (bækˈlɪt) ADJECTIVE illuminated from behind: *a backlit screen.*

backlog (ˈbækˌlɒg) NOUN 1 an accumulation of uncompleted work, unsold stock, etc., to be dealt with. 2 *Chiefly US and Canadian* a large log at the back of a fireplace.

backlot (ˈbækˌlɒt) NOUN an area outside a film or television studio used for outdoor filming.

back marker NOUN a competitor who is at the back of a field in a race.

back matter NOUN the parts of a book, such as the index and appendices, that follow the main text. Also called: **end matter.**

backmost (ˈbækˌməʊst) ADJECTIVE furthest back.

back mutation NOUN *Genetics* the reversion of a mutant to the original phenotype.

back number NOUN 1 an issue of a newspaper, magazine, etc., that appeared on a previous date. 2 *Informal* a person or thing considered to be old-fashioned.

back o' Bourke (bɜːk) ADVERB *Austral* in a remote or backward place.
▷HISTORY from *Bourke*, a town in New South Wales

back off VERB (*adverb*) *Informal* 1 (*intr*) to retreat. 2 (*tr*) to abandon (an intention, objective, etc.).

back office NOUN **a** the administrative and support staff of a financial institution or other business. **b** (*as modifier*): *back-office operations.*

back out VERB (*intr, adverb;* often followed by *of*) to withdraw (from an agreement, etc.).

backpack (ˈbækˌpæk) NOUN 1 a rucksack or knapsack. 2 a pack carried on the back of an astronaut, containing oxygen cylinders, essential supplies, etc. ◆ VERB 3 (*intr*) to travel about or go hiking with a backpack. 4 (*tr*) to transport (food or equipment) by backpack.
▸ **ˈbackˌpacker** NOUN ▸ **ˈbackˌpacking** NOUN

back passage NOUN 1 the rectum. 2 an interior passageway towards the back of a building.

back pay NOUN pay received by an employee from an increase awarded retrospectively.

back-pedal VERB **-pedals, -pedalling, -pedalled** *or US* **-pedals, -pedaling, -pedaled.** (*intr*) 1 to turn the pedals of a bicycle backwards. 2 to retract or modify a previous opinion, principle, etc. 3 *Boxing* to take backward steps.

back pressure NOUN 1 *Engineering* **a** the pressure that opposes the motion of a piston on its exhaust stroke in an internal-combustion engine. **b** the exhaust pressure in external combustion engines. 2 *Med* the local pressure that builds up when fluid flow is obstructed in the cardiovascular or urinary systems.

back projection NOUN a method of projecting pictures onto a translucent screen so that they are viewed from the opposite side, used esp in films to create the illusion that the actors in the foreground are moving. Also called: **background projection.**

back rest NOUN a support for the back of something.

Back River NOUN a river in N Canada, flowing northeast through Nunavut to the Arctic Ocean. Length: about 966 km (600 miles).

back room NOUN **a** a place where research or planning is done, esp secret research in wartime. **b** (*as modifier*): *back-room boys.*

Backs (bæks) PLURAL NOUN **the.** the grounds between the River Cam and certain Cambridge colleges.

back saw NOUN a small handsaw stiffened along its upper edge by a metal section.

back scatter NOUN *Physics* 1 the scattering of particles or radiation, such as sound waves, X-rays, or alpha-particles, by the atoms of the medium through which they pass, in the backward direction. 2 the radiation or particles so scattered. 3 a technique whereby very long-range radars locate targets hidden by the curvature of the earth. Radar beams are reflected off the underside of the troposphere onto the target and the return beams, similarly reflected, are measured.

backscratcher (ˈbækˌskrætʃə) NOUN 1 an implement with a long handle, used for scratching one's own back. 2 *Informal* a person who provides a service, corporate or public money etc., for another, in order to receive a similar service or reward in return.
▸ **ˈbackˌscratching** NOUN

back seat NOUN 1 a seat at the back, esp of a vehicle. 2 *Informal* a subordinate or inconspicuous position (esp in the phrase **take a back seat**).

back-seat driver NOUN *Informal* 1 a passenger in a car who offers unwanted advice to the driver. 2 a person who offers advice on or tries to direct matters that are not his or her concern.

backsheesh (ˈbækʃiːʃ) NOUN a variant spelling of **baksheesh.**

back shift NOUN *Brit* 1 a group of workers who work a shift from late afternoon to midnight in an industry or occupation where a day shift or a night shift is also worked. 2 the period worked. ◆ US and Canadian name: **swing shift.**

backside (ˌbækˈsaɪd) NOUN 1 the back of something. 2 (ˈbækˌsaɪd) *Informal* the buttocks.

backsight (ˈbækˌsaɪt) NOUN 1 the sight of a rifle nearer the stock. 2 *Surveying* a reading taken looking backwards to a previously occupied station. Compare **foresight** (sense 4).

back slang NOUN a type of slang in which words are spelled and, as far as possible, pronounced backwards.

back-slapping ADJECTIVE energetically jovial; hearty.

backslash NOUN a solidus which slopes to the left (\).

backslide (ˈbækˌslaɪd) VERB **-slides, -sliding, -slid; -slid** *or* **-slidden.** (*intr*) to lapse into bad habits or vices from a state of virtue, religious faith, etc.
▸ **ˈbackˌslider** NOUN

backspace (ˈbækˌspeɪs) VERB 1 to move a (typewriter carriage) backwards. ◆ NOUN 2 a typewriter key that effects such a movements.

backspin (ˈbækˌspɪn) NOUN *Sport* a backward spinning motion imparted to a ball to reduce its speed at impact. Compare **topspin.**

backstage (ˌbækˈsteɪdʒ) ADVERB 1 behind the part of the theatre in view of the audience; in the dressing rooms, wings, etc. 2 towards the rear of the stage. ◆ ADJECTIVE 3 situated backstage. 4 *Informal* away from public view.

backstairs (ˈbækˈstɛəz) PLURAL NOUN 1 a secondary staircase in a house, esp one originally for the use of servants. ◆ ADJECTIVE *also* **backstair.** 2 underhand: *backstairs gossip.*

backstay (ˈbækˌsteɪ) NOUN 1 *Nautical* a stay leading aft from the upper part of a mast to the deck or stern. 2 *Machinery* a supporting piece or arresting part. 3 anything that supports or strengthens the back of something, such as leather covering the back seam of a shoe.

backstitch (ˈbækˌstɪtʃ) NOUN 1 a strong sewing stitch made by starting the next stitch at the middle or beginning of the preceding one. ◆ VERB 2 to sew using this stitch.

backstop (ˈbækˌstɒp) NOUN 1 *Sport* a screen or fence to prevent balls leaving the playing area. 2 a block or catch to prevent excessive backward movement, such as one on the sliding seat of a rowing boat. ◆ VERB **-stops, -stopping, -stopped.** (*tr*) 3 *US* to provide with backing or support.

back story NOUN the events which take place before, and which help to bring about, the events portrayed in a film.

back straight NOUN a straight part of a circuit, esp of an athletics track, furthest from the finishing point.

backstreet (ˈbækˌstriːt) NOUN 1 a street in a town remote from the main roads. 2 (*modifier*) denoting illicit activities regarded as likely to take place in such a street: *a backstreet abortion.*

back stretch NOUN a horse-racing term for **back straight.**

backstroke (ˈbækˌstrəʊk) NOUN 1 Also called: **back crawl.** *Swimming* **a** a stroke performed on the back, using backward circular strokes of each arm and flipper movements of the feet. **b** (*as modifier*): *the backstroke champion.* 2 a return stroke or blow. 3 *Chiefly US* a backhanded stroke. 4 *Bell-ringing* the upward movement of the bell rope as the bell swings back and forth. Compare **handstroke.** ◆ VERB 5 (*intr*) to swim the backstroke.

backswept (ˈbækˌswɛpt) ADJECTIVE 1 slanting backwards. 2 another word for **sweptback.**

backsword (ˈbækˌsɔːd) NOUN 1 another name for **broadsword.** 2 Also called: **backswordsman.** a person who uses the backsword. 3 a fencing stick with a basket-like protective hilt.

back-to-back ADJECTIVE (*usually postpositive*) 1 facing in opposite directions, often with the backs touching. 2 *Chiefly Brit* (of urban houses) built so that their backs are joined or separated only by a narrow alley. 3 *Informal* consecutive. 4 *Commerce* **a** denoting a credit arrangement in which a finance house acts as an intermediary to conceal the identity of the seller from the buyer. **b** denoting a loan from one company to another in a different country using a finance house to provide the loan but not the funding. ◆ NOUN 5 a house or terrace built in back-to-back style.

backtrack (ˈbækˌtræk) VERB (*intr*) 1 to return by the same route by which one has come. 2 to retract or reverse one's opinion, action, policy, etc.
▸ **ˈbackˌtracking** NOUN

back up VERB (*adverb*) 1 (*tr*) to support or assist. 2 (*intr*) *Cricket* (of a nonstriking batsman) to move down the wicket in readiness for a run as a ball is bowled. 3 (of water) to accumulate. 4 (of traffic) to become jammed behind an accident or other obstruction. 5 *Computing* to make a copy of (a data file), esp for storage in another place as a security copy. 6 *Printing* to print the second side of (a sheet). 7 (*intr,* usually foll by *on*) *Austral* to repeat an action immediately. ◆ NOUN **backup.** 8 a support or reinforcement. 9 **a** a reserve or substitute. **b** (*as modifier*): *backup troops.* 10 the overflow from a blocked drain or pipe. 11 *Computing* a file or set of files copied for security purposes.

back-up light NOUN a US and Canadian name for **reversing light.**

backward ('bækwəd) ADJECTIVE [1] (*usually prenominal*) directed towards the rear: *a backward glance.* [2] retarded in physical, material, or intellectual development: *backward countries; a backward child.* [3] **a** of or relating to the past; conservative or reactionary. **b** (*in combination*): *backward-looking.* [4] reluctant or bashful: *a backward lover.* [5] *Chess* (of a pawn) behind neighbouring pawns and unable to be supported by them. ◆ ADVERB [6] a variant of **backwards.**
▸ **'backwardly** ADVERB ▸ **'backwardness** NOUN

backwardation (ˌbækwə'deɪʃən) NOUN *Commerce* [1] the difference between the spot price for a commodity, including rent and interest, and the forward price. [2] (formerly, on the Stock Exchange) postponement of delivery by a seller of securities until the next settlement period.

backwards ('bækwədz) *or* **backward** ADVERB [1] towards the rear. [2] with the back foremost. [3] in the reverse of usual order or direction. [4] to or towards the past. [5] into a worse state: *the patient was slipping backwards.* [6] towards the point of origin. [7] **bend, lean,** *or* **fall over backwards.** *Informal* to make a special effort, esp in order to please. [8] **know backwards.** *Informal* to understand completely.

backwash ('bækˌwɒʃ) NOUN [1] a sucking movement of water, such as that of retreating waves. Compare **swash.** [2] water washed backwards by the motion of oars or other propelling devices. [3] the backward flow of air set up by an aircraft's engines. [4] a condition resulting from a previous event; repercussion. ◆ VERB [5] (*tr*) to remove oil from (combed wool).

backwater ('bækˌwɔːtə) NOUN [1] a body of stagnant water connected to a river. [2] water held or driven back, as by a dam, flood, or tide. [3] an isolated, backward, or intellectually stagnant place or condition. ◆ VERB **back water.** [4] (*intr*) to reverse the direction of a boat, esp to push the oars of a rowing boat.

backwoods ('bækwʊdz) PLURAL NOUN [1] *Chiefly US and Canadian* partially cleared, sparsely populated forests. [2] any remote sparsely populated place. [3] (*modifier*) of, from, or like the backwoods. [4] (*modifier*) uncouth; rustic.

backwoodsman ('bækˌwʊdzmən) NOUN, *plural* **-men.** [1] a person from the backwoods. [2] *US informal* an uncouth or rustic person. [3] *Brit informal* a peer who rarely attends the House of Lords.

backword ('bækˌwɜːd) NOUN *Brit dialect* the act or an instance of failing to keep a promise or commitment (esp in the phrase **give (someone) backword**).

back yard NOUN [1] a yard at the back of a house, etc. [2] **in one's own back yard. a** close at hand. **b** involving or implicating one.

baclava ('bɑːkləˌvɑː) NOUN a variant spelling of **baklava.**

Bacolod (bə'kɒləd) NOUN a town in the Philippines, on the NW coast of Negros Island. Pop.: 429 076 (2000).

bacon ('beɪkən) NOUN [1] meat from the back and sides of a pig, dried, salted, and usually smoked. [2] **bring home the bacon.** *Informal* **a** to achieve success. **b** to provide material support. [3] **save (someone's) bacon.** *Brit informal* to help (someone) to escape from danger.
▷**HISTORY** C12: from Old French *bacon,* from Old High German *bahho;* related to Old Saxon *baco;* see BACK[1]

bacon-and-eggs NOUN another name for **bird's-foot trefoil.**

bacon beetle NOUN See **dermestid.**

baconer ('beɪkənə) NOUN a pig that weighs between 83 and 101 kg, from which bacon is cut.

Baconian (beɪ'kəʊnɪən) ADJECTIVE [1] of or relating to Francis Bacon, Baron Verulam, Viscount St. Albans (1561–1626), the English philosopher, statesman, and essayist, or to his inductive method of reasoning. ◆ NOUN [2] a follower of Bacon's philosophy. [3] one who believes that plays attributed to Shakespeare were written by Bacon.

BACS (bæks) NOUN ACRONYM FOR Bankers Automated Clearing System; a method of making payments direct to a creditor's bank without using a cheque.

bacteraemia *or US* **bacteremia** (ˌbæktə'riːmɪə) NOUN *Pathol* the presence of bacteria in the blood.

bacteria (bæk'tɪərɪə) PLURAL NOUN, *singular* **-rium** (-rɪəm). a very large group of microorganisms comprising one of the three domains of living organisms. They are prokaryotic, unicellular, and either free-living in soil or water or parasites of plants or animals. See also **prokaryote.**
▷**HISTORY** C19: plural of New Latin *bacterium,* from Greek *baktērion,* literally: a little stick, from *baktron* rod, staff
▸ **bac'terial** ADJECTIVE ▸ **bac'terially** ADVERB

bacteria bed NOUN a layer of sand or gravel used to expose sewage effluent, in its final stages, to air and the action of microorganisms. Compare **filter bed** (sense 1).

bacterial plaque NOUN another term for **dental plaque.**

bactericide (bæk'tɪərɪˌsaɪd) NOUN a substance able to destroy bacteria.
▸ **bacˌteri'cidal** ADJECTIVE

bacterin ('bæktərɪn) NOUN *Obsolete* a vaccine prepared from bacteria.

bacterio-, bacteri-, *or sometimes before a vowel* **bacter-** COMBINING FORM indicating bacteria or an action or condition relating to bacteria: *bacteriology; bactericide; bacteroid.*
▷**HISTORY** New Latin, from BACTERIA

bacteriol. ABBREVIATION FOR: [1] bacteriological. [2] bacteriology.

bacteriological warfare NOUN another term for **germ warfare.**

bacteriology (bækˌtɪərɪ'ɒlədʒɪ) NOUN the branch of science concerned with the study of bacteria.
▸ **bacteriological** (bækˌtɪərɪə'lɒdʒɪkᵊl) ADJECTIVE
▸ **bacˌterio'logically** ADVERB ▸ **bacˌteri'ologist** NOUN

bacteriolysis (bækˌtɪərɪ'ɒlɪsɪs) NOUN the destruction or disintegration of bacteria.
▸ **bacteriolytic** (bækˌtɪərɪə'lɪtɪk) ADJECTIVE

bacteriophage (bæk'tɪərɪəˌfeɪdʒ) NOUN a virus that is parasitic in a bacterium and multiplies within its host, which is destroyed when the new viruses are released. Often shortened to: **phage.**
▸ **bacteriophagic** (bækˌtɪərɪə'fædʒɪk) ADJECTIVE
▸ **bacteriophagous** (bækˌtɪərɪ'ɒfəgəs) ADJECTIVE

bacteriostasis (bækˌtɪərɪəʊ'steɪsɪs, -'stæsɪs) NOUN, *plural* **-stases** (-'steɪsiːz, -'stæsiːz). inhibition of the growth and reproduction of bacteria, esp by the action of a chemical agent.
▸ **bacteriostatic** (bækˌtɪərɪəʊ'stætɪk) ADJECTIVE
▸ **bacˌterio'statically** ADVERB

bacteriostat (bæk'tɪərɪəʊˌstæt) NOUN any substance that arrests the growth or reproduction of bacteria but does not kill them.

bacteriotoxin (bækˌtɪərɪəʊ'tɒksɪn) NOUN [1] any toxin that kills bacteria. [2] a toxin produced by bacteria.

bacterium (bæk'tɪərɪəm) NOUN the singular of **bacteria.**

bacteriuria (bækˌtɪərɪ'jʊərɪə) *or* **bacteruria** (ˌbæktə'rjʊərɪə) NOUN the presence of bacteria in the urine.

bacteroid ('bæktəˌrɔɪd) ADJECTIVE [1] resembling a bacterium. ◆ NOUN [2] any rodlike bacterium of the genus *Bacteroides,* occurring in the gut of man and animals.

Bactria ('bæktrɪə) NOUN an ancient country of SW Asia, between the Hindu Kush mountains and the Oxus River: forms the present Balkh region in N Afghanistan.

Bactrian ('bæktrɪən) ADJECTIVE [1] of or relating to Bactria. ◆ NOUN [2] a native or inhabitant of Bactria.

Bactrian camel NOUN a two-humped camel, *Camelus bactrianus,* used as a beast of burden in the cold deserts of central Asia. Compare **Arabian camel.**

baculiform (bə'kjuːlɪˌfɔːm, 'bækjuː-) ADJECTIVE *Biology* shaped like a rod: *baculiform fungal spores.*
▷**HISTORY** C19: from *baculi-,* from Latin *baculum* walking stick + -FORM

baculum ('bækjʊləm) NOUN, *plural* **-la** (-lə) *or* **-lums.** a bony support in the penis of certain mammals, esp the carnivores.
▷**HISTORY** C20: New Latin, from Latin: stick, staff

bad[1] (bæd) ADJECTIVE **worse, worst.** [1] not good; of poor quality; inadequate; inferior: *bad workmanship; bad soil; bad light for reading.* [2] (often foll by *at*) lacking skill or talent; incompetent: *a bad painter; bad at sports.* [3] (often foll by *for*) harmful: *bad air; smoking is bad for you.* [4] immoral; evil: *a bad life.* [5] naughty; mischievous; disobedient: *a bad child.* [6] rotten; decayed; spoiled: *a bad egg.* [7] severe; intense: *a bad headache.* [8] incorrect; wrong; faulty: *bad pronunciation.* [9] ill or in pain (esp in the phrase **feel bad**). [10] regretful, sorry, or upset (esp in the phrase **feel bad about**). [11] unfavourable; distressing: *bad news; a bad business.* [12] offensive; unpleasant; disagreeable: *bad language; bad temper.* [13] not valid or sound; void: *a bad cheque.* [14] not recoverable: *a bad debt.* [15] (**badder, baddest**) *Slang* good; excellent. [16] **go from bad to worse.** to deteriorate even more. [17] **go bad.** to putrefy; spoil. [18] **in a bad way.** *Informal* **a** seriously ill, through sickness or injury. **b** in trouble of any kind. [19] **in someone's bad books.** See **book** (sense 21). [20] **make the best of a bad job.** to manage as well as possible in unfavourable circumstances. [21] **not bad** *or* **not so bad.** *Informal* passable; fair; fairly good. [22] **not half bad.** *Informal* very good. [23] **too bad.** *Informal* (often used dismissively) regrettable. ◆ NOUN [24] unfortunate or unpleasant events collectively (often in the phrase **take the bad with the good**). [25] an immoral or degenerate state (often in the phrase **go to the bad**). [26] the debit side of an account: *£200 to the bad.* ◆ ADVERB [27] *Not standard* badly: *to want something bad.*
▷**HISTORY** C13: probably from *bæd-,* as the first element of Old English *bǣddel* hermaphrodite, *bǣdling* sodomite
▸ **'baddish** ADJECTIVE ▸ **'badness** NOUN

bad[2] (bæd) VERB a variant of **bade.**

Badajoz ('bædəˌhɒz; *Spanish* ba'ðaxoθ) NOUN a city in SW Spain: strategically positioned near the frontier with Portugal. Pop.: 134 710 (1998 est.).

Badalona (*Spanish* baða'lona) NOUN a port in NE Spain: an industrial suburb of Barcelona. Pop.: 209 606 (1995 est.).

badass ('bædˌæs) *Slang, chiefly US* ◆ NOUN [1] a tough or aggressive person: *the meanest badass in town.* ◆ ADJECTIVE [2] tough or aggressive: *a badass rock band.* [3] excellent: *a real badass watch.*

bad blood NOUN a feeling of intense hatred or hostility; enmity.

baddeleyite ('bædlɪˌaɪt) NOUN a mineral consisting largely of zirconium dioxide: a source of zirconium. Formula: ZrO_2.
▷**HISTORY** C19: named after J. *Baddeley,* British geologist

badderlocks ('bædəˌlɒks) NOUN a seaweed, *Alaria esculenta,* that has long brownish-green fronds and is eaten in parts of N Europe.
▷**HISTORY** C18: of unknown origin

baddie *or* **baddy** ('bædɪ) NOUN, *plural* **-dies.** a bad character in a story, film, etc., esp an opponent of the hero.

bade (bæd, beɪd) *or* **bad** VERB past tense of **bid.**

Baden ('bɑːdən) NOUN a former state of West Germany, now part of Baden-Württemberg.

Baden-Baden NOUN a spa in SW Germany, in Baden-Württemberg. Pop.: 52 520 (1991).

Baden-Württemberg (*German* 'baːdən'vyrtəmbɛrk) NOUN a state of SW Germany; formerly in West Germany. Capital: Stuttgart. Pop.: 10 475 900 (2000 est.). Area: 35 742 sq. km (13 800 sq. miles).

bad faith NOUN [1] intention to deceive; treachery or dishonesty (esp in the phrase **in bad faith**). [2] Also called: **mauvaise foi.** (in the philosophy of the 20th-century French philosopher Jean-Paul Sartre) self-deception, as when an agent regards his actions as conditioned by circumstances or conventions in order to evade his own responsibility for choosing them freely.

badge (bædʒ) NOUN [1] a distinguishing emblem or mark worn to signify membership, employment, achievement, etc. [2] any revealing feature or mark.
▷**HISTORY** C14: from Norman French *bage;* related to Anglo-Latin *bagia*

badger ('bædʒə) NOUN [1] any of various stocky omnivorous musteline mammals of the subfamily *Melinae,* such as *Meles meles* (**Eurasian badger**), occurring in Europe, Asia, and North America: order *Carnivora* (carnivores). They are typically large burrowing animals, with strong claws and a thick

coat striped black and white on the head. Compare **ferret badger, hog badger.** 2 **honey badger.** another name for **ratel.** ◆ VERB 3 *(tr)* to pester or harass.
▷**HISTORY** C16: variant of *badgeard*, probably from BADGE (from the white mark on its forehead) + -ARD

Bad Godesberg (*German* baːt 'goːdəsbɛrk) NOUN the official name for **Godesberg.**

bad hair day NOUN *Informal* 1 a day on which one's hair is untidy and unmanageable. 2 a day of mishaps and general irritation.

badinage ('bædɪˌnɑːʒ) NOUN playful or frivolous repartee or banter.
▷**HISTORY** C17: from French, from *badiner* to jest, banter, from Old Provençal *badar* to gape

badinerie (bəˌdɪnə'riː) NOUN *Music* a name given in the 18th century to a type of quick, light movement in a suite.
▷**HISTORY** French: a pleasantry

badlands ('bædˌlændz) PLURAL NOUN any deeply eroded barren area.

Bad Lands PLURAL NOUN a deeply eroded barren region of SW South Dakota and NW Nebraska.

badly ('bædlɪ) ADVERB **worse, worst.** 1 poorly; defectively; inadequately: *the chair is badly made.* 2 unfavourably; unsuccessfully; unfortunately: *our scheme worked out badly.* 3 severely; gravely: *he was badly hurt.* 4 incorrectly or inaccurately: *to speak German badly.* 5 improperly; naughtily; wickedly: *to behave badly.* 6 without humanity; cruelly: *to treat badly.* 7 very much (esp in the phrases **need badly, badly in need of, want badly**). 8 regretfully: *he felt badly about it.* 9 **badly off.** poor; impoverished. ◆ ADJECTIVE 10 *(postpositive) Northern English dialect* ill; poorly.

badman ('bædˌmæn) NOUN, *plural* **-men.** *Chiefly US* a hired gunman, outlaw, or criminal.

badminton ('bædmɪntən) NOUN 1 a game played with rackets and a shuttlecock, which is hit back and forth across a high net. 2 Also called: **badminton cup.** a long refreshing drink of claret with soda water and sugar.
▷**HISTORY** C19: named after BADMINTON House, where the game was first played

Badminton ('bædmɪntən) NOUN a village in SW England, in South Gloucestershire unitary authority, Gloucestershire: site of Badminton House, seat of the Duke of Beaufort; annual horse trials.

bad-mouth VERB *(tr) Slang* to speak unfavourably about.

bad news NOUN *Slang* someone or something regarded as undesirable: *he's bad news around here.*

bad-tempered ADJECTIVE angry, irritable, or ungracious.

bad trot NOUN *Austral slang* a period of ill fortune.

Baedeker ('beɪdɪkə) NOUN 1 any of a series of travel guidebooks issued by the German publisher Karl Baedeker (1801–59) or his firm. 2 any guidebook.

Baedeker raid NOUN *Informal* one of the German air raids in 1942 on places of cultural and historical importance in England.

bael ('beɪəl) NOUN 1 a spiny Indian rutaceous tree, *Aegle marmelos.* 2 the edible thick-shelled fruit of this tree.
▷**HISTORY** C17: from Hindi *bel*

BAF ABBREVIATION FOR British Athletic Federation.

Bafana bafana (ba'fɑːna) PLURAL NOUN *South African* an African name for the South African national soccer team.
▷**HISTORY** C20: from Nguni *bafana* the boys

baffies ('bæfɪz) PLURAL NOUN *Scot dialect* slippers.

Baffin Bay ('bæfɪn) NOUN part of the Northwest Passage, situated between Baffin Island and Greenland.
▷**HISTORY** named after William *Baffin*, 17th-century English navigator

Baffin Island NOUN the largest island of the Canadian Arctic, between Greenland and Hudson Bay. Area: 476 560 sq. km (184 000 sq. miles).

baffle ('bæfᵊl) VERB *(tr)* 1 to perplex; bewilder; puzzle. 2 to frustrate (plans, efforts, etc.). 3 to check, restrain, or regulate (the flow of a fluid or the emission of sound or light). 4 to provide with a baffle. 5 *Obsolete* to cheat or trick. ◆ NOUN Also called: **baffle board, baffle plate.** a plate or mechanical device designed to restrain or regulate the flow of a fluid, the emission of light or sound, or the distribution of sound, esp in a loudspeaker or microphone.
▷**HISTORY** C16: perhaps from Scottish dialect *bachlen* to condemn publicly; perhaps related to French *bafouer* to disgrace
▸ '**bafflement** NOUN ▸ '**baffler** NOUN

baffling ('bæflɪŋ) ADJECTIVE impossible to understand; perplexing; bewildering; puzzling.
▸ '**bafflingly** ADVERB

BAFTA ('bæftə) NOUN ACRONYM FOR British Academy of Film and Television Arts.

bag (bæg) NOUN 1 a flexible container with an opening at one end. 2 Also called: **bagful.** the contents of or amount contained in such a container. 3 any of various measures of quantity, such as a bag containing 1 hundredweight of coal. 4 a piece of portable luggage. 5 short for **handbag.** 6 anything that hangs loosely, sags, or is shaped like a bag, such as a loose fold of skin under the eyes or the bulging part of a sail. 7 any pouch or sac forming part of the body of an animal, esp the udder of a cow. 8 *Hunting* the quantity of quarry taken in a single hunting trip or by a single hunter. 9 *Derogatory slang* an ugly or bad-tempered woman or girl (often in the phrase **old bag**). 10 *Slang* a measure of marijuana, heroin, etc., in folded paper. 11 *Slang* a person's particular taste, field of skill, interest, activity, etc.: *blues is his bag.* 12 **bag and baggage.** *Informal* **a** with all one's belongings. **b** entirely. 13 **a bag of bones.** a lean creature. 14 **in the bag.** *Slang* almost assured of succeeding or being obtained. 15 **the (whole) bag of tricks.** *Informal* every device; everything. ◆ VERB **bags, bagging, bagged.** 16 *(tr)* to put into a bag. 17 to bulge or cause to bulge; swell. 18 *(tr)* to capture or kill, as in hunting. 19 *(tr)* to catch, seize, or steal. 20 *(intr)* to hang loosely; sag. 21 *(tr)* to achieve or accomplish: *she bagged seven birdies.* 22 *(tr) Brit informal* to reserve or secure the right to do or to have something: *he bagged the best chair.* 23 *(tr) Austral slang* to criticize; disparage. See also **bags.**
▷**HISTORY** C13: probably from Old Norse *baggi*; related to Old French *bague* bundle, pack, Medieval Latin *baga* chest, sack, Flemish *bagge*

Baganda (bə'gændə, -'gɑːn-) NOUN *(functioning as plural)* a Negroid people of E Africa living chiefly in Uganda. See also **Ganda, Luganda.**

bagasse (bə'gæs) NOUN 1 the pulp remaining after the extraction of juice from sugar cane or similar plants: used as fuel and for making paper, etc. 2 Also called: **megass, megasse.** a type of paper made from bagasse fibres.
▷**HISTORY** C19: from French, from Spanish *bagazo* dregs, refuse, from *baga* husk, from Latin *bāca* berry

bagassosis (ˌbægə'səʊsɪs) NOUN an allergic response to the dust of bagasse, causing breathlessness and fever.

bagatelle (ˌbægə'tɛl) NOUN 1 something of little value or significance; trifle. 2 a board game in which balls are struck into holes, with pins as obstacles; pinball. 3 another name for **bar billiards.** 4 a short light piece of music, esp for piano.
▷**HISTORY** C17: from French, from Italian *bagattella*, from (dialect) *bagatta* a little possession, from *baga* a possession, probably from Latin *bāca* berry

Bagdad (bæg'dæd) NOUN a variant spelling of **Baghdad.**

bagel *or* **beigel** ('beɪgᵊl) NOUN a hard ring-shaped bread roll, characteristic of Jewish baking.
▷**HISTORY** C20: from Yiddish *beygel*, ultimately from Old High German *boug* ring

baggage ('bægɪdʒ) NOUN 1 **a** suitcases, bags, etc., packed for a journey; luggage. **b** *Chiefly US and Canadian (as modifier)*: *baggage car.* 2 an army's portable equipment. 3 *Informal, old-fashioned* **a** a pert young woman. **b** an immoral woman or prostitute. 4 *Irish informal* a cantankerous old woman. 5 *Informal* previous knowledge and experience that a person may use or be influenced by in new circumstances: *cultural baggage.*
▷**HISTORY** C15: from Old French *bagage*, from *bague* a bundle, perhaps of Scandinavian origin; compare Old Norse *baggi* BAG

bagging ('bægɪŋ) NOUN coarse woven cloth; sacking.

baggy[1] ('bægɪ) ADJECTIVE **-gier, -giest.** (of clothes) hanging loosely; puffed out.
▸ '**baggily** ADVERB ▸ '**bagginess** NOUN

baggy[2] ('bægɪ) NOUN, *plural* **-gies.** a variant spelling of **bagie.**

baggy green NOUN *Austral informal* 1 the Australian Test cricket cap. 2 **don** *or* **wear the baggy green.** to represent Australia at Test cricket.

bagh (bɑːg) NOUN (in India and Pakistan) a garden.
▷**HISTORY** Urdu

Baghdad *or* **Bagdad** (bæg'dæd) NOUN the capital of Iraq, on the River Tigris: capital of the Abbasid Caliphate (762–1258). Pop.: 4 478 000 (1995 est.).

bagie ('beɪgɪ) *or* **baggy** NOUN, *plural* **-gies.** *Northumbrian dialect* a turnip.
▷**HISTORY** perhaps from RUTABAGA

bag lady NOUN a woman who is homeless and wanders city streets with all her possessions in shopping bags. Also called (in full): **shopping bag lady.**

bagless ('bæglɪs) ADJECTIVE (esp of a vacuum cleaner) not containing a bag.

bagman ('bægmən) NOUN, *plural* **-men.** 1 *Brit informal* a travelling salesman. 2 *Slang, chiefly US* a person who collects or distributes money for racketeers. 3 *Informal, chiefly Canadian* a person who solicits money or subscriptions for a political party. 4 *Austral history* a tramp or swagman, esp one on horseback. 5 Also called: **bagswinger.** *Austral slang* someone who takes money for a bookmaker.

bag moth NOUN *NZ* a moth, the larvae of which develop in bags or cases.

bagna cauda (ˌbɑːnjə 'kaʊdə) NOUN a dip made from garlic, anchovies, butter, and olive oil, usually served hot over a spirit burner, with raw vegetables.
▷**HISTORY** from Italian *bagno caldo*, literally: hot bath

bagnette ('bægnɛt) NOUN a variant of **baguette** (sense 3).

bagnio ('bɑːnjəʊ) NOUN, *plural* **-ios.** 1 a brothel. 2 *Obsolete* an oriental prison for slaves. 3 *Obsolete* an Italian or Turkish bathhouse.
▷**HISTORY** C16: from Italian *bagno*, from Latin *balneum* bath, from Greek *balaneion*

bagpipe ('bægˌpaɪp) NOUN *(modifier)* of or relating to the bagpipes: *a bagpipe maker.*

bagpipes ('bægˌpaɪps) PLURAL NOUN any of a family of musical wind instruments in which sounds are produced in reed pipes supplied with air from a bag inflated either by the player's mouth, as in the **Irish bagpipes** or **Highland bagpipes** of Scotland, or by arm-operated bellows, as in the **Northumbrian bagpipes.**

bags (bægz) PLURAL NOUN 1 *Informal* a lot; a great deal. 2 short for **Oxford bags.** 3 *Brit informal* any pair of trousers. ◆ INTERJECTION 4 Also: **bags I.** *Children's slang, Brit and Austral* an indication of the desire to do, be, or have something. 5 **rough as bags** *or* **sacks.** *Austral and NZ* uncouth.

bagswinger ('bægˌswɪŋə) NOUN *Austral slang* another term for **bagman.**

baguette *or* **baguet** (bæ'gɛt) NOUN 1 a narrow French stick loaf. 2 a small gem cut as a long rectangle. 3 the shape of such a gem. 4 *Architect* a small moulding having a semicircular cross section.
▷**HISTORY** C18: from French, from Italian *bacchetta* a little stick, from *bacchio* rod, from Latin *baculum* walking stick

Baguio ('bægɪˌəʊ) NOUN a city in the N Philippines, on N Luzon: summer capital of the Republic. Pop.: 252 386 (2000).

bagwash ('bægˌwɒʃ) NOUN *Old-fashioned* 1 a laundry that washes clothes without drying or pressing them. 2 the clothes so washed.

bagwig ('bægˌwɪg) NOUN an 18th-century wig with hair pushed back into a bag.

bagworm ('bægˌwɜːm) NOUN 1 the larva of moths of the family *Psychidae*, which forms a protective case of silk covered with grass, leaves, etc. 2 **bagworm moth.** any moth of the family *Psychidae.*

bah (bɑː, bæ) INTERJECTION an expression of contempt or disgust.

bahadur (bə'hɑːdə) NOUN *(often in combination)* a title formerly conferred by the British on distinguished Indians.

▷**HISTORY** C18: from Hindi *bahādur* hero, from Persian: valiant

Baha'í (bə'hɑːɪ) NOUN 1 an adherent of the Baha'í Faith. ♦ ADJECTIVE 2 of or relating to the Baha'í Faith.
▷**HISTORY** from Persian *bahā'ī*, literally: of glory, from *bahā' u'llāh* glory of God, from Arabic

Baha'í Faith *or* **Baha'í** NOUN a religious system founded in 1863 by Baha'ullah, based on Babism and emphasizing the value of all religions and the spiritual unity of all mankind.
▸**Ba'ha'ist** *or* **Ba'ha'ite** ADJECTIVE, NOUN

Baha'ísm (ba'hɑːˌɪzəm) NOUN another name, not in Baha'í use, for the **Baha'í Faith**.

Bahamas (bə'hɑːməz) *or* **Bahama Islands** PLURAL NOUN **the**. a group of over 700 coral islands (about 20 of which are inhabited) in the Caribbean: a British colony from 1783 until 1964; an independent nation within the Commonwealth from 1973. Language: English. Currency: Bahamian dollar. Capital: Nassau. Pop.: 298 000 (2001 est.). Area: 13 939 sq. km (5381 sq. miles).

Bahamian (bə'heɪmɪən, -'hɑː-) ADJECTIVE 1 of or relating to the Bahamas. ♦ NOUN 2 a native or inhabitant of the Bahamas.

Bahasa Indonesia (bɑː'hɑːsə) NOUN the official language of Indonesia: developed from the form of Malay formerly widely used as a trade language in SE Asia.

Bahawalpur (ˌbæhə'wɒlpə) NOUN an industrial city in Pakistan: cotton, soap. Pop. (urban area): 403 408 (1998).

Bahia (bə'hiːə; *Portuguese* bə'iːə) NOUN 1 a state of E Brazil, on the Atlantic coast. Capital: Salvador. Pop.: 13 066 764 (2000). Area: about 562 000 sq. km (217 000 sq. miles). 2 the former name of **San Salvador**.

Bahía Blanca (*Spanish* ba'ia 'blanka) NOUN a port in E Argentina. Pop.: 281 161 (1999 est.).

Bahia de los Cochinos (ba'ia de los ko'tʃinos) NOUN the Spanish name for the **Bay of Pigs**.

Bahrain *or* **Bahrein** (bɑː'reɪn) NOUN an independent sheikhdom on the Persian Gulf, consisting of several islands: under British protection until the declaration of independence in 1971. It has large oil reserves. Language: Arabic. Religion: Muslim. Currency: dinar. Capital: Manama. Pop.: 701 000 (2001 est.). Area: 678 sq. km (262 sq. miles).

Bahraini *or* **Bahreini** (bɑː'reɪnɪ) ADJECTIVE 1 of or relating to Bahrain. ♦ NOUN 2 a native or inhabitant of Bahrain.

baht (bɑːt) NOUN, *plural* **bahts** *or* **baht**. the standard monetary unit of Thailand, divided into 100 satang.
▷**HISTORY** from Thai *bāt*

bahuvrihi (ˌbɑːhuː'vriːhiː) NOUN *Linguistics* 1 a class of compound words consisting of two elements the first of which is a specific feature of the second. 2 a compound word of this type, such as *hunchback, bluebell, highbrow*.
▷**HISTORY** C19: from Sanskrit *bahuvrīhi*, itself this type of compound, from *bahu* much + *vrīh* rice

Baikal (baɪ'kɑːl, -'kæl) NOUN **Lake**. a lake in Russia, in SE Siberia: the largest freshwater lake in Eurasia and the deepest in the world. Greatest depth: over 1500 m (5000 ft.). Area: about 33 670 sq. km (13 000 sq. miles).

bail[1] (beɪl) *Law* ♦ NOUN 1 a sum of money by which a person is bound to take responsibility for the appearance in court of another person or himself, forfeited if the person fails to appear. 2 the person or persons so binding themselves; surety. 3 the system permitting release of a person from custody where such security has been taken: *he was released on bail*. 4 **jump bail** *or* (*formal*) **forfeit bail**. to fail to appear in court to answer to a charge. 5 **stand** *or* **go bail**. to act as surety (for someone). ♦ VERB (*tr*) 6 (often foll by *out*) to release or obtain the release of (a person) from custody, security having been made. ♦ See also **bail out**.
▷**HISTORY** C14: from Old French: custody, from *baillier* to hand over, from Latin *bājulāre* to carry burdens, from *bājulus* carrier, of obscure origin

bail[2] *or* **bale** (beɪl) VERB (often foll by *out*) to remove (water) from (a boat).
▷**HISTORY** C13: from Old French *baille* bucket, from Latin *bājulus* carrier
▸**'bailer** *or* **'baler** NOUN

bail[3] (beɪl) NOUN 1 *Cricket* either of two small wooden bars placed across the tops of the stumps to form the wicket. 2 *Agriculture* **a** a partition between stalls in a stable or barn, for horses. **b** a portable dairy house built on wheels or skids. 3 *Austral and NZ* a framework in a cowshed used to secure the head of a cow during milking. ♦ VERB 4 See **bail up**.
▷**HISTORY** C18: from Old French *baile* stake, fortification, probably from Latin *baculum* stick

bail[4] *or* **bale** (beɪl) NOUN 1 the semicircular handle of a kettle, bucket, etc. 2 a semicircular support for a canopy. 3 a movable bar on a typewriter that holds the paper against the platen.
▷**HISTORY** C15: probably of Scandinavian origin; compare Old Norse *beygja* to bend

bailable ('beɪləbᵊl) ADJECTIVE *Law* 1 eligible for release on bail. 2 admitting of bail: *a bailable offence*.

bail bandit NOUN a person who commits a crime having been released on bail to await trial for another offence.

bail bond NOUN a document in which a prisoner and one or more sureties guarantee that the prisoner will attend the court hearing of the charges against him if he is released on bail.

Baile Átha Cliath (blɑː'klɪə) NOUN the Irish Gaelic name for **Dublin**.

bailee (beɪ'liː) NOUN *Contract law* a person to whom the possession of goods is transferred under a bailment.

bailey ('beɪlɪ) NOUN the outermost wall or court of a castle.
▷**HISTORY** C13: from Old French *baille* enclosed court, from *bailler* to enclose; see BAIL[3]

Bailey bridge NOUN a temporary bridge made of prefabricated steel panels that can be rapidly assembled.
▷**HISTORY** C20: named after Sir Donald Coleman *Bailey* (1901–85), its English designer

bailie ('beɪlɪ) NOUN 1 (in Scotland) a municipal magistrate. 2 an obsolete or dialect spelling of **bailiff**.
▷**HISTORY** C13: from Old French *bailli*, from earlier *baillif* BAILIFF

bailiff ('beɪlɪf) NOUN 1 *Brit* the agent or steward of a landlord or landowner. 2 a sheriff's officer who serves writs and summonses, makes arrests, and ensures that the sentences of the court are carried out. 3 *Chiefly Brit* (formerly) a high official having judicial powers. 4 *Chiefly US* an official having custody of prisoners appearing in court.
▷**HISTORY** C13: from Old French *baillif*, from *bail* custody; see BAIL[1]

bailiwick ('beɪlɪwɪk) NOUN 1 *Law* the area over which a bailiff has jurisdiction. 2 a person's special field of interest, authority, or skill.
▷**HISTORY** C15: from BAILIE + WICK[2]

bailment ('beɪlmənt) NOUN 1 *Contract law* a contractual delivery of goods in trust to a person for a specific purpose. 2 *Criminal law* the act of granting bail.

bailor ('beɪlə, beɪ'lɔː) NOUN *Contract law* a person who retains ownership of goods but entrusts possession of them to another under a bailment.

bail out *or* **bale out** VERB (*adverb*) 1 (*intr*) to make an emergency parachute jump from an aircraft. 2 (*tr*) *Informal* to help (a person, organization, etc.) out of a predicament: *the government bailed the company out*. 3 (*intr*) *Informal* to escape from a predicament.

bail up VERB (*adverb*) 1 *Austral and NZ informal* to confine (a cow) or (of a cow) to be confined by the head in a bail. See **bail**[3]. 2 (*tr*) *Austral history* (of a bushranger) to hold under guard in order to rob. 3 (*intr*) *Austral* to submit to robbery without offering resistance. 4 (*tr*) *Austral informal* to accost or detain, esp in conversation; buttonhole.

Baily ('beɪlɪ) NOUN one of the largest craters on the moon, about 293 kilometres in diameter, lying in the SE quadrant.

Baily's beads ('beɪlɪz) PLURAL NOUN the brilliant points of sunlight that appear briefly around the moon, just before and after a total eclipse.
▷**HISTORY** C19: named after Francis *Baily* (died 1844), English astronomer who described them

báinín *or* **bawneen** ('bɑːniːn) NOUN *Irish* 1 a collarless revers-less unlined man's jacket made of white close-woven wool. 2 the material for such a jacket. 3 **báinín skirt**. a skirt made of this material. 4 **báinín wool**. white woollen thread.
▷**HISTORY** C20: from Irish Gaelic *báinín*, diminutive of *bán* white

bainite ('beɪnaɪt) NOUN a mixture of iron and iron carbide found in incompletely hardened steels, produced when austenite is transformed at temperatures between the pearlite and martensite ranges.
▷**HISTORY** C20: named after Edgar C. *Bain* (1891–1971), American physicist; see -ITE[1]

bain-marie *French* (bẽmari) NOUN, *plural* ***bains-marie*** (bẽmari). a vessel for holding hot water, in which sauces and other dishes are gently cooked or kept warm.
▷**HISTORY** C19: from French, from Medieval Latin *balneum Mariae*, literally: bath of Mary, inaccurate translation of Medieval Greek *kaminos Marios*, literally: furnace of *Miriam*, alleged author of a treatise on alchemy

Bairam (baɪ'ræm, 'baɪræm) NOUN either of two Muslim festivals, one (**Lesser Bairam**) falling at the end of Ramadan, the other (**Greater Bairam**) 70 days later at the end of the Islamic year.
▷**HISTORY** from Turkish *bayrām*

bairn (bɛən; *Scot* bern) NOUN *Scot and northern English* a child.
▷**HISTORY** Old English *bearn*; related to *bearm* lap, Old Norse, Old High German *barn* child

Baisakhi (baɪ'sækiː) NOUN an annual Sikh festival commemorating the founding (1699) of the Order of the Khalsa by Gobind Singh.
▷**HISTORY** from Sanskrit, *Baisakh* (month of the year)

bait[1] (beɪt) NOUN 1 something edible, such as soft bread paste, worms, pieces of meat, etc., fixed to a hook or in a trap to attract fish or animals. 2 an enticement; temptation. 3 a variant spelling of **bate**[4]. 4 *Northern English dialect* food, esp a packed lunch. 5 *Archaic* a short stop for refreshment during a journey. ♦ VERB 6 (*tr*) to put a piece of food on or in (a hook or trap). 7 (*tr*) to persecute or tease. 8 (*tr*) to entice; tempt. 9 (*tr*) to set dogs upon (a bear, etc.). 10 (*tr*) *Archaic* to feed (a horse), esp during a break in a journey. 11 (*intr*) *Archaic* to stop for rest and refreshment during a journey.
▷**HISTORY** C13: from Old Norse *beita* to hunt, persecute; related to Old English *bǣtan* to restrain, hunt, Old High German *beizen*

Language note The phrase *with bated breath* is sometimes wrongly spelled *with baited breath*.

bait[2] (beɪt) VERB a variant spelling of **bate**[2].

baize (beɪz) NOUN 1 a woollen fabric resembling felt, usually green, used mainly for the tops of billiard tables. ♦ VERB 2 (*tr*) to line or cover with such fabric.
▷**HISTORY** C16: from Old French *baies*, plural of *baie* baize, from *bai* reddish brown, BAY[5], perhaps the original colour of the fabric

Baja California ('baehɑɑ) NOUN the Spanish name for **Lower California**.

Baja California Norte ('nɔːteɪ) NOUN a state of NW Mexico, in the N part of the Lower California peninsula. Capital: Mexicali. Pop.: 2 487 700 (2000). Area: about 71 500 sq. km (27 600 sq. miles).

Baja California Sur NOUN a state of NW Mexico, in the S part of the Lower California peninsula. Capital: La Paz. Pop.: 423 516 (2000). Area: 73 475 sq. km (28 363 sq. miles).

Bajan ('beɪdʒən) *Caribbean informal* ♦ NOUN 1 a native of Barbados. ♦ ADJECTIVE 2 of or relating to Barbados or its inhabitants.
▷**HISTORY** C20: variant of *Badian*, a shortened form of *Barbadian*

BAK *Text messaging* ABBREVIATION FOR back at keyboard.

bake (beɪk) VERB 1 (*tr*) to cook by dry heat in or as if in an oven. 2 (*intr*) to cook bread, pastry, etc., in an oven. 3 to make or become hardened by heat.

4 (*intr*) *Informal* to be extremely hot, as in the heat of the sun. ◆ NOUN 5 *US* a party at which the main dish is baked. 6 a batch of things baked at one time. 7 *Scot* a kind of biscuit. 8 *Caribbean* a small flat fried cake.
▷HISTORY Old English *bacan*; related to Old Norse *baka*, Old High German *bahhan* to bake, Greek *phōgein* to parch, roast

bakeapple ('beɪk,æpᵊl) NOUN *Canadian* the fruit of the cloudberry.

baked Alaska NOUN a dessert consisting of cake and ice cream covered with meringue and cooked very quickly in a hot oven.

baked beans PLURAL NOUN haricot beans, baked and tinned in tomato sauce.

bakehouse ('beɪk,haʊs) NOUN another word for **bakery**.

Bakelite ('beɪkə,laɪt) NOUN *Trademark* any one of a class of thermosetting resins used as electric insulators and for making plastic ware, telephone receivers, etc.
▷HISTORY C20: named after L. H. *Baekeland* (1863–1944), Belgian-born US inventor; see -ITE[1]

baker ('beɪkə) NOUN 1 a person whose business or employment is to make or sell bread, cakes, etc. 2 a portable oven. 3 **on the baker's list.** *Irish informal* in good health.

baker's dozen NOUN thirteen.
▷HISTORY C16: from the bakers' former practice of giving thirteen rolls where twelve were requested, to protect themselves against accusations of giving light weight

bakery ('beɪkərɪ) NOUN, *plural* **-eries.** 1 Also called: **bakehouse.** a room or building equipped for baking. 2 a shop in which bread, cakes, etc., are sold.

Bakewell tart ('beɪkwɛl) NOUN *Brit* an open tart having a pastry base and a layer of jam and filled with almond-flavoured sponge cake.
▷HISTORY C19: named after *Bakewell*, Derbyshire

Bakhtaran (,bæktə'rɑːn, -'ræn) NOUN a city in W Iran, in the valley of the Qareh Su: oil refinery. Pop.: 692 986 (1996). Former name (until 1987): **Kermanshah.**

baking ('beɪkɪŋ) NOUN 1 **a** the process of cooking bread, cakes, etc. **b** (*as modifier*): *a baking dish.* 2 the bread, cakes, etc., cooked at one time. ◆ ADJECTIVE 3 (esp of weather) very hot and dry.

baking powder NOUN any of various powdered mixtures that contain sodium bicarbonate, starch (usually flour), and one or more slightly acidic compounds, such as cream of tartar: used in baking as a substitute for yeast.

bakkie ('bʌkiː) NOUN *South African* a small truck with an open body and low sides.
▷HISTORY C20: from Afrikaans *bak* container

baklava *or* **baclava** ('bɑːklə,vɑː) NOUN a rich cake of Middle Eastern origin consisting of thin layers of pastry filled with nuts and honey.
▷HISTORY from Turkish

bakra ('bækrə) *Caribbean* ◆ NOUN, *plural* **-ra** *or* **-ras.** 1 a White person, esp one from Britain. ◆ ADJECTIVE 2 (of people) White, esp British.
▷HISTORY of African origin

baksheesh *or* **backsheesh** ('bækʃiːʃ) (in some Eastern countries, esp formerly) NOUN 1 money given as a tip, a present, or alms. ◆ VERB 2 to give such money to (a person).
▷HISTORY C17: from Persian *bakhshīsh*, from *bakhshīdan* to give; related to Sanskrit *bhaksati* he enjoys

Baku (*Russian* ba'ku) NOUN the capital of Azerbaijan, a port on the Caspian Sea: important for its extensive oilfields. Pop.: 1 727 200 (1997 est.).

BAL ABBREVIATION FOR British anti-lewisite. See **dimercaprol.**

Bala ('bælə) NOUN **Lake.** a narrow lake in Gwynedd: the largest natural lake in Wales. Length: 6 km (4 miles).

Balaam ('beɪlæm) NOUN *Old Testament* a Mesopotamian diviner who, when summoned to curse the Israelites, prophesied future glories for them instead, after being reproached by his ass (Numbers 22–23).

Balaclava *or* **Balaclava helmet** (,bælə'klɑːvə) NOUN (*often not capitals*) a close-fitting woollen hood that covers the ears and neck, as originally worn by soldiers in the Crimean War.
▷HISTORY C19: named after BALAKLAVA

Balaklava *or* **Balaclava** (,bælə'klɑːvə; *Russian* bəla'klavə) NOUN a small port in the Ukraine, in S Crimea: scene of an inconclusive battle (1854), which included the charge of the Light Brigade, during the Crimean War.

balalaika (,bælə'laɪkə) NOUN a plucked musical instrument, usually having a triangular body and three strings: used chiefly for Russian folk music.
▷HISTORY C18: from Russian

balance ('bæləns) NOUN 1 a weighing device, generally consisting of a horizontal beam pivoted at its centre, from the ends of which two pans are suspended. The substance to be weighed is placed in one pan and known weights are placed in the other until the beam returns to the horizontal. See also **microbalance.** 2 an imagined device for events, actions, motives, etc., in relation to each other (esp in the phrases **weigh in the balance, hang in the balance**). 3 a state of equilibrium. 4 something that brings about such a state. 5 equilibrium of the body; steadiness: *to lose one's balance.* 6 emotional stability; calmness of mind. 7 harmony in the parts of a whole: *balance in an artistic composition.* 8 the act of weighing factors, quantities, etc., against each other. 9 the power to influence or control: *he held the balance of power.* 10 something that remains or is left: *let me have the balance of what you owe me.* 11 *Accounting* **a** equality of debit and credit totals in an account. **b** a difference between such totals. 12 *Chem* the state of a chemical equation in which the number, kind, electrical charges, etc., of the atoms on opposite sides are equal. 13 a balancing movement. 14 short for **spring balance.** 15 **in the balance.** in an uncertain or undecided condition. 16 **on balance.** after weighing up all the factors. 17 **strike a balance.** to make a compromise. ◆ VERB 18 (*tr*) to weigh in or as if in a balance. 19 (*intr*) to be or come into equilibrium. 20 (*tr*) to bring into or hold in equilibrium. 21 (*tr*) to assess or compare the relative weight, importance, etc., of. 22 (*tr*) to act so as to equalize; be equal to. 23 (*tr*) to compose or arrange so as to create a state of harmony. 24 (*tr*) to bring (a chemical or mathematical equation) into balance. 25 (*tr*) *Accounting* **a** to compute the credit and debit totals of (an account) in order to determine the difference. **b** to equalize the credit and debit totals of (an account) by making certain entries. **c** to settle or adjust (an account) by paying any money due. 26 (*intr*) (of a business account, balance sheet, etc.) to have the debit and credit totals equal. 27 to match or counter (one's dancing partner or his or her steps) by moving towards and away from him or her.
▷HISTORY C13: from Old French, from Vulgar Latin *bilancia* (unattested), from Late Latin *bilanx* having two scalepans, from BI-[1] + *lanx* scale
▸'**balanceable** ADJECTIVE

Balance ('bæləns) NOUN **the.** the constellation Libra, the seventh sign of the zodiac.

balance bridge NOUN another name for **bascule bridge** (see **bascule** (sense1)).

balanced ('bælənst) ADJECTIVE 1 having weight equally distributed. 2 (of a person) mentally and emotionally stable. 3 (of a discussion, programme, etc.) presenting opposing points of view fairly and without bias. 4 (of a diet) consisting of all essential nutrients in suitable form and amounts to maintain health. 5 (of a budget) having expenditure no greater than income. 6 *Electronics* (of signals or circuitry) symmetrically disposed about earth or other reference potential. 7 (of a chemical equation) having the correct relative number of moles of reactants and products.

balance of nature NOUN the stable state in which natural communities of animals and plants exist, maintained by adaptation, competition, and other interactions between members of the community and their nonliving environment.

balance of payments NOUN the difference over a given time between total payments to foreign nations, arising from imports of goods and services and transfers abroad of capital, interest, grants, etc., and total receipts from foreign nations, arising from exports of goods and services and transfers from abroad of capital, interest, grants, etc.

balance of power NOUN 1 the distribution of power among countries so that no one nation can seriously threaten the fundamental interests of another. 2 any similar distribution of power or influence.

balance of trade NOUN the difference in value between total exports and total imports of goods. Also called: **visible balance.** Compare **invisible balance.**

balance pipe NOUN *Engineering* a pipe between two points used to equalize pressure.

balancer ('bælənsə) NOUN 1 a person or thing that balances. 2 *Entomol* another name for **haltere.**

balance sheet NOUN a statement that shows the financial position of a business enterprise at a specified date by listing the asset balances and the claims on such assets.

balance weight NOUN *Engineering* a weight used in machines to counterbalance a part, as of a crankshaft. Also called: **bobweight.**

balance wheel NOUN a wheel oscillating against the hairspring of a timepiece, thereby regulating its beat.

balancing act ('bælənsɪŋ) NOUN 1 a circus act in which a performer displays his or her balancing ability. 2 a situation requiring careful balancing of opposing groups, views, or activities: *a delicate balancing act between Greek and Turkish interests.*

balanitis (,bælə'naɪtɪs) NOUN *Med* inflammation of the glans penis, usually due to infection.
▷HISTORY from New Latin *balanus*, from Greek *balanos* acorn + -ITIS

balas ('bæləs, 'beɪ-) NOUN a red variety of spinel, used as a gemstone. Also called: **balas ruby.**
▷HISTORY C15: from Old French *balais*, from Arabic *bālakhsh*, from *Badhakhshān*, region in Afghanistan where the gem is found

balata ('bælətə) NOUN 1 a tropical American sapotaceous tree, *Manilkara bidentata*, yielding a latex-like sap. 2 a rubber-like gum obtained from this sap: used as a substitute for gutta-percha.
▷HISTORY from American Spanish, of Carib origin

Balaton (*Hungarian* 'bɔlɔtɔn) NOUN **Lake.** a large shallow lake in W Hungary. Area: 689 sq. km (266 sq. miles).

balboa (bæl'bəʊə) NOUN the standard currency unit of Panama, divided into 100 centesimos.
▷HISTORY named after Vasco Núñez de *Balboa* (?1475–1519), Spanish explorer

Balboa (bæl'bəʊə; *Spanish* bal'βoa) NOUN a port in Panama at the Pacific end of the Panama Canal: the administrative centre of the former Canal Zone. Pop.: 2750 (1990).

balbriggan (bæl'brɪgən) NOUN 1 a knitted unbleached cotton fabric. 2 (*often plural*) underwear made of this.
▷HISTORY C19: from *Balbriggan*, Ireland, where it was originally made

balconette (,bælkə'nɛt) NOUN a lightly padded bra that is designed to lift and enhance the appearance of a woman's bust.

balcony ('bælkənɪ) NOUN, *plural* **-nies.** 1 a platform projecting from the wall of a building with a balustrade or railing along its outer edge, often with access from a door or window. 2 a gallery in a theatre or auditorium, above the dress circle. 3 *US and Canadian* any circle or gallery in a theatre or auditorium including the dress circle.
▷HISTORY C17: from Italian *balcone*, probably from Old High German *balko* beam; see BALK
▸'**balconied** ADJECTIVE

bald (bɔːld) ADJECTIVE 1 having no hair or fur, esp (of a man) having no hair on all or most of the scalp. 2 lacking natural growth or covering. 3 plain or blunt: *a bald statement.* 4 bare or simple; unadorned. 5 Also: **baldfaced.** (of certain birds and other animals) having white markings on the head and face. 6 (of a tyre) having a worn tread.
▷HISTORY C14 *ballede* (literally: having a white spot); related to Danish *bældet*, Greek *phalaros* having a white spot
▸'**baldish** ADJECTIVE ▸'**baldly** ADVERB ▸'**baldness** NOUN

baldachin, baldaquin ('bɔːldəkɪn), *or* **baldachino** (,bɔːldə'kiːnəʊ) NOUN 1 a richly ornamented silk and gold brocade. 2 a canopy of fabric or stone over an altar, shrine, or throne in a Christian church or carried in Christian religious processions over an object of veneration.

▷HISTORY Old English *baldekin*, from Italian *baldacchino*, literally: stuff from Baghdad, from *Baldacco* Baghdad, noted for its brocades

bald cypress NOUN another name for **swamp cypress.**

bald eagle NOUN a large eagle, *Haliaeetus leucocephalus*, of North America, having a white head and tail, a yellow bill, and dark wings and body. It is the US national bird (see also **American eagle**).

Balder ('bɔːldə) NOUN *Norse myth* a god, son of Odin and Frigg, noted for his beauty and sweet nature. He was killed by a bough of mistletoe thrown by the blind god Höd, misled by the malicious Loki.

balderdash ('bɔːldəˌdæʃ) NOUN stupid or illogical talk; senseless rubbish.
▷HISTORY C16: of unknown origin

baldhead ('bɔːldˌhɛd) NOUN a person with a bald head.

baldheaded (ˌbɔːld'hɛdɪd) ADJECTIVE having a bald head.

balding ('bɔːldɪŋ) ADJECTIVE somewhat bald or becoming bald.

baldmoney ('bɔːldˌmʌnɪ) NOUN another name for **spignel.**

baldpate ('bɔːldˌpeɪt) NOUN [1] a person with a bald head. [2] another name for the **American wigeon** (see **wigeon** (sense 2)).

baldric ('bɔːldrɪk) NOUN a wide silk sash or leather belt worn over the right shoulder to the left hip for carrying a sword, etc.
▷HISTORY C13: from Old French *baudrei*, of Frankish origin

baldy ('bɔːldɪ) *Informal* ◆ ADJECTIVE [1] bald. ◆ NOUN, *plural* **baldies.** [2] a bald person.

bale¹ (beɪl) NOUN [1] a large bundle, esp of a raw or partially processed material, bound by ropes, wires, etc., for storage or transportation: *bale of hay.* [2] a large package or carton of goods. [3] *US* 500 pounds of cotton. [4] a group of turtles. [5] *Austral and NZ* See **wool bale.** ◆ VERB [6] to make (hay, etc.) into a bale or bales. [7] to put (goods) into packages or cartons. [8] *Austral and NZ* to pack and compress (wool) into wool bales. ◆ See also **bail out.**
▷HISTORY C14: probably from Old French *bale*, from Old High German *balla* BALL¹

bale² (beɪl) NOUN *Archaic* [1] evil; injury. [2] woe; suffering; pain.
▷HISTORY Old English *bealu*; related to Old Norse *böl* evil, Gothic *balwa*, Old High German *balo*

bale³ (beɪl) VERB a variant spelling of **bail².**

bale⁴ (beɪl) NOUN a variant spelling of **bail⁴.**

Bâle (bɑl) NOUN the French name for **Basel.**

Balearic Islands (ˌbælɪ'ærɪk) PLURAL NOUN a group of islands in the W Mediterranean, consisting of Majorca, Minorca, Ibiza, Formentera, Cabrera, and 11 islets: a province of Spain. Capital: Palma, on Majorca. Pop.: 845 630 (2000 est.). Area: 5012 sq. km (1935 sq. miles). Spanish name: **Baleares** (bale'ares).

baleen (bə'liːn) NOUN whalebone.
▷HISTORY C14: from Latin *bālaena* whale; related to Greek *phalaina* whale

baleen whale NOUN another name for **whalebone whale.**

balefire ('beɪlˌfaɪə) NOUN *Archaic* [1] a bonfire. [2] a beacon fire. [3] a funeral pyre.
▷HISTORY C14 *bale*, from Old English *bǣl* pyre; related to Old Norse *bāl* flame, pyre, Sanskrit *bhāla* brightness

baleful ('beɪlfʊl) ADJECTIVE [1] harmful, menacing, or vindictive. [2] *Archaic* dejected.
▸ **'balefully** ADVERB ▸ **'balefulness** NOUN

baler ('beɪlə) NOUN an agricultural machine for making bales of hay, etc. Also called: **baling machine.**

Balfour Declaration ('bælfə) NOUN the statement made by British foreign secretary Arthur Balfour (1848–1930) in 1917 of British support for the setting up of a national home for the Jews in Palestine, provided that the rights of "existing non-Jewish communities" in Palestine could be safeguarded.

Bali ('bɑːlɪ) NOUN an island in Indonesia, east of Java: mountainous, rising over 3000 m (10 000 ft.). Capital: Denpasar. Pop.: 2 902 200 (1995 est.). Area: 5558 sq. km (2146 sq. miles).

balibuntal (ˌbælɪ'bʌntᵊl) NOUN [1] closely woven fine straw, used for making hats in the Philippines. [2] a hat of this straw.
▷HISTORY C20: changed from *Baliuag buntal*, from *Baliuag* in the Philippines, where such hats were made

Balikpapan (ˌbɑːlɪk'pɑːpɑːn) NOUN a city in Indonesia, on the SE coast of Borneo. Pop.: 416 200 (1995 est.).

Balinese (ˌbɑːlɪ'niːz) ADJECTIVE [1] of or relating to Bali, its people, or their language. ◆ NOUN [2] (*plural* **-nese**) a native or inhabitant of Bali. [3] the language of the people of Bali, belonging to the Malayo-Polynesian family. [4] See **Balinese cat.**

Balinese cat NOUN a breed of cat with medium-length silky hair, a plumed tail, blue eyes, large ears, and a dark mask, tail, and paws.

balk *or* **baulk** (bɔːk, bɔːlk) VERB [1] (*intr;* usually foll by *at*) to stop short, esp suddenly or unexpectedly; jib: *the horse balked at the jump.* [2] (*intr;* foll by *at*) to turn away abruptly; recoil: *he balked at the idea of murder.* [3] (*tr*) to thwart, check, disappoint, or foil: *he was balked in his plans.* [4] (*tr*) to avoid deliberately: *he balked the question.* [5] (*tr*) to miss unintentionally. ◆ NOUN [6] a roughly squared heavy timber beam. [7] a timber tie beam of a roof. [8] an unploughed ridge to prevent soil erosion or mark a division on common land. [9] an obstacle; hindrance; disappointment. [10] *Baseball* an illegal motion by a pitcher towards the plate or towards the base when there are runners on base, esp without delivering the ball. ◆ See also **baulk.**
▷HISTORY Old English *balca*; related to Old Norse *bálkr* partition, Old High German *balco* beam
▸ **'balker** *or* **'baulker** NOUN

Balkan ('bɔːlkən) ADJECTIVE of, denoting, or relating to the Balkan States or their inhabitants, the Balkan Peninsula, or the Balkan Mountains.

Balkanize *or* **Balkanise** ('bɔːlkəˌnaɪz) VERB [1] (*tr*) to divide (a territory) into small warring states. [2] to divide (a group or organization) into small factions.
▸ **ˌBalkani'zation** *or* **ˌBalkani'sation** NOUN ▸ **'Balkaˌnized** *or* **'Balkaˌnised** ADJECTIVE

Balkan Mountains PLURAL NOUN a mountain range extending across Bulgaria from the Black Sea to the eastern border. Highest peak: Mount Botev, 2376 m (7793 ft.).

Balkan Peninsula NOUN a large peninsula in SE Europe, between the Adriatic and Aegean Seas.

Balkan States PLURAL NOUN the countries of the Balkan Peninsula: the former Yugoslavian Republics, Romania, Bulgaria, Albania, Greece, and the European part of Turkey. Also called: **the Balkans.**

Balkh (bɑːlk) NOUN a region of N Afghanistan, corresponding to ancient Bactria. Chief town: Mazar-i-Sharif.

Balkhash (*Russian* bal'xaʃ) NOUN **Lake.** a salt lake in SE Kazakhstan: fed by the Ili River. Area: about 18 000 sq. km (7000 sq. miles).

balky *or* **baulky** ('bɔːkɪ, 'bɔːlkɪ) ADJECTIVE **balkier, balkiest** *or* **baulkier, baulkiest.** inclined to stop abruptly and unexpectedly: *a balky horse.*
▸ **'balkily** *or* **'baulkily** ADVERB ▸ **'balkiness** *or* **'baulkiness** NOUN

ball¹ (bɔːl) NOUN [1] a spherical or nearly spherical body or mass: *a ball of wool.* [2] a round or roundish body, either solid or hollow, of a size and composition suitable for any of various games, such as football, golf, billiards, etc. [3] a ball propelled in a particular way in a sport: *a high ball.* [4] any of various rudimentary games with a ball: *to play ball.* [5] *Cricket* a single delivery of the ball by the bowler to the batsman. [6] *Baseball* a single delivery of the ball by a pitcher outside certain limits and not swung at by the batter. [7] **a** a solid nonexplosive projectile for a firearm. Compare **shell** (sense 6). **b** such projectiles collectively. [8] any more or less rounded part or protuberance: *the ball of the foot.* [9] *Slang* a testicle. See **balls.** [10] *Vet science* another word for **bolus.** [11] *Horticulture* the hard mass of roots and earth removed with the rest of the plant during transplanting. [12] **ball of muscle.** *Austral* a very strong, fit, or forceful person. [13] **have the ball at one's feet.** to have the chance of doing something. [14] **keep the ball rolling.** to maintain the progress of a project, plan, etc. [15] **on the ball.** *Informal* alert; informed. [16] **play ball.** *Informal* to cooperate. [17] **set** *or* **start the ball rolling.** to open or initiate (an action, discussion, movement, etc.). [18] **the ball is in your court.** you are obliged to make the next move. ◆ VERB [19] (*tr*) to make, form, wind, etc., into a ball or balls: *to ball wool.* [20] (*intr*) to gather into a ball or balls. [21] *Taboo slang, chiefly US* to copulate (with).
▷HISTORY C13: from Old Norse *böllr*; related to Old High German *balla*, Italian *palla* French *balle*

> **Language note** Sense 9 of this word was formerly considered to be taboo, and it was labelled as such in previous editions of *Collins English Dictionary*. However, it has now become acceptable in speech, although some older or more conservative people may object to its use.

ball² (bɔːl) NOUN [1] a social function for dancing, esp one that is lavish or formal. [2] *Informal* a very enjoyable time (esp in the phrase **have a ball**).
▷HISTORY C17: from French *bal* (n), from Old French *baller* (vb), from Late Latin *ballāre* to dance, from Greek *ballizein*

ballad ('bæləd) NOUN [1] a narrative song with a recurrent refrain. [2] a narrative poem in short stanzas of popular origin, originally sung to a repeated tune. [3] a slow sentimental song, esp a pop song.
▷HISTORY C15: from Old French *balade*, from Old Provençal *balada* song accompanying a dance, from *balar* to dance, from Late Latin *ballāre*; see BALL²

ballade (bæ'lɑːd; *French* balad) NOUN [1] *Prosody* a verse form consisting of three stanzas and an envoy, all ending with the same line. The first three stanzas commonly have eight or ten lines each and the same rhyme scheme. [2] *Music* an instrumental composition, esp for piano, based on or intended to evoke a narrative.

balladeer (ˌbælə'dɪə) NOUN a singer of ballads.

ballad metre NOUN the metre of a ballad stanza.

balladmonger ('bælədˌmʌŋgə) NOUN [1] (formerly) a seller of ballads, esp on broadsheets. [2] *Derogatory* a writer of mediocre poetry.

ballad opera NOUN an opera consisting of popular tunes to which appropriate words have been set, interspersed with spoken dialogue.

balladry ('bælədrɪ) NOUN [1] ballad poetry or songs. [2] the art of writing, composing, or performing ballads.

ballad stanza NOUN a four-line stanza, often used in ballads, in which the second and fourth lines rhyme and have three stresses each and the first and third lines are unrhymed and have four stresses each.

ball ammunition NOUN live small-arms ammunition.

ball and chain NOUN [1] (formerly) a heavy iron ball attached to a chain and fastened to a prisoner. [2] a heavy restraint. [3] *Slang* one's wife.

ball-and-socket joint *or* **ball joint** NOUN [1] a coupling between two rods, tubes, etc., that consists of a spherical part fitting into a spherical socket, allowing free movement within a specific conical volume. [2] Also called: **multiaxial joint.** *Anatomy* a bony joint, such as the hip joint, in which a rounded head fits into a rounded cavity, allowing a wide range of movement.

Ballarat ('bæləˌræt, ˌbælə'ræt) NOUN a town in SE Australia, in S central Victoria: originally the centre of a gold-mining region. Pop.: 64 980 (1991). See also **Eureka Stockade.**

ballast ('bæləst) NOUN [1] any dense heavy material, such as lead or iron pigs, used to stabilize a vessel, esp one that is not carrying cargo. [2] crushed rock, broken stone, etc., used for the foundation of a road or railway track. [3] coarse aggregate of sandy gravel, used in making concrete. [4] anything that provides stability or weight. [5] *Electronics* a device for maintaining the current in a circuit. ◆ VERB (*tr*) [6] to give stability or weight to.
▷HISTORY C16: probably from Low German; related to Old Danish, Old Swedish *barlast*, literally: bare load (without commercial value), from *bar* bare, mere + *last* load, burden

ball bearing NOUN [1] a bearing consisting of a

number of hard steel balls rolling between a metal sleeve fitted over the rotating shaft and an outer sleeve held in the bearing housing, so reducing friction between moving parts while providing support for the shaft. [2] a metal ball, esp one used in such a bearing.

ball boy NOUN (esp in tennis) a person who retrieves balls that go out of play.

ballbreaker (ˈbɔːlˌbreɪkə) NOUN *Slang* a person, esp a woman, whose character and behaviour may be regarded as threatening a man's sense of power.
▷HISTORY C20: from BALL[1] (in the sense: testicle) + BREAKER[1]

ball cock NOUN a device for regulating the flow of a liquid into a tank, cistern, etc., consisting of a floating ball mounted at one end of an arm and a valve on the other end that opens and closes as the ball falls and rises.

ballerina (ˌbæləˈriːnə) NOUN [1] a female ballet dancer. [2] *US* the principal female dancer of a ballet company.
▷HISTORY C18: from Italian, feminine of *ballerino* dancing master, from *ballare* to dance, from Late Latin *ballāre*: see BALL[2]

ballet (ˈbæleɪ, bæˈleɪ) NOUN [1] **a** a classical style of expressive dancing based on precise conventional steps with gestures and movements of grace and fluidity. **b** (*as modifier*): *ballet dancer*. [2] a theatrical representation of a story or theme performed to music by ballet dancers. [3] a troupe of ballet dancers. [4] a piece of music written for a ballet.
▷HISTORY C17: from French, from Italian *balletto* literally: a little dance, from *ballare* to dance; see BALL[2]
▸**balletic** (bæˈlɛtɪk) ADJECTIVE

balletomania (ˌbælɪtəʊˈmeɪnɪə) NOUN passionate enthusiasm for ballet.
▷HISTORY C20: from BALLET + -O- + -MANIA
▸**balletomane** (ˈbælɪtəʊˌmeɪn) NOUN

ballflower (ˈbɔːlˌflaʊə) NOUN *Architect* a carved ornament in the form of a ball enclosed by the three petals of a circular flower.

ball game NOUN [1] any game played with a ball. [2] *US and Canadian* a game of baseball. [3] *Informal* a situation; state of affairs (esp in the phrase **a whole new ball game**).

ballicatter (ˌbælɪˈkætə) NOUN (in Newfoundland) ice that forms along a shore from waves and freezing spray.

ballista (bəˈlɪstə) NOUN, *plural* **-tae** (-tiː). [1] an ancient catapult for hurling stones, etc. [2] an ancient form of large crossbow used to propel a spear.
▷HISTORY C16: from Latin, ultimately from Greek *ballein* to throw

ballistic (bəˈlɪstɪk) ADJECTIVE [1] of or relating to ballistics. [2] denoting or relating to the flight of projectiles after power has been cut off, moving under their own momentum and the external forces of gravity and air resistance. [3] (of a measurement or measuring instrument) depending on a brief impulse or current that causes a movement related to the quantity to be measured: *a ballistic pendulum*. [4] **go ballistic.** *Informal* to become enraged or frenziedly violent. [5] (of materials) strong enough to resist damage by projectile weapons: *ballistic nylon*.
▸**balˈlistically** ADVERB

ballistic galvanometer NOUN *Physics* a type of galvanometer for measuring surges of current. After deflection the instrument returns slowly to its original reading.

ballistic missile NOUN a missile that has no wings or fins and that follows a ballistic trajectory when its propulsive power is discontinued.

ballistics (bəˈlɪstɪks) NOUN (*functioning as singular*) the study of the flight dynamics of projectiles, either through the interaction of the forces of propulsion, the aerodynamics of the projectile, atmospheric resistance, and gravity (**exterior ballistics**), or through these forces along with the means of propulsion, and the design of the propelling weapon and projectile (**interior ballistics**).

ballistospore (bəˈlɪstəˌspɔː) NOUN *Botany* a spore, esp a fungal spore, that is forcefully ejected from its source.

ball joint NOUN another name for **ball-and-socket joint.**

ball lightning NOUN *Meteorol* a luminous electrically charged ball occasionally seen during electrical storms.

ball mill NOUN *Engineering* a horizontal cylinder or cone in which a substance, such as a mineral, is ground by rotation with steel or ceramic balls.

ballocks (ˈbɒləks, ˈbæl-) PLURAL NOUN, INTERJECTION, VERB a variant spelling of **bollocks.**

ball of fire NOUN *Informal* a very lively person.

ballon d'essai (bæˈlɔ̃ dɛˈseɪ) NOUN, *plural* **ballons d'essai** (bæˈlɔ̃ dɛˈseɪ). a project or policy put forward experimentally to gauge reactions to it. Compare **trial balloon.**
▷HISTORY C19: from French, literally: trial balloon

ballonet (ˌbæləˈnɛt) NOUN an air or gas compartment in a balloon or nonrigid airship, used to control buoyancy and shape.
▷HISTORY C20: from French *ballonnet* a little BALLOON

balloon (bəˈluːn) NOUN [1] an inflatable rubber bag of various sizes, shapes, and colours: usually used as a plaything or party decoration. [2] a large impermeable bag inflated with a lighter-than-air gas, designed to rise and float in the atmosphere. It may have a basket or gondola for carrying passengers, etc. See also **barrage balloon, hot-air balloon.** [3] a circular or elliptical figure containing the words or thoughts of a character in a cartoon. [4] *Brit* **a** a kick or stroke that propels a ball high into the air. **b** (*as modifier*): *a balloon shot*. [5] *Chem* a round-bottomed flask. [6] a large rounded brandy glass. [7] *Commerce* **a** a large sum paid as an irregular instalment of a loan repayment. **b** (*as modifier*): *a balloon loan*. [8] *Surgery* **a** an inflatable plastic tube used for dilating obstructed blood vessels or parts of the alimentary canal. **b** (*as modifier*): *balloon angioplasty*. [9] **go down like a lead balloon.** *Informal* to be completely unsuccessful or unpopular. [10] **when the balloon goes up.** *Informal* when the trouble or action begins. ◆ VERB [11] (*intr*) to go up or fly in a balloon. [12] (*intr*) to increase or expand significantly and rapidly: *losses ballooned to £278 million*. [13] to inflate or be inflated; distend; swell: *the wind ballooned the sails*. [14] (*tr*) *Brit* to propel (a ball) high into the air.
▷HISTORY C16 (in the sense: ball, ball game): from Italian dialect *ballone*, from *balla*, of Germanic origin; compare Old High German *balla* BALL[1]
▸**balˈlooning** NOUN ▸**balˈloonist** NOUN ▸**balˈloon-ˌlike** ADJECTIVE

balloon loan NOUN a loan in respect of which interest and capital are paid off in instalments at irregular intervals.

balloon sail NOUN *Nautical* a large light bellying sail used in light winds. Compare **spinnaker.**

balloon sleeve NOUN a sleeve fitting tightly from wrist to elbow and becoming fully rounded from elbow to shoulder.

balloon tyre NOUN a pneumatic tyre containing air at a relatively low pressure and having a wide tread.

balloon vine NOUN a tropical tendril-climbing sapindaceous plant, *Cardiospermum halicacabum*, cultivated for its ornamental balloon-like seed capsules.

ballot (ˈbælət) NOUN [1] the democratic practice of selecting a representative, a course of action, or deciding some other choice by submitting the options to a vote of all qualified persons. [2] an instance of voting, usually in secret using ballot papers or a voting machine. [3] the paper on which a vote is recorded. [4] a list of candidates standing for office. [5] the number of votes cast in an election. [6] a random selection of successful applicants for something in which the demand exceeds the supply, esp for shares in an oversubscribed new issue. [7] *NZ* the allocation by ballot of farming land among eligible candidates, such as ex-servicemen. [8] *NZ* a low-interest housing loan allocated by building societies by drawing lots among its eligible members. ◆ VERB **-lots, -loting, -loted.** [9] to vote or elicit a vote from: *we balloted the members on this issue*. [10] (*tr*; usually foll by *for*) to select (officials, etc.) by lot or ballot or to select (successful applicants) at random. [11] (*tr*; often foll by *for*) to vote or decide (on an issue, etc.).
▷HISTORY C16: from Italian *ballotta*, literally: a little ball, from *balla* BALL[1]

ballot box NOUN a box into which ballot papers are dropped after voting.

ballotini (ˌbæləˈtiːnɪ) PLURAL NOUN small glass beads used in reflective paints.
▷HISTORY C20: from Italian *ballottini* small balls

ballot paper NOUN a paper used for voting in a ballot, esp (in a parliamentary or local government election) one having the names of the candidates printed on it.

ballottement (bəˈlɒtmənt) NOUN *Med* a technique of feeling for a movable object in the body, esp confirmation of pregnancy by feeling the rebound of the fetus following a quick digital tap on the wall of the uterus.
▷HISTORY C19: from French, literally: a tossing, shaking, from *ballotter* to toss, from *ballotte* a little ball, from Italian *ballotta*; see BALLOT

ballpark (ˈbɔːlˌpɑːk) NOUN [1] *US and Canadian* a stadium used for baseball games. [2] *Informal* **a** approximate range: *in the right ballpark*. **b** (*as modifier*): *a ballpark figure*. [3] *Informal* a situation; state of affairs: *its a whole new ballpark for him*.

ball-peen hammer NOUN a hammer that has one end of its head shaped in a hemisphere for beating metal, etc.

ballplayer (ˈbɔːlˌpleɪə) NOUN [1] a player, esp in soccer, with outstanding ability to control the ball. [2] *US and Canadian* a baseball player, esp a professional.

ballpoint, ballpoint pen (ˈbɔːlˌpɔɪnt), *or* **ball pen** NOUN a pen having a small ball bearing as a writing point. Also called (Brit): **Biro.**

ball race NOUN *Engineering* [1] a ball bearing. [2] one of the metal rings having a circular track within which the balls of the bearing roll.

ballroom (ˈbɔːlˌruːm, -ˌrʊm) NOUN a large hall for dancing.

ballroom dancing NOUN social dancing, popular since the beginning of the 20th century, to dances in conventional rhythms (**ballroom dances**) such as the foxtrot and the quickstep.

balls (bɔːlz) *Slang* ◆ PLURAL NOUN [1] the testicles. [2] **by the balls.** so as to be rendered powerless. [3] nonsense; rubbish. [4] courage; forcefulness. ◆ INTERJECTION [5] an exclamation of strong disagreement, contempt, annoyance, etc.

> **Language note** Both its anatomical senses and its various extended senses nowadays have far less impact than they used to, and seen unlikely to cause offence, though some older or more conservative people may object. Interestingly, its use in the sense of courage is exactly paralleled in the Spanish term "cojones".

balls-up *or US* **ballup** (ˈbɔːlʌp) *Slang* ◆ NOUN [1] something botched or muddled. ◆ VERB **balls up,** *or US* **ball up.** [2] (*tr, adverb*) to muddle or botch.

ballsy (ˈbɔːlzɪ) ADJECTIVE *Slang* courageous and spirited.
▷HISTORY C20: from BALLS meaning courage, forcefulness

ball tearer NOUN *Austral slang* something exceptional in its class, for good or bad qualities.

ball valve NOUN a one-way valve consisting of a metal ball with a cylindrical hole fitting into a concave seat over an opening.

bally[1] (ˈbælɪ) ADJECTIVE, ADVERB (intensifier) *Brit slang* a euphemistic word for **bloody** (sense 6).

bally[2] (ˈbælɪ) NOUN *Northern English dialect* a thumb.

ballyhoo (ˌbælɪˈhuː) NOUN *Informal* [1] a noisy, confused, or nonsensical situation or uproar. [2] sensational or blatant advertising or publicity. ◆ VERB **-hoos, -hooing, -hooed.** [3] (*tr*) *Chiefly US* to advertise or publicize by sensational or blatant methods.
▷HISTORY C19: of uncertain origin

Ballymena (ˌbælɪˈmiːnə) NOUN a district in central Northern Ireland, in Co. Antrim. Pop.: 58 610 (2001). Area: 634 sq. km (247 sq. miles).

Ballymoney (ˌbælɪˈmʌnɪ) NOUN a district in N Northern Ireland, in Co. Antrim. Pop.: 26 894 (2001). Area: 417 sq. km (161 sq. miles).

ballyrag (ˈbælɪˌræg) VERB **-rags, -ragging, -ragged.** a variant of **bullyrag.**

balm (bɑːm) NOUN [1] any of various oily aromatic resinous substances obtained from certain tropical trees and used for healing and soothing. See also **balsam** (sense 1). [2] any plant yielding such a substance, esp the balm of Gilead. [3] something comforting or soothing: *soft music is a balm.* [4] any aromatic or oily substance used for healing or soothing. [5] Also called: **lemon balm.** an aromatic Eurasian herbaceous plant, *Melissa officinalis*, having clusters of small fragrant white two-lipped flowers: family *Lamiaceae* (labiates). [6] a pleasant odour.
▷HISTORY C13: from Old French *basme*, from Latin *balsamum* BALSAM
▸ˈ**balmˌlike** ADJECTIVE

balmacaan (ˌbælməˈkɑːn) NOUN a man's knee-length loose flaring overcoat with raglan sleeves.
▷HISTORY C19: after *Balmacaan*, near Inverness, Scotland

Balmain bug (ˈbælmeɪn) NOUN a flattish edible Australian shellfish, *Ibacus peronii*, similar to the Moreton Bay bug.
▷HISTORY named after *Balmain*, a suburb of Sydney, Australia

Balmer series (*German* ˈbalmər) NOUN a series of lines in the hydrogen spectrum, discovered by Johann Jakob Balmer (1825–98) in 1885.

balm of Gilead NOUN [1] any of several trees of the burseraceous genus *Commiphora*, esp *C. opobalsamum* of Africa and W Asia, that yield a fragrant oily resin (see **balm** (sense 1)). Compare **myrrh** (sense 1). [2] the resin exuded by these trees. [3] a North American hybrid female poplar tree, *Populus gileadensis* (or *P. candicans*), with broad heart-shaped leaves. [4] a fragrant resin obtained from the balsam fir. See also **Canada balsam.**

Balmoral[1] (bælˈmɒrəl) NOUN (*sometimes not capital*) [1] a laced walking shoe. [2] a 19th-century woollen petticoat, worn showing below the skirt. [3] Also called: **bluebonnet.** a Scottish brimless hat traditionally of dark blue wool with a cockade and plume on one side.
▷HISTORY C19: named after BALMORAL Castle

Balmoral[2] (bælˈmɒrəl) NOUN a castle in NE Scotland, in SW Aberdeenshire: a private residence of the British sovereign.

Balmung (ˈbælmʊŋ) *or* **Balmunc** (ˈbælmʊŋk) NOUN (in the *Nibelungenlied*) Siegfried's sword.

balmy (ˈbɑːmɪ) ADJECTIVE **balmier, balmiest.** [1] (of weather) mild and pleasant. [2] having the qualities of balm; fragrant or soothing. [3] a variant spelling of **barmy.**
▸ˈ**balmily** ADVERB ▸ˈ**balminess** NOUN

balneal (ˈbælnɪəl) *or* **balneary** (ˈbælnɪərɪ) ADJECTIVE *Rare* of or relating to baths or bathing.
▷HISTORY C17: from Latin *balneum* bath, from Greek *balaneion*

balneology (ˌbælnɪˈɒlədʒɪ) NOUN the branch of medical science concerned with the therapeutic value of baths, esp those taken with natural mineral waters.
▷HISTORY C19: from Latin *balneum* bath
▸**balneological** (ˌbælnɪəˈlɒdʒɪkᵊl) ADJECTIVE
▸ˌ**balneˈologist** NOUN

balneotherapy (ˌbælnɪəˈθɛrəpɪ) NOUN the treatment of disease by bathing, esp to improve limb mobility in arthritic and neuromuscular disorders.

baloney *or* **boloney** (bəˈləʊnɪ) NOUN [1] *Informal* foolish talk; nonsense. [2] *Chiefly US* another name for **bologna sausage.**
▷HISTORY C20: changed from *Bologna* (sausage)

BALPA (ˈbælpə) NOUN ACRONYM FOR British Airline Pilots' Association.

balsa (ˈbɔːlsə) NOUN [1] a bombacaceous tree, *Ochroma lagopus*, of tropical America. [2] Also called: **balsawood.** the very light wood of this tree, used for making rafts, etc. [3] a light raft.
▷HISTORY C18: from Spanish: raft

balsam (ˈbɔːlsəm) NOUN [1] any of various fragrant oleoresins, such as balm or tolu, obtained from any of several trees and shrubs and used as a base for medicines and perfumes. [2] any of various similar substances used as medicinal or ceremonial ointments. [3] any of certain aromatic resinous turpentines. See also **Canada balsam.** [4] any plant yielding balsam. [5] Also called: **busy Lizzie.** any of several balsaminaceous plants of the genus *Impatiens*, esp *I. balsamina*, cultivated for its brightly coloured flowers. [6] anything healing or soothing.
▷HISTORY C15: from Latin *balsamum*, from Greek *balsamon*, from Hebrew *bāśām* spice
▸**balsamic** (bɔːlˈsæmɪk) ADJECTIVE ▸ˈ**balsamy** ADJECTIVE

balsam apple NOUN an ornamental cucurbitaceous vine, *Momordica balsamina*, of the Old World tropics, with yellow flowers and orange egg-shaped fruits.

balsam fir NOUN a fir tree, *Abies balsamea*, of NE North America, that yields Canada balsam. Also called: **balsam, Canada balsam.** See also **balm of Gilead.**

balsamic vinegar NOUN a type of dark-coloured sweet Italian vinegar made from white grapes and aged in wooden barrels over a number of years.

balsamiferous (ˌbɔːlsəˈmɪfərəs) ADJECTIVE yielding or producing balsam.

balsaminaceous (ˌbɔːlsəmɪˈneɪʃəs) ADJECTIVE of, relating to, or belonging to the *Balsaminaceae*, a family of flowering plants, including balsam and touch-me-not, that have irregular flowers and explosive capsules.

balsam of Peru NOUN an aromatic balsam that is obtained from the tropical South American leguminous tree *Myroxylon pereirae* and is similar to balsam of Tolu. Also called: **Peru balsam.**

balsam of Tolu NOUN the full name of **tolu.**

balsam poplar NOUN a poplar tree, *Populus balsamifera*, of NE North America, having resinous buds and broad heart-shaped leaves. See also **tacamahac.**

balsam spruce NOUN either of two North American coniferous trees of the genus *Picea*, *P. pungens* (the blue spruce) or *P. engelmanni.*

Balt (bɔːlt) NOUN a member of any of the Baltic-speaking peoples of the Baltic States.

Balthazar[1] (ˈbælθəˌzɑː, bælˈθæzə) NOUN a wine bottle holding the equivalent of sixteen normal bottles (approximately 12 litres).
▷HISTORY C20: named after Balthazar (BELSHAZZAR) from his drinking wine at a great feast (Daniel 5:1)

Balthazar[2] (ˈbælθəˌzɑː, bælˈθæzə) NOUN one of the Magi, the others being Caspar and Melchior.

balti (ˈbɔːltɪ, ˈbæltɪ) NOUN **a** a spicy Indian dish, stewed until most of the liquid has evaporated, and served in a woklike pot. **b** (*as modifier*): *a balti house.*
▷HISTORY from Urdu *bāltī* pail

Baltic (ˈbɔːltɪk) ADJECTIVE [1] denoting or relating to the Baltic Sea or the Baltic States. [2] of, denoting, or characteristic of Baltic as a group of languages. [3] *Brit informal* extremely cold. ◆ NOUN [4] a branch of the Indo-European family of languages consisting of Lithuanian, Latvian, and Old Prussian. [5] short for **Baltic Sea.** [6] Also called: **Baltic Exchange.** a freight-chartering market in the City of London, which formerly also dealt in some commodities.

Baltics (ˈbɔːltɪks) PLURAL NOUN **the.** another name for the **Baltic States.**

Baltic Sea NOUN a sea in N Europe, connected with the North Sea by the Skaggerak, Kattegat, and Öresund; shallow, with low salinity and small tides.

Baltic Shield NOUN the wide area of ancient rock in Scandinavia. Also called: **Scandinavian Shield.** See **shield** (sense 7).

Baltic States PLURAL NOUN the republics of Estonia, Latvia, and Lithuania, which became constituent republics of the former Soviet Union in 1940, regaining their independence in 1991. Sometimes shortened to: **the Baltics.**

Baltimore (ˈbɔːltɪˌmɔː) NOUN a port in N Maryland, on Chesapeake Bay. Pop.: 651 154 (2000).

Baltimore oriole NOUN a North American oriole, *Icterus galbula*, the male of which has orange and black plumage.

Balto-Slavonic *or* **Balto-Slavic** NOUN a hypothetical subfamily of Indo-European languages consisting of Baltic and Slavonic. It is now generally believed that similarities between them result from geographical proximity rather than any special relationship.

Baluchi (bəˈluːtʃɪ) *or* **Balochi** (bəˈləʊtʃɪ) NOUN [1] (*plural* **-chis** *or* **-chi**) a member of a Muslim people living chiefly in coastal Pakistan and Iran. [2] the language of this people, belonging to the West Iranian branch of the Indo-European family. ◆ ADJECTIVE [3] of or relating to Baluchistan, its inhabitants, or their language.

Baluchistan (bəˈluːtʃɪˌstɑːn, -ˌstæn) *or* **Balochistan** (bəˈlɒtʃɪˌstɑːn, -ˌstæn) NOUN [1] a mountainous region of SW Asia, in SW Pakistan and SE Iran. [2] a province of SW Pakistan: a former territory of British India (until 1947). Capital: Quetta. Pop.: 6 511 000 (1998).

balun (ˈbælən) NOUN *Electronics* a device for coupling two electrical circuit elements, such as an aerial and its feeder cable, where one is balanced and the other is unbalanced.
▷HISTORY C20: shortened from *bal(ance to) un(balance transformer)*

baluster (ˈbæləstə) NOUN [1] any of a set of posts supporting a rail or coping. ◆ ADJECTIVE [2] (of a shape) swelling at the base and rising in a concave curve to a narrow stem or neck: *a baluster goblet stem.*
▷HISTORY C17: from French *balustre*, from Italian *balaustro* pillar resembling a pomegranate flower, ultimately from Greek *balaustion*

balustrade (ˈbæləˌstreɪd) NOUN an ornamental rail or coping with its supporting set of balusters.
▷HISTORY C17: from French, from *balustre* BALUSTER

Bamako (ˌbæməˈkəʊ) NOUN the capital of Mali, in the south, on the River Niger. Pop.: 809 552 (1996 est.).

Bambara (bɑːmˈbɑːrə) NOUN [1] (*plural* **-ra** *or* **-ras**) a member of a Negroid people of W Africa living chiefly in Mali and by the headwaters of the River Niger in Guinea. [2] the language of this people, belonging to the Mande branch of the Niger-Congo family.

Bamberg (ˈbæmbɜːg; *German* ˈbambɛrk) NOUN a town in S Germany, in N Bavaria: seat of independent prince-bishops of the Holy Roman Empire (1007–1802). Pop.: 70 690 (1991).

bambi (ˈbæmbɪ) NOUN ACRONYM FOR born-again middle-aged biker: an affluent middle-aged man who rides a powerful motorbike.

bambino (bæmˈbiːnəʊ) NOUN, *plural* **-nos** *or* **-ni** (-niː). [1] *Informal* a young child, esp an Italian one. [2] a representation of the infant Jesus.
▷HISTORY C18: from Italian

bamboo (bæmˈbuː) NOUN [1] any tall treelike tropical or semitropical fast-growing grass of the genus *Bambusa*, having hollow woody-walled stems with ringed joints and edible young shoots (**bamboo shoots**). [2] the stem of any of these plants, used for building, poles, and furniture. [3] any of various bamboo-like grasses of the genera *Arundinaria*, *Phyllostachys* or *Dendrocalamus*. [4] (*modifier*) made of bamboo: *a bamboo fence.*
▷HISTORY C16: probably from Malay *bambu*

bamboo curtain NOUN (esp in the 1950s and 1960s) the political and military barrier to communications around the People's Republic of China.

bamboo network NOUN a network of close-knit Chinese entrepreneurs with large corporate empires in southeast Asia.

bamboozle (bæmˈbuːzᵊl) VERB (*tr*) *Informal* [1] to cheat; mislead. [2] to confuse.
▷HISTORY C18: of unknown origin
▸**bamˈboozler** NOUN ▸**bamˈboozlement** NOUN

ban[1] (bæn) VERB **bans, banning, banned.** [1] (*tr*) to prohibit, esp officially, from action, display, entrance, sale, etc.; forbid: *to ban a book; to ban smoking.* [2] (*tr*) (formerly in South Africa) to place (a person suspected of illegal political activity) under a government order restricting his movement and his contact with other people. [3] *Archaic* to curse. ◆ NOUN [4] an official prohibition or interdiction. [5] *Law* an official proclamation or public notice, esp of prohibition. [6] a public proclamation or edict, esp of outlawry. [7] *Archaic* public censure or condemnation. [8] *Archaic* a curse; imprecation.
▷HISTORY Old English *bannan* to proclaim; compare Old Norse *banna* to forbid, Old High German *bannan* to command

ban² (bæn) NOUN (in feudal England) the summoning of vassals to perform their military obligations.
▷HISTORY C13: from Old French *ban*, of Germanic origin; related to Old High German *ban* command, Old Norse *bann* BAN¹

ban³ (bæn) NOUN, *plural* **bani** ('bɑːnɪ). a monetary unit of Romania and Moldova worth one hundredth of a leu.
▷HISTORY from Romanian, from Serbo-Croat *bān* lord

Banaba (bə'nɑːbə) NOUN an island in the SW Pacific, in the Republic of Kiribati. Phosphates were mined by Britain (1900–79). Area: about 5 sq. km (2 sq. miles). Pop.: 284 (1990). Also called: **Ocean Island.**

Banaban (bə'nɑːbən) ADJECTIVE [1] of or relating to the SW Pacific island of Banaba. ◆ NOUN [2] a native or inhabitant of Banaba.

banak ('bænək) NOUN [1] a tree of the genus *Virola*, of Central America: family *Myristicaceae*. [2] the timber of this tree, used esp in Honduras for turning and construction.
▷HISTORY C20: Honduran name

banal (bə'nɑːl) ADJECTIVE lacking force or originality; trite; commonplace.
▷HISTORY C18: from Old French: relating to compulsory feudal service, hence common to all, commonplace, from *ban* BAN²
▸**banality** (bə'nælɪtɪ) NOUN ▸**ba'nally** ADVERB

banana (bə'nɑːnə) NOUN [1] any of several tropical and subtropical herbaceous treelike plants of the musaceous genus *Musa*, esp *M. sapientum*, a widely cultivated species propagated from suckers and having hanging clusters of edible fruit. [2] the crescent-shaped fruit of any of these plants. Compare **plantain²**.
▷HISTORY C16: from Spanish or Portuguese, of African origin

banana belt NOUN *Canadian informal* a region with a warm climate, esp one in Canada.

Banana bender NOUN *Austral slang, offensive* a native or inhabitant of Queensland. Also called: **Bananalander** (bə'nɑːnə,lændə).

banana oil NOUN [1] a solution of cellulose nitrate in pentyl acetate or a similar solvent, which has a banana-like smell. [2] a nontechnical name for **pentyl acetate.**

banana plug NOUN *Electrical engineering* a small single-conductor electrical plug having a curved metal spring along its shank used to hold it in its socket.

banana prawn NOUN *Austral* a prawn of the genus *Penaeus*, fished commercially in tropical waters of N Australia.

banana republic NOUN *Informal and derogatory* a small country, esp in Central America, that is politically unstable and has an economy dominated by foreign interest, usually dependent on one export, such as bananas.

bananas (bə'nɑːnəz) ADJECTIVE *Slang* crazy (esp in the phrase **go bananas**).

banana skin NOUN [1] the soft outer covering of a banana. [2] *Informal* something unforeseen that causes an obvious and embarrassing mistake.
▷HISTORY sense 2 from the common slapstick joke of a person slipping after treading on a banana skin

banana split NOUN a dish of ice cream and banana cut in half lengthwise, usually topped with syrup, nuts, whipped cream, etc.

Banaras (bə'nɑːrəz) NOUN a variant spelling of **Benares.**

Banat ('bænɪt, 'bɑːnɪt) NOUN a fertile plain extending through Hungary, Romania, and Serbia.

banausic (bə'nɔːsɪk) ADJECTIVE merely mechanical; materialistic; utilitarian.
▷HISTORY C19: from Greek *banausikos* for mechanics, from *baunos* forge

Banbridge ('bænbrɪdʒ) NOUN a district in S Northern Ireland, in Co. Down. Pop.: 41 392 (2001). Area: 442 sq. km (170 sq. miles).

Banbury ('bænbərɪ) NOUN a town in central England, in N Oxfordshire: telecommunications, financial services. Pop.: 39 906 (1991).

Banbury cake NOUN *Brit* a cake consisting of a pastry base filled with currants, raisins, candied peel, and sugar, with a criss-cross pattern on the top.

banc (bæŋk) NOUN **in banc.** *Law* sitting as a full court.
▷HISTORY C18: from Anglo-French: bench

bancassurance ('bæŋkə,ʃʊərəns) NOUN the selling of insurance products by a bank to its customers.
▷HISTORY from French *banc* bank + *assurance* assurance

banco ('bæŋkəʊ) INTERJECTION a call in gambling games such as chemin de fer and baccarat by a player or bystander who wishes to bet against the entire bank.
▷HISTORY C18: from French from Italian: bank

band¹ (bænd) NOUN [1] a company of people having a common purpose; group: *a band of outlaws.* [2] a group of musicians playing either brass and percussion instruments only (**brass band**) or brass, woodwind, and percussion instruments (**concert band** or **military band**). [3] a group of musicians who play popular music, jazz, etc., often for dancing. [4] a group of instrumentalists generally; orchestra. [5] *Canadian* a formally recognized group of Indians on a reserve. [6] *Anthropol* a division of a tribe; a family group or camp group. [7] *US and Canadian* a flock or herd. ◆ VERB [8] (usually foll by *together*) to unite; assemble.
▷HISTORY C15: from French *bande* probably from Old Provençal *banda* of Germanic origin; compare Gothic *bandwa* sign, BANNER

band² (bænd) NOUN [1] a thin flat strip of some material, used esp to encircle objects and hold them together: *a rubber band.* [2] **a** a strip of fabric or other material used as an ornament, distinguishing mark, or to reinforce clothing. **b** (*in combination*): *waistband; hairband; hatband.* [3] a stripe of contrasting colour or texture. See also **chromosome band.** [4] a driving belt in machinery. [5] a range of values that are close or related in number, degree, or quality. [6] **a** *Physics* a range of frequencies or wavelengths between two limits. **b** *Radio* such a range allocated to a particular broadcasting station or service. [7] short for **energy band.** [8] *Computing* one or more tracks on a magnetic disk or drum. [9] *Anatomy* any structure resembling a ribbon or cord that connects, encircles, or binds different parts. [10] the cords to which the folded sheets of a book are sewn. [11] a thin layer or seam of ore. [12] *Architect* a strip of flat panelling, such as a fascia or plinth, usually attached to a wall. [13] a large white collar, sometimes edged with lace, worn in the 17th century. [14] either of a pair of hanging extensions of the collar, forming part of academic, legal, or (formerly) clerical dress. [15] a ring for the finger (esp in phrases such as **wedding band, band of gold,** etc.). ◆ VERB (*tr*) [16] to fasten or mark with a band. [17] *US and Canadian* to ring (birds). See **ring¹** (sense 22).
▷HISTORY C15: from Old French *bende*, of Germanic origin; compare Old High German *binda* fillet; see BAND³

band³ (bænd) NOUN an archaic word for **bond** (senses 1, 3, 4).
▷HISTORY C13: from Old Norse *band*; related to Old High German *bant* fetter; see BEND¹, BOND

bandage ('bændɪdʒ) NOUN [1] a piece of material used to dress a wound, bind a broken limb, etc. [2] a strip of any soft material used for binding, etc. ◆ VERB [3] to cover or bind with a bandage.
▷HISTORY C16: from French, from *band* strip, BAND²

bandanna *or* **bandana** (bæn'dænə) NOUN a large silk or cotton handkerchief or neckerchief.
▷HISTORY C18: from Hindi *bāndhnū* tie-dyeing, from *bāndhnā* to tie, from Sanskrit *bandhnāti* he ties

Bandar Seri Begawan ('bɑːndɑː 'sɛrɪ bə'gɑːwən) NOUN the capital of Brunei. Pop.: 21 484 (1991). Former name: **Brunei.**

Banda Sea NOUN a part of the Pacific in Indonesia, between Sulawesi and New Guinea.

B & B ABBREVIATION FOR bed and breakfast.

bandbox ('bænd,bɒks) NOUN a lightweight usually cylindrical box used for holding small articles, esp hats.

bandeau ('bændəʊ) NOUN, *plural* **-deaux** (-dəʊz). a narrow band of ribbon, velvet, etc., worn round the head.
▷HISTORY C18: from French, from Old French *bandel* a little BAND²

banderilla (,bændə'riːə, -'riːljə) NOUN *Bullfighting* a decorated barbed dart, thrust into the bull's neck or shoulder.
▷HISTORY Spanish, literally: a little banner, from *bandera* BANNER

banderillero (,bændəriː'ɛərəʊ, -riː'ljeərəʊ) NOUN, *plural* **-ros.** a bullfighter's assistant who sticks banderillas into the bull.

banderole, banderol ('bændə,rəʊl), *or* **bannerol** NOUN [1] a long narrow flag, usually with forked ends, esp one attached to the masthead of a ship; pennant. [2] a square flag draped over a tomb or carried at a funeral. [3] a ribbon-like scroll or sculptured band bearing an inscription, found esp in Renaissance architecture. [4] a streamer on a knight's lance.
▷HISTORY C16: from Old French, from Italian *banderuola*, literally: a little banner, from *bandiera* BANNER

band-gala ('bʌndgəlɑː) ADJECTIVE (in India) (of a coat) closed at the neck.
▷HISTORY from Hindi

bandh *or* **bundh** (bʌnd) NOUN (in India) a general strike.
▷HISTORY Hindi, literally: a tying up

bandicoot ('bændɪ,kuːt) NOUN [1] any agile terrestrial marsupial of the family *Peramelidae* of Australia and New Guinea. They have a long pointed muzzle and a long tail and feed mainly on small invertebrates. [2] **bandicoot rat.** Also called: **mole rat.** any of three burrowing rats of the genera *Bandicota* and *Nesokia*, of S and SE Asia: family *Muridae*.
▷HISTORY C18: from Telugu *pandikokku*, from *pandi* pig + *kokku* bandicoot

banding ('bændɪŋ) NOUN *Brit* the practice of grouping schoolchildren according to ability to ensure a balanced intake at different levels of ability to secondary school.

bandit ('bændɪt) NOUN, *plural* **-dits** *or* **-ditti** (-'dɪtɪ). a robber, esp a member of an armed gang; brigand.
▷HISTORY C16: from Italian *bandito*, literally: banished man, from *bandire* to proscribe, from *bando* edict, BAN¹
▸**'banditry** NOUN

Bandjarmasin *or* **Bandjermasin** (,bændʒə'mɑːsɪn) NOUN variant spellings of **Banjarmasin.**

bandmaster ('bænd,mɑːstə) NOUN the conductor of a band.

bandobust *or* **bundobust** ('bʌndəʊbəst) NOUN (in India and Pakistan) an arrangement.
▷HISTORY Hindi *band-o-bast* tying and binding, from Persian

Band of Hope NOUN a society promoting lifelong abstention from alcohol among young people: founded in Britain in 1847.

bandolier *or* **bandoleer** (,bændə'lɪə) NOUN a soldier's broad shoulder belt having small pockets or loops for cartridges.
▷HISTORY C16: from Old French *bandouliere*, from Old Spanish *bandolera*, *bandolero* guerrilla, from Catalan *bandoler*, from *bandol* band, from Spanish *bando*; see BAND¹

bandoline ('bændə,liːn) NOUN a glutinous hair dressing, used (esp formerly) to keep the hair in place.
▷HISTORY C19: *bando-*, from French BANDEAU + *-line*, from Latin *linere* to smear

bandoneon (bæn'dəʊnɪən) NOUN a type of square concertina, esp used in Argentina.
▷HISTORY C20: from Spanish, from German *Bandonion*, from Heinrich *Band*, its inventor

bandore (bæn'dɔː, 'bændɔː) NOUN a 16th-century plucked musical instrument resembling a lute but larger and fitted with seven pairs of metal strings. Also called: **pandore, pandora.**
▷HISTORY C16: from Spanish *bandurria*, from Late Latin *pandūra* three-stringed instrument, from Greek *pandoura*

band-pass filter NOUN [1] *Electronics* a filter that transmits only those currents having a frequency lying within specified limits. Compare **high-pass filter, low-pass filter.** [2] an optical device, consisting of absorbing filters, for transmitting electromagnetic waves of predetermined wavelengths.

B and S NOUN *Austral informal* a dance held for young people in country areas, usually in a field or barn.
▷HISTORY abbreviation for BACHELOR AND SPINSTER

band saw NOUN a power-operated saw consisting of an endless toothed metal band running over and driven by two wheels.

bandsman ('bændzmən) NOUN, *plural* **-men**. a player in a musical band, esp a brass or military band.

band spectrum NOUN a spectrum consisting of a number of bands of closely spaced lines that are associated with emission or absorption of radiation by molecules.

bandspreading ('bænd,sprɛdɪŋ) NOUN an additional tuning control in some radio receivers whereby a selected narrow band of frequencies can be spread over a wider frequency band, in order to give finer control of tuning.

bandstand ('bænd,stænd) NOUN a platform for a band, usually out of doors and roofed.

band theory NOUN *Physics* a theory of the electrical properties of metals, semiconductors, and insulators based on energy bands.

Bandung ('bændʊŋ) NOUN a city in Indonesia, in SW Java. Pop.: 2 356 120 (1995 est.).

B & W ABBREVIATION FOR black and white.

bandwagon ('bænd,wægən) NOUN [1] *US* a wagon, usually high and brightly coloured, for carrying the band in a parade. [2] **jump, climb,** *or* **get on the bandwagon.** to join or give support to a party or movement that seems to be assured of success.

bandwidth ('bænd,wɪdθ) NOUN [1] the range of frequencies within a given waveband used for a particular transmission. [2] the range of frequencies over which a receiver or amplifier should not differ by more than a specified amount. [3] the range of frequencies used in a specific telecommunications signal.

bandy ('bændɪ) ADJECTIVE **-dier, -diest.** [1] Also: **bandy-legged.** having legs curved outwards at the knees. [2] (of legs) curved outwards at the knees. [3] **knock (someone) bandy.** *Austral informal* to amaze or astound. ◆ VERB **-dies, -dying, -died.** *(tr)* [4] to exchange (words) in a heated or hostile manner. [5] to give and receive (blows). [6] (often foll by *about*) to circulate (a name, rumour, etc.). [7] to throw or strike to and fro; toss about. ◆ NOUN, *plural* **-dies.** [8] an early form of hockey, often played on ice. [9] a stick, curved at one end, used in the game of bandy. [10] an old form of tennis.
▷HISTORY C16: probably from Old French *bander* to hit the ball back and forth at tennis

bandy-bandy ('bændɪ'bændɪ) NOUN, *plural* **-bandies.** a small Australian elapid snake, *Vermicella annulata*, ringed with black and yellow.

bandy legs PLURAL NOUN another term for **bow legs.**

Bandywallop ('bændɪ,wɒləp) NOUN *Austral informal* an imaginary town, far from civilization.

bane[1] (beɪn) NOUN [1] a person or thing that causes misery or distress (esp in the phrase **bane of one's life**). [2] something that causes death or destruction. [3] **a** a fatal poison. **b** *(in combination)*: *ratsbane.* [4] *Archaic* ruin or distress.
▷HISTORY Old English *bana*; related to Old Norse *bani* death, Old High German *bano* destruction, death

bane[2] (ben, beɪn) NOUN a Scot word for **bone.**

baneberry ('beɪnbərɪ) NOUN, *plural* **-ries.** [1] Also called: (Brit) **herb Christopher,** (US) **cohosh.** any ranunculaceous plant of the genus *Actaea*, esp *A. spicata*, which has small white flowers and red or white poisonous berries. [2] a berry of any of these plants.

baneful ('beɪnfʊl) ADJECTIVE *Archaic* destructive, poisonous, or fatal.
▸ **'banefully** ADVERB ▸ **'banefulness** NOUN

Banff (bæmf) NOUN [1] a town in NE Scotland, in Aberdeenshire. Pop.: 6230 (1991). [2] a town in Canada, in SW Alberta, in the Rocky Mountains: surrounded by **Banff National Park.** Pop.: 5700 (1991).

Banffshire ('bæmf,ʃɪə, -ʃə) NOUN (until 1975) a county of NE Scotland: formerly (1975–96) part of Grampian region, now part of Aberdeenshire.

bang[1] (bæŋ) NOUN [1] a short loud explosive noise, as of the bursting of a balloon or the report of a gun. [2] a hard blow or knock, esp a noisy one; thump: *he gave the ball a bang.* [3] *Informal* a startling or sudden effect: *he realized with a bang that he was late.* [4] *Slang* an injection of heroin or other narcotic. [5] *Taboo slang* an act of sexual intercourse. [6] **get a bang out of.** *US and Canadian slang* to experience a thrill or excitement from. [7] **with a bang.** successfully: *the party went with a bang.* ◆ VERB [8] to hit or knock, esp with a loud noise; bump: *to bang one's head.* [9] to move noisily or clumsily: *to bang about the house.* [10] to close (a door, window, etc.) or (of a door, etc.) be closed noisily; slam. [11] *(tr)* to cause to move by hitting vigorously: *he banged the ball over the fence.* [12] to make or cause to make a loud noise, as of an explosion. [13] *(tr) Brit* **a** to cause (stock prices) to fall by rapid selling. **b** to sell rapidly in (a stock market), thus causing prices to fall. [14] *Taboo slang* to have sexual intercourse with. [15] *(intr) Slang* to inject heroin, etc. [16] **bang for one's buck.** *Informal* value for money: *this option offers more bang for your buck.* [17] **bang goes.** *Informal* that is the end of: *bang goes my job in Wapping.* [18] **bang one's head against a brick wall.** to try to achieve something impossible. ◆ ADVERB [19] with a sudden impact or effect: *bang went his hopes of winning; the car drove bang into a lamp-post.* [20] precisely: *bang in the middle of the road.* [21] **bang to rights.** *Slang* caught red-handed. [22] **go bang.** to burst, shut, etc., with a loud noise. See also **bang up.**
▷HISTORY C16: from Old Norse *bang, banga* hammer; related to Low German *bangen* to beat; all of imitative origin

bang[2] (bæŋ) NOUN [1] a fringe or section of hair cut straight across the forehead. ◆ VERB *(tr)* [2] to cut (the hair) in such a style. [3] to dock (the tail of a horse, etc.).
▷HISTORY C19: probably short for *bangtail* short tail

bang[3] (bæŋ) NOUN a variant spelling of **bhang.**

bangalay ('bæŋgəleɪ, bæŋ'gælɪ) NOUN a myrtaceous Australian tree, *Eucalyptus botryoides*, valued for its hard red wood.
▷HISTORY from a native Australian language

Bangalore (,bæŋgə'lɔː) NOUN a city in S India, capital of Karnataka state: printing, textiles, pharmaceuticals. Pop.: 2 660 088 (1991).

bangalore torpedo NOUN an explosive device in a long metal tube, used to blow gaps in barbed-wire barriers.
▷HISTORY C20: named after BANGALORE, where it was developed

bangalow ('bæŋgələʊ) NOUN an Australian palm, *Archontophoenix cunninghamiana*, native to New South Wales and Queensland. Also called: **bangalow palm.**
▷HISTORY from a native Australian language

bang-bang NOUN *Informal* war and fighting, esp involving ammunition.

banger ('bæŋə) NOUN *Brit* [1] *Slang* a sausage. [2] *Informal* **a** an old decrepit car. **b** *(as modifier)*: *banger racing.* [3] a type of firework that explodes loudly.

bangin' ('bæŋɪn) *or* **banging** ('bæŋɪŋ) ADJECTIVE *Slang* excellent: *the island boasts a bangin' selection of clubs.*

Bangka *or* **Banka** ('bæŋkə) NOUN an island in Indonesia, separated from Sumatra by the **Bangka Strait.** Chief town: Pangkalpinang. Area: about 11 914 sq. km (4600 sq. miles).

Bangkok ('bæŋkɒk, bæŋ'kɒk) NOUN the capital and chief port of Thailand, on the Chao Phraya River: became a royal city and the capital in 1782. Pop.: 6 320 174 (1999 est.). Thai name: **Krung Thep** ('krʊŋ 'teɪp).

Bangla ('bæŋlə) NOUN another name for **Bengali** (sense 2).

Bangladesh (,bɑːŋglə'dɛʃ, ,bæŋ-) NOUN a republic in S Asia: formerly the Eastern Province of Pakistan; became independent in 1971 after civil war and the defeat of Pakistan by India; consists of the plains and vast deltas of the Ganges and Brahmaputra Rivers; prone to flooding: economy based on jute and jute products (over 70 per cent of world production); a member of the Commonwealth. Language: Bengali. Religion: Muslim. Currency: taka. Capital: Dhaka. Pop.: 131 270 000 (2001 est.). Area: 142 797 sq. km (55 126 sq. miles).

Bangladeshi (,bɑːŋglə'dɛʃɪ, ,bæŋ-) ADJECTIVE [1] of or relating to Bangladesh. ◆ NOUN [2] a native or inhabitant of Bangladesh.

bangle ('bæŋgᵊl) NOUN [1] a bracelet, usually without a clasp, often worn high up round the arm or sometimes round the ankle. [2] a disc or charm hanging from a bracelet, necklace, etc.
▷HISTORY C19: from Hindi *bangrī*

bang on ADJECTIVE, ADVERB *Brit informal* [1] with absolute accuracy. [2] excellent or excellently. ◆ Also (US): **bang up.**

Bangor ('bæŋgɔː, -gə) NOUN [1] a university town in NW Wales, in Gwynedd, on the Menai Strait. Pop.: 12 330 (1991). [2] a town in SE Northern Ireland, in North Down district, Co. Down, on Belfast Lough. Pop.: 52 437 (1991).

bangtail ('bæŋ,teɪl) NOUN [1] a horse's tail cut straight across but not through the bone. [2] a horse with a tail cut in this way. [3] *Marketing* a type of envelope used in direct marketing in which a perforated tail can be used as an order form or response note.
▷HISTORY C19: from *bangtail* short tail

bangtail muster NOUN *Austral history* a roundup of cattle to be counted, each one having the hairs on its tail docked as it is counted.

Bangui (*French* bɑ̃gi) NOUN the capital of the Central African Republic, in the south part, on the Ubangi River. Pop.: 553 000 (1995 est.).

bang up VERB *(tr, adverb) Prison slang* to lock up (a prisoner) in his cell, esp for the night.

Bangweulu (,bæŋwɪ'uːluː) NOUN **Lake.** a shallow lake in NE Zambia, discovered by David Livingstone, who died there in 1873. Area: about 9850 sq. km (3800 sq. miles), including swamps.

bani ('bɑːnɪ) NOUN the plural of **ban**[3].

banian ('bænjən) NOUN a variant spelling of **banyan.**

banish ('bænɪʃ) VERB *(tr)* [1] to expel from a place, esp by an official decree as a punishment. [2] to drive away: *to banish gloom.*
▷HISTORY C14: from Old French *banir*, of Germanic origin; compare Old High German *ban* BAN[2]
▸ **'banishment** NOUN

banisters *or* **bannisters** ('bænɪstəz) PLURAL NOUN the railing and supporting balusters on a staircase; balustrade.
▷HISTORY C17: altered from BALUSTER

Banja Luka (*Serbo-Croat* 'baːnjaː ,luːka) NOUN a city in NW Bosnia-Herzegovina, on the Vrbas River: scene of battles between the Austrians and Turks in 1527, 1688, and 1737; besieged by Serb forces (1992–95). Pop.: 160 000 (1997 est.).

Banjarmasin, Banjermasin, Bandjarmasin, *or* **Bandjermasin** (,bændʒə'mɑːsɪn) NOUN a port in Indonesia, in SW Borneo. Pop.: 534 600 (1995 est.).

banjo ('bændʒəʊ) NOUN, *plural* **-jos** *or* **-joes.** [1] a stringed musical instrument with a long neck (usually fretted) and a circular drumlike body overlaid with parchment, plucked with the fingers or a plectrum. [2] *Slang* any banjo-shaped object, esp a frying pan. [3] *Austral and NZ slang* a long-handled shovel with a wide blade. [4] *(modifier)* banjo-shaped: *a banjo clock.*
▷HISTORY C18: variant (US Southern pronunciation) of BANDORE
▸ **'banjoist** NOUN

Banjul (bæn'dʒuːl) NOUN the capital of The Gambia, a port at the mouth of the Gambia River. Pop.: 42 407 (1993). Former name (until 1973): **Bathurst.**

bank[1] (bæŋk) NOUN [1] an institution offering certain financial services, such as the safekeeping of money, conversion of domestic into and from foreign currencies, lending of money at interest, and acceptance of bills of exchange. [2] the building used by such an institution. [3] a small container used at home for keeping money. [4] the funds held by a gaming house or a banker or dealer in some gambling games. [5] (in various games) **a** the stock, as of money, pieces, tokens, etc., on which players may draw. **b** the player holding this stock. [6] any supply, store, or reserve, for future use: *a data bank; a blood bank.* ◆ VERB [7] *(tr)* to deposit (cash, cheques,

etc.) in a bank. [8] (*intr*) to transact business with a bank. [9] (*intr*) to engage in the business of banking. [10] (*intr*) to hold the bank in some gambling games. ◆ See also **bank on.**
▷**HISTORY** C15: probably from Italian *banca* bench, moneychanger's table, of Germanic origin; compare Old High German *banc* BENCH

bank[2] (bæŋk) NOUN [1] a long raised mass, esp of earth; mound; ridge. [2] a slope, as of a hill. [3] the sloping side of any hollow in the ground, esp when bordering a river: *the left bank of a river is on a spectator's left looking downstream.* [4] **a** an elevated section, rising to near the surface, of the bed of a sea, lake, or river. **b** (*in combination*): *sandbank; mudbank.* [5] **a** the area around the mouth of the shaft of a mine. **b** the face of a body of ore. [6] the lateral inclination of an aircraft about its longitudinal axis during a turn. [7] Also called: **banking, camber, cant, superelevation.** a bend on a road or on a railway, athletics, cycling, or other track having the outside built higher than the inside in order to reduce the effects of centrifugal force on vehicles, runners, etc., rounding it at speed and in some cases to facilitate drainage. [8] the cushion of a billiard table. ◆ VERB [9] (when *tr*, often foll by *up*) to form into a bank or mound. [10] (*tr*) to border or enclose (a road, etc.) with a bank. [11] (*tr*, sometimes foll by *up*) to cover (a fire) with ashes, fresh fuel, etc., so that it will burn slowly. [12] to cause (an aircraft) to tip laterally about its longitudinal axis or (of an aircraft) to tip in this way, esp. while turning. [13] to travel round a bank, esp. at high speed. [14] (*tr*) *Billiards* to drive (a ball) into the cushion.
▷**HISTORY** C12: of Scandinavian origin; compare Old Icelandic *bakki* hill, Old Danish *banke*, Swedish *backe*

bank[3] (bæŋk) NOUN [1] an arrangement of objects, esp similar objects, in a row or in tiers: *a bank of dials.* [2] **a** a tier of oars in a galley. **b** a bench for the rowers in a galley. [3] a grade of lightweight writing and printing paper used for airmail letters, etc. [4] *Telephony* (in automatic switching) an assembly of fixed electrical contacts forming a rigid unit in a selector or similar device. ◆ VERB [5] (*tr*) to arrange in a bank.
▷**HISTORY** C17: from Old French *banc* bench, of Germanic origin; see BANK[1]

Banka (ˈbæŋkə) NOUN a variant spelling of **Bangka.**

bankable (ˈbæŋkəbᵊl) ADJECTIVE [1] appropriate for receipt by a bank. [2] dependable or reliable: *a bankable promise.* [3] (esp of a star) likely to ensure the financial success of a film.
▶ ˌ**bankaˈbility** NOUN

bank acceptance NOUN a bill of exchange or draft drawn on and endorsed by a bank. Also called: **banker's acceptance.**

bank account NOUN [1] an account created by the deposit of money at a bank by a customer. [2] the amount of money credited to a depositor at a bank.

bank annuities PLURAL NOUN another term for **consols.**

bank bill NOUN [1] Also called: **bank draft.** a bill of exchange drawn by one bank on another. [2] Also called: **banker's bill.** *US* a banknote.

bankbook (ˈbæŋkˌbʊk) NOUN a book held by depositors at certain banks, in which the bank enters a record of deposits, withdrawals, and earned interest. Also called: **passbook.**

bank clerk NOUN *Brit* an employee of a bank.

bank discount NOUN interest on a loan deducted from the principal amount when the loan is made and based on the loan's face value.

bank draft NOUN a cheque drawn by a bank on itself, which is bought by a person to pay a supplier unwilling to accept a normal cheque. Also called: **banker's cheque.**

banker[1] (ˈbæŋkə) NOUN [1] a person who owns or is an executive in a bank. [2] an official or player in charge of the bank in any of various games, esp gambling games. [3] a result that has been forecast identically in a series of entries on a football pool coupon. [4] a person or thing that appears certain to win or be successful.

banker[2] (ˈbæŋkə) NOUN [1] a fishing vessel of Newfoundland. [2] a fisherman in such a vessel. [3] *Austral and NZ informal* a stream almost overflowing its banks (esp in the phrase **run a banker**). [4] Also called: **bank engine.** *Brit* a locomotive that is used to help a heavy train up a steep gradient.

banker[3] (ˈbæŋkə) NOUN [1] a craftsman's workbench. [2] a timber board used as a base for mixing building materials.

banker's order NOUN another name for **standing order** (sense 1).

banket (ˈbæŋkɪt) NOUN a gold-bearing conglomerate found in South Africa.
▷**HISTORY** C19: from Dutch: a kind of almond hardbake, alluding to its appearance

Bank Giro NOUN a British giro system operated by clearing banks to enable customers to pay sums of money to others by credit transfer.

bank holiday NOUN (in Britain) any of several weekdays on which banks are closed by law and which are observed as national holidays.

banking[1] (ˈbæŋkɪŋ) NOUN the business engaged in by a bank.

banking[2] (ˈbæŋkɪŋ) NOUN [1] an embankment of a river. [2] another word for **bank[1]** (sense 7). [3] fishing on a sea bank, esp off the coast of Newfoundland. [4] the manoeuvre causing an aircraft to bank.

bank manager NOUN a person who directs the business of a local branch of a bank.

banknote (ˈbæŋkˌnəʊt) NOUN a promissory note issued by a central bank, serving as money.

Bank of England NOUN the central bank of the United Kingdom, which acts as banker to the government and the commercial banks. It is responsible for managing the government's debt and implementing its policy on other monetary matters: established in 1694, nationalized in 1946; in 1997 the government restored the authority to set interest rates to the Bank.

bank on VERB (*intr, preposition*) to expect or rely with confidence on: *you can bank on him always arriving on time.*

bank rate NOUN another name for **base rate.**

bankroll (ˈbæŋkˌrəʊl) *Chiefly US and Canadian* ◆ NOUN [1] a roll of currency notes. [2] the financial resources of a person, organization, etc. ◆ VERB [3] (*tr*) *Slang* to provide the capital for; finance.

bankroller (ˈbæŋkˌrəʊlə) NOUN the person or organization that provides the finance for a project, business, etc.

bankrupt (ˈbæŋkrʌpt, -rəpt) NOUN [1] a person adjudged insolvent by a court, his property being transferred to a trustee and administered for the benefit of his creditors. [2] any person unable to discharge all his debts. [3] a person whose resources in a certain field are exhausted or nonexistent: *a spiritual bankrupt.* ◆ ADJECTIVE [4] adjudged insolvent. [5] financially ruined. [6] depleted in resources or having completely failed: *spiritually bankrupt.* [7] (foll by *of*) *Brit* lacking: *bankrupt of intelligence.* ◆ VERB [8] (*tr*) to make bankrupt.
▷**HISTORY** C16: from Old French *banqueroute*, from Old Italian *bancarotta*, from *banca* BANK[1] + *rotta* broken, from Latin *ruptus*, from *rumpere* to break

bankruptcy (ˈbæŋkrʌptsɪ, -rəptsɪ) NOUN, *plural* **-cies.** the state, condition, or quality of being or becoming bankrupt.

bankruptcy order NOUN *Law* a court order appointing a receiver to manage the property of a debtor or bankrupt. Former name: **receiving order.**

banksia (ˈbæŋksɪə) NOUN any shrub or tree of the Australian genus *Banksia*, having long leathery evergreen leaves and dense cylindrical heads of flowers that are often red or yellowish: family *Proteaceae*. See also **honeysuckle** (sense 3).
▷**HISTORY** C19: New Latin, named after Sir Joseph Banks (1743–1820), British botanist and explorer

Banks Island NOUN [1] an island of N Canada, in the Northwest Territories: the westernmost island of the Arctic Archipelago. Area: about 67 340 sq. km (26 000 sq. miles). [2] an island of W Canada, off British Columbia. Length: about 72 km (45 miles).

banksman (ˈbæŋksmən) NOUN a crane driver's helper, who signals instructions to the driver for the movement of the crane and its jib.

bank statement NOUN a statement of transactions in a bank account, esp one of a series sent at regular intervals to the depositor.

banlieue *French* (bɑ̃ljø) NOUN a suburb of a city.

banner (ˈbænə) NOUN [1] a long strip of flexible material displaying a slogan, advertisement, etc., esp one suspended between two points. [2] a placard or sign carried in a procession or demonstration. [3] something that represents a belief or principle: *a commitment to nationalization was the banner of British socialism.* [4] the flag of a nation, army, etc., used as a standard or ensign. [5] (formerly) the standard of an emperor, knight, etc. [6] Also called: **banner headline.** a large headline in a newspaper, etc., extending across the page, esp the front page. [7] an advertisement that extends across the width of a web page. [8] a square flag, often charged with the arms of its bearer. ◆ VERB [9] (*tr*) (of a newspaper headline) to display (a story) prominently. ◆ ADJECTIVE [9] *US* outstandingly successful: *a banner year for orders.*
▷**HISTORY** C13: from Old French *baniere*, of Germanic origin; compare Gothic *bandwa* sign; influenced by Medieval Latin *bannum* BAN[1], *bannīre* to BANISH
▶ ˈ**bannered** ADJECTIVE

banner ad NOUN [1] a banner advertising a product. [2] an advert along the top of a page of a website.

banneret (ˈbænərɪt, -əˌrɛt) NOUN (in the Middle Ages) [1] Also called: **knight banneret.** a knight who was entitled to command other knights and men-at-arms under his own banner. [2] a title of knighthood conferred by the king for valour on the battlefield.
▷**HISTORY** C14: from Old French *banerete* a small BANNER

bannerette *or* **banneret** (ˌbænəˈrɛt) NOUN a small banner.
▷**HISTORY** C13: from Old French *baneret*, from *banere* BANNER

bannerol (ˈbænəˌrəʊl) NOUN a variant of **banderole.**

bannisters (ˈbænɪstəz) PLURAL NOUN a variant spelling of **banisters.**

bannock (ˈbænək) NOUN a round flat unsweetened cake originating in Scotland, made from oatmeal or barley and baked on a griddle.
▷**HISTORY** Old English *bannuc*; of Celtic origin; compare Gaelic *bannach*, Cornish *banna* a drop, bit; perhaps related to Latin *pānicium*, from *pānis* bread

Bannockburn (ˈbænəkˌbɜːn) NOUN a village in central Scotland, south of Stirling: nearby is the site of a victory (1314) of the Scots, led by Robert the Bruce, over the English. Pop.: 2675 (1991).

banns *or* **bans** (bænz) PLURAL NOUN [1] the public declaration of an intended marriage, usually formally announced on three successive Sundays in the parish churches of both the betrothed. [2] **forbid the banns.** to raise an objection to a marriage announced in this way.
▷**HISTORY** C14: plural of *bann* proclamation; see BAN[1]

banoffee *or* **banoffi** (bəˈnɒfɪ) NOUN a filling for a pie, consisting of toffee and banana.
▷**HISTORY** C20: from BAN(ANA) + (T)OFFEE

banquet (ˈbæŋkwɪt) NOUN [1] a lavish and sumptuous meal; feast. [2] a ceremonial meal for many people, often followed by speeches. ◆ VERB **-quets, -queting, -queted.** [3] (*intr*) to hold or take part in a banquet. [4] (*tr*) to entertain or honour (a person) with a banquet.
▷**HISTORY** C15: from Old French, from Italian *banchetto*, from *banco* a table, of Germanic origin; see BANK[1]
▶ ˈ**banqueter** NOUN

banquette (bæŋˈkɛt) NOUN [1] an upholstered bench. [2] (formerly) a raised part behind a parapet. [3] a footbridge.
▷**HISTORY** C17: from French, from Provençal *banqueta*, literally: a little bench, from *banc* bench; see BANK[3]

bans (bænz) PLURAL NOUN a variant spelling of **banns.**

bansela (banˈsɛlə) NOUN a variant of **bonsela.**

banshee (ˈbænʃiː, bænˈʃiː) NOUN (in Irish folklore) a female spirit whose wailing warns of impending death.
▷**HISTORY** C18: from Irish Gaelic *bean sídhe*, literally: woman of the fairy mound

Banstead (ˈbænˌstɛd) NOUN a town in S England,

in NE Surrey: a dormitory town for London. Pop.: 37 245 (1991).

bant (bænt) NOUN *Lancashire dialect* 1 string. 2 strength or springiness of material.
▷HISTORY probably a dialect pronunciation of BAND[2]

bantam ('bæntəm) NOUN 1 any of various very small breeds of domestic fowl. 2 a small but aggressive person. 3 *Boxing* short for **bantamweight**. 4 *Canadian* **a** an age level of between 13 and 15 in amateur sport, esp ice hockey. **b** (*as modifier*): *bantam hockey*.
▷HISTORY C18: after *Bantam* village in Java, said to be the original home of this fowl

bantamweight ('bæntəm,weɪt) NOUN 1 **a** a professional boxer weighing 112–118 pounds (51–53.5 kg). **b** an amateur boxer weighing 51–54 kg (112–119 pounds). **c** (*as modifier*): *the bantamweight champion*. 2 a wrestler in a similar weight category (usually 115–126 pounds (52–57 kg)).

banter ('bæntə) VERB 1 to speak to or tease lightly or jokingly. ♦ NOUN 2 light, teasing, or joking language or repartee.
▷HISTORY C17: of unknown origin
▸**'banterer** NOUN

banting ('bæntɪŋ) NOUN *Obsolete* slimming by avoiding eating sugar, starch, and fat.
▷HISTORY C19: named after William *Banting* (1797–1878), London undertaker who popularized this diet

bantling ('bæntlɪŋ) NOUN *Archaic, disparaging* a young child; brat.
▷HISTORY C16: perhaps from German *Bänkling* illegitimate child, from *Bank* bench + -LING[1]

Bantoid ('bɑːntɔɪd, 'bæn-) ADJECTIVE denoting or relating to languages, esp in Cameroon and Nigeria, that possess certain Bantu characteristics. See also **Semi-Bantu**.

Bantu ('bɑːntuː, 'bæntuː, bæn'tuː) NOUN 1 a group of languages of Africa, including most of the principal languages spoken from the equator to the Cape of Good Hope, but excluding the Khoisan family: now generally regarded as part of the Benue-Congo branch of the Niger-Congo family. 2 (*plural* **-tu** *or* **-tus**) *South African derogatory* a Black speaker of a Bantu language. ♦ ADJECTIVE 3 denoting, relating to, or belonging to this group of peoples or to any of their languages.
▷HISTORY C19: from Bantu *Ba-ntu* people

Bantu beer NOUN *South African* a malted drink made from partly fermented and germinated millet.

Bantustan ('bɑːntuː,stɑːn, ,bæntuː'stɑːn) NOUN (formerly, in South Africa) an area reserved for occupation by a Black African people, with limited self-government; abolished in 1993. Official name: **homeland**.

banyan *or* **banian** ('bænjən) NOUN 1 a moraceous tree, *Ficus benghalensis*, of tropical India and the East Indies, having aerial roots that grow down into the soil forming additional trunks. 2 a member of the Hindu merchant caste of N and W India. 3 a loose-fitting shirt, jacket, or robe, worn originally in India.
▷HISTORY C16: from Hindi *baniyā*, from Sanskrit *vānija* merchant

Banyana banyana (bə'njɑːnə bə'njɑːnə) PLURAL NOUN the South Africa women's national soccer team.
▷HISTORY C20: from Nguni *banyana* the girls

banzai ('bɑːnzaɪ, bɑː'nzaɪ) INTERJECTION a patriotic cheer, battle cry, or salutation.
▷HISTORY Japanese: literally, (may you live for) ten thousand years

banzai attack NOUN a mass attack of troops, without concern for casualties, as practised by the Japanese in World War II.

baobab ('beɪəʊ,bæb) NOUN a bombacaceous tree, *Adansonia digitata*, native to Africa, that has a very thick trunk, large white flowers, and a gourdlike fruit with an edible pulp called monkey bread. Also called: **bottle tree, monkey bread tree**.
▷HISTORY C17: probably from a native African word

Baoding ('baʊ'dɪŋ), **Paoting,** *or* **Pao-ting** NOUN a city in NE China, in N Hebei province. Pop.: 570 167 (1999 est.). Former name: **Ch'ing-yüan** *or* **Tsingyuan**.

BAOR ABBREVIATION FOR British Army of the Rhine.

Baotou ('baʊ'tuː) *or* **Paotow** NOUN an industrial city in N China, in the central Inner Mongolia AR on the Yellow River. Pop.: 1 092 819 (1999 est.).

bap (bæp) NOUN *Brit* a large soft bread roll.
▷HISTORY C16: of unknown origin

bapt. ABBREVIATION FOR: 1 baptism. 2 baptized.

baptism ('bæp,tɪzəm) NOUN 1 a Christian religious rite consisting of immersion in or sprinkling with water as a sign that the subject is cleansed from sin and constituted as a member of the Church. 2 the act of baptizing or of undergoing baptism. 3 any similar experience of initiation, regeneration, or dedication.
▸**bap'tismal** ADJECTIVE ▸**bap'tismally** ADVERB

baptism of fire NOUN 1 a soldier's first experience of battle. 2 any initiating ordeal or experience. 3 *Christianity* the penetration of the Holy Ghost into the human spirit to purify, consecrate, and strengthen it, as was believed to have occurred initially at Pentecost.

Baptist ('bæptɪst) NOUN 1 a member of any of various Christian sects that affirm the necessity of baptism (usually of adults and by immersion) following a personal profession of the Christian faith. 2 **the Baptist**. See **John the Baptist**. ♦ ADJECTIVE 3 denoting, relating to, or characteristic of any Christian sect that affirms the necessity of baptism following a personal profession of the Christian faith.

baptistry *or* **baptistery** ('bæptɪstrɪ) NOUN, *plural* **-ries** *or* **-eries**. 1 a part of a Christian church in which baptisms are carried out. 2 a tank in a Baptist church in which baptisms are carried out.

baptize *or* **baptise** (bæp'taɪz) VERB 1 *Christianity* to immerse (a person) in water or sprinkle water on (a person) as part of the rite of baptism. 2 (*tr*) to give a name to; christen. 3 (*tr*) to cleanse; purify.
▷HISTORY C13: from Late Latin *baptīzāre*, from Greek *baptizein*, from *baptein* to bathe, dip

bar[1] (bɑː) NOUN 1 a rigid usually straight length of metal, wood, etc., that is longer than it is wide or thick, used esp as a barrier or as a structural or mechanical part: *a bar of a gate*. 2 a solid usually rectangular block of any material: *a bar of soap*. 3 anything that obstructs or prevents. 4 **a** an offshore ridge of sand, mud, or shingle lying near the shore and parallel to it, across the mouth of a river, bay, or harbour, or linking an island to the mainland. **b** *US and Canadian* an alluvial deposit in a stream, river, or lake. 5 a counter or room where alcoholic drinks are served. 6 a counter, room, or establishment where a particular range of goods, food, services, etc., are sold: *a coffee bar; a heel bar*. 7 a narrow band or stripe, as of colour or light. 8 a heating element in an electric fire. 9 (in England) the area in a court of law separating the part reserved for the bench and Queen's Counsel from the area occupied by junior barristers, solicitors, and the general public. See also **Bar**. 10 the place in a court of law where the accused stands during his trial: *the prisoner at the bar*. 11 a particular court of law. 12 *Brit* (in the House of Lords and House of Commons) the boundary where nonmembers wishing to address either House appear and where persons are arraigned. 13 a plea showing that a plaintiff has no cause of action, as when the case has already been adjudicated upon or the time allowed for bringing the action has passed. 14 anything referred to as an authority or tribunal: *the bar of decency*. 15 Also called: **measure**. *Music* **a** a group of beats that is repeated with a consistent rhythm throughout a piece or passage of music. The number of beats in the bar is indicated by the time signature. **b** another word for **bar line**. 16 **a** *Brit* insignia added to a decoration indicating a second award. **b** *US* a strip of metal worn with uniform, esp to signify rank or as an award for service. 17 a variant spelling of **barre**. 18 *Sport* See **crossbar**. 19 *Gymnastics* See **horizontal bar**. 20 **a** part of the metal mouthpiece of a horse's bridle. **b** the space between the horse's teeth in which such a part fits. 21 either of two horny extensions that project forwards and inwards from the rear of the outer layer of a horse's hoof. 22 See **crowbar** and **glazing-bar**. 23 *Lacemaking, needlework* another name for **bride**[2]. 24 *Heraldry* an ordinary consisting of a horizontal line across a shield, typically narrower than a fesse, and usually appearing in twos or threes. 25 *Maths* a superscript line ¯ placed over a letter symbol to indicate, for example, a mean value or the complex conjugate of a complex number. 26 **behind bars.** in prison. 27 **won't** (*or* **wouldn't**) **have a bar of.** *Austral and NZ informal* cannot tolerate; dislike. ♦ VERB **bars, barring, barred.** (*tr*) 28 to fasten or secure with a bar: *to bar the door*. 29 to shut in or out with or as if with barriers: *to bar the entrances*. 30 to obstruct; hinder: *the fallen tree barred the road*. 31 (usually foll by *from*) to prohibit; forbid: *to bar a couple from meeting*. 32 (usually foll by *from*) to keep out; exclude: *to bar a person from membership*. 33 to mark with a bar or bars. 34 *Law* to prevent or halt (an action) by showing that the claimant has no cause. 35 to mark off (music) into bars with bar lines. ♦ PREPOSITION 36 except for: *the best recital bar last night's*. 37 **bar none.** without exception.
▷HISTORY C12: from Old French *barre*, from Vulgar Latin *barra* (unattested) bar, rod, of unknown origin

bar[2] (bɑː) NOUN a cgs unit of pressure equal to 10^6 dynes per square centimetre. 1 bar is equivalent to 10^5 newtons per square metre.
▷HISTORY C20: from Greek *baros* weight

bar[3] (bɑː) *Southwest English dialect* ♦ NOUN 1 immunity from being caught or otherwise penalized in a game. ♦ INTERJECTION 2 a cry for such immunity.
▷HISTORY variant of BARLEY[2]

Bar (bɑː) NOUN **the.** 1 (in England and elsewhere) barristers collectively. 2 *US* the legal profession collectively. 3 **be called to** *or* **go to the Bar.** *Brit* to become a barrister. 4 **be called within the Bar.** *Brit* to be appointed as a Queen's Counsel.

BAR ABBREVIATION FOR Browning Automatic Rifle.

bar. ABBREVIATION FOR: 1 barometer. 2 barometric. 3 barrel (container or unit of measure). 4 barrister.

Bar- (bar, bɑː) PREFIX (before Jewish patronymic names) son of: *Bar-Kochba*.

Barabbas (bə'ræbəs) NOUN *New Testament* a condemned robber who was released at the Passover instead of Jesus (Matthew 27:16).

barachois (,bærə'ʃwɑː) NOUN (in the Atlantic Provinces of Canada) a shallow lagoon formed by a sand bar.
▷HISTORY French

baraesthesia *or* *US* **baresthesia** (,bærɪs'θiːzɪə) NOUN *Physiol* the ability to sense pressure.
▷HISTORY C20: from Greek *baros* weight + AESTHESIA

Baranof Island ('bærənɔf) NOUN an island off SE Alaska, in the western part of the Alexander Archipelago. Area: 4162 sq. km (1607 sq. miles).

Bárány test (*German* 'bɑːranɪ) NOUN a test which detects diseases of the semicircular canals of the inner ear, devised by Robert Bárány (1876–1936).

barathea (,bærə'θɪə) NOUN a fabric made of silk and wool or cotton and rayon, used esp for coats.
▷HISTORY C19: of unknown origin

baraza (ba'raza) NOUN *E African* 1 a place where public meetings are held. 2 a palaver or meeting.
▷HISTORY C19: from Swahili

barb[1] (bɑːb) NOUN 1 a subsidiary point facing in the opposite direction to the main point of a fish-hook, harpoon, arrow, etc., intended to make extraction difficult. 2 any of various pointed parts, as on barbed wire. 3 a cutting remark; gibe. 4 any of the numerous hairlike filaments that form the vane of a feather. 5 a beardlike growth in certain animals. 6 a hooked hair or projection on certain fruits. 7 any small cyprinid fish of the genus *Barbus* (or *Puntius*) and related genera, such as *B. conchonius* (**rosy barb**). 8 (*usually plural*) any of the small fleshy protuberances beneath the tongue in horses and cattle. 9 a white linen cloth forming part of a headdress extending from the chin to the upper chest, originally worn by women in the Middle Ages, now worn by nuns of some orders. 10 *Obsolete* a beard. ♦ VERB 11 (*tr*) to provide with a barb or barbs.
▷HISTORY C14: from Old French *barbe* beard, point, from Latin *barba* beard
▸**barbed** ADJECTIVE

barb[2] (bɑːb) NOUN a breed of horse of North African origin, similar to the Arab but less spirited.
▷HISTORY C17: from French *barbe*, from Italian *barbero* a Barbary (horse)

barb[3] (bɑːb) NOUN *Austral* a black kelpie (see **kelpie**[1]).
▷HISTORY C19: named after one that was named *Barb* after a winning racehorse

BARB (bɑːb) NOUN (in Britain) ◆ ACRONYM FOR Broadcasters' Audience Research Board.

Barbadian (bɑːˈbeɪdɪən) ADJECTIVE [1] of or relating to Barbados or its inhabitants. ◆ NOUN [2] a native or inhabitant of Barbados.

Barbados (bɑːˈbeɪdəʊs, -dəʊz, -dɒs) NOUN an island in the Caribbean, in the E Lesser Antilles: a British colony from 1628 to 1966, now an independent state within the Commonwealth. Language: English. Currency: Barbados dollar. Capital: Bridgetown. Pop.: 269 000 (2001). Area: 430 sq. km (166 sq. miles).

Barbados earth NOUN a diatomaceous marl found in Barbados.

barbarian (bɑːˈbɛərɪən) NOUN [1] a member of a primitive or uncivilized people. [2] a coarse, insensitive, or uncultured person. [3] a vicious person. ◆ ADJECTIVE [4] of an uncivilized culture. [5] insensitive, uncultured, or brutal.
▷HISTORY C16: see BARBAROUS
▸**barˈbarianism** NOUN

barbaric (bɑːˈbærɪk) ADJECTIVE [1] of or characteristic of barbarians. [2] primitive or unsophisticated; unrestrained. [3] brutal.
▷HISTORY C15: from Latin *barbaricus* foreign, outlandish; see BARBAROUS
▸**barˈbarically** ADVERB

barbarism (ˈbɑːbəˌrɪzəm) NOUN [1] a brutal, coarse, or ignorant act. [2] the condition of being backward, coarse, or ignorant. [3] a substandard or erroneously constructed or derived word or expression; solecism. [4] any act or object that offends against accepted taste.
▷HISTORY C16: from Latin *barbarismus* error of speech, from Greek *barbarismos*, from *barbaros* BARBAROUS

barbarity (bɑːˈbærɪtɪ) NOUN, *plural* **-ties**. [1] the state or condition of being barbaric or barbarous. [2] a brutal or vicious act. [3] a crude or unsophisticated quality, style, expression, etc.

barbarize *or* **barbarise** (ˈbɑːbəˌraɪz) VERB [1] to make or become barbarous. [2] to use barbarisms in (language).
▸**ˌbarbariˈzation** *or* **ˌbarbariˈsation** NOUN

barbarous (ˈbɑːbərəs) ADJECTIVE [1] uncivilized; primitive. [2] brutal or cruel. [3] lacking refinement.
▷HISTORY C15: via Latin from Greek *barbaros* barbarian, non-Greek, in origin imitative of incomprehensible speech; compare Sanskrit *barbara* stammering, non-Aryan
▸**ˈbarbarously** ADVERB ▸**ˈbarbarousness** NOUN

Barbary (ˈbɑːbərɪ) NOUN a region of N Africa, extending from W Egypt to the Atlantic and including the former **Barbary States** of Tripolitania, Tunisia, Algeria, and Morocco.

Barbary ape NOUN a tailless macaque, *Macaca sylvana*, that inhabits rocky cliffs and forests in NW Africa and Gibraltar: family *Cercopithecidae*, order *Primates*.

Barbary Coast NOUN **the**. the Mediterranean coast of North Africa: a centre of piracy against European shipping from the 16th to the 19th centuries.

barbastelle (ˌbɑːbəˈstɛl) NOUN an insectivorous forest bat, *Barbastella barbastellus*, widely distributed across Eurasia, having a wrinkled face and prominent ears: roosts in trees or caves.
▷HISTORY French: from Italian *barbastello*, from Latin *vespertilio* bat; see PIPISTRELLE

barbate (ˈbɑːbeɪt) ADJECTIVE *Chiefly biology* having tufts of long hairs; bearded.
▷HISTORY C19: from Latin *barba* a beard

barbecue (ˈbɑːbɪˌkjuː) NOUN [1] a meal cooked out of doors over an open fire. [2] an outdoor party or picnic at which barbecued food is served. [3] a grill or fireplace used in barbecuing. [4] the food so cooked. ◆ VERB **-cues, -cuing, -cued**. (*tr*) [5] to cook (meat, fish, etc.) on a grill, usually over charcoal and often with a highly seasoned sauce. [6] to cook (meat, fish, etc.) in a highly seasoned sauce.
▷HISTORY C17: from American Spanish *barbacoa*, probably from Taino: frame made of sticks

barbed wire NOUN strong wire with sharply pointed barbs at close intervals. Also called (US): **barbwire**.

barbed-wire grass NOUN *Austral* an aromatic grass, *Cymbopogon refractus*, with groups of seed heads resembling barbed wire.

barbel (ˈbɑːbᵊl) NOUN [1] any of several slender tactile spines or bristles that hang from the jaws of certain fishes, such as the catfish and carp. [2] any of several European cyprinid fishes of the genus *Barbus*, esp *B. barbus*, that resemble the carp but have a longer body and pointed snout.
▷HISTORY C14: from Old French, from Latin *barbus*, from *barba* beard

barbell (ˈbɑːˌbɛl) NOUN a metal rod to which heavy discs are attached at each end for weightlifting exercises.

barbellate (ˈbɑːbɪˌleɪt, bɑːˈbɛlɪt, -eɪt) ADJECTIVE [1] (of plants or plant organs) covered with barbs, hooks, or bristles. [2] (of animals) possessing bristles or barbels.
▷HISTORY C19: from New Latin *barbellātus*, from *barbella* short stiff hair, from Latin *barbula* a little beard, from Latin *barba*

barber (ˈbɑːbə) NOUN [1] a person whose business is cutting men's hair and shaving or trimming beards. ◆ VERB (*tr*) [2] to cut the hair of. [3] to shave or trim the beard of.
▷HISTORY C13: from Old French *barbeor*, from *barbe* beard, from Latin *barba*

barberry (ˈbɑːbərɪ) NOUN, *plural* **-ries**. [1] any spiny berberidaceous shrub of the widely distributed genus *Berberis*, esp *B. vulgaris*, having clusters of yellow flowers and orange or red berries: widely cultivated as hedge plants. [2] the fruit of any of these plants.
▷HISTORY C15: from Old French *berberis*, from Arabic *barbāris*

barbershop (ˈbɑːbəˌʃɒp) NOUN [1] *Now chiefly US* the premises of a barber. [2] (*modifier*) denoting or characterized by a type of close four-part harmony for male voices, popular in romantic and sentimental songs of the 1920s and 1930s: *a barbershop quartet*.

barber's itch *or* **rash** NOUN any of various fungal infections of the bearded portion of the neck and face. Technical name: **tinea barbae**.

barber's pole NOUN a sign outside a barber's shop consisting of a pole painted with red and white spiral stripes.

Barberton daisy (ˈbɑːbətən) NOUN See **gerbera**.
▷HISTORY from *Barberton*, a town in Mpumulanga Province, South Africa

barbet (ˈbɑːbɪt) NOUN any small tropical brightly coloured bird of the family *Capitonidae*, having short weak wings and a sharp stout bill with tuftlike feathers at its base: order *Piciformes* (woodpeckers, etc.).
▷HISTORY C18: from French, ultimately from Latin *barbātus* bearded, BARBATE

barbette (bɑːˈbɛt) NOUN [1] (formerly) an earthen platform inside a parapet, from which heavy guns could fire over the top. [2] an armoured cylinder below a turret on a warship that protects the revolving structure and foundation of the turret.
▷HISTORY C18: from French, diminutive of *barbe* a nun's BARB[1], from a fancied similarity between the earthwork around a cannon and this part of a nun's habit

barbican (ˈbɑːbɪkən) NOUN [1] a walled outwork or tower to protect a gate or drawbridge of a fortification. [2] a watchtower projecting from a fortification.
▷HISTORY C13: from Old French *barbacane*, from Medieval Latin *barbacana*, of unknown origin

Barbican (ˈbɑːbɪkən) NOUN **the**. a building complex in the City of London: includes residential developments and the Barbican Arts Centre (completed 1982) housing concert and exhibition halls, theatres, cinemas, etc.

barbicel (ˈbɑːbɪˌsɛl) NOUN *Ornithol* any of the minute hooks on the barbules of feathers that interlock with those of adjacent barbules.
▷HISTORY C19: from New Latin *barbicella*, literally: a small beard, from Latin *barba* beard

barbie *or* **barby** (ˈbɑːbɪ) NOUN *Informal, chiefly Austral* short for **barbecue**.

Barbie doll *or* **Barbie** (ˈbɑːbɪ) NOUN [1] *Trademark* a teenage doll with numerous sets of clothes and accessories. [2] *Slang, usually derogatory* a superficially attractive but insipid young woman.

bar billiards NOUN (*functioning as singular*) *Brit* a table game in pubs, etc., in which short cues are used to pocket balls into holes scoring various points and guarded by wooden pegs that incur penalties if they are knocked over.

barbitone (ˈbɑːbɪˌtəʊn) *or US* **barbital** (ˈbɑːbɪˌtæl) NOUN a long-acting barbiturate used medicinally, usually in the form of the sodium salt, as a sedative or hypnotic.
▷HISTORY C20: from BARBIT(URIC ACID) + -ONE

barbiturate (bɑːˈbɪtjʊrɪt, -ˌreɪt) NOUN a derivative of barbituric acid, such as phenobarbital, used in medicine as a sedative, hypnotic, or auticonvulsant.

barbituric acid (ˌbɑːbɪˈtjʊərɪk) NOUN a white crystalline solid used in the preparation of barbiturate drugs. Formula: $C_4H_4N_2O_3$. Systematic name: **2,4,6-trioxypyrimidine**. Also called: **malonylurea**.
▷HISTORY C19: partial translation of German *Barbitursäure*, perhaps from the name *Barbara* + URIC + *Säure* acid

Barbizon School (ˈbɑːbɪˌzɒn) NOUN a group of French painters of landscapes of the 1840s, including Théodore Rousseau, Daubigny, Diaz, Corot, and Millet.
▷HISTORY C19: from *Barbizon* a village near Paris and a favourite haunt of the painters

Barbour jacket *or* **Barbour** (ˈbɑːbə) NOUN *Trademark* a hard-wearing waterproof waxed jacket.

Barbuda (bɑːˈbuːdə) NOUN a coral island in the E Caribbean, in the Leeward Islands: part of the independent state of Antigua and Barbuda. Area: 160 sq. km (62 sq. miles).

barbule (ˈbɑːbjuːl) NOUN [1] a very small barb. [2] *Ornithol* any of the minute hairs that project from a barb and in some feathers interlock by hooks and grooves, forming a flat vane.
▷HISTORY C19: from Latin *barbula* a little beard, from *barba* beard

Barca (ˈbɑːkə) NOUN the surname of several noted Carthaginian generals, including Hamilcar, Hasdrubal, and Hannibal.
▸**ˈBarcan** ADJECTIVE

barcarole *or* **barcarolle** (ˈbɑːkəˌrəʊl, -ˌrɒl, ˌbɑːkəˈrəʊl) NOUN [1] a Venetian boat song in a time of six or twelve quaver beats to the bar. [2] an instrumental composition resembling this.
▷HISTORY C18: from French, from Italian *barcarola*, from *barcaruolo* boatman, from *barca* boat; see BARQUE

Barce (ˈbartʃe) *or* **Barca** (ˈbarka) NOUN the Italian name for **Al Marj**.

Barcelona (ˌbɑːsɪˈləʊnə) NOUN the chief port of Spain, on the NE Mediterranean coast: seat of the Republican government during the Civil War (1936–39); the commercial capital of Spain. Pop.: 1 505 581 (1998 est.). Ancient name: **Barcino** (bɑːˈsiːnəʊ).

BArch ABBREVIATION FOR Bachelor of Architecture.

barchan, barkhan, barchane, *or* **barkan** (bɑːˈkɑːn) NOUN a crescent-shaped shifting sand dune, convex on the windward side and steeper and concave on the leeward.

bar chart NOUN another name for **bar graph**.

bar code NOUN *Commerce* a machine-readable arrangement of numbers and parallel lines of different widths printed on a package, which can be electronically scanned at a checkout to register the price of the goods and to activate computer stock-checking and reordering. Also called: **Universal Product Code, UPC**.

Barcoo River (bɑːˈkuː) NOUN a river in E central Australia, in SW Queensland: joins with the Thomson River to form Cooper Creek.

Barcoo salute NOUN *Austral informal* a movement of the hand to brush flies away from the face.

bard[1] (bɑːd) NOUN [1] **a** (formerly) one of an ancient Celtic order of poets who recited verses about the exploits, often legendary, of their tribes. **b** (in modern times) a poet who wins a verse competition at a Welsh eisteddfod. [2] *Archaic or literary* any poet, esp one who writes lyric or heroic verse or is of national importance.
▷HISTORY C14: from Scottish Gaelic; related to Welsh *bardd*

▸ **ˈbardic** ADJECTIVE ▸ **ˈbardism** NOUN

bard[2] *or* **barde** (bɑːd) NOUN [1] a piece of larding bacon or pork fat placed on game or lean meat during roasting to prevent drying out. [2] an ornamental caparison for a horse. ◆ VERB (*tr*) [3] to place a bard on.
▷HISTORY C15: from Old French *barde*, from Old Italian *barda*, from Arabic *barda'ah* packsaddle

Bard (bɑːd) NOUN **the.** an epithet of William Shakespeare (1564–1616), the English dramatist and poet.

bar diagram NOUN another name for **bar graph.**

bardie (ˈbɑːdiː) NOUN [1] an edible white wood-boring grub of Australia. [2] **starve the bardies!** *Austral slang* an exclamation of surprise or protest.
▷HISTORY from a native Australian language

bardo (ˈbɑːdəʊ) NOUN (*often capital*) (in Tibetan Buddhism) the state of the soul between its death and its rebirth.
▷HISTORY Tibetan *bardo* between two

bardolatry (bɑːˈdɒlətrɪ) NOUN *Facetious* idolatry or excessive admiration of William Shakespeare (1564–1616), the English dramatist and poet.

Bardolino (ˌbɑːdəˈliːnəʊ) NOUN, *plural* **-nos.** a light dry red wine produced around Verona in NE Italy.

bare[1] (bɛə) ADJECTIVE [1] unclothed; exposed: used esp of a part of the body. [2] without the natural, conventional, or usual covering or clothing: *a bare tree.* [3] lacking appropriate furnishings, etc.: *a bare room.* [4] unembellished; simple: *the bare facts.* [5] (*prenominal*) just sufficient; mere: *he earned the bare minimum.* [6] **with one's bare hands.** without a weapon or tool. ◆ VERB [7] (*tr*) to make bare; uncover; reveal.
▷HISTORY Old English *bær*; compare Old Norse *berr*, Old High German *bar* naked, Old Slavonic *bosŭ* barefoot
▸ **ˈbareness** NOUN

bare[2] (bɛə) VERB *Archaic* a past tense of **bear[1]**.

bareback (ˈbɛəˌbæk) *or* **barebacked** ADJECTIVE, ADVERB [1] (of horse-riding) without a saddle. [2] (of sex) without a condom. ◆ VERB [3] (*intr*) to practise unprotected sex.

barefaced (ˈbɛəˌfeɪst) ADJECTIVE [1] unconcealed or shameless: *a barefaced lie.* [2] with the face uncovered or shaven.
▸ **barefacedly** (ˈbɛəˌfeɪsɪdlɪ) ADVERB ▸ **ˈbareˌfacedness** NOUN

barefoot (ˈbɛəˌfʊt) *or* **barefooted** ADJECTIVE, ADVERB with the feet uncovered.

barefoot doctor NOUN (esp in developing countries) a worker trained as a medical auxiliary in a rural area who dispenses medicine, gives first aid, assists at childbirth, etc.
▷HISTORY C20: translation of Chinese *chijiao yisheng*, officially translated as primary health worker

barège *French* (barɛʒ) NOUN [1] a light silky gauze fabric made of wool. ◆ ADJECTIVE [2] made of such a fabric.
▷HISTORY C19: named after *Barèges*, France, where it was originally made

barehanded (ˌbɛəˈhændɪd) ADVERB, ADJECTIVE [1] without weapons, tools, etc. [2] with hands uncovered.

bareheaded (ˌbɛəˈhɛdɪd) ADJECTIVE, ADVERB with head uncovered.

Bareilly (bəˈreɪlɪ) NOUN a city in N India, in N central Uttar Pradesh. Pop.: 587 211 (1991).

bare-knuckle ADJECTIVE [1] without boxing gloves: *a bare-knuckle fight.* [2] aggressive and without reservations: *a bare-knuckle confrontation.*

barely (ˈbɛəlɪ) ADVERB [1] only just; scarcely: *barely enough for their needs.* [2] *Informal* not quite; nearly: *barely old enough.* [3] scantily; poorly: *barely furnished.* [4] *Archaic* openly.

> **Language note** See at **hardly.**

Barents Sea (ˈbærənts) NOUN a part of the Arctic Ocean, bounded by Norway, Russia, and the islands of Novaya Zemlya, Spitsbergen, and Franz Josef Land.
▷HISTORY named after Willem *Barents* (1550–97) Dutch navigator and explorer

baresark (ˈbɛəˌsɑːk) NOUN another word for **berserk** (sense 2).
▷HISTORY C19: literally: bare shirt

barf (bɑːf) *Slang* ◆ VERB (*tr*) [1] to vomit. ◆ NOUN [2] the act of vomiting. [3] the matter ejected in vomiting.
▷HISTORY C20: probably of imitative origin

barfly (ˈbɑːflaɪ) NOUN, *plural* **-flies.** *Informal* a person who frequents bars.

bargain (ˈbɑːgɪn) NOUN [1] an agreement or contract establishing what each party will give, receive, or perform in a transaction between them. [2] something acquired or received in such an agreement. [3] **a** something bought or offered at a low price: *a bargain at an auction.* **b** (*as modifier*): *a bargain price.* [4] **into** *or US* **in the bargain.** in excess of what has been stipulated; besides. [5] **make** *or* **strike a bargain.** to agree on terms. ◆ VERB [6] (*intr*) to negotiate the terms of an agreement, transaction, etc. [7] (*tr*) to exchange, as in a bargain. [8] to arrive at (an agreement or settlement).
▷HISTORY C14: from Old French *bargaigne*, from *bargaignier* to trade, of Germanic origin; compare Medieval Latin *barcāniāre* to trade, Old English *borgian* to borrow
▸ **ˈbargainer** NOUN ▸ **ˈbargaining** NOUN, ADJECTIVE

bargain away VERB (*tr, adverb*) to lose or renounce (freedom, rights, etc.) in return for something valueless or of little value.

bargain basement NOUN part of a shop where goods are sold at reduced prices.

bargain for VERB (*intr, preposition*) to expect; anticipate (a style of behaviour, change in fortune, etc.): *he got more than he bargained for.*

bargaining agent NOUN an organization, usually a trade union, that acts or bargains on behalf of a group of employees in collective bargaining.

bargaining level NOUN the level within an organizational hierarchy, such as company level, national level, etc., at which collective bargaining takes place.

bargaining scope NOUN the range of topics within the scope of a particular set of negotiations leading to a collective agreement.

bargaining unit NOUN a specific group of employees who are covered by the same collective agreement or set of agreements and represented by the same bargaining agent or agents.

bargain on VERB (*intr, preposition*) to rely or depend on (something): *he bargained on her support.*

barge (bɑːdʒ) NOUN [1] a vessel, usually flat-bottomed and with or without its own power, used for transporting freight, esp on canals. [2] a vessel, often decorated, used in pageants, for state occasions, etc. [3] *Navy* a boat allocated to a flag officer, used esp for ceremonial occasions and often carried on board his flagship. [4] *Informal and derogatory* any vessel, esp an old or clumsy one. [5] *Austral informal* a heavy or cumbersome surfboard. ◆ VERB [6] (*intr;* foll by *into*) *Informal* to bump (into). [7] (*tr*) *Informal* to push (someone or one's way) violently. [8] (*intr;* foll by *into* or *in*) *Informal* to interrupt rudely or clumsily: *to barge into a conversation.* [9] (*tr*) *Sailing* to bear down on (another boat or boats) at the start of a race. [10] (*tr*) to transport by barge. [11] (*intr*) *Informal* to move slowly or clumsily.
▷HISTORY C13: from Old French, from Medieval Latin *barga*, probably from Late Latin *barca* a small boat; see BARQUE

bargeboard (ˈbɑːdʒˌbɔːd) NOUN a board, often decorated with carved ornaments, placed along the gable end of a roof. Also called: **vergeboard.**

barge couple NOUN either of a pair of outside rafters along the gable end of a roof.

barge course NOUN [1] the overhang of the gable end of a roof. [2] a course of bricks laid on edge to form the coping of a wall.

bargee (bɑːˈdʒiː) *or US and Canadian* **bargeman** (ˈbɑːdʒmən) NOUN, *plural* **bargees** *or* **bargemen.** a person employed on or in charge of a barge.

bargepole (ˈbɑːdʒˌpəʊl) NOUN [1] a long pole used to propel a barge. [2] **not touch with a bargepole.** *Informal* to refuse to have anything to do with.

bar girl NOUN *Chiefly US* an attractive girl employed by the management of a bar to befriend male customers and encourage them to buy drinks.

bar graph NOUN a graph consisting of vertical or horizontal bars whose lengths are proportional to amounts or quantities. Also called: **bar chart, bar diagram.**

Bari (ˈbɑːrɪ) NOUN a port in SE Italy, capital of Apulia, on the Adriatic coast. Pop.: 331 848 (2000 est.).

baric[1] (ˈbɛərɪk, ˈbærɪk) ADJECTIVE of or containing barium.

baric[2] (ˈbærɪk) ADJECTIVE of or concerned with weight, esp that of the atmosphere as indicated by barometric pressure.

barilla (bəˈrɪlə) NOUN [1] an impure mixture of sodium carbonate and sodium sulphate obtained from the ashes of certain plants, such as the saltworts. [2] either of two chenopodiaceous plants, *Salsola kali* (or *soda*) or *Halogeton soda*, formerly burned to obtain a form of sodium carbonate. See also **saltwort.**
▷HISTORY C17: from Spanish *barrilla*, literally: a little bar, from *barra* BAR[1]

barista (bəˈrɪstə) NOUN a person who makes and serves coffee in a coffee bar.
▷HISTORY C20: Italian: literally, bartender

barit. ABBREVIATION FOR baritone.

barite (ˈbɛəraɪt) NOUN the usual US and Canadian name for **barytes.**
▷HISTORY C18: from BAR(IUM) + -ITE[1]

baritone (ˈbærɪˌtəʊn) NOUN [1] the second lowest adult male voice, having a range approximately from G an eleventh below middle C to F a fourth above it. [2] a singer with such a voice. [3] the second lowest instrument in the families of the saxophone, horn, oboe, etc. ◆ ADJECTIVE [4] relating to or denoting a baritone: *a baritone part.* [5] denoting the second lowest instrument in a family: *the baritone horn.*
▷HISTORY C17: from Italian *baritono* a deep voice, from Greek *barutonos* deep-sounding, from *barus* heavy, low + *tonos* TONE

barium (ˈbɛərɪəm) NOUN a soft silvery-white metallic element of the alkaline earth group. It is used in bearing alloys and compounds are used as pigments. Symbol: Ba; atomic no.: 56; atomic wt.: 137.327; valency: 2; relative density: 3.5; melting pt.: 729°C; boiling pt.: 1805°C.
▷HISTORY C19: from BAR(YTA) + -IUM

barium enema NOUN an injection into the rectum of a preparation of barium sulphate, which is opaque to X-rays, before X-raying the lower alimentary canal.

barium hydroxide NOUN a white poisonous crystalline solid, used in the manufacture of organic compounds and in the preparation of beet sugar. Formula: $Ba(OH)_2$. Also called: **baryta.**

barium meal NOUN a preparation of barium sulphate, which is opaque to X-rays, swallowed by a patient before X-ray examination of the upper part of the alimentary canal.

barium oxide NOUN a white or yellowish-white poisonous heavy powder used esp as a dehydrating agent. Formula: BaO. Also called: **baryta.**

barium sulphate NOUN a white insoluble fine dense powder, used as a pigment, as a filler for paper, rubber, etc., and in barium meals. Formula: $BaSO_4$. Also called: **blanc fixe.**

barium titanate NOUN a crystalline ceramic used in capacitors and piezoelectric devices. Formula: $BaTiO_3$.

bark[1] (bɑːk) NOUN [1] the loud abrupt usually harsh or gruff cry of a dog or any of certain other animals. [2] a similar sound, such as one made by a person, gun, etc. [3] **his bark is worse than his bite.** he is bad-tempered but harmless. ◆ VERB [4] (*intr*) (of a dog or any of certain other animals) to make its typical loud abrupt cry. [5] (*intr*) (of a person, gun, etc.) to make a similar loud harsh sound. [6] to say or shout in a brusque, peremptory, or angry tone: *he barked an order.* [7] *US informal* to advertise (a show, merchandise, etc.) by loudly addressing passers-by. [8] **bark up the wrong tree.** *Informal* to misdirect one's attention, efforts, etc.; be mistaken.
▷HISTORY Old English *beorcan*; related to Lithuanian *burgėti* to quarrel, growl

bark[2] (bɑːk) NOUN [1] a protective layer of dead corky cells on the outside of the stems of woody plants. [2] any of several varieties of this substance that can be used in tanning, dyeing, or in

medicine. [3] an informal name for **cinchona.** ◆ VERB (*tr*) [4] to scrape or rub off skin, as in an injury. [5] to remove the bark or a circle of bark from (a tree or log). [6] to cover or enclose with bark. [7] to tan (leather), principally by the tannins in barks.
▷HISTORY C13: from Old Norse *börkr*; related to Swedish, Danish *bark*, German *Borke*; compare Old Norse *björkr* BIRCH

bark[3] (bɑːk) NOUN a variant spelling (esp US) of **barque.**

bark beetle NOUN any small beetle of the family *Scolytidae*, which bore tunnels in the bark and wood of trees, causing great damage. They are closely related to the weevils.

bark cloth NOUN a papery fabric made from the fibrous inner bark of various trees, esp of the moraceous genus *Ficus* and the leguminous genus *Brachystegia*.

barkeeper ('bɑːˌkiːpə) NOUN another name (esp US) for **barman.**

barkentine *or* **barkantine** ('bɑːkənˌtiːn) NOUN the usual US and Canadian spellings of **barquentine.**

barker[1] ('bɑːkə) NOUN [1] an animal or person that barks. [2] a person who stands at a show, fair booth, etc., and loudly addresses passers-by to attract customers.

barker[2] ('bɑːkə) NOUN a person or machine that removes bark from trees or logs or prepares it for tanning.

barkhan *or* **barkan** (bɑː'kɑːn) NOUN variant spellings of **barchan.**

Barkhausen effect (*German* 'barkhauzᵊn) NOUN the phenomenon that ferromagnetic material in an increasing magnetic field becomes magnetized in discrete jumps, discovered by Heinrich Georg Barkhausen (1881–1956).

barking ('bɑːkɪŋ) *Slang* ◆ ADJECTIVE [1] mad; crazy. ◆ ADVERB [2] (intensifier): *barking mad.*

Barking and Dagenham ('bɑːkɪŋ) NOUN a borough of E Greater London. Pop.: 163 944 (2001). Area: 34 sq. km (13 sq. miles).

barking deer NOUN another name for **muntjac.**

Barletta (*Italian* bar'letta) NOUN a port in SE Italy, in Apulia. Pop.: 88 750 (1990).

barley[1] ('bɑːlɪ) NOUN [1] any of various erect annual temperate grasses of the genus *Hordeum*, esp *H. vulgare*, that have short leaves and dense bristly flower spikes and are widely cultivated for grain and forage. [2] the grain of any of these grasses, used in making beer and whisky and for soups, puddings, etc. See also **pearl barley.**
▷HISTORY Old English *bærlīc* (adj); related to *bere* barley, Old Norse *barr* barley, Gothic *barizeins* of barley, Latin *farīna* flour

barley[2] ('bɑːlɪ) SENTENCE SUBSTITUTE *Dialect* a cry for truce or respite from the rules of a game.
▷HISTORY C18: probably changed from PARLEY

barleycorn ('bɑːlɪˌkɔːn) NOUN [1] a grain of barley, or barley itself. [2] an obsolete unit of length equal to one third of an inch.

barley sugar NOUN a brittle clear amber-coloured sweet made by boiling sugar, originally with a barley extract.

barley water NOUN a drink made from an infusion of barley, usually flavoured with lemon or orange.

barley wine NOUN *Brit* an exceptionally strong beer.

bar line *or* **bar** NOUN *Music* the vertical line marking the boundary between one bar and the next.

barm (bɑːm) NOUN [1] the yeasty froth on fermenting malt liquors. [2] an archaic or dialect word for **yeast.**
▷HISTORY Old English *beorm*; related to *beran* to BEAR, Old Norse *barmr* barm, Gothic *barms*, Old High German *barm* see FERMENT

barmaid ('bɑːˌmeɪd) NOUN a woman who serves in a pub.

barman ('bɑːmən) NOUN, *plural* **-men.** a man who serves in a pub.

barmbrack ('bɑːmˌbræk) NOUN *Irish* a loaf of bread with currants in it. Also: **barnbrack.** Often shortened to: **brack.**
▷HISTORY from Irish Gaelic *bairín breac* speckled loaf

barm cake NOUN *Lancashire dialect* a round flat soft bread roll.

Barmecide ('bɑːmɪˌsaɪd) *or* **Barmecidal** ADJECTIVE lavish or plentiful in imagination only; illusory; sham: *a Barmecide feast.*
▷HISTORY C18: from the name of a prince in *The Arabian Nights* who served empty plates to beggars, alleging that they held sumptuous food

Bar Mitzvah (bɑː 'mɪtsvə) (*sometimes not capitals*) *Judaism* ◆ ADJECTIVE [1] (of a Jewish boy) having assumed full religious obligations, being at least thirteen years of age. ◆ NOUN [2] the occasion, ceremony, or celebration of that event. [3] the boy himself on that day.
▷HISTORY Hebrew: son of the law

barmy ('bɑːmɪ) ADJECTIVE **-mier, -miest.** *Slang* insane. Also: **balmy.**
▷HISTORY C16: originally, full of BARM, hence frothing, excited, flighty, etc.

barn[1] (bɑːn) NOUN [1] a large farm outbuilding, used chiefly for storing hay, grain, etc., but also for housing livestock. [2] *US and Canadian* a large shed for sheltering railroad cars, trucks, etc. [3] any large building, esp an unattractive one. [4] (*modifier*) relating to a system of poultry farming in which birds are allowed to move freely within a barn: *barn eggs.*
▷HISTORY Old English *beren*, from *bere* barley + *ærn* room; see BARLEY[1]

barn[2] (bɑːn) NOUN a unit of nuclear cross section equal to 10^{-28} square metre. Symbol: b.
▷HISTORY C20: from BARN[1]; so called because of the relatively large cross section

Barnabas ('bɑːnəbəs) NOUN **Saint.** *New Testament* original name: *Joseph.* a Cypriot Levite who supported Saint Paul in his apostolic work (Acts 4:36, 37). Feast day: June 11.

barnacle ('bɑːnəkᵊl) NOUN [1] any of various marine crustaceans of the subclass *Cirripedia* that, as adults, live attached to rocks, ship bottoms, etc. They have feathery food-catching cirri protruding from a hard shell. See **acorn barnacle, goose barnacle.** [2] a person or thing that is difficult to get rid of.
▷HISTORY C16: related to Late Latin *bernicla*, of obscure origin
▸**'barnacled** ADJECTIVE

barnacle goose NOUN [1] a N European goose, *Branta leucopsis*, that has a black-and-white head and body and grey wings. [2] a former name for **brent goose.**
▷HISTORY C13 *bernekke*, related to Late Latin *bernaca*, from the belief that the goose developed from a shellfish; ultimate origin obscure

Barnard's star NOUN a red dwarf star in the constellation Ophiuchus having the largest proper motion known.
▷HISTORY C20: named after Edward Emerson Barnard (1857–1923), US astronomer

Barnaul (*Russian* bərna'ul) NOUN a city in S Russia, on the River Ob. Pop.: 586 200 (1999 est.).

barn dance NOUN [1] *Brit* a progressive round country dance. [2] *US and Canadian* a party with hoedown music and square-dancing. [3] a party featuring country dancing. [4] a disco or party held in a barn.

barn door NOUN [1] the door of a barn. [2] *Informal* a target so large that it cannot be missed. [3] *Photog, television, theatre* an adjustable flap over the front of a studio or theatre lamp.

barnet *or* **barnet fair** ('bɑːnɪt) NOUN *Brit slang* hair.
▷HISTORY C19: from rhyming slang *Barnet Fair* hair

Barnet ('bɑːnɪt) NOUN a borough of N Greater London: scene of a Yorkist victory (1471) in the Wars of the Roses. Pop.: 314 561 (2001). Area: 89 sq. km (34 sq. miles).

barney ('bɑːnɪ) *Informal* ◆ NOUN [1] a noisy argument. ◆ VERB (*intr*) [2] *Chiefly Austral and NZ* to argue or quarrel.
▷HISTORY C19: of unknown origin

barn owl NOUN any owl of the genus *Tyto*, esp *T. alba*, having a pale brown and white plumage, long slender legs, and a heart-shaped face: family *Tytonidae*.

Barnsley ('bɑːnzlɪ) NOUN [1] an industrial town in N England, in Barnsley unitary authority, South Yorkshire. Pop.: 75 120 (1991). [2] a unitary authority in N England, in South Yorkshire. Pop.: 218 062 (2001). Area: 329 sq. km (127 sq. miles).

Barnstaple ('bɑːnstəpᵊl) NOUN a town in SW England, in Devon, on the estuary of the River Taw: tourism, agriculture. Pop.: 27 691 (1991).

barnstorm ('bɑːnˌstɔːm) VERB (*intr*) [1] to tour rural districts putting on shows, esp theatrical, athletic, or acrobatic shows. [2] *Chiefly US and Canadian* to tour rural districts making speeches in a political campaign.
▷HISTORY C19: from BARN[1] + STORM (*vb*); from the performances often being in barns
▸**'barnˌstormer** NOUN ▸**'barnˌstorming** NOUN, ADJECTIVE

barn swallow NOUN the US and Canadian name for the common swallow, *Hirundo rustica.* See **swallow**[2]**.**

barnyard ('bɑːnˌjɑːd) NOUN [1] a yard adjoining a barn, in which farm animals are kept. [2] (*modifier*) belonging to or characteristic of a barnyard. [3] (*modifier*) crude or earthy: *barnyard humour.*

baro COMBINING FORM indicating weight or pressure: *barometer.*
▷HISTORY from Greek *baros* weight; related to Latin *gravis* heavy

Baroda (bə'rəʊdə) NOUN [1] a former state of W India, part of Gujarat since 1960. [2] the former name (until 1976) of **Vadodara.**

barognosis (ˌbærəg'nəʊsɪs) NOUN *Physiol* the ability to judge weight.
▷HISTORY C20: from Greek *baros* weight + *gnosis* knowledge

barogram ('bærəˌgræm) NOUN *Meteorol* the record of atmospheric pressure traced by a barograph or similar instrument.

barograph ('bærəˌgrɑːf, -ˌgræf) NOUN *Meteorol* a self-recording aneroid barometer.
▸**barographic** (ˌbærə'græfɪk) ADJECTIVE

Barolo (bə'rəʊləʊ) NOUN (*sometimes not capital*) a dry red wine produced in the Piedmont region of Italy.

barometer (bə'rɒmɪtə) NOUN [1] an instrument for measuring atmospheric pressure, usually to determine altitude or weather changes. [2] anything that shows change or impending change: *the barometer of social change.*
▸**barometric** (ˌbærə'metrɪk) *or* ˌ**baro'metrical** ADJECTIVE
▸ˌ**baro'metrically** ADVERB ▸**ba'rometry** NOUN

barometric pressure NOUN atmospheric pressure as indicated by a barometer.

baron ('bærən) NOUN [1] a member of a specific rank of nobility, esp the lowest rank in the British Isles. [2] (in Europe from the Middle Ages) originally any tenant-in-chief of a king or other overlord, who held land from his superior by honourable service; a land-holding nobleman. [3] a powerful businessman or financier: *a press baron.* [4] *English law* (formerly) the title held by judges of the Court of Exchequer. [5] short for **baron of beef.**
▷HISTORY C12: from Old French, of Germanic origin; compare Old High German *baro* freeman, Old Norse *berjask* to fight

baronage ('bærənɪdʒ) NOUN [1] barons collectively. [2] the rank or dignity of a baron.

baroness ('bærənɪs) NOUN [1] the wife or widow of a baron. [2] a woman holding the rank of baron in her own right.

baronet ('bærənɪt, -ˌnet) NOUN (in Britain) a commoner who holds the lowest hereditary title of honour, ranking below a baron. Abbreviations: **Bart.** *or* **Bt.**
▷HISTORY C15: order instituted 1611, from BARON + -ET

baronetage ('bærənɪtɪdʒ) NOUN [1] the order of baronets; baronets collectively. [2] the rank of a baronet; baronetcy.

baronetcy ('bærənɪtsɪ, -ˌnet-) NOUN, *plural* **-cies.** the rank, position, or patent of a baronet.

barong (bæ'rɒŋ) NOUN a broad-bladed cleaver-like knife used in the Philippines.
▷HISTORY from Moro; see PARANG

baronial (bə'rəʊnɪəl) ADJECTIVE of, relating to, or befitting a baron or barons.

baron of beef NOUN a cut of beef consisting of a double sirloin joined at the backbone.

Barons' War NOUN either of two civil wars in 13th-century England. The **First Barons' War** (1215–

17) was precipitated by King John's failure to observe the terms of Magna Carta: many of the Barons' grievances were removed by his death (1216) and peace was concluded in 1217. The **Second Barons' War** (1264–67) was caused by Henry III's refusal to accept limitations on his authority: the rebel Barons (led (1264–65) by Simon de Montfort), initially successful, were defeated at the battle of Evesham (1265); sporadic resistance continued until 1267.

barony ('bærənɪ) NOUN, *plural* **-nies.** [1] **a** the domain of a baron. **b** (in Ireland) a division of a county. **c** (in Scotland) a large estate or manor. [2] the rank or dignity of a baron. [3] a sphere of influence dominated by an industrial magnate or other powerful individual.

barophilic (ˌbærə'fɪlɪk) ADJECTIVE (of living organisms) growing best in conditions of high atmospheric pressure.
▸**barophile** ('bærəˌfaɪl) NOUN

barophoresis (ˌbærəfə'riːsɪs) NOUN *Chem* the diffusion of suspended particles at a rate dependent on external forces.

baroque (bə'rɒk, bə'rəʊk) NOUN (*often capital*) [1] a style of architecture and decorative art that flourished throughout Europe from the late 16th to the early 18th century, characterized by extensive ornamentation. [2] a 17th-century style of music characterized by extensive use of the thorough bass and of ornamentation. [3] any ornate or heavily ornamented style. ◆ ADJECTIVE [4] denoting, being in, or relating to the baroque. [5] (of pearls) irregularly shaped.
▷HISTORY C18: from French, from Portuguese *barroco* a rough or imperfectly shaped pearl

baroreceptor ('bærəʊrɪˌsɛptə) *or* **baroceptor** NOUN a collection of sensory nerve endings, principally in the carotid sinuses and the aortic arch, that monitor blood pressure changes in the body.

baroscope ('bærəˌskəʊp) NOUN any instrument for measuring atmospheric pressure, esp a manometer with one side open to the atmosphere.
▸**baroscopic** (ˌbærə'skɒpɪk) ADJECTIVE

barostat ('bærəʊˌstæt) NOUN a device for maintaining constant pressure, such as one used in an aircraft cabin.

Barotse (bə'rɒtsɪ) NOUN [1] (*plural* **-se** *or* **-ses**) a member of a Negroid people of central Africa living chiefly in SW Zambia. [2] the language spoken by this people; Lozi.

barouche (bə'ruːʃ) NOUN a four-wheeled horse-drawn carriage, popular in the 19th century, having a retractable hood over the rear half, seats inside for two couples facing each other, and a driver's seat outside at the front.
▷HISTORY C19: from German (dialect) *Barutsche*, from Italian *baroccio*, from Vulgar Latin *birotium* (unattested) vehicle with two wheels, from Late Latin *birotus* two-wheeled, from BI-[1] + *rota* wheel

barperson ('bɑːˌpɜːsᵊn) NOUN, *plural* **-persons.** a person who serves in a pub: used esp in advertisements.

barque *or esp US* **bark** (bɑːk) NOUN [1] a sailing ship of three or more masts having the foremasts rigged square and the aftermast rigged fore-and-aft. [2] *Poetic* any boat, esp a small sailing vessel.
▷HISTORY C15: from Old French, from Old Provençal *barca*, from Late Latin, of unknown origin

barquentine *or* **barquantine** ('bɑːkənˌtiːn) NOUN a sailing ship of three or more masts rigged square on the foremast and fore-and-aft on the others. Usual US and Canadian spelling: **barkentine.**
▷HISTORY C17: from BARQUE + (BRIG)ANTINE

Barquisimeto (*Spanish* barkisi'meto) NOUN a city in NW Venezuela. Pop.: 875 790 (2000 est.).

barra ('bærə) NOUN *Austral informal* a barramundi.

Barra ('bærə) NOUN an island in NW Scotland, in the Outer Hebrides: fishing, crofting, tourism. Pop.: 1200 (latest est.).

barrack[1] ('bærək) VERB to house (people, esp soldiers) in barracks.

barrack[2] ('bærək) VERB *Brit, Austral, and NZ informal* [1] to criticize loudly or shout against (a player, team, speaker, etc.); jeer. [2] (*intr*; foll by *for*) to shout support (for).
▷HISTORY C19: from northern Irish: to boast
▸'**barracker** NOUN ▸'**barracking** NOUN, ADJECTIVE

barrack-room lawyer NOUN a person who freely offers opinions, esp in legal matters, that he is unqualified to give.

barracks ('bærəks) PLURAL NOUN (*sometimes singular; when plural, sometimes functions as singular*) [1] a building or group of buildings used to accommodate military personnel. [2] any large building used for housing people, esp temporarily. [3] a large and bleak building.
▷HISTORY C17: from French *baraque*, from Old Catalan *barraca* hut, of uncertain origin

barracoon (ˌbærə'kuːn) NOUN (formerly) a temporary place of confinement for slaves or convicts, esp those awaiting transportation.
▷HISTORY C19: from Spanish *barracón*, from *barraca* hut, from Catalan

barracouta (ˌbærə'kuːtə) NOUN a large predatory Pacific fish, *Thyrsites atun*, with a protruding lower jaw and strong teeth: family *Gempylidae*.
▷HISTORY C17: variant of BARRACUDA

barracuda (ˌbærə'kjuːdə) NOUN, *plural* **-da** *or* **-das.** any predatory marine teleost fish of the mostly tropical family *Sphyraenidae*, esp *Sphyraena barracuda*. They have an elongated body, strong teeth, and a protruding lower jaw.
▷HISTORY C17: from American Spanish, of unknown origin

barrage ('bærɑːʒ) NOUN [1] *Military* the firing of artillery to saturate an area, either to protect against an attack or to support an advance. [2] an overwhelming and continuous delivery of something, as words, questions, or punches. [3] a usually gated construction, similar to a low dam, across a watercourse, esp one to increase the depth of water to assist navigation or irrigation. [4] *Fencing* a heat or series of bouts in a competition. ◆ VERB [5] (*tr*) to attack or confront with a barrage: *the speaker was barraged with abuse.*
▷HISTORY C19: from French, from *barrer* to obstruct; see BAR[1]

barrage balloon NOUN one of a number of tethered balloons with cables or net suspended from them, used to deter low-flying air attack.

barramunda (ˌbærə'mʌndə) NOUN, *plural* **-das** *or* **-da.** the edible Australian lungfish, *Neoceratodus forsteri*, having paddle-like fins and a long body covered with large scales.
▷HISTORY from a native Australian language

barramundi (ˌbærə'mʌndɪ) NOUN, *plural* **-dis, -dies** *or* **-di.** any of several large edible Australian fishes esp the percoid species *Lates calcarifer* (family Centropomidae) of NE coastal waters or the freshwater species *Scleropages leichardti* (family Osteoglossidae) of Queensland.

barranca (bə'ræŋkə) *or* **barranco** (bə'ræŋkəʊ) NOUN, *plural* **-cas** *or* **-cos.** *Southwestern US* a ravine or precipice.
▷HISTORY C19: from Spanish, of uncertain origin

Barranquilla (*Spanish* barran'kiʎa) NOUN a port in N Colombia, on the Magdalena River. Pop.: 1 223 260 (1999 est.).

barrator ('bærətə) NOUN a person guilty of barratry.
▷HISTORY C14: from Old French *barateor*, from *barater* to BARTER

barratry *or* **barretry** ('bærətrɪ) NOUN [1] *Criminal law* (formerly) the vexatious stirring up of quarrels or bringing of lawsuits. [2] *Maritime law* a fraudulent practice committed by the master or crew of a ship to the prejudice of the owner or charterer. [3] *Scots law* the crime committed by a judge in accepting a bribe. [4] the purchase or sale of public or Church offices.
▷HISTORY C15: from Old French *baraterie* deception, from *barater* to BARTER
▸'**barratrous** *or* '**barretrous** ADJECTIVE ▸'**barratrously** *or* '**barretrously** ADVERB

barre *French* (bar) NOUN a rail at hip height used for ballet practice and leg exercises.
▷HISTORY literally: bar

barré ('bæreɪ) NOUN [1] the act of laying the index finger over some or all of the strings of a guitar, lute, or similar instrument, so that the pitch of each stopped string is simultaneously raised. Compare **capo**[1]. [2] the playing of chords in this manner. ◆ VERB [3] to execute (chords) in this manner. ◆ ADVERB [4] by using the barré.
▷HISTORY C19: from French, from *barrer* BAR[1]

barrel ('bærəl) NOUN [1] a cylindrical container usually bulging outwards in the middle and held together by metal hoops; cask. [2] Also called: **barrelful.** the amount that a barrel can hold. [3] a unit of capacity used in brewing, equal to 36 Imperial gallons. [4] a unit of capacity used in the oil and other industries, normally equal to 42 US gallons or 35 Imperial gallons. [5] a thing or part shaped like a barrel, esp a tubular part of a machine. [6] the tube through which the projectile of a firearm is discharged. [7] *Horology* the cylindrical drum in a watch or clock that is rotated by the mainspring. [8] the trunk of a four-legged animal: *the barrel of a horse.* [9] the quill of a feather. [10] *Informal* a large measure; a great deal (esp in the phrases **barrel of fun, barrel of laughs**). [11] *Austral informal* the hollow inner side of a wave. [12] **over a barrel.** *Informal* powerless. [13] **scrape the barrel.** *Informal* to be forced to use one's last and weakest resource. ◆ VERB **-rels, -relling, -relled** *or US* **-rels, -reling, -reled.** [14] (*tr*) to put into a barrel or barrels. [15] (*intr*; foll by *along, in,* etc.) *Informal* to travel or move very fast. (*intr*) [16] *Austral informal* to ride on the inside of a wave.
▷HISTORY C14: from Old French *baril* perhaps from *barre* BAR[1]

barrel-chested ADJECTIVE having a large rounded chest.

barrel distortion NOUN *Photog* distortion of an image produced by an optical system that causes straight lines at image margins to bulge outwards.

barrelhouse ('bærəlˌhaʊs) NOUN [1] *US* a cheap and disreputable drinking establishment. [2] **a** a vigorous and unpolished style of jazz for piano, originating in the barrelhouses of New Orleans. **b** (*as modifier*): *barrelhouse blues.*

barrel organ NOUN [1] an instrument consisting of a cylinder turned by a handle and having pins on it that interrupt the air flow to certain pipes, thereby playing any of a number of tunes. See also **hurdy-gurdy.** [2] a similar instrument in which the projections on a rotating barrel pluck a set of strings.

barrel roll NOUN [1] a flight manoeuvre in which an aircraft rolls about its longitudinal axis while following a spiral course in line with the direction of flight. ◆ VERB **barrel-roll.** [2] (*intr*) (of an aircraft) to perform a barrel roll.

barrel vault NOUN *Architect* a vault in the form of a half cylinder. Also called: **wagon vault, tunnel vault.**

barren ('bærən) ADJECTIVE [1] incapable of producing offspring, seed, or fruit; sterile: *a barren tree.* [2] unable to support the growth of crops, etc.; unproductive; bare: *barren land.* [3] lacking in stimulation or ideas; dull: *a rather barren play.* [4] not producing worthwhile results; unprofitable: *a barren period in a writer's life.* [5] (foll by *of*) totally lacking (in); devoid (of): *his speech was barren of wit.* [6] (of rock strata) having no fossils.
▷HISTORY C13: from Old French *brahain*, of uncertain origin
▸'**barrenly** ADVERB ▸'**barrenness** NOUN

Barren Lands PLURAL NOUN **the.** a region of tundra in N Canada, extending westwards from Hudson Bay: sparsely inhabited, chiefly by Inuit. Also called: **Barren Grounds.**

barrens ('bærənz) PLURAL NOUN (*sometimes singular*) (in North America) a stretch of usually level land that is sparsely vegetated or barren.

barrenwort ('bærənˌwɜːt) NOUN a herbaceous European berberidaceous plant, *Epimedium alpinum*, having red-and-yellow star-shaped flowers.

barret ('bærɪt) NOUN a small flat cap resembling a biretta.
▷HISTORY C19: from French *barrette*, from Italian *berretta* BIRETTA; compare BERET

barrette (bə'rɛt) NOUN a clasp or pin for holding women's hair in place.
▷HISTORY C20: from French: a little bar, from *barre* BAR[1]

barricade (ˌbærɪ'keɪd, 'bærɪˌkeɪd) NOUN [1] a barrier for defence, esp one erected hastily, as during street fighting. ◆ VERB (*tr*) [2] to erect a barricade across (an entrance, passageway, etc.) or at points of access to (a room, district of a town,

etc.): *they barricaded the door.* 3 (*usually passive*) to obstruct; block: *his mind was barricaded against new ideas.*
▷HISTORY C17: from Old French, from *barriquer* to barricade, from *barrique* a barrel, from Spanish *barrica*, from *barril* BARREL
▸ˈbarriˌcader NOUN

barrie (ˈbærɪ) ADJECTIVE *Scot dialect* very good; attractive.
▷HISTORY from Romany

barrier (ˈbærɪə) NOUN 1 anything serving to obstruct passage or to maintain separation, such as a fence or gate. 2 anything that prevents or obstructs passage, access, or progress: *a barrier of distrust.* 3 anything that separates or hinders union: *a language barrier.* 4 **a** an exposed offshore sand bar separated from the shore by a lagoon. **b** (*as modifier*): *a barrier beach.* 5 (*sometimes capital*) that part of the Antarctic icecap extending over the sea.
▷HISTORY C14: from Old French *barriere*, from *barre* BAR[1]

barrier cream NOUN a cream used to protect the skin, esp the hands, from dirt and from the action of oils or solvents.

barrier-nurse VERB (*tr*) to tend (infectious patients) in isolation, to prevent the spread of infection.
▸**barrier nursing** NOUN

barrier of ideas NOUN *Philosophy* the representations of objects which certain accounts of perception interpose between the objects themselves and our awareness of them, so that, as critics argue, we can never know whether there is in reality anything which resembles our perceptions. See **representationalism** (sense 1).

barrier reef NOUN a long narrow coral reef near and lying parallel to the shore, separated from it by deep water. See **Great Barrier Reef.**

barring (ˈbɑːrɪŋ) PREPOSITION unless (something) occurs; except for: *barring rain, the match will be held tomorrow.*

barrio (ˈbærɪəʊ; *Spanish* ˈbarrjo) NOUN, *plural* **-rios.** 1 a Spanish-speaking quarter in a town or city, esp in the US. 2 a Spanish-speaking community.
▷HISTORY from Spanish, from Arabic *barrī* of open country, from *barr* open country

barrister (ˈbærɪstə) NOUN 1 Also called: **barrister-at-law.** (in England) a lawyer who has been called to the bar and is qualified to plead in the higher courts. Compare **solicitor.** See also **advocate, counsel.** 2 (in Canada) a lawyer who pleads in court. 3 *US* a less common word for **lawyer.**
▷HISTORY C16: from BAR[1]

barro (ˈbærəʊ) ADJECTIVE *Austral slang* embarrassing.

barroom (ˈbɑːˌruːm, -ˌrʊm) NOUN *US* a room or building where alcoholic drinks are served over a counter.

barrow[1] (ˈbærəʊ) NOUN 1 See **wheelbarrow, handbarrow.** 2 Also called: **barrowful.** the amount contained in or on a barrow. 3 *Chiefly Brit* a handcart, typically having two wheels and a canvas roof, used esp by street vendors. 4 *Northern English dialect* concern or business (esp in the phrases **that's not my barrow, that's just my barrow**). 5 **into one's barrow.** *Irish and Scot dialect* suited to one's interests or desires.
▷HISTORY Old English *bearwe*; related to Old Norse *barar* BIER, Old High German *bāra*

barrow[2] (ˈbærəʊ) NOUN a heap of earth placed over one or more prehistoric tombs, often surrounded by ditches. **Long barrows** are elongated Neolithic mounds usually covering stone burial chambers; **round barrows** are Bronze Age, covering burials or cremations.
▷HISTORY Old English *beorg*; related to Old Norse *bjarg*, Gothic *bairgahei* hill, Old High German *berg* mountain

barrow[3] (ˈbærəʊ) NOUN a castrated pig.
▷HISTORY Old English *bearg*; related to Old Norse *börgr*, Old High German *barug*

Barrow (ˈbærəʊ) NOUN 1 a river in SE Ireland, rising in the Slieve Bloom Mountains and flowing south to Waterford Harbour. Length: about 193 km (120 miles). 2 See **Barrow-in-Furness** and **Barrow Point.**

barrow boy NOUN *Brit* a man who sells his wares from a barrow; street vendor.

Barrow-in-Furness NOUN an industrial town in NW England, in S Cumbria. Pop.: 48 947 (1991).

Barrow Point NOUN the northernmost tip of Alaska, on the Arctic Ocean.

barry *or* **Barry Crocker** (ˈbærɪ) NOUN *Austral slang* a mistake or blunder; a disappointing performance.
▷HISTORY rhyming slang for SHOCKER

Barry (ˈbærɪ) NOUN a port in SE Wales, in Vale of Glamorgan county borough on the Bristol Channel. Pop.: 49 887 (1991).

Barsac (ˈbɑːsæk; *French* barsak) NOUN a sweet French white wine produced around the town of Barsac in the Gironde.

bar sinister NOUN 1 (not in heraldic usage) another name for **bend sinister.** 2 the condition, implication, or stigma of being of illegitimate birth.

Bart. ABBREVIATION FOR Baronet.

bartender (ˈbɑːˌtɛndə) NOUN another name (esp US and Canadian) for **barman.**

barter (ˈbɑːtə) VERB 1 to trade (goods, services, etc.) in exchange for other goods, services, etc., rather than for money: *the refugees bartered for food.* 2 (*intr*) to haggle over the terms of such an exchange; bargain. ◆ NOUN 3 trade by the exchange of goods.
▷HISTORY C15: from Old French *barater* to cheat; perhaps related to Greek *prattein* to do
▸ˈ**barterer** NOUN

Barthian (ˈbɑːtɪən, -θɪən) ADJECTIVE 1 of or relating to Karl Barth (1886–1968), the Swiss Protestant theologian, or his ideas. ◆ NOUN 2 a person who supports or believes in the ideas of Karl Barth.

Bartholin's glands (ˈbɑːθəlɪnz) PLURAL NOUN *Anatomy* two small reddish-yellow glands, one on each side of the vaginal orifice, that secrete a mucous lubricating substance during sexual stimulation in females. Compare **Cowper's glands.**
▷HISTORY named by Caspar *Bartholin* (1655–1738), Danish anatomist, in honour of his father, Thomas

Bartholomew (bɑːˈθɒləˌmjuː) NOUN *New Testament* **Saint.** one of the twelve apostles (Matthew 10:3). Feast day: Aug. 24 or June 11.

bartizan (ˈbɑːtɪzən, ˌbɑːtɪˈzæn) NOUN a small turret projecting from a wall, parapet, or tower.
▷HISTORY C19: variant of *bertisene*, erroneously for *bretising*, from *bretasce* parapet; see BRATTICE
▸**bartizaned** (ˈbɑːtɪzənd, ˌbɑːtɪˈzænd) ADJECTIVE

Bartlett *or* **Bartlett pear** (ˈbɑːtlɪt) NOUN another name for **Williams pear**: used esp in the US and generally of tinned pears.
▷HISTORY named after Enoch *Bartlett* (1779–1860), of Dorchester, Mass., who marketed it in the US

barton (ˈbɑːtᵊn) NOUN *Archaic* a farmyard.
▷HISTORY Old English *beretūn*, from *bere* barley + *tūn* stockade; see TOWN

bartsia (ˈbɑːtsɪə) NOUN any of several species of semiparasitic scrophulariaceous plants, including **red bartsia** (*Odontites verna*), a pink-flowered weed of cornfields.
▷HISTORY C18: New Latin, named after Johann *Bartsch* (died 1738), German botanist

Baruch (ˈbɛərʊk, ˈbɑː-) NOUN *Bible* **a** a disciple of Jeremiah (Jeremiah 32–36). **b** the book of the Apocrypha said to have been written by him.

barycentre (ˈbærɪˌsɛntə) NOUN a centre of mass, esp of the earth-moon system or the solar system.
▷HISTORY C20: from Greek *barus* heavy + CENTRE
▸ˌ**baryˈcentric** ADJECTIVE

barye (ˈbærɪ) NOUN a unit of pressure in the cgs system equal to one dyne per square centimetre. 1 barye is equivalent to 1 microbar.
▷HISTORY C19: from French, from Greek *barus* heavy

baryon (ˈbærɪˌɒn) NOUN any of a class of elementary particles that have a mass greater than or equal to that of the proton, participate in strong interactions, and have a spin of ½. Baryons are either nucleons or hyperons. The **baryon number** is the number of baryons in a system minus the number of antibaryons.
▷HISTORY C20: *bary-*, from Greek *barus* heavy + -ON

baryonic (ˌbærɪˈɒnɪk) ADJECTIVE of or relating to a baryon.

barysphere (ˈbærɪˌsfɪə) NOUN a former name for **core** (sense 4).
▷HISTORY C20: from Greek *barus* heavy + SPHERE

baryta (bəˈraɪtə) NOUN another name for **barium oxide** or **barium hydroxide.**
▷HISTORY C19: New Latin, from Greek *barutēs* weight, from *barus* heavy
▸**barytic** (bəˈrɪtɪk) ADJECTIVE

barytes (bəˈraɪtiːz) NOUN a colourless or white mineral consisting of barium sulphate in orthorhombic crystalline form, occurring in sedimentary rocks and with sulphide ores: a source of barium. Formula: $BaSO_4$. Also called: (esp US and Canadian) **barite, heavy spar.**
▷HISTORY C18: from Greek *barus* heavy + *-itēs* -ITE[1]

baryton (ˈbærɪˌtəʊn) NOUN a bass viol with sympathetic strings as well as its six main strings.
▷HISTORY C18: from French: BARITONE

barytone[1] (ˈbærɪˌtəʊn) NOUN a less common spelling of **baritone.**

barytone[2] (ˈbærɪˌtəʊn) (in ancient Greek) ADJECTIVE 1 having the last syllable unaccented. ◆ NOUN 2 a word in which the last syllable is unaccented. Compare **oxytone.**
▷HISTORY C19: from Greek *barutonos* heavy-sounding, from *barus* heavy + *tonos* TONE

basal (ˈbeɪsᵊl) ADJECTIVE 1 at, of, or constituting a base. 2 of or constituting a foundation or basis; fundamental; essential.
▸ˈ**basally** ADVERB

basal anaesthesia NOUN preliminary and incomplete anaesthesia induced to prepare a surgical patient for total anaesthesia with another agent.

basal ganglia PLURAL NOUN the thalamus together with other closely related masses of grey matter, situated near the base of the brain.

basal metabolic rate NOUN the rate at which heat is produced by the body at rest, 12 to 14 hours after eating, measured in kilocalories per square metre of body surface per hour. Abbreviation: **BMR.**

basal metabolism NOUN the amount of energy required by an individual in the resting state, for such functions as breathing and circulation of the blood. See **basal metabolic rate.**

basalt (ˈbæsɔːlt) NOUN 1 a fine-grained dark basic igneous rock consisting of plagioclase feldspar, a pyroxene, and olivine: the most common volcanic rock and usually extrusive. See **flood basalt.** 2 a form of black unglazed pottery resembling basalt.
▷HISTORY C18: from Late Latin *basaltēs*, variant of *basanītēs*, from Greek *basanitēs* touchstone, from *basanos*, of Egyptian origin
▸**baˈsaltic** ADJECTIVE

basaltware (ˈbæsɔːltˌwɛə, ˈbeɪsɔːlt-) NOUN hard fine-grained black stoneware, made in Europe, esp in England, in the late 18th century.

basanite (ˈbæsəˌnaɪt) NOUN a black basaltic rock containing plagioclase, augite, olivine, and nepheline, leucite, or analcite, formerly used as a touchstone.
▷HISTORY C18: see BASALT

bas bleu *French* (bɑ blø) NOUN, *plural* ***bas bleus*** (bɑ blø). a bluestocking; intellectual woman.
▷HISTORY C18: from French translation of English BLUESTOCKING

bascinet (ˌbæsɪˈnɛt, ˈbæsɪˌnɛt) NOUN *Armour* a variant spelling of **basinet.**

bascule (ˈbæskjuːl) NOUN 1 Also called: **balance bridge, counterpoise bridge.** a bridge with a movable section hinged about a horizontal axis and counterbalanced by a weight. Compare **drawbridge.** 2 a movable roadway forming part of such a bridge: *Tower Bridge has two bascules.*
▷HISTORY C17: from French: seesaw, from *bas* low + *cul* rump; see BASE[2], CULET

base[1] (beɪs) NOUN 1 the bottom or supporting part of anything. 2 the fundamental or underlying principle or part, as of an idea, system, or organization; basis. 3 **a** a centre of operations, organization, or supply: *the climbers made a base at 8000 feet.* **b** (*as modifier*): *base camp.* 4 a centre from which military activities are coordinated. 5 anything from which a process, as of measurement, action, or thought, is or may be begun; starting point: *the new discovery became the base for further research.* 6 the main ingredient of a mixture: *to use*

rice as a base in cookery. 7 a chemical compound that combines with an acid to form a salt and water. A solution of a base in water turns litmus paper blue, produces hydroxyl ions, and has a pH greater than 7. Bases are metal oxides or hydroxides or amines. See also **Lewis base.** 8 *Biochem* any of the nitrogen-containing constituents of nucleic acids: adenine, thymine (in DNA), uracil (in RNA), guanine, or cytosine. 9 a medium such as oil or water in which the pigment is dispersed in paints, inks, etc.; vehicle. 10 the inorganic material on which the dye is absorbed in lake pigments; carrier. 11 *Biology* **a** the part of an organ nearest to its point of attachment. **b** the point of attachment of an organ or part. 12 the bottommost layer or part of anything. 13 *Architect* **a** the lowest division of a building or structure. **b** the lower part of a column or pier. 14 another word for **baseline** (sense 2). 15 the lower side or face of a geometric construction. 16 *Maths* **a** the number of distinct single-digit numbers in a counting system, and so the number represented as *10* in a place-value system: *the binary system has two digits, 0 and 1, and 10 to base two represents 2.* See **place-value. b** (of a logarithm or exponential) the number whose powers are expressed: *since* $1000 = 10^3$, *the logarithm of 1000 to base 10 is 3.* **c** (of a mathematical structure) a substructure from which the given system can be generated. **d** the initial instance from which a generalization is proven by mathematical induction. 17 *Logic, maths* Also called: **base clause.** the initial element of a recursive definition, that defines the first element of the infinite sequence generated thereby. 18 *Linguistics* **a** a root or stem. **b** See **base component.** 19 *Electronics* the region in a transistor between the emitter and collector. 20 *Photog* the glass, paper, or cellulose-ester film that supports the sensitized emulsion with which it is coated. 21 *Heraldry* the lower part of the shield. 22 *Jewellery* the quality factor used in pricing natural pearls. 23 a starting or finishing point in any of various games. 24 *Baseball* any of the four corners of the diamond, which runners have to reach in order to score. 25 the main source of a certain commodity or element: *a customer base; their fan base.* 26 **get to first base.** *US and Canadian informal* to accomplish the first stage in a project or a series of objectives. 27 **off base.** *US and Canadian informal* wrong or badly mistaken. 28 **touch base.** to make contact. ◆ VERB 29 (*tr* foll by *on* or *upon*) to use as a basis (for); found (on): *your criticisms are based on ignorance.* 30 (often foll by *at* or *in*) to station, post, or place (a person or oneself).
▷HISTORY C14: from Old French, from Latin *basis* pedestal; see BASIS

base² (beɪs) ADJECTIVE 1 devoid of honour or morality; ignoble; contemptible. 2 of inferior quality or value. 3 debased; alloyed; counterfeit: *base currency.* 4 *English history* **a** (of land tenure) held by villein or other ignoble service. **b** holding land by villein or other ignoble service. 5 *Archaic* born of humble parents; plebeian. 6 *Archaic* illegitimate. ◆ ADJECTIVE, NOUN 7 *Music* an obsolete spelling of **bass.**
▷HISTORY C14: from Old French *bas*, from Late Latin *bassus* of low height, perhaps from Greek *bassōn* deeper
▸**'basely** ADVERB ▸**'baseness** NOUN

baseball ('beɪsˌbɔːl) NOUN 1 a team game with nine players on each side, played on a field with four bases connected to form a diamond. The object is to score runs by batting the ball and running round the bases. 2 the hard rawhide-covered ball used in this game.

baseball cap NOUN a close-fitting thin cap with a deep peak.

baseband ('beɪsˌbænd) NOUN a transmission technique using a narrow range of frequencies that allows only one message to be telecommunicated at a time. See also **broadband.**

baseboard ('beɪsˌbɔːd) NOUN 1 a board functioning as the base of anything. 2 the usual US and Canadian word for **skirting board.**

baseborn ('beɪsˌbɔːn) ADJECTIVE *Archaic* 1 born of humble parents. 2 illegitimate. 3 mean; contemptible.

baseburner ('beɪsˌbɜːnə) NOUN *US* a stove into which coal is automatically fed from a hopper above the fire chamber.

base component NOUN the system of rules in a transformational grammar that specify the deep structure of the language.

base head NOUN *Slang* a person who is addicted to cocaine.

base hospital NOUN *Austral* a hospital serving a large rural area.

base jumping NOUN a sport in which a participant parachutes from any of a variety of fixed objects such as high buildings, cliffs, etc.
▷HISTORY C20: *b(uilding), a(ntennae), s(pan, and) e(arthbound object)*

Basel ('bɑːzᵊl) NOUN a variant spelling of **Basle.**

baseless ('beɪslɪs) ADJECTIVE not based on fact; unfounded: *a baseless supposition.*
▸**'baselessly** ADVERB ▸**'baselessness** NOUN

base level NOUN the lowest level to which a land surface can be eroded by streams, which is, ultimately, sea level.

baseline ('beɪsˌlaɪn) NOUN 1 *Surveying* a measured line through a survey area from which triangulations are made. 2 an imaginary line, standard of value, etc., by which things are measured or compared. 3 a line at each end of a tennis court that marks the limit of play.

base load NOUN the more or less constant part of the total load on an electrical power-supply system. Compare **peak load.**

baseman ('beɪsmən) NOUN, *plural* **-men.** *Baseball* a fielder positioned near a base.

basement ('beɪsmənt) NOUN 1 **a** a partly or wholly underground storey of a building, esp the one immediately below the main floor. Compare **cellar. b** (*as modifier*): *a basement flat.* 2 the foundation or substructure of a wall or building. 3 *Geology* a part of the earth's crust formed of hard igneous or metamorphic rock that lies beneath the cover of soft sedimentary rock, sediment, and soil.

base metal NOUN any of certain common metals such as copper, lead, zinc, and tin, as distinct from the precious metals, gold, silver, and platinum.

basenji (bəˈsɛndʒɪ) NOUN a small smooth-haired breed of dog of African origin having a tightly curled tail and an inability to bark.
▷HISTORY C20: from a Bantu language

base pairing NOUN *Biochem* the hydrogen bonding that occurs between complementary nitrogenous bases in the two polynucleotide chains of a DNA molecule.

base period NOUN *Statistics* a neutral period used as a standard for comparison in constructing an index to express a variable factor: 100 is usually taken as the index number for the variable in the base period.

base rate NOUN 1 *Brit* the rate of interest used by individual commercial banks as a basis for their lending rates. 2 *Brit informal* the rate at which the Bank of England lends to the discount houses, which effectively controls the interest rates charged throughout the banking system. 3 *Statistics* the average number of times an event occurs divided by the average number of times on which it might occur.

base rate fallacy NOUN *Statistics* the tendency, when making judgments of the probability with which an event will occur, to ignore the base rate and to concentrate on other information.

bases¹ ('beɪsiːz) NOUN the plural of **basis.**

bases² ('beɪsɪz) NOUN the plural of **base¹.**

base speed NOUN *Slang* a pure pinkish-grey form of the drug amphetamine with a putty-like consistency.

base station NOUN a fixed transmitter that forms part of an otherwise mobile radio network.

base unit NOUN *Physics* any of the fundamental units in a system of measurement. The base SI units are the metre, kilogram, second, ampere, kelvin, candela, and mole.

bash (bæʃ) *Informal* ◆ VERB 1 (*tr*) to strike violently or crushingly. 2 (*tr;* often foll by *in, down,* etc.) to smash, break, etc., with a crashing blow: *to bash a door down.* 3 (*intr;* foll by *into*) to crash (into); collide (with): *to bash into a lamppost.* 4 to dent or be dented: *this tin is bashed; this cover won't bash easily.* ◆ NOUN 5 a heavy blow, as from a fist. 6 a dent; indentation. 7 a party. 8 **have a bash.** *Informal* to make an attempt. ◆ See also **bash up.**
▷HISTORY C17: of uncertain origin

Bashan ('beɪʃæn) NOUN *Old Testament* a region to the east of the Jordan, renowned for its rich pasture (Deuteronomy 32:14).

bashaw (bəˈʃɔː) NOUN 1 a rare spelling of **pasha.** 2 an important or pompous person.
▷HISTORY C16: from Turkish *başa*, from *bas* head, chief

bashful ('bæʃfʊl) ADJECTIVE 1 disposed to attempt to avoid notice through shyness or modesty; diffident; timid. 2 indicating or characterized by shyness or modesty.
▷HISTORY C16: from *bash*, short for ABASH + -FUL
▸**'bashfully** ADVERB ▸**'bashfulness** NOUN

bashibazouk (ˌbæʃɪbəˈzuːk) NOUN (in the 19th century) one of a group of irregular Turkish soldiers notorious for their brutality.
▷HISTORY C19: from Turkish *başibozuk* irregular soldier, from *bas* head + *bozuk* corrupt

-bashing NOUN AND ADJECTIVE COMBINING FORM *Informal or slang* **a** indicating a malicious attack on members of a particular group: *queer-bashing; union-bashing.* **b** indicating any of various other activities: *Bible-bashing; spud-bashing; square-bashing.*
▸**-basher** NOUN COMBINING FORM

Bashkir (bæʃˈkɪə) NOUN 1 (*plural* **-kir** *or* **-kirs**) a member of a Mongoloid people of E central Russia, living chiefly in the Bashkir Republic. 2 the language of this people, belonging to the Turkic branch of the Altaic family.

Bashkir Republic NOUN a constituent republic of E central Russia, in the S Urals: established as the first Soviet autonomous republic in 1919; rich mineral resources. Capital: Ufa. Pop.: 4 117 000 (2000 est.). Area: 143 600 sq. km (55 430 sq. miles). Also called: **Bashkiria** (bæʃˈkɪərɪə), **Bashkortostan** (bæʃˈkɔːtɔˌstɑːn; *Russian* baʃkərtəˈstɑːn).

basho ('bæʃəʊ) NOUN, *plural* **basho.** a grand tournament in sumo wrestling.
▷HISTORY C20: from Japanese

bash up VERB (*tr, adverb*) *Brit slang* to thrash; beat violently.

basic ('beɪsɪk) ADJECTIVE 1 of, relating to, or forming a base or basis; fundamental; underlying. 2 elementary or simple: *a few basic facts.* 3 excluding additions or extras: *basic pay.* 4 *Chem* **a** of, denoting, or containing a base; alkaline. **b** (of a salt) containing hydroxyl or oxide groups not all of which have been replaced by an acid radical: *basic lead carbonate,* $2PbCO_3.Pb(OH)_2$. 5 *Metallurgy* of, concerned with, or made by a process in which the furnace or converter is made of a basic material, such as magnesium oxide. 6 (of such igneous rocks as basalt) containing between 52 and 45 per cent silica. 7 *Military* primary or initial: *basic training.* ◆ NOUN 8 (*usually plural*) a fundamental principle, fact, etc.

BASIC *or* **Basic** ('beɪsɪk) NOUN a computer programming language that uses common English terms.
▷HISTORY C20: acronym of *b(eginner's) a(ll-purpose) s(ymbolic) i(nstruction) c(ode)*

basically ('beɪsɪklɪ) ADVERB 1 in a fundamental or elementary manner; essentially: *strident and basically unpleasant.* 2 (*sentence modifier*) in essence; in summary; put simply: *basically we had underestimated mother nature.*

Basic Curriculum NOUN *Brit education* the National Curriculum plus religious education.

basic education NOUN (in India) education in which all teaching is correlated with the learning of a craft.

basic English NOUN a simplified form of English, proposed by C. K. Ogden and I. A. Richards, containing a vocabulary of approximately 850 of the commonest English words, intended as an international language.

basic industry NOUN an industry which is highly important in a nation's economy.

basicity (beɪˈsɪsɪtɪ) NOUN *Chem* **a** the state of being a base. **b** the extent to which a substance is basic.

basicranial (ˌbæsɪˈkreɪnɪᵊl) ADJECTIVE *Anatomy* of or relating to the base of the skull.

basic rate NOUN the standard or lowest level on a scale of money payable, esp in taxation.

basic slag NOUN a furnace slag produced in steel-making, containing large amounts of calcium phosphate: used as a fertilizer.

basidiocarp (bæ'sɪdɪəʊˌkɑːp) NOUN the fruiting body of basidiomycetous fungi; the mushroom of agarics.

basidiomycete (bæˌsɪdɪəʊmaɪ'siːt) NOUN any fungus of the phylum Basidiomycota (formerly class *Basidiomycetes*), in which the spores are produced in basidia. The group includes boletes, puffballs, smuts, and rusts.
▷HISTORY C19: from BASIDI(UM) + -MYCETE
▸**baˌsidiomy'cetous** ADJECTIVE

basidiospore (bæ'sɪdɪəʊˌspɔː) NOUN one of the spores, usually four in number, produced in a basidium.
▸**baˌsidio'sporous** ADJECTIVE

basidium (bæ'sɪdɪəm) NOUN, *plural* **-ia** (-ɪə). the structure, produced by basidiomycetous fungi after sexual reproduction, in which spores are formed at the tips of projecting slender stalks.
▷HISTORY C19: from New Latin, from Greek *basidion*; see BASIS, -IUM
▸**ba'sidial** ADJECTIVE

basifixed ('beɪsɪˌfɪxt) ADJECTIVE *Botany* (of an anther) attached to the filament by its base.

basifugal (beɪ'sɪfjʊgᵊl) ADJECTIVE *Botany* a less common word for **acropetal**.

basify ('beɪsɪˌfaɪ) VERB **-fies, -fying, -fied.** (*tr*) to make basic.

basil ('bæzᵊl) NOUN [1] Also called: **sweet basil.** a Eurasian plant, *Ocimum basilicum*, having spikes of small white flowers and aromatic leaves used as herbs for seasoning: family *Lamiaceae* (labiates). [2] Also called: **wild basil.** a European plant, *Satureja vulgaris* (or *Clinopodium vulgare*), with dense clusters of small pink or whitish flowers: family *Lamiaceae*. [3] **basil-thyme.** a European plant, *Acinos arvensis*, having clusters of small violet-and-white flowers: family *Lamiaceae*.
▷HISTORY C15: from Old French *basile*, from Late Latin *basilicum*, from Greek *basilikon*, from *basilikos* royal, from *basileus* king

Basilan (bə'siːlɑːn, bæ'siːlæn) NOUN [1] a group of islands in the Philippines, SW of Mindanao. [2] the main island of this group, separated from Mindanao by the **Basilan Strait**. Area: 1282 sq. km (495 sq. miles). [3] a city on Basilan Island. Pop.: 201 407 (1980).

basilar ('bæsɪlə) ADJECTIVE *Chiefly anatomy* of or situated at a base: *basilar artery* (at the base of the skull). Also: **basilary** ('bæsɪlərɪ, -sɪlrɪ).
▷HISTORY C16: from New Latin *basilaris*, from Latin *basis* BASE[1]; compare Medieval Latin *bassile* pelvis

Basildon ('bæzɪldən) NOUN a town in SE England, in S Essex: designated a new town in 1955. Pop.: 100 924 (1991).

Basilian (bə'zɪlɪən) NOUN a monk of the Eastern Christian order of St. Basil, founded in Cappadocia in the 4th century A.D.

basilica (bə'zɪlɪkə) NOUN [1] a Roman building, used for public administration, having a large rectangular central nave with an aisle on each side and an apse at the end. [2] a rectangular early Christian or medieval church, usually having a nave with clerestories, two or four aisles, one or more vaulted apses, and a timber roof. [3] a Roman Catholic church having special ceremonial rights.
▷HISTORY C16: from Latin, from Greek *basilikē* hall, from *basilikē oikia* the king's house, from *basileus* king; see BASIL
▸**ba'silican** *or* **ba'silic** ADJECTIVE

Basilicata (*Italian* bazili'kata) NOUN a region of S Italy, between the Tyrrhenian Sea and the Gulf of Taranto. Capital: Potenza. Pop.: 606 183 (2000 est.). Area: 9985 sq. km (3855 sq. miles).

basilic vein (bə'zɪlɪk) NOUN a large vein situated on the inner side of the arm.
▷HISTORY C18: from Latin *basilicus* kingly; see BASIL

basilisk ('bæzɪˌlɪsk) NOUN [1] (in classical legend) a serpent that could kill by its breath or glance. [2] any small arboreal semiaquatic lizard of the genus *Basiliscus* of tropical America: family *Iguanidae* (iguanas). The males have an inflatable head crest, used in display. [3] a 16th-century medium cannon, usually made of brass.
▷HISTORY C14: from Latin *basiliscus*, from Greek *basiliskos* royal child, from *basileus* king

basin ('beɪsᵊn) NOUN [1] a round container open and wide at the top with sides sloping inwards towards the bottom or base, esp one in which liquids are mixed or stored. [2] Also called: **basinful.** the amount a basin will hold. [3] a washbasin or sink. [4] any partially enclosed or sheltered area where vessels may be moored or docked. [5] the catchment area of a particular river and its tributaries or of a lake or sea. [6] a depression in the earth's surface. [7] *Geology* a part of the earth's surface consisting of rock strata that slope down to a common centre.
▷HISTORY C13: from Old French *bacin*, from Late Latin *bacchīnon*, from Vulgar Latin *bacca* (unattested) container for water; related to Latin *bāca* berry

basinet *or* **bascinet** ('bæsɪnɪt, -ˌnɛt) NOUN a close-fitting medieval helmet of light steel usually with a visor.
▷HISTORY C14: from Old French *bacinet*, a little basin, from *bacin* BASIN

Basingstoke ('beɪzɪŋˌstəʊk) NOUN a town in S England, in N Hampshire. Pop.: 77 837 (1991).

basion ('beɪsɪən) NOUN *Anatomy* the midpoint on the forward border of the foramen magnum.
▷HISTORY C19: from New Latin, from Latin *basis* BASE[1]

basipetal (beɪ'sɪpɪtᵊl) ADJECTIVE (of leaves and flowers) produced in order from the apex downwards so that the youngest are at the base. Compare **acropetal**.

basis ('beɪsɪs) NOUN, *plural* **-ses** (-siːz). [1] something that underlies, supports, or is essential to something else, esp an abstract idea. [2] a principle on which something depends or from which something has issued. [3] *Maths* (of a vector space) a maximal set of linearly independent vectors, in terms of which all the elements of the space are uniquely expressible, and the number of which is the dimension of the space: *the vectors* ***x****,* ***y*** *and* ***z*** *form a basis of the 3-dimensional space all members of which can be written as* ***ax*** *+* ***by*** *+* ***cz***.
▷HISTORY C14: via Latin from Greek: step, from *bainein* to step, go

bask (bɑːsk) VERB (*intr; usually foll by in*) [1] to lie in or be exposed to pleasant warmth, esp that of the sun. [2] to flourish or feel secure under some benevolent influence or favourable condition.
▷HISTORY C14: from Old Norse *bathask* to BATHE

Baskerville ('bæskəˌvɪl) NOUN a style of type.
▷HISTORY C18: named after John *Baskerville* (1706–1775), English printer

basket ('bɑːskɪt) NOUN [1] a container made of interwoven strips of pliable materials, such as cane, straw, thin wood, or plastic, and often carried by means of a handle or handles. [2] Also called: **basketful.** the amount a basket will hold. [3] something resembling such a container in appearance or function, such as the structure suspended from a balloon. [4] *Basketball* **a** an open horizontal metal hoop fixed to the backboard, through which a player must throw the ball to score points. **b** a point or points scored in this way. [5] a group or collection of similar of related things: *a basket of currencies*. [6] *Informal* a euphemism for **bastard** (senses 1, 2).
▷HISTORY C13: probably from Old Northern French *baskot* (unattested), from Latin *bascauda* basketwork holder, of Celtic origin

basketball ('bɑːskɪtˌbɔːl) NOUN [1] a game played by two opposing teams of five men (or six women) each, usually on an indoor court. Points are scored by throwing the ball through an elevated horizontal metal hoop. [2] the inflated ball used in this game.

basket case NOUN *Slang* [1] *Chiefly US and Canadian* a person who has had both arms and both legs amputated. [2] a person who is suffering from extreme nervous strain; nervous wreck. [3] **a** someone or something that is incapable of functioning normally. **b** (*as modifier*): *a basket-case economy*.

basket chair NOUN a chair made of wickerwork; a wicker chair.

basket clause NOUN an all-inclusive or comprehensive clause in a contract.

basket hilt NOUN a hilt fitted to a broadsword, with a generally padded basket-shaped guard to protect the hand.
▸**'basket-ˌhilted** ADJECTIVE

Basket Maker NOUN a member of an early American Indian people of the southwestern US, preceding the Pueblo people, known for skill in basket-making.

basketry ('bɑːskɪtrɪ) NOUN [1] the art or practice of making baskets. [2] baskets collectively.

basket-star NOUN any of several echinoderms of the genus *Gorgonocephalus*, in which long slender arms radiate from a central disc: order *Ophiuroidea* (brittle-stars).

basket weave NOUN a weave of two or more yarns together, resembling that of a basket, esp in wool or linen fabric.

basketweaver ('bɑːskɪtˌwiːvə) NOUN *Austral derogatory slang* a person who advocates simple, natural, and unsophisticated living.

basketwork ('bɑːskɪtˌwɜːk) NOUN another word for **wickerwork**.

basking shark NOUN a very large plankton-eating shark, *Cetorhinus maximus*, often floating at the sea surface: family *Cetorhinidae*. Also called: **sailfish**.

Basle (bɑːl) *or* **Basel** ('bɑːzᵊl) NOUN [1] a canton of NW Switzerland, divided into the demicantons of **Basle-Landschaft** and **Basle-Stadt**. Pops.: 258 600 and 188 500 (2000 est.). Areas: 427 sq. km (165 sq. miles) and 36 sq. km (14 sq. miles) respectively. [2] a city in NW Switzerland, capital of Basle canton, on the Rhine: oldest university in Switzerland. Pop.: 174 007 (1996 est.). French name: **Bâle**.

basmati rice (bəz'mætɪ) NOUN a variety of long-grain rice with slender aromatic grains, used for savoury dishes.
▷HISTORY from Hindi, literally: aromatic

Bas Mitzvah (bɑːs 'mɪtsvə) NOUN (*sometimes not capitals*) a variant of **Bat Mitzvah**.

basophil ('beɪsəfɪl) *or* **basophile** ADJECTIVE *also* **basophilic** (ˌbeɪsə'fɪlɪk). [1] (of cells or cell contents) easily stained by basic dyes. ◆ NOUN [2] a basophil cell, esp a leucocyte.
▷HISTORY C19: from Greek; see BASE[1] + -PHILE

basophilia (ˌbeɪsə'fɪlɪə) NOUN [1] an abnormal increase of basophil leucocytes in the blood. [2] the affinity of a biological specimen for basic dyes.

Basotho (bə'suːtuː, -'səʊtəʊ) NOUN, *plural* **-tho** *or* **-thos.** a member of the subgroup of the Sotho people who chiefly inhabit Lesotho. Former name: **Basuto**.

Basotho-Qwaqwa (bə'suːtuː'kwɑːkwə, -'səʊtəʊ-) NOUN (formerly) a Bantustan in South Africa, in the Orange Free State; the only Bantustan without exclaves: abolished in 1993. Also called: **Qwaqwa**. Former name (until 1972): **Basotho-Ba-Borwa**.

basque (bæsk, bɑːsk) NOUN [1] a short extension below the waist to the bodice of a woman's jacket, etc. [2] a tight-fitting bodice for women.
▷HISTORY C19: perhaps from BASQUE

Basque (bæsk, bɑːsk) NOUN [1] a member of a people of unknown origin living around the W Pyrenees in France and Spain. [2] the language of this people, of no known relationship with any other language. ◆ ADJECTIVE [3] relating to, denoting, or characteristic of this people or their language.
▷HISTORY C19: from French, from Latin *Vascō* a Basque

Basque Provinces NOUN an autonomous region of N Spain, comprising the provinces of Álava, Guipúzcoa, and Viscaya: inhabited mainly by Basques, who retained virtual autonomy from the 9th to the 19th century. Pop.: 2 098 596 (2000 est.). Area: about 7250 sq. km (2800 sq. miles).

Basra, Basrah ('bæzrə), **Busra,** *or* **Busrah** ('bʌsrə) NOUN a port in SE Iraq, on the Shatt-al-Arab. Pop.: 406 296 (1987).

bas-relief (ˌbɑːrɪ'liːf, ˌbæs-, 'bɑːrɪˌliːf, 'bæs-) NOUN sculpture in low relief, in which the forms project slightly from the background but no part is completely detached from it. Also called (Italian): **basso rilievo**.
▷HISTORY C17: from French, from Italian *basso rilievo* low relief; see BASE[2], RELIEF

Bas-Rhin (*French* barɛ̃) NOUN a department of NE France in Alsace region. Capital: Strasbourg. Pop.:

1 026 120 (1999). Area: 4793 sq. km (1869 sq. miles).

bass[1] (beɪs) NOUN 1 the lowest adult male voice usually having a range from E a 13th below middle C to D a tone above it. 2 a singer with such a voice. 3 **the bass.** the lowest part in a piece of harmony. See also **thorough bass.** 4 *Informal* short for **bass guitar, double bass.** 5 **a** the low-frequency component of an electrical audio signal, esp in a record player or tape recorder. **b** the knob controlling this on such an instrument. ◆ ADJECTIVE 6 relating to or denoting the bass: *bass pitch*; *the bass part.* 7 denoting the lowest and largest instrument in a family: *a bass trombone.*
▷HISTORY C15 *bas* BASE[1]; modern spelling influenced by BASSO

bass[2] (bæs) NOUN 1 any of various sea perches, esp *Morone labrax*, a popular game fish with one large spiny dorsal fin separate from a second smaller one. See also **sea bass, stone bass.** 2 another name for the **European perch** (see **perch**[2] (sense 1)). 3 any of various predatory North American freshwater percoid fishes, such as *Micropterus salmoides*, (**largemouth bass**): family *Centrarchidae* (sunfishes, etc.). See also **black bass, rock bass.**
▷HISTORY C15: changed from BASE[2], influenced by Italian *basso* low

bass[3] (bæs) NOUN 1 another name for **bast** (sense 1). 2 short for **basswood.** 3 Also called: **fish bass.** a bast fibre bag for holding an angler's catch.
▷HISTORY C17: changed from BAST

bass clef (beɪs) NOUN the clef that establishes F a fifth below middle C on the fourth line of the staff. Symbol: 𝄢. Also called: **F clef.**

bass drum (beɪs) NOUN a large shallow drum of low and indefinite pitch. Also called: **gran cassa.**

Bassein (bɑːˈseɪn) NOUN a city in Myanmar, on the Irrawaddy delta: a port on the **Bassein River** (the westernmost distributary of the Irrawaddy). Pop.: 183 900 (1993 est.).

Basse-Normandie (*French* basnɔrmɑ̃di) NOUN a region of NW France, on the English Channel: consists of the Cherbourg peninsula in the west rising to the Normandy hills in the east; mainly agricultural.

Bassenthwaite (ˈbæsᵊnˌθweɪt) NOUN a lake in NW England, in Cumbria near Keswick. Length: 6 km (4 miles).

Basses-Alpes (*French* basalp) NOUN the former name for **Alpes-de-Haute-Provence.**

Basses-Pyrénées (*French* baspirene) PLURAL NOUN the former name for **Pyrénées (Atlantiques).**

basset[1] (ˈbæsɪt) NOUN a long low smooth-haired breed of hound with short strong legs and long ears. Also called: **basset hound.**
▷HISTORY C17: from French, from *basset* short, from *bas* low; see BASE[2]

basset[2] (ˈbæsɪt) VERB **-sets, -seting, -seted,** NOUN a rare word for **outcrop.**
▷HISTORY C17: perhaps from French: low stool, see BASSET[1]

Basseterre (bæsˈtɛə; *French* bastɛr) NOUN a port in the Caribbean, on St Kitts in the Leeward Islands: the capital of St Kitts-Nevis. Pop.: 12 605 (1994 est.).

Basse-Terre (ˈbæsˈtɛə; *French* bastɛr) NOUN 1 a mountainous island in the Caribbean, in the Leeward Islands, comprising part of Guadeloupe. Area: 848 sq. km (327 sq. miles). 2 a port in W Guadeloupe, on Basse-Terre Island: the capital of the French Overseas Department of Guadeloupe. Pop.: 12 549 (1999).

basset horn NOUN an obsolete woodwind instrument of the clarinet family.
▷HISTORY C19: probably from German *Bassetthorn*, from Italian *bassetto*, diminutive of BASSO + HORN

bass guitar (beɪs) NOUN a guitar that has the same pitch and tuning as a double bass, usually electrically amplified.

bassinet (ˌbæsɪˈnɛt) NOUN a wickerwork or wooden cradle or pram, usually hooded.
▷HISTORY C19: from French: little basin, from *bassin* BASIN; associated in folk etymology with French *barcelonnette* a little cradle, from *berceau* cradle

bassist (ˈbeɪsɪst) NOUN a player of a double bass, esp in a jazz band.

basso (ˈbæsəʊ) NOUN, *plural* **-sos** *or* **-si** (-sɪ). (esp in operatic or solo singing) a singer with a bass voice.
▷HISTORY C19: from Italian, from Late Latin *bassus* low; see BASE[2]

basso continuo NOUN another term for **thorough bass.** Often shortened to: **continuo.**
▷HISTORY Italian, literally: continuous bass

bassoon (bəˈsuːn) NOUN 1 a woodwind instrument, the tenor of the oboe family. Range: about three and a half octaves upwards from the B flat below the bass staff. 2 an orchestral musician who plays the bassoon.
▷HISTORY C18: from French *basson*, from Italian *bassone*, from *basso* deep; see BASE[2]
▸**bassoonist** NOUN

basso profundo (prəʊˈfʌndəʊ; *Italian* proˈfundo) NOUN, *plural* **-dos.** (esp in operatic solo singing) a singer with a very deep bass voice.
▷HISTORY Italian, literally: deep bass

basso rilievo (*Italian* ˈbasso riˈljevo) NOUN, *plural* **-vos.** Italian name for **bas-relief.**

bass response (beɪs) NOUN the response of an audio reproduction system or component to low frequencies.

Bass Strait (bæs) NOUN a channel between mainland Australia and Tasmania, linking the Indian Ocean and the Tasman Sea.

bass viol (beɪs) NOUN 1 another name for **viola da gamba.** 2 *US* a less common name for **double bass** (sense 1).

basswood (ˈbæsˌwʊd) NOUN 1 any of several North American linden trees, esp *Tilia americana*. Sometimes shortened to: **bass.** 2 the soft light-coloured wood of any of these trees, used for furniture.
▷HISTORY C19: from BASS[3]; see BAST

bast (bæst) NOUN 1 Also called: **bass.** fibrous material obtained from the phloem of jute, hemp, flax, lime, etc., used for making rope, matting, etc. 2 *Botany* another name for **phloem.**
▷HISTORY Old English *bæst*; related to Old Norse, Middle High German *bast*

bastard (ˈbɑːstəd, ˈbæs-) NOUN 1 *Informal, offensive* an obnoxious or despicable person. 2 *Informal, often humorous or affectionate* a person, esp a man: *lucky bastard.* 3 *Informal* something extremely difficult or unpleasant: *that job is a real bastard.* 4 *Old-fashioned or offensive* a person born of unmarried parents; an illegitimate baby, child, or adult. 5 something irregular, abnormal, or inferior. 6 a hybrid, esp an accidental or inferior one. ◆ ADJECTIVE (*prenominal*) 7 *Old-fashioned or offensive* illegitimate by birth. 8 irregular, abnormal, or inferior in shape, size, or appearance. 9 resembling a specified thing, but not actually being such: *a bastard cedar.* 10 counterfeit; spurious.
▷HISTORY C13: from Old French *bastart*, perhaps from *bast* in the phrase *fils de bast* son of the packsaddle (that is, of an unlawful and not the marriage bed), from Medieval Latin *bastum* packsaddle, of uncertain origin
▸ˈ**bastardly** ADJECTIVE

bastard cut ADJECTIVE *Mechanical engineering* (of a file) having medium teeth; intermediate between a coarse cut and a fine cut.

bastardization *or* **bastardisation** (ˌbɑːstədaɪˈzeɪʃən, ˌbæs-) NOUN 1 the act of bastardizing. 2 *Austral* **a** an initiation ceremony in a school or military unit, esp one involving brutality. **b** brutality or bullying.

bastardize *or* **bastardise** (ˈbɑːstəˌdaɪz, ˈbæs-) VERB (*tr*) 1 to debase; corrupt. 2 *Archaic* to declare illegitimate.

bastard measles NOUN *Pathol* an informal name for **rubella.**

bastardry (ˈbɑːstədrɪ, ˈbæs-) NOUN *Slang, chiefly Austral* malicious or cruel behaviour.

bastard title NOUN another name for **half-title** (of a book).

bastard wing NOUN a tuft of feathers attached to the first digit of a bird, distinct from the wing feathers attached to the other digits and the ulna. Also called: **alula.**

bastardy (ˈbɑːstədɪ, ˈbæs-) NOUN *Archaic* the condition of being a bastard; illegitimacy.

baste[1] (beɪst) VERB (*tr*) to sew with loose temporary stitches.
▷HISTORY C14: from Old French *bastir* to build, of Germanic origin; compare Old High German *besten* to sew with BAST

baste[2] (beɪst) VERB to moisten (meat) during cooking with hot fat and the juices produced.
▷HISTORY C15: of uncertain origin

baste[3] (beɪst) VERB (*tr*) to beat thoroughly; thrash.
▷HISTORY C16: probably from Old Norse *beysta*

basti, bustee, *or* **busti** (ˈbʌstɪ) NOUN (in India) a slum inhabited by poor people.
▷HISTORY Urdu: settlement

Bastia (ˈbɑːstjə) NOUN a port in NE Corsica: the main commercial and industrial town of the island: capital of Haute-Corse department. Pop.: 38 728 (1990).

Bastille (bæˈstiːl; *French* bastij) NOUN a fortress in Paris, built in the 14th century: a prison until its destruction in 1789, at the beginning of the French Revolution.
▷HISTORY C14: from Old French *bastile* fortress, from Old Provençal *bastida*, from *bastir* to build, of Germanic origin; see BASTE[1]

Bastille Day NOUN (in France) an annual holiday on July 14, commemorating the fall of the Bastille.

bastinado (ˌbæstɪˈneɪdəʊ) NOUN, *plural* **-does.** 1 punishment or torture in which the soles of the feet are beaten with a stick. 2 a blow or beating with a stick. 3 a stick; cudgel. ◆ VERB **-does, -doing, -doed.** (*tr*) 4 to beat (a person) on the soles of the feet.
▷HISTORY C16: from Spanish *bastonada*, from *baston* stick, from Late Latin *bastum* see BATON

basting (ˈbeɪstɪŋ) NOUN 1 loose temporary stitches; tacking. 2 sewing with such stitches.

bastion (ˈbæstɪən) NOUN 1 a projecting work in a fortification designed to permit fire to the flanks along the face of the wall. 2 any fortified place. 3 a thing or person regarded as upholding or defending an attitude, principle, etc.: *the last bastion of opposition.*
▷HISTORY C16: from French, from earlier *bastillon* bastion, from *bastille* BASTILLE

bastnaesite *or* **bastnasite** (ˈbæstnəˌsaɪt) NOUN a rare yellow to reddish-brown mineral consisting of a carbonate of fluorine and several lanthanide metals. It occurs in association with zinc and is a source of the lanthanides. Formula: $LaFCO_3$.
▷HISTORY C19: from Swedish *bastnäsit*, after *Bastnäs*, Sweden, where it was found

Bastogne (bæˈstəʊn; *French* bastɔɲ) NOUN a town in SE Belgium: of strategic importance to Allied defences during the Battle of the Bulge; besieged by the Germans during the winter of 1944–45. Pop.: 7000 (1991 est.).

Basuto (bəˈsuːtəʊ) NOUN, *plural* **-tos** *or* **-to.** a former name for **Sotho** (senses 3, 4).

Basutoland (bəˈsuːtəʊˌlænd) NOUN the former name (until 1966) of **Lesotho.**

BASW (ˈbæzwə) NOUN (in Britain) ◆ ACRONYM FOR British Association of Social Workers.

bat[1] (bæt) NOUN 1 any of various types of club with a handle, used to hit the ball in certain sports, such as cricket, baseball, or table tennis. 2 a flat round club with a short handle, resembling a table-tennis bat, used by a man on the ground to guide the pilot of an aircraft when taxiing. 3 *Cricket* short for **batsman.** 4 any stout stick, esp a wooden one. 5 *Informal* a blow from such a stick. 6 *Austral* a small board used for tossing the coins in the game of two-up. 7 *US and Canadian slang* a drinking spree; binge. 8 *Slang* speed; rate; pace: *they went at a fair bat.* 9 another word for **batting** (sense 1). 10 **carry one's bat.** *Cricket* (of a batsman) to reach the end of an innings without being dismissed. 11 **off one's own bat. a** of one's own accord; without being prompted by someone else. **b** by one's own unaided efforts. 12 (**right**) **off the bat.** *US and Canadian informal* immediately; without hesitation. ◆ VERB **bats, batting, batted.** 13 (*tr*) to strike with or as if with a bat. 14 (*intr*) *Sport* (of a player or a team) to take a turn at batting. ◆ See also **bat around.**
▷HISTORY Old English *batt* club, probably of Celtic origin; compare Gaelic *bat*, Russian *bat*

bat[2] (bæt) NOUN 1 any placental mammal of the order *Chiroptera*, being a nocturnal mouselike animal flying with a pair of membranous wings

(patagia). The group is divided into the *Megachiroptera* (**fruit bats**) and *Microchiroptera* (**insectivorous bats**). Related adjective: **chiropteran.** [2] *Slang* an irritating or eccentric woman (esp in the phrase **old bat**). [3] **blind as a bat.** having extremely poor eyesight. [4] **have bats in the** (*or* **one's**) **belfry.** *Informal* to be mad or eccentric; have strange ideas. [5] **like a bat out of hell.** *Slang* very quickly.
▷HISTORY C14 *bakke*, probably of Scandinavian origin; compare Old Norse *ledhrblaka* leather-flapper, Swedish dialect *natt-batta* night bat
▸ **'batlike** ADJECTIVE

bat[3] (bæt) VERB **bats, batting, batted.** (*tr*) [1] to wink or flutter (one's eyelids). [2] **not bat an eye** *or* **eyelid.** *Informal* to show no surprise or concern.
▷HISTORY C17: probably a variant of BATE[2]

Bataan (bəˈtæn, -ˈtɑːn) NOUN a peninsula in the Philippines, in W Luzon: scene of the surrender of US and Philippine forces to the Japanese during World War II, later retaken by American forces.

Batangas (bəˈtæŋgæs) NOUN a port in the Philippines, in SW Luzon. Pop.: 190 627 (1994 est.).

Batan Islands (bəˈtɑːn) PLURAL NOUN a group of islands in the Philippines, north of Luzon. Capital: Basco. Pop.: 12 091 (latest est.). Area: 197 sq. km (76 sq. miles).

bat around VERB [1] (*tr, adverb*) *US and Canadian slang* to discuss (an idea, proposition, etc.) informally. [2] (*intr*) Also: **bat along.** *Dialect, US and Canadian slang* to wander or move about.

batata (bəˈtɑːtə) NOUN another name for **sweet potato.**
▷HISTORY C16: from Spanish, from Taino

batavia (bəˈteɪvɪə) NOUN a variety of lettuce with smooth pale green leaves. Also called: **Batavian endive, Batavian lettuce.**

Batavia (bəˈteɪvɪə) NOUN [1] an ancient district of the Netherlands, on an island at the mouth of the Rhine. [2] an archaic or literary name for **Holland**[1]. [3] a former name for **Jakarta.**

Batavian (bəˈteɪvɪən) ADJECTIVE [1] of or relating to Batavia (a former name for Holland or Jakarta) or its inhabitants. ◆ NOUN [2] a native or inhabitant of Batavia.

batch[1] (bætʃ) NOUN [1] a group or set of usually similar objects or people, esp if sent off, handled, or arriving at the same time. [2] the bread, cakes, etc., produced at one baking. [3] the amount of a material needed for an operation. [4] Also called: **batch loaf.** a tall loaf having a close texture and a thick crust on the top and bottom, baked as part of a batch: the sides of each loaf are greased so that they will pull apart after baking to have pale crumby sides; made esp in Scotland and Ireland. Compare **pan loaf.** ◆ VERB (*tr*) [5] to group (items) for efficient processing. [6] to handle by batch processing.
▷HISTORY C15 *bache*; related to Old English *bacan* to BAKE; compare Old English *gebæc* batch, German *Gebäck*

batch[2] *or* **bach** (bætʃ) VERB *Austral and NZ informal* [1] (*intr*) (of a man) to do his own cooking and housekeeping. [2] to live alone.

Bat Chayil (bɑːt ˈxajil) NOUN (*sometimes not capitals*) *Judaism* [1] (in some congregations) a ceremony of confirmation for a girl of at least Bat Mitzvah age. [2] the girl herself. ◆ Also: **Bat Hayil.**
▷HISTORY from Hebrew, literally: daughter of valour

batch processing NOUN [1] manufacturing products or treating materials in batches, by passing the output of one process to subsequent processes. Compare **continuous processing.** [2] a system by which the computer programs of a number of individual users are submitted to the computer as a single batch. Compare **time sharing** (sense 2).

bate[1] (beɪt) VERB [1] another word for **abate.** [2] **with bated breath.** holding one's breath in suspense or fear.

bate[2] (beɪt) VERB (*intr*) (of hawks) to jump violently from a perch or the falconer's fist, often hanging from the leash while struggling to escape.
▷HISTORY C13: from Old French *batre* to beat, from Latin *battuere*; related to BAT[1]

bate[3] (beɪt) VERB (*tr*) [1] to soak (skin or hides) in a special solution to soften them and remove chemicals used in previous treatments. ◆ NOUN [2] the solution used.
▷HISTORY Old English *bǣtan* to BAIT[1]

bate[4] (beɪt) NOUN *Brit slang* a bad temper or rage.
▷HISTORY C19: from BAIT[1], alluding to the mood of a person who is being baited

bateau (bæˈtəʊ; *French* bato) NOUN, *plural* **-teaux** (-təʊz; *French* -to). a light flat-bottomed boat used on rivers in Canada and the northern US.
▷HISTORY C18: from French: boat, from Old French *batel*, from Old English *bāt*; see BOAT

bateleur eagle (ˈbætələː) NOUN an African crested bird of prey, *Terathopius ecaudatus*, with a short tail and long wings: subfamily *Circaetinae*, family *Accipitridae* (hawks, etc.).
▷HISTORY C19: from French *bateleur* juggler

Batesian mimicry (ˈbeɪtsɪən) NOUN *Zoology* mimicry in which a harmless species is protected from predators by means of its resemblance to a harmful or inedible species.
▷HISTORY C19: named after H. W. *Bates* (1825–92), British naturalist and explorer

batfish (ˈbætˌfɪʃ) NOUN, *plural* **-fish** *or* **-fishes.** any angler of the family *Ogcocephalidae*, having a flattened scaleless body and moving on the sea floor by means of fleshy pectoral and pelvic fins.

batfowl (ˈbætˌfaʊl) VERB (*intr*) to catch birds by temporarily blinding them with light.
▸ **ˈbatˌfowler** NOUN

bath[1] (bɑːθ) NOUN, *plural* **baths** (bɑːðz). [1] a large container, esp one made of enamelled iron or plastic, used for washing or medically treating the body. Related adjective: **balneal.** [2] the act or an instance of washing in such a container. [3] the amount of liquid contained in a bath. [4] **run a bath.** to turn on the taps to fill a bath with water for bathing oneself. [5] (*usually plural*) a place that provides baths or a swimming pool for public use. [6] **a** a vessel in which something is immersed to maintain it at a constant temperature, to process it photographically, electrolytically, etc., or to lubricate it. **b** the liquid used in such a vessel. ◆ VERB [7] *Brit* to wash in a bath.
▷HISTORY Old English *bæth*; compare Old High German *bad*, Old Norse *bath*; related to Swedish *basa* to clean with warm water, Old High German *bāen* to warm

bath[2] (bæθ) NOUN an ancient Hebrew unit of liquid measure equal to about 8.3 Imperial gallons or 10 US gallons.
▷HISTORY Hebrew

Bath (bɑːθ) NOUN a city in SW England, in Bath and North East Somerset unitary authority, Somerset, on the River Avon: famous for its hot springs; a fashionable spa in the 18th century; Roman remains, notably the baths; university (1966). Pop.: 85 202 (1991). Latin name: **Aquae Sulis** (ˈækwiːˈsuːlɪs).

Ba'th (bɑːθ) *or* **Ba'ath** NOUN an Arab Socialist party, esp in Iraq and Syria, founded by Michel Aflaq in 1941. It attempts to combine Marxism with pan-Islamic nationalism.
▷HISTORY C20: from Arabic: resurgence
▸ **'Ba'thi** ADJECTIVE ▸ **'Ba'thism** NOUN ▸ **'Ba'thist** NOUN

Bath and North East Somerset (ˈsʌməset) NOUN a unitary authority in SW England, in Somerset; formerly (1974–96) part of the county of Avon. Pop.: 169 045 (2001). Area: 351 sq. km (136 sq. miles).

Bat Hayil (bɑːt ˈxajil) NOUN a variant spelling of **Bat Chayil.**

bath bun NOUN *Brit* a sweet bun containing spices and dried fruit.
▷HISTORY C19: from BATH, where it was originally made

Bath chair NOUN a wheelchair for invalids, often with a hood.

Bath chap NOUN the lower part of the cheek of a pig, cooked and eaten, usually cold.

bath cube NOUN a cube of soluble scented material for use in a bath.

bathe (beɪð) VERB [1] (*intr*) to swim or paddle in a body of open water or a river, esp for pleasure. [2] (*tr*) to apply liquid to (skin, a wound, etc.) in order to cleanse or soothe. [3] to immerse or be immersed in a liquid: *to bathe machine parts in oil.* [4] *Chiefly US and Canadian* to wash in a bath. [5] (*tr; often passive*) to suffuse: *her face was bathed with radiance.* [6] (*tr*) (of water, the sea, etc.) to lap; wash: *waves bathed the shore.* ◆ NOUN [7] *Brit* a swim or paddle in a body of open water or a river.
▷HISTORY Old English *bathian*; related to Old Norse *batha*, Old High German *badōn*
▸ **'bather** NOUN

bathers (ˈbeɪðəz) PLURAL NOUN *Austral* a swimming costume.

bathetic (bəˈθetɪk) ADJECTIVE containing or displaying bathos.

bathhouse (ˈbɑːθˌhaʊs) NOUN a building containing baths, esp for public use.

bathing beauty (ˈbeɪðɪŋ) NOUN an attractive girl in a swimming costume. Also called (old-fashioned): **bathing belle.**

bathing cap (ˈbeɪðɪŋ) NOUN a tight rubber cap worn by a swimmer to keep the hair dry.

bathing costume (ˈbeɪðɪŋ) NOUN another name for **swimming costume.**

bathing machine (ˈbeɪðɪŋ) NOUN a small hut, on wheels so that it could be pulled to the sea, used in the 18th and 19th centuries for bathers to change their clothes.

bathing suit (ˈbeɪðɪŋ) NOUN [1] a garment worn for bathing, esp an old-fashioned one that covers much of the body. [2] another name for **swimming costume.**

batho- COMBINING FORM a variant of **bathy-.**

bathochromic (ˌbæθəˈkrəʊmɪk) ADJECTIVE *Chem* denoting or relating to a shift to a longer wavelength in the absorption spectrum of a compound.
▸ **ˈbathoˌchrome** NOUN

batholith (ˈbæθəlɪθ) *or* **batholite** (ˈbæθəˌlaɪt) NOUN a very large irregular-shaped mass of igneous rock, esp granite, formed from an intrusion of magma at great depth, esp one exposed after erosion of less resistant overlying rocks.
▸ **ˌbathoˈlithic** *or* **ˌbathoˈlitic** ADJECTIVE

Bath Oliver NOUN *Brit* a kind of unsweetened biscuit.
▷HISTORY C19: named after William *Oliver* (1695–1764), a physician at Bath

bathometer (bəˈθɒmɪtə) NOUN an instrument for measuring the depth of water.
▸ **bathometric** (ˌbæθəˈmetrɪk) ADJECTIVE
▸ **ˌbathoˈmetrically** ADVERB ▸ **bathometry** (bəˈθɒmɪtrɪ) NOUN

Bathonian (bəˈθəʊnɪən) ADJECTIVE [1] of or relating to Bath. [2] *Geology* of or denoting a stage of the Jurassic system in NW Europe. ◆ NOUN [3] a native or resident of Bath. [4] the Bathonian period or rock system.

bathophilous (bæˈθɒfɪləs) ADJECTIVE (of an organism) living in very deep water.

bathos (ˈbeɪθɒs) NOUN [1] a sudden ludicrous descent from exalted to ordinary matters or style in speech or writing. [2] insincere or excessive pathos. [3] triteness; flatness. [4] the lowest point; nadir.
▷HISTORY C18: from Greek: depth, from *bathus* deep

bathrobe (ˈbɑːθˌrəʊb) NOUN [1] a loose-fitting garment of towelling, for wear before or after a bath or swimming. [2] *US and Canadian* a dressing gown.

bathroom (ˈbɑːθˌruːm, -ˌrʊm) NOUN [1] a room containing a bath or shower and usually a washbasin and lavatory. [2] *US and Canadian* another name for **lavatory.**

bath salts PLURAL NOUN soluble scented salts for use in a bath.

Bathsheba (bæθˈʃiːbə, ˈbæθʃɪbə) NOUN *Old Testament* the wife of Uriah, who committed adultery with David and later married him and became the mother of his son Solomon (II Samuel 11–12).

Bath stone NOUN *Brit* a kind of limestone used as a building material, esp at Bath in England.

bathtub (ˈbɑːθˌtʌb) NOUN a bath, esp one not permanently fixed.

bathtub race NOUN *Canadian* a sailing race between bathtubs fitted with outboard motors.

Bathurst (ˈbæθəst) NOUN [1] a city in SE Australia, in E New South Wales: scene of a gold rush in 1851. Pop.: 24 682 (1991). [2] a port in E Canada, in NE New Brunswick: rich mineral resources discovered in 1953. Pop.: 15 890 (1991). 3 the former name (until 1973) of **Banjul.**

Bathurst burr NOUN an Australian plant, *Xanthium spinosum*, having numerous hooked burrs that became entangled in sheep's wool.
▷HISTORY C19: from Bathurst region of New South Wales

bathy- *or* **batho-** COMBINING FORM indicating depth: *bathysphere; bathometer.*
▷HISTORY from Greek *bathus* deep

bathyal ('bæθɪəl) ADJECTIVE denoting or relating to an ocean depth of between 200 and 2000 metres (about 100 and 1000 fathoms), corresponding to the continental slope.

bathylimnetic (ˌbæθɪlɪm'nɛtɪk) ADJECTIVE (of an organism) living in the depths of lakes and marshes.

bathymetry (bə'θɪmɪtrɪ) NOUN measurement of the depth of an ocean or other large body of water.
▸**bathymetric** (ˌbæθɪ'mɛtrɪk) ADJECTIVE
▸**ˌbathy'metrically** ADVERB

bathypelagic (ˌbæθɪpə'lædʒɪk) ADJECTIVE of, relating to, or inhabiting the lower depths of the ocean between approximately 1000 and 4000 metres.

bathyscaph ('bæθɪˌskæf), **bathyscaphe** ('bæθɪˌskeɪf, -ˌskæf), *or* **bathyscape** ('bæθɪˌskæp) NOUN a submersible vessel having a flotation compartment with an observation capsule underneath, capable of reaching ocean depths of over 10 000 metres (about 5000 fathoms).
▷HISTORY C20: from BATHY- + *-scaph*, from Greek *skaphē* light boat

bathysphere ('bæθɪˌsfɪə) NOUN a strong steel deep-sea diving sphere, lowered by cable.

batik *or* **battik** ('bætɪk) NOUN **a** a process of printing fabric in which parts not to be dyed are covered by wax. **b** fabric printed in this way. **c** (*as modifier*): *a batik shirt.*
▷HISTORY C19: via Malay from Javanese: painted

batiste (bæ'tiːst) NOUN a fine plain-weave cotton fabric: used esp for shirts and dresses.
▷HISTORY C17: from French, from Old French *toile de baptiste*, probably after *Baptiste* of Cambrai, 13th-century French weaver, its reputed inventor

Batley ('bætlɪ) NOUN a town in N England, in Kirklees unitary authority, West Yorkshire. Pop.: 48 030 (1991).

batman ('bætmən) NOUN, *plural* **-men.** an officer's personal servant in any of the armed forces.
▷HISTORY C18: from Old French *bat, bast*, from Medieval Latin *bastum* packsaddle

Batman ('bætˌmæn) NOUN a character in an American comic strip and several films who secretly assumes a batlike costume in order to fight crime.

Bat Mitzvah (bɑːt 'mɪtsvə) (*sometimes not capitals*) *Judaism* ◆ ADJECTIVE 1 (of a Jewish girl) having attained religious majority at the age of twelve. ◆ NOUN 2 the date of, or, in some congregations, a ceremony marking, this event. 3 the girl herself on that day. ◆ Also called: **Bas Mitzvah.**
▷HISTORY from Hebrew, literally: daughter of the commandment

baton ('bætən, -tɒn) NOUN 1 a thin stick used by the conductor of an orchestra, choir, etc., to indicate rhythm or expression. 2 **a** a short stick carried for use as a weapon, as by a policeman; truncheon. **b** (*as modifier*): *a baton charge.* 3 *Athletics* a short bar carried by a competitor in a relay race and transferred to the next runner at the end of each stage. 4 a long stick with a knob on one end, carried, twirled, and thrown up and down by a drum major or drum majorette, esp at the head of a parade. 5 a staff or club carried by an official as a symbol of authority. 6 *Heraldry* a single narrow diagonal line superimposed on all other charges, esp one curtailed at each end, signifying a bastard line.
▷HISTORY C16: from French *bâton*, from Late Latin *bastum* rod, probably ultimately from Greek *bastazein* to lift up, carry

bâton de commandement *French* (bɑtɔ̃ də kɔmɑ̃dmɑ̃) NOUN an antler object found in Upper Palaeolithic sites from the Aurignacian period onwards, consisting of a rod, often ornately decorated, with a hole through the thicker end.
▷HISTORY literally: baton of command, although the object was probably actually used in making shafts for arrows and spears

Baton Rouge ('bætᵊn 'ruːʒ) NOUN the capital of Louisiana, in the SE part on the Mississippi River. Pop.: 227 818 (2000).

baton round NOUN the official name for **plastic bullet.**

batrachian (bə'treɪkɪən) NOUN 1 any amphibian, esp a frog or toad. ◆ ADJECTIVE 2 of or relating to the frogs and toads.
▷HISTORY C19: from New Latin *Batrachia*, from Greek *batrakhos* frog

bats (bæts) ADJECTIVE *Informal* crazy; very eccentric.
▷HISTORY from BATS-IN-THE-BELFRY (sense 2)

bats-in-the-belfry NOUN (*functioning as singular*) 1 a hairy Eurasian campanulaceous plant, *Campanula trachelium*, with bell-shaped blue-purple flowers. ◆ ADJECTIVE 2 *Slang* mad; demented.

batsman ('bætsmən) NOUN, *plural* **-men.** 1 *Cricket* **a** a person who bats or whose turn it is to bat. **b** a player who specializes in batting. 2 a person on the ground who uses bats to guide the pilot of an aircraft when taxiing.
▸**'batsmanˌship** NOUN

bats-wing coral-tree NOUN a small tree, *Erythrina verspertilio*, of tropical and subtropical Australia with red flowers and leaves shaped like the wings of a bat.

batt (bæt) NOUN 1 *Textiles* another word for **batting** (sense 1). 2 *Austral and NZ* a slab-shaped piece of insulating material used in building houses.

battalion (bə'tæljən) NOUN 1 a military unit comprised of three or more companies or formations of similar size. 2 (*usually plural*) any large array.
▷HISTORY C16: from French *bataillon*, from Old Italian *battaglione*, from *battaglia* company of soldiers, BATTLE

battels ('bætᵊlz) PLURAL NOUN (at some universities) the account of a member of a college for board, provisions, and other college expenses.
▷HISTORY C16: perhaps from obsolete *battle* to feed, fatten, of uncertain origin

battement (*French* batmɑ̃) NOUN *Ballet* extension of one leg forwards, sideways, or backwards, either once or repeatedly.
▷HISTORY C19: French, literally: beating

batten¹ ('bætᵊn) NOUN 1 a sawn strip of wood used in building to cover joints, provide a fixing for tiles or slates, support lathing, etc. 2 a long narrow board used for flooring. 3 a narrow flat length of wood or plastic inserted in pockets of a sail to give it proper shape. 4 a lath used for holding a tarpaulin along the side of a raised hatch on a ship. 5 *Theatre* **a** a row of lights. **b** the strip or bar supporting them. 6 Also called: **dropper.** *NZ* an upright part of a fence made of wood or other material, designed to keep wires at equal distances apart. ◆ VERB 7 (*tr*) to furnish or strengthen with battens. 8 **batten down the hatches. a** to use battens in nailing a tarpaulin over a hatch on a ship to make it secure. **b** to prepare for action, a crisis, etc.
▷HISTORY C15: from French *bâton* stick; see BATON
▸**'battening** NOUN

batten² ('bætᵊn) VERB (*intr;* usually foll by *on*) to thrive, esp at the expense of someone else: *to batten on the needy.*
▷HISTORY C16: probably from Old Norse *batna* to improve; related to Old Norse *betr* BETTER¹, Old High German *bazzen* to get better

Battenburg ('bætᵊnˌbɜːg) NOUN an oblong sponge cake divided longitudinally into four square sections, two coloured pink and two yellow, with an outer coating of marzipan.
▷HISTORY perhaps named after *Battenberg*, a village in Prussia

batten plate NOUN (in structural design) a horizontal rectangular plate that is used to connect pairs of steel sections by being riveted or welded across them to form a composite section.

Batten's disease ('bætᵊnz) NOUN a rare hereditary disease in which lipids accumulate in the nervous system, leading to mental deterioration, spasticity, and blindness that start in early childhood.
▷HISTORY C20: named after F. E. *Batten* (1865–1918), British neurologist

batter¹ ('bætə) VERB 1 to hit (someone or something) repeatedly using heavy blows, as with a club or other heavy instrument; beat heavily. 2 (*tr; often passive*) to damage or injure, as by blows, heavy wear, etc. 3 (*tr*) *Social welfare* to subject (a person, esp a close relative living in the same house) to repeated physical violence. 4 (*tr*) to subject (a person, opinion, or theory) to harsh criticism; attack.
▷HISTORY C14 *bateren*, probably from *batten* to BAT¹

batter² ('bætə) NOUN a mixture of flour, eggs, and milk, used to make cakes, pancakes, etc., and to coat certain foods before frying.
▷HISTORY C15 *bater*, probably from *bateren* to BATTER¹

batter³ ('bætə) NOUN *Sport* a player who bats.

batter⁴ ('bætə) NOUN 1 the slope of the face of a wall that recedes gradually backwards and upwards. ◆ VERB 2 (*intr*) to have such a slope.
▷HISTORY C16 (vb: to incline): of uncertain origin

batter⁵ ('bætə) NOUN a spree or debauch.
▷HISTORY C19: of unknown origin

battered ('bætəd) ADJECTIVE subjected to persistent physical violence, esp by a close relative living in the same house: *a battered baby.*

batterer ('bætərə) NOUN **a** a person who batters someone. **b** (*in combination*): *baby-batterer; wife-batterer.*

batterie de cuisine (*French* batri də kɥizin) NOUN cooking utensils collectively; pots and pans, etc.
▷HISTORY C18: literally: battery of kitchen

battering ('bætərɪŋ) NOUN **a** the act or practice of battering someone. **b** (*in combination*): *baby-battering; granny-battering.*

battering ram NOUN (esp formerly) a large beam used to break down the walls or doors of fortifications.

Battersea ('bætəsɪ) NOUN a district in London, in Wandsworth: noted for its dogs' home, power station (being developed into a leisure centre), and park.

battery ('bætərɪ) NOUN, *plural* **-teries.** 1 **a** two or more primary cells connected together, usually in series, to provide a source of electric current. **b** short for **dry battery.** 2 another name for **accumulator** (sense 1). 3 a number of similar things occurring together: *a battery of questions.* 4 *Criminal law* unlawful beating or wounding of a person or mere touching in a hostile or offensive manner. See also **assault and battery.** 5 a fortified structure on which artillery is mounted. 6 a group of guns, missile launchers, searchlights, or torpedo tubes of similar type or size operated as a single entity. 7 a small tactical unit of artillery usually consisting of two or more troops, each of two, three or four guns. 8 *Chiefly Brit* **a** a large group of cages for intensive rearing of poultry. **b** (*as modifier*): *battery hens.* 9 *Psychol* a series of tests. 10 *Chess* two men of the same colour placed so that one can unmask an attack by the other by moving. 11 the percussion section in an orchestra. 12 *Baseball* the pitcher and the catcher considered together.
▷HISTORY C16: from Old French *batterie* beating, from *battre* to beat, from Latin *battuere*

battik ('bætɪk) NOUN a variant spelling of **batik.**

batting ('bætɪŋ) NOUN 1 Also called: **batt.** cotton or woollen wadding used in quilts, mattresses, etc. 2 the action of a person or team that hits with a bat, esp in cricket or baseball.

battle ('bætᵊl) NOUN 1 a fight between large armed forces; military or naval engagement; combat. 2 conflict; contention; struggle: *his battle for recognition.* 3 **do, give,** *or* **join battle.** to start fighting. ◆ VERB 4 (when *intr*, often foll by *against, for,* or *with*) to fight in or as if in military combat; contend (with): *she battled against cancer.* 5 to struggle in order to achieve something or arrive somewhere: *he battled through the crowd.* 6 (*intr*) *Austral* to scrape a living, esp by doing odd jobs.
▷HISTORY C13: from Old French *bataile*, from Late Latin *battālia* exercises performed by soldiers, from *battuere* to beat
▸**'battler** NOUN

Battle ('bætᵊl) NOUN a town in SE England, in East Sussex: site of the Battle of Hastings (1066); medieval abbey. Pop.: 5234 (1991).

battle-axe NOUN 1 (formerly) a large broad-headed axe. 2 *Informal* an argumentative domineering woman.

battle-axe block NOUN *Austral* a block of land behind another, with access from the street through a narrow drive.

battlebus ('bætəlˌbʌs) NOUN the coach that transports politicians and their advisers round the country during an election campaign.

battle cruiser NOUN a warship of battleship size but with lighter armour and fewer guns and capable of high speed.

battle cry NOUN 1 a shout uttered by soldiers going into battle. 2 a slogan used to rally the supporters of a campaign, movement, etc.

battledore ('bætəlˌdɔː) NOUN 1 Also called: **battledore and shuttlecock.** an ancient racket game. 2 a light racket, smaller than a tennis racket, used for striking the shuttlecock in this game. 3 (formerly) a wooden utensil used for beating clothes, in baking, etc.
▷HISTORY C15 *batyldoure*, perhaps from Old Provençal *batedor* a beater, from Old French *battre* to beat, BATTER[1]

battledress ('bætəlˌdrɛs) NOUN the ordinary uniform of a soldier, consisting of tunic and trousers.

battle fatigue NOUN *Psychol* a type of mental disorder, characterized by anxiety, depression, and loss of motivation, caused by the stress of active warfare. Also called: **combat fatigue.** See also **shell shock.**

battlefield ('bætəlˌfiːld) *or* **battleground** ('bætəlˌgraʊnd) NOUN the place where a battle is fought; an area of conflict.

battle line NOUN 1 the line along which troops are positioned for battle. 2 **the battle lines are drawn.** conflict or argument is about to occur between opposing people or groups.

battlement ('bætəlmənt) NOUN a parapet or wall with indentations or embrasures, originally for shooting through.
▷HISTORY C14: from Old French *batailles*, plural of *bataille* BATTLE
▸'**battlemented** ADJECTIVE

Battle of Britain NOUN **the.** from August to October 1940, the prolonged bombing of S England by the German Luftwaffe and the successful resistance by the RAF Fighter Command, which put an end to the German plan of invading Britain.

Battle of the Atlantic NOUN the struggle for control of the sea routes around the United Kingdom during World War II, esp 1940–43.

battlepiece ('bætəlˌpiːs) NOUN a painting, relief, mosaic, etc., depicting a battle, usually commemorating an actual event.

battle royal NOUN 1 a fight, esp with fists or cudgels, involving more than two combatants; melee. 2 a long violent argument.

battleship ('bætəlˌʃɪp) NOUN 1 a heavily armoured warship of the largest type having many large-calibre guns. 2 (formerly) a warship of sufficient size and armament to take her place in the line of battle; ship of the line.

battue (bæ'tuː, -'tjuː; *French* baty) NOUN 1 the beating of woodland or cover to force game to flee in the direction of hunters. 2 **a** an organized shooting party using this method. **b** the game disturbed or shot by this method. 3 indiscriminate slaughter, as of a defenceless crowd.
▷HISTORY C19: from French, feminine of *battu* beaten, from *battre* to beat, from Latin *battuere*

batty ('bætɪ) ADJECTIVE **-tier, -tiest.** *Slang* 1 insane; crazy. 2 odd; eccentric.
▷HISTORY C20: from BAT[2]; compare the phrase *have bats in the belfry*

batty boy *or* **man** NOUN *Chiefly Brit derogatory slang* a male homosexual.
▷HISTORY C20: from Caribbean slang *batty* bottom, buttocks

Batum (bɑː'tuːm) *or* **Batumi** (bɑː'tuːmɪ) NOUN a city in Georgia: capital of the Adzhar Autonomous Republic; a major Black Sea port. Pop.: 137 100 (1997 est.).

batwing ('bætˌwɪŋ) ADJECTIVE shaped like the wings of a bat, as a black tie, collar, etc.

batwing sleeve NOUN a sleeve of a garment with a deep armhole and a tight wrist.

batwoman ('bætwʊmən) NOUN, *plural* **-women.** a female servant in any of the armed forces.

bauble ('bɔːbəl) NOUN 1 a showy toy or trinket of little value; trifle. 2 (formerly) a mock staff of office carried by a court jester.
▷HISTORY C14: from Old French *baubel* plaything, of obscure origin

Bauchi ('baʊtʃɪ) NOUN 1 a state of N Nigeria: formed in 1976 from part of North-Eastern State; tin mining. Capital: Bauchi. Pop.: 4 801 569 (1995 est.). Area: 64 605 sq. km (24 944 sq. miles). 2 a town in N central Nigeria, capital of Bauchi state. Pop.: 76 070 (1991 est.).

bauchle ('bɒxəl) NOUN *Scot* 1 an old worn shoe. 2 a worthless or clumsy person. 3 a useless object. 4 a trout-fisher's term for a **perch**[2].
▷HISTORY C18: of unknown origin

Baucis ('bɔːsɪs) NOUN *Greek myth* a poor peasant woman who, with her husband Philemon, was rewarded for hospitality to the disguised gods Zeus and Hermes.

baud (bɔːd) NOUN a unit used to measure the speed of electronic code transmissions, equal to one unit interval per second.
▷HISTORY C20: named after J. M. E. *Baudot* (1845–1903), French inventor

bauera ('baʊərə) NOUN any small evergreen Australian shrub of the genus *Bauera*, having pink or purple flowers.
▷HISTORY C19: named after Franz (1758–1840) and Ferdinand (1760–1826) *Bauer*, Australian botanical artists

Bauhaus ('baʊˌhaʊs) NOUN **a** a German school of architecture and applied arts founded in 1919 by Walter Gropius on experimental principles of functionalism and truth to materials. After being closed by the Nazis in 1933, its ideas were widely disseminated by its students and staff, including Kandinsky, Klee, Feininger, Moholy-Nagy, and Mies van der Rohe. **b** (*as modifier*): *Bauhaus wallpaper*.
▷HISTORY C20: German, literally: building house

bauhinia (bɔː'hɪnɪə, bəʊ-) NOUN any climbing or shrubby leguminous plant of the genus *Bauhinia*, of tropical and warm regions, widely cultivated for ornament.
▷HISTORY C18: New Latin, named after Jean and Gaspard *Bauhin*, 16th-century French herbalists

baulk (bɔːk; *usually for sense 1* bɔːlk) NOUN 1 Also (US): **balk.** *Billiards* **a** (in billiards) the space, usually 29 inches deep, between the baulk line and the bottom cushion. **b** (in baulk-line games) one of the spaces between the cushions and the baulk lines. **c in baulk.** inside one of these spaces. 2 *Archaeol* a strip of earth left between excavation trenches for the study of the complete stratigraphy of a site. 3 *Croquet* either of two lines (**A baulk** and **B baulk**) at diagonally opposite ends of the court, from which the ball is struck into play. ◆ VERB, NOUN 4 a variant spelling of **balk.**

baulk line *or US* **balk line** NOUN *Billiards* 1 Also called: **string line.** a straight line across a billiard table behind which the cue balls are placed at the start of a game. 2 **a** one of four lines parallel to the cushions dividing the table into a central panel and eight smaller ones (the baulks). **b** a type of game using these lines as restrictions.

Baumé scale (bəʊ'meɪ, 'bəʊmeɪ) NOUN a scale for calibrating hydrometers used for measuring the specific gravity of liquids. 1 degree Baumé is equal to 144.3((*s*–1)/*s*), where *s* is specific gravity.
▷HISTORY C19: named after Antoine *Baumé* (1728–1804), French chemist

Bautzen ('baʊtsən) NOUN a city in E Germany, in Saxony: site of an indecisive battle in 1813 between Napoleon's army and an allied army of Russians and Prussians. Pop.: 52 390 (latest est.).

bauxite ('bɔːksaɪt) NOUN a white, red, yellow, or brown amorphous claylike substance comprising aluminium oxides and hydroxides, often with such impurities as iron oxides. It is the chief ore of aluminium. General formula: $Al_2O_3.nH_2O$.
▷HISTORY C19: from French, from (*Les*) *Baux* in southern France, where it was originally found

Bavaria (bə'vɛərɪə) NOUN a state of S Germany: a former duchy and kingdom; mainly wooded highland, with the Alps in the south. Capital: Munich. Pop.: 12 155 000 (2000 est.). Area: 70 531 sq. km (27 232 sq. miles). German name: **Bayern.**

Bavarian (bə'vɛərɪən) ADJECTIVE 1 of or relating to Bavaria or its inhabitants. ◆ NOUN 2 a native or inhabitant of Bavaria.

Bavarian cream NOUN a cold dessert consisting of a rich custard set with gelatine and flavoured in various ways. Also called: **bavarois** (*French* bavarwa).

bawbee (bɔː'biː) NOUN 1 a former Scottish silver coin. 2 *Scot* an informal word for **halfpenny** (sense 2).
▷HISTORY C16: named after Alexander Orok of *Sillebawby*, master of the mint

bawcock ('bɔːˌkɒk) NOUN *Archaic* a fine fellow.
▷HISTORY C16: from French *beau coq*, from *beau* handsome + *coq* COCK[1]

bawd (bɔːd) NOUN *Archaic* 1 a person who runs a brothel, esp a woman. 2 a prostitute.
▷HISTORY C14: from Old French *baude*, feminine of *baud* merry, of Germanic origin; compare Old High German *bald* BOLD

bawdry ('bɔːdrɪ) NOUN *Archaic* obscene talk or language.

bawdy ('bɔːdɪ) ADJECTIVE **bawdier, bawdiest.** 1 (of language, plays, etc.) containing references to sex, esp to be humorous. ◆ NOUN 2 obscenity or eroticism, esp in writing or drama.
▸'**bawdily** ADVERB ▸'**bawdiness** NOUN

bawdyhouse ('bɔːdɪˌhaʊs) NOUN an archaic word for **brothel.**

bawl (bɔːl) VERB 1 (*intr*) to utter long loud cries, as from pain or frustration; wail. 2 to shout loudly, as in anger. ◆ NOUN 3 a loud shout or cry.
▷HISTORY C15: probably from Icelandic *baula* to low; related to Medieval Latin *baulāre* to bark, Swedish *böla* to low; all of imitative origin
▸'**bawler** NOUN ▸'**bawling** NOUN

bawl out VERB (*tr, adverb*) *Informal* to scold loudly.

bawneen ('bɑːniːn) NOUN *Irish* a variant spelling of **báinín.**

bay[1] (beɪ) NOUN 1 a wide semicircular indentation of a shoreline, esp between two headlands or peninsulas. 2 an extension of lowland into hills that partly surround it. 3 *US* an extension of prairie into woodland.
▷HISTORY C14: from Old French *baie*, perhaps from Old French *baer* to gape, from Medieval Latin *batāre* to yawn

bay[2] (beɪ) NOUN 1 an alcove or recess in a wall. 2 any partly enclosed compartment, as one in which hay is stored in a barn. 3 See **bay window.** 4 an area off a road in which vehicles may park or unload, esp one adjacent to a shop, factory, etc. 5 a compartment in an aircraft, esp one used for a specified purpose: *the bomb bay*. 6 *Nautical* a compartment in the forward part of a ship between decks, often used as the ship's hospital. 7 *Brit* a tracked recess in the platform of a railway station, esp one forming the terminus of a branch line.
▷HISTORY C14: from Old French *baee* gap or recess in a wall, from *baer* to gape; see BAY[1]

bay[3] (beɪ) NOUN 1 a deep howl or growl, esp of a hound on the scent. 2 **at bay. a** (of a person or animal) forced to turn and face attackers: *the dogs held the deer at bay*. **b** at a distance: *to keep a disease at bay*. 3 **bring to bay.** to force into a position from which retreat is impossible. ◆ VERB 4 (*intr*) to howl (at) in deep prolonged tones. 5 (*tr*) to utter in a loud prolonged tone. 6 (*tr*) to drive to or hold at bay.
▷HISTORY C13: from Old French *abaiier* to bark, of imitative origin

bay[4] (beɪ) NOUN 1 Also called: **bay laurel, sweet bay.** a small evergreen Mediterranean laurel, *Laurus nobilis*, with glossy aromatic leaves, used for flavouring in cooking, and small blackish berries. See **laurel** (sense 1). 2 any of various other trees with strongly aromatic leaves used in cooking, esp a member of the genera *Myrica* or *Pimenta*. 3 any of several magnolias. See **sweet bay.** 4 any of certain other trees or shrubs, esp bayberry. 5 (*plural*) a wreath of bay leaves. See **laurel** (sense 6).
▷HISTORY C14: from Old French *baie* laurel berry, from Latin *bāca* berry

bay[5] (beɪ) NOUN 1 **a** a moderate reddish-brown colour. **b** (*as adjective*): *a bay horse*. 2 an animal of this colour, esp a horse.

▷HISTORY C14: from Old French *bai*, from Latin *badius*

bayadere (ˌbaɪəˈdɪə, -ˈdɛə) NOUN 1 a dancing girl, esp one serving in a Hindu temple. 2 a fabric or design with horizontal stripes, esp of a bright colour. ◆ ADJECTIVE 3 (of fabric, etc.) having horizontal stripes.
▷HISTORY C18: via French from Portuguese *bailadeira* dancing girl, from *bailar* to dance, from Latin *ballāre*; see BALL²

Bayamón (*Spanish* bajaˈmon) NOUN a city in NE central Puerto Rico, south of San Juan. Pop.: 203 499 (2000).

Bayard (ˈbeɪəd) NOUN a legendary horse that figures prominently in medieval romance.

bayberry (ˈbeɪbərɪ) *or* **bay** NOUN, *plural* **-ries.** 1 any of several North American aromatic shrubs or small trees of the genus *Myrica*, that bear grey waxy berries: family *Myricaceae*. See also **wax myrtle.** 2 Also called: **bay rum tree.** a tropical American myrtaceous tree, *Pimenta racemosa*, that yields an oil used in making bay rum. 3 the fruit of any of these plants.

Bayern (ˈbaiərn) NOUN the German name for **Bavaria.**

Bayesian (ˈbeɪzɪən) ADJECTIVE (of a theory) presupposing known a priori probabilities which may be subjectively assessed and which can be revised in the light of experience in accordance with Bayes' theorem. A hypothesis is thus confirmed by an experimental observation which is likely given the hypothesis and unlikely without it. Compare **maximum likelihood.**

Bayes' theorem (beɪz) NOUN *Statistics* the fundamental result which expresses the conditional probability $P(E/A)$ of an event E given an event A as $P(A/E).P(E)/P(A)$; more generally, where E_n is one of a set of values E_i which partition the sample space, $P(E_n/A) = P(A/E_n)P(E_n)/\Sigma P(A/E_i)P(E_i)$. This enables prior estimates of probability to be continually revised in the light of observations.
▷HISTORY C20: named after Thomas *Bayes* (1702–61), English mathematician and Presbyterian minister

Bayeux (*French* bajø) NOUN a town in NW France, on the River Aure: its museum houses the Bayeux tapestry and there is a 13th-century cathedral: dairy foods, plastic. Pop.: 14 704 (1990).

Bayeux tapestry NOUN an 11th- or 12th-century tapestry in Bayeux, nearly 70.5 m (231 ft.) long by 50 cm (20 inches) high, depicting the Norman conquest of England.

bay leaf NOUN a leaf, usually dried, of the Mediterranean laurel, *Laurus nobilis*, used in cooking to flavour soups and stews.

bay lynx NOUN another name for **bobcat.**

Bay of Pigs NOUN a bay on the SW coast of Cuba: scene of an unsuccessful invasion of Cuba by US-backed troops (April 17, 1961). Spanish name: **Bahia de los Cochinos.**

bayonet (ˈbeɪənɪt) NOUN 1 a blade that can be attached to the muzzle of a rifle for stabbing in close combat. 2 a type of fastening in which a cylindrical member is inserted into a socket against spring pressure and turned so that pins on its side engage in slots in the socket. ◆ VERB **-nets, -neting, -neted** *or* **-nets, -netting, -netted.** 3 (*tr*) to stab or kill with a bayonet.
▷HISTORY C17: from French *baïonnette*, from BAYONNE where it originated

Bayonne (*French* bajɔn) NOUN a port in SW France: a commercial centre for the Basque region. Pop.: 41 846 (1990).

bayou (ˈbaɪjuː) NOUN (in the southern US) a sluggish marshy tributary of a lake or river.
▷HISTORY C18: from Louisiana French, from Choctaw *bayuk*

Bayreuth (*German* baiˈrɔyt) NOUN a city in E Germany, in NE Bavaria: home and burial place of Richard Wagner; annual festivals of his music. Pop.: 72 780 (1991).

bay rum NOUN 1 an aromatic liquid, used in medicines and cosmetics, originally obtained by distilling the leaves of the bayberry tree (*Pimenta racemosa*) with rum: now also synthesized from alcohol, water, and various oils. 2 **bay rum tree.** another name for **bayberry** (sense 2).

Bay Street NOUN (in Canada) 1 the financial centre of Toronto, in which Canada's largest stock exchange is situated. 2 the financial interests and powers of Toronto.

bay tree NOUN another name for **bay**⁴ (sense 1).

bay window NOUN a window projecting from the wall of a building and forming an alcove of a room. Sometimes shortened to: **bay.** See also **bow window, oriel window.**

baywood (ˈbeɪˌwʊd) NOUN the light soft wood of a tropical American mahogany tree, *Swietenia macrophylla*, of the bay region of SE Mexico.

bazaar *or* **bazar** (bəˈzɑː) NOUN 1 (esp in the Orient) a market area, esp a street of small stalls. 2 a sale in aid of charity, esp of miscellaneous secondhand or handmade articles. 3 a shop where a large variety of goods is sold.
▷HISTORY C16: from Persian *bāzār*, from Old Persian *abēcharish*

bazoo (bəˈzuː) NOUN a US slang word for **mouth.**
▷HISTORY C19: of unknown origin

bazooka (bəˈzuːkə) NOUN a portable tubular rocket-launcher that fires a projectile capable of piercing armour: used by infantrymen as a short-range antitank weapon.
▷HISTORY C20: named after a pipe instrument invented by Bob Burns (1896–1956), American comedian

bb THE INTERNET DOMAIN NAME FOR Barbados.

BB 1 ABBREVIATION FOR Boys' Brigade. 2 (on Brit pencils) ◆ SYMBOL FOR double black: denoting a very soft lead.

B2B ABBREVIATION FOR business to business; denoting trade between commercial organizations rather than between businesses and private customers. ◆ Compare **B2C, B2E.**

BBBC ABBREVIATION FOR British Boxing Board of Control.

BBC ABBREVIATION FOR British Broadcasting Corporation.

BBFC ABBREVIATION FOR British Board of Film Classification.

BBL *Text messaging* ABBREVIATION FOR be back later.

B-boy (ˈbiːˌbɔɪ) NOUN a male rap-music fan, who typically can be identified by his casual style of dress.
▷HISTORY C20: from *Bronx boy*

BBQ ABBREVIATION FOR barbecue.

BBS *Text messaging* ABBREVIATION FOR be back soon.

BBSRC (in Britain) ABBREVIATION FOR Biotechnology and Biological Sciences Research Council.

B bursary NOUN *NZ* the lower of two bursaries available for students entering university, polytechnic, etc. Compare **A bursary.**

BC (*esp in postal addresses*) ABBREVIATION FOR British Columbia.

B2C ABBREVIATION FOR business to consumer: denoting an Internet communication channel between a business and consumers. ◆ Compare **B2B, B2E.**

B.C. *or* **BC** ABBREVIATION FOR (indicating years numbered back from the supposed year of the birth of Christ) before Christ: *in 54* B.C. *Caesar came.* Compare **A.D.**

Language note See at **A.D.**

BCA (in New Zealand) ABBREVIATION FOR Bachelor of Commerce and Administration.

BCAR ABBREVIATION FOR **British Civil Airworthiness Requirements.**

BCC ABBREVIATION FOR British Coal Corporation (formerly the National Coal Board).

BCD ABBREVIATION FOR **binary-coded decimal.**

BCE ABBREVIATION FOR Before Common Era (used, esp by non-Christians, in numbering years B.C.).

B-cell NOUN another name for **B-lymphocyte.**

BCF ABBREVIATION FOR: 1 British Chess Federation. 2 British Cycling Federation.

BCG ABBREVIATION FOR bacille Calmette-Guérin (antituberculosis vaccine).

BCh ABBREVIATION FOR Bachelor of Surgery.
▷HISTORY from Latin *Baccalaureus Chirurgiae*

BCL ABBREVIATION FOR Bachelor of Civil Law.

BCNU *Text messaging* ABBREVIATION FOR be seeing you.

BCNZ ABBREVIATION FOR (the former) Broadcasting Corporation of New Zealand.

BCom ABBREVIATION FOR Bachelor of Commerce.

B complex NOUN short for **vitamin B complex.**

B.C.S. (in the US and Canada) ABBREVIATION FOR Bachelor of Computer Science.

bd¹ ABBREVIATION FOR: 1 board. 2 *Insurance, finance* bond.

bd² THE INTERNET DOMAIN NAME FOR Bangladesh.

BD ABBREVIATION FOR: 1 Bachelor of Divinity. 2 *Commerce* bills discounted. ◆ 3 INTERNATIONAL CAR REGISTRATION FOR Bangladesh.

B/D ABBREVIATION FOR: 1 bank draft. 2 *Commerce* bills discounted. 3 Also: **b/d.** *Book-keeping* brought down.

BDA ABBREVIATION FOR British Dental Association.

Bde *or* **bde** ABBREVIATION FOR brigade.

bdellium (ˈdɛlɪəm) NOUN 1 any of several African or W Asian trees of the burseraceous genus *Commiphora* that yield a gum resin. 2 the aromatic gum resin, similar to myrrh, produced by any of these trees.
▷HISTORY C16: from Latin, from Greek *bdellion*, perhaps from Hebrew *bĕdhōlah*

bdl ABBREVIATION FOR bundle.

bds ABBREVIATION FOR bundles.

BDS 1 ABBREVIATION FOR Bachelor of Dental Surgery. ◆ 2 INTERNATIONAL CAR REGISTRATION FOR Barbados.

be¹ (biː; *unstressed* bɪ) VERB, *present singular 1st person* **am**; *2nd person* **are**; *3rd person* **is,** *present plural* **are,** *past singular 1st person* **was**; *2nd person* **were**; *3rd person* **was,** *past plural* **were,** *present participle* **being,** *past participle* **been.** (*intr*) 1 to have presence in the realm of perceived reality; exist; live: *I think, therefore I am; not all that is can be understood.* 2 (*used in the perfect or past perfect tenses only*) to pay a visit; go: *have you been to Spain?* 3 to take place; occur: *my birthday was last Thursday.* 4 (*copula*) used as a linking verb between the subject of a sentence and its noun or adjective complement or complementing phrase. In this case *be* expresses the relationship of either essential or incidental equivalence or identity (*John is a man; John is a musician*) or specifies an essential or incidental attribute (*honey is sweet; Susan is angry*). It is also used with an adverbial complement to indicate a relationship of location in space or time (*Bill is at the office; the dance is on Saturday*). 5 (*takes a present participle*) forms the progressive present tense: *the man is running.* 6 (*takes a past participle*) forms the passive voice of all transitive verbs and (archaically) certain intransitive ones: *a good film is being shown on television tonight; I am done.* 7 (*takes an infinitive*) expresses intention, expectation, supposition, or obligation: *the president is to arrive at 9.30; you are not to leave before I say so.* 8 (*takes a past participle*) forms the perfect or past perfect tense of certain intransitive verbs of motion, such as **go** or **come**: *the last train is gone.* 9 **be that as it may.** the facts concerning (something) are of no importance.
▷HISTORY Old English *bēon*; related to Old High German *bim* am, Latin *fui* I have been, Greek *phuein* to bring forth, Sanskrit *bhavati* he is

be² THE INTERNET DOMAIN NAME FOR Belgium.

Be THE CHEMICAL SYMBOL FOR beryllium.

Bé ABBREVIATION FOR Baumé.

BE ABBREVIATION FOR: 1 bill of exchange. 2 (in the US) Board of Education. 3 Bachelor of Education. 4 Bachelor of Engineering.

B2E ABBREVIATION FOR business to employee: denoting an Internet communication channel between a company and its employers. ◆ Compare **B2B, B2C.**

be- PREFIX FORMING TRANSITIVE VERBS 1 (*from nouns*) to surround completely; cover on all sides: *befog.* 2 (*from nouns*) to affect completely or excessively: *bedazzle.* 3 (*from nouns*) to consider as or cause to be: *befool; befriend.* 4 (*from nouns*) to provide or cover with: *bejewel.* 5 (*from verbs*) at, for, against, on, or over: *bewail; berate.*
▷HISTORY Old English *be-, bi-*, unstressed variant of *bī* BY

B/E, BE, *or* **b.e.** ABBREVIATION FOR bill of exchange.

BEA (formerly) ABBREVIATION FOR British European Airways.

beach (biːtʃ) NOUN 1 an extensive area of sand or shingle sloping down to a sea or lake, esp the area between the high- and low-water marks on a seacoast. Related adjective: **littoral.** ◆ VERB 2 to run or haul (a boat) onto a beach.
▷HISTORY C16: perhaps related to Old English *bæce* river, BECK[2]

beach ball NOUN a large light brightly coloured ball for playing with on a beach.

beach buggy NOUN a low car, often open and with balloon tyres, for driving on sand. Also called: **dune buggy.**

beachcomber (ˈbiːtʃˌkəʊmə) NOUN 1 a person who searches shore debris for anything of worth, esp a vagrant living on a beach. 2 a long high wave rolling onto a beach.
▸ **ˈbeachˌcombing** NOUN

beach flea NOUN another name for the **sand hopper.**

beachhead (ˈbiːtʃˌhɛd) NOUN *Military* 1 an area on a beach that has been captured from the enemy and on which troops and equipment are landed. 2 the object of an amphibious operation.
▷HISTORY C20: modelled on BRIDGEHEAD

Beach-la-Mar (ˌbiːtʃləˈmɑː) NOUN an English-based creole language spoken in Vanuatu and Fiji, and formerly much more widespread. Also called: **Biche-la-mar.**
▷HISTORY C19: quasi-French, from BÊCHE-DE-MER (trepang, this being a major trading commodity in the SW Pacific; hence the name was applied to the trading language)

beach plum NOUN 1 a rosaceous shrub, *Prunus maritima*, of coastal regions of E North America. 2 its edible plumlike fruit.

Beachy Head (ˈbiːtʃɪ) NOUN a headland in East Sussex, on the English Channel, consisting of chalk cliffs 171 m (570 ft.) high.

beacon (ˈbiːkən) NOUN 1 a signal fire or light on a hill, tower, etc., esp one used formerly as a warning of invasion. 2 a hill on which such fires were lit. 3 a lighthouse, signalling buoy, etc., used to warn or guide ships in dangerous waters. 4 short for **radio beacon.** 5 a radio or other signal marking a flight course in air navigation. 6 short for **Belisha beacon.** 7 a person or thing that serves as a guide, inspiration, or warning. 8 a stone set by a surveyor to mark a corner or line of a site boundary, etc. ◆ VERB 9 to guide or warn. 10 (*intr*) to shine.
▷HISTORY Old English *beacen* sign; related to Old Frisian *bāken*, Old Saxon *bōcan*, Old High German *bouhhan*

beacon school NOUN *Brit* a notably successful school whose methods and practices are brought to the attention of the education service as a whole in order that they may be adopted by other schools.

Beaconsfield (ˈbɛkənzˌfiːld, ˈbiːk-) NOUN a town in SE England, in Buckinghamshire: a residential centre for London. Pop.: 12 292 (1991).

beacon status NOUN *Brit* a ranking awarded by the government to an organization, rendering it eligible for extra funding, and aimed at encouraging organizations to share good practice with each other.

bead (biːd) NOUN 1 a small usually spherical piece of glass, wood, plastic, etc., with a hole through it by means of which it may be strung with others to form a necklace, etc. 2 a small drop of moisture: *a bead of sweat.* 3 a small bubble in or on a liquid. 4 a small metallic knob acting as the sight of a firearm. 5 **draw a bead on.** to aim a rifle or pistol at. 6 Also called: **astragal.** *Architect, furniture* a small convex moulding having a semicircular cross section. 7 *Chem* a small solid globule made by fusing a powdered sample with borax or a similar flux on a platinum wire. The colour of the globule serves as a test for the presence of certain metals (**bead test**). 8 *Metallurgy* a deposit of welding metal on the surface of a metal workpiece, often used to examine the structure of the weld zone. 9 *RC Church* one of the beads of a rosary. 10 **count, say,** *or* **tell one's beads.** to pray with a rosary. ◆ VERB 11 (*tr*) to decorate with beads. 12 to form into beads or drops.
▷HISTORY Old English *bed* prayer; related to Old High German *gibet* prayer
▸ **ˈbeaded** ADJECTIVE

beadblast (ˈbiːdˌblɑːst) NOUN 1 a jet of small glass beads blown from a nozzle under air or steam pressure. ◆ VERB 2 (*tr*) to clean or treat (a surface) with a beadblast.
▸ **ˈbeadˌblaster** NOUN

beading (ˈbiːdɪŋ) NOUN 1 another name for **bead** (sense 6). 2 Also called: **beadwork** (ˈbiːdˌwɜːk). a narrow strip of some material used for edging or ornamentation.

beadle (ˈbiːdᵊl) NOUN 1 (formerly, in the Church of England) a minor parish official who acted as an usher and kept order. 2 (in Scotland) a church official attending on the minister. 3 *Judaism* a synagogue attendant. See also **shammes.** 4 an official in certain British universities and other institutions.
▷HISTORY Old English *bydel*; related to Old High German *butil* bailiff
▸ **ˈbeadleship** NOUN

beadledom (ˈbiːdᵊldəm) NOUN petty officialdom.

beadroll (ˈbiːdˌrəʊl) NOUN *Archaic* a list of persons for whom prayers are to be offered.

bead-ruby NOUN, *plural* **-bies.** a N temperate liliaceous plant with small white bell-shaped flowers and small red berries.

beadsman *or* **bedesman** (ˈbiːdzmən) NOUN, *plural* **-men.** 1 a person who prays for another's soul, esp one paid or fed for doing so. 2 a person kept in an almshouse.

beady (ˈbiːdɪ) ADJECTIVE **beadier, beadiest.** 1 small, round, and glittering: used esp of eyes. 2 resembling or covered with beads.
▸ **ˈbeadily** ADVERB ▸ **ˈbeadiness** NOUN

beady eye NOUN *Informal* keen watchfulness that may be somewhat hostile: *he's got his beady eye on you.*
▸ **ˌbeady-ˈeyed** ADJECTIVE

beagle (ˈbiːgᵊl) NOUN 1 a small sturdy breed of hound, having a smooth dense coat usually of white, tan, and black; often used (esp formerly) for hunting hares. 2 *Archaic* a person who spies on others. ◆ VERB 3 (*intr*) to hunt with beagles, normally on foot.
▷HISTORY C15: of uncertain origin

beak[1] (biːk) NOUN 1 the projecting jaws of a bird, covered with a horny sheath; bill. 2 any beaklike mouthpart in other animals, such as turtles. 3 *Slang* a person's nose, esp one that is large, pointed, or hooked. 4 any projecting part, such as the pouring lip of a bucket. 5 *Architect* the upper surface of a cornice, which slopes out to throw off water. 6 *Chem* the part of a still or retort through which vapour passes to the condenser. 7 *Nautical* another word for **ram** (sense 5).
▷HISTORY C13: from Old French *bec*, from Latin *beccus*, of Gaulish origin
▸ **beaked** (biːkt) ADJECTIVE ▸ **ˈbeakless** ADJECTIVE
▸ **ˈbeakˌlike** ADJECTIVE ▸ **ˈbeaky** ADJECTIVE

beak[2] (biːk) NOUN a Brit slang word for **judge, magistrate, headmaster** or **schoolmaster.**
▷HISTORY C19: originally thieves' jargon

beaker (ˈbiːkə) NOUN 1 a cup usually having a wide mouth: *a plastic beaker.* 2 a cylindrical flat-bottomed container used in laboratories, usually made of glass and having a pouring lip. 3 the amount a beaker holds.
▷HISTORY C14: from Old Norse *bikarr*; related to Old High German *behhāri*, Middle Dutch *bēker* beaker, Greek *bikos* earthenware jug

Beaker folk NOUN a prehistoric people thought to have originated in the Iberian peninsula and spread to central Europe and Britain during the second millennium B.C.
▷HISTORY C20: named after the beakers found among their remains

beaky-nosed ADJECTIVE having a nose that is large, pointed, or hooked.

be-all and end-all NOUN *Informal* 1 the ultimate aim or justification: *to provide help for others is the be-all and end-all of this group.* 2 *Often humorous* a person or thing considered to be beyond improvement.

beam (biːm) NOUN 1 a long thick straight-sided piece of wood, metal, concrete, etc., esp one used as a horizontal structural member. 2 any rigid member or structure that is loaded transversely. 3 the breadth of a ship or boat taken at its widest part, usually amidships. 4 a ray or column of light, as from a beacon. 5 a broad smile. 6 one of the two cylindrical rollers on a loom, one of which holds the warp threads before weaving, the other the finished work. 7 the main stem of a deer's antler from which the smaller branches grow. 8 the central shaft of a plough to which all the main parts are attached. 9 a narrow unidirectional flow of electromagnetic radiation or particles: *a beam of light; an electron beam.* 10 the horizontal centrally pivoted bar in a balance. 11 *Informal* the width of the hips (esp in the phrase **broad in the beam**). 12 **a beam in one's eye.** a fault or grave error greater in oneself than in another person. 13 **off (the) beam. a** not following a radio beam to maintain a course. **b** *Informal* wrong, mistaken, or irrelevant. 14 **on the beam. a** following a radio beam to maintain a course. **b** *Nautical* opposite the beam of a vessel; abeam. **c** *Informal* correct, relevant, or appropriate. ◆ VERB 15 to send out or radiate (rays of light). 16 (*tr*) to divert or aim (a radio signal or broadcast, light, etc.) in a certain direction: *to beam a programme to Tokyo.* 17 (*intr*) to smile broadly with pleasure or satisfaction.
▷HISTORY Old English *beam*; related to Gothic *bagms* tree, Old High German *boum* tree
▸ **beamed** ADJECTIVE ▸ **ˈbeaming** ADJECTIVE, NOUN
▸ **ˈbeamless** ADJECTIVE ▸ **ˈbeamˌlike** ADJECTIVE ▸ **ˈbeamy** ADJECTIVE

beam aerial NOUN an aerial system, such as a Yagi aerial, having directional properties. Also called (esp US): **beam antenna.**

beam compass NOUN an instrument for drawing large circles or arcs, consisting of a horizontal beam along which two vertical legs slide. Also called: **trammel.**

beam-ends PLURAL NOUN 1 the ends of a vessel's beams. 2 **on her beam-ends.** (of a vessel) heeled over through an angle of 90°. 3 **on one's beam-ends. a** out of resources; destitute. **b** desperate.

beam engine NOUN an early type of steam engine, in which a pivoted beam is vibrated by a vertical steam cylinder at one end, so that it transmits motion to the workload, such as a pump, at the other end.

beamer (ˈbiːmə) NOUN *Cricket* a full-pitched ball bowled at the batsman's head.

beam riding NOUN a method of missile guidance in which the missile steers itself along the axis of a conically scanned microwave beam.
▸ **beam rider** NOUN

beam splitter NOUN a system that divides a beam of light, electrons, etc., into two or more paths.

bean (biːn) NOUN 1 any of various leguminous plants of the widely cultivated genus *Phaseolus* producing edible seeds in pods. See **French bean, lima bean, scarlet runner, string bean.** 2 any of several other leguminous plants that bear edible pods or seeds, such as the broad bean and soya bean. 3 any of various other plants whose seeds are produced in pods or podlike fruits. 4 the seed or pod of any of these plants. 5 any of various beanlike seeds, such as coffee. 6 *US and Canadian slang* another word for **head.** 7 **not have a bean.** *Slang* to be without money: *I haven't got a bean.* 8 **full of beans.** *Informal* **a** full of energy and vitality. **b** *US* mistaken; erroneous. 9 **spill the beans.** *Informal* to disclose something confidential. ◆ VERB 10 *Chiefly US and Canadian slang* (*tr*) to hit (a person) on the head.
▷HISTORY Old English *bēan*; related to Old Norse *baun*, Old Frisian *bāne*, Old High German *bōna* bean

beanbag (ˈbiːnˌbæg) NOUN 1 a small cloth bag filled with dried beans and thrown in games. 2 a very large cushion loosely filled with foam rubber or polystyrene granules so that it moulds into a comfortable shape: used as an informal low seat.

beanbag gun NOUN a gun that fires a fabric bag containing lead shot, designed to stun or knock the target to the ground.

bean caper NOUN a shrub, *Zygophyllum fabago*, of E Mediterranean regions, whose flower buds are eaten as a substitute for capers: family *Zygophyllaceae.*

bean-counter NOUN *Informal* an accountant.

bean curd NOUN another name for **tofu.**

beanery (ˈbiːnərɪ) NOUN, *plural* **-eries.** *US informal* a cheap restaurant.

beanfeast (ˈbiːnˌfiːst) NOUN *Brit informal* 1 an annual dinner given by employers to employees. 2 any festive or merry occasion.

beanie *or* **beany** (ˈbiːnɪ) NOUN, *plural* **beanies.** a round close-fitting hat resembling a skullcap.

beano (ˈbiːnəʊ) NOUN, *plural* **beanos.** *Brit slang* a celebration, party, or other enjoyable time.

beanpole (ˈbiːnˌpəʊl) NOUN 1 a tall stick or pole used to support bean plants. 2 *Slang* a tall thin person.

bean sprout NOUN the sprout of a newly germinated mung bean, eaten as a vegetable, esp in Chinese dishes.

beanstalk (ˈbiːnˌstɔːk) NOUN the stem of a bean plant.

bean tree NOUN any of various trees having beanlike pods, such as the catalpa and carob.

bear¹ (bɛə) VERB **bears, bearing, bore, borne.** (*mainly tr*) 1 to support or hold up; sustain. 2 to bring or convey: *to bear gifts.* 3 to take, accept, or assume the responsibility of: *to bear an expense.* 4 (*past participle* **born** in passive use except when foll by *by*) to give birth to: *to bear children.* 5 (*also intr*) to produce by or as if by natural growth: *to bear fruit.* 6 to tolerate or endure: *she couldn't bear him.* 7 to admit of; sustain: *his story does not bear scrutiny.* 8 to hold in the conscious mind or in one's feelings: *to bear a grudge; I'll bear that idea in mind.* 9 to show or be marked with: *he still bears the scars.* 10 to transmit or spread: *to bear gossip.* 11 to render or supply (esp. in the phrase **bear witness**). 12 to conduct or manage (oneself, the body, etc.): *she bore her head high.* 13 to have, be, or stand in (relation or comparison): *his account bears no relation to the facts.* 14 (*intr*) to move, be located, or lie in a specified direction: *the way bears east.* 15 to have by right; be entitled to (esp. in the phrase **bear title**). 16 **bear a hand.** to give assistance. 17 **bring to bear.** to bring into operation or effect: *he brought his knowledge to bear on the situation.* ◆ See also **bear down, bear off, bear on, bear out, bear up, bear with, born.**
▷HISTORY Old English *beran*; related to Old Norse *bera*, Old High German *beran* to carry, Latin *ferre*, Greek *pherein* to bear, Sanskrit *bharati* he carries

bear² (bɛə) NOUN, *plural* **bears** *or* **bear.** 1 any plantigrade mammal of the family *Ursidae*: order *Carnivora* (carnivores). Bears are typically massive omnivorous animals with a large head, a long shaggy coat, and strong claws. See also **black bear, brown bear, polar bear.** Related adjective: **ursine.** 2 any of various bearlike animals, such as the koala and the ant bear. 3 a clumsy, churlish, or ill-mannered person. 4 a teddy bear. 5 *Stock Exchange* **a** a speculator who sells in anticipation of falling prices to make a profit on repurchase. **b** (*as modifier*): *a bear market.* Compare **bull**¹ (sense 5). ◆ VERB **bears, bearing, beared.** 6 (*tr*) to lower or attempt to lower the price or prices of (a stock market or a security) by speculative selling.
▷HISTORY Old English *bera*; related to Old Norse *bjorn*, Old High German *bero*

Bear (bɛə) NOUN **the.** 1 the English name for either **Ursa Major** (**Great Bear**) or **Ursa Minor** (**Little Bear**). 2 an informal name for **Russia.**

bearable (ˈbɛərəbᵊl) ADJECTIVE endurable; tolerable.
▸ˈ**bearably** ADVERB

bear-baiting NOUN (formerly) an entertainment in which dogs attacked and enraged a chained bear.

bearberry (ˈbɛəbərɪ) NOUN, *plural* **-ries.** 1 a trailing evergreen ericaceous shrub, *Arctostaphylos uva-ursi*, with small pinkish-white flowers, red berries, and astringent leaves. 2 **alpine** *or* **black bearberry.** a related species, *A. alpina* of European mountains, having black berries.

bearcat (ˈbɛəˌkæt) NOUN another name for **lesser panda.** ◆ See **panda** (sense 2).

beard (bɪəd) NOUN 1 the hair growing on the lower parts of a man's face. 2 any similar growth in animals. 3 a tuft of long hairs in plants such as barley and wheat; awn. 4 the gills of an oyster. 5 a barb, as on an arrow or fish-hook. 6 *Slang* a woman who accompanies a homosexual man to give the impression that he is heterosexual. 7 *Printing* the part of a piece of type that connects the face with the shoulder. ◆ VERB (*tr*) 8 to oppose boldly or impertinently. 9 to pull or grasp the beard of.
▷HISTORY Old English *beard*; related to Old Norse *barth*, Old High German *bart*, Latin *barba*
▸ˈ**bearded** ADJECTIVE

bearded collie NOUN a medium-sized breed of dog having a profuse long straight coat, usually grey or fawn and often with white on the head, legs, and chest, a long tail, and a distinctive beard.

bearded dragon NOUN 1 a large Australian lizard, *Amphibolurus barbatus*, with an erectile frill around the neck. Also called: **bearded lizard, jew lizard.** 2 another name for **frill-necked lizard.**

bearded tit NOUN another name for **reedling.**

bearded vulture NOUN another name for **lammergeier.**

beardless (ˈbɪədlɪs) ADJECTIVE 1 without a beard. 2 too young to grow a beard; immature.
▸ˈ**beardlessness** NOUN

bear down VERB (*intr, adverb*; often foll by *on* or *upon*) 1 to press or weigh down. 2 to approach in a determined or threatening manner. 3 (of a vessel) to make an approach (to another vessel, obstacle, etc.) from windward. 4 (of a woman during childbirth) to exert a voluntary muscular pressure to assist delivery.

beard-stroking NOUN 1 deep thought: *the response involved much beard-stroking.* ◆ ADJECTIVE 2 boringly intellectual: *a beard-stroking bore.*

bearer (ˈbɛərə) NOUN 1 a person or thing that bears, presents, or upholds. 2 a person who presents a note or bill for payment. 3 (formerly, in Africa, India, etc.) **a** a native carrier, esp on an expedition. **b** a native servant. 4 See **pallbearer.** 5 the holder of a rank, position, office, etc. 6 (*modifier*) *Finance* payable to the person in possession: *bearer bonds.*

bear garden NOUN 1 (formerly) a place where bears were exhibited and where bear-baiting took place. 2 a place or scene of tumult and disorder.

bear hug NOUN 1 a wrestling hold in which the arms are locked tightly round an opponent's chest and arms. 2 any similar tight embrace. 3 *Commerce* an approach to the board of one company by another to indicate that an offer is to be made for their shares.

bearing (ˈbɛərɪŋ) NOUN 1 a support, guide, or locating piece for a rotating or reciprocating mechanical part. 2 (foll by *on* or *upon*) relevance (to): *it has no bearing on this problem.* 3 a person's general social conduct, esp in manners, dress, and behaviour. 4 **a** the act, period, or capability of producing fruit or young. **b** an amount produced; yield. 5 the part of a beam or lintel that rests on a support. 6 anything that carries weight or acts as a support. 7 the angular direction of a line, point, or course measured from true north or south (**true bearing**), magnetic north or south (**magnetic bearing**), or one's own position. 8 (*usually plural*) the position or direction, as of a ship, fixed with reference to two or more known points. 9 (*usually plural*) a sense of one's relative position or situation; orientation (esp in the phrases **lose, get,** *or* **take one's bearings**). 10 *Heraldry* **a** a device or emblem on a heraldic shield; charge. **b** another name for **coat of arms.**

bearing pedestal NOUN an independent support for a bearing, usually incorporating a bearing housing.

bearing pile NOUN a foundation pile that supports weight vertically. Compare **sheet pile.**

bearing rein NOUN *Chiefly Brit* a rein from the bit to the saddle, designed to keep the horse's head in the desired position. Usual US word: **checkrein.**

bearish (ˈbɛərɪʃ) ADJECTIVE 1 like a bear; rough; clumsy; churlish. 2 *Stock Exchange* causing, expecting, or characterized by a fall in prices: *a bearish market.*
▸ˈ**bearishly** ADVERB ▸ˈ**bearishness** NOUN

Béarnaise (ˌbeɪəˈneɪz) NOUN a rich sauce made from egg yolks, lemon juice or wine vinegar, butter, shallots, herbs, and seasoning.
▷HISTORY C19: French, from *Béarn* in SW France

bear off VERB (*adverb*) *Nautical* (of a vessel) to avoid hitting an obstacle, another vessel, etc., by swerving onto a different course.

bear on VERB (*intr, preposition*) 1 to be relevant to; relate to. 2 to be burdensome to or afflict: *his misdeeds bore heavily on his conscience.*

bear out VERB (*tr, adverb*) to show to be true or truthful; confirm: *the witness will bear me out.*

bear paw NOUN *Canadian* a type of small round snowshoe.

bear raid NOUN an attempt to force down the price of a security or commodity by sustained selling.

bear's-breech *or* **bear's-breeches** NOUN a widely cultivated S European acanthus plant, *Acanthus mollis*, having whitish purple-veined flowers.

bear's-ear NOUN another name for **auricula** (sense 1).

bear's-foot NOUN either of two Eurasian hellebore plants, *Helleborus foetidus* or *H. viridis*, having leaves shaped like the foot and claws of a bear.

bearskin (ˈbɛəˌskɪn) NOUN 1 the pelt of a bear, esp when used as a rug. 2 a tall helmet of black fur worn by certain regiments in the British Army. 3 a rough shaggy woollen cloth, used for overcoats.

bear up VERB (*intr, adverb*) to endure cheerfully.

bear with VERB (*intr, preposition*) to be patient with: *bear with me while I tell you my story.*

bearwood (ˈbɛəˌwʊd) NOUN another name for **cascara** (sense 2).

beast (biːst) NOUN 1 any animal other than man, esp a large wild quadruped. 2 savage nature or characteristics: *the beast in man.* 3 a brutal, uncivilized, or filthy person.
▷HISTORY C13: from Old French *beste*, from Latin *bestia*, of obscure origin

beastie (ˈbiːstɪ) NOUN 1 *Scot* a small animal. 2 *Informal* an insect.

beastings (ˈbiːstɪŋz) NOUN a US spelling of **beestings.**

beastly (ˈbiːstlɪ) ADJECTIVE **-lier, -liest.** 1 *Informal* unpleasant; disagreeable; nasty: *beastly weather.* 2 *Obsolete* of or like a beast; bestial. ◆ ADVERB 3 *Informal* (intensifier): *the weather is so beastly hot.*
▸ˈ**beastliness** NOUN

beast of burden NOUN an animal, such as a donkey or ox, used for carrying loads.

beast of prey NOUN any animal that hunts other animals for food.

beastoid (ˈbiːstɔɪd) NOUN an autonomous robot which can perform some of the tasks of animals.
▷HISTORY C20: from BEAST and ANDROID

beat (biːt) VERB **beats, beating, beat; beaten** *or* **beat.** 1 (when *intr*, often foll by *against, on*, etc) to strike with or as if with a series of violent blows; dash or pound repeatedly (against). 2 (*tr*) to punish by striking; flog. 3 to move or cause to move up and down; flap: *the bird beat its wings heavily.* 4 (*intr*) to throb rhythmically; pulsate: *her heart beat fast.* 5 (*tr*) to make (one's way) by or as if by blows: *she beat her way out of the crowd.* 6 (*tr*; sometimes foll by *up*) *Cookery* to stir or whisk (an ingredient or mixture) vigorously. 7 (*tr*; sometimes foll by *out*) to shape, make thin, or flatten (a piece of metal) by repeated blows. 8 (*tr*) *Music* to indicate (time) by the motion of one's hand, baton, etc., or by the action of a metronome. 9 (when *tr*, sometimes foll by *out*) to produce (a sound or signal) by or as if by striking a drum. 10 to sound or cause to sound, by or as if by beating: *beat the drums!* 11 to overcome (an opponent) in a contest, battle, etc. 12 (*tr*; often foll by *back, down, off* etc.) to drive, push, or thrust. 13 (*tr*) to arrive or finish before (someone or something);anticipate or forestall: *they set off early to beat the rush hour.* 14 (*tr*) to form (a path or track) by repeatedly walking or riding over it. 15 to scour (woodlands, coverts, or undergrowth) so as to rouse game for shooting. 16 (*tr*) *Slang* to puzzle or baffle: *it beats me how he can do that.* 17 (*intr*) *Physics* (of sounds or electrical signals) to combine and produce a pulsating sound or signal. 18 (*intr*) *Nautical* to steer a sailing vessel as close as possible to the direction from which the wind is blowing. 19 (*tr*) *Slang, chiefly US* to cheat or defraud: *he beat his brother out of the inheritance.* 20 **beat about the bush.** to avoid the point at issue; prevaricate. 21 **beat a retreat.** to withdraw or depart in haste. 22 **beat it.** *Slang* (*often imperative*) to go away. 23 **beat one's breast.** See **breast** (sense 10). 24 **beat someone's brains**

out. *Slang* to kill by knocking severely about the head. 25 **beat someone to it.** *Informal* to reach a place or achieve an objective before someone else. 26 **beat the bounds.** *Brit* (formerly) to define the boundaries of a parish by making a procession around them and hitting the ground with rods. 27 **can you beat it** *or* **that?** *Slang* an expression of utter amazement or surprise. ◆ NOUN 28 a stroke or blow. 29 the sound made by a stroke or blow. 30 a regular sound or stroke; throb. 31 **a** an assigned or habitual round or route, as of a policeman or sentry. **b** (*as modifier*): *beat police officers*. 32 the basic rhythmic unit in a piece of music, usually grouped in twos, threes, or fours. 33 **a** pop or rock music characterized by a heavy rhythmic beat. **b** (*as modifier*): *a beat group*. 34 *Physics* the low regular frequency produced by combining two sounds or electrical signals that have similar frequencies. 35 *Horology* the impulse given to the balance wheel by the action of the escapement. 36 *Prosody* the accent, stress, or ictus in a metrical foot. 37 *Nautical* a course that steers a sailing vessel as close as possible to the direction from which the wind is blowing. 38 **a** the act of scouring for game by beating. **b** the organized scouring of a particular woodland so as to rouse the game in it. **c** the woodland where game is so roused. 39 short for **beatnik.** 40 *Fencing* a sharp tap with one's blade on an opponent's blade to deflect it. 41 (*modifier, often capital*) of, characterized by, or relating to the Beat Generation: *a beat poet; beat philosophy*. ◆ ADJECTIVE 42 (*postpositive*) *Slang* totally exhausted. See also **beat down, beat up.**
▷HISTORY Old English *bēatan*; related to Old Norse *bauta*, Old High German *bōzan*
▸ ˈ**beatable** ADJECTIVE

beatbox (ˈbiːtˌbɒks) NOUN *Informal* a drum machine.

beat down VERB (*adverb*) 1 (*tr*) *Informal* to force or persuade (a seller) to accept a lower price: *I beat him down three pounds*. 2 (*intr*) (of the sun) to shine intensely; be very hot.

beaten (ˈbiːtᵊn) ADJECTIVE 1 defeated or baffled. 2 shaped or made thin by hammering: *a bowl of beaten gold*. 3 much travelled; well trodden (esp in the phrase **the beaten track**). 4 **off the beaten track. a** in or into unfamiliar territory. **b** out of the ordinary; unusual. 5 (of food) mixed by beating; whipped. 6 tired out; exhausted. 7 *Hunting* (of woods, undergrowth, etc.) scoured so as to rouse game.

beater (ˈbiːtə) NOUN 1 a person who beats or hammers: *a panel beater*. 2 an instrument or device used for beating: *a carpet beater*. 3 a person who rouses wild game from woodland, undergrowth, etc.

Beat Generation NOUN (*functioning as singular or plural*) 1 members of the generation that came to maturity in the 1950s, whose rejection of the social and political systems of the West was expressed through contempt for regular work, possessions, traditional dress, etc., and espousal of anarchism, communal living, drugs, etc. 2 a group of US writers, notably Jack Kerouac, Allen Ginsberg, and William Burroughs, who emerged in the 1950s.

beatific (ˌbiːəˈtɪfɪk) ADJECTIVE 1 displaying great happiness, calmness, etc: *a beatific smile*. 2 of, conferring, or relating to a state of celestial happiness.
▷HISTORY C17: from Late Latin *beātificus*, from Latin *beātus*, from *beāre* to bless + *facere* to make
▸ ˌ**beaˈtifically** ADVERB

beatify (bɪˈætɪˌfaɪ) VERB **-fies, -fying, -fied.** 1 (*tr*) *RC Church* (of the pope) to declare formally that (a deceased person) showed a heroic degree of holiness in his or her life and therefore is worthy of public veneration: the first step towards canonization. 2 (*tr*) to make extremely happy.
▷HISTORY C16: from Old French *beatifier*, from Late Latin *beātificāre* to make blessed; see BEATIFIC
▸ **beatification** (bɪˌætɪfɪˈkeɪʃən) NOUN

beating (ˈbiːtɪŋ) NOUN 1 a whipping or thrashing, as in punishment. 2 a defeat or setback. 3 **take some** *or* **a lot of beating.** to be difficult to improve upon.

beatitude (bɪˈætɪˌtjuːd) NOUN 1 supreme blessedness or happiness. 2 an honorific title of the Eastern Christian Church, applied to those of patriarchal rank.
▷HISTORY C15: from Latin *beātitūdō*, from *beātus* blessed; see BEATIFIC

Beatitude (bɪˈætɪˌtjuːd) NOUN *New Testament* any of eight distinctive sayings of Jesus in the Sermon on the Mount (Matthew 5:3–11) in which he declares that the poor, the meek, those that mourn, the merciful, the peacemakers, the pure of heart, those that thirst for justice, and those that are persecuted will, in various ways, receive the blessings of heaven.

beatnik (ˈbiːtnɪk) NOUN 1 a member of the Beat Generation (sense 1). 2 *Informal* any person with long hair and shabby clothes.
▷HISTORY C20: from BEAT (n) + -NIK, by analogy with SPUTNIK

beat up *Informal* ◆ VERB 1 (*tr, adverb*) to strike or kick (a person), usually repeatedly, so as to inflict severe physical damage. 2 **beat oneself up.** *Informal* to reproach oneself. ◆ ADJECTIVE **beat-up.** 3 worn-out; dilapidated.

beaty (ˈbiːtɪ) ADJECTIVE *Informal* (of music) having a strong rhythm: *funky, beaty rock tracks*.

beau (bəʊ) NOUN, *plural* **beaux** (bəʊ, bəʊz) *or* **beaus** (bəʊz). 1 a lover, sweetheart, or escort of a girl or woman. 2 a man who is greatly concerned with his clothes and appearance; dandy.
▷HISTORY C17: from French, from Old French *biau*, from Latin *bellus* handsome, charming

Beaufort scale NOUN *Meteorol* an international scale of wind velocities ranging for practical purposes from 0 (calm) to 12 (hurricane force). In the US an extension of the scale, from 13 to 17 for winds over 64 knots, is used.
▷HISTORY C19: after Sir Francis *Beaufort* (1774–1857), British admiral and hydrographer who devised it

Beaufort Sea NOUN part of the Arctic Ocean off the N coast of North America.

beau geste *French* (bo ʒɛst) NOUN, *plural* ***beaux gestes*** (bo ʒɛst). a noble or gracious gesture or act, esp one that is meaningless.
▷HISTORY literally: beautiful gesture

beau idéal *French* (bo ideal) NOUN, *plural* ***beaux idéals*** (boz ideal). perfect beauty or excellence.
▷HISTORY literally: ideal beauty

beaujolais (ˈbəʊʒəˌleɪ) NOUN (*sometimes capital*) a popular fresh-tasting red or white wine from southern Burgundy in France.

Beaulieu (ˈbjuːlɪ) NOUN a village in S England, in Hampshire: site of Palace House, seat of Lord Montagu and once the gatehouse of the ruined 13th-century abbey; the National Motor Museum is in its grounds. Pop.: 1200 (latest est.).

Beaumaris (bəʊˈmærɪs) NOUN a resort in N Wales, on the island of Anglesey: 13th-century castle. Pop.: 1561 (1991).

beau monde (ˈbəʊ ˈmɒnd; *French* bo mɔ̃d) NOUN the world of fashion and society.
▷HISTORY C18: French, literally: fine world

Beaumont (ˈbəʊmɒnt) NOUN a city in SE Texas. Pop.: 113 866 (2000).

Beaune (bəʊn) NOUN 1 a city in E France, near Dijon: an important trading centre for Burgundy wines. Pop.: 22 170 (1990). 2 a wine produced in this district.

beaut (bjuːt) *Slang, chiefly Austral and NZ* ◆ NOUN 1 a person or thing that is outstanding or distinctive. 2 a kind, friendly, or trustworthy person. ◆ ADJECTIVE 3 good or excellent. ◆ INTERJECTION 4 Also: **you beaut!** an exclamation of joy or pleasure.

beauteous (ˈbjuːtɪəs) ADJECTIVE a poetic word for **beautiful.**
▸ ˈ**beauteously** ADVERB ▸ ˈ**beauteousness** NOUN

beautician (bjuːˈtɪʃən) NOUN a person who works in or manages a beauty salon.

beautiful (ˈbjuːtɪfʊl) ADJECTIVE 1 possessing beauty; aesthetically pleasing. 2 highly enjoyable; very pleasant: *the party was beautiful*.
▸ ˈ**beautifulness** NOUN

beautifully (ˈbjuːtɪflɪ) ADVERB 1 in a beautiful manner. 2 *Informal* (intensifier): *you did beautifully well in the race*.

beautiful people PLURAL NOUN (*sometimes capitals*; preceded by *the*) rich, fashionable people in international high society.

beautify (ˈbjuːtɪˌfaɪ) VERB **-fies, -fying, -fied.** to make or become beautiful.
▸ **beautification** (ˌbjuːtɪfɪˈkeɪʃən) NOUN ▸ ˈ**beautiˌfier** NOUN

beauty (ˈbjuːtɪ) NOUN, *plural* **-ties.** 1 the combination of all the qualities of a person or thing that delight the senses and please the mind. 2 a very attractive and well-formed girl or woman. 3 *Informal* an outstanding example of its kind: *the horse is a beauty*. 4 *Informal* an advantageous feature: *one beauty of the job is the short hours*. 5 *Informal, old-fashioned* a light-hearted and affectionate term of address: *hello, my old beauty!* ◆ INTERJECTION 6 (*NZ* ˈbjuːdɪ) an expression of approval or agreement. Also (Scot, Austral, and NZ): **you beauty.**
▷HISTORY C13: from Old French *biauté*, from *biau* beautiful; see BEAU

beauty contest NOUN 1 a competition in which the participants, usually women, are judged on their attractiveness, with a prize, and often a title, awarded to the winner. 2 *Informal* any contest decided on the basis of superficial attractiveness, popularity, etc: *the referendum might turn into a party political beauty contest*.

beauty queen NOUN an attractive young woman, esp one who has won a beauty contest.

beauty salon *or* **parlour** NOUN an establishment providing women with services to improve their beauty, such as hairdressing, manicuring, facial treatment, and massage.

beauty sleep NOUN *Informal* sleep, esp sleep before midnight.

beauty spot NOUN 1 a place of outstanding beauty. 2 a small dark-coloured patch or spot worn on a lady's face as an adornment or as a foil to her complexion. 3 a mole or other similar natural mark on the skin.

beauty therapist NOUN a person whose job is to carry out treatments to improve a person's appearance, such as facials, manicures, removal of unwanted hair, etc.

Beauvais (*French* bovɛ) NOUN a market town in N France, 64 km (40 miles) northwest of Paris. Pop.: 56 280 (1990).

beaux (bəʊ, bəʊz) NOUN a plural of **beau.**

beaux-arts (bəʊˈzɑː) PLURAL NOUN 1 another word for **fine art.** 2 (*modifier*) relating to the classical decorative style, esp that of the École des Beaux-Arts in Paris: *beaux-arts influences*.
▷HISTORY C19: French, literally: fine arts

beaver¹ (ˈbiːvə) NOUN 1 a large amphibious rodent, *Castor fiber*, of Europe, Asia, and North America: family *Castoridae*. It has soft brown fur, a broad flat hairless tail, and webbed hind feet, and constructs complex dams and houses (lodges) in rivers. 2 the fur of this animal. 3 **mountain beaver.** a burrowing rodent, *Aplodontia rufa*, of W North America: family *Aplodontidae*. 4 a tall hat of beaver fur or a fabric resembling it, worn, esp by men, during the 19th century. 5 a woollen napped cloth resembling beaver fur, formerly much used for overcoats, etc. 6 a greyish- or yellowish-brown. 7 *Obsolete* a full beard. 8 a bearded man. 9 (*modifier*) having the colour of beaver or made of beaver fur or some similar material: *a beaver lamb coat; a beaver stole*. ◆ VERB 10 (*intr*; usually foll by *away*) to work industriously or steadily.
▷HISTORY Old English *beofor*; compare Old Norse *biōrr*, Old High German *bibar*, Latin *fiber*, Sanskrit *babhrú* red-brown

beaver² (ˈbiːvə) NOUN a movable piece on a medieval helmet used to protect the lower part of the face.
▷HISTORY C15: from Old French *baviere*, from *baver* to dribble

Beaver (ˈbiːvə) NOUN a member of a **Beaver Colony,** the youngest group of boys (aged 6–8 years) in the Scout Association.

beaverboard (ˈbiːvəˌbɔːd) NOUN a stiff light board of compressed wood fibre, used esp to surface partitions.

beaver fever NOUN *Canadian* an infectious disease caused by drinking water that has been contaminated by wildlife.

Beaver Tail NOUN *Trademark* a flat oval doughnut served fried and sugared.

bebeerine (bəˈbɪəriːn, -rɪn) NOUN an alkaloid, resembling quinine, obtained from the bark of the greenheart and other plants.
▷HISTORY C19: from German *Bebeerin*; see BEBEERU, -INE^2

bebeeru (bəˈbɪəruː) NOUN another name for **greenheart** (sense 1).
▷HISTORY C19: from Spanish *bibirú*, of Carib origin

Bebington (ˈbɛbɪŋtən) NOUN a town in NW England, in Wirral unitary authority, Merseyside: docks and chemical works. Pop.: 60 148 (1991).

bebop (ˈbiːbɒp) NOUN the full name for **bop^1** (sense 1).
▷HISTORY C20: imitative of the rhythm of the music
▸ **ˈbebopper** NOUN

becalmed (bɪˈkɑːmd) ADJECTIVE (of a sailing boat or ship) motionless through lack of wind.

became (bɪˈkeɪm) VERB the past tense of **become**.

because (bɪˈkɒz, -ˈkəz) CONJUNCTION 1 (*subordinating*) on account of the fact that; on account of being; since: *because it's so cold we'll go home*. 2 **because of.** (*preposition*) on account of: *I lost my job because of her*.
▷HISTORY C14 *bi cause*, from *bi* BY + CAUSE

> **Language note** See at **reason**.

beccafico (ˌbɛkəˈfiːkəʊ) NOUN, *plural* **-cos**. any of various European songbirds, esp warblers of the genus *Sylvia*, eaten as a delicacy in Italy and other countries.
▷HISTORY C17: from Italian, from *beccare* to peck + *fico* fig, from Latin *ficus*

béchamel sauce (ˌbeɪʃəˈmɛl) NOUN a thick white sauce flavoured with onion and seasonings.
▷HISTORY C18: named after the Marquis of *Béchamel*, steward of Louis XIV of France and its creator

bechance (bɪˈtʃɑːns) VERB (*intr*) *Archaic* to happen (to).

Béchar (*French* beʃar) NOUN a city in NW Algeria: an oasis. Pop.: 131 010 (1998). Former name: **Colomb-Béchar**.

bêche-de-mer (ˌbeɪʃdəˈmɛə) NOUN, *plural* **bêches-de-mer** (ˌbeɪʃdəˈmɛə) *or* **bêche-de-mer**. 1 another name for **trepang**. 2 See **Beach-la-Mar**.
▷HISTORY C19: quasi-French, from earlier English *biche de mer*, from Portuguese *bicho do mar* worm of the sea

Bechuana (bɛˈtʃwɑːnə, ˌbɛtʃʊˈɑːnə, ˌbɛkjʊ-) NOUN, *plural* **-na** *or* **-nas**. 1 a former name for **Tswana**. 2 a former name for a member of the Bantu people of Botswana.

Bechuanaland (bɛˈtʃwɑːnəˌlænd, ˌbɛtʃʊˈɑːnəˌlænd, ˌbɛkjʊ-) NOUN the former name (until 1966) of **Botswana**.

beck^1 (bɛk) NOUN 1 a nod, wave, or other gesture or signal. 2 **at (someone's) beck and call.** ready to obey (someone's) orders instantly; subject to (someone's) slightest whim.
▷HISTORY C14: short for *becnen* to BECKON

beck^2 (bɛk) NOUN (in N England) a stream, esp a swiftly flowing one.
▷HISTORY Old English *becc*, from Old Norse *bekkr*; related to Old English *bece*, Old Saxon *beki*, Old High German *bah* brook, Sanskrit *bhanga* wave

becket (ˈbɛkɪt) NOUN *Nautical* 1 a clevis forming part of one end of a sheave, used for securing standing lines by means of a thimble. 2 a short line with a grommet or eye at one end and a knot at the other, used for securing spars or other gear in place.
▷HISTORY C18: of unknown origin

becket bend NOUN another name for **sheet bend**.

beckon (ˈbɛkən) VERB 1 to summon with a gesture of the hand or head. 2 to entice or lure. ◆ NOUN 3 a summoning gesture.
▷HISTORY Old English *bīecnan*, from *bēacen* sign; related to Old Saxon *bōknian*; see BEACON
▸ **ˈbeckoner** NOUN ▸ **ˈbeckoning** ADJECTIVE, NOUN

becloud (bɪˈklaʊd) VERB (*tr*) 1 to cover or obscure with a cloud. 2 to confuse or muddle: *to becloud the issues*.

become (bɪˈkʌm) VERB **-comes, -coming, -came, -come.** (*mainly intr*) 1 (*copula*) to come to be; develop or grow into: *he became a monster*. 2 (foll by *of; usually used in a question*) to fall to or be the lot (of); happen (to): *what became of him?* 3 (*tr*) (of clothes, etc.) to enhance the appearance of (someone); suit: *that dress becomes you*. 4 (*tr*) to be appropriate; befit: *it ill becomes you to complain*.
▷HISTORY Old English *becuman* to happen; related to Old High German *biqueman* to come to, Gothic *biquiman* to appear suddenly

becoming (bɪˈkʌmɪŋ) ADJECTIVE 1 suitable; appropriate. ◆ NOUN 2 any process of change. 3 (in the philosophy of Aristotle) any change from the lower level of potentiality to the higher level of actuality.
▸ **beˈcomingly** ADVERB ▸ **beˈcomingness** NOUN

becquerel (ˌbɛkəˈrɛl) NOUN the derived SI unit of radioactivity equal to one disintegration per second. Symbol: Bq.
▷HISTORY C20: named after Antoine Henri Becquerel (1852–1908), French physicist

BECTU (ˈbɛktuː) (in Britain) NOUN ABBREVIATION OR ACRONYM FOR Broadcasting, Entertainment, Cinematograph and Theatre Union.

bed (bɛd) NOUN 1 a piece of furniture on which to sleep. 2 the mattress and bedclothes on such a piece of furniture: *an unmade bed*. 3 sleep or rest: *time for bed*. 4 any place in which a person or animal sleeps or rests. 5 *Med* a unit of potential occupancy in a hospital or residential institution. 6 *Informal* a place for sexual intercourse. 7 *Informal* sexual intercourse. 8 a plot of ground in which plants are grown, esp when considered together with the plants in it: *a flower bed*. 9 the bottom of a river, lake, or sea. 10 a part of this used for cultivation of a plant or animal: *oyster beds*. 11 a layer of crushed rock, gravel, etc., used as a foundation for a road, railway, etc. 12 a layer of mortar in a masonry wall. 13 the underside of a brick, tile, slate, etc., when in position. Compare **back^1** (sense 12). 14 any underlying structure or part. 15 a layer of rock, esp sedimentary rock. 16 the flat part of a letterpress printing press onto or against which the type forme is placed. 17 a layer of solid particles of an absorbent, catalyst, or reagent through which a fluid is passed during the course of a chemical reaction or other process. 18 a machine base on which a moving part carrying a tool or workpiece slides: *lathe bed*. 19 **a bed of roses.** a situation of comfort or ease. 20 **to be brought to bed (of).** *Archaic* to give birth (to). 21 **bed of nails. a** a situation or position of extreme difficulty. **b** a bed studded with nails on which a fakir lies. 22 **get out of bed on the wrong side.** *Informal* to be ill-tempered from the start of the day. 23 **go to bed. a** (often foll by *with*) to have sexual intercourse (with). **b** *Journalism, printing* (of a newspaper, magazine, etc.) to go to press; start printing. 24 **put to bed. a** *Journalism* to finalize work on (a newspaper, magazine, etc.) so that it is ready to go to press. **b** *Printing* to lock up the type forme of (a publication) in the press before printing. 25 **take to one's bed.** to remain in bed, esp because of illness. ◆ VERB **beds, bedding, bedded.** 26 (usually foll by *down*) to go to or put into a place to sleep or rest. 27 (*tr*) to have sexual intercourse with. 28 (*tr*) to place, fix, or sink firmly into position; embed. 29 *Geology* to form or be arranged in a distinct layer; stratify. 30 (*tr*; often foll by *out*) to plant in a bed of soil. See also **bed in**.
▷HISTORY Old English *bedd*; related to Old Norse *bethr*, Old High German *betti*, Gothic *badi*

BEd ABBREVIATION FOR Bachelor of Education.

bed and board NOUN 1 sleeping accommodation and meals. 2 **divorce from bed and board.** *US law* a form of divorce whereby the parties are prohibited from living together but the marriage is not dissolved.

bed and breakfast *Chiefly Brit* ◆ NOUN 1 (in a hotel, boarding house, etc.) overnight accommodation and breakfast. ◆ ADJECTIVE 2 (of a stock-exchange transaction) establishing a loss for tax purposes, shares being sold after hours one evening and bought back the next morning when the market opens.

bed and PEP ADJECTIVE *Brit* (of a stock-exchange transaction) complying with regulations for self-select PEPs, a shareholding being sold in the evening and bought back the next morning for the shareholder's own PEP.

bedaub (bɪˈdɔːb) VERB (*tr*) 1 to smear all over with something thick, sticky, or dirty. 2 to ornament in a gaudy or vulgar fashion.

bedazzle (bɪˈdæzəl) VERB (*tr*) to dazzle or confuse, as with brilliance.
▸ **beˈdazzlement** NOUN

bed bath NOUN another name for **blanket bath**.

bed-blocking NOUN *Brit* the use of hospital beds by elderly patients cannot leave hospital because they have no place in a residential care home.
▸ **ˈbed-ˌblocker** NOUN

bedbug (ˈbɛdˌbʌg) NOUN any of several bloodsucking insects of the heteropterous genus *Cimex*, esp *C. lectularius* of temperate regions, having an oval flattened wingless body and infesting dirty houses: family *Cimicidae*.

bedchamber (ˈbɛdˌtʃeɪmbə) NOUN an archaic word for **bedroom**.

bedclothes (ˈbɛdˌkləʊðz) PLURAL NOUN sheets, blankets, and other coverings of a bed.

beddable (ˈbɛdəbəl) ADJECTIVE sexually attractive.

bedder (ˈbɛdə) NOUN 1 *Brit* (at some universities) a college servant employed to keep students' rooms in order. 2 a plant that may be grown in a garden bed.

bedding (ˈbɛdɪŋ) NOUN 1 bedclothes, sometimes considered together with a mattress. 2 litter, such as straw, for animals. 3 something acting as a foundation, such as mortar under a brick. 4 the arrangement of a mass of rocks into distinct layers; stratification.

bedding plant NOUN a plant that may be grown in a garden bed.

bedeck (bɪˈdɛk) VERB (*tr*) to cover with decorations; adorn.

bedel *or* **bedell** (ˈbiːdəl) NOUN archaic spellings of **beadle** (sense 4).

bedesman (ˈbiːdzmən) NOUN, *plural* **-men.** a variant spelling of **beadsman**.

bedevil (bɪˈdɛvəl) VERB **-ils, -illing, -illed** *or US* **-ils, -iling, -iled.** (*tr*) 1 to harass or torment. 2 to throw into confusion. 3 to possess, as with a devil.
▸ **beˈdevilment** NOUN

bedew (bɪˈdjuː) VERB (*tr*) to wet or cover with or as if with drops of dew.

bedfast (ˈbɛdˌfɑːst) ADJECTIVE an archaic word for **bedridden**.

bedfellow (ˈbɛdˌfɛləʊ) NOUN 1 a person with whom one shares a bed. 2 a temporary ally or associate.

Bedford (ˈbɛdfəd) NOUN 1 a town in SE central England, administrative centre of Bedfordshire, on the River Ouse. Pop.: 73 917 (1991). 2 short for **Bedfordshire**.

Bedford cord NOUN a heavy corded cloth, similar to corduroy.
▷HISTORY C19: named after BEDFORD

Bedfordshire (ˈbɛdfədˌʃɪə, -ʃə) NOUN a county of S central England: mainly low-lying, with the Chiltern Hills in the south: the geographical county includes Luton, which became a separate unitary authority in 1997. Administrative centre: Bedford. Pop. (excluding Luton): 381 571 (2001). Area (excluding Luton): 1192 sq. km (460 sq. miles). Abbreviation: **Beds.**

bedight (bɪˈdaɪt) *Archaic* ◆ VERB **-dights, -dighting, -dight** *or* **-dighted.** 1 (*tr*) to array or adorn. ◆ ADJECTIVE 2 (*past participle of the verb*) adorned or bedecked.
▷HISTORY C14: from DIGHT

bedim (bɪˈdɪm) VERB **-dims, -dimming, -dimmed.** (*tr*) to make dim or obscure.

bed in VERB 1 (*preposition*) *Engineering* to fit (parts) together accurately or (of parts) to be fitted together, either through machining or use, as in fitting a bearing to its shaft. 2 (*preposition*) to make or become settled and able to work efficiently in harmony.

Bedivere (ˈbɛdɪˌvɪə) NOUN **Sir.** (in Arthurian legend) a knight who took the dying King Arthur to the barge in which he was carried to Avalon.

bedizen (bɪˈdaɪzən, -ˈdɪzən) VERB (*tr*) *Archaic* to dress or decorate gaudily or tastelessly.
▷HISTORY C17: from BE- + obsolete *dizen* to dress up, of uncertain origin
▸ **beˈdizenment** NOUN

bed jacket NOUN a woman's short upper garment worn over a nightgown when sitting up in bed.

bedlam ('bɛdləm) NOUN [1] a noisy confused place or situation; state of uproar: *his speech caused bedlam.* [2] *Archaic* a lunatic asylum; madhouse.
▷**HISTORY** C13 *bedlem, bethlem,* after the Hospital of St Mary of *Bethlehem* in London

bedlamite ('bɛdləˌmaɪt) NOUN *Archaic* a lunatic; insane person.

bed linen NOUN sheets and pillowcases for a bed.

Bedlington terrier ('bɛdlɪŋtən) NOUN a lithe, graceful breed of terrier having a long tapering head with no stop and a thick fleecy coat. Often shortened to: **Bedlington.**
▷**HISTORY** C19: named after the town *Bedlington* in Northumberland, where they were first bred

Bedloe's Island ('bɛdləʊz) *or* **Bedloe Island** NOUN the former name (until 1956) of **Liberty Island.**

bed moulding NOUN *Architect* [1] a moulding in an entablature between the corona and the frieze. [2] any moulding below a projection.

Bedouin *or* **Beduin** ('bɛdʊɪn) NOUN [1] (*plural* **-ins** *or* **-in**) a member of any of the nomadic tribes of Arabs inhabiting the deserts of Arabia, Jordan, and Syria, as well as parts of the Sahara. [2] a wanderer or rover. ◆ ADJECTIVE [3] of or relating to the Bedouins. [4] wandering or roving.
▷**HISTORY** C14: from Old French *beduin,* from Arabic *badāwī,* plural of *badwi,* from *badw* desert

bedpan ('bɛdˌpæn) NOUN [1] a shallow vessel placed under a bedridden patient to collect faeces and urine. [2] another name for **warming pan.**

bedplate ('bɛdˌpleɪt) NOUN a heavy metal platform or frame to which an engine or machine is attached.

bedpost ('bɛdˌpəʊst) NOUN [1] any of the four vertical supports at the corners of a bedstead. [2] **between you and me and the bedpost.** *Informal* confidentially; in secret.

bedraggle (bɪ'dræɡᵊl) VERB (*tr*) to make (hair, clothing, etc.) limp, untidy, or dirty, as with rain or mud.

bedraggled (bɪ'dræɡᵊld) ADJECTIVE (of hair, clothing, etc.) limp, untidy, or dirty, as with rain or mud.

bedrail ('bɛdˌreɪl) NOUN a rail or board along the side of a bed that connects the headboard with the footboard.

bedridden ('bɛdˌrɪdᵊn) ADJECTIVE confined to bed because of illness, esp for a long or indefinite period.
▷**HISTORY** Old English *bedreda,* from *bedd* BED + *-rida* rider, from *rīdan* to RIDE

bedrock ('bɛdˌrɒk) NOUN [1] the solid unweathered rock that lies beneath the loose surface deposits of soil, alluvium, etc. [2] basic principles or facts (esp in the phrase **get down to bedrock**). [3] the lowest point, level, or layer.

bedroll ('bɛdˌrəʊl) NOUN a portable roll of bedding, such as a sleeping bag, used esp for sleeping in the open.

bedroom ('bɛdˌruːm, -ˌrʊm) NOUN [1] a room furnished with beds or used for sleeping. [2] (*modifier*) containing references to sex: *a bedroom comedy.*

Beds ABBREVIATION FOR Bedfordshire.

bedside ('bɛdˌsaɪd) NOUN **a** the space by the side of a bed, esp of a sick person. **b** (*as modifier*): *a bedside lamp; a doctor's bedside manner.*

bedsit ('bɛdˌsɪt) NOUN a furnished sitting room containing sleeping accommodation and sometimes cooking and washing facilities. Also called: **bedsitter, bedsitting room.**

bedsore ('bɛdˌsɔː) NOUN the nontechnical name for **decubitus ulcer.**

bedspread ('bɛdˌsprɛd) NOUN a top cover on a bed over other bedclothes.

bedstead ('bɛdˌstɛd) NOUN the framework of a bed, usually including a headboard and springs but excluding the mattress and other coverings.

bedstraw ('bɛdˌstrɔː) NOUN any of numerous rubiaceous plants of the genus *Galium,* which have small white or yellow flowers and prickly or hairy fruits: some species formerly used as straw for beds as they are aromatic when dry. See also **lady's bedstraw.**

bed tea NOUN (in some Asian countries) tea served to a guest in bed in the morning.

bedtime ('bɛdˌtaɪm) NOUN **a** the time when one usually goes to bed. **b** (*as modifier*): *a bedtime story.*

bedwarmer ('bɛdˌwɔːmə) NOUN a metal pan containing hot coals, formerly used to warm a bed.

bed-wetting NOUN the act or habit of involuntarily urinating in bed. Technical term: **enuresis.**
▸ **'bed-ˌwetter** NOUN

Bedworth ('bɛdwəθ) NOUN a town in central England, in N Warwickshire. Pop.: 31 932 (1991).

bee[1] (biː) NOUN [1] any hymenopterous insect of the superfamily *Apoidea,* which includes social forms such as the honeybee and solitary forms such as the carpenter bee. See also **bumblebee, mason bee.** Related adjective: **apian.** [2] **busy bee.** a person who is industrious or has many things to do. [3] **have a bee in one's bonnet.** to be preoccupied or obsessed with an idea.
▷**HISTORY** Old English *bīo;* related to Old Norse *bý,* Old High German *bīa,* Dutch *bij,* Swedish *bi*

bee[2] (biː) NOUN [1] a social gathering for a specific purpose, as to carry out a communal task or hold competitions: *quilting bee.* [2] See **spelling bee.**
▷**HISTORY** C18: perhaps from dialect *bean* neighbourly help, from Old English *bēn* boon

bee[3] (biː) NOUN *Nautical* a small sheave with one cheek removed and the pulley and other cheek fastened flat to a boom or another spar, used for reeving outhauls or stays.
▷**HISTORY** Old English *bēag;* related to Old High German *boug* ring, Old Norse *bogi* a bow

Beeb (biːb) NOUN **the.** an informal name for the **BBC.**

bee beetle NOUN a European beetle, *Trichodes apiarius,* that is often parasitic in beehives: family *Cleridae.*

beebread ('biːˌbrɛd) NOUN a mixture of pollen and nectar prepared by worker bees and fed to the larvae. Also called: **ambrosia.**

beech (biːtʃ) NOUN [1] any N temperate tree of the genus *Fagus,* esp *F. sylvatica* of Europe, having smooth greyish bark: family *Fagaceae.* [2] any tree of the related genus *Nothofagus,* of temperate Australasia and South America. [3] the hard wood of any of these trees, used in making furniture, etc. [4] See **copper beech.**
▷**HISTORY** Old English *bēce;* related to Old Norse *bók,* Old High German *buohha,* Middle Dutch *boeke,* Latin *fāgus* beech, Greek *phēgos* edible oak
▸ **'beechen** *or* **'beechy** ADJECTIVE

beech fern NOUN a fern, *Thelypteris phegopteris,* that grows in damp N temperate woods and hills: family *Polypodiaceae.*

beech marten NOUN another name for **stone marten.**

beechnut ('biːtʃˌnʌt) NOUN the small brown triangular edible nut of the beech tree. Collectively, the nuts are often termed **beech mast,** esp when lying on the ground.

bee-eater NOUN any insectivorous bird of the family *Meropidae* of tropical and subtropical regions of the Old World, having a long downward-curving bill and long pointed wings and tail: order *Coraciiformes* (kingfishers, etc.).

beef (biːf) NOUN [1] the flesh of various bovine animals, esp the cow, when killed for eating. [2] (*plural* **beeves** (biːvz)) an adult ox, bull, cow, etc., reared for its meat. [3] *Informal* human flesh, esp when muscular. [4] (*plural* **beefs**) a complaint. ◆ VERB [5] (*intr*) *Slang* to complain, esp repeatedly: *he was beefing about his tax.* [6] (*tr;* often foll by *up*) *Informal* to strengthen; reinforce.
▷**HISTORY** C13: from Old French *boef,* from Latin *bōs* ox; see COW[1]

beefburger ('biːfˌbɜːɡə) NOUN a flat fried cake of minced beef; hamburger.

beefcake ('biːfˌkeɪk) NOUN *Slang* men displayed for their muscular bodies, esp in photographs. Compare **cheesecake** (sense 2).

beefeater ('biːfˌiːtə) NOUN a nickname often applied to the Yeomen of the Guard and the Yeomen Warders at the Tower of London.

bee fly NOUN any hairy beelike nectar-eating dipterous fly of the family *Bombyliidae,* whose larvae are parasitic on those of bees and related insects.

beef road NOUN *Austral* a road used for transporting cattle.

beefsteak ('biːfˌsteɪk) NOUN a piece of beef that can be grilled, fried, etc., cut from any lean part of the animal.

beefsteak fungus NOUN an edible reddish bracket fungus, *Fistulina hepatica,* that grows esp on oak trees and oozes a bloodlike juice.

beef stroganoff NOUN a dish of thin strips of beef cooked with onions, mushrooms, and seasonings, served in a sour-cream sauce.
▷**HISTORY** C19: named after Count Paul *Stroganoff,* 19th-century Russian diplomat

beef tea NOUN a drink made by boiling pieces of lean beef: often given to invalids to stimulate the appetite.

beef tomato NOUN a very large fleshy variety of tomato. Also called: **beefsteak tomato.**

beefwood ('biːfˌwʊd) NOUN [1] any of various trees that produce very hard wood, esp the Australian tree *Casuarina equisetifolia* (see **casuarina**), widely planted in warm regions. [2] the wood of any of these trees.
▷**HISTORY** from the red colour and grain

beefy ('biːfɪ) ADJECTIVE **beefier, beefiest.** [1] like beef. [2] *Informal* muscular; brawny. [3] *Informal* fleshy; obese.
▸ **'beefily** ADVERB ▸ **'beefiness** NOUN

bee glue NOUN another name for **propolis.**

beehive ('biːˌhaɪv) NOUN [1] a man-made receptacle used to house a swarm of bees. [2] a dome-shaped hair style in which the hair is piled high on the head. [3] a place where busy people are assembled.

Beehive ('biːˌhaɪv) NOUN **the.** *Informal* [1] the dome-shaped building that houses sections of Parliament in Wellington, New Zealand. [2] the New Zealand government.

beehive house NOUN a prehistoric circular building found in various parts of Europe, usually of stone and having a dome-shaped roof.

beekeeper ('biːˌkiːpə) NOUN a person who keeps bees for their honey; apiarist.
▸ **'beeˌkeeping** NOUN

bee killer NOUN another name for **robber fly.**

beeline ('biːˌlaɪn) NOUN the most direct route between two places (esp in the phrase **make a beeline for**).

Beelzebub (bɪ'ɛlzɪˌbʌb) NOUN [1] *Old Testament* a god of the Philistines (2 Kings 1:2). [2] Satan or any devil or demon.
▷**HISTORY** Old English *Belzebub,* ultimately from Hebrew *bá'al zebūb,* literally: lord of flies

bee moth NOUN any of various pyralid moths, such as the wax moth, whose larvae live in the nests of bees or wasps, feeding on nest materials and host larvae.

been (biːn, bɪn) VERB the past participle of **be.**

been-there done-that INTERJECTION an exclamation expressing familiarity and boredom with a situation, experience, etc.

beento ('biːntuː, 'bɪntʊ) *W African informal* ◆ NOUN, *plural* **-tos.** [1] a person who has resided in Britain, esp during part of his education. ◆ ADJECTIVE [2] of, relating to, or characteristic of such a person.
▷**HISTORY** C20: from BEEN + TO

bee orchid NOUN [1] a European orchid, *Ophrys apifera,* whose flower resembles a bumble bee in shape and colour. [2] any of several other orchids with beelike flowers.

beep (biːp) NOUN [1] a short high-pitched sound, esp one made by the horn of a car, bicycle, etc., or by electronic apparatus. ◆ VERB [2] to make or cause to make such a noise.
▷**HISTORY** C20: of imitative origin
▸ **'beeper** NOUN

bee plant NOUN any of various plants much visited by bees for nectar and pollen.

beer (bɪə) NOUN [1] an alcoholic drink brewed from malt, sugar, hops, and water and fermented with yeast. Compare **ale.** [2] a slightly fermented drink made from the roots or leaves of certain plants: *ginger beer; nettle beer.* [3] (*modifier*) relating to or used in the drinking of beer: *beer glass; beer mat.* [4]

(*modifier*) in which beer is drunk, esp (of licensed premises) having a licence to sell beer: *beer house; beer cellar; beer garden*.
▷HISTORY Old English *beor*; related to Old Norse *bjōrr*, Old Frisian *biār*, Old High German *bior*

beer and skittles NOUN (*functioning as singular*) *Informal* enjoyment or pleasure.

beer belly NOUN *Informal* a protruding belly caused by excessive beer drinking. Also called: **beer gut**.

beer goggles PLURAL NOUN **with one's beer goggles on**. *Informal* seeing people and things as becoming increasingly attractive as one's alcohol intake rises.

beer parlour *or* **parlor** NOUN *Canadian* a room in a tavern, hotel, etc. in which beer is served.

Beersheba (bɪə'ʃi:bə) NOUN a town in S Israel: commercial centre of the Negev. In biblical times it marked the southern limit of Palestine. Pop.: 163 700 (1999 est.).

beer-up NOUN *Austral dated slang* a drinking bout.

beery ('bɪərɪ) ADJECTIVE **beerier, beeriest**. **1** smelling or tasting of beer. **2** given to drinking beer.
▸'**beerily** ADVERB ▸'**beeriness** NOUN

bee's knees NOUN **the**. (*functioning as singular*) *Informal* an excellent or ideally suitable person or thing.

beestings, biestings, *or US* **beastings** ('bi:stɪŋz) NOUN (*functioning as singular*) the first milk secreted by the mammary glands of a cow or similar animal immediately after giving birth; colostrum.
▷HISTORY Old English *bȳsting*, from *bēost* beestings; related to Middle Dutch *biest*

bee-stung ADJECTIVE (of the lips) pouting and sensuous.

beeswax ('bi:z,wæks) NOUN **1** **a** a yellowish or dark brown wax secreted by honeybees for constructing honeycombs. **b** this wax after refining, purifying, etc., used in polishes, ointments, and for modelling. ◆ VERB **2** (*tr*) to polish with such wax.

beeswing ('bi:z,wɪŋ) NOUN **1** a light filmy crust of tartar that forms in port and some other wines after long keeping in the bottle. **2** a port or other wine containing beeswing.

beet (bi:t) NOUN **1** any chenopodiaceous plant of the genus *Beta*, esp the Eurasian species *B. vulgaris*, widely cultivated in such varieties as the sugar beet, mangelwurzel, beetroot, and spinach beet. See also **chard**. **2** the leaves of any of several varieties of this plant, which are cooked and eaten as a vegetable. **3** **red beet**. the US name for **beetroot**.
▷HISTORY Old English *bēte*, from Latin *bēta*

beetfly ('bi:t,flaɪ) NOUN, *plural* **-flies**. a muscid fly, *Pegomyia hyoscyami*: a common pest of beets and mangel-wurzels. Also called: **mangold fly**.

beetle[1] ('bi:tᵊl) NOUN **1** any insect of the order *Coleoptera*, having biting mouthparts and forewings modified to form shell-like protective elytra. Related adjective: **coleopteran**. **2** a game played with dice in which the players draw or assemble a beetle-shaped form. ◆ VERB (*intr*; foll by *along, off,* etc.) **3** *Informal* to scuttle or scurry; hurry.
▷HISTORY Old English *bitela*; related to *bitol* teeth, BIT, *bītan* to BITE

beetle[2] ('bi:tᵊl) NOUN **1** a heavy hand tool, usually made of wood, used for ramming, pounding, or beating. **2** a machine used to finish cloth by stamping it with wooden hammers. ◆ VERB (*tr*) **3** to beat or pound with a beetle. **4** to finish (cloth) by means of a beetle.
▷HISTORY Old English *bīetel*, from *bēatan* to BEAT; related to Middle Low German *bētel* chisel, Old Norse *beytill* penis

beetle[3] ('bi:tᵊl) VERB **1** (*intr*) to overhang; jut. ◆ ADJECTIVE **2** overhanging; prominent.
▷HISTORY C14: perhaps related to BEETLE[1]
▸'**beetling** ADJECTIVE

beetle-browed ADJECTIVE **1** having bushy or overhanging eyebrows. **2** sullen in appearance; scowling.

beetle drive NOUN a social occasion at which a progressive series of games of beetle is played. See **beetle[1]** (sense 2).

beetroot ('bi:t,ru:t) NOUN **1** a variety of the beet plant, *Beta vulgaris*, that has a bulbous dark red root that may be eaten as a vegetable, in salads, or pickled. **2** the root of this plant. ◆ US name: **red beet**.

beet sugar NOUN the sucrose obtained from sugar beet, identical in composition to cane sugar.

beeves (bi:vz) NOUN *Archaic* the plural of **beef** (sense 2).

beezer ('bi:zə) *Slang* ◆ NOUN **1** *Brit old-fashioned* a person or chap. **2** *Brit old-fashioned* the nose. **3** *Scot* an extreme example of its kind. ◆ ADJECTIVE **4** *Brit old-fashioned* excellent; most attractive.
▷HISTORY C20: of uncertain origin

BEF ABBREVIATION FOR British Expeditionary Force, the British armies that served in France and Belgium 1914–18 and in France 1939–40.

befall (bɪ'fɔ:l) VERB **-falls, -falling, -fell, -fallen**. *Archaic or literary* **1** (*intr*) to take place; come to pass. **2** (*tr*) to happen to. **3** (*intr*; usually foll by *to*) to be due, as by right.
▷HISTORY Old English *befeallan*; related to Old High German *bifallan*, Dutch *bevallen*; see BE-, FALL

befit (bɪ'fɪt) VERB **-fits, -fitting, -fitted**. (*tr*) to be appropriate to or suitable for.
▷HISTORY C15: from BE- + FIT[1]
▸**be'fitting** ADJECTIVE ▸**be'fittingly** ADVERB

befog (bɪ'fɒg) VERB **-fogs, -fogging, -fogged**. (*tr*) **1** to surround with fog. **2** to make confused, vague, or less clear.

befool (bɪ'fu:l) VERB (*tr*) to make a fool of.

before (bɪ'fɔ:) CONJUNCTION (*subordinating*) **1** earlier than the time when. **2** rather than: *he'll resign before he agrees to it*. ◆ PREPOSITION **3** preceding in space or time; in front of; ahead of: *standing before the altar*. **4** when confronted by: *to withdraw before one's enemies*. **5** in the presence of: *to be brought before a judge*. **6** in preference to: *to put friendship before money*. ◆ ADVERB **7** at an earlier time; previously; beforehand; in front.
▷HISTORY Old English *beforan*; related to Old Frisian *befara*, Old High German *bifora*

beforehand (bɪ'fɔ:,hænd) ADJECTIVE (*postpositive*), ADVERB early; in advance; in anticipation: *she came an hour beforehand*.

beforetime (bɪ'fɔ:,taɪm) ADVERB *Archaic* formerly.

befoul (bɪ'faʊl) VERB (*tr*) to make dirty or foul; soil; defile.
▸**be'fouler** NOUN ▸**be'foulment** NOUN

befriend (bɪ'frɛnd) VERB (*tr*) to be a friend to; assist; favour.

befuddle (bɪ'fʌdᵊl) VERB (*tr*) **1** to confuse, muddle, or perplex. **2** to make stupid with drink.
▸**be'fuddlement** NOUN

beg[1] (bɛg) VERB **begs, begging, begged**. **1** (when *intr*, often foll by *for*) to solicit (for money, food, etc.), esp in the street. **2** to ask (someone) for (something or leave to do something) formally, humbly, or earnestly: *I beg forgiveness; I beg to differ*. **3** (*intr*) (of a dog) to sit up with forepaws raised expectantly. **4** to leave unanswered or unresolved: *to beg a point*. **5** **beg the question**. **a** to evade the issue. **b** to assume the thing under examination as proved. **c** to suggest that a question needs to be asked: *the firm's success begs the question: why aren't more companies doing the same?* **6** **go (a-)begging**. to be unwanted or unused. See also **beg off**.
▷HISTORY C13: probably from Old English *bedecian*; related to Gothic *bidagwa* BEGGAR

> **Language note** The use of *beg the question* to mean that a question needs to be asked is considered by some people to be incorrect.

beg[2] (bɛg) NOUN a variant of **bey**.

begad (bɪ'gæd) INTERJECTION *Archaic slang* an emphatic exclamation.
▷HISTORY C18: euphemistic alteration of *by God!*

began (bɪ'gæn) VERB the past tense of **begin**.

begat (bɪ'gæt) VERB *Archaic* a past tense of **beget**.

beget (bɪ'gɛt) VERB **-gets, -getting, -got** *or* **-gat; -gotten** *or* **-got**. (*tr*) **1** to father. **2** to cause or create.
▷HISTORY Old English *begietan*; related to Old Saxon *bigetan*, Old High German *pigezzan*, Gothic *bigitan* to find; see BE-, GET
▸**be'getter** NOUN

beggar ('bɛgə) NOUN **1** a person who begs, esp one who lives by begging. **2** a person who has no money or resources; pauper. **3** *Ironic or jocular, chiefly Brit* fellow: *lucky beggar!* ◆ VERB (*tr*) **4** to be beyond the resources of (esp in the phrase **to beggar description**). **5** to impoverish; reduce to begging.
▸'**beggar,hood** *or* '**beggardom** NOUN

beggarly ('bɛgəlɪ) ADJECTIVE meanly inadequate; very poor: *beggarly living conditions*.
▸'**beggarliness** NOUN

beggar-my-neighbour NOUN **1** a card game in which one player tries to win all the cards of the other player. **2** (*modifier*) relating to or denoting an advantage gained by one side at the expense of the other: *beggar-my-neighbour policies*.

beggar's-lice NOUN (*functioning as singular*) **1** any of several plants, esp the stickseed, having small prickly fruits that adhere to clothing, fur, etc. **2** the seed or fruit of any of these plants.

beggar-ticks *or* **beggar's-ticks** NOUN (*functioning as singular*) **1** any of various plants, such as the bur marigold and tick trefoil, having fruits or seeds that cling to clothing, fur, etc. **2** the seed or fruit of any of these plants.

beggarweed ('bɛgə,wi:d) NOUN any of various leguminous plants of the genus *Desmodium*, esp *D. purpureum* of the Caribbean, grown in the southern US as forage plants and to improve the soil. See also **tick trefoil**.

beggary ('bɛgərɪ) NOUN **1** extreme poverty or need. **2** the condition of being a beggar.

begging bowl NOUN a bowl carried by a beggar, esp a Franciscan or other friar or a Buddhist monk, to receive food or alms.

begging letter NOUN a letter asking for money sent esp by a stranger to someone known to be rich.

Beghard ('bɛgəd, bɪ'gɑ:d) NOUN a member of a Christian brotherhood that was founded in Flanders in the 13th century and followed a life based on that of the Beguines. Also called: **Beguin**.
▷HISTORY C17: from Medieval Latin *beghardus*, from BEG(UINE) + -ARD; compare Old French *bégard*, Middle Dutch *beggaert*, Middle High German *beghart*

begin (bɪ'gɪn) VERB **-gins, -ginning, -gan, -gun**. **1** to start or cause to start (something or to do something). **2** to bring or come into being for the first time; arise or originate. **3** to start to say or speak. **4** (*used with a negative*) to have the least capacity (to do something): *he couldn't begin to compete with her*. **5** **to begin with**. in the first place.
▷HISTORY Old English *beginnan*; related to Old High German *biginnan*, Gothic *duginnan*

beginner (bɪ'gɪnə) NOUN a person who has just started to do or learn something; novice.

beginning (bɪ'gɪnɪŋ) NOUN **1** a start; commencement. **2** (*often plural*) a first or early part or stage. **3** the place where or time when something starts. **4** an origin; source.

begird (bɪ'gɜ:d) VERB **-girds, -girding, -girt** *or* **-girded**. (*tr*) *Poetic* **1** to surround; gird around. **2** to bind.
▷HISTORY Old English *begierdan*; see BE-, GIRD[1]

beg off VERB (*intr, adverb*) to ask to be released from an engagement, obligation, etc.

begone (bɪ'gɒn) SENTENCE SUBSTITUTE go away!
▷HISTORY C14: from BE (imperative) + GONE

begonia (bɪ'gəʊnjə) NOUN any plant of the genus *Begonia*, of warm and tropical regions, widely cultivated for their ornamental leaves and waxy flowers: family *Begoniaceae*.
▷HISTORY C18: New Latin, named after Michel *Bégon* (1638–1710), French patron of science

begorra (bɪ'gɒrə) INTERJECTION an emphatic exclamation, regarded as a characteristic utterance of Irishmen.
▷HISTORY C19: euphemistic alteration of *by God!*

begot (bɪ'gɒt) VERB a past tense and past participle of **beget**.

begotten (bɪ'gɒtᵊn) VERB a past participle of **beget**.

begrime (bɪ'graɪm) VERB (*tr*) to make dirty; soil.

begrudge (bɪ'grʌdʒ) VERB (*tr*) **1** to give, admit, or allow unwillingly or with a bad grace. **2** to envy (someone) the possession of (something).
▸**be'grudgingly** ADVERB

beguile (bɪ'gaɪl) VERB **-guiles, -guiling, -guiled**. (*tr*) **1** to charm; fascinate. **2** to delude; influence by slyness. **3** (often foll by *of* or *out of*) to deprive (someone) of something by trickery; cheat (someone) of. **4** to pass pleasantly; while away.
▸**be'guilement** NOUN ▸**be'guiler** NOUN

beguiling (bɪˈgaɪlɪŋ) ADJECTIVE 1 charming or fascinating. 2 using slyness to delude someone.
▸**beˈguilingly** ADVERB

Beguin (ˈbɛgɪn; *French* begɛ̃) NOUN another word for **Beghard.**

beguine (bɪˈgiːn) NOUN 1 a dance of South American origin in bolero rhythm. 2 a piece of music in the rhythm of this dance. 3 a variant of **biggin**[1].
▹HISTORY C20: from Louisiana French, from French *béguin* flirtation

Beguine (ˈbegiːn) NOUN a member of a Christian sisterhood that was founded in Liège in the 12th century, and, though not taking religious vows, followed an austere life.
▹HISTORY C15: from Old French, perhaps after *Lambert le Bègue* (the Stammerer), 12th-century priest of Liège, who founded the sisterhood

begum (ˈbeɪgəm) NOUN (in Pakistan and certain other Muslim countries) a woman of high rank, esp the widow of a prince.
▹HISTORY C18: from Urdu *begam*, from Turkish *begim*; see BEY

begun (bɪˈgʌn) VERB the past participle of **begin.**

behalf (bɪˈhɑːf) NOUN interest, part, benefit, or respect (only in the phrases **on (someone's) behalf, on** *or US and Canadian* **in behalf of, in this** (*or* **that**) **behalf**).
▹HISTORY Old English *be halfe* from *be* by + *halfe* side; compare Old Norse *af halfu*

behave (bɪˈheɪv) VERB 1 (*intr*) to act or function in a specified or usual way. 2 to conduct (oneself) in a specified way: *he behaved badly towards her.* 3 to conduct (oneself) properly or as desired: *the child behaved himself all day.*
▹HISTORY C15: see BE-, HAVE

behaviour *or US* **behavior** (bɪˈheɪvjə) NOUN 1 manner of behaving or conducting oneself. 2 **on one's best behaviour.** behaving with careful good manners. 3 *Psychol* **a** the aggregate of all the responses made by an organism in any situation. **b** a specific response of a certain organism to a specific stimulus or group of stimuli. 4 the action, reaction, or functioning of a system, under normal or specified circumstances.
▹HISTORY C15: from BEHAVE; influenced in form by Middle English *havior*, from Old French *havoir*, from Latin *habēre* to have
▸**beˈhavioural** *or US* **beˈhavioral** ADJECTIVE

behavioural contagion NOUN the spread of a particular type of behaviour, such as crying, through a crowd or group of people.

behavioural science NOUN the application of scientific methods to the study of the behaviour of organisms.

behavioural sink NOUN *Psychol* a small area in which people or animals live in overcrowded conditions.

behaviourism *or US* **behaviorism** (bɪˈheɪvjəˌrɪzəm) NOUN 1 a school of psychology that regards the objective observation of the behaviour of organisms (usually by means of automatic recording devices) as the only proper subject for study and that often refuses to postulate any intervening mechanisms between the stimulus and the response. 2 the doctrine that the mind has no separate existence but that statements about the mind and mental states can be analysed into statements about actual and potential behaviour. Compare **materialism** (sense 2). See also **mind-body problem.**
▸**beˈhaviourist** *or US* **beˈhaviorist** ADJECTIVE, NOUN
▸**beˌhaviourˈistic** *or US* **beˌhaviorˈistic** ADJECTIVE

behaviour therapy NOUN any of various means of treating psychological disorders, such as desensitization, aversion therapy, and instrumental conditioning, that depend on the patient systematically learning new modes of behaviour.

behead (bɪˈhɛd) VERB (*tr*) to remove the head from; decapitate.
▹HISTORY Old English *behēafdian*, from BE- + *heafod* HEAD; related to Middle High German *behoubeten*

beheld (bɪˈhɛld) VERB the past tense and past participle of **behold.**

behemoth (bɪˈhiːmɒθ) NOUN 1 *Old Testament* a gigantic beast, probably a hippopotamus, described in Job 40:15. 2 a huge or monstrous person or thing.
▹HISTORY C14: from Hebrew *bĕhēmōth*, plural of *bĕhēmāh* beast

behest (bɪˈhɛst) NOUN an authoritative order or earnest request.
▹HISTORY Old English *behǣs*, from *behātan*; see BE-, HEST

behind (bɪˈhaɪnd) PREPOSITION 1 in or to a position further back than; at the rear of; at the back of. 2 in the past in relation to: *I've got the exams behind me now.* 3 late according to; not keeping up with: *running behind schedule.* 4 concerning the circumstances surrounding: *the reasons behind his departure.* 5 backing or supporting: *I'm right behind you in your application.* ♦ ADVERB 6 in or to a position further back; following. 7 remaining after someone's departure: *he left it behind.* 8 in debt; in arrears: *to fall behind with payments.* ♦ ADJECTIVE 9 (*postpositive*) in a position further back; retarded: *the man behind prodded me.* ♦ NOUN 10 *Informal* the buttocks. 11 *Australian Rules football* a score of one point made by kicking the ball over the **behind line** between a goalpost and one of the smaller outer posts (**behind posts**).
▹HISTORY Old English *behindan*

behindhand (bɪˈhaɪndˌhænd) ADJECTIVE (*postpositive*), ADVERB 1 remiss in fulfilling an obligation. 2 in debt; in arrears. 3 delayed in development; backward. 4 late; behind time.

Behistun (ˌbeɪhɪˈstuːn), **Bisitun,** *or* **Bisutun** NOUN a village in W Iran by the ancient road from Ecbatana to Babylon. On a nearby cliff is an inscription by Darius in Old Persian, Elamite, and Babylonian describing his enthronement.

behold (bɪˈhəʊld) VERB **-holds, -holding, -held.** (often used in the imperative to draw attention to something) *Archaic or literary* to look (at); observe.
▹HISTORY Old English *bihealdan*; related to Old High German *bihaltan*, Dutch *behouden*; see BE-, HOLD
▸**beˈholder** NOUN

beholden (bɪˈhəʊldᵊn) ADJECTIVE indebted; obliged; under a moral obligation.
▹HISTORY Old English *behealden*, past participle of *behealdan* to BEHOLD

behoof (bɪˈhuːf) NOUN, *plural* **-hooves.** *Rare* advantage or profit.
▹HISTORY Old English *behōf*; related to Middle High German *behuof* something useful; see BEHOVE

behove (bɪˈhəʊv) *or US* **behoove** (bɪˈhuːv) VERB (*tr; impersonal*) *Archaic* to be necessary or fitting for: *it behoves me to arrest you.*
▹HISTORY Old English *behōfian*; related to Middle Low German *behōven*

beige (beɪʒ) NOUN 1 **a** a very light brown, sometimes with a yellowish tinge, similar to the colour of undyed wool. **b** (*as adjective*): *beige gloves.* 2 a fabric made of undyed or unbleached wool.
▹HISTORY C19: from Old French, of obscure origin

beigel (ˈbeɪgᵊl) NOUN a variant spelling of **bagel.**

beignet (ˈbɛnjeɪ) NOUN *Chiefly US and Canadian* a square deep-fried pastry served hot and sprinkled with icing sugar.
▹HISTORY C19: French *bignet* filled pastry, from *buyne*, literally: bump or lump

Beijing (ˈbeɪˈdʒɪŋ) NOUN the capital of the People's Republic of China, in the northeast in central Hebei province: dates back to the 12th century B.C.; consists of two central walled cities, the Outer City (containing the commercial quarter) and the Inner City, which contains the Imperial City, within which is the Purple or Forbidden City; three universities. Pop.: 6 633 929 (1999 est.). Former English name: **Peking.**

being (ˈbiːɪŋ) NOUN 1 the state or fact of existing; existence. 2 essential nature; self: *she put her whole being into the part.* 3 something that exists or is thought to exist, esp something that cannot be assigned to any category: *a being from outer space.* 4 a person; human being. 5 (in the philosophy of Aristotle) actuality. Compare **becoming** (sense 3).

Beira (ˈbaɪərə) NOUN a port in E Mozambique: terminus of a transcontinental railway from Lobito, Angola, through the Democratic Republic of Congo (formerly Zaïre), Zambia, and Zimbabwe. Pop.: 298 847 (1991 est.).

Beirut *or* **Beyrouth** (ˌbeɪˈruːt) NOUN the capital of Lebanon, a port on the Mediterranean: part of the Ottoman Empire from the 16th century until 1918; four universities (Lebanese, American, French, and Arab). Pop.: 1 500 000 (1998 est.).

Beit Knesset *or* **Beth Knesseth** (bɛt ˈknɛsɛt) NOUN a synagogue: often used in the names of congregations.
▹HISTORY from Hebrew, literally: house of assembly

bejesus (bɪˈdʒeɪzəz) *Informal* ♦ INTERJECTION 1 an exclamation of surprise, emphasis, etc., regarded as a characteristic utterance of Irish people. ♦ NOUN 2 **the bejesus.** (intensifier) used in such phrases as **beat the bejesus out of, scare the bejesus out of,** etc.
▹HISTORY C20: alteration of *by Jesus!*

bejewel (bɪˈdʒuːəl) VERB **-els, -elling, -elled** *or US* **-els, -eling, -eled.** (*tr*) to decorate with or as if with jewels.

bejewelled *or US* **bejeweled** (bɪˈdʒuːəld) ADJECTIVE decorated with or as if with jewels.

Bekaa *or* **Beqaa** (bɪˈkɑː) NOUN a broad valley in central Lebanon, between the Lebanon and Anti-Lebanon Mountains. Ancient name: **Coelesyria** (ˌsiːliːˈsɪrɪə).

bel (bɛl) NOUN a unit for comparing two power levels, equal to the logarithm to the base ten of the ratio of the two powers. Symbols: **B, b.** See also **decibel.**
▹HISTORY C20: named after Alexander Graham Bell (1847–1922), Scots-born US scientist

Bel (beɪl) NOUN (in Babylonian and Assyrian mythology) the god of the earth.

belabour *or US* **belabor** (bɪˈleɪbə) VERB (*tr*) 1 to beat severely; thrash. 2 to attack verbally; criticize harshly. 3 an obsolete word for **labour.**

belah *or* **belar** (ˈbiːlɑː) NOUN an Australian casuarina tree, *Casuarina glauca*, yielding a useful timber.

Belarus (ˈbɛləˌrʌs, -ˌrʊs), **Byelorussia,** *or* **Belorussia** (ˌbjɛləʊˈrʌʃə, ˌbɛl-) NOUN a republic in E Europe; part of the medieval Lithuanian and Polish empires before occupied by Russia; a Soviet republic (1919–91); in 1997 formed a close political and economic union with Russia: mainly low-lying and forested. Languages: Belarussian; Russian. Religion: believers are mostly Christian. Currency: rouble. Capital: Minsk. Pop.: 9 986 000 (2001 est.). Area: 207 600 sq. km (80 134 sq. miles). Also called: **Byelorussian Republic, Bielorussia, White Russia.**

Belarussian, Belarusian, Byelorussian, *or* **Belorussian** (ˌbɛləʊˈrʌʃən, ˌbjɛl-) ADJECTIVE 1 of, relating to, or characteristic of Belarus, its people, or their language. ♦ NOUN 2 the official language of Belarus: an East Slavonic language closely related to Russian. 3 a native or inhabitant of Belarus. ♦ Also called: **White Russian.**

belated (bɪˈleɪtɪd) ADJECTIVE late or too late: *belated greetings.*
▸**beˈlatedly** ADVERB ▸**beˈlatedness** NOUN

Belau (bəˈlaʊ) NOUN **Republic of.** a republic comprising a group of islands in the W Pacific, in the W Caroline Islands; administratively part of the UN Trust Territory of the Pacific Islands 1947–87; entered into an agreement of free association with the US (1980); became fully independent in 1994. Chief island: Babelthuap. Capital: Koror. Pop.: 19 700 (2001 est.). Area: 476 sq. km (184 sq. miles). Former names: **Pelew Islands, Palau Islands** (until 1981).

belay (bɪˈleɪ) VERB **-lays, -laying, -layed.** 1 *Nautical* to make fast (a line) by securing to a pin, cleat, or bitt. 2 (*usually imperative*) *Nautical* to stop; cease. 3 (ˈbiːˌleɪ) *Mountaineering* to secure (a climber) to a mountain by tying the rope off round a rock spike, piton, nut, etc. ♦ NOUN 4 (ˈbiːˌleɪ) *Mountaineering* the attachment (of a climber) to a mountain by tying the rope off round a rock spike, piton, nut, etc., to safeguard the party in the event of a fall. See also **running belay.**
▹HISTORY Old English *belecgan*; related to Old High German *bileggen*, Dutch *beleggen*

belaying pin NOUN *Nautical* a cylindrical, sometimes tapered pin, usually of metal or wood, that fits into a hole in a pin or fife rail: used for belaying.

bel canto (ˈbɛl ˈkæntəʊ) NOUN *Music* **a** a style of singing characterized by beauty of tone rather than dramatic power. **b** (*as modifier*): *a bel canto aria.*
▹HISTORY C19: Italian, literally: beautiful singing

belch (bɛltʃ) VERB 1 (*usually intr*) to expel wind from the stomach noisily through the mouth;

eructate. [2] to expel or be expelled forcefully from inside: *smoke belching from factory chimneys.* [3] to say (curses, insults, etc.) violently or bitterly. ◆ NOUN [4] an act of belching; eructation.
▷HISTORY Old English *bialcan*; related to Middle Low German *belken* to shout, Dutch *balken* to bray

beldam *or* **beldame** (ˈbɛldəm) NOUN [1] *Archaic* an old woman, esp an ugly or malicious one; hag. [2] an obsolete word for **grandmother.**
▷HISTORY C15: from *bel-* grand (as in *grandmother*), from Old French *bel* beautiful, from Latin *bellus* + *dam* mother, variant of DAME

beleaguer (bɪˈliːɡə) VERB (*tr*) [1] to trouble persistently; harass. [2] to lay siege to.
▷HISTORY C16: from BE- + LEAGUER[1]

Belém (*Portuguese* bəˈlẽi) NOUN a port in N Brazil, the capital of Pará state, on the Pará River: major trading centre for the Amazon basin. Pop.: 1 271 615 (2000).

belemnite (ˈbɛləmˌnaɪt) NOUN [1] any extinct marine cephalopod mollusc of the order *Belemnoidea*, related to the cuttlefish. [2] the long pointed conical internal shell of any of these animals: a common Mesozoic fossil.
▷HISTORY C17: from Greek *belemnon* dart

belemnoid (ˈbɛləmˌnɔɪd) ADJECTIVE *Anatomy, zoology* shaped like a dart.

bel esprit *French* (bɛl ɛspri) NOUN, *plural* ***beaux esprits*** (boz ɛspri). a witty or clever person.
▷HISTORY literally: fine wit

Belfast (ˈbɛlfɑːst, bɛlˈfɑːst) NOUN [1] the capital of Northern Ireland, a port on Belfast Lough in Belfast district, Co. Antrim and Co. Down: became the centre of Irish Protestantism and of the linen industry in the 17th century; seat of the Northern Ireland assembly and executive. Pop.: 279 237 (1991). [2] a district of W Northern Ireland, in Co. Antrim and Co. Down. Pop.: 277 391 (2001). Area: 115 sq. km (44 sq. miles).

Belfort (*French* bɛlfɔr) NOUN [1] **Territoire de** (tɛritwar də). a department of E France, now in Franche-Comté region: the only part of Alsace remaining to France after 1871. Capital: Belfort. Pop.: 137 408 (1999). Area: 608 sq. km (237 sq. miles). [2] a fortress town in E France: strategically situated in the **Belfort Gap** between the Vosges and the Jura mountains. Pop.: 50 125 (1990).

belfry (ˈbɛlfrɪ) NOUN, *plural* **-fries.** [1] the part of a tower or steeple in which bells are hung. [2] a tower or steeple. Compare **campanile.** [3] the timber framework inside a tower or steeple on which bells are hung. [4] (formerly) a movable tower for attacking fortifications.
▷HISTORY C13: from Old French *berfrei*, of Germanic origin; compare Middle High German *bercfrit* fortified tower, Medieval Latin *berfredus* tower

Belg. *or* **Bel.** ABBREVIATION FOR: [1] Belgian. [2] Belgium.

belga (ˈbɛlɡə) NOUN a former Belgian monetary unit worth five francs.

Belgae (ˈbɛldʒiː, ˈbɛlɡaɪ) NOUN an ancient Celtic people who in Roman times inhabited present-day Belgium and N France.
▸ **ˈBelgic** ADJECTIVE

Belgaum (bɛlˈɡaum) NOUN a city in India, in Karnataka: cotton, furniture, leather. Pop.: 326 399 (1991).

Belgian (ˈbɛldʒən) NOUN [1] a native, citizen, or inhabitant of Belgium. See also **Fleming**[1], **Walloon.** ◆ ADJECTIVE [2] of, relating to, or characteristic of Belgium or the Belgians. [3] of or relating to the Walloon French or the Flemish languages.

Belgian Congo NOUN a former name (1908–60) of (Democratic Republic of) **Congo** (sense 1).

Belgian hare NOUN a large red breed of domestic rabbit.

Belgian shepherd dog NOUN a medium-sized well-proportioned dog of a breed that resembles an Alsatian in appearance and is often used as a sheepdog or a guard dog.

Belgium (ˈbɛldʒəm) NOUN a federal kingdom in NW Europe: at various times under the rulers of Burgundy, Spain, Austria, France, and the Netherlands before becoming an independent kingdom in 1830. It formed the Benelux customs union with the Netherlands and Luxembourg in 1947 and was a founder member of the EEC (now the EU). It consists chiefly of a low-lying region of sand, woods, and heath (the Campine) in the north and west, and a fertile undulating central plain rising to the Ardennes Mountains in the southeast. Languages: French, Flemish (Dutch), German. Religion: Roman Catholic majority. Currency: euro. Capital: Brussels. Pop.: 10 268 000 (2001 est.). Area: 30 513 sq. km (11 778 sq. miles).

Belgorod-Dnestrovski *or* **Byelgorod-Dnestrovski** (*Russian* ˈbjɛlɡərət-dnjɪˈstrɔfskij) NOUN a port in the SW Ukraine, on the Dniester estuary: belonged to Romania from 1918 until 1940; under Soviet rule (1944–91). Pop.: 56 800 (1991 est.). Romanian name: **Cetatea Albă.** Former name (until 1946): **Akkerman.**

Belgrade (bɛlˈɡreɪd, ˈbɛlɡreɪd) NOUN the capital of the Union of Serbia and Montenegro and of Serbia, in the E part at the confluence of the Danube and Sava Rivers: became the capital of Serbia in 1878 and of Yugoslavia in 1929. Pop.: 1 194 878 (1991). Serbo-Croat name: **Beograd.**

Belgravia (bɛlˈɡreɪvɪə) NOUN a fashionable residential district of W central London, around Belgrave Square.

Belial (ˈbiːlɪəl) NOUN [1] a demon mentioned frequently in apocalyptic literature: identified in the Christian tradition with the devil or Satan. [2] (in the Old Testament and rabbinical literature) worthlessness or wickedness.
▷HISTORY C13: from Hebrew *bəlīyya'al*, from *bəlīy* without + *ya'al* worth

belie (bɪˈlaɪ) VERB **-lies, -lying, -lied.** (*tr*) [1] to show to be untrue; contradict. [2] to misrepresent; disguise the nature of: *the report belied the real extent of the damage.* [3] to fail to justify; disappoint.
▷HISTORY Old English *belēogan*; related to Old Frisian *biliuga*, Old High German *biliugan*; see BE-, LIE[1]
▸ **beˈlier** NOUN

belief (bɪˈliːf) NOUN [1] a principle, proposition, idea, etc., accepted as true. [2] opinion; conviction. [3] religious faith. [4] trust or confidence, as in a person or a person's abilities, probity, etc.

believe (bɪˈliːv) VERB [1] (*tr; may take a clause as object*) to accept (a statement, supposition, or opinion) as true: *I believe God exists.* [2] (*tr*) to accept the statement or opinion of (a person) as true. [3] (*intr; foll by in*) to be convinced of the truth or existence (of): *to believe in fairies.* [4] (*intr*) to have religious faith. [5] (*when tr, takes a clause as object*) to think, assume, or suppose: *I believe that he has left already.* [6] (*tr; foll by of; used with can, could, would,* etc) to think that someone is able to do (a particular action): *I wouldn't have believed it of him.*
▷HISTORY Old English *beliefan*
▸ **beˌlievaˈbility** NOUN ▸ **beˈlievable** ADJECTIVE ▸ **beˈlievably** ADVERB ▸ **beˈliever** NOUN ▸ **beˈlieving** NOUN, ADJECTIVE

belike (bɪˈlaɪk) ADVERB *Archaic or dialect* perhaps; maybe.

Belisha beacon (bəˈliːʃə) NOUN a flashing light in an orange globe mounted on a post, indicating a pedestrian crossing on a road.
▷HISTORY C20: named after Leslie Hore-*Belisha* (1893–1957), British politician

belittle (bɪˈlɪtᵊl) VERB (*tr*) [1] to consider or speak of (something) as less valuable or important than it really is; disparage. [2] to cause to make small; dwarf.
▸ **beˈlittlement** NOUN ▸ **beˈlittler** NOUN ▸ **beˈlittlingly** ADVERB

Belitung (bɪˈliːtuŋ) NOUN another name for **Billiton.**

Belize (bəˈliːz) NOUN a state in Central America, on the Caribbean Sea: site of a Mayan civilization until the 9th century A.D.; colonized by the British from 1638; granted internal self-government in 1964; became an independent state within the Commonwealth in 1981. Official language: English; Carib and Spanish are also spoken. Currency: Belize dollar. Capital: Belmopan. Pop.: 247 000 (2001 est.). Area: 22 965 sq. km (8867 sq. miles). Former name (until 1973): **British Honduras.**

Belizean (bəˈliːzən) ADJECTIVE [1] of or relating to Belize or its inhabitants. ◆ NOUN [2] a native or inhabitant of Belize.

Belize City NOUN a port and the largest city in Belize, on the Caribbean coast: capital until 1973, when it was abandoned as hurricane-prone. Pop.: 48 655 (1994).

bell[1] (bɛl) NOUN [1] a hollow, usually metal, cup-shaped instrument that emits a musical ringing sound when struck, often by a clapper hanging inside it. [2] the sound made by such an instrument or device, as for showing the hours or marking the beginning or end of a period of time. [3] an electrical device that rings or buzzes as a signal. [4] the bowl-shaped termination of the tube of certain musical wind instruments, such as the trumpet or oboe. [5] any musical percussion instrument emitting a ringing tone, such as a glockenspiel, one of a set of hand bells, etc. Compare **chime**[1] (sense 3). [6] *Nautical* a signal rung on a ship's bell to count the number of half-hour intervals during each of six four-hour watches reckoned from midnight. Thus, one bell may signify 12.30, 4.30, or 8.30 a.m. or p.m. [7] See **diving bell.** [8] *Biology* a structure resembling a bell in shape, such as the corolla of certain flowers or the body of a jellyfish. [9] *Brit slang* a telephone call (esp in the phrase **give someone a bell**). [10] **bell, book, and candle. a** instruments used formerly in excommunications and other ecclesiastical acts. **b** *Informal* the solemn ritual ratification of such acts. [11] **ring a bell.** to sound familiar; recall to the mind something previously experienced, esp indistinctly. [12] **sound as a bell.** in perfect condition. [13] **the bells.** the ringing of bells, in a church or other public building, at midnight on December 31st, symbolizing the beginning of a new year. ◆ VERB [14] to be or cause to be shaped like a bell. [15] (*tr*) to attach a bell or bells to. [16] **bell the cat.** to undertake a dangerous mission.
▷HISTORY Old English *belle*; related to Old Norse *bjalla*, Middle Low German *bell*; see BELL[2]

bell[2] (bɛl) NOUN [1] a bellowing or baying cry, esp that of a hound or a male deer in rut. ◆ VERB [2] to utter (such a cry).
▷HISTORY Old English *bellan*; related to Old Norse *belja* to bellow, Old High German *bellan* to roar, Sanskrit *bhāsate* he talks; see BELLOW

belladonna (ˌbɛləˈdɒnə) NOUN [1] either of two alkaloid drugs, atropine or hyoscyamine, obtained from the leaves and roots of the deadly nightshade. [2] another name for **deadly nightshade.**
▷HISTORY C16: from Italian, literally: beautiful lady; supposed to refer to its use by women as a cosmetic

belladonna lily NOUN another name for **amaryllis.**

bellarmine (ˈbɛlɑːˌmiːn) NOUN a large stoneware or earthenware jug for ale or spirits, bearing a bearded mask.
▷HISTORY C18: named after Saint Robert Bellarmine (1542–1621), Italian Jesuit theologian and cardinal, whom these jugs were intended to caricature

Bellatrix (ˈbɛlətrɪks) NOUN the third brightest star in the constellation Orion.

bellbird (ˈbɛlˌbɜːd) NOUN [1] any of several tropical American passerine birds of the genus *Procnias* having a bell-like call: family *Cotingidae* (cotingas). [2] either of two other birds with a bell-like call: an Australian flycatcher, *Oreoica gutturalis* (**crested bellbird**), or a New Zealand honeyeater, *Anthornis melanura*.

bell-bottoms PLURAL NOUN trousers that flare from the knee and have wide bottoms.
▸ **ˈbell-ˌbottomed** ADJECTIVE

bellboy (ˈbɛlˌbɔɪ) NOUN a man or boy employed in a hotel, club, etc., to carry luggage and answer calls for service; page; porter. Also called (US and Canadian): **bellhop.**

bell bronze NOUN an alloy of copper and tin that contains a high proportion (at least 20 per cent) of tin: used for bell founding.

bell buoy NOUN a navigational buoy fitted with a bell, the clapper of which strikes when the waves move the buoy.

bell captain NOUN *US and Canadian* another name for **captain** (sense 9).

bell crank NOUN *Engineering* a lever with two arms having a common fulcrum at their junction.

belle (bɛl) NOUN [1] a beautiful girl or woman. [2] the most attractive or admired girl or woman at a place, function, etc. (esp in the phrase **the belle of the ball**).
▷HISTORY C17: from French, feminine of BEAU

Belleau Wood ('bɛləʊ; *French* bɛlo) NOUN a forest in N France: site of a battle (1918) in which the US Marines halted a German advance on Paris.

Belleek (bə'li:k) NOUN *Trademark* **a** a kind of thin fragile porcelain with a lustrous glaze. **b** (*as modifier*): *a Belleek vase*.
▷HISTORY named after *Belleek*, a town in Northern Ireland where such porcelain is made

belle époque *French* (bɛl epɔk) NOUN the period of comfortable well-established life before World War I.
▷HISTORY literally: fine period

Belle Isle NOUN an island in the Atlantic, at the N entrance to the **Strait of Belle Isle**, between Labrador and Newfoundland. Area: about 39 sq. km (15 sq. miles).

Bellerophon (bə'lɛrə,fɒn) NOUN *Greek myth* a hero of Corinth who performed many deeds with the help of the winged horse Pegasus, notably the killing of the monster Chimera.

belles-lettres (*French* bɛllɛtrə) NOUN (*functioning as singular*) literary works, esp essays and poetry, valued for their aesthetic rather than their informative or moral content.
▷HISTORY C17: from French: fine letters

belletrist (bɛl'lɛtrɪst) NOUN a writer of belles-lettres.
▸**bel'letrism** NOUN ▸**belletristic** (,bɛlɪ'trɪstɪk) ADJECTIVE

bellflower ('bɛl,flaʊə) NOUN another name for **campanula.**

bellfounder ('bɛl,faʊndə) NOUN a foundry worker who casts bells.
▸**'bell,foundry** NOUN

bell glass NOUN another name for **bell jar.**

bell heather NOUN an ericaceous shrub, *Erica cinerea*. See **heath** (sense 2).

bellhop ('bɛl,hɒp) NOUN *US and Canadian* another name for **bellboy.**

bellicose ('bɛlɪ,kəʊs, -,kəʊz) ADJECTIVE warlike; aggressive; ready to fight.
▷HISTORY C15: from Latin *bellicōsus*, from *bellum* war
▸**'belli,cosely** ADVERB ▸**bellicosity** (,bɛlɪ'kɒsɪtɪ) NOUN

belligerati (bɪ,lɪdʒə'rɑ:tɪ) PLURAL NOUN intellectuals, such as writers, who advocate war or imperialism.
▷HISTORY C20: from BELLIG(ERENT) + *-ati* as in LITERATI

belligerence (bɪ'lɪdʒərəns) NOUN the act or quality of being belligerent or warlike; aggressiveness.

belligerency (bɪ'lɪdʒərənsɪ) NOUN the state of being at war.

belligerent (bɪ'lɪdʒərənt) ADJECTIVE [1] marked by readiness to fight or argue; aggressive: *a belligerent tone*. [2] relating to or engaged in a legally recognized war or warfare. ◆ NOUN [3] a person or country engaged in fighting or war.
▷HISTORY C16: from Latin *belliger*, from *bellum* war + *gerere* to wage

Bellingshausen Sea ('bɛlɪŋz,haʊzᵊn) NOUN an area of the S Pacific Ocean off the coast of Antarctica.
▷HISTORY named after Fabian Gottlieb *Bellingshausen* (1778–1852), Russian explorer

Bellinzona (*Italian* bellin'tsona) NOUN a town in SE central Switzerland, capital of Ticino canton. Pop.: 35 860 (1990).

bell jar NOUN a bell-shaped glass cover used to protect flower arrangements or fragile ornaments or to cover apparatus in experiments, esp to prevent gases escaping.

bell magpie NOUN another name for **currawong.**

bellman ('bɛlmən) NOUN, *plural* **-men.** a man who rings a bell, esp (formerly) a town crier.

bell metal NOUN an alloy of copper and tin, with some zinc and lead, used in casting bells.

bell moth NOUN any moth of the family *Tortricidae*, which when at rest resemble the shape of a bell.

bellock ('bɛlək) VERB *Midland English dialect* to shout.

Bellona (bə'ləʊnə) NOUN the Roman goddess of war.

bellow ('bɛləʊ) VERB [1] (*intr*) to make a loud deep raucous cry like that of a bull; roar. [2] to shout (something) unrestrainedly, as in anger or pain; bawl. ◆ NOUN [3] the characteristic noise of a bull. [4] a loud deep sound, as of pain or anger.
▷HISTORY C14: probably from Old English *bylgan*; related to *bellan* to BELL[2]
▸**'bellower** NOUN

bellows ('bɛləʊz) NOUN (*functioning as singular or plural*) [1] Also called: **pair of bellows.** an instrument consisting of an air chamber with flexible sides or end, a means of compressing it, an inlet valve, and a constricted outlet that is used to create a stream of air, as for producing a draught for a fire or for sounding organ pipes. [2] *Photog* a telescopic light-tight sleeve, connecting the lens system of some cameras to the body of the instrument. [3] a flexible corrugated element used as an expansion joint, pump, or means of transmitting axial motion.
▷HISTORY C16: from plural of Old English *belig* BELLY

bellows fish NOUN another name for **snipefish.**

bell pull NOUN a handle, rope, or cord pulled to operate a doorbell or servant's bell.

bell punch NOUN a machine that issues or stamps a ticket, etc., ringing a bell as it does so.

bell push NOUN a button pressed to operate an electric bell.

bell-ringer NOUN [1] a person who rings church bells. [2] a person who plays musical handbells.
▸**'bell-,ringing** NOUN

bells and whistles PLURAL NOUN [1] additional features or accessories which are nonessential but very attractive: *my car has all the latest bells and whistles*. [2] additions, such as options or warranties, made to a financial product to increase its market appeal.
▷HISTORY C20: from the bells and whistles which used to decorate fairground organs

bell sheep NOUN *Austral* a sheep that a shearer is just starting to shear (and which he is allowed to finish) as the bell rings for the end of a work period.

bells of Ireland NOUN (*functioning as singular*) an annual garden plant, *Moluccella laevis*, whose flowers have a green cup-shaped calyx: family *Lamiaceae* (labiates).

Bell's palsy NOUN a usually temporary paralysis of the muscles of the face, normally on one side.
▷HISTORY C19: named after Sir Charles *Bell* (1774–1842), British anatomist

bell tent NOUN a cone-shaped tent having a single central supporting pole.

bell-topper NOUN *NZ obsolete, informal* a tall silk hat.

bellwether ('bɛl,wɛðə) NOUN [1] a sheep that leads the herd, often bearing a bell. [2] a leader, esp one followed blindly.

bellwort ('bɛl,wɜ:t) NOUN *US* [1] any plant of the North American liliaceous genus *Uvularia*, having slender bell-shaped yellow flowers. [2] another name for **campanula.**

belly ('bɛlɪ) NOUN, *plural* **-lies.** [1] the lower or front part of the body of a vertebrate, containing the intestines and other abdominal organs; abdomen. Related adjective: **ventral.** [2] the stomach, esp when regarded as the seat of gluttony. [3] a part, line, or structure that bulges deeply: *the belly of a sail*. [4] the inside or interior cavity of something: *the belly of a ship*. [5] the front or inner part or underside of something. [6] the surface of a stringed musical instrument over which the strings are stretched. [7] the thick central part of certain muscles. [8] *Austral and NZ* the wool from a sheep's belly. [9] *Tanning* the portion of a hide or skin on the underpart of an animal. [10] *Archery* the surface of the bow next to the bowstring. [11] *Archaic* the womb. [12] **go belly up.** *Informal* to die, fail, or come to an end. ◆ VERB **-lies, -lying, -lied.** [13] to swell out or cause to swell out; bulge.
▷HISTORY Old English *belig*; related to Old High German *balg*, Old Irish *bolg* sack, Sanskrit *barhi* chaff

bellyache ('bɛlɪ,eɪk) NOUN [1] an informal term for **stomachache.** ◆ VERB [2] (*intr*) *Slang* to complain repeatedly.
▸**'belly,acher** NOUN

bellyband ('bɛlɪ,bænd) NOUN a strap around the belly of a draught animal, holding the shafts of a vehicle.

bellybutton ('bɛlɪ,bʌtᵊn) NOUN an informal name for the **navel.**

belly dance NOUN [1] a sensuous and provocative dance of Middle Eastern origin, performed by women, with undulating movements of the hips and abdomen. ◆ VERB **belly-dance.** [2] (*intr*) to perform such a dance.
▸**belly dancer** NOUN

belly flop NOUN [1] a dive into water in which the body lands horizontally. [2] another name for **belly landing.** ◆ VERB **belly-flop, -flops, -flopping, -flopped.** [3] (*intr*) to perform a belly flop.

bellyful ('bɛlɪ,fʊl) NOUN [1] as much as one wants or can eat. [2] *Slang* more than one can tolerate.

belly landing NOUN the landing of an aircraft on its fuselage without use of its landing gear.

belly laugh NOUN a loud deep hearty laugh.

Belmopan (,bɛlmə'pæn) NOUN (since 1973) the capital of Belize, about 50 miles inland: founded in 1970. Pop.: 6490 (1996 est.).

Belo Horizonte (*Portuguese* 'bɛ:lori'zõ:ntə) NOUN a city in SE Brazil, the capital of Minas Gerais state. Pop.: 2 229 697 (2000).

belong (bɪ'lɒŋ) VERB (*intr*) [1] (foll by *to*) to be the property or possession (of). [2] (foll by *to*) to be bound to (a person, place, or club) by ties of affection, dependence, allegiance, or membership. [3] (foll by *to, under, with*, etc.) to be classified (with): *this plant belongs to the daisy family*. [4] (foll by *to*) to be a part or adjunct (of): *this top belongs to the smaller box*. [5] to have a proper or usual place: *that plate belongs in the cupboard*. [6] *Informal* to be suitable or acceptable, esp socially: *although they were rich, they just didn't belong*.
▷HISTORY C14 *belongen*, from BE- (intensive) + *longen*; related to Old High German *bilangēn* to reach; see LONG[3]

belonging (bɪ'lɒŋɪŋ) NOUN secure relationship; affinity (esp in the phrase **a sense of belonging**).

belongings (bɪ'lɒŋɪŋz) PLURAL NOUN (*sometimes singular*) the things that a person owns or has with him; possessions; effects.

Belorussia (,bjɛləʊ'rʌʃə, ,bɛl-) NOUN a variant spelling of **Belarus.**

Belorussian NOUN, ADJECTIVE a variant spelling of **Belarussian.**

Belostok (bjɪla'stɔk) NOUN transliteration of the Russian name for **Białystok.**

beloved (bɪ'lʌvɪd, -'lʌvd) ADJECTIVE [1] dearly loved. ◆ NOUN [2] a person who is dearly loved, such as a wife or husband.

Belovo (*Russian* 'bjɛləvə) NOUN a variant spelling of **Byelovo.**

below (bɪ'ləʊ) PREPOSITION [1] at or to a position lower than; under. [2] less than in quantity or degree. [3] south of. [4] downstream of. [5] unworthy of; beneath. ◆ ADVERB [6] at or to a lower position or place. [7] at a later place (in something written): *see below*. [8] *Archaic* beneath heaven; on earth or in hell.
▷HISTORY C14: *biloghe*, from *bi* BY + *looghe* LOW[1]

below stairs ADVERB (formerly) at or in the basement of a large house, considered as the place where the servants live and work.

below-the-line ADJECTIVE [1] denoting the entries printed below the horizontal line on a company's profit-and-loss account that show how any profit is to be distributed. [2] (of an advertising campaign) employing sales promotions, direct marketing, in-store exhibitions and displays, trade shows, sponsorship, and merchandising that do not involve an advertising agency. [3] (in national accounts) below the horizontal line separating revenue from capital transactions. Compare **above-the-line.**

Bel Paese ('bɛl pɑ:'eɪzɪ) NOUN a mild creamy Italian cheese.
▷HISTORY C20: from Italian, literally: beautiful country

Belsen ('bɛlsᵊn; *German* 'bɛlzən) NOUN a village in NE Germany: with Bergen, the site of a Nazi concentration camp (1943–45).

Belshazzar (bɛl'ʃæzə) NOUN 6th century B.C., the son of Nabonidus, coregent of Babylon with his father for eight years: referred to as king and son of Nebuchadnezzar in the Old Testament (Daniel 5:1, 17; 8:1); described as having received a divine message of doom written on a wall at a banquet (**Belshazzar's Feast**).

belt (bɛlt) NOUN 1 a band of cloth, leather, etc., worn, usually around the waist, to support clothing, carry tools, weapons, or ammunition, or as decoration. 2 a narrow band, circle, or stripe, as of colour. 3 an area, esp an elongated one, where a specific thing or specific conditions are found; zone: *the town belt; a belt of high pressure.* 4 a belt worn as a symbol of rank (as by a knight or an earl), or awarded as a prize (as in boxing or wrestling), or to mark particular expertise (as in judo or karate). 5 See **seat belt.** 6 a band of flexible material between rotating shafts or pulleys to transfer motion or transmit goods: *a fan belt; a conveyer belt.* 7 short for **beltcourse** (see **cordon**(sense 4)). 8 *Informal* a sharp blow, as with a bat or the fist. 9 **below the belt. a** *Boxing* below the waist, esp in the groin. **b** *Informal* in an unscrupulous or cowardly way. 10 **tighten one's belt.** to take measures to reduce expenditure. 11 **under one's belt. a** (of food or drink) in one's stomach. **b** in one's possession. **c** as part of one's experience: *he had a linguistics degree under his belt.* ◆ VERB 12 (*tr*) to fasten or attach with or as if with a belt. 13 (*tr*) to hit with a belt. 14 (*tr*) *Slang* to give a sharp blow; punch. 15 (*intr; often foll by along*) *Slang* to move very fast, esp in a car: *belting down the motorway.* 16 (*tr*) *Rare* to mark with belts, as of colour. 17 (*tr*) *Rare* to encircle; surround.
◆ See also **belt out, belt up.**
▷HISTORY Old English, from Latin *balteus*

belt-and-braces ADJECTIVE providing double security, in case one security measure should fail: *a belt-and-braces policy.*

Beltane (ˈbɛlteɪn, -tən) NOUN an ancient Celtic festival with a sacrificial bonfire on May Day. It is also celebrated by modern pagans.
▷HISTORY C15: from Scottish Gaelic *bealltainn*

beltcourse (ˈbɛltˌkɔːs) NOUN another name for **cordon** (sense 4).

belt drive NOUN *Engineering* a transmission system using a flexible belt to transfer power.

belter (ˈbɛltə) NOUN *Slang* 1 an event, person, quality, etc., that is admirable, outstanding, or thrilling: *a real belter of a match.* 2 **a** a rousing or spirited popular song that is sung loudly and enthusiastically. **b** a person who sings popular songs in a loud and spirited manner.

belting (ˈbɛltɪŋ) NOUN 1 the material used to make a belt or belts. 2 belts collectively. 3 *Informal* a beating.

belt man NOUN *Austral and NZ* (formerly) the member of a beach life-saving team who swam out with a line attached to his belt.

belt out VERB (*tr, adverb*) *Informal* to sing loudly or emit (sound, esp pop music) loudly: *a jukebox belting out the latest hits.*

belt up VERB (*adverb*) 1 *Slang* to become or cause to become silent; stop talking: often used in the imperative. 2 to fasten with or by a belt, esp a seat belt.

beltway (ˈbɛltˌweɪ) NOUN 1 the usual US name for a **ring road.** 2 (*usually with capital*) **a** the people and institutions located in the area bounded by the Washington Beltway, taken to be politically and socially out of touch with the rest of America and much given to political intrigue. **b** (*as modifier*): *Beltway Cassandras.*

beluga (bɪˈluːgə) NOUN 1 a large white sturgeon, *Acipenser* (or *Huso*) *huso*, of the Black and Caspian Seas: a source of caviar and isinglass. 2 another name for **white whale.**
▷HISTORY C18: from Russian *byeluga*, from *byely* white

belvedere (ˈbɛlvɪˌdɪə, ˌbɛlvɪˈdɪə) NOUN a building, such as a summerhouse or roofed gallery, sited to command a fine view. See also **gazebo.**
▷HISTORY C16: from Italian: beautiful sight

Belvoir Castle (ˈbiːvə) NOUN a castle in Leicestershire, near Grantham (in Lincolnshire): seat of the Dukes of Rutland; rebuilt by James Wyatt in 1816.

BEM ABBREVIATION FOR British Empire Medal.

bema, bimah, *or* **bima** (ˈbiːmə) NOUN 1 the speaker's platform in the assembly in ancient Athens. 2 *Christian Orthodox Church* a raised area surrounding the altar in a church; the sanctuary. 3 *Judaism* another word for **almemar.**
▷HISTORY C17: via Late Latin, from Greek *bēma*, from *bainein* to go

Bemba (ˈbɛmbə) NOUN 1 (*plural* **-ba** *or* **-bas**) a member of a Negroid people of Africa, living chiefly in Zambia on a high infertile plateau. 2 the language of this people, belonging to the Bantu group of the Niger-Congo family.

Bembo (ˈbɛmbəʊ) NOUN a style of type.
▷HISTORY C20: named after Pietro *Bembo* (1470–1547), Italian scholar, poet, and cardinal, because the design of the typeface was based on one used for an edition of his tract *De ætna* by the printer Aldus Manutius

bemean (bɪˈmiːn) VERB a less common word for **demean.**

bemire (bɪˈmaɪə) VERB (*tr*) 1 to soil with or as if with mire. 2 (*usually passive*) to stick fast in mud or mire.

bemoan (bɪˈməʊn) VERB to grieve over (a loss, etc.); mourn; lament (esp in the phrase **bemoan one's fate**).
▷HISTORY Old English *bemǣnan*; see BE-, MOAN

bemuse (bɪˈmjuːz) VERB (*tr*) to confuse; bewilder.
▸**beˈmusement** NOUN ▸**beˈmusing** ADJECTIVE

bemused (bɪˈmjuːzd) ADJECTIVE preoccupied; lost in thought.
▸**bemusedly** (bɪˈmjuːzɪdlɪ) ADVERB

ben[1] (bɛn) *Scot* ◆ NOUN 1 an inner room in a house or cottage. ◆ PREPOSITION, ADVERB 2 in; within; inside; into the inner part (of a house). ◆ ADJECTIVE 3 inner. Compare **but**[2].
▷HISTORY Old English *binnan*, from BE- + *innan* inside

ben[2] (bɛn) NOUN 1 any of several Asiatic trees of the genus *Moringa*, esp *M. oleifera* of Arabia and India, whose seeds yield **oil of ben**, used in manufacturing perfumes and cosmetics, lubricating delicate machinery, etc.: family *Moringaceae*. 2 the seed of such a tree.
▷HISTORY C15: from Arabic *bān*

ben[3] (bɛn) NOUN *Scot, Irish* a mountain peak (esp in place names): *Ben Lomond.*
▷HISTORY C18: from Gaelic *beinn*, from *beann*

Benadryl (ˈbɛnədrɪl) NOUN *Trademark* an antihistamine drug used in sleeping tablets; diphenhydramine. Formula: $C_{17}H_{21}NO$.

bename (bɪˈneɪm) VERB **-names, -naming, -named; -named** *or* **-nempt.** an archaic word for **name** (sense 12).
▷HISTORY Old English *benemnan*; see BE-, NAME

Benares (bɪˈnɑːrɪz) *or* **Banaras** NOUN the former name of **Varanasi.**

bench (bɛntʃ) NOUN 1 a long seat for more than one person, usually lacking a back or arms. 2 a plain stout worktable. 3 **the bench.** (*sometimes capital*) **a** a judge or magistrate sitting in court in a judicial capacity. **b** judges or magistrates collectively. 4 *Sport* the seat on which reserve players and officials sit during a game. 5 *Geology* a flat narrow platform of land, esp one marking a former shoreline. 6 a ledge in a mine or quarry from which work is carried out. 7 a platform on which dogs or other domestic animals are exhibited at shows. 8 *NZ* a hollow on a hillside formed by sheep. ◆ VERB (*tr*) 9 to provide with benches. 10 to exhibit (a dog, etc.) at a show. 11 *NZ* to form (a track) up a hill by excavating a flattened area. 12 *US and Canadian sport* to take or keep (a player) out of a game, often for disciplinary reasons.
▷HISTORY Old English *benc*; related to Old Norse *bekkr*, Old High German *bank*, Danish, Swedish *bänk*; see BANK[3]

bencher (ˈbɛntʃə) NOUN (*often plural*) *Brit* 1 a member of the governing body of one of the Inns of Court, usually a judge or a Queen's Counsel. 2 See **backbencher.**

benchmark (ˈbɛntʃˌmɑːk) NOUN 1 a mark on a stone post or other permanent feature, at a point whose exact elevation and position is known: used as a reference point in surveying. Abbreviation: **BM.** 2 **a** a criterion by which to measure something; standard; reference point. **b** (*as modifier*): *a benchmark test.* ◆ VERB 3 to measure or test against a benchmark: *the firm benchmarked its pay against that in industry.*

benchmark position NOUN *NZ* a public service job used for comparison with a similar position, such as a position in commerce, for wage settlements.

bench press NOUN 1 a weight-training exercise in which a person lies on a bench and pushes a barbell upwards with both hands from chest level until the arms are straight, then lowers it again. ◆ VERB **bench-press.** 2 (*intr*) to carry out one or more bench presses.

bench test NOUN the critical evaluation of a new or repaired component, device, apparatus, etc., prior to installation to ensure that it is in perfect condition.

bench warrant NOUN a warrant issued by a judge or court directing that an offender be apprehended.

benchy (ˈbɛntʃɪ) ADJECTIVE *NZ* (of a hillside) hollowed out in benches.

bend[1] (bɛnd) VERB **bends, bending, bent.** 1 to form or cause to form a curve, as by pushing or pulling. 2 to turn or cause to turn from a particular direction: *the road bends left past the church.* 3 (*intr; often foll by down*, etc.) to incline the body; stoop; bow. 4 to submit or cause to submit: *to bend before superior force.* 5 (*tr*) to turn or direct (one's eyes, steps, attention, etc.). 6 (*tr*) to concentrate (the mind); apply oneself closely. 7 (*tr*) *Nautical* to attach or fasten, as a sail to a boom or a line to a cleat. 8 **bend over backwards.** *Informal* to make a special effort, esp in order to please: *he bends over backwards to accommodate his customers.* 9 **bend (someone's) ear.** *Informal* to speak at length to an unwilling listener, esp to voice one's troubles. 10 **bend the rules.** *Informal* to ignore rules or change them to suit one's own convenience. ◆ NOUN 11 a curved part, as in a road or river. 12 *Nautical* a knot or eye in a line for joining it to another or to an object. 13 the act or state of bending. 14 *Brit slang* **round the bend.** mad; crazy; eccentric. ◆ See also **bends.**
▷HISTORY Old English *bendan*; related to Old Norse *benda*, Middle High German *benden*; see BIND, BAND[3]

bend[2] (bɛnd) NOUN *Heraldry* an ordinary consisting of a diagonal line traversing a shield.
▷HISTORY Old English *bend* BAND[2]; see BEND[1]

Ben Day process NOUN *Printing* a method of adding texture, shading, or detail to line drawings by overlaying a transparent sheet of dots or any other pattern during platemaking.
▷HISTORY C20: named after *Benjamin Day* (1838–1916), American printer

bender (ˈbɛndə) NOUN 1 *Informal* a drinking bout. 2 *Brit derogatory slang* a male homosexual. 3 *Informal* a makeshift shelter constructed by placing tarpaulin or plastic sheeting over bent saplings or woven branches.

Bendigo (ˈbɛndɪˌgəʊ) NOUN a city in SE Australia, in central Victoria: founded in 1851 after the discovery of gold. Pop.: 57 427 (1991).

bending moment NOUN the algebraic sum of all the moments to one side of a cross-section of a beam or other structural support.

bends (bɛndz) PLURAL NOUN **the.** (*functioning as singular or plural*) a nontechnical name for **decompression sickness.**

bend sinister NOUN *Heraldry* a diagonal line bisecting a shield from the top right to the bottom left, typically indicating a bastard line.

bendy[1] (ˈbɛndɪ) ADJECTIVE **bendier, bendiest.** 1 flexible or pliable. 2 having many bends: *a bendy road.*

bendy[2] *or* **bendee** (ˈbɛndɪ) ADJECTIVE (*usually postpositive*) *Heraldry* striped diagonally.

beneath (bɪˈniːθ) PREPOSITION 1 below, esp if covered, protected, or obscured by. 2 not as great or good as would be demanded by: *beneath his dignity.* ◆ ADVERB 3 below; underneath.
▷HISTORY Old English *beneothan*, from BE- + *neothan* low; see NETHER

benedicite (ˌbɛnɪˈdaɪsɪtɪ) NOUN 1 (esp in Christian religious orders) a blessing or grace. ◆ INTERJECTION 2 *Obsolete* an expression of surprise.
▷HISTORY C13: from Latin, from *benedīcere*, from *bene* well + *dīcere* to speak

Benedicite (ˌbɛnɪˈdaɪsɪtɪ) NOUN *Christianity* a canticle that originated as part of the *Song of the*

Three Holy Children in the secondary addition to the Book of Daniel, beginning *Benedicite omnia opera Domini Domino* in Latin, and *O all ye Works of the Lord* in English.

Benedictine NOUN 1 (ˌbɛnɪˈdɪktɪn, -taɪn) a monk or nun who is a member of a Christian religious community founded by or following the rule of Saint Benedict (?480–?547 A.D.), the Italian monk. 2 (ˌbɛnɪˈdɪktiːn) a greenish-yellow liqueur made from a secret formula developed at the Benedictine monastery at Fécamp in France in about 1510. ◆ ADJECTIVE 3 (ˌbɛnɪˈdɪktɪn, -taɪn) of or relating to Saint Benedict, his order, or his rule.

benediction (ˌbɛnɪˈdɪkʃən) NOUN 1 an invocation of divine blessing, esp at the end of a Christian religious ceremony. 2 a Roman Catholic service in which the congregation is blessed with the sacrament. 3 the state of being blessed.
▷HISTORY C15: from Latin *benedictio*, from *benedīcere* to bless; see BENEDICITE
▸ˌ**beneˈdictory** ADJECTIVE

Benedict's solution *or* **reagent** NOUN a chemical solution used to detect the presence of glucose and other reducing sugars. Medically, it is used to test the urine of diabetics.
▷HISTORY named after S. R. *Benedict* (1884–1936), US chemist

Benedictus (ˌbɛnɪˈdɪktəs) NOUN (*sometimes not capital*) *Christianity* 1 a short canticle beginning *Benedictus qui venit in nomine Domini* in Latin and *Blessed is he that cometh in the name of the Lord* in English. 2 a canticle beginning *Benedictus Dominus Deus Israel* in Latin and *Blessed be the Lord God of Israel* in English.

benefaction (ˌbɛnɪˈfækʃən) NOUN 1 the act of doing good, esp by giving a donation to charity. 2 the donation or help given.
▷HISTORY C17: from Late Latin *benefactiō*, from Latin *bene* well + *facere* to do

benefactor (ˈbɛnɪˌfæktə, ˌbɛnɪˈfæk-) NOUN a person who supports or helps a person, institution, etc., esp by giving money; patron.
▸ˈ**beneˌfactress** FEMININE NOUN

benefic (bɪˈnɛfɪk) ADJECTIVE a rare word for **beneficent**.

benefice (ˈbɛnɪfɪs) NOUN 1 *Christianity* an endowed Church office yielding an income to its holder; a Church living. 2 the property or revenue attached to such an office. 3 (in feudal society) a tenement (piece of land) held by a vassal from a landowner on easy terms or free, esp in return for military support. See also **vassalage.** ◆ VERB 4 (*tr*) to provide with a benefice.
▷HISTORY C14: from Old French, from Latin *beneficium* benefit, from *beneficus*, from *bene* well + *facere* to do

beneficence (bɪˈnɛfɪsəns) NOUN 1 the act of doing good; kindness. 2 a charitable act or gift.

beneficent (bɪˈnɛfɪsᵊnt) ADJECTIVE charitable; generous.
▷HISTORY C17: from Latin *beneficent-*, from *beneficus*; see BENEFICE
▸**beˈneficently** ADVERB

beneficial (ˌbɛnɪˈfɪʃəl) ADJECTIVE 1 (sometimes foll by *to*) causing a good result; advantageous. 2 *Law* entitling a person to receive the profits or proceeds of property: *a beneficial interest in land.*
▷HISTORY C15: from Late Latin *beneficiālis*, from Latin *beneficium* kindness
▸ˌ**beneˈficially** ADVERB

beneficiary (ˌbɛnɪˈfɪʃərɪ) NOUN, *plural* **-ciaries.** 1 a person who gains or benefits in some way from something. 2 *Law* a person entitled to receive funds or other property under a trust, will, or insurance policy. 3 the holder of an ecclesiastical or other benefice. 4 *NZ* a person who receives government assistance: *social security beneficiary.* ◆ ADJECTIVE 5 of or relating to a benefice or the holder of a benefice.

benefit (ˈbɛnɪfɪt) NOUN 1 something that improves or promotes. 2 advantage or sake: *this is for your benefit.* 3 *Brit* **a** an allowance paid by the government as for sickness, unemployment, etc., to which a person is entitled under social security or the national insurance scheme. **b** any similar allowance in various other countries. 4 (*sometimes plural*) a payment or series of payments made by an institution, such as an insurance company or trade union, to a person who is ill, unemployed, etc. 5 a theatrical performance, sports event, etc., to raise money for a charity. ◆ VERB **-fits, -fiting, -fited** *or esp US* **-fits, -fitting, -fitted.** 6 to do or receive good; profit.
▷HISTORY C14: from Anglo-French *benfet*, from Latin *benefactum*, from *bene facere* to do well

benefit in kind NOUN a nonpecuniary benefit, such as a company car or medical insurance, given to an employee.

benefit of clergy NOUN *Christianity* 1 sanction by the church: *marriage without benefit of clergy.* 2 (in the Middle Ages) a privilege that placed the clergy outside the jurisdiction of secular courts and entitled them to trial in ecclesiastical courts.

benefit society NOUN a US term for **friendly society.**

Benelux (ˈbɛnɪˌlʌks) NOUN 1 the customs union formed by Belgium, the Netherlands, and Luxembourg in 1948; became an economic union in 1960. 2 these countries collectively.

benempt (bɪˈnɛmpt) VERB *Archaic* a past participle of **bename.**

Benevento (ˌbɛnəˈvɛntəʊ) NOUN a city in S Italy, in N Campania: at various times under Samnite, Roman, Lombard, Saracen, Norman, and papal rule. Pop.: 64 690 (1990). Ancient name: **Beneventum** (ˌbɛnəˈvɛntʊm).

benevolence (bɪˈnɛvələns) NOUN 1 inclination or tendency to help or do good to others; charity. 2 an act of kindness. 3 (in the Middle Ages) a forced loan or contribution exacted by English kings from their nobility and subjects.

benevolent (bɪˈnɛvələnt) ADJECTIVE 1 intending or showing goodwill; kindly; friendly: *a benevolent smile; a benevolent old man.* 2 doing good or giving aid to others, rather than making profit; charitable: *a benevolent organization.*
▷HISTORY C15: from Latin *benevolēns*, from *bene* well + *velle* to wish
▸**beˈnevolently** ADVERB

Benfleet (ˈbɛnˌfliːt) NOUN a town in SE England, in S Essex on an inlet of the Thames estuary. Pop.: 49 701 (1991).

BEng ABBREVIATION FOR Bachelor of Engineering.

Bengal (bɛnˈgɔːl, bɛŋ-) NOUN 1 a former province of NE India, in the great deltas of the Ganges and Brahmaputra Rivers: in 1947 divided into West Bengal (belonging to India) and East Bengal (Bangladesh). 2 **Bay of.** a wide arm of the Indian Ocean, between India and Myanmar. 3 a breed of medium-large cat with a spotted or marbled coat.

Bengali (bɛnˈgɔːlɪ, bɛŋ-) NOUN 1 a member of a people living chiefly in Bangladesh and in West Bengal. The West Bengalis are mainly Hindus; the East Bengalis of Bangladesh are mainly Muslims. 2 the language of this people: the official language of Bangladesh and the chief language of West Bengal; it belongs to the Indic branch of the Indo-European family. Also called: **Bangla.** ◆ ADJECTIVE 3 of or relating to Bengal, the Bengalis, or their language.

bengaline (ˈbɛŋgəˌliːn, ˌbɛŋgəˈliːn) NOUN a heavy corded fabric, esp silk with woollen or cotton cord.
▷HISTORY C19: from French; see BENGAL, -INE[1]; first produced in Bengal

Bengal light NOUN a firework or flare that burns with a steady bright blue light, formerly used as a signal.

Bengbu (ˈbɛŋˈbuː), **Pengpu,** *or* **Pang-fou** NOUN a city in E China, in Anhui province. Pop.: 506 239 (1999 est.).

Benghazi *or* **Bengasi** (bɛnˈgɑːzɪ) NOUN a port in N Libya, on the Gulf of Sidra: centre of Italian colonization (1911–42); scene of much fighting in World War II. Pop.: 650 000 (1995 est.). Ancient names: **Hesperides, Berenice** (bɛrəˈnaɪsɪ).

Benguela (bɛŋˈgwɛlə) NOUN a port in W Angola: founded in 1617; a terminus (with Lobito) of the railway that runs from Beira in Mozambique through the Copper Belt of Zambia and Zimbabwe. Pop.: 41 000 (latest est.).

Beni (*Spanish* ˈbeni) NOUN a river in N Bolivia, rising in the E Cordillera of the Andes and flowing north to the Marmoré River. Length: over 1600 km (1000 miles).

benighted (bɪˈnaɪtɪd) ADJECTIVE 1 lacking cultural, moral, or intellectual enlightenment; ignorant. 2 *Archaic* overtaken by night.
▸**beˈnightedly** ADVERB ▸**beˈnightedness** NOUN

benign (bɪˈnaɪn) ADJECTIVE 1 showing kindliness; genial. 2 (of soil, climate, etc.) mild; gentle. 3 favourable; propitious. 4 *Pathol* (of a tumour, etc.) not threatening to life or health; not malignant.
▷HISTORY C14: from Old French *benigne*, from Latin *benignus*, from *bene* well + *gignere* to produce
▸**beˈnignly** ADVERB

benignant (bɪˈnɪgnənt) ADJECTIVE 1 kind; gracious, as a king to his subjects. 2 a less common word for **benign** (senses 3, 4).
▸**beˈnignancy** NOUN ▸**beˈnignantly** ADVERB

benignity (bɪˈnɪgnɪtɪ) NOUN, *plural* **-ties.** 1 the quality of being benign; favourable attitude. 2 a kind or gracious act.

Beni Hasan (ˈbɛnɪ hæˈsɑːn) NOUN a village in central Egypt, on the Nile, with cliff-cut tombs dating from 2000 B.C.

Benin (bɛˈniːn) NOUN 1 a republic in W Africa, on the **Bight of Benin,** a section of the Gulf of Guinea: in the early 19th century a powerful kingdom, famed for its women warriors; became a French colony in 1893, gaining independence in 1960. It consists chiefly of coastal lagoons and swamps in the south, a fertile plain and marshes in the centre, and the Atakora Mountains in the northwest. Official language: French. Religion: animist majority. Currency: franc. Capital: Porto Novo (the government is based in Cotonou). Pop.: 6 591 000 (2001 est.). Area: 112 622 sq. km (43 474 sq. miles). Former name (until 1975): **Dahomey.** 2 a former kingdom of W Africa, powerful from the 14th to the 17th centuries: now a province of S Nigeria: noted for its bronzes.

Benin City NOUN a city in S Nigeria, capital of Edo state: former capital of the kingdom of Benin. Pop.: 229 400 (1996 est.).

Beninese (ˌbɛniːˈniːz) ADJECTIVE 1 of or relating to Benin or its people. ◆ NOUN 2 a native or inhabitant of Benin. Also: **Beninois** (ˌbɛniːˈnwɑː).

Benioff zone (ˈbɛnɪəf) NOUN a long narrow region, usually adjacent to a continent, along which earthquake foci lie on a plane which dips downwards at about 45° and along which the oceanic lithosphere is thought to be descending into the earth's interior. Compare **subduction zone.**
▷HISTORY C20: named after Hugo *Benioff* (1899–1968), American seismologist, who first discovered the phenomenon

benison (ˈbɛnɪzᵊn, -sᵊn) NOUN *Archaic* a blessing, esp a spoken one.
▷HISTORY C13: from Old French *beneison*, from Latin *benedictiō* BENEDICTION

benjamin (ˈbɛndʒəmɪn) NOUN 1 another name for **benzoin** (sense 1). 2 **benjamin bush.** another name for **spicebush.**
▷HISTORY C16: variant of *benzoin*; influenced in form by the name *Benjamin*

Benjamin (ˈbɛndʒəmɪn) NOUN 1 *Old Testament* **a** the youngest and best-loved son of Jacob and Rachel (Genesis 35:16–18; 42:4). **b** the tribe descended from this patriarch. **c** the territory of this tribe, northwest of the Dead Sea. 2 *Archaic* a youngest and favourite son.

Ben Lomond (bɛn ˈləʊmənd) NOUN 1 a mountain in W central Scotland, on the E side of Loch Lomond. Height: 973 m (3192 ft.). 2 a mountain in NE Tasmania. Height: 1527 m (5010 ft.). 3 a mountain in SE Australia, in NE New South Wales. Height: 1520 m (4986 ft.).

benne (ˈbɛnɪ) NOUN 1 another name for **sesame.** 2 **benne oil.** the edible oil obtained from sesame seeds.
▷HISTORY C18: from Malay *bene*; compare Bambara *bene*

bennet (ˈbɛnɪt) NOUN short for **herb bennet.**

Ben Nevis (bɛn ˈnɛvɪs) NOUN a mountain in W Scotland, in the Grampian mountains: highest peak in Great Britain. Height: 1343 m (4406 ft.).

Bennington (ˈbɛnɪŋtən) NOUN a town in SW Vermont: the site of a British defeat (1777) in the War of American Independence. Pop.: 16 451 (1990).

benny[1] (ˈbɛnɪ) NOUN, *plural* **-nies.** *Dated slang* an amphetamine tablet, esp benzedrine: a stimulant.
▷HISTORY C20: shortened from BENZEDRINE

benny[2] ('bɛnɪ) NOUN, *plural* **-nies.** *US slang* a man's overcoat.
▷HISTORY C19: from *Benjamin*, perhaps from a tailor's name

benomyl ('bɛnəmɪl) NOUN a fungicide derived from imidazole, used on cereal and fruit crops: suspected of being carcinogenic.

Benoni (bɪ'nəʊnɪ) NOUN a city in NE South Africa: gold mines. Pop.: 365 467 (1996).

bent[1] (bɛnt) ADJECTIVE [1] not straight; curved. [2] (foll by *on*) fixed (on a course of action); resolved (to); determined (to). [3] *Slang* **a** dishonest; corrupt. **b** (of goods) stolen. **c** crazy; mad. **d** sexually deviant, esp homosexual. ◆ NOUN [4] personal inclination, propensity, or aptitude. [5] capacity of endurance (esp in the phrase **to the top of one's bent**). [6] *Civil engineering* a framework placed across a structure to stiffen it.

bent[2] (bɛnt) NOUN [1] short for **bent grass.** [2] a stalk of bent grass. [3] *Archaic* any stiff grass or sedge. [4] *Archaic, or, Scot and northern English dialect* heath or moorland.
▷HISTORY Old English *bionot*; related to Old Saxon *binet*, Old High German *binuz* rush

bent grass NOUN any perennial grass of the genus *Agrostis*, esp *A. tenuis*, which has a spreading panicle of tiny flowers. Some species are planted for hay or in lawns. Sometimes shortened to: **bent.**

Benthamism ('bɛnθəˌmɪzəm) NOUN the philosophy of utilitarianism as first expounded by the British philosopher and jurist Jeremy Bentham (1748–1832) in terms of an action being good that has a greater tendency to augment the happiness of the community than to diminish it.
▸**'Benthaˌmite** NOUN, ADJECTIVE

benthos ('bɛnθɒs) *or* **benthon** NOUN [1] the animals and plants living at the bottom of a sea or lake. [2] the bottom of a sea or lake.
▷HISTORY C19: from Greek: depth; related to *bathus* deep
▸**'benthic** *or* **'benthal** *or* **ben'thonic** ADJECTIVE

bento *or* **bento box** ('bɛntəʊ) NOUN, *plural* **-tos.** a thin box, made of plastic or lacquered wood, divided into compartments which contain small separate dishes comprising a Japanese meal, esp lunch.
▷HISTORY Japanese *bentō* box lunch

bentonite ('bɛntəˌnaɪt) NOUN a valuable clay, formed by the decomposition of volcanic ash, that swells as it absorbs water: used as a filler in the building, paper, and pharmaceutical industries.
▷HISTORY C19: from Fort *Benton*, Montana, USA, where found, + -ITE[1]

bentwood ('bɛntˌwʊd) NOUN **a** wood bent in moulds after being heated by steaming, used mainly for furniture. **b** (*as modifier*): *a bentwood chair.*

Benue ('bɛnʊˌeɪ) NOUN [1] a state of SE Nigeria, formed in 1976 from part of Benue-Plateau state. Capital: Makurdi. Pop.: 3 108 754 (1995 est.). Area: 34 059 sq. km (13 150 sq. miles). [2] a river in W Africa, rising in N Cameroon and flowing west across Nigeria: chief tributary of the River Niger. Length: 1400 km (870 miles).

Benue-Congo NOUN [1] a branch of the Niger-Congo family of African languages, consisting of the Bantu languages together with certain other languages of W Africa. ◆ ADJECTIVE [2] relating or belonging to this group of languages.

benumb (bɪ'nʌm) VERB (*tr*) [1] to make numb or powerless; deaden physical feeling in, as by cold. [2] (*usually passive*) to make inactive; stupefy (the mind, senses, will, etc.).
▸**be'numbingly** ADVERB

Benxi ('bɛn'ʃiː), **Penchi,** *or* **Penki** NOUN an industrial city in SE China, in S Liaoning province. Pop.: 827 203 (1999 est.).

benzaldehyde (bɛn'zældɪˌhaɪd) NOUN a yellowish fragrant volatile oil occurring in almond kernels and used in the manufacture of dyes, perfumes, and flavourings and as a solvent for oils and resins. Formula: C_6H_5CHO. Systematic name: **benzenecarbaldehyde.**

Benzedrine ('bɛnzɪˌdriːn, -drɪn) NOUN a trademark for **amphetamine.**

benzene ('bɛnziːn, bɛn'ziːn) NOUN a colourless flammable toxic aromatic liquid used in the manufacture of styrene, phenol, etc., as a solvent for fats, resins, etc., and as an insecticide. Formula: C_6H_6. See also **benzene ring.**

benzenecarbaldehyde (ˌbɛnziːnkɑː'bældɪˌhaɪd) NOUN the systematic name for **benzaldehyde.**

benzenecarbonyl (ˌbɛnziːn'kɑːbɒnaɪl) NOUN (*modifier*) the systematic name for **benzoyl.**

benzenecarboxylate (ˌbɛnziːnkɑː'bɒksɪˌleɪt) NOUN the systematic name for **benzoate.**

benzenecarboxylic acid (ˌbɛnziːnˌkɑːbɒk'sɪlɪk) NOUN the systematic name for **benzoic acid.**

benzene hexachloride NOUN another name for **hexachlorocyclohexane.**

benzene ring NOUN the hexagonal ring of bonded carbon atoms in the benzene molecule or its derivatives. Also called: **benzene nucleus.** See also **Kekulé formula.**

benzidine ('bɛnzɪˌdiːn, -dɪn) NOUN a grey or reddish poisonous crystalline powder that is used mainly in the manufacture of dyes, esp Congo red. Formula: $NH_2(C_6H_4)_2NH_2$.

benzine ('bɛnziːn, bɛn'ziːn) *or* **benzin** ('bɛnzɪn) NOUN a volatile mixture of the lighter aliphatic hydrocarbon constituents of petroleum. See **ligroin, petroleum ether.**

benzo- *or sometimes before a vowel* **benz-** COMBINING FORM [1] indicating a benzene ring fused to another ring in a polycyclic compound: *benzofuran.* [2] indicating derivation from benzene or benzoic acid or the presence of phenyl groups: *benzophenone.*
▷HISTORY from BENZOIN

benzoate ('bɛnzəʊˌeɪt, -ɪt) NOUN any salt or ester of benzoic acid, containing the group C_6H_5COO– or the ion $C_6H_5COO^-$. Systematic name: **benzenecarboxylate.**

benzoate of soda NOUN another name for **sodium benzoate.**

benzocaine ('bɛnzəʊˌkeɪn) NOUN a white crystalline ester used as a local anaesthetic; ethyl *para*-aminobenzoate. Formula: $C_9H_{11}NO_2$.

benzodiazepine (ˌbɛnzəʊdaɪ'eɪzəˌpiːn) NOUN any of a group of chemical compounds that are used as minor tranquillizers, such as diazepam (Valium) and chlordiazepoxide (Librium).
▷HISTORY C20: from BENZO- + DI-[1] + AZA- + EP- + -INE[2]

benzofuran (ˌbɛnzəʊ'fjʊəræn) NOUN a colourless insoluble aromatic liquid obtained from coal tar and used in the manufacture of synthetic resins. Formula: C_8H_6O. Also called: **coumarone, cumarone.**

benzoic (bɛn'zəʊɪk) ADJECTIVE of, containing, or derived from benzoic acid or benzoin.

benzoic acid NOUN a white crystalline solid occurring in many natural resins, used in the manufacture of benzoates, plasticizers, and dyes and as a food preservative (**E210**). Formula: C_6H_5COOH. Systematic name: **benzenecarboxylic acid.**

benzoin ('bɛnzɔɪn, -zəʊɪn, bɛn'zəʊɪn) NOUN [1] Also called: **benjamin.** a gum resin containing benzoic acid, obtained from various trees of the genus *Styrax*, esp *S. benzoin* of Java and Sumatra, and used in ointments, perfume, etc. [2] a white or yellowish crystalline compound with a camphor-like odour used as an antiseptic and flavouring; 2-hydroxy-2-phenylacetophenone. Formula: $C_6H_5CHOHCOC_6H_5$. [3] any lauraceous aromatic shrub or tree of the genus *Lindera*, esp *L. benzoin* (spicebush).
▷HISTORY C16: from French *benjoin*, from Old Catalan *benjui*, from Arabic *lubān jāwī*, literally: frankincense of Java

benzol *or* **benzole** ('bɛnzɒl) NOUN [1] a crude form of benzene, containing toluene, xylene, and other hydrocarbons, obtained from coal tar or coal gas and used as a fuel. [2] an obsolete name for **benzene.**

benzophenone (ˌbɛnzəʊfɪ'nəʊn) NOUN a white sweet-smelling crystalline solid used mainly in the manufacture of organic compounds and in perfume. Formula: $C_6H_5COC_6H_5$. Also called: **diphenylketone.**

benzoquinone (ˌbɛnzəʊkwɪ'nəʊn, -'kwɪnəʊn) NOUN a yellow crystalline water-soluble unsaturated ketone manufactured from aniline and used in the production of dyestuffs. Formula: $C_6H_4O_2$. Also called: **quinone.** Systematic name: **cyclohexadiene-1,4-quinone.**

benzoyl ('bɛnzəʊɪl) NOUN (*modifier*) of, consisting of, or containing the monovalent group C_6H_5CO-: *benzoyl group or radical.* Systematic name: **benzenecarbonyl.**

benzyl ('bɛnzaɪl) NOUN (*modifier*) of, consisting of, or containing the monovalent group $C_6H_5CH_2$–: *benzyl alcohol.* Systematic name: **phenylmethyl.**

Beograd (bɛ'ɔgrad) NOUN the Serbo-Croat name for **Belgrade.**

Beothuk (bɪ'ɒθʊk) NOUN a member of an extinct Native Canadian people formerly living in Newfoundland.

Beowulf ('beɪəˌwʊlf) NOUN an anonymous Old English epic poem in alliterative verse, believed to have been composed in the 8th century A.D.

bequeath (bɪ'kwiːð, -'kwiːθ) VERB (*tr*) [1] *Law* to dispose of (property, esp personal property) by will. Compare **devise** (sense 2). [2] to hand down; pass on, as to following generations.
▷HISTORY Old English *becwethan*; related to Old Norse *kvetha* to speak, Gothic *qithan*, Old High German *quethan*
▸**be'queather** NOUN

bequest (bɪ'kwɛst) NOUN [1] **a** the act of bequeathing. **b** something that is bequeathed. [2] *Law* a gift of property by will, esp personal property. Compare **devise** (senses 4, 5).
▷HISTORY C14: BE- + Old English *-cwiss* degree; see BEQUEATH

Berar (bɛ'rɑː) NOUN a region of W central India: part of Maharashtra state since 1956; important for cotton growing.

berate (bɪ'reɪt) VERB (*tr*) to scold harshly.

Berber ('bɜːbə) NOUN [1] a member of a Caucasoid Muslim people of N Africa. [2] the language of this people, forming a subfamily of the Afro-Asiatic family of languages. There are extensive differences between dialects. ◆ ADJECTIVE [3] of or relating to this people or their language.

Berbera ('bɜːbərə) NOUN a port in N Somalia, on the Gulf of Aden. Pop.: 70 000 (latest est.).

berbere (beə'beə) NOUN a hot-tasting Ethiopian paste made from garlic, cayenne pepper, coriander, and other spices, often used in stews.
▷HISTORY French

berberidaceous (ˌbɜːbərɪ'deɪʃəs) ADJECTIVE of, relating to, or belonging to the *Berberidaceae*, a mainly N temperate family of flowering plants (mostly shrubs), including barberry and barrenwort.
▷HISTORY C19: from Medieval Latin *berberis*, from Arabic *barbārīs* BARBERRY

berberine ('bɜːbəˌriːn) NOUN a yellow bitter-tasting alkaloid obtained from barberry and other plants and used medicinally, esp in tonics. Formula: $C_{20}H_{19}NO_5$.
▷HISTORY C19: from German *Berberin*, from New Latin *berberis* BARBERRY

berberis ('bɜːbərɪs) NOUN any shrub of the berberidaceous genus *Berberis*. See **barberry.**
▷HISTORY C19: from Medieval Latin, of unknown origin

berbice chair ('bɜːbiːs) NOUN a large armchair with long arms that can be folded inwards to act as leg rests.
▷HISTORY C20: named after *Berbice*, a river and former county in Guyana

berceuse (*French* bɛrsøz) NOUN [1] a cradlesong or lullaby. [2] an instrumental piece suggestive of this, in six-eight time.
▷HISTORY C19: from French: lullaby, from *bercer* to rock

Berchtesgaden (*German* 'bɛrçtəsgaːdən) NOUN a town in Germany, in SE Bavaria: site of the fortified mountain retreat of Adolf Hitler. Pop.: 7865 (1992 est.).

bereave (bɪ'riːv) VERB (*tr*) [1] (usually foll by *of*) to deprive (of) something or someone valued, esp through death. [2] *Obsolete* to remove by force. ◆ See also **bereft.**
▷HISTORY Old English *bereafian*; see REAVE[1]

bereaved (bɪ'riːvd) ADJECTIVE having been deprived of something or someone valued, esp through death.

bereavement (bɪ'riːvmənt) NOUN [1] the

condition having been deprived of something or someone valued, esp through death. **2** a death.

bereft (bɪ'rɛft) ADJECTIVE (usually foll by *of*) deprived; parted (from): *bereft of hope*.

beret ('bɛreɪ) NOUN a round close-fitting brimless cap of soft wool material or felt.
▷ HISTORY C19: from French *béret*, from Old Provençal *berret*, from Medieval Latin *birrettum* cap; see BIRETTA

Berezina (*Russian* bɪrɪzi'na) NOUN a river in Belarus, rising in the north and flowing south to the River Dnieper: linked with the River Dvina and the Baltic Sea by the **Berezina Canal**. Length: 563 km (350 miles).

Berezniki (*Russian* bɪrɪzni'ki) NOUN a city in E Russia: chemical industries. Pop.: 182 200 (1999 est.).

berg[1] (bɜ:g) NOUN short for **iceberg**.

berg[2] (bɜ:g) NOUN a South African word for **mountain**.

Bergamo (*Italian* 'bɛrgamo) NOUN a walled city in N Italy, in Lombardy. Pop.: 117 837 (2000 est.).

bergamot ('bɜ:gəˌmɒt) NOUN **1** Also called: **bergamot orange**. a small Asian spiny rutaceous tree, *Citrus bergamia*, having sour pear-shaped fruit. **2** **essence of bergamot**. a fragrant essential oil from the fruit rind of this plant, used in perfumery and some teas (including Earl Grey). **3** a Mediterranean mint, *Mentha citrata*, that yields an oil similar to essence of bergamot. **4** **a wild bergamot**. a North American plant, *Monarda fistulosa*, with clusters of purple flowers: family *Lamiaceae* (labiates). **b** a garden plant of the same genus, usually *M. didyma* (bee balm), grown for its scarlet or pink flowers. **5** a variety of pear.
▷ HISTORY C17: from French *bergamote*, from Italian *bergamotta*, of Turkic origin; related to Turkish *bey-armudu* prince's pear; see BEY

Bergdama (ˌbɜ:g'dɑ:mə) NOUN another name for a **Damara**.

bergen ('bɜ:gən) NOUN a large rucksack with a capacity of over 50 litres.

Bergen NOUN **1** (*Norwegian* 'bærgən) a port in SW Norway: chief city in medieval times. Pop.: 229 496 (2000 est.). **2** ('bɛrxən) the Flemish name for **Mons**.

bergère (bɜ:'ʒɛə) NOUN **1** a type of French armchair made from about 1725 having a wide deep seat and upholstered sides and back. In later examples, woven cane is often used instead of upholstery. **2** a sofa of a similar design.
▷ HISTORY French, literally: shepherdess

Bergie ('bɜ:gɪ) NOUN *South African informal* a vagabond, esp one living on the slopes of Table Mountain in the Western Cape province of South Africa.
▷ HISTORY from Afrikaans *berg* mountain

bergschrund ('bɛrkʃrʊnt, 'bɜ:gʃru:nd) NOUN a crevasse at the head of a glacier. Also called: **rimaye**.
▷ HISTORY C19: German: mountain crack

Bergsonian (bɜ:g'səʊnɪən) ADJECTIVE **1** of or relating to Henri Bergson, the French philosopher (1859–1941). ◆ NOUN **2** a follower or admirer of Bergson.

Bergsonism ('bɜ:gsəˌnɪzəm) NOUN the philosophy of Henri Bergson, the French philosopher (1859–1941), which emphasizes duration as the basic element of experience and asserts the existence of a life-giving force that permeates the entire natural order. Compare **élan vital**.

berg wind NOUN a hot dry wind in South Africa blowing from the plateau down to the coast.

beriberi (ˌbɛrɪ'bɛrɪ) NOUN a disease, endemic in E and S Asia, caused by dietary deficiency of thiamine (vitamin B_1). It affects the nerves to the limbs, producing pain, paralysis, and swelling.
▷ HISTORY C19: from Sinhalese, by reduplication from *beri* weakness

berimbau (berĩ'bɒw) NOUN a Brazilian single-stringed bowed instrument, used to accompany capoeira.
▷ HISTORY from the quimbundo (an Angolan language) word *mbirimbau*

Bering Sea NOUN a part of the N Pacific Ocean, between NE Siberia and Alaska. Area: about 2 275 000 sq. km (878 000 sq. miles).

Bering Strait NOUN a strait between Alaska and Russia, connecting the Bering Sea and the Arctic Ocean.

berk *or* **burk** (bɜ:k) NOUN *Brit slang* a stupid person; fool.
▷ HISTORY C20: shortened from *Berkeley* or *Berkshire Hunt* rhyming slang for *cunt*

Berkeleian (bɑ:'klɪən) ADJECTIVE **1** denoting or relating to the philosophy of George Berkeley, the Irish philosopher and Anglican bishop (1685–1753). ◆ NOUN **2** a follower of his teachings.

Berkeleianism (bɑ:'klɪəˌnɪzəm) NOUN the philosophical system of George Berkeley, the Irish philosopher and Anglican bishop (1685–1753), holding that objects exist only when perceived, that God's perception sustains the universe, and that there is no independent substratum or substance in which these perceptions inhere.

Berkeley ('bɜ:klɪ) NOUN a city in W California, on San Francisco Bay: seat of the University of California. Pop.: 102 743 (2000).

Berkeley Castle ('bɑ:klɪ) NOUN a castle in Gloucestershire: scene of the murder of Edward II in 1327.

berkelium (bɜ:'ki:lɪəm, 'bɜ:klɪəm) NOUN a metallic transuranic element produced by bombardment of americium. Symbol: Bk; atomic no.: 97; half-life of most stable isotope, ^{247}Bk: 1400 years; valency: 3 or 4; relative density: 14 (est.).
▷ HISTORY C20: named after BERKELEY, where it was discovered

berko ('bɜ:kəʊ) ADJECTIVE *Austral slang* berserk.

Berks (bɑ:ks) ABBREVIATION FOR Berkshire.

Berkshire ('bɑ:kʃɪə, -ʃə) NOUN **1** a historic county of S England: since reorganization in 1974 the River Thames has marked the N boundary while the **Berkshire Downs** occupy central parts; the county council was replaced by six unitary authorities in 1998. Area: 1259 sq. km (486 sq. miles). Abbreviation: **Berks**. **2** a rare breed of pork and bacon pig having a black body and white points.

berley *or* **burley** ('bɜ:lɪ) *Austral* ◆ NOUN **1** bait scattered on water to attract fish. **2** *Slang* rubbish; nonsense. ◆ VERB (*tr*) **3** to scatter (bait) on water. **4** to hurry (someone); urge on.
▷ HISTORY origin unknown

berlin (bə'lɪn, 'bɜ:lɪn) NOUN **1** (*sometimes capital*) Also called: **berlin wool**. a fine wool yarn used for tapestry work, etc. **2** a four-wheeled two-seated covered carriage, popular in the 18th century. **3** a limousine with a glass partition between the front and rear seats. ◆ Also called (for senses 2, 3): **berline** (bə'li:n, 'bɜ:li:n).
▷ HISTORY C18: named after BERLIN

Berlin (bɜ:'lɪn; *German* bɛr'li:n) NOUN the capital of Germany (1871–1945 and from 1990), formerly divided (1945–90) into the eastern sector, capital of East Germany, and the western sectors, which formed an exclave in East German territory closely affiliated with West Germany: a wall dividing the sectors was built in 1961 by the East German authorities to stop the flow of refugees from east to west; demolition of the wall began in 1989 and the city was formally reunited in 1990: formerly (1618–1871) the capital of Brandenburg and Prussia. Pop.: 3 392 900 (1999 est.).

Berliner (bɜ:'lɪnə) NOUN a native or inhabitant of Berlin.

berm *or* **berme** (bɜ:m) NOUN **1** a narrow path or ledge at the edge of a slope, road, or canal. **2** *NZ* the grass verge of a suburban street, usually kept mown. **3** *Fortifications* a narrow path or ledge between a moat and a rampart. **4** *Military* a man-made ridge of sand, designed as an obstacle to tanks, which, in crossing it, have to expose their vulnerable underparts.
▷ HISTORY C18: from French *berme*, from Dutch *berm*, probably from Old Norse *barmr* BRIM

Bermejo (*Spanish* ber'mexo) NOUN a river in Argentina, rising in the northwest and flowing southeast to the Paraguay River. Length: about 1600 km (1000 miles).

Bermuda (bə'mju:də) NOUN a UK Overseas Territory consisting of a group of over 150 coral islands (**the Bermudas**) in the NW Atlantic: discovered in about 1503, colonized by the British by 1612, although not acquired by the British crown until 1684. Capital: Hamilton. Pop.: 63 500 (2001 est.). Area: 53 sq. km (20 sq. miles).

Bermuda grass NOUN a widely distributed grass, *Cynodon dactylon*, with wiry creeping rootstocks and several purplish spikes of flowers arising from a single point: used for lawns, pasturage, binding sand dunes, etc. Also called: **scutch grass, wire grass**.

Bermuda rig NOUN a fore-and-aft sailing boat rig characterized by a tall mainsail (**Bermudian mainsail**) that tapers to a point.
▸ **Ber'muda-'rigged** ADJECTIVE

Bermuda shorts PLURAL NOUN close-fitting shorts that come down to the knees. Also called: **Bermudas**.

Bermuda Triangle NOUN an area in the Atlantic Ocean bounded by Bermuda, Puerto Rico, and Florida where ships and aeroplanes are alleged to have disappeared mysteriously.

Bermudian (bə'mju:dɪən) NOUN **1** a native or inhabitant of Bermuda. ◆ ADJECTIVE **2** of or relating to Bermuda or its inhabitants.

Bern (bɜ:n; *German* bɛrn) NOUN **1** the capital of Switzerland, in the W part, on the Aar River: entered the Swiss confederation in 1353 and became the capital in 1848. Pop.: 123 254 (1999 est.). **2** a canton of Switzerland, between the French frontier and the Bernese Alps. Capital: Bern. Pop.: 943 400 (2000 est.). Area: 6884 sq. km (2658 sq. miles). French name: **Berne** (bɛrn).

Bernardine ('bɜ:nədɪn, -ˌdi:n) NOUN **1** a monk of one of the reformed and stricter branches of the Cistercian order. ◆ ADJECTIVE **2** **a** of or relating to this branch of the Cistercians. **b** of or relating to Saint Bernard of Clairvaux (?1090–1153), French abbot and theologian.

Bernese Alps *or* **Oberland** ('bɜ:ni:z) NOUN a mountain range in SW Switzerland, the N central part of the Alps. Highest peak: Finsteraarhorn, 4274 m (14 022 ft.).

Bernese mountain dog NOUN a strong sturdy dog of a breed with a bushy tail and a long silky black coat with reddish-brown and white markings, often used as a working farm dog.

bernicle goose ('bɜ:nɪkᵊl) NOUN a former name for the **brent goose** or **barnacle goose**.

Bernina (bə'ni:nə; *Italian* ber'nina) NOUN **Piz**. a mountain in SE Switzerland, the highest peak of the **Bernina Alps** in the S Rhaetian Alps. Height: 4049 m (13 284 ft.).

Bernina Pass NOUN a pass in the Alps between SE Switzerland and N Italy, east of Piz Bernina. Height: 2323 m (7622 ft.).

Bernoulli's principle *or* **law** NOUN *Physics* the principle that in a liquid flowing through a pipe the pressure difference that accelerates the flow when the bore changes is equal to the product of half the density times the change of the square of the speed, provided friction is negligible.
▷ HISTORY C19: named after Daniel Bernoulli (1700–82), Swiss mathematician and physicist

Bernoulli trial NOUN *Statistics* one of a sequence of independent experiments each of which has the same probability of success, such as successive throws of a die, the outcome of which is described by a binomial distribution. See also **binomial experiment**.
▷ HISTORY named after Jacques Bernoulli (1654–1705), Swiss mathematician

berretta (bɪ'rɛtə) NOUN a variant spelling of **biretta**.

berrigan ('bɛrɪgən) NOUN an Australian tree, *Pittosporum phylliraeoides*, with hanging branches.

berry ('bɛrɪ) NOUN, *plural* **-ries**. **1** any of various small edible fruits such as the blackberry and strawberry. **2** *Botany* an indehiscent fruit with two or more seeds and a fleshy pericarp, such as the grape or gooseberry. **3** any of various seeds or dried kernels, such as a coffee bean. **4** the egg of a lobster, crayfish, or similar animal. ◆ VERB **-ries, -rying, -ried**. (*intr*) **5** to bear or produce berries. **6** to gather or look for berries.
▷ HISTORY Old English *berie*; related to Old High German *beri*, Dutch *bezie*
▸ **'berried** ADJECTIVE

bersagliere (ˌbɛəsɑ:'ljɛərɪ) NOUN, *plural* **-ri** (-ri:). a member of a rifle regiment in the Italian Army.
▷ HISTORY C19: from Italian, from *bersaglio* target, from Old French *bersail*, from *berser* to fire at

berseem (bɜ:'si:m) NOUN a Mediterranean clover,

Trifolium alexandrinum, grown as a forage crop and to improve the soil in the southwestern US and the Nile valley. Also called: **Egyptian clover.**
▷HISTORY C20: from Arabic *barsīm*, from Coptic *bersīm*

berserk (bəˈzɜːk, -ˈsɜːk) ADJECTIVE 1 frenziedly violent or destructive (esp in the phrase **go berserk**). ◆ NOUN 2 Also called: **berserker.** a member of a class of ancient Norse warriors who worked themselves into a frenzy before battle and fought with insane fury and courage.
▷HISTORY C19: Icelandic *berserkr*, from *björn* bear + *serkr* shirt

berth (bɜːθ) NOUN 1 a bed or bunk in a vessel or train, usually narrow and fixed to a wall. 2 *Nautical* a place assigned to a ship at a mooring. 3 *Nautical* sufficient distance from the shore or from other ships or objects for a ship to manoeuvre. 4 **give a wide berth to.** to keep clear of; avoid. 5 *Nautical* accommodation on a ship. 6 *Informal* a job, esp as a member of a ship's crew. ◆ VERB 7 *(tr) Nautical* to assign a berth to (a vessel). 8 *Nautical* to dock (a vessel). 9 *(tr)* to provide with a sleeping place, as on a vessel or train. 10 *(intr) Nautical* to pick up a mooring in an anchorage.
▷HISTORY C17: probably from BEAR[1] + -TH[1]

bertha (ˈbɜːθə) NOUN a wide deep capelike collar, often of lace, usually to cover up a low neckline.
▷HISTORY C19: from French *berthe*, from *Berthe*, 8th-century Frankish queen, mother of Charlemagne

Bertillon system (ˈbɜːtɪˌlɒn; *French* bɛrtijɔ̃) NOUN a system formerly in use for identifying persons, esp criminals, by means of a detailed record of physical characteristics.
▷HISTORY C19: named after Alphonse *Bertillon* (1853–1914), French criminal investigator

Berwickshire (ˈbɛrɪkˌʃɪə, -ʃə) NOUN (until 1975) a county of SE Scotland: part of the Borders region from 1975 to 1996, now part of Scottish Borders council area.

Berwick-upon-Tweed (twiːd) NOUN a town in N England, in N Northumberland at the mouth of the Tweed: much involved in border disputes between England and Scotland between the 12th and 16th centuries; neutral territory 1551–1885. Pop.: 13 544 (1991). Also called: **Berwick.**

beryl (ˈbɛrɪl) NOUN a white, blue, yellow, green, or pink mineral, found in coarse granites and igneous rocks. It is a source of beryllium and used as a gemstone; the green variety is emerald, the blue is aquamarine. Composition: beryllium aluminium silicate. Formula: $Be_3Al_2Si_6O_{18}$. Crystal structure: hexagonal.
▷HISTORY C13: from Old French, from Latin *bēryllus*, from Greek *bērullos*, of Indic origin
▸ˈ**beryline** ADJECTIVE

beryllium (bɛˈrɪlɪəm) NOUN a corrosion-resistant toxic silvery-white metallic element that occurs chiefly in beryl and is used mainly in X-ray windows and in the manufacture of alloys. Symbol: Be; atomic no.: 4; atomic wt.: 9.012; valency: 2; relative density: 1.848; melting pt.: 1289°C; boiling pt.: 2472°C. Former names: **glucinum, glucinium.**
▷HISTORY C19: from Latin *bēryllus*, from Greek *bērullos*

Bes (bɛs) NOUN an ancient Egyptian god represented as a grotesque hairy dwarf: the patron of music and pleasure.

Besançon (*French* bəzɑ̃sɔ̃) NOUN a city in E France, on the Doubs River: university (1422). Pop.: 117 304 (1999).

beseech (bɪˈsiːtʃ) VERB **-seeches, -seeching, -sought** *or* **-seeched.** *(tr)* to ask (someone) earnestly (to do something *or* for something); beg.
▷HISTORY C12: see BE-, SEEK; related to Old Frisian *besēka*
▸**beˈseecher** NOUN ▸**beˈseeching** ADJECTIVE
▸**beˈseechingly** ADVERB

beseem (bɪˈsiːm) VERB *Archaic* to be suitable for; befit.

beset (bɪˈsɛt) VERB **-sets, -setting, -set.** *(tr)* 1 (esp of dangers, temptations, or difficulties) to trouble or harass constantly. 2 to surround or attack from all sides. 3 *Archaic* to cover with, esp with jewels.
▸**beˈsetter** NOUN

besetting (bɪˈsɛtɪŋ) ADJECTIVE tempting, harassing, or assailing (esp in the phrase **besetting sin**).

beshrew (bɪˈʃruː) VERB *(tr) Archaic* to wish evil on; curse (used in mild oaths such as **beshrew me**).
▷HISTORY C14: see BE-, SHREW

beside (bɪˈsaɪd) PREPOSITION 1 next to; at, by, or to the side of. 2 as compared with. 3 away from; wide of: *beside the point.* 4 *Archaic* besides. 5 **beside oneself.** *(postpositive;* often foll by *with)* overwhelmed; overwrought: *beside oneself with grief.* ◆ ADVERB 6 at, by, to, or along the side of something or someone.
▷HISTORY Old English *be sīdan*; see BY, SIDE

besides (bɪˈsaɪdz) PREPOSITION 1 apart from; even considering: *besides costing too much, the scheme is impractical.* ◆ SENTENCE CONNECTOR 2 anyway; moreover. ◆ ADVERB 3 as well.

besiege (bɪˈsiːdʒ) VERB *(tr)* 1 to surround (a fortified area, esp a city) with military forces to bring about its surrender. 2 to crowd round; hem in. 3 to overwhelm, as with requests or queries.
▸**beˈsieger** NOUN

besmear (bɪˈsmɪə) VERB *(tr)* 1 to smear over; daub. 2 to sully; defile (often in the phrase **besmear (a person's) reputation**).

besmirch (bɪˈsmɜːtʃ) VERB *(tr)* 1 to make dirty; soil. 2 to reduce the brightness or lustre of. 3 to sully (often in the phrase **besmirch (a person's) name**).

besom[1] (ˈbiːzəm) NOUN 1 a broom, esp one made of a bundle of twigs tied to a handle. 2 *Curling* a broom or brush used to sweep the ice in front of the stone to make it slide farther. ◆ VERB *(tr)* 3 to sweep with a besom.
▷HISTORY Old English *besma*; related to Old High German *besmo* broom

besom[2] (ˈbɪzəm, ˈbizəm) NOUN *Scot and northern English dialect* a derogatory term for a **woman.**
▷HISTORY perhaps from Old English *bysen* example; related to Old Norse *bysn* wonder

besotted (bɪˈsɒtɪd) ADJECTIVE 1 stupefied with drink; intoxicated. 2 infatuated; doting. 3 foolish; muddled.

besought (bɪˈsɔːt) VERB the past tense and past participle of **beseech.**

bespangle (bɪˈspæŋgᵊl) VERB *(tr)* to cover or adorn with or as if with spangles.

bespatter (bɪˈspætə) VERB *(tr)* 1 to splash all over, as with dirty water. 2 to defile; slander; besmirch.

bespeak (bɪˈspiːk) VERB **-speaks, -speaking, -spoke; -spoken** *or* **-spoke.** *(tr)* 1 to engage, request, or ask for in advance. 2 to indicate or suggest: *this act bespeaks kindness.* 3 *Poetic* to speak to; address. 4 *Archaic* to foretell.

bespectacled (bɪˈspɛktəkᵊld) ADJECTIVE wearing spectacles.

bespoke (bɪˈspəʊk) ADJECTIVE *Chiefly Brit* 1 (esp of a suit, jacket, etc.) made to the customer's specifications. 2 making or selling such suits, jackets, etc.: *a bespoke tailor.*

bespread (bɪˈsprɛd) VERB **-spreads, -spreading, -spread.** *(tr)* to cover (a surface) with something.

besprent (bɪˈsprɛnt) ADJECTIVE *Poetic* sprinkled over.
▷HISTORY C14: past participle of Old English *besprengan* to BESPRINKLE

besprinkle (bɪˈsprɪŋkᵊl) VERB *(tr)* to sprinkle all over with liquid, powder, etc.

Bessarabia (ˌbɛsəˈreɪbɪə) NOUN a region in E Europe, mostly in Moldova and the Ukraine: long disputed by the Turks and Russians; a province of Romania from 1918 until 1940. Area: about 44 300 sq. km (17 100 sq. miles).

Bessemer converter (ˈbɛsɪmə) NOUN a refractory-lined furnace used to convert pig iron into steel by the Bessemer process.

Bessemer process NOUN 1 (formerly) a process for producing steel by blowing air through molten pig iron at about 1250°C in a Bessemer converter: silicon, manganese, and phosphorus impurities are removed and the carbon content is controlled. 2 a similar process for removing sulphur and iron from copper matte.
▷HISTORY C19: named after Sir Henry *Bessemer* (1813–98), English engineer

best (bɛst) ADJECTIVE 1 the superlative of **good.** 2 most excellent of a particular group, category, etc. 3 most suitable, advantageous, desirable, attractive, etc. 4 **the best part of.** most of: *the best part of an hour.* 5 **put one's best foot forward.** a to do one's utmost to make progress. b to hurry. ◆ ADVERB 6 the superlative of **well.** 7 in a manner surpassing all others; most excellently, advantageously, attractively, etc. 8 *(in combination)* in or to the greatest degree or extent; most: *the best-loved hero.* 9 **as best one can** *or* **may.** as effectively as possible within one's limitations. 10 **had best.** would be wise, sensible, etc., to: *you had best go now.* ◆ NOUN 11 **the best.** the most outstanding or excellent person, thing, or group in a category. 12 (often preceded by *at*) the most excellent, pleasing, or skilled quality or condition: *journalism at its best.* 13 the most effective effort of which a person or group is capable: *even their best was inadequate.* 14 a winning majority: *the best of three games.* 15 Also: **all the best.** best wishes: *she sent him her best.* 16 a person's smartest outfit of clothing. 17 **at best.** a in the most favourable interpretation. b under the most favourable conditions. 18 **for the best.** a for an ultimately good outcome. b with good intentions: *he meant it for the best.* 19 **get** *or* **have the best of.** to surpass, defeat, or outwit; better. 20 **give (someone) the best.** to concede (someone's) superiority. 21 **make the best of.** to cope as well as possible in the unfavourable circumstances of (often in the phrases **make the best of a bad job, make the best of it**). 22 **six of the best.** *Informal* six strokes with a cane on the buttocks or hand. ◆ VERB 23 *(tr)* to gain the advantage over or defeat.
▷HISTORY Old English *betst*; related to Gothic *batista*, Old High German *bezzist*

best-ball ADJECTIVE *Golf* of, relating to, or denoting a match in which one player competes against the best individual totals of two or more other players at each hole.

best boy NOUN *Chiefly US* the assistant to the senior electrician or to the key grip in a film crew.

best end NOUN the end of the neck of lamb, pork, etc., nearest to the ribs.

best girl NOUN *Archaic* one's sweetheart.

bestial (ˈbɛstɪəl) ADJECTIVE 1 brutal or savage. 2 sexually depraved; carnal. 3 lacking in refinement; brutish. 4 of or relating to a beast.
▷HISTORY C14: from Late Latin *bestiālis*, from Latin *bestia* BEAST
▸ˈ**bestially** ADVERB

bestiality (ˌbɛstɪˈælɪtɪ) NOUN, *plural* **-ties.** 1 bestial behaviour, character, or action. 2 sexual activity between a person and an animal.

bestialize *or* **bestialise** (ˈbɛstɪəˌlaɪz) VERB *(tr)* to make bestial or brutal.

bestiary (ˈbɛstɪərɪ) NOUN, *plural* **-aries.** a moralizing medieval collection of descriptions of real and/or mythical animals.

bestir (bɪˈstɜː) VERB **-stirs, -stirring, -stirred.** *(tr)* to cause (oneself, or, rarely, another person) to become active; rouse.

best man NOUN the (male) attendant of the bridegroom at a wedding.

bestow (bɪˈstəʊ) VERB *(tr)* 1 to present (a gift) or confer (an award or honour). 2 *Archaic* to apply (energy, resources, etc.). 3 *Archaic* to house (a person) or store (goods).
▸**beˈstowal** *or* **beˈstowment** NOUN ▸**beˈstower** NOUN

bestrew (bɪˈstruː) VERB **-strews, -strewing, -strewed; -strewn** *or* **-strewed.** *(tr)* to scatter or lie scattered over (a surface).

bestride (bɪˈstraɪd) VERB **-strides, -striding, -strode** *or archaic* **-strid, -stridden** *or archaic* **-strid.** *(tr)* 1 to have or put a leg on either side of. 2 to extend across; span. 3 to stride over or across.

bestseller (ˌbɛstˈsɛlə) NOUN 1 a book, record, CD, or other product that has sold in great numbers, esp over a short period. 2 the author of one or more such books, etc.
▸ˌ**bestˈselling** ADJECTIVE

bet (bɛt) NOUN 1 an agreement between two parties that a sum of money or other stake will be paid by the loser to the party who correctly predicts the outcome of an event. 2 the money or stake risked. 3 the predicted result in such an agreement: *his bet was that the horse would win.* 4 a person, event, etc., considered as likely to succeed or occur: *it's a good bet that they will succeed.* 5 a course of action (esp in the phrase **one's best bet**). 6 *Informal* an opinion; view: *my bet is that you've been up to no good.* ◆ VERB **bets, betting, bet** *or* **betted.** 7

(when *intr* foll by *on* or *against*) to make or place a bet with (a person or persons). [8] (*tr*) to stake (money, etc.) in a bet. [9] (*tr; may take a clause as object*) *Informal* to predict (a certain outcome): *I bet she fails.* [10] **you bet.** *Informal* of course; naturally.
▷HISTORY C16: probably short for ABET

beta ('bi:tə) NOUN [1] the second letter in the Greek alphabet (Β or β), a consonant, transliterated as *b*. [2] the second highest grade or mark, as in an examination. [3] (*modifier*) **a** involving or relating to electrons: *beta emitter*. **b** relating to one of two or more allotropes or crystal structures of a solid: *beta iron*. **c** relating to one of two or more isomeric forms of a chemical compound.
▷HISTORY from Greek *bēta*, from Hebrew; see BETH

Beta ('bi:tə) NOUN (*foll by the genitive case of a specified constellation*) a star in a constellation, usually the second brightest: *Beta Persei*.

beta-blocker NOUN any of a class of drugs, such as propranolol, that inhibit the activity of the nerves that are stimulated by adrenaline; they therefore decrease the contraction and speed of the heart: used in the treatment of high blood pressure and angina pectoris.

Betacam ('bi:təˌkæm) NOUN *Trademark* a high-quality professional video system.

betacarotene (ˌbi:tə'kærəˌti:n) NOUN the most important form of the plant pigment carotene, which occurs in milk, vegetables, and other foods and, when eaten by man and animals, is converted in the body to vitamin A.

beta coefficient NOUN *Stock Exchange* a measure of the extent to which a particular security rises or falls in value in response to market movements.

betacyanin (ˌbi:tə'saɪənɪn) NOUN any one of a group of red nitrogenous pigments found in certain plants, such as beetroot.

beta decay NOUN the radioactive transformation of an atomic nucleus accompanying the emission of an electron. It involves unit change of atomic number but none in mass number. Also called: **beta transformation** *or* **process.**

beta globulin NOUN another name for **transferrin.**

betaine ('bi:təˌi:n, -ɪn, bɪ'teɪi:n, -ɪn) NOUN [1] a sweet-tasting alkaloid that occurs in the sugar beet and other plants and in animals. Formula: $C_5H_{11}NO_2$. [2] (*plural*) a group of chemical compounds that resemble betaine and are slightly basic zwitterions.
▷HISTORY C19: from New Latin *Bēta* beet + -INE²

beta iron NOUN a nonmagnetic allotrope of pure iron stable between 770°C and 910°C.

betake (bɪ'teɪk) VERB **-takes, -taking, -took, -taken.** (*tr*) [1] **betake oneself.** to go; move. [2] *Archaic* to apply (oneself) to.

beta particle NOUN a high-speed electron or positron emitted by a nucleus during radioactive decay or nuclear fission.

beta ray NOUN a stream of beta particles.

beta rhythm *or* **wave** NOUN *Physiol* the normal electrical activity of the cerebral cortex, occurring at a frequency of 13 to 30 hertz and detectable with an electroencephalograph. See also **brain wave.**

beta stock NOUN any of the second rank of active securities on the Stock Exchange, of which there are about 500. Continuous display of prices by market makers is required but not immediate publication of transactions.

beta-test NOUN [1] a test of a new or modified piece of computer software by customers who volunteer to do so. ◆ VERB (*tr*) [2] to test (software) in this way. Compare **alpha-test.**

betatopic (ˌbi:tə'tɒpɪk) ADJECTIVE (of atoms) differing in proton number by one, theoretically as a result of emission of a beta particle.

betatron ('bi:təˌtrɒn) NOUN a type of particle accelerator for producing high-energy beams of electrons, having an alternating magnetic field to keep the electrons in a circular orbit of fixed radius and accelerate them by magnetic induction. It produces energies of up to about 300 MeV.

betel ('bi:tᵊl) NOUN an Asian piperaceous climbing plant, *Piper betle*, the leaves of which are chewed, with the betel nut, by the peoples of SE Asia.
▷HISTORY C16: from Portuguese, from Malayalam *vettila*

Betelgeuse *or* **Betelgeux** (ˌbi:tᵊl'dʒɜ:z, 'bi:tᵊlˌdʒɜ:z) NOUN a very remote luminous red supergiant, Alpha Orionis: the second brightest star in the constellation Orion. It is a variable star.
▷HISTORY C18: from French, from Arabic *bīt al-jauzā'* literally: shoulder of the giant, that is, of Orion

betel nut NOUN the seed of the betel palm, chewed with betel leaves and lime by people in S and SE Asia as a digestive stimulant and narcotic.

betel palm NOUN a tropical Asian feather palm, *Areca catechu*, with scarlet or orange fruits. See **betel nut.**

bête noire *French* (bɛt nwar) NOUN, *plural* ***bêtes noires*** (bɛt nwar). a person or thing that one particularly dislikes or dreads.
▷HISTORY literally: black beast

beth (bɛt) NOUN the second letter of the Hebrew alphabet (ב) transliterated as *b*.
▷HISTORY from Hebrew *bēth-, bayith* house

Bethany ('bɛθənɪ) NOUN a village in the West Bank, near Jerusalem at the foot of the Mount of Olives: in the New Testament, the home of Lazarus and the lodging place of Jesus during Holy Week.

Beth Din *or* **Bet Din** (bɛθ dɪn; *Hebrew* bet din) NOUN *Judaism* a rabbinical court, consisting of at least three dayanim, and having authority over such matters as divorce and conversion and other communal ecclesiastical matters such as Kashruth. It may also try civil disputes with the consent of both parties.
▷HISTORY from Hebrew, literally: house of judgment

Bethel ('bɛθəl) NOUN [1] an ancient town in the West Bank, near Jerusalem: in the Old Testament, the place where the dream of Jacob occurred (Genesis 28:19). [2] a chapel of any of certain Nonconformist Christian sects. [3] a seamen's chapel.
▷HISTORY C17: from Hebrew *bēth 'Ēl* house of God

Bethesda (bə'θɛzdə) NOUN [1] *New Testament* a pool in Jerusalem reputed to have healing powers, where a paralytic was healed by Jesus (John 5:2). [2] a chapel of any of certain Nonconformist Christian sects.

bethink (bɪ'θɪŋk) VERB **-thinks, -thinking, -thought.** *Archaic or dialect* [1] to cause (oneself) to consider or meditate. [2] (*tr*; often foll by *of*) to remind (oneself).

Bethlehem ('bɛθlɪˌhɛm, -lɪəm) NOUN a town in the West Bank, near Jerusalem: birthplace of Jesus and early home of King David.

bethought (bɪ'θɔ:t) VERB the past tense and past participle of **bethink.**

Bethsaida (bɛθ'seɪdə) NOUN a ruined town in N Israel, near the N shore of the Sea of Galilee.

betide (bɪ'taɪd) VERB to happen or happen to; befall (often in the phrase **woe betide** (**someone**)).
▷HISTORY C13: see BE-, TIDE²

betimes (bɪ'taɪmz) ADVERB *Archaic* [1] in good time; early. [2] in a short time; soon.
▷HISTORY C14 *bitimes*; see BY, TIME

bêtise (bɛ'ti:z) NOUN *Rare* folly or lack of perception.
▷HISTORY French, from *bête* foolish, from *bête* (n) stupid person, BEAST

betoken (bɪ'təʊkən) VERB (*tr*) [1] to indicate; signify: *black clothes betoken mourning.* [2] to portend; augur.

betony ('bɛtənɪ) NOUN, *plural* **-nies.** [1] a Eurasian plant, *Stachys* (or *Betonica*) *officinalis*, with a spike of reddish-purple flowers, formerly used in medicine and dyeing: family *Lamiaceae* (labiates). [2] any of several related plants of the genus *Stachys*. [3] **wood betony.** a North American scrophulariaceous plant, *Pedicularis canadensis*. See also **lousewort.**
▷HISTORY C14: from Old French *betoine*, from Latin *betonica*, variant of *vettonica*, probably named after the *Vettones*, an ancient Iberian tribe

betook (bɪ'tʊk) VERB the past tense of **betake.**

betray (bɪ'treɪ) VERB (*tr*) [1] to aid an enemy of (one's nation, friend, etc.); be a traitor to: *to betray one's country.* [2] to hand over or expose (one's nation, friend, etc.) treacherously to an enemy. [3] to disclose (a secret, confidence, etc.) treacherously. [4] to break (a promise) or be disloyal to (a person's trust). [5] to disappoint the expectations of; fail: *his tired legs betrayed him.* [6] to show signs of; indicate: *if one taps china, the sound betrays any faults.* [7] to reveal unintentionally: *his grin betrayed his satisfaction.* [8] **betray oneself.** to reveal one's true character, intentions, etc. [9] to lead astray; deceive. [10] *Euphemistic* to seduce and then forsake (a woman).
▷HISTORY C13: from BE- + *trayen* from Old French *trair*, from Latin *trādere*
▸**be'trayal** NOUN ▸**be'trayer** NOUN

betroth (bɪ'trəʊð) VERB (*tr*) *Archaic* to promise to marry or to give in marriage.
▷HISTORY C14 *betreuthen*, from BE- + *treuthe* TROTH, TRUTH

betrothal (bɪ'trəʊðəl) NOUN [1] engagement to be married. [2] a mutual promise to marry.

betrothed (bɪ'trəʊðd) ADJECTIVE [1] engaged to be married: *he was betrothed to her.* ◆ NOUN [2] the person to whom one is engaged; fiancé or fiancée.

betta ('bɛtə) NOUN another name for **fighting fish.**
▷HISTORY C19: from New Latin, of unknown origin

better¹ ('bɛtə) ADJECTIVE [1] the comparative of **good.** [2] more excellent than other members of a particular group, category, etc. [3] more suitable, advantageous, attractive, etc. [4] improved in health. [5] fully recovered in health. [6] in more favourable circumstances, esp financially. [7] **the better part of.** a large part of: *the better part of a day.* ◆ ADVERB [8] the comparative of **well.** [9] in a more excellent manner; more advantageously, attractively, etc. [10] in or to a greater degree or extent; more: *she is better loved than her sister.* [11] **go one better.** (*Brit intr; US tr*) to outdo (a person) or improve upon (someone else's effort). [12] **had better.** would be wise, sensible, etc. to: *I had better be off.* [13] **know better than to.** not to be so stupid as to. [14] **think better of.** **a** to change one's course of action after reconsideration. **b** to rate (a person) more highly. ◆ NOUN [15] **the better.** something that is the more excellent, useful, etc., of two such things. [16] (*usually plural*) a person who is superior, esp in social standing or ability. [17] **all the better for.** improved as a result of. [18] **all the better to.** more suitable to. [19] **for better for worse.** whatever the subsequent events or changes may be. [20] **for the better.** by way of improvement: *a change for the better.* [21] **get the better of.** to defeat, outwit, or surpass. [22] **the better of.** *Irish* having recovered from: *I'm not the better of it yet.* ◆ VERB [23] to make or become better. [24] (*tr*) to improve upon; surpass.
▷HISTORY Old English *betera*; related to Old Norse *betri*, Gothic *batiza*, Old High German *beziro*

better² *or esp US* **bettor** ('bɛtə) NOUN a person who bets.

better half NOUN *Humorous* one's spouse.

betterment ('bɛtəmənt) NOUN [1] a change for the better; improvement. [2] *Property law* an improvement effected on real property that enhances the value of the property.

betting shop NOUN (in Britain) a licensed bookmaker's premises not on a racecourse.

bettong (bɛ'tɒŋ) NOUN a species of rat kangaroo of Australia having a short nose.
▷HISTORY C19: from a native Australian language

betulaceous (ˌbɛtjʊ'leɪʃəs) ADJECTIVE of, relating to, or belonging to the *Betulaceae*, a family of mostly N temperate catkin-bearing trees and shrubs such as birch and alder, some species of which reach the northern limits of tree growth.
▷HISTORY C19: from Latin *betula* birch

between (bɪ'twi:n) PREPOSITION [1] at a point or in a region intermediate to two other points in space, times, degrees, etc. [2] in combination; together: *between them, they saved enough money to buy a car.* [3] confined or restricted to: *between you and me.* [4] indicating a reciprocal relation or comparison: *an argument between a man and his wife.* [5] indicating two or more alternatives: *a choice between going now and staying all night.* ◆ ADVERB *also* **in between.** [6] between one specified thing and another: *two houses with a garage between.*
▷HISTORY Old English *betwēonum*; related to Gothic *tweihnai* two together; see TWO, TWAIN

Language note After *distribute* and words with a similar meaning, *among* should be used rather than *between*: *this enterprise issued shares which were distributed among its workers.*

between-subjects design NOUN *(modifier)* *Statistics* (of an experiment) concerned with measuring the value of the dependent variable for distinct and unrelated groups subjected to each of the experimental conditions. Compare **within-subjects design, matched-pairs design.**

betweentimes (bɪˈtwiːnˌtaɪmz) *or* **betweenwhiles** (bɪˈtwiːnˌwaɪlz) ADVERB between other activities; during intervals.

betwixt (bɪˈtwɪkst) PREPOSITION, ADVERB 1 *Archaic* another word for **between.** 2 **betwixt and between.** in an intermediate, indecisive, or middle position.
▷HISTORY Old English *betwix*; related to Old High German *zwiski* two each

Betws-y-Coed (ˌbɛtsɪˈkɔɪd) NOUN a village in N Wales, in Conwy county borough, on the River Conwy: noted for its scenery. Pop.: 2860 (1991).

Beulah (ˈbjuːlə) NOUN *Old Testament* the land of Israel (Isaiah 62:4).
▷HISTORY Hebrew, literally: married woman

Beuthen (ˈbɔytən) NOUN the German name for **Bytom.**

BeV (in the US) ABBREVIATION FOR gigaelectronvolts (GeV).
▷HISTORY C20: from *b(illion) e(lectron) v(olts)*

Bevan (ˈbɛvən) *or* **Bev** (bɛv) NOUN *Austral slang* 1 a stupid or unfashionable male. 2 an aggressive and surly youth.
▷HISTORY from the boy's name *Bevan*

Bev curls (bɛv) PLURAL NOUN *Austral slang* long locks of hair, considered to be typical of a certain kind of unfashionable male.
▷HISTORY C20: see BEVAN

bevel (ˈbɛvᵊl) NOUN 1 **a** Also called: **cant.** a surface that meets another at an angle other than a right angle. Compare **chamfer** (sense 1). **b** *(as modifier)*: *a bevel edge; bevel square.* ◆ VERB **-els, -elling, -elled** *or US* **-els, -eling, -eled.** 2 *(intr)* to be inclined; slope. 3 *(tr)* to cut a bevel on (a piece of timber, etc.).
▷HISTORY C16: from Old French *bevel* (unattested), from *baïf*, from *baer* to gape; see BAY[1]
▸ˈ**bevelled** *or US* ˈ**beveled** ADJECTIVE ▸ˈ**beveller** *or US* ˈ**beveler** NOUN

bevel gear NOUN a gear having teeth cut into a conical surface known as the pitch zone. Two such gears mesh together to transmit power between two shafts at an angle to each other.

bevel square NOUN a woodworker's square with an adjustable arm that can be set to mark out an angle or to check the slope of a surface.

beverage (ˈbɛvərɪdʒ, ˈbɛvrɪdʒ) NOUN any drink, usually other than water.
▷HISTORY C13: from Old French *bevrage*, from *beivre* to drink, from Latin *bibere*

beverage room NOUN *Canadian* a room in a tavern, hotel, etc. in which alcoholic drinks are served.

Beverley (ˈbɛvəlɪ) NOUN a market town in NE England, the administrative centre of the East Riding of Yorkshire. Pop.: 23 632 (1991).

Beverley pills PLURAL NOUN *Mainly US slang* a recreational drug consisting of the prescription painkiller Vicodin. Also called: **Vikes.**
▷HISTORY C20: a play on BEVERLEY HILLS, referring to the drug's supposed popularity in the US entertainment industry

Beverly Hills (ˈbɛvəlɪ) NOUN a city in SW California, near Los Angeles: famous as the home of film stars. Pop.: 31 970 (1990).

Bevin boy NOUN (in Britain during World War II) a young man selected by ballot to work in a coal mine instead of doing conventional military service.
▷HISTORY C20: named after Ernest Bevin (1881–1951), British Labour statesman and trade unionist, who originated the scheme

bevvy (ˈbɛvɪ) *Dialect* ◆ NOUN, *plural* **-vies.** 1 a drink, esp an alcoholic one: *we had a few bevvies last night.* 2 a session of drinking. ◆ VERB **-vies, -vying, -vied.** *(intr)* 3 to drink alcohol.
▷HISTORY probably from Old French *bevee, buvee* drinking
▸ˈ**bevvied** ADJECTIVE

bevy (ˈbɛvɪ) NOUN, *plural* **bevies.** 1 a flock of quails. 2 a group, esp of girls. 3 a group of roedeer.
▷HISTORY C15: of uncertain origin

bewail (bɪˈweɪl) VERB to express great sorrow over (a person or thing); lament.
▸**beˈwailed** ADJECTIVE ▸**beˈwailer** NOUN ▸**beˈwailing** NOUN, ADJECTIVE ▸**beˈwailingly** ADVERB

beware (bɪˈwɛə) VERB *(usually used in the imperative or infinitive,* often foll by *of)* to be cautious or wary (of); be on one's guard (against).
▷HISTORY C13 *be war*, from BE (imperative) + *war* WARY

bewhiskered (bɪˈwɪskəd) ADJECTIVE having whiskers on the cheeks.

Bewick's swan NOUN a white Old World swan, *Cygnus bewickii*, having a black bill with a small yellow base.
▷HISTORY named after Thomas *Bewick* (1753–1828), English engraver noted esp for his woodcuts of birds

bewilder (bɪˈwɪldə) VERB *(tr)* 1 to confuse utterly; puzzle. 2 *Archaic* to cause to become lost.
▷HISTORY C17: see BE-, WILDER

bewildering (bɪˈwɪldərɪŋ) ADJECTIVE causing utter confusion; puzzling.
▸**beˈwilderingly** ADVERB

bewitch (bɪˈwɪtʃ) VERB *(tr)* 1 to attract and fascinate; enchant. 2 to cast a spell over.
▷HISTORY C13 *bewicchen*; see BE-, WITCH
▸**beˈwitching** ADJECTIVE ▸**beˈwitchingly** ADVERB

bewray (bɪˈreɪ) VERB *(tr)* an obsolete word for **betray.**
▷HISTORY C13: from BE- + Old English *wrēgan* to accuse; related to Gothic *wrōhjan*
▸**beˈwrayer** NOUN

Bexhill(-on-Sea) (ˌbɛksˈhɪl) NOUN a resort in S England, in East Sussex on the English Channel. Pop.: 38 905 (1991).

Bexley (ˈbɛkslɪ) NOUN a borough of SE Greater London. Pop.: 218 307 (2001). Area: 61 sq. km (23 sq. miles).

bey (beɪ) NOUN 1 (in the Ottoman Empire) a title given to senior officers, provincial governors, certain other officials or nobles, and (sometimes) Europeans. 2 (in modern Turkey) a title of address, corresponding to *Mr.* Also called: **beg.**
▷HISTORY C16: Turkish: lord

Beyoğlu (ˈbeɪɔːluː) NOUN a district of Istanbul, north of the Golden Horn: the European quarter. Former name: **Pera.**

beyond (bɪˈjɒnd) PREPOSITION 1 at or to a point on the other side of; at or to the further side of: *beyond those hills there is a river.* 2 outside the limits or scope of: *beyond this country's jurisdiction.* ◆ ADVERB 3 at or to the other or far side of something. 4 outside the limits of something. ◆ NOUN 5 **the beyond.** the unknown; the world outside the range of man's perception, esp life after death in certain religious beliefs.
▷HISTORY Old English *begeondan*; see BY, YONDER

Beyrouth (beɪˈruːt, ˈbeɪruːt) NOUN a variant spelling of **Beirut.**

bezant, bezzant (ˈbɛzᵊnt, bɪˈzænt), *or* **byzant** NOUN 1 a medieval Byzantine gold coin. 2 *Architect* an ornament in the form of a flat disc. 3 *Heraldry* a small gold circle.
▷HISTORY C13: from Old French *besant*, from Medieval Latin *Bȳzantius* Byzantine (coin)

bezel (ˈbɛzᵊl) NOUN 1 the sloping face adjacent to the working edge of a cutting tool. 2 the upper oblique faces of a cut gem. 3 a grooved ring or part holding a gem, watch crystal, etc. 4 a retaining outer rim used in vehicle instruments, e.g. in tachometers and speedometers. 5 a small indicator light used in vehicle instrument panels.
▷HISTORY C17: probably from French *biseau*, perhaps from Latin *bis* twice

Béziers (*French* bezje) NOUN a city in S France: scene of a massacre (1209) during the Albigensian Crusade. It is a centre of the wine trade. Pop.: 70 996 (1990).

bezique (bɪˈziːk) NOUN 1 a card game for two or more players with tricks similar to whist but with additional points scored for honours and sequences: played with two packs with nothing below a seven. 2 (in this game) the queen of spades and jack of diamonds declared together.
▷HISTORY C19: from French *bésigue*, of unknown origin

bezoar (ˈbiːzɔː) NOUN a hard mass, such as a stone or hairball, in the stomach and intestines of animals, esp ruminants, and man: formerly thought to be an antidote to poisons.
▷HISTORY C15: from Old French *bézoard*, from Arabic *bāzahr*, from Persian *bādzahr*, from *bād* against + *zahr* poison

bezonian (bɪˈzəʊnɪən) NOUN *Archaic* a knave or rascal.
▷HISTORY C16: from Italian *bisogno* ill-equipped raw recruit; literally, need

Bezwada (ˈbeɪzˌwɑːdə) NOUN the former name of **Vijayawada.**

bf THE INTERNET DOMAIN NAME FOR Burkina Faso.

B/F *or* **b/f** *Book-keeping* ABBREVIATION FOR brought forward.

B.F.A. (in the US and Canada) ABBREVIATION FOR Bachelor of Fine Arts.

BFI ABBREVIATION FOR British Film Institute.

BFN *Text messaging* ABBREVIATION FOR bye for now.

BFPO ABBREVIATION FOR British Forces Post Office.

bg THE INTERNET DOMAIN NAME FOR Bulgaria.

BG INTERNATIONAL CAR REGISTRATION FOR Bulgaria.

bh THE INTERNET DOMAIN NAME FOR Bahrain.

BH INTERNATIONAL CAR REGISTRATION FOR Belize.
▷HISTORY from *British Honduras*

Bhagalpur (ˈbɑːgəlˌpʊə) NOUN a city in India, in Bihar: agriculture, textiles, university (1960). Pop.: 253 225 (1991).

Bhagavad-Gita (ˈbʌgəvədˈgiːtə) NOUN a sacred Hindu text composed about 200 B.C. and incorporated into the *Mahabharata*, a Sanskrit epic.
▷HISTORY from Sanskrit: song of the Blessed One, from *bhaga* blessing + *gītā* a song

Bhai (baɪ) NOUN a title or form of address prefixed to the names of distinguished Sikhs.
▷HISTORY from Hindi *bhāī*, from Sanskrit *bhrātr* BROTHER

bhajan (ˈbʌdʒən) NOUN *Hinduism, Sikhism* the singing of devotional songs and hymns.
▷HISTORY from Sanskrit, literally: adoration, worship

bhaji (ˈbɑːdʒɪ) NOUN an Indian savoury made of chopped vegetables mixed in a spiced batter and deep-fried.
▷HISTORY C19: from Hindi *bhājī* fried vegetables

bhakti (ˈbʌktɪ) NOUN *Hinduism* loving devotion to God leading to nirvana.
▷HISTORY from Sanskrit: portion, from *bhajati* he allocates

bhang *or* **bang** (bæŋ) NOUN a preparation of the leaves and flower tops of Indian hemp, which has psychoactive properties: much used in India. See also **cannabis.**
▷HISTORY C16: from Hindi *bhāng*

bhangra (ˈbæŋgrə) NOUN a type of Asian pop music that combines elements of traditional Punjabi music with Western pop.
▷HISTORY C20: from Hindi

bharal *or* **burhel** (ˈbʌrəl) NOUN a wild Himalayan sheep, *Pseudois nayaur*, with a bluish-grey coat and round backward-curving horns.
▷HISTORY Hindi

Bharat (ˈbʌrʌt) NOUN transliteration of the Hindi name for **India.**

Bharatiya (ˈbɑːrəˌtiːjə) ADJECTIVE of or relating to India; Indian.

Bharat Natyam (ˈbʌrət ˈnɑːtjəm) NOUN a form of Indian classical ballet.
▷HISTORY from Sanskrit *bharatanātya* Bharata's dancing, from *Bharata* the sage supposed to have written of dramatic art and dancing + *nātya* dancing

Bhatpara (bɑːtˈpɑːrə) NOUN a city in NE India, in West Bengal on the Hooghly River: jute and cotton mills. Pop.: 304 952 (1991).

bhavan (ˈbʌvən) *or* **bhawan** NOUN (in India) a large house or building.

Bhavnagar (ˈbɑːvnəgə) NOUN a port in W India, in S Gujarat. Pop.: 402 338 (1991).

bhikhu (ˈbiːˌku) NOUN a fully ordained Buddhist monk.
▷HISTORY Pali, literally: beggar

bhikkhuni (ˈbiːkuˌni) NOUN a fully ordained Buddhist nun.
▷HISTORY Pali, literally: beggar

bhindi (ˈbɪndɪ) NOUN the okra as used in Indian

cooking: its green pods are eaten as vegetables. Also called: **lady's finger.**
▷HISTORY Hindi

bhishti *or* **bheesty** ('bi:stɪ) NOUN, *plural* **-ties.** (formerly in India) a water-carrier.
▷HISTORY C18: from Hindi *bhīstī*, from Persian *bihishtī* heavenly one, from *bihisht* paradise

Bhopal (bəʊ'pɑ:l) NOUN a city in central India, the capital of Madhya Pradesh state and of the former state of Bhopal: site of a poisonous gas leak from a US-owned factory, which killed over 2000 people in 1984. Pop.: 1 062 771 (1991).

B horizon NOUN the layer of a soil profile immediately below the A horizon, containing deposits of leached material.

bhp ABBREVIATION FOR brake horsepower.

BHP (in Australia) ABBREVIATION FOR Broken Hill Proprietary.

Bhubaneswar (ˌbʊbə'neɪʃwə) NOUN an ancient city in E India, the capital of Orissa state: many temples built between the 7th and 16th centuries. Pop.: 411 542 (1991).

Bhutan (bu:'tɑ:n) NOUN a kingdom in central Asia: disputed by Tibet, China, India, and Britain since the 18th century, the conflict now being chiefly between China and India (which is responsible for Bhutan's external affairs); contains inaccessible stretches of the E Himalayas in the north. Official language: Dzongka; Nepali is also spoken. Official religion: Mahayana Buddhist. Currencies: ngultrum and Indian rupee. Capital: Thimbu. Pop.: 692 000 (2001 est.). Area: about 46 600 sq. km (18 000 sq. miles).

Bhutanese (ˌbu:tɑ:n'ɪ:z) NOUN [1] a native or inhabitant of Bermuda. ◆ ADJECTIVE [2] of or relating to Bhutan or its inhabitants.

bi¹ (baɪ) ADJECTIVE, NOUN *Slang* short for **bisexual** (senses 1, 6).

bi² THE INTERNET DOMAIN NAME FOR Burundi.

Bi THE CHEMICAL SYMBOL FOR bismuth.

bi-¹ *or sometimes before a vowel* **bin-** COMBINING FORM [1] two; having two: *bifocal.* [2] occurring every two; lasting for two: *biennial.* [3] on both sides, surfaces, directions, etc.: *bilateral.* [4] occurring twice during: *biweekly.* [5] **a** denoting an organic compound containing two identical cyclic hydrocarbon systems: *biphenyl.* **b** (rare in technical usage) indicating an acid salt of a dibasic acid: *sodium bicarbonate.* **c** (not in technical usage) equivalent of **di-¹** (sense 2a).
▷HISTORY from Latin, from *bis* TWICE

bi-² COMBINING FORM a variant of **bio-**.

Biafra (bɪ'æfrə) NOUN [1] a region of E Nigeria, formerly a local government region: seceded as an independent republic (1967–70) during the Civil War, but defeated by Nigerian government forces. [2] **Bight of.** former name (until 1975) of (the Bight of) **Bonny.**

Biafran (bɪ'æfrən) ADJECTIVE [1] of or relating to Biafra or its inhabitants. ◆ NOUN [2] a native or inhabitant of Biafra.

Biak (bi:'jɑ:k) NOUN an island in Indonesia, north of West Irian: the largest of the Schouten Islands. Area: 2455 sq. km (948 sq. miles).

Białystok (*Polish* bja'wɪstɔk) NOUN a city in E Poland: belonged to Prussia (1795–1807) and to Russia (1807–1919). Pop.: 283 937 (1999 est.). Russian name: **Belostock.**

biannual (baɪ'ænjʊəl) ADJECTIVE occurring twice a year. Compare **biennial.**
▸**bi'annually** ADVERB

biannulate (baɪ'ænjʊlɪt, -ˌleɪt) ADJECTIVE *Zoology* having two bands, esp of colour.

Biarritz ('bɪərɪts, bɪə'rɪts; *French* bjarits) NOUN a town in SW France, on the Bay of Biscay: famous resort, patronized by Napoleon III and by Queen Victoria and Edward VII of Great Britain and Ireland. Pop.: 28 890 (1990).

bias ('baɪəs) NOUN [1] mental tendency or inclination, esp an irrational preference or prejudice. [2] a diagonal line or cut across the weave of a fabric. [3] *Electronics* the voltage applied to an electronic device or system to establish suitable working conditions. [4] *Bowls* **a** a bulge or weight inside one side of a bowl. **b** the curved course of such a bowl on the green. [5] *Statistics* **a** an extraneous latent influence on, unrecognized conflated variable in, or selectivity in a sample which influences its distribution and so renders it unable to reflect the desired population parameters. **b** if T is an estimator of the parameter θ, the expected value of $(T - \theta)$. [6] an inaudible high-frequency signal used to improve the quality of a tape recording. ◆ ADJECTIVE [7] slanting obliquely; diagonal: *a bias fold.* ◆ ADVERB [8] obliquely; diagonally. ◆ VERB **-ases, -asing, -ased** *or* **-asses, -assing, -assed.** (*tr*) [9] (*usually passive*) to cause to have a bias; prejudice; influence.
▷HISTORY C16: from Old French *biais*, from Old Provençal, perhaps ultimately from Greek *epikarsios* oblique
▸**'biased** *or* **'biassed** ADJECTIVE

bias binding NOUN a strip of material cut on the bias for extra stretch and often doubled, used for binding hems, interfacings, etc., or for decoration.

biathlon (baɪ'æθlən, -lɒn) NOUN *Sport* a contest in which skiers with rifles shoot at four targets along a 20-kilometre (12.5-mile) cross-country course.

biauriculate (ˌbaɪɔ:'rɪkjʊlɪt, -ˌleɪt) *or* **biauricular** ADJECTIVE having two auricles or earlike parts.

biaxial (baɪ'æksɪəl) ADJECTIVE (esp of a crystal) having two axes.

bib (bɪb) NOUN [1] a piece of cloth or plastic worn, esp by babies, to protect their clothes while eating. [2] the upper part of some aprons, dungarees, etc., that covers the upper front part of the body. [3] Also called: **pout, whiting pout.** a light-brown European marine gadoid food fish, *Gadus* (or *Trisopterus*) *luscus*, with a barbel on its lower jaw. [4] short for **bibcock.** [5] **stick one's bib in.** *Austral informal* to interfere. ◆ VERB **bibs, bibbing, bibbed.** [6] *Archaic* to drink (something); tipple.
▷HISTORY C14 *bibben* to drink, probably from Latin *bibere*

bib and brace NOUN a work garment consisting of trousers and an upper front part supported by straps over the shoulders.

bib and tucker NOUN *Informal* an outfit of clothes (esp in the phrase **best bib and tucker**).

bibb (bɪb) NOUN *Nautical* a wooden support on a mast for the trestletrees.
▷HISTORY C18: variant of BIB

bibber ('bɪbə) NOUN a drinker; tippler (esp in the expression **wine-bibber**).

bibble ('bɪbᵊl) NOUN *Midland English dialect* a pebble.

bibcock ('bɪbˌkɒk) *or* **bib** NOUN a tap having a nozzle bent downwards and supplied from a horizontal pipe.

bibelot ('bɪbləʊ; *French* biblo) NOUN [1] an attractive or curious trinket. [2] a miniature book.
▷HISTORY C19: from French, from Old French *beubelet*, perhaps from a reduplication of *bel* beautiful

Bible ('baɪbᵊl) NOUN [1] **a the.** the sacred writings of the Christian religion, comprising the Old and New Testaments and, in the Roman Catholic Church, the Apocrypha. **b** (*as modifier*): *a Bible reading.* [2] (*often not capital*) any book containing the sacred writings of a religion. [3] (*usually not capital*) a book regarded as authoritative: *the angler's bible.*
▷HISTORY C13: from Old French, from Medieval Latin *biblia* books, from Greek, plural of *biblion* book, diminutive of *biblos* papyrus, from *Bublos* Phoenician port from which Greece obtained Egyptian papyrus

Bible Belt NOUN **the.** those states of the S US where Protestant fundamentalism is dominant.

Bible paper NOUN [1] a thin tough opaque paper used for Bibles, prayer books, and reference books. [2] (not in technical usage) another name for **India paper.**

Bible-thumper NOUN *Slang* an enthusiastic or aggressive exponent of the Bible. Also called: **Bible-basher, Bible-pounder, Bible-puncher.**
▸**'Bible-ˌthumping** NOUN, ADJECTIVE

biblical ('bɪblɪkᵊl) ADJECTIVE [1] of, occurring in, or referring to the Bible. [2] resembling the Bible in written style.
▸**'biblically** ADVERB

Biblical Aramaic NOUN the form of Aramaic that was the common language of Palestine in New Testament times. It was widespread throughout the Persian Empire from the 5th century and is found in the later books of the Old Testament (esp Daniel 2:4–7:28).

Biblical Latin NOUN the form of Latin used in versions of the Bible, esp the form used in the Vulgate. See also **Late Latin.**

Biblicist ('bɪblɪsɪst) *or* **Biblist** NOUN [1] a biblical scholar. [2] a person who takes the Bible literally.

biblio- COMBINING FORM indicating book or books: *bibliography; bibliomania.*
▷HISTORY from Greek *biblion* book

bibliog. ABBREVIATION FOR: [1] bibliographer. [2] bibliography.

bibliography (ˌbɪblɪ'ɒgrəfɪ) NOUN, *plural* **-phies.** [1] a list of books or other material on a subject. [2] a list of sources used in the preparation of a book, thesis, etc. [3] a list of the works of a particular author or publisher. [4] **a** the study of the history, classification, etc., of literary material. **b** a work on this subject.
▸**ˌbibli'ographer** NOUN ▸**bibliographic** (ˌbɪblɪəʊ'græfɪk) *or* **ˌbiblio'graphical** ADJECTIVE ▸**ˌbiblio'graphically** ADVERB

bibliolatry (ˌbɪblɪ'ɒlətrɪ) NOUN [1] excessive devotion to or reliance on the Bible. [2] extreme fondness for books.

bibliomancy ('bɪblɪəʊˌmænsɪ) NOUN prediction of the future by interpreting a passage chosen at random from a book, esp the Bible.

bibliomania (ˌbɪblɪəʊ'meɪnɪə) NOUN extreme fondness for books.
▸**ˌbiblio'maniˌac** NOUN, ADJECTIVE

bibliophile ('bɪblɪəˌfaɪl) *or* **bibliophil** ('bɪblɪəfɪl) NOUN a person who collects or is fond of books.
▸**bibliophilism** (ˌbɪblɪ'ɒfəˌlɪzəm) NOUN ▸**ˌbibliˌophi'listic** ADJECTIVE

bibliopole ('bɪblɪəʊˌpəʊl) *or* **bibliopolist** (ˌbɪblɪ'ɒpəlɪst) NOUN a dealer in books, esp rare or decorative ones.
▷HISTORY C18: from Latin *bibliopōla*, from Greek *bibliopōlēs* bookseller, from BIBLIO- + *pōlein* to sell
▸**ˌbibli'opoly** NOUN

bibliotheca (ˌbɪblɪəʊ'θi:kə) NOUN, *plural* **-cas** *or* **-cae** (-ki:). [1] a library or collection of books. [2] a printed catalogue compiled by a bibliographer.
▷HISTORY Latin: library, from Greek *bibliothēkē*, from BIBLIO- + *thēkē* receptacle

bibulous ('bɪbjʊləs) ADJECTIVE addicted to alcohol.
▷HISTORY C17: from Latin *bibulus*, from *bibere* to drink
▸**'bibulously** ADVERB ▸**'bibulousness** NOUN

bicameral (baɪ'kæmərəl) ADJECTIVE (of a legislature) consisting of two chambers.
▷HISTORY C19: from BI-¹ + Latin *camera* CHAMBER
▸**bi'cameralˌism** NOUN ▸**bi'cameralist** NOUN

bicapsular (baɪ'kæpsjʊlə) ADJECTIVE (of plants) having two capsules or one capsule with two chambers.

bicarb ('baɪkɑ:b) NOUN short for **bicarbonate of soda.** See **sodium bicarbonate.**

bicarbonate (baɪ'kɑ:bənɪt, -ˌneɪt) NOUN [1] a salt of carbonic acid containing the ion HCO_3^-; an acid carbonate. [2] (*modifier*) consisting of, containing, or concerned with the ion HCO_3^-: *a bicarbonate compound.* Systematic name: **hydrogen carbonate.** [3] short for **bicarbonate of soda.**

bicarbonate of soda NOUN sodium bicarbonate, esp when used as a medicine or as a raising agent in baking.

bicarpellary (ˌbaɪkɑ:'pelərɪ) ADJECTIVE *Botany* (of an ovary) having two carpels.

bice (baɪs) NOUN [1] Also called: **bice blue.** a medium blue colour; azurite. [2] Also called: **bice green.** a yellowish-green colour; malachite.
▷HISTORY C14: from Old French *bis* dark grey, of uncertain origin

bicentenary (ˌbaɪsen'ti:nərɪ) *or US* **bicentennial** (ˌbaɪsen'tenɪəl) ADJECTIVE [1] marking a 200th anniversary. [2] occurring every 200 years. [3] lasting 200 years. ◆ NOUN, *plural* **-naries.** [4] a 200th anniversary.

bicephalous (baɪ'sefələs) ADJECTIVE [1] *Biology* having two heads. [2] crescent-shaped.

biceps ('baɪseps) NOUN, *plural* **-ceps.** *Anatomy* any muscle having two heads or origins, esp the muscle that flexes the forearm. Related adjective: **bicipital.**

▷HISTORY C17: from Latin: having two heads, from BI-[1] *caput* head

Biche-la-mar (ˌbiːtʃlə'mɑː) NOUN another name for **Beach-la-Mar.**

bichloride (baɪ'klɔːraɪd) NOUN another name for **dichloride.**

bichloride of mercury NOUN another name for **mercuric chloride.**

bichon frise ('biːʃɒn 'friːzeɪ) NOUN, *plural* **bichon frises.** a small white poodle-like dog of European origin, with a silky, loosely curling coat.
▷HISTORY C20: French, literally: curly toy dog

bichromate (baɪ'krəʊˌmeɪt, -mɪt) NOUN another name for **dichromate.**

bicipital (baɪ'sɪpɪtəl) ADJECTIVE [1] having two heads. [2] of or relating to a biceps muscle.
▷HISTORY C17: see BICEPS, -AL[1]

bicker ('bɪkə) VERB (*intr*) [1] to argue over petty matters; squabble. [2] *Poetic* **a** (esp of a stream) to run quickly. **b** to flicker; glitter. ◆ NOUN [3] a petty squabble.
▷HISTORY C13: of unknown origin
▸**'bickerer** NOUN ▸**'bickering** NOUN, ADJECTIVE

bickie ('bɪkɪ) NOUN *Informal* [1] short for **biscuit** (sense 1). [2] **big bickies.** *Austral slang* a large sum of money.

bicoastal (baɪ'kəʊstəl) ADJECTIVE relating to both the east and west coasts of the US: *she had a bicoastal upbringing.*

bicollateral (ˌbaɪkɒ'lætərəl) ADJECTIVE *Botany* (of a vascular bundle) having two phloem groups to the inside and outside, respectively, of the xylem.

bicolour ('baɪˌkʌlə), **bicoloured,** *or US* **bicolor, bicolored** ADJECTIVE two-coloured.

biconcave (baɪ'kɒnkeɪv, ˌbaɪkɒn'keɪv) ADJECTIVE (of a lens) having concave faces on both sides; concavo-concave.
▸**biconcavity** (ˌbaɪkɒn'kævɪtɪ) NOUN

biconditional (ˌbaɪkən'dɪʃənəl) NOUN another name for **equivalence** (sense 2).

biconvex (baɪ'kɒnvɛks, ˌbaɪkɒn'vɛks) ADJECTIVE (of a lens) having convex faces on both sides; convexo-convex.

bicorn ('baɪkɔːn), **bicornate** (baɪ'kɔːnɪt, -ˌneɪt), *or* **bicornuate** (baɪ'kɔːnjʊɪt, -ˌeɪt) ADJECTIVE having two horns or hornlike parts.
▷HISTORY C19: from Latin *bicornis*, from BI-[1] + *cornu* horn

bi-curious ADJECTIVE considering experimenting with bisexuality.

bicuspid (baɪ'kʌspɪd) *or* **bicuspidate** (baɪ'kʌspɪˌdeɪt) ADJECTIVE [1] having or terminating in two cusps or points. ◆ NOUN [2] a bicuspid tooth; premolar.

bicuspid valve NOUN another name for **mitral valve.**

bicycle ('baɪsɪkəl) NOUN [1] a vehicle with a tubular metal frame mounted on two spoked wheels, one behind the other. The rider sits on a saddle, propels the vehicle by means of pedals that drive the rear wheel through a chain, and steers with handlebars on the front wheel. Often shortened to: **cycle,** (informal) **bike.** ◆ VERB [2] (*intr*) to ride a bicycle; cycle.
▷HISTORY C19: from BI-[1] + Late Latin *cyclus*, from Greek *kuklos* wheel
▸**'bicyclist** *or* **'bicycler** NOUN

bicycle chain NOUN a chain that transmits power from the pedals to the driving wheel of a bicycle.

bicycle clip NOUN one of a pair of clips worn around the ankles by cyclists to keep the trousers tight and out of the chain.

bicycle pump NOUN a hand pump for pumping air into the tyres of a bicycle.

bicyclic (baɪ'saɪklɪk, -'sɪklɪk) *or* **bicyclical** ADJECTIVE [1] of, forming, or formed by two circles, cycles, etc. [2] (of stamens, petals, etc.) arranged in two whorls. [3] (of a chemical compound) having atoms arranged in two rings fused together with at least two atoms common to each ring: *naphthalene is bicyclic.*

bid (bɪd) VERB **bids; bidding; bad, bade** *or esp for senses 1, 2, 5, 7* **bid; bidden** *or esp for senses 1, 2, 5, 7* **bid.** [1] (often foll by *for* or *against*) to offer (an amount) in attempting to buy something, esp in competition with others as at an auction. [2] *Commerce* to respond to an offer by a seller by stating (the more favourable terms) on which one is willing to make a purchase. [3] (*tr*) to say (a greeting, blessing, etc.): *to bid farewell.* [4] to order; command: *do as you are bid!* [5] (*intr;* usually foll by *for*) to attempt to attain power, etc. [6] (*tr*) to invite; ask kindly: *she bade him sit down.* [7] *Bridge, etc* to declare in the auction before play how many tricks one expects to make. [8] **bid defiance.** to resist boldly. [9] **bid fair.** to seem probable. ◆ NOUN [10] **a** an offer of a specified amount, as at an auction. **b** the price offered. [11] *Commerce* **a** a statement by a buyer, in response to an offer by a seller, of the more favourable terms that would be acceptable. **b** the price or other terms so stated. [12] an attempt, esp an attempt to attain power. [13] *Bridge, etc* **a** the number of tricks a player undertakes to make. **b** a player's turn to make a bid. [14] short for **bid price.** ◆ See also **bid in, bid up.**
▷HISTORY Old English *biddan*; related to German *bitten*
▸**'bidder** NOUN

b.i.d. (in prescriptions) ABBREVIATION FOR bis in die.
▷HISTORY Latin: twice a day

Bida ('baɪdɑː) *or* **El Beda** (ɛl 'beɪdɑː) NOUN the former name of **Doha.**

bidarka (baɪ'dɑːkə) *or* **bidarkee** (baɪ'dɑːkiː) NOUN a canoe covered in animal skins, esp sealskin, used by the Eskimos of Alaska.
▷HISTORY C19: from Russian *baidarka*, diminutive of *baidara* umiak

biddable ('bɪdəbəl) ADJECTIVE [1] having sufficient value to be bid on, as a hand or suit at bridge. [2] docile; obedient.
▸**'biddableness** NOUN ▸**'biddably** ADVERB

bidden ('bɪdən) VERB a past participle of **bid.**

bidding ('bɪdɪŋ) NOUN [1] an order; command (often in the phrases **do** *or* **follow the bidding of, at someone's bidding**). [2] an invitation; summons. [3] the act of making bids, as at an auction or in bridge. [4] *Bridge* a group of bids considered collectively, esp those made on a particular deal.

biddy[1] ('bɪdɪ) NOUN, *plural* **-dies.** a dialect word for **chicken** or **hen.**
▷HISTORY C17: perhaps imitative of calling chickens

biddy[2] ('bɪdɪ) NOUN, *plural* **-dies.** *Informal* a woman, esp an old gossipy or interfering one.
▷HISTORY C18: from pet form of *Bridget*

biddy-biddy *or* **biddi-biddi** ('bɪdɪˌbɪdɪ) NOUN, *plural* **-biddies.** [1] a low-growing rosaceous plant, *Acaena viridior* of New Zealand, having prickly burs. [2] the burs of this plant. ◆ Also: (NZ) **biddy-bid,** (Austral) **bidgee-widgee** ('bɪdʒɪˌwɪdʒɪ).
▷HISTORY from Maori *piri piri*

bide (baɪd) VERB **bides, biding, bided** *or* **bode, bided.** [1] (*intr*) *Archaic or dialect* to continue in a certain place or state; stay. [2] (*intr*) *Archaic or dialect* to live; dwell. [3] (*tr*) *Archaic or dialect* to tolerate; endure. [4] **bide a wee.** *Scot* to stay a little. [5] **bide by.** *Scot* to abide by. [6] **bide one's time.** to wait patiently for an opportunity. ◆ Also: (Scot) **byde.**
▷HISTORY Old English *bīdan*; related to Old Norse *bítha* to wait, Gothic *beidan*, Old High German *bītan*

bidentate (baɪ'dɛnˌteɪt) ADJECTIVE [1] having two teeth or toothlike parts or processes. [2] *Chem* (of a ligand) having two atoms from which electrons can be donated to the central coordinated atom.

bidet ('biːdeɪ) NOUN a small low basin for washing the genitals and anal area.
▷HISTORY C17: from French: small horse, probably from Old French *bider* to trot

bidie-in (ˌbaɪdɪ'ɪn) NOUN *Scot* a live-in sexual partner.

bid in VERB (*adverb*) (in an auction) to outbid all previous offers for (one's own property) to retain ownership or increase the final selling price.

bidirectional (ˌbaɪdɪ'rɛkʃənəl) ADJECTIVE *Computing* (of a printhead) capable of printing from left to right and from right to left.

bid price NOUN *Stock Exchange* the price at which a stockjobber is prepared to purchase a specific security. Compare **offer price.**

bid up VERB (*adverb*) to increase the market price of (a commodity) by making artificial bids.

Biedermeier ('biːdəˌmaɪə) ADJECTIVE [1] of or relating to a decorative and furnishing style in mid-19th-century Germany, characterized by solidity and conventionality. [2] boringly conventional in outlook; bourgeois.
▷HISTORY C19: after Gottlieb *Biedermeier*, a fictitious character portrayed as a conventional unimaginative bourgeois and the author of poems actually written by several satirical poets

Biel (biːl) NOUN [1] a town in NW Switzerland, on Lake Biel. Pop.: 52 197 (1994). French name: **Bienne.** [2] **Lake.** a lake in NW Switzerland: remains of lake dwellings were discovered here in the 19th century. Area: 39 sq. km (15 sq. miles). German name: **Bielersee** ('biːləzeː).

bield (biːld) *Scot and northern English dialect* ◆ NOUN [1] a shelter; house. ◆ VERB [2] to shelter or take shelter.
▷HISTORY Old English *bieldo, byldo* boldness (hence: refuge); related to Gothic *balthei*, Old English *beald* BOLD

Bielefeld (*German* 'biːləfɛlt) NOUN a city in Germany, in NE North Rhine-Westphalia: food, textiles. Pop.: 321 600 (1999 est.).

Bielsko-Biała (*Polish* 'bjɛlskɔ'bjawa) NOUN a town in S Poland: created in 1951 by the union of Bielsko and Biala Krakowska; a leading textile centre since the 16th century. Pop.: 180 307 (1999 est.).

Bien Hoa ('bjɛn 'həʊə) NOUN a town in S Vietnam: a former capital of Cambodia. Pop.: 273 879 (1992 est.).

Bienne (bjɛn) NOUN the French name for **Biel.**

biennial (baɪ'ɛnɪəl) ADJECTIVE [1] occurring every two years. [2] lasting two years. Compare **biannual.** ◆ NOUN [3] a plant, such as the carrot, that completes its life cycle within two years, developing vegetative storage parts during the first year and flowering and fruiting in its second year. Compare **annual** (sense 3), **perennial** (sense 3). [4] an event that takes place every two years.
▸**bi'ennially** ADVERB

bien-pensant *French* (bjɛ̃pɑ̃sɑ̃) ADJECTIVE [1] right-thinking; orthodox. ◆ NOUN ***bien pensant,*** *plural* ***bien pensants*** (bjɛ̃pɑ̃sɑ̃) [2] a right-thinking person.
▷HISTORY literally: well-thinking

bier (bɪə) NOUN a platform or stand on which a corpse or a coffin containing a corpse rests before burial.
▷HISTORY Old English *bǣr*; related to *beran* to BEAR[1], Old High German *bāra* bier, Sanskrit *bhārá* a burden

bierkeller ('bɪəˌkɛlə) NOUN *Brit* a public house decorated in German style, selling German beers.
▷HISTORY C20: German, literally: beer cellar

biestings ('biːstɪŋz) NOUN a variant spelling of **beestings.**

bifacial (baɪ'feɪʃəl) ADJECTIVE [1] having two faces or surfaces. [2] *Botany* (of leaves, etc.) having upper and lower surfaces differing from each other. [3] *Archaeol* (of flints) flaked by percussion from two sides along the chopping edge.

bifarious (baɪ'fɛərɪəs) ADJECTIVE *Botany* having parts arranged in two rows on either side of a central axis.
▷HISTORY C17: from Latin *bifārius* double
▸**bi'fariously** ADVERB

biff (bɪf) *Slang* ◆ NOUN [1] a blow with the fist. [2] *Irish school slang* a blow to the palm of the hand with a strap or cane as a punishment. ◆ VERB [3] (*tr*) to give (someone) such a blow.
▷HISTORY C20: probably of imitative origin

biffer ('bɪfə) NOUN *Informal* [1] someone, such as a sportsperson, who has a reputation for hitting hard. [2] an implement used to serve blows.

BIFFEX ('bɪfɛks) acronym ◆ ABBREVIATION FOR Baltic International Freight Futures Exchange.

biffin ('bɪfɪn) NOUN *Brit* a variety of red cooking apple.
▷HISTORY C18: from *beefin* ox for slaughter, from BEEF; referring to the apple's colour

biffo ('bɪfəʊ) *Austral slang* ◆ NOUN [1] fighting or aggressive behaviour: *he enjoys a bit of biffo now and then.* ◆ ADJECTIVE [2] aggressive; pugnacious.

bifid ('baɪfɪd) ADJECTIVE divided into two lobes by a median cleft: *bifid leaves.*
▷HISTORY C17: from Latin *bifidus* from BI-[1] + *-fidus*, from *findere* to split
▸**bi'fidity** NOUN ▸**'bifidly** ADVERB

bifilar (baɪ'faɪlə) ADJECTIVE [1] having two parallel threads, as in the suspension of certain measuring instruments. [2] of or relating to a resistor in which

the wire is wound in a loop around a coil, the two leads being parallel, to reduce the inductance.
▸**bi'filarly** ADVERB

biflagellate (baɪ'flædʒɪˌleɪt, -lɪt) ADJECTIVE *Biology* having two flagella: *biflagellate protozoans.*

bifocal (baɪ'fəʊkᵊl) ADJECTIVE [1] *Optics* having two different focuses. [2] relating to a compound lens permitting near and distant vision.

bifocals (baɪ'fəʊkᵊlz) PLURAL NOUN a pair of spectacles with bifocal lenses.

bifoliate (baɪ'fəʊlɪˌeɪt, -ɪt) ADJECTIVE having only two leaves.

bifoliolate (baɪ'fəʊlɪəʊˌleɪt, -lɪt) ADJECTIVE (of compound leaves) consisting of two leaflets.

biforate ('baɪfəˌreɪt) ADJECTIVE *Biology* having two openings, pores, or perforations.
▷**HISTORY** C19: from New Latin *biforātus*, from BI-[1] + *forāre* to pierce

biform ('baɪˌfɔːm) *or* **biformed** ADJECTIVE having or combining the characteristics of two forms, as a centaur.

Bifrost ('bɪvrɒst, 'biːfrɒst) NOUN *Norse myth* the rainbow bridge of the gods from their realm Asgard to earth.
▷**HISTORY** from Icelandic, from *bifa* to shake + *rost* path

bifter ('bɪftə) NOUN *Slang* a cannabis cigarette.

bifurcate VERB ('baɪfəˌkeɪt) [1] to fork or divide into two parts or branches. ◆ ADJECTIVE ('baɪfəˌkeɪt, -kɪt) [2] forked or divided into two sections or branches.
▷**HISTORY** C17: from Medieval Latin *bifurcātus*, from Latin *bifurcus*, from BI-[1] + *furca* fork
▸ˌ**bifur'cation** NOUN

big[1] (bɪg) ADJECTIVE **bigger, biggest.** [1] of great or considerable size, height, weight, number, power, or capacity. [2] having great significance; important: *a big decision.* [3] important through having power, influence, wealth, authority, etc.: *the big four banks.* [4] (intensifier usually qualifying something undesirable): *a big dope.* [5] *Informal* considerable in extent or intensity (esp in the phrase **in a big way**). [6] **a** elder: *my big brother.* **b** grown-up: *when you're big, you can stay up later.* [7] **a** generous; magnanimous: *that's very big of you.* **b** (*in combination*): *big-hearted.* [8] (often foll by *with*) brimming; full: *my heart is big with sadness.* [9] extravagant; boastful: *he's full of big talk.* [10] **too big for one's boots** *or* **breeches.** conceited; unduly self-confident. [11] in an advanced stage of pregnancy (esp in the phrase **big with child**). [12] **big on.** *Informal* enthusiastic about: *that company is big on research.* ◆ ADVERB *Informal* [13] boastfully; pretentiously (esp in the phrase **talk big**). [14] in an exceptional way; well: *his talk went over big with the audience.* [15] on a grand scale (esp in the phrase **think big**). See also **big up.**
▷**HISTORY** C13: perhaps of Scandinavian origin; compare Norwegian dialect *bugge* big man
▸'**biggish** ADJECTIVE ▸'**bigness** NOUN

big[2] (bɪg) VERB **bigs, bigging, bigged** *or* **bug** (bʌg). *Scot* [1] to build. [2] to excavate (earth) into a pile.
▷**HISTORY** from Old Norse *byggja*; related to Old English *būian* to inhabit

bigamy ('bɪgəmɪ) NOUN, *plural* **-mies.** the crime of marrying a person while one is still legally married to someone else.
▷**HISTORY** C13: via French from Medieval Latin *bigamus*; see BI-[1], -GAMY
▸'**bigamist** NOUN ▸'**bigamous** ADJECTIVE ▸'**bigamously** ADVERB

Big Apple NOUN **the.** *Informal* New York City.
▷**HISTORY** C20: probably from US jazzmen's earlier use to mean any big, esp northern, city; of obscure origin

bigarreau ('bɪgəˌrəʊ, ˌbɪgə'rəʊ) NOUN any of several heart-shaped varieties of sweet cherry that have firm flesh.
▷**HISTORY** C17: from French, from *bigarré* mottled

big band NOUN a large jazz or dance band, popular esp in the 1930s to the 1950s.

big bang NOUN [1] any sudden forceful beginning or radical change. [2] (*modifier*) of or relating to the big-bang theory. [3] (*sometimes capitals*) the major modernization that took place on the London Stock Exchange on Oct. 27 1986, after which the distinction between jobbers and brokers was abolished and operations became fully computerized.

big-bang theory NOUN a cosmological theory postulating that approximately 12 billion years ago all the matter of the universe, packed into a small superdense mass, was hurled in all directions by a cataclysmic explosion. As the fragments slowed down, the galaxies and stars evolved but the universe is still expanding. Compare **steady-state theory.**

big beast NOUN *Informal* an important or powerful person.

big beat NOUN **a** an eclectic type of dance music in which heavy beats and samples are layered over the songs or instrumental tracks of other performers or bands. **b** (*as modifier*): *a big-beat compilation.*

Big Ben NOUN [1] the bell in the clock tower of the Houses of Parliament, London. [2] the clock in this tower. [3] the tower.
▷**HISTORY** C19: named after Sir *Benjamin* Hall, Chief Commissioner of Works in 1856 when it was cast

Big Bertha NOUN any of three large German guns of World War I used to bombard Paris.
▷**HISTORY** C20: approximate translation of German *dicke Bertha*: fat Bertha; named after *Bertha* Krupp, at whose works in Essen a very effective 42 cm mortar was made

Big Board NOUN *US informal* [1] the quotation board in the New York Stock Exchange. [2] the New York Stock Exchange.

Big Brother NOUN [1] a person, organization, etc., that exercises total dictatorial control. [2] a television gameshow format in which a small number of people living in accomodation sealed off from the outside world are constantly monitored by TV cameras. Viewers vote each week to expel a person from the group until there is only one person left, who wins a cash prize.
▷**HISTORY** C20: after a character in the novel *1984* (1949) by English writer George Orwell (1903–1950)

big bucks PLURAL NOUN *Informal, chiefly US* [1] large quantities of money. [2] the power and influence of people or organizations that control large quantities of money.

big bud NOUN a serious disease of plants, esp of blackcurrants, in which the buds swell up as a result of attack by the gall mite *Cecidophyopsis ribis.*

big business NOUN large commercial organizations collectively, esp when considered as exploitative or socially harmful.

big cheese NOUN *Slang* an important person.

big Chief *or* **big Daddy** NOUN *Informal* other terms for **big White Chief.**

big deal INTERJECTION *Slang* an exclamation of scorn, derision, etc., used esp to belittle a claim or offer.

big dipper NOUN (in amusement parks) a narrow railway with open carriages that run swiftly over a route of sharp curves and steep inclines. Also called: **roller coaster.**

Big Dipper NOUN the US and Canadian name for the **Plough** (constellation).

big end NOUN *Brit* [1] Also called (in vertical engines): **bottom end.** the larger end of a connecting rod in an internal-combustion engine. Compare **little end.** [2] the bearing surface between the larger end of a connecting rod and the crankpin of the crankshaft.

bigener ('baɪdʒɪnə) NOUN *Biology* a hybrid between individuals of different genera.
▷**HISTORY** C20: back formation from *bigeneric*; see BI-[1], GENUS

bigeneric (ˌbaɪdʒə'nɛrɪk) ADJECTIVE (of a hybrid plant) derived from parents of two different genera.

bigeye ('bɪgˌaɪ) NOUN, *plural* **-eye** *or* **-eyes.** any tropical or subtropical red marine percoid fish of the family *Priacanthidae*, having very large eyes and rough scales.

big fish NOUN *Informal* [1] an important or powerful person. [2] **a big fish in a small pond.** the most important or powerful person in a small group.

Big Five NOUN **the.** [1] the five countries considered to be the major world powers. In the period immediately following World War II, the US, Britain, the Soviet Union, China, and France were regarded as the Big Five. [2] the lion, the elephant, the rhinoceros, the buffalo, and the leopard: considered to be the five principal African wild animals, esp as sought by those on safari. [3] a small powerful group, as of banks, companies, etc. Also: **Big Four, Big Three.**

big game NOUN [1] large animals that are hunted or fished for sport. [2] *Informal* the objective of an important or dangerous undertaking.

biggin[1] *or* **biggon** ('bɪgɪn) NOUN a plain close-fitting cap, often tying under the chin, worn in the Middle Ages and by children in the 17th century.
▷**HISTORY** C16: from French *béguin*; see BEGUINE

biggin[2] ('bɪgən) NOUN *Scot* a construction, esp a house or cottage.
▷**HISTORY** see BIG[2]

big gun NOUN *Informal* an important or influential person.

bighead ('bɪgˌhɛd) NOUN [1] *Informal* a conceited person. [2] *US and Canadian informal* conceit; egotism. [3] *Vet science* **a** an abnormal bulging or increase in the size of an animal's skull, as from osteomalacia. **b** any of various diseases of sheep characterized by swelling of the head, esp any caused by infection with *Clostridium* bacteria.
▸ˌ**big'headed** ADJECTIVE ▸ˌ**big'headedly** ADVERB
▸ˌ**big'headedness** NOUN

big-hearted ADJECTIVE warmly generous.
▸ˌ**big-'heartedness** NOUN

big hitter NOUN [1] a sportsperson who is capable of hitting the ball long or hard. [2] *Informal* an influential and important person: *one of the government's big hitters.*

bighorn ('bɪgˌhɔːn) NOUN, *plural* **-horns** *or* **-horn.** a large wild sheep, *Ovis canadensis*, inhabiting mountainous regions in North America and NE Asia: family *Bovidae*, order *Artiodactyla*. The male has massive curved horns, and the species is well adapted for climbing and leaping.

bight (baɪt) NOUN [1] a wide indentation of a shoreline, or the body of water bounded by such a curve. [2] the slack middle part of an extended rope. [3] a curve or loop in a rope. ◆ VERB [4] (*tr*) to fasten or bind with a bight.
▷**HISTORY** Old English *byht*; see BOW[2]

Bight NOUN **the.** *Austral informal* the major indentation of the S coast of Australia, from Cape Pasley in W Australia to the Eyre Peninsula in S Australia. In full: **the Great Australian Bight.**

big money NOUN large sums of money: *there's big money in professional golf.*

bigmouth ('bɪgˌmaʊθ) NOUN *Slang* a noisy, indiscreet, or boastful person.
▸'**big-ˌmouthed** ADJECTIVE

big name NOUN *Informal* **a** a famous person. **b** (*as modifier*): *a big-name performer.*

big noise NOUN *Informal* an important person.

bignonia (bɪg'nəʊnɪə) NOUN any tropical American bignoniaceous climbing shrub of the genus *Bignonia* (or *Doxantha*), cultivated for their trumpet-shaped yellow or reddish flowers. See also **cross vine.**
▷**HISTORY** C19: from New Latin, named after the Abbé Jean-Paul *Bignon* (1662–1743)

bignoniaceous (bɪgˌnəʊnɪ'eɪʃəs) ADJECTIVE of, relating to, or belonging to the *Bignoniaceae*, a chiefly tropical family of trees, shrubs, and lianas, including jacaranda, bignonia, and catalpa.

big-note VERB *Austral informal* to boast about (oneself).

bigot ('bɪgət) NOUN a person who is intolerant of any ideas other than his or her own, esp on religion, politics, or race.
▷**HISTORY** C16: from Old French: name applied contemptuously to the Normans by the French, of obscure origin
▸'**bigoted** ADJECTIVE

bigotry ('bɪgətrɪ) NOUN, *plural* **-ries.** the attitudes, behaviour, or way of thinking of a bigot; prejudice; intolerance.

big science NOUN scientific research that requires a large investment of capital.

big screen NOUN an informal name for the **cinema.**

big shot NOUN *Informal* an important or influential person.

Big Smoke NOUN **the.** *Informal* a large city, esp London.

big stick NOUN *Informal* force or the threat of using force.

big tent NOUN **a** a political approach in which a party claims to be open to a wide spectrum of constituents and groups. **b** (*as modifier*): *big-tent politics.*

big time NOUN *Informal* **a the.** the highest or most profitable level of an occupation or profession, esp the entertainment business. **b** (*as modifier*): *a big-time comedian.*
▸ **'big-'timer** NOUN

big top NOUN *Informal* 1 the main tent of a circus. 2 the circus itself.

big tree NOUN a giant Californian coniferous tree, *Sequoiadendron giganteum*, with a wide tapering trunk and thick spongy bark: family *Taxodiaceae*. It often reaches a height of 90 metres. Also called: **giant sequoia, wellingtonia.** See also **sequoia.**

biguanide (baɪ'gwɑːnaɪd) NOUN any of a class of compounds some of which are used in the treatment of certain forms of diabetes. See also **phenformin.**
▹ HISTORY C19: from BI-[1] + GUANIDINE + -IDE

big up VERB **bigs, bigging, bigged.** (*tr, adverb*) *Slang, chiefly Caribbean* to make important, prominent, or famous: *we'll do our best to big you up.*

big wheel NOUN 1 another name for a **Ferris wheel.** 2 *Informal* an important person.

big White Chief NOUN *Informal* an important person, boss, or leader. Also called: **big Chief, big Daddy.**

bigwig ('bɪgˌwɪg) NOUN *Informal* an important person.

Bihar (bɪ'hɑː) NOUN a state of NE India: consists of part of the Ganges plain; important for rice: lost the S to the new state of Jharkand in 2000. Capital: Patna. Pop.: 82 878 796 (2001). Area: 99 225 sq. km (38 301 sq. miles).

Bihari (bɪ'hɑːrɪ) NOUN 1 (*plural* **Bihari** *or* **Biharis**) a member of an Indian people living chiefly in Bihar but also in other parts of NW India and Bangladesh. 2 the language of this people, comprising a number of highly differentiated dialects, belonging to the Indic branch of the Indo-European family. ◆ ADJECTIVE 3 of or relating to this people, their language, or Bihar.

Biisk (*Russian* bijsk) NOUN a variant spelling of **Biysk.**

Bijapur (bɪ'dʒɑːpʊə) NOUN an ancient city in W India, in N Mysore: capital of a former kingdom, which fell at the end of the 17th century: cotton. Pop.: 186 939 (1991).

bijection (baɪ'dʒɛkʃən) NOUN a mathematical function or mapping that is both an injection and a surjection and therefore has an inverse. See also **injection** (sense 5), **surjection.**

bijective (baɪ'dʒɛktɪv) ADJECTIVE *Maths* (of a function, relation, etc.) associating two sets in such a way that every member of each set is uniquely paired with a member of the other: *the mapping from the set of married men to the set of married women is bijective in a monogamous society.*

bijou ('biːʒuː) NOUN, *plural* **-joux** (-ʒuːz). 1 something small and delicately worked, such as a trinket. 2 (*modifier*) *Often ironic* small but elegant and tasteful: *a bijou residence.*
▹ HISTORY C19: from French, from Breton *bizou* finger ring, from *biz* finger; compare Welsh *bys* finger, Cornish *bis*

bijouterie (biː'ʒuːtərɪ) NOUN 1 jewellery esteemed for the delicacy of the work rather than the value of the materials. 2 a collection of such jewellery.

bijugate ('baɪdʒʊˌgeɪt, baɪ'dʒuːgeɪt) *or* **bijugous** ADJECTIVE (of compound leaves) having two pairs of leaflets.

Bikaner ('biːkəˌnɪə) NOUN a walled city in NW India, in Rajasthan: capital of the former state of Bikaner, on the edge of the Thar Desert. Pop.: 416 289 (1991).

bike[1] (baɪk) NOUN, VERB 1 *Informal* short for **bicycle** or **motorcycle.** 2 **on your bike.** *Brit slang* away you go. 3 **get off one's bike.** *Austral and NZ slang* to lose one's self-control. ◆ NOUN 4 *Slang* a promiscuous woman: *the town bike.*

bike[2] *or* **byke** (bəɪk, baɪk) *Scot* ◆ NOUN 1 a wasps' or bees' nest. ◆ VERB (*intr*) 2 to swarm.
▹ HISTORY C14: of uncertain origin

biker ('baɪkə) NOUN *Informal* a member of a motorcyle gang.

biker jacket NOUN a short, close-fitting leather jacket with zips and studs, often worn by motorcyclists.

bikie ('baɪkɪ) NOUN *Austral and NZ slang* a member of a motorcycle gang.

bikini (bɪ'kiːnɪ) NOUN, *plural* **-nis.** a woman's very brief two-piece swimming costume.
▹ HISTORY C20: after Bikini atoll, from a comparison between the devastating effect of the atomic-bomb test and the effect caused by women wearing bikinis

Bikini (bɪ'kiːnɪ) NOUN an atoll in the N Pacific; one of the Marshall Islands: site of a US atomic-bomb test in 1946.

bilabial (baɪ'leɪbɪəl) ADJECTIVE 1 of, relating to, or denoting a speech sound articulated using both lips: *(p) is a bilabial stop, (w) a bilabial semivowel.* ◆ NOUN 2 a bilabial speech sound.

bilabiate (baɪ'leɪbɪˌeɪt, -ɪt) ADJECTIVE *Botany* divided into two lips: *the snapdragon has a bilabiate corolla.*

bilander ('bɪləndə) NOUN a small two-masted cargo ship.
▹ HISTORY C17: from Dutch, literally: by-lander, because used on canals

bilateral (baɪ'lætərəl) ADJECTIVE 1 having or involving two sides. 2 affecting or undertaken by two parties; mutual: *a bilateral treaty.* 3 denoting or relating to bilateral symmetry. 4 having identical sides or parts on each side of an axis; symmetrical. 5 *Sociol* relating to descent through both maternal and paternal lineage. Compare **unilateral** (sense 5). 6 *Brit* relating to an education that combines academic and technical courses. 7 a bilateral meeting.
▸ **bi'laterally** ADVERB

bilateral symmetry NOUN the property of an organism or part of an organism such that, if cut in only one plane, the two cut halves are mirror images of each other. See also **radial symmetry.**

bilateral trade NOUN a system of trading between two countries in which each country attempts to balance its trade with that of the other.

Bilbao (bɪl'bɑːəʊ; *Spanish* bil'βau) NOUN a port in N Spain, on the Bay of Biscay: the largest city in the Basque Provinces: famous since medieval times for the production of iron and steel goods: modern buildings include the Guggenheim Art Museum (1997). Pop.: 358 467 (1998 est.).

bilberry ('bɪlbərɪ) NOUN, *plural* **-ries.** 1 any of several ericaceous shrubs of the genus *Vaccinium*, having edible blue or blackish berries. See also **blueberry.** 2 **a** the fruit of any of these plants. **b** (*as modifier*): *bilberry pie.*
▹ HISTORY C16: probably of Scandinavian origin; compare Danish *böllebær*, from *bölle* bilberry + *bær* BERRY

bilbo ('bɪlbəʊ) NOUN, *plural* **-bos** *or* **-boes.** (formerly) a sword with a marked temper and elasticity.
▹ HISTORY C16: from *Bilboa*, variant (in English) of *Bilbao*, Spain, noted for its blades

bilboes ('bɪlbəʊz) PLURAL NOUN a long iron bar with two sliding shackles, formerly used to confine the ankles of a prisoner.
▹ HISTORY C16: perhaps changed from BILBAO

bilby ('bɪlbɪ) NOUN, *plural* **-bies.** a burrowing marsupial of the genus *Macrotis* of Australia having long pointed ears and grey fur. Also called: **rabbit bandicoot, dalgyte.**

Bildungsroman *German* ('bɪldʊŋsromaːn) NOUN a novel concerned with a person's formative years and development.
▹ HISTORY literally: education novel

bile[1] (baɪl) NOUN 1 a bitter greenish to golden brown alkaline fluid secreted by the liver and stored in the gall bladder. It is discharged during digestion into the duodenum, where it aids the emulsification and absorption of fats. 2 irritability or peevishness. 3 *Archaic* either of two bodily humours, one of which (**black bile**) was thought to cause melancholy and the other (**yellow bile**) anger.
▹ HISTORY C17: from French, from Latin *bīlis*, probably of Celtic origin; compare Welsh *bustl* bile

bile[2] (bəɪl) VERB a Scot word for **boil.**

bilection (baɪ'lɛkʃən) NOUN another word for **bolection.**

bilestone ('baɪlˌstəʊn) NOUN another name for **gallstone.**

bilge (bɪldʒ) NOUN 1 *Nautical* the parts of a vessel's hull where the vertical sides curve inwards to form the bottom. 2 (*often plural*) the parts of a vessel between the lowermost floorboards and the bottom. 3 Also called: **bilge water.** the dirty water that collects in a vessel's bilge. 4 *Informal* silly rubbish; nonsense. 5 the widest part of the belly of a barrel or cask. ◆ VERB 6 (*intr*) *Nautical* (of a vessel) to take in water at the bilge. 7 (*tr*) *Nautical* to damage (a vessel) in the bilge, causing it to leak.
▹ HISTORY C16: probably a variant of BULGE
▸ **'bilgy** ADJECTIVE

bilge keel NOUN one of two keel-like projections along the bilges of some vessels to improve sideways stability.

bilharzia (bɪl'hɑːtsɪə) NOUN 1 another name for a **schistosome.** 2 another name for **schistosomiasis.**
▹ HISTORY C19: New Latin, named after Theodor *Bilharz* (1825–62), German parasitologist who discovered schistosomes

bilharziasis (ˌbɪlhɑː'tsaɪəsɪs) *or* **bilharziosis** (bɪlˌhɑːtsɪ'əʊsɪs) NOUN another name for **schistosomiasis.**

biliary ('bɪlɪərɪ) ADJECTIVE of or relating to bile, to the ducts that convey bile, or to the gall bladder.

bilinear (baɪ'lɪnɪə) ADJECTIVE 1 of or referring to two lines. 2 of or relating to a function of two variables that is linear in each independently, as $f(x, y) = xy$.

bilingual (baɪ'lɪŋgwəl) ADJECTIVE 1 able to speak two languages, esp with fluency. 2 written or expressed in two languages. ◆ NOUN 3 a bilingual person.
▸ **bi'lingualˌism** NOUN ▸ **bi'lingually** ADVERB

bilious ('bɪlɪəs) ADJECTIVE 1 of or relating to bile. 2 affected with or denoting any disorder related to excess secretion of bile. 3 *Informal* (esp of colours) extremely distasteful; nauseating: *a bilious green.* 4 *Informal* bad-tempered; irritable.
▹ HISTORY C16: from Latin *bīliōsus* full of BILE[1]
▸ **'biliousness** NOUN

bilirubin (ˌbɪlɪ'ruːbɪn, ˌbaɪ-) NOUN an orange-yellow pigment in the bile formed as a breakdown product of haemoglobin. Excess amounts in the blood produce the yellow appearance associated with jaundice. Formula: $C_{32}H_{36}O_6N_4$.
▹ HISTORY C19: from BILE[1] + Latin *ruber* red + -IN

biliverdin (ˌbɪlɪ'vɜːdɪn) NOUN a dark green pigment in the bile formed by the oxidation of bilirubin. Formula: $C_{33}H_{34}O_6N_4$.
▹ HISTORY C19: coined in Swedish, from Latin *bīlis* bile + Old French *verd* green + -IN

bilk (bɪlk) VERB (*tr*) 1 to balk; thwart. 2 (often foll by *of*) to cheat or deceive, esp to avoid making payment to. 3 to escape from; elude. 4 *Cribbage* to play a card that hinders (one's opponent) from scoring in his crib. ◆ NOUN 5 a swindle or cheat. 6 a person who swindles or cheats.
▹ HISTORY C17: perhaps variant of BALK
▸ **'bilker** NOUN

bill[1] (bɪl) NOUN 1 money owed for goods or services supplied: *an electricity bill.* 2 a written or printed account or statement of money owed. 3 *Chiefly Brit* such an account for food and drink in a restaurant, hotel, etc. Usual US and Canadian word: **check.** 4 any printed or written list of items, events, etc., such as a theatre programme: *who's on the bill tonight?* 5 **fit** *or* **fill the bill.** *Informal* to serve or perform adequately. 6 a statute in draft, before it becomes law. 7 a printed notice or advertisement; poster. 8 *US and Canadian* a piece of paper money; note. 9 an obsolete name for **promissory note.** 10 *Law* See **bill of indictment.** 11 See **bill of exchange.** 12 See **bill of fare.** 13 *Archaic* any document. ◆ VERB (*tr*) 14 to send or present an account for payment to (a person). 15 to enter (items, goods, etc.) on an account or statement. 16 to advertise by posters.

[17] to schedule as a future programme: *the play is billed for next week.*
▷HISTORY C14: from Anglo-Latin *billa*, alteration of Late Latin *bulla* document, BULL[3]

bill² (bɪl) NOUN [1] the mouthpart of a bird, consisting of projecting jaws covered with a horny sheath; beak. It varies in shape and size according to the type of food eaten and may also be used as a weapon. [2] any beaklike mouthpart in other animals. [3] a narrow promontory: *Portland Bill.* [4] *Nautical* the pointed tip of the fluke of an anchor. ◆ VERB (*intr*) (esp in the phrase **bill and coo**) [5] (of birds, esp doves) to touch bills together. [6] (of lovers) to kiss and whisper amorously.
▷HISTORY Old English *bile*; related to *bill* BILL[3]

bill³ (bɪl) NOUN [1] a pike or halberd with a narrow hooked blade. [2] short for **billhook.**
▷HISTORY Old English *bill* sword, related to Old Norse *bīldr* instrument used in blood-letting, Old High German *bil* pickaxe

bill⁴ (bɪl) NOUN *Ornithol* another word for **boom¹** (sense 4).
▷HISTORY C18: from dialect *beel* BELL[2] (vb)

billabong ('bɪlə,bɒŋ) NOUN *Austral* [1] a backwater channel that forms a lagoon or pool. [2] a branch of a river running to a dead end.
▷HISTORY C19: from a native Australian language, from *billa* river + *bong* dead

billboard¹ ('bɪl,bɔːd) NOUN another name for **hoarding.**
▷HISTORY C19: from BILL[1] + BOARD

billboard² ('bɪl,bɔːd) NOUN a fitting at the bow of a vessel for securing an anchor.
▷HISTORY C19: from BILL[2] + BOARD

bill broker NOUN a person whose business is the purchase and sale of bills of exchange.

biller ('bɪlə) NOUN *Southwest English dialect* the stem of a plant.

billet¹ ('bɪlɪt) NOUN [1] accommodation, esp for a soldier, in civilian lodgings. [2] the official requisition for such lodgings. [3] a space or berth allocated, esp for slinging a hammock, in a ship. [4] *Informal* a job. [5] *Archaic* a brief letter or document. ◆ VERB **-lets, -leting, -leted.** [6] (*tr*) to assign a lodging to (a soldier). [7] (*tr*) *Informal* to assign to a post or job. [8] to lodge or be lodged.
▷HISTORY C15: from Old French *billette*, from *bulle* a document; see BULL[3]
▸ **,billet'ee** NOUN ▸ **'billeter** NOUN

billet² ('bɪlɪt) NOUN [1] a chunk of wood, esp for fuel. [2] *Metallurgy* **a** a metal bar of square or circular cross section. **b** an ingot cast into the shape of a prism. [3] *Architect* a carved ornament in a moulding, with short cylinders or blocks evenly spaced.
▷HISTORY C15: from Old French *billette* a little log, from *bille* log, probably of Celtic origin

billet-doux (,bɪlɪ'duː; *French* bijɛdu) NOUN, *plural* **billets-doux** (,bɪlɪ'duːz; *French* bijɛdu). *Old-fashioned or jocular* a love letter.
▷HISTORY C17: from French, literally: a sweet letter, from *billet* (see BILLET[1]) + *doux* sweet, from Latin *dulcis*

billfish ('bɪl,fɪʃ) NOUN, *plural* **-fish, -fishes.** *US* any of various fishes having elongated jaws, esp any fish of the family *Istiophoridae*, such as the spearfish and marlin.

billfold ('bɪl,fəʊld) NOUN a US and Canadian word for **wallet.**

billhook ('bɪl,hʊk) NOUN a cutting tool with a wooden handle and a curved blade terminating in a hook at its tip, used for pruning, chopping, etc. Also called: **bill.**

billiard ('bɪljəd) NOUN (*modifier*) of or relating to billiards: *a billiard table; a billiard cue; a billiard ball.*

billiards ('bɪljədz) NOUN (*functioning as singular*) [1] any of various games in which long cues are used to drive balls now made of composition or plastic. It is played on a rectangular table covered with a smooth tight-fitting cloth and having raised cushioned edges. [2] a version of this, played on a rectangular table having six pockets let into the corners and the two longer sides. Points are scored by striking one of three balls with the cue to contact the other two or one of the two. Compare **pool²** (sense 5), **snooker.**

▷HISTORY C16: from Old French *billard* curved stick, from Old French *bille* log; see BILLET[2]

billing ('bɪlɪŋ) NOUN [1] *Theatre* the relative importance of a performer or act as reflected in the prominence given in programmes, advertisements, etc. [2] *Chiefly US and Canadian* public notice or advertising (esp in the phrase **advance billing**).

billingsgate ('bɪlɪŋz,geɪt) NOUN obscene or abusive language.
▷HISTORY C17: after BILLINGSGATE, which was notorious for such language

Billingsgate ('bɪlɪŋz,geɪt) NOUN the largest fish market in London, on the N bank of the River Thames; moved to new site on the Isle of Dogs in 1982.

Billings method NOUN a natural method of birth control that involves examining the colour and viscosity of the cervical mucus to discover when ovulation is occurring. Also called: **ovulation method, mucus method.**
▷HISTORY C20: devised by Drs John and Evelyn *Billings* in the 1960s

billion ('bɪljən) NOUN, *plural* **-lions** *or* **-lion.** [1] one thousand million: it is written as 1 000 000 000 or 10^9. [2] (formerly, in Britain) one million million: it is written as 1 000 000 000 000 or 10^{12}. [3] (*often plural*) any exceptionally large number. ◆ DETERMINER [4] (preceded by *a* or a cardinal number) **a** amounting to a billion: *it seems like a billion years ago.* **b** (*as pronoun*): *we have a billion here.*
▷HISTORY C17: from French, from BI-[1] + *-llion* as in *million*
▸ **'billionth** ADJECTIVE, NOUN

billionaire (,bɪljə'nɛə) NOUN a person whose assets are worth over a billion of the monetary units of his country.

Billiton ('bɪlɪtɒn, bɪ'liːtɒn) NOUN an island of Indonesia, in the Java Sea between Borneo and Sumatra. Chief town: Tandjungpandan. Area: 4833 sq. km (1866 sq. miles). Also called: **Belitung.**

bill of adventure NOUN a certificate made out by a merchant to show that goods handled by him and his agents are the property of another party at whose risk the dealing is done.

bill of attainder NOUN (formerly) a legislative act finding a person guilty without trial of treason or felony and declaring him attainted. See also **attainder** (sense 1).

bill of exchange NOUN (now chiefly in foreign transactions) a document, usually negotiable, containing an instruction to a third party to pay a stated sum of money at a designated future date or on demand.

bill of fare NOUN another name for **menu.**

bill of health NOUN [1] a certificate, issued by a port officer, that attests to the health of a ship's company. [2] **clean bill of health.** *Informal* **a** a good report of one's physical condition. **b** a favourable account of a person's or a company's financial position.

bill of indictment NOUN *Criminal law* a formal document accusing a person or persons of crime, formerly presented to a grand jury for certification as a true bill but now signed by a court official.

bill of lading NOUN (in foreign trade) a document containing full particulars of goods shipped or for shipment. Usual US and Canadian name: **waybill.**

bill of quantities NOUN a document drawn up by a quantity surveyor providing details of the prices, dimensions, etc., of the materials required to build a large structure, such as a factory.

Bill of Rights NOUN [1] an English statute of 1689 guaranteeing the rights and liberty of the individual subject. [2] the first ten amendments to the US Constitution, added in 1791, which guarantee the liberty of the individual. [3] (in Canada) a statement of basic human rights and freedoms enacted by Parliament in 1960. [4] (*usually not capitals*) any charter or summary of basic human rights.

bill of sale NOUN *Law* a deed transferring personal property, either outright or as security for a loan or debt.

billon ('bɪlən) NOUN [1] an alloy consisting of gold or silver and a base metal, usually copper, used esp for coinage. [2] any coin made of such an alloy.

▷HISTORY C18: from Old French: ingot, from *bille* log; see BILLET[2]

billow ('bɪləʊ) NOUN [1] a large sea wave. [2] a swelling or surging mass, as of smoke or sound. [3] a large atmospheric wave, usually in the lee of a hill. [4] (*plural*) *Poetic* the sea itself. ◆ VERB [5] to rise up, swell out, or cause to rise up or swell out.
▷HISTORY C16: from Old Norse *bylgja*; related to Swedish *bōlja*, Danish *bölg*, Middle High German *bulge*; see BELLOW, BELLY
▸ **'billowing** ADJECTIVE, NOUN

billowy ('bɪləʊɪ) ADJECTIVE full of or forming billows: *a billowy sea.*
▸ **'billowiness** NOUN

billposter ('bɪl,pəʊstə) *or* **billsticker** NOUN a person who is employed to stick advertising posters to walls, fences, etc.
▸ **'bill,posting** *or* **'bill,sticking** NOUN

billy¹ ('bɪlɪ) NOUN, *plural* **-lies.** *US and Canadian* a wooden club esp a policeman's truncheon.
▷HISTORY C19: special use of the name *Billy*, pet form of *William*

billy² ('bɪlɪ) *or* **billycan** ('bɪlɪ,kæn) NOUN, *plural* **-lies** *or* **-lycans.** [1] a metal can or pot for boiling water, etc., over a campfire. [2] *Austral and NZ* (*as modifier*): *billy-tea.* [3] *Austral and NZ informal* to make tea.
▷HISTORY C19: from Scot *billypot* cooking vessel

billy-bread NOUN *NZ* bread baked in a billy over a camp fire.

billycock ('bɪlɪkɒk) NOUN *Rare, chiefly Brit* any of several round-crowned brimmed hats of felt, such as the bowler.
▷HISTORY C19: named after *William Coke*, Englishman for whom it was first made

billy goat NOUN a male goat. Compare **nanny goat.**

Billy No-Mates NOUN *Slang* a person with no friends.

billyo *or* **billyoh** ('bɪlɪ,əʊ) NOUN **like billyo.** *Informal* (intensifier): *snowing like billyo.*
▷HISTORY C19: of unknown origin

bilobate (baɪ'ləʊ,beɪt) *or* **bilobed** ('baɪ,ləʊbd) ADJECTIVE divided into or having two lobes: *a bilobate leaf.*

bilocular (baɪ'lɒkjʊlə) *or* **biloculate** ADJECTIVE *Biology* divided into two chambers or cavities: *some flowering plants have bilocular ovaries.*

biltong ('bɪl,tɒŋ) NOUN *South African* strips of meat dried and cured in the sun.
▷HISTORY C19: Afrikaans, from Dutch *bil* buttock + *tong* TONGUE

Bim (bɪm) NOUN *Informal* a native or inhabitant of Barbados.
▷HISTORY C19: of unknown origin

BIM ABBREVIATION FOR British Institute of Management.

bimah *or* **bima** ('biːmə) NOUN variant spellings of **bema.**

bimanous ('bɪmənəs, baɪ'meɪ-) ADJECTIVE (of man and the higher primates) having two hands distinct in form and function from the feet.
▷HISTORY C19: from New Latin *bimana* two handed, from BI-[1] + Latin *manus* hand

bimanual (baɪ'mænjʊəl) ADJECTIVE using or requiring both hands.
▸ **bi'manually** ADVERB

bimble box ('bɪmbᵊl) NOUN a dense Australian tree, *Eucalyptus populnea*, with shiny green leaves, valued for its hard wood.
▷HISTORY *bimble* from a native Australian language + BOX[3]

bimbo ('bɪmbəʊ) NOUN, *plural* **-bos** *or* **-boes.** [1] an attractive but empty-headed young woman. [2] a fellow; person esp a foolish one.
▷HISTORY C20: from Italian: little child, perhaps via Polari

bimestrial (baɪ'mɛstrɪəl) ADJECTIVE [1] lasting for two months. [2] a less common word for **bimonthly** (sense 1).
▷HISTORY C19: from Latin *bimēstris*, from BI-[1] + *mēnsis* month
▸ **bi'mestrially** ADVERB

bimetallic (,baɪmɪ'tælɪk) ADJECTIVE [1] consisting of two metals. [2] of, relating to, or based on bimetallism.

bimetallic strip NOUN a strip consisting of two

metals of different coefficients of expansion welded together so that it buckles on heating: used in thermostats, etc.

bimetallism (baɪˈmɛtəˌlɪzəm) NOUN 1 the use of two metals, esp gold and silver, in fixed relative values as the standard of value and currency. 2 the economic policies or doctrine supporting a bimetallic standard.
▸ **biˈmetallist** NOUN

bimillenary (ˌbaɪmɪˈliːnərɪ, baɪˈmɪlɪnərɪ) ADJECTIVE 1 marking a two-thousandth anniversary. ◆ NOUN, *plural* **-naries.** 2 a two-thousandth anniversary.

bimodal distribution (baɪˈməʊdᵊl) NOUN *Statistics* a frequency distribution with two modes.

bimolecular (ˌbaɪməˈlɛkjʊlə) ADJECTIVE (of a chemical complex, collision, etc.) having or involving two molecules.

bimonthly (baɪˈmʌnθlɪ) ADJECTIVE, ADVERB 1 every two months. 2 (often avoided because of confusion with sense 1) twice a month; semimonthly. See **bi-**[1]. ◆ NOUN, *plural* **-lies.** 3 a periodical published every two months.

bimorph (ˈbaɪmɔːf) *or* **bimorph cell** NOUN *Electronics* an assembly of two piezoelectric crystals cemented together so that an applied voltage causes one to expand and the other to contract, converting electrical signals into mechanical energy. Conversely, bending can generate a voltage: used in loudspeakers, gramophone pick-ups, etc.

bin (bɪn) NOUN 1 a large container or enclosed space for storing something in bulk, such as coal, grain, or wool. 2 Also called: **bread bin.** a small container for bread. 3 Also called: **dustbin, rubbish bin.** a container for litter, rubbish, etc. 4 *Brit* **a** a storage place for bottled wine. **b** one particular bottling of wine. ◆ VERB **bins, binning, binned.** 5 (*tr*) to store in a bin. 6 (*tr*) to put in a wastepaper bin.
▹ HISTORY Old English *binne* basket, probably of Celtic origin; related to *bindan* to BIND

bin- PREFIX a variant, esp before a vowel, of **bi-**[1]: *binocular.*

binal (ˈbaɪnᵊl) ADJECTIVE twofold; double.
▹ HISTORY C17: from New Latin *bīnālis;* see BIN-

binary (ˈbaɪnərɪ) ADJECTIVE 1 composed of, relating to, or involving two; dual. 2 *Maths, computing* of, relating to, or expressed in binary notation or binary code. 3 (of a compound or molecule) containing atoms of two different elements. 4 *Metallurgy* (of an alloy) consisting of two components or phases. 5 (of an educational system) consisting of two parallel forms of education such as the grammar school and the secondary modern in Britain. 6 *Maths, logic* (of a relation, expression, or operation) applying to two elements of its domain; having two argument places; dyadic. ◆ NOUN, *plural* **-ries.** 7 something composed of two parts or things. 8 *Astronomy* See **binary star.** 9 short for **binary weapon.**
▹ HISTORY C16: from Late Latin *bīnārius;* see BIN-

binary code NOUN *Computing* the representation of each one of a set of numbers, letters, etc., as a unique sequence of bits, as in ASCII.

binary-coded decimal NOUN a number in binary code written in groups of four bits, each group representing one digit of the corresponding decimal number. Abbreviation: **BCD.**

binary digit NOUN either of the two digits 0 or 1, used in binary notation. See also **bit**[4].

binary fission NOUN asexual reproduction in unicellular organisms by division into two daughter cells.

binary form NOUN *Music* a structure consisting of two sections, each being played twice.

binary notation *or* **system** NOUN a number system having a base of two, numbers being expressed by sequences of the digits 0 and 1: used in computing, as 0 and 1 can be represented electrically as *off* and *on.*

binary number NOUN a number expressed in binary notation, as $1101.101 = 1 \times 2^3 + 1 \times 2^2 + 0 \times 2^1 + 1 \times 2^0 + 1 \times 2^{-1} + 0 \times 2^{-2} + 1 \times 2^{-3} = 13\ 5/8$.

binary star NOUN a double star system comprising two stars orbiting around their common centre of mass. A **visual binary** can be seen through a telescope. A **spectroscopic binary** can only be observed by the spectroscopic Doppler shift as each star moves towards or away from the earth. Sometimes shortened to: **binary.** See also **optical double star, eclipsing binary.**

binary weapon NOUN a chemical weapon consisting of a projectile containing two substances separately that mix to produce a lethal agent when the projectile is fired.

binate (ˈbaɪˌneɪt) ADJECTIVE *Botany* occurring in two parts or in pairs: *binate leaves.*
▹ HISTORY C19: from New Latin *bīnātus,* probably from Latin *combīnātus* united
▸ **ˈbiˌnately** ADVERB

binaural (baɪˈnɔːrəl, bɪn-) ADJECTIVE 1 relating to, having, or hearing with both ears. 2 employing two separate channels for recording or transmitting sound; so creating an impression of depth: *a binaural recording.*
▸ **binˈaurally** ADVERB

bind (baɪnd) VERB **binds, binding, bound.** 1 to make or become fast or secure with or as if with a tie or band. 2 (*tr;* often foll by *up*) to encircle or enclose with a band: *to bind the hair.* 3 (*tr*) to place (someone) under obligation; oblige. 4 (*tr*) to impose legal obligations or duties upon (a person or party to an agreement). 5 (*tr*) to make (a bargain, agreement, etc.) irrevocable; seal. 6 (*tr*) to restrain or confine with or as if with ties, as of responsibility or loyalty. 7 (*tr*) to place under certain constraints; govern. 8 (*tr;* often foll by *up*) to bandage or swathe: *to bind a wound.* 9 to cohere or stick or cause to cohere or stick: *egg binds fat and flour.* 10 to make or become compact, stiff, or hard: *frost binds the earth.* 11 **a** (*tr*) to enclose and fasten (the pages of a book) between covers. **b** (*intr*) (of a book) to undergo this process. 12 (*tr*) to provide (a garment, hem, etc.) with a border or edging, as for decoration or to prevent fraying. 13 (*tr;* sometimes foll by *out* or *over*) to employ as an apprentice; indenture. 14 (*intr*) *Slang* to complain. 15 (*tr*) *Logic* to bring (a variable) into the scope of an appropriate quantifier. See also **bound**[1] (sense 9). ◆ NOUN 16 something that binds. 17 the act of binding or state of being bound. 18 *Informal* a difficult or annoying situation. 19 another word for **bine.** 20 *Music* another word for **tie** (sense 17). 21 *Mining* clay between layers of coal. 22 *Fencing* a pushing movement with the blade made to force one's opponent's sword from one line into another. 23 *Chess* a position in which one player's pawns have a hold on the centre that makes it difficult for the opponent to advance there. ◆ See also **bind over.**
▹ HISTORY Old English *bindan;* related to Old Norse *binda,* Old High German *bintan,* Latin *offendix* BAND[2], Sanskrit *badhnāti* he binds

binder (ˈbaɪndə) NOUN 1 a firm cover or folder with rings or clasps for holding loose sheets of paper together. 2 a material used to bind separate particles together, give an appropriate consistency, or facilitate adhesion to a surface. 3 **a** a person who binds books; bookbinder. **b** a machine that is used to bind books. 4 something used to fasten or tie, such as rope or twine. 5 *NZ informal* a square meal. 6 Also called: **reaper binder.** *Obsolete* a machine for cutting grain and binding it into bundles or sheaves. Compare **combine harvester.** 7 an informal agreement giving insurance coverage pending formal issue of a policy. 8 a tie, beam, or girder, used to support floor joists. 9 a stone for binding masonry; bondstone. 10 the nonvolatile component of the organic media in which pigments are dispersed in paint. 11 (in systemic grammar) a word that introduces a bound clause; a subordinating conjunction or a relative pronoun. Compare **linker** (sense 2).

bindery (ˈbaɪndərɪ) NOUN, *plural* **-eries.** a place in which books are bound.

bindi *or* **bindhi** (ˈbɪndɪ) NOUN a decorative dot worn in the middle of the forehead, esp by Hindu women.
▹ HISTORY Hindi

bindi-eye (ˈbɪndɪˌaɪ) NOUN *Austral* 1 any of various small weedy Australian herbaceous plants of the genus *Calotis,* with burlike fruits: family *Asteraceae* (composites). 2 any bur or prickle.
▹ HISTORY C20: perhaps from a native Australian language

binding (ˈbaɪndɪŋ) NOUN 1 anything that binds or fastens. 2 the covering within which the pages of a book are bound. 3 the material or tape used for binding hems, etc. ◆ ADJECTIVE 4 imposing an obligation or duty: *a binding promise.* 5 causing hindrance; restrictive.

binding energy NOUN *Physics* 1 the energy that must be supplied to a stable nucleus before it can undergo fission. It is equal to the mass defect. 2 the energy required to remove a particle from a system, esp an electron from an atom.

bind over VERB (*tr, adverb*) to place (a person) under a legal obligation, such as one to keep the peace.

bindweed (ˈbaɪndˌwiːd) NOUN 1 any convolvulaceous plant of the genera *Convolvulus* and *Calystegia* that twines around a support. See also **convolvulus.** 2 any of various other trailing or twining plants, such as black bindweed.

bine (baɪn) NOUN 1 the climbing or twining stem of any of various plants, such as the woodbine or bindweed. 2 any plant with such a stem.
▹ HISTORY C19: variant of BIND

Binet-Simon scale (ˈbiːneɪˈsaɪmən) NOUN *Psychol* a test comprising questions and tasks, used to determine the mental age of subjects, usually children. Also called: **Binet scale** *or* **test.** See also **Stanford-Binet test.**
▹ HISTORY C20: named after Alfred *Binet* (1857–1911) + Théodore *Simon* (1873–1961), French psychologists

bing (bɪŋ) NOUN *Dialect* a heap or pile, esp of spoil from a mine.
▹ HISTORY C16: from Old Norse *bingr* heap

binge (bɪndʒ) NOUN *Informal* 1 a bout of excessive eating or drinking. 2 excessive indulgence in anything: *a shopping binge.* ◆ VERB **binges, bingeing** *or* **binging, binged.** (*intr*) 3 to indulge in a binge (esp of eating or drinking).
▹ HISTORY C19: probably Lincolnshire dialect *binge* to soak

binge drinking NOUN the practice of drinking excessive amounts of alcohol regularly.

Bingen (ˈbɪŋən) NOUN a town in W Germany on the Rhine: wine trade and tourist centre. Pop.: 23 141 (latest est.).

bingle (ˈbɪŋgᵊl) NOUN *Austral old-fashioned informal* a minor crash or upset, as in a car or on a surfboard.
▹ HISTORY C20: of uncertain origin

bingo (ˈbɪŋgəʊ) NOUN, *plural* **-gos.** 1 a gambling game, usually played with several people, in which numbers selected at random are called out and the players cover the numbers on their individual cards. The first to cover a given arrangement of numbers is the winner. Compare **lotto.** ◆ SENTENCE SUBSTITUTE 2 a cry by the winner of a game of bingo. 3 an expression of surprise at a sudden occurrence or the successful completion of something: *and bingo! the lights went out.*
▹ HISTORY C19: perhaps from *bing,* imitative of a bell ringing to mark the win

Bini *or* **Beni** (bəˈniː) NOUN, *plural* **-ni** *or* **-nis.** other names for **Edo.**

biniou (binju) (*noun*) a small high-pitched Breton bagpipe.
▹ HISTORY from Breton *beniou*

binman (ˈbɪnˌmæn, ˈbɪnmən) NOUN, *plural* **-men.** another name for **dustman.**

binnacle (ˈbɪnəkᵊl) NOUN a housing for a ship's compass.
▹ HISTORY C17: changed from C15 *bitakle,* from Portuguese *bitácula,* from Late Latin *habitāculum* dwelling-place, from Latin *habitāre* to inhabit; spelling influenced by BIN

binocular (bɪˈnɒkjʊlə, baɪ-) ADJECTIVE involving, relating to, seeing with or intended for both eyes: *binocular vision.*
▹ HISTORY C18: from BI-[1] + Latin *oculus* eye

binocular disparity NOUN *Physiol* the small differences in the positions of the parts of the images falling on each eye that results when each eye views the scene from a slightly different position; these differences make stereoscopic vision possible.

binocular rivalry NOUN *Psychol* the inability to see simultaneously different images presented one to each eye; usually in some areas of the eye the image presented to the left eye is seen, in others that presented to the right eye. Also called: **retinal rivalry.**

binoculars (bɪˈnɒkjʊləz, baɪ-) PLURAL NOUN an

optical instrument for use with both eyes, consisting of two small telescopes joined together. Also called: **field glasses.**

binomial (baɪˈnəʊmɪəl) NOUN [1] a mathematical expression consisting of two terms, such as $3x + 2y$. [2] a two-part taxonomic name for an animal or plant. See **binomial nomenclature.** ◆ ADJECTIVE [3] referring to two names or terms.
▷**HISTORY** C16: from Medieval Latin *binōmius* from BI-[1] + Latin *nōmen* NAME
▸**biˈnomially** ADVERB

binomial coefficient NOUN *Maths* any of the numerical factors which multiply the successive terms in a binomial expansion; any term of the form $n!/(n-k)!k!$: written $\binom{n}{k}$, ^nC_k, or $C^n{}_k$. See also **combination** (sense 6).

binomial distribution NOUN a statistical distribution giving the probability of obtaining a specified number of successes in a specified number of independent trials of an experiment with a constant probability of success in each. Symbol: *Bi* (n, p), where n is the number of trials and p the probability of success in each.

binomial experiment NOUN *Statistics* an experiment consisting of a fixed number of independent trials each with two possible outcomes, success and failure, and the same probability of success. The probability of a given number of successes is described by a binominal distribution. See also **Bernoulli trial.**

binomial nomenclature *or* **binominal** NOUN a system for naming plants and animals by means of two Latin names: the first indicating the genus and the second the species to which the organism belongs, as in *Panthera leo* (the lion).

binomial theorem NOUN a mathematical theorem that gives the expansion of any binomial raised to a positive integral power, n. It contains $n + 1$ terms: $(x + a)^n = x^n + nx^{n-1}a + [n(n-1)/2]x^{n-2}a^2 + \ldots + \binom{n}{k}x^{n-k}a^k + \ldots + a^n$, where $\binom{n}{k} = n!/(n-k)!k!$, the number of combinations of k items selected from n.

binominal (baɪˈnɒmɪn(ə)l) *Biology* ◆ ADJECTIVE [1] of or denoting the binomial nomenclature. ◆ NOUN [2] a two-part taxonomic name; binomial.

binovular (bɪˈnɒvjʊlə) ADJECTIVE relating to or derived from two different ova: *binovular fertilization; binovular twins.*

bins (bɪnz) PLURAL NOUN *Northern English dialect* a pair of glasses.

bint (bɪnt) NOUN *Slang* a derogatory term for **girl** or **woman.**
▷**HISTORY** C19: from Arabic, literally: daughter

binturong (ˈbɪntjʊˌrɒŋ, bɪnˈtjʊərɒŋ) NOUN an arboreal SE Asian viverrine mammal, *Arctictis binturong*, closely related to the palm civets but larger and having long shaggy black hair.
▷**HISTORY** from Malay

binucleate (baɪˈnjuːklɪˌeɪt, -ɪt) ADJECTIVE *Biology* having two nuclei: *a binucleate cell.* Also: **binuclear, binucleated.**

bio (ˈbaɪəʊ) NOUN, *plural* **bios.** short for **biography.**

bio- *or before a vowel* **bi-** COMBINING FORM [1] indicating or involving life or living organisms: *biogenesis; biolysis.* [2] indicating a human life or career: *biography; biopic.*
▷**HISTORY** from Greek *bios* life

bioaccumulate (ˌbaɪəʊəˈkjuːmʊˌleɪt) VERB (*intr*) (of substances, esp toxins) to build up within the tissues of organisms.
▸**ˌbioacˌcumuˈlation** NOUN

bioaeration (ˌbaɪəʊɛəˈreɪʃən) NOUN the oxidative treatment of raw sewage by aeration.

bioaeronautics (ˌbaɪəʊˌɛərəˈnɔːtɪks) NOUN (*functioning as singular*) the use of aircraft in the discovery, development, and protection of natural and biological resources.

bioassay NOUN (ˌbaɪəʊəˈseɪ, -ˈæseɪ) [1] a method of determining the concentration, activity, or effect of a change to substance by testing its effect on a living organism and comparing this with the activity of an agreed standard. ◆ VERB (ˌbaɪəʊəˈseɪ) [2] (*tr*) to subject to a bioassay.

bioastronautics (ˌbaɪəʊˌæstrəˈnɔːtɪks) NOUN (*functioning as singular*) the study of the effects of space flight on living organisms. See **space medicine.**

bioavailability (ˌbaɪəʊəˌveɪləˈbɪlɪtɪ) NOUN the extent to which a drug or other substance is taken up by a specific tissue or organ after administration; the proportion of the dose of a drug that reaches the systemic circulation intact after administration by a route other than intravenous. Also called: **systemic availability.**
▸**ˌbioaˈvailable** ADJECTIVE

Bío-Bío (*Spanish* ˈbiːoˈbiːo) NOUN a river in central Chile, rising in the Andes and flowing northwest to the Pacific. Length: about 390 km (240 miles).

biocatalyst (ˌbaɪəʊˈkætəlɪst) NOUN a chemical, esp an enzyme, that initiates or increases the rate of a biochemical reaction.
▸**biocatalytic** (ˌbaɪəʊˌkætəˈlɪtɪk) ADJECTIVE

biocellate (baɪˈɒsɪˌleɪt, ˌbaɪəʊˈsɛlɪt) ADJECTIVE (of animals and plants) marked with two eyelike spots or ocelli.
▷**HISTORY** C19: from BI-[1] + *ocellate*, from Latin *ocellus*, diminutive of *oculus* eye

biochemical oxygen demand NOUN a measure of the organic pollution of water: the amount of oxygen, in mg per litre of water, absorbed by a sample kept at 20°C for five days. Abbreviation: **BOD.**

biochemistry (ˌbaɪəʊˈkɛmɪstrɪ) NOUN the study of the chemical compounds, reactions, etc., occurring in living organisms.
▸**biochemical** (ˌbaɪəʊˈkɛmɪk(ə)l) ADJECTIVE ▸**ˌbioˈchemically** ADVERB ▸**ˌbioˈchemist** NOUN

biochip (ˈbaɪəˌtʃɪp) NOUN a small glass or silicon plate containing an array of biochemical molecules or structures, used as a biosensor or in gene sequencing.

biocide (ˈbaɪəˌsaɪd) NOUN a chemical, such as a pesticide, capable of killing living organisms.
▸**ˌbioˈcidal** ADJECTIVE

bioclastic (ˌbaɪəʊˈklæstɪk) ADJECTIVE (of deposits, esp limestones) derived from shell fragments or similar organic remains.

bioclimatology (ˌbaɪəʊˌklaɪməˈtɒlədʒɪ) NOUN the study of the effects of climatic conditions on living organisms.
▸**ˌbioˌclimaˈtologist** NOUN

biocoenology *or* **biocenology** (ˌbaɪəʊsɪˈnɒlədʒɪ) NOUN the branch of ecology concerned with the relationships and interactions between the members of a natural community.
▷**HISTORY** C20: from BIO- + *ceno-*, from Greek *koinos* common + -LOGY

biocoenosis *or* **biocenosis** (ˌbaɪəʊsɪˈnəʊsɪs) NOUN a diverse community inhabiting a single biotope.
▸**ˌbiocoeˈnotic** *or* **ˌbioceˈnotic** ADJECTIVE

bioconversion (ˌbaɪəʊkənˈvɜːʃən) NOUN the use of biological processes or materials to change organic substances into a new form, such as the conversion of waste into methane by fermentation.

biocycle (ˈbaɪəʊˌsaɪk(ə)l) NOUN *Ecology* the cycling of chemicals through the biosphere.

biodata (ˈbaɪəʊˌdeɪtə, -ˌdɑːtə) NOUN information regarding an individual's education and work history, esp in the context of a selection process.
▷**HISTORY** C20: from BIO(GRAPHICAL) + DATA

biodegradable (ˌbaɪəʊdɪˈgreɪdəb(ə)l) ADJECTIVE (of sewage constituents, packaging material, etc.) capable of being decomposed by bacteria or other biological means.
▸**biodegradation** (ˌbaɪəʊˌdɛgrəˈdeɪʃən) NOUN
▸**biodegradability** (ˌbaɪəʊˌdɛgreɪdɪˈbɪlɪtɪ) NOUN

biodiesel (ˈbaɪəʊˌdiːz(ə)l) NOUN a biofuel intended for use in diesel engines.

biodiversity (ˌbaɪəʊdaɪˈvɜːsɪtɪ) NOUN the existence of a wide variety of plant and animal species in their natural environments, which is the aim of conservationists concerned about the indiscriminate destruction of rainforests and other habitats.

biodot (ˈbaɪəʊˌdɒt) NOUN a temperature-sensitive device stuck to the skin in order to monitor stress.

biodynamics (ˌbaɪəʊdaɪˈnæmɪks, -dɪ-) NOUN (*functioning as singular*) the branch of biology that deals with the energy production and activities of organisms.
▸**ˌbiodyˈnamic** *or* **ˌbiodyˈnamical** ADJECTIVE

bioecology (ˌbaɪəʊɪˈkɒlədʒɪ) NOUN another word for **ecology** (sense 1).
▸**bioecological** (ˌbaɪəʊˌiːkəˈlɒdʒɪk(ə)l) ADJECTIVE
▸**ˌbioˌecoˈlogically** ADVERB ▸**ˌbioeˈcologist** NOUN

bioelectricity (ˌbaɪəʊˌɪlɛkˈtrɪsɪtɪ) NOUN electricity generated by a living organism.
▸**ˌbioeˈlectric** ADJECTIVE

bioenergetics (ˌbaɪəʊˌɛnəˈdʒɛtɪks) NOUN (*functioning as singular*) the study of energy transformations in living organisms and systems.
▸**ˌbioˌenerˈgetic** ADJECTIVE

bioengineering (ˌbaɪəʊˌɛndʒɪˈnɪərɪŋ) NOUN [1] the design and manufacture of aids, such as artificial limbs, to rectify defective body functions. [2] the design, manufacture, and maintenance of engineering equipment used in biosynthetic processes, such as fermentation.
▸**ˌbioˌengiˈneer** NOUN

bioethics (ˌbaɪəʊˈɛθɪks) NOUN (*functioning as singular*) the study of ethical problems arising from biological research and its applications in such fields as organ transplantation, genetic engineering, or artificial insemination.
▸**ˌbioˈethical** ADJECTIVE ▸**bioethicist** (ˌbaɪəʊˈɛθɪsɪst) NOUN

biofact (ˈbaɪəʊfækt) NOUN [1] an item of biological information. [2] an item of biographical information.

biofeedback (ˌbaɪəʊˈfiːdˌbæk) NOUN *Physiol, psychol* a technique for teaching the control of autonomic functions, such as the rate of heartbeat or breathing, by recording the activity and presenting it (usually visually) so that the person can know the state of the autonomic function he is learning to control.

bioflavonoid (ˌbaɪəʊˈfleɪvəˌnɔɪd) NOUN another name for **vitamin P.**

biofuel (ˈbaɪəʊˌfjʊəl) NOUN a gaseous, liquid, or solid substance of biological origin that is used as a fuel.

biog. ABBREVIATION FOR: [1] biographical. [2] biography.

biogas (ˈbaɪəʊˌgæs) NOUN a gas that is produced by the action of bacteria on organic waste matter: used as a fuel.

biogen (ˈbaɪədʒən) NOUN a hypothetical protein assumed to be the basis of the formation and functioning of body cells and tissues.

biogenesis (ˌbaɪəʊˈdʒɛnɪsɪs) NOUN the principle that a living organism must originate from a parent organism similar to itself. Compare **abiogenesis.**
▸**ˌbiogeˈnetic** *or* **ˌbiogeˈnetical** *or* **biogenous** (baɪˈɒdʒənəs) ADJECTIVE ▸**ˌbiogeˈnetically** ADVERB

biogenic (ˌbaɪəʊˈdʒɛnɪk) ADJECTIVE produced or originating from a living organism.

biogeography (ˌbaɪəʊdʒɪˈɒgrəfɪ) NOUN the branch of biology concerned with the geographical distribution of plants and animals.
▸**biogeographical** (ˌbaɪəʊˌdʒɪəˈgræfɪk(ə)l) ADJECTIVE
▸**ˌbioˌgeoˈgraphically** ADVERB

biographize *or* **biographise** (baɪˈɒgrəˌfaɪz) VERB (*tr*) to write a biography of: *the maverick duo were not easy to biographize.*

biography (baɪˈɒgrəfɪ) NOUN, *plural* **-phies.** [1] an account of a person's life by another. [2] such accounts collectively.
▸**biˈographer** NOUN ▸**biographical** (ˌbaɪəˈgræfɪk(ə)l) *or* (*archaic*) **ˌbioˈgraphic** ADJECTIVE ▸**ˌbioˈgraphically** ADVERB

biohazard (ˌbaɪəʊˈhæzəd) NOUN material of biological origin that is hazardous to humans.
▸**ˌbioˈhazardous** ADJECTIVE

bioherm (ˈbaɪəʊˌhɜːm) NOUN [1] a mound of material laid down by sedentary marine organisms, esp a coral reef. [2] the fossilized remains of such a mound.
▷**HISTORY** C20: from BIO- + Greek *herma* submerged rock

bioinformatics (ˌbaɪəʊˌɪnfəˈmætɪks) NOUN (*functioning as singular*) the branch of information science concerned with large databases of biochemical or pharmaceutical information.

Bioko (baɪˈəʊkəʊ) NOUN an island in the Gulf of Guinea, off the coast of Cameroon: part of Equatorial Guinea. Capital: Malabo. Area: 2017 sq. km (786 sq. miles). Former names: **Fernando Po** (until 1973), **Macías Nguema** (1973–79).

biol. ABBREVIATION FOR: [1] biological. [2] biology.

biological (ˌbaɪəˈlɒdʒɪk(ə)l) *or archaic* **biologic** ADJECTIVE [1] of or relating to biology. [2] (of a detergent) containing enzymes said to be capable of

removing stains of organic origin from items to be washed. ◆ NOUN 3 (*usually plural*) a drug, such as a vaccine, that is derived from a living organism.
▸ ˌbioˈlogically ADVERB

biological clock NOUN 1 an inherent periodicity in the physiological processes of living organisms that is not dependent on the periodicity of external factors. 2 the hypothetical mechanism responsible for this periodicity. ◆ See also **circadian.**

biological control NOUN the control of destructive organisms by the use of other organisms, such as the natural predators of the pests.

biological marker NOUN a substance, physiological characteristic, gene, etc. that indicates, or may indicate, the presence of disease, a physiological abnormality or a psychological condition. Also called: **biomarker.**

biological shield NOUN a protective shield impervious to radiation, esp the thick concrete wall surrounding the core of a nuclear reactor.

biological warfare NOUN the use of living organisms or their toxic products to induce death or incapacity in humans and animals and damage to plant crops, etc. Abbreviation: **BW.**

biology (baɪˈɒlədʒɪ) NOUN 1 the study of living organisms, including their structure, functioning, evolution, distribution, and interrelationships. 2 the structure, functioning, etc., of a particular organism or group of organisms. 3 the animal and plant life of a particular region.
▸ biˈologist NOUN

bioluminescence (ˌbaɪəʊˌluːmɪˈnɛsəns) NOUN the production of light by living organisms as a result of the oxidation of a light-producing substance (luciferin) by the enzyme luciferase: occurs in many marine organisms, insects such as the firefly, etc.
▸ ˌbioˌlumiˈnescent ADJECTIVE

biolysis (baɪˈɒlɪsɪs) NOUN 1 the death and dissolution of a living organism. 2 the disintegration of organic matter by the action of bacteria etc.
▸ biolytic (ˌbaɪəˈlɪtɪk) ADJECTIVE

biomarker (ˈbaɪəʊˌmɑːkə) NOUN another name for **biological marker.**

biomass (ˈbaɪəʊˌmæs) NOUN 1 the total number of living organisms in a given area, expressed in terms of living or dry weight per unit area. 2 vegetable matter used as a source of energy.

biomathematics (ˌbaɪəʊˌmæθəˈmætɪks, -ˌmæθˈmæt-) NOUN (*functioning as singular*) the study of the application of mathematics to biology.

biome (ˈbaɪˌəʊm) NOUN a major ecological community, extending over a large area and usually characterized by a dominant vegetation. See **formation** (sense 6).
▹ HISTORY C20: from BIO- + -OME

biomechanics (ˌbaɪəʊmɪˈkænɪks) NOUN (*functioning as singular*) the study of the mechanics of the movement of living organisms.

biomedical (ˌbaɪəʊˈmɛdɪkᵊl) ADJECTIVE of or relating to biology and medicine or biomedicine.

biomedicine (ˌbaɪəʊˈmɛdɪsɪn, -ˈmɛdsɪn) NOUN 1 the medical study of the effects of unusual environmental stress on human beings, esp in connection with space travel. 2 the study of herbal remedies.

biometeorology (ˌbaɪəʊˌmiːtɪəˈrɒlədʒɪ) NOUN the study of the effect of weather conditions on living organisms.

biometry (baɪˈɒmɪtrɪ) *or* **biometrics** (ˌbaɪəˈmɛtrɪks) NOUN (*functioning as singular*) 1 the analysis of biological data using mathematical and statistical methods. 2 the statistical calculation of the probable duration of human life.
▸ biometric (ˌbaɪəˈmɛtrɪk) ADJECTIVE ▸ ˌbioˈmetrically ADVERB

biomimetic (ˌbaɪəʊmɪˈmɛtɪk) ADJECTIVE (of a human-made product) imitating nature or a natural process.

biomimicry (ˌbaɪəʊmɪˈmɪkrɪ) NOUN the mimicking of life using imitation biological systems.

bionic (baɪˈɒnɪk) ADJECTIVE 1 of or relating to bionics. 2 (in science fiction) having certain physiological functions augmented or replaced by electronic equipment: *the bionic man.*

bionics (baɪˈɒnɪks) NOUN (*functioning as singular*) 1 the study of certain biological functions, esp those relating to the brain, that are applicable to the development of electronic equipment, such as computer hardware, designed to operate in a similar manner. 2 the technique of replacing a limb or body part by an artificial limb or part that is electronically or mechanically powered.
▹ HISTORY C20: from BIO- + (ELECTR)ONICS

bionomics (ˌbaɪəˈnɒmɪks) NOUN (*functioning as singular*) a less common name for **ecology** (senses 1, 2).
▹ HISTORY C19: from BIO- + *nomics* on pattern of ECONOMICS
▸ ˌbioˈnomic ADJECTIVE ▸ ˌbioˈnomically ADVERB ▸ bionomist (baɪˈɒnəmɪst) NOUN

biopharmaceutical (ˌbaɪəʊˌfɑːməˈsjuːtɪkᵊl) ADJECTIVE of or relating to drugs produced using biotechnology.

biophilia (ˌbaɪəʊˈfɪlɪə) NOUN an innate love for the natural world, supposed to be felt universally by humankind.
▹ HISTORY C20: BIO + -PHILIA

biophysics (ˌbaɪəʊˈfɪzɪks) NOUN (*functioning as singular*) the physics of biological processes and the application of methods used in physics to biology.
▸ ˌbioˈphysical ADJECTIVE ▸ ˌbioˈphysically ADVERB
▸ biophysicist (ˌbaɪəʊˈfɪzɪsɪst) NOUN

biopic (ˈbaɪəʊˌpɪk) NOUN *Informal* a film based on the life of a famous person, esp one giving a popular treatment.
▹ HISTORY C20: from *bio(graphical)* + *pic(ture)*

biopiracy (ˈbaɪəʊˌpaɪrəsɪ) NOUN the use of wild plants by international companies to develop medicines, without recompensing the countries from which they are taken.

bioplasm (ˈbaɪəʊˌplæzəm) NOUN *Now rare* living matter; protoplasm.
▸ ˌbioˈplasmic ADJECTIVE

biopoiesis (ˌbaɪəʊpɔɪˈiːsɪs) NOUN the development of living matter from nonliving matter, esp considered as an evolutionary process.

bioprospecting (ˌbaɪəʊˈprɒspɛktɪŋ) NOUN searching for plant or animal species for use as a source of commercially exploitable products, such as medicinal drugs.

biopsy (ˈbaɪɒpsɪ) NOUN, *plural* **-sies.** 1 examination, esp under a microscope, of tissue from a living body to determine the cause or extent of a disease. 2 the sample taken for such an examination.
▹ HISTORY C20: from BIO- + Greek *opsis* sight
▸ bioptic (baɪˈɒptɪk) ADJECTIVE

bioreagent (ˈbaɪəʊriːˌeɪdʒənt) NOUN a reagent of biological origin, such as an enzyme.

bioremediation (ˌbaɪəʊrɪˌmiːdɪˈeɪʃən) NOUN the use of plants to extract heavy metals from contaminated soils and water. Also called: **phytoremediation.**

biorhythm (ˈbaɪəʊˌrɪðəm) NOUN a cyclically recurring pattern of physiological states in an organism or organ, such as alpha rhythm or circadian rhythm; believed by some to affect physical and mental states and behaviour.
▸ ˌbioˈrhythmic ADJECTIVE ▸ ˌbioˈrhythmically ADVERB

biorhythmics (ˌbaɪəʊˈrɪðmɪks) NOUN (*functioning as singular*) the study of biorhythms.

biosafety (ˌbaɪəʊˈseɪftɪ) NOUN the precautions taken to control the cultivation and distribution of genetically modified crops and products.

bioscience (ˈbaɪəʊˌsaɪəns) NOUN 1 another name for a **life science.** 2 the life sciences collectively.
▸ ˌbioscienˈtific ADJECTIVE ▸ ˌbioˈscientist NOUN

bioscope (ˈbaɪəˌskəʊp) NOUN 1 a kind of early film projector. 2 a South African word for **cinema.**

bioscopy (baɪˈɒskəpɪ) NOUN, *plural* **-pies.** examination of a body to determine whether it is alive.

bio-security NOUN the precautions taken to protect against the spread of lethal or harmful organisms and diseases.
▸ bio-secure ADJECTIVE

-biosis NOUN COMBINING FORM indicating a specified mode of life: *symbiosis.*
▹ HISTORY New Latin, from Greek *biōsis*; see BIO-, -OSIS
▸ -biotic ADJECTIVE COMBINING FORM

biosphere (ˈbaɪəˌsfɪə) NOUN the part of the earth's surface and atmosphere inhabited by living things.

biostatics (ˌbaɪəʊˈstætɪks) NOUN (*functioning as singular*) the branch of biology that deals with the structure of organisms in relation to their function.
▸ ˌbioˈstatic ADJECTIVE ▸ ˌbioˈstatically ADVERB

biostrome (ˈbaɪəˌstrəʊm) NOUN a rock layer consisting of a deposit of organic material, such as fossils.
▹ HISTORY C20: from BIO- + Greek *strōma* covering

biosurgery (ˈbaɪəʊˌsɜːdʒərɪ) NOUN the use of live sterile maggots to treat patients with infected wounds.

biosynthesis (ˌbaɪəʊˈsɪnθɪsɪs) NOUN the formation of complex compounds from simple substances by living organisms.
▸ biosynthetic (ˌbaɪəʊsɪnˈθɛtɪk) ADJECTIVE
▸ ˌbiosynˈthetically ADVERB

biosystematics (ˌbaɪəʊˌsɪstɪˈmætɪks) NOUN (*functioning as singular*) the study of the variation and evolution of a population of organisms in relation to their taxonomic classification.

biota (baɪˈəʊtə) NOUN the plant and animal life of a particular region or period.
▹ HISTORY C20: from New Latin, from Greek *biotē* way of life, from *bios* life

biotech (ˈbaɪəʊˌtɛk) NOUN *Informal* short for **biotechnology.**

biotech (ˈbaɪəʊˌtɛk) NOUN **a** short for **biotechnology. b** (*as modifier*): *a biotech company.*

biotechnology (ˌbaɪəʊtɛkˈnɒlədʒɪ) NOUN 1 (in industry) the technique of using microorganisms, such as bacteria, to perform chemical processing, such as waste recycling, or to produce other materials, such as beer and wine, cheese, antibiotics, and (using genetic engineering) hormones, vaccines, etc. 2 another name for **ergonomics.**
▸ biotechnological (ˌbaɪəʊˌtɛknəˈlɒdʒɪkᵊl) ADJECTIVE
▸ ˌbioˌtechnoˈlogically ADVERB ▸ ˌbiotechˈnologist NOUN

biotelemetry (ˌbaɪəʊtɪˈlɛmɪtrɪ) NOUN the monitoring of biological functions in humans or animals by means of a miniature transmitter that sends data to a distant point to be read by electronic instruments.
▸ biotelemetric (ˌbaɪəʊtɛlɪˈmɛtrɪk) ADJECTIVE

bio-terrorism *or* **bio-terror** NOUN the use of living organisms and their toxic products to kill or incapacitate, esp as a political weapon.
▸ ˈbio-ˌterrorist ADJECTIVE, NOUN

biotic (baɪˈɒtɪk) ADJECTIVE 1 of or relating to living organisms. 2 (of a factor in an ecosystem) produced by the action of living organisms. Compare **edaphic.**
▹ HISTORY C17: from Greek *biotikos*, from *bios* life

biotin (ˈbaɪətɪn) NOUN a vitamin of the B complex, abundant in egg yolk and liver, deficiency of which causes dermatitis and loss of hair. Formula: $C_{10}H_{16}N_2O_3S$. See also **avidin.**
▹ HISTORY C20: *biot-* from Greek *biotē* life, way of life + -IN

biotite (ˈbaɪəˌtaɪt) NOUN a black or dark green mineral of the mica group, found in igneous and metamorphic rocks. Composition: hydrous magnesium iron potassium aluminium silicate. General formula: $K(Mg,Fe)_3(Al,Fe)Si_3O_{10}(OH)_2$. Crystal structure: monoclinic.
▸ biotitic (ˌbaɪəˈtɪtɪk) ADJECTIVE

biotope (ˈbaɪəˌtəʊp) NOUN *Ecology* a small area, such as the bark of a tree, that supports its own distinctive community.
▹ HISTORY C20: from BIO- + Greek *topos* place

biotroph (ˈbaɪəʊˌtrəʊf) NOUN a parasitic organism, esp a fungus.

biotype (ˈbaɪəˌtaɪp) NOUN a group of genetically identical plants within a species, produced by apomixis. Also called: **microspecies.**
▸ biotypic (ˌbaɪəˈtɪpɪk) ADJECTIVE

bio-warfare NOUN another name for **biological warfare.**

bioweapon (ˈbaɪəʊˌwɛpən) NOUN a living organism or a toxic product manufactured from it, used to kill or incapacitate.

biparietal (ˌbaɪpəˈraɪɪtᵊl) ADJECTIVE *Anatomy* relating to or connected to both parietal bones.

biparous (ˈbɪpərəs) ADJECTIVE [1] *Zoology* producing offspring in pairs. [2] *Botany* (esp of an inflorescence) producing two branches from one stem.

bipartisan (ˌbaɪpɑːtɪˈzæn, baɪˈpɑːtɪˌzæn) ADJECTIVE consisting of or supported by two political parties.
▸**ˌbipartiˈsanship** NOUN

bipartite (baɪˈpɑːtaɪt) ADJECTIVE [1] consisting of or having two parts. [2] affecting or made by two parties; bilateral: *a bipartite agreement.* [3] *Botany* (esp of some leaves) divided into two parts almost to the base.
▸**biˈpartitely** ADVERB ▸**bipartition** (ˌbaɪpɑːˈtɪʃən) NOUN

biped (ˈbaɪpɛd) NOUN [1] any animal with two feet. ◆ ADJECTIVE *also* **bipedal** (baɪˈpiːdᵊl, -ˈpɛdᵊl). [2] having two feet.

bipetalous (baɪˈpɛtələs) ADJECTIVE having two petals.

biphasic (baɪˈfeɪzɪk) ADJECTIVE [1] having two phases. [2] See **two-phase.**

biphenyl (baɪˈfenᵊl, -ˈfiː-) NOUN [1] a white or colourless crystalline solid used as a heat-transfer agent, as a fungicide, as an antifungal food preservative (**E230**) on the skins of citrus fruit, and in the manufacture of dyes, etc. Formula: $C_6H_5C_6H_5$. [2] any substituted derivative of biphenyl. Also called: **diphenyl.**

bipinnate (baɪˈpɪnˌeɪt) ADJECTIVE (of pinnate leaves) having the leaflets themselves divided into smaller leaflets.
▸**biˈpinˌnately** ADVERB

biplane (ˈbaɪˌpleɪn) NOUN a type of aeroplane having two sets of wings, one above the other. Compare **monoplane.**

bipod (ˈbaɪpɒd) NOUN a two-legged support or stand.

bipolar (baɪˈpəʊlə) ADJECTIVE [1] having two poles: *a bipolar dynamo; a bipolar neuron.* [2] relating to or found at the North and South Poles. [3] having or characterized by two opposed opinions, natures, etc. [4] (of a transistor) utilizing both majority and minority charge carriers. [5] suffering from bipolar manic-depressive disorder.
▸**bipoˈlarity** NOUN

bipolar manic-depressive disorder *or* **bipolar syndrome** NOUN See **manic-depressive.**

biprism (ˈbaɪˌprɪzəm) NOUN a prism having a highly obtuse angle to facilitate beam splitting.

bipropellant (ˌbaɪprəˈpɛlənt) NOUN a rocket propellant consisting of two substances, usually a fuel and an oxidizer. Also called: **dipropellant.** Compare **monopropellant.**

bipyramid (ˌbaɪˈpɪrəmɪd) NOUN a geometrical form consisting of two pyramids with a common polygonal base.

biquadrate (baɪˈkwɒdreɪt, -rɪt) NOUN *Maths* the fourth power.

biquadratic (ˌbaɪkwɒˈdrætɪk) *Maths* ◆ ADJECTIVE *also* **quartic.** [1] of or relating to the fourth power. ◆ NOUN [2] a biquadratic equation, such as $x^4 + x + 6 = 0$.

biquarterly (baɪˈkwɔːtəlɪ) ADJECTIVE occurring twice every three months.

biracial (baɪˈreɪʃəl) ADJECTIVE for, representing, or including members of two races, esp White and Black.
▸**biˈracialism** NOUN ▸**biˈracially** ADVERB

biradial (baɪˈreɪdɪəl) ADJECTIVE showing both bilateral and radial symmetry, as certain sea anemones.

biramous (ˈbɪrəməs) ADJECTIVE divided into two parts, as the appendages of crustaceans.

birch (bɜːtʃ) NOUN [1] any betulaceous tree or shrub of the genus *Betula*, having thin peeling bark. See also **silver birch.** [2] the hard close-grained wood of any of these trees. [3] **the birch.** a bundle of birch twigs or a birch rod used, esp formerly, for flogging offenders. ◆ ADJECTIVE [4] of, relating to, or belonging to the birch. [5] consisting or made of birch. ◆ VERB [6] (*tr*) to flog with a birch.
▷**HISTORY** Old English *bierce*; related to Old High German *birihha*, Sanskrit *bhūrja*
▸**ˈbirchen** ADJECTIVE

birchbark biting (ˈbɜːtʃˌbɑːk) NOUN a Native Canadian craft in which designs are bitten onto bark from birch trees.

Bircher (ˈbɜːtʃə), **Birchist,** *or* **Birchite** NOUN a member or supporter of the John Birch Society.
▸**ˈBirchˌism** NOUN

bird (bɜːd) NOUN [1] any warm-blooded egg-laying vertebrate of the class *Aves*, characterized by a body covering of feathers and forelimbs modified as wings. Birds vary in size between the ostrich and the humming bird. Related adjectives: **avian, ornithic.** [2] *Informal* a person (usually preceded by a qualifying adjective, as in the phrases **rare bird, odd bird, clever bird**). [3] *Slang, chiefly Brit* a girl or young woman, esp one's girlfriend. [4] *Slang* prison or a term in prison (esp in the phrase **do bird**; shortened from *birdlime*, rhyming slang for *time*). [5] **a bird in the hand.** something definite or certain. [6] **the bird has flown.** *Informal* the person in question has fled or escaped. [7] **the birds and the bees.** *Euphemistic or jocular* sex and sexual reproduction. [8] **birds of a feather.** people with the same characteristics, ideas, interests, etc. [9] **get the bird.** *Informal* **a** to be fired or dismissed. **b** (esp of a public performer) to be hissed at, booed, or derided. [10] **give (someone) the bird.** *Informal* to tell (someone) rudely to depart; scoff at; hiss. [11] **kill two birds with one stone.** to accomplish two things with one action. [12] **like a bird.** without resistance or difficulty. [13] **a little bird.** a (supposedly) unknown informant: *a little bird told me it was your birthday.* [14] **(strictly) for the birds.** *Informal* deserving of disdain or contempt; not important.
▷**HISTORY** Old English *bridd*, of unknown origin
▸**ˈbirdlike** ADJECTIVE

birdbath (ˈbɜːdˌbɑːθ) NOUN a small basin or trough for birds to bathe in, usually in a garden.

bird-brained ADJECTIVE *Informal* silly; stupid.

birdcage (ˈbɜːdˌkeɪdʒ) NOUN [1] a wire or wicker cage in which captive birds are kept. [2] any object of a similar shape, construction, or purpose. [3] *Austral and NZ* an area on a racecourse where horses parade before a race.

bird call NOUN [1] the characteristic call or song of a bird. [2] an imitation of this. [3] an instrument imitating the call of a bird, used esp by hunters or bird-catchers.

bird cherry NOUN a small Eurasian rosaceous tree, *Prunus padus*, with clusters of white flowers and small black fruits. See also **cherry** (sense 1).

bird colonel NOUN *US military slang* a full colonel in the US Army.
▷**HISTORY** from the eagle insignia of rank

bird dog *US and Canadian* ◆ NOUN [1] *Hunting* a dog used or trained to retrieve game birds after they are shot. ◆ VERB **bird-dog, -dogs, -dogging, -dogged.** [2] *Informal* to control closely with unceasing vigilance.

birder (ˈbɜːdə) NOUN an informal name for a **bird-watcher.**
▸**ˈbirding** NOUN

birdhouse (ˈbɜːdˌhaʊs) NOUN *US* [1] a small shelter or box for birds to nest in. [2] an enclosure or large cage for captive birds; aviary.

birdie (ˈbɜːdɪ) NOUN [1] *Golf* a score of one stroke under par for a hole. [2] *Informal* a bird, esp a small bird. ◆ VERB [3] (*tr*) *Golf* to play (a hole) in one stroke under par.

birdlime (ˈbɜːdˌlaɪm) NOUN [1] a sticky substance, prepared from holly, mistletoe, or other plants, smeared on twigs to catch small birds. ◆ VERB [2] (*tr*) to smear (twigs) with birdlime to catch (small birds).

birdman (ˈbɜːdˌmæn, -mən) NOUN, *plural* **-men.** [1] a man concerned with birds, such as a fowler or ornithologist. [2] a man who attempts to fly using his own muscle power. [3] an obsolete informal name for **airman.**

bird-nesting *or* **birds'-nesting** NOUN searching for birds' nests as a hobby, often to steal the eggs.

bird of paradise NOUN [1] any songbird of the family *Paradisaeidae* of New Guinea and neighbouring regions, the males of which have brilliantly coloured ornate plumage. [2] **bird-of-paradise flower.** any of various banana-like plants of the genus *Strelitzia*, esp *S. reginae*, that are native to tropical southern Africa and South America and have purple bracts and large orange or yellow flowers resembling birds' heads: family *Strelitziaceae.*

bird of passage NOUN [1] a bird that migrates seasonally. [2] a transient person or one who roams about.

bird of peace NOUN a figurative name for **dove**[1] (sense 1).

bird of prey NOUN a bird, such as a hawk, eagle, or owl, that hunts and kills other animals, esp vertebrates, for food. It has strong talons and a sharp hooked bill. Related adjective: **raptorial.**

bird pepper NOUN [1] a tropical solanaceous plant, *Capsicum frutescens*, thought to be the ancestor of the sweet pepper and many hot peppers. [2] the narrow podlike hot-tasting fruit of this plant.

birdseed (ˈbɜːdˌsiːd) NOUN a mixture of various kinds of seeds for feeding cagebirds. Also called: **canary seed.**

bird's-eye ADJECTIVE [1] **a** seen or photographed from high above. **b** summarizing the main points of a topic; summary (esp in the phrase **bird's-eye view**). [2] having markings resembling birds' eyes. ◆ NOUN [3] **bird's-eye primrose.** a Eurasian primrose, *Primula farinosa*, having clusters of purplish flowers with yellow centres. [4] **bird's-eye speedwell.** the usual US name for **germander speedwell.** [5] any of several other plants having flowers of two contrasting colours. [6] a pattern in linen and cotton fabrics, made up of small diamond shapes with a dot in the centre of each. [7] a linen or cotton fabric with such a pattern.

bird's-eye chilli NOUN a small red hot-tasting chilli.

bird's-foot *or* **bird-foot** NOUN, *plural* **-foots.** [1] a European leguminous plant, *Ornithopus perpusillus*, with small red-veined white flowers and curved pods resembling a bird's claws. [2] any of various other plants whose flowers, leaves, or pods resemble a bird's foot or claw.

bird's-foot trefoil NOUN any of various creeping leguminous Eurasian plants of the genus *Lotus*, esp *L. corniculatus*, with red-tipped yellow flowers and seed pods resembling the claws of a bird. Also called: **bacon-and-eggs.**

birdshot (ˈbɜːdˌʃɒt) NOUN small pellets designed for shooting birds.

bird's-nest VERB (*intr*) to search for the nests of birds in order to collect the eggs.

bird's-nest fungus NOUN any fungus of the family *Nidulariaceae*, having a nestlike spore-producing body containing egglike spore-filled structures.

bird's-nest orchid NOUN [1] a brown parasitic Eurasian orchid, *Neottia nidus-avis*, whose thick fleshy roots resemble a bird's nest and contain a fungus on which the orchid feeds. [2] a parasitic Eurasian plant, *Monotropa hypopitys*, whose thick fleshy roots resemble a bird's nest and contain a fungus on which the plant feeds: family *Monotropaeceae.*

bird's-nest soup NOUN a rich spicy Chinese soup made from the outer part of the nests of SE Asian swifts of the genus *Collocalia.*

birdsong (ˈbɜːdˌsɒŋ) NOUN the musical call of a bird or birds.

bird spider NOUN any large hairy predatory bird-eating spider of the family *Aviculariidae*, of tropical America.

bird strike NOUN a collision of an aircraft with a bird.

bird table NOUN a table or platform in the open on which food for birds may be placed.

bird-watcher NOUN a person who studies wild birds in their natural surroundings.
▸**ˈbird-ˌwatching** NOUN

birefringence (ˌbaɪrɪˈfrɪndʒəns) NOUN another name for **double refraction.**
▸**ˌbireˈfringent** ADJECTIVE

bireme (ˈbaɪriːm) NOUN an ancient galley having two banks of oars.
▷**HISTORY** C17: from Latin *birēmus*, from BI-[1] + *-rēmus* oar

biretta *or* **berretta** (bɪˈrɛtə) NOUN *RC Church* a stiff clerical cap having either three or four upright pieces projecting outwards from the centre to the

edge: coloured black for priests, purple for bishops, red for cardinals, and white for certain members of religious orders.
▷HISTORY C16: from Italian *berretta*, from Old Provençal *berret*, from Late Latin *birrus* hooded cape

biriani (ˌbɪrɪˈɑːnɪ) NOUN a variant spelling of **biryani**.

birk (bɪrk, bɜːk) *Chiefly Scot* ◆ NOUN 1 a birch tree. 2 (*plural*) a birch wood. ◆ ADJECTIVE 3 consisting or made of birch.
▷HISTORY C14: from Old Norse; compare BIRCH

Birkenhead (ˌbɜːkənˈhɛd) NOUN a port in NW England, in Wirral unitary authority, Merseyside: former shipbuilding centre. Pop.: 93 087 (1991).

birkie (ˈbɪrkɪ) NOUN *Scot* 1 a spirited or lively person. 2 a foolish posturer.
▷HISTORY C18: perhaps related to Old English *beorcan* to bark; compare Old Norse *berkia*

birl[1] (bɜːl; *Scot* bɪrl) VERB 1 *Scot* to spin; twirl. 2 *US and Canadian* to cause (a floating log) to spin using the feet while standing on it, esp as a sport among lumberjacks. ◆ NOUN 3 a variant spelling of **burl**[2].
▷HISTORY C18: probably imitative and influenced by WHIRL and HURL

birl[2] (bɜːl; *Scot* bɪrl) VERB *Archaic, Scot* to ply (one's guests, etc.) with drink.
▷HISTORY Old English *byrelian*; related to *byrele* cup-bearer

Birman (ˈbɜːmən) NOUN a breed of large long-haired cat having a light-coloured coat with dark face, tail, and legs, and white feet.
▷HISTORY variant of *Burman*, a Burmese cat

Birmingham (ˈbɜːmɪŋəm) NOUN 1 an industrial city in central England, in Birmingham unitary authority, in the West Midlands: the second largest city in Great Britain; two cathedrals; three universities (1900, 1966, 1992). Pop.: 965 928 (1994 est.). Related adjective: **Brummie**. 2 a unitary authority in central England, in the West Midlands. Pop.: 977 091 (2001). Area: 283 sq. km (109 sq. miles). 3 (ˈbɜːmɪŋˌhæm) an industrial city in N central Alabama: rich local deposits of coal, iron ore, and other minerals. Pop.: 242 820 (2000).

Biro (ˈbaɪrəʊ) NOUN, *plural* **-ros**. *Trademark, Brit* a kind of ballpoint.
▷HISTORY C20: named after Laszlo *Bíró* (1900–85), Hungarian inventor

Birobidzhan *or* **Birobijan** (*Russian* birəbidˈʒan) NOUN 1 a city in SE Russia: capital of the Jewish Autonomous Region. Pop.: 82 000 (1994). 2 another name for the **Jewish Autonomous Region**.

birr[1] (bɜː) *Chiefly US and Scot* ◆ VERB 1 to make or cause to make a whirring sound. ◆ NOUN 2 a whirring sound. 3 force, as of wind. 4 vigour; energy.
▷HISTORY Old English *byre* storm, related to Old Norse *byrr* favourable wind

birr[2] (bɜː) NOUN the standard monetary unit of Ethiopia, divided into 100 cents.
▷HISTORY C20: from Amharic

birth (bɜːθ) NOUN 1 the process of bearing young; parturition; childbirth. Related adjective: **natal**. 2 the act or fact of being born; nativity. 3 the coming into existence of something; origin. 4 ancestry; lineage: *of high birth*. 5 noble ancestry: *a man of birth*. 6 natural or inherited talent: *an artist by birth*. 7 *Archaic* the offspring or young born at a particular time or of a particular mother. 8 **give birth (to)**. **a** to bear (offspring). **b** to produce, originate, or create (an idea, plan, etc.). ◆ VERB (*tr*) *Rare* 9 to bear or bring forth (a child).
▷HISTORY C12: from Old Norse *byrth*; related to Gothic *gabaurths*, Old Swedish *byrdh*, Old High German *berd* child; see BEAR[1], BAIRN

birth certificate NOUN an official form giving details of the time and place of a person's birth, and his or her name, sex, mother's name and (usually) father's name.

birth control NOUN limitation of child-bearing by means of contraception. See also **family planning**.

birthday (ˈbɜːθˌdeɪ) NOUN 1 **a** an anniversary of the day of one's birth. **b** (*as modifier*): *birthday present*. 2 the day on which a person was born. 3 any anniversary.

Birthday honours PLURAL NOUN (in Britain) honorary titles conferred on the official birthday of the sovereign.

birthday suit NOUN *Informal, humorous* a state of total nakedness, as at birth.

birthing ball NOUN a large soft rubber ball used by women during childbirth to give support and to aid pain relief.

birthing centre (ˈbɜːθɪŋ) NOUN *NZ* a private maternity hospital.

birthing chair NOUN a chair constructed to allow a woman in labour to give birth in a sitting position.

birthing pool NOUN a large bath in which a woman can give birth.

birthmark (ˈbɜːθˌmɑːk) NOUN a blemish or new growth on skin formed before birth, usually brown or dark red; naevus.

birth mother NOUN the woman who gives birth to a child, regardless of whether she is the genetic mother or subsequently brings up the child.

birthplace (ˈbɜːθˌpleɪs) NOUN the place where someone was born or where something originated.

birth rate NOUN the ratio of live births in a specified area, group, etc., to the population of that area, etc., usually expressed per 1000 population per year.

birthright (ˈbɜːθˌraɪt) NOUN 1 privileges or possessions that a person has or is believed to be entitled to as soon as he is born. 2 the privileges or possessions of a first-born son. 3 inheritance; patrimony.

birthroot (ˈbɜːθˌruːt) NOUN any of several North American plants of the genus *Trillium*, esp *T. erectum*, whose tuber-like roots were formerly used by the American Indians as an aid in childbirth: family *Trilliaceae*.

birthstone (ˈbɜːθˌstəʊn) NOUN a precious or semiprecious stone associated with a month or sign of the zodiac and thought to bring luck if worn by a person born in that month or under that sign.

birthwort (ˈbɜːθˌwɜːt) NOUN any of several climbing plants of the genus *Aristolochia*, esp *A. clematitis* of Europe, once believed to ease childbirth: family *Aristolochiaceae*.

biryani *or* **biriani** (ˌbɪrɪˈɑːnɪ) NOUN any of a variety of Indian dishes made with rice, highly flavoured and coloured with saffron or turmeric, mixed with meat or fish.
▷HISTORY from Urdu

bis (bɪs) ADVERB 1 twice; for a second time (used in musical scores to indicate a part to be repeated). ◆ SENTENCE SUBSTITUTE 2 encore! again!
▷HISTORY C19: via Italian from Latin, from Old Latin *duis*

BIS 1 ABBREVIATION FOR Bank for International Settlements: an institution, based in Basel, Switzerland, that accepts deposits, makes loans for national central banks, and assists in offsetting speculative movements of funds between the major currencies; set up in 1930. ◆ 2 INTERNATIONAL CAR REGISTRATION FOR Bosnia-Herzegovina.

Bisayan (bɪˈsɑːjən) NOUN a variant of **Visayan**.

Bisayas (biˈsajas) PLURAL NOUN the Spanish name for the **Visayan Islands**.

Biscay (ˈbɪskeɪ, -kɪ) NOUN **Bay of**. a large bay of the Atlantic Ocean between W France and N Spain: notorious for storms.

biscuit (ˈbɪskɪt) NOUN 1 *Brit* a small flat dry sweet or plain cake of many varieties, baked from a dough. US and Canadian word: **cookie**. 2 *US and Canadian* a kind of small roll similar to a muffin. 3 **a** a pale brown or yellowish-grey colour. **b** (*as adjective*): *biscuit gloves*. 4 Also called: **bisque**. earthenware or porcelain that has been fired but not glazed. 5 **take the biscuit**. *Slang* to be regarded (by the speaker) as the most surprising thing that could have occurred.
▷HISTORY C14: from Old French, from (*pain*) *bescuit* twice-cooked (bread), from *bes* BIS + *cuire* to cook, from Latin *coquere*

bise (biːz) NOUN a cold dry northerly wind in Switzerland and the neighbouring parts of France and Italy, usually in the spring.
▷HISTORY C14: from Old French, of Germanic origin; compare Old Swedish *bīsa* whirlwind

bisect (baɪˈsɛkt) VERB 1 (*tr*) *Maths* to divide into two equal parts. 2 to cut or split into two.
▷HISTORY C17: BI-[1] + *-sect* from Latin *secāre* to cut
▸**bisection** (baɪˈsɛkʃən) NOUN

bisector (baɪˈsɛktə) NOUN *Maths* 1 a straight line or plane that bisects an angle. 2 a line or plane that bisects another line.

bisectrix (baɪˈsɛktrɪks) NOUN, *plural* **bisectrices** (baɪˈsɛktrɪˌsiːz). 1 another name for **bisector**. 2 the bisector of the angle between the optic axes of a crystal.

biseriate (ˌbaɪˈsɪərɪɪt) ADJECTIVE (of plant parts, such as petals) arranged in two whorls, cycles, rows, or series.

biserrate (baɪˈsɛreɪt, -ɪt) ADJECTIVE 1 *Botany* (of leaf margins, etc.) having serrations that are themselves serrate. 2 *Zoology* serrated on both sides, as the antennae of some insects.

bi sex NOUN sex with both male and female partners.

bisexual (baɪˈsɛksjʊəl) ADJECTIVE 1 sexually attracted by both men and women. 2 showing characteristics of both sexes: *a bisexual personality*. 3 (of some plants and animals) having both male and female reproductive organs. 4 of or relating to both sexes. ◆ NOUN 5 a bisexual organism; a hermaphrodite. 6 a bisexual person.
▸**bisexuality** (baɪˌsɛksjʊˈælɪtɪ) *or esp US* **biˈsexualism** NOUN ▸**biˈsexually** ADVERB

bish (bɪʃ) NOUN *Brit slang* a mistake.
▷HISTORY C20: of unknown origin

Bishkek (bɪʃˈkɛk) NOUN the capital of Kyrgyzstan. Pop.: 619 000 (1999 est.). Also called: **Pishpek**. Former name (1926–91): **Frunze**.

bishop (ˈbɪʃəp) NOUN 1 (in the Roman Catholic, Anglican, and Greek Orthodox Churches) a clergyman having spiritual and administrative powers over a diocese or province of the Church. See also **suffragan**. Related adjective: **episcopal**. 2 (in some Protestant Churches) a spiritual overseer of a local church or a number of churches. 3 a chesspiece, capable of moving diagonally over any number of unoccupied squares of the same colour. 4 mulled wine, usually port, spiced with oranges, cloves, etc.
▷HISTORY Old English *biscop*, from Late Latin *epīscopus*, from Greek *episkopos*, from EPI- + *skopos* watcher

Bishop Auckland NOUN a town in N England, in central Durham: seat of the bishops of Durham since the 12th century: light industries. Pop.: 23 154 (1991).

bishopbird (ˈbɪʃəpˌbɜːd) NOUN any African weaverbird of the genus *Euplectes* (or *Pyromelana*), the males of which have black plumage marked with red or yellow.

bishopric (ˈbɪʃəprɪk) NOUN the see, diocese, or office of a bishop.

bishop's-cap NOUN another name for **mitrewort**.

bishop sleeve NOUN a full sleeve gathered at the wrist.

bishop's mitre NOUN a European heteropterous bug, *Aelia acuminata*, whose larvae are a pest of cereal grasses: family *Pentatomidae*.

bishop's weed NOUN another name for **goutweed**.

Bisitun (ˌbiːsɪˈtuːn) NOUN another name for **Behistun**.

bisk (bɪsk) NOUN a less common spelling of **bisque**[1].

Bisk (*Russian* bijsk) NOUN a variant spelling of **Biysk**.

Biskra (ˈbɪskrɑː) NOUN a town and oasis in NE Algeria, in the Sahara. Pop.: 170 956 (1998).

Bisley (ˈbɪzlɪ) NOUN a village in SE England, in Surrey: annual meetings of the National Rifle Association.

Bismarck (ˈbɪzmɑːk) NOUN a city in North Dakota, on the Missouri River: the state capital. Pop.: 49 256 (1990).

Bismarck Archipelago NOUN a group of over 200 islands in the SW Pacific, northeast of New Guinea: part of Papua New Guinea. Main islands: New Britain, New Ireland, Lavongai, and the Admiralty Islands. Chief town: Rabaul, on New Britain. Pop.: 424 000 (1995 est.). Area: 49 658 sq. km (19 173 sq. miles).

Bismarck herring NOUN marinaded herring, served cold.

Bismillah (ˌbɪsmɪˈlaː) INTERJECTION the words which preface all except one of the surahs of the Koran, used by Muslims as a blessing before eating or some other action.
▷HISTORY shortened from *Bismillah-ir-Rahman-ir-Rahim*, from Arabic, literally: in the name of God, the merciful and compassionate

bismuth (ˈbɪzməθ) NOUN a brittle pinkish-white crystalline metallic element having low thermal and electrical conductivity, which expands on cooling. It is widely used in alloys, esp low-melting alloys in fire safety devices; its compounds are used in medicines. Symbol: Bi; atomic no.: 83; atomic wt.: 208.98037; valency: 3 or 5; relative density: 9.747; melting pt.: 271.4°C; boiling pt.: 1564±5°C.
▷HISTORY C17: from New Latin *bisemūtum*, from German *Wismut*, of unknown origin
▸**bismuthal** (ˈbɪzməθəl) ADJECTIVE

bismuthic (bɪzˈmjuːθɪk, -ˈmʌθɪk) ADJECTIVE of or containing bismuth in the pentavalent state.

bismuthinite (bɪzˈmʌθɪˌnaɪt) *or* **bismuth glance** NOUN a grey mineral consisting of bismuth sulphide in orthorhombic crystalline form. It occurs in veins associated with tin, copper, silver, lead, etc., and is a source of bismuth. Formula: Bi_2S_3.

bismuthous (ˈbɪzməθəs) ADJECTIVE of or containing bismuth in the trivalent state.

bison (ˈbaɪsᵊn) NOUN, *plural* **-son.** [1] Also called: **American bison, buffalo.** a member of the cattle tribe, *Bison bison*, formerly widely distributed over the prairies of W North America but now confined to reserves and parks, with a massive head, shaggy forequarters, and a humped back. [2] Also called: **wisent, European bison.** a closely related and similar animal, *Bison bonasus*, formerly widespread in Europe.
▷HISTORY C14: from Latin *bisōn*, of Germanic origin; related to Old English *wesand*, Old Norse *vīsundr*

bisphosphonate (ˌbɪsˈfɒsfəneɪt) NOUN any drug of a class that inhibits the resorption of bone; used in treating certain bone disorders, esp osteoporosis.

bisque¹ (bɪsk) NOUN a thick rich soup made from shellfish.
▷HISTORY C17: from French

bisque² (bɪsk) NOUN [1] **a** a pink to yellowish tan colour. **b** (*as adjective*): *a bisque tablecloth.* [2] *Ceramics* another name for **biscuit** (sense 4).
▷HISTORY C20: shortened from BISCUIT

bisque³ (bɪsk) NOUN *Tennis, golf, croquet* an extra point, stroke, or turn allowed to an inferior player, usually taken when desired.
▷HISTORY C17: from French, of obscure origin

Bissau (bɪˈsaʊ) *or* **Bissão** (*Portuguese* biˈsɐ̃u) NOUN the capital of Guinea-Bissau, a port on the Atlantic: until 1974 the capital of Portuguese Guinea. Pop.: 274 000 (1999 est.).

bissextile (bɪˈsɛkstaɪl) ADJECTIVE [1] (of a month or year) containing the extra day of a leap year. ◆ NOUN [2] a rare name for **leap year.**
▷HISTORY C16: from Late Latin *bissextilis annus* leap year, from Latin *bissextus*, from BI-¹ + *sextus* sixth; referring to February 24, the 6th day before the Calends of March

bist (bɪst) VERB *Archaic or dialect* a form of the second person singular of **be.**

bistable (baɪˈsteɪbᵊl) ADJECTIVE [1] having two stable states: *bistable circuit.* ◆ NOUN [2] *Computing* another name for **flip-flop** (sense 2).

Bisto (ˈbɪstəʊ) NOUN *Trademark* a preparation for thickening, flavouring, and browning gravy.

bistort (ˈbɪstɔːt) NOUN [1] Also called: **snakeroot, snakeweed, Easter-ledges.** a Eurasian polygonaceous plant, *Polygonum bistorta*, having leaf stipules fused to form a tube around the stem and a spike of small pink flowers. [2] Also called: **snakeroot.** a related plant, *Polygonum bistortoides*, of W North America, with oval clusters of pink or white flowers. [3] any of several other plants of the genus *Polygonum*.
▷HISTORY C16: from French *bistorte*, from Latin *bis* twice + *tortus* from *torquēre* to twist

bistoury (ˈbɪstərɪ) NOUN, *plural* **-ries.** a long surgical knife with a narrow blade.
▷HISTORY C15: from Old French *bistorie* dagger, of unknown origin

bistre *or US* **bister** (ˈbɪstə) NOUN [1] a transparent water-soluble brownish-yellow pigment made by boiling the soot of wood, used for pen and wash drawings. [2] **a** a yellowish-brown to dark brown colour. **b** (*as adjective*): *bistre paint.*
▷HISTORY C18: from French, of unknown origin

bistro (ˈbiːstrəʊ) NOUN, *plural* **-tros.** a small restaurant.
▷HISTORY French: of obscure origin; perhaps from Russian *bistro* fast

bisulcate (baɪˈsʌlˌkeɪt) ADJECTIVE [1] marked by two grooves. [2] *Zoology* **a** cleft or cloven, as a hoof. **b** having cloven hoofs.

bisulphate (baɪˈsʌlˌfeɪt) NOUN [1] a salt or ester of sulphuric acid containing the monovalent group $-HSO_4$ or the ion HSO_4^-. [2] (*modifier*) consisting of, containing, or concerned with the group $-HSO_4$ or the ion HSO_4^-: *bisulphate ion.* ◆ Systematic name: **hydrogen sulphate.**

bisulphide (baɪˈsʌlfaɪd) NOUN another name for **disulphide.**

bisulphite (baɪˈsʌlfaɪt) NOUN [1] a salt or ester of sulphurous acid containing the monovalent group $-HSO_3$ or the ion HSO_3^-. [2] (*modifier*) consisting of or containing the group $-HSO_3$ or the ion HSO_3^-: *bisulphite ion.* ◆ Systematic name: **hydrogen sulphite.**

Bisutun (ˌbiːsʊˈtuːn) NOUN another name for **Behistun.**

bisymmetric (ˌbaɪsɪˈmɛtrɪk) *or* **bisymmetrical** ADJECTIVE [1] *Botany* showing symmetry in two planes at right angles to each other. [2] (of plants and animals) showing bilateral symmetry.
▸ˌ**bisymˈmetrically** ADVERB ▸**bisymmetry** (baɪˈsɪmɪtrɪ) NOUN

bit¹ (bɪt) NOUN [1] a small piece, portion, or quantity. [2] a short time or distance. [3] *US and Canadian informal* the value of an eighth of a dollar: spoken of only in units of two: *two bits.* [4] any small coin. [5] short for **bit part.** [6] *Informal* way of behaving, esp one intended to create a particular impression: *she's doing the prima donna bit.* [7] **a bit.** rather; somewhat: *a bit dreary.* [8] **a bit of. a** rather: *a bit of a dope.* **b** a considerable amount: *that must take quite a bit of courage.* [9] **a bit of all right, bit of crumpet, bit of stuff,** *or* **bit of tail.** *Brit slang* a sexually attractive woman. [10] **bit by bit.** gradually. [11] **bit on the side.** *Informal* an extramarital affair. [12] **do one's bit.** to make one's expected contribution. [13] **every bit.** (foll by *as*) to the same degree: *she was every bit as clever as her brother.* [14] **not a bit** (**of it**). not in the slightest; not at all. [15] **to bits.** completely apart: *to fall to bits.*
▷HISTORY Old English *bite* action of biting; see BITE

bit² (bɪt) NOUN [1] a metal mouthpiece, for controlling a horse on a bridle. [2] anything that restrains or curbs. [3] **take** *or* **have the bit in** *or* **between one's teeth. a** to undertake a task with determination. **b** to rebel against control. [4] a cutting or drilling tool, part, or head in a brace, drill, etc. [5] the blade of a woodworking plane. [6] the part of a pair of pincers designed to grasp an object. [7] the copper end of a soldering iron. [8] the part of a key that engages the levers of a lock. ◆ VERB **bits, bitting, bitted.** (*tr*) [9] to put a bit in the mouth of (a horse). [10] to restrain; curb.
▷HISTORY Old English *bita*; related to Old English *bītan* to BITE

bit³ (bɪt) VERB the past tense and (archaic) past participle of **bite.**

bit⁴ (bɪt) NOUN *Maths, computing* [1] a single digit of binary notation, represented either by 0 or by 1. [2] the smallest unit of information, indicating the presence or absence of a single feature. [3] a unit of capacity of a computer, consisting of an element of its physical structure capable of being in either of two states, such as a switch with *on* and *off* positions, or a microscopic magnet capable of alignment in two directions.
▷HISTORY C20: from abbreviation of BINARY DIGIT

bitartrate (baɪˈtɑːˌtreɪt) NOUN (not in technical usage) a salt or ester of tartaric acid containing the monovalent group $-HC_4H_4O_6$ or the ion $HC_4H_4O_6^-$. Also called: **hydrogen tartrate.**

bitch (bɪtʃ) NOUN [1] a female dog or other female canine animal, such as a wolf. [2] *Slang, derogatory* a malicious, spiteful, or coarse woman. [3] *Informal* a complaint. [4] *Informal* a difficult situation or problem. ◆ VERB *Informal* [5] (*intr*) to complain; grumble. [6] to behave (towards) in a spiteful or malicious manner. [7] (*tr*, often foll by *up*) to botch; bungle.
▷HISTORY Old English *bicce*

bitchfest (ˈbɪtʃˌfest) NOUN *Slang* a malicious and spiteful discussion of people, events, etc.

bitchin' (ˈbɪtʃɪn) *or* **bitching** (ˈbɪtʃɪŋ) *US slang* ◆ ADJECTIVE [1] wonderful or excellent. ◆ ADVERB [2] extremely: *bitchin' good.*

bitch-slap VERB **-slaps, -slapped, -slapping.** (*tr*) *Slang* to strike (someone) with one's open hand.

bitchy (ˈbɪtʃɪ) ADJECTIVE **bitchier, bitchiest.** *Informal* characteristic of or behaving like a bitch; malicious; snide.
▸ˈ**bitchily** ADVERB ▸ˈ**bitchiness** NOUN

bite (baɪt) VERB **bites, biting, bit, bitten.** [1] to grip, cut off, or tear with or as if with the teeth or jaws. [2] (of animals, insects, etc.) to injure by puncturing or tearing (the skin or flesh) with the teeth, fangs, etc., esp as a natural characteristic. [3] (*tr*) to cut or penetrate, as with a knife. [4] (of corrosive material such as acid) to eat away or into. [5] to smart or cause to smart; sting: *mustard bites the tongue.* [6] (*intr*) *Angling* (of a fish) to take or attempt to take the bait or lure. [7] to take firm hold of or act effectively upon. [8] to grip or hold (a workpiece) with a tool or chuck. [9] (of a screw, thread, etc.) to cut into or grip (an object, material, etc.). [10] (*tr*) *Informal* to annoy or worry: *what's biting her?* [11] (*often passive*) *Slang* to cheat. [12] (*tr*; often foll by *for*) *Austral and NZ slang* to ask (for); scrounge from. [13] **bite off more than one can chew.** *Informal* to attempt a task beyond one's capability. [14] **bite the bullet.** to face up to (pain, trouble, etc.) with fortitude; be stoical. [15] **bite someone's head off.** to respond harshly and rudely (to). [16] **bite the dust.** See **dust** (sense 11). [17] **bite the hand that feeds one.** to repay kindness with injury or ingratitude. [18] **once bitten, twice shy.** after an unpleasant experience one is cautious in similar situations. [19] **put the bite on** (**someone**). *Austral slang* to ask (someone) for money. ◆ NOUN [20] the act of biting. [21] a thing or amount bitten off. [22] a wound, bruise, or sting inflicted by biting. [23] *Angling* an attempt by a fish to take the bait or lure. [24] *Informal* an incisive or penetrating effect or quality: *tthat's a question with a bite.* [25] a light meal; snack. [26] a cutting, stinging, or smarting sensation. [27] the depth of cut of a machine tool. [28] the grip or hold applied by a tool or chuck to a workpiece. [29] *Dentistry* the angle or manner of contact between the upper and lower teeth when the mouth is closed naturally. [30] the surface of a file or rasp with cutting teeth. [31] the corrosive action of acid, as on a metal etching plate.
▷HISTORY Old English *bītan*; related to Latin *findere* to split, Sanskrit *bhedati* he splits
▸ˈ**biter** NOUN

bite back VERB (*tr, adverb*) to restrain (a hurtful, embarrassing, or indiscreet remark); avoid saying.

Bithynia (bɪˈθɪnɪə) NOUN an ancient country on the Black Sea in NW Asia Minor.

biting (ˈbaɪtɪŋ) ADJECTIVE [1] piercing; keen: *a biting wind.* [2] sarcastic; incisive: *a biting comment.*
▸ˈ**bitingly** ADVERB

biting *or* **bird louse** NOUN See **louse** (sense 2).

biting midge NOUN any small fragile dipterous fly of the family *Ceratopogonidae*, most of which suck the blood of mammals, birds, or other insects.

biting point NOUN [1] (in driving) the point at which the plates of the clutch connect as the clutch pedal is released. [2] a point at which success is achieved.

bitmap (ˈbɪtˌmæp) NOUN *Computing* [1] a picture created on a visual display unit where each pixel corresponds to one or more bits in memory, the number of bits per pixel determining the number of available colours. ◆ VERB **-maps, -mapping, -mapped.** [2] (*tr*) to create a bitmap of.

Bitolj (*Serbo-Croat* ˈbitɔlj) *or* **Bitola** (ˈbiːtəʊlə) NOUN a city in SW Macedonia: under Turkish rule from 1382 until 1913 when it was taken by the Serbs. Pop.: 75 386 (1994).

bit part NOUN a very small acting role with few lines to speak.

bit rate NOUN *Computing* the rate of flow of binary digits in a digital data-processing system, usually expressed as the number of bits per second.

bitser ('bɪtsə) NOUN *Austral informal* a mongrel dog.
▷HISTORY C20: from *bits o'* bits of, as in *his dog is bits o' this and bits o' that*

bit slice ADJECTIVE *Computing* (of central processing units) able to be built up in sections to form complete central processing units with various word lengths.

bitstock ('bɪtˌstɒk) NOUN the handle or stock of a tool into which a drilling bit is fixed.

bitt (bɪt) *Nautical* ◆ NOUN 1 one of a pair of strong posts on the deck of a ship for securing mooring and other lines. 2 another word for **bollard** (sense 1). ◆ VERB 3 (*tr*) to secure (a line) by means of a bitt.
▷HISTORY C14: probably of Scandinavian origin; compare Old Norse *biti* cross beam, Middle High German *bizze* wooden peg

bitten ('bɪtᵊn) VERB the past participle of **bite**.

bitter ('bɪtə) ADJECTIVE 1 having or denoting an unpalatable harsh taste, as the peel of an orange or coffee dregs. Compare **sour** (sense 1). 2 showing or caused by strong unrelenting hostility or resentment: *he was still bitter about the divorce*. 3 difficult or unpleasant to accept or admit: *a bitter blow*. 4 cutting; sarcastic: *bitter words*. 5 bitingly cold: *a bitter night*. ◆ ADVERB 6 very; extremely (esp in the phrase **bitter cold**). ◆ NOUN 7 a thing that is bitter. 8 *Brit* beer with a high hop content, with a slightly bitter taste. ◆ VERB 9 to make or become bitter. ◆ See also **bitters**.
▷HISTORY Old English *biter*; related to *bītan* to BITE
▸'**bitterly** ADVERB ▸'**bitterness** NOUN

bitter apple NOUN another name for **colocynth**.

bitterbark ('bɪtəˌba:k) NOUN an Australian tree, *Alstonia constricta*, with bitter-tasting bark that is used in preparing tonic medicines.

bittercress ('bɪtəˌkrɛs) NOUN one of several perennial or annual plants of the genus *Cardamine*, that are related to lady's-smock, including **hairy bittercress** (*C. hirsuta*), a common weed resembling shepherd's purse, with which it is often confused: family: *Brassicaceae* (crucifers).

bitter end NOUN 1 *Nautical* the end of a line, chain, or cable, esp the end secured in the chain locker of a vessel. 2 **a to the bitter end.** until the finish of a task, job, or undertaking, however unpleasant or difficult. **b** until final defeat or death.
▷HISTORY C19: in both senses perhaps from BITT

Bitter Lakes PLURAL NOUN two lakes, the **Great Bitter Lake** and **Little Bitter Lake** in NE Egypt: part of the Suez Canal.

bitterling ('bɪtəlɪŋ) NOUN a small brightly coloured European freshwater cyprinid fish, *Rhodeus sericeus*: a popular aquarium fish.
▷HISTORY C19: from German; see BITTER + -LING[1]

bittern[1] ('bɪtən) NOUN any wading bird of the genera *Ixobrychus* and *Botaurus*, related and similar to the herons but with shorter legs and neck, a stouter body, and a booming call: family *Ardeidae*, order *Ciconiiformes*.
▷HISTORY C14: from Old French *butor*, perhaps from Latin *būtiō* bittern + *taurus* bull; referring to its cry

bittern[2] ('bɪtən) NOUN the bitter liquid remaining after common salt has been crystallized out of sea water: a source of magnesium, bromine, and iodine compounds.
▷HISTORY C17: variant of *bittering*; see BITTER

bitternut ('bɪtəˌnʌt) NOUN 1 an E North American hickory tree, *Carya cordiformis*, with thin-shelled nuts and bitter kernels. 2 the nut of this plant.

bitter orange NOUN another name for **Seville orange**.

bitter principle NOUN any of various bitter-tasting substances, such as aloin, usually extracted from plants.

bitters ('bɪtəz) PLURAL NOUN 1 bitter-tasting spirits of varying alcoholic content flavoured with plant extracts. 2 a similar liquid containing a bitter-tasting substance, used as a tonic to stimulate the appetite or improve digestion.

bittersweet ('bɪtəˌswi:t) NOUN 1 any of several North American woody climbing plants of the genus *Celastrus*, esp *C. scandens*, having orange capsules that open to expose scarlet-coated seeds: family *Celastraceae*. 2 another name for **woody nightshade.** ◆ ADJECTIVE 3 tasting of or being a mixture of bitterness and sweetness. 4 pleasant but tinged with sadness.

bitterweed ('bɪtəˌwi:d) NOUN any of various plants that contain a bitter-tasting substance.

bitterwood ('bɪtəˌwʊd) NOUN any of several simaroubaceous trees of the genus *Picrasma* of S and SE Asia and the Caribbean, whose bitter bark and wood are used in medicine as a substitute for quassia.

bitty ('bɪtɪ) ADJECTIVE **-tier, -tiest**. 1 lacking unity; disjointed. 2 containing bits, sediment, etc.
▸'**bittiness** NOUN

bitumen ('bɪtjʊmɪn) NOUN 1 any of various viscous or solid impure mixtures of hydrocarbons that occur naturally in asphalt, tar, mineral waxes, etc.: used as a road surfacing and roofing material. 2 the constituents of coal that can be extracted by an organic solvent. 3 any liquid suitable for coating aggregates. 4 **the bitumen. a** *Austral and NZ informal* any road with a bitumen surface. **b** (*capital*) *Austral informal* the road in the Northern Territory between Darwin and Alice Springs. 5 a transparent brown pigment or glaze made from asphalt.
▷HISTORY C15: from Latin *bitūmen*, perhaps of Celtic origin
▸**bituminous** (bɪ'tju:mɪnəs) ADJECTIVE

bituminize *or* **bituminise** (bɪ'tju:mɪˌnaɪz) VERB (*tr*) to treat with or convert into bitumen.
▸**biˌtuminiˈzation** *or* **biˌtuminiˈsation** NOUN

bituminous coal NOUN a soft black coal, rich in volatile hydrocarbons, that burns with a smoky yellow flame. Fixed carbon content: 46–86 per cent; calorific value: $1.93 \times 10^7 - 3.63 \times 10^7$ J/kg. Also called: **soft coal.**

bivalence (baɪ'veɪləns, 'bɪvə-) NOUN *Logic, philosophy* the semantic principle that there are exactly two truth values, so that every meaningful statement is either true or false. Compare **many-valued logic.**

bivalent (baɪ'veɪlənt, 'bɪvə-) ADJECTIVE 1 *Chem* another word for **divalent.** 2 (of homologous chromosomes) associated together in pairs. ◆ NOUN 3 a structure formed during meiosis consisting of two homologous chromosomes associated together.
▸**bi'valency** NOUN

bivalve ('baɪˌvælv) NOUN 1 Also called: **pelecypod, amellibranch.** any marine or freshwater mollusc of the class *Pelecypoda* (formerly *Bivalvia* or *Lamellibranchia*), having a laterally compressed body, a shell consisting of two hinged valves, and gills for respiration. The group includes clams, cockles, oysters, and mussels. ◆ ADJECTIVE 2 Also: **pelecypod, lamellibranch.** of, relating to, or belonging to the *Pelecypoda*. 3 Also: **bivalvate** (baɪ'vælveɪt). *Biology* having or consisting of two valves or similar parts: *a bivalve seed capsule*.
▸**bi'valvular** ADJECTIVE

bivariate (baɪ'vɛərɪɪt) ADJECTIVE *Statistics* (of a distribution) involving two random variables, not necessarily independent of one another.

bivouac ('bɪvʊˌæk, 'bɪvwæk) NOUN 1 a temporary encampment with few facilities, as used by soldiers, mountaineers, etc. ◆ VERB **-acs, -acking, -acked.** 2 (*intr*) to make such an encampment.
▷HISTORY C18: from French *bivuac*, probably from Swiss German *Beiwacht*, literally: BY + WATCH

bivvy ('bɪvɪ) NOUN, *plural* **-vies**. *Slang* a small tent or shelter.
▷HISTORY C20: shortened from BIVOUAC

biweekly (baɪ'wi:klɪ) ADJECTIVE, ADVERB 1 every two weeks. 2 (often avoided because of confusion with sense 1) twice a week; semiweekly. See **bi-[1]**. ◆ NOUN, *plural* **-lies**. 3 a periodical published every two weeks.

biyearly (baɪ'jɪəlɪ) ADJECTIVE, ADVERB 1 every two years; biennial or biennially. 2 (often avoided because of confusion with sense 1) twice a year; biannual or biannually. See **bi-[1]**.

Biysk, Biisk, *or* **Bisk** (*Russian* bijsk) NOUN a city in SW Russia, at the foot of the Altai Mountains. Pop: 225 700 (1999 est.).

biz (bɪz) NOUN *Informal* short for **business**.

biz AN INTERNET DOMAIN NAME FOR a business.

bizarre (bɪ'zɑ:) ADJECTIVE odd or unusual, esp in an interesting or amusing way.
▷HISTORY C17: from French: from Italian *bizzarro* capricious, of uncertain origin
▸**bi'zarrely** ADVERB ▸**bi'zarreness** NOUN

bizarrerie (bɪ'zɑ:rərɪ) NOUN 1 the quality of being bizarre. 2 a bizarre act.

Bizerte (bɪ'zɜ:tə; *French* bizɛrt) *or* **Bizerta** NOUN a port in N Tunisia, on the Mediterranean at the canalized outlet of **Lake Bizerte**. Pop.: 98 900 (1994).

bizzo ('bɪzəʊ) NOUN *Austral informal* 1 empty and irrelevant talk or ideas; nonsense: *all that bizzo*. 2 a businessman's club.

bizzy ('bɪzɪ) NOUN, *plural* **-zies**. *Brit slang, chiefly Liverpudlian* a policeman.
▷HISTORY C20: from BUSY

bj THE INTERNET DOMAIN NAME FOR Benin.

B.J. (in the US and Canada) ABBREVIATION FOR Bachelor of Journalism.

Björneborg (bjœrnə'bɔrj) NOUN the Swedish name for **Pori**.

bk ABBREVIATION FOR: 1 bank. 2 book.

Bk THE CHEMICAL SYMBOL FOR berkelium.

bkcy ABBREVIATION FOR bankruptcy.

bkg ABBREVIATION FOR banking.

bkpt ABBREVIATION FOR bankrupt.

bks ABBREVIATION FOR: 1 barracks. 2 books.

bl ABBREVIATION FOR barrel.

BL ABBREVIATION FOR: 1 Bachelor of Law. 2 Bachelor of Letters. 3 Barrister-at-Law. 4 **British Library**.

B/L, b/l, *or* **b.l.** *plural* **Bs/L, bs/l** *or* **bs.l** ABBREVIATION FOR bill of lading.

blab (blæb) VERB **blabs, blabbing, blabbed.** 1 to divulge (secrets) indiscreetly. 2 (*intr*) to chatter thoughtlessly; prattle. ◆ NOUN 3 a less common word for **blabber** (senses 1, 2).
▷HISTORY C14: of Germanic origin; compare Old High German *blabbizōn*, Icelandic *blabbra*
▸'**blabbing** NOUN, ADJECTIVE

blabber ('blæbə) NOUN 1 a person who blabs. 2 idle chatter. ◆ VERB 3 (*intr*) to talk without thinking; chatter.
▷HISTORY C15 *blabberen*, probably of imitative origin

blabbermouth ('blæbəˌmaʊθ) NOUN *Informal* a person who talks too much or indiscreetly.

black (blæk) ADJECTIVE 1 of the colour of jet or carbon black, having no hue due to the absorption of all or nearly all incident light. Compare **white** (sense 1). 2 without light; completely dark. 3 without hope or alleviation; gloomy: *the future looked black*. 4 very dirty or soiled: *black factory chimneys*. 5 angry or resentful: *she gave him black looks*. 6 (of a play or other work) dealing with the unpleasant realities of life, esp in a pessimistic or macabre manner: *black comedy*. 7 (of coffee or tea) without milk or cream. 8 causing, resulting from, or showing great misfortune: *black areas of unemployment*. 9 **a** wicked or harmful: *a black lie*. **b** (*in combination*): *black-hearted*. 10 causing or deserving dishonour or censure: *a black crime*. 11 (of the face) purple, as from suffocation. 12 *Brit* (of goods, jobs, works, etc.) being subject to boycott by trade unionists, esp in support of industrial action elsewhere. ◆ NOUN 13 a black colour. 14 a dye or pigment of or producing this colour. 15 black clothing, worn esp as a sign of mourning. 16 *Chess, draughts* **a** a black or dark-coloured piece or square. **b** (*usually capital*) the player playing with such pieces. 17 complete darkness: *the black of the night*. 18 a black ball in snooker, etc. 19 (in roulette and other gambling games) one of two colours on which players may place even bets, the other being red. 20 **in the black.** in credit or without debt. 21 *Archery* a black ring on a target, between the outer and the blue, scoring three points. ◆ VERB 22 another word for **blacken.** 23 (*tr*) to polish (shoes, etc.) with blacking. 24 (*tr*) to bruise so as to make black: *he blacked her eye*. 25 (*tr*) *Brit, Austral, and NZ* (of trade unionists) to organize a boycott of (specified goods, jobs, work, etc.), esp in support of industrial action elsewhere. See also **blackout.**
▷HISTORY Old English *blæc*; related to Old Saxon *blak* ink, Old High German *blakra* to blink
▸'**blackish** ADJECTIVE ▸'**blackishly** ADVERB ▸'**blackly** ADVERB ▸'**blackness** NOUN

Black (blæk) NOUN 1 *Sometimes derogatory* a

member of a dark-skinned race, esp someone of Negroid or Australoid origin. ◆ ADJECTIVE [2] of or relating to a Black or Blacks: *a Black neighbourhood.*

blackamoor (ˈblækəˌmʊə, -ˌmɔː) NOUN *Archaic* a Black or other person with dark skin.
▷**HISTORY** C16: see BLACK, MOOR

black-and-blue ADJECTIVE [1] (of the skin) discoloured, as from a bruise. [2] feeling pain or soreness, as from a beating.

black and tan NOUN a mixture of stout or porter and ale.

Black and Tans PLURAL NOUN **the.** a specially recruited armed auxiliary police force sent to Ireland in 1921 by the British Government to combat Sinn Féin.
▷**HISTORY** name suggested by the colour of their uniforms and the *Black and Tans* hunt in Munster

black-and-tan terrier NOUN a less common name for **Manchester terrier.**

black-and-white NOUN [1] **a** a photograph, picture, sketch, etc., in black, white, and shades of grey rather than in colour. **b** (*as modifier*): *black-and-white film.* [2] the neutral tones of black, white, and intermediate shades of grey. Compare **colour** (sense 2). [3] **in black and white. a** in print or writing. **b** in extremes: *he always saw things in black and white.*

black art NOUN **the.** another name for **black magic.**

black-backed gull NOUN either of two common black-and-white European coastal gulls, *Larus fuscus* (**lesser black-backed gull**) and *L. marinus* (**great black-backed gull**).

blackball (ˈblækˌbɔːl) NOUN [1] a negative vote or veto. [2] a black wooden ball used to indicate disapproval or to veto in a vote. [3] *NZ* a hard boiled sweet with black-and-white stripes. ◆ VERB (*tr*) [4] to vote against in a ballot. [5] to exclude (someone) from a group, profession, etc.; ostracize.
▷**HISTORY** C18: see sense 2

black bass (bæs) NOUN any of several predatory North American percoid freshwater game fishes of the genus *Micropterus*: family *Centrarchidae* (sunfishes, etc.).

black bean NOUN an Australian leguminous tree, *Castanospermum australe*, having thin smooth bark and yellow or reddish flowers: used in furniture manufacture. Also called: **Moreton Bay chestnut.**

black bear NOUN [1] **American black bear.** a bear, *Euarctos* (or *Ursus*) *americanus*, inhabiting forests of North America. It is smaller and less ferocious than the brown bear. [2] **Asiatic black bear.** a bear, *Selenarctos thibetanus*, of central and E Asia, whose coat is black with a pale V-shaped mark on the chest.

black beetle NOUN another name for the **oriental cockroach** (see **cockroach**).

black belt NOUN [1] *Martial Arts* **a** a black belt worn by an instructor or expert competitor in the dan grades, usually from first to fifth dan. **b** a person entitled to wear this. [2] **the.** a region of the southern US extending from Georgia across central Alabama and Mississippi, in which the population contains a large number of Blacks: also noted for its fertile black soil.

blackberry (ˈblækbərɪ) NOUN, *plural* **-ries.** [1] Also called: **bramble.** any of several woody plants of the rosaceous genus *Rubus*, esp *R. fruticosus*, that have thorny stems and black or purple glossy edible berry-like fruits (drupelets). [2] **a** the fruit of any of these plants. **b** (*as modifier*): *blackberry jam.* [3] **blackberry lily.** an ornamental Chinese iridaceous plant, *Belamcanda chinensis*, that has red-spotted orange flowers and clusters of black seeds that resemble blackberries. ◆ VERB **-ries, -rying, -ried.** [4] (*intr*) to gather blackberries.

black bile NOUN *Archaic* one of the four bodily humours; melancholy. See **humour** (sense 8).

black bindweed NOUN a twining polygonaceous European plant, *Polygonum convolvulus*, with heart-shaped leaves and triangular black seed pods.

blackbird (ˈblækˌbɜːd) NOUN [1] a common European thrush, *Turdus merula*, in which the male has a black plumage and yellow bill and the female is brown. [2] any of various American orioles having a dark plumage, esp any of the genus *Agelaius.* [3] *History* a person, esp a South Sea Islander, who was kidnapped and sold as a slave, esp in Australia. ◆ VERB [4] (*tr*) (formerly) to kidnap and sell into slavery.

Black Bloc *or* **Black Block** NOUN an informal grouping of militant, mainly anarchist, protesters who act together during anti-capitalism, anti-war, etc., protests, often wearing black hoods and black clothing.

blackboard (ˈblækˌbɔːd) NOUN a hard or rigid surface made of a smooth usually dark substance, used for writing or drawing on with chalk, esp in teaching.

black body NOUN *Physics* a hypothetical body that would be capable of absorbing all the electromagnetic radiation falling on it. Also called: **full radiator.**

black book NOUN [1] a book containing the names of people to be punished, blacklisted, etc. [2] **in someone's black books.** *Informal* out of favour with someone.

black bottom NOUN a dance of the late 1920s that originated in America, involving a sinuous rotation of the hips.

black box NOUN [1] a self-contained unit in an electronic or computer system whose circuitry need not be known to understand its function. [2] an informal name for **flight recorder.**

black boy *or* **blackboy** (ˈblækˌbɔɪ) NOUN another name for **grass tree** (sense 1).

black bread NOUN a kind of very dark coarse rye bread.

black bream NOUN [1] another name for **luderick.** [2] a dark-coloured food and game fish, *Acanthopagrus australis*, of E Australian seas.

black bryony NOUN a climbing herbaceous Eurasian plant, *Tamus communis*, having small greenish flowers and poisonous red berries: family *Dioscoreaceae.*

blackbuck (ˈblækˌbʌk) NOUN an Indian antelope, *Antilope cervicapra*, the male of which has spiral horns, a dark back, and a white belly.

black bun NOUN *Scot* a very rich dark fruitcake, usually in a pastry case. Also called: **currant bun.**

Blackburn (ˈblækbɜːn) NOUN [1] a city in NW England, in Blackburn with Darwen unitary authority, Lancashire: formerly important for textiles, now has mixed industries. Pop: 105 994 (1991). [2] **Mount.** a mountain in SE Alaska, the highest peak in the Wrangell Mountains. Height: 5037 m (16 523 ft.).

Blackburn with Darwen (ˈdɑːwɛn) NOUN a unitary authority in NW England, in Lancashire. Pop.: 137 471 (2001). Area: 137 sq. km (53 sq. miles).

blackbutt (ˈblækˌbʌt) NOUN any of various Australian eucalyptus trees having rough fibrous bark and hard wood used as timber.

blackcap (ˈblækˌkæp) NOUN [1] a brownish-grey Old World warbler, *Sylvia atricapilla*, the male of which has a black crown. [2] any of various similar birds, such as the black-capped chickadee (*Parus atricapillus*). [3] *US* a popular name for **raspberry** (sense 3). [4] *Brit* (formerly) the cap worn by a judge when passing a death sentence.

Black Caps PLURAL NOUN **the.** the international cricket team of New Zealand.
▷**HISTORY** C20: so named because of the players' black caps

black-coated ADJECTIVE *Brit* (esp formerly) (of a worker) clerical or professional, as distinguished from commercial or industrial.

blackcock (ˈblækˌkɒk) NOUN the male of the black grouse. Also called: **heath cock.** Compare **greyhen.**

Black Country NOUN **the.** the formerly heavily industrialized region of central England, northwest of Birmingham.

black cuckoo NOUN *Austral* another name for **koel.**

blackcurrant (ˌblækˈkʌrənt) NOUN [1] a N temperate shrub, *Ribes nigrum*, having red or white flowers and small edible black berries: family *Grossulariaceae.* [2] **a** the fruit of this shrub. **b** (*as modifier*): *blackcurrant jelly.*

blackdamp (ˈblækˌdæmp) NOUN air that is low in oxygen content and high in carbon dioxide as a result of an explosion in a mine. Also called: **chokedamp.**

Black Death NOUN **the.** a form of bubonic plague pandemic in Europe and Asia during the 14th century, when it killed over 50 million people. See **bubonic plague.**

black diamond NOUN [1] another name for **carbonado**[2]. [2] (*usually plural*) a figurative expression for **coal.**

black disc NOUN a conventional black vinyl gramophone record as opposed to a compact disc.

black disease NOUN *Vet science* an infectious necrotic hepatitis in sheep and occasionally cattle caused by to toxins produced by infection with species of *Clostridial.* Secondary to liver fluke infestation, the disease is characterized by sudden death. So-called because of the black discolouration of subcutaneous tissues due to congestion and haemorrhage seen at post-mortem.

black dog NOUN *Informal* depression or melancholy.

black earth NOUN another name for **chernozem.**

black economy NOUN that portion of the income of a nation that remains illegally undeclared either as a result of payment in kind or as a means of tax avoidance.

blacken (ˈblækən) VERB [1] to make or become black or dirty. [2] (*tr*) to defame; slander (esp in the phrase **blacken someone's name**).

black eye NOUN bruising round the eye.

black-eyed pea NOUN another name for **cowpea** (sense 2).

black-eyed Susan NOUN [1] any of several North American plants of the genus *Rudbeckia*, esp *R. hirta*, having flower heads of orange-yellow rays and brown-black centres: family *Asteraceae* (composites). [2] a climbing plant, *Thunbergia alata*, native to tropical Africa but widely naturalized elsewhere, having yellow flowers with purple centres, grown as a greenhouse annual.

blackface (ˈblækˌfeɪs) NOUN [1] **a** a performer made up to imitate a Black person. **b** the make-up used by such a performer, usually consisting of burnt cork. [2] a breed of sheep having a dark face.

Black Ferns PLURAL NOUN **the.** the women's international Rugby Union football team of New Zealand.

blackfish (ˈblækˌfɪʃ) NOUN, *plural* **-fish, -fishes.** [1] a minnow-like Alaskan freshwater fish, *Dallia pectoralis*, related to the pikes and thought to be able to survive prolonged freezing. [2] a female salmon that has recently spawned. Compare **redfish** (sense 1). [3] any of various other dark fishes, esp the luderick, a common edible Australian estuary fish. [4] another name for **pilot whale.**

black flag NOUN another name for the **Jolly Roger.**

blackfly (ˈblækˌflaɪ) NOUN, *plural* **-flies.** a black aphid, *Aphis fabae*, that infests beans, sugar beet, and other plants. Also called: **bean aphid.**

black fly NOUN any small blackish stout-bodied dipterous fly of the family *Simuliidae*, which sucks the blood of man, mammals, and birds. See also **buffalo gnat.**

Blackfoot (ˈblækˌfʊt) NOUN [1] (*plural* **-feet** *or* **-foot**) a member of a warlike group of North American Indian peoples formerly living in the northwestern Plains. [2] any of the languages of these peoples, belonging to the Algonquian family.
▷**HISTORY** C19: translation of Blackfoot *Siksika*

Black Forest NOUN **the.** a hilly wooded region of SW Germany, in Baden-Württemberg: a popular resort area. German name: **Schwarzwald.**

Black Friar NOUN a Dominican friar.

black frost NOUN a frost without snow or rime that is severe enough to blacken vegetation.

black game NOUN another name for **black grouse** (sense 1).

black grouse NOUN [1] Also called: **black game.** a large N European grouse, *Lyrurus tetrix*, the male of which has a bluish-black plumage and lyre-shaped tail. [2] a related and similar species, *Lyrurus mlokosiewiczi*, of W Asia.

blackguard (ˈblægɑːd, -gəd) NOUN [1] **a** an unprincipled contemptible person; scoundrel. **b** (*as modifier*): *blackguard language.* ◆ VERB [2] (*tr*) to

ridicule or denounce with abusive language. [3] (*intr*) to behave like a blackguard.
▷HISTORY C16: originally a collective noun referring to the lowest menials in court, camp followers, vagabonds; see BLACK, GUARD
▸ **'blackguardism** NOUN ▸ **'blackguardly** ADJECTIVE

black guillemot NOUN a common guillemot, *Cepphus grylle*: its summer plumage is black with white wing patches and its winter plumage white with greyish wings.

Black Hand NOUN [1] a group of Sicilian blackmailers and terrorists formed in the 1870s and operating in the US in the early 20th century. [2] (in 19th-century Spain) an organization of anarchists.

black hat NOUN *Informal* **a** a computer hacker who carries out illegal malicious hacking work. **b** (*as modifier*): *black-hat hackers*. Compare **white hat.**

blackhead ('blæk,hɛd) NOUN [1] a black-tipped plug of fatty matter clogging a pore of the skin, esp the duct of a sebaceous gland. Technical name: **comedo.** [2] an infectious and often fatal disease of turkeys and some other fowl caused by the parasitic protozoa *Histomonas meleagridis*. Technical name: **infectious enterohepatitis.** [3] any of various birds, esp gulls or ducks, with black plumage on the head.

blackheart ('blæk,hɑ:t) NOUN [1] an abnormal darkening of the woody stems of some plants, thought to be caused by extreme cold. [2] any of various diseases of plants, such as the potato, in which the central tissues are blackened. [3] a variety of cherry that has large sweet fruit with purplish flesh and an almost black skin.

black heat NOUN heat emitted by an electric element made from low-resistance thick wire that does not glow red.

Blackheath ('blækhi:θ) NOUN a residential district in SE London, mainly in the boroughs of Lewisham and Greenwich: a large heath formerly notorious for highwaymen.

Black Hills PLURAL NOUN a group of mountains in W South Dakota and NE Wyoming: famous for the gigantic sculptures of US presidents on the side of Mount Rushmore. Highest peak: Harney Peak, 2207 m (7242 ft.).

black hole *Astronomy* ◆ NOUN [1] an object in space so dense that its escape velocity exceeds the speed of light. [2] any place regarded as resembling a black hole in that items or information entering it cannot be retrieved.

Black Hole of Calcutta NOUN [1] a small dungeon in which in 1756 the Nawab of Bengal reputedly confined 146 English prisoners, of whom only 23 survived. [2] *Informal, chiefly Brit* any uncomfortable or overcrowded place.

black horehound NOUN a hairy unpleasant-smelling chiefly Mediterranean plant, *Ballota nigra*, having clusters of purple flowers: family *Lamiaceae* (labiates).

black house NOUN a type of thatched house, usually made of turf, formerly found in the highlands and islands of Scotland.

black ice NOUN a thin transparent layer of new ice on a road or similar surface.

blacking ('blækɪŋ) NOUN any preparation, esp one containing lampblack, for giving a black finish to shoes, metals, etc.

Black Isle NOUN **the.** a peninsula in NE Scotland, in Highland council area, between the Cromarty and Moray Firths.
▷HISTORY so called because until the late 18th century much of it was uncultivated black moor

blackjack¹ ('blæk,dʒæk) *Chiefly US and Canadian* ◆ NOUN [1] a truncheon of leather-covered lead with a flexible shaft. ◆ VERB [2] (*tr*) to hit with or as if with a blackjack. [3] (*tr*) to compel (a person) by threats.
▷HISTORY C19: from BLACK + JACK¹ (implement)

blackjack² ('blæk,dʒæk) NOUN *Cards* [1] pontoon or any of various similar card games. [2] the ace of spades.
▷HISTORY C20: from BLACK + JACK¹ (the knave)

blackjack³ ('blæk,dʒæk) NOUN a dark iron-rich variety of the mineral sphalerite.
▷HISTORY C18: from BLACK + JACK¹ (originally a miner's name for this useless ore)

blackjack⁴ ('blæk,dʒæk) NOUN a small oak tree, *Quercus marilandica*, of the southeastern US, with blackish bark and fan-shaped leaves. Also called: **blackjack oak.**
▷HISTORY C19: from BLACK + JACK¹ (from the proper name, popularly used in many plant names)

blackjack⁵ ('blæk,dʒæk) NOUN a tarred leather tankard or jug.
▷HISTORY C16: from BLACK + JACK³

black japan NOUN a black bituminous varnish.

black knight NOUN *Commerce* a person or firm that makes an unwelcome takeover bid for a company. Compare **grey knight, white knight.**

black knot NOUN a fungal disease of plums and cherries caused by *Dibotryon morbosum*, characterized by rough black knotlike swellings on the twigs and branches.

black lead (lɛd) NOUN another name for **graphite.**

blackleg ('blækˌlɛg) NOUN [1] Also called: **scab.** *Brit* **a** a person who acts against the interests of a trade union, as by continuing to work during a strike or taking over a striker's job. **b** (*as modifier*): *blackleg labour*. [2] Also called: **black quarter.** an acute infectious disease of cattle, sheep, and pigs, characterized by gas-filled swellings, esp on the legs, caused by *Clostridium* bacteria. [3] *Plant pathol* **a** a fungal disease of cabbages and related plants caused by *Phoma lingam*, characterized by blackening and decay of the lower stems. **b** a similar disease of potatoes, caused by bacteria. [4] a person who cheats in gambling, esp at cards or in racing. ◆ VERB **-legs, -legging, -legged.** [5] *Brit* to act against the interests of a trade union, esp by refusing to join a strike.

black letter NOUN *Printing* another name for **Gothic** (sense 10).

black light NOUN the invisible electromagnetic radiation in the ultraviolet and infrared regions of the spectrum.

blacklist ('blæk,lɪst) NOUN [1] a list of persons or organizations under suspicion, or considered untrustworthy, disloyal, etc., esp one compiled by a government or an organization. ◆ VERB [2] (*tr*) to put on a blacklist.
▸ **'black,listing** NOUN

black lung NOUN another name for **pneumoconiosis.**

black magic NOUN magic used for evil purposes by invoking the power of the devil.

blackmail ('blæk,meɪl) NOUN [1] the act of attempting to obtain money by intimidation, as by threats to disclose discreditable information. [2] the exertion of pressure or threats, esp unfairly, in an attempt to influence someone's actions. ◆ VERB (*tr*) [3] to exact or attempt to exact (money or anything of value) from (a person) by threats or intimidation; extort. [4] to attempt to influence the actions of (a person), esp by unfair pressure or threats.
▷HISTORY C16: see BLACK, MAIL³
▸ **'blackmailer** NOUN

Black Maria (mə'raɪə) NOUN a police van for transporting prisoners.

black mark NOUN an indication of disapproval, failure, etc.

black market NOUN [1] **a** any system in which goods or currencies are sold and bought illegally, esp in violation of controls or rationing. **b** (*as modifier*): *black market lamb*. [2] the place where such a system operates. ◆ VERB **black-market.** [3] to sell (goods) on the black market.
▸ **black marketeer** NOUN

black mass NOUN (*sometimes capitals*) a blasphemous travesty of the Christian Mass, performed by practitioners of black magic.

black measles PLURAL NOUN (*often functioning as singular*) a severe form of measles characterized by dark eruptions caused by bleeding under the skin.

black medick NOUN a small European leguminous plant, *Medicago lupulina*, with trifoliate leaves, small yellow flowers, and black pods. Also called: **nonesuch.**

black money NOUN [1] that part of a nation's income that relates to its black economy. [2] any money that a person or organization acquires illegally, as by a means that involves tax evasion. [3] *US* money to fund a government project that is concealed in the cost of some other project.

Black Monk NOUN a Benedictine monk.

black mould NOUN another name for **bread mould.**

Black Mountain NOUN **the.** a mountain range in S Wales, in E Carmarthenshire and W Powys. Highest peak: Carmarthen Van, 802 m (2632 ft.).

Black Mountains PLURAL NOUN a mountain range running from N Monmouthshire and SE Powys (Wales) to SW Herefordshire (England). Highest peak: Waun Fach, 811 m (2660 ft.).

Black Muslim NOUN (esp in the US) a member of a political and religious movement of Black people who adopt the religious practices of Islam and seek to establish a new Black nation. Official name: **Nation of Islam.**

black mustard NOUN a Eurasian plant, *Brassica* (or *Sinapsis*) *nigra*, with clusters of yellow flowers and pungent seeds from which the condiment mustard is made: family *Brassicaceae* (crucifers).

black nightshade NOUN a poisonous solanaceous plant, *Solanum nigrum*, a common weed in cultivated land, having small white flowers with backward-curved petals and black berry-like fruits.

black opal NOUN any opal of a dark coloration, not necessarily black.

blackout ('blækaʊt) NOUN [1] the extinguishing or hiding of all artificial light, esp in a city visible to an enemy attack from the air. [2] a momentary loss of consciousness, vision, or memory. [3] a temporary electrical power failure or cut. [4] *Electronics* a temporary loss of sensitivity in a valve following a short strong pulse. [5] a temporary loss of radio communications between a spacecraft and earth, esp on re-entry into the earth's atmosphere. [6] the suspension of radio or television broadcasting, as by a strike or for political reasons. ◆ VERB **black out.** (*adverb*) [7] (*tr*) to obliterate or extinguish (lights). [8] (*tr*) to create a blackout in (a city etc.). [9] (*intr*) to lose vision, consciousness, or memory temporarily. [10] (*tr, adverb*) to stop (news, a television programme) from being released or broadcast.

black pad NOUN *Midland English dialect* a rough road or track.

Black Panther NOUN (in the US) a member of a militant Black political party founded in 1965 to end the political dominance of Whites.

black pepper NOUN a pungent condiment made by grinding the dried unripe berries, together with their black husks, of the pepper plant *Piper nigrum*.

black pine NOUN See **matai.**

blackpoll ('blæk,pəʊl) NOUN a North American warbler, *Dendroica striata*, the male of which has a black-and-white head.

Blackpool ('blæk,pu:l) NOUN [1] a town and resort in NW England, in Blackpool unitary authority, Lancashire on the Irish Sea: famous for its tower, 158 m (518 ft.) high, and its illuminations. Pop.: 146 262 (1991). [2] a unitary authority in NW England, in Lancashire. Pop.: 142 284 (2001). Area: 35 sq. km (13 sq. miles).

black powder NOUN another name for **gunpowder.**

Black Power NOUN a social, economic, and political movement of Black people, esp in the US, to obtain equality with Whites.

black propaganda NOUN propaganda that does not come from the source it claims to come from. Compare **grey propaganda, white propaganda.**

black pudding NOUN a kind of black sausage made from minced pork fat, pig's blood, and other ingredients. Also called: **blood pudding.** Usual US and Canadian name: **blood sausage.**

black quarter NOUN another name for **blackleg** (sense 2).

black rat NOUN a common rat, *Rattus rattus*: a household pest that has spread from its native Asia to all countries.

Black Rod NOUN [1] (in Britain) an officer of the House of Lords and of the Order of the Garter, whose main duty is summoning the Commons at the opening and proroguing of Parliament. [2] a similar officer in any of certain other legislatures.

black rot NOUN any of various plant diseases of fruits and vegetables, producing blackening, rotting, and shrivelling and caused by bacteria (including *Xanthomonas campestris*) and fungi (such as *Physalospora malorum*).

black run NOUN *Skiing* an extremely difficult run, suitable for expert skiers.

black rust NOUN a stage in any of several diseases of cereals and grasses caused by rust fungi in which black masses of spores appear on the stems or leaves.

Black Sash NOUN (formerly, in South Africa) an organization of women opposed to apartheid.

Black Sea NOUN an inland sea between SE Europe and Asia: connected to the Aegean Sea by the Bosporus, the Sea of Marmara, and the Dardanelles, and to the Sea of Azov by the Kerch Strait. Area: about 415 000 sq. km (160 000 sq. miles). Also called: **Euxine Sea.** Ancient name: **Pontus Euxinus.**

black section NOUN (in Britain) an unofficial group within the Labour Party in any constituency that represents the interests of local Black people.

black sheep NOUN a person who is regarded as a disgrace or failure by his family or peer group.

Blackshirt ('blæk,ʃɜːt) NOUN (in Europe) a member of a fascist organization, esp a member of the Italian Fascist party before and during World War II.

blacksmith ('blæk,smɪθ) NOUN an artisan who works iron with a furnace, anvil, hammer, etc.
▷HISTORY C14: see BLACK, SMITH

blacksnake ('blæk,sneɪk) NOUN 1 any of several Old World black venomous elapid snakes, esp *Pseudechis porphyriacus* (**Australian blacksnake**). 2 any of various dark nonvenomous snakes, such as *Coluber constrictor* (black racer). 3 *US and Canadian* a long heavy pliant whip of braided leather or rawhide.

black spot NOUN 1 a place on a road where accidents frequently occur. 2 any dangerous or difficult place. 3 a disease of roses, *Diplocarpon rosae*, that causes circular black blotches on the leaves.

black spruce NOUN a coniferous tree, *Picea mariana*, of the northern regions of North America, growing mostly in cold bogs and having dark green needles. Also called: **spruce pine.**

blackstrap molasses ('blæk,stræp) PLURAL NOUN (*functioning as singular*) the molasses remaining after the maximum quantity of sugar has been extracted from the raw material.

black stump NOUN 1 **the.** *Austral* an imaginary marker of the extent of civilization (esp in the phrase **beyond the black stump**). 2 *NZ* a long way off.

black swan NOUN a large Australian swan, *Cygnus atratus*, that has a black plumage and red bill.

blacktail ('blæk,teɪl) NOUN a variety of mule deer having a black tail.

blackthorn ('blæk,θɔːn) NOUN 1 Also called: **sloe.** a thorny Eurasian rosaceous shrub, *Prunus spinosa*, with black twigs, white flowers, and small sour plumlike fruits. 2 a walking stick made from its wood.

black tie NOUN 1 a black bow tie worn with a dinner jacket. 2 (*modifier*) denoting an occasion when a dinner jacket should be worn. ◆ Compare **white tie.**

blacktop ('blæk,tɒp) NOUN *Chiefly US and Canadian* 1 a bituminous mixture used for paving. 2 a road paved with this mixture.

black tracker NOUN *Austral* an Aboriginal tracker working for the police.

black treacle NOUN *Brit* another term for **treacle** (sense 1).

black velvet NOUN 1 a mixture of stout and champagne in equal proportions. 2 *Austral slang* Aboriginal women as sexual partners.

Black Volta NOUN a river in W Africa, rising in SW Burkina-Faso and flowing northeast, then south into Lake Volta: forms part of the border of Ghana with Burkina-Faso and with the Ivory Coast. Length: about 800 km (500 miles).

black vomit NOUN 1 vomit containing blood, often a manifestation of disease, such as yellow fever. 2 *Informal* yellow fever.

Blackwall hitch ('blæk,wɔːl) NOUN a knot for hooking tackle to the end of a rope, holding fast when pulled but otherwise loose.
▷HISTORY C19: named after *Blackwall*, former docks in London

black walnut NOUN 1 a North American walnut tree, *Juglans nigra*, with hard dark wood and edible oily nuts. 2 the valuable wood of this tree, used for cabinet work. 3 the nut of this tree. ◆ Compare **butternut** (senses 1–4).

Black Watch NOUN **the.** the Royal Highland Regiment in the British army.
▷HISTORY so called for their dark tartan

black-water fever NOUN *Vet science* a form of babesiosis seen in cattle, deer, bison, water buffalo, African buffalo, and reindeer; characterized by fever, depression, jaundice, dark red-black discolouration of the urine, anaemia, and death. Also called: **Texas fever.**

blackwater rafting NOUN *NZ* the sport of riding through underground caves on a large rubber tube. Also called: **cave tubing.**

black wattle NOUN 1 a small Australian acacia tree, *A. mearnsii*, with yellow flowers. 2 a tall Australian shrub, *Callicoma serratifolia*.

black whale NOUN another name for **pilot whale.**

black widow NOUN an American spider, *Latrodectus mactans*, the female of which is black with red markings, highly venomous, and commonly eats its mate.

blackwood ('blæk,wʊd) NOUN 1 Also called: **Sally Wattle.** a tall Australian acacia tree, *A. melanoxylon*, having small clusters of flowers and curved pods and yielding highly valued black timber. 2 any of various trees or shrubs of the leguminous genus *Dalbergia*, esp *D. melanoxylon* (of Africa) or *D. latifolia* (of India), yielding black wood used for carving and musical instruments. 3 the wood of any of these trees.

Blackwood ('blæk,wʊd) NOUN *Bridge* a conventional bidding sequence of four and five no-trumps, which are requests to the partner to show aces and kings respectively.
▷HISTORY C20: named after Easeley F. *Blackwood*, its American inventor

bladder ('blædə) NOUN 1 *Anatomy* a distensible membranous sac, usually containing liquid or gas, esp the urinary bladder. Related adjective: **vesical.** 2 an inflatable part of something. 3 a blister, cyst, vesicle, etc., usually filled with fluid. 4 a hollow vesicular or saclike part or organ in certain plants, such as the bladderwort or bladderwrack.
▷HISTORY Old English *blǣdre*
▸'**bladdery** ADJECTIVE

bladder campion NOUN a European caryophyllaceous plant, *Silene vulgaris*, having white flowers with an inflated calyx.

bladdered ('bladəd) ADJECTIVE *Slang* intoxicated; drunk.

bladder fern NOUN a small fern, *Cystoperis fragilis*, with graceful lanceolate leaves, typically growing on limestone rocks and walls.
▷HISTORY C19: named from the bladder-shaped indusium

bladder ketmia ('kɛtmɪə) NOUN another name for **flower-of-an-hour.**

bladdernose ('blædə,nəʊz) NOUN another name for **hooded seal.**

bladdernut ('blædə,nʌt) NOUN 1 any temperate shrub or small tree of the genus *Staphylea*, esp *S. pinnata* of S Europe, that has bladder-like seed pods: family *Staphyleaceae*. 2 the pod of any such tree.

bladder senna NOUN a Eurasian leguminous plant, *Colutea arborescens*, with yellow and red flowers and membranous inflated pods.

bladder worm NOUN an encysted saclike larva of the tapeworm. The main types are cysticercus, hydatid and coenurus.

bladderwort ('blædə,wɜːt) NOUN any aquatic plant of the genus *Utricularia*, some of whose leaves are modified as small bladders to trap minute aquatic animals: family *Lentibulariaceae*.

bladderwrack ('blædə,ræk) NOUN any of several seaweeds of the genera *Fucus* and *Ascophyllum*, esp *F. vesiculosus*, that grow in the intertidal regions of rocky shores and have branched brown fronds with air bladders.

blade (bleɪd) NOUN 1 the part of a sharp weapon, tool, etc., that forms the cutting edge. 2 (*plural*) *Austral and NZ* hand shears used for shearing sheep. 3 the thin flattish part of various tools, implements, etc., as of a propeller, turbine, etc. 4 the flattened expanded part of a leaf, sepal, or petal. 5 the long narrow leaf of a grass or related plant. 6 the striking surface of a bat, club, stick, or oar. 7 the metal runner on an ice skate. 8 *Archaeol* a long thin flake of flint, possibly used as a tool. 9 the upper part of the tongue lying directly behind the tip. 10 *Archaic* a dashing or swaggering young man. 11 short for **shoulder blade.** 12 a poetic word for a **sword** or **swordsman.**
▷HISTORY Old English *blæd*; related to Old Norse *blath* leaf, Old High German *blat*, Latin *folium* leaf
▸'**bladed** ADJECTIVE

blade grader NOUN another name for **grader** (sense 2).

blade-shearing NOUN *NZ* the shearing of sheep using hand shears.
▸'**blade-**,**shearer** NOUN

blade slap NOUN the regular noise beat generated by the rotor blades of a helicopter.

blading NOUN the act or an instance of skating with in-line skates.

blady grass ('bleɪdɪ) NOUN a coarse leafy Australasian grass, *Imperata cylindrica*.

blae (ble, bleɪ) ADJECTIVE *Scot* bluish-grey; slate-coloured.
▷HISTORY from Old Norse *blár*

blaeberry ('bleɪbərɪ) NOUN, *plural* **-ries.** *Brit* another name for **bilberry** (senses 1, 2).
▷HISTORY C15: from BLAE + BERRY

Blaenau Gwent ('blaɪ,naʊ 'gwɛnt) NOUN a county borough of SE Wales, created in 1996 from NW Gwent. Administrative centre: Ebbw Vale. Pop.: 76 058 (2001). Area: 109 sq. km (42 sq. miles).

blaes (blez, bleɪz) NOUN *Scot* **a** hardened clay or shale, esp when crushed and used to form the top layer of a sports pitch: bluish-grey or reddish in colour. **b** (*as modifier*): *a blaes pitch*.
▷HISTORY C18: from BLAE

blag (blæg) *Slang* ◆ NOUN 1 a robbery, esp with violence. ◆ VERB **blags, blagging, blagged.** (*tr*) 2 to obtain by wheedling or cadging: *she blagged free tickets from her mate.* 3 to snatch (wages, someone's handbag, etc.); steal. 4 to rob (esp a bank or post office).
▷HISTORY C19: of unknown origin
▸'**blagger** NOUN

Blagoveshchensk (*Russian* bləga'vjeʃtʃɪnsk) NOUN a city and port in E Russia, in Siberia on the Amur River. Pop.: 220 900 (1999 est.).

blague (blɑːg) NOUN pretentious but empty talk; nonsense.
▷HISTORY C19: from French
▸'**blaguer** NOUN

blah *or* **blah blah** (blɑː) *Slang* ◆ NOUN 1 worthless or silly talk; claptrap. ◆ ADJECTIVE 2 uninteresting; insipid. ◆ VERB 3 (*intr*) to talk nonsense or boringly.

blain (bleɪn) NOUN a blister, blotch, or sore on the skin.
▷HISTORY Old English *blegen*; related to Middle Low German *bleine*

Blairite ('blɛəraɪt) ADJECTIVE 1 of or relating to the modernizing policies of Tony Blair (full name *Anthony Charles Lynton Blair*; born 1953), British Labour politician and prime minister from 1997. ◆ NOUN 2 a supporter of the modernizing policies of Tony Blair.

Blair's babes PLURAL NOUN *Informal* (in Britain) the female Members of Parliament elected as part of Prime Minister Tony Blair's Labour government in 1997.

blame (bleɪm) NOUN 1 responsibility for something that is wrong or deserving censure; culpability. 2 an expression of condemnation; reproof. 3 **be to blame.** to be at fault or culpable. ◆ VERB (*tr*) 4 (usually foll by *for*) to attribute responsibility to; accuse: *I blame him for the failure.* 5 (usually foll by *on*) to ascribe responsibility for (something) to: *I blame the failure on him.* 6 to find fault with.
▷HISTORY C12: from Old French *blasmer*, ultimately from Late Latin *blasphēmāre* to BLASPHEME
▸'**blamable** *or* '**blameable** ADJECTIVE ▸'**blamably** *or* '**blameably** ADVERB

blamed (bleɪmd) ADJECTIVE, ADVERB *Chiefly US* a euphemistic word for **damned** (senses 2, 3).

blameful ('bleɪmfʊl) ADJECTIVE deserving blame; guilty.

▸'**blamefully** ADVERB ▸'**blamefulness** NOUN

blameless ('bleɪmlɪs) ADJECTIVE free from blame; innocent.
▸'**blamelessly** ADVERB ▸'**blamelessness** NOUN

blameworthy ('bleɪm,wɜːðɪ) ADJECTIVE deserving disapproval or censure.
▸'**blame,worthiness** NOUN

Blanc (*French* blɑ̃) NOUN [1] **Mont**. See **Mont Blanc**. [2] **Cape**. a headland in N Tunisia: the northernmost point of Africa. [3] **Cape**. Also called: **Cape Blanco** ('blæŋkəʊ). a peninsula in Mauritania, on the Atlantic coast.

blanc fixe *French* (blɑ̃ fiks) NOUN another name for **barium sulphate**.
▷HISTORY literally: fixed white

blanch (blɑːntʃ) VERB (*mainly tr*) [1] (*also intr*) to remove colour from, or (of colour) to be removed; whiten; fade: *the sun blanched the carpet; over the years the painting blanched*. [2] (*usually intr*) to become or cause to become pale, as with sickness or fear. [3] to plunge tomatoes, nuts, etc., into boiling water to loosen the skin. [4] to plunge (meat, green vegetables, etc.) in boiling water or bring to the boil in water in order to whiten, preserve the natural colour, or reduce or remove a bitter or salty taste. [5] to cause (celery, chicory, etc.) to grow free of chlorophyll by the exclusion of sunlight. [6] *Metallurgy* to whiten (a metal), usually by treating it with an acid or by coating it with tin. [7] (*tr*, usually foll by *over*) to attempt to conceal something.
▷HISTORY C14: from Old French *blanchir* from *blanc* white; see BLANK

blancmange (blə'mɒnʒ) NOUN a jelly-like dessert, stiffened usually with cornflour and set in a mould.
▷HISTORY C14: from Old French *blanc manger*, literally: white food

bland (blænd) ADJECTIVE [1] devoid of any distinctive or stimulating characteristics; uninteresting; dull: *bland food*. [2] gentle and agreeable; suave. [3] (of the weather) mild and soothing. [4] unemotional or unmoved: *a bland account of atrocities*. ◆ See also **bland out**.
▷HISTORY C15: from Latin *blandus* flattering
▸'**blandly** ADVERB ▸'**blandness** NOUN

blandish ('blændɪʃ) VERB (*tr*) to seek to persuade or influence by mild flattery; coax.
▷HISTORY C14: from Old French *blandir* from Latin *blandīrī*

blandishments ('blændɪʃmənts) PLURAL NOUN (*rarely singular*) flattery intended to coax or cajole.

bland out VERB (*intr, adverb*) *Informal* to become bland.

blank (blæŋk) ADJECTIVE [1] (of a writing surface) bearing no marks; not written on. [2] (of a form, etc.) with spaces left for details to be filled in. [3] without ornament or break; unrelieved: *a blank wall*. [4] not filled in; empty; void: *a blank space*. [5] exhibiting no interest or expression: *a blank look*. [6] lacking understanding; confused: *he looked blank even after the explanations*. [7] absolute; complete: *blank rejection*. [8] devoid of ideas or inspiration: *his mind went blank in the exam*. [9] unproductive; barren. ◆ NOUN [10] an emptiness; void; blank space. [11] an empty space for writing in, as on a printed form. [12] a printed form containing such empty spaces. [13] something characterized by incomprehension or mental confusion: *my mind went a complete blank*. [14] a mark, often a dash, in place of a word, esp a taboo word. [15] short for **blank cartridge**. [16] a plate or plug used to seal an aperture. [17] a piece of material prepared for stamping, punching, forging, etc. [18] *Archery* the white spot in the centre of a target. [19] **draw a blank**. **a** to choose a lottery ticket that fails to win. **b** to get no results from something. ◆ VERB (*tr*) [20] (usually foll by *out*) to cross out, blot, or obscure. [21] *Slang* to ignore or be unresponsive towards (someone): *the crowd blanked her for the first four numbers*. [22] to forge, stamp, punch, or cut (a piece of material) in preparation for forging, die-stamping, or drawing operations. [23] (often foll by *off*) to seal (an aperture) with a plate or plug. [24] *US and Canadian informal* to prevent (an opponent) from scoring in a game.
▷HISTORY C15: from Old French *blanc* white, of Germanic origin; related to Old English *blanca* a white horse
▸'**blankly** ADVERB ▸'**blankness** NOUN

blank cartridge NOUN a cartridge containing powder but no bullet: used in battle practice or as a signal.

blank cheque NOUN [1] a signed cheque on which the amount payable has not been specified. [2] complete freedom of action.

blank endorsement NOUN an endorsement on a bill of exchange, cheque, etc., naming no payee and thus making the endorsed sum payable to the bearer. Also called: **endorsement in blank**.

blanket ('blæŋkɪt) NOUN [1] a large piece of thick cloth for use as a bed covering, animal covering, etc., enabling a person or animal to retain much of his natural body heat. [2] a concealing cover or layer, as of smoke, leaves, or snow. [3] a rubber or plastic sheet wrapped round a cylinder, used in offset printing to transfer the image from the plate, stone, or forme to the paper. [4] *Physics* a layer of a fertile substance placed round the core of a nuclear reactor as a reflector or absorber and often to breed new fissionable fuel. [5] (*modifier*) applying to or covering a wide group or variety of people, conditions, situations, etc.: *blanket insurance against loss, injury, and theft*. [6] (**born**) **on the wrong side of the blanket**. *Informal* illegitimate. ◆ VERB (*tr*) [7] to cover with or as if with a blanket; overlie. [8] to cover a very wide area, as in a publicity campaign; give blanket coverage. [9] (usually foll by *out*) to obscure or suppress: *the storm blanketed out the TV picture*. [10] *Nautical* to prevent wind from reaching the sails of (another sailing vessel) by passing to windward of it.
▷HISTORY C13: from Old French *blancquete*, from *blanc*; see BLANK

blanket bath NOUN an all-over wash given to a person confined to bed.

blanket bog NOUN a very acid peat bog, low in nutrients, extending widely over a flat terrain, found in cold wet climates.

blanket finish NOUN *Athletics, horse racing* a finish so close that a blanket would cover all the contestants involved.

blanket stitch NOUN a strong reinforcing stitch for the edges of blankets and other thick material.

blankety ('blæŋkɪtɪ) ADJECTIVE, ADVERB a euphemism for any taboo word.
▷HISTORY C20: from BLANK

blank verse NOUN *Prosody* unrhymed verse, esp in iambic pentameters.

blanquette de veau (blæŋ'ket də 'vəʊ) NOUN a ragout or stew of veal in a white sauce.
▷HISTORY French

Blantyre-Limbe (blæn'taɪə'lɪmbeɪ) NOUN a city in S Malawi: largest city in the country; formed in 1956 from the adjoining towns of Blantyre and Limbe. Pop.: 478 155 (1998 est.).

blare (bleə) VERB [1] to sound loudly and harshly. [2] to proclaim loudly and sensationally. ◆ NOUN [3] a loud and usually harsh or grating noise.
▷HISTORY C14: from Middle Dutch *bleren*; of imitative origin

blarney ('blɑːnɪ) NOUN [1] flattering talk. ◆ VERB [2] to cajole with flattery; wheedle.
▷HISTORY C19: after the BLARNEY STONE

Blarney Stone NOUN a stone in **Blarney Castle**, in the SW Republic of Ireland, said to endow whoever kisses it with skill in flattery.

blart (blæt) VERB (*intr*) *English dialect* to sound loudly and harshly.

blasé ('blɑːzeɪ) ADJECTIVE [1] indifferent to something because of familiarity or surfeit. [2] lacking enthusiasm; bored.
▷HISTORY C19: from French, past participle of *blaser* to cloy

blaspheme (blæs'fiːm) VERB [1] (*tr*) to show contempt or disrespect for (God, a divine being, or sacred things), esp in speech. [2] (*intr*) to utter profanities, curses, or impious expressions.
▷HISTORY C14: from Late Latin *blasphēmāre*, from Greek *blasphēmein* from *blasphēmos* BLASPHEMOUS
▸**blas'phemer** NOUN

blasphemous ('blæsfɪməs) ADJECTIVE expressing or involving impiousness or gross irreverence towards God, a divine being, or something sacred.
▷HISTORY C15: via Late Latin, from Greek *blasphēmos* evil-speaking, from *blapsis* evil + *phēmē* speech

▸'**blasphemously** ADVERB

blasphemy ('blæsfɪmɪ) NOUN, *plural* **-mies**. [1] blasphemous behaviour or language. [2] Also called: **blasphemous libel**. *Law* the crime committed if a person insults, offends, or vilifies the deity, Christ, or the Christian religion.

blast (blɑːst) NOUN [1] an explosion, as of dynamite. [2] **a** the rapid movement of air away from the centre of an explosion, combustion of rocket fuel, etc. **b** a wave of overpressure caused by an explosion; shock wave. [3] the charge of explosive used in a single explosion. [4] a sudden strong gust of wind or air. [5] a sudden loud sound, as of a trumpet. [6] a violent verbal outburst, as of criticism. [7] a forcible jet or stream of air, esp one used to intensify the heating effect of a furnace, increase the draught in a steam engine, or break up coal at a coalface. [8] any of several diseases of plants and animals, esp one producing withering in plants. [9] *US slang* a very enjoyable or thrilling experience: *the party was a blast*. [10] (**at**) **full blast**. at maximum speed, volume etc. ◆ INTERJECTION [11] *Slang* an exclamation of annoyance (esp in phrases such as **blast it! blast him!**). ◆ VERB [12] to destroy or blow up with explosives, shells, etc. [13] to make or cause to make a loud harsh noise. [14] (*tr*) to remove, open, etc., by an explosion: *to blast a hole in a wall*. [15] (*tr*) to ruin; shatter: *the rain blasted our plans for a picnic*. [16] to wither or cause to wither; blight or be blighted. [17] to criticize severely. [18] to shoot or shoot at: *he blasted the hat off her head; he blasted away at the trees*. ◆ See also **blastoff**.
▷HISTORY Old English *blǣst*, related to Old Norse *blāstr*
▸'**blaster** NOUN

-blast NOUN COMBINING FORM (in biology) indicating an embryonic cell or formative layer: *mesoblast*.
▷HISTORY from Greek *blastos* bud

blasted ('blɑːstɪd) ADJECTIVE [1] blighted or withered. ◆ ADJECTIVE (*prenominal*), ADVERB [2] *Slang* (intensifier): *a blasted idiot*.

blastema (blæ'stiːmə) NOUN, *plural* **-mas** *or* **-mata** (-mətə). a mass of undifferentiated animal cells that will develop into an organ or tissue: present at the site of regeneration of a lost part.
▷HISTORY C19: from New Latin, from Greek: offspring, from *blastos* bud
▸**blastemic** (blæ'stiːmɪk, -'stem-) ADJECTIVE

blast furnace NOUN a vertical cylindrical furnace for smelting iron, copper, lead, and tin ores. The ore, scrap, solid fuel, and slag-forming materials are fed through the top and a blast of preheated air is forced through the charge from the bottom. Metal and slag are run off from the base.

blast-furnace cement NOUN a type of cement made from a blend of ordinary Portland cement and crushed slag from a blast furnace. It has lower setting properties than ordinary Portland cement.

blasting ('blɑːstɪŋ) NOUN a distortion of sound caused by overloading certain components of a radio system.

blast injection NOUN the injection of liquid fuel directly into the cylinder of an internal-combustion engine using a blast of high-pressure air to atomize the spray of fuel. Compare **solid injection**.

blasto- COMBINING FORM (in biology) indicating an embryo or bud or the process of budding: *blastoderm*.
▷HISTORY from Greek *blastos*. See -BLAST

blastocoel *or* **blastocoele** ('blæstəʊ,siːl) NOUN *Embryol* the cavity within a blastula. Also called: **segmentation cavity**.

blastocyst ('blæstəʊ,sɪst) NOUN *Embryol* [1] Also called: **blastosphere**. the blastula of mammals: a sphere of cells (trophoblast) enclosing an inner mass of cells and a fluid-filled cavity (blastocoel). [2] another name for **germinal vesicle**.

blastoderm ('blæstəʊ,dɜːm) NOUN *Embryol* [1] the layer of cells that surrounds the blastocoel of a blastula. [2] a flat disc of cells formed after cleavage in a heavily yolked egg, such as a bird's egg. Also called: **blastodisc**.
▸,**blasto'dermic** ADJECTIVE

blastodisc ('blæstəʊ,dɪsk) NOUN another name for **blastoderm**.

blastoff ('blɑːst,ɒf) NOUN [1] the launching of a rocket under its own power. [2] the time at which this occurs. ◆ VERB **blast off**. [3] (*adverb; when tr*, usually passive) (of a rocket, spacemen, etc.) to be launched.

blastogenesis (ˌblæstəʊˈdʒɛnɪsɪs) NOUN 1 the theory that inherited characteristics are transmitted only by germ plasm. See also **pangenesis.** 2 asexual reproduction, esp budding.
▸ ˌ**blastoˈgenic** *or* ˌ**blastogeˈnetic** ADJECTIVE

blastoma (ˌblæsˈtəʊmə) NOUN, *plural* **-mata** *or* **-mas.** *Pathol* **a** a tumour composed of embryonic tissue that has not yet developed a specialized function. **b** (*in combination*): *neuroblastoma*.
▹HISTORY C20: New Latin, from BLASTO- + -OMA

blastomere (ˈblæstəʊˌmɪə) NOUN *Embryol* any of the cells formed by cleavage of a fertilized egg.
▸ **blastomeric** (ˌblæstəʊˈmɛrɪk) ADJECTIVE

blastopor (ˈblæstəʊˌpɔː) NOUN *Embryol* the opening of the archenteron in the gastrula that develops into the anus of some animals.
▸ ˌ**blastoˈporic** *or* ˌ**blastoˈporal** ADJECTIVE

blastosphere (ˈblæstəʊˌsfɪə) NOUN 1 another name for **blastula.** 2 another name for **blastocyst** (sense 1).

blastospore (ˈblæstəʊˌspɔː) NOUN *Botany* a spore formed by budding, as in certain fungi.

blastula (ˈblæstjʊlə) NOUN, *plural* **-las** *or* **-lae** (-liː). an early form of an animal embryo that develops from a morula, consisting of a sphere of cells with a central cavity. Also called: **blastosphere.**
▹HISTORY C19: New Latin; see BLASTO-
▸ ˈ**blastular** ADJECTIVE

blastulation (ˌblæstjʊˈleɪʃən) NOUN *Embryol* the process of blastula formation.

blat (blæt) VERB **blats, blatting, blatted.** *US and Canadian* 1 (*intr*) to cry out or bleat like a sheep. 2 (*tr*) to utter indiscreetly in a loud voice.
▹HISTORY C19: of imitative origin

blatant (ˈbleɪtᵊnt) ADJECTIVE 1 glaringly conspicuous or obvious: *a blatant lie*. 2 offensively noticeable: *blatant disregard for a person's feelings*. 3 offensively noisy.
▹HISTORY C16: coined by Edmund Spenser; probably influenced by Latin *blatīre* to babble; compare Middle Low German *pladderen*
▸ ˈ**blatancy** NOUN ▸ ˈ**blatantly** ADVERB

blather (ˈblæðə) *or Scot* **blether** VERB 1 (*intr*) to speak foolishly. ◆ NOUN 2 foolish talk; nonsense. 3 a person who blathers.
▹HISTORY C15: from Old Norse *blathra*, from *blathr* nonsense

blatherskite (ˈblæðəˌskaɪt) NOUN 1 a talkative silly person. 2 foolish talk; nonsense.
▹HISTORY C17: see BLATHER, SKATE[3]

blatted (ˈblætɪd) ADJECTIVE *Slang* drunk.
▹HISTORY C20: of uncertain origin

Blaue Reiter *German* (ˈblauə ˈraitər) NOUN **der.** a group of German expressionist painters formed in Munich in 1911, including Kandinsky and Klee, who sought to express the spiritual side of man and nature, which they felt had been neglected by impressionism.
▹HISTORY C20: literally: blue rider, name adopted by Kandinsky and Marc because they liked the colour blue, horses, and riders

blaxploitation (ˌblæksplɔɪˈteɪʃən) NOUN a genre of films featuring Black stereotypes.
▹HISTORY C20: from BLA(CK) + (E)XPLOITATION

Blaydon (ˈbleɪdᵊn) NOUN an industrial town in NE England, in Gateshead unitary authority, Tyne and Wear. Pop: 15 510 (1991).

blaze[1] (bleɪz) NOUN 1 a strong fire or flame. 2 a very bright light or glare. 3 an outburst (of passion, acclaim, patriotism, etc.). 4 brilliance; brightness. ◆ VERB (*intr*) 5 to burn fiercely. 6 to shine brightly. 7 (often foll by *up*) to become stirred, as with anger or excitement. 8 (usually foll by *away*) to shoot continuously. ◆ See also **blazes.**
▹HISTORY Old English *blæse*

blaze[2] (bleɪz) NOUN 1 a mark, usually indicating a path, made on a tree, esp by chipping off the bark. 2 a light-coloured marking on the face of a domestic animal, esp a horse. ◆ VERB (*tr*) 3 to indicate or mark (a tree, path, etc.) with a blaze. 4 **blaze a trail.** to explore new territories, areas of knowledge, etc., in such a way that others can follow.
▹HISTORY C17: probably from Middle Low German *bles* white marking; compare BLEMISH

blaze[3] (bleɪz) VERB (*tr*; often foll by *abroad*) to make widely known; proclaim.
▹HISTORY C14: from Middle Dutch *blāsen*, from Old High German *blāsan*; related to Old Norse *blāsa*

blazer (ˈbleɪzə) NOUN a fairly lightweight jacket, often striped or in the colours of a sports club, school, etc.

blazes (ˈbleɪzɪz) PLURAL NOUN 1 *Slang* a euphemistic word for **hell** (esp in the phrase **go to blazes**). 2 *Informal* (intensifier): *to run like blazes; what the blazes are you doing?*

blazing star NOUN *US* 1 a North American liliaceous plant, *Chamaelirium luteum*, with a long spike of small white flowers. 2 any plant of the North American genus *Liatris*, having clusters of small red or purple flowers: family *Asteraceae* (composites).

blazon (ˈbleɪzᵊn) VERB (*tr*) 1 (often foll by *abroad*) to proclaim loudly and publicly. 2 *Heraldry* to describe (heraldic arms) in proper terms. 3 to draw and colour (heraldic arms) conventionally. ◆ NOUN 4 *Heraldry* a conventional description or depiction of heraldic arms. 5 any description or recording, esp of good qualities.
▹HISTORY C13: from Old French *blason* coat of arms
▸ ˈ**blazoner** NOUN

blazonry (ˈbleɪzənrɪ) NOUN, *plural* **-ries.** 1 the art or process of describing heraldic arms in proper form. 2 heraldic arms collectively. 3 colourful or ostentatious display.

bldg ABBREVIATION FOR building.

bleach (bliːtʃ) VERB 1 to make or become white or colourless, as by exposure to sunlight, by the action of chemical agents, etc. ◆ NOUN 2 a bleaching agent. 3 the degree of whiteness resulting from bleaching. 4 the act of bleaching.
▹HISTORY Old English *blǣcan*; related to Old Norse *bleikja*, Old High German *bleih* pale
▸ ˈ**bleachable** ADJECTIVE ▸ ˈ**bleacher** NOUN

bleachers (ˈbliːtʃəz) PLURAL NOUN 1 (*sometimes singular*) a tier of seats in a sports stadium, etc., that are unroofed and inexpensive. 2 the people occupying such seats.

bleaching powder NOUN a white powder with the odour of chlorine, consisting of chlorinated calcium hydroxide with an approximate formula $CaCl(OCl).4H_2O$. It is used in solution as a bleaching agent and disinfectant. Also called: **chloride of lime, chlorinated lime.**

bleak[1] (bliːk) ADJECTIVE 1 exposed and barren; desolate. 2 cold and raw. 3 offering little hope or excitement; dismal: *a bleak future*.
▹HISTORY Old English *blāc* bright, pale; related to Old Norse *bleikr* white, Old High German *bleih* pale
▸ ˈ**bleakly** ADVERB ▸ ˈ**bleakness** NOUN

bleak[2] (bliːk) NOUN any slender silvery European cyprinid fish of the genus *Alburnus*, esp *A. lucidus*, occurring in slow-flowing rivers.
▹HISTORY C15: probably from Old Norse *bleikja* white colour; related to Old High German *bleiche* BLEACH

blear (blɪə) *Archaic* ◆ VERB 1 (*tr*) to make (eyes or sight) dim with or as if with tears; blur. ◆ ADJECTIVE 2 a less common word for **bleary.**
▹HISTORY C13: *blere* to make dim; related to Middle High German *blerre* blurred vision

bleary (ˈblɪərɪ) ADJECTIVE **blearier, bleariest.** 1 (of eyes or vision) dimmed or blurred, as by tears or tiredness. 2 indistinct or unclear. 3 exhausted; tired.
▸ ˈ**blearily** ADVERB ▸ ˈ**bleariness** NOUN

bleary-eyed *or* **blear-eyed** ADJECTIVE 1 with eyes blurred, as with old age or after waking. 2 physically or mentally unperceptive.

bleat (bliːt) VERB 1 (*intr*) (of a sheep, goat, or calf) to utter its characteristic plaintive cry. 2 (*intr*) to speak with any similar sound. 3 to whine; whimper. ◆ NOUN 4 the characteristic cry of sheep, goats, and young calves. 5 any sound similar to this. 6 a weak complaint or whine.
▹HISTORY Old English *blǣtan*; related to Old High German *blāzen*, Dutch *blaten*, Latin *flēre* to weep; see BLARE
▸ ˈ**bleater** NOUN ▸ ˈ**bleating** NOUN, ADJECTIVE

bleb (blɛb) NOUN 1 a fluid-filled blister on the skin. 2 a small air bubble.
▹HISTORY C17: variant of BLOB

▸ ˈ**blebby** ADJECTIVE

bleed (bliːd) VERB **bleeds, bleeding, bled.** 1 (*intr*) to lose or emit blood. 2 (*tr*) to remove or draw blood from (a person or animal). 3 (*intr*) to be injured or die, as for a cause or one's country. 4 (of plants) to exude (sap or resin), esp from a cut. 5 (*tr*) *Informal* to obtain relatively large amounts of money, goods, etc., esp by extortion. 6 (*tr*) to draw liquid or gas from (a container or enclosed system): *to bleed the hydraulic brakes*. 7 (*intr*) (of dye or paint) to run or become mixed, as when wet. 8 to print or be printed so that text, illustrations, etc., run off the trimmed page. 9 (*tr*) to trim (the edges of a printed sheet) so closely as to cut off some of the printed matter. 10 (*intr*) *Civil engineering, building trades* (of a mixture) to exude (a liquid) during compaction, such as water from cement. 11 **bleed (someone or something) dry.** to extort gradually all the resources of (a person or thing). 12 **one's heart bleeds.** used to express sympathetic grief, but often used ironically. ◆ NOUN 13 *Printing* **a** an illustration or sheet trimmed so that some matter is bled. **b** (*as modifier*): *a bleed page*. 14 *Printing* the trimmings of a sheet that has been bled.
▹HISTORY Old English *blēdan*; see BLOOD

bleeder (ˈbliːdə) NOUN 1 *Slang* **a** *Derogatory* a despicable person: *a rotten bleeder*. **b** any person; fellow: *where's the bleeder gone?* 2 *Pathol* a nontechnical name for a **haemophiliac.**

bleeder resistor NOUN a resistor connected across the output terminals of a power supply in order to improve voltage regulation and to discharge filter capacitors.

bleeder's disease NOUN a nontechnical name for **haemophilia.**

bleeding (ˈbliːdɪŋ) ADJECTIVE, ADVERB *Brit slang* (intensifier): *a bleeding fool; it's bleeding beautiful*.

bleeding edge NOUN the very forefront of technological development.

bleeding heart NOUN 1 any of several plants of the genus *Dicentra*, esp the widely cultivated Japanese species *D. spectabilis*, which has finely divided leaves and heart-shaped nodding pink flowers: family *Fumariaceae*. 2 *Informal* **a** a person who is excessively softhearted. **b** (*as modifier*): *a bleeding-heart liberal*.

bleed valve NOUN a valve for running off a liquid from a tank, tube, etc., or for allowing accumulations of gas in a liquid to blow off. Also called: **bleed nipple.**

bleep (bliːp) NOUN 1 a short high-pitched signal made by an electronic apparatus; beep. 2 another word for **bleeper.** ◆ VERB 3 (*intr*) to make such a noise. 4 (*tr*) to call (someone) by triggering the bleeper he or she is wearing.
▹HISTORY C20: of imitative origin

bleeper (ˈbliːpə) NOUN a small portable radio receiver, carried esp by doctors, that sounds a coded bleeping signal to call the carrier. Also called: **bleep.**

blemish (ˈblɛmɪʃ) NOUN 1 a defect; flaw; stain. ◆ VERB 2 (*tr*) to flaw the perfection of; spoil; tarnish.
▹HISTORY C14: from Old French *blemir* to make pale, probably of Germanic origin

blench[1] (blɛntʃ) VERB (*intr*) to shy away, as in fear; quail.
▹HISTORY Old English *blencan* to deceive

blench[2] (blɛntʃ) VERB to make or become pale or white.
▹HISTORY C19: variant of BLANCH

blend (blɛnd) VERB 1 to mix or mingle (components) together thoroughly. 2 (*tr*) to mix (different grades or varieties of tea, whisky, tobacco, etc.) to produce a particular flavour, consistency, etc. 3 (*intr*) to look good together; harmonize. 4 (*intr*) (esp of colours) to shade imperceptibly into each other. ◆ NOUN 5 a mixture or type produced by blending. 6 the act of blending. 7 Also called: **portmanteau word.** a word formed by joining together the beginning and the end of two other words: *"brunch" is a blend of "breakfast" and "lunch"*.
▹HISTORY Old English *blandan*; related to *blendan* to deceive, Old Norse *blanda*, Old High German *blantan*

blende (blɛnd) NOUN 1 another name for **sphalerite.** 2 any of several sulphide ores, such as antimony sulphide.
▹HISTORY C17: German *Blende*, from *blenden* to

deceive, BLIND; so called because it is easily mistaken for galena

blended learning NOUN *Education* the use of both classroom teaching and on-line learning in education.

blender (ˈblɛndə) NOUN [1] a person or thing that blends. [2] Also called: **liquidizer.** a kitchen appliance with blades used for puréeing vegetables, blending liquids, etc.

Blenheim[1] (ˈblɛnɪm) NOUN a village in SW Germany, site of a victory of Anglo-Austrian forces under the Duke of Marlborough and Prince Eugène of Savoy that saved Vienna from the French and Bavarians (1704) during the War of the Spanish Succession. Modern name: **Blindheim.**

Blenheim[2] (ˈblɛnɪm) NOUN [1] a type of King Charles spaniel having red-and-white markings. [2] Also called: **Blenheim orange. a** a type of apple tree bearing gold-coloured apples. **b** the fruit of this tree.
▷HISTORY C19: named after BLENHEIM PALACE

Blenheim Palace NOUN a palace in Woodstock in Oxfordshire: built (1705–22) by Sir John Vanbrugh for the 1st Duke of Marlborough as a reward from the nation for his victory at Blenheim; gardens laid out by Henry Wise and Capability Brown; birthplace of Sir Winston Churchill (1874).

blennioid (ˈblɛnɪˌɔɪd) ADJECTIVE [1] of, relating to, or belonging to the *Blennioidea*, a large suborder of small mainly marine spiny-finned fishes having an elongated body with reduced pelvic fins. The group includes the blennies, butterfish, and gunnel. ◆ NOUN [2] any fish belonging to the *Blennioidea*.

blennorrhoea *or US* **blennorrhea** (ˌblɛnəˈrɪə) NOUN *Pathol* an excessive discharge of watery mucus, esp from the urethra or the vagina.

blenny (ˈblɛnɪ) NOUN, *plural* **-nies.** [1] any blennioid fish of the family *Blenniidae* of coastal waters, esp of the genus *Blennius*, having a tapering scaleless body, a long dorsal fin, and long raylike pelvic fins. [2] any of various related fishes.
▷HISTORY C18: from Latin *blennius*, from Greek *blennos* slime; from the mucus that coats its body

blent (blɛnt) VERB *Archaic or literary* a past participle of **blend.**

blepharism (ˈblɛfərɪzəm) NOUN spasm of the eyelids, causing rapid involuntary blinking.

blepharitis (ˌblɛfəˈraɪtɪs) NOUN inflammation of the eyelids.
▷HISTORY C19: from Greek *blephar(on)* eyelid + -ITIS
▸**blepharitic** (ˌblɛfəˈrɪtɪk) ADJECTIVE

blepharoplasty (ˈblɛfərəʊˌplæstɪ) NOUN cosmetic surgery performed on the eyelid.
▷HISTORY C20: from Greek *blepharo(n)* eyelid + -PLASTY

blepharospasm (ˈblɛfərəʊˌspæzəm) NOUN spasm of the muscle of the eyelids, causing the eyes to shut tightly, either as a response to painful stimuli or occurring as a form of dystonia.
▷HISTORY C19: from Greek *blepharo(n)* eyelid + SPASM

blert (blɜːt) NOUN *Northern English dialect* a foolish person.

blesbok *or* **blesbuck** (ˈblɛsˌbʌk) NOUN, *plural* **-boks, -bok** *or* **-bucks, -buck.** an antelope, *Damaliscus dorcas* (or *albifrons*), of southern Africa. The coat is a deep reddish-brown with a white blaze between the eyes; the horns are lyre-shaped.
▷HISTORY C19: Afrikaans, from Dutch *bles* BLAZE[2] + *bok* goat, BUCK[1]

bless (blɛs) VERB **blesses, blessing, blessed** *or* **blest.** (*tr*) [1] to consecrate or render holy, beneficial, or prosperous by means of a religious rite. [2] to give honour or glory to (a person or thing) as divine or holy. [3] to call upon God to protect; give a benediction to. [4] to worship or adore (God); call or hold holy. [5] (*often passive*) to grant happiness, health, or prosperity to: *they were blessed with perfect peace.* [6] (*usually passive*) to endow with a talent, beauty, etc.: *she was blessed with an even temper.* [7] *Rare* to protect against evil or harm. [8] **bless!** (*interjection*) an exclamation of well-wishing. [9] **bless you!** (*interjection*) **a** a traditional phrase said to a person who has just sneezed. **b** an exclamation of well-wishing or surprise. [10] **bless me!** *or* **(God) bless my soul!** (*interjection*) an exclamation of surprise. [11] **not have a penny to bless oneself with.** to be desperately poor.
▷HISTORY Old English *blǣdsian* to sprinkle with sacrificial blood; related to *blōd* BLOOD

blessed (ˈblɛsɪd, blɛst) ADJECTIVE [1] made holy by religious ceremony; consecrated. [2] worthy of deep reverence or respect. [3] *RC Church* (of a person) beatified by the pope. [4] characterized by happiness or good fortune: *a blessed time.* [5] bringing great happiness or good fortune. [6] a euphemistic word for **damned**, used in mild oaths: *I'm blessed if I know.* ◆ NOUN [7] **the blessed.** *Christianity* the dead who are already enjoying heavenly bliss.
▸ˈ**blessedly** ADVERB ▸ˈ**blessedness** NOUN

Blessed Sacrament NOUN *Chiefly RC Church* the consecrated elements of the Eucharist.

Blessed Virgin NOUN *Chiefly RC Church* another name for **Mary** (sense 1a).

blessing (ˈblɛsɪŋ) NOUN [1] the act of invoking divine protection or aid. [2] the words or ceremony used for this. [3] a short prayer of thanksgiving before or after a meal; grace. [4] *Judaism* Also called: **brachah, brocho. a** a short prayer prescribed for a specific occasion and beginning "Blessed art thou, O Lord...". **b** a section of the liturgy including a similar formula. [5] approval; good wishes: *her father gave his blessing to the marriage.* [6] the bestowal of a divine gift or favour. [7] a happy event or state of affairs: *a blessing in disguise.*

blest (blɛst) VERB a past tense and past participle of **bless.**

blet (blɛt) NOUN a state of softness or decay in certain fruits, such as the medlar, brought about by overripening.
▷HISTORY C19: from French *blettir* to become overripe

blether (ˈblɛðə) VERB, NOUN *Scot* a variant spelling of **blather.**
▷HISTORY C16: from Old Norse *blathra*, from *blathr* nonsense

blethered (ˈblɛðəd) ADJECTIVE *Northern English dialect* weary.

blew (bluː) VERB the past tense of **blow**[1].

blewits (ˈbluːɪts) NOUN (*functioning as singular*) an edible saprotroph agaricaceous fungus, *Tricholoma saevum*, having a pale brown cap and bluish stalk.
▷HISTORY C19: probably based on BLUE

Blida (ˈbliːdə) NOUN a city in N Algeria, on the edge of the Mitidja Plain. Pop. (urban area): 226 512 (1998).

blight (blaɪt) NOUN [1] any plant disease characterized by withering and shrivelling without rotting. ◆ See also **potato blight.** [2] any factor, such as bacterial attack or air pollution, that causes the symptoms of blight in plants. [3] a person or thing that mars or prevents growth, improvement, or prosperity. [4] an ugly urban district. [5] the state or condition of being blighted or spoilt. ◆ VERB [6] to cause or suffer a blight. [7] (*tr*) to frustrate or disappoint. [8] (*tr*) to spoil; destroy.
▷HISTORY C17: perhaps related to Old English *blǣce* rash; compare BLEACH

blighter (ˈblaɪtə) NOUN *Brit informal* [1] a fellow: *where's the blighter gone?* [2] a despicable or irritating person or thing.

blighty *or* **blighty bird** (ˈblaɪtɪ) NOUN *NZ* another name for **white-eye.**

Blighty (ˈblaɪtɪ) NOUN (*sometimes not capital*) *Brit slang* (used esp by troops serving abroad) [1] England; home. [2] (esp in World War I) **a** Also called: **a blighty one.** a slight wound that causes the recipient to be sent home to England. **b** leave in England.
▷HISTORY C20: from Hindi *bilāyatī* foreign land, England, from Arabic *wilāyat* country, from *waliya* he rules

blimey (ˈblaɪmɪ) INTERJECTION *Brit slang* an exclamation of surprise or annoyance.
▷HISTORY C19: short for *gorblimey* God blind me

blimp[1] (blɪmp) NOUN [1] a small nonrigid airship, esp one used for observation or as a barrage balloon. [2] *Films* a soundproof cover fixed over a camera during shooting. ◆ See also **blimp out.**
▷HISTORY C20: probably from (*type*) *B-limp*

blimp[2] (blɪmp) NOUN (*often capital*) *Chiefly Brit* a person, esp a military officer, who is stupidly complacent and reactionary. Also called: **Colonel Blimp.**
▷HISTORY C20: after a character created by Sir David Low (1891–1963), New Zealand-born British political cartoonist

blimp out VERB (*intr, adverb*) *Slang* to become greatly overweight.

blin (blɪn) ADJECTIVE a Scot word for **blind.**

blind (blaɪnd) ADJECTIVE [1] **a** unable to see; sightless. **b** (*as collective noun*; preceded by *the*): *the blind.* [2] (usually foll by *to*) unable or unwilling to understand or discern. [3] not based on evidence or determined by reason: *blind hatred.* [4] acting or performed without control or preparation. [5] done without being able to see, relying on instruments for information. [6] hidden from sight: *a blind corner; a blind stitch.* [7] closed at one end: *a blind alley.* [8] completely lacking awareness or consciousness: *a blind stupor.* [9] *Informal* very drunk. [10] having no openings or outlets: *a blind wall.* [11] without having been seen beforehand: *a blind purchase.* [12] (of cultivated plants) having failed to produce flowers or fruits. [13] (intensifier): *not a blind bit of notice.* [14] **turn a blind eye (to).** to disregard deliberately or pretend not to notice (something, esp an action of which one disapproves). ◆ ADVERB [15] without being able to see ahead or using only instruments: *to drive blind; flying blind.* [16] without adequate knowledge or information; carelessly: *to buy a house blind.* [17] (intensifier) (in the phrase **blind drunk**). [18] **bake blind.** to bake (the empty crust of a pie, pastry, etc.) by half filling with dried peas, crusts of bread, etc., to keep it in shape. ◆ VERB (*mainly tr*) [19] to deprive of sight permanently or temporarily. [20] to deprive of good sense, reason, or judgment. [21] to darken; conceal. [22] (foll by *with*) to overwhelm by showing detailed knowledge: *to blind somebody with science.* [23] (*intr*) *Brit slang* to drive very fast. [24] (*intr*) *Brit slang* to curse (esp in the phrase **effing and blinding**). ◆ NOUN [25] (*modifier*) for or intended to help the blind: *a blind school.* [26] a shade for a window, usually on a roller. [27] any obstruction or hindrance to sight, light, or air. [28] a person, action, or thing that serves to deceive or conceal the truth. [29] a person who acts on behalf of someone who does not wish his identity or actions to be known. [30] *Brit slang* Also called: **blinder.** a drunken orgy; binge. [31] *Poker* a stake put up by a player before he examines his cards. [32] *Hunting chiefly US and Canadian* a screen of brush or undergrowth, in which hunters hide to shoot their quarry. Brit name: **hide.** [33] *Military* a round or demolition charge that fails to explode.
▷HISTORY Old English *blind*; related to Old Norse *blindr*, Old High German *blint*; Lettish *blendu* to see dimly; see BLUNDER
▸ˈ**blindly** ADVERB ▸ˈ**blindness** NOUN

> **Language note** See at **disabled.**

blindage (ˈblaɪndɪdʒ) NOUN *Military* (esp formerly) a protective screen or structure, as over a trench.

blind alley NOUN [1] an alley open at one end only; cul-de-sac. [2] *Informal* a situation in which no further progress can be made.

blind blocking NOUN *Bookbinding* another name for **blind stamping.**

blind date NOUN *Informal* [1] a social meeting between a man and a woman who have not met before. [2] either of the persons involved.

blinder (ˈblaɪndə) NOUN [1] an outstanding performance in sport. [2] *Brit slang* another name for **blind** (sense 30).

blinders (ˈblaɪndəz) PLURAL NOUN the usual US and Canadian word for **blinkers.**

blindfish (ˈblaɪndˌfɪʃ) NOUN, *plural* **-fish** *or* **-fishes.** any of various small fishes, esp the cavefish, that have rudimentary or functionless eyes and occur in subterranean streams.

blindfold (ˈblaɪndˌfəʊld) VERB (*tr*) [1] to prevent (a person or animal) from seeing by covering (the eyes). [2] to prevent from perceiving or understanding. ◆ NOUN [3] a piece of cloth, bandage, etc., used to cover the eyes. [4] any interference to sight. ◆ ADJECTIVE, ADVERB [5] having the eyes covered with a cloth or bandage. [6] *Chess* not seeing the board and pieces. [7] rash; inconsiderate.
▷HISTORY changed (C16) through association with FOLD[1] from Old English *blindfellian* to strike blind; see BLIND, FELL[2]

Blind Freddie NOUN *Austral informal* an imaginary person representing the highest degree of incompetence (esp in the phrase **Blind Freddie could see that!**).

blind gut NOUN *Informal* another name for the **caecum.**

Blindheim (ˈblɪntˌhaɪm) NOUN the German name for **Blenheim**[1].

blinding (ˈblaɪndɪŋ) NOUN 1 sand or grit spread over a road surface to fill up cracks. 2 the process of laying blinding. 3 Also called: **mattress.** a layer of concrete made with little cement spread over soft ground to seal it so that reinforcement can be laid on it. ◆ ADJECTIVE 4 making one blind or as if blind: *blinding snow.* 5 most noticeable; brilliant or dazzling: *a blinding display of skill.*
▸ **ˈblindingly** ADVERB

blind man's buff NOUN a game in which a blindfolded person tries to catch and identify the other players.
▷ HISTORY C16: buff, perhaps from Old French *buffe* a blow; see BUFFET[2]

blind register NOUN (in the United Kingdom) a list of those who are blind and are therefore entitled to financial and other benefits.

blind side NOUN 1 *Rugby* the side of the field between the scrum and the nearer touchline. 2 the side on which a person's vision is obscured. ◆ VERB **blind-side.** 3 (*tr*) *US* to take (someone) by surprise.

blindsight (ˈblaɪndˌsaɪt) NOUN the ability to respond to visual stimuli without having any conscious visual experience; it can occur after some forms of brain damage.

blind snake NOUN any burrowing snake of the family *Typhlopidae* and related families of warm and tropical regions, having very small or vestigial eyes.

blind spot NOUN 1 a small oval-shaped area of the retina in which vision is not experienced. It marks the nonphotosensitive site of entrance into the eyeball of the optic nerve. See **optic disc.** 2 a place or area, as in an auditorium or part of a road, where vision is completely or partially obscured or hearing is difficult or impossible. 3 a subject about which a person is ignorant or prejudiced, or an occupation in which he is inefficient. 4 a location within the normal range of a radio transmitter with weak reception.

blind staggers NOUN (*functioning as singular*) *Vet science* another name for **staggers.**

blind stamping NOUN *Bookbinding* an impression on a book cover without using colour or gold leaf. Also called: **blind blocking.**

blindstorey *or* **blindstory** (ˈblaɪndˌstɔːrɪ) NOUN, *plural* **-reys** *or* **-ries.** a storey without windows, such as a gallery in a Gothic church. Compare **clerestory.**

blind trust NOUN a trust fund that manages the financial affairs of a person without informing him or her of any investments made, usually so that the beneficiary cannot be accused of using public office for private gain.

blindworm (ˈblaɪndˌwɜːm) NOUN another name for **slowworm.**

bling-bling (ˈblɪŋˌblɪŋ) *or* **bling** ADJECTIVE 1 *Slang* flashy; ostentatious; glitzy. ◆ NOUN 2 ostentatious jewellery.
▷ HISTORY C20: imitative of jewellery clashing together or of light reflecting off jewellery

blini (ˈblɪnɪ), **bliny,** *or* **blinis** (ˈblɪnɪz) PLURAL NOUN Russian pancakes made of buckwheat flour and yeast.
▷ HISTORY C19: from Russian: plural of *blin*, from Old Russian *mlinŭ*, related to Russian *molot'* to grind

blink (blɪŋk) VERB 1 to close and immediately reopen (the eyes or an eye), usually involuntarily. 2 (*intr*) to look with the eyes partially closed, as in strong sunlight. 3 to shine intermittently, as in signalling, or unsteadily. 4 (*tr*; foll by *away, from,* etc) to clear the eyes of (dust, tears, etc.). 5 (when *tr*, usually foll by *at*) to be surprised or amazed: *he blinked at the splendour of the ceremony.* 6 (when *intr*, foll by *at*) to pretend not to know or see (a fault, injustice, etc.). ◆ NOUN 7 the act or an instance of blinking. 8 a glance; glimpse. 9 short for **iceblink** (sense 1). 10 **on the blink.** *Slang* not working properly.
▷ HISTORY C14: variant of BLENCH[1]; related to Middle Dutch *blinken* to glitter, Danish *blinke* to wink, Swedish *blinka*

blinker (ˈblɪŋkə) NOUN 1 a flashing light for sending messages, as a warning device, etc., such as a direction indicator on a road vehicle. 2 (*often plural*) a slang word for **eye**[1]. ◆ VERB (*tr*) 3 to provide (a horse) with blinkers. 4 to obscure with or as if with blinkers.

blinkered (ˈblɪŋkəd) ADJECTIVE 1 considering only a narrow point of view. 2 (of a horse) wearing blinkers.

blinkers (ˈblɪŋkəz) PLURAL NOUN 1 (*sometimes singular*) *Chiefly Brit* leather sidepieces attached to a horse's bridle to prevent sideways vision. Usual US and Canadian word: **blinders.** 2 a slang word for **goggle** (sense 4).

blinking (ˈblɪŋkɪŋ) ADJECTIVE, ADVERB *Informal* (intensifier): *a blinking fool; a blinking good film.*

blinks (blɪŋks) NOUN (*functioning as singular*) a small temperate portulacaceous plant, *Montia fontana* with small white flowers.
▷ HISTORY C19: from BLINK, because the flowers do not fully open and thus seem to blink at the light

blintz *or* **blintze** (blɪnts) NOUN a thin pancake folded over a filling usually of apple, cream cheese, or meat.
▷ HISTORY C20: from Yiddish *blintse*, from Russian *blinyets* little pancakes; see BLINI

blip (blɪp) NOUN 1 a repetitive sound, such as that produced by an electronic device, by dripping water, etc. 2 Also called: **pip.** the spot of light or a sharply peaked pulse on a radar screen indicating the position of an object. 3 a temporary irregularity recorded in performance of something. ◆ VERB **blips, blipping, blipped.** 4 (*intr*) to produce such a noise.
▷ HISTORY C20: of imitative origin

blipvert (ˈblɪpˌvɜːt) NOUN a very short television advertisement.
▷ HISTORY (C20: from BLIP + (AD)VERT

bliss (blɪs) NOUN 1 perfect happiness; serene joy. 2 the ecstatic joy of heaven.
▷ HISTORY Old English *blīths*; related to *blīthe* BLITHE, Old Saxon *blīdsea* bliss
▸ **ˈblissless** ADJECTIVE

blissful (ˈblɪsful) ADJECTIVE 1 serenely joyful or glad. 2 **blissful ignorance.** unawareness or inexperience of something unpleasant.
▸ **ˈblissfully** ADVERB ▸ **ˈblissfulness** NOUN

B list NOUN **a** a category considered to be slightly below the most socially desirable. **b** (*as modifier*): *B-list celebrities.* ◆ Compare **A list.**

blister (ˈblɪstə) NOUN 1 a small bubble-like elevation of the skin filled with serum, produced as a reaction to a burn, mechanical irritation, etc. 2 a swelling containing air or liquid, as on a painted surface. 3 a transparent dome or any bulge on the fuselage of an aircraft, such as one used for observation. 4 *Slang* an irritating person. 5 *NZ slang* a rebuke. ◆ VERB 6 to have or cause to have blisters. 7 (*tr*) to attack verbally with great scorn or sarcasm.
▷ HISTORY C13: from Old French *blestre*, probably from Middle Dutch *bluyster* blister; see BLAST
▸ **ˈblistered** ADJECTIVE ▸ **ˈblistery** ADJECTIVE

blister beetle NOUN any beetle of the family *Meloidae*, many of which produce a secretion that blisters the skin. See also **Spanish fly.**

blister copper NOUN an impure form of copper having a blister-like surface due to the release of gas during cooling.

blistering (ˈblɪstərɪŋ, -trɪŋ) ADJECTIVE 1 (of weather) extremely hot. 2 (of criticism) extremely harsh.
▸ **ˈblisteringly** ADVERB

blister pack NOUN a type of packet in which small items are displayed and sold, consisting of a transparent dome of plastic or similar material mounted on a firm backing such as cardboard. Also called: **bubble pack.**

blister rust NOUN a disease of certain pines caused by rust fungi of the genus *Cronartium*, causing swellings on the bark from which orange masses of spores are released.

BLit ABBREVIATION FOR Bachelor of Literature.

blithe (blaɪð) ADJECTIVE 1 very happy or cheerful. 2 heedless; casual and indifferent.
▷ HISTORY Old English *blīthe*
▸ **ˈblithely** ADVERB ▸ **ˈblitheness** NOUN

blithering (ˈblɪðərɪŋ) ADJECTIVE 1 talking foolishly; jabbering. 2 *Informal* stupid; foolish: *you blithering idiot.*
▷ HISTORY C19: variant of BLATHER + -ING[2]

blithesome (ˈblaɪðsəm) ADJECTIVE *Literary* cheery; merry.
▸ **ˈblithesomely** ADVERB ▸ **ˈblithesomeness** NOUN

BLitt ABBREVIATION FOR Bachelor of Letters.
▷ HISTORY Latin *Baccalaureus Litterarum*

blitz (blɪts) NOUN 1 a violent and sustained attack, esp with intensive aerial bombardment. 2 any sudden intensive attack or concerted effort. 3 *American football* a defensive charge on the quarterback. ◆ VERB 4 (*tr*) to attack suddenly and intensively.
▷ HISTORY C20: shortened from German *Blitzkrieg* lightning war

Blitz (blɪts) NOUN **the.** the systematic night-time bombing of the British in 1940–41 by the German Luftwaffe.

blitzkrieg (ˈblɪtsˌkriːg) NOUN a swift intensive military attack, esp using tanks supported by aircraft, designed to defeat the opposition quickly.
▷ HISTORY C20: from German: lightning war

blizzard (ˈblɪzəd) NOUN a strong bitterly cold wind accompanied by a widespread heavy snowfall.
▷ HISTORY C19: of uncertain origin

BLL ABBREVIATION FOR Bachelor of Laws.

BL Lac object NOUN an extremely compact violently variable form of active galaxy.
▷ HISTORY C20: named after BL Lacertae, first identified example found in the constellation Lacerta and originally thought to be a variable star

bloat (bləut) VERB 1 to swell or cause to swell, as with a liquid, air, or wind. 2 to become or cause to be puffed up, as with conceit. 3 (*tr*) to cure (fish, esp herring) by half-drying in smoke. ◆ NOUN 4 *Vet science* an abnormal distention of the abdomen in cattle, sheep, etc., caused by accumulation of gas in the stomach.
▷ HISTORY C17: probably related to Old Norse *blautr* soaked, Old English *blāt* pale

bloated (ˈbləutɪd) ADJECTIVE 1 swollen, as with a liquid, air, or wind. 2 puffed up, as with conceit.

bloater (ˈbləutə) NOUN 1 a herring, or sometimes a mackerel, that has been salted in brine, smoked, and cured. 2 *Brit slang* a fat or greedy person.

blob (blɒb) NOUN 1 a soft mass or drop, as of some viscous liquid. 2 a spot, dab, or blotch of colour, ink, etc. 3 a indistinct or shapeless form or object. 4 a slang word for **condom.** ◆ VERB **blobs, blobbing, blobbed.** 5 (*tr*) to put blobs, as of ink or paint, on.
▷ HISTORY C15: perhaps of imitative origin; compare BUBBLE
▸ **ˈblobby** ADJECTIVE

bloc (blɒk) NOUN a group of people or countries combined by a common interest or aim: *the Soviet bloc.*
▷ HISTORY C20: from French: BLOCK

block (blɒk) NOUN 1 a large solid piece of wood, stone, or other material with flat rectangular sides, as for use in building. 2 any large solid piece of wood, stone, etc., usually having at least one face fairly flat. 3 such a piece on which particular tasks may be done, as chopping, cutting, or beheading. 4 Also called: **building block.** one of a set of wooden or plastic cubes as a child's toy. 5 a form on which things are shaped or displayed: *a wig block.* 6 *Slang* a person's head (esp in the phrase **knock someone's block off**). 7 **do one's block.** *Austral and NZ slang* to become angry. 8 a dull, unemotional, or hardhearted person. 9 a large building of offices, flats, etc. 10 **a** a group of buildings in a city bounded by intersecting streets on each side. **b** the area or distance between such intersecting streets. 11 *Austral and NZ* an area of land for a house, farm, etc. 12 *Austral and NZ* a log, usually a willow, fastened to a timber base and used in a wood-chopping competition. 13 an area of land, esp one to be divided for building or settling. 14 See **cylinder block.** 15 **a** a piece of wood, metal, or other material having an engraved, cast, or carved design in relief, used either for printing or for stamping book covers, etc. **b** *Brit* a letterpress

printing plate, esp one mounted type-high on wood or metal. 16 a casing housing one or more freely rotating pulleys. See also **block and tackle.** 17 **on the block.** *Chiefly US and Canadian* up for auction. 18 the act of obstructing or condition of being obstructed, as in sports. 19 an obstruction or hindrance. 20 *Pathol* **a** interference in the normal physiological functioning of an organ or part. **b** See **heart block. c** See **nerve block.** 21 *Psychol* a short interruption of perceptual or thought processes. 22 obstruction of an opponent in a sport. 23 **a** a section or quantity, as of tickets or shares, handled or considered as a single unit. **b** (*as modifier*): *a block booking; block voting.* 24 **a** a stretch of railway in which only one train may travel at a time. **b** (*as modifier*): *a block signal.* 25 an unseparated group of four or more postage stamps. Compare **strip**[1] (sense 3). 26 a pad of paper. 27 *Computing* a group of words on tape, disk, etc., treated as a unit of data. 28 *Athletics* short for **starting block.** 29 *Cricket* a mark made near the popping crease by a batsman to indicate his position in relation to the wicket. 30 **a chip off the old block.** *Informal* a person who resembles one of his or her parents in behaviour. ◆ VERB (*mainly tr*) 31 to shape or form (something) into a block. 32 to fit with or mount on a block. 33 to shape by use of a block: *to block a hat.* 34 (often foll by *up*) to obstruct (a passage, channel, etc.) or prevent or impede the motion or flow of (something or someone) by introducing an obstacle: *to block the traffic; to block up a pipe.* 35 to impede, retard, or prevent (an action, procedure, etc.). 36 to stamp (a title, design, etc.) on (a book cover, etc.) by means of a block (see sense 15a.), esp using gold leaf or other foil. 37 (esp of a government or central bank) to limit the use or conversion of assets or currency. 38 (*also intr*) *Sport* to obstruct or impede movement by (an opponent). 39 (*intr*) to suffer a psychological block. 40 to interrupt a physiological function, as by use of an anaesthetic. 41 (*also intr*) *Cricket* to play (a ball) defensively. See also **block in, block out.**
▷HISTORY C14: from Old French *bloc*, from Dutch *blok*; related to Old High German *bloh*
▸ˈ**blocker** NOUN

blockade (blɒˈkeɪd) NOUN 1 *Military* the interdiction of a nation's sea lines of communications, esp of an individual port by the use of sea power. 2 something that prevents access or progress. 3 *Med* the inhibition of the effect of a hormone or a drug, a transport system, or the action of a nerve by a drug. ◆ VERB (*tr*) 4 to impose a blockade on. 5 to obstruct the way to.
▷HISTORY C17: from BLOCK + *-ade*, as in AMBUSCADE
▸**blockˈader** NOUN

blockage (ˈblɒkɪdʒ) NOUN 1 the act of blocking or state of being blocked. 2 an object causing an obstruction.

block and tackle NOUN a hoisting device in which a rope or chain is passed around a pair of blocks containing one or more pulleys. The upper block is secured overhead and the lower block supports the load, the effort being applied to the free end of the rope or chain.

blockboard (ˈblɒkˌbɔːd) NOUN a type of plywood in which soft wood strips are bonded together and sandwiched between two layers of veneer.

blockbuster (ˈblɒkˌbʌstə) NOUN *Informal* 1 a large bomb used to demolish extensive areas or strengthened targets. 2 a very successful, effective, or forceful person, thing, etc.

blockbusting (ˈblɒkˌbʌstɪŋ) NOUN *US informal* the act or practice of inducing the sale of property cheaply by exploiting the owners' fears of lower prices if racial minorities live in the area.

block capital NOUN another term for **block letter.**

block diagram NOUN 1 a diagram showing the interconnections between the parts of an industrial process. 2 a three-dimensional drawing representing a block of the earth's crust, showing geological structure. 3 *Computing* a diagram showing the interconnections between electronic components or parts of a program.

blocked (blɒkt) ADJECTIVE *Slang* functionally impeded by amphetamine.

blocked shoe NOUN a dancing shoe with a stiffened toe that enables a ballet dancer to dance on the tips of the toes.

blocker NOUN 1 a person or thing that acts as a block. 2 *Physiol* an agent that blocks a physiological function, such as the transport of an ion across an ion channel.

block grant NOUN (in Britain) an annual grant made by the government to a local authority to help to pay for the public services it provides, such as health, education, and housing.

blockhead (ˈblɒkˌhɛd) NOUN *Derogatory* a stupid person.
▸ˈ**blockˌheaded** ADJECTIVE ▸ˈ**blockˌheadedly** ADVERB
▸ˈ**blockˌheadedness** NOUN

blockhouse (ˈblɒkˌhaʊs) NOUN 1 (formerly) a wooden fortification with ports or loopholes for defensive fire, observation, etc. 2 a concrete structure strengthened to give protection against enemy fire, with apertures to allow defensive gunfire. 3 a building constructed of logs or squared timber. 4 a reinforced concrete building close to a rocket-launching site for protecting personnel and equipment during launching.

blockie (ˈblɒkɪ) NOUN *Austral informal* an owner of a small property, esp a farm.

block in VERB (*tr, adverb*) to sketch in outline, with little detail.

blocking (ˈblɒkɪŋ) NOUN 1 *Electronics* the interruption of anode current in a valve because of the application of a high negative voltage to the grid. 2 internal congestion in a communication system that prevents the transmission of information.

blockish (ˈblɒkɪʃ) ADJECTIVE lacking vivacity or imagination; stupid.
▸ˈ**blockishly** ADVERB ▸ˈ**blockishness** NOUN

block lava NOUN volcanic lava occurring as rough-surfaced jagged blocks.

block letter NOUN Also called: **block capital.** a plain capital letter.

block out VERB (*tr, adverb*) 1 to plan or describe (something) in a general fashion. 2 to prevent the entry or consideration of (something). 3 *Photog, printing* to mask part of (a negative), in order that light may not pass through it.

block plane NOUN a carpenter's small plane used to cut across the end grain of wood.

block printing NOUN printing from hand engraved or carved blocks of wood or linoleum.

block release NOUN *Brit* the release of industrial trainees from work for study at a college for several weeks.

block sampling NOUN the selection of a corpus for statistical literary analysis by random selection of a starting point and consideration of the continuous passage following it. Compare **spread sampling.**

block tin NOUN pure tin, esp when cast into ingots.

block vote NOUN *Brit* (at a conference, esp of trade unionists) the system whereby each delegate's vote has a value in proportion to the number of people he represents.

blocky ADJECTIVE like a block, esp in shape and solidity.
▸ˈ**blockiness** NOUN

Bloc Quebecois (blɒk keɪbɛˈkwɑː) NOUN (in Canada) a political party that advocates autonomy for Quebec.

Bloemfontein (ˈbluːmfɒnˌteɪn) NOUN a city in central South Africa: capital of Free State province and judicial capital of the country. Pop. (urban area): 333 769 (1996).

blog (blɒg) NOUN *Informal* short for **weblog.**
▸ˈ**blogger** NOUN

Blois (*French* blwa) NOUN a city in N central France, on the Loire: 13th-century castle. Pop.: 51 550 (1990).

bloke (bləʊk) NOUN *Brit and Austral* an informal word for **man.**
▷HISTORY C19: from Shelta

blokeish *or* **blokish** (ˈbləʊkɪʃ) ADJECTIVE *Informal, sometimes derogatory* denoting or exhibiting the characteristics believed typical of an ordinary man. Also: **blokey** (ˈbləʊkɪ).
▸ˈ**blokeishness** *or* ˈ**blokishness** NOUN

blond (blɒnd) ADJECTIVE 1 (of men's hair) of a light colour; fair. 2 (of a person, people or a race) having fair hair, a light complexion, and, typically, blue or grey eyes. 3 (of soft furnishings, wood, etc.) light in colour. ◆ NOUN 4 a person, esp a man, having light-coloured hair and skin.
▷HISTORY C15: from Old French *blond*, probably of Germanic origin; related to Late Latin *blundus* yellow, Italian *biondo*, Spanish *blondo*
▸ˈ**blondness** NOUN

> **Language note** Although *blond* and *blonde* correspond to masculine and feminine forms in French, this distinction is not consistently made in English. *Blonde* is the commoner form both as a noun and an adjective, and is more frequently used to refer to women than men. The less common variant *blond* occurs usually as an adjective, occasionally as a noun, and is the preferred form when referring to men with fair hair.

blonde (blɒnd) ADJECTIVE 1 (of women's hair) of a light colour; fair. 2 (of a person, people or a race) having fair hair, a light complexion, and, typically, blue or grey eyes. 3 (of soft furnishings, wood, etc.) light in colour. ◆ NOUN 4 a person, esp a woman, having light-coloured hair and skin. 5 Also called: **blonde lace.** a French pillow lace, originally of unbleached cream-coloured Chinese silk, later of bleached or black-dyed silk.
▷HISTORY C15: from Old French *blond* (fem *blonde*), probably of Germanic origin; related to Late Latin *blundus* yellow, Italian *biondo*, Spanish *blondo*
▸ˈ**blondeness** NOUN

blonding (ˈblɒndɪŋ) NOUN **a** the act or an instance of dyeing hair blonde. **b** (*as modifier*): *blonding sprays.*

blood (blʌd) NOUN 1 a reddish fluid in vertebrates that is pumped by the heart through the arteries and veins, supplies tissues with nutrients, oxygen, etc., and removes waste products. It consists of a fluid (see **blood plasma**) containing cells (erythrocytes, leucocytes, and platelets). Related adjectives: **haemal, haematic, sanguineous.** 2 a similar fluid in such invertebrates as annelids and arthropods. 3 bloodshed, esp when resulting in murder. 4 the guilt or responsibility for killing or injuring (esp in the phrase **to have blood on one's hands** *or* **head**). 5 life itself; lifeblood. 6 relationship through being of the same family, race, or kind; kinship. 7 **blood, sweat and tears.** *Informal* hard work and concentrated effort. 8 **flesh and blood. a** near kindred or kinship, esp that between a parent and child. **b** human nature (esp in the phrase **it's more than flesh and blood can stand**). 9 ethnic or national descent: *of Spanish blood.* 10 **in one's blood.** as a natural or inherited characteristic or talent. 11 **the blood.** royal or noble descent: *a prince of the blood.* 12 temperament; disposition; temper. 13 **a** good or pure breeding; pedigree. **b** (*as modifier*): *blood horses.* 14 people viewed as members of a group, esp as an invigorating force (in the phrases **new blood, young blood**). 15 *Chiefly Brit rare* a dashing young man; dandy; rake. 16 the sensual or carnal nature of man. 17 *Obsolete* one of the four bodily humours. See **humour** (sense 8). 18 **bad blood.** hatred; ill feeling. 19 **blood is thicker than water.** family duties and loyalty outweigh other ties. 20 **have** *or* **get one's blood up.** to be or cause to be angry or inflamed. 21 **in cold blood.** showing no passion; deliberately; ruthlessly. 22 **make one's blood boil.** to cause to be angry or indignant. 23 **make one's blood run cold.** to fill with horror. ◆ VERB (*tr*) 24 *Hunting* to cause (young hounds) to taste the blood of a freshly killed quarry and so become keen to hunt. 25 *Hunting* to smear the cheeks or forehead of (a person) with the blood of the kill as an initiation in hunting. 26 to initiate (a person) to war.
▷HISTORY Old English *blōd*; related to Old Norse *blōth*, Old High German *bluot*

blood-and-thunder ADJECTIVE denoting or relating to a melodramatic adventure story.

blood bank NOUN a place where whole blood, blood plasma, or other blood products are stored until required in transfusion.

blood bath NOUN indiscriminate slaughter; a massacre.

blood brother NOUN 1 a brother by birth. 2 a man or boy who has sworn to treat another as his brother, often in a ceremony in which their blood is mingled.

blood cell NOUN any of the cells that circulate in the blood. See **erythrocyte, leucocyte.**

blood count NOUN the number of red and white blood corpuscles and platelets in a specific sample of blood. See **haemocytometer.**

bloodcurdling (ˈblʌdˌkɜːdlɪŋ) ADJECTIVE terrifying; horrifying.
▸ **ˈbloodˌcurdlingly** ADVERB

blood donor NOUN a person who gives his or her blood to be used for transfusion.

blood doping NOUN the illegal practice of removing a quantity of blood from an athlete long before a race and reinjecting it shortly before a race, so boosting oxygenation of the blood.

blood-drop emlets (ˈɛmlɪts) NOUN (*functioning as singular*) a Chilean scrophulariaceous plant, *Mimulus luteus*, naturalized in Europe, having red-spotted yellow flowers. See also **monkey flower, musk** (sense 3).

blooded (ˈblʌdɪd) ADJECTIVE [1] (of horses, cattle, etc.) of good breeding. [2] (*in combination*) having blood or temperament as specified: *hot-blooded, cold-blooded, warm-blooded, red-blooded, blue-blooded.*

blood feud NOUN a feud in which the members of hostile families or clans murder each other.

bloodfin (ˈblʌdˌfɪn) NOUN a silvery red-finned South American freshwater fish, *Aphyocharax rubripinnis*: a popular aquarium fish: family *Characidae* (characins).

blood fluke NOUN any parasitic flatworm, such as a schistosome, that lives in the blood vessels of man and other vertebrates: class *Digenea*. See also **trematode.**

blood group NOUN any one of the various groups into which human blood is classified on the basis of its agglutinogens. Also called: **blood type.**

blood guilt NOUN guilt of murder or shedding blood.
▸ **ˈblood-ˌguilty** ADJECTIVE ▸ **ˈblood-ˌguiltiness** NOUN

blood heat NOUN the normal temperature of the human body, 98.4°F or 37°C.

bloodhound (ˈblʌdˌhaʊnd) NOUN [1] a large breed of hound having a smooth glossy coat of red, tan, or black and loose wrinkled skin on its head: formerly much used in tracking and police work. [2] *Informal* a detective.

bloodless (ˈblʌdlɪs) ADJECTIVE [1] without blood. [2] conducted without violence (esp in the phrase **bloodless revolution**). [3] anaemic-looking; pale. [4] lacking vitality; lifeless. [5] lacking in emotion; cold; unfeeling.
▸ **ˈbloodlessly** ADVERB ▸ **ˈbloodlessness** NOUN

Bloodless Revolution NOUN **the.** another name for the **Glorious Revolution.**

blood-letting (ˈblʌdˌlɛtɪŋ) NOUN [1] the therapeutic removal of blood, as in relieving congestive heart failure. See also **phlebotomy.** [2] bloodshed, esp in a blood feud.

bloodline (ˈblʌdˌlaɪn) NOUN all the members of a family group over generations, esp regarding characteristics common to that group; pedigree.

bloodmobile (ˈblʌdməˌbiːl) NOUN *US* a motor vehicle equipped for collecting blood from donors.

blood money NOUN [1] compensation paid to the relatives of a murdered person. [2] money paid to a hired murderer. [3] a reward for information about a criminal, esp a murderer.

blood orange NOUN a variety of orange all or part of the pulp of which is dark red when ripe.

blood plasma NOUN [1] the pale yellow fluid portion of the blood; blood from which red and white blood cells and platelets have been removed. [2] a sterilized preparation of this fluid for use in transfusions.

blood poisoning NOUN a nontechnical term for **septicaemia.**

blood pressure NOUN the pressure exerted by the blood on the inner walls of the arteries, being relative to the elasticity and diameter of the vessels and the force of the heartbeat.

blood pudding NOUN another name for **black pudding.**

blood red NOUN **a** a deep red colour. **b** (*as adjective*): *blood-red roses.*

blood relation *or* **relative** NOUN a person related to another by birth, as distinct from one related by marriage.

bloodroot (ˈblʌdˌruːt) NOUN [1] Also called: **red puccoon.** a North American papaveraceous plant, *Sanguinaria canadensis*, having a single whitish flower and a fleshy red root that yields a red dye. [2] another name for **tormentil.**

blood sausage NOUN another term (esp US and Canadian) for **black pudding.**

blood serum NOUN blood plasma from which the clotting factors have been removed.

bloodshed (ˈblʌdˌʃɛd) NOUN slaughter; killing.

bloodshot (ˈblʌdˌʃɒt) ADJECTIVE (of an eye) inflamed.

blood sport NOUN any sport involving the killing of an animal, esp hunting.

bloodstain (ˈblʌdˌsteɪn) NOUN a dark discoloration caused by blood, esp dried blood.

bloodstained (ˈblʌdˌsteɪnd) ADJECTIVE stained by or covered in blood.

bloodstock (ˈblʌdˌstɒk) NOUN thoroughbred horses, esp those bred for racing.

bloodstock industry NOUN the breeding and training of racehorses.

bloodstone (ˈblʌdˌstəʊn) NOUN a dark-green variety of chalcedony with red spots: used as a gemstone. Also called: **heliotrope.**

bloodstream (ˈblʌdˌstriːm) NOUN the flow of blood through the vessels of a living body.

blood substitute NOUN a substance such as plasma, albumin, or dextran, used to replace lost blood or increase the blood volume.

bloodsucker (ˈblʌdˌsʌkə) NOUN [1] an animal that sucks blood, esp a leech or mosquito. [2] a person or thing that preys upon another person, esp by extorting money.

blood sugar NOUN *Med* the glucose concentration in the blood: the normal fasting value is between 3.9 and 5.6 mmol/l.

blood test NOUN analysis of a blood sample to determine blood group, alcohol concentration, etc.

bloodthirsty (ˈblʌdˌθɜːstɪ) ADJECTIVE **-thirstier, -thirstiest.** [1] murderous; cruel. [2] taking pleasure in bloodshed or violence. [3] describing or depicting killing and violence; gruesome: *a bloodthirsty film.*
▸ **ˈbloodˌthirstily** ADVERB ▸ **ˈbloodˌthirstiness** NOUN

blood type NOUN another name for **blood group.**

blood vessel NOUN an artery, capillary, or vein.

blood volume NOUN *Med* the total quantity of blood in the body.

bloodwood (ˈblʌdˌwʊd) NOUN any of several species of Australian eucalyptus that exude a red sap.

bloodworm (ˈblʌdˌwɜːm) NOUN [1] the red wormlike aquatic larva of the midge, *Chironomus plumosus*, which lives at the bottom of stagnant pools and ditches. [2] a freshwater oligochaete tubifex worm. [3] any of several small reddish worms used as angling bait.

bloody (ˈblʌdɪ) ADJECTIVE **bloodier, bloodiest.** [1] covered or stained with blood. [2] resembling or composed of blood. [3] marked by much killing and bloodshed: *a bloody war.* [4] cruel or murderous: *a bloody tyrant.* [5] of a deep red colour; blood-red. ◆ ADVERB, ADJECTIVE [6] *Slang, chiefly Brit* (intensifier): *a bloody fool; bloody fine food.* ◆ VERB **bloodies, bloodying, bloodied.** [7] (*tr*) to stain with blood.
▸ **ˈbloodily** ADVERB ▸ **ˈbloodiness** NOUN

Bloody Mary NOUN a drink consisting of tomato juice and vodka.

bloody-minded ADJECTIVE *Brit informal* deliberately obstructive and unhelpful.

bloody-nosed beetle NOUN a beetle, *Timarcha tenebricosa*, that exudes bright red blood when alarmed: family *Chrysomelidae.*

bloom[1] (bluːm) NOUN [1] a blossom on a flowering plant; a flower. [2] the state, time, or period when flowers open (esp in the phrases **in bloom, in full bloom**). [3] open flowers collectively: *a tree covered with bloom.* [4] a healthy, vigorous, or flourishing condition; prime (esp in the phrase **the bloom of youth**). [5] youthful or healthy rosiness in the cheeks or face; glow. [6] a fine whitish coating on the surface of fruits, leaves, etc., consisting of minute grains of a waxy substance. [7] any coating similar in appearance, such as that on new coins. [8] *Ecology* a visible increase in the algal constituent of plankton, which may be seasonal or due to excessive organic pollution. [9] Also called: **chill.** a dull area formed on the surface of gloss paint, lacquer, or varnish. ◆ VERB (*mainly intr*) [10] (of flowers) to open; come into flower. [11] to bear flowers; blossom. [12] to flourish or grow. [13] to be in a healthy, glowing, or flourishing condition. [14] (*tr*) *Physics* to coat (a lens) with a thin layer of a substance, often magnesium fluoride, to eliminate surface reflection.
▷ **HISTORY** C13: of Germanic origin; compare Old Norse *blōm* flower, Old High German *bluomo*, Middle Dutch *bloeme*; see BLOW[3]

bloom[2] (bluːm) NOUN [1] a rectangular mass of metal obtained by rolling or forging a cast ingot. See also **billet**[1] (sense 2). ◆ VERB [2] (*tr*) to convert (an ingot) into a bloom by rolling or forging.
▷ **HISTORY** Old English *blōma* lump of metal

bloomed (bluːmd) ADJECTIVE *Photog, optics* (of a lens) coated with a thin film of magnesium fluoride or some other substance to reduce the amount of light lost by reflection. Also: **coated.**

bloomer[1] (ˈbluːmə) NOUN a plant that flowers, esp in a specified way: *a night bloomer.*

bloomer[2] (ˈbluːmə) NOUN *Brit informal* a stupid mistake; blunder.
▷ **HISTORY** C20: from BLOOMING

bloomer[3] (ˈbluːmə) NOUN *Brit* a medium-sized loaf, baked on the sole of the oven, glazed and notched on top.
▷ **HISTORY** C20: of uncertain origin

bloomers (ˈbluːməz) PLURAL NOUN [1] *Informal* women's or girls' baggy knickers. [2] (formerly) loose trousers gathered at the knee worn by women for cycling and athletics. [3] *History* Also called: **rational dress.** long loose trousers gathered at the ankle and worn under a shorter skirt.
▷ **HISTORY** from *bloomer*, a garment introduced in about 1850 and publicized by Mrs A. *Bloomer* (1818–94), US social reformer

bloomery (ˈbluːmərɪ) NOUN, *plural* **-eries.** a place in which malleable iron is produced directly from iron ore.

blooming (ˈbluːmɪŋ) ADVERB, ADJECTIVE *Brit informal* (intensifier): *a blooming genius; blooming painful.*
▷ **HISTORY** C19: euphemistic for BLOODY

Bloomington (ˈbluːmɪŋtən) NOUN a city in central Indiana: seat of the University of Indiana (1820). Pop.: 60 633 (1990).

Bloomsbury (ˈbluːmzbərɪ, -brɪ) NOUN [1] a district of central London in the borough of Camden: contains the British Museum, part of the University of London, and many publishers' offices. ◆ ADJECTIVE [2] relating to or characteristic of the Bloomsbury Group.

Bloomsbury Group NOUN a group of writers, artists, and intellectuals living and working in and around Bloomsbury in London from about 1907 to 1930. Influenced by the philosophy of G. E. Moore, they included Leonard and Virginia Woolf, Clive and Vanessa Bell, Roger Fry, E. M. Forster, Lytton Strachey, Duncan Grant, and John Maynard Keynes.

bloomy (ˈbluːmɪ) ADJECTIVE **bloomier, bloomiest.** having a fine whitish coating on the surface, such as on the rind of a cheese.

blooper (ˈbluːpə) NOUN *Informal, chiefly US and Canadian* a blunder; bloomer; stupid mistake.
▷ **HISTORY** C20: from *bloop* (imitative of an embarrassing sound) + -ER[1]

blossom (ˈblɒsəm) NOUN [1] the flower or flowers of a plant, esp conspicuous flowers producing edible fruit. [2] the time or period of flowering (esp in the phrases **in blossom, in full blossom**). ◆ VERB (*intr*) [3] (of plants) to come into flower. [4] to develop or come to a promising stage: *youth had blossomed into maturity.*
▷ **HISTORY** Old English *blōstm*; related to Middle Low German *blōsem*, Latin *flōs* flower
▸ **ˈblossoming** NOUN, ADJECTIVE ▸ **ˈblossomless** ADJECTIVE ▸ **ˈblossomy** ADJECTIVE

blot[1] (blɒt) NOUN [1] a stain or spot of ink, paint, dirt, etc. [2] something that spoils or detracts from

the beauty or worth of something. [3] a blemish or stain on one's character or reputation. ◆ VERB **blots, blotting, blotted.** [4] (of ink, dye, etc.) to form spots or blobs on (a material) or (of a person) to cause such spots or blobs to form on (a material). [5] **blot one's copybook.** *Informal* to spoil one's reputation by making a mistake, offending against social customs, etc. [6] (*intr*) to stain or become stained or spotted. [7] (*tr*) to cause a blemish in or on; disgrace. [8] to soak up (excess ink, etc.) by using blotting paper or some other absorbent material. [9] (of blotting paper or some other absorbent material) to absorb (excess ink, etc.). [10] (*tr;* often foll by *out*) **a** to darken or hide completely; obscure; obliterate. **b** to destroy; annihilate.
▷HISTORY C14: probably of Germanic origin; compare Middle Dutch *bluyster* BLISTER

blot² (blɒt) NOUN [1] *Backgammon* a man exposed by being placed alone on a point and therefore able to be taken by the other player. [2] *Archaic* a weak spot.
▷HISTORY C16: perhaps from Middle Dutch *bloot* poor

blot analysis NOUN *Biochem* a technique for analysing biological molecules, such as proteins (**Western blot analysis**), DNA (**Southern blot analysis**), and RNA (**Northern blot analysis**), involving their separation by gel electrophoresis, transfer to a nitrocellulose sheet, and subsequent analysis by autoradiography. Also called: **blotting.**

blotch (blɒtʃ) NOUN [1] an irregular spot or discoloration, esp a dark and relatively large one such as an ink stain. ◆ VERB [2] to become or cause to become marked by such discoloration. [3] (*intr*) (of a pen or ink) to write or flow unevenly in blotches.
▷HISTORY C17: probably from BOTCH, influenced by BLOT¹

blotchy (ˈblɒtʃɪ) ADJECTIVE covered in or marked by blotches.
▸ˈ**blotchily** ADVERB ▸ˈ**blotchiness** NOUN

blotter (ˈblɒtə) NOUN [1] something used to absorb excess ink or other liquid, esp a sheet of blotting paper with a firm backing. [2] *US* a daily record of events, such as arrests, in a police station (esp in the phrase **police blotter**).

blotting paper NOUN a soft absorbent unsized paper, used esp for soaking up surplus ink.

blotto (ˈblɒtəʊ) ADJECTIVE *Slang* unconscious, esp through drunkenness.
▷HISTORY C20: from BLOT¹ (vb); compare *blot out*

blouse (blaʊz) NOUN [1] a woman's shirtlike garment made of cotton, nylon, etc. [2] a loose-fitting smocklike garment, often knee length and belted, worn esp by E European peasants. [3] a loose-fitting waist-length belted jacket worn by soldiers. ◆ VERB [4] to hang or make so as to hang in full loose folds.
▷HISTORY C19: from French, of unknown origin

blouson (ˈbluːzɒn) NOUN a short jacket or top having the shape of a blouse.
▷HISTORY C20: French

blow¹ (bləʊ) *Archaic* ◆ VERB **blows, blowing, blew, blown.** [1] (of a current of air, the wind, etc.) to be or cause to be in motion. [2] (*intr*) to move or be carried by or as if by wind or air: *a feather blew in through the window.* [3] to expel (air, cigarette smoke, etc.) through the mouth or nose. [4] to force or cause (air, dust, etc.) to move (into, in, over, etc.) by using an instrument or by expelling breath. [5] (*intr*) to breathe hard; pant. [6] (sometimes foll by *up*) to inflate with air or the breath. [7] (*intr*) (of wind, a storm, etc.) to make a roaring or whistling sound. [8] to cause (a whistle, siren, etc.) to sound by forcing air into it, as a signal, or (of a whistle, etc.) to sound thus. [9] (*tr*) to force air from the lungs through (the nose) to clear out mucus or obstructing matter. [10] (often foll by *up, down, in,* etc.) to explode, break, or disintegrate completely: *the bridge blew down in the gale.* [11] *Electronics* to burn out (a fuse, valve, etc.) because of excessive current or (of a fuse, valve, etc.) to burn out. [12] **blow a fuse.** *Slang* to lose one's temper. [13] (*intr*) (of a whale) to spout water or air from the lungs. [14] (*tr*) to wind (a horse) by making it run excessively. [15] to cause (a wind instrument) to sound by forcing one's breath into the mouthpiece, or (of such an instrument) to sound in this way. [16] (*intr*) *Jazz, slang* to play in a jam session. [17] (*intr*) (of flies) to lay eggs (in). [18] to shape (glass, ornaments, etc.) by forcing air or gas through the material when molten. [19] (*intr*) *Chiefly Scot, Austral, and NZ* to boast or brag. [20] (*tr*) *Slang* **a** to spend (money) freely. **b** *US* to treat or entertain. [21] (*tr*) *Slang* to use (an opportunity) ineffectively. [22] *Slang* to go suddenly away (from). [23] (*tr*) *Slang* to expose or betray (a person or thing meant to be kept secret). [24] (*tr*) *US slang* to inhale (a drug). [25] (*intr*) *Slang* to masturbate. [26] (*past participleiciple* **blowed**) *Informal* another word for **damn** (esp in the phrases **I'll be blowed, blow it!, blow me down!**). [27] *Draughts* another word for **huff** (sense 4). [28] **blow hot and cold.** to vacillate. [29] **blow a kiss** *or* **kisses.** to kiss one's hand, then blow across it as if to carry the kiss through the air to another person. [30] **blow one's own trumpet.** to boast of one's own skills or good qualities. [31] **blow someone's mind.** *Slang* **a** (of a drug, esp LSD) to alter someone's mental state. **b** to astound or surprise someone. [32] **blow one's top** *or* (esp US and Canadian) **lid** *or* **stack.** *Informal* to lose one's temper. ◆ NOUN [33] the act or an instance of blowing. [34] the sound produced by blowing. [35] a blast of air or wind. [36] *Metallurgy* **a** a stage in the Bessemer process in which air is blasted upwards through molten pig iron. **b** the quantity of metal treated in a Bessemer converter. [37] *Mining* **a** a rush of air into a mine. **b** the collapse of a mine roof. [38] *Jazz, slang* a jam session. [39] **a** *Brit* a slang name for **cannabis** (sense 2). **b** *US* a slang name for **cocaine.** ◆ See also **blow away, blow in, blow into, blow off, blow on, blow out, blow over, blow through. blow up.**
▷HISTORY Old English *blāwan,* related to Old Norse *blǣr* gust of wind, Old High German *blāen,* Latin *flāre*

blow² (bləʊ) NOUN [1] a powerful or heavy stroke with the fist, a weapon, etc. [2] **at one** *or* **a blow.** by or with only one action; all at one time. [3] a sudden setback; unfortunate event: *to come as a blow.* [4] **come to blows. a** to fight. **b** to result in a fight. [5] an attacking action: *a blow for freedom.* [6] *Austral and NZ* a stroke of the shears in sheep-shearing.
▷HISTORY C15: probably of Germanic origin; compare Old High German *bliuwan* to beat

blow³ (bləʊ) VERB **blows, blowing, blew, blown.** [1] (*intr*) (of a plant or flower) to blossom or open out. [2] (*tr*) to produce (flowers). ◆ NOUN [3] a mass of blossoms. [4] the state or period of blossoming (esp in the phrase **in full blow**).
▷HISTORY Old English *blōwan;* related to Old Frisian *blōia* to bloom, Old High German *bluoen,* Latin *flōs* flower; see BLOOM¹

blow away VERB (*tr, adverb*) *Slang, chiefly US* [1] to kill (someone) by shooting. [2] to defeat decisively.

blowback (ˈbləʊˌbæk) NOUN [1] the escape to the rear of gases formed during the firing of a weapon or in a boiler, internal-combustion engine, etc. [2] the action of a light automatic weapon in which the expanding gases of the propellant force back the bolt, thus reloading the weapon.

blow-by NOUN the leakage of gas past the piston of an engine at maximum pressure.

blow-by-blow ADJECTIVE (*prenominal*) explained in great detail: *a blow-by-blow account of the argument.*

blowdown (ˈbləʊˌdaʊn) NOUN [1] an accident in a nuclear reactor in which a cooling pipe bursts causing the loss of essential coolant. ◆ VERB [2] to open a valve in a steam boiler to eject any sediment that has collected.

blow-dry VERB **-dries, -drying, -dried.** (*tr*) [1] to style (hair) while drying it with a hand-held hairdryer. ◆ NOUN [2] this method of styling the hair.

blower (ˈbləʊə) NOUN [1] a mechanical device, such as a fan, that blows. [2] a low-pressure rotary compressor, esp in a furnace or internal-combustion engine. See also **supercharger.** [3] an informal name for **telephone.** [4] an informal name for **speaking tube.** [5] an informal name for a **whale.** [6] *Mining* a discharge of firedamp from a crevice.

blowfish (ˈbləʊˌfɪʃ) NOUN, *plural* **-fish** *or* **-fishes.** a popular name for **puffer** (sense 2).

blowfly (ˈbləʊˌflaɪ) NOUN, *plural* **-flies.** any of various dipterous flies of the genus *Calliphora* and related genera that lay their eggs in rotting meat, dung, carrion, and open wounds: family *Calliphoridae.* Also called: **bluebottle.**

blowgun (ˈbləʊˌɡʌn) NOUN the US word for **blowpipe** (sense 1).

blowhard (ˈbləʊˌhɑːd) *Informal* ◆ NOUN [1] a boastful person. ◆ ADJECTIVE [2] blustering or boastful.

blowhole (ˈbləʊˌhəʊl) NOUN [1] the nostril, paired or single, of whales, situated far back on the skull. [2] a hole in ice through which whales, seals, etc., breathe. [3] **a** a vent for air or gas, esp to release fumes from a tunnel, passage, etc. **b** *NZ* a hole emitting gas or steam in a volcanic region. [4] a bubble-like defect in an ingot resulting from gas being trapped during solidification. [5] *Geology* a hole in a cliff top leading to a sea cave through which air is forced by the action of the sea.

blowie (ˈbləʊɪ) NOUN *Austral informal* a blowfly.

blow in VERB (*intr, adverb*) *Informal* to arrive or enter suddenly.

blow-in NOUN *Austral informal* an unwelcome newcomer or stranger.

blow into VERB (*intr, preposition*) *Informal* to arrive in or enter (a room, etc.) suddenly.

blow job NOUN a slang term for **fellatio.**

> **Language note** This word was formerly considered to be taboo, and it was labelled as such in previous editions of *Collins English Dictionary.* However, it has now become acceptable in speech, although some older or more conservative people may object to its use.

blowlamp (ˈbləʊˌlæmp) NOUN another name for **blowtorch.**

blow moulding NOUN a process for moulding single-piece plastic objects in which a thermoplastic is extruded into a split mould and blown against its sides.

blown (bləʊn) VERB the past participle of **blow¹** and **blow³.**

blow off VERB (*adverb*) [1] to permit (a gas under pressure, esp steam) to be released. [2] (*intr*) *Brit slang* to emit wind noisily from the anus. [3] (*tr*) *Informal* to reject or jilt (someone). [4] **blow off steam.** See **steam** (sense 6). ◆ NOUN **blow-off.** [5] a discharge of a surplus fluid, such as steam, under pressure. [6] a device through which such a discharge is made.

blow on VERB (*intr, preposition*) to defame or discredit (a person).

blow out VERB (*adverb*) [1] to extinguish (a flame, candle, etc.) or (of a flame, candle, etc.) to become extinguished. [2] (*intr*) (of a tyre) to puncture suddenly, esp at high speed. [3] (*intr*) (of a fuse) to melt suddenly. [4] (*tr; often reflexive*) to diminish or use up the energy of: *the storm blew itself out.* [5] (*intr*) (of an oil or gas well) to lose oil or gas in an uncontrolled manner. [6] (*tr*) *Slang* to cancel: *the band had to blow out the gig.* [7] **blow one's brains out.** to kill oneself by shooting oneself in the head. ◆ NOUN **blowout.** [8] the sudden melting of an electrical fuse. [9] a sudden burst in a tyre. [10] the uncontrolled escape of oil or gas from an oil or gas well. [11] the failure of a jet engine, esp when in flight. [12] *Slang* a large filling meal or lavish entertainment.

blow over VERB (*intr, adverb*) [1] to cease or be finished: *the storm blew over.* [2] to be forgotten: *the scandal will blow over.*

blowpipe (ˈbləʊˌpaɪp) NOUN [1] a long tube from which pellets, poisoned darts, etc., are shot by blowing. US word: **blowgun.** [2] Also called: **blow tube.** a tube for blowing air or oxygen into a flame to intensify its heat and direct it onto a small area. [3] a long narrow iron pipe used to gather molten glass and blow it into shape.

blowsy *or* **blowzy** (ˈblaʊzɪ) ADJECTIVE **blowsier, blowsiest** *or* **blowzier, blowziest.** [1] (esp of a woman) untidy in appearance; slovenly or sluttish. [2] (of a woman) ruddy in complexion; red-faced.
▷HISTORY C18: from dialect *blowze* beggar girl, of unknown origin
▸ˈ**blowsily** *or* ˈ**blowzily** ADVERB ▸ˈ**blowsiness** *or* ˈ**blowziness** NOUN

blow through VERB (*intr, adverb*) *Austral informal* to leave; make off.

blowtorch (ˈbləʊˌtɔːtʃ) NOUN a small burner that produces a very hot flame, used to remove old paint, melt soft metal, etc.

blow up VERB (*adverb*) [1] to explode or cause to explode. [2] (*tr*) to increase the importance of (something): *they blew the whole affair up.* [3] (*intr*) to come into consideration: *we lived well enough before this thing blew up.* [4] (*intr*) to come into existence with sudden force: *a storm had blown up.* [5] *Informal* to lose one's temper (with a person). [6] (*tr*) *Informal* to reprimand (someone). [7] (*tr*) *Informal* to enlarge the size or detail of (a photograph). ◆ NOUN **blow-up.** [8] an explosion. [9] *Informal* an enlarged photograph or part of a photograph. [10] *Informal* a fit of temper or argument. [11] Also called: **blowing up.** *Informal* a reprimand.

blowy ('bləʊɪ) ADJECTIVE **blowier, blowiest**. another word for **windy** (sense 1).

blub (blʌb) VERB **blubs, blubbing, blubbed**. *Brit* a slang word for **blubber** (senses 1–3).

blubber ('blʌbə) VERB [1] to sob without restraint. [2] to utter while sobbing. [3] (*tr*) to make (the face) wet and swollen or disfigured by crying. ◆ NOUN [4] a thick insulating layer of fatty tissue below the skin of aquatic mammals such as the whale: used by man as a source of oil. [5] *Informal* excessive and flabby body fat. [6] the act or an instance of weeping without restraint. [7] *Austral* an informal name for **jellyfish.** ◆ ADJECTIVE [8] (*often in combination*) swollen or fleshy: *blubber-faced; blubber-lips.*
▷**HISTORY** C12: perhaps from Low German *blubbern* to BUBBLE, of imitative origin
▸ **'blubberer** NOUN

blubbery ('blʌbərɪ) ADJECTIVE **-ier, -iest.** [1] of, containing, or like blubber; fat. [2] weeping or with the face disfigured by weeping.

blucher ('bluːkə, -tʃə) NOUN *Obsolete* a high shoe with laces over the tongue.
▷**HISTORY** C19: named after Gebhard Leberecht von Blücher (1742–1819), Prussian field marshal, who commanded the Prussian army against Napoleon at Waterloo (1815)

bludge (blʌdʒ) *Austral and NZ informal* ◆ VERB [1] (when *intr*, often foll by *on*) to scrounge from (someone). [2] (*intr*) to evade work. [3] (*intr*) *Archaic* to act as a pimp. ◆ NOUN [4] a very easy task; undemanding employment.
▷**HISTORY** C19: back formation from slang *bludger* pimp, from BLUDGEON

bludgeon ('blʌdʒən) NOUN [1] a stout heavy club, typically thicker at one end. [2] a person, line of argument, etc., that is effective but unsubtle. ◆ VERB (*tr*) [3] to hit or knock down with or as with a bludgeon. [4] (often foll by *into*) to force; bully; coerce: *they bludgeoned him into accepting the job.*
▷**HISTORY** C18: of uncertain origin
▸ **'bludgeoner** NOUN

bludger ('blʌdʒə) NOUN *Austral and NZ informal* [1] a person who scrounges. [2] a person who avoids work. [3] a person in authority regarded as ineffectual by those working under him.

blue (bluː) NOUN [1] any of a group of colours, such as that of a clear unclouded sky, that have wavelengths in the range 490–445 nanometres. Blue is the complementary colour of yellow and with red and green forms a set of primary colours. Related adjective: **cyanic.** [2] a dye or pigment of any of these colours. [3] blue cloth or clothing: *dressed in blue.* [4] **a** a sportsman who represents or has represented Oxford or Cambridge University and has the right to wear the university colour (dark blue for Oxford, light blue for Cambridge): *an Oxford blue.* **b** the honour of so representing one's university. [5] *Brit* an informal name for **Tory.** [6] any of numerous small blue-winged butterflies of the genera *Lampides, Polyommatus*, etc.: family *Lycaenidae.* [7] *Archaic* short for **bluestocking.** [8] *Slang* a policeman. [9] *Archery* a blue ring on a target, between the red and the black, scoring five points. [10] a blue ball in snooker, etc. [11] another name for **blueing.** [12] *Austral and NZ slang* an argument or fight: *he had a blue with a taxi driver.* [13] Also: **bluey.** *Austral and NZ slang* a court summons, esp for a traffic offence. [14] *Austral and NZ informal* a mistake; error. [15] **out of the blue.** apparently from nowhere; unexpectedly: *the opportunity came out of the blue.* [16] **into the blue.** into the unknown or the far distance. ◆ ADJECTIVE **bluer, bluest.** [17] of the colour blue. [18] (of the flesh) having a purple tinge, as from cold or contusion. [19] depressed, moody, or unhappy. [20] dismal or depressing: *a blue day.* [21] indecent, titillating, or pornographic: *blue films.* [22] bluish in colour or having parts or marks that are bluish: *a blue fox; a blue whale.* [23] *Rare* aristocratic; noble; patrician: *a blue family.* See **blue blood.** ◆ VERB **blues, blueing.** *or* **bluing blued** [24] to make, dye, or become blue. [25] (*tr*) to treat (laundry) with blueing. [26] (*tr*) *Slang* to spend extravagantly or wastefully; squander. ◆ See also **blues.**
▷**HISTORY** C13: from Old French *bleu*, of Germanic origin; compare Old Norse *blār*, Old High German *blāo*, Middle Dutch *blā*; related to Latin *flāvus* yellow
▸ **'bluely** ADVERB ▸ **'blueness** NOUN

Blue (bluː) *or* **Bluey** NOUN *Austral informal* a person with red hair.

blue-arsed fly NOUN [1] *Informal* a blowfly; bluebottle. [2] **like a blue-arsed fly.** *Informal* in a state of frenzied activity.

blue baby NOUN a baby born with a bluish tinge to the skin because of lack of oxygen in the blood, esp caused by a congenital defect of the heart.

blue bag NOUN (in Britain) [1] a fabric bag for a barrister's robes. [2] a small bag containing blueing for laundering.

Bluebeard ('bluːˌbɪəd) NOUN [1] a villain in European folk tales who marries several wives and murders them in turn. In many versions the seventh and last wife escapes the fate of the others. [2] a man who has had several wives.

bluebeat ('bluːˌbiːt) NOUN a type of West Indian pop music of the 1960s; a precursor of reggae.

bluebell ('bluːˌbɛl) NOUN [1] Also called: **wild** *or* **wood hyacinth.** a European liliaceous woodland plant, *Hyacinthoides* (or *Endymion*) *non-scripta*, having a one-sided cluster of blue bell-shaped flowers. [2] Also called: **Spanish bluebell.** a similar and related plant, *hispanica*, widely grown in gardens and becoming naturalized. [3] a Scot name for **harebell.** [3] any of various other plants with blue bell-shaped flowers.

blue beret NOUN an informal name for a soldier of a United Nations peacekeeping force.

blueberry ('bluːbərɪ, -brɪ) NOUN, *plural* **-ries.** [1] Also called: **huckleberry.** any of several North American ericaceous shrubs of the genus *Vaccinium*, such as *V. pennsylvanicum*, that have blue-black edible berries with tiny seeds. See also **bilberry.** [2] **a** the fruit of any of these plants. **b** (*as modifier*): *blueberry pie.*

bluebill ('bluːˌbɪl) NOUN *US* another name for **scaup.**

blue billy NOUN *NZ* an informal name for **dove prion.**
▷**HISTORY** probably from the name *Billy*

bluebird ('bluːˌbɜːd) NOUN [1] any North American songbird of the genus *Sialia*, having a blue or partly blue plumage: subfamily *Turdinae* (thrushes). [2] **fairy bluebird.** any songbird of the genus *Irena*, of S and SE Asia, having a blue-and-black plumage: family *Irenidae.* [3] any of various other birds having a blue plumage.

blue blood NOUN royal or aristocratic descent.
▷**HISTORY** C19: translation of Spanish *sangre azul*
▸ **'blue-'blooded** ADJECTIVE

bluebonnet ('bluːˌbɒnɪt) *or* **bluecap** ('bluːˌkæp) NOUN other names for **Balmoral**[1] (sense 3).

bluebook NOUN [1] (in Britain) a government publication bound in a stiff blue paper cover: usually the report of a royal commission or a committee. [2] *Informal, chiefly US* a register of well-known people. [3] (in Canada) an annual statement of government accounts.

bluebottle ('bluːˌbɒtᵊl) NOUN [1] another name for the **blowfly.** [2] any of various blue-flowered plants, esp the cornflower. [3] *Brit* an informal word for a **policeman.** [4] *Austral and NZ* an informal name for **Portuguese man-of-war.**

blue box NOUN *Canadian* a blue plastic container for domestic refuse that is to be collected and recycled.

blue buck NOUN another name for the **blaubok.**

bluebush ('bluːˌbʊʃ) NOUN any of various blue-grey herbaceous Australian shrubs of the genus *Maireana.*

blue cattle dog NOUN an Australian breed of dog with a bluish coat, developed for herding cattle. Also called: **Australian cattle dog, blue heeler.**

blue cheese NOUN cheese containing a blue mould, esp Stilton, Roquefort, or Danish blue. Also called (Austral and NZ): **blue vein.**

blue chip NOUN [1] a gambling chip with the highest value. [2] *Finance* **a** a stock considered reliable with respect to both dividend income and capital value. **b** (*as modifier*): *a blue-chip company.* [3] (*modifier*) denoting something considered to be a valuable asset.

blue cod NOUN a common marine spiny-finned food fish, *Parapercis colias*, of the sub-Antarctic waters of New Zealand, esp at the Chatham Islands, which is greenish blue with brown marbling and inhabits rocky bottoms. Its smoked flesh is considered a delicacy. Also called: **rock cod, pakirikiri, patutuki.**

blue-collar ADJECTIVE of, relating to, or designating manual industrial workers: *a blue-collar union.* Compare **white-collar, pink-collar.**

blue devils PLURAL NOUN [1] a fit of depression or melancholy. [2] an attack of delirium tremens.

blue duck NOUN a mountain duck, *Hymenolaimus malacorhynchos*, of New Zealand having a mostly lead-blue plumage.

Blue Ensign NOUN an ensign having the Union Jack on a blue background at the upper corner of the vertical edge alongside the hoist: flown by Royal Navy auxiliary vessels, and, with some extra distinguishing mark or insignia, by certain yacht clubs. Compare **Red Ensign, White Ensign.**

blue-eyed boy NOUN *Informal, chiefly Brit* the favourite or darling of a person or group. Usual US equivalent: **fair-haired boy.**

blue-eyed grass NOUN any of various mainly North American iridaceous marsh plants of the genus *Sisyrinchium* that have grasslike leaves and small flat starlike blue flowers.

blue-eyed Mary NOUN a blue-flowered boraginaceous plant, *Omphalodes verna*, native to S Europe and cultivated in Britain.

blue-eyed soul NOUN *Informal* soul music written and performed by White singers in a style derived from the blues.

bluefin ('bluːˌfɪn) *or* **bluefin tuna** another name for **tunny.**

bluefish ('bluːˌfɪʃ) NOUN, *plural* **-fish** *or* **-fishes.** [1] Also called: **snapper.** a bluish marine percoid food and game fish, *Pomatomus saltatrix*, related to the horse mackerel: family *Pomatomidae.* [2] any of various other bluish fishes.

Blue Flag NOUN an award given to a seaside resort that meets EU standards of cleanliness of beaches and purity of water in bathing areas.

blue fox NOUN [1] a variety of the arctic fox that has a pale grey winter coat and is bred for its fur. [2] the fur of this animal.

blue funk NOUN *Slang* a state of great terror or loss of nerve.

bluegill ('bluːˌgɪl) NOUN a common North American freshwater sunfish, *Lepomis macrochirus*: an important food and game fish.

blue goose NOUN a variety of the snow goose that has a bluish-grey body and white head and neck.

bluegrass ('bluːˌgrɑːs) NOUN [1] any of several North American bluish-green grasses of the genus *Poa*, esp *P. pratensis* (**Kentucky bluegrass**), grown for forage. [2] a type of folk music originating in Kentucky, characterized by a simple harmonized accompaniment.

blue-green algae PLURAL NOUN the former name for **cyanobacteria.**

blue ground NOUN *Mineralogy* another name for **kimberlite.**

blue grouse NOUN a grouse, *Dendragapus obscurus*, of W North America, having a bluish-grey plumage with a black tail.

blue gum NOUN [1] a tall fast-growing widely cultivated Australian myrtaceous tree, *Eucalyptus globulus*, having aromatic leaves containing a medicinal oil, bark that peels off in shreds, and hard timber. The juvenile leaves are bluish in colour. [2] any of several other eucalyptus trees. ◆ See also **red gum** (sense 1).

blue heeler NOUN *Austral and NZ* a cattle dog that controls cattle by biting their heels. Also called: **heeler.**

blueing *or* **bluing** (ˈbluːɪŋ) NOUN [1] a blue material, such as indigo, used in laundering to counteract yellowing. [2] the formation of a film of blue oxide on a steel surface.

bluejacket (ˈbluːˌdʒækɪt) NOUN a sailor in the Navy.

blue jay NOUN a common North American jay, *Cyanocitta cristata*, having bright blue plumage with greyish-white underparts.

blue john NOUN a blue or purple fibrous variety of fluorspar occurring only in Derbyshire: used for vases, etc.

blue laws PLURAL NOUN *US history* a number of repressive puritanical laws of the colonial period, forbidding any secular activity on Sundays.

blue lias NOUN a type of rock composed of alternating layers of bluish shale or clay and grey argillaceous limestone. See also **Lias**.

Blue Mantle NOUN one of the four pursuivants of the British College of Arms.

blue merle NOUN See **merle**[2].

blue moon NOUN [1] the second full moon occurring within a calendar month. [2] **once in a blue moon**. *Informal* very rarely; almost never.

blue mould NOUN [1] Also called: **green mould**. any fungus of the genus *Penicillium* that forms a bluish mass on decaying food, leather, etc. [2] any fungal disease of fruit trees characterized by necrosis and a bluish growth on the affected tissue: mostly caused by *Penicillium* species.

Blue Mountains PLURAL NOUN [1] a mountain range in the US, in NE Oregon and SE Washington. Highest peak: Rock Creek Butte, 2773 m (9097 ft.). [2] a mountain range in the Caribbean, in E Jamaica: Blue Mountain coffee is grown on its slopes. Highest peak: Blue Mountain Peak, 2256 m (7402 ft.). [3] a plateau in SE Australia, in E New South Wales: part of the Great Dividing Range. Highest part: about 1134 m (3871 ft.).

blue murder NOUN *Informal* a great outcry, noise; horrible din (esp in such phrases as **cry, howl, scream,** etc., **blue murder**).

Blue Nile NOUN a river in E Africa, rising in central Ethiopia as the Abbai and flowing southeast, then northwest to join the White Nile. Length: about 1530 km (950 miles).

bluenose (ˈbluːˌnəʊz) NOUN [1] *US slang* a puritanical or prudish person. [2] (*often capital*) *Informal* a native or inhabitant of Nova Scotia.

blue note NOUN *Jazz* a flattened third or seventh, used frequently in the blues.

blue pencil NOUN [1] deletion, alteration, or censorship of the contents of a book or other work. ◆ VERB **blue-pencil, -cils, -cilling, -cilled** *or US* **-cils, -ciling, -ciled**. [2] (*tr*) to alter or delete parts of (a book, film, etc.), esp to censor.

blue peter NOUN a signal flag of blue with a white square at the centre, displayed by a vessel about to leave port.
▷HISTORY C19: from the name *Peter*

blue pointer NOUN a large shark, *Isuropsis mako*, of Australian coastal waters, having a blue back and pointed snout.

blueprint (ˈbluːˌprɪnt) NOUN [1] Also called: **cyanotype**. a photographic print of plans, technical drawings, etc., consisting of white lines on a blue background. [2] an original plan or prototype that influences subsequent design or practice: *the Montessori method was the blueprint for education in the 1940s*. ◆ VERB [3] (*tr*) to make a blueprint of (a plan).

blue racer NOUN a long slender blackish-blue fast-moving colubrid snake, *Coluber constrictor flaviventris*, of the US.

blue riband *or* **ribband** NOUN [1] (*sometimes capitals*) Also called (esp US): **blue ribbon**. the record for the fastest sea journey between two places, esp (in the 1920s and 30s) for a passenger liner between New York and Southampton. [2] **a** the most distinguished achievement in any field. **b** (*as modifier*): *the blue-riband event of the meeting*.

blue ribbon NOUN [1] (in Britain) a badge of blue silk worn by members of the Order of the Garter. [2] a badge awarded as the first prize in a competition. [3] *US* a badge worn by a member of a temperance society.

blue-ribbon jury NOUN a US name for a **special jury**.

Blue Ridge Mountains PLURAL NOUN a mountain range in the eastern US, extending from West Virginia into Georgia: part of the Appalachian mountains. Highest peak: Mount Mitchell, 2038 m (6684 ft.).

blue-ringed octopus NOUN a highly venomous octopus, *Octopus maculosus*, of E Australia which exhibits blue bands on its tentacles when disturbed.

blue rinse NOUN [1] a rinse for tinting grey hair a silvery-blue colour. ◆ ADJECTIVE **blue-rinse**. [2] denoting or typifying an elderly, well-groomed, socially active, and comparatively wealthy woman.

Blue Rod NOUN *Brit* officer of the Order of St Michael and St George. Full title: **Gentleman Usher of the Blue Rod**.

blue run NOUN *Skiing* an easy run, suitable for beginners.

blues (bluːz) PLURAL NOUN (*sometimes functioning as singular*) **the**. [1] a feeling of depression or deep unhappiness. [2] a type of folk song devised by Black Americans at the beginning of the 20th century, usually employing a basic 12-bar chorus, the tonic, subdominant, and dominant chords, frequent minor intervals, and blue notes.
► ˈ**bluesy** ADJECTIVE

Blues (bluːz) PLURAL NOUN **the**. *Brit* the Royal Horse Guards.

blue schist NOUN a metamorphic rock formed under conditions of high pressure and relatively low temperature.

blue screen NOUN a special effects film technique involving filming actors against a blue screen on which effects such as computerized graphics can be added later and integrated into a single sequence.

blueshift (ˈbluːˌʃɪft) NOUN a shift in the spectral lines of a stellar spectrum towards the blue end of the visible region relative to the wavelengths of these lines in the terrestrial spectrum: a result of the **Doppler effect** caused by stars approaching the solar system. Compare **redshift**.

blue-singlet ADJECTIVE *Austral* working-class.

blue-sky *or* **blue-skies** NOUN (*modifier*) of or denoting theoretical research without regard to any future application of its result: *a blue-sky project*.

blue-sky law NOUN *US* a state law regulating the trading of securities: intended to protect investors from fraud.

blue spruce NOUN a spruce tree, *Picea pungens glauca*, native to the Rocky Mountains of North America, having blue-green needle-like leaves. Also called: **balsam spruce**.

blue stain NOUN *Forestry* a bluish discoloration of sapwood caused by growth of fungi.

bluestocking (ˈbluːˌstɒkɪŋ) NOUN *Usually disparaging* a scholarly or intellectual woman.
▷HISTORY from the blue worsted stockings worn by members of a C18 literary society

bluestone (ˈbluːˌstəʊn) NOUN [1] a blue-grey sandstone containing much clay, used for building and paving. [2] the blue crystalline form of copper sulphate. [3] a blue variety of basalt found in Australia and used as a building stone.

blue swimmer NOUN [1] an edible bluish Australian swimming crab, *Portunus pelagicus*. [2] *Austral informal* an Australian ten-dollar note.

bluet (ˈbluːɪt) NOUN a North American rubiaceous plant, *Houstonia caerulea*, with small four-petalled blue flowers.

bluethroat (ˈbluːˌθrəʊt) NOUN a small brownish European songbird, *Cyanosylvia svecica*, related to the thrushes, the male of which has a blue throat: family *Muscicapidae*.

bluetit (ˈbluːˌtɪt) NOUN a common European tit, *Parus caeruleus*, having a blue crown, wings, and tail, yellow underparts, and a black and grey head.

bluetongue (ˌbluːˈtʌŋ) NOUN an Australian lizard, *Tiliqua scincoides*, having a cobalt-blue tongue.

bluetongue (ˌbluːˈtʌŋ) NOUN *Vet science* a viral disease of domestic and wild ruminants transmitted by arthropods and characterized by reproductive problems or vasculitis. Sheep, which are most frequently affected, develop swelling of the face and a cyanotic tongue.

blue vein NOUN *Austral and NZ* another name for **blue cheese**.

blue vitriol NOUN the fully hydrated blue crystalline form of copper sulphate.

blueweed (ˈbluːˌwiːd) NOUN *US* another name for **viper's bugloss**.

blue whale NOUN the largest mammal: a widely distributed bluish-grey whalebone whale, *Sibbaldus* (or *Balaenoptera*) *musculus*, closely related and similar to the rorquals: family *Balaenopteridae*. Also called: **sulphur-bottom**.

bluey (ˈbluːɪ) NOUN *Austral informal* [1] a blanket. [2] a swagman's bundle. [3] **hump (one's) bluey**. to carry one's bundle; tramp. [4] *Slang* a variant of **blue** (sense 13). [5] a cattle dog. [6] a red-headed person.
▷HISTORY (for senses 1, 2, 5) C19: from BLUE (on account of their colour) + -Y[2]

Bluey (ˈbluːɪ) NOUN a variant of **Blue**.

bluff[1] (blʌf) VERB [1] to pretend to be confident about an uncertain issue or to have undisclosed resources, in order to influence or deter (someone). ◆ NOUN [2] deliberate deception intended to create the impression of a stronger position or greater resources than one actually has. [3] **call someone's bluff**. to challenge someone to give proof of his claims.
▷HISTORY C19: originally US poker-playing term, from Dutch *bluffen* to boast
► ˈ**bluffer** NOUN

bluff[2] (blʌf) NOUN [1] a steep promontory, bank, or cliff, esp one formed by river erosion on the outside bend of a meander. [2] *Canadian* a clump of trees on the prairie; copse. ◆ ADJECTIVE [3] good-naturedly frank and hearty. [4] (of a bank, cliff, etc.) presenting a steep broad face.
▷HISTORY C17 (in the sense: nearly perpendicular): perhaps from Middle Dutch *blaf* broad
► ˈ**bluffly** ADVERB ► ˈ**bluffness** NOUN

bluish *or* **blueish** (ˈbluːɪʃ) ADJECTIVE somewhat blue.
► ˈ**bluishness** *or* ˈ**blueishness** NOUN

blunder (ˈblʌndə) NOUN [1] a stupid or clumsy mistake. [2] a foolish tactless remark. ◆ VERB (*mainly intr*) [3] to make stupid or clumsy mistakes. [4] to make foolish tactless remarks. [5] (often foll by *about, into,* etc) to act clumsily; stumble: *he blundered into a situation he knew nothing about*. [6] (*tr*) to mismanage; botch.
▷HISTORY C14: of Scandinavian origin; compare Old Norse *blunda* to close one's eyes, Norwegian dialect *blundra*; see BLIND
► ˈ**blunderer** NOUN ► ˈ**blundering** NOUN, ADJECTIVE
► ˈ**blunderingly** ADVERB

blunderbuss (ˈblʌndəˌbʌs) NOUN [1] an obsolete short musket with large bore and flared muzzle, used to scatter shot at short range. [2] *Informal* a clumsy unsubtle person.
▷HISTORY C17: changed (through the influence of BLUNDER) from Dutch *donderbus*; from *donder* THUNDER + obsolete *bus* gun

blunge (blʌndʒ) VERB (*tr*) to mix (clay or a similar substance) with water in order to form a suspension for use in ceramics.
▷HISTORY C19: probably from BLEND + PLUNGE

blunger (ˈblʌndʒə) NOUN a large vat in which the contents, esp clay and water, are mixed by rotating arms.

blunt (blʌnt) ADJECTIVE [1] (esp of a knife or blade) lacking sharpness or keenness; dull. [2] not having a sharp edge or point: *a blunt instrument*. [3] (of people, manner of speaking, etc.) lacking refinement or subtlety; straightforward and uncomplicated. [4] outspoken; direct and to the point: *a blunt Yorkshireman*. ◆ VERB (*tr*) [5] to make less sharp. [6] to diminish the sensitivity or perception of; make dull. ◆ NOUN [7] *Slang* a cannabis cigarette.
▷HISTORY C12: probably of Scandinavian origin; compare Old Norse *blundr* dozing, *blunda* to close one's eyes; see BLUNDER, BLIND
► ˈ**bluntly** ADVERB ► ˈ**bluntness** NOUN

blur (blɜː) VERB **blurs, blurring, blurred**. [1] to make or become vague or less distinct: *heat haze blurs the hills; education blurs class distinctions*. [2] to smear or smudge. [3] (*tr*) to make (the judgment, memory, or perception) less clear; dim. ◆ NOUN [4] something vague, hazy, or indistinct. [5] a smear or smudge.
▷HISTORY C16: perhaps variant of BLEAR

▸**blurred** (blɜːd) ADJECTIVE ▸**blurredly** (ˈblɜːrɪdlɪ, ˈblɜːd-) ADVERB ▸ˈ**blurredness** NOUN ▸ˈ**blurriness** NOUN ▸ˈ**blurry** ADJECTIVE

blurb (blɜːb) NOUN a promotional description, as found on the jackets of books.
▷HISTORY C20: coined by Gelett Burgess (1866–1951), US humorist and illustrator

blurt (blɜːt) VERB (*tr; often foll by out*) to utter suddenly and involuntarily.
▷HISTORY C16: probably of imitative origin

blush (blʌʃ) VERB [1] (*intr*) to become suddenly red in the face from embarrassment, shame, modesty, or guilt; redden. [2] to make or become reddish or rosy. ◆ NOUN [3] a sudden reddening of the face from embarrassment, shame, modesty, or guilt. [4] a rosy glow: *the blush of a peach.* [5] a reddish or pinkish tinge. [6] a cloudy area on the surface of freshly applied gloss paint. [7] **at first blush.** when first seen; as a first impression.
▷HISTORY Old English *blȳscan*; related to *blȳsian* to burn, Middle Low German *blüsen* to light a fire
▸ˈ**blushful** ADJECTIVE ▸ˈ**blushing** NOUN, ADJECTIVE ▸ˈ**blushingly** ADVERB

blusher (ˈblʌʃə) NOUN a cosmetic applied to the face to give a rosy colour.

bluster (ˈblʌstə) VERB [1] to speak or say loudly or boastfully. [2] to act in a bullying way. [3] (*tr*, foll by *into*) to force or attempt to force (a person) into doing something by behaving thus. [4] (*intr*) (of the wind) to be noisy or gusty. ◆ NOUN [5] boisterous talk or action; swagger. [6] empty threats or protests. [7] a strong wind; gale.
▷HISTORY C15: probably from Middle Low German *blüsteren* to storm, blow violently
▸ˈ**blusterer** NOUN ▸ˈ**blustering** NOUN, ADJECTIVE ▸ˈ**blusteringly** *or* ˈ**blusterously** ADVERB ▸ˈ**blustery** *or* ˈ**blusterous** ADJECTIVE

Blu-tack (ˈbluːtæk) NOUN [1] *Trademark* a type of blue, malleable, sticky material used to attach paper, card, etc. to walls and other surfaces. ◆ VERB [2] (*tr*) to attach (paper, card, etc.) to a wall or other surface by means of this material.

Blvd ABBREVIATION FOR Boulevard.

B-lymphocyte NOUN a type of lymphocyte, originating in bone marrow, that produces antibodies. Also called: **B-cell**. See also **T-lymphocyte**.

Blyth (blaɪð) NOUN a port in N England, in SE Northumberland, on the North Sea. Pop.: 35 327 (1991).

bm[1] ABBREVIATION FOR: [1] board measure. [2] bowel movement.

bm[2] THE INTERNET DOMAIN NAME FOR Bermuda.

BM ABBREVIATION FOR: [1] Bachelor of Medicine. [2] *Surveying* benchmark. [3] **British Museum.**

BMA ABBREVIATION FOR British Medical Association.

BMI ABBREVIATION FOR: [1] body mass index. [2] Broadcast Music Incorporated.

BMJ ABBREVIATION FOR British Medical Journal.

B-movie NOUN a film originally made (esp in Hollywood in the 1940s and 50s) as a supporting film, now often considered as a genre in its own right.

BMR ABBREVIATION FOR **basal metabolic rate**.

BMus ABBREVIATION FOR Bachelor of Music.

BMX ABBREVIATION FOR: [1] bicycle motocross; stunt riding on rough ground or over an obstacle course on a bicycle. [2] a bicycle designed for bicycle motocross.

bn[1] ABBREVIATION FOR billion.

bn[2] THE INTERNET DOMAIN NAME FOR Brunei Darussalam.

Bn ABBREVIATION FOR: [1] Baron. [2] Also: **bn** Battalion.

B4N *Text messaging* ABBREVIATION FOR bye for now.

BNA (in Canada) ABBREVIATION FOR British North America.

B'nai B'rith (bəˈneɪ bəˈriːθ, brɪθ) NOUN a Jewish fraternal organization founded in New York in 1843, having moral, philanthropic, social, educational, and political aims.
▷HISTORY from Hebrew *benē brīth* sons of the covenant

BNFL ABBREVIATION FOR British Nuclear Fuels Limited.

BNP ABBREVIATION FOR British National Party.

bo *or* **boh** (bəʊ) INTERJECTION [1] Also: **boh.** an exclamation uttered to startle or surprise someone, esp a child in a game. [2] *Slang* an exclamation of encouragement or an expression of enthusiasm.

bo THE INTERNET DOMAIN NAME FOR Bolivia.

BO ABBREVIATION FOR: [1] *Informal* body odour. [2] box office.

b.o. ABBREVIATION FOR: [1] back order. [2] branch office. [3] broker's order. [4] buyer's option.

B/O ABBREVIATION FOR: [1] *Book-keeping* brought over. [2] buyer's option.

boa (ˈbəʊə) NOUN [1] any large nonvenomous snake of the family *Boidae*, most of which occur in Central and South America and the Caribbean. They have vestigial hind limbs and kill their prey by constriction. [2] a woman's long thin scarf, usually of feathers or fur.
▷HISTORY C19: from New Latin, from Latin: a large Italian snake, water snake

boab (ˈbəʊæb) NOUN *Austral* short for **baobab**.

BOAC (formerly) ABBREVIATION FOR British Overseas Airways Corporation.

boa constrictor NOUN a very large snake, *Constrictor constrictor*, of tropical America and the Caribbean, that kills its prey by constriction: family *Boidae* (boas).

boak (bok, bəʊk) VERB, NOUN a variant spelling of **boke.**

Boanerges (ˌbəʊəˈnɜːdʒiːz) NOUN [1] *New Testament* a nickname applied by Jesus to James and John in Mark 3:17. [2] a fiery preacher, esp one with a powerful voice.
▷HISTORY C17: from Hebrew *benē reghesh* sons of thunder

boar (bɔː) NOUN [1] an uncastrated male pig. [2] See **wild boar.**
▷HISTORY Old English *bār*; related to Old High German *bēr*

board (bɔːd) NOUN [1] a long wide flat relatively thin piece of sawn timber. [2] **a** a smaller flat piece of rigid material for a specific purpose: *ironing board.* **b** (*in combination*): *breadboard; cheeseboard.* [3] a person's food or meals, provided regularly for money or sometimes as payment for work done (esp in the phrases **full board, board and lodging**). [4] *Archaic* a table, esp one used for eating at, and esp when laden with food. [5] **a** (*sometimes functioning as plural*) a group of people who officially administer a company, trust, etc: *a board of directors.* **b** (*as modifier*): *a board meeting.* [6] any other committee or council: *a board of interviewers.* [7] **the boards.** (*plural*) the acting profession; the stage. [8] short for **blackboard, chessboard, notice board, printed circuit board** (see **printed circuit**), **springboard, surfboard.** [9] stiff cardboard or similar material covered with paper, cloth, etc., used for the outside covers of a book. [10] a flat thin rectangular sheet of composite material, such as plasterboard or chipboard. [11] *Chiefly US* **a** a list on which stock-exchange securities and their prices are posted. **b** *Informal* the stock exchange itself. [12] *Nautical* **a** the side of a ship. **b** the leg that a sailing vessel makes on a beat to windward. [13] *Austral and NZ* the part of the floor of a sheep-shearing shed, esp a raised part, where the shearers work. [14] *NZ* the killing floor of an abattoir or freezing works. [15] **a** any of various portable surfaces specially designed for indoor games such as chess, backgammon, etc. **b** (*as modifier*): *board games.* [16] **a** a set of hands in duplicate bridge. **b** a wooden or metal board containing four slots, or often nowadays, a plastic wallet, in which the four hands are placed so that the deal may be replayed with identical hands. [17] the hull of a sailboard, usually made of plastic, to which the mast is jointed and on which a windsurfer stands. [18] See **above board.** [19] **go by the board.** to be in disuse, neglected, or lost: *in these days courtesy goes by the board.* [20] **on board.** on or in a ship, boat, aeroplane, or other vehicle. [21] **sweep the board. a** (in gambling) to win all the cards or money. **b** to win every event or prize in a contest. [22] **take on board.** to accept (new ideas, situations, theories, etc.). ◆ VERB [23] to go aboard (a vessel, train, aircraft, or other vehicle). [24] *Nautical* to come alongside (a vessel) before attacking or going aboard. [25] to attack (a ship) by forcing one's way aboard. [26] (*tr; often foll by up, in,* etc.) to cover or shut with boards. [27] (*intr*) to give or receive meals or meals and lodging in return for money or work. [28] (sometimes foll by *out*) to receive or arrange for (someone, esp a child) to receive food and lodging away from home, usually in return for payment.
▷HISTORY Old English *bord*; related to Old Norse *borth* ship's side, table, Old High German *bort* ship's side, Sanskrit *bardhaka* a cutting off
▸ˈ**boardable** ADJECTIVE

board-and-shingle NOUN *Caribbean* a small dwelling with wooden walls and a shingle roof.

board bridge NOUN another name for **duplicate bridge.**

boarder (ˈbɔːdə) NOUN [1] *Brit* a pupil who lives at school during term time. [2] *US* a child who lives away from its parents and is cared for by a person or organization receiving payment. [3] another word for **lodger.** [4] a person who boards a ship, esp one who forces his way aboard in an attack: *stand by to repel boarders.* [5] *Informal* a person who takes part in sailboarding or snowboarding.

board foot NOUN a unit of board measure: the cubic content of a piece of wood one foot square and one inch thick.

boarding (ˈbɔːdɪŋ) NOUN [1] a structure of boards, such as a floor or fence. [2] timber boards collectively. [3] **a** the act of embarking on an aircraft, train, ship, etc. **b** (*as modifier*): *a boarding pass.* [4] a process used in tanning to accentuate the natural grain of hides, in which the surface of a softened leather is lightly creased by folding grain to grain and the fold is worked to and fro across the leather.

boarding house NOUN [1] a private house in which accommodation and meals are provided for paying guests. [2] *Austral* a house for boarders at a school. See also **house** (sense 10).

boarding out NOUN *Social welfare Brit* **a** the local-authority practice of placing a client in a foster family or voluntary establishment and paying for it. **b** (*as modifier*): *boarding-out allowances.*

boarding school NOUN a school providing living accommodation for some or all of its pupils.

board measure NOUN a system of units for measuring wood based on the board foot. 1980 board feet equal one standard.

board of trade NOUN *US and Canadian* another name for a **chamber of commerce.**

Board of Trade NOUN (in the United Kingdom) a ministry within the Department of Trade: responsible for the supervision of commerce and the promotion of export trade.

Board of Trade Unit NOUN a unit of electrical energy equal to 1 kilowatt-hour. Abbreviation: **BTU.**

boardroom (ˈbɔːdˌruːm, -ˌrʊm) NOUN **a** a room where the board of directors of a company meets. **b** (*as modifier*): *a boardroom power struggle.*

board rule NOUN a measuring device for estimating the number of board feet in a quantity of wood.

boardsailing (ˈbɔːdˌseɪlɪŋ) NOUN another name for **windsurfing.**
▸ˈ**boardˌsailor** NOUN

board school NOUN *Brit* (formerly) a school managed by a board elected by local ratepayers.

boardwalk (ˈbɔːdˌwɔːk) NOUN *US and Canadian* a promenade, esp along a beach, usually made of planks.

boarfish (ˈbɔːˌfɪʃ) NOUN, *plural* **-fish** *or* **-fishes.** any of various spiny-finned marine teleost fishes of the genera *Capros, Antigonia,* etc., related to the dories, having a deep compressed body, a long snout, and large eyes.

boarish (ˈbɔːrɪʃ) ADJECTIVE coarse, cruel, or sensual.
▸ˈ**boarishly** ADVERB ▸ˈ**boarishness** NOUN

boart (bɔːt) NOUN a variant spelling of **bort.**

boast[1] (bəʊst) VERB [1] (*intr; sometimes foll by of or about*) to speak in exaggerated or excessively proud terms of one's possessions, skills, or superior qualities; brag. [2] (*tr*) to possess (something to be proud of): *the city boasts a fine cathedral.* ◆ NOUN [3] a bragging statement. [4] a possession, attribute, attainment, etc., that is or may be bragged about.
▷HISTORY C13: of uncertain origin
▸ˈ**boaster** NOUN ▸ˈ**boasting** NOUN, ADJECTIVE ▸ˈ**boastingly** ADVERB

boast[2] (bəʊst) VERB (*tr*) to shape or dress (stone) roughly with a broad chisel.

▷**HISTORY** C19: of unknown origin

boast[3] (bəʊst) *Squash* ◆ NOUN [1] a stroke in which the ball is hit on to one of the side walls before hitting the front wall. ◆ VERB [2] to hit (the ball) in this way or make such a stroke.
▷**HISTORY** C19: perhaps from French *bosse* the place where the ball hits the wall
▸ **'boasted** ADJECTIVE

boastful ('bəʊstfʊl) ADJECTIVE tending to boast; characterized by boasting.
▸ **'boastfully** ADVERB ▸ **'boastfulness** NOUN

boat (bəʊt) NOUN [1] a small vessel propelled by oars, paddle, sails, or motor for travelling, transporting goods, etc., esp one that can be carried aboard a larger vessel. [2] (not in technical use) another word for **ship**. [3] *Navy* a submarine. [4] a container for gravy, sauce, etc. [5] a small boat-shaped container for incense, used in some Christian churches. [6] **in the same boat.** sharing the same problems. [7] **burn one's boats.** See **burn**[1] (sense 19). [8] **miss the boat.** to lose an opportunity. [9] **push the boat out.** *Brit informal* to celebrate, esp lavishly and expensively. [10] **rock the boat.** *Informal* to cause a disturbance in the existing situation. ◆ VERB [11] (*intr*) to travel or go in a boat, esp as a form of recreation. [12] (*tr*) to transport or carry in a boat.
▷**HISTORY** Old English *bāt*; related to Old Norse *beit* boat

boatbill ('bəʊt,bɪl) *or* **boat-billed heron** NOUN a nocturnal tropical American wading bird, *Cochlearius cochlearius*, similar to the night herons but with a broad flattened bill: family *Ardeidae*, order *Ciconiiformes*.

boat deck NOUN the deck of a ship on which the lifeboats are kept.

boat drill NOUN practice in launching the lifeboats and taking off the passengers and crew of a ship.

boatel *or* **botel** (bəʊ'tɛl) NOUN [1] a waterside hotel catering for boating people. [2] a ship that functions as a hotel.
▷**HISTORY** C20: from BOAT + (HOT)EL

boater ('bəʊtə) NOUN a stiff straw hat with a straight brim and flat crown.

boathook ('bəʊt,hʊk) NOUN a pole with a hook at one end, used aboard a vessel for fending off other vessels or obstacles or for catching a line or mooring buoy.

boathouse ('bəʊt,haʊs) NOUN a shelter by the edge of a river, lake, etc., for housing boats.

boatie ('bəʊtɪ) NOUN *Austral and NZ informal* a boating enthusiast.

boating ('bəʊtɪŋ) NOUN the practice of rowing, sailing, or cruising in boats as a form of recreation.

boatload ('bəʊt,ləʊd) NOUN the amount of cargo or number of people held by a boat or ship.

boatman ('bəʊtmən) NOUN, *plural* **-men.** [1] a man who works on, hires out, repairs, or operates a boat or boats. [2] short for **water boatman.**

boat neck NOUN a high slitlike neckline of a garment that extends onto the shoulders. Also called: **bateau neckline.**

boat people PLURAL NOUN refugees, esp from Vietnam in the late 1970s, who leave by boat hoping to be picked up by ships of another country.

boat race NOUN **the.** *Brit* a rowing event held annually in the spring, in which an eight representing Oxford University rows against one representing Cambridge University on the Thames between Putney and Mortlake.

boatswain, bosun, *or* **bo's'n** ('bəʊsᵊn) NOUN a petty officer on a merchant ship or a warrant officer on a warship who is responsible for the maintenance of the ship and its equipment.
▷**HISTORY** Old English *bātswegen*; see BOAT, SWAIN

boatswain's chair NOUN *Nautical* a seat consisting of a short flat board slung from ropes, used to support a person working on the side of a vessel or in its rigging.

boat train NOUN a train scheduled to take passengers to or from a particular ship.

Boa Vista (*Portuguese* 'boːə 'viʃtə) NOUN a town in N Brazil, capital of the federal territory of Roraima, on the Rio Branco. Pop.: 196 942 (2000).

Boaz ('bəʊæz) NOUN *Old Testament* a kinsman of Naomi, who married her daughter-in-law Ruth (Ruth 2–4); one of David's ancestors.

bob[1] (bɒb) VERB **bobs, bobbing, bobbed.** [1] to move or cause to move up and down repeatedly, as while floating in water. [2] to move or cause to move with a short abrupt movement, as of the head. [3] to make (a bow or curtsy): *the little girl bobbed before the visitor.* [4] (*intr;* usually foll by *up*) to appear or emerge suddenly. [5] (*intr;* foll by *under, below,* etc.) to disappear suddenly, as beneath a surface. [6] (*intr;* usually foll by *for*) to attempt to get hold (of a floating or hanging object, esp an apple) in the teeth as a game. ◆ NOUN [7] a short abrupt movement, as of the head. [8] a quick curtsy or bow. [9] *Bell-ringing* a particular set of changes. [10] *Angling* **a** short for **bobfloat. b** the topmost fly on a cast of three, often fished bobbing at the surface. **c** this position on a wet-fly cast.
▷**HISTORY** C14: of uncertain origin

bob[2] (bɒb) NOUN [1] a hairstyle for women and children in which the hair is cut short evenly all round the head. [2] a dangling or hanging object, such as the weight on a pendulum or on a plumb line. [3] a polishing disc on a rotating spindle. It is usually made of felt, leather, etc., impregnated with an abrasive material. [4] short for **bob skate** or **bobsleigh.** [5] a runner or pair of runners on a bobsled. [6] *Angling* a small knot of worms, maggots, etc., used as bait. [7] a very short line of verse at the end of a stanza or preceding a rhyming quatrain (the wheel) at the end of a stanza. [8] a refrain or burden with such a short line or lines. [9] a docked tail, esp of a horse. [10] *Brit dialect* a hanging cluster, as of flowers or ribbons. ◆ VERB **bobs, bobbing, bobbed.** [11] (*tr*) to cut (the hair) in a bob. [12] (*tr*) to cut short (something, esp the tail of an animal); dock or crop. [13] (*intr*) to ride on a bobsled.
▷**HISTORY** C14 *bobbe* bunch of flowers, perhaps of Celtic origin

bob[3] (bɒb) VERB **bobs, bobbing, bobbed.** [1] to tap or cause to tap or knock lightly (against). ◆ NOUN [2] a light knock; tap.
▷**HISTORY** C13 *bobben* to rap, beat; see BOP[2]

bob[4] (bɒb) NOUN, *plural* **bob.** *Brit* (formerly) an informal word for a **shilling.**
▷**HISTORY** C19: of unknown origin

Bob (bɒb) NOUN **Bob's your uncle.** *Slang* everything is or will turn out all right.
▷**HISTORY** C19: perhaps from pet form of *Robert*

bobbejaan ('bɒbə,jɑːn) NOUN *South African* [1] a baboon. [2] a large black spider. [3] a monkey wrench.
▷**HISTORY** Afrikaans

bobbery ('bɒbərɪ) NOUN, *plural* **-beries.** [1] Also called: **bobbery pack.** a mixed pack of hunting dogs, often not belonging to any of the hound breeds. [2] *Informal* a noisy commotion. ◆ ADJECTIVE [3] *Informal* noisy or excitable.
▷**HISTORY** C19: from Hindi *bāp re*, literally: oh father!

bobbin ('bɒbɪn) NOUN [1] a spool or reel on which thread or yarn is wound, being unwound as required; spool; reel. [2] narrow braid or cord used as binding or for trimming. [3] a device consisting of a short bar and a length of string, used to control a wooden door latch. [4] **a** a spool on which insulated wire is wound to form the coil of a small electromagnetic device, such as a bell or buzzer. **b** the coil of such a spool. [5] (*plural*) *Brit slang* matter that is worthless or of inferior quality; rubbish.
▷**HISTORY** C16: from Old French *bobine*, of unknown origin

bobbinet (,bɒbɪ'nɛt) NOUN a netted fabric of hexagonal mesh, made on a lace machine.
▷**HISTORY** C19: see BOBBIN, NET[1]

bobbin lace NOUN lace made with bobbins rather than with needle and thread (needlepoint lace); pillow lace.

bobble ('bɒbᵊl) NOUN [1] a short jerky motion, as of a cork floating on disturbed water; bobbing movement. [2] a tufted ball, usually for ornament, as on a knitted hat. [3] any small dangling ball or bundle. ◆ VERB [4] (*intr*) *Sport* (of a ball) to bounce with a rapid erratic motion due to an uneven playing surface. [5] *US informal* to handle (something) ineptly; muff; bungle: *he bobbled the ball and lost the game.*
▷**HISTORY** C19: from BOB[1] (vb)

bobble hat NOUN a knitted hat with a tufted woollen ball on top.

bobby ('bɒbɪ) NOUN, *plural* **-bies.** *Informal* a British policeman.
▷**HISTORY** C19: from *Bobby* after Sir *Robert* Peel (1788–1850), British Conservative statesman, who, as Home Secretary, set up the Metropolitan Police Force in 1828

bobby calf NOUN an unweaned calf culled for slaughter.

bobby-dazzler NOUN *Dialect* anything outstanding, striking, or showy, esp an attractive girl.
▷**HISTORY** C19: expanded form of *dazzler* something striking or attractive

bobby pin NOUN *US, Canadian, Austral, and NZ* a metal hairpin bent in order to hold the hair in place. Brit terms: **hairgrip, kirby grip.**

bobby socks PLURAL NOUN ankle-length socks worn by teenage girls, esp in the US in the 1940s.

bobbysoxer ('bɒbɪ,sɒksə) NOUN *Informal, chiefly US* an adolescent girl wearing bobby socks, esp in the 1940s.

bobcat ('bɒb,kæt) NOUN a North American feline mammal, *Lynx rufus*, closely related to but smaller than the lynx, having reddish-brown fur with dark spots or stripes, tufted ears, and a short tail. Also called: **bay lynx.**
▷**HISTORY** C19: from BOB[2] (referring to its short tail) + CAT[1]

bobfloat ('bɒb,fləʊt) NOUN *Angling* a small buoyant float, usually consisting of a quill stuck through a piece of cork.

boblet ('bɒblɪt) NOUN a two-man bobsleigh.
▷**HISTORY** C20: from BOB[2] + -LET

Bobo-Dioulasso ('bəʊbəʊdjuː'læsəʊ) NOUN a city in W Burkina-Faso. Pop.: 300 000 (1993 est.).

bobol ('bʌbɔːl) *E Caribbean* ◆ NOUN [1] a fraud carried out by one or more persons with access to public funds in collusion with someone in a position of authority. ◆ VERB [2] (*intr*) to commit a bobol.
▷**HISTORY** C20: of uncertain origin

bobolink ('bɒbə,lɪŋk) NOUN an American songbird, *Dolichonyx oryzivorus*, the male of which has a white back and black underparts in the breeding season: family *Icteridae* (American orioles). Also called (US): **reedbird, ricebird.**
▷**HISTORY** C18: of imitative origin

bobotie (bʊ'bʊtɪ) NOUN a South African dish consisting of curried mincemeat with a topping of beaten egg baked to a crust.
▷**HISTORY** C19: from Afrikaans, probably from Malay

bobowler ('bɒb,aʊlə) NOUN *Midland English dialect* a large moth.
▷**HISTORY** of uncertain origin

Bobruisk *or* **Bobruysk** (bɔ'bruːɪsk) NOUN a port in Belarus, on the River Berezina: engineering, timber, tyre manufacturing. Pop.: 227 000 (1998 est.).

bob skate NOUN *Chiefly US and Canadian* an ice skate with two parallel blades.
▷**HISTORY** C20: from *bob(sled)* + SKATE[1]

bobsleigh ('bɒb,sleɪ) NOUN [1] a racing sledge for two or more people, with a steering mechanism enabling the driver to direct it down a steeply banked ice-covered run. [2] (esp formerly) **a** a sleigh made of two short sledges joined one behind the other. **b** one of these two short sledges. ◆ VERB [3] (*intr*) to ride on a bobsleigh. Also called (esp US and Canadian): **bobsled** ('bɒb,slɛd).
▷**HISTORY** C19: BOB[2] + SLEIGH

bobstay ('bɒb,steɪ) NOUN a strong stay between a bowsprit and the stem of a vessel for holding down the bowsprit.
▷**HISTORY** C18: perhaps from BOB[1] + STAY[3]

bobsy-die ('bɒbzɪ,daɪ) NOUN *NZ informal* fuss; confusion; pandemonium (esp in the phrases **kick up bobsy-die, play bobsy-die**).
▷**HISTORY** from C19 *bob's a-dying*

bobtail ('bɒb,teɪl) NOUN [1] a docked or diminutive tail. [2] an animal with such a tail. ◆ ADJECTIVE *also* **bobtailed.** [3] having the tail cut short. ◆ VERB (*tr*) [4] to dock the tail of. [5] to cut short; curtail.
▷**HISTORY** C16: from BOB[2] + TAIL[1]

bobweight ('bɒb,weɪt) NOUN another name for **balance weight.**

bobwhite ('bɒb,waɪt) NOUN a brown North American quail, *Colinus virginianus*, the male of which has white markings on the head: a popular game bird.
▷**HISTORY** C19: of imitative origin

bocage (bɒ'kɑːʒ) NOUN [1] the wooded countryside characteristic of northern France, with small irregular-shaped fields and many hedges and copses. [2] woodland scenery represented in ceramics.
▷**HISTORY** C17: from French, from Old French *bosc*; see BOSCAGE

boccie, bocci, bocce ('bɒtʃiː), *or* **boccia** ('bɒtʃə) NOUN an Italian version of bowls played on a lawn smaller than a bowling green.
▷**HISTORY** from Italian *bocce* bowls, plural of *boccia* ball; see BOSS[2]

Boche (bɒʃ) NOUN *Derogatory slang* (esp in World Wars I and II) [1] a German, esp a German soldier. [2] **the.** (*usually functioning as plural*) Germans collectively, esp German soldiers regarded as the enemy.
▷**HISTORY** C20: from French, probably shortened from *alboche* German, from *allemand* German + *caboche* pate

Bochum (*German* 'boːxum) NOUN an industrial city in NW Germany, in W North Rhine-Westphalia: university (1965). Pop.: 392 900 (1999 est.).

bock (bok, bəʊk) VERB, NOUN a variant spelling of **boke.**

bock beer *or* **bock** (bɒk) NOUN [1] *US and Canadian* heavy dark strong beer. [2] (in France) a light beer.
▷**HISTORY** C19: from German *Bock bier*, literally: buck beer, name given through folk etymology to beer brewed in *Einbeck*, near Hanover

bockedy ('bɒkədɪ) ADJECTIVE *Irish* (of a structure, piece of furniture, etc.) unsteady.
▷**HISTORY** from Irish Gaelic *bacaideach* limping

bod (bɒd) NOUN *Informal* [1] a fellow; chap: *he's a queer bod.* [2] another word for **body** (sense 1).
▷**HISTORY** C18: short for BODY

BOD ABBREVIATION FOR **biochemical oxygen demand.**

bodacious (bəʊ'deɪʃəs) ADJECTIVE *Slang, chiefly US* impressive or remarkable; excellent.
▷**HISTORY** C19: from English dialect; blend of BOLD + AUDACIOUS

bode[1] (bəʊd) VERB [1] to be an omen of (good or ill, esp of ill); portend; presage. [2] (*tr*) *Archaic* to predict; foretell.
▷**HISTORY** Old English *bodian*; related to Old Norse *botha* to proclaim, Old Frisian *bodia* to invite
▸ **'boding** NOUN, ADJECTIVE ▸ **'bodement** NOUN

bode[2] (bəʊd) VERB the past tense of **bide.**

bodega (bəʊ'diːgə; *Spanish* bo'ðeɣa) NOUN a shop selling wine and sometimes groceries, esp in a Spanish-speaking country.
▷**HISTORY** C19: from Spanish, ultimately from Greek *apothēkē* storehouse, from *apotithenai* to store, put away

Bodensee ('boːdənzeː) NOUN the German name for (Lake) **Constance.**

Bode's law (bəʊdz) NOUN *Astronomy* an empirical rule relating the distances of the planets from the sun, based on the numerical sequence 0, 3, 6, 12, 24,.... Adding 4 to each number and dividing by 10 gives the sequence 0.4, 0.7, 1, 1.6, 2.8,..., which is a reasonable representation of distances in astronomical units for most planets if the minor planets are counted as a single entity at 2.8.
▷**HISTORY** named after Johann Elert *Bode* (1747–1826), who in 1772 published the law, formulated by Johann Titius in 1766

bodge (bɒdʒ) VERB [1] *Informal* to make a mess of; botch. [2] *Austral informal* to make or adjust in a false or clumsy way: *I bodged the figures.*
▷**HISTORY** C16: changed from BOTCH

bodger ('bɒdʒə) ADJECTIVE [1] *Austral informal* worthless or second-rate. [2] a labourer who traditionally lived and worked in the forest, making chairs from felling trees.
▷**HISTORY** C20: from BODGE

bodgie ('bɒdʒɪ) *Austral and NZ* ◆ NOUN [1] an unruly or uncouth young man, esp in the 1950s; teddy boy. ◆ ADJECTIVE [2] inferior; worthless.
▷**HISTORY** C20: from BODGE

Bodh Gaya ('bɒd gə'jɑː) NOUN a variant spelling of **Buddh Gaya.**

Bodhisattva (,bəʊdɪ'sætvə, -wə, ,bɒd-, ,bəʊdiː'sʌtvə) NOUN (in Mahayana Buddhism) a divine being worthy of nirvana who remains on the human plane to help men to salvation. Compare **arhat.**
▷**HISTORY** Sanskrit, literally: one whose essence is enlightenment, from *bodhi* enlightenment + *sattva* essence

Bodhi Tree (,bəʊdɪ) NOUN the sacred peepul at Buddh Gaya under which Gautama Siddhartha attained enlightenment and became the Buddha.
▷**HISTORY** Sanskrit *bodhi* enlightenment

bodhrán (baʊ'rɑːn, 'bɔːrɑːn) NOUN a shallow one-sided drum popular in Irish and Scottish folk music.
▷**HISTORY** Irish Gaelic

bodice ('bɒdɪs) NOUN [1] the upper part of a woman's dress, from the shoulder to the waist. [2] a tight-fitting corset worn laced over a blouse, as in certain national costumes, or (formerly) as a woman's undergarment.
▷**HISTORY** C16: originally Scottish *bodies*, plural of BODY

bodice ripper NOUN *Informal* a romantic novel, usually on a historical theme, that involves some sex and violence.

Bo Diddley beat (,bəʊ 'dɪdlɪ 'biːt) NOUN a type of syncopated Black rhythm, frequently used in rock music.
▷**HISTORY** C20: named after *Bo Diddley* (born 1929), US rhythm-and-blues performer and songwriter

-bodied ADJECTIVE (*in combination*) having a body or bodies as specified: *able-bodied; long-bodied; many-bodied.*

bodiless ('bɒdɪlɪs) ADJECTIVE having no body or substance; incorporeal or insubstantial.

bodily ('bɒdɪlɪ) ADJECTIVE [1] relating to or being a part of the human body. ◆ ADVERB [2] by taking hold of the body: *he threw him bodily from the platform.* [3] in person; in the flesh.

bodkin ('bɒdkɪn) NOUN [1] a blunt large-eyed needle used esp for drawing tape through openwork. [2] *Archaic* a dagger. [3] *Printing* a pointed steel tool used for extracting characters when correcting metal type. [4] *Archaic* a long ornamental hairpin.
▷**HISTORY** C14: probably of Celtic origin; compare Gaelic *biodag* dagger

Bodleian (bɒd'liːən, 'bɒdlɪ-) NOUN the principal library of Oxford University: a copyright deposit library.
▷**HISTORY** C17: named after Sir Thomas *Bodley* (1545–1613), English scholar who founded it in 1602

Bodmin ('bɒdmɪn) NOUN a market town in SW England, in Cornwall, near **Bodmin Moor**, a granite upland rising to 420 m (1375 ft.). Pop.: 12 553 (1991).

Bodoni (bə'dəʊnɪ) NOUN a style of type designed by the Italian printer Giambattista *Bodoni* (1740–1813).

body ('bɒdɪ) NOUN, *plural* **bodies.** [1] **a** the entire physical structure of an animal or human being. Related adjectives: **corporeal, physical. b** (*as modifier*): *body odour.* [2] the flesh, as opposed to the spirit: *while we are still in the body.* [3] the trunk or torso, not including the limbs, head, or tail. [4] a dead human or animal; corpse. [5] the largest or main part of anything: *the body of a vehicle; the body of a plant.* [6] a separate or distinct mass of water or land. [7] the main part; majority: *the body of public opinion.* [8] the central part of a written work: *the body of a thesis as opposed to the footnotes.* [9] a number of individuals regarded as a single entity; group: *the student body; they marched in a body.* [10] *Maths* a three-dimensional region with an interior. [11] *Physics* an object or substance that has three dimensions, a mass, and is distinguishable from surrounding objects. [12] fullness in the appearance of the hair. [13] the characteristic full quality of certain wines, determined by the density and the content of alcohol or tannin: *a Burgundy has a heavy body.* [14] substance or firmness, esp of cloth. [15] the sound box of a guitar, violin, or similar stringed instrument. [16] a woman's close-fitting one-piece garment for the torso. [17] the part of a dress covering the body from the shoulders to the waist. [18] another name for **shank** (sense 11). [19] **a** the pigment contained in or added to paint, dye, etc. **b** the opacity of a paint in covering a surface. **c** the apparent viscosity of a paint. [20] (in watercolour painting) **a** a white filler mixed with pigments to make them opaque. **b** (*as modifier*): *body colour.* See also **gouache.** [21] *Printing* the measurement from top to bottom of a piece of type, usually ascender to descender. [22] an informal or dialect word for a **person.** [23] **keep body and soul together.** to manage to keep alive; survive. [24] (*modifier*) of or relating to the main reading matter of a book as distinct from headings, illustrations, appendices, etc.: *the body text.* ◆ VERB **bodies, bodying, bodied.** (*tr*) [25] (usually foll by *forth*) to give a body or shape to.
▷**HISTORY** Old English *bodig*; related to Old Norse *buthkr* box, Old High German *botah* body

body bag NOUN *Military* a large heavy-duty plastic bag used to contain and transport human remains, esp those of battle casualties.

body beautiful NOUN (usually with *the*) **a** a beautiful body. **b** idealized physical beauty.

body blow NOUN [1] *Boxing* Also called: **body punch.** a blow to the body of an opponent. [2] a severe disappointment or setback: *unavailability of funds was a body blow to the project.*

bodyboard ('bɒdɪ,bɔːd) NOUN a surfboard that is shorter and blunter than the standard board and on which the surfer lies rather than stands.

bodyboarding ('bɒdɪ,bɔːdɪŋ) NOUN the sport of surfing using a bodyboard.

body building NOUN the practice of performing regular exercises designed to make the muscles of the body conspicuous.

body cavity NOUN the internal cavity of any multicellular animal that contains the digestive tract, heart, kidneys, etc. In vertebrates it develops from the coelom.

body-centred ADJECTIVE (of a crystal) having a lattice point at the centre of each unit cell as well as at the corners. Compare **face-centred.**

bodycheck ('bɒdɪ,tʃɛk) NOUN [1] *Sport* obstruction of another player. [2] *Wrestling* the act of blocking a charging opponent with the body. ◆ VERB [3] (*tr*) to deliver a bodycheck to (an opponent).

body corporate NOUN *Law* a group of persons incorporated to carry out a specific enterprise. See **corporation** (sense 1).

body double NOUN *Films* a person who substitutes for a star for the filming of a scene that involves shots of the body rather than the face.

body dysmorphic disorder NOUN a psychological disorder characterized by a strong feeling that one's appearance or health would be improved by the removal of a healthy body part.

bodyguard ('bɒdɪ,gɑːd) NOUN a person or group of people who escort and protect someone, esp a political figure.

body horror NOUN a horror film genre in which the main feature is the graphically depicted destruction or degeneration of a human body or bodies.

body image NOUN *Psychol* an individual's concept of his own body.

body language NOUN the nonverbal imparting of information by means of conscious or subconscious bodily gestures, posture, etc.

body-line ADJECTIVE *Cricket* denoting or relating to fast bowling aimed at the batsman's body.

body mass index NOUN an index used to indicate whether a person is over- or underweight. It is obtained by dividing a person's weight in kilograms by the square of their height in metres. An index of 20–25 is normal. Abbreviation: **BMI.**

body modification NOUN any method of permanently adorning the body, including tattooing and piercing.

Body of Christ NOUN the Christian Church.

body-packer NOUN a person who smuggles illicit drugs in balloons, condoms, or similar plastic bags which have either been swallowed or inserted in the rectum or vagina.

body politic NOUN **the.** the people of a nation or the nation itself considered as a political entity; the state.

body search NOUN [1] a form of search by police, customs officials, etc., that involves examination of a prisoner's or suspect's bodily orifices. ♦ VERB **body-search.** [2] (*tr*) to search (a prisoner or suspect) in this manner.

bodyshell ('bɒdɪˌʃɛl) NOUN the external shell of a motor vehicle.

body shop NOUN a place where the bodywork of motor vehicles is built or repaired.

body snatcher NOUN (formerly) a person who robbed graves and sold the corpses for dissection.
▸**body snatching** NOUN

body stocking NOUN a one-piece undergarment for women, usually of nylon, covering the torso.

bodysuit ('bɒdɪˌsuːt, -ˌsjuːt) NOUN [1] another name for **body** (sense 16). [2] a one-piece undergarment for a baby.

body-surf VERB (*intr*) [1] to ride a wave by lying on it without a surfboard. [2] (*intr*) *Informal* to fling oneself prone onto a crowd of people, for examaple on a dance floor or at a rock concert, and move or be carried over their heads.
▸**'body,surfer** NOUN ▸**'body,surfing** NOUN

body swerve NOUN [1] *Sport* (esp in football games) the act or an instance of swerving past an opponent. [2] *Scot* the act or an instance of avoiding (a situation considered unpleasant): *I think I'll give the meeting a body swerve.* ♦ VERB **body-swerve.** [3] *Sport* (esp in football games) to pass (an opponent) using a body swerve. [4] *Scot* to avoid (a situation or person considered unpleasant).

body warmer NOUN a sleeveless type of jerkin, usually quilted, worn as an outer garment for extra warmth.

bodywork ('bɒdɪˌwɜːk) NOUN [1] the external shell of a motor vehicle. [2] any form of therapy in which parts of the body are manipulated, such as massage.

body wrap NOUN a beauty treatment in which the body is covered in lotion and wrapped tightly in strips of cloth in order to promote weight loss or improve skin tone.

Boehmite ('bɜːmaɪt) NOUN a grey, red, or brown mineral that consists of alumina in rhombic crystalline form and occurs in bauxite. Formula: AlO(OH).
▷**HISTORY** C20: from German *Böhmit*, after J. *Böhm*, 20th-century German scientist

Boeotia (bɪ'əʊʃɪə) NOUN [1] a region of ancient Greece, northwest of Athens. It consisted of ten city-states, which formed the Boeotian League, led by Thebes: at its height in the 4th century B.C. [2] transliteration of the Modern Greek name for **Voiotia.**

Boeotian (bɪ'əʊʃɪən) NOUN [1] a native or inhabitant of Boeotia, a region of ancient Greece. ♦ ADJECTIVE [2] of or relating to Boeotia or its inhabitants.

Boer (bʊə, 'bəʊə, bɔː) NOUN, ADJECTIVE **a** a descendant of any of the Dutch or Huguenot colonists who settled in South Africa, mainly in Cape Colony, the Orange Free State, and the Transvaal. **b** (*as modifier*): *a Boer farm.*
▷**HISTORY** C19: from Dutch *Boer*; see BOOR

boerbul ('bʊəˌbʊl) NOUN *South African* a crossbred mastiff used esp as a watchdog.
▷**HISTORY** from Afrikaans *boerboel* a breed of mastiff

boere- (bʊə, 'bəʊə, bɔː) COMBINING FORM *South African* rustic or country-style: *boeremusiek.*
▷**HISTORY** Afrikaans

boeremusiek ('bʊərəˌmjuːzɪk) NOUN *South African* a special variety of light music associated with the culture of the Afrikaners.
▷**HISTORY** Afrikaans

boerewors ('bʊərəˌvɒs) NOUN *South African* a highly seasoned traditional sausage made from minced or pounded meat.
▷**HISTORY** Afrikaans

Boer War NOUN either of two conflicts between Britain and the South African Boers, the first (1880–1881) when the Boers sought to regain the independence given up for British aid against the Zulus, the second (1899–1902) when the Orange Free State and Transvaal declared war on Britain.

boet (bʊt) NOUN *South African* brother; mate, chum.
▷**HISTORY** Afrikaans

boeuf bourguignon (*French* bœf burgiɲɔ̃) NOUN a casserole of beef, vegetables, herbs, etc., cooked in red wine. Also called: **boeuf à la bourguignonne.**
▷**HISTORY** French: Burgundy beef

boff (bɒf) NOUN *Informal* short for **boffin.**

boffin ('bɒfɪn) NOUN [1] *Brit informal* a scientist, esp one carrying out military research. [2] a person who has extensive skill or knowledge in a particular field: *a Treasury boffin.* [3] *Informal* someone who is considered to be very clever, often to the exclusion of all non-academic interests.
▷**HISTORY** C20: of uncertain origin

boffo ('bɒfəʊ) ADJECTIVE [1] *Slang* very good; highly successful. [2] a person who has extensive skill or knowledge in a particular field: *a Treasury boffin.*
▷**HISTORY** C20: of uncertain origin

Bofors gun ('bəʊfəz) NOUN an automatic single- or double-barrelled anti-aircraft gun with 40 millimetre bore.
▷**HISTORY** C20: named after *Bofors*, Sweden, where it was first made

bog (bɒg) NOUN [1] wet spongy ground consisting of decomposing vegetation, which ultimately forms peat. [2] an area of such ground. [3] a place or thing that prevents or slows progress or improvement. [4] a slang word for **lavatory** (sense 1). [5] *Austral slang* the act or an instance of defecating. See also **bog down, bog in, bog off.**
▷**HISTORY** C13: from Gaelic *bogach* swamp, from *bog* soft
▸**'boggy** ADJECTIVE ▸**'bogginess** NOUN

bogan[1] ('bəʊgən) NOUN *Canadian* (esp in the Maritime Provinces) a sluggish side stream. Also called: **logan, pokelogan.**
▷**HISTORY** of Algonquian origin

bogan[2] ('bəʊgən) NOUN *Austral informal* [1] a fool. [2] a hooligan.
▷**HISTORY** C20: of unknown origin

bogart ('bəʊgɑːt) VERB (*tr*) *Slang* to monopolize or keep (something, esp a marijuana cigarette) to oneself selfishly.
▷**HISTORY** C20: after the US film actor Humphrey *Bogart* (1899–1957), on account of his alleged greed for marijuana

bog asphodel NOUN either of two liliaceous plants, *Narthecium ossifragum* of Europe or *N. americanum* of North America, that grow in boggy places and have small yellow flowers and grasslike leaves.

Boğazköy (*Turkish* bɔːˈɑzkœi) NOUN a village in central Asia Minor: site of the ancient Hittite capital.

bogbean ('bɒgˌbiːn) NOUN another name for **buckbean.**

bog cotton NOUN another name for **cotton grass.**

bog deal NOUN pine wood found preserved in peat bogs.

bog down VERB **bogs, bogging, bogged.** (*adverb*; when *tr, often passive*) to impede or be impeded physically or mentally.

bogey[1] *or* **bogy** ('bəʊgɪ) NOUN [1] an evil or mischievous spirit. [2] something that worries or annoys. [3] *Golf* **a** a score of one stroke over par on a hole. Compare **par** (sense 5). **b** *Obsolete* a standard score for a hole or course, regarded as one that a good player should make. [4] *Slang* a piece of dried mucus discharged from the nose. [5] *Air Force, slang* an unidentified or hostile aircraft. [6] *Slang* a detective; policeman. ♦ VERB [7] (*tr*) *Golf* to play (a hole) in one stroke over par.
▷**HISTORY** C19: probably related to BUG[2] and BOGLE[1]; compare BUGABOO

bogey[2] *or* **bogie** ('bəʊgɪ) *Austral* ♦ VERB [1] to bathe or swim. ♦ NOUN [2] a bathe or swim.
▷**HISTORY** C19: from a native Australian language

bogey hole NOUN *Austral* a natural pool used for swimming.

bogeyman ('bəʊgɪˌmæn) NOUN, *plural* **-men.** a person, real or imaginary, used as a threat, esp to children.

boggart ('bɒgət) NOUN *Northern English dialect* a ghost or poltergeist.
▷**HISTORY** perhaps from *bog*, variant of BUG[2] + -ARD

bogger (bɒgə) NOUN *Austral slang* a lavatory.

bogging ('bɒgɪŋ) ADJECTIVE *Scot informal* filthy; covered in dirt and grime.

boggle ('bɒgᵊl) VERB (*intr*; often foll by *at*) [1] to be surprised, confused, or alarmed (esp in the phrase **the mind boggles**). [2] to hesitate or be evasive when confronted with a problem. [3] (*tr*) to baffle; bewilder; puzzle.
▷**HISTORY** C16: probably variant of BOGLE[1]

bogie[1] *or* **bogy** ('bəʊgɪ) NOUN [1] an assembly of four or six wheels forming a pivoted support at either end of a railway coach. It provides flexibility on curves. [2] *Chiefly Brit* a small railway truck of short wheelbase, used for conveying coal, ores, etc. [3] a Scot word for **soapbox** (sense 3).
▷**HISTORY** C19: of unknown origin

bogie[2] ('bəʊgɪ) NOUN a variant spelling of **bogey**[2].

bog in VERB **bogs, bogging, bogged.** (*intr, adverb*) *Austral and NZ informal* [1] to start energetically on a task. [2] to start eating; tuck in. ♦ Also (preposition): **bog into.**

bogle[1] ('bəʊgᵊl, 'bɒg-) NOUN [1] a dialect or archaic word for **bogey**[1] (sense 1). [2] *Scot* a scarecrow.
▷**HISTORY** C16: from Scottish *bogill*, perhaps from Gaelic; compare Welsh *bygel*; see BUG[2]

bogle[2] ('bəʊgᵊl) NOUN [1] a rhythmic dance, originating in the early 1990s, performed to ragga music. ♦ VERB [2] (*intr*) to perform such a dance.

bogman ('bɒgˌmæn) NOUN, *plural* **-men.** *Archaeol* the body of a person found preserved in a peat bog.

bog moss NOUN another name for **peat moss.**

bog myrtle NOUN another name for **sweet gale.**

Bognor Regis ('bɒgnə 'riːdʒɪs) NOUN a resort in S England, in West Sussex on the English Channel: electronics industries. *Regis* was added to the name after King George V's convalescence there in 1929. Pop.: 56 744 (1991).

bog oak NOUN oak or other wood found preserved in peat bogs; bogwood.

BOGOF ('bɒgɒf) ACRONYM FOR buy one, get one free.

bog off *Brit slang* ♦ INTERJECTION [1] go away! ♦ VERB **bogs, bogging, bogged.** [2] (*intr, adverb*) to go away.

bogong ('bəʊˌgɒŋ) *or* **bugong** ('buːˌgɒŋ) NOUN an edible dark-coloured Australian noctuid moth, *Agrotis infusa.*

Bogor ('bəʊgɔː) NOUN a city in Indonesia, in W Java: botanical gardens and research institutions. Pop.: 285 114 (1995 est.). Former name: **Buitenzorg.**

bog orchid NOUN an orchid, *Hammarbya* (or *Malaxis*) *paludosa*, growing in sphagnum bogs in the N hemisphere. It has greenish-yellow flowers and its leaves bear a fringe of tiny bulbils.

Bogotá (ˌbəʊgə'tɑː; *Spanish* boɣo'ta) NOUN the capital of Colombia, on a central plateau of the E Andes: originally the centre of Chibcha civilization; founded as a city in 1538 by the Spaniards. Pop.: 6 260 862 (1999 est.).

bog rosemary NOUN another name for **marsh andromeda.**

bog rush NOUN a blackish tufted cyperaceous plant, *Schoenus nigricans*, growing on boggy ground.

bog-standard NOUN *Informal* completely ordinary; run-of-the-mill.

bogtrotter ('bɒgˌtrɒtə) NOUN a derogatory term for an Irishman, esp an Irish peasant.

bogus ('bəʊgəs) ADJECTIVE spurious or counterfeit; not genuine: *a bogus note.*
▷**HISTORY** C19: from *bogus* apparatus for making counterfeit money; perhaps related to BOGEY[1]
▸**'bogusly** ADVERB ▸**'bogusness** NOUN

bogwood ('bɒgˌwʊd) NOUN another name for **bog oak.**

bogy ('bəʊgɪ) NOUN, *plural* **-gies.** a variant spelling of **bogey**[1] or **bogie**[1].

boh (bəʊ) INTERJECTION a variant spelling of **bo.**

Bohai ('bɔː'haɪ) *or* **Pohai** NOUN a large inlet of the Yellow Sea on the coast of NE China. Also called: (Gulf of) **Chihli.**

bohea (bəʊ'hiː) NOUN a black Chinese tea, once regarded as the choicest, but now as an inferior grade.
▷**HISTORY** C18: from Chinese (Fukien dialect) *bu-i*, from Mandarin Chinese *Wu-i Shan* range of hills on which this tea was grown

Bohemia (bəʊ'hiːmɪə) NOUN [1] a former kingdom

of central Europe, surrounded by mountains: independent from the 9th to the 13th century; belonged to the Hapsburgs from 1526 until 1918. [2] an area of the W Czech Republic, formerly a province of Czechoslovakia (1918–1949). From 1939 until 1945 it formed part of the German protectorate of **Bohemia-Moravia**. Czech name: **Čechy**. German name: **Böhmen** ('bø:mən). [3] a district frequented by unconventional people, esp artists or writers.

Bohemian (bəʊ'hi:mɪən) NOUN [1] a native or inhabitant of Bohemia, esp of the old kingdom of Bohemia; a Czech. [2] *(often not capital)* a person, esp an artist or writer, who lives an unconventional life. [3] the Czech language. ◆ ADJECTIVE [4] of, relating to, or characteristic of Bohemia, its people, or their language. [5] unconventional in appearance, behaviour, etc.

Bohemian Brethren PLURAL NOUN a Protestant Christian sect formed in the 15th century from various Hussite groups, which rejected oaths and military service and advocated a pure and disciplined spiritual life. It was reorganized in 1722 as the Moravian Church. Also called: **Unitas Fratrem** ('ju:nɪtæs 'frætrɛm).

Bohemian Forest NOUN a mountain range between the SW Czech Republic and SE Germany. Highest peak: Arber, 1457 m (4780 ft.). Czech name: **Český Les** ('tʃɛski: 'lɛs). German name: **Böhmerwald** ('bø:mər,valt).

Bohemianism (bəʊ'hi:mɪə,nɪzəm) NOUN unconventional behaviour or appearance, esp of an artist.

Böhm flute NOUN a type of flute in which the holes are covered with keys; the standard type of modern flute.
▷HISTORY C19: named after Theobald *Böhm* (1793–1881), German flautist who invented it

boho ('bəʊhəʊ) NOUN, *plural* **-hos**, ADJECTIVE *Informal* short for **Bohemian** (senses 2, 5).

Bohol (bəʊ'hɔ:l) NOUN an island of the central Philippines. Chief town: Tagbilaran. Pop.: 948 000 (1990). Area: about 3900 sq. km (1500 sq. miles).

bohrium ('bɒrɪəm) NOUN a transuranic element artificially produced in minute quantities by bombarding ^{204}Bi atoms with ^{54}Cr nuclei. Symbol: Bh; atomic no.: 107. Former names: **element 107, unnilheptium.**
▷HISTORY C20: after Neils *Bohr* (1885–1962), Danish physicist

Bohr theory NOUN a theory of atomic structure that explains the spectrum of hydrogen atoms. It assumes that the electron orbiting around the nucleus can exist only in certain energy states, a jump from one state to another being accompanied by the emission or absorption of a quantum of radiation.
▷HISTORY C20: after Niels *Bohr* (1885–1962), Danish physicist

bohunk ('bəʊ,hʌŋk) NOUN *US and Canadian derogatory slang* a labourer from east or central Europe.
▷HISTORY C20: blend of *Bo(hemian)* + *Hung(arian)*, with alteration of *g* to *k*

boil[1] (bɔɪl) VERB [1] to change or cause to change from a liquid to a vapour so rapidly that bubbles of vapour are formed copiously in the liquid. Compare **evaporate.** [2] to reach or cause to reach boiling point. [3] to cook or be cooked by the process of boiling. [4] *(intr)* to bubble and be agitated like something boiling; seethe: *the ocean was boiling.* [5] *(intr)* to be extremely angry or indignant (esp in the phrase **make one's blood boil**): *she was boiling at his dishonesty.* [6] *(intr)* to contain a boiling liquid: *the pot is boiling.* ◆ NOUN [7] the state or action of boiling (esp in the phrases **on the boil, off the boil**). ◆ See also **boil away, boil down, boil off, boil over, boil up.**
▷HISTORY C13: from Old French *boillir*, from Latin *bullīre* to bubble, from *bulla* a bubble
▸**'boilable** ADJECTIVE

boil[2] (bɔɪl) NOUN a red painful swelling with a hard pus-filled core caused by bacterial infection of the skin and subcutaneous tissues, esp at a hair follicle. Technical name: **furuncle.**
▷HISTORY Old English *byle*; related to Old Norse *beyla* swelling, Old High German *būlla* bladder, Gothic *ufbauljan* to inflate

boil away VERB *(adverb)* to cause (liquid) to evaporate completely by boiling or (of liquid) to evaporate completely.

boil down VERB *(adverb)* [1] to reduce or be reduced in quantity and usually altered in consistency by boiling: *to boil a liquid down to a thick glue.* [2] **boil down to. a** *(intr)* to be the essential element in something. **b** *(tr)* to summarize; reduce to essentials.

boiled shirt NOUN *Informal* a dress shirt with a stiff front.

boiled sweet NOUN *Brit* a hard sticky sweet of boiled sugar with any of various flavourings.

boiler ('bɔɪlə) NOUN [1] a closed vessel or arrangement of enclosed tubes in which water is heated to supply steam to drive an engine or turbine or provide heat. [2] a domestic device burning solid fuel, gas, or oil, to provide hot water, esp for central heating. [3] a large tub for boiling laundry. [4] a tough old chicken for cooking by boiling.

boilermaker ('bɔɪlə,meɪkə) NOUN [1] a person who works with metal in heavy industry; plater or welder. [2] *Brit slang* a beer drink consisting of half of draught mild and half of bottled brown ale. [3] *US slang* a drink of whisky followed by a beer chaser.

boilerplate ('bɔɪlə,pleɪt) NOUN [1] a form of mild-steel plate used in the production of boiler shells. [2] a copy made with the intention of making other copies from it. [3] a set of instructions incorporated in several places in a computer program or a standard form of words used repeatedly in drafting contracts, guarantees, etc. [4] a draft contract that can easily be modified to cover various types of transaction.

boiler room NOUN [1] any room in a building (often in the basement) that contains a boiler for central heating, etc. [2] the part of a steam ship that houses the boilers and furnaces. [3] the room or department in which the real work of an organization goes on unseen. [4] *(Chiefly US)* an office used by a team of telephone salespeople, esp of stocks and shares, operating under high pressure. [5] **a** a fraudulent scheme in which investors are encouraged to buy non-existent, worthless, or over-priced shares. **b** *(as modifier)*: *a boiler-room scam.*

boiler suit NOUN *Brit* a one-piece work garment consisting of overalls and a shirt top usually worn over ordinary clothes to protect them.

boiling ('bɔɪlɪŋ) ADJECTIVE, ADVERB [1] very warm: *a boiling hot day.* ◆ NOUN [2] **the whole boiling.** *Slang* the whole lot.

boiling point NOUN [1] the temperature at which a liquid boils at a given pressure, usually atmospheric pressure at sea level; the temperature at which the vapour pressure of a liquid equals the external pressure. [2] *Informal* the condition of being angered or highly excited.

boiling-water reactor NOUN a nuclear reactor using water as coolant and moderator, steam being produced in the reactor itself: enriched uranium oxide cased in zirconium is the fuel. Abbreviation: **BWR.**

boil off VERB to remove or be removed (from) by boiling: *to boil off impurities.*

boilover ('bɔɪl,əʊvə) NOUN *Austral* [1] a surprising result in a sporting event, esp in a horse race. [2] a sudden conflict.

boil over VERB *(adverb)* [1] to overflow or cause to overflow while boiling. [2] *(intr)* to burst out in anger or excitement: *she boiled over at the mention of his name.*

boil up VERB *(intr, adverb) Austral and NZ* to make tea.

bois-brûlé (,bwɑ:bru:'leɪ) NOUN *(sometimes capital) Canadian archaic* a mixed-race person of Indian and White (usually French Canadian) ancestry; Métis. Also called: **Brule.**
▷HISTORY French, literally: burnt wood

Bois de Boulogne *(French* bwa də bulɔɲ) NOUN a large park in W Paris, formerly a forest: includes the racecourses of Auteuil and Longchamp.

Boise *or* **Boise City** ('bɔɪzɪ, -sɪ) NOUN a city in SW Idaho: the state capital. Pop.: 185 787 (2000).

Bois-le-Duc (bwa lə dyk) NOUN the French name for **'s Hertogenbosch.**

boisterous ('bɔɪstərəs, -strəs) ADJECTIVE [1] noisy and lively; unrestrained or unruly. [2] (of the wind, sea, etc.) turbulent or stormy.
▷HISTORY C13 *boistuous*, of unknown origin
▸**'boisterously** ADVERB ▸**'boisterousness** NOUN

Bok (bɒk) NOUN *mainly S. African* short for **Springbok.**

bok choy ('bɒk 'tʃɔɪ) NOUN a Chinese plant, *Brassica chinensis*, that is related to the cabbage and has edible stalks and leaves. Also called: **Chinese cabbage, Chinese leaf, pak-choi cabbage.**
▷HISTORY from Chinese dialect, literally: white vegetable

boke, boak, *or* **bock** (bok, bəʊk) *Scot* ◆ VERB [1] to retch or vomit. ◆ NOUN [2] a retch; vomiting fit.
▷HISTORY Middle English *bolken*; related to BELCH, German *bölken* to roar

Bokhara (bʊ'xɑ:rə) NOUN a variant spelling of **Bukhara.**

bokmakierie (,bɒkmə'kɪərɪ) NOUN *South African* a large yellow shrike, *Telephorus zeylonus*, of southern Africa, known for its melodious song.
▷HISTORY C19: from Afrikaans, imitative of its call

Bokmål *(Norwegian* 'bu:kmo:l) NOUN one of the two official forms of written Norwegian, closely related to Danish. Also called: **Dano-Norwegian.** Formerly called: **Riksmål.** Compare **Nynorsk.**
▷HISTORY Norwegian, literally: book language

BOL INTERNATIONAL CAR REGISTRATION FOR Bolivia.

Bol. ABBREVIATION FOR Bolivia(n).

bola ('bəʊlə) *or* **bolas** ('bəʊləs) NOUN, *plural* **-las** *or* **-lases.** a missile used by gauchos and Indians of South America, consisting of two or more heavy balls on a cord. It is hurled at a running quarry, such as an ox or emu, so as to entangle its legs.
▷HISTORY Spanish: ball, from Latin *bulla* knob

Boland ('bʊəlant) NOUN an area of high altitude in S South Africa.

Bolan Pass (bəʊ'lɑ:n) NOUN a mountain pass in W central Pakistan through the Brahui Range, between Sibi and Quetta, rising to 1800 m (5900 ft.).

bold (bəʊld) ADJECTIVE [1] courageous, confident, and fearless; ready to take risks. [2] showing or requiring courage: *a bold plan.* [3] immodest or impudent: *she gave him a bold look.* [4] standing out distinctly; conspicuous: *a figure carved in bold relief.* [5] very steep: *the bold face of the cliff.* [6] imaginative in thought or expression: *the novel's bold plot.* [7] *Printing* set in bold face. ◆ NOUN [8] *Printing* short for **bold face.**
▷HISTORY Old English *beald*; related to Old Norse *ballr* dangerous, terrible, *baldinn* defiant, Old High German *bald* bold
▸**'boldly** ADVERB ▸**'boldness** NOUN

bold face NOUN [1] *Printing* a weight of type characterized by thick heavy lines, as the entry words in this dictionary. Compare **light face.** ◆ ADJECTIVE **boldface.** [2] (of type) having this weight.

bole[1] (bəʊl) NOUN the trunk of a tree.
▷HISTORY C14: from Old Norse *bolr*; related to Middle High German *bole* plank

bole[2] (bəʊl) *or* **bolus** NOUN [1] a reddish soft variety of clay used as a pigment. [2] a moderate reddish-brown colour.
▷HISTORY C13: from Late Latin *bōlus* lump, from Greek *bōlos*

bolection (bəʊ'lɛkʃən) NOUN *Architect* a stepped moulding covering and projecting beyond the joint between two members having surfaces at different levels. Also called: **bilection.**
▷HISTORY C18: of unknown origin

bolero (bə'lɛərəʊ) NOUN, *plural* **-ros.** [1] a Spanish dance, often accompanied by the guitar and castanets, usually in triple time. [2] a piece of music composed for or in the rhythm of this dance. [3] *(also* 'bɒlərəʊ) a kind of short jacket not reaching the waist, with or without sleeves and open at the front: worn by men in Spain and by women elsewhere.
▷HISTORY C18: from Spanish; perhaps related to *bola* ball

boletus (bəʊ'li:təs) NOUN, *plural* **-tuses** *or* **-ti** (-,taɪ). any saprotroph basidiomycetous fungus of the genus *Boletus*, having a brownish umbrella-shaped cap with spore-bearing tubes in the underside: family *Boletaceae*. Many species are edible.

▷HISTORY C17: from Latin: variety of mushroom, from Greek *bōlitēs*; perhaps related to Greek *bōlos* lump

bolide (ˈbəʊlaɪd, -lɪd) NOUN a large exceptionally bright meteor that often explodes. Also called: **fireball.**
▷HISTORY C19: from French, from *bolis* missile; see BALLISTA

boline (ˈbəʊliːn) NOUN (in Wicca) a knife, usually sickle-shaped and with a white handle, used for gathering herbs and carving symbols.

bolívar (ˈbɒlɪˌvɑː; *Spanish* boˈliβar) NOUN, *plural* **-vars** *or* **-vares** (-βares). the standard monetary unit of Venezuela, equal to 100 céntimos.
▷HISTORY named after Simon *Bolívar* (1783–1830), South American soldier and liberator

Bolivia (bəˈlɪvɪə) NOUN an inland republic in central S America: original Aymará Indian population conquered by the Incas in the 13th century; colonized by Spain from 1538; became a republic in 1825; consists of low plains in the east, with ranges of the Andes rising to over 6400 m (21 000 ft.) and the Altiplano, a plateau averaging 3900 m (13 000 ft.) in the west; contains some of the world's highest inhabited regions; important producer of tin and other minerals. Official languages: Spanish, Quechua, and Aymara. Religion: Roman Catholic. Currency: boliviano. Capital: La Paz (administrative); Sucre (judicial). Pop.: 8 516 000 (2001 est.). Area: 1 098 580 sq. km (424 260 sq. miles).

Bolivian (bəˈlɪvɪən) ADJECTIVE [1] of or relating to Bolivia or its inhabitants. ◆ NOUN [2] a native or inhabitant of Bolivia.

boliviano (bəˌlɪvɪˈɑːnəʊ; *Spanish* boliˈβjano) NOUN, *plural* **-nos** (-nəʊz; *Spanish* -nos). (until 1963 and from 1987) the standard monetary unit of Bolivia, equal to 100 centavos.

boll (bəʊl) NOUN the fruit of such plants as flax and cotton, consisting of a rounded capsule containing the seeds.
▷HISTORY C13: from Dutch *bolle*; related to Old English *bolla* BOWL[1]

bollard (ˈbɒlɑːd, ˈbɒləd) NOUN [1] a strong wooden or metal post mounted on a wharf, quay, etc., used for securing mooring lines. [2] *Brit* a small post or marker placed on a kerb or traffic island to make it conspicuous to motorists. [3] *Mountaineering* an outcrop of rock or pillar of ice that may be used to belay a rope.
▷HISTORY C14: perhaps from BOLE[1] + -ARD

bollocking (ˈbɒləkɪŋ) NOUN *Slang* a severe telling-off; dressing-down.
▷HISTORY from bollock (vb) (in the sense: to reprimand)

bollocks (ˈbɒləks), **ballocks,** *or US* **bollix** (ˈbɒlɪks) *Slang* ◆ PLURAL NOUN [1] another word for **testicles.** [2] nonsense; rubbish. ◆ INTERJECTION [3] an exclamation of annoyance, disbelief, etc. [4] **the (dog's) bollocks.** something excellent. ◆ VERB (usually foll by *up*) [5] to muddle or botch.
▷HISTORY Old English *beallucas*, diminutive (pl) of *beallu* (unattested); see BALL[1]

> **Language note** Both its anatomical senses and its various extended senses nowadays have far less impact than they used to, and seem unlikely to cause offence, though some older or more conservative people may object. The fact that shops displaying the Sex Pistols' album containing this word were charged with offences defined in 19th century Indecent Advertisement and Vagrancy Acts now seems hard to credit.

boll weevil NOUN a greyish weevil, *Anthonomus grandis*, of the southern US and Mexico, whose larvae live in and destroy cotton bolls. See also **weevil** (sense 1).

bollworm (ˈbəʊlˌwɜːm) NOUN any of various moth caterpillars, such as *Pectinophora* (or *Platyedra*) *gossypiella* (**pink bollworm**), that feed on and destroy cotton bolls.

Bollywood (ˈbɒlɪˌwʊd) NOUN *Informal* **a** the Indian film industry. **b** (*as modifier*): *a Bollywood star.*
▷HISTORY C20: from BO(MBAY) + (HO)LLYWOOD

bolo (ˈbəʊləʊ) NOUN, *plural* **-los.** a large single-edged knife, originating in the Philippines.
▷HISTORY Philippine Spanish, probably from a native word

Bologna (bəˈləʊnjə; *Italian* boˈloɲɲa) NOUN a city in N Italy, at the foot of the Apennines: became a free city in the Middle Ages; university (1088). Pop.: 381 161 (2000 est.). Ancient name: **Bononia** (bəˈnəʊnɪə).

bologna sausage NOUN *Chiefly US and Canadian* a large smoked sausage made of seasoned mixed meats. Also called: **baloney, boloney,** (esp Brit) **polony.**

Bolognese (ˌbɒləˈniːz, -ˈneɪz) ADJECTIVE [1] of or relating to Bologna or its inhabitants. ◆ NOUN [2] a native or inhabitant of Bologna.

bolometer (bəʊˈlɒmɪtə) NOUN a sensitive instrument for measuring radiant energy by the increase in the resistance of an electrical conductor.
▷HISTORY C19: from *bol-*, from Greek *bolē* ray of light, stroke, from *ballein* to throw + -METER
▸**bolometric** (ˌbəʊləˈmɛtrɪk) ADJECTIVE ▸ˌ**boloˈmetrically** ADVERB ▸**boˈlometry** NOUN

boloney (bəˈləʊnɪ) NOUN [1] a variant spelling of **baloney.** [2] *Chiefly US* another name for **bologna sausage.**

Bolshevik (ˈbɒlʃɪvɪk) NOUN, *plural* **-viks** *or* **-viki** (-ˈviːkɪ). [1] (formerly) a Russian Communist. Compare **Menshevik.** [2] any Communist. [3] (*often not capital*) *Informal and derogatory* any political radical, esp a revolutionary.
▷HISTORY C20: from Russian *Bol'shevik* majority, from *bol'shoi* great; from the fact that this group formed a majority of the Russian Social Democratic Party in 1903
▸ˈ**Bolsheˌvism** NOUN ▸ˈ**Bolshevist** ADJECTIVE, NOUN ▸ˌ**Bolsheˈvistic** ADJECTIVE

bolshie *or* **bolshy** (ˈbɒlʃɪ) (*sometimes capital*) *Brit informal* ◆ ADJECTIVE [1] difficult to manage; rebellious. [2] politically radical or left-wing. ◆ NOUN, *plural* **-shies.** [3] *Derogatory* any political radical.
▷HISTORY C20: shortened from BOLSHEVIK

bolson (bəʊlˈsəʊn) NOUN *Southwestern US* a desert valley surrounded by mountains, with a shallow lake at the centre.
▷HISTORY C19: from American Spanish *bolsón*, from Spanish *bolsa* purse, from Late Latin *bursa* bag; see PURSE

bolster (ˈbəʊlstə) VERB (*tr*) [1] (often foll by *up*) to support or reinforce; strengthen: *to bolster morale.* [2] to prop up with a pillow or cushion. [3] to add padding to: *to bolster a dress.* ◆ NOUN [4] a long narrow pillow or cushion. [5] any pad or padded support. [6] *Architect* a short horizontal length of timber fixed to the top of a post to increase the bearing area and reduce the span of the supported beam. [7] a cold chisel having a broad blade splayed towards the cutting edge, used for cutting stone slabs, etc.
▷HISTORY Old English *bolster*; related to Old Norse *bolstr*, Old High German *bolstar*, Dutch *bulster*
▸ˈ**bolsterer** NOUN ▸ˈ**bolstering** NOUN, ADJECTIVE

bolt[1] (bəʊlt) NOUN [1] a bar that can be slid into a socket to lock a door, gate, etc. [2] a bar or rod that forms part of a locking mechanism and is moved by a key or a knob. [3] a metal rod or pin that has a head at one end and a screw thread at the other to take a nut. [4] a sliding bar in a breech-loading firearm that ejects the empty cartridge, replaces it with a new one, and closes the breech. [5] a flash of lightning. [6] a sudden start or movement, esp in order to escape: *they made a bolt for the door.* [7] *US* a sudden desertion, esp from a political party. [8] a roll of something, such as cloth, wallpaper, etc. [9] an arrow, esp for a crossbow. [10] *Printing* a folded edge on a sheet of paper that is removed when cutting to size. [11] *Mechanical engineering* short for **expansion bolt.** [12] **a bolt from the blue.** a sudden, unexpected, and usually unwelcome event. [13] **shoot one's bolt.** to exhaust one's effort: *the runner had shot his bolt.* ◆ VERB [14] (*tr*) to secure or lock with or as with a bolt or bolts: *bolt your doors.* [15] (*tr*) to eat hurriedly: *don't bolt your food.* [16] (*intr;* usually foll by *from* or *out*) to move or jump suddenly: *he bolted from the chair.* [17] (*intr*) (esp of a horse) to start hurriedly and run away without warning. [18] (*tr*) to roll or make (cloth, wallpaper, etc.) into bolts. [19] *US* to desert (a political party, etc.). [20] (*intr*) (of cultivated plants) to produce flowers and seeds prematurely. [21] (*tr*) to cause (a wild animal) to leave its lair; start: *terriers were used for bolting rats.* ◆ ADVERB [22] stiffly, firmly, or rigidly (archaic except in the phrase **bolt upright**).
▷HISTORY Old English *bolt* arrow; related to Old High German *bolz* bolt for a crossbow

bolt[2] *or* **boult** (bəʊlt) VERB (*tr*) [1] to pass (flour, a powder, etc.) through a sieve. [2] to examine and separate.
▷HISTORY C13: from Old French *bulter*, probably of Germanic origin; compare Old High German *būtil* bag
▸ˈ**bolter** *or* ˈ**boulter** NOUN

bolter (ˈbəʊltə) NOUN *Austral informal* [1] an outsider in a contest or race. [2] *History* an escaped convict; bushranger.

bolt hole NOUN a place of escape from danger.

bolt-on ADJECTIVE supplementary or additional: *a bolt-on prologue.*

boltonia (bəʊlˈtəʊnɪə) NOUN any North American plant of the genus *Boltonia*, having daisy-like flowers with white, violet, or pinkish rays: family *Compositae* (composites).
▷HISTORY C18: New Latin, named after James *Bolton*, C18 English botanist

boltrope (ˈbəʊltˌrəʊp) NOUN *Nautical* a rope sewn to the foot or luff of a sail to strengthen it.
▷HISTORY C17: from BOLT[1] + ROPE

Boltzmann constant NOUN *Physics* the ratio of the gas constant to the Avogadro constant, equal to $1.380\ 650 \times 10^{-23}$ joule per kelvin. Symbol: *k*.

bolus (ˈbəʊləs) NOUN, *plural* **-luses.** [1] a small round soft mass, esp of chewed food. [2] an intravenous injection of a single dose of a drug over a short period. [3] *Obsolete* a large pill or tablet used in veterinary and clinical medicine. [4] another word for **bole[2]**.
▷HISTORY C17: from New Latin, from Greek *bōlos* clod, lump

Bolzano (*Italian* bolˈtsano) NOUN a city in NE Italy, in Trentino-Alto Adige: belonged to Austria until 1919. Pop.: 100 380 (1990). German name: **Bozen.**

boma (ˈboːma) NOUN (in central and E Africa) [1] an enclosure, esp a palisade or fence of thorn bush, set up to protect a camp, herd of animals, etc. [2] **a** a police post. **b** a magistrate's office.
▷HISTORY C19: from Swahili

Boma (ˈbəʊmə) NOUN a port in the Democratic Republic of Congo (formerly Zaïre), on the Congo River, capital of the Belgian Congo until 1926: forest products. Pop.: 135 284 (1994 est.).

bomb (bɒm) NOUN [1] **a** a hollow projectile containing explosive, incendiary, or other destructive substance, esp one carried by aircraft. **b** (*as modifier*): *bomb disposal; a bomb bay.* **c** (*in combination*): *a bombload; bombproof.* [2] any container filled with explosive: *a car bomb; a letter bomb.* [3] **the bomb. a** a hydrogen or atomic bomb considered as the ultimate destructive weapon. **b** *Slang* something excellent: *it's the bomb.* [4] a round or pear-shaped mass of volcanic rock, solidified from molten lava that has been thrown into the air. [5] *Med* a container for radioactive material, applied therapeutically to any part of the body: *a cobalt bomb.* [6] *Brit slang* a large sum of money (esp in the phrase **make a bomb**). [7] *US and Canadian slang* a disastrous failure: *the new play was a total bomb.* [8] *Austral and NZ slang* an old or dilapidated motorcar. [9] *American football* a very long high pass. [10] (in rugby union) another term for **up-and-under.** [11] **like a bomb.** *Brit and NZ informal* with great speed or success; very well (esp in the phrase **go like a bomb**). ◆ VERB [12] to attack with or as if with a bomb or bombs; drop bombs (on). [13] (*intr; often foll by off, along,* etc.) *Informal* to move or drive very quickly. [14] (*intr*) *Slang* to fail disastrously; be a flop: *the new play bombed.* See also **bomb out.**
▷HISTORY C17: from French *bombe*, from Italian *bomba*, probably from Latin *bombus* a booming sound, from Greek *bombos*, of imitative origin; compare Old Norse *bumba* drum

bombacaceous (ˌbɒmbəˈkeɪʃəs) ADJECTIVE of, relating to, or belonging to the *Bombacaceae*, a family of tropical trees, including the kapok tree and baobab, that have very thick stems, often with water-storing tissue.
▷HISTORY C19: from New Latin *Bombācāceae*, from Medieval Latin *bombāx* cotton, from Latin *bombyx* silkworm, silk, from Greek *bombux*

bombard VERB (bɒmˈbɑːd) (*tr*) [1] to attack with

concentrated artillery fire or bombs. [2] to attack with vigour and persistence: *the boxer bombarded his opponent with blows to the body.* [3] to attack verbally, esp with questions: *the journalists bombarded her with questions.* [4] *Physics* to direct high-energy particles or photons against (atoms, nuclei, etc.) esp to produce ions or nclear transformations. ◆ NOUN ('bɒmbɑ:d) [5] an ancient type of cannon that threw stone balls.
▷HISTORY C15: from Old French *bombarder* to pelt, from *bombarde* stone-throwing cannon, probably from Latin *bombus* booming sound; see BOMB
▸**bom'bardment** NOUN

bombarde ('bɒm,bɑ:d) NOUN an alto wind instrument similar to the oboe or medieval shawm, used mainly in Breton traditional music.
▷HISTORY French, from BOMBARD, in the sense of booming sound

bombardier (,bɒmbə'dɪə) NOUN [1] the member of a bomber aircrew responsible for aiming and releasing the bombs. [2] *Brit* a noncommissioned rank below the rank of sergeant in the Royal Artillery. [3] Also called: **bombardier beetle.** any of various small carabid beetles of the genus *Brachinus*, esp *B. crepitans* of Europe, which defend themselves by ejecting a jet of volatile fluid.
▷HISTORY C16: from Old French: one directing a bombard; see BOMBARD

Bombardier (,bɒmbə'dɪə) NOUN *Trademark Canadian* a snow tractor, typically having caterpillar tracks at the rear and skis at the front.
▷HISTORY C20: named after J. A. *Bombardier*, Canadian inventor and manufacturer

bombardon ('bɒmbədən, bɒm'bɑ:dᵊn) NOUN [1] a brass instrument of the tuba type, similar to a sousaphone. [2] a 16-foot bass reed stop on an organ.
▷HISTORY C19: from Italian *bombardone*; see BOMBARD

bombast ('bɒmbæst) NOUN [1] pompous and grandiloquent language. [2] *Obsolete* material used for padding.
▷HISTORY C16: from Old French *bombace*, from Medieval Latin *bombāx* cotton; see BOMBACACEOUS
▸**bom'bastic** ADJECTIVE ▸**bom'bastically** ADVERB

Bombay (bɒm'beɪ) NOUN [1] a port in W India, capital of Maharashtra state, on the Arabian Sea: ceded by Portugal to England in 1661 and of major importance in British India; commercial and industrial centre, esp for cotton. Pop.: 9 925 891 (1991). Official and Hindi name: **Mumbai.** [2] a breed of black short-haired medium-sized cat.

Bombay duck NOUN a teleost fish, *Harpodon nehereus*, that resembles and is related to the lizard fishes: family *Harpodontidae*. It is eaten dried with curry dishes as a savoury. Also called: **bummalo.**
▷HISTORY C19: changed from *bombil* (see BUMMALO) through association with Bombay, from which it was exported

Bombay Hills PLURAL NOUN a row of hills marking the southern boundary of greater Auckland on the North Island, New Zealand.

bombazine *or* **bombasine** (,bɒmbə'zi:n, 'bɒmbə,zi:n) NOUN a twilled fabric, esp one with a silk warp and worsted weft, formerly worn dyed black for mourning.
▷HISTORY C16: from Old French *bombasin*, from Latin *bombȳcinus* silken, from *bombyx* silkworm, silk; see BOMBACACEOUS

bomb calorimeter NOUN *Chem* a device for determining heats of combustion by igniting a sample in a high pressure of oxygen in a sealed vessel and measuring the resulting rise in temperature: used for measuring the calorific value of foods.

bombe (bɒmb) NOUN [1] Also called: **bombe glacée.** a dessert of ice cream lined or filled with custard, cake crumbs, etc. [2] a mould shaped like a bomb in which this dessert is made.
▷HISTORY C19: from French, literally: BOMB; from its rounded shape

bombé (bɒm'beɪ; *French* bɔ̃be) ADJECTIVE (of furniture) having a projecting swollen shape.
▷HISTORY French, literally: bomb-shaped, from *bombe* BOMB

bombed (bɒmd) ADJECTIVE *Slang* under the influence of alcohol or drugs (esp in the phrase **bombed out of one's mind** *or* **skull**).

bomber ('bɒmə) NOUN [1] a military aircraft designed to carry out bombing missions. [2] a person who plants bombs. [3] *Navy, slang* a Polaris submarine.

bomber jacket NOUN a short jacket finishing at the waist with an elasticated band, usually having a zip front and cuffed sleeves.

bombinate ('bɒmbɪ,neɪt) VERB (*intr*) *Literary* to make a buzzing noise. Also (rare): **bombilate.**
▷HISTORY C19: from Latin *bombināre*, variant of *bombilāre* to buzz
▸,**bombi'nation** NOUN

bombing run NOUN the part of a flight of a bomber aircraft that brings it to the point over a target at which its bombs are released.

bombora (bɒm'bɔ:rə) NOUN *Austral* [1] a submerged reef. [2] a turbulent area of sea over such a reef.
▷HISTORY from a native Australian language

bomb out VERB (*adverb; tr, usually passive*) to make homeless by bombing: *24 families in this street have been bombed out.*

bombshell ('bɒm,ʃel) NOUN [1] (esp formerly) a bomb or artillery shell. [2] a shocking or unwelcome surprise: *the news of his death was a bombshell.* [3] *Informal* an attractive girl or woman (esp in the phrase **blonde bombshell**).

bombsight ('bɒm,saɪt) NOUN a mechanical or electronic device in an aircraft for aiming bombs.

bomb site NOUN an area where the buildings have been destroyed by bombs.

bombycid ('bɒmbɪsɪd) NOUN [1] any moth, including the silkworm moth, of the family *Bombycidae*, most of which occur in Africa and SE Asia. ◆ ADJECTIVE [2] of, relating to, or belonging to the *Bombycidae*.
▷HISTORY C19: from Latin *bombyx* silkworm

Bomu ('bəumu:) *or* **Mbomu** (ᵊm'bəumu:) NOUN a river in central Africa, rising in the SE Central African Republic and flowing west into the Uele River, forming the Ubangi River. Length: about 800 km (500 miles).

Bon[1] (bɔ:n) NOUN [1] Also called: **Feast** (*or* **Festival**) **of Lanterns.** an annual festival celebrated by Japanese Buddhists. [2] **a** the pre-Buddhist priests of Tibet or one such priest. **b** their religion.
▷HISTORY from Japanese *bon*, originally *Urabon*, from Sanskrit *ullambana* hanging upside down

Bon[2] (bɒn) NOUN **Cape.** a peninsula of NE Tunisia.

Bona ('bəunə) NOUN **Mount.** a mountain in S Alaska, in the Wrangell Mountains. Height: 5005 m (16 420 ft.).

bona fide ADJECTIVE ('bəunə 'faɪdɪ) [1] real or genuine: *a bona fide manuscript.* [2] undertaken in good faith: *a bona fide agreement.* ◆ NOUN ('bɔ:nə faɪd) [3] *Irish informal* a public house licensed to remain open after normal hours to serve bona fide travellers.
▷HISTORY C16: from Latin

bona fides ('bəunə 'faɪdi:z) NOUN *Law* good faith; honest intention.
▷HISTORY Latin

Bonaire (bɒn'ɛə) NOUN an island in the S Caribbean, in the E Netherlands Antilles: one of the Leeward Islands. Chief town: Kralendijk. Pop.: 12 533 (1994 est.). Area: about 288 sq. km (111 sq. miles).

bonanza (bə'nænzə) NOUN [1] a source, usually sudden and unexpected, of luck or wealth. [2] *US and Canadian* a mine or vein rich in ore.
▷HISTORY C19: from Spanish, literally: calm sea, hence, good luck, from Medieval Latin *bonacia*, from Latin *bonus* good + *malacia* dead calm, from Greek *malakia* softness

Bonapartism ('bəunəpɑ:,tɪzəm) NOUN [1] a political system resembling the rules of the Bonapartes, esp Napoleon I (1769–1821; Emperor of the French 1804–15) and Napoleon III (1808–73; Emperor of the French 1852–70): centralized government by a military dictator, who enjoys popular support given expression in plebiscites. [2] (esp in France) support for the government or dynasty of Napoleon Bonaparte.
▸'**Bona,partist** NOUN

bona vacantia ('bəunə və'kæntɪə) PLURAL NOUN *Law* unclaimed goods.

bonbon ('bɒnbɒn) NOUN a sweet.

▷HISTORY C19: from French, originally a children's word from *bon* good

bonce (bɒns) NOUN *Brit slang* the head.
▷HISTORY C19 (originally: a type of large playing marble): of unknown origin

bond (bɒnd) NOUN [1] something that binds, fastens, or holds together, such as a chain or rope. [2] (*often plural*) something that brings or holds people together; tie: *a bond of friendship.* [3] (*plural*) something that restrains or imprisons; captivity or imprisonment. [4] something that governs behaviour; obligation; duty. [5] a written or spoken agreement, esp a promise: *marriage bond.* [6] adhesive quality or strength. [7] *Finance* a certificate of debt issued in order to raise funds. It carries a fixed rate of interest and is repayable with or without security at a specified future date. [8] *Law* a written acknowledgment of an obligation to pay a sum or to perform a contract. [9] *Insurance US and Canadian* a policy guaranteeing payment of a stated sum to an employer in compensation for financial losses incurred through illegal or unauthorized acts of an employee. [10] any of various arrangements of bricks or stones in a wall in which they overlap so as to provide strength. [11] See **chemical bond.** [12] See **bond paper.** [13] **in bond.** *Commerce* deposited in a bonded warehouse. ◆ VERB (*mainly tr*) [14] (*also intr*) to hold or be held together, as by a rope or an adhesive; bind; connect. [15] *Aeronautics* to join (metallic parts of an aircraft) together such that they are electrically interconnected. [16] to put or hold (goods) in bond. [17] *Law* to place under bond. [18] *Finance* to issue bonds on; mortgage. [19] to arrange (bricks, etc.) in a bond.
▷HISTORY C13: from Old Norse *band*; see BAND[2]

bondage ('bɒndɪdʒ) NOUN [1] slavery or serfdom; servitude. [2] Also called: **villeinage.** (in medieval Europe) the condition and status of unfree peasants who provided labour and other services for their lord in return for holdings of land. [3] a sexual practice in which one partner is physically bound.

bonded ('bɒndɪd) ADJECTIVE [1] *Finance* consisting of, secured by, or operating under a bond or bonds. [2] *Commerce* deposited in a bonded warehouse; placed or stored in bond.

bonded warehouse NOUN a warehouse in which dutiable goods are deposited until duty is paid or the goods are cleared for export.

bondholder ('bɒnd,həuldə) NOUN an owner of one or more bonds issued by a company or other institution.

Bondi Beach ('bɒndaɪ) NOUN a beach in Sydney, Australia, popular with surfers.

bonding ('bɒndɪŋ) NOUN the process by which individuals become emotionally attached to one another. See also **pair bond.**

bondmaid ('bɒnd,meɪd) NOUN an unmarried female serf or slave.

bond paper NOUN a superior quality of strong white paper, used esp for writing and typing.

bondservant ('bɒnd,sɜ:vənt) NOUN a serf or slave.

bondsman ('bɒndzmən) NOUN, *plural* **-men.** [1] *Law* a person bound by bond to act as surety for another. [2] another word for **bondservant.**

bondstone ('bɒnd,stəun) NOUN a long stone or brick laid in a wall as a header. Also called: **bonder.**

bond washing NOUN a series of deals in bonds made with the intention of avoiding taxation.

bone (bəun) NOUN [1] any of the various structures that make up the skeleton in most vertebrates. [2] the porous rigid tissue of which these parts are made, consisting of a matrix of collagen and inorganic salts, esp calcium phosphate, interspersed with canals and small holes. Related adjectives: **osseous, osteal.** [3] something consisting of bone or a bonelike substance. [4] (*plural*) the human skeleton or body: *they laid his bones to rest; come and rest your bones.* [5] a thin strip of whalebone, light metal, plastic, etc., used to stiffen corsets and brassieres. [6] (*plural*) the essentials (esp in the phrase **the bare bones**): *to explain the bones of a situation.* [7] (*plural*) dice. [8] (*plural*) an informal nickname for a **doctor.** [9] **close to** *or* **near the bone. a** risqué or indecent: *his jokes are rather close to the bone.* **b** in poverty; destitute. [10] **feel in one's bones.** to have an intuition of. [11] **have a bone to pick.** to have grounds for a quarrel. [12] **make no bones about. a** to be direct and candid about. **b** to have no scruples about. [13] **point**

the bone. (often foll by *at*) *Austral* **a** to wish bad luck (on). **b** to threaten to bring about the downfall (of). ◆ VERB (*mainly tr*) [14] to remove the bones from (meat for cooking, etc.). [15] to stiffen (a corset, etc.) by inserting bones. [16] to fertilize with bone meal. [17] *Taboo slang* to have sexual intercourse with. [18] *Brit* a slang word for **steal.** ◆ See also **bone up.**
▷HISTORY Old English *bān*; related to Old Norse *bein*, Old Frisian *bēn*, Old High German *bein*
▸ **'boneless** ADJECTIVE

Bône (*French* bon) NOUN a former name of **Annaba.**

bone ash NOUN the residue obtained when bones are burned in air, consisting mainly of calcium phosphate. It is used as a fertilizer and in the manufacture of bone china.

bone bed NOUN *Geology* a sediment containing large quantities of fossilized animal remains, such as bones, teeth, scales, etc.

boneblack ('bəʊnˌblæk) NOUN a black residue from the destructive distillation of bones, containing about 10 per cent carbon and 80 per cent calcium phosphate, used as a decolorizing agent and pigment.

bone china NOUN porcelain containing bone ash.

bone-dry ADJECTIVE *Informal* **a** completely dry: *a bone-dry well.* **b** (*postpositive*): *the well was bone dry.*

bonefish ('bəʊnˌfɪʃ) NOUN, *plural* **-fish** *or* **-fishes.** [1] a silvery marine clupeoid game fish, *Albula vulpes*, occurring in warm shallow waters: family *Albulidae*. [2] a similar related fish, *Dixonina nemoptera*, of the Pacific Ocean.

bonehead ('bəʊnˌhɛd) NOUN *Slang* a stupid or obstinate person.
▸ **ˌbone'headed** ADJECTIVE

bone idle ADJECTIVE very idle; extremely lazy.

bone marrow NOUN See **marrow**[1] (sense 1).

bone meal NOUN the product of dried and ground animal bones, used as a fertilizer or in stock feeds.

bone of contention NOUN the grounds or subject of a dispute.

bone oil NOUN a dark brown pungent oil, containing pyridine and hydrocarbons, obtained by the destructive distillation of bones.

boner ('bəʊnə) NOUN [1] *Slang* a blunder. [2] *NZ* a low-grade slaughtered animal suitable for use in pies, sausages, etc.

boneset ('bəʊnˌsɛt) NOUN any of various North American plants of the genus *Eupatorium*, esp *E. perfoliatum*, which has flat clusters of small white flowers: family *Asteraceae* (composites). Also called: **agueweed, feverwort, thoroughwort.**

bonesetter ('bəʊnˌsɛtə) NOUN a person who sets broken or dislocated bones, esp one who has no formal medical qualifications.

boneshaker ('bəʊnˌʃeɪkə) NOUN [1] an early type of bicycle having solid tyres and no springs. [2] *Slang* any decrepit or rickety vehicle.

bone turquoise NOUN fossilized bone or tooth stained blue with iron phosphate and used as a gemstone. Also called: **odontolite.**

bone up VERB (*adverb; when intr*, usually foll by *on*) *Informal* to study intensively.

boneyard ('bəʊnˌjɑːd) NOUN an informal name for a **cemetery.**

bonfire ('bɒnˌfaɪə) NOUN a large outdoor fire.
▷HISTORY C15: alteration (through influence of French *bon* good) of *bone-fire*; from the use of bones as fuel

bong[1] (bɒŋ) NOUN [1] a deep reverberating sound, as of a large bell. ◆ VERB (*intr*) [2] to make a deep reverberating sound.
▷HISTORY C20: of imitative origin

bong[2] (bɒŋ) NOUN a type of water pipe for smoking marijuana, crack, etc.
▷HISTORY C20: of unknown origin

bongo[1] ('bɒŋgəʊ) NOUN, *plural* **-go** *or* **-gos.** a rare spiral-horned antelope, *Boocercus* (or *Taurotragus*) *eurycerus*, inhabiting forests of central Africa. The coat is bright red-brown with narrow cream stripes.
▷HISTORY of African origin

bongo[2] ('bɒŋgəʊ) NOUN, *plural* **-gos** *or* **-goes.** a small bucket-shaped drum, usually one of a pair, played by beating with the fingers.
▷HISTORY American Spanish, probably of imitative origin

bonham ('bɒnəv) NOUN *Irish* a piglet.
▷HISTORY C19: from Irish Gaelic *banbh*

bonhomie ('bɒnəmiː; *French* bɔnɔmi) NOUN exuberant friendliness.
▷HISTORY C18: from French, from *bonhomme* good-humoured fellow, from *bon* good + *homme* man

bonhomous ('bɒnəməs) ADJECTIVE exhibiting bonhomie.

Bonin Islands ('bəʊnɪn) PLURAL NOUN a group of 27 volcanic islands in the W Pacific: occupied by the US after World War II; returned to Japan in 1968. Largest island: Chichijima. Area: 103 sq. km (40 sq. miles). Japanese name: **Ogasawara Gunto.**

bonism ('bəʊˌnɪzəm) NOUN the doctrine that the world is good, although not the best of all possible worlds.
▷HISTORY C19: from Latin *bonus* good + -ISM
▸ **'bonist** NOUN, ADJECTIVE

bonito (bə'niːtəʊ) NOUN, *plural* **-tos.** [1] any of various small tunny-like marine food fishes of the genus *Sarda*, of warm Atlantic and Pacific waters: family *Scombridae* (tunnies and mackerels). [2] any of various similar or related fishes, such as *Katsuwonus pelamis* (**oceanic bonito**), the flesh of which is dried and flaked and used in Japanese cookery.
▷HISTORY C16: from Spanish *bonito*, from Latin *bonus* good

bonk (bɒŋk) VERB *Informal* [1] (*tr*) to hit. [2] to have sexual intercourse (with).
▷HISTORY C20: probably of imitative origin
▸ **'bonking** NOUN

bonkbuster NOUN ('bɒŋkˌbʌstə) *Informal* a novel characterized by graphic descriptions of the heroine's frequent sexual encounters.
▷HISTORY C20: from BONK (sense 2) + (BLOCK)BUSTER

bonkers ('bɒŋkəz) ADJECTIVE *Slang, chiefly Brit* mad; crazy.
▷HISTORY C20 (originally in the sense: slightly drunk, tipsy): of unknown origin

bon mot (*French* bɔ̃ mo) NOUN, *plural* **bons mots** (bɔ̃ mo). a clever and fitting remark.
▷HISTORY French, literally: good word

Bonn (bɒn; *German* bɔn) NOUN a city in W Germany, in North Rhine-Westphalia on the Rhine: the former capital (1949–90) of West Germany; university (1786). Pop.: 304 100 (1999 est.).

bonne *French* (bɔn) NOUN a housemaid or female servant.
▷HISTORY C18: from feminine of *bon* good

bonne bouche *French* (bɔn buʃ) NOUN, *plural* ***bonnes bouches*** (bɔn buʃ). a tasty titbit or morsel.
▷HISTORY literally: good mouth(ful)

bonnet ('bɒnɪt) NOUN [1] any of various hats worn, esp formerly, by women and girls, usually framing the face and tied with ribbons under the chin. [2] (in Scotland) Also called: **bunnet** ('bʌnɪt). **a** a soft cloth cap. **b** formerly, a flat brimless cap worn by men. [3] the hinged metal part of a motor vehicle body that provides access to the engine, or to the luggage space in a rear-engined vehicle. [4] a cowl on a chimney. [5] *Nautical* a piece of sail laced to the foot of a foresail to give it greater area in light winds. [6] (in the US and Canada) a headdress of feathers worn by some tribes of American Indians, esp formerly as a sign of war.
▷HISTORY C14: from Old French *bonet*, from Medieval Latin *abonnis*, of unknown origin

bonnet monkey NOUN an Indian macaque, *Macaca radiata*, with a bonnet-like tuft of hair.

bonnet rouge *French* (bɔnɛ ruʒ) NOUN [1] a red cap worn by ardent supporters of the French Revolution. [2] an extremist or revolutionary.
▷HISTORY literally: red cap

bonny ('bɒnɪ) ADJECTIVE **-nier, -niest.** [1] *Scot and northern English dialect* beautiful or handsome: *a bonny lass.* [2] merry or lively: *a bonny family.* [3] good or fine: *a bonny house.* [4] (esp of babies) plump. [5] *Scot and northern English dialect* considerable; to be reckoned with: *cost a bonny penny.* ◆ ADVERB [6] *Informal* agreeably or well: *to speak bonny.*
▷HISTORY C15: of uncertain origin; perhaps from Old French *bon* good, from Latin *bonus*
▸ **'bonnily** ADVERB

Bonny ('bɒnɪ) NOUN **Bight of.** a wide bay at the E end of the Gulf of Guinea off the coasts of Nigeria and Cameroon. Former name (until 1975): **Bight of Biafra.**

bonobo (bɒn'əbʊ) NOUN an anthropoid ape, *Pan paniscus*, of central W Africa: similar to the chimpanzee but much smaller and having a black face. Also called: **pygmy chimpanzee.**
▷HISTORY C20: from W African language

bonsai ('bɒnsaɪ) NOUN, *plural* **-sai.** [1] the art of growing dwarfed ornamental varieties of trees or shrubs in small shallow pots or trays by selective pruning, etc. [2] a tree or shrub grown by this method.
▷HISTORY C20: Japanese: plant grown in a pot, from *bon* basin, bowl + *sai* to plant

bonsela (bɒn'sɛlə) NOUN *South African informal* a present or gratuity. Also called: **bansela, pasela** (pə'sɛlə).
▷HISTORY from Zulu *Ibanselo* a gift

bonspiel ('bɒnˌspiːl, -spəl) NOUN a curling match.
▷HISTORY C16: probably from Low German; compare Flemish *bonespel* children's game; see SPIEL

bontebok ('bɒntɪˌbʌk) NOUN, *plural* **-boks** *or* **-bok.** an antelope, *Damaliscus pygargus* (or *dorcas*), of southern Africa, having a deep reddish-brown coat with a white blaze, tail, and rump patch.
▷HISTORY C18: Afrikaans, from *bont* pied + *bok* BUCK[1]

bon ton *French* (bɔ̃ tɔ̃) NOUN *Literary* [1] sophisticated manners or breeding. [2] fashionable society.
▷HISTORY literally: good tone

bonus ('bəʊnəs) NOUN [1] something given, paid, or received above what is due or expected: *a Christmas bonus for all employees.* [2] *Chiefly Brit* an extra dividend allotted to shareholders out of profits. [3] *Insurance Brit* a dividend, esp a percentage of net profits, distributed to policyholders either annually or when the policy matures. [4] *Brit* a slang word for a **bribe.**
▷HISTORY C18: from Latin *bonus* (adj) good

bonus issue NOUN *Brit* an issue of shares made by a company without charge and distributed pro rata among existing shareholders. Also called: **scrip issue.**

bon vivant *French* (bɔ̃ vivɑ̃) NOUN, *plural* ***bons vivants*** (bɔ̃ vivɑ̃). a person who enjoys luxuries, esp good food and drink. Also called (but not in French): **bon viveur** (ˌbɒn viː'vɜː).
▷HISTORY literally: good living (man)

bon voyage (*French* bɔ̃ vwajaʒ) SENTENCE SUBSTITUTE a phrase used to wish a traveller a pleasant journey.
▷HISTORY French, literally: good journey

bonxie ('bɒŋksɪ) NOUN a name, originally Shetland, for the **great skua** (see **skua**).
▷HISTORY C19: probably of Scandinavian origin: compare Norwegian *bunke* heap, something dumpy

bony ('bəʊnɪ) ADJECTIVE **bonier, boniest.** [1] resembling or consisting of bone or bones. [2] having many bones. [3] having prominent bones: *bony cheeks.* [4] thin or emaciated: *a bony old woman.*
▸ **'boniness** NOUN

bony bream NOUN an Australian freshwater clupeid fish, *Fluvialosa richardsonii*.

bony fish NOUN, NOUN any fish of the class *Osteichthyes*, including most of the extant species, having a skeleton of bone rather than cartilage.

bonze (bɒnz) NOUN a Chinese or Japanese Buddhist priest or monk.
▷HISTORY C16: from French, from Portuguese *bonzo*, from Japanese *bonsō*, from Sanskrit *bon* + *sō* priest or monk

bonzer ('bɒnzə) ADJECTIVE *Austral and NZ slang, archaic* excellent; very good.
▷HISTORY C20: of uncertain origin; perhaps from BONANZA

boo (buː) INTERJECTION [1] an exclamation uttered to startle or surprise someone, esp a child. [2] a shout uttered to express disgust, dissatisfaction, or contempt, esp at a theatrical production, political meeting, etc. [3] **would not say boo to a goose.** is extremely timid or diffident. ◆ VERB **boos, booing, booed.** [4] to shout "boo" at (someone or something), esp as an expression of disgust, dissatisfaction, or disapproval: *to boo the actors.*

boob[1] (buːb) *Slang* ◆ NOUN [1] an ignorant or foolish person; booby. [2] *Brit* an embarrassing

mistake; blunder. [3] a female breast. ◆ VERB [4] *(intr)* *Brit* to make a blunder.
▷**HISTORY** C20: back formation from BOOBY

boob² (bu:b) NOUN *Austral slang* [1] a prison. ◆ ADJECTIVE [2] of poor quality, similar to that provided in prison: *boob coffee*.
▷**HISTORY** from the US colloquial sense of *booby hatch* meaning jail

boob happy ADJECTIVE *Austral slang* suffering from the mental strain caused by the difficulties of prison life.

boobhead ('bu:bˌhɛd) NOUN *Austral slang* a repeat offender in a prison.

boobialla (ˌbu:bɪ'ælə) NOUN *Austral* [1] another name for **golden wattle** (sense 2). [2] any of various trees or shrubs of the genus *Myoporum*, esp *M. insulare*.
▷**HISTORY** from a native Australian language

boo-boo NOUN, *plural* **-boos.** *Informal* an embarrassing mistake; blunder.
▷**HISTORY** C20: perhaps from nursery talk; compare BOOHOO

boobook ('bu:bʊk) NOUN a small spotted brown Australian owl, *Ninox boobook*.

boob tube NOUN *Slang* [1] a close-fitting strapless top, worn by women. [2] *Austral* a strapless, boneless, shapeless brassiere made of a stretch fabric. [3] *Chiefly US and Canadian* a television receiver.

booby ('bu:bɪ) NOUN, *plural* **-bies.** [1] an ignorant or foolish person. [2] *Brit* the losing player in a game. [3] any of several tropical marine birds of the genus *Sula*: family *Sulidae*, order *Pelecaniformes* (pelicans, cormorants, etc.). They have a straight stout bill and the plumage is white with darker markings. Compare **gannet**.
▷**HISTORY** C17: from Spanish *bobo*, from Latin *balbus* stammering

booby hatch NOUN [1] a hoodlike covering for a hatchway on a ship. [2] *US slang* a mental hospital.

booby prize NOUN a mock prize given to the person having the lowest score or giving the worst performance in a competition.

booby trap NOUN [1] a hidden explosive device primed in such a way as to be set off by an unsuspecting victim. [2] a trap for an unsuspecting person, esp one intended as a practical joke, such as an object balanced above a door to fall on the person who opens it. ◆ VERB **booby-trap, traps, -trapping, -trapped.** [3] *(tr)* to set a booby trap in or on (a building or object) or for (a person).

boodle ('bu:dᵊl) *Slang* ◆ NOUN [1] money or valuables, esp when stolen, counterfeit, or used as a bribe. [2] *Chiefly US* another word for **caboodle.** ◆ VERB [3] to give or receive money corruptly or illegally.
▷**HISTORY** C19: from Dutch *boedel* all one's possessions, from Old Frisian *bōdel* movable goods, inheritance; see CABOODLE

boofhead ('bʊfhɛd) NOUN *Slang, chiefly Austral* [1] a stupid person. [2] a person or animal with a large head.

boofy ('bʊfɪ) ADJECTIVE *Austral informal* [1] muscular and strong but stupid. [2] (of the hair) voluminous. [3] puffed out: *boofy sleeves*.

boogie ('bu:gɪ) *Slang* ◆ VERB **-gies, -gieing, -gied.** *(intr)* [1] to dance to pop music. [2] to make love. ◆ NOUN [3] a session of dancing to pop music.
▷**HISTORY** C20: originally African-American slang, perhaps from Kongo *mbugi* devilishly good

boogie-woogie ('bʊgɪ'wʊgɪ, 'bu:gɪ'wu:gɪ) NOUN a style of piano jazz using a dotted bass pattern, usually with eight notes in a bar and the harmonies of the 12-bar blues.

boohai (bu:'haɪ) NOUN **up the boohai.** *NZ informal* thoroughly lost.
▷**HISTORY** from the remote township of *Puhoi*

boohoo (ˌbu:'hu:) VERB **-hoos, -hooing, -hooed.** [1] to sob or pretend to sob noisily. ◆ NOUN, *plural* **-hoos.** [2] *(sometimes plural)* distressed or pretended sobbing.
▷**HISTORY** C20: nursery talk

boo-hurrah theory NOUN *Philosophy* an informal term for **emotivism.**

book (bʊk) NOUN [1] a number of printed or written pages bound together along one edge and usually protected by thick paper or stiff pasteboard covers. See also **hardback, paperback.** [2] **a** a written work or composition, such as a novel, technical manual, or dictionary. **b** *(as modifier)*: *the book trade; book reviews*. **c** *(in combination)*: *bookseller; bookshop; bookshelf; bookrack*. [3] a number of blank or ruled sheets of paper bound together, used to record lessons, keep accounts, etc. [4] *(plural)* a record of the transactions of a business or society. [5] the script of a play or the libretto of an opera, musical, etc. [6] a major division of a written composition, as of a long novel or of the Bible. [7] a number of tickets, sheets, stamps, etc., fastened together along one edge. [8] *Bookmaking* a record of the bets made on a horse race or other event. [9] (in card games) the number of tricks that must be taken by a side or player before any trick has a scoring value: *in bridge, six of the 13 tricks form the book*. [10] strict or rigid regulations, rules, or standards (esp in the phrases **according to the book, by the book**). [11] a source of knowledge or authority: *the book of life*. [12] a telephone directory (in the phrase **in the book**). [13] **the book.** *(sometimes capital)* the Bible. [14] **an open book.** a person or subject that is thoroughly understood. [15] **a closed book.** a person or subject that is unknown or beyond comprehension: *chemistry is a closed book to him*. [16] **bring to book.** to reprimand or require (someone) to give an explanation of his conduct. [17] **close the book on.** to bring to a definite end: *we have closed the book on apartheid*. [18] **close the books.** *Book-keeping* to balance accounts in order to prepare a statement or report. [19] **cook the books.** *Informal* to make fraudulent alterations to business or other accounts. [20] **in my book.** according to my view of things. [21] **in someone's good** *or* **bad books.** regarded by someone with favour (or disfavour). [22] **keep the books.** to keep written records of the finances of a business or other enterprise. [23] **on the books. a** enrolled as a member. **b** registered or recorded. [24] **read (someone) like a book.** to understand (a person, his motives, character, etc.) thoroughly and clearly. [25] **throw the book at. a** to charge with every relevant offence. **b** to inflict the most severe punishment on. ◆ VERB [26] to reserve (a place, passage, etc.) or engage the services of (a performer, driver, etc.) in advance: *to book a flight; to book a band*. [27] *(tr)* to take the name and address of (a person guilty of a minor offence) with a view to bringing a prosecution: *he was booked for ignoring a traffic signal*. [28] *(tr)* (of a football referee) to take the name of (a player) who grossly infringes the rules while playing, two such acts resulting in the player's dismissal from the field. [29] *(tr)* *Archaic* to record in a book. ◆ See also **book in, book into, book out, book up.**
▷**HISTORY** Old English *bōc*; related to Old Norse *bōk*, Old High German *buoh* book, Gothic *bōka* letter; see BEECH (the bark of which was used as a writing surface)

bookbinder ('bʊkˌbaɪndə) NOUN a person whose business or craft is binding books.
▸ **'bookˌbinding** NOUN

bookbindery ('bʊkˌbaɪndərɪ) NOUN, *plural* **-eries.** a place in which books are bound. Often shortened to: **bindery.**

bookcase ('bʊkˌkeɪs) NOUN a piece of furniture containing shelves for books, often fitted with glass doors.

book club NOUN a club that sells books at low prices to members, usually by mail order, esp on condition that they buy a minimum number.

booked up ADJECTIVE unable to offer any appointments or accept any reservations, etc.; fully booked; full up.

book end NOUN one of a pair of usually ornamental supports for holding a row of books upright.

Booker Prize ('bʊkə) NOUN an annual prize for a work of British, Commonwealth, or Irish fiction of £50,000, awarded since 1969 by the Booker food -trading company. Official name from 2002: **Man Booker Prize.**

book group NOUN another name for **reading group.**

bookie ('bʊkɪ) NOUN *Informal* short for **bookmaker.**

book in VERB *(adverb)* [1] to reserve a room for (oneself or someone else) at a hotel. [2] *Chiefly Brit* to record something in a book or register, esp one's arrival at a hotel.

booking ('bʊkɪŋ) NOUN [1] *Chiefly Brit* **a** a reservation, as of a table or room in a hotel, seat in a theatre, or seat on a train, aircraft, etc. **b** *(as modifier)*: *the booking office at a railway station*. [2] *Theatre* an engagement for the services of an actor or acting company.

book into VERB *(preposition)* to reserve a room for (oneself or someone else) at (a hotel).

bookish ('bʊkɪʃ) ADJECTIVE [1] fond of reading; studious. [2] consisting of or forming opinions or attitudes through reading rather than direct personal experience; academic: *a bookish view of life*. [3] of or relating to books: *a bookish career in publishing*.
▸ **'bookishly** ADVERB ▸ **'bookishness** NOUN

book-keeping NOUN the skill or occupation of systematically recording business transactions.
▸ **'book-ˌkeeper** NOUN

book-learning NOUN [1] knowledge gained from books rather than from direct personal experience. [2] formal education.

booklet ('bʊklɪt) NOUN a thin book, esp one having paper covers; pamphlet.

booklight ('bʊkˌlaɪt) NOUN a small light that can be clipped onto a book for reading by.

booklouse ('bʊkˌlaʊs) NOUN, *plural* **-lice.** any small insect of the order *Psocoptera*, esp *Trogium pulsatorium* (**common booklouse**), a wingless species that feeds on bookbinding paste, etc.

bookmaker ('bʊkˌmeɪkə) NOUN a person who as an occupation accepts bets, esp on horseraces, and pays out to winning betters.
▸ **'bookˌmaking** NOUN

bookmark ('bʊkˌmɑ:k) NOUN [1] Also called: **bookmarker.** a strip or band of some material, such as leather or ribbon, put between the pages of a book to mark a place. [2] *Computing* **a** an address for a website stored on a computer so that the user can easily return to the site. **b** an identifier placed in a document so that part of the document can be accessed easily. ◆ VERB [3] *(tr)* *Computing* **a** to identify and store (a website) so that one can return to it quickly and easily. **b** to place a bookmark in (a document).

bookmobile ('bʊkməˌbi:l) NOUN the US and Canadian word for **mobile library.**

book of account NOUN another name for **journal** (sense 4a).

Book of Changes NOUN another name for the **I Ching.**

Book of Common Prayer NOUN the official book of church services of the Church of England, until 1980, when the Alternative Service Book was sanctioned.

book of hours NOUN *(often capitals)* a book used esp in monasteries during the Middle Ages that contained the prayers and offices of the canonical hours.

Book of Kells NOUN See **Kells.**

Book of Mormon NOUN a sacred book of the Mormon Church, believed by Mormons to be a history of certain ancient peoples in America, written on golden tablets (now lost) and revealed by the prophet Mormon to Joseph Smith.

book of original entry NOUN another name for **journal** (sense 4a).

book out VERB *(usually intr, adverb)* to leave or cause to leave a hotel.

bookplate ('bʊkˌpleɪt) NOUN a label bearing the owner's name and an individual design or coat of arms, pasted into a book.

book scorpion NOUN any of various small arachnids of the order *Pseudoscorpionida* (false scorpions), esp *Chelifer cancroides*, which are sometimes found in old books, etc.

bookstall ('bʊkˌstɔ:l) NOUN a stall or stand where periodicals, newspapers, or books are sold. US word: **newsstand.**

booksy ('bʊksɪ) ADJECTIVE inclined to be bookish or literary.

book token NOUN *Brit* a gift token to be exchanged for books.

book up VERB *(adverb)* [1] to make a reservation (for); book. [2] See **booked up.**

book value NOUN [1] the value of an asset of a business according to its books. [2] **a** the net capital value of an enterprise as shown by the excess of book assets over book liabilities. **b** the value of a share computed by dividing the net capital value of an enterprise by its issued shares. Compare **par value, market value.**

bookworm ('bʊkˌwɜːm) NOUN [1] a person excessively devoted to studying. [2] any of various small insects that feed on the binding paste of books, esp the book louse.

bool (bul) *Scot* ◆ NOUN [1] a bowling bowl. [2] a playing marble. [3] (*plural*) the game of bowls or marbles. ◆ VERB (*intr*) [4] to play bowls.
▷HISTORY Scot variant of BOWL[2]

Boolean algebra ('buːlɪən) NOUN a system of symbolic logic devised by George Boole to codify logical operations. It is used in computers.

boom[1] (buːm) VERB [1] to make a deep prolonged resonant sound, as of thunder or artillery fire. [2] to prosper or cause to prosper vigorously and rapidly: *business boomed.* ◆ NOUN [3] a deep prolonged resonant sound: *the boom of the sea.* [4] the cry of certain animals, esp the bittern. [5] a period of high economic growth characterized by rising wages, profits, and prices, full employment, and high levels of investment, trade, and other economic activity. Compare **depression** (sense 5).
▷HISTORY C15: perhaps from Dutch *bommen*, of imitative origin

boom[2] (buːm) NOUN [1] *Nautical* a spar to which a sail is fastened to control its position relative to the wind. [2] a beam or spar pivoting at the foot of the mast of a derrick, controlling the distance from the mast at which a load is lifted or lowered. [3] a pole, usually extensible, carrying an overhead microphone and projected over a film or television set. [4] **a** a barrier across a waterway, usually consisting of a chain of connected floating logs, to confine free-floating logs, protect a harbour from attack, etc. **b** the area so barred off.
▷HISTORY C16: from Dutch *boom* tree, BEAM

boomer ('buːmə) NOUN [1] *Austral* a large male kangaroo. [2] *Austral and NZ informal* anything exceptionally large.
▷HISTORY from English dialect

boomerang ('buːməˌræŋ) NOUN [1] a curved flat wooden missile of native Australians, which can be made to return to the thrower. [2] an action or statement that recoils on its originator. ◆ VERB [3] (*intr*) to recoil or return unexpectedly, causing harm to its originator; backfire.
▷HISTORY C19: from a native Australian language

boomerang generation NOUN young adults who, after having lived on their own for a time, return to live in their parental home, usually due to financial problems caused by unemployment or the high cost of living independently.

boomkin ('buːmkɪn) NOUN *Nautical* a short boom projecting from the deck of a ship, used to secure the main-brace blocks or to extend the lower edge of the foresail.
▷HISTORY C17: from Dutch *boomken*, from *boom* tree; see BEAM, -KIN

boomslang ('buːmˌslæŋ) NOUN a large greenish venomous arboreal colubrid snake, *Dispholidus typus*, of southern Africa.
▷HISTORY C18: from Afrikaans, from *boom* tree + *slang* snake

boom town NOUN a town that is enjoying sudden prosperity or has grown rapidly.

boon[1] (buːn) NOUN [1] something extremely useful, helpful, or beneficial; a blessing or benefit: *the car was a boon to him.* [2] *Archaic* a favour; request: *he asked a boon of the king.*
▷HISTORY C12: from Old Norse *bōn* request; related to Old English *bēn* prayer

boon[2] (buːn) ADJECTIVE [1] close, special, or intimate (in the phrase **boon companion**). [2] *Archaic* jolly or convivial.
▷HISTORY C14: from Old French *bon* from Latin *bonus* good

boondocks ('buːnˌdɒks) PLURAL NOUN **the.** *US and Canadian slang* [1] wild, desolate, or uninhabitable country. [2] a remote rural or provincial area. Sometimes shortened to: **the Boonies.**
▷HISTORY C20: from Tagalog *bundok* mountain

boondoggle ('buːnˌdɒgᵊl) *Informal, chiefly US and Canadian* ◆ VERB [1] (*intr*) to do futile and unnecessary work. ◆ NOUN [2] a futile and unnecessary project or work.
▷HISTORY C20: said to have been coined by R. H. Link, American scoutmaster
▸ 'boonˌdoggler NOUN

boong (buːŋ) NOUN *Austral offensive* a Black person.
▷HISTORY C20: perhaps of native Australian origin

boonga (buːŋə) NOUN *NZ offensive* a Pacific Islander.
▷HISTORY perhaps of native Australian origin, from BOONG

boongary ('buːŋgærɪ) NOUN a tree kangaroo, *Dendrolagus lumholtzi*, of northeastern Queensland.
▷HISTORY from a native Australian language

boor (bʊə) NOUN an ill-mannered, clumsy, or insensitive person.
▷HISTORY Old English *gebūr*; related to Old High German *gibūr* farmer, dweller, Albanian *būr* man; see NEIGHBOUR

boorish ('bʊərɪʃ) ADJECTIVE ill-mannered, clumsy, or insensitive; rude.
▸ 'boorishly ADVERB ▸ 'boorishness NOUN

booshit ('buːʃɪt) ADJECTIVE *Austral slang* very good; excellent.

boost (buːst) NOUN [1] encouragement, improvement, or help: *a boost to morale.* [2] an upward thrust or push: *he gave him a boost over the wall.* [3] an increase or rise: *a boost in salary.* [4] a publicity campaign; promotion. [5] the amount by which the induction pressure of a supercharged internal-combustion engine exceeds that of the ambient pressure. ◆ VERB (*tr*) [6] to encourage, assist, or improve: *to boost morale.* [7] to lift by giving a push from below or behind. [8] to increase or raise: *to boost the voltage in an electrical circuit.* [9] to cause to rise; increase: *to boost sales.* [10] to advertise on a big scale. [11] to increase the induction pressure of (an internal-combustion engine) above that of the ambient pressure; supercharge.
▷HISTORY C19: of unknown origin

booster ('buːstə) NOUN [1] a person or thing that supports, assists, or increases power or effectiveness. [2] Also called: **launch vehicle.** the first stage of a multistage rocket. [3] *Radio, television* **a** a radio-frequency amplifier connected between an aerial and a receiver to amplify weak incoming signals. **b** a radio-frequency amplifier that amplifies incoming signals, retransmitting them at higher power. [4] another name for **supercharger.** [5] short for **booster dose.** [6] *Slang, chiefly US* a shoplifter.

booster dose NOUN a supplementary injection of a vaccine given to maintain the immunization provided by an earlier dose.

boosterish ('buːstərɪʃ) ADJECTIVE designed to boost business; optimistic.

boosterism ('buːstəˌrɪzəm) NOUN the practice of actively promoting a city, region, etc., and its local businesses.

boot[1] (buːt) NOUN [1] a strong outer covering for the foot; shoe that extends above the ankle, often to the knee. See also **chukka boot, top boot, Wellington boot, surgical boot.** [2] *Brit* an enclosed compartment of a car for holding luggage, etc., usually at the rear. US and Canadian name: **trunk.** [3] a protective covering over a mechanical device, such as a rubber sheath protecting a coupling joining two shafts. [4] *US and Canadian* a rubber patch used to repair a puncture in a tyre. [5] an instrument of torture used to crush the foot and lower leg. [6] a protective covering for the lower leg of a horse. [7] a kick: *he gave the door a boot.* [8] *Brit slang* an ugly person (esp in the phrase **old boot**). [9] *US slang* a navy or marine recruit, esp one in training. [10] *Computing* short for **bootstrap** (sense 4a). [11] **bet one's boots.** to be certain: *you can bet your boots he'll come.* [12] See **boots and all.** [13] **die with one's boots on. a** to die while still active. **b** to die in battle. [14] **lick the boots of.** to be servile, obsequious, or flattering towards. [15] **put the boot in.** *Slang* **a** to kick a person, esp when he is already down. **b** to harass someone or aggravate a problem. **c** to finish off (something) with unnecessary brutality. [16] **the boot.** *Slang* dismissal from employment; the sack. [17] **the boot is on the other foot** *or* **leg.** the situation is or has now reversed. [18] **too big for one's boots.** self-important or conceited. ◆ VERB [19] (*tr*) (esp in football) to kick. [20] (*tr*) to equip with boots. [21] (*tr*) *Informal* **a** (often foll by *out*) to eject forcibly. **b** to dismiss from employment. [22] Also: **boot up.** to start up the operating system of (a computer) or (of a computer) to begin operating. ◆ See also **boots.**
▷HISTORY C14 *bote*, from Old French, of uncertain origin

boot[2] (buːt) VERB (*usually impersonal*) [1] *Archaic* to be of advantage or use to (a person): *what boots it to complain?* ◆ NOUN [2] *Obsolete* an advantage. [3] *Dialect* something given in addition, esp to equalize an exchange: *a ten pound boot to settle the bargain.* [4] **to boot.** as well; in addition: *it's cold and musty, and damp to boot.*
▷HISTORY Old English *bōt* compensation; related to Old Norse *bōt* remedy, Gothic *bōta*, Old High German *buoza* improvement

bootblack ('buːtˌblæk) NOUN *Chiefly US* another word for **shoeblack.**

boot boy NOUN a member of a gang of hooligans who usually wear heavy boots.

boot camp NOUN [1] *US slang* a basic training camp for new recruits to the US Navy or Marine Corps. [2] a centre for juvenile offenders, with a strict disciplinary regime, hard physical exercise, and community labour programmes.

boot-cut ADJECTIVE (of trousers) slightly flared at the bottom of the legs.

booted ('buːtɪd) ADJECTIVE [1] wearing boots. [2] *Ornithol* **a** (of birds) having an undivided tarsus covered with a horny sheath. **b** (of poultry) having a feathered tarsus.

bootee ('buːtiː, buː'tiː) NOUN [1] a soft shoe for a baby, esp a knitted one. [2] a boot for women and children, esp an ankle-length one.

Boötes (bəʊ'əʊtiːz) NOUN, *Latin genitive* **Boötis** (bəʊ'əʊtɪs). a constellation in the N hemisphere lying near Ursa Major and containing the first magnitude star Arcturus.
▷HISTORY C17: via Latin from Greek: ploughman, from *boōtein* to plough, from *bous* ox

booth (buːð, buːθ) NOUN, *plural* **booths** (buːðz). [1] a stall for the display or sale of goods, esp a temporary one at a fair or market. [2] a small enclosed or partially enclosed room or cubicle, such as one containing a telephone (**telephone booth**) or one in which a person casts his vote at an election (**polling booth**). [3] two long high-backed benches with a long table between, used esp in bars and inexpensive restaurants. [4] (formerly) a temporary structure for shelter, dwelling, storage, etc.
▷HISTORY C12: of Scandinavian origin; compare Old Norse *buth*, Swedish, Danish *bod* shop, stall; see BOWER[1]

Boothia Peninsula ('buːθɪə) NOUN a peninsula of N Canada: the northernmost part of the mainland of North America, lying west of the **Gulf of Boothia**, an arm of the Arctic Ocean.

bootie ('buːtɪ) NOUN *Brit slang* a Royal Marine.
▷HISTORY C20: from *bootneck*, so called from the leather tab used to close their tunic collars

bootjack ('buːtˌdʒæk) NOUN a device that grips the heel of a boot to enable the foot to be withdrawn easily.

bootlace ('buːtˌleɪs) NOUN a strong lace for fastening a boot.

bootlace fungus NOUN another name for **honey fungus.**

bootlace worm NOUN a nemertean worm, *Linens longissimus*, that inhabits shingly shores and attains lengths of over 6 m (20 ft.).

Bootle ('buːtᵊl) NOUN a port in NW England, in Sefton unitary authority, Merseyside; on the River Mersey adjoining Liverpool. Pop.: 65 454 (1991).

bootleg ('buːtˌlɛg) VERB **-legs, -legging, -legged.** [1] to make, carry, or sell (illicit goods, esp alcohol). ◆ NOUN [2] something made or sold illicitly, such as alcohol during Prohibition in the US. [3] an illegally made copy of a CD, tape, etc. ◆ ADJECTIVE [4] produced, distributed, or sold illicitly: *bootleg whisky; bootleg tapes.*
▷HISTORY C17: see BOOT[1], LEG; from the practice of smugglers of carrying bottles of liquor concealed in their boots
▸ 'bootˌlegger NOUN

bootless ('buːtlɪs) ADJECTIVE of little or no use; vain; fruitless: *a bootless search.*
▷HISTORY Old English *bōtlēas*, from *bōt* compensation; Old Norse *bótalauss*
▸ 'bootlessly ADVERB

bootlick ('bu:t,lɪk) VERB *Informal* to seek favour by servile or ingratiating behaviour towards (someone, esp someone in authority); toady.
▸ **'boot,licker** NOUN

bootloader ('bu:t,ləʊdə) NOUN *Computing* short for **bootstrap loader**. See **bootstrap** (sense 4).

boot money NOUN *Informal* unofficial bonuses in the form of illegal cash payments made by a professional sports club to its players.

boots (bu:ts) NOUN, *plural* **boots**. *Brit* (formerly) a shoeblack who cleans the guests' shoes in a hotel.

boots and all *Austral and NZ informal* ◆ ADVERB [1] making every effort; with no holds barred. ◆ ADJECTIVE (**boots-and-all** *when prenominal*) [2] behaving or conducted in such a manner.

boots and saddles NOUN a bugle call formerly used in the US Cavalry to summon soldiers to mount.

bootstrap ('bu:t,stræp) NOUN [1] a leather or fabric loop on the back or side of a boot for pulling it on. [2] **by one's (own) bootstraps**. by one's own efforts; unaided. [3] (*modifier*) self-acting or self-sufficient, as an electronic amplifier that uses its output voltage to bias its input. [4] **a** a technique for loading the first few program instructions into a computer main store to enable the rest of the program to be introduced from an input device. **b** (*as modifier*): *a bootstrap loader*. [5] *Commerce* an offer to purchase a controlling interest in a company, esp with the intention of purchasing the remainder of the equity at a lower price.

boot topping NOUN *Nautical* [1] the part of a ship's hull that is between the load line and the water line when the ship is not loaded. [2] a coating applied to this part of a ship to remove marine growth.

boot tree NOUN [1] a shoetree for a boot, often having supports to stretch the leg of the boot. [2] a last for making boots.

booty[1] ('bu:tɪ) NOUN, *plural* **-ties**. any valuable article or articles, esp when obtained as plunder.
▷HISTORY C15: from Old French *butin*, from Middle Low German *buite* exchange; related to Old Norse *býta* to exchange, *býti* barter

booty[2] ('bu:tɪ) NOUN *Slang* the buttocks.
▷HISTORY C20: from BUTT[1] buttocks

booty call NOUN *Slang* a meeting arranged for the purpose of having sex.

bootylicious (,bu:tɪ'lɪʃəs) ADJECTIVE *Slang* sexually attractive, esp with curvaceous buttocks.
▷HISTORY C:20 from BOOTY[2] + (DE)LICIOUS

boo-word ('bu:,wɜ:d) NOUN any word that seems to cause irrational fear: *"communism" became a boo-word in the McCarthy era*.

booze (bu:z) *Informal* ◆ NOUN [1] alcoholic drink. [2] a drinking bout or party. ◆ VERB [3] (*usually intr*) to drink (alcohol), esp in excess.
▷HISTORY C13: from Middle Dutch *būsen*
▸ **boozed** ADJECTIVE ▸ **'boozing** NOUN

booze cruise NOUN *Brit informal* a day trip to a foreign country, esp from England across the English Channel to France, for the purposes of buying cheap alcohol, cigarettes, etc.

boozed-up ADJECTIVE *Slang* intoxicated; drunk.

boozer ('bu:zə) NOUN *Informal* [1] a person who is fond of drinking. [2] *Brit, Austral, and NZ* a bar or pub.

booze hag NOUN *NZ slang* a girl or woman who drinks to excess.

booze-up NOUN *Brit, Austral, and NZ slang* a drinking spree.

boozy ('bu:zɪ) ADJECTIVE **boozier, booziest**. *Informal* inclined to or involving excessive drinking of alcohol; drunken: *a boozy lecturer; a boozy party*.
▸ **'booziness** NOUN

bop[1] (bɒp) NOUN [1] a form of jazz originating in the 1940s, characterized by rhythmic and harmonic complexity and instrumental virtuosity. Originally called: **bebop**. [2] *Informal* a session of dancing to pop music. ◆ VERB **bops, bopping, bopped**. [3] (*intr*) *Informal* to dance to pop music.
▷HISTORY C20: shortened from BEBOP
▸ **'bopper** NOUN

bop[2] (bɒp) *Informal* ◆ VERB **bops, bopping, bopped**. [1] (*tr*) to strike; hit. ◆ NOUN [2] a blow.
▷HISTORY C19: of imitative origin

bo-peep (,bəʊ'pi:p) NOUN [1] a game for very young children, in which one hides (esp hiding one's face in one's hands) and reappears suddenly. [2] *Austral and NZ informal* a look (esp in the phrase **have a bo-peep**).

Bophuthatswana (,bəʊpu:tɑ:t'swɑ:nə) NOUN (formerly) a Bantu homeland in N South Africa: consists of six separate areas; granted independence by South Africa in 1977 although this was not internationally recognized; abolished in 1993. Capital: Mmabatho.

bora[1] ('bɔ:rə) NOUN (*sometimes capital*) a violent cold north wind blowing from the mountains to the E coast of the Adriatic, usually in winter.
▷HISTORY C19: from Italian (Venetian dialect), from Latin *borēas* the north wind

bora[2] ('bɔ:rə) NOUN an initiation ceremony of native Australians, introducing youths to manhood.
▷HISTORY from a native Australian language

Bora Bora ('bɔ:rə 'bɔ:rə) NOUN an island in the S Pacific, in French Polynesia, in the Society Islands: one of the Leeward Islands. Area: 39 sq. km (15 sq. miles).

boracic (bə'ræsɪk) ADJECTIVE another word for **boric**.

boracite ('bɔ:rə,saɪt) NOUN a white mineral that forms salt deposits of magnesium borate and chloride in orthorhombic crystalline form. Formula: $Mg_3ClB_7O_{13}$.

borage ('bɒrɪdʒ, 'bʌrɪdʒ) NOUN [1] a European boraginaceous plant, *Borago officinalis*, with star-shaped blue flowers. The young leaves have a cucumber-like flavour and are sometimes used in salads or as seasoning. [2] any of several related plants.
▷HISTORY C13: from Old French *bourage*, perhaps from Arabic *abū 'āraq* literally: father of sweat, from its use as a diaphoretic

boraginaceous (bə,rædʒɪ'neɪʃəs) ADJECTIVE of, relating to, or belonging to the *Boraginaceae*, a family of temperate and tropical typically hairy-leaved flowering plants that includes forget-me-not, lungwort, borage, comfrey, and heliotrope.
▷HISTORY C19: from New Latin *Borāginācea*e, from *Borāgō* genus name; see BORAGE

borak ('bɔ:rək) *or* **borax** ('bɔ:ræks) NOUN *Austral and NZ slang, archaic* [1] rubbish; nonsense. [2] **poke borak at (someone)**. to jeer at (someone).
▷HISTORY from a native Australian language

borane ('bɔ:reɪn) NOUN any compound of boron and hydrogen, used in the synthesis of other boron compounds and as high-energy fuels.
▷HISTORY C20: from BOR(ON) + -ANE

Borås (*Swedish* bu'ro:s) NOUN a city in SW Sweden, chiefly producing textiles. Pop.: 96 123 (1994).

borate NOUN ('bɔ:reɪt, -ɪt) [1] a salt or ester of boric acid. Salts of boric acid consist of BO_3 and BO_4 units linked together. ◆ VERB ('bɔ:reɪt) [2] (*tr*) to treat with borax, boric acid, or borate.

borax ('bɔ:ræks) NOUN, *plural* **-raxes, -races** (-rə,si:z). [1] Also called: **tincal**. a soluble readily fusible white mineral consisting of impure hydrated disodium tetraborate in monoclinic crystalline form, occurring in alkaline soils and salt deposits. Formula: $Na_2B_4O_7.10H_2O$. [2] pure disodium tetraborate.
▷HISTORY C14: from Old French *boras*, from Medieval Latin *borax*, from Arabic *būraq*, from Persian *būrah*

borazon ('bɔ:rə,zɒn, -zᵊn) NOUN an extremely hard form of boron nitride.
▷HISTORY C20: from BOR(ON) + AZO- + -ON

borborygmus (,bɔ:bə'rɪgməs) NOUN, *plural* **-mi** (-maɪ). rumbling of the stomach.
▷HISTORY C18: from Greek
▸ **,borbo'rygmal** *or* **,borbo'rygmic** ADJECTIVE

Bordeaux (bɔ:'dəʊ; *French* bɔrdo) NOUN [1] a port in SW France, on the River Garonne: a major centre of the wine trade. Pop.: 215 118 (1999). [2] any of several red, white, or rosé wines produced around Bordeaux. Related adjective: **Bordelais**.

Bordeaux mixture NOUN *Horticulture* a fungicide consisting of a solution of equal quantities of copper sulphate and quicklime.
▷HISTORY C19: loose translation of French *bouillie bordelaise*, from *bouillir* to boil + *bordelais* of BORDEAUX

Bordelaise (,bɔ:də'leɪz; *French* bɔrdəlɛz) ADJECTIVE *Cookery* denoting a brown sauce flavoured with red wine and sometimes mushrooms.
▷HISTORY French: of BORDEAUX

bordello (bɔ:'dɛləʊ) NOUN, *plural* **-los**. a brothel. Also called (archaic): **bordel** ('bɔ:dᵊl).
▷HISTORY C16: from Italian, from Old French *borde* hut, cabin

border ('bɔ:də) NOUN [1] a band or margin around or along the edge of something. [2] the dividing line or frontier between political or geographic regions. [3] **a** a region straddling such a boundary. **b** (*as modifier*): *border country*. [4] **a** a design or ornamental strip around the edge or rim of something, such as a printed page or dinner plate. **b** (*as modifier*): *a border illustration*. [5] a long narrow strip of ground planted with flowers, shrubs, trees, etc., that skirts a path or wall or surrounds a lawn or other area: *a herbaceous border*. ◆ VERB [6] (*tr*) to decorate or provide with a border. [7] (when *intr*, foll by *on* or *upon*) **a** to be adjacent (to); lie along the boundary (of): *his land borders on mine*. **b** to be nearly the same (as); verge (on): *his stupidity borders on madness*.
▷HISTORY C14: from Old French *bordure*, from *border* to border, from *bort* side of a ship, of Germanic origin; see BOARD

Border ('bɔ:də) NOUN **the**. [1] (*often plural*) the area straddling the border between England and Scotland. [2] the area straddling the border between Northern Ireland and the Republic of Ireland. [3] the region in S South Africa around East London.

Border collie NOUN a medium-sized breed of collie with a silky usually black-and-white coat: used mainly as sheepdogs.

border disease NOUN *Vet science* a congenital infectious disease of sheep and goats caused by a *Togavirus* and characterized by abortion, infertility, and deformity of lambs.

bordereau (,bɔ:də'rəʊ; *French* bɔrdəro) NOUN, *plural* **-reaux** (-'rəʊ, -'rəʊz; *French* -ro). a memorandum or invoice prepared for a company by an underwriter, containing a list of reinsured risks.
▷HISTORY C20: from French

borderer ('bɔ:dərə) NOUN a person who lives in a border area, esp the border between England and Scotland.

borderland ('bɔ:də,lænd) NOUN [1] land located on or near a frontier or boundary. [2] an indeterminate region: *the borderland between intellect and intelligence*.

Border Leicester NOUN a breed of sheep originally developed in the border country between Scotland and England by crossing English Leicesters with Cheviots: large numbers in Scotland, Australia, and New Zealand. It has a long white fleece with no wool on the head.

borderline ('bɔ:də,laɪn) NOUN [1] a border; dividing line; line of demarcation. [2] an indeterminate position between two conditions or qualities: *the borderline between friendship and love*. ◆ ADJECTIVE [3] on the edge of one category and verging on another: *a borderline failure in the exam*.

Borders Region NOUN a former local government region in S Scotland, formed in 1975 from Berwick, Peebles, Roxburgh, Selkirk, and part of Midlothian; replaced in 1996 by Scottish Borders council area.

border terrier NOUN a small rough-coated breed of terrier that originated in Britain.

bordure ('bɔ:djʊə) NOUN *Heraldry* the outer edge of a shield, esp when decorated distinctively.
▷HISTORY C15: from Old French; see BORDER

bore[1] (bɔ:) VERB [1] to produce (a hole) in (a material) by use of a drill, auger, or other cutting tool. [2] to increase the diameter of (a hole), as by an internal turning operation on a lathe or similar machine. [3] (*tr*) to produce (a hole in the ground, tunnel, mine shaft, etc.) by digging, drilling, cutting, etc. [4] (*intr*) *Informal* (of a horse or athlete in a race) to push other competitors, esp in order to try to get them out of the way. ◆ NOUN [5] a hole or tunnel in the ground, esp one drilled in search of minerals, oil, etc. [6] **a** a circular hole in a material produced by drilling, turning, or drawing. **b** the diameter of such a hole. [7] **a** the hollow part of a

tube or cylinder, esp of a gun barrel. **b** the diameter of such a hollow part; calibre. [8] *Austral* an artesian well.
▷HISTORY Old English *borian*; related to Old Norse *bora*, Old High German *borōn* to bore, Latin *forāre* to pierce, Greek *pharos* ploughing, *pháranx* PHARYNX

bore² (bɔː) VERB [1] *(tr)* to tire or make weary by being dull, repetitious, or uninteresting. ◆ NOUN [2] a dull, repetitious, or uninteresting person, activity, or state.
▷HISTORY C18: of unknown origin
▸**bored** ADJECTIVE

bore³ (bɔː) NOUN a high steep-fronted wave moving up a narrow estuary, caused by the tide.
▷HISTORY C17: from Old Norse *bāra* wave, billow

bore⁴ (bɔː) VERB the past tense of **bear¹**.

boreal (ˈbɔːrɪəl) ADJECTIVE of or relating to the north or the north wind.
▷HISTORY C15: from Latin *boreās* the north wind

Boreal (ˈbɔːrɪəl) ADJECTIVE [1] of or denoting the coniferous forests in the north of the N hemisphere. [2] designating a climatic zone having snowy winters and short summers. [3] designating a dry climatic period from about 7500 to 5500 B.C., characterized by cold winters, warm summers, and a flora dominated by pines and hazels.

Boreas (ˈbɔːrɪəs) NOUN *Greek myth* the god personifying the north wind.
▷HISTORY C14: via Latin from Greek

borecole (ˈbɔːkəʊl) NOUN another name for **kale**.

boredom (ˈbɔːdəm) NOUN the state of being bored; tedium.

boree (ˈbɔːriː) NOUN *Austral* another name for **myall**.
▷HISTORY from a native Australian language

boreen (ˈboːriːn) NOUN *Irish* a country lane or narrow road.
▷HISTORY C19: from Irish Gaelic *bóithrín*, diminutive of *bóthar* road

borehole (ˈbɔːˌhəʊl) NOUN a hole driven into the ground to obtain geological information, release water, etc.

borer (ˈbɔːrə) NOUN [1] a machine or hand tool for boring holes. [2] any of various insects, insect larvae, molluscs, or crustaceans that bore into rock or plant material, esp wood. See also **woodborer, corn borer, marine borer, rock borer.**

borer bomb NOUN *NZ* a device that emits pesticide fumes.

Borgerhout (*Flemish* bɔrxərˈhɔut) NOUN a city in N Belgium, near Antwerp. Pop.: 44 000 (latest est.).

boric (ˈbɔːrɪk) ADJECTIVE of or containing boron. Also: **boracic.**

boric acid NOUN [1] Also called: **orthoboric acid.** Systematic name: **trioxoboric(III) acid.** a white soluble weakly acid crystalline solid used in the manufacture of heat-resistant glass and porcelain enamels, as a fireproofing material, and as a mild antiseptic. Formula: H_3BO_3. [2] any other acid containing boron.

boride (ˈbɔːraɪd) NOUN a compound in which boron is the most electronegative element, esp a compound of boron and a metal.
▷HISTORY C19: from BOR(ON) + -IDE

boring¹ (ˈbɔːrɪŋ) NOUN [1] **a** the act or process of making or enlarging a hole. **b** the hole made in this way. [2] *(often plural)* a fragment, particle, chip, etc., produced during boring.

boring² (ˈbɔːrɪŋ) ADJECTIVE dull; repetitious; uninteresting.
▸ˈ**boringly** ADVERB

boring mill NOUN *Engineering* a large vertical lathe having a rotating table on which work is secured. Tools are held on a fixed post and the work is rotated around it. Also called (informal): **roundabout.**

borlotti bean (bɔːˈlɒtɪ) NOUN a variety of kidney bean with a pinkish-brown speckled skin that turns brown when cooked: grown in southern Europe, East Africa, and Taiwan.
▷HISTORY from Italian, plural of *borlotto* kidney bean

borm (bɔːm) VERB *(tr) Midland English dialect* to smear with paint, oil, etc.

born (bɔːn) VERB [1] the past participle (in most passive uses) of **bear¹** (sense 4). [2] **was not born yesterday.** is not gullible or foolish. ◆ ADJECTIVE [3] possessing or appearing to have possessed certain qualities from birth: *a born musician.* [4] **a** being at birth in a particular social status or other condition as specified: *ignobly born.* **b** *(in combination)*: *lowborn.* [5] **in all one's born days.** *Informal* so far in one's life.

> **Language note** Care should be taken not to use *born* where *borne* is intended: *he had borne (not born) his ordeal with great courage; the following points should be borne in mind.*

borna disease (ˈbɔːnə) NOUN *Vet science* a viral disease of mammals, especially horses, caused by a member of the *Flaviviridae* and characterized by the development of encephalitis.

born-again (ˈbɔːnəˌgɛn) ADJECTIVE [1] having experienced conversion, esp to evangelical Christianity. [2] showing the enthusiasm of one newly converted to any cause: *a born-again monetarist.* ◆ NOUN [3] a person who shows fervent enthusiasm for a new-found cause, belief, etc.

borne (bɔːn) VERB [1] the past participle of **bear¹** (for all active uses of the verb; also for all passive uses except sense 4 unless followed by *by*). [2] **be borne in on** *or* **upon.** (of a fact) to be realized by (someone): *it was borne in on us how close we had been to disaster.*

Bornean (ˈbɔːnɪən) ADJECTIVE [1] of or relating to Borneo or its inhabitants. ◆ NOUN [2] a native or inhabitant of Borneo.

Borneo (ˈbɔːnɪˌəʊ) NOUN an island in the W Pacific, between the Sulu and Java Seas, part of the Malay Archipelago: divided into Kalimantan (**Indonesian Borneo**), the Malaysian states of Sarawak and Sabah, and the British-protected sultanate of Brunei; mountainous and densely forested. Area: about 750 000 sq. km (290 000 sq. miles).

borneol (ˈbɔːnɪˌɒl) NOUN a white solid terpene alcohol extracted from the Malaysian tree *Dryobalanops aromatica*, used in perfume and in the manufacture of organic esters. Formula: $C_{10}H_{17}OH$. Also called: **bornyl alcohol.**
▷HISTORY C19: from BORNE(O) + -OL¹

Bornholm (*Danish* bɔrnˈhɔlm) NOUN an island in the Baltic Sea, south of Sweden: administratively part of Denmark. Chief town: Rønne. Pop.: 44 126 (2001). Area: 588 sq. km (227 sq. miles).

Bornholm disease (ˈbɔːnˌhɒlm) NOUN an epidemic virus infection characterized by pain round the base of the chest.
▷HISTORY C20: named after BORNHOLM, where it was first described

bornite (ˈbɔːnaɪt) NOUN a mineral consisting of a sulphide of copper and iron that tarnishes to purple or dark red. It occurs in copper deposits. Formula: Cu_5FeS_4. Also called: **peacock ore.**
▷HISTORY C19: named after I. von *Born* (1742–91), Austrian mineralogist; see -ITE¹

Borno (ˈbɔːnəʊ) NOUN a state of NE Nigeria, on Lake Chad: the second largest state, formed in 1976 from part of North-Eastern State. Capital: Maiduguri. Pop.: 2 903 238 (1995 est.). Area: 70 898 sq. km (27 374 sq. miles).

Borodino (ˌbɒrəˈdiːnəʊ; *Russian* bərədiˈnɔ) NOUN a village in E central Russia, about 110 km (70 miles) west of Moscow: scene of a battle (1812) in which Napoleon defeated the Russians but irreparably weakened his army.

boron (ˈbɔːrɒn) NOUN a very hard almost colourless crystalline metalloid element that in impure form exists as a brown amorphous powder. It occurs principally in borax and is used in hardening steel. The naturally occurring isotope **boron-10** is used in nuclear control rods and neutron detection instruments. Symbol: B; atomic no.: 5; atomic wt.: 10.81; valency: 3; relative density: 2.34 (crystalline), 2.37 (amorphous); melting pt.: 2092°C; boiling pt.: 4002°C.
▷HISTORY C19: from BOR(AX) + (CARB)ON

boron carbide NOUN a black extremely hard inert substance having a high capture cross section for thermal neutrons. It is used as an abrasive and refractory and in control rods in nuclear reactors. Formula: B_4C.

boronia (bəˈrəʊnɪə) NOUN any aromatic rutaceous shrub of the Australian genus *Boronia*.

boron nitride NOUN a white inert crystalline solid existing both in a graphite-like form and in an extremely hard diamond-like form (borazon). It is used as a refractory, high temperature lubricant and insulator, and heat shield. Formula BN.

borosilicate (ˌbɔːrəʊˈsɪlɪkɪt, -ˌkeɪt) NOUN a salt of boric and silicic acids.

borosilicate glass NOUN any of a range of heat- and chemical-resistant glasses, such as Pyrex, prepared by fusing together boron(III) oxide, silicon dioxide, and, usually, a metal oxide.

borough (ˈbʌrə) NOUN [1] a town, esp (in Britain) one that forms the constituency of an MP or that was originally incorporated by royal charter. See also **burgh.** [2] any of the 32 constituent divisions that together with the City of London make up Greater London. [3] any of the five constituent divisions of New York City. [4] (in the US) a self-governing incorporated municipality. [5] (in medieval England) a fortified town or village or a fort. [6] (in New Zealand) a small municipality with a governing body.
▷HISTORY Old English *burg*; related to *beorgan* to shelter, Old Norse *borg* wall, Gothic *baurgs* city, Old High German *burg* fortified castle

borough-English NOUN *English law* (until 1925) a custom in certain English boroughs whereby the youngest son inherited land to the exclusion of his older brothers. Compare **primogeniture, gavelkind.**
▷HISTORY C14: from Anglo-French *tenure en burgh Engloys* tenure in an English borough; so called because the custom was unknown in France

borrow (ˈbɒrəʊ) VERB [1] to obtain or receive (something, such as money) on loan for temporary use, intending to give it, or something equivalent or identical, back to the lender. [2] to adopt (ideas, words, etc.) from another source; appropriate. [3] *Not standard* to lend. [4] *Golf* to putt the ball uphill of the direct path to the hole. [5] *(intr) Golf* (of a ball) to deviate from a straight path because of the slope of the ground. ◆ NOUN [6] *Golf* a deviation of a ball from a straight path because of the slope of the ground: *a left borrow.* [7] material dug from a borrow pit to provide fill at another. [8] **living on borrowed time. a** living an unexpected extension of life. **b** close to death.
▷HISTORY Old English *borgian*; related to Old High German *borgēn* to take heed, give security
▸ˈ**borrower** NOUN

> **Language note** The use of *off* after *borrow* was formerly considered incorrect, but is now acceptable in informal contexts.

borrow pit NOUN *Civil engineering* an excavation dug to provide fill to make up ground elsewhere.

Bors (bɔːs) NOUN **Sir.** (in Arthurian legend) [1] one the knights of the Round Table, nephew of Lancelot. [2] an illegitimate son of King Arthur.

borscht (bɔːʃt), **borsch** (bɔːʃ), *or* **borshch** (bɔːʃtʃ) NOUN a Russian and Polish soup based on beetroot.
▷HISTORY C19: from Russian *borshch*

borsic (ˈbɔːsɪk) NOUN *Aeronautics* a strong light composite material of boron fibre and silicon carbide used in aviation.

borstal (ˈbɔːstəl) NOUN [1] (formerly in Britain) an informal name for an establishment in which offenders aged 15 to 21 could be detained for corrective training. Since the Criminal Justice Act 1982, they have been replaced by **youth custody centres** (now known as **young offender institutions**). [2] (formerly) a similar establishment in Australia and New Zealand.
▷HISTORY C20: named after *Borstal*, village in Kent where the first institution was founded

bort, boart (bɔːt), *or* **bortz** (bɔːts) NOUN an inferior grade of diamond used for cutting and drilling or, in powdered form, as an industrial abrasive.
▷HISTORY Old English *gebrot* fragment; related to Old Norse *brot* piece, Old High German *broz* bud
▸ˈ**borty** ADJECTIVE

borzoi (ˈbɔːzɔɪ) NOUN, *plural* **-zois.** a tall graceful fast-moving breed of dog with a long silky coat, originally used in Russia for hunting wolves. Also called: **Russian wolfhound.**

▷**HISTORY** C19: from Russian *borzoi*, literally: swift; related to Old Slavonic *brŭzŭ* swift

bosberaad ('bɒsbə,rɑːd) NOUN *South African* a meeting in an isolated venue to break a political deadlock.
▷**HISTORY** C20: Afrikaans, from *bos* bush + *beraad* council

boscage *or* **boskage** ('bɒskɪdʒ) NOUN *Literary* a mass of trees and shrubs; thicket.
▷**HISTORY** C14: from Old French *bosc*, probably of Germanic origin; see BUSH[1], -AGE

Bosch process NOUN *Obsolete* an industrial process for manufacturing hydrogen by the catalytic reduction of steam with carbon monoxide.
▷**HISTORY** C20: named after Carl *Bosch* (1874–1940), German chemist

boschvark ('bɒʃ,vɑːk) NOUN *South African* another name for **bushpig**.
▷**HISTORY** Afrikaans

Bose-Einstein statistics PLURAL NOUN *(functioning as singular) Physics* the branch of quantum statistics applied to systems of particles of zero or integral spin that do not obey the exclusion principle. Compare **Fermi-Dirac statistics**.

bosh[1] (bɒʃ) NOUN *Informal* empty or meaningless talk or opinions; nonsense.
▷**HISTORY** C19: from Turkish *boş* empty

bosh[2] (bɒʃ) NOUN 1 the lower tapering portion of a blast furnace, situated immediately above the air-inlet tuyères. 2 the deposit of siliceous material that occurs on the surfaces of vessels in which copper is refined. 3 a water tank for cooling glass-making tools, etc. 4 *South Wales dialect* a kitchen sink or wash basin.
▷**HISTORY** C17: probably from German; compare *böschen* to slope, *Böschung* slope

bosk (bɒsk) NOUN *Literary* a small wood of bushes and small trees.
▷**HISTORY** C13: variant of *busk* BUSH[1]

bosket *or* **bosquet** ('bɒskɪt) NOUN a clump of small trees or bushes; thicket.
▷**HISTORY** C18: from French *bosquet*, from Italian *boschetto*, from *bosco* wood, forest; see BUSH[1]

Boskop ('bɒskɒp) NOUN **a** a prehistoric race of the late Pleistocene period in sub-Saharan Africa. **b** *(as modifier)*: *Boskop man*.
▷**HISTORY** C20: named after *Boskop*, in the Transvaal, where remains of this race were first discovered

bosky ('bɒskɪ) ADJECTIVE **boskier, boskiest**. *Literary* containing or consisting of bushes or thickets: *a bosky wood*.

Bosman ruling ('bɒzmən) NOUN *Soccer* an EU ruling that allows out-of-contract footballers to leave their clubs without the clubs receiving a transfer fee.
▷**HISTORY** C20: named after Jean-Marc *Bosman* (born 1964), Belgian footballer whose court case brought about the ruling

bo's'n ('bəʊs^{ə}n) NOUN *Nautical* a variant spelling of **boatswain**.

Bosnia ('bɒznɪə) NOUN a region of central Bosnia-Herzegovina: belonged to Turkey (1463–1878), to Austria-Hungary (1879–1918), then to Yugoslavia (1918–91).

Bosnia-Herzegovina *or esp US* **Bosnia and Herzegovina** NOUN a country in SW Europe; a constituent republic of Yugoslavia until 1991; in a state of civil war (1992–95); Serbian and Croatian forces were also involved: mostly barren and mountainous, with forests in the east. Language: Serbo-Croatian. Religion: Muslim, Serbian Orthodox, and Roman Catholic. Currency: euro. Capital: Sarajevo. Pop.: 3 922 000 (2001 est.). Area: 51 129 sq. km (19 737 sq. miles).

Bosnian ('bɒznɪən) ADJECTIVE 1 of or relating to Bosnia or its inhabitants. ◆ NOUN 2 a native or inhabitant of Bosnia.

bosom ('bʊzəm) NOUN 1 the chest or breast of a person, esp the female breasts. 2 the part of a woman's dress, coat, etc., that covers the chest. 3 a protective centre or part: *the bosom of the family*. 4 the breast considered as the seat of emotions. 5 *(modifier)* very dear; intimate: *a bosom friend*. ◆ VERB *(tr)* 6 to embrace. 7 to conceal or carry in the bosom.
▷**HISTORY** Old English *bōsm*; related to Old High German *buosam*

bosomy ('bʊzəmɪ) ADJECTIVE (of a woman) having large breasts.

boson ('bəʊzɒn) NOUN any of a group of elementary particles, such as a photon or pion, that has zero or integral spin and obeys the rules of Bose-Einstein statistics. Compare **fermion**.
▷**HISTORY** C20: named after Satyendra Nath *Bose* (1894–1974), Indian physicist; see -ON

Bosporus ('bɒspərəs) *or* **Bosphorus** ('bɒsfərəs) NOUN **the**. a strait between European and Asian Turkey, linking the Black Sea and the Sea of Marmara.

bosquet ('bɒskɪt) NOUN a variant spelling of **bosket**.

boss[1] (bɒs) *Informal* ◆ NOUN 1 a person in charge of or employing others. 2 *Chiefly US* a professional politician who controls a party machine or political organization, often using devious or illegal methods. ◆ VERB 3 to employ, supervise, or be in charge of. 4 (usually foll by *around* or *about*) to be domineering or overbearing towards (others). ◆ ADJECTIVE 5 *Slang* excellent; fine: *a boss hand at carpentry; that's boss!*
▷**HISTORY** C19: from Dutch *baas* master; probably related to Old High German *basa* aunt, Frisian *baes* master

boss[2] (bɒs) NOUN 1 a knob, stud, or other circular rounded protuberance, esp an ornamental one on a vault, a ceiling, or a shield. 2 *Biology* any of various protuberances or swellings in plants and animals. 3 **a** an area of increased thickness, usually cylindrical, that strengthens or provides room for a locating device on a shaft, hub of a wheel, etc. **b** a similar projection around a hole in a casting or fabricated component. 4 an exposed rounded mass of igneous or metamorphic rock, esp the uppermost part of an underlying batholith. ◆ VERB *(tr)* 5 to ornament with bosses; emboss.
▷**HISTORY** C13: from Old French *boce*, from Vulgar Latin *bottia* (unattested); related to Italian *bozza* metal knob, swelling

boss[3] (bɒs) *or* **bossy** NOUN, *plural* **bosses** *or* **bossies**. a calf or cow.
▷**HISTORY** C19: from dialect *buss* calf, perhaps ultimately from Latin *bōs* cow, ox

BOSS (bɒs) NOUN (formerly) ACRONYM FOR Bureau of State Security; a branch of the South African security police.

bossa nova ('bɒsə 'nəʊvə) NOUN 1 a dance similar to the samba, originating in Brazil. 2 a piece of music composed for or in the rhythm of this dance.
▷**HISTORY** C20: Portuguese, literally: new voice

bossboy ('bɒs,bɔɪ) NOUN *South African* a Black African foreman of a gang of workers.

boss cocky NOUN *Austral informal* a boss or person in power.

bosset ('bɒsɪt) NOUN either of the rudimentary antlers found in young deer.
▷**HISTORY** C19: from French *bossette* a small protuberance, from *bosse* BOSS[2]

boss-eyed ADJECTIVE *Informal* having a squint.
▷**HISTORY** C19: from *boss* to miss or bungle a shot at a target (dialect)

bossing ('bɒsɪŋ) NOUN *Civil engineering* the act of shaping malleable metal, such as lead cladding, with mallets to fit a surface.

bossism ('bɒs,ɪzəm) NOUN *US* the domination or the system of domination of political organizations by bosses.

boss screen NOUN a screen image within a computer game that can be activated instantly, designed to hide the evidence of game-playing, especially at work.

bossy[1] ('bɒsɪ) ADJECTIVE **bossier, bossiest**. *Informal* domineering, overbearing, or authoritarian.
▸ **'bossily** ADVERB ▸ **'bossiness** NOUN

bossy[2] ('bɒsɪ) ADJECTIVE (of furniture) ornamented with bosses.

bosthoon ('bɒsduːn) NOUN *Irish* a boor.
▷**HISTORY** C19: from Irish Gaelic *bastún*, from Old French *baston* penis

boston ('bɒstən) NOUN 1 a card game for four, played with two packs. 2 *Chiefly US* a slow gliding dance, a variation of the waltz.

Boston ('bɒstən) NOUN 1 a port in E Massachusetts, the state capital. Pop.: 589 141 (2000). 2 a port in E England, in SE Lincolnshire. Pop.: 34 606 (1991).

Boston bluefish NOUN *Canadian* another name for **pollack**.

Boston crab NOUN a wrestling hold in which a wrestler seizes both or one of his opponent's legs, turns him face downwards, and exerts pressure over his back.

Boston ivy NOUN the US name for **Virginia creeper** (sense 2).

Boston matrix NOUN a two-dimensional matrix, used in planning the business strategy of a large organization, that identifies those business units in the organization that generate cash and those that use it.
▷**HISTORY** C20: from the Boston Consultancy Group, a leading firm of strategic consultants, who developed it

Boston Tea Party NOUN *US history* a raid in 1773 made by citizens of Boston (disguised as Indians) on three British ships in the harbour as a protest against taxes on tea and the monopoly given to the East India Company. The contents of several hundred chests of tea were dumped into the harbour.

Boston terrier *or* **Boston bull terrier** NOUN a short stocky smooth-haired breed of terrier with a short nose, originally developed by crossing the French and English bulldogs with the English bull terrier.

bosun ('bəʊs^{ə}n) NOUN *Nautical* a variant spelling of **boatswain**.

Boswellian (bɒz'wɛlɪən) ADJECTIVE of or relating to James Boswell, the Scottish author and lawyer (1740–95).

Bosworth Field ('bɒzwɜːθ, -wəθ) NOUN *English history* the site, two miles south of Market Bosworth in Leicestershire, of the battle that ended the Wars of the Roses (August, 1485). Richard III was killed and Henry Tudor was crowned king as Henry VII.

bot[1] *or* **bott** (bɒt) NOUN 1 the larva of a botfly, which typically develops inside the body of a horse, sheep, or man. 2 any similar larva. 3 *NZ informal* a mild illness in humans. ◆ See also **bots**.
▷**HISTORY** C15: probably from Low German; related to Dutch *bot*, of obscure origin

bot[2] (bɒt) *Austral informal* ◆ VERB 1 to scrounge or borrow. 2 *(intr;* often foll by *on)* to scrounge (from); impose (on). ◆ NOUN 3 a scrounger. 4 **on the bot (for)**. wanting to scrounge: *he's on the bot for a cigarette*.
▷**HISTORY** C20: perhaps from BOTFLY, alluding to the creature's bite; see BITE (sense 12)

bot[3] (bɒt) NOUN *Computing* an autonomous computer program that performs time-consuming tasks, esp on the Internet.
▷**HISTORY** C20: from (RO)BOT

BOT ABBREVIATION FOR Board of Trade.

bot. ABBREVIATION FOR: 1 botanical. 2 botany.

botanical (bə'tænɪk^{ə}l) *or* **botanic** ADJECTIVE 1 of or relating to botany or plants. ◆ NOUN 2 any drug or pesticide that is made from parts of a plant.
▷**HISTORY** C17: from Medieval Latin *botanicus*, from Greek *botanikos* relating to plants, from *botanē* plant, pasture, from *boskein* to feed; perhaps related to Latin *bōs* ox, cow
▸ **bo'tanically** ADVERB

botanic garden NOUN a place in which plants are grown, studied, and exhibited.

botanize *or* **botanise** ('bɒtə,naɪz) VERB 1 *(intr)* to collect or study plants. 2 *(tr)* to explore and study the plants in (an area or region).

botany ('bɒtənɪ) NOUN, *plural* **-nies**. 1 the study of plants, including their classification, structure, physiology, ecology, and economic importance. 2 the plant life of a particular region or time. 3 the biological characteristics of a particular group of plants.
▷**HISTORY** C17: from BOTANICAL; compare ASTRONOMY, ASTRONOMICAL
▸ **'botanist** NOUN

Botany Bay NOUN 1 an inlet of the Tasman Sea, on the SE coast of Australia: surrounded by the suburbs of Sydney. 2 (in the 19th century) a

British penal settlement that was in fact at Port Jackson, New South Wales.

Botany wool NOUN a fine wool from the merino sheep.
▷HISTORY C19: from BOTANY BAY, where the wool came from originally

botargo (bə'tɑːgəʊ) NOUN, *plural* **-gos** *or* **-goes.** a relish consisting of the roe of mullet or tunny, salted and pressed into rolls.
▷HISTORY C15: from obsolete Italian, from Arabic *butarkhah*

botch (bɒtʃ) VERB (*tr*; often foll by *up*) [1] to spoil through clumsiness or ineptitude. [2] to repair badly or clumsily. ◆ NOUN [3] Also called: **botch-up.** a badly done piece of work or repair (esp in the phrase **make a botch of (something)**).
▷HISTORY C14: of unknown origin
▸'**botcher** NOUN

botchy ('bɒtʃɪ) ADJECTIVE **botchier, botchiest.** clumsily done or made.
▸'**botchily** ADVERB ▸'**botchiness** NOUN

botel (bəʊ'tɛl) NOUN a variant spelling of **boatel.**

botfly ('bɒtˌflaɪ) NOUN, *plural* **-flies.** any of various stout-bodied hairy dipterous flies of the families *Oestridae* and *Gasterophilidae*, the larvae of which are parasites of man, sheep, and horses.

both (bəʊθ) DETERMINER [1] **a** the two; two considered together: *both dogs were dirty.* **b** (*as pronoun*): *both are to blame.* ◆ CONJUNCTION [2] (*coordinating*) used preceding words, phrases, or clauses joined by *and*, used to emphasize that not just one, but also the other of the joined elements is included: *both Ellen and Keith enjoyed the play; both new and exciting.*
▷HISTORY C12: from Old Norse *bāthir*; related to Old High German *bēde*, Latin *ambō*, Greek *amphō*

bother ('bɒðə) VERB [1] (*tr*) to give annoyance, pain, or trouble to; irritate: *his bad leg is bothering him again.* [2] (*tr*) to trouble (a person) by repeatedly disturbing; pester: *stop bothering your father!* [3] (*intr*) to take the time or trouble; concern oneself: *don't bother to come with me.* [4] (*tr*) to make (a person) alarmed or confused: *the thought of her husband's return clearly bothered her.* ◆ NOUN [5] a state of worry, trouble, or confusion. [6] a person or thing that causes fuss, trouble, or annoyance. [7] *Informal* a disturbance or fight; trouble (esp in the phrase **a spot of bother**). ◆ INTERJECTION [8] *Chiefly Brit* an exclamation of slight annoyance.
▷HISTORY C18: perhaps from Irish Gaelic *bodhar* deaf, vexed; compare Irish Gaelic *buairim* I vex

botheration (ˌbɒðə'reɪʃən) NOUN, INTERJECTION *Informal* another word for **bother** (senses 5, 8).

bothersome ('bɒðəsəm) ADJECTIVE causing bother; troublesome.

Bothnia ('bɒθnɪə) NOUN **Gulf of.** an arm of the Baltic Sea, extending north between Sweden and Finland.

both ways ADJECTIVE, ADVERB [1] another term for **each way.** [2] **have it both ways.** (*usually with a negative*) to try to get the best of a situation, argument, etc., by chopping and changing between alternatives or opposites.

bothy ('bɒθɪ) NOUN, *plural* **bothies.** *Chiefly Scot* [1] a cottage or hut. [2] (esp in NE Scotland) a farmworker's summer quarters. [3] a mountain shelter.
▷HISTORY C18: perhaps related to BOOTH

bothy ballad NOUN *Scot* a folk song, esp one from the farming community of NE Scotland.

Botox ('bəʊtɒks) NOUN *Trademark* a preparation of botulinum toxin used to treat muscle spasm and to remove wrinkles.
▷HISTORY C20: from BOT(ULINUM) (T)OX(IN)

bo tree (bəʊ) NOUN another name for the **peepul.**
▷HISTORY C19: from Sinhalese, from Pali *bodhitaru* tree of wisdom, from Sanskrit *bodhi* wisdom, awakening; see BODHISATTVA

botryoidal (ˌbɒtrɪ'ɔɪd^{ə}l) *or* **botryose** ('bɒtrɪˌəʊs, -ˌəʊz) ADJECTIVE (of minerals, parts of plants, etc.) shaped like a bunch of grapes.
▷HISTORY C18: from Greek *botruoeidēs*, from *botrus* cluster of grapes; see -OID

botrytis (bɒt'raɪtɪs) NOUN [1] any of a group of fungi of the genus *Botrytis*, several of which cause plant diseases. [2] *Winemaking* a fungus of this genus, *Botrytis cinerea*, which causes noble rot.

bots (bɒts) NOUN (*functioning as singular*) a digestive disease of horses and some other animals caused by the presence of botfly larvae in the stomach.

Botswana (bʊ'tʃwɑːnə, bʊt'swɑːnə, bɒt-) NOUN a republic in southern Africa: established as the British protectorate of Bechuanaland in 1885 as a defence against the Boers; became an independent state within the Commonwealth in 1966; consists mostly of a plateau averaging 1000 m (3300 ft.), with the extensive Okavango swamps in the northwest and the Kalahari Desert in the southwest. Languages: English and Tswana. Religion: animist majority. Currency: pula. Capital: Gaborone. Pop.: 1 586 000 (2001 est.). Area: about 570 000 sq. km (220 000 sq. miles).

bott (bɒt) NOUN a variant spelling of **bot^{1}.**

botte *French* (bɔt) NOUN *Fencing* a thrust or hit.

bottine (bɒ'tiːn) NOUN a light boot for women or children; half-boot.
▷HISTORY C19: from French: little boot, from *botte* boot

bottle^{1} ('bɒt^{ə}l) NOUN [1] **a** a vessel, often of glass and typically cylindrical with a narrow neck that can be closed with a cap or cork, for containing liquids. **b** (*as modifier*): *a bottle rack.* [2] Also called: **bottleful.** the amount such a vessel will hold. [3] **a** a container equipped with a teat that holds a baby's milk or other liquid; nursing bottle. **b** the contents of such a container: *the baby drank his bottle.* [4] *Brit slang* nerve; courage (esp in the phrase **lose one's bottle**). [5] *Brit slang* money collected by street entertainers or buskers. [6] **full bottle.** *Austral slang* well-informed and enthusiastic about something. [7] **the bottle.** *Informal* drinking of alcohol, esp to excess. ◆ VERB (*tr*) [8] to put or place (wine, beer, jam, etc.) in a bottle or bottles. [9] to store (gas) in a portable container under pressure. [10] *Slang* to injure by thrusting a broken bottle into (a person). [11] *Brit slang* (of a busker) to collect money from the bystanders. See also **bottle out, bottle up.**
▷HISTORY C14: from Old French *botaille*, from Medieval Latin *butticula* literally: a little cask, from Late Latin *buttis* cask, BUTT^{4}

bottle^{2} ('bɒt^{ə}l) NOUN *Dialect* a bundle, esp of hay.
▷HISTORY C14: from Old French *botel*, from *botte* bundle, of Germanic origin

bottle bank NOUN a large container into which the public may throw glass bottles for recycling.

bottlebrush ('bɒt^{ə}lˌbrʌʃ) NOUN [1] a cylindrical brush on a thin shaft, used for cleaning bottles. [2] Also called: **callistemon.** any of various Australian myrtaceous shrubs or trees of the genera *Callistemon* and *Melaleuca*, having dense spikes of large red flowers with protruding brushlike stamens. [3] any of various similar trees or shrubs.

bottled *or* **bottle gas** NOUN butane or propane gas liquefied under pressure in portable containers and used in camping stoves, blowtorches, etc.

bottle-feed VERB **-feeds, -feeding, -fed.** to feed (a baby) with milk from a bottle instead of breast-feeding.

bottle glass NOUN glass used for making bottles, consisting of a silicate of sodium, calcium, and aluminium.

bottle gourd NOUN [1] an Old World cucurbitaceous climbing plant, *Lagenaria siceraria*, having large hard-shelled gourds as fruits. [2] the fruit of this plant. ◆ Also called: **calabash.**

bottle green NOUN, ADJECTIVE **a** a dark green colour. **b** (*as adjective*): *a bottle-green car.*

bottle-jack NOUN *NZ* a large jack used for heavy lifts.

bottleneck ('bɒt^{ə}lˌnɛk) NOUN [1] **a** a narrow stretch of road or a junction at which traffic is or may be held up. **b** the hold up. [2] something that holds up progress, esp of a manufacturing process. [3] *Music* **a** the broken-off neck of a bottle placed over a finger and used to produce a buzzing effect in a style of guitar-playing originally part of the American blues tradition. **b** the style of guitar playing using a bottleneck. ◆ VERB [4] (*tr*) *US* to be or cause an obstruction in.

bottlenose dolphin ('bɒt^{ə}lˌnəʊz) NOUN any dolphin of the genus *Tursiops*, esp *T. truncatus*, some of which have been kept in captivity and trained to perform tricks.

bottle-o *or* **bottle-oh** NOUN *Austral and NZ history informal* a dealer in empty bottles.

bottle out VERB (*intr, adverb*) *Brit slang* to lose one's nerve.

bottle party NOUN a party to which guests bring drink.

bottler ('bɒt^{ə}lə) NOUN *Austral and NZ informal* an excellent or outstanding person or thing.

bottle shop NOUN *Austral and NZ* a shop or part of a hotel where alcohol is sold in unopened containers for consumption elsewhere. Also called: **bottle store.**

bottle tree NOUN [1] any of several Australian sterculiaceous trees of the genus *Sterculia* (or *Brachychiton*) that have a bottle-shaped swollen trunk. [2] another name for **baobab.**

bottle up VERB (*tr, adverb*) [1] to restrain (powerful emotion). [2] to keep (an army or other force) contained or trapped: *the French fleet was bottled up in Le Havre.*

bottle-washer NOUN *Informal* a menial or factotum.

bottom ('bɒtəm) NOUN [1] the lowest, deepest, or farthest removed part of a thing: *the bottom of a hill.* [2] the least important or successful position: *the bottom of a class.* [3] the ground underneath a sea, lake, or river. [4] **touch bottom.** to run aground. [5] the inner depths of a person's true feelings (esp in the phrase **from the bottom of one's heart**). [6] the underneath part of a thing. [7] *Nautical* the parts of a vessel's hull that are under water. [8] (in literary or commercial contexts) a boat or ship. [9] *Billiards, snooker* a strike in the centre of the cue ball. [10] a dry valley or hollow. [11] (*often plural*) *US and Canadian* the low land bordering a river. [12] the lowest level worked in a mine. [13] (esp of horses) staying power; stamina. [14] importance, seriousness, or influence: *his views all have weight and bottom.* [15] *Informal* the buttocks. [16] **at bottom.** in reality; basically or despite appearances to the contrary: *he's a kind man at bottom.* [17] **be at the bottom of.** to be the ultimate cause of. [18] **get to the bottom of.** to discover the real truth about. [19] **knock the bottom out of.** to destroy or eliminate. ◆ ADJECTIVE (*prenominal*) [20] lowest or last: *the bottom price.* [21] **bet** (*or* **put**) **one's bottom dollar on.** to be absolutely sure of (one's opinion, a person, project, etc.). [22] of, relating to, or situated at the bottom or a bottom: *the bottom shelf.* [23] fundamental; basic. ◆ VERB [24] (*tr*) to provide (a chair, etc.) with a bottom or seat. [25] (*tr*) to discover the full facts or truth of; fathom. [26] (usually foll by *on* or *upon*) to base or be founded (on an idea, etc.). [27] (*intr*) *Nautical* to strike the ground beneath the water with a vessel's bottom. [28] *Austral mining* **a** to mine (a hole, claim, etc.) deep enough to reach any gold there is. **b** (*intr*; foll by *on*) to reach (gold, mud, etc.) on bottoming. [29] *Electronics* to saturate a transistor so that further increase of input produces no change in output. ◆ See also **bottom out.**
▷HISTORY Old English *botm*; related to Old Norse *botn*, Old High German *bodam*, Latin *fundus*, Greek *puthmēn*

bottom dead centre NOUN *Engineering* the position of the crank of a reciprocating engine when the piston is at its nearest point to the crankshaft. Also called: **outer dead centre.**

bottom drawer NOUN *Brit* a young woman's collection of clothes, linen, cutlery, etc., in anticipation of marriage. US & Canadian equivalent: **hope chest.**

bottom end NOUN (in vertical engines) another name for **big end** (sense 1).

bottom feeder NOUN [1] a fish that feeds on material at the bottom of a river, lake, sea, etc. [2] an objectionable and unimpressive person or thing.

bottom fishing NOUN investing in low-priced shares that show prospects of recovery or in shares that are low-priced because of a general market decline in the hope of making a profit.

bottom house NOUN *Caribbean* [1] the open space beneath a house built upon high pillars. [2] such a space partially enclosed and floored for use as servants' quarters.

bottoming ('bɒtəmɪŋ) NOUN the lowest level of foundation material for a road or other structure.

bottomless ('bɒtəmlɪs) ADJECTIVE [1] having no bottom. [2] unlimited; inexhaustible. [3] very deep.

bottom line NOUN [1] the last line of a financial statement that shows the net profit or loss of a company or organization. [2] the final outcome of a process, discussion, etc. [3] the most important or fundamental aspect of a situation.

bottommost ('bɒtəm,məʊst) ADJECTIVE lowest or most fundamental.

bottom out VERB (*intr, adverb*) to reach the lowest point and level out: *the recession shows no sign of bottoming out.*

bottomry ('bɒtəmrɪ) NOUN, *plural* **-ries.** *Maritime law* a contract whereby the owner of a ship borrows money to enable the vessel to complete the voyage and pledges the ship as security for the loan.
▷HISTORY C16: from Dutch *bodemerij*, from *bodem* BOTTOM (hull of a ship) + *-erij* -RY

bottomset bed ('bɒtəm,sɛt) NOUN the fine sediment deposited at the front of a growing delta.

bottoms up INTERJECTION an informal drinking toast.

bottom-up ADJECTIVE from the lowest level of a hierarchy or process to the top: *a bottom-up approach to corporate decision-making.*

bottom-up processing NOUN a processing technique, either in the brain or in a computer, in which incoming information is analysed in successive steps and later-stage processing does not affect processing in earlier stages.

Bottrop (*German* 'bɔtrɔp) NOUN an industrial city in W Germany, in North Rhine-Westphalia in the Ruhr. Pop.: 121 500 (1999 est.).

botulin ('bɒtjʊlɪn) NOUN a potent toxin produced by the bacterium *Clostridium botulinum* in imperfectly preserved food, etc., causing botulism.
▷HISTORY C19: from BOTULINUS

botulinum toxin (,bɒtjʊ'laɪnəm) NOUN a pharmaceutical formulation of botulin used in minute doses to treat various forms of muscle spasm and for the cosmetic removal of wrinkles. See **Botox.**

botulinus (,bɒtjʊ'laɪnəs) NOUN, *plural* **-nuses.** an anaerobic bacterium, *Clostridium botulinum*, whose toxins (botulins) cause botulism: family *Bacillaceae.*
▷HISTORY C19: from New Latin, from Latin *botulus* sausage

botulism ('bɒtjʊ,lɪzəm) NOUN severe poisoning from ingestion of botulin, which affects the central nervous system producing difficulty in swallowing, visual disturbances, and respiratory paralysis: often fatal.
▷HISTORY C19: first formed as German *Botulismus* literally: sausage poisoning, from Latin *botulus* sausage

Bouaké (*French* bwake) NOUN a market town in S central Côte d'Ivoire. Pop.: 330 000 (1995 est.).

boubou *or* **bubu** ('bu:bu:) NOUN a long flowing garment worn by men and women in Mali, Nigeria, Senegal, and some other parts of Africa.
▷HISTORY a native name in Mali

bouchée (bu:'ʃeɪ) NOUN a small pastry case filled with a savoury mixture, served hot with cocktails or as an hors d'oeuvre.
▷HISTORY C19: from French: mouthful

Bouches-du-Rhône (*French* buʃdyron) NOUN a department of S central France, in Provence-Alpes-Côte d'Azur region. Capital: Marseille. Pop.: 1 835 719 (1999 est.). Area: 5284 sq. km (2047 sq. miles).

bouclé ('bu:kleɪ) NOUN [1] a curled or looped yarn or fabric giving a thick knobbly effect. ◆ ADJECTIVE [2] of or designating such a yarn or fabric: *a bouclé wool coat.*
▷HISTORY C19: from French *bouclé* curly, from *boucle* a curl, BUCKLE

bouclée ('bu:kleɪ) NOUN a support for a cue in billiards formed by doubling the first finger so that its tip is aligned with the thumb at its second joint, to form a loop through which the cue may slide.
▷HISTORY from French, literally: curled

boudin (*French* budɛ̃) NOUN a French version of a black pudding.
▷HISTORY C20: French

boudoir ('bu:dwɑ:, -dwɔ:) NOUN a woman's bedroom or private sitting room.
▷HISTORY C18: from French, literally: room for sulking in, from *bouder* to sulk

boudoir grand NOUN a domestic grand piano between 5 and 6 feet in length. Compare **baby grand, concert grand.**

bouffant ('bu:fɒŋ) ADJECTIVE [1] (of a hair style) having extra height and width through back-combing; puffed out. [2] (of sleeves, skirts, etc.) puffed out. ◆ NOUN [3] a bouffant hair style.
▷HISTORY C20: from French, from *bouffer* to puff up

bouffe (bu:f) NOUN See **opéra bouffe.**

Bougainville ('bu:gən,vɪl) NOUN an island in the W Pacific, in Papua New Guinea: the largest of the Solomon Islands: unilaterally declared independence in 1990; occupied by government troops in 1992, and granted autonomy in 2001. Chief town: Kieta. Area: 10 049 sq. km (3880 sq. miles).

bougainvillea *or* **bougainvillaea** (,bu:gən'vɪlɪə) NOUN any tropical woody nyctaginaceous widely cultivated climbing plant of the genus *Bougainvillea*, having inconspicuous flowers surrounded by showy red or purple bracts.
▷HISTORY C19: New Latin, named after Louis Antoine de *Bougainville* (1729–1811), French navigator

bough (baʊ) NOUN any of the main branches of a tree.
▷HISTORY Old English *bōg* arm, twig; related to Old Norse *bōgr* shoulder, ship's bow, Old High German *buog* shoulder, Greek *pēkhus* forearm, Sanskrit *bāhu*; see BOW[3], ELBOW

bought (bɔ:t) VERB [1] the past tense and past participle of **buy.** ◆ ADJECTIVE [2] purchased from a shop; not homemade.

boughten ('bɔ:tᵊn) ADJECTIVE a dialect word for **bought** (sense 2).

bougie ('bu:ʒi:, bu:'ʒi:) NOUN *Med* a long slender semiflexible cylindrical instrument for inserting into body passages, such as the rectum or urethra, to dilate structures, introduce medication, etc.
▷HISTORY C18: from French, originally a wax candle from *Bougie* (Bujiya), Algeria

bouillabaisse (,bu:jə'bɛs) NOUN a rich stew or soup of fish and vegetables flavoured with spices, esp saffron.
▷HISTORY C19: from French, from Provençal *bouiabaisso*, literally: boil down

bouillon ('bu:jɒn) NOUN a plain unclarified broth or stock.
▷HISTORY C18: from French, from *bouillir* to BOIL[1]

boulder ('bəʊldə) NOUN [1] a smooth rounded mass of rock that has a diameter greater than 25cm and that has been shaped by erosion and transported by ice or water from its original position. [2] *Geology* a rock fragment with a diameter greater than 256 mm and thus bigger than a cobble.
▷HISTORY C13: probably of Scandinavian origin; compare Swedish dialect *bullersten*, from Old Swedish *bulder* rumbling + *sten* STONE
▸ **'bouldery** ADJECTIVE

boulder clay NOUN an unstratified glacial deposit consisting of fine clay, boulders, and pebbles. See also **till**[4].

Boulder Dam NOUN the former name (1933–47) of **Hoover Dam.**

bouldering ('bəʊldərɪŋ) NOUN rock climbing on large boulders or small outcrops either as practice or as a sport in its own right.

boule[1] ('bu:li:) NOUN [1] the parliament in modern Greece. [2] the senate of an ancient Greek city-state.
▷HISTORY C19: from Greek *boulē* senate

boule[2] (bu:l) NOUN a pear-shaped imitation ruby, sapphire, etc., made from synthetic corundum.
▷HISTORY C19: from French: ball

boules *French* (bul) PLURAL NOUN (*functioning as singular*) a game, popular in France, in which metal bowls are thrown to land as near as possible to a target ball. It is played on rough surfaces.
▷HISTORY plural of *boule* BALL[1]; see BOWL[2]

boulevard ('bu:lvɑ:, -vɑ:d) NOUN [1] **a** a wide usually tree-lined road in a city, often used as a promenade. **b** (*capital as part of a street name*): *Sunset Boulevard.* [2] *Chiefly Canadian* **a** a grass strip between the pavement and road. **b** the strip of ground between the edge of a private property and the road. **c** the centre strip of a road dividing traffic travelling in different directions.
▷HISTORY C18: from French, from Middle Dutch *bolwerc* BULWARK; so called because originally often built on the ruins of an old rampart

boulevardier (bu:l'vɑ:dɪ,eɪ) NOUN (originally in Paris) a fashionable man, esp one who frequents public places.

boulle, boule, *or* **buhl** (bu:l) ADJECTIVE [1] denoting or relating to a type of marquetry of patterned inlays of brass and tortoiseshell, occasionally with other metals such as pewter, much used on French furniture from the 17th century. ◆ NOUN [2] Also called: **boullework.** something ornamented with such marquetry.
▷HISTORY C18: named after André Charles *Boulle* (1642–1732), French cabinet-maker

Boulogne (bʊ'lɔɪn; *French* bulɔɲ) NOUN a port in N France, on the English Channel. Pop.: 44 244 (1990). Official name: **Boulogne-sur-Mer** (*French* bulɔɲsyrmɛr).

Boulogne-Billancourt (*French* bulɔɲbijɑ̃kur) NOUN an industrial suburb of SW Paris. Pop.: 106 367 (1999). Also called: **Boulogne-sur-Seine** (*French* bulɔɲsyrsɛn).

boult (bəʊlt) VERB a variant spelling of **bolt**[2].

bounce (baʊns) VERB [1] (*intr*) (of an elastic object, such as a ball) to rebound from an impact. [2] (*tr*) to cause (such an object) to hit a solid surface and spring back. [3] to rebound or cause to rebound repeatedly. [4] to move or cause to move suddenly, excitedly, or violently; spring: *she bounced up from her chair.* [5] *Slang* (of a bank) to send (a cheque) back or (of a cheque) to be sent back unredeemed because of lack of funds in the drawer's account. [6] (of an Internet service provider) to send (an email message) back or (of an email message) to be sent back to the sender, for example because the recipient's email account is full. [7] (*tr*) *Slang* to force (a person) to leave (a place or job); throw out; eject. [8] (*tr*) *Brit* to hustle (a person) into believing or doing something. ◆ NOUN [9] the action of rebounding from an impact. [10] a leap; jump; bound. [11] the quality of being able to rebound; springiness. [12] *Informal* vitality; vigour; resilience. [13] *Brit* swagger or impudence. [14] **the bounce.** *Australian Rules football* the start of play at the beginning of each quarter or after a goal. [15] **get** *or* **give the bounce.** *US informal* to dismiss or be dismissed from a job. [16] **on the bounce.** *Informal* in succession; one after the other: *they have lost nine games on the bounce.*
▷HISTORY C13: probably of imitative origin; compare Low German *bunsen* to beat, Dutch *bonken* to thump

bounce back VERB [1] (*intr, adverb*) to recover one's health, good spirits, confidence, etc., easily after a setback. ◆ NOUN **bounce-back.** [2] a recovery following a setback.

bounce game NOUN (esp in soccer) a non-competitive game played as part of training.

bouncer ('baʊnsə) NOUN [1] *Slang* a man employed at a club, pub, disco, etc., to throw out drunks or troublemakers and stop those considered undesirable from entering. [2] *Slang* a dishonoured cheque. [3] *Cricket* another word for **bumper**[1]. [4] a person or thing that bounces.

bouncing ('baʊnsɪŋ) ADJECTIVE (when *postpositive*, foll by *with*) vigorous and robust (esp in the phrase **a bouncing baby**).

bouncing Bet (bɛt) NOUN another name for **soapwort.**

bouncy ('baʊnsɪ) ADJECTIVE **bouncier, bounciest.** [1] lively, exuberant, or self-confident. [2] having the capability or quality of bouncing: *a bouncy ball.* [3] responsive to bouncing; springy: *a bouncy bed.*
▸ **'bouncily** ADVERB ▸ **'bounciness** NOUN

bouncy castle NOUN a very large inflatable model, usually of a castle, on which children may bounce at fairs, etc.

bound[1] (baʊnd) VERB [1] the past tense and past participle of **bind.** ◆ ADJECTIVE [2] in bonds or chains; tied with or as if with a rope: *a bound prisoner.* [3] (*in combination*) restricted; confined: *housebound; fogbound.* [4] (*postpositive*, foll by an infinitive) destined; sure; certain: *it's bound to happen.* [5] (*postpositive*, often foll by *by*) compelled or obliged to act, behave, or think in a particular way, as by duty, circumstance, or convention. [6] (of a book) secured within a cover or binding: *to deliver bound books*. See also **half-bound**. [7] (*postpositive*, foll by *on*) *US* resolved; determined: *bound on winning*. [8] *Linguistics* **a** denoting a morpheme, such as the prefix *non-*, that occurs only as part of another word and not as a separate word in itself. Compare **free** (sense 21). **b** (in systemic grammar) denoting a clause that has a nonfinite predicator or that is introduced by a binder, and that occurs only together with a freestanding clause. [9] *Logic* (of a variable) occurring within the scope of a quantifier that indicates the degree of generality of the open sentence in which the variable occurs: in (*x*) (*Fx* → *bxy*), *x* is bound and *y* is free. Compare **free** (sense 22). [10] **bound up with.** closely or inextricably linked with: *his irritability is bound up with his work*. [11] **I'll be bound.** I am sure (something) is true.

bound[2] (baʊnd) VERB [1] to move forwards or make (one's way) by leaps or jumps. [2] to bounce; spring away from an impact. ◆ NOUN [3] a jump upwards or forwards. [4] **by leaps and bounds.** with unexpectedly rapid progess: *her condition improved by leaps and bounds*. [5] a sudden pronounced sense of excitement: *his heart gave a sudden bound when he saw her*. [6] a bounce, as of a ball.
▷HISTORY C16: from Old French *bond* a leap, from *bondir* to jump, resound, from Vulgar Latin *bombitīre* (unattested) to buzz, hum, from Latin *bombus* booming sound

bound[3] (baʊnd) VERB [1] (*tr*) to place restrictions on; limit. [2] (when *intr*, foll by *on*) to form a boundary of (an area of land or sea, political or administrative region, etc.). ◆ NOUN [3] *Maths* **a** a number which is greater than all the members of a set of numbers (an **upper bound**), or less than all its members (a **lower bound**). See also **bounded** (sense 1). **b** more generally, an element of an ordered set that has the same ordering relation to all the members of a given subset. **c** whence, an estimate of the extent of some set. [4] See **bounds.**
▷HISTORY C13: from Old French *bonde*, from Medieval Latin *bodina*, of Gaulish origin

bound[4] (baʊnd) ADJECTIVE **a** (*postpositive*, often foll by *for*) going or intending to go towards; on the way to: *a ship bound for Jamaica*; *homeward bound*. **b** (*in combination*): *northbound traffic*.
▷HISTORY C13: from Old Norse *buinn*, past participle of *būa* to prepare

boundary ('baʊndərɪ, -drɪ) NOUN, *plural* **-ries.** [1] something that indicates the farthest limit, as of an area; border. [2] *Cricket* **a** the marked limit of the playing area. **b** a stroke that hits the ball beyond this limit. **c** the four runs scored with such a stroke, or the six runs if the ball crosses the boundary without touching the ground.

Boundary Commission NOUN (in Britain) a body established by statute to undertake periodic reviews of the boundaries of parliamentary constituencies and to recommend changes to take account of population shifts.

boundary layer NOUN the layer of fluid closest to the surface of a solid past which the fluid flows: it has a lower rate of flow than the bulk of the fluid because of its adhesion to the solid.

boundary rider NOUN *Austral* an employee on a sheep or cattle station whose job is to maintain fences in good repair and to prevent stock from straying.

bounded ('baʊndɪd) ADJECTIVE *Maths* [1] (of a set) having a bound, esp where a measure is defined in terms of which all the elements of the set, or the differences between all pairs of members, are less than some value, or else all its members lie within some other well-defined set. [2] (of an operator, function, etc.) having a bounded set of values.

bounden ('baʊndən) ADJECTIVE morally obligatory (archaic except in the phrase **bounden duty**).

bounder ('baʊndə) NOUN [1] *Old-fashioned, Brit slang* a morally reprehensible person; cad. [2] a person or animal that bounds.

boundless ('baʊndlɪs) ADJECTIVE unlimited; vast: *boundless energy*.
▸ **'boundlessly** ADVERB ▸ **'boundlessness** NOUN

bounds (baʊndz) PLURAL NOUN [1] (*sometimes singular*) a limit; boundary (esp in the phrase **know no bounds**). [2] something that restrains or confines, esp the standards of a society: *within the bounds of modesty*. [3] **beat the bounds.** See **beat** (sense 26). ◆ See also **out of bounds.**

bounteous ('baʊntɪəs) ADJECTIVE *Literary* [1] giving freely; generous: *the bounteous goodness of God*. [2] plentiful; abundant.
▸ **'bounteously** ADVERB ▸ **'bounteousness** NOUN

bountiful ('baʊntɪfʊl) ADJECTIVE [1] plentiful; ample (esp in the phrase **a bountiful supply**). [2] giving freely; generous.
▸ **'bountifully** ADVERB ▸ **'bountifulness** NOUN

bounty ('baʊntɪ) NOUN, *plural* **-ties.** [1] generosity in giving to others; liberality. [2] a generous gift; something freely provided. [3] a payment made by a government, as, formerly, to a sailor on enlisting or to a soldier after a campaign. [4] any reward or premium: *a bounty of 20p for every rat killed*.
▷HISTORY C13 (in the sense: goodness): from Old French *bontet*, from Latin *bonitās* goodness, from *bonus* good

Bounty ('baʊntɪ) NOUN a British naval ship commanded by Captain William Bligh, which was on a scientific voyage in 1789 between Tahiti and the West Indies when her crew mutinied.

bouquet NOUN [1] (bəʊ'keɪ, buː-) a bunch of flowers, esp a large carefully arranged one. [2] (buː'keɪ) Also called: **nose.** the characteristic aroma or fragrance of a wine or liqueur. [3] a compliment or expression of praise.
▷HISTORY C18: from French: thicket, from Old French *bosc* forest, wood, probably of Germanic origin; see BUSH[1]

bouquet garni ('buːkeɪ gɑː'niː) NOUN, *plural* **bouquets garnis** ('buːkeɪz gɑː'niː). a bunch of herbs tied together and used for flavouring soups, stews, etc.
▷HISTORY C19: from French, literally: garnished bouquet

Bourbaki ('bɔːbəkɪ) NOUN **Nicholas.** the pseudonym of a group of mainly French mathematicians that, since 1939, has been producing a monumental work on advanced mathematics, *Eléments de Mathématique*.

bourbon ('bɜːbᵊn) NOUN a whiskey distilled, chiefly in the US, from maize, esp one containing at least 51 per cent maize (the rest being malt and rye) and aged in charred white-oak barrels.
▷HISTORY C19: named after *Bourbon* county, Kentucky, where it was first made

Bourbon biscuit NOUN a rich chocolate-flavoured biscuit with a chocolate-cream filling.

Bourbonism ('bʊəbəˌnɪzəm) NOUN [1] support for the rule of the Bourbons, the European royal line that ruled in France from 1589 to 1793 and 1815–48, and in Spain (1700–1808; 1813–1931) and Naples and Sicily (1734–1806; 1815–1860). [2] *US* extreme political and social conservatism.

bourdon ('bʊədᵊn, 'bɔːdᵊn) NOUN [1] a 16-foot organ stop of the stopped diapason type. [2] the drone of a bagpipe. [3] a drone or pedal point in the bass of a harmonized melody.
▷HISTORY C14: from Old French: drone (of a musical instrument), of imitative origin

Bourdon gauge NOUN a type of aneroid pressure gauge consisting of a flattened curved tube attached to a pointer that moves around a dial. As the pressure in the tube increases the tube tends to straighten and the pointer indicates the applied pressure.
▷HISTORY C19: named after Eugène *Bourdon* (1808–84), French hydraulic engineer, who invented it

bourg (bʊəg; *French* bur) NOUN a French market town, esp one beside a castle.
▷HISTORY C15: French, from Old French *borc*, from Late Latin *burgus* castle, of Germanic origin; see BOROUGH

bourgeois[1] ('bʊəʒwɑː, bʊə'ʒwɑː) *Often disparaging* ◆ NOUN, *plural* **-geois.** [1] a member of the middle class, esp one regarded as being conservative and materialistic or (in Marxist thought) a capitalist exploiting the working class. [2] a mediocre, unimaginative, or materialistic person. ◆ ADJECTIVE [3] characteristic of, relating to, or comprising the middle class. [4] conservative or materialistic in outlook: *a bourgeois mentality*. [5] (in Marxist thought) dominated by capitalists or capitalist interests.
▷HISTORY C16: from Old French *borjois*, *burgeis* burgher, citizen, from *bourg* town; see BURGESS
▸ **bourgeoise** ('bʊəʒwɑːz, bʊə'ʒwɑːz) FEMININE NOUN

bourgeois[2] (bə'dʒɔɪs) NOUN (formerly) a size of printer's type approximately equal to 9 point.
▷HISTORY C19: perhaps from its size, midway between long primer and brevier

bourgeoisie (ˌbʊəʒwɑː'ziː) NOUN **the.** [1] the middle classes. [2] (in Marxist thought) the ruling class of the two basic classes of capitalist society, consisting of capitalists, manufacturers, bankers, and other employers. The bourgeoisie owns the most important of the means of production, through which it exploits the working class.

bourgeon ('bɜːdʒən) NOUN, VERB a variant spelling of **burgeon.**

Bourges (*French* burʒ) NOUN a city in central France. Pop.: 75 609 (1990).

Bourgogne (burgɔɲ) NOUN the French name for **Burgundy.**

bourn[1] *or* **bourne** (bɔːn) NOUN *Archaic* [1] a destination; goal. [2] a boundary.
▷HISTORY C16: from Old French *borne*; see BOUND[3]

bourn[2] (bɔːn) NOUN *Chiefly southern Brit* a stream, esp an intermittent one in chalk areas. Compare **burn**[2].
▷HISTORY C16: from Old French *bodne* limit; see BOUND[3]

Bournemouth ('bɔːnməθ) NOUN [1] a resort in S England, in Bournemouth unitary authority, Dorset, on the English Channel. Pop.: 155 488 (1991). [2] a unitary authority in SE Dorset. Pop.: 163 441 (2001). Area: 46 sq. km (17 sq. miles).

bourrée ('bʊəreɪ) NOUN [1] a traditional French dance in fast duple time, resembling a gavotte. [2] a piece of music composed in the rhythm of this dance.
▷HISTORY C18: from French *bourrée* a bundle of faggots (it was originally danced round a fire of faggots)

Bourse (bʊəs) NOUN a stock exchange of continental Europe, esp Paris.
▷HISTORY C19: from French, literally: purse, from Medieval Latin *bursa*, ultimately from Greek: leather

bouse *or* **bowse** (baʊz) VERB (*tr*) *Nautical* to raise or haul with a tackle.
▷HISTORY C16: of unknown origin

boustrophedon (ˌbuːstrə'fiːdᵊn, ˌbaʊ-) ADJECTIVE having alternate lines written from right to left and from left to right.
▷HISTORY C17: from Greek, literally: turning as in ploughing with oxen, from *bous* ox + *-strophēdon* from *strephein* to turn; see STROPHE

bout (baʊt) NOUN [1] **a** a period of time spent doing something, such as drinking. **b** a period of illness. [2] a contest or fight, esp a boxing or wrestling match.
▷HISTORY C16: variant of obsolete *bought* turn; related to German *Bucht* BIGHT; see ABOUT

boutade (buː'tɑːd) NOUN an outburst; sally.
▷HISTORY C17: from French, from *bouter* to thrust

boutique (buː'tiːk) NOUN [1] a shop, esp a small one selling fashionable clothes and other items. [2] (*modifier*) of or denoting a small specialized producer or business: *a boutique operation*; *a boutique winery*. [3] a small specialized stall or shopping area within a supermarket, esp selling fresh meat, seafood, etc.
▷HISTORY C18: from French, probably from Old Provençal *botica*, ultimately from Greek *apothēkē* storehouse; see APOTHECARY

boutonniere (ˌbuːtɒnɪ'ɛə) NOUN another name for **buttonhole** (sense 2).
▷HISTORY C19: from French: buttonhole, from *bouton* BUTTON

bouvier ('buːvɪeɪ) NOUN a large powerful dog of a Belgian breed, having a rough shaggy coat: used esp for cattle herding and guarding.
▷HISTORY C20: from French, literally: cowherd

bouzouki (buː'zuːkɪ) NOUN a Greek long-necked stringed musical instrument related to the mandolin.
▷HISTORY C20: from Modern Greek *mpouzouki*, perhaps from Turkish *büjük* large

bovid ('bəʊvɪd) ADJECTIVE [1] of, relating to, or belonging to the *Bovidae*, a family of ruminant artiodactyl hollow-horned mammals including

sheep, goats, cattle, antelopes, and buffalo. ◆ NOUN 2 any bovid animal.
▷HISTORY C19: from New Latin *Bovidae*, from Latin *bōs* ox

bovine ('bəʊvaɪn) ADJECTIVE 1 of, relating to, or belonging to the *Bovini* (cattle), a bovid tribe including domestic cattle. 2 (of people) dull; sluggish; stolid. ◆ NOUN 3 any animal belonging to the *Bovini*.
▷HISTORY C19: from Late Latin *bovīnus* concerning oxen or cows, from Latin *bōs* ox, cow
▸'**bovinely** ADVERB

bovine somatotrophin NOUN the full name for **BST** (sense 1).

bovine spongiform encephalopathy NOUN the full name for **BSE**.

Bovril ('bɒvrɪl) NOUN *Trademark* a concentrated beef extract, used for flavouring, as a stock, etc.

bovver ('bɒvə) NOUN *Brit slang* **a** rowdiness, esp caused by gangs of teenage youths. **b** (*as modifier*): *a bovver boy*.
▷HISTORY C20: slang pronunciation of BOTHER

bovver boots PLURAL NOUN *Brit slang* heavy boots worn by some teenage youths in Britain, used in gang fights.

bow[1] (baʊ) VERB 1 to lower (one's head) or bend (one's knee or body) as a sign of respect, greeting, assent, or shame. 2 to bend or cause to bend; incline downwards. 3 (*intr*; usually foll by *to* or *before*) to comply or accept: *bow to the inevitable*. 4 (*tr*; foll by *in, out, to* etc.) to usher (someone) into or out of a place with bows and deference: *the manager bowed us to our car*. 5 (*tr*; usually foll by *down*) to bring (a person, nation, etc.) to a state of submission. 6 **bow and scrape.** to behave in an excessively deferential or obsequious way. ◆ NOUN 7 a lowering or inclination of the head or body as a mark of respect, greeting, or assent. 8 **take a bow.** to acknowledge or receive applause or praise. ◆ See also **bow out**.
▷HISTORY Old English *būgan*, related to Old Norse *bjūgr* bent, Old High German *biogan* to bend, Dutch *buigen*

bow[2] (bəʊ) NOUN 1 a weapon for shooting arrows, consisting of an arch of flexible wood, plastic, metal, etc. bent by a string (**bowstring**) fastened at each end. See also **crossbow**. 2 **a** a long slightly curved stick across which are stretched strands of horsehair, used for playing the strings of a violin, viola, cello, or related instrument. **b** a stroke with such a stick. 3 **a** a decorative interlacing of ribbon or other fabrics, usually having two loops and two loose ends. **b** the knot forming such an interlacing; bowknot. 4 **a** something that is curved, bent, or arched. **b** (*in combination*): *rainbow; oxbow; saddlebow*. 5 a person who uses a bow and arrow; archer. 6 *US* **a** a frame of a pair of spectacles. **b** a sidepiece of the frame of a pair of spectacles that curls round behind the ear. 7 a metal ring forming the handle of a pair of scissors or of a large old-fashioned key. 8 *Architect* part of a building curved in the form of a bow. See also **bow window**. ◆ VERB 9 to form or cause to form a curve or curves. 10 to make strokes of a bow across (violin strings).
▷HISTORY Old English *boga* arch, bow; related to Old Norse *bogi* a bow, Old High German *bogo*, Old Irish *bocc*, and BOW[1]

bow[3] (baʊ) NOUN 1 *Chiefly nautical* **a** (*often plural*) the forward end or part of a vessel. **b** (*as modifier*): *the bow mooring line*. 2 *Rowing* short for **bowman**[2]. 3 **on the port** (*or* **starboard**) **bow.** *Nautical* within 45 degrees to the port (or starboard) of straight ahead. 4 **a shot across someone's bows.** *Informal* a warning.
▷HISTORY C15: probably from Low German *boog*; related to Dutch *boeg*, Danish *bov* ship's bow, shoulder; see BOUGH

bow collector (bəʊ) NOUN a sliding current collector, consisting of a bow-shaped strip mounted on a hinged framework, used on trains, etc., to collect current from an overhead-wire. Compare **skate**[1] (sense 4).

bow compass (bəʊ) NOUN a compass for drawing, in which the legs are joined by a flexible metal bow-shaped spring rather than a hinge, the angle being adjusted by a screw. Also called: **bow-spring compass**.

bowdlerize *or* **bowdlerise** ('baʊdləˌraɪz) VERB (*tr*) to remove passages or words regarded as indecent from (a play, novel, etc.); expurgate.
▷HISTORY C19: after Thomas Bowdler (1754–1825), English editor who published an expurgated edition of Shakespeare
▸ˌ**bowdleri'zation** *or* ˌ**bowdleri'sation** NOUN
▸'**bowdlerˌizer** *or* '**bowdlerˌiser** NOUN ▸'**bowdlerism** NOUN

bowed (baʊd) ADJECTIVE 1 lowered; bent forward; curved: *bowed head; bowed back*. 2 **bowed down.** (foll by *by* or *with*) weighed down; troubled: *bowed down by grief*.

bowel ('baʊəl) NOUN 1 an intestine, esp the large intestine in man. 2 (*plural*) innards; entrails. 3 (*plural*) the deep or innermost part (esp in the phrase **the bowels of the earth**). 4 (*plural*) *Archaic* the emotions, esp of pity or sympathy.
▷HISTORY C13: from Old French *bouel*, from Latin *botellus* a little sausage, from *botulus* sausage

bowel movement NOUN 1 the discharge of faeces; defecation. 2 the waste matter discharged; faeces.

bower[1] ('baʊə) NOUN 1 a shady leafy shelter or recess, as in a wood or garden; arbour. 2 *Literary* a lady's bedroom or apartments, esp in a medieval castle; boudoir. 3 *Literary* a country cottage, esp one regarded as charming or picturesque.
▷HISTORY Old English *būr* dwelling; related to Old Norse *būr* pantry, Old High German *būr* dwelling
▸'**bowery** ADJECTIVE

bower[2] ('baʊə) NOUN *Nautical* a vessel's bow anchor.
▷HISTORY C18: from BOW[3] + -ER[1]

bower[3] ('baʊə) NOUN a jack in euchre and similar card games.
▷HISTORY C19: from German *Bauer* peasant, jack (in cards)

bowerbird ('baʊəˌbɜːd) NOUN 1 any of various songbirds of the family *Ptilonorhynchidae*, of Australia and New Guinea. The males build bower-like display grounds in the breeding season to attract the females. 2 *Informal, chiefly Austral* a person who collects miscellaneous objects.

Bowery ('baʊərɪ) NOUN **the.** a street in New York City noted for its cheap hotels and bars, frequented by vagrants and drunks.
▷HISTORY C17: from Dutch *bouwerij*, from *bouwen* to farm + *erij* -ERY; see BOOR, BOER

bowfin ('bəʊˌfɪn) NOUN a primitive North American freshwater bony fish, *Amia calva*, with an elongated body and a very long dorsal fin: family *Amiidae*.

bowhead ('bəʊˌhɛd) NOUN a large-mouthed arctic whale, *Balaena mysticetus*, that has become rare through overfishing but is now a protected species.

bowie knife ('bəʊɪ) NOUN a stout hunting knife with a short hilt and a guard for the hand.
▷HISTORY C19: named after Jim Bowie (1796–1836), US frontiersman, who popularized it

bowing ('bəʊɪŋ) NOUN the technique of using the bow in playing a violin, viola, cello, or related instrument.

bowknot ('bəʊˌnɒt) NOUN a decorative knot usually having two loops and two loose ends; bow.

bowl[1] (bəʊl) NOUN 1 a round container open at the top, used for holding liquid, keeping fruit, serving food, etc. 2 Also: **bowlful.** the amount a bowl will hold. 3 the rounded or hollow part of an object, esp of a spoon or tobacco pipe. 4 any container shaped like a bowl, such as a sink or lavatory. 5 *Chiefly US* a bowl-shaped building or other structure, such as a football stadium or amphitheatre. 6 a bowl-shaped depression of the land surface. See also **dust bowl**. 7 *Literary* **a** a drinking cup. **b** intoxicating drink.
▷HISTORY Old English *bolla*; related to Old Norse *bolli*, Old Saxon *bollo*

bowl[2] (bəʊl) NOUN 1 a wooden ball used in the game of bowls, having flattened sides, one side usually being flatter than the other in order to make it run on a curved course. 2 a large heavy ball with holes for gripping with the fingers and thumb, used in tenpin bowling. ◆ VERB 3 to roll smoothly or cause to roll smoothly, esp by throwing underarm along the ground. 4 (*intr*; usually foll by *along*) to move easily and rapidly, as in a car. 5 *Cricket* **a** to send (a ball) down the pitch from one's hand towards the batsman, keeping the arm straight while doing so. **b** Also: **bowl out.** to dismiss (a batsman) by delivering a ball that breaks his wicket. 6 (*intr*) to play bowls or tenpin bowling. 7 (*tr*) (in tenpin bowling) to score (a specified amount): *he bowled 120*. ◆ See also **bowl over, bowls**.
▷HISTORY C15: from French *boule*, ultimately from Latin *bulla* bubble

bow legs (bəʊ) PLURAL NOUN a condition in which the legs curve outwards like a bow between the ankle and the thigh. Also called: **bandy legs**.
▸**bow-legged** (bəʊ'lɛgɪd, bəʊ'lɛgd) ADJECTIVE

bowler[1] ('bəʊlə) NOUN 1 one who bowls in cricket. 2 a player at the game of bowls.

bowler[2] ('bəʊlə) NOUN a stiff felt hat with a rounded crown and narrow curved brim. US and Canadian name: **derby**.
▷HISTORY C19: named after John Bowler, 19th-century London hatter

bowler[3] ('baʊlə) NOUN *Dublin dialect* a dog.
▷HISTORY perhaps from B(OW-WOW) + (H)OWLER

bowline ('bəʊlɪn) NOUN *Nautical* 1 a line for controlling the weather leech of a square sail when a vessel is close-hauled. 2 **on a bowline.** beating close to the wind. 3 a knot used for securing a loop that will not slip at the end of a piece of rope.
▷HISTORY C14: probably from Middle Low German *bōlīne*, equivalent to BOW[3] + LINE[1]

bowling ('bəʊlɪŋ) NOUN 1 any of various games in which a heavy ball is rolled down a special alley, usually made of wood, at a group of wooden pins, esp the games of tenpin bowling (tenpins) and skittles (ninepins). 2 the game of bowls. 3 *Cricket* the act of delivering the ball to the batsman. 4 (*modifier*) of or relating to bowls or bowling: *a bowling team*.

bowling alley NOUN 1 **a** a long narrow wooden lane down which the ball is rolled in tenpin bowling. **b** a similar lane or alley, usually with raised sides, for playing skittles (ninepins). 2 a building having several lanes for tenpin bowling.

bowling crease NOUN *Cricket* a line marked at the wicket, over which a bowler must not advance fully before delivering the ball.

bowling green NOUN an area of closely mown turf on which the game of bowls is played.

bowl over VERB (*tr, adverb*) 1 *Informal* to surprise (a person) greatly, esp in a pleasant way; astound; amaze: *he was bowled over by our gift*. 2 to knock (a person or thing) down; cause to fall over.

bowls (bəʊlz) NOUN (*functioning as singular*) 1 **a** a game played on a bowling green in which a small bowl (the jack) is pitched from a mark and two opponents or opposing teams take turns to roll biased wooden bowls towards it, the object being to finish as near the jack as possible. **b** (*as modifier*): *a bowls tournament*. 2 skittles or tenpin bowling.

bowman[1] ('bəʊmən) NOUN, *plural* **-men.** an archer.

bowman[2] ('baʊmən) NOUN, *plural* **-men.** *Nautical* an oarsman at the bow of a boat. Also called: **bow oar**.

bow out (baʊ) VERB (*adverb; usually tr*; often foll by *of*) to retire or withdraw gracefully.

bowsaw ('bəʊˌsɔː) NOUN a saw with a thin blade in a bow-shaped frame.

bowse (baʊz) VERB a variant spelling of **bouse**.

bowser ('baʊzə) NOUN 1 a tanker containing fuel for aircraft, military vehicles, etc. 2 *Austral and NZ obsolete* a petrol pump at a filling station.
▷HISTORY originally a US proprietary name, from S. F. *Bowser*, US inventor, who made the first one in 1885

bowshot ('bəʊˌʃɒt) NOUN the distance an arrow travels from the bow.

bowsie ('baʊziː) NOUN *Irish* a low-class mean or obstreperous person.
▷HISTORY of unknown origin

bowsprit ('bəʊsprɪt) NOUN *Nautical* a spar projecting from the bow of a vessel, esp a sailing vessel, used to carry the headstay as far forward as possible.
▷HISTORY C13: from Middle Low German *bōchsprēt*, from *bōch* BOW[3] + *sprēt* pole

Bow Street runner (bəʊ) NOUN (in Britain from 1749 to 1829) an officer at Bow Street magistrates' court, London, whose duty was to pursue and arrest criminals.

bowstring ('bəʊˌstrɪŋ) NOUN the string of an

archer's bow, usually consisting of three strands of hemp.

bowstring hemp NOUN a hemplike fibre obtained from the sansevieria.

bow tie (bəʊ) NOUN a man's tie tied in a bow, now chiefly in plain black for formal evening wear.

bow weight (bəʊ) NOUN *Archery* the poundage required to draw a bow to the full length of the arrow.

bow window (bəʊ) NOUN a bay window in the shape of a curve.

bow-wow (ˈbaʊˌwaʊ, -ˈwaʊ) NOUN [1] a child's word for **dog.** [2] an imitation of the bark of a dog. ◆ VERB [3] (*intr*) to bark or imitate a dog's bark.

bowyangs (ˈbəʊjæŋz) PLURAL NOUN *Austral and NZ history* a pair of strings or straps secured round each trouser leg below the knee, worn esp by sheep-shearers and other labourers.
▷HISTORY C19: from English dialect *bowy-yanks* leggings

bowyer (ˈbəʊjə) NOUN a person who makes or sells archery bows.

box¹ (bɒks) NOUN [1] a receptacle or container made of wood, cardboard, etc., usually rectangular and having a removable or hinged lid. [2] Also called: **boxful.** the contents of such a receptacle or the amount it can contain: *he ate a whole box of chocolates.* [3] any of various containers for a specific purpose: *a money box; letter box.* [4] (*often in combination*) any of various small cubicles, kiosks, or shelters: *a telephone box or callbox; a sentry box; a signal box on a railway.* [5] a separate compartment in a public place for a small group of people, as in a theatre or certain restaurants. [6] an enclosure within a courtroom. See **jury box, witness box.** [7] a compartment for a horse in a stable or a vehicle. See **loosebox, horsebox.** [8] *Brit* a small country house occupied by sportsmen when following a field sport, esp shooting. [9] **a** a protective housing for machinery or mechanical parts. **b** the contents of such a box. **c** (*in combination*): *a gearbox.* [10] a shaped device of light tough material worn by sportsmen to protect the genitals, esp in cricket. [11] a section of printed matter on a page, enclosed by lines, a border, or white space. [12] a central agency to which mail is addressed and from which it is collected or redistributed: *a post-office box; to reply to a box number in a newspaper advertisement.* [13] the central part of a computer or the casing enclosing it. [14] short for **penalty box.** [15] *Baseball* either of the designated areas for the batter or the pitcher. [16] the raised seat on which the driver sits in a horse-drawn coach. [17] *NZ* a wheeled container for transporting coal in a mine. [18] *Austral and NZ* an accidental mixing of herds or flocks. [19] a hole cut into the base of a tree to collect the sap. [20] short for **Christmas box.** [21] a device for dividing water into two or more ditches in an irrigation system. [22] an informal name for a **coffin.** [23] *Austral taboo slang* the female genitals. [24] **be a box of birds.** *NZ* to be very well indeed. [25] **the box.** *Brit informal* television. [26] **think out of the box.** to think in a different, innovative, or original manner, esp with regard to business practices, products, systems, etc. [27] **out of the box.** *Austral informal* outstanding or excellent: *a day out of the box.* ◆ VERB [28] (*tr*) to put into a box. [29] (*tr*; usually foll by *in* or *up*) to prevent from moving freely; confine. [30] (*tr*; foll by *in*) *Printing* to enclose (text) within a ruled frame. [31] (*tr*) to make a cut in the base of (a tree) in order to collect the sap. [32] (*tr*) *Austral and NZ* to mix (flocks or herds) accidentally. [33] (*tr*; sometimes foll by *up*) *NZ* to confuse: *I am all boxed up.* [34] *Nautical* short for **boxhaul.** [35] **box the compass.** *Nautical* to name the compass points in order.
▷HISTORY Old English *box*, from Latin *buxus* from Greek *puxos* BOX³
▸ˈ**box,like** ADJECTIVE

box² (bɒks) VERB [1] (*tr*) to fight (an opponent) in a boxing match. [2] (*intr*) to engage in boxing. [3] (*tr*) to hit (a person) with the fist; punch or cuff. [4] **box clever.** to behave in a careful and cunning way. ◆ NOUN [5] a punch with the fist, esp on the ear.
▷HISTORY C14: of uncertain origin; perhaps related to Dutch *boken* to shunt, push into position

box³ (bɒks) NOUN [1] a dense slow-growing evergreen tree or shrub of the genus *Buxus*, esp *B. sempervirens*, which has small shiny leaves and is used for hedges, borders, and garden mazes: family *Buxaceae.* [2] the wood of this tree. See **boxwood** (sense 1). [3] any of several trees the timber or foliage of which resembles this tree, esp various species of *Eucalyptus* with rough bark.
▷HISTORY Old English, from Latin *buxus*

box beam NOUN another name for **box girder.**

boxberry (ˈbɒksbərɪ) NOUN, *plural* **-ries.** [1] the fruit of the partridgeberry or wintergreen. [2] another name for **partridgeberry** and **wintergreen** (sense 1).

boxboard (ˈbɒksˌbɔːd) NOUN a tough paperboard made from wood and wastepaper pulp: used for making boxes, etc.

box calf NOUN black calfskin leather, tanned with chromium salts, having a pattern of fine creases formed by boarding.
▷HISTORY C20: named after Joseph *Box*, London shoemaker

box camera NOUN a simple box-shaped camera having an elementary lens, shutter, and viewfinder.

box canyon NOUN *Western US* a canyon with vertical or almost vertical walls.

boxcar (ˈbɒksˌkɑː) NOUN *US and Canadian* a closed railway freight van.

box chronometer NOUN *Nautical* a ship's chronometer, supported on gimbals in a wooden box.

box coat NOUN [1] a plain short coat that hangs loosely from the shoulders. [2] a heavy overcoat, worn formerly by coachmen.

box cutter NOUN a knife-like tool with a short retractable blade.

box elder NOUN a medium-sized fast-growing widely cultivated North American maple, *Acer negundo*, which has compound leaves with lobed leaflets. Also called: **ash-leaved maple.**

boxer (ˈbɒksə) NOUN [1] a person who boxes, either professionally or as a hobby; pugilist. [2] a medium-sized smooth-haired breed of dog with a short nose and a docked tail.

Boxer (ˈbɒksə) NOUN **a** a member of a nationalistic Chinese secret society that led an unsuccessful rebellion in 1900 against foreign interests in China. **b** (*as modifier*): *the Boxer Rebellion.*
▷HISTORY C18: rough translation of Chinese *I Ho Ch'üan*, literally: virtuous harmonious fist, altered from *I Ho T'uan* virtuous harmonious society

boxercise (ˈbɒksəˌsaɪz) NOUN a system of sustained exercises combining boxing movements with aerobic activities.

boxer shorts PLURAL NOUN men's underpants shaped like shorts but having a front opening. Also called: **boxers.**

boxfish (ˈbɒksˌfɪʃ) NOUN, *plural* **-fish** *or* **-fishes.** another name for **trunkfish.**

box-fresh ADJECTIVE unused or unspoiled; straight from the packaging.

box girder NOUN **a** a girder that is hollow and square or rectangular in shape. **b** (*as modifier*): *a box-girder bridge.* Also called: **box beam.**

Boxgrove man (ˈbɒksgrəʊv) NOUN a type of primitive man, probably *Homo heidelbergensis* (see **Heidelberg man**) and probably dating from the Middle Palaeolithic period some 500 000 years ago; remains were found at Boxgrove in West Sussex in 1993 and 1995.

boxhaul (ˈbɒksˌhɔːl) VERB *Nautical* to bring (a square-rigger) onto a new tack by backwinding the foresails and steering hard round.

boxing (ˈbɒksɪŋ) NOUN **a** the act, art, or profession of fighting with the fists, esp the modern sport practised under Queensberry rules. **b** (*as modifier*): *a boxing enthusiast.*

Boxing Day NOUN *Brit* the first day (traditionally and strictly, the first weekday) after Christmas, observed as a holiday.
▷HISTORY C19: from the custom of giving Christmas boxes to tradesmen and staff on this day

boxing glove NOUN one of a pair of thickly padded mittens worn for boxing.

box jellyfish NOUN any of various highly venomous jellyfishes of the order *Cubomedusae*, esp *Chironex fleckeri*, of Australian tropical waters, having a cuboidal body with tentacles hanging from each of the lower corners. Also called (Austral): **sea wasp.**

box junction NOUN (in Britain) a road junction having yellow cross-hatching painted on the road surface. Vehicles may only enter the hatched area when their exit is clear.

box kite NOUN a kite with a boxlike frame open at both ends.

box number NOUN [1] the number of an individual pigeonhole at a newspaper to which replies to an advertisement may be addressed. [2] the number of an individual pigeonhole at a post office from which mail may be collected.

box office NOUN [1] an office at a theatre, cinema, etc., where tickets are sold. [2] the receipts from a play, film, etc. [3] **a** the public appeal of an actor or production: *the musical was bad box office.* **b** (*as modifier*): *a box-office success.*

box pleat NOUN a flat double pleat made by folding under the fabric on either side of it.

boxroom (ˈbɒksˌruːm, -ˌrʊm) NOUN a small room or large cupboard in which boxes, cases, etc., may be stored.

box seat NOUN [1] a seat in a theatre box. [2] **in the box seat.** *Brit, Austral, and NZ* in the best position.

box spanner NOUN a spanner consisting of a steel cylinder with a hexagonal end that fits over a nut: used esp to turn nuts in positions that are recessed or difficult of access.

box spring NOUN a coiled spring contained in a boxlike frame, used as base for mattresses, chairs, etc.

boxthorn (ˈbɒksˌθɔːn) NOUN another name for **matrimony vine.**

boxwood (ˈbɒksˌwʊd) NOUN [1] the hard close-grained yellow wood of the box tree, used to make tool handles, small turned or carved articles, etc. [2] the box tree.

boxy (ˈbɒksɪ) ADJECTIVE squarish or chunky in style or appearance: *a boxy square-cut jacket.*

boy (bɔɪ) NOUN [1] a male child; lad; youth. [2] a man regarded as immature or inexperienced: *he's just a boy when it comes to dealing with women.* [3] See **old boy.** [4] *Informal* a group of men, esp a group of friends. [5] *Usually derogatory* (esp in former colonial territories) a Black or native male servant of any age. [6] *Austral* a jockey or apprentice. [7] short for **boyfriend.** [8] **boys will be boys.** youthful indiscretion or exuberance must be expected and tolerated. [9] **jobs for the boys.** *Informal* appointment of one's supporters to posts, without reference to their qualifications or ability. [10] **the boy.** *Irish informal* the right tool for a particular task: *that's the boy to cut it.* ◆ INTERJECTION [11] an exclamation of surprise, pleasure, contempt, etc.
▷HISTORY C13 (in the sense: male servant; C14: young male): of uncertain origin; perhaps from Anglo-French *abuié* fettered (unattested), from Latin *boia* fetter

boyar (ˈbəʊjɑː, ˈbɔɪə) NOUN a member of an old order of Russian nobility, ranking immediately below the princes: abolished by Peter the Great.
▷HISTORY C16: from Old Russian *boyarin*, from Old Slavic *boljarinŭ*, probably from Old Turkic *boila* a title

boy band NOUN an all-male vocal pop group created to appeal to a young audience.

boycott (ˈbɔɪkɒt) VERB [1] (*tr*) to refuse to have dealings with (a person, organization, etc.) or refuse to buy (a product) as a protest or means of coercion: *to boycott foreign produce.* ◆ NOUN [2] an instance or the use of boycotting.
▷HISTORY C19: after Captain C. C. *Boycott* (1832–97), Irish land agent for the Earl of Erne, County Mayo, Ireland, who was a victim of such practices for refusing to reduce rents

boyf (bɔɪf) NOUN *Slang* a boyfriend.

boyfriend (ˈbɔɪˌfrɛnd) NOUN a male friend with whom a person is romantically or sexually involved; sweetheart or lover.

boyhood (ˈbɔɪhʊd) NOUN the state or time of being a boy: *his boyhood was happy.*

boyish (ˈbɔɪɪʃ) ADJECTIVE of or like a boy in looks, behaviour, or character, esp when regarded as attractive or endearing: *a boyish smile.*
▸ˈ**boyishly** ADVERB ▸ˈ**boyishness** NOUN

Boyle's law NOUN the principle that the pressure of a gas varies inversely with its volume at constant temperature.

▷HISTORY C18: named after Robert *Boyle* (1627–91), Irish scientist

boy-meets-girl ADJECTIVE conventionally or trivially romantic: *a boy-meets-girl story*.

Boyne (bɔɪn) NOUN a river in the E Republic of Ireland, rising in the Bog of Allen and flowing northeast to the Irish Sea: William III of England defeated the deposed James II in a battle (**Battle of the Boyne**) on its banks in 1690, completing the overthrow of the Stuart cause in Ireland. Length: about 112 km (70 miles).

boyo ('bɔɪəʊ) NOUN *Brit informal* a boy or young man: often used in direct address.
▷HISTORY from Irish and Welsh

Boyoma Falls (bɔɪ'əʊmə) PLURAL NOUN a series of seven cataracts in the NE Democratic Republic of Congo (formerly Zaïre), on the upper River Congo: forms an unnavigable stretch of 90 km (56 miles), which falls 60 m (200 ft.). Former name: **Stanley Falls.**

boy racer NOUN *Informal* **a** a young man who drives his car aggressively and at inappropriately high speeds. **b** (*as modifier*): *the boy-racer market*.

Boys' Brigade NOUN (in Britain) an organization for boys, founded in 1883, with the aim of promoting discipline and self-respect.

boy scout NOUN See **Scout.**

boysenberry ('bɔɪzənbərɪ) NOUN, *plural* **-ries.** [1] a type of bramble: a hybrid of the loganberry and various blackberries and raspberries. [2] the large red edible fruit of this plant.
▷HISTORY C20: named after Rudolph *Boysen*, American botanist who developed it

boysy ('bɔɪzɪ) ADJECTIVE *Informal* suited to or typical of boys or young men: *done in a matey, boysy way*.

Bozcaada (ˌbɔzdʒaa'da) NOUN the Turkish name for **Tenedos.**

Bozen ('bo:tsən) NOUN the German name for **Bolzano.**

bozo ('bəʊzəʊ) NOUN, *plural* **-zos.** *US slang* a man, esp a stupid one.
▷HISTORY C20: of uncertain origin; perhaps based on BEAU

bp ABBREVIATION FOR: [1] (of alcoholic density) below proof. [2] boiling point. [3] bishop.

BP ABBREVIATION FOR: [1] blood pressure. [2] British Pharmacopoeia.

BPC ABBREVIATION FOR British Pharmaceutical Codex.

B.P.E. (in the US and Canada) ABBREVIATION FOR Bachelor of Physical Education.

BPharm ABBREVIATION FOR Bachelor of Pharmacy.

BPhil ABBREVIATION FOR Bachelor of Philosophy.

bpi ABBREVIATION FOR bits per inch (used of a computer tape or disk surface).

BPR ABBREVIATION FOR **business process re-engineering.**

bps *Computing* ABBREVIATION FOR bits per second (of transmitted information).

b.pt. ABBREVIATION FOR boiling point.

Bq SYMBOL FOR becquerel(s).

br ABBREVIATION FOR: [1] brother. [2] Also: **B/R.** bills receivable. ◆ [3] THE INTERNET DOMAIN NAME FOR Brazil.

Br [1] ABBREVIATION FOR (in a religious order) Brother. ◆ [2] THE CHEMICAL SYMBOL FOR bromine.

BR [1] (formerly) ABBREVIATION FOR British Rail. ◆ [2] INTERNATIONAL CAR REGISTRATION FOR Brazil.

Br. ABBREVIATION FOR: [1] Britain. [2] British.

B/R *or* **br** ABBREVIATION FOR bills receivable.

bra (brɑ:) NOUN short for **brassiere.**

braai (braɪ) *South African* ◆ VERB [1] to grill or roast (meat) over open coals. ◆ NOUN [2] short for **braaivleis.**
▷HISTORY Afrikaans

braaivleis ('braɪˌfleɪs) NOUN *South African* [1] a picnic at which meat is cooked over an open fire; a barbecue. [2] the meat cooked at such a barbecue.
▷HISTORY from Afrikaans *braai* roast + *vleis* meat

braata ('brɑ:tə) *or* **braatas** ('brɑ:təs) NOUN *Caribbean* a small portion added to a purchase of food by a market vendor, to encourage the customer to return. Also called: **broughta, broughtas.**
▷HISTORY perhaps from Spanish *barata* a bargain

Brabant (brə'bænt) NOUN [1] a former duchy of W Europe: divided when Belgium became independent (1830), the south forming the Belgian provinces of Antwerp and Brabant and the north forming the province of North Brabant in the Netherlands. [2] a former province of central Belgium; replaced in 1995 by the provinces of **Flemish Brabant** and **Walloon Brabant.**

brabble ('bræbəl) VERB, NOUN a rare word for **squabble.**
▷HISTORY C16: from Middle Dutch *brabbelen* to jabber
▸'**brabbler** NOUN

braccate ('brækeɪt) ADJECTIVE (of birds) having feathered legs.
▷HISTORY from Latin *braccātus*, from *brăccae* breeches + -ATE[1]

brace (breɪs) NOUN [1] In full: **hand brace.** a hand tool for drilling holes, with a socket to hold the drill at one end and a cranked handle by which the tool can be turned. See also **brace and bit.** [2] something that steadies, binds, or holds up another thing. [3] a structural member, such as a beam or prop, used to stiffen a framework. [4] a sliding loop, usually of leather, attached to the cords of a drum: used to change its tension. [5] a pair; two, esp of game birds: *a brace of partridges*. [6] either of a pair of characters, { }, used for connecting lines of printing or writing or as a third sign of aggregation in complex mathematical or logical expressions that already contain parentheses and square brackets. [7] Also called: **accolade.** a line or bracket connecting two or more staves of music. [8] (*often plural*) an appliance of metal bands and wires that can be tightened to maintain steady pressure on the teeth for correcting uneven alignment. [9] *Med* any of various appliances for supporting the trunk, a limb, or teeth. [10] another word for **bracer[2].** [11] (in square-rigged sailing ships) a rope that controls the movement of a yard and thus the position of a sail. [12] See **braces.** ◆ VERB (*mainly tr*) [13] to provide, strengthen, or fit with a brace. [14] to steady or prepare (oneself or something) as before an impact. [15] (*also intr*) to stimulate; freshen; invigorate: *sea air is bracing*. [16] to control the horizontal movement of (the yards of a square-rigged sailing ship).
▷HISTORY C14: from Old French: the two arms, from Latin *bracchia* arms

brace and bit NOUN a hand tool for boring holes, consisting of a cranked handle into which a drilling bit is inserted.

bracelet ('breɪslɪt) NOUN [1] an ornamental chain worn around the arm or wrist. [2] an expanding metal band for a wristwatch. Related adjective: **armillary.**
▷HISTORY C15: from Old French, from *bracel*, literally: a little arm, from Latin *bracchium* arm; see BRACE

bracelets ('breɪslɪts) PLURAL NOUN a slang name for **handcuffs.**

bracer[1] ('breɪsə) NOUN [1] a person or thing that braces. [2] *Informal* a tonic, esp an alcoholic drink taken as a tonic.

bracer[2] ('breɪsə) NOUN *Archery, fencing* a leather guard worn to protect the arm.
▷HISTORY C14: from Old French *braciere*, from *braz* arm, from Latin *bracchium* arm

braces ('breɪsɪz) PLURAL NOUN *Brit* a pair of straps worn over the shoulders by men for holding up the trousers. US and Canadian word: **suspenders.**

brach (brætʃ) *or* **brachet** ('brætʃɪt) NOUN *Archaic* a bitch hound.
▷HISTORY C14: back formation from *brachez* hunting dogs, from Old French, plural of *brachet*, of Germanic origin; compare Old High German *braccho* hound

brachah (bra'xa) *or* **brocho** NOUN *Judaism* Hebrew terms usually translated as "blessing". See **blessing** (sense 4).

brachial ('breɪkɪəl, 'bræk-) ADJECTIVE of or relating to the arm or to an armlike part or structure.

brachiate ADJECTIVE ('breɪkɪɪt, -ˌeɪt, 'bræk-) [1] *Botany* having widely divergent paired branches. ◆ VERB ('breɪkɪˌeɪt, 'bræk-) [2] (*intr*) (of some arboreal apes and monkeys) to swing by the arms from one hold to the next.
▷HISTORY C19: from Latin *bracchiātus* with armlike branches
▸ˌ**brachi'ation** NOUN

brachio- *or before a vowel* **brachi-** COMBINING FORM indicating a brachium: *brachiopod*.

brachiocephalic (ˌbreɪkɪəsɪ'fælɪk) ADJECTIVE of, relating to, or supplying the arm and head: *brachiocephalic artery*.

brachiopod ('breɪkɪəˌpɒd, 'bræk-) NOUN any marine invertebrate animal of the phylum *Brachiopoda*, having a ciliated feeding organ (lophophore) and a shell consisting of dorsal and ventral valves. Also called: **lamp shell.** See also **bryozoan.**
▷HISTORY C19: from New Latin *Brachiopoda*; see BRACHIUM, -POD

brachiosaurus (ˌbreɪkɪə'sɔ:rəs, ˌbræk-) NOUN a dinosaur of the genus *Brachiosaurus*, up to 30 metres long: the largest land animal ever known. See also **sauropod.**

brachistochrone (brə'kɪstəˌkrəʊn) NOUN *Maths* the curve between two points through which a body moves under the force of gravity in a shorter time than for any other curve; the path of quickest descent.
▷HISTORY C18: from Greek *brakhistos*, superlative of *brakhus* short + *chronos* time

brachium ('breɪkɪəm, 'bræk-) NOUN, *plural* **-chia** (-kɪə). [1] *Anatomy* the arm, esp the upper part. [2] a corresponding part, such as a wing, in an animal. [3] *Biology* a branching or armlike part.
▷HISTORY C18: New Latin, from Latin *bracchium* arm, from Greek *brakhiōn*

brachy- COMBINING FORM indicating something short: *brachycephalic*.
▷HISTORY from Greek *brakhus* short

brachycephalic (ˌbrækɪsɪ'fælɪk) ADJECTIVE *also* **brachycephalous** (ˌbrækɪ'sɛfələs). [1] having a head nearly as broad from side to side as from front to back, esp one with a cephalic index over 80. ◆ NOUN [2] an individual with such a head. ◆ Compare **dolichocephalic, mesocephalic.**
▸ˌ**brachy'cephaly** *or* ˌ**brachy'cephalism** NOUN

brachycerous (bræ'kɪsərəs) ADJECTIVE (of insects) having short antennae.

brachydactylic (ˌbrækɪdæk'tɪlɪk) *or* **brachydactylous** (ˌbrækɪ'dæktɪləs) ADJECTIVE having abnormally short fingers or toes.
▸ˌ**brachy'dactyly** *or* ˌ**brachy'dactylˌism** NOUN

brachylogy (bræ'kɪlədʒɪ) NOUN, *plural* **-gies.** [1] a concise style in speech or writing. [2] a colloquial shortened form of expression that is not the result of a regular grammatical process: *the omission of "good" in the expression "Afternoon" is a brachylogy*.
▸**bra'chylogous** ADJECTIVE

brachyodont ('brækɪəˌdɒnt) ADJECTIVE (of mammals, such as humans) having teeth with short crowns.

brachypterous (bræ'kɪptərəs) ADJECTIVE having very short or incompletely developed wings: *brachypterous insects*.
▸**bra'chypterism** NOUN

brachyuran (ˌbrækɪ'jʊərən) NOUN [1] any decapod crustacean of the group (formerly suborder) *Brachyura*, which includes the crabs. ◆ ADJECTIVE [2] of, relating to, or belonging to the *Brachyura*.
▷HISTORY C19: from New Latin *Brachyura* (literally: short-tailed creatures), from BRACHY- + Greek *oura* tail

bracing ('breɪsɪŋ) ADJECTIVE [1] refreshing; stimulating; invigorating: *the air here is bracing*. ◆ NOUN [2] a system of braces used to strengthen or support: *the bracing supporting the building is perfectly adequate*.
▸'**bracingly** ADVERB

bracken ('brækən) NOUN [1] Also called: **brake.** any of various large coarse ferns, esp *Pteridium aquilinum*, having large fronds with spore cases along the undersides and extensive underground stems. [2] a clump of any of these ferns.
▷HISTORY C14: of Scandinavian origin; compare Swedish *bräken*, Danish *bregne*

bracket ('brækɪt) NOUN [1] an L-shaped or other support fixed to a wall to hold a shelf, etc. [2] one or more wall shelves carried on brackets. [3] *Architect* a support projecting from the side of a wall or other structure. See also **corbel, ancon, console[2].** [4] Also called: **square bracket.** either of a pair of characters, [ ], used to enclose a section of writing or printing to separate it from the main text. [5] a

general name for **parenthesis**, **square bracket** and **brace** (sense 6). [6] a group or category falling within or between certain defined limits: *the lower income bracket.* [7] the distance between two preliminary shots of artillery fire in range-finding. [8] a skating figure consisting of two arcs meeting at a point, tracing the shape ⋎. ◆ VERB (*tr*) **-kets, -keting, -keted** [9] to fix or support by means of a bracket or brackets. [10] to put (written or printed matter) in brackets, esp as being irrelevant, spurious, or bearing a separate relationship of some kind to the rest of the text. [11] to couple or join (two lines of text, etc.) with a brace. [12] (often foll by *with*) to group or class together: *to bracket Marx with the philosophers.* [13] to adjust (artillery fire) until the target is hit.
▷HISTORY C16: from Old French *braguette* codpiece, diminutive of *bragues* breeches, from Old Provençal *braga*, from Latin *brāca* breeches

bracket fungus NOUN any saprotroph or parasitic fungus of the basidiomycetous family *Polyporaceae*, growing as a shelflike mass (bracket) from tree trunks and producing spores in vertical tubes in the bracket.

bracketing ('brækɪtɪŋ) NOUN [1] a set of brackets. [2] *Photog* a technique in which a series of test pictures are taken at different exposure levels in order to obtain the optimum exposure.

brackish ('brækɪʃ) ADJECTIVE (of water) slightly briny or salty.
▷HISTORY C16: from Middle Dutch *brac* salty; see -ISH
▸ **'brackishness** NOUN

Bracknell ('bræknəl) NOUN a town in SE England, in Bracknell Forest unitary authority, Berkshire, designated a new town in 1949. Pop.: 60 895 (1991).

Bracknell Forest NOUN a unitary authority in SE England, in E Berkshire. Pop.: 109 606 (2001). Area: 109 sq. km (42 sq. miles).

bract (brækt) NOUN a specialized leaf, usually smaller than the foliage leaves, with a single flower or inflorescence growing in its axil.
▷HISTORY C18: from New Latin *bractea*, Latin: thin metal plate, gold leaf, variant of *brattea*, of obscure origin
▸ **'bracteal** ADJECTIVE ▸ **'bractless** ADJECTIVE

bracteate ('bræktɪɪt, -ˌeɪt) ADJECTIVE [1] (of a plant) having bracts. ◆ NOUN [2] *Archaeol* a fine decorated dish or plate of precious metal.
▷HISTORY C19: from Latin *bracteātus* gold-plated; see BRACT

bracteole ('bræktɪˌəʊl) NOUN a secondary bract subtending a flower within an inflorescence. Also called: **bractlet**.
▷HISTORY C19: from New Latin *bracteola*, from *bractea* thin metal plate; see BRACT
▸ **bracteolate** ('bræktɪəlɪt, -ˌleɪt) ADJECTIVE

brad (bræd) NOUN a small tapered nail having a small head that is either symmetrical or formed on one side only.
▷HISTORY Old English *brord* point, prick; related to Old Norse *broddr* spike, sting, Old High German *brort* edge

bradawl ('brædˌɔːl) NOUN an awl used to pierce wood, leather, or other materials for the insertion of brads, screws, etc.

Bradford ('brædfəd) NOUN [1] an industrial city in N England, in Bradford unitary authority, West Yorkshire: a centre of the woollen industry from the 14th century and of the worsted trade from the 18th century; university (1966). Pop.: 289 376 (1991). [2] a unitary authority in West Yorkshire. Pop.: 467 668 (2001). Area: 370 sq. km (143 sq. miles).

Bradford score NOUN a measure of the amount of time during which an employee is absent from work, based on assigning a number of points according to the frequency and length of absences.

Bradshaw ('brædˌʃɔː) NOUN a British railway timetable, published annually from 1839 to 1961.
▷HISTORY C19: named after its original publisher, George *Bradshaw* (1801–53)

brady- COMBINING FORM indicating slowness: *bradycardia*.
▷HISTORY from Greek *bradus* slow

bradycardia (ˌbrædɪ'kɑːdɪə) NOUN *Pathol* an abnormally low rate of heartbeat. Compare **tachycardia**.
▸ **bradycardiac** (ˌbrædɪ'kɑːdɪˌæk) ADJECTIVE

bradykinesia (ˌbrædɪkɪ'niːzɪə) NOUN *Physiol* abnormal slowness of physical movement, esp as an effect of Parkinson's disease.
▷HISTORY C20: from BRADY- + Greek *kinēsis* motion

bradykinin (ˌbrædɪ'kaɪnɪn, ˌbreɪdɪ-) NOUN a peptide in blood plasma that dilates blood vessels and causes contraction of smooth muscles. Formula: $C_{50}H_{73}N_{15}O_{11}$.
▷HISTORY C20: from BRADY- + Greek *kin(ēsis)* motion + -IN

brae (breɪ; *Scot* bre) NOUN *Scot* [1] a hill or hillside; slope. [2] (*plural*) an upland area: *the Gleniffer Braes.*
▷HISTORY C14 *bra*; related to Old Norse *brā* eyelash, Old High German *brāwa* eyelid, eyebrow; compare BROW

Braeburn ('breɪˌbɜːn) NOUN a variety of eating apple from New Zealand having sweet flesh and green and red skin.

braeheid (bre'hiːd) NOUN *Scot* the summit of a hill or slope.

Braemar (ˌbreɪ'mɑː) NOUN a village in NE Scotland, in Aberdeenshire; Balmoral Castle is nearby: site of the Royal Braemar Gathering, an annual Highland Games meeting.

brag (bræg) VERB **brags, bragging, bragged.** [1] to speak of (one's own achievements, possessions, etc.) arrogantly and boastfully. ◆ NOUN [2] boastful talk or behaviour, or an instance of this. [3] something boasted of: *his brag was his new car.* [4] a braggart; boaster. [5] a card game: an old form of poker.
▷HISTORY C13: of unknown origin
▸ **'bragger** NOUN ▸ **'bragging** NOUN, ADJECTIVE
▸ **'braggingly** ADVERB

Braga (*Portuguese* 'brɑːgə) NOUN a city in N Portugal: capital of the Roman province of Lusitania; 12th-century cathedral, seat of the Primate of Portugal. Pop.: 105 000 (2001). Ancient name: **Bracara Augusta.**

braggadocio (ˌbrægə'dəʊtʃɪˌəʊ) NOUN, *plural* **-os.** [1] vain empty boasting. [2] a person who boasts; braggart.
▷HISTORY C16: from *Braggadocchio*, name of a boastful character in Spenser's *Faerie Queene*; probably from BRAGGART + Italian *-occhio* (augmentative suffix)

braggadocious (ˌbrægə'dəʊʃəs) ADJECTIVE *US informal* boastful.
▷HISTORY C20: from BRAGGADOCIO

braggart ('brægət) NOUN [1] a person who boasts loudly or exaggeratedly; bragger. ◆ ADJECTIVE [2] boastful.
▷HISTORY C16: see BRAG

Bragg's law NOUN the principle that when a beam of X-rays of wavelength λ enters a crystal, the maximum intensity of the reflected ray occurs when sin θ = *n*λ/2*d*, where θ is the complement of the angle of incidence, *n* is a whole number, and *d* is the distance between layers of atoms.
▷HISTORY C20: named after Sir William Henry *Bragg* (1862–1942), and his son, Sir Lawrence *Bragg* (1890–1971), British physicists

Bragi ('brɑːgɪ) *or* **Brage** ('brɑːgə) NOUN *Norse myth* the god of poetry and music, son of Odin.

Brahma[1] ('brɑːmə) NOUN [1] a Hindu god: in later Hindu tradition, the Creator who, with Vishnu, the Preserver, and Shiva, the Destroyer, constitutes the triad known as the Trimurti. [2] another name for **Brahman** (sense 2).
▷HISTORY from Sanskrit, from *brahman* praise

Brahma[2] ('brɑːmə, 'breɪ-) NOUN a heavy breed of domestic fowl with profusely feathered legs and feet.
▷HISTORY C19: shortened from *Brahmaputra* (river); from its having been imported originally from Lakhimpur, a town on the Brahmaputra

Brahman ('brɑːmən) NOUN, *plural* **-mans.** [1] (*sometimes not capital*) Also called (esp formerly): **Brahmin.** a member of the highest or priestly caste in the Hindu caste system. [2] *Hinduism* the ultimate and impersonal divine reality of the universe, from which all being originates and to which it returns. [3] another name for **Brahma**[1].
▷HISTORY C14: from Sanskrit *brāhmana*, from *brahman* prayer
▸ **Brahmanic** (brɑː'mænɪk) *or* **Brah'manical** ADJECTIVE

Brahmana ('brɑːmənə) NOUN *Hinduism* any of a number of sacred treatises added to each of the Vedas.

Brahmani ('brɑːmənɪ) NOUN, *plural* **-nis.** (*sometimes not capital*) a woman of the Brahman caste.

Brahmanism ('brɑːməˌnɪzəm) *or* **Brahminism** NOUN (*sometimes not capital*) [1] the religious and social system of orthodox Hinduism, characterized by diversified pantheism, the caste system, and the sacrifices and family ceremonies of Hindu tradition. [2] the form of Hinduism prescribed in the Vedas, Brahmanas, and Upanishads.
▸ **'Brahmanist** *or* **'Brahminist** NOUN

Brahmaputra (ˌbrɑːmə'puːtrə) NOUN a river in S Asia, rising in SW Tibet as the Tsangpo and flowing through the Himalayas and NE India to join the Ganges at its delta in Bangladesh. Length: about 2900 km (1800 miles).

Brahmin ('brɑːmɪn) NOUN, *plural* **-min** *or* **-mins.** [1] the older spelling of **Brahman** (a Hindu priest). [2] (in the US) a highly intelligent or socially exclusive person, esp a member of one of the older New England families. [3] an intellectual or social snob.
▸ **Brah'minic** *or* **Brah'minical** ADJECTIVE

Brahui (brɑː'huːɪ) NOUN [1] a language spoken in Pakistan, forming an isolated branch of the Dravidian family. [2] (*plural* **-hui** *or* **-huis**) a member of the people that speaks this language.

braid[1] (breɪd) VERB (*tr*) [1] to interweave several strands of (hair, thread, etc.); plait. [2] to make by such weaving: *to braid a rope.* [3] to dress or bind (the hair) with a ribbon, etc. [4] to decorate with an ornamental trim or border: *to braid a skirt.* ◆ NOUN [5] a length of hair, fabric, etc., that has been braided; plait. [6] narrow ornamental tape of woven silk, wool, etc.
▷HISTORY Old English *bregdan* to move suddenly, weave together; compare Old Norse *bregtha*, Old High German *brettan* to draw a sword
▸ **'braider** NOUN

braid[2] (bred, breɪd) *Scot* ◆ ADJECTIVE [1] broad. ◆ ADVERB [2] broadly; frankly.
▷HISTORY Scot variant of BROAD

braided ('breɪdɪd) ADJECTIVE (of a river or stream) flowing in several shallow interconnected channels separated by banks of deposited material.

braiding ('breɪdɪŋ) NOUN [1] braids collectively. [2] work done in braid. [3] a piece of braid.

brail (breɪl) *Nautical* ◆ NOUN [1] one of several lines fastened to the leech of a fore-and-aft sail to aid in furling it. ◆ VERB [2] (*tr*; sometimes foll by *up*) to furl (a fore-and-aft sail) using brails.
▷HISTORY C15: from Old French *braiel*, from Medieval Latin *brācāle* belt for breeches, from Latin *brāca* breeches

Braille (breɪl) NOUN [1] a system of writing for the blind consisting of raised dots that can be interpreted by touch, each dot or group of dots representing a letter, numeral, or punctuation mark. [2] any writing produced by this method. Compare **Moon**[1]. ◆ VERB [3] (*tr*) to print or write using this method.

brain (breɪn) NOUN [1] the soft convoluted mass of nervous tissue within the skull of vertebrates that is the controlling and coordinating centre of the nervous system and the seat of thought, memory, and emotion. It includes the cerebrum, brainstem, and cerebellum. Technical name: **encephalon.** Related adjectives: **cerebral, encephalic.** [2] the main neural bundle or ganglion of certain invertebrates. [3] (*often plural*) *Informal* intellectual ability: *he's got brains.* [4] *Informal* shrewdness or cunning. [5] *Informal* an intellectual or intelligent person. [6] (*usually plural; functioning as singular*) *Informal* a person who plans and organizes an undertaking or is in overall control of an organization, etc. [7] an electronic device, such as a computer, that performs apparently similar functions to the human brain. [8] **on the brain.** constantly in mind: *I had that song on the brain.* [9] **pick someone's brain.** to obtain information or ideas from someone. ◆ VERB (*tr*) [10] to smash the skull of. [11] *Slang* to hit hard on the head.
▷HISTORY Old English *brægen*; related to Old Frisian *brein*, Middle Low German *bregen*, Greek *brekhmos* forehead

brainbox ('breɪnˌbɒks) NOUN *Slang* [1] the skull. [2] a clever person.

brain candy NOUN *Informal* something that is entertaining or enjoyable but lacks depth or significance.

brainchild (ˈbreɪnˌtʃaɪld) NOUN, *plural* **-children.** *Informal* an idea or plan produced by creative thought; invention.

brain coral NOUN a stony coral of the genus *Meandrina*, in which the polyps lie in troughlike thecae resembling the convoluted surface of a human brain.

braindead (ˈbreɪnˌdɛd) ADJECTIVE 1 having suffered brain death. 2 *Informal* not using or showing intelligence; stupid.

brain death NOUN irreversible cessation of respiration due to irreparable brain damage, even though the heart may continue beating with the aid of a mechanical ventilator: widely considered as the criterion of death.

brain drain NOUN *Informal* the emigration of scientists, technologists, academics, etc., for better pay, equipment, or conditions.

brain fever NOUN inflammation of the brain or its covering membranes.

brain-fever bird NOUN an Indian cuckoo, *Cuculus varius*, that utters a repetitive call.

brain gain NOUN *Informal* the immigration into a country of scientists, technologists, academics, etc., attracted by better pay, equipment, or conditions.

brainiac (ˈbreɪnɪˌæk) NOUN *Informal* a highly intelligent person.
▷HISTORY C20: from a super-intelligent character in an American comic strip

brainless (ˈbreɪnlɪs) ADJECTIVE stupid or foolish.
▸ **ˈbrainlessly** ADVERB ▸ **ˈbrainlessness** NOUN

brainpan (ˈbreɪnˌpæn) NOUN *Informal* the skull.

brainpower (ˈbreɪnˌpaʊə) NOUN intelligence; mental ability.

brainsick (ˈbreɪnˌsɪk) ADJECTIVE relating to or caused by insanity; crazy; mad.
▸ **ˈbrainˌsickly** ADVERB ▸ **ˈbrainˌsickness** NOUN

brainstem (ˈbreɪnˌstɛm) NOUN the stalklike part of the brain consisting of the medulla oblongata, the midbrain, and the pons Varolii.

brainstorm (ˈbreɪnˌstɔːm) NOUN 1 a severe outburst of excitement, often as the result of a transitory disturbance of cerebral activity. 2 *Brit informal* a sudden mental aberration. 3 *Informal* another word for **brainwave.**

brainstorming (ˈbreɪnˌstɔːmɪŋ) NOUN intensive discussion to solve problems or generate ideas.

brains trust NOUN 1 a group of knowledgeable people who discuss topics in public or on radio or television. 2 Also called: **brain trust.** *US* a group of experts who advise the government.

brain-teaser *or* **brain-twister** NOUN *Informal* a difficult problem.

brain up VERB (*tr*) to make more intellectually demanding or sophisticated: *we need to brain up the curriculum.*

brainwash (ˈbreɪnˌwɒʃ) VERB (*tr*) to effect a radical change in the ideas and beliefs of (a person), esp by methods based on isolation, sleeplessness, hunger, extreme discomfort, pain, and the alternation of kindness and cruelty.
▸ **ˈbrainˌwasher** NOUN ▸ **ˈbrainˌwashing** NOUN

brainwave NOUN (ˈbreɪnˌweɪv), NOUN *Informal* a sudden inspiration or idea. Also: **brainstorm.**

brain wave NOUN any of the fluctuations of electrical potential in the brain as represented on an electroencephalogram. They vary in frequency from 1 to 30 hertz. See also **alpha rhythm, beta rhythm, delta rhythm.**

brainy (ˈbreɪnɪ) ADJECTIVE **brainier, brainiest.** *Informal* clever; intelligent.
▸ **ˈbrainily** ADVERB ▸ **ˈbraininess** NOUN

braise (breɪz) VERB to cook (meat, vegetables, etc.) by lightly browning in fat and then cooking slowly in a closed pan with a small amount of liquid.
▷HISTORY C18: from French *braiser*, from Old French *brese* live coals, probably of Germanic origin; compare Old English *brædan*, Old High German *brātan* to roast

brak (brak) ADJECTIVE *South African* (of water) brackish or salty.
▷HISTORY C19: Afrikaans

brake¹ (breɪk) NOUN 1 **a** (*often plural*) a device for slowing or stopping a vehicle, wheel, shaft, etc., or for keeping it stationary, esp by means of friction. See also **drum brake, disc brake, hydraulic brake, air brake, handbrake. b** (*as modifier*): *the brake pedal.* 2 a machine or tool for crushing or breaking flax or hemp to separate the fibres. 3 Also called: **brake harrow.** a heavy harrow for breaking up clods. 4 short for **brake van.** 5 short for **shooting brake.** 6 Also spelt: **break.** an open four-wheeled horse-drawn carriage. 7 an obsolete word for the **rack** (an instrument of torture). ◆ VERB 8 to slow down or cause to slow down, by or as if by using a brake. 9 (*tr*) to crush or break up using a brake.
▷HISTORY C18: from Middle Dutch *braeke*; related to *breken* to BREAK
▸ **ˈbrakeless** ADJECTIVE

brake² (breɪk) NOUN an area of dense undergrowth, shrubs, brushwood, etc.; thicket.
▷HISTORY Old English *bracu*; related to Middle Low German *brake*, Old French *bracon* branch

brake³ (breɪk) NOUN another name for **bracken** (sense 1). See also **rock brake.**

brake⁴ (breɪk) VERB *Archaic, chiefly biblical* a past tense of **break.**

brake band NOUN a strip of fabric, leather, or metal tightened around a pulley or shaft to act as a brake.

brake drum NOUN the cast-iron drum attached to the hub of a wheel of a motor vehicle fitted with drum brakes. See also **brake shoe.**

brake-fade NOUN the decrease in efficiency of braking of a motor vehicle due to overheating of the brakes.

brake fluid NOUN an oily liquid used to transmit pressure in a hydraulic brake or clutch system.

brake horsepower NOUN the rate at which an engine does work, expressed in horsepower. It is measured by the resistance of an applied brake. Abbreviation: **bhp.**

brake light NOUN a red light attached to the rear of a motor vehicle that lights up when the brakes are applied, serving as a warning to following drivers. Also called: **stoplight.**

brake lining NOUN a curved thin strip of an asbestos composition riveted to a brake shoe to provide it with a renewable surface.

brakeman (ˈbreɪkmən) NOUN, *plural* **-men.** 1 *US and Canadian* a crew member of a goods or passenger train. His duties include controlling auxiliary braking power and inspecting the train. 2 the man at the back of a two- or four-man bobsleigh, who operates the brake.

brake pad NOUN the flat metal casting, together with the bound friction material, in a disc brake.

brake parachute NOUN a parachute attached to the rear of a vehicle and opened to assist braking. Also called: **brake chute, parachute brake, parabrake.**

brake shoe NOUN 1 the curved metal casting to which the brake lining is riveted in a drum brake. 2 the curved metal casting together with the attached brake lining. Sometimes (for both senses) shortened to: **shoe.**

brakesman (ˈbreɪksmən) NOUN, *plural* **-men.** a pithead winch operator.

brake van NOUN *Railways Brit* the coach or vehicle from which the guard applies the brakes; guard's van.

Brakpan (ˈbrækˌpæn) NOUN a city in E South Africa: gold-mining centre. Pop.: 46 416 (latest est.).

bramble (ˈbræmbᵊl) NOUN 1 any of various prickly herbaceous plants or shrubs of the rosaceous genus *Rubus*, esp the blackberry. See also **stone bramble.** 2 *Scot* **a** a blackberry. **b** (*as modifier*): *bramble jelly.* 3 any of several similar and related shrubs. ◆ VERB (*intr*) 4 to gather blackberries.
▷HISTORY Old English *brǣmbel*; related to Old Saxon *brāmal*, Old High German *brāmo*
▸ **ˈbrambly** ADJECTIVE

brambling (ˈbræmblɪŋ) NOUN a Eurasian finch, *Fringilla montifringilla*, with a speckled head and back and, in the male, a reddish brown breast and darker wings and tail.

Bramley (ˈbræmlɪ) *or* **Bramley's seedling** NOUN a variety of cooking apple having juicy firm flesh.
▷HISTORY C19: named after Matthew *Bramley*, 19th-century English butcher, said to have first grown it

bran (bræn) NOUN 1 husks of cereal grain separated from the flour by sifting. 2 food prepared from these husks. Related adjective: **furfuraceous.**
▷HISTORY C13: from Old French, probably of Gaulish origin

branch (brɑːntʃ) NOUN 1 a secondary woody stem arising from the trunk or bough of a tree or the main stem of a shrub. 2 a subdivision of the stem or root of any other plant. 3 an offshoot or secondary part: *a branch of a deer's antlers.* 4 **a** a subdivision or subsidiary section of something larger or more complex: *branches of learning; branch of the family.* **b** (*as modifier*): *a branch office.* 5 *US* any small stream. 6 *Maths* a section of a curve separated from the rest of the curve by discontinuities or special points. 7 Also called: **jump.** *Computing* a departure from the normal sequence of programmed instructions into a separate program area. 8 an alternative route in an atomic or nuclear decay series. ◆ VERB 9 (*intr*) (of a tree or other plant) to produce or possess branches. 10 (*intr*; usually foll by *from*) (of stems, roots, etc.) to grow and diverge (from another part). 11 to divide or be divided into subsidiaries or offshoots. 12 (*intr*; often foll by *off*) to diverge from the main way, road, topic, etc. ◆ See also **branch out.**
▷HISTORY C13: from Old French *branche*, from Late Latin *branca* paw, foot
▸ **ˈbranchless** ADJECTIVE ▸ **ˈbranchˌlike** ADJECTIVE
▸ **ˈbranchy** ADJECTIVE

branch- ADJECTIVE AND NOUN COMBINING FORM (in zoology) indicating gills: *lamellibranch.*
▷HISTORY from Latin: BRANCHIA

branched chain NOUN *Chem* an open chain of atoms with one or more side chains attached to it. Compare **straight chain.**

branchia (ˈbræŋkɪə) NOUN, *plural* **-chiae** (-kɪˌiː). a gill in aquatic animals.
▸ **ˈbranchiˌate** ADJECTIVE

branchial (ˈbræŋkɪəl) ADJECTIVE 1 of or relating to the gills of an aquatic animal, esp a fish. 2 of or relating to homologous structures in higher vertebrates: *branchial cyst.*

branching (ˈbrɑːntʃɪŋ) NOUN *Physics* the occurrence of several decay paths (**branches**) in the disintegration of a particular nuclide or the de-excitation of an excited atom. The **branching fraction** (nuclear) or **branching ratio** (atomic) is the proportion of the disintegrating nuclei that follow a particular branch to the total number of disintegrating nuclides.

branch instruction NOUN *Computing* a machine-language or assembly-language instruction that causes the computer to branch to another instruction.

branchiopod (ˈbræŋkɪəˌpɒd) NOUN any crustacean of the mainly freshwater subclass *Branchiopoda*, having flattened limblike appendages for swimming, feeding, and respiration. The group includes the water fleas.

branchiostegal (ˌbræŋkɪəˈstiːgᵊl) ADJECTIVE *Zoology* of or relating to the operculum covering the gill slits of fish: *branchiostegal membrane; branchiostegal rays.*
▷HISTORY from BRANCHIA + Greek *stegos* roof

branch line NOUN *Railways* a secondary route to a place or places not served by a main line.

branch officer NOUN (in the British navy since 1949) any officer who holds warrant.

branch out VERB (*intr, adverb*; often foll by *into*) to expand or extend one's interests: *our business has branched out into computers now.*

branch plant *or* **factory** NOUN *Canadian* a plant or factory in Canada belonging to a company whose headquarters are in another country.

brand (brænd) NOUN 1 a particular product or a characteristic that serves to identify a particular product. 2 a trade name or trademark. 3 a particular kind or variety: *he had his own brand of humour.* 4 an identifying mark made, usually by burning, on the skin of animals or (formerly) slaves or criminals, esp as a proof of ownership. 5 an iron heated and used for branding animals, etc. 6 a mark of disgrace or infamy; stigma: *he bore the brand of a coward.* 7 a burning or burnt piece of wood, as

in a fire. 8 *Archaic or poetic* **a** a flaming torch. **b** a sword. 9 a fungal disease of garden plants characterized by brown spots on the leaves, caused by the rust fungus *Puccinia arenariae*. ◆ VERB (*tr*) 10 to label, burn, or mark with or as with a brand. 11 to place indelibly in the memory: *the scene of slaughter was branded in their minds*. 12 to denounce; stigmatize: *they branded him a traitor*. 13 to give a product a distinctive identity by means of characteristic design, packaging, etc.
▷HISTORY Old English *brand-*, related to Old Norse *brandr*, Old High German *brant*; see BURN[1]
▸ **'brander** NOUN

brand awareness NOUN *Marketing* the extent to which consumers are aware of a particular product or service.

brand contamination NOUN the process by which the reputation of a particular brand or product becomes tarnished by adverse publicity.

branded ('brændɪd) ADJECTIVE identifiable as being the product of a particular manufacturer or marketing company.

Brandenburg ('brændən,bɜːg; *German* 'brandənburk) NOUN 1 a state in NE Germany, part of East Germany until 1990. A former electorate, it expanded under the Hohenzollerns to become the kingdom of Prussia (1701). The district east of the Oder River became Polish in 1945. Capital: Potsdam. Pop.: 2 601 200 (2000 est.). Area: 29 481 sq. km (11 219 sq. miles). 2 a city in NE Germany: former capital of the Prussian province of Brandenburg. Pop.: 93 660 (latest est.).

brand extension NOUN *Marketing* the practice of using a well-known brand name to promote new products or services in unrelated fields. Also called: **brand stretching.**

brand image NOUN the attributes of a brand as perceived by potential and actual customers.

brandish ('brændɪʃ) VERB (*tr*) 1 to wave or flourish (a weapon) in a triumphant, threatening, or ostentatious way. ◆ NOUN 2 a threatening or defiant flourish.
▷HISTORY C14: from Old French *brandir*, from *brand* sword, of Germanic origin; compare Old High German *brant* weapon
▸ **'brandisher** NOUN

brand leader NOUN *Marketing* a product with the highest number of total sales within its category.

brandling ('brændlɪŋ) NOUN a small red earthworm, *Eisenia foetida* (or *Helodrilus foetidus*), found in manure and used as bait by anglers.
▷HISTORY C17: from BRAND + -LING[1]

brand name NOUN another name for **brand** (sense 2).

brand-new ADJECTIVE absolutely new.
▷HISTORY C16: from BRAND (n) + NEW, likened to newly forged iron

brand stretching NOUN *Marketing* another name for **brand extension.**

brandy ('brændɪ) NOUN, *plural* **-dies.** 1 an alcoholic drink consisting of spirit distilled from grape wine. 2 a distillation of wines made from other fruits: *plum brandy*.
▷HISTORY C17: from earlier *brandewine*, from Dutch *brandewijn* burnt wine, from *bernen* to burn or distil + *wijn* WINE; compare German *Branntwein*

brandy bottle NOUN another name for a **yellow water lily.**

brandy butter NOUN butter and sugar creamed together with brandy and served with Christmas pudding, etc.

brandy snap NOUN a crisp sweet biscuit, rolled into a cylinder after baking and often filled with whipped cream.

branks (bræŋks) PLURAL NOUN (formerly) an iron bridle used to restrain scolding women.
▷HISTORY C16: of unknown origin

branle ('bræn[ə]l) NOUN an old French country dance performed in a linked circle.
▷HISTORY C17: from Old French *branler* to shake, variant of *brandir* to BRANDISH

brant (brænt) NOUN, *plural* **brants** *or* **brant.** another name (esp US and Canadian) for **brent goose.**

Brantford ('bræntfəd) NOUN a city in central Canada, in SW Ontario. Pop.: 84 764 (1996).

bran tub NOUN (in Britain) a tub containing bran in which small wrapped gifts are hidden, used at parties, fairs, etc.

brasco ('bræskəʊ) NOUN *Austral slang* a lavatory.
▷HISTORY from a toilet manufacturer named *Brass Co.*

brash[1] (bræʃ) ADJECTIVE 1 tastelessly or offensively loud, showy, or bold. 2 hasty; rash. 3 impudent.
▷HISTORY C19: perhaps influenced by RASH[1]
▸ **'brashly** ADVERB ▸ **'brashness** NOUN

brash[2] (bræʃ) NOUN loose rubbish, such as broken rock, hedge clippings, etc.; debris.
▷HISTORY C18: of unknown origin

brash[3] (bræʃ) NOUN *Pathol* another name for **heartburn.**
▷HISTORY C16: perhaps of imitative origin

brashy ('bræʃɪ) ADJECTIVE **brashier, brashiest.** 1 loosely fragmented; rubbishy. 2 (of timber) brittle.
▸ **'brashiness** NOUN

brasier ('breɪzɪə) NOUN a less common spelling of **brazier.**

brasil (brə'zɪl) NOUN a variant spelling of **brazil.**

Brasil (brə'ziːl) NOUN the Portuguese spelling of **Brazil.**

brasilein (brə'zɪlɪɪn) NOUN a variant spelling of **brazilein.**

Brasília (brə'zɪljə; *Portuguese* brəzi'liːa) NOUN the capital of Brazil (since 1960), on the central plateau: the former capital was Rio de Janeiro. Pop.: 1 954 442 (2000).

brasilin ('bræzɪlɪn) NOUN a variant spelling of **brazilin.**

Braşov (*Romanian* bra'ʃov) NOUN an industrial city in central Romania: formerly a centre for expatriate Germans; ceded by Hungary to Romania in 1920. Pop.: 317 772 (1997 est.). Former name (1950–61): **Stalin.** German name: **Kronstadt.** Hungarian name: **Brassó.**

brass (brɑːs) NOUN 1 an alloy of copper and zinc containing more than 50 per cent of copper. **Alpha brass** (containing less than 35 per cent of zinc) is used for most engineering materials requiring forging, pressing, etc. **Alpha-beta brass** (35–45 per cent zinc) is used for hot working and extrusion. **Beta brass** (45–50 per cent zinc) is used for castings. Small amounts of other metals, such as lead or tin, may be added. Compare **bronze** (sense 1). 2 an object, ornament, or utensil made of brass. 3 **a** the large family of wind instruments including the trumpet, trombone, French horn, etc., each consisting of a brass tube blown directly by means of a cup- or funnel-shaped mouthpiece. **b** (*sometimes functioning as plural*) instruments of this family forming a section in an orchestra. **c** (*as modifier*): *a brass ensemble*. 4 a renewable sleeve or bored semicylindrical shell made of brass or bronze, used as a liner for a bearing. 5 (*functioning as plural*) *Informal* important or high-ranking officials, esp military officers: *the top brass*. See also **brass hat.** 6 *Northern English dialect* money: *where there's muck, there's brass!* 7 *Brit* an engraved brass memorial tablet or plaque, set in the wall or floor of a church. 8 *Informal* bold self-confidence; cheek; nerve: *he had the brass to ask for more time*. 9 *Slang* a prostitute. 10 (*modifier*) of, consisting of, or relating to brass or brass instruments: *a brass ornament*; *a brass band*. Related adjective: **brazen.**
▷HISTORY Old English *bræs*; related to Old Frisian *bres* copper, Middle Low German *bras* metal

brassard ('bræsɑːd) *or* **brassart** ('bræsət) NOUN 1 an identifying armband or badge. 2 a piece of armour for the upper arm.
▷HISTORY C19: from French, from *bras* arm, from Latin BRACHIUM

brass band NOUN See **band[1]** (sense 2).

brassbound ('brɑːs,baʊnd) ADJECTIVE inflexibly entrenched: *brassbound traditions*.

brassed off ADJECTIVE *Brit slang* fed up; disgruntled.

brasserie ('bræsərɪ) NOUN 1 a bar in which drinks and often food are served. 2 a small and usually cheap restaurant.
▷HISTORY C19: from French, from *brasser* to stir, brew

brass farthing NOUN *Brit informal* something of little or no value: *his opinion isn't worth a brass farthing*.
▷HISTORY C18: probably coined when farthings were first minted in bronze rather than silver

brass hat NOUN *Brit informal* a top-ranking official, esp a military officer.
▷HISTORY C20: from the gold leaf decoration on the peaks of caps worn by officers of high rank

brassica ('bræsɪkə) NOUN any plant of the genus *Brassica*, such as cabbage, rape, turnip, and mustard: family *Brassicaceae* (crucifers).
▷HISTORY C19: from Latin: cabbage
▸ **brassicaceous** (,bræsɪ'keɪʃəs) ADJECTIVE

brassie *or* **brassy** ('bræsɪ, 'brɑː-) NOUN, *plural* **brassies.** *Golf* a former name for a club, a No. 2 wood, originally having a brass-plated sole and with a shallower face than a driver to give more loft.

brassiere ('bræsɪə, 'bræz-) NOUN a woman's undergarment for covering and supporting the breasts. Often shortened to: **bra.**
▷HISTORY C20: from C17 French: bodice, from Old French *braciere* a protector for the arm, from *braz* arm

brass neck NOUN *Brit informal* effrontery; nerve.

Brassó ('brɔʃʃoː) NOUN the Hungarian name for **Braşo.**

brass rubbing NOUN 1 the taking of an impression of an engraved brass tablet or plaque by placing a piece of paper over it and rubbing the paper with graphite, heelball, or chalk. 2 an impression made in this way.

brass tacks PLURAL NOUN *Informal* basic realities; hard facts (esp in the phrase **get down to brass tacks**).

brassy ('brɑːsɪ) ADJECTIVE **brassier, brassiest.** 1 insolent; brazen. 2 flashy; showy. 3 (of sound) harsh, strident, or resembling the sound of a brass instrument. 4 like brass, esp in colour. 5 decorated with or made of brass. 6 a variant spelling of **brassie.**
▸ **'brassily** ADVERB ▸ **'brassiness** NOUN

brat[1] (bræt) NOUN a child, esp one who is ill-mannered or unruly: used contemptuously or playfully.
▷HISTORY C16: perhaps special use of earlier *brat* rag, from Old English *bratt* cloak, of Celtic origin; related to Old Irish *bratt* cloth, BRAT[2]

brat[2] (bræt) NOUN *Northern English dialect* an apron or overall.
▷HISTORY from Old English *brat* cloak; related to Old Irish *bratt* cloth used to cover the body

Bratislava (,brætɪ'slɑːvə) NOUN the capital of Slovakia since 1918, a port on the River Danube; capital of Hungary (1541–1784) and seat of the Hungarian parliament until 1848. Pop.: 448 292 (2000 est.). German name: **Pressburg.** Hungarian name: **Pozsony.**

bratpack ('bræt,pæk) NOUN 1 a group of precocious and successful young actors, writers, etc. 2 a group of ill-mannered young people.
▸ **'brat,packer** NOUN

brattice ('brætɪs) NOUN 1 a partition of wood or treated cloth used to control ventilation in a mine. 2 *Medieval fortifications* a fixed wooden tower or parapet. ◆ VERB 3 (*tr*) *Mining* to fit with a brattice.
▷HISTORY C13: from Old French *bretesche* wooden tower, from Medieval Latin *breteschia*, probably from Latin *Britō* a Briton

brattishing ('brætɪʃɪŋ) NOUN *Architect* decorative work along the coping or on the cornice of a building.
▷HISTORY C16: variant of *bratticing*; see BRATTICE

bratwurst ('brɑːt,wɜːst; *German* 'braːtvurst) NOUN a type of small pork sausage.
▷HISTORY C20: German, from Old High German, from *brāto* meat + *wurst* sausage; related to Old Saxon *brādo* ham

braunite ('braʊnaɪt) NOUN a brown or black mineral that consists of manganese oxide and silicate and is a source of manganese. Formula: $3Mn_2O_3.MnSiO_3$.
▷HISTORY C19: named after A. E. *Braun* (1809–56), German official in the treasury at Gotha

bravado (brə'vɑːdəʊ) NOUN, *plural* **-does** *or* **-dos.** vaunted display of courage or self-confidence; swagger.
▷HISTORY C16: from Spanish *bravada* (modern *bravata*), from Old Italian *bravare* to challenge, provoke, from *bravo* wild, BRAVE

Bravais lattice (ˈbrævei, brəˈvei) NOUN *Crystallog* any of 14 possible space lattices found in crystals.
▷HISTORY named after Auguste *Bravais*, 19th-century French physicist

brave (breiv) ADJECTIVE 1 **a** having or displaying courage, resolution, or daring; not cowardly or timid. **b** (*as collective noun* preceded by *the*): *the brave*. 2 fine; splendid: *a brave sight; a brave attempt*. 3 *Archaic* excellent or admirable. ◆ NOUN 4 a warrior of a North American Indian tribe. 5 an obsolete word for **bully**[1]. ◆ VERB (*tr*) 6 to dare or defy: *to brave the odds*. 7 to confront with resolution or courage: *to brave the storm*. 8 *Obsolete* to make splendid, esp in dress.
▷HISTORY C15: from French, from Italian *bravo* courageous, wild, perhaps ultimately from Latin *barbarus* BARBAROUS
▸ˈ**bravely** ADVERB ▸ˈ**braveness** NOUN ▸ˈ**bravery** NOUN

bravissimo (brɑːˈvisiˌməʊ) INTERJECTION very well done! excellent!
▷HISTORY C18: from Italian, superlative of BRAVO

bravo INTERJECTION 1 (brɑːˈvəʊ) well done! ◆ NOUN 2 (brɑːˈvəʊ) (*plural* **-vos**) a cry of "bravo". 3 (ˈbrɑːvəʊ) (*plural* **-voes** *or* **-vos**) a hired killer or assassin.
▷HISTORY C18: from Italian: splendid!; see BRAVE

Bravo (ˈbrɑːvəʊ) NOUN *Communications* a code word for the letter *b*.

bravura (brəˈvjʊərə, -ˈvʊərə) NOUN 1 a display of boldness or daring. 2 *Music* **a** brilliance of execution. **b** (*as modifier*): *a bravura passage*.
▷HISTORY C18: from Italian: spirit, courage, from *bravare* to show off, see BRAVADO

braw (brɔː, brɑː) *Chiefly Scot* ◆ ADJECTIVE 1 fine or excellent, esp in appearance or dress. ◆ PLURAL NOUN 2 best clothes.
▷HISTORY C16: Scottish variant of BRAVE
▸ˈ**brawly** ADVERB

brawl[1] (brɔːl) NOUN 1 a loud disagreement or fight. 2 *US slang* an uproarious party. ◆ VERB (*intr*) 3 to quarrel or fight noisily; squabble. 4 (esp of water) to flow noisily.
▷HISTORY C14: probably related to Dutch *brallen* to boast, behave aggressively
▸ˈ**brawler** NOUN ▸ˈ**brawling** NOUN, ADJECTIVE

brawl[2] (brɔːl) NOUN a dance: the English version of the branle.

brawn (brɔːn) NOUN 1 strong well-developed muscles. 2 physical strength, esp as opposed to intelligence. 3 *Brit* a seasoned jellied loaf made from the head and sometimes the feet of a pig or calf.
▷HISTORY C14: from Old French *braon* slice of meat, of Germanic origin; compare Old High German *brāto*, Old English *brǣd* flesh

brawny (ˈbrɔːni) ADJECTIVE **brawnier, brawniest**. muscular and strong.
▸ˈ**brawnily** ADVERB ▸ˈ**brawniness** NOUN

Braxton Hicks contractions (ˈbrækstən ˈhiks) PLURAL NOUN painless intermittent contractions of the womb that occur in pregnancy, becoming stronger towards full term.
▷HISTORY C19: named after J. *Braxton Hicks* (1823–97), British obstetrician

braxy (ˈbræksi) NOUN an acute and usually fatal bacterial disease of sheep characterized by high fever, coma, and inflammation of the fourth stomach, caused by infection with *Clostridium septicum*.
▷HISTORY C18: of unknown origin

bray[1] (brei) VERB 1 (*intr*) (of a donkey) to utter its characteristic loud harsh sound; heehaw. 2 (*intr*) to make a similar sound, as in laughing: *he brayed at the joke*. 3 (*tr*) to utter with a loud harsh sound. ◆ NOUN 4 the loud harsh sound uttered by a donkey. 5 a similar loud cry or uproar: *a bray of protest*.
▷HISTORY C13: from Old French *braire*, probably of Celtic origin
▸ˈ**brayer** NOUN

bray[2] (brei) VERB 1 (*tr*) to distribute (ink) over printing type or plates. 2 (*tr*) to pound into a powder, as in a mortar. 3 *Northern English dialect* to hit or beat (someone or something) hard; bang.
▷HISTORY C14: from Old French *breier* of Germanic origin; see BREAK
▸ˈ**brayer** NOUN

Braz. ABBREVIATION FOR Brazil(ian).

braze[1] (breiz) VERB (*tr*) 1 to decorate with, make like, or make of brass. 2 to make like brass, as in hardness.
▷HISTORY Old English *bræsen*, from *bræs* BRASS

braze[2] (breiz) VERB 1 (*tr*) to make a joint between (two metal surfaces) by fusing a layer of brass or high-melting solder between them. ◆ 2 NOUN the high-melting solder or alloy used in brazing.
▷HISTORY C16: from Old French: to burn, of Germanic origin; see BRAISE
▸ˈ**brazer** NOUN

brazen (ˈbreizᵊn) ADJECTIVE 1 shameless and bold. 2 made of or resembling brass. 3 having a ringing metallic sound like that of a brass trumpet. ◆ VERB (*tr*) 4 (usually foll by *out* or *through*) to face and overcome boldly or shamelessly: *the witness brazened out the prosecutor's questions*. 5 to make (oneself, etc.) bold or brash.
▷HISTORY Old English *bræsen*, from *bræs* BRASS
▸ˈ**brazenly** ADVERB ▸ˈ**brazenness** NOUN

brazen-faced ADJECTIVE shameless and impudent.

brazier[1] *or* **brasier** (ˈbreiziə) NOUN a person engaged in brass-working or brass-founding.
▷HISTORY C14: from Old English *bræsian* to work in brass + -ER[1]
▸ˈ**braziery** NOUN

brazier[2] *or* **brasier** (ˈbreiziə) NOUN a portable metal receptacle for burning charcoal or coal, used for cooking, heating, etc.
▷HISTORY C17: from French *brasier*, from *braise* live coals; see BRAISE

brazil *or* **brasil** (brəˈzil) NOUN 1 Also called: **brazil wood**. the red wood obtained from various tropical leguminous trees of the genus *Caesalpinia*, such as *C. echinata* of America: used for cabinetwork. 2 the red or purple dye extracted from any of these woods. See also **brazilin**. 3 short for **brazil nut**.
▷HISTORY C14: from Old Spanish *brasil*, from *brasa* glowing coals, of Germanic origin; referring to the redness of the wood; see BRAISE

Brazil (brəˈzil) NOUN a republic in South America, comprising about half the area and half the population of South America: colonized by the Portuguese from 1500 onwards; became independent in 1822 and a republic in 1889; consists chiefly of the tropical Amazon basin in the north, semiarid scrub in the northeast, and a vast central tableland; an important producer of coffee and minerals, esp iron ore. Official language: Portuguese. Religion: Roman Catholic majority. Currency: real. Capital: Brasília. Pop.: 172 118 000 (2001 est.). Area: 8 511 957 sq. km (3 286 470 sq. miles).

brazilein *or* **brasilein** (brəˈziliin) NOUN a red crystalline solid obtained by the oxidation of brazilin and used as a dye. Formula: $C_{16}H_{12}O_5$.
▷HISTORY C19: from German *Brasilein*, from BRAZILIN

Brazilian (brəˈziljən) ADJECTIVE 1 of or relating to Brazil or its inhabitants. ◆ NOUN 2 a native or inhabitant of Brazil.

Brazilian bikini wax (brəˈziliən) NOUN the act or instance of removing all or almost all of a woman's pubic hair for cosmetic reasons.
▷HISTORY C20: reference to the popularity of this treatment in Brazil

brazilin *or* **brasilin** (ˈbræzilin) NOUN a pale yellow soluble crystalline solid, turning red in alkaline solution, extracted from brazil wood and sappanwood and used in dyeing and as an indicator. Formula: $C_{16}H_{14}O_5$.
▷HISTORY C19: from French *brésiline*, from *brésil* brazil wood

brazil nut NOUN 1 a tropical South American tree, *Bertholletia excelsa*, producing large globular capsules, each containing several closely packed triangular nuts: family *Lecythidaceae*. 2 the nut of this tree, having an edible oily kernel and a woody shell. ◆ Often shortened to: **brazil**.

Brazzaville (*French* brazavil) NOUN the capital of Congo-Brazzaville, in the south on the River Congo. Pop.: 937 579 (1995 est.).
▷HISTORY C19: named after Pierre de *Brazza* (1852–1905), French explorer

BRB *Text messaging* ABBREVIATION FOR be right back.

BRCS ABBREVIATION FOR British Red Cross Society.

BRE (in Britain) ABBREVIATION FOR Building Research Establishment.

breach (briːtʃ) NOUN 1 a crack, break, or rupture. 2 a breaking, infringement, or violation of a promise, obligation, etc. 3 any severance or separation: *there was a breach between the two factions of the party*. 4 a gap in an enemy's fortifications or line of defence created by bombardment or attack. 5 the act of a whale in breaking clear of the water. 6 the breaking of sea waves on a shore or rock. 7 an obsolete word for **wound**[1]. ◆ VERB 8 (*tr*) to break through or make an opening, hole, or incursion in. 9 (*tr*) to break a promise, law, etc. 10 (*intr*) (of a whale) to break clear of the water.
▷HISTORY Old English *bræc*; influenced by Old French *brèche*, from Old High German *brecha*, from *brechan* to BREAK

breach of promise NOUN *Law* (formerly) failure to carry out one's promise to marry.

breach of the peace NOUN *Law* an offence against public order causing an unnecessary disturbance of the peace.

breach of trust NOUN *Law* a violation of duty by a trustee or any other person in a fiduciary position.

bread (brɛd) NOUN 1 a food made from a dough of flour or meal mixed with water or milk, usually raised with yeast or baking powder and then baked. 2 necessary food; nourishment: *give us our daily bread*. 3 a slang word for **money**. 4 *Christianity* a small loaf, piece of bread, or wafer of unleavened bread used in the Eucharist. 5 **bread and circuses**. something offered as a means of distracting attention from a problem or grievance. 6 **break bread**. See **break** (sense 46). 7 **cast one's bread upon the waters**. to do good without expectation of advantage or return. 8 **to know which side one's bread is buttered**. to know what to do in order to keep one's advantages. 9 **take the bread out of (someone's) mouth**. to deprive (someone) of a livelihood. ◆ VERB 10 (*tr*) to cover with breadcrumbs before cooking: *breaded veal*.
▷HISTORY Old English *brēad*; related to Old Norse *braud*, Old Frisian *brād*, Old High German *brōt*

bread and butter *Informal* ◆ NOUN 1 a means of support or subsistence; livelihood: *the inheritance was their bread and butter*. ◆ MODIFIER 2 **bread-and-butter**. **a** providing a basic means of subsistence: *a bread-and-butter job*. **b** solid, reliable, or practical: *a bread-and-butter player*. **c** expressing gratitude, as for hospitality (esp in the phrase **bread-and-butter letter**).

bread and honey NOUN *Brit slang* money.
▷HISTORY C20: rhyming slang

breadbasket (ˈbrɛdˌbɑːskit) NOUN 1 a basket for carrying bread or rolls. 2 a slang word for **stomach**.

breadboard (ˈbrɛdˌbɔːd) NOUN 1 a wooden board on which dough is kneaded or bread is sliced. 2 an experimental arrangement of electronic circuits giving access to components so that modifications can be carried out easily.

breadcrumb (ˈbrɛdˌkrʌm) NOUN 1 the soft inner part of bread. 2 (*plural*) bread crumbled into small fragments, as for use in cooking. ◆ VERB (*tr*) 3 to coat (food) with breadcrumbs: *egg and breadcrumb the escalopes*.

breadfruit (ˈbrɛdˌfruːt) NOUN, *plural* **-fruits** *or* **-fruit**. 1 a moraceous tree, *Artocarpus communis* (or *A. altilis*), of the Pacific Islands, having large round edible starchy usually seedless, fruit. 2 the fruit of this tree, which is eaten baked or roasted and has a texture like bread.

bread-headed ADJECTIVE *Slang* greatly or excessively concerned about money.

breadline (ˈbrɛdˌlain) NOUN 1 a queue of people waiting for free food given out by a government agency or a charity organization. 2 **on the breadline**. impoverished; living at subsistence level.

bread mould *or* **black mould** NOUN a black saprotrophic zygomycete fungus, *Rhizopus nigricans*, occurring on decaying bread and vegetable matter.

breadnut (ˈbrɛdˌnʌt) NOUN 1 a moraceous tree, *Brosimum alicastrum*, of Central America and the Caribbean. 2 the nutlike fruit of this tree, ground to produce a substitute for wheat flour, esp in the West Indies.

breadroot (ˈbrɛdˌruːt) NOUN a leguminous plant, *Psoralea esculenta*, of central North America, having an edible starchy root. Also called: **prairie turnip**.

bread sauce NOUN a milk sauce thickened with

breadcrumbs and served with roast poultry, esp chicken.

breadth (brɛdθ, brɛtθ) NOUN [1] the linear extent or measurement of something from side to side; width. [2] a piece of fabric having a standard or definite width. [3] distance, extent, size, or dimension. [4] openness and lack of restriction, esp of viewpoint or interest; liberality.
▷HISTORY C16: from obsolete *brēde* (from Old English *brǣdu*, from *brād* BROAD) + -TH[1]; related to Gothic *braidei*, Old High German *breitī*

breadthways ('brɛdθˌweɪz, 'brɛtθ-) *or esp US* **breadthwise** ('brɛdθˌwaɪz, 'brɛtθ-) ADVERB from side to side.

breadwinner ('brɛdˌwɪnə) NOUN a person supporting a family with his or her earnings.
▸ **'bread,winning** NOUN, ADJECTIVE

break (breɪk) VERB **breaks, breaking, broke, broken.** [1] to separate or become separated into two or more pieces: *this cup is broken.* [2] to damage or become damaged so as to be inoperative: *my radio is broken.* [3] to crack or become cracked without separating. [4] to burst or cut the surface of (skin, etc.). [5] to discontinue or become discontinued: *they broke for lunch; to break a journey.* [6] to disperse or become dispersed: *the clouds broke.* [7] (*tr*) to fail to observe (an agreement, promise, law, etc.): *to break one's word.* [8] (foll by *with*) to discontinue an association (with). [9] to disclose or be disclosed: *he broke the news gently.* [10] (*tr*) to fracture (a bone) in (a limb, etc.). [11] (*tr*) to divide (something complete or perfect): *to break a set of books.* [12] to bring or come to an end: *the summer weather broke at last.* [13] (*tr*) to bring to an end by or as if by force: *to break a strike.* [14] (when *intr*, often foll by *out*) to escape (from): *he broke jail; he broke out of jail.* [15] to weaken or overwhelm or be weakened or overwhelmed, as in spirit. [16] (*tr*) to cut through or penetrate: *a cry broke the silence.* [17] (*tr*) to improve on or surpass: *to break a record.* [18] (*tr*; often foll by *in*) to accustom (a horse) to the bridle and saddle, to being ridden, etc. [19] (*tr*; often foll by *of*) to cause (a person) to give up (a habit): *this cure will break you of smoking.* [20] (*tr*) to weaken the impact or force of: *this net will break his fall.* [21] (*tr*) to decipher: *to break a code.* [22] (*tr*) to lose the order of: *to break ranks.* [23] (*tr*) to reduce to poverty or the state of bankruptcy. [24] (when *intr*, foll by *into*) to obtain, give, or receive smaller units in exchange for; change: *to break a pound note.* [25] (*tr*) *Chiefly military* to demote to a lower rank. [26] (*intr*; often foll by *from* or *out of*) to proceed suddenly. [27] (*intr*) to come into being: *light broke over the mountains.* [28] (*intr*; foll by *into* or *out into*) to burst into song, laughter, etc. [29] (*tr*) to open with explosives: *to break a safe.* [30] (*intr*) (of waves) **a** (often foll by *against*) to strike violently. **b** to collapse into foam or surf. [31] (*intr*) (esp of fish) to appear above the surface of the water. [32] (*intr*) (of the amniotic fluid surrounding an unborn baby) to be released when the amniotic sac ruptures in the first stage of labour: *her waters have broken.* [33] (*intr*) *Informal, chiefly US* to turn out in a specified manner: *things are breaking well.* [34] (*intr*) (of prices, esp stock exchange quotations) to fall sharply. [35] (*intr*) to make a sudden effort, as in running, horse racing, etc. [36] (*intr*) *Cricket* (of a ball) to change direction on bouncing. [37] (*tr*) *Cricket* (of a player) to knock down at least one bail from (a wicket). [38] (*intr*) *Billiards, snooker* to scatter the balls at the start of a game. [39] (*intr*) *Horse racing* to commence running in a race: *they broke even.* [40] (*intr*) *Boxing, wrestling* (of two fighters) to separate from a clinch. [41] (*intr*) *Music* **a** (of the male voice) to undergo a change in register, quality, and range at puberty. **b** (of the voice or some instruments) to undergo a change in tone, quality, etc., when changing registers. [42] (*intr*) *Phonetics* (of a vowel) to turn into a diphthong, esp. as a development in the language. [43] (*tr*) to open the breech of (certain firearms) by snapping the barrel away from the butt on its hinge. [44] (*tr*) to interrupt the flow of current in (an electrical circuit). Compare **make**[1] (sense 27). [45] (*intr*) *Informal, chiefly US* to become successful; make a breakthrough. [46] **break bread. a** to eat a meal, esp. with others. **b** *Christianity* to administer or participate in Holy Communion. [47] **break camp.** to pack up equipment and leave a camp. [48] **break (new) ground.** to do something that has not been done before. [49] **break one's back** *or* (*Slang*) **balls.** to overwork or work very hard. [50] **break the back of.** to complete the greatest or hardest part of (a task). [51] **break the bank.** to ruin financially or deplete the resources of a bank (as in gambling). [52] **break the ice. a** to relieve shyness or reserve, esp. between strangers. **b** to be the first of a group to do something. [53] **break the mould.** to make a change that breaks an established habit, pattern, etc. [54] **break service.** *Tennis* to win a game in which an opponent is serving. [55] **break wind.** to emit wind from the anus. ◆ NOUN [56] the act or result of breaking; fracture. [57] a crack formed as the result of breaking. [58] a brief respite or interval between two actions: *a break from one's toil.* [59] a sudden rush, esp. to escape: *to make a break for freedom.* [60] a breach in a relationship: *she has made a break from her family.* [61] any sudden interruption in a continuous action. [62] *Brit* a short period between classes at school. US and Canadian equivalent: **recess.** [63] *Informal* a fortunate opportunity, esp. to prove oneself. [64] *Informal* a piece of (good or bad) luck. [65] (esp. in a stock exchange) a sudden and substantial decline in prices. [66] *Prosody* a pause in a line of verse; caesura. [67] *Billiards, snooker* **a** a series of successful shots during one turn. **b** the points scored in such a series. [68] *Billiards, snooker* **a** the opening shot with the cue ball that scatters the placed balls. **b** the right to take this first shot. [69] Also called: **service break, break of serve.** *Tennis* the act or instance of breaking an opponent's service. [70] one of the intervals in a sporting contest. [71] *Horse racing* the start of a race: *an even break.* [72] (in tenpin bowling) failure to knock down all the pins after the second attempt. [73] **a** *Jazz* a short usually improvised solo passage. **b** an instrumental passage in a pop song. [74] a discontinuity in an electrical circuit. [75] access to a radio channel by a citizens' band operator. [76] a variant spelling of **brake**[1] (sense 6). ◆ INTERJECTION [77] *Boxing, wrestling* a command by a referee for two opponents to separate. ◆ See also **breakaway, break down, break even, break in, break into, break off, break out, break through, break up, break with.**
▷HISTORY Old English *brecan*; related to Old Frisian *breka*, Gothic *brikan*, Old High German *brehhan*, Latin *frangere* Sanskrit *bhráj* bursting forth

breakable ('breɪkəbᵊl) ADJECTIVE [1] capable of being broken. ◆ NOUN [2] (*usually plural*) a fragile easily broken article.

breakage ('breɪkɪdʒ) NOUN [1] the act or result of breaking. [2] the quantity or amount broken: *the total breakage was enormous.* [3] compensation or allowance for goods damaged while in use, transit, etc.

breakaway ('breɪkəˌweɪ) NOUN [1] **a** loss or withdrawal of a group of members from an association, club, etc. **b** (*as modifier*): *a breakaway faction.* [2] *Sport* **a** a sudden attack, esp from a defensive position, in football, hockey, etc. **b** an attempt to get away from the rest of the field in a race. [3] *Austral* a stampede of cattle, esp at the smell of water. ◆ VERB **break away.** (*intr, adverb*) [4] (often foll by *from*) to leave hastily or escape. [5] to withdraw or secede. [6] *Sport* to make a breakaway. [7] *Horse racing* to start prematurely.

breakbeat ('breɪkˌbiːt) NOUN a type of electronic dance music.

breakbone fever ('breɪkˌbəʊn) NOUN another name for **dengue.**

break dance NOUN [1] an acrobatic dance style originating in the 1980s. ◆ VERB **break-dance.** [2] (*intr*) to perform a break dance.
▸ **break dancer** NOUN ▸ **break dancing** NOUN

break down VERB (*adverb*) [1] (*intr*) to cease to function; become ineffective: *communications had broken down.* [2] to yield or cause to yield, esp to strong emotion or tears: *she broke down in anguish.* [3] (*tr*) to crush or destroy. [4] (*intr*) to have a nervous breakdown. [5] to analyse or be subjected to analysis. [6] to separate or cause to separate into simpler chemical elements; decompose. [7] (*tr*) *NZ* to saw (a large log) into planks. [8] **break it down.** *Austral and NZ informal* **a** stop it. **b** don't expect me to believe that; come off it. ◆ NOUN **breakdown.** [9] an act or instance of breaking down; collapse. [10] short for **nervous breakdown.** [11] an analysis or classification of something into its component parts: *he prepared a breakdown of the report.* [12] the sudden electrical discharge through an insulator or between two electrodes in a vacuum or gas discharge tube. [13] *Electrical engineering* the sudden transition, dependent on the bias magnitude, from a high to a low dynamic resistance in a semiconductor device. [14] a lively American country dance.

breakdown van *or* **truck** NOUN a motor vehicle equipped for towing away wrecked or disabled cars. US and Canadian names: **wrecker, tow truck.**

breaker[1] ('breɪkə) NOUN [1] a person or thing that breaks something, such as a person or firm that breaks up old cars, etc. [2] a large wave with a white crest on the open sea or one that breaks into foam on the shore. [3] *Electronics* short for **circuit breaker.** [4] a machine or plant for crushing rocks or coal. [5] Also called: **breaking plough.** a plough with a long shallow mouldboard for turning virgin land or sod land. [6] *Textiles* a machine for extracting fibre preparatory to carding. [7] an operator on citizens' band radio.

breaker[2] ('breɪkə) NOUN a small water cask for use in a boat.
▷HISTORY C19: anglicized variant of Spanish *barrica*, from French (Gascon dialect) *barrique*

break even VERB [1] (*intr, adverb*) to attain a level of activity, as in commerce, or a point of operation, as in gambling, at which there is neither profit nor loss. ◆ NOUN **breakeven.** [2] *Accounting* **a** the level of commercial activity at which the total cost and total revenue of a business enterprise are equal. **b** (*as modifier*): *breakeven prices.*

breakeven chart ('breɪkˌiːvᵊn) NOUN *Accounting* a graph measuring the value of an enterprise's revenue and costs against some index of its activity, such as percentage capacity. The intersection of the total revenue and total cost curves gives the breakeven point.

breakfast ('brɛkfəst) NOUN [1] **a** the first meal of the day. **b** (*as modifier*): *breakfast cereal; a breakfast room.* [2] the food at this meal. [3] (in the Caribbean) a midday meal. ◆ VERB [4] to eat or supply with breakfast.
▷HISTORY C15: from BREAK + FAST[2]
▸ **'breakfaster** NOUN

break feeding NOUN *NZ* the feeding of animals on paddocks where feeding space is controlled by the frequent movement of an electric fence.

breakfront ('breɪkˌfrʌnt) ADJECTIVE (*prenominal*) (of a bookcase, bureau, etc.) having a slightly projecting central section.

break in VERB (*adverb*) [1] (sometimes foll by *on*) to interrupt. [2] (*intr*) to enter a house, etc., illegally, esp by force. [3] (*tr*) to accustom (a person or animal) to normal duties or practice. [4] (*tr*) to use or wear (shoes, new equipment, etc.) until comfortable or running smoothly. [5] (*tr*) *Austral and NZ* to bring (new land) under cultivation. ◆ NOUN **break-in.** [6] **a** the illegal entering of a building, esp by thieves. **b** (*as modifier*): *the break-in plans.*

breaking ('breɪkɪŋ) NOUN *Linguistics* (in Old English, Old Norse, etc.) the change of a vowel into a diphthong.
▷HISTORY C19: translation of German *Brechung*

breaking and entering NOUN (formerly) the gaining of unauthorized access to a building with intent to commit a crime or, having committed the crime, the breaking out of the building.

breaking point NOUN [1] the point at which something or someone gives way under strain. [2] the moment of crisis in a situation.

break into VERB (*intr, preposition*) [1] to enter (a house, etc.) illegally, esp by force. [2] to change abruptly from a slower to a faster speed: *the horse broke into a gallop.* [3] to consume (supplies held in reserve): *at the end of the exercise the soldiers had to break into their iron rations.*

breakneck ('breɪkˌnɛk) ADJECTIVE (*prenominal*) (of speed, pace, etc.) excessive and dangerous.

break of day NOUN another term for **dawn** (sense 1).

break off VERB [1] to sever or detach or be severed or detached: *it broke off in my hands; he broke a piece off the bar of chocolate.* [2] (*adverb*) to end (a relationship, association, etc.) or (of a relationship, etc.) to be ended. [3] (*intr, adverb*) to stop abruptly; halt: *he broke off in the middle of his speech.* ◆ NOUN **breakoff.** [4] the act or an instance of breaking off or stopping.

break out VERB 1 (*intr, adverb*) to begin or arise suddenly: *panic broke out.* 2 (*intr, adverb*) to make an escape, esp from prison or confinement. 3 (*intr, adverb,* foll by *in*) (of the skin) to erupt (in a rash, pimples, etc.). 4 (*tr, adverb*) to launch or introduce (a new product). 5 (*tr, adverb*) to open and start using: *break out the champagne.* ◆ NOUN **break-out.** 6 an escape, esp from prison or confinement. 7 **a** a great success, esp following relatively disappointing performance. **b** (*as modifier*): *a breakout year.*

break-out group NOUN a group of people who detach themselves from a larger group or meeting in order to hold separate discussions.

breakpoint ('breɪk,pɔɪnt) NOUN *Computing* **a** an instruction inserted by a debug program causing a return to the debug program. **b** the point in a program at which such an instruction operates.

break point NOUN *Tennis* a point which allows the receiving player to break the service of the server.

break through VERB 1 (*intr*) to penetrate. 2 (*intr, adverb*) to achieve success, make a discovery, etc., esp after lengthy efforts. ◆ NOUN **breakthrough.** 3 a significant development or discovery, esp in science. 4 the penetration of an enemy's defensive position or line in depth and strength.

break up VERB (*adverb*) 1 to separate or cause to separate. 2 to put an end to (a relationship) or (of a relationship) to come to an end. 3 to dissolve or cause to dissolve; disrupt or be disrupted: *the meeting broke up at noon.* 4 (*intr*) *Brit* (of a school) to close for the holidays. 5 *Informal* to lose or cause to lose control of the emotions: *the news of his death broke her up.* 6 *Slang* to be or cause to be overcome with laughter. ◆ NOUN **break-up.** 7 a separation or disintegration.

break-up value NOUN *Commerce* 1 the value of an organization assuming that it will not continue to trade. 2 the value of a share in a company based only on the value of its assets.

breakwater ('breɪk,wɔːtə) NOUN 1 Also called: **mole.** a massive wall built out into the sea to protect a shore or harbour from the force of waves. 2 another name for **groyne.**

break with VERB (*intr, preposition*) to end a relationship or association with (someone or an organization or social group).

bream¹ (briːm; *Austral* brɪm) *or Austral* **brim** (brɪm) NOUN, *plural* **bream** *or* **brim.** 1 any of several Eurasian freshwater cyprinid fishes of the genus *Abramis*, esp *A. brama*, having a deep compressed body covered with silvery scales. 2 **white** *or* **silver bream.** a similar cyprinid, *Blicca bjoerkna.* 3 short for **sea bream.**
▷HISTORY C14: from Old French *bresme*, of Germanic origin; compare Old High German *brahsema*; perhaps related to *brehan* to glitter

bream² (briːm) VERB *Nautical* (formerly) to clean debris from (the bottom of a vessel) by heating to soften the pitch.
▷HISTORY C15: probably from Middle Dutch *bremme* broom; from using burning broom as a source of heat

breast (brɛst) NOUN 1 the front part of the body from the neck to the abdomen; chest. 2 either of the two soft fleshy milk-secreting glands on the chest in sexually mature human females. Related adjective: **mammary.** 3 a similar organ in certain other mammals. 4 anything that resembles a breast in shape or position: *the breast of the hill.* 5 a source of nourishment: *the city took the victims to its breast.* 6 the source of human emotions. 7 the part of a garment that covers the breast. 8 a projection from the side of a wall, esp that formed by a chimney. 9 *Mining* the face being worked at the end of a tunnel. 10 **beat one's breast.** to display guilt and remorse publicly or ostentatiously. 11 **make a clean breast of.** to make a confession of. ◆ VERB (*tr*) 12 to confront boldly; face: *breast the storm.* 13 to oppose with the breast or meet at breast level: *breasting the waves.* 14 to come alongside of: *breast the ship.* 15 to reach the summit of: *breasting the mountain top.*
▷HISTORY Old English *brēost*; related to Old Norse *brjōst*, Old High German *brust*, Dutch *borst*, Swedish *bräss*, Old Irish *brū* belly, body

breastbone ('brɛst,bəʊn) NOUN the nontechnical name for **sternum.**

breast-feed VERB **-feeds, -feeding, -fed.** to feed (a baby) with milk from the breast; suckle.
▸**'breast-,fed** ADJECTIVE ▸**'breast-,feeding** NOUN

breastpin ('brɛst,pɪn) NOUN a brooch worn on the breast, esp to close a garment.

breastplate ('brɛst,pleɪt) NOUN 1 a piece of armour covering the chest. 2 the strap of a harness covering a horse's breast. 3 *Judaism* an ornamental silver plate hung on the scrolls of the Torah. 4 *Old Testament* a square vestment ornamented with 12 precious stones, representing the 12 tribes of Israel, worn by the high priest when praying before the holy of holies. 5 *Zoology* a nontechnical name for **plastron.**

breast pump NOUN a device for extracting and collecting milk from the breast during lactation.

breaststroke ('brɛst,strəʊk) NOUN a swimming stroke in which the arms are extended in front of the head and swept back on either side while the legs are drawn up beneath the body and thrust back together.

breastwork ('brɛst,wɜːk) NOUN *Fortifications* a temporary defensive work, usually breast-high. Also called: **parapet.**

breath (brɛθ) NOUN 1 the intake and expulsion of air during respiration. 2 the air inhaled or exhaled during respiration. 3 a single respiration or inhalation of air, etc. 4 the vapour, heat, or odour of exhaled air: *his breath on the window melted the frost.* 5 a slight gust of air. 6 a short pause or rest: *take a breath for five minutes.* 7 a brief time: *it was done in a breath.* 8 a suggestion or slight evidence; suspicion: *a breath of scandal.* 9 a whisper or soft sound. 10 life, energy, or vitality: *the breath of new industry.* 11 *Phonetics* the passage of air through the completely open glottis without vibration of the vocal cords, as in exhaling or pronouncing fricatives such as (f) or (h) or stops such as (p) or (k). Compare **voice** (sense 11). 12 **a breath of fresh air.** a refreshing change from what one is used to. 13 **catch one's breath.** to rest until breathing is normal, esp after exertion. 14 **hold one's breath.** to wait expectantly or anxiously. 15 **in the same breath.** done or said at the same time. 16 **out of breath.** gasping for air after exertion. 17 **save one's breath.** to refrain from useless talk. 18 **take one's breath away.** to overwhelm with surprise, etc. 19 **under** or **below one's breath.** in a quiet voice or whisper.
▷HISTORY Old English *brǣth*; related to *brǣdan* to burn, Old High German *brādam* heat, breath

breathable ('briːðəbᵊl) ADJECTIVE 1 (of air) fit to be breathed. 2 (of a material) allowing air to pass through so that perspiration can evaporate.

breathalyse *or US* **breathalyze** ('brɛθə,laɪz) VERB (*tr*) to apply a Breathalyser test to (someone).

Breathalyser *or* **Breathalyzer** ('brɛθə,laɪzə) NOUN *Trademark* a device for estimating the amount of alcohol in the breath: used in testing people suspected of driving under the influence of alcohol.
▷HISTORY C20: BREATH + (AN)ALYSER

breatharian (,brɛθ'ɛərɪən) NOUN 1 a person who believes that it is possible to subsist healthily on air alone. ◆ ADJECTIVE 2 of or relating to a breatharian: *a breatharian purification programme.*
▸**breath'arian,ism** NOUN

breathe (briːð) VERB 1 to take in oxygen from (the surrounding medium, esp air) and give out carbon dioxide; respire. 2 (*intr*) to exist; be alive: *every animal that breathes on earth.* 3 (*intr*) to rest to regain breath, composure, etc.: *stop your questions, and give me a chance to breathe.* 4 (*intr*) (esp of air) to blow lightly: *the wind breathed through the trees.* 5 (*intr*) *Machinery* **a** to take in air, esp for combustion: *the engine breathes through this air filter.* **b** to equalize the pressure within a container, chamber, etc., with atmospheric pressure: *the crankcase breathes through this duct.* 6 (*tr*) *Phonetics* to articulate (a speech sound) without vibration of the vocal cords. Compare **voice** (sense 19). 7 to exhale or emit: *the dragon breathed fire.* 8 (*tr*) to impart; instil: *to breathe confidence into the actors.* 9 (*tr*) to speak softly; whisper: *to breathe words of love.* 10 (*tr*) to permit to rest: *to breathe a horse.* 11 (*intr*) (of a material) to allow air to pass through so that perspiration can evaporate. 12 **breathe again, freely** *or* **easily.** to feel relief: *I could breathe again after passing the exam.* 13 **breathe down (someone's) neck.** to stay close to (someone), esp to oversee what they are doing. 14 **breathe one's last.** to die or be finished or defeated.
▷HISTORY C13: from BREATH

breathed (brɛθt, briːðd) ADJECTIVE *Phonetics* relating to or denoting a speech sound for whose articulation the vocal cords are not made to vibrate. Compare **voiced.**

breather ('briːðə) NOUN 1 *Informal* a short pause for rest. 2 a person who breathes in a specified way: *a deep breather.* 3 a vent in a container to equalize internal and external pressure, such as the pipe in the crankcase of an internal-combustion engine. 4 a small opening in a room, container, cover, etc., supplying air for ventilation.

breathing ('briːðɪŋ) NOUN 1 the passage of air into and out of the lungs to supply the body with oxygen. 2 a single breath: *a breathing between words.* 3 an utterance: *a breathing of hate.* 4 a soft movement, esp of air. 5 a rest or pause. 6 *Phonetics* **a** expulsion of breath (**rough breathing**) or absence of such expulsion (**smooth breathing**) preceding the pronunciation of an initial vowel or rho in ancient Greek. **b** either of two symbols indicating this.

breathing space NOUN 1 enough area to permit freedom of movement: *the country gives us some breathing space.* 2 a pause for rest, etc.: *a coffee break was their only breathing space.*

breathless ('brɛθlɪs) ADJECTIVE 1 out of breath; gasping, etc. 2 holding one's breath or having it taken away by excitement, etc.: *a breathless confrontation.* 3 (esp of the atmosphere) motionless and stifling. 4 *Rare* lifeless; dead.
▸**'breathlessly** ADVERB ▸**'breathlessness** NOUN

breathtaking ('brɛθ,teɪkɪŋ) ADJECTIVE causing awe or excitement: *a breathtaking view.*
▸**'breath,takingly** ADVERB

breath test NOUN *Brit* a chemical test of a driver's breath to determine the amount of alcohol he has consumed.

breathy ('brɛθɪ) ADJECTIVE **breathier, breathiest.** 1 (of the speaking voice) accompanied by an audible emission of breath. 2 (of the singing voice) lacking resonance.
▸**'breathily** ADVERB ▸**'breathiness** NOUN

breccia ('brɛtʃɪə) NOUN a rock consisting of angular fragments embedded in a finer matrix, formed by erosion, impact, volcanic activity, etc.
▷HISTORY C18: from Italian, from Old High German *brecha* a fragment; see BREACH
▸**'brecci,ated** ADJECTIVE

Brechtian ('brɛxtɪən) ADJECTIVE 1 of or relating to Bertolt Brecht, the German dramatist, theatrical producer, and poet (1898–1956). ◆ NOUN 2 a follower or admirer of Brecht.

Brecon ('brɛkən) *or* **Brecknock** ('brɛknɒk) NOUN 1 a town in SE Wales, in Powys: textile and leather industries. Pop.: 7523 (1991). 2 short for **Breconshire.**

Breconshire ('brɛkən,ʃɪə, -ʃə) *or* **Brecknockshire** ('brɛknɒk,ʃɪə, -ʃə) NOUN (until 1974) a county of SE Wales, now mainly in Powys: over half its area forms the **Brecon Beacons National Park.**

bred (brɛd) VERB 1 the past tense and past participle of **breed.** ◆ NOUN 2 *Austral slang* a person who lives in a small remote place.
▷HISTORY sense 2: diminutive form of *inbred*

Breda ('briːdə; *Dutch* bre'daː) NOUN a city in the S Netherlands, in North Brabant province: residence of Charles II of England during his exile. Pop.: 159 042 (1999 est.).

brede (briːd) NOUN, VERB an archaic spelling of **braid¹.**

bredie ('briːdɪ) NOUN *South African* a meat and vegetable stew.
▷HISTORY C19: from Portuguese *bredo* ragout

bree¹ *or* **brie** (briː) NOUN *Scot* broth, stock, or juice.
▷HISTORY Old English *brīg*, variant of *brīw* pottage; related to Old High German *brīo* soup, Old English *brīwan* to cook, Middle Irish *brēo* flame

bree² (briː) NOUN a Scot word for **brunt.**
▷HISTORY C19: perhaps from earlier *bree* brow

breech NOUN (briːtʃ) 1 the lower dorsal part of the human trunk; buttocks; rump. 2 the lower part or bottom of something: *the breech of the bridge.*

3 the lower portion of a pulley block, esp the part to which the rope or chain is secured. 4 the part of a firearm behind the barrel or bore. 5 *Obstetrics* short for **breech delivery.** ◆ VERB (briːtʃ, brɪtʃ) (*tr*) 6 to fit (a gun) with a breech. 7 *Archaic* to clothe in breeches or any other clothing. ◆ See also **breeches.**
▷HISTORY Old English *brēc*, plural of *brōc* leg covering; related to Old Norse *brōk*, Old High German *bruoh*

> **Language note** *Breech* is sometimes wrongly used as a verb where *breach* is meant: *the barrier/agreement was breached* (not *breeched*).

breechblock (ˈbriːtʃˌblɒk) NOUN a metal block in breech-loading firearms that is withdrawn to insert the cartridge and replaced to close the breech before firing.

breechcloth (ˈbriːtʃˌklɒθ) *or* **breechclout** (ˈbriːtʃˌklaʊt) NOUN other names for **loincloth.**

breech delivery NOUN birth of a baby with the feet or buttocks appearing first.

breeches (ˈbrɪtʃɪz, ˈbriː-) PLURAL NOUN 1 trousers extending to the knee or just below, worn for riding, mountaineering, etc. 2 *Informal or dialect* any trousers. 3 **too big for one's breeches.** conceited; unduly self-confident.

breeches buoy NOUN a ring-shaped life buoy with a support in the form of a pair of short breeches, in which a person is suspended for safe transfer from a ship.

breeching (ˈbrɪtʃɪŋ, ˈbriː-) NOUN 1 the strap of a harness that passes behind a horse's haunches. 2 *Naval* (formerly) the rope used to check the recoil run of a ship's guns or to secure them against rough weather. 3 the parts comprising the breech of a gun.

breech-loader (ˈbriːtʃˌləʊdə) NOUN a firearm that is loaded at the breech.

breech-loading (ˈbriːtʃˌləʊdɪŋ) ADJECTIVE (of a firearm) loaded at the breech.

breed (briːd) VERB **breeds, breeding, bred.** 1 to bear (offspring). 2 (*tr*) to bring up; raise. 3 to produce or cause to produce by mating; propagate. 4 to produce and maintain new or improved strains of (domestic animals and plants). 5 to produce or be produced; generate: *to breed trouble; violence breeds in densely populated areas.* ◆ NOUN 6 a group of organisms within a species, esp a group of domestic animals, originated and maintained by man and having a clearly defined set of characteristics. 7 a lineage or race: *a breed of Europeans.* 8 a kind, sort, or group: *a special breed of hatred.*
▷HISTORY Old English *brēdan*, of Germanic origin; related to BROOD

breeder (ˈbriːdə) NOUN 1 a person who breeds plants or animals. 2 something that reproduces, esp to excess: *rabbits are persistent breeders.* 3 an animal kept for breeding purposes. 4 a source or cause: *a breeder of discontent.* 5 short for **breeder reactor.**

breeder reactor NOUN a type of nuclear reactor that produces more fissionable material than it consumes. Compare **converter reactor.** See also **fast-breeder reactor.**

breeding (ˈbriːdɪŋ) NOUN 1 the process of bearing offspring; reproduction. 2 the process of producing plants or animals by sexual reproduction. 3 the result of good training, esp the knowledge of correct social behaviour; refinement: *a man of breeding.* 4 a person's line of descent: *his breeding was suspect.* 5 *Physics* a process occurring in a nuclear reactor as a result of which more fissionable material is produced than is used up.

Breed's Hill (briːdz) NOUN a hill in E Massachusetts, adjoining Bunker Hill: site of the Battle of Bunker Hill (1775).

breeks (briːks) PLURAL NOUN *Scot* trousers.
▷HISTORY Scot variant of BREECHES

breenge *or* **breinge** (briːndʒ) *Scot* ◆ VERB (*intr*) 1 to lunge forward; move violently or dash. ◆ NOUN 2 a violent movement.
▷HISTORY of unknown origin

breeze[1] (briːz) NOUN 1 a gentle or light wind. 2 *Meteorol* a wind of force two to six inclusive on the Beaufort scale. 3 *Informal* an easy task or state of ease: *being happy here is a breeze.* 4 *Informal, chiefly Brit* a disturbance, esp a lively quarrel. 5 **shoot the breeze.** *Informal* to chat. ◆ VERB (*intr*) 6 to move quickly or casually: *he breezed into the room.* 7 (of wind) to blow: *the south wind breezed over the fields.*
▷HISTORY C16: probably from Old Spanish *briza* northeast wind

breeze[2] (briːz) NOUN an archaic or dialect name for the **gadfly.**
▷HISTORY Old English *briosa*, of unknown origin

breeze[3] (briːz) NOUN ashes of coal, coke, or charcoal used to make breeze blocks.
▷HISTORY C18: from French *braise* live coals; see BRAISE

breeze block NOUN a light building brick made from the ashes of coal, coke, etc., bonded together by cement and used esp for walls that bear relatively small loads. Usual US names: **cinder block, clinker block.**

breezeway (ˈbriːzˌweɪ) NOUN a roofed passageway connecting two buildings, sometimes with the sides enclosed.

breezy (ˈbriːzɪ) ADJECTIVE **breezier, breeziest.** 1 fresh; windy: *a breezy afternoon.* 2 casual or carefree; lively; light-hearted: *her breezy nature.* 3 lacking substance; light: *a breezy conversation.*
▸ˈ**breezily** ADVERB ▸ˈ**breeziness** NOUN

bregma (ˈbrɛgmə) NOUN, *plural* **-mata** (-mətə). the point on the top of the skull where the coronal and sagittal sutures meet: in infants this corresponds to the anterior fontanelle.
▷HISTORY C16: New Latin from Greek: front part of the head

brei (breɪ) VERB **breis, breiing, breid.** (*intr*) *South African informal* to speak with a uvular *r*, esp in Afrikaans. Also: **brey.** Compare **burr**[2].
▷HISTORY C20: from Afrikaans; compare BRAY[1]

breid (briːd) NOUN a Scot word for **bread.**

breist *or* **breest** (briːst) NOUN a Scot word for **breast.**

brekky (ˈbrɛkɪ) NOUN a slang word for **breakfast.**

Bremen (ˈbreɪmən) NOUN 1 a state of NW Germany, centred on the city of Bremen and its outport Bremerhaven; formerly in West Germany. Pop.: 663 100 (2000 est.). Area: 404 sq. km (156 sq. miles). 2 an industrial city and port in NW Germany, on the Weser estuary. Pop.: 542 300 (1999 est.).

Bremerhaven (*German* breːmərˈhaːfən) NOUN a port in NW Germany: an outport for Bremen. Pop.: 123 800 (1999 est.). Former name (until 1947): **Wesermünde.**

bremsstrahlung (ˈbrɛmzˌʃtrɑːləŋ) NOUN the radiation produced when an electrically charged particle, especially an electron, is slowed down by the electric field of an atomic nucleus or an atomic ion.
▷HISTORY C20: German: braking radiation

Bren gun (brɛn) NOUN an air-cooled gas-operated light machine gun taking .303 calibre ammunition: used by British and Commonwealth forces in World War II.
▷HISTORY C20: after *Br(no)*, now in the Czech Republic, where it was first made and *En(field)*, England, where manufacture was continued

Brenner Pass (ˈbrɛnə) NOUN a pass over the E Alps, between Austria and Italy. Highest point: 1372 m (4501 ft.).

Brent (brɛnt) NOUN a borough of NW Greater London. Pop.: 263 463 (2001). Area: 44 sq. km (17 sq. miles).

brent goose (brɛnt) NOUN a small goose, *Branta bernicla*, that has a dark grey plumage and short neck and occurs in most northern coastal regions. also called: **brent,** (esp US and Canadian) **brant.**
▷HISTORY C16: perhaps of Scandinavian origin; compare Old Norse *brandgās* sheldrake

Brentwood (ˈbrɛntˌwʊd) NOUN a residential town in SE England, in SW Essex near London. Pop.: 49 463 (1991).

br'er (brɜː, brɛə) NOUN *Southern African-American dialect* brother: usually prefixed to a name: *Br'er Jones.*

Brescia (*Italian* ˈbreʃʃa) NOUN a city in N Italy, in Lombardy: at its height in the 16th century. Pop.: 191 317 (2000 est.). Ancient name: **Brixia** (ˈbrɪksɪə).

Breslau (ˈbrɛzlaʊ) NOUN the German name for **Wrocław.**

Brest (brɛst) NOUN 1 a port in NW France, in Brittany: chief naval station of the country, planned by Richelieu in 1631 and fortified by Vauban. Pop.: 149 634 (1999). 2 a city in SW Belarus: Polish until 1795 and from 1921 to 1945. Pop.: 297 000 (1998 est.). Former name (until 1921): **Brest Litovsk** (brɛst lɪˈtɔfsk). Polish name: **Brześć nad Bugiem.**

Bretagne (brətaɲ) NOUN the French name for **Brittany.**

brethren (ˈbrɛðrɪn) PLURAL NOUN *Archaic except when referring to fellow members of a religion, sect, society, etc* a plural of **brother.**

Breton (ˈbrɛtᵊn; *French* brətɔ̃) ADJECTIVE 1 of, relating to, or characteristic of Brittany, its people, or their language. ◆ NOUN 2 a native or inhabitant of Brittany, esp one who speaks the Breton language. 3 the indigenous language of Brittany, belonging to the Brythonic subgroup of the Celtic family of languages.

Bretton Woods Conference (ˈbrɛtᵊn) NOUN an international monetary conference held in 1944 at Bretton Woods in New Hampshire, which resulted in the establishment of the World Bank and the International Monetary Fund.

breunnerite (ˈbrɔɪnəˌraɪt) NOUN an iron-containing type of magnesite used in the manufacture of refractory bricks.
▷HISTORY C19: named after Count *Breunner*, Austrian nobleman, + -ITE[1]

breve (briːv) NOUN 1 an accent, (˘), placed over a vowel to indicate that it is of short duration or is pronounced in a specified way. 2 *Music* a note, now rarely used, equivalent in time value to two semibreves. 3 *RC Church* a less common word for **brief** (papal letter).
▷HISTORY C13: from Medieval Latin *breve*, from Latin *brevis* short; see BRIEF

brevet (ˈbrɛvɪt) NOUN 1 a document entitling a commissioned officer to hold temporarily a higher military rank without the appropriate pay and allowances. ◆ VERB **-vets, -vetting, -vetted** *or* **-vets, -veting, -veted.** 2 (*tr*) to promote by brevet.
▷HISTORY C14: from Old French *brievet* a little letter, from *brief* letter; see BRIEF
▸ˈ**brevetcy** NOUN

breviary (ˈbriːvjərɪ) NOUN, *plural* **-ries.** 1 *RC Church* a book of psalms, hymns, prayers, etc., to be recited daily by clerics in major orders and certain members of religious orders as part of the divine office. 2 a similar book in the Orthodox Church.
▷HISTORY C16: from Latin *breviārium* an abridged version, from *breviāre* to shorten, from *brevis* short

brevier (brəˈvɪə) NOUN (formerly) a size of printer's type approximately equal to 8 point.
▷HISTORY C16: probably from Dutch, literally: BREVIARY; so called because this type size was used for breviaries

brevity (ˈbrɛvɪtɪ) NOUN, *plural* **-ties.** 1 conciseness of expression; lack of verbosity. 2 a short duration; brief time.
▷HISTORY C16: from Latin *brevitās* shortness, from *brevis* BRIEF

brew[1] (bruː) VERB 1 to make (beer, ale, etc.) from malt and other ingredients by steeping, boiling, and fermentation. 2 to prepare (a drink, such as tea) by boiling or infusing. 3 (*tr*) to devise or plan: *to brew a plot.* 4 (*intr*) to be in the process of being brewed: *the tea was brewing in the pot.* 5 (*intr*) to be impending or forming: *there's a storm brewing.* ◆ NOUN 6 a beverage produced by brewing, esp tea or beer: *a strong brew.* 7 an instance or time of brewing: *last year's brew.* 8 a mixture: *an eclectic brew of mysticism and political discontent.* See also **brew up.**
▷HISTORY Old English *brēowan*; related to Old Norse *brugga*, Old Saxon *breuwan*, Old High German *briuwan*
▸ˈ**brewer** NOUN

brew[2] (bruː) NOUN *Northern English dialect* a hill.

brewage (ˈbruːɪdʒ) NOUN 1 a product of brewing; brew. 2 the process of brewing.

brewer's grain NOUN an exhausted malt occurring as a by-product of brewing and used as a feedstuff for cattle, pigs, and sheep.

brewer's yeast NOUN 1 a yeast, *Saccharomyces*

cerevisiae, used in brewing. See **yeast** (sense 3). 2 yeast obtained as a by-product of brewing.

brewery ('brʊərɪ) NOUN, *plural* **-eries**. a place where beer, ale, etc., is brewed.

brewing ('bruːɪŋ) NOUN a quantity of a beverage brewed at one time.

brewis ('bruːɪs) *or* **brevis** ('brɛvɪs) NOUN *Dialect, chiefly northern English, Canadian, and US* 1 bread soaked in broth, gravy, etc. 2 thickened broth. 3 (bruːz) *Canadian* a Newfoundland stew of cod or pork, hardtack, and potatoes.
▷**HISTORY** C16: from Old French *broez*, from *broet*, diminutive of *breu* BROTH

brewpub ('bruːˌpʌb) NOUN a pub that incorporates a brewery on its premises.

brew up *Brit and NZ informal* ◆ VERB (*intr, adverb*) 1 to make tea, esp out of doors or in informal circumstances. ◆ NOUN **brew-up.** 2 a making of tea.

brey (breɪ) VERB (*intr*) *South African informal* a variant spelling of **brei.**

briar[1] *or* **brier** ('braɪə) NOUN 1 Also called: **tree heath.** an ericaceous shrub, *Erica arborea*, of S Europe, having a hard woody root (briarroot). 2 a tobacco pipe made from the root of this plant.
▷**HISTORY** C19: from French *bruyère* heath, from Late Latin *brūcus*, of Gaulish origin
▸'**briary** *or* '**briery** ADJECTIVE

briar[2] ('braɪə) NOUN a variant spelling of **brier**[1].

briard (briːˈɑːd, briːˈɑː) NOUN a medium-sized dog of an ancient French sheep-herding breed having a long rough coat of a single colour.
▷**HISTORY** French, literally: of *Brie* (region in N France)

Briareus (braɪˈɛərɪəs) NOUN *Greek myth* a giant with a hundred arms and fifty heads who aided Zeus and the Olympians against the Titans.
▸**Bri'arean** ADJECTIVE

briarroot *or* **brierroot** ('braɪəˌruːt) NOUN 1 the hard woody root of the briar, used for making tobacco pipes. 2 any of several other woods used to make tobacco pipes. Also called: **briarwood, brierwood.**

bribe (braɪb) VERB 1 to promise, offer, or give something, usually money, to (a person) to procure services or gain influence, esp illegally. ◆ NOUN 2 a reward, such as money or favour, given or offered for this purpose. 3 any persuasion or lure. 4 a length of flawed or damaged cloth removed from the main piece.
▷**HISTORY** C14: from Old French *briber* to beg, of obscure origin
▸'**bribable** *or* '**bribeable** ADJECTIVE ▸'**briber** NOUN

bribery ('braɪbərɪ) NOUN, *plural* **-eries**. the process of giving or taking bribes.

bric-a-brac ('brɪkəˌbræk) NOUN miscellaneous small objects, esp furniture and curios, kept because they are ornamental or rare.
▷**HISTORY** C19: from French; phrase based on *bric* piece

bricht (brixt) ADJECTIVE a Scot word for **bright.**

brick (brɪk) NOUN 1 **a** a rectangular block of clay mixed with sand and fired in a kiln or baked by the sun, used in building construction. **b** (*as modifier*): *a brick house.* 2 the material used to make such blocks. 3 any rectangular block: *a brick of ice.* 4 bricks collectively. 5 *Informal* a reliable, trustworthy, or helpful person. 6 *Brit* a child's building block. 7 short for **brick red.** 8 **drop a brick.** *Brit informal* to make a tactless or indiscreet remark. 9 **like a ton of bricks.** *Informal* (used esp of the manner of punishing or reprimanding someone) with great force; severely: *when he spotted my mistake he came down on me like a ton of bricks.* ◆ VERB (*tr*) 10 (usually foll by *in, up* or *over*) to construct, line, pave, fill, or wall up with bricks: *to brick up a window; brick over a patio.* 11 *Slang* to attack (a person) with a brick or bricks.
▷**HISTORY** C15: from Old French *brique*, from Middle Dutch *bricke*; related to Middle Low German *brike*, Old English *brecan* to BREAK

brickbat ('brɪkˌbæt) NOUN 1 a piece of brick or similar material, esp one used as a weapon. 2 blunt criticism: *the critic threw several brickbats at the singer.*

brickearth ('brɪkˌɜːθ) NOUN a clayey alluvium suitable for the making of bricks: specifically, such a deposit in southern England, yielding a fertile soil.

brickie *or* **bricky** ('brɪkɪ) NOUN *Brit informal* a bricklayer.

bricking ('brɪkɪŋ) NOUN *Austral slang* the falsification of evidence in order to bring a criminal charge.

bricklayer ('brɪkˌleɪə) NOUN a person trained or skilled in laying bricks.

bricklaying ('brɪkˌleɪɪŋ) NOUN the technique or practice of laying bricks.

brick red NOUN, ADJECTIVE **a** a reddish-brown colour. **b** (*as adjective*): *a brick-red carpet.*

bricks and clicks NOUN 1 a combination of traditional business carried out on physical premises and Internet trading. ◆ MODIFIER **bricks-and-clicks.** 2 combining traditional business carried out on physical premises and Internet trading: *bricks-and-clicks companies.*
▷**HISTORY** C20: from BRICKS AND MORTAR and *click*, meaning an act of pressing and releasing a computer mouse button

bricks and mortar NOUN 1 **a** a building or buildings: *he invested in bricks and mortar rather than stocks and shares.* **b** (*modifier*). **bricks-and-mortar.** 2 a physical business premises rather than an Internet presence: *bricks-and-mortar firms.*

brick veneer NOUN (in Australia) a timber-framed house with a brick exterior.

brickwork ('brɪkˌwɜːk) NOUN 1 a structure, such as a wall, built of bricks. 2 construction using bricks.

bricky ('brɪkɪ) ADJECTIVE 1 made of bricks, or like a brick. ◆ NOUN 2 a variant spelling of **brickie.**

brickyard ('brɪkˌjɑːd) NOUN a place in which bricks are made, stored, or sold.

bricolage ('brɪkəˌlɑːʒ; *French* brikɔlaʒ) NOUN *Architect* 1 the jumbled effect produced by the close proximity of buildings from different periods and in different architectural styles. 2 the deliberate creation of such an effect in certain modern developments: *the post-modernist bricolage of the new shopping centre.*

bricole (brɪˈkəʊl, 'brɪkᵊl) NOUN 1 *Billiards* a shot in which the cue ball touches a cushion after striking the object ball and before touching another ball. 2 (in ancient and medieval times) a military catapult for throwing stones, etc. 3 (esp formerly) a harness worn by soldiers for dragging guns or carrying stretchers. 4 an indirect or unexpected action.
▷**HISTORY** C16: from Old French: catapult, from Medieval Latin *bricola*, of uncertain origin

bridal ('braɪdᵊl) ADJECTIVE 1 of or relating to a bride or a wedding; nuptial. ◆ NOUN 2 *Obsolete* a wedding or wedding feast.
▷**HISTORY** Old English *brȳdealu*, literally: "bride ale", that is, wedding feast

bridal wreath NOUN any of several N temperate rosaceous shrubs of the genus *Spiraea*, esp *S. prunifolia*, cultivated for their sprays of small white flowers.

bride[1] (braɪd) NOUN a woman who has just been or is about to be married.
▷**HISTORY** Old English *brȳd*; related to Old Norse *brūthr*, Gothic *brūths* daughter-in-law, Old High German *brūt*

bride[2] (braɪd) NOUN *Lacemaking, needlework* a thread or loop that joins parts of a pattern. Also called: **bar.**
▷**HISTORY** C19: from French, literally: BRIDLE, probably of Germanic origin

bridegroom ('braɪdˌɡruːm, -ˌɡrʊm) NOUN a man who has just been or is about to be married.
▷**HISTORY** C14: changed (through influence of GROOM) from Old English *brȳdguma*, from *brȳd* BRIDE[1] + *guma* man; related to Old Norse *brūthgumi*, Old High German *brūtigomo*

bride price *or* **wealth** NOUN (in some societies) money, property, or services given by a bridegroom to the kinsmen of his bride in order to establish his rights over the woman.

bridesmaid ('braɪdzˌmeɪd) NOUN a girl or young unmarried woman who attends a bride at her wedding. Compare **matron of honour, maid of honour.**

bridewell ('braɪdˌwɛl, -wəl) NOUN a house of correction; jail, esp for minor offences.
▷**HISTORY** C16: after *Bridewell* (originally, *St Bride's Well*), a house of correction in London

bridge[1] (brɪdʒ) NOUN 1 a structure that spans and provides a passage over a road, railway, river, or some other obstacle. 2 something that resembles this in shape or function: *his letters provided a bridge across the centuries.* 3 **a** the hard ridge at the upper part of the nose, formed by the underlying nasal bones. **b** any anatomical ridge or connecting structure. Compare **pons.** 4 the part of a pair of glasses that rests on the nose. 5 Also called: **bridgework.** a dental plate containing one or more artificial teeth that is secured to the surrounding natural teeth. 6 a platform athwartships and above the rail, from which a ship is piloted and navigated. 7 a piece of wood, usually fixed, supporting the strings of a violin, guitar, etc., and transmitting their vibrations to the sounding board. 8 Also called: **bridge passage.** a passage in a musical, literary, or dramatic work linking two or more important sections. 9 Also called: **bridge circuit.** *Electronics* any of several networks, such as a Wheatstone bridge, consisting of two branches across which a measuring device is connected. The resistance, capacitance, etc., of one component can be determined from the known values of the others when the voltage in each branch is balanced. 10 *Computing* a device that connects networks and sends packets between them. 11 *Billiards, snooker* **a** a support for a cue made by placing the fingers on the table and raising the thumb. **b** a cue rest with a notched end for shots beyond normal reach. 12 *Theatre* **a** a platform of adjustable height above or beside the stage for the use of stagehands, light operators, etc. **b** *Chiefly Brit* a part of the stage floor that can be raised or lowered. 13 a partition in a furnace or boiler to keep the fuel in place. 14 **build bridges.** to promote reconciliation or cooperation between hostile groups or people. 15 **burn one's bridges.** See **burn**[1] (sense 19). 16 **cross a bridge when (one) comes to it.** to deal with a problem only when it arises; not to anticipate difficulties. ◆ VERB (*tr*) 17 to build or provide a bridge over something; span: *to bridge a river.* 18 to connect or reduce the distance between: *let us bridge our differences.*
▷**HISTORY** Old English *brycg*; related to Old Norse *bryggja* gangway, Old Frisian *bregge*, Old High German *brucka*, Danish, Swedish *bro*
▸'**bridgeable** ADJECTIVE ▸'**bridgeless** ADJECTIVE

bridge[2] (brɪdʒ) NOUN a card game for four players, based on whist, in which one hand (the dummy) is exposed and the trump suit decided by bidding between the players. See also **contract bridge, duplicate bridge, rubber bridge, auction bridge.**
▷**HISTORY** C19: of uncertain origin, but compare Turkish *bir-üç* (unattested phrase) one-three (said perhaps to refer to the one exposed hand and the three players' hands)

bridgeboard ('brɪdʒˌbɔːd) NOUN a board on both sides of a staircase that is cut to support the treads and risers. Also called: **cut string.**

bridgehead ('brɪdʒˌhɛd) NOUN *Military* 1 an area of ground secured or to be taken on the enemy's side of an obstacle, esp a defended river. 2 a fortified or defensive position at the end of a bridge nearest to the enemy. 3 an advantageous position gained for future expansion.

Bridgend (ˌbrɪdʒˈɛnd) NOUN a county borough in S Wales, created in 1996 from S Mid Glamorgan. Administrative centre: Bridgend. Pop.: 128 650 (2001). Area: 264 sq. km (102 sq. miles).

Bridge of Sighs NOUN a covered 16th-century bridge in Venice, between the Doges' Palace and the prisons, through which prisoners were formerly led to trial or execution.

bridge passage NOUN See **bridge**[1] (sense 8).

Bridgeport ('brɪdʒˌpɔːt) NOUN a port in SW Connecticut, on Long Island Sound. Pop.: 139 529 (2000).

bridge rectifier NOUN *Electrical engineering* a full-wave rectifier consisting of a bridge with a similar rectifier in each of the four arms.

bridge roll NOUN *Brit* a soft bread roll in a long thin shape.
▷**HISTORY** C20: from BRIDGE[2] or perhaps BRIDGE[1]

Bridgetown ('brɪdʒˌtaʊn) NOUN the capital of Barbados, a port on the SW coast. Pop.: 6070 (1990).

bridgework ('brɪdʒˌwɜːk) NOUN 1 **a** a partial denture attached to the surrounding teeth. See **bridge**[1] (sense 5). **b** the technique of making such appliances. 2 the process or occupation of constructing bridges.

bridging ('brɪdʒɪŋ) NOUN 1 one or more timber struts fixed between floor or roof joists to stiffen the construction and distribute the loads. [2] *Mountaineering* a technique for climbing a wide chimney by pressing left hand and foot against one side of it and right hand and foot against the other side.

bridging loan NOUN a loan made to cover the period between two transactions, such as the buying of another house before the sale of the first is completed.

Bridgwater ('brɪdʒˌwɔːtə) NOUN a town in SW England, in central Somerset. Pop.: 34 610 (1991).

bridie ('braɪdɪ; *Scot* 'brəɪdɪ) NOUN *Scot* a semicircular pie containing meat and onions.
▷HISTORY of unknown origin

bridle ('braɪdᵊl) NOUN [1] a headgear for a horse, etc., consisting of a series of buckled straps and a metal mouthpiece (bit) by which the animal is controlled through the reins. [2] something that curbs or restrains; check. [3] a Y-shaped cable, rope, or chain, used for holding, towing, etc. [4] *Machinery* a device by which the motion of a component is limited, often in the form of a linkage or flange. ◆ VERB [5] *(tr)* to put a bridle on (a horse, mule, etc.). [6] *(intr)* (of a horse) to respond correctly to the pull of the reins. [7] *(tr)* to restrain; curb: *he bridled his rage.* [8] *(intr; often foll by at)* to show anger, scorn, or indignation.
▷HISTORY Old English *brigdels*; related to *bregdan* to BRAID[1], Old High German *brittil*, Middle Low German *breidel*
▸ **'bridler** NOUN

bridle path NOUN a path suitable for riding or leading horses. Also called (NZ): **bridle track.**

bridlewise ('braɪdᵊlˌwaɪz) ADJECTIVE *US* (of a horse) obedient to the pressure of the reins on the neck rather than to the bit.

bridoon (brɪ'duːn) NOUN a horse's bit: a small snaffle used in double bridles.
▷HISTORY C18: from French *bridon*, from *bride* bridle; compare Middle English *bride*

brie (briː) NOUN a variant spelling of **bree[1]**.

Brie (briː) NOUN [1] a soft creamy white cheese, similar to Camembert but milder. [2] a mainly agricultural area in N France, between the Rivers Marne and Seine: noted esp for its cheese.

brief (briːf) ADJECTIVE [1] short in duration: *a brief holiday.* [2] short in length or extent; scanty: *a brief bikini.* [3] abrupt in manner; brusque: *the professor was brief with me this morning.* [4] terse or concise; containing few words: *he made a brief statement.* ◆ NOUN [5] a condensed or short statement or written synopsis; abstract. [6] *Law* a document containing all the facts and points of law of a case by which a solicitor instructs a barrister to represent a client. [7] *RC Church* a letter issuing from the Roman court written in modern characters, as contrasted with a papal bull; papal brief. [8] short for **briefing.** [9] a paper outlining the arguments and information on one side of a debate. [10] *Brit slang* a lawyer, esp a barrister. [11] **hold a brief for.** to argue for; champion. [12] **in brief.** in short; to sum up. ◆ VERB *(tr)* [13] to prepare or instruct by giving a summary of relevant facts. [14] to make a summary or synopsis of. [15] *English law* **a** to instruct (a barrister) by brief. **b** to retain (a barrister) as counsel. [16] *(intr; foll by against)* to supply potentially damaging or negative information regarding somone, as to the media, a politician, etc. See also **briefs.**
▷HISTORY C14: from Old French *bref*, from Latin *brevis*; related to Greek *brakhus*
▸ **'briefly** ADVERB ▸ **'briefness** NOUN

briefcase ('briːfˌkeɪs) NOUN a flat portable case, often of leather, for carrying papers, books, etc.

briefing ('briːfɪŋ) NOUN [1] a meeting at which detailed information or instructions are given, as for military operations, etc. [2] the facts presented during such a meeting.

briefless ('briːflɪs) ADJECTIVE (said of a barrister) without clients.

briefs (briːfs) PLURAL NOUN men's underpants or women's pants without legs.

brier[1] *or* **briar** ('braɪə) NOUN any of various thorny shrubs or other plants, such as the sweetbrier and greenbrier.
▷HISTORY Old English *brēr*, *brǣr*, of obscure origin
▸ **'briery** *or* **'briary** ADJECTIVE

brier[2] ('braɪə) NOUN a variant spelling of **briar[1]**.

brierroot ('braɪəˌruːt) NOUN a variant spelling of **briarroot.** Also called: **'brierˌwood.**

brig[1] (brɪg) NOUN [1] *Nautical* a two-masted square-rigger. [2] *Chiefly US* a prison, esp in a navy ship.
▷HISTORY C18: shortened from BRIGANTINE

brig[2] (brɪg) NOUN a Scot and northern English word for a **bridge[1]**.

Brig. ABBREVIATION FOR Brigadier.

brigade (brɪ'geɪd) NOUN [1] a formation of fighting units, together with support arms and services, smaller than a division and usually commanded by a brigadier. [2] a group of people organized for a certain task: *a rescue brigade.* ◆ VERB *(tr)* [3] to organize into a brigade. [4] to put or group together.
▷HISTORY C17: from Old French, from Old Italian, from *brigare* to fight, perhaps of Celtic origin; see BRIGAND

brigadier (ˌbrɪgə'dɪə) NOUN [1] an officer of the British Army or Royal Marines who holds a rank junior to a major general but senior to a colonel, usually commanding a brigade. [2] an equivalent rank in other armed forces. [3] *US army* short for **brigadier general.** [4] *History* a noncommissioned rank in the armies of Napoleon I.
▷HISTORY C17: from French, from BRIGADE

brigadier general NOUN, *plural* **brigadier generals.** [1] an officer of the US Army, Air Force, or Marine Corps who holds a rank junior to a major general but senior to a colonel, usually commanding a brigade. [2] the former name for a **brigadier** (sense 1).

brigalow ('brɪgələʊ) NOUN *Austral* **a** any of various acacia trees. **b** *(as modifier)*: *brigalow country.*
▷HISTORY C19: from a native Australian language

brigand ('brɪgənd) NOUN a bandit or plunderer, esp a member of a gang operating in mountainous areas.
▷HISTORY C14: from Old French, from Old Italian *brigante* fighter, from *brigare* to fight, from *briga* strife, of Celtic origin
▸ **'brigandage** *or* **'brigandry** NOUN

brigandine ('brɪgənˌdiːn, -ˌdaɪn) NOUN a coat of mail, invented in the Middle Ages to increase mobility, consisting of metal rings or sheets sewn on to cloth or leather.
▷HISTORY C15: from Old French, from BRIGAND + -INE[1]

brigantine ('brɪgənˌtiːn, -ˌtaɪn) NOUN a two-masted sailing ship, rigged square on the foremast and fore-and-aft with square topsails on the mainmast.
▷HISTORY C16: from Old Italian *brigantino* pirate ship, from *brigante* BRIGAND

Brig. Gen. ABBREVIATION FOR brigadier general.

Brighouse ('brɪgˌhaʊs) NOUN a town in N England, in Calderdale unitary authority, West Yorkshire: machine tools, textiles, engineering. Pop.: 32 198 (1991).

bright (braɪt) ADJECTIVE [1] emitting or reflecting much light; shining. [2] (of colours) intense or vivid. [3] full of promise: *a bright future.* [4] full of animation; cheerful: *a bright face.* [5] *Informal* quick witted or clever: *a bright child.* [6] magnificent; glorious: *a bright victory.* [7] polished; glistening: *a bright finish.* [8] (of the voice) distinct and clear. [9] (of a liquid) translucent and clear: *a circle of bright water.* [10] **bright and early.** very early in the morning. ◆ NOUN [11] a thin flat paintbrush with a straight sharp edge used for highlighting in oil painting. [12] *Poetic* brightness or splendour: *the bright of his armour.* ◆ ADVERB [13] brightly: *the fire was burning bright.* ◆ See also **brights.**
▷HISTORY Old English *beorht*; related to Old Norse *bjartr*, Gothic *bairhts* clear, Old High German *beraht*, Norwegian *bjerk*, Swedish *brokig* pied
▸ **'brightly** ADVERB

bright-blindness NOUN *Vet science* blindness occurring in sheep grazing pastures heavily infested with bracken.

brighten ('braɪtᵊn) VERB [1] to make or become bright or brighter. [2] to make or become cheerful.
▸ **'brightener** NOUN

brightening agent NOUN a compound applied to a textile to increase its brightness by the conversion of ultraviolet radiation to visible (blue) light, used in detergents.

bright-eyed ADJECTIVE [1] eager; fresh and enthusiastic. [2] **bright-eyed and bushy-tailed.** *Informal* keen, confident, and alert.

bright lights PLURAL NOUN **the.** places of entertainment in a city.

brightness ('braɪtnɪs) NOUN [1] the condition of being bright. [2] *Physics* a former name for **luminosity** (sense 4). [3] *Psychol* the experienced intensity of light.

Brighton ('braɪtᵊn) NOUN a coastal resort in S England, in Brighton and Hove unitary authority, East Sussex: patronized by the Prince Regent, who had the Royal Pavilion built (1782); seat of the University of Sussex (1966) and the University of Brighton (1992). Pop.: 124 851 (1991).

Brighton and Hove (həʊv) NOUN a city and unitary authority in S England, in East Sussex. Pop.: 247 820 (2001). Area: 72 sq. km (28 sq. miles).

brights (braɪts) PLURAL NOUN *US* the high beam of the headlights of a motor vehicle.

Bright's disease (braɪts) NOUN chronic inflammation of the kidneys; chronic nephritis.
▷HISTORY C19: named after Richard *Bright* (1789–1858), British physician

brightwork ('braɪtˌwɜːk) NOUN [1] shiny metal trimmings or fittings on ships, cars, etc. [2] varnished or plain woodwork on a vessel.

brik (brɪk) NOUN a Tunisian deep-fried spicy pastry filled with fish or meat and sometimes an egg.
▷HISTORY Arabic

brill (brɪl) NOUN, *plural* **brill** *or* **brills.** a European food fish, *Scophthalmus rhombus*, a flatfish similar to the turbot but lacking tubercles on the body: family *Bothidae.*
▷HISTORY C15: probably from Cornish *brȳthel* mackerel, from Old Cornish *brȳth* speckled; related to Welsh *brith* spotted

brilliance ('brɪljəns) *or* **brilliancy** NOUN [1] great brightness; radiance. [2] excellence or distinction in physical or mental ability; exceptional talent. [3] splendour; magnificence: *the brilliance of the royal court.* [4] *Physics* a former term for **luminance.**

brilliant ('brɪljənt) ADJECTIVE [1] shining with light; sparkling. [2] (of a colour) having a high saturation and reflecting a considerable amount of light; vivid. [3] outstanding; exceptional: *a brilliant success.* [4] splendid; magnificent: *a brilliant show.* [5] of outstanding intelligence or intellect: *a brilliant mind; a brilliant idea.* [6] *Music* **a** (of the tone of an instrument) having a large proportion of high harmonics above the fundamental. **b** Also: **brilliant** (*French* brijɑ̃), **brilliante** (*French* brijɑ̃t). with spirit; lively. ◆ NOUN [7] Also called: **brilliant cut. a** a popular circular cut for diamonds and other gemstones in the form of two many-faceted pyramids (the top one truncated) joined at their bases. **b** a diamond of this cut. [8] (formerly) a size of a printer's type approximately equal to 4 point.
▷HISTORY C17: from French *brillant* shining, from *briller* to shine, from Italian *brillare*, from *brillo* BERYL
▸ **'brilliantly** ADVERB

brilliantine ('brɪljənˌtiːn) NOUN [1] a perfumed oil used to make the hair smooth and shiny. [2] *Chiefly US* a glossy fabric made of mohair and cotton.
▷HISTORY C19: from French, from *brillant* shining

brim (brɪm) NOUN [1] the upper rim of a vessel: *the brim of a cup.* [2] a projecting rim or edge: *the brim of a hat.* [3] the brink or edge of something. ◆ VERB **brims, brimming, brimmed.** [4] to fill or be full to the brim: *eyes brimming with tears.*
▷HISTORY C13: from Middle High German *brem*, probably from Old Norse *barmr*; see BERM
▸ **'brimless** ADJECTIVE

brimful *or* **brimfull** (ˌbrɪm'fʊl) ADJECTIVE *(postpositive, foll by of)* filled up to the brim (with).

brimmer ('brɪmə) NOUN a vessel, such as a glass or bowl, filled to the brim.

brimstone ('brɪmˌstəʊn) NOUN [1] an obsolete name for **sulphur.** [2] a common yellow butterfly, *Gonepteryx rhamni*, of N temperate regions of the Old World: family *Pieridae.* [3] *Archaic* a scolding nagging woman; virago.
▷HISTORY Old English *brynstān*; related to Old Norse *brennistein*; see BURN[1], STONE

Brindisi (*Italian* 'brindizi) NOUN a port in SE Italy, in SE Apulia: important naval base in Roman times and a centre of the Crusades in the Middle Ages. Pop.: 93 290 (1991). Ancient name: **Brundisium.**

brindle ('brɪndᵊl) NOUN [1] a brindled animal. [2] a brindled colouring.

▷**HISTORY** C17: back formation from BRINDLED

brindled (ˈbrɪndᵊld) ADJECTIVE brown or grey streaked or patched with a darker colour: *a brindled dog.*
▷**HISTORY** C17: changed from C15 *brended*, literally: branded, probably of Scandinavian origin; compare Old Norse *bröndottr*; see BRAND

brine (braɪn) NOUN 1 a strong solution of salt and water, used for salting and pickling meats, etc. 2 the sea or its water. 3 *Chem* **a** a concentrated solution of sodium chloride in water. **b** any solution of a salt in water: *a potassium chloride brine.* ◆ VERB 4 (*tr*) to soak in or treat with brine.
▷**HISTORY** Old English *brīne*; related to Middle Dutch *brīne*, Old Slavonic *bridŭ* bitter, Sanskrit *bibhrāya* burnt
▸ˈ**brinish** ADJECTIVE

brinelling (ˈbrɪnelɪŋ) NOUN a localized surface corrosion; a cause of damage to bearings.

Brinell hardness number *or* **Brindell (hardness) number** (brɪˈnɛl) NOUN a measure of the hardness of a material obtained by pressing a hard steel ball into its surface; it is expressed as the ratio of the load on the ball in kilograms to the area of the depression made by the ball in square millimetres.
▷**HISTORY** C19: named after Johann A. *Brinell* (1849–1925), Swedish engineer

bring (brɪŋ) VERB **brings, bringing, brought.** (*tr*) 1 to carry, convey, or take (something or someone) to a designated place or person: *bring that book to me; will you bring Jessica to Tom's party?* 2 to cause to happen or occur to (oneself or another): *to bring disrespect on oneself.* 3 to cause to happen as a consequence: *responsibility brings maturity.* 4 to cause to come to mind: *it brought back memories.* 5 to cause to be in a certain state, position, etc.: *the punch brought him to his knees.* 6 to force, persuade, or make (oneself): *I couldn't bring myself to do it.* 7 to sell for; fetch: *the painting brought 20 pounds.* 8 *Law* **a** to institute (proceedings, charges, etc.). **b** to put (evidence, etc.) before a tribunal. 9 **bring forth.** to give birth to. 10 **bring home to. a** to convince of: *his account brought home to us the gravity of the situation.* **b** to place the blame on. 11 **bring to bear.** See **bear**[1] (sense 17). ◆ See also **bring about, bring down, bring forward, bring in, bring off, bring on, bring out, bring over, bring round, bring to, bring up.**
▷**HISTORY** Old English *bringan*; related to Gothic *briggan*, Old High German *bringan*
▸ˈ**bringer** NOUN

bring about VERB (*tr, adverb*) 1 to cause to happen: *to bring about a change in the law.* 2 to turn (a ship) around.

bring-and-buy sale NOUN *Brit and NZ* an informal sale, often conducted for charity, to which people bring items for sale and buy those that others have brought.

bring down VERB (*tr, adverb*) 1 to cause to fall: *the fighter aircraft brought the enemy down; the ministers agreed to bring down the price of oil.* 2 (*usually passive*) *Slang* to cause to be elated and then suddenly depressed, as from using drugs.

bring forward VERB (*tr, adverb*) 1 to present or introduce (a subject) for discussion. 2 *Book-keeping* to transfer (a figure representing the sum of the figures on a page or in a column) to the top of the next page or column. 3 to move to an earlier time or date: *the kickoff has been brought forward to 2 p.m.*

bring in VERB (*tr, adverb*) 1 to yield (income, profit, or cash): *his investments brought him in £100.* 2 to produce or return (a verdict). 3 to put forward or introduce (a legislative bill, etc.).

bringing-up NOUN another term for **upbringing.**

bring off VERB (*tr, adverb*) 1 to succeed in achieving (something), esp with difficulty or contrary to expectations: *he managed to bring off the deal.* 2 *Slang* to cause to have an orgasm.

> **Language note** The second sense of this word was formerly considered to be taboo, and it was labelled as such in previous editions of *Collins English Dictionary*. However, it has now become acceptable in speech, although some older or more conservative people may object to its use.

bring on VERB (*tr, adverb*) 1 to induce or cause: *these pills will bring on labour.* 2 *Slang* to cause sexual excitement in; stimulate.

> **Language note** The second sense of this word was formerly considered to be taboo, and it was labelled as such in previous editions of *Collins English Dictionary*. However, it has now become acceptable in speech, although some older or more conservative people may object to its use.

bring out VERB (*tr, adverb*) 1 to produce or publish or have published: *when are you bringing out a new dictionary?* 2 to expose, reveal, or cause to be seen: *she brought out the best in me.* 3 to encourage (a shy person) to be less reserved (often in the phrase **bring (someone) out of himself** *or* **herself**). 4 *Brit* (of a trade union, provocative action by management, misunderstanding, etc.) to cause (workers) to strike. 5 (foll by *in*) to cause (a person) to become covered (with spots, a rash, etc.). 6 *Brit* to introduce (a girl) formally into society as a debutante.

bring over VERB (*tr, adverb*) to cause (a person) to change allegiances.

bring round *or* **around** VERB (*tr, adverb*) 1 to restore (a person) to consciousness, esp after a faint. 2 to convince (another person, usually an opponent) of an opinion or point of view.

bring to VERB (*tr*) 1 (*adverb*) to restore (a person) to consciousness. 2 (*adverb*) to cause (a ship) to turn into the wind and reduce her headway. 3 (*preposition*) to make (something) equal to (an amount of money): *that brings your bill to £17.*

bring up VERB (*tr, adverb*) 1 to care for and train (a child); rear: *we had been brought up to go to church.* 2 to raise (a subject) for discussion; mention. 3 to vomit (food). 4 (foll by *against*) to cause (a person) to face or confront. 5 (foll by *to*) to cause (something) to be of a required standard.

brinjal (ˈbrɪndʒəl) NOUN (in India and Africa) another name for the **aubergine.**
▷**HISTORY** C17: from Portuguese *berinjela*, from Arabic; see AUBERGINE

brink (brɪŋk) NOUN 1 the edge, border, or verge of a steep place: *the brink of the precipice.* 2 the highest point; top: *the sun fell below the brink of the hill.* 3 the land at the edge of a body of water. 4 the verge of an event or state: *the brink of disaster.*
▷**HISTORY** C13: from Middle Dutch *brinc*, of Germanic origin; compare Old Norse *brekka* slope, Middle Low German *brink* edge of a field

brinkmanship (ˈbrɪŋkmənˌʃɪp) NOUN the art or practice of pressing a dangerous situation, esp in international affairs, to the limit of safety and peace in order to win an advantage from a threatening or tenacious foe.

brinny (ˈbrɪnɪ) NOUN, *plural* **-nies.** *Austral children's slang, old-fashioned* a stone, esp when thrown.

briny (ˈbraɪnɪ) ADJECTIVE **brinier, briniest.** 1 of or resembling brine; salty. ◆ NOUN 2 (preceded by *the*) an informal name for the **sea.**
▸ˈ**brininess** NOUN

brio (ˈbriːəʊ) NOUN liveliness or vigour; spirit. See also **con brio.**
▷**HISTORY** C19: from Italian, of Celtic origin

brioche (ˈbriːəʊʃ, -ɒʃ; *French* briɔʃ) NOUN a soft roll or loaf made from a very light yeast dough, sometimes mixed with currants.
▷**HISTORY** C19: from Norman dialect, from *brier* to knead, of Germanic origin; compare French *broyer* to pound, BREAK

briolette (ˌbriːəʊˈlɛt) NOUN a pear-shaped gem cut with long triangular facets.
▷**HISTORY** C19: from French, alteration of *brillolette*, from *brignolette* little dried plum, after *Brignoles*, France, where these plums are produced

briony (ˈbraɪənɪ) NOUN, *plural* **-nies.** a variant spelling of **bryony.**

briquette *or* **briquet** (brɪˈkɛt) NOUN 1 a small brick made of compressed coal dust, sawdust, charcoal, etc., used for fuel. 2 a small brick of any substance: *an ice-cream briquette.* ◆ VERB 3 (*tr*) to make into the form of a brick or bricks: *to briquette clay.*
▷**HISTORY** C19: from French: a little brick, from *brique* BRICK

bris (ˈbrɪs) *or* **brith** (ˈbrɪt) NOUN *Judaism* ritual circumcision of male babies, usually at eight days old, regarded as the formal entry of the child to the Jewish community.
▷**HISTORY** from Hebrew, literally: covenant

brisance (ˈbriːzəns; *French* brizɑ̃s) NOUN the shattering effect or power of an explosion or explosive.
▷**HISTORY** C20: from French, from *briser* to break, ultimately of Celtic origin; compare Old Irish *brissim* I break
▸ˈ**brisant** ADJECTIVE

Brisbane (ˈbrɪzbən) NOUN a port in E Australia, the capital of Queensland: founded in 1824 as a penal settlement; vast agricultural hinterland. Pop.: 848 741 (1998 est.).

brise-soleil (ˌbriːzsəʊˈleɪ) NOUN a structure used in hot climates to protect a window from the sun, usually consisting of horizontal or vertical strips of wood, concrete, etc.
▷**HISTORY** C20: French: break-sun, from *briser* to break + *soleil* sun

brisk (brɪsk) ADJECTIVE 1 lively and quick; vigorous: *a brisk walk; trade was brisk.* 2 invigorating or sharp: *brisk weather.* ◆ VERB 3 (often foll by *up*) to enliven; make or become brisk.
▷**HISTORY** C16: probably variant of BRUSQUE
▸ˈ**briskly** ADVERB ▸ˈ**briskness** NOUN

brisken (ˈbrɪskən) VERB to make or become more lively or brisk.

brisket (ˈbrɪskɪt) NOUN 1 the breast of a four-legged animal. 2 the meat from this part, esp of beef.
▷**HISTORY** C14: probably of Scandinavian origin; related to Old Norse *brjōsk* gristle, Norwegian and Danish *brusk*

brisling (ˈbrɪslɪŋ) NOUN another name for a **sprat**, esp a Norwegian sprat seasoned, smoked, and canned in oil
▷**HISTORY** C20: from Norwegian; related to obsolete Danish *bretling*, German *Breitling*

Brisso (ˈbrɪzəʊ) NOUN *Austral informal* a person who lives in Brisbane.

bristle (ˈbrɪsᵊl) NOUN 1 any short stiff hair of an animal or plant. 2 something resembling these hair: *toothbrush bristle.* ◆ VERB 3 (when *intr*, often foll by *up*) to stand up or cause to stand up like bristles: *the angry cat's fur bristled.* 4 (*intr*; sometimes foll by *up*) to show anger, indignation, etc.: *she bristled at the suggestion.* 5 (*intr*) to be thickly covered or set: *the target bristled with arrows.* 6 (*intr*) to be in a state of agitation or movement: *the office was bristling with activity.* 7 (*tr*) to provide with a bristle or bristles.
▷**HISTORY** C13 *bristil, brustel*, from earlier *brust*, from Old English *byrst*; related to Old Norse *burst*, Old High German *borst*
▸ˈ**bristly** ADJECTIVE

bristlecone pine (ˈbrɪsᵊlˌkəʊn) NOUN a coniferous tree, *Pinus aristata*, of the western US, bearing cones with bristle-like prickles: one of the longest-lived trees, useful in radiocarbon dating.

bristle-grass NOUN any of various grasses of the genus *Setaria*, such as *S. viridis*, having a bristly inflorescence.

bristletail (ˈbrɪsᵊlˌteɪl) NOUN any primitive wingless insect of the orders *Thysanura* and *Diplura*, such as the silverfish and firebrat, having a flattened body and long tail appendages.

bristle worm NOUN a popular name for a **polychaete.**

Bristol (ˈbrɪstᵊl) NOUN 1 **City of.** a port and industrial city in SW England, mainly in Bristol unitary authority, on the River Avon seven miles from its mouth on the Bristol Channel: a major port, trading with America, in the 17th and 18th centuries; the modern port consists chiefly of docks at Avonmouth and Portishead; noted for the **Clifton Suspension Bridge** (designed by I. K. Brunel, 1834) over the Avon gorge; Bristol university (1909) and University of the West of England (1992). Pop.: 407 992 (1991). 2 **City of.** a unitary authority in SW England, created in 1996 from part of Avon county. Pop.: 380 615 (2001). Area: 110 sq. km (42 sq. miles).

Bristol board NOUN a heavy smooth cardboard of fine quality, used for printing and drawing.

Bristol Channel NOUN an inlet of the Atlantic, between S Wales and SW England, merging into the Severn estuary. Length: about 137 km (85 miles).

Bristol fashion ADVERB, ADJECTIVE (*postpositive*) 1 *Nautical* clean and neat, with newly painted and scrubbed surfaces, brass polished, etc. 2 **shipshape and Bristol fashion.** in good order; efficiently arranged.

bristols (ˈbrɪstᵊlz) PLURAL NOUN *Brit slang* a woman's breasts.
▷HISTORY C20: short for *Bristol Cities*, rhyming slang for *titties*

brit (brɪt) NOUN (*functioning as singular or plural*) 1 the young of a herring, sprat, or similar fish. 2 minute marine crustaceans, esp copepods, forming food for many fishes and whales.
▷HISTORY C17: perhaps from Cornish *brȳthel* mackerel; see BRILL

Brit (brɪt) NOUN *Informal* a British person.

Brit. ABBREVIATION FOR: 1 Britain. 2 British.

Britain (ˈbrɪtᵊn) NOUN another name for **Great Britain** or the **United Kingdom.**

Britannia (brɪˈtænɪə) NOUN 1 a female warrior carrying a trident and wearing a helmet, personifying Great Britain or the British Empire. 2 (in the ancient Roman Empire) the S part of Great Britain. 3 short for **Britannia coin.**

Britannia coin NOUN any of four British gold coins introduced in 1987 for investment purposes; their denominations are £100, £50, £25, and £10.

Britannia metal NOUN an alloy of low melting point consisting of tin with 5–10 per cent antimony, 1–3 per cent copper, and sometimes small quantities of zinc, lead, or bismuth: used for decorative purposes and for bearings.

Britannic (brɪˈtænɪk) ADJECTIVE of Britain; British (esp in the phrases **His** *or* **Her Britannic Majesty**).

Britart (ˈbrɪt,ɑːt) NOUN a movement in modern British art beginning in the late 1980s, often conceptual or using controversial materials, including such artists as Damien Hirst and Rachel Whiteread.
▷HISTORY C20: *Brit* short for *British*

britches (ˈbrɪtʃɪz) PLURAL NOUN a variant spelling of **breeches.**

brith (brit) NOUN a variant of **bris.**

Briticism (ˈbrɪtɪ,sɪzəm) NOUN a custom, linguistic usage, or other feature peculiar to Britain or its people.

British (ˈbrɪtɪʃ) ADJECTIVE 1 relating to, denoting, or characteristic of Britain or any of the natives, citizens, or inhabitants of the United Kingdom. 2 relating to or denoting the English language as spoken and written in Britain, esp the S dialect generally regarded as standard. See also **Southern British English, Received Pronunciation.** 3 relating to or denoting the ancient Britons. ◆ NOUN 4 (*functioning as plural*) the natives or inhabitants of Britain. 5 the extinct Celtic language of the ancient Britons. See also **Brythonic.**
▸ **ˈBritishness** NOUN

British Antarctic Territory NOUN a UK Overseas Territory in the S Atlantic: created in 1962 and consisting of the South Shetland Islands, the South Orkney Islands, and Graham Land; formerly part of the Falkland Islands Dependencies.

British Association screw thread NOUN *Engineering* a system of screw sizes designated from 0 to 25. Now superseded by standard metric sizes. Abbreviation: **BA.**

British Cameroons PLURAL NOUN a former British trust territory of West Africa. See **Cameroon.**

British Civil Airworthiness Requirements PLURAL NOUN (in Britain) documents specifying aerodynamic, engineering design, construction, and performance requirements, which must be met before an aircraft is given permission to fly.

British Columbia NOUN a province of W Canada, on the Pacific coast: largely mountainous with extensive forests, rich mineral resources, and important fisheries. Capital: Victoria. Pop.: 4 095 900 (2001 est.). Area: 930 532 sq. km (359 279 sq. miles). Abbreviation: **BC.**

British Columbian ADJECTIVE 1 of or relating to British Columbia or its inhabitants. ◆ NOUN 2 a native or inhabitant of British Columbia.

British Commonwealth of Nations NOUN the former name of the **Commonwealth.**

British Council NOUN an organization founded (1934) to extend the influence of British culture and education throughout the world.

British disease NOUN (usually preceded by *the*) the pattern of strikes and industrial unrest in the 1970s and early 1980s supposed by many during this time to be endemic in Britain and to weaken the British economy.

British East Africa NOUN the former British possessions of Uganda, Kenya, Tanganyika, and Zanzibar, before their independence in the 1960s.

British Empire NOUN (formerly) the United Kingdom and the territories under its control, which reached its greatest extent at the end of World War I when it embraced over a quarter of the world's population and more than a quarter of the world's land surface.

Britisher (ˈbrɪtɪʃə) NOUN (not used by the British) 1 a native or inhabitant of Great Britain. 2 any British subject.

British Guiana NOUN the former name (until 1966) of **Guyana.**

British Honduras NOUN the former name of **Belize.**

British India NOUN the 17 provinces of India formerly governed by the British under the British sovereign: ceased to exist in 1947 when the independent states of India and Pakistan were created.

British Indian Ocean Territory NOUN a UK Overseas Territory in the Indian Ocean: consists of the Chagos Archipelago (formerly a dependency of Mauritius) and formerly included (until 1976) Aldabra, Farquhar, and Des Roches, now administratively part of the Seychelles. Diego Garcia is an important US naval base.

British Isles PLURAL NOUN a group of islands in W Europe, consisting of Great Britain, Ireland, the Isle of Man, Orkney, the Shetland Islands, the Channel Islands belonging to Great Britain, and the islands adjacent to these.

Britishism (ˈbrɪtɪ,ʃɪzəm) NOUN a variant of **Briticism.**

British Legion NOUN *Brit* a shortened form of **Royal British Legion.**

British Library NOUN the British national library, formed in 1973 from the British Museum library and other national collections: housed mainly in the British Museum until 1997 when a purpose-built library in St Pancras, London, was completed.

British List NOUN a list, maintained by the British Ornithologists' Union, of birds accepted as occurring at least once in the British Isles.

British longhair (ˈlɒŋ,hеə) NOUN a breed of large cat with a semi-long thick soft coat.

British lop NOUN a breed of large white pig with large drooping ears, originating from Wales, Cumberland, and Ulster. Former name: **long white lop-eared.**

British Museum NOUN a museum in London, founded in 1753: contains one of the world's richest collections of antiquities and (until 1997) most of the British Library.

British National Party NOUN (in Britain) a neo-Nazi political party. Abbreviation: **BNP.**

British North America NOUN (formerly) Canada or its constituent regions or provinces that formed part of the British Empire.

British shorthair (ˈʃɔːt,hеə) NOUN a breed of large cat with a short dense coat.

British Somaliland NOUN a former British protectorate (1884–1960) in E Africa, on the Gulf of Aden: united with Italian Somaliland in 1960 to form the Somali Republic.

British Standard brass thread NOUN *Engineering* a Whitworth screw thread having 26 threads per inch, used for thin-walled tubing and designated by the diameter of the tubing. Abbreviation: **BSB.**

British Standard fine thread NOUN *Engineering* a screw thread having a Whitworth profile but a finer pitch for a given diameter. Abbreviation: **BSF.**

British Standard pipe thread NOUN *Engineering* a screw thread of Whitworth profile used for piping and designated by the bore of the pipe. Abbreviation: **BSP.**

British Standards Institution NOUN an association, founded in London in 1901, that establishes and maintains standards for units of measurements, clothes sizes, technical terminology, etc., as used in Britain. Abbreviation: **BSI.** Compare **National Bureau of Standards, International Standards Organization.**

British Standard Time NOUN the standard time used in Britain all the year round from 1968 to 1971, set one hour ahead of Greenwich Mean Time and equalling Central European Time.

British Standard Whitworth thread NOUN See **Whitworth screw thread.** Abbreviation: **BSW.**

British Summer Time NOUN time set one hour ahead of Greenwich Mean Time: used in Britain from the end of March to the end of October, providing an extra hour of daylight in the evening. Abbreviation: **BST.** Compare **daylight-saving time.**

British Technology Group NOUN an organization formed in 1981 by the merger of the National Enterprise Board and the National Research and Development Corporation to encourage and finance technological innovation: privatized in 2000. Abbreviation: **BTG.**

British thermal unit NOUN a unit of heat in the fps system equal to the quantity of heat required to raise the temperature of 1 pound of water by 1°F. 1 British thermal unit is equivalent to 1055.06 joules or 251.997 calories. Abbrevs: **btu, BThU.**

British Union of Fascists NOUN the British fascist party founded by Sir Oswald Mosley (1932), which advocated a strong corporate state and promoted anti-Semitism.

British Virgin Islands PLURAL NOUN a UK Overseas Territory in the Caribbean, consisting of 36 islands in the E Virgin Islands: formerly part of the Federation of the Leeward Islands (1871–1956). Capital: Road Town, on Tortola. Pop.: 19 000 (1997 est.). Area: 153 sq. km (59 sq. miles).

British warm NOUN an army officer's short thick overcoat.

British West Africa NOUN the former British possessions of Nigeria, The Gambia, Sierra Leone, and the Gold Coast, and the former trust territories of Togoland and Cameroons.

British West Indies PLURAL NOUN the states in the Caribbean that are members of the Commonwealth: the Bahamas, Barbados, Jamaica, Trinidad and Tobago, Antigua and Barbuda, Saint Kitts-Nevis, Dominica, Grenada, Saint Lucia, and Saint Vincent and the Grenadines.

British White NOUN a British breed of medium-sized white cattle with black points, bred mainly for meat.

Brit Lit *or* **Britlit** (ˈbrɪt,lɪt) NOUN British literature, esp current fashionable writing.

brit milah (ˈbrit miˈlɑː, ˈmilɑ) NOUN *Judaism* a Hebrew term usually translated as **circumcision.**

Britneyfication (,brɪtnɪfɪˈkeɪʃən) NOUN the effect on clothes and fashions of following the revealing styles favoured by the US pop singer Britney Spears (born 1981).

Briton (ˈbrɪtᵊn) NOUN 1 a native or inhabitant of Britain. 2 a citizen of the United Kingdom. 3 *History* any of the early Celtic inhabitants of S Britain who were largely dispossessed by the Anglo-Saxon invaders after the 5th century A.D.
▷HISTORY C13: from Old French *Breton*, from Latin *Britto*, of Celtic origin

Britpack (ˈbrɪt,pæk) NOUN **a** a group of young and successful British actors, directors, artists, etc. **b** (*as modifier*): *Britpack talent.*
▷HISTORY C20: a play on BRATPACK

Britpop (ˈbrɪt,pɒp) NOUN the characteristic pop music performed by some British bands of the mid 1990s.

Brittany[1] (ˈbrɪtənɪ) NOUN a region of NW France, the peninsula between the English Channel and the Bay of Biscay: settled by Celtic refugees from Wales and Cornwall during the Anglo-Saxon invasions; disputed between England and France until 1364. Breton name: **Breiz** (braɪz). French name: **Bretagne.** Related adjective: **Breton.**

Brittany² NOUN, *plural* **-nies.** a medium-sized strongly-built variety of retriever with a slightly wavy coat usu. in tan and white, liver and white, or black and white.

brittle (ˈbrɪtᵊl) ADJECTIVE [1] easily cracked, snapped, or broken; fragile. [2] curt or irritable: *a brittle reply.* [3] hard or sharp in quality. ◆ NOUN [4] a crunchy sweet made with treacle and nuts: *peanut brittle.*
▷HISTORY C14: from Old English *brytel* (unattested); related to *brytsen* fragment, *brēotan* to break
▸ˈ**brittlely** *or* ˈ**brittly** ADVERB

brittle bone disease NOUN the nontechnical name for **osteogenesis imperfecta.**

brittleness (ˈbrɪtᵊlnɪs) NOUN [1] the quality of being brittle. [2] *Metallurgy* the tendency of a metal to break without being significantly distorted or exposed to a high level of stress. Compare **toughness** (sense 2), **softness** (sense 2).

brittle-star NOUN any echinoderm of the class *Ophiuroidea*, occurring on the sea bottom and having five long slender arms radiating from a small central disc. See also **basket-star.**

Brittonic (brɪˈtɒnɪk) NOUN, ADJECTIVE another word for **Brythonic.**

britzka *or* **britska** (ˈbrɪtskə) NOUN a long horse-drawn carriage with a folding top over the rear seat and a rear-facing front seat.
▷HISTORY C19: from German, variant of *Britschka*, from Polish *bryczka* a little cart, from *bryka* cart

Brix scale (brɪks) NOUN a scale for calibrating hydrometers used for measuring the concentration and density of sugar solutions at a given temperature.
▷HISTORY C19: named after A. F. W. *Brix*, 19th-century German inventor

BRN INTERNATIONAL CAR REGISTRATION FOR Bahrain.

Brno (ˈbɜːnəʊ; *Czech* ˈbrnɔ) NOUN a city in the Czech Republic; formerly the capital of Moravia: the country's second largest city. Pop.: 383 569 (2000 est.). German name: **Brünn.**

bro¹ (brəʊ) NOUN [1] *NZ* a family member. [2] a close associate.

bro² (bruː) NOUN *South African informal* a friend, often used in direct address.
▷HISTORY C20: from Afrikaans *broer* brother

bro. (brəʊ) ABBREVIATION FOR brother.

broach¹ (brəʊtʃ) VERB [1] *(tr)* to initiate (a topic) for discussion: *to broach a dangerous subject.* [2] *(tr)* to tap or pierce (a container) to draw off (a liquid): *to broach a cask; to broach wine.* [3] *(tr)* to open in order to begin to use: *to broach a shipment.* [4] *(intr)* to break the surface of the water: *the trout broached after being hooked.* [5] *(tr) Machinery* to enlarge and finish (a hole) by reaming. ◆ NOUN [6] a long tapered toothed cutting tool for enlarging holes. [7] a spit for roasting meat, etc. [8] a roof covering the corner triangle on the top of a square tower having an octagonal spire. [9] a pin, forming part of some types of lock, that registers in the hollow bore of a key. [10] a tool used for tapping casks. [11] a less common spelling of **brooch.**
▷HISTORY C14: from Old French *broche*, from Vulgar Latin *brocca* (unattested), from Latin *brochus* projecting
▸ˈ**broacher** NOUN

broach² (brəʊtʃ) VERB *Nautical* (usually foll by *to*) to cause (a sailing vessel) to swerve sharply and dangerously or (of a sailing vessel) to swerve sharply and dangerously in a following sea, so as to be broadside to the waves.
▷HISTORY C18: perhaps from BROACH¹ in obsolete sense of turn on a spit

broad (brɔːd) ADJECTIVE [1] having relatively great breadth or width. [2] of vast extent; spacious: *a broad plain.* [3] *(postpositive)* from one side to the other: *four miles broad.* [4] of great scope or potential: *that invention had broad applications.* [5] not detailed; general: *broad plans.* [6] clear and open; full (esp in the phrase **broad daylight**). [7] obvious or plain: *broad hints.* [8] liberal; tolerant: *a broad political stance.* [9] widely spread; extensive: *broad support.* [10] outspoken or bold: *a broad manner.* [11] vulgar; coarse; indecent: *a broad joke.* [12] unrestrained; free: *broad laughter.* [13] (of a dialect or pronunciation) consisting of a large number of speech sounds characteristic of a particular geographical area: *a broad Yorkshire accent.* [14] *Finance* denoting an assessment of liquidity as including notes and coin in circulation with the public, banks' till money and balances, most private-sector bank deposits, and sterling bank-deposit certificates: *broad money.* Compare **narrow** (sense 7). [15] *Phonetics* **a** of or relating to a type of pronunciation transcription in which symbols correspond approximately to phonemes without taking account of allophonic variations. **b** **broad a.** the long vowel in English words such as *father, half*, as represented in the received pronunciation of Southern British English. [16] **as broad as it is long.** amounting to the same thing; without advantage either way. ◆ NOUN [17] the broad part of something. [18] *Slang, chiefly US and Canadian* **a** a girl or woman. **b** a prostitute. [19] *Brit dialect* a river spreading over a lowland. See also **Broads.** [20] *East Anglian dialect* a shallow lake. [21] a wood-turning tool used for shaping the insides and bottoms of cylinders. ◆ ADVERB [22] widely or fully: *broad awake.*
▷HISTORY Old English *brād*; related to Old Norse *breithr*, Old Frisian *brēd*, Old High German *breit*, Gothic *braiths*
▸ˈ**broadly** ADVERB ▸ˈ**broadness** NOUN

B-road NOUN (in Britain) a secondary road.

broad arrow NOUN [1] a mark shaped like a broad arrowhead designating British government property and formerly used on prison clothing. [2] an arrow with a broad head.

broadband (ˈbrɔːdˌbænd) NOUN a transmission technique using a wide range of frequencies that enables messages to be sent simultaneously, used in fast Internet connections. See also **baseband.**

broad bean NOUN [1] an erect annual Eurasian bean plant, *Vicia faba*, cultivated for its large edible flattened seeds, used as a vegetable. [2] the seed of this plant. Also called: **horse bean.**

broadbill (ˈbrɔːdˌbɪl) NOUN [1] any passerine bird of the family *Eurylaimidae*, of tropical Africa and Asia, having bright plumage and a short wide bill. [2] *US* any of various wide-billed birds, such as the scaup and shoveler. [3] *US* another name for **swordfish.**

broadbrim (ˈbrɔːdˌbrɪm) NOUN a broad-brimmed hat, esp one worn by the Quakers in the 17th century.

broadbrush (ˈbrɔːdˌbrʌʃ) ADJECTIVE lacking full detail or information; incomplete or rough: *anything other than a broadbrush strategy for the industry will be overloaded with detail.*

broadcast (ˈbrɔːdˌkɑːst) VERB **-casts, -casting, -cast** *or* **-casted.** [1] to transmit (announcements or programmes) on radio or television. [2] *(intr)* to take part in a radio or television programme. [3] *(tr)* to make widely known throughout an area: *to broadcast news.* [4] *(tr)* to scatter (seed, etc.) over an area, esp by hand. ◆ NOUN [5] **a** a transmission or programme on radio or television. **b** *(as modifier)*: *a broadcast signal.* [6] **a** the act of scattering seeds. **b** *(as modifier)*: *the broadcast method of sowing.* ◆ ADJECTIVE [7] dispersed over a wide area: *broadcast seeds.* ◆ ADVERB [8] far and wide: *seeds to be sown broadcast.*
▸ˈ**broadˌcaster** NOUN ▸ˈ**broadˌcasting** NOUN

Broad Church NOUN [1] a party within the Church of England which favours a broad and liberal interpretation of Anglican formularies and rubrics and objects to positive definition in theology. Compare **High Church, Low Church.** [2] *(usually not capitals)* a group or movement which embraces a wide and varied number of views, approaches, and opinions. ◆ ADJECTIVE **Broad-Church.** [3] of or relating to this party in the Church of England.

broadcloth (ˈbrɔːdˌklɒθ) NOUN [1] fabric woven on a wide loom. [2] a closely woven fabric of wool, worsted, cotton, or rayon with lustrous finish, used for clothing.

broaden (ˈbrɔːdᵊn) VERB to make or become broad or broader; widen.

broad gauge NOUN [1] a railway track with a greater distance between the lines than the standard gauge of 56½ inches (about 1.44 metres) used now by most mainline railway systems. ◆ ADJECTIVE **broad-gauge.** [2] of, relating to, or denoting a railway having this track.

broad jump NOUN a US and Canadian term for **long jump.**

Broadlands (ˈbrɔːdləndz) NOUN a Palladian mansion near Romsey in Hampshire: formerly the home of Lord Palmerston and Lord Mountbatten.

broadleaf (ˈbrɔːdˌliːf) NOUN, *plural* **-leaves.** any tobacco plant having broad leaves, used esp in making cigars.

broad-leaved ADJECTIVE denoting trees other than conifers, most of which have broad rather than needle-shaped leaves.

broadloom (ˈbrɔːdˌluːm) NOUN *(modifier)* of or designating carpets or carpeting woven on a wide loom to obviate the need for seams.

broad-minded ADJECTIVE [1] tolerant of opposing viewpoints; not prejudiced; liberal. [2] not easily shocked by permissive sexual habits, pornography, etc.
▸ˌ**broad-ˈmindedly** ADVERB ▸ˌ**broad-ˈmindedness** NOUN

Broadmoor (ˈbrɔːdˌmɔː) NOUN an institution in Berkshire, England, for housing and treating mentally ill criminals.

Broads (brɔːdz) PLURAL NOUN **the.** [1] a group of shallow navigable lakes, connected by a network of rivers, in E England, in Norfolk and Suffolk. [2] the region around these lakes: a tourist centre; several bird sanctuaries.

broad seal NOUN the official seal of a nation and its government.

broadsheet (ˈbrɔːdˌʃiːt) NOUN [1] a newspaper having a large format, approximately 15 by 24 inches (38 by 61 centimetres). Compare **tabloid.** [2] another word for **broadside** (sense 4).

broadside (ˈbrɔːdˌsaɪd) NOUN [1] *Nautical* the entire side of a vessel, from stem to stern and from waterline to rail. [2] *Naval* **a** all the armament fired from one side of a warship. **b** the simultaneous discharge of such armament. [3] a strong or abusive verbal or written attack. [4] Also called: **broadside ballad.** a ballad or popular song printed on one side of a sheet of paper and sold by hawkers, esp in 16th-century England. [5] any standard size of paper before cutting or folding: *demy broadside.* [6] another name for **broadsheet** (sense 1). [7] a large flat surface: *the broadside of the barn.* ◆ ADVERB [8] with a broader side facing an object; sideways: *the train hit the lorry broadside.*

broad-spectrum NOUN *(modifier)* effective against a wide variety of diseases or microorganisms: *a broad-spectrum antibiotic.*

broadsword (ˈbrɔːdˌsɔːd) NOUN a broad-bladed sword used for cutting rather than stabbing. Also called: **backsword.**

broadtail (ˈbrɔːdˌteɪl) NOUN [1] the highly valued black wavy fur obtained from the skins of newly born karakul lambs; caracul. [2] another name for **karakul.**

Broadway (ˈbrɔːdˌweɪ) NOUN [1] a thoroughfare in New York City, famous for its theatres: the centre of the commercial theatre in the US. ◆ ADJECTIVE [2] of or relating to or suitable for the commercial theatre, esp on Broadway.

Brobdingnagian (ˌbrɒbdɪŋˈnægɪən) ADJECTIVE gigantic; huge; immense.
▷HISTORY C18: from *Brobdingnag*, an imaginary country of giants in Swift's *Gulliver's Travels* (1726)

brocade (brəʊˈkeɪd) NOUN [1] **a** a rich fabric woven with a raised design, often using gold or silver threads. **b** *(as modifier)*: *brocade curtains.* ◆ VERB [2] *(tr)* to weave with such a design.
▷HISTORY C17: from Spanish *brocado*, from Italian *broccato* embossed fabric, from *brocco* spike, from Latin *brochus* projecting; see BROACH¹

Broca's area *or* **centre** (ˈbrɒkəz) NOUN the region of the cerebral cortex of the brain concerned with speech; the speech centre.
▷HISTORY C19: named after Paul *Broca* (1824–80), French surgeon and anthropologist

brocatelle *or US* **brocatel** (ˌbrɒkəˈtɛl) NOUN [1] a heavy brocade with the design in deep relief, used chiefly in upholstery. [2] a type of variegated marble from France and Italy.
▷HISTORY C17: from French, from Italian *broccatello*, diminutive of *broccato* BROCADE

broccoli (ˈbrɒkəlɪ) NOUN [1] a cultivated variety of

cabbage, *Brassica oleracea italica*, having branched greenish flower heads. 2 the flower head of this plant, eaten as a vegetable before the buds have opened. 3 a variety of this plant that does not form a head, whose stalks are eaten as a vegetable.
▷HISTORY C17: from Italian, plural of *broccolo* a little sprout, from *brocco* sprout, spike; see BROCADE

broch (brɒk, brɒx) NOUN (in Scotland) a circular dry-stone tower large enough to serve as a fortified home; they date from the Iron Age and are found esp in the north and the islands.
▷HISTORY C17: from Old Norse *borg*; related to Old English *burh* settlement, burgh

broché (brəʊˈʃeɪ; *French* brɔʃe) ADJECTIVE woven with a raised design, as brocade.
▷HISTORY C19: from French *brocher* to brocade, stitch; see BROACH[1]

brochette (brɒˈʃɛt; *French* brɔʃɛt) NOUN a skewer or small spit, used for holding pieces of meat, etc., while roasting or grilling.
▷HISTORY C19: from Old French *brochete* small pointed tool; see BROACH[1]

brocho (ˈbrɔɔx) NOUN a variant of **brachah**.

brochure (ˈbrəʊʃjʊə, -ʃə) NOUN a pamphlet or booklet, esp one containing summarized or introductory information or advertising.
▷HISTORY C18: from French, from *brocher* to stitch (a book)

brock (brɒk) NOUN a Brit. name for **badger** (sense 1): used esp as a form of address in stories, etc.
▷HISTORY Old English *broc*, of Celtic origin; compare Welsh *broch*

Brocken (*German* ˈbrɔkən) NOUN a mountain in central Germany, formerly in East Germany: the highest peak of the Harz Mountains; important in German folklore. Height: 1142 m (3747 ft.). The **Brocken Bow** or **Brocken Spectre** is an atmospheric phenomenon in which an observer, when the sun is low, may see his enlarged shadow against the clouds, often surrounded by coloured lights.

brocket (ˈbrɒkɪt) NOUN any small deer of the genus *Mazama*, of tropical America, having small unbranched antlers.
▷HISTORY C15: from Anglo-French *broquet*, from *broque* horn, from Vulgar Latin *brocca* (unattested); see BROACH[1]

broddle (ˈbrɒdᵊl) VERB (*tr*) *Yorkshire dialect* to poke or pierce (something).
▷HISTORY perhaps from BRADAWL

broderie anglaise (ˌbrəʊdəri: ɑːŋˈglɛz) NOUN open embroidery on white cotton, fine linen, etc.
▷HISTORY C19: French: English embroidery

Broederbond (ˈbrʊdəˌbɔːnt, ˈbruːdəˌbɒnt) NOUN (in South Africa) a secret society of Afrikaner Nationalists committed to securing and maintaining Afrikaner control over important areas of government.
▷HISTORY Afrikaans: band of brothers

broekies (ˈbrʊkiːz) PLURAL NOUN *South African informal* underpants.
▷HISTORY C19: Afrikaans

brog (brɒg, brɔːg, brog) NOUN *Scot* a bradawl.
▷HISTORY C19: of uncertain origin

brogan (ˈbrəʊgən) NOUN a heavy laced usually ankle-high work boot.
▷HISTORY C19: from Gaelic *brōgan* a little shoe, from *brōg* shoe; see BROGUE[2]

brogue[1] (brəʊg) NOUN a broad gentle-sounding dialectal accent, esp that used by the Irish in speaking English.
▷HISTORY C18: probably from BROGUE[2], alluding to the footwear of the peasantry

brogue[2] (brəʊg) NOUN 1 a sturdy walking shoe, often with ornamental perforations. 2 an untanned shoe worn formerly in Ireland and Scotland.
▷HISTORY C16: from Irish Gaelic *bróg* boot, shoe, probably from Old Norse *brōk* leg covering

broider (ˈbrɔɪdə) VERB (*tr*) an archaic word for **embroider**.
▷HISTORY C15: from Old French *brosder*, of Germanic origin; see EMBROIDER

broil[1] (brɔɪl) VERB 1 the usual US and Canadian word for **grill**[1] (sense 1). 2 to become or cause to become extremely hot. 3 (*intr*) to be furious. ◆ NOUN 4 the process of broiling. 5 something broiled.
▷HISTORY C14: from Old French *bruillir* to burn, of uncertain origin

broil[2] (brɔɪl) *Archaic* ◆ NOUN 1 a loud quarrel or disturbance; brawl. ◆ VERB 2 (*intr*) to brawl; quarrel.
▷HISTORY C16: from Old French *brouiller* to mix, from *breu* broth; see BREWIS, BROSE

broiler (ˈbrɔɪlə) NOUN 1 a young tender chicken suitable for roasting. 2 *Chiefly US* a pan, grate, etc. for broiling food. 3 a very hot day.

broiler house NOUN a building in which broiler chickens are reared in confined conditions.

broke (brəʊk) VERB 1 the past tense of **break**. ◆ ADJECTIVE 2 *Informal* having no money; bankrupt. 3 **go for broke**. *Slang* to risk everything in a gambling or other venture.

broken (ˈbrəʊkən) VERB 1 the past participle of **break**. ◆ ADJECTIVE 2 fractured, smashed, or splintered: *a broken vase*. 3 imperfect or incomplete; fragmentary: *a broken set of books*. 4 interrupted; disturbed; disconnected: *broken sleep*. 5 intermittent or discontinuous: *broken sunshine*. 6 varying in direction or intensity, as of pitch: *a broken note; a broken run*. 7 not functioning: *a broken radio*. 8 spoilt or ruined by divorce (esp in the phrases **broken home**, **broken marriage**). 9 (of a trust, promise, contract, etc.) violated; infringed. 10 overcome with grief or disappointment: *a broken heart*. 11 (of the speech of a foreigner) imperfect in grammar, vocabulary, and pronunciation: *broken English*. 12 *Also* **broken-in**. made tame or disciplined by training: *a broken horse; a broken recruit*. 13 exhausted or weakened as through ill-health or misfortune. 14 confused or disorganized: *broken ranks of soldiers*. 15 breached or opened: *broken defensive lines*. 16 irregular or rough; uneven: *broken ground*. 17 bankrupt or out of money: *a broken industry*. 18 (of colour) having a multicoloured decorative effect, as by stippling paint onto a surface.
▸ **ˈbrokenly** ADVERB

broken chord NOUN *Music* a chord played as an arpeggio.

broken consort NOUN See **consort** (sense 4).

broken-down ADJECTIVE 1 worn out, as by age or long use; dilapidated: *a broken-down fence*. 2 not in working order: *a broken-down tractor*. 3 physically or mentally ill.

brokenhearted (ˌbrəʊkənˈhɑːtɪd) ADJECTIVE overwhelmed by grief or disappointment.
▸ **ˌbrokenˈheartedly** ADVERB ▸ **ˌbrokenˈheartedness** NOUN

Broken Hill NOUN a city in SE Australia, in W New South Wales: mining centre for lead, silver, and zinc. Pop.: 24 500 (latest est.).

broken wind (wɪnd) NOUN *Vet science* another name for **heaves** (sense 1).

broker (ˈbrəʊkə) NOUN 1 an agent who, acting on behalf of a principal, buys or sells goods, securities, etc., in return for a commission: *insurance broker*. 2 (formerly) short for **stockbroker**. 3 a dealer in second-hand goods. ◆ VERB 4 to act as a broker (in).
▷HISTORY C14: from Anglo-French *brocour* broacher (of casks, hence, one who sells, agent), from Old Northern French *broquier* to tap a cask, from *broque* tap of a cask; see BROACH[1]

brokerage (ˈbrəʊkərɪdʒ) NOUN 1 commission charged by a broker to his principals. 2 a broker's business or office.

broker-dealer NOUN another name for **stockbroker**.

broking (ˈbrəʊkɪŋ) ADJECTIVE 1 acting as a broker. ◆ NOUN 2 the business of a broker.
▷HISTORY C16: from obsolete verb *broke*; see BROKER

brolga (ˈbrɒlgə) NOUN a large grey Australian crane, *Grus rubicunda*, having a red-and-green head and a trumpeting call. Also called: **Australian crane**, **native companion**.
▷HISTORY C19: from a native Australian language

brolly (ˈbrɒlɪ) NOUN, *plural* **-lies**. an informal Brit name for **umbrella** (sense 1).

bromal (ˈbrəʊməl) NOUN a yellowish oily synthetic liquid formerly used medicinally as a sedative and hypnotic; tribromoacetaldehyde. Formula: Br_3CCHO.
▷HISTORY C19: from BROM(INE) + AL(COHOL)

bromate (ˈbrəʊmeɪt) NOUN 1 any salt or ester of bromic acid, containing the monovalent group $-BrO_3$ or ion BrO_3^-. ◆ VERB 2 to add bromate to (a product), as in the treatment of flour.
▷HISTORY C19: probably from German *Bromat*; see BROMO-, -ATE[1]

brome grass *or* **brome** (brəʊm) NOUN any of various grasses of the genus *Bromus*, having small flower spikes in loose drooping clusters. Some species are used for hay.
▷HISTORY C18: via Latin from Greek *bromos* oats, of obscure origin

bromeliad (brəʊˈmiːlɪˌæd) NOUN any plant of the tropical American family *Bromeliaceae*, typically epiphytes with a rosette of fleshy leaves. The family includes the pineapple and Spanish moss.
▷HISTORY C19: from New Latin *Bromelia* type genus, after Olaf *Bromelius* (1639–1705), Swedish botanist
▸ **broˌmeliˈaceous** ADJECTIVE

bromelin (ˈbrəʊməlɪn) NOUN a protein-digesting enzyme (see **endopeptidase**) found in pineapple and extracted for use in treating joint pain and inflammation, hay fever, and various other conditions.
▷HISTORY C20: from *Bromelia* type genus of pineapple family (see BROMELIAD) + -IN

bromeosin (brəʊˈmiːəsɪn) NOUN *Chem* another name for **eosin**.
▷HISTORY C20: from BROMO- + EOSIN

bromic (ˈbrəʊmɪk) ADJECTIVE of or containing bromine in the trivalent or pentavalent state.

bromic acid NOUN a colourless unstable water-soluble liquid used as an oxidizing agent in the manufacture of dyes and pharmaceuticals. Formula: $HBrO_3$.

bromide (ˈbrəʊmaɪd) NOUN 1 any salt of hydrobromic acid, containing the monovalent ion Br^- (**bromide ion**). 2 any compound containing a bromine atom, such as methyl bromide. 3 a dose of sodium or potassium bromide given as a sedative. 4 **a** a trite saying; platitude. **b** a dull or boring person.
▷HISTORY C19, C20 (cliché): from BROM(INE) + -IDE

bromide paper NOUN a type of photographic paper coated with an emulsion of silver bromide usually containing a small quantity of silver iodide.

bromidic (brəʊˈmɪdɪk) ADJECTIVE ordinary; dull.

brominate (ˈbrəʊmɪˌneɪt) VERB to treat or react with bromine. Also: **bromate**.
▸ **ˌbrominˈation** NOUN

bromine (ˈbrəʊmiːn, -mɪn) NOUN a pungent dark red volatile liquid element of the halogen series that occurs in natural brine and is used in the production of chemicals, esp ethylene dibromide. Symbol: Br; atomic no.: 35; atomic wt.: 79.904; valency: 1, 3, 5, or 7; relative density 3.12; density (gas): 7.59 kg/m^3; melting pt.: –7.2°C; boiling pt.: 58.78°C.
▷HISTORY C19: from French *brome* bromine, from Greek *brōmos* bad smell + -INE[2], of uncertain origin

bromism (ˈbrəʊˌmɪzəm) *or US* **brominism** NOUN poisoning caused by the excessive intake of bromine or compounds containing bromine.

Bromley (ˈbrɒmlɪ) NOUN a borough of SE Greater London. Pop.: 295 530 (2001). Area: 153 sq. km (59 sq. miles).

bromo- *or before a vowel* **brom-** COMBINING FORM indicating the presence of bromine: *bromoform*.

bromoform (ˈbrəʊməˌfɔːm) NOUN a heavy colourless liquid substance with a sweetish taste and an odour resembling that of chloroform. Formula: $CHBr_3$. Systematic name: **tribromomethane**.

Bromsgrove (ˈbrɒmzˌgrəʊv) NOUN a town in W central England, in N Worcestershire. Pop.: 26 366 (1991).

bronchi (ˈbrɒŋkaɪ) NOUN the plural of **bronchus**.

bronchia (ˈbrɒŋkɪə) PLURAL NOUN another name for **bronchial tubes**.
▷HISTORY C17: from Late Latin, from Greek *bronkhia*, plural of *bronkhion*, diminutive of *bronkhus* windpipe, throat

bronchial (ˈbrɒŋkɪəl) ADJECTIVE of or relating to the bronchi or the bronchial tubes.
▸ **ˈbronchially** ADVERB

bronchial tubes PLURAL NOUN the bronchi or their smaller divisions.

bronchiectasis (ˌbrɒŋkɪˈɛktəsɪs) NOUN chronic

dilation of the bronchi or bronchial tubes, which often become infected.
▷HISTORY C19: from BRONCHO- + Greek *ektasis* a stretching

bronchiole (ˈbrɒŋkɪˌəʊl) NOUN any of the smallest bronchial tubes, usually ending in alveoli.
▷HISTORY C19: from New Latin *bronchiolum*, diminutive of Late Latin *bronchium*, singular of BRONCHIA
▸**bronchiolar** (ˌbrɒŋkɪˈəʊlə) ADJECTIVE

bronchiolitis (ˌbrɒŋkiəʊˈlaɪtɪs) NOUN a condition in which the small airways in the lungs become inflamed by a virus. It is most common in infants, who become breathless in severe cases. Recurrent attacks may lead to asthma.

bronchitis (brɒŋˈkaɪtɪs) NOUN inflammation of the bronchial tubes, characterized by coughing, difficulty in breathing, etc., caused by infection or irritation of the respiratory tract.
▸**bronchitic** (brɒŋˈkɪtɪk) ADJECTIVE, NOUN

broncho- *or before a vowel* **bronch-** COMBINING FORM indicating or relating to the bronchi: *bronchitis*.
▷HISTORY from Greek: BRONCHUS

bronchodilator (ˈbrɒŋkəʊdaɪˌleɪtə) NOUN any drug or other agent that causes dilation of the bronchial tubes by relaxing bronchial muscle: used, esp in the form of aerosol sprays, for the relief of asthma.

bronchography (brɒŋˈkɒgrəfɪ) NOUN radiography of the bronchial tubes after the introduction of a radiopaque medium into the bronchi.

bronchopneumonia (ˌbrɒŋkəʊnjuːˈməʊnɪə) NOUN inflammation of the lungs, originating in the bronchioles.

bronchoscope (ˈbrɒŋkəˌskəʊp) NOUN an instrument for examining and providing access to the interior of the bronchial tubes.
▸**bronchoscopic** (ˌbrɒŋkəˈskɒpɪk) ADJECTIVE
▸**bronchoscopist** (brɒŋˈkɒskəpɪst) NOUN ▸**bronˈchoscopy** NOUN

bronchus (ˈbrɒŋkəs) NOUN, *plural* **-chi** (-kaɪ). either of the two main branches of the trachea, which contain cartilage within their walls.
▷HISTORY C18: from New Latin, from Greek *bronkhos* windpipe

bronco *or* **broncho** (ˈbrɒŋkəʊ) NOUN, *plural* **-cos** *or* **-chos**. (in the US and Canada) a wild or partially tamed pony or mustang of the western plains.
▷HISTORY C19: from Mexican Spanish, short for Spanish *potro bronco* unbroken colt, probably from Latin *broccus* projecting (as knots on wood), hence, rough, wild

broncobuster (ˈbrɒŋkəʊˌbʌstə) NOUN (in the western US and Canada) a cowboy who breaks in broncos or wild horses.

brontosaurus (ˌbrɒntəˈsɔːrəs) *or* **brontosaur** (ˈbrɒntəˌsɔː) NOUN any very large herbivorous quadrupedal dinosaur of the genus *Apatosaurus*, common in North America during Jurassic times, having a long neck and long tail: suborder *Sauropoda* (sauropods).
▷HISTORY C19: from New Latin, from Greek *brontē* thunder + *sauros* lizard

Bronx (brɒŋks) NOUN **the.** a borough of New York City, on the mainland, separated from Manhattan by the Harlem River. Pop.: 1 203 789 (1990).

Bronx cheer NOUN *Chiefly US* a loud noise, imitating a fart, made with the lips and tongue and expressing derision or contempt; raspberry.

bronze (brɒnz) NOUN [1] **a** any hard water-resistant alloy consisting of copper and smaller proportions of tin and sometimes zinc and lead. **b** any similar copper alloy containing other elements in place of tin, such as aluminium bronze, beryllium bronze, etc. See also **phosphor bronze, gunmetal.** Compare **brass** (sense 1). [2] a yellowish-brown colour or pigment. [3] a statue, medal, or other object made of bronze. [4] short for **bronze medal.** ◆ ADJECTIVE [5] made of or resembling bronze. [6] of a yellowish-brown colour: *a bronze skin.* ◆ VERB [7] (esp of the skin) to make or become brown; tan. [8] (*tr*) to give the appearance of bronze to.
▷HISTORY C18: from French, from Italian *bronzo*, perhaps ultimately from Latin *Brundisium* Brindisi, famed for its bronze
▸ˈ**bronzy** ADJECTIVE

bronze age NOUN *Classical myth* a period of man's existence marked by war and violence, following the golden and silver ages and preceding the iron age.

Bronze Age NOUN *Archaeol* **a** a technological stage between the Stone and Iron Ages, beginning in the Middle East about 4500 B.C. and lasting in Britain from about 2000 to 500 B.C., during which weapons and tools were made of bronze and there was intensive trading. **b** (*as modifier*): *a Bronze-Age tool.*

bronze medal NOUN a medal of bronze, awarded to a competitor who comes third in a contest or race. Compare **gold medal, silver medal.**

bronzer (ˈbrɒnzə) NOUN a cosmetic applied to the skin to simulate a sun tan.

bronze whaler NOUN a shark, *Carcharhinus brachyurus*, of southern Australian waters, having a bronze-coloured back.

bronzing (ˈbrɒnzɪŋ) NOUN *Building trades* [1] blue pigment producing a metallic lustre when ground into paint media at fairly high concentrations. [2] the application of a mixture of powdered metal or pigments of a metallic lustre, and a binding medium, such as gold size, to a surface.

bronzite (ˈbrɒnzaɪt) NOUN a type of orthopyroxene often having a metallic or pearly sheen.

brooch (brəʊtʃ) NOUN an ornament with a hinged pin and catch, worn fastened to clothing.
▷HISTORY C13: from Old French *broche*; see BROACH[1]

brood (bruːd) NOUN [1] a number of young animals, esp birds, produced at one hatching. [2] all the offspring in one family: often used jokingly or contemptuously. [3] a group of a particular kind; breed. [4] (*as modifier*) kept for breeding: *a brood mare.* ◆ VERB [5] (of a bird) **a** to sit on or hatch (eggs). **b** (*tr*) to cover (young birds) protectively with the wings. [6] (when *intr*, often foll by *on, over* or *upon*) to ponder morbidly or persistently.
▷HISTORY Old English *brōd*; related to Middle High German *bruot*, Dutch *broed*; see BREED
▸ˈ**brooding** NOUN, ADJECTIVE ▸ˈ**broodingly** ADVERB

brooder (ˈbruːdə) NOUN [1] an enclosure or other structure, usually heated, used for rearing young chickens or other fowl. [2] a person or thing that broods.

brood pouch NOUN [1] a pouch or cavity in certain animals, such as frogs and fishes, in which their eggs develop and hatch. [2] another name for **marsupium.**

broody (ˈbruːdɪ) ADJECTIVE **broodier, broodiest.** [1] moody; meditative; introspective. [2] (of poultry) wishing to sit on or hatch eggs. [3] *Informal* (of a woman) wishing to have a baby of her own.
▸ˈ**broodiness** NOUN

brook[1] (brʊk) NOUN a natural freshwater stream smaller than a river.
▷HISTORY Old English *brōc*; related to Old High German *bruoh* swamp, Dutch *broek*

brook[2] (brʊk) VERB (*tr; usually used with a negative*) to bear; tolerate.
▷HISTORY Old English *brūcan*; related to Gothic *brūkjan* to use, Old High German *brūhhan*, Latin *fruī* to enjoy
▸ˈ**brookable** ADJECTIVE

Brook Farm NOUN an experimental communist community established by writers and scholars in West Roxbury, Massachusetts, from 1841 to 1847.

brookite (ˈbrʊkaɪt) NOUN a reddish-brown to black mineral consisting of titanium oxide in orthorhombic crystalline form: occurs in silica veins. Formula: TiO_2.
▷HISTORY C19: named after Henry J. *Brooke* (died 1857), English mineralogist

brooklet (ˈbrʊklɪt) NOUN a small brook.

brooklime (ˈbrʊkˌlaɪm) NOUN either of two blue-flowered scrophulariaceous trailing plants, *Veronica americana* of North America or *V. beccabunga* of Europe and Asia, growing in moist places. See also **speedwell.**
▷HISTORY C16: variant of C15 *brokelemk* speedwell, from BROOK[1] + *-lemk*, from Old English *hleomoce*; influenced by *lime*

Brooklyn (ˈbrʊklɪn) NOUN a borough of New York City, on the SW end of Long Island. Pop.: 2 291 664 (1990).

Brooks Range (brʊks) NOUN a mountain range in N Alaska. Highest peak: Mount Isto, 2761 m (9058 ft.).

brook trout NOUN a North American freshwater trout, *Salvelinus fontinalis*, introduced in Europe and valued as a food and game fish. Also called: **speckled trout.**

brookweed (ˈbrʊkˌwiːd) NOUN either of two white-flowered primulaceous plants, *Samolus valerandi* of Europe or *S. floribundus* of North America, growing in moist places. Also called: **water pimpernel.** See also **pimpernel.**

broom (bruːm, brʊm) NOUN [1] an implement for sweeping consisting of a long handle to which is attached either a brush of straw, bristles, or twigs, bound together, or a solid head into which are set tufts of bristles or fibres. [2] any of various yellow-flowered Eurasian leguminous shrubs of the genera *Cytisus, Genista,* and *Spartium*, esp *C. scoparius.* [3] **new broom.** a newly appointed official, etc., eager to make changes. ◆ VERB [4] (*tr*) to sweep with a broom.
▷HISTORY Old English *brōm*; related to Old High German *brāmo*, Middle Dutch *bremme*

broomcorn (ˈbruːmˌkɔːn, ˈbrʊm-) NOUN a variety of sorghum, *Sorghum vulgare technicum*, the long stiff flower stalks of which have been used for making brooms.

broomrape (ˈbruːmˌreɪp, ˈbrʊm-) NOUN any orobanchaceous plant of the genus *Orobanche*: brownish small-flowered leafless parasites on the roots of other plants, esp on legumes.
▷HISTORY C16: adaptation and partial translation of Medieval Latin *rāpum genistae* tuber (hence: root nodule) of Genista (a type of broom plant)

broomstick (ˈbruːmˌstɪk, ˈbrʊm-) NOUN the long handle of a broom.

bros. *or* **Bros.** ABBREVIATION FOR brothers.

brose (brəʊz) NOUN *Scot* oatmeal or pease porridge, sometimes with butter or fat added. See also **Atholl brose.**
▷HISTORY C13 *broys*, from Old French *broez*, from *breu* broth, of Germanic origin

bro talk NOUN [1] *NZ* Maori English. [2] *NZ* English spoken with a Maori accent.
▷HISTORY C20: BRO[1] (sense 1) + TALK

broth (brɒθ) NOUN [1] a soup made by boiling meat, fish, vegetables, etc., in water. [2] another name for **stock** (sense 19).
▷HISTORY Old English *broth*; related to Old Norse *broth*, Old High German *brod*, German *brodeln* to boil; see BREW

brothel (ˈbrɒθəl) NOUN [1] a house or other place where men pay to have sexual intercourse with prostitutes. [2] *Austral informal* any untidy or messy place.
▷HISTORY C16: short for *brothel-house*, from C14 *brothel* useless person, from Old English *brēothan* to deteriorate; related to *briethel* worthless

brother (ˈbrʌðə) NOUN, *plural* **brothers** *or (archaic except when referring to fellow members of a religion, sect, society, etc.)* **brethren.** [1] a male person having the same parents as another person. [2] short for **half-brother** or **stepbrother.** [3] **a** a male person belonging to the same group, profession, nationality, trade union, etc., as another or others; fellow member. **b** (*as modifier*): *brother workers.* [4] comrade; friend: used as a form of address. [5] *Christianity* **a** a member of a male religious order who undertakes work for the order without actually being in holy orders. **b** a lay member of a male religious order. Related adjective: **fraternal.** ◆ INTERJECTION [6] *Slang* an exclamation of amazement, disgust, surprise, disappointment, etc.
▷HISTORY Old English *brōthor*; related to Old Norse *brōthir*, Old High German *bruoder*, Latin *frāter*, Greek *phratēr*, Sanskrit *bhrātar*

brotherhood (ˈbrʌðəˌhʊd) NOUN [1] the state of being related as a brother or brothers. [2] an association or fellowship, such as a trade union. [3] all persons engaged in a particular profession, trade, etc. [4] the belief, feeling, or hope that all men should regard and treat one another as brothers.

brother-in-law NOUN, *plural* **brothers-in-law.** [1] the brother of one's wife or husband. [2] the husband of one's sister.

brotherly (ˈbrʌðəlɪ) ADJECTIVE [1] of, resembling, or suitable to a brother, esp in showing loyalty and

affection; fraternal. ◆ ADVERB [2] in a brotherly way; fraternally.
► 'brotherliness NOUN

brougham ('bru:əm, bru:m) NOUN [1] a four-wheeled horse-drawn closed carriage having a raised open driver's seat in front. [2] *Obsolete* a large car with an open compartment at the front for the driver. [3] *Obsolete* an early electric car.
▷HISTORY C19: named after Henry Peter, Lord *Brougham* (1778–1868)

brought (brɔ:t) VERB the past tense and past participle of **bring**.

broughta ('brɔ:tə) *or* **broughtas** ('brɔ:təs) NOUN variants of **braata**.

brouhaha ('bru:hɑ:hɑ:) NOUN a loud confused noise; commotion; uproar.
▷HISTORY French, of imitative origin

brow (braʊ) NOUN [1] the part of the face from the eyes to the hairline; forehead. [2] short for **eyebrow**. [3] the expression of the face; countenance: *a troubled brow*. [4] the top of a mine shaft; pithead. [5] the jutting top of a hill, etc. [6] *Northern English dialect* a steep slope on a road.
▷HISTORY Old English *brū*; related to Old Norse *brūn* eyebrow, Lithuanian *bruvis*, Greek *ophrus*, Sanskrit *bhrūs*

browband ('braʊ,bænd) NOUN the strap of a horse's bridle that goes across the forehead.

browbeat ('braʊ,bi:t) VERB **-beats, -beating, -beat, -beaten**. (*tr*) to discourage or frighten with threats or a domineering manner; intimidate.
► 'brow,beater NOUN

-browed ADJECTIVE (*in combination*) having a brow or brows as specified: *dark-browed*.

brown (braʊn) NOUN [1] any of various colours, such as those of wood or earth, produced by low intensity light in the wavelength range 620–585 nanometres. [2] a dye or pigment producing these colours. [3] brown cloth or clothing: *dressed in brown*. [4] any of numerous mostly reddish-brown butterflies of the genera *Maniola, Lasiommata*, etc., such as *M. jurtina* (**meadow brown**): family *Satyridae*. ◆ ADJECTIVE [5] of the colour brown. [6] (of bread) made from a flour that has not been bleached or bolted, such as wheatmeal or wholemeal flour. [7] deeply tanned or sunburnt. ◆ VERB [8] to make (esp food as a result of cooking) brown or (esp of food) to become brown.
▷HISTORY Old English *brūn*; related to Old Norse *brūnn*, Old High German *brūn*, Greek *phrunos* toad, Sanskrit *babhru* reddish-brown
► 'brownish *or* 'browny ADJECTIVE ► 'brownness NOUN

brown algae PLURAL NOUN any algae of the phylum *Phaeophyta*, such as the wracks and kelps, which contain a brown pigment in addition to chlorophyll.

brown bag *US* ◆ NOUN [1] a bag made of brown paper, often used for carrying a packed lunch or alcohol. ◆ VERB **brown-bag, -bags, -bagging, -bagged**. (*intr*) [2] to take a packed lunch in a brown bag. [3] to carry alcohol in a brown bag.

brown bagging NOUN the practice of eating one's lunch or drinking a bottle of alcohol from a brown bag.

brown bear NOUN a large ferocious brownish bear, *Ursus arctos*, inhabiting temperate forests of North America, Europe, and Asia. See also **grizzly bear, Kodiak bear**.

brown coal NOUN a low-quality coal intermediate in grade between peat and lignite.

brown cow NOUN *South African* a drink made by mixing cola and milk.

brown creeper NOUN a small bush bird, *Finschia novaeseelandiae*, of South Island, New Zealand. Also called: **bush canary**.

brown dwarf NOUN a type of celestial body midway in mass between a large planet and a small star.

brown earth NOUN an intrazonal soil of temperate humid regions typically developed under deciduous forest into a dark rich layer (mull): characteristic of much of southern and central England.

browned-off ADJECTIVE *Informal* thoroughly discouraged or disheartened; fed up.

brown fat NOUN tissue composed of a type of fat cell that dissipates as heat most of the energy released when food is oxidized; brown adipose tissue. It is present in hibernating animals and human babies and is thought to be important in adult weight control.

brownfield ('braʊn,fi:ld) NOUN (*modifier*) denoting or located in an urban area that has previously been built on: *Hampshire has many brownfield developments*.

brown goods PLURAL NOUN *Marketing* consumer goods such as televisions, radios, or videos. Compare **white goods** (sense 1).

Brownian movement ('braʊnɪən) NOUN random movement of microscopic particles suspended in a fluid, caused by bombardment of the particles by molecules of the fluid. First observed in 1827, it provided strong evidence in support of the kinetic theory of molecules.
▷HISTORY C19: named after Robert *Brown* (1773–1858), Scottish botanist

brownie ('braʊnɪ) NOUN [1] (in folklore) an elf said to do helpful work at night, esp household chores. [2] a small square nutty chocolate cake. [3] *Austral history* a bread made with currants.
▷HISTORY C16: diminutive of BROWN (that is, a small brown man)

Brownie ('braʊnɪ) NOUN [1] another name for **Brownie Guide**. [2] *Trademark* (formerly) a popular make of simple box camera.

Brownie Guide *or* **Brownie** ('braʊnɪ) NOUN a member of the Brownie Guides, one of the junior branches (aged 7–10 years) in The Guide Association.

Brownie Guider NOUN the adult leader of a pack of Brownie Guides. Former name: **Brown Owl**.

Brownie point NOUN a notional mark to one's credit earned for being seen to do the right thing.
▷HISTORY C20: from the mistaken notion that Brownie Guides earn points for good deeds

browning ('braʊnɪŋ) NOUN *Brit* a substance used to darken soups, gravies, etc.

Browning ('braʊnɪŋ) NOUN [1] Also called: **Browning automatic rifle**. a portable gas-operated air-cooled automatic rifle using .30 calibre ammunition and capable of firing between 200 and 350 rounds per minute. Abbreviation: **BAR**. [2] Also called: **Browning machine gun**. a water-cooled automatic machine gun using .30 or .50 calibre ammunition and capable of firing over 500 rounds per minute.
▷HISTORY C20: named after John M. *Browning* (1855–1926), American designer of firearms

Brownist ('braʊnɪst) NOUN a person who supported the principles of church government advocated by Robert Browne and adopted in modified form by the Independents or Congregationalists.
▷HISTORY C16: named after Robert *Browne* (?1550–1633), English Puritan
► 'Brownism NOUN

brown lung disease NOUN another name for **byssinosis**.

brown nose NOUN *Vet science* a form of light sensitization in cattle.

brown-nose *Slang* ◆ VERB [1] to be abjectly subservient (to); curry favour (with). ◆ NOUN [2] an abjectly subservient person; sycophant.
▷HISTORY C20: from the notion that a subservient person kisses the backside of the person with whom he is currying favour

brownout ('braʊn,aʊt) NOUN *Chiefly US* [1] a dimming or reduction in the use of electric lights in a city, esp to conserve electric power or as a defensive precaution in wartime. [2] a temporary reduction in electrical power. Compare **blackout** (sense 3). [3] a temporary slowing down of the workings of the Internet caused when too many users attempt to access it at the same time.

brown owl NOUN another name for **tawny owl**.

Brown Owl NOUN a name (no longer in official use) for **Brownie Guider**.

brown paper NOUN a coarse unbleached paper used for wrapping.

brown rat NOUN a common brownish rat, *Rattus norvegicus*: a serious pest in all parts of the world. Also called: **Norway rat**.

brown rice NOUN unpolished rice, in which the grains retain the outer yellowish-brown layer (bran).

brown rot NOUN [1] a disease of apples, peaches, etc., caused by fungi of the genus *Sclerotinia* and characterized by yellowish-brown masses of spores on the plant surface. [2] decay of timber caused by the action of fungi on the cellulose.

brown seaweed NOUN another term for **brown algae**.

Brown Shirt NOUN [1] (in Nazi Germany) a storm trooper. [2] a member of any fascist party or group.

brown snake NOUN *Austral* any of various common venomous snakes of the genus *Pseudonaja*.

brown-state ADJECTIVE (of linen and lace fabrics) undyed.

brownstone ('braʊn,stəʊn) NOUN *US* [1] a reddish-brown iron-rich sandstone used for building. [2] a house built of or faced with this stone.

brown study NOUN a mood of deep absorption or thoughtfulness; reverie.

brown sugar NOUN sugar that is unrefined or only partially refined.

brown-tail moth NOUN a small brown-and-white European moth, *Euproctis phaeorrhoea*, naturalized in the eastern US where it causes damage to shade trees: family *Lymantriidae* (or *Liparidae*). See also **tussock moth**.

brown toast NOUN *Canadian* toasted wholemeal bread.

brown trout NOUN a common brownish variety of the trout *Salmo trutta* that occurs in the rivers of N Europe and has been successfully introduced in North America. Compare **sea trout** (sense 1).

browse (braʊz) VERB [1] to look through (a book, articles for sale in a shop, etc.) in a casual leisurely manner. [2] *Computing* to search for and read hypertext, esp on the World Wide Web. [3] (of deer, goats, etc.) to feed upon (vegetation) by continual nibbling. ◆ NOUN [4] the act or an instance of browsing. [5] the young twigs, shoots, leaves, etc., on which certain animals feed.
▷HISTORY C15: from French *broust, brost* (modern French *brout*) bud, of Germanic origin; compare Old Saxon *brustian* to bud

browser ('braʊzə) NOUN [1] a person or animal that browses. [2] *Computing* a software package that enables a user to find and read hypertext files, esp on the World Wide Web.

BRT *Text messaging* ABBREVIATION FOR be right there.

BRU INTERNATIONAL CAR REGISTRATION FOR Brunei.

Bruce (bru:s) NOUN *Brit* a jocular name for an Australian man.

brucellosis (,bru:sɪ'ləʊsɪs) NOUN an infectious disease of cattle, goats, dogs, and pigs, caused by bacteria of the genus *Brucella* and transmittable to man (e.g. by drinking contaminated milk): symptoms include fever, chills, and severe headache. Also called: **undulant fever**.
▷HISTORY C20: from New Latin *Brucella*, named after Sir David *Bruce* (1855–1931), Australian bacteriologist and physician

brucine ('bru:si:n, -sin) NOUN bitter poisonous alkaloid resembling strychnine and obtained from the tree *Strychnos nuxvomica*: used mainly in the denaturation of alcohol. Formula: $C_{23}H_{26}N_2O_4$.
▷HISTORY C19: named after James *Bruce* (1730–94), Scottish explorer of Africa

Brücke (*German* 'brykə) NOUN **die** (di:). a group of German Expressionist painters (1905–13), including Karl Schmidt-Rottluff, Fritz Bleyl, Erich Heckel, and Ernst Ludwig Kirchner. In 1912 they exhibited with *der Blaue Reiter*.
▷HISTORY German: literally, the bridge

Bruges (bru:ʒ; *French* bryʒ) NOUN a city in NW Belgium, capital of West Flanders province: centre of the medieval European wool and cloth trade. Pop.: 116 246 (2000 est.). Flemish name: **Brugge** ('bryxə).

brugmansia (brʊg'mænsɪə) NOUN any of various solanaceous plants of the genus *Brugmansia*, native to tropical American regions and closely related to daturas, having sweetly scented flowers.

bruin ('bru:ɪn) NOUN a name for a bear, used in children's tales, fables, etc.

▷**HISTORY** C17: from Dutch *bruin* brown, the name of the bear in the epic *Reynard the Fox*

bruise (bru:z) VERB (*mainly tr*) 1 (*also intr*) to injure (tissues) without breaking the skin, usually with discoloration, or (of tissues) to be injured in this way. 2 to offend or injure (someone's feelings) by an insult, unkindness, etc. 3 to damage the surface of (something), as by a blow. 4 to crush (food, etc.) by pounding or pressing. ◆ NOUN 5 a bodily injury without a break in the skin, usually with discoloration; contusion.
▷**HISTORY** Old English *brȳsan*, of Celtic origin; compare Irish *brūigim* I bruise

bruiser ('bru:zə) NOUN a strong tough person, esp a boxer or a bully.

bruising ('bru:zɪŋ) ADJECTIVE 1 causing bruises, as by a blow. 2 aggressively antagonistic; hurtful: *four months of bruising negotiation*. ◆ NOUN 3 a bruise or bruises.

bruit (bru:t) VERB 1 (*tr; often passive*; usually foll by *about*) to report; rumour: *it was bruited about that the king was dead*. ◆ NOUN 2 *Med* an abnormal sound heard within the body during auscultation, esp a heart murmur. 3 *Archaic* **a** a rumour. **b** a loud outcry; clamour.
▷**HISTORY** C15: via French from Medieval Latin *brūgītus*, probably from Vulgar Latin *bragere* (unattested) to yell + Latin *rugīre* to roar

Brule *or* **Brûlé** (bru:'leɪ) NOUN (*sometimes not capital*) short for **bois-brûlé**.

Brumaire *French* (brymɛr) NOUN the month of mist: the second month of the French revolutionary calendar, extending from Oct. 23 to Nov. 21.
▷**HISTORY** C19: from *brume* mist, from Latin *brūma* winter; see BRUME

brumal ('bru:məl) ADJECTIVE of, characteristic of, or relating to winter; wintry.

brumby ('brʌmbɪ) NOUN, *plural* **-bies**. *Austral* 1 a wild horse, esp one descended from runaway stock. 2 *Informal* a wild or unruly person.
▷**HISTORY** C19: of unknown origin

brume (bru:m) NOUN *Poetic* heavy mist or fog.
▷**HISTORY** C19: from French: mist, winter, from Latin *brūma*, contracted from *brevissima diēs* the shortest day
▸'**brumous** ADJECTIVE

Brummagem ('brʌmədʒəm) NOUN 1 an informal name for **Birmingham**. Often shortened to: **Brum.** 2 (*sometimes not capital*) something that is cheap and flashy, esp imitation jewellery. ◆ ADJECTIVE 3 (*sometimes not capital*) cheap and gaudy; tawdry.
▷**HISTORY** C17: from earlier *Bromecham*, local variant of BIRMINGHAM

Brummie ('brʌmɪ) NOUN 1 *Informal* a native or inhabitant of Birmingham. ◆ ADJECTIVE 2 of or relating to Birmingham.
▷**HISTORY** C20: from BRUMMAGEM

brunch (brʌntʃ) NOUN a meal eaten late in the morning, combining breakfast with lunch.
▷**HISTORY** C20: from BR(EAKFAST) + (L)UNCH

Brundisium (brʌn'dɪzɪəm) NOUN the ancient name for **Brindisi**.

Brunei (bru:'naɪ, 'bru:naɪ) NOUN 1 a sultanate in NW Borneo, consisting of two separate areas on the South China Sea, otherwise bounded by Sarawak: controlled all of Borneo and parts of the Philippines and the Sulu Islands in the 16th century; under British protection since 1888; internally self-governing since 1971; became independent in 1984 as a member of the Commonwealth. The economy depends chiefly on oil and natural gas. Official language: Malay; English is also widely spoken. Religion: Muslim. Currency: Brunei dollar. Capital: Bandar Seri Begawan. Pop.: 344 000 (2001 est.). Area: 5765 sq. km (2226 sq. miles). 2 the former name of **Bandar Seri Begawan**.

brunette (bru:'nɛt) NOUN 1 a girl or woman with dark brown hair. ◆ ADJECTIVE *also* **brunet.** 2 dark brown: *brunette hair*.
▷**HISTORY** C17: from French, feminine of *brunet* dark, brownish, from *brun* brown, of Germanic origin; see BROWN

Brunhild ('brʊnhɪld, -hɪlt) *or* **Brünnhilde** (*German* bryn'hɪldə) NOUN (in the *Nibelungenlied*) a legendary queen won for King Gunther by the magic of Siegfried: corresponds to Brynhild in Norse mythology.

Brunswick ('brʌnzwɪk) NOUN 1 a former duchy (1635–1918) and state (1918–46) of central Germany, now part of the state of Lower Saxony; formerly (1949–90) part of West Germany. 2 a city in central Germany: formerly capital of the duchy and state of Brunswick. Pop.: 246 800 (1999 est.). German name: **Braunschweig.**

brunt (brʌnt) NOUN the main force or shock of a blow, attack, etc. (esp in the phrase **bear the brunt of**).
▷**HISTORY** C14: of unknown origin

bruschetta (bru'ʃɛtə) NOUN an Italian open sandwich of toasted bread topped with olive oil and tomatoes, olives, etc.
▷**HISTORY** C20: from Italian *bruscare*, from *abbrustolire* to toast

brush[1] (brʌʃ) NOUN 1 a device made of bristles, hairs, wires, etc., set into a firm back or handle: used to apply paint, clean or polish surfaces, groom the hair, etc. 2 the act or an instance of brushing. 3 a light stroke made in passing; graze. 4 a brief encounter or contact, esp an unfriendly one; skirmish. 5 the bushy tail of a fox, often kept as a trophy after a hunt, or of certain breeds of dog. 6 an electric conductor, esp one made of carbon, that conveys current between stationary and rotating parts of a generator, motor, etc. 7 a dark brush-shaped region observed when a biaxial crystal is viewed through a microscope, caused by interference between beams of polarized light. ◆ VERB 8 (*tr*) to clean, polish, scrub, paint, etc., with a brush. 9 (*tr*) to apply or remove with a brush or brushing movement: *brush the crumbs off the table*. 10 (*tr*) to touch lightly and briefly. 11 (*intr*) to move so as to graze or touch something lightly. ◆ See also **brush aside, brush off, brush up.**
▷**HISTORY** C14: from Old French *broisse*, perhaps from *broce* BRUSH[2]
▸'**brusher** NOUN ▸'**brush,like**

brush[2] (brʌʃ) NOUN 1 a thick growth of shrubs and small trees; scrub. 2 land covered with scrub. 3 broken or cut branches or twigs; brushwood. 4 wooded sparsely populated country; backwoods.
▷**HISTORY** C16 (dense undergrowth), C14 (cuttings of trees): from Old French *broce*, from Vulgar Latin *bruscia* (unattested) brushwood

brush aside *or* **away** VERB (*tr, adverb*) to dismiss without consideration; disregard.

brush border NOUN *Physiol* a layer of tightly packed minute finger-like protuberances on cells that line absorptive surfaces, such as those of the intestine and kidney. See also **microvillus.**

brush discharge NOUN a slightly luminous electrical discharge between points of high charge density when the charge density is insufficient to cause a spark or around sharp points on a highly charged conductor because of ionization of air molecules in their vicinity.

brushed (brʌʃt) ADJECTIVE *Textiles* treated with a brushing process to raise the nap and give a softer, warmer finish: *brushed nylon*.

brush fire NOUN 1 a fire in bushes and scrub. 2 a minor local war.

brush flower NOUN a flower or inflorescence with numerous long stamens, usually pollinated by birds or bats.

brushmark ('brʌʃ,mɑ:k) NOUN the indented lines sometimes left by the bristles of a brush on a painted surface.

brush off *Slang* ◆ VERB (*tr, adverb*) 1 to dismiss and ignore (a person), esp curtly. ◆ NOUN **brushoff.** 2 an abrupt dismissal or rejection.

brush-tailed phalanger NOUN *Austral* another name for **tuan**[2].

brush-tailed possum *or* **brush-tail possum** NOUN any of several widely-distributed Australian possums of the genus *Trichosurus*.

brush turkey NOUN any of several gallinaceous birds, esp *Alectura lathami*, of New Guinea and Australia, having a black plumage: family *Megapodidae* (megapodes).

brush up VERB (*adverb*) 1 (*tr*; often foll by *on*) to refresh one's knowledge, skill, or memory of (a subject). 2 to make (a person or oneself) tidy, clean, or neat as after a journey. ◆ NOUN **brush-up.** 3 *Brit* the act or an instance of tidying one's appearance (esp in the phrase **wash and brush-up**).

brushwood ('brʌʃ,wʊd) NOUN 1 cut or broken-off tree branches, twigs, etc. 2 another word for **brush**[2] (sense 1).

brushwork ('brʌʃ,wɜ:k) NOUN 1 a characteristic manner of applying paint with a brush: *that is not Rembrandt's brushwork*. 2 work done with a brush.

brushy[1] ('brʌʃɪ) ADJECTIVE **brushier, brushiest.** like a brush; thick and furry.

brushy[2] ('brʌʃɪ) ADJECTIVE **brushier, brushiest.** covered or overgrown with brush.

brusque (bru:sk, brʊsk) ADJECTIVE blunt or curt in manner or speech.
▷**HISTORY** C17: from French, from Italian *brusco* sour, rough, from Medieval Latin *bruscus* butcher's broom
▸'**brusquely** ADVERB ▸'**brusqueness** *or* (*less commonly*) **brusquerie** ('bru:skərɪ) NOUN

Brussels ('brʌsəlz) NOUN the capital of Belgium, in the central part: became capital of Belgium in 1830; seat of the European Commission. Pop. (urban area): 1 121 000 (2000 est.). Flemish name: **Brussel** ('brysəl). French name: **Bruxelles.**

Brussels carpet NOUN a worsted carpet with a heavy pile formed by uncut loops of wool on a linen warp.

Brussels lace NOUN a fine lace with a raised or appliqué design.

Brussels sprout NOUN 1 a variety of cabbage, *Brassica oleracea gemmifera*, having a stout stem studded with budlike heads of tightly folded leaves, resembling tiny cabbages. 2 the head of this plant, eaten as a vegetable.

brussen ('brʌsən) ADJECTIVE *Northern English dialect* bold.

brut (bru:t; *French* bryt) ADJECTIVE (of champagne) not sweet; dry.
▷**HISTORY** C19: from French raw, rough, from Latin *brūtus* heavy; see BRUTE

brutal ('bru:təl) ADJECTIVE 1 cruel; vicious; savage. 2 extremely honest or coarse in speech or manner. 3 harsh; severe; extreme: *brutal cold*.
▸**bru'tality** NOUN ▸'**brutally** ADVERB

brutalism ('bru:tə,lɪzəm) NOUN an austere style of architecture characterized by emphasis on such structural materials as undressed concrete and unconcealed service pipes. Also called: **new brutalism.**
▸'**brutalist** NOUN, ADJECTIVE

brutalize *or* **brutalise** ('bru:tə,laɪz) VERB 1 to make or become brutal. 2 (*tr*) to treat brutally.
▸,**brutali'zation** *or* ,**brutali'sation** NOUN

brute (bru:t) NOUN 1 **a** any animal except man; beast; lower animal. **b** (*as modifier*): *brute nature*. 2 a brutal person. ◆ ADJECTIVE (*prenominal*) 3 wholly instinctive or physical (esp in the phrases **brute strength, brute force**). 4 without reason or intelligence. 5 coarse and grossly sensual.
▷**HISTORY** C15: from Latin *brūtus* heavy, irrational; related to *gravis* heavy

brutify ('bru:tɪ,faɪ) VERB **-fies, -fying, -fied.** a less common word for **brutalize** (sense 1).

brutish ('bru:tɪʃ) ADJECTIVE 1 of, relating to, or resembling a brute or brutes; animal. 2 coarse; cruel; stupid.
▸'**brutishly** ADVERB ▸'**brutishness** NOUN

Bruxelles (brysɛl) NOUN the French name for **Brussels.**

bruxism ('brʌksɪzəm) NOUN the habit of grinding the teeth, esp unconsciously.
▷**HISTORY** irregularly formed from Greek *brykein* to gnash the teeth + -ISM

Brynhild ('brɪnhɪld) NOUN *Norse myth* a Valkyrie won as the wife of Gunnar by Sigurd who wakes her from an enchanted sleep: corresponds to Brunhild in the *Nibelungenlied*.

bryology (braɪ'ɒlədʒɪ) NOUN the branch of botany concerned with the study of bryophytes.
▸**bryological** (,braɪə'lɒdʒɪkəl) ADJECTIVE ▸**bry'ologist** NOUN

bryony *or* **briony** ('braɪənɪ) NOUN, *plural* **-nies.** any of several herbaceous climbing plants of the cucurbitaceous genus *Bryonia*, of Europe and N Africa. See also **black bryony, white bryony.**
▷**HISTORY** Old English *bryōnia*, from Latin, from Greek *bruōnia*

bryophyte ('braɪəˌfaɪt) NOUN any plant of the phyla *Bryophyta* (mosses), *Hepatophyta* (liverworts), or *Anthocerophyta* (hornworts), having stems and leaves but lacking true vascular tissue and roots and reproducing by spores.
▷HISTORY C19: New Latin, from Greek *bruon* moss + -PHYTE
▸**bryophytic** (ˌbraɪə'fɪtɪk) ADJECTIVE

bryozoan (ˌbraɪə'zəʊən) NOUN [1] any aquatic invertebrate animal of the phylum *Bryozoa*, forming colonies of polyps each having a ciliated feeding organ (lophophore). Popular name: **sea mat**. ◆ ADJECTIVE [2] of, relating to, or belonging to the *Bryozoa*. ◆ Also: **polyzoan, ectoproct.**
▷HISTORY C19: from Greek *bruon* moss + *zōion* animal

Brython ('brɪθən) NOUN a Celt who speaks a Brythonic language. Compare **Goidel.**
▷HISTORY C19: from Welsh; see BRITON

Brythonic (brɪ'θɒnɪk) NOUN [1] the S group of Celtic languages, consisting of Welsh, Cornish, and Breton. ◆ ADJECTIVE [2] of, relating to, or characteristic of this group of languages. ◆ Also called: **Brittonic.**

bs THE INTERNET DOMAIN NAME FOR Bahamas.

BS ABBREVIATION FOR: [1] Bachelor of Surgery. [2] British Standard(s) (indicating the catalogue or publication number of the British Standards Institution). ◆ [3] INTERNATIONAL CAR REGISTRATION FOR Bahamas.

B.S. (in the US and Canada) ABBREVIATION FOR Bachelor of Science.

B/S *or* **b/s** ABBREVIATION FOR: [1] bags. [2] bales. [3] bill of sale.

BSB ABBREVIATION FOR: [1] British Sky Broadcasting (formerly for British Satellite Broadcasting). [2] **British Standard brass thread.**

BSc ABBREVIATION FOR Bachelor of Science.

BSC ABBREVIATION FOR: [1] (the former) British Steel Corporation. [2] (in Britain) Broadcasting Standards Commission.

BSE ABBREVIATION FOR bovine spongiform encephalopathy: a fatal slow-developing disease of cattle, affecting the nervous system. It is caused by a prion protein and is thought to be transmissable to humans, causing a variant form of Creutzfeldt-Jakob disease. Informal name: **mad cow disease.**

B-setting NOUN *Photog* a shutter setting in which the shutter remains open until the shutter control is released.

BSF ABBREVIATION FOR **British Standard fine thread.**

BSI ABBREVIATION FOR **British Standards Institution.**

B-side NOUN the less important side of a gramophone record. Also called: **flip side.**

bsl ABBREVIATION FOR below sea level.

BSL ABBREVIATION FOR British Sign Language.

Bs/L ABBREVIATION FOR bills of lading.

BSP ABBREVIATION FOR **British Standard pipe thread.**

B Special NOUN a member of a part-time largely Protestant police force formerly functioning in Northern Ireland.

BSS ABBREVIATION FOR British Standards Specification.

BSSc *or* **BSocSc** ABBREVIATION FOR Bachelor of Social Science.

BST ABBREVIATION FOR: [1] bovine somatotrophin: a growth hormone that can be used to increase milk production in dairy cattle. [2] **British Summer Time.**

BSW ABBREVIATION FOR **British Standard Whitworth thread.**

bt THE INTERNET DOMAIN NAME FOR Bhutan.

Bt ABBREVIATION FOR Baronet.

BT ABBREVIATION FOR British Telecom.
▷HISTORY C20: shortened from TELECOMMUNICATIONS

BTEC ('bɪˌtɛk) (in Britain) NOUN ACRONYM FOR: [1] Business and Technology Council. [2] a certificate or diploma in a vocational subject awarded by this body.

BTG ABBREVIATION FOR **British Technology Group.**

B.Th. (in the US and Canada) ABBREVIATION FOR Bachelor of Theology.

btl. ABBREVIATION FOR bottle.

btu *or* **BThU** ABBREVIATION FOR British thermal unit. US abbreviation: **BTU.**

BTU ABBREVIATION FOR **Board of Trade Unit.**

BTW ABBREVIATION FOR by the way: used esp in e-mails, text messages, etc.

bty *or* **btry.** *Military* ABBREVIATION FOR battery.

bub (bʌb) NOUN [1] *US informal* fellow; youngster: used as a form of address. [2] *Austral and NZ slang* **a** a baby. **b bubs grade.** the first grade of schooling; nursery school.
▷HISTORY C20: perhaps from German *Bube* boy

bubal ('bju:bᵊl) *or* **bubalis** ('bju:bəlɪs) NOUN any of various antelopes, esp an extinct N African variety of hartebeest.
▷HISTORY C15: from Latin *būbalus* African gazelle, from Greek *boubalos*, from Greek *bous* ox

bubaline ('bju:bəˌlaɪn, -lɪn) ADJECTIVE [1] (of antelopes) related to or resembling the bubal. [2] resembling or relating to the buffalo.
▷HISTORY C19: from New Latin, from Latin *būbalus*; see BUBAL

bubble ('bʌbᵊl) NOUN [1] a thin film of liquid forming a hollow globule around air or a gas: *a soap bubble*. [2] a small globule of air or a gas in a liquid or a solid, as in carbonated drinks, glass, etc. [3] the sound made by a bubbling liquid. [4] something lacking substance, stability, or seriousness. [5] an unreliable scheme or enterprise. [6] a dome, esp a transparent glass or plastic one. ◆ VERB [7] to form or cause to form bubbles. [8] (*intr*) to move or flow with a gurgling sound. [9] (*intr*; often foll by *over*) to overflow (with excitement, anger, etc.). [10] (*intr*) *Scot* to snivel; blubber. ◆ See also **bubble under.**
▷HISTORY C14: probably of Scandinavian origin; compare Swedish *bubbla*, Danish *boble*, Dutch *bobbel*, all of imitative origin

bubble and squeak NOUN (in Britain and Australia) a dish of leftover boiled cabbage, potatoes, and sometimes cooked meat fried together.
▷HISTORY C18: so called from the sounds of this dish cooking

bubble bath NOUN [1] a powder, liquid, or crystals used to scent, soften, and foam in bath water. [2] a bath to which such a substance has been added.

bubble car NOUN (in Britain, formerly) a small car, often having three wheels, with a transparent bubble-shaped top.

bubble chamber NOUN a device that enables the tracks of ionizing particles to be photographed as a row of bubbles in a superheated liquid. Immediately before the particles enter the chamber the pressure is reduced so that the ionized particles act as centres for small vapour bubbles.

bubble float NOUN *Angling* a hollow spherical float that can be weighted with water to aid casting.

bubble gum NOUN [1] a type of chewing gum that can be blown into large bubbles. [2] *Slang* **a** crassly commercial pop music aimed at the very young. **b** (*as modifier*): *a bubble-gum hit*.

bubble memory NOUN *Computing* a method of storing high volumes of data by the use of minute pockets of magnetism (bubbles) in a semiconducting material: the bubbles may be caused to migrate past a read head or to a buffer area for storage.

bubble pack NOUN another term for **blister pack.**

bubble point NOUN *Chem* the temperature at which bubbles just start to appear in a heated liquid mixture.

bubbler ('bʌblə) NOUN [1] a drinking fountain in which the water is forced in a stream from a small vertical nozzle. [2] *Chem* any device for bubbling gas through a liquid.

bubble under VERB (*intr, adverb*) [1] to remain just beneath a particular level. [2] to continue in the background or under the surface.

bubble wrap NOUN a type of polythene wrapping containing many small air pockets, used as a protective covering when transporting breakable goods.

bubbly ('bʌblɪ) ADJECTIVE **-blier, -bliest.** [1] full of or resembling bubbles. [2] lively; animated; excited: *a bubbly personality*. ◆ NOUN [3] an informal name for **champagne.**

bubo ('bju:bəʊ) NOUN, *plural* **-boes.** *Pathol* inflammation and swelling of a lymph node, often with the formation of pus, esp in the region of the armpit or groin.
▷HISTORY C14: from Medieval Latin *bubō* swelling, from Greek *boubōn* groin, glandular swelling
▸**bubonic** (bju:'bɒnɪk) ADJECTIVE

bubonic plague NOUN an acute infectious febrile disease characterized by chills, prostration, delirium, and formation of buboes: caused by the bite of a rat flea infected with the bacterium *Yersinia pestis*. See also **plague.**

bubonocele (bju:'bɒnəˌsi:l) NOUN an incomplete hernia in the groin; partial inguinal hernia.
▷HISTORY C17: from Greek *boubōn* groin + *kēlē* tumour

bubu ('bu:bu:) NOUN a variant spelling of **boubou.**

buccal ('bʌkᵊl) ADJECTIVE [1] of or relating to the cheek. [2] of or relating to the mouth; oral: *buccal lesion*.
▷HISTORY C19: from Latin *bucca* cheek

buccaneer (ˌbʌkə'nɪə) NOUN [1] a pirate, esp one who preyed on the Spanish colonies and shipping in America and the Caribbean in the 17th and 18th centuries. ◆ VERB (*intr*) [2] to be or act like a buccaneer.
▷HISTORY C17: from French *boucanier*, from *boucaner* to smoke meat, from Old French *boucan* frame for smoking meat, of Tupian origin; originally applied to French and English hunters of wild oxen in the Caribbean

buccinator ('bʌksɪˌneɪtə) NOUN a thin muscle that compresses the cheeks and holds them against the teeth during chewing, etc.
▷HISTORY C17: from Latin, from *buccināre* to sound the trumpet, from *buccina* trumpet

bucentaur (bju:'sɛntɔ:) NOUN the state barge of Venice from which the doge and other officials dropped a ring into the sea on Ascension Day to symbolize the ceremonial marriage of the state with the Adriatic.
▷HISTORY C17: from Italian *bucentoro*, of uncertain origin

Bucephalus (bju:'sɛfələs) NOUN the favourite horse of Alexander the Great.
▷HISTORY C17: from Latin, from Greek *Boukephalos*, from *bous* ox + *kephalē* head

Bucharest (ˌbu:kə'rɛst, ˌbju:-) NOUN the capital of Romania, in the southeast. Pop.: 2 027 512 (1997 est.). Romanian name: **Bucureşti.**

Buchenwald (*German* 'bu:xənvalt) NOUN a village in E central Germany, near Weimar; site of a Nazi concentration camp (1937–45).

Buchmanism ('bʊkməˌnɪzəm) NOUN another name for **Moral Rearmament.**
▷HISTORY C20: named after Frank *Buchman* (1878–1961), US evangelist who founded it
▸**'Buchmanˌite** NOUN, ADJECTIVE

Buchner funnel ('bʌknə) NOUN a laboratory filter funnel used under reduced pressure. It consists of a shallow porcelain cylinder with a flat perforated base.
▷HISTORY named after its inventor, Eduard *Buchner* (1860–1917), German chemist

buchu ('bu:ku:) NOUN any of several S. African rutaceous shrubs of the genus *Barosma*, esp *B. betulina*, whose leaves are used as an antiseptic and diuretic.
▷HISTORY C18: from a South African Bantu name

buck[1] (bʌk) NOUN [1] **a** the male of various animals including the goat, hare, kangaroo, rabbit, and reindeer. **b** (*as modifier*): *a buck antelope*. [2] *South African* an antelope or deer of either sex. [3] *US informal* a young man. [4] *Archaic* a robust spirited young man. [5] *Archaic* a dandy; fop. [6] the act of bucking. ◆ VERB [7] (*intr*) (of a horse or other animal) to jump vertically, with legs stiff and back arched. [8] (*tr*) (of a horse, etc.) to throw (its rider) by bucking. [9] (when *intr*, often foll by *against*) *Informal, chiefly US and Canadian* to resist or oppose obstinately: *to buck against change; to buck change*. [10] (*tr; usually passive*) *Informal* to cheer or encourage: *I was very bucked at passing the exam*. [11] *US and Canadian informal* (esp of a car) to move forward jerkily; jolt. [12] *US and Canadian* to charge against (something) with the head down; butt. ◆ See also **buck up.**

▷HISTORY Old English *bucca* he-goat; related to Old Norse *bukkr*, Old High German *bock*, Old Irish *bocc*
▸'**bucker** NOUN

buck² (bʌk) NOUN [1] *US, Canadian, and Austral informal* a dollar. [2] *South African informal* a rand. [3] **a fast buck.** easily gained money. [4] **bang for one's buck.** See **bang¹** (sense 15).
▷HISTORY C19: of obscure origin

buck³ (bʌk) NOUN [1] *Gymnastics* a type of vaulting horse. [2] a US and Canadian word for **sawhorse.** ◆ VERB [3] *(tr) US and Canadian* to cut (a felled or fallen tree) into lengths.
▷HISTORY C19: short for SAWBUCK

buck⁴ (bʌk) NOUN [1] *Poker* a marker in the jackpot to remind the winner of some obligation when his turn comes to deal. [2] **pass the buck.** *Informal* to shift blame or responsibility onto another. [3] **the buck stops here.** *Informal* the ultimate responsibility lies here.
▷HISTORY C19: probably from *buckhorn knife*, placed before a player in poker to indicate that he was the next dealer

buck and wing NOUN *US* a boisterous tap dance, derived from Black and Irish clog dances.

buckaroo ('bʌkəˌruː, ˌbʌkə'ruː) NOUN, *plural* **-roos.** *Southwestern US* a cowboy.
▷HISTORY C19: variant of Spanish *vaquero*, from *vaca* cow, from Latin *vacca*

buckbean ('bʌkˌbiːn) NOUN a marsh plant, *Menyanthes trifoliata*, with white or pink flowers: family *Menyanthaceae*. Also called: **bogbean.**

buckboard ('bʌkˌbɔːd) NOUN *US and Canadian* an open four-wheeled horse-drawn carriage with the seat attached to a flexible board between the front and rear axles.

buckeen (bʌ'kiːn) NOUN (in Ireland) a poor young man who aspires to the habits and dress of the wealthy.
▷HISTORY C18: from Irish Gaelic *boicín*, diminutive of *boc* an important person

bucket ('bʌkɪt) NOUN [1] an open-topped roughly cylindrical container; pail. [2] Also called: **bucketful.** the amount a bucket will hold. [3] any of various bucket-like parts of a machine, such as the scoop on a mechanical shovel. [4] a cupped blade or bucket-like compartment on the outer circumference of a water wheel, paddle wheel, etc. [5] *Computing* a unit of storage on a direct-access device from which data can be retrieved. [6] *Chiefly US* a turbine rotor blade. [7] *Austral and NZ* an ice cream container. [8] **kick the bucket.** *Slang* to die. ◆ VERB **-kets, -keting, -keted.** [9] *(tr)* to carry in or put into a bucket. [10] *(intr; often foll by down)* (of rain) to fall very heavily: *it bucketed all day.* [11] *(intr; often foll by along) Chiefly Brit* to travel or drive fast. [12] *(tr) Chiefly Brit* to ride (a horse) hard without consideration. [13] *(tr) Austral slang* to criticize severely.
▷HISTORY C13: from Anglo-French *buket*, from Old English *būc*; compare Old High German *būh* belly, German *Bauch* belly

bucket about VERB *(intr) Brit* (esp of a boat in a storm) to toss or shake violently.

bucket ladder NOUN **a** a series of buckets that move in a continuous chain, used to dredge riverbeds, etc., or to excavate land. **b** (*as modifier*): *a bucket-ladder dredger.*

bucket out VERB *(tr)* to empty out with or as if with a bucket.

bucket seat NOUN a seat in a car, aircraft, etc., having curved sides that partially enclose and support the body.

bucket shop NOUN [1] an unregistered firm of stockbrokers that engages in speculation with clients' funds. [2] *Chiefly Brit* any small business that cannot be relied upon, esp one selling cheap airline tickets.

buckeye ('bʌkˌaɪ) NOUN any of several North American trees of the genus *Aesculus*, esp *A. glabra* (Ohio buckeye), having erect clusters of white or red flowers and prickly fruits: family *Hippocastanaceae*. See also **horse chestnut.**

Buckfast ('bʌkˌfɑːst) NOUN *Trademark* a fortified tonic wine.
▷HISTORY from *Buckfast* Abbey, Devon, England where it is produced

buck fever NOUN nervous excitement felt by inexperienced hunters at the approach of game.

buckhorn ('bʌkˌhɔːn) NOUN [1] **a** horn from a buck, used for knife handles, etc. **b** (*as modifier*): *a buckhorn knife.* [2] Also called: **buck's horn plantain.** a Eurasian plant, *Plantago coronopus*, having leaves resembling a buck's horn: family *Plantaginaceae*.

buckhound ('bʌkˌhaʊnd) NOUN a hound, smaller than a staghound, used for hunting the smaller breeds of deer, esp fallow deer.

buckie ('bʌkɪ) NOUN *Scot* [1] a whelk or its shell. [2] a lively or boisterous person, esp a youngster.
▷HISTORY related to Latin *buc(c)inum* whelk, from *buc(c)ina* trumpet, horn

Buckingham ('bʌkɪŋəm) NOUN a town in S central England, in Buckinghamshire; university (1975). Pop.: 2786 (1991).

Buckingham Palace NOUN the London residence of the British sovereign: built in 1703, rebuilt by John Nash in 1821–36 and partially redesigned in the early 20th century.

Buckinghamshire ('bʌkɪŋəmˌʃɪə, -ʃə) NOUN a county in SE central England, containing the Vale of Aylesbury and parts of the Chiltern Hills: the geographic and ceremonial county includes Milton Keynes, which became an independent unitary authority in 1997. Administrative centre: Aylesbury. Pop. (excluding Milton Keynes): 479 028 (2001). Area (excluding Milton Keynes): 1568 sq. km (605 sq. miles). Abbreviation: **Bucks.**

buckjumper ('bʌkˌdʒʌmpə) NOUN *Austral* an untamed horse.

buckjumping ('bʌkˌdʒʌmpɪŋ) NOUN *Austral* a competitive event for buckjumpers in a rodeo.

buckle ('bʌkᵊl) NOUN [1] a clasp for fastening together two loose ends, esp of a belt or strap, usually consisting of a frame with an attached movable prong. [2] an ornamental representation of a buckle, as on a shoe. [3] a kink, bulge, or other distortion: *a buckle in a railway track.* ◆ VERB [4] to fasten or be fastened with a buckle. [5] to bend or cause to bend out of shape, esp as a result of pressure or heat.
▷HISTORY C14: from Old French *bocle*, from Latin *buccula* a little cheek, hence, cheek strap of a helmet, from *bucca* cheek

buckle down VERB *(intr, adverb) Informal* to apply oneself with determination: *to buckle down to a job.*

buckler ('bʌklə) NOUN [1] a small round shield worn on the forearm or held by a short handle. [2] a means of protection; defence. ◆ VERB [3] *(tr) Archaic* to defend.
▷HISTORY C13: from Old French *bocler*, from *bocle* shield boss; see BUCKLE, BOSS²

buckler fern NOUN any of various ferns of the genus *Dryopteris*, such as *D. dilatata* (broad buckler fern): family *Polypodiaceae*.

Buckley's chance ('bʌklɪz) NOUN *Austral and NZ slang* no chance at all. Often shortened to: **Buckley's.**
▷HISTORY C19: of obscure origin

buckling ('bʌklɪŋ) NOUN another name for a **bloater.**
▷HISTORY C20: from German *Bückling*

buckminsterfullerene (ˌbʌkmɪnstə'fʊləˌriːn) NOUN a form of carbon that contains molecules having 60 carbon atoms arranged at the vertices of a polyhedron with hexagonal and pentagonal faces. It is produced in carbon arcs and occurs naturally in small amounts in certain minerals. Also called: **fullerene.**
▷HISTORY C20: named after (Richard) *Buckminster Fuller* (1895–1983), US architect and engineer

bucko ('bʌkəʊ) NOUN, *plural* **-oes.** *Irish* a lively young fellow: often a term of address.

buckra ('bʌkrə) NOUN (used contemptuously by Black people, esp in the US) a White man.
▷HISTORY C18: probably from Efik *mba-ka-ra* master

buck rabbit *or* **rarebit** NOUN *Brit* Welsh rabbit with either an egg or a piece of toast on top.

buckram ('bʌkrəm) NOUN [1] **a** cotton or linen cloth stiffened with size, etc., used in lining or stiffening clothes, bookbinding, etc. **b** (*as modifier*): *a buckram cover.* [2] *Archaic* stiffness of manner. ◆ VERB **-rams, -raming, -ramed.** [3] *(tr)* to stiffen with buckram.
▷HISTORY C14: from Old French *boquerant*, from Old Provençal *bocaran*, ultimately from BUKHARA, once an important source of textiles

Bucks (bʌks) ABBREVIATION FOR Buckinghamshire.

bucksaw ('bʌkˌsɔː) NOUN a woodcutting saw having its blade set in a frame and tensioned by a turnbuckle across the back of the frame.

buck's fizz NOUN a cocktail made of champagne and orange juice.

buckshee (ˌbʌk'ʃiː) ADJECTIVE *Brit slang* without charge; free.
▷HISTORY C20: from BAKSHEESH

buckshot ('bʌkˌʃɒt) NOUN lead shot of large size used in shotgun shells, esp for hunting game.
▷HISTORY C15 (original sense: the distance at which a buck can be shot)

buckskin ('bʌkˌskɪn) NOUN [1] the skin of a male deer. [2] **a** a strong greyish-yellow suede leather, originally made from deerskin but now usually made from sheepskin. **b** (*as modifier*): *buckskin boots.* [3] *US (sometimes capital)* a person wearing buckskin clothes, esp an American soldier of the Civil War. [4] a stiffly starched cotton cloth. [5] a strong satin-woven woollen fabric. ◆ ADJECTIVE [6] greyish-yellow.

buckskins ('bʌkˌskɪnz) PLURAL NOUN (in the US and Canada) breeches, shoes, or a suit of buckskin.

buck's party *or* **night** NOUN the Austral name for **stag party.**

buckthorn ('bʌkˌθɔːn) NOUN any of several thorny small-flowered shrubs of the genus *Rhamnus*, esp the Eurasian species *R. cathartica*, whose berries were formerly used as a purgative: family *Rhamnaceae*. See also **sea buckthorn.**
▷HISTORY C16: from BUCK¹ (from the spiny branches, imagined as resembling antlers) + THORN

bucktooth ('bʌkˌtuːθ) NOUN, *plural* **-teeth.** *Derogatory* a projecting upper front tooth.
▷HISTORY C18: from BUCK¹ (deer) + TOOTH
▸'**buck-toothed** ADJECTIVE

buck up VERB *(adverb) Informal* [1] to make or cause to make haste. [2] to make or become more cheerful, confident, etc.

buckwheat ('bʌkˌwiːt) NOUN [1] any of several polygonaceous plants of the genus *Fagopyrum*, esp *F. esculentum*, which has fragrant white flowers and is cultivated, esp in the US, for its seeds. [2] the edible seeds of this plant, ground into flour or used as animal fodder. [3] the flour obtained from these seeds.
▷HISTORY C16: from Middle Dutch *boecweite*, from *boeke* BEECH + *weite* WHEAT, from the resemblance of their seeds to beechnuts

buckyball ('bʌkɪˌbɔːl) NOUN *Informal* a ball-like polyhedral carbon molecule of the type found in buckminsterfullerene and other fullerenes.
▷HISTORY C20: from BUCK(MINSTERFULLERENE) + Y² + BALL¹

buckytube ('bʌkɪˌtjuːb) NOUN *Informal* a tube of carbon atoms structurally similar to buckminsterfullerene.

bucolic (bjuː'kɒlɪk) ADJECTIVE *also* **bucolical.** [1] of or characteristic of the countryside or country life; rustic. [2] of or relating to shepherds; pastoral. ◆ NOUN [3] *(sometimes plural)* a pastoral poem, often in the form of a dialogue. [4] a rustic; farmer or shepherd.
▷HISTORY C16: from Latin *būcolicus*, from Greek *boukolikos*, from *boukolos* cowherd, from *bous* ox
▸**bu'colically** ADVERB

Bucureşti (buku'reʃtj) NOUN the Romanian name for **Bucharest.**

bud¹ (bʌd) NOUN [1] a swelling on a plant stem consisting of overlapping immature leaves or petals. [2] **a** a partially opened flower. **b** (*in combination*): *rosebud.* [3] any small budlike outgrowth: *taste buds.* [4] something small or immature. [5] an asexually produced outgrowth in simple organisms, such as yeasts, and the hydra that develops into a new individual. [6] a slang word for **marijuana.** [7] **in bud.** at the stage of producing buds. [8] **nip in the bud.** to put an end to (an idea, movement, etc.) in its initial stages. ◆ VERB **buds, budding, budded.** [9] *(intr)* (of plants and some animals) to produce buds. [10] *(intr)* to begin to develop or grow. [11] *(tr) Horticulture* to graft (a bud) from one plant onto another, usually by insertion under the bark.

▷HISTORY C14 *budde*, of Germanic origin; compare Icelandic *budda* purse, Dutch *buidel*

bud² (bʌd) NOUN *Informal, chiefly US* short for **buddy**: used as a term of address.

Budapest (ˌbjuːdəˈpɛst; *Hungarian* ˈbudɔpɛʃt) NOUN the capital of Hungary, on the River Danube: formed in 1873 from the towns of Buda and Pest. Traditionally Buda, the old Magyar capital, was the administrative and Pest the trade centre: suffered severely in the Russian siege of 1945 and in the unsuccessful revolt against the Communist regime (1956). Pop.: 1 811 552 (2000 est.).

buddha (ˈbʊdə) NOUN [1] *Buddhism (often capital)* a person who has achieved a state of perfect enlightenment. [2] an image or picture of the Buddha.
▷HISTORY C17: from Sanskrit: awakened, enlightened, from *budh* to awake, know

Buddha (ˈbʊdə) NOUN **the.** ?563–483 B.C., a title applied to Gautama Siddhartha, a nobleman and religious teacher of N India, regarded by his followers as the most recent rediscoverer of the path to enlightenment: the founder of Buddhism.

Buddh Gaya (ˈbʊd gəˈjɑː), **Buddha Gaya,** *or* **Bodh Gaya** NOUN a village in NE India, in Bihar: site of the sacred bo tree under which Gautama Siddhartha attained enlightenment and became the Buddha; pilgrimage centre. Pop.: 21 686 (1991 est.).

Buddhism (ˈbʊdɪzəm) NOUN a religious teaching propagated by the Buddha and his followers, which declares that by destroying greed, hatred, and delusion, which are the causes of all suffering, man can attain perfect enlightenment. See **nirvana.**
▸ˈ**Buddhist** NOUN, ADJECTIVE

budding (ˈbʌdɪŋ) ADJECTIVE at an early stage of development but showing promise or potential: *a budding genius.*

buddle (ˈbʌdᵊl) NOUN [1] a sloping trough in which ore is washed. ◆ VERB [2] *(tr)* to wash (ore) in a buddle.
▷HISTORY C16: of unknown origin

buddleia (ˈbʌdlɪə) NOUN any ornamental shrub of the genus *Buddleia*, esp *B. davidii*, which has long spikes of mauve flowers and is frequently visited by butterflies: family *Buddleiaceae*. Also called: **butterfly bush.**
▷HISTORY C19: named after A. *Buddle* (died 1715), British botanist

buddy (ˈbʌdɪ) NOUN, *plural* **-dies.** [1] *Chiefly US and Canadian* an informal word for **friend.** Also called (as a term of address): **bud.** [2] a volunteer who visits and gives help and support to a person suffering from AIDS. [3] a volunteer who gives help and support to a person who has become disabled but is returning to work. ◆ VERB **-dying, -died.** [4] *(intr)* to act as a buddy to a person suffering from AIDS.
▷HISTORY C19: probably a baby-talk variant (US) of BROTHER

buddy-buddy ADJECTIVE *Informal, chiefly US* on friendly or intimate terms.

buddy movie *or* **film** NOUN a genre of film dealing with the relationship and adventures of two friends.

budge¹ (bʌdʒ) VERB *(usually used with a negative)* [1] to move, however slightly: *the car won't budge.* [2] to change or cause to change opinions, etc.
▷HISTORY C16: from Old French *bouger*, from Vulgar Latin *bullicāre* (unattested) to bubble, from Latin *bullīre* to boil, from *bulla* bubble

budge² (bʌdʒ) NOUN a lambskin dressed for the fur to be worn on the outer side.
▷HISTORY C14: from Anglo-French *bogee*, of obscure origin

budgerigar (ˈbʌdʒərɪˌgɑː) NOUN a small green Australian parrot, *Melopsittacus undulatus*: a popular cagebird that is bred in many different coloured varieties. Often (informal) shortened to: **budgie.**
▷HISTORY C19: from a native Australian language

budget (ˈbʌdʒɪt) NOUN [1] an itemized summary of expected income and expenditure of a country, company, etc., over a specified period, usually a financial year. [2] an estimate of income and a plan for domestic expenditure of an individual or a family, often over a short period, such as a month or a week. [3] a restriction on expenditure (esp in the phrase **on a budget**). [4] *(modifier)* economical; inexpensive: *budget meals for a family.* [5] the total amount of money allocated for a specific purpose during a specified period. [6] *Archaic* a stock, quantity, or supply. ◆ VERB **-gets, -geting, -geted.** [7] *(tr)* to enter or provide for in a budget. [8] to plan the expenditure of (money, time, etc.). [9] *(intr)* to make a budget.
▷HISTORY C15 (meaning: leather pouch, wallet): from Old French *bougette*, diminutive of *bouge*, from Latin *bulga*, of Gaulish origin; compare Old English *bælg* bag
▸ˈ**budgetary** ADJECTIVE

Budget (ˈbʌdʒɪt) NOUN **the.** an estimate of British government expenditures and revenues and the financial plans for the ensuing fiscal year presented annually to the House of Commons by the Chancellor of the Exchequer.

budget account NOUN [1] an account with a department store, etc., enabling a customer to make monthly payments to cover his past and future purchases. [2] a bank account for paying household bills, being credited with regular or equal monthly payments from the customer's current account.

budgetary control NOUN a system of managing a business by applying a financial value to each forecast activity. Actual performance is subsequently compared with the estimates.

budget deficit NOUN the amount by which government expenditure exceeds income from taxation, customs duties, etc., in any one fiscal year.

budget for VERB *(tr, preposition)* to allocate, save, or set aside money for (a particular purpose, period, etc.): *we need to budget for a fuel increase this winter.*

budgie (ˈbʌdʒɪ) NOUN *Informal* short for **budgerigar.**

bud scale NOUN one of the hard protective sometimes hairy or resinous specialized leaves surrounding the buds of certain plants, such as the rhododendron.

bud sport NOUN *Horticulture* a shoot, inflorescence, etc., that differs from another such structure on a plant and is caused by a somatic mutation; the differences can be retained by vegetative propagation.

Buenos Aires (ˈbweɪnɒs ˈaɪrɪz; *Spanish* ˈbwenos ˈaires) NOUN the capital of Argentina, a major port and industrial city on the Río de la Plata estuary: became capital in 1880; university (1821). Pop. (urban area): 2 904 192 (1999 est.).

BUF ABBREVIATION FOR (formerly) **British Union of Fascists.**

buff¹ (bʌf) NOUN [1] **a** a soft thick flexible undyed leather made chiefly from the skins of buffalo, oxen, and elk. **b** *(as modifier)*: *a buff coat.* [2] **a** a dull yellow or yellowish-brown colour. **b** *(as adjective)*: *buff paint.* [3] Also called: **buffer. a** a cloth or pad of material used for polishing an object. **b** a flexible disc or wheel impregnated with a fine abrasive for polishing metals, etc., with a power tool. [4] *Informal* one's bare skin (esp in the phrase **in the buff**). ◆ VERB [5] to clean or polish (a metal, floor, shoes, etc.) with a buff. [6] to remove the grain surface of (a leather). ◆ ADJECTIVE [7] *US informal* in a condition of high physical fitness and body tone, maintained by regular exercise.
▷HISTORY C16: from Old French *buffle*, from Old Italian *bufalo*, from Late Latin *būfalus* BUFFALO

buff² (bʌf) VERB [1] *(tr)* to deaden the force of. ◆ NOUN [2] *Archaic* a blow or buffet (now only in the phrase **blind man's buff**).
▷HISTORY C15: back formation from BUFFET²

buff³ (bʌf) NOUN *Informal* an expert on or devotee of a given subject: *a cheese buff.*
▷HISTORY C20: originally US: an enthusiastic fire watcher, from the buff-coloured uniforms worn by volunteer firemen in New York City

buffalo (ˈbʌfəˌləʊ) NOUN, *plural* **-loes** *or* **-lo.** [1] Also called: **Cape buffalo.** a member of the cattle tribe, *Syncerus caffer*, mostly found in game reserves in southern and eastern Africa and having upward-curving horns. [2] short for **water buffalo.** [3] a US and Canadian name for **bison** (sense 1). Related adjective: **bubaline.** ◆ VERB *(tr) US and Canadian informal* [4] *(often passive)* to confuse. [5] to intimidate.
▷HISTORY C16: from Italian *bufalo*, from Late Latin *būfalus*, alteration of Latin *būbalus*; see BUBAL

Buffalo (ˈbʌfəˌləʊ) NOUN a port in W New York State, at the E end of Lake Erie. Pop.: 292 648 (2000).

buffalo fish NOUN any of several freshwater North American hump-backed cyprinoid fishes of the genus *Ictiobus*: family *Catostomidae* (suckers).

buffalo gnat NOUN any of various small North American blood-sucking dipterous insects of the genus *Simulium* and related genera: family *Simuliidae*. Also called: **black fly.**

buffalo grass NOUN [1] a short grass, *Buchloë dactyloides*, growing on the dry plains of the central US. [2] *Austral* a grass, *Stenotaphrum americanum*, introduced from North America.

buffel grass (ˈbʌfəl) NOUN *Austral* a pasture grass, *Cenchrus ciliaris*, native to Africa and India, introduced in N Australia.

buffer¹ (ˈbʌfə) NOUN [1] one of a pair of spring-loaded steel pads attached at both ends of railway vehicles and at the end of a railway track to reduce shock due to contact. [2] a person or thing that lessens shock or protects from damaging impact, circumstances, etc. [3] *Chem* **a** an ionic compound, usually a salt of a weak acid or base, added to a solution to resist changes in its acidity or alkalinity and thus stabilize its pH. **b** Also called: **buffer solution.** a solution containing such a compound. [4] *Computing* a memory device for temporarily storing data. [5] *Electronics* an isolating circuit used to minimize the reaction between a driving and a driven circuit. [6] short for **buffer state.** [7] **hit the buffers.** *Informal* to finish or be stopped, esp unexpectedly. ◆ VERB *(tr)* [8] to insulate against or protect from shock; cushion. [9] *Chem* to add a buffer to (a solution).
▷HISTORY C19: from BUFF²

buffer² (ˈbʌfə) NOUN [1] any device used to shine, polish, etc.; buff. [2] a person who uses such a device.

buffer³ (ˈbʌfə) NOUN *Brit informal* a stupid or bumbling man (esp in the phrase **old buffer**).
▷HISTORY C18: perhaps from Middle English *buffer* stammerer

buffer state NOUN a small neutral state between two rival powers.

buffer stock NOUN *Commerce* a stock of a commodity built up by a government or trade organization with the object of using it to stabilize prices.

buffet¹ NOUN [1] (ˈbʊfeɪ) a counter where light refreshments are served. [2] (ˈbʊfeɪ) **a** a meal at which guests help themselves from a number of dishes and often eat standing up. **b** *(as modifier)*: *a buffet lunch.* [3] (ˈbʌfɪt, ˈbʊfeɪ) a piece of furniture used from medieval times to the 18th century for displaying plates, etc. and typically comprising one or more cupboards and some open shelves. [4] (ˈbʌfɪ) *Scot and northern English dialect* a kind of low stool, pouffe, or hassock.
▷HISTORY C18: from French, of unknown origin

buffet² (ˈbʌfɪt) VERB **-fets, -feting, -feted.** [1] *(tr)* to knock against or about; batter: *the wind buffeted the boat.* [2] *(tr)* to hit, esp with the fist; cuff. [3] to force (one's way), as through a crowd. [4] *(intr)* to struggle; battle. ◆ NOUN [5] a blow, esp with a fist or hand. [6] aerodynamic excitation of an aircraft structure by separated flows.
▷HISTORY C13: from Old French *buffeter*, from *buffet* a light blow, from *buffe*, of imitative origin
▸ˈ**buffeter** NOUN

buffet car (ˈbʊfeɪ) NOUN *Brit* a railway coach where light refreshments are served.

buffeting (ˈbʌfɪtɪŋ) NOUN response of an aircraft structure to buffet, esp an irregular oscillation of the tail.

buffing wheel NOUN a wheel covered with a soft material, such as lamb's wool or leather, used for shining and polishing. Also called: **buff wheel.**

bufflehead (ˈbʌfᵊlˌhɛd) NOUN a small North American diving duck, *Bucephala* (or *Glaucionetta*) *albeola*: the male has black-and-white plumage and a fluffy head. Also called: **butterball.**
▷HISTORY C17 *buffle* from obsolete *buffle* wild ox (see BUFF¹), referring to the duck's head

buffo (ˈbʊfəʊ; *Italian* ˈbuffo) NOUN, *plural* **-fi** (-fɪ) *or* **-fos.** [1] (in Italian opera of the 18th century) a comic part, esp one for a bass. [2] Also called: **buffo**

bass, basso buffo (*Italian* 'basso 'buffo). a bass singer who performs such a part.
▷HISTORY C18: from Italian (adj): comic, from *buffo* (n) BUFFOON

buffoon (bə'fu:n) NOUN [1] a person who amuses others by ridiculous or odd behaviour, jokes, etc. [2] a foolish person.
▷HISTORY C16: from French *bouffon*, from Italian *buffone*, from Medieval Latin *būfō*, from Latin: toad
▸ **buf'foonery** NOUN

Buffs (bʌfs) PLURAL NOUN **the.** the Third Regiment of Foot, esp the Royal East Kent Regiment.
▷HISTORY C19: from their buff-coloured facings

buff-tip moth NOUN a large European moth, *Phalera bucephala*, having violet-brown buff-tipped forewings held at rest around the body so that it resembles a snapped-off twig.

bufotalin (ˌbu:fəʊ'tælɪn) NOUN the principal poisonous substance in the skin and saliva of the common European toad.

bug[1] (bʌg) NOUN [1] any insect of the order *Hemiptera*, esp any of the suborder *Heteroptera*, having piercing and sucking mouthparts specialized as a beak (rostrum). See also **assassin bug, bedbug, chinch bug.** [2] *Chiefly US and Canadian* any insect, such as the June bug or the Croton bug. [3] *Informal* **a** a microorganism, esp a bacterium, that produces disease. **b** a disease, esp a stomach infection, caused by a microorganism. [4] *Informal* an obsessive idea, hobby, etc.; craze (esp in the phrases **get the bug, be bitten by the bug, the bug bites,** etc.). [5] *Informal* a person having such a craze; enthusiast. [6] (*often plural*) *Informal* an error or fault, as in a machine or system, esp in a computer or computer program. [7] *Informal* a concealed microphone used for recording conversations, as in spying. [8] *US* (in poker) a joker used as an ace or wild card to complete a straight or flush. ◆ VERB **bugs, bugging, bugged.** *Informal* [9] (*tr*) to irritate; bother. [10] (*tr*) to conceal a microphone in (a room, etc.). [11] (*intr*) *US* (of eyes) to protrude. See also **bug out.**
▷HISTORY C16: of uncertain origin; perhaps related to Old English *budda* beetle

bug[2] (bʌg) NOUN *Obsolete* an evil spirit or spectre; hobgoblin.
▷HISTORY C14 *bugge*, perhaps from Middle Welsh *bwg* ghost. See also BUGBEAR, BUGABOO

bug[3] (bʌg) VERB a past tense and past participle of **big**[2].

Bug (*Russian* buk) NOUN [1] Also called: **Southern Bug.** a river in E Europe, rising in the W Ukraine and flowing southeast to the Dnieper estuary and the Black Sea. Length: 853 km (530 miles). [2] Also called: **Western Bug.** a river in E Europe, rising in the SW Ukraine and flowing northwest to the River Vistula in Poland, forming part of the border between Poland and the Ukraine. Length: 724 km (450 miles).

bugaboo ('bʌgəˌbu:) NOUN, *plural* **-boos.** an imaginary source of fear; bugbear; bogey.
▷HISTORY C18: probably of Celtic origin; compare Cornish *buccaboo* the devil

bugbane ('bʌgˌbeɪn) NOUN any of several ranunculaceous plants of the genus *Cimicifuga*, esp *C. foetida* of Europe, whose flowers are reputed to repel insects.

bugbear ('bʌgˌbɛə) NOUN [1] a thing that causes obsessive fear or anxiety. [2] (in English folklore) a goblin said to eat naughty children and thought to be in the form of a bear.
▷HISTORY C16: from BUG[2] + BEAR[2]; compare BUGABOO

bugger ('bʌgə) NOUN [1] a person who practises buggery. [2] *Slang* a person or thing considered to be contemptible, unpleasant, or difficult. [3] *Slang* a humorous or affectionate term for a man or child: *a silly old bugger; a friendly little bugger.* [4] **bugger all.** *Slang* nothing. [5] **play silly buggers.** *Slang* to fool around and waste time. ◆ VERB [6] to practise buggery (with). [7] (*tr*) *Slang, chiefly Brit* to ruin, complicate, or frustrate. [8] *Slang* to tire; weary: *he was absolutely buggered.* ◆ INTERJECTION [9] *Slang* an exclamation of annoyance or disappointment.
▷HISTORY C16: from Old French *bougre*, from Medieval Latin *Bulgarus* Bulgarian; from the condemnation of the Eastern Orthodox Bulgarians as heretics

bugger about *or* **around** VERB (*adverb*) *Brit slang* [1] (*intr*) to fool about and waste time. [2] (*tr*) to create difficulties or complications for (a person).

bugger off VERB (*intr, adverb*) *Brit slang* to go away; depart.

buggery ('bʌgərɪ) NOUN anal intercourse between a man and another man, a woman, or an animal. Compare **sodomy.**

Buggins' turn ('bʌgɪnz) *or* **Buggins's turn** NOUN *Brit slang* the principle of awarding an appointment to members of a group in turn, rather than according to merit.
▷HISTORY C20: origin unknown

buggy[1] ('bʌgɪ) NOUN, *plural* **-gies.** [1] a light horse-drawn carriage having either four wheels (esp in the US and Canada) or two wheels (esp in Britain and India). [2] short for **beach buggy.** [3] short for **baby buggy.** [4] a small motorized vehicle designed for a particular purpose: *golf buggy; moon buggy.*
▷HISTORY C18: of unknown origin

buggy[2] ('bʌgɪ) ADJECTIVE **-gier, -giest.** [1] infested with bugs. [2] *US slang* insane.
▸ **'bugginess** NOUN

bughouse ('bʌgˌhaʊs) *Offensive slang, chiefly US* ◆ NOUN [1] a mental hospital or asylum. ◆ ADJECTIVE [2] insane; crazy.
▷HISTORY C20: from BUG[1] + (MAD)HOUSE

bugle[1] ('bju:g(ə)l) NOUN [1] *Music* a brass instrument similar to the cornet but usually without valves: used for military fanfares, signal calls, etc. ◆ VERB [2] (*intr*) to play or sound (on) a bugle.
▷HISTORY C14: short for *bugle horn* ox horn (musical instrument), from Old French *bugle*, from Latin *būculus* young bullock, from *bōs* ox
▸ **'bugler** NOUN

bugle[2] ('bju:g(ə)l) NOUN any of several Eurasian plants of the genus *Ajuga*, esp *A. reptans*, having small blue or white flowers: family *Lamiaceae* (labiates). Also called: **bugleweed.** See also **ground pine.**
▷HISTORY C13: from Late Latin *bugula*, of uncertain origin

bugle[3] ('bju:g(ə)l) NOUN a tubular glass or plastic bead sewn onto clothes for decoration.
▷HISTORY C16: of unknown origin

bugleweed ('bju:g(ə)lˌwi:d) NOUN [1] Also called: **water horehound.** *US* any aromatic plant of the genus *Lycopus*, having small whitish or pale blue flowers: family *Lamiaceae* (labiates). See also **gipsywort.** [2] another name for **bugle**[2].

bugloss ('bju:glɒs) NOUN any of various hairy Eurasian boraginaceous plants of the genera *Anchusa*, *Lycopsis*, and *Echium*, esp *L. arvensis*, having clusters of blue flowers. See also **viper's bugloss.**
▷HISTORY C15: from Latin *būglōssa*, from Greek *bouglōssos* ox-tongued, from *bōs* ox + *glōssa* tongue

bugong ('bu:gɒŋ) NOUN another name for **bogong.**

bug out VERB (*intr, adverb*) *Slang, chiefly US* to depart hurriedly; run away; retreat.

buhl (bu:l) ADJECTIVE, NOUN the usual US spelling of **boulle.**

buhrstone, burstone, *or* **burrstone** ('bɜ:ˌstəʊn) NOUN [1] a hard tough rock containing silica, fossils, and cavities, formerly used as a grindstone. [2] a grindstone or millstone made of this rock.
▷HISTORY C18 *burr*, perhaps identical to BURR[1] (alluding to roughness)

BUI INTERNATIONAL CAR REGISTRATION FOR (British) Virgin Islands.

buibui ('buɪ'buɪ) NOUN a piece of black cloth worn as a shawl by Muslim women, esp on the E African coast.
▷HISTORY from Swahili

build (bɪld) VERB **builds, building, built.** [1] to make, construct, or form by joining parts or materials: *to build a house.* [2] (*intr*) to be a builder by profession. [3] (*tr*) to order the building of: *the government builds most of our hospitals.* [4] (foll by *on* or *upon*) to base; found: *his theory was not built on facts.* [5] (*tr*) to establish and develop: *it took ten years to build a business.* [6] (*tr*) to make in a particular way or for a particular purpose: *the car was not built for speed.* [7] (*intr*; often foll by *up*) to increase in intensity: *the wind was building.* [8] *Cards* **a** to add cards to each other to form (a sequence or set). **b** (*intr*) to add to the layout of cards on the table from one's hand. ◆ NOUN [9] physical form, figure, or proportions: *a man with an athletic build.* See also **build in, build into, build up.**
▷HISTORY Old English *byldan*; related to *bylda* farmer, *bold* building, Old Norse *bōl* farm, dwelling; see BOWER[1]

buildable ('bɪldəb(ə)l) ADJECTIVE suitable for building on.

builder ('bɪldə) NOUN [1] a person who builds, esp one who contracts for and supervises the construction or repair of buildings. [2] a substance added to a soap or detergent as a filler or abrasive.

build in VERB (*tr, adverb*) to incorporate or construct as an integral part: *to build in safety features.*

building ('bɪldɪŋ) NOUN [1] something built with a roof and walls, such as a house or factory. [2] the act, business, occupation, or art of building houses, boats, etc.

building and loan association NOUN a US name for **building society.**

building block NOUN [1] a block of stone or other material, larger than a brick, used in building. [2] a component that fits with others to form a whole: *standardized software building blocks.* [3] another name for **block** (the child's toy).

building line NOUN the boundary line along a street beyond which buildings must not project.

building paper NOUN any of various types of heavy-duty paper that usually consist of bitumen reinforced with fibre sandwiched between two sheets of kraft paper: used in damp-proofing or as insulation between the soil and a road surface.

building society NOUN a cooperative organization that accepts deposits of money from savers and uses them to make loans, secured by mortgages, to house buyers. Since 1986 they have been empowered to offer banking services.

build into VERB (*tr, preposition*) to make (something) a definite part of (a contract, agreement, etc.).

build up VERB (*adverb*) [1] (*tr*) to construct gradually, systematically, and in stages. [2] to increase, accumulate, or strengthen, esp by degrees: *the murmur built up to a roar.* [3] (*intr*) to prepare for or gradually approach a climax. [4] (*tr*) to improve the health or physique of (a person). [5] (*tr, usually passive*) to cover (an area) with buildings. [6] (*tr*) to cause (a person, enterprise, etc.) to become better known; publicize: *they built several actresses up into stars.* ◆ NOUN **build-up.** [7] progressive increase in number, size, etc.: *the build-up of industry.* [8] a gradual approach to a climax or critical point. [9] extravagant publicity or praise, esp in the form of a campaign. [10] *Military* the process of attaining the required strength of forces and equipment, esp prior to an operation.

built (bɪlt) VERB the past tense and past participle of **build.**

built cane NOUN *Angling* another name for **split cane.**

built-in ADJECTIVE [1] made or incorporated as an integral part: *a built-in cupboard; a built-in escape clause.* [2] essential; inherent. ◆ NOUN [3] *Austral* a built-in cupboard or wardrobe.

built-in obsolescence NOUN See **planned obsolescence.**

built-up ADJECTIVE [1] having many buildings (esp in the phrase **built-up area**). [2] denoting a beam, girder, or stanchion constructed of sections welded, riveted, or bolted together, etc. [3] increased by the addition of parts: *built-up heels.*

Bujumbura (ˌbu:dʒəm'bʊərə) NOUN the capital of Burundi, a port at the NE end of Lake Tanganyika. Pop.: 300 000 (1994 est.). Former name: **Usumbura.**

Bukhara *or* **Bokhara** (bʊ'xɑ:rə) NOUN [1] a city in S Uzbekistan. Pop.: 220 000 (1998 est.). [2] a former emirate of central Asia: a powerful kingdom and centre of Islam; became a territory of the Soviet Union (1920) and was divided between the former Uzbek, Tajik, and Turkmen Soviet Socialist Republics.

Bukhara rug *or* **Bokhara rug** NOUN a kind of rug, typically having a black-and-white geometrical pattern on a reddish ground.

Bul (bu:l) NOUN the eighth month of the Old Hebrew calendar, corresponding to Heshvan of the

Babylonian or post-exilic Jewish calendar: a period from mid-October to mid-November.
▷HISTORY from Hebrew *būl*, of Canaanite origin

bul. ABBREVIATION FOR bulletin.

Bulawayo (ˌbʊləˈweɪəʊ) NOUN a city in SW Zimbabwe founded (1893) on the site of the kraal of Lobengula, the last Matabele king; the country's main industrial centre. Pop.: 790 000 (1998 est.).

bulb (bʌlb) NOUN 1 a rounded organ of vegetative reproduction in plants such as the tulip and onion: a flattened stem bearing a central shoot surrounded by fleshy nutritive inner leaves and thin brown outer leaves. Compare **corm.** 2 a plant, such as a hyacinth or daffodil, that grows from a bulb. 3 See **light bulb.** 4 a rounded part of an instrument such as a syringe or thermometer. 5 *Anatomy* a rounded expansion of a cylindrical organ or part, such as the medulla oblongata. 6 Also called: **bulbous bow.** a bulbous protuberance at the forefoot of a ship to reduce turbulence.
▷HISTORY C16: from Latin *bulbus*, from Greek *bolbos* onion

bulbar (ˈbʌlbə) ADJECTIVE *Chiefly anatomy* of or relating to a bulb, esp the medulla oblongata.

bulb fly NOUN a hoverfly the larvae of which live in bulbs and can become serious pests, esp the yellow and black **narcissus bulb fly** (*Meridon equestris*).

bulbiferous (bʌlˈbɪfərəs) ADJECTIVE (of plants) producing bulbs.

bulbil (ˈbʌlbɪl) *or* **bulbel** (ˈbʌlbᵊl) NOUN 1 a small bulblike organ of vegetative reproduction growing in leaf axils or on flower stalks of plants such as the onion and tiger lily. 2 any small bulb of a plant. 3 any small bulblike structure in an animal.
▷HISTORY C19: from New Latin *bulbillus*, from Latin *bulbus* BULB

bulb mite NOUN a widespread mite, *Rhizaglophus eclinops*, that tunnels in the bulbs of lilies and other plants.

bulbous (ˈbʌlbəs) ADJECTIVE 1 shaped like a bulb; swollen; bulging. 2 growing from or bearing bulbs.
▸ˈ**bulbously** ADVERB

bulbul (ˈbʊlbʊl) NOUN 1 any songbird of the family *Pycnonotidae* of tropical Africa and Asia, having brown plumage and, in many species, a distinct crest. 2 a songbird, taken to be the nightingale, often mentioned in Persian poetry.
▷HISTORY C18: via Persian from Arabic

Bulg. ABBREVIATION FOR Bulgaria(n).

Bulgar (ˈbʌlgɑː, ˈbʊl-) NOUN 1 a member of a group of non-Indo-European peoples that settled in SE Europe in the late 7th century A.D. and adopted the language and culture of their Slavonic subjects. 2 a rare name for a **Bulgarian.**

Bulgaria (bʌlˈgɛərɪə, bʊl-) NOUN a republic in SE Europe, on the Balkan Peninsula on the Black Sea: under Turkish rule from 1395 until 1878; became an independent kingdom in 1908 and a republic in 1946; consists chiefly of the Danube valley in the north, the Balkan Mountains in the central part, separated from the Rhodope Mountains of the south by the valley of the Maritsa River. Language: Bulgarian. Religion: Christian (Bulgarian Orthodox) majority. Currency: lev. Capital: Sofia. Pop.: 7 953 000 (2001 est.). Area: 110 911 sq. km (42 823 sq. miles).

Bulgarian (bʌlˈgɛərɪən, bʊl-) ADJECTIVE 1 of, relating to, or characteristic of Bulgaria, its people, or their language. ◆ NOUN 2 the official language of Bulgaria, belonging to the S Slavonic branch of the Indo-European family. 3 a native, inhabitant, or citizen of Bulgaria.

bulge (bʌldʒ) NOUN 1 a swelling or an outward curve. 2 a sudden increase in number or volume, esp of population. 3 *Brit* another name for **baby boom.** 4 *Brit* the projecting part of an army's front line; salient. ◆ VERB 5 to swell outwards.
▷HISTORY C13: from Old French *bouge*, from Latin *bulga* bag, probably of Gaulish origin
▸ˈ**bulging** ADJECTIVE ▸ˈ**bulgingly** ADVERB ▸ˈ**bulgy** ADJECTIVE
▸ˈ**bulginess** NOUN

Bulge (bʌldʒ) NOUN **Battle of the.** (in World War II) the final major German counteroffensive in 1944 when the Allied forces were pushed back into NE Belgium; the Germans were repulsed by Jan. 1945.

bulgur (ˈbʌlgə) NOUN Also called: **burghul.** a kind of dried cracked wheat.
▷HISTORY C20: from Turkish, from Arabic *burghul*, from Persian

bulimia (bjuːˈlɪmɪə) NOUN 1 pathologically insatiable hunger, esp when caused by a brain lesion. 2 Also called: **bulimia nervosa.** a disorder characterized by compulsive overeating followed by vomiting: sometimes associated with anxiety about gaining weight.
▷HISTORY C17: from New Latin, from Greek *boulimia*, from *bous* ox + *limos* hunger
▸**buˈlimic** NOUN, ADJECTIVE

bulk (bʌlk) NOUN 1 volume, size, or magnitude, esp when great. 2 the main part: *the bulk of the work is repetitious.* 3 a large body, esp of a person: *he eased his bulk out of the chair.* 4 unpackaged cargo or goods. 5 a ship's cargo or hold. 6 *Printing* **a** the thickness of a number of sheets of paper or cardboard. **b** the thickness of a book excluding its covers. 7 (*plural*) copies of newspapers sold in bulk at a discounted price to hotels, airlines, etc. which issue them free to their customers. 8 **in bulk. a** in large quantities. **b** (of a cargo, etc.) unpackaged. ◆ VERB 9 to cohere or cause to cohere in a mass. 10 to place, hold, or transport (several cargoes of goods) in bulk. 11 **bulk large.** to be or seem important or prominent: *the problem bulked large in his mind.*
▷HISTORY C15: from Old Norse *bulki* cargo

> **Language note** The use of a plural noun after *bulk* was formerly considered incorrect, but is now acceptable.

bulk buying NOUN 1 the purchase at one time, and often at a reduced price, of a large quantity of a particular commodity. 2 the purchase of the whole or greater part of the output of a commodity of a country or state by a single buyer, usually another country or state; state trading.

bulk carrier NOUN a ship that carries unpackaged cargo, usually consisting of a single dry commodity, such as coal or grain. Also called: **bulker.**

bulkhead (ˈbʌlkˌhɛd) NOUN 1 any upright wall-like partition in a ship, aircraft, vehicle, etc. 2 a wall or partition built to hold back earth, fire, water, etc.
▷HISTORY C15: probably from *bulk* projecting framework, from Old Norse *bálkr* partition + HEAD

bulking (ˈbʌlkɪŋ) NOUN 1 the expansion of excavated material to a volume greater than that of the excavation from which it came. 2 an increase in the volume of dry sand when its moisture content is increased.

bulk modulus NOUN a coefficient of elasticity of a substance equal to minus the ratio of the applied stress (*p*) to the resulting fractional change in volume (d*V*/*V*) in a specified reference state (d*V*/*V* is the **bulk strain**). Symbol: *K*.

bulk up VERB (*adverb*) to increase or cause to increase in size or importance.

bulky (ˈbʌlkɪ) ADJECTIVE **bulkier, bulkiest.** very large and massive, esp so as to be unwieldy.
▸ˈ**bulkily** ADVERB ▸ˈ**bulkiness** NOUN

bull¹ (bʊl) NOUN 1 any male bovine animal, esp one that is sexually mature. Related adjective: **taurine.** 2 the uncastrated adult male of any breed of domestic cattle. 3 the male of various other animals including the elephant and whale. 4 a very large, strong, or aggressive person. 5 *Stock Exchange* **a** a speculator who buys in anticipation of rising prices in order to make a profit on resale. **b** (*as modifier*): *a bull market.* Compare **bear¹** (sense 5). 6 *Chiefly Brit* short for **bull's-eye** (senses 1, 2). 7 *Slang* short for **bullshit.** 8 short for **bulldog, bull terrier.** 9 **a bull in a china shop.** a clumsy person. 10 **shoot the bull.** *US and Canadian slang* **a** to pass time talking lightly. **b** to boast or exaggerate. 11 **take the bull by the horns.** to face and tackle a difficulty without shirking. ◆ ADJECTIVE 12 male; masculine: *a bull elephant.* 13 large; strong. ◆ VERB 14 (*tr*) to raise or attempt to raise the price or prices of (a stock market or a security) by speculative buying. 15 (*intr*) (of a cow) to be on heat. 16 (*intr*) *US slang* to talk lightly or foolishly.
▷HISTORY Old English *bula*, from Old Norse *boli*; related to Middle Low German *bulle*, Middle Dutch *bolle*

bull² (bʊl) NOUN a ludicrously self-contradictory or inconsistent statement. Also called: **Irish bull.**
▷HISTORY C17: of uncertain origin

bull³ (bʊl) NOUN a formal document issued by the pope, written in antiquated characters and often sealed with a leaden bulla.
▷HISTORY C13: from Medieval Latin *bulla* seal attached to a bull, from Latin: round object

Bull (bʊl) NOUN **the.** the constellation Taurus, the second sign of the zodiac.

bulla (ˈbʊlə, ˈbʌlə) NOUN, *plural* **-lae** (-liː). 1 a leaden seal affixed to a papal bull, having a representation of Saints Peter and Paul on one side and the name of the reigning pope on the other. 2 an ancient Roman rounded metal or leather box containing an amulet, worn around the neck. 3 *Pathol* another word for **blister** (sense 1). 4 *Anatomy* a rounded bony projection.
▷HISTORY C19: from Latin: round object, bubble

bullace (ˈbʊlɪs) NOUN a small Eurasian rosaceous tree, *Prunus domestica insititia* (or *P. insititia*), of which the damson is the cultivated form. See also **plum¹** (sense 1).
▷HISTORY C14: from Old French *beloce*, from Medieval Latin *bolluca*, perhaps of Gaulish origin

Bullamakanka (ˌbuːləməˈkæŋkə) NOUN *Austral slang* an imaginary very remote and backward place.

bull ant NOUN another name for **bulldog ant.**

bullate (ˈbʌleɪt, -ɪt, ˈbʊl-) ADJECTIVE *Botany, anatomy* puckered or blistered in appearance: *the bullate leaves of the primrose.*
▷HISTORY C19: from Medieval Latin *bullātus* inflated, from Latin *bulla* bubble

bull bars PLURAL NOUN a large protective metal grille on the front of some vehicles, esp four-wheel-drive vehicles.

bullbat (ˈbʊlˌbæt) NOUN another name for **nighthawk** (sense 1).

bulldog (ˈbʊlˌdɒg) NOUN 1 a sturdy thickset breed of dog with an undershot jaw, short nose, broad head, and a muscular body. 2 (at Oxford University) an official who accompanies the proctors on ceremonial occasions. 3 *Commerce* a fixed-interest bond issued in Britain by a foreign borrower.

bulldog ant NOUN any large Australian ant of the genus *Myrmecia*, having a powerful stinging bite: subfamily *Ponerinae*. Sometimes shortened to: **bull ant.**

bulldog clip NOUN *Trademark* a clip for holding papers together, consisting of two T-shaped metal clamps held in place by a cylindrical spring.

bulldoze (ˈbʊlˌdəʊz) VERB (*tr*) 1 to move, demolish, flatten, etc., with a bulldozer. 2 *Informal* to force; push: *he bulldozed his way through the crowd.* 3 *Informal* to intimidate or coerce.
▷HISTORY C19: probably from BULL¹ + DOSE

bulldozer (ˈbʊlˌdəʊzə) NOUN 1 a powerful tractor fitted with caterpillar tracks and a blade at the front, used for moving earth, rocks, etc. 2 *Informal* a person who bulldozes.

bull dust NOUN *Austral* 1 fine dust. 2 *Slang* nonsense.

bull dyke NOUN *Slang* a lesbian who is markedly masculine.

bullet (ˈbʊlɪt) NOUN 1 **a** a small metallic missile enclosed in a cartridge, used as the projectile of a gun, rifle, etc. **b** the entire cartridge. 2 something resembling a bullet, esp in shape or effect. 3 *Stock Exchange* a fixed interest security with a single maturity date. 4 *Commerce* a security that offers a fixed interest and matures on a fixed date. 5 *Commerce* **a** the final repayment of a loan that repays the whole of the sum borrowed, as interim payments have been for interest only. **b** (*as modifier*): *a bullet loan.* 6 *Brit slang* dismissal, sometimes without notice (esp in the phrases **get** *or* **give the bullet**). 7 *Printing* See **centred dot.** 8 **bite the bullet.** See **bite** (sense 14).
▷HISTORY C16: from French *boulette*, diminutive of *boule* ball; see BOWL²
▸ˈ**bullet-ˌlike** ADJECTIVE

bulletin (ˈbʊlɪtɪn) NOUN 1 an official statement on a matter of public interest, such as the illness of

a public figure. [2] a broadcast summary of the news. [3] a periodical publication of an association, etc. ◆ VERB [4] *(tr)* to make known by bulletin.
▷HISTORY C17: from French, from Italian *bullettino*, from *bulletta*, diminutive of *bulla* papal edict, BULL³

bulletin board NOUN [1] the US and Canadian name for **notice board.** [2] *Computing* a facility on a computer network allowing any user to leave messages that can be read by any other user, and to download software and information to the user's own computer.

bullet point NOUN any of a number of items printed in a list, each after a centred dot, usually the most important points in a longer piece of text.

bulletproof (ˈbʊlɪtˌpruːf) ADJECTIVE [1] not penetrable by bullets: *bulletproof glass.* ◆ VERB [2] *(tr)* to make bulletproof.

bulletwood (ˈbʊlɪtˌwʊd) NOUN the wood of a tropical American sapotaceous tree, *Manilkara bidentata*, widely used for construction due to its durability and toughness.

bullfight (ˈbʊlˌfaɪt) NOUN a traditional Spanish, Portuguese, and Latin American spectacle in which a matador, assisted by banderilleros and mounted picadors, baits and usually kills a bull in an arena.
▸ **ˈbullˌfighter** NOUN ▸ **ˈbullˌfighting** NOUN

bullfinch¹ (ˈbʊlˌfɪntʃ) NOUN [1] a common European finch, *Pyrrhula pyrrhula*: the male has a bright red throat and breast, black crown, wings, and tail, and a grey-and-white back. [2] any of various similar finches.
▷HISTORY C14: see BULL¹, FINCH; probably so called from its stocky shape and thick neck

bullfinch² (ˈbʊlˌfɪntʃ) NOUN *Brit* a high thick hedge too difficult for a horse and rider to jump.
▷HISTORY C19: perhaps changed from the phrase *bull fence*

bullfrog (ˈbʊlˌfrɒg) NOUN any of various large frogs, such as *Rana catesbeiana* (**American bullfrog**), having a loud deep croak.

bullhead (ˈbʊlˌhɛd) NOUN [1] any of various small northern mainly marine scorpaenoid fishes of the family *Cottidae* that have a large head covered with bony plates and spines. [2] any freshwater North American catfish of the genus *Ameiurus* (or *Ictalurus*), having a large head bearing several long barbels. [3] a scorpion fish, *Scorpaena guttata*, of North American Pacific coastal waters. [4] *Informal* a stupidly stubborn or unintelligent person.

bull-headed ADJECTIVE blindly obstinate; stubborn, headstrong, or stupid.
▸ **ˌbull-ˈheadedly** ADVERB ▸ **ˌbull-ˈheadedness** NOUN

bullhead rail NOUN *Railways* a rail having a cross section with a bulbous top and bottom, the top being larger. Now largely superseded by **flat-bottomed rail.**

bullhorn (ˈbʊlˌhɔːn) NOUN the US and Canadian name for **loud-hailer.**

bullion (ˈbʊljən) NOUN [1] gold or silver in mass. [2] gold or silver in the form of bars and ingots, suitable for further processing. [3] Also called: **bullion fringe.** a thick gold or silver wire or fringed cord used as a trimming, as on military uniforms.
▷HISTORY C14 (in the sense: melted gold or silver): from Anglo-French: mint, probably from Old French *bouillir* to boil, from Latin *bullīre*

bullish (ˈbʊlɪʃ) ADJECTIVE [1] like a bull. [2] *Stock Exchange* causing, expecting, or characterized by a rise in prices: *a bullish market.* [3] *Informal* cheerful and optimistic: *the prime minister was in a bullish mood.*
▸ **ˈbullishness** NOUN

bull kelp NOUN any of various large brown seaweeds of Pacific and Antarctic waters.

bull mastiff NOUN a large powerful breed of dog with a short usually fawn or brindle coat, developed by crossing the bulldog with the mastiff.

bull-necked ADJECTIVE having a short thick neck.

bull nose NOUN [1] Also called: **atrophic rhinitis.** a disease of pigs resulting in deformity of the nose, caused by infection with the bacterium *Bordatella bronchiseptica*. [2] a rounded edge of a brick, step, etc. [3] a rounded exterior angle, as where two walls meet.

bull-nosed ADJECTIVE having a rounded end.

bullock (ˈbʊlək) NOUN [1] a gelded bull; steer. [2] *Archaic* a bull calf. ◆ VERB [3] *(intr) Austral and NZ informal* to work hard and long.
▷HISTORY Old English *bulluc*;see BULL¹, -OCK

bullock's heart NOUN another name for **custard apple** (senses 1, 2).

bullocky (ˈbʊləkɪ) NOUN, *plural* **-ockies.** *Austral and NZ informal* the driver of a team of bullocks.

bullpen (ˈbʊlˌpɛn) NOUN [1] *US informal* a large cell where prisoners are confined together temporarily. [2] *Baseball* a part of a baseball field where relief pitchers warm up.

bullring (ˈbʊlˌrɪŋ) NOUN an arena for bullfighting.

bullroarer (ˈbʊlˌrɔːrə) NOUN a wooden slat attached to a thong that makes a roaring sound when the thong is whirled: used esp by native Australians in religious rites.

Bull Run NOUN **Battles of.** two battles fought at Manassas Junction near a stream named Bull Run, during the American Civil War (July, 1861 and August, 1862), in both of which the Federal army was routed by the Confederates. Also called: **First and Second Manassas.** See also **Manassas.**

bull session NOUN *Informal, chiefly US and Canadian* an informal discussion, often among men.
▷HISTORY C20: from BULL²

bull's-eye NOUN [1] the small central disc of a target, usually the highest valued area. [2] a shot hitting this. [3] *Informal* something that exactly achieves its aim. [4] a small circular or oval window or opening. [5] a thick disc of glass set into a ship's deck, etc., to admit light. [6] the glass boss at the centre of a sheet of blown glass. [7] **a** a small thick plano-convex lens used as a condenser. **b** a lamp or lantern containing such a lens. [8] a peppermint-flavoured, usually striped, boiled sweet. [9] *Nautical* a circular or oval wooden block with a groove around it for the strop of a shroud and a hole at its centre for a line. Compare **deadeye.** [10] *Meteorol* the eye or centre of a cyclone.

bullshit (ˈbʊlʃɪt) *Slang* ◆ NOUN [1] exaggerated or foolish talk; nonsense. [2] (in the British Army) exaggerated zeal, esp for ceremonial drill, cleaning, polishing, etc. Usually shortened to: **bull.** ◆ VERB **-shits, -shitting, -shitted.** [3] *(intr)* to talk in an exaggerated or foolish manner.
▸ **ˈbullshitter** NOUN

> **Language note** This word was formerly considered to be taboo, and it was labelled as such in previous editions of *Collins English Dictionary*. However, it has now become acceptable in speech, although some older or more conservative people may object to its use.

bull snake NOUN any burrowing North American nonvenomous colubrid snake of the genus *Pituophis*, typically having yellow and brown markings. Also called: **gopher snake.**

bull's wool NOUN *Austral and NZ informal* nonsense.

bull terrier NOUN a breed of terrier having a muscular body and thick neck, with a short smooth often white coat: developed by crossing the bulldog with various terriers. See also **pit bull terrier, Staffordshire bull terrier.**

bull tongue NOUN *Chiefly US* [1] a heavy plough used in growing cotton, having an almost vertical mouldboard. [2] a plough or cultivator with a single shovel.

bull trout NOUN any large trout, esp the salmon trout.

bullwhip (ˈbʊlˌwɪp) NOUN [1] a long tapering heavy whip, esp one of plaited rawhide. ◆ VERB **-whips, -whipping, -whipped.** [2] *(tr)* to whip with a bullwhip.

bully¹ (ˈbʊlɪ) NOUN, *plural* **-lies.** [1] a person who hurts, persecutes, or intimidates weaker people. [2] *Archaic* a hired ruffian. [3] *Obsolete* a procurer; pimp. [4] *Obsolete* a fine fellow or friend. [5] *Obsolete* a sweetheart; darling. ◆ VERB **-lies, -lying, -lied.** [6] (when *tr*, often foll by *into*) to hurt, intimidate, or persecute (a weaker or smaller person), esp to make him do something. ◆ ADJECTIVE [7] dashing; jolly: *my bully boy.* [8] *Informal* very good; fine. ◆ INTERJECTION [9] Also: **bully for you, him,** etc. *Informal* well done! bravo!
▷HISTORY C16 (in the sense: sweetheart, hence fine fellow, hence swaggering coward): probably from Middle Dutch *boele* lover, from Middle High German *buole*, perhaps childish variant of *bruoder* BROTHER

bully² (ˈbʊlɪ) NOUN any of various small freshwater fishes of the genera *Gobiomorphus* and *Philynodon* of New Zealand. Also called (NZ): **pakoko, titarakura, toitoi.**
▷HISTORY C20: short for COCKABULLY

bully beef NOUN tinned corned beef. Often shortened to: **bully.**
▷HISTORY C19 *bully*, anglicized version of French *bouilli*, from *boeuf bouilli* boiled beef

bullyboy (ˈbʊlɪˌbɔɪ) NOUN **a** a ruffian or tough, esp a hired one. **b** (*as modifier*): *bullyboy tactics.*

bully-off *Hockey* ◆ NOUN [1] a method by which a game is restarted after a stoppage. Two opposing players stand with the ball between them and alternately strike their sticks together and against the ground three times before trying to hit the ball. ◆ VERB **bully off.** [2] *(intr, adverb)* to restart play after a stoppage with a bully-off. ◆ Often shortened to: **bully.** Compare **face-off.**
▷HISTORY C19: perhaps from *bully* scrum in Eton football; of unknown origin

bullyrag (ˈbʊlɪˌræg) VERB **-rags, -ragging, -ragged.** *(tr)* to bully, esp by means of cruel practical jokes. Also: **ballyrag.**
▷HISTORY C18: of unknown origin

bulnbuln (ˈbʊlnˈbʊln) NOUN *Austral* another name for **lyrebird.**
▷HISTORY C19: from a native Australian language

bulrush (ˈbʊlˌrʌʃ) NOUN [1] a grasslike cyperaceous marsh plant, *Scirpus lacustris*, used for making mats, chair seats, etc. [2] a popular name for **reed mace** (sense 1): the name derived from Alma-Tadema's painting of the finding of the infant Moses in the "bulrushes" — actually reed mace. [3] a biblical word for **papyrus** (the plant).
▷HISTORY C15 *bulrish, bul-* perhaps from BULL¹ + *rish* RUSH², referring to the largeness of the plant

bulwaddy, bullwaddy, bullwaddie, *or* **bulwaddee** (bʊlˈwɒdɪ) NOUN a N Australian tree, *Macropteranthes kekwickii*, growing in dense thickets.
▷HISTORY of uncertain origin

bulwark (ˈbʊlwək) NOUN [1] a wall or similar structure used as a fortification; rampart. [2] a person or thing acting as a defence against injury, annoyance, etc. [3] *(often plural) Nautical* a solid vertical fencelike structure along the outward sides of a deck. [4] a breakwater or mole. ◆ VERB [5] *(tr)* to defend or fortify with or as if with a bulwark.
▷HISTORY C15: via Dutch from Middle High German *bolwerk*, from *bol* plank, BOLE¹ + *werk* WORK

bum¹ (bʌm) NOUN *Brit slang* the buttocks or anus.
▷HISTORY C14: of uncertain origin

bum² (bʌm) *Informal* ◆ NOUN [1] a disreputable loafer or idler. [2] a tramp; hobo. [3] an irresponsible, unpleasant, or mean person. [4] a person who spends a great deal of time on a specified sport: *baseball bum.* [5] **on the bum. a** living as a loafer or vagrant. **b** out of repair; broken. ◆ VERB **bums, bumming, bummed.** [6] *(tr)* to get by begging; cadge: *to bum a lift.* [7] *(intr;* often foll by *around)* to live by begging or as a vagrant or loafer. [8] *(intr;* usually foll by *around)* to spend time to no good purpose; loaf; idle. [9] **bum (someone) off.** *US and Canadian slang* to disappoint, annoy, or upset (someone). ◆ ADJECTIVE [10] *(prenominal)* of poor quality; useless. [11] wrong or inappropriate: *a bum note.*
▷HISTORY C19: probably shortened from earlier *bummer* a loafer, probably from German *bummeln* to loaf

bum bag NOUN a small bag worn on a belt round the waist.

bumbailiff (ˌbʌmˈbeɪlɪf) NOUN *Brit derogatory* (formerly) an officer employed to collect debts and arrest debtors for nonpayment.
▷HISTORY C17: from BUM¹ + bailiff, so called because he follows hard behind debtors

bumble¹ (ˈbʌmbᵊl) VERB [1] to speak or do in a clumsy, muddled, or inefficient way: *he bumbled his way through his speech.* [2] *(intr)* to proceed unsteadily; stumble. ◆ NOUN [3] a blunder or botch.

▷HISTORY C16: perhaps a blend of BUNGLE + STUMBLE
▸'**bumbler** NOUN ▸'**bumbling** NOUN, ADJECTIVE

bumble[2] ('bʌmbᵊl) VERB (*intr*) to make a humming sound.
▷HISTORY C14 *bomblen* to buzz, boom, of imitative origin

bumblebee ('bʌmbᵊlˌbiː) *or* **humblebee** NOUN any large hairy social bee of the genus *Bombus* and related genera, of temperate regions: family *Apidae*.
▷HISTORY C16: from BUMBLE[2] + BEE[1]

bumbledom ('bʌmbəldəm) NOUN self-importance in a minor office.
▷HISTORY C19: after *Bumble*, name of the beadle in Dickens' *Oliver Twist* (1837–38)

bumble-foot NOUN *Vet science* an inflammatory condition of the feet of birds, usually caused by an infection.

bumble-puppy NOUN [1] a game in which a ball, attached by string to a post, is hit so that the string winds round the post. [2] (*modifier*) (of whist or bridge) played unskilfully.

bumboat ('bʌmˌbəʊt) NOUN any small boat used for ferrying supplies or goods for sale to a ship at anchor or at a mooring.
▷HISTORY C17 (in the sense: scavenger's boat) *bum*, from Dutch *boomschip* canoe (from *bom* tree) + BOAT

bumf *or* **bumph** (bʌmf) NOUN *Brit* [1] *Informal, derogatory* official documents, forms, etc. [2] *Slang* toilet paper.
▷HISTORY C19: short for earlier *bumfodder*; see BUM[1]

bumfluff ('bʌmˌflʌf) NOUN *Informal* the soft and fluffy growth of hair on the chin of an adolescent.

bumfreezer ('bʌmˌfriːzə) NOUN [1] a slang name for an **Eton jacket.** [2] *Slang* any of various similar styles of short jacket worn by men.

bumkin ('bʌmkɪn) NOUN a variant spelling of **boomkin.**

bummalo ('bʌməˌləʊ) NOUN, *plural* **-lo.** another name for **Bombay duck.**
▷HISTORY C17: from Marathi *bombīla*

bummaree (ˌbʌmə'riː) NOUN *Brit* (formerly) [1] a dealer at Billingsgate fish market. [2] a porter at Smithfield meat market.
▷HISTORY C18: of unknown origin

bummer ('bʌmə) NOUN *Slang* [1] an unpleasant or disappointing experience. [2] *Chiefly US* a vagrant or idler. [3] an adverse reaction to a drug, characterized by panic or fear.

bump (bʌmp) VERB [1] (when *intr*, usually foll by *against* or *into*) to knock or strike with a jolt. [2] (*intr*; often foll by *along*) to travel or proceed in jerks and jolts. [3] (*tr*) to hurt by knocking: *he bumped his head on the ceiling.* [4] (*tr*) to knock out of place; dislodge: *the crash bumped him from his chair.* [5] (*tr*) *Brit* to throw (a child) into the air, one other child holding each limb, and let him down again to touch the ground. [6] (in rowing races, esp at Oxford and Cambridge) to catch up with and touch (another boat that started a fixed distance ahead). [7] *Cricket* to bowl (a ball) so that it bounces high on pitching or (of a ball) to bounce high when bowled. [8] (*intr*) *Chiefly US and Canadian* to dance erotically by thrusting the pelvis forward (esp in the phrase **bump and grind**). [9] (*tr*) *Poker* to raise (someone). [10] (*tr*) *Informal* to exclude a ticket-holding passenger from a flight as a result of overbooking. ◆ NOUN [11] (*tr*) *Informal* to displace (someone or something) from a previously allocated position: *the story was bumped from the front page.* [12] an impact; knock; jolt; collision. [13] a dull thud or other noise from an impact or collision. [14] the shock of a blow or collision. [15] a lump on the body caused by a blow. [16] a protuberance, as on a road surface. [17] any of the natural protuberances of the human skull, said by phrenologists to indicate underlying faculties and character. [18] a rising current of air that gives an aircraft a severe upward jolt. [19] (*plural*) the act of bumping a child. See sense 5. [20] *Rowing* the act of bumping. See **bumping race.** [21] *Cricket* **bump ball.** a ball that bounces into the air after being hit directly into the ground by the batsman. ◆ See also **bump into, bump off, bump up.**
▷HISTORY C16: probably of imitative origin

bumper[1] ('bʌmpə) NOUN [1] a horizontal metal bar attached to the front or rear end of a car, lorry, etc., to protect against damage from impact. [2] a person or machine that bumps. [3] *Cricket* a ball bowled so that it bounces high on pitching; bouncer.

bumper[2] ('bʌmpə) NOUN [1] a glass, tankard, etc., filled to the brim, esp as a toast. [2] an unusually large or fine example of something. ◆ ADJECTIVE [3] unusually large, fine, or abundant: *a bumper crop.* ◆ VERB [4] (*tr*) to toast with a bumper. [5] (*tr*) to fill to the brim. [6] (*intr*) to drink bumpers.
▷HISTORY C17 (in the sense: a brimming glass): probably from *bump* (obsolete vb) to bulge; see BUMP

bumper[3] ('bʌmpə) NOUN *Austral old-fashioned informal* a cigarette end.
▷HISTORY C19: perhaps from a blend of BUTT[1] and STUMP

bumper car NOUN a low-powered electrically propelled vehicle driven and bumped against similar cars in a special rink at a funfair. Also called: **Dodgem.**

bumper sticker NOUN a label affixed to the rear windscreen or bumper of a motor vehicle displaying an advertisement or slogan.

bumph (bʌmf) NOUN a variant spelling of **bumf.**

bumping race NOUN (esp at Oxford and Cambridge) a race in which rowing eights start an equal distance one behind the other and each tries to bump the boat in front.

bump into VERB (*intr, preposition*) *Informal* to meet by chance; encounter unexpectedly.

bumpkin[1] ('bʌmpkɪn) NOUN an awkward simple rustic person (esp in the phrase **country bumpkin**).
▷HISTORY C16 (perhaps originally applied to Dutchmen): perhaps from Dutch *boomken* small tree, or from Middle Dutch *boomekijn* small barrel, alluding to a short or squat person

bumpkin[2] ('bʌmpkɪn) *or* **bumkin** NOUN variant spellings of **boomkin.**

bump off VERB (*tr, adverb*) *Slang* to murder; kill.

bump start *Brit* ◆ NOUN [1] a method of starting a motor vehicle by engaging a low gear with the clutch depressed and pushing it or allowing it to run down a hill until sufficient momentum has been acquired to turn the engine by releasing the clutch. ◆ VERB **bump-start.** [2] (*tr*) to start (a motor vehicle) using this method.

bumptious ('bʌmpʃəs) ADJECTIVE offensively self-assertive or conceited.
▷HISTORY C19: perhaps a blend of BUMP + FRACTIOUS
▸'**bumptiously** ADVERB ▸'**bumptiousness** NOUN

bump up VERB (*tr, adverb*) *Informal* to raise or increase: *prices are being bumped up daily.*

bumpy ('bʌmpɪ) ADJECTIVE **bumpier, bumpiest.** [1] having an uneven surface: *a bumpy road.* [2] full of jolts; rough: *a bumpy flight.*
▸'**bumpily** ADVERB ▸'**bumpiness** NOUN

bum rap NOUN *US slang* [1] a trumped-up or false charge. [2] an unjust punishment.

bum's rush NOUN *Slang* [1] forcible ejection, as from a gathering. [2] rapid dismissal, as of an idea.

bum steer NOUN *Slang, chiefly US* false or misleading information or advice.

bumsters ('bʌmstəz) PLURAL NOUN *Brit* trousers cut so that the top lies just above the cleft of the buttocks.

bumsucking ('bʌmˌsʌkɪŋ) NOUN *Brit slang* obsequious behaviour; toadying.
▸'**bum,sucker** NOUN

bun (bʌn) NOUN [1] a small roll, similar to bread but usually containing sweetening, currants, spices, etc. [2] any of various types of small round sweet cakes. [3] a hairstyle in which long hair is gathered into a bun shape at the back of the head. [4] **have a bun in the oven.** *Slang* to be pregnant.
▷HISTORY C14: of unknown origin

Buna ('buːnə, 'bjuː-) NOUN *Trademark* a synthetic rubber formed by polymerizing butadiene or by copolymerizing it with such compounds as acrylonitrile or styrene.

bunch (bʌntʃ) NOUN [1] a number of things growing, fastened, or grouped together: *a bunch of grapes; a bunch of keys.* [2] a collection; group: *a bunch of queries.* [3] *Informal* a group or company: *a bunch of boys.* [4] *Archaic* a protuberance. ◆ VERB [5] (sometimes foll by *up*) to group or be grouped into a bunch. ◆ See also **bunches.**
▷HISTORY C14: of obscure origin

bunchberry ('bʌntʃˌbərɪ) NOUN, *plural* **-ries.** a dwarf variety of dogwood native to North America, *Cornus canadensis*, having red berries.

bunches ('bʌntʃɪz) PLURAL NOUN *Brit* a hairstyle in which hair is tied into two sections on either side of the head at the back.

bunchy ('bʌntʃɪ) ADJECTIVE **bunchier, bunchiest.** [1] composed of or resembling bunches. [2] bulging.
▸'**bunchiness** NOUN

bunco *or* **bunko** ('bʌŋkəʊ) *US informal* ◆ NOUN, *plural* **-cos** *or* **-kos.** [1] a swindle, esp one by confidence tricksters. ◆ VERB **-cos, -coing, -coed** *or* **-kos, -koing, -koed.** [2] (*tr*) to swindle; cheat.
▷HISTORY C19: perhaps from Spanish *banca* bank (in gambling), from Italian *banca* BANK[1]

buncombe ('bʌŋkəm) NOUN a variant spelling (esp US) of **bunkum.**

bund (bʌnd) NOUN (in India and the Far East) [1] an embankment; dyke. [2] an embanked road or quay.
▷HISTORY C19: from Hindi *band*, from Persian; related to Sanskrit *bandha* BAND[1]

Bund (bʊnd; *German* bʊnt) NOUN, *plural* **Bunds** *or* **Bünde** (*German* 'byndə). [1] (*sometimes not capital*) a federation or league. [2] short for **German American Bund**, an organization of US Nazis and Nazi sympathizers in the 1930s and 1940s. [3] an organization of socialist Jewish workers in Russia founded in 1897. [4] the confederation of N German states, which existed from 1867–71.
▷HISTORY C19: German; related to BAND[2], BIND

Bundaberg ('bʌndəˌbɜːg) NOUN a city in E Australia, near the E coast of Queensland: centre of a sugar-growing area, with a nearby deep-water port. Pop.: 52 267 (1993).

Bundesrat ('bʊndəsˌrɑːt) NOUN [1] (in Germany and formerly in West Germany) the council of state ministers with certain legislative and administrative powers, representing the state governments at federal level. [2] (in Austria) an assembly with some legislative power that represents state interests at the federal level. [3] (in Switzerland) the executive council of the confederation. [4] (in the German empire from 1871–1918) the council representing the governments of the constituent states, with administrative, judicial, and legislative powers.
▷HISTORY C19: German, from *Bund* federation + *Rat* council

Bundestag ('bʊndəsˌtɑːg) NOUN (in Germany and formerly in West Germany) the legislative assembly, which is elected by universal adult suffrage and elects the federal chancellor.
▷HISTORY C19: German, from *Bund* federation + *-tag*, from *tagen* to meet

bundh (bʌnd) NOUN a variant spelling of **bandh.**

bundle ('bʌndᵊl) NOUN [1] a number of things or a quantity of material gathered or loosely bound together: *a bundle of sticks.* Related adjective: **fascicular.** [2] something wrapped or tied for carrying; package. [3] *Slang* a large sum of money. [4] **go a bundle on.** *Slang* to be extremely fond of. [5] *Biology* a collection of strands of specialized tissue such as nerve fibres. [6] *Botany* short for **vascular bundle.** [7] *Textiles* a measure of yarn or cloth; 60 000 yards of linen yarn; 5 or 10 pounds of cotton hanks. [8] **drop one's bundle.** *Austral and NZ slang* to panic or give up hope. ◆ VERB [9] (*tr*; often foll by *up*) to make into a bundle. [10] (foll by *out, off, into* etc) to go or cause to go, esp roughly or unceremoniously: *we bundled him out of the house.* [11] (*tr*; usually foll by *into*) to push or throw, esp quickly and untidily: *to bundle shirts into a drawer.* [12] (*tr*) to sell (computer hardware and software) as one indivisible package. [13] (*tr*) to give away (a relatively cheap product) when selling an expensive one to attract business: *several free cassettes are often bundled with music centres.* [14] (*intr*) to sleep or lie in one's clothes on the same bed as one's betrothed: formerly a custom in New England, Wales, and elsewhere.
▷HISTORY C14: probably from Middle Dutch *bundel*; related to Old English *bindele* bandage; see BIND, BOND
▸'**bundler** NOUN

bundle up VERB (*adverb*) [1] to dress (somebody) warmly and snugly. [2] (*tr*) to make (something) into a bundle or bundles, esp by tying.

bundobust ('bʌndəbʌst) NOUN a variant spelling of **bandobust.**

bundu ('bʊndʊ) NOUN *South African and*

Zimbabwean slang **a** a largely uninhabited wild region far from towns. **b** (*as modifier*): *a bundu hat.*
▷**HISTORY** C20: from a Bantu language

bundwall (ˈbʌndˌwɔːl) NOUN a concrete or earth wall surrounding a storage tank containing crude oil or its refined product, designed to hold the contents of the tank in the event of a rupture or leak.
▷**HISTORY** C20: from BUND + WALL

bundy (ˈbʌndɪ) NOUN, *plural* **-dies.** *Austral* 1 a time clock. 2 *Informal* **punch the bundy. a** to start work. **b** to be in regular employment. ◆ VERB 3 (*intr; foll by on or off*) to arrive or depart from work, esp when it involves registering the time of arrival or departure on a card.
▷**HISTORY** from a trademark

bunfight (ˈbʌnˌfaɪt) NOUN *Brit slang* 1 a tea party. 2 *Ironic* an official function. 3 a petty squabble or argument.

bung[1] (bʌŋ) NOUN 1 a stopper, esp of cork or rubber, for a cask, piece of laboratory glassware, etc. 2 short for **bunghole.** ◆ VERB (*tr*) 3 (often foll by *up*) to close or seal with or as with a bung: *the car's exhaust was bunged up with mud.* 4 *Brit slang* to throw; sling.
▷**HISTORY** C15: from Middle Dutch *bonghe*, from Late Latin *puncta* PUNCTURE

bung[2] (bʌŋ) *Brit slang* ◆ NOUN 1 a gratuity; tip. 2 a bribe. ◆ VERB 3 (*tr*) to give (someone) a tip or bribe.
▷**HISTORY** C16 (originally in the sense: a purse): perhaps from Old English *pung*, changed through the influence of BUNG[1]

bung[3] (bʌŋ) ADJECTIVE *Austral and NZ informal* 1 useless. 2 **go bung.** to fail or collapse.
▷**HISTORY** C19: from a native Australian language

bungalow (ˈbʌŋɡəˌləʊ) NOUN 1 a one-storey house, sometimes with an attic. 2 (in India) a one-storey house, usually surrounded by a veranda.
▷**HISTORY** C17: from Hindi *banglā* (house) of the Bengal type

bungee jumping *or* **bungy jumping** (ˈbʌndʒɪ) NOUN a sport in which a participant jumps from a high bridge, building, etc., secured only by a rubber cord attached to the ankles.
▷**HISTORY** C20: from *bungie*, slang for India rubber, of unknown origin

bunger (ˈbʌŋə) NOUN *Austral slang* a firework.

bunghole (ˈbʌŋˌhəʊl) NOUN a hole in a cask, barrel, etc., through which liquid can be poured or drained.

bungle (ˈbʌŋɡəl) VERB 1 (*tr*) to spoil (an operation) through clumsiness, incompetence, etc.; botch. ◆ NOUN 2 a clumsy or unsuccessful performance or piece of work; mistake; botch.
▷**HISTORY** C16: perhaps of Scandinavian origin; compare dialect Swedish *bangla* to work without results
▶ˈ**bungler** NOUN ▶ˈ**bungling** ADJECTIVE, NOUN

bungwall (ˈbʌŋwɔl) NOUN an Australian fern, *Blechnum indicum*, having an edible rhizome.
▷**HISTORY** from a native Australian language

bunion (ˈbʌnjən) NOUN swelling of the first joint of the big toe, which is displaced to one side. An inflamed bursa forms over the joint.
▷**HISTORY** C18: perhaps from obsolete *bunny* a swelling, of uncertain origin

bunk[1] (bʌŋk) NOUN 1 a narrow shelflike bed fixed along a wall. 2 short for **bunk bed.** 3 *Informal* any place where one sleeps. ◆ VERB 4 (*intr; often foll by down*) to prepare to sleep: *he bunked down on the floor.* 5 (*intr*) to occupy a bunk or bed. 6 (*tr*) to provide with a bunk or bed.
▷**HISTORY** C19: probably short for BUNKER

bunk[2] (bʌŋk) NOUN *Informal* short for **bunkum** (sense 1).

bunk[3] (bʌŋk) *Brit slang* ◆ NOUN 1 a hurried departure, usually under suspicious circumstances (esp in the phrase **do a bunk**). ◆ VERB 2 (usually foll by *off*) to play truant from (school, work, etc.).
▷**HISTORY** C19: perhaps from BUNK[1] (in the sense: to occupy a bunk, hence a hurried departure, as on a ship)

bunk bed NOUN one of a pair of beds constructed one above the other.

bunker (ˈbʌŋkə) NOUN 1 a large storage container or tank, as for coal. 2 Also called (esp US and Canadian): **sand trap.** an obstacle on a golf course, usually a sand-filled hollow bordered by a ridge. 3 an underground shelter, often of reinforced concrete and with a bank and embrasures for guns above ground. ◆ VERB 4 (*tr*) *Golf* **a** to drive (the ball) into a bunker. **b** (*passive*) to have one's ball trapped in a bunker. 5 (*tr*) *Nautical* **a** to fuel (a ship). **b** to transfer (cargo) from a ship to a storehouse.
▷**HISTORY** C16 (in the sense: chest, box): from Scottish *bonkar*, of unknown origin

Bunker Hill NOUN the first battle of the American Revolution, actually fought on Breed's Hill, next to Bunker Hill, near Boston, on June 17, 1775. Though defeated, the colonists proved that they could stand against British regular soldiers.

bunkhouse (ˈbʌŋkˌhaʊs) NOUN (in the US and Canada) a building containing the sleeping quarters of workers on a ranch.

bunko (ˈbʌŋkəʊ) NOUN, VERB a variant spelling of **bunco.**

bunkum *or* **buncombe** (ˈbʌŋkəm) NOUN 1 empty talk; nonsense. 2 *Chiefly US* empty or insincere speechmaking by a politician to please voters or gain publicity.
▷**HISTORY** C19: after *Buncombe*, a county in North Carolina, alluded to in an inane speech by its Congressional representative Felix Walker (about 1820)

bunny (ˈbʌnɪ) NOUN, *plural* **-nies.** 1 Also called: **bunny rabbit.** a child's word for **rabbit** (sense 1). 2 Also called: **bunny girl.** a night-club hostess whose costume includes rabbit-like tail and ears. 3 *Austral informal* a mug; dupe. 4 *Slang* a devotee of a specified pastime or activity: *gym bunny; disco bunny.* 5 *Brit slang* talk, esp when inconsequential; chatter. 6 **not a happy bunny.** *Slang* deeply dissatisfied or discontented.
▷**HISTORY** C17: from Scottish Gaelic *bun* scut of a rabbit; sense 5 from RABBIT (sense 4)

bunny boiler NOUN *Slang* a woman who is considered to be emotionally unstable and likely to be dangerously vengeful.
▷**HISTORY** C20: from the 1987 film *Fatal Attraction*, in which a female character boils a pet rabbit to terrorize the family of the lover who spurns her

bunny hug NOUN 1 a ballroom dance with syncopated rhythm, popular in America in the early 20th century. 2 a piece of music in the rhythm of this dance.

bunodont (ˈbjuːnəˌdɒnt) ADJECTIVE (of the teeth of certain mammals) having cusps that are separate and rounded.
▷**HISTORY** from Greek *bounos* hill + -ODONT

bunraku (bʊnˈrɑːkuː) NOUN a Japanese form of puppet theatre in which the puppets are usually about four feet high, with moving features as well as limbs and each puppet is manipulated by up to three puppeteers who remain onstage.
▷**HISTORY** C20: Japanese

buns (bʌnz) PLURAL NOUN *Informal, chiefly US* the buttocks.

Bunsen burner NOUN a gas burner, widely used in scientific laboratories, consisting of a metal tube with an adjustable air valve at the base.
▷**HISTORY** C19: named after its inventor Robert Wilhelm *Bunsen* (1811–99), German chemist

bunt[1] (bʌnt) VERB 1 (of an animal) to butt (something) with the head or horns. 2 to cause (an aircraft) to fly in part of an inverted loop or (of an aircraft) to fly in such a loop. 3 *US and Canadian* (in baseball) to hit (a pitched ball) very gently. ◆ NOUN 4 the act or an instance of bunting.
▷**HISTORY** C19: perhaps nasalized variant of BUTT[3]

bunt[2] (bʌnt) NOUN *Nautical* the baggy centre of a fishing net or other piece of fabric, such as a square sail.
▷**HISTORY** C16: perhaps from Middle Low German *bunt* BUNDLE

bunt[3] (bʌnt) NOUN a disease of cereal plants caused by smut fungi (genus *Tilletia*).
▷**HISTORY** C17: of unknown origin

buntal (ˈbʌntəl) NOUN straw obtained from leaves of the talipot palm.
▷**HISTORY** C20: from Tagalog

bunting[1] (ˈbʌntɪŋ) NOUN 1 a coarse, loosely woven cotton fabric used for flags, etc. 2 decorative flags, pennants, and streamers. 3 flags collectively, esp those of a boat.
▷**HISTORY** C18: of unknown origin

bunting[2] (ˈbʌntɪŋ) NOUN any of numerous seed-eating songbirds of the families *Fringillidae* (finches, etc.) or *Emberizidae*, esp those of the genera *Emberiza* of the Old World and *Passerina* of North America. They all have short stout bills.
▷**HISTORY** C13: of unknown origin

buntline (ˈbʌntlɪn, -ˌlaɪn) NOUN *Nautical* one of several lines fastened to the foot of a square sail for hauling it up to the yard when furling.
▷**HISTORY** C17: from BUNT[2] + LINE[1]

bunt order NOUN the order of precedence within a group of cattle or pigs, based on their ability to butt or bunt with the head or horns.

bunya (ˈbʌnjə) NOUN a tall dome-shaped Australian coniferous tree, *Araucaria bidwillii*, having edible cones (**bunya nuts**) and thickish flattened needles. Also called: **bunya-bunya, bunya-bunya pine.**
▷**HISTORY** C19: from a native Australian language

bunyip (ˈbʌnjɪp) NOUN *Austral* a legendary monster said to inhabit swamps and lagoons of the Australian interior.
▷**HISTORY** C19: from a native Australian language

buoy (bɔɪ; *US* ˈbuːɪ) NOUN 1 a distinctively shaped and coloured float, anchored to the bottom, for designating moorings, navigable channels, or obstructions in a body of water. See also **life buoy.** ◆ VERB 2 (*tr; usually foll by up*) to prevent from sinking: *the belt buoyed him up.* 3 (*tr; usually foll by up*) to raise the spirits of; hearten. 4 (*tr*) *Nautical* to mark (a channel or obstruction) with a buoy or buoys. 5 (*intr*) to rise to the surface.
▷**HISTORY** C13: probably of Germanic origin; compare Middle Dutch *boeie, boeye*; see BEACON

buoyage (ˈbɔɪɪdʒ) NOUN 1 a system of buoys. 2 the buoys used in such a system. 3 the providing of buoys.

buoyancy (ˈbɔɪənsɪ) NOUN 1 the ability to float in a liquid or to rise in a fluid. 2 the property of a fluid to exert an upward force (upthrust) on a body that is wholly or partly submerged in it. 3 the ability to recover quickly after setbacks; resilience. 4 cheerfulness.

buoyancy bags PLURAL NOUN another term for **flotation bags.**

buoyant (ˈbɔɪənt) ADJECTIVE 1 able to float in or rise to the surface of a liquid. 2 (of a liquid or gas) able to keep a body afloat or cause it to rise. 3 cheerful or resilient.
▷**HISTORY** C16: probably from Spanish *boyante*, from *boyar* to float, from *boya* buoy, ultimately of Germanic origin

BUPA (ˈbuːpə) NOUN ACRONYM FOR The British United Provident Association Limited: a company which provides private medical insurance.

bupivacaine (bjuːˈpɪvəkeɪn) NOUN a local anaesthetic of long duration, used for nerve blocks.
▷**HISTORY** C20: perhaps from BU(TYL) + *pi(pecoloxylidide)*, the drug's chemical components + *-vacaine*, from (NO)VOCAINE

buppie (ˈbʌpɪ) NOUN *Informal* (*sometimes capital*) an affluent young Black person.
▷**HISTORY** C20: from B(LACK) + (Y)UPPIE

buprenorphine (bjuːˈprɛnɔːfiːn) NOUN an opiate used medicinally as a powerful analgesic.

buprestid (bjuːˈprɛstɪd) NOUN 1 any beetle of the mainly tropical family *Buprestidae*, the adults of which are brilliantly coloured and the larvae of which bore into and cause damage to trees, roots, etc. ◆ ADJECTIVE 2 of, relating to, or belonging to the family *Buprestidae*.
▷**HISTORY** C19: from Latin *buprestis* poisonous beetle, causing the cattle who eat it to swell up, from Greek, from *bous* ox + *prēthein* to swell up

bur (bɜː) NOUN 1 a seed vessel or flower head, as of burdock, having hooks or prickles. 2 any plant that produces burs. 3 a person or thing that clings like a bur. 4 a small surgical or dental drill. 5 a variant spelling of **burr**[3], **burr**[4]. ◆ VERB **burs, burring, burred.** 6 (*tr*) to remove burs from. ◆ Also (for senses 1–4, 6): **burr.**
▷**HISTORY** C14: probably of Scandinavian origin; compare Danish *burre* bur, Swedish *kardborre* burdock

BUR INTERNATIONAL CAR REGISTRATION FOR Myanmar (Burma).

Bur. ABBREVIATION FOR Myanmar (Burma).

buran (bu:'rɑ:n) *or* **bura** (bu:'rɑ:) NOUN (in central Asia) 1 a blizzard, with the wind blowing from the north and reaching gale force. 2 a summer wind from the north, causing dust storms.
▷HISTORY C19: from Russian, of Turkic origin; related to Kazan Tatar *buran*

Burberry ('bɜ:bərɪ) NOUN, *plural* **-ries**. *Trademark* a light good-quality raincoat, esp of gabardine.

burble ('bɜ:bᵊl) VERB 1 to make or utter with a bubbling sound; gurgle. 2 (*intr*; often foll by *away* or *on*) to talk quickly and excitedly. 3 (*intr*) (of the airflow around a body) to become turbulent. ♦ NOUN 4 a bubbling or gurgling sound. 5 a flow of excited speech. 6 turbulence in the airflow around a body.
▷HISTORY C14: probably of imitative origin; compare Spanish *borbollar* to bubble, gush, Italian *borbugliare*
▸'**burbler** NOUN

burbot ('bɜ:bət) NOUN, *plural* **-bots** *or* **-bot**. a freshwater gadoid food fish, *Lota lota*, that has barbels around its mouth and occurs in Europe, Asia, and North America.
▷HISTORY C14: from Old French *bourbotte*, from *bourbeter* to wallow in mud, from *bourbe* mud, probably of Celtic origin

'burbs *or* **burbs** (bɜ:bz) PLURAL NOUN *Informal* short for **suburbs.**

burden[1] ('bɜ:dᵊn) NOUN 1 something that is carried; load. 2 something that is exacting, oppressive, or difficult to bear: *the burden of responsibility*. Related adjective: **onerous.** 3 *Nautical* **a** the cargo capacity of a ship. **b** the weight of a ship's cargo. ♦ VERB (*tr*) 4 (sometimes foll by *up*) to put or impose a burden on; load. 5 to weigh down; oppress: *the old woman was burdened with cares*.
▷HISTORY Old English *byrthen*; related to *beran* to BEAR[1], Old Frisian *berthene* burden, Old High German *burdin*

burden[2] ('bɜ:dᵊn) NOUN 1 a line of words recurring at the end of each verse of a ballad or similar song; chorus or refrain. 2 the principal or recurrent theme of a speech, book, etc. 3 another word for **bourdon.**
▷HISTORY C16: from Old French *bourdon* bass horn, droning sound, of imitative origin

burden of proof NOUN *Law* the obligation, in criminal cases resting initially on the prosecution, to provide evidence that will convince the court or jury of the truth of one's contention.

burdensome ('bɜ:dᵊnsəm) ADJECTIVE hard to bear; onerous.

burdizzo (bɜ:'dɪzəʊ) NOUN *Vet science* a surgical instrument used to castrate animals.

burdock ('bɜ:ˌdɒk) NOUN a coarse weedy Eurasian plant of the genus *Arctium*, having large heart-shaped leaves, tiny purple flowers surrounded by hooked bristles, and burlike fruits: family *Asteraceae* (composites).
▷HISTORY C16: from BUR + DOCK[4]

bureau ('bjʊərəʊ) NOUN, *plural* **-reaus** *or* **-reaux** (-rəʊz). 1 *Chiefly Brit* a writing desk with pigeonholes, drawers, etc., against which the writing surface can be closed when not in use. 2 *US* a chest of drawers. 3 an office or agency, esp one providing services for the public. 4 **a** a government department. **b** a branch of a government department.
▷HISTORY C17: from French: desk, office, originally: type of cloth used for covering desks and tables, from Old French *burel*, from Late Latin *burra* shaggy cloth

bureaucracy (bjʊə'rɒkrəsɪ) NOUN, *plural* **-cies**. 1 a system of administration based upon organization into bureaus, division of labour, a hierarchy of authority, etc.: designed to dispose of a large body of work in a routine manner. 2 government by such a system. 3 government or other officials collectively. 4 any administration in which action is impeded by unnecessary official procedures and red tape.

bureaucrat ('bjʊərəˌkræt) NOUN 1 an official in a bureaucracy. 2 an official who adheres to bureaucracy, esp rigidly.
▸**bureaucratism** (bjʊə'rɒkrəˌtɪzəm) NOUN

bureaucratic (ˌbjʊərə'krætɪk) ADJECTIVE of or relating to bureaucrats; characterized by bureaucracy.
▸ˌ**bureau'cratically** ADVERB

bureaucratize *or* **bureaucratise** (bjʊə'rɒkrəˌtaɪz) VERB (*tr*) to administer by or transform into a bureaucracy.
▸**buˌreaucrati'zation** *or* **buˌreaucrati'sation** NOUN

burette *or US* **buret** (bjʊ'rɛt) NOUN a graduated glass tube with a stopcock on one end for dispensing and transferring known volumes of fluids, esp liquids.
▷HISTORY C15: from French: cruet, oil can, from Old French *buire* ewer, of Germanic origin; compare Old English *būc* pitcher, belly

burg (bɜ:g) NOUN 1 *History* a fortified town. 2 *US informal* a town or city.
▷HISTORY C18 (in the sense: fortress): from Old High German *burg* fortified town; see BOROUGH

burgage ('bɜ:gɪdʒ) NOUN *History* 1 (in England) tenure of land or tenement in a town or city, which originally involved a fixed money rent. 2 (in Scotland) the tenure of land direct from the crown in Scottish royal burghs in return for watching and warding.
▷HISTORY C14: from Medieval Latin *burgāgium*, from *burgus*, from Old English *burg*; see BOROUGH

burgee ('bɜ:dʒi:) NOUN *Nautical* a triangular or swallow-tailed flag flown from the mast of a merchant ship for identification and from the mast of a yacht to indicate its owner's membership of a particular yacht club.
▷HISTORY C18: perhaps from French (Jersey dialect) *bourgeais* shipowner, from Old French *borgeis*; see BOURGEOIS[1], BURGESS

burgeon *or* **bourgeon** ('bɜ:dʒən) VERB 1 (often foll by *forth* or *out*) (of a plant) to sprout (buds). 2 (*intr*; often foll by *forth* or *out*) to develop or grow rapidly; flourish. ♦ NOUN 3 a bud of a plant.
▷HISTORY C13: from Old French *burjon*, perhaps ultimately from Late Latin *burra* shaggy cloth; from the downiness of certain buds

burger ('bɜ:gə) NOUN *Informal* **a** short for **hamburger.** **b** (*in combination*): *a cheeseburger*.

burgess ('bɜ:dʒɪs) NOUN 1 (in England) **a** a citizen or freeman of a borough. **b** any inhabitant of a borough. 2 *English history* a Member of Parliament from a borough, corporate town, or university. 3 a member of the colonial assembly of Maryland or Virginia.
▷HISTORY C13: from Old French *burgeis*, from *borc* town, from Late Latin *burgus*, of Germanic origin; see BOROUGH

Burgess Shale NOUN a bed of Cambrian sedimentary rock in the Rocky Mountains in British Columbia containing many unique invertebrate fossils.
▷HISTORY named after the *Burgess* Pass, where the bed is exposed

burgh ('bʌrə) NOUN 1 (in Scotland) a town, esp one incorporated by charter, that enjoyed a degree of self-government until the local-government reorganization of 1975. 2 an archaic form of **borough** (sense 1).
▷HISTORY C14: Scottish form of BOROUGH
▸**burghal** ('bɜ:gᵊl) ADJECTIVE

burgher ('bɜ:gə) NOUN 1 a member of the trading or mercantile class of a medieval city. 2 a respectable citizen; bourgeois. 3 *Archaic* a citizen or inhabitant of a corporate town, esp on the Continent. 4 *South African history* **a** a citizen of the Cape Colony or of one of the Transvaal and Free State republics. **b** (*as modifier*): *burgher troops*.
▷HISTORY C16: from German *Bürger*, or Dutch *burger* freeman of a BOROUGH

Burghley House NOUN an Elizabethan mansion near Stamford in Lincolnshire: seat of the Cecil family; site of the annual Burghley Horse Trials.

burghul (bɜ:'gu:l) NOUN another name for **bulgur.**

burglar ('bɜ:glə) NOUN a person who commits burglary; housebreaker.
▷HISTORY C15: from Anglo-French *burgler*, from Medieval Latin *burglātor*, probably from *burgāre* to thieve, from Latin *burgus* castle, fortress, of Germanic origin

burglarize *or* **burglarise** ('bɜ:gləˌraɪz) VERB (*tr*) *US and Canadian* to break into (a place) and steal from (someone); burgle.

burglary ('bɜ:glərɪ) NOUN, *plural* **-ries**. *English criminal law* the crime of either entering a building as a trespasser with the intention of committing theft, rape, grievous bodily harm, or damage, or, having entered as a trespasser, of committing one or more of these offences.
▸**burglarious** (bɜ:'glɛərɪəs) ADJECTIVE

burgle ('bɜ:gᵊl) VERB to commit burglary upon (a house, etc.).

burgomaster ('bɜ:gəˌmɑ:stə) NOUN 1 the chief magistrate of a town in Austria, Belgium, Germany, or the Netherlands; mayor. 2 a popular name for the **glaucous gull.**
▷HISTORY C16: partial translation of Dutch *burgemeester*; see BOROUGH, MASTER

burgonet ('bɜ:gəˌnɛt) NOUN a light 16th-century helmet, usually made of steel, with hinged cheekpieces.
▷HISTORY C16: from French *bourguignotte*, from *bourguignot* of Burgundy, from *Bourgogne* Burgundy

burgoo ('bɜ:gu:, bɜ:'gu:) NOUN, *plural* **-goos**. 1 *Nautical, slang* porridge. 2 *Southern US* **a** a thick highly seasoned soup or stew of meat and vegetables. **b** a picnic or gathering at which such soup is served.
▷HISTORY C18: perhaps from Arabic *burghul* crushed grain

burgrave ('bɜ:greɪv) NOUN 1 the military governor of a German town or castle, esp in the 12th and 13th centuries. 2 a nobleman ruling a German town or castle by hereditary right.
▷HISTORY C16: from German *Burggraf*, from Old High German *burg* BOROUGH + *grāve* count

Burgundian (bɜ:'gʌndɪən) ADJECTIVE 1 of or relating to Burgundy or its inhabitants. ♦ NOUN 2 a native or inhabitant of Burgundy.

Burgundy ('bɜ:gəndɪ) NOUN, *plural* **-dies**. 1 a region of E France famous for its wines, lying west of the Saône: formerly a semi-independent duchy; annexed to France in 1482. French name: **Bourgogne.** 2 **Free County of.** another name for **Franche-Comté.** 3 a monarchy (1384–1477) of medieval Europe, at its height including the Low Countries, the duchy of Burgundy, and Franche-Comté. 4 **Kingdom of.** a kingdom in E France, established in the early 6th century A.D., eventually including the later duchy of Burgundy, Franche-Comté, and the Kingdom of Provence: known as the Kingdom of Arles from the 13th century. 5 **a** any red or white wine produced in the region of Burgundy, around Dijon. **b** any heavy red table wine. 6 (*often not capital*) a blackish-purple to purplish-red colour.

burhel ('bʌrəl) NOUN a variant spelling of **bharal.**

burial ('bɛrɪəl) NOUN the act of burying, esp the interment of a dead body.
▷HISTORY Old English *byrgels* burial place, tomb; see BURY, -AL[2]

burial ground NOUN a graveyard or cemetery.

Buridan's ass ('bjʊərɪdənz) NOUN *Philosophy* an example intended to show the deficiency of reason. An ass standing equidistant from two identical heaps of oats starves to death because reason provides no grounds for choosing to eat one rather than the other.
▷HISTORY named after Jean *Buridan*, 14th-century French philosopher, to whom it was incorrectly attributed

burier ('bɛrɪə) NOUN a person or thing that buries.

burin ('bjʊərɪn) NOUN 1 a chisel of tempered steel with a sharp lozenge-shaped point, used for engraving furrows in metal, wood, or marble. 2 an engraver's individual style. 3 *Archaeol* a prehistoric flint tool with a very small transverse edge.
▷HISTORY C17: from French, perhaps from Italian *burino*, of Germanic origin: compare Old High German *boro* auger; see BORE[1]

burk (bɜ:k) NOUN *Brit slang* a variant spelling of **berk.**

burka ('bɜ:kə) NOUN a variant spelling of **burqa.**
▷HISTORY C19: from Arabic

burke (bɜ:k) VERB (*tr*) 1 to murder in such a way as to leave no marks on the body, usually by suffocation. 2 to get rid of, silence, or suppress.
▷HISTORY C19: named after William *Burke* (1792–1829), Irish murderer and body snatcher, associate

of William Hare; executed in Edinburgh for a murder of this type

Burkinabé (ˌbɜːkɪnəˈbeɪ) ADJECTIVE [1] of or relating to Burkina-Faso or its inhabitants. ◆ NOUN [2] a native or inhabitant of Burkina-Faso.

Burkina-Faso (bɜːˈkiːnəˈfæsəʊ) NOUN an inland republic in W Africa: dominated by Mossi kingdoms (10th–19th centuries); French protectorate established in 1896; became an independent republic in 1960; consists mainly of a flat savanna plateau. Official language: French; Mossi and other African languages also widely spoken. Religion: mostly animist, with a large Muslim minority. Currency: franc. Capital: Ouagadougou. Pop.: 12 272 000 (2001 est.). Area: 273 200 sq. km (105 900 sq. miles). Former name (until 1984): **Upper Volta.**

Burkitt lymphoma (ˈbɜːkɪt) *or* **Burkitt's lymphoma** (ˈbɜːkɪts) NOUN a rare type of tumour of the white blood cells, occurring mainly in Africa and associated with infection by Epstein-Barr virus.
▷HISTORY named after Dennis *Burkitt* (1911–93), British surgeon who first described the tumour

burl[1] (bɜːl) NOUN [1] a small knot or lump in wool. [2] a roundish warty outgrowth from the trunk, roots, or branches of certain trees. ◆ VERB [3] (*tr*) to remove the burls from (cloth).
▷HISTORY C15: from Old French *burle* tuft of wool, probably ultimately from Late Latin *burra* shaggy cloth
▸ˈ**burler** NOUN

burl[2] *or* **birl** (bɜːl) NOUN *Informal* [1] *Scot, Austral, and NZ* an attempt; try (esp in the phrase **give it a burl**). [2] *Austral and NZ* a ride in a car.
▷HISTORY C20: perhaps from BIRL[1] in the Scot sense: a twist or turn

burlap (ˈbɜːlæp) NOUN a coarse fabric woven from jute, hemp, or the like.
▷HISTORY C17: from *borel* coarse cloth, from Old French *burel* (see BUREAU) + LAP[1]

burlesque (bɜːˈlɛsk) NOUN [1] an artistic work, esp literary or dramatic, satirizing a subject by caricaturing it. [2] a ludicrous imitation or caricature. [3] a play of the 17th–19th centuries that parodied some contemporary dramatic fashion or event. [4] Also: **burlesk.** *US and Canadian theatre* a bawdy comedy show of the late 19th and early 20th centuries: the striptease eventually became one of its chief elements. Slang name: **burleycue.** ◆ ADJECTIVE [5] of, relating to, or characteristic of a burlesque. ◆ VERB **-lesques, -lesquing, -lesqued.** [6] to represent or imitate (a person or thing) in a ludicrous way; caricature.
▷HISTORY C17: from French, from Italian *burlesco*, from *burla* a jest, piece of nonsense
▸**burˈlesquer** NOUN

burley[1] (ˈbɜːlɪ) NOUN, VERB a variant spelling of **berley.**

burley[2] (ˈbɜːlɪ) NOUN a light thin-leaved tobacco, grown esp in Kentucky.
▷HISTORY C19: probably from the name *Burley*

Burlington (ˈbɜːlɪŋtən) NOUN [1] a city in S Canada on Lake Ontario, northeast of Hamilton. Pop.: 136 976 (1996). [2] a city in NW Vermont on Lake Champlain: largest city in the state; University of Vermont (1791). Pop.: 39 127 (1990).

burly (ˈbɜːlɪ) ADJECTIVE **-lier, -liest.** large and thick of build; sturdy; stout.
▷HISTORY C13: of Germanic origin; compare Old High German *burlīh* lofty
▸ˈ**burliness** NOUN

Burma (ˈbɜːmə) NOUN the former name (until 1989) of **Myanmar.**

bur marigold NOUN any plant of the genus *Bidens* that has yellow flowers and pointed fruits that cling to fur and clothing: family *Asteraceae* (composites). Also called: **beggar-ticks, sticktight.**

Burma Road NOUN the route extending from Lashio in Burma (now Myanmar) to Chongqing in China, which was used by the Allies during World War II to supply military equipment to Chiang Kai-shek's forces in China.

Burmese (bɜːˈmiːz) ADJECTIVE *also* **Burman.** [1] of, relating to, or characteristic of Burma (Myanmar), its people, or their language. ◆ NOUN, *plural* **-mese.** [2] a native or inhabitant of Burma (Myanmar). [3] the official language of Burma (Myanmar), belonging to the Sino-Tibetan family.

Burmese cat NOUN a breed of cat similar in shape to the Siamese but typically having a dark brown or blue-grey coat.

burn[1] (bɜːn) VERB **burns, burning, burnt** *or* **burned.** [1] to undergo or cause to undergo combustion. [2] to destroy or be destroyed by fire. [3] (*tr*) to damage, injure, or mark by heat: *he burnt his hand; she was burnt by the sun.* [4] to die or put to death by fire: *to burn at the stake.* [5] (*intr*) to be or feel hot: *my forehead burns.* [6] to smart or cause to smart: *brandy burns one's throat.* [7] (*intr*) to feel strong emotion, esp anger or passion. [8] (*tr*) to use for the purposes of light, heat, or power: *to burn coal.* [9] (*tr*) to form by or as if by fire: *to burn a hole.* [10] to char or become charred: *the potatoes are burning in the saucepan.* [11] (*tr*) to brand or cauterize. [12] (*tr*) to cut (metal) with an oxygen-rich flame. [13] to produce by or subject to heat as part of a process: *to burn charcoal.* [14] (*tr*) to copy information onto (a CD-ROM). [15] *Astronomy* to convert (a lighter element) to a heavier one by nuclear fusion in a star: *to burn hydrogen.* [16] *Cards chiefly Brit* to discard or exchange (one or more useless cards). [17] (*tr; usually passive*) *Informal* to cheat, esp financially. [18] *Slang, chiefly US* to electrocute or be electrocuted. [19] (*tr*) *Austral slang* to drive fast (esp in the phrase **go for a burn**). [20] **burn one's bridges** *or* **boats.** to commit oneself to a particular course of action with no possibility of turning back. [21] **burn the candle at both ends.** See **candle** (sense 3). [22] **burn one's fingers.** to suffer from having meddled or been rash. ◆ NOUN [23] an injury caused by exposure to heat, electrical, chemical, or radioactive agents. Burns are classified according to the depth of tissue affected: **first-degree burn**: skin surface painful and red; **second-degree burn**: blisters appear on the skin; **third-degree burn**: destruction of both epidermis and dermis. [24] a mark, e.g. on wood, caused by burning. [25] a controlled use of rocket propellant, esp for a course correction. [26] a hot painful sensation in a muscle, experienced during vigorous exercise: *go for the burn!* [27] *Austral and NZ* a controlled fire to clear an area of scrub. [28] *Slang* tobacco or a cigarette. ◆ See also **burn in, burn off, burn out.**
▷HISTORY Old English *beornan* (intr), *bærnan* (tr); related to Old Norse *brenna* (tr or intr), Gothic *brinnan* (intr), Latin *fervēre* to boil, seethe

burn[2] (bɜːn; *Scot* bʌrn) NOUN *Scot and northern English* a small stream; brook.
▷HISTORY Old English *burna*; related to Old Norse *brunnr* spring, Old High German *brunno*, Lithuanian *briáutis* to burst forth

burned (bɜːnd) ADJECTIVE *Slang* having been cheated in a sale of drugs.

burner (ˈbɜːnə) NOUN [1] the part of a stove, lamp, etc., that produces flame or heat. [2] an apparatus for burning something, as fuel or refuse: *an oil burner.*

burnet (ˈbɜːnɪt) NOUN [1] a plant of the rosaceous genus *Sanguisorba* (or *Poterium*), such as *S. minor* (or *P. sanguisorba*) (**salad burnet**), which has purple-tinged green flowers and leaves that are sometimes used for salads. [2] **burnet rose.** Also called: **Scotch rose.** a very prickly Eurasian rose, *Rosa pimpinellifolia*, with white flowers and purplish-black fruits. [3] **burnet saxifrage.** a Eurasian umbelliferous plant of the genus *Pimpinella*, having umbrella-like clusters of white or pink flowers. [4] a moth of the genus *Zygaena*, having red-spotted dark green wings and antennae with enlarged tips: family *Zygaenidae*.
▷HISTORY C14: from Old French *burnete*, variant of *brunete* dark brown (see BRUNETTE); so called from the colour of the flowers of some of the plants

Burnham scale (ˈbɜːnəm) NOUN the salary scale for teachers in English state schools, which is revised periodically.
▷HISTORY C20: named after Lord *Burnham* (1862–1933), chairman of the committee that originally set it up

burn in VERB (*tr, adverb*) to darken (areas on a photographic print) by exposing them to light while masking other regions.

burning (ˈbɜːnɪŋ) ADJECTIVE [1] intense; passionate. [2] urgent; crucial: *a burning problem.* ◆ NOUN [3] a form of heat treatment used to harden and finish ceramic materials or to prepare certain ores for further treatment by calcination. [4] overheating of an alloy during heat treatment in which local fusion or excessive oxide formation and penetration occur, weakening the alloy. [5] the heat treatment of particular kinds of gemstones to change their colour.
▸ˈ**burningly** ADVERB

burning bush NOUN [1] a rutaceous shrub, *Dictamnus fraxinella*, of S Europe and Asia, whose glands release a volatile inflammable oil that can burn without harming the plant: identified as the bush from which God spoke to Moses (Exodus 3:2–4). [2] any of several shrubs or trees, esp the wahoo, that have bright red fruits or seeds. [3] another name for **gas plant.** [4] any of several plants, esp kochia, with a bright red autumn foliage.

burning glass NOUN a convex lens for concentrating the sun's rays into a small area to produce heat or fire.

burnish (ˈbɜːnɪʃ) VERB [1] to make or become shiny or smooth by friction; polish. ◆ NOUN [2] a shiny finish; lustre.
▷HISTORY C14 *burnischen*, from Old French *brunir* to make brown, from *brun* BROWN
▸ˈ**burnishable** ADJECTIVE ▸ˈ**burnisher** NOUN

Burnley (ˈbɜːnlɪ) NOUN an industrial town in NW England, in E Lancashire. Pop.: 74 661 (1991).

burn off VERB (*tr, adverb*) [1] to clear (land) of vegetation by burning. [2] to get rid of (unwanted gas at an oil well, etc.) by burning. ◆ NOUN **burn-off.** [3] an act or the process of burning off.

burnous, burnouse, *or US* **burnoose** (bɜːˈnuːs, -ˈnuːz) NOUN a long circular cloak with a hood attached, worn esp by Arabs.
▷HISTORY C17: via French *burnous* from Arabic *burnus*, from Greek *birros* cloak
▸**burˈnoused** *or US* **burˈnoosed** ADJECTIVE

burn out VERB (*adverb*) [1] to become or cause to become worn out or inoperative as a result of heat or friction: *the clutch burnt out.* [2] (*intr*) (of a rocket, jet engine, etc.) to cease functioning as a result of exhaustion of the fuel supply. [3] (*tr; usually passive*) to destroy by fire. [4] to become or cause to become exhausted through overwork or dissipation. ◆ NOUN **burnout.** [5] the failure of a mechanical device from excessive heating. [6] a total loss of energy and interest and an inability to function effectively, experienced as a result of excessive demands upon one's resources or chronic overwork.

burnsides (ˈbɜːnˌsaɪdz) PLURAL NOUN *US* thick side whiskers worn with a moustache and clean-shaven chin.
▷HISTORY C19: named after General A. E. *Burnside* (1824–81), Union general in the US Civil War

burnt (bɜːnt) VERB [1] a past tense and past participle of **burn**[1]. ◆ ADJECTIVE [2] affected by or as if by burning; charred. [3] (of various pigments, such as ochre and orange) calcined, with a resultant darkening of colour.

burnt almond NOUN a sweet consisting of an almond enclosed in burnt sugar.

burnt offering NOUN a sacrificial offering burnt, usually on an altar, to honour, propitiate, or supplicate a deity.

burnt shale NOUN carbonaceous shale formed by destructive distillation of oil shale or by spontaneous combustion of shale after it has been some years in a tip: sometimes used in road making.

burnt sienna NOUN [1] a reddish-brown dye or pigment obtained by roasting raw sienna in a furnace. [2] a dark reddish-orange to reddish-brown colour.

burnt-tip orchid NOUN a small orchid, *Orchis ustulata*, resembling the lady orchid, having dark reddish-brown hoods that give a burnt look to the tip of the flower spike.

burnt umber NOUN [1] a brown pigment obtained by heating umber. [2] a dark brown colour.

burn-up NOUN *Slang* a period of fast driving.

bur oak NOUN an E North American oak, *Quercus macrocarpa*, having fringed acorn cups and durable timber.

buroo (bəˈruː, bruː) NOUN, *plural* **-roos.** *Scot and Irish dialect* [1] the government office from which unemployment benefit is distributed. [2] the unemployment benefit itself (esp in the phrase **on the buroo**).
▷HISTORY C20: from BUREAU

burp (bɜ:p) NOUN [1] *Informal* a belch. ♦ VERB [2] (*intr*) *Informal* to belch. [3] (*tr*) to cause (a baby) to burp to relieve flatulence after feeding.
▷HISTORY C20: of imitative origin

burp gun NOUN *US slang* an automatic pistol or submachine gun.

burqa *or* **burka** ('bɜ:kə) NOUN a long enveloping garment worn by Muslim women in public.
▷HISTORY C19: from Arabic

burr[1] (bɜ:) NOUN [1] a small power-driven hand-operated rotary file, esp for removing burrs or for machining recesses. [2] a rough edge left on a workpiece after cutting, drilling, etc. [3] a rough or irregular protuberance, such as a burl on a tree. [4] *Brit* a burl on the trunk or root of a tree, sliced across for use as decorative veneer. ♦ NOUN, VERB [5] a variant spelling of **bur.** ♦ VERB (*tr*) [6] to form a rough edge on (a workpiece). [7] to remove burrs from (a workpiece) by grinding, filing, etc.; deburr.
▷HISTORY C14: variant of BUR

burr[2] (bɜ:) NOUN [1] *Phonetics* an articulation of (r) characteristic of certain English dialects, esp the uvular fricative trill of Northumberland or the retroflex *r* of the West of England. [2] a whirring sound. ♦ VERB [3] to pronounce (words) with a burr. [4] to make a whirring sound.
▷HISTORY C18: either special use of BUR (in the sense: rough sound) or of imitative origin

burr[3] *or* **bur** (bɜ:) NOUN [1] a washer fitting around the end of a rivet. [2] a blank punched out of sheet metal.
▷HISTORY C16 (in the sense: broad ring on a spear): variant of *burrow* (in obsolete sense: BOROUGH)

burr[4], buhr, *or* **bur** (bɜ:) NOUN [1] short for **buhrstone.** [2] a mass of hard siliceous rock surrounded by softer rock.
▷HISTORY C18: probably from BUR, from its qualities of roughness

burramys ('bʌrəmɪs) NOUN the very rare mountain pigmy possum, *Burramys parvus*, of Australia. It is about the size of a rat and restricted in habitat to very high altitudes, mainly Mt Hotham, Victoria. Until 1966 it was known only as a fossil.

burrawang ('bʌrəwæŋ) NOUN any of several Australian cycads of the genus *Macrozamia*, having an edible nut.
▷HISTORY C19: from Mount *Budawang*, New South Wales

bur reed NOUN a marsh plant of the genus *Sparganium*, having narrow leaves, round clusters of small green flowers, and round prickly fruit: family *Sparganiaceae*.

Burrell Collection ('bʌrəl) NOUN a gallery in Glasgow, noted for its collection of paintings, textiles, furniture, ceramics, etc.
▷HISTORY C20: named after Sir William *Burrell* (1861–1958), Scottish shipping magnate, and his wife Constance, who founded the collection

Burren ('bʌrən) NOUN **the.** a limestone area on the North Clare coast in the Irish Republic, famous for its wild flowers, caves, and dolmens.

burrito (bə'ri:təʊ) NOUN, *plural* **-tos.** *Mexican cookery* a tortilla folded over a filling of minced beef, chicken, cheese, or beans.
▷HISTORY C20: from Mexican Spanish, from Spanish: literally, a young donkey

burro ('bʊrəʊ) NOUN, *plural* **-ros.** a donkey, esp one used as a pack animal.
▷HISTORY C19: Spanish, from Portuguese, from *burrico* donkey, ultimately from Latin *burrīcus* small horse

burrow ('bʌrəʊ) NOUN [1] a hole or tunnel dug in the ground by a rabbit, fox, or other small animal, for habitation or shelter. [2] a small snug place affording shelter or retreat. ♦ VERB [3] to dig (a burrow) in, through, or under (ground). [4] (*intr*; often foll by *through*) to move through by or as by digging: *to burrow through the forest.* [5] (*intr*) to hide or live in a burrow. [6] (*intr*) to delve deeply: *he burrowed into his pockets.* [7] to hide (oneself).
▷HISTORY C13: probably a variant of BOROUGH
▸ **'burrower** NOUN

burrstone ('bɜ:ˌstəʊn) NOUN a variant spelling of **buhrstone.**

burry ('bɜ:rɪ) ADJECTIVE **-rier, -riest.** [1] full of or covered in burs. [2] resembling burs; prickly.

bursa ('bɜ:sə) NOUN, *plural* **-sae** (-si:) *or* **-sas.** [1] a small fluid-filled sac that reduces friction between movable parts of the body, esp at joints. [2] *Zoology* any saclike cavity or structure.
▷HISTORY C19: from Medieval Latin: bag, pouch, from Greek: skin, hide; see PURSE
▸ **'bursal** ADJECTIVE

bursar ('bɜ:sə) NOUN [1] an official in charge of the financial management of a school, college, or university. [2] *Chiefly Scot and NZ* a student holding a bursary.
▷HISTORY C13: from Medieval Latin *bursārius* keeper of the purse, from *bursa* purse

bursarial (bɜ:'sɛərɪəl) ADJECTIVE of, relating to, or paid by a bursar or bursary.

bursary ('bɜ:sərɪ) NOUN, *plural* **-ries.** [1] Also called: **bursarship.** a scholarship or grant awarded esp in Scottish and New Zealand schools, universities etc. [2] *Brit* **a** the treasury of a college, etc. **b** the bursar's room in a college.

Burschenschaft *German* ('bʊrʃənʃaft) NOUN a students' fraternity, originally one concerned with Christian ideals, patriotism, etc.
▷HISTORY literally: youth association

burse (bɜ:s) NOUN [1] *Chiefly RC Church* a flat case used at Mass as a container for the corporal. [2] *Scot* **a** a fund providing allowances for students. **b** the allowance provided.
▷HISTORY C19: from Medieval Latin *bursa* purse

burseraceous (ˌbɜ:sə'reɪʃəs) ADJECTIVE of, relating to, or belonging to the *Burseraceae*, a tropical family of trees and shrubs having compound leaves and resin or balsam in their stems. The family includes bdellium and some balsams.
▷HISTORY C19: from New Latin *Bursera* type genus, named after J. *Burser* (1593–1649), German botanist

bursicon ('bɜ:sɪkɒn) NOUN a hormone, produced by the insect brain, that regulates processes associated with ecdysis, such as darkening of the cuticle.

bursiform ('bɜ:sɪˌfɔ:m) ADJECTIVE shaped like a pouch or sac.
▷HISTORY C19: from Latin *bursa* bag + -FORM

bursitis (bɜ:'saɪtɪs) NOUN inflammation of a bursa, esp one in the shoulder joint.

burst (bɜ:st) VERB **bursts, bursting, burst.** [1] to break or cause to break open or apart suddenly and noisily, esp from internal pressure; explode. [2] (*intr*) to come, go, etc., suddenly and forcibly: *he burst into the room.* [3] (*intr*) to be full to the point of breaking open. [4] (*intr*) to give vent (to) suddenly or loudly: *to burst into song.* [5] to cause or suffer the rupture of: *to burst a blood vessel.* ♦ NOUN [6] a sudden breaking open or apart; explosion. [7] a break; breach; rupture. [8] a sudden display or increase of effort or action; spurt: *a burst of speed.* [9] a sudden and violent emission, occurrence, or outbreak: *a burst of heavy rain; a burst of applause.* [10] a volley of fire from a weapon or weapons. ♦ ADJECTIVE [11] broken apart; ruptured: *a burst pipe.*
▷HISTORY Old English *berstan*; related to Old Norse *bresta*, Old Frisian *bersta*, Old High German *brestan*; compare BREAK
▸ **'burster** NOUN

burstone ('bɜ:ˌstəʊn) NOUN a variant spelling of **buhrstone.**

burthen ('bɜ:ðən) NOUN, VERB an archaic word for **burden[1].**
▸ **'burthensome** ADJECTIVE

burton ('bɜ:tᵊn) NOUN [1] *Nautical* a kind of light hoisting tackle. [2] **go for a burton.** *Brit slang* **a** to be broken, useless, or lost. **b** to die.
▷HISTORY C15: of uncertain origin

Burton-upon-Trent NOUN a town in W central England, in E Staffordshire: famous for brewing. Pop.: 60 525 (1991).

Burundi (bə'rʊndɪ) NOUN a republic in E central Africa: inhabited chiefly by the Hutu, Tutsi, and Twa (Pygmy); made part of German East Africa in 1899; part of the Belgian territory of Ruanda-Urundi from 1923 until it became independent in 1962; ethnic violence has continued since independence; consists mainly of high plateaus along the main Nile-Congo dividing range, dropping rapidly to the Great Rift Valley in the west. Official languages: Kirundi and French. Religion: Christian majority. Currency: Burundi franc. Capital: Bujumbura. Pop.: 6 224 000 (2001 est.). Area: 27 731 sq. km (10 707 sq. miles). Former name (until 1962): **Urundi.**

Burundian (bə'rʊndɪən) ADJECTIVE [1] of or relating to Burundi or its inhabitants. ♦ NOUN [2] a native or inhabitant of Burundi.

burweed ('bɜ:ˌwi:d) NOUN any of various plants that bear burs, such as the burdock.

bury ('bɛrɪ) VERB **buries, burying, buried.** (*tr*) [1] to place (a corpse) in a grave, usually with funeral rites; inter. [2] to place in the earth and cover with soil. [3] to lose through death. [4] to cover from sight; hide. [5] to embed; sink: *to bury a nail in plaster.* [6] to occupy (oneself) with deep concentration; engross: *to be buried in a book.* [7] to dismiss from the mind; abandon: *to bury old hatreds.* [8] **bury the hatchet.** to cease hostilities and become reconciled. [9] **bury one's head in the sand.** to refuse to face a problem.
▷HISTORY Old English *byrgan* to bury, hide; related to Old Norse *bjarga* to save, preserve, Old English *beorgan* to defend

Bury ('bɛrɪ) NOUN [1] a town in NW England, in Bury unitary authority, Greater Manchester: an early textile centre. Pop.: 62 633 (1991). [2] a unitary authority in NW England, in Greater Manchester. Pop.: 180 612 (2001). Area: 99 sq. km (38 sq. miles).

Buryat *or* **Buriat** (bʊə'jɑ:t, bʊərɪ'ɑ:t) NOUN [1] a member of a Mongoloid people living chiefly in the Buryat Republic. [2] the language of this people, belonging to the Mongolic branch of the Altaic family.

Buryat Republic *or* **Buryatia** (bʊə'jɑ:tɪə; *Russian* bu'rjatija) NOUN a constituent republic of SE central Russia, on Lake Baikal: mountainous, with forests covering over half the total area. Capital: Ulan-Ude. Pop.: 1 035 000 (2000 est.). Area: 351 300 sq. km (135 608 sq. miles).

burying beetle NOUN a beetle of the genus *Necrophorous*, which buries the dead bodies of small animals by excavating beneath them, using the corpses as food for themselves and their larvae: family *Silphidae*. Also called: **sexton.**

Bury St Edmunds ('bɛrɪ sənt 'ɛdməndz) NOUN a market town in E England, in Suffolk. Pop.: 31 237 (1991).

bus (bʌs) NOUN, *plural* **buses** *or* **busses.** [1] a large motor vehicle designed to carry passengers between stopping places along a regular route. More formal name: **omnibus.** Sometimes called: **motorbus.** [2] short for **trolleybus.** [3] (*modifier*) of or relating to a bus or buses: *a bus driver; a bus station.* [4] *Informal* a car or aircraft, esp one that is old and shaky. [5] *Electronics, computing* short for **busbar.** [6] the part of a MIRV missile payload containing the re-entry vehicles and guidance and thrust devices. [7] *Astronautics* a platform in a space vehicle used for various experiments and processes. [8] **miss the bus.** to miss an opportunity; be too late. ♦ VERB **buses, busing, bused** *or* **busses, bussing, bussed.** [9] to travel or transport by bus. [10] *Chiefly US and Canadian* to transport (children) by bus from one area to a school in another in order to create racially integrated classes.
▷HISTORY C19: short for OMNIBUS

busbar ('bʌzˌbɑ:) NOUN [1] an electrical conductor, maintained at a specific voltage and capable of carrying a high current, usually used to make a common connection between several circuits in a system. [2] a group of such electrical conductors at a low voltage, used for carrying data in binary form between the various parts of a computer or its peripherals. ♦ Sometimes shortened to: **bus.**

bus boy NOUN *US and Canadian* a waiter's assistant.

busby ('bʌzbɪ) NOUN, *plural* **-bies.** [1] a tall fur helmet with a bag hanging from the top to the right side, worn by certain soldiers, usually hussars, as in the British Army. [2] (not in official usage) another name for **bearskin** (the hat).
▷HISTORY C18 (in the sense: large bushy wig): perhaps from a proper name

busera (bʊ'sɛrə) NOUN [1] a Ugandan alcoholic drink made from millet: sometimes mixed with honey. [2] a porridge made out of millet.
▷HISTORY from Rukiga, a language of SW Uganda

bush[1] (bʊʃ) NOUN [1] a dense woody plant, smaller than a tree, with many branches arising from the lower part of the stem; shrub. [2] a dense cluster of

such shrubs; thicket. [3] something resembling a bush, esp in density: *a bush of hair.* [4] **a** (often preceded by *the*) an uncultivated or sparsely settled area, esp in Africa, Australia, New Zealand, or Canada: usually covered with trees or shrubs, varying from open shrubby country to dense rainforest. **b** (*as modifier*): *bush flies.* [5] *Canadian* an area of land on a farm on which timber is grown and cut. Also called: **bush lot, woodlot.** [6] a forested area; woodland. [7] (often preceded by *the*) *Informal* the countryside, as opposed to the city: *out in the bush.* [8] a fox's tail; brush. [9] *Obsolete* **a** a bunch of ivy hung as a vintner's sign in front of a tavern. **b** any tavern sign. [10] **beat about the bush.** to avoid the point at issue; prevaricate. ◆ ADJECTIVE [11] *West African informal* ignorant or stupid, esp as considered typical of unwesternized rustic life. [12] *US and Canadian informal* unprofessional, unpolished, or second-rate. [13] **go bush.** *Informal, Austral and NZ* **a** to abandon city amenities and live rough. **b** to run wild. ◆ VERB [14] (*intr*) to grow thick and bushy. [15] (*tr*) to cover, decorate, support, etc., with bushes.
▷HISTORY C13: of Germanic origin; compare Old Norse *buski*, Old High German *busc*, Middle Dutch *bosch*; related to Old French *bosc* wood, Italian *bosco*

bush^{2} (bʊʃ) NOUN [1] Also called (esp US and Canadian): **bushing.** a thin metal sleeve or tubular lining serving as a bearing or guide. ◆ VERB [2] to fit a bush to (a casing, bearing, etc.).
▷HISTORY C15: from Middle Dutch *busse* box, bush; related to German *Büchse* tin, Swedish *hjulbössa* wheel-box, Late Latin *buxis* BOX^{1}

bushbaby (ˈbʊʃˌbeɪbɪ) NOUN, *plural* **-babies.** any agile nocturnal arboreal prosimian primate of the genera *Galago* and *Euoticus*, occurring in Africa south of the Sahara: family *Lorisidae* (lorises). They have large eyes and ears and a long tail. Also called: **galago.**

bush ballad NOUN an old Australian bush poem in a ballad metre dealing with aspects of life and characters in the bush.

bush-bash VERB *Austral slang* (*intr*) [1] to clear scrubland. [2] to drive through thick scrubland. ◆ Also called: scrub-bash:

bushbashing (ˈbʊʃˌbæʃɪŋ) NOUN *Austral and NZ slang* the process of forcing a path through the bush.

bushbuck (ˈbʊʃˌbʌk) *or* **boschbok** NOUN, *plural* **-bucks, -buck** *or* **-boks, -bok.** a small nocturnal spiral-horned antelope, *Tragelaphus scriptus*, of the bush and tropical forest of Africa. Its coat is reddish-brown with a few white markings.

bush canary NOUN *NZ* another name for **brown creeper.**

bush carpenter NOUN *Austral and NZ slang* a rough-and-ready unskilled workman.

bushcraft (ˈbʊʃˌkrɑːft) NOUN *Austral and NZ* ability and experience in matters concerned with living in the bush.

bushed (bʊʃt) ADJECTIVE *Informal* [1] (*postpositive*) extremely tired; exhausted. [2] *Canadian* mentally disturbed from living in isolation, esp in the north. [3] *Austral and NZ* lost or bewildered, as in the bush.

bushel^{1} (ˈbʊʃəl) NOUN [1] a Brit unit of dry or liquid measure equal to 8 Imperial gallons. 1 Imperial bushel is equivalent to 0.036 37 cubic metres. [2] a US unit of dry measure equal to 64 US pints. 1 US bushel is equivalent to 0.035 24 cubic metres. [3] a container with a capacity equal to either of these quantities. [4] *US informal* a large amount; great deal. [5] **hide one's light under a bushel.** to conceal one's abilities or good qualities.
▷HISTORY C14: from Old French *boissel*, from *boisse* one sixth of a bushel, of Gaulish origin

bushel^{2} (ˈbʊʃəl) VERB **-els, -elling, -elled** *or* **-els, -eling, -eled.** (*tr*) *US* to alter or mend (a garment).
▷HISTORY C19: probably from German *bosseln* to do inferior work, patch, from Middle High German *bōzeln* to beat, from Old High German *bōzan*
▸ **ˈbusheller** *or* **ˈbusheler** *or* **ˈbushelman** NOUN

bushfire (ˈbʊʃˌfaɪə) NOUN an uncontrolled fire in the bush; a scrub or forest fire.

bushfly (ˈbʊʃˌflaɪ) NOUN, *plural* **-flies.** any of various small black dipterous flies of Australia, esp *Musca vetustissima*, that breed in faeces and dung: family *Calliphoridae*.

bush grass NOUN a coarse reedlike grass, *Calamagrostis epigejos*, 1–1½ metres (3–4½ ft.) high that grows on damp clay soils in Europe and temperate parts of Asia.

bushhammer (ˈbʊʃˌhæmə) NOUN a hammer with small pyramids projecting from its working face, used for dressing stone.
▷HISTORY C19: from German *Bosshammer*, from *bossen* to beat + HAMMER

bush house NOUN *Chiefly Austral* a shed or hut in the bush or a garden.

Bushido (ˌbuːʃɪˈdəʊ) NOUN (*sometimes not capital*) the feudal code of the Japanese samurai, stressing self-discipline, courage and loyalty.
▷HISTORY C19: from Japanese *bushi* warrior (from Chinese *wushih*) + *dō* way (from Chinese *tao*)

bushie (ˈbʊʃɪ) NOUN a variant spelling of **bushy^{2}.**

Bushie (ˈbʊʃɪ) NOUN a supporter of US President George W. Bush or a member of his administration.

bushing (ˈbʊʃɪŋ) NOUN [1] another word for **bush^{2}** (sense 1). [2] an adaptor having ends of unequal diameters, often with internal screw threads, used to connect pipes of different sizes. [3] a layer of electrical insulation enabling a live conductor to pass through an earthed wall, etc.

Bushism (ˈbʊʃɪzəm) NOUN an apparently fatuous statement attributed to George W. Bush (born 1946), 43rd President of the USA.

bush jacket *or* **shirt** NOUN a casual jacket or shirt having four patch pockets and a belt.

bush lawyer NOUN *Austral and NZ* [1] any of several prickly trailing plants of the genus *Rubus*. [2] *Informal* a person who gives opinions but is not qualified to do so.

bush-line NOUN *NZ* the contour at which the growth of the bush ceases.

bush lot NOUN *Canadian* another name for **bush^{1}** (sense 5).

bushman (ˈbʊʃmən) NOUN, *plural* **-men.** *Austral and NZ* a person who lives or travels in the bush, esp one versed in bush lore.

Bushman (ˈbʊʃmən) NOUN, *plural* **-man** *or* **-men.** [1] a member of a hunting and gathering people of southern Africa, esp the Kalahari region, typically having leathery yellowish skin, short stature, and prominent buttocks. [2] any language of this people, belonging to the Khoisan family.
▷HISTORY C18: from Afrikaans *boschjesman*

bushman's singlet NOUN *NZ* a sleeveless heavy black woollen singlet, used as working clothing by timber fellers.

bushmaster (ˈbʊʃˌmɑːstə) NOUN a large greyish-brown highly venomous snake, *Lachesis muta*, inhabiting wooded regions of tropical America: family *Crotalidae* (pit vipers).

bushmeat (ˈbʊʃˌmiːt) NOUN meat taken from any animal native to African forests, including species that may be endangered or not usually eaten outside Africa.

bush oyster NOUN *Austral euphemistic* a bull's testicle when cooked and eaten.

bushpig (ˈbʊʃˌpɪg) NOUN a wild pig, *Potamochoerus porcus*, inhabiting forests in tropical Africa and Madagascar. It is brown or black, with pale markings on the face. Also called: **boschvark.**

bushranger (ˈbʊʃˌreɪndʒə) NOUN [1] *Austral history* an escaped convict or robber living in the bush. [2] *US* a person who lives away from civilization; backwoodsman.

bush shrike NOUN [1] any shrike of the African subfamily *Malaconotinae*, such as *Chlorophoneus nigrifrons* (**black-fronted bush shrike**). [2] another name for **ant bird.**

bush sickness NOUN *NZ and Austral* an animal disease caused by a cobalt deficiency in old bush country.
▸ **ˈbush-ˌsick** ADJECTIVE

bush sickness NOUN *Vet science* a cobalt deficiency in stock animals.

bush tea NOUN [1] a leguminous shrub of the genus *Cyclopia*, of southern Africa. [2] a beverage prepared from the dried leaves of any of these plants.

bush telegraph NOUN [1] a means of communication between primitive peoples over large areas, as by drum beats. [2] a means of spreading rumour, gossip, etc.

bushtit (ˈbʊʃˌtɪt) NOUN any small grey active North American songbird of the genus *Psaltriparus*, such as *P. minimus* (**common bushtit**): family *Paridae* (titmice).

bush tram NOUN *NZ* a railway line in the bush to facilitate the entry of workers and the removal of timber.

bushveld (ˈbʊʃˌfɛlt, -ˌvɛlt) NOUN **the.** an area of low altitude in N South Africa, having scrub vegetation. Also called: **lowveld.**

bushwalking (ˈbʊʃˌwɔːkɪŋ) NOUN *Austral* an expedition on foot in the bush.

bushwhack (ˈbʊʃˌwæk) VERB [1] (*tr*) *US, Canadian, and Austral* to ambush. [2] (*intr*) *US, Canadian, and Austral* to cut or beat one's way through thick woods. [3] (*intr*) *US, Canadian, and Austral* to range or move around in woods or the bush. [4] (*intr*) *US and Canadian* to fight as a guerrilla in wild or uncivilized regions. [5] (*intr*) *NZ* to work in the bush, esp at timber felling.

bushwhacker (ˈbʊʃˌwækə) NOUN [1] *US, Canadian, and Austral* a person who travels around or lives in thinly populated woodlands. [2] *Austral informal* an unsophisticated person; boor. [3] a Confederate guerrilla during the American Civil War. [4] *US* any guerrilla. [5] *NZ* a person who works in the bush, esp at timber felling.

bush wren NOUN a wren, *Xenicus longipes*, occurring in New Zealand: family *Xenicidae*. See also **rifleman** (sense 2).

bushy^{1} (ˈbʊʃɪ) ADJECTIVE **bushier, bushiest.** [1] covered or overgrown with bushes. [2] thick and shaggy: *bushy eyebrows.*
▸ **ˈbushily** ADVERB ▸ **ˈbushiness** NOUN

bushy^{2} *or* **bushie** (ˈbʊʃɪ) NOUN, *plural* **bushies.** *Austral informal* [1] a person who lives in the bush. [2] an unsophisticated uncouth person. [3] a member of a bush fire brigade.

busily (ˈbɪzɪlɪ) ADVERB in a busy manner; industriously.

business (ˈbɪznɪs) NOUN [1] a trade or profession. [2] an industrial, commercial, or professional operation; purchase and sale of goods and services: *the tailoring business.* [3] a commercial or industrial establishment, such as a firm or factory. [4] commercial activity; dealings (esp in the phrase **do business**). [5] volume or quantity of commercial activity: *business is poor today.* [6] commercial policy or procedure: *overcharging is bad business.* [7] proper or rightful concern or responsibility (often in the phrase **mind one's own business**). [8] a special task; assignment. [9] a matter or matters to be attended to: *the business of the meeting.* [10] an affair; matter: *a queer business; I'm tired of the whole business.* [11] serious work or activity: *get down to business.* [12] a complicated affair; rigmarole. [13] *Informal* a vaguely defined collection or area: *jets, fast cars, and all that business.* [14] Also called: **stage business.** *Theatre* an incidental action, such as lighting a pipe, performed by an actor for dramatic effect. [15] **like nobody's business.** *Informal* extremely well or fast. [16] **mean business.** to be in earnest. [17] a euphemistic word for **defecation** (esp in the phrase **do one's business**). [18] a slang word for **prostitution.**
▷HISTORY Old English *bisignis* solicitude, attentiveness, from *bisig* BUSY + *-nis* -NESS

business angel NOUN *Informal* an investor in a business venture, esp one in its early stages.

business casual NOUN *Informal* a style of casual clothing worn by businesspeople at work instead of more formal attire.

business class NOUN [1] a class of air travel which is less luxurious than first class but superior to economy class, intended for business passengers. ◆ ADJECTIVE **business-class.** [2] of or relating to this class of travel.

business college NOUN a college providing courses in secretarial studies, business management, accounting, commerce, etc.

business cycle NOUN another name (esp US and Canadian) for **trade cycle.**

business end NOUN *Informal* the part of a tool or weapon that does the work, as contrasted with the handle.

businesslike (ˈbɪznɪsˌlaɪk) ADJECTIVE [1] efficient and methodical. [2] earnest or severe.

businessman (ˈbɪznɪsˌmæn, -mən) NOUN, *plural*

-men. a person, esp a man, engaged in commercial or industrial business, esp as an owner or executive.

business park NOUN an area specially designated and landscaped to accommodate business offices, warehouses, light industry, etc.

businessperson ('bɪznɪsˌpɜrsən) NOUN, *plural* **-people** *or* **-persons**. a person engaged in commercial or industrial business, esp as an owner or executive.

business plan NOUN a detailed plan setting out the objectives of a business, the strategy and tactics planned to achieve them, and the expected profits, usually over a period of three to ten years.

business process re-engineering NOUN restructuring an organization by means of a radical reassessment of its core processes and predominant competencies. Abbreviation: **BPR**.

businesswoman ('bɪznɪsˌwʊmən) NOUN, *plural* **-women**. a woman engaged in commercial or industrial business, esp as an owner or executive.

businessy ('bɪznɪsɪ) ADJECTIVE of, relating to, typical of, or suitable for the world of commercial or industrial business: *well-heeled, businessy types.*

busk[1] (bʌsk) NOUN [1] a strip of whalebone, wood, steel, etc., inserted into the front of a corset to stiffen it. [2] *Archaic or dialect* the corset itself.
▷HISTORY C16: from Old French *busc*, probably from Old Italian *busco* splinter, stick, of Germanic origin

busk[2] (bʌsk) VERB *(intr) Brit* to make money by singing, dancing, acting, etc., in public places, as in front of theatre queues.
▷HISTORY C20: perhaps from Spanish *buscar* to look for
▸'**busker** NOUN ▸'**busking** NOUN

busk[3] (bʌsk) VERB *(tr) Scot* [1] to make ready; prepare. [2] to dress or adorn.
▷HISTORY C14: from Old Norse *būask*, from *būa* to make ready, dwell; see BOWER[1]

buskin ('bʌskɪn) NOUN [1] (formerly) a sandal-like covering for the foot and leg, reaching the calf and usually laced. [2] Also called: **cothurnus**. a thick-soled laced half boot resembling this, worn esp by actors of ancient Greece. [3] (usually preceded by *the*) *Chiefly literary* tragic drama.
▷HISTORY C16: perhaps from Spanish *borzeguí*; related to Old French *bouzequin*, Italian *borzacchino*, of obscure origin

bus lane NOUN one track of a road marked for use by buses only.

busman's holiday ('bʌsmənz) NOUN *Informal* a holiday spent doing the same sort of thing as one does at work.
▷HISTORY C20: alluding to a bus driver having a driving holiday

Busra *or* **Busrah** ('bʌsrə) NOUN variant spellings of **Basra**.

buss (bʌs) NOUN, VERB an archaic or dialect word for **kiss**.
▷HISTORY C16: probably of imitative origin; compare French *baiser*, German dialect *Bussi* little kiss

bus shelter NOUN a covered structure at a bus stop providing protection against the weather for people waiting for a bus.

bus stop NOUN a place on a bus route, usually marked by a sign, at which buses stop for passengers to alight and board.

bust[1] (bʌst) NOUN [1] the chest of a human being, esp a woman's bosom. [2] a sculpture of the head, shoulders, and upper chest of a person.
▷HISTORY C17: from French *buste*, from Italian *busto* a sculpture, of unknown origin

bust[2] (bʌst) *Informal* ◆ VERB **busts, busting, busted** *or* **bust**. [1] to burst or break. [2] to make or become bankrupt. [3] *(tr)* (of the police) to raid, search, or arrest: *the girl was busted for drugs.* [4] *(tr) US and Canadian* to demote, esp in military rank. [5] *(tr) US and Canadian* to break or tame (a horse, etc.). [6] *(tr) Chiefly US* to punch; hit. [7] **bust a gut**. See **gut** (sense 9). ◆ NOUN [8] a raid, search, or arrest by the police. [9] *Chiefly US* a punch; hit. [10] *US and Canadian* a failure, esp a financial one; bankruptcy. [11] a drunken party. ◆ ADJECTIVE [12] broken. [13] bankrupt. [14] **go bust**. to become bankrupt.
▷HISTORY C19: from a dialect pronunciation of BURST

bustard ('bʌstəd) NOUN any terrestrial bird of the family *Otididae*, inhabiting open regions of the Old World: order *Gruiformes* (cranes, rails, etc.). They have long strong legs, a heavy body, a long neck, and speckled plumage.
▷HISTORY C15: from Old French *bistarde*, influenced by Old French *oustarde*, both from Latin *avis tarda* slow bird

busted ('bʌstəd) ADJECTIVE *Informal* caught out doing something wrong and therefore in trouble: *you are so busted.*

bustee *or* **busti** ('bʌsti:) NOUN variant spellings of **basti**.

buster ('bʌstə) NOUN *Slang* [1] *(in combination)* a person or thing destroying something as specified: *dambuster.* [2] *US and Canadian* a term of address for a boy or man. [3] *US and Canadian* a person who breaks horses. [4] *Chiefly US and Canadian* a spree, esp a drinking bout.

buster collar NOUN a round collar, similar to a lampshade in shape, that is fitted round the neck of an animal or bird, for example to prevent it removing or interfering with a dressing or other treatment.

bustier ('bu:stɪeɪ) NOUN a type of close-fitting usually strapless top worn by women.

bustle[1] ('bʌsᵊl) VERB [1] (when *intr*, often foll by *about*) to hurry or cause to hurry with a great show of energy or activity. ◆ NOUN [2] energetic and noisy activity.
▷HISTORY C16: probably from obsolete *buskle* to make energetic preparation, from dialect *busk* from Old Norse *būask* to prepare
▸'**bustler** NOUN ▸'**bustling** ADJECTIVE

bustle[2] ('bʌsᵊl) NOUN a cushion or a metal or whalebone framework worn by women in the late 19th century at the back below the waist in order to expand the skirt.
▷HISTORY C18: of unknown origin

bust-up *Informal* ◆ NOUN [1] a quarrel, esp a serious one ending a friendship, etc. [2] *Brit* a disturbance or brawl. ◆ VERB **bust up**. *(adverb)* [3] *(intr)* to quarrel and part. [4] *(tr)* to disrupt (a meeting), esp violently.

busty ('bʌstɪ) ADJECTIVE **bustier, bustiest**. (of a woman) having a prominent bust.

busuuti (bu:'su:tɪ) NOUN a long garment with short sleeves and a square neckline, worn by Ugandan women, esp in S Uganda.
▷HISTORY C20: from Luganda

busy ('bɪzɪ) ADJECTIVE **busier, busiest**. [1] actively or fully engaged; occupied. [2] crowded with or characterized by activity: *a busy day.* [3] *Chiefly US and Canadian* (of a room, telephone line, etc.) in use; engaged. [4] overcrowded with detail: *a busy painting.* [5] meddlesome; inquisitive; prying. ◆ VERB **busies, busying, busied**. [6] *(tr)* to make or keep (someone, esp oneself) busy; occupy.
▷HISTORY Old English *bisig*; related to Middle Dutch *besich*, perhaps to Latin *festīnāre* to hurry
▸'**busyness** NOUN

busybody ('bɪzɪˌbɒdɪ) NOUN, *plural* **-bodies**. a meddlesome, prying, or officious person.
▸'**busyˌbodying** NOUN

busy Lizzie ('lɪzɪ) NOUN a balsaminaceous plant, *Impatiens balsamina*, that has pink, red, or white flowers and is often grown as a pot plant.

busy signal NOUN US and Canadian equivalent of **engaged tone**.

but[1] (bʌt; *unstressed* bət) CONJUNCTION *(coordinating)* [1] contrary to expectation: *he cut his knee but didn't cry.* [2] in contrast; on the contrary: *I like opera but my husband doesn't.* [3] *(usually used after a negative)* other than: *we can't do anything but wait.* [4] only: *I can but try.* ◆ CONJUNCTION *(subordinating)* [5] *(usually used after a negative)* without it happening or being the case that: *we never go out but it rains.* [6] (foll by *that*) except that: *nothing is impossible but that we live forever.* [7] *Archaic* if not; unless. ◆ SENTENCE CONNECTOR [8] *Informal* used to introduce an exclamation: *my, but you're nice.* ◆ PREPOSITION [9] except; save: *they saved all but one of the pigs.* [10] **but for**. were it not for: *but for you, we couldn't have managed.* ◆ ADVERB [11] just; merely: *he was but a child.* [12] *Scot, Austral and NZ informal* though; however: *it's a rainy day: warm, but.* [13] **all but**. almost; practically: *he was all but dead when we found him.* ◆ NOUN [14] an objection (esp in the phrase **ifs and buts**).
▷HISTORY Old English *būtan* without, outside, except, from *be* BY + *ūtan* OUT; related to Old Saxon *biūtan*, Old High German *biūzan*

but[2] (bʌt) *Scot* ◆ NOUN [1] the outer room of a two-roomed cottage: usually the kitchen. ◆ PREPOSITION, ADVERB [2] in or into the outer part (of a house). Compare **ben**[1].
▷HISTORY C18: from *but* (adv) outside, hence, outer room; see BUT[1]

butadiene (ˌbju:tə'daɪi:n) NOUN a colourless easily liquefiable flammable gas that polymerizes readily and is used mainly in the manufacture of synthetic rubbers. Formula: CH_2:CHCH:CH_2. Systematic name: **buta-1,3-diene.**
▷HISTORY C20: from BUTA(NE) + DI-[1] + -ENE

but and ben NOUN *Scot* a two-roomed cottage consisting of an outer room or kitchen (**but**) and an inner room (**ben**).

butane ('bju:teɪn, bju:'teɪn) NOUN a colourless flammable gaseous alkane that exists in two isomeric forms, both of which occur in natural gas. The stable isomer, *n*-butane, is used mainly in the manufacture of rubber and fuels (such as Calor Gas). Formula: C_4H_{10}.
▷HISTORY C19: from BUT(YL) + -ANE

butanol ('bju:təˌnɒl) NOUN a colourless substance existing in four isomeric forms. The three liquid isomers are used as solvents for resins, lacquers, etc., and in the manufacture of organic compounds. Formula: C_4H_9OH. Also called: **butyl alcohol.**
▷HISTORY C19: from BUTAN(E) + -OL[1]

butanone ('bju:təˌnəʊn) NOUN a colourless soluble flammable liquid used mainly as a solvent for resins, as a paint remover, and in lacquers, cements, and adhesives. Formula: $CH_3COC_2H_5$. Also called: **methyl ethyl ketone.**
▷HISTORY C20: from BUTAN(E) + -ONE

butch (bʊtʃ) *Slang* ◆ ADJECTIVE [1] (of a woman or man) markedly or aggressively masculine. ◆ NOUN [2] a lesbian who is noticeably masculine. [3] a strong rugged man.
▷HISTORY C18: back formation from BUTCHER

butcher ('bʊtʃə) NOUN [1] a retailer of meat. [2] a person who slaughters or dresses meat for market. [3] an indiscriminate or brutal murderer. [4] a person who destroys, ruins, or bungles something. ◆ VERB *(tr)* [5] to slaughter or dress (animals) for meat. [6] to kill indiscriminately or brutally. [7] to make a mess of; botch; ruin.
▷HISTORY C13: from Old French *bouchier*, from *bouc* he-goat, probably of Celtic origin; see BUCK[1]; compare Welsh *bwch* he-goat

butcherbird ('bʊtʃəˌbɜ:d) NOUN [1] a shrike, esp one of the genus *Lanius*. [2] any of several Australian magpies of the genus *Cracticus* that impale their prey on thorns.

butcher's ('bʊtʃəz) *or* **butcher's hook** NOUN *Brit slang* a look.
▷HISTORY C19: rhyming slang

butcher's-broom NOUN a liliaceous evergreen shrub, *Ruscus aculeatus*, that has stiff prickle-tipped flattened green stems, which resemble and function as true leaves. The plant was formerly used for making brooms.

butchery ('bʊtʃərɪ) NOUN, *plural* **-eries**. [1] the business or work of a butcher. [2] wanton and indiscriminate slaughter; carnage. [3] a less common word for **slaughterhouse**.

Bute[1] (bju:t) NOUN an island off the coast of SW Scotland, in Argyll and Bute council area: situated in the Firth of Clyde, separated from the Cowal peninsula by the **Kyles of Bute**. Chief town: Rothesay. Pop.: 8000 (latest est.). Area: 121 sq. km (47 sq. miles).

butene ('bju:ti:n) NOUN a pungent colourless gas existing in four isomeric forms, all of which are used in the manufacture of organic compounds. Formula: C_4H_8. Also called: **butylene.**
▷HISTORY C20: from BUT(YL) + -ENE

butenedioic acid (ˌbju:ti:ndaɪ'əʊɪk) NOUN either of two geometrical isomers with the formula HOOCCH:CHCOOH. See **fumaric acid, maleic acid.**

Buteshire ('bju:tˌʃɪə, -ʃə) NOUN (until 1975) a county of SW Scotland, consisting of islands in the Firth of Clyde and Kilbrannan Sound: formerly part of Strathclyde region (1975–96), now part of Argyll and Bute council area.

Buteyko method (ˌbuːˈteɪkəʊ) NOUN a breath control technique used to prevent hyperventilation and treat asthma without drugs.
▷HISTORY C20: named after Konstantin P. *Buteyko* (born 1923), Russian physician

butler (ˈbʌtlə) NOUN the male servant of a household in charge of the wines, table, etc.: usually the head servant.
▷HISTORY C13: from Old French *bouteillier*, from *bouteille* BOTTLE[1]

butlery (ˈbʌtlərɪ) NOUN, *plural* **-leries.** 1 a butler's room. 2 another name for **buttery**[2] (sense 1).

butsudan (ˈbʊtsəˌdæn) NOUN, *plural* **butsudan, -dans.** 1 (in Buddhism) a small household altar. 2 (in Nichiren Buddhism) an ornate cabinet which holds the Gohonzon.
▷HISTORY from Japanese *butsu* Buddha (from Chinese *fu*) + *dan* shelf

butt[1] (bʌt) NOUN 1 the thicker or blunt end of something, such as the end of the stock of a rifle. 2 the unused end of something, esp of a cigarette; stub. 3 *Tanning* the portion of a hide covering the lower backside of the animal. 4 *US and Canadian informal* the buttocks. 5 *US* a slang word for **cigarette.** 6 *Building trades* short for **butt joint** or **butt hinge.**
▷HISTORY C15 (in the sense: thick end of something, buttock): related to Old English *buttuc* end, ridge, Middle Dutch *bot* stumpy

butt[2] (bʌt) NOUN 1 a person or thing that is the target of ridicule, wit, etc. 2 *Shooting, archery* **a** a mound of earth behind the target on a target range that stops bullets or wide shots. **b** the target itself. **c** (*plural*) the target range. 3 a low barrier, usually of sods or peat, behind which sportsmen shoot game birds, esp grouse. 4 *Archaic* goal; aim. ◆ VERB 5 (usually foll by *on* or *against*) to lie or be placed end on to; abut: *to butt a beam against a wall.*
▷HISTORY C14 (in the sense: mark for archery practice): from Old French *but*; related to French *butte* knoll, target

butt[3] (bʌt) VERB 1 to strike or push (something) with the head or horns. 2 (*intr*) to project; jut. 3 (*intr*; foll by *in* or *into*) to intrude, esp into a conversation; interfere; meddle. 4 **butt out.** *Informal, chiefly US and Canadian* to stop interfering or meddling. ◆ NOUN 5 a blow with the head or horns.
▷HISTORY C12: from Old French *boter*, of Germanic origin; compare Middle Dutch *botten* to strike; see BEAT, BUTTON
▸ **ˈbutter** NOUN

butt[4] (bʌt) NOUN 1 a large cask, esp one with a capacity of two hogsheads, for storing wine or beer. 2 a US unit of liquid measure equal to 126 US gallons.
▷HISTORY C14: from Old French *botte*, from Old Provençal *bota*, from Late Latin *buttis* cask, perhaps from Greek *butinē* chamber pot

butte (bjuːt) NOUN *Western US and Canadian* an isolated steep-sided flat-topped hill.
▷HISTORY C19: from French, from Old French *bute* mound behind a target, from *but* target; see BUTT[2]

butter (ˈbʌtə) NOUN 1 **a** an edible fatty whitish-yellow solid made from cream by churning, for cooking and table use. **b** (*as modifier*): *butter icing.* Related adjective: **butyraceous.** 2 any substance with a butter-like consistency, such as peanut butter or vegetable butter. 3 **look as if butter wouldn't melt in one's mouth.** to look innocent, although probably not so. ◆ VERB (*tr*) 4 to put butter on or in. 5 to flatter. ◆ See also **butter up.**
▷HISTORY Old English *butere*, from Latin *būtyrum*, from Greek *bouturon*, from *bous* cow + *turos* cheese

butter-and-eggs NOUN (*functioning as singular*) any of various plants, such as toadflax, the flowers of which are of two shades of yellow.

butterball (ˈbʌtəˌbɔːl) NOUN *US* 1 another name for **bufflehead.** 2 *Informal* a chubby or fat person.

butter bean NOUN a variety of lima bean that has large pale flat edible seeds and is grown in the southern US.

butterbur (ˈbʌtəˌbɜː) NOUN a plant of the Eurasian genus *Petasites* with fragrant whitish or purple flowers, woolly stems, and leaves formerly used to wrap butter: family *Asteraceae* (composites).

buttercup (ˈbʌtəˌkʌp) NOUN any of various yellow-flowered ranunculaceous plants of the genus *Ranunculus*, such as *R. acris* (meadow buttercup), which is native to Europe but common throughout North America. See also **crowfoot, goldilocks** (sense 2), **spearwort, lesser celandine.**

butterfat (ˈbʌtəˌfæt) NOUN the fatty substance of milk from which butter is made, consisting of a mixture of glycerides, mainly butyrin, olein, and palmitin.

butterfat cheque NOUN **the.** *NZ* the total annual cash return for operations on a dairy farm.

butterfingers (ˈbʌtəˌfɪŋɡəz) NOUN (*functioning as singular*) *Informal* a person who drops things inadvertently or fails to catch things.
▸ **ˈbutterˌfingered** ADJECTIVE

butterfish (ˈbʌtəˌfɪʃ) NOUN, *plural* **-fish** *or* **-fishes.** 1 an eel-like blennioid food fish, *Pholis gunnellus*, occurring in North Atlantic coastal regions: family *Pholidae* (gunnels). It has a slippery scaleless golden brown skin with a row of black spots along the base of the long dorsal fin. 2 Also called: **greenbone,** (Maori) **marari.** an edible reef fish, *Coridodax pullus*, of esp S New Zealand. It has a slippery purplish-grey to olive-green skin and is often found browsing on kelp.

butterflies (ˈbʌtəˌflaɪz) PLURAL NOUN *Informal* tremors in the stomach region due to nervousness.

butterfly (ˈbʌtəˌflaɪ) NOUN, *plural* **-flies.** 1 any diurnal insect of the order *Lepidoptera* that has a slender body with clubbed antennae and typically rests with the wings (which are often brightly coloured) closed over the back. Compare **moth.** Related adjective: **lepidopteran.** 2 a person who never settles with one group, interest, or occupation for long. 3 a swimming stroke in which the arms are plunged forward together in large circular movements. 4 *Commerce* the simultaneous purchase and sale of traded call options, at different exercise prices or with different expiry dates, on a stock exchange or commodity market.
▷HISTORY Old English *buttorflēoge*; the name perhaps is based on a belief that butterflies stole milk and butter

butterfly ballot NOUN *US* a ballot paper in the form of two leaves extending from a central spine.
▷HISTORY C20: from its resemblance to a butterfly's wings

butterfly bush NOUN another name for **buddleia.**

butterfly collar NOUN the Irish name for **wing collar.**

butterfly diagram NOUN *Astronomy* a graphical butterfly-shaped representation of the sunspot density on the solar disc in the 11-year sunspot cycle.

butterfly effect NOUN the idea, used in chaos theory, that a very small difference in the initial state of a physical system can make a significant difference to the state at some later time.
▷HISTORY C20: from the theory that a butterfly flapping its wings in one part of the world might ultimately cause a hurricane in another part of the world

butterfly fish NOUN any small tropical marine percoid fish of the genera *Chaetodon, Chelmon*, etc., that has a deep flattened brightly coloured body and brushlike teeth: family *Chaetodontidae.* See also **angelfish** (sense 1).

butterfly nut NOUN another name for **wing nut.**

butterfly valve NOUN 1 a disc that acts as a valve by turning about a diameter, esp one used as the throttle valve in a carburettor. 2 a non-return valve consisting of two semicircular plates hinged about a common central spindle.

butterfly weed NOUN a North American asclepiadaceous plant, *Asclepias tuberosa* (or *A. decumbens*), having flat-topped clusters of bright orange flowers. Also called: **orange milkweed, pleurisy root.**

butterine (ˈbʌtəˌriːn, -rɪn) NOUN an artificial butter made partly from milk.

Buttermere (ˈbʌtəˌmɪə) NOUN a lake in NW England, in Cumbria, in the Lake District, southwest of Keswick. Length: 2 km (1.25 miles).

buttermilk (ˈbʌtəˌmɪlk) NOUN the sourish liquid remaining after the butter has been separated from milk, often used for making scones and soda bread.

butter muslin NOUN a fine loosely woven cotton material originally used for wrapping butter.

butternut (ˈbʌtəˌnʌt) NOUN 1 a walnut tree, *Juglans cinerea* of E North America. Compare **black walnut.** 2 the oily edible egg-shaped nut of this tree. 3 the hard brownish-grey wood of this tree. 4 the bark of this tree or an extract from it, formerly used as a laxative. 5 a brownish colour or dye. 6 *NZ* short for **butternut pumpkin.** ◆ Also called (for senses 1–4): **white walnut.**

butternut pumpkin NOUN *Austral* a variety of pumpkin, eaten as vegetable. Also called (NZ): **butternut.**

butterscotch (ˈbʌtəˌskɒtʃ) NOUN 1 a kind of hard brittle toffee made with butter, brown sugar, etc. 2 **a** a flavouring made from these ingredients. **b** (*as modifier*): *butterscotch icing.*
▷HISTORY C19: perhaps first made in Scotland

butter tart NOUN *Canadian* a kind of tart made with butter, brown sugar, and raisins.

butter up VERB (*tr, adverb*) to flatter.

butterwort (ˈbʌtəˌwɜːt) NOUN a plant of the genus *Pinguicula*, esp *P. vulgaris*, that grows in wet places and has violet-blue spurred flowers and fleshy greasy glandular leaves on which insects are trapped and digested: family *Lentibulariaceae.*

buttery[1] (ˈbʌtərɪ) ADJECTIVE 1 containing, like, or coated with butter. 2 *Informal* grossly or insincerely flattering; obsequious.
▸ **ˈbutteriness** NOUN

buttery[2] (ˈbʌtərɪ) NOUN, *plural* **-teries.** 1 a room for storing foods or wines. 2 *Brit* (in some universities) a room in which food is supplied or sold to students.
▷HISTORY C14: from Anglo-French *boterie*, from Anglo-Latin *buteria*, probably from *butta* cask, BUTT[4]

butt hinge NOUN a hinge made of two matching leaves, one recessed into a door and the other into the jamb so that they are in contact when the door is shut. sometimes shortened to: **butt.**

butt joint NOUN a joint between two plates, planks, bars, sections, etc., when the components are butted together and do not overlap or interlock. The joint may be strapped with jointing plates laid across it or welded (**butt weld**). Sometimes shortened to: **butt.**

buttock (ˈbʌtək) NOUN 1 either of the two large fleshy masses of thick muscular tissue that form the human rump. See also **gluteus.** Related adjectives: **gluteal, natal.** 2 the analogous part in some mammals.
▷HISTORY C13: perhaps from Old English *buttuc* round slope, diminutive of *butt* (unattested) strip of land; see BUTT[1] -OCK

buttock-clenching ADJECTIVE *Informal* making one tighten the buttocks through extreme fear or embarrassment: *buttock-clenching embarrassment.*

button (ˈbʌtᵊn) NOUN 1 a disc or knob of plastic, wood, etc., attached to a garment, etc., usually for fastening two surfaces together by passing it through a buttonhole or loop. 2 a small round object, such as any of various sweets, decorations, or badges. 3 a small disc that completes an electric circuit when pushed, as one that operates a doorbell or machine. 4 a symbolic representation of a button on the screen of a computer that is notionally depressed by manipulating the mouse to initiate an action. 5 *Biology* any rounded knoblike part or organ, such as an unripe mushroom. 6 *Fencing* the protective knob fixed to the point of a foil. 7 a small amount of metal, usually lead, with which gold or silver is fused, thus concentrating it during assaying. 8 the piece of a weld that pulls out during the destructive testing of spot welds. 9 *Rowing* a projection around the loom of an oar that prevents it slipping through the rowlock. 10 *Brit* an object of no value (esp in the phrase **not worth a button**). 11 *Slang* intellect; mental capacity (in such phrases as **a button short, to have all one's buttons,** etc.). 12 **on the button.** *Informal* exactly; precisely. ◆ VERB 13 to fasten with a button or buttons. 14 (*tr*) to provide with buttons. 15 (*tr*) *Fencing* to hit (an opponent) with the button of one's foil. 16 **button (up) one's lip** *or* **mouth.** to stop talking: often imperative. ◆ See also **buttons, button up.**

▷HISTORY C14: from Old French *boton*, from *boter* to thrust, butt, of Germanic origin; see BUTT[3] ▸'**buttoner** NOUN ▸'**buttonless** ADJECTIVE ▸'**buttony** ADJECTIVE

buttonball ('bʌtᵊnˌbɔːl) NOUN *US and Canadian* a North American plane tree, *Platanus occidentalis*. See **plane tree.**

button-down ADJECTIVE [1] (of a collar) having points that are fastened to the garment with buttons. [2] (of a shirt) having a button-down collar. [3] Also: **buttoned-down.** conventional or conservative: *a button-down corporate culture.*

buttonhole ('bʌtᵊnˌhəʊl) NOUN [1] a slit in a garment, etc., through which a button is passed to fasten two surfaces together. [2] a flower or small bunch of flowers worn pinned to the lapel or in the buttonhole, esp at weddings, formal dances, etc. US name: **boutonniere.** ◆ VERB (*tr*) [3] to detain (a person) in conversation. [4] to make buttonholes in. [5] to sew with buttonhole stitch.

buttonhole stitch NOUN a reinforcing looped stitch for the edge of material, such as around a buttonhole.

buttonhook ('bʌtᵊnˌhʊk) NOUN a thin tapering hooked instrument formerly used for pulling buttons through the buttonholes of gloves, shoes, etc.

buttonmould ('bʌtᵊnˌməʊld) NOUN the small core of plastic, wood, or metal that is the base for buttons covered with fabric, leather, etc.

button quail NOUN any small quail-like terrestrial bird of the genus *Turnix*, such as *T. sylvatica* (striped button quail), occurring in tropical and subtropical regions of the Old World: family *Turnicidae*, order *Gruiformes* (cranes, rails, etc.). Also called: **hemipode.**

buttons ('bʌtᵊnz) NOUN (*functioning as singular*) *Brit informal* a page boy.

button-through ADJECTIVE (of a dress or skirt) fastened with buttons from top to hem.

button tow NOUN a kind of ski lift for one person consisting of a pole that has a circular plate at the bottom and is attached to a moving cable. The person places the pole between his legs so that the plate takes his weight.

button up VERB (*tr, adverb*) [1] to fasten (a garment) with a button or buttons. [2] *Informal* to conclude (business) satisfactorily. [3] **buttoned up.** *Slang* taciturn; silent and somewhat tense.

buttonwood ('bʌtᵊnˌwʊd) *or* **button tree** NOUN [1] Also called: **buttonball.** a North American plane tree, *Platanus occidentalis*. See **plane tree.** [2] a small West Indian tree, *Conocarpus erectus*, with button-like fruits and heavy hard compact wood: family *Combretaceae*.

butt plate NOUN a plate made usually of metal and attached to the butt end of a gunstock.

buttress ('bʌtrɪs) NOUN [1] Also called: **pier.** a construction, usually of brick or stone, built to support a wall. See also **flying buttress.** [2] any support or prop. [3] something shaped like a buttress, such as a projection from a mountainside. [4] either of the two pointed rear parts of a horse's hoof. ◆ VERB (*tr*) [5] to support (a wall) with a buttress. [6] to support or sustain.
▷HISTORY C13: from Old French *bouterez*, short for *ars bouterez* thrusting arch, from *bouter* to thrust, BUTT[3]

buttress root NOUN a tree root that extends above ground as a platelike outgrowth of the trunk supporting the tree. Buttress roots are mainly found in trees of tropical rain forests.

buttress thread NOUN a screw thread having one flank that is vertical while the other is inclined, and a flat top and bottom: used in machine tools and designed to withstand heavy thrust in one direction.

butt shaft NOUN a blunt-headed unbarbed arrow.

butt weld NOUN See **butt joint.**

butty[1] ('bʌtɪ) NOUN, *plural* **-ties.** *Chiefly northern English dialect* a sandwich: *a jam butty.*
▷HISTORY C19: from *buttered* (*bread*)

butty[2] ('bʌtɪ) NOUN, *plural* **-ties.** *English dialect* (esp in mining parlance) a friend or workmate.
▷HISTORY C19: perhaps from obsolete *booty* sharing, from BOOT[2], later applied to a middleman in a mine

Butung ('buːtʊŋ) NOUN an island of Indonesia, southeast of Sulawesi: hilly and forested. Chief town: Baubau. Pop.: 317 124 (latest est.). Area: 4555 sq. km (1759 sq. miles).

butut (bʊ'tʊt) NOUN a Gambian monetary unit worth one hundredth of a dalasi.

butyl ('bjuːˌtaɪl, -tɪl) NOUN (*modifier*) of, consisting of, or containing any of four isomeric forms of the group C_4H_9–: *butyl rubber.*
▷HISTORY C19: from BUT(YRIC ACID) + -YL

butyl acetate NOUN a colourless liquid with a fruity odour, existing in four isomeric forms. Three of the isomers are important solvents for cellulose lacquers. Formula: $CH_3COOC_4H_9$.

butyl alcohol NOUN another name for **butanol.**

butylene ('bjuːtɪˌliːn) NOUN another name for **butene.**

butyl rubber NOUN a copolymer of isobutene and isoprene, used in tyres and as a waterproofing material.

butyraceous (ˌbjuːtɪ'reɪʃəs) ADJECTIVE of, containing, or resembling butter.
▷HISTORY C17 *butyr-*, from Latin *būtyrum* BUTTER + -ACEOUS

butyraldehyde (ˌbjuːtɪ'rældɪˌhaɪd) NOUN a colourless flammable pungent liquid used in the manufacture of resins. Formula: $CH_3(CH_2)_2CHO$.
▷HISTORY C20: from BUTYR(IC ACID) + ALDEHYDE

butyrate ('bjuːtɪˌreɪt) NOUN any salt or ester of butyric acid, containing the monovalent group C_3H_7COO- or ion $C_3H_7COO^-$.

butyric acid (bjuː'tɪrɪk) NOUN a carboxylic acid existing in two isomeric forms, one of which produces the smell in rancid butter. Its esters are used in flavouring. Formula: $C_3(CH_2)_2COOH$.
▷HISTORY C19 *butyric*, from Latin *būtyrum* BUTTER

butyrin ('bjuːtɪrɪn) NOUN a colourless liquid ester or oil found in butter. It is formed from butyric acid and glycerine.
▷HISTORY C20: from BUTYR(IC ACID + GLYCER)IN(E)

buxom ('bʌksəm) ADJECTIVE [1] (esp of a woman) healthily plump, attractive, and vigorous. [2] (of a woman) full-bosomed.
▷HISTORY C12: *buhsum* compliant, pliant, from Old English *būgan* to bend, BOW[1]; related to Middle Dutch *būchsam* pliant, German *biegsam* ▸'**buxomly** ADVERB ▸'**buxomness** NOUN

Buxton ('bʌkstən) NOUN a town in N England, in NW Derbyshire in the Peak District: thermal springs. Pop.: 19 854 (1991).

buy (baɪ) VERB **buys, buying, bought.** (*mainly tr*) [1] to acquire by paying or promising to pay a sum of money or the equivalent; purchase. [2] to be capable of purchasing: *money can't buy love.* [3] to acquire by any exchange or sacrifice: *to buy time by equivocation.* [4] (*intr*) to act as a buyer. [5] to bribe or corrupt; hire by or as by bribery. [6] *Slang* to accept as true, practical, etc. [7] (*intr*; foll by *into*) to purchase shares of (a company): *we bought into General Motors.* [8] (*tr*) *Theol* (esp of Christ) to ransom or redeem (a Christian or the soul of a Christian). [9] **have bought it.** *Slang* to be killed. ◆ NOUN [10] a purchase (often in the phrases **good** or **bad buy**). ◆ See also **buy in, buy into, buy off, buy out, buy up.**
▷HISTORY Old English *bycgan*; related to Old Norse *byggja* to let out, lend, Gothic *bugjan* to buy

> **Language note** The use of *off* after *buy* as in *I bought this off my neighbour* was formerly considered incorrect, but is now acceptable in informal contexts.

buy-back ('baɪˌbæk) NOUN *Commerce* the repurchase by a company of some or all of its shares from an investor, who acquired them by putting venture capital into the company when it was formed.

buyer ('baɪə) NOUN [1] a person who buys; purchaser; customer. [2] a person employed to buy merchandise, materials, etc., as for a shop or factory.

buyers' market NOUN a market in which supply exceeds demand and buyers can influence prices.

buy in VERB (*adverb*) [1] (*tr*) to buy back for the owner (an item in an auction) at or below the reserve price. [2] (*intr*) to purchase shares in a company. [3] (*intr*) to buy goods or securities on the open market against a defaulting seller, charging this seller with any market differences. [4] (*tr*) Also: **buy into.** *US informal* to pay money to secure a position or place for (someone, esp oneself) in some organization, esp a business or club. [5] to purchase (goods, etc.) in large quantities: *to buy in for the winter.* ◆ NOUN **buy-in.** [6] the purchase of a company by a manager or group who does not work for that company.

buy into VERB (*intr, preposition*) [1] to agree with or accept as valid (an argument, theory, etc.). [2] *Austral and NZ informal* to get involved in (an argument, fight, etc.).

buy off VERB (*tr, adverb*) to pay (a person or group) to drop a charge, end opposition, relinquish a claim, etc.

buy out VERB (*tr, adverb*) [1] to purchase the ownership, controlling interest, shares, etc., of (a company, etc.). [2] to gain the release of (a person) from the armed forces by payment of money. [3] to pay (a person) once and for all to give up (property, interest, etc.). ◆ NOUN **buyout.** [4] the purchase of a company, esp by its former management or staff. See also **leveraged buyout, management buyout.**

Buys Ballot's Law (baɪs bə'lɒts, bɔɪs) NOUN a law stating that if an observer stands with his back to the wind in the N hemisphere, atmospheric pressure is lower on his left, and vice versa in the S hemisphere.
▷HISTORY named after C. H. D. *Buys Ballot* (1817–90), Dutch meteorologist

buy-to-let (bɔɪs) (*modifier*) NOUN of or relating to the practice of buying a property to let to tenants rather than to live in onself: *the buy-to-let boom.*

buy up VERB (*tr, adverb*) [1] to purchase all, or all that is available, of (something). [2] *Commerce* to purchase a controlling interest in (a company, etc.), as by the acquisition of shares.

buzkashi (ˌbuz'kæʃɪ) NOUN a game played in Aghanistan, in which opposing teams of horsemen strive for possession of the headless carcass of a goat.

buzz (bʌz) NOUN [1] a rapidly vibrating humming sound, as that of a prolonged *z* or of a bee in flight. [2] a low sound, as of many voices in conversation. [3] a rumour; report; gossip. [4] *Informal* a telephone call: *I'll give you a buzz.* [5] *Slang* **a** a pleasant sensation, as from a drug such as cannabis. **b** a sense of excitement; kick. ◆ VERB [6] (*intr*) to make a vibrating sound like that of a prolonged *z.* [7] (*intr*) to talk or gossip with an air of excitement or urgency: *the town buzzed with the news.* [8] (*tr*) to utter or spread (a rumour). [9] (*intr*; often foll by *about*) to move around quickly and busily; bustle. [10] (*tr*) to signal or summon with a buzzer. [11] (*tr*) *Informal* to call by telephone. [12] (*tr*) *Informal* **a** to fly an aircraft very low over (an object): *to buzz a ship.* **b** to fly an aircraft very close to or across the path of (another aircraft), esp to warn or intimidate. [13] (*tr*) (esp of insects) to make a buzzing sound with (wings, etc.). ◆ See also **buzz in.**
▷HISTORY C16: of imitative origin ▸'**buzzing** NOUN, ADJECTIVE

buzzard ('bʌzəd) NOUN [1] any diurnal bird of prey of the genus *Buteo*, typically having broad wings and tail and a soaring flight: family *Accipitridae* (hawks, etc.). See **honey buzzard.** Compare **turkey buzzard.** [2] a mean or cantankerous person.
▷HISTORY C13: from Old French *buisard*, variant of *buison* buzzard, from Latin *būteō* hawk, falcon

buzz bomb NOUN another name for the **V-1.**
▷HISTORY C20: from the sound of its engine

buzzer ('bʌzə) NOUN [1] a person or thing that buzzes. [2] a device that produces a buzzing sound, esp one similar to an electric bell without a hammer or gong. [3] *NZ* a wood planing machine.

buzz in VERB (*tr, adverb*) *Informal* to admit (someone) to a building by activating an electronically-controlled door.

buzz off VERB (*intr, adverb; often imperative*) *Informal, chiefly Brit* to go away; leave; depart.

buzz phrase NOUN *Informal* a phrase that comes into vogue in the same way as a buzz word.

buzz saw NOUN *US and Canadian* a power-operated circular saw.

buzz word NOUN *Informal* a word, often

originating in a particular jargon, that becomes a vogue word in the community as a whole or among a particular group.

bv THE INTERNET DOMAIN NAME FOR Bouvet Island.

BV ABBREVIATION FOR: **1** Beata Virgo. **2** bene vale.
▷HISTORY (for sense 1) Latin: Blessed Virgin; (for sense 2) Latin: farewell

BVA ABBREVIATION FOR British Veterinary Association.

BVM ABBREVIATION FOR Beata Virgo Maria.
▷HISTORY Latin: Blessed Virgin Mary

bw THE INTERNET DOMAIN NAME FOR Botswana.

BW ABBREVIATION FOR biological warfare.

B/W *Photog* ABBREVIATION FOR black and white.

bwana (ˈbwɑːnə) NOUN (in E Africa) a master, often used as a respectful form of address corresponding to *sir*.
▷HISTORY Swahili, from Arabic *abūna* our father

BWD *Text messaging* ABBREVIATION FOR backward.

BWG ABBREVIATION FOR Birmingham Wire Gauge: a notation for the diameters of metal rods, ranging from 0 (0.340 inch) to 36 (0.004 inch).

BWR ABBREVIATION FOR **boiling-water reactor**.

BWV (*preceding a number*) *Music* ABBREVIATION FOR Bach Werke-Verzeichnis: indicating the serial number in the catalogue of the works of J. S. Bach made by Wolfgang Schmieder (born 1901), published in 1950.

bx ABBREVIATION FOR box.

by (baɪ) PREPOSITION **1** used to indicate the agent after a passive verb: *seeds eaten by the birds*. **2** used to indicate the person responsible for a creative work: *this song is by Schubert*. **3** via; through: *enter by the back door*. **4** followed by a gerund to indicate a means used: *he frightened her by hiding behind the door*. **5** beside; next to; near: *a tree by the house*. **6** passing the position of; past: *he drove by the old cottage*. **7** not later than; before: *return the books by Tuesday*. **8** used to indicate extent, after a comparative: *it is hotter by five degrees than it was yesterday*. **9** (esp in oaths) invoking the name of: *I swear by all the gods*. **10** multiplied by: *four by three equals twelve*. **11** (*in habitual sentences*) during the passing of (esp in the phrases **by day**, **by night**). **12** placed between measurements of the various dimensions of something: *a plank fourteen inches by seven*. ◆ ADVERB **13** near: *the house is close by*. **14** away; aside: *he put some money by each week for savings*. **15** passing a point near something; past: *he drove by*. **16** *Scot* past; over and done with: *that's a' by now*. **17** *Scot* aside; behind one: *you must put that by you*. ◆ NOUN, *plural* **byes**. **18** a variant spelling of **bye**.
▷HISTORY Old English *bī*; related to Gothic *bi*, Old High German *bī*, Sanskrit *abhi* to, towards

by THE INTERNET DOMAIN NAME FOR Belarus.

by- *or* **bye-** PREFIX **1** near: *bystander*. **2** secondary or incidental: *by-effect*; *by-election*; *by-path*; *by-product*.
▷HISTORY from BY

by and by ADVERB **1** presently or eventually. ◆ NOUN **by-and-by**. **2** *US and Canadian* a future time or occasion.

by and large ADVERB in general; on the whole.
▷HISTORY C17: originally nautical (meaning: to the wind and off it)

by-bidder NOUN a bidder at an auction who bids up the price of an item for the benefit of a seller.

by-blow NOUN **1** a passing or incidental blow. **2** an archaic word for a **bastard**.

by-catch NOUN unwanted fish and other sea animals caught in a fishing net along with the desired kind of fish.

byde (bəɪd) VERB *Scot* a variant spelling of **bide**.

Bydgoszcz (*Polish* ˈbidgɔʃtʃ) NOUN an industrial city and port in N Poland: under Prussian rule from 1772 to 1919. Pop.: 386 855 (1999 est.). German name: **Bromberg**.

bye[1] (baɪ) NOUN **1** *Sport* the situation in which a player or team in an eliminatory contest wins a preliminary round by virtue of having no opponent. **2** *Golf* one or more holes of a stipulated course that are left unplayed after the match has been decided. **3** *Cricket* a run scored off a ball not struck by the batsman: allotted to the team as an extra and not to the individual batsman. See also **leg bye**. **4** something incidental or secondary. **5** **by the bye**. incidentally; by the way: used as a sentence connector.
▷HISTORY C16: a variant of BY

bye[2] *or* **bye-bye** SENTENCE SUBSTITUTE *Brit informal* goodbye.

bye-byes NOUN (*functioning as singular*) an informal word for **sleep**, used esp in addressing children (as in the phrase **go to bye-byes**).

by-election *or* **bye-election** NOUN **1** (in the United Kingdom and other countries of the Commonwealth) an election held during the life of a parliament to fill a vacant seat in the lower chamber. **2** (in the US) a special election to fill a vacant elective position with an unexpired term.

Byelorussia NOUN a variant spelling of **Belarus**.

Byelorussian ADJECTIVE, NOUN a variant spelling of **Belarussian**.

by-form NOUN a subsidiary or variant form.

bygone (ˈbaɪˌɡɒn) ADJECTIVE **1** (*usually prenominal*) past; former. ◆ NOUN **2** (*often plural*) a past occurrence. **3** (*often plural*) an artefact, implement, etc., of former domestic or industrial use, now often collected for interest. **4** **let bygones be bygones**. to agree to forget past quarrels.

byke (bəɪk, baɪk) NOUN *Scot* a variant spelling of **bike**[2].

bylane (ˈbaɪˌleɪn) NOUN a side lane or alley off a road.

bylaw *or* **bye-law** (ˈbaɪˌlɔː) NOUN **1** a rule made by a local authority for the regulation of its affairs or management of the area it governs. **2** a regulation of a company, society, etc. **3** a subsidiary law.
▷HISTORY C13: probably of Scandinavian origin; compare Old Norse *bȳr* dwelling, town; see BOWER[1], LAW[1]

by-line NOUN **1** *Journalism* a line under the title of a newspaper or magazine article giving the author's name. **2** *Soccer* another word for **touchline**.

by-numbers ADJECTIVE *Informal* done in an uninspired, simplistic, or formulaic way.
▷HISTORY C20: from *painting by numbers*, a method of painting a picture in which the colours to be used are indicated by numbers

BYO NOUN *Austral and NZ* an unlicensed restaurant at which diners may drink their own wine, etc.
▷HISTORY C20: from the phrase *bring your own*

BYOB ABBREVIATION FOR: **1** bring your own beer. **2** bring your own booze. **3** bring your own bottle.

bypass (ˈbaɪˌpɑːs) NOUN **1** a main road built to avoid a city or other congested area. **2** any system of pipes or conduits for redirecting the flow of a liquid. **3** a means of redirecting the flow of a substance around an appliance through which it would otherwise pass. **4** *Surgery* **a** the redirection of blood flow, either to avoid a diseased blood vessel or in order to perform heart surgery. See **coronary bypass**. **b** (*as modifier*): *bypass surgery*. **5** *Electronics* **a** an electrical circuit, esp one containing a capacitor, connected in parallel around one or more components, providing an alternative path for certain frequencies. **b** (*as modifier*): *a bypass capacitor*. ◆ VERB **-passes, -passing, -passed** *or* **-past**. (*tr*) **6** to go around or avoid (a city, obstruction, problem, etc.). **7** to cause (traffic, fluid, etc.) to go through a bypass. **8** to proceed without reference to (regulations, a superior, etc.); get round; avoid.

bypass engine NOUN a gas turbine in which a part of the compressor delivery bypasses the combustion zone, flowing directly into or around the main exhaust gas flow to provide additional thrust. Compare **turbofan**.

bypass ratio NOUN *Aeronautics* the ratio of the amount of air that bypasses the combustion chambers of an aircraft gas turbine to that passing through them.

bypath (ˈbaɪˌpɑːθ) NOUN a little-used path or track, esp in the country.

by-play NOUN secondary action or talking carried on apart while the main action proceeds, esp in a play.

by-product NOUN **1** a secondary or incidental product of a manufacturing process. **2** a side effect.

byre (baɪə) NOUN *Brit* a shelter for cows.
▷HISTORY Old English *bȳre*; related to *būr* hut, cottage; see BOWER[1]

byrnie (ˈbɜːnɪ) NOUN an archaic word for **coat of mail**.
▷HISTORY Old English *byrne*; related to Old Norse *brynja*, Gothic *brunjō*, Old High German *brunnia* coat of mail, Old Irish *bruinne* breast

byroad (ˈbaɪˌrəʊd) NOUN a secondary or side road.

Byronic (baɪˈrɒnɪk) ADJECTIVE **1** of or relating to **George Gordon**, 6th Baron Byron, the British Romantic poet (1788–1824). **2** dark and romantically brooding.
▸**Byˈronically** ADVERB ▸**ˈByronˌism** NOUN

byssinosis (ˌbɪsɪˈnəʊsɪs) NOUN a lung disease caused by prolonged inhalation of fibre dust in textile factories.
▷HISTORY C19: from New Latin, from Greek *bussinos* of linen (see BYSSUS) + -OSIS

byssus (ˈbɪsəs) NOUN, *plural* **byssuses** *or* **byssi** (ˈbɪsaɪ). a mass of strong threads secreted by a sea mussel or similar mollusc that attaches the animal to a hard fixed surface.
▷HISTORY C17: from Latin, from Greek *bussos* linen, flax, ultimately of Egyptian origin

bystander (ˈbaɪˌstændə) NOUN a person present but not involved; onlooker; spectator.

bystreet (ˈbaɪˌstriːt) NOUN an obscure or secondary street.

byte (baɪt) NOUN *Computing* **1** a group of bits, usually eight, processed as a single unit of data. **2** the storage space in a memory or other storage device that is allocated to such a group of bits. **3** a subdivision of a word.
▷HISTORY C20: probably a blend of BIT[4] + BITE

byway (ˈbaɪˌweɪ) NOUN **1** a secondary or side road, esp in the country. **2** an area, field of study, etc., that is very obscure or of secondary importance.

byword (ˈbaɪˌwɜːd) NOUN **1** a person, place, or thing regarded as a perfect or proverbial example of something: *their name is a byword for good service*. **2** an object of scorn or derision. **3** a common saying; proverb.
▷HISTORY Old English *bīwyrde*; see BY, WORD; compare Old High German *pīwurti*, from Latin *prōverbium* proverb

by-your-leave NOUN a request for permission (esp in the phrase **without so much as a by-your-leave**).

Byzantine (bɪˈzænˌtaɪn, -ˌtiːn, baɪ-, ˈbɪzənˌtiːn) (-ˌtaɪn) ADJECTIVE **1** of, characteristic of, or relating to Byzantium or the Byzantine Empire. **2** of, relating to, or characterizing the Orthodox Church or its rites and liturgy. **3** of or relating to the highly coloured stylized form of religious art developed in the Byzantine Empire. **4** of or relating to the style of architecture developed in the Byzantine Empire, characterized by massive domes with square bases, rounded arches, spires and minarets, and the extensive use of mosaics. **5** denoting the Medieval Greek spoken in the Byzantine Empire. **6** (of attitudes, etc.) inflexible or complicated. ◆ NOUN **7** an inhabitant of Byzantium.
▸**Byzantinism** (bɪˈzæntaɪˌnɪzəm, -tiː-, baɪ-, ˈbɪzəntiːˌnɪzəm) (-taɪ-) NOUN

Byzantine Church NOUN another name for the **Orthodox Church**.

Byzantine Empire NOUN the continuation of the Roman Empire in the East, esp after the deposition of the last emperor in Rome (476 A.D.). It was finally extinguished by the fall of Constantinople, its capital, in 1453. See also **Eastern Roman Empire**.

Byzantium (bɪˈzæntɪəm, baɪ-) NOUN an ancient Greek city on the Bosphorus: founded about 660 B.C.; rebuilt by Constantine I in 330 A.D. and called Constantinople; present-day Istanbul.

bz THE INTERNET DOMAIN NAME FOR Belize.

Bz *or* **Bz.** ABBREVIATION FOR benzene.

Cc

c *or* **C** (siː) NOUN, *plural* **c's, C's** *or* **Cs.** 1 the third letter and second consonant of the modern English alphabet. 2 a speech sound represented by this letter, in English usually either a voiceless alveolar fricative, as in *cigar,* or a voiceless velar stop, as in *case.* 3 the third in a series, esp the third highest grade in an examination. 4 **a** something shaped like a C. **b** (*in combination*): *a C-spring.*

c SYMBOL FOR: 1 centi-. 2 cubic. 3 cycle. 4 *Maths* constant. 5 specific heat capacity. 6 the speed of light and other types of electromagnetic radiation in a vacuum. 7 *Chess* See **algebraic notation.**

C SYMBOL FOR: 1 *Music* **a** a note having a frequency of 261.63 hertz (**middle C**) or this value multiplied or divided by any power of 2; the first degree of a major scale containing no sharps or flats (**C major**). **b** a key, string, or pipe producing this note. **c** the major or minor key having this note as its tonic. **d** a time signature denoting four crotchet beats to the bar. See also **alla breve** (sense 2), **common time.** 2 *Chem* carbon. 3 *Biochem* cytosine. 4 capacitance. 5 heat capacity. 6 cold (water). 7 *Physics* compliance. 8 Celsius. 9 centigrade. 10 century: *C20.* 11 coulomb. ◆ 12 THE ROMAN NUMERAL FOR 100. See **Roman numerals.** ◆ 13 INTERNATIONAL CAR REGISTRATION FOR Cuba. ◆ NOUN 14 a computer programming language combining the advantages of a high-level language with the ability to address the computer at a level comparable with that of an assembly language.

c. ABBREVIATION FOR: 1 carat. 2 *Cricket* caught. 3 cent(s). 4 century or centuries. 5 (used esp preceding a date) circa: *c. 1800.*
▷**HISTORY** (for sense 4) Latin: about

C. ABBREVIATION FOR: 1 (on maps as part of name) Cape. 2 Catholic. 3 Celtic. 4 Conservative. 5 Corps.

c/- *Austral* (in addresses) ABBREVIATION FOR care of.

C- (of US military aircraft) ABBREVIATION FOR cargo transport: *C-5.*

© SYMBOL FOR copyright.

C1 NOUN **a** a person whose job is supervisory or clerical, or who works in junior management. **b** (*as adjective*): *C1 worker.* ◆ See also **occupation groupings.**

C2 NOUN **a** a skilled manual worker, or a manual worker with responsibility for other people. **b** (*as adjective*): *C2 worker.* ◆ See also **occupation groupings.**

C3 *or* **C-3** ADJECTIVE 1 in poor health or having a poor physique. 2 *Informal* inferior; worthless. Compare **A1.**

C4 NOUN *US* a type of plastic explosive.
▷**HISTORY** C20: from *C(omposition) 4*

ca THE INTERNET DOMAIN NAME FOR Canada.

Ca THE CHEMICAL SYMBOL FOR calcium.

CA ABBREVIATION FOR: 1 California. 2 Central America. 3 chartered accountant. 4 chief accountant. 5 consular agent. 6 (in Britain) Consumers' Association.

ca. ABBREVIATION FOR circa.
▷**HISTORY** Latin: about

C/A ABBREVIATION FOR: 1 capital account. 2 credit account. 3 current account.

caa[1] *or* **ca'** (kɔː) VERB, NOUN a Scot word for **call.**

caa[2] *or* **ca'** (kɔː) VERB *Scot* 1 to drive or propel. 2 to knock. 3 **caa** *or* **ca' canny.** to proceed cautiously; go slow. 4 **caa** *or* **ca' the feet frae.** to send (a person) sprawling.
▷**HISTORY** see CAA[1]

CAA (in Britain) ABBREVIATION FOR Civil Aviation Authority.

Caaba (ˈkɑːbə) NOUN a variant spelling of **Kaaba.**

cab[1] (kæb) NOUN 1 **a** a taxi. **b** (*as modifier*): *a cab rank.* 2 the enclosed compartment of a lorry, locomotive, crane, etc., from which it is driven or operated. 3 (formerly) a light horse-drawn vehicle used for public hire. 4 **first cab off the rank.** *Austral informal* the first person, etc., to do or take advantage of something.
▷**HISTORY** C19: shortened from CABRIOLET

cab[2] *or* **kab** (kæb) NOUN an ancient Hebrew measure equal to about 2.3 litres (4 pints).
▷**HISTORY** C16: from Hebrew *qabh* container, something hollowed out

CAB ABBREVIATION FOR: 1 (in Britain) Citizens' Advice Bureau. 2 (in the US) Civil Aeronautics Board.

cabal (kəˈbæl) NOUN 1 a small group of intriguers, esp one formed for political purposes. 2 a secret plot, esp a political one; conspiracy; intrigue. 3 a secret or exclusive set of people; clique. ◆ VERB **-bals, -balling, -balled.** (*intr*) 4 to form a cabal; conspire; plot.
▷**HISTORY** C17: from French *cabale,* from Medieval Latin *cabala;* see CABBALA

Cabal (kəˈbæl) NOUN **the.** *English history* a group of ministers of Charles II that governed from 1667–73: consisting of Clifford, Ashley, Buckingham, Arlington, and Lauderdale.
▷**HISTORY** see CABBALA; by a coincidence, the initials of Charles II's ministers can be arranged to form this word

cabala (kəˈbɑːlə) NOUN a variant spelling of **cabbala.**
▸**cabalism** (ˈkæbəˌlɪzəm) NOUN ▸**ˈcabalist** NOUN ▸**ˌcabaˈlistic** ADJECTIVE

caballero (ˌkæbəˈljɛərəʊ; *Spanish* kaβaˈʎero) NOUN, *plural* **-ros** (-rəʊz; *Spanish* -ros). 1 a Spanish gentleman. 2 a southwestern US word for **horseman.**
▷**HISTORY** C19: from Spanish: gentleman, horseman, from Late Latin *caballārius* rider, groom, from *caballus* horse; compare CAVALIER

cabana (kəˈbɑːnə) NOUN *Chiefly US* a tent used as a dressing room by the sea.
▷**HISTORY** from Spanish *cabaña:* CABIN

cabaret (ˈkæbəˌreɪ) NOUN 1 a floor show of dancing, singing, or other light entertainment at a nightclub or restaurant. 2 *Chiefly US* a nightclub or restaurant providing such entertainment.
▷**HISTORY** C17: from Norman French: tavern, probably from Late Latin *camera* an arched roof, CHAMBER

cabbage[1] (ˈkæbɪdʒ) NOUN 1 Also called: **cole.** any of various cultivated varieties of the plant *Brassica oleracea capitata,* typically having a short thick stalk and a large head of green or reddish edible leaves: family *Brassicaceae* (crucifers). See also **brassica, savoy.** Compare **skunk cabbage, Chinese cabbage.** 2 **wild cabbage.** a European plant, *Brassica oleracea,* with broad leaves and a long spike of yellow flowers: the plant from which the cabbages, cauliflower, broccoli, and Brussels sprout have been bred. 3 **a** the head of a cabbage. **b** the edible leaf bud of the cabbage palm. 4 *Informal* a dull or unimaginative person. 5 *Informal* a person who has no mental faculties and is dependent on others for his subsistence.
▷**HISTORY** C14: from Norman French *caboche* head; perhaps related to Old French *boce* hump, bump, Latin *caput* head

cabbage[2] (ˈkæbɪdʒ) *Brit slang* ◆ NOUN 1 snippets of cloth appropriated by a tailor from a customer's material. ◆ VERB 2 to steal; pilfer.
▷**HISTORY** C17: of uncertain origin; perhaps related to Old French *cabas* theft

cabbage bug NOUN another name for the **harlequin bug.**

cabbage lettuce NOUN any of several varieties of lettuce that have roundish flattened heads resembling cabbages.

cabbage moth NOUN a common brownish noctuid moth, *Mamestra brassicae,* the larva of which is destructive of cabbages and other plants.

cabbage palm *or* **tree** NOUN 1 a West Indian palm, *Roystonea* (or *Oreodoxa*) *oleracea,* whose leaf buds are eaten like cabbage. 2 a similar Brazilian palm, *Euterpe oleracea.* 3 an Australian palm tree, *Livistona australis.* 4 any of several plants of the genus *Cordyline,* grown as ornamentals: family *Agavaceae.*

cabbage palmetto NOUN a tropical American fan palm, *Sabal palmetto,* with edible leaf buds and leaves used in thatching.

cabbage root fly NOUN a dipterous fly, *Erioischia brassicae,* whose larvae feed on the roots and stems of cabbages and other brassicas: family *Muscidae* (houseflies, etc.).

cabbage rose NOUN a rose, *Rosa centifolia,* with a round compact full-petalled head.

cabbagetown (ˈkæbɪdʒˌtaʊn) NOUN *Canadian* a city slum.
▷**HISTORY** C20: from *Cabbagetown,* a depressed area of Toronto, where the Anglo-Saxon population was thought to exist on cabbage

cabbage tree NOUN 1 Also called: **ti.** a tree, *Cordyline australis,* of New Zealand having a tall branchless trunk and a palmlike top. 2 any of several other similar trees of the genus *Cordyline.*

cabbage white NOUN any large white butterfly of the genus *Pieris,* esp the Eurasian species *P. brassicae,* the larvae of which feed on the leaves of cabbages and related vegetables: family *Pieridae.*

cabbageworm (ˈkæbɪdʒˌwɜːm) NOUN *US* any caterpillar that feeds on cabbages, esp that of the cabbage white.

cabbala, cabala, kabbala, *or* **kabala** (kəˈbɑːlə) NOUN 1 an ancient Jewish mystical tradition based on an esoteric interpretation of the Old Testament. 2 any secret or occult doctrine or science.
▷**HISTORY** C16: from Medieval Latin, from Hebrew *qabbālāh* tradition, what is received, from *qābal* to receive
▸**cabbalism, cabalism, kabbalism,** *or* **kabalism** (ˈkæbəˌlɪzəm) NOUN ▸**ˈcabbalist, ˈcabalist, ˈkabbalist,** *or* **ˈkabalist** NOUN ▸**ˌcabbaˈlistic, ˌcabaˈlistic, ˌkabbaˈlistic,** *or* **ˌkabaˈlistic** ADJECTIVE

cabbie *or* **cabby** (ˈkæbɪ) NOUN, *plural* **-bies.** *Informal* a cab driver.

CABE (in Britain) ABBREVIATION FOR Commission for Architecture and the Built Environment.

caber (ˈkeɪbə; *Scot* ˈkebər) NOUN *Scot* a heavy section of trimmed tree trunk thrown in competition at Highland games (**tossing the caber**).
▷**HISTORY** C16: from Gaelic *cabar* pole

Cabernet Sauvignon (ˈkæbəneɪ ˈsəʊvɪnjɒn; *French* kabɛrnɛ soviɲɔ̃) NOUN (*sometimes not capitals*) 1 a black grape originally grown in the Bordeaux area of France, and now throughout the wine-producing world. 2 any of various red wines made from this grape.
▷**HISTORY** French

cabezon (ˈkæbɪzɒn) *or* **cabezone** (ˈkæbɪˌzəʊn) NOUN a large food fish, *Scorpaenichthys marmoratus,* of North American Pacific coastal waters, having greenish flesh: family *Cottidae* (bullheads and sea scorpions).
▷**HISTORY** Spanish, from *cabeza* head, ultimately from Latin *caput*

Cabimas (*Spanish* kaˈβimas) NOUN a town in NW Venezuela, on the NE shore of Lake Maracaibo. Pop.: 214 000 (2000 est.).

cabin (ˈkæbɪn) NOUN 1 a small simple dwelling; hut. 2 a simple house providing accommodation for travellers or holiday-makers at a motel or holiday camp. 3 a room used as an office or living quarters in a ship. 4 a covered compartment used for shelter or living quarters in a small boat. 5 (in a warship) the compartment or room reserved for the commanding officer. 6 *Brit* another name for **signal box.** 7 **a** the enclosed part of a light aircraft in which the pilot and passengers sit. **b** the part of an airliner in which the passengers are carried. **c** the

section of an aircraft used for cargo. ◆ VERB [8] to confine in a small space.
▷HISTORY C14: from Old French *cabane,* from Old Provençal *cabana,* from Late Latin *capanna* hut

cabin boy NOUN a boy who waits on the officers and passengers of a ship.

cabin class NOUN a class of accommodation on a passenger ship between first class and tourist class.

cabin cruiser NOUN a power boat fitted with a cabin and comforts for pleasure cruising or racing.

Cabinda (kəˈbiːndə) NOUN an exclave of Angola, separated from the rest of the country by part of the Democratic Republic of Congo (formerly Zaïre). Pop.: 174 000 (1993 est.). Area: 7270 sq. km (2807 sq. miles).

cabinet (ˈkæbɪnɪt) NOUN [1] **a** a piece of furniture containing shelves, cupboards, or drawers for storage or display. **b** (*as modifier*): *cabinet teak.* [2] the outer case of a television, radio, etc. [3] **a** (*often capital*) the executive and policy-making body of a country, consisting of all government ministers or just the senior ministers. **b** (*sometimes capital*) an advisory council to a president, sovereign, governor, etc. **c** (*as modifier*): *a cabinet reshuffle; a cabinet minister.* [4] **a** a standard size of paper, 6 × 4 inches (15 × 10 cm) or 6½ × 4¼ inches (16.5 × 10.5 cm), for mounted photographs. **b** (*as modifier*): *a cabinet photograph.* [5] *Printing* an enclosed rack for holding cases of type, etc. [6] *Archaic* a private room. [7] (*modifier*) suitable in size, value, decoration, etc., for a display cabinet: *a cabinet edition of Shakespeare.* [8] (*modifier*) (of a drawing or projection of a three-dimensional object) constructed with true horizontal and vertical representation of scale but with oblique distances reduced to about half scale to avoid the appearance of distortion. [9] (*modifier*) (of a wine) specially selected and usually rare.
▷HISTORY C16: from Old French, diminutive of *cabine,* of uncertain origin

cabinet beetle NOUN See **dermestid.**

cabinet-maker NOUN a craftsman specializing in the making of fine furniture.
▸**ˈcabinet-ˌmaking** NOUN

cabinet pudding NOUN a steamed suet pudding containing dried fruit.

cabinetwork (ˈkæbɪnɪtˌwɜːk) NOUN [1] the making of furniture, esp of fine quality. [2] an article made by a cabinet-maker.

cabin fever NOUN *Chiefly Canadian* acute depression resulting from being isolated or sharing cramped quarters in the wilderness, esp during the long northern winter.

cable (ˈkeɪbᵊl) NOUN [1] a strong thick rope, usually of twisted hemp or steel wire. [2] *Nautical* an anchor chain or rope. [3] **a** a unit of distance in navigation, equal to one tenth of a sea mile (about 600 feet). **b** Also called: **cable length, cable's length.** a unit of length in nautical use that has various values, including 100 fathoms (600 feet). [4] a wire or bundle of wires that conducts electricity: *a submarine cable.* See also **coaxial cable.** [5] Also called: **overseas** *or* **international telegram, cablegram.** a telegram sent abroad by submarine cable, radio, communications satellite, or by telephone line. [6] See **cable stitch.** [7] short for **cable television.** ◆ VERB [8] to send (a message) to (someone) by cable. [9] (*tr*) to fasten or provide with a cable or cables. [10] (*tr*) to supply (a place) with or link (a place) to cable television.
▷HISTORY C13: from Old Norman French, from Late Latin *capulum* halter

cable car NOUN [1] a cabin suspended from and moved by an overhead cable in a mountain area. [2] a cableway. [3] a passenger car on a cable railway.

cablegram (ˈkeɪbᵊlˌgræm) NOUN a more formal name for **cable** (sense 5).

cable-laid ADJECTIVE (of a rope) made of three plain-laid ropes twisted together in a left-handed direction.

cable railway NOUN a railway on which individual cars are drawn along by a strong cable or metal chain operated by a stationary motor.

cable release NOUN a short length of flexible cable, used to operate the shutter of a camera without shaking it.

cable-stayed bridge NOUN a type of suspension bridge in which the supporting cables are connected directly to the bridge deck without the use of suspenders.

cable stitch NOUN **a** a pattern or series of knitting stitches producing a design like a twisted rope. **b** (*as modifier*): *a cable-stitch sweater.* Sometimes shortened to **cable.**

cablet (ˈkeɪblɪt) NOUN a small cable, esp a cable-laid rope that has a circumference of less than 25 centimetres (ten inches).

cable television NOUN a television service in which programmes are distributed to subscribers' televisions by cable rather than by broadcast transmission.

cableway (ˈkeɪbᵊlˌweɪ) NOUN a system for moving people or bulk materials in which suspended cars, buckets, etc., run on cables that extend between terminal towers.

cabman (ˈkæbmən) NOUN, *plural* **-men.** the driver of a cab.

cabob (kəˈbɒb) NOUN a variant of **kebab.**

cabochon (ˈkæbəˌʃɒn; *French* kabɔʃɔ̃) NOUN a smooth domed gem, polished but unfaceted.
▷HISTORY C16: from Old French, from Old Norman French *caboche* head; see CABBAGE[1]

caboodle (kəˈbuːdᵊl) NOUN *Informal* a lot, bunch, or group (esp in the phrases **the whole caboodle, the whole kit and caboodle**).
▷HISTORY C19: probably contraction of KIT[1] and BOODLE

caboose (kəˈbuːs) NOUN [1] *US informal* short for **calaboose.** [2] *Railways, US and Canadian* a guard's van, esp one with sleeping and eating facilities for the train crew. [3] *Nautical* **a** a deckhouse for a galley aboard ship or formerly in Canada, on a lumber raft. **b** *Chiefly Brit* the galley itself. [4] *Canadian* **a** a mobile bunkhouse used by lumbermen, etc. **b** an insulated cabin on runners, equipped with a stove.
▷HISTORY C18: from Dutch *cabūse,* of unknown origin

Cabora Bassa (kəˈbɔːrə ˈbæsə) NOUN the site on the Zambezi River in N Mozambique of the largest dam in southern Africa.

cabotage (ˈkæbəˌtɑːʒ) NOUN [1] *Nautical* coastal navigation or shipping, esp within the borders of one country. [2] reservation to a country's carriers of its internal traffic, esp air traffic.
▷HISTORY C19: from French, from *caboter* to sail near the coast, apparently from Spanish *cabo* CAPE[2]

cabover (ˈkæbˌəʊvə) ADJECTIVE of or denoting a truck or lorry in which the cab is over the engine.

cab rank rule NOUN *Brit* the rule that obliges barristers to take on any client in strict rotation.
▷HISTORY C20: from the idea of a queue of taxis, each taking the first customer who comes along

cabretta (kəˈbrɛtə) NOUN *Chiefly US* a soft leather obtained from the skins of certain South American or African sheep.
▷HISTORY from Spanish *cabra* she-goat

cabrilla (kəˈbrɪlə) NOUN any of various serranid food fishes, esp *Epinephelus analogus,* occurring in warm seas around Florida and the Caribbean.
▷HISTORY Spanish, literally: little goat

cabriole (ˈkæbrɪˌəʊl) NOUN [1] Also called: **cabriole leg.** a type of furniture leg, popular in the first half of the 18th century, in which an upper convex curve descends tapering to a concave curve. [2] *Ballet* a leap in the air with one leg outstretched and the other beating against it.
▷HISTORY C18: from French, from *cabrioler* to caper; from its being based on the leg of a capering animal; see CABRIOLET

cabriolet (ˌkæbrɪəʊˈleɪ) NOUN [1] a small two-wheeled horse-drawn carriage with two seats and a folding hood. [2] a former name for a **drophead coupé.**
▷HISTORY C18: from French, literally: a little skip, from *cabriole,* from Latin *capreolus* wild goat, from *caper* goat; referring to the lightness of movement

ca'canny (ˌkɔːˈkænɪ) NOUN *Scot* [1] moderation or wariness. [2] **a** a policy of restricting the output of work; a go-slow. **b** (*as modifier*): *a ca'canny policy.* See also **caa**[2].
▷HISTORY C19: literally, *call canny* to drive gently

cacao (kəˈkɑːəʊ, -ˈkeɪəʊ) NOUN [1] a small tropical American evergreen tree, *Theobroma cacao,* having yellowish flowers and reddish-brown seed pods from which cocoa and chocolate are prepared: family *Sterculiaceae.* [2] **cacao bean.** another name for **cocoa bean.** [3] **cacao butter.** another name for **cocoa butter.**
▷HISTORY C16: from Spanish, from Nahuatl *cacauatl* cacao beans

cacciatore (ˌkɑːtʃəˈtɔːrɪ, ˌkætʃ-) *or* **cacciatora** ADJECTIVE (*immediately postpositive*) prepared with tomatoes, mushrooms, herbs, and other seasonings.
▷HISTORY Italian, literally: hunter

Cáceres (*Spanish* ˈkaθeres) NOUN a city in W Spain: held by the Moors (1142–1229). Pop.: 71 745 (1991).

cachalot (ˈkæʃəˌlɒt) NOUN another name for **sperm whale.**
▷HISTORY C18: from French, from Portuguese, *cachalote,* of unknown origin

cache (kæʃ) NOUN [1] a hidden store of provisions, weapons, treasure, etc. [2] the place where such a store is hidden. [3] *Computing* a small high-speed memory that improves computer performance. ◆ VERB [4] (*tr*) to store in a cache.
▷HISTORY C19: from French, from *cacher* to hide

cache memory NOUN *Computing* a small area of memory in a computer that can be accessed very quickly.

cachepot (ˈkæʃˌpɒt, ˌkæʃˈpəʊ) NOUN an ornamental container for a flowerpot.
▷HISTORY French: pot-hider

cachet (ˈkæʃeɪ) NOUN [1] an official seal on a document, letter, etc. [2] a distinguishing mark; stamp. [3] prestige; distinction. [4] *Philately* **a** a mark stamped by hand on mail for commemorative purposes. **b** a small mark made by dealers and experts on the back of postage stamps. Compare **overprint** (sense 3), **surcharge** (sense 5). [5] a hollow wafer, formerly used for enclosing an unpleasant-tasting medicine.
▷HISTORY C17: from Old French, from *cacher* to hide

cachexia (kəˈkɛksɪə) *or* **cachexy** NOUN a generally weakened condition of body or mind resulting from any debilitating chronic disease.
▷HISTORY C16: from Late Latin from Greek *kakhexia,* from *kakos* bad + *hexis* condition, habit
▸**cachectic** (kəˈkɛktɪk) ADJECTIVE

cachinnate (ˈkækɪˌneɪt) VERB (*intr*) to laugh loudly.
▷HISTORY C19: from Latin *cacchinăre,* probably of imitative origin
▸**ˌcachinˈnatory** ADJECTIVE

cachinnation (ˌkækɪˈneɪʃən) NOUN [1] raucous laughter. [2] *Psychiatry* inappropriate laughter, sometimes found in schizophrenia.

cachou (ˈkæʃuː, kæˈʃuː) NOUN [1] a lozenge eaten to sweeten the breath. [2] another name for **catechu.**
▷HISTORY C18: via French from Portuguese, from Malay *kāchu*

cachucha (kəˈtʃuːtʃə) NOUN [1] a graceful Spanish solo dance in triple time. [2] music composed for this dance.
▷HISTORY C19: from Spanish

cacique (kəˈsiːk) *or* **cazique** (kəˈziːk) NOUN [1] an American Indian chief in a Spanish-speaking region. [2] (esp in Spanish America) a local political boss. [3] any of various tropical American songbirds of the genus *Cacicus* and related genera: family *Icteridae* (American orioles).
▷HISTORY C16: from Spanish, of Arawak origin; compare Taino *cacique* chief

caciquism (kəˈsiːkˌɪzəm) NOUN (esp in Spanish America) government by local political bosses.

cackermander (ˈkækəˌmɑːndə) NOUN *Southeast English dialect* a friend.

cack-handed (ˌkækˈhændɪd) ADJECTIVE *Informal* [1] left-handed. [2] clumsy.
▷HISTORY from dialect *cack* excrement, from the fact that clumsy people usually make a mess; via Middle Low German or Middle Dutch from Latin *cacāre* to defecate

cackle (ˈkækᵊl) VERB [1] (*intr*) (esp of a hen) to squawk with shrill notes. [2] (*intr*) to laugh or chatter raucously. [3] (*tr*) to utter in a cackling manner. ◆ NOUN [4] the noise or act of cackling. [5] noisy chatter. [6] **cut the cackle.** *Informal* to stop chattering; be quiet.

▷HISTORY C13: probably from Middle Low German *kākelen,* of imitative origin
▸'**cackler** NOUN

cacky ('kækɪ) ADJECTIVE *Informal* **cackier, cackiest** [1] of or like excrement. [2] dirty, worthless, or contemptible.
▷HISTORY from dialect *cack* excrement

caco- COMBINING FORM bad, unpleasant, or incorrect: *cacophony*.
▷HISTORY from Greek *kakos* bad

cacodemon *or* **cacodaemon** (ˌkækə'di:mən) NOUN an evil spirit or devil.
▷HISTORY C16: from Greek *kakodaimōn* evil genius

cacodyl ('kækədaɪl) NOUN an oily poisonous liquid with a strong garlic smell; tetramethyldiarsine. Formula: $[(CH_3)_2As]_2$.
▷HISTORY C19: from Greek *kakōdēs* evil-smelling (from *kakos* CACO- + *ozein* to smell) + -YL
▸**cacodylic** (ˌkækə'dɪlɪk) ADJECTIVE

cacoepy (kə'kəʊɪpɪ) NOUN bad or mistaken pronunciation.
▷HISTORY C19: from Greek *kakoepeia*
▸**cacoepistic** (kəˌkəʊɪ'pɪstɪk) ADJECTIVE

cacoethes (ˌkækəʊ'i:θi:z) NOUN an uncontrollable urge or desire, esp for something harmful; mania: *a cacoethes for smoking*.
▷HISTORY C16: from Latin *cacoēthes* malignant disease, from Greek *kakoēthēs* of an evil disposition, from *kakos* CACO- + *ēthos* character
▸**cacoethic** (ˌkækəʊ'ɛθɪk) ADJECTIVE

cacogenics (ˌkækəʊ'dʒɛnɪks) NOUN another name for **dysgenics.**
▷HISTORY C20: from CACO- + EUGENICS
▸ˌ**caco'genic** ADJECTIVE

cacography (kæ'kɒgrəfɪ) NOUN [1] bad handwriting. Compare **calligraphy.** [2] incorrect spelling. Compare **orthography.**
▸**ca'cographer** NOUN ▸**cacographic** (ˌkækə'græfɪk) *or* ˌ**caco'graphical** ADJECTIVE

cacology (kə'kɒlədʒɪ) NOUN a bad choice of words; faulty speech.
▷HISTORY C17 (in the sense: ill report): from Greek *kakologia*

cacomistle ('kækəˌmɪsᵊl) *or* **cacomixle** ('kækəˌmɪksᵊl) NOUN [1] a catlike omnivorous mammal, *Bassariscus astutus,* of S North America, related to but smaller than the raccoons: family *Procyonidae,* order *Carnivora* (carnivores). It has yellowish-grey fur and a long bushy tail banded in black and white. [2] a related smaller animal, *Jentinkia* (or *Bassariscus*) *sumichrasti,* of Central America.
▷HISTORY C19: from Mexican Spanish, from Nahuatl *tlacomiztli,* from *tlaco* half + *miztli* cougar

cacophonous (kə'kɒfənəs) *or* **cacophonic** (ˌkækə'fɒnɪk) ADJECTIVE jarring in sound; discordant; harsh.
▸**ca'cophonously** *or* ˌ**caco'phonically** ADVERB

cacophony (kə'kɒfənɪ) NOUN, *plural* **-nies.** [1] harsh discordant sound; dissonance. [2] the use of unharmonious or dissonant speech sounds in language. Compare **euphony.**

cactoblastis (ˌkæktəʊ'blɑ:stɪs) NOUN a moth, *Cactoblastis cactorum,* that was introduced into Australia to act as a biological control on the prickly pear.

cactus ('kæktəs) NOUN, *plural* **-tuses** *or* **-ti** (-taɪ). [1] any spiny succulent plant of the family *Cactaceae* of the arid regions of America. Cactuses have swollen tough stems, leaves reduced to spines or scales, and often large brightly coloured flowers. [2] **cactus dahlia.** a double-flowered variety of dahlia.
▷HISTORY C17: from Latin: prickly plant, from Greek *kaktos* cardoon
▸**cactaceous** (kæk'teɪʃəs) ADJECTIVE

cacuminal (kæ'kju:mɪnᵊl) *Phonetics* ◆ ADJECTIVE [1] Also called: **cerebral.** relating to or denoting a consonant articulated with the tip of the tongue turned back towards the hard palate. ◆ NOUN [2] a consonant articulated in this manner.
▷HISTORY C19: from Latin *cacūmen* point, top

cad (kæd) NOUN *Brit informal, old-fashioned* a man who does not behave in a gentlemanly manner towards others.
▷HISTORY C18: shortened from CADDIE
▸'**caddish** ADJECTIVE

CAD ACRONYM FOR computer-aided design.

cadagi (kə'dɑ:dʒɪ) *or* **cadaga** (kə'dɑ:gə) NOUN a eucalyptus tree, *E. torelliana,* of tropical and subtropical Australia, having a smooth green trunk.
▷HISTORY of uncertain origin

cadaster *or* **cadastre** (kə'dæstə) NOUN an official register showing details of ownership, boundaries, and value of real property in a district, made for taxation purposes.
▷HISTORY C19: from French, from Provençal *cadastro,* from Italian *catastro,* from Late Greek *katastikhon* register, from *kata stikhon* line by line, from *kata* (see CATA-) + *stikhos* line, STICH
▸**ca'dastral** ADJECTIVE

cadaver (kə'deɪvə, -'dɑ:v-) NOUN *Med* a corpse.
▷HISTORY C16: from Latin, from *cadere* to fall
▸**ca'daveric** ADJECTIVE

cadaverine (kə'dævəˌri:n) NOUN a toxic diamine with an unpleasant smell, produced by protein hydrolysis during putrefaction of animal tissue. Formula: $NH_2(CH_2)_5NH_2$.

cadaverous (kə'dævərəs) ADJECTIVE [1] of or like a corpse, esp in being deathly pale; ghastly. [2] thin and haggard; gaunt.
▸**ca'daverously** ADVERB ▸**ca'daverousness** NOUN

CADCAM ('kædˌkæm) NOUN ACRONYM FOR computer-aided design and manufacture.

caddie *or* **caddy** ('kædɪ) NOUN, *plural* **-dies.** [1] *Golf* an attendant who carries clubs, etc., for a player. ◆ VERB **-dies, -dying, -died.** [2] (*intr*) to act as a caddie.
▷HISTORY C17 (originally: a gentleman learning the military profession by serving in the army without a commission, hence C18 (Scottish): a person looking for employment, an errand-boy): from French CADET

caddie car *or* **caddie cart** NOUN *Golf* a small light two-wheeled trolley for carrying clubs.

caddis *or* **caddice** ('kædɪs) NOUN a type of coarse woollen yarn, braid, or fabric.

caddis fly NOUN any small mothlike insect of the order *Trichoptera,* having two pairs of hairy wings and aquatic larvae (caddis worms).
▷HISTORY C17: of unknown origin

caddis worm *or* **caddis** NOUN the aquatic larva of a caddis fly, which constructs a protective case around itself made of silk, sand, stones, etc. Also called: **caseworm, strawworm.**

Caddoan ('kædəʊən) NOUN a family of North American Indian languages, including Pawnee, formerly spoken in a wide area of the Midwest, and probably distantly related to Siouan.

caddy¹ ('kædɪ) NOUN, *plural* **-dies.** *Chiefly Brit* a small container, esp for tea.
▷HISTORY C18: from Malay *kati;* see CATTY²

caddy² ('kædɪ) NOUN, *plural* **-dies,** VERB **-dies, -dying, -died.** a variant spelling of **caddie.**

cade¹ (keɪd) NOUN a juniper tree, *Juniperus oxycedrus* of the Mediterranean region, the wood of which yields an oily brown liquid (**oil of cade**) used to treat skin ailments.
▷HISTORY C16: via Old French from Old Provençal, from Medieval Latin *catanus*

cade² (keɪd) ADJECTIVE (of a young animal) left by its mother and reared by humans, usually as a pet.
▷HISTORY C15: of unknown origin

-cade NOUN COMBINING FORM indicating a procession of a specified kind: *motorcade*.
▷HISTORY abstracted from CAVALCADE

cadelle (kə'dɛl) NOUN a widely distributed beetle, *Tenebroides mauritanicus,* that feeds on flour, grain, and other stored foods: family *Trogositidae*.
▷HISTORY French, from Provençal *cadello,* from Latin *catellus* a little dog

cadence ('keɪdᵊns) *or* **cadency** NOUN, *plural* **-dences** *or* **-dencies.** [1] the beat or measure of something rhythmic. [2] a fall in the pitch of the voice, as at the end of a sentence. [3] modulation of the voice; intonation. [4] a rhythm or rhythmic construction in verse or prose; measure. [5] the close of a musical phrase or section.
▷HISTORY C14: from Old French, from Old Italian *cadenza,* literally: a falling, from Latin *cadere* to fall

cadency ('keɪdᵊnsɪ) NOUN, *plural* **-cies.** [1] the line of descent from a younger member of a family. [2] another word for **cadence.**

cadent ('keɪdᵊnt) ADJECTIVE [1] having cadence; rhythmic. [2] *Archaic* falling; descending.
▷HISTORY C16: from Latin *cadēns* falling, from *cadere* to fall

cadenza (kə'dɛnzə) NOUN [1] a virtuoso solo passage occurring near the end of a piece of music, formerly improvised by the soloist but now usually specially composed. [2] *South African informal* a fit or convulsion.
▷HISTORY C19: from Italian; see CADENCE

cadet (kə'dɛt) NOUN [1] a young person undergoing preliminary training, usually before full entry to the uniformed services, police, etc., esp for officer status. [2] a school pupil receiving elementary military training in a school corps. [3] (in England and in France before 1789) a gentleman, usually a younger son, who entered the army to prepare for a commission. [4] a younger son or brother. [5] **cadet branch.** the family or family branch of a younger son. [6] (in New Zealand) a person learning sheep farming on a sheep station.
▷HISTORY C17: from French, from dialect (Gascon) *capdet* captain, ultimately from Latin *caput* head
▸**ca'detship** NOUN

cadge (kædʒ) VERB [1] to get (food, money, etc.) by sponging or begging. ◆ NOUN [2] *Brit* a person who cadges. [3] **on the cadge.** *Brit informal* engaged in cadging.
▷HISTORY C17: of unknown origin

cadger NOUN [1] ('kædʒə) *Brit* a person who cadges. [2] ('kædʒər) *Scot* a pedlar or carrier.

cadi *or* **kadi** ('kɑ:dɪ, 'keɪdɪ) NOUN, *plural* **-dis.** a judge in a Muslim community.
▷HISTORY C16: from Arabic *qādī* judge

Cádiz (kə'dɪz; *Spanish* 'kaðiθ) NOUN a port in SW Spain, on a narrow peninsula that forms the **Bay of Cádiz** at the E end of the **Gulf of Cádiz** founded about 1100 B.C. as a Phoenician trading colony; centre of trade with America from the 16th to 18th centuries. Pop.: 143 121 (1998 est.).

Cadmean victory ('kædmɪən) NOUN another name for **Pyrrhic victory.**

cadmium ('kædmɪəm) NOUN a malleable ductile toxic bluish-white metallic element that occurs in association with zinc ores. It is used in electroplating, alloys, and as a neutron absorber in the control of nuclear fission. Symbol: Cd; atomic no.: 48; atomic wt.: 112.411; valency: 2; relative density: 8.65; melting pt.: 321.1°C; boiling pt.: 767°C.
▷HISTORY C19: from New Latin, from Latin *cadmīa* zinc ore, CALAMINE, referring to the fact that both calamine and cadmium are found in the ore

cadmium cell NOUN [1] a photocell with a cadmium electrode that is especially sensitive to ultraviolet radiation. [2] a former name for **Weston standard cell.**

cadmium sulphide NOUN an orange or yellow insoluble solid used as a pigment in paints, etc. (**cadmium yellow**). Formula: CdS.

Cadmus ('kædməs) NOUN *Greek myth* a Phoenician prince who killed a dragon and planted its teeth, from which sprang a multitude of warriors who fought among themselves until only five remained, who joined Cadmus to found Thebes.
▸'**Cadmean** ADJECTIVE

cadre ('kɑ:də) NOUN [1] the nucleus of trained professional servicemen forming the basis for the training of new units or other military expansion. [2] a basic unit or structure, esp of specialists or experts; nucleus; core. [3] a group of revolutionaries or other political activists, esp when taking part in military or terrorist activities. [4] a member of a cadre.
▷HISTORY C19: from French, from Italian *quadro,* from Latin *quadrum* square

caduceus (kə'dju:sɪəs) NOUN, *plural* **-cei** (-sɪˌaɪ). [1] *Classical myth* a staff entwined with two serpents and bearing a pair of wings at the top, carried by Hermes (Mercury) as messenger of the gods. [2] an insignia resembling this staff used as an emblem of the medical profession. Compare **staff of Aesculapius.**
▷HISTORY C16: from Latin, from Doric Greek *karukeion,* from *karux* herald

caducibranchiate (kəˌdju:sɪ'bræŋkɪˌeɪt) ADJECTIVE (of many amphibians, such as frogs) having gills during one stage of the life cycle only.
▷HISTORY from Latin *cadūcus* CADUCOUS + BRANCHIA

caducity (kə'dju:sɪtɪ) NOUN [1] perishableness. [2] senility.

▷HISTORY C18: from French, from Latin *cadūcus* CADUCOUS

caducous (kəˈdjuːkəs) ADJECTIVE *Biology* (of parts of a plant or animal) shed during the life of the organism.
▷HISTORY C17: from Latin *cadūcus* falling, from *cadere* to fall

CAE ABBREVIATION FOR **computer-aided engineering.**

caecilian (siːˈsɪlɪən) NOUN any tropical limbless cylindrical amphibian of the order *Apoda* (or *Gymnophiona*), resembling earthworms and inhabiting moist soil.
▷HISTORY C19: from Latin *caecilia* a kind of lizard, from *caecus* blind

caecum *or US* **cecum** (ˈsiːkəm) NOUN, *plural* **-ca** (-kə). *Anatomy* any structure or part that ends in a blind sac or pouch, esp the pouch that marks the beginning of the large intestine.
▷HISTORY C18: short for Latin *intestinum caecum* blind intestine, translation of Greek *tuphlon enteron*
▸ˈ**caecal** *or US* ˈ**cecal** ADJECTIVE

Caelian (ˈsiːlɪən) NOUN the southeasternmost of the Seven Hills of Rome.

Caelum (ˈsiːləm) NOUN, *Latin genitive* **Caeli** (ˈsiːlaɪ). a small faint constellation in the S hemisphere close to Eridanus.
▷HISTORY Latin: the sky, heaven

Caen (kɒŋ; *French* kɑ̃) NOUN an industrial city in NW France. Pop.: 113 987 (1999).

caenogenesis (ˌsiːnəʊˈdʒɛnɪsɪs), **cainogenesis, kainogenesis,** *or US* **cenogenesis, kenogenesis** NOUN the development of structures and organs in an embryo or larva that are adaptations to its way of life and are not retained in the adult form. Compare **recapitulation** (sense 2).
▸**caenogenetic** (ˌsiːnəʊdʒɪˈnɛtɪk) ▸ˌ**cainogeˈnetic,** ˌ**kainogeˈnetic,** *or US* ˌ**cenogeˈnetic,** ˌ**kenogeˈnetic** ADJECTIVE ▸ˌ**caenogeˈnetically,** ˌ**cainogeˈnetically,** *or* ˌ**kainogeˈnetically,** *or US* ˌ**cenogeˈnetically,** ˌ**kenogeˈnetically** ADVERB

Caenozoic (ˌsiːnəˈzəʊɪk) ADJECTIVE a variant spelling of **Cenozoic.**

caeoma (siːˈəʊmə) NOUN an aecium in some rust fungi that has no surrounding membrane.
▷HISTORY New Latin, from Greek *kaiein* to burn; referring to its glowing colour

Caerleon (kɑːˈlɪən) NOUN a town in SE Wales, in Newport county borough on the River Usk: traditionally the seat of King Arthur's court. Pop.: 8931 (1991).

Caernarfon, Caernarvon, *or* **Carnarvon** (kɑːˈnɑːvᵊn) NOUN a port and resort in NW Wales, in Gwynedd on the Menai Strait: 13th-century castle. Pop.: 9695 (1991).

Caernarvonshire (kɑːˈnɑːvᵊnˌʃɪə, -ʃə) NOUN (until 1974) a county of NW Wales, now part of Gwynedd.

Caerphilly (kɛəˈfɪlɪ) NOUN 1 a market town in SE Wales, in Caerphilly county borough: site of the largest castle in Wales (13th–14th centuries). Pop.: 28 481 (1991). 2 a county borough in SE Wales, created in 1996 from parts of Mid Glamorgan and Gwent. Pop.: 169 521 (2001). Area: 275 sq. km (106 sq. miles). 3 a creamy white mild-flavoured cheese.

Caesar (ˈsiːzə) NOUN 1 any Roman emperor. 2 (*sometimes not capital*) any emperor, autocrat, dictator, or other powerful ruler. 3 a title of the Roman emperors from Augustus to Hadrian. 4 (in the Roman Empire) **a** a title borne by the imperial heir from the reign of Hadrian. **b** the heir, deputy, and subordinate ruler to either of the two emperors under Diocletian's system of government.
▷HISTORY from Gaius Julius Caesar (100–44 B.C.), Roman general and statesman

Caesaraugusta (ˌsiːzərɔːˈgʌstə) NOUN the Latin name for **Zaragoza.**

Caesarea (ˌsiːzəˈrɪə) NOUN an ancient port in NW Israel, capital of Roman Palestine: founded by Herod the Great.

Caesarea Mazaca (ˈmæzəkə) NOUN the ancient name of **Kayseri.**

Caesarean, Caesarian, *or US* **Cesarean, Cesarian** (sɪˈzɛərɪən) ADJECTIVE 1 of or relating to any of the Caesars, esp Julius Caesar (100–44 B.C.), Roman general, statesman, and historian. ◆ NOUN 2 (*sometimes not capital*) *Surgery* **a** a short for **Caesarean section. b** (*as modifier*): *Caesarean birth; Caesarean operation.*

Caesarean section NOUN surgical incision through the abdominal and uterine walls in order to deliver a baby.
▷HISTORY C17: from the belief that Julius Caesar was so delivered, the name allegedly being derived from *caesus,* past participle of *caedere* to cut

Caesarism (ˈsiːzəˌrɪzəm) NOUN an autocratic system of government. See also **Bonapartism.**
▸ˈ**Caesarist** NOUN ▸ˌ**Caesarˈistic** ADJECTIVE

caesious *or US* **cesious** (ˈsiːzɪəs) ADJECTIVE *Botany* having a waxy bluish-grey coating.
▷HISTORY C19: from Latin *caesius* bluish grey

caesium *or US* **cesium** (ˈsiːzɪəm) NOUN a ductile silvery-white element of the alkali metal group that is the most electropositive metal. It occurs in pollucite and lepidolite and is used in photocells. The radioisotope **caesium-137,** with a half-life of 30.2 years, is used in radiotherapy. Symbol: Cs; atomic no.: 55; atomic wt.: 132.90543; valency: 1; relative density: 1.873; melting pt.: 28.39±0.01°C; boiling pt.: 671°C.

caesium clock NOUN a type of atomic clock that uses the frequency of radiation absorbed in changing the spin of electrons in caesium atoms. See also **second**[2].

caespitose *or US* **cespitose** (ˈsɛspɪˌtəʊs) ADJECTIVE *Botany* growing in dense tufts.
▷HISTORY C19: from New Latin *caespitōsus,* from *caespitem* turf
▸ˈ**caespiˌtosely** *or US* ˈ**cespiˌtosely** ADVERB

caesura (sɪˈzjʊərə) NOUN, *plural* **-ras** *or* **-rae** (-riː). 1 (in modern prosody) a pause, esp for sense, usually near the middle of a verse line. Usual symbol: ‖ 2 (in classical prosody) a break between words within a metrical foot, usually in the third or fourth foot of the line.
▷HISTORY C16: from Latin, literally: a cutting, from *caedere* to cut
▸**caeˈsural** ADJECTIVE

CAF ABBREVIATION FOR cost and freight.

cafard (*French* kafar) NOUN a feeling of severe depression.
▷HISTORY C20: from French, literally: cockroach, hypocrite

café (ˈkæfeɪ, ˈkæfɪ) NOUN 1 a small or inexpensive restaurant or coffee bar, serving light meals and refreshments. 2 *South African* a corner shop or grocer.
▷HISTORY C19: from French: COFFEE

café au lait *French* (kafe o lɛ) NOUN 1 coffee with milk. 2 a light brown colour.

café-au-lait spot NOUN a brown patch on the skin that can occur normally in small numbers or in neurofibromatosis, when they are more numerous.

café noir *French* (kafe nwar) NOUN black coffee.

cafeteria (ˌkæfɪˈtɪərɪə) NOUN a self-service restaurant.
▷HISTORY C20: from American Spanish: coffee shop

cafetiere (ˌkæfəˈtjɛə, ˌkæfəˈtɪə) NOUN a kind of coffeepot in which boiling water is poured onto ground coffee and a plunger fitted with a metal filter is pressed down, forcing the grounds to the bottom.
▷HISTORY C20: from French *cafetière* coffeepot

caff (kæf) NOUN a slang word for **café.**

caffeinated (ˈkæfɪˌneɪtəd) ADJECTIVE 1 **a** with no natural caffeine removed. **b** with added caffeine. 2 highly stimulated by caffeine.

caffeine *or* **caffein** (ˈkæfiːn, ˈkæfɪˌiːn) NOUN a white crystalline bitter alkaloid responsible for the stimulant action of tea, coffee, and cocoa: a constituent of many tonics and analgesics. Formula: $C_8H_{10}N_4O_2$. See also **xanthine** (sense 2).
▷HISTORY C19: from German *Kaffein,* from *Kaffee* COFFEE

caftan (ˈkæfˌtæn, -ˌtɑːn) NOUN a variant spelling of **kaftan.**

cag (kæg) NOUN *Mountaineering* short for **cagoule.**

caganer (*Catalan* kagaˈne) NOUN a figure of a squatting defecating person, a traditional character in Catalan Christmas crèche scenes.
▷HISTORY C20: from Catalan *cagar* shit

cage (keɪdʒ) NOUN 1 **a** an enclosure, usually made with bars or wire, for keeping birds, monkeys, mice, etc. **b** (*as modifier*): *cagebird.* 2 a thing or place that confines or imprisons. 3 something resembling a cage in function or structure: *the rib cage.* 4 the enclosed platform of a lift, esp as used in a mine. 5 *Engineering* a skeleton ring device that ensures that the correct amount of space is maintained between the individual rollers or balls in a rolling bearing. 6 *Informal* the basket used in basketball. 7 *Informal* the goal in ice hockey. 8 *US* a steel framework on which guns are supported. 9 **rattle someone's cage.** *Informal* to upset or anger someone. ◆ VERB 10 (*tr*) to confine in or as in a cage.
▷HISTORY C13: from Old French, from Latin *cavea* enclosure, from *cavus* hollow

cageling (ˈkeɪdʒlɪŋ) NOUN a bird kept in a cage.

cagey *or* **cagy** (ˈkeɪdʒɪ) ADJECTIVE **-ier, -iest.** *Informal* not open or frank; cautious; wary.
▷HISTORY C20: of unknown origin
▸ˈ**cagily** ADVERB ▸ˈ**caginess** NOUN

cag-handed (ˌkægˈhændɪd) ADJECTIVE *Dialect* a variant of **cack-handed.**

Cagliari (kælˈjɑːrɪ; *Italian* kaʎˈʎari) NOUN a port in Italy, the capital of Sardinia, on the S coast. Pop.: 165 926 (2000 est.).

cagmag (ˈkægˌmæg) *Midland English dialect* ◆ ADJECTIVE 1 done shoddily; left incomplete. ◆ VERB **-mags, -magging, -magged.** (*intr*) 2 to chat idly; gossip.
▷HISTORY C18: of uncertain origin

cagoule (kəˈguːl) NOUN a lightweight usually knee-length type of anorak. Also spelt: **kagoul, kagoule.** Sometimes shortened to **cag.**
▷HISTORY C20: from French

cahier *French* (kaje) NOUN 1 a notebook. 2 a written or printed report, esp of the proceedings of a meeting.

Cahokia Mounds (kəˈhəʊkɪə) PLURAL NOUN the largest group of prehistoric Indian earthworks in the US, located northeast of East St Louis.

cahoots (kəˈhuːts) PLURAL NOUN (*sometimes singular*) *Informal* 1 *US* partnership; league (esp in the phrases **go in cahoots with, go cahoot**). 2 **in cahoots.** in collusion.
▷HISTORY C19: of uncertain origin

CAI ABBREVIATION FOR computer-aided instruction.

Caiaphas (ˈkaɪəˌfæs) NOUN *New Testament* the high priest at the beginning of John the Baptist's preaching and during the trial of Jesus (Luke 3:2; Matthew 26).

Caicos Islands (ˈkeɪkəs) PLURAL NOUN a group of islands in the Caribbean: part of the British dependency of the **Turks and Caicos Islands.**

cailleach (ˈkæljəx) NOUN *Scot* an old woman.
▷HISTORY Gaelic

caiman (ˈkeɪmən) NOUN, *plural* **-mans.** a variant spelling of **cayman.**

cain *or* **kain** (keɪn) NOUN *History* (in Scotland and Ireland) payment in kind, usually farm produce paid as rent.
▷HISTORY C12: from Scottish Gaelic *cāin* rent, perhaps ultimately from Late Latin *canōn* tribute (see CANON); compare Middle Irish *cāin* law

Cain (keɪn) NOUN **raise Cain. a** to cause a commotion. **b** to react or protest heatedly.
▷HISTORY from Cain, the first son of Adam and Eve, who killed his brother Abel (Genesis 4:1–16), used as a euphemism for hell or the devil

cainogenesis (ˌkaɪnəʊˈdʒɛnɪsɪs) NOUN a variant spelling of **caenogenesis.**
▸**cainogenetic** (ˌkaɪnəʊdʒɪˈnɛtɪk) ADJECTIVE
▸ˌ**cainogeˈnetically** ADVERB

Cainozoic (ˌkaɪnəʊˈzəʊɪk, ˌkeɪ-) ADJECTIVE a variant of **Cenozoic.**

caïque (kaɪˈiːk) NOUN 1 a long narrow light rowing skiff used on the Bosporus. 2 a sailing vessel of the E Mediterranean with a sprit mainsail, square topsail, and two or more jibs or other sails.
▷HISTORY C17: from French, from Italian *caicco,* from Turkish *kayik*

caird (kɛəd; *Scot* kerd) NOUN *Scot obsolete* a travelling tinker; vagrant.
▷HISTORY C17: from Scottish Gaelic; related to Welsh *cerdd* craft

Caird Coast (kɛəd) NOUN a region of Antarctica: a

part of Coats Land on the SE coast of the Weddell Sea; now included in the British Antarctic Territory.

Cairene ('kaıri:n) ADJECTIVE 1 of or relating to Cairo or its inhabitants. ◆ NOUN 2 a native or inhabitant of Cairo.

cairn (kɛən) NOUN 1 a mound of stones erected as a memorial or marker. 2 Also called: **cairn terrier.** a small rough-haired breed of terrier originally from Scotland.
▷HISTORY C15: from Gaelic *carn*

cairngorm ('kɛən,gɔ:m, ,kern'gɒrm) NOUN a smoky yellow, grey, or brown variety of quartz, used as a gemstone. Also called: **smoky quartz.**
▷HISTORY C18: from *Cairn Gorm* (literally: blue cairn), mountain in Scotland where it is found

Cairngorm Mountains PLURAL NOUN a mountain range of NE Scotland: part of the Grampians. Highest peak: Ben Macdhui, 1309 m (4296 ft.). Also called: **the Cairngorms.**

Cairns (kænz, kɛənz) NOUN a port in NE Australia, in Queensland. Pop.: 100 900 (1995 est.).

Cairo ('kaırəʊ) NOUN the capital of Egypt, on the Nile: the largest city in Africa and in the Middle East; industrial centre; site of the university and mosque of Al Azhar (founded in 972). Pop.: 6 789 479 (1996). Arabic name: **El Qahira** (ɛl 'kahi:rɔ).
▸'**Cairene** NOUN, ADJECTIVE

caisson (kə'su:n, 'keıs°n) NOUN 1 a watertight chamber open at the bottom and containing air under pressure, used to carry out construction work under water. 2 a similar unpressurized chamber. 3 a watertight float filled with air, used to raise sunken ships. See also **camel** (sense 2). 4 a watertight structure placed across the entrance of a basin, dry dock, etc., to exclude water from it. 5 **a** a box containing explosives, formerly used as a mine. **b** an ammunition chest. **c** a two-wheeled vehicle containing an ammunition chest. 6 another name for **coffer** (sense 3).
▷HISTORY C18: from French, assimilated to *caisse* CASE[2]

caisson disease NOUN another name for **decompression sickness.**

Caithness (keıθ'nɛs, 'keıθnɛs) NOUN (until 1975) a county of NE Scotland, now part of Highland.

caitiff ('keıtıf) *Archaic or poetic* ◆ NOUN 1 a cowardly or base person. ◆ ADJECTIVE 2 cowardly; base.
▷HISTORY C13: from Old French *caitif* prisoner, from Latin *captīvus* CAPTIVE

cajeput ('kædʒə,pʊt) NOUN a variant spelling of **cajuput.**

cajole (kə'dʒəʊl) VERB to persuade (someone) by flattery or pleasing talk to do what one wants; wheedle; coax.
▷HISTORY C17: from French *cajoler* to coax, of uncertain origin
▸**ca'jolement** NOUN ▸**ca'joler** NOUN ▸**ca'jolery** NOUN ▸**ca'jolingly** ADVERB

Cajun ('keıdʒən) NOUN 1 a native of Louisiana descended from 18th-century Acadian immigrants. 2 the dialect of French spoken by such people. 3 the music of this ethnic group, combining blues and European folk music. ◆ ADJECTIVE 4 denoting or relating to such people, their language, or their music.
▷HISTORY C19: alteration of ACADIAN; compare *Injun* for *Indian*

cajuput *or* **cajeput** ('kædʒə,pʊt) NOUN 1 a small myrtaceous tree or shrub, *Melaleuca leucadendron*, native to the East Indies and Australia, with whitish flowers and leaves. 2 a green aromatic oil derived from this tree, used to treat skin diseases. 3 a lauraceous tree, *Umbellularia californica*, whose aromatic leaves are used in medicine.
▷HISTORY C18: from Malay *kayu puteh*, from *kayu* wood + *puteh* white

cake (keık) NOUN 1 a baked food, usually in loaf or layer form, typically made from a mixture of flour, sugar, and eggs. 2 a flat thin mass of bread, esp unleavened bread. 3 a shaped mass of dough or other food of similar consistency: *a fish cake.* 4 a mass, slab, or crust of a solidified or compressed substance, as of soap or ice. 5 **have one's cake and eat it.** to enjoy both of two desirable but incompatible alternatives. 6 **go** *or* **sell like hot cakes.** *Informal* to be sold very quickly or in large quantities. 7 **piece of cake.** *Informal* something that is easily achieved or obtained. 8 **take the cake.** *Informal* to surpass all others, esp in stupidity, folly, etc. 9 *Informal* the whole or total of something that is to be shared or divided: *the miners are demanding a larger slice of the cake; that is a fair method of sharing the cake.* ◆ VERB 10 (*tr*) to cover with a hard layer; encrust: *the hull was caked with salt.* 11 to form or be formed into a hardened mass.
▷HISTORY C13: from Old Norse *kaka;* related to Danish *kage,* German *Kuchen*
▸'**cakey** *or* '**caky** ADJECTIVE

cakewalk ('keık,wɔ:k) NOUN 1 a dance based on a march with intricate steps, originally performed by African-Americans with the prize of a cake for the best performers. 2 a piece of music composed for this dance. 3 *Informal* an easily accomplished task. ◆ VERB 4 (*intr*) to perform the cakewalk.
▸'**cake,walker** NOUN

CAL ABBREVIATION FOR computer-aided (or -assisted) learning.

cal. ABBREVIATION FOR: 1 calibre. 2 calorie (small).

Cal. ABBREVIATION FOR: 1 Calorie (large). 2 California.

Calabar ('kælə,bɑ:) NOUN a port in SE Nigeria, capital of Cross River state. Pop.: 174 400 (1996 est.).

Calabar bean (,kælə'bɑ:, 'kælə,bɑ:) NOUN the dark brown very poisonous seed of a leguminous woody climbing plant, *Physostigma venenosum* of tropical Africa, used as a source of the drug physostigmine.

calabash ('kælə,bæʃ) NOUN 1 Also called: **calabash tree.** a tropical American evergreen tree, *Crescentia cujete,* that produces large round gourds: family *Bignoniaceae.* 2 another name for the **bottle gourd.** 3 the gourd of either of these plants. 4 the dried hollow shell of a gourd used as the bowl of a tobacco pipe, a bottle, rattle, etc. 5 **calabash nutmeg.** a tropical African shrub, *Monodora myristica,* whose oily aromatic seeds can be used as nutmegs: family *Annonaceae.*
▷HISTORY C17: from obsolete French *calabasse,* from Spanish *calabaza,* perhaps from Arabic *qar'ah yābisah* dry gourd, from *qar'ah* gourd + *yābisah* dry

calabogus (,kælə'bəʊgəs) NOUN *Canadian* a mixed drink containing rum, spruce beer, and molasses.
▷HISTORY C18: of unknown origin

calaboose ('kælə,bu:s) NOUN *US informal* a prison; jail.
▷HISTORY C18: from Creole French, from Spanish *calabozo* dungeon, of unknown origin

calabrese (,kælə'breızı) NOUN a variety of green sprouting broccoli.
▷HISTORY C20: from Italian: Calabrian

Calabria (kə'læbrıə) NOUN 1 a region of SW Italy: mostly mountainous and subject to earthquakes. Chief town: Reggio di Calabria. Pop.: 2 050 478 (2000 est.). Area: 15 080 sq. km (5822 sq. miles). 2 an ancient region of extreme SE Italy (3rd century B.C. to about 668 A.D.); now part of Apulia.

Calabrian (kə'læbrıən) ADJECTIVE 1 of or relating to Calabria or its inhabitants. ◆ NOUN 2 a native or inhabitant of Calabria.

caladium (kə'leıdıəm) NOUN any of various tropical plants of the aroid genus *Caladium,* which are widely cultivated as potted plants for their colourful variegated foliage.
▷HISTORY C19: from New Latin, from Malay *kĕladi* araceous plant

Calais ('kæleı, 'kælı; *French* kalɛ) NOUN a port in N France, on the Strait of Dover: the nearest French port to England; belonged to England 1347–1558. Pop.: 75 309 (1990).

calalu *or* **calaloo** ('kæləlu:) NOUN *Caribbean* the edible leaves of various plants, used as greens or in making thick soups.
▷HISTORY probably of African origin

calamanco (,kælə'mæŋkəʊ) NOUN a glossy woollen fabric woven with a checked design that shows on one side only.
▷HISTORY C16: of unknown origin

calamander ('kælə,mændə) NOUN the hard black-and-brown striped wood of several trees of the genus *Diospyros,* esp *D. quaesita* of India and Sri Lanka, used in making furniture: family *Ebenaceae.* See also **ebony** (sense 2).
▷HISTORY C19: metathetic variant of *coromandel* in COROMANDEL COAST

calamari (,kælə'mɑ:rı) NOUN squid cooked for eating, esp cut into rings and fried in batter.
▷HISTORY C20: from Italian, pl of *calamaro* squid, from Latin *calamarium* pen-case, referring to the squid's internal shell, from Greek *kalamos* reed

calamata olive (,kælə'mɑ:tə) NOUN a variant spelling of **kalamata olive.**

calamine ('kælə,maın) NOUN 1 a pink powder consisting of zinc oxide and ferric oxide, (iron(III) oxide), used medicinally in the form of soothing lotions or ointments. 2 *US* another name for **smithsonite** or **hemimorphite.**
▷HISTORY C17: from Old French, from Medieval Latin *calamīna,* from Latin *cadmīa;* see CADMIUM

calamint ('kælə,mınt) NOUN any aromatic Eurasian plant of the genus *Satureja* (or *Calamintha*), having clusters of purple or pink flowers: family *Lamiaceae* (labiates).
▷HISTORY C14: from Old French *calament* (but influenced by English MINT[1]), from Medieval Latin *calamentum,* from Greek *kalaminthē*

calamite ('kælə,maıt) NOUN any extinct treelike plant of the genus *Calamites,* of Carboniferous times, related to the horsetails.
▷HISTORY C19: from New Latin *Calamītes* type genus, from Greek *kalamitēs* reedlike, from *kalamos* reed

calamitous (kə'læmıtəs) ADJECTIVE causing, involving, or resulting in a calamity; disastrous.
▸**ca'lamitously** ADVERB ▸**ca'lamitousness** NOUN

calamity (kə'læmıtı) NOUN, *plural* **-ties.** 1 a disaster or misfortune, esp one causing extreme havoc, distress, or misery. 2 a state or feeling of deep distress or misery.
▷HISTORY C15: from French *calamité,* from Latin *calamitās;* related to Latin *incolumis* uninjured

calamondin ('kælə,mʌndın) *or* **calamondin orange** NOUN 1 a small citrus tree, *Citrus mitis,* of the Philippines. 2 the acid-tasting fruit of this tree, resembling a small orange.
▷HISTORY from Tagalog *kalamunding*

calamus ('kæləməs) NOUN, *plural* **-mi** (-,maı). 1 any tropical Asian palm of the genus *Calamus,* some species of which are a source of rattan and canes. 2 another name for **sweet flag.** 3 the aromatic root of the sweet flag. 4 *Ornithol* the basal hollow shaft of a feather; quill.
▷HISTORY C14: from Latin, from Greek *kalamos* reed, cane, stem

calando (kə'lændəʊ) ADJECTIVE, ADVERB *Music* (to be performed) with gradually decreasing tone and speed.
▷HISTORY Italian: dropping, from *calare* to lower, to drop

calandria (kə'lændrıə) NOUN a cylindrical vessel through which vertical tubes pass, esp one forming part of an evaporator, heat exchanger, or nuclear reactor.
▷HISTORY C20: arbitrarily named, from Spanish, literally: lark

calash (kə'læʃ) *or* **calèche** NOUN 1 a horse-drawn carriage with low wheels and a folding top. 2 the folding top of such a carriage. 3 a woman's folding hooped hood worn in the 18th century.
▷HISTORY C17: from French *calèche,* from German *Kalesche,* from Czech *kolesa* wheels

calathea (,kælə'θıə) NOUN any plant of the S. American perennial genus *Calathea,* many species of which are grown as greenhouse or house plants for their decorative variegated leaves, esp the zebra plant (*C. zebrina*), the leaves of which are purplish below and dark green with lighter stripes above: family *Marantaceae.*
▷HISTORY New Latin, from Greek *kalathos* a basket

calathus ('kæləθəs) NOUN, *plural* **-thi** (-,θaı). a vase-shaped basket represented in ancient Greek art, used as a symbol of fruitfulness.
▷HISTORY C18: from Latin, from Greek *kalathos*

calaverite (kə'lævə,raıt) NOUN a metallic pale yellow mineral consisting of a telluride of gold in the form of elongated striated crystals. It is a source of gold in Australia and North America. Formula: $AuTe_2$.
▷HISTORY C19: named after *Calaveras,* county in California where it was discovered

calc- COMBINING FORM a variant of **calci-** before a vowel.

calcaneus (kæl'keɪnɪəs) *or* **calcaneum** NOUN, *plural* **-nei** (-nɪˌaɪ) *or* **-nea** (-nɪə). [1] the largest tarsal bone, forming the heel in man. Nontechnical name: **heel bone.** [2] the corresponding bone in other vertebrates.
▷HISTORY C19: from Late Latin: heel, from Latin *calx* heel
▸**cal'caneal** *or* **cal'canean** ADJECTIVE

calcar ('kælˌkɑː) NOUN, *plural* **calcaria** (kæl'kɛərɪə). a spur or spurlike process, as on the leg of a bird or the corolla of a flower.
▷HISTORY C19: from Latin, from *calx* heel

calcareous (kæl'kɛərɪəs) ADJECTIVE of, containing, or resembling calcium carbonate; chalky.
▷HISTORY C17: from Latin *calcārius,* from *calx* lime

calcariferous (ˌkælkə'rɪfərəs) ADJECTIVE *Biology* having a spur or spurs.

calceiform ('kælsɪɪˌfɔːm, kæl'siː-) *or* **calceolate** ('kælsɪəˌleɪt) ADJECTIVE *Botany* shaped like a shoe or slipper.
▷HISTORY C19: from Latin *calceus* shoe

calceolaria (ˌkælsɪə'lɛərɪə) NOUN any tropical American scrophulariaceous plant of the genus *Calceolaria:* cultivated for its speckled slipper-shaped flowers. Also called: **slipperwort.**
▷HISTORY C18: from Latin *calceolus* small shoe, from *calceus*

calces ('kælsiːz) NOUN a plural of **calx.**

Calchas ('kælkæs) NOUN *Greek myth* a soothsayer who assisted the Greeks in the Trojan War.

calci- *or before a vowel* **calc-** COMBINING FORM indicating lime or calcium: *calcify.*
▷HISTORY from Latin *calx, calc-* limestone

calcic ('kælsɪk) ADJECTIVE of, containing, or concerned with lime or calcium.
▷HISTORY C19: from Latin *calx* lime

calcicole ('kælsɪˌkəʊl) NOUN any plant that thrives in lime-rich soils.
▷HISTORY C20: from CALCI- + *-cole,* from Latin *colere* to dwell
▸**calcicolous** (kæl'sɪkələs) ADJECTIVE

calciferol (kæl'sɪfəˌrɒl) NOUN a fat-soluble steroid, found esp in fish-liver oils, produced by the action of ultraviolet radiation on ergosterol. It increases the absorption of calcium from the intestine and is used in the treatment of rickets. Formula: $C_{28}H_{43}OH$. Also called: **vitamin D_2.**
▷HISTORY C20: from CALCIF(EROUS + ERGOST)EROL

calciferous (kæl'sɪfərəs) ADJECTIVE forming or producing salts of calcium, esp calcium carbonate.

calcific (kæl'sɪfɪk) ADJECTIVE forming or causing to form lime or chalk.

calcification (ˌkælsɪfɪ'keɪʃən) NOUN [1] the process of calcifying or becoming calcified. [2] *Pathol* a tissue hardened by deposition of lime salts. [3] any calcified object or formation.

calcifuge ('kælsɪˌfjuːdʒ) NOUN any plant that thrives in acid soils but not in lime-rich soils.
▸**calcifugal** (ˌkælsɪ'fjuːgəl) ADJECTIVE ▸**calcifugous** (kæl'sɪfjəgəs) ADJECTIVE

calcify ('kælsɪˌfaɪ) VERB **-fies, -fying, -fied.** [1] to convert or be converted into lime. [2] to harden or become hardened by impregnation with calcium salts.

calcimine ('kælsɪˌmaɪn, -mɪn) *or* **kalsomine** NOUN [1] a white or pale tinted wash for walls. ◆ VERB [2] (*tr*) to cover with calcimine.
▷HISTORY C19: changed from *Kalsomine,* a trademark

calcine ('kælsaɪn, -sɪn) VERB [1] (*tr*) to heat (a substance) so that it is oxidized, reduced, or loses water. [2] (*intr*) to oxidize as a result of heating.
▷HISTORY C14: from Medieval Latin *calcināre* to heat, from Latin *calx* lime
▸**calcination** (ˌkælsɪ'neɪʃən) NOUN

calcinosis (ˌkælsɪ'nəʊsɪs) NOUN the abnormal deposition of calcium salts in the tissues of the body.

calcite ('kælsaɪt) NOUN a colourless or white mineral (occasionally tinged with impurities), found in sedimentary and metamorphic rocks, in veins, in limestone, and in stalagmites and stalactites. It is used in the manufacture of cement, plaster, paint, glass, and fertilizer. Composition: calcium carbonate. Formula: $CaCO_3$. Crystal structure: hexagonal (rhombohedral).
▸**calcitic** (kæl'sɪtɪk) ADJECTIVE

calcitonin (ˌkælsɪ'təʊnɪn) NOUN a hormone secreted by the thyroid that inhibits the release of calcium from the skeleton and prevents a build-up of calcium in the blood. Also called: **thyrocalcitonin.** Compare **parathyroid hormone.**
▷HISTORY C20: from CALCI- + TON(IC) + -IN

calcium ('kælsɪəm) NOUN a malleable silvery-white metallic element of the alkaline earth group; the fifth most abundant element in the earth's crust (3.6 per cent), occurring esp as forms of calcium carbonate. It is an essential constituent of bones and teeth and is used as a deoxidizer in steel. Symbol: Ca; atomic no.: 20; atomic wt.: 40.078; valency: 2; relative density: 1.55; melting pt.: 842±2°C; boiling pt.: 1494°C.
▷HISTORY C19: from New Latin, from Latin *calx* lime

calcium antagonist NOUN another name for **calcium channel blocker.**

calcium carbide NOUN a grey salt of calcium used in the production of acetylene (by its reaction with water) and calcium cyanamide. Formula: CaC_2. Sometimes shortened to **carbide.**

calcium carbonate NOUN a white crystalline salt occurring in limestone, chalk, marble, calcite, coral, and pearl: used in the production of lime and cement. Formula: $CaCO_3$.

calcium channel blocker NOUN any drug that prevents the influx of calcium ions into cardiac and smooth muscle: used to treat high blood pressure and angina. Also called: **calcium antagonist.**

calcium chloride NOUN a white deliquescent salt occurring naturally in seawater and used in the de-icing of roads and as a drying agent. Formula: $CaCl_2$.

calcium cyanamide NOUN a white crystalline compound formed by heating calcium carbide with nitrogen. It is important in the fixation of nitrogen and can be hydrolysed to ammonia or used as a fertilizer. Formula: $CaCN_2$.

calcium hydroxide NOUN a white crystalline slightly soluble alkali with many uses, esp in cement, water softening, and the neutralization of acid soils. Formula: $Ca(OH)_2$. Also called: **lime, slaked lime, hydrated lime, calcium hydrate, caustic lime, lime hydrate.**

calcium light NOUN another name for **limelight.**

calcium oxide NOUN a white crystalline base used in the production of calcium hydroxide and bleaching powder and in the manufacture of glass, paper, and steel. Formula: CaO. Also called: **lime, quicklime, calx, burnt lime, calcined lime, fluxing lime.**

calcium phosphate NOUN [1] the insoluble nonacid calcium salt of orthophosphoric acid (phosphoric(V) acid): it occurs in bones and is the main constituent of bone ash. Formula: $Ca_3(PO_4)_2$. [2] any calcium salt of a phosphoric acid. Calcium phosphates are found in many rocks and used esp in fertilizers.

calcrete ('kælkriːt) NOUN another name for **caliche** (sense 1).

calcsinter ('kælkˌsɪntə) NOUN another name for **travertine.**
▷HISTORY C19: from German *Kalksinter,* from *Kalk* lime + *sinter* dross; see CHALK, SINTER

calcspar ('kælkˌspɑː) NOUN another name for **calcite.**
▷HISTORY C19: partial translation of Swedish *kalkspat,* from *kalk* lime (ultimately from Latin *calx*) + *spat* SPAR[3]

calc-tufa ('kælkˌtuːfə) *or* **calc-tuff** ('kælkˌtʌf) NOUN another name for **tufa.**

calculable ('kælkjʊləbəl) ADJECTIVE [1] that may be computed or estimated. [2] predictable; dependable.
▸ˌ**calcula'bility** NOUN ▸'**calculably** ADVERB

calculate ('kælkjʊˌleɪt) VERB [1] to solve (one or more problems) by a mathematical procedure; compute. [2] (*tr; may take a clause as object*) to determine beforehand by judgment, reasoning, etc.; estimate. [3] (*tr; usually passive*) to design specifically; aim: *the car was calculated to appeal to women.* [4] (*intr;* foll by *on* or *upon*) to depend; rely. [5] (*tr; may take a clause as object*) *US dialect* **a** to suppose; think. **b** to intend (to do something).
▷HISTORY C16: from Late Latin *calculāre,* from *calculus* pebble used as a counter; see CALCULUS
▸**calculative** ('kælkjʊlətɪv) ADJECTIVE

calculated ('kælkjʊˌleɪtɪd) ADJECTIVE (*usually prenominal*) [1] undertaken after considering the likelihood of success or failure: *a calculated risk.* [2] deliberately planned; premeditated: *a calculated insult.*

calculating ('kælkjʊˌleɪtɪŋ) ADJECTIVE [1] selfishly scheming. [2] shrewd; cautious.
▸'**calcuˌlatingly** ADVERB

calculation (ˌkælkjʊ'leɪʃən) NOUN [1] the act, process, or result of calculating. [2] an estimation of probability; forecast. [3] careful planning or forethought, esp for selfish motives.

calculator ('kælkjʊˌleɪtə) NOUN [1] a device for performing mathematical calculations, esp an electronic device that can be held in the hand. [2] a person or thing that calculates. [3] a set of tables used as an aid to calculations.

calculous ('kælkjʊləs) ADJECTIVE *Pathol* of or suffering from a calculus.

calculus ('kælkjʊləs) NOUN, *plural* **-luses.** [1] a branch of mathematics, developed independently by Newton and Leibniz. Both **differential calculus** and **integral calculus** are concerned with the effect on a function of an infinitesimal change in the independent variable as it tends to zero. [2] any mathematical system of calculation involving the use of symbols. [3] *Logic* an uninterpreted formal system. Compare **formal language** (sense 2). [4] (*plural* **-li** (-ˌlaɪ)) *Pathol* a stonelike concretion of minerals and salts found in ducts or hollow organs of the body.
▷HISTORY C17: from Latin: pebble, stone used in reckoning, from *calx* small stone, counter

calculus of variations NOUN a branch of calculus concerned with maxima and minima of definite integrals.

Calcutta (kæl'kʌtə) NOUN a port in E India, capital of West Bengal state, on the Hooghly River: former capital of the country (1833–1912); major commercial and industrial centre; three universities. Pop.: 4 399 819 (1991). Official name: **Kolkata.**

caldarium (kæl'dɛərɪəm) NOUN, *plural* **-daria** (-'dɛərɪə). (in ancient Rome) a room for taking hot baths.
▷HISTORY C18: from Latin, from *calidus* warm, from *calēre* to be warm

caldera (kæl'dɛərə, 'kɔːldərə) NOUN a large basin-shaped crater at the top of a volcano, formed by the collapse or explosion of the cone. See **cirque.**
▷HISTORY C19: from Spanish *Caldera* (literally: CAULDRON), name of a crater in the Canary Islands

Calderdale ('kɔːldəˌdeɪl) NOUN a unitary authority in N England, in West Yorkshire. Pop.: 192 396 (2001). Area: 364 sq. km (140 sq. miles).

caldron ('kɔːldrən) NOUN a variant spelling of **cauldron.**

calèche (*French* kalɛʃ) NOUN a variant of **calash.**

Caledonia (ˌkælɪ'dəʊnɪə) NOUN the Roman name for **Scotland**: used poetically in later times.

Caledonian (ˌkælɪ'dəʊnɪən) ADJECTIVE [1] of or relating to Scotland. [2] of or denoting a period of mountain building in NW Europe in the Palaeozoic era. ◆ NOUN [3] *Literary* a native or inhabitant of Scotland.

Caledonian Canal NOUN a canal in N Scotland, linking the Atlantic with the North Sea through the Great Glen: built 1803–47; now little used.

calefacient (ˌkælɪ'feɪʃənt) ADJECTIVE [1] causing warmth. ◆ NOUN [2] *Med, obsolete* an agent that warms, such as a mustard plaster.
▷HISTORY C17: from Latin *calefaciēns,* from *calefacere* to heat
▸**calefaction** (ˌkælɪ'fækʃən) NOUN

calefactory (ˌkælɪ'fæktərɪ, -trɪ) ADJECTIVE [1] giving warmth. ◆ NOUN, *plural* **-ries.** [2] a heated sitting room in a monastery.
▷HISTORY C16: from Latin *calefactōrius,* from *calefactus* made warm; see CALEFACIENT

calendar ('kælɪndə) NOUN [1] a system for determining the beginning, length, and order of years and their divisions. See also **Gregorian calendar, Jewish calendar, Julian calendar, Revolutionary calendar, Roman calendar.** [2] a table showing any such

arrangement, esp as applied to one or more successive years. [3] a list, register, or schedule of social events, pending court cases, appointments, etc. ◆ VERB [4] (*tr*) to enter in a calendar; schedule; register.
▷**HISTORY** C13: via Norman French from Medieval Latin *kalendārium* account book, from *Kalendae* the CALENDS, when interest on debts became due
▸**calendrical** (kæ'lɛndrɪkᵊl) *or* **ca'lendric** ADJECTIVE

calendar day NOUN See **day** (sense 1).

calendar month NOUN See **month** (sense 1).

calendar year NOUN See **year** (sense 1).

calender¹ ('kælɪndə) NOUN [1] a machine in which paper or cloth is glazed or smoothed by passing between rollers. ◆ VERB [2] (*tr*) to subject (material) to such a process.
▷**HISTORY** C17: from French *calandre,* of unknown origin

calender² ('kælɪndə) NOUN a member of a mendicant order of dervishes in Turkey, Iran, and India.
▷**HISTORY** from Persian *kalandar*

calends *or* **kalends** ('kælɪndz) PLURAL NOUN the first day of each month in the ancient Roman calendar.
▷**HISTORY** C14: from Latin *kalendae;* related to Latin *calāre* to proclaim

calendula (kæ'lɛndjʊlə) NOUN [1] any Eurasian plant of the genus *Calendula,* esp the pot marigold, having orange-and-yellow rayed flowers: family *Asteraceae* (composites). [2] the dried flowers of the pot marigold, formerly used medicinally and for seasoning.
▷**HISTORY** C19: from Medieval Latin, from Latin *kalendae* CALENDS; perhaps from its supposed efficacy in curing menstrual disorders

calenture ('kælən,tjʊə) NOUN a mild fever of tropical climates, similar in its symptoms to sunstroke.
▷**HISTORY** C16: from Spanish *calentura* fever, ultimately from Latin *calēre* to be warm

calf¹ (kɑːf) NOUN, *plural* **calves.** [1] the young of cattle, esp domestic cattle. Related adjective: **vituline.** [2] the young of certain other mammals, such as the buffalo, elephant, giraffe, and whale. [3] a large piece of floating ice detached from an iceberg, etc. [4] **kill the fatted calf.** to celebrate lavishly, esp as a welcome. [5] another name for **calfskin.**
▷**HISTORY** Old English *cealf;* related to Old Norse *kālfr,* Gothic *kalbō,* Old High German *kalba*

calf² (kɑːf) NOUN, *plural* **calves.** the thick fleshy part of the back of the leg between the ankle and the knee. Related adjective: **sural.**
▷**HISTORY** C14: from Old Norse *kalfi*

calf diphtheria NOUN *Vet science* a disease of the throat in young calves caused by *Fusobacterium necrophorum,* resulting in breathing difficulty and a painful cough.

calf love NOUN temporary infatuation or love of an adolescent for a member of the opposite sex. Also called: **puppy love.**

calf's-foot jelly NOUN a jelly made from the stock of boiled calves' feet and flavourings, formerly often served to invalids.

calfskin ('kɑːf,skɪn) NOUN [1] the skin or hide of a calf. [2] Also called: **calf. a** fine leather made from this skin. **b** (*as modifier*): *calfskin boots.*

Calgary ('kælgərɪ) NOUN a city in Canada, in S Alberta: centre of a large agricultural region; oilfields. Pop.: 768 082 (1996).

Calgon ('kælgɒn) NOUN *Trademark* a chemical compound, sodium hexametaphosphate, with water-softening properties, used in detergents.

Cali (*Spanish* 'kali) NOUN a city in SW Colombia: commercial centre in a rich agricultural region. Pop.: 2 077 386 (1999 est.).

Caliban ('kælɪ,bæn) NOUN a brutish or brutalized man.
▷**HISTORY** C19: after a character in Shakespeare's *The Tempest* (1611)

calibrate ('kælɪ,breɪt) VERB (*tr*) [1] to measure the calibre of (a gun, mortar, etc.). [2] to mark (the scale of a measuring instrument) so that readings can be made in appropriate units. [3] to determine the accuracy of (a measuring instrument, etc.). [4] to determine or check the range and accuracy of (a piece of artillery).
▸**,cali'bration** NOUN ▸**'cali,brator** *or* **'cali,brater** NOUN

calibre *or US* **caliber** ('kælɪbə) NOUN [1] the diameter of a cylindrical body, esp the internal diameter of a tube or the bore of a firearm. [2] the diameter of a shell or bullet. [3] ability; distinction: *a musician of high calibre.* [4] personal character: *a man of high calibre.*
▷**HISTORY** C16: from Old French, from Italian *calibro,* from Arabic *qālib* shoemaker's last, mould
▸**'calibred** *or US* **'calibered** ADJECTIVE

calices ('kælɪ,siːz) NOUN the plural of **calix.**

caliche (kæ'liːtʃɪ) NOUN [1] a bed of sand or clay in arid regions cemented by calcium carbonate, sodium chloride, and other soluble minerals. [2] a surface layer of soil encrusted with calcium carbonate, occurring in arid regions. also called **calcrete, duricrust.**
▷**HISTORY** C20: from American Spanish, from Latin *calx* lime

calicle ('kælɪkᵊl) NOUN a variant spelling of **calycle.**
▸**calicular** (kə'lɪkjʊlə) ADJECTIVE

calico ('kælɪ,kəʊ) NOUN, *plural* **-coes** *or* **-cos.** [1] a white or unbleached cotton fabric with no printed design. [2] *Chiefly US* a coarse printed cotton fabric. [3] (*modifier*) made of calico.
▷**HISTORY** C16: based on *Calicut,* town in India

calico bush NOUN another name for **mountain laurel.**

Calicut ('kælɪ,kʌt) NOUN the former name for **Kozhikode.**

calif ('keɪlɪf, 'kæl-) NOUN a variant spelling of **caliph.**

Calif. ABBREVIATION FOR California.

califate ('keɪlɪ,feɪt, -fɪt, 'kæl-) NOUN a variant spelling of **caliphate.**

califont ('kælɪ,fɒnt) NOUN *NZ* a gas water heater.
▷**HISTORY** from a trade name

California (,kælɪ'fɔːnɪə) NOUN [1] a state on the W coast of the US: the third largest state in area and the largest in population; consists of a narrow, warm coastal plain rising to the Coast Range, deserts in the south, the fertile central valleys of the Sacramento and San Joaquin Rivers, and the mountains of the Sierra Nevada in the east; major industries include the growing of citrus fruits and grapes, fishing, oil production, electronics, information technology, and films. Capital: Sacramento. Pop.: 33 871 648 (2000 est.). Area: 411 015 sq. km (158 693 sq. miles). Abbreviations: **Cal., Calif.,** (with zip code) **CA.** [2] **Gulf of.** an arm of the Pacific Ocean, between Sonora and Lower California.

Californian (,kælɪ'fɔːnɪən) ADJECTIVE [1] of or relating to California or its inhabitants. ◆ NOUN [2] a native or inhabitant of California.

Californian Spangled cat NOUN a breed of short-haired cat with a spotted coat, bred in California to resemble a leopard in appearance.

California poppy NOUN a papaveraceous plant, *Eschscholtzia californica,* of the Pacific coast of North America, having yellow or orange flowers and finely divided bluish-green leaves.

californium (,kælɪ'fɔːnɪəm) NOUN a metallic transuranic element artificially produced from curium. Symbol: Cf; atomic no.: 98; half-life of most stable isotope, ^{251}Cf: 800 years (approx.).
▷**HISTORY** C20: New Latin; discovered at the University of *California*

caliginous (kə'lɪdʒɪnəs) ADJECTIVE *Archaic* dark; dim.
▷**HISTORY** C16: from Latin *cālīginōsus,* from *cālīgō* darkness
▸**caliginosity** (kə,lɪdʒɪ'nɒsɪtɪ) NOUN

Calimere ('kælɪ,mɪə) NOUN **Point.** a cape on the SE coast of India, on the Palk Strait.

calipash *or* **callipash** ('kælɪ,pæʃ) NOUN the greenish glutinous edible part of the turtle found next to the upper shell, considered a delicacy.
▷**HISTORY** C17: perhaps changed from Spanish *carapacho* CARAPACE

calipee ('kælɪ,piː) NOUN the yellow glutinous edible part of the turtle found next to the lower shell, considered a delicacy.
▷**HISTORY** C17: perhaps a variant of CALIPASH

caliper ('kælɪpə) NOUN the usual US spelling of **calliper.**

caliph, calif, kalif, *or* **khalif** ('keɪlɪf, 'kæl-) NOUN *Islam* the title of the successors of Mohammed as rulers of the Islamic world, later assumed by the Sultans of Turkey.
▷**HISTORY** C14: from Old French, from Arabic *khalīfa* successor

caliphate, califate, *or* **kalifate** ('keɪlɪ,feɪt, -fɪt, 'kæl-) NOUN the office, jurisdiction, or reign of a caliph.

calisaya (,kælɪ'seɪə) NOUN the bark of any of several tropical trees of the rubiaceous genus *Cinchona,* esp *C. calisaya,* from which quinine is extracted. Also called: **calisaya bark, yellowbark, cinchona.**
▷**HISTORY** C19: from Spanish, from the name of a Bolivian Indian who taught the uses of quinine to the Spanish

calisthenics (,kælɪs'θɛnɪks) NOUN a variant spelling (esp US) of **callisthenics.**
▸**,calis'thenic** ADJECTIVE

calix ('keɪlɪks, 'kæ-) NOUN, *plural* **calices** ('kælɪ,siːz). a cup; chalice.
▷**HISTORY** C18: from Latin: CHALICE

calk¹ (kɔːk) VERB a variant spelling of **caulk.**

calk² (kɔːk) *or* **calkin** ('kɔːkɪn, 'kæl-) NOUN [1] a metal projection on a horse's shoe to prevent slipping. [2] *Chiefly US and Canadian* a set of spikes or a spiked plate attached to the sole of a boot, esp by loggers, to prevent slipping. ◆ VERB (*tr*) [3] to provide with calks. [4] to wound with a calk.
▷**HISTORY** C17: from Latin *calx* heel

calk³ (kɔːk) VERB (*tr*) to transfer (a design) by tracing it with a blunt point from one sheet backed with loosely fixed colouring matter onto another placed underneath.
▷**HISTORY** C17: from French *calquer* to trace; see CALQUE

call (kɔːl) VERB [1] (often foll by *out*) to speak or utter (words, sounds, etc.) loudly so as to attract attention: *he called out her name.* [2] (*tr*) to ask or order to come: *to call a policeman.* [3] (*intr;* sometimes foll by *on*) to make a visit (to): *she called on him.* [4] (often foll by *up*) to telephone (a person): *he called back at nine.* [5] (*tr*) to summon to a specific office, profession, etc.: *he was called to the ministry.* [6] (of animals or birds) to utter (a characteristic sound or cry). [7] (*tr*) to summon (a bird or animal) by imitating its cry. [8] (*tr*) to name or style: *they called the dog Rover.* [9] (*tr*) to designate: *they called him a coward.* [10] (*tr*) *Brit dialect* to speak ill of or scold. [11] (*tr*) to regard in a specific way: *I call it a foolish waste of time.* [12] (*tr*) to attract (attention). [13] (*tr*) to read (a list, register, etc.) aloud to check for omissions or absentees. [14] (when *tr,* usually foll by *for*) to give an order (for): *to call a strike.* [15] (*intr*) to try to predict the result of tossing a coin. [16] (*tr*) to awaken: *I was called early this morning.* [17] (*tr*) to cause to assemble: *to call a meeting.* [18] (*tr*) *Sport* (of an umpire, referee, etc.) to pass judgment upon (a shot, player, etc.) with a call. [19] (*tr*) *Austral and NZ* to broadcast a commentary on (a horse race or other sporting event). [20] (*tr*) to demand repayment of (a loan, redeemable bond, security, etc.). [21] (*tr;* often foll by *up*) *Accounting* to demand payment of (a portion of a share issue not yet paid by subscribers). [22] (*tr*) *Brit* to award (a student at an Inn of Court) the degree of barrister (esp in the phrase **call to the bar**). [23] (*tr*) *Computing* to transfer control to (a named subprogram). [24] (*tr*) *Poker* to demand that (a player) expose his hand, after equalling his bet. [25] (*intr*) *Bridge* to make a bid. [26] (in square-dancing) to call out (instructions) to the dancers. [27] *Billiards* to ask (a player) to say what kind of shot he will play or (of a player) to name his shot. [28] (*intr;* foll by *for*) **a** to require: *this problem calls for study.* **b** to come or go (for) in order to fetch: *I will call for my book later.* [29] (*intr;* foll by *on* or *upon*) to make an appeal or request (to): *they called upon him to reply.* [30] (*tr*) to predict the outcome of an event: *we don't know yet if the plan has succeeded because it's too soon to call.* [31] **call into being.** to create. [32] **call into play.** to begin to operate. [33] **call in** *or* **into question.** See **question** (sense 12). [34] **call it a day.** to stop work or other activity. [35] **too close to call.** (of the outcome of a competition, election, match, etc.) unable to be predicted. [36] **call to mind.** to remember or cause to be remembered. ◆ NOUN [37] a cry or shout. [38] the characteristic cry of a bird or animal. [39] a device, such as a whistle,

intended to imitate the cry of a bird or animal. 40 a summons or invitation. 41 a summons or signal sounded on a horn, bugle, etc. 42 *Hunting* any of several notes or patterns of notes, blown on a hunting horn as a signal. 43 *Hunting* **a** an imitation of the characteristic cry of a wild animal or bird to lure it to the hunter. **b** an instrument for producing such an imitation. 44 a short visit: *the doctor made six calls this morning.* 45 an inner urge to some task or profession; vocation. 46 allure or fascination, esp of a place: *the call of the forest.* 47 *Brit* the summons to the bar of a student member of an Inn of Court. 48 need, demand, or occasion: *there is no call to shout; we don't get much call for stockings these days.* 49 demand or claim (esp in the phrase **the call of duty**). 50 *Theatre* a notice to actors informing them of times of rehearsals. 51 (in square dancing) an instruction to execute new figures. 52 a conversation or a request for a connection by telephone. 53 *Commerce* **a** a demand for repayment of a loan. **b** (*as modifier*): *call money.* 54 *Finance* **a** a demand for redeemable bonds or shares to be presented for repayment. **b** a demand for an instalment payment on the issue price of bonds or shares. 55 *Billiards* a demand to an opponent to say what kind of shot he will play. 56 *Poker* a demand for a hand or hands to be exposed. 57 *Bridge* a bid, or a player's turn to bid. 58 a decision or judgment: *it's your call.* 59 *Sport* a decision of an umpire or referee regarding a shot, pitch, etc. 60 *Austral* a broadcast commentary on a horse race or other sporting event. 61 Also called: **call option.** *Stock Exchange* an option to buy a stated amount of securities at a specified price during a specified period. Compare **put** (sense 20). 62 See **roll call.** 63 **call for margin.** *Stock Exchange* a demand made by a stockbroker for partial payment of a client's debt due to decreasing value of the collateral. 64 **call of nature.** See **nature** (sense 16). 65 **on call. a** (of a loan, etc.) repayable on demand. **b** available to be called for work outside normal working hours. 66 **within call.** within range; accessible. ◆ See also **call down, call forth, call in, call off, call out, call up.**
▷HISTORY Old English *ceallian;* related to Old Norse *kalla,* Old High German *kallōn,* Old Slavonic *glasŭ* voice

calla ('kælə) NOUN 1 Also called: **calla lily, arum lily.** any southern African plant of the aroid genus *Zantedeschia,* esp *Z. aethiopica,* which has a white funnel-shaped spathe enclosing a yellow spadix. 2 an aroid plant, *Calla palustris,* that grows in wet places and has a white spathe enclosing a greenish spadix, and red berries.
▷HISTORY C19: from New Latin, probably from Greek *kalleia* wattles on a cock, probably from *kallos* beauty

callable ('kɔːləbᵊl) ADJECTIVE 1 (of a security) subject to redemption before maturity. 2 (of money loaned) repayable on demand.

callais (kə'leɪɪs) NOUN a green stone found as beads and ornaments in the late Neolithic and early Bronze Age of W Europe.
▷HISTORY C19: from Greek *kallais*

call alarm NOUN **a** an electronic device that sends an alarm signal, usually to a distant monitoring centre. **b** (*as modifier*): *a call-alarm system.*

call-and-response NOUN a form of interaction between a speaker and one or more listeners, in which every utterance of the speaker elicits a verbal or non-verbal response from the listener or listeners.

Callanetics (ˌkælə'nɛtɪks) NOUN (*functioning as singular*) *Trademark* a system of exercise involving frequent repetition of small muscular movements and squeezes, designed to improve muscle tone.
▷HISTORY C20: named after *Callan* Pinckney (born 1939), its US inventor

callant ('kælənt) *or* **callan** ('kælən) NOUN *Scot* a youth; lad.
▷HISTORY C16: from Dutch or Flemish *kalant* customer, fellow

Callao (*Spanish* ka'ʎao) NOUN a port in W Peru, near Lima, on **Callao Bay:** chief import centre of Peru. Pop.: 407 904 (1998 est.).

call box NOUN a soundproof enclosure for a public telephone. Also called: **telephone box, telephone kiosk.**

callboy ('kɔːlˌbɔɪ) NOUN a person who notifies actors when it is time to go on stage.

call centre NOUN an office where staff carry out an organization's telephone transactions.

call down VERB (*tr, adverb*) to request or invoke: *to call down God's anger.*

caller¹ ('kɔːlə) NOUN a person or thing that calls, esp a person who makes a brief visit.

caller² ('kælə; *Scot* 'kælər, 'kɒlər) ADJECTIVE *Scot* 1 (of food, esp fish) fresh. 2 cool: *a caller breeze.*
▷HISTORY C14: perhaps a Scottish variant of *calver* to prepare fresh salmon or trout in a certain way; perhaps from Old English *calwer* curds, from a fancied resemblance with the flaked flesh of the fish

call forth VERB (*tr, adverb*) to cause (something) to come into action or existence: *she called forth all her courage.*

call girl NOUN a prostitute with whom appointments are made by telephone.

calli- COMBINING FORM beautiful: *calligraphy.*
▷HISTORY from Greek *kalli-,* from *kallos* beauty

calligraphy (kə'lɪgrəfɪ) NOUN handwriting, esp beautiful handwriting considered as an art. Also called: **chirography.**
▸**cal'ligrapher** *or* **cal'ligraphist** NOUN ▸**calligraphic** (ˌkælɪ'græfɪk) ADJECTIVE ▸**ˌcalli'graphically** ADVERB

call in VERB (*adverb*) 1 (*intr;* often foll by *on*) to pay a visit, esp a brief or informal one: *call in if you are in the neighbourhood.* 2 (*tr*) to demand payment of: *to call in a loan.* 3 (*tr*) to take (something) out of circulation, because it is defective or no longer useful. 4 (*tr*) to summon to one's assistance: *they had to call in a specialist.*

calling ('kɔːlɪŋ) NOUN 1 a strong inner urge to follow an occupation, etc.; vocation. 2 an occupation, profession, or trade.

calling card NOUN a small card bearing the name and usually the address of a person, esp for giving to business or social acquaintances. Also called: **visiting card.**

calliope (kə'laɪəpɪ) NOUN *US and Canadian* a steam organ.
▷HISTORY C19: after CALLIOPE (literally: beautiful-voiced)

Calliope (kə'laɪəpɪ) NOUN *Greek myth* the Muse of epic poetry.

calliopsis (ˌkælɪ'ɒpsɪs) NOUN another name for **coreopsis.**

callipash ('kælɪˌpæʃ) NOUN a variant spelling of **calipash.**

calliper *or US* **caliper** ('kælɪpə) NOUN 1 (*often plural*) Also called: **calliper compasses.** an instrument for measuring internal or external dimensions, consisting of two steel legs hinged together. 2 Also called: **calliper splint.** *Med* a splint consisting of two metal rods with straps attached, for supporting or exerting tension on the leg. ◆ VERB 3 (*tr*) to measure the dimensions of (an object) with callipers.
▷HISTORY C16: variant of CALIBRE

calliper rule NOUN a measuring instrument having two parallel jaws, one fixed at right angles to the end of a calibrated scale and the other sliding along it.

callipygian (ˌkælɪ'pɪdʒɪən) *or* **callipygous** (ˌkælɪ'paɪgəs) ADJECTIVE having beautifully shaped buttocks.
▷HISTORY C19: from Greek *kallipugos,* epithet of a statue of Aphrodite, from CALLI- + *pugē* buttocks

callistemon (kə'lɪstəmən) NOUN another name for **bottlebrush** (sense 2).

callisthenics *or* **calisthenics** (ˌkælɪs'θɛnɪks) NOUN 1 (*functioning as plural*) light exercises designed to promote general fitness, develop muscle tone, etc. 2 (*functioning as singular*) the practice of callisthenic exercises.
▷HISTORY C19: from CALLI- + Greek *sthenos* strength
▸**ˌcallis'thenic** *or* **ˌcalis'thenic** ADJECTIVE

Callisto¹ (kə'lɪstəʊ) NOUN *Greek myth* a nymph who attracted the love of Zeus and was changed into a bear by Hera. Zeus then set her in the sky as the constellation Ursa Major.

Callisto² (kə'lɪstəʊ) NOUN the second largest (but faintest) of the four Galilean satellites of Jupiter, discovered in 1610 by Galileo. Approximate diameter: 4800 km; orbital radius: 1 883 000 km. See also **Galilean satellite.**

call letters PLURAL NOUN the call sign of an American or Canadian radio station, esp that of a commercial broadcasting station.

call loan NOUN a loan that is repayable on demand. Also called: **demand loan.** Compare **time loan.**

call money NOUN money loaned by banks and recallable on demand.

call number NOUN the number given to a book in a library, indicating its shelf location. Also called: **call mark.**

call off VERB (*tr, adverb*) 1 to cancel or abandon: *the game was called off because of rain.* 2 to order (an animal or person) to desist or summon away: *the man called off his dog.* 3 to stop (something) or give the order to stop.

callop ('kæləp) NOUN an edible freshwater fish, *Plectroplites ambiguus,* of Australia, often golden or pale yellow in colour.
▷HISTORY from a native Australian language

callose ('kæləʊz) NOUN a carbohydrate, a polymer of glucose, found in plants, esp in the sieve tubes.

callosity (kə'lɒsɪtɪ) NOUN, *plural* **-ties.** 1 hardheartedness. 2 another name for **callus** (sense 1).

callous ('kæləs) ADJECTIVE 1 unfeeling; insensitive. 2 (of skin) hardened and thickened. ◆ VERB 3 *Pathol* to make or become callous.
▷HISTORY C16: from Latin *callōsus;* see CALLUS
▸**'callously** ADVERB ▸**'callousness** NOUN

call out VERB (*adverb*) 1 to utter aloud, esp loudly. 2 (*tr*) to summon. 3 (*tr*) to order (workers) to strike. 4 (*tr*) to summon (an employee) to work at a time outside his normal working hours, usually in an emergency.

callow ('kæləʊ) ADJECTIVE 1 lacking experience of life; immature. 2 *Rare* (of a young bird) unfledged and usually lacking feathers.
▷HISTORY Old English *calu;* related to Old High German *kalo,* Old Slavonic *golŭ* bare, naked, Lithuanian *galva* head, Latin *calvus* bald
▸**'callowness** NOUN

call rate NOUN the interest rate on a call loan.

call sign NOUN a group of letters and numbers identifying a radio transmitting station, esp an amateur radio station. Compare **call letters.**

call slip NOUN a form for requesting a library book by title and call number. Also called: **call card, requisition form.**

call up VERB (*adverb*) 1 to summon to report for active military service, as in time of war. 2 (*tr*) to recall (something); evoke: *his words called up old memories.* 3 (*tr*) to bring or summon (people, etc.) into action: *to call up reinforcements.* ◆ NOUN **call-up.** 4 **a** a general order to report for military service. **b** the number of men so summoned.

callus ('kæləs) NOUN, *plural* **luses.** 1 Also called: **callosity.** an area of skin that is hard or thick, esp on the palm of the hand or sole of the foot, as from continual friction or pressure. 2 an area of bony tissue formed during the healing of a fractured bone. 3 *Botany* **a** a mass of hard protective tissue produced in woody plants at the site of an injury. **b** an accumulation of callose in the sieve tubes. 4 *Biotechnology* a mass of undifferentiated cells produced as the first stage in tissue culture. ◆ VERB 5 to produce or cause to produce a callus.
▷HISTORY C16: from Latin, variant of *callum* hardened skin

calm (kɑːm) ADJECTIVE 1 almost without motion; still: *a calm sea.* 2 *Meteorol* of force 0 on the Beaufort scale; without wind. 3 not disturbed, agitated, or excited; under control: *he stayed calm throughout the confusion.* 4 tranquil; serene: *a calm voice.* ◆ NOUN 5 an absence of disturbance or rough motion; stillness. 6 absence of wind. 7 tranquillity. ◆ VERB 8 (often foll by *down*) to make or become calm.
▷HISTORY C14: from Old French *calme,* from Old Italian *calma,* from Late Latin *cauma* heat, hence a rest during the heat of the day, from Greek *kauma* heat, from *kaiein* to burn
▸**'calmly** ADVERB ▸**'calmness** NOUN

calmative ('kælmətɪv, 'kɑːmə-) ADJECTIVE 1 (of a remedy or agent) sedative. ◆ NOUN 2 a sedative remedy or drug.

calmodulin (kəl'mɒdjʊlɪn) NOUN *Biochem* a

protein found in most living cells; it regulates many enzymic processes that are dependent on calcium.
▷**HISTORY** from CAL(CIUM) + MODUL(ATE) + -IN

calomel ('kælə,mɛl, -məl) NOUN a colourless tasteless powder consisting chiefly of mercurous chloride, used medicinally, esp as a cathartic. Formula: Hg_2Cl_2.
▷**HISTORY** C17: perhaps from New Latin *calomelas* (unattested), literally: beautiful black (perhaps so named because it was originally sublimed from a black mixture of mercury and mercuric chloride), from Greek *kalos* beautiful + *melas* black

calorescence (,kælə'rɛsəns) NOUN *Physics* the absorption of radiation by a body, subsequently re-emitted at a higher frequency (lower wavelength).
▸**,calo'rescent** ADJECTIVE

Calor Gas ('kælə) NOUN *Trademark* butane gas liquefied under pressure in portable containers for domestic use.

caloric (kə'lɒrɪk, 'kælərɪk) ADJECTIVE [1] of or concerned with heat or calories. ◆ NOUN [2] *Obsolete* a hypothetical elastic fluid formerly postulated as the embodiment of heat.
▸**caloricity** (,kælə'rɪsɪtɪ) NOUN

calorie *or* **calory** ('kælərɪ) NOUN, *plural* **-ries.** a unit of heat, equal to 4.1868 joules (**International Table calorie**): formerly defined as the quantity of heat required to raise the temperature of 1 gram of water by 1°C under standard conditions. It has now largely been replaced by the joule for scientific purposes. Abbreviation: **cal.** Also called: **gram calorie, small calorie.** Compare **Calorie.**
▷**HISTORY** C19: from French, from Latin *calor* heat

Calorie ('kælərɪ) NOUN [1] Also called: **kilogram calorie, kilocalorie, large calorie.** a unit of heat, equal to one thousand calories, often used to express the heat output of an organism or the energy value of food. Abbreviation: **Cal.** [2] the amount of a specific food capable of producing one thousand calories of energy.

calorific (,kælə'rɪfɪk) ADJECTIVE of, concerning, or generating heat.
▸**,calo'rifically** ADVERB

calorific value NOUN the quantity of heat produced by the complete combustion of a given mass of a fuel, usually expressed in joules per kilogram.

calorimeter (,kælə'rɪmɪtə) NOUN an apparatus for measuring amounts of heat, esp to find specific heat capacities, calorific values, etc.
▸**calorimetric** (,kælərɪ'mɛtrɪk) *or* **,calori'metrical** ADJECTIVE ▸**,calori'metrically** ADVERB ▸**,calo'rimetry** NOUN

calorize ('kælə,raɪz) VERB (*tr*) to coat (a ferrous metal) by spraying with aluminium powder and then heating.

calotte (kə'lɒt) NOUN [1] a skullcap worn by Roman Catholic clergy. [2] *Architect* a concavity in the form of a niche or cup, serving to reduce the apparent height of an alcove or chapel.
▷**HISTORY** C17: from French, from Provençal *calota,* perhaps from Greek *kaluptra* hood

calotype ('kæləʊ,taɪp) NOUN [1] an early photographic process invented by W. H. Fox Talbot, in which the image was produced on paper treated with silver iodide and developed by sodium thiosulphite. [2] a photograph made by this process.
▷**HISTORY** C19: from Greek *kalos* beautiful + -TYPE

caloyer ('kælɔɪə) NOUN a monk of the Greek Orthodox Church, esp of the Basilian Order.
▷**HISTORY** C17: from French, from Medieval Greek *kalogēros* venerable, from Greek *kalos* beautiful + *gēras* old age

calpac, calpack, *or* **kalpak** ('kælpæk) NOUN a large black brimless hat made of sheepskin or felt, worn by men in parts of the Near East.
▷**HISTORY** C16: from Turkish *kalpāk*

Calpe ('kælpɪ) NOUN the ancient name for (the Rock of) **Gibraltar.**

calque (kælk) NOUN [1] another word for **loan translation.** ◆ VERB **calques, calquing, calqued.** [2] (*tr*) another word for **calk**[3].
▷**HISTORY** C20: from French: a tracing, from *calquer,* from Latin *calcāre* to tread

Caltanissetta (*Italian* kaltanis'sɛtta) NOUN a city in central Sicily: sulphur mines. Pop.: 60 000 (latest est.).

Caltech ('kæl,tɛk) NOUN the California Institute of Technology.

caltrop, caltrap ('kæltrəp), *or* **calthrop** ('kælθrəp) NOUN [1] any tropical or subtropical plant of the zygophyllaceous genera *Tribulus* and *Kallstroemia* that have spiny burs or bracts. [2] **water caltrop.** another name for **water chestnut** (sense 1). [3] another name for the **star thistle.** [4] *Military* a four-spiked iron ball or four joined spikes laid upon the ground as a device to lame cavalry horses, puncture tyres, etc.
▷**HISTORY** Old English *calcatrippe* (the plant), from Medieval Latin *calcatrippa,* probably from Latin *calx* heel + *trippa* TRAP[1]

calumet ('kælju,mɛt) NOUN a less common name for **peace pipe.**
▷**HISTORY** C18: from Canadian French, from French (Normandy dialect): straw, from Late Latin *calamellus* a little reed, from Latin: CALAMUS

calumniate (kə'lʌmnɪ,eɪt) VERB (*tr*) to slander.
▸**ca'lumniable** ADJECTIVE ▸**ca,lumni'ation** NOUN
▸**ca'lumni,ator** NOUN

calumnious (kə'lʌmnɪəs) *or* **calumniatory** (kə'lʌmnɪətərɪ, -trɪ) ADJECTIVE [1] of or using calumny. [2] (of a person) given to calumny.

calumny ('kæləmnɪ) NOUN, *plural* **-nies.** [1] the malicious utterance of false charges or misrepresentation; slander; defamation. [2] such a false charge or misrepresentation.
▷**HISTORY** C15: from Latin *calumnia* deception, slander

calutron ('kælju,trɒn) NOUN a device used for the separation of isotopes.
▷**HISTORY** C20: from Cal(ifornia) U(niversity) + -TRON

Calvados ('kælvə,dɒs) NOUN [1] a department of N France in the Basse-Normandie region. Capital: Caen. Pop.: 648 385 (1999). Area: 5693 sq. km (2198 sq. miles). [2] an apple brandy distilled from cider in this region.

calvaria (kæl'vɛərɪə) NOUN the top part of the skull of vertebrates. Nontechnical name: **skullcap.**
▷**HISTORY** C14: from Late Latin: (human) skull, from Latin *calvus* bald

calvary ('kælvərɪ) NOUN, *plural* **-ries.** [1] (*often capital*) a representation of Christ's crucifixion, usually sculptured and in the open air. [2] any experience involving great suffering.

Calvary ('kælvərɪ) NOUN the place just outside the walls of Jerusalem where Jesus was crucified. Also called: **Golgotha.**
▷**HISTORY** from Late Latin *Calvāria,* translation of Greek *kranion* skull, translation of Aramaic *gulgulta* Golgotha

Calvary cross NOUN a Latin cross with a representation of three steps beneath it.

calve (kɑːv) VERB [1] to give birth to (a calf). [2] (of a glacier or iceberg) to release (masses of ice) in breaking up.

calves (kɑːvz) NOUN the plural of **calf**[1] and **calf**[2].

Calvin cycle NOUN *Botany* a series of reactions, occurring during photosynthesis, in which glucose is synthesized from carbon dioxide.
▷**HISTORY** C20: named after Melvin *Calvin* (1911–97), US chemist, who elucidated it

Calvinism ('kælvɪ,nɪzəm) NOUN the theological system of John Calvin (original name *Jean Cauvin, Caulvin,* or *Chauvin.*; 1509–64), the French theologian and leader of the Protestant Reformation, and his followers, characterized by emphasis on the doctrines of predestination, the irresistibility of grace, and justification by faith.
▸**'Calvinist** NOUN, ADJECTIVE ▸**,Calvin'istic** *or* **,Calvin'istical** ADJECTIVE

calvities (kæl'vɪʃɪ,iːz) NOUN baldness.
▷**HISTORY** C17: from Late Latin, from Latin *calvus* bald

calx (kælks) NOUN, *plural* **calxes** *or* **calces** ('kælsiːz). [1] the powdery metallic oxide formed when an ore or mineral is roasted. [2] another name for **calcium oxide.** [3] *Anatomy* the heel.
▷**HISTORY** C15: from Latin: lime, from Greek *khalix* pebble

calyces ('kælɪ,siːz, 'keɪlɪ-) NOUN a plural of **calyx.**

calycine ('kælɪ,saɪn) *or* **calycinal** (kə'lɪsɪnᵊl) ADJECTIVE relating to, belonging to, or resembling a calyx.

calycle, calicle ('kælɪkᵊl), *or* **calyculus** (kə'lɪkjʊləs) NOUN [1] *Zoology* a cup-shaped structure, as in the coral skeleton. [2] *Botany* another name for **epicalyx.**
▷**HISTORY** C18: from Latin, diminutive of CALYX
▸**calycular** (kə'lɪkjʊlə) ADJECTIVE

Calydonian boar (,kælɪ'dəʊnɪən) NOUN *Greek myth* a savage boar sent by Artemis to destroy Calydon, a city in Aetolia, because its king had neglected to sacrifice to her. It was killed by Meleager, the king's son.

calypso[1] (kə'lɪpsəʊ) NOUN, *plural* **-sos.** [1] a popular type of satirical, usually topical, West Indian ballad, esp from Trinidad, usually extemporized to a percussive syncopated accompaniment. [2] a dance done to the rhythm of this song.
▷**HISTORY** C20: probably from CALYPSO

calypso[2] (kə'lɪpsəʊ) NOUN, *plural* **-sos.** a rare N temperate orchid, *Calypso* (or *Cytherea*) *bulbosa,* whose flower is pink or white with purple and yellow markings.
▷**HISTORY** C19: named after CALYPSO

Calypso (kə'lɪpsəʊ) NOUN *Greek myth* (in Homer's *Odyssey*) a sea nymph who detained Odysseus on the island of Ogygia for seven years.

calypsonian (,kælɪp'səʊnɪən) NOUN a performer or writer of calypsos.

calyptra (kə'lɪptrə) NOUN *Botany* [1] a membranous hood covering the spore-bearing capsule of mosses and liverworts. [2] any hoodlike structure, such as a root cap.
▷**HISTORY** C18: from New Latin, from Greek *kaluptra* hood, from *kaluptein* to cover
▸**calyptrate** (kə'lɪp,treɪt) ADJECTIVE

calyptrogen (kə'lɪptrədʒən) NOUN a layer of rapidly dividing cells at the tip of a plant root, from which the root cap is formed. It occurs in grasses and many other plants.
▷**HISTORY** C19: from CALYPTRA + -GEN

calyx ('keɪlɪks, 'kælɪks) NOUN, *plural* **calyxes** *or* **calyces** ('kælɪ,siːz, 'keɪlɪ-). [1] the sepals of a flower collectively, forming the outer floral envelope that protects the developing flower bud. Compare **corolla.** [2] any cup-shaped cavity or structure, esp any of the divisions of the human kidney (**renal calyx**) that form the renal pelvis.
▷**HISTORY** C17: from Latin, from Greek *kalux* shell, from *kaluptein* to cover, hide
▸**calycate** ('kælɪ,keɪt) ADJECTIVE

calzone (kæl'tsəʊnɪ) NOUN a dish of Italian origin consisting of pizza dough folded over a filling of cheese and tomatoes, herbs, ham, etc.
▷**HISTORY** C20: Italian, literally: trouser leg, from *calzoni* trousers

-cam NOUN COMBINING FORM camera: *webcam.*

cam (kæm) NOUN a slider or roller attached to a rotating shaft to give a particular type of reciprocating motion to a part in contact with its profile.
▷**HISTORY** C18: from Dutch *kam* comb

Cam (kæm) NOUN a river in E England, in Cambridgeshire, flowing through Cambridge to the River Ouse. Length: about 64 km (40 miles).

CAM ABBREVIATION FOR [1] computer-aided manufacture. [2] *Botany* **a** crassulacean acid metabolism: a form of photosynthesis, first described in crassulaceous plants, in which carbon dioxide is taken up only at night. **b** (*as modifier*): *a CAM plant.* [3] complementary and alternative medicine. ◆ [4] INTERNATIONAL CAR REGISTRATION FOR Cameroon.

cama ('kɑːmə) NOUN the hybrid offspring of a camel and a llama.

Camagüey ('kæmə,gweɪ; *Spanish* kama'ɣwej) NOUN a city in E central Cuba. Pop.: 293 961 (1994 est.).

camail ('kæmeɪl) NOUN *Armour* a neck and shoulders covering of mail worn with and laced to the basinet.

caman ('kæmən) NOUN *Shinty* the wooden stick used to hit the ball.
▷**HISTORY** C19: from Gaelic

camaraderie (,kæmə'rɑːdərɪ) NOUN a spirit of familiarity and trust existing between friends.
▷**HISTORY** C19: from French, from COMRADE

Camargue (kæ'mɑːg) NOUN **la** (la). a delta region in S France, between the channels of the Grand and

Petit Rhône: cattle, esp bulls for the Spanish bullrings, and horses are reared.

camarilla (ˌkæməˈrɪlə; *Spanish* kamaˈriʎa) NOUN a group of confidential advisers, esp formerly, to the Spanish kings; cabal.
▷HISTORY C19: from Spanish: literally: a little room

camass *or* **camas** (ˈkæmæs) NOUN [1] Also called: **quamash.** any of several North American plants of the liliaceous genus *Camassia,* esp *C. quamash,* which has a cluster of blue or white flowers and a sweet edible bulb. [2] **death camass.** any liliaceous plant of the genus *Zygadenus* (or *Zigadenus*), of the western US, that is poisonous to livestock, esp sheep.
▷HISTORY C19: from Chinook Jargon *kamass,* from Nootka *chamas* sweet

Camb. ABBREVIATION FOR Cambridge.

Cambay (kæmˈbeɪ) NOUN **Gulf of.** an inlet of the Arabian Sea on the W coast of India, southeast of the Kathiawar Peninsula.

camber (ˈkæmbə) NOUN [1] a slight upward curve to the centre of the surface of a road, ship's deck, etc. [2] another name for **bank**[2] (sense 7). [3] an outward inclination of the front wheels of a road vehicle so that they are slightly closer together at the bottom than at the top. [4] Also called: **hog.** a small arching curve of a beam or girder provided to lessen deflection and improve appearance. [5] aerofoil curvature expressed by the ratio of the maximum height of the aerofoil mean line to its chord. ◆ VERB [6] to form or be formed with a surface that curves upwards to its centre.
▷HISTORY C17: from Old French (northern dialect) *cambre* curved, from Latin *camurus;* related to *camera* CHAMBER

Camberwell beauty (ˈkæmbəˌwel, -wəl) NOUN a nymphalid butterfly, *Nymphalis antiopa,* of temperate regions, having dark purple wings with cream-yellow borders. US name: **mourning cloak.**
▷HISTORY C19: named after *Camberwell,* a district of S London

Camberwell carrot NOUN *Informal* a large, almost conical, marijuana cigarette.

cambist (ˈkæmbɪst) NOUN *Finance* [1] a dealer or expert in foreign exchange. [2] a manual of currency exchange rates and similar equivalents of weights and measures.
▷HISTORY C19: from French *cambiste,* from Italian *cambista,* from *cambio* (money) exchange
▸ **ˈcambistry** NOUN

cambium (ˈkæmbɪəm) NOUN, *plural* **-biums** *or* **-bia** (-bɪə). *Botany* a meristem that increases the girth of stems and roots by producing additional xylem and phloem. See also **cork cambium.**
▷HISTORY C17: from Medieval Latin: exchange, from Late Latin *cambiāre* to exchange, barter
▸ **ˈcambial** ADJECTIVE

Cambodia (kæmˈbəʊdɪə) NOUN a country in SE Asia: became part of French Indochina in 1887; achieved self-government in 1949 and independence in 1953; civil war (1970–74) ended in victory for the Khmer Rouge, who renamed the country Kampuchea (1975); Vietnamese forces ousted the Khmer Rouge in 1979 and set up a pro-Vietnamese government who reverted (1981) to the name Cambodia; in 1982 exiled factions formed the Coalition Government of Democratic Kampuchea (CGDK); after the Vietnamese withdrawal in 1989 CGDK guerrillas continued to engage government forces; a peace settlement was followed in 1993 by elections and the adoption of a democratic monarchist constitution restoring Sihanouk to the throne: contains the central plains of the Mekong River and the Cardamom Mountains in the SW. Official language: Khmer; French is also widely spoken. Currency: riel. Capital: Phnom Penh. Pop.: 12 720 000 (2001 est.). Area: 181 000 sq. km (69 895 sq. miles).

Cambodian (kæmˈbəʊdɪən) ADJECTIVE [1] of or relating to Cambodia or its inhabitants. ◆ NOUN [2] a native or inhabitant of Cambodia.

cambogia (kæmˈbəʊdʒɪə) NOUN another name for **gamboge** (senses 1, 2).

camboose (kæmˈbuːs) NOUN (formerly, in Canada) [1] a cabin built as living quarters for a gang of lumbermen. [2] an open fireplace in such a cabin.
▷HISTORY C19: from Canadian French, from French *cambuse* hut, store, from Dutch *kambuis*

Camborne-Redruth (ˈkæmbɔːnˈrɛdˌruːθ) NOUN a former (until 1974) urban district in SW England, in Cornwall: formed in 1934 by the amalgamation of the neighbouring towns of Camborne and Redruth. Pop.: 35 915 (1991).

Cambrai (*French* kɑ̃brɛ) NOUN a town in NE France: textile industry: scene of a battle in which massed tanks were first used and broke through the German line (November, 1917). Pop.: 34 210 (1990).

cambrel (ˈkæmbrəl) NOUN a variant of **gambrel.**

Cambria (ˈkæmbrɪə) NOUN the Medieval Latin name for **Wales.**

Cambrian (ˈkæmbrɪən) ADJECTIVE [1] of, denoting, or formed in the first 65 million years of the Palaeozoic era, during which marine invertebrates, esp trilobites, flourished. [2] of or relating to Wales. ◆ NOUN [3] **the.** the Cambrian period or rock system. [4] a Welshman.

Cambrian Mountains PLURAL NOUN a mountain range in Wales, extending from Carmarthenshire in the S to Denbighshire in the N. Highest peak: Aran Fawddwy, 891 m (2970 ft.).

cambric (ˈkeɪmbrɪk) NOUN a fine white linen or cotton fabric.
▷HISTORY C16: from Flemish *Kamerijk* CAMBRAI

Cambridge (ˈkeɪmbrɪdʒ) NOUN [1] a city in E England, administrative centre of Cambridgeshire, on the River Cam: centred around the university, founded in the 12th century: electronics, biotechnology. Pop.: 113 800 (1994 est.). Medieval Latin name: **Cantabrigia.** [2] short for **Cambridgeshire.** [3] a city in the US, in E Massachusetts: educational centre, with Harvard University (1636) and the Massachusetts Institute of Technology. Pop.: 101 355 (2000). Related adjective: **Cantabrigian.**

Cambridge blue NOUN [1] **a** a lightish blue colour. **b** (*as adjective*): *a Cambridge-blue scarf.* [2] a person who has been awarded a blue from Cambridge University.

Cambridgeshire (ˈkeɪmbrɪdʒˌʃɪə, -ʃə) NOUN a county of E England, in East Anglia: includes the former counties of the Isle of Ely and Huntingdon and lies largely in the Fens: Peterborough became an independent unitary authority in 1998. Administrative centre: Cambridge. Pop. (excluding Peterborough): 552 655 (2001). Area (excluding Peterborough): 3068 sq. km (184 sq. miles).

Cambs ABBREVIATION FOR Cambridgeshire.

camcorder (ˈkæmˌkɔːdə) NOUN a video camera and recorder combined in a portable unit.

Camden (ˈkæmdən) NOUN a borough of N Greater London. Pop.: 198 027 (2001 est.). Area: 21 sq. km (8 sq. miles).

came[1] (keɪm) VERB the past tense of **come.**

came[2] (keɪm) NOUN a grooved strip of lead used to join pieces of glass in a stained-glass window or a leaded light.
▷HISTORY C17: of unknown origin

camel (ˈkæməl) NOUN [1] either of two cud-chewing artiodactyl mammals of the genus *Camelus* (see **Arabian camel, Bactrian camel**): family *Camelidae.* They are adapted for surviving long periods without food or water in desert regions, esp by using humps on the back for storing fat. [2] a float attached to a vessel to increase its buoyancy. See also **caisson** (sense 3). [3] a raft or float used as a fender between a vessel and a wharf. [4] **a** a fawn colour. **b** (*as adjective*): *a camel dress.*
▷HISTORY Old English, from Latin *camēlus,* from Greek *kamēlos,* of Semitic origin; related to Arabic *jamal*

cameleer (ˌkæmɪˈlɪə) NOUN a camel-driver.

camel hair *or* **camel's hair** NOUN [1] the hair of the camel or dromedary, used in clothing, rugs, etc. [2] **a** soft cloth made of or containing this hair or a substitute, usually tan in colour. **b** (*as modifier*): *a camelhair coat.* [3] **a** the hair of the squirrel's tail, used for paintbrushes. **b** (*as modifier*): *a camelhair brush.*

camelid (kəˈmɛlɪd) ADJECTIVE [1] of or relating to camels. [2] belonging to the camel family, *Camelidae.* ◆ NOUN [3] any animal of the camel family.

camellia (kəˈmiːlɪə) NOUN any ornamental shrub of the Asian genus *Camellia,* esp *C. japonica,* having glossy evergreen leaves and showy roselike flowers, usually white, pink or red in colour: family *Theaceae.* Also called: **japonica.**
▷HISTORY C18: New Latin, named after Georg Josef *Kamel* (1661–1706), Moravian Jesuit missionary, who introduced it to Europe

camelopard (ˈkæmɪləˌpɑːd, kəˈmɛl-) NOUN an obsolete word for **giraffe.**
▷HISTORY C14: from Medieval Latin *camēlopardus,* from Greek *kamēlopardalis,* from *kamēlos* CAMEL + *pardalis* LEOPARD, because the giraffe was thought to have a head like a camel's and spots like a leopard's

Camelopardus (kəˌmɛləˈpɑːdəs) *or* **Camelopardalis** (kəˌmɛləˈpɑːdəlɪs) NOUN, *Latin genitive* **Camelopardi** (kəˌmɛləˈpɑːdaɪ) *or* **Camelopardalis** (kəˌmɛləˈpɑːdəlɪs). a faint extensive constellation in the N hemisphere close to Ursa Major and Cassiopeia.

Camelot (ˈkæmɪˌlɒt) NOUN [1] (in Arthurian legend) the English town where King Arthur's palace and court were situated. [2] (in the US) the supposedly golden age of the presidency of John F. Kennedy, 1961–63.

camel's hair NOUN See **camel hair.**

Camembert (ˈkæməmˌbɛə; *French* kamɑ̃bɛr) NOUN a rich soft creamy cheese.
▷HISTORY French, from *Camembert,* a village in Normandy where it originated

Camenae (kəˈmiːniː) PLURAL NOUN *Roman myth* a group of nymphs originally associated with a sacred spring in Rome, later identified with the Greek Muses.

cameo (ˈkæmɪˌəʊ) NOUN, *plural* **cameos.** [1] **a** a medallion, as on a brooch or ring, with a profile head carved in relief. **b** (*as modifier*): *a cameo necklace.* [2] an engraving upon a gem or other stone of at least two differently coloured layers, such as sardonyx, so carved that the background is of a different colour from the raised design. [3] a stone with such an engraving. [4] **a** a single and often brief dramatic scene played by a well-known actor or actress in a film or television play. **b** (*as modifier*): *a cameo role.* [5] **a** a short literary work or dramatic sketch. **b** (*as modifier*): *a cameo sketch.*
▷HISTORY C15: from Italian *cammeo,* of uncertain origin

cameo ware NOUN jasper ware with applied decoration of classical motifs, resembling a cameo.

camera (ˈkæmərə, ˈkæmrə) NOUN [1] an optical device consisting of a lens system set in a light-proof construction inside which a light-sensitive film or plate can be positioned. See also **cine camera, digital camera.** [2] *Television* the equipment used to convert the optical image of a scene into the corresponding electrical signals. [3] See **camera obscura.** [4] (*plural* **-erae** (-əˌriː)) a judge's private room. [5] **in camera. a** *Law* relating to a hearing from which members of the public are excluded. **b** in private. [6] **off camera.** not within an area being filmed. [7] **on camera.** (esp of an actor) being filmed.
▷HISTORY C18: from Latin: vault, from Greek *kamara*

cameral (ˈkæmərəl) ADJECTIVE of or relating to a judicial or legislative chamber.
▷HISTORY C18: from Medieval Latin *camerālis;* see CAMERA

camera lucida (ˈluːsɪdə) NOUN an instrument attached to a microscope, etc. to enable an observer to view simultaneously the image and a drawing surface to facilitate the sketching of the image.
▷HISTORY New Latin: light chamber

cameraman (ˈkæmərəˌmæn, ˈkæmrə-) NOUN, *plural* **-men.** a person who operates a film or television camera.

camera obscura (ɒbˈskjʊərə) NOUN a darkened chamber or small building in which images of outside objects are projected onto a flat surface by a convex lens in an aperture. Sometimes shortened to **camera.**
▷HISTORY New Latin: dark chamber

camera-ready copy NOUN *Printing* type matter ready to be photographed for plate-making without further alteration. Also called: **mechanical.**

camera-shy ADJECTIVE having an aversion to being photographed or filmed.

caméra stylo (*French* kamera stilo) NOUN *Films* the use of the camera as a means of personal expression, especially as practised by some directors of the New Wave.
▷HISTORY French, literally: camera stylograph

camera tube NOUN the part of a television camera that converts an optical image into an electrical signal. See also **image orthicon, vidicon, Plumbicon, iconoscope.**

camerlengo (ˌkæməˈlɛŋgəʊ) *or* **camerlingo** (ˌkæməˈlɪŋgəʊ) NOUN, *plural* **-gos.** *RC Church* a cardinal who acts as the pope's financial secretary and the papal treasurer.
▷HISTORY C17: from Italian *camerlingo,* of Germanic origin; compare CHAMBERLAIN

Cameroon (ˌkæməˈruːn, ˈkæməˌruːn) NOUN 1 a republic in West Africa, on the Gulf of Guinea: became a German colony in 1884; divided in 1919 into the **Cameroons** (administered by Britain) and **Cameroun** (administered by France); Cameroun and the S part of the Cameroons formed a republic in 1961 (the N part joined Nigeria); became a member of the Commonwealth in 1995. Official languages: French and English. Religions: Christian, Muslim, and animist. Currency: franc. Capital: Yaoundé. Pop.: 15 803 000 (2001 est.). Area: 475 500 sq. km (183 591 sq. miles). French name: **Cameroun.** German name: **Kamerun.** 2 an active volcano in W Cameroon: the highest peak on the West African coast. Height: 4070 m (13 352 ft.).

Cameroun (kamrun) NOUN the French name for **Cameroon.**

cam follower NOUN *Engineering* the slider or roller in contact with the cam that transmits the movement dictated by the cam profile.

camiknickers (ˈkæmɪˌnɪkəz) PLURAL NOUN women's knickers attached to a camisole top. Often shortened to **camiknicks.**

camion (ˈkæmɪən; *French* kamjɔ̃) NOUN a lorry, or, esp formerly, a large dray.
▷HISTORY C19: from French, of obscure origin

camisado (ˌkæmɪˈsɑːdəʊ) *or* **camisade** (ˌkæmɪˈseɪd) NOUN, *plural* **-sados** *or* **-sades.** (formerly) an attack made under cover of darkness.
▷HISTORY C16: from obsolete Spanish *camisada,* literally: an attack in one's shirt (worn over the armour as identification), from *camisa* shirt

camise (kəˈmiːz) NOUN a loose light shirt, smock, or tunic originally worn in the Middle Ages.
▷HISTORY C19: from Arabic *qamīs,* from Late Latin *camīsia*

camisole (ˈkæmɪˌsəʊl) NOUN 1 a woman's underbodice with shoulder straps, originally designed as a cover for a corset. 2 a woman's dressing jacket or short negligée. 3 (*modifier*) resembling a camisole (the underbodice), as in fitting snugly around the bust and having a straight neckline: *a camisole slip*; *a camisole top.*
▷HISTORY C19: from French, from Provençal *camisola,* from *camisa* shirt, from Late Latin *camīsia*

camlet (ˈkæmlɪt) NOUN 1 a tough waterproof cloth. 2 a garment or garments made from such cloth. 3 a soft woollen fabric used in medieval Asia.
▷HISTORY C14: from Old French *camelot,* perhaps from Arabic *hamlat* plush fabric

camo (ˈkæməʊ) NOUN *Informal* short for **camouflage** (sense 2): *camo fatigues.*

camogie (kaˈmoːgiː) NOUN *Irish* a form of hurling played by women.
▷HISTORY from Irish Gaelic *camógaíocht,* from *camóg* crooked stick

camomile *or* **chamomile** (ˈkæməˌmaɪl) NOUN 1 any aromatic plant of the Eurasian genus *Anthemis,* esp *A. nobilis,* whose finely dissected leaves and daisy-like flowers are used medicinally: family *Asteraceae* (composites). 2 any plant of the related genus *Matricaria,* esp *M. chamomilla* (**German** or **wild camomile**). 3 **camomile tea.** a medicinal beverage made from the fragrant leaves and flowers of any of these plants.
▷HISTORY C14: from Old French *camomille,* from Medieval Latin *chamomilla,* from Greek *khamaimēlon,* literally, earth-apple (referring to the apple-like scent of the flowers)

camoodi (kæˈmuːdɪ) NOUN a Caribbean name for **anaconda.**
▷HISTORY C19: from an American Indian language of Guyana

Camorra (kəˈmɒrə) NOUN 1 a secret society organized in about 1820 in Naples, which thrives on blackmail and extortion. 2 any similar clandestine group.
▷HISTORY C19: from Italian, probably from Spanish: quarrel

camouflage (ˈkæməˌflɑːʒ) NOUN 1 the exploitation of natural surroundings or artificial aids to conceal or disguise the presence of military units, equipment, etc. 2 (*modifier*) (of fabric or clothing) having a design of irregular patches of dull colours (such as browns and greens), as used in military camouflage. 3 the means by which animals escape the notice of predators, usually because of a resemblance to their surroundings: includes cryptic and apatetic coloration. 4 a device or expedient designed to conceal or deceive. ◆ VERB 5 (*tr*) to conceal by camouflage.
▷HISTORY C20: from French, from *camoufler,* from Italian *camuffare* to disguise, deceive, of uncertain origin

camp¹ (kæmp) NOUN 1 a place where tents, cabins, or other temporary structures are erected for the use of military troops, for training soldiers, etc. 2 the military life. 3 tents, cabins, etc., used as temporary lodgings by a group of travellers, holiday-makers, Scouts, Gypsies, etc. 4 the group of people living in such lodgings. 5 *South African* a field or paddock fenced off as pasture. 6 a group supporting a given doctrine or theory: *the socialist camp.* 7 (*modifier*) suitable for use in temporary quarters, on holiday, etc., esp by being portable and easy to set up: *a camp bed*; *a camp chair.* ◆ VERB 8 (*intr*; often foll by *down*) to establish or set up a camp. 9 (*intr*; often foll by *out*) to live temporarily in or as if in a tent. 10 (*tr*) to put in a camp.
▷HISTORY C16: from Old French, ultimately from Latin *campus* field
▶ˈ**camping** NOUN

camp² (kæmp) *Informal* ◆ ADJECTIVE 1 effeminate; affected in mannerisms, dress, etc. 2 homosexual. 3 consciously artificial, exaggerated, vulgar, or mannered; self-parodying, esp when in dubious taste. ◆ VERB 4 (*tr*) to perform or invest with a camp quality. 5 **camp it up. a** to seek to focus attention on oneself by making an ostentatious display, overacting, etc. **b** to flaunt one's homosexuality. ◆ NOUN 6 a camp quality, style, etc.
▷HISTORY C20: of uncertain origin

campagna (kæmˈpɑːnjə) NOUN another word for **champaign** (sense 1).

Campagna (kæmˈpɑːnjə) NOUN a low-lying plain surrounding Rome, Italy: once fertile, it deteriorated to malarial marshes; recently reclaimed. Area: about 2000 sq. km (800 sq. miles). Also called: **Campagna di Roma** (dɪ ˈrəʊmə).

campaign (kæmˈpeɪn) NOUN 1 a series of coordinated activities, such as public speaking and demonstrating, designed to achieve a social, political, or commercial goal: *a presidential campaign; an advertising campaign.* 2 *Military* a number of complementary operations aimed at achieving a single objective, usually constrained by time or geographic area. ◆ VERB 3 (*intr*; often foll by *for*) to conduct, serve in, or go on a campaign.
▷HISTORY C17: from French *campagne* open country, from Italian *campagna,* from Late Latin *campānia,* from Latin *campus* field
▶**camˈpaigner** NOUN

Campania (kæmˈpeɪnɪə; *Italian* kamˈpaɲɲa) NOUN a region of SW Italy: includes the islands of Capri and Ischia. Chief town: Naples. Pop.: 5 780 958 (2000 est.). Area: 13 595 sq. km (5248 sq. miles).

campanile (ˌkæmpəˈniːlɪ) NOUN (esp in Italy) a bell tower, not usually attached to another building. Compare **belfry.**
▷HISTORY C17: from Italian, from *campana* bell

campanology (ˌkæmpəˈnɒlədʒɪ) NOUN the art or skill of ringing bells musically.
▷HISTORY C19: from New Latin *campānologia,* from Late Latin *campāna* bell
▶**campanological** (ˌkæmpənəˈlɒdʒɪkᵊl) ADJECTIVE
▶ˌ**campaˈnologist** *or* ˌ**campaˈnologer** NOUN

campanula (kæmˈpænjʊlə) NOUN any N temperate plant of the campanulaceous genus *Campanula,* typically having blue or white bell-shaped flowers. Also called: **bellflower.** See also **Canterbury bell, harebell.**
▷HISTORY C17: from New Latin: a little bell, from Late Latin *campāna* bell; see CAMPANILE

campanulaceous (kəmˌpænjʊˈleɪʃəs) ADJECTIVE of, relating to, or belonging to the *Campanulaceae,* a family of temperate and subtropical plants, including the campanulas, having bell-shaped nodding flowers.

campanulate (kæmˈpænjʊlɪt, -ˌleɪt) ADJECTIVE (esp of flower corollas) shaped like a bell.
▷HISTORY C17: from New Latin *campanulātus;* see CAMPANULA

Campbell-Stokes recorder (ˌkæmbəlˈstəʊks) NOUN an instrument for recording hours of sunshine per day, consisting of a solid glass sphere that focuses rays of sunlight onto a light-sensitive card on which a line is burnt.

Camp David (ˈdeɪvɪd) NOUN the US president's retreat in the Appalachian Mountains, Maryland: scene of the **Camp David Agreement** (Sept., 1978) between Anwar Sadat of Egypt and Menachem Begin of Israel, mediated by Jimmy Carter, which outlined a framework for establishing peace in the Middle East. This agreement was the basis of the peace treaty between Israel and Egypt signed in Washington (March, 1979).

camp-drafting NOUN *Austral* a competitive test, esp at an agricultural show, of horsemen's skill in drafting cattle.

Campeche (*Spanish* kamˈpetʃe) NOUN 1 a state of SE Mexico, on the SW of the Yucatán peninsula: forestry and fishing. Capital: Campeche. Pop.: 689 656 (2000 est.). Area: 56 114 sq. km (21 666 sq. miles). 2 a port in SE Mexico, capital of Campeche state. Pop.: 195 000 (2000 est.). 3 **Bay of.** Also called: **Gulf of Campeche.** the SW part of the Gulf of Mexico.

camper (ˈkæmpə) NOUN 1 a person who lives or temporarily stays in a tent, cabin, etc. 2 a vehicle equipped for camping out.

camper van NOUN a motor caravan.

campestral (kæmˈpɛstrəl) ADJECTIVE of or relating to open fields or country.
▷HISTORY C18: from Latin *campester,* from *campus* field

campfire (ˈkæmpˌfaɪə) NOUN an outdoor fire in a camp, esp one used for cooking or as a focal point for community events.

camp follower NOUN 1 any civilian, esp a prostitute, who unofficially provides services to military personnel. 2 a nonmember who is sympathetic to a particular group, theory, etc.

camphene (ˈkæmfiːn) NOUN a colourless crystalline insoluble optically active terpene derived from pinene and present in many essential oils. Formula: $C_{10}H_{16}$.
▷HISTORY C19: from CAMPH(OR) + -ENE

camphire (ˈkæmfaɪə) NOUN an archaic name for **henna** (senses 1, 2).

camphor (ˈkæmfə) NOUN a whitish crystalline aromatic terpene ketone obtained from the wood of the camphor tree or made from pinene: used in the manufacture of celluloid and in medicine as a liniment and treatment for colds. Formula: $C_{10}H_{16}O$.
▷HISTORY C15: from Old French *camphre,* from Medieval Latin *camphora,* from Arabic *kāfūr,* from Malay *kāpūr* chalk; related to Khmer *kāpōr* camphor
▶**camphoric** (kæmˈfɒrɪk) ADJECTIVE

camphorate (ˈkæmfəˌreɪt) VERB (*tr*) to apply, treat with, or impregnate with camphor.

camphorated oil NOUN a liniment consisting of camphor and peanut oil, used as a counterirritant.

camphor ball NOUN another name for **mothball** (sense 1).

camphor ice NOUN an ointment consisting of camphor, white wax, spermaceti, and castor oil, used to treat skin ailments, esp chapped skin.

camphor laurel NOUN an Australian name for the camphor tree, now occurring in the wild in parts of Australia.

camphor tree NOUN 1 a lauraceous evergreen E Asian tree, *Cinnamomum camphora,* whose aromatic wood yields camphor. 2 any similar tree, such as the dipterocarpaceous tree *Dryobalanops aromatica* of Borneo.

campimetry (kæm'pɪmɪtrɪ) NOUN a technique for assessing the central part of the visual field.
▷HISTORY C20: from New Latin, from Latin *campus* field + *-metry;* see -METER

Campina Grande (*Portuguese* kəm'pi:nə 'grɐ:ndə) NOUN a city in NE Brazil, in E Paraíba state. Pop.: 336 218 (2000).

Campinas (kæm'pi:nəs; *Portuguese* kəm'pi:nəʃ) NOUN a city in SE Brazil, in São Paulo state: centre of a rich agricultural region, producing esp coffee. Pop.: 951 824 (2000).

camping ground NOUN another word for **camp site.**

campion ('kæmpɪən) NOUN any of various caryophyllaceous plants of the genera *Silene* and *Lychnis,* having red, pink, or white flowers. See also **bladder campion.**
▷HISTORY C16: probably from *campion,* obsolete variant of CHAMPION, perhaps so called because originally applied to *Lychnis coronaria,* the leaves of which were used to crown athletic champions

CAM plant (kæm) NOUN any plant that undergoes a form of photosynthesis known as crassulacean acid metabolism, in which carbon dioxide is taken up only at night.
▷HISTORY *C(rassulacean) A(cid) M(etabolism) plant*

camp meeting NOUN *Chiefly US* a religious meeting held in a large tent or outdoors, often lasting several days.

campo ('kæmpəʊ) NOUN, *plural* **-pos.** (*often plural*) level or undulating savanna country, esp in the uplands of Brazil.
▷HISTORY American Spanish, from Latin *campus*

Campobello (ˌkæmpə'bɛləʊ) NOUN an island in the Bay of Fundy, off the coast of SE Canada: part of New Brunswick province. Area: about 52 sq. km (20 sq. miles). Pop.: 1317 (1991).

Campo Formio (*Italian* 'kampo 'fɔrmjo) NOUN a village in NE Italy, in Friuli-Venezia Giulia: scene of the signing of a treaty in 1797 that ended the war between revolutionary France and Austria. Modern name: **Campoformido** (kampo'fɔrmido).

Campo Grande (*Portuguese* 'kə:mpu 'grɐ:ndə) NOUN a city in SW Brazil, capital of Mato Grosso do Sul state on the São Paulo–Corumbá railway: market centre. Pop.: 654 832 (2000).

camporee (ˌkæmpə'ri:) NOUN a local meeting or assembly of Scouts.
▷HISTORY C20: from CAMP[1] + (JAMB)OREE

Campos (*Portuguese* 'kə:mpuʃ) NOUN a city in E Brazil, in E Rio de Janeiro state on the Paraíba River. Pop.: 363 489 (2000).

camp oven NOUN *Austral and NZ* a metal pot or box with a heavy lid, used for baking over an open fire.

camp pie NOUN *Austral history* tinned meat.

camp site NOUN an area on which holiday-makers may pitch a tent, etc. Also called: **camping site.**

campus ('kæmpəs) NOUN, *plural* **-puses.** [1] the grounds and buildings of a university. [2] *Chiefly US* the outside area of a college, university, etc.
▷HISTORY C18: from Latin: field

campus university NOUN *Brit* a university in which the buildings, often including shops and cafés, are all on one site. Compare **redbrick.**

campy ('kæmpɪ) ADJECTIVE **campier, campiest.** *Informal* [1] effeminate; affected in mannerisms, dress, etc. [2] relating to or considered characteristic of homosexuals. [3] consciously artificial, exaggerated, vulgar, or mannered; self-parodying, esp when in dubious taste.

campylobacter (ˌkæmpɪləʊ'bæktə) NOUN a rod-shaped bacterium that causes infections in cattle and man. Unpasteurized milk infected with campylobacter is a common cause of gastroenteritis.
▷HISTORY from Greek *kampulos* bent + BACTER(IUM)

CAMRA ('kæmrə) NOUN ACRONYM FOR Campaign for Real Ale.

Cam Ranh ('kæm 'ræn) NOUN a port in SE Vietnam: large natural harbour, in recent years used as a naval base by French, Japanese, US, and Russian forces successively. Pop.: 114 041 (1992 est.).

camshaft ('kæmˌʃɑ:ft) NOUN a shaft having one or more cams attached to it, esp one used to operate the valves of an internal-combustion engine.

camwood ('kæmˌwʊd) NOUN [1] a W African leguminous tree, *Baphia nitida,* whose hard wood was formerly used in making a red dye. [2] the wood of this tree.
▷HISTORY C20: perhaps from Temne

can^1 (kæn; *unstressed* kən) VERB, *past* **could.** (takes an infinitive without *to* or an implied infinitive) (*intr*) used as an auxiliary: [1] to indicate ability, skill, or fitness to perform a task: *I can run a mile in under four minutes.* [2] to indicate permission or the right to something: *can I have a drink?* [3] to indicate knowledge of how to do something: *he can speak three languages fluently.* [4] to indicate the possibility, opportunity, or likelihood: *my trainer says I can win the race if I really work hard.*
▷HISTORY Old English *cunnan;* related to Old Norse *kunna,* Old High German *kunnan,* Latin *cognōscere* to know, Sanskrit *jānāti* he knows; see KEN, UNCOUTH

Language note See at **may.**

can^2 (kæn) NOUN [1] a container, esp for liquids, usually of thin sheet metal: *a petrol can; beer can.* [2] another name (esp US) for **tin** (metal container). [3] Also called: **canful.** the contents of a can or the amount a can will hold. [4] a slang word for **prison.** [5] *US and Canadian* a slang word for **toilet** or **buttocks.** [6] *US navy* a slang word for **destroyer.** [7] *Naval, slang* a depth charge. [8] a shallow cylindrical metal container of varying size used for storing and handling film. [9] **can of worms.** *Informal* a complicated problem. [10] **carry the can.** See **carry** (sense 37). [11] **in the can. a** (of a film, piece of music, etc.) having been recorded, processed, edited, etc. **b** *Informal* arranged or agreed: *the contract is almost in the can.* ◆ VERB **cans, canning, canned.** [12] to put (food, etc.) into a can or cans; preserve in a can. [13] (*tr*) *US slang* to dismiss from a job. [14] (*tr*) *US informal* to stop (doing something annoying or making an annoying noise) (esp in the phrase **can it!**). [15] (*tr*) *Informal* to reject or discard.
▷HISTORY Old English *canne;* related to Old Norse, Old High German *kanna,* Irish *gann,* Swedish *kana* sled

Can. ABBREVIATION FOR: [1] Canada. [2] Canadian.

Cana ('keɪnə) NOUN *New Testament* the town in Galilee, north of Nazareth, where Jesus performed his first miracle by changing water into wine (John 2:1, 11).

Canaan ('keɪnən) NOUN an ancient region between the River Jordan and the Mediterranean, corresponding roughly to Israel: the Promised Land of the Israelites.

Canaan dog NOUN a strongly-built medium-sized dog of a breed with erect ears, a dense coat, and a bushy tail carried curled over its back.

Canaanite ('keɪnəˌnaɪt) NOUN [1] a member of an ancient Semitic people who occupied the land of Canaan before the Israelite conquest. [2] the extinct language of this people, belonging to the Canaanitic branch of the Semitic subfamily of the Afro-Asiatic family. [3] (in later books of the Old Testament) a merchant or trader (Job 40:30; Proverbs 31:24).

Canaanitic (ˌkeɪnə'nɪtɪk) NOUN [1] a group of ancient languages belonging to the Semitic subfamily of the Afro-Asiatic family and including Canaanite, Phoenician, Ugaritic, and Hebrew. ◆ ADJECTIVE [2] denoting, relating to, or belonging to this group of languages.

Canada ('kænədə) NOUN a country in North America: the second largest country in the world; first permanent settlements made by the French from 1605; ceded to Britain in 1763 after a series of colonial wars; established as the Dominion of Canada in 1867; a member of the Commonwealth. It consists generally of sparsely inhabited tundra regions, rich in natural resources, in the north, the Rocky Mountains in the west, the Canadian Shield in the east, and vast central prairies; the bulk of the population is concentrated along the US border and the Great Lakes in the south. Languages: English and French. Religion: Christian majority. Currency: Canadian dollar. Capital: Ottawa. Pop.: 31 081 900 (2001 est.). Area: 9 976 185 sq. km (3 851 809 sq. miles).

Canada balsam NOUN [1] a yellow transparent resin obtained from the balsam fir. Because its refractive index is similar to that of glass, it is used as an adhesive in optical devices and as a mounting medium for microscope specimens. [2] another name for **balsam fir.**

Canada Day NOUN (in Canada) July 1, the anniversary of the day in 1867 when Canada became the first British colony to receive dominion status: a bank holiday. Former name: **Dominion Day.**

Canada goose NOUN a large common greyish-brown North American goose, *Branta canadensis,* with a black neck and head and a white throat patch.

Canada jay NOUN a large common jay of North America, *Perisoreus canadensis,* with a grey body, and a white-and-black crestless head.

Canada lily NOUN a lily, *Lilium canadense,* of NE North America, with small orange funnel-shaped nodding flowers. Also called: **meadow lily.**

Canadarm ('kænədˌɑ:m) NOUN a type of robotic arm, developed in Canada, used on space vehicles.

Canada thistle NOUN the US and Canadian name for **creeping thistle.**

Canadian (kə'neɪdɪən) ADJECTIVE [1] of or relating to Canada or its people. ◆ NOUN [2] a native, citizen, or inhabitant of Canada.

Canadian Alliance NOUN a Canadian right-wing federal political party, founded in 2000.

Canadian bacon NOUN the US name for **back bacon.**

Canadian English NOUN the English language as spoken in Canada.

Canadian football NOUN a game resembling American football, played on a grass pitch between two teams of 12 players.

Canadian Forces PLURAL NOUN the official name for the military forces of Canada.

Canadian French NOUN [1] the French language as spoken in Canada, esp in Quebec. ◆ ADJECTIVE [2] denoting this language or a French-speaking Canadian.

Canadianism (kə'neɪdɪəˌnɪzəm) NOUN [1] the Canadian national character or spirit. [2] loyalty to Canada, its political independence, culture, etc. [3] a linguistic usage, custom, or other feature peculiar to or characteristic of Canada, its people, or their culture.

Canadian pondweed NOUN a North American aquatic plant, *Elodea* (or *Anacharis*) *canadensis,* naturalized in Europe, having crowded dark green leaves: family *Hydrocharitaceae.* It is used in aquariums.

Canadian River NOUN a river in the southern US, rising in NE New Mexico and flowing east to the Arkansas River in E Oklahoma. Length: 1458 km (906 miles).

Canadian Shield NOUN (in Canada) the wide area of Precambrian rock extending west from the Labrador coast to the basin of the Mackenzie and north from the Great Lakes to Hudson Bay and the Arctic: rich in minerals. Also called: **Laurentian Shield, Laurentian Plateau.** See **shield** (sense 7).

canaigre (kə'naɪgə) NOUN a dock, *Rumex hymenosepalus,* of the southern US, the root of which yields a substance used in tanning.
▷HISTORY C19: from Mexican Spanish

canaille *French* (kanɑj) NOUN the masses; mob; rabble.
▷HISTORY C17: from French, from Italian *canaglia* pack of dogs

canakin ('kænɪkɪn) NOUN a variant spelling of **cannikin.**

canal (kə'næl) NOUN [1] an artificial waterway constructed for navigation, irrigation, water power, etc. [2] any of various tubular passages or ducts: *the alimentary canal.* [3] any of various elongated intercellular spaces in plants. [4] *Astronomy* any of the indistinct surface features of Mars originally thought to be a network of channels but not seen on close-range photographs. They are caused by an optical illusion in which faint geological features appear to have a geometric structure. ◆ VERB **-nals, -nalling, -nalled** *or US* **-nals, -naling, -naled.** (*tr*) [5] to dig a canal through. [6] to provide with a canal or canals.

▹HISTORY C15 (in the sense: pipe, tube): from Latin *canālis* channel, water pipe, from *canna* reed, CANE[1]

canal boat NOUN a long narrow boat used on canals, esp for carrying freight.

canaliculus (ˌkænəˈlɪkjʊləs) NOUN, *plural* **-li** (-ˌlaɪ). a small channel, furrow, or groove, as in some bones and parts of plants.
▹HISTORY C16: from Latin: a little channel, from *canālis* CANAL
▸ **ˌcanaˈlicular** *or* **canaliculate** (ˌkænəˈlɪkjʊlɪt, -ˌleɪt) *or* **ˌcanaˈlicuˌlated** ADJECTIVE

canalize *or* **canalise** (ˈkænəˌlaɪz) VERB (*tr*) [1] to provide with or convert into a canal or canals. [2] to give a particular direction to or provide an outlet for; channel. [3] to divide a channel into separate reaches controlled by dams and weirs to aid navigation, control water levels, generate power, etc.
▸ **ˌcanaliˈzation** *or* **ˌcanaliˈsation** NOUN

canal ray NOUN *Physics* a stream of positive ions produced in a discharge tube by allowing them to pass through holes in the cathode.

Canal Zone NOUN a former administrative region of the US, on the Isthmus of Panama around the Panama Canal: bordered on each side by the Republic of Panama, into which it was incorporated in 1979. Also called: **Panama Canal Zone.**

canapé (ˈkænəpɪ, -ˌpeɪ; *French* kanape) NOUN [1] a small piece of bread, toast, etc., spread with a savoury topping. [2] (in French cabinetwork) a sofa.
▹HISTORY C19: from French: sofa

Canara (kəˈnɑːrə) NOUN a variant spelling of **Kanara.**

canard (kæˈnɑːd; *French* kanar) NOUN [1] a false report; rumour or hoax. [2] an aircraft in which the tailplane is mounted in front of the wing.
▹HISTORY C19: from French: a duck, hoax, from Old French *caner* to quack, of imitative origin

Canarese (ˌkænəˈriːz) NOUN, *plural* **-rese,** ADJECTIVE a variant spelling of **Kanarese.**

canary (kəˈnɛərɪ) NOUN, *plural* **-naries.** [1] a small finch, *Serinus canaria,* of the Canary Islands and Azores: a popular cagebird noted for its singing. Wild canaries are streaked yellow and brown, but most domestic breeds are pure yellow. [2] See **canary yellow.** [3] *Austral history* a convict. [4] *Archaic* a sweet wine from the Canary Islands similar to Madeira.
▹HISTORY C16: from Old Spanish *canario* of or from the Canary Islands

canary creeper NOUN a climbing plant, *Tropaeolum peregrinum,* similar to the nasturtium but with smaller yellow flowers and lobed leaves.

canary grass NOUN [1] any of various grasses of the genus *Phalaris,* esp *P. canariensis,* that is native to Europe and N Africa and has straw-coloured seeds used as birdseed. [2] **reed canary grass.** a related plant, *Phalaris arundinacea,* used as fodder throughout the N hemisphere.

Canary Islands *or* **Canaries** PLURAL NOUN a group of mountainous islands in the Atlantic off the NW coast of Africa, forming an Autonomous Community of Spain. Pop.: 1 716 276 (2000 est.).

canary seed NOUN another name for **birdseed.**

canary yellow NOUN **a** a moderate yellow colour, sometimes with a greenish tinge. **b** (*as adjective*): *a canary-yellow car.* Sometimes shortened to **canary.**

canasta (kəˈnæstə) NOUN [1] a card game for two to six players who seek to amass points by declaring sets of cards. [2] Also called: **meld.** a declared set in this game, containing seven or more like cards, worth 500 points if the canasta is pure or 300 if wild (containing up to three jokers).
▹HISTORY C20: from Spanish: basket (because two packs, or a basketful, of cards are required), variant of *canastro,* from Latin *canistrum;* see CANISTER

canaster (ˈkænəstə) NOUN coarsely broken dried tobacco leaves.
▹HISTORY C19: (meaning: rush basket in which tobacco was packed): from Spanish *canastro;* see CANISTER

Canaveral (kəˈnævərəl) NOUN **Cape.** a cape on the E coast of Florida: site of the US Air Force Missile Test Centre, from which the majority of US space missions have been launched. Former name (1963–73): Cape **Kennedy.**

Canberra (ˈkænbərə, -brə) NOUN the capital of Australia, in Australian Capital Territory: founded in 1913 as a planned capital. Pop.: 306 600 (1998 est.).

can buoy NOUN *Nautical* a buoy with a flat-topped cylindrical shape above water, marking the left side of a channel leading into a harbour: red in British waters but green (occasionally black) in US waters. Compare **nun buoy.**

cancan (ˈkænˌkæn) NOUN a high-kicking dance performed by a female chorus, originating in the music halls of 19th-century Paris.
▹HISTORY C19: from French, of uncertain origin

cancel (ˈkænsᵊl) VERB **-cels, -celling, -celled** *or US* **-cels, -celing, -celed.** (*mainly tr*) [1] to order (something already arranged, such as a meeting or event) to be postponed indefinitely; call off. [2] to revoke or annul: *the order for the new television set was cancelled.* [3] to delete (writing, numbers, etc.); cross out: *he cancelled his name and substituted hers.* [4] to mark (a cheque, postage stamp, ticket, etc.) with an official stamp or by a perforation to prevent further use. [5] (*also intr;* usually foll by *out*) to counterbalance; make up for (a deficiency, etc.): *his generosity cancelled out his past unkindness.* [6] **a** to close (an account) by discharging any outstanding debts. **b** (sometimes foll by *out*) *Accounting* to eliminate (a debit or credit) by making an offsetting entry on the opposite side of the account. [7] *Maths* **a** to eliminate (numbers, quantities, or terms) as common factors from both the numerator and denominator of a fraction or as equal terms from opposite sides of an equation. **b** (*intr*) to be able to be eliminated in this way. ◆ NOUN [8] a new leaf or section of a book replacing a defective one, one containing errors, or one that has been omitted. [9] a less common word for **cancellation.** [10] *Music* a US word for **natural** (sense 19a).
▹HISTORY C14: from Old French *canceller,* from Medieval Latin *cancellāre,* from Late Latin: to strike out, make like a lattice, from Latin *cancellī* lattice, grating
▸ **ˈcanceller** *or US* **ˈcanceler** NOUN

cancellate (ˈkænsɪˌleɪt), **cancellous** (ˈkænsɪləs), *or* **cancellated** ADJECTIVE [1] *Anatomy* having a spongy or porous internal structure: *cancellate bones.* [2] *Botany* forming a network; reticulate: *a cancellate venation.*
▹HISTORY C17: from Latin *cancellāre* to make like a lattice; see CANCEL

cancellation (ˌkænsɪˈleɪʃən) NOUN [1] the fact or an instance of cancelling. [2] something that has been cancelled, such as a theatre ticket, esp when it is available for another person to take: *we have a cancellation in the stalls.* [3] the marks or perforation made by cancelling.

cancer (ˈkænsə) NOUN [1] any type of malignant growth or tumour, caused by abnormal and uncontrolled cell division: it may spread through the lymphatic system or blood stream to other parts of the body. [2] the condition resulting from this. [3] an evil influence that spreads dangerously. ◆ Related prefix: **carcino-.**
▹HISTORY C14: from Latin: crab, a creeping tumour; related to Greek *karkinos* crab, Sanskrit *karkata*
▸ **ˈcancerous** ADJECTIVE ▸ **ˈcancerously** ADVERB

Cancer (ˈkænsə) NOUN, *Latin genitive* **Cancri** (ˈkæŋkriː). [1] *Astronomy* a small faint zodiacal constellation in the N hemisphere, lying between Gemini and Leo on the ecliptic and containing the star cluster Praesepe. [2] *Astrology* **a** Also called: **the Crab.** the fourth sign of the zodiac, symbol ♋, having a cardinal water classification and ruled by the moon. The sun is in this sign between about June 21 and July 22. **b** a person born during a period when the sun is in this sign. [3] **tropic of Cancer.** See **tropic** (sense 1). ◆ ADJECTIVE [4] *Astrology* born under or characteristic of Cancer. ◆ Also (for senses 2b, 4): **Cancerian** (kænˈsɪərɪən).

cancerophobia (ˌkænsərəʊˈfəʊbɪə) NOUN a morbid dread of being afflicted by cancer.

cancer stick NOUN a slang name for **cigarette.**

cancrizans (ˈkænkrɪˌzæns, ˈkæŋ-) ADJECTIVE See **crab canon.**
▹HISTORY Medieval Latin: moving backwards, from *cancrizāre* to move crabwise

cancroid (ˈkæŋkrɔɪd) ADJECTIVE [1] resembling a cancerous growth. [2] resembling a crab. ◆ NOUN [3] a skin cancer, esp one of only moderate malignancy.

c & b *Cricket* ABBREVIATION FOR caught and bowled (by).

candela (kænˈdiːlə, -ˈdeɪlə) NOUN the basic SI unit of luminous intensity; the luminous intensity in a given direction of a source that emits monochromatic radiation of frequency 540×10^{12} hertz and that has a radiant intensity in that direction of (1/683) watt per steradian. Symbol: cd. Also called: **candle, standard candle.**
▹HISTORY C20: from Latin: CANDLE

candelabrum (ˌkændɪˈlɑːbrəm) *or* **candelabra** NOUN, *plural* **-bra** (-brə), **-brums,** *or* **-bras.** a large branched candleholder or holder for overhead lights.
▹HISTORY C19: from Latin, from *candēla* CANDLE

candent (ˈkændənt) ADJECTIVE an archaic word for **incandescent.**
▹HISTORY C16: from Latin *candēre* to shine

candescent (kænˈdesᵊnt) ADJECTIVE *Rare* glowing or starting to glow with heat.
▹HISTORY C19: from Latin *candescere,* from *candēre* to be white, shine
▸ **canˈdescence** NOUN ▸ **canˈdescently** ADVERB

c & f ABBREVIATION FOR cost and freight.

C & G ABBREVIATION FOR City and Guilds.

Candia (ˈkandja) NOUN the Italian name for **Iráklion.**

candid (ˈkændɪd) ADJECTIVE [1] frank and outspoken: *he was candid about his dislike of our friends.* [2] without partiality; unbiased. [3] unposed or informal: *a candid photograph.* [4] *Obsolete* **a** white. **b** clear or pure.
▹HISTORY C17: from Latin *candidus* white, from *candēre* to be white
▸ **ˈcandidly** ADVERB ▸ **ˈcandidness** NOUN

candida (ˈkændɪdə) NOUN any yeastlike parasitic fungus of the genus *Candida,* esp *C. albicans,* which causes thrush (**candidiasis**).
▹HISTORY New Latin, feminine of *candidus* white

candidate (ˈkændɪˌdeɪt, -dɪt) NOUN [1] a person seeking or nominated for election to a position of authority or honour or selection for a job, promotion, etc. [2] a person taking an examination or test. [3] a person or thing regarded as suitable or likely for a particular fate or position: *this wine is a candidate for his cellar.*
▹HISTORY C17: from Latin *candidātus* clothed in white (because the candidate wore a white toga), from *candidus* white
▸ **candidacy** (ˈkændɪdəsɪ) *or* **candidature** (ˈkændɪdətʃə) NOUN

candid camera NOUN **a** a small camera that may be used to take informal photographs of people, usually without their knowledge. **b** (*as modifier*): *a candid-camera photograph.*

candied (ˈkændɪd) ADJECTIVE [1] impregnated or encrusted with or as if with sugar or syrup: *candied peel.* [2] (of sugar, honey, etc.) crystallized.

Candiot (ˈkændɪˌɒt) *or* **Candiote** (ˈkændɪˌəʊt) ADJECTIVE [1] of or relating to Candia (Iráklion) or Crete; Cretan. ◆ NOUN [2] a native or inhabitant of Crete; a Cretan.

candle (ˈkændᵊl) NOUN [1] a cylindrical piece of wax, tallow, or other fatty substance surrounding a wick, which is burned to produce light. [2] *Physics* **a** See **international candle. b** another name for **candela.** [3] **burn the candle at both ends.** to exhaust oneself, esp by being up late and getting up early to work. [4] **not hold a candle to.** *Informal* to be inferior or contemptible in comparison with: *your dog doesn't hold a candle to mine.* [5] **not worth the candle.** *Informal* not worth the price or trouble entailed (esp in the phrase **the game's not worth the candle**). ◆ VERB [6] (*tr*) to examine (eggs) for freshness or the likelihood of being hatched by viewing them against a bright light.
▹HISTORY Old English *candel,* from Latin *candēla,* from *candēre* to be white, glitter
▸ **ˈcandler** NOUN

candleberry (ˈkændᵊlbərɪ) NOUN, *plural* **-ries.** another name for **wax myrtle.**

candlefish (ˈkændᵊlˌfɪʃ) NOUN, *plural* **-fish** *or* **-fishes.** a salmonoid food fish, *Thaleichthys pacificus,* that occurs in the N Pacific and has oily flesh. Also called: **eulachon.**

candlelight (ˈkændᵊlˌlaɪt) NOUN [1] **a** the light

from a candle or candles: *they ate by candlelight.* **b** (*as modifier*): *a candlelight dinner.* [2] dusk; evening.

Candlemas ('kændəlməs) NOUN *Christianity* Feb. 2, the Feast of the Purification of the Virgin Mary and the presentation of Christ in the Temple: the day on which the church candles are blessed. In Scotland it is one of the four quarter days.

candlenut ('kændəlˌnʌt) NOUN [1] a euphorbiaceous tree, *Aleurites mollucana,* of tropical Asia and Polynesia. [2] the nut of this tree, which yields an oil used in paints and varnishes. In their native regions the nuts are strung together and burned as candles.

candlepin ('kændəlˌpɪn) NOUN a bowling pin, as used in skittles, tenpin bowling, candlepins, etc.

candlepins ('kændəlˌpɪnz) NOUN (*functioning as singular*) a type of bowling game, employing a smaller ball than tenpins, in which three balls are allowed to a frame and fallen pins are not removed from the alley.

candlepower ('kændəlˌpaʊə) NOUN the luminous intensity of a source of light in a given direction: now expressed in candelas but formerly in terms of the international candle.

candlestick ('kændəlˌstɪk) *or* **candleholder** ('kændəlˌhəʊldə) NOUN a holder, usually ornamental, with a spike or socket for a candle.

candle-tree NOUN another name for **wax myrtle.**

candlewick ('kændəlˌwɪk) NOUN [1] unbleached cotton or muslin into which loops of yarn are hooked and then cut to give a tufted pattern. It is used for bedspreads, dressing gowns, etc. [2] the wick of a candle. [3] (*modifier*) being or made of candlewick fabric.

candlewood ('kændəlˌwʊd) NOUN [1] the resinous wood of any of several trees, used for torches and candle substitutes. [2] any tree or shrub, such as ocotillo, that produces this wood.

C & M ABBREVIATION FOR: [1] care and maintenance. [2] clicks and mortar (company).

can-do ADJECTIVE confident and resourceful in the face of challenges: *a can-do attitude.*

Candomblé (*Portuguese* kæn'dəʊmbleɪ, kændɒm'bleɪ) NOUN any of a number of similar religious cults in Brazil that combine elements of Roman Catholicism with elements of West African, especially Yoruba, and South American Indian religions.

candour *or US* **candor** ('kændə) NOUN [1] the quality of being open and honest; frankness. [2] fairness; impartiality. [3] *Obsolete* purity or brightness.
▷HISTORY C17: from Latin *candor,* from *candēre* to be white, shine

C & W ABBREVIATION FOR country and western.

candy ('kændɪ) NOUN, *plural* **-dies.** [1] *Chiefly US and Canadian* confectionery in general; sweets, chocolate, etc. [2] a person or thing that is regarded as being attractive but superficial: *arm candy.* [3] **like taking candy from a baby.** *Informal* very easy to accomplish. ◆ VERB **-dies, -dying, -died.** [4] to cause (sugar, etc.) to become crystalline, esp by boiling or (of sugar) to become crystalline through boiling. [5] to preserve (fruit peel, ginger, etc.) by boiling in sugar. [6] to cover with any crystalline substance, such as ice or sugar.
▷HISTORY C18: from Old French *sucre candi* candied sugar, from Arabic *qandi* candied, from *qand* cane sugar, of Dravidian origin

candyfloss ('kændɪˌflɒs) NOUN *Brit* a very light fluffy confection made from coloured spun sugar, usually held on a stick. US and Canadian name: **cotton candy.** Austral name: **fairyfloss.**

candy store NOUN a US and Canadian term for **sweet shop.**

candy-striped ADJECTIVE (esp of clothing fabric) having narrow coloured stripes on a white background.
▸**candy stripe** NOUN

candytuft ('kændɪˌtʌft) NOUN either of two species of *Iberis* grown as annual garden plants for their umbels ("tufts") of white, red, or purplish flowers. See **iberis.**
▷HISTORY C17: from *Candy,* obsolete variant of CANDIA (Crete) + TUFT

cane[1] (keɪn) NOUN [1] **a** the long jointed pithy or hollow flexible stem of the bamboo, rattan, or any similar plant. **b** any plant having such a stem. [2] **a** strips of such stems, woven or interlaced to make wickerwork, the seats and backs of chairs, etc. **b** (*as modifier*): *a cane chair.* [3] the woody stem of a reed, young grapevine, blackberry, raspberry, or loganberry. [4] any of several grasses with long stiff stems, esp *Arundinaria gigantea* of the southeastern US. [5] a flexible rod with which to administer a beating as a punishment, as to schoolboys. [6] a slender rod, usually wooden and often ornamental, used for support when walking; walking stick. [7] See **sugar cane.** [8] a slender rod or cylinder, as of glass. ◆ VERB (*tr*) [9] to whip or beat with or as if with a cane. [10] to make or repair with cane. [11] *Informal* to defeat: *we got well caned in the match.* [12] **cane it.** *Slang* to do something with great power, force, or speed or consume something such as alcohol in large quantities: *you can do it in ten minutes if you really cane it.*
▷HISTORY C14: from Old French, from Latin *canna,* from Greek *kanna,* of Semitic origin; related to Arabic *qanāh* reed
▸'**caner** NOUN

cane[2] (keɪn) NOUN *Dialect* a female weasel.
▷HISTORY C18: of unknown origin

Canea (kæ'nɪə) *or* **Chania** ('hɑːnɪə) NOUN the chief port of Crete, on the NW coast. Pop.: 50 000 (latest est.). Greek name: **Khaniá.**

canebrake ('keɪnˌbreɪk) NOUN *US* a thicket of canes.

cane grass NOUN *Austral* any of several tall perennial hard-stemmed grasses, esp *Eragrostis australasica,* of inland swamps.

canella (kə'nɛlə) NOUN the fragrant cinnamon-like inner bark of a West Indian tree, *Canella winterana* (family *Canellaceae*) used as a spice and in medicine.
▷HISTORY C17: from Medieval Latin: cinnamon, from Latin *canna* cane, reed

cane piece NOUN (in the Caribbean) a field of sugar cane, esp a peasant's isolated field.

cane rat NOUN [1] Also called (in W Africa): **cutting grass.** a tropical African cavy-like hystricomorph rodent, *Thryonomys swinderianus,* that lives in swampy regions: family *Thryonomyidae.* [2] a similar but smaller species, *T. gregorianus.*

canescent (kə'nɛsənt) ADJECTIVE [1] *Biology* white or greyish due to the presence of numerous short white hairs. [2] becoming hoary, white, or greyish.
▷HISTORY C19: from Latin *cānescere* to grow white, become hoary, from *cānēre* to be white
▸**ca'nescence** NOUN

cane sugar NOUN [1] the sucrose obtained from sugar cane, which is identical to that obtained from sugar beet. See also **beet sugar.** [2] another name for **sucrose.**

Canes Venatici ('kɑːniːz vɪ'nætɪˌsaɪ) NOUN, *Latin genitive* **Canum Venaticorum** ('kɑːnəm vɪˌnætɪ'kɔːrəm). a small faint constellation in the N hemisphere near Ursa Major that contains the globular cluster M3 and the spiral whirlpool galaxy M51.
▷HISTORY Latin: hunting dogs

cane toad NOUN a large toad, *Bufo marinus,* native to Central and South America but introduced into many countries to control insects and other pests of sugar-cane plantations. Also called: **giant toad, marine toad.**

canfield ('kænˌfiːld) NOUN *Cards* a gambling game adapted from a type of patience.
▷HISTORY C20: named after R. A. *Canfield* (1855–1914), US gambler

cangue *or* **cang** (kæŋ) NOUN (formerly in China) a large wooden collar worn by petty criminals as a punishment.
▷HISTORY C18: from French, from Portuguese *canga* yoke

Canicula (kə'nɪkjʊlə) NOUN another name for **Sirius.**
▷HISTORY Latin, literally: little dog, from *canis* dog

canicular (kə'nɪkjʊlə) ADJECTIVE of or relating to the star Sirius or its rising.

canikin ('kænɪkɪn) NOUN a variant spelling of **cannikin.**

canine ('keɪnaɪn, 'kæn-) ADJECTIVE [1] of or resembling a dog; doglike. [2] of, relating to, or belonging to the *Canidae,* a family of mammals, including dogs, jackals, wolves, and foxes, typically having a bushy tail, erect ears, and a long muzzle: order *Carnivora* (carnivores). [3] of or relating to any of the four teeth, two in each jaw, situated between the incisors and the premolars. ◆ NOUN *also* **canid** ('kænɪd). [4] any animal of the family *Canidae.* [5] a canine tooth.
▷HISTORY C17: from Latin *canīnus,* from *canis* dog

canine distemper NOUN See **distemper**[1].

canine parvovirus NOUN *Vet science* a highly contagious viral disease of dogs characterized by vomiting, haemorrhagic diarrhoea, depression, and, in severe cases, death.

caning ('keɪnɪŋ) NOUN [1] a beating with a cane as a punishment. [2] *Informal* a severe defeat.

Canis Major ('keɪnɪs) NOUN, *Latin genitive* **Canis Majoris** (mə'dʒɔːrɪs). a constellation in the S hemisphere close to Orion, containing Sirius, the brightest star in the sky. Also called: **the Great Dog.**
▷HISTORY Latin: the greater dog

Canis Minor NOUN, *Latin genitive* **Canis Minoris** (maɪ'nɔːrɪs). a small constellation in the N hemisphere close to Orion, containing the first magnitude star Procyon. Also called: **the Little Dog.**
▷HISTORY Latin: the lesser dog

canister ('kænɪstə) NOUN [1] a container, usually made of metal, in which dry food, such as tea or coffee, is stored. [2] (formerly) **a** a type of shrapnel shell for firing from a cannon. **b** Also called: **canister shot, case shot.** the shot or shrapnel packed inside this.
▷HISTORY C17: from Latin *canistrum* basket woven from reeds, from Greek *kanastron,* from *kanna* reed, CANE[1]

canker ('kæŋkə) NOUN [1] an ulceration, esp of the lips or lining of the oral cavity. [2] *Vet science* **a** a disease of horses in which the horn of the hoofs becomes soft and spongy. **b** an inflammation of the lining of the external ear, esp in dogs and cats, resulting in a discharge and sometimes ulceration. **c** ulceration or abscess of the mouth, eyelids, ears, or cloaca of birds. [3] an open wound in the stem of a tree or shrub, caused by injury or parasites. [4] something evil that spreads and corrupts. ◆ VERB [5] to infect or become infected with or as if with canker.
▷HISTORY Old English *cancer,* from Latin *cancer* crab, cancerous sore

cankerous ('kæŋkərəs) ADJECTIVE [1] having cankers. [2] infectious; corrupting.

cankerworm ('kæŋkəˌwɜːm) NOUN the larva of either of two geometrid moths, *Paleacrita vernata* or *Alsophila pometaria,* which feed on and destroy fruit and shade trees in North America.

CanLit (ˌkæn'lɪt) NOUN ACRONYM FOR Canadian Literature.

canna ('kænə) NOUN any of various tropical plants constituting the genus *Canna,* having broad leaves and red or yellow showy flowers for which they are cultivated: family *Cannaceae.*
▷HISTORY C17: from New Latin CANE[1]

cannabin ('kænəbɪn) NOUN a greenish-black poisonous resin obtained from the Indian hemp plant. Also called: **cannabis resin.**

cannabinoid ('kænəbɪˌnɔɪd) NOUN any of the narcotic chemical substances found in cannabin.

cannabis ('kænəbɪs) NOUN [1] another name for **hemp** (the plant), esp Indian hemp (*Cannabis indica*). [2] the drug obtained from the dried leaves and flowers of the hemp plant, which is smoked or chewed for its psychoactive properties. It produces euphoria and relaxation; repeated use may lead to psychological dependence. See also **cannabin, hashish, marijuana, bhang.**
▷HISTORY C18: from Latin, from Greek *kannabis;* see HEMP
▸'**cannabic** ADJECTIVE

Cannae ('kæniː) NOUN an ancient city in SE Italy: scene of a victory by Hannibal over the Romans (216 B.C.).

canned (kænd) ADJECTIVE [1] preserved and stored in airtight cans or tins: *canned meat.* [2] *Informal* prepared or recorded in advance; artificial; not spontaneous: *canned music.* [3] a slang word for **drunk** (sense 1).

cannel coal *or* **cannel** ('kænəl) NOUN a dull coal having a high volatile content and burning with a smoky luminous flame.

▷HISTORY C16: from Northern English dialect *cannel* candle: so called from its bright flame

cannelloni *or* **canneloni** (ˌkænɪˈləʊnɪ) PLURAL NOUN tubular pieces of pasta filled with meat or cheese.
▷HISTORY Italian, plural of *cannellone,* from *cannello* stalk, from *canna* CANE^{1}

cannelure (ˈkænəˌlʊə) NOUN a groove or fluting, esp one around the cylindrical part of a bullet.
▷HISTORY C18: from French, ultimately from Latin *canālis* CANAL

canner (ˈkænə) NOUN a person or organization whose job is to can foods.

cannery (ˈkænərɪ) NOUN, *plural* **-neries**. a place where foods are canned.

Cannes (kæn, kænz; *French* kan) NOUN a port and resort in SE France: developed in the 19th century from a fishing village; annual film festival. Pop.: 335 647 (1990).

cannibal (ˈkænɪbəl) NOUN **1** **a** a person who eats the flesh of other human beings. **b** (*as modifier*): *cannibal tribes*. **2** an animal that feeds on the flesh of others of its kind.
▷HISTORY C16: from Spanish *Canibales,* name used by Columbus to designate the Caribs of Cuba and Haiti, from Arawak *caniba,* variant of CARIB

cannibalism (ˈkænɪbəˌlɪzəm) NOUN **1** the act of eating human flesh or the flesh of one's own kind. **2** savage and inhuman cruelty.
▸ˌ**cannibalˈistic** ADJECTIVE ▸ˌ**cannibalˈistically** ADVERB

cannibalize *or* **cannibalise** (ˈkænɪbəˌlaɪz) VERB (*tr*) to use (serviceable parts from one machine or vehicle) to repair another, esp as an alternative to using new parts.
▸ˌ**cannibaliˈzation** *or* ˌ**cannibaliˈsation** NOUN

cannikin, canakin, *or* **canikin** (ˈkænɪkɪn) NOUN a small can, esp one used as a drinking vessel.
▷HISTORY C16: from Middle Dutch *kanneken;* see CAN^{2}, -KIN

canning (ˈkænɪŋ) NOUN the process or business of sealing food in cans or tins to preserve it.

Canning Basin NOUN an arid basin in NW Western Australia, largely unexplored. Area: 400 000 sq. km (150 000 sq. miles).

Cannock (ˈkænək) NOUN a town in W central England, in S Staffordshire: **Cannock Chase** (a public area of heathland, once a royal preserve) is just to the east. Pop.: 60 106 (1991).

cannon (ˈkænən) NOUN, *plural* **-nons** *or* **-non**. **1** an automatic aircraft gun of large calibre. **2** *History* a heavy artillery piece consisting of a metal tube mounted on a carriage. **3** a heavy tube or drum, esp one that can rotate freely on the shaft by which it is supported. **4** the metal loop at the top of a bell, from which it is suspended. **5** See **cannon bone**. **6** *Billiards* **a** a shot in which the cue ball is caused to contact one object ball after another. **b** the points scored by this. Usual US and Canadian word: **carom**. **7** a rebound or bouncing back, as of a ball off a wall. **8** either of the two parts of a vambrace. ◆ VERB **9** (*intr;* often foll by *into*) to collide (with). **10** short for **cannonade**. **11** (*intr*) *Billiards* to make a cannon.
▷HISTORY C16: from Old French *canon,* from Italian *cannone* cannon, large tube, from *canna* tube, CANE^{1}

cannonade (ˌkænəˈneɪd) NOUN **1** an intense and continuous artillery bombardment. ◆ VERB **2** to attack (a target) with cannon.

cannonball (ˈkænənˌbɔːl) NOUN **1** a projectile fired from a cannon: usually a solid round metal shot. **2** *Tennis* **a** a very fast low serve. **b** (*as modifier*): *a cannonball serve*. **3** a jump into water by a person who has his arms tucked into the body to form a ball. ◆ VERB (*intr*) **4** (often foll by *along,* etc.) to rush along, like a cannonball. **5** to execute a cannonball jump. ◆ ADJECTIVE **6** very fast or powerful.

cannon bone NOUN a bone in the legs of horses and other hoofed animals consisting of greatly elongated fused metatarsals or metacarpals.

cannoneer (ˌkænəˈnɪə) NOUN (formerly) a soldier who served and fired a cannon; artilleryman.

cannon fodder NOUN men regarded as expendable because they are part of a huge army.

cannonry (ˈkænənrɪ) NOUN, *plural* **-ries**. *Rare* **1** a volley of artillery fire. **2** artillery in general.

cannot (ˈkænɒt, kæˈnɒt) VERB an auxiliary verb expressing incapacity, inability, withholding permission, etc.; can not.

cannula *or* **canula** (ˈkænjʊlə) NOUN, *plural* **-las** *or* **-lae** (-ˌliː). *Surgery* a narrow tube for insertion into a bodily cavity, as for draining off fluid, introducing medication, etc.
▷HISTORY C17: from Latin: a small reed, from *canna* a reed

cannulate *or* **canulate** VERB (ˈkænjʊˌleɪt) **1** to insert a cannula into. ◆ ADJECTIVE (ˈkænjʊˌleɪt, -ˌlɪt) *also* **cannular** *or* **canular**. **2** shaped like a cannula.
▸ˌ**cannuˈlation** *or* ˌ**canuˈlation** NOUN

canny (ˈkænɪ) ADJECTIVE **-nier, -niest**. **1** shrewd, esp in business; astute or wary; knowing. **2** *Scot and Northeast English dialect* good or nice: used as a general term of approval. **3** *Scot* lucky or fortunate. ◆ ADVERB **4** *Scot and Northeast English dialect* quite; rather: *a canny long while*.
▷HISTORY C16: from CAN^{1} (in the sense: to know how) + -Y^{1}
▸ˈ**cannily** ADVERB ▸ˈ**canniness** NOUN

canoe (kəˈnuː) NOUN **1** a light narrow open boat, propelled by one or more paddles. **2** *NZ* another word for **waka** (sense 1). **3** **in the same canoe**. *NZ* of the same tribe. ◆ VERB **-noes, -noeing, -noed**. **4** to go in a canoe or transport by canoe.
▷HISTORY C16: from Spanish *canoa,* of Carib origin
▸**caˈnoeing** NOUN ▸**caˈnoeist** NOUN

canoewood (kəˈnuːˌwʊd) NOUN another name for the **tulip tree**.

canola (kəˈnəʊlə) NOUN a cooking oil extracted from a variety of rapeseed developed in Canada.
▷HISTORY C20: from CAN(ADA) + *-ola,* from OLEUM

canon^{1} (ˈkænən) NOUN **1** *Christianity* a Church decree enacted to regulate morals or religious practices. **2** (*often plural*) a general rule or standard, as of judgment, morals, etc. **3** (*often plural*) a principle or accepted criterion applied in a branch of learning or art. **4** *RC Church* the complete list of the canonized saints. **5** *RC Church* the prayer in the Mass in which the Host is consecrated. **6** a list of writings, esp sacred writings, officially recognized as genuine. **7** a piece of music in which an extended melody in one part is imitated successively in one or more other parts. See also **round** (sense 31), **catch** (sense 33). **8** a list of the works of an author that are accepted as authentic. **9** (formerly) a size of printer's type equal to 48 point.
▷HISTORY Old English, from Latin, from Greek *kanōn* rule, rod for measuring, standard; related to *kanna* reed, CANE^{1}

canon^{2} (ˈkænən) NOUN **1** one of several priests on the permanent staff of a cathedral, who are responsible for organizing services, maintaining the fabric, etc. **2** *RC Church* Also called: **canon regular**. a member of either of two religious orders, the Augustinian or Premonstratensian Canons, living communally as monks but performing clerical duties.
▷HISTORY C13: from Anglo-French *canunie,* from Late Latin *canonicus* one living under a rule, from CANON^{1}

cañon (ˈkænjən) NOUN a variant spelling of **canyon**.

canoness (ˈkænənɪs) NOUN *RC Church* a woman belonging to any one of several religious orders and living under a rule but not under a vow.

canonical (kəˈnɒnɪkəl) *or* **canonic** ADJECTIVE **1** belonging to or included in a canon of sacred or other officially recognized writings. **2** belonging to or in conformity with canon law. **3** according to recognized law; accepted. **4** *Music* in the form of a canon. **5** of or relating to a cathedral chapter. **6** of or relating to a canon (clergyman).
▸**caˈnonically** ADVERB

canonical hour NOUN **1** *RC Church* **a** one of the seven prayer times appointed for each day by canon law. **b** the services prescribed for these times, namely matins, prime, terce, sext, nones, vespers, and compline. **2** *Church of England* any time between 8:00 a.m. and 6:00 p.m. at which marriages may lawfully be celebrated.

canonicals (kəˈnɒnɪkəlz) PLURAL NOUN the vestments worn by clergy when officiating.

canonicate (kəˈnɒnɪˌkeɪt, -kɪt) NOUN the office or rank of a canon; canonry.

canonicity (ˌkænəˈnɪsɪtɪ) NOUN the fact or quality of being canonical.

canonist (ˈkænənɪst) NOUN a specialist in canon law.

canonize *or* **canonise** (ˈkænəˌnaɪz) VERB (*tr*) **1** *RC Church* to declare (a person) to be a saint and thus admit to the canon of saints. **2** to regard as holy or as a saint. **3** to sanction by canon law; pronounce valid.
▸ˌ**canoniˈzation** *or* ˌ**canoniˈsation** NOUN

canon law NOUN the law governing the affairs of a Christian Church, esp the law created or recognized by papal authority in the Roman Catholic Church. See **Corpus Juris Canonici, Codex Juris Canonici**.

canonry (ˈkænənrɪ) NOUN, *plural* **-ries**. **1** the office, benefice, or status of a canon. **2** canons collectively.
▷HISTORY C15: from CANON^{2} + -RY

canoodle (kəˈnuːdəl) VERB (*intr;* often foll by *with*) *Slang* to kiss and cuddle; pet; fondle.
▷HISTORY C19: of unknown origin
▸**caˈnoodler** NOUN

can-opener NOUN another name for **tin-opener**.

Canopic jar, urn, *or* **vase** (kəˈnəʊpɪk) NOUN (in ancient Egypt) one of four containers with tops in the form of animal heads of the gods, for holding the entrails of a mummy.

Canopus^{1} (kəˈnəʊpəs) NOUN the brightest star in the constellation Carina and the second brightest star in the sky. Visual magnitude: -0.7; spectral type: F0II; distance: 313 light years.

Canopus^{2} (kəˈnəʊpəs) NOUN a port in ancient Egypt east of Alexandria where granite monuments have been found inscribed with the name of Rameses II and written in languages similar to those of the Rosetta stone.
▸**Caˈnopic** ADJECTIVE

canopy (ˈkænəpɪ) NOUN, *plural* **-pies**. **1** an ornamental awning above a throne or bed or held over a person of importance on ceremonial occasions. **2** a rooflike covering over an altar, niche, etc. **3** a roofed structure serving as a sheltered passageway or area. **4** a large or wide covering, esp one high above: *the sky was a grey canopy*. **5** the nylon or silk hemisphere that forms the supporting surface of a parachute. **6** the transparent cover of an aircraft cockpit. **7** the highest level of branches and foliage in a forest, formed by the crowns of the trees. ◆ VERB **-pies, -pying, -pied**. **8** (*tr*) to cover with or as if with a canopy.
▷HISTORY C14: from Medieval Latin *canōpeum* mosquito net, from Latin *cōnōpeum* gauze net, from Greek *kōnōpeion* bed with protective net, from *kōnōps* mosquito

canorous (kəˈnɔːrəs) ADJECTIVE *Rare* tuneful; melodious.
▷HISTORY C17: from Latin *canōrus,* from *canere* to sing
▸**caˈnorously** ADVERB ▸**caˈnorousness** NOUN

Canossa (kəˈnɒsə; *Italian* kaˈnɔssa) NOUN a ruined castle in N Italy, in Emilia near Reggio nell'Emilia: scene of the penance done by the Holy Roman Emperor Henry IV before Pope Gregory VII.

cans (kænz) PLURAL NOUN an informal name for **headphones**.

Canso (ˈkænsəʊ) NOUN **1** a cape in Canada, at the NE tip of Nova Scotia. **2** **Strait of Canso**. Also called: **Gut of Canso**. a channel in Canada, between the Nova Scotia mainland and S Cape Breton Island.

canst (kænst) VERB *Archaic* the form of **can^{1}** used with the pronoun *thou* or its relative form.

cant^{1} (kænt) NOUN **1** insincere talk, esp concerning religion or morals; pious platitudes. **2** stock phrases that have become meaningless through repetition. **3** specialized vocabulary of a particular group, such as thieves, journalists, or lawyers; jargon. **4** singsong whining speech, as used by beggars. ◆ VERB **5** (*intr*) to speak in or use cant.
▷HISTORY C16: probably via Norman French *canter* to sing, from Latin *cantāre;* used disparagingly, from the 12th century, of chanting in religious services
▸ˈ**canter** NOUN ▸ˈ**cantingly** ADVERB

cant^{2} (kænt) NOUN **1** inclination from a vertical or horizontal plane; slope; slant. **2** a sudden movement that tilts or turns something. **3** the angle or tilt thus caused. **4** a corner or outer angle,

esp of a building. 5 an oblique or slanting surface, edge, or line. ◆ VERB (tr) 6 to tip, tilt, or overturn, esp with a sudden jerk. 7 to set in an oblique position. 8 another word for **bevel** (sense 1). ◆ ADJECTIVE 9 oblique; slanting. 10 having flat surfaces and without curves.
▷HISTORY C14 (in the sense: edge, corner): perhaps from Latin *canthus* iron hoop round a wheel, of obscure origin
▸**'cantic** ADJECTIVE

cant³ (kɑ:nt) ADJECTIVE *Scot and Northern English dialect* lusty; merry; hearty.
▷HISTORY C14: related to Low German *kant* bold, merry

Cant. ABBREVIATION FOR: 1 Canterbury. 2 *Bible* Canticles.

can't (kɑ:nt) VERB CONTRACTION OF cannot.

Cantab. (kæn'tæb) ABBREVIATION FOR Cantabrigiensis.
▷HISTORY Latin: of Cambridge

cantabile (kæn'tɑ:bɪlɪ) *Music* ◆ ADJECTIVE, ADVERB 1 (to be performed) in a singing style, i.e. flowingly and melodiously. ◆ NOUN 2 a piece or passage performed in this way.
▷HISTORY Italian, from Late Latin *cantābilis,* from Latin *cantāre* to sing

Cantabrian Mountains (kæn'teɪbrɪən) PLURAL NOUN a mountain chain along the N coast of Spain, consisting of a series of high ridges that rise over 2400 m (8000 ft.): rich in minerals (esp coal and iron).

Cantabrigian (ˌkæntə'brɪdʒɪən) ADJECTIVE 1 of, relating to, or characteristic of Cambridge or Cambridge University, or of Cambridge, Massachusetts, or Harvard University. ◆ NOUN 2 a member or graduate of Cambridge University or Harvard University. 3 an inhabitant or native of Cambridge.
▷HISTORY C17: from Medieval Latin *Cantabrigia*

Cantal (*French* kɑ̃tal) NOUN 1 a department of S central France, in the Auvergne region. Capital: Aurillac. Pop.: 150 778 (1999). Area: 5779 sq. km (2254 sq. miles). 2 a hard strong cheese made in this area.

cantala (kæn'tɑ:lə) NOUN 1 a tropical American plant, *Agave cantala,* similar to the century plant: family *Agavaceae* (agaves). 2 the coarse tough fibre of this plant, used in making twine.
▷HISTORY of unknown origin

cantaloupe *or* **cantaloup** ('kæntəˌlu:p) NOUN 1 a cultivated variety of muskmelon, *Cucumis melo cantalupensis,* with ribbed warty rind and orange flesh. 2 any of several other muskmelons.
▷HISTORY C18: from French, from *Cantaluppi,* former papal villa near Rome, where it was first cultivated in Europe

cantankerous (kæn'tæŋkərəs) ADJECTIVE quarrelsome; irascible.
▷HISTORY C18: perhaps from C14 (obsolete) *conteckour* a contentious person, from *conteck* strife, from Anglo-French *contek,* of obscure origin
▸**can'tankerously** ADVERB ▸**can'tankerousness** NOUN

cantata (kæn'tɑ:tə) NOUN a musical setting of a text, esp a religious text, consisting of arias, duets, and choruses interspersed with recitatives.
▷HISTORY C18: from Italian, from *cantare* to sing, from Latin

cantatrice (*French* kɑ̃tatris) NOUN a female singer, esp a professional soloist.

canteen (kæn'ti:n) NOUN 1 a restaurant attached to a factory, school, etc., providing meals for large numbers of people. 2 **a** a small shop that provides a limited range of items, such as toilet requisites, to a military unit. **b** a recreation centre for military personnel. 3 a soldier's eating and drinking utensils. 4 a temporary or mobile stand at which food is provided. 5 **a** a box in which a set of cutlery is laid out. **b** the cutlery itself. 6 a flask or canister for carrying water or other liquids, as used by soldiers or travellers.
▷HISTORY C18: from French *cantine,* from Italian *cantina* wine cellar, from *canto* corner, from Latin *canthus* iron hoop encircling chariot wheel; see CANT²

canteen culture NOUN the alleged clannishness of the police force, whereby the prevalent attitudes inhibit officers from reporting or speaking out against malpractice, racism, etc.

canter ('kæntə) NOUN 1 an easy three-beat gait of horses, etc., between a trot and a gallop in speed. 2 **at a canter.** easily; without effort: *he won at a canter.* ◆ VERB 3 to move or cause to move at a canter.
▷HISTORY C18: short for *Canterbury trot,* the supposed pace at which pilgrims rode to Canterbury

canterbury ('kæntəbərɪ, -brɪ) NOUN, *plural* **-buries.** *Antiques* 1 a late 18th-century low wooden stand with partitions for holding cutlery and plates: often mounted on casters. 2 a similar 19th-century stand used for holding sheet music, music books, or magazines.

Canterbury ('kæntəbərɪ, -brɪ) NOUN 1 a city in SE England, in E Kent: starting point for St Augustine's mission to England (597 A.D.); cathedral where St Thomas à Becket was martyred (1170); seat of the archbishop and primate of England; seat of the University of Kent (1965). Pop.: 36 464 (1991). Latin name: **Durovernum** (ˌdu:rəʊ'vɜ:nəm, ˌdjuə-). 2 a regional council area of New Zealand, on E central South Island on **Canterbury Bight**: mountainous with coastal lowlands; agricultural. Chief town: Christchurch. Pop.: 491 565 (2001). Area: 43 371 sq. km (16 742 sq. miles).

Canterbury bell NOUN a campanulaceous biennial European plant, *Campanula medium,* widely cultivated for its blue, violet, or white flowers.

Canterbury lamb NOUN New Zealand lamb exported chilled or frozen to the United Kingdom.

Canterbury Pilgrims PLURAL NOUN 1 the pilgrims whose stories are told in Chaucer's *Canterbury Tales.* 2 *NZ* the early settlers in Christchurch, Canterbury region.

cantharid ('kænθərɪd) NOUN any beetle of the family *Cantharidae,* having a soft elongated body; though found frequenting flowers, they are carnivorous.

cantharides (kæn'θærɪˌdi:z) PLURAL NOUN, *singular* **cantharis** ('kænθərɪs). a diuretic and urogenital stimulant or irritant prepared from the dried bodies of Spanish fly (family *Meloidae,* not *Cantharidae*), once thought to be an aphrodisiac. Also called: **Spanish fly.**
▷HISTORY C15: from Latin, plural of *cantharis,* from Greek *kantharis* Spanish fly

Can Tho ('kʌn 'təʊ, 'kæn) NOUN a town in S Vietnam, on the River Mekong. Pop.: 215 587 (1992 est.).

cant hook *or* **dog** NOUN *Forestry* a wooden pole with a blunt steel tip and an adjustable hook at one end, used for handling logs.

canthus ('kænθəs) NOUN, *plural* **-thi** (-θaɪ). the inner or outer corner or angle of the eye, formed by the natural junction of the eyelids.
▷HISTORY C17: from New Latin, from Latin: iron tyre
▸**'canthal** ADJECTIVE

canticle ('kæntɪkᵊl) NOUN 1 a nonmetrical hymn, derived from the Bible and used in the liturgy of certain Christian churches. 2 a song, poem, or hymn, esp one that is religious in character.
▷HISTORY C13: from Latin *canticulum,* diminutive of *canticus* a song, from *canere* to sing

Canticle of Canticles NOUN another name for the **Song of Solomon**, used in the Douay Bible

cantilena (ˌkæntɪ'leɪnə) NOUN a smooth flowing style in the writing of vocal music.
▷HISTORY C18: Italian, from Latin *cantilēna* a song

cantilever ('kæntɪˌli:və) NOUN 1 **a** a beam, girder, or structural framework that is fixed at one end and is free at the other. **b** (*as modifier*): *a cantilever wing.* 2 a wing or tailplane of an aircraft that has no external bracing or support. 3 a part of a beam or a structure projecting outwards beyond its support. ◆ VERB 4 (*tr*) to construct (a building member, beam, etc.) so that it is fixed at one end only. 5 (*intr*) to project like a cantilever.
▷HISTORY C17: perhaps from CANT² + LEVER

cantilever bridge NOUN a bridge having spans that are constructed as cantilevers and often a suspended span or spans, each end of which rests on one end of a cantilever span.

cantillate ('kæntɪˌleɪt) VERB 1 to chant (passages of the Hebrew Scriptures) according to the traditional Jewish melody. 2 to intone or chant.
▷HISTORY C19: from Late Latin *cantillāre* to sing softly, from Latin *cantāre* to sing

cantillation (ˌkæntɪ'leɪʃən) NOUN 1 the traditional notation representing the various traditional Jewish melodies to which scriptural passages are chanted. 2 chanting or intonation.

cantina (kæn'ti:nə) NOUN a bar or wine shop, esp in a Spanish-speaking country.
▷HISTORY from Spanish

canting arms PLURAL NOUN *Heraldry* a coat of arms making visual reference to the surname of its owner.

cantle ('kæntᵊl) NOUN 1 the back part of a saddle that slopes upwards. 2 a slice; a broken-off piece.
▷HISTORY C14: from Old Northern French *cantel,* from *cant* corner; see CANT²

canto ('kæntəʊ) NOUN, *plural* **-tos.** 1 *Music* another word for **cantus** (sense 2). 2 a main division of a long poem.
▷HISTORY C16: from Italian: song, from Latin *cantus,* from *canere* to sing

canto fermo ('kæntəʊ 'fɜ:məʊ) *or* **cantus firmus** ('kæntəs 'fɜ:məs) NOUN 1 a melody that is the basis to which other parts are added in polyphonic music. 2 the traditional plainchant as prescribed by use and regulation in the Christian Church.
▷HISTORY Italian, from Medieval Latin, literally: fixed song

canton NOUN ('kæntɒn, kæn'tɒn) 1 any of the 23 political divisions of Switzerland. 2 a subdivision of a French arrondissement. 3 ('kæntən) *Heraldry* a small square or oblong charge on a shield, usually in the top left corner. ◆ VERB 4 (kæn'tɒn) (*tr*) to divide into cantons. 5 (kən'tu:n) (esp formerly) to allocate accommodation to (military personnel).
▷HISTORY C16: from Old French: corner, division, from Italian *cantone,* from *canto* corner, from Latin *canthus* iron rim; see CANT²
▸**'cantonal** ADJECTIVE

Canton NOUN 1 (kæn'tɒn) a port in SE China, capital of Guangdong province, on the Zhu Jiang (Pearl River): the first Chinese port open to European trade. Pop.: 3 306 277 (1999 est.). Chinese names: **Guangzhou, Kwangchow.** 2 ('kæntən) a city in the US, in NE Ohio. Pop.: 80 806 (2000).

Canton crepe ('kæntɒn, -tən) NOUN a fine crinkled silk or rayon crepe fabric, slightly heavier than crepe de Chine.
▷HISTORY C19: named after *Canton,* China, where it was originally made

Cantonese (ˌkæntə'ni:z) NOUN 1 the Chinese language spoken in the city of Canton, Guangdong and Guanxi provinces, Hong Kong, and elsewhere outside China. 2 (*plural* **-ese**) a native or inhabitant of the city of Canton or Guangdong province. ◆ ADJECTIVE 3 of or relating to the city of Canton, Guangdong province, or the Chinese language spoken there.

Canton flannel ('kæntɒn, -tən) NOUN another name for **cotton flannel.**
▷HISTORY C19: named after *Canton,* China

cantonment (kən'tu:nmənt) NOUN *Military* (esp formerly) 1 a large training camp. 2 living accommodation, esp the winter quarters of a campaigning army. 3 *History* a permanent military camp in British India.

Canton River (kæn'tɒn) NOUN another name for the **Zhu Jiang.**

cantor ('kæntɔ:) NOUN 1 *Judaism* Also called: **chazan.** a man employed to lead synagogue services, esp to traditional modes and melodies. 2 *Christianity* the leader of the singing in a church choir.
▷HISTORY C16: from Latin: singer, from *canere* to sing

cantorial (kæn'tɔ:rɪəl) ADJECTIVE 1 of or relating to a precentor. 2 (of part of a choir) on the same side of a cathedral, etc., as the precentor; on the N side of the choir. Compare **decanal.**

cantoris (kæn'tɔ:rɪs) ADJECTIVE (in antiphonal music) to be sung by the cantorial side of a choir. Compare **decani.**
▷HISTORY Latin: genitive of *cantor* precentor

Cantor's paradox ('kæntɔ:z) NOUN *Logic* the paradox derived from the supposition of an all-inclusive universal set, since every set has more

subsets than members while every subset of such a universal set would be a member of it.
▷HISTORY named after Georg *Cantor* (1845–1918), German mathematician, born in Russia

cantrip ('kæntrɪp) *Scot* ◆ NOUN [1] a magic spell. [2] (*often plural*) a mischievous trick. ◆ ADJECTIVE [3] (of an effect) produced by black magic.
▷HISTORY C18: Scottish, of unknown origin

Cantuar. ('kæntjʊˌɑː) ABBREVIATION FOR Cantuariensis.
▷HISTORY Latin: (Archbishop) of Canterbury

cantus ('kæntəs) NOUN, *plural* **-tus.** [1] a medieval form of church singing; chant. [2] Also called: **canto.** the highest part in a piece of choral music. [3] (in 15th- or 16th-century music) a piece of choral music, usually secular, in polyphonic style.
▷HISTORY Latin: song, from *canere* to sing

canty ('kæntɪ, 'kɑːn-) ADJECTIVE **cantier, cantiest.** *Scot and Northern English dialect* lively; brisk; in good spirits.
▷HISTORY C18: see CANT[3]
▸'**cantily** ADVERB ▸'**cantiness** NOUN

Canuck (kə'nʌk) NOUN *US and Canadian informal* **a** a Canadian. **b** (formerly) esp a French Canadian.
▷HISTORY C19: of uncertain origin

canula ('kænjʊlə) NOUN, *plural* **-las** *or* **-lae** (-ˌliː). *Surgery* a variant spelling of **cannula.**

canvas ('kænvəs) NOUN [1] **a** a heavy durable cloth made of cotton, hemp, or jute, used for sails, tents, etc. **b** (*as modifier*): *a canvas bag.* [2] **a** a piece of canvas or a similar material on which a painting is done, usually in oils. **b** a painting on this material, esp in oils. [3] a tent or tents collectively. [4] *Nautical* any cloth of which sails are made. [5] *Nautical* the sails of a vessel collectively. [6] any coarse loosely woven cloth on which embroidery, tapestry, etc., is done. [7] (preceded by *the*) the floor of a boxing or wrestling ring. [8] *Rowing* the tapering covered part at either end of a racing boat, sometimes referred to as a unit of length: *to win by a canvas.* [9] **under canvas. a** in tents. **b** *Nautical* with sails unfurled.
▷HISTORY C14: from Norman French *canevas,* ultimately from Latin *cannabis* hemp

canvasback ('kænvəsˌbæk) NOUN, *plural* **-backs** *or* **-back.** a North American diving duck, *Aythyra valisineria,* the male of which has a white body and reddish-brown head.

canvass ('kænvəs) VERB [1] to solicit votes, orders, advertising, etc., from. [2] to determine the feelings and opinions of (voters before an election, etc.), esp by conducting a survey. [3] to investigate (something) thoroughly, esp by discussion or debate. [4] *Chiefly US* to inspect (votes) officially to determine their validity. ◆ NOUN [5] a solicitation of opinions, votes, sales orders, etc. [6] close inspection; scrutiny.
▷HISTORY C16: probably from obsolete sense of CANVAS (to toss someone in a canvas sheet, hence, to harass, criticize); the development of current senses is unexplained
▸'**canvasser** NOUN ▸'**canvassing** NOUN

canyon *or* **cañon** ('kænjən) NOUN a gorge or ravine, esp in North America, usually formed by the down-cutting of a river in a dry area where there is insufficient rainfall to erode the sides of the valley.
▷HISTORY C19: from Spanish *cañon,* from *caña* tube, from Latin *canna* cane

canzona (kæn'zəʊnə) NOUN a type of 16th- or 17th-century contrapuntal music, usually for keyboard, lute, or instrumental ensemble.
▷HISTORY C19: from Italian, from Latin *cantiō* song, from *canere* to sing

canzone (kæn'zəʊnɪ) NOUN, *plural* **-ni** (-nɪ). [1] a Provençal or Italian lyric, often in praise of love or beauty. [2] **a** a song, usually of a lyrical nature. **b** (in 16th-century choral music) a polyphonic song from which the madrigal developed.
▷HISTORY C16: from Italian: song, from Latin *cantiō,* from *canere* to sing

canzonetta (ˌkænzə'nɛtə) *or* **canzonet** (ˌkænzə'nɛt) NOUN a short cheerful or lively song, typically of the 16th to 18th centuries.
▷HISTORY C16: Italian *canzonetta,* diminutive of CANZONE

caoutchouc ('kaʊtʃʊːk, -tʃʊk, kaʊ'tʃuːk, -'tʃʊk) NOUN another name for **rubber**[1] (sense 1).

▷HISTORY C18: from French, from obsolete Spanish *cauchuc,* from Quechua

cap (kæp) NOUN [1] a covering for the head, esp a small close-fitting one made of cloth or knitted. [2] such a covering serving to identify the wearer's rank, occupation, etc.: *a nurse's cap.* [3] something that protects or covers, esp a small lid or cover: *lens cap.* [4] an uppermost surface or part: *the cap of a wave.* [5] **a** See **percussion cap. b** a small amount of explosive enclosed in paper and used in a toy gun. [6] *Sport, chiefly Brit* **a** an emblematic hat or beret given to someone chosen for a representative team: *he has won three England caps.* **b** a player chosen for such a team. [7] the upper part of a pedestal in a classical order. [8] the roof of a windmill, sometimes in the form of a dome. [9] *Botany* the pileus of a mushroom or toadstool. [10] *Hunting* **a** money contributed to the funds of a hunt by a follower who is neither a subscriber nor a farmer, in return for a day's hunting. **b** a collection taken at a meet of hounds, esp for a charity. [11] *Anatomy* **a** the natural enamel covering a tooth. **b** an artificial protective covering for a tooth. [12] See **Dutch cap** (sense 2). [13] an upper financial limit. [14] a mortarboard when worn with a gown at an academic ceremony (esp in the phrase **cap and gown**). [15] *Meteorol* **a** the cloud covering the peak of a mountain. **b** the transient top of detached clouds above an increasing cumulus. [16] **cap in hand.** humbly, as when asking a favour. [17] **if the cap fits.** *Brit* the allusion or criticism seems to be appropriate to a particular person. [18] **set one's cap for** *or* **at.** (of a woman) to be determined to win as a husband or lover. ◆ VERB **caps, capping, capped.** (*tr*) [19] to cover, as with a cap: *snow capped the mountain tops.* [20] *Informal* to outdo; excel: *your story caps them all; to cap an anecdote.* [21] **to cap it all.** to provide the finishing touch: *we had sun, surf, cheap wine, and to cap it all a free car.* [22] *Sport, Brit* to select (a player) for a representative team: *he was capped 30 times by Scotland.* [23] to seal off (an oil or gas well). [24] to impose an upper limit on the level of increase of (a tax, such as the council tax): *rate-capping.* [25] *Hunting* to ask (hunt followers) for a cap. [26] *Chiefly Scot and NZ* to award a degree to.
▷HISTORY Old English *cæppe,* from Late Latin *cappa* hood, perhaps from Latin *caput* head
▸'**capper** NOUN

CAP ABBREVIATION FOR Common Agricultural Policy: (in the EU) the system for supporting farm incomes by maintaining agricultural prices at agreed levels.

cap. ABBREVIATION FOR: [1] capital. [2] capitalize. [3] capitalization. [4] capital letter.
▷HISTORY Latin: chapter

capability (ˌkeɪpə'bɪlɪtɪ) NOUN, *plural* **-ties.** [1] the quality of being capable; ability. [2] the quality of being susceptible to the use or treatment indicated: *the capability of a metal to be fused.* [3] (*usually plural*) a characteristic that may be developed; potential aptitude.

capable ('keɪpəb[ə]l) ADJECTIVE [1] having ability, esp in many different fields; competent. [2] (*postpositive;* foll by *of*) able or having the skill (to do something): *she is capable of hard work.* [3] (*postpositive;* foll by *of*) having the temperament or inclination (to do something): *he seemed capable of murder.*
▷HISTORY C16: from French, from Late Latin *capābilis* able to take in, from Latin *capere* to take
▸'**capableness** NOUN ▸'**capably** ADVERB

capacious (kə'peɪʃəs) ADJECTIVE capable of holding much; roomy; spacious.
▷HISTORY C17: from Latin *capāx,* from Latin *capere* to take
▸**ca'paciously** ADVERB ▸**ca'paciousness** NOUN

capacitance (kə'pæsɪtəns) NOUN [1] the property of a system that enables it to store electric charge. [2] a measure of this, equal to the charge that must be added to such a system to raise its electrical potential by one unit. Symbol: *C.* Former name: **capacity.**
▷HISTORY C20: from CAPACIT(Y) + -ANCE
▸**ca'pacitive** ADJECTIVE ▸**ca'pacitively** ADVERB

capacitate (kə'pæsɪˌteɪt) VERB (*tr*) [1] to make legally competent. [2] *Rare* to make capable.
▸**caˌpaci'tation** NOUN

capacitor (kə'pæsɪtə) NOUN a device for accumulating electric charge, usually consisting of two conducting surfaces separated by a dielectric. Former name: **condenser.**

capacity (kə'pæsɪtɪ) NOUN, *plural* **-ties.** [1] the ability or power to contain, absorb, or hold. [2] the amount that can be contained; volume: *a capacity of six gallons.* [3] **a** the maximum amount something can contain or absorb (esp in the phrase **filled to capacity**). **b** (*as modifier*): *a capacity crowd.* [4] the ability to understand or learn; aptitude; capability: *he has a great capacity for Greek.* [5] the ability to do or produce (often in the phrase **at capacity**): *the factory's output was not at capacity.* [6] a specified position or function: *he was employed in the capacity of manager.* [7] a measure of the electrical output of a piece of apparatus such as a motor, generator, or accumulator. [8] *Electronics* a former name for **capacitance.** [9] *Computing* **a** the number of words or characters that can be stored in a particular storage device. **b** the range of numbers that can be processed in a register. [10] the bit rate that a communication channel or other system can carry. [11] legal competence: *the capacity to make a will.*
▷HISTORY C15: from Old French *capacite,* from Latin *capācitās,* from *capāx* spacious, from *capere* to take

cap and bells NOUN the traditional garb of a court jester, including a cap with bells attached to it.

cap-a-pie (ˌkæpə'piː) ADVERB (dressed, armed, etc.) from head to foot.
▷HISTORY C16: from Old French

caparison (kə'pærɪs[ə]n) NOUN [1] a decorated covering for a horse or other animal, esp (formerly) for a warhorse. [2] rich or elaborate clothing and ornaments. ◆ VERB [3] (*tr*) to put a caparison on.
▷HISTORY C16: via obsolete French from Old Spanish *caparazón* saddlecloth, probably from *capa* CAPE[1]

cape[1] (keɪp) NOUN [1] a sleeveless garment like a cloak but usually shorter. [2] a strip of material attached to a coat or other garment so as to fall freely, usually from the shoulders.
▷HISTORY C16: from French, from Provençal *capa,* from Late Latin *cappa;* see CAP

cape[2] (keɪp) NOUN a headland or promontory.
▷HISTORY C14: from Old French *cap,* from Old Provençal, from Latin *caput* head

Cape (keɪp) NOUN **the.** [1] the SW region of South Africa, in Western Cape province. [2] See **Cape of Good Hope.**

Cape Barren goose NOUN a greyish Australian goose, *Cereopsis novaehollandiae,* having a black bill with a greenish cere.
▷HISTORY C19: named after *Cape Barren* Island in the Bass Strait

Cape Breton Island NOUN an island off SE Canada, in NE Nova Scotia, separated from the mainland by the Strait of Canso: its easternmost point is **Cape Breton.** Pop.: 120 098 (1991). Area: 10 280 sq. km (3970 sq. miles).

Cape buffalo NOUN another name for **buffalo** (sense 1).

Cape cart NOUN *South African* a two-wheeled horse-drawn vehicle sometimes with a canvas hood.

Cape Cod NOUN [1] a long sandy peninsula in SE Massachusetts, between **Cape Cod Bay** and the Atlantic. [2] Also called: **Cape Cod cottage.** a one-storey cottage of timber construction with a simple gable roof and a large central chimney: originated on Cape Cod in the 18th century.

Cape Colony NOUN the name from 1652 until 1910 of the former **Cape Province** of South Africa.

Cape Coloured NOUN (in South Africa) another name for a **Coloured** (sense 2).

Cape doctor NOUN *South African informal* a strong fresh SE wind blowing in the vicinity of Cape Town, esp in the summer.

Cape Dutch NOUN [1] an obsolete name for **Afrikaans.** [2] (in South Africa) a distinctive style of furniture or architecture.

Cape Flats PLURAL NOUN the strip of low-lying land in South Africa joining the Cape Peninsula proper to the African mainland.

cape gooseberry NOUN another name for **strawberry tomato.**

Cape Horn NOUN a rocky headland on an island

at the extreme S tip of South America, belonging to Chile. It is notorious for gales and heavy seas; until the building of the Panama Canal it lay on the only sea route between the Atlantic and the Pacific. Also called: **the Horn.**

Cape jasmine NOUN a widely cultivated gardenia shrub, *Gardenia jasminoides.* See **gardenia.**

capelin ('kæpəlɪn) *or* **caplin** NOUN a small marine food fish, *Mallotus villosus,* occurring in northern and Arctic seas: family *Osmeridae* (smelts).
▷HISTORY C17: from French *capelan,* from Old Provençal, literally: CHAPLAIN

Capella (kə'pɛlə) NOUN the brightest star in the constellation Auriga; it is a yellow giant and a spectroscopic binary. Visual magnitude: 0.08; spectral type: G6III and G2III; distance: 42 light years.
▷HISTORY C17: New Latin, from Latin, diminutive of *capra* she-goat, from *caper* goat

capellmeister *or* **kapellmeister** (kæ'pɛlˌmaɪstə) NOUN a person in charge of an orchestra, esp in an 18th-century princely household. See also **maestro di cappella.**
▷HISTORY from German, from *Kapelle* chapel + *Meister* MASTER

Cape of Good Hope NOUN a cape in SW South Africa south of Cape Town.

Cape Peninsula NOUN (in South Africa) the peninsula and the part of the mainland on which Cape Town and most of its suburbs are located.

Cape pigeon NOUN a species of seagoing petrel, *Daption capensis,* with characteristic white wing patches: a common winter visitor off the coasts of southern Africa: family *Diomedeidae.* Also called: **pintado petrel.**

Cape primrose NOUN See **streptocarpus.**

Cape Province NOUN a former province of S South Africa; replaced in 1994 by the new provinces of Northern Cape, Western Cape, Eastern Cape and part of North-West. Capital: Cape Town. Official name: **Cape of Good Hope Province.** Former name (1652–1910): **Cape Colony.**

caper¹ ('keɪpə) NOUN 1 a playful skip or leap. 2 a high-spirited escapade. 3 **cut a caper** *or* **capers. a** to skip or jump playfully. **b** to act or behave playfully; frolic. 4 *Slang* a crime, esp an organized robbery. 5 *Austral informal* a job or occupation. 6 *Austral informal* a person's behaviour. ◆ VERB 7 *(intr)* to leap or dance about in a light-hearted manner.
▷HISTORY C16: probably from CAPRIOLE
▸ 'caperer NOUN ▸ 'caperingly ADVERB

caper² ('keɪpə) NOUN 1 a spiny trailing Mediterranean capparidaceous shrub, *Capparis spinosa,* with edible flower buds. 2 any of various similar plants or their edible parts. See also **bean caper, capers.**
▷HISTORY C15: from earlier *capers, capres* (assumed to be plural), from Latin *capparis,* from Greek *kapparis*

capercaillie (ˌkæpə'keɪljɪ) *or* **capercailzie** (ˌkæpə'keɪljɪ, -'keɪlzɪ) NOUN a large European woodland grouse, *Tetrao urogallus,* having a black plumage and fan-shaped tail in the male.
▷HISTORY C16: from Scottish Gaelic *capull coille* horse of the woods

Capernaum (kə'pɜːnɪəm) NOUN a ruined town in N Israel, on the NW shore of the Sea of Galilee: closely associated with Jesus Christ during his ministry.

capers ('keɪpəz) PLURAL NOUN the flower buds of the caper plant, which are pickled and used as a condiment.

capeskin ('keɪpˌskɪn) NOUN 1 a soft leather obtained from the skins of a type of lamb or sheep having hairlike wool. ◆ ADJECTIVE 2 made of this leather.
▷HISTORY C19: named after the *Cape of Good Hope*

Cape smoke NOUN *South African informal* South African brandy.

Cape sparrow NOUN a sparrow, *Passer melanurus,* very common in southern Africa: family *Ploceidae.* Also called (esp South African): **mossie.**

Capetian (kə'piːʃən) NOUN 1 a member of the dynasty founded by Hugh Capet (?938–996 A.D.), king of France (987–96), which ruled France from 987–1328 A.D. ◆ ADJECTIVE 2 of, or relating to, the Capetian kings or their rule.

Cape Town NOUN the legislative capital of South Africa and capital of Western Cape province, situated in the southwest on Table Bay: founded in 1652, the first White settlement in southern Africa; important port. Pop. (urban area): 2 415 408 (1996).

Cape Verde (vɜːd) NOUN a republic in the Atlantic off the coast of West Africa, consisting of a group of ten islands and five islets: an overseas territory of Portugal until 1975, when the islands became independent. Official language: Portuguese. Religion: Christian (Roman Catholic) majority; animist minority. Currency: Cape Verdean escudo. Capital: Praia. Pop.: 446 000 (2001 est.). Area: 4033 sq. km (1557 sq. miles).

Cape Verdean ('vɜːdɪən) ADJECTIVE 1 of or relating to Cape Verde or its inhabitants. ◆ NOUN 2 a native or inhabitant of Cape Verde.

Cape York NOUN the northernmost point of the Australian mainland, in N Queensland on the Torres Strait at the tip of **Cape York Peninsula** (a peninsula between the Coral Sea and the Gulf of Carpentaria).

Cap-Haitien (*French* kapaisjɛ̃, -tjɛ̃) NOUN a port in N Haiti: capital during the French colonial period. Pop.: 107 026 (1997 est.). Also called: **le Cap** (lə kap).

capias ('keɪpɪˌæs, 'kæp-) NOUN *Law* (formerly) a writ directing a sheriff or other officer to arrest a named person.
▷HISTORY C15: from Latin, literally: you must take, from *capere*

capillaceous (ˌkæpɪ'leɪʃəs) ADJECTIVE 1 having numerous filaments resembling hairs or threads. 2 resembling a hair; capillary.
▷HISTORY C18: from Latin *capillāceus* hairy, from *capillus* hair

capillarity (ˌkæpɪ'lærɪtɪ) NOUN a phenomenon caused by surface tension and resulting in the distortion, elevation, or depression of the surface of a liquid in contact with a solid. Also called: **capillary action.**

capillary (kə'pɪlərɪ) ADJECTIVE 1 resembling a hair; slender. 2 (of tubes) having a fine bore. 3 *Anatomy* of or relating to any of the delicate thin-walled blood vessels that form an interconnecting network between the arterioles and the venules. 4 *Physics* of or relating to capillarity. ◆ NOUN, *plural* **-laries.** 5 *Anatomy* any of the capillary blood vessels. 6 a fine hole or narrow passage in any substance.
▷HISTORY C17: from Latin *capillāris,* from *capillus* hair

capillary tube NOUN a glass tube with a fine bore and thick walls, used in thermometers, etc.

capita ('kæpɪtə) NOUN 1 See **per capita.** 2 *Anatomy* the plural of **caput.**

capital¹ ('kæpɪtᵊl) NOUN 1 **a** the seat of government of a country or other political unit. **b** *(as modifier)*: *a capital city.* 2 material wealth owned by an individual or business enterprise. 3 wealth available for or capable of use in the production of further wealth, as by industrial investment. 4 **make capital (out) of.** to get advantage from. 5 *(sometimes capital)* the capitalist class or their interests: *capital versus labour.* 6 *Accounting* **a** the ownership interests of a business as represented by the excess of assets over liabilities. **b** the nominal value of the authorized or issued shares. **c** *(as modifier)*: *capital issues.* 7 any assets or resources, esp when used to gain profit or advantage. 8 **a** a capital letter. Abbreviations: **cap, cap. b** *(as modifier)*: *capital B.* 9 **with a capital A, B,** etc. (used to give emphasis to a statement): *he is mean with a capital M.* ◆ ADJECTIVE 10 *(prenominal) Law* involving or punishable by death: *a capital offence.* 11 very serious; fatal: *a capital error.* 12 primary, chief, or principal: *our capital concern is that everyone be fed.* 13 of, relating to, or designating the large modern majuscule letter used chiefly as the initial letter in personal names and place names and other uniquely specificatory nouns, and often for abbreviations and acronyms. Compare **small** (sense 9). See also **upper case.** 14 *Chiefly Brit* excellent; first-rate: *a capital idea.*
▷HISTORY C13: from Latin *capitālis* (adjective) concerning the head, chief, from *caput* head; compare Medieval Latin *capitāle* (noun) wealth, from *capitālis* (adjective)

capital² ('kæpɪtᵊl) NOUN the upper part of a column or pier that supports the entablature. Also called: **chapiter, cap.**
▷HISTORY C14: from Old French *capitel,* from Late Latin *capitellum,* diminutive of *caput* head

capital account NOUN 1 *Economics* that part of a balance of payments composed of movements of capital and international loans and grants. Compare **current account** (sense 2). 2 *Accounting* a financial statement showing the net value of a company at a specified date. It is defined as total assets minus total liabilities and represents ownership interests. 3 *US* an account of fixed assets.

capital allowance NOUN the allowing of a certain amount of money spent by a company on fixed assets to be taken off the profits of the company before tax is imposed.

capital assets PLURAL NOUN another name for **fixed assets.**

capital expenditure NOUN expenditure on acquisitions of or improvements to fixed assets.

capital gain NOUN the amount by which the selling price of a financial asset exceeds its cost.

capital gains tax NOUN a tax on the profit made from the sale of an asset. Abbreviation: **CGT.**

capital goods PLURAL NOUN *Economics* goods that are themselves utilized in the production of other goods rather than being sold to consumers. Also called: **producer goods.** Compare **consumer goods.**

capitalism ('kæpɪtəˌlɪzəm) NOUN an economic system based on the private ownership of the means of production, distribution, and exchange, characterized by the freedom of capitalists to operate or manage their property for profit in competitive conditions. Also called: **free enterprise, private enterprise.** Compare **socialism** (sense 1).

capitalist ('kæpɪtəlɪst) NOUN 1 a person who owns capital, esp capital invested in a business. 2 *Politics* a supporter of capitalism. 3 *Informal, usually derogatory* a rich person. ◆ ADJECTIVE 4 of or relating to capital, capitalists, or capitalism.
▸ ˌcapital'istic ADJECTIVE

capitalization *or* **capitalisation** (ˌkæpɪtəlaɪ'zeɪʃən) NOUN 1 **a** the act of capitalizing. **b** the sum so derived. 2 *Accounting* the par value of the total share capital issued by a company, including the loan capital and sometimes reserves. 3 the act of estimating the present value of future payments, earnings, etc. 4 the act of writing or printing in capital letters.

capitalization issue NOUN another name for **rights issue.**

capitalize *or* **capitalise** ('kæpɪtəˌlaɪz) VERB *(mainly tr)* 1 *(intr;* foll by *on)* to take advantage (of); profit (by). 2 to write or print (text) in capital letters or with the first letter of (a word or words) in capital letters. 3 to convert (debt or retained earnings) into capital stock. 4 to authorize (a business enterprise) to issue a specified amount of capital stock. 5 to provide with capital. 6 *Accounting* to treat (expenditures) as assets. 7 **a** to estimate the present value of (a periodical income). **b** to compute the present value of (a business) from actual or potential earnings.

capital levy NOUN a tax on capital or property as contrasted with a tax on income.

capitally ('kæpɪtəlɪ) ADVERB *Chiefly Brit* in an excellent manner; admirably.

capital market NOUN the financial institutions collectively that deal with medium-term and long-term capital and loans. Compare **money market.**

capital punishment NOUN the punishment of death for a crime; death penalty.

capital ship NOUN one of the largest and most heavily armed ships in a naval fleet.

capital stock NOUN 1 the par value of the total share capital that a company is authorized to issue. 2 the total physical capital existing in an economy at any moment of time.

capital surplus NOUN another name (esp US) for **share premium.**

capital transfer tax NOUN (in Britain) a tax payable from 1974 to 1986 at progressive rates on the cumulative total of gifts of money or property made during the donor's lifetime or after his death. It was replaced by inheritance tax.

capitate ('kæpɪˌteɪt) ADJECTIVE 1 *Botany* shaped like a head, as certain flowers or inflorescences. 2 *Zoology* having an enlarged headlike end: *a capitate bone*.
▷HISTORY C17: from Latin *capitātus* having a (large) head, from *caput* head

capitation (ˌkæpɪ'teɪʃən) NOUN 1 a tax levied on the basis of a fixed amount per head. 2 **capitation grant.** a grant of money given to every person who qualifies under certain conditions. 3 the process of assessing or numbering by counting heads.
▷HISTORY C17: from Late Latin *capitātiō*, from Latin *caput* head
▸**'capitative** ADJECTIVE

capitellum (ˌkæpɪ'tɛləm) NOUN, *plural* **-la** (-lə). *Anatomy* an enlarged knoblike structure at the end of a bone that forms an articulation with another bone; capitulum.
▷HISTORY C19: from Latin, diminutive of CAPITULUM

Capitol ('kæpɪtᵊl) NOUN 1 **a** another name for the **Capitoline. b** the temple on the Capitoline. 2 **the.** the main building of the US Congress. 3 (*sometimes not capital*) Also called: **statehouse.** (in the US) the building housing any state legislature.
▷HISTORY C14: from Latin *Capitōlium*, from *caput* head

Capitoline ('kæpɪtᵊˌlaɪn, kə'pɪtəʊ-) NOUN 1 **the.** the most important of the Seven Hills of Rome. The temple of Jupiter was on the southern summit and the ancient citadel on the northern summit. ◆ ADJECTIVE 2 of or relating to the Capitoline or the temple of Jupiter.

capitular (kə'pɪtjʊlə) ADJECTIVE 1 of or associated with a cathedral chapter. 2 of or relating to a capitulum.
▷HISTORY C17: from Medieval Latin *capitulāris*, from *capitulum* CHAPTER
▸**ca'pitularly** ADVERB

capitulary (kə'pɪtjʊlərɪ) NOUN, *plural* **-laries.** any of the collections of ordinances promulgated by the Frankish kings (8th–10th centuries A.D.).
▷HISTORY C17: from Medieval Latin *capitulāris*; see CAPITULAR

capitulate (kə'pɪtjʊˌleɪt) VERB (*intr*) to surrender, esp under agreed conditions.
▷HISTORY C16 (meaning: to arrange under heads, draw up in order; hence, to make terms of surrender): from Medieval Latin *capitulare* to draw up under heads, from *capitulum* CHAPTER
▸**ca'pituˌlator** NOUN

capitulation (kəˌpɪtjʊ'leɪʃən) NOUN 1 the act of capitulating. 2 a document containing terms of surrender. 3 a statement summarizing the main divisions of a subject.
▸**ca'pitulatory** ADJECTIVE

capitulum (kə'pɪtjʊləm) NOUN, *plural* **-la** (-lə). 1 a racemose inflorescence in the form of a disc of sessile flowers, the youngest at the centre. It occurs in the daisy and related plants. 2 *Anatomy, zoology* a headlike part, esp the enlarged knoblike terminal part of a long bone, antenna, etc.
▷HISTORY C18: from Latin, literally: a little head, from *caput* head

capiz ('kæpɪz) NOUN the bivalve shell of a mollusc (*Placuna placenta*) found esp in the Philippines and having a smooth translucent shiny interior: used in jewellery, ornaments, lampshades, etc. Also called: **jingle shell, window shell.**
▷HISTORY from the native name in the Philippines

caplet ('kæplɪt) NOUN a medicinal tablet, usually oval in shape, coated in a soluble substance.
▷HISTORY C20: CAP(SULE) + (TAB)LET

caplin ('kæplɪn) NOUN a variant of **capelin.**

capo¹ ('keɪpəʊ, 'kæpəʊ) NOUN, *plural* **-pos.** a device fitted across all the strings of a guitar, lute, etc., so as to raise the pitch of each string simultaneously. Compare **barré.** Also called: **capo tasto** ('kæpəʊ 'tæstəʊ).
▷HISTORY from Italian *capo tasto* head stop

capo² ('kæpəʊ; *Italian* 'kapo) NOUN, *plural* **-pos.** the presumed title of a leader in the Mafia.
▷HISTORY Italian: head

capoeira (ˌkæpʊ'eɪrə) NOUN a movement discipline combining martial art and dance, which originated among African slaves in 19th-century Brazil.
▷HISTORY C20: from Portuguese

cap of maintenance NOUN a ceremonial cap or hat worn or carried as a symbol of office, rank, etc.

capon ('keɪpən) NOUN a castrated cock fowl fattened for eating.
▷HISTORY Old English *capun*, from Latin *cāpō* capon; related to Greek *koptein* to cut off

caponize *or* **caponise** ('keɪpəˌnaɪz) VERB (*tr*) to make (a cock) into a capon.

caporal (ˌkæpə'rɑːl) NOUN a strong coarse dark tobacco.
▷HISTORY C19: from French *tabac du caporal* corporal's tobacco, denoting its superiority to *tabac du soldat* soldier's tobacco

Caporetto (kapo'retto) NOUN the Italian name for **Kobarid.**

capot (kə'pɒt) NOUN *Piquet* the winning of all the tricks by one player.
▷HISTORY C17: from French

capote (kə'pəʊt; *French* kapɔt) NOUN a long cloak or soldier's coat, usually with a hood.
▷HISTORY C19: from French: cloak, from *cape*; see CAPE[1]

Cappadocia (ˌkæpə'dəʊsɪə) NOUN an ancient region of E Asia Minor famous for its horses.

Cappadocian (ˌkæpə'dəʊsɪən) ADJECTIVE 1 of or relating to Cappadocia (an ancient region of E Asia Minor) or its inhabitants. ◆ NOUN 2 a native or inhabitant of Cappadocia.

capparidaceous (ˌkæpærɪ'deɪʃəs) ADJECTIVE of, relating to, or belonging to the *Capparidaceae* (or (*Capparaceae*), a family of plants, mostly shrubs including the caper, of warm tropical regions.
▷HISTORY C19: from New Latin *Capparidaceae*, from Latin *capparis* caper

cappelletti (ˌkæpə'lɛtɪ) NOUN small squares of pasta containing a savoury mixture of meat, cheese, or vegetables.
▷HISTORY C19: Italian, plural of *cappelletto*, literally: little hat

cappuccino (ˌkæpʊ'tʃiːnəʊ) NOUN, *plural* **-nos.** coffee with steamed milk, sometimes served with whipped cream or sprinkled with powdered chocolate.
▷HISTORY Italian: CAPUCHIN

capreolate ('kæprɪəˌleɪt, kə'priː-) ADJECTIVE *Biology* possessing or resembling tendrils.
▷HISTORY C18: from Latin *capreolus* tendril

Capri (kə'priː; *Italian* 'kapri) NOUN an island off W Italy, in the Bay of Naples: resort since Roman times. Pop.: 8000 (latest est.). Area: about 13 sq. km (5 sq. miles).

capric acid ('kæprɪk) NOUN another name for **decanoic acid.**
▷HISTORY C19: from Latin *caper* goat, so named from its smell

capriccio (kə'prɪtʃɪˌəʊ) *or* **caprice** NOUN, *plural* **-priccios, -pricci** (-'priːtʃɪ), *or* **-prices.** *Music* a lively piece composed freely and without adhering to the rules for any specific musical form.
▷HISTORY C17: from Italian: CAPRICE

capriccioso (kəˌprɪtʃɪ'əʊzəʊ) ADVERB *Music* to be played in a free and lively style.
▷HISTORY Italian: from *capriccio* CAPRICE

caprice (kə'priːs) NOUN 1 a sudden or unpredictable change of attitude, behaviour, etc.; whim. 2 a tendency to such changes. 3 another word for **capriccio.**
▷HISTORY C17: from French, from Italian *capriccio* a shiver, caprice, from *capo* head + *riccio* hedgehog, suggesting a convulsive shudder in which the hair stood on end like a hedgehog's spines; meaning also influenced by Italian *capra* goat, by folk etymology

capricious (kə'prɪʃəs) ADJECTIVE characterized by or liable to sudden unpredictable changes in attitude or behaviour; impulsive; fickle.
▸**ca'priciously** ADVERB ▸**ca'priciousness** NOUN

Capricorn ('kæprɪˌkɔːn) NOUN 1 *Astrology* **a** Also called: **the Goat, Capricornus.** the tenth sign of the zodiac, symbol ♑, having a cardinal earth classification and ruled by the planet Saturn. The sun is in this sign between about Dec. 22 and Jan. 19. **b** a person born during the period when the sun is in this sign. 2 *Astronomy* another name for **Capricornus.** 3 **tropic of Capricorn.** See **tropic** (sense 1). ◆ ADJECTIVE 4 *Astrology* born under or characteristic of Capricorn. ◆ Also (for senses 1b, 4): **Capricornean** (ˌkæprɪ'kɔːnɪən).
▷HISTORY C14: from Latin *Capricornus* (translating Greek *aigokerōs* goat-horned), from *caper* goat + *cornū* horn

Capricornia (ˌkæprɪ'kɔːnɪə) NOUN the regions of Australia in the tropic of Capricorn.

Capricornus (ˌkæprɪ'kɔːnəs) NOUN, *Latin genitive* **-ni** (-naɪ). a faint zodiacal constellation in the S hemisphere, lying between Sagittarius and Aquarius.

caprification (ˌkæprɪfɪ'keɪʃən) NOUN a method of pollinating the edible fig by hanging branches of caprifig flowers in edible fig trees. Parasitic wasps in the caprifig flowers transfer pollen to the edible fig flowers.
▷HISTORY C17: from Latin *caprificātiō*, from *caprificāre* to pollinate figs by this method, from *caprificus* CAPRIFIG

caprifig ('kæprɪˌfɪg) NOUN a wild variety of fig, *Ficus carica sylvestris*, of S Europe and SW Asia, used in the caprification of the edible fig.
▷HISTORY C15: from Latin *caprificus* literally: goat fig, from *caper* goat + *fīcus* FIG[1]

caprifoliaceous (ˌkæprɪˌfəʊlɪ'eɪʃəs) ADJECTIVE of, relating to, or belonging to the *Caprifoliaceae*, a family of N temperate shrubs, small trees, and climbers including honeysuckle, elder, and guelder-rose.
▷HISTORY C19: from New Latin *caprifoliāceae*, from *caprifolium* type genus, from Medieval Latin: honeysuckle, from Latin *caper* goat + *folium* leaf

caprine ('kæpraɪn) ADJECTIVE of or resembling a goat.
▷HISTORY C17: from Latin *caprīnus*, from *caper* goat

capriole ('kæprɪˌəʊl) NOUN 1 *Dressage* a high upward but not forward leap made by a horse with all four feet off the ground. 2 *Dancing* a leap from bent knees. ◆ VERB 3 (*intr*) to perform a capriole.
▷HISTORY C16: from French, from Old Italian *capriola*, from *capriolo* roebuck, from Latin *capreolus*, *caper* goat

Capri pants *or* **Capris** PLURAL NOUN women's tight-fitting trousers.

cap rock NOUN 1 a layer of rock that overlies a salt dome and consists of limestone, gypsum, etc. 2 a layer of relatively impervious rock overlying an oil- or gas-bearing rock.

caproic acid (kə'prəʊɪk) NOUN another name for **hexanoic acid.**
▷HISTORY C19: *caproic*, from Latin *caper* goat, alluding to its smell

caprolactam (ˌkæprəʊ'læktæm) NOUN a white crystalline cyclic imine used in the manufacture of nylon. Formula: $C_5H_{10}NHCO$.
▷HISTORY C20: from CAPRO(IC ACID) + LACTAM

caps. ABBREVIATION FOR capital letters.

capsaicin (kæp'seɪɪsɪn) NOUN a colourless crystalline bitter alkaloid found in capsicums and used as a flavouring in vinegar and pickles. Formula: $C_{18}H_{27}O_3N$.
▷HISTORY C19 *capsicine*, from CAPSICUM + -INE[2]; modern form refashioned from Latin *capsa* box, case + -IN

cap screw NOUN a screwed bolt with a cylindrical head having a hexagonal recess. The bolt is turned using a wrench of hexagonal cross section.

Capsian ('kæpsɪən) NOUN 1 a late Palaeolithic culture, dating from about 12 000 B.C., found mainly around the salt lakes of Tunisia. The culture is characterized by the presence of microliths, backed blades, and engraved limestone slabs. ◆ ADJECTIVE 2 of or relating to this culture.
▷HISTORY C20: from French *capsien*, from *Capsa*, Latinized form of *Gafsa*, Tunisia

capsicum ('kæpsɪkəm) NOUN 1 any tropical American plant of the solanaceous genus *Capsicum*, such as *C. frutescens*, having mild or pungent seeds enclosed in a pod-shaped or bell-shaped fruit. 2 the fruit of any of these plants, used as a vegetable or ground to produce a condiment. ◆ See also **pepper** (sense 4).
▷HISTORY C18: from New Latin, from Latin *capsa* box, CASE[2]

capsid¹ ('kæpsɪd) NOUN any heteropterous bug of the family *Miridae* (formerly *Capsidae*), most of

which feed on plant tissues, causing damage to crops.
▷HISTORY C19: from New Latin *Capsus* (genus)

capsid² (ˈkæpsɪd) NOUN the outer protein coat of a mature virus.
▷HISTORY C20: from French *capside,* from Latin *capsa* box

capsize (kæpˈsaɪz) VERB to overturn accidentally; upset.
▷HISTORY C18: of uncertain origin
▸**capˈsizal** NOUN

capsomere (ˈkæpsəˌmɪə) NOUN any of the protein units that together form the capsid of a virus.

capstan (ˈkæpstən) NOUN [1] a machine with a drum that rotates round a vertical spindle and is turned by a motor or lever, used for hauling in heavy ropes, etc. [2] any similar device, such as the rotating shaft in a tape recorder that pulls the tape past the head.
▷HISTORY C14: from Old Provençal *cabestan,* from Latin *capistrum* a halter, from *capere* to seize

capstan bar NOUN a lever, often wooden, for turning a capstan.

capstan lathe NOUN a lathe for repetitive work, having a rotatable turret resembling a capstan to hold tools for successive operations. Also called: **turret lathe.**

capstone (ˈkæpˌstəʊn) *or* **copestone** (ˈkəʊpˌstəʊn) NOUN [1] one of a set of slabs on the top of a wall, building, etc. [2] *Mountaineering* a chockstone occurring at the top of a gully or chimney. [3] a crowning achievement; peak.

capsulate (ˈkæpsjʊˌleɪt, -lɪt) *or* **capsulated** ADJECTIVE within or formed into a capsule.
▸ˌ**capsuˈlation** NOUN

capsule (ˈkæpsjuːl) NOUN [1] a soluble case of gelatine enclosing a dose of medicine. [2] a thin metal cap, seal, or cover, such as the foil covering the cork of a wine bottle. [3] *Botany* **a** a dry fruit that liberates its seeds by splitting, as in the violet, or through pores, as in the poppy. **b** the spore-producing organ of mosses and liverworts. [4] *Bacteriol* a gelatinous layer of polysaccharide or protein surrounding the cell wall of some bacteria: thought to be responsible for the virulence in pathogens. [5] *Anatomy* **a** a cartilaginous, fibrous, or membranous envelope surrounding any of certain organs or parts. **b** a broad band of white fibres (**internal capsule**) near the thalamus in each cerebral hemisphere. [6] See **space capsule.** [7] an aeroplane cockpit that can be ejected in a flight emergency, complete with crew, instruments, etc. [8] (*modifier*) in a highly concise form: *a capsule summary.* [9] (*modifier*) (in the fashion industry) consisting of a few important representative items: *a capsule collection.*
▷HISTORY C17: from French, from Latin *capsula,* diminutive of *capsa* box

capsule range NOUN a small range of clothes by a particular designer, intended to be representative of the full range.

capsule wardrobe NOUN a collection of clothes and accessories that includes only items considered essential.

capsulize *or* **capsulise** (ˈkæpsjʊˌlaɪz) VERB (*tr*) [1] to state (information) in a highly condensed form. [2] to enclose in a capsule.

Capt. ABBREVIATION FOR Captain.

captain (ˈkæptɪn) NOUN [1] the person in charge of and responsible for a vessel. [2] an officer of the navy who holds a rank junior to a rear admiral but senior to a commander. [3] an officer of the army, certain air forces, and the marine corps who holds a rank junior to a major but senior to a lieutenant. [4] the officer in command of a civil aircraft, usually the senior pilot. [5] the leader of a team in games. [6] a person in command over a group, organization, etc.; leader: *a captain of industry.* [7] *US* a policeman in charge of a precinct. [8] *US and Canadian* (formerly) a head waiter. [9] Also called: **bell captain.** *US and Canadian* a supervisor of bellboys in a hotel. [10] *Austral informal* a person who is buying drinks for people in a bar. ◆ VERB [11] (*tr*) to be captain of.
▷HISTORY C14: from Old French *capitaine,* from Late Latin *capitāneus* chief, from Latin *caput* head
▸ˈ**captaincy** *or* ˈ**captainˌship** NOUN

Captain Cooker (ˈkʊkə) NOUN *NZ* a wild pig.
▷HISTORY from Captain James Cook (1728–79), British navigator and explorer, who first released pigs in the New Zealand bush

captain's biscuit NOUN a type of hard fancy biscuit.

caption (ˈkæpʃən) NOUN [1] a title, brief explanation, or comment accompanying an illustration; legend. [2] a heading, title, or headline of a chapter, article, etc. [3] graphic material, usually containing lettering, used in television presentation. [4] another name for **subtitle** (sense 2). [5] the formal heading of a legal document stating when, where, and on what authority it was taken or made. ◆ VERB [6] to provide with a caption or captions.
▷HISTORY C14 (meaning: seizure, an arrest; later, heading of a legal document): from Latin *captiō* a seizing, from *capere* to take

captious (ˈkæpʃəs) ADJECTIVE apt to make trivial criticisms; fault-finding; carping.
▷HISTORY C14 (meaning: catching in error): from Latin *captiōsus,* from *captiō* a seizing; see CAPTION
▸ˈ**captiously** ADVERB ▸ˈ**captiousness** NOUN

captivate (ˈkæptɪˌveɪt) VERB (*tr*) [1] to hold the attention of by fascinating; enchant. [2] an obsolete word for **capture.**
▷HISTORY C16: from Late Latin *captivāre,* from *captīvus* CAPTIVE
▸ˈ**captiˌvatingly** ADVERB ▸ˌ**captiˈvation** NOUN ▸ˈ**captiˌvator** NOUN

captive (ˈkæptɪv) NOUN [1] a person or animal that is confined or restrained, esp a prisoner of war. [2] a person whose behaviour is dominated by some emotion: *a captive of love.* ◆ ADJECTIVE [3] held as prisoner. [4] held under restriction or control; confined: *captive water held behind a dam.* [5] captivated; enraptured. [6] unable by circumstances to avoid speeches, advertisements, etc. (esp in the phrase **captive audience**).
▷HISTORY C14: from Latin *captīvus,* from *capere* to take

captive market NOUN a group of consumers who are obliged through lack of choice to buy a particular product, thus giving the supplier a monopoly.

captivity (kæpˈtɪvɪtɪ) NOUN, *plural* **-ties.** [1] the condition of being captive; imprisonment. [2] the period of imprisonment.

captopril (ˈkæptəprɪl) NOUN an ACE inhibitor used to treat high blood pressure and congestive heart failure.

captor (ˈkæptə) NOUN a person or animal that holds another captive.
▷HISTORY C17: from Latin, from *capere* to take

capture (ˈkæptʃə) VERB (*tr*) [1] to take prisoner or gain control over: *to capture an enemy; to capture a town.* [2] (in a game or contest) to win control or possession of: *to capture a pawn in chess.* [3] to succeed in representing or describing (something elusive): *the artist captured her likeness.* [4] *Physics* (of an atom, molecule, ion, or nucleus) to acquire (an additional particle). [5] to insert or transfer (data) into a computer. ◆ NOUN [6] the act of taking by force; seizure. [7] the person or thing captured; booty. [8] *Physics* a process by which an atom, molecule, ion, or nucleus acquires an additional particle. [9] Also called: **piracy.** *Geography* the process by which the headwaters of one river are diverted into another through erosion caused by the second river's tributaries. [10] the act or process of inserting or transferring data into a computer.
▷HISTORY C16: from Latin *captūra* a catching, that which is caught, from *capere* to take
▸ˈ**capturer** NOUN

Capua (ˈkæpjʊə; *Italian* ˈkapua) NOUN a town in S Italy, in NW Campania: strategically important in ancient times, situated on the Appian Way. Pop.: 19 520 (1990).

capuche *or* **capouch** (kəˈpuːʃ) NOUN a large hood or cowl, esp that worn by Capuchin friars.
▷HISTORY C17: from French, from Italian *cappuccio* hood, from Late Latin *cappa* cloak

capuchin (ˈkæpjʊtʃɪn, -ʃɪn) NOUN [1] any agile intelligent New World monkey of the genus *Cebus,* inhabiting forests in South America, typically having a cowl of thick hair on the top of the head. [2] a woman's hooded cloak. [3] (*sometimes capital*) a rare variety of domestic fancy pigeon.
▷HISTORY C16: from French, from Italian *cappuccino,* from *cappuccio* hood; see CAPUCHE

Capuchin (ˈkæpjʊtʃɪn, ˈkæpjʊʃɪn) NOUN **a** a friar belonging to a strict and autonomous branch of the Franciscan order founded in 1525. **b** (*as modifier*): *a Capuchin friar.*
▷HISTORY C16: from French; see CAPUCHE

caput (ˈkeɪpət, ˈkæp-) NOUN, *plural* **capita** (ˈkæpɪtə). [1] *Anatomy* a technical name for the **head.** [2] the main or most prominent part of an organ or structure.
▷HISTORY C18: from Latin

capybara (ˌkæpɪˈbɑːrə) NOUN the largest rodent: a pig-sized amphibious hystricomorph, *Hydrochoerus hydrochaeris,* resembling a guinea pig and inhabiting river banks in Central and South America: family *Hydrochoeridae.*
▷HISTORY C18: from Portuguese *capibara,* from Tupi

Caquetà (*Spanish* kakeˈta) NOUN the Japurá River from its source in Colombia to the border with Brazil.

car (kɑː) NOUN [1] **a** Also called: **motorcar, automobile.** a self-propelled road vehicle designed to carry passengers, esp one with four wheels that is powered by an internal-combustion engine. **b** (*as modifier*): *car coat.* [2] a conveyance for passengers, freight, etc., such as a cable car or the carrier of an airship or balloon. [3] *Brit* a railway vehicle for passengers only, such as a sleeping car or buffet car. [4] *Chiefly US and Canadian* a railway carriage or van. [5] *Chiefly US* the enclosed platform of a lift. [6] a poetic word for **chariot.**
▷HISTORY C14: from Anglo-French *carre,* ultimately related to Latin *carra, carrum* two-wheeled wagon, probably of Celtic origin; compare Old Irish *carr*

CAR ABBREVIATION FOR **compound annual return.**

carabao (ˌkærəˈbeɪəʊ) NOUN, *plural* **-os.** another name for **water buffalo.**
▷HISTORY from Visayan *karabáw;* compare Malay *karbaw*

carabid (ˈkærəbɪd) NOUN [1] any typically dark-coloured beetle of the family *Carabidae,* including the bombardier and other ground beetles. ◆ ADJECTIVE [2] of, relating to, or belonging to the *Carabidae.*
▷HISTORY C19: from New Latin, from Latin *cārabus* a kind of crab (name applied to these beetles)

carabin (ˈkærəbɪn) *or* **carabine** (ˈkærəˌbaɪn) NOUN variants of **carbine** (sense 2).

carabineer *or* **carabinier** (ˌkærəbɪˈnɪə) NOUN variants of **carbineer.**

carabiner (ˌkærəˈbiːnə) NOUN a variant spelling of **karabiner.**

carabiniere *Italian* (karabiˈnjɛːre) NOUN, *plural* **-ri** (-ri). an Italian national policeman.

caracal (ˈkærəˌkæl) NOUN [1] Also called: **desert lynx.** a lynxlike feline mammal, *Lynx caracal,* inhabiting deserts of N Africa and S Asia, having long legs, a smooth coat of reddish fur, and black-tufted ears. [2] the fur of this animal.
▷HISTORY C18: from French, from Turkish *kara kūlāk,* literally: black ear

caracara (ˌkɑːrəˈkɑːrə) NOUN any of various large carrion-eating diurnal birds of prey of the genera *Caracara, Polyborus,* etc., of S North, Central, and South America, having long legs and naked faces: family *Falconidae* (falcons).
▷HISTORY C19: from Spanish or Portuguese, from Tupi; of imitative origin

Caracas (kəˈrækəs, -ˈrɑː-; *Spanish* kaˈrakas) NOUN the capital of Venezuela, in the north: founded in 1567; major industrial and commercial centre, notably for oil companies. Pop.: 1 975 787 (2000 est.).

caracole (ˈkærəˌkəʊl) *or* **caracol** (ˈkærəˌkɒl) NOUN [1] *Dressage* a half turn to the right or left. [2] a spiral staircase. ◆ VERB (*intr*) [3] *Dressage* to execute a half turn to the right or left.
▷HISTORY C17: from French, from Spanish *caracol* snail, spiral staircase, turn

caracul (ˈkærəˌkʌl) NOUN [1] Also called: **Persian lamb.** the black loosely curled fur obtained from the skins of newly born lambs of the karakul sheep. [2] a variant spelling of **karakul.**

carafe (kəˈræf, -ˈrɑːf) NOUN **a** an open-topped glass container for serving water or wine at table. **b** (*as modifier*): *a carafe wine.*

▷HISTORY C18: from French, from Italian *caraffa,* from Spanish *garrafa,* from Arabic *gharrāfah* vessel

carageen ('kærə,gi:n) NOUN a variant spelling of **carrageen.**

carambola (,kærəm'bəʊlə) NOUN [1] a tree, *Averrhoa carambola,* probably native to Brazil but cultivated in the tropics, esp SE Asia, for its edible fruit. [2] Also called: **star fruit.** the smooth-skinned yellow fruit of this tree, which is star-shaped on cross section.
▷HISTORY C18: Spanish *carambola* a sour greenish fruit, from Portuguese, from Marathi *karambal*

caramel ('kærəməl, -,mɛl) NOUN [1] burnt sugar, used for colouring and flavouring food. [2] a chewy sweet made from sugar, butter, milk, etc. ◆ See also **crème caramel.**
▷HISTORY C18: from French, from Spanish *caramelo,* of uncertain origin

caramelize *or* **caramelise** ('kærəmə,laɪz) VERB to convert or be converted into caramel.

carangid (kə'rændʒɪd, -'ræŋgɪd) *or* **carangoid** (kə'ræŋgɔɪd) NOUN [1] any marine percoid fish of the family *Carangidae,* having a compressed body and deeply forked tail. The group includes the jacks, horse mackerel, pompano, and pilot fish. ◆ ADJECTIVE [2] of, relating to, or belonging to the *Carangidae.*
▷HISTORY C19: from New Latin *Carangidae,* from *Caranx* type genus, from French *carangue* shad, from Spanish *caranga,* of obscure origin

carapace ('kærə,peɪs) NOUN the thick hard shield, made of chitin or bone, that covers part of the body of crabs, lobsters, tortoises, etc.
▷HISTORY C19: from French, from Spanish *carapacho,* of unknown origin

carat ('kærət) NOUN [1] a measure of the weight of precious stones, esp diamonds. It was formerly defined as 3.17 grains, but the international carat is now standardized as 0.20 grams. [2] Usual US spelling: **karat.** a measure of the proportion of gold in an alloy, expressed as the number of parts of gold in 24 parts of the alloy.
▷HISTORY C16: from Old French, from Medieval Latin *carratus,* from Arabic *qīrāt* weight of four grains, carat, from Greek *keration* a little horn, from *keras* horn

caravan ('kærə,væn) NOUN [1] **a** a large enclosed vehicle capable of being pulled by a car or lorry and equipped to be lived in. US and Canadian name: **trailer. b** (*as modifier*): *a caravan site.* [2] (esp in some parts of Asia and Africa) a company of traders or other travellers journeying together, often with a train of camels, through the desert. [3] a group of wagons, pack mules, camels, etc., esp travelling in single file. [4] a large covered vehicle, esp a gaily coloured one used by Gypsies, circuses, etc. ◆ VERB **-vans, -vanning, -vanned.** [5] (*intr*) *Brit* to travel or have a holiday in a caravan.
▷HISTORY C16: from Italian *caravana,* from Persian *kārwān*
▸ **'cara,vanning** NOUN

caravanserai (,kærə'vænsə,raɪ, -,reɪ) *or* **caravansary** (,kærə'vænsərɪ) NOUN, *plural* **-rais** *or* **-ries.** (in some Eastern countries esp formerly) a large inn enclosing a courtyard providing accommodation for caravans.
▷HISTORY C16: from Persian *kārwānsarāī* caravan inn

caravel ('kærə,vɛl) *or* **carvel** NOUN a two- or three-masted sailing ship, esp one with a broad beam, high poop deck, and lateen rig that was used by the Spanish and Portuguese in the 15th and 16th centuries.
▷HISTORY C16: from Portuguese *caravela,* diminutive of *caravo* ship, ultimately from Greek *karabos* crab, horned beetle

caraway ('kærə,weɪ) NOUN [1] an umbelliferous Eurasian plant, *Carum carvi,* having finely divided leaves and clusters of small whitish flowers. [2] **caraway seed.** the pungent aromatic one-seeded fruit of this plant, used in cooking and in medicine.
▷HISTORY C14: probably from Medieval Latin *carvi,* from Arabic *karawyā,* from Greek *karon*

carbamate ('kɑ:bə,meɪt) NOUN a salt or ester of carbamic acid. The salts contain the monovalent ion NH_2COO^-, and the esters contain the group NH_2COO–.

carbamazepine (,kɑ:bə'mæzə,pi:n) NOUN an anticonvulsant drug used in the management of epilepsy.

carbamic acid (kɑ:'bæmɪk) NOUN a hypothetical compound known only in the form of carbamate salts and esters. Formula: NH_2COOH.

carbamide ('kɑ:bə,maɪd) NOUN another name for **urea.**

carbamidine (kɑ:'bæmɪ,daɪn) NOUN another name for **guanidine.**

carbanion (kɑ:'bænaɪən) NOUN *Chem* a negatively charged organic ion in which most of the negative charge is localized on a carbon atom. Compare **carbonium ion.**

carbaryl ('kɑ:bərɪl) NOUN an organic compound of the carbamate group: used as an insecticide, esp to treat head lice.

carbazole ('kɑ:bə,zəʊl) NOUN a colourless insoluble solid obtained from coal tar and used in the production of some dyes. Formula: $C_{12}H_9N$. Also called: **diphenylenimine** (daɪ,fi:naɪ'lɛnɪmi:n).

carbeen ('kɑ:bi:n) NOUN an Australian eucalyptus tree, *E. tessellaris,* having drooping branches and grey bark. Also called: **Moreton Bay ash.**
▷HISTORY from a native Australian language

carbene ('kɑ:bi:n) NOUN *Chem* a neutral divalent free radical, such as methylene: CH_2.

carbide ('kɑ:baɪd) NOUN [1] a binary compound of carbon with a more electropositive element. See also **acetylide.** [2] See **calcium carbide.**

carbimazole (kɑ:'bɪmə,zəʊl) NOUN a drug that inhibits the synthesis of the hormone thyroxine, used in the management of hyperthyroidism.

carbine ('kɑ:baɪn) NOUN [1] a light automatic or semiautomatic rifle of limited range. [2] Also called: **carabin, carabine.** a light short-barrelled shoulder rifle formerly used by cavalry.
▷HISTORY C17: from French *carabine,* from Old French *carabin* carabineer, perhaps variant of *escarrabin* one who prepares corpses for burial, from *scarabée,* from Latin *scarabaeus* SCARAB

carbineer (,kɑ:bɪ'nɪə), **carabineer,** *or* **carabinier** (,kærəbɪ'nɪə) NOUN (formerly) a soldier equipped with a carbine.

carbo- *or before a vowel* **carb-** COMBINING FORM carbon: *carbohydrate; carbonate.*

carbocyclic (,kɑ:bəʊ'saɪklɪk) ADJECTIVE (of a chemical compound) containing a closed ring of carbon atoms.

carbohydrate (,kɑ:bəʊ'haɪdreɪt) NOUN any of a large group of organic compounds, including sugars, such as sucrose, and polysaccharides, such as cellulose, glycogen, and starch, that contain carbon, hydrogen, and oxygen, with the general formula $C_m(H_2O)_n$: an important source of food and energy for animals.

carbolated ('kɑ:bə,leɪtɪd) ADJECTIVE containing carbolic acid.

carbolic acid (kɑ:'bɒlɪk) NOUN another name for **phenol,** esp when it is used as an antiseptic or disinfectant
▷HISTORY C19: *carbolic,* from CARBO- + -OL[1] + -IC

carbolize *or* **carbolise** ('kɑ:bə,laɪz) VERB (*tr*) another word for **phenolate.**

carbon ('kɑ:bᵊn) NOUN [1] **a** a nonmetallic element existing in the three crystalline forms: graphite, diamond, and buckminsterfullerene: occurring in carbon dioxide, coal, oil, and all organic compounds. The isotope **carbon-12** has been adopted as the standard for atomic wt.; **carbon-14,** a radioisotope with a half-life of 5700 years, is used in radiocarbon dating and as a tracer. Symbol: C; atomic no.: 6; atomic wt.: 12.011; valency: 2, 3, or 4; relative density: 1.8–2.1 (amorphous), 1.9–2.3 (graphite), 3.15–3.53 (diamond); sublimes at 3367±25°C; boiling pt.: 4827°C. **b** (*as modifier*): *a carbon compound.* [2] short for **carbon paper** or **carbon copy.** [3] a carbon electrode used in a carbon-arc light or in carbon-arc welding. [4] a rod or plate, made of carbon, used in some types of battery.
▷HISTORY C18: from French *carbone,* from Latin *carbō* charcoal, dead or glowing coal
▸ **'carbonous** ADJECTIVE

carbonaceous (,kɑ:bə'neɪʃəs) ADJECTIVE of, resembling, or containing carbon.

carbonade (,kɑ:bə'neɪd, -'nɑ:d) NOUN a stew of beef and onions cooked in beer.
▷HISTORY C20: from French

carbonado[1] (,kɑ:bə'neɪdəʊ, -'nɑ:dəʊ) NOUN, *plural* **-does** *or* **-dos.** [1] a piece of meat, fish, etc., scored and grilled. ◆ VERB **-dos, -doing, -doed.** (*tr*) [2] to score and grill (meat, fish, etc.). [3] *Archaic* to hack or slash.
▷HISTORY C16: from Spanish *carbonada,* from *carbón* charcoal; see CARBON

carbonado[2] (,kɑ:bə'neɪdəʊ, -'nɑ:dəʊ) NOUN, *plural* **-dos** *or* **-does.** an inferior dark massive variety of diamond used in industry for polishing and drilling. Also called: **black diamond.**
▷HISTORY Portuguese, literally: carbonated

carbon arc NOUN [1] **a** an electric arc produced between two carbon electrodes, formerly used as a light source. **b** (*as modifier*): *carbon-arc light.* [2] **a** an electric arc produced between a carbon electrode and material to be welded. **b** (*as modifier*): *carbon-arc welding.*

Carbonari (,kɑ:bə'nɑ:rɪ) PLURAL NOUN, *singular* **-naro** (-'nɑ:rəʊ). members of a secret political society with liberal republican aims, originating in S Italy about 1811 and particularly engaged in the struggle for Italian unification.
▷HISTORY C19: from Italian, plural of *carbonaro* seller or burner of charcoal, name adopted by the society

carbonate NOUN ('kɑ:bə,neɪt, -nɪt) [1] a salt or ester of carbonic acid. Carbonate salts contain the divalent ion CO_3^{2-}. ◆ VERB ('kɑ:bə,neɪt) [2] to form or turn into a carbonate. [3] (*tr*) to treat with carbon dioxide or carbonic acid, as in the manufacture of soft drinks.
▷HISTORY C18: from French, from *carbone* CARBON

carbonation (,kɑ:bə'neɪʃən) NOUN [1] absorption of or reaction with carbon dioxide. [2] another word for **carbonization.**

carbon bisulphide NOUN (not in technical usage) another name for **carbon disulphide.**

carbon black NOUN a black finely divided form of amorphous carbon produced by incomplete combustion of natural gas or petroleum: used to reinforce rubber and in the manufacture of pigments and ink.

carbon brush NOUN a small block of carbon used to convey current between the stationary and moving parts of an electric generator, motor, etc.

carbon copy NOUN [1] a duplicate copy of writing, typewriting, or drawing obtained by using carbon paper. Often shortened to **carbon.** [2] *Informal* a person or thing that is identical or very similar to another.

carbon credit NOUN a certificate showing that a government or company has paid to have a certain amount of carbon dioxide removed from the environment.

carbon cycle NOUN [1] the circulation of carbon between living organisms and their surroundings. Carbon dioxide from the atmosphere is synthesized by plants into plant tissue, which is ingested and metabolized by animals and converted to carbon dioxide again during respiration and decay. [2] four thermonuclear reactions believed to be the source of energy in many stars. Carbon nuclei function as catalysts in the fusion of protons to form helium nuclei.

carbon dating NOUN short for **radiocarbon dating.**

carbon dioxide NOUN a colourless odourless incombustible gas present in the atmosphere and formed during respiration, the decomposition and combustion of organic compounds, and in the reaction of acids with carbonates: used in carbonated drinks, fire extinguishers, and as dry ice for refrigeration. Formula: CO_2. Also called: **carbonic-acid gas.**

carbon dioxide snow NOUN solid carbon dioxide, used as a refrigerant.

carbon disulphide NOUN a colourless slightly soluble volatile flammable poisonous liquid commonly having a disagreeable odour due to the presence of impurities: used as an organic solvent and in the manufacture of rayon and carbon tetrachloride. Formula: CS_2. Also called (not in technical usage): **carbon bisulphide.**

carbonette (,kɑ:bə'nɛt) NOUN *NZ* a ball of compressed coal dust used as fuel.

carbon fibre NOUN a black silky thread of pure

carbon made by heating and stretching textile fibres and used because of its lightness and strength at high temperatures for reinforcing resins, ceramics, and metals, esp in turbine blades and for fishing rods.

carbon fixation NOUN the process by which plants assimilate carbon from carbon dioxide in the atmosphere to form metabolically active compounds.

carbon-14 dating NOUN another name for **radiocarbon dating.**

carbonic (kɑːˈbɒnɪk) ADJECTIVE (of a compound) containing carbon, esp tetravalent carbon.

carbonic acid NOUN a weak acid formed when carbon dioxide combines with water: obtained only in aqueous solutions, never in the pure state. Formula: H_2CO_3.

carbonic-acid gas NOUN another name for **carbon dioxide.**

carbonic anhydrase NOUN an enzyme in blood cells that catalyses the decomposition of carbonic acid into carbon dioxide and water, facilitating the transport of carbon dioxide from the tissues to the lungs.

carboniferous (ˌkɑːbəˈnɪfərəs) ADJECTIVE yielding coal or carbon.

Carboniferous (ˌkɑːbəˈnɪfərəs) ADJECTIVE 1 of, denoting, or formed in the fifth period of the Palaeozoic era, between the Devonian and Permian periods, lasting for nearly 64 million years during which coal measures were formed. ◆ NOUN 2 **the.** the Carboniferous period or rock system.

carbonium ion (kɑːˈbəʊnɪəm) NOUN *Chem* a positively charged organic ion in which most of the positive charge is localized on a carbon atom. Compare **carbanion.**

carbonize *or* **carbonise** (ˈkɑːbəˌnaɪz) VERB 1 to turn or be turned into carbon as a result of heating, fossilization, chemical treatment, etc. 2 (*tr*) to enrich or coat (a substance) with carbon. 3 (*intr*) to react or unite with carbon. ◆ Also (for senses 2, 3): **carburize.**
▸ **ˌcarboniˈzation** *or* **ˌcarboniˈsation** NOUN ▸ **ˈcarbonˌizer** *or* **ˈcarbonˌiser** NOUN

carbonless paper NOUN a sheet of paper impregnated with dye which transfers writing or typing onto the copying surface below without the necessity for carbon pigment. See **carbon paper.**

carbon microphone NOUN a microphone in which a diaphragm, vibrated by sound waves, applies a varying pressure to a container packed with carbon granules, altering the resistance of the carbon. A current flowing through the carbon is thus modulated at the frequency of the sound waves.

carbon monoxide NOUN a colourless odourless poisonous flammable gas formed when carbon compounds burn in insufficient air and produced by the action of steam on hot carbon: used as a reducing agent in metallurgy and as a fuel. Formula: CO.

carbon paper NOUN 1 a thin sheet of paper coated on one side with a dark waxy pigment, often containing carbon, that is transferred by the pressure of writing or of typewriter keys onto the copying surface below. Often shortened to **carbon.** 2 another name for **carbon tissue.**

carbon process *or* **printing** NOUN a photographic process for producing positive prints by exposing sensitized carbon tissue to light passing through a negative. Washing removes the unexposed gelatine leaving the pigmented image in the exposed insoluble gelatine.

carbon sequestration NOUN the prevention of greenhouse gas build-up in the earth's atmosphere by methods such as planting trees to absorb carbon dioxide or pumping carbon dioxide into underground reservoirs.

carbon sink NOUN areas of vegetation, especially forests, and the phytoplankton-rich seas that absorb the carbon dioxide produced by the burning of fossil fuels.

carbon steel NOUN steel whose characteristics are determined by the amount of carbon it contains.

carbon tax NOUN a tax on the emissions caused by the burning of coal, gas, and oil, aimed at reducing the production of greenhouse gases.

carbon tetrachloride NOUN a colourless volatile nonflammable sparingly soluble liquid made from chlorine and carbon disulphide; tetrachloromethane. It is used as a solvent, cleaning fluid, and insecticide. Formula: CCl_4.

carbon tissue NOUN a sheet of paper coated with pigmented gelatine, used in the carbon process. Also called: **carbon paper.**

carbon trading NOUN the trading by a country with a relatively low level of carbon dioxide emission of part of its emission entitlement to a country that has a higher level of emission.

carbon value NOUN *Chem* an empirical measurement of the tendency of a lubricant to form carbon when in use.

carbonyl (ˈkɑːbəˌnaɪl, -nɪl) NOUN *Chem* 1 (*modifier*) of, consisting of, or containing the divalent group =CO: *a carbonyl group or radical.* 2 any one of a class of inorganic complexes in which carbonyl groups are bound directly to metal atoms.
▸ **carbonylic** (ˌkɑːbəˈnɪlɪk) ADJECTIVE

carbonyl chloride NOUN (not in technical usage) another name for **phosgene.**

car-boot sale NOUN a sale of goods from car boots in a site hired for the occasion.

Carborundum (ˌkɑːbəˈrʌndəm) NOUN *Trademark* **a** any of various abrasive materials, esp one consisting of silicon carbide. **b** (*as modifier*): *a Carborundum wheel.*

carboxyhaemoglobin *or US* **carboxyhemoglobin** (kɑːˌbɒksɪˌhiːməʊˈgləʊbɪn, -ˌhem-) NOUN haemoglobin coordinated with carbon monoxide, formed as a result of carbon monoxide poisoning. As carbon monoxide is bound in preference to oxygen, tissues are deprived of oxygen.

carboxylase (kɑːˈbɒksɪˌleɪz) NOUN any enzyme that catalyses the release of carbon dioxide from certain acids.

carboxylate (kɑːˈbɒksɪˌleɪt) NOUN any salt or ester of a carboxylic acid having a formula of the type $M(RCOO)_x$, where M is a metal and R an organic group, or R^1COOR^2, where R^1 and R^2 are organic groups.

carboxyl group *or* **radical** (kɑːˈbɒksaɪl, -sɪl) NOUN the monovalent group –COOH, consisting of a carbonyl group bound to a hydroxyl group: the functional group in organic acids.
▷HISTORY C19 *carboxyl,* from CARBO- + OXY-^{2} + -YL

carboxylic acid (ˌkɑːbɒkˈsɪlɪk) NOUN any of a class of organic acids containing the carboxyl group. See also **fatty acid.**

carboy (ˈkɑːˌbɔɪ) NOUN a large glass or plastic bottle, usually protected by a basket or box, used for containing corrosive liquids such as acids.
▷HISTORY C18: from Persian *qarāba*

carbuncle (ˈkɑːˌbʌŋkᵊl) NOUN 1 an extensive skin eruption, similar to but larger than a boil, with several openings: caused by staphylococcal infection. 2 a rounded gemstone, esp a garnet cut without facets. 3 a dark reddish-greyish-brown colour.
▷HISTORY C13: from Latin *carbunculus* diminutive of *carbō* coal
▸ **ˈcarˌbuncled** ADJECTIVE ▸ **carbuncular** (kɑːˈbʌŋkjʊlə) ADJECTIVE

carburation (ˌkɑːbjʊˈreɪʃən) NOUN the process of mixing a hydrocarbon fuel with a correct amount of air to make an explosive mixture for an internal-combustion engine.

carburet (ˈkɑːbjʊˌrɛt, ˌkɑːbjʊˈrɛt, -bə-) VERB **-rets, -retting, -retted** *or US* **-rets, -reting, -reted.** (*tr*) to combine or mix (a gas) with carbon or carbon compounds.
▷HISTORY C18: from CARB(ON) + -URET

carburettor, carburetter (ˌkɑːbjʊˈrɛtə, ˈkɑːbjʊˌrɛtə, -bə-), *or US* **carburetor** (ˈkɑːbjʊˌreɪtə, -bə-) NOUN a device used in petrol engines for atomizing the petrol, controlling its mixture with air, and regulating the intake of the air-petrol mixture into the engine. Compare **fuel injection.**

carburize *or* **carburise** (ˈkɑːbjʊˌraɪz, -bə-) VERB 1 another word for **carbonize** (senses 2, 3). 2 (*tr*) to increase the carbon content of (the surface of a low-carbon steel) so that the surface can be hardened by heat treatment.
▸ **ˌcarburiˈzation** *or* **ˌcarburiˈsation** NOUN

carby (ˈkɑːbɪ) NOUN, *plural* **-bies.** *Austral informal* short for **carburettor.**

carbylamine (ˌkɑːbɪləˈmiːn, -ˈæmɪn) NOUN another name for **isocyanide.**

carcajou (ˈkɑːkəˌdʒuː, -ˌʒuː) NOUN a North American name for **wolverine.**
▷HISTORY C18: from Canadian French, from Algonquian *karkajou*

carcanet (ˈkɑːkəˌnɛt, -nɪt) NOUN *Archaic* a jewelled collar or necklace.
▷HISTORY C16: from French *carcan,* of Germanic origin; compare Old Norse *kverkband* chin strap

carcass *or* **carcase** (ˈkɑːkəs) NOUN 1 the dead body of an animal, esp one that has been slaughtered for food, with the head, limbs, and entrails removed. 2 *Informal, usually facetious or derogatory* a person's body. 3 the skeleton or framework of a structure. 4 the remains of anything when its life or vitality is gone; shell.
▷HISTORY C14: from Old French *carcasse,* of obscure origin

Carcassonne (*French* karkasɔn) NOUN a city in SW France: extensive remains of medieval fortifications. Pop.: 44 990 (1990).

Carchemish (ˈkɑːkəmɪʃ, kɑːˈkiː-) NOUN an ancient city in Syria on the Euphrates, lying on major trade routes; site of a victory of the Babylonians over the Egyptians (605 B.C.).

carcinogen (kɑːˈsɪnədʒən, ˈkɑːsɪnəˌdʒɛn) NOUN *Pathol* any substance that produces cancer.
▷HISTORY C20: from Greek *karkinos* CANCER + -GEN
▸ **ˌcarcinoˈgenic** ADJECTIVE ▸ **ˌcarcinogenˈicity** NOUN

carcinogenesis (ˌkɑːsɪnəʊˈdʒɛnɪsɪs) NOUN *Pathol* the development of cancerous cells from normal ones.

carcinoma (ˌkɑːsɪˈnəʊmə) NOUN, *plural* **-mas** *or* **-mata** (-mətə). *Pathol* 1 any malignant tumour derived from epithelial tissue. 2 another name for **cancer** (sense 1).
▷HISTORY C18: from Latin, from Greek *karkinōma,* from *karkinos* CANCER
▸ **ˌcarciˈnomaˌtoid** *or* **ˌcarciˈnomatous** ADJECTIVE

carcinomatosis (ˌkɑːsɪˌnəʊməˈtəʊsɪs) NOUN *Pathol* a condition characterized by widespread dissemination of carcinomas or by a carcinoma that affects a large area. Also called: **carcinosis** (ˌkɑːsɪˈnəʊsɪs).

car-crash TV NOUN television programmes that show deliberately controversial, disturbing, or horrific material.
▷HISTORY C20: from their eliciting in the viewer a similar horrified fascination to that experienced by people watching scenes of cars crashing

card¹ (kɑːd) NOUN 1 a piece of stiff paper or thin cardboard, usually rectangular, with varied uses, as for filing information in an index, bearing a written notice for display, entering scores in a game, etc. 2 such a card used for identification, reference, proof of membership, etc.: *library card; identity card; visiting card.* 3 such a card used for sending greetings, messages, or invitations, often bearing an illustration, printed greetings, etc.: *Christmas card; birthday card.* 4 one of a set of small pieces of cardboard, variously marked with significant figures, symbols, etc., used for playing games or for fortune-telling. 5 **a** short for **playing card. b** (*as modifier*): *a card game.* **c** (*in combination*): *cardsharp.* 6 *Informal* a witty, entertaining, or eccentric person. 7 short for **cheque card** or **credit card.** 8 See **compass card.** 9 Also called: **race card.** *Horse racing* a daily programme of all the races at a meeting, listing the runners, riders, weights to be carried, distances to be run, and conditions of each race. 10 a thing or action used in order to gain an advantage, esp one that is concealed and kept in reserve until needed (esp in the phrase **a card up one's sleeve**). 11 short for **printed circuit card.** See **printed circuit.** ◆ See also **cards.**
▷HISTORY C15: from Old French *carte,* from Latin *charta* leaf of papyrus, from Greek *khartēs,* probably of Egyptian origin

card² (kɑːd) VERB 1 (*tr*) to comb out and clean fibres of wool or cotton before spinning. ◆ NOUN 2 (formerly) a machine or comblike tool for carding fabrics or for raising the nap on cloth.
▷HISTORY C15: from Old French *carde* card, teasel, from Latin *carduus* thistle
▸ **ˈcarding** NOUN ▸ **ˈcarder** NOUN

Card. ABBREVIATION FOR Cardinal.

cardamom, cardamum (ˈkɑːdəməm), *or* **cardamon** NOUN [1] a tropical Asian zingiberaceous plant, *Elettaria cardamomum,* that has large hairy leaves. [2] the seeds of this plant, used esp as a spice or condiment. [3] a related East Indian plant, *Amomum cardamomum,* whose seeds are used as a substitute for cardamom seeds.
▷HISTORY C15: from Latin *cardamōmum,* from Greek *kardamōmon,* from *kardamon* cress + *amōmon* an Indian spice

cardan joint (ˈkɑːdæn) NOUN *Engineering* a type of universal joint in a shaft that enables it to rotate when out of alignment.
▷HISTORY C20: named after Geronimo *Cardan* (1501–76), Italian mathematician

cardboard (ˈkɑːdˌbɔːd) NOUN [1] **a** a thin stiff board made from paper pulp and used esp for making cartons. **b** (*as modifier*): *cardboard boxes.* ◆ ADJECTIVE [2] (*prenominal*) without substance: *a cardboard smile; a cardboard general.*

cardboard city NOUN *Informal* an area of a city in which homeless people sleep rough, often in cardboard boxes.

cardboardy (ˈkɑːdˌbɔːdɪ) ADJECTIVE like cardboard, esp in stiffness, texture, or taste: *it becomes cardboardy if cooked too long.*

card-carrying ADJECTIVE being an official member of a specified organization: *a card-carrying union member; a card-carrying Communist.*

card catalogue NOUN a catalogue of books, papers, etc., filed on cards.

card file NOUN another term for **card index.**

cardiac (ˈkɑːdɪˌæk) ADJECTIVE [1] of or relating to the heart. [2] of or relating to the portion of the stomach connected to the oesophagus. ◆ NOUN [3] a person with a heart disorder. [4] *Obsolete* a drug that stimulates the heart muscle.
▷HISTORY C17: from Latin *cardiacus,* from Greek, from *kardia* heart

cardiac arrest NOUN failure of the pumping action of the heart, resulting in loss of consciousness and absence of pulse and breathing: a medical emergency requiring immediate resuscitative treatment.

cardialgia (ˌkɑːdɪˈældʒɪə, -dʒə) NOUN [1] *Obsolete* pain in or near the heart. [2] a technical name for **heartburn.**
▸ˌcardiˈalgic ADJECTIVE

cardie *or* **cardy** (ˈkɑːdɪ) NOUN *Informal* short for **cardigan.**

Cardiff (ˈkɑːdɪf) NOUN [1] the capital of Wales, situated in the southeast, in Cardiff county borough: formerly an important port; seat of the Welsh assembly (1999); university (1883). Pop.: 272 129 (1991). [2] a county borough in SE Wales, created in 1996 from part of South Glamorgan. Pop.: 305 340 (2001). Area: 139 sq. km (54 sq. miles).

cardigan (ˈkɑːdɪgən) NOUN a knitted jacket or sweater with buttons up the front.
▷HISTORY C19: named after James Thomas Brudenell, 7th Earl of Cardigan (1797–1868), British cavalry officer

Cardigan (ˈkɑːdɪgən) NOUN the larger variety of corgi, having a long tail.

Cardigan Bay NOUN an inlet of St George's Channel, on the W coast of Wales.

Cardiganshire (ˈkɑːdɪgənˌʃɪə, -ʃə) NOUN a former county of W Wales: became part of Dyfed in 1974; reinstated as **Ceredigion** in 1996.

cardinal (ˈkɑːdɪnᵊl) NOUN [1] *RC Church* any of the members of the Sacred College, ranking next after the pope, who elect the pope and act as his chief counsellors. [2] Also called: **cardinal red.** a deep vivid red colour. [3] See **cardinal number.** [4] Also called: **cardinal grosbeak,** (US) **redbird.** a crested North American bunting, *Richmondena* (or *Pyrrhuloxia*) *cardinalis,* the male of which has a bright red plumage and the female a brown one. [5] a fritillary butterfly, *Pandoriana pandora,* found in meadows of southern Europe. [6] a woman's hooded shoulder cape worn in the 17th and 18th centuries. ◆ ADJECTIVE [7] (*usually prenominal*) fundamentally important; principal. [8] of a deep vivid red colour. [9] *Astrology* of or relating to the signs Aries, Cancer, Libra, and Capricorn. Compare **mutable** (sense 2), **fixed** (sense 10).
▷HISTORY C13: from Latin *cardinālis,* literally: relating to a hinge, hence, that on which something depends, principal, from *cardō* hinge
▸ˈcardinally ADVERB

cardinalate (ˈkɑːdɪnᵊˌleɪt) *or* **cardinalship** NOUN [1] the rank, office, or term of office of a cardinal. [2] the cardinals collectively.

cardinal beetle NOUN any of various large N temperate beetles of the family *Pyrochroidae,* such as *Pyrochroa serraticornis,* typically scarlet or partly scarlet in colour.

cardinal flower NOUN a campanulaceous plant, *Lobelia cardinalis* of E North America, that has brilliant scarlet, pink, or white flowers.

cardinality (ˌkɑːdɪˈnælɪtɪ) NOUN [1] *Maths* the property of possessing a cardinal number. [2] *Maths, logic* (of a class) the cardinal number associated with the given class. Two classes have the same cardinality if they can be put in one-to-one correspondence.

cardinal number *or* **numeral** NOUN [1] a number denoting quantity but not order in a set. Sometimes shortened to **cardinal.** [2] *Maths, logic* **a** a measure of the size of a set that does not take account of the order of its members. Compare **natural number. b** a particular number having this function. ◆ Compare **ordinal number.**

cardinal points PLURAL NOUN the four main points of the compass: north, south, east, and west.

cardinal spider NOUN a large house spider, *Tegenaria parietina.*

cardinal virtues PLURAL NOUN the most important moral qualities, traditionally justice, prudence, temperance, and fortitude.

cardinal vowels PLURAL NOUN a set of theoretical vowel sounds, based on the shape of the mouth needed to articulate them, that can be used to classify the vowel sounds of any speaker in any language.

card index *or* **file** NOUN [1] an index in which each item is separately listed on systematically arranged cards. ◆ VERB **card-index.** (*tr*) [2] to make such an index of (a book).

carding (ˈkɑːdɪŋ) NOUN the process of preparing the fibres of cotton, wool, etc., for spinning.

cardio- *or before a vowel* **cardi-** COMBINING FORM heart: *cardiogram.*
▷HISTORY from Greek *kardia* heart

cardiocentesis (ˌkɑːdɪəʊsɛnˈtiːsɪs) NOUN *Med* surgical puncture of the heart.

cardiogram (ˈkɑːdɪəʊˌgræm) NOUN short for **electrocardiogram.**

cardiograph (ˈkɑːdɪəʊˌgrɑːf, -ˌgræf) NOUN [1] an instrument for recording the mechanical force and form of heart movements. [2] short for **electrocardiograph.**
▸**cardiographer** (ˌkɑːdɪˈɒgrəfə) NOUN ▸**cardiographic** (ˌkɑːdɪəʊˈgræfɪk) *or* ˌ**cardioˈgraphical** ADJECTIVE ▸ˌ**cardioˈgraphically** ADVERB ▸ˌ**cardiˈography** NOUN

cardioid (ˈkɑːdɪˌɔɪd) NOUN a heart-shaped curve generated by a fixed point on a circle as it rolls around another fixed circle of equal radius, *a.* Equation: $r = a(1 - \cos \phi)$, where r is the radius vector and ϕ is the polar angle.

cardiology (ˌkɑːdɪˈɒlədʒɪ) NOUN the branch of medical science concerned with the heart and its diseases.
▸**cardiological** (ˌkɑːdɪəˈlɒdʒɪkᵊl) ADJECTIVE ▸ˌ**cardiˈologist** NOUN

cardiomegaly (ˌkɑːdɪəʊˈmɛgəlɪ) NOUN *Pathol* another name for **megalocardia.**

cardiomyopathy (ˌkɑːdɪəʊmaɪˈɒpəθɪ) NOUN *Pathol* a disease of the heart muscle usually caused by a biochemical defect or a toxin such as alcohol.

cardioplegia (ˌkɑːdɪəʊˈpliːdʒɪə) NOUN *Med* deliberate arrest of the action of the heart, as by hypothermia or the injection of chemicals, to enable complex heart surgery to be carried out.

cardiopulmonary (ˌkɑːdɪəʊˈpʌlmənərɪ, -mənrɪ, -ˈpʊl-) ADJECTIVE of, relating to, or affecting the heart and lungs.

cardiopulmonary resuscitation NOUN an emergency measure to revive a patient whose heart has stopped beating, in which compressions applied with the hands to the patient's chest are alternated with mouth-to-mouth respiration. Abbreviation: **CPR.**

cardiovascular (ˌkɑːdɪəʊˈvæskjʊlə) ADJECTIVE of or relating to the heart and the blood vessels.

carditis (kɑːˈdaɪtɪs) NOUN inflammation of the heart.

cardoon (kɑːˈduːn) NOUN a thistle-like S European plant, *Cynara cardunculus,* closely related to the artichoke, with spiny leaves, purple flowers, and a leafstalk that may be blanched and eaten: family *Asteraceae* (composites).
▷HISTORY C17: from French *cardon,* ultimately from Latin *carduus* thistle, artichoke

cardphone (ˈkɑːdfəʊn) NOUN a public telephone operated by the insertion of a phonecard instead of coins.

card punch NOUN [1] a device, no longer widely used, controlled by a computer, for transferring information from the central processing unit onto punched cards. Compare **card reader.** [2] another name for **key punch.**

card reader NOUN a device, no longer widely used, for reading information on a punched card and transferring it to a computer. Compare **card punch.**

cards (kɑːdz) NOUN [1] (*usually functioning as singular*) **a** any game or games played with cards, esp playing cards. **b** the playing of such a game. [2] an employee's national insurance and other documents held by the employer. [3] **get one's cards.** to be told to leave one's employment. [4] **on the cards.** possible or likely. US equivalent: **in the cards.** [5] **play one's cards.** to carry out one's plans; take action (esp in the phrase **play one's cards right**). [6] **put** *or* **lay one's cards on the table.** Also: **show one's cards.** to declare one's intentions, resources, etc.

cardsharp (ˈkɑːdˌʃɑːp) *or* **cardsharper** NOUN a professional card player who cheats.
▸ˈ**cardˌsharping** NOUN

card surfing NOUN *Slang* a form of cash-card fraud in which one person watches another using a cash dispenser, notes his or her personal identification number, and, after an accomplice has stolen the card, uses the card to withdraw cash.

card vote NOUN *Brit* a vote by delegates, esp at a trade-union conference, in which each delegate's vote counts as a vote by all his constituents.

cardy (ˈkɑːdɪ) NOUN, *plural* **-dies.** *Informal* a variant spelling of **cardie.**

care (kɛə) VERB [1] (when *tr, may take a clause as object*) to be troubled or concerned; be affected emotionally: *he is dying, and she doesn't care.* [2] (*intr;* foll by *for* or *about*) to have regard, affection, or consideration (for): *he cares more for his hobby than his job.* [3] (*intr;* foll by *for*) to have a desire or taste (for): *would you care for some tea?* [4] (*intr;* foll by *for*) to provide physical needs, help, or comfort (for): *the nurse cared for her patients.* [5] (*tr*) to agree or like (to do something): *would you care to sit down, please?* [6] **for all I care** *or* **I couldn't care less.** I am completely indifferent. ◆ NOUN [7] careful or serious attention: *under her care the plant flourished; he does his work with care.* [8] protective or supervisory control: *in the care of a doctor.* [9] (*often plural*) trouble; anxiety; worry. [10] an object of or cause for concern: *the baby's illness was her only care.* [11] caution: *handle with care.* [12] **care of.** at the address of: written on envelopes. Usual abbreviation: **c/o.** [13] **in** (*or* **into**) **care.** *Social welfare* made the legal responsibility of a local authority by order of a court.
▷HISTORY Old English *cearu* (noun), *cearian* (verb), of Germanic origin; compare Old High German *chara* lament, Latin *garrīre* to gossip

CARE (kɛə) NOUN ACRONYM FOR: [1] Cooperative for American Relief Everywhere, Inc.; a federation of US charities, giving financial and technical assistance to many regions of the world. [2] communicated authenticity, regard, empathy: the three qualities believed to be essential in the therapist practising client-centred therapy.

care and maintenance NOUN *Commerce* the state of a building, ship, machinery, etc., that is not in current use although it is kept in good condition to enable it to be quickly brought into service if there is demand for it. Abbreviation: **C & M.**

care attendant NOUN *Social welfare* (in Britain) a person who is paid to look after one or more severely handicapped people by visiting them frequently and staying when needed, but who does not live in.

careen (kəˈriːn) VERB [1] to sway or cause to sway dangerously over to one side. [2] (*tr*) *Nautical* to cause (a vessel) to keel over to one side, esp in order to clean or repair its bottom. [3] (*intr*) *Nautical* (of a vessel) to keel over to one side.
▷HISTORY C17: from French *carène* keel, from Italian *carena,* from Latin *carīna* keel
▸**caˈreenage** NOUN ▸**caˈreener** NOUN

career (kəˈrɪə) NOUN [1] a path or progress through life or history. [2] a profession or occupation chosen as one's life's work. [3] (*modifier*) having or following a career as specified: *a career diplomat.* [4] a course or path, esp a swift or headlong one. ◆ VERB [5] (*intr*) to move swiftly along; rush in an uncontrolled way.
▷HISTORY C16: from French *carrière,* from Late Latin *carrāria* carriage road, from Latin *carrus* two-wheeled wagon, CAR

career girl *or* **woman** NOUN a girl or woman, often unmarried, who follows a career or profession.

careerist (kəˈrɪərɪst) NOUN a person who values success in his career above all else and seeks to advance it by any possible means.
▸**caˈreerism** NOUN

careers adviser *or* **advisor** NOUN a person trained in giving vocational advice, esp in secondary, further, or higher education.

careers master NOUN a male teacher who gives pupils advice and information about careers.

careers mistress NOUN a female teacher who gives pupils advice and information about careers.

Careers Officer NOUN a person trained in giving vocational advice, esp to school leavers.

carefree (ˈkɛəˌfriː) ADJECTIVE without worry or responsibility.
▸**ˈcareˌfreeness** NOUN

careful (ˈkɛəfʊl) ADJECTIVE [1] cautious in attitude or action; prudent. [2] painstaking in one's work; thorough: *he wrote very careful script.* [3] (*usually postpositive;* foll by *of, in,* or *about*) solicitous; protective: *careful of one's reputation.* [4] *Archaic* full of care; anxious. [5] *Brit* mean or miserly.
▸**ˈcarefully** ADVERB ▸**ˈcarefulness** NOUN

caregiver (ˈkɛəˌgɪvə) NOUN the usual US and Canadian term for **carer.**

careless (ˈkɛəlɪs) ADJECTIVE [1] done with or acting with insufficient attention; negligent. [2] (often foll by *in, of,* or *about*) unconcerned in attitude or action; heedless; indifferent (to): *she's very careless about her clothes.* [3] (*usually prenominal*) carefree. [4] (*usually prenominal*) unstudied; artless: *an impression of careless elegance.*
▸**ˈcarelessly** ADVERB ▸**ˈcarelessness** NOUN

careline (ˈkɛəlaɪn) NOUN a telephone service set up by a company or other organization to provide its customers or clients with information about its products or services.

care plan NOUN a plan for the medical care of a particular patient or the welfare of a child in care.

carer (ˈkɛərə) NOUN *Social welfare* a person who has accepted responsibility for looking after a vulnerable neighbour or relative. See also **caretaker** (sense 3). Usual US and Canadian term: **caregiver.**

caress (kəˈrɛs) NOUN [1] a gentle touch or embrace, esp one given to show affection. ◆ VERB [2] (*tr*) to touch or stroke gently with affection or as with affection: *the wind caressed her face.*
▷HISTORY C17: from French *caresse,* from Italian *carezza,* from Latin *cārus* dear
▸**caˈresser** NOUN ▸**caˈressingly** ADVERB

caret (ˈkærɪt) NOUN a symbol (‸) used to indicate the place in written or printed matter at which something is to be inserted.
▷HISTORY C17: from Latin, literally: there is missing, from *carēre* to lack

caretaker (ˈkɛəˌteɪkə) NOUN [1] a person who is in charge of a place or thing, esp in the owner's absence: *the caretaker of a school.* [2] (*modifier*) holding office temporarily; interim: *a caretaker government.* [3] *Social welfare* a person who takes care of a vulnerable person, often a close relative. See also **carer.**
▸**ˈcareˌtaking** NOUN

careworn (ˈkɛəˌwɔːn) ADJECTIVE showing signs of care, stress, worry, etc.

Carey Street (ˈkɛərɪ) NOUN [1] (formerly) the street in which the London bankruptcy court was situated. [2] the state of bankruptcy.

carfare (ˈkɑːˌfɛə) NOUN *US and Canadian* the fare that a passenger is charged for a ride on a bus, etc.

carfax (ˈkɑːfæks) NOUN a place where principal roads or streets intersect, esp a place in a town where four roads meet.
▷HISTORY C14: from Anglo-French *carfuks,* from Old French *carrefures,* from Latin *quadrifurcus* four-forked

carfuffle (kəˈfʌfᵊl) NOUN *Informal, chiefly Brit* a variant spelling of **kerfuffle.**
▷HISTORY C20: of unknown origin

cargo (ˈkɑːgəʊ) NOUN, *plural* **-goes** *or* **-gos.** [1] **a** goods carried by a ship, aircraft, or other vehicle; freight. **b** (*as modifier*): *a cargo vessel.* [2] any load: *the train pulled in with its cargo of new arrivals.*
▷HISTORY C17: from Spanish: from *cargar* to load, from Late Latin *carricāre* to load a vehicle, from *carrus* CAR

cargo cult NOUN a religious movement of the SW Pacific, characterized by expectation of the return of spirits in ships or aircraft carrying goods that will provide for the needs of the followers.

cargo pants *or* **trousers** PLURAL NOUN loose trousers with a large external pocket on the side of each leg.

carhop (ˈkɑːˌhɒp) NOUN *US and Canadian informal* a waiter or waitress at a drive-in restaurant.

Caria (ˈkɛərɪə) NOUN an ancient region of SW Asia Minor, on the Aegean Sea: chief cities were Halicarnassus and Cnidus: corresponds to the present-day Turkish districts of S Aydin and W Muğla.

Carib (ˈkærɪb) NOUN [1] (*plural* **-ibs** *or* **-ib**) a member of a group of American Indian peoples of NE South America and the Lesser Antilles. [2] the family of languages spoken by these peoples.
▷HISTORY C16: from Spanish *Caribe,* from Arawak
▸**ˈCariban** ADJECTIVE

Caribbean (ˌkærɪˈbiːən; *US* kəˈrɪbɪən) ADJECTIVE [1] of, or relating to, the Caribbean Sea and its islands. [2] of, or relating to, the Carib or any of their languages. ◆ NOUN [3] **the.** the states and islands of the Caribbean Sea, including the West Indies, when considered as a geopolitical region. [4] short for the **Caribbean Sea.** [5] a member of any of the peoples inhabiting the islands of the Caribbean Sea, such as a West Indian or a Carib.

Caribbean Sea NOUN an almost landlocked sea, part of the Atlantic Ocean, bounded by the Caribbean islands, Central America, and the N coast of South America. Area: 2 718 200 sq. km (1 049 500 sq. miles).

Caribbee bark (ˈkærɪˌbiː) NOUN the bark of any of various tropical American and Caribbean rubiaceous trees of the genus *Exostema,* used as a substitute for cinchona bark.

Caribbees (ˈkærɪˌbiːz) PLURAL NOUN **the.** another name for the **Lesser Antilles.**

Cariboo (ˈkærɪˌbuː) NOUN **the.** *Canadian* a region in the W foothills of the Cariboo Mountains, scene of a gold rush beginning in 1860.

Cariboo Mountains PLURAL NOUN a mountain range in SW Canada, in SE British Columbia. Highest peak: Mount Sir Wilfrid Laurier, 3582 m (11 750 ft.).

caribou (ˈkærɪˌbuː) NOUN, *plural* **-bou** *or* **-bous.** a large deer, *Rangifer tarandus,* of Arctic regions of North America, having large branched antlers in the male and female: also occurs in Europe and Asia, where it is called a reindeer. Also called (Canadian): **tuktu.**
▷HISTORY C18: from Canadian French, of Algonquian origin; compare Micmac *khalibu* literally: scratcher

Caribou (ˈkærɪˌbuː) NOUN *Canadian* a mixed drink containing wine and grain alcohol.

Caribou Eskimo NOUN a member of any of the Inuit peoples who inhabit the Barren Lands of N Canada.

caricature (ˈkærɪkəˌtjʊə) NOUN [1] a pictorial, written, or acted representation of a person, which exaggerates his characteristic traits for comic effect. [2] a ludicrously inadequate or inaccurate imitation: *he is a caricature of a statesman.* ◆ VERB [3] (*tr*) to represent in caricature or produce a caricature of.
▷HISTORY C18: from Italian *caricatura* a distortion, exaggeration, from *caricare* to load, exaggerate; see CARGO
▸**ˈcaricaˌtural** ADJECTIVE ▸**ˈcaricaˌturist** NOUN

CARICOM (ˈkærɪˌkɒm) NOUN ACRONYM FOR Caribbean Community and Common Market.

caries (ˈkɛəriːz) NOUN, *plural* **-ies.** progressive decay of a bone or a tooth.
▷HISTORY C17: from Latin: decay; related to Greek *kēr* death

CARIFTA (kæˈrɪftə) NOUN ACRONYM FOR Caribbean Free Trade Area.

carillon (kəˈrɪljən) NOUN *Music* [1] a set of bells usually hung in a tower and played either by keys and pedals or mechanically. [2] a tune played on such bells. [3] an organ stop giving the effect of a bell. [4] a form of celesta or keyboard glockenspiel. ◆ VERB **-lons, -lonning, -lonned.** [5] (*intr*) to play a carillon.
▷HISTORY C18: from French: set of bells, from Old French *quarregnon,* ultimately from Latin *quattuor* four

carillonneur (kəˌrɪljəˈnɜː) NOUN a person who plays a carillon.

carina (kəˈriːnə, -ˈraɪ-) NOUN, *plural* **-nae** (-niː) *or* **-nas.** a keel-like part or ridge, as in the breastbone of birds or the fused lower petals of a leguminous flower.
▷HISTORY C18: from Latin: keel

Carina (kəˈriːnə, -ˈraɪ-) NOUN, *Latin genitive* **Carinae** (kəˈriːniː, -ˈraɪ-). a large conspicuous constellation in the S hemisphere close to the Southern Cross that contains Canopus, the second brightest star in the sky. It was originally considered part of Argo.

carinate (ˈkærɪˌneɪt) *or* **carinated** ADJECTIVE *Biology* having a keel or ridge; shaped like a keel.
▷HISTORY C17: from Latin *carīnāre* to furnish with a keel or shell, from *carīna* keel

caring (ˈkɛərɪŋ) ADJECTIVE [1] feeling or showing care and compassion: *a caring attitude.* [2] of or relating to professional social or medical care: *nursing is a caring job.* ◆ NOUN [3] the practice or profession of providing social or medical care.

Carinthia (kəˈrɪnθɪə) NOUN a state of S Austria: an independent duchy from 976 to 1276; mainly mountainous, with many lakes and resorts. Capital: Klagenfurt. Pop.: 561 114 (2001). Area: 9533 sq. km (3681 sq. miles). German name: **Kärnten.**

carioca (ˌkærɪˈəʊkə) NOUN [1] a Brazilian dance similar to the samba. [2] a piece of music composed for this dance.
▷HISTORY C19: from Brazilian Portuguese

Cariocan (ˌkærɪˈəʊkən) *or* **Carioca** NOUN a native of Rio de Janeiro, Brazil.

cariogenic (ˌkɛərɪəʊˈdʒɛnɪk) ADJECTIVE (of a substance) producing caries, esp in the teeth.

cariole *or* **carriole** (ˈkærɪˌəʊl) NOUN [1] a small open two-wheeled horse-drawn vehicle. [2] a covered cart.
▷HISTORY C19: from French *carriole,* ultimately from Latin *carrus;* see CAR

carious (ˈkɛərɪəs) *or* **cariose** (ˈkɛərɪˌəʊz) ADJECTIVE (of teeth or bone) affected with caries; decayed.
▸**cariosity** (ˌkærɪˈɒsɪtɪ, ˌkɛərɪ-) *or* **ˈcariousness** NOUN

Carisbrooke Castle (ˈkærɪzˌbrʊk) NOUN a castle near Newport on the Isle of Wight: Charles I was held prisoner here from 1647 until his execution in 1649.

carjack (ˈkɑːˌdʒæk) VERB (*tr*) to attack (a driver in a car) in order to rob the driver or to steal the car for another crime.
▷HISTORY C20: CAR + (HI)JACK
▸**ˈcarˌjacker** NOUN

cark[1] (kɑːk) NOUN, VERB an archaic word for **worry** (senses 1, 2, 11, 13).
▷HISTORY C13 *carken* to burden, from Old Northern French *carquier,* from Late Latin *carricāre* to load

cark[2] (kɑːk) VERB (*intr*) *Austral slang* to break down; die.
▷HISTORY perhaps from the cry of the crow, as a carrion feeding bird

carl *or* **carle** (kɑːl) NOUN *Archaic* another word for **churl.**
▷HISTORY Old English, from Old Norse *karl*

carlin (ˈkɑːlɪn) NOUN another name for **pug**[1].
▷HISTORY C18: named after a French actor who played Harlequin, because of the resemblance of the dog's face to the black mask of the Harlequin

carline[1] (ˈkɑːlɪn) NOUN a Eurasian thistle-like plant, *Carlina vulgaris,* having spiny leaves and flower heads surrounded by raylike whitish bracts: family *Asteraceae* (composites). Also called: **carline thistle.**
▷HISTORY C16: from French, probably from Latin *cardō* thistle

carline[2] *or* **carlin** (ˈkɑːlɪn) NOUN [1] *Chiefly Scot* an old woman, hag, or witch. [2] a variant of **carling.**
▷HISTORY C14: from Old Norse *kerling* old woman, diminutive of *karl* man, CHURL

carling (ˈkɑːlɪŋ) *or* **carline** NOUN a fore-and-aft beam in a vessel, used for supporting the deck, esp around a hatchway or other opening.
▷HISTORY C14: from Old Norse *kerling* old woman, CARLINE[2]

Carlisle (kɑːˈlaɪl, ˈkɑːlaɪl) NOUN a city in NW England, administrative centre of Cumbria: railway and industrial centre. Pop.: 72 439 (1991). Latin name: **Luguvallum** (ˌluːguːˈvæləm).

Carlist (ˈkɑːlɪst) NOUN [1] (in Spain) a supporter of Don Carlos or his descendants as the rightful kings of Spain. [2] (in France) a supporter of Charles X or his descendants.
▸ˈ**Carlism** NOUN

Carlovingian (ˌkɑːləʊˈvɪndʒɪən) ADJECTIVE, NOUN *History* a variant of **Carolingian.**

Carlow (ˈkɑːləʊ) NOUN [1] a county of SE Republic of Ireland, in Leinster: mostly flat, with barren mountains in the southeast. County town: Carlow. Pop.: 41 616 (1996). Area: 896 sq. km (346 sq. miles). [2] a town in SE Republic of Ireland, county town of Co. Carlow. Pop.: 11 275 (1991).

Carlsbad (ˈkarlsbaːt) NOUN a variant spelling of the German name for **Karlovy Vary.**

Carlton (ˈkɑːltən) NOUN a town in N central England, in S Nottinghamshire. Pop.: 47 302 (1991).

carmagnole (ˌkɑːmənˈjəʊl; *French* karmaɲɔl) NOUN [1] a dance and song popular during the French Revolution. [2] the costume worn by many French Revolutionaries, consisting of a short jacket with wide lapels, black trousers, a red liberty cap, and a tricoloured sash.
▷HISTORY C18: from French, probably named after *Carmagnola,* Italy, taken by French Revolutionaries in 1792

carman (ˈkɑːmən) NOUN, *plural* **-men.** [1] a man who drives a car or cart; carter. [2] a man whose business is the transport of goods; haulier. [3] *US and Canadian* a tram driver.

Carmarthen (kɑːˈmɑːðən) NOUN a market town in S Wales, the administrative centre of Carmarthenshire: Norman castle. Pop.: 13 524 (1991).

Carmarthenshire (kɑːˈmɑːðənˌʃɪə, -ʃə) NOUN a county of S Wales, formerly part of Dyfed (1974–96): on Carmarthen Bay, with the Cambrian Mountains in the N: generally agricultural (esp dairying). Administrative centre: Carmarthen. Pop.: 173 635 (2001). Area: 2398 sq. km (926 sq. miles).

Carme[1] (ˈkɑːmɪ) NOUN *Greek myth* a nymph who was one of Diana's attendants and mother of Britomaris by Jupiter.

Carme[2] (ˈkɑːmɪ) NOUN a small outer satellite of the planet Jupiter with a retrograde orbit.

Carmel (ˈkɑːməl) NOUN **Mount.** a mountain ridge in NW Israel, extending from the Samarian Hills to the Mediterranean. Highest point: about 540 m (1800 ft.).

Carmelite (ˈkɑːməˌlaɪt) NOUN *RC Church* [1] a member of an order of mendicant friars founded about 1154; a White Friar. [2] a member of a corresponding order of nuns founded in 1452, noted for its austere rule. [3] (*modifier*) of or relating to the Carmelite friars or nuns.
▷HISTORY C14: from French; named after Mount CARMEL, where the order was founded

carminative (ˈkɑːmɪnətɪv) ADJECTIVE [1] able to relieve flatulence. ◆ NOUN [2] a carminative drug.
▷HISTORY C15: from French *carminatif,* from Latin *carmināre* to card wool, remove impurities, from *cārere* to card

carmine (ˈkɑːmaɪn) NOUN [1] **a** a vivid red colour, sometimes with a purplish tinge. **b** (*as adjective*): *carmine paint.* [2] a pigment of this colour obtained from cochineal.
▷HISTORY C18: from Medieval Latin *carmīnus,* from Arabic *qirmiz* KERMES

Carnac (ˈkɑːnæk) NOUN a village in NW France: noted for its many megalithic monuments, including alignments of stone menhirs.

carnage (ˈkɑːnɪdʒ) NOUN extensive slaughter, esp of human beings in battle.
▷HISTORY C16: from French, from Italian *carnaggio,* from Medieval Latin *carnāticum,* from Latin *carō* flesh

carnal (ˈkɑːnᵊl) ADJECTIVE relating to the appetites and passions of the body; sensual; fleshly.
▷HISTORY C15: from Late Latin: relating to flesh, from Latin *carō* flesh
▸ˈ**carnalist** NOUN ▸**car**ˈ**nality** NOUN ▸ˈ**carnally** ADVERB

carnal knowledge NOUN *Chiefly law* [1] sexual intercourse. [2] **have carnal knowledge of.** to have sexual intercourse with.

carnallite (ˈkɑːnəˌlaɪt) NOUN a white or sometimes coloured mineral consisting of a hydrated chloride of potassium and magnesium in orthorhombic crystalline form: a source of potassium and also used as a fertilizer. Formula: $KCl.MgCl_2.6H_2O$.
▷HISTORY C19: named after Rudolf von *Carnall* (1804–74), German mining engineer; see -ITE[1]

carnaroli (ˌkɑːnəˈrəʊlɪ) NOUN a variety of short-grain rice used for risotto.
▷HISTORY Italian

Carnarvon (kɑːˈnɑːvᵊn) NOUN a variant spelling of **Caernarfon.**

carnassial (kɑːˈnæsɪəl) ADJECTIVE [1] *Zoology* of, relating to, or designating the last upper premolar and first lower molar teeth of carnivores, which have sharp edges for tearing flesh. ◆ NOUN [2] a carnassial tooth.
▷HISTORY C19: from French *carnassier* meat-eating, from Provençal, from *carnasso* abundance of meat, from *carn* meat, flesh, from Latin *carō*

Carnatic (kɑːˈnætɪk) NOUN a region of S India, between the Eastern Ghats and the Coromandel Coast: originally the country of the Kanarese; historically important as a rich and powerful trading centre; now part of Madras state.

carnation (kɑːˈneɪʃən) NOUN [1] Also called: **clove pink.** a Eurasian caryophyllaceous plant, *Dianthus caryophyllus,* cultivated in many varieties for its white, pink, or red flowers, which have a fragrant scent of cloves. [2] the flower of this plant. [3] **a** a pink or reddish-pink colour. **b** (*as adjective*): *a carnation dress.* [4] (*often plural*) a flesh tint in painting.
▷HISTORY C16: from French: flesh colour, from Late Latin *carnātiō* fleshiness, from Latin *carō* flesh

carnauba (kɑːˈnaubə) NOUN [1] Also called: **wax palm.** a Brazilian fan palm, *Copernicia cerifera.* [2] Also called: **carnauba wax.** the wax obtained from the young leaves of this tree, used esp as a polish.
▷HISTORY from Brazilian Portuguese, probably of Tupi origin

Carnegie Hall (ˈkɑːnəgɪ) NOUN a famous concert hall in New York (opened 1891); endowed by Andrew Carnegie (1835–1919), Scots-born US steel manufacturer and philanthropist.

carnelian (kɑːˈniːljən) NOUN a red or reddish-yellow translucent variety of chalcedony, used as a gemstone.
▷HISTORY C17: variant of *cornelian,* from Old French *corneline,* of uncertain origin; *car-* spelling influenced by Latin *carneus* flesh-coloured

carnet (ˈkɑːneɪ) NOUN [1] **a** a customs licence authorizing the temporary importation of a motor vehicle. **b** an official document permitting motorists to cross certain frontiers. [2] a book of tickets, travel coupons, etc.
▷HISTORY French: notebook, from Old French *quernet,* ultimately from Latin *quaternī* four at a time; see QUIRE[1]

carnify (ˈkɑːnɪˌfaɪ) VERB **-fies, -fying, -fied.** (*intr*) *Pathol* (esp of lung tissue, as the result of pneumonia) to be altered so as to resemble skeletal muscle.
▷HISTORY C17: from Latin *carō* flesh + *facere* to make
▸**carnification** (ˌkɑːnɪfɪˈkeɪʃən) NOUN

Carniola (ˌkɑːnɪˈəʊlə) NOUN a region of N Slovenia: a former duchy and crownland of Austria (1335–1919); divided between Yugoslavia and Italy in 1919; part of Yugoslavia (1947–92). German name: **Krain** (krain). Slovene name: **Kranj.**

carnival (ˈkɑːnɪvᵊl) NOUN [1] **a** a festive occasion or period marked by merrymaking, processions, etc.: esp in some Roman Catholic countries, the period just before Lent. **b** (*as modifier*): *a carnival atmosphere.* [2] a travelling fair having merry-go-rounds, etc. [3] a show or display arranged as an amusement. [4] *Austral* a sports meeting.
▷HISTORY C16: from Italian *carnevale,* from Old Italian *carnelevare* a removing of meat (referring to the Lenten fast)

carnivalesque (ˌkɑːnɪvᵊˈlɛsk) ADJECTIVE characteristic of, suitable for, or like a carnival.

carnivore (ˈkɑːnɪˌvɔː) NOUN [1] any placental mammal of the order *Carnivora,* typically having large pointed canine teeth and sharp molars and premolars, specialized for eating flesh. The order includes cats, dogs, bears, raccoons, hyenas, civets, and weasels. [2] any other animal or any plant that feeds on animals. [3] *Informal* an aggressively ambitious person.
▷HISTORY C19: probably back formation from CARNIVOROUS

carnivorous (kɑːˈnɪvərəs) ADJECTIVE [1] (esp of animals) feeding on flesh. [2] (of plants such as the pitcher plant and sundew) able to trap and digest insects and other small animals. [3] of or relating to the *Carnivora.* [4] *Informal* aggressively ambitious or reactionary.
▷HISTORY C17: from Latin *carnivorus,* from *carō* flesh + *vorāre* to consume
▸**car**ˈ**nivorously** ADVERB ▸**car**ˈ**nivorousness** NOUN

Carnot cycle NOUN an idealized reversible heat-engine cycle giving maximum efficiency and consisting of an isothermal expansion, an adiabatic expansion, an isothermal compression, and an adiabatic compression back to the initial state.

carnotite (ˈkɑːnəˌtaɪt) NOUN a radioactive yellow mineral consisting of hydrated uranium potassium vanadate: occurs in sedimentary rocks and is a source of uranium, radium, and vanadium. Formula: $K_2(UO_2)_2(VO_4)_2.3H_2O$.
▷HISTORY C20: named after A. *Carnot* (died 1920), French inspector general of mines

Carnot principle NOUN the principle that no heat engine can be more efficient than one operating on a Carnot cycle of reversible changes.

carny[1] *or* **carney** (ˈkɑːnɪ) VERB **-nies, -nying, -nied** *or* **-neys, -neying, -neyed.** *Brit informal* to coax or cajole or act in a wheedling manner.
▷HISTORY C19: of unknown origin

carny[2], **carney,** *or* **carnie** (ˈkɑːnɪ) NOUN, *plural* **-nies.** *US and Canadian slang* [1] short for **carnival.** [2] a person who works in a carnival.

carob (ˈkærəb) NOUN [1] Also called: **algarroba.** an evergreen leguminous Mediterranean tree, *Ceratonia siliqua,* with compound leaves and edible pods. [2] Also called: **algarroba, Saint John's bread.** the long blackish sugary pod of this tree, used as a substitute for chocolate and for animal fodder.
▷HISTORY C16: from Old French *carobe,* from Medieval Latin *carrūbium,* from Arabic *al kharrūbah*

caroche (kəˈrɒʃ) NOUN a stately ceremonial carriage used in the 16th and 17th centuries.
▷HISTORY C16: from French, ultimately from Latin *carrus* CAR

carol (ˈkærəl) NOUN [1] a joyful hymn or religious song, esp one (a **Christmas carol**) celebrating the birth of Christ. [2] *Archaic* an old English circular dance. ◆ VERB **-ols, -olling, -olled** *or US* **-ols, -oling, -oled.** [3] (*intr*) to sing carols at Christmas. [4] to sing (something) in a joyful manner.
▷HISTORY C13: from Old French, of uncertain origin
▸ˈ**caroler** *or* ˈ**caroller** NOUN ▸ˈ**caroling** *or* ˈ**carolling** NOUN

Carolina (ˌkærəˈlaɪnə) NOUN a former English colony on the E coast of North America, first established in 1663: divided in 1729 into North and South Carolina, which are often referred to as **the Carolinas.**

Caroline (ˈkærəˌlaɪn) *or* **Carolean** (ˌkærəˈliːən) ADJECTIVE [1] Also called: **Carolinian.** characteristic of or relating to Charles I (1600–49) or Charles II (1630–85), Stuart kings of England, Scotland, and

Ireland, the society over which they ruled, or their government. [2] of or relating to any other king called Charles.

Caroline Islands PLURAL NOUN an archipelago of over 500 islands and islets in the W Pacific Ocean east of the Philippines, all are now part of the Federated States of Micronesia, except for the Belau group: formerly part of the US Trust Territory of the Pacific Islands; centre of a typhoon zone. Area: (land) 1183 sq. km (457 sq. miles).

Carolingian (ˌkærəˈlɪndʒɪən) ADJECTIVE [1] of or relating to the Frankish dynasty founded by Pepin the Short (died 768 A.D.), son of Charles Martel (?688–741 A.D.), which ruled in France from 751–987 A.D. and in Germany until 911 A.D. ◆ NOUN [2] a member of the dynasty of the Carolingian Franks. ◆ Also: **Carlovingian, Carolinian.**

Carolinian[1] (ˌkærəˈlɪnɪən) ADJECTIVE, NOUN a variant of **Caroline** or **Carolingian.**

Carolinian[2] (ˌkærəˈlɪnɪən) ADJECTIVE [1] of or relating to North or South Carolina. ◆ NOUN [2] a native or inhabitant of North or South Carolina.

carolus (ˈkærələs) NOUN, *plural* **-luses** *or* **-li** (-ˌlaɪ). any of several coins struck in the reign of a king called Charles, esp an English gold coin from the reign of Charles I.

carom (ˈkærəm) NOUN *Billiards* another word (esp US and Canadian) for **cannon** (sense 6).
▷HISTORY C18: from earlier *carambole* (taken as *carom ball*), from Spanish CARAMBOLA

Caro's acid (ˈkærəʊz, ˈkɑː-) NOUN another name for **peroxysulphuric acid.**
▷HISTORY C19: named after Heinrich *Caro* (died 1910), German chemist

carotene (ˈkærəˌtiːn) *or* **carotin** (ˈkærətɪn) NOUN any of four orange-red isomers of an unsaturated hydrocarbon present in many plants (β-carotene is the orange pigment of carrots) and converted to vitamin A in the liver. Formula: $C_{40}H_{56}$.
▷HISTORY C19 carotin, from Latin *carōta* CARROT; see -ENE

carotenoid *or* **carotinoid** (kəˈrɒtɪˌnɔɪd) NOUN [1] any of a group of red or yellow pigments, including carotenes, found in plants and certain animal tissues. ◆ ADJECTIVE [2] of or resembling carotene or a carotenoid.

carotid (kəˈrɒtɪd) NOUN [1] either one of the two principal arteries that supply blood to the head and neck. ◆ ADJECTIVE [2] of or relating to either of these arteries.
▷HISTORY C17: from French, from Greek *karōtides*, from *karoun* to stupefy; so named by Galen, because pressure on them produced unconsciousness
▸**caˈrotidal** ADJECTIVE

carousal (kəˈraʊzᵊl) NOUN a merry drinking party.

carouse (kəˈraʊz) VERB [1] (*intr*) to have a merry drinking spree; drink freely. ◆ NOUN [2] another word for **carousal.**
▷HISTORY C16: via French *carrousser* from German (*trinken*) *gar aus* (to drink) right out
▸**caˈrouser** NOUN

carousel (ˌkærəˈsɛl, -ˈzɛl) NOUN [1] a circular magazine in which slides for a projector are held: it moves round as each slide is shown. [2] a rotating conveyor belt for luggage, as at an airport. [3] the usual US and Canadian name for **merry-go-round.** [4] *History* a tournament in which horsemen took part in races and various manoeuvres in formation.
▷HISTORY C17: from French *carrousel*, from Italian *carosello*, of uncertain origin

carp[1] (kɑːp) NOUN, *plural* **carp** *or* **carps.** [1] a freshwater teleost food fish, *Cyprinus carpio*, having a body covered with cycloid scales, a naked head, one long dorsal fin, and two barbels on each side of the mouth: family *Cyprinidae*. [2] any other fish of the family *Cyprinidae*; a cyprinid. Related adjectives: **cyprinid, cyprinoid.**
▷HISTORY C14: from Old French *carpe*, of Germanic origin; compare Old High German *karpfo*, Old Norse *karfi*

carp[2] (kɑːp) VERB (*intr*; often foll by *at*) to complain or find fault; nag pettily.
▷HISTORY C13: from Old Norse *karpa* to boast; related to Latin *carpere* to pluck
▸**ˈcarper** NOUN

-carp NOUN COMBINING FORM (in botany) fruit or a reproductive structure that develops into a particular part of the fruit: *epicarp*.
▷HISTORY from New Latin *-carpium*, from Greek *-karpion*, from *karpos* fruit

carpaccio (ˌkɑːˈpætʃɪəʊ; *Italian* karˈpattʃo) NOUN, *plural* **-os.** an Italian dish of thin slices of raw meat or fish.
▷HISTORY possibly after the Italian painter Vittore Carpaccio (?1460–?1525)

carpal (ˈkɑːpᵊl) NOUN **a** any bone of the wrist. **b** (*as modifier*): *carpal bones*. Also: **carpale** (kɑːˈpeɪlɪ).
▷HISTORY C18: from New Latin *carpālis*, from Greek *karpos* wrist

carpal tunnel syndrome NOUN a condition characterized by pain and tingling in the fingers, caused by pressure on a nerve as it passes under the ligament situated across the front of the wrist.

car park NOUN an area or building reserved for parking cars. Usual US and Canadian term: **parking lot.**

Carpathian Mountains (kɑːˈpeɪθɪən) *or* **Carpathians** PLURAL NOUN a mountain system of central and E Europe, extending from Slovakia to central Romania: mainly forested, with rich iron ore resources. Highest peak: Gerlachovka, 2663 m (8788 ft.).

Carpatho-Ukraine (kɑːˈpeɪθəʊjuːˈkreɪn) NOUN another name for **Ruthenia.**

carpe diem *Latin* (ˈkɑːpɪ ˈdiːɛm) enjoy the pleasures of the moment, without concern for the future.
▷HISTORY literally: seize the day!

carpel (ˈkɑːpᵊl) NOUN the female reproductive organ of flowering plants, consisting of an ovary, style (sometimes absent), and stigma. The carpels are separate or fused to form a single pistil.
▷HISTORY C19: from New Latin *carpellum*, from Greek *karpos* fruit
▸**ˈcarpellary** ADJECTIVE ▸**carpellate** (ˈkɑːpɪˌleɪt) ADJECTIVE

Carpentaria (ˌkɑːpənˈtɛərɪə) NOUN **Gulf of.** a shallow inlet of the Arafura Sea, in N Australia between Arnhem Land and Cape York Peninsula.

carpenter (ˈkɑːpɪntə) NOUN [1] a person skilled in woodwork, esp in buildings, ships, etc. ◆ VERB [2] (*intr*) to do the work of a carpenter. [3] (*tr*) to make or fit together by or as if by carpentry.
▷HISTORY C14: from Anglo-French, from Latin *carpentārius* wagon-maker, from *carpentum* wagon; of Celtic origin

carpenter bee NOUN any large solitary bee of the genus *Xylocopa* and related genera that lays its eggs in tunnels bored into wood or in plant stems: family *Apidae*.

carpenter moth NOUN any of various large moths of the family *Cossidae*, the larvae of which bore beneath and cause damage to tree bark.

carpentry (ˈkɑːpɪntrɪ) NOUN [1] the art or technique of working wood. [2] the work produced by a carpenter; woodwork.

carpet (ˈkɑːpɪt) NOUN [1] **a** a heavy fabric for covering floors. **b** (*as modifier*): *a carpet sale*. [2] a covering like a carpet: *a carpet of leaves*. [3] **on the carpet.** *Informal* **a** before authority to be reproved for misconduct or error. **b** under consideration. ◆ VERB (*tr*) **-pets, -peting, -peted** [4] to cover with or as if with a carpet. [5] *Informal* to reprimand.
▷HISTORY C14: from Old French *carpite*, from Old Italian *carpita*, from Late Latin *carpeta*, literally: (wool) that has been carded, from Latin *carpere* to pluck, card

carpetbag (ˈkɑːpɪtˌbæg) NOUN a travelling bag originally made of carpeting.

carpetbagger (ˈkɑːpɪtˌbægə) NOUN [1] a politician who seeks public office in a locality where he has no real connections. [2] *Brit* a person who makes a short-term investment in a mutual savings or life-assurance organization in order to benefit from free shares issued following the organization's conversion to a public limited company. [3] *US* a Northern White who went to the South after the Civil War to profit from Reconstruction.

carpet beetle *or US* **carpet bug** NOUN any of various beetles of the genus *Anthrenus*, the larvae of which feed on carpets, furnishing fabrics, etc.: family *Dermestidae*.

carpet bombing NOUN systematic intensive bombing of an area.

carpet bowling NOUN a form of bowls played indoors on a strip of carpet, at the centre of which lies an obstacle round which the bowl has to pass.

carpeting (ˈkɑːpɪtɪŋ) NOUN carpet material or carpets in general.

carpet knight NOUN *Disparaging* a soldier who spends his life away from battle; idler.

carpet moth NOUN any of several geometrid moths with black- (or brown-)and-white mottled wings.
▷HISTORY C19: so named from the patterns on their wings

carpet plot NOUN *Maths* the graphed values of a function of more than one variable, read from an ordinate at points located by the intersection of curves of constant values of each of the variables.
▷HISTORY C20: from the shape of the graph, thought to resemble a flying carpet

carpet shark NOUN any of various sharks of the family *Orectolobidae*, having two dorsal fins and a patterned back, typically marked with white and brown.

carpet slipper NOUN one of a pair of slippers, originally one made with woollen uppers resembling carpeting.

carpet snake *or* **python** NOUN a large nonvenomous Australian snake, *Morelia variegata*, having a carpetlike pattern on its back.

carpet-sweeper NOUN a household device with a revolving brush for sweeping carpets.

carpet tiles PLURAL NOUN small pieces of carpeting laid as tiles to cover a floor.

car phone NOUN a telephone that operates by cellular radio for use in a car.

carpi (ˈkɑːpaɪ) NOUN the plural of **carpus.**

-carpic ADJECTIVE COMBINING FORM a variant of **-carpous.**

carping (ˈkɑːpɪŋ) ADJECTIVE tending to make petty complaints; fault-finding.
▸**ˈcarpingly** ADVERB

carpo-[1] COMBINING FORM (in botany) indicating fruit or a reproductive structure that develops into part of the fruit: *carpophore*; *carpogonium*.
▷HISTORY from Greek *karpos* fruit

carpo-[2] COMBINING FORM carpus or carpal bones: *carpometacarpus*.

carpogonium (ˌkɑːpəˈgəʊnɪəm) NOUN, *plural* **-nia** (-nɪə). the female sex organ of red algae, consisting of a swollen base containing the ovum and a long neck down which the male gametes pass.
▸**ˌcarpoˈgonial** ADJECTIVE

carpology (kɑːˈpɒlədʒɪ) NOUN the branch of botany concerned with the study of fruits and seeds.
▸**carpological** (ˌkɑːpəˈlɒdʒɪkᵊl) ADJECTIVE ▸**carˈpologist** NOUN

carpometacarpus (ˌkɑːpəʊˌmɛtəˈkɑːpəs) NOUN a bone in the wing of a bird that consists of the metacarpal bones and some of the carpal bones fused together.

carpophagous (kɑːˈpɒfəgəs) ADJECTIVE *Zoology* feeding on fruit: *carpophagous bats*.

carpophore (ˈkɑːpəˌfɔː) NOUN [1] the central column surrounded by carpels in such flowers as the geranium. [2] a spore-bearing structure in some of the higher fungi.

carport (ˈkɑːˌpɔːt) NOUN a shelter for a car usually consisting of a roof built out from the side of a building and supported by posts.

carpospore (ˈkɑːpəʊˌspɔː) NOUN a sexual spore produced by red algae after fertilization of the carpogonium.

-carpous *or* **-carpic** ADJECTIVE COMBINING FORM (in botany) indicating a certain kind or number of fruit: *apocarpous*.
▷HISTORY from New Latin *-carpus*, from Greek *karpos* fruit

carpus (ˈkɑːpəs) NOUN, *plural* **-pi** (-paɪ). [1] the technical name for **wrist.** [2] the eight small bones of the human wrist that form the joint between the arm and the hand. [3] the corresponding joint in other tetrapod vertebrates.
▷HISTORY C17: New Latin, from Greek *karpos*

carr (kɑː) NOUN *Brit* an area of bog or fen in which scrub, esp willow, has become established.
▷HISTORY C15: from Old Norse

carrack ('kærək) NOUN a galleon sailed in the Mediterranean as a merchantman in the 15th and 16th centuries.
▷HISTORY C14: from Old French *caraque,* from Old Spanish *carraca,* from Arabic *qarāqīr* merchant ships

carrageen, carragheen, *or* **carageen** ('kærə,gi:n) NOUN an edible red seaweed, *Chondrus crispus,* of North America and N Europe. Also called: **Irish moss.**
▷HISTORY C19: from *Carragheen,* near Waterford, Ireland, where it is plentiful

carrageenan, carragheenan, *or* **carageenan** (,kærə'gi:nən) NOUN a carbohydrate extracted from carrageen, used to make a beverage, medicine, and jelly, and as an emulsifying and gelling agent (**E407**) in various processed desserts and drinks.

Carrantuohill *or* **Carrauntoohill** (,kærən'tu:l) NOUN a mountain in SW Republic of Ireland, in Macgillicuddy's Reeks in Kerry: the highest peak in Ireland. Height: 1041 m (3414 ft.).

Carrara (kə'rɑ:rə; *Italian* kar'ra:ra) NOUN a town in NW Italy, in NW Tuscany: famous for its marble. Pop.: 68 480 (1990).

carrefour ('kærə,fɔ:) NOUN [1] a rare word for **crossroads.** [2] a public square, esp one at the intersection of several roads.
▷HISTORY C15: from Old French *quarrefour,* ultimately from Latin *quadrifurcus* having four forks

carrel *or* **carrell** ('kærəl) NOUN a small individual study room or private desk, often in a library, where a student or researcher can work undisturbed.
▷HISTORY C16: a variant of CAROL

carriage ('kærɪdʒ) NOUN [1] *Brit* a railway coach for passengers. [2] the manner in which a person holds and moves his head and body; bearing. [3] a four-wheeled horse-drawn vehicle for persons. [4] the moving part of a machine that bears another part: *a typewriter carriage; a lathe carriage.* [5] ('kærɪdʒ, 'kærɪɪdʒ) **a** the act of conveying; carrying. **b** the charge made for conveying (esp in the phrases **carriage forward,** when the charge is to be paid by the receiver, and **carriage paid**).
▷HISTORY C14: from Old Northern French *cariage,* from *carier* to CARRY

carriage bolt NOUN *Chiefly US and Canadian* another name for **coach bolt.**

carriage clock NOUN a portable clock, usually in a rectangular case with a handle on the top, of a type originally used by travellers.

carriage dog NOUN a former name for **Dalmatian.**

carriage line NOUN another term for **coach line.**

carriage trade NOUN trade from the wealthy part of society.

carriageway ('kærɪdʒ,weɪ) NOUN *Brit* the part of a road along which traffic passes in a single line moving in one direction only: *a dual carriageway.*

carrick bend ('kærɪk) NOUN a knot used for joining two ropes or cables together.
▷HISTORY C19: perhaps variant of CARRACK

carrick bitt NOUN *Nautical* either of a pair of strong posts used for supporting a windlass.

Carrickfergus (,kærɪk'fɜ:gəs) NOUN [1] a town in E Northern Ireland, in Carrickfergus district, Co. Antrim; historic settlement of Scottish Protestants on Belfast Lough; Norman castle. Pop.: 22 885 (1991). [2] a district of E Northern Ireland, in Co. Antrim. Pop.: 37 659 (2001). Area: 83 sq. km (32 sq. miles).

carrier ('kærɪə) NOUN [1] a person, thing, or organization employed to carry goods, passengers, etc. [2] a mechanism by which something is carried or moved, such as a device for transmitting rotation from the faceplate of a lathe to the workpiece. [3] *Pathol* another name for **vector** (sense 3). [4] *Pathol* a person or animal that, without having any symptoms of a disease, is capable of transmitting it to others. [5] Also called: **charge carrier.** *Physics* an electron, ion, or hole that carries the charge in a conductor or semiconductor. [6] short for **carrier wave.** [7] *Chem* **a** the inert solid on which a dyestuff is adsorbed in forming a lake. **b** a substance, such as kieselguhr or asbestos, used to support a catalyst. **c** an inactive substance containing a radioisotope used in radioactive tracing. **d** an inert gas used to transport the sample through a gas-chromatography column. **e** a catalyst that effects the transfer of an atom or group from one molecule to another. [8] See **aircraft carrier.** [9] a breed of domestic fancy pigeon having a large walnut-shaped wattle over the beak; a distinct variety of pigeon from the homing or carrier pigeon. See also **carrier pigeon.** [10] a US name for **roof rack.**

Carrier ('kærɪə) NOUN a member of an Athapaskan Native North American people of British Columbia.

carrier bag NOUN *Brit* a large paper or plastic bag for carrying shopping.

carrier pigeon NOUN any homing pigeon, esp one used for carrying messages.

carrier wave NOUN *Radio* a wave of fixed amplitude and frequency that is modulated in amplitude, frequency, or phase in order to carry a signal in radio transmission, etc. See **amplitude modulation, frequency modulation.**

carriole ('kærɪ,əʊl) NOUN a variant spelling of **cariole.**

carrion ('kærɪən) NOUN [1] dead and rotting flesh. [2] *(modifier)* eating carrion: *carrion beetles.* [3] something rotten or repulsive.
▷HISTORY C13: from Anglo-French *caroine,* ultimately from Latin *carō* flesh

carrion beetle NOUN any beetle of the family *Silphidae* that track carrion by a keen sense of smell: best known are the **burying** or **sexton beetles.**

carrion crow NOUN a common predatory and scavenging European crow, *Corvus corone,* similar to the rook but having a pure black bill. See also **hooded crow.**

carrion flower NOUN [1] a liliaceous climbing plant, *Smilax herbacea* of E North America, whose small green flowers smell like decaying flesh. [2] any of several other plants, esp any of the genus *Stapelia,* whose flowers have an unpleasant odour.

carronade (,kærə'neɪd) NOUN an obsolete naval gun of short barrel and large bore.
▷HISTORY C18: named after *Carron,* Scotland, where it was first cast; see -ADE

carron oil ('kærən) NOUN an ointment of limewater and linseed oil, formerly used to treat burns.
▷HISTORY C19: named after *Carron,* Scotland, where it was used among the ironworkers

carrot ('kærət) NOUN [1] an umbelliferous plant, *Daucus carota sativa,* with finely divided leaves and flat clusters of small white flowers. See also **wild carrot.** [2] the long tapering orange root of this plant, eaten as a vegetable. [3] **a** something offered as a lure or incentive. **b carrot and stick.** reward and punishment as methods of persuasion.
▷HISTORY C16: from Old French *carotte,* from Late Latin *carōta,* from Greek *karōton;* perhaps related to Greek *karē* head

carrot fly NOUN a dipterous insect, *Psila rosae,* that is a serious pest of carrots. The larvae tunnel into the root to feed.

carroty ('kærətɪ) ADJECTIVE [1] of a reddish or yellowish-orange colour. [2] having red hair.

carrousel (,kærə'sɛl, -'zɛl) NOUN a variant spelling of **carousel.**

carry ('kærɪ) VERB **-ries, -rying, -ried.** *(mainly tr)* [1] *(also intr)* to take or bear (something) from one place to another: *to carry a baby in one's arms.* [2] to transfer for consideration; take: *he carried his complaints to her superior.* [3] to have on one's person: *he always carries a watch.* [4] *(also intr)* to be transmitted or serve as a medium for transmitting: *sound carries best over water.* [5] to contain or be capable of containing: *the jug carries water.* [6] to bear or be able to bear the weight, pressure, or responsibility of: *her efforts carry the whole production.* [7] to have as an attribute or result: *this crime carries a heavy penalty.* [8] to bring or communicate: *to carry news.* [9] *(also intr)* to be pregnant with (young): *she is carrying her third child.* [10] to bear (the head, body, etc.) in a specified manner: *she carried her head high.* [11] to conduct or bear (oneself) in a specified manner: *she carried herself well in a difficult situation.* [12] to continue or extend: *the war was carried into enemy territory.* [13] to cause to move or go: *desire for riches carried him to the city.* [14] to influence, esp by emotional appeal: *his words carried the crowd.* [15] to secure the passage of (a bill, motion, etc.). [16] to win (an election). [17] to obtain victory for (a candidate or measure) in an election. [18] *Chiefly US* to win a plurality or majority of votes in (a district, legislative body, etc.): *the candidate carried 40 states.* [19] to capture: *our troops carried the town.* [20] (of communications media) to include as the content: *this newspaper carries no book reviews.* [21] Also (esp US): **carry over.** *Book-keeping* to transfer (an item) to another account, esp to transfer to the following year's account instead of writing off against profit and loss: *to carry a loss.* [22] *Maths* to transfer (a number) from one column of figures to the next, as from units to tens in multiplication and addition. [23] (of a shop, trader, etc.) to keep in stock: *to carry confectionery.* [24] to support (a musical part or melody) against the other parts. [25] to sustain (livestock): *this land will carry twelve ewes to the acre.* [26] to maintain (livestock) in good health but without increasing their weight or obtaining any products from them. [27] *(intr)* (of a ball, projectile, etc.) to travel through the air or reach a specified point: *his first drive carried to the green.* [28] *Sport, esp golf* (of a ball) to travel beyond: *the drive carried the trees.* [29] *(intr)* (of a gun) to have a range as specified: *this rifle carries for 1200 yards.* [30] to retain contact with and pursue (a line of scent). [31] *(intr)* (of ground) to be in such a condition that scent lies well upon it. [32] *Ice hockey* to move (the puck) forwards, keeping it against the blade of the stick. [33] *Informal* to imbibe (alcoholic drink) without showing ill effects. [34] *(intr) Slang* to have drugs on one's person. [35] **carry all before (one).** to win unanimous support or approval for (oneself). [36] **carry a tune.** to be able to sing in tune. [37] **carry the can (for).** *Informal* to take the responsibility for some misdemeanour, etc. (on behalf of). [38] **carry the day.** to win a contest or competition; succeed. ◆ NOUN, *plural* **-ries.** [39] the act of carrying. [40] *US and Canadian* a portion of land over which a boat must be portaged. [41] the range of a firearm or its projectile. [42] the distance travelled by a ball, etc., esp (in golf) the distance from where the ball is struck to where it first touches the ground.
▷HISTORY C14 *carien,* from Old Northern French *carier* to move by vehicle, from *car,* from Latin *carrum* transport wagon; see CAR

carryall¹ ('kærɪ,ɔ:l) NOUN a light four-wheeled horse-drawn carriage usually designed to carry four passengers.

carryall² ('kærɪ,ɔ:l) NOUN the usual US and Canadian name for a **holdall.**

carry away VERB *(tr, adverb)* [1] to remove forcefully. [2] *(usually passive)* to cause (a person) to lose self-control. [3] *(usually passive)* to delight or enrapture: *he was carried away by the music.*

carry back *Tax accounting* ◆ VERB [1] *(tr, adverb)* to apply (a legally permitted credit, esp an operating loss) to the taxable income of previous years in order to ease the overall tax burden. ◆ NOUN **carry-back.** [2] an amount carried back.

carrycot ('kærɪ,kɒt) NOUN a light cot with handles, similar to but smaller than the body of a pram and often attachable to an unsprung wheeled frame.

carry forward VERB *(tr, adverb)* [1] *Book-keeping* to transfer (a balance) to the next page, column, etc. [2] *Tax accounting* to apply (a legally permitted credit, esp an operating loss) to the taxable income of following years to ease the overall tax burden. ◆ Also: **carry over.** ◆ NOUN **carry-forward.** [3] Also called: **carry-over.** *Tax accounting* an amount carried forward.

carry-in ADJECTIVE of or relating to a type of after-sales service in which the customer must take the product to the service provider for repair: *carry-in warranty.*

carrying capacity NOUN *Ecology* the maximum number of individuals that an area of land can support, usually determined by their food requirements.

carrying charge NOUN the opportunity cost of unproductive assets, such as goods stored in a warehouse.

carrying-on NOUN, *plural* **carryings-on.** *Informal* [1] unconventional or questionable behaviour. [2] excited or flirtatious behaviour, esp when regarded as foolish.

carrying place NOUN *Canadian* another name for **portage.**

carry off VERB *(tr, adverb)* [1] to remove forcefully. [2] to win: *he carried off all the prizes.* [3] to manage or handle (a situation) successfully: *he carried off the introductions well.* [4] to cause to die: *he was carried off by pneumonia.*

carry on VERB *(adverb)* [1] *(intr)* to continue or persevere: *we must carry on in spite of our difficulties.* [2] *(tr)* to manage or conduct: *to carry on a business.* [3] *(intr; often foll by with) Informal* to have an affair. [4] *(intr) Informal* to cause a fuss or commotion. ◆ NOUN **carry-on.** [5] *Informal, chiefly Brit* a fuss or commotion.

carry out VERB *(tr, adverb)* [1] to perform or cause to be implemented: *I wish he could afford to carry out his plan.* [2] to bring to completion; accomplish. ◆ NOUN **carry-out.** *Chiefly Scot* [3] alcohol bought at a pub or off-licence for consumption elsewhere. [4] **a** hot cooked food bought at a shop or restaurant for consumption elsewhere. **b** a shop or restaurant that sells such food: *we'll get something from the Chinese carry-out.* **c** *(as modifier): a carry-out shop.*

carry over VERB *(tr, adverb)* [1] to postpone or defer. [2] *Book-keeping, tax accounting* another term for **carry forward.** [3] (on the London Stock Exchange) to postpone (payment or settlement) until the next account day. ◆ NOUN [4] something left over for future use, esp goods to be sold. [5] *Book-keeping* a sum or balance carried forward. [6] another name for **contango.** [7] *Tax accounting* another name for **carry-forward.**

carry through VERB *(tr, adverb)* [1] to bring to completion. [2] to enable to endure (hardship, trouble, etc.); support.

carse (kɑːs; *Scot* kærs) NOUN *Scot* a riverside area of flat fertile alluvium.
▷**HISTORY** C14: of uncertain origin; perhaps from a plural form of CARR

carsick (ˈkɑːˌsɪk) ADJECTIVE nauseated from riding in a car or other vehicle.
▸ˈ**car,sickness** NOUN

Carson City (ˈkɑːsᵊn) NOUN a city in W Nevada, capital of the state. Pop.: 46 770 (1995 est.).

Carstensz (ˈkɑːstənz) NOUN **Mount.** a former name of (Mount) **Jaya.**

cart[1] (kɑːt) NOUN [1] a heavy open vehicle, usually having two wheels and drawn by horses, used in farming and to transport goods. [2] a light open horse-drawn vehicle having two wheels and springs, for business or pleasure. [3] any small vehicle drawn or pushed by hand, such as a trolley. [4] **put the cart before the horse.** to reverse the usual or natural order of things. ◆ VERB [5] *(usually tr)* to use or draw a cart to convey (goods, etc.): *to cart groceries.* [6] *(tr)* to carry with effort; haul: *to cart wood home.*
▷**HISTORY** C13: from Old Norse *kartr;* related to Old English *cræt* carriage, Old French *carete;* see CAR
▸ˈ**cartable** ADJECTIVE ▸ˈ**carter** NOUN

cart[2] (kɑːt) NOUN *Radio, television* short for **cartridge** (sense 4).

CART ABBREVIATION FOR Championship Auto Racing Teams.

cartage (ˈkɑːtɪdʒ) NOUN the process or cost of carting.

Cartagena (ˌkɑːtəˈdʒiːnə; *Spanish* kartaˈxena) NOUN [1] a port in NW Colombia, on the Caribbean: centre for the Inquisition and the slave trade in the 16th century; chief oil port of Colombia. Pop.: 805 757 (1999 est.). [2] a port in SE Spain, on the Mediterranean: important since Carthaginian and Roman times for its minerals. Pop.: 175 628 (1998 est.).

carte (kɑːt) NOUN a variant spelling of **quarte** (in fencing).

carte blanche (ˈkɑːt ˈblɑːntʃ; *French* kart blɑ̃ʃ) NOUN, *plural* **cartes blanches** (ˈkɑːts ˈblɑːntʃ; *French* kart blɑ̃ʃ). [1] complete discretion or authority: *the government gave their negotiator carte blanche.* [2] *Cards* a piquet hand containing no court cards: scoring ten points.
▷**HISTORY** C18: from French: blank paper

carte du jour (ˈkɑːt də ˈʒʊə, duː; *French* kart dy ʒur) NOUN, *plural* **cartes du jour** (ˈkɑːts də ˈʒʊə, duː; *French* kart dy ʒur). a menu listing dishes available on a particular day.
▷**HISTORY** French, literally: card of the day

cartel (kɑːˈtɛl) NOUN [1] Also called: **trust.** a collusive international association of independent enterprises formed to monopolize production and distribution of a product or service, control prices, etc. [2] *Politics* an alliance of parties or interests to further common aims.
▷**HISTORY** C20: from German *Kartell,* from French, from Italian *cartello* a written challenge, public notice, diminutive of *carta* CARD[1]

cartelize *or* **cartelise** (ˈkɑːtəlaɪz) VERB to form or be formed into a cartel.
▸ˌ**carteliˈzation** *or* ˌ**carteliˈsation** NOUN

Cartesian (kɑːˈtiːzɪən, -ʒən) ADJECTIVE [1] of or relating to the works of René Descartes (1596–1650), the French philosopher and mathematician. [2] of, relating to, or used in Descartes' mathematical system: *Cartesian coordinates.* [3] of, relating to, or derived from Descartes' philosophy, esp his contentions that personal identity consists in the continued existence of a unique mind and that the mind and body are connected causally. See also **dualism** (sense 2). ◆ NOUN [4] a follower of the teachings and methods of Descartes.
▸**Carˈtesian,ism** NOUN

Cartesian coordinates PLURAL NOUN a system of representing points in space in terms of their distance from a given origin measured along a set of mutually perpendicular axes. Written *(x,y,z)* with reference to three axes.

Cartesian product NOUN *Maths, logic* the set of all ordered pairs of members of two given sets. The product $A \times B$ is the set of all pairs $< a, b >$ where *a* is a member of *A* and *b* is a member of *B*. Also called: **cross product.**

cartful (ˈkɑːtˌfʊl) NOUN the amount a cart can hold.

Carthage (ˈkɑːθɪdʒ) NOUN an ancient city state, on the N African coast near present-day Tunis. Founded about 800 B.C. by Phoenician traders, it grew into an empire dominating N Africa and the Mediterranean. Destroyed and then rebuilt by Rome, it was finally razed by the Arabs in 697 A.D. See also **Punic Wars.**

Carthaginian (ˌkɑːθəˈdʒɪnɪən) ADJECTIVE [1] of or relating to Carthage (an ancient N African city state) or its inhabitants. ◆ NOUN [2] a native or inhabitant of Carthage.

carthorse (ˈkɑːtˌhɔːs) NOUN a large heavily built horse kept for pulling carts or carriages.

Carthusian (kɑːˈθjuːzɪən) NOUN *RC Church* **a** a member of an austere monastic order founded by Saint Bruno in 1084 near Grenoble, France. **b** *(as modifier): a Carthusian monastery.*
▷**HISTORY** C14: from Medieval Latin *Carthusianus,* from Latin *Carthusia* Chartreuse, near Grenoble

cartilage (ˈkɑːtɪlɪdʒ, ˈkɑːtlɪdʒ) NOUN a tough elastic tissue composing most of the embryonic skeleton of vertebrates. In the adults of higher vertebrates it is mostly converted into bone, remaining only on the articulating ends of bones, in the thorax, trachea, nose, and ears. Nontechnical name: **gristle.**
▷**HISTORY** C16: from Latin *cartilāgō*
▸**cartilaginous** (ˌkɑːtɪˈlædʒɪnəs) ADJECTIVE

cartilage bone NOUN any bone that develops within cartilage rather than in a fibrous tissue membrane. Compare **membrane bone.**

cartilaginous fish NOUN any fish of the class *Chondrichthyes,* including the sharks, skates, and rays, having a skeleton composed entirely of cartilage.

cartload (ˈkɑːtˌləʊd) NOUN [1] the amount a cart can hold. [2] a quantity of rubble, ballast, etc., of between one quarter and one half of a cubic yard.

cart off, away, *or* **out** VERB *(tr, adverb) Informal* to carry or remove brusquely or by force.

cartogram (ˈkɑːtəˌɡræm) NOUN a map showing statistical information in diagrammatic form.
▷**HISTORY** C20: from French *cartogramme,* from *carte* map, CHART; see -GRAM

cartography *or* **chartography** (kɑːˈtɒɡrəfɪ) NOUN the art, technique, or practice of compiling or drawing maps or charts.
▷**HISTORY** C19: from French *cartographie,* from *carte* map, CHART
▸**carˈtographer** *or* **charˈtographer** NOUN ▸**cartographic** (ˌkɑːtəˈɡræfɪk), ˌ**cartoˈgraphical,** *or* ˌ**chartoˈgraphic,** ˌ**chartoˈgraphical** ADJECTIVE ▸ˌ**cartoˈgraphically** *or* ˌ**chartoˈgraphically** ADVERB

cartomancy (ˈkɑːtəˌmænsɪ) NOUN the telling of fortunes with playing cards.
▷**HISTORY** C19: from French *carte* card + -MANCY

carton (ˈkɑːtᵊn) NOUN [1] a cardboard box for containing goods. [2] a container of waxed paper or plastic in which liquids, such as milk, are sold. [3] *Shooting* **a** a white disc at the centre of a target. **b** a shot that hits this disc. ◆ VERB *(tr)* [4] to enclose (goods) in a carton.
▷**HISTORY** C19: from French, from Italian *cartone* pasteboard, from *carta* CARD[1]

cartoon (kɑːˈtuːn) NOUN [1] a humorous or satirical drawing, esp one in a newspaper or magazine, concerning a topical event. [2] Also called: **comic strip.** a sequence of drawings in a newspaper, magazine, etc., relating a comic or adventurous situation. [3] See **animated cartoon.** [4] a full-size preparatory sketch for a fresco, tapestry, mosaic, etc., from which the final work is traced or copied.
▷**HISTORY** C17: from Italian *cartone* pasteboard, sketch on stiff paper; see CARTON
▸**carˈtoonist** NOUN

cartoonish (ˌkɑːˈtuːnɪʃ) ADJECTIVE like a cartoon, esp in being one-dimensional, brightly coloured, or exaggerated.

cartophily (kɑːˈtɒfɪlɪ) NOUN the hobby of collecting cigarette cards.
▷**HISTORY** C20: from French *carte* card + -O- + *-phily* from Greek *philos* loving
▸**carˈtophilist** NOUN

cartouche *or* **cartouch** (kɑːˈtuːʃ) NOUN [1] a carved or cast ornamental tablet or panel in the form of a scroll, sometimes having an inscription. [2] an oblong figure enclosing characters expressing royal or divine names in Egyptian hieroglyphics. [3] the paper case holding combustible materials in certain fireworks. [4] *Now rare* a cartridge or a box for cartridges.
▷**HISTORY** C17: from French: scroll, cartridge, from Italian *cartoccio,* from *carta* paper; see CARD[1]

cartridge (ˈkɑːtrɪdʒ) NOUN [1] a cylindrical, usually metal casing containing an explosive charge and often a bullet, for a rifle or other small arms. [2] a case for an explosive, such as a blasting charge. [3] an electromechanical transducer in the pick-up of a record player, usually either containing a piezoelectric crystal (**crystal cartridge**) or an electromagnet (**magnetic cartridge**). [4] a container for magnetic tape that is inserted into a tape deck in audio or video systems. It is about four times the size of a cassette. [5] Also called: **cassette, magazine.** *Photog* a light-tight film container that enables a camera to be loaded and unloaded in normal light. [6] *Computing* a removable unit in a computer, such as an integrated circuit, containing software.
▷**HISTORY** C16: from earlier *cartage,* variant of CARTOUCHE (cartridge)

cartridge belt NOUN a belt with pockets for cartridge clips or loops for cartridges.

cartridge clip NOUN a metallic container holding cartridges for an automatic firearm.

cartridge paper NOUN [1] an uncoated type of drawing or printing paper, usually made from bleached sulphate wood pulp with an addition of esparto grass. [2] a heavy paper used in making cartridges or as drawing or printing paper.

cartridge pen NOUN a pen having a removable ink reservoir that is replaced when empty.

cart track NOUN a rough track or road in a rural area. Also called: **cart road.**

cartulary (ˈkɑːtjʊlərɪ) *or* **chartulary** (ˈtʃɑːtjʊlərɪ) NOUN, *plural* **-laries.** *Law* **a** a collection of charters or records, esp relating to the title to an estate or monastery. **b** any place where records are kept.
▷**HISTORY** C16: from Medieval Latin *cartulārium,* from Latin *chartula* a little paper, from *charta* paper; see CARD[1]

cartwheel (ˈkɑːtˌwiːl) NOUN [1] the wheel of a cart, usually having wooden spokes and metal tyres. [2] an acrobatic movement in which the body makes a sideways revolution supported on the hands with arms and legs outstretched. [3] *US slang* a large coin, esp the silver dollar.

cartwheel flower NOUN another name for **giant hogweed.**

cartwright ('kɑːtˌraɪt) NOUN a person who makes carts.

caruncle ('kærəŋkᵊl, kə'rʌŋ-) NOUN 1 a fleshy outgrowth on the heads of certain birds, such as a cock's comb. 2 an outgrowth near the hilum on the seeds of some plants. 3 any small fleshy mass in or on the body, either natural or abnormal.
▷HISTORY C17: from obsolete French *caruncule,* from Latin *caruncula* a small piece of flesh, from *carō* flesh
▸**caruncular** (kə'rʌŋkjʊlə) *or* **ca'runculous** ADJECTIVE
▸**carunculate** (kə'rʌŋkjʊlɪt, -ˌleɪt) *or* **ca'runcuˌlated** ADJECTIVE

carve (kɑːv) VERB 1 (*tr*) to cut or chip in order to form something: *to carve wood.* 2 to decorate or form (something) by cutting or chipping: *to carve statues.* 3 to slice (meat) into pieces: *to carve a turkey.*
▷HISTORY Old English *ceorfan;* related to Old Frisian *kerva,* Middle High German *kerben* to notch

carvel ('kɑːvᵊl) NOUN another word for **caravel.**

carvel-built ADJECTIVE (of a vessel) having a hull with planks made flush at the seams. Compare **clinker-built.**

carven ('kɑːvᵊn) VERB an archaic or literary past participle of **carve.**

carve out VERB (*tr, adverb*) to make or create (a career): *he carved out his own future.*

carver ('kɑːvə) NOUN 1 a carving knife. 2 (*plural*) a large matched knife and fork for carving meat. 3 *Brit* a chair having arms that forms part of a set of dining chairs.

carvery ('kɑːvərɪ) NOUN, *plural* **-veries.** an eating establishment at which customers pay a set price and may then have unrestricted helpings of food from a variety of meats, salads, and other vegetables.

carve up VERB (*tr, adverb*) 1 to cut (something) into pieces. 2 to divide or dismember (a country, land, etc.). ◆ NOUN **carve-up.** 3 *Informal* an act or instance of dishonestly prearranging the result of a competition. 4 *Slang* the distribution of something, as of booty.

carving ('kɑːvɪŋ) NOUN a figure or design produced by carving stone, wood, etc. Related adjective: **glyptic.**

carving knife NOUN a long-bladed knife for carving cooked meat for serving.

caryatid (ˌkærɪ'ætɪd) NOUN, *plural* **-ids** *or* **-ides** (-ɪˌdiːz). a column, used to support an entablature, in the form of a draped female figure. Compare **telamon.**
▷HISTORY C16: from Latin *Caryātides,* from Greek *Karuatides* priestesses of Artemis at *Karuai* (Caryae), village in Laconia
▸ **ˌcary'atidal, ˌcaryˌati'dean, ˌcary'atic,** *or* **caryatidic** (ˌkærɪə'tɪdɪk) ADJECTIVE

caryo- COMBINING FORM a variant of **karyo-.**

caryophyllaceous (ˌkærɪəʊfɪ'leɪʃəs) ADJECTIVE of, relating to, or belonging to the *Caryophyllaceae,* a family of flowering plants including the pink, carnation, sweet william, and chickweed.
▷HISTORY C19: from New Latin *Caryophyllāceae,* from *Caryophyllus* former type genus, from Greek *karuophullon* clove tree, from *karuon* nut + *phullon* leaf

caryopsis (ˌkærɪ'ɒpsɪs) NOUN, *plural* **-ses** (-siːz) *or* **-sides** (-sɪˌdiːz). a dry seedlike fruit having the pericarp fused to the seed coat of the single seed: produced by the grasses.
▷HISTORY C19: New Latin; see KARYO-, -OPSIS

CAS (in Canada) ABBREVIATION FOR Children's Aid Society.

casaba *or* **cassaba** (kə'sɑːbə) NOUN a kind of winter muskmelon having a yellow rind and sweet juicy flesh.
▷HISTORY from *Kassaba,* former name of Turgutlu, Turkey

Casablanca (ˌkæsə'blæŋkə) NOUN a port in NW Morocco, on the Atlantic: largest city in the country; industrial centre. Pop.: 523 279 (1994).

Casanova (ˌkæsə'nəʊvə) NOUN any man noted for his amorous adventures; a rake.
▷HISTORY from Giovanni Jacopo *Casanova* (1725–98), Italian adventurer

casbah ('kæzbɑː) NOUN (*sometimes capital*) a variant spelling of **kasbah.**

cascabel ('kæskəˌbel) NOUN 1 a knoblike protrusion on the rear part of the breech of an obsolete muzzle-loading cannon. 2 the rear part itself.
▷HISTORY C17: from Spanish: small bell, rattle, of uncertain origin

cascade (kæs'keɪd) NOUN 1 a waterfall or series of waterfalls over rocks. 2 something resembling this, such as folds of lace. 3 **a** a consecutive sequence of chemical or physical processes. **b** (*as modifier*): *cascade liquefaction.* 4 **a** a series of stages in the processing chain of an electrical signal where each operates the next in turn. **b** (*as modifier*): *a cascade amplifier.* 5 the cumulative process responsible for the formation of an electrical discharge, cosmic-ray shower, or Geiger counter avalanche in a gas. 6 the sequence of spontaneous decays by an excited atom or ion. ◆ VERB 7 (*intr*) to flow or fall in or like a cascade.
▷HISTORY C17: from French, from Italian *cascata,* from *cascare* to fall, ultimately from Latin *cadere* to fall

Cascade Range NOUN a chain of mountains in the US and Canada: a continuation of the Sierra Nevada range from N California through Oregon and Washington to British Columbia. Highest peak: Mount Rainier, 4392 m (14 408 ft.).

cascara (kæs'kɑːrə) NOUN 1 See **cascara sagrada.** 2 Also called: **cascara buckthorn, bearwood.** a shrub or small tree, *Rhamnus purshiana* of NW North America, whose bark is a source of cascara sagrada: family *Rhamnaceae.*
▷HISTORY C19: from Spanish: bark, from *cascar* to break, from Vulgar Latin *quassicāre* (unattested) to shake violently, shatter, from Latin *quassāre* to dash to pieces

cascara sagrada (sə'grɑːdə) NOUN the dried bark of the cascara buckthorn, used as a stimulant and laxative. Often shortened to **cascara.**
▷HISTORY Spanish, literally: sacred bark

cascarilla (ˌkæskə'rɪlə) NOUN 1 a West Indian euphorbiaceous shrub, *Croton eluteria,* whose bitter aromatic bark is used as a tonic. 2 the bark of this shrub.
▷HISTORY C17: from Spanish, diminutive of *cáscara* bark; see CASCARA

case¹ (keɪs) NOUN 1 a single instance, occurrence, or example of something. 2 an instance of disease, injury, hardship, etc. 3 a question or matter for discussion: *the case before the committee.* 4 a specific condition or state of affairs; situation. 5 a set of arguments supporting a particular action, cause, etc. 6 **a** a person attended or served by a doctor, social worker, solicitor, etc.; patient or client. **b** (*as modifier*): *a case study.* 7 **a** an action or suit at law or something that forms sufficient grounds for bringing an action: *he has a good case.* **b** the evidence offered in court to support a claim. 8 *Grammar* **a** a set of grammatical categories of nouns, pronouns, and adjectives, marked by inflection in some languages, indicating the relation of the noun, adjective, or pronoun to other words in the sentence. **b** any one of these categories: *the nominative case.* 9 *Informal* a person in or regarded as being in a specified condition: *the accident victim was a hospital case; he's a mental case.* 10 *Informal* a person of a specified character (esp in the phrase **a hard case**). 11 *Informal* an odd person; eccentric. 12 *US informal* love or infatuation. 13 short for **case shot.** See **canister** (sense 2b). 14 **as the case may be.** according to the circumstances. 15 **in any case.** (*adverb*) no matter what; anyhow: *we will go in any case.* 16 **in case.** (*adverb*) **a** in order to allow for eventualities. **b** (*as conjunction*) in order to allow for the possibility that: *take your coat in case it rains.* **c** *US* if. 17 **in case of.** (*preposition*) in the event of. 18 **in no case.** (*adverb*) under no circumstances: *in no case should you fight back.*
▷HISTORY Old English *casus* (grammatical) case, associated also with Old French *cas* a happening; both from Latin *cāsus,* a befalling, occurrence, from *cadere* to fall

case² (keɪs) NOUN 1 **a** a container, such as a box or chest. **b** (*in combination*): *suitcase; briefcase.* 2 an outer cover or sheath, esp for a watch. 3 a receptacle and its contents: *a case of ammunition.* 4 a pair or brace, esp of pistols. 5 *Architect* another word for **casing** (sense 3). 6 a completed cover ready to be fastened to a book to form its binding. 7 *Printing* a tray divided into many compartments in which a compositor keeps individual metal types of a particular size and style. Cases were originally used in pairs, one (the **upper case**) for capitals, the other (the **lower case**) for small letters. 8 *Metallurgy* the surface of a piece of steel that has been case-hardened. ◆ VERB (*tr*) 9 to put into or cover with a case: *to case the machinery.* 10 *Slang* to inspect carefully (esp a place to be robbed).
▷HISTORY C13: from Old French *casse,* from Latin *capsa,* from *capere* to take, hold

casease ('keɪsɪˌeɪz) NOUN a proteolytic enzyme formed by certain bacteria that activates the solution of albumin and casein in milk and cheese.
▷HISTORY C20: from CASE(IN) + -ASE

caseate ('keɪsɪˌeɪt) VERB (*intr*) *Pathol* to undergo caseation.
▷HISTORY C19: from Latin *cāseus* CHEESE¹

caseation (ˌkeɪsɪ'eɪʃən) NOUN 1 the formation of cheese from casein during the coagulation of milk. 2 *Pathol* the degeneration of dead tissue into a soft cheeselike mass.

casebook ('keɪsˌbʊk) NOUN a book in which records of legal or medical cases are kept.

casebound ('keɪsˌbaʊnd) ADJECTIVE another word for **hardback.**

casefy ('keɪsɪˌfaɪ) VERB **-fies, -fying, -fied.** to make or become similar to cheese.
▷HISTORY C20: from Latin *cāseus* CHEESE¹ + -FY

case grammar NOUN *Linguistics* a system of grammatical description based on the functional relations that noun groups have to the main verb of a sentence. Compare **systemic grammar, transformational grammar.**

case-harden VERB (*tr*) 1 *Metallurgy* to form a hard surface layer of high carbon content on (a steel component) by heating in a carburizing environment with subsequent quenching or heat treatment. 2 to harden the spirit or disposition of; make callous: *experience had case-hardened the judge.*

case history NOUN a record of a person's background, medical history, etc., esp one used for determining medical treatment.

casein ('keɪsiːn, -siːn) NOUN a phosphoprotein, precipitated from milk by the action of rennin, forming the basis of cheese: used in the manufacture of plastics and adhesives. Also called (US): **paracasein.**
▷HISTORY C19: from Latin *cāseus* cheese + -IN

caseinogen (ˌkeɪsɪ'ɪnədʒən, keɪ'siːnə-) NOUN the principal protein of milk, converted to casein by rennin. Sometimes called (US): **casein.**

case knife NOUN another name for **sheath knife.**

case law NOUN law established by following judicial decisions given in earlier cases. Compare **statute law.** See also **precedent** (sense 1).

caseload ('keɪsləʊd) NOUN the number of cases constituting the work of a doctor, solicitor, social worker, etc. over a specified period.

casemate ('keɪsˌmeɪt) NOUN an armoured compartment in a ship or fortification in which guns are mounted.
▷HISTORY C16: from French, from Italian *casamatta,* perhaps from Greek *khasmata* apertures, plural of *khasma* CHASM
▸ **'caseˌmated** ADJECTIVE

casement ('keɪsmənt) NOUN 1 a window frame that is hinged on one side. 2 a window containing frames hinged at the side or at the top or bottom. 3 a poetic word for **window.**
▷HISTORY C15: probably from Old Northern French *encassement* frame, from *encasser* to frame, encase, from *casse* framework, crate, CASE²

caseose ('keɪsɪˌəʊz, -ˌəʊs) NOUN a peptide produced by the peptic digestion of casein.
▷HISTORY C20: from Latin *cāseus* cheese + -OSE²

caseous ('keɪsɪəs) ADJECTIVE of or like cheese.
▷HISTORY C17: from Latin *cāseus* CHEESE¹

casern *or* **caserne** (kə'zɜːn) NOUN (formerly) a billet or accommodation for soldiers in a town.
▷HISTORY C17: from French *caserne,* from Old Provençal *cazerna* group of four men, ultimately from Latin *quattuor* four

Caserta (*Italian* ka'zerta) NOUN a town in S Italy, in Campania: centre of Garibaldi's campaigns for the unification of Italy (1860); Allied headquarters in World War II. Pop.: 69 350 (1990).

case shot NOUN another name for **canister** (sense 2b).

case stated NOUN *Law* a statement of the facts of a case prepared by one court for the opinion or judgment of another court. Also called: **stated case.**

case study NOUN the act or an instance of analysing one or more particular cases or case histories with a view to making generalizations.

casework (ˈkeɪsˌwɜːk) NOUN social work based on close study of the personal histories and circumstances of individuals and families.
▸ **ˈcaseˌworker** NOUN

caseworm (ˈkeɪsˌwɜːm) NOUN another name for a **caddis worm.**

cash¹ (kæʃ) NOUN 1 banknotes and coins, esp in hand or readily available; money or ready money. 2 immediate payment, in full or part, for goods or services (esp in the phrase **cash down**). 3 (*modifier*) of, for, or paid by cash: *a cash transaction.* 4 (usually preceded by *the*) *Canadian* a checkout counter. ◆ VERB 5 (*tr*) to obtain or pay ready money for: *to cash a cheque.* ◆ See also **cash in, cash up.**
▷HISTORY C16: from Old Italian *cassa* money box, from Latin *capsa* CASE²
▸ **ˈcashable** ADJECTIVE

cash² (kæʃ) NOUN, *plural* **cash.** any of various Chinese, Indonesian, or Indian coins of low value.
▷HISTORY C16: from Portuguese *caixa,* from Tamil *kāsu,* from Sanskrit *karsa* weight of gold or silver

cash-and-carry ADJECTIVE, ADVERB 1 sold or operated on a basis of cash payment for merchandise that is not delivered but removed by the purchaser. ◆ NOUN 2 a wholesale store, esp for groceries, that operates on this basis. 3 an operation on a commodities futures market in which spot goods are purchased and sold at a profit on a futures contract.

cashback (ˈkæʃˌbæk) NOUN 1 **a** a discount offered in return for immediate payment. **b** (*as modifier*): *cashback price £519.99 — save £30!* 2 **a** a service provided by some supermarkets in which customers paying by debit card can draw cash. **b** the cash so drawn.

cash-book NOUN *Book-keeping* a journal in which all cash or cheque receipts and disbursements are recorded.

cash card NOUN an embossed plastic card bearing the name and account details of a bank or building-society customer, used with a personal identification number to obtain money from a cash dispenser: may also function as a cheque card or debit card or both. Also called: **cash-point card.**

cash cow NOUN a product, acquisition, etc., that produces a steady flow of cash, esp one with a well-known brand name commanding a high market share.

cash crop NOUN a crop grown for sale rather than for subsistence.

cash desk NOUN a counter or till in a shop where purchases are paid for.

cash discount NOUN a discount granted to a purchaser who pays before a stipulated date.

cash dispenser NOUN a computerized device outside a bank that supplies cash or account information when the user inserts his cash card and keys in his identification number. Also called: **automated teller machine.**

cashed up ADJECTIVE *Austral informal* having plenty of money.

cashew (ˈkæʃuː, kæˈʃuː) NOUN 1 a tropical American anacardiaceous evergreen tree, *Anacardium occidentale,* bearing kidney-shaped nuts that protrude from a fleshy receptacle. 2 Also called: **cashew nut.** the edible nut of this tree.
▷HISTORY C18: from Portuguese *cajú,* from Tupi *acajú*

cash flow NOUN 1 the movement of money into and out of a business. 2 a prediction of such movement over a given period.

cash-for-questions ADJECTIVE *Brit* of, involved in, or relating to a scandal in which some MPs were accused of accepting bribes to ask particular questions in Parliament.

cashier¹ (kæˈʃɪə) NOUN 1 a person responsible for receiving payments for goods, services, etc., as in a shop. 2 Also called: **teller.** an employee of a bank responsible for receiving deposits, cashing cheques, and other financial transactions; bank clerk. 3 any person responsible for handling cash or maintaining records of its receipt and disbursement.
▷HISTORY C16: from Dutch *cassier* or French *caissier,* from *casse* money chest; see CASE²

cashier² (kæˈʃɪə) VERB (*tr*) 1 to dismiss with dishonour, esp from the armed forces. 2 *Rare* to put away or discard; reject.
▷HISTORY C16: from Middle Dutch *kasseren,* from Old French *casser,* from Latin *quassāre* to QUASH

cash in VERB (*adverb*) 1 (*tr*) to give (something) in exchange, esp for money. 2 (*intr;* often foll by *on*) *Informal* **a** to profit (from). **b** to take advantage (of). 3 (*intr*) a slang expression for **die¹**.

cashless (ˈkæʃlɪs) ADJECTIVE functioning, operated, or performed without using coins or banknotes for money transactions but instead using credit cards or electronic transfer of funds: *cashless shopping.*

cash limit NOUN (*often plural*) a limit imposed as a method of curtailing overall expenditure without specifying the precise means of budgetary control.

cashmere *or* **kashmir** (ˈkæʃmɪə) NOUN 1 a fine soft wool from goats of the Kashmir area. 2 **a** cloth or knitted material made from this or similar wool. **b** (*as modifier*): *a cashmere sweater.*

Cashmere (kæʃˈmɪə) NOUN a variant spelling of **Kashmir.**

cash on delivery NOUN a service entailing cash payment to the carrier on delivery of merchandise. Abbreviation: **COD.**

cashpoint (ˈkæʃˌpɔɪnt) NOUN a cash dispenser.

cash ratio NOUN the ratio of cash on hand to total deposits that by law or custom commercial banks must maintain. Also called: **liquidity ratio.**

cash register NOUN a till with a keyboard that operates a mechanism for displaying and adding the amounts of cash received in individual sales.

cash up VERB (*intr, adverb*) *Brit* (of cashiers, shopkeepers, etc.) to add up the money taken, esp at the end of a working day.

casimere (ˈkæsɪˌmɪə) NOUN a variant spelling of **cassimere.**

casing (ˈkeɪsɪŋ) NOUN 1 a protective case or cover. 2 material for a case or cover. 3 Also called: **case.** a frame containing a door, window, or staircase. 4 the intestines of cattle, pigs, etc., or a synthetic substitute, used as a container for sausage meat. 5 the outer cover of a pneumatic tyre. 6 a pipe or tube used to line a hole or shaft. 7 the outer shell of a steam or gas turbine.

casino (kəˈsiːnəʊ) NOUN, *plural* **-nos.** 1 a public building or room in which gaming takes place, esp roulette and card games such as baccarat and chemin de fer. 2 a variant spelling of **cassino.**
▷HISTORY C18: from Italian, diminutive of *casa* house, from Latin

cask (kɑːsk) NOUN 1 a strong wooden barrel used mainly to hold alcoholic drink: *a wine cask.* 2 any barrel. 3 the quantity contained in a cask. 4 *Austral* a lightweight cardboard container with plastic lining and a small tap, used to hold and serve wine. 5 *Engineering* another name for **flask** (sense 6).
▷HISTORY C15: from Spanish *casco* helmet, perhaps from *cascar* to break

casket (ˈkɑːskɪt) NOUN 1 a small box or chest for valuables, esp jewels. 2 *Chiefly US* another name for **coffin** (sense 1).
▷HISTORY C15: probably from Old French *cassette* little box; see CASE²

Caslon (ˈkæzlən) NOUN a style of type designed by William Caslon, English type founder (1692–1766).

Caspar (ˈkæspə, ˈkæspɑː) *or* **Gaspar** NOUN (in Christian tradition) one of the Magi, the other two being Melchior and Balthazar.

Casparian strip (kæˈspeərɪən) NOUN *Botany* a band of suberized material around the radial walls of endodermal cells: impervious to gases and liquids.
▷HISTORY C20: named after Robert *Caspary,* 19th-century German botanist

Caspian Sea (ˈkæspɪən) NOUN a salt lake between SE Europe and Asia: the largest inland sea in the world; fed mainly by the River Volga. Area: 394 299 sq. km (152 239 sq. miles).

casque (kæsk) NOUN *Zoology* a helmet or a helmet-like process or structure, as on the bill of most hornbills.
▷HISTORY C17: from French, from Spanish *casco;* see CASK
▸ **casqued** ADJECTIVE

cassaba (kəˈsɑːbə) NOUN a variant spelling of **casaba.**

Cassandra (kəˈsændrə) NOUN 1 *Greek myth* a daughter of Priam and Hecuba, endowed with the gift of prophecy but fated never to be believed. 2 anyone whose prophecies of doom are unheeded.

cassareep (ˈkæsəˌriːp) NOUN the juice of the bitter cassava root, boiled down to a syrup and used as a flavouring, esp in West Indian cookery.
▷HISTORY C19: of Carib origin

cassata (kəˈsɑːtə) NOUN an ice cream, originating in Italy, usually containing nuts and candied fruit.
▷HISTORY from Italian

cassation (kæˈseɪʃən) NOUN *Chiefly law* (esp in France) annulment, as of a judicial decision by a higher court.
▷HISTORY C15: from Old French, from Medieval Latin *cassātiō,* from Late Latin *cassāre* to cancel, from Latin *quassāre* to QUASH

cassava (kəˈsɑːvə) NOUN 1 Also called: **manioc.** any tropical euphorbiaceous plant of the genus *Manihot,* esp the widely cultivated American species *M. esculenta* (or *utilissima*) (**bitter cassava**) and *M. dulcis* (**sweet cassava**). 2 a starch derived from the root of this plant: an important food in the tropics and a source of tapioca.
▷HISTORY C16: from Spanish *cazabe* cassava bread, from Taino *caçábi*

Cassegrain telescope (ˈkæsɪˌgreɪn) NOUN an astronomical reflecting telescope in which incident light is reflected from a large concave paraboloid mirror onto a smaller convex hyperboloid mirror and then back through a hole in the concave mirror to form the image.
▷HISTORY C19: named after N. *Cassegrain,* 17th-century French scientist who invented it

Cassel (*German* ˈkasəl) NOUN a variant spelling of **Kassel.**

casserole (ˈkæsəˌrəʊl) NOUN 1 a covered dish of earthenware, glass, etc., in which food is cooked and served. 2 any food cooked and served in such a dish: *chicken casserole.* ◆ VERB 3 to cook or be cooked in a casserole.
▷HISTORY C18: from French, from Old French *casse* ladle, pan for dripping, from Old Provençal *cassa,* from Late Latin *cattia* dipper, from Greek *kuathion,* diminutive of *kuathos* cup

cassette (kæˈsɛt) NOUN 1 **a** a plastic container for magnetic tape, as one inserted into a tape deck. **b** (*as modifier*): *a cassette recorder.* 2 *Photog* another term for **cartridge** (sense 5). 3 *Films* a container for film used to facilitate the loading of a camera or projector, esp when the film is used in the form of a loop.
▷HISTORY C18: from French: little box; see CASE²

cassia (ˈkæsɪə) NOUN 1 any plant of the mainly tropical leguminous genus *Cassia,* esp *C. fistula,* whose pods yield **cassia pulp,** a mild laxative. See also **senna.** 2 a lauraceous tree, *Cinnamomum cassia,* of tropical Asia. 3 **cassia bark.** the cinnamon-like bark of this tree, used as a spice.
▷HISTORY Old English, from Latin *casia,* from Greek *kasia,* of Semitic origin; related to Hebrew *qesīʿāh* cassia

cassimere *or* **casimere** (ˈkæsɪˌmɪə) NOUN a woollen suiting cloth of plain or twill weave.
▷HISTORY C18: variant of *cashmere,* from KASHMIR

Cassini's division (kæˈsiːnɪz) NOUN the gap that divides Saturn's rings into two parts, discovered by Giovanni Domenico Cassini (1625–1712) in 1675.

cassino *or* **casino** (kəˈsiːnəʊ) NOUN a card game for two to four players in which players pair cards from their hands with others exposed on the table.

Cassino (*Italian* kasˈsiːno) NOUN a town in central Italy, in Latium at the foot of Monte Cassino: an ancient Volscian (and later Roman) town and citadel. Pop.: 34 590 (1990). Latin name: **Casinum.**

Cassiopeia¹ (ˌkæsɪəˈpiːə) NOUN *Greek myth* the wife of Cepheus and mother of Andromeda.

Cassiopeia² (ˌkæsɪəˈpiːə) NOUN, *Latin genitive* **Cassiopeiae** (ˌkæsɪəˈpiːiː). a very conspicuous

W-shaped constellation near the Pole Star. **Cassiopeia A** is a very strong radio and X-ray source, identified as the remnant of a supernova thought to have occurred in the late 17th century.
▸ **ˌCassioˈpeian** ADJECTIVE

cassis (kɑːˈsiːs) NOUN a blackcurrant cordial.
▷**HISTORY** C19: from French

cassiterite (kəˈsɪtəˌraɪt) NOUN a black or brown mineral, found in igneous rocks and hydrothermal veins. It is a source of tin. Composition: tin oxide. Formula: SnO_2. Crystal structure: tetragonal. Also called: **tinstone.**
▷**HISTORY** C19: from Greek *kassiteros* tin

cassock (ˈkæsək) NOUN *Christianity* an ankle-length garment, usually black, worn by priests and choristers.
▷**HISTORY** C16: from Old French *casaque,* from Italian *casacca* a long coat, of uncertain origin
▸ **ˈcassocked** ADJECTIVE

cassoulet (ˌkæsəˈleɪ) NOUN a stew originating from France, made from haricot beans and goose, duck, pork, etc.
▷**HISTORY** French, related to *casse* saucepan, bowl

cassowary (ˈkæsəˌwɛərɪ) NOUN, *plural* **-waries.** any large flightless bird of the genus *Casuarius,* inhabiting forests in NE Australia, New Guinea, and adjacent islands, having a horny head crest, black plumage, and brightly coloured neck and wattles: order *Casuariiformes* (see **ratite**).
▷**HISTORY** C17: from Malay *kĕsuari*

casspir (ˈkæspɜː) NOUN *South African* an armoured military vehicle.
▷**HISTORY** C20: coined from an anagram of *CSIR* (Council for Scientific and Industrial Research) and *SAP* (South African Police)

cast (kɑːst) VERB **casts, casting, cast.** (*mainly tr*) [1] to throw or expel with violence or force. [2] to throw off or away: *she cast her clothes to the ground.* [3] to reject or dismiss: *he cast the idea from his mind.* [4] to shed or drop: *the snake cast its skin; the horse cast a shoe; the ship cast anchor.* [5] **be cast.** *NZ* (of a sheep) to have fallen and been unable to rise. [6] to cause to appear: *to cast a shadow.* [7] to express (doubts, suspicions, etc.) or cause (them) to be felt. [8] to direct (a glance, attention, etc.): *cast your eye over this.* [9] to place, esp in a violent manner: *he was cast into prison.* [10] (*also intr*) *Angling* to throw (a line) into the water. [11] to draw or choose (lots). [12] to give or deposit (a vote). [13] to select (actors) to play parts in (a play, film, etc.). [14] **a** to shape (molten metal, glass, etc.) by pouring or pressing it into a mould. **b** to make (an object) by such a process. [15] (*also intr; often foll by up*) to compute (figures or a total). [16] to predict: *the old woman cast my fortune.* [17] *Astrology* to draw on (a horoscope) details concerning the positions of the planets in the signs of the zodiac at a particular time for interpretation in terms of human characteristics, behaviour. [18] to contrive (esp in the phrase **cast a spell**). [19] to formulate: *he cast his work in the form of a chart.* [20] (*also intr*) to twist or cause to twist. [21] (*also intr*) *Nautical* to turn the head of (a sailing vessel) or (of a sailing vessel) to be turned away from the wind in getting under way. [22] *Hunting* to direct (a pack of hounds) over (ground) where their quarry may recently have passed. [23] (*intr*) (of birds of prey) to eject from the crop and bill a pellet consisting of the indigestible parts of birds or animals previously eaten. [24] *Falconry* to hold the body of a hawk between the hands so as to perform some operation upon it. [25] *Printing* to stereotype or electrotype. [26] **cast** *or* **throw in one's lot with.** to share in the activities or fortunes of (someone else). ◆ NOUN [27] the act of casting or throwing. [28] **a** Also called: **casting.** something that is shed, dropped, or egested, such as the coil of earth left by an earthworm. **b** another name for **pellet** (sense 4). [29] an object that is thrown. [30] the distance an object is or may be thrown. [31] **a** a throw at dice. **b** the resulting number shown. [32] *Angling* **a** a trace with a fly or flies attached. **b** the act or an instance of casting. [33] the wide sweep made by a sheepdog to get behind a flock of sheep or by a hunting dog in search of a scent. [34] **a** the actors in a play collectively. **b** (*as modifier*): *a cast list.* [35] **a** an object made of metal, glass, etc., that has been shaped in a molten state by being poured or pressed into a mould. **b** the mould used to shape such an object. [36] form or appearance. [37] sort, kind, or style. [38] a fixed twist or defect, esp in the eye. [39] a distortion of shape. [40] *Surgery* a rigid encircling casing, often made of plaster of Paris, for immobilizing broken bones while they heal. [41] *Pathol* a mass of fatty, waxy, cellular, or other material formed in a diseased body cavity, passage, etc. [42] the act of casting a pack of hounds. [43] *Falconry* a pair of falcons working in combination to pursue the same quarry. [44] *Archery* the speed imparted to an arrow by a particular bow. [45] a slight tinge or trace, as of colour. [46] a computation or calculation. [47] a forecast or conjecture. [48] fortune or a stroke of fate. [49] *Palaeontol* a replica of an organic object made of nonorganic material, esp a lump of sediment that indicates the internal or external surface of a shell or skeleton. [50] *Palaeontol* a sedimentary structure representing the infilling of a mark or depression in a soft layer of sediment (or bed). ◆ See also **cast about, castaway, cast back, cast down, cast-off, cast on, cast out, cast up.**
▷**HISTORY** C13: from Old Norse *kasta*

castable (ˈkɑːstəbᵊl) ADJECTIVE [1] able to be cast; suitable for casting. [2] (of an actor) able or likely to be selected to play a part in a play, film, etc.

cast about *or* **around** VERB (*intr, adverb*) to make a mental or visual search: *to cast about for an idea for a book.*

Castalia (kæˈsteɪlɪə) NOUN a spring on Mount Parnassus: in ancient Greece sacred to Apollo and the Muses and believed to be a source of inspiration.
▸ **Casˈtalian** ADJECTIVE

castanets (ˌkæstəˈnɛts) PLURAL NOUN curved pieces of hollow wood, usually held between the fingers and thumb and made to click together: used esp by Spanish dancers.
▷**HISTORY** C17 *castanet,* from Spanish *castañeta,* diminutive of *castaña* CHESTNUT

castaway (ˈkɑːstəˌweɪ) NOUN [1] a person who has been shipwrecked. [2] something thrown off or away; castoff. ◆ ADJECTIVE (*prenominal*) [3] shipwrecked or put adrift. [4] thrown away or rejected. ◆ VERB **cast away.** [5] (*tr, adverb; often passive*) to cause (a ship, person, etc.) to be shipwrecked or abandoned.

cast back VERB (*adverb*) to turn (the mind) to the past.

cast down VERB (*tr, adverb*) to make (a person) discouraged or dejected.

caste (kɑːst) NOUN [1] **a** any of the four major hereditary classes, namely the **Brahman, Kshatriya, Vaisya,** and **Sudra** into which Hindu society is divided. **b** Also called: **caste system.** the system or basis of such classes. **c** the social position or rank conferred by this system. [2] any social class or system based on such distinctions as heredity, rank, wealth, profession, etc. [3] the position conferred by such a system. [4] *Entomol* any of various types of specialized individual, such as the worker, in social insects (hive bees, ants, etc.).
▷**HISTORY** C16: from Portuguese *casta* race, breed, ancestry, from *casto* pure, chaste, from Latin *castus*

Castellammare di Stabia (*Italian* kastɛllamˈmaːre di ˈstabja) NOUN a port and resort in SW Italy, in Campania on the Bay of Naples: site of the Roman resort of Stabiae, which was destroyed by the eruption of Vesuvius in 79 A.D. Pop.: 67 974 (1993 est.).

castellan (ˈkæstɪlən) NOUN *Rare* a keeper or governor of a castle. Also called: **chatelain.**
▷**HISTORY** C14: from Latin *castellānus,* from *castellum* CASTLE

castellated (ˈkæstɪˌleɪtɪd) ADJECTIVE [1] having turrets and battlements, like a castle. [2] having indentations similar to battlements: *a castellated nut; a castellated filament.*
▷**HISTORY** C17: from Medieval Latin *castellātus,* from *castellāre* to fortify as a CASTLE
▸ **ˌcastelˈlation** NOUN

Castellón de la Plana (*Spanish* kasteˈʎon de la ˈplana) NOUN a port in E Spain. Pop.: 137 741 (1998 est.).

caster (ˈkɑːstə) NOUN [1] a person or thing that casts. [2] Also: **castor.** a bottle with a perforated top for sprinkling sugar, etc., or a stand containing such bottles. [3] Also: **castor.** a small wheel mounted on a swivel so that the wheel tends to turn into its plane of rotation.

caster action NOUN the tendency, caused by the design of the mounting, of a wheel to turn into its plane of rotation.

caster sugar (ˈkɑːstə) NOUN finely ground white sugar.

castigate (ˈkæstɪˌɡeɪt) VERB (*tr*) to rebuke or criticize in a severe manner; chastise.
▷**HISTORY** C17: from Latin *castīgāre* to correct, punish, from *castum* pure + *agere* to compel (to be)
▸ **ˌcastiˈgation** NOUN ▸ **ˈcastiˌgator** NOUN ▸ **ˌcastiˈgatory** ADJECTIVE

Castile (kæˈstiːl) *or* **Castilla** (*Spanish* kasˈtiʎa) NOUN a former kingdom comprising most of modern Spain: originally part of León, it became an independent kingdom in the 10th century and united with Aragon (1469), the first step in the formation of the Spanish state.

Castile soap NOUN a hard soap made from olive oil and sodium hydroxide.

Castilian (kæˈstɪljən) NOUN [1] the Spanish dialect of Castile; the standard form of European Spanish. [2] a native or inhabitant of Castile. ◆ ADJECTIVE [3] denoting, relating to, or characteristic of Castile, its inhabitants, or the standard form of European Spanish.

Castilla la Vieja (kasˈtiʎa la ˈbjexa) NOUN the Spanish name for **Old Castile.**

casting (ˈkɑːstɪŋ) NOUN [1] an object or figure that has been cast, esp in metal from a mould. [2] the process of transferring molten steel to a mould. [3] the choosing of actors for a production. [4] *Hunting* the act of directing a pack of hounds over ground where their quarry may recently have passed so that they can quest for, discover, or recapture its scent. [5] *Zoology* another word for **cast** (sense 28) or **pellet** (sense 4).

casting couch NOUN *Informal* a couch on which a casting director is said to seduce women seeking a part in a film or play.

casting vote NOUN the deciding vote used by the presiding officer of an assembly when votes cast on both sides are equal in number.

cast iron NOUN [1] iron containing so much carbon (1.7 to 4.5 per cent) that it cannot be wrought and must be cast into shape. ◆ ADJECTIVE **cast-iron.** [2] made of cast iron. [3] rigid, strong, or unyielding: *a cast-iron decision.*

castle (ˈkɑːsᵊl) NOUN [1] a fortified building or set of buildings, usually permanently garrisoned, as in medieval Europe. [2] any fortified place or structure. [3] a large magnificent house, esp when the present or former home of a nobleman or prince. [4] the citadel and strongest part of the fortifications of a medieval town. [5] *Chess* another name for **rook²**. ◆ VERB [6] *Chess* to move (the king) two squares laterally on the first rank and place the nearest rook on the square passed over by the king, either towards the king's side (**castling short**) or the queen's side (**castling long**).
▷**HISTORY** C11: from Latin *castellum,* diminutive of *castrum* fort

Castlebar (ˌkɑːsᵊlˈbɑː) NOUN the county town of Co. Mayo, Republic of Ireland; site of the battle (1798) between the French and British known as Castlebar Races. Pop.: 6070 (1991).

castled (ˈkɑːsᵊld) ADJECTIVE [1] like a castle in construction; castellated: *a castled mansion.* [2] (of an area) having many castles.

Castleford (ˈkɑːsᵊlfəd) NOUN a town in N England, in Wakefield unitary authority, West Yorkshire on the River Aire. Pop.: 38 536 (1991).

Castle Howard (ˈhaʊəd) NOUN a mansion near York in Yorkshire: designed in 1700 by Sir John Vanbrugh and Nicholas Hawksmoor; the grounds include the Temple of the Four Winds and a mausoleum.

castle in the air *or* **in Spain** NOUN a hope or desire unlikely to be realized; daydream.

castle nut NOUN a hexagonal nut with six slots in the head, two of which take a locking pin to hold it firmly in position.

Castlereagh (ˈkɑːsᵊlˌreɪ) NOUN a district of E Northern Ireland, in Co. Down. Pop.: 66 488 (2001). Area.: 85 sq. km (33 sq. miles).

Castner process (ˈkæstnə) NOUN a process for

extracting sodium from sodium hydroxide, devised by Hamilton Young Castner (1858–98).

cast-off ADJECTIVE 1 (*prenominal*) thrown away; abandoned: *cast-off shoes.* ◆ NOUN **castoff.** 2 a person or thing that has been discarded or abandoned. 3 *Printing* an estimate of the amount of space that a piece of copy will occupy when printed in a particular size and style of type. ◆ VERB **cast off.** (*adverb*) 4 to remove (mooring lines) that hold (a vessel) to a dock. 5 to knot (a row of stitches, esp the final row) in finishing off knitted or woven material. 6 *Printing* to estimate the amount of space that will be taken up by (a book, piece of copy, etc.) when it is printed in a particular size and style of type. 7 (*intr*) (in Scottish country dancing) to perform a progressive movement during which each partner of a couple dances separately behind one line of the set and then reunites with the other in their original position in the set or in a new position.

cast on VERB (*adverb*) to form (the first row of stitches) in knitting and weaving.

castor[1] ('kɑːstə) NOUN 1 the brownish aromatic secretion of the anal glands of a beaver, used in perfumery and medicine. 2 the fur of the beaver. 3 a hat made of beaver or similar fur. 4 a less common name for **beaver**[1] (sense 1).
▷**HISTORY** C14: from Latin, from Greek *kastōr* beaver

castor[2] ('kɑːstə) NOUN a variant spelling of **caster** (senses 2, 3).

Castor ('kɑːstə) NOUN 1 the second brightest star, Alpha Geminorum, in the constellation Gemini: a multiple star consisting of six components lying close to the star Pollux. Distance: 52 light years. 2 *Classical myth* See **Castor and Pollux.**

Castor and Pollux NOUN *Classical myth* the twin sons of Leda: Pollux was fathered by Zeus, Castor by the mortal Tyndareus. After Castor's death, Pollux spent half his days with his half-brother in Hades and half with the gods in Olympus.

castor bean NOUN *US and Canadian* 1 another name for **castor-oil plant.** 2 the seed of this plant.

castor oil NOUN a colourless or yellow glutinous oil obtained from the seeds of the castor-oil plant and used as a fine lubricant and as a cathartic.

castor-oil plant NOUN a tall euphorbiaceous Indian plant, *Ricinus communis,* cultivated in tropical regions for ornament and for its poisonous seeds, from which castor oil is extracted. Also called (US and Canadian): **castor bean.**

cast out VERB (*intr, adverb*) *Scot* to quarrel; be no longer friends.

castrate (kæ'streɪt) VERB (*tr*) 1 to remove the testicles of; emasculate; geld. 2 to deprive of vigour, masculinity, etc. 3 to remove the ovaries of; spay. 4 to expurgate or censor (a book, play, etc.).
▷**HISTORY** C17: from Latin *castrāre* to emasculate, geld
▸**cas'tration** NOUN ▸**cas'trator** NOUN

castration complex NOUN *Psychoanal* an unconscious fear of having one's genitals removed, as a punishment for wishing to have sex with a parent.

castrato (kæ'strɑːtəʊ) NOUN, *plural* **-ti** (-tɪ) *or* **-tos.** (in 17th- and 18th-century opera) a male singer whose testicles were removed before puberty, allowing the retention of a soprano or alto voice.
▷**HISTORY** C18: from Italian, from Latin *castrātus* castrated

Castries (kæs'triːs) NOUN the capital and chief port of St Lucia. Pop.: 13 615 (1992 est.).

Castrop-Rauxel *or* **Kastrop-Rauxel** (*German* 'kastrɔp'rauksəl) NOUN an industrial city in W Germany, in North Rhine-Westphalia. Pop.: 80 000 (latest est.).

cast steel NOUN steel containing varying amounts of carbon, manganese, phosphorus, silicon, and sulphur that is cast into shape rather than wrought.

cast stone NOUN *Building trades* a building component, such as a block or lintel, made from cast concrete with a facing that resembles natural stone.

cast up VERB (*tr, adverb*) 1 (of the sea) to cast ashore. 2 to compute (figures or a total). 3 to bring up as a reproach against a person.

casual ('kæʒjʊəl) ADJECTIVE 1 happening by accident or chance: *a casual meeting.* 2 offhand; not premeditated: *a casual remark.* 3 shallow or superficial: *a casual affair.* 4 being or seeming unconcerned or apathetic: *he assumed a casual attitude.* 5 (esp of dress) for informal wear: *a casual coat.* 6 occasional or irregular: *casual visits; a casual labourer.* 7 *Biology* another term for **adventive.** ◆ NOUN 8 (*usually plural*) an informal article of clothing or footwear. 9 an occasional worker. 10 *Biology* another term for an **adventive.** 11 (*usually plural*) a young man dressed in expensive casual clothes who goes to football matches in order to start fights.
▷**HISTORY** C14: from Late Latin *cāsuālis* happening by chance, from Latin *cāsus* event, from *cadere* to fall; see CASE[1]
▸**'casually** ADVERB ▸**'casualness** NOUN

casualization *or* **casualisation** (ˌkæʒjʊəlaɪ'zeɪʃən) NOUN the altering of working practices so that regular workers are re-employed on a casual or short-term basis.

casualty ('kæʒjʊəltɪ) NOUN, *plural* **-ties.** 1 a serviceman who is killed, wounded, captured, or missing as a result of enemy action. 2 a person who is injured or killed in an accident. 3 a hospital department in which victims of accidents, violence, etc., are treated. 4 anything that is lost, damaged, or destroyed as the result of an accident, etc.

casuarina (ˌkæsjʊə'riːnə) NOUN any tree of the genus *Casuarina,* of Australia and the East Indies, having jointed leafless branchlets: family *Casuarinaceae.* See also **beefwood, she-oak.**
▷**HISTORY** C19: from New Latin, from Malay *kĕsuari* CASSOWARY, referring to the resemblance of the branches to the feathers of the cassowary

casuist ('kæzjʊɪst) NOUN 1 a person, esp a theologian, who attempts to resolve moral dilemmas by the application of general rules and the careful distinction of special cases. 2 a person who is oversubtle in his analysis of fine distinctions; sophist.
▷**HISTORY** C17: from French *casuiste,* from Spanish *casuista,* from Latin *cāsus* CASE[1]
▸ˌ**casu'istic** *or* ˌ**casu'istical** ADJECTIVE ▸ˌ**casu'istically** ADVERB

casuistry ('kæzjʊɪstrɪ) NOUN, *plural* **-ries.** 1 *Philosophy* the resolution of particular moral dilemmas, esp those arising from conflicting general moral rules, by careful distinction of the cases to which these rules apply. 2 reasoning that is specious, misleading, or oversubtle.

casus belli *Latin* ('kɑːsʊs 'bɛliː) NOUN, *plural* ***casus belli*** ('kɑːsʊs 'bɛliː). 1 an event or act used to justify a war. 2 the immediate cause of a quarrel.
▷**HISTORY** literally: occasion of war

cat[1] (kæt) NOUN 1 Also called: **domestic cat.** a small domesticated feline mammal, *Felis catus* (or *domesticus*), having thick soft fur and occurring in many breeds in which the colour of the fur varies greatly: kept as a pet or to catch rats and mice. 2 Also called: **big cat.** any of the larger felines, such as a lion or tiger. 3 any wild feline mammal of the genus *Felis,* such as the lynx or serval, resembling the domestic cat. ◆ Related adjective: **feline.** 4 *Informal* a woman who gossips maliciously. 5 *Slang* a man; guy. 6 *Nautical* a heavy tackle for hoisting an anchor to the cathead. 7 a short sharp-ended piece of wood used in the game of tipcat. 8 short for **catboat.** 9 *Informal* short for **Caterpillar.** 10 short for **cat-o'-nine-tails.** 11 **a bag of cats.** *Irish informal* a bad-tempered person: *she's a real bag of cats this morning.* 12 **fight like Kilkenny cats.** to fight until both parties are destroyed. 13 **let the cat out of the bag.** to disclose a secret, often by mistake. 14 **like a cat on a hot tin roof** *or* **on hot bricks.** in an uneasy or agitated state. 15 **like cat and dog.** quarrelling savagely. 16 **look like something the cat brought in.** to appear dishevelled or bedraggled. 17 **not a cat in hell's chance.** no chance at all. 18 **not have room to swing a cat.** to have very little space. 19 **play cat and mouse.** to play with a person or animal in a cruel or teasing way, esp before a final act of cruelty or unkindness. 20 **put, set,** etc., **the cat among the pigeons.** to introduce some violently disturbing new element. 21 **rain cats and dogs.** to rain very heavily. ◆ VERB **cats, catting, catted.** 22 (*tr*) to flog with a cat-o'-nine-tails. 23 (*tr*) *Nautical* to hoist (an anchor) to the cathead. 24 (*intr*) a slang word for **vomit.**
▷**HISTORY** Old English *catte,* from Latin *cattus;* related to Old Norse *köttr,* Old High German *kazza,* Old French *chat,* Russian *kot*
▸**'cat**ˌ**like** ADJECTIVE ▸**'cattish** ADJECTIVE

cat[2] (kæt) NOUN *Informal* short for **catamaran** (sense 1).

cat[3] (kæt) NOUN 1 **a** short for **catalytic converter. b** (*as modifier*): *a cat car.* ◆ ADJECTIVE 2 short for **catalytic:** *a cat cracker.*

CAT ABBREVIATION FOR: 1 computer-aided teaching. 2 computer-assisted trading.

cat. ABBREVIATION FOR: 1 catalogue. 2 catamaran.

cata-, kata-, *before an aspirate* **cath-,** *or before a vowel* **cat-** PREFIX 1 down; downwards; lower in position: *catadromous; cataphyll.* 2 indicating reversal, opposition, degeneration, etc.: *cataplasia; catatonia.*
▷**HISTORY** from Greek *kata-,* from *kata.* In compound words borrowed from Greek, *kata-* means: down (*catabolism*), away, off (*catalectic*), against (*category*), according to (*catholic*), and thoroughly (*catalogue*)

catabasis (kə'tæbəsɪs) NOUN, *plural* **-ses** (-ˌsiːz). 1 a descent or downward movement. 2 the decline of a disease.
▸**catabatic** (ˌkætə'bætɪk) ADJECTIVE

catabolism *or* **katabolism** (kə'tæbəˌlɪzəm) NOUN a metabolic process in which complex molecules are broken down into simple ones with the release of energy; destructive metabolism. Compare **anabolism.**
▷**HISTORY** C19 *katabolism,* from Greek *katabolē* a throwing down, from *kataballein,* from *kata-* down + *ballein* to throw
▸**catabolic** *or* **katabolic** (ˌkætə'bɒlɪk) ADJECTIVE
▸ˌ**cata'bolically** *or* ˌ**kata'bolically** ADVERB

catabolite (kə'tæbəˌlaɪt) NOUN a substance produced as a result of catabolism.

catacaustic (ˌkætə'kɔːstɪk, -'kɒs-) *Physics* ◆ ADJECTIVE 1 (of a caustic curve or surface) formed by reflected light rays. Compare **diacaustic.** ◆ NOUN 2 a catacaustic curve or surface.

catachresis (ˌkætə'kriːsɪs) NOUN the incorrect use of words, as *luxuriant* for *luxurious.*
▷**HISTORY** C16: from Latin, from Greek *katakhrēsis* a misusing, from *katakhrēsthai,* from *khrēsthai* to use
▸**catachrestic** (ˌkætə'krestɪk) *or* ˌ**cata'chrestical** ADJECTIVE ▸ˌ**cata'chrestically** ADVERB

cataclasis (ˌkætə'kleɪsɪs) NOUN, *plural* **-ses** (-siːz). *Geology* the deformation of rocks by crushing and shearing.
▷**HISTORY** C19: New Latin, from Greek, from CATA- + *klasis* a breaking
▸**cataclastic** (ˌkætə'klæstɪk) ADJECTIVE

cataclinal (ˌkætə'klaɪnəl) ADJECTIVE (of streams, valleys, etc.) running in the direction of the dip of the surrounding rock strata.

cataclysm ('kætəˌklɪzəm) NOUN 1 a violent upheaval, esp of a political, military, or social nature. 2 a disastrous flood; deluge. 3 *Geology* another name for **catastrophe** (sense 4).
▷**HISTORY** C17: via French from Latin, from Greek *kataklusmos* deluge, from *katakluzein* to flood, from *kluzein* to wash
▸ˌ**cata'clysmic** *or* ˌ**cata'clysmal** ADJECTIVE
▸ˌ**cata'clysmically** ADVERB

catacomb ('kætəˌkəʊm, -ˌkuːm) NOUN 1 (*usually plural*) an underground burial place, esp the galleries at Rome, consisting of tunnels with vaults or niches leading off them for tombs. 2 a series of interconnected underground tunnels or caves.
▷**HISTORY** Old English *catacumbe,* from Late Latin *catacumbas* (singular), name of the cemetery under the Basilica of St Sebastian, near Rome; origin unknown

catadioptric (ˌkætədaɪ'ɒptrɪk) ADJECTIVE involving a combination of reflecting and refracting components: *a catadioptric telescope.*
▷**HISTORY** C18: from CATA- + DIOPTRIC

catadromous (kə'tædrəməs) ADJECTIVE (of fishes such as the eel) migrating down rivers to the sea in order to breed. Compare **anadromous.**

▷**HISTORY** C19: from Greek *katadromos,* from *kata-* down + *dromos,* from *dremein* to run

catafalque ('kætəˌfælk) NOUN a temporary raised platform on which a body lies in state before or during a funeral.
▷**HISTORY** C17: from French, from Italian *catafalco,* of uncertain origin; compare SCAFFOLD

Catalan ('kætəˌlæn, -lən) NOUN [1] a language of Catalonia, quite closely related to Spanish and Provençal, belonging to the Romance group of the Indo-European family. [2] a native or inhabitant of Catalonia. ◆ ADJECTIVE [3] denoting, relating to, or characteristic of Catalonia, its inhabitants, or their language.

catalase ('kætəˌleɪs) NOUN an enzyme that catalyses the decomposition of hydrogen peroxide.

catalectic (ˌkætə'lɛktɪk) ADJECTIVE *Prosody* (of a line of verse) having an incomplete final foot.
▷**HISTORY** C16: via Late Latin from Greek *katalēktikos* incomplete, from *katalēgein,* from *kata-* off + *lēgein* to stop

catalepsy ('kætəˌlɛpsɪ) NOUN a state of prolonged rigid posture, occurring for example in schizophrenia or in hypnotic trances.
▷**HISTORY** C16: from Medieval Latin *catalēpsia,* variant of Late Latin *catalēpsis,* from Greek *katalēpsis,* literally: a seizing, from *katalambanein* to hold down, from *kata-* down + *lambanein* to grasp
▸**ˌcata'leptic** ADJECTIVE

Catalina Island (ˌkætə'li:nə) NOUN another name for **Santa Catalina.**

catalo ('kætəˌləʊ) NOUN, *plural* **-loes** *or* **-los.** a variant spelling of **cattalo.**

catalogue *or US* **catalog** ('kætəˌlɒg) NOUN [1] a complete, usually alphabetical list of items, often with notes giving details. [2] a book, usually illustrated, containing details of items for sale, esp as used by mail-order companies. [3] a list of all the books or resources of a library. [4] *US and Canadian* a publication issued by a university, college, etc., listing courses offered, regulations, services, etc. [5] *NZ* a list of wool lots prepared for auction. ◆ VERB **-logues, -loguing, -logued** *or US* **-logs, -loging, -loged.** [6] to compile a catalogue of (a library). [7] to add (books, items, etc.) to an existing catalogue.
▷**HISTORY** C15: from Late Latin *catalogus,* from Greek *katalogos,* from *katalegein* to list, from *kata-* completely + *legein* to collect
▸**'cataˌloguer** *or* **'cataˌloguist** NOUN

catalogue raisonné *French* (katalɔg rɛzɔne) NOUN a descriptive catalogue, esp one covering works of art in an exhibition or collection.

Catalonia (ˌkætə'ləʊnɪə) NOUN a region of NE Spain, with a strong separatist tradition: became an autonomous region with its own parliament in 1979; an important agricultural and industrial region, with many resorts. Pop.: 6 261 999 (2000 est.). Area: 31 929 sq. km (12 328 sq. miles). Catalan name: **Catalunya** (ˌkatə'lu:nɪə). Spanish name: **Cataluña** (kata'luɲa).

catalpa (kə'tælpə) NOUN any bignoniaceous tree of the genus *Catalpa* of North America and Asia, having large leaves, bell-shaped whitish flowers, and long slender pods.
▷**HISTORY** C18: New Latin, from Carolina Creek *kutuhlpa,* literally: winged head, referring to the appearance of the flowers

catalyse *or US* **catalyze** ('kætəˌlaɪz) VERB (*tr*) to influence (a chemical reaction) by catalysis.
▸**'cataˌlyser** *or US* **'cataˌlyzer** NOUN

catalysis (kə'tælɪsɪs) NOUN, *plural* **-ses** (-ˌsi:z). acceleration of a chemical reaction by the action of a catalyst.
▷**HISTORY** C17: from New Latin, from Greek *katalusis,* from *kataluein* to dissolve

catalyst ('kætəlɪst) NOUN [1] a substance that increases the rate of a chemical reaction without itself suffering any permanent chemical change. Compare **inhibitor** (sense 2). [2] a person or thing that causes a change.

catalytic (ˌkætə'lɪtɪk) ADJECTIVE of or relating to catalysis; involving a catalyst.
▸**ˌcata'lytically** ADVERB

catalytic converter NOUN a device using three-way catalysts to reduce the obnoxious and poisonous components of the products of combustion (mainly oxides of nitrogen, carbon monoxide, and unburnt hydrocarbons) from the exhausts of motor vehicles.

catalytic cracker NOUN a unit in an oil refinery in which mineral oils with high boiling points are converted to fuels with lower boiling points by a catalytic process. Often shortened to **cat cracker.**

catamaran (ˌkætəmə'ræn) NOUN [1] a sailing, or sometimes motored, vessel with twin hulls held parallel by a rigid framework. [2] a primitive raft made of logs lashed together. [3] *Informal* a quarrelsome woman.
▷**HISTORY** C17: from Tamil *kattumaram* tied timber

catamenia (ˌkætə'mi:nɪə) PLURAL NOUN *Physiol* another word for **menses.**
▷**HISTORY** C18: from New Latin, from Greek *katamēnia* menses
▸**ˌcata'menial** ADJECTIVE

catamite ('kætəˌmaɪt) NOUN a boy kept for homosexual purposes.
▷**HISTORY** C16: from Latin *Catamītus,* variant of *Ganymēdēs* GANYMEDE[1]

catamount ('kætəˌmaʊnt) *or* **catamountain** NOUN any of various medium-sized felines, such as the puma or lynx.
▷**HISTORY** C17: short for *cat of the mountain*

catananche (ˌkætə'næŋkɪ) NOUN any of the hardy perennial genus *Catananche,* from S Europe; some, esp *C. caerulea,* are grown for their blue-and-white flowers that can be dried as winter decoration: family *Asteraceae.* Also called: **cupid's dart.**
▷**HISTORY** from Greek *katanangkē* a spell (from their use in love potions)

Catania (*Italian* ka'ta:nja) NOUN a port in E Sicily, near Mount Etna. Pop.: 337 862 (2000 est.).

Catanzaro (*Italian* katan'dza:ro) NOUN a city in S Italy, in Calabria. Pop.: 103 800 (1990).

cataphora (kə'tæfərə) NOUN *Grammar* the use of a word such as a pronoun that has the same reference as a word used subsequently in the same discourse. Compare **anaphora.**
▷**HISTORY** from CATA- + Greek *pherein* to bear
▸**cataphoric** (ˌkætə'fɒrɪk) ADJECTIVE

cataphoresis (ˌkætəfə'ri:sɪs) NOUN another name for **electrophoresis.**
▸**cataphoretic** (ˌkætəfə'rɛtɪk) ADJECTIVE
▸**ˌcatapho'retically** ADVERB

cataphyll ('kætəˌfɪl) NOUN a simplified form of plant leaf, such as a scale leaf or cotyledon.

cataplasia (ˌkætə'pleɪzɪə) NOUN the degeneration of cells and tissues to a less highly developed form.
▸**cataplastic** (ˌkætə'plæstɪk) ADJECTIVE

cataplasm ('kætəˌplæzəm) NOUN *Med* another name for **poultice.**
▷**HISTORY** C16: from Latin *cataplasma,* from Greek, from *kataplassein* to cover with a plaster, from *plassein* to shape

cataplexy ('kætəˌplɛksɪ) NOUN [1] sudden temporary paralysis, brought on by severe shock. [2] a state of complete absence of movement assumed by animals while shamming death.
▷**HISTORY** C19: from Greek *kataplēxis* amazement, from *kataplēssein* to strike down (with amazement), confound, from *kata-* down + *plēssein* to strike
▸**ˌcata'plectic** ADJECTIVE

catapult ('kætəˌpʌlt) NOUN [1] a Y-shaped implement with a loop of elastic fastened to the ends of the two prongs, used mainly by children for shooting small stones, etc. US and Canadian name: **slingshot.** [2] a heavy war engine used formerly for hurling stones, etc. [3] a device installed in warships to launch aircraft. ◆ VERB [4] (*tr*) to shoot forth from or as if from a catapult. [5] (foll by *over, into,* etc.) to move precipitately: *she was catapulted to stardom overnight.*
▷**HISTORY** C16: from Latin *catapulta,* from Greek *katapeltēs,* from *kata-* down + *pallein* to hurl

cataract ('kætəˌrækt) NOUN [1] a large waterfall or rapids. [2] a deluge; downpour. [3] *Pathol* **a** a partial or total opacity of the crystalline lens of the eye. **b** the opaque area.
▷**HISTORY** C15: from Latin *catarracta,* from Greek *katarrhaktēs,* from *katarassein* to dash down, from *arassein* to strike

catarrh (kə'tɑ:) NOUN [1] inflammation of a mucous membrane with increased production of mucus, esp affecting the nose and throat in the common cold. [2] the mucus so formed.
▷**HISTORY** C16: via French from Late Latin *catarrhus,* from Greek *katarrous,* from *katarrhein* to flow down, from *kata-* down + *rhein* to flow
▸**ca'tarrhal** *or* **ca'tarrhous** ADJECTIVE

catarrhine ('kætəˌraɪn) ADJECTIVE [1] (of apes and Old World monkeys) having the nostrils set close together and opening to the front of the face. [2] Also: **leptorrhine.** (of humans) having a thin or narrow nose. ◆ NOUN [3] an animal or person with this characteristic. ◆ Compare **platyrrhine.**
▷**HISTORY** C19: from New Latin *Catarrhina* (for sense 1), all ultimately from Greek *katarrhin* having a hooked nose, from *kata-* down + *rhis* nose

catastrophe (kə'tæstrəfɪ) NOUN [1] a sudden, extensive, or notable disaster or misfortune. [2] the denouement of a play, esp a classical tragedy. [3] a final decisive event, usually causing a disastrous end. [4] Also called: **cataclysm.** any sudden and violent change in the earth's surface caused by flooding, earthquake, or some other rapid process.
▷**HISTORY** C16: from Greek *katastrophē,* from *katastrephein* to overturn, from *strephein* to turn
▸**catastrophic** (ˌkætə'strɒfɪk) ADJECTIVE
▸**ˌcata'strophically** ADVERB

catastrophe theory NOUN **a** a mathematical theory that classifies surfaces according to their form. **b** the popular application of this theory to the explanation of abruptly changing phenomena, as by the discontinuity of a line on the topmost fold of a folded surface.

catastrophism (kə'tæstrəˌfɪzəm) NOUN [1] an old doctrine, now discarded, that the earth was created and has subsequently been shaped by sudden divine acts which have no logical connection with each other rather than by gradual evolutionary processes. [2] Also called: **neo-catastrophism.** a modern doctrine that the gradual evolutionary processes shaping the earth have been supplemented in the past by the effects of huge natural catastrophes. See **uniformitarianism.** Compare **gradualism** (sense 2).
▸**ca'tastrophist** NOUN

catatonia (ˌkætə'təʊnɪə) NOUN a state of muscular rigidity and stupor, sometimes found in schizophrenia.
▷**HISTORY** C20: New Latin, from German *Katatonie,* from CATA- + *-tonia,* from Greek *tonos* tension
▸**catatonic** (ˌkætə'tɒnɪk) ADJECTIVE, NOUN

Catawba (kə'tɔ:bə) NOUN [1] (*plural* **-ba** *or* **-bas**) a member of a North American Indian people, formerly of South Carolina, now almost extinct. [2] their language, belonging to the Siouan family. [3] a cultivated variety of red North American grape, widely grown in the eastern US. [4] the wine made from these grapes.

catbird ('kætˌbɜ:d) NOUN [1] any of several North American songbirds of the family *Mimidae* (mockingbirds), esp *Dumetella carolinensis,* whose call resembles the mewing of a cat. [2] any of several Australian bowerbirds of the genera *Ailuroedus* and *Scenopoeetes,* having a catlike call.

catboat ('kætˌbəʊt) NOUN a sailing vessel with a single mast, set well forward and often unstayed, and a large sail, usually rigged with a gaff. Shortened form: **cat.**

cat brier NOUN another name for **greenbrier.**

cat burglar NOUN a burglar who enters buildings by climbing through upper windows, skylights, etc.

catcall ('kætˌkɔ:l) NOUN [1] a shrill whistle or cry expressing disapproval, as at a public meeting, etc. ◆ VERB [2] to utter such a call (at); deride with catcalls.
▸**'catˌcaller** NOUN

catch (kætʃ) VERB **catches, catching, caught.** [1] (*tr*) to take hold of so as to retain or restrain: *he caught the ball.* [2] (*tr*) to take, seize, or capture, esp after pursuit. [3] (*tr*) to ensnare or deceive, as by trickery. [4] (*tr*) to surprise or detect in an act: *he caught the dog rifling the larder.* [5] (*tr*) to reach with a blow: *the stone caught him on the side of the head.* [6] (*tr*) to overtake or reach in time to board: *if we hurry we should catch the next bus.* [7] (*tr*) to see or hear; attend: *I didn't catch the Ibsen play.* [8] (*tr*) to be infected with: *to catch a cold.* [9] to hook or entangle or become hooked or entangled: *her dress caught on a nail.* [10] to fasten or be fastened with or as if with a latch or other device. [11] (*tr*) to attract or arrest: *she tried to catch his eye.* [12] (*tr*) to comprehend: *I didn't*

catch his meaning. 13 (*tr*) to hear accurately: *I didn't catch what you said.* 14 (*tr*) to captivate or charm. 15 (*tr*) to perceive and reproduce accurately: *the painter managed to catch his model's beauty.* 16 (*tr*) to hold back or restrain: *he caught his breath in surprise.* 17 (*intr*) to become alight: *the fire won't catch.* 18 (*tr*) *Cricket* to dismiss (a batsman) by intercepting and holding a ball struck by him before it touches the ground. 19 (*intr; often foll by at*) **a** to grasp or attempt to grasp. **b** to take advantage (of), esp eagerly: *he caught at the chance.* 20 (*intr; used passively*) *Informal* to make pregnant. 21 **catch it.** *Informal* to be scolded or reprimanded. 22 **catch oneself on.** *Slang* to realize that one's actions are mistaken. ◆ NOUN 23 the act of catching or grasping. 24 a device that catches and fastens, such as a latch. 25 anything that is caught, esp something worth catching. 26 the amount or number caught. 27 *Informal* a person regarded as an eligible matrimonial prospect. 28 a check or break in the voice. 29 a break in a mechanism. 30 *Informal* **a** a concealed, unexpected, or unforeseen drawback or handicap. **b** (*as modifier*): *a catch question.* 31 a game in which a ball is thrown from one player to another. 32 *Cricket* the catching of a ball struck by a batsman before it touches the ground, resulting in him being out. 33 *Music* a type of round popular in the 17th, 18th, and 19th centuries, having a humorous text that is often indecent or bawdy and hard to articulate. See **round** (sense 31), **canon**[1] (sense 7). ◆ See also **catch on, catch out, catch up.**
▷**HISTORY** C13 *cacchen* to pursue, from Old Northern French *cachier,* from Latin *captāre* to snatch, from *capere* to seize
▸ ˈ**catchable** ADJECTIVE

catch-all NOUN **a** something designed to cover a variety of situations or possibilities. **b** (*as modifier*): *a catch-all clause.*

catch-as-catch-can NOUN 1 a style of wrestling in which trips, holds below the waist, etc., are allowed. ◆ ADJECTIVE, ADVERB 2 *Chiefly US and Canadian* using any method or opportunity that comes to hand.

catch basin NOUN the US and Canadian name for **catch pit.**

catch crop NOUN a quick-growing crop planted between two regular crops grown in consecutive seasons, or between two rows of regular crops in the same season.

catcher (ˈkætʃə) NOUN 1 a person or thing that catches, esp in a game or sport. 2 *Baseball* a fielder who stands behind home plate and catches pitched balls not hit by the batter.

catchfly (ˈkætʃˌflaɪ) NOUN, *plural* **-flies.** any of several caryophyllaceous plants of the genus *Silene* that have sticky calyxes and stems on which insects are sometimes trapped.

catching (ˈkætʃɪŋ) ADJECTIVE 1 infectious. 2 attractive; captivating.

catching pen NOUN *Austral and NZ* a pen adjacent to a shearer's stand containing the sheep ready for shearing.

catchment (ˈkætʃmənt) NOUN 1 the act of catching or collecting water. 2 a structure in which water is collected. 3 the water so collected. 4 *Brit* the intake of a school from one catchment area.

catchment area NOUN 1 the area of land bounded by watersheds draining into a river, basin, or reservoir. Also called: **catchment basin, drainage area, drainage basin.** 2 the area from which people are allocated to a particular school, hospital, etc.

Catchment board NOUN *NZ* a public body concerned with the conservation and organization of water supply from a catchment area.

catch on VERB (*intr, adverb*) *Informal* 1 to become popular or fashionable. 2 to grasp mentally; understand.

catch out VERB (*tr, adverb*) *Informal, chiefly Brit* to trap (a person), esp in an error or doing something reprehensible.

catchpenny (ˈkætʃˌpɛnɪ) ADJECTIVE 1 (*prenominal*) designed to have instant appeal, esp in order to sell quickly and easily without regard for quality: *catchpenny ornaments.* ◆ NOUN, *plural* **-nies.** 2 an item or commodity that is cheap and showy.

catch phrase NOUN a well-known frequently used phrase, esp one associated with a particular group, etc.

catch pit NOUN a pit in a drainage system in which matter that might otherwise block a sewer is collected so that it may periodically be removed. US and Canadian name: **catch basin.**

catch points PLURAL NOUN railway points designed to derail a train running back in the wrong direction to prevent collision with a following train.

catchpole *or* **catchpoll** (ˈkætʃˌpəʊl) NOUN (in medieval England) a sheriff's officer who arrested debtors.
▷**HISTORY** Old English *cæcepol,* from Medieval Latin *cacepollus* tax-gatherer, literally: chicken-chaser, from *cace-* CATCH + *pollus* (from Latin *pullus* chick)

catch-22 NOUN 1 a situation in which a person is frustrated by a paradoxical rule or set of circumstances that preclude any attempt to escape from them. 2 a situation in which any move that a person can make will lead to trouble.
▷**HISTORY** C20: from the title of a novel (1961) by J. Heller

catchup (ˈkætʃəp, ˈkɛtʃ-) NOUN a variant spelling (esp US) of **ketchup.**

catch up VERB (*adverb*) 1 (*tr*) to seize and take up (something) quickly. 2 (when *intr,* often foll by *with*) to reach or pass (someone or something), after following: *he soon caught him up.* 3 (*intr;* usually foll by *on* or *with*) to make up for lost ground or deal with a backlog (in some specified task or activity). 4 (*tr; often passive*) to absorb or involve: *she was caught up in her reading.* 5 (*tr*) to raise by or as if by fastening: *the hem of her dress was caught up with ribbons.*

catchwater drain (ˈkætʃˌwɔːtə) NOUN a channel cut along the edge of high ground to catch surface water from it and divert it away from low-lying ground.

catchweight (ˈkætʃˌweɪt) ADJECTIVE *Wrestling* of or relating to a contest in which normal weight categories have been waived by agreement.

catchword (ˈkætʃˌwɜːd) NOUN 1 a word or phrase made temporarily popular, esp by a political campaign; slogan. 2 a word printed as a running head in a reference book. 3 *Theatre* an actor's cue to speak or enter. 4 the first word of a printed or typewritten page repeated at the bottom of the page preceding.

catchy (ˈkætʃɪ) ADJECTIVE **catchier, catchiest.** 1 (of a tune, etc.) pleasant and easily remembered or imitated. 2 tricky or deceptive: *a catchy question.* 3 irregular: *a catchy breeze.*
▸ ˈ**catchiness** NOUN

cat cracker NOUN an informal name for **catalytic cracker.**

cat door NOUN a small door or flap in a larger door through which a cat can pass.

catechetical (ˌkætɪˈkɛtɪkəl) *or* **catechetic** ADJECTIVE of or relating to teaching by question and answer.
▸ ˌ**cateˈchetically** ADVERB

catechin (ˈkætəkɪn) NOUN a soluble yellow solid substance found in catechu and mahogany wood and used in tanning and dyeing. Formula: $C_{15}H_{14}O_6$.
▷**HISTORY** C19: from CATECHU + -IN

catechism (ˈkætɪˌkɪzəm) NOUN 1 instruction by a series of questions and answers, esp a book containing such instruction on the religious doctrine of a Christian Church. 2 rigorous and persistent questioning, as in a test or interview.
▷**HISTORY** C16: from Late Latin *catēchismus,* ultimately from Greek *katēkhizein* to CATECHIZE
▸ ˌ**cateˈchismal** ADJECTIVE

catechize *or* **catechise** (ˈkætɪˌkaɪz) VERB (*tr*) 1 to teach or examine by means of questions and answers. 2 to give oral instruction in Christianity, esp by using a catechism. 3 to put questions to (someone).
▷**HISTORY** C15: from Late Latin *catēchizāre,* from Greek *katēkhizein,* from *katēkhein* to instruct orally, literally: to shout down, from *kata-* down + *ēkhein* to sound
▸ ˈ**catechist,** ˈ**cateˌchizer,** *or* ˈ**cateˌchiser** NOUN
▸ ˌ**cateˈchistic** *or* ˌ**cateˈchistical** ADJECTIVE
▸ ˌ**cateˈchistically** ADVERB ▸ ˌ**catechiˈzation** *or* ˌ**catechiˈsation** NOUN

catechol (ˈkætɪˌtʃɒl, -ˌkɒl) NOUN a colourless crystalline phenol found in resins and lignins; 1,2-dihydroxybenzene. It is used as a photographic developer. Formula: $C_6H_4(OH)_2$. Also called: **pyrocatechol.**
▷**HISTORY** C20: from CATECHU + -OL[1]

catecholamine (ˌkætəˈkɒləˌmiːn) NOUN any of a group of hormones that are catechol derivatives, esp adrenaline and noradrenaline.
▷**HISTORY** C20: from CATECHU + -OL[1] + AMINE

catechu (ˈkætɪˌtʃuː), **cachou,** *or* **cutch** NOUN a water-soluble astringent resinous substance obtained from any of certain tropical plants, esp the leguminous tree *Acacia catechu* of S Asia, and used in medicine, tanning, and dyeing. See also **gambier.**
▷**HISTORY** C17: probably from Malay *kachu,* of Dravidian origin

catechumen (ˌkætɪˈkjuːmɛn) NOUN *Christianity* a person, esp in the early Church, undergoing instruction prior to baptism.
▷**HISTORY** C15: via Old French, from Late Latin, from Greek *katēkhoumenos* one being instructed verbally, from *katēkhein;* see CATECHIZE
▸ ˌ**cateˈchumenal** *or* **catechumenical** (ˌkætəkjʊˈmɛnɪkəl) ADJECTIVE ▸ ˌ**cateˈchumenate** NOUN ▸ ˌ**cateˈchumenism** NOUN

categorial (ˌkætɪˈgɔːrɪəl) ADJECTIVE 1 of or relating to a category. 2 *Logic* (of a statement) consisting of a subject, S, and a predicate, P, each of which denotes a class, and having one of the following forms: *all S are P* (universal affirmative); *some S are P* (particular affirmative); *some S are not P* (particular negative); *no S are P* (universal negative). See **syllogism.**

categorial grammar NOUN a theory that characterizes syntactic categories in terms of functions between classes of expressions. The basic classes are names (*N*) and sentences (*S*). Intransitive verbs are symbols for functions which take a name and yield a sentence (written *S/N*), adverbs form compound verbs from verbs (for example, *run fast*) and so are (*S/N*)/(*S/N*), etc.

categorical (ˌkætɪˈgɒrɪkəl) *or* **categoric** ADJECTIVE 1 unqualified; positive; unconditional: *a categorical statement.* 2 relating to or included in a category. 3 *Logic* another word for **categorial.**
▸ ˌ**cateˈgorically** ADVERB ▸ ˌ**cateˈgoricalness** NOUN

categorical imperative NOUN (in the ethics of Kant) the unconditional moral principle that one's behaviour should accord with universalizable maxims which respect persons as ends in themselves; the obligation to do one's duty for its own sake and not in pursuit of further ends. Compare **hypothetical imperative.**

categorize *or* **categorise** (ˈkætɪgəˌraɪz) VERB (*tr*) to place in a category; classify.
▸ ˌ**categoriˈzation** *or* ˌ**categoriˈsation** NOUN

category (ˈkætɪgərɪ) NOUN, *plural* **-ries.** 1 a class or group of things, people, etc., possessing some quality or qualities in common; a division in a system of classification. 2 *Metaphysics* any one of the most basic classes into which objects and concepts can be analysed. 3 **a** (in the philosophy of Aristotle) any one of ten most fundamental modes of being, such as quantity, quality, and substance. **b** (in the philosophy of Kant) one of twelve concepts required by human beings to interpret the empirical world. **c** any set of objects, concepts, or expressions distinguished from others within some logical or linguistic theory by the intelligibility of a specific set of statements concerning them. See also **category mistake.**
▷**HISTORY** C15: from Late Latin *catēgoria,* from Greek *katēgoria,* from *kategorein* to accuse, assert

Category A ADJECTIVE *Brit* 1 (of a prisoner) regarded as highly dangerous and therefore requiring constant observation and maximum security. 2 (of a prison or prison unit) designed for such prisoners.

Category D ADJECTIVE *Brit* 1 (of a prisoner) regarded as sufficiently trustworthy to be kept under open prison conditions. 2 (of a prison or prison unit) designed for such prisoners.

category killer NOUN a person, product, or business that dominates a particular market.

category management NOUN *Marketing* the management of a range of related products in a way designed to increase sales of all of the products.

category mistake NOUN *Philosophy, logic* a sentence that says of something in one category what can only intelligibly be said of something in another, as when speaking of the mind located in space.

catena (kəˈtiːnə) NOUN, *plural* **-nae** (-niː). a connected series, esp of patristic comments on the Bible.
▷HISTORY C17: from Latin: chain

catenaccio *Italian* (kateˈnattʃo) NOUN *Football* an extremely defensive style of play.
▷HISTORY C20: from Latin *catena* chain

catenane (ˈkætɪˌneɪn) NOUN a type of chemical compound in which the molecules have two or more rings that are interlocked like the links of a chain.
▷HISTORY C20: from Latin *catena* chain + -ANE

catenary (kəˈtiːnərɪ) NOUN, *plural* **-ries.** [1] the curve assumed by a heavy uniform flexible cord hanging freely from two points. When symmetrical about the y-axis and intersecting it at $y = a$, the equation is $y = a \cosh x/a$. [2] the hanging cable between pylons along a railway track, from which the trolley wire is suspended. ◆ ADJECTIVE *also* **catenarian** (ˌkætɪˈnɛərɪən). [3] of, resembling, relating to, or constructed using a catenary or suspended chain.
▷HISTORY C18: from Latin *catēnārius* relating to a chain

catenate (ˈkætɪˌneɪt) VERB [1] *Biology* to arrange or be arranged in a series of chains or rings. ◆ ADJECTIVE [2] another word for **catenulate.**
▷HISTORY C17: from Latin *catēnāre* to bind with chains
▸ **ˌcateˈnation** NOUN

catenoid (ˈkætəˌnɔɪd) NOUN the geometrical surface generated by rotating a catenary about its axis.

catenulate (kəˈtɛnjʊˌleɪt, -lɪt) ADJECTIVE (of certain spores) formed in a row or chain.
▷HISTORY C19: from Latin *catēnula,* diminutive of *catēna* chain

cater (ˈkeɪtə) VERB [1] (*intr;* foll by *for* or *to*) to provide what is required or desired (for): *to cater for a need; cater to your tastes.* [2] (when *intr,* foll by *for*) to provide food, services, etc. (for): *we cater for parties; to cater a banquet.*
▷HISTORY C16: from earlier *catour* purchaser, variant of *acatour,* from Anglo-Norman *acater* to buy, ultimately related to Latin *acceptāre* to ACCEPT

cateran (ˈkætərən) NOUN (formerly) a member of a band of brigands and marauders in the Scottish highlands.
▷HISTORY C14: probably from Scottish Gaelic *ceathairneach* robber, plunderer

cater-cornered (ˈkætəˌkɔːnəd) ADJECTIVE, ADVERB *US and Canadian informal* diagonally placed; diagonal. Also: **catty-cornered, kitty-cornered.**
▷HISTORY C16 *cater,* from dialect *cater* (adverb) diagonally, from obsolete *cater* (noun) four-spot of dice, from Old French *quatre* four, from Latin *quattuor*

cater-cousin (ˈkeɪtəˌkʌzᵊn) NOUN *Archaic* a close friend.
▷HISTORY C16: perhaps from obsolete *cater* caterer; for sense, compare FOSTER, as in *foster brother,* etc.

caterer (ˈkeɪtərə) NOUN a person who caters, esp one who as a profession provides food for large social events, etc.

catering (ˈkeɪtərɪŋ) NOUN [1] the trade of a professional caterer. [2] the food, etc., provided at a function by a caterer.

caterpillar (ˈkætəˌpɪlə) NOUN the wormlike larva of butterflies and moths, having numerous pairs of legs and powerful biting jaws. It may be brightly coloured, hairy, or spiny.
▷HISTORY C15 *catyrpel,* probably from Old Northern French *catepelose,* literally: hairy cat

Caterpillar (ˈkætəˌpɪlə) NOUN *Trademark* [1] an endless track, driven by sprockets or wheels, used to propel a heavy vehicle and enable it to cross soft or uneven ground. [2] a vehicle, such as a tractor, tank, bulldozer, etc., driven by such tracks.

caterpillar hunter NOUN any of various carabid beetles of the genus *Calosoma,* of Europe and North America, which prey on the larvae of moths and butterflies.

caterwaul (ˈkætəˌwɔːl) VERB (*intr*) [1] to make a yowling noise, as a cat on heat. ◆ NOUN [2] a shriek or yell made by or sounding like a cat on heat.
▷HISTORY C14: of imitative origin
▸ **ˈcaterˌwauler** NOUN

cates (keɪts) PLURAL NOUN (*sometimes singular*) *Archaic* choice dainty food; delicacies.
▷HISTORY C15: variant of *acates* purchases, from Old Northern French *acater* to buy, from Vulgar Latin *accaptāre* (unattested); ultimately related to Latin *acceptāre* to ACCEPT

catfall (ˈkætˌfɔːl) NOUN *Nautical* the line used in a cat.

catfight (ˈkætˌfaɪt) NOUN *Informal* a fight between two women.

catfish (ˈkætˌfɪʃ) NOUN, *plural* **-fish** *or* **-fishes.** [1] any of numerous mainly freshwater teleost fishes having whisker-like barbels around the mouth, esp the silurids of Europe and Asia and the horned pouts of North America. [2] another name for **wolffish.**

cat flu NOUN *Vet science* an upper respiratory-tract infection in cats, resulting in sneezing, ocular and nasal discharges, and coughs.

catgut (ˈkætˌgʌt) NOUN a strong cord made from the dried intestines of sheep and other animals that is used for stringing certain musical instruments and sports rackets, and, when sterilized, as surgical ligatures. Often shortened to **gut.**

cath- PREFIX a variant of **cata-** before an aspirate: *cathode.*

Cathar (ˈkæθə) *or* **Catharist** (ˈkæθərɪst) NOUN, *plural* **-ars, -ari** (-ərɪ), *or* **-arists.** a member of a Christian sect in Provence in the 12th and 13th centuries who believed the material world was evil and only the spiritual was good.
▷HISTORY from Medieval Latin *Cathari,* from Greek *katharoi* the pure
▸ **ˈCatharˌism** NOUN

catharsis (kəˈθɑːsɪs) NOUN, *plural* **-ses.** [1] (in Aristotelian literary criticism) the purging or purification of the emotions through the evocation of pity and fear, as in tragedy. [2] *Psychoanal* the bringing of repressed ideas or experiences into consciousness, thus relieving tensions. See also **abreaction.** [3] purgation, esp of the bowels.
▷HISTORY C19: New Latin, from Greek *katharsis,* from *kathairein* to purge, purify

cathartic (kəˈθɑːtɪk) ADJECTIVE [1] purgative. [2] effecting catharsis. ◆ NOUN [3] a purgative drug or agent.
▸ **caˈthartically** ADVERB

Cathay (kæˈθeɪ) NOUN a literary or archaic name for **China.**
▷HISTORY C14: from Medieval Latin *Cataya,* of Turkic origin

cathead (ˈkætˌhɛd) NOUN a fitting at the bow of a vessel for securing the anchor when raised.

cathectic (kəˈθɛktɪk) ADJECTIVE of or relating to cathexis.

cathedra (kəˈθiːdrə) NOUN [1] a bishop's throne. [2] the office or rank of a bishop. [3] See **ex cathedra.**
▷HISTORY from Latin: chair

cathedral (kəˈθiːdrəl) NOUN **a** the principal church of a diocese, containing the bishop's official throne. **b** (*as modifier*): *a cathedral city; cathedral clergy.*
▷HISTORY C13: from Late Latin (*ecclesia*) *cathedrālis* cathedral (church), from *cathedra* bishop's throne, from Greek *kathedra* seat

cathepsin (kəˈθɛpsɪn) NOUN a proteolytic enzyme responsible for the autolysis of cells after death.
▷HISTORY C20: from Greek *kathepsein* to boil down, soften

Catherine wheel NOUN [1] Also called: **pinwheel.** a type of firework consisting of a powder-filled spiral tube, mounted with a pin through its centre. When lit it rotates quickly, producing a display of sparks and coloured flame. [2] a circular window having ribs radiating from the centre.
▷HISTORY C16: named after St Catherine of Alexandria (died 307 A.D.), legendary Christian martyr who was tortured on a spiked wheel and beheaded

catheter (ˈkæθɪtə) NOUN *Med* a long slender flexible tube for inserting into a natural bodily cavity or passage for introducing or withdrawing fluid, such as urine or blood.
▷HISTORY C17: from Late Latin, from Greek *kathetēr,* from *kathienai* to send down, insert

catheterize *or* **catheterise** (ˈkæθɪtəˌraɪz) VERB (*tr*) to insert a catheter into.
▸ **ˌcatheteriˈzation** *or* **ˌcatheteriˈsation** NOUN

cathexis (kəˈθɛksɪs) NOUN, *plural* **-thexes** (-ˈθɛksiːz). *Psychoanal* concentration of psychic energy on a single goal.
▷HISTORY C20: from New Latin, from Greek *kathexis,* from *katekhein* to hold fast, intended to render German *Besetzung* a taking possession of

Catho (ˈkæθəʊ) NOUN, *plural* **Cathos.** *Austral slang* a member of the Catholic Church.

cathode (ˈkæθəʊd) NOUN [1] the negative electrode in an electrolytic cell; the electrode by which electrons enter a device from an external circuit. [2] the negatively charged electron source in an electronic valve. [3] the positive terminal of a primary cell. ◆ Compare **anode.**
▷HISTORY C19: from Greek *kathodos* a descent, from *kata-* down + *hodos* way
▸ **cathodal** (kæˈθəʊdᵊl) ▸ **cathodic** (kæˈθɒdɪk, -ˈθəʊ-) *or* **caˈthodical** ADJECTIVE

cathode rays PLURAL NOUN a stream of electrons emitted from the surface of a cathode in a valve.

cathode-ray tube NOUN a valve in which a beam of high-energy electrons is focused onto a fluorescent screen to give a visible spot of light. The device, with appropriate deflection equipment, is used in television receivers, visual display units, oscilloscopes, etc. Abbreviation: **CRT.**

cathodic protection NOUN *Metallurgy* a technique for protecting metal structures, such as steel ships and pipelines, from electrolytic corrosion by making the structure the cathode in a cell, either by applying an electromotive force directly or by putting it into contact with a more electropositive metal. See also **sacrificial anode.**

cathodoluminescence (ˌkæθədəʊˌluːmɪˈnɛsəns) NOUN *Physics* luminescence caused by irradiation with electrons (cathode rays).

cat hole NOUN one of a pair of holes in the after part of a ship through which hawsers are passed for steadying the ship or heaving astern.

catholic (ˈkæθəlɪk, ˈkæθlɪk) ADJECTIVE [1] universal; relating to all men; all-inclusive. [2] comprehensive in interests, tastes, etc.; broad-minded; liberal.
▷HISTORY C14: from Latin *catholicus,* from Greek *katholikos* universal, from *katholou* in general, from *kata-* according to + *holos* whole
▸ **catholically** *or* **catholicly** (kəˈθɒlɪklɪ) ADVERB

Catholic (ˈkæθəlɪk, ˈkæθlɪk) ADJECTIVE *Christianity* [1] denoting or relating to the entire body of Christians, esp to the Church before separation into the Greek or Eastern and Latin or Western Churches. [2] denoting or relating to the Latin or Western Church after this separation. [3] denoting or relating to the Roman Catholic Church. [4] denoting or relating to any church, belief, etc., that claims continuity with or originates in the ancient undivided Church. ◆ NOUN [5] a member of any of the Churches regarded as Catholic, esp the Roman Catholic Church.

Catholic Church NOUN [1] short for **Roman Catholic Church.** [2] any of several Churches claiming to have maintained continuity with the ancient and undivided Church.

Catholic Epistles PLURAL NOUN *New Testament* the epistles of James, I and II Peter, I John, and Jude, which were addressed to the universal Church rather than to an individual or a particular church.

Catholicism (kəˈθɒlɪˌsɪzəm) NOUN [1] short for **Roman Catholicism.** [2] the beliefs, practices, etc., of any Catholic Church.

catholicity (ˌkæθəˈlɪsɪtɪ) NOUN [1] a wide range of interests, tastes, etc.; liberality. [2] universality; comprehensiveness.

Catholicity (ˌkæθəˈlɪsɪtɪ) NOUN the beliefs, etc., of the Catholic Church.

catholicize *or* **catholicise** (kəˈθɒlɪˌsaɪz) VERB [1] to make or become catholic. [2] (*often capital*) to convert to or become converted to Catholicism.
▸ **caˌtholiciˈzation** *or* **caˌtholiciˈsation** NOUN

catholicon (kəˈθɒlɪkən) NOUN a remedy for all ills; panacea.
▷HISTORY C15: from Medieval Latin; see CATHOLIC

Catholicos (kəˈθɒlɪkɒs) NOUN the patriarch of the Armenian Church.
▷HISTORY C17: from Greek *katholikos*; see CATHOLIC

cathouse (ˈkætˌhaʊs) NOUN *US and Canadian* a slang word for **brothel**.

cation (ˈkætaɪən) NOUN a positively charged ion; an ion that is attracted to the cathode during electrolysis. Compare **anion**.
▷HISTORY C19: from CATA- + ION
▸**cationic** (ˌkætaɪˈɒnɪk) ADJECTIVE

cationic detergent NOUN a type of detergent in which the active part of the molecule is a positive ion (cation). Cationic detergents are usually quaternary ammonium salts and often also have bactericidal properties.

catkin (ˈkætkɪn) NOUN an inflorescence consisting of a spike, usually hanging, of much reduced flowers of either sex: occurs in birch, hazel, etc. Also called: **ament**.
▷HISTORY C16: from obsolete Dutch *katteken* kitten, identical in meaning with French *chaton*, German *Kätzchen*

catling (ˈkætlɪŋ) NOUN 1 a long double-edged surgical knife for amputations. 2 *Rare* catgut or a string made from it. 3 an archaic word for **kitten**.
▷HISTORY C17: from CAT[1] + -LING[1]

cat litter NOUN absorbent material, often in a granular form, that is used to line a receptacle in which a domestic cat can urinate and defecate indoors.

catmint (ˈkætˌmɪnt) NOUN a Eurasian plant, *Nepeta cataria*, having spikes of purple-spotted white flowers and scented leaves of which cats are fond: family *Lamiaeae* (labiates). Also called: **catnip**.

catnap (ˈkætˌnæp) NOUN 1 a short sleep or doze. ◆ VERB **-naps, -napping, -napped**. 2 (*intr*) to sleep or doze for a short time or intermittently.

catnip (ˈkætˌnɪp) NOUN another name for **catmint**.

catolyte (ˈkætəʊˌlaɪt) *or* **catholyte** (ˈkæθəʊˌlaɪt) NOUN *Electronics* the part of the electrolyte that surrounds the cathode in an electrolytic cell.

cat-o'-mountain NOUN another name for **catamount**.

cat-o'-nine-tails NOUN, *plural* **-tails**. a rope whip consisting of nine knotted thongs, used formerly to flog prisoners. Often shortened to **cat**.

catoptrics (kəˈtɒptrɪks) NOUN (*functioning as singular*) the branch of optics concerned with reflection, esp the formation of images by mirrors.
▷HISTORY C18: from Greek *katoptrikos*, from *katoptron* mirror
▸**caˈtoptric** *or* **caˈtoptrical** ADJECTIVE

cat rig NOUN the rig of a catboat.
▸**ˈcatˌrigged** ADJECTIVE

CATS (kæts) NOUN ACRONYM FOR credit accumulation transfer scheme: a scheme enabling school-leavers and others to acquire transferable certificates for relevant work experience and study towards a recognized qualification.

CAT scanner (kæt) NOUN former name for **CT scanner**.
▷HISTORY C20: (*C*)*omputerized* (*A*)*xial* (*T*)*omography*

cat's cradle NOUN a game played by making intricate patterns with a loop of string between the fingers.

cat-scratch fever NOUN a disease of humans caused by an organism, *Bartonella henselae*, usually resulting from a scratch by a cat and characterized by lymph node enlargement.

cat's-ear NOUN any of various European plants of the genus *Hypochoeris*, esp *H. radicata*, having dandelion-like heads of yellow flowers: family *Asteraceae* (composites).

cat's-eye NOUN any of a group of gemstones, esp a greenish-yellow variety of chrysoberyl, that reflect a streak of light when cut in a rounded unfaceted shape.

Catseye (ˈkætsˌaɪ) NOUN *Trademark, Brit* a glass reflector set into a small fixture, placed at intervals along roads to indicate traffic lanes at night.

cat's-foot NOUN, *plural* **-feet**. a European plant, *Antennaria dioica*, with whitish woolly leaves and heads of typically white flowers: family *Asteraceae* (composites). Also called: **mountain everlasting**.

Catskill Mountains (ˈkætskɪl) PLURAL NOUN a mountain range in SE New York State: resort. Highest peak: Slide Mountain, 1261 m (4204 ft.). Also called: **Catskills**.

cat's-paw NOUN 1 a person used by another as a tool; dupe. 2 *Nautical* a hitch in the form of two loops, or eyes, in the bight of a line, used for attaching it to a hook. 3 a pattern of ripples on the surface of water caused by a light wind.
▷HISTORY (sense 1) C18: so called from the tale of the monkey who used a cat's paw to draw chestnuts out of a fire

cat's-tail NOUN 1 another name for **reed mace** (sense 1). 2 another name for **catkin**.

CAT standard NOUN (in Britain) a standard accepted voluntarily by building societies relating to charges, access, etc., against which Individual Savings Accounts can be judged.
▷HISTORY C20: *C*(*harges*) *A*(*ccess*) *T*(*erms*)

catsuit (ˈkætˌsuːt) NOUN a one-piece usually close-fitting trouser suit.

catsup (ˈkætsəp) NOUN a variant (esp US) of **ketchup**.

cat's whisker NOUN 1 a pointed wire used to make contact with the crystal in a crystal radio receiver. 2 any wire used to make contact with a semiconductor.

cat's whiskers *or* **cat's pyjamas** NOUN **the.** *Slang* a person or thing that is excellent or superior.

cattalo *or* **catalo** (ˈkætəˌləʊ) NOUN, *plural* **-loes** *or* **-los**. a hardy breed of cattle developed by crossing the American bison with domestic cattle.
▷HISTORY C20: from CATT(LE + BUFF)ALO

Cattegat (ˈkætɪˌgæt) NOUN a variant spelling of **Kattegat**.

Catterick (ˈkætərɪk) NOUN a village in N England, in North Yorkshire on the River Swale: site of an important army garrison and a racecourse.

cattery (ˈkætərɪ) NOUN, *plural* **-teries**. a place where cats are bred or looked after.

cattle (ˈkætᵊl) NOUN (*functioning as plural*) 1 bovid mammals of the tribe *Bovini* (bovines), esp those of the genus *Bos*. 2 Also called: **domestic cattle**. any domesticated bovine mammals, esp those of the species *Bos taurus* (domestic ox). ◆ Related adjective: **bovine**.
▷HISTORY C13: from Old Northern French *catel*, Old French *chatel* CHATTEL

cattle-cake NOUN concentrated food for cattle in the form of cakes.

cattle dog NOUN *Austral informal* a catalogue.
▷HISTORY supposedly imitative of CATALOGUE

cattle-grid NOUN a grid of metal bars covering a hollow or hole dug in a roadway, intended to prevent the passage of livestock while allowing vehicles, etc., to pass unhindered.

cattleman (ˈkætᵊlmən) NOUN, *plural* **-men**. 1 a person who breeds, rears, or tends cattle. 2 *Chiefly US and Canadian* a person who owns or rears cattle on a large scale, usually for beef, esp the owner of a cattle ranch.

cattle market NOUN *Brit slang* a situation or place, such as a beauty contest or nightclub, in which women are felt to be, or feel themselves to be, on display and judged solely by their appearance.

cattle plague NOUN another name for **rinderpest**.

cattle prod NOUN a hand-held electrified rod with low voltage used to control cattle.

cattle-stop NOUN the NZ name for **cattle-grid**.

cattle truck NOUN a railway wagon designed for carrying livestock. US and Canadian equivalent: **stock car**.

cattleya (ˈkætlɪə) NOUN any tropical American orchid of the genus *Cattleya*, cultivated for their purplish-pink or white showy flowers.
▷HISTORY C19: New Latin, named after William *Cattley* (died 1832), English botanist

cat-train *or* **cat-swing** NOUN *Canadian* a train of sleds, cabooses, etc., pulled by a caterpillar tractor, used chiefly in the north during winter to transport freight.

catty[1] (ˈkætɪ) *or* **cattish** ADJECTIVE **-tier, -tiest**. 1 *Informal* spiteful: *a catty remark*. 2 of or resembling a cat.
▸**ˈcattily** *or* **ˈcattishly** ADVERB ▸**ˈcattiness** *or* **ˈcattishness** NOUN

catty[2] *or* **cattie** (ˈkætɪ) NOUN, *plural* **-ties**. a unit of weight, used esp in China, equal to about one and a half pounds or about 0.67 kilogram.
▷HISTORY C16: from Malay *kati*

catty-cornered ADJECTIVE a variant of **cater-cornered**.

CATV ABBREVIATION FOR community antenna television.

catwalk (ˈkætˌwɔːk) NOUN 1 a narrow ramp extending from the stage into the audience in a theatre, nightclub, etc., esp as used by models in a fashion show. 2 a narrow pathway over the stage of a theatre, along a bridge, etc.

catworm (ˈkætˌwɜːm) NOUN an active carnivorous polychaete worm, *Nephthys hombergi*, that is about 10cm (4in) long, having a pearly sheen to its body: often dug for bait. Also called: **white worm, white cat**.

Cauca (*Spanish* ˈkauka) NOUN a river in W Colombia, rising in the northwest and flowing north to the Magdalena River. Length: about 1350 km (840 miles).

Caucasia (kɔːˈkeɪzɪə, -ʒə) NOUN a region in SW Russia, Georgia, Armenia, and Azerbaijan, between the Caspian Sea and the Black Sea: contains the Caucasus Mountains, dividing it into Ciscaucasia in the north and Transcaucasia in the south; one of the most complex ethnic areas in the world, with over 50 different peoples. Also called: **the Caucasus**.

Caucasian (kɔːˈkeɪzɪən, -ʒən) *or* **Caucasic** (kɔːˈkeɪzɪk) ADJECTIVE 1 another word for **Caucasoid**. 2 of or relating to the Caucasus. ◆ NOUN 3 a member of the Caucasoid race; a white man. 4 a native or inhabitant of Caucasia. 5 any of three possibly related families of languages spoken in the Caucasus: **North-West Caucasian**, including Circassian and Abkhaz, **North-East Caucasian**, including Avar, and **South Caucasian** including Georgian.

Caucasoid (ˈkɔːkəˌzɔɪd) ADJECTIVE 1 denoting, relating to, or belonging to the light-complexioned racial group of mankind, which includes the peoples indigenous to Europe, N Africa, SW Asia, and the Indian subcontinent and their descendants in other parts of the world. ◆ NOUN 2 a member of this racial group.

Caucasus (ˈkɔːkəsəs) NOUN **the.** 1 a mountain range in SW Russia, running along the N borders of Georgia and Azerbaijan, between the Black Sea and the Caspian Sea: mostly over 2700 m (9000 ft.). Highest peak: Mount Elbrus, 5642 m (18 510 ft.). Also called: **Caucasus Mountains**. 2 another name for **Caucasia**.

caucus (ˈkɔːkəs) NOUN, *plural* **-cuses**. 1 *Chiefly US and Canadian* **a** a closed meeting of the members of one party in a legislative chamber, etc., to coordinate policy, choose candidates, etc. **b** such a bloc of politicians: *the Democratic caucus in Congress*. 2 *Chiefly US* **a** a group of leading politicians of one party. **b** a meeting of such a group. 3 *Chiefly US* a local meeting of party members. 4 *Brit* a group or faction within a larger group, esp a political party, who discuss tactics, choose candidates, etc. 5 *Austral* a meeting of the members of the Federal parliamentary Labor Party. 6 *NZ* a formal meeting of all Members of Parliament belonging to one political party. ◆ VERB 7 (*intr*) to hold a caucus.
▷HISTORY C18: probably of Algonquian origin; related to *caucauasu* adviser

cauda (ˈkɔːdə) NOUN 1 *Zoology* the area behind the anus of an animal; tail. 2 *Anatomy* **a** any tail-like structure. **b** the posterior part of an organ.
▷HISTORY Latin: tail

caudad (ˈkɔːdæd) ADVERB *Anatomy* towards the tail or posterior part. Compare **cephalad**.
▷HISTORY C19: from CAUDA + -AD[2]

caudal (ˈkɔːdᵊl) ADJECTIVE 1 *Anatomy* of or towards the posterior part of the body. 2 *Zoology* relating to, resembling, or in the position of the tail.
▷HISTORY C17: from New Latin *caudālis*, from CAUDA
▸**ˈcaudally** ADVERB

caudal fin NOUN the tail fin of fishes and some other aquatic vertebrates, used for propulsion during locomotion.

caudate ('kɔːdeɪt) *or* **caudated** ADJECTIVE having a tail or a tail-like appendage.
▷HISTORY C17: from New Latin *caudātus,* from CAUDA
▸**cau'dation** NOUN

caudex ('kɔːdɛks) NOUN, *plural* **-dices** (-dɪˌsiːz) *or* **-dexes.** 1 the thickened persistent stem base of some herbaceous perennial plants. 2 the woody stem of palms and tree ferns.
▷HISTORY C19: from Latin

caudillo (kɔː'diːljəʊ; *Spanish* kau'ðiʎo) NOUN, *plural* **-los** (-jəʊz; *Spanish* -ʎos). (in Spanish-speaking countries) a military or political leader.
▷HISTORY Spanish, from Late Latin *capitellum,* diminutive of Latin *caput* head

Caudine Forks ('kɔːdaɪn) PLURAL NOUN a narrow pass in the Apennines, in S Italy, between Capua and Benevento: scene of the defeat of the Romans by the Samnites (321 B.C.).

caudle ('kɔːdᵊl) NOUN a hot spiced wine drink made with gruel, formerly used medicinally.
▷HISTORY C13: from Old Northern French *caudel,* from Medieval Latin *caldellum,* from Latin *calidus* warm

caught (kɔːt) VERB the past tense and past participle of **catch**.

caul (kɔːl) NOUN *Anatomy* 1 a portion of the amniotic sac sometimes covering a child's head at birth. 2 a large fold of peritoneum hanging from the stomach across the intestines; the large omentum.
▷HISTORY C13: from Old French *cale,* back formation from *calotte* close-fitting cap, of Germanic origin

cauld (kɔːld) ADJECTIVE, NOUN a Scot word for **cold**.

cauldrife ('kɔːldrɪf) ADJECTIVE *Scot* 1 susceptible to cold; chilly. 2 lifeless.
▷HISTORY C18: from CAULD + RIFE

cauldron *or* **caldron** ('kɔːldrən) NOUN a large pot used for boiling, esp one with handles.
▷HISTORY C13: from earlier *cauderon,* from Anglo-French, from Latin *caldārium* hot bath, from *calidus* warm

caulescent (kɔː'lɛsᵊnt) ADJECTIVE having a stem clearly visible above the ground.
▷HISTORY C18: from Latin *caulis* stalk

caulicle ('kɔːlɪkᵊl) NOUN *Botany* a small stalk or stem.
▷HISTORY C17: from Latin *cauliculus,* from *caulis* stem

cauliflory ('kɔːlɪˌflɔːrɪ) NOUN *Botany* the production of flowers on the trunk, branches, etc., of a woody plant, as opposed to the ends of the twigs.
▷HISTORY C20: from Latin *caulis* stem + *-flory,* from *flōs* flower
▸ˌ**cauli'florous** ADJECTIVE

cauliflower ('kɒlɪˌflaʊə) NOUN 1 a variety of cabbage, *Brassica oleracea botrytis,* having a large edible head of crowded white flowers on a very short thick stem. 2 the flower head of this plant, used as a vegetable.
▷HISTORY C16: from Italian *caoli fiori,* literally: cabbage flowers, from *cavolo* cabbage (from Latin *caulis*) + *fiore* flower (from Latin *flōs*)

cauliflower cheese NOUN a dish of cauliflower with a cheese sauce, eaten hot.

cauliflower ear NOUN permanent swelling and distortion of the external ear as the result of ruptures of the blood vessels: usually caused by blows received in boxing. Also called: **boxer's ear.** Technical name: **aural haematoma.**

cauline ('kɔːlɪn, -laɪn) ADJECTIVE relating to or growing from a plant stem.
▷HISTORY C18: from New Latin *caulīnus,* from Latin *caulis* stem

caulis ('kɔːlɪs) NOUN, *plural* **-les** (-liːz). *Rare* the main stem of a plant.
▷HISTORY C16: from Latin

caulk *or* **calk** (kɔːk) VERB 1 to stop up (cracks, crevices, etc.) with a filler. 2 *Nautical* to pack (the seams) between the planks of the bottom of (a vessel) with waterproof material to prevent leakage.
▷HISTORY C15: from Old Northern French *cauquer* to press down, from Latin *calcāre* to trample, from *calx* heel
▸'**caulker** *or* '**calker** NOUN

causal ('kɔːzᵊl) ADJECTIVE 1 acting as or being a cause. 2 stating, involving, or implying a cause: *the causal part of the argument.* 3 *Philosophy* (of a theory) explaining a phenomenon or analysing a concept in terms of some causal relation.
▸'**causally** ADVERB

causalgia (kɔː'zældʒɪə) NOUN *Pathol* a burning sensation along the course of a peripheral nerve together with local changes in the appearance of the skin.
▷HISTORY C19: from New Latin, from Greek *kausos* fever + -ALGIA

causality (kɔː'zælɪtɪ) NOUN, *plural* **-ties.** 1 **a** the relationship of cause and effect. **b** the principle that nothing can happen without being caused. 2 causal agency or quality.

causation (kɔː'zeɪʃən) NOUN 1 the act or fact of causing; the production of an effect by a cause. 2 the relationship of cause and effect.
▸**cau'sational** ADJECTIVE

causative ('kɔːzətɪv) ADJECTIVE 1 *Grammar* relating to a form or class of verbs, such as *persuade,* that express causation. 2 (*often postpositive* and foll by *of*) producing an effect. ◆ NOUN 3 the causative form or class of verbs.
▸'**causatively** ADVERB ▸'**causativeness** NOUN

cause (kɔːz) NOUN 1 a person, thing, event, state, or action that produces an effect. 2 grounds for action; motive; justification: *she had good cause to shout like that.* 3 the ideals, etc., of a group or movement: *the Communist cause.* 4 the welfare or interests of a person or group in a dispute: *they fought for the miners' cause.* 5 a matter of widespread concern or importance: *the cause of public health.* 6 **a** a ground for legal action; matter giving rise to a lawsuit. **b** the lawsuit itself. 7 (in the philosophy of Aristotle) any of four requirements for a thing's coming to be, namely material (material cause), its nature (formal cause), an agent (efficient cause), and a purpose (final cause). 8 **make common cause with.** to join with (a person, group, etc.) for a common objective. ◆ VERB 9 (*tr*) to be the cause of; bring about; precipitate; be the reason for.
▷HISTORY C13: from Latin *causa* cause, reason, motive
▸'**causable** ADJECTIVE ▸ˌ**causa'bility** NOUN ▸'**causeless** ADJECTIVE ▸'**causer** NOUN

cause célèbre ('kɔːz sə'lɛbrə, -'lɛb; *French* koz selɛbrə) NOUN, *plural* **causes célèbres** ('kɔːz sə'lɛbrəz, -'lɛb, 'kɔːzɪz sə'lɛbrə, -'lɛbz) (*French* koz selɛbrə). a famous lawsuit, trial, or controversy.
▷HISTORY C19: from French: famous case

cause list NOUN *Brit* a list of cases awaiting a hearing.

causerie ('kəʊzərɪ; *French* kozri) NOUN an informal talk or conversational piece of writing.
▷HISTORY C19: from French, from *causer* to chat

causeway ('kɔːzˌweɪ) NOUN 1 a raised path or road crossing water, marshland, sand, etc. 2 a paved footpath. 3 a road surfaced with setts.
▷HISTORY C15 *cauciwey* (from *cauci* + WAY); *cauci* paved road, from Medieval Latin (*via*) *calciāta, calciātus* paved with limestone, from Latin *calx* limestone

causey ('kɔːzɪ) NOUN 1 an archaic or dialect word for **causeway.** 2 *Scot* a cobbled street. 3 *Scot* a cobblestone.

caustic ('kɔːstɪk) ADJECTIVE 1 capable of burning or corroding by chemical action: *caustic soda.* 2 sarcastic; cutting: *a caustic reply.* 3 of, relating to, or denoting light that is reflected or refracted by a curved surface. ◆ NOUN 4 Also called: **caustic surface.** a surface that envelopes the light rays reflected or refracted by a curved surface. 5 Also called: **caustic curve.** a curve formed by the intersection of a caustic surface with a plane. 6 *Chem* a caustic substance, esp an alkali.
▷HISTORY C14: from Latin *causticus,* from Greek *kaustikos,* from *kaiein* to burn
▸'**caustical** ADJECTIVE ▸'**caustically** ADVERB ▸'**causticness** *or* **causticity** (kɔː'stɪsɪtɪ) NOUN

caustic potash NOUN another name for **potassium hydroxide.**

caustic soda NOUN another name for **sodium hydroxide.**

cauterant ('kɔːtərənt) ADJECTIVE 1 caustic; cauterizing. ◆ NOUN 2 another name for **cautery** (sense 2).

cauterize *or* **cauterise** ('kɔːtəˌraɪz) VERB (*tr*) (esp in the treatment of a wound) to burn or sear (body tissue) with a hot iron or caustic agent.
▷HISTORY C14: from Old French *cauteriser,* from Late Latin *cautērizāre,* from *cautērium* branding iron, from Greek *kautērion,* from *kaiein* to burn
▸ˌ**cauteri'zation** *or* ˌ**cauteri'sation** NOUN

cautery ('kɔːtərɪ) NOUN, *plural* **-teries.** 1 the coagulation of blood or destruction of body tissue by cauterizing. 2 Also called: **cauterant.** an instrument or chemical agent for cauterizing.
▷HISTORY C14: from Old French *cautère,* from Latin *cautērium;* see CAUTERIZE

caution ('kɔːʃən) NOUN 1 care, forethought, or prudence, esp in the face of danger; wariness. 2 something intended or serving as a warning; admonition. 3 *Law, chiefly Brit* a formal warning given to a person suspected or accused of an offence that his words will be taken down and may be used in evidence. 4 a notice entered on the register of title to land that prevents a proprietor from disposing of his land without a notice to the person who entered the caution. 5 *Informal* an amusing or surprising person or thing: *she's a real caution.* ◆ VERB 6 (*tr*) to urge or warn (a person) to be careful. 7 (*tr*) *Law, chiefly Brit* to give a caution to (a person). 8 (*intr*) to warn, urge, or advise: *he cautioned against optimism.*
▷HISTORY C13: from Old French, from Latin *cautiō,* from *cavēre* to beware
▸'**cautioner** NOUN

cautionary ('kɔːʃənərɪ) ADJECTIVE serving as a warning; intended to warn: *a cautionary tale.*

caution money NOUN *Chiefly Brit* a sum of money deposited as security for good conduct, against possible debts, etc.

cautious ('kɔːʃəs) ADJECTIVE showing or having caution; wary; prudent.
▸'**cautiously** ADVERB ▸'**cautiousness** NOUN

Cauvery *or* **Kaveri** ('kɔːvərɪ) NOUN a river in S India, rising in the Western Ghats and flowing southeast to the Bay of Bengal. Length: 765 km (475 miles).

CAV *or* **Cur. adv. vult** *Law* ABBREVIATION FOR Curia advisari vult: used in English law to indicate that a court has decided to consider a case privately before giving judgment, as when time is needed to consider arguments or submissions made to it. Compare **avizandum.**
▷HISTORY Medieval Latin: the court wishes to consider

cava ('kɑːvə) NOUN a Spanish sparkling wine produced by a method similar to that used for champagne.
▷HISTORY from Spanish

cavalcade (ˌkævəl'keɪd) NOUN 1 a procession of people on horseback, in cars, etc. 2 any procession: *a cavalcade of guests.*
▷HISTORY C16: from French, from Italian *cavalcata,* from *cavalcare* to ride on horseback, from Late Latin *caballicāre,* from *caballus* horse

cavalier (ˌkævə'lɪə) ADJECTIVE 1 showing haughty disregard; offhand. ◆ NOUN 2 a gallant or courtly gentleman, esp one acting as a lady's escort. 3 *Archaic* a horseman, esp one who is armed.
▷HISTORY C16: from Italian *cavaliere,* from Old Provençal *cavalier,* from Late Latin *caballārius* rider, from *caballus* horse, of obscure origin
▸ˌ**cava'lierly** ADVERB

Cavalier (ˌkævə'lɪə) NOUN a supporter of Charles I during the English Civil War. Compare **Roundhead.**

cavalier King Charles spaniel NOUN See **King Charles spaniel.**

Cavalier poets PLURAL NOUN a group of mid-17th-century English lyric poets, mostly courtiers of Charles I. Chief among them were Robert Herrick, Thomas Carew, Sir John Suckling, and Richard Lovelace.

cavalla (kə'vælə) *or* **cavally** NOUN, *plural* **-la, -las,** *or* **-lies.** any of various tropical carangid fishes, such as *Gnathanodon speciosus* (golden cavalla).
▷HISTORY C19: from Spanish *caballa,* from Late Latin, feminine of *caballus* horse

cavalry ('kævəlrɪ) NOUN, *plural* **-ries.** 1 (esp formerly) the part of an army composed of mounted troops. 2 the armoured element of a modern army. 3 (*as modifier*): *a cavalry unit; a cavalry charge.*

▷HISTORY C16: from French *cavallerie,* from Italian *cavalleria,* from *cavaliere* horseman; see CAVALIER
▸ˈ**cavalryman** NOUN

cavalry twill NOUN a strong woollen twill fabric used for trousers, etc.

Cavan (ˈkævᵊn) NOUN [1] a county of N Republic of Ireland: hilly, with many small lakes and bogs. County town: Cavan. Pop.: 52 944 (1996). Area: 1890 sq. km (730 sq. miles). [2] a market town in N Republic of Ireland, county town of Co. Cavan. Pop.: 4500 (latest est.).

cavatina (ˌkævəˈtiːnə) NOUN, *plural* **-ne** (-nɪ). [1] a solo song resembling a simple aria. [2] an instrumental composition reminiscent of this.
▷HISTORY C19: from Italian

cave[1] (keɪv) NOUN [1] an underground hollow with access from the ground surface or from the sea, often found in limestone areas and on rocky coastlines. [2] *Brit history* a secession or a group seceding from a political party on some issue. See **Adullamite.** [3] (*modifier*) living in caves. ◆ VERB [4] (*tr*) to hollow out. ◆ See also **cave in, caving.**
▷HISTORY C13: from Old French, from Latin *cava,* plural of *cavum* cavity, from *cavus* hollow

cave[2] (ˈkeɪvɪ) *Brit school slang* ◆ NOUN [1] guard or lookout (esp in the phrase **keep cave**). ◆ SENTENCE SUBSTITUTE [2] watch out!
▷HISTORY from Latin *cavē!* beware!

caveat (ˈkeɪvɪˌæt, ˈkæv-) NOUN [1] *Law* a formal notice requesting the court or officer to refrain from taking some specified action without giving prior notice to the person lodging the caveat. [2] a warning; caution.
▷HISTORY C16: from Latin, literally: let him beware

caveat emptor (ˈɛmptɔː) NOUN the principle that the buyer must bear the risk for the quality of goods purchased unless they are covered by the seller's warranty.
▷HISTORY Latin: let the buyer beware

caveator (ˈkeɪvɪˌeɪtə, ˈkæv-) NOUN *Law* a person who enters a caveat.

cavefish (ˈkeɪvˌfɪʃ) NOUN, *plural* **-fish** *or* **-fishes.** any of various small freshwater cyprinodont fishes of the genera *Amblyopsis, Chologaster,* etc., living in subterranean and other waters in S North America. See also **blindfish.**

cave in VERB (*intr, adverb*) [1] to collapse; subside. [2] *Informal* to yield completely, esp under pressure. ◆ NOUN **cave-in.** [3] the sudden collapse of a roof, piece of ground, etc., into a hollow beneath it; subsidence. [4] the site of such a collapse, as at a mine or tunnel. [5] *Informal* an instance of yielding completely, esp under pressure.

cavel (ˈkeɪvᵊl) NOUN *NZ* a drawing of lots among miners for an easy and profitable place at the coalface.
▷HISTORY C19: from English dialect *cavel* to cast lots, apportion

caveman (ˈkeɪvˌmæn) NOUN, *plural* **-men.** [1] a man of the Palaeolithic age; cave dweller. [2] *Informal and facetious* a man who is primitive or brutal in behaviour, etc.

cavendish (ˈkævəndɪʃ) NOUN tobacco that has been sweetened and pressed into moulds to form bars.
▷HISTORY C19: perhaps from the name of the first maker

cavern (ˈkævᵊn) NOUN [1] a cave, esp when large and formed by underground water, or a large chamber in a cave. ◆ VERB (*tr*) [2] to shut in or as if in a cavern. [3] to hollow out.
▷HISTORY C14: from Old French *caverne,* from Latin *caverna,* from *cavus* hollow; see CAVE[1]

cavernous (ˈkævənəs) ADJECTIVE [1] suggestive of a cavern in vastness, darkness, etc.: *cavernous hungry eyes.* [2] filled with small cavities; porous. [3] (of rocks) containing caverns or cavities.
▸ˈ**cavernously** ADVERB

cavesson (ˈkævɪsən) NOUN a kind of hard noseband, used (esp formerly) in breaking a horse in.
▷HISTORY C16: via French from Italian *cavezzone,* from *cavezza* halter, ultimately related to Latin *caput* head

cavetto (kəˈvɛtəʊ; *Italian* kaˈvetto) NOUN, *plural* **-ti** (-tɪ; *Italian* -ti). *Architect* a concave moulding, shaped to a quarter circle in cross section.
▷HISTORY C17: from Italian, from *cavo* hollow, from Latin *cavus*

cave tubing NOUN *NZ* another name for **blackwater rafting.**

caviar *or* **caviare** (ˈkævɪˌɑː, ˌkævɪˈɑː) NOUN the salted roe of sturgeon, esp the beluga, usually served as an hors d'oeuvre.
▷HISTORY C16: from earlier *cavery,* from Old Italian *caviari,* plural of *caviaro* caviar, from Turkish *havyār*

CAVIAR (ˈkævɪˌɑː) NOUN ACRONYM FOR Cinema and Video Industry Audience Research.

cavicorn (ˈkævɪˌkɔːn) ADJECTIVE (of sheep, goats, etc.) having hollow horns as distinct from the solid antlers of deer.
▷HISTORY C19: from Latin *cavus* hollow + *cornū* horn

cavie (ˈkeɪvɪ) NOUN *Scot* a hen coop.
▷HISTORY C18: via Dutch or Flemish *kavie,* from Latin *cavea* cavity

cavil (ˈkævɪl) VERB **-ils, -illing, -illed** *or US* **-ils, -iling, -iled.** [1] (*intr;* foll by *at* or *about*) to raise annoying petty objections; quibble; carp. ◆ NOUN [2] a captious trifling objection.
▷HISTORY C16: from Old French *caviller,* from Latin *cavillārī* to jeer, from *cavilla* raillery
▸ˈ**caviller** NOUN ▸ˈ**cavilling** ADJECTIVE

caving (ˈkeɪvɪŋ) NOUN the sport of climbing in and exploring caves.
▸ˈ**caver** NOUN

cavitation (ˌkævɪˈteɪʃən) NOUN [1] the formation of vapour- or gas-filled cavities in a flowing liquid when tensile stress is superimposed on the ambient pressure. [2] the formation of cavities in a structure.

Cavite (kəˈviːtɪ, -teɪ) NOUN a port in the N Philippines, in S Luzon on Manila Bay: US naval base. Pop.: 103 422 (1994 est.).

cavity (ˈkævɪtɪ) NOUN, *plural* **-ties.** [1] a hollow space; hole. [2] *Dentistry* a soft decayed area on a tooth. See **caries.** [3] any empty or hollow space within the body: *the oral cavity.* [4] *Electronics* See **cavity resonator.**
▷HISTORY C16: from French *cavité,* from Late Latin *cavitās,* from Latin *cavus* hollow

cavity block NOUN a precast concrete block that contains a cavity or cavities.

cavity resonator NOUN *Electronics* a conducting surface enclosing a space in which an oscillating electromagnetic field can be maintained, the dimensions of the cavity determining the resonant frequency of the oscillations. It is used in microwave devices for frequencies exceeding 300 megahertz. Also called: **resonant cavity, rhumbatron.**

cavity wall NOUN a wall that consists of two separate walls, joined by wall-ties, with an airspace between them.

cavolo nero (ˈkɑːvəˌləʊ ˈnɛrəʊ) NOUN an Italian variety of cabbage with dark green leaves.
▷HISTORY from Italian, black cabbage

cavo-relievo *or* **cavo-rilievo** (ˌkɑːvəʊrɪˈliːvəʊ, ˌkeɪ-) NOUN, *plural* **-vos** *or* **-vi** (-vɪ). a relief sculpture in which the highest point in the carving is below the level of the original surface.
▷HISTORY Italian, literally: hollow relief

cavort (kəˈvɔːt) VERB (*intr*) to prance; caper.
▷HISTORY C19: perhaps from CURVET
▸**caˈvorter** NOUN

cavy (ˈkeɪvɪ) NOUN, *plural* **-vies.** any small South American hystricomorph rodent of the family *Caviidae,* esp any of the genus *Cavia,* having a thickset body and very small tail. See also **guinea pig.**
▷HISTORY C18: from New Latin *Cavia,* from Galibi *cabiai*

caw (kɔː) NOUN [1] the cry of a crow, rook, or raven. ◆ VERB [2] (*intr*) to make this cry.
▷HISTORY C16: of imitative origin

CAW ABBREVIATION FOR Canadian Auto Workers (trade union).

Cawnpore (ˌkɔːnˈpɔː) *or* **Cawnpur** (ˌkɔːnˈpʊə) NOUN the former name of **Kanpur.**

Caxton (ˈkækstən) NOUN [1] a book printed by William Caxton. [2] a style of type, imitating the Gothic, that Caxton used in his books.

cay (keɪ, kiː) NOUN a small low island or bank composed of sand and coral fragments, esp in the Caribbean area. Also called: **key.**
▷HISTORY C18: from Spanish *cayo,* probably from Old French *quai* QUAY

Cayenne (keɪˈɛn) NOUN the capital of French Guiana, on an island at the mouth of the Cayenne River: French penal settlement from 1854 to 1938. Pop.: 50 594 (1999).

cayenne pepper (keɪˈɛn) NOUN a very hot condiment, bright red in colour, made from the dried seeds and pods of various capsicums. Often shortened to **cayenne.** Also called: **red pepper.**
▷HISTORY C18: ultimately from Tupi *quiynha*

Cayes (keɪ; *French* kaj) NOUN short for **Les Cayes.**

cayman *or* **caiman** (ˈkeɪmən) NOUN, *plural* **-mans.** any tropical American crocodilian of the genus *Caiman* and related genera, similar to alligators but with a more heavily armoured belly: family *Alligatoridae* (alligators, etc.).
▷HISTORY C16: from Spanish *caimán,* from Carib *cayman,* probably of African origin

Cayman Islands (ˈkeɪmən) PLURAL NOUN three coral islands in the Caribbean Sea northwest of Jamaica: a dependency of Jamaica until 1962, now a UK Overseas Territory. Capital: Georgetown. Pop.: 38 000 (1998 est.). Area: about 260 sq. km (100 sq. miles).

Cayuga (keɪˈjuːgə, kaɪ-) NOUN [1] (*plural* **-gas** *or* **-ga**) a member of a North American Indian people (one of the Iroquois peoples) formerly living around Cayuga Lake. [2] the language of this people, belonging to the Iroquoian family.

cayuse (ˈkaɪuːs) NOUN *Western US and Canadian* a small American Indian pony used by cowboys.
▷HISTORY C19: from a Chinookan language

caz (kæʒ) ADJECTIVE *Slang* short for **casual.**

cb ABBREVIATION FOR centre of buoyancy (of a boat, etc.).

Cb THE CHEMICAL SYMBOL FOR columbium.

CB ABBREVIATION FOR: [1] **Citizens' Band.** [2] Companion of the (Order of the) Bath (an English title). [3] County Borough. [4] (in Canada) Cape Breton Island.

CBC ABBREVIATION FOR Canadian Broadcasting Corporation.

CBD *or* **cbd** ABBREVIATION FOR: [1] cash before delivery. [2] central business district.

CBE ABBREVIATION FOR Commander of the (Order of the) British Empire.

CBI ABBREVIATION FOR Confederation of British Industry.

CBR (of weapons or warfare) ABBREVIATION FOR chemical, bacteriological, and radiation.

CBS ABBREVIATION FOR Columbia Broadcasting System.

CBSO ABBREVIATION FOR City of Birmingham Symphony Orchestra.

CBT ABBREVIATION FOR computer-based training.

cc[1] *or* **c.c.** ABBREVIATION FOR: [1] carbon copy *or* copies. [2] *South African* close corporation. [3] cubic centimetre(s).

cc[2] THE INTERNET DOMAIN NAME FOR Cocos Islands.

CC ABBREVIATION FOR: [1] City Council. [2] (in Britain) Competition Commission. [3] County Council. [4] Cricket Club. [5] Companion of the Order of Canada.

cc. ABBREVIATION FOR chapters.

CCANZ ABBREVIATION FOR Council of Churches in Aotearoa/New Zealand.

c.c.c. ABBREVIATION FOR cwmni cyfyngedig cyhoeddus; a public limited company in Wales.

CCD *Electronics* ABBREVIATION FOR **charge-coupled device.**

CCEA ABBREVIATION FOR Northern Ireland Council for the Curriculum, Examinations and Assessment.

CCF (in Britain) ABBREVIATION FOR Combined Cadet Force.

CCJ (in England) ABBREVIATION FOR county court judgment.

C clef NOUN *Music* a symbol (𝄡), placed at the beginning of the staff, establishing middle C as being on its centre line. See **alto clef, soprano clef, tenor clef.**

CCMA (in South Africa) ABBREVIATION FOR Council for Conciliation, Mediation and Arbitration.

CCRC ABBREVIATION FOR Criminal Cases Review

Commission: a British government body established in 1997 to investigate alleged miscarriages of justice.

CCTA (in Britain) ABBREVIATION FOR Central Computer and Telecommunications Agency.

CCTV ABBREVIATION FOR **closed-circuit television.**

cd[1] [1] ABBREVIATION FOR cash discount. ◆ [2] SYMBOL FOR candela.

cd[2] THE INTERNET DOMAIN NAME FOR Democratic Republic of Congo.

Cd [1] (in Britain) ABBREVIATION FOR command (paper). ◆ [2] THE CHEMICAL SYMBOL FOR cadmium.

CD ABBREVIATION FOR: [1] compact disc. [2] Civil Defence (Corps). [3] Corps Diplomatique (Diplomatic Corps). [4] Conference on Disarmament: a United Nations standing conference, held in Geneva, to negotiate a global ban on chemical weapons. [5] (in the US and Canada) certificate of deposit. Also: **C.D.**

c/d *Book-keeping* ABBREVIATION FOR carried down.

CDC ABBREVIATION FOR: [1] (in the US) Center for Disease Control. [2] Commonwealth Development Corporation.

CDE ABBREVIATION FOR compact disc erasable: a compact disc that can be used to record and rerecord. Compare **CDR.**

cdf *Statistics* ABBREVIATION FOR cumulative distribution function.

Cdn ABBREVIATION FOR Canadian.

CDN INTERNATIONAL CAR REGISTRATION FOR Canada.

cDNA ABBREVIATION FOR complementary DNA; a form of DNA artificially synthesized from a messenger RNA template and used in genetic engineering to produce gene clones.

CD player NOUN a device for playing compact discs. In full: **compact-disc player.**

Cdr *Military* ABBREVIATION FOR Commander.

CDR ABBREVIATION FOR compact disc recordable: a compact disc that can be used to record only once. Compare **CDE.**

Cdre ABBREVIATION FOR Commodore.

CD-ROM (-ˈrɒm) NOUN compact disc read-only memory; a compact disc used with a computer system as a read-only optical disk.

CD-RW NOUN compact disc rewritable; a compact disc that can be used to record and rerecord.

CDT ABBREVIATION FOR: [1] *US and Canadian* Central Daylight Time. [2] Craft, Design, and Technology: a subject on the GCSE syllabus, related to the National Curriculum.

CDU ABBREVIATION FOR Christlich-Demokratische Union: a German (until 1990 West German) political party.
▷HISTORY German: Christian Democratic Union

CDV ABBREVIATION FOR: [1] **CD-video.** [2] **compact video disc.**

CD-video NOUN a compact-disc player that, when connected to a television and hi-fi, produces high-quality stereo sound and synchronized pictures from a disc resembling a large compact audio disc. In full: **compact-disc video.**

Ce THE CHEMICAL SYMBOL FOR cerium.

CE ABBREVIATION FOR: [1] chief engineer. [2] Church of England. [3] civil engineer. [4] **Common Entrance.** [5] **Common Era.** [6] Communauté Européenne (European Union).

ceanothus (ˌsiːəˈnəʊθəs) NOUN any shrub of the North American rhamnaceous genus *Ceanothus:* grown for their ornamental, often blue, flower clusters.
▷HISTORY C19: New Latin, from Greek *keanōthos* a kind of thistle

Ceará (*Portuguese* siaˈra) NOUN [1] a state of NE Brazil: sandy coastal plain, rising to a high plateau. Capital: Fortaleza. Pop.: 7 417 402 (2000). Area: 150 630 sq. km (58 746 sq. miles). [2] another name for **Fortaleza.**

cease (siːs) VERB [1] (when *tr,* may take a gerund or an infinitive as object) to bring or come to an end; desist from; stop. ◆ NOUN [2] **without cease.** without stopping; incessantly.
▷HISTORY C14: from Old French *cesser,* from Latin *cessāre,* frequentative of *cēdere* to yield, CEDE

cease-fire *Chiefly military* ◆ NOUN [1] a period of truce, esp one that is temporary and a preliminary step to establishing a more permanent peace on agreed terms. ◆ INTERJECTION, NOUN [2] the order to stop firing.

ceaseless (ˈsiːslɪs) ADJECTIVE without stop or pause; incessant.
▸ˈ**ceaselessly** ADVERB

Cebú (sɪˈbuː) NOUN [1] an island in the central Philippines. Pop.: 2 091 602 (latest est.). Area: 4422 sq. km (1707 sq. miles). [2] a port in the Philippines, on E Cebú island. Pop.: 718 821 (2000).

Čechy (ˈtʃɛxi) NOUN the Czech name for **Bohemia.**

cecity (ˈsiːsɪtɪ) NOUN a rare word for **blindness.**
▷HISTORY C16: from Latin *caecitās,* from *caecus* blind

cecropia moth (sɪˈkrəʊpɪə) NOUN a large North American saturniid moth, *Hyalophora* (or *Samia*) *cecropia,* with brightly coloured wings and feathery antennae.
▷HISTORY C19: New Latin, from Latin *Cecropius* belonging to CECROPS

Cecrops (ˈsiːkrɒps) NOUN (in ancient Greek tradition) the first king of Attica, represented as half-human, half-dragon.

cecum (ˈsiːkəm) NOUN, *plural* **-ca** (-kə). *US* a variant spelling of **caecum.**
▸ˈ**cecal** ADJECTIVE

cedar (ˈsiːdə) NOUN [1] any Old World coniferous tree of the genus *Cedrus,* having spreading branches, needle-like evergreen leaves, and erect barrel-shaped cones: family *Pinaceae*. See also **cedar of Lebanon, deodar.** [2] any of various other conifers, such as the red cedars and white cedars. [3] the wood of any of these trees. [4] any of certain other plants, such as thr Spanish cedar. ◆ ADJECTIVE [5] made of the wood of a cedar tree.
▷HISTORY C13: from Old French *cedre,* from Latin *cedrus,* from Greek *kedros*

cedar of Lebanon NOUN a cedar, *Cedrus libani,* of SW Asia with level spreading branches and fragrant wood.

Cedar Rapids NOUN a city in the US, in E Iowa. Pop.: 120 758 (2000).

cede (siːd) VERB [1] (when *intr,* often foll by *to*) to transfer, make over, or surrender (something, esp territory or legal rights): *the lands were ceded by treaty.* [2] (*tr*) to allow or concede (a point in an argument, etc.).
▷HISTORY C17: from Latin *cēdere* to yield, give way
▸ˈ**ceder** NOUN

cedi (ˈseɪdɪ) NOUN, *plural* **-di.** the standard monetary unit of Ghana, divided into 100 pesewas.

cedilla (sɪˈdɪlə) NOUN a character (¸) placed underneath a *c* before *a, o,* or *u,* esp in French, Portuguese, or Catalan, denoting that it is to be pronounced (s), not (k). The same character is used in the scripts of other languages, as in Turkish under *s.*
▷HISTORY C16: from Spanish: little *z,* from *ceda* zed, from Late Latin *zeta;* a small *z* was originally written after *c* in Spanish, to indicate a sibilant

Ceefax (ˈsiːˌfæks) NOUN *Trademark* the BBC Teletext service. See **Teletext.**

CEGB *Brit* ABBREVIATION FOR (the former) Central Electricity Generating Board.

ceiba (ˈseɪbə) NOUN [1] any bombacaceous tropical tree of the genus *Ceiba,* such as the silk-cotton tree. [2] silk cotton; kapok.
▷HISTORY C19: from New Latin, from Spanish, of Arawak origin

ceil (siːl) VERB (*tr*) [1] to line (a ceiling) with plaster, boarding, etc. [2] to provide with a ceiling.
▷HISTORY C15 *celen,* perhaps back formation from CEILING

ceilidh (ˈkeɪlɪ) NOUN (esp in Scotland and Ireland) an informal social gathering with folk music, singing, dancing, and storytelling.
▷HISTORY C19: from Gaelic

ceiling (ˈsiːlɪŋ) NOUN [1] the inner upper surface of a room. [2] **a** an upper limit, such as one set by regulation on prices or wages. **b** (*as modifier*): *ceiling prices.* [3] the upper altitude to which an aircraft can climb measured under specified conditions. See also **service ceiling, absolute ceiling.** [4] *Meteorol* the highest level in the atmosphere from which the earth's surface is visible at a particular time, usually the base of a cloud layer. [5] a wooden or metal surface fixed to the interior frames of a vessel for rigidity.
▷HISTORY C14: of uncertain origin

ceilometer (siːˈlɒmɪtə) NOUN a device for determining the cloud ceiling, esp by means of a reflected light beam.
▷HISTORY C20: from CEILING + -METER

cel *or* **cell** (sɛl) NOUN short for **celluloid** (senses 2b, 2c).

celadon (ˈsɛləˌdɒn) NOUN [1] a type of porcelain having a greyish-green glaze: mainly Chinese. [2] a pale greyish-green colour, sometimes somewhat yellow.
▷HISTORY C18: from French, from the name of the shepherd hero of *L'Astrée* (1610), a romance by Honoré d'Urfé

Celaeno (sɛˈliːnəʊ) NOUN *Greek myth* one of the Pleiades.

celandine (ˈsɛlənˌdaɪn) NOUN either of two unrelated plants, *Chelidonium majus* (see **greater celandine**) or *Ranunculus ficaria* (see **lesser celandine**).
▷HISTORY C13: earlier *celydon,* from Latin *chelīdonia* (the plant), from *chelīdonius* of the swallow, from Greek *khelidōn* swallow; the plant's season was believed to parallel the migration of swallows

Celaya (*Spanish* θeˈlaja) NOUN a city in central Mexico, in Guanajuato state: market town, famous for its sweetmeats; textile-manufacturing. Pop.: 270 000 (2000).

-cele NOUN COMBINING FORM tumour or hernia: *hydrocele.*
▷HISTORY from Greek *kēlē* tumour

celeb (sɪˈlɛb) NOUN *Informal* a celebrity.

Celebes (ˈsɛlɪbiːz, sɛˈliːbɪz) NOUN the English name for **Sulawesi.**

Celebes Sea NOUN the part of the Pacific Ocean between Sulawesi, Borneo, and Mindanao.

celebrant (ˈsɛlɪbrənt) NOUN [1] a person participating in a religious ceremony. [2] *Christianity* an officiating priest, esp at the Eucharist.

celebrate (ˈsɛlɪˌbreɪt) VERB [1] to rejoice in or have special festivities to mark (a happy day, event, etc.). [2] (*tr*) to observe (a birthday, anniversary, etc.): *she celebrates her ninetieth birthday next month.* [3] (*tr*) to perform (a solemn or religious ceremony), esp to officiate at (Mass). [4] (*tr*) to praise publicly; proclaim.
▷HISTORY C15: from Latin *celebrāre,* from *celeber* numerous, thronged, renowned
▸ˌ**celeˈbration** NOUN ▸ˈ**celebrative** ADJECTIVE
▸ˈ**celeˌbrator** NOUN ▸ˈ**celeˌbratory** ADJECTIVE

celebrated (ˈsɛlɪˌbreɪtɪd) ADJECTIVE (*usually prenominal*) famous: *a celebrated pianist; a celebrated trial.*

celebrity (sɪˈlɛbrɪtɪ) NOUN, *plural* **-ties.** [1] a famous person: *a show-business celebrity.* [2] fame or notoriety.

celeriac (sɪˈlɛrɪˌæk) NOUN a variety of celery, *Apium graveolens rapaceum,* with a large turnip-like root, used as a vegetable.
▷HISTORY C18: from CELERY + *-ac,* of unexplained origin

celerity (sɪˈlɛrɪtɪ) NOUN rapidity; swiftness; speed.
▷HISTORY C15: from Old French *celerite,* from Latin *celeritās,* from *celer* swift

celery (ˈsɛlərɪ) NOUN [1] an umbelliferous Eurasian plant, *Apium graveolens dulce,* whose blanched leafstalks are used in salads or cooked as a vegetable. See also **celeriac.** [2] **wild celery.** a related and similar plant, *Apium graveolens.*
▷HISTORY C17: from French *céleri,* from Italian (Lombardy) dialect *selleri* (plural), from Greek *selinon* parsley

celery pine NOUN a New Zealand gymnosperm tree, *Phyllocladus trichomanoides,* with celerylike shoots and useful wood: family *Phyllocladaceae.*

celesta (sɪˈlɛstə) *or* **celeste** (sɪˈlɛst) NOUN *Music* a keyboard percussion instrument consisting of a set of steel plates of graduated length that are struck with key-operated hammers. The tone is an ethereal tinkling sound. Range: four octaves upwards from middle C.
▷HISTORY C19: from French, Latinized variant of *céleste* heavenly

celestial (sɪˈlɛstɪəl) ADJECTIVE [1] heavenly; divine; spiritual: *celestial peace.* [2] of or relating to the sky: *celestial bodies.*

▷HISTORY C14: from Medieval Latin *cēlestiālis,* from Latin *caelestis,* from *caelum* heaven
▸**ce'lestially** ADVERB

Celestial Empire NOUN an archaic or literary name for the **Chinese Empire.**

celestial equator NOUN the great circle lying on the celestial sphere the plane of which is perpendicular to the line joining the north and south celestial poles. Also called: **equinoctial, equinoctial circle.**

celestial globe NOUN a spherical model of the celestial sphere showing the relative positions of stars, constellations, etc.

celestial guidance NOUN the guidance of a spacecraft or missile by reference to the position of one or more celestial bodies.

celestial horizon NOUN See **horizon** (sense 2b).

celestial latitude NOUN the angular distance of a celestial body north or south from the ecliptic. Also called: **ecliptic latitude.**

celestial longitude NOUN the angular distance measured eastwards from the vernal equinox to the intersection of the ecliptic with the great circle passing through a celestial body and the poles of the ecliptic. Also called: **ecliptic longitude.**

celestial mechanics NOUN the study of the motion of celestial bodies under the influence of gravitational fields.

celestial navigation NOUN navigation by observation of the positions of the stars. Also called: **astronavigation.**

celestial pole NOUN either of the two points at which the earth's axis, extended to infinity, would intersect the celestial sphere. Sometimes shortened to **pole.**

celestial sphere NOUN an imaginary sphere of infinitely large radius enclosing the universe so that all celestial bodies appear to be projected onto its surface.

celestite ('sɛlɪˌstaɪt) *or* **celestine** ('sɛlɪstɪn, -ˌstaɪn) NOUN a white, red, or blue mineral consisting of strontium sulphate in orthorhombic crystalline form: a source of strontium compounds. Formula: $SrSO_4$.
▷HISTORY C19: from German *Zölestin,* from Latin *caelestis* CELESTIAL (referring to the blue colour) + -ITE[1]

celiac ('siːlɪˌæk) ADJECTIVE *Anatomy* the usual US spelling of **coeliac.**

celibate ('sɛlɪbɪt) NOUN [1] a person who is unmarried, esp one who has taken a religious vow of chastity. ◆ ADJECTIVE [2] unmarried, esp by vow. [3] abstaining from sexual intercourse.
▷HISTORY C17: from Latin *caelibātus,* from *caelebs* unmarried, of obscure origin
▸**'celibacy** NOUN

cell[1] (sɛl) NOUN [1] a small simple room, as in a prison, convent, monastery, or asylum; cubicle. [2] any small compartment: *the cells of a honeycomb.* [3] *Biology* the basic structural and functional unit of living organisms. It consists of a nucleus, containing the genetic material, surrounded by the cytoplasm in which are mitochondria, lysosomes, ribosomes, and other organelles. All cells are bounded by a cell membrane; plant cells have an outer cell wall in addition. [4] *Biology* any small cavity or area, such as the cavity containing pollen in an anther. [5] a device for converting chemical energy into electrical energy, usually consisting of a container with two electrodes immersed in an electrolyte. See also **primary cell, secondary cell, dry cell, wet cell, fuel cell.** [6] short for **electrolytic cell.** [7] a small religious house dependent upon a larger one. [8] a small group of persons operating as a nucleus of a larger political, religious, or other organization: *Communist cell.* [9] *Maths* a small unit of volume in a mathematical coordinate system. [10] *Zoology* one of the areas on an insect wing bounded by veins. [11] the geographical area served by an individual transmitter in a cellular radio network.
▷HISTORY C12: from Medieval Latin *cella* monk's cell, from Latin: room, storeroom; related to Latin *cēlāre* to hide
▸**'cell-ˌlike** ADJECTIVE

cell[2] (sɛl) NOUN a variant spelling of **cel.**

cella ('sɛlə) NOUN, *plural* **-lae** (-liː). the inner room of a classical temple, esp the room housing the statue of a deity. Also called: **naos.**

▷HISTORY C17: from Latin: room, shrine; see CELL[1]

cellar ('sɛlə) NOUN [1] an underground room, rooms, or storey of a building, usually used for storage. Compare **basement.** [2] a place where wine is stored. [3] a stock of bottled wines. ◆ VERB [4] (*tr*) to store in a cellar.
▷HISTORY C13: from Anglo-French, from Latin *cellārium* food store, from *cella* CELLA

cellarage ('sɛlərɪdʒ) NOUN [1] an area of a cellar. [2] a charge for storing goods in a cellar, etc.

cellar dwellers PLURAL NOUN *Austral slang* the team at the bottom of a sports league.

cellarer ('sɛlərə) NOUN a monastic official responsible for food, drink, etc.

cellaret (ˌsɛlə'rɛt) NOUN a case, cabinet, or sideboard with compartments for holding wine bottles.

cell cycle NOUN the growth cycle of eukaryotic cells. It is divided into five stages, known as G_0, in which the cell is quiescent, G_1 and G_2, in which it increases in size, S, in which it duplicates its DNA, and M, in which it undergoes mitosis and divides.

cell division NOUN *Cytology* the division of a cell into two new cells during growth or reproduction. See **amitosis, meiosis, mitosis.**

Celle (*German* 'tsɛlə) NOUN a city in N Germany, on the Aller River in Lower Saxony: from 1378 to 1705 the residence of the Dukes of Brunswick-Lüneburg. Pop.: 71 050 (1989 est.).

cellentani (ˌtʃɛlən'tɑːnɪ) NOUN pasta in the form of corkscrews.
▷HISTORY Italian

cell line NOUN *Biology* a clone of animal or plant cells that can be grown in a suitable nutrient culture medium in the laboratory.

cell lineage NOUN *Biology* the developmental history of a tissue or part of an organism from particular cells in the fertilized egg or embryo through to their fully differentiated state.

cell membrane NOUN a very thin membrane, composed of lipids and protein, that surrounds the cytoplasm of a cell and controls the passage of substances into and out of the cell. Also called: **plasmalemma, plasma membrane.**

cello ('tʃɛləʊ) NOUN, *plural* **-los.** *Music* a bowed stringed instrument of the violin family. Range: more than four octaves upwards from C below the bass staff. It has four strings, is held between the knees, and has an extendible metal spike at the lower end, which acts as a support. Full name: **violoncello.**
▸**'cellist** NOUN

cellobiose (ˌsɛləʊ'baɪəʊz) *or* **cellose** ('sɛləʊz) NOUN a disaccharide obtained by the hydrolysis of cellulose by cellulase. Formula: $C_{12}H_{22}O_{11}$.
▷HISTORY C20: from CELLULOSE + BI-[1] + -OSE[2]

celloidin (sə'lɔɪdɪn) NOUN a nitrocellulose compound derived from pyroxylin, used in a solution of alcohol and ether for embedding specimens before cutting sections for microscopy.
▷HISTORY C20: from CELLULOSE + -OID + -IN

Cellophane ('sɛləˌfeɪn) NOUN *Trademark* a flexible thin transparent sheeting made from wood pulp and used as a moisture-proof wrapping.
▷HISTORY C20: from CELLULOSE + -PHANE

Cellosolve ('sɛləʊˌsɒlv) NOUN *Trademark* an organic compound used as a solvent in the plastics industry; 2-ethoxyethan-1-ol. Formula: $C_2H_5OCH_2CH_2OH$.

cellphone ('sɛlˌfəʊn) NOUN a portable telephone operated by cellular radio. In full: **cellular telephone.**

cellular ('sɛljʊlə) ADJECTIVE [1] of, relating to, resembling, or composed of a cell or cells. [2] having cells or small cavities; porous. [3] divided into a network of cells. [4] *Textiles* woven with an open texture: *a cellular blanket.* [5] designed for or involving cellular radio.
▸**cellularity** (ˌsɛljʊ'lærɪtɪ) NOUN

cellular radio NOUN radio communication based on a network of transmitters each serving a small area known as a cell: used in personal communications systems in which the mobile receiver switches frequencies automatically as it passes from one cell to another.

cellulase ('sɛljʊˌleɪz) NOUN any enzyme that converts cellulose to the disaccharide cellobiose.
▷HISTORY C20: from CELLULOSE + -ASE

cellule ('sɛljuːl) NOUN a very small cell.
▷HISTORY C17: from Latin *cellula,* diminutive of *cella* CELL[1]

cellulite ('sɛljʊˌlaɪt) NOUN a name sometimes given to subcutaneous fat alleged to resist dieting.
▷HISTORY C20: from French, from *cellule* cell

cellulitis (ˌsɛljʊ'laɪtɪs) NOUN inflammation of any of the tissues of the body, characterized by fever, pain, swelling, and redness of the affected area.
▷HISTORY C19: from Latin *cellula* CELLULE + -ITIS

celluloid ('sɛljʊˌlɔɪd) NOUN [1] a flammable thermoplastic material consisting of cellulose nitrate mixed with a plasticizer, usually camphor: used in sheets, rods, and tubes for making a wide range of articles. [2] **a** a cellulose derivative used for coating film. **b** one of the transparent sheets on which the constituent drawings of an animated film are prepared. **c** a transparent sheet used as an overlay in artwork. **d** cinema film.

cellulose ('sɛljʊˌləʊz, -ˌləʊs) NOUN a polysaccharide consisting of long unbranched chains of linked glucose units: the main constituent of plant cell walls and used in making paper, rayon, and film.
▷HISTORY C18: from French *cellule* cell (see CELLULE) + -OSE[2]
▸ˌ**cellu'losic** ADJECTIVE, NOUN

cellulose acetate NOUN nonflammable material made by acetylating cellulose: used in the manufacture of film, dopes, lacquers, and artificial fibres.

cellulose nitrate NOUN a compound made by treating cellulose with nitric and sulphuric acids, used in plastics, lacquers, and explosives: a nitrogen-containing ester of cellulose. Also called (not in chemical usage): **nitrocellulose.** See also **guncotton.**

cell wall NOUN the outer layer of a cell, esp the structure in plant cells that consists of cellulose, lignin, etc., and gives mechanical support to the cell.

celom ('siːləm) NOUN a less frequent US spelling of **coelom.**

celosia (sə'ləʊsɪə) NOUN See **cockscomb** (sense 2).
▷HISTORY New Latin, from Greek *kēlos* dry, burnt (from the appearance of the flowers of some species)

Celsius ('sɛlsɪəs) ADJECTIVE denoting a measurement on the Celsius scale. Symbol: C.
▷HISTORY C18: named after Anders *Celsius* (1701–44), Swedish astronomer who invented it

Celsius scale NOUN a scale of temperature in which 0° represents the melting point of ice and 100° represents the boiling point of water. See also **centigrade.** Compare **Fahrenheit scale.**

celt (sɛlt) NOUN *Archaeol* a stone or metal axelike instrument with a bevelled edge.
▷HISTORY C18: from Late Latin *celtes* chisel, of obscure origin

Celt (kɛlt, sɛlt) *or* **Kelt** NOUN [1] a person who speaks a Celtic language. [2] a member of an Indo-European people who in pre-Roman times inhabited Britain, Gaul, Spain, and other parts of W and central Europe.

Celtiberian (ˌkɛltɪ'bɪərɪən, -taɪ-, ˌsɛl-) NOUN [1] a member of a Celtic people (**Celtiberi**) who inhabited the Iberian peninsula during classical times. [2] the extinct language of this people, possibly belonging to the Celtic branch of the Indo-European family, recorded in a number of inscriptions.

Celtic ('kɛltɪk, 'sɛl-) *or* **Keltic** NOUN [1] a branch of the Indo-European family of languages that includes Gaelic, Welsh, and Breton, still spoken in parts of Scotland, Ireland, Wales, and Brittany. Modern Celtic is divided into the Brythonic (southern) and Goidelic (northern) groups. ◆ ADJECTIVE [2] of, relating to, or characteristic of the Celts or the Celtic languages.
▸**'Celtically** *or* **'Keltically** ADVERB ▸**Celticism** ('kɛltɪˌsɪzəm, 'sɛl-) *or* **'Keltiˌcism** NOUN ▸**'Celticist, 'Celtist,** *or* **'Kelticist, 'Keltist** NOUN

Celtic cross NOUN a Latin cross with a broad ring surrounding the point of intersection.

cembalo ('tʃɛmbələʊ) NOUN, *plural* **-li** (-lɪ) *or* **-los.** another word for **harpsichord.**
▷HISTORY C19: shortened from CLAVICEMBALO
▸**'cembalist** NOUN

cement (sɪ'mɛnt) NOUN 1 a fine grey powder made of a mixture of calcined limestone and clay, used with water and sand to make mortar, or with water, sand, and aggregate, to make concrete. 2 a binder, glue, or adhesive. 3 something that unites or joins; bond. 4 *Dentistry* any of various materials used in filling teeth. 5 mineral matter, such as silica and calcite, that binds together particles of rock, bones, etc., to form a solid mass of sedimentary rock. 6 another word for **cementum.** ◆ VERB (*tr*) 7 to reinforce or consolidate: *once a friendship is cemented it will last for life.* 8 to join, bind, or glue together with or as if with cement. 9 to coat or cover with cement.
▷HISTORY C13: from Old French *ciment,* from Latin *caementum* stone from the quarry, from *caedere* to hew
▸**ce'menter** NOUN

cementation (ˌsiːmɛn'teɪʃən) NOUN 1 the process of heating a solid with a powdered material to modify the properties of the solid, esp the heating of wrought iron, surrounded with charcoal, to 750–900°C to produce steel. 2 the process of cementing or being cemented. 3 *Civil engineering* the injection of cement grout into fissured rocks to make them watertight.

cementite (sɪ'mɛntaɪt) NOUN the hard brittle compound of iron and carbon that forms in carbon steels and some cast irons. Formula: Fe_3C.

cementum (sɪ'mɛntəm) NOUN a thin bonelike tissue that covers the dentine in the root of a tooth.
▷HISTORY C19: New Latin, from Latin: CEMENT

cemetery ('sɛmɪtrɪ) NOUN, *plural* **-teries.** a place where the dead are buried, esp one not attached to a church.
▷HISTORY C14: from Late Latin *coemētērium,* from Greek *koimētērion* room for sleeping, from *koiman* to put to sleep

cenacle *or* **coenacle** ('sɛnəkᵊl) NOUN 1 a supper room, esp one on an upper floor. 2 (*capital*) the room in which the Last Supper took place.
▷HISTORY C14: from Old French, from Late Latin *cēnāculum,* from *cēna* supper

-cene NOUN AND ADJECTIVE COMBINING FORM denoting a recent geological period: *Miocene.*
▷HISTORY from Greek *kainos* new

CENELEC ('sɛnəˌlɛk) NOUN ACRONYM FOR Commission Européenne de Normalisation Électrique: the EU standards organization for electrical goods. Also called: **CEN.**

cenesthesia (ˌsiːnɪs'θiːzɪə) NOUN *Psychol* a variant spelling (esp US) of **coenaesthesia.**

CEng ABBREVIATION FOR chartered engineer.

Cenis (*French* səni) NOUN **Mont.** a pass over the Graian Alps in SE France, between Lanslebourg (France) and Susa (Italy): nearby tunnel, opened in 1871. Highest point: 2082 m (6831 ft.). Italian name: **Monte Cenisio** ('monte tʃe'niːzjo).

cenobite ('siːnəʊˌbaɪt) NOUN a variant spelling of **coenobite.**

cenogenesis (ˌsiːnəʊ'dʒɛnɪsɪs) NOUN a US spelling of **caenogenesis.**

cenospecies ('siːnəˌspiːʃiːz) NOUN, *plural* **-species.** a species related to another by the ability to interbreed: *dogs and wolves are cenospecies.*
▷HISTORY C20: from Greek *koinos* common + SPECIES

cenotaph ('sɛnəˌtɑːf) NOUN a monument honouring a dead person or persons buried elsewhere.
▷HISTORY C17: from Latin *cenotaphium,* from Greek *kenotaphion,* from *kenos* empty + *taphos* tomb
▸**ˌceno'taphic** ADJECTIVE

Cenotaph ('sɛnəˌtɑːf) NOUN **the.** the monument in Whitehall, London, honouring the dead of both World Wars: designed by Sir Edwin Lutyens: erected in 1920.

cenote (sɪ'nəʊteɪ) NOUN (esp in the Yucatán peninsula) a natural well formed by the collapse of an overlying limestone crust: often used as a sacrificial site by the Mayas.
▷HISTORY C19: via Mexican Spanish from Maya *conot*

Cenozoic, Caenozoic (ˌsiːnəʊ'zəʊɪk), *or* **Cainozoic** ADJECTIVE 1 of, denoting, or relating to the most recent geological era, which began 65 000 000 years ago: characterized by the development and increase of the mammals. ◆ NOUN 2 **the.** the Cenozoic era.
▷HISTORY C19: from Greek *kainos* new, recent + *zōikos,* from *zōion* animal

cense (sɛns) VERB (*tr*) to burn incense near or before (an altar, shrine, etc.).
▷HISTORY C14: from Old French *encenser;* see INCENSE[1]

censer ('sɛnsə) NOUN a container for burning incense, esp one swung at religious ceremonies. Also called: **thurible.**

censor ('sɛnsə) NOUN 1 a person authorized to examine publications, theatrical presentations, films, letters, etc., in order to suppress in whole or part those considered obscene, politically unacceptable, etc. 2 any person who controls or suppresses the behaviour of others, usually on moral grounds. 3 (in republican Rome) either of two senior magistrates elected to keep the list of citizens up to date, control aspects of public finance, and supervise public morals. 4 *Psychoanal* the postulated factor responsible for regulating the translation of ideas and desires from the unconscious to the conscious mind. See also **superego.** ◆ VERB (*tr*) 5 to ban or cut portions of (a publication, film, letter, etc.). 6 to act as a censor of (behaviour, etc.).
▷HISTORY C16: from Latin, from *cēnsēre* to consider, assess
▸**'censorable** ADJECTIVE ▸**censorial** (sɛn'sɔːrɪəl) ADJECTIVE

censorious (sɛn'sɔːrɪəs) ADJECTIVE harshly critical; fault-finding.
▸**cen'soriously** ADVERB ▸**cen'soriousness** NOUN

censorship ('sɛnsəˌʃɪp) NOUN 1 a policy or programme of censoring. 2 the act or system of censoring. 3 *Psychoanal* the activity of the mind in regulating impulses, etc., from the unconscious so that they are modified before reaching the conscious mind.

censurable ('sɛnʃərəbᵊl) ADJECTIVE deserving censure, condemnation, or blame.
▸**'censurableness** *or* **ˌcensura'bility** NOUN ▸**'censurably** ADVERB

censure ('sɛnʃə) NOUN 1 severe disapproval; harsh criticism. ◆ VERB 2 to criticize (someone or something) severely; condemn.
▷HISTORY C14: from Latin *cēnsūra,* from *cēnsēre* to consider, assess
▸**'censurer** NOUN

census ('sɛnsəs) NOUN, *plural* **-suses.** 1 an official periodic count of a population including such information as sex, age, occupation, etc. 2 any offical count: *a traffic census.* 3 (in ancient Rome) a registration of the population and a property evaluation for purposes of taxation.
▷HISTORY C17: from Latin, from *cēnsēre* to assess
▸**'censual** ADJECTIVE

cent (sɛnt) NOUN 1 a monetary unit of American Samoa, Andorra, Antigua and Barbuda, Aruba, Australia, Austria, the Bahamas, Barbados, Belgium, Belize, Bermuda, Bosnia and Hercegovina, Brunei, Canada, the Cayman Islands, Cyprus, Dominica, East Timor, Ecuador, El Salvador, Ethiopia, Fiji, Finland, France, French Guiana, Germany, Greece, Grenada, Guadeloupe, Guam, Guyana, Hong Kong, Ireland, Jamaica, Kenya, Kiribati, Kosovo, Liberia, Luxembourg, Malaysia, Malta, the Marshall Islands, Martinique, Mauritius, Mayotte, Micronesia, Monaco, Montenegro, Namibia, Nauru, the Netherlands, the Netherlands Antilles, New Zealand, the Northern Mariana Islands, Palau, Portugal, Puerto Rico, Réunion, Saint Kitts and Nevis, Saint Lucia, Saint Vincent and the Grenadines, San Marino, the Seychelles, Sierra Leone, Singapore, the Solomon Islands, Somalia, South Africa, Spain, Sri Lanka, Surinam, Swaziland, Taiwan, Tanzania, Trinidad and Tobago, Tuvalu, Uganda, the United States, the Vatican City, the Virgin Islands, and Zimbabwe. It is worth one hundredth of their respective standard units. 2 an interval of pitch between two frequencies f_2 and f_1 equal to 3986.31 log (f_2/f_1); one twelve-hundredth of the interval between two frequencies having the ratio 1:2 (an octave).
▷HISTORY C16: from Latin *centēsimus* hundredth, from *centum* hundred

cental ('sɛntᵊl) NOUN a unit of weight equal to 100 pounds (45.3 kilograms).
▷HISTORY C19: from Latin *centum* hundred

centas ('tsæntæs) NOUN, *plural* **centai** ('tsæntaɪ). a monetary unit of Lithuania, worth one hundredth of a litas.

centaur ('sɛntɔː) NOUN *Greek myth* one of a race of creatures with the head, arms, and torso of a man, and the lower body and legs of a horse.
▷HISTORY C14: from Latin, from Greek *kentauros,* of unknown origin

centaurea (ˌsɛntɔː'rɪə, sɛn'tɔːrɪə) NOUN any plant of the genus *Centaurea,* which includes the cornflower and knapweed.
▷HISTORY C19: ultimately from Greek *Kentauros* the Centaur; see CENTAURY

Centaurus (sɛn'tɔːrəs) NOUN, *Latin genitive* **Centauri** (sɛn'tɔːraɪ). a conspicuous extensive constellation in the S hemisphere, close to the Southern Cross, that contains two first magnitude stars, Alpha Centauri and Beta Centauri, and the globular cluster Omega Centauri. Also called: **The Centaur.**

centaury ('sɛntɔːrɪ) NOUN, *plural* **-ries.** any Eurasian plant of the genus *Centaurium,* esp *C. erythraea,* having purplish-pink flowers and formerly believed to have medicinal properties: family *Gentianaceae.*
▷HISTORY C14: ultimately from Greek *Kentauros* the Centaur; from the legend that Chiron the Centaur divulged its healing properties

centavo (sɛn'tɑːvəʊ) NOUN, *plural* **-vos.** 1 a monetary unit of Argentina, Bolivia, Brazil, Cape Verde, Chile, Colombia, Cuba, the Dominican Republic, Guatemala, Guinea-Bissau, Honduras, Mexico, Mozambique, Nicaragua, and the Philippines. It is worth one hundredth of their respective standard units. 2 a former monetary unit of Ecuador, El Salvador, and Portugal, worth one hundredth of their former standard units.
▷HISTORY Spanish: one hundredth part

centenarian (ˌsɛntɪ'nɛərɪən) NOUN 1 a person who is at least 100 years old. ◆ ADJECTIVE 2 being at least 100 years old. 3 of or relating to a centenarian.

centenary (sɛn'tiːnərɪ) ADJECTIVE 1 of or relating to a period of 100 years. 2 occurring once every 100 years. ◆ NOUN, *plural* **-naries.** 3 a 100th anniversary or its celebration.
▷HISTORY C17: from Latin *centēnārius* of a hundred, from *centēnī* a hundred each, from *centum* hundred

centennial (sɛn'tɛnɪəl) ADJECTIVE 1 relating to, lasting for, or completing a period of 100 years. 2 occurring every 100 years. ◆ NOUN 3 *Chiefly US and Canadian* another name for **centenary.**
▷HISTORY C18: from Latin *centum* hundred, on the model of BIENNIAL
▸**cen'tennially** ADVERB

center ('sɛntə) NOUN, VERB the US spelling of **centre.**

centering ('sɛntərɪŋ) NOUN a US spelling of **centring.**

centesimal (sɛn'tɛsɪməl) NOUN 1 hundredth. ◆ ADJECTIVE 2 relating to division into hundredths.
▷HISTORY C17: from Latin *centēsimus,* from *centum* hundred
▸**cen'tesimally** ADVERB

centesimo (sɛn'tɛsɪˌməʊ) NOUN, *plural* **-mos** *or* **-mi.** a former monetary unit of Italy, San Marino, and the Vatican City worth one hundredth of a lira.
▷HISTORY C19: from Italian, from Latin *centēsimus* hundredth, from *centum* hundred

centésimo (sɛn'tɛsɪˌməʊ) NOUN, *plural* **-mos** *or* **-mi.** a monetary unit of Panama and Uruguay. It is worth one hundredth of their respective standard units.
▷HISTORY C19: from Spanish; see CENTESIMO

centi- *or before a vowel* **cent-** PREFIX 1 denoting one hundredth: *centimetre.* Symbol: c. 2 *Rare* denoting a hundred: *centipede.*
▷HISTORY from French, from Latin *centum* hundred

centiare ('sɛntɪˌɛə; *French* sɑ̃tjar) *or* **centare** ('sɛntɛə; *French* sɑ̃tar) NOUN a unit of area equal to one square metre.
▷HISTORY French, from CENTI- + *are* from Latin *ārea;* see ARE[2], AREA

centigrade ('sɛntɪˌgreɪd) ADJECTIVE 1 a former

name for **Celsius.** ◆ NOUN [2] a unit of angle equal to one hundredth of a grade.

> **Language note** Although still used in meteorology, *centigrade*, when indicating the Celsius scale of temperature, is now usually avoided because of its possible confusion with the hundredth part of a grade.

centigram *or* **centigramme** (ˈsɛntɪˌɡræm) NOUN one hundredth of a gram.

centile (ˈsɛntaɪl) NOUN another word for **percentile.**

centilitre *or US* **centiliter** (ˈsɛntɪˌliːtə) NOUN one hundredth of a litre.

centillion (sɛnˈtɪljən) NOUN, *plural* **-lions** *or* **-lion.** [1] (in Britain and Germany) the number represented as one followed by 600 zeros (10^{600}). [2] (in the US, Canada, and France) the number represented as one followed by 303 zeros (10^{303}).

centime (ˈsɒnˌtiːm; *French* sɑ̃tim) NOUN [1] a monetary unit of Algeria, Benin, Burkina-Faso, Burundi, Cameroon, the Central African Republic, Chad, Comoros, Democratic Republic of Congo, Congo-Brazzaville, Côte d'Ivoire, Djibouti, Equatorial Guinea, French Polynesia, Gabon, Guinea, Guinea-Bissau, Haiti, Liechtenstein, Madagascar, Mali, Mayotte, Morocco, New Caledonia, Niger, Rwanda, Senegal, Switzerland, and Togo. It is worth one hundredth of their respective standard units. [2] a former monetary unit of Andorra, Belgium, France, French Guiana, Guadeloupe, Luxembourg, Martinique, Monaco, and Réunion, worth one hundredth of a franc.
▷**HISTORY** C18: from French, from Old French *centiesme* from Latin *centēsimus* hundredth, from *centum* hundred

centimetre *or US* **centimeter** (ˈsɛntɪˌmiːtə) NOUN one hundredth of a metre.

centimetre-gram-second NOUN See **cgs units.**

céntimo (ˈsɛntɪˌməʊ) NOUN, *plural* **-mos.** [1] a monetary unit of Costa Rica, Paraguay, Peru, and Venezuela. It is worth one hundredth of their respective standard currency units. [2] a former monetary unit of Andorra and Spain, worth one hundredth of a peseta.
▷**HISTORY** from Spanish; see CENTIME

cêntimo (ˈsɛntɪˌməʊ) NOUN, *plural* **-mos.** a monetary unit of Sao Tomê e Principe, worth one hundredth of a dobra.

centimorgan (ˈsɛntɪˌmɔːɡən) NOUN *Genetics* a unit of chromosome length, used in genetic mapping, equal to the length of chromosome over which crossing over occurs with 1 per cent frequency.
▷**HISTORY** C20: named after Thomas Hunt *Morgan* (1866–1945), US biologist

centipede (ˈsɛntɪˌpiːd) NOUN any carnivorous arthropod of the genera *Lithobius, Scutigera,* etc., having a body of between 15 and 190 segments, each bearing one pair of legs: class *Chilopoda.* See also **myriapod.**

centipoise (ˈsɛntɪˌpɔɪz) NOUN one hundredth of a poise. 1 centipoise is equal to 0.001 newton second per square metre.

centner (ˈsɛntnə) NOUN [1] Also called (esp US): **short hundredweight.** a unit of weight equivalent to 100 pounds (45.3 kilograms). [2] (in some European countries) a unit of weight equivalent to 50 kilograms (110.23 pounds). [3] a unit of weight equivalent to 100 kilograms.
▷**HISTORY** C17: from German *Zentner,* ultimately from Latin *centēnārius* of a hundred; see CENTENARY

cento (ˈsɛntəʊ) NOUN, *plural* **-tos.** a piece of writing, esp a poem, composed of quotations from other authors.
▷**HISTORY** C17: from Latin, literally: patchwork garment

CENTO (ˈsɛntəʊ) NOUN ACRONYM FOR Central Treaty Organization; an organization for military and economic cooperation formed in 1959 by the UK, Iran, Pakistan, and Turkey as a successor to the Baghdad Pact: disbanded 1979.

centra (ˈsɛntrə) NOUN a plural of **centrum.**

central (ˈsɛntrəl) ADJECTIVE [1] in, at, of, from, containing, or forming the centre of something: *the central street in a city; the central material of a golf ball.* [2] main, principal, or chief; most important: *the central cause of a problem.* [3] **a** of or relating to the central nervous system. **b** of or relating to the centrum of a vertebra. [4] of, relating to, or denoting a vowel articulated with the tongue held in an intermediate position halfway between the positions for back and front vowels, as for the *a* of English *soda.* [5] (of a force) directed from or towards a point. [6] *Informal* (*immediately postpositive*) used to describe a place where a specified thing, quality, etc. is to be found in abundance: *nostalgia central.*
▶ˈ**centrally** ADVERB

Central African Federation NOUN another name for the **Federation of Rhodesia and Nyasaland.**

Central African Republic NOUN a landlocked country of central Africa: joined with Chad as a territory of French Equatorial Africa in 1910; became an independent republic in 1960; a parliamentary monarchy (1976–79); consists of a huge plateau, mostly savanna, with dense forests in the south; drained chiefly by the Shari and Ubangi Rivers. Official language: French; Sango is the national language. Religion: Christian and animist. Currency: franc. Capital: Bangui. Pop.: 3 577 000 (2001 est.). Area: 622 577 sq. km (240 376 sq. miles). Former names: **Ubangi-Shari** (until 1958), **Central African Empire** (1976–79). French name: **République Centrafricaine** (repyblik sɑ̃trafrikɛn).

Central America NOUN an isthmus joining the continents of North and South America, extending from the S border of Mexico to the NW border of Colombia and consisting of Belize, Guatemala, Honduras, El Salvador, Nicaragua, Costa Rica, and Panama. Area: about 518 000 sq. km (200 000 sq. miles).

Central American ADJECTIVE [1] of or relating to Central America or its inhabitants. ◆ NOUN [2] a native or inhabitant of Central America.

central angle NOUN an angle whose vertex is at the centre of a circle.

central bank NOUN a national bank that does business mainly with a government and with other banks: it regulates the volume and cost of credit.

Central Committee NOUN (in Communist parties) the body responsible for party policy between meetings of the party congress: in practice, it is in charge of day-to-day operations of the party bureaucracy.

Central European Time NOUN the standard time adopted by Western European countries one hour ahead of Greenwich Mean Time, corresponding to British Summer Time. Abbreviation: **CET.**

central heating NOUN a system for heating the rooms of a building by means of radiators or air vents connected by pipes or ducts to a central source of heat.

Central India Agency NOUN a former group of 89 states in India, under the supervision of a British political agent until 1947: most important were Indore, Bhopal, and Rewa.

Central Intelligence Agency NOUN See **CIA.**

centralism (ˈsɛntrəˌlɪzəm) NOUN the principle or act of bringing something under central control; centralization.
▶ˈ**centralist** NOUN, ADJECTIVE ▶ˌ**centralˈistic** ADJECTIVE

centrality (sɛnˈtrælɪtɪ) NOUN, *plural* **-ties.** the state or condition of being central.

centralize *or* **centralise** (ˈsɛntrəˌlaɪz) VERB [1] to draw or move (something) to or towards a centre. [2] to bring or come under central control, esp governmental control.
▶ˌ**centraliˈzation** *or* ˌ**centraliˈsation** NOUN ▶ˈ**centralˌizer** *or* ˈ**centralˌiser** NOUN

Central Karoo (kəˈruː) NOUN an arid plateau of S central South Africa, in Cape Province, separated from the Little Karoo to the southwest by the Swartberg range. Average height: 750 m (2500 ft.).

central limit theorem NOUN *Statistics* the fundamental result that the sum (or mean) of independent identically distributed random variables with finite variance approaches a normally distributed random variable as their number increases, whence in particular if enough samples are repeatedly drawn from any population, the sum of the sample values can be thought of, approximately, as an outcome from a normally distributed random variable.

central locking NOUN a system by which all the doors of a motor vehicle can be locked simultaneously when the driver's door is locked.

central nervous system NOUN the mass of nerve tissue that controls and coordinates the activities of an animal. In vertebrates it consists of the brain and spinal cord. Abbreviation: **CNS.** Compare **autonomic nervous system.**

Central Powers PLURAL NOUN *European history* **a** (before World War I) Germany, Italy, and Austria-Hungary after they were linked by the Triple Alliance in 1882. **b** (during World War I) Germany and Austria-Hungary, together with their allies Turkey and Bulgaria.

central processing unit NOUN the part of a computer that performs logical and arithmetical operations on the data as specified in the instructions. Abbreviation: **CPU.**

Central Provinces PLURAL NOUN **the.** the Canadian provinces of Ontario and Quebec.

Central Provinces and Berar (bɛˈrɑː) NOUN a former province of central India: renamed Madhya Pradesh in 1950, Berar being transferred to Maharashtra in 1956.

Central Region NOUN a former local government region in central Scotland, formed in 1975 from Clackmannanshire, most of Stirlingshire, and parts of Perthshire, West Lothian, Fife, and Kinross-shire; in 1996 it was replaced by the council areas of Stirling, Clackmannanshire, and Falkirk.

central reserve *or* **reservation** NOUN *Brit* the strip, often covered with grass, that separates the two sides of a motorway or dual carriageway. US and Austral name: **median strip.** Canadian name: **median.**

Central Standard Time NOUN [1] one of the standard times used in North America, based on the local time of the 90° meridian, six hours behind Greenwich Mean Time. [2] one of the standard times used in Australia. Abbreviation: **CST.**

central sulcus NOUN a deep cleft in each hemisphere of the brain separating the frontal lobe from the parietal lobe.

central tendency NOUN *Statistics* the tendency of the values of a random variable to cluster around the mean, median, and mode.

centre *or US* **center** (ˈsɛntə) NOUN [1] *Geometry* **a** the midpoint of any line or figure, esp the point within a circle or sphere that is equidistant from any point on the circumference or surface. **b** the point within a body through which a specified force may be considered to act, such as the centre of gravity. [2] the point, axis, or pivot about which a body rotates. [3] a point, area, or part that is approximately in the middle of a larger area or volume. [4] a place at which some specified activity is concentrated: *a shopping centre.* [5] a person or thing that is a focus of interest. [6] a place of activity or influence: *a centre of power.* [7] a person, group, policy, or thing in the middle. [8] (*usually capital*) *Politics* **a** a political party or group favouring moderation, esp the moderate members of a legislative assembly. **b** (*as modifier*): *a Centre-Left alliance.* [9] *Physiol* any part of the central nervous system that regulates a specific function: *respiratory centre.* [10] a bar with a conical point upon which a workpiece or part may be turned or ground. [11] a punch mark or small conical hole in a part to be drilled, which enables the point of the drill to be located accurately. [12] *Sport* **a** a player who plays in the middle of the forward line. **b** the act or an instance of passing the ball from a wing to the middle of the field, court, etc. [13] *Basketball* **a** the position of a player who jumps for the ball at the start of play. **b** the player in this position. [14] *Archery* **a** the ring around the bull's eye. **b** a shot that hits this ring. ◆ VERB [15] to move towards, mark, put, or be at a centre. [16] (*tr*) to focus or bring together: *to centre one's thoughts.* [17] (*intr;* often foll by *on*) to have as a main point of view or theme: *the novel centred on crime.* [18] (*tr*) to adjust or locate (a workpiece or part) using a centre. [19] (*intr;* foll by *on* or *round*) to have as a centre. [20] (*tr*) *Sport* to pass (the ball) into the middle of the field or court.
▷**HISTORY** C14: from Latin *centrum* the stationary

point of a compass, from Greek *kentron* needle, from *kentein* to prick

Centre NOUN [1] ('sɛntə) **the.** the sparsely inhabited central region of Australia. [2] (*French* sɑ̃trə) a region of central France: generally low-lying; drained chiefly by the Rivers Loire, Loir, and Cher.

centre bit NOUN a drilling bit with a central projecting point and two side cutters.

centreboard ('sɛntəˌbɔːd) NOUN a supplementary keel for a sailing vessel, which may be adjusted by raising and lowering. Compare **daggerboard.**

centred dot NOUN *Printing* [1] Also called (esp US and Canadian): **bullet.** a heavy dot (•) used to draw attention to a particular paragraph. [2] a dot placed at a central level in a line of type or writing.

centre-fire ADJECTIVE [1] (of a cartridge) having the primer in the centre of the base. [2] (of a firearm) adapted for such cartridges. ◆ Compare **rim-fire.**

centrefold *or US* **centerfold** ('sɛntəˌfəʊld) NOUN [1] a large coloured illustration folded so that it forms the central spread of a magazine. [2] a photograph of a nude or nearly nude woman (or man) in a magazine on such a spread.

centre forward NOUN *Sport* the central forward in the attack.

centre half *or* **centre back** NOUN *Soccer* a defender who plays in the middle of the defence.

centre of curvature NOUN the point on the normal at a given point on a curve on the concave side of the curve whose distance from the point on the curve is equal to the radius of curvature.

centre of gravity NOUN the point through which the resultant of the gravitational forces on a body always acts.

centre of mass NOUN the point at which the mass of a system could be concentrated without affecting the behaviour of the system under the action of external linear forces.

centre of pressure NOUN [1] *Physics* the point in a body at which the resultant pressure acts when the body is immersed in a fluid. [2] *Aeronautics* the point at which the resultant aerodynamic forces intersect the chord line of the aerofoil.

centre pass NOUN *Hockey* a push or hit made in any direction to start the game or to restart the game after a goal has been scored.

centrepiece ('sɛntəˌpiːs) NOUN an object used as the centre of something, esp for decoration.

centre punch NOUN a small steel tool with a conical tip used to punch a small indentation at the location of the centre of a hole to be drilled.

centre spread NOUN [1] the pair of two facing pages in the middle of a magazine, newspaper, etc., often illustrated. [2] a photograph of a nude or nearly nude woman (or man) in a magazine on such pages.

centre stage NOUN [1] the centre point on a stage. [2] the main focus of attention.

centre three-quarter NOUN *Rugby* either of two middle players on the three-quarter line.

centri- COMBINING FORM a variant of **centro-.**

centric ('sɛntrɪk) *or* **centrical** ADJECTIVE [1] being central or having a centre. [2] relating to or originating at a nerve centre. [3] *Botany* **a** Also: **concentric.** (of vascular bundles) having one type of tissue completely surrounding the other. **b** (of leaves, such as those of the onion) cylindrical.
▸ **'centrically** ADVERB ▸ **centricity** (sɛn'trɪsɪtɪ) NOUN

-centric SUFFIX FORMING ADJECTIVES having a centre as specified: *heliocentric.*
▷ **HISTORY** abstracted from ECCENTRIC, CONCENTRIC, etc.

centrifugal (sɛn'trɪfjʊgᵊl, 'sɛntrɪˌfjuːgᵊl) ADJECTIVE [1] acting, moving, or tending to move away from a centre. Compare **centripetal.** [2] of, concerned with, or operated by centrifugal force: *centrifugal pump.* [3] *Botany* (esp of certain inflorescences) developing outwards from a centre. [4] *Physiol* another word for **efferent.** ◆ NOUN [5] any device that uses centrifugal force for its action. [6] the rotating perforated drum in a centrifuge.
▷ **HISTORY** C18: from New Latin *centrifugus,* from CENTRI- + Latin *fugere* to flee
▸ **cen'trifugally** ADVERB

centrifugal brake NOUN a safety mechanism on a hoist, crane, etc., that consists of revolving brake shoes that are driven outwards by centrifugal force into contact with a fixed brake drum when the rope drum revolves at excessive speed.

centrifugal clutch NOUN *Engineering* an automatic clutch in which the friction surfaces are engaged by weighted levers acting under centrifugal force at a certain speed of rotation.

centrifugal force NOUN a fictitious force that can be thought of as acting outwards on any body that rotates or moves along a curved path.

centrifugal pump NOUN a pump having a high-speed rotating impeller whose blades throw the water outwards.

centrifuge ('sɛntrɪˌfjuːdʒ) NOUN [1] any of various rotating machines that separate liquids from solids or dispersions of one liquid in another, by the action of centrifugal force. [2] any of various rotating devices for subjecting human beings or animals to varying accelerations for experimental purposes. ◆ VERB [3] (*tr*) to subject to the action of a centrifuge.
▸ **centrifugation** (ˌsɛntrɪfjʊ'geɪʃən) NOUN

centring ('sɛntrɪŋ) *or US* **centering** NOUN a temporary structure, esp one made of timber, used to support an arch during construction.

centriole ('sɛntrɪˌəʊl) NOUN either of two rodlike bodies in most animal cells that form the poles of the spindle during mitosis.
▷ **HISTORY** C19: from New Latin *centriolum,* diminutive of Latin *centrum* CENTRE

centripetal (sɛn'trɪpɪtᵊl, 'sɛntrɪˌpiːtᵊl) ADJECTIVE [1] acting, moving, or tending to move towards a centre. Compare **centrifugal.** [2] of, concerned with, or operated by centripetal force. [3] *Botany* (esp of certain inflorescences) developing from the outside towards the centre. [4] *Physiol* another word for **afferent.**
▷ **HISTORY** C17: from New Latin *centripetus* seeking the centre; see CENTRI-, -PETAL
▸ **cen'tripetally** ADVERB

centripetal force NOUN a force that acts inwards on any body that rotates or moves along a curved path and is directed towards the centre of curvature of the path or the axis of rotation. Compare **centrifugal force.**

centrist ('sɛntrɪst) NOUN a person holding moderate political views.
▸ **'centrism** NOUN

centro-, centri-, *or before a vowel* **centr-** COMBINING FORM denoting a centre: *centroclinal; centromere; centrosome; centrosphere; centrist.*
▷ **HISTORY** from Greek *kentron* CENTRE

centrobaric (ˌsɛntrəʊ'bærɪk) ADJECTIVE of or concerned with a centre of gravity.
▷ **HISTORY** C18: from Late Greek *kentrobarikos,* from Greek *kentron bareos* centre of gravity

centroclinal (ˌsɛntrəʊ'klaɪnᵊl) ADJECTIVE *Geology* of, relating to, or designating a rock formation in which the strata slope down and in towards a central point or area.

centroid ('sɛntrɔɪd) NOUN **a** the centre of mass of an object of uniform density, esp of a geometric figure. **b** (of a finite set) the point whose coordinates are the mean values of the coordinates of the points of the set.

centrolecithal (ˌsɛntrəʊ'lɛsɪθəl) ADJECTIVE *Zoology* (of animal eggs) having a centrally located yolk.

centromere ('sɛntrəˌmɪə) NOUN the dense nonstaining region of a chromosome that attaches it to the spindle during mitosis.
▸ **centromeric** (ˌsɛntrə'mɛrɪk, -'mɪərɪk) ADJECTIVE

centrosome ('sɛntrəˌsəʊm) NOUN a small body in a cell where microtubules are produced. In animal cells it surrounds the centriole. Also called: **centrosphere.**
▸ **centrosomic** (ˌsɛntrə'sɒmɪk) ADJECTIVE

centrosphere ('sɛntrəˌsfɪə) NOUN [1] a former name for **core (sense 4).** [2] another name for **centrosome.**

centrum ('sɛntrəm) NOUN, *plural* **-trums** *or* **-tra** (-trə). the main part or body of a vertebra.
▷ **HISTORY** C19: from Latin: CENTRE

centum ('sɛntəm) ADJECTIVE denoting or belonging to the Indo-European languages in which original velar stops (*k*) were not palatalized, namely languages of the Hellenic, Italic, Celtic, Germanic, Anatolian, and Tocharian branches. Compare **satem.**
▷ **HISTORY** Latin: HUNDRED, chosen because the *c* represents the Indo-European *k*

centuplicate VERB (sɛn'tjuːplɪˌkeɪt) [1] (*tr*) to increase 100 times. ◆ ADJECTIVE (sɛn'tjuːplɪkɪt, -ˌkeɪt) [2] increased a hundredfold. ◆ NOUN (sɛn'tjuːplɪkɪt, -ˌkeɪt) [3] one hundredfold. ◆ Also: **centuple** ('sɛntjʊpᵊl).
▷ **HISTORY** C17: from Late Latin *centuplicāre,* from *centuplex* hundredfold, from Latin *centum* hundred + *-plex* -fold
▸ **cenˌtupli'cation** NOUN

centurial (sɛn'tjʊərɪəl) ADJECTIVE [1] of or relating to a Roman century. [2] *Rare* involving a period of 100 years.

centurion (sɛn'tjʊərɪən) NOUN the officer commanding a Roman century.
▷ **HISTORY** C14: from Latin *centuriō,* from *centuria* CENTURY

century ('sɛntʃərɪ) NOUN, *plural* **-ries.** [1] a period of 100 years. [2] one of the successive periods of 100 years dated before or after an epoch or event, esp the birth of Christ. [3] **a** a score or grouping of 100: *to score a century in cricket.* **b** *Chiefly US* (*as modifier*): *the basketball team passed the century mark in their last game.* [4] (in ancient Rome) a unit of foot soldiers, originally 100 strong, later consisting of 60 to 80 men. See also **maniple.** [5] (in ancient Rome) a division of the people for purposes of voting. [6] (*often capital*) a style of type.
▷ **HISTORY** C16: from Latin *centuria,* from *centum* hundred

century plant NOUN an agave, *Agave americana,* native to tropical America but naturalized elsewhere, having very large spiny greyish leaves and greenish flowers on a tall fleshy stalk. It blooms only once in its life, after 10 to 30 years (formerly thought to flower after a century). Also called: **American aloe.**

ceorl (tʃɛəl) NOUN a freeman of the lowest class in Anglo-Saxon England.
▷ **HISTORY** Old English; see CHURL
▸ **'ceorlish** ADJECTIVE

cep (sɛp) NOUN another name for **porcino.**
▷ **HISTORY** C19: from French *cèpe,* from Gascon dialect *cep,* from Latin *cippus* stake

cepaceous (sɪ'peɪʃəs) ADJECTIVE *Botany* having an onion-like smell or taste.
▷ **HISTORY** from Latin *caepa* onion + -ACEOUS

cephalad ('sɛfəˌlæd) ADVERB *Anatomy* towards the head or anterior part. Compare **caudad.**

cephalalgia (ˌsɛfə'lældʒɪə, -dʒə) NOUN a technical name for **headache.**

cephalic (sɪ'fælɪk) ADJECTIVE [1] of or relating to the head. [2] situated in, on, or near the head.

-cephalic *or* **-cephalous** ADJECTIVE COMBINING FORM indicating skull or head; -headed: *brachycephalic.*
▷ **HISTORY** from Greek *-kephalos*
▸ **-cephaly** *or* **-cephalism** NOUN COMBINING FORM

cephalic index NOUN the ratio of the greatest width of the human head to its greatest length, multiplied by 100.

cephalic version NOUN another name for **version** (sense 5).

cephalin ('sɛfəlɪn, 'kɛf-) *or* **kephalin** ('kɛfəlɪn) NOUN a phospholipid, similar to lecithin, that occurs in the nerve tissue and brain. Systematic name: **phosphatidylethanolamine.**

cephalization *or* **cephalisation** (ˌsɛfəlaɪ'zeɪʃən) NOUN (in the evolution of animals) development of a head by the concentration of feeding and sensory organs and nervous tissue at the anterior end.

cephalo- *or before a vowel* **cephal-** COMBINING FORM indicating the head: *cephalopod.*
▷ **HISTORY** via Latin from Greek *kephalo-,* from *kephale* head

cephalochordate (ˌsɛfələʊ'kɔːdeɪt) NOUN [1] any chordate animal of the subphylum *Cephalochordata,* having a fishlike body and no vertebral column; a lancelet. ◆ ADJECTIVE [2] of, relating to, or belonging to the *Cephalochordata.*

cephalometer (ˌsɛfə'lɒmɪtə) NOUN an instrument for positioning the human head for X-ray examination in cephalometry.

cephalometry (ˌsɛfəˈlɒmɪtrɪ) NOUN 1 measurement of the dimensions of the human head by radiography: used mainly in orthodontics. 2 measurement of the dimensions of the fetal head by radiography or ultrasound.
▸**cephalometric** (ˌsɛfələʊˈmɛtrɪk) ADJECTIVE

Cephalonia (ˌsɛfəˈləʊnɪə) NOUN a mountainous island in the Ionian Sea, the largest of the Ionian Islands, off the W coast of Greece. Pop.: 32 474 (1991). Area: 935 sq. km (365 sq. miles). Modern Greek name: **Kephallinía.**

cephalopod (ˈsɛfələˌpɒd) NOUN 1 any marine mollusc of the class *Cephalopoda*, characterized by well-developed head and eyes and a ring of sucker-bearing tentacles. The group also includes the octopuses, squids, cuttlefish, and pearly nautilus. ◆ ADJECTIVE *also* **cephalopodic, cephalopodous** (ˌsɛfəˈlɒpədəs). 2 of, relating to, or belonging to the *Cephalopoda*.
▸ˌ**cephaˈlopodan** ADJECTIVE, NOUN

cephalosporin (ˌsɛfələʊˈspɔːrɪn) NOUN any of a group of broad-spectrum antibiotics obtained from fungi of the genus *Cephalosporium*.

cephalothorax (ˌsɛfələʊˈθɔːræks) NOUN, *plural* **-raxes** *or* **-races** (-rəˌsiːz). the anterior part of many crustaceans and some other arthropods consisting of a united head and thorax.
▸**cephalothoracic** (ˌsɛfələʊθəˈræsɪk) ADJECTIVE

-cephalus NOUN COMBINING FORM denoting a cephalic abnormality: *hydrocephalus*.
▷HISTORY New Latin *-cephalus;* see -CEPHALIC

Cepheid variable (ˈsiːfɪɪd) NOUN *Astronomy* any of a class of variable stars with regular cycles of variations in luminosity (most ranging from three to fifty days). There is a relationship between the periods of variation and the absolute magnitudes, which is used for measuring the distance of such stars.

Cepheus[1] (ˈsiːfjuːs) NOUN, *Latin genitive* **Cephei** (ˈsiːfɪˌaɪ). a faint constellation in the N hemisphere near Cassiopeia and the Pole Star. See also **Cepheid variable.**
▷HISTORY from Latin *Cēpheus* named after the mythical king

Cepheus[2] (ˈsiːfjuːs) NOUN *Greek myth* a king of Ethiopia, father of Andromeda and husband of Cassiopeia.

CER ABBREVIATION FOR Closer Economic Relations: a trade agreement between Australia and New Zealand signed in 1983.

ceraceous (sɪˈreɪʃəs) ADJECTIVE waxlike or waxy.
▷HISTORY C18: from Latin *cēra* wax

Ceram (sɪˈræm) NOUN a variant spelling of **Seram.**

ceramal (səˈreɪməl) NOUN another name for **cermet.**
▷HISTORY C20: from CERAM(IC) + AL(LOY)

ceramic (sɪˈræmɪk) NOUN 1 a hard brittle material made by firing clay and similar substances. 2 an object made from such a material. ◆ ADJECTIVE 3 of, relating to, or made from a ceramic: *this vase is ceramic*. 4 of or relating to ceramics: *ceramic arts and crafts*.
▷HISTORY C19: from Greek *keramikos*, from *keramos* potter's clay, pottery

ceramic hob NOUN (on an electric cooker) a flat ceramic cooking surface having heating elements fitted on the underside, usually patterned to show the areas where heat is produced.

ceramic oxide NOUN a compound of oxygen with nonorganic material: recently discovered to act as a high-temperature superconductor.

ceramics (sɪˈræmɪks) NOUN (*functioning as singular*) the art and techniques of producing articles of clay, porcelain, etc.
▸**ceramist** (ˈsɛrəmɪst) *or* **ceˈramicist** NOUN

ceramide (ˈsɛrəˌmaɪd) NOUN any of a class of biologically important compounds used as moisturizers in skin-care preparations.

cerargyrite (sɪˈrɑːdʒɪˌraɪt) NOUN another name for **chloroargyrite.**
▷HISTORY C19: from Greek *keras* horn + *arguros* silver + -ITE[1]

cerastes (səˈræstiːz) NOUN, *plural* **-tes.** any venomous snake of the genus *Cerastes*, esp the horned viper.
▷HISTORY C16: from Latin: horned serpent, from Greek *kerastēs* horned, from *keras* horn

cerate (ˈsɪərɪt, -reɪt) NOUN a hard ointment or medicated paste consisting of lard or oil mixed with wax or resin.
▷HISTORY C16: from Latin *cērātum*, from *cēra* wax

cerated (ˈsɪəreɪtɪd) ADJECTIVE (of certain birds, such as the falcon) having a cere.

cerato- *or before a vowel* **cerat-** COMBINING FORM 1 denoting horn or a hornlike part: *ceratodus*. 2 *Anatomy* denoting the cornea. ◆ Also: **kerato-.**
▷HISTORY from Greek *kerat-*, *keras* horn

ceratodus (sɪˈrætədəs, ˌsɛrəˈtəʊdəs) NOUN, *plural* **-duses.** any of various extinct lungfish constituting the genus *Ceratodus*, common in Cretaceous and Triassic times. Compare **barramunda.**
▷HISTORY C19: New Latin, from CERATO- + Greek *odous* tooth

ceratoid (ˈsɛrəˌtɔɪd) ADJECTIVE having the shape or texture of animal horn.

Cerberus (ˈsɜːbərəs) NOUN 1 *Greek myth* a dog, usually represented as having three heads, that guarded the entrance to Hades. 2 **a sop to Cerberus.** a bribe or something given to propitiate a potential source of danger or problems.
▸**Cerberean** (səˈbɪərɪən) ADJECTIVE

cercal (ˈsɜːkəl) ADJECTIVE *Zoology* 1 of or relating to a tail. 2 of or relating to the cerci.

cercaria (səˈkɛərɪə) NOUN, *plural* **-iae** (-ɪˌiː). one of the larval forms of trematode worms. It has a short forked tail and resembles an immature adult.
▷HISTORY C19: New Latin, literally: tailed creature, from Greek *kerkos* tail
▸**cerˈcarial** ADJECTIVE ▸**cerˈcarian** ADJECTIVE, NOUN

cercis (ˈsɜːsɪs) NOUN any tree or shrub of the leguminous genus *Cercis*, which includes the redbud and Judas tree.
▷HISTORY C19: New Latin, from Greek *kerkis* weaver's shuttle, Judas tree

cercopithecoid (ˌsɜːkəʊpɪˈθiːkɔɪd) ADJECTIVE 1 of, relating to, or belonging to the primate superfamily *Cercopithecoidea* (Old World monkeys). ◆ NOUN *also* **cercopithecid** (ˌsɜːkəʊpɪˈθiːsɪd). 2 an Old World monkey.
▷HISTORY C19: from Latin *cercopithēcus* monkey with a tail (from Greek *kerkopithēkos*, from *kerkos* tail + *pithēkos* ape) + -OID

cercus (ˈsɜːkəs) NOUN, *plural* **-ci** (-siː). one of a pair of sensory appendages at the tip of the abdomen of some insects and other arthropods.
▷HISTORY C19: from New Latin, from Greek *kerkos* tail

cere[1] (sɪə) NOUN a soft waxy swelling, containing the nostrils, at the base of the upper beak in such birds as the parrot.
▷HISTORY C15: from Old French *cire* wax, from Latin *cēra*

cere[2] (sɪə) VERB (*tr*) to wrap (a corpse) in a cerecloth.
▷HISTORY C15: from Latin *cērāre*, from *cēra* wax

cereal (ˈsɪərɪəl) NOUN 1 any grass that produces an edible grain, such as oat, rye, wheat, rice, maize, sorghum, and millet. 2 the grain produced by such a plant. 3 any food made from this grain, esp breakfast food. 4 (*modifier*) of or relating to any of these plants or their products: *cereal farming*.
▷HISTORY C19: from Latin *cereālis* concerning agriculture, of CERES[1]

cerebellar syndrome NOUN a disease of the cerebellum characterized by unsteady movements and mispronunciation of words. Also called: **Nonne's syndrome.**

cerebellum (ˌsɛrɪˈbɛləm) NOUN, *plural* **-lums** *or* **-la** (-lə). one of the major divisions of the vertebrate brain, situated in man above the medulla oblongata and beneath the cerebrum, whose function is coordination of voluntary movements and maintenance of bodily equilibrium.
▷HISTORY C16: from Latin, diminutive of CEREBRUM
▸ˌ**cereˈbellar** ADJECTIVE

cerebral (ˈsɛrɪbrəl; *US also* səˈriːbrəl) ADJECTIVE 1 of or relating to the cerebrum or to the entire brain. 2 involving intelligence rather than emotions or instinct. 3 *Phonetics* another word for **cacuminal.** ◆ NOUN 4 *Phonetics* a consonant articulated in the manner of a cacuminal consonant.
▸ˈ**cerebrally** ADVERB

cerebral dominance NOUN the normal tendency for one half of the brain, usually the left cerebral hemisphere in right-handed people, to exercise more control over certain functions (e.g. handedness and language) than the other.

cerebral haemorrhage NOUN bleeding from an artery in the brain, which in severe cases causes a stroke.

cerebral hemisphere NOUN either half of the cerebrum.

cerebral palsy NOUN a nonprogressive impairment of muscular function and weakness of the limbs, caused by lack of oxygen to the brain immediately after birth, brain injury during birth, or viral infection.

cerebrate (ˈsɛrɪˌbreɪt) VERB (*intr*) *Usually facetious* to use the mind; think; ponder; consider.

cerebration (ˌsɛrɪˈbreɪʃən) NOUN the act of thinking; consideration; thought.
▷HISTORY C19: from Latin *cerebrum* brain

cerebro- *or before a vowel* **cerebr-** COMBINING FORM indicating the brain: *cerebrospinal*.
▷HISTORY from CEREBRUM

cerebroside (ˈsɛrɪbrəʊˌsaɪd) NOUN *Biochem* any glycolipid in which *N*-acyl sphingosine is combined with glucose or galactose: occurs in the myelin sheaths of nerves.

cerebrospinal (ˌsɛrɪbrəʊˈspaɪnəl) ADJECTIVE of or relating to the brain and spinal cord.

cerebrospinal fluid NOUN the clear colourless fluid in the spaces inside and around the spinal cord and brain. Abbreviation: **CSF.**

cerebrospinal meningitis *or* **fever** NOUN an acute infectious form of meningitis caused by the bacterium *Neisseria meningitidis*, characterized by high fever, skin rash, delirium, stupor, and sometimes coma. Also called: **epidemic meningitis.**

cerebrotonia (ˌsɛrɪbrəʊˈtəʊnɪə) NOUN a personality type characterized by restraint, alertness, and an intellectual approach to life: said to be correlated with an ectomorph body type. Compare **somatotonia, viscerotonia.**

cerebrovascular (ˌsɛrɪbrəʊˈvæskjʊlə) ADJECTIVE of or relating to the blood vessels and the blood supply of the brain.

cerebrovascular accident *or* **cerebral vascular accident** NOUN a sudden interruption of the blood supply to the brain caused by rupture of an artery in the brain (**cerebral haemorrhage**) or the blocking of a blood vessel, as by a clot of blood (**cerebral occlusion**). See **apoplexy, stroke** (sense 4).

cerebrum (ˈsɛrɪbrəm) NOUN, *plural* **-brums** *or* **-bra** (-brə). 1 the anterior portion of the brain of vertebrates, consisting of two lateral hemispheres joined by a thick band of fibres: the dominant part of the brain in man, associated with intellectual function, emotion, and personality. See **telencephalon.** 2 the brain considered as a whole. 3 the main neural bundle or ganglion of certain invertebrates.
▷HISTORY C17: from Latin: the brain
▸ˈ**cereˌbroid** ADJECTIVE ▸**cerebric** (ˈsɛrɪbrɪk) ADJECTIVE

cerecloth (ˈsɪəˌklɒθ) NOUN waxed waterproof cloth of a kind formerly used as a shroud.
▷HISTORY C15: from earlier *cered cloth*, from Latin *cērāre* to wax; see CERE[2]

Ceredigion (ˌkɛrəˈdɪgjən) NOUN a county of W Wales, on Cardigan Bay: created in 1996 from part of Dyfed; corresponds to the former Cardiganshire (abolished 1974): mainly agricultural, with the Cambrian Mountains in the E and N. Administrative centre: Aberaeron. Pop.: 75 384 (2001). Area: 1793 sq. km (692 sq. miles).

cerement (ˈsɪəmənt) NOUN 1 another name for **cerecloth.** 2 any burial clothes.
▷HISTORY C17: from French *cirement*, from *cirer* to wax; see CERE[2]

ceremonial (ˌsɛrɪˈməʊnɪəl) ADJECTIVE 1 involving or relating to ceremony or ritual. ◆ NOUN 2 the observance of formality, esp in etiquette. 3 a plan for formal observances on a particular occasion; ritual. 4 *Christianity* **a** the prescribed order of rites and ceremonies. **b** a book containing this.
▸ˌ**cereˈmonialism** NOUN ▸ˌ**cereˈmonialist** NOUN
▸ˌ**cereˈmonially** ADVERB

ceremonious (ˌsɛrɪˈməʊnɪəs) ADJECTIVE 1 especially or excessively polite or formal. 2 observing ceremony; involving formalities.
▸ˌ**cereˈmoniously** ADVERB ▸ˌ**cereˈmoniousness** NOUN

ceremony ('sɛrɪmənɪ) NOUN, *plural* **-nies.** 1 a formal act or ritual, often set by custom or tradition, performed in observation of an event or anniversary: *a ceremony commemorating Shakespeare's birth.* 2 a religious rite or series of rites. 3 a courteous gesture or act: *the ceremony of toasting the Queen.* 4 ceremonial observances or gestures collectively: *the ceremony of a monarchy.* 5 **stand on ceremony.** to insist on or act with excessive formality. 6 **without ceremony.** in a casual or informal manner.
▷**HISTORY** C14: from Medieval Latin *cēremōnia,* from Latin *caerimōnia* what is sacred, a religious rite

Ceres[1] ('sɪəri:z) NOUN the Roman goddess of agriculture. Greek counterpart: **Demeter.**

Ceres[2] ('sɪəri:z) NOUN the largest asteroid and the first to be discovered. It has a diameter of 930 kilometres.

ceresin ('sɛrɪsɪn) NOUN a white wax extracted from ozocerite.
▷**HISTORY** C19: irregularly from Latin *cēra* wax

cereus ('sɪərɪəs) NOUN 1 any tropical American cactus of the genus *Cereus,* esp *C. jamacaru* of N Brazil, which grows to a height of 13 metres (40 feet). 2 any of several similar and related cacti, such as the night-blooming cereus.
▷**HISTORY** C18: from New Latin, from Latin *cēreus* a wax taper, from *cēra* wax

ceria ('sɪərɪə) NOUN another name (not in technical usage) for **ceric oxide.**
▷**HISTORY** New Latin, from CERIUM

ceric ('sɪərɪk) ADJECTIVE of or containing cerium in the tetravalent state.

ceric oxide NOUN a white or yellow solid used in ceramics, enamels, and radiation shields. Formula: CeO_2. Also called: **cerium dioxide, ceria.**

ceriferous (sɪ'rɪfərəs) ADJECTIVE *Biology* producing or bearing wax.

cerise (sə'ri:z, -'ri:s) NOUN **a** a moderate to dark red colour. **b** (*as adjective*): *a cerise scarf.*
▷**HISTORY** C19: from French: CHERRY

cerium ('sɪərɪəm) NOUN a malleable ductile steel-grey element of the lanthanide series of metals, used in lighter flints and as a reducing agent in metallurgy. Symbol: Ce; atomic no.: 58; atomic wt.: 140.115; valency: 3 or 4; relative density: 6.770; melting pt.: 798°C; boiling pt.: 3443°C.
▷**HISTORY** C19: New Latin, from CERES (the asteroid) + -IUM

cerium metals PLURAL NOUN the metals lanthanum, cerium, praseodymium, neodymium, promethium, and samarium, forming a sub-group of the lanthanides.

cermet ('sɜ:mɪt) NOUN any of several materials consisting of a metal matrix with ceramic particles disseminated through it. They are hard and resistant to high temperatures. Also called: **ceramal.**
▷**HISTORY** C20: from CER(AMIC) + MET(AL)

CERN (sɜ:n) NOUN ACRONYM FOR Conseil Européen pour la Recherche Nucléaire; an organization of European states with a centre in Geneva for research in high-energy particle physics, now called the European Laboratory for Particle Physics.

Cernăuţi (tʃernə'utsj) NOUN the Romanian name for **Chernovtsy.**

cernuous ('sɜ:njʊəs) ADJECTIVE *Botany* (of some flowers or buds) drooping.
▷**HISTORY** C17: from Latin *cernuus* leaning forwards, of obscure origin

cero ('sɪərəʊ, 'sɪrəʊ) NOUN, *plural* **-ro** *or* **-ros.** 1 a large spiny-finned food fish, *Scomberomorus regalis,* of warm American coastal regions of the Atlantic: family *Scombridae* (mackerels, tunnies, etc.). 2 any similar or related fish.
▷**HISTORY** C19: from Spanish: saw, sawfish, altered spelling of SIERRA

cero- COMBINING FORM indicating the use of wax: *ceroplastic.*
▷**HISTORY** from Greek *kēros* wax

Ceroc (sə'rɒk) NOUN *Trademark* a form of dance combining elements of jive and salsa.

cerography (sɪə'rɒgrəfɪ) NOUN the art of engraving on a waxed plate on which a printing surface is created by electrotyping.
▸**cerographic** (ˌsɪərəʊ'græfɪk) *or* ˌ**cero'graphical** ADJECTIVE ▸**ce'rographist** NOUN

ceroplastic (ˌsɪərəʊ'plæstɪk) ADJECTIVE 1 relating to wax modelling. 2 modelled in wax.

ceroplastics (ˌsɪərəʊ'plæstɪks) NOUN (*functioning as singular*) the art of wax modelling.

cerotic acid (sɪ'rɒtɪk) NOUN another name (not in technical usage) for **hexacosanoic acid.**

cerotype ('sɪərəˌtaɪp) NOUN a process for preparing a printing plate by engraving a wax-coated copper plate and then using this as a mould for an electrotype.

cerous ('sɪərəs) ADJECTIVE of or containing cerium in the trivalent state.
▷**HISTORY** C19: from CERIUM + -OUS

Cerro de Pasco (*Spanish* 'θɛrrɔ ðe 'pasko) NOUN a town in central Peru, in the Andes: one of the highest towns in the world, 4400 m (14 436 ft.) above sea level; mining centre. Pop.: 62 749 (1993).

Cerro Gordo (*Spanish* 'θɛrrɔ 'gorðo) NOUN a mountain pass in E Mexico, between Veracruz and Jalapa: site of a battle in the Mexican War (1847) in which American forces under General Scott decisively defeated the Mexicans.

cert (sɜ:t) NOUN *Informal* something that is a certainty, esp a horse that is certain to win a race (esp in the phrase **a dead cert**).

certain ('sɜ:tən) ADJECTIVE 1 (*postpositive*) positive and confident about the truth of something; convinced: *I am certain that he wrote a book.* 2 (*usually postpositive*) definitely known: *it is certain that they were on the bus.* 3 (*usually postpositive*) sure; bound; destined: *he was certain to fail.* 4 decided or settled upon; fixed: *the date is already certain for the invasion.* 5 unfailing; reliable: *his judgment is certain.* 6 moderate or minimum: *to a certain extent.* 7 **make certain of.** to ensure (that one will get something); confirm. ◆ ADVERB 8 **for certain.** definitely; without a doubt: *he will win for certain.* ◆ DETERMINER 9 **a** known but not specified or named: *certain people may doubt this.* **b** (*as pronoun; functioning as plural*): *certain of the members have not paid their subscriptions.* 10 named but not known: *he had written to a certain Mrs Smith.*
▷**HISTORY** C13: from Old French, from Latin *certus* sure, fixed, from *cernere* to discern, decide

certainly ('sɜ:tənlɪ) ADVERB 1 with certainty; without doubt: *he certainly rides very well.* ◆ SENTENCE SUBSTITUTE 2 by all means; definitely: used in answer to questions.

certainty ('sɜ:təntɪ) NOUN, *plural* **-ties.** 1 the condition of being certain. 2 something established as certain or inevitable. 3 **for a certainty.** without doubt.

CertEd (in Britain) ABBREVIATION FOR Certificate in Education.

certes ('sɜ:tɪz) ADVERB *Archaic* with certainty; truly.
▷**HISTORY** C13: from Old French, ultimately from Latin *certus* CERTAIN

certifiable ('sɜ:tɪˌfaɪəbəl) ADJECTIVE 1 capable of being certified. 2 fit to be certified as insane.
▸'**certiˌfiably** ADVERB

certificate NOUN (sə'tɪfɪkɪt) 1 an official document attesting the truth of the facts stated, as of birth, marital status, death, health, completion of an academic course, ability to practise a profession, etc. 2 short for **share certificate.** ◆ VERB (sə'tɪfɪˌkeɪt) 3 (*tr*) to authorize by or present with an official document.
▷**HISTORY** C15: from Old French *certificat,* from *certifier* CERTIFY
▸**cer'tificatory** ADJECTIVE

certificate of deposit NOUN a negotiable certificate issued by a bank in return for a deposit of money for a term of up to five years. Abbreviation: **CD.**

certificate of incorporation NOUN *Company law* a signed statement by the Registrar of Companies that a company is duly incorporated.

certificate of origin NOUN a document stating the name of the country that produced a specified shipment of goods: often required before importation of goods.

Certificate of Secondary Education NOUN See **CSE.**

certificate of unruliness NOUN (in Britain) the decision of a juvenile court that a young person on remand is too unmanageable for local-authority care and should be taken into custody.

certification (ˌsɜ:tɪfɪ'keɪʃən) NOUN 1 the act of certifying or state of being certified. 2 *Law* a document attesting the truth of a fact or statement.

certified ('sɜ:tɪˌfaɪd) ADJECTIVE 1 holding or guaranteed by a certificate. 2 endorsed or guaranteed: *a certified cheque.* 3 (of a person) declared legally insane.

certified accountant NOUN (in Britain) a member of the Chartered Association of Certified Accountants, who is authorized to audit company accounts. Compare **chartered accountant, certified public accountant.**

certified public accountant NOUN (in the US) a public accountant certified to have met state legal requirements. Compare **certified accountant.**

certify ('sɜ:tɪˌfaɪ) VERB **-fies, -fying, -fied.** 1 to confirm or attest (to), usually in writing: *the letter certified her age.* 2 (*tr*) to endorse or guarantee (that certain required standards have been met). 3 to give reliable information or assurances: *he certified that it was Walter's handwriting.* 4 (*tr*) to declare legally insane. 5 (*tr*) *US and Canadian* (of a bank) to state in writing on (a cheque) that payment is guaranteed.
▷**HISTORY** C14: from Old French *certifier,* from Medieval Latin *certificāre* to make certain, from Latin *certus* CERTAIN + *facere* to make
▸'**certiˌfier** NOUN

certiorari (ˌsɜ:tɪɔ:'rɛəraɪ) NOUN *Law* an order of a superior court directing that a record of proceedings in a lower court be sent up for review. See also **mandamus, prohibition.**
▷**HISTORY** C15: from legal Latin: to be informed

certitude ('sɜ:tɪˌtju:d) NOUN confidence; certainty.
▷**HISTORY** C15: from Church Latin *certitūdō,* from Latin *certus* CERTAIN

cerulean (sɪ'ru:lɪən) NOUN **a** a deep blue colour; azure. **b** (*as adjective*): *a cerulean sea.*
▷**HISTORY** C17: from Latin *caeruleus,* probably from *caelum* sky

cerumen (sɪ'ru:mɛn) NOUN the soft brownish-yellow wax secreted by glands in the auditory canal of the external ear. Nontechnical name: **earwax.**
▷**HISTORY** C18: from New Latin, from Latin *cēra* wax + ALBUMEN
▸**ce'ruminous** ADJECTIVE

ceruse (sə'ru:s) NOUN another name for **white lead** (sense 1).
▷**HISTORY** C14: from Old French *céruse,* from Latin *cērussa,* perhaps ultimately from Greek *kēros* wax

cerussite *or* **cerusite** ('sɪərəˌsaɪt) NOUN a usually white mineral, found in veins. It is a source of lead. Composition: lead carbonate. Formula: $PbCO_3$. Crystal structure: orthorhombic. Also called: **white lead ore.**
▷**HISTORY** C19: from Latin *cērussa* (see CERUSE) + -ITE[1]

cervelat ('sɜ:vəˌlæt, -ˌlɑ:) NOUN a smoked sausage made from pork and beef.
▷**HISTORY** C17: via obsolete French from Italian *cervellata*

cervena (ˌsɜ:'vɛnə) NOUN *Trademark NZ* farm-produced venison.

cervical ('sɜ:vɪkəl, sə'vaɪ-) ADJECTIVE of or relating to the neck or cervix.
▷**HISTORY** C17: from New Latin *cervīcālis,* from Latin *cervīx* neck

cervical smear NOUN *Med* a smear of cellular material taken from the neck (cervix) of the uterus for detection of cancer. Also called: **Pap test** *or* **smear.**

cervicitis (ˌsɜ:vɪ'saɪtɪs) NOUN inflammation of the neck of the uterus.

cervicography (ˌsɜ:vɪ'kɒgrəfɪ) NOUN *Med* a method of cervical screening in which the neck of the uterus is photographed to facilitate the early detection of cancer.

cervicum ('sɜ:vɪkəm, sə'vaɪ-) NOUN *Zoology* the flexible region between the prothorax and head in insects.

cervid ('sɜ:vɪd) NOUN 1 any ruminant mammal of the family *Cervidae,* including the deer, characterized by the presence of antlers. ◆ ADJECTIVE 2 of, relating to, or belonging to the *Cervidae.*
▷**HISTORY** C19: from New Latin *Cervidae,* from Latin *cervus* deer

Cervin (sɛrvɛ̃) NOUN **Mont.** the French name for the **Matterhorn.**

cervine ('sɜːvaɪn) ADJECTIVE [1] resembling or relating to a deer. [2] of a dark yellowish-brown colour.
▷HISTORY C19: from Latin *cervīnus,* from *cervus* a deer

cervix ('sɜːvɪks) NOUN, *plural* **cervixes** *or* **cervices** (sə'vaɪsiːz). [1] the technical name for **neck.** [2] any necklike part of an organ, esp the lower part of the uterus that extends into the vagina.
▷HISTORY C18: from Latin

Cesarean *or* **Cesarian** (sɪ'zeərɪən) ADJECTIVE *US* variant spellings of **Caesarean.**

Cesena (*Italian* tʃe'zeːna) NOUN a city in N Italy, in Emilia-Romagna. Pop.: 89 500 (1990).

cesium ('siːzɪəm) NOUN the usual US spelling of **caesium.**

České Budějovice (*Czech* 'tʃɛskɛː 'budjɛjɔvitsɛ) NOUN a city in the S Czech Republic, on the Vltava (Moldau) River. Pop.: 175 000 (1993). German name: **Budweis.**

Československo ('tʃɛskɔslɔvɛnskɔ) NOUN the Czech name for **Czechoslovakia.**

Cesky terrier ('tʃɛskɪ) NOUN a sturdy long-bodied short-legged variety of terrier with a wavy grey or light brown coat.

cespitose ('sɛspɪˌtəʊs) ADJECTIVE a variant spelling (esp US) of **caespitose.**
▸**'cespiˌtosely** ADVERB

cess¹ (sɛs) NOUN [1] *Brit* any of several special taxes, such as a land tax in Scotland. [2] (formerly, in Ireland) **a** the obligation to provide the soldiers and household of the lord deputy with supplies at fixed prices. **b** any military exaction. ◆ VERB [3] *(tr) Brit* to tax or assess for taxation. [4] *(tr)* (formerly in Ireland) to impose (soldiers) upon a population, to be supported by them.
▷HISTORY C16: short for ASSESSMENT

cess² (sɛs) NOUN an Irish slang word for **luck** (esp in the phrase **bad cess to you!**).
▷HISTORY C19: probably from CESS¹ (sense 2)

cess³ (sɛs) NOUN short for **cesspool.**

cessation (sɛ'seɪʃən) NOUN a ceasing or stopping; discontinuance; pause: *temporary cessation of hostilities.*
▷HISTORY C14: from Latin *cessātiō* a delaying, inactivity, from *cessāre* to be idle, desist from, from *cēdere* to yield, CEDE

cesser ('sɛsə) NOUN *Law* the coming to an end of a term interest or annuity.

cession ('sɛʃən) NOUN [1] the act of ceding, esp of ceding rights, property, or territory. [2] something that is ceded, esp land or territory.
▷HISTORY C14: from Latin *cessiō,* from *cēdere* to yield

cessionary ('sɛʃənərɪ) NOUN, *plural* **-aries.** *Law* a person to whom something is transferred; assignee; grantee.

cesspool ('sɛsˌpuːl) *or* **cesspit** ('sɛsˌpɪt) NOUN [1] Also called: **sink, sump.** a covered cistern, etc., for collecting and storing sewage or waste water. [2] a filthy or corrupt place: *a cesspool of iniquity.*
▷HISTORY C17: changed (through influence of POOL¹) from earlier *cesperalle,* from Old French *souspirail* vent, air, from *soupirer* to sigh; see SUSPIRE

c'est la vie *French* (sɛ la vi) that's life.

cestode ('sɛstəʊd) NOUN any parasitic flatworm of the class *Cestoda,* which includes the tapeworms.
▷HISTORY C19: from New Latin *Cestoidea* ribbon-shaped creatures, from Latin *cestus* belt, girdle; see CESTUS¹

cestoid ('sɛstɔɪd) ADJECTIVE (esp of tapeworms and similar animals) ribbon-like in form.

cestus¹ ('sɛstəs) *or* **cestos** ('sɛstɒs) NOUN *Classical myth* the girdle of Aphrodite (Venus) decorated to cause amorousness.
▷HISTORY C16: from Latin, from Greek *kestos* belt, from *kentein* to stitch

cestus² *or* **caestus** ('sɛstəs) NOUN, *plural* **-tus** *or* **-tuses.** (in classical Roman boxing) a pugilist's gauntlet of bull's hide loaded or studded with metal.
▷HISTORY C18: from Latin *caestus,* probably from *caedere* to strike, slay

cesura (sɪ'zjʊərə) NOUN, *plural* **-ras** *or* **-rae** (-riː). *Prosody* a variant spelling of **caesura.**
▸**ce'sural** ADJECTIVE

CET ABBREVIATION FOR: [1] **Central European Time.** [2] Common External Tariff.

cetacean (sɪ'teɪʃən) ADJECTIVE *also* **cetaceous.** [1] of, relating to, or belonging to the *Cetacea,* an order of aquatic placental mammals having no hind limbs and a blowhole for breathing: includes toothed whales (dolphins, porpoises, etc.) and whalebone whales (rorquals, right whales, etc.). ◆ NOUN [2] a whale.
▷HISTORY C19: from New Latin *Cētācea,* ultimately from Latin *cētus* whale, from Greek *kētos*

cetane ('siːteɪn) NOUN a colourless insoluble liquid alkane hydrocarbon used in the determination of the cetane number of diesel fuel. Formula: $C_{16}H_{34}$. Also called: **hexadecane.**
▷HISTORY C19: from Latin *cētus* whale + -ANE, so called because related compounds are found in sperm whale oil

cetane number NOUN a measure of the quality of a diesel fuel expressed as the percentage of cetane in a mixture of cetane and 1-methylnapthalene of the same quality as the given fuel. Also called: **cetane rating.** Compare **octane number.**

Cetatea Albă (tʃe'tatea 'albə) NOUN the Romanian name for **Byelgorod-Dnestrovski.**

cete (siːt) NOUN a group of badgers.
▷HISTORY C15: perhaps from Latin *coetus* assembly, from *coīre* to come together

ceteris paribus ('kɛtərɪs 'pɑːrɪbʊs) other things being equal.
▷HISTORY C17: Latin

Cetinje (*Serbo-Croat* 'tsɛtinjɛ) NOUN a city in Serbia and Montenegro, in SW Montenegro: former capital of Montenegro (until 1945); palace and fortified monastery, residences of Montenegrin prince-bishops. Pop.: 15 924 (1991).

Cetnik ('tʃɛtnɪk, tʃɛt'niːk) NOUN a variant spelling of **Chetnik.**

cetology (siː'tɒlədʒɪ) NOUN the branch of zoology concerned with the study of whales (cetaceans).
▷HISTORY C19: from Latin *cētus* whale
▸**cetological** (ˌsiːtə'lɒdʒɪkᵊl) ADJECTIVE ▸**ce'tologist** NOUN

cetrimide ('sɛtrɪˌmaɪd) NOUN a quaternary ammonium compound used as a detergent and, having powerful antiseptic properties, for sterilizing surgical instruments, cleaning wounds, etc.

Cetti's warbler ('tʃɛtɪz) NOUN a reddish-brown Eurasian warbler, *Cettia cetti,* with a distinctive song.
▷HISTORY C19: after F. *Cetti,* 18th-century Italian ornithologist

Cetus ('siːtəs) NOUN, *Latin genitive* **Ceti** ('siːtaɪ). a large constellation on the celestial equator near Pisces and Aquarius. It contains the variable star Mira Ceti.
▷HISTORY Latin: whale

Ceuta (*Spanish* 'θeuta) NOUN an enclave in Morocco on the Strait of Gibraltar, consisting of a port and military station: held by Spain since 1580. Pop.: 75 241 (2000 est.).

Cévennes (*French* sevɛn) NOUN a mountain range in S central France, on the SE edge of the Massif Central. Highest peak: 1754 m (5755 ft.).

Ceylon (sɪ'lɒn) NOUN [1] the former name (until 1972) of **Sri Lanka.** [2] an island in the Indian Ocean, off the SE coast of India: consists politically of the republic of Sri Lanka. Area: 64 644 sq. km (24 959 sq. miles).

Ceylonese (ˌsɛlə'niːz, ˌsiːlə-) ADJECTIVE of or relating to Ceylon or its inhabitants.

Ceylon moss NOUN a red East Indian seaweed, *Gracilaria lichenoides,* from which agar is made.

Ceyx ('siːɪks) NOUN *Greek myth* a king of Trachis in Thessaly and the husband of Alcyone. He died in a shipwreck and his wife drowned herself in grief. Compare **Alcyone¹** (sense 1).

cf¹ *or* **CF** ABBREVIATION FOR cost and freight. Also: **c & f.**

cf² THE INTERNET DOMAIN NAME FOR Central African Republic.

Cf THE CHEMICAL SYMBOL FOR californium.

CF *Chiefly Brit* ABBREVIATION FOR Chaplain to the Forces.

cf. ABBREVIATION FOR confer.

▷HISTORY Latin: compare

c/f *Book-keeping* ABBREVIATION FOR carried forward.

CFB (in Canada) ABBREVIATION FOR Canadian Forces Base.

CFC ABBREVIATION FOR chlorofluorocarbon.

CFD ABBREVIATION FOR computational fluid dynamics.

CFE ABBREVIATION FOR: [1] College of Further Education. [2] Conventional Forces in Europe: negotiations between NATO and the Warsaw Pact to reduce conventional forces located between the Atlantic and the Urals.

cfi *or* **CFI** ABBREVIATION FOR cost, freight, and insurance (included in the price quoted). Also: **c.i.f.**

CFL ABBREVIATION FOR Canadian Football League.

CFS ABBREVIATION FOR chronic fatigue syndrome.

cg¹ [1] ABBREVIATION FOR centre of gravity. ◆ [2] SYMBOL FOR centigram.

cg² THE INTERNET DOMAIN NAME FOR Republic of Congo.

CG ABBREVIATION FOR: [1] captain general. [2] coastguard. [3] Coldstream Guards. [4] computer-generated. [5] consul general.

CGBR ABBREVIATION FOR Central Government Borrowing Requirement.

CGI ABBREVIATION FOR: [1] computer-generated image *or* imagery. [2] common gateway interface.

CGM *Chiefly Brit* ABBREVIATION FOR Conspicuous Gallantry Medal.

CGS (in Britain) ABBREVIATION FOR Chief of General Staff.

cgs units PLURAL NOUN a metric system of units based on the centimetre, gram, and second. For scientific and technical purposes these units have been replaced by SI units.

CGT ABBREVIATION FOR capital gains tax.

ch [1] ABBREVIATION FOR custom house. ◆ [2] THE INTERNET DOMAIN NAME FOR Switzerland.

CH [1] ABBREVIATION FOR Companion of Honour (a Brit. title). ◆ [2] INTERNATIONAL CAR REGISTRATION FOR Switzerland.
▷HISTORY from French *Confédération Helvétique*

ch. ABBREVIATION FOR: [1] chain (unit of measure). [2] chapter. [3] *Chess* check. [4] chief. [5] church.

chabazite ('kæbəˌzaɪt) NOUN a pink, white, or colourless zeolite mineral consisting of a hydrated silicate of calcium, sodium, potassium, and aluminium in hexagonal crystalline form. Formula: $Ca_2Al_2Si_4O_{12}.6H_2O$.
▷HISTORY C19: from French *chabazie* from Late Greek *khabazios,* erroneous for *khalazios* stone similar to a hailstone, from Greek *khalazios* of hail, from *khalaza* hailstone + -ITE¹

Chablis ('ʃæblɪ; *French* ʃabli) NOUN *(sometimes not capitals)* a dry white burgundy wine made around Chablis, in central France.

cha-cha-cha (ˌtʃɑːtʃɑː'tʃɑː) *or* **cha-cha** NOUN [1] a Latin-American ballroom dance with small steps and swaying hip movements. [2] a piece of music composed for this dance. ◆ VERB *(intr)* [3] to perform this dance.
▷HISTORY C20: from American (Cuban) Spanish

chacma ('tʃækmə) NOUN a baboon, *Papio* (or *Chaeropithecus*) *ursinus,* having coarse greyish hair and occurring in southern and eastern Africa.
▷HISTORY C19: from Khoikhoi

Chaco (*Spanish* 'tʃako) NOUN See **Gran Chaco.**

chaconne (ʃə'kɒn; *French* ʃakɔn) NOUN [1] a musical form consisting of a set of continuous variations upon a ground bass. See also **passacaglia.** [2] *Archaic* a dance in slow triple time probably originating in Spain.
▷HISTORY C17: from French, from Spanish *chacona,* probably imitative of the castanet accompaniment

chacun à son goût *French* (ʃakœ̃n a sɔ̃ gu) each to his own taste.

chad (tʃæd) NOUN the small pieces of cardboard or paper removed during the punching of holes in computer printer paper, paper tape, etc.
▷HISTORY C20: perhaps based on CHAFF¹

Chad (tʃæd) NOUN [1] a republic in N central Africa: made a territory of French Equatorial Africa in 1910; became independent in 1960; contains much desert and the Tibesti Mountains, with Lake Chad in the west; produces chiefly cotton and livestock;

has suffered intermittent civil war from 1963 and prolonged drought. Official languages: Arabic; French. Religion: Muslim majority, also Christian and animist. Currency: franc. Capital: Ndjamena. Pop.: 8 707 000 (2001 est.). Area: 1 284 000 sq. km (495 750 sq. miles). French name: **Tchad.** [2] **Lake.** a lake in N central Africa: fed chiefly by the Shari River, it has no apparent outlet. Area: 10 000 to 26 000 sq. km (4000 to 10 000 sq. miles), varying seasonally.

Chadderton (ˈtʃædətᵊn) NOUN a town in NW England, in Oldham unitary authority, in Greater Manchester. Pop.: 34 026 (1991).

Chadic (ˈtʃædɪk) NOUN [1] a subfamily of the Afro-Asiatic family of languages, spoken in an area west and south of Lake Chad, the chief member of which is Hausa. ◆ ADJECTIVE [2] denoting, relating to, or belonging to this group of languages.

chado (ˈtʃɑːdəʊ), **sado** (ˈsɑːdəʊ), *or* **chanoyu** (ˌtʃɑːnɔːˈjuː) NOUN the Japanese tea ceremony.
▷HISTORY from Japanese *cha* or *sa* tea (from Chinese *cha*) + *dō* way (from Chinese *tao*); *chanoyu* literally: tea's hot water

chador (ˈtʃʌdə) NOUN a variant spelling of **chuddar.**

chadri (ˈtʃædriː) NOUN a shroud which covers the body from heat to foot, usually worn by females in Islamic countries.

chaebol (ˈtʃeɪbɒl) NOUN a large, usually family-owned, business group in South Korea.
▷HISTORY C20: from Korean, literally: money clan

Chaeronea (ˌkɛrəˈniːə) NOUN an ancient Greek town in W Boeotia: site of the victory of Philip of Macedon over the Athenians and Thebans (338 B.C.) and of Sulla over Mithridates (86 B.C.).

chaeta (ˈkiːtə) NOUN, *plural* **-tae** (-tiː). any of the chitinous bristles on the body of such annelids as the earthworm and the lugworm: used in locomotion; a seta.
▷HISTORY C19: New Latin, from Greek *khaitē* long hair

chaetiferous (kiːˈtɪfərəs) ADJECTIVE *Zoology* having bristles.

chaetognath (ˈkiːtɒgˌnæθ) NOUN any small wormlike marine invertebrate of the phylum *Chaetognatha,* including the arrowworms, having a coelom and a ring of bristles around the mouth.
▷HISTORY C19: New Latin *Chaetognatha,* literally: hair-jaw, from CHAETA + Greek *gnathos* jaw

chaetopod (ˈkiːtəˌpɒd) NOUN any annelid worm of the classes *Oligochaeta* or *Polychaeta.* See **oligochaete, polychaete.**
▷HISTORY C19: from New Latin *Chaetopoda;* see CHAETA, -POD

chafe (tʃeɪf) VERB [1] to make or become sore or worn by rubbing. [2] (*tr*) to warm (the hands, etc.) by rubbing. [3] to irritate or be irritated or impatient: *he was chafed because he was not allowed out.* [4] (*intr;* often foll by *on, against,* etc.) to cause friction; rub. [5] **chafe at the bit.** See **champ**[1] (sense 3). ◆ NOUN [6] a soreness or irritation caused by friction.
▷HISTORY C14: from Old French *chaufer* to warm, ultimately from Latin *calefacere,* from *calēre* to be warm + *facere* to make

chafer (ˈtʃeɪfə) NOUN any of various scarabaeid beetles, such as the cockchafer and rose chafer.
▷HISTORY Old English *ceafor;* related to Old Saxon *kevera,* Old High German *chevar*

chaff[1] (tʃɑːf) NOUN [1] the mass of husks, etc., separated from the seeds during threshing. [2] finely cut straw and hay used to feed cattle. [3] something of little worth; rubbish (esp in the phrase **separate the wheat from the chaff**). [4] the dry membranous bracts enclosing the flowers of certain composite plants. [5] thin strips of metallic foil released into the earth's atmosphere to confuse radar signals and prevent detection.
▷HISTORY Old English *ceaf;* related to Old High German *keva* husk
▸ˈ**chaffy** ADJECTIVE

chaff[2] (tʃɑːf) NOUN [1] light-hearted teasing or joking; banter. ◆ VERB [2] to tease good-naturedly; banter.
▷HISTORY C19: probably slang variant of CHAFE, perhaps influenced by CHAFF[1]
▸ˈ**chaffer** NOUN

chaffer (ˈtʃæfə) VERB [1] (*intr*) to haggle or bargain. [2] to chatter, talk, or say idly; bandy (words). [3] (*tr*) *Obsolete* to deal in; barter. ◆ NOUN [4] haggling or bargaining.
▷HISTORY C13 *chaffare,* from *chep* bargain + *fare* journey; see CHEAP, FARE
▸ˈ**chafferer** NOUN

chaffinch (ˈtʃæfɪntʃ) NOUN a common European finch, *Fringilla coelebs,* with black and white wings and, in the male, a reddish body and blue-grey head.
▷HISTORY Old English *ceaffinc,* from *ceaf* CHAFF[1] + *finc* FINCH

chafing dish (ˈtʃeɪfɪŋ) NOUN a vessel with a heating apparatus beneath it, for cooking or keeping food warm at the table.

Chagas' disease (ˈʃɑːgəs) NOUN a form of trypanosomiasis found in South America, caused by the protozoan *Trypanosoma cruzi,* characterized by fever and, often, inflammation of the heart muscles. Also called: **(South) American trypanosomiasis.** Compare **sleeping sickness.**
▷HISTORY C20: named after Carlos *Chagas* (1879–1934), Brazilian physician who first described it

Chagres (*Spanish* ˈtʃaɣres) NOUN a river in Panama, flowing southwest through Gatún Lake, then northwest to the Caribbean Sea.

chagrin (ˈʃægrɪn) NOUN [1] a feeling of annoyance or mortification. ◆ VERB (*tr*) [2] to embarrass and annoy; mortify.
▷HISTORY C17: from French *chagrin, chagriner,* of unknown origin
▸ˈ**chagrined** ADJECTIVE

chai (tʃaɪ) NOUN tea, esp as made in India with added spices.
▷HISTORY C20: Indian

chain (tʃeɪn) NOUN [1] a flexible length of metal links, used for confining, connecting, pulling, etc., or in jewellery. [2] (*usually plural*) anything that confines, fetters, or restrains: *the chains of poverty.* [3] (*usually plural*) Also called: **snow chains.** a set of metal links that fit over the tyre of a motor vehicle to increase traction and reduce skidding on an icy surface. [4] **a** a number of establishments such as hotels, shops, etc., having the same owner or management. **b** (*as modifier*): *a chain store.* [5] a series of related or connected facts, events, etc. [6] (of reasoning) a sequence of arguments each of which takes the conclusion of the preceding as a premise. See (as an example) **sorites.** [7] Also called: **Gunter's chain.** a unit of length equal to 22 yards. [8] Also called: **engineer's chain.** a unit of length equal to 100 feet. [9] *Chem* two or more atoms or groups bonded together so that the configuration of the resulting molecule, ion, or radical resembles a chain. See also **open chain, ring**[1] (sense 18). [10] *Geography* a series of natural features, esp approximately parallel mountain ranges. [11] **off the chain.** *Austral and NZ informal* free from responsibility. [12] **yank (someone's) chain.** *Informal* to tease, mislead, or harass (someone). ◆ VERB [13] *Surveying* to measure with a chain or tape. [14] (*tr;* often foll by *up*) to confine, tie, or make fast with or as if with a chain. [15] short for **chain-stitch.**
▷HISTORY C13: from Old French *chaine,* ultimately from Latin; see CATENA

chain drive NOUN *Engineering* a chain of links passing over sprockets that transmits rotation from one shaft to another.

chain gang NOUN *US* a group of convicted prisoners chained together, usually while doing hard labour.

chain grate NOUN a type of mechanical stoker for a furnace, in which the grate consists of an endless chain that draws the solid fuel into the furnace as it rotates.

chain letter NOUN a letter, often with a request for and promise of money, that is sent to many people who add to or recopy it and send it on to others: illegal in many countries.

chain lightning NOUN another name for **forked lightning.**

chain mail NOUN another term for **mail**[2] (sense 1).

chainman (ˈtʃeɪnmən) NOUN, *plural* **-men.** *Surveying* a person who does the chaining in a survey.

chainplate (ˈtʃeɪnˌpleɪt) NOUN a metal plate on the side of a vessel, to which the shrouds are attached.

chain printer NOUN a line printer in which the type is on a continuous chain, used to print computer output.

chain-react VERB (*intr*) to undergo a chain reaction.

chain reaction NOUN [1] a process in which a neutron colliding with an atomic nucleus causes fission and the ejection of one or more other neutrons, which induce other nuclei to split. [2] a chemical reaction in which the product of one step is a reactant in the following step. [3] a series of rapidly occurring events, each of which precipitates the next.

chain rule NOUN *Maths* a theorem that may be used in the differentiation of the function of a function. It states that $du/dx = (du/dy)(dy/dx)$, where y is a function of x and u a function of y.

chain saw NOUN a motor-driven saw, usually portable, in which the cutting teeth form links in a continuous chain.

chain shot NOUN cannon shot comprising two balls or half balls joined by a chain, much used formerly, esp in naval warfare to destroy rigging.

chain-smoke VERB to smoke (cigarettes, etc.) continually, esp lighting one from the preceding one.
▸**chain smoker** NOUN

chain stitch NOUN [1] an ornamental looped embroidery stitch resembling the links of a chain. ◆ VERB **chain-stitch.** [2] to sew (something) with this stitch.

chain store NOUN one of several retail enterprises under the same ownership and management. Also called: **multiple store.**

chain wheel NOUN *Engineering* a toothed wheel that meshes with a roller chain to transmit motion.

chair (tʃɛə) NOUN [1] a seat with a back on which one person sits, typically having four legs and often having arms. [2] an official position of authority: *a chair on the board of directors.* [3] the chairman of a debate or meeting: *the speaker addressed the chair.* [4] a professorship: *the chair of German.* [5] *Railways* an iron or steel cradle bolted to a sleeper in which the rail sits and is locked in position. [6] short for **sedan chair.** [7] **in the chair.** chairing a debate or meeting. [8] **take the chair.** to preside as chairman for a meeting, etc. [9] **the chair.** an informal name for **electric chair.** ◆ VERB (*tr*) [10] to preside over (a meeting). [11] *Brit* to carry aloft in a sitting position after a triumph or great achievement. [12] to provide with a chair of office. [13] to install in a chair.
▷HISTORY C13: from Old French *chaiere,* from Latin *cathedra,* from Greek *kathedra,* from *kata-* down + *hedra* seat; compare CATHEDRAL

chairborne (ˈtʃɛəˌbɔːn) ADJECTIVE *Informal* having an administrative or desk job rather than a more active one.

chairbound (ˈtʃɛəˌbaʊnd) ADJECTIVE *Social welfare* unable to walk; dependent on a wheelchair for mobility.

chairlift (ˈtʃɛəˌlɪft) NOUN a series of chairs suspended from a power-driven cable for conveying people, esp skiers, up a mountain.

chairman (ˈtʃɛəmən) NOUN, *plural* **-men.** [1] Also called: **chairperson,** (feminine) **chairwoman.** a person who presides over a company's board of directors, a committee, a debate, an administrative department, etc. [2] *History* someone who carries a sedan chair.
▸ˈ**chairmanˌship** NOUN

> **Language note** *Chairman* can seem inappropriate when applied to a woman, while *chairwoman* can be offensive. *Chair* and *chairperson* can be applied to either a man or a woman; *chair* is generally preferred to *chairperson.*

chairperson (ˈtʃɛəˌpɜːsᵊn) NOUN another word for **chairman** (sense 1).

> **Language note** See at **chairman.**

chaise (ʃeɪz) NOUN [1] a light open horse-drawn carriage, esp one with two wheels designed for two passengers. [2] short for **post chaise** and **chaise longue.** [3] a gold coin first issued in France in the 14th century, depicting the king seated on a throne.

▷HISTORY C18: from French, variant of Old French *chaiere* CHAIR

chaise longue (ˈʃeɪz ˈlɒŋ; *French* ʃɛz lɔ̃g) NOUN, *plural* **chaise longues** *or* **chaises longues** (ˈʃeɪz ˈlɒŋ; *French* ʃɛz lɔ̃g). a long low chair for reclining, with a back and single armrest.
▷HISTORY C19: from French: long chair

chakalaka (ˌʃakaˈlaka) NOUN *South African* a relish made from tomatoes, onions, and spices.
▷HISTORY of unknown origin

chakra (ˈtʃækrə, ˈtʃʌkrə) NOUN (in yoga) any of the seven major energy centres in the body.
▷HISTORY C19: from Sanskrit *cakra* wheel, circle

chalaza (kəˈleɪzə) NOUN, *plural* **-zas** *or* **-zae** (-ziː). 1 one of a pair of spiral threads of albumen holding the yolk of a bird's egg in position. 2 the basal part of a plant ovule, where the integuments and nucellus are joined.
▷HISTORY C18: New Latin, from Greek: hailstone
▸**chaˈlazal** ADJECTIVE

chalazion (kəˈleɪzɪən) NOUN a small cyst on the eyelid resulting from chronic inflammation of a meibomian gland. Also called: **meibomian cyst.**
▷HISTORY C18: from Greek: a small CHALAZA

chalcanthite (kælˈkænθaɪt) NOUN a blue secondary mineral consisting of hydrated copper sulphate in triclinic crystalline form. Formula: $CuSO_4.5H_2O$.
▷HISTORY C19: via German from Latin *chalcanthum* copper sulphate solution, from Greek *khalkanthon,* from *khalkos* copper + *anthos* flower; see -ITE[1]

chalcedony (kælˈsɛdənɪ) NOUN, *plural* **-nies**. a microcrystalline often greyish form of quartz with crystals arranged in parallel fibres: a gemstone. Formula: SiO_2.
▷HISTORY C15: from Late Latin *chalcēdōnius,* from Greek *khalkēdōn* a precious stone (Revelation 21:19), perhaps named after *Khalkēdōn* Chalcedon, town in Asia Minor
▸**chalcedonic** (ˌkælsɪˈdɒnɪk) ADJECTIVE

chalcid *or* **chalcid fly** (ˈkælsɪd) NOUN any tiny hymenopterous insect of the family *Chalcididae* and related families, whose larvae are parasites of other insects.
▷HISTORY C19: from New Latin *Chalcis* type genus, from Greek *khalkos* copper, referring to its metallic sheen

Chalcidice (kælˈsɪdɪsɪ) NOUN a peninsula of N central Greece, in Macedonia Central, ending in the three promontories of Kassandra, Sithonia, and Akti. Area: 2945 sq. km (1149 sq. miles). Modern Greek name: **Khalkidíki.**

Chalcis (ˈkælsɪs) NOUN a city in SE Greece, at the narrowest point of the Euripus strait: important since the 7th century B.C., founding many colonies in ancient times. Pop.: 47 600 (1995 est.). Modern Greek name: **Khalkís.** Medieval English name: **Negropont.**

chalco- *or before a vowel* **chalc-** COMBINING FORM indicating copper or a copper alloy: *chalcopyrite; chalcolithic.*
▷HISTORY from Greek *khalkos* copper

chalcocite (ˈkælkəˌsaɪt) NOUN a lead-grey or black mineral, found as a copper ore or in veins. It is a source of copper. Composition: copper sulphide. Formula: Cu_2S. Crystal structure: orthorhombic.
▷HISTORY C19: changed from earlier *chalcosine,* from Greek *khalkos* copper + -ITE[1]

chalcogen (ˈkælkəˌdʒɛn) NOUN any of the elements oxygen, sulphur, selenium, tellurium, or polonium, of group 6A of the periodic table.
▷HISTORY C20: from CHALCO(PYRITE) + -GEN

chalcography (kælˈkɒgrəfɪ) NOUN the art of engraving on copper or brass.
▸**chalˈcographer** *or* **chalˈcographist** NOUN ▸**chalcographic** (ˌkælkəˈgræfɪk) *or* ˌ**chalcoˈgraphical** ADJECTIVE

chalcolithic (ˌkælkəˈlɪθɪk) ADJECTIVE *Archaeol* of or relating to a period characterized by the use of both stone and bronze implements.

chalcopyrite (ˌkælkəˈpaɪraɪt, -ˈpaɪə-) NOUN a widely distributed yellow mineral consisting of a sulphide of copper and iron in tetragonal crystalline form: the principal ore of copper. Formula: $CuFeS_2$. Also called: **copper pyrites.**

Chaldea *or* **Chaldaea** (kælˈdiːə) NOUN 1 an ancient region of Babylonia; the land lying between the Euphrates delta, the Persian Gulf, and the Arabian desert. 2 another name for **Babylonia.**

Chaldean *or* **Chaldaean** (kælˈdiːən) NOUN 1 a member of an ancient Semitic people who controlled S Babylonia from the late 8th to the late 7th century B.C. 2 the dialect of Babylonian spoken by this people. ◆ ADJECTIVE 3 of or relating to the ancient Chaldeans or their language.

Chaldee (kælˈdiː) NOUN 1 a nontechnical term for **Biblical Aramaic**, once believed to be the language of the ancient Chaldeans 2 the actual language of the ancient Chaldeans. See also **Chaldean** (sense 2). 3 an inhabitant of ancient Chaldea; a Chaldean. ◆ Also (for senses 1, 2): **Chaldaic** (kælˈdeɪɪk).

chaldron (ˈtʃɔːldrən) NOUN a unit of capacity equal to 36 bushels. Formerly used in the US for the measurement of solids, being equivalent to 1.268 cubic metres. Used in Britain for both solids and liquids, it is equivalent to 1.309 cubic metres.
▷HISTORY C17: from Old French *chauderon* CAULDRON

chalet (ˈʃæleɪ; *French* ʃalɛ) NOUN 1 a type of wooden house of Swiss origin, typically low, with wide projecting eaves. 2 a similar house used esp as a ski lodge, garden house, etc.
▷HISTORY C19: from French (Swiss dialect)

chalice (ˈtʃælɪs) NOUN 1 *Poetic* a drinking cup; goblet. 2 *Christianity* a gold or silver cup containing the wine at Mass. 3 the calyx of a flower, esp a cup-shaped calyx.
▷HISTORY C13: from Old French, from Latin *calix* cup; related to Greek *kalux* calyx

chaliced (ˈtʃælɪst) ADJECTIVE (of plants) having cup-shaped flowers.

chalicothere (ˈkælɪkəʊˌθɪə) NOUN any of various very large extinct Tertiary horselike perissodactyl mammals that had clawed feet but otherwise resembled titanotheres.
▷HISTORY C19: from New Latin *Chalicotherium* type genus, from Greek *khalix* gravel + Greek *thērion* a little beast, from *thēr* wild animal

chalk (tʃɔːk) NOUN 1 a soft fine-grained white sedimentary rock consisting of nearly pure calcium carbonate, containing minute fossil fragments of marine organisms, usually without a cementing material. 2 a piece of chalk or a substance like chalk, often coloured, used for writing and drawing on a blackboard. 3 a line, mark, etc. made with chalk. 4 *Billiards, snooker* a small cube of prepared chalk or similar substance for rubbing the tip of a cue. 5 *Brit* a score, tally, or record. 6 **as alike** (*or* **different**) **as chalk and cheese.** *Informal* totally different in essentials. 7 **by a long chalk.** *Brit informal* by far. 8 **can't tell** (*or* **doesn't know**) **chalk from cheese.** to be unable to judge or appreciate important differences. 9 **not by a long chalk.** *Brit informal* by no means; not possibly. 10 (*modifier*) made of chalk. ◆ VERB 11 to draw or mark (something) with chalk. 12 (*tr*) to mark, rub, or whiten with or as if with chalk. 13 (*intr*) (of paint) to become chalky; powder. 14 (*tr*) to spread chalk on (land) as a fertilizer. ◆ See also **chalk out, chalk up.**
▷HISTORY Old English *cealc,* from Latin *calx* limestone, from Greek *khalix* pebble
▸ˈ**chalk**ˌ**like** ADJECTIVE ▸ˈ**chalky** ADJECTIVE ▸ˈ**chalkiness** NOUN

chalk and talk NOUN *Sometimes derogatory* a formal method of teaching, in which the focal points are the blackboard and the teacher's voice, as contrasted with more informal child-centred activities.

chalkboard (ˈtʃɔːkˌbɔːd) NOUN a US and Canadian word for **blackboard.**

chalkface (ˈtʃɔːkˌfeɪs) NOUN *Brit informal* **a** the work or art of teaching in a school, esp classroom teaching as distinct from organizational responsibilities (esp in the phrase **at the chalkface**). **b** (*as modifier*): *chalkface experience.*

chalk out VERB (*tr, adverb*) to outline (a plan, scheme, etc.); sketch.

chalkpit (ˈtʃɔːkˌpɪt) NOUN a quarry for chalk.

chalkstone (ˈtʃɔːkˌstəʊn) NOUN *Pathol* another name for **tophus.**

chalk talk NOUN *US and Canadian* an informal lecture with pertinent points, explanatory diagrams, etc., shown on a blackboard.

chalk up VERB (*tr, adverb*) *Informal* 1 to score or register (something): *we chalked up 100 in the game.* 2 to credit (money) to an account etc. (esp in the phrase **chalk it up**).

challah *or* **hallah** (ˈhɑːlə; *Hebrew* xaˈla) NOUN, *plural* **-lahs** *or* **-loth** (*Hebrew* -ˈlɔt). bread, usually in the form of a plaited loaf, traditionally eaten by Jews to celebrate the Sabbath.
▷HISTORY from Hebrew *hallāh*

challenge (ˈtʃælɪndʒ) VERB (*mainly tr*) 1 to invite or summon (someone to do something, esp to take part in a contest). 2 (*also intr*) to call (something) into question; dispute. 3 to make demands on; stimulate: *the job challenges his ingenuity.* 4 to order (a person) to halt and be identified or to give a password. 5 *Law* to make formal objection to (a juror or jury). 6 to lay claim to (attention, etc.). 7 (*intr*) *Hunting* (of a hound) to cry out on first encountering the scent of a quarry. 8 to inject (an experimental animal immunized with a test substance) with disease microorganisms to test for immunity to the disease. ◆ NOUN 9 a call to engage in a fight, argument, or contest. 10 a questioning of a statement or fact; a demand for justification or explanation. 11 a demanding or stimulating situation, career, object, etc. 12 a demand by a sentry, watchman, etc., for identification or a password. 13 *US* an assertion that a person is not entitled to vote or that a vote is invalid. 14 *Law* a formal objection to a person selected to serve on a jury (**challenge to the polls**) or to the whole body of jurors (**challenge to the array**).
▷HISTORY C13: from Old French *chalenge,* from Latin *calumnia* CALUMNY
▸ˈ**challengeable** ADJECTIVE ▸ˈ**challenger** NOUN

challenging (ˈtʃælɪndʒɪŋ) ADJECTIVE demanding or stimulating: *a challenging new job.*

challis (ˈʃælɪ, -lɪs) *or* **challie** (ˈʃælɪ) NOUN a lightweight plain-weave fabric of wool, cotton, etc., usually with a printed design.
▷HISTORY C19: probably from a surname

chalone (ˈkæləʊn) NOUN any internal secretion that inhibits a physiological process or function.
▷HISTORY C20: from Greek *khalōn,* from *khalan* to slacken

Châlons-sur-Marne (*French* ʃalɔ̃syrmarn) NOUN a city in NE France, on the River Marne: scene of Attila's defeat by the Romans (451 A.D.). Pop.: 51 530 (1990). Shortened form: **Châlons.**

Chalon-sur-Saône (*French* ʃalɔ̃syrson) NOUN an industrial city in E central France, on the Saône River. Pop.: 54 575 (1990). Shortened form: **Chalon.**

chalutz *or* ***halutz*** *Hebrew* (xaˈluts; *English* hɑːˈluts) NOUN, *plural* **-lutzim** (-luːˈtsiːm; *English* -ˈluːtsɪm). a member of an organization of immigrants to Israeli agricultural settlements.
▷HISTORY literally: pioneer, fighter

chalybeate (kəˈlɪbɪɪt) ADJECTIVE 1 containing or impregnated with iron salts. ◆ NOUN 2 any drug containing or tasting of iron.
▷HISTORY C17: from New Latin *chalybēātus,* ultimately from *khalups* iron

chalybite (ˈkælɪˌbaɪt) NOUN another name for **siderite** (sense 1).

cham (kæm) NOUN an archaic word for **khan**[1] (sense 1).
▷HISTORY C16: from French, from Persian *khān;* see KHAN[1]

Cham (tʃæm) NOUN 1 (*plural* **Cham** *or* **Chams**) a member of a people of Indonesian stock living in Cambodia and central Vietnam. 2 the language of this people, belonging to the Malayo-Polynesian family.

chamade (ʃəˈmɑːd) NOUN *Military* (formerly) a signal by drum or trumpet inviting an enemy to a parley.
▷HISTORY C17: from French, from Portuguese *chamada,* from *chamar* to call, from Latin *clamāre*

Chamaeleon (kəˈmiːlɪən) NOUN, *Latin genitive* **Chamaeleontis** (kəˌmiːlɪˈɒntɪs). a faint constellation lying between Volans and the South celestial pole.

chamaephyte (ˈkæməˌfaɪt) NOUN a plant whose buds are close to the ground.
▷HISTORY C20: from Greek *khamai* on the ground + -PHYTE

chamber (ˈtʃeɪmbə) NOUN 1 a meeting hall, esp one used for a legislative or judicial assembly. 2 a

reception room or audience room in an official residence, palace, etc. 3 *Archaic or poetic* a room in a private house, esp a bedroom. 4 **a** a legislative, deliberative, judicial, or administrative assembly. **b** any of the houses of a legislature. 5 an enclosed space; compartment; cavity: *the smallest chamber in the caves.* 6 the space between two gates of the locks of a canal, dry dock, etc. 7 an enclosure for a cartridge in the cylinder of a revolver or for a shell in the breech of a cannon. 8 *Obsolete* a place where the money of a government, corporation, etc., was stored; treasury. 9 short for **chamber pot**. 10 *NZ* the freezing room in an abattoir. 11 (*modifier*) of, relating to, or suitable for chamber music: *a chamber concert.* ◆ VERB 12 (*tr*) to put in or provide with a chamber. ◆ See also **chambers**.
▷HISTORY C13: from Old French *chambre,* from Late Latin *camera* room, Latin: vault, from Greek *kamara*

chamber counsel *or* **counsellor** NOUN a counsel who advises in private and does not plead in court.

chambered nautilus NOUN another name for the **pearly nautilus**.

chamberhand (ˈtʃeɪmbəˌhænd) NOUN *NZ* a worker in the cold storage area of a slaughterhouse.

chamberlain (ˈtʃeɪmbəlɪn) NOUN 1 an officer who manages the household of a king. 2 the steward of a nobleman or landowner. 3 the treasurer of a municipal corporation.
▷HISTORY C13: from Old French *chamberlayn,* of Frankish origin; related to Old High German *chamarling* chamberlain, Latin *camera* CHAMBER
▸ˈ**chamberlainˌship** NOUN

chambermaid (ˈtʃeɪmbəˌmeɪd) NOUN a woman or girl employed to clean and tidy bedrooms, now chiefly in hotels.

chamber music NOUN music for performance by a small group of instrumentalists.

chamber of commerce NOUN (*sometimes capitals*) an organization composed mainly of local businessmen to promote, regulate, and protect their interests.

chamber of trade NOUN (*sometimes capitals*) a national organization representing local chambers of commerce.

chamber orchestra NOUN a small orchestra of about 25 players, used for the authentic performance of baroque and early classical music as well as modern music written specifically for a small orchestra.

chamber organ NOUN *Music* a small compact organ used esp for the authentic performance of preclassical music.

chamber pot NOUN a vessel for urine, used in bedrooms.

chambers (ˈtʃeɪmbəz) PLURAL NOUN 1 a judge's room for hearing cases not taken in open court. 2 (in England) the set of rooms occupied by barristers where clients are interviewed (in London, mostly in the Inns of Court). 3 *Brit archaic* a suite of rooms; apartments. 4 (in the US) the private office of a judge. 5 **in chambers.** *Law* **a** in the privacy of a judge's chambers. **b** in a court not open to the public. Former name for sense 5: **in camera**.

Chambertin (*French* ʃɑ̃bɛrtɛ̃) NOUN a dry red burgundy wine produced in Gevrey-Chambertin in E France.

Chambéry (*French* ʃɑ̃beri) NOUN a city in SE France, in the Alps: skiing centre; former capital of the duchy of Savoy. Pop.: 54 120 (1990).

Chambord (*French* ʃɑ̃bɔr) NOUN a village in N central France: site of a famous Renaissance chateau.

chambray (ˈʃæmbreɪ) NOUN a smooth light fabric of cotton, linen, etc., with white weft and a coloured warp.
▷HISTORY C19: after *Cambrai;* see CAMBRIC

chambré (ˈʃɑ̃breɪ) ADJECTIVE (of wine) at room temperature.
▷HISTORY from French, from *chambrer* to bring (wine) to room temperature, from *chambre* room

chameleon (kəˈmiːlɪən) NOUN 1 any lizard of the family *Chamaeleontidae* of Africa and Madagascar, having long slender legs, a prehensile tail and tongue, and the ability to change colour. 2 a changeable or fickle person.
▷HISTORY C14: from Latin *chamaeleon,* from Greek *khamaileōn,* from *khamai* on the ground + *leōn* LION
▸**chameleonic** (kəˌmiːlɪˈɒnɪk) ADJECTIVE
▸**chaˈmeleon-ˌlike** ADJECTIVE

chametz *or* ***chometz*** *Hebrew* (xaˈmɛtʒ; *Yiddish* ˈxɔmətʒ) NOUN *Judaism* leavened food which may not be eaten during Passover.

chamfer (ˈtʃæmfə) NOUN 1 a narrow flat surface at the corner of a beam, post, etc., esp one at an angle of 45°. Compare **bevel** (sense 1). ◆ VERB (*tr*) 2 to cut such a surface on (a beam, etc.). 3 another word for **chase**[2] (sense 4).
▷HISTORY C16: back formation from *chamfering,* from Old French *chamfrein,* from *chant* edge (see CANT[2]) + *fraindre* to break, from Latin *frangere*
▸ˈ**chamferer** NOUN

chamfron, chamfrain (ˈtʃæmfrən), *or* **chanfron** NOUN a piece of armour for a horse's head.
▷HISTORY C14: from Old French *chanfrein,* from *chafresner* to harness, from *chief* head + *frener* to bridle

chamois (ˈʃæmɪ; *French* ʃamwa) NOUN, *plural* **-ois**. 1 (ˈʃæmwɑː) a sure-footed goat antelope, *Rupicapra rupicapra,* inhabiting mountains of Europe and SW Asia, having vertical horns with backward-pointing tips. 2 a soft suede leather formerly made from the hide of this animal, now obtained from the skins of sheep and goats. 3 Also called: **chamois leather, shammy (leather), chammy (leather)** (ˈʃæmɪ). a piece of such leather or similar material used for polishing, etc. 4 (ˈʃæmwɑː) a yellow to greyish-yellow colour. ◆ VERB (*tr*) 5 to dress (leather or skin) like chamois. 6 to polish with a chamois.
▷HISTORY C16: from Old French, from Late Latin *camox* of uncertain origin

chamomile (ˈkæməˌmaɪl) NOUN a variant spelling of **camomile**.

Chamonix (ˈʃæmənɪ; *French* ʃamɔni) NOUN a town in SE France, in the Alps at the foot of Mont Blanc: skiing and tourist centre. Pop.: 9255 (latest est.).

champ[1] (tʃæmp) VERB 1 to munch (food) noisily like a horse. 2 (when *intr,* often foll by *on, at,* etc.) to bite (something) nervously or impatiently; gnaw. 3 **champ** (*or* **chafe**) **at the bit.** *Informal* to be impatient to start work, a journey, etc. ◆ NOUN 4 the act or noise of champing. 5 *Ulster dialect* a dish, originating in Ireland, of mashed potatoes and spring onions or leeks.
▷HISTORY C16: probably of imitative origin
▸ˈ**champer** NOUN

champ[2] (tʃæmp) NOUN *Informal* short for **champion** (sense 1).

champac *or* **champak** (ˈtʃæmpæk, ˈtʃʌmpʌk) NOUN a magnoliaceous tree, *Michelia champaca,* of India and the East Indies. Its fragrant yellow flowers yield an oil used in perfumes and its wood is used for furniture.
▷HISTORY C18: from Hindi *campak,* from Sanskrit *campaka,* of Dravidian origin

champagne (ʃæmˈpeɪn) NOUN 1 (*sometimes capital*) a white sparkling wine produced around Reims and Epernay, France. 2 (loosely) any effervescent white wine. 3 **a** a colour varying from a pale orange-yellow to a greyish-yellow. **b** (*as adjective*): *a champagne carpet.* 4 (*modifier*) denoting a luxurious lifestyle: *a champagne capitalist.*

Champagne-Ardenne (ʃæmˈpeɪnɑːˈdɛn; *French* ʃɑ̃paɲardɛn) NOUN a region of NE France: a countship and commercial centre in medieval times; it consists of a great plain, with sheep and dairy farms and many vineyards.

champagne socialist NOUN a professed socialist who enjoys an extravagant lifestyle.

champaign (ʃæmˈpeɪn) NOUN 1 Also called: **campagna**. an expanse of open level or gently undulating country. 2 an obsolete word for **battlefield**.
▷HISTORY C14: from Old French *champaigne,* from Late Latin *campānia;* see CAMPAIGN

champers (ˈʃæmpəz) NOUN a slang name for **champagne**.

champerty (ˈtʃæmpətɪ) NOUN, *plural* **-ties**. *Law* (formerly) an illegal bargain between a party to litigation and an outsider whereby the latter agrees to pay for the action and thereby share in any proceeds recovered. See also **maintenance**.
▷HISTORY C14: from Anglo-French *champartie,* from Old French *champart* share of produce, from *champ* field + *part* share (a feudal lord's)
▸ˈ**champertous** ADJECTIVE

champignon (tʃæmˈpɪnjən) NOUN any of various agaricaceous edible mushrooms, esp *Marasmius oreades* (**fairy ring champignon**) and the meadow mushroom.
▷HISTORY C16: from French, perhaps from Vulgar Latin *campīnus* (unattested) of the field, from Latin *campus* plain, field

Champigny-sur-Marne (*French* ʃɑ̃piɲisyrmarn) NOUN a suburb of Paris, on the River Marne. Pop.: 80 290 (latest est.).

champion (ˈtʃæmpɪən) NOUN 1 **a** a person who has defeated all others in a competition: *a chess champion.* **b** (*as modifier*): *a champion team.* 2 **a** a plant or animal that wins first place in a show, etc. **b** (*as modifier*): *a champion marrow.* 3 a person who defends a person or cause: *champion of the underprivileged.* 4 (formerly) a warrior or knight who did battle for another, esp a king or queen, to defend their rights or honour. ◆ ADJECTIVE 5 *Northern English dialect* first rate; excellent. ◆ ADVERB 6 *Northern English dialect* very well; excellently. ◆ VERB (*tr*) 7 to support; defend: *we champion the cause of liberty.*
▷HISTORY C13: from Old French, from Late Latin *campiō,* from Latin *campus* field, battlefield

championship (ˈtʃæmpɪənˌʃɪp) NOUN 1 (*sometimes plural*) any of various contests held to determine a champion. 2 the title or status of being a champion. 3 support for or defence of a cause, person, etc.

Champlain (ʃæmˈpleɪn) NOUN **Lake.** a lake in the northeastern US, between the Green Mountains and the Adirondack Mountains: linked by the **Champlain Canal** to the Hudson River and by the Richelieu River to the St Lawrence; a major communications route in colonial times.

champlevé *French* (ʃɑ̃lve; *English* ˌʃæmpləˈveɪ) ADJECTIVE 1 of or relating to a process of enamelling by which grooves are cut into a metal base and filled with enamel colours. ◆ NOUN 2 an object enamelled by this process.
▷HISTORY C19: from *champ* field (level surface) + *levé* raised

Champs Elysées (ʃɒnz eɪˈliːzeɪ; *French* ʃɑ̃z elize) NOUN a major boulevard in Paris, leading from the Arc de Triomphe: site of the Elysées Palace and government offices.

chance (tʃɑːns) NOUN 1 **a** the unknown and unpredictable element that causes an event to result in a certain way rather than another, spoken of as a real force. **b** (*as modifier*): *a chance meeting.* Related adjective: **fortuitous**. 2 fortune; luck; fate. 3 an opportunity or occasion. 4 a risk; gamble: *you take a chance with his driving.* 5 the extent to which an event is likely to occur; probability. 6 an unpredicted event, esp a fortunate one: *that was quite a chance, finding him here.* 7 *Archaic* an unlucky event; mishap. 8 **by chance. a** accidentally: *he slipped by chance.* **b** perhaps: *do you by chance have a room?* 9 **(the) chances are....** it is likely (that) .... 10 **on the chance.** acting on the possibility; in case. 11 **the main chance.** the opportunity for personal gain (esp in the phrase **an eye to the main chance**). ◆ VERB 12 (*tr*) to risk; hazard: *I'll chance the worst happening.* 13 to happen by chance; be the case by chance: *I chanced to catch sight of her as she passed.* 14 **chance on** (*or* **upon**). to come upon by accident: *he chanced on the solution to his problem.* 15 **chance one's arm.** to attempt to do something although the chance of success may be slight.
▷HISTORY C13: from Old French *cheance,* from *cheoir* to fall, occur, from Latin *cadere*
▸ˈ**chanceful** ADJECTIVE ▸ˈ**chanceless** ADJECTIVE

chancel (ˈtʃɑːnsəl) NOUN the part of a church containing the altar, sanctuary, and choir, usually separated from the nave and transepts by a screen.
▷HISTORY C14: from Old French, from Latin *cancellī* (plural) lattice

chancellery *or* **chancellory** (ˈtʃɑːnsələrɪ, -slərɪ) NOUN, *plural* **-leries** *or* **-lories**. 1 the building or room occupied by a chancellor's office. 2 the position, rank, or office of a chancellor. 3 *US* **a** the residence or office of an embassy or legation. **b** the office of a consulate. 4 *Brit* another name for a diplomatic **chancery**.

▷**HISTORY** C14: from Anglo-French *chancellerie,* from Old French *chancelier* CHANCELLOR

chancellor ('tʃɑːnsələ, -slə) NOUN 1 the head of the government in several European countries. 2 *US* the president of a university or, in some colleges, the chief administrative officer. 3 *Brit and Canadian* the honorary head of a university. Compare **vice chancellor** (sense 1). 4 *US* (in some states) the presiding judge of a court of chancery or equity. 5 *Brit* the chief secretary of an embassy. 6 *Christianity* a clergyman acting as the law officer of a bishop. 7 *Archaic* the chief secretary of a prince, nobleman, etc.
▷**HISTORY** C11: from Anglo-French *chanceler,* from Late Latin *cancellārius* porter, secretary, from Latin *cancellī* lattice; see CHANCEL
▸'**chancellor,ship** NOUN

Chancellor of the Duchy of Lancaster NOUN *Brit* a minister of the crown, nominally appointed as representative of the Queen (who is the Duke, not Duchess, of Lancaster), but in practice chiefly employed on parliamentary work determined by the prime minister.

Chancellor of the Exchequer NOUN *Brit* the cabinet minister responsible for finance.

chance-medley NOUN *Law* a sudden quarrel in which one party kills another; unintentional but not blameless killing.
▷**HISTORY** C15: from Anglo-French *chance medlee* mixed chance

chancer ('tʃɑːnsə) NOUN *Slang* an unscrupulous or dishonest opportunist who is prepared to try any dubious scheme for making money or furthering his own ends.
▷**HISTORY** C19: from CHANCE + -ER[1]

chancery ('tʃɑːnsərɪ) NOUN, *plural* **-ceries.** 1 Also called: **Chancery Division.** (in England) the Lord Chancellor's court, now a division of the High Court of Justice. 2 Also called: **court of chancery.** (in the US) a court of equity. 3 *Brit* the political section or offices of an embassy or legation. 4 another name for **chancellery.** 5 a court of public records; archives. 6 *Christianity* a diocesan office under the supervision of a bishop's chancellor, having custody of archives, issuing official enactments, etc. 7 **in chancery. a** *Law* (of a suit) pending in a court of equity. **b** *Wrestling, boxing* (of a competitor's head) locked under an opponent's arm. **c** in an awkward or helpless situation.
▷**HISTORY** C14: shortened from CHANCELLERY

chancre ('ʃæŋkə) NOUN *Pathol* a small hard nodular growth, which is the first diagnostic sign of acquired syphilis.
▷**HISTORY** C16: from French, from Latin: CANCER
▸'**chancrous** ADJECTIVE

chancroid ('ʃæŋkrɔɪd) NOUN 1 a soft venereal ulcer, esp of the male genitals, caused by infection with the bacillus *Haemophilus ducreyi.* ◆ ADJECTIVE 2 relating to or resembling a chancroid or chancre.
▸**chan'croidal** ADJECTIVE

chancy *or* **chancey** ('tʃɑːnsɪ) ADJECTIVE **chancier, chanciest.** *Informal* of uncertain outcome or temperament; risky.
▸'**chancily** ADVERB ▸'**chanciness** NOUN

chandelier (ˌʃændɪ'lɪə) NOUN an ornamental hanging light with branches and holders for several candles or bulbs.
▷**HISTORY** C17: from French: candleholder, from Latin CANDELABRUM

chandelle (ʃæn'dɛl; *French* ʃɑ̃dɛl) NOUN 1 *Aeronautics* an abrupt climbing turn almost to the point of stalling, in which an aircraft's momentum is used to increase its rate of climb. ◆ VERB 2 *(intr)* to carry out a chandelle.
▷**HISTORY** French, literally: CANDLE

Chandernagore (ˌtʃʌndənə'gɔː) NOUN a port in E India, in S West Bengal on the Hooghly River: a former French settlement (1686–1950). Pop.: 120 378 (1991).

Chandigarh (ˌtʃʌndɪ'gɑː) NOUN a city and Union Territory of N India, joint capital of the Punjab and Haryana: modern city planned in the 1950s by Le Corbusier. Pop.: 504 094 (1991), of city; 900 414 (2001), of union territory. Area (of union territory): 114 sq. km (44 sq. miles).

chandler ('tʃɑːndlə) NOUN 1 a dealer in a specified trade or merchandise: *corn chandler; ship's chandler.* 2 a person who makes or sells candles. 3 *Brit obsolete* a retailer of grocery provisions; shopkeeper.
▷**HISTORY** C14: from Old French *chandelier* one who makes or deals in candles, from *chandelle* CANDLE

chandlery ('tʃɑːndlərɪ) NOUN, *plural* **-dleries.** 1 the business, warehouse, or merchandise of a chandler. 2 a place where candles are kept.

Chandrasekhar limit (ˌtʃændrə'siːkə) NOUN *Astronomy* the upper limit to the mass of a white dwarf, equal to 1.44 solar masses. A star having a mass above this limit will continue to collapse to form a neutron star.
▷**HISTORY** C20: named after Subrahmanyan Chandrasekhar (1910–95), Indian-born US astronomer, who calculated it

Chang (tʃæŋ) NOUN another name for the **Yangtze.**

Changan ('tʃæŋ'ɑːn) NOUN a former name of **Xi An.**

Changchiakow *or* **Changchiak'ou** ('tʃæŋ'tʃjɑː'kaʊ) NOUN a variant transliteration of the Chinese name for **Zhangjiakou.**

Changchow *or* **Ch'ang-chou** ('tʃæŋ'tʃaʊ) NOUN a variant transliteration of the Chinese name for **Zhangzhou.**

Changchun *or* **Ch'ang Ch'un** ('tʃæŋ'tʃʊn) NOUN a city in NE China, capital of Jilin province: as **Hsinking,** capital of the Japanese state of Manchukuo (1932–45). Pop.: 2 072 324 (1999 est.).

Changde ('tʃæŋ'deɪ), **Changteh,** *or* **Ch'ang-te** NOUN a port in SE central China, in N Hunan province, near the mouth of the Yuan River: severely damaged by the Japanese in World War II. Pop.: 384 433 (1999 est.).

change (tʃeɪndʒ) VERB 1 to make or become different; alter. 2 *(tr)* to replace with or exchange for another: *to change one's name.* 3 (sometimes foll by *to* or *into*) to transform or convert or be transformed or converted. 4 to give and receive (something) in return; interchange: *to change places with someone.* 5 *(tr)* to give or receive (money) in exchange for the equivalent sum in a smaller denomination or different currency. 6 *(tr)* to remove or replace the coverings of: *to change a baby.* 7 (when *intr,* may be foll by *into* or *out of*) to put on other clothes. 8 *(intr)* (of the moon) to pass from one phase to the following one. 9 to operate (the gear lever of a motor vehicle) in order to change the gear ratio: *to change gear.* 10 to alight from (one bus, train, etc.) and board another. 11 **change face.** to rotate the telescope of a surveying instrument through 180° horizontally and vertically, taking a second sighting of the same object in order to reduce error. 12 **change feet.** *Informal* to put on different shoes, boots, etc. 13 **change front. a** *Military* to redeploy (a force in the field) so that its main weight of weapons points in another direction. **b** to alter one's attitude, opinion, etc. 14 **change hands.** to pass from one owner to another. 15 **change one's mind.** to alter one's decision or opinion. 16 **change one's tune.** to alter one's attitude or tone of speech. ◆ NOUN 17 the act or fact of changing or being changed. 18 a variation, deviation, or modification. 19 the substitution of one thing for another; exchange. 20 anything that is or may be substituted for something else. 21 variety or novelty (esp in the phrase **for a change**): *I want to go to France for a change.* 22 a different or fresh set, esp of clothes. 23 money given or received in return for its equivalent in a larger denomination or in a different currency. 24 the balance of money given or received when the amount tendered is larger than the amount due. 25 coins of a small denomination regarded collectively. 26 *(often capital) Archaic* a place where merchants meet to transact business; an exchange. 27 the act of passing from one state or phase to another. 28 the transition from one phase of the moon to the next. 29 the order in which a peal of bells may be rung. 30 *Sport* short for **changeover** (sense 3b). 31 *Slang* desirable or useful information. 32 *Obsolete* fickleness or caprice. 33 **change of heart.** a profound change of outlook, opinion, etc. 34 **get no change out of (someone).** *Slang* not to be successful in attempts to exploit or extract information from (someone). 35 **ring the changes.** to vary the manner or performance of an action that is often repeated. ◆ See also **change down, changeover, change round, change up.**
▷**HISTORY** C13: from Old French *changier,* from Latin *cambīre* to exchange, barter
▸'**changeless** ADJECTIVE ▸'**changelessly** ADVERB ▸'**changelessness** NOUN ▸'**changer** NOUN

changeable ('tʃeɪndʒəb^əl) ADJECTIVE 1 able to change or be changed; fickle: *changeable weather.* 2 varying in colour when viewed from different angles or in different lights.
▸ˌ**changea'bility** *or* '**changeableness** NOUN ▸'**changeably** ADVERB

change down VERB *(intr, adverb)* to select a lower gear when driving.

changeful ('tʃeɪndʒfʊl) ADJECTIVE often changing; inconstant; variable.
▸'**changefully** ADVERB ▸'**changefulness** NOUN

changeling ('tʃeɪndʒlɪŋ) NOUN 1 a child believed to have been exchanged by fairies for the parents' true child. 2 *Archaic* **a** an idiot. **b** a fickle or changeable person.

change of life NOUN a nontechnical name for **menopause.**

change of venue NOUN *Law* the removal of a trial out of one jurisdiction into another.

changeover ('tʃeɪndʒˌəʊvə) NOUN 1 an alteration or complete reversal from one method, system, or product to another: *a changeover to decimal currency.* 2 a reversal of a situation, attitude, etc. 3 *Sport* **a** the act of transferring to or being relieved by a team-mate in a relay race, as by handing over a baton, etc. **b** Also called: **change, takeover.** the point in a relay race at which the transfer is made. 4 *Sport, chiefly Brit* the exchange of ends by two teams, esp at half time. ◆ VERB **change over.** *(adverb)* 5 to adopt (a completely different position or attitude): *the driver and navigator changed over after four hours.* 6 *(intr) Sport, chiefly Brit* (of two teams) to exchange ends of a playing field, etc., as after half time.

change point NOUN *Surveying* a point to which a foresight and backsight are taken in levelling; turning point.

change-ringing NOUN 1 the art of bell-ringing in which a set of bells is rung in an established order which is then changed. 2 variations on a topic or theme.

change round VERB *(adverb)* 1 to place in or adopt a different or opposite position. ◆ NOUN **changeround.** 2 the act of changing to a different position.

change up VERB 1 *(intr, adverb)* to select a higher gear when driving. ◆ NOUN **change-up.** 2 *Baseball* an unexpectedly slow ball thrown in order to surprise the batter.

Changsha *or* **Ch'ang-sha** ('tʃæŋ'ʃɑː) NOUN a port in SE China, capital of Hunan province, on the Xiang River. Pop.: 1 334 036 (1999 est.).

Changteh *or* **Ch'ang-te** ('tʃæŋ'teɪ) NOUN a variant transliteration of the Chinese name for **Changde.**

Chania *or* **Hania** ('hɑːnɪə) NOUN the chief port of Crete, on the NW coast. Pop.: 50 000 (latest est.). Greek name: **Khaniá.**

channel[1] ('tʃæn^əl) NOUN 1 a broad strait connecting two areas of sea. 2 the bed or course of a river, stream, or canal. 3 a navigable course through a body of water. 4 *(often plural)* a means or agency of access, communication, etc.: *to go through official channels.* 5 a course into which something can be directed or moved: *a new channel of thought.* 6 *Electronics* **a** a band of radio frequencies assigned for a particular purpose, esp the broadcasting of a television signal. **b** a path for an electromagnetic signal: *a stereo set has two channels.* **c** a thin semiconductor layer between the source and drain of a field-effect transistor, the conductance of which is controlled by the gate voltage. 7 a tubular or trough-shaped passage for fluids. 8 a groove or flute, as in the shaft of a column. 9 *Computing* **a** a path along which data can be transmitted between a central processing unit and one or more peripheral devices. **b** one of the lines along the length of a paper tape on which information can be stored in the form of punched holes. 10 short for **channel iron.** ◆ VERB **-nels, -nelling, -nelled** *or US* **-nels, -neling, -neled.** 11 to provide or be provided with a channel or channels; make or cut channels in (something). 12 *(tr)* to guide into or convey through a channel or channels: *information was channelled through to them.* 13 to serve as a medium through whom the spirit of (a person of a former age) allegedly communicates with the

living. [14] (*tr*) to form a groove or flute in (a column, etc.).
▷HISTORY C13: from Old French *chanel,* from Latin *canālis* pipe, groove, conduit; see CANAL
▸ 'channeller NOUN

channel² ('tʃænᵊl) NOUN *Nautical* a flat timber or metal ledge projecting from the hull of a vessel above the chainplates to increase the angle of the shrouds.
▷HISTORY C18: variant of earlier *chainwale;* see CHAIN, WALE¹ (planking)

Channel ('tʃænᵊl) NOUN **the.** short for **English Channel.**

channel captain NOUN *Marketing* the most powerful member, and often the one that decides specifications, in a channel for distributing goods (which usually consists of a manufacturer, wholesaler, and retailer). The channel captain is sometimes the manufacturer but in the case of a chain store it may be the retailer.

Channel Country NOUN **the.** an area of E central Australia, in SW Queensland: crossed by intermittent rivers and subject to both flooding and long periods of drought.

channel-hop VERB **-hops, -hopping, -hopped.** (*intr*) to change television channels repeatedly using a remote control device.

channel iron *or* **bar** NOUN a rolled-steel bar with a U-shaped cross section. Sometimes shortened to **channel.**

Channel Islands PLURAL NOUN a group of islands in the English Channel, off the NW coast of France, consisting of Jersey, Guernsey, Alderney, Brechou, Great Sark, Little Sark, Herm, Jethou, and Lihou (British crown dependencies), and the Roches Douvres and the Iles Chausey (which belong to France): the only part of the duchy of Normandy remaining to Britain. Pop.: 153 700 (2001 est.). Area: 194 sq. km (75 sq. miles).

channelize *or* **channelise** ('tʃænəlaɪz) VERB (*tr*) to guide through or as if through a channel; provide a channel for.

Channel Tunnel NOUN the Anglo-French railway tunnel that runs beneath the English Channel, between Folkestone and Coquelles, near Calais; opened in 1994. Also called: **Chunnel, Eurotunnel.**

chanoyo (ˌtʃɑːnɔːˈjuː) NOUN a variant of **chado.**

chanson de geste *French* (ʃɑ̃sɔ̃ də ʒɛst) NOUN one of a genre of Old French epic poems celebrating heroic deeds, the most famous of which is the *Chanson de Roland.*
▷HISTORY literally: song of exploits

chant (tʃɑːnt) NOUN [1] a simple song or melody. [2] a short simple melody in which several words or syllables are assigned to one note, as in the recitation of psalms. [3] a psalm or canticle performed by using such a melody. [4] a rhythmic or repetitious slogan, usually spoken or sung, as by sports supporters, etc. [5] monotonous or singsong intonation in speech. ◆ VERB [6] to sing or recite (a psalm, prayer, etc.) as a chant. [7] to intone (a slogan) rhythmically or repetitiously. [8] to speak or say monotonously as if intoning a chant.
▷HISTORY C14: from Old French *chanter* to sing, from Latin *cantāre,* frequentative of *canere* to sing
▸ 'chantingly ADVERB

chanter ('tʃɑːntə) NOUN [1] a person who chants. [2] the pipe on a set of bagpipes that is provided with finger holes and on which the melody is played.

chanterelle (ˌtʃæntəˈrɛl) NOUN any saprotrophic basidiomycetous fungus of the genus *Cantharellus,* esp *C. cibarius,* having an edible yellow funnel-shaped mushroom: family *Cantharellaceae.*
▷HISTORY C18: from French, from New Latin *cantharella,* diminutive of Latin *cantharus* drinking vessel, from Greek *kantharos*

chanteuse (*French* ʃɑ̃tøz) NOUN a female singer, esp in a nightclub or cabaret.
▷HISTORY French: singer

chantey ('ʃæntɪ, 'tʃæn-) NOUN, *plural* **-teys.** the usual US spelling of **shanty².**

chanticleer (ˌtʃæntɪˈklɪə) *or* **chantecler** (ˌtʃæntɪˈklɛə) NOUN a name for a cock, used esp in fables.
▷HISTORY C13: from Old French *Chantecler,* from *chanter cler* to sing clearly

Chantilly (ʃænˈtɪlɪ; *French* ʃɑ̃tiji) NOUN [1] a town in N France, near the **Forest of Chantilly** formerly famous for lace and porcelain. Pop.: 11 341 (1990). [2] Also called: **Tiffany.** a breed of medium-sized cat with silky semi-long hair. ◆ ADJECTIVE [3] (of cream) lightly sweetened and whipped.

Chantilly lace NOUN (*sometimes not capital*) a delicate ornamental lace.

chantry ('tʃɑːntrɪ) NOUN, *plural* **-tries.** *Christianity* [1] an endowment for the singing of Masses for the soul of the founder or others designated by him. [2] a chapel or altar so endowed. [3] (*as modifier*): *a chantry priest.*
▷HISTORY C14: from Old French *chanterie,* from *chanter* to sing; see CHANT

chanty ('ʃæntɪ, 'tʃæn-) NOUN, *plural* **-ties.** a variant of **shanty².**

Chanukah ('hɑːnəkə, -nʊˌkɑː; *Hebrew* xanuˈka) NOUN a variant spelling of **Hanukkah.**

chanukiah ('hɑːnʊkɪə; *Hebrew* xanuˈkiːa) NOUN a variant spelling of **hanukiah.**

Chaoan ('tʃaʊˈɑːn) NOUN a city in SE China, in E Guangdong province, on the Han River: river port. Pop.: 313 469 (1990). Also called: **Chaochow.**

Chaochow ('tʃaʊˈtʃəʊ) NOUN another name for **Chaoan.**

chaology (keɪˈɒlədʒɪ) NOUN the study of chaos theory.
▸ cha'ologist NOUN

Chao Phraya ('tʃaʊ prəˈjɑː) NOUN a river in N Thailand, rising in the N highlands and flowing south to the Gulf of Siam. Length: (including the headstreams Nan and Ping) 1200 km (750 miles). Also called: **Menam.**

chaos ('keɪɒs) NOUN [1] complete disorder; utter confusion. [2] (*usually capital*) the disordered formless matter supposed to have existed before the ordered universe. [3] an obsolete word for **abyss.**
▷HISTORY C15: from Latin, from Greek *khaos;* compare CHASM, yawn
▸ **chaotic** (keɪˈɒtɪk) ADJECTIVE ▸ cha'otically ADVERB

chaos theory NOUN a theory, applied in various branches of science, that apparently random phenomena have underlying order.

chap¹ (tʃæp) VERB **chaps, chapping, chapped.** [1] (of the skin) to make or become raw and cracked, esp by exposure to cold. [2] *Scot* (of a clock) to strike (the hour). [3] *Scot* to knock (at a door, window, etc.). ◆ NOUN [4] (*usually plural*) a cracked or sore patch on the skin caused by chapping. [5] *Scot* a knock.
▷HISTORY C14: probably of Germanic origin; compare Middle Dutch, German *kappen* to chop off

chap² (tʃæp) NOUN *Informal* a man or boy; fellow.
▷HISTORY C16 (in the sense: buyer): shortened from CHAPMAN

chap³ (tʃɒp, tʃæp) NOUN a less common word for **chop³.**

chap. ABBREVIATION FOR: [1] chaplain. [2] chapter.

chaparejos (ˌʃæpəˈreɪəʊs; *Spanish* tʃapaˈrexos) *or* **chaparajos** (ˌʃæpəˈreɪəʊs; *Spanish* tʃapaˈraxos) PLURAL NOUN another name for **chaps.**
▷HISTORY from Mexican Spanish

chaparral (ˌtʃæpəˈræl, ˌʃæp-) NOUN (in the southwestern US) a dense growth of shrubs and trees, esp evergreen oaks.
▷HISTORY C19: from Spanish, from *chaparra* evergreen oak

chaparral cock NOUN another name for **roadrunner.**

chaparral pea NOUN a thorny leguminous Californian shrub, *Pickeringia montana,* with reddish-purple showy flowers.

chapati *or* **chapatti** (tʃəˈpætɪ, -ˈpʌtɪ, -ˈpɑːtɪ) NOUN, *plural* **-ti, -tis,** *or* **-ties.** (in Indian cookery) a flat coarse unleavened bread resembling a pancake.
▷HISTORY from Hindi

chapbook ('tʃæpˌbʊk) NOUN a book of popular ballads, stories, etc., formerly sold by chapmen or pedlars.

chape (tʃeɪp) NOUN [1] a metal tip or trimming for a scabbard. [2] the metal tongue of a buckle.
▷HISTORY C14: from Old French: hood, metal cover, from Late Latin *cappa* CAP
▸ 'chapeless ADJECTIVE

chapeau ('ʃæpəʊ; *French* ʃapo) NOUN, *plural* **-peaux** (-pəʊ, -pəʊz; *French* -po) *or* **-peaus.** a hat.
▷HISTORY C16: from French, from Late Latin *cappellus* hood, from *cappa* CAP

chapel ('tʃæpᵊl) NOUN [1] a place of Christian worship in a larger building, esp a place set apart, with a separate altar, in a church or cathedral. [2] a similar place of worship in or attached to a large house or institution, such as a college, hospital or prison. [3] a church subordinate to a parish church. [4] (in Britain) **a** a Nonconformist place of worship. **b** Nonconformist religious practices or doctrine. **c** (*as adjective*): *he is chapel, but his wife is church.* Compare **church** (sense 8). [5] (in Scotland) a Roman Catholic church. [6] the members of a trade union in a particular newspaper office, printing house, etc. [7] a printing office.
▷HISTORY C13: from Old French *chapele,* from Late Latin *cappella,* diminutive of *cappa* cloak (see CAP); originally denoting the sanctuary where the cloak of St Martin of Tours was kept as a relic

chapel of ease NOUN a church built to accommodate those living at a distance from the parish church.

chapelry NOUN, *plural* **-ries.** the district legally assigned to and served by an Anglican chapel.

chaperon *or* **chaperone** ('ʃæpəˌrəʊn) NOUN [1] (esp formerly) an older or married woman who accompanies or supervises a young unmarried woman on social occasions. [2] someone who accompanies and supervises a group, esp of young people, usually when in public places. ◆ VERB [3] to act as a chaperon to.
▷HISTORY C14: from Old French, from *chape* hood, protective covering; see CAP
▸ **chaperonage** ('ʃæpərənɪdʒ) NOUN

chapess (tʃæpˈɛs) NOUN *Brit informal* a woman.

chapfallen ('tʃæpˌfɔːlən) *or* **chopfallen** ADJECTIVE dejected; downhearted; crestfallen.
▷HISTORY C16: from CHOPS + FALLEN

chapiter ('tʃæpɪtə) NOUN *Architect* another name for **capital².**
▷HISTORY C15: from Old French *chapitre,* from Latin *capitellum* CAPITAL²

chaplain ('tʃæplɪn) NOUN a Christian clergyman attached to a private chapel of a prominent person or institution or ministering to a military body, professional group, etc: *a military chaplain; a prison chaplain.*
▷HISTORY C12: from Old French *chapelain,* from Late Latin *cappellānus,* from *cappella* CHAPEL
▸ 'chaplaincy, 'chaplainˌship, *or* 'chaplainry NOUN

chaplet ('tʃæplɪt) NOUN [1] an ornamental wreath of flowers, beads, etc., worn on the head. [2] a string of beads or something similar. [3] *RC Church* **a** a string of prayer beads constituting one third of the rosary. **b** the prayers counted on this string. [4] a narrow convex moulding in the form of a string of beads; astragal. [5] a metal support for the core in a casting mould, esp for the core of a cylindrical pipe.
▷HISTORY C14: from Old French *chapelet* garland of roses, from *chapel* hat; see CHAPEAU
▸ 'chapleted ADJECTIVE

chapman ('tʃæpmən) NOUN, *plural* **-men.** *Archaic* a trader, esp an itinerant pedlar.
▷HISTORY Old English *cēapman,* from *cēap* buying and selling (see CHEAP)
▸ 'chapmanˌship NOUN

Chapman Stick ('tʃæpmən) NOUN an electronically amplified musical instrument with ten or twelve strings and a fretted neck, which is played by striking the strings against the frets with the fingers. Often shortened to **Stick.**
▷HISTORY C20: named after its inventor, Emmett H. *Chapman* (born 1936), US guitarist

chappal ('tʃʌpᵊl) NOUN one of a pair of sandals, usually of leather, worn in India.
▷HISTORY from Hindi

chappie ('tʃæpɪ) NOUN *Informal* another word for **chap².**

chaps (tʃæps, ʃæps) PLURAL NOUN leather overalls without a seat, worn by cowboys. Also called: **chaparejos, chaparajos.**
▷HISTORY C19: shortened from CHAPAREJOS

chapstick ('tʃæpˌstɪk) NOUN *Chiefly US and Canadian* a cylinder of a substance for preventing or soothing chapped lips.
▷HISTORY C20: from a trademark

chaptalize *or* **chaptalise** (ˈtʃæptəˌlaɪz) VERB (*tr*) to add sugar to (a fermenting wine) to increase the alcohol content.
▷HISTORY C19: after J. A. *Chaptal* (1756–1832), French chemist who originated the process
▸ˌ**chaptaliˈzation** *or* ˌ**chaptaliˈsation** NOUN

chapter (ˈtʃæptə) NOUN [1] a division of a written work, esp a narrative, usually titled or numbered. [2] a sequence of events having a common attribute: *a chapter of disasters*. [3] **chapter of accidents. a** a series of misfortunes. **b** the unforeseeable course of events. [4] an episode or period in a life, history, etc. [5] a numbered reference to that part of a Parliamentary session which relates to a specified Act of Parliament. [6] a branch of some societies, clubs, etc., esp of a secret society. [7] the collective body or a meeting of the canons of a cathedral or collegiate church or of the members of a monastic or knightly order. Related adjective: **capitular.** [8] a general assembly of some organization. [9] **chapter and verse.** exact authority for an action or statement. ◆ VERB [10] (*tr*) to divide into chapters.
▷HISTORY C13: from Old French *chapitre,* from Latin *capitulum,* literally: little head, hence, section of writing, from *caput* head; in Medieval Latin: chapter of scripture or of a religious rule, a gathering for the reading of this, hence, assemblage of clergy

chapter 7 NOUN *US* the statute regarding liquidation proceedings that empowers a court to appoint a trustee to operate a failing business to prevent further loss.
▷HISTORY C20: from *chapter 7* of the Bankruptcy Reform Act (1978)

chapter 11 NOUN *US* the statute regarding the reorganization of a failing business empowering a court to allow the debtors to remain in control of the business to attempt to save it: *they are in chapter 11.*
▷HISTORY C20: from *chapter 11* of the Bankruptcy Reform Act (1978)

chapterhouse (ˈtʃæptəˌhaʊs) NOUN [1] the building attached to a cathedral, collegiate church, or religious house in which the chapter meets. [2] *US* the meeting place of a college fraternity or sorority.

chapter stop NOUN any of several markers placed at intervals on a DVD film, enabling the viewer to find and select particular scenes.

char¹ (tʃɑː) VERB **chars, charring, charred.** [1] to burn or be burned partially, esp so as to blacken the surface; scorch. [2] (*tr*) to reduce (wood) to charcoal by partial combustion.
▷HISTORY C17: short for CHARCOAL

char² *or* **charr** (tʃɑː) NOUN, *plural* **char, chars** *or* **charr, charrs.** any of various troutlike fishes of the genus *Salvelinus,* esp *S. alpinus,* occurring in cold lakes and northern seas: family *Salmonidae* (salmon).
▷HISTORY C17: of unknown origin

char³ (tʃɑː) NOUN [1] *Informal* short for **charwoman.** ◆ VERB **chars, charring, charred.** [2] *Brit informal* to do housework, cleaning, etc., as a job.
▷HISTORY C18: from Old English *cerr*

char⁴ (tʃɑː) NOUN *Brit* a slang word for **tea.**
▷HISTORY from Chinese *ch'a*

charabanc (ˈʃærəˌbæŋ; *French* ʃarabɑ̃) NOUN *Brit obsolete* a motor coach, esp one used for sightseeing tours.
▷HISTORY C19: from French *char-à-bancs,* wagon with seats

characin (ˈkærəsɪn) *or* **characid** NOUN any small carnivorous freshwater cyprinoid fish of the family *Characidae,* of Central and South America and Africa. They are similar to the carps but more brightly coloured.
▷HISTORY C19: from New Latin *Characinidae,* from *characinus,* from Greek *kharax* a fish, probably the sea bream

character (ˈkærɪktə) NOUN [1] the combination of traits and qualities distinguishing the individual nature of a person or thing. [2] one such distinguishing quality; characteristic. [3] moral force; integrity: *a man of character.* [4] **a** reputation, esp a good reputation. **b** (*as modifier*): *character assassination.* [5] a summary or account of a person's qualities and achievements; testimonial: *my last employer gave me a good character.* [6] capacity, position, or status: *he spoke in the character of a friend rather than a father.* [7] a person represented in a play, film, story, etc.; role. [8] an outstanding person: *one of the great characters of the century.* [9] *Informal* an odd, eccentric, or unusual person: *he's quite a character.* [10] an informal word for **person:** *a shady character.* [11] a symbol used in a writing system, such as a letter of the alphabet. [12] Also called: **sort.** *Printing* any single letter, numeral, punctuation mark, or symbol cast as a type. [13] *Computing* any letter, numeral, etc., which is a unit of information and can be represented uniquely by a binary pattern. [14] a style of writing or printing. [15] *Genetics* any structure, function, attribute, etc., in an organism, which may or may not be determined by a gene or group of genes. [16] a short prose sketch of a distinctive type of person, usually representing a vice or virtue. [17] **in** (*or* **out of**) **character.** typical (or not typical) of the apparent character of a person or thing. ◆ VERB (*tr*) [18] to write, print, inscribe, or engrave. [19] *Rare* to portray or represent.
▷HISTORY C14: from Latin: distinguishing mark, from Greek *kharaktēr* engraver's tool, from *kharassein* to engrave, stamp
▸ˈ**characterful** ADJECTIVE ▸ˈ**characterless** ADJECTIVE

character actor NOUN an actor who specializes in playing odd or eccentric characters.

character armour NOUN *Psychol* the defence an individual exhibits to others and to himself to disguise his underlying weaknesses: a term coined by William Reich.

character assassination NOUN the act of deliberately attempting to destroy a person's reputation by defamatory remarks.

character code NOUN *Computing* a machine-readable code that identifies a specified character or a set of such codes.

characteristic (ˌkærɪktəˈrɪstɪk) NOUN [1] a distinguishing quality, attribute, or trait. [2] *Maths* **a** the integral part of a common logarithm, indicating the order of magnitude of the associated number: *the characteristic of 2.4771 is 2.* Compare **mantissa. b** another name for **exponent** (sense 4), esp in number representation in computing ◆ ADJECTIVE [3] indicative of a distinctive quality, etc.; typical.
▸ˌ**characterˈistically** ADVERB

characteristic curve NOUN *Photog* a graph of the density of a particular photographic material plotted against the logarithm of the exposure producing this density.

characteristic function NOUN [1] *Maths* a function that assigns the value 1 to the members of a given set and the value 0 to its nonmembers. [2] *Statistics* a function derived from the probability distribution function that enables the distribution of the sum of given random variables to be analysed.

characterization *or* **characterisation** (ˌkærɪktəraɪˈzeɪʃən) NOUN [1] description of character, traits, etc. [2] the act of characterizing.

characterize *or* **characterise** (ˈkærɪktəˌraɪz) VERB (*tr*) [1] to be a characteristic of: *loneliness characterized the place.* [2] to distinguish or mark as a characteristic. [3] to describe or portray the character of.
▸ˈ**characterˌizable** *or* ˈ**characterˌisable** ADJECTIVE
▸ˈ**characterˌizer** *or* ˈ**characterˌiser** NOUN

character recognition NOUN *Computing* a magnetic or optical process used to detect the shape of individual characters printed or written on paper.

character sketch NOUN a brief description or portrayal of a person's character, qualities, etc.

character type NOUN *Psychol* a cluster of personality traits commonly occurring together in an individual.

charactery (ˈkærɪktərɪ, -trɪ) NOUN, *plural* **-teries.** *Archaic* [1] the use of symbols to express thoughts. [2] the group of symbols so used.

charade (ʃəˈrɑːd) NOUN [1] an episode or act in the game of charades. [2] *Chiefly Brit* an absurd act; travesty.

charades (ʃəˈrɑːdz) NOUN (*functioning as singular*) a parlour game in which one team acts out each syllable of a word, the other team having to guess the word.
▷HISTORY C18: from French *charade* entertainment, from Provençal *charrado* chat, from *charra* chatter, of imitative origin

charanga (ˌtʃæˈræŋgə) NOUN a type of orchestra used in performing traditional Cuban music.
▷HISTORY Spanish

charas (ˈtʃɑːrəs) NOUN another name for **hashish.**
▷HISTORY C19: from Hindi

charcoal (ˈtʃɑːˌkəʊl) NOUN [1] a black amorphous form of carbon made by heating wood or other organic matter in the absence of air: used as a fuel, in smelting metal ores, in explosives, and as an absorbent. See **activated carbon.** [2] a stick or pencil of this for drawing. [3] a drawing done in charcoal. [4] short for **charcoal grey.** ◆ VERB [5] (*tr*) to write, draw, or blacken with charcoal.
▷HISTORY C14: from *char* (origin obscure) + COAL

charcoal-burner NOUN (formerly) a person whose work was making charcoal by burning wood.

charcoal grey NOUN **a** a very dark grey colour. **b** (*as adjective*): *charcoal-grey trousers.*

charcuterie (ʃɑːˈkuːtəriː) NOUN [1] cooked cold meats. [2] a shop selling cooked cold meats.
▷HISTORY French

chard (tʃɑːd) NOUN a variety of beet, *Beta vulgaris cicla,* with large succulent leaves and thick stalks, used as a vegetable. Also called: **Swiss chard, leaf beet, seakale beet.**
▷HISTORY C17: probably from French *carde* edible leafstalk of the artichoke, but associated also with French *chardon* thistle, both ultimately from Latin *carduus* thistle; see CARDOON

Chardonnay (ˈʃɑːdəˌneɪ) NOUN (*sometimes not capital*) [1] a white grape originally grown in the Burgundy region of France, and now throughout the wine-producing world. [2] any of various white wines made from this grape.
▷HISTORY French

Charente (*French* ʃarɑ̃t) NOUN [1] a department of W central France, in Poitou-Charentes region. Capital: Angoulême. Pop.: 339 628 (1999). Area: 5972 sq. km (2329 sq. miles). [2] a river in W France, flowing west to the Bay of Biscay. Length: 362 km (225 miles).

Charente-Maritime (*French* ʃarɑ̃tmaritim) NOUN a department of W France, in Poitou-Charentes region. Capital: La Rochelle. Pop.: 557 024 (1999). Area: 7232 sq. km (2820 sq. miles).

charge (tʃɑːdʒ) VERB [1] to set or demand (a price): *he charges too much for his services.* [2] (*tr*) to hold financially liable; enter a debit against. [3] (*tr*) to enter or record as an obligation against a person or his account. [4] (*tr*) to accuse or impute a fault to (a person, etc.), as formally in a court of law. [5] (*tr*) to command; place a burden upon or assign responsibility to: *I was charged to take the message to headquarters.* [6] to make a rush at or sudden attack upon (a person or thing). [7] (*tr*) to fill (a receptacle) with the proper or appropriate quantity. [8] (often foll by *up*) to cause (an accumulator, capacitor, etc.) to take or store electricity or (of an accumulator) to have electricity fed into it. [9] to fill or suffuse or to be filled or suffused with matter by dispersion, solution, or absorption: *to charge water with carbon dioxide.* [10] (*tr*) to fill or suffuse with feeling, emotion, etc.: *the atmosphere was charged with excitement.* [11] (*tr*) *Law* (of a judge) to address (a jury) authoritatively. [12] (*tr*) to load (a firearm). [13] (*tr*) to aim (a weapon) in position ready for use. [14] (*tr*) *Heraldry* to paint (a shield, banner, etc.) with a charge. [15] (*intr*) (of hunting dogs) to lie down at command. ◆ NOUN [16] a price charged for some article or service; cost. [17] a financial liability, such as a tax. [18] a debt or a book entry recording it. [19] an accusation or allegation, such as a formal accusation of a crime in law. [20] **a** an onrush, attack, or assault. **b** the call to such an attack in battle. [21] custody or guardianship. [22] a person or thing committed to someone's care. [23] **a** a cartridge or shell. **b** the explosive required to discharge a firearm or other weapon. **c** an amount of explosive material to be detonated at any one time. [24] the quantity of anything that a receptacle is intended to hold. [25] *Physics* **a** the attribute of matter by which it responds to electromagnetic forces responsible for all electrical phenomena, existing in two forms to which the signs negative and positive are arbitrarily assigned. **b** a similar property of a body or system determined by the

extent to which it contains an excess or deficiency of electrons. **c** a quantity of electricity determined by the product of an electric current and the time for which it flows, measured in coulombs. **d** the total amount of electricity stored in a capacitor. **e** the total amount of electricity held in an accumulator, usually measured in ampere-hours. Symbol: *q or Q*. 26 a load or burden. 27 a duty or responsibility; control. 28 a command, injunction, or order. 29 *Slang* a thrill. 30 *Law* the address made by a judge to the jury at the conclusion of the evidence. 31 *Heraldry* a design, device, or image depicted on heraldic arms: *a charge of three lions.* 32 the solid propellant used in rockets, sometimes including the inhibitor. 33 **in charge.** in command. 34 **in charge of. a** having responsibility for. **b** *US* under the care of.
▷HISTORY C13: from Old French *chargier* to load, from Late Latin *carricāre;* see CARRY

chargeable ('tʃɑːdʒəbᵊl) ADJECTIVE 1 charged or liable to be charged. 2 liable to result in a legal charge.
▸**'chargeableness** *or* **ˌchargea'bility** NOUN ▸**'chargeably** ADVERB

chargeable asset NOUN any asset that can give rise to assessment for capital gains tax on its disposal. Exempt assets include principal private residences, cars, investments held in a personal equity plan, and government securities.

chargeable transfer NOUN a transfer of value made as a gift during a person's lifetime that is not covered by a specific exemption and therefore gives rise to liability under inheritance tax.

charge account NOUN another term for **credit account.**

charge-cap ('tʃɑːdʒˌkæp) VERB (*tr*) **-caps, -capping, -capped** (in Britain) to impose on (a local authority) an upper limit on the community charge it may levy.
▸**'charge-ˌcapping** NOUN

charge card NOUN a card issued by a chain store, shop, or organization, that enables customers to obtain goods and services for which they pay at a later date.

charge carrier NOUN an electron, hole, or ion that transports the electric charge in an electric current.

charge-coupled device NOUN *Computing* an electronic device, used in imaging and signal processing, in which information is represented as packets of electric charge that are stored in an array of tiny closely spaced capacitors and can be moved from one capacitor to another in a controlled way. Abbreviation: **CCD.**

chargé d'affaires ('ʃɑːʒeɪ dæ'fɛə; *French* ʃarʒe dafɛr) NOUN, *plural* **chargés d'affaires** ('ʃɑːʒeɪ, -ʒeɪz; *French* ʃarʒe). 1 the temporary head of a diplomatic mission in the absence of the ambassador or minister. 2 the head of a diplomatic mission of the lowest level.
▷HISTORY C18: from French: (one) charged with affairs

charge density NOUN the electric charge per unit volume of a medium or body or per unit area of a surface.

charge hand NOUN *Brit* a workman whose grade of responsibility is just below that of a foreman.

charge nurse NOUN *Brit* a nurse in charge of a ward in a hospital: the male equivalent of **sister.**

charge of quarters NOUN *US* a member of the armed forces who handles administration in his unit, esp after duty hours.

charger[1] ('tʃɑːdʒə) NOUN 1 a person or thing that charges. 2 a large strong horse formerly ridden into battle. 3 a device for charging or recharging an accumulator or rechargeable battery.

charger[2] ('tʃɑːdʒə) NOUN *Antiques* a large dish for serving at table or for display.
▷HISTORY C14 *chargeour* something to bear a load, from *chargen* to CHARGE

charge sheet NOUN *Brit* a document on which a police officer enters details of the charge against a prisoner and the court in which he will appear.

char-grilled ADJECTIVE (of food) grilled over charcoal.

Chari ('tʃɑːrɪ) *or* **Shari** NOUN a river in N central Africa, rising in the N Central African Republic and flowing north to Lake Chad. Length: about 2250 km (1400 miles).

charidee ('tʃærɪdiː) NOUN *Informal* a jocular spelling of charity, as pronounced in a mid-Atlantic accent.

charily ('tʃɛərɪlɪ) ADVERB 1 cautiously; carefully. 2 sparingly.

chariness ('tʃɛərɪnɪs) NOUN the state of being chary.

Charing Cross ('tʃærɪŋ) NOUN a district of London, in the city of Westminster: the modern cross (1863) in front of Charing Cross railway station replaces the one erected by Edward I (1290), the last of twelve marking the route of the funeral procession of his queen, Eleanor.

Chari-Nile ('tʃɑːrɪ'naɪl) NOUN 1 a group of languages of E Africa, now generally regarded as a branch of the Nilo-Saharan family, spoken in parts of the Sudan, the Democratic Republic of Congo (formerly Zaïre), Uganda, Kenya, Tanzania, and adjacent countries. ◆ ADJECTIVE 2 relating to or belonging to this group of languages.

chariot ('tʃærɪət) NOUN 1 a two-wheeled horse-drawn vehicle used in ancient Egypt, Greece, Rome, etc., in war, races, and processions. 2 a light four-wheeled horse-drawn ceremonial carriage. 3 *Poetic* any stately vehicle.
▷HISTORY C14: from Old French, augmentative of *char* CAR

charioteer (ˌtʃærɪə'tɪə) NOUN the driver of a chariot.

charisma (kə'rɪzmə) *or* **charism** ('kærɪzəm) NOUN 1 a special personal quality or power of an individual making him capable of influencing or inspiring large numbers of people. 2 a quality inherent in a thing which inspires great enthusiasm and devotion. 3 *Christianity* a divinely bestowed power or talent.
▷HISTORY C17: from Church Latin, from Greek *kharisma,* from *kharis* grace, favour
▸**charismatic** (ˌkærɪz'mætɪk) ADJECTIVE

charismatic movement NOUN *Christianity* any of various groups, within existing denominations, that emphasize communal prayer and the charismatic gifts of speaking in tongues, healing, etc.

charitable ('tʃærɪtəbᵊl) ADJECTIVE 1 generous in giving to the needy. 2 kind or lenient in one's attitude towards others. 3 concerned with or involving charity.
▸**'charitableness** NOUN ▸**'charitably** ADVERB

charitable trust NOUN a trust set up for the benefit of a charity that complies with the regulations of the Charity Commissioners to enable it to be exempt from paying income tax.

charity ('tʃærɪtɪ) NOUN, *plural* **-ties.** 1 **a** the giving of help, money, food, etc., to those in need. **b** (*as modifier*): *a charity show.* 2 **a** an institution or organization set up to provide help, money, etc., to those in need. **b** (*as modifier*): *charity funds.* 3 the help, money, etc., given to the needy; alms. 4 a kindly and lenient attitude towards people. 5 love of one's fellow men.
▷HISTORY C13: from Old French *charite,* from Latin *cāritās* affection, love, from *cārus* dear

Charity Commissioners PLURAL NOUN (in Britain) members of a commission constituted to keep a register of charities and control charitable trusts.

charivari (ˌʃɑːrɪ'vɑːrɪ), **shivaree,** *or esp US* **chivaree** NOUN 1 a discordant mock serenade to newlyweds, made with pans, kettles, etc. 2 a confused noise; din.
▷HISTORY C17: from French, from Late Latin *caribaria* headache, from Greek *karēbaria,* from *karē* head + *barus* heavy

charkha *or* **charka** ('tʃɑːkə) NOUN (in India) a spinning wheel, esp for cotton.
▷HISTORY from Hindi

charlady ('tʃɑːˌleɪdɪ) NOUN, *plural* **-dies.** another name for **charwoman.**

charlatan ('ʃɑːlətᵊn) NOUN someone who professes knowledge or expertise, esp in medicine, that he does not have; quack.
▷HISTORY C17: from French, from Italian *ciarlatano,* from *ciarlare* to chatter
▸**'charlatanˌism** *or* **'charlatanry** NOUN ▸**ˌcharlatan'istic** ADJECTIVE

Charleroi (*French* ʃarlərwa) NOUN a town in SW Belgium, in Hainaut province: centre of an industrial region. Pop.: 200 827 (2000 est.).

Charles' law (tʃɑːlz) NOUN the principle that all gases expand equally for the same rise of temperature if they are held at constant pressure: also that the pressures of all gases increase equally for the same rise of temperature if they are held at constant volume. The law is now known to be only true for ideal gases. Also called: **Gay-Lussac's law.**
▷HISTORY C18: named after Jacques A. C. *Charles* (1746–1823), French physicist who first formulated it

Charles's Wain (weɪn) NOUN another name for the **Plough.**
▷HISTORY Old English *Carles wægn,* from *Carl* Charlemagne (?742–814 A.D.), king of the Franks and Holy Roman Emperor + *wægn* WAIN

charleston ('tʃɑːlstən) NOUN a fast rhythmic dance of the 1920s, characterized by kicking and by twisting of the legs from the knee down.
▷HISTORY C20: named after CHARLESTON, South Carolina

Charleston ('tʃɑːlstən) NOUN 1 a city in central West Virginia: the state capital. Pop.: 59 371 (1985 est.). 2 a port in SE South Carolina, on the Atlantic: scene of the first action in the Civil War. Pop.: 96 650 (2000).

Charleville-Mézières (*French* ʃarləvilmezjɛr) NOUN twin towns on opposite sides of the River Meuse in NE France. Pop.: 59 440 (1990). See **Mézières.**

charley horse ('tʃɑːlɪ) NOUN *US and Canadian informal* muscle stiffness or cramp following strenuous athletic exercise.
▷HISTORY C19: of uncertain origin

charlie ('tʃɑːlɪ) NOUN 1 *Brit informal* a silly person; fool. 2 *Austral informal* a girl or woman.
▷HISTORY C20: for sense 1: shortened from *Charlie Hunt,* rhyming slang for CUNT; sense 2 is shortened from *Charlie Wheeler,* rhyming slang for SHEILA

Charlie[1] ('tʃɑːlɪ) NOUN *Communications* a code word for the letter *c.*

Charlie[2] *or* **Charley** ('tʃɑːlɪ) NOUN *US and Austral military slang* a member of the Vietcong or the Vietcong collectively: *Charlie hit us with rockets.*
▷HISTORY shortened from *Victor Charlie,* communications code for *VC,* abbreviation of *Vietcong*

Charlie[3] ('tʃɑːlɪ) NOUN *Slang* cocaine.

charlier shoe ('tʃɑːlɪə) NOUN a special light type of horseshoe that does not have a toe clip; it is applied by a farrier before a horse is turned out.

charlock ('tʃɑːlɒk) NOUN 1 Also called: **wild mustard.** a weedy Eurasian plant, *Sinapis arvensis* (or *Brassica kaber*), with hairy stems and foliage and yellow flowers: family: *Brassicaceae* (crucifers). 2 **white charlock.** Also called: **wild radish, runch** (rʌntʃ). a related plant, *Raphanus raphanistrum,* with yellow, mauve, or white flowers and podlike fruits.
▷HISTORY Old English *cerlic,* of obscure origin

charlotte ('ʃɑːlət) NOUN 1 a baked dessert served hot or cold, commonly made with fruit and layers or a casing of bread or cake crumbs, sponge cake, etc.: *apple charlotte.* 2 short for **charlotte russe.**
▷HISTORY C19: from French, from the name *Charlotte*

Charlotte ('ʃɑːlət) NOUN a city in S North Carolina: the largest city in the state. Pop.: 540 828 (2000).

Charlotte Amalie ('ʃɑːlət ə'mɑːlɪə) NOUN the capital of the Virgin Islands of the United States, a port on St Thomas Island. Pop.: 12 331 (1990). Former name (1921–37): **Saint Thomas.**

Charlottenburg (*German* ʃar'lɔtənburk) NOUN a district of Berlin (of West Berlin until 1990), formerly an independent city. Pop.: 145 564 (latest est.).

charlotte russe (ruːs) NOUN a cold dessert made in a mould with sponge fingers enclosing a mixture of whipped cream, custard, etc.
▷HISTORY French: Russian charlotte

Charlottetown ('ʃɑːlətˌtaʊn) NOUN a port in SE Canada, capital of the province of Prince Edward Island. Pop.: 15 396 (1991).

charm[1] (tʃɑːm) NOUN [1] the quality of pleasing, fascinating, or attracting people. [2] a pleasing or attractive feature. [3] a small object worn or kept for supposed magical powers of protection; amulet; talisman. [4] a trinket worn on a bracelet. [5] a magic spell; enchantment. [6] a formula or action used in casting such a spell. [7] *Physics* an internal quantum number of certain elementary particles, used to explain some scattering experiments. [8] **like a charm.** perfectly; successfully. ◆ VERB [9] to attract or fascinate; delight greatly. [10] to cast a magic spell on. [11] to protect, influence, or heal, supposedly by magic. [12] (*tr*) to influence or obtain by personal charm: *he charmed them into believing him.*
▷ HISTORY C13: from Old French *charme,* from Latin *carmen* song, incantation, from *canere* to sing

charm[2] (tʃɑːm) NOUN *Southwest English dialect* a loud noise, as of a number of people chattering or of birds singing.
▷ HISTORY C16: variant of CHIRM

charmed (tʃɑːmd) ADJECTIVE [1] delighted or fascinated: *a charmed audience.* [2] seemingly protected by a magic spell: *he bears a charmed life.* [3] *Physics* possessing charm: *a charmed quark.*

charmer (ˈtʃɑːmə) NOUN [1] an attractive person. [2] a person claiming or seeming to have magical powers.

Charmeuse (ʃɑːˈmuːz; *French* ʃarmøz) NOUN *Trademark* a lightweight fabric with a satin-like finish.

Charminar (ˌtʃɑːmɪˈnɑː) NOUN a 16th-century monument with four minarets at Hyderabad, India.

charming (ˈtʃɑːmɪŋ) ADJECTIVE delightful; pleasant; attractive.
▸ **ˈcharmingly** ADVERB

charm offensive NOUN a concentrated attempt to gain favour or respectability by conspicuously cooperative or obliging behaviour.

charnel (ˈtʃɑːnᵊl) NOUN [1] short for **charnel house.** ◆ ADJECTIVE [2] ghastly; sepulchral; deathly.
▷ HISTORY C14: from Old French: burial place, from Latin *carnālis* fleshly, CARNAL

charnel house NOUN (esp formerly) a building or vault where corpses or bones are deposited.

Charolais (ˈʃærəˌleɪ) NOUN a breed of large white beef cattle that originated in France.
▷ HISTORY C19: from French: named after Monts du *Charollais,* E France

Charon[1] (ˈkɛərən) NOUN *Greek myth* the ferryman who brought the dead across the rivers Styx or Acheron to Hades.

Charon[2] (ˈkɛərən) NOUN the only known satellite of Pluto, discovered in 1978.

charpoy (ˈtʃɑːpɔɪ) *or* **charpai** (ˈtʃɑːpaɪ) NOUN a bedstead of woven webbing or hemp stretched on a wooden frame on four legs, common in India.
▷ HISTORY C19: from Urdu *cārpāī*

charqui (ˈtʃɑːkɪ) NOUN meat, esp beef, cut into strips and dried.
▷ HISTORY C18: from Spanish, from Quechuan
▸ **charquid** (ˈtʃɑːkɪd) ADJECTIVE

charr (tʃɑː) NOUN, *plural* **charr** *or* **charrs.** a variant spelling of **char** (the fish).

chart (tʃɑːt) NOUN [1] a map designed to aid navigation by sea or air. [2] an outline map, esp one on which weather information is plotted. [3] a sheet giving graphical, tabular, or diagrammatical information. [4] another name for **graph** (sense 1). [5] *Astrology* another word for **horoscope** (sense 3). [6] **the charts.** *Informal* the lists produced weekly from various sources of the bestselling pop singles and albums or the most popular videos. ◆ VERB [7] (*tr*) to make a chart of. [8] (*tr*) to make a detailed plan of. [9] (*tr*) to plot or outline the course of. [10] (*intr*) (of a record or video) to appear in the charts (sense 6).
▷ HISTORY C16: from Latin, from Greek *khartēs* papyrus, literally: something on which to make marks; related to Greek *kharattein* to engrave
▸ **ˈchartable** ADJECTIVE

charter (ˈtʃɑːtə) NOUN [1] a formal document from the sovereign or state incorporating a city, bank, college, etc., and specifying its purposes and rights. [2] (*sometimes capital*) a formal document granting or demanding from the sovereign power of a state certain rights or liberties. [3] a document issued by a society or an organization authorizing the establishment of a local branch or chapter. [4] a special privilege or exemption. [5] (*often capital*) the fundamental principles of an organization; constitution: *the Charter of the United Nations.* [6] **a** the hire or lease of transportation. **b** the agreement or contract regulating this. **c** (*as modifier*): *a charter flight.* [7] a law, policy, or decision containing a loophole which allows a specified group to engage more easily in an activity considered undesirable: *a beggars' charter.* [8] *Maritime law* another word for **charterparty.** ◆ VERB (*tr*) [9] to lease or hire by charterparty. [10] to hire (a vehicle, etc.). [11] to grant a charter of incorporation or liberties to (a group or person).
▷ HISTORY C13: from Old French *chartre,* from Latin *chartula* a little paper, from *charta* leaf of papyrus; see CHART
▸ **ˈcharterer** NOUN

charter colony NOUN *US history* a colony, such as Virginia or Massachusetts, created by royal charter under the control of an individual, trading company, etc., and exempt from interference by the Crown.

chartered (ˈtʃɑːtəd) ADJECTIVE (of a professional person) having attained certain professional qualifications or standards and acquired membership of a particular professional body.

chartered accountant NOUN (in Britain) an accountant who has passed the professional examinations of the Institute of Chartered Accountants in England and Wales, the Institute of Chartered Accountants of Scotland, or the Institute of Chartered Accountants in Ireland. Abbreviation: **CA.**

chartered club NOUN *NZ* a private club licensed to serve alcohol to members.

chartered engineer NOUN (in Britain) an engineer who is registered with the Engineering Council as having the scientific and technical knowledge and practical experience to satisfy its professional requirements. Abbreviation: **CEng.**

chartered librarian NOUN (in Britain) a librarian who has obtained a qualification from the Library Association in addition to a degree or diploma in librarianship.

chartered surveyor NOUN (in Britain) a surveyor who is registered with the Royal Institution of Chartered Surveyors as having the qualifications, training, and experience to satisfy their professional requirements.

chartered teacher NOUN (in Scotland) a teacher with extensive qualifications and experience paid at a higher rate to remain as a classroom teacher rather than seek promotion to an administrative post.

Charterhouse (ˈtʃɑːtəˌhaʊs) NOUN a Carthusian monastery.
▷ HISTORY C16: changed by folk etymology from Anglo-French *chartrouse,* after *Chartosse* (now Saint-Pierre-de-Chartreuse), village near Grenoble, France, the original home of the Carthusian order

charter member NOUN an original or founder member of a society or organization.

charterparty (ˈtʃɑːtəˌpɑːtɪ) NOUN, *plural* **-parties.** [1] *Maritime law* an agreement for the hire of all or part of a ship for a specified voyage or period of time. [2] an individual or group that charters a ship, etc.

Chartism (ˈtʃɑːˌtɪzəm) NOUN *English history* the principles of the reform movement in England from 1838 to 1848, which included manhood suffrage, payment of Members of Parliament, equal electoral districts, annual parliaments, voting by ballot, and the abolition of property qualifications for MPs.
▷ HISTORY named after the *People's Charter,* a document which stated their aims
▸ **ˈChartist** NOUN, ADJECTIVE

chartist (ˈtʃɑːtɪst) NOUN a stock market specialist who analyses and predicts market trends from graphs of recent price and volume movements of selected securities.

chartless (ˈtʃɑːtlɪs) ADJECTIVE not mapped; uncharted.

chartography (kɑːˈtɒgrəfɪ) NOUN *Rare* a variant spelling of **cartography.**
▸ **charˈtographer** NOUN ▸ **chartographic** (ˌkɑːtəˈgræfɪk) *or* **ˌchartoˈgraphical** ADJECTIVE ▸ **ˌchartoˈgraphically** ADVERB

Chartres (ˈʃɑːtrə, ʃɑːt; *French* ʃartrə) NOUN a city in NW France: Gothic cathedral; market town. Pop.: 41 850 (1990).

chartreuse (ʃɑːˈtrɜːz; *French* ʃartrøz) NOUN [1] either of two liqueurs, green or yellow, made from herbs and flowers. [2] **a** a colour varying from a clear yellowish-green to a strong greenish-yellow. **b** (*as adjective*): *a chartreuse dress.*
▷ HISTORY C19: from French, after *La Grande Chartreuse,* monastery near Grenoble, where the liqueur is produced

Chartreux (ʃɑːˈtrɜː; *French* ʃartrø) NOUN, *plural* **-treux** (-ˈtrɜː; *French* -trø). a breed of sturdy cat with short dense woolly fur.

chartulary (ˈtʃɑːtjʊlərɪ) NOUN, *plural* **-laries.** a variant of **cartulary.**

Chartwell (ˈtʃɑːtˌwɛl) NOUN a house near Westerham in Kent: home for 40 years of Sir Winston Churchill.

charver (ˈʃɑːvə) NOUN *Northumbrian English dialect, derogatory* a young woman.

charwoman (ˈtʃɑːˌwʊmən) NOUN, *plural* **-women.** *Brit* a woman who is hired to clean, tidy, etc., in a house or office.

chary (ˈtʃɛərɪ) ADJECTIVE **charier, chariest.** [1] wary; careful. [2] choosy; finicky. [3] shy. [4] sparing; mean.
▷ HISTORY Old English *cearig;* related to *caru* CARE, Old High German *charag* sorrowful

Charybdis (kəˈrɪbdɪs) NOUN a ship-devouring monster in classical mythology, identified with a whirlpool off the north coast of Sicily, lying opposite Scylla on the Italian coast. Compare **Scylla.**
▸ **Chaˈrybdian** ADJECTIVE

chase[1] (tʃeɪs) VERB [1] to follow or run after (a person, animal, or goal) persistently or quickly. [2] (*tr; often foll by out, away,* or *off*) to force to run (away); drive (out). [3] (*tr*) *Informal* to court (a member of the opposite sex) in an unsubtle manner. [4] (*tr; often foll by up*) *Informal* to pursue persistently and energetically in order to obtain results, information, etc.: *chase up the builders and get a delivery date.* [5] (*intr*) *Informal* to hurry; rush. ◆ NOUN [6] the act of chasing; pursuit. [7] any quarry that is pursued. [8] *Brit* an unenclosed area of land where wild animals are preserved to be hunted. [9] *Brit* the right to hunt a particular quarry over the land of others. [10] **the chase.** the act or sport of hunting. [11] short for **steeplechase.** [12] *Real Tennis* a ball that bounces twice, requiring the point to be played again. [13] **cut to the chase.** *Informal, chiefly US* to start talking about the important aspects of something. [14] **give chase.** to pursue (a person, animal, or thing) actively.
▷ HISTORY C13: from Old French *chacier,* from Vulgar Latin *captiāre* (unattested), from Latin *captāre* to pursue eagerly, from *capere* to take; see CATCH
▸ **ˈchaseable** ADJECTIVE

chase[2] (tʃeɪs) NOUN [1] *Printing* a rectangular steel or cast-iron frame into which metal type and blocks making up pages are locked for printing or plate-making. [2] the part of a gun barrel from the front of the trunnions to the muzzle. [3] a groove or channel, esp one that is cut in a wall to take a pipe, cable, etc. ◆ VERB (*tr*) [4] Also: **chamfer.** to cut a groove, furrow, or flute in (a surface, column, etc.).
▷ HISTORY C17 (in the sense: frame for letterpress matter): probably from French *châsse* frame (in the sense: bore of a cannon, etc.): from Old French *chas* enclosure, from Late Latin *capsus* pen for animals; both from Latin *capsa* CASE[2]

chase[3] (tʃeɪs) VERB (*tr*) [1] Also: **enchase.** to ornament (metal) by engraving or embossing. [2] to form or finish (a screw thread) with a chaser.
▷ HISTORY C14: from Old French *enchasser* ENCHASE

chaser[1] (ˈtʃeɪsə) NOUN [1] a person or thing that chases. [2] a drink drunk after another of a different kind, as beer after spirits. [3] a cannon on a vessel situated either at the bow (**bow chaser**) or the stern (**stern chaser**) and used during pursuit by or of another vessel.

chaser[2] (ˈtʃeɪsə) NOUN [1] a person who engraves. [2] a lathe cutting tool for accurately finishing a screw thread, having a cutting edge consisting of several repetitions of the thread form.

chasm (ˈkæzəm) NOUN [1] a deep cleft in the ground; abyss. [2] a break in continuity; gap. [3] a wide difference in interests, feelings, etc.

▷**HISTORY** C17: from Latin *chasma,* from Greek *khasma;* related to Greek *khainein* to gape
▸**chasmal** ('kæzməl) *or* '**chasmic** ADJECTIVE

chasmogamy (kæz'mɒgəmɪ) NOUN *Botany* the production of flowers that open, so as to expose the reproductive organs and allow cross-pollination. Compare **cleistogamy.**
▷**HISTORY** C20: from New Latin *(flores) chasmogami* from Greek *khasma* CHASM + -GAMY
▸**chas'mogamous** ADJECTIVE

chassé ('ʃæseɪ) NOUN [1] one of a series of gliding steps in ballet in which the same foot always leads. [2] three consecutive dance steps, two fast and one slow, to four beats of music. ◆ VERB **-sés, -séing, -séd.** [3] *(intr)* to perform either of these steps.
▷**HISTORY** C19: from French: a chasing

chassepot ('ʃæspəʊ; *French* ʃaspo) NOUN a breech-loading bolt-action rifle formerly used by the French Army.
▷**HISTORY** C19: named after A. A. *Chassepot* (1833–1905), French gunsmith who invented it

chasseur (ʃæ'sɜː; *French* ʃasœr) NOUN [1] *French army* a member of a unit specially trained and equipped for swift deployment. [2] (in some parts of Europe, esp formerly) a uniformed attendant, esp one in the livery of a huntsman. ◆ ADJECTIVE [3] *(often postpositive)* designating or cooked in a sauce consisting of white wine and mushrooms.
▷**HISTORY** C18: from French: huntsman

Chassid, Chasid, Hassid, *or* **Hasid** ('hæsɪd; *Hebrew* xa'sid) NOUN, *plural* **Chassidim, Chasidim, Hassidim** *or* **Hasidim** ('hæsɪˌdiːm, -dɪm; *Hebrew* xasɪ'dim). [1] a sect of Jewish mystics founded in Poland about 1750, characterized by religious zeal and a spirit of prayer, joy, and charity. [2] a Jewish sect of the 2nd century B.C., formed to combat Hellenistic influences.
▸**Chassidic, Chasidic** *or* **Hassidic, Hasidic** (hə'sɪdɪk) ADJECTIVE ▸'**Chassidˌism,** '**Chasidˌism** *or* '**Hassidˌism,** '**Hasidˌism** NOUN

chassis ('ʃæsɪ) NOUN, *plural* **-sis** (-sɪz). [1] the steel frame, wheels, engine, and mechanical parts of a motor vehicle, to which the body is attached. [2] *Electronics* a mounting for the circuit components of an electrical or electronic device, such as a radio or television. [3] the landing gear of an aircraft. [4] *Obsolete* a wooden framework for a window, screen, etc. [5] the frame on which a cannon carriage moves backwards and forwards. [6] *Slang* the body of a person, esp a woman.
▷**HISTORY** C17 (meaning: window frame): from French *châssis* frame, from Vulgar Latin *capsicum* (unattested), ultimately from Latin *capsa* CASE[2]

chaste (tʃeɪst) ADJECTIVE [1] not having experienced sexual intercourse; virginal. [2] abstaining from unlawful or immoral sexual intercourse. [3] (of conduct, speech, etc.) pure; decent; modest. [4] (of style or taste) free from embellishment; simple; restrained.
▷**HISTORY** C13: from Old French, from Latin *castus* pure; compare CASTE
▸'**chastely** ADVERB ▸'**chasteness** NOUN

chasten ('tʃeɪsᵊn) VERB *(tr)* [1] to bring to a state of submission; subdue; tame. [2] to discipline or correct by punishment. [3] to moderate; restrain; temper.
▷**HISTORY** C16: from Old French *chastier,* from Latin *castigāre;* see CASTIGATE
▸'**chastener** NOUN ▸'**chasteningly** ADVERB

chaste tree NOUN a small ornamental verbenaceous tree, *Vitex agnus-castus,* of S Europe and SW Asia, with spikes of pale blue flowers.

chastise (tʃæs'taɪz) VERB *(tr)* [1] to discipline or punish, esp by beating. [2] to scold severely.
▷**HISTORY** C14 *chastisen,* irregularly from *chastien* to CHASTEN
▸**chas'tisable** ADJECTIVE ▸**chastisement** ('tʃæstɪzmənt, tʃæs'taɪz-) NOUN ▸**chas'tiser** NOUN

chastity ('tʃæstɪtɪ) NOUN [1] the state of being chaste; purity. [2] abstention from sexual intercourse; virginity or celibacy: *a vow of chastity.*
▷**HISTORY** C13: from Old French *chasteté,* from Latin *castitās,* from *castus* CHASTE

chastity belt NOUN a locking beltlike device with a loop designed to go between a woman's legs in order to prevent her from having sexual intercourse.

chasuble ('tʃæzjʊbᵊl) NOUN *Christianity* a long sleeveless outer vestment worn by a priest when celebrating Mass.
▷**HISTORY** C13: from French, from Late Latin *casubla* garment with a hood, apparently from *casula* cloak, literally: little house, from Latin *casa* cottage

chat[1] (tʃæt) NOUN [1] informal conversation or talk conducted in an easy familiar manner. [2] any Old World songbird of the subfamily *Turdinae* (thrushes, etc.) having a harsh chattering cry. See also **stonechat, whinchat.** [3] any of various North American warblers, such as *Icteria virens* (**yellow-breasted chat**). [4] any of various Australian wrens (family *Muscicapidae*) of the genus *Ephthianura* and other genera. ◆ VERB **chats, chatting, chatted.** *(intr)* [5] to talk in an easy familiar way. ◆ See also **chat up.**
▷**HISTORY** C16: short for CHATTER

chat[2] (tʃæt) NOUN *Archaic or dialect* a catkin, esp a willow catkin.
▷**HISTORY** C15: from French *chat* cat, referring to the furry appearance

chatbot ('tʃætˌbɒt) NOUN a computer program in the form of a virtual e-mail correspondent that can reply to messages from computer users.
▷**HISTORY** C20: from CHAT[1] + (RO)BOT

chateau *or* **château** ('ʃætəʊ; *French* ʃato) NOUN, *plural* **-teaux** (-təʊ, -təʊz; *French* -to) *or* **-teaus.** [1] a country house, castle, or manor house, esp in France. [2] (in Quebec) the residence of a seigneur or (formerly) a governor. [3] (in the name of a wine) estate or vineyard.
▷**HISTORY** C18: from French, from Old French *chastel,* from Latin *castellum* fortress, CASTLE

Chateaubriand (*French* ʃatobrijɑ̃) NOUN a thick steak cut from the fillet of beef.
▷**HISTORY** C19: named after François René, Vicomte de Chateaubriand (1768–1848), French writer and statesman

chateau cardboard NOUN *NZ informal* wine sold in a winebox.

Châteauroux (*French* ʃatoru) NOUN a city in central France: tenth-century castle (**Château-Raoul**). Pop.: 52 950 (1990).

Château-Thierry ('ʃætəʊ'tɪərɪ; *French* ʃatotjɛri) NOUN a town in N central France, on the River Marne: scene of the second battle of the Marne (1918) during World War I. Pop.: 15 830 (1990).

chateau wine NOUN a wine produced from any of certain vineyards in the Bordeaux region of France.

chatelain ('ʃætᵊˌleɪn; *French* ʃatlɛ̃) NOUN the keeper or governor of a castle.
▷**HISTORY** C16: from French, from Latin *castellānus* occupant of a CASTLE

chatelaine ('ʃætəˌleɪn; *French* ʃatlɛn) NOUN [1] (esp formerly) the mistress of a castle or fashionable household. [2] a chain or clasp worn at the waist by women in the 16th to the 19th centuries, with handkerchief, keys, etc., attached. [3] a decorative pendant worn on the lapel.

Chatham ('tʃætəm) NOUN [1] a town in SE England, in N Kent on the River Medway: formerly royal naval dockyard. Pop.: 71 691 (1991). [2] a city in SE Canada, in SE Ontario on the Thames River. Pop.: 43 557 (1991).

Chatham Island NOUN another name for **San Cristóbal** (sense 1).

Chatham Islands PLURAL NOUN a group of islands in the S Pacific Ocean, forming a county of South Island, New Zealand: consists of the main islands of Chatham, Pitt, and several rocky islets. Chief settlement: Waitangi. Pop.: 769 (1991). Area: 963 sq. km (372 sq. miles).

chatline ('tʃætˌlaɪn) NOUN a telephone service enabling callers to join in general conversation with each other.

chatoyant (ʃə'tɔɪənt) ADJECTIVE [1] having changeable lustre; twinkling. [2] (of a gem, esp a cabochon) displaying a band of light reflected off inclusions of other minerals. ◆ NOUN [3] a gemstone with a changeable lustre, such as a **cat's eye.**
▷**HISTORY** C18: from French, from *chatoyer* to gleam like a cat's eyes, from *chat* CAT[1]
▸**cha'toyancy** NOUN

chatroom ('tʃætˌruːm, -ˌrʊm) NOUN a site on the Internet, or another computer network, where users have group discussions by electronic mail, typically about one subject.

chat show NOUN *Brit* a television or radio show in which guests, esp celebrities, are interviewed informally. US name: **talk show.**

Chatsworth House ('tʃætswɜːθ) NOUN a mansion near Bakewell in Derbyshire: seat of the Dukes of Devonshire; built (1687–1707) in the classical style.

Chattanooga (ˌtʃætᵊ'nuːgə) NOUN a city in SE Tennessee, on the Tennessee River: scene of two battles during the Civil War, in which the North defeated the Confederates, cleared Tennessee, and opened the way to Georgia (1863). Pop.: 155 554 (2000).

chattel ('tʃætᵊl) NOUN [1] *(often plural) Property law* **a chattel personal.** an item of movable personal property, such as furniture, domestic animals, etc. **b chattel real.** an interest in land less than a freehold, such as a lease. [2] **goods and chattels.** personal property.
▷**HISTORY** C13: from Old French *chatel* personal property, from Medieval Latin *capitāle* wealth; see CAPITAL[1]

chattel house NOUN (esp in Barbados) a movable wooden dwelling, usually set on a foundation of loose stones on rented land.

chattel mortgage NOUN *US and Canadian* a mortgage on movable personal property.

chatter ('tʃætə) VERB [1] to speak (about unimportant matters) rapidly and incessantly; prattle. [2] *(intr)* (of birds, monkeys, etc.) to make rapid repetitive high-pitched noises resembling human speech. [3] *(intr)* (of the teeth) to click together rapidly through cold or fear. [4] *(intr)* to make rapid intermittent contact with a component, as in machining, causing irregular cutting. ◆ NOUN [5] idle or foolish talk; gossip. [6] the high-pitched repetitive noise made by a bird, monkey, etc. [7] the rattling of objects, such as parts of a machine. [8] the undulating pattern of marks in a machined surface from the vibration of the tool or workpiece. Also called: **chatter mark.**
▷**HISTORY** C13: of imitative origin
▸'**chattery** ADJECTIVE

chatterati (ˌtʃætə'rɑːtiː) NOUN *Informal* another word for **chattering classes.**
▷**HISTORY** C20: from CHATTER + *-ati* as in LITERATI

chatterbox ('tʃætəˌbɒks) NOUN *Informal* a person who talks constantly, esp about trivial matters.

chatterer ('tʃætərə) NOUN [1] someone or something that chatters. [2] another name for **cotinga.**

chattering classes PLURAL NOUN *Informal, often derogatory* (usually preceded by *the*) the educated sections of society, considered as enjoying discussion of political, social, and cultural issues.

chatter mark NOUN [1] any of a series of grooves, pits, and scratches on the surface of a rock, usually made by the movement of a glacier. [2] another name for **chatter** (sense 8).

chatty ('tʃætɪ) ADJECTIVE **-tier, -tiest.** [1] full of trivial conversation; talkative. [2] informal and friendly; gossipy: *a chatty letter.*
▸'**chattily** ADVERB ▸'**chattiness** NOUN

chat up VERB *(tr, adverb) Brit informal* [1] to talk flirtatiously to (a person), esp with the intention of seducing him or her. [2] to talk persuasively to (a person), esp with an ulterior motive.

Chaucerian (tʃɔː'sɪərɪən) ADJECTIVE [1] of, relating to, or characteristic of the writings of Geoffrey Chaucer (?1340–1400), the English poet. ◆ NOUN [2] an imitator of Chaucer, esp one of a group of 15th-century Scottish writers who took him as a model. [3] **a** an admirer of Chaucer's works. **b** a specialist in the study or teaching of Chaucer.

chaudfroid *French* (ʃofrwa) NOUN a sweet or savoury jellied sauce used to coat cold meat, chicken, etc.
▷**HISTORY** literally: hot-cold (because prepared as hot dish, but served cold)

chauffer *or* **chaufer** ('tʃɔːfə) NOUN a small portable heater or stove.
▷**HISTORY** C19: from French *chauffoir,* from *chauffer* to heat

chauffeur ('ʃəʊfə, ʃəʊ'fɜː) NOUN [1] a person employed to drive a car. ◆ VERB [2] to act as driver

for (a person): *he chauffeured me to the stadium; he chauffeurs for the Duke.*
▷HISTORY C20: from French, literally: stoker, from *chauffer* to heat
▸**chauffeuse** (ʃəʊˈfɜːz) FEMININE NOUN

chaulmoogra (tʃɔːlˈmuːɡrə) NOUN 1 a tropical Asian tree, *Taraktogenos* (or *Hydnocarpus*) *kurzii*: family *Flacourtiaceae*. 2 oil from the seed of this tree, used in treating leprosy. 3 any of several similar or related trees.
▷HISTORY from Bengali *cāulmugrā*, from *cāul* rice + *mugrā* hemp

chaunt (tʃɔːnt) NOUN, VERB a less common variant of **chant**.
▸ˈ**chaunter** NOUN

chausses (ʃəʊs) NOUN (*functioning as singular*) a tight-fitting medieval garment covering the feet and legs, usually made of chain mail.
▷HISTORY C15: from Old French *chauces*, plural of *chauce* leg-covering, from Medieval Latin *calcea*, from Latin *calceus* shoe, from *calx* heel

chautauqua (ʃəˈtɔːkwə) NOUN (in the US, formerly) a summer school or educational meeting held in the summer.
▷HISTORY C19: named after *Chautauqua*, a lake in New York near which such a school was first held

chauvinism (ˈʃəʊvɪˌnɪzəm) NOUN 1 aggressive or fanatical patriotism; jingoism. 2 enthusiastic devotion to a cause. 3 smug irrational belief in the superiority of one's own race, party, sex, etc.: *male chauvinism.*
▷HISTORY C19: from French *chauvinisme*, after Nicolas *Chauvin*, legendary French soldier under Napoleon, noted for his vociferous and unthinking patriotism
▸ˈ**chauvinist** NOUN ▸ˌ**chauvinˈistic** ADJECTIVE ▸ˌ**chauvinˈistically** ADVERB

chaw (tʃɔː) *Dialect* ◆ VERB 1 to chew (tobacco), esp without swallowing it. ◆ NOUN 2 something chewed, esp a plug of tobacco.
▸ˈ**chawer** NOUN

chawk (tʃɔːk) NOUN *Southwest English dialect* a jackdaw.

chayote (tʃɑːˈjəʊteɪ, tʃaɪˈəʊtɪ) NOUN 1 a tropical American cucurbitaceous climbing plant, *Sechium edule*, that has edible pear-shaped fruit enclosing a single enormous seed. 2 the fruit of this plant, which is cooked and eaten as a vegetable.
▷HISTORY from Spanish, from Nahuatl *chayotli*

chazan, hazan, *or* ***hazzan*** *Hebrew* (xaˈzan; *English* ˈhɑːzᵊn) NOUN, *plural* **chazanim** (xazaˈnim; *English* hɑːˈzɔːniːm) *or English* **chazans**. a person who leads synagogue services, esp as a profession; cantor.

ChB ABBREVIATION FOR Bachelor of Surgery.
▷HISTORY Latin: *Chirurgiae Baccalaureus*

ChE ABBREVIATION FOR Chemical Engineer.

CHE (tʃiː) NOUN (in New Zealand, formerly) ACRONYM FOR Crown Health Enterprise: an agency supervising health expenditure in a district.

cheap (tʃiːp) ADJECTIVE 1 costing relatively little; inexpensive; good value. 2 charging low prices: *a cheap hairdresser.* 3 of poor quality; shoddy: *cheap furniture; cheap and nasty.* 4 worth relatively little: *promises are cheap.* 5 not worthy of respect; vulgar. 6 ashamed; embarrassed: *to feel cheap.* 7 stingy; miserly. 8 *Informal* mean; despicable: *a cheap liar.* 9 **cheap as chips.** See **chip** (sense 11). 10 **dirt cheap.** *Informal* extremely inexpensive. ◆ NOUN 11 **on the cheap.** *Brit informal* at a low cost. ◆ ADVERB 12 at very little cost.
▷HISTORY Old English *ceap* barter, bargain, price, property; related to Old Norse *kaup* bargain, Old High German *kouf* trade, Latin *caupō* innkeeper
▸ˈ**cheapish** ADJECTIVE ▸ˈ**cheaply** ADVERB ▸ˈ**cheapness** NOUN

cheapen (ˈtʃiːpᵊn) VERB 1 to make or become lower in reputation, quality, etc.; degrade or be degraded. 2 to make or become cheap or cheaper.
▸ˈ**cheapener** NOUN

cheap-jack *Informal* ◆ NOUN 1 a person who sells cheap and shoddy goods. ◆ ADJECTIVE 2 shoddy or inferior.
▷HISTORY C19: from CHEAP + *Jack* (name used to typify a person)

cheapo (ˈtʃiːpəʊ) ADJECTIVE, NOUN, *plural* **cheapos**. *Informal* very cheap and possibly shoddy.

cheapskate (ˈtʃiːpˌskeɪt) NOUN *Informal* a miserly person.

cheat (tʃiːt) VERB 1 to deceive or practise deceit, esp for one's own gain; trick or swindle (someone). 2 (*intr*) to obtain unfair advantage by trickery, as in a game of cards. 3 (*tr*) to escape or avoid (something unpleasant) by luck or cunning: *to cheat death.* 4 (when *intr*, usually foll by *on*) *Informal* to be sexually unfaithful to (one's wife, husband, or lover). ◆ NOUN 5 a person who cheats. 6 a deliberately dishonest transaction, esp for gain; fraud. 7 *Informal* sham. 8 *Law* the obtaining of another's property by fraudulent means. 9 the usual US name for **rye-brome.**
▷HISTORY C14: short for ESCHEAT
▸ˈ**cheatable** ADJECTIVE ▸ˈ**cheater** NOUN ▸ˈ**cheatingly** ADVERB

Cheb (*Czech* xɛp) NOUN a town in the W Czech Republic, in W Bohemia on the Ohře River: 12th-century castle where Wallenstein was murdered (1634); a centre of the Sudeten-German movement after World War I. Pop.: 31 847 (1991). German name: **Eger.**

Cheboksary (*Russian* tʃɪbakˈsari) NOUN a port in W central Russia on the River Volga: capital of the Chuvash Republic. Pop.: 458 000 (1999 est.).

Chebyshev's inequality (ˈtʃɛbɪˌʃɒfs) NOUN *Statistics* the fundamental theorem that the probability that a random variable differs from its mean by more than k standard deviations is less than or equal to $1/k^2$.
▷HISTORY named after P. L. *Chebyshev* (1821–94), Russian mathematician

Chechen (ˈtʃɛtʃɛn) NOUN, *plural* **-chens** *or* **-chen.** a member of a people of Russia, speaking a Circassian language and chiefly inhabiting the Chechen Republic.

Chechen Republic NOUN a constituent republic of S Russia, on the N slopes of the Caucasus Mountains: major oil and natural gas resources; formed an Autonomous Republic with Ingushetia from 1936 until 1944 and from 1957 until 1991; declared independence from Ingushetia in 1992; fighting between Chechen separatists and Russian forces (1994–96) led to de facto independence: reoccupied by Russia in 1999–2000. Capital: Grozny. Pop.: 574 000 (2000 est.). Area (including Ingushetia): 19 300 sq. km (7450 sq. miles). Also called: **Chechenia** (tʃɪˈtʃɛnɪə), **Chechnya** (tʃɪˈtʃnɪə).

check (tʃɛk) VERB 1 to pause or cause to pause, esp abruptly. 2 (*tr*) to restrain or control: *to check one's tears.* 3 (*tr*) to slow the growth or progress of; retard. 4 (*tr*) to rebuke or rebuff. 5 (when *intr*, often foll by *on* or *up on*) to examine, investigate, or make an inquiry into (facts, a product, etc.) for accuracy, quality, or progress, esp rapidly or informally. 6 (*tr*) *Chiefly US and Canadian* to mark off so as to indicate approval, correctness, or preference. Usual Brit word: **tick.** 7 (*intr*; often foll by *with*) *Chiefly US and Canadian* to correspond or agree: *this report checks with the other.* 8 (*tr*) *Chiefly US, Canadian, and NZ* to leave in or accept (clothing or property) for temporary custody. 9 *Chess* to place (an opponent's king) in check. 10 (*tr*) to mark with a pattern of squares or crossed lines. 11 to crack or cause to crack. 12 *Agriculture* short for **checkrow.** 13 (*tr*) *Ice hockey* to impede (an opponent). 14 (*intr*) *Hunting* (of hounds) to pause in the pursuit of quarry while relocating a lost scent. 15 (*intr*; foll by *at*) *Falconry* to change from one quarry to another while in flight. 16 (*intr*) to decline the option of opening the betting in a round of poker. 17 **check the helm.** *Nautical* to swing back the helm of a vessel to prevent it from turning too quickly or too far. ◆ NOUN 18 a break in progress; stoppage. 19 a restraint or rebuff. 20 **a** a person or thing that restrains, halts, etc. **b** (*as modifier*): *a check line.* 21 **a** a control, esp a rapid or informal one, designed to ensure accuracy, progress, etc. **b** (*as modifier*): *a check list.* 22 a means or standard to ensure against fraud or error. 23 the US word for **tick**[1]. 24 the US spelling of **cheque.** 25 *Chiefly US* the bill in a restaurant. 26 *Chiefly US and Canadian* a ticket or tag used to identify clothing or property deposited for custody. 27 a pattern of squares or crossed lines. 28 a single square in such a pattern. 29 **a** a fabric with a pattern of squares or crossed lines. **b** (*as modifier*): *a check suit.* 30 *Chess* the state or position of a king under direct attack, from which it must be moved or protected by another piece. 31 a small crack, as one in veneer or one that occurs in timber during seasoning. 32 part of the action of a piano that arrests the backward motion of a hammer after it has struck a string and holds it until the key is released. 33 a chip or counter used in some card and gambling games. 34 *Hunting* a pause by the hounds in the pursuit of their quarry owing to loss of its scent. 35 *Angling* a ratchet fitted to a fishing reel to check the free running of the line. 36 *Ice hockey* the act of impeding an opponent with one's body or stick. 37 **in check.** under control or restraint. ◆ INTERJECTION 38 *Chess* a call made to an opponent indicating that his king is in check. 39 *Chiefly US and Canadian* an expression of agreement. ◆ See also **check in, check off, check out, checkup.**
▷HISTORY C14: from Old French *eschec* a check at chess, hence, a pause (to verify something), via Arabic from Persian *shāh* the king! (in chess)
▸ˈ**checkable** ADJECTIVE

check digit NOUN *Computing* a digit derived from and appended to a string of data digits, used to detect corruption of the data string during transmission or transcription.

checked (tʃɛkt) ADJECTIVE 1 having a pattern of small squares. 2 *Phonetics* (of a syllable) ending in a consonant.

checker[1] (ˈtʃɛkə) NOUN, VERB 1 the usual US spelling of **chequer.** ◆ NOUN 2 *Textiles* a variant spelling of **chequer** (sense 2). 3 the US and Canadian name for **draughtsman** (sense 3). ◆ See also **checkers.**

checker[2] (ˈtʃɛkə) NOUN *Chiefly US and Canadian* 1 a cashier, esp in a supermarket. 2 an attendant in a cloakroom, left-luggage office, etc.

checkerberry (ˈtʃɛkəbərɪ, -brɪ) NOUN, *plural* **-ries.** 1 the fruit of any of various plants, esp the wintergreen (*Gaultheria procumbens*). 2 any plant bearing this fruit.

checkerbloom (ˈtʃɛkəˌbluːm) NOUN a Californian malvaceous plant, *Sidalcea malvaeflora*, with pink or purple flowers.

checkerboard (ˈtʃɛkəˌbɔːd) NOUN the US and Canadian name for a **draughtboard.**

checkers (ˈtʃɛkəz) NOUN (*functioning as singular*) the US and Canadian name for **draughts.**

check in VERB (*adverb*) 1 (*intr*) to record one's arrival, as at a hotel or for work; sign in or report. 2 (*tr*) to register the arrival of (passengers, etc.). ◆ NOUN **check-in.** 3 **a** the formal registration of arrival, as at an airport or a hotel. **b** (*as modifier*): *check-in time.* 4 the place where one registers arrival at an airport, etc.

checking account NOUN the US name for **current account.**

check list NOUN a list of items, facts, names, etc., to be checked or referred to for comparison, identification, or verification.

checkmate (ˈtʃɛkˌmeɪt) NOUN 1 *Chess* **a** the winning position in which an opponent's king is under attack and unable to escape. **b** the move by which this position is achieved. 2 utter defeat. ◆ VERB (*tr*) 3 *Chess* to place (an opponent's king) in checkmate. 4 to thwart or render powerless. ◆ INTERJECTION 5 *Chess* a call made when placing an opponent's king in checkmate.
▷HISTORY C14: from Old French *eschec mat*, from Arabic *shāh māt*, the king is dead; see CHECK

check off VERB (*tr, adverb*) 1 to mark with a tick. 2 to deduct (union contributions) directly from an employee's pay. ◆ NOUN **check-off.** 3 a procedure whereby an employer deducts union contributions directly from an employee's pay and pays the money to the union.

check out VERB (*adverb*) 1 (*intr*) to pay the bill and depart, esp from a hotel. 2 (*intr*) to depart from a place; record one's departure from work. 3 to investigate or prove to be in order after investigation: *the police checked out all the statements; their credentials checked out.* 4 (*tr*) *Informal* to have a look at; inspect: *check out the wally in the pink shirt.* ◆ NOUN **checkout.** 5 **a** the latest time for vacating a room in a hotel, etc. **b** (*as modifier*): *checkout time.* 6 a counter, esp in a supermarket, where customers pay.

checkpoint (ˈtʃɛkˌpɔɪnt) NOUN a place, as at a frontier or in a motor rally, where vehicles or travellers are stopped for official identification, inspection, etc.

checkrail ('tʃɛk,reɪl) NOUN *Brit* another word for **guardrail** (sense 2).

checkrein ('tʃɛk,reɪn) NOUN the usual US word for **bearing rein.**

checkroom ('tʃɛk,ruːm, -,rʊm) NOUN the US and Canadian name for **left-luggage office.**

checkrow ('tʃɛk,rəʊ) *US agriculture* ◆ NOUN [1] a row of plants, esp corn, in which the spaces between adjacent plants are equal to those between adjacent rows to facilitate cultivation. ◆ VERB [2] (*tr*) to plant in checkrows.

checks and balances PLURAL NOUN *Government, chiefly US* competition and mutual restraint among the various branches of government.

checkup ('tʃɛk,ʌp) NOUN [1] an examination to see if something is in order. [2] *Med* a medical examination, esp one taken at regular intervals to verify a normal state of health or discover a disease in its early stages. ◆ VERB **check up.** [3] (*intr, adverb; sometimes foll by on*) to investigate or make an inquiry into (a person's character, evidence, etc.), esp when suspicions have been aroused.

check valve NOUN a valve that closes by fluid pressure to prevent return flow. Also called: **nonreturn valve.**

checky ('tʃɛkɪ) ADJECTIVE (*usually postpositive*) *Heraldry* having squares of alternating tinctures or furs; checked.

Cheddar ('tʃɛdə) NOUN [1] (*sometimes not capital*) any of several types of smooth hard yellow or whitish cheese. [2] a village in SW England, in N Somerset: situated near **Cheddar Gorge**, a pass through the Mendip Hills renowned for its stalactitic caverns and rare limestone flora. Pop.: 4484 (1991).

cheddite ('tʃɛdaɪt, 'ʃɛd-) NOUN an explosive made by mixing a powdered chlorate or perchlorate with a fatty substance, such as castor oil.
▷HISTORY C20: from *Chedde* town in Savoy, France, where it was first made

cheder *or* ***heder*** *Hebrew* ('xedɛr; *English* 'heɪdə) NOUN, *plural* ***chadarim*** (xadaˈriːm) *or English* **cheders.** *Judaism* [1] (in Western countries) elementary religious education classes, usually outside normal school hours. [2] more traditionally, a full-time elementary religious school. [3] *Informal* a place of corrective instruction; prison.
▷HISTORY literally: room

chee-chee ('tʃiː,tʃiː) NOUN a less common spelling of **chichi**[2].

cheek (tʃiːk) NOUN [1] **a** either side of the face, esp that part below the eye. **b** either side of the oral cavity; side of the mouth. Related adjectives: **buccal, genal, malar.** [2] *Informal* impudence; effrontery. [3] (*often plural*) *Informal* either side of the buttocks. [4] (*often plural*) a side of a door jamb. [5] *Nautical* one of the two fore-and-aft supports for the trestletrees on a mast of a sailing vessel, forming part of the hounds. [6] one of the jaws of a vice. [7] **cheek by jowl.** close together; intimately linked. [8] **turn the other cheek.** to be submissive and refuse to retaliate even when provoked or treated badly. [9] **with (one's) tongue in (one's) cheek.** See **tongue** (sense 19). ◆ VERB [10] (*tr*) *Informal* to speak or behave disrespectfully to; act impudently towards.
▷HISTORY Old English *ceace;* related to Middle Low German *kāke*, Dutch *kaak*
▸ **'cheekless** ADJECTIVE

cheekbone ('tʃiːk,bəʊn) NOUN the nontechnical name for **zygomatic bone.** Related adjective: **malar.**

cheekpiece ('tʃiːk,piːs) NOUN either of the two straps of a bridle that join the bit to the crownpiece.

cheek pouch NOUN a membranous pouch inside the mouth of many rodents and some other mammals: used for holding food.

cheeky ('tʃiːkɪ) ADJECTIVE **cheekier, cheekiest.** disrespectful in speech or behaviour; impudent: *a cheeky child.*
▸ **'cheekily** ADVERB ▸ **'cheekiness** NOUN

cheep (tʃiːp) NOUN [1] the short weak high-pitched cry of a young bird; chirp. ◆ VERB [2] (*intr*) (of young birds) to utter characteristic shrill sounds.
▸ **'cheeper** NOUN

cheer (tʃɪə) VERB [1] (usually foll by *up*) to make or become happy or hopeful; comfort or be comforted. [2] to applaud with shouts. [3] (when *tr*, sometimes foll by *on*) to encourage (a team, person, etc.) with shouts, esp in contests. ◆ NOUN [4] a shout or cry of approval, encouragement, etc., often using such words as **hurrah!** or **rah! rah! rah!** [5] **three cheers.** three shouts of hurrah given in unison by a group to honour someone or celebrate something. [6] happiness; good spirits. [7] state of mind; spirits (archaic, except in the phrases **be of good cheer, with good cheer**). [8] *Archaic* provisions for a feast; fare. ◆ See also **cheers.**
▷HISTORY C13 (in the sense: face, welcoming aspect): from Old French *chere*, from Late Latin *cara* face, from Greek *kara* head
▸ **'cheerer** NOUN ▸ **'cheeringly** ADVERB

cheerful ('tʃɪəfʊl) ADJECTIVE [1] having a happy disposition; in good spirits. [2] pleasantly bright; gladdening: *a cheerful room.* [3] hearty; ungrudging; enthusiastic: *cheerful help.*
▸ **'cheerfully** ADVERB ▸ **'cheerfulness** NOUN

cheerio (,tʃɪərɪ'əʊ) SENTENCE SUBSTITUTE *Informal, chiefly Brit* [1] a farewell greeting. [2] a drinking toast. ◆ NOUN [3] *NZ* a type of small sausage.

cheerleader ('tʃɪə,liːdə) NOUN a person who leads a crowd in formal cheers, esp at sports events.

cheerless ('tʃɪəlɪs) ADJECTIVE dreary, gloomy, or pessimistic.
▸ **'cheerlessly** ADVERB ▸ **'cheerlessness** NOUN

cheerly ('tʃɪəlɪ) ADJECTIVE, ADVERB *Archaic* cheerful or cheerfully.

cheers (tʃɪəz) SENTENCE SUBSTITUTE *Informal, chiefly Brit* [1] a drinking toast. [2] goodbye! cheerio! [3] thanks!

cheery ('tʃɪərɪ) ADJECTIVE **cheerier, cheeriest.** showing or inspiring cheerfulness.
▸ **'cheerily** ADVERB ▸ **'cheeriness** NOUN

cheese[1] (tʃiːz) NOUN [1] the curd of milk separated from the whey and variously prepared as a food. [2] a mass or complete cake of this substance. [3] any of various substances of similar consistency, etc.: *lemon cheese.* [4] **big cheese.** *Slang* an important person. [5] **as alike** (*or* **different**) **as chalk and cheese.** See **chalk** (sense 6).
▷HISTORY Old English *cēse*, from Latin *cāseus* cheese; related to Old Saxon *kāsi*

cheese[2] (tʃiːz) VERB *Slang* [1] (*tr*) to stop; desist. [2] (*intr*) *Prison slang* to act in a grovelling manner.
▷HISTORY C19: of unknown origin

cheeseboard ('tʃiːz,bɔːd) NOUN a board from which cheese is served at a meal.

cheeseburger ('tʃiːz,bɜːgə) NOUN a hamburger cooked with a slice of cheese on top of it.

cheesecake ('tʃiːz,keɪk) NOUN [1] a rich tart with a biscuit base, filled with a mixture of cream cheese, cream, sugar, and often sultanas, sometimes having a fruit topping. [2] *Slang* women displayed for their sex appeal, as in photographs in magazines, newspapers, or films. Compare **beefcake.**

cheesecloth ('tʃiːz,klɒθ) NOUN a loosely woven cotton cloth formerly used only for wrapping cheese.

cheese cutter NOUN [1] a board with a wire attached for cutting cheese. [2] *Nautical* a keel that may be drawn up into the boat when not in use. [3] a nautical peaked cap worn without a badge.

cheesed off ADJECTIVE (*usually postpositive*) *Brit slang* bored, disgusted, or angry.
▷HISTORY C20: from CHEESE[2]

cheese-head ADJECTIVE denoting or relating to a screw or bolt with a cylindrical slotted head.

cheese mite NOUN a white soft-bodied free-living mite, *Tyrophagus* (or *Tyroglyphus*) *longior,* sometimes found in decaying cheese.

cheesemonger ('tʃiːz,mʌŋgə) NOUN a person dealing in cheese, butter, etc.

cheeseparing ('tʃiːz,pɛərɪŋ) ADJECTIVE [1] penny-pinching; stingy. ◆ NOUN [2] **a** a paring of cheese rind. **b** anything similarly worthless. [3] stinginess.

cheese skipper NOUN a dipterous fly, *Piophila casei,* whose larvae feed on cheese and move by jumping: family *Piophilidae.*

cheese straw NOUN a long thin cheese-flavoured strip of pastry.

cheesewood ('tʃiːz,wʊd) NOUN *Austral rare* the tough yellowish wood of Australian trees of the genus *Pittosporum:* family *Pittosporaceae.*

cheesy ('tʃiːzɪ) ADJECTIVE **cheesier, cheesiest.** [1] like cheese in flavour, smell, or consistency. [2] *Informal* (of a smile) broad but possibly insincere: *a big cheesy grin.* [3] *Informal* banal or trite; in poor taste.
▸ **'cheesiness** NOUN

cheetah *or* **chetah** ('tʃiːtə) NOUN a large feline mammal, *Acinonyx jubatus,* of Africa and SW Asia: the swiftest mammal, having very long legs, nonretractile claws, and a black-spotted light-brown coat.
▷HISTORY C18: from Hindi *cītā*, from Sanskrit *citrakāya* tiger, from *citra* bright, speckled + *kāya* body

chef (ʃɛf) NOUN a cook, esp the principal cook in a restaurant.
▷HISTORY C19: from French, from Old French *chief* head, CHIEF

chef-d'oeuvre *French* (ʃɛdœvrə) NOUN, *plural* ***chefs-d'oeuvre*** (ʃɛdœvrə). a masterpiece.

Chefoo ('tʃiː'fuː) NOUN another name for **Yantai.**

cheiro- COMBINING FORM a variant spelling of **chiro-.**

Cheiron ('kaɪrɒn, -rən) NOUN a variant spelling of **Chiron.**

Cheju ('tʃɛ'dʒuː) NOUN a volcanic island in the N East China Sea, southwest of Korea: constitutes a province (Cheju-do) of South Korea. Capital: Cheju. Pop.: 513 000 (2000). Area: 1792 sq. km (692 sq. miles). Also called: **Quelpart.**

Cheka *Russian* ('tʃɛka) NOUN *Russian history* the secret police set up in 1917 by the Bolshevik government: reorganized in the Soviet Union in Dec. 1922 as the GPU.
▷HISTORY C20: from Russian, acronym of *Chrezvychainaya Komissiya* Extraordinary Commission (to combat Counter-Revolution)

Chekhovian *or* **Chekovian** (tʃɛ'kəʊvɪən) ADJECTIVE of or relating to Anton Pavlovich Chekhov, the Russian dramatist and short-story writer (1860–1904).

Chekiang ('tʃɛ'kjæŋ, -kaɪ'æŋ) NOUN a variant transliteration of the Chinese name for **Zhejiang.**

chela[1] ('kiːlə) NOUN, *plural* **lae** (-liː). a large pincer-like claw of such arthropods as the crab and scorpion.
▷HISTORY C17: New Latin, from Greek *khēlē* claw
▸ **cheliferous** (kɪ'lɪfərəs) ADJECTIVE

chela[2] ('tʃeɪlə) NOUN *Hinduism* a disciple of a religious teacher.
▷HISTORY C19: from Hindi *celā*, from Sanskrit *ceta* servant, slave
▸ **'chela,ship** NOUN

chelate ('kiːleɪt) NOUN [1] *Chem* a coordination compound in which a metal atom or ion is bound to a ligand at two or more points on the ligand, so as to form a heterocyclic ring containing a metal atom. ◆ ADJECTIVE [2] *Zoology* of or possessing chelae. [3] *Chem* of or denoting a chelate. ◆ VERB [4] (*intr*) *Chem* to form a chelate.
▷HISTORY C20: from CHELA[1]
▸ **che'lation** NOUN

chelating agent NOUN a chemical compound that coordinates with a metal to form a chelate, often used to trap or remove heavy metal ions.

chelicera (kɪ'lɪsərə) NOUN, *plural* **-erae** (-ə,riː). one of a pair of appendages on the head of spiders and other arachnids: often modified as food-catching claws.
▷HISTORY C19: from New Latin, from French *chélicère*, from *chél-* see CHELA[1] + *-cère* from Greek *keras* horn
▸ **che'liceral** ADJECTIVE

chelicerate (kɪ'lɪsə,reɪt) ADJECTIVE [1] of, relating to, or belonging to the *Chelicerata,* a subphylum of arthropods, including arachnids and the horseshoe crab, in which the first pair of limbs are modified as chelicerae. ◆ NOUN [2] any arthropod belonging to the *Chelicerata.*

cheliform ('kiːlɪ,fɔːm) ADJECTIVE shaped like a chela; pincer-like.

Chellean ('ʃɛlɪən) NOUN, ADJECTIVE *Archaeol* (*no longer in technical usage*) another word for **Abbevillian.**
▷HISTORY C19: from French *chelléen*, from *Chelles*, France, where various items were found

chellup ('tʃɛləp) NOUN *Northern and Midland English dialect* noise.

Chelmsford ('tʃɛlmzfəd) NOUN a city in SE England, administrative centre of Essex: electronics, retail; university (1992). Pop.: 197 451 (1991).

cheloid ('ki:lɔɪd) NOUN *Pathol* a variant spelling of **keloid**.
▸**che'loidal** ADJECTIVE

chelone (kə'ləʊnɪ) NOUN any plant of the hardy N American genus *Chelone*, grown for its white, rose, or purple flower spikes: family *Scrophulariaceae*.
▷**HISTORY** New Latin, from Greek *chelōnē* a tortoise, from a fancied resemblance between a tortoise's head and the shape of the flower

chelonian (kɪ'ləʊnɪən) NOUN 1 any reptile of the order *Chelonia*, including the tortoises and turtles, in which most of the body is enclosed in a protective bony capsule. ◆ ADJECTIVE 2 of, relating to, or belonging to the *Chelonia*.
▷**HISTORY** C19: from New Latin *Chelōnia*, from Greek *khelōnē* tortoise

chelp (tʃɛlp) VERB (*intr*) *Northern and Midland English dialect* 1 (esp of women or children) to chatter or speak out of turn: *she's always chelping at the teacher*. 2 (of birds) to squeak or chirp.
▷**HISTORY** C19: perhaps from *ch(irp)* + *(y)elp*

Chelsea ('tʃɛlsɪ) NOUN a residential district of SW London, in the Royal Borough of Kensington and Chelsea: site of the Chelsea Royal Hospital for old and invalid soldiers (**Chelsea Pensioners**).

Chelsea bun NOUN a rolled yeast currant bun decorated with sugar.

Cheltenham ('tʃɛltᵊnəm) NOUN 1 a town in W England, in central Gloucestershire: famous for its schools, racecourse, and saline springs (discovered in 1716). Pop.: 91 301 (1991). 2 a style of type.

Chelyabinsk (*Russian* tʃɪ'ljabinsk) NOUN an industrial city in SW Russia. Pop.: 1 086 300 (1999 est.).

Chelyuskin (*Russian* tʃɪ'ljuskin) NOUN **Cape.** a cape in N central Russia, in N Siberia at the end of the Taimyr Peninsula: the northernmost point of Asia.

chem. ABBREVIATION FOR: 1 chemical. 2 chemist. 3 chemistry.

chem- COMBINING FORM variant of **chemo-** before a vowel.

chemautotroph (ˌki:məʊ'ɔ:tətrəʊf) *or* **chemoautroph** (ˌki:məʊ'ɔ:trəʊf, ˌkɛm-) NOUN *Biology* an organism, such as a bacterium, that obtains its energy from inorganic reactions using simple compounds, such as ammonia or hydrogen sulphide. Also called: **chemolithotroph.**
▸**chemautotrophic** (ˌki:məʊˌɔ:tə'trɒfɪk, ˌkɛm-) ADJECTIVE

chemical ('kɛmɪkᵊl) NOUN 1 any substance used in or resulting from a reaction involving changes to atoms or molecules. ◆ ADJECTIVE 2 of or used in chemistry: *chemical balance*. 3 of, made from, or using chemicals: *chemical fertilizer*.
▸'**chemically** ADVERB

chemical bond NOUN a mutual attraction between two atoms resulting from a redistribution of their outer electrons. See also **covalent bond, electrovalent bond, coordinate bond.**

chemical engineering NOUN the branch of engineering concerned with the design, operation, maintenance, and manufacture of the plant and machinery used in industrial chemical processes.
▸**chemical engineer** NOUN

chemical equation NOUN a representation of a chemical reaction using symbols of the elements to indicate the amount of substance, usually in moles, of each reactant and product.

chemical machining NOUN the shaping of a metal part by controlled removal of unwanted metal by a flow of chemical solutions.

chemical peeling NOUN a cosmetic process in which a substance containing a chemical (esp alpha-hydroxy acids) is applied to the skin of the face and peeled away to remove a layer of dead cells.

chemical potential NOUN a thermodynamic function of a substance in a system that is the partial differential of the Gibbs function of the system with respect to the number of moles of the substance. Symbol: μ.

chemical reaction NOUN a process that involves changes in the structure and energy content of atoms, molecules, or ions but not their nuclei. Compare **nuclear reaction.**

chemical warfare NOUN warfare in which chemicals other than explosives are used as weapons, esp warfare using asphyxiating or nerve gases, poisons, defoliants, etc.

chemico- COMBINING FORM chemical: *chemicophysical*.

chemiluminescence (ˌkɛmɪˌlu:mɪ'nɛsəns) NOUN the phenomenon in which a chemical reaction leads to the emission of light without incandescence.
▸ˌ**chemiˌlumi'nescent** ADJECTIVE

chemin de fer (ʃə'mæn də 'fɛə; *French* ʃəmɛ̃dfɛr) NOUN a gambling game, a variation of baccarat.
▷**HISTORY** French: railway, referring to the fast tempo of the game

chemiosmosis (ˌkɛmɪɒz'məʊsɪs) *or* **chemosmosis** NOUN 1 *Biochem* the mechanism by which the synthesis and utilization of the biochemical energy source ATP is regulated: the energy generated by oxidative phosphorylation generates a proton gradient across the membrane of the mitochondrion that drives the enzymic resynthesis of ATP. 2 a chemical reaction between two compounds after osmosis through an intervening semipermeable membrane.

chemise (ʃə'mi:z) NOUN 1 an unwaisted loose-fitting dress hanging straight from the shoulders. 2 a loose shirtlike undergarment. ◆ Also called: **shift.**
▷**HISTORY** C14: from Old French: shirt, from Late Latin *camisa*, perhaps of Celtic origin

chemisette (ˌʃɛmɪ'zɛt) NOUN an underbodice of lawn, lace, etc., worn to fill in a low-cut dress.
▷**HISTORY** C19: from French, diminutive of CHEMISE

chemism ('kɛmɪzəm) NOUN *Obsolete* chemical action.

chemisorb (ˌkɛmɪ'sɔ:b) *or* **chemosorb** VERB (*tr*) to take up (a substance) by chemisorption.

chemisorption (ˌkɛmɪ'sɔ:pʃən) NOUN an adsorption process in which an adsorbate is held on the surface of an adsorbent by chemical bonds.

chemist ('kɛmɪst) NOUN 1 *Brit* a shop selling medicines, cosmetics, etc. 2 *Brit* a qualified dispenser of prescribed medicines. 3 a person studying, trained in, or engaged in chemistry. 4 an obsolete word for **alchemist.**
▷**HISTORY** C16: from earlier *chimist*, from New Latin *chimista*, shortened from Medieval Latin *alchimista* ALCHEMIST

chemistry ('kɛmɪstrɪ) NOUN, *plural* **-tries.** 1 the branch of physical science concerned with the composition, properties, and reactions of substances. See also **inorganic chemistry, organic chemistry, physical chemistry.** 2 the composition, properties, and reactions of a particular substance. 3 the nature and effects of any complex phenomenon: *the chemistry of humour*. 4 *Informal* a reaction, taken to be instinctual, between two persons.
▷**HISTORY** C17: from earlier *chimistrie*, from *chimist* CHEMIST

chemmy ('ʃɛmɪ) NOUN *Cards* short for **chemin de fer.**

Chemnitz (*German* 'kɛmnɪts) NOUN a city in E Germany, in Saxony, at the foot of the Erzgebirge: textiles, engineering. Pop.: 266 000 (1999 est.). Also called (1953–90): **Karl-Marx-Stadt.**

chemo ('ki:məʊ) NOUN *Informal* short for **chemotherapy.**

chemo-, chemi-, *or before a vowel* **chem-** COMBINING FORM indicating that chemicals or chemical reactions are involved: *chemotherapy*.
▷**HISTORY** New Latin, from Late Greek *khēmeia*; see ALCHEMY

chemoattractant (ˌkɛməʊə'træktənt) NOUN a chemical substance that provokes chemotaxis, esp one that causes a bacterium to move in the direction in which its concentration is increasing.

chemoautroph (ˌki:məʊ'ɔ:trəʊf) NOUN a variant of **chemautotroph.**

chemoheterotroph (ˌki:məʊ'hɛtərəʊtrəʊf, ˌkɛm-) NOUN *Biology* an organism that obtains its energy from the oxidation of organic compounds. Also called: **chemo-organotroph.**
▸**chemoheterotrophic** (ˌki:məʊˌhɛtərəʊ'trɒfɪk, ˌkɛm-) ADJECTIVE

chemokinesis (ˌkɛməʊkaɪ'ni:sɪs) NOUN *Immunol* the random movement of cells, such as leucocytes, stimulated by substances in their environment.

chemolithotroph (ˌki:məʊ'lɪθətrəʊf, ˌkɛm-) NOUN another name for **chemoautotroph.**

chemonasty ('kɛməʊˌnæstɪ) NOUN *Botany* the nastic movement of a plant in response to a chemical stimulus.

chemo-organotroph (ˌki:məʊɔ:'gænətrəʊf, ˌkɛm-) NOUN another name for **chemoheterotroph.**

chemoprophylaxis (ˌkɛməʊˌprəʊfə'læksɪs, -ˌprɒfə-) NOUN the prevention of disease using chemical drugs.
▸ˌ**chemoˌprophy'lactic** ADJECTIVE

chemoreceptor (ˌkɛməʊrɪ'sɛptə) *or* **chemoceptor** NOUN a sensory receptor in a biological cell membrane to which an external molecule binds to generate a smell or taste sensation.

chemosmosis (ˌkɛmɒz'məʊsɪs) NOUN a variant spelling of **chemiosmosis.**
▸**chemosmotic** (ˌkɛmɒz'mɒtɪk) ADJECTIVE

chemosphere ('kɛməˌsfɪə) NOUN *Meteorol* a rare name for **thermosphere.**
▸**chemospheric** (ˌkɛmə'sfɛrɪk) ADJECTIVE

chemostat ('ki:məʊˌstæt, 'kɛm-) NOUN an apparatus for growing bacterial cultures at a constant rate by controlling the supply of nutrient medium.

chemosynthesis (ˌkɛməʊ'sɪnθɪsɪs) NOUN the formation of organic material by certain bacteria using energy derived from simple chemical reactions.
▸**chemosynthetic** (ˌkɛməʊsɪn'θɛtɪk) ADJECTIVE
▸ˌ**chemosyn'thetically** ADVERB

chemotaxis (ˌkɛməʊ'tæksɪs) NOUN the movement of a microorganism or cell in response to a chemical stimulus.
▸ˌ**chemo'tactic** ADJECTIVE ▸ˌ**chemo'tactically** ADVERB

chemotherapy (ˌki:məʊ'θɛrəpɪ, ki:mə-) NOUN treatment of disease, esp cancer, by means of chemical agents. Compare **radiotherapy.**
▸ˌ**chemo'therapist** NOUN

chemotropism (ˌkɛməʊ'trəʊˌpɪzəm) NOUN the growth response of an organism, esp a plant, to a chemical stimulus.
▸**chemotropic** (ˌkɛməʊ'trɒpɪk) ADJECTIVE
▸ˌ**chemo'tropically** ADVERB

chempaduk ('tʃɛmpəˌdʌk) NOUN 1 an evergreen moraceous tree, *Artocarpus champeden* (or *A. integer*), of Malaysia, similar to the jackfruit. 2 the fruit of this tree, edible when cooked, having yellow starchy flesh and a leathery rind.
▷**HISTORY** from Malay

Chemulpo (ˌtʃɛmʊl'pəʊ) NOUN a former name of **Inchon.**

chemurgy ('kɛmɜ:dʒɪ) NOUN the branch of chemistry concerned with the industrial use of organic raw materials, esp materials of agricultural origin.
▸**chem'urgic** *or* **chem'urgical** ADJECTIVE

Chenab (tʃɪ'næb) NOUN a river rising in the Himalayas and flowing southwest to the Sutlej River in Pakistan. Length: 1087 km (675 miles).

Cheng-chiang ('tʃɛŋ'tʃæŋ) NOUN a variant transliteration of the Chinese name for **Jinjiang.**

Chengchow *or* **Cheng-chou** ('tʃɛŋ'tʃaʊ) NOUN a variant transliteration of the Chinese name for **Zhengzhou.**

Chengde, Chengteh, *or* **Ch'eng-te** ('tʃɛŋ'teɪ) NOUN a city in NE China, in Hebei on the Luan River: summer residence of the Manchu emperors. Pop.: 298 895 (1999 est.).

Chengdu, Chengtu, *or* **Ch'eng-tu** ('tʃɛŋ'tu:) NOUN a city in S central China, capital of Sichuan province. Pop.: 2 146 126 (1999 est.).

chenille (ʃə'ni:l) NOUN 1 a thick soft tufty silk or worsted velvet cord or yarn used in embroidery and for trimmings, etc. 2 a fabric of such yarn. 3 a rich and hard-wearing carpet of such fabric.
▷**HISTORY** C18: from French, literally: hairy caterpillar, from Latin *canicula*, diminutive of *canis* dog

Chennai (tʃɪ'naɪ) NOUN the official name for **Madras.**

chenopod ('ki:nəˌpɒd, 'kɛn-) NOUN any flowering

plant of the family *Chenopodiaceae,* which includes the beet, mangel-wurzel, spinach, and goosefoot.
▷HISTORY C16: from Greek *khēn* goose + *pous* foot
▶**chenopodiaceous** (ˌkiːnəˌpəʊdɪˈeɪʃəs, ˌkɛn-) ADJECTIVE

cheongsam (ˈtʃɒŋˈsæm) NOUN a straight dress, usually of silk or cotton, with a stand-up collar and a slit in one side of the skirt, worn by Chinese women.
▷HISTORY from Chinese (Cantonese), variant of Mandarin *ch'ang shan* long jacket

Chepstow (ˈtʃɛpstəʊ) NOUN a town in S Wales, in Monmouthshire on the River Wye: tourism, light industry. Pop.: 9461 (1991).

cheque *or US* **check** (tʃɛk) NOUN [1] a bill of exchange drawn on a bank by the holder of a current account; payable into a bank account, if crossed, or on demand, if uncrossed. [2] *Austral and NZ* the total sum of money received for contract work or a crop. [3] *Austral and NZ* wages.
▷HISTORY C18: from CHECK, in the sense: a means of verification

cheque account NOUN an account at a bank or a building society upon which cheques can be drawn.

chequebook *or US* **checkbook** (ˈtʃɛkˌbʊk) NOUN a book containing detachable blank cheques and issued by a bank or building society to holders of cheque accounts.

chequebook journalism NOUN the practice of securing exclusive rights to material for newspaper stories by paying a high price for it, regardless of any moral implications such as paying people to boast of criminal or morally reprehensible activities.

cheque card NOUN a card issued by a bank or building society, guaranteeing payment of a customer's cheques up to a stated value: may also function as a cash card or debit card or both.

chequer *or US* **checker** (ˈtʃɛkə) NOUN [1] any of the marbles, pegs, or other pieces used in the game of Chinese chequers. [2] **a** a pattern consisting of squares of different colours, textures, or materials. **b** one of the squares in such a pattern. ◆ VERB *(tr)* [3] to make irregular in colour or character; variegate. [4] to mark off with alternating squares of colour. ◆ See also **chequers.**
▷HISTORY C13: chessboard, from Anglo-French *escheker,*from *eschec* CHECK

chequerboard (ˈtʃɛkəˌbɔːd) NOUN another name for a **draughtboard.**

chequered *or esp US* **checkered** (ˈtʃɛkəd) ADJECTIVE marked by fluctuations of fortune (esp in the phrase **a chequered career**).

chequered flag NOUN the black-and-white checked flag traditionally shown to the winner and all finishers at the end of a motor race by a senior race official.

chequers (ˈtʃɛkəz) NOUN *(functioning as singular)* another name for **draughts.**

Chequers (ˈtʃɛkəz) NOUN an estate and country house in S England, in central Buckinghamshire: the official country residence of the British prime minister.

chequing account (ˈtʃɛkɪŋ) NOUN the Canadian name for **current account.**

Cher *(French* ʃɛr) NOUN [1] a department of central France, in E Centre region. Capital: Bourges. Pop.: 314 428 (1999 est.). Area: 7304 sq. km (2849 sq. miles). [2] a river in central France, rising in the Massif Central and flowing northwest to the Loire. Length: 354 km (220 miles).

Cherbourg (ˈʃɛəbʊəg; *French* ʃɛrbur) NOUN a port in NW France, on the English Channel. Pop.: 28 773 (1990).

Cheremiss *or* **Cheremis** (ˌtʃɛərəˈmɪs, -ˈmiːs, ˈtʃɛərəˌmɪs, -ˌmiːs) NOUN [1] *(plural* **-miss** *or* **-mis)** a member of an Ugrian people of the Volga region, esp of the Mari El Republic. [2] Also called: **Mari.** the language of this people, belonging to the Finno-Ugric family.

Cherenkov radiation (tʃɪˈrɛŋkɒf) NOUN the electromagnetic radiation produced when a charged particle moves through a medium at a greater velocity than the velocity of light in that medium.
▷HISTORY C20: named after Pavel Alekseyevich Cherenkov (1904–90), Soviet physicist

Cheribon (ˈtʃɪərəˌbɒn) NOUN a variant spelling of **Tjirebon.**

cherish (ˈtʃɛrɪʃ) VERB *(tr)* [1] to show great tenderness for; treasure. [2] to cling fondly to (a hope, idea, etc.); nurse: *to cherish ambitions.*
▷HISTORY C14: from Old French *cherir,* from *cher* dear, from Latin *cārus*
▶ˈ**cherishable** ADJECTIVE ▶ˈ**cherisher** NOUN ▶ˈ**cherishingly** ADVERB

Chernigov (ˈtʃɜːnɪgɒf) NOUN a city in the N central Ukraine, on the River Desna: tyres, pianos, consumer goods. Pop.: 310 800 (1998 est.).

Chernobyl (tʃɜːˈnəʊbᵊl, -ˈnɒbᵊl) NOUN a town in the N Ukraine; site of a nuclear power station accident in 1986.

Chernovtsy *(Russian* tʃɪrnafˈtsi) NOUN a city in the Ukraine on the Prut River: formerly under Polish, Austro-Hungarian, and Romanian rule; part of the Soviet Union (1947–91). Pop.: 259 000 (1998 est.). German name: **Czernowitz.** Romanian name: **Cernăuţi.**

chernozem *or* **tschernosem** (ˈtʃɜːnəʊˌzɛm) NOUN a black soil, rich in humus and carbonates, in cool or temperate semiarid regions, as the grasslands of Russia.
▷HISTORY from Russian, contraction of *chernaya zemlya* black earth

Cherokee (ˈtʃɛrəˌkiː, ˌtʃɛrəˈkiː) NOUN [1] *(plural* **-kees** *or* **-kee)** a member of a North American Indian people formerly living in and around the Appalachian Mountains, now chiefly in Oklahoma; one of the Iroquois peoples. [2] the language of this people, belonging to the Iroquoian family.

Cherokee rose NOUN an evergreen climbing Chinese rose, *Rosa laevigata,* that now grows wild in the southern US, having large white fragrant flowers.

cheroot (ʃəˈruːt) NOUN a cigar with both ends cut off squarely.
▷HISTORY C17: from Tamil *curuttu* curl, roll

cherry (ˈtʃɛrɪ) NOUN, *plural* **-ries.** [1] any of several trees of the rosaceous genus *Prunus,* such as *P. avium* **(sweet cherry)**, having a small fleshy rounded fruit containing a hard stone. See also **bird cherry.** [2] the fruit or wood of any of these trees. [3] any of various unrelated plants, such as the ground cherry and Jerusalem cherry. [4] **a** a bright red colour; cerise. **b** *(as adjective)*: *a cherry coat.* [5] *Slang* virginity or the hymen as its symbol. [6] *(modifier)* of or relating to the cherry fruit or wood: *cherry tart.*
▷HISTORY C14: back formation from Old English *ciris* (mistakenly thought to be plural), ultimately from Late Latin *ceresia,* perhaps from Latin *cerasus* cherry tree, from Greek *kerasios*
▶ˈ**cherry-**ˌ**like** ADJECTIVE

cherry brandy NOUN a red liqueur made of brandy flavoured with cherries.

cherry laurel NOUN a Eurasian rosaceous evergreen shrub, *Prunus laurocerasus,* having glossy aromatic leaves, white flowers, and purplish-black fruits.

cherry-pick VERB *(tr)* to choose or take the best or most profitable of (a number of things), esp for one's own benefit or gain: *cherry-pick the best routes.*

cherry picker NOUN a hydraulic crane, esp one mounted on a lorry, that has an elbow joint or telescopic arm supporting a basket-like platform enabling a person to service high power lines or to carry out similar operations above the ground.

cherry-pie NOUN a widely planted garden heliotrope, *Heliotropium peruvianum.*

cherry plum NOUN a small widely planted Asian rosaceous tree, *Prunus cerasifera,* with white flowers and red or yellow cherry-like fruit. Also called: **myrobalan.**

cherry tomato NOUN a miniature tomato not much bigger than a cherry.

chersonese (ˈkɜːsəˌniːs) NOUN **a** a poetic or rhetorical word for **peninsula. b** *(capital when part of a name)*: *Thracian Chersonese.*
▷HISTORY C17: from Latin, from Greek *khersonēsos,* from *khersos* dry (land) + *nēsos* island

chert (tʃɜːt) NOUN a microcrystalline form of silica usually occurring as bands or layers of pebbles in sedimentary rock. Formula: SiO_2. Varieties include flint, lyddite (Lydian stone). Also called: **hornstone.**
▷HISTORY C17: of obscure origin
▶ˈ**cherty** ADJECTIVE

Chertsey (ˈtʃɜːtsɪ) NOUN a town in S England, in N Surrey on the River Thames. Pop.: 11 786 (1991).

cherub (ˈtʃɛrəb) NOUN, *plural* **cherubs** *or* **cherubim** (ˈtʃɛrəbɪm, -ʊbɪm). [1] *Theol* a member of the second order of angels, whose distinctive gift is knowledge, often represented as a winged child or winged head of a child. [2] an innocent or sweet child.
▷HISTORY Old English, from Hebrew *kĕrūbh*
▶**cherubic** (tʃəˈruːbɪk) *or* **cheˈrubical** ADJECTIVE
▶**cheˈrubically** ADVERB

chervil (ˈtʃɜːvɪl) NOUN [1] an aromatic umbelliferous Eurasian plant, *Anthriscus cerefolium,* with small white flowers and aniseed-flavoured leaves used as herbs in soups and salads. [2] **bur chervil.** a similar and related plant, *Anthriscus caucalis.* [3] a related plant, *Chaerophyllum temulentum,* having a hairy purple-spotted stem.
▷HISTORY Old English *cerfelle,* from Latin *caerephylla,* plural of *caerephyllum* chervil, from Greek *khairephullon,* from *khairein* to enjoy + *phullon* leaf

chervonets (tʃəˈvɔːnɛts) NOUN (formerly) a Soviet monetary unit and gold coin worth ten roubles.
▷HISTORY from Old Russian *červonyi,* from Old Polish *czerwony* golden, purple

Ches. ABBREVIATION FOR Cheshire.

Chesapeake Bay (ˈtʃɛsəˌpiːk) NOUN the largest inlet of the Atlantic in the coast of the US: bordered by Maryland and Virginia.

Chesapeake Bay retriever NOUN a strongly built variety of retriever with a short thick, slightly wavy coat in straw colour, reddish gold, or brown.

Cheshire (ˈtʃɛʃə, ˈtʃɛʃɪə) NOUN a county of NW England: low-lying and undulating, bordering on the Pennines in the east; mainly agricultural: the geographic and ceremonial county includes Warrington and Halton, which became independent unitary authorities in 1998. Administrative centre: Chester. Pop. (excluding unitary authorities): 673 777 (2001). Area (excluding unitary authorites): 2077 sq. km (802 sq. miles). Abbreviation: **Ches.**

Cheshire cheese NOUN a mild-flavoured cheese with a crumbly texture, originally made in Cheshire.

Cheshunt (ˈtʃɛʃənt) NOUN a town in SE England, in SE Hertfordshire: a dormitory town of London. Pop.: 51 998 (1991).

Cheshvan *or* **Heshvan** (xɛʃˈvan) NOUN (in the Jewish calendar) the eighth month of the year according to biblical reckoning and the second month of the civil year, usually falling within October and November. Also called: **Marcheshvan.**
▷HISTORY from Hebrew

chess[1] (tʃɛs) NOUN a game of skill for two players using a chessboard on which chessmen are moved. Initially each player has one king, one queen, two rooks, two bishops, two knights, and eight pawns, which have different types of moves according to kind. The object is to checkmate the opponent's king.
▷HISTORY C13: from Old French *esches,* plural of *eschec* check (at chess); see CHECK

chess[2] (tʃɛs) NOUN *US* a less common name for **rye-brome.**
▷HISTORY C18: of unknown origin

chess[3] (tʃɛs) NOUN, *plural* **chess** *or* **chesses.** a floorboard of the deck of a pontoon bridge.
▷HISTORY C15 (in the sense: layer, tier): from Old French *chasse* frame, from Latin *capsa* box

chessboard (ˈtʃɛsˌbɔːd) NOUN a square board divided into 64 squares of two alternating colours, used for playing chess or draughts.

chessel (ˈtʃɛsᵊl) NOUN a mould used in cheese-making.
▷HISTORY C18: probably from CHEESE[1] + WELL[2]

chessman (ˈtʃɛsˌmæn, -mən) NOUN, *plural* **-men.** any of the eight pieces and eight pawns used by each player in a game of chess.
▷HISTORY C17: back formation from *chessmen,* from Middle English *chessemeyne* chess company, from *meynie, menye* company, body of men, from Old French *meyné*

chesspiece (ˈtʃɛsˌpiːs) NOUN any of the eight pieces (excluding the pawns) used by each player in a game of chess.

chest (tʃɛst) NOUN 1 **a** the front part of the trunk from the neck to the belly. Related adjective: **pectoral. b** (*as modifier*): *a chest cold.* 2 **get (something) off one's chest.** *Informal* to unburden oneself of troubles, worries, etc., by talking about them. 3 a box, usually large and sturdy, used for storage or shipping: *a tea chest.* 4 Also: **chestful.** the quantity a chest holds. 5 *Rare* **a** the place in which a public or charitable institution deposits its funds. **b** the funds so deposited. 6 a sealed container or reservoir for a gas: *a wind chest; a steam chest.*
▷HISTORY Old English *cest,* from Latin *cista* wooden box, basket, from Greek *kistē* box
▸ **'chested** ADJECTIVE

Chester ('tʃɛstə) NOUN a city in NW England, administrative centre of Cheshire, on the River Dee: intact surrounding walls; 16th- and 17th-century double-tier shops. Pop.: 80 110 (1991). Latin name: **Deva.**

chesterfield ('tʃɛstəˌfiːld) NOUN 1 a man's knee-length overcoat, usually with a fly front to conceal the buttons and having a velvet collar. 2 a large tightly stuffed sofa, often upholstered in leather, with straight upholstered arms of the same height as the back.
▷HISTORY C19: named after a 19th-century Earl of *Chesterfield*

Chesterfield ('tʃɛstəˌfiːld) NOUN an industrial town in N central England, in Derbyshire: famous 14th-century church with twisted spire. Pop.: 71 945 (1991).

Chesterfieldian (ˌtʃɛstə'fiːldɪən) ADJECTIVE of or like Lord Chesterfield; suave; elegant; polished.

chestnut ('tʃɛsˌnʌt) NOUN 1 any N temperate fagaceous tree of the genus *Castanea,* such as *C. sativa* (**sweet** or **Spanish chestnut**), which produce flowers in long catkins and nuts in a prickly bur. Compare **horse chestnut, water chestnut, dwarf chestnut.** 2 the edible nut of any of these trees. 3 the hard wood of any of these trees, used in making furniture, etc. 4 **a** a reddish-brown to brown colour. **b** (*as adjective*): *chestnut hair.* 5 a horse of a yellow-brown or golden-brown colour. 6 a small horny callus on the inner surface of a horse's leg. 7 *Informal* an old or stale joke.
▷HISTORY C16: from earlier *chesten nut: chesten,* from Old French *chastaigne,* from Latin *castanea,* from Greek *kastanea*

chest of drawers NOUN a piece of furniture consisting of a frame, often on short legs, containing a set of drawers.

chest of viols NOUN a set of viols of different sizes, usually six in number, used in consorts.

chest-on-chest NOUN another term for **tallboy.**

chest voice *or* **register** NOUN a voice of the lowest speaking or singing register. Compare **head voice.**

chesty ('tʃɛstɪ) ADJECTIVE **chestier, chestiest.** *Informal* 1 *Brit* suffering from or symptomatic of chest disease: *a chesty cough.* 2 having a large well-developed chest or bosom.
▸ **'chestiness** NOUN

chetah ('tʃiːtə) NOUN a variant spelling of **cheetah.**

Chetnik ('tʃɛtnɪk, tʃɛt'niːk) NOUN 1 a Serbian nationalist belonging to a group that fought against the Turks before World War I and engaged in guerrilla warfare during both World Wars. 2 a member of a Serbian nationalist paramilitary group fighting to retain Serbian influence in the countries which formerly constituted Yugoslavia.
▷HISTORY from Serbian *četnik, from četa* troop

cheval-de-frise (ʃəˌvældə'friːz) NOUN, *plural* **chevaux-de-frise** (ʃəˌvəʊdə'friːz). 1 a portable barrier of spikes, sword blades, etc., used to obstruct the passage of cavalry. 2 a row of spikes or broken glass set as an obstacle on top of a wall.
▷HISTORY C17: from French, literally: horse from Friesland (where it was first used)

cheval glass (ʃə'væl) NOUN a full-length mirror mounted so as to swivel within a frame.
▷HISTORY C19: from French *cheval* support (literally: horse)

chevalier (ˌʃɛ'vælɪə) NOUN 1 a member of certain orders of merit, such as the French Legion of Honour. 2 *French history* **a** a mounted soldier or knight, esp a military cadet. **b** the lowest title of rank in the old French nobility. 3 an archaic word for **knight.** 4 a chivalrous man; gallant.
▷HISTORY C14: from Old French, from Medieval Latin *caballārius* horseman, CAVALIER

chevet (ʃə'veɪ) NOUN a semicircular or polygonal east end of a church, esp a French Gothic church, often with a number of attached apses.
▷HISTORY C19: from French: pillow, from Latin *capitium,* from *caput* head

Cheviot ('tʃiːvɪət, 'tʃɛv-) NOUN 1 a large British breed of sheep reared for its wool. 2 (*often not capital*) a rough twill-weave woollen suiting fabric.

Cheviot Hills PLURAL NOUN a range of hills on the border between England and Scotland, mainly in Northumberland.

Chevra Kadisha *Hebrew* (xɛv'rɑ kɑdɪ'ʃɑ; *Yiddish* 'xɛvrə kɑ'dɪʃə) NOUN a Jewish burial society, usually composed of unpaid volunteers who provide funerals for members of their congregation.
▷HISTORY literally: Holy Company

chèvre ('ʃɛvrə) NOUN any cheese made from goats' milk.
▷HISTORY C20: from French, literally: goat

chevrette (ʃə'vrɛt) NOUN 1 the skin of a young goat. 2 the leather made from this skin.
▷HISTORY C18: from French: kid, from *chèvre* goat, from Latin *capra*

chevron ('ʃɛvrən) NOUN 1 *Military* a badge or insignia consisting of one or more V-shaped stripes to indicate a noncommissioned rank or length of service. 2 *Heraldry* an inverted V-shaped charge on a shield, one of the earliest ordinaries found in English arms. 3 (*usually plural*) a pattern of horizontal black and white V-shapes on a road sign indicating a sharp bend. 4 any V-shaped pattern or device. 5 Also called: **dancette.** an ornamental moulding having a zigzag pattern.
▷HISTORY C14: from Old French, ultimately from Latin *caper* goat; compare Latin *capreoli* two pieces of wood forming rafters (literally: little goats)

chevrotain ('ʃɛvrəˌteɪn, -tɪn) NOUN any small timid ruminant artiodactyl mammal of the genera *Tragulus* and *Hyemoschus,* of S and SE Asia: family *Tragulidae.* They resemble rodents, and the males have long tusklike upper canines. Also called: **mouse deer.**
▷HISTORY C18: from French, from Old French *chevrot* kid, from *chèvre* goat, from Latin *capra,* feminine of *caper* goat

chevy ('tʃɛvɪ) NOUN, VERB a variant of **chivy.**

chew (tʃuː) VERB 1 to work the jaws and teeth in order to grind (food); masticate. 2 to bite repeatedly: *she chewed her nails anxiously.* 3 (*intr*) to use chewing tobacco. 4 **chew the fat** *or* **rag.** *Slang* **a** to argue over a point. **b** to talk idly; gossip. ◆ NOUN 5 the act of chewing. 6 something that is chewed: *a chew of tobacco.* ◆ See also **chew out, chew over, chew up.**
▷HISTORY Old English *ceowan;* related to Old High German *kiuwan,* Dutch *kauwen,* Latin *gingīva* a gum
▸ **'chewable** ADJECTIVE ▸ **'chewer** NOUN

Chewa ('tʃeɪwə) NOUN 1 (*plural* **-was** *or* **-wa**) a member of a Negroid people of Malawi, E Zambia, and N Zimbabwe, related to the Bemba. 2 the language of this people. See **Chichewa.**

chewie ('tʃuːɪ) NOUN *Austral informal* chewing gum.

chewing gum NOUN a preparation for chewing, usually made of flavoured and sweetened chicle or such substitutes as polyvinyl acetate.

chew-'n'-spew *or* **chew and spew** NOUN *Austral slang* any fast-food restaurant considered to be serving poor quality food.

chew out VERB (*tr, adverb*) *Informal, chiefly US and Canadian* to reprimand.

chew over VERB (*tr, adverb*) to consider carefully; ruminate on.

chew up VERB (*tr, adverb*) 1 to damage or destroy (something) by or as by chewing or grinding. 2 (*usually passive*) *Slang* to cause (a person) to be nervous or worried: *he was all chewed up about the interview.*

chewy ('tʃuːɪ) ADJECTIVE **chewier, chewiest.** of a consistency requiring chewing; somewhat firm and sticky.

Cheyenne[1] (ʃaɪ'æn) NOUN 1 (*plural* **-enne** *or* **-ennes**) a member of a North American Indian people of the western Plains, now living chiefly in Montana and Oklahoma. 2 the language of this people, belonging to the Algonquian family.
▷HISTORY via Canadian French from Dakota *Shaiyena,* from *shaia* to speak incoherently, from *sha* red + *ya* to speak

Cheyenne[2] (ʃaɪ'æn, -'ɛn) NOUN a city in SE Wyoming, capital of the state. Pop.: 50 008 (1990).

Cheyne-Stokes breathing ('tʃeɪn'stəʊks) NOUN *Pathol* alternating shallow and deep breathing, as in comatose patients.
▷HISTORY C19: named after John *Cheyne* (1777–1836), Scottish physician, and William *Stokes* (1804–78), Irish physician

chez *French* (ʃe) PREPOSITION 1 at the home of. 2 with, among, or in the manner of.

chg. *Commerce, finance* ABBREVIATION FOR charge.

Chhattisgarh (ˌtʃʌtɪs'gɑː) NOUN a state of E central India, created from the SE part of Madhya Pradesh in 2000: consists of a hilly plateau, with extensive forests; agricultural. Capital: Raipur. Pop.: 20 795 956 (2001). Area: 135 194 sq. km (52 199 sq. miles). Abbreviation: **Ches.**

chi[1] (kaɪ) NOUN the 22nd letter of the Greek alphabet (Χ, χ), a consonant, transliterated as *ch* or rarely *kh.*

chi[2], **ch'i** (tʃiː), *or* **qi** NOUN (*sometimes capital*) (in Oriental medicine, martial arts, etc.) vital energy believed to circulate round the body in currents.
▷HISTORY Chinese, literally: energy

chiack *or* **chyack** ('tʃaɪæk) *Austral informal* ◆ VERB (*tr*) 1 to tease or banter. ◆ NOUN 2 good-humoured banter.
▷HISTORY C19: from *chi-hike,* a shout or greeting

Chian ('kaɪən) ADJECTIVE 1 of or relating to Chios. ◆ NOUN 2 a native or inhabitant of Chios.

chianti (kɪ'æntɪ) NOUN (*sometimes capital*) a dry red wine made from this Chianti region of Italy.

Chianti (*Italian* 'kjanti) PLURAL NOUN a mountain range in central Italy, in Tuscany, rising over 870 m (2900 ft.): part of the Apennines.

Chiapas (*Spanish* 'tʃjapas) NOUN a state of S Mexico: mountainous and forested; Maya ruins in the northeast; rich mineral resources. Capital: Tuxtla Gutiérrez. Pop.: 3 920 515 (2000). Area: 73 887 sq. km (28 816 sq. miles).

chiaroscuro (kɪˌɑːrə'skʊərəʊ) NOUN, *plural* **-ros.** 1 the artistic distribution of light and dark masses in a picture. 2 monochrome painting using light and dark only, as in grisaille.
▷HISTORY C17: from Italian, from *chiaro* CLEAR + *oscuro* OBSCURE
▸ **chiˌaro'scurist** NOUN ▸ **chiˌaro'scurism** NOUN

chiasma (kaɪ'æzmə) *or* **chiasm** ('kaɪæzəm) NOUN, *plural* **-mas, -mata** (-mətə) *or* **-asms.** 1 *Cytology* the cross-shaped connection produced by the crossing over of pairing chromosomes during meiosis. 2 *Anatomy* the crossing over of two parts or structures, such as the fibres of the optic nerves in the brain.
▷HISTORY C19: from Greek *khiasma* wooden crosspiece, from *khiazein* to mark with an X, from *khi* CHI[1]
▸ **chi'asmal** *or* **chi'asmic** ADJECTIVE

chiasmus (kaɪ'æzməs) NOUN, *plural* **-mi** (-maɪ). *Rhetoric* reversal of the order of words in the second of two parallel phrases: *he came in triumph and in defeat departs.*
▷HISTORY C19: from New Latin, from Greek *khiasmos* crisscross arrangement; see CHIASMA
▸ **chiastic** (kaɪ'æstɪk) ADJECTIVE

chiastolite (kaɪ'æstəˌlaɪt) NOUN a variety of andalusite containing carbon impurities. Also called: **macle.**
▷HISTORY C19: from German *Chiastolith,* from Greek *khiastos* crossed, marked with a chi + *lithos* stone

Chiba ('tʃiːba) NOUN an industrial city in central Japan, in SE Honshu on Tokyo Bay. Pop.: 856 882 (1995).

Chibchan ('tʃɪbtʃən) NOUN 1 a family of Indian languages found in Colombia and elsewhere in South America. ◆ ADJECTIVE 2 belonging or relating to this family of languages.

chibol ('tʃɪbᵊl) NOUN *English dialect* a spring onion.
▷HISTORY see SYBO

chibouk *or* **chibouque** (tʃɪ'buːk) NOUN a Turkish tobacco pipe with an extremely long stem.
▷HISTORY C19: from French *chibouque,* from Turkish *çubuk* pipe

chic (ʃiːk, ʃɪk) ADJECTIVE 1 (esp of fashionable clothes, women, etc.) stylish or elegant. ♦ NOUN 2 stylishness, esp in dress; modishness; fashionable good taste.
▷HISTORY C19: from French, of uncertain origin
▸ˈ**chicly** ADVERB

Chicago (ʃɪˈkɑːgəʊ) NOUN a port in NE Illinois, on Lake Michigan: the third largest city in the US; it is a major railway and air traffic centre. Pop.: 2 896 016 (1996 est.).

chicalote (ˌtʃiːkɑːˈləʊteɪ) NOUN a poppy, *Argemone platyceras*, of the southwestern US and Mexico with prickly leaves and white or yellow flowers.
▷HISTORY from Spanish, from Nahuatl *chicalotl*

chicane (ʃɪˈkeɪn) NOUN 1 a bridge or whist hand without trumps. 2 *Motor racing* a short section of sharp narrow bends formed by barriers placed on a motor-racing circuit to provide an additional test of driving skill. 3 a less common word for **chicanery.** ♦ VERB 4 (*tr*) to deceive or trick by chicanery. 5 (*tr*) to quibble about; cavil over. 6 (*intr*) to use tricks or chicanery.
▷HISTORY C17: from French *chicaner* to quibble, of obscure origin
▸chiˈ**caner** NOUN

chicanery (ʃɪˈkeɪnərɪ) NOUN, *plural* **-eries.** 1 verbal deception or trickery, esp in legal quibbling; dishonest or sharp practice. 2 a trick, deception, or quibble.

chicano (tʃɪˈkɑːnəʊ) NOUN, *plural* **-nos.** an American citizen of Mexican origin.
▷HISTORY C20: from Spanish *mejicano* Mexican

chiccory (ˈtʃɪkərɪ) NOUN, *plural* **-ries.** a variant spelling of **chicory.**

Chichagof Island (ˈtʃɪtʃəˌgɔːf) NOUN an island of Alaska, in the Alexander Archipelago. Area: 5439 sq. km (2100 sq. miles).

Chichen Itzá (*Spanish* tʃiˈtʃen itˈsa) NOUN a village in Yucatán state in Mexico: site of important Mayan ruins.

Chichester (ˈtʃɪtʃɪstə) NOUN a city in S England, administrative centre of West Sussex: Roman ruins; 11th-century cathedral; Festival Theatre. Pop.: 26 572 (1991).

Chichewa (tʃɪˈtʃeɪwə) NOUN the language of the Chewa people of central Africa, widely used as a lingua franca in Malawi. It belongs to the Bantu group of the Niger-Congo family.

chichi¹ (ˈʃiːˌʃiː) ADJECTIVE 1 affectedly pretty or stylish. ♦ NOUN 2 the quality of being affectedly pretty or stylish.
▷HISTORY C20: from French

chichi² (ˈtʃiːˌtʃiː) NOUN, *plural* **chichis.** (formerly, in India) **a** a person of mixed British and Indian descent; Anglo-Indian. **b** (*as modifier*): *a chichi accent.* ♦ Also (less common): **chee-chee.**
▷HISTORY C18: perhaps from Hindi *chhī-chhī,* literally: dirt, or perhaps imitative of their supposed singsong speech

Chichihaerh *or* **Ch'i-ch'i-haerh** (ˈtʃiːˌtʃiːˈhɑː) NOUN a variant transliteration of the Chinese name for **Qiqihar.**

chick (tʃɪk) NOUN 1 the young of a bird, esp of a domestic fowl. 2 *Slang* a girl or young woman, esp an attractive one. 3 a young child: used as a term of endearment.
▷HISTORY C14: short for CHICKEN

chickabiddy (ˈtʃɪkəˌbɪdɪ) NOUN, *plural* **-dies.** a term of endearment, esp for a child.
▷HISTORY C18: from CHICK + BIDDY¹

chickadee (ˈtʃɪkəˌdiː) NOUN any of various small North American songbirds of the genus *Parus,* such as *P. atricapillus* (**black-capped chickadee**), typically having grey-and-black plumage: family *Paridae* (titmice).
▷HISTORY C19: imitative of its note

chickaree (ˈtʃɪkəˌriː) NOUN another name for **American red squirrel** (see **squirrel** (sense 1)).

Chickasaw (ˈtʃɪkəˌsɔː) NOUN 1 (*plural* **-saws** *or* **-saw**) a member of a North American Indian people of N Mississippi. 2 the language of this people, belonging to the Muskogean family and closely related to Choctaw.

chicken (ˈtʃɪkɪn) NOUN 1 a domestic fowl bred for its flesh or eggs, esp a young one. 2 the flesh of such a bird used for food. 3 any of various similar birds, such as a prairie chicken. 4 *Slang* a cowardly person. 5 *Slang* a young inexperienced person. 6 *Slang* an underage boy or girl regarded as a potential target for sexual abuse. 7 *Informal* any of various, often dangerous, games or challenges in which the object is to make one's opponent lose his nerve. 8 **count one's chickens before they are hatched.** to be overoptimistic in acting on expectations which are not yet fulfilled. 9 **like a headless chicken.** *Brit informal* disorganized and uncontrolled. 10 **no (spring) chicken.** *Slang* no longer young: *she's no chicken.* ♦ ADJECTIVE 11 *Slang* easily scared; cowardly; timid.
▷HISTORY Old English *ciecen;* related to Old Norse *kjūklingr* gosling, Middle Low German *küken* chicken

chicken breast NOUN *Pathol* another name for **pigeon breast.**
▸ˌ**chicken-**ˈ**breasted** ADJECTIVE

chicken feed NOUN *Slang* a trifling amount of money.

chicken fillet NOUN 1 a fillet cut from a chicken. 2 a gel-filled pad inserted under clothing to enlarge the appearance of a woman's breast.

chicken-hearted *or* **chicken-livered** ADJECTIVE easily frightened; cowardly.
▸ˌ**chicken-**ˈ**heartedly** ADVERB ▸ˌ**chicken-**ˈ**heartedness** NOUN

chicken louse NOUN a louse, *Menopon pallidum* (or *gallinae*); a parasite of poultry: order *Mallophaga* (bird lice).

chicken out VERB (*intr, adverb*) *Informal* to fail to do something through fear or lack of conviction.

chickenpox (ˈtʃɪkɪnˌpɒks) NOUN a highly communicable viral disease most commonly affecting children, characterized by slight fever and the eruption of a rash.

chicken wire NOUN wire netting with a hexagonal mesh.

chick flick NOUN *Informal, derogatory* a film aimed at or appealing to women.
▷HISTORY C20: from CHICK (sense 2) + FLICK²

chick lit NOUN **a** a genre of fiction concentrating on young working women and their emotional lives. **b** (*as modifier*): *chick-lit romances.*

chickpea (ˈtʃɪkˌpiː) NOUN 1 a bushy leguminous plant, *Cicer arietinum,* cultivated for its edible pealike seeds in the Mediterranean region, central Asia, and Africa. 2 Also called: **garbanzo.** the seed of this plant.
▷HISTORY C16 *ciche peasen,* from *ciche* (from French *chiche,* from Latin *cicer* chickpea) + *peasen;* see PEA

chickweed (ˈtʃɪkˌwiːd) NOUN 1 any of various caryophyllaceous plants of the genus *Stellaria,* esp *S. media,* a common garden weed with small white flowers. 2 **mouse-ear chickweed.** any of various similar and related plants of the genus *Cerastium.*

Chiclayo (*Spanish* tʃiˈklajo) NOUN a city in NW Peru. Pop.: 469 200 (1998 est.).

chicle (ˈtʃɪkᵊl) NOUN a gumlike substance obtained from the sapodilla; the main ingredient of chewing gum. Also called: **chicle gum.**
▷HISTORY from Spanish, from Nahuatl *chictli*

chico (ˈtʃiːkəʊ) NOUN, *plural* **-cos.** another name for **greasewood** (sense 1).

chicory (ˈtʃɪkərɪ) NOUN, *plural* **-ries.** 1 Also called: **succory.** a blue-flowered plant, *Cichorium intybus,* cultivated for its leaves, which are used in salads, and for its roots: family *Asteraceae* (composites). 2 the root of this plant, roasted, dried, and used as a coffee substitute. ♦ Compare **endive.**
▷HISTORY C15: from Old French *chicorée,* from Latin *cichorium,* from Greek *kikhōrion*

chide (tʃaɪd) VERB **chides, chiding, chided** *or* **chid; chided, chid** *or* **chidden.** 1 to rebuke or scold. 2 (*tr*) to goad into action.
▷HISTORY Old English *cīdan*
▸ˈ**chider** NOUN ▸ˈ**chidingly** ADVERB

chief (tʃiːf) NOUN 1 the head, leader, or most important individual in a group or body of people. 2 another word for **chieftain** (sense 1). 3 *Heraldry* the upper third of a shield. 4 **in chief.** primarily; especially. ♦ ADJECTIVE 5 (*prenominal*) **a** most important; principal. **b** highest in rank or authority. ♦ ADVERB 6 *Archaic* principally.
▷HISTORY C13: from Old French, from Latin *caput* head

Chief Education Officer NOUN *Brit* an official who is the chief administrative officer of a Local Education Authority. Also called: **Director of Education.**

chief executive NOUN the person with overall responsibility for the efficient running of a company, organization, etc.

chief justice NOUN 1 (in any of several Commonwealth countries) the judge presiding over a supreme court. 2 (in the US) the presiding judge of a court composed of a number of members. ♦ See also **Lord Chief Justice.**
▸**chief justiceship** NOUN

chiefly (ˈtʃiːflɪ) ADVERB 1 especially or essentially; above all. 2 in general; mainly; mostly. ♦ ADJECTIVE 3 of or relating to a chief or chieftain.

Chief of Staff NOUN 1 the senior staff officer under the commander of a major military formation or organization. 2 the senior officer of each service of the armed forces. Abbreviations: **C of S, COS.**

chief petty officer NOUN the senior naval rank for personnel without commissioned or warrant rank. Abbreviation: **CPO.**

Chief Rabbi NOUN the chief religious minister of a national Jewish community.

chieftain (ˈtʃiːftən, -tɪn) NOUN 1 the head or leader of a tribe or clan. 2 the chief of a group of people.
▷HISTORY C14: from Old French *chevetaine,* from Late Latin *capitāneus* commander; see CAPTAIN
▸ˈ**chieftaincy** *or* ˈ**chieftain**ˌ**ship** NOUN

chief technician NOUN a noncommissioned officer in the Royal Air Force junior to a flight sergeant.

chiel (tʃiːl) NOUN *Scot* a young man; lad.
▷HISTORY C14: a Scot variant of CHILD

Chiengmai (ˈtʃɪɛŋˈmaɪ) *or* **Chiang Mai** NOUN a town in NW Thailand: teak, silver, silk industries: university (1964). Pop.: 171 594 (1999 est.).

chiffchaff (ˈtʃɪfˌtʃæf) NOUN a common European warbler, *Phylloscopus collybita,* with a yellowish-brown plumage.
▷HISTORY C18: imitative of its call

chiffon (ʃɪˈfɒn, ˈʃɪfɒn) NOUN 1 a fine transparent or almost transparent plain-weave fabric of silk, nylon, etc. 2 (*often plural*) *Now rare* feminine finery. ♦ ADJECTIVE 3 made of chiffon. 4 (of soufflés, pies, cakes, etc.) having a very light fluffy texture.
▷HISTORY C18: from French, from *chiffe* rag; probably related to CHIP
▸ˈ**chiffony** ADJECTIVE

chiffonade (ˌʃɪfəˈnɑːd) NOUN finely shredded leaf vegetables used as a base for a dish or as a garnish.

chiffonier *or* **chiffonnier** (ˌʃɪfəˈnɪə) NOUN 1 a tall, elegant chest of drawers, originally intended for holding needlework. 2 a wide low open-fronted cabinet, sometimes fitted with two grille doors and shelves.
▷HISTORY C19: from French, from *chiffon* rag; see CHIFFON

chigetai (ˌtʃɪgɪˈtaɪ) NOUN a variety of the Asiatic wild ass, *Equus hemionus,* of Mongolia. Also spelt: **dziggetai.**
▷HISTORY from Mongolian *tchikhitei* long-eared, from *tchikhi* ear

chigger (ˈtʃɪgə) NOUN 1 Also called: **chigoe, redbug.** *US and Canadian* the parasitic larva of any of various free-living mites of the family *Trombidiidae,* which causes intense itching of human skin. 2 another name for the **chigoe** (sense 1).

chignon (ˈʃiːnjɒn; *French* ʃiɲɔ̃) NOUN an arrangement of long hair in a roll or knot at the back of the head.
▷HISTORY C18: from French, from Old French *chaignon* link, from *chaine* CHAIN; influenced also by Old French *tignon* coil of hair, from *tigne,* moth, from Latin *tinea* moth
▸ˈ**chignoned** ADJECTIVE

chigoe (ˈtʃɪgəʊ) NOUN 1 Also called: **chigger, jigger, sand flea.** a tropical flea, *Tunga penetrans,* the female of which lives on or burrows into the skin of its host, which includes man. 2 another name for **chigger** (sense 1).
▷HISTORY C17: from Carib *chigo*

Chigwell (ˈtʃɪgwəl) NOUN a town in S England, in W Essex. Pop.: 10 332 (1991).

Chihli (ˈtʃiːˈliː) NOUN **Gulf of.** another name for the **Bohai.**

Chihuahua (tʃɪˈwɑːwɑː, -wə) NOUN 1 a state of N Mexico: mostly high plateau; important mineral resources, with many silver mines. Capital: Chihuahua. Pop.: 3 047 867 (2000). Area: 247 087 sq. km (153 194 sq. miles). 2 a city in N Mexico, capital of Chihuahua state. Pop.: 650 000 (2000 est.). 3 a breed of tiny dog originally from Mexico, having short smooth hair, large erect ears, and protruding eyes.

chi kung (ˈtʃiː ˈgɒŋ) NOUN a variant spelling of **qi gong**.

chilblain (ˈtʃɪlˌbleɪn) NOUN *Pathol* (*usually plural*) an inflammation of the fingers, toes, or ears, caused by prolonged exposure to moisture and cold. Technical name: **pernio**.
▷HISTORY C16: from CHILL (noun) + BLAIN
▸ˈ**chilˌblained** ADJECTIVE

child (tʃaɪld) NOUN, *plural* **children**. 1 **a** a boy or girl between birth and puberty. **b** (*as modifier*): *child labour*. 2 a baby or infant. 3 an unborn baby. Related prefix: **paedo-**. 4 **with child**. another term for **pregnant**. 5 a human offspring; a son or daughter. Related adjective: **filial**. 6 a childish or immature person. 7 a member of a family or tribe; descendant: *a child of Israel*. 8 a person or thing regarded as the product of an influence or environment: *a child of nature*. 9 *Midland and Western English dialect* a female infant.
▷HISTORY Old English *cild*; related to Gothic *kilthei* womb, Sanskrit *jathara* belly, *jartu* womb
▸ˈ**childless** ADJECTIVE ▸ˈ**childlessness** NOUN ▸ˈ**childly** ADJECTIVE

child abuse NOUN physical, sexual, or emotional ill-treatment or neglect of a child, esp by those responsible for its welfare. See also **nonaccidental injury**.

child-abuse register NOUN *Social welfare* (in Britain) a list of children deemed to be at risk of abuse or injury from their parents or guardians, compiled and held by a local authority, area health authority, or NSPCC Special Unit. Also called: **NAI register**.

child-bearing NOUN **a** the act or process of carrying and giving birth to a child. **b** (*as modifier*): *of child-bearing age*.

childbed (ˈtʃaɪldˌbɛd) NOUN **a** (often preceded by *in*) the condition of giving birth to a child. **b** (*as modifier*): *childbed fever*.

child benefit NOUN (in Britain and New Zealand) a regular government payment to the parents of children up to a certain age.

childbirth (ˈtʃaɪldˌbɜːθ) NOUN the act of giving birth to a child. Related adjective: **obstetric**.

childcare (ˈtʃaɪldˌkɛə) NOUN *Brit* 1 care provided for children without homes (or with a seriously disturbed home life) by a local authority. 2 care and supervision of children whose parents are working, provided by a childminder or local authority.

childe (tʃaɪld) NOUN *Archaic* a young man of noble birth.
▷HISTORY C13: variant of CHILD

childermas (ˈtʃɪldəˌmæs) NOUN *Archaic* Holy Innocents Day, Dec. 28.
▷HISTORY Old English *cylda-mæsse*, from *cildra*, genitive plural of CHILD, + *mæsse* MASS

child guidance NOUN the counselling of emotionally disturbed children.

childhood (ˈtʃaɪldhʊd) NOUN the condition of being a child; the period of life before puberty.

childish (ˈtʃaɪldɪʃ) ADJECTIVE 1 in the manner of, belonging to, or suitable to a child. 2 foolish or petty; puerile: *childish fears*.
▸ˈ**childishly** ADVERB ▸ˈ**childishness** NOUN

child labour NOUN the full-time employment of children below a minimum age laid down by statute.

childlike (ˈtʃaɪldˌlaɪk) ADJECTIVE like or befitting a child, as in being innocent, trustful, etc. Compare **childish** (sense 2).

child minder NOUN a person who looks after children, esp those whose parents are working.

children (ˈtʃɪldrən) NOUN the plural of **child**.

Children's Panel NOUN (in Scotland) a group of representatives of relevant agencies, with the power to deal with a child under sixteen who is in criminal or family trouble. Its hearings are private and replace most of the functions of juvenile courts.

child's play NOUN *Informal* something that is easy to do.

chile (ˈtʃɪlɪ) NOUN a variant spelling of **chilli**.

Chile (ˈtʃɪlɪ) NOUN a republic in South America, on the Pacific, with a total length of about 4090 km (2650 miles) and an average width of only 177 km (110 miles): gained independence from Spain in 1818; the government of President Allende (elected 1970) attempted the implementation of Marxist policies within a democratic system until overthrown by a military coup (1973); democracy restored 1988. Chile consists chiefly of the Andes in the east, the Atacama Desert in the north, a central fertile region, and a huge S region of almost uninhabitable mountains, glaciers, fjords, and islands; an important producer of copper, iron ore, nitrates, etc. Language: Spanish. Religion: Roman Catholic majority. Currency: peso. Capital: Santiago. Pop.: 15 402 000 (2001 est.). Area: 756 945 sq. km (292 256 sq. miles).

Chilean (ˈtʃɪlɪən) ADJECTIVE 1 of or relating to Chile or its inhabitants. ◆ NOUN 2 a native or inhabitant of Chile.

Chilean firebush (ˈfaɪəˌbʊʃ) NOUN another name for **embrothrium**.

Chile pine NOUN another name for the **monkey puzzle**.

Chile saltpetre *or* **nitre** NOUN a naturally occurring form of sodium nitrate: a soluble white or colourless mineral occurring in arid regions, esp in Chile and Peru. Also called: **soda nitre**.

chiliad (ˈkɪlɪˌæd) NOUN 1 a group of one thousand. 2 one thousand years.
▷HISTORY C16: from Greek *khilias*, from *khilioi* a thousand
▸ˌ**chiliˈadal** *or* ˌ**chiliˈadic** ADJECTIVE

chiliasm (ˈkɪlɪˌæzəm) NOUN *Christian theol* another term for **millenarianism** or the **millennium**.
▷HISTORY C17: from Greek *khiliasmos*, from *khilioi* a thousand
▸ˈ**chiliˌast** NOUN ▸ˌ**chiliˈastic** ADJECTIVE

Chilkoot Pass (ˈtʃɪlkuːt) NOUN a mountain pass in North America between SE Alaska and NW British Columbia, over the Coast Range.

chill (tʃɪl) NOUN 1 a moderate coldness. 2 a sensation of coldness resulting from a cold or damp environment, or from a sudden emotional reaction. 3 a feverish cold. 4 a check on enthusiasm or joy. 5 a metal plate placed in a sand mould to accelerate cooling and control local grain growth. 6 another name for **bloom**[1] (sense 9). ◆ ADJECTIVE 7 another word for **chilly**. ◆ VERB 8 to make or become cold. 9 (*tr*) to cool or freeze (food, drinks, etc.). 10 (*tr*) **a** to depress (enthusiasm, etc.). **b** to discourage. 11 (*tr*) to cool (a casting or metal object) rapidly in order to prevent the formation of large grains in the metal. 12 (*intr*) *Slang, chiefly US* to relax; calm oneself. ◆ See also **chill out**.
▷HISTORY Old English *ciele*; related to *calan* to COOL, Latin *gelidus* icy
▸ˈ**chillingly** ADVERB ▸ˈ**chillness** NOUN

Chillán (*Spanish* tʃiˈʎan) NOUN a city in central Chile. Pop.: 162 969 (1999 est.).

chilled (tʃɪld) ADJECTIVE 1 (of a person) feeling cold. 2 (of food or drink) kept cool. 3 *Informal* Also: **chilled-out**. relaxed or easy-going in character or behaviour.

chiller (ˈtʃɪlə) NOUN 1 *Informal* short for **spine-chiller**. 2 *NZ* a refrigerated storage area for meat.

chiller cabinet NOUN a cupboard or chest in a shop where chilled foods and drinks are displayed and kept cool.

chilli *or* **chili** (ˈtʃɪlɪ) NOUN, *plural* **chillies** *or* **chilies**. the small red hot-tasting pod of a type of capsicum used for flavouring sauces, pickles, etc.
▷HISTORY C17: from Spanish *chile*, from Nahuatl *chilli*

chilli con carne (kɒn ˈkɑːnɪ) NOUN a highly seasoned Mexican dish of meat, onions, beans, and chilli powder.
▷HISTORY from Spanish *chile con carne* chilli with meat

chilli powder NOUN ground chilli blended with other spices.

chilli sauce NOUN a highly seasoned sauce made of tomatoes cooked with chilli and other spices and seasonings.

Chillon (ʃɪˈlɒn; *French* ʃijɔ̃) NOUN a castle in W Switzerland, in Vaud at the E end of Lake Geneva.

chill out *Informal* ◆ VERB 1 (*intr, adverb*) to relax, esp after energetic dancing or a spell of hard work. ◆ ADJECTIVE **chill-out**. 2 suitable for relaxation after energetic dancing or hard work: *a chill-out area; chill-out music*.

chill pill NOUN *Informal* an imaginary medicinal pill with a calming, relaxing effect: *take a chill pill*.

chillum (ˈtʃɪləm) NOUN a short pipe, usually of clay, used esp for smoking cannabis.
▷HISTORY C18: from Hindi *cilam*, from Persian *chilam*

chilly (ˈtʃɪlɪ) ADJECTIVE **-lier, -liest**. 1 causing or feeling cool or moderately cold. 2 without warmth; unfriendly. 3 (of people) sensitive to cold.
▸ˈ**chilliness** NOUN

chilly bin NOUN *NZ informal* a portable insulated container with provision for packing food and drink in ice.

Chiloé Island (ˌtʃɪləʊˈeɪ) NOUN an island administered by Chile, off the W coast of South America in the Pacific Ocean: timber. Pop.: 116 000 (latest est.). Area: 8394 sq. km (3240 sq. miles).

chilopod (ˈkaɪləˌpɒd) NOUN any arthropod of the class *Chilopoda*, which includes the centipedes. See also **myriapod**.
▷HISTORY C19: from New Latin *Chilopoda*, from Greek *kheilos* lip + *pous* foot; referring to the modification of the first pair of legs into jawlike claws
▸**chilopodan** (kaɪˈlɒpədᵊn) NOUN, ADJECTIVE
▸**chiˈlopodous** ADJECTIVE

Chilpancingo (*Spanish* tʃilpanˈθiŋgo) NOUN a town in S Mexico, capital of Guerrero state, in the Sierra Madre del Sur. Pop.: 140 000 (2000 est.).

Chiltern Hills (ˈtʃɪltən) PLURAL NOUN a range of low chalk hills in SE England extending northwards from the Thames valley. Highest point: 260 m (852 ft.).

Chiltern Hundreds PLURAL NOUN (in Britain) short for **Stewardship of the Chiltern Hundreds**; a nominal office that an MP applies for in order to resign his seat.

Chilung *or* **Chi-lung** (ˈtʃiːˈlʊŋ) NOUN a port in N Taiwan: fishing and industrial centre. Pop.: 385 201 (2000 est.). Also called: **Keelung, Kilung**.

chimaera (kaɪˈmɪərə, kɪ-) NOUN 1 any tapering smooth-skinned cartilaginous deep-sea fish of the subclass *Holocephali* (or *Bradyodonti*), esp any of the genus *Chimaera*. They have a skull in which the upper jaw is fused to the cranium. See also **rabbitfish** (sense 1). 2 *Greek myth* a variant spelling of **chimera** (sense 1).

chimb (tʃaɪm) NOUN a variant spelling of **chime**[2].

Chimborazo (ˌtʃɪmbəˈrɑːzəʊ, -ˈreɪ-; *Spanish* tʃimboˈraθo) NOUN an extinct volcano in central Ecuador, in the Andes: the highest peak in Ecuador. Height: 6267 m (20 561 ft.).

Chimbote (*Spanish* tʃimˈbote) NOUN a port in N central Peru: contains Peru's first steelworks (1958), using hydroelectric power from the Santa River. Pop.: 298 800 (1998 est.).

chime[1] (tʃaɪm) NOUN 1 an individual bell or the sound it makes when struck. 2 (*often plural*) the machinery employed to sound a bell in this way. 3 Also called: **bell**. a percussion instrument consisting of a set of vertical metal tubes of graduated length, suspended in a frame and struck with a hammer. 4 a harmonious or ringing sound: *the chimes of children's laughter*. 5 agreement; concord. ◆ VERB 6 **a** to sound (a bell) or (of a bell) to be sounded by a clapper or hammer. **b** to produce (music or sounds) by chiming. 7 (*tr*) to indicate or show (time or the hours) by chiming. 8 (*tr*) to summon, announce, or welcome by ringing bells. 9 (*intr*; foll by *with*) to agree or harmonize. 10 to speak or recite in a musical or rhythmic manner.
▷HISTORY C13: probably shortened from earlier *chymbe bell*, ultimately from Latin *cymbalum* CYMBAL
▸ˈ**chimer** NOUN

chime[2], **chimb** (tʃaɪm), *or* **chine** NOUN the projecting edge or rim of a cask or barrel.

▷HISTORY Old English *cimb-;* related to Middle Low German *kimme* outer edge, Swedish *kimb*

chime in VERB *(intr, adverb) Informal* [1] to join in or interrupt (a conversation), esp repeatedly and unwelcomely. [2] to voice agreement.

chimera *or* **chimaera** (kaɪˈmɪərə, kɪ-) NOUN [1] *(often capital) Greek myth* a fire-breathing monster with the head of a lion, body of a goat, and tail of a serpent. [2] a fabulous beast made up of parts taken from various animals. [3] a wild and unrealistic dream or notion. [4] *Biology* an organism, esp a cultivated plant, consisting of at least two genetically different kinds of tissue as a result of mutation, grafting, etc.
▷HISTORY C16: from Latin *chimaera,* from Greek *khimaira* she-goat, from *khimaros* he-goat

chimere (tʃɪˈmɪə, ʃɪ-), **chimer,** *or* **chimar** (ˈtʃɪmə, ˈʃɪm-) NOUN *Anglican Church* a sleeveless red or black gown, part of a bishop's formal dress though not a vestment.
▷HISTORY C14: perhaps from Medieval Latin *chimēra* (see CHIMERA) and related to Spanish *zamarra* sheepskin coat

chimerical (kaɪˈmɛrɪkəl, kɪ-) *or* **chimeric** ADJECTIVE [1] wildly fanciful; imaginary. [2] given to or indulging in fantasies.
▸**chiˈmerically** ADVERB ▸**chiˈmericalness** NOUN

Chimkent (tʃɪmˈkɛnt) NOUN a city in S Kazakhstan; a major railway junction. Pop.: 360 100 (1999 est.).

chimney (ˈtʃɪmnɪ) NOUN [1] a vertical structure of brick, masonry, or steel that carries smoke or steam away from a fire, engine, etc. [2] another name for **flue**[1] (sense 1). [3] short for **chimney stack.** [4] an open-ended glass tube fitting around the flame of an oil or gas lamp in order to exclude draughts. [5] *Brit* a fireplace, esp an old and large one. [6] *Geology* **a** a cylindrical body of an ore, which is usually oriented vertically. **b** the vent of a volcano. [7] *Mountaineering* a vertical fissure large enough for a person's body to enter. [8] anything resembling a chimney in shape or function.
▷HISTORY C14: from Old French *cheminée,* from Late Latin *camīnāta,* from Latin *camīnus* furnace, from Greek *kaminos* fireplace, oven

chimney breast NOUN the wall or walls that surround the base of a chimney or fireplace.

chimney corner NOUN a recess that contains a seat in a large open fireplace; inglenook.

chimneypiece (ˈtʃɪmnɪˌpiːs) NOUN another name (esp Brit) for **mantelpiece** (sense 1).

chimneypot (ˈtʃɪmnɪˌpɒt) NOUN a short pipe on the top of a chimney, which increases the draught and directs the smoke upwards.

chimney stack NOUN the part of a chimney that rises above the roof of a building.

chimney swallow NOUN [1] another name for **common swallow** (see **swallow**[2]). [2] a less common name for **chimney swift.**

chimney sweep *or* **sweeper** NOUN a person whose job is the cleaning out of soot from chimneys.

chimney swift NOUN a North American swift, *Chaetura pelagica,* that nests in chimneys and similar hollows.

chimp (tʃɪmp) NOUN *Informal* short for **chimpanzee.**

chimpanzee (ˌtʃɪmpænˈziː) NOUN a gregarious and intelligent anthropoid ape, *Pan troglodytes,* inhabiting forests in central W Africa.
▷HISTORY C18: from Kongo dialect

chin (tʃɪn) NOUN [1] the protruding part of the lower jaw. [2] the front part of the face below the lips. Related adjectives: **genial, menal.** [3] **keep one's chin up.** to keep cheerful under difficult circumstances. Sometimes shortened to **chin up!** [4] **take it on the chin.** *Informal* to face squarely up to a defeat, adversity, etc. ◆ VERB **chins, chinning, chinned.** [5] *Gymnastics* to raise one's chin to (a horizontal bar, etc.) when hanging by the arms. [6] *(tr) Informal* to punch or hit (someone) on the chin.
▷HISTORY Old English *cinn;* related to Old Norse *kinn,* Old High German *kinni,* Latin *gena* cheek, Old Irish *gin* mouth, Sanskrit *hanu*

Chin. ABBREVIATION FOR: [1] China. [2] Chinese.

china[1] (ˈtʃaɪnə) NOUN [1] ceramic ware of a type originally from China. [2] any porcelain or similar ware. [3] cups, saucers, etc., collectively. [4] *(modifier)* made of china.
▷HISTORY C16 *chiny,* from Persian *chīnī*

china[2] (ˈtʃaɪnə) NOUN *Brit and South African informal* a friend or companion.
▷HISTORY C19: originally Cockney rhyming slang: *china plate, mate*

China (ˈtʃaɪnə) NOUN [1] **People's Republic of.** Also called: **Communist China, Red China.** a republic in E Asia: the third largest and the most populous country in the world; the oldest continuing civilization (beginning over 2000 years B.C.); republic established in 1911 after the overthrow of the Manchu dynasty by Sun Yat-sen; People's Republic formed in 1949; the 1980s and 1990s saw economic liberalization but a rejection of political reform; contains vast deserts, steppes, great mountain ranges (Himalayas, Kunlun, Tian Shan, and Nan Shan), a central rugged plateau, and intensively cultivated E plains. Language: Chinese in various dialects, the chief of which is Mandarin. Religion: nonreligious majority; Buddhist and Taoist minorities. Currency: yuan. Capital: Beijing. Pop.: 1 274 915 000 (2001 est.). Area: 9 560 990 sq. km (3 691 502 sq. miles). [2] **Republic of.** Also called: **Nationalist China, Taiwan.** a republic (recognized as independent by less than 40 nations) in E Asia occupying the island of Taiwan, 13 nearby islands, and 64 islands of the Penghu (Pescadores) group: established in 1949 by the Nationalist government of China under Chiang Kai-shek after its expulsion by the Communists from the mainland; under US protection 1954–79; lost its seat at the U.N. to the People's Republic of China in 1971; state of war with the People's Republic of China formally ended in 1991. Language: Mandarin Chinese. Religion: nonreligious majority; Buddhist and Taoist minorities. Currency: New Taiwan dollar. Capital: Taipei. Pop.: 22 340 000 (2001). Area: 35 981 sq. km (13 892 sq. miles). Former name: **Formosa.** Related adjective: **Sinitic.**

China aster NOUN a Chinese plant, *Callistephus chinensis,* widely cultivated for its aster-like flowers: family *Asteraceae* (composites).

china bark NOUN another name for **cinchona** (sense 2).

chinaberry (ˈtʃaɪnəbərɪ) NOUN, *plural* **-ries.** [1] Also called: **China tree, azedarach.** a spreading Asian meliaceous tree, *Melia azedarach,* widely grown in the US for its ornamental white or purple flowers and beadlike yellow fruits. [2] another name for **soapberry.** [3] the fruit of any of these trees.

china clay *or* **stone** NOUN another name for **kaolin.**

Chinagraph (ˈtʃaɪnəˌgrɑːf, -ˌgræf) NOUN *Trademark* **a** a coloured pencil used for writing on china, glass, etc. **b** *(as modifier): a Chinagraph pencil.*

China ink NOUN another name for **Indian ink.**

Chinaman (ˈtʃaɪnəmən) NOUN, *plural* **-men.** [1] *Archaic or derogatory* a native or inhabitant of China. [2] *(often not capital) Cricket* a ball bowled by a left-handed bowler to a right-handed batsman that spins from off to leg.

Chinan *or* **Chi-nan** (ˈtʃiːˈnæn) NOUN a variant transliteration of the Chinese name for **Jinan.**

China rose NOUN [1] a rosaceous shrub, *Rosa chinensis* (or *R. indica*), with red, pink, or white fragrant flowers: the ancestor of many cultivated roses. [2] a related dwarf plant, *Rosa semperflorens,* having crimson flowers. [3] another name for **hibiscus.**

China Sea NOUN part of the Pacific Ocean off the coast of China: divided by Taiwan into the East China Sea in the north and the South China Sea in the south.

china stone NOUN [1] a type of kaolinized granitic rock containing unaltered plagioclase. [2] any of certain limestones having a very fine grain and smooth texture.

Chinatown (ˈtʃaɪnəˌtaʊn) NOUN a quarter of any city or town outside China with a predominantly Chinese population.

China tree NOUN another name for **chinaberry** (sense 1).

chinaware (ˈtʃaɪnəˌwɛə) NOUN [1] articles made of china, esp those made for domestic use. [2] *(modifier)* made of china.

chin ball NOUN *NZ* a device fastened under the chin of a bull to mark cows he has mounted.

chincapin (ˈtʃɪŋkəpɪn) NOUN a variant spelling of **chinquapin.**

chinch (tʃɪntʃ) NOUN *Southern US* another name for a **bedbug.**
▷HISTORY C17: from Spanish *chinche,* from Latin *cīmex* bug

chinch bug NOUN [1] a black-and-white tropical American heteropterous insect, *Blissus leucopterus,* that is very destructive to grasses and cereals in the US: family *Lygaeidae.* [2] a related and similar European insect, *Ischnodemus sabuleti.*

chincherinchee (ˌtʃɪntʃərɪnˈtʃiː, -ˈrɪntʃɪ) NOUN a bulbous South African liliaceous plant, *Ornithogalum thyrsoides,* having long spikes of white or yellow long-lasting flowers.
▷HISTORY of unknown origin

chinchilla (tʃɪnˈtʃɪlə) NOUN [1] a small gregarious hystricomorph rodent, *Chinchilla laniger,* inhabiting mountainous regions of South America: family *Chinchillidae.* It has a stocky body and is bred in captivity for its soft silvery grey fur. [2] the highly valued fur of this animal. [3] **mountain chinchilla.** Also called: **mountain viscacha.** any of several long-tailed rodents of the genus *Lagidium,* having coarse poor quality fur. [4] a breed of rabbit with soft silver-grey fur. [5] a thick napped woollen cloth used for coats.
▷HISTORY C17: from Spanish, perhaps from Aymara

chin-chin SENTENCE SUBSTITUTE *Informal* a greeting, farewell, or toast.
▷HISTORY C18: from Chinese (Peking) *ch'ing-ch'ing* please-please

Chin-Chou *or* **Chin-chow** (ˈtʃɪnˈtʃaʊ) NOUN a variant transliteration of the Chinese name for **Jinzhou.**

chin cough NOUN another name for **whooping cough.**
▷HISTORY C16: changed (through influence from CHINE[1] and CHIN) from earlier *chink-cough,* from CHINK[2] + COUGH

Chindit (ˈtʃɪndɪt) NOUN a member of the Allied forces commanded by Orde Wingate fighting behind the Japanese lines in Burma (1943–45).
▷HISTORY C20: from Burmese *chinthé* a fabulous lion a symbol of which was their badge; adoption of title perhaps influenced by CHINDWIN

Chindwin (ˈtʃɪnˈdwɪn) NOUN a river in N Myanmar, rising in the Kumôn Range and flowing northwest then south to the Irrawaddy, of which it is the main tributary. Length: about 966 km (600 miles).

chine[1] (tʃaɪn) NOUN [1] the backbone. [2] the backbone of an animal with adjoining meat, cut for cooking. [3] a ridge or crest of land. [4] (in some boats) a corner-like intersection where the bottom meets the side. ◆ VERB [5] *(tr)* to cut (meat) along or across the backbone.
▷HISTORY C14: from Old French *eschine,* of Germanic origin; compare Old High German *scina* needle, shinbone; see SHIN[1]

chine[2] (tʃaɪn) NOUN another word for **chime**[2].

chine[3] (tʃaɪn) NOUN *Southern English dialect* a deep fissure in the wall of a cliff.
▷HISTORY Old English *cīnan* to crack

chiné (ˈʃiːneɪ) ADJECTIVE *Textiles* having a mottled pattern.
▷HISTORY C19: from French *chiner* to make in the Chinese fashion, from *Chine* China

Chinee (tʃaɪˈniː) NOUN *Informal* a Chinaman.

Chinese (tʃaɪˈniːz) ADJECTIVE [1] of, relating to, or characteristic of China, its people, or their languages. ◆ NOUN [2] *(plural* **-nese***)* a native or inhabitant of China or a descendant of one. [3] any of the languages of China belonging to the Sino-Tibetan family, sometimes regarded as dialects of one language. They share a single writing system that is not phonetic but ideographic. A phonetic system using the Roman alphabet was officially adopted by the Chinese government in 1966. See also **Mandarin Chinese, Pekingese, Cantonese.** Related prefix: **Sino-.**

Chinese block NOUN a percussion instrument consisting of a hollow wooden block played with a drumstick.

Chinese burn NOUN a minor torture inflicted by

twisting the skin of a person's wrist or arm in two different directions simultaneously.

Chinese cabbage NOUN 1 Also called: **pe-tsai cabbage.** a Chinese plant, *Brassica pekinensis,* that is related to the cabbage and has crisp edible leaves growing in a loose cylindrical head. 2 another name for **bok choy.**

Chinese chequers NOUN (*functioning as singular*) a board game played with marbles or pegs.

Chinese Chippendale NOUN **a** a branch of Chippendale style in which Chinese styles and motifs are used. **b** (*as modifier*): *a Chinese Chippendale cabinet.*

Chinese copy NOUN an exact copy of an original.

Chinese crested NOUN a small dog of a Chinese breed having long slender legs and a hairless body with hair only on the feet, head, and tail.

Chinese eddo NOUN another name for **taro.**

Chinese Empire NOUN China as ruled by the emperors until the establishment of the republic in 1911–12.

Chinese gooseberry NOUN another name for **kiwi fruit.**

Chinese ink NOUN another name for **Indian ink.**

Chinese lantern NOUN 1 a collapsible lantern made of thin coloured paper. 2 an Asian solanaceous plant, *Physalis franchetii,* cultivated for its attractive orange-red inflated calyx. See also **winter cherry.**

Chinese leaf PLURAL NOUN the edible leaves of a Chinese cabbage.

Chinese puzzle NOUN 1 an intricate puzzle, esp one consisting of boxes within boxes. 2 a complicated problem.

Chinese red NOUN **a** a bright red colour. **b** (*as adjective*): *a Chinese-red bag.*

Chinese restaurant syndrome NOUN a group of symptoms such as dizziness, headache, and flushing thought to be caused in some people by consuming large amounts of monosodium glutamate, esp as used in Chinese food.

Chinese Revolution NOUN 1 the overthrow of the last Manchu emperor and the establishment of a republic in China (1911–12). 2 the transformation of China (esp in the 1940s and 1950s) under the Chinese Communist Party.

Chinese sacred lily NOUN a Chinese amaryllidaceous plant, *Narcissus tazetta orientalis,* widely grown as a house plant for its fragrant yellow and white flowers. See also **polyanthus** (sense 2).

Chinese Turkestan NOUN the E part of the central Asian region of Turkestan: corresponds generally to the present-day Xinjiang Uygur Autonomous Region of China.

Chinese wall NOUN 1 a notional barrier between the parts of a business, esp between the market makers and brokers of a stock-exchange business, across which no information should pass to the detriment of clients. 2 an insurmountable obstacle.

Chinese water deer NOUN a small Chinese or Korean deer, *Hydropotes inermis,* having tusks and no antlers: introduced into England and France.

Chinese water torture NOUN a form of torture in which water is made to drip onto a victim's forehead to drive him insane.

Chinese wax *or* **treewax** ('triːˌwæks) NOUN a yellowish wax secreted by an oriental scale insect, *Ceroplastes ceriferus,* and used commercially.

Chinese whispers NOUN (*functioning as singular*) 1 a game in which a message is passed on, in a whisper, by each of a number of people, so that the final version of the message is often radically changed from the original. 2 any situation where information is passed on in turn by a number of people, often becoming distorted in the process.

Chinese white NOUN white zinc oxide, formerly used in paints. Also called: **zinc white.**

Chinese windlass NOUN another name for **differential windlass.**

Chinese wood oil NOUN another name for **tung oil.**

Ching *or* **Ch'ing** (tʃɪŋ) ADJECTIVE of, relating to, or designating the Manchu dynasty (1644–1912) of China.

Chinghai *or* **Ch'ing-hai** ('tʃɪŋ'haɪ) NOUN a variant transliteration of the Chinese name for **Qinghai.**

Chingtao *or* **Ch'ing-tao** ('tʃɪŋ'taʊ) NOUN a variant transliteration of the Chinese name for **Qingdao.**

Ch'ing-yüan ('tʃɪŋ'juːɑːn) NOUN a former name of **Baoding.**

Chin Hills (tʃɪn) PLURAL NOUN a mountainous region of W Myanmar; part of the Arakan Yoma system. Highest peak: Mount Victoria, 3053 m (10 075 ft.).

Chin-Hsien ('tʃɪn'ʃjɛn) NOUN the former name (1913–47) of **Jinzhou.**

chink[1] (tʃɪŋk) NOUN 1 a small narrow opening, such as a fissure or crack. 2 **chink in one's armour.** a small but fatal weakness. ◆ VERB 3 (*tr*) *Chiefly US and Canadian* to fill up or make cracks in.
▷HISTORY C16: perhaps variant of earlier *chine,* from Old English *cine* crack; related to Middle Dutch *kene,* Danish *kin*
► '**chinky** ADJECTIVE

chink[2] (tʃɪŋk) VERB 1 to make or cause to make a light ringing sound, as by the striking of glasses or coins. ◆ NOUN 2 such a sound.
▷HISTORY C16: of imitative origin

Chink (tʃɪŋk) *or* **Chinky** ('tʃɪŋkɪ) NOUN, *plural* **Chinks** *or* **Chinkies,** ADJECTIVE a derogatory term for **Chinese.**
▷HISTORY C20: probably from *Chinese,* influenced by CHINK[1] (referring to the characteristic shape of the Chinese eye)

chinkapin ('tʃɪŋkəpɪn) NOUN a variant spelling of **chinquapin.**

Chinkiang ('tʃɪn'kjæŋ, -kaɪ'æŋ) NOUN a variant transliteration of the Chinese name for **Jinjiang.**

chinless ('tʃɪnlɪs) ADJECTIVE 1 having a receding chin. 2 weak or ineffectual.

chinless wonder NOUN *Brit informal* a person, esp an upper-class one, lacking strength of character.

chino ('tʃiːnəʊ) NOUN, *plural* **-nos.** *US* a durable cotton twill cloth.
▷HISTORY C20: from American Spanish, of obscure origin

Chino- COMBINING FORM of or relating to China. See also **Sino-.**

chinoiserie (ʃiːnˌwɑːzə'riː, -'wɑːzərɪ) NOUN 1 a style of decorative or fine art based on imitations of Chinese motifs. 2 an object or objects in this style.
▷HISTORY French, from *chinois* CHINESE; see -ERY

chinook (tʃɪ'nuːk, -'nʊk) NOUN 1 Also called: **snow eater.** a warm dry southwesterly wind blowing down the eastern slopes of the Rocky Mountains. 2 Also called: **wet chinook.** a warm moist wind blowing onto the Washington and Oregon coasts from the sea.
▷HISTORY C19: from Salish *c'inuk*

Chinook (tʃɪ'nuːk, -'nʊk) NOUN 1 (*plural* **-nook** *or* **-nooks**) a North American Indian people of the Pacific coast near the Columbia River. 2 the language of this people, probably forming a separate branch of the Penutian phylum.

Chinook Jargon NOUN a pidgin language containing elements of North American Indian languages, English, and French: formerly used among fur traders and Indians on the NW coast of North America.

Chinook salmon NOUN a Pacific salmon, *Oncorhynchus tschawytscha,* valued as a food fish. Also called: **quinnat salmon, king salmon.**

chinos ('tʃiːnəʊz) PLURAL NOUN trousers made of chino.

chinquapin, chincapin, *or* **chinkapin** ('tʃɪŋkəpɪn) NOUN 1 a dwarf chestnut tree, *Castanea pumila,* of the eastern US, yielding edible nuts. 2 Also called: **giant chinquapin.** a large evergreen fagaceous tree, *Castanopsis chrysophylla,* of W North America. 3 the nut of either of these trees. ◆ Compare **water chinquapin.**
▷HISTORY C17: of Algonquian origin; compare Algonquian *chechinkamin* chestnut

chintz (tʃɪnts) NOUN 1 a printed, patterned cotton fabric, with glazed finish. 2 a painted or stained Indian calico.
▷HISTORY C17: from Hindi *chīnt,* from Sanskrit *citra* gaily-coloured

chintzy ('tʃɪntsɪ) ADJECTIVE **chintzier, chintziest.** 1 of, resembling, or covered with chintz. 2 *Brit informal* typical of the decor associated with the use of chintz soft furnishings, as in a country cottage.

chinwag ('tʃɪnˌwæg) NOUN *Brit informal* a chat or gossipy conversation.

chionodoxa (kaɪˌɒnə'dɒksə) NOUN any plant of the liliaceous genus *Chionodoxa,* of S Europe and W Asia. See **glory-of-the-snow.**
▷HISTORY C19: New Latin, from Greek *khiōn* snow + *doxa* glory

Chios ('kaɪɒs, -əʊs, 'kiː-) NOUN 1 an island in the Aegean Sea, off the coast of Turkey: belongs to Greece. Capital: Chios. Pop.: 52 184 (1991). Area: 904 sq. km (353 sq. miles). 2 a port on the island of Chios: in ancient times, one of the 12 Ionian city-states. Pop.: 54 000 (1995 est.). Modern Greek name: **Khíos.**

chip (tʃɪp) NOUN 1 a small piece removed by chopping, cutting, or breaking. 2 a mark left after a small piece has been chopped, cut, or broken off something. 3 (in some games) a counter used to represent money. 4 a thin strip of potato fried in deep fat. 5 the US, Canadian, and Austral name for **crisp** (sense 10). 6 a small piece or thin slice of food. 7 *Sport* a shot, kick, etc., lofted into the air, esp over an obstacle or an opposing player's head, and travelling only a short distance. 8 *Electronics* a tiny wafer of semiconductor material, such as silicon, processed to form a type of integrated circuit or component such as a transistor. 9 a thin strip of wood or straw used for making woven hats, baskets, etc. 10 *NZ* a container for soft fruit, made of thin sheets of wood; punnet. 11 **cheap as chips.** *Brit informal* inexpensive; good value. 12 **chip off the old block.** *Informal* a person who resembles one of his or her parents in behaviour. 13 **have a chip on one's shoulder.** *Informal* to be aggressively sensitive about a particular thing or bear a grudge. 14 **have had one's chips.** *Brit informal* to be defeated, condemned to die, killed, etc. 15 **when the chips are down.** *Informal* at a time of crisis or testing. ◆ VERB **chips, chipping, chipped.** 16 to break small pieces from or become broken off in small pieces: *will the paint chip?* 17 (*tr*) to break or cut into small pieces: *to chip ice.* 18 (*tr*) to shape by chipping. 19 *Sport* to strike or kick (a ball) in a high arc.
▷HISTORY Old English *cipp* (noun), *cippian* (verb), of obscure origin
► '**chipper** NOUN

chip-based ('tʃɪpˌbeɪst) ADJECTIVE (of electronic equipment or components) using or incorporating microchips.

chip basket NOUN 1 a wire basket for holding potato chips, etc., while frying in deep fat. 2 a basket made of thin strips of wood, used esp for packing fruit.

chipboard ('tʃɪpˌbɔːd) NOUN a thin rigid sheet made of compressed wood chips bound with a synthetic resin.

chip in VERB (*adverb*) *Informal* 1 to contribute (money, time, etc.) to a cause or fund. 2 (*intr*) to interpose a remark or interrupt with a remark.

chip log NOUN *Nautical* a log for determining a vessel's speed, consisting of a wooden chip tossed overboard at the end of a line that is marked off in lengths of 47 feet 3 inches; the speed is calculated by counting the number of such intervals that pass overboard in a 28-second interval.

chipmunk ('tʃɪpˌmʌŋk) NOUN any burrowing sciurine rodent of the genera *Tamias* of E North America and *Eutamias* of W North America and Asia, typically having black-striped yellowish fur and cheek pouches for storing food.
▷HISTORY C19: of Algonquian origin; compare Ojibwa *atchitamon* squirrel, literally: headfirst, referring to its method of descent from trees

chipolata (ˌtʃɪpə'lɑːtə) NOUN *Chiefly Brit* a small sausage in a narrow casing.
▷HISTORY via French from Italian *cipollata* an onion-flavoured dish, from *cipolla* onion

chip pan NOUN a deep pan for frying potato chips, etc.

Chippendale ('tʃɪpᵊnˌdeɪl) ADJECTIVE (of furniture)

designed by, made by, or in the style of Thomas Chippendale (?1718–79) English cabinet-maker and furniture designer, characterized by the use of Chinese and Gothic motifs, cabriole legs, and massive carving.

chipper[1] (ˈtʃɪpə) ADJECTIVE *Informal* 1 cheerful; lively. 2 smartly dressed.

chipper[2] (ˈtʃɪpər) NOUN *Irish and Scot informal* a fish-and-chip shop.

Chippewa (ˈtʃɪpɪˌwɑː) *or* **Chippeway** (ˈtʃɪpɪˌweɪ) NOUN, *plural* **-was, -wa** *or* **-ways, -way.** another name for **Ojibwa.**

chipping (ˈtʃɪpɪŋ) NOUN another name for **chip** (sense 1).

chipping sparrow NOUN a common North American sparrow, *Spizella passerina,* having brown-and-grey plumage and a white eye stripe.

chippy[1] (ˈtʃɪpɪ) NOUN, *plural* **-pies.** 1 *Brit informal* a fish-and-chip shop. 2 *Brit and NZ* a slang word for **carpenter.** 3 *NZ* a potato crisp.
▷HISTORY C19: from CHIP (noun)

chippy[2] (ˈtʃɪpɪ) ADJECTIVE **-pier, -piest.** *Informal* resentful or oversensitive about being perceived as inferior: *a chippy miner's son.*
▷HISTORY C20: from CHIP (sense 12)
▸ˈ**chippiness** NOUN

chippy[3] *or* **chippie** (ˈtʃɪpɪ) NOUN, *plural* **-pies.** an informal name for **chipmunk** or **chipping sparrow.**

chippy[4] *or* **chippie** (ˈtʃɪpɪ) NOUN, *plural* **-pies.** *Informal, chiefly US and Canadian* a promiscuous woman.
▷HISTORY C19: perhaps from CHIP (noun)

chippy[5] (ˈtʃɪpɪ) ADJECTIVE **-pier, -piest.** belligerent or touchy.
▷HISTORY C19: from CHIP (noun), sense probably developing from: as dry as a chip of wood, hence irritable, touchy

chip shot NOUN *Golf* a short approach shot to the green, esp one that is lofted.

chip wagon NOUN *Canadian* a small van in which chips are cooked and sold.

chirality (kaɪˈrælɪtɪ) NOUN the configuration or handedness (left or right) of an asymmetric, optically active chemical compound. Also called: **dissymmetry.**
▷HISTORY C19: from Greek *kheir* hand + -AL[1] + -ITY
▸ˈ**chiral** ADJECTIVE

chirm (tʃɜːm) NOUN 1 the chirping of birds. ◆ VERB 2 (*intr*) (esp of a bird) to chirp.
▷HISTORY Old English *cierm* noise; related to Old Saxon *karm*

chiro (ˈkaɪrəʊ) NOUN, *plural* **chiros.** an informal name for **chiropractor.**

chiro- *or* **cheiro-** COMBINING FORM indicating the hand; of or by means of the hand: *chiromancy.*
▷HISTORY via Latin from Greek *kheir* hand

chirography (kaɪˈrɒɡrəfɪ) NOUN another name for **calligraphy.**
▸**chiˈrographer** NOUN ▸**chirographic** (ˌkaɪrəˈɡræfɪk) *or* **ˌchiroˈgraphical** ADJECTIVE

chiromancy (ˈkaɪrəˌmænsɪ) NOUN another word for **palmistry.**
▸ˈ**chiroˌmancer** NOUN

Chiron *or* **Cheiron** (ˈkaɪrɒn, -rən) NOUN 1 *Greek myth* a wise and kind centaur who taught many great heroes in their youth, including Achilles, Actaeon, and Jason. 2 a minor planet, discovered by Charles Kowal in 1977, revolving round the sun between the orbits of Saturn and Uranus.

chironomid (kaɪˈrɒnəmɪd) NOUN 1 a member of the *Chironomidae,* a family of nonbiting midges. ◆ ADJECTIVE 2 of or relating to this family.
▷HISTORY C19: from New Latin *chironomus,* from Greek *kheironomos* a gesturer, from *kheir* hand + *nomos* manager + -ID[2]

chiropody (kɪˈrɒpədɪ) NOUN the treatment of the feet, esp the treatment of corns, verrucas, etc.
▸**chiˈropodist** NOUN ▸**chiropodial** (ˌkaɪrəʊˈpəʊdɪəl) ADJECTIVE

chiropractic (ˌkaɪrəˈpræktɪk) NOUN a system of treating bodily disorders by manipulation of the spine and other parts, based on the belief that the cause is the abnormal functioning of a nerve.
▷HISTORY C20: from CHIRO- + *-practic,* from Greek *praktikos* effective, PRACTICAL
▸ˈ**chiroˌpractor** NOUN

chiropteran (kaɪˈrɒptərən) ADJECTIVE 1 of, relating to, or belonging to the *Chiroptera,* an order of placental mammals comprising the bats. ◆ NOUN 2 Also called: **chiropter** (kaɪˈrɒptə). a bat.

chirp (tʃɜːp) VERB (*intr*) 1 (esp of some birds and insects) to make a short high-pitched sound. 2 to speak in a lively fashion. ◆ NOUN 3 a chirping sound, esp that made by a bird.
▷HISTORY C15 (as *chirpinge,* gerund): of imitative origin
▸ˈ**chirper** NOUN

CHIRP (tʃɜːp) NOUN ACRONYM FOR Confidential Human Incidents Reporting Programme: a system, run by the RAF Institute of Medicine, by which commercial pilots can comment on safety trends without the knowledge of their employers.

chirpy (ˈtʃɜːpɪ) ADJECTIVE **chirpier, chirpiest.** *Informal* cheerful; lively.
▸ˈ**chirpily** ADVERB ▸ˈ**chirpiness** NOUN

chirr, chirre, *or* **churr** (tʃɜː) VERB 1 (*intr*) (esp of certain insects, such as crickets) to make a shrill trilled sound. ◆ NOUN 2 the sound of chirring.
▷HISTORY C17: of imitative origin

chirrup (ˈtʃɪrəp) VERB (*intr*) 1 (esp of some birds) to chirp repeatedly. 2 to make clucking sounds with the lips. ◆ NOUN 3 such a sound.
▷HISTORY C16: variant of CHIRP
▸ˈ**chirruper** NOUN ▸ˈ**chirrupy** ADJECTIVE

chiru (ˈtʃɪruː) NOUN a Tibetan antelope, *Pantholops hodgsoni,* having a dense woolly pinkish-brown fleece prized as the source of shahtoosh wool: now close to extinction due to illegal slaughter for its fleece.
▷HISTORY C19: probably from Tibetan

chirurgeon (kaɪˈrɜːdʒən) NOUN an archaic word for **surgeon.**
▷HISTORY C13: from Old French *cirurgeon*
▸**chiˈrurgery** NOUN

chisel (ˈtʃɪzᵊl) NOUN 1 **a** a hand tool for working wood, consisting of a flat steel blade with a cutting edge attached to a handle of wood, plastic, etc. It is either struck with a mallet or used by hand. **b** a similar tool without a handle for working stone or metal. ◆ VERB **-els, -elling, -elled** *or US* **-els, -eling, -eled.** 2 to carve (wood, stone, metal, etc.) or form (an engraving, statue, etc.) with or as with a chisel. 3 *Slang* to cheat or obtain by cheating.
▷HISTORY C14: via Old French, from Vulgar Latin *cīsellus* (unattested), from Latin *caesus* cut, from *caedere* to cut

chiselled *or US* **chiseled** (ˈtʃɪzᵊld) ADJECTIVE 1 carved or formed with or as if with a chisel. 2 clear-cut: *finely chiselled features.*

chiseller (ˈtʃɪzᵊlə) NOUN 1 a person who uses a chisel. 2 *Informal* a cheat. 3 *Dublin slang* a child.

Chishima (ˌtʃiːʃiːˈmɑ) NOUN the Japanese name for the **Kuril Islands.**

Chisimaio (ˌkiːzɪˈmɑːjəʊ) NOUN a port in S Somalia, on the Indian Ocean. Pop.: 200 000 (latest est.). Also called: **Kismayu.**

Chişinău (kiʃiˈnəu) NOUN the Romanian name for **Kishinev.**

chi-square distribution (ˈkaɪˌskwɛə) NOUN *Statistics* a continuous single-parameter distribution derived as a special case of the gamma distribution and used esp to measure goodness of fit and to test hypotheses and obtain confidence intervals for the variance of a normally distributed variable.

chi-square test NOUN *Statistics* a test derived from the chi-square distribution to compare the goodness of fit of theoretical and observed frequency distributions or to compare nominal data derived from unmatched groups of subjects.

chit[1] (tʃɪt) NOUN 1 a voucher for a sum of money owed, esp for food or drink. 2 Also called: **chitty** (ˈtʃɪtɪ). *Chiefly Brit* **a** a note or memorandum. **b** a requisition or receipt.
▷HISTORY C18: from earlier *chitty,* from Hindi *cittha* note, from Sanskrit *citra* brightly-coloured

chit[2] (tʃɪt) NOUN *Facetious or derogatory* a pert, impudent, or self-confident girl or child: *a young chit of a thing.*
▷HISTORY C14 (in the sense: young of an animal, kitten): of obscure origin

Chita (*Russian* tʃiˈta) NOUN an industrial city in SE Russia, on the Trans-Siberian railway. Pop.: 314 300 (1995 est.).

chital (ˈtʃiːtᵊl) NOUN another name for **axis**[2] (the deer).
▷HISTORY from Hindi

chitarrone (ˌkɪtɑːˈrəʊnɪ, ˌtʃɪt-) NOUN, *plural* **-ni** (-nɪ). a large lute with a double neck in common use during the baroque period, esp in Italy.
▷HISTORY Italian, from *chitarra,* from Greek *kithara* lyre

chitchat (ˈtʃɪtˌtʃæt) NOUN 1 talk of a gossipy nature. ◆ VERB **-chats, -chatting, -chatted.** 2 (*intr*) to gossip.

chitin (ˈkaɪtɪn) NOUN a polysaccharide that is the principal component of the exoskeletons of arthropods and of the bodies of fungi.
▷HISTORY C19: from French *chitine,* from Greek *khitōn* CHITON + -IN
▸ˈ**chitinous** ADJECTIVE ▸ˈ**chitinˌoid** ADJECTIVE

chiton (ˈkaɪtᵊn, -tɒn) NOUN 1 (in ancient Greece and Rome) a loose woollen tunic worn knee length by men and full length by women. 2 Also called: **coat-of-mail shell.** any small primitive marine mollusc of the genus *Chiton* and related genera, having an elongated body covered with eight overlapping shell plates: class *Amphineura.*
▷HISTORY C19: from Greek *khitōn* coat of mail, of Semitic origin; related to Hebrew *kethōnet*

Chittagong (ˈtʃɪtəˌɡɒŋ) NOUN a port in E Bangladesh, on the Bay of Bengal: industrial centre. Pop.: 1 599 000 (1991).

chitter (ˈtʃɪtə) VERB (*intr*) 1 *Chiefly US* to twitter or chirp. 2 a dialect word for **shiver**[1] or (of the teeth) **chatter.**
▷HISTORY C14: of imitative origin

chitterlings (ˈtʃɪtəlɪŋz), **chitlins** (ˈtʃɪtlɪnz), *or* **chitlings** (ˈtʃɪtlɪŋz) PLURAL NOUN (*sometimes singular*) the intestines of a pig or other animal prepared as a dish.
▷HISTORY C13: of uncertain origin; perhaps related to Middle High German *kutel*

chiv (tʃɪv, ʃɪv) *or* **shiv** (ʃɪv) *Slang* ◆ NOUN 1 a knife. ◆ VERB **chivs, chivving, chivved** *or* **shivs, shivving, shivved.** 2 to stab (someone).
▷HISTORY C17: perhaps from Romany *chiv* blade

chivalrous (ˈʃɪvəlrəs) ADJECTIVE 1 gallant; courteous. 2 involving chivalry.
▷HISTORY C14: from Old French *chevalerous,* from CHEVALIER
▸ˈ**chivalrously** ADVERB ▸ˈ**chivalrousness** NOUN

chivalry (ˈʃɪvəlrɪ) NOUN, *plural* **-ries.** 1 the combination of qualities expected of an ideal knight, esp courage, honour, justice, and a readiness to help the weak. 2 courteous behaviour, esp towards women. 3 the medieval system and principles of knighthood. 4 knights, noblemen, etc., collectively.
▷HISTORY C13: from Old French *chevalerie,* from CHEVALIER
▸ˈ**chivalric** ADJECTIVE

chivaree (ˌʃɪvəˈriː, ˈʃɪvəˌriː) NOUN a US spelling of **charivari.**

chive (tʃaɪv) NOUN a small Eurasian purple-flowered alliaceous plant, *Allium schoenoprasum,* whose long slender hollow leaves are used in cooking to flavour soups, stews, etc. Also called: **chives.**
▷HISTORY C14: from Old French *cive,* ultimately from Latin *caepa* onion

chivy, chivvy (ˈtʃɪvɪ), *or* **chevy** *Brit* ◆ VERB **chivies, chivying, chivied, chivvies, chivvying, chivvied** *or* **chevies, chevying, chevied.** 1 (*tr*) to harass or nag. 2 (*tr*) to hunt. 3 (*intr*) to run about. ◆ NOUN, *plural* **chivies, chivvies,** *or* **chevies.** 4 a hunt. 5 *Obsolete* a hunting cry.
▷HISTORY C19: variant of *chevy,* probably from *Chevy Chase,* title of a Scottish border ballad

Chkalov (*Russian* ˈtʃkaləf) NOUN the former name (1938–57) of **Orenburg.**

Chladni figure (ˈklɑːdnɪ) NOUN *Physics* a pattern formed by fine powder placed on a vibrating surface, used to display the positions of nodes and antinodes.
▷HISTORY C19: named after Ernst *Chladni* (1756–1827), German physicist

chlamydate (ˈklæmɪˌdeɪt) ADJECTIVE (of some molluscs) possessing a mantle.
▷HISTORY C19: from Latin *chlamydātus* wearing a mantle, from Greek *khlamus* mantle

chlamydeous (klə'mɪdɪəs) ADJECTIVE (of plants) relating to or possessing sepals and petals.

chlamydia (klə'mɪdɪə) NOUN any Gram-negative bacteria of the genus *Chlamydia*, which are obligate intracellular parasites and are responsible for such diseases as trachoma, psittacosis, and some sexually transmitted diseases.
▷HISTORY C20: New Latin, from Greek *khlamus* mantle + -IA

chlamydospore (klə'mɪdəˌspɔː) NOUN a thick-walled asexual spore of many fungi: capable of surviving adverse conditions.

chloanthite (kləʊ'ænθaɪt) NOUN a form of nickel arsenide having commercial importance as a nickel ore.
▷HISTORY C19: from Greek *khloanthēs* budding, sprouting + -ITE[1]

chloasma (kləʊ'æzmə) NOUN, *plural* **chloasmata** (kləʊ'æzmətə). *Med* the appearance on a person's skin, esp of the face, of patches of darker colour: associated with hormonal changes caused by liver disease or the use of oral contraceptives.
▷HISTORY C19: from New Latin, from Greek *khloasma* greenness

Chloe ('kləʊɪ) NOUN See **Daphnis and Chloe.**

chlor- COMBINING FORM a variant of **chloro-** before a vowel.

chloracne (klɔː'ræknɪ) NOUN a disfiguring skin disease that results from contact with or ingestion or inhalation of certain chlorinated aromatic hydrocarbons.
▷HISTORY C20: from CHLORO- + ACNE

chloral ('klɔːrəl) NOUN [1] a colourless oily liquid with a pungent odour, made from chlorine and acetaldehyde and used in preparing chloral hydrate and DDT; trichloroacetaldehyde. [2] short for **chloral hydrate.**

chloral hydrate NOUN a colourless crystalline soluble solid produced by the reaction of chloral with water and used as a sedative and hypnotic; 2,2,2-trichloro-1,1-ethanediol. Formula: $CCl_3CH(OH)_2$.

chlorambucil (klɔː'ræmbjʊsɪl) NOUN an alkylating drug derived from nitrogen mustard, administered orally in the treatment of leukaemia and other malignant diseases. Formula: $C_{14}H_{19}Cl_2NO_2$.

chloramine ('klɔːrəˌmiːn) NOUN [1] an unstable colourless liquid with a pungent odour, made by the reaction of sodium hypochlorite and ammonia. Formula: NH_2Cl. [2] any compound produced by replacing hydrogen atoms in an azo or amine group with chlorine atoms.

chloramphenicol (ˌklɔːræm'fɛnɪˌkɒl) NOUN a broad-spectrum antibiotic used esp in treating typhoid fever and rickettsial infections: obtained from the bacterium *Streptomyces venezuelae* or synthesized. Formula: $C_{11}H_{12}N_2O_5Cl_2$.
▷HISTORY C20: from CHLORO- + AM(IDO)- + PHE(NO)- + NI(TRO)- + (GLY)COL

chlorate ('klɔːˌreɪt, -rɪt) NOUN any salt of chloric acid, containing the monovalent ion ClO_3^-.

chlordane ('klɔːdeɪn) *or* **chlordan** ('klɔːdæn) NOUN a white insoluble toxic solid existing in several isomeric forms and usually used, as an insecticide, in the form of a brown impure liquid. Formula: $C_{10}H_6Cl_8$.
▷HISTORY C20: from CHLORO- + (IN)D(ENE) + -ANE

chlordiazepoxide (ˌklɔːdaɪˌeɪzɪ'pɒksaɪd) NOUN a chemical compound used as a tranquillizer and muscle relaxant and in the treatment of delirium tremens. Formula: $C_{16}H_{14}ClN_3O$.

chlorella (klɔː'rɛlə, klə-) NOUN any microscopic unicellular green alga of the genus *Chlorella:* some species are used in the preparation of human food.
▷HISTORY C19: from New Latin, from CHLORO- + Latin *-ella*, diminutive suffix

chlorenchyma (klə'rɛŋkɪmə) NOUN plant tissue consisting of parenchyma cells that contain chlorophyll.
▷HISTORY C19: from CHLOR(OPHYLL) + -ENCHYMA

chlorhexidine (klɔː'hɛksɪdiːn) NOUN an antiseptic compound used in skin cleansers, mouthwashes, etc.
▷HISTORY C20: from CHLOR(O)- + HEX(ANE) + -I(DE) + (AM)INE

chloric ('klɔːrɪk) ADJECTIVE of or containing chlorine in the pentavalent state.

chloric acid NOUN a strong acid with a pungent smell, known only in solution and in the form of chlorate salts. Formula: $HClO_3$.

chloride ('klɔːraɪd) NOUN [1] any salt of hydrochloric acid, containing the chloride ion Cl^-. [2] any compound containing a chlorine atom, such as methyl chloride (chloromethane), CH_3Cl.
▸**chloridic** (klə'rɪdɪk) ADJECTIVE

chloride of lime *or* **chlorinated lime** NOUN another name for **bleaching powder.**

chlorinate ('klɔːrɪˌneɪt) VERB (*tr*) [1] to combine or treat (a substance) with chlorine. [2] to disinfect (water) with chlorine.
▸ˌ**chlorin'ation** NOUN ▸'**chlorinˌator** NOUN

chlorine ('klɔːriːn) *or* **chlorin** ('klɔːrɪn) NOUN a toxic pungent greenish-yellow gas of the halogen group; the 15th most abundant element in the earth's crust, occurring only in the combined state, mainly in common salt: used in the manufacture of many organic chemicals, in water purification, and as a disinfectant and bleaching agent. Symbol: Cl; atomic no.: 17; atomic wt.: 35.4527; valency: 1, 3, 5, or 7; density: 3.214 kg/m^3; relative density: 1.56; melting pt.: –101.03°C; boiling pt.: –33.9°C.
▷HISTORY C19 (coined by Sir Humphrey Davy): from CHLORO- + -INE[2], referring to its colour

chlorite[1] ('klɔːraɪt) NOUN any of a group of green soft secondary minerals consisting of the hydrated silicates of aluminium, iron, and magnesium in monoclinic crystalline form: common in metamorphic rocks.
▷HISTORY C18: from Latin *chlōrītis* precious stone of a green colour, from Greek *khlōritis*, from *khlōros* greenish yellow
▸**chloritic** (klɔː'rɪtɪk) ADJECTIVE

chlorite[2] ('klɔːraɪt) NOUN any salt of chlorous acid, containing the monovalent ion ClO_2^-.

chloro- *or before a vowel* **chlor-** COMBINING FORM [1] indicating the colour green: *chlorophyll.* [2] chlorine: *chloroform.*

chloroacetic acid (ˌklɔːrəʊə'siːtɪk) *or* **chloracetic acid** (ˌklɔːrə'siːtɪk) NOUN [1] a colourless crystalline soluble strong acid prepared by chlorinating acetic acid and used as an intermediate in the manufacture of many chemicals; monochloracetic acid. Formula: $CH_2ClCOOH$. [2] either of two related compounds: **dichloracetic acid,** $CHCl_2COOH$, or **trichloracetic acid,** CCl_3COOH.

chloroargyrite (ˌklɔːrəʊɑːdʒɪˌraɪt) NOUN a greyish-yellow or colourless soft secondary mineral consisting of silver chloride in cubic crystalline form: a source of silver. Formula: AgCl. Also called: **cerargyrite, horn silver.**
▷HISTORY C19: from Greek *keras* horn + *arguros* silver + -ITE[1]

chlorobenzene (ˌklɔːrəʊ'bɛnziːn) NOUN a colourless volatile flammable insoluble liquid with an almond-like odour, made from chlorine and benzene and used as a solvent and in the preparation of many organic compounds, esp phenol and DDT. Formula: C_6H_5Cl.

chlorofluorocarbon (ˌklɔːrəˌflʊərəʊ'kɑːbᵊn) NOUN *Chem* any of various gaseous compounds of carbon, hydrogen, chlorine, and fluorine, used as refrigerants, aerosol propellants, solvents, and in foam: some cause a breakdown of ozone in the earth's atmosphere. Abbreviation: **CFC.**

chloroform ('klɔːrəˌfɔːm) NOUN a heavy volatile liquid with a sweet taste and odour, used as a solvent and cleansing agent and in refrigerants: formerly used as an inhalation anaesthetic. Formula: $CHCl_3$. Systematic name: **trichloromethane.**
▷HISTORY C19: from CHLORO- + FORM(YL) (in an obsolete sense that applied to a CH radical)

chlorohydrin (ˌklɔːrəʊ'haɪdrɪn) NOUN [1] any of a class of organic compounds containing a hydroxyl group and a chlorine atom. [2] a colourless unstable hygroscopic liquid that is used mainly as a solvent; 3-chloropropane-1,2-diol. Formula: $CH_2OHCHOHCH_2Cl$.
▷HISTORY C20: from CHLORO- + HYDRO- + -IN

Chloromycetin (ˌklɔːrəʊmaɪ'siːtɪn) NOUN *Trademark* a brand of **chloramphenicol.**

chlorophyll *or US* **chlorophyl** ('klɔːrəfɪl) NOUN the green pigment of plants and photosynthetic algae and bacteria that traps the energy of sunlight for photosynthesis and exists in several forms, the most abundant being **chlorophyll a** ($C_{55}H_{72}O_5N_4Mg$): used as a colouring agent in medicines or food (**E140**).
▸'**chloroˌphylloid** ADJECTIVE ▸ˌ**chloro'phyllous** ADJECTIVE

chlorophytum (ˌklɔːrə'faɪtəm) NOUN any plant of the genus *Chlorophytum*, esp *C. elatum variegatum*, grown as a pot plant for its long narrow leaves with a light central stripe, and characterized by the production of offsets at the end of long scapes: family *Liliaceae*. Also called: **spider plant.**
▷HISTORY New Latin, from Greek *chlōros* green + *phyton* plant

chloropicrin (ˌklɔːrəʊ'pɪkrɪn) *or* **chlorpicrin** (klɔː'pɪkrɪn) NOUN a colourless insoluble toxic lachrymatory liquid used as a pesticide and a tear gas; nitrotrichloromethane. Formula: CCl_3NO_2.
▷HISTORY C20: from CHLORO- + PICRO- + -IN

chloroplast ('klɔːrəʊˌplæst) NOUN a plastid containing chlorophyll and other pigments, occurring in plants and algae that carry out photosynthesis.
▸ˌ**chloro'plastic** ADJECTIVE

chloroprene ('klɔːrəʊˌpriːn) NOUN a colourless liquid derivative of butadiene that is used in making neoprene rubbers; 2-chloro-1,2-butadiene. Formula: CH_2:CHCCl:CH_2.
▷HISTORY C20: from CHLORO- + (ISO)PRENE

chloroquine ('klɔːrəʊˌkwiːn) NOUN a synthetic drug administered orally to treat malaria. Formula: $C_{18}H_{26}ClN_3$.
▷HISTORY C20: from CHLORO- + QUIN(OLINE)

chlorosis (klɔː'rəʊsɪs) NOUN [1] Also called: **greensickness.** *Pathol* a disorder, formerly common in adolescent girls, characterized by pale greenish-yellow skin, weakness, and palpitation and caused by insufficient iron in the body. [2] *Botany* a deficiency of chlorophyll in green plants caused by mineral deficiency, lack of light, disease, etc., the leaves appearing uncharacteristically pale.
▷HISTORY C17: from CHLORO- + -OSIS
▸**chlorotic** (klɔː'rɒtɪk) ADJECTIVE

chlorothiazide (ˌklɔːrə'θaɪəˌzaɪd) NOUN a diuretic drug administered orally in the treatment of chronic heart and kidney disease and hypertension. Formula: $C_7H_6ClN_3O_4S_2$.
▷HISTORY C20: from CHLORO- + THI(O-) + (DI)AZ(INE + DIOX)IDE

chlorous ('klɔːrəs) ADJECTIVE [1] of or containing chlorine in the trivalent state. [2] of or containing chlorous acid.

chlorous acid NOUN an unstable acid that is a strong oxidizing agent. Formula: $HClO_2$.

chlorpromazine (klɔː'prɒməˌziːn) NOUN a drug derived from phenothiazine, used as a tranquillizer and sedative, esp in psychotic disorders. Formula: $C_{17}H_{19}ClN_2S$.
▷HISTORY C20: from CHLORO- + PRO(PYL + A)M(INE) + AZINE

chlorpropamide (klɔː'prəʊpəˌmaɪd) NOUN a sulfonylurea drug that reduces blood glucose and is administered orally in the treatment of diabetes mellitus. Formula: $C_{10}H_{13}ClN_2O_3S$.

chlortetracycline (klɔːˌtɛtrə'saɪkliːn) NOUN an antibiotic used in treating many bacterial and rickettsial infections: obtained from the bacterium *Streptomyces aureofaciens*. Formula: $C_{22}H_{23}ClN_2O_8$.

chlorthalidone (klɔː'θælɪdəʊn) NOUN a diuretic used in the treatment of congestive heart failure and hypertension.
▷HISTORY C20: from CHLOR(O)- + TH(IAZINE) + -AL[3] + -ID(E) + -ONE

ChM ABBREVIATION FOR Master of Surgery.
▷HISTORY Latin *Chirurgiae Magister*

choanocyte ('kəʊənəˌsaɪt) NOUN any of the flagellated cells in sponges that maintain a flow of water through the body. A collar of protoplasm surrounds the base of the flagellum. Also called: **collar cell.**
▷HISTORY C19: from Greek *khoanē* funnel (from *khein* to pour) + -CYTE

choccy ('tʃɒkɪ) *Informal* ◆ NOUN, *plural* **-cies.** [1] a chocolate. ◆ ADJECTIVE [2] made of, tasting of, smelling of, or resembling chocolate: *a delicious choccy taste.*

choc-ice (ˈtʃɒkˌaɪs) NOUN an ice cream covered with a thin layer of chocolate.

chock (tʃɒk) NOUN 1 a block or wedge of wood used to prevent the sliding or rolling of a heavy object. 2 *Nautical* **a** a fairlead consisting of a ringlike device with an opening at the top through which a rope is placed. **b** a cradle-like support for a boat, barrel, etc. 3 *Mountaineering* See **nut** (sense 10). ◆ VERB (*tr*) 4 (usually foll by *up*) *Brit* to cram full: *chocked up with newspapers.* 5 to fit with or secure by a chock. 6 to support (a boat, barrel, etc.) on chocks. ◆ ADVERB 7 as closely or tightly as possible: *chock against the wall.*
▷**HISTORY** C17: of uncertain origin; perhaps related to Old French *çoche* log; compare Provençal *soca* tree stump

chock-a-block ADJECTIVE, ADVERB 1 filled to capacity; in a crammed state. 2 *Nautical* with the blocks brought close together, as when a tackle is pulled as tight as possible.

chocker (ˈtʃɒkə) ADJECTIVE 1 *Informal* full up; packed. 2 *Brit slang* irritated; fed up.
▷**HISTORY** C20: from CHOCK-A-BLOCK

chock-full, choke-full, *or* **chuck-full** ADJECTIVE (*postpositive*) completely full.
▷**HISTORY** C17 *choke-full;* see CHOKE, FULL

chockstone (ˈtʃɒkˌstəʊn) NOUN *Mountaineering* 1 a stone securely jammed in a crack. It may vary in size from a pebble to a large boulder. 2 another name for **chock** (sense 3).

choco *or* **chocko** (ˈtʃɒkəʊ) NOUN, *plural* **chocos** *or* **chockos.** *Austral slang* (in World War II) **a** a member of the citizen army; militiaman. **b** a conscript.
▷**HISTORY** C20: shortened from *chocolate soldier*

chocoholic *or* **chocaholic** (ˌtʃɒkəˈhɒlɪk) NOUN *Informal* **a** someone who is very fond of eating chocolate. **b** (*as modifier*): *the chocoholic British.*
▷**HISTORY** C20: from CHOCO(LATE) + -HOLIC

chocolate (ˈtʃɒkəlɪt, ˈtʃɒklɪt, -lət) NOUN 1 a food preparation made from roasted ground cacao seeds, usually sweetened and flavoured. 2 a drink or sweetmeat made from this. 3 **a** a moderate to deep brown colour. **b** (*as adjective*): *a chocolate carpet.*
▷**HISTORY** C17: from Spanish, from Aztec *xocolatl,* from *xococ* sour, bitter + *atl* water
▸ˈ**chocolaty** ADJECTIVE

chocolate-box NOUN (*modifier*) *Informal* sentimentally pretty or appealing.

chocolate soldier NOUN *Informal* a person who mistakenly believes that he or she is very powerful, important, or impressive.

chocolatier (ˌtʃɒkəˈlætɪə; *French* ʃɔkɔlatje) NOUN a person or company that makes or sells chocolate.
▷**HISTORY** French

choctaw (ˈtʃɒktɔː) NOUN *Skating* a turn from the inside edge of one skate to the outside edge of the other or vice versa.
▷**HISTORY** C19: after CHOCTAW

Choctaw (ˈtʃɒktɔː) NOUN 1 (*plural* **-taws** *or* **-taw**) a member of a North American Indian people of Alabama. 2 the language of this people, belonging to the Muskogean family.
▷**HISTORY** C18: from Choctaw *Chahta*

chog (ˈtʃɒg) NOUN *Northern English dialect* the core of a piece of fruit: *an apple chog.*

Chogyal (ˈtʃɒgjɑːl) NOUN the title of the ruler of Sikkim.

choice (tʃɔɪs) NOUN 1 the act or an instance of choosing or selecting. 2 the opportunity or power of choosing. 3 a person or thing chosen or that may be chosen: *he was a possible choice.* 4 an alternative action or possibility: *what choice did I have?* 5 a supply from which to select: *a poor choice of shoes.* 6 **of choice.** preferred; favourite. ◆ ADJECTIVE 7 of superior quality; excellent: *choice wine.* 8 carefully chosen, appropriate: *a few choice words will do the trick.* 9 vulgar or rude: *choice language.*
▷**HISTORY** C13: from Old French *chois,* from *choisir* to CHOOSE
▸ˈ**choicely** ADVERB ▸ˈ**choiceness** NOUN

choir (kwaɪə) NOUN 1 an organized group of singers, esp for singing in church services. 2 **a** the part of a cathedral, abbey, or church in front of the altar, lined on both sides with benches, and used by the choir and clergy. Compare **chancel. b** (*as modifier*): *choir stalls.* 3 a number of instruments of the same family playing together: *a brass choir.* 4 Also called: **choir organ.** one of the manuals on an organ controlling a set of soft sweet-toned pipes. Compare **great** (sense 21), **swell** (sense 16). 5 any of the nine orders of angels in medieval angelology. Archaic spelling: **quire.**
▷**HISTORY** C13 *quer,* from Old French *cuer,* from Latin CHORUS
▸ˈ**choir**ˌ**like** ADJECTIVE

choirboy (ˈkwaɪəˌbɔɪ) NOUN one of a number of young boys who sing the treble part in a church choir.

choir loft NOUN a gallery in a cathedral, abbey, or church used by the choir.

choirmaster (ˈkwaɪəˌmɑːstə) NOUN a person who trains, leads, or conducts a choir.

choir school NOUN (in Britain) a school, esp a preparatory school attached to a cathedral, college, etc., offering general education to boys whose singing ability is good.

Choiseul (*French* ʃwazœl) NOUN an island in the SW Pacific Ocean, in the Solomon Islands: hilly and densely forested. Area: 3885 sq. km (1500 sq. miles).

choke (tʃəʊk) VERB 1 (*tr*) to hinder or stop the breathing of (a person or animal), esp by constricting the windpipe or by asphyxiation. 2 (*intr*) to have trouble or fail in breathing, swallowing, or speaking. 3 (*tr*) to block or clog up (a passage, pipe, street, etc.). 4 (*tr*) to retard the growth or action of: *the weeds are choking my plants.* 5 (*tr*) to suppress (emotion): *she choked her anger.* 6 (*intr*) *Slang* to die. 7 (*tr*) to enrich the petrol-air mixture by reducing the air supply to (a carburettor, petrol engine, etc.). 8 (*intr*) (esp in sport) to be seized with tension and fail to perform well. ◆ NOUN 9 the act or sound of choking. 10 a device in the carburettor of a petrol engine that enriches the petrol-air mixture by reducing the air supply. 11 any constriction or mechanism for reducing the flow of a fluid in a pipe, tube, etc. 12 Also called: **choke coil.** *Electronics* an inductor having a relatively high impedance, used to prevent the passage of high frequencies or to smooth the output of a rectifier. 13 the inedible centre of the head of an artichoke. ◆ See also **choke back, choke up.**
▷**HISTORY** Old English *ācēocian,* of Germanic origin; related to CHEEK
▸ˈ**chokeable** ADJECTIVE

choke back *or* **down** VERB (*tr, adverb*) to suppress (anger, tears, etc.).

chokeberry (ˈtʃəʊkbərɪ, -brɪ) NOUN, *plural* **-ries.** 1 any of various North American rosaceous shrubs of the genus *Aronia.* 2 the red or purple bitter fruit of any of these shrubs.

chokebore (ˈtʃəʊkˌbɔː) NOUN 1 a shotgun bore that becomes narrower towards the muzzle so that the shot is not scattered. 2 a shotgun having such a bore.

choke chain NOUN a collar and lead for a dog so designed that if the dog drags on the lead the collar tightens round its neck.

chokecherry (ˈtʃəʊkˌtʃerɪ) NOUN, *plural* **-ries.** 1 any of several North American species of cherry, esp *Prunus virginiana,* having very astringent dark red or black fruit. 2 the fruit of any of these trees.

choke coil NOUN another name for **choke** (sense 12).

choked (tʃəʊkt) ADJECTIVE *Brit informal* annoyed or disappointed.

chokedamp (ˈtʃəʊkˌdæmp) NOUN another word for **blackdamp.**

choke-full ADJECTIVE a less common spelling of **chock-full.**

choker (ˈtʃəʊkə) NOUN 1 a woman's high collar, popular esp in the late 19th century. 2 any neckband or necklace worn tightly around the throat. 3 a high clerical collar; stock. 4 a person who chokes. 5 something that causes a person to choke.

choke up VERB (*tr, adverb*) 1 to block (a drain, pipe, etc.) completely. 2 *Informal* (*usually passive*) to overcome (a person) with emotion, esp without due cause.

chokey *or* **choky** (ˈtʃəʊkɪ) NOUN *Brit* a slang word for **prison.**
▷**HISTORY** C17: from Anglo-Indian, from Hindi *caukī* a shed or lockup

choko (ˈtʃəʊkəʊ) NOUN, *plural* **-kos.** the cucumber-like fruit of a tropical American cucurbitaceous vine, *Sechium edule:* eaten as a vegetable in the Caribbean, Australia, and New Zealand.
▷**HISTORY** C18: from a Brazilian Indian name

choky *or* **chokey** (ˈtʃəʊkɪ) ADJECTIVE **chokier, chokiest.** involving, caused by, or causing choking.

cholagogue (ˈkɒləgɒg) NOUN a drug or other substance that promotes the flow of bile from the gall bladder into the duodenum.
▸ˌ**chola**ˈ**gogic** ADJECTIVE

cholangiography (kəˌlændʒɪˈɒgrəfɪ) NOUN radiographic examination of the bile ducts after the introduction into them of a contrast medium.

chole- *or before a vowel* **chol-** COMBINING FORM indicating bile or gall: *cholesterol.*
▷**HISTORY** from Greek *kholē*

cholecalciferol (ˌkəʊlɪkælˈsɪfəˌrɒl) NOUN a compound occurring naturally in fish-liver oils, used to treat rickets. Formula: $C_{27}H_{44}O$. Also called: **vitamin D_3.** See also **calciferol.**

cholecyst (ˈkɒlɪsɪst) NOUN *Rare* another name for **gall bladder.**

cholecystectomy (ˌkɒlɪsɪˈstɛktəmɪ) NOUN, *plural* **-mies.** surgical removal of the gall bladder.

cholecystitis (ˌkɒlɪsɪsˈtaɪtɪs) NOUN inflammation of the gall bladder, due to bacterial infection or the presence of gallstones.

cholecystography (ˌkɒlɪsɪsˈtɒgrəfɪ) NOUN *Med* radiography of the gall bladder after administration of a contrast medium.

cholecystokinin (ˌkɒlɪˌsɪstəˈkaɪnɪn) NOUN a hormone secreted by duodenal cells that stimulates the contraction of the gall bladder and secretion of pancreatic enzymes. Also called: **pancreozymin.**

cholent (ˈtʃɒlənt) NOUN *Judaism* a meal usually consisting of a stew of meat, potatoes, and pulses prepared before the Sabbath on Friday and left to cook until eaten for Sabbath lunch.

choler (ˈkɒlə) NOUN 1 anger or ill humour. 2 *Archaic* one of the four bodily humours; yellow bile. See **humour** (sense 8). 3 *Obsolete* biliousness.
▷**HISTORY** C14: from Old French *colère,* from Medieval Latin *cholera,* from Latin: jaundice, CHOLERA

cholera (ˈkɒlərə) NOUN an acute intestinal infection characterized by severe diarrhoea, cramp, etc.: caused by ingestion of water or food contaminated with the bacterium *Vibrio comma.* Also called: **Asiatic cholera, epidemic cholera, Indian cholera.**
▷**HISTORY** C14: from Latin, from Greek *kholera* jaundice, from *kholē* bile
▸ˈ**chole**ˌ**roid** ADJECTIVE

choleric (ˈkɒlərɪk) ADJECTIVE 1 bad-tempered. 2 bilious or causing biliousness.
▸ˈ**cholerically** *or* ˈ**cholericly** ADVERB

cholesterol (kəˈlɛstəˌrɒl) NOUN a sterol found in all animal tissues, blood, bile, and animal fats: a precursor of other body steroids. A high level of cholesterol in the blood is implicated in some cases of atherosclerosis, leading to heart disease. Formula: $C_{27}H_{45}OH$. Former name: **cholesterin** (kəˈlɛstərɪn).
▷**HISTORY** C19: from CHOLE- + Greek *stereos* hard, solid, so called because first observed in gallstones

cholesterolaemia *or US* **cholesterolemia** (kəˌlɛstərəˈliːmɪə) NOUN the presence of abnormally high levels of cholesterol in the blood.

Chol Hamoed *Hebrew* (xol hɑˈmoed; *Yiddish* xaʊl həˈmaʊəd) NOUN *Judaism* the middle days of the festivals of Passover and Sukkoth, on which necessary work is permitted.
▷**HISTORY** literally: the weekdays of the festival

choli (ˈkəʊlɪ) NOUN, *plural* **-lis.** a short-sleeved bodice, as worn by Indian women.
▷**HISTORY** from Hindi

cholic acid (ˈkəʊlɪk) NOUN a crystalline insoluble acid present in bile: used as an emulsifying agent and an intermediate in the synthesis of organic compounds. Formula: $C_{24}H_{40}O_5$.
▷**HISTORY** C19: from Greek *kholikos;* see CHOLE-

choline (ˈkəʊliːn, -ɪn, ˈkɒl-) NOUN a colourless viscous soluble alkaline substance present in animal tissues, esp as a constituent of lecithin: used as a supplement to the diet of poultry and in medicine

for preventing the accumulation of fat in the liver. Formula: $[(CH_3)_3NCH_2CH_2OH]^+OH^-$.
▷HISTORY C19: from CHOLE- + -INE^{2}, so called because of its action in the liver

cholinergic (ˌkəʊlɪˈnɜːdʒɪk) ADJECTIVE [1] denoting nerve fibres that release acetylcholine when stimulated. [2] of or relating to the type of chemical activity associated with acetylcholine and similar substances.
▷HISTORY C20: from (ACETYL)CHOLIN(E) + Greek *ergon* work

cholinesterase (ˌkəʊlɪˈnɛstəˌreɪs, ˌkɒl-) NOUN an enzyme that hydrolyses acetylcholine to choline and acetic acid.

cholla (ˈtʃəʊljɑː; *Spanish* ˈtʃoʎa) NOUN any of several spiny cacti of the genus *Opuntia* that grow in the southwestern US and Mexico and have cylindrical stem segments. See also **prickly pear.**
▷HISTORY Mexican Spanish, from Spanish: head, perhaps from Old French (dialect) *cholle* ball, of Germanic origin

chollers (ˈtʃɒləz) PLURAL NOUN *Northeast English dialect* the jowls or cheeks.
▷HISTORY C18: perhaps from Old English *ceolur* throat. See JOWL^{2}

Cholon (tʃəˈlʌn; *French* ʃɔlɔ̃) NOUN a city in S Vietnam: a suburb of Ho Chi Minh City.

Cholula (*Spanish* tʃoˈlula) NOUN a town in S Mexico, in Puebla state: ancient ruins, notably a pyramid, 53 m (177 ft.) high. Pop.: 37 791 (1990).

choma (ˈtʃɒmə) NOUN *South African informal* a friend, used esp by Black males.
▷HISTORY probably from Afrikaans *tjommie*, from CHUM^{1}

chometz *Hebrew* (xaˈmɛtʒ; *Yiddish* ˈxɔmətʒ) NOUN a variant spelling of **chametz.**

chomophyte (ˈkɒməʊˌfaɪt) NOUN any plant that grows on rocky ledges or in fissures and crevices.

chomp (tʃɒmp) *or* **chump** VERB [1] to chew (food) noisily; champ. ◆ NOUN [2] the act or sound of chewing in this manner.
▷HISTORY variant of CHAMP^{1}

Chomskyan (ˈtʃɒmskɪən) ADJECTIVE of or relating to (Avram) Noam Chomsky, the US linguist and political critic (born 1928).

chon (tʃəʊn) NOUN, *plural* **chon.** a North and South Korean monetary unit worth one hundredth of a won.

chondral (ˈkɒndrəl) ADJECTIVE of or relating to cartilage.

chondrichthyan (kɒnˈdrɪkθɪən) NOUN *Zoology* a technical name for a **cartilaginous fish.**
▷HISTORY New Latin, from Greek *khondros* grain, cartilage + *ikhthus* fish

chondrify (ˈkɒndrɪˌfaɪ) VERB **-fies, -fying, -fied.** to become or convert into cartilage.
▸ˌ**chondrifiˈcation** NOUN

chondrin (ˈkɒndrɪn) NOUN a resilient translucent bluish-white substance that forms the matrix of cartilage.

chondriosome (ˈkɒndrɪəˌsəʊm) NOUN another name for **mitochondrion.**
▸ˌ**chondrioˈsomal** ADJECTIVE

chondrite (ˈkɒndraɪt) NOUN a stony meteorite consisting mainly of silicate minerals in the form of chondrules. Compare **achondrite.**
▸**chondritic** (kɒnˈdrɪtɪk) ADJECTIVE

chondro-, chondri-, *or before a vowel* **chondr-** COMBINING FORM [1] indicating cartilage: *chondroma.* [2] grain or granular: *chondrule.*
▷HISTORY from Greek *khondros* grain, cartilage

chondroma (kɒnˈdrəʊmə) NOUN, *plural* **-mas** *or* **-mata** (-mətə). *Pathol* a benign cartilaginous growth or neoplasm.
▸**chonˈdromatous** ADJECTIVE

chondroskeleton (ˈkɒndrəʊˌskɛlɪtən) NOUN the cartilaginous part of the skeleton of vertebrates.

chondrule (ˈkɒndruːl) NOUN one of the small spherical masses of mainly silicate minerals present in chondrites.

Chŏngjin *or* **Chungjin** (ˈtʃʌŋˈdʒɪn) NOUN a port in E North Korea, on the Sea of Japan. Pop.: 520 000 (latest est.).

Chongqing (ˈtʃʊŋˈtʃɪŋ), **Chungking,** *or* **Ch'ung-ch'ing** NOUN a port in SW China, in Sichuan province at the confluence of the Yangtze and Jialing rivers: site of a city since the 3rd millennium B.C.; wartime capital of China (1938–45); major trade centre for W China. Pop.: 3 193 889 (1999 est.). Also called: **Pahsien.**

Chŏnju (ˈtʃʌnˈdʒuː) NOUN a city in SW South Korea: centre of large rice-growing region. Pop.: 563 406 (1995).

choo-choo (ˈtʃuːˌtʃuː) NOUN *Brit* a child's name for a railway train.
▷HISTORY C20: of imitative origin

choof off (tʃʊf) VERB (*intr, adverb*) *Austral slang* to go away; make off.

chook (tʃʊk) VERB [1] See **jook.** ◆ NOUN [2] Also called: **chookie.** *Austral informal* a hen or chicken. [3] *Austral informal* a woman. ◆ INTERJECTION [4] *Austral* a exclamation used to attract chickens.

chook chaser NOUN *Austral derogatory slang* [1] a small motorcycle, esp for off-road use. [2] a person who rides such a motorcycle.

choom (tʃʊm) NOUN (*often capital*) *Old-fashioned, Austral slang* an Englishman.

choose (tʃuːz) VERB **chooses, choosing, chose, chosen.** [1] to select (a person, thing, course of action, etc.) from a number of alternatives. [2] (*tr; takes a clause as object or an infinitive*) to consider it desirable or proper: *I don't choose to read that book.* [3] (*intr*) to like; please: *you may stand if you choose.* [4] **cannot choose but.** to be obliged to: *we cannot choose but vote for him.* [5] **nothing** *or* **little to choose between.** (of two people or objects) almost equal.
▷HISTORY Old English *ceosan;* related to Old Norse *kjōsa,* Old High German *kiosan*
▸ˈ**chooser** NOUN

choosy (ˈtʃuːzɪ) ADJECTIVE **choosier, choosiest.** *Informal* particular in making a choice; difficult to please.

chop^{1} (tʃɒp) VERB **chops, chopping, chopped.** [1] (often foll by *down* or *off*) to cut (something) with a blow from an axe or other sharp tool. [2] (*tr*) to produce or make in this manner: *to chop firewood.* [3] (*tr;* often foll by *up*) to cut into pieces. [4] (*tr*) *Brit informal* to dispense with or reduce. [5] (*intr*) to move quickly or violently. [6] *Sport* to hit (a ball) sharply downwards. [7] *Boxing, martial Arts* to punch or strike (an opponent) with a short sharp blow. [8] *West African* an informal word for **eat.** ◆ NOUN [9] a cutting blow. [10] the act or an instance of chopping. [11] a piece chopped off. [12] a slice of mutton, lamb, or pork, generally including a rib. [13] *Austral and NZ slang* a share (esp in the phrase **get** *or* **hop in for one's chop**). [14] *West African* an informal word for **food.** [15] *Austral and NZ* a competition of skill and speed in chopping logs. [16] *Sport* a sharp downward blow or stroke. [17] **not much chop.** *Austral and NZ informal* not much good; poor. [18] **the chop.** *Slang* dismissal from employment.
▷HISTORY C16: variant of CHAP^{1}

chop^{2} (tʃɒp) VERB **chops, chopping, chopped.** [1] (*intr*) to change direction suddenly; vacillate (esp in the phrase **chop and change**). [2] *Obsolete* to barter. [3] **chop logic.** to use excessively subtle or involved logic or argument.
▷HISTORY Old English *ceapian* to barter; see CHEAP, CHAPMAN

chop^{3} (tʃɒp) NOUN a design stamped on goods as a trademark, esp in the Far East.
▷HISTORY C17: from Hindi *chhāp*

chop chop ADVERB pidgin English for **quickly.**
▷HISTORY C19: from Chinese dialect; related to Cantonese *kap kap*

chopfallen (ˈtʃɒpˌfɔːlən) ADJECTIVE a variant of **chapfallen.**

chophouse^{1} (ˈtʃɒpˌhaʊs) NOUN a restaurant specializing in steaks, grills, chops, etc.

chophouse^{2} (ˈtʃɒpˌhaʊs) NOUN (formerly) a customs house in China.

chopine (tʃɒˈpiːn) *or* **chopin** (ˈtʃɒpɪn) NOUN a sandal-like shoe on tall wooden or cork bases popular in the 18th century.
▷HISTORY C16: from Old Spanish *chapín,* probably imitative of the sound made by the shoe when walking

chopper (ˈtʃɒpə) NOUN [1] *Chiefly Brit* a small hand axe. [2] a butcher's cleaver. [3] a person or thing that cuts or chops. [4] an informal name for a **helicopter.** [5] *Chiefly Brit* a slang name for **penis.** [6] a device for periodically interrupting an electric current or beam of radiation to produce a pulsed current or beam. See also **vibrator** (sense 2). [7] a type of bicycle or motorcycle with very high handlebars and an elongated saddle. [8] *NZ* a child's bicycle. [9] *Obsolete slang, chiefly US* a sub-machine-gun.

chopper tool NOUN a core tool of flint or stone, with a transverse cutting edge, characteristic of cultures in Asia and parts of the Middle East and Europe.

choppy (ˈtʃɒpɪ) ADJECTIVE **-pier, -piest.** (of the sea, weather, etc.) fairly rough.
▸ˈ**choppily** ADVERB ▸ˈ**choppiness** NOUN

chops (tʃɒps) PLURAL NOUN [1] the jaws or cheeks; jowls. [2] the mouth. [3] *Slang* **a** *Music* embouchure. **b** *Jazz* skill. [4] **lick one's chops.** *Informal* to anticipate with pleasure.
▷HISTORY C16: of uncertain origin

chopsticks (ˈtʃɒpstɪks) PLURAL NOUN a pair of thin sticks, of ivory, wood, etc., used as eating utensils by the Chinese, Japanese, and other people of East Asia.
▷HISTORY C17: from pidgin English, from *chop* quick, of Chinese dialect origin + STICK^{1}

chop suey (ˈsuːɪ) NOUN a Chinese-style dish originating in the US, consisting of meat or chicken, bean sprouts, etc., stewed and served with rice.
▷HISTORY C19: from Chinese (Cantonese) *tsap sui* odds and ends

choragus (kɔːˈreɪgəs) NOUN, *plural* **-gi** (-dʒaɪ) *or* **-guses.** [1] (in ancient Greek drama) **a** the leader of a chorus. **b** a sponsor of a chorus. [2] a conductor of a festival.
▷HISTORY C17: from Latin, from Greek *khoragos,* from *khoros* CHORUS + *agein* to lead
▸**choragic** (kɔːˈrædʒɪk, -ˈreɪ-) ADJECTIVE

choral ADJECTIVE (ˈkɔːrəl) [1] relating to, sung by, or designed for a chorus or choir. ◆ NOUN (kɒˈrɑːl) [2] a variant spelling of **chorale.**
▸ˈ**chorally** ADVERB

chorale *or* **choral** (kɒˈrɑːl) NOUN [1] a slow stately hymn tune, esp of the Lutheran Church. [2] *Chiefly US* a choir or chorus.
▷HISTORY C19: from German *Choralgesang,* translation of Latin *cantus chorālis* choral song

chorale prelude NOUN a composition for organ using a chorale as a cantus firmus or as the basis for variations.

chord^{1} (kɔːd) NOUN [1] *Maths* **a** a straight line connecting two points on a curve or curved surface. **b** the line segment lying between two points of intersection of a straight line and a curve or curved surface. [2] *Engineering* one of the principal members of a truss, esp one that lies along the top or the bottom. [3] *Anatomy* a variant spelling of **cord.** [4] an emotional response, esp one of sympathy: *the story struck the right chord.* [5] an imaginary straight line joining the leading edge and the trailing edge of an aerofoil. [6] *Archaic* the string of a musical instrument.
▷HISTORY C16: from Latin *chorda,* from Greek *khordē* gut, string; see CORD
▸ˈ**chorded** ADJECTIVE

chord^{2} (kɔːd) NOUN [1] the simultaneous sounding of a group of musical notes, usually three or more in number. See **concord** (sense 4), **discord** (sense 3). ◆ VERB [2] (*tr*) to provide (a melodic line) with chords.
▷HISTORY C15: short for ACCORD; spelling influenced by CHORD^{1}
▸ˈ**chordal** ADJECTIVE

chordate (ˈkɔːˌdeɪt) NOUN [1] any animal of the phylum *Chordata,* including the vertebrates and protochordates, characterized by a notochord, dorsal tubular nerve cord, and pharyngeal gill slits. ◆ ADJECTIVE [2] of, relating to, or belonging to the *Chordata.*
▷HISTORY C19: from Medieval Latin *chordata;* see CHORD^{1} + -ATE^{1}

chording (ˈkɔːdɪŋ) NOUN *Music* [1] the distribution of chords throughout a piece of harmony. [2] the intonation of a group of instruments or voices.

chordophone (ˈkɔːdəˌfəʊn) NOUN any musical instrument producing sounds through the vibration of strings, such as the piano, harp, violin, or guitar.

chord symbol NOUN *Music* any of a series of letters and numerals, used as a shorthand indication of chords, esp in jazz, folk, or pop music: *B7 indicates the dominant seventh chord in the key of E.*

chordwise ('kɔːdˌwaɪz) ADVERB [1] in the direction of an aerofoil chord. ◆ ADJECTIVE [2] moving in this direction: *chordwise force.*

chore (tʃɔː) NOUN [1] a small routine task, esp a domestic one. [2] an unpleasant task.
▷**HISTORY** C19: variant of Middle English *chare;* related to CHAR[3]

-chore NOUN COMBINING FORM (in botany) indicating a plant distributed by a certain means: *anemochore.*
▷**HISTORY** from Greek *khōrein* to move
▸**-chorous** *or* **-choric** ADJECTIVE COMBINING FORM

chorea (kɒ'rɪə) NOUN a disorder of the central nervous system characterized by uncontrollable irregular brief jerky movements. See **Huntington's disease, Sydenham's chorea.**
▷**HISTORY** C19: from New Latin, from Latin: dance, from Greek *khoreia,* from *khoros* dance; see CHORUS
▸**cho'real** *or* **cho'reic** ADJECTIVE

choreo- COMBINING FORM indicating the art of dancing or ballet: *choreodrama; choreography.*
▷**HISTORY** from Greek *khoreios,* from *khoros* dance

choreodrama (ˌkɒrɪəʊ'drɑːmə) NOUN *Dancing* dance drama performed by a group.

choreograph ('kɒrɪəˌgræf) VERB *(tr)* to compose the steps and dances for (a piece of music or ballet).

choreography (ˌkɒrɪ'ɒgrəfɪ) *or* **choregraphy** (kɒ'rɛgrəfɪ) NOUN [1] the composition of dance steps and sequences for ballet and stage dancing. [2] the steps and sequences of a ballet or dance. [3] the notation representing such steps. [4] the art of dancing.
▷**HISTORY** C18: from Greek *khoreia* dance + -GRAPHY
▸**ˌchore'ographer** *or* **cho'regrapher** NOUN ▸**choreographic** (ˌkɒrɪə'græfɪk) *or* **choregraphic** (ˌkɒrə'græfɪk) ADJECTIVE
▸**ˌchoreo'graphically** *or* **ˌchore'graphically** ADVERB

choriamb ('kɒrɪˌæmb) *or* **choriambus** (ˌkɒrɪ'æmbəs) NOUN, *plural* **-ambs** *or* **-ambi** (-'æmbaɪ). *Prosody* a metrical foot used in classical verse consisting of four syllables, two short ones between two long ones (–⏑⏑–).
▷**HISTORY** C19: from Late Latin *choriambus,* from Greek *khoriambos,* from *khoreios* trochee, of a chorus, from *khoros* CHORUS
▸**ˌchori'ambic** ADJECTIVE

choric ('kɒrɪk) ADJECTIVE of, like, for, or in the manner of a chorus, esp of singing, dancing, or the speaking of verse.

chorion ('kɔːrɪən) NOUN the outer of two membranes (see also **amnion**) that form a sac around the embryonic reptile, bird, or mammal: contributes to the placenta in mammals.
▷**HISTORY** C16: from Greek *khorion* afterbirth
▸**ˌchori'onic** *or* **'chorial** ADJECTIVE

chorionic gonadotrophin NOUN a hormone secreted by the chorionic villi of the placenta in mammals, esp **human chorionic gonadotrophin.** It promotes the secretion of progesterone by the corpus luteum and its presence in the urine is an indication of pregnancy.

chorionic villus sampling NOUN a method of diagnosing genetic disorders early in pregnancy by the removal by catheter through the cervix or abdomen of a tiny sample of tissue from the chorionic villi. Abbreviation: **CVS.**

chorister ('kɒrɪstə) NOUN a singer in a choir, esp a choirboy.
▷**HISTORY** C14: from Medieval Latin *chorista*

chorizo (tʃɔː'riːzəʊ) NOUN, *plural* **-zos.** a kind of highly seasoned pork sausage of Spain or Mexico.
▷**HISTORY** C19: Spanish

C horizon NOUN the layer of a soil profile immediately below the B horizon and above the bedrock, composed of weathered rock little affected by soil-forming processes.

Chorley ('tʃɔːlɪ) NOUN a town in NW England, in S Lancashire: cotton textiles. Pop.: 33 536 (1991).

chorography (kɒ'rɒgrəfɪ) NOUN *Geography* [1] the technique of mapping regions. [2] *(plural* **-phies**) a description or map of a region, as opposed to a small area.
▷**HISTORY** C16: via Latin from Greek *khōrographia,* from *khōros* place, country + -GRAPHY
▸**cho'rographer** NOUN ▸**chorographic** (ˌkɒrə'græfɪk) *or* **ˌchoro'graphical** ADJECTIVE ▸**ˌchoro'graphically** ADVERB

choroid ('kɔːrɔɪd) *or* **chorioid** ('kɔːrɪˌɔɪd) ADJECTIVE [1] resembling the chorion, esp in being vascular. ◆ NOUN [2] the brownish vascular membrane of the eyeball between the sclera and the retina.
▷**HISTORY** C18: from Greek *khoroeidēs,* erroneously for *khorioeidēs,* from CHORION

choroid plexus NOUN a multilobed vascular membrane, projecting into the cerebral ventricles, that secretes cerebrospinal fluid.

chorology (kə'rɒlədʒɪ) NOUN [1] the study of the causal relations between geographical phenomena occurring within a particular region. [2] the study of the spatial distribution of organisms.
▷**HISTORY** C20: from German *Chorologie,* from Greek *khōros* place + -LOGY
▸**cho'rologist** NOUN

choropleth ('kɔːrəˌplɛθ) NOUN **a** a symbol or marked and bounded area on a map denoting the distribution of some property. **b** *(as modifier)*: *a choropleth map.*
▷**HISTORY** C20: from Gk *khōra* place + *plēthos* multitude

chorrie ('tʃɒrɪ) NOUN *South African informal* a dilapidated old car.
▷**HISTORY** C20: from Afrikaans *tjor* a crock

chortle ('tʃɔːtᵊl) VERB [1] *(intr)* to chuckle gleefully. ◆ NOUN [2] a gleeful chuckle.
▷**HISTORY** C19: coined (1871) by Lewis Carroll in *Through the Looking-glass;* probably a blend of CHUCKLE + SNORT
▸**'chortler** NOUN

chorus ('kɔːrəs) NOUN, *plural* **-ruses.** [1] a large choir of singers or a piece of music composed for such a choir. [2] a body of singers or dancers who perform together, in contrast to principals or soloists. [3] a section of a song in which a soloist is joined by a group of singers, esp in a recurring refrain. [4] an intermediate section of a pop song, blues, etc., as distinct from the verse. [5] *Jazz* any of a series of variations on a theme. [6] (in ancient Greece) **a** a lyric poem sung by a group of dancers, originally as a religious rite. **b** an ode or series of odes sung by a group of actors. [7] **a** (in classical Greek drama) the actors who sang the chorus and commented on the action of the play. **b** actors playing a similar role in any drama. [8] **a** (esp in Elizabethan drama) the actor who spoke the prologue, etc. **b** the part of the play spoken by this actor. [9] a group of people or animals producing words or sounds simultaneously. [10] any speech, song, or other utterance produced by a group of people or animals simultaneously: *a chorus of sighs; the dawn chorus.* [11] **in chorus.** in unison. ◆ VERB [12] to speak, sing, or utter (words, etc.) in unison.
▷**HISTORY** C16: from Latin, from Greek *khoros*

chorus girl NOUN a girl who dances or sings in the chorus of a musical comedy, revue, etc.

chorusmaster ('kɔːrəsˌmɑːstə) NOUN the conductor of a choir.

chorus pedal NOUN *Music* an electronic device that creates the effect of more than one sound from a single source by combining a short delay with slight deviations in pitch.

Chorzów (*Polish* 'ɔxʒuf) NOUN an industrial city in SW Poland: under German administration from 1794 to 1921. Pop.: 121 708 (1999 est.). German name: **Königshütte.**

chose[1] (tʃəʊz) VERB the past tense of **choose.**

chose[2] (ʃəʊz) NOUN *Law* an article of personal property.
▷**HISTORY** C17: from French: thing, from Latin *causa* cause, case, reason

chosen ('tʃəʊzᵊn) VERB [1] the past participle of **choose.** ◆ ADJECTIVE [2] selected or picked out, esp for some special quality.

Chosen ('tʃəʊ'sɛn) NOUN the official name for **Korea** as a Japanese province (1910–45).

chosen people PLURAL NOUN any of various peoples believing themselves to be chosen by God, esp the Jews.

Chosŏn ('tʃəʊ'sɒn) NOUN the Korean name for **North Korea.**

Chota Nagpur ('tʃəʊtə 'nɑːgpʊə) NOUN a plateau in E India, mainly in Jharkand state since 2000: forested, with rich mineral resources and much heavy industry; produces chiefly lac (world's leading supplier), coal (half India's total output), and mica.

chott (ʃɒt) NOUN a variant spelling of **shott.**

chou (ʃuː) NOUN, *plural* **choux** (ʃuː). [1] a type of cabbage. [2] a rosette. [3] a round cream bun.
▷**HISTORY** C18 (a bun): from French, from Latin *caulis* cabbage

Chou (tʃəʊ) *or* **Zhou** NOUN the imperial dynasty of China from about 1126 to 255 B.C.

chough (tʃʌf) NOUN [1] a large black passerine bird, *Pyrrhocorax pyrrhocorax,* of parts of Europe, Asia, and Africa, with a long downward-curving red bill: family *Corvidae* (crows). [2] **alpine chough.** a smaller related bird, *Pyrrhocorax graculus,* with a shorter yellow bill.
▷**HISTORY** C14: of uncertain origin; probably related to Old French *cauwe,* Old English *cēo*

choux pastry (ʃuː) NOUN a very light pastry made with eggs, used for eclairs, etc.
▷**HISTORY** partial translation of French *pâte choux* cabbage dough (from its round shape)

chow (tʃaʊ) NOUN [1] *Informal* food. [2] short for **chow-chow** (sense 1). ◆ See also **chow down.**

chow-chow NOUN [1] a thick-coated breed of the spitz type of dog with a curled tail and a characteristic blue-black tongue; it came originally from China. Often shortened to **chow.** [2] a Chinese preserve of ginger, orange peel, etc. in syrup. [3] a mixed vegetable pickle.
▷**HISTORY** C19: from pidgin English, probably based on Mandarin Chinese *cha* miscellaneous

chowder ('tʃaʊdə) NOUN a thick soup or stew containing clams or fish.
▷**HISTORY** C18: from French *chaudière* kettle, from Late Latin *caldāria;* see CAULDRON

chow down VERB *(intr, adverb;* foll by *on) Informal* to eat heartily.

chowk (tʃaʊk) NOUN (in the Indian subcontinent) [1] *(often in place names)* a marketplace or market area: *Vijay Chowk.* [2] a courtyard. [3] a road junction or roundabout.
▷**HISTORY** from Hindi *cauk*

chow mein (meɪn) NOUN a Chinese-American dish, consisting of mushrooms, meat, shrimps, etc., served with fried noodles.
▷**HISTORY** from Chinese (Cantonese), variant of Mandarin *ch'ao mien* fried noodles

chrematistic (ˌkriːmə'tɪstɪk) ADJECTIVE of, denoting, or relating to money-making.
▷**HISTORY** C18: from Greek, from *khrēmatizein* to make money, from *khrēma* money
▸**ˌchrema'tistics** NOUN

chresard ('krɛsəd) NOUN the amount of water present in the soil that is available to plants.
▷**HISTORY** C20: from Greek *khrēsis* use (from *khrēsthai* to use) + *ardein* to water

chrestomathy (krɛs'tɒməθɪ) NOUN, *plural* **-thies.** *Rare* a collection of literary passages, used in the study of language.
▷**HISTORY** C19: from Greek *khrēstomatheia,* from *khrēstos* useful + *mathein* to learn
▸**chrestomathic** (ˌkrɛstəʊ'mæθɪk) ADJECTIVE

Chrimbo *or* **Crimbo** ('krɪmbəʊ) NOUN *Brit* an informal word for **Christmas.**

chrism *or* **chrisom** ('krɪzəm) NOUN a mixture of olive oil and balsam used for sacramental anointing in the Greek Orthodox and Roman Catholic Churches.
▷**HISTORY** Old English *crisma,* from Medieval Latin, from Greek *khrisma* unction, from *khriein* to anoint
▸**chrismal** ('krɪzməl) ADJECTIVE

chrismation (ˌkrɪz'meɪʃən) NOUN *Greek Orthodox Church* a rite of initiation involving anointing with chrism and taking place at the same time as baptism.

chrismatory ('krɪzmətərɪ, -trɪ) NOUN, *plural* **-ries.** *RC Church* a small receptacle containing the three kinds of consecrated oil used in the sacraments.

chrisom ('krɪzəm) NOUN [1] *Christianity* a white robe put on an infant at baptism and formerly used as a burial shroud if the infant died soon afterwards. [2] *Archaic* an infant wearing such a robe. [3] a variant spelling of **chrism.**

Chrissie ('krɪsɪ) NOUN *Chiefly Austral* a slang name for **Christmas.**

Christ (kraɪst) NOUN [1] Jesus of Nazareth (Jesus

Christ), regarded by Christians as fulfilling Old Testament prophecies of the Messiah. 2 the Messiah or anointed one of God as the subject of Old Testament prophecies. 3 an image or picture of Christ. ◆ INTERJECTION 4 *Taboo slang* an oath expressing annoyance, surprise, etc. ◆ See also **Jesus.**
▷HISTORY Old English *Crīst,* from Latin *Chrīstus,* from Greek *khristos* anointed one (from *khriein* to anoint), translating Hebrew *māshīah* MESSIAH
▸**ˈChristly** ADJECTIVE

Christadelphian (ˌkrɪstəˈdɛlfɪən) NOUN 1 a member of a Christian millenarian sect founded in the US about 1848, holding that only the just will enter eternal life, that the wicked will be annihilated, and that the ignorant, the unconverted, and infants will not be raised from the dead. ◆ ADJECTIVE 2 of or relating to this body or its beliefs and practices.
▷HISTORY C19: from Late Greek *khristadelphos,* from *khristos* CHRIST + *adelphos* brother

Christchurch (ˈkraɪstˌtʃɜːtʃ) NOUN 1 a city in New Zealand, on E South Island: manufacturing centre of a rich agricultural region. Pop. (urban area): 324 300 (1999 est.). 2 a town and resort in S England, in SE Dorset. Pop.: 36 379 (1991).

christcross (ˈkrɪsˌkrɒs) NOUN *Archaic* 1 **a** the mark of a cross formerly placed in front of the alphabet in hornbooks. **b** the alphabet itself. 2 a cross used in place of a signature by someone unable to sign his name.

christen (ˈkrɪsən) VERB (*tr*) 1 to give a Christian name to in baptism as a sign of incorporation into a Christian Church. 2 another word for **baptize.** 3 to give a name to (anything), esp with some ceremony. 4 *Informal* to use for the first time.
▷HISTORY Old English *cristnian,* from *Crīst* CHRIST
▸**ˈchristener** NOUN

Christendom (ˈkrɪsəndəm) NOUN 1 the collective body of Christians throughout the world or throughout history. 2 an obsolete word for **Christianity.**

christening (ˈkrɪsənɪŋ) NOUN the Christian sacrament of baptism or the ceremony in which this is conferred.

Christhood (ˈkraɪsthʊd) NOUN the state of being the Christ, the anointed one of God.

Christian (ˈkrɪstʃən) NOUN 1 **a** a person who believes in and follows Jesus Christ. **b** a member of a Christian Church or denomination. 2 *Informal* a person who possesses Christian virtues, esp practical ones. ◆ ADJECTIVE 3 of, relating to, or derived from Jesus Christ, his teachings, example, or his followers. 4 (*sometimes not capital*) exhibiting kindness or goodness.
▸**ˈchristianly** ADJECTIVE, ADVERB

Christian Action NOUN an inter-Church movement formed in 1946 to promote Christian ideals in society at large.

Christian Brothers PLURAL NOUN *RC Church* a religious congregation of laymen founded in France in 1684 for the education of the poor. Also called: **Brothers of the Christian Schools.**

Christian Democracy NOUN the beliefs, principles, practices, or programme of a Christian Democratic party.
▸**Christian Democratic** ADJECTIVE

Christian Democrat NOUN 1 a member or supporter of a Christian Democratic party. ◆ ADJECTIVE 2 of or relating to a Christian Democratic party.

Christian Democratic Party NOUN any of various political parties in Europe and Latin America which combine moderate conservatism with historical links to the Christian Church.

Christian Era NOUN the period beginning with the year of Christ's birth. Dates in this era are labelled A.D., those previous to it B.C. Also called: **Common Era.**

Christiania (ˌkrɪstɪˈɑːnɪə) NOUN a former name (1624–1877) of **Oslo.**

Christianity (ˌkrɪstɪˈænɪtɪ) NOUN 1 the Christian religion. 2 Christian beliefs, practices or attitudes. 3 a less common word for **Christendom** (sense 1).

Christianize *or* **Christianise** (ˈkrɪstʃəˌnaɪz) VERB (*tr*) 1 to make Christian or convert to Christianity. 2 to imbue with Christian principles, spirit, or outlook.
▸**ˌChristianiˈzation** *or* **ˌChristianiˈsation** NOUN
▸**ˈChristianˌizer** *or* **ˈChristianˌiser** NOUN

Christian name NOUN a personal name formally given to Christians at christening. The term is loosely used to mean any person's first name as distinct from his or her surname. Also called: **first name, forename, given name.**

Christiansand (ˈkrɪstʃənˌsænd; *Norwegian* kristianˈsan) NOUN a variant spelling of **Kristiansand.**

Christian Science NOUN the religious system and teaching of the Church of Christ, Scientist. It was founded by Mary Baker Eddy (1866) and emphasizes spiritual healing and the unreality of matter.
▸**Christian Scientist** NOUN

Christingle (ˌkrɪsˈtɪŋgəl) NOUN (in Britain) a Christian service for children held shortly before Christmas, in which each child is given a decorated fruit with a lighted candle in it.
▷HISTORY C20: from CHRISTMAS + INGLE

Christlike (ˈkraɪstˌlaɪk) ADJECTIVE resembling or showing the spirit of Jesus Christ.
▸**ˈChristˌlikeness** NOUN

Christmas (ˈkrɪsməs) NOUN 1 **a** the annual commemoration by Christians of the birth of Jesus Christ on Dec. 25. **b** Also called: **Christmas Day.** Dec. 25, observed as a day of secular celebrations when gifts and greetings are exchanged. **c** (*as modifier*): *Christmas celebrations.* 2 Also called: **Christmas Day.** (in England, Wales and Ireland) Dec. 25, one of the four quarter days. Compare **Lady Day, Midsummer's Day, Michaelmas.** 3 Also called: **Christmastide.** the season of Christmas extending from Dec. 24 (Christmas Eve) to Jan. 6 (the festival of the Epiphany or Twelfth Night).
▷HISTORY Old English *Crīstes mæsse* MASS of CHRIST

Christmas beetle NOUN any of various greenish-gold Australian scarab beetles of the genus *Anoplognathus,* which are common in summer.

Christmas box NOUN a tip or present given at Christmas, esp to postmen, tradesmen, etc.

Christmas cactus NOUN a Brazilian cactus, *Schlumbergera* (formerly *Zygocactus*) *truncatus,* widely cultivated as an ornamental for its showy red flowers.

Christmas card NOUN a greeting card sent at Christmas.

Christmas disease NOUN a relatively mild type of haemophilia, caused by lack of a protein (**Christmas factor**) implicated in the process of blood clotting.
▷HISTORY C20: named after S. *Christmas,* the first patient suffering from the disease who was examined in detail

Christmas Eve NOUN the evening or the whole day before Christmas Day.

Christmas Island NOUN 1 the former name (until 1981) of **Kiritimati.** 2 an island in the Indian Ocean, south of Java: administered by Singapore (1900–58), now by Australia; phosphate mining. Pop.: 2500 (1994 est.). Area: 135 sq. km (52 sq. miles).

Christmas pudding NOUN *Brit* a rich steamed pudding containing suet, dried fruit, spices, brandy, etc., served at Christmas. Also called: **plum pudding.**

Christmas rose NOUN an evergreen ranunculaceous plant, *Helleborus niger,* of S Europe and W Asia, with white or pinkish winter-blooming flowers. Also called: **hellebore, winter rose.**

Christmas stocking NOUN a stocking hung up by children on Christmas Eve for Santa Claus to fill with presents.

Christmassy (ˈkrɪsməsɪ) ADJECTIVE of, relating to, or suitable for Christmas.

Christmastide (ˈkrɪsməsˌtaɪd) NOUN another name for **Christmas** (sense 3).

Christmas tree NOUN 1 an evergreen tree or an imitation of one, decorated as part of Christmas celebrations. 2 Also called: **Christmas bush.** *Austral* any of various trees or shrubs flowering at Christmas and used for decoration.

Christo- COMBINING FORM indicating or relating to Christ: *Christology.*

Christology (krɪˈstɒlədʒɪ, kraɪ-) NOUN the branch of theology concerned with the person, attributes, and deeds of Christ.
▸**Christological** (ˌkrɪstəˈlɒdʒɪkəl) ADJECTIVE
▸**Chrisˈtologist** NOUN

Christ's-thorn NOUN any of several rhamnaceous plants of SW Asia, such as *Paliurus spina-christi* or the jujube, that have thorny stems and are popularly believed to have been used for Christ's Crown of Thorns.

Christy *or* **Christie** (ˈkrɪstɪ) NOUN, *plural* **-ties.** (*sometimes not capital*) *Skiing* a turn in which the body is swung sharply round with the skis parallel, originating in Norway and used for stopping, slowing down, or changing direction quickly.
▷HISTORY C20: shortened from CHRISTIANIA

chroma (ˈkrəʊmə) NOUN 1 the attribute of a colour that enables an observer to judge how much chromatic colour it contains irrespective of achromatic colour present. See also **saturation** (sense 4). 2 (in colour television) the colour component in a composite coded signal.
▷HISTORY C19: from Greek *khrōma* colour

chromakey (ˈkrəʊməˌkiː) NOUN (in colour television) a special effect in which a coloured background can be eliminated and a different background substituted. Also called: **colour separation overlay.**

chromate (ˈkrəʊˌmeɪt) NOUN any salt or ester of chromic acid. Simple chromate salts contain the divalent ion, CrO_4^{2-}, and are orange.

chromatic (krəˈmætɪk) ADJECTIVE 1 of, relating to, or characterized by a colour or colours. 2 *Music* **a** involving the sharpening or flattening of notes or the use of such notes in chords and harmonic progressions. **b** of or relating to the chromatic scale or an instrument capable of producing it: *a chromatic harmonica.* **c** of or relating to chromaticism. Compare **diatonic.**
▷HISTORY C17: from Greek *khrōmatikos,* from *khrōma* colour
▸**chroˈmatically** ADVERB ▸**chroˈmaticism** NOUN

chromatic aberration NOUN a defect in a lens system in which different wavelengths of light are focused at different distances because they are refracted through different angles. It produces a blurred image with coloured fringes.

chromatic adaptation NOUN *Botany* the alteration by photosynthesizing organisms of the proportions of their photosynthetic pigments in response to the intensity and colour of the available light, as shown by algae in the littoral zone, which change from green to red as the zone is descended.

chromatic colour NOUN *Physics* a formal term for **colour** (sense 2).

chromaticity (ˌkrəʊməˈtɪsɪtɪ) NOUN the quality of a colour or light with reference to its purity and its dominant wavelength.

chromaticity coordinates PLURAL NOUN *Physics* three numbers used to specify a colour, each of which is equal to one of the three tristimulus values divided by their sum. Symbols: ***x, y, z.***

chromaticity diagram NOUN *Physics* a diagram in which values of two chromaticity coordinates are marked on a pair of rectangular axes, a point in the plane of these axes representing the chromaticity of any colour.

chromaticness (krəʊˈmætɪknɪs) NOUN *Physics* the attribute of colour that involves both hue and saturation.

chromatics (krəʊˈmætɪks) *or* **chromatology** (ˌkrəʊməˈtɒlədʒɪ) NOUN (*functioning as singular*) the science of colour.
▸**chromatist** (ˈkrəʊmətɪst) *or* **ˌchromaˈtologist** NOUN

chromatic scale NOUN a twelve-note scale including all the semitones of the octave.

chromatid (ˈkrəʊmətɪd) NOUN either of the two strands into which a chromosome divides during mitosis. They separate to form daughter chromosomes at anaphase.

chromatin (ˈkrəʊmətɪn) NOUN *Cytology* the part of the nucleus that consists of DNA and proteins, forms the chromosomes, and stains with basic dyes. See also **euchromatin, heterochromatin.**
▸**ˌchromaˈtinic** ADJECTIVE ▸**ˈchromaˌtoid** ADJECTIVE

chromato- *or before a vowel* **chromat-** COMBINING FORM 1 indicating colour or coloured:

chromatophore. [2] indicating chromatin: *chromatolysis*.
▷HISTORY from Greek *khrōma, khrōmat-* colour

chromatogram ('krəʊmətəˌgræm, krəʊ'mæt-) NOUN [1] a column or strip of material containing constituents of a mixture separated by chromatography. [2] a graph showing the quantity of a substance leaving a chromatography column as a function of time.

chromatography (ˌkrəʊmə'tɒgrəfɪ) NOUN the technique of separating and analysing the components of a mixture of liquids or gases by selective adsorption in, for example, a column of powder (**column chromatography**) or on a strip of paper (**paper chromatography**). See also **gas chromatography**.
▸ **ˌchroma'tographer** NOUN ▸**chromatographic** (ˌkrəʊmətə'græfɪk) ADJECTIVE ▸ **ˌchromato'graphically** ADVERB

chromatology (ˌkrəʊmə'tɒlədʒɪ) NOUN another name for **chromatics**.

chromatolysis (ˌkrəʊmə'tɒlɪsɪs) NOUN *Cytology* the dissolution of stained material, such as chromatin in injured cells.

chromatophore ('krəʊmətəˌfɔː) NOUN [1] a cell in the skin of frogs, chameleons, etc., in which pigment is concentrated or dispersed, causing the animal to change colour. [2] another name for **chromoplast**.
▸ **ˌchromato'phoric** *or* **chromatophorous** (ˌkrəʊmə'tɒfərəs) ADJECTIVE

chrome (krəʊm) NOUN [1] **a** another word for **chromium**, esp when present in a pigment or dye. **b** (*as modifier*): *a chrome dye*. [2] anything plated with chromium, such as fittings on a car body. [3] a pigment or dye that contains chromium. ◆ VERB [4] to plate or be plated with chromium, usually by electroplating. [5] to treat or be treated with a chromium compound, as in dyeing or tanning.
▷HISTORY C19: via French from Greek *khrōma* colour

-chrome NOUN AND ADJECTIVE COMBINING FORM colour, coloured, or pigment: *monochrome*.
▷HISTORY from Greek *khrōma* colour

chrome alum NOUN a violet-red crystalline substance, used as a mordant in dyeing. Formula: $KCr(SO_4)_2.12H_2O$.

chrome dioxide NOUN another name for **chromium dioxide**.

chrome green NOUN [1] any green pigment made by mixing lead chromate with Prussian blue. [2] any green pigment containing chromic oxide.

chromel ('krəʊmɛl) NOUN a nickel-based alloy containing about 10 per cent chromium, used in heating elements.
▷HISTORY C20: from CHRO(MIUM) + ME(TA)L

chrome red NOUN any red pigment used in paints, consisting of a mixture of lead chromate and lead oxide; basic lead chromate.

chrome steel NOUN any of various hard rust-resistant steels containing chromium. Also called: **chromium steel**.

chrome tape NOUN magnetic recording tape coated with chrome dioxide.

chrome yellow NOUN any yellow pigment consisting of lead chromate mixed with lead sulphate.

chromic ('krəʊmɪk) ADJECTIVE [1] of or containing chromium in the trivalent state. [2] of or derived from chromic acid.

chromic acid NOUN an unstable dibasic oxidizing acid known only in solution and in the form of chromate salts. Formula: H_2CrO_4.

chrominance ('krəʊmɪnəns) NOUN [1] the quality of light that causes the sensation of colour. It is determined by comparison with a reference source of the same brightness and of known chromaticity. [2] the information that defines the colour (hue and saturation) of a television image, but not the brightness.
▷HISTORY C20: from CHROMO- + LUMINANCE

chromite ('krəʊmaɪt) NOUN [1] a brownish-black mineral consisting of a ferrous chromic oxide in cubic crystalline form, occurring principally in basic igneous rocks: the only commercial source of chromium and its compounds. Formula: $FeCr_2O_4$. [2] a salt of chromous acid.

chromium ('krəʊmɪəm) NOUN a hard grey metallic element that takes a high polish, occurring principally in chromite: used in steel alloys and electroplating to increase hardness and corrosion-resistance. Symbol: Cr; atomic no.: 24; atomic wt.: 51.9961; valency: 2, 3, or 6; relative density: 7.18–7.20; melting pt.: 1863±20°C; boiling pt.: 2672°C.
▷HISTORY C19: from New Latin, from French: CHROME

chromium dioxide NOUN a chemical compound used as a magnetic coating on cassette tapes; chromium(IV) oxide. Formula: CrO_2. Also called (not in technical usage): **chrome dioxide**.

chromium steel NOUN another name for **chrome steel**.

chromo ('krəʊməʊ) NOUN, *plural* **-mos**. short for **chromolithograph**.

chromo- *or before a vowel* **chrom-** COMBINING FORM [1] indicating colour, coloured, or pigment: *chromogen*. [2] indicating chromium: *chromyl*.
▷HISTORY from Greek *khrōma* colour

chromogen ('krəʊmədʒən) NOUN [1] a compound that forms coloured compounds on oxidation. [2] a substance that can be converted to a dye. [3] a bacterium that produces a pigment.

chromogenic (ˌkrəʊmə'dʒɛnɪk) ADJECTIVE [1] producing colour. [2] of or relating to a chromogen. [3] *Photog* involving the use of chromogens rather than silver halide during processing to produce the image: *chromogenic film*.

chromolithograph (ˌkrəʊməʊ'lɪθəˌgrɑːf, -ˌgræf) NOUN a picture produced by chromolithography.

chromolithography (ˌkrəʊməʊlɪ'θɒgrəfɪ) NOUN the process of making coloured prints by lithography.
▸ **ˌchromoli'thographer** NOUN ▸**chromolithographic** (ˌkrəʊməʊlɪθə'græfɪk) ADJECTIVE

chromomere ('krəʊməˌmɪə) NOUN *Cytology* any of the dense areas of chromatin along the length of a chromosome during the early stages of cell division.

chromonema (ˌkrəʊmə'niːmə) NOUN, *plural* **-mata** (-mətə). *Cytology* [1] the coiled mass of threads visible within a nucleus at the start of cell division. [2] a coiled chromatin thread within a single chromosome.
▷HISTORY C20: from CHROMO- + Greek *nēma* thread, yarn
▸ **ˌchromo'nemal, chromonematic** (ˌkrəʊməʊnɪ'mætɪk), *or* **ˌchromo'nemic** ADJECTIVE

chromophore ('krəʊməˌfɔː) NOUN a group of atoms in a chemical compound that are responsible for the colour of the compound.
▸ **ˌchromo'phoric** *or* **ˌchromo'phorous** ADJECTIVE

chromoplast ('krəʊməˌplæst) NOUN a coloured plastid in a plant cell, esp one containing carotenoids.

chromoprotein (ˌkrəʊməʊ'prəʊtiːn) NOUN any of a group of conjugated proteins, such as haemoglobin, in which the protein is joined to a coloured compound, such as a metal-containing porphyrin.

chromosome ('krəʊməˌsəʊm) NOUN any of the microscopic rod-shaped structures that appear in a cell nucleus during cell division, consisting of nucleoprotein arranged into units (genes) that are responsible for the transmission of hereditary characteristics. See also **homologous chromosomes**.
▸ **ˌchromo'somal** ADJECTIVE ▸ **ˌchromo'somally** ADVERB

chromosome band NOUN any of the transverse bands that appear on a chromosome after staining. The banding pattern is unique to each type of chromosome, allowing characterization.

chromosome map NOUN a graphic representation of the positions of genes on chromosomes, obtained by observation of chromosome bands or by determining the degree of linkage between genes. See also **genetic map**.
▸**chromosome mapping** NOUN

chromosome number NOUN the number of chromosomes present in each somatic cell, which is constant for any one species of plant or animal. In the reproductive cells this number is halved. See also **diploid** (sense 1), **haploid**.

chromosphere ('krəʊməˌsfɪə) NOUN a gaseous layer of the sun's atmosphere extending from the photosphere to the corona and visible during a total eclipse of the sun.
▸**chromospheric** (ˌkrəʊmə'sfɛrɪk) ADJECTIVE

chromous ('krəʊməs) ADJECTIVE of or containing chromium in the divalent state.

chromyl ('krəʊmɪl) NOUN (*modifier*) of, consisting of, or containing the divalent radical CrO_2.

Chron. *Bible* ABBREVIATION FOR Chronicles.

chronaxie *or* **chronaxy** ('krəʊnæksɪ) NOUN *Physiol* the minimum time required for excitation of a nerve or muscle when the stimulus is double the minimum (threshold) necessary to elicit a basic response. Compare **rheobase**.
▷HISTORY C20: from French, from CHRONO- + Greek *axia* worth, from *axios* worthy, of equal weight

chronic ('krɒnɪk) ADJECTIVE [1] continuing for a long time; constantly recurring. [2] (of a disease) developing slowly, or of long duration. Compare **acute** (sense 7). [3] inveterate; habitual: *a chronic smoker*. [4] *Informal* **a** very bad: *the play was chronic*. **b** very serious: *he left her in a chronic condition*.
▷HISTORY C15: from Latin *chronicus* relating to time, from Greek *khronikos*, from *khronos* time
▸ **'chronically** ADVERB ▸**chronicity** (krɒ'nɪsɪtɪ) NOUN

chronic fatigue syndrome NOUN another name for **myalgic encephalopathy**. Abbreviation: **CFS**.

chronicle ('krɒnɪkᵊl) NOUN [1] a record or register of events in chronological order. ◆ VERB [2] (*tr*) to record in or as if in a chronicle.
▷HISTORY C14: from Anglo-French *cronicle*, via Latin *chronica* (pl), from Greek *khronika* annals, from *khronikos* relating to time; see CHRONIC
▸ **'chronicler** NOUN

chronicle play NOUN a drama based on a historical subject.

Chronicles ('krɒnɪkᵊlz) NOUN (*functioning as singular*) either of two historical books (**I** and **II Chronicles**) of the Old Testament.

chrono- *or before a vowel* **chron-** COMBINING FORM indicating time: *chronology; chronometer*.
▷HISTORY from Greek *khronos* time

chronobiology (ˌkrɒnəbaɪ'ɒlədʒɪ, ˌkrəʊnə-) NOUN the branch of biology concerned with the periodicity occurring in living organisms. See also **biological clock, circadian**.
▸ **ˌchronobi'ologist** NOUN

chronogram ('krɒnəˌgræm, 'krəʊnə-) NOUN [1] a phrase or inscription in which letters such as M, C, X, L and V can be read as Roman numerals giving a date. [2] a record kept by a chronograph.
▸**chronogrammatic** (ˌkrɒnəʊgrə'mætɪk) *or* **ˌchronogram'matical** ADJECTIVE ▸ **ˌchronogram'matically** ADVERB

chronograph ('krɒnəˌgrɑːf, -ˌgræf, 'krəʊnə-) NOUN [1] an accurate instrument for recording small intervals of time. [2] any timepiece, esp a wristwatch designed for maximum accuracy.
▸**chronographer** (krə'nɒgrəfə) NOUN ▸**chronographic** (ˌkrɒnə'græfɪk) ADJECTIVE ▸ **ˌchrono'graphically** ADVERB

chronological (ˌkrɒnə'lɒdʒɪkᵊl, ˌkrəʊ-) *or* **chronologic** ADJECTIVE [1] (esp of a sequence of events) arranged in order of occurrence. [2] relating to or in accordance with chronology.
▸ **ˌchrono'logically** ADVERB

chronology (krə'nɒlədʒɪ) NOUN, *plural* **-gies**. [1] the determination of the proper sequence of past events. [2] the arrangement of dates, events, etc., in order of occurrence. [3] a table or list of events arranged in order of occurrence.
▸**chro'nologist** NOUN

chronometer (krə'nɒmɪtə) NOUN a timepiece designed to be accurate in all conditions of temperature, pressure, etc., used esp at sea.
▸**chronometric** (ˌkrɒnə'mɛtrɪk) *or* **ˌchrono'metrical** ADJECTIVE ▸ **ˌchrono'metrically** ADVERB

chronometry (krə'nɒmɪtrɪ) NOUN the science or technique of measuring time with extreme accuracy.

chronon ('krəʊnɒn) NOUN a unit of time equal to the time that a photon would take to traverse the diameter of an electron: about 10^{-24} seconds.

chronoscope ('krɒnəˌskəʊp, 'krəʊnə-) NOUN an instrument that registers small intervals of time on a dial, cathode-ray tube, etc.
▸**chronoscopic** (ˌkrɒnə'skɒpɪk, ˌkrəʊnə-) ADJECTIVE ▸ **ˌchrono'scopically** ADVERB

-chroous *or* **-chroic** ADJECTIVE COMBINING FORM coloured in a specified way: *isochroous.*
▷HISTORY from Greek *khrōs* skin, complexion, colour

chrysalid (ˈkrɪsəlɪd) NOUN [1] another name for **chrysalis.** ◆ ADJECTIVE *also* **chrysalidal** (krɪˈsælɪdᵊl). [2] of or relating to a chrysalis.

chrysalis (ˈkrɪsəlɪs) NOUN, *plural* **chrysalises** *or* **chrysalides** (krɪˈsælɪˌdiːz). [1] the obtect pupa of a moth or butterfly. [2] anything in the process of developing.
▷HISTORY C17: from Latin *chrȳsallis,* from Greek *khrusallis,* from *khrusos* gold, of Semitic origin; compare Hebrew *harūz* gold

chrysanthemum (krɪˈsænθəməm) NOUN [1] any widely cultivated plant of the genus *Chrysanthemum,* esp *C. morifolium* of China, having brightly coloured showy flower heads: family *Asteraceae* (composites). [2] any other plant of the genus *Chrysanthemum,* such as oxeye daisy.
▷HISTORY C16: from Latin: marigold, from Greek *khrusanthemon,* from *khrusos* gold + *anthemon* flower

chrysarobin (ˌkrɪsəˈrəʊbɪn) NOUN a tasteless odourless powder containing anthraquinone derivatives of araroba, formerly used medicinally to treat chronic skin conditions.
▷HISTORY C20: from CHRYSO- (referring to its golden colour) + ARAROBA + -IN

chryselephantine (ˌkrɪselɪˈfæntɪn) ADJECTIVE (of ancient Greek statues) made of or overlaid with gold and ivory.
▷HISTORY C19: from Greek *khruselephantinos,* from *khrusos* gold + *elephas* ivory; see ELEPHANT

chryso- *or before a vowel* **chrys-** COMBINING FORM indicating gold or the colour of gold: *chryselephantine; chrysolite.*
▷HISTORY from Greek *khrusos* gold

chrysoberyl (ˈkrɪsəˌberɪl) NOUN a rare very hard greenish-yellow mineral consisting of beryllium aluminate in orthorhombic crystalline form and occurring in coarse granite: used as a gemstone in the form of cat's eye and alexandrite. Formula: $BeAl_2O_4$.

chrysolite (ˈkrɪsəˌlaɪt) NOUN another name for **olivine.**
▸**chrysolitic** (ˌkrɪsəˈlɪtɪk) ADJECTIVE

chrysoprase (ˈkrɪsəˌpreɪz) NOUN an apple-green variety of chalcedony: a gemstone.
▷HISTORY C13 *crisopace,* from Old French, from Latin *chrȳsoprasus,* from Greek *khrusoprasos,* from CHRYSO- + *prason* leek

chrysotile (ˈkrɪsətɪl) NOUN a green, grey, or white fibrous mineral, a variety of serpentine, that is an important source of commercial asbestos. Formula: $Mg_3Si_2O_5(OH)_4$.
▷HISTORY C20: from CHRYSO- + Greek *tilos* something plucked, shred, thread, from *tillein* to pluck

chthonian (ˈθəʊnɪən) *or* **chthonic** (ˈθɒnɪk) ADJECTIVE of or relating to the underworld.
▷HISTORY C19: from Greek *khthonios* in or under the earth, from *khthōn* earth

chub (tʃʌb) NOUN, *plural* **chub** *or* **chubs.** [1] a common European freshwater cyprinid game fish, *Leuciscus* (or *Squalius*) *cephalus,* having a cylindrical dark greenish body. [2] any of various North American fishes, esp certain whitefishes and minnows.
▷HISTORY C15: of unknown origin

Chubb (tʃʌb) NOUN *Trademark* a type of patent lock containing a device that sets the bolt immovably if the lock is picked.

chubby (ˈtʃʌbɪ) ADJECTIVE **-bier, -biest.** (esp of the human form) plump and round.
▷HISTORY C17: perhaps from CHUB, with reference to the plump shape of the fish
▸ˈ**chubbiness** NOUN

Chu Chiang (ˈtʃuː ˈkjæŋ, kaɪˈæŋ) NOUN a variant transliteration of the Chinese name for the **Zhu Jiang.**

chuck¹ (tʃʌk) VERB (*mainly tr*) [1] *Informal* to throw. [2] to pat affectionately, esp under the chin. [3] (sometimes foll by *in* or *up*) *Informal* to give up; reject: *he chucked up his job; she chucked her boyfriend.* [4] (*intr;* usually foll by *up*) *Slang, chiefly US* to vomit. [5] **chuck off at.** *Austral* and *NZ informal* to abuse or make fun of. ◆ NOUN [6] a throw or toss. [7] a playful pat under the chin. [8] **the chuck.** *Informal* dismissal. ◆ See also **chuck in, chuck out.**
▷HISTORY C16: of unknown origin

chuck² (tʃʌk) NOUN [1] Also called: **chuck steak.** a cut of beef extending from the neck to the shoulder blade. [2] **a** Also called: **three jaw chuck.** a device that holds a workpiece in a lathe or tool in a drill, having a number of adjustable jaws geared to move in unison to centralize the workpiece or tool. **b** Also called: **four jaw chuck, independent jaw chuck.** a similar device having independently adjustable jaws for holding an unsymmetrical workpiece.
▷HISTORY C17: variant of CHOCK

chuck³ (tʃʌk) VERB [1] (*intr*) a less common word for **cluck** (sense 2). ◆ NOUN [2] a clucking sound. [3] a term of endearment.
▷HISTORY C14 *chukken* to cluck, of imitative origin

chuck⁴ (tʃʌk) NOUN *Canadian W coast* [1] a large body of water. [2] short for **saltchuck** (the sea).
▷HISTORY C19: from Chinook Jargon, from Nootka *chauk*

chucker (ˈtʃʌkə) NOUN [1] a person who throws something. [2] *Cricket, informal* a bowler whose arm action is illegal.

chuck-full ADJECTIVE a less common spelling of **chock-full.**

chuckie (ˈtʃʌkɪ) NOUN *Scot and NZ* a small stone.
▷HISTORY probably from CHUCK¹

chuck in VERB (*adverb*) *Informal* [1] (*tr*) *Brit* to abandon or give up: *ready to chuck in a hopeless attempt.* [2] (*intr*) *Austral* to contribute to the cost of something.

chuckle (ˈtʃʌkᵊl) VERB (*intr*) [1] to laugh softly or to oneself. [2] (of animals, esp hens) to make a clucking sound. ◆ NOUN [3] a partly suppressed laugh.
▷HISTORY C16: probably from CHUCK³
▸ˈ**chuckler** NOUN ▸ˈ**chucklingly** ADVERB

chucklehead (ˈtʃʌkᵊlˌhed) NOUN *Informal* a stupid person; blockhead; dolt.
▸ˈ**chuckleˌheaded** ADJECTIVE ▸ˈ**chuckleˌheadedness** NOUN

chuck out VERB (*tr, adverb;* often foll by *of*) *Informal* to eject forcibly (from); throw out (of): *he was chucked out of the lobby.*

chuck wagon NOUN a wagon carrying provisions and cooking utensils for men, such as cowboys, who work in the open.
▷HISTORY C19: perhaps from CHUCK² (beef, food)

chuckwalla (ˈtʃʌkˌwɒlə) NOUN a lizard, *Sauromalus obesus,* that has an inflatable body and inhabits desert regions of the southwestern US: family *Iguanidae* (iguanas).
▷HISTORY from Mexican Spanish *chacahuala,* from Shoshonean *tcaxxwal*

chuck-will's-widow NOUN a large North American nightjar, *Caprimulgus carolinensis,* similar to the whippoorwill.

chuddar, chudder, chuddah, *or* **chador** (ˈtʃʌdə) NOUN a large shawl or veil worn by Muslim or Hindu women that covers them from head to foot.
▷HISTORY from Hindi *caddar,* from Persian *chaddar*

chuddies (ˈtʃʌdɪz) PLURAL NOUN *Indian informal* underpants.
▷HISTORY C20: possibly from CHUDDAR

Chudskoye Ozero (*Russian* ˈtʃutskəjɪ ˈɔzɪrə) NOUN the Russian name for Lake **Peipus.**

chufa (ˈtʃuːfə) NOUN a sedge, *Cyperus esculentus,* of warm regions of the Old World, with nutlike edible tubers.
▷HISTORY C19: from Old Spanish: a morsel, joke, from *chufar* to joke, from *chuflar* to deride, ultimately from Latin *sībilāre* to whistle

chuff¹ (tʃʌf) NOUN [1] a puffing sound of or as if of a steam engine. ◆ VERB [2] (*intr*) to move while emitting such sounds: *the train chuffed on its way.*
▷HISTORY C20: of imitative origin

chuff² (tʃʌf) NOUN *Dialect* a boor; churl; sullen fellow.
▷HISTORY C17: from obsolete *chuff* (noun) fat cheek, of obscure origin

chuff³ (tʃʌf) VERB (*tr; usually passive*) *Brit slang* to please or delight: *he was chuffed by his pay rise.*
▷HISTORY probably from *chuff* (adjective) pleased, happy (earlier: chubby), from C16 *chuff* (obsolete noun) a fat cheek, of unknown origin

chuffed (tʃʌft) ADJECTIVE *Brit slang* pleased or delighted: *none too chuffed.*

chuffing (ˈtʃʌfɪŋ) ADJECTIVE (*prenominal*), ADVERB *Brit slang* (intensifier): *that is the chuffing noise we hear: chuffing marvellous.*
▷HISTORY C20: from N English *chuff,* a euphemism for *fuck*

chug (tʃʌg) NOUN [1] a short dull sound, esp one that is rapidly repeated, such as that made by an engine. ◆ VERB **chugs, chugging, chugged.** [2] (*intr*) (of an engine, etc.) to operate while making such sounds.
▷HISTORY C19: of imitative origin

chukar (tʃʌˈkɑː) NOUN a common Indian partridge, *Alectoris chukar* (or *graeca*), having red legs and bill and a black-barred sandy plumage.
▷HISTORY from Hindi *cakor,* from Sanskrit *cakora,* probably of imitative origin

Chukchi *or* **Chukchee** (ˈtʃʊktʃɪ) NOUN [1] (*plural* **-chi, -chis** *or* **-chee, -chees**) a member of a people of the Chukchi Peninsula. [2] the language of this people, related only to some of the smaller aboriginal languages of Siberia.

Chukchi Peninsula NOUN a peninsula in the extreme NE of Russia, in NE Siberia: mainly tundra. Also called: **Chukots Peninsula** (ˈtʃʊkɒts).

Chukchi Sea NOUN part of the Arctic Ocean, north of the Bering Strait between Asia and North America. Russian name: **Chukotskoye More** (tʃuˈkɔtskəji ˈmɔrji). Also called: **Chukots Sea** (ˈtʃʊkɒts).

Chu Kiang (ˈtʃuː ˈkjæŋ, kaɪˈæŋ) NOUN a variant transliteration of the Chinese name for the **Zhu Jiang.**

chukka *or US* **chukker** (ˈtʃʌkə) NOUN *Polo* a period of continuous play, generally lasting 7½ minutes.
▷HISTORY C20: from Hindi *cakkar,* from Sanskrit *cakra* wheel, circle

chukka boot *or* **chukka** NOUN an ankle-high boot made of suede or rubber and worn for playing polo.

chum¹ (tʃʌm) NOUN [1] *Informal* a close friend. ◆ VERB **chums, chumming, chummed.** [2] (*intr;* usually foll by *up with*) to be or become an intimate friend (of). [3] (*tr*) *Scot* to accompany: *If you like I'll chum you home.*
▷HISTORY C17 (meaning: a person sharing rooms with another): probably shortened from *chamber fellow,* originally student slang (Oxford); compare CRONY

chum² (tʃʌm) NOUN *Angling chiefly US and Canadian* chopped fish, meal, etc., used as groundbait.
▷HISTORY C19: origin uncertain

chum³ (tʃʊm) NOUN a Pacific salmon, *Oncorhynchus keta.*
▷HISTORY from Chinook Jargon *tsum* spots, marks, from Chinook

chumash *Hebrew* (xuˈmaʃ; *Yiddish* ˈxuməʃ) NOUN *Judaism* a printed book containing one of the Five Books of Moses.
▷HISTORY literally: a fifth (part of the Torah)

chummy (ˈtʃʌmɪ) ADJECTIVE **-mier, -miest.** *Informal* friendly.
▸ˈ**chummily** ADVERB ▸ˈ**chumminess** NOUN

chump¹ (tʃʌmp) NOUN [1] *Informal* a stupid person: *what sort of a chump would put Adam in charge?.* [2] a thick heavy block of wood. [3] **a** the thick blunt end of anything, esp of a piece of meat. **b** (*as modifier*): *a chump chop.* [4] *Brit slang* the head (esp in the phrase **off one's chump**).
▷HISTORY C18: perhaps a blend of CHUNK and LUMP¹

chump² (tʃʌmp) VERB a less common word for **chomp.**

chumping (ˈtʃʌmpɪŋ) NOUN *Yorkshire dialect* collecting wood for bonfires on Guy Fawkes Day.
▷HISTORY from CHUMP¹ (sense 2)

chunder (ˈtʃʌndə) *Slang, chiefly Austral* ◆ VERB (*intr*) [1] to vomit. ◆ NOUN [2] vomit.
▷HISTORY C20: of uncertain origin

chunderous (ˈtʃʌndərəs) ADJECTIVE *Austral slang* nauseating.

Chungjin (ˈtʃʌŋˈdʒɪn) NOUN a variant spelling of **Chŏngjin.**

Chungking (ˈtʃʊŋˈkɪŋ, ˈtʃʌŋ-) *or* **Ch'ung-ch'ing**

('tʃuŋ'tʃɪŋ, 'tʃʌŋ-) NOUN a variant transliteration of the Chinese name for **Chongqing.**

chunk (tʃʌŋk) NOUN [1] a thick solid piece, as of meat, wood, etc. [2] a considerable amount.
▷HISTORY C17: variant of CHUCK[2]

chunking ('tʃʌŋkɪŋ) NOUN *Psychol* the grouping together of a number of items by the mind, after which they can be remembered as a single item, such as a word or a musical phrase.

chunky ('tʃʌŋkɪ) ADJECTIVE **chunkier, chunkiest.** [1] thick and short. [2] consisting of or containing thick pieces: *chunky dog food.* [3] *Chiefly Brit* (of clothes, esp knitwear) made of thick bulky material.
▸'**chunkily** ADVERB ▸'**chunkiness** NOUN

Chunnel ('tʃʌnᵊl) NOUN *Informal* a rail tunnel beneath the English Channel, linking England and France, opened in 1994.
▷HISTORY C20: from CH(ANNEL) + (T)UNNEL

chunter ('tʃʌntə) VERB (*intr; often foll by on*) *Brit informal* to mutter or grumble incessantly in a meaningless fashion.
▷HISTORY C16: probably of imitative origin

chupatti *or* **chupatty** (tʃə'pætɪ, -'pʌtɪ, -'pɑːtɪ) NOUN, *plural* **-patti, -pattis,** *or* **-patties.** variant spellings of **chapati.**

chuppah *or* **huppah** ('hʊpə) NOUN *Judaism* [1] the canopy under which a marriage is performed. [2] the wedding ceremony as distinct from the celebration.
▷HISTORY from Hebrew

Chuquisaca (*Spanish* tʃuki'saka) NOUN the former name (until 1839) of **Sucre**[1].

Chur (*German* kuːr) NOUN a city in E Switzerland, capital of Grisons canton. Pop.: 30 236 (1990). Ancient name: **Curia Rhaetorum** ('kuːrɪə riː'təʊrəm, 'kjuː-). French name: **Coire.**

Churban *or* ***Hurban*** *Hebrew* (xuː'rbɒn; *Yiddish* 'xuːrbᵊn) NOUN *Judaism* [1] the destruction of the Temple in Jerusalem, first by the Babylonians in 587 B.C. and again by the Romans in 70 A.D. [2] another name for **holocaust** (sense 2).
▷HISTORY literally: destruction

church (tʃɜːtʃ) NOUN [1] a building designed for public forms of worship, esp Christian worship. [2] an occasion of public worship. [3] the clergy as distinguished from the laity. [4] (*usually capital*) institutionalized forms of religion as a political or social force: *conflict between Church and State.* [5] (*usually capital*) the collective body of all Christians. [6] (*often capital*) a particular Christian denomination or group of Christian believers. [7] (*often capital*) the Christian religion. [8] (in Britain) the practices or doctrines of the Church of England and similar denominations. Compare **chapel** (sense 4b). Related adjective: **ecclesiastical.** ◆ VERB (*tr*) [9] *Church of England* to bring (someone, esp a woman after childbirth) to church for special ceremonies. [10] *US* to impose church discipline upon.
▷HISTORY Old English *cirice,* from Late Greek *kurikon,* from Greek *kuriakon* (*dōma*) the Lord's (house), from *kuriakos* of the master, from *kurios* master, from *kuros* power

Church Army NOUN a voluntary Anglican organization founded in 1882 to assist the parish clergy.

Church Commissioners PLURAL NOUN *Brit* a group of representatives of Church and State that administers the endowments and property of the Church of England.

churchgoer ('tʃɜːtʃˌgəʊə) NOUN [1] a person who attends church regularly. [2] an adherent of an established Church in contrast to a Nonconformist.
▸'**church͵going** NOUN, ADJECTIVE

Churchill ('tʃɜːtʃɪl) NOUN [1] a river in E Canada, rising in SE Labrador and flowing north and southeast over Churchill Falls, then east to the Atlantic. Length: about 1000 km (600 miles). Former name: **Hamilton River.** [2] a river in central Canada, rising in NW Saskatchewan and flowing east through several lakes to Hudson Bay. Length: about 1600 km (1000 miles).

Churchill Falls PLURAL NOUN a waterfall in E Canada, in SW Labrador on the Churchill River: site of one of the largest hydroelectric power projects in the world. Height: 75 m (245 ft.). Former name: **Grand Falls.**

church key NOUN *US* a device with a triangular point at one end for making holes in the tops of cans.

churchly ('tʃɜːtʃlɪ) ADJECTIVE appropriate to, associated with, or suggestive of church life and customs.
▸'**churchliness** NOUN

churchman ('tʃɜːtʃmən) NOUN, *plural* **-men.** [1] a clergyman. [2] a male practising member of a church.
▸'**churchmanly** ADJECTIVE ▸'**churchman͵ship** NOUN

church mode NOUN *Music* a less common name for **mode** (sense 3a).

Church of Christ, Scientist NOUN the official name for the **Christian Scientists.**

Church of England NOUN the reformed established state Church in England, Catholic in order and basic doctrine, with the Sovereign as its temporal head.

Church of Jesus Christ of Latter-Day Saints NOUN the official name for the Mormon Church.

Church of Rome NOUN another name for the **Roman Catholic Church.**

Church of Scotland NOUN the established church in Scotland, Calvinist in doctrine and Presbyterian in constitution.

church parade NOUN a parade by servicemen or members of a uniformed organization for the purposes of attending religious services.

Church Slavonic *or* **Slavic** NOUN Old Church Slavonic, esp as preserved in the liturgical use of the Orthodox church.

church text NOUN a heavy typeface in Gothic style.

churchwarden (ˌtʃɜːtʃ'wɔːdᵊn) NOUN [1] *Church of England, Episcopal Church* one of two assistants of a parish priest who administer the secular affairs of the church. [2] a long-stemmed tobacco pipe made of clay.

churchwoman ('tʃɜːtʃˌwʊmən) NOUN, *plural* **-women.** a female practising member of a church.

churchy ('tʃɜːtʃɪ) ADJECTIVE **churchier, churchiest.** [1] like a church, church service, etc. [2] excessively religious.

churchyard ('tʃɜːtʃˌjɑːd) NOUN the grounds surrounding a church, usually used as a graveyard.

churchyard beetle NOUN a blackish nocturnal ground beetle, *Blaps mucronata,* found in cellars and similar places.

churidars ('tʃuːrɪˌdɑːz) PLURAL NOUN long tight-fitting trousers, worn by Indian men and women. Also called: **churidar pyjamas.**
▷HISTORY from Hindi

churinga (tʃə'rɪŋgə) NOUN, *plural* **-ga** *or* **-gas.** a sacred amulet of the native Australians.
▷HISTORY from a native Australian language

churl (tʃɜːl) NOUN [1] a surly ill-bred person. [2] *Archaic* a farm labourer. [3] a variant spelling of **ceorl.**
▷HISTORY Old English *ceorl;* related to Old Norse *karl,* Middle Low German *kerle,*Greek *gerōn* old man

churlish ('tʃɜːlɪʃ) ADJECTIVE [1] rude or surly. [2] of or relating to peasants. [3] miserly.
▸'**churlishly** ADVERB ▸'**churlishness** NOUN

churn (tʃɜːn) NOUN [1] *Brit* a large container for milk. [2] a vessel or machine in which cream or whole milk is vigorously agitated to produce butter. [3] any similar device. ◆ VERB [4] the number of customers who switch from one supplier to another. [5] **a** to stir or agitate (milk or cream) in order to make butter. **b** to make (butter) by this process. [6] (sometimes foll by *up*) to move or cause to move with agitation: *ideas churned in his head.* [7] (of a bank, broker, etc.) to encourage an investor or policyholder to change investments, endowment policies, etc., to increase commissions at the client's expense. [8] (of a government) to pay benefits to a wide category of people and claw it back by taxation from the well off. [9] to promote the turnover of existing subscribers leasing, and new subscribers joining, a cable television system or mobile phone company.
▷HISTORY Old English *ciern;* related to Old Norse *kjarni,* Middle Low German *kerne* churn, German dialect *Kern* cream
▸'**churner** NOUN

churning ('tʃɜːnɪŋ) NOUN [1] the quantity of butter churned at any one time. [2] the act, process, or effect of someone or something that churns.

churn out VERB (*tr, adverb*) *Informal* [1] to produce (something) at a rapid rate: *to churn out ideas.* [2] to perform (something) mechanically: *to churn out a song.*

churr (tʃɜː) VERB, NOUN a variant spelling of **chirr.**

churrigueresque (ˌtʃʊərɪgə'rɛsk) *or* **churrigueresco** ADJECTIVE of or relating to a style of baroque architecture of Spain in the late 17th and early 18th centuries.
▷HISTORY C19: from Spanish *churrigueresco* in the style of José *Churriguera* (1650–1725), Spanish architect and sculptor

chute[1] (ʃuːt) NOUN [1] an inclined channel or vertical passage down which water, parcels, coal, etc., may be dropped. [2] a steep slope, used as a slide as for toboggans. [3] a slide into a swimming pool. [4] a narrow passageway through which animals file for branding, spraying, etc. [5] a rapid or waterfall.
▷HISTORY C19: from Old French *cheoite,* feminine past participle of *cheoir* to fall, from Latin *cadere;* in some senses, a variant spelling of SHOOT

chute[2] (ʃuːt) NOUN, VERB *Informal* short for **parachute.**
▸'**chutist** NOUN

chutney ('tʃʌtnɪ) NOUN [1] a pickle of Indian origin, made from fruit, vinegar, spices, sugar, etc.: *mango chutney.* [2] a type of music popular in the Caribbean Asian community, much influenced by calypso.
▷HISTORY C19: from Hindi *catni,* of uncertain origin

chutzpah *or* **hutzpah** ('xʊtspə) NOUN *Informal* shameless audacity; impudence.
▷HISTORY C20: from Yiddish

Chuvash (tʃʊ'vɑːʃ) NOUN [1] (*plural* **-vash** *or* **-vashes**) a member of a Mongoloid people of Russia, living chiefly in the middle Volga region. [2] the language of this people, generally classed within the Turkic branch of the Altaic family.

Chuvash Republic NOUN a constituent republic of W central Russia, in the middle Volga valley: generally low-lying with undulating plains and large areas of forest. Capital: Cheboksary. Pop.: 1 357 000 (2000 est.). Area: 18 300 sq. km (7064 sq. miles). Also called: **Chuvashia** (tʃuː'vɑːʃɪə).

chyack ('tʃaɪæk) VERB a variant spelling of **chiack.**

chyle (kaɪl) NOUN a milky fluid composed of lymph and emulsified fat globules, formed in the small intestine during digestion.
▷HISTORY C17: from Late Latin *chȳlus,* from Greek *khulos* juice pressed from a plant; related to Greek *khein* to pour
▸**chylaceous** (kaɪ'leɪʃəs) *or* '**chylous** ADJECTIVE

chylomicron (ˌkaɪləʊ'maɪkrɒn) NOUN *Biochem* a minute droplet of fat, found in blood and chyle, that is the form in which dietary fat is carried in these fluids.

chyme (kaɪm) NOUN the thick fluid mass of partially digested food that leaves the stomach.
▷HISTORY C17: from Late Latin *chȳmus,* from Greek *khumos* juice; compare CHYLE
▸'**chymous** ADJECTIVE

chymosin ('kaɪməsɪn) NOUN another name for **rennin.**
▷HISTORY C20: from CHYME + -OSE[2] + -IN

chymotrypsin (ˌkaɪməʊ'trɪpsɪn) NOUN a powerful proteolytic enzyme secreted from the pancreas in the form of chymotrypsinogen, being converted to the active form by trypsin.
▷HISTORY C20: from CHYME + TRYPSIN

chymotrypsinogen (ˌkaɪməʊtrɪp'sɪnədʒɪn) NOUN the inactive precursor of chymotrypsin.
▷HISTORY C20: from CHYMOTRYPSIN + -GEN

chypre *French* (ʃiprə) NOUN a perfume made from sandalwood.
▷HISTORY literally: Cyprus, where it perhaps originated

ci THE INTERNET DOMAIN NAME FOR Côte d'Ivoire.

Ci SYMBOL FOR curie.

CI [1] ABBREVIATION FOR Channel Islands. ◆ [2] INTERNATIONAL CAR REGISTRATION FOR Côte d'Ivoire.

CIA ABBREVIATION FOR Central Intelligence Agency; a

federal US bureau created in 1947 to coordinate and conduct espionage and intelligence activities.

ciabatta (tʃəˈbætə) NOUN a type of open-textured bread made with olive oil.
▷HISTORY C20: from Italian, literally: slipper

ciao *Italian* (tʃau) SENTENCE SUBSTITUTE an informal word for **hello** or **goodbye.**

CIB (in New Zealand) ABBREVIATION FOR Criminal Investigation Branch (of New Zealand police).

ciborium (sɪˈbɔːrɪəm) NOUN, *plural* **-ria** (-rɪə). *Christianity* [1] a goblet-shaped lidded vessel used to hold consecrated wafers in Holy Communion. [2] a freestanding canopy fixed over an altar and supported by four pillars.
▷HISTORY C17: from Medieval Latin, from Latin: drinking cup, from Greek *kibōrion* cup-shaped seed vessel of the Egyptian lotus, hence, a cup

CICA (in Britain) ABBREVIATION FOR Criminal Injuries Compensation Authority.

cicada (sɪˈkɑːdə) *or* **cicala** NOUN, *plural* **-das, -dae** (-diː) *or* **-las, -le** (-leɪ). any large broad insect of the homopterous family *Cicadidae,* most common in warm regions. Cicadas have membranous wings and the males produce a high-pitched drone by vibration of a pair of drumlike abdominal organs.
▷HISTORY C19: from Latin

cicala (sɪˈkɑːlə; *Italian* tʃiˈkala) NOUN, *plural* **-las** *or* **-le** (-leɪ; *Italian* -le). another name for **cicada.**
▷HISTORY C19: from Italian, from Latin: CICADA

cicatricle (ˈsɪkəˌtrɪkᵊl) NOUN [1] *Zoology* the blastoderm in the egg of a bird. [2] *Biology* any small scar or mark.
▷HISTORY C17: from Latin *cicātrīcula* a little scar, from CICATRIX

cicatrix (ˈsɪkətrɪks) NOUN, *plural* **cicatrices** (ˌsɪkəˈtraɪsiːz). [1] the tissue that forms in a wound during healing; scar. [2] a scar on a plant indicating the former point of attachment of a part, esp a leaf.
▷HISTORY C17: from Latin: scar, of obscure origin
▸**cicatricial** (ˌsɪkəˈtrɪʃəl) ADJECTIVE ▸**cicatricose** (sɪˈkætrɪˌkəʊs, ˈsɪkə-) ADJECTIVE

cicatrize *or* **cicatrise** (ˈsɪkəˌtraɪz) VERB (of a wound or defect in tissue) to close or be closed by scar formation; heal.
▸ˌ**cicaˈtrizant** *or* ˌ**cicaˈtrisant** ADJECTIVE ▸ˌ**cicatriˈzation** *or* ˌ**cicatriˈsation** NOUN ▸ˈ**ciсaˌtrizer** *or* ˈ**cicaˌtriser** NOUN

cicely (ˈsɪsəlɪ) NOUN, *plural* **-lies.** short for **sweet cicely.**
▷HISTORY C16: from Latin *seselis,* from Greek, of obscure origin; influenced in spelling by the English proper name *Cicely*

cicero (ˈsɪsəˌrəʊ) NOUN, *plural* **-ros.** a measure for type that is somewhat larger than the pica.
▷HISTORY C19: from its first being used in a 15th-century edition of the writings of Marcus Tullius *Cicero* (106–43 B.C.), the Roman consul, orator, and writer

cicerone (ˌsɪsəˈrəʊnɪ, ˌtʃɪtʃ-) NOUN, *plural* **-nes** *or* **-ni** (-nɪ). a person who conducts and informs sightseers.
▷HISTORY C18: from Italian: antiquarian scholar, guide, after Marcus Tullius Cicero (106–43 B.C.), Roman consul, orator, and writer, alluding to the eloquence and erudition of these men

Ciceronian (ˌsɪsəˈrəʊnɪən) ADJECTIVE [1] of or resembling Marcus Tullius Cicero (106–43 B.C.), Roman consul, orator, and writer, or his rhetorical style; eloquent. [2] (of literary style) characterized by the use of antithesis and long periods.

cichlid (ˈsɪklɪd) NOUN [1] any tropical freshwater percoid fish of the family *Cichlidae,* which includes the mouthbrooders. Cichlids are popular aquarium fishes. ◆ ADJECTIVE [2] of, relating to, or belonging to the *Cichlidae.*
▷HISTORY C19: from New Latin *Cichlidae,* ultimately from Greek *kikhlē* a sea fish
▸ˈ**cichloid** ADJECTIVE

cicisbeo *Italian* (tʃitʃizˈbɛːo) NOUN, *plural* **-bei** (-ˈbɛːi). the escort or lover of a married woman, esp in 18th-century Italy.
▷HISTORY C18: Italian, of uncertain origin

ciclosporin *or* **cyclosporin** (ˌsaɪkləʊˈspɔːrɪn) NOUN a drug extracted from a fungus and used after organ transplantation to suppress the body's immune mechanisms, and so prevent rejection of an organ.

CID (in Britain) ABBREVIATION FOR Criminal Investigation Department; the detective division of a police force.

-cide NOUN COMBINING FORM [1] indicating a person or thing that kills: *insecticide.* [2] indicating a killing; murder: *homicide.*
▷HISTORY from Latin *-cīda* (agent), *-cīdium* (act), from *caedere* to kill
▸**-cidal** ADJECTIVE COMBINING FORM

cider *or* **cyder** (ˈsaɪdə) NOUN [1] Also called (US): **hard cider.** an alcoholic drink made from the fermented juice of apples. [2] Also called: **sweet cider.** *US and Canadian* an unfermented drink made from apple juice.
▷HISTORY C14: from Old French *cisdre,* via Medieval Latin, from Late Greek *sikera* strong drink, from Hebrew *shēkhār*

ci-devant *French* (sidəvɑ̃) ADJECTIVE (esp of an office-holder) former; recent.
▷HISTORY literally: heretofore

Cie ABBREVIATION FOR compagnie.
▷HISTORY French: company

CIE ABBREVIATION FOR: [1] Commission Internationale de l'Éclairage. [2] Companion of the Indian Empire. [3] (in the Irish Republic) Coras Iompair Eireann.
▷HISTORY (for sense 2) French: International Lighting Commission; (for sense 3) Irish Gaelic: Transport Organization of Ireland

Cienfuegos (*Spanish* θjenˈfueɣos) NOUN a port in S Cuba, on **Cienfuegos Bay.** Pop.: 132 038 (1994 est.).

c.i.f. *or* **CIF** ABBREVIATION FOR cost, insurance, and freight (included in the price quoted).

c.i.f.c.i. ABBREVIATION FOR cost, insurance, freight, commission, and interest (included in the price quoted).

CIFE (in Britain) ABBREVIATION FOR Colleges and Institutes for Further Education.

cig (sɪg) *or* **ciggy** (ˈsɪgɪ) NOUN, *plural* **cigs** *or* **ciggies.** *Informal* a cigarette.

cigar (sɪˈgɑː) NOUN a cylindrical roll of cured tobacco leaves, for smoking.
▷HISTORY C18: from Spanish *cigarro,* perhaps from Mayan *sicar* to smoke

cigarette *or sometimes US* **cigaret** (ˌsɪgəˈrɛt) NOUN a short tightly rolled cylinder of tobacco, wrapped in thin paper and often having a filter tip, for smoking. Shortened forms: **cig, ciggy.**
▷HISTORY C19: from French, literally: a little CIGAR

cigarette card NOUN a small picture card, formerly given away with cigarettes, now collected as a hobby.

cigarette end NOUN the part of a cigarette that is held in the mouth and that remains unsmoked after it is finished.

cigarette holder NOUN a mouthpiece of wood, ivory, etc., used for holding a cigarette while it is smoked.

cigarette lighter NOUN See **lighter**[1].

cigarette paper NOUN a piece of thin paper rolled around tobacco to form a cigarette.

cigarillo (ˌsɪgəˈrɪləʊ) NOUN, *plural* **-los.** a small cigar often only slightly larger than a cigarette.

CIGS (formerly, in Britain) ABBREVIATION FOR Chief of the Imperial General Staff.

cilantro (sɪˈlæntrəʊ) NOUN the US and Canadian word for **coriander.**
▷HISTORY C20: Spanish

cilia (ˈsɪlɪə) NOUN the plural of **cilium.**

ciliary (ˈsɪlɪərɪ) ADJECTIVE [1] of or relating to cilia. [2] of or relating to the ciliary body.

ciliary body NOUN the part of the vascular tunic of the eye that connects the choroid with the iris.

ciliate (ˈsɪlɪɪt, -eɪt) ADJECTIVE [1] Also: ˈ**ciliˌated.** possessing or relating to cilia: *a ciliate epithelium.* [2] of or relating to protozoans of the phylum *Ciliophora,* which have an outer layer of cilia. ◆ NOUN [3] a protozoan of the phylum *Ciliophora.*
▸ˌ**ciliˈation** NOUN

cilice (ˈsɪlɪs) NOUN a haircloth fabric or garment.
▷HISTORY Old English *cilic,* from Latin *cilicium* shirt made of Cilician goats' hair, from Greek *kilikion,* from *Kilikia* CILICIA

Cilicia (sɪˈlɪʃɪə) NOUN an ancient region and former kingdom of SE Asia Minor, between the Taurus Mountains and the Mediterranean: corresponds to the region around present-day Adana.

Cilician (sɪˈlɪʃɪən) ADJECTIVE [1] of or relating to Cilicia (an ancient region of SE Asia Minor) or its inhabitants. ◆ NOUN [2] a native or inhabitant of Cilicia.

Cilician Gates PLURAL NOUN a pass in S Turkey, over the Taurus Mountains. Turkish name: **Gülek Bogaz.**

ciliolate (ˈsɪlɪəlɪt, -ˌleɪt) ADJECTIVE covered with minute hairs, as some plants.
▷HISTORY C19: from New Latin *ciliolum,* diminutive of CILIUM

cilium (ˈsɪlɪəm) NOUN, *plural* **cilia** (ˈsɪlɪə). [1] any of the short thread-like projections on the surface of a cell, organism, etc., whose rhythmic beating causes movement of the organism or of the surrounding fluid. [2] the technical name for **eyelash.**
▷HISTORY C18: New Latin, from Latin: (lower) eyelid, eyelash

cill (sɪl) NOUN *Brit* a variant spelling (used in the building industry) for **sill** (senses 1–4).

CIM ABBREVIATION FOR: [1] computer input on microfilm. [2] computer integrated manufacture.

cimbalom *or* **cymbalom** (ˈtsɪmbələm) NOUN a type of dulcimer, esp of Hungary. See **dulcimer** (sense 1).
▷HISTORY C19: Hungarian, from Italian *cembalo;* see CEMBALO

Cimbri (ˈsɪmbriː, ˈkɪm-) PLURAL NOUN a Germanic people from N Jutland who migrated southwards in the 2nd century B.C.: annihilated by Marius in the Po valley (101 B.C.).
▸**Cimbrian** (ˈsɪmbrɪən) NOUN, ADJECTIVE ▸ˈ**Cimbric** ADJECTIVE

Ciment Fondu (ˈsiːmɒŋ fɒnˈduː; *French* simɑ̃ fɔ̃dy) NOUN *Trademark* a type of quick-hardening refractory cement having a high alumina content. Also called: **aluminous cement.**

cimetidine (saɪˈmɛtɪdiːn) NOUN a drug used to suppress the formation of acid by the stomach and so to encourage the healing of gastric and duodenal ulcers. Formula: $C_{10}H_{16}$-N_6S.

cimex (ˈsaɪmɛks) NOUN, *plural* **cimices** (ˈsɪmɪˌsiːz). any of the heteropterous insects of the genus *Cimex,* esp the bedbug.
▷HISTORY C16: from Latin: bug

Cimmerian (sɪˈmɪərɪən) ADJECTIVE [1] (*sometimes not capital*) very dark; gloomy. ◆ NOUN [2] *Greek myth* one of a people who lived in a land of darkness at the edge of the world.

C in C *or* **C.-in-C.** *Military* ABBREVIATION FOR Commander in Chief.

cinch[1] (sɪntʃ) NOUN [1] *Slang* an easy task. [2] *Slang* a certainty. [3] a US and Canadian name for **girth** (sense 3). [4] *Informal* a firm grip. ◆ VERB [5] (often foll by *up*) *US and Canadian* to fasten a girth around (a horse). [6] *(tr) Informal* to make sure of. [7] *(tr) Informal* to get a firm grip on.
▷HISTORY C19: from Spanish *cincha* saddle girth, from Latin *cingula* girdle, from *cingere* to encircle

cinch[2] (sɪntʃ) NOUN a card game in which the five of trumps ranks highest.
▷HISTORY C19: probably from CINCH[1]

cinchona (sɪŋˈkəʊnə) NOUN [1] any tree or shrub of the South American rubiaceous genus *Cinchona,* esp *C. calisaya,* having medicinal bark. [2] Also called: **cinchona bark, Peruvian bark, calisaya, china bark.** the dried bark of any of these trees, which yields quinine and other medicinal alkaloids. [3] any of the drugs derived from cinchona bark.
▷HISTORY C18: New Latin, named after the Countess of *Chinchón* (1576–1639), vicereine of Peru
▸**cinchonic** (sɪŋˈkɒnɪk) ADJECTIVE

cinchonidine (sɪŋˈkɒnɪˌdiːn) NOUN an alkaloid that is a stereoisomer of cinchonine, with similar properties and uses.

cinchonine (ˈsɪŋkəˌniːn) NOUN an insoluble crystalline alkaloid isolated from cinchona bark, used to treat malaria. Formula: $C_{19}H_{22}N_2O$.

cinchonism (ˈsɪŋkəˌnɪzəm) NOUN a condition resulting from an excessive dose of cinchona bark or its alkaloids, characterized chiefly by headache, ringing in the ears, and vomiting.

cinchonize *or* **cinchonise** (ˈsɪŋkəˌnaɪz) VERB *(tr)*

to treat (a patient) with cinchona or one of its alkaloids, esp quinine.
▸ **ˌcinchoniˈzation** *or* **ˌcinchoniˈsation** NOUN

Cincinnati (ˌsɪnsɪˈnætɪ) NOUN a city in SW Ohio, on the Ohio River. Pop.: 331 285 (2000).

cincture (ˈsɪŋktʃə) NOUN something that encircles or surrounds, esp a belt, girdle, or border.
▷ HISTORY C16: from Latin *cinctūra,* from *cingere* to gird

cinder (ˈsɪndə) NOUN 1 a piece of incombustible material left after the combustion of coal, coke, etc.; clinker. 2 a piece of charred material that burns without flames; ember. 3 Also called: **sinter.** any solid waste from smelting or refining. 4 (*plural*) fragments of volcanic lava; scoriae. ◆ VERB 5 (*tr*) *Rare* to burn to cinders.
▷ HISTORY Old English *sinder;* related to Old Norse *sindr,* Old High German *sintar,* Old Slavonic *sedra* stalactite
▸ **ˈcindery** ADJECTIVE

cinder block NOUN the usual US name for **breeze block.**

Cinderella (ˌsɪndəˈrɛlə) NOUN 1 a girl who achieves fame after being obscure. 2 **a** a poor, neglected, or unsuccessful person or thing. **b** (*as modifier*): *a Cinderella service within the NHS.* 3 (*modifier*) relating to dramatic success: *a Cinderella story.*
▷ HISTORY C19: after *Cinderella,* the heroine of a fairy tale who is aided by a fairy godmother

cinder track NOUN a racetrack covered with fine cinders.

cine- COMBINING FORM indicating motion picture or cinema: *cine camera; cinephotography.*

cineaste (ˈsɪnɪˌæst) NOUN an enthusiast for films.
▷ HISTORY C20: French, from CINEMA + *-aste,* as *-ast* in *enthusiast*

cine camera (ˈsɪnɪ) NOUN *Brit* a camera in which a strip of film moves past the lens, usually to give 16 or 24 exposures per second, thus enabling moving pictures to be taken. US and Canadian term: **movie camera.**

cine film NOUN *Brit* photographic film, wound on a spool, usually 8, 16, or 35 millimetres wide, up to several hundred metres long, and having one or two lines of sprocket holes along its length enabling it to be used in a cine camera. US and Canadian term: **movie film.**

cinema (ˈsɪnɪmə) NOUN 1 *Chiefly Brit* **a** a place designed for the exhibition of films. **b** (*as modifier*): *a cinema seat.* 2 **the cinema. a** the art or business of making films. **b** films collectively.
▷ HISTORY C19 (earlier spelling *kinema*): shortened from CINEMATOGRAPH
▸ **cinematic** (ˌsɪnɪˈmætɪk) ADJECTIVE ▸ **ˌcineˈmatically** ADVERB

CinemaScope (ˈsɪnɪməˌskəʊp) NOUN *Trademark* an anamorphic process of wide-screen film projection in which an image of approximately twice the usual width is squeezed into a 35mm frame and then screened by a projector having complementary lenses.

cinematheque (ˌsɪnɪməˈtɛk) NOUN a small intimate cinema.
▷ HISTORY C20: from French *cinémathèque* film library, from CINEMA + (*biblio*)*thèque* library

cinematograph (ˌsɪnɪˈmætəˌgrɑːf, -ˌgræf) *Chiefly Brit* ◆ NOUN 1 a combined camera, printer, and projector. ◆ VERB 2 to take pictures (of) with a film camera.
▷ HISTORY C19 (earlier spelling *kinematograph*): from Greek *kinēmat-, kinēma* motion + -GRAPH
▸ **cinematographer** (ˌsɪnɪməˈtɒgrəfə) NOUN
▸ **cinematographic** (ˌsɪnɪˌmætəˈgræfɪk) ADJECTIVE
▸ **ˌcineˌmatoˈgraphically** ADVERB ▸ **ˌcinemaˈtography** NOUN

cinéma vérité (*French* sinema verite) NOUN films characterized by subjects, actions, etc., that have the appearance of real life.
▷ HISTORY French, literally: cinema truth

cineol (ˈsɪnɪˌɒl) *or* **cineole** (ˈsɪnɪˌəʊl) NOUN another name for **eucalyptol.**
▷ HISTORY C19: changed from New Latin *oleum cinae,* literally: oil of wormseed

Cinerama (ˌsɪnəˈrɑːmə) NOUN *Trademark* wide-screen presentation of films using either three separate 35mm projectors or one 70mm projector to produce an image on a large deeply curved screen.

cineraria (ˌsɪnəˈrɛərɪə) NOUN a plant, *Senecio cruentus,* of the Canary Islands, widely cultivated for its blue, purple, red, or variegated daisy-like flowers: family *Asteraceae* (composites).
▷ HISTORY C16: from New Latin, from Latin *cinerārius* of ashes, from *cinis* ashes; from its downy leaves

cinerarium (ˌsɪnəˈrɛərɪəm) NOUN, *plural* **-raria** (-ˈrɛərɪə). a place for keeping the ashes of the dead after cremation.
▷ HISTORY C19: from Latin, from *cinerārius* relating to ashes; see CINERARIA
▸ **cinerary** (ˈsɪnərərɪ) ADJECTIVE

cinerator (ˈsɪnəˌreɪtə) NOUN another name (esp US) for **cremator** (sense 1).
▸ **ˌcineˈration** NOUN

cinereous (sɪˈnɪərɪəs) *or* **cineritious** (ˌsɪnəˈrɪʃəs) ADJECTIVE 1 of a greyish colour. 2 resembling or consisting of ashes.
▷ HISTORY C17: from Latin *cinereus,* from *cinis* ashes

cinerin (ˈsɪnərɪn) NOUN either of two similar organic compounds found in pyrethrum and used as insecticides. Formulas: $C_{20}H_{28}O_3$ (**cinerin I**), $C_{21}H_{28}O_5$ (**cinerin II**).
▷ HISTORY C20: from Latin *ciner-, cinis* ashes + -IN

cingulum (ˈsɪŋgjʊləm) NOUN, *plural* **-la** (-lə). *Anatomy* a girdle-like part, such as the ridge round the base of a tooth or the band of fibres connecting parts of the cerebrum.
▷ HISTORY C19: from Latin: belt, from *cingere* to gird
▸ **cingulate** (ˈsɪŋgjʊlɪt, -ˌleɪt) *or* **ˈcinguˌlated** ADJECTIVE

cinnabar (ˈsɪnəˌbɑː) NOUN 1 a bright red or brownish-red mineral form of mercuric sulphide (mercury(II) sulphide), found close to areas of volcanic activity and hot springs. It is the main commercial source of mercury. Formula: HgS. Crystal structure: hexagonal. 2 the red form of mercuric sulphide (mercury(II) sulphide), esp when used as a pigment. 3 a bright red to reddish-orange; vermilion. 4 a large red-and-black European moth, *Callimorpha jacobaeae:* family *Arctiidae* (tiger moths, etc.).
▷ HISTORY C15: from Old French *cenobre,* from Latin *cinnābaris,* from Greek *kinnabari,* of Oriental origin

cinnamic acid (sɪˈnæmɪk) NOUN a white crystalline water-insoluble weak organic acid existing in two isomeric forms; 3-phenylpropenoic acid. The *trans-* form occurs naturally and its esters are used in perfumery. Formula: $C_6H_5CH{:}CHCOOH$.
▷ HISTORY C19: from CINNAM(ON) + -IC; from its being found in cinnamon oil

cinnamon (ˈsɪnəmən) NOUN 1 a tropical Asian lauraceous tree, *Cinnamomum zeylanicum,* having aromatic yellowish-brown bark. 2 the spice obtained from the bark of this tree, used for flavouring food and drink. 3 **Saigon cinnamon.** an E Asian lauraceous tree, *Cinnamomum loureirii,* the bark of which is used as a cordial and to relieve flatulence. 4 any of several similar or related trees or their bark. See **cassia** (sense 2). 5 a light yellowish brown.
▷ HISTORY C15: from Old French *cinnamome,* via Latin and Greek, from Hebrew *qinnāmōwn*
▸ **cinˈnamic** *or* **cinnamonic** (ˌsɪnəˈmɒnɪk) ADJECTIVE

cinnamon bear NOUN a reddish-brown variety of the American black bear. See **black bear** (sense 1).

cinnamon sedge NOUN an angler's name for a small caddis fly, *Limnephilus lunatus,* having pale hind wings, that frequents sluggish water.

cinnamon stone NOUN another name for **hessonite or grossular.**

cinquain (sɪŋˈkeɪn, ˈsɪŋkeɪn) NOUN a stanza of five lines.
▷ HISTORY C18 (in the sense: a military company of five): from French *cinq* five, from Latin *quinque;* compare QUATRAIN

cinque (sɪŋk) NOUN the number five in cards, dice, etc.
▷ HISTORY C14: from Old French *cinq* five

cinquecento (ˌtʃɪŋkwɪˈtʃɛntəʊ) NOUN the 16th century, esp in reference to Italian art, architecture, or literature.
▷ HISTORY C18: Italian, shortened from *milcinquecento* 1500
▸ **ˌcinqueˈcentist** NOUN

cinquefoil (ˈsɪŋkˌfɔɪl) NOUN 1 any plant of the N temperate rosaceous genus *Potentilla,* typically having five-lobed compound leaves. 2 an ornamental carving in the form of five arcs arranged in a circle and separated by cusps. 3 *Heraldry* a charge representing a five-petalled flower.
▷ HISTORY C13 *sink foil,* from Old French *cincfoille,* from Latin *quinquefolium* plant with five leaves, translating Greek *pentaphullon* from *pente* five + *phullon* leaf

Cinque Ports (sɪŋk) PLURAL NOUN an association of ports on the SE coast of England, originally consisting of Hastings, Romney, Hythe, Dover, and Sandwich, which from late Anglo-Saxon times provided ships for the king's service in return for the profits of justice in their courts. The Cinque Ports declined with the growth of other ports and surrendered their charters in 1685.

Cintra (ˈsɪntrə) NOUN the former name for **Sintra.**

Cinzano (tʃɪnˈzɑːnəʊ) NOUN *Trademark* an Italian vermouth.

CIO *US* ABBREVIATION FOR **Congress of Industrial Organizations.** See also **AFL-CIO.**

Cipango (sɪˈpæŋgəʊ) NOUN (in medieval legend) an island E of Asia: called Zipangu by Marco Polo and sought by Columbus; identified with Japan.

cipher *or* **cypher** (ˈsaɪfə) NOUN 1 a method of secret writing using substitution or transposition of letters according to a key. 2 a secret message. 3 the key to a secret message. 4 an obsolete name for **zero** (sense 1). 5 any of the Arabic numerals (0, 1, 2, 3, etc., to 9) or the Arabic system of numbering as a whole. 6 a person or thing of no importance; nonentity. 7 a design consisting of interwoven letters; monogram. 8 *Music* a defect in an organ resulting in the continuous sounding of a pipe, the key of which has not been depressed. ◆ VERB 9 to put (a message) into secret writing. 10 (*intr*) (of an organ pipe) to sound without having the appropriate key depressed. 11 *Rare* to perform (a calculation) arithmetically.
▷ HISTORY C14: from Old French *cifre* zero, from Medieval Latin *cifra,* from Arabic *sifr* zero, empty

cipolin (ˈsɪpəlɪn) NOUN an Italian marble with alternating white and green streaks.
▷ HISTORY C18: from French, from Italian *cipollino* a little onion, from *cipolla* onion, from Late Latin *cēpulla,* diminutive of Latin *cēpa* onion; from its likeness to the layers of an onion

ciprofloxacin (ˌsɪprəʊˈflɒksəsɪn) NOUN a broad-spectrum antibiotic used against Gram-negative bacteria. It is effective against anthrax.

cir. *or* **circ.** ABBREVIATION FOR (preceding a date) circa.

circa (ˈsɜːkə) PREPOSITION (used with a date) at the approximate time of: *circa 1182 B.C.* Abbreviations: ***c., ca.***
▷ HISTORY Latin: about; related to Latin *circus* circle, CIRCUS

circadian (sɜːˈkeɪdɪən) ADJECTIVE of or relating to biological processes that occur regularly at about 24-hour intervals, even in the absence of periodicity in the environment. See also **biological clock.**
▷ HISTORY C20: from Latin *circa* about + *diēs* day

Circassia (sɜːˈkæsɪə) NOUN a region of S Russia, on the Black Sea north of the Caucasus Mountains.

Circassian (sɜːˈkæsɪən) NOUN 1 a native of Circassia. 2 a language or languages spoken in Circassia, belonging to the North-West Caucasian family. See also **Adygei, Kabardian.** ◆ ADJECTIVE *also* **Circassic.** 3 relating to Circassia, its people, or language.

Circe (ˈsɜːsɪ) NOUN *Greek myth* an enchantress who detained Odysseus on her island and turned his men into swine.
▸ **Circean** (sɜːˈsɪən) ADJECTIVE

circinate (ˈsɜːsɪˌneɪt) ADJECTIVE 1 *Botany* (of part of a plant, such as a young fern) coiled so that the tip is at the centre. 2 *Anatomy* resembling a ring or a circle.
▷ HISTORY C19: from Latin *circināre* to make round, from *circinus* pair of compasses, from *circus,* see CIRCUS
▸ **ˈcirciˌnately** ADVERB

Circinus ('sɜːsɪnəs) NOUN, *Latin genitive* **Circini** ('sɜːsɪˌnaɪ). a small faint constellation in the S hemisphere close to Centaurus and the Southern Cross.
▷HISTORY C19: from Latin, a pair of compasses

circle ('sɜːkᵊl) NOUN 1 *Maths* a closed plane curve every point of which is equidistant from a given fixed point, the centre. Equation: $(x-h)^2 + (y-k)^2 = r^2$ where r is the radius and (h, k) are the coordinates of the centre; area πr^2; circumference: $2\pi r$. 2 the figure enclosed by such a curve. 3 *Theatre* the section of seats above the main level of the auditorium, usually comprising the dress circle and the upper circle. 4 something formed or arranged in the shape of a circle. 5 a group of people sharing an interest, activity, upbringing, etc.; set: *golf circles; a family circle.* 6 a domain or area of activity, interest, or influence. 7 a circuit. 8 a process or chain of events or parts that forms a connected whole; cycle. 9 a parallel of latitude. See also **great circle, small circle.** 10 the ring of a circus. 11 one of a number of Neolithic or Bronze Age rings of standing stones, such as Stonehenge, found in Europe and thought to be associated with some form of ritual or astronomical measurement. 12 *Hockey* See **striking circle.** 13 a circular argument. See **vicious circle** (sense 2). 14 **come full circle.** to arrive back at one's starting point. See also **vicious circle.** 15 **go** *or* **run round in circles.** to engage in energetic but fruitless activity. ◆ VERB 16 to move in a circle (around): *we circled the city by car.* 17 (*tr*) to enclose in a circle; encircle.
▷HISTORY C14: from Latin *circulus* a circular figure, from *circus* ring, circle
▸'**circler** NOUN

circlet ('sɜːklɪt) NOUN a small circle or ring, esp a circular ornament worn on the head.
▷HISTORY C15: from Old French *cerclet* a little CIRCLE

circlip ('sɜːˌklɪp) NOUN *Engineering* a flat spring ring split at one point so that it can be sprung open, passed over a shaft or spindle, and allowed to close into a closely fitting annular recess to form a collar on the shaft. A similar design can be closed to pass into a bore and allowed to spring out into an annular recess to form a shoulder in the bore. Also called: **retaining ring.**

Circlorama (ˌsɜːklə'rɑːmə) NOUN *Trademark* a system of film projection in which a number of projectors and screens are employed to produce a picture that surrounds the viewer.

circs (sɜːks) NOUN *Brit informal* short for **circumstances** (see **circumstance** (sense 1)).

circuit ('sɜːkɪt) NOUN 1 **a** a complete route or course, esp one that is curved or circular or that lies around an object. **b** the area enclosed within such a route. 2 the act of following such a route: *we made three circuits of the course.* 3 **a** a complete path through which an electric current can flow. **b** (*as modifier*): *a circuit diagram.* 4 **a** a periodical journey around an area, as made by judges, salesmen, etc. **b** the route traversed or places visited on such a journey. **c** the persons making such a journey. 5 an administrative division of the Methodist Church comprising a number of neighbouring churches. 6 *English law* one of six areas into which England is divided for the administration of justice. 7 a number of theatres, cinemas, etc., under one management or in which the same film is shown or in which a company of performers plays in turn. 8 *Sport* **a** a series of tournaments in which the same players regularly take part: *the international tennis circuit.* **b** (usually preceded by *the*) the contestants who take part in such a series. 9 *Chiefly Brit* a motor racing track, usually of irregular shape. ◆ VERB 10 to make or travel in a circuit around (something).
▷HISTORY C14: from Latin *circuitus* a going around, from *circumīre,* from *circum* around + *īre* to go
▸'**circuital** ADJECTIVE

circuit binding NOUN a style of limp-leather binding, used esp for Bibles and prayer books, in which the edges of the cover bend over to protect the edges of the pages.

circuit board NOUN short for **printed circuit board.** See **printed circuit.**

circuit breaker NOUN a device that under abnormal conditions, such as a short circuit, interrupts the flow of current in an electrical circuit. Sometimes shortened to **breaker.** Compare **fuse²** (sense 6).

circuit judge NOUN *Brit* a judge presiding over a county court or crown court.

circuitous (sə'kjuːɪtəs) ADJECTIVE indirect and lengthy; roundabout: *a circuitous route.*
▸**cir'cuitously** ADVERB ▸**cir'cuitousness** NOUN

circuit rider NOUN *US and Canadian* (formerly) a minister of religion who preached from place to place along an established circuit.

circuitry ('sɜːkɪtrɪ) NOUN 1 the design of an electrical circuit. 2 the system of circuits used in an electronic device.

circuit training NOUN a form of athletic training in which a number of exercises are performed in turn.

circuity (sə'kjuːɪtɪ) NOUN, *plural* **-ties.** (of speech, reasoning, etc.) a roundabout or devious quality.

circular ('sɜːkjʊlə) ADJECTIVE 1 of, involving, resembling, or shaped like a circle. 2 circuitous. 3 (of arguments) futile because the truth of the premises cannot be established independently of the conclusion. 4 travelling or occurring in a cycle. 5 (of letters, announcements, etc.) intended for general distribution. ◆ NOUN 6 a printed or duplicated advertisement or notice for mass distribution.
▸**circularity** (ˌsɜːkjʊ'lærɪtɪ) *or* '**circularness** NOUN
▸'**circularly** ADVERB

circular breathing NOUN a technique for sustaining a phrase on a wind instrument, using the cheeks to force air out of the mouth while breathing in through the nose.

circular function NOUN another name for **trigonometric function** (sense 1).

circularize *or* **circularise** ('sɜːkjʊləˌraɪz) VERB (*tr*) 1 to distribute circulars to. 2 to canvass or petition (people), as for support, votes, etc., by distributing letters, etc. 3 to make circular.
▸ˌ**circulari'zation** *or* ˌ**circulari'sation** NOUN ▸'**circularˌizer** *or* '**circularˌiser** NOUN

circular measure NOUN the measurement of an angle in radians.

circular mil NOUN a unit of area of cross section of wire, equal to the area of a circle whose diameter is one thousandth of an inch. 1 circular mil is equal to 0.785×10^{-6} square inch or 0.2×10^{-9} square metre.

circular polarization NOUN electromagnetic radiation (esp light) in which the electric field vector describes a circle about the direction of propagation at any point in the path of the radiation.

circular saw NOUN a power-driven saw in which a circular disc with a toothed edge is rotated at high speed.

circular triangle NOUN a triangle in which each side is the arc of a circle.

circulate ('sɜːkjʊˌleɪt) VERB 1 to send, go, or pass from place to place or person to person: *don't circulate the news.* 2 to distribute or be distributed over a wide area. 3 to move or cause to move through a circuit, system, etc., returning to the starting point: *blood circulates through the body.* 4 to move in a circle: *the earth circulates around the sun.*
▷HISTORY C15: from Latin *circulārī* to assemble in a circle, from *circulus* CIRCLE
▸'**circuˌlative** ADJECTIVE ▸'**circuˌlator** NOUN ▸'**circulatory** ADJECTIVE

circulating decimal NOUN another name for **recurring decimal.**

circulating library NOUN 1 another name (esp US) for **lending library.** 2 a small library circulated in turn to a group of schools or other institutions. 3 a rare name for **subscription library.**

circulating medium NOUN *Finance* currency serving as a medium of exchange.

circulation (ˌsɜːkjʊ'leɪʃən) NOUN 1 the transport of oxygenated blood through the arteries to the capillaries, where it nourishes the tissues, and the return of oxygen-depleted blood through the veins to the heart, where the cycle is renewed. 2 the flow of sap through a plant. 3 any movement through a closed circuit. 4 the spreading or transmission of something to a wider group of people or area. 5 (of air and water) free movement within an area or volume. 6 **a** the distribution of newspapers, magazines, etc. **b** the number of copies of an issue of such a publication that are distributed. 7 *Library science* **a** a book loan, as from a library lending department. **b** each loan transaction of a particular book. **c** the total issue of library books over a specified period. 8 a rare term for **circulating medium.** 9 **in circulation. a** (of currency) serving as a medium of exchange. **b** (of people) active in a social or business context.

circulatory system NOUN *Anatomy, zoology* the system concerned with the transport of blood and lymph, consisting of the heart, blood vessels, lymph vessels, etc.

circum- PREFIX around; surrounding; on all sides: *circumlocution; circumrotate.*
▷HISTORY from Latin *circum* around, from *circus* circle

circumambient (ˌsɜːkəm'æmbɪənt) ADJECTIVE surrounding.
▷HISTORY C17: from Late Latin *circumambīre,* from CIRCUM- + *ambīre* to go round
▸ˌ**circum'ambience** *or* ˌ**circum'ambiency** NOUN

circumambulate (ˌsɜːkəm'æmbjʊˌleɪt) VERB 1 to walk around (something). 2 (*intr*) to avoid the point.
▷HISTORY C17: from Late Latin CIRCUM- + *ambulāre* to walk
▸ˌ**circumˌambu'lation** NOUN ▸ˌ**circum'ambuˌlator** NOUN
▸ˌ**circum'ambulatory** ADJECTIVE

circumbendibus (ˌsɜːkəm'bɛndɪbəs) NOUN *Humorous* a circumlocution.
▷HISTORY C17: coined from CIRCUM- + BEND¹, with a pseudo-Latin ending

circumcise ('sɜːkəmˌsaɪz) VERB (*tr*) 1 to remove the foreskin of (a male). 2 to incise surgically the skin over the clitoris of (a female). 3 to remove the clitoris of (a female). 4 to perform the religious rite of circumcision on (someone).
▷HISTORY C13: from Latin *circumcīdere,* from CIRCUM- + *caedere* to cut
▸'**circumˌciser** NOUN

circumcision (ˌsɜːkəm'sɪʒən) NOUN 1 **a** surgical removal of the foreskin of males. **b** surgical incision into the skin covering the clitoris in females. **c** removal of the clitoris. 2 the act of circumcision, performed as a religious rite by Jews and Muslims. 3 *RC Church* the festival celebrated on Jan. 1 in commemoration of the circumcision of Jesus.

circumference (sə'kʌmfərəns) NOUN 1 the boundary of a specific area or geometric figure, esp of a circle. 2 the length of a closed geometric curve, esp of a circle. The circumference of a circle is equal to the diameter multiplied by π.
▷HISTORY C14: from Old French *circonference,* from Latin *circumferre* to carry around, from CIRCUM- + *ferre* to bear
▸**circumferential** (səˌkʌmfə'rɛnʃəl) ADJECTIVE
▸**cirˌcumfer'entially** ADVERB

circumflex ('sɜːkəmˌflɛks) NOUN 1 a mark (^) placed over a vowel to show that it is pronounced with rising and falling pitch, as in ancient Greek, as a long vowel rather than a short one, as in French, or with some other different quality. ◆ ADJECTIVE 2 (of certain nerves, arteries, or veins) bending or curving around.
▷HISTORY C16: from Latin *circumflexus,* from *circumflectere* to bend around, from CIRCUM- + *flectere* to bend
▸ˌ**circum'flexion** NOUN

circumfluous (sə'kʌmflʊəs) ADJECTIVE 1 Also: **circumfluent.** flowing all around. 2 surrounded by or as if by water.
▷HISTORY C17: from Latin *circumfluere* to flow around, from CIRCUM- + *fluere* to flow
▸**cir'cumfluence** NOUN

circumfuse (ˌsɜːkəm'fjuːz) VERB (*tr*) 1 to pour or spread (a liquid, powder, etc.) around. 2 to surround with a substance, such as a liquid.
▷HISTORY C16: from Latin *circumfūsus,* from *circumfundere* to pour around, from CIRCUM- + *fundere* to pour
▸**circumfusion** (ˌsɜːkəm'fjuːʒən) NOUN

circumlocution (ˌsɜːkəmlə'kjuːʃən) NOUN 1 an indirect way of expressing something. 2 an indirect expression.
▸**circumlocutory** (ˌsɜːkəm'lɒkjʊtərɪ, -trɪ) ADJECTIVE

circumlunar (ˌsɜːkəm'luːnə) ADJECTIVE around or revolving around the moon: *a circumlunar orbit.*

circumnavigate (ˌsɜːkəmˈnævɪˌgeɪt) VERB *(tr)* to sail or fly completely around.
▸ **ˌcircumˈnavigable** ADJECTIVE ▸ **ˌcircumˌnaviˈgation** NOUN ▸ **ˌcircumˈnaviˌgator** NOUN

circumnutation (ˌsɜkəmnjuːˈteɪʃən) NOUN another name for **nutation** (sense 3).
▹ HISTORY C19: from CIRCUM- + *-nutate,* from Latin *nūtāre* to nod repeatedly, sway

circumpolar (ˌsɜːkəmˈpəʊlə) ADJECTIVE 1 (of a star or constellation) visible above the horizon at all times at a specified locality on the earth's surface. 2 surrounding or located at or near either of the earth's poles.

circumscissile (ˌsɜːkəmˈsɪsaɪl) ADJECTIVE (of the dry dehiscent fruits of certain plants) opening completely by a transverse split.
▹ HISTORY C19: from CIRCUM- + Latin *scissilis* capable of splitting, from *scindere* to split

circumscribe (ˌsɜːkəmˈskraɪb, ˈsɜːkəmˌskraɪb) VERB *(tr)* 1 to restrict within limits. 2 to mark or set the bounds of. 3 to draw a geometric construction around (another construction) so that the two are in contact but do not intersect. Compare **inscribe** (sense 4). 4 to draw a line round.
▹ HISTORY C15: from Latin *circumscrībere,* from CIRCUM- + *scrībere* to write
▸ **ˌcircumˈscribable** ADJECTIVE ▸ **ˌcircumˈscriber** NOUN

circumscription (ˌsɜːkəmˈskrɪpʃən) NOUN 1 the act of circumscribing or the state of being circumscribed. 2 something that limits or encloses. 3 a circumscribed space. 4 an inscription around a coin or medal.
▸ **ˌcircumˈscriptive** ADJECTIVE ▸ **ˌcircumˈscriptively** ADVERB

circumsolar (ˌsɜːkəmˈsəʊlə) ADJECTIVE surrounding or rotating around the sun.

circumspect (ˈsɜːkəmˌspɛkt) ADJECTIVE cautious, prudent, or discreet.
▹ HISTORY C15: from Latin *circumspectus,* from CIRCUM- + *specere* to look
▸ **ˌcircumˈspection** NOUN ▸ **ˌcircumˈspective** ADJECTIVE ▸ **ˈcircumˌspectly** ADVERB

circumstance (ˈsɜːkəmstəns) NOUN 1 *(usually plural)* a condition of time, place, etc., that accompanies or influences an event or condition. 2 an incident or occurrence, esp a chance one. 3 accessory information or detail. 4 formal display or ceremony (archaic except in the phrase **pomp and circumstance**). 5 **under** *or* **in no circumstances.** in no case; never. 6 **under the circumstances.** because of conditions; this being the case. 7 **in good** (*or* **bad**) **circumstances.** (of a person) in a good (or bad) financial situation. ◆ VERB *(tr)* 8 to place in a particular condition or situation. 9 *Obsolete* to give in detail.
▹ HISTORY C13: from Old French *circonstance,* from Latin *circumstantia,* from *circumstāre* to stand around, from CIRCUM- + *stāre* to stand

circumstantial (ˌsɜːkəmˈstænʃəl) ADJECTIVE 1 of or dependent on circumstances. 2 fully detailed. 3 incidental.
▸ **ˌcircumˌstantiˈality** NOUN ▸ **ˌcircumˈstantially** ADVERB

circumstantial evidence NOUN indirect evidence that tends to establish a conclusion by inference. Compare **direct evidence.**

circumstantiate (ˌsɜːkəmˈstænʃɪˌeɪt) VERB *(tr)* to support by giving particulars.
▸ **ˌcircumˌstantiˈation** NOUN

circumvallate (ˌsɜːkəmˈvæleɪt) VERB *(tr)* to surround with a defensive fortification.
▹ HISTORY C19: from Latin *circumvallāre,* from CIRCUM- + *vallum* rampart
▸ **ˌcircumvalˈlation** NOUN

circumvent (ˌsɜːkəmˈvɛnt) VERB *(tr)* 1 to evade or go around. 2 to outwit. 3 to encircle (an enemy) so as to intercept or capture.
▹ HISTORY C15: from Latin *circumvenīre,* from CIRCUM- + *venīre* to come
▸ **ˌcircumˈventer** *or* **ˌcircumˈventor** NOUN ▸ **ˌcircumˈvention** NOUN ▸ **ˌcircumˈventive** ADJECTIVE

circumvolution (ˌsɜːkəmvəˈluːʃən) NOUN 1 the act of turning, winding, or folding around a central axis. 2 a single complete turn, cycle, or fold. 3 anything winding or sinuous. 4 a roundabout course or procedure.
▹ HISTORY C15: from Medieval Latin *circumvolūtiō,* from Latin *circumvolvere,* from CIRCUM- + *volvere* to roll
▸ **ˌcircumvoˈlutory** ADJECTIVE

circus (ˈsɜːkəs) NOUN, *plural* **-cuses.** 1 a travelling company of entertainers such as acrobats, clowns, trapeze artistes, and trained animals. 2 a public performance given by such a company. 3 an oval or circular arena, usually tented and surrounded by tiers of seats, in which such a performance is held. 4 a travelling group of professional sportsmen: *a cricket circus.* 5 (in ancient Rome) **a** an open-air stadium, usually oval or oblong, for chariot races or public games. **b** the games themselves. 6 *Brit* **a** an open place, usually circular, in a town, where several streets converge. **b** *(capital when part of a name)*: *Piccadilly Circus.* 7 *Informal* noisy or rowdy behaviour. 8 *Informal* a person or group of people whose behaviour is wild, disorganized, or (esp unintentionally) comic.
▹ HISTORY C16: from Latin, from Greek *kirkos* ring

Circus Maximus (ˈmæksɪməs) NOUN an amphitheatre in Rome, used in ancient times for chariot races, public games, etc.

ciré (ˈsɪəreɪ) ADJECTIVE 1 (of fabric) treated with a heat or wax process to make it smooth. ◆ NOUN 2 such a surface on a fabric. 3 a fabric having such a surface.
▹ HISTORY C20: French, from *cirer* to wax, from *cire,* from Latin *cēra* wax

Cirenaica (ˌsaɪrəˈneɪɪkə, ˌsɪrə-) NOUN a variant spelling of **Cyrenaica.**

Cirencester (ˈsaɪrənˌsɛstə) NOUN a market town in S England, in Gloucestershire: Roman amphitheatre. Pop.: 15 221 (1991). Latin name: **Corinium.**

cire perdue *French* (sir pɛrdy) NOUN a method of casting bronze, in which a mould is formed around a wax pattern, which is subsequently melted and drained away.
▹ HISTORY literally: lost wax

cirque (sɜːk) NOUN 1 Also called: **corrie, cwm.** a semicircular or crescent-shaped basin with steep sides and a gently sloping floor formed in mountainous regions by the erosive action of a glacier. 2 *Archaeol* an obsolete term for **circle** (sense 11). 3 *Poetic* a circle, circlet, or ring.
▹ HISTORY C17: from French, from Latin *circus* ring, circle, CIRCUS

cirrate (ˈsɪreɪt), **cirrose,** *or* **cirrous** ADJECTIVE *Biology* bearing or resembling cirri.
▹ HISTORY C19: from Latin *cirrātus* curled, from CIRRUS

cirrhosis (sɪˈrəʊsɪs) NOUN any of various progressive diseases of the liver, characterized by death of liver cells, irreversible fibrosis, etc.: caused by inadequate diet, excessive alcohol, chronic infection, etc. Also called: **cirrhosis of the liver.**
▹ HISTORY C19: New Latin, from Greek *kirrhos* orange-coloured + -OSIS; referring to the appearance of the diseased liver
▸ **cirˈrhosed** ADJECTIVE ▸ **cirrhotic** (sɪˈrɒtɪk) ADJECTIVE

cirri (ˈsɪraɪ) NOUN the plural of **cirrus.**

cirripede (ˈsɪrɪˌpiːd) *or* **cirriped** (ˈsɪrɪˌpɛd) NOUN 1 any marine crustacean of the subclass *Cirripedia,* including the barnacles, the adults of which are sessile or parasitic. ◆ ADJECTIVE 2 of, relating to, or belonging to the *Cirripedia.*

cirro- *or* **cirri-** COMBINING FORM indicating cirrus or cirri: *cirrocumulus; cirriped.*

cirrocumulus (ˌsɪrəʊˈkjuːmjʊləs) NOUN, *plural* **-li** (-ˌlaɪ). *Meteorol* a high cloud of ice crystals grouped into small separate globular masses, usually occurring above 6000 metres (20 000 feet). See also **mackerel sky.**

cirrose (ˈsɪrəʊs, sɪˈrəʊs) *or* **cirrous** (ˈsɪrəs) ADJECTIVE 1 *Biology* another word for **cirrate.** 2 characteristic of cirrus clouds.

cirrostratus (ˌsɪrəʊˈstrɑːtəs) NOUN, *plural* **-ti** (-taɪ). a uniform layer of cloud above about 6000 metres (20 000 feet).
▸ **ˌcirroˈstrative** ADJECTIVE

cirrus (ˈsɪrəs) NOUN, *plural* **-ri** (-raɪ). 1 *Meteorol* a thin wispy fibrous cloud at high altitudes, composed of ice particles. 2 a plant tendril or similar part. 3 *Zoology* **a** a slender tentacle or filament in barnacles and other marine invertebrates. **b** a hairlike structure in other animals, such as a filament on the appendage of an insect or a barbel of a fish.
▹ HISTORY C18: from Latin: curl, tuft, fringe

cirsoid (ˈsɜːsɔɪd) ADJECTIVE *Pathol* resembling a varix. Also: **varicoid.**
▹ HISTORY C19: from Greek *kirsoeidēs,* from *kirsos* swollen vein + -OID

cis- PREFIX 1 on this or the near side of: *cisalpine.* 2 (often in italics) indicating that two groups of atoms in an unsaturated compound lie on the same side of a double bond: *cis*-butadiene. Compare **trans-** (sense 5).
▹ HISTORY from Latin

CIS ABBREVIATION FOR **Commonwealth of Independent States.**

cisalpine (sɪsˈælpaɪn) ADJECTIVE 1 on this (the southern) side of the Alps, as viewed from Rome. 2 relating to a movement in the Roman Catholic Church to minimize the authority of the pope and to emphasize the independence of branches of the Church. Compare **ultramontane** (sense 2).

Cisalpine Gaul NOUN (in the ancient world) that part of Gaul between the Alps and the Apennines.

Ciscaucasia (ˌsɪskɔːˈkeɪzɪə, -ʒə) NOUN the part of Caucasia north of the Caucasus Mountains.

cisco (ˈsɪskəʊ) NOUN, *plural* **-coes** *or* **-cos.** any of various whitefish, esp *Coregonus artedi* (also called **lake herring**), of cold deep lakes of North America.
▹ HISTORY C19: short for Canadian French *ciscoette,* from Ojibwa *pemitewiskawet* fish with oily flesh

Ciskei (ˈsɪskaɪ) NOUN (formerly) a Bantustan in SE South Africa; granted independence in 1981 but this was not recognized outside South Africa; abolished in 1993. Capital: Bisho.

cislunar (sɪsˈluːnə) ADJECTIVE of or relating to the space between the earth and the moon. Compare **translunar.**

cismontane (sɪsˈmɒnteɪn) ADJECTIVE on this (the writer's or speaker's) side of the mountains, esp the Alps. Compare **ultramontane** (sense 1).
▹ HISTORY C18: from Latin CIS- + *montānus* of the mountains, from *mōns* mountain

cispadane (ˈsɪspəˌdeɪn, sɪsˈpeɪdeɪn) ADJECTIVE on this (the southern) side of the River Po, as viewed from Rome. Compare **transpadane.**
▹ HISTORY from Latin CIS- + *Padānus* of the Po

cisplatin (sɪsˈplætɪn) NOUN a cytotoxic drug that acts by preventing DNA replication and hence cell division, used in the treatment of tumours, esp of the ovary and testis.
▹ HISTORY C20: from CIS- + PLATIN(UM)

cissing (ˈsɪsɪŋ) NOUN *Building trades* the appearance of pinholes, craters, etc., in paintwork due to poor adhesion of the paint to the surface.

cissoid (ˈsɪsɔɪd) NOUN 1 a geometric curve whose two branches meet in a cusp at the origin and are asymptotic to a line parallel to the *y*-axis. Its equation is $y^2(2a - x)=x^3$ where 2a is the distance between the *y*-axis and this line. ◆ ADJECTIVE 2 contained between the concave sides of two intersecting curves. Compare **sistroid.**
▹ HISTORY C17: from Greek *kissoeidēs,* literally: ivy-shaped, from *kissos* ivy

cissus (ˈsɪsəs) NOUN any plant of the climbing genus *Cissus,* some species of which, esp the kangaroo vine (*C. antarctica*) from Australia, are grown as greenhouse or house plants for their shiny green or mottled leaves: family *Vitaceae.*
▹ HISTORY New Latin, from Greek *kissos* ivy

cissy (ˈsɪsɪ) NOUN a variant spelling of **sissy.**

cist[1] (sɪst) NOUN a wooden box for holding ritual objects used in ancient Rome and Greece.
▹ HISTORY C19: from Latin *cista* box, chest, basket, from Greek *kistē*

cist[2] (sɪst) *or* **kist** NOUN *Archaeol* a box-shaped burial chamber made from stone slabs or a hollowed tree trunk.
▹ HISTORY C19: from Welsh: chest, from Latin *cista* box; see CIST[1]

cistaceous (sɪˈsteɪʃəs) ADJECTIVE of, relating to, or belonging to the *Cistaceae,* a family of shrubby or herbaceous plants that includes the rockroses.
▹ HISTORY C19: from New Latin *Cistaceae,* from Greek *kistos* rockrose

Cistercian (sɪˈstɜːʃən) NOUN **a** a member of a Christian order of monks and nuns founded in 1098, which follows an especially strict form of the Benedictine rule. Also called: **White Monk. b** *(as modifier)*: *a Cistercian monk.*
▹ HISTORY C17: from French *Cistercien,* from

Medieval Latin *Cisterciānus,* from *Cistercium* (modern *Cîteaux*), original home of the order

cistern ('sɪstən) NOUN 1 a tank for the storage of water, esp on or within the roof of a house or connected to a WC. 2 an underground reservoir for the storage of a liquid, esp rainwater. 3 *Anatomy* another name for **cisterna.**
▷HISTORY C13: from Old French *cisterne,* from Latin *cisterna* underground tank, from *cista* box
▸**cisternal** (sɪ'stɜːnᵊl) ADJECTIVE

cisterna (sɪ'stɜːnə) NOUN, *plural* **-nae** (-niː). a sac or partially closed space containing body fluid, esp lymph or cerebrospinal fluid.
▷HISTORY New Latin, from Latin; see CISTERN

cis-trans test ('sɪs'trɑːnz) NOUN *Genetics* a test to define the unit of genetic function, based on whether two mutations of the same character occur in a single chromosome (the cis position) or in different cistrons in each chromosome of a homologous pair (the trans position).
▷HISTORY C20: see CIS-, TRANS-

cistron ('sɪstrən) NOUN *Genetics* the section of a chromosome that encodes a single polypeptide chain.
▷HISTORY C20: from *cis-trans;* see CIS-TRANS TEST

cistus ('sɪstəs) NOUN any plant of the genus *Cistus.* See **rockrose.**
▷HISTORY C16: New Latin, from Greek *kistos*

CIT (in New Zealand) ABBREVIATION FOR Central Institute of Technology.

cit. ABBREVIATION FOR: 1 citation. 2 cited.

citadel ('sɪtədᵊl, -ˌdɛl) NOUN 1 a stronghold within or close to a city. 2 any strongly fortified building or place of safety; refuge. 3 a specially strengthened part of the hull of a warship. 4 (*often capital*) the headquarters of the Salvation Army.
▷HISTORY C16: from Old French *citadelle,* from Old Italian *cittadella* a little city, from *cittade* city, from Latin *cīvitās*

citation (saɪ'teɪʃən) NOUN 1 the quoting of a book or author in support of a fact. 2 a passage or source cited for this purpose. 3 a listing or recounting, as of facts. 4 an official commendation or award, esp for bravery or outstanding service, work, etc., usually in the form of a formal statement made in public. 5 *Law* **a** an official summons to appear in court. **b** the document containing such a summons. 6 *Law* the quoting of decided cases to serve as guidance to a court.
▸**citatory** ('saɪtətərɪ, -trɪ) ADJECTIVE

cite (saɪt) VERB (*tr*) 1 to quote or refer to (a passage, book, or author) in substantiation as an authority, proof, or example. 2 to mention or commend (a soldier, etc.) for outstanding bravery or meritorious action. 3 to summon to appear before a court of law. 4 to enumerate: *he cited the king's virtues.*
▷HISTORY C15: from Old French *citer* to summon, from Latin *citāre* to rouse, from *citus* quick, from *ciēre* to excite
▸**'citable** *or* **'citeable** ADJECTIVE ▸**'citer** NOUN

CITES ABBREVIATION FOR Convention on International Trade in Endangered Species.

cithara ('sɪθərə) *or* **kithara** NOUN a stringed musical instrument of ancient Greece and elsewhere, similar to the lyre and played with a plectrum.
▷HISTORY C18: from Greek *kithara*

cither ('sɪθə) *or* **cithern** ('sɪθən) NOUN variants of **cittern.**
▷HISTORY C17: from Latin *cithara,* from Greek *kithara* lyre

citified *or* **cityfied** ('sɪtɪˌfaɪd) ADJECTIVE *Often derogatory* having the customs, manners, or dress of city people.

citify *or* **cityfy** ('sɪtɪˌfaɪ) VERB **-fies, -fying, -fied.** (*tr*) 1 to cause to conform to or adopt the customs, habits, or dress of city people. 2 to make urban.
▸**ˌcitifi'cation** *or* **ˌcityfi'cation** NOUN

citizen ('sɪtɪzᵊn) NOUN 1 a native registered or naturalized member of a state, nation, or other political community. Compare **alien.** 2 an inhabitant of a city or town. 3 a native or inhabitant of any place. 4 a civilian, as opposed to a soldier, public official, etc. Related adjective: **civil.**
▷HISTORY C14: from Anglo-French *citesein,* from Old French *citeien,* from *cité,* CITY
▸**citizeness** ('sɪtɪzənɪs, -ˌnɛs) FEMININE NOUN ▸**'citizenly** ADJECTIVE

citizenry ('sɪtɪzənrɪ) NOUN, *plural* **-ries.** citizens collectively.

citizen's arrest NOUN an arrest carried out by an ordinary member of the public rather than an officer of the law.

Citizens' Band NOUN a range of radio frequencies assigned officially for use by the public for private communication. Abbreviation: **CB.**

Citizen's Charter NOUN (formerly, in Britain) a government document setting out standards of service for public and private sector bodies, such as schools, hospitals, railway companies, water and energy suppliers, etc.

citizenship ('sɪtɪzənˌʃɪp) NOUN 1 the condition or status of a citizen, with its rights and duties. 2 a person's conduct as a citizen: *an award for good citizenship.*

Citlaltépetl (ˌsiːtlɑːl'teɪpɛtᵊl) NOUN a volcano in SE Mexico, in central Veracruz state: the highest peak in the country. Height: 5699 m (18 698 ft.). Spanish name: **Pico de Orizaba** (piko de ori'saba).

citole ('sɪtəʊl, sɪ'təʊl) NOUN a rare word for **cittern.**
▷HISTORY C14: from Old French, probably from Latin *cithara* CITHER

citral ('sɪtrəl) NOUN a yellow volatile liquid with a lemon-like odour, found in oils of lemon grass, orange, and lemon and used in perfumery: a terpene aldehyde consisting of the *cis-* isomer (**citral-a** or **geranial**) and the *trans-* isomer (**citral-b** or **neral**). Formula: $(CH_3)_2C{:}CH(CH_2)_2C(CH_3){:}CHCHO$.
▷HISTORY C19: from CITR(US) + -AL[3]

citrate ('sɪtreɪt, -rɪt, 'saɪtreɪt) NOUN any salt or ester of citric acid. Salts of citric acid are used in beverages and pharmaceuticals.
▷HISTORY C18: from CITR(US) + -ATE[1]

citreous ('sɪtrɪəs) ADJECTIVE of a greenish-yellow colour; citron.

citric ('sɪtrɪk) ADJECTIVE of or derived from citrus fruits or citric acid.

citric acid NOUN a water-soluble weak tribasic acid found in many fruits, esp citrus fruits, and used in pharmaceuticals and as a flavouring (**E330**). It is extracted from citrus fruits or made by fermenting molasses and is an intermediate in carbohydrate metabolism. Formula: $CH_2(COOH)C(OH)(COOH)CH_2COOH$.

citric acid cycle NOUN another name for **Krebs cycle.**

citriculture ('sɪtrɪˌkʌltʃə) NOUN the cultivation of citrus fruits.
▸**ˌcitri'culturist** NOUN

citrin ('sɪtrɪn) NOUN another name for **vitamin P.**

citrine ('sɪtrɪn) NOUN 1 a brownish-yellow variety of quartz: a gemstone; false topaz. 2 the yellow colour of a lemon.

citron ('sɪtrən) NOUN 1 a small Asian rutaceous tree, *Citrus medica,* having lemon-like fruit with a thick aromatic rind. See also **citron wood.** 2 the fruit of this tree. 3 Also called: **citron melon.** a variety of watermelon, *Citrullus vulgaris citroides,* that has an inedible fruit with a hard rind. 4 the rind of either of these fruits, candied and used for decoration and flavouring of foods. 5 a greenish-yellow colour.
▷HISTORY C16: from Old French, from Old Provençal, from Latin *citrus* citrus tree

citronella (ˌsɪtrə'nɛlə) NOUN 1 Also called: **citronella grass.** a tropical Asian grass, *Cymbopogon* (or *Andropogon*) *nardus,* with bluish-green lemon-scented leaves. 2 Also called: **citronella oil.** the yellow aromatic oil obtained from this grass, used in insect repellents, soaps, perfumes, etc.
▷HISTORY C19: New Latin, from French *citronnelle* lemon balm, from *citron* lemon

citronellal (ˌsɪtrə'nɛlæl) NOUN a colourless slightly water-soluble liquid with a lemon-like odour, a terpene aldehyde found esp in citronella and certain eucalyptus oils: used as a flavouring and in soaps and perfumes. Formula: $(CH_3)_2C{:}CH(CH_2)_2CH(CH_3)CH_2CHO$. Also called: **rhodinal.**

citron wood NOUN 1 the wood of the citron tree. 2 the wood of the sandarac.

citrulline ('sɪtrəˌliːn) NOUN an amino acid that occurs in watermelons and is an intermediate in the formation of urea. Formula: $NH_2CONH(CH_2)_3CHNH_2COOH$.
▷HISTORY C20: from Medieval Latin *citrullus* a kind of watermelon, from Latin *citron,* referring to its colour

citrus ('sɪtrəs) NOUN, *plural* **-ruses.** 1 any tree or shrub of the tropical and subtropical rutaceous genus *Citrus,* which includes the orange, lemon, lime, grapefruit, citron, and calamondin. ◆ ADJECTIVE *also* **citrous.** 2 of, relating to, or belonging to the genus *Citrus* or to the fruits of plants of this genus.
▷HISTORY C19: from Latin: citrus tree, sandarac tree; related to Greek *kedros* cedar

citrussy ('sɪtrəsɪ) ADJECTIVE having or resembling the taste or colour of a citrus fruit.

Città del Vaticano (tʃit'ta del vati'kaːno) NOUN the Italian name for **Vatican City.**

cittern ('sɪtɜːn), **cither,** *or* **cithern** NOUN a medieval stringed instrument resembling a lute but having wire strings and a flat back. Compare **gittern.**
▷HISTORY C16: perhaps a blend of CITHER + GITTERN

city ('sɪtɪ) NOUN, *plural* **cities.** 1 any large town or populous place. 2 (in Britain) a large town that has received this title from the Crown: usually the seat of a bishop. 3 (in the US) an incorporated urban centre with its own government and administration established by state charter. 4 (in Canada) a similar urban municipality incorporated by the provincial government. 5 an ancient Greek city-state; polis. 6 the people of a city collectively. 7 (*modifier*) in or characteristic of a city: *a city girl; city habits.* ◆ Related adjectives: **civic, urban, municipal.**
▷HISTORY C13: from Old French *cité,* from Latin *cīvitās* citizenship, state, from *cīvis* citizen

City ('sɪtɪ) NOUN **the.** 1 short for **City of London**: the original settlement of London on the N bank of the Thames; a municipality governed by the Lord Mayor and Corporation. Resident pop.: 7186 (2001). 2 the area in central London in which the United Kingdom's major financial business is transacted. 3 the various financial institutions located in this area.

City and Guilds of London Institute NOUN (in Britain) an examining body for technical and craft skills, many of the examinations being at a lower standard than for a degree. Often shortened to **City and Guilds.**

city blues NOUN (*functioning as singular*) *Jazz* another name for **urban blues.**

City Code NOUN (in Britain) short for **City Code on Takeovers and Mergers**: a code laid down in 1968 (later modified) to control takeover bids and mergers.

City Company NOUN (in Britain) a corporation that represents one of the historic trade guilds of London.

city desk NOUN 1 *Brit* the department of a newspaper office dealing with financial and commercial news. 2 *US and Canadian* the department of a newspaper office dealing with local news.

city editor NOUN (on a newspaper) 1 *Brit* the editor in charge of financial and commercial news. 2 *US and Canadian* the editor in charge of local news.

city father NOUN a person who is active or prominent in the public affairs of a city, such as an alderman.

city hall NOUN 1 the building housing the administrative offices of a city or municipal government. 2 *Chiefly US and Canadian* **a** municipal government. **b** the officials of a municipality collectively. 3 *US informal* bureaucracy.

city manager NOUN (in the US) an administrator hired by a municipal council to manage its affairs. See also **council-manager plan.**

City of God NOUN 1 *Christianity* heaven conceived of as the New Jerusalem. 2 the Church in contrast to the world, as described by St Augustine.

city planning NOUN the US term for **town planning.**
▸**city planner** NOUN

cityscape ('sɪtɪskeɪp) NOUN an urban landscape; view of a city.

city slicker NOUN *Informal* [1] a person with the sophistication often attributed to city people. [2] a smooth tricky untrustworthy person.

city-state NOUN a state consisting of a sovereign city and its dependencies. Among the most famous are the great independent cities of the ancient world, such as Athens, Sparta, Carthage, and Rome.

city technology college NOUN (in Britain) a type of senior secondary school specializing in technological subjects, set up in inner-city areas with funding from industry as well as the government. Abbreviation: **CTC.**

Ciudad Bolívar (*Spanish* θiu'ðað bo'liβar) NOUN a port in E Venezuela, on the Orinoco River: accessible to ocean-going vessels. Pop.: 312 691 (2000 est.). Former name (1764–1846): **Angostura.**

Ciudad Guayana (*Spanish* θiu'ðað gwa'jana) NOUN an industrial conurbation in E Venezuela, on the River Orinoco: iron and steel processing, gold mining. Pop. (urban area): 704 168 (2000 est.). Former name: **Santo Tomé de Guayana.**

Ciudad Juárez (*Spanish* θiu'ðað 'xwareθ) NOUN a city in N Mexico, in Chihuahua state on the Río Grande, opposite El Paso, Texas. Pop. (urban area): 1 190 000 (2000 est.). Former name (until 1888): **El Paso del Norte** (ɛl 'paso del 'nɔrte).

Ciudad Real (*Spanish* θiu'ðað re'al) NOUN a market town in S central Spain. Pop.: 59 400 (1991).

Ciudad Trujillo (*Spanish* θiu'ðað tru'xiʎo) NOUN the former name (1936–61) of **Santo Domingo.**

Ciudad Victoria (*Spanish* θiu'ðað bik'torja) NOUN a city in E central Mexico, capital of Tamaulipas state. Pop.: 248 000 (2000 est.).

civet ('sɪvɪt) NOUN [1] any catlike viverrine mammal of the genus *Viverra* and related genera, of Africa and S Asia, typically having blotched or spotted fur and secreting a powerfully smelling fluid from anal glands. [2] the yellowish fatty secretion of such an animal, used as a fixative in the manufacture of perfumes. [3] the fur of such an animal. [4] short for **palm civet.**
▷HISTORY C16: from Old French *civette,* from Italian *zibetto,* from Arabic *zabād* civet perfume

civic ('sɪvɪk) ADJECTIVE of or relating to a city, citizens, or citizenship: *civic duties.*
▷HISTORY C16: from Latin *cīvicus,* from *cīvis* citizen
▸ **'civically** ADVERB

civic centre NOUN *Brit* the public buildings of a town, including recreational facilities and offices of local administration.

civics ('sɪvɪks) NOUN (*functioning as singular*) [1] the study of the rights and responsibilities of citizenship. [2] *US and Canadian* the study of government and its workings.

civic university NOUN (in Britain) a university originally instituted as a higher education college serving a particular city.

civies ('sɪvɪz) PLURAL NOUN *Informal* a variant spelling of **civvies.**

civil ('sɪvᵊl) ADJECTIVE [1] of the ordinary life of citizens as distinguished from military, legal, or ecclesiastical affairs. [2] of or relating to the citizen as an individual: *civil rights.* [3] of or occurring within the state or between citizens: *civil strife.* [4] polite or courteous. [5] a less common word for **civic.** [6] of or in accordance with Roman law. [7] relating to the private rights of citizens.
▷HISTORY C14: from Old French, from Latin *cīvīlis,* from *cīvis* citizen
▸ **'civilly** ADVERB ▸ **'civilness** NOUN

civil day NOUN another name for **calendar day.** See **day** (sense 1).

civil death NOUN *Law* (formerly) the loss of all civil rights because of a serious conviction. See also **attainder.**

civil defence NOUN the organizing of civilians to deal with enemy attacks.

civil disobedience NOUN a refusal to obey laws, pay taxes, etc.: a nonviolent means of protesting or of attempting to achieve political goals.

civil engineer NOUN a person qualified to design, construct, and maintain public works, such as roads, bridges, harbours, etc.
▸ **civil engineering** NOUN

civilian (sɪ'vɪljən) NOUN **a** a person whose primary occupation is civil or nonmilitary. **b** (*as modifier*): *civilian life.*
▷HISTORY C14 (originally: a practitioner of civil law): from *civile* (from the Latin phrase *jūs cīvīle* civil law) + -IAN

civilianize *or* **civilianise** (sɪ'vɪljə,naɪz) VERB (*tr*) to change the status of (an armed force, a base, etc.) from military to nonmilitary.

civility (sɪ'vɪlɪtɪ) NOUN, *plural* **-ties.** [1] politeness or courtesy, esp when formal. [2] (*often plural*) an act of politeness.

civilization *or* **civilisation** (,sɪvɪlaɪ'zeɪʃən) NOUN [1] a human society that has highly developed material and spiritual resources and a complex cultural, political, and legal organization; an advanced state in social development. [2] the peoples or nations collectively who have achieved such a state. [3] the total culture and way of life of a particular people, nation, region, or period: *classical civilization.* [4] the process of bringing or achieving civilization. [5] intellectual, cultural, and moral refinement. [6] cities or populated areas, as contrasted with sparsely inhabited areas, deserts, etc.

civilize *or* **civilise** ('sɪvɪ,laɪz) VERB (*tr*) [1] to bring out of savagery or barbarism into a state characteristic of civilization. [2] to refine, educate, or enlighten.
▸ **'civi,lizable** *or* **'civi,lisable** ADJECTIVE ▸ **'civi,lizer** *or* **'civi,liser** NOUN

civilized *or* **civilised** ('sɪvɪ,laɪzd) ADJECTIVE [1] having a high state of culture and social development. [2] cultured; polite: *everything had been done in a civilized manner.*

civil law NOUN [1] the law of a state relating to private and civilian affairs. [2] the body of law in force in ancient Rome, esp the law applicable to private citizens. [3] any system of law based on the Roman system as distinguished from the common law and canon law. [4] the law of a state as distinguished from international law.

civil liberty NOUN the right of an individual to certain freedoms of speech and action.

civil list NOUN (in Britain) the annuities voted by Parliament for the support of the royal household and the royal family.

civil marriage NOUN *Law* a marriage performed by some official other than a clergyman.

civil partnership NOUN a legal union or contract, similar to a marriage, between two people of the same sex.

civil rights PLURAL NOUN [1] the personal rights of the individual citizen, in most countries upheld by law, as in the US. [2] (*modifier*) of, relating to, or promoting equality in social, economic, and political rights.

civil servant NOUN a member of the civil service.

civil service NOUN [1] the service responsible for the public administration of the government of a country. It excludes the legislative, judicial, and military branches. Members of the civil service have no official political allegiance and are not generally affected by changes of governments. [2] the members of the civil service collectively.

civil society NOUN the elements such as freedom of speech, an independent judiciary, etc., that make up a democratic society.

civil war NOUN war between parties, factions, or inhabitants of different regions within the same nation.

Civil War NOUN [1] *English history* the conflict between Charles I and the Parliamentarians resulting from disputes over their respective prerogatives. Parliament gained decisive victories at Marston Moor in 1644 and Naseby in 1645, and Charles was executed in 1649. [2] *US history* the war fought from 1861 to 1865 between the North and the South, sparked off by Lincoln's election as president but with deep-rooted political and economic causes, exacerbated by the slavery issue. The advantages of the North in terms of population, finance, and communications brought about the South's eventual surrender at Appomattox.

civil year NOUN another name for **calendar year.** See **year** (sense 1).

civism ('sɪvɪzəm) NOUN *Rare* good citizenship.
▷HISTORY C18: from French *civisme,* from Latin *cīvis* citizen

civvy ('sɪvɪ) NOUN, *plural* **civvies.** *Slang* [1] a civilian. [2] (*plural*) civilian dress as opposed to uniform. [3] **civvy street.** civilian life.

CJ ABBREVIATION FOR Chief Justice.

CJA (in Britain) ABBREVIATION FOR Criminal Justice Act.

CJD ABBREVIATION FOR **Creutzfeldt-Jakob disease.**

ck THE INTERNET DOMAIN NAME FOR Cook Islands.

cl[1] SYMBOL FOR centilitre.

cl[2] THE INTERNET DOMAIN NAME FOR Chile.

Cl THE CHEMICAL SYMBOL FOR chlorine.

CL INTERNATIONAL CAR REGISTRATION FOR Sri Lanka.
▷HISTORY from *Ceylon*

clabby-doo (,klæbɪ'du:) NOUN *Scot* a variant of **clappy-doo.**

clachan (*Gaelic* 'klaxən; *English* 'klæ-) NOUN *Scot and Irish dialect* a small village; hamlet.
▷HISTORY C15: from Scottish Gaelic: probably from *clach* stone

clack (klæk) VERB [1] to make or cause to make a sound like that of two pieces of wood hitting each other. [2] (*intr*) to jabber. [3] a less common word for **cluck.** ◆ NOUN [4] a short sharp sound. [5] a person or thing that produces this sound. [6] chatter. [7] Also called: **clack valve.** a simple nonreturn valve using either a hinged flap or a ball.
▷HISTORY C13: probably from Old Norse *klaka* to twitter, of imitative origin

clacker ('klækə) NOUN [1] an object that makes a clacking sound. [2] *Northern English dialect* the mouth.

Clackmannan (klæk'mænən) NOUN a town in E central Scotland, in Clackmannanshire. Pop.: 3420 (1991).

Clackmannanshire (klæk'mænən,ʃɪə, -ʃə) NOUN a council area and historical county of central Scotland; became part of the Central region in 1975 but reinstated as an independent unitary authority in 1996; mainly agricultural. Administrative centre: Alloa. Pop.: 48 077 (2001). Area: 142 sq. km (55 sq. miles).

Clacton *or* **Clacton-on-Sea** ('klæktən) NOUN a town and resort in SE England, in E Essex. Pop.: 45 065 (1991).

Clactonian (klæk'təʊnɪən) NOUN [1] one of the Lower Palaeolithic cultures found in England, characterized by the use of chopper tools. ◆ ADJECTIVE [2] of, designating, or relating to this culture.
▷HISTORY after CLACTON, Essex, where the tools of this culture were first found

clad[1] (klæd) VERB a past participle of **clothe.**
▷HISTORY Old English *clāthode* clothed, from *clāthian* to CLOTHE

clad[2] (klæd) VERB **clads, cladding, clad.** (*tr*) to bond a metal to (another metal), esp to form a protective coating.
▷HISTORY C14 (in the obsolete sense: to clothe): special use of CLAD[1]

Claddagh ring ('klædə) NOUN *Irish* any of various elaborately designed rings, esp one in the shape of two hands embracing a heart, given as a token of lasting affection.
▷HISTORY from *Claddagh,* a small fishing village on the edge of Galway city

cladding ('klædɪŋ) NOUN [1] the process of protecting one metal by bonding a second metal to its surface. [2] the protective coating so bonded to metal. [3] the material used for the outside facing of a building, etc.

clade (kleɪd) NOUN *Biology* a group of organisms considered as having evolved from a common ancestor.
▷HISTORY C20: from Greek *klados* branch, shoot

cladistics (klə'dɪstɪks) NOUN (*functioning as singular*) *Biology* a method of grouping animals that makes use of lines of descent rather than structural similarities.
▷HISTORY C20: New Latin, from Greek *klādos* branch, shoot
▸ **cladism** ('klædɪzəm) NOUN ▸ **cladist** ('klædɪst) NOUN

cladoceran (klə'dɒsərən) NOUN [1] any minute freshwater crustacean of the order *Cladocera,* which

includes the water fleas. ◆ ADJECTIVE [2] of, relating to, or belonging to the *Cladocera.*
▷HISTORY C19: from New Latin *Cladocera,* from Greek *klados* shoot + *keras* horn

cladode ('klædəʊd) NOUN *Botany* a flattened stem resembling and functioning as a leaf, as in butcher's-broom. Also called: **cladophyll, phylloclade.**
▷HISTORY C19: from New Latin *cladōdium,* from Late Greek *kladōdēs* having many shoots

cladogram ('kleɪdəʊˌɡræm) NOUN *Biology* a treelike diagram illustrating the development of a clade.
▷HISTORY C20: from CLADE + -O- + -GRAM

cladophyll ('klædəfɪl) NOUN another name for **cladode.**
▷HISTORY C19: from Greek *klados* branch + *phullon* leaf

claes (klez) PLURAL NOUN a Scot word for **clothes.**

clag (klæɡ) *Dialect* ◆ NOUN [1] sticky mud. ◆ VERB *(intr)* **clags, clagged, clagging** [2] to stick, as mud.
▷HISTORY C16: perhaps of Scandinavian origin, related to Danish *klag* sticky mud

claggy ('klæɡɪ) ADJECTIVE **-gier, -giest.** *Chiefly dialect* stickily clinging, as mud.

claim (kleɪm) VERB *(mainly tr)* [1] to demand as being due or as one's property; assert one's title or right to: *he claimed the record.* [2] *(takes a clause as object or an infinitive)* to assert as a fact; maintain against denial: *he claimed to be telling the truth.* [3] to call for or need; deserve: *this problem claims our attention.* [4] to take: *the accident claimed four lives.* ◆ NOUN [5] an assertion of a right; a demand for something as due. [6] an assertion of something as true, real, or factual: *he made claims for his innocence.* [7] a right or just title to something; basis for demand: *a claim to fame.* [8] **lay claim to** *or* **stake a claim to.** to assert one's possession of or right to. [9] anything that is claimed, esp in a formal or legal manner, such as a piece of land staked out by a miner. [10] *Law* a document under seal, issued in the name of the Crown or a court, commanding the person to whom it is addressed to do or refrain from doing some specified act. Former name: **writ.** [11] **a** a demand for payment in connection with an insurance policy, etc. **b** the sum of money demanded.
▷HISTORY C13: from Old French *claimer* to call, appeal, from Latin *clāmāre* to shout
▶'**claimable** ADJECTIVE ▶'**claimer** NOUN

claimant ('kleɪmᵊnt) NOUN [1] a person who makes a claim. [2] a person who brings a civil action in a court of law. Formerly called: **plaintiff.** Compare **defendant** (sense 1).

claiming race NOUN *US and Canadian horse racing* a race in which each owner declares beforehand the price at which his horse will be offered for sale after the race.

clairaudience (ˌklɛər'ɔːdɪəns) NOUN *Psychol* the postulated ability to hear sounds beyond the range of normal hearing. Compare **clairvoyance.**
▷HISTORY C19: from French *clair* clear + AUDIENCE, after CLAIRVOYANCE
▶ˌ**clair'audient** ADJECTIVE, NOUN

clair-obscure (ˌklɛərəb'skjʊə) NOUN another word for **chiaroscuro.**
▷HISTORY C18: from French, literally: clear-obscure

clairvoyance (klɛə'vɔɪəns) NOUN [1] the alleged power of perceiving things beyond the natural range of the senses. See also **extrasensory perception.** [2] keen intuitive understanding.
▷HISTORY C19: from French: clear-seeing, from *clair* clear, from Latin *clārus* + *voyance,* from *voir* to see, from Latin *vidēre*

clairvoyant (klɛə'vɔɪənt) ADJECTIVE [1] of, possessing, or relating to clairvoyance. [2] having great insight or second sight. ◆ NOUN [3] a person claiming to have the power to foretell future events.
▶**clair'voyantly** ADVERB

clam[1] (klæm) NOUN [1] any of various burrowing bivalve molluscs of the genera *Mya, Venus,* etc. Many species, such as the quahog and soft-shell clam, are edible and *Tridacna gigas* is the largest known bivalve, nearly 1.5 metres long. [2] the edible flesh of such a mollusc. [3] *Informal* a reticent person. ◆ VERB **clams, clamming, clammed.** [4] *(intr) Chiefly US* to gather clams. ◆ See also **clam up.**
▷HISTORY C16: from earlier *clamshell,* that is, shell that clamps; related to Old English *clamm* fetter, Old High German *klamma* constriction; see CLAMP[1]

clam[2] (klæm) VERB **clams, clamming, clammed.** a variant of **clem.**

clamant ('kleɪmənt) ADJECTIVE [1] noisy. [2] calling urgently.
▷HISTORY C17: from Latin *clāmāns,* from *clāmāre* to shout

clamatorial (ˌklæmə'tɔːrɪəl) ADJECTIVE of or relating to the American flycatchers (family *Tyrannidae*). See **flycatcher** (sense 2).
▷HISTORY C19: from New Latin *clāmātōres,* plural of Latin *clāmātor* one who shouts; see CLAMANT

clambake ('klæmˌbeɪk) NOUN *US and Canadian* [1] a picnic, often by the sea, at which clams, etc., are baked. [2] an informal party.

clamber ('klæmbə) VERB [1] (usually foll by *up, over,* etc.) to climb (something) awkwardly, esp by using both hands and feet. ◆ NOUN [2] a climb performed in this manner.
▷HISTORY C15: probably a variant of CLIMB
▶'**clamberer** NOUN

clam-diggers PLURAL NOUN calf-length trousers.

clammy ('klæmɪ) ADJECTIVE **-mier, -miest.** [1] unpleasantly sticky; moist: *clammy hands.* [2] (of the weather, atmosphere, etc.) close; humid.
▷HISTORY C14: from Old English *clǣman* to smear; related to Old Norse *kleima,* Old High German *kleimen*
▶'**clammily** ADVERB ▶'**clamminess** NOUN

clamour *or US* **clamor** ('klæmə) NOUN [1] a loud persistent outcry, as from a large number of people. [2] a vehement expression of collective feeling or outrage: *a clamour against higher prices.* [3] a loud and persistent noise: *the clamour of traffic.* ◆ VERB [4] *(intr;* often foll by *for* or *against)* to make a loud noise or outcry; make a public demand. [5] *(tr)* to move, influence, or force by outcry: *the people clamoured him out of office.*
▷HISTORY C14: from Old French *clamour,* from Latin *clāmor,* from *clāmāre* to cry out
▶'**clamourer** *or US* '**clamorer** NOUN ▶'**clamorous** ADJECTIVE ▶'**clamorously** ADVERB ▶'**clamorousness** NOUN

clamp[1] (klæmp) NOUN [1] a mechanical device with movable jaws with which an object can be secured to a bench or with which two objects may be secured together. [2] a means by which a fixed joint may be strengthened. [3] *Nautical* a horizontal beam fastened to the ribs for supporting the deck beams in a wooden vessel. ◆ VERB *(tr)* [4] to fix or fasten with or as if with a clamp. [5] to immobilize (a car) by means of a wheel clamp. [6] to inflict or impose forcefully: *they clamped a curfew on the town.*
▷HISTORY C14: from Dutch or Low German *klamp;* related to Old English *clamm* bond, fetter, Old Norse *kleppr* lump

clamp[2] (klæmp) *Brit agriculture* ◆ NOUN [1] a mound formed out of a harvested root crop, covered with straw and earth to protect it from winter weather. [2] a pile of bricks ready for processing in a furnace. ◆ VERB [3] *(tr)* to enclose (a harvested root crop) in a mound.
▷HISTORY C16: from Middle Dutch *klamp* heap; related to CLUMP

clamp down VERB *(intr, adverb;* often foll by *on)* [1] to behave repressively; attempt to repress something regarded as undesirable. ◆ NOUN **clampdown.** [2] a sudden restrictive measure.

clamper ('klæmpə) NOUN a spiked metal frame fastened to the sole of a shoe to prevent slipping on ice.

clamshell ('klæmˌʃɛl) NOUN [1] *Chiefly US* a dredging bucket that is hinged like the shell of a clam. [2] *Aeronautics* **a** an aircraft cockpit canopy hinged at the front and rear. **b** the hinged door of a cargo aircraft. **c** another name for **eyelid** (sense 2). [3] any of a variety of objects hinged like the shell of a clam, such as a container for takeaway food, a portable computer, etc.

clam up VERB *(intr, adverb) Informal* to keep or become silent or withhold information.

clamworm ('klæmˌwɜːm) NOUN the US name for the **ragworm.**

clan (klæn) NOUN [1] a group of people interrelated by ancestry or marriage. [2] a group of families with a common surname and a common ancestor, acknowledging the same leader, esp among the Scots and the Irish. [3] a group of people united by common characteristics, aims, or interests.
▷HISTORY C14: from Scottish Gaelic *clann* family, descendants, from Latin *planta* sprout, PLANT[1]

clandestine (klæn'dɛstɪn) ADJECTIVE secret and concealed, often for illicit reasons; furtive.
▷HISTORY C16: from Latin *clandestīnus,* from *clam* secretly; related to Latin *celāre* to hide
▶**clan'destinely** ADVERB ▶**clan'destineness** NOUN

clang (klæŋ) VERB [1] to make or cause to make a loud resounding noise, as metal when struck. [2] *(intr)* to move or operate making such a sound. ◆ NOUN [3] a resounding metallic noise. [4] the harsh cry of certain birds.
▷HISTORY C16: from Latin *clangere*

clang association NOUN *Psychol* the association made between two words because they sound similar; for example *cling* and *ring.*

clanger ('klæŋə) NOUN [1] *Informal* a conspicuous mistake (esp in the phrase **drop a clanger**). [2] something that clangs or causes a clang.
▷HISTORY C20: from CLANG, referring to a mistake whose effects seem to clang

clangour *or US* **clangor** ('klæŋɡə, 'klæŋə) NOUN [1] a loud resonant often-repeated noise. [2] an uproar. ◆ VERB [3] *(intr)* to make or produce a loud resonant noise.
▷HISTORY C16: from Latin *clangor* a noise, from *clangere* to CLANG
▶'**clangorous** ADJECTIVE ▶'**clangorously** ADVERB

clank (klæŋk) NOUN [1] an abrupt harsh metallic sound. ◆ VERB [2] to make or cause to make such a sound. [3] *(intr)* to move or operate making such a sound.
▷HISTORY C17: of imitative origin
▶'**clankingly** ADVERB

clannish ('klænɪʃ) ADJECTIVE [1] of or characteristic of a clan. [2] tending to associate closely within a limited group to the exclusion of outsiders; cliquish.
▶'**clannishly** ADVERB ▶'**clannishness** NOUN

clansman ('klænzmən) NOUN, *plural* **-men.** a man belonging to a clan.

clanswoman ('klænzˌwʊmən) NOUN, *plural* **-women.** a woman belonging to a clan.

clap[1] (klæp) VERB **claps, clapping, clapped.** [1] to make or cause to make a sharp abrupt sound, as of two nonmetallic objects struck together. [2] to applaud (someone or something) by striking the palms of the hands together sharply. [3] *(tr)* to strike (a person) lightly with an open hand, in greeting, encouragement, etc. [4] *(tr)* to place or put quickly or forcibly: *they clapped him into jail.* [5] (of certain birds) to flap (the wings) noisily. [6] *(tr;* foll by *up* or *together)* to contrive or put together hastily: *they soon clapped up a shed.* [7] **clap eyes on.** *Informal* to catch sight of. [8] **clap hold of.** *Informal* to grasp suddenly or forcibly. ◆ NOUN [9] the sharp abrupt sound produced by striking the hands together. [10] the act of clapping, esp in applause: *he deserves a good clap.* [11] a sudden sharp sound, esp of thunder. [12] a light blow. [13] *Archaic* a sudden action or mishap.
▷HISTORY Old English *clæppan;* related to Old High German *klepfen,* Middle Dutch *klape* rattle, Dutch *klepel* clapper; all of imitative origin

clap[2] (klæp) NOUN (usually preceded by *the)* a slang word for **gonorrhoea.**
▷HISTORY C16: from Old French *clapoir* venereal sore, from *clapier* brothel, from Old Provençal, from *clap* heap of stones, of obscure origin

clapboard ('klæpˌbɔːd, 'klæbəd) NOUN [1] **a** a long thin timber board with one edge thicker than the other, used esp in the US and Canada in wood-frame construction by lapping each board over the one below. **b** *(as modifier): a clapboard house.* ◆ VERB [2] *(tr)* to cover with such boards.
▷HISTORY C16: partial translation of Low German *klappholt,* from *klappen* to crack + *holt* wood; related to Dutch *claphout;* see BOARD

Clapham Sect ('klæpəm) NOUN a group of early 19th-century Church of England evangelicals advocating personal piety, the abolition of slavery, etc.
▷HISTORY C19: named after *Clapham,* a district of London

clap-net NOUN a net, used esp by entomologists, that can be closed instantly by pulling a string.

clapometer (ˌklæˈpɒmɪtə) NOUN a device that measures applause.

clap on VERB *(tr)* to don hastily: *they clapped on their armour.*

clapped out ADJECTIVE (**clapped-out** *when prenominal) Brit, Austral, and NZ informal* (esp of machinery) worn out; dilapidated.

clapper (ˈklæpə) NOUN [1] a person or thing that claps. [2] a contrivance for producing a sound of clapping, as for scaring birds. [3] Also called: **tongue.** a small piece of metal suspended within a bell that causes it to sound when made to strike against its side. [4] a slang word for **tongue** (sense 1). [5] **go (run,** *or* **move) like the clappers.** *Brit informal* to move extremely fast.

clapperboard (ˈklæpəˌbɔːd) NOUN a pair of boards clapped together during film shooting in order to aid sound synchronization.

clapper bridge NOUN a primitive type of bridge in which planks or slabs of stone rest on piles of stones.

clapperclaw (ˈklæpəˌklɔː) VERB *(tr) Archaic* [1] to claw or scratch with the hands and nails. [2] to revile; abuse.
▷HISTORY C16: perhaps from CLAPPER + CLAW
▸ˈ**clapperˌclawer** NOUN

clappy-doo (ˌklæpɪˈduː) *or* **clabby-doo** NOUN *Scot* a large black mussel.
▷HISTORY C19: probably from Scottish Gaelic *clab* enormous mouth + *dubh* black

claptrap (ˈklæpˌtræp) NOUN *Informal* [1] contrived but foolish talk. [2] insincere and pretentious talk: *politicians' claptrap.*
▷HISTORY C18 (in the sense: something contrived to elicit applause): from CLAP[1] + TRAP[1]

claque (klæk) NOUN [1] a group of people hired to applaud. [2] a group of fawning admirers.
▷HISTORY C19: from French, from *claquer* to clap, of imitative origin

clarabella *or* **claribella** (ˌklærəˈbɛlə) NOUN an eight-foot flute stop on an organ.
▷HISTORY C19: from Latin *clāra,* feminine of *clārus* clear + *bella,* feminine of *bellus* beautiful

Clare (klɛə) NOUN a county of W Republic of Ireland, in Munster between Galway Bay and the Shannon estuary. County town: Ennis. Pop.: 94 006 (1996). Area: 3188 sq. km (1231 sq. miles).

clarence (ˈklærəns) NOUN a closed four-wheeled horse-drawn carriage, having a glass front.
▷HISTORY C19: named after the Duke of *Clarence* (1765–1837)

Clarenceux (ˈklærənsuː) NOUN *Heraldry* the second King-of-Arms in England.

clarendon (ˈklærəndən) NOUN *Printing* a style of boldface roman type.
▷HISTORY C20: named after the Clarendon Press at Oxford University

Clarendon (ˈklærəndən) NOUN a village near Salisbury in S England: site of a council held by Henry II in 1164 that produced a code of laws (the **Constitutions of Clarendon**) defining relations between church and state.

Clarendon Code NOUN *English history* four acts passed by the Cavalier Parliament between 1661 and 1665 to deal with the religious problems of the Restoration.
▷HISTORY C17: named after Edward Hyde, first Earl of Clarendon (1609–74), English statesman and historian, who was not, however, a supporter of the code

claret (ˈklærət) NOUN [1] *Chiefly Brit* a red wine, esp one from the Bordeaux district of France. [2] **a** a purplish-red colour. **b** *(as adjective): a claret carpet.*
▷HISTORY C14: from Old French *(vin) claret* clear (wine), from Medieval Latin *clārātum,* from *clārāre* to make clear, from Latin *clārus* CLEAR

claret cup NOUN an iced drink made of claret, brandy, lemon, sugar, and sometimes sherry, Curaçao, etc.

clarify (ˈklærɪˌfaɪ) VERB **-fies, -fying, -fied.** [1] to make or become clear or easy to understand. [2] to make or become free of impurities. [3] to make (fat, butter, etc.) clear by heating, etc., or (of fat, etc.) to become clear as a result of such a process.
▷HISTORY C14: from Old French *clarifier,* from Late Latin *clārificāre,* from Latin *clārus* clear + *facere* to make
▸ˌ**clarifiˈcation** NOUN ▸ˈ**clariˌfier** NOUN

clarinet (ˌklærɪˈnɛt) NOUN *Music* [1] a keyed woodwind instrument with a cylindrical bore and a single reed. It is a transposing instrument, most commonly pitched in A or B flat. Obsolete name: **clarionet** (ˌklærɪəˈnɛt). [2] an orchestral musician who plays the clarinet.
▷HISTORY C18: from French *clarinette,* probably from Italian *clarinetto,* from *clarino* trumpet
▸ˌ**clariˈnettist** *or* ˌ**clariˈnetist** NOUN

clarino (klæˈriːnəʊ) ADJECTIVE [1] of or relating to a high passage for the trumpet in 18th-century music. ◆ NOUN, *plural* **-nos** *or* **-ni** (-nɪ). [2] the high register of the trumpet. [3] an organ stop similar to the high register of the trumpet. [4] a trumpet or clarion.

clarion (ˈklærɪən) NOUN [1] a four-foot reed stop of trumpet quality on an organ. [2] an obsolete, high-pitched, small-bore trumpet. [3] the sound of such an instrument or any similar sound. ◆ ADJECTIVE [4] *(prenominal)* clear and ringing; inspiring: *a clarion call to action.* ◆ VERB [5] to proclaim loudly.
▷HISTORY C14: from Medieval Latin *clāriō* trumpet, from Latin *clārus* clear

clarity (ˈklærɪtɪ) NOUN [1] clearness, as of expression. [2] clearness, as of water.
▷HISTORY C16: from Latin *clāritās,* from *clārus* CLEAR

Clark cell (klɑːk) NOUN *Physics* a cell having a mercury cathode surrounded by a paste of mercuric sulphate and a zinc anode in a saturated solution of zinc sulphate. Formerly used as a standard, its emf is 1.4345 volts.
▷HISTORY C19: named after Hosiah *Clark* (died 1898), English scientist

clarkia (ˈklɑːkɪə) NOUN any North American onagraceous plant of the genus *Clarkia:* cultivated for their red, purple, or pink flowers.
▷HISTORY C19: New Latin, named after William Clark (1770–1838), US explorer and frontiersman, who discovered it

claro (ˈklɑːrəʊ) NOUN, *plural* **-ros** *or* **-roes.** a mild light-coloured cigar.
▷HISTORY from Spanish: CLEAR

clarsach (ˈklɑrsəx, ˈklɑːsək) NOUN the Celtic harp of Scotland and Ireland.
▷HISTORY C15: *clareschaw,* from Scottish Gaelic *clarsach,* Irish Gaelic *cláirsach* harp

clarthead (ˈklɑːtˌhɛd) NOUN *Northern English dialect* a slow-witted or stupid person.

clarts (klɑːts; *Scot* klærts) PLURAL NOUN *Scot and Northern English dialect* lumps of mud, esp on shoes.
▷HISTORY of unknown origin

clarty (ˈklɑːtɪ; *Scot* ˈklærtɪ) ADJECTIVE **clartier, clartiest.** *Scot and Northern English dialect* dirty, esp covered in mud; filthy.

clary (ˈklɛərɪ) NOUN, *plural* **claries.** any of several European plants of the genus *Salvia,* having aromatic leaves and blue flowers: family *Lamiaceae* (labiates).
▷HISTORY C14: from earlier *sclarreye,* from Medieval Latin *sclareia,* of obscure origin

-clase NOUN COMBINING FORM (in mineralogy) indicating a particular type of cleavage: *plagioclase.*
▷HISTORY via French from Greek *klasis* a breaking, from *klan* to break

clash (klæʃ) VERB [1] to make or cause to make a loud harsh sound, esp by striking together. [2] *(intr)* to be incompatible; conflict. [3] *(intr)* to engage together in conflict or contest. [4] *(intr)* (of dates or events) to coincide. [5] *(intr)* (of colours) to look ugly or inharmonious together. ◆ NOUN [6] a loud harsh noise. [7] a collision or conflict. [8] *Scot* gossip; tattle.
▷HISTORY C16: of imitative origin
▸ˈ**clasher** NOUN ▸ˈ**clashingly** ADVERB

clasp (klɑːsp) NOUN [1] a fastening, such as a catch or hook, used for holding things together. [2] a firm grasp, hold, or embrace. [3] *Military* a bar or insignia on a medal ribbon, to indicate either a second award or the battle, campaign, or reason for its award. ◆ VERB *(tr)* [4] to hold in a firm grasp. [5] to grasp firmly with the hand. [6] to fasten together with or as if with a clasp.
▷HISTORY C14: of uncertain origin; compare Old English *clyppan* to embrace
▸ˈ**clasper** NOUN

claspers (ˈklɑːspəz) PLURAL NOUN *Zoology* [1] a paired organ of male insects, used to clasp the female during copulation. [2] a paired organ of male sharks and related fish, used to assist the transfer of spermatozoa into the body of the female during copulation.

clasp knife NOUN a large knife with one or more blades or other devices folding into the handle.

class (klɑːs) NOUN [1] a collection or division of people or things sharing a common characteristic, attribute, quality, or property. [2] a group of persons sharing a similar social position and certain economic, political, and cultural characteristics. [3] (in Marxist theory) a group of persons sharing the same relationship to the means of production. [4] **a** the pattern of divisions that exist within a society on the basis of rank, economic status, etc. **b** *(as modifier): the class struggle; class distinctions.* [5] **a** a group of pupils or students who are taught and study together. **b** a meeting of a group of students for tuition. [6] *Chiefly US* a group of students who graduated in a specified year: *the class of '53.* [7] *(in combination and as modifier) Brit* a grade of attainment in a university honours degree: *second-class honours.* [8] one of several standards of accommodation in public transport. See also **first class, second class, third class.** [9] **a** *Informal* excellence or elegance, esp in dress, design, or behaviour: *that girl's got class.* **b** *(as modifier): a class act.* [10] **a** outstanding speed and stamina in a racehorse. **b** *(as modifier): the class horse in the race.* [11] *Biology* any of the taxonomic groups into which a phylum is divided and which contains one or more orders. *Amphibia, Reptilia,* and *Mammalia* are three classes of phylum *Chordata.* [12] *Maths, logic* **a** another name for **set**[2] (sense 3). **b proper class.** a class which cannot itself be a member of other classes. [13] **in a class of its own** *or* **in a class by oneself.** unequalled; unparalleled. ◆ VERB [14] to have or assign a place within a group, grade, or class.
▷HISTORY C17: from Latin *classis* class, rank, fleet; related to Latin *calāre* to summon
▸ˈ**classable** ADJECTIVE ▸ˈ**classer** NOUN

class-A amplifier NOUN an electronic amplifier in which the output current flows for the whole of the input signal cycle.

class action NOUN *US law* a legal action undertaken by one or more people representing the interests of a large group of people with the same grievance.

class A drug NOUN *Law* (in Britain) any of the most dangerous group of controlled drugs, including heroin, cocaine, and MDMA. Compare **class B drug, class C drug.**

class-B amplifier NOUN an electronic amplifier in which the output flows for half of the input signal cycle.

class B drug NOUN *Law* (in Britain) any of the second most dangerous group of controlled drugs, including amphetamine. Compare **class A drug, class C drug.**

class-C amplifier NOUN an electronic amplifier in which the output current flows for less than half of the input cycle.

class C drug NOUN *Law* (in Britain) any of the least dangerous group of controlled drugs, including temazepam. Compare **class A drug, class B drug.**

class-conscious ADJECTIVE aware of belonging to a particular social rank or grade, esp in being hostile or proud because of class distinctions.
▸ˌ**class-ˈconsciousness** NOUN

classic (ˈklæsɪk) ADJECTIVE [1] of the highest class, esp in art or literature. [2] serving as a standard or model of its kind; definitive. [3] adhering to an established set of rules or principles in the arts or sciences: *a classic proof.* [4] characterized by simplicity, balance, regularity, and purity of form; classical. [5] of lasting interest or significance. [6] continuously in fashion because of its simple and basic style: *a classic day dress.* ◆ NOUN [7] an author, artist, or work of art of the highest excellence. [8] a creation or work considered as definitive. [9] *Horse racing* **a** any of the five principal races for three-year-old horses in Britain, namely the One Thousand Guineas, Two Thousand Guineas, Derby, Oaks, and Saint Leger. **b** a race equivalent to any of these in other countries. ◆ See also **classics.**

▷**HISTORY** C17: from Latin *classicus* of the first rank, from *classis* division, rank, CLASS

classical (ˈklæsɪkəl) ADJECTIVE 1 of, relating to, or characteristic of the ancient Greeks and Romans or their civilization, esp in the period of their ascendancy. 2 designating, following, or influenced by the art or culture of ancient Greece or Rome: *classical architecture.* 3 *Music* **a** of, relating to, or denoting any music or its period of composition marked by stability of form, intellectualism, and restraint. Compare **romantic** (sense 5). **b** accepted as a standard: *the classical suite.* **c** denoting serious art music in general. Compare **pop** (sense 2). 4 *Music* of or relating to a style of music composed, esp at Vienna, during the late 18th and early 19th centuries. This period is marked by the establishment, esp by Haydn and Mozart, of sonata form. 5 denoting or relating to a style in any of the arts characterized by emotional restraint and conservatism: *a classical style of painting.* See **classicism** (sense 1). 6 well versed in the art and literature of ancient Greece and Rome. 7 (of an education) based on the humanities and the study of Latin and Greek. 8 *Physics* **a** not involving the quantum theory or the theory of relativity: *classical mechanics.* **b** obeying the laws of Newtonian mechanics or 19th-century physics: *a classical gas.* 9 another word for **classic** (senses 2, 4). 10 (of a logical or mathematical system) according with the law of excluded middle, so that every statement is known to be either true or false even if it is not known which.
▸ˌ**classiˈcality** *or* ˈ**classicalness** NOUN ▸ˈ**classically** ADVERB

classical college NOUN (in Quebec) a college offering a programme that emphasizes the classics and leads to university entrance.

classical conditioning NOUN *Psychol* the alteration in responding that occurs when two stimuli are regularly paired in close succession: the response originally given to the second stimulus comes to be given to the first. See also **conditioned response.**

classical probability NOUN another name for **mathematical probability.**

Classical school NOUN economic theory based on the works of Adam Smith and David Ricardo, which explains the creation of wealth and advocates free trade.

classic blues NOUN (*functioning as singular or plural*) *Jazz* a type of city blues performed by a female singer accompanied by a small group.

classic car NOUN *Chiefly Brit* a car that is more than twenty-five years old. Compare **veteran car, vintage car.**

classicism (ˈklæsɪˌsɪzəm) *or* **classicalism** (ˈklæsɪkəˌlɪzəm) NOUN 1 a style based on the study of Greek and Roman models, characterized by emotional restraint and regularity of form, associated esp with the 18th century in Europe; the antithesis of romanticism. Compare **neoclassicism.** 2 knowledge or study of the culture of ancient Greece and Rome. 3 **a** a Greek or Latin form or expression. **b** an expression in a modern language, such as English, that is modelled on a Greek or Latin form.

classicist (ˈklæsɪsɪst) *or* **classicalist** (ˈklæsɪkəlɪst) NOUN 1 **a** a student of ancient Latin and Greek. **b** a person who advocates the study of ancient Latin and Greek. 2 an adherent of classicism in literature or art.
▸ˌ**classiˈcistic** ADJECTIVE

classicize *or* **classicise** (ˈklæsɪˌsaɪz) VERB 1 (*tr*) to make classic. 2 (*intr*) to imitate classical style.

classics (ˈklæsɪks) PLURAL NOUN 1 **the.** a body of literature regarded as great or lasting, esp that of ancient Greece or Rome. 2 **the.** the ancient Greek and Latin languages. 3 (*functioning as singular*) ancient Greek and Roman culture considered as a subject for academic study.

classification (ˌklæsɪfɪˈkeɪʃən) NOUN 1 systematic placement in categories. 2 one of the divisions in a system of classifying. 3 *Biology* **a** the placing of animals and plants in a series of increasingly specialized groups because of similarities in structure, origin, molecular composition, etc., that indicate a common relationship. The major groups are domain or superkingdom, kingdom, phylum (in animals) or division (in plants), class, order, family, genus, and species. **b** the study of the principles and practice of this process; taxonomy. 4 *Government* the designation of an item of information as being secret and not available to people outside a restricted group.
▷**HISTORY** C18: from French; see CLASS, -IFY, -ATION
▸ˌ**classifiˈcational** ADJECTIVE ▸ˌ**classifiˈcatory** ADJECTIVE

classification schedule NOUN *Library science* the printed scheme of a system of classification.

classified (ˈklæsɪˌfaɪd) ADJECTIVE 1 arranged according to some system of classification. 2 *Government* (of information) not available to people outside a restricted group, esp for reasons of national security. 3 (of information) closely concealed or secret. 4 (of advertisements in newspapers, etc.) arranged according to type. 5 *Brit* (of newspapers) containing sports results, esp football results. 6 (of British roads) having a number in the national road system. If the number is preceded by an M the road is a motorway, if by an A it is a first-class road, and if by a B it is a secondary road.

classify (ˈklæsɪˌfaɪ) VERB **-fies, -fying, -fied.** (*tr*) 1 to arrange or order by classes; categorize. 2 *Government* to declare (information, documents, etc.) of possible aid to an enemy and therefore not available to people outside a restricted group.
▷**HISTORY** C18: back formation from CLASSIFICATION
▸ˈ**classiˌfiable** ADJECTIVE ▸ˈ**classiˌfier** NOUN

class interval NOUN *Statistics* one of the intervals into which the range of a variable of a distribution is divided, esp one of the divisions of the base line of a bar chart or histogram.

classis (ˈklæsɪs) NOUN, *plural* **classes** (ˈklæsiːz). (in some Reformed Churches) 1 a governing body of elders or pastors. 2 the district or group of local churches directed by such a body.
▷**HISTORY** C16: from Latin; see CLASS

classism (ˈklɑːsɪzəm) NOUN the belief that people from certain social or economic classes are superior to others.
▸ˈ**classist** ADJECTIVE

classless (ˈklɑːslɪs) ADJECTIVE 1 not belonging to or forming a class. 2 characterized by the absence of economic and social distinctions.
▸ˈ**classlessness** NOUN

class list NOUN (in Britain) a list categorizing students according to the class of honours they have obtained in their degree examination.

class mark NOUN 1 *Statistics* a value within a class interval, esp its midpoint or the nearest integral value, used to represent the interval for computational convenience. 2 Also called: **class number.** *Library science* a symbol on a book or other publication indicating its subject field, shelf position, etc.

classmate (ˈklɑːsˌmeɪt) NOUN a friend or contemporary of the same class in a school, college, etc.

classroom (ˈklɑːsˌruːm, -ˌrʊm) NOUN a room in which classes are conducted, esp in a school or college.

classroom assistant NOUN a person whose job is to help a schoolteacher in the classroom.

class struggle NOUN **the.** *Marxism* the continual conflict between the capitalist and working classes for economic and political power. Also called: **class war.**

classy (ˈklɑːsɪ) ADJECTIVE **classier, classiest.** *Slang* elegant; stylish.
▸ˈ**classily** ADVERB ▸ˈ**classiness** NOUN

clastic (ˈklæstɪk) ADJECTIVE 1 (of sedimentary rock, etc.) composed of fragments of pre-existing rock that have been transported some distance from their points of origin. 2 *Biology* dividing into parts: *a clastic cell.* 3 able to be dismantled for study or observation: *a clastic model of the brain.*
▷**HISTORY** C19: from Greek *klastos* shattered, from *klan* to break

clat (klæt) NOUN *Dialect* an irksome or troublesome task.

clathrate (ˈklæθreɪt) ADJECTIVE 1 resembling a net or lattice. ◆ NOUN 2 *Chem* a solid compound in which molecules of one substance are physically trapped in the crystal lattice of another.
▷**HISTORY** C17: from Latin *clāthrāre* to provide with a lattice, from Greek *klēthra,* from *klaithron* a bar

clatter (ˈklætə) VERB 1 to make or cause to make a rattling noise, esp as a result of movement. 2 (*intr*) to chatter. ◆ NOUN 3 a rattling sound or noise. 4 a noisy commotion, such as one caused by loud chatter.
▷**HISTORY** Old English *clatrung* clattering (gerund); related to Dutch *klateren* to rattle, German *klatschen* to smack, Norwegian *klattra* to knock
▸ˈ**clatterer** NOUN ▸ˈ**clatteringly** ADVERB ▸ˈ**clattery** ADJECTIVE

claudication (ˌklɔːdɪˈkeɪʃən) NOUN 1 limping; lameness. 2 *Pathol* short for **intermittent claudication.**
▷**HISTORY** C18: from Latin *claudicātiō,* from *claudicāre,* from *claudus* lame

clause (klɔːz) NOUN 1 *Grammar* a group of words, consisting of a subject and a predicate including a finite verb, that does not necessarily constitute a sentence. See also **main clause, subordinate clause, coordinate clause.** 2 a section of a legal document such as a contract, will, or draft statute.
▷**HISTORY** C13: from Old French, from Medieval Latin *clausa* a closing (of a rhetorical period), back formation from Latin *clausula,* from *claudere* to close
▸ˈ**clausal** ADJECTIVE

claustral (ˈklɔːstrəl) ADJECTIVE a less common variant of **cloistral.**

claustrophobia (ˌklɔːstrəˈfəʊbɪə, ˌklɒs-) NOUN an abnormal fear of being closed in or of being in a confined space.
▷**HISTORY** C19: from *claustro-,* from Latin *claustrum* CLOISTER + -PHOBIA
▸ˈ**claustroˌphobe** NOUN

claustrophobic (ˌklɔːstrəˈfəʊbɪk, ˌklɒs-) ADJECTIVE 1 suffering from claustrophobia. 2 unpleasantly cramped, confined, or closed in: *narrow claustrophobic spaces.*
▸ˌ**claustroˈphobically** ADVERB

clavate (ˈkleɪveɪt, -vɪt) *or* **claviform** ADJECTIVE shaped like a club with the thicker end uppermost.
▷**HISTORY** C19: from Latin *clāva* club
▸ˈ**clavately** ADVERB

clave[1] (kleɪv, klɑːv) NOUN *Music* one of a pair of hardwood sticks struck together to make a hollow sound, esp to mark the beat of Latin-American dance music.
▷**HISTORY** C20: from American Spanish, from Latin *clavis* key

clave[2] (kleɪv) VERB *Archaic* a past tense of **cleave.**

clave[3] (kleɪv) NOUN *Zoology* a clublike thickening at the upper end of an organ, esp of the antenna of an insect.
▷**HISTORY** C19: from Latin *clāva* club

claver (ˈkleɪvə) VERB (*intr*) 1 to talk idly; gossip. ◆ NOUN 2 (*often plural*) idle talk; gossip.
▷**HISTORY** C13: of uncertain origin

clavicembalo (ˌklævɪˈtʃɛmbələʊ) NOUN, *plural* **-los.** another name for **harpsichord.**
▷**HISTORY** C18: from Italian, from Medieval Latin *clāvis* key + *cymbalum* CYMBAL

clavichord (ˈklævɪˌkɔːd) NOUN a keyboard instrument consisting of a number of thin wire strings struck from below by brass tangents. The instrument is noted for its delicate tones, since the tangents do not rebound from the string until the key is released.
▷**HISTORY** C15: from Medieval Latin *clāvichordium,* from Latin *clāvis* key + *chorda* string, CHORD[1]
▸ˈ**claviˌchordist** NOUN

clavicle (ˈklævɪkəl) NOUN 1 either of the two bones connecting the shoulder blades with the upper part of the breastbone. Nontechnical name: **collarbone.** 2 the corresponding structure in other vertebrates.
▷**HISTORY** C17: from Medieval Latin *clāvicula,* from Latin *clāvis* key
▸**clavicular** (kləˈvɪkjʊlə) ADJECTIVE ▸**claviculate** (kləˈvɪkjʊˌleɪt) ADJECTIVE

clavicorn (ˈklævɪˌkɔːn) NOUN 1 any beetle of the group *Clavicornia,* including the ladybirds, characterized by club-shaped antennae. ◆ ADJECTIVE 2 of, relating to, or belonging to the *Clavicornia.*
▷**HISTORY** C19: from New Latin *Clavicornia,* from Latin *clāva* club + *cornū* horn

clavier (kləˈvɪə, ˈklævɪə) NOUN **a** any keyboard instrument. **b** the keyboard itself.

▷**HISTORY** C18: from French: keyboard, from Old French (in the sense: key bearer), from Latin *clāvis* key

claviform ('klævɪˌfɔːm) ADJECTIVE another word for **clavate.**
▷**HISTORY** C19: from Latin *clāva* club

Clavius ('kleɪvɪəs) NOUN one of the largest of the craters on the moon, about 230 kilometres (145 miles) in diameter, whose walls have peaks up to 5700 metres (19 000 feet) above the floor. It lies in the SE quadrant.

claw (klɔː) NOUN [1] a curved pointed horny process on the end of each digit in birds, some reptiles, and certain mammals. [2] a corresponding structure in some invertebrates, such as the pincer of a crab. [3] a part or member like a claw in function or appearance. [4] *Botany* the narrow basal part of certain petals and sepals. ◆ VERB [5] to scrape, tear, or dig (something or someone) with claws, etc. [6] (*tr*) to create by scratching as with claws: *to claw an opening.*
▷**HISTORY** Old English *clawu;* related to Old High German *kluwi,* Sanskrit *glau-* ball, sphere
▸**'clawer** NOUN ▸**'clawless** ADJECTIVE

claw back VERB (*tr, adverb*) [1] to get back (something) with difficulty. [2] to recover (a sum of money), esp by taxation or a penalty. ◆ NOUN **clawback.** [3] the recovery of a sum of money, esp by taxation or a penalty. [4] the sum so recovered.

claw hammer NOUN a hammer with a cleft at one end of the head for extracting nails. Also called: **carpenter's hammer.**

claw hatchet NOUN a hatchet with a claw at one end of its head for extracting nails.

claw off VERB (*adverb, usually tr*) *Nautical* to avoid the dangers of (a lee shore or other hazard) by beating.

claw setting NOUN *Brit* a jewellery setting with clawlike prongs. US equivalent: **Tiffany setting.**

clay (kleɪ) NOUN [1] a very fine-grained material that consists of hydrated aluminium silicate, quartz, and organic fragments and occurs as sedimentary rocks, soils, and other deposits. It becomes plastic when moist but hardens on heating and is used in the manufacture of bricks, cement, ceramics, etc. Related adjective: **figuline.** [2] earth or mud in general. [3] *Poetic* the material of the human body. ◆ VERB [4] (*tr*) to cover or mix with clay.
▷**HISTORY** Old English *clǣg;* related to Old High German *klīa,* Norwegian *kli,* Latin *glūs* glue, Greek *gloios* sticky oil
▸**'clayey, 'clayish,** *or* **'clayˌlike** ADJECTIVE

claybank ('kleɪˌbæŋk) NOUN *US* **a** a dull brownish-orange colour. **b** (*as adjective*): *a claybank horse.*

clay court NOUN a tennis court with a playing surface topped by a layer of crushed shale, brick, or stone.

claymation (ˌkleɪ'meɪʃən) NOUN the techniques of animation applied to clay models.
▷**HISTORY** C20: from CLAY + (ANI)MATION

clay mineral NOUN any of a group of minerals consisting of hydrated aluminium silicates: the major constituents of clays.

claymore ('kleɪˌmɔː; *Scot* ˌkle'mor) NOUN [1] a large two-edged broadsword used formerly by Scottish Highlanders. [2] a US type of antipersonnel mine.
▷**HISTORY** C18: from Gaelic *claidheamh mōr* great sword

claypan ('kleɪˌpæn) NOUN a layer of stiff impervious clay situated just below the surface of the ground, which holds water after heavy rain.

clay pigeon NOUN [1] a disc of baked clay hurled into the air from a machine as a target to be shot at. [2] *US slang* a person in a defenceless position; sitting duck.

clay road NOUN *NZ* an unsealed and unmetalled road in a rural area.

claystone ('kleɪˌstəʊn) NOUN a compact very fine-grained rock consisting of consolidated clay particles.

claytonia (kleɪ'təʊnɪə) NOUN any low-growing North American succulent portulacaceous plant of the genus *Claytonia.*
▷**HISTORY** C18: named after John *Clayton* (1693–1773), American botanist

CLC ABBREVIATION FOR Canadian Labour Congress.

-cle SUFFIX FORMING NOUNS indicating smallness: *cubicle; particle.*
▷**HISTORY** via Old French from Latin *-culus.* See -CULE

clean (kliːn) ADJECTIVE [1] without dirt or other impurities; unsoiled. [2] without anything in it or on it: *a clean page.* [3] without extraneous or foreign materials. [4] without defect, difficulties, or problems: *a clean test flight.* [5] **a** (of a nuclear weapon) producing little or no radioactive fallout or contamination. **b** uncontaminated. Compare **dirty** (sense 11). [6] (of a wound, etc.) having no pus or other sign of infection. [7] pure; morally sound. [8] without objectionable language or obscenity: *a clean joke.* [9] (of printer's proofs, etc.) relatively free from errors; easily readable: *clean copy.* [10] thorough or complete: *a clean break.* [11] dexterous or adroit: *a clean throw.* [12] *Sport* played fairly and without fouls. [13] simple in design: *a ship's clean lines.* [14] *Aeronautics* causing little turbulence; streamlined. [15] (of an aircraft) having no projections, such as rockets, flaps, etc., into the airstream. [16] honourable or respectable. [17] habitually neat. [18] (esp of a driving licence) showing or having no record of offences. [19] *Slang* **a** innocent; not guilty. **b** not carrying illegal drugs, weapons, etc. [20] *Nautical* (of a vessel) **a** having its bottom clean. **b** having a satisfactory bill of health. [21] *Old Testament* **a** (of persons) free from ceremonial defilement. **b** (of animals, birds, and fish) lawful to eat. [22] *New Testament* morally and spiritually pure. ◆ VERB [23] to make or become free of dirt, filth, etc.: *the stove cleans easily.* [24] (*tr*) to remove in making clean: *to clean marks off the wall.* [25] (*tr*) to prepare (fish, poultry, etc.) for cooking: *to clean a chicken.* ◆ ADVERB [26] in a clean way; cleanly. [27] *Not standard* (intensifier): *clean forgotten; clean dead.* [28] **clean bowled.** *Cricket* bowled by a ball that breaks the wicket without hitting the batsman or his bat. [29] **come clean.** *Informal* to make a revelation or confession. ◆ NOUN [30] the act or an instance of cleaning: *he gave his shoes a clean.* [31] **clean sweep.** See **sweep** (sense 33). ◆ See also **clean out, clean up.**
▷**HISTORY** Old English *clǣne;* related to Old Frisian *klēne* small, neat, Old High German *kleini*
▸**'cleanable** ADJECTIVE ▸**'cleanness** NOUN

clean-cut ADJECTIVE [1] clearly outlined; neat: *clean-cut lines of a ship.* [2] definite: *a clean-cut decision in boxing.*

cleaner ('kliːnə) NOUN [1] a person, device, chemical agent, etc., that removes dirt, as from clothes or carpets. [2] (*usually plural*) a shop, etc. that provides a dry-cleaning service. [3] **take (a person) to the cleaners.** *Informal* to rob or defraud (a person) of all of his money.

clean-limbed ADJECTIVE having well-proportioned limbs.

cleanly ADVERB ('kliːnlɪ) [1] in a fair manner. [2] easily or smoothly: *the screw went into the wood cleanly.* ◆ ADJECTIVE ('klɛnlɪ) **-lier, -liest.** [3] habitually clean or neat.
▸**cleanlily** ('klɛnlɪlɪ) ADVERB ▸**cleanliness** ('klɛnlɪnɪs) NOUN

clean out VERB (*tr, adverb*) [1] (foll by *of* or *from*) to remove (something) (from or away from). [2] *Slang* to leave (someone) with no money: *gambling had cleaned him out.* [3] *Informal* to exhaust (stocks, goods, etc.) completely.

cleanse (klɛnz) VERB (*tr*) [1] to remove dirt, filth, etc., from. [2] to remove guilt from. [3] to remove a group of people from (an area) by means of ethnic cleansing.
▷**HISTORY** Old English *clǣnsian;* related to Middle Low German *klēnsen;* see CLEAN
▸**'cleansable** ADJECTIVE

cleanser ('klɛnzə) NOUN a cleansing agent, such as a detergent.

clean-shaven ADJECTIVE (of men) having the facial hair shaved off.

clean sheet NOUN *Sport* an instance of conceding no goals or points in a match or competition (esp in the phrase **keep a clean sheet**).

cleanskin ('kliːnˌskɪn) NOUN *Austral* [1] an unbranded animal. [2] *Slang* a person without a criminal record.

clean up VERB (*adverb*) [1] to rid (something) of dirt, filth, or other impurities. [2] to make (someone or something) orderly or presentable. [3] (*tr*) to rid (a place) of undesirable people or conditions: *the campaign against vice had cleaned up the city.* [4] (*intr*) *Informal* to make a great profit. ◆ NOUN **cleanup.** [5] **a** the process of cleaning up or eliminating something. **b** (*as modifier*): *a cleanup campaign.* [6] *Informal, chiefly US* a great profit.

clean wool NOUN wool that has been scoured to remove wax.

clear (klɪə) ADJECTIVE [1] free from darkness or obscurity; bright. [2] (of weather) free from dullness or clouds. [3] transparent: *clear water.* [4] even and pure in tone or colour: *clear blue.* [5] without discoloration, blemish, or defect: *a clear skin.* [6] easy to see or hear; distinct. [7] free from doubt or confusion: *his instructions are not clear.* [8] (*postpositive*) certain in the mind; sure: *are you clear?* [9] evident or obvious: *it is clear that he won't come now.* [10] (of sounds or the voice) not harsh or hoarse. [11] serene; calm. [12] without qualification or limitation; complete: *a clear victory.* [13] free of suspicion, guilt, or blame: *a clear conscience.* [14] free of obstruction; open: *a clear passage.* [15] free from debt or obligation. [16] (of money, profits, etc.) without deduction; net. [17] emptied of freight or cargo. [18] (of timber) having a smooth, unblemished surface. [19] Also: **in clear.** (of a message, etc.) not in code. [20] Also: **light.** *Phonetics* denoting an (l) in whose articulation the main part of the tongue is brought forward giving the sound of a front-vowel timbre. [21] *Showjumping* (of a round) ridden without any fences being knocked down or any points being lost. ◆ ADVERB [22] in a clear or distinct manner. [23] completely or utterly. [24] (*postpositive;* often foll by *of*) not in contact (with); free: *stand clear of the gates.* ◆ NOUN [25] a clear space. [26] another word for **clearance.** [27] **in the clear. a** free of suspicion, guilt, or blame. **b** *Sport* able to receive a pass without being tackled. ◆ VERB [28] to make or become free from darkness, obscurity, etc. [29] (*intr*) **a** (of the weather) to become free from dullness, fog, rain, etc. **b** (of mist, fog, etc.) to disappear. [30] (*tr*) to free from impurity or blemish. [31] (*tr*) to free from doubt or confusion: *to clear one's mind.* [32] (*tr*) to rid of objects, obstructions, etc. [33] (*tr*) to make or form (a path, way, etc.) by removing obstructions. [34] (*tr*) to free or remove (a person or thing) from something, such as suspicion, blame, or guilt. [35] (*tr*) to move or pass by or over without contact or involvement: *he cleared the wall easily.* [36] (*tr*) to rid (the throat) of phlegm or obstruction. [37] (*tr*) to make or gain (money) as profit. [38] (*tr;* often foll by *off*) to discharge or settle (a debt). [39] (*tr*) to free (a debtor) from obligation. [40] (*intr*) (of a cheque) to pass through one's bank and be charged against one's account. [41] *Banking* to settle accounts by exchanging (commercial documents) in a clearing house. [42] to permit (ships, aircraft, cargo, passengers, etc.) to unload, disembark, depart, etc., after fulfilling the customs and other requirements, or (of ships, etc.) to be permitted to unload, etc. [43] to obtain or give (clearance). [44] (*tr*) to obtain clearance from. [45] (*tr*) *Microscopy* to make (specimens) transparent by immersion in a fluid such as xylene. [46] (*tr*) to permit (a person, company, etc.) to see or handle classified information. [47] (*tr*) *Military* **a** to achieve transmission of (a signalled message) and acknowledgment of its receipt at its destination. **b** to decode (a message, etc.). [48] (*tr*) *Sport* to hit, kick, carry, or throw (the ball) out of the defence area. [49] (*tr*) *Computing* to remove data from a storage device and replace it with particular characters that usually indicate zero. [50] (*tr*) *NZ* to remove (trees, scrub, etc.) from land. [51] **clear the air.** See **air** (sense 11). [52] **clear the decks.** to prepare for action, as by removing obstacles from a field of activity or combat. ◆ See also **clear away, clear off, clear out, clear up.**
▷**HISTORY** C13 *clere,* from Old French *cler,* from Latin *clārus* clear, bright, brilliant, illustrious
▸**'clearable** ADJECTIVE ▸**'clearer** NOUN ▸**'clearness** NOUN

clearance ('klɪərəns) NOUN [1] **a** the process or an instance of clearing: *slum clearance.* **b** (*as modifier*): *a clearance order.* [2] space between two parts in motion or in relative motion. [3] permission for an aircraft, ship, passengers, etc., to proceed. [4] *Banking* the exchange of commercial documents drawn on the members of a clearing house. [5] **a** the disposal of merchandise at reduced prices. **b** (*as modifier*): *a clearance sale.* 6 *Sport* **a** the act of hitting or kicking a ball out of the defensive area, as in football. **b** an instance of this. 7 the act of clearing an area of land of its inhabitants by mass eviction. See **Highland Clearances.** 8 *Dentistry* the extraction of all of a person's teeth. 9 a less common word for **clearing.**

clear away VERB (*adverb*) to remove (objects) from (the table) after a meal.

clearcole ('klɪəkəʊl) NOUN 1 a type of size containing whiting. ◆ VERB 2 (*tr*) to paint (a wall) with this size.
▷HISTORY C19: from French *claire colle* clear size

clear-cut ADJECTIVE (**clear cut** *when postpositive*) 1 definite; not vague: *a clear-cut proposal.* 2 clearly outlined. ◆ VERB 3 (*tr*) another term for **clear-fell.**

clear-eyed ADJECTIVE 1 discerning; perceptive. 2 having clear eyes or sharp vision.

clear-fell VERB (*tr*) to cut down all of the trees in (a wood, part of a wood, or throughout an area of land).

clear-headed ADJECTIVE mentally alert; sensible; judicious.
▸ **ˌclear-ˈheadedly** ADVERB ▸ **ˌclear-ˈheadedness** NOUN

clearing ('klɪərɪŋ) NOUN an area with few or no trees or shrubs in wooded or overgrown land.

clearing bank NOUN (in Britain) any bank that makes use of the central clearing house in London for the transfer of credits and cheques between banks.

clearing house NOUN 1 *Banking* an institution where cheques and other commercial papers drawn on member banks are cancelled against each other so that only net balances are payable. 2 a central agency for the collection and distribution of information or materials.

clearing sale NOUN *Austral* the auction of plant, stock, and effects of a country property, esp after the property has changed hands.

clearly ('klɪəlɪ) ADVERB 1 in a clear, distinct, or obvious manner: *I could see everything quite clearly.* 2 (*sentence modifier*) it is obvious that; evidently: *clearly the social services must be flexible.*

clear off VERB (*intr, adverb*) *Informal* to go away: often used imperatively.

clear out VERB (*adverb*) 1 (*intr*) *Informal* to go away: often used imperatively. 2 (*tr*) to remove and sort the contents of (a room, container, etc.). 3 (*tr*) *Slang* to leave (someone) with no money. 4 (*tr*) *Slang* to exhaust (stocks, goods, etc.) completely.

clear-sighted ADJECTIVE 1 involving accurate perception or judgment: *a clear-sighted compromise.* 2 having clear vision.
▸ **ˌclear-ˈsightedly** ADVERB ▸ **ˌclear-ˈsightedness** NOUN

clearstory ('klɪəˌstɔːrɪ) NOUN a variant spelling of **clerestory.**
▸ **ˈclearˌstoried** ADJECTIVE

clear up VERB (*adverb*) 1 (*tr*) to explain or solve (a mystery, misunderstanding, etc.). 2 to put (a place or thing that is disordered) in order. 3 (*intr*) (of the weather) to become brighter. ◆ NOUN **clear-up** ('klɪərˌʌp). 4 the act or an instance of clearing up.

clearway ('klɪəˌweɪ) NOUN 1 *Brit* a stretch of road on which motorists may stop only in an emergency. 2 an area at the end of a runway over which an aircraft taking off makes its initial climb: it is under the control of the airport.

clearwing *or* **clearwing moth** ('klɪəˌwɪŋ) NOUN any moth of the family *Sesiidae* (or *Aegeriidae*), characterized by the absence of scales from the greater part of the wings. They are day-flying and some, such as the **hornet clearwing** (*Sesia apiformis*), resemble wasps and other hymenopterans.

cleat (kliːt) NOUN 1 a wedge-shaped block, usually of wood, attached to a structure to act as a support. 2 a device consisting of two hornlike prongs projecting horizontally in opposite directions from a central base, used for securing lines on vessels, wharves, etc. 3 a short length of angle iron used as a bracket. 4 a piece of metal, leather, etc., attached to the sole of a shoe to prevent wear or slipping. 5 a small triangular-shaped nail used in glazing. 6 any of the main cleavage planes in a coal seam. ◆ VERB (*tr*) 7 to supply or support with a cleat or cleats. 8 to secure (a line) on a cleat.
▷HISTORY C14: of Germanic origin, compare Old High German *chlōz* clod, lump, Dutch *kloot* ball

cleavage ('kliːvɪdʒ) NOUN 1 *Informal* the separation between a woman's breasts, esp as revealed by a low-cut dress. 2 a division or split. 3 (of crystals) the act of splitting or the tendency to split along definite planes so as to yield smooth surfaces. 4 Also called: **segmentation.** *Embryol* (in animals) the repeated division of a fertilized ovum into a solid ball of cells (a morula), which later becomes hollow (a blastula). 5 the breaking of a chemical bond in a molecule to give smaller molecules or radicals. 6 *Geology* the natural splitting of certain rocks, or minerals such as slates, or micas along the planes of weakness.

cleave[1] (kliːv) VERB **cleaves, cleaving; cleft, cleaved,** *or* **clove; cleft, cleaved,** *or* **cloven.** 1 to split or cause to split, esp along a natural weakness. 2 (*tr*) to make by or as if by cutting: *to cleave a path.* 3 (when *intr,* foll by *through*) to penetrate or traverse.
▷HISTORY Old English *clēofan;* related to Old Norse *kljūfa,* Old High German *klioban,* Latin *glūbere* to peel
▸ **ˈcleavable** ADJECTIVE ▸ **ˌcleavaˈbility** NOUN

cleave[2] (kliːv) VERB (*intr;* foll by *to*) to cling or adhere.
▷HISTORY Old English *cleofian;* related to Old High German *klebēn* to stick

cleaver ('kliːvə) NOUN a heavy knife or long-bladed hatchet, esp one used by butchers.

cleavers ('kliːvəz) NOUN (*functioning as singular*) a Eurasian rubiaceous plant, *Galium aparine,* having small white flowers and prickly stems and fruits. Also called: **goosegrass, hairif, sticky willie.**
▷HISTORY Old English *clīfe;* related to *clīfan* to CLEAVE[2]

cleck[1] (klɛk) VERB (*tr*) *Scot* 1 (of birds) to hatch. 2 to lay or hatch (a plot or scheme).
▷HISTORY C15: from Old Norse *klekja*

cleck[2] (klɛk) *South Wales dialect* ◆ VERB 1 (*intr;* often foll by *on*) to gossip (about); tell (on). ◆ NOUN 2 (*often plural*) a piece of gossip.
▷HISTORY from Welsh, from *clecan* to gossip, and *clec* gossip
▸ **ˈclecky** ADJECTIVE

cleek *or* **cleik** (kliːk) NOUN 1 *Chiefly Scot* a large hook, such as one used to land fish. 2 *Golf* a former name for a club, corresponding to the modern No. 1 or No. 2 iron, used for long low shots.
▷HISTORY C15: of uncertain origin

Cleethorpes ('kliːθɔːps) NOUN a resort in E England, in North East Lincolnshire unitary authority, Lincolnshire. Pop.: 32 719 (1991).

clef (klef) NOUN one of several symbols placed on the left-hand side beginning of each stave indicating the pitch of the music written after it. See also **alto clef, bass clef, C clef, soprano clef, tenor clef, treble clef.**
▷HISTORY C16: from French: key, clef, from Latin *clāvis;* related to Latin *claudere* to close

cleft (klɛft) VERB 1 the past tense and a past participle of **cleave**[1]. ◆ NOUN 2 a fissure or crevice. 3 an indentation or split in something, such as the chin, palate, etc. ◆ ADJECTIVE 4 split; divided. 5 (of leaves) having one or more incisions reaching nearly to the midrib.
▷HISTORY Old English *geclyft* (noun); related to Old High German *kluft* tongs, German *Kluft* gap, fissure; see CLEAVE[1]

cleft palate NOUN a congenital crack or fissure in the midline of the hard palate, often associated with a harelip.

cleg (klɛg) NOUN another name for a **horsefly**, esp one of the genus *Haematopota*
▷HISTORY C15: from Old Norse *kleggi*

cleidoic egg (klaɪˈdəʊɪk) NOUN the egg of birds and insects, which is enclosed in a protective shell limiting the exchange of water, gases, etc.
▷HISTORY C20: from Greek *kleidoun* to lock up, from *kleid-, kleis* key

cleistogamy (klaɪˈstɒgəmɪ) NOUN self-pollination and fertilization of an unopened flower, as in the flowers of the violet produced in summer. Compare **chasmogamy.**
▸ **cleisˈtogamous** *or* **cleistogamic** (ˌklaɪstəˈgæmɪk) ADJECTIVE

clem (klɛm) *or* **clam** VERB **clems, clemming, clemmed** *or* **clams, clamming, clammed.** (when *tr, usually passive*) *English dialect* to be hungry or cause to be hungry.
▷HISTORY C16: of Germanic origin; related to Dutch, German *klemmen* to pinch, cramp; compare Old English *beclemman* to shut in

clematis ('klɛmətɪs, kləˈmeɪtɪs) NOUN any N temperate ranunculaceous climbing plant or erect shrub of the genus *Clematis,* having plumelike fruits. Many species are cultivated for their large colourful flowers. See also **traveller's joy.**
▷HISTORY C16: from Latin, from Greek *klēmatis* climbing plant, brushwood, from *klēma* twig

clemency ('klɛmənsɪ) NOUN, *plural* **-cies.** 1 mercy or leniency. 2 mildness, esp of the weather.
▷HISTORY C15: from Latin *clēmentia,* from *clēmēns* gentle

clement ('klɛmənt) ADJECTIVE 1 merciful. 2 (of the weather) mild.
▷HISTORY C15: from Latin *clēmēns* mild; probably related to Greek *klinein* to lean
▸ **ˈclemently** ADVERB

clementine ('klɛmənˌtiːn, -ˌtaɪn) NOUN a citrus fruit thought to be either a variety of tangerine or a hybrid between a tangerine and sweet orange.
▷HISTORY C20: from French *clémentine,* perhaps from the female Christian name

Clementines ('klɛmənˌtiːnz, -ˌtaɪnz) PLURAL NOUN *RC Church* an official compilation of decretals named after Clement V and issued in 1317 which forms part of the Corpus Juris Canonici.

clench (klɛntʃ) VERB (*tr*) 1 to close or squeeze together (the teeth, a fist, etc.) tightly. 2 to grasp or grip firmly. ◆ NOUN 3 a firm grasp or grip. 4 a device that grasps or grips, such as a clamp. ◆ NOUN, VERB 5 another word for **clinch.**
▷HISTORY Old English *beclencan,* related to Old High German *klenken* to tie, Middle High German *klank* noose, Dutch *klinken* rivet

cleome (klɪˈəʊmɪ) NOUN any herbaceous or shrubby plant of the mostly tropical capparidaceous genus *Cleome,* esp *C. spinosa,* cultivated for their clusters of white or purplish flowers with long stamens.
▷HISTORY C19: New Latin, of obscure origin

cleopatra (ˌkliːəˈpætrə, -ˈpɑː-) NOUN a yellow butterfly, *Gonepteryx cleopatra,* the male of which has its wings flushed with orange.

Cleopatra's Needle (ˌkliːəˈpætrəz, -ˈpɑː-) NOUN either of two Egyptian obelisks, originally set up at Heliopolis about 1500 B.C.: one was moved to the Thames Embankment, London, in 1878, the other to Central Park, New York, in 1880.

clepe (kliːp) VERB **clepes, cleping; cleped** (kliːpt, klɛpt), **clept, ycleped,** *or* **yclept.** (*tr*) *Archaic* to call by the name of.
▷HISTORY Old English *cleopian;* related to Middle Low German *kleperen* to rattle

clepsydra ('klɛpsɪdrə) NOUN, *plural* **-dras** *or* **-drae** (-ˌdriː). an ancient device for measuring time by the flow of water or mercury through a small aperture. Also called: **water clock.**
▷HISTORY C17: from Latin, from Greek *klepsudra,* from *kleptein* to steal + *hudōr* water

cleptomania (ˌklɛptəʊˈmeɪnɪə, -ˈmeɪnjə) NOUN a variant spelling of **kleptomania.**
▸ **ˌcleptoˈmaniˌac** NOUN

clerestory *or* **clearstory** ('klɪəˌstɔːrɪ) NOUN, *plural* **-ries.** 1 a row of windows in the upper part of the wall of a church that divides the nave from the aisle, set above the aisle roof. 2 the part of the wall in which these windows are set. Compare **blindstorey.**
▷HISTORY C15: from CLEAR + STOREY
▸ **ˈclereˌstoried** *or* **ˈclearˌstoried** ADJECTIVE

clergy ('klɜːdʒɪ) NOUN, *plural* **-gies.** the collective body of men and women ordained as religious ministers, esp of the Christian Church. Related adjectives: **clerical, pastoral.**
▷HISTORY C13: from Old French *clergie,* from *clerc* ecclesiastic, CLERK

clergyman ('klɜːdʒɪmən) NOUN, *plural* **-men.** a member of the clergy.

cleric ('klɛrɪk) NOUN a member of the clergy.
▷HISTORY C17: from Church Latin *clēricus* priest, CLERK

clerical ('klɛrɪkəl) ADJECTIVE 1 relating to or

associated with the clergy: *clerical dress.* 2 of or relating to office clerks or their work: *a clerical error.* 3 supporting or advocating clericalism.
▸ 'clerically ADVERB

clerical collar NOUN a stiff white collar with no opening at the front that buttons at the back of the neck; the distinctive mark of the clergy in certain Churches. Informal name: **dog collar.**

clericalism ('klɛrɪkəˌlɪzəm) NOUN 1 a policy of upholding the power of the clergy. 2 the power of the clergy esp when excessively strong.
▸ 'clericalist NOUN

clericals ('klɛrɪkəlz) PLURAL NOUN the distinctive dress of a clergyman.

clerihew ('klɛrɪˌhjuː) NOUN a form of comic or satiric verse, consisting of two couplets of metrically irregular lines, containing the name of a well-known person.
▷HISTORY C20: named after Edmund *Clerihew* Bentley (1875–1956), English writer who invented it

clerk (klɑːk; *US and Canadian* klɜːrk) NOUN 1 a worker, esp in an office, who keeps records, files, etc. 2 **clerk to the justices.** (in England) a legally qualified person who sits in court with lay justices to advise them on points of law. 3 an employee of a court, legislature, board, corporation, etc., who keeps records and accounts, etc.: *a town clerk.* 4 Also called: **clerk of the House.** *Brit* a senior official of the House of Commons. 5 Also called: **clerk in holy orders.** a cleric. 6 *US and Canadian* short for **salesclerk.** 7 Also called: **desk clerk.** *US and Canadian* a hotel receptionist. 8 *Archaic* a scholar. ◆ VERB 9 (*intr*) to serve as a clerk.
▷HISTORY Old English *clerc,* from Church Latin *clēricus,* from Greek *klērikos* cleric, relating to the heritage (alluding to the Biblical Levites, whose inheritance was the Lord), from *klēros* heritage
▸ 'clerkdom NOUN ▸ 'clerkish ADJECTIVE ▸ 'clerkship NOUN

clerkess (klɑːˈkɛs) NOUN a female office clerk.

clerkly ('klɑːklɪ) ADJECTIVE **-lier, -liest.** 1 of or like a clerk. 2 *Obsolete* learned. ◆ ADVERB 3 *Obsolete* in the manner of a clerk.
▸ 'clerkliness NOUN

clerk of works NOUN an employee who supervises building work in progress or the upkeep of existing buildings.

Clermont-Ferrand (*French* klɛrmɔ̃ferɑ̃) NOUN a city in S central France: capital of Puy-de-Dôme department; industrial centre. Pop.: 137 140 (1999).

cleruchy ('klɛəˌruːkɪ) NOUN, *plural* **-chies.** (in the ancient world) a special type of Athenian colony, in which settlers (**cleruchs**) retained their Athenian citizenship and the community remained a political dependency of Athens.
▸ cleruchial (klɪ'ruːkɪəl) ADJECTIVE

cleveite ('kliːvaɪt) NOUN a crystalline variety of the mineral uranitite.
▷HISTORY C19: named after P. T. *Cleve* (1840–1905), Swedish chemist; see -ITE[1]

Cleveland ('kliːvlənd) NOUN 1 a former county of NE England formed in 1974 from parts of E Durham and N Yorkshire; replaced in 1996 by the unitary authorities of Hartlepool (Durham), Stockton-on-Tees (Durham), Middlesbrough (North Yorkshire) and Redcar and Cleveland (North Yorkshire). 2 a port in NE Ohio, on Lake Erie: major heavy industries. Pop.: 478 403 (2000). 3 a hilly region of NE England, extending from the **Cleveland Hills** to the River Tees.

Cleveland Bay NOUN one of the oldest British breeds of clean-legged, light draught farm and carriage horse, originating from Yorkshire.

clever ('klɛvə) ADJECTIVE 1 displaying sharp intelligence or mental alertness. 2 adroit or dexterous, esp with the hands. 3 smart in a superficial way. 4 *Brit informal* sly; cunning. 5 (*predicative; used with a negative*) *Dialect* healthy; fit.
▷HISTORY C13 *cliver* (in the sense: quick to seize, adroit), of uncertain origin
▸ 'cleverish ADJECTIVE ▸ 'cleverly ADVERB ▸ 'cleverness NOUN

clever-clever ADJECTIVE *Informal* clever in a showy manner; artful; overclever.

clever Dick *or* **cleverdick** ('klɛvəˌdɪk) NOUN *Informal* a person considered to have an unwarrantably high opinion of his own ability.

clevis ('klɛvɪs) NOUN the U-shaped component of a shackle for attaching a drawbar to a plough or similar implement.
▷HISTORY C16: related to CLEAVE[1]

clew (kluː) NOUN 1 a ball of thread, yarn, or twine. 2 *Nautical* either of the lower corners of a square sail or the after lower corner of a fore-and-aft sail. 3 (*usually plural*) the rigging of a hammock. 4 a rare variant of **clue.** ◆ VERB 5 (*tr*) to coil or roll into a ball.
▷HISTORY Old English *cliewen* (verb); related to Old High German *kliu* ball

clew line NOUN *Nautical* any of several lines fastened to the clews of a square sail and used for furling it.

clew up VERB (*adverb*) *Nautical* to furl (a square sail) by gathering its clews up to the yard by means of clew lines.

clianthus (klɪ'ænθəs) NOUN any Australian or New Zealand plant of the leguminous genus *Clianthus,* with ornamental clusters of slender scarlet flowers. See also **desert pea.**
▷HISTORY C19: New Latin, probably from Greek *klei-, kleos* glory + *anthos* flower

cliché ('kliːʃeɪ) NOUN 1 a word or expression that has lost much of its force through overexposure, as for example the phrase: *it's got to get worse before it gets better.* 2 an idea, action, or habit that has become trite from overuse. 3 *Printing, chiefly Brit* a stereotype or electrotype plate.
▷HISTORY C19: from French, from *clicher* to stereotype; imitative of the sound made by the matrix when it is dropped into molten metal
▸ 'clichéd *or* 'cliché'd ADJECTIVE

Clichy (kliː'ʃiː) NOUN an industrial suburb of NW Paris: residence of the Merovingian kings (7th century). Pop.: 48 204 (1990). Official name: **Clichy-la-Garenne** (*French* kliʃilagarɛn).

click (klɪk) NOUN 1 a short light often metallic sound. 2 **a** the locking member of a ratchet mechanism, such as a pawl or detent. **b** the movement of such a mechanism between successive locking positions. 3 *Phonetics* any of various stop consonants, found in Khoisan and as borrowings in southern Bantu languages, that are produced by the suction of air into the mouth. 4 *US and Canadian slang* a kilometre. 5 *Computing* an act of pressing and releasing a button on a mouse. ◆ VERB 6 to make or cause to make a clicking sound: *to click one's heels.* 7 (usually foll by *on*) *Computing* to press and release (a button on a mouse) or to select (a particular function) by pressing and releasing a button on a mouse. 8 (*intr*) *Slang* to be a great success: *that idea really clicked.* 9 (*intr*) *Informal* to become suddenly clear. 10 (*intr*) *Slang* to go or fit together with ease.
▷HISTORY C17: of imitative origin
▸ 'clicker NOUN

clickable ('klɪkəbəl) ADJECTIVE (of a website) having links that can be accessed by clicking a computer mouse: *a clickable map.*

click beetle NOUN any beetle of the family *Elateridae,* which have the ability to right themselves with a snapping movement when placed on their backs. Also called: **snapping beetle, skipjack.** See also **wireworm.**

clicker ('klɪkə) NOUN 1 a person or thing that clicks. 2 *Informal* a foreman in a shoe factory or printing works.

clicks and mortar ADJECTIVE making use of traditional trading methods in conjunction with Internet trading. Abbreviation: **C & M.**
▷HISTORY C20: pun on *bricks and mortar,* with CLICK referring to the computing sense

clickstream ('klɪkˌstriːm) NOUN a record of the path taken by users through a website, enabling designers to access the use being made of their website.

click through VERB 1 (*tr, adverb*) to navigate around (a website) using the links provided to move onto different pages. ◆ ADJECTIVE **click-through.** 2 (of a website) able to be navigated by means of links between different pages.

client ('klaɪənt) NOUN 1 a person, company, etc., that seeks the advice of a professional man or woman. 2 a customer. 3 a person who is registered with or receiving services or financial aid from a welfare agency. 4 *Computing* a program or work station that requests data or information from a server. 5 a person depending on another's patronage.
▷HISTORY C14: from Latin *cliēns* retainer, dependant; related to Latin *clīnāre* to lean
▸ cliental (klaɪ'ɛntəl) ADJECTIVE

client-centred therapy NOUN *Psychol* a form of psychotherapy in which the therapist makes no attempt to interpret what the patient says but encourages him to develop his own attitudes and insights, often by questioning him.

clientele (ˌkliːɒn'tɛl) *or* **clientage** ('klaɪəntɪdʒ) NOUN customers or clients collectively.
▷HISTORY C16: from Latin *clientēla,* from *cliēns* CLIENT

Clifden nonpareil ('klɪftən) NOUN a handsome nocturnal moth, *Catocala fraxini,* that is brown with bluish patches on the hindwings: related to the red underwing.

cliff (klɪf) NOUN a steep high rock face, esp one that runs along the seashore and has the strata exposed.
▷HISTORY Old English *clif;* related to Old Norse *kleif,* Middle Low German *klēf,* Dutch *klif;* see CLEAVE[2]
▸ 'cliffy ADJECTIVE

cliffhanger ('klɪfˌhæŋə) NOUN 1 **a** a situation of imminent disaster usually occurring at the end of each episode of a serialized film. **b** the serialized film itself. 2 a situation that is dramatic or uncertain.
▸ 'cliffˌhanging ADJECTIVE

cliff swallow NOUN an American swallow, *Petrochelidon pyrrhonota,* that has a square-tipped tail and builds nests of mud on cliffs, walls, etc.

climacteric (klaɪ'mæktərɪk, ˌklaɪmæk'tɛrɪk) NOUN 1 a critical event or period. 2 another name for **menopause.** 3 the period in the life of a man corresponding to the menopause, chiefly characterized by diminished sexual activity. 4 *Botany* the period during which certain fruits, such as apples, ripen, marked by a rise in the rate of respiration. ◆ ADJECTIVE *also* **climacterical** (ˌklaɪmæk'tɛrɪkəl). 5 involving a crucial event or period.
▷HISTORY C16: from Latin *clīmactēricus,* from Greek *klimaktērikos,* from *klimakter* rung of a ladder, from *klimax* ladder; see CLIMAX
▸ ˌclimac'terically ADVERB

climactic (klaɪ'mæktɪk) *or* **climactical** ADJECTIVE consisting of, involving, or causing a climax.
▸ cli'mactically ADVERB

> **Language note** See at **climate.**

climate ('klaɪmɪt) NOUN 1 the long-term prevalent weather conditions of an area, determined by latitude, position relative to oceans or continents, altitude, etc. 2 an area having a particular kind of climate. 3 a prevailing trend or current of feeling: *the political climate.*
▷HISTORY C14: from Late Latin *clima,* from Greek *klima* inclination, region; related to Greek *klinein* to lean
▸ climatic (klaɪ'mætɪk), cli'matical, *or* 'climatal ADJECTIVE ▸ cli'matically ADVERB

> **Language note** *Climatic* is sometimes wrongly used where *climactic* is meant. *Climatic* is properly used to talk about things relating to climate; *climactic* is used to describe something which forms a climax.

climatic zone NOUN any of the eight principal zones, roughly demarcated by lines of latitude, into which the earth can be divided on the basis of climate.

climatology (ˌklaɪmə'tɒlədʒɪ) NOUN the study of climate.
▸ climatologic (ˌklaɪmətə'lɒdʒɪk) *or* ˌclimato'logical ADJECTIVE ▸ ˌclimato'logically ADVERB ▸ ˌclima'tologist NOUN

climax ('klaɪmæks) NOUN 1 the most intense or highest point of an experience or of a series of events: *the party was the climax of the week.* 2 a decisive moment in a dramatic or other work. 3 a

rhetorical device by which a series of sentences, clauses, or phrases are arranged in order of increasing intensity. [4] *Ecology* the stage in the development of a community during which it remains stable under the prevailing environmental conditions. [5] Also called: **sexual climax.** (esp in referring to women) another word for **orgasm.** ◆ VERB [6] to reach or bring to a climax.
▷HISTORY C16: from Late Latin, from Greek *klimax* ladder

climb (klaɪm) VERB (*mainly intr*) [1] (*also tr;* often foll by *up*) to go up or ascend (stairs, a mountain, etc.). [2] (often foll by *along*) to progress with difficulty: *to climb along a ledge.* [3] to rise to a higher point or intensity: *the temperature climbed.* [4] to incline or slope upwards: *the road began to climb.* [5] to ascend in social position. [6] (of plants) to grow upwards by twining, using tendrils or suckers, etc. [7] *Informal* (foll by *into*) to put (on) or get (into). [8] to be a climber or mountaineer. ◆ NOUN [9] the act or an instance of climbing. [10] a place or thing to be climbed, esp a route in mountaineering. ◆ Related adjective: **scansorial.**
▷HISTORY Old English *climban;* related to Old Norse *klembra* to squeeze, Old High German *climban* to clamber
▸'**climbable** ADJECTIVE

climb down VERB (*intr, adverb*) [1] to descend. [2] (often foll by *from*) to retreat (from an opinion, position, etc.). ◆ NOUN **climb-down.** [3] a retreat from an opinion, etc.

climber ('klaɪmə) NOUN [1] a person or thing that climbs. [2] a plant that lacks rigidity and grows upwards by twining, scrambling, or clinging with tendrils and suckers. [3] *Chiefly Brit* short for **social climber.**

climbing fish *or* **perch** NOUN an Asian labyrinth fish, *Anabas testudineus,* that resembles a perch and can travel over land on its spiny gill covers and pectoral fins.

climbing frame NOUN a structure of wood or metal tubing used by children for climbing.

climbing irons PLURAL NOUN spiked steel frames worn on the feet to assist in climbing trees, ice slopes, etc.

climbing wall NOUN *Mountaineering* a specially constructed wall with recessed and projecting holds to give practice in rock climbing; a feature of many sports centres.

clime (klaɪm) NOUN *Poetic* a region or its climate.
▷HISTORY C16: from Late Latin *clima;* see CLIMATE

clinandrium (klɪ'nændrɪəm) NOUN, *plural* **-dria** (-drɪə). *Botany* a cavity in the upper part of the column of an orchid flower that contains the anthers. Also called: **androclinium.**
▷HISTORY C19: from New Latin, literally: bed for stamen, from Greek *klinē* couch + *anēr* man + -IUM

clinch (klɪntʃ) VERB [1] (*tr*) to secure (a driven nail) by bending the protruding point over. [2] (*tr*) to hold together in such a manner: *to clinch the corners of the frame.* [3] (*tr*) to settle (something, such as an argument, bargain, etc.) in a definite way. [4] (*tr*) *Nautical* to fasten by means of a clinch. [5] (*intr*) to engage in a clinch, as in boxing or wrestling. ◆ NOUN [6] the act of clinching. [7] **a** a nail with its point bent over. **b** the part of such a nail, etc., that has been bent over. [8] *Boxing, wrestling* an act or an instance in which one or both competitors hold on to the other to avoid punches, regain wind, etc. [9] *Slang* a lovers' embrace. [10] *Nautical* a loop or eye formed in a line by seizing the end to the standing part. ◆ Also (for senses 1, 2, 4, 7, 8, 10): **clench.**
▷HISTORY C16: variant of CLENCH

clincher ('klɪntʃə) NOUN [1] *Informal* something decisive, such as a fact, score, etc. [2] a person or thing that clinches.

cline (klaɪn) NOUN a continuous variation in form between members of a species having a wide variable geographical or ecological range.
▷HISTORY C20: from Greek *klinein* to lean
▸'**clinal** ADJECTIVE ▸'**clinally** ADVERB

-cline NOUN COMBINING FORM indicating a slope: *anticline.*
▷HISTORY back formation from INCLINE
▸**-clinal** ADJECTIVE COMBINING FORM

cling (klɪŋ) VERB **clings, clinging, clung.** (*intr*) [1] (often foll by *to*) to hold fast or adhere closely (to something), as by gripping or sticking. [2] (foll by *together*) to remain in contact (with each other). [3] to be or remain physically or emotionally close: *to cling to outmoded beliefs.* ◆ NOUN [4] *Agriculture chiefly US* the tendency of cotton fibres in a sample to stick to each other. [5] *Agriculture, obsolete* diarrhoea or scouring in animals. [6] short for **clingstone.**
▷HISTORY Old English *clingan;* related to CLENCH
▸'**clinger** NOUN ▸'**clingingly** ADVERB ▸'**clingy** ADJECTIVE
▸'**clinginess** *or* '**clingingness** NOUN

clingfilm ('klɪŋˌfɪlm) NOUN a thin polythene material that clings closely to any surface around which it is placed: used for wrapping food.

clingfish ('klɪŋˌfɪʃ) NOUN, *plural* **-fish** *or* **-fishes.** any small marine teleost fish of the family *Gobiesocidae,* having a flattened elongated body with a sucking disc beneath the head for clinging to rocks, etc.

clinging vine NOUN *US and Canadian informal* a woman who displays excessive emotional dependence on a man.

clingstone ('klɪŋˌstəʊn) NOUN **a** a fruit, such as certain peaches, in which the flesh tends to adhere to the stone. **b** (*as modifier*): *a clingstone peach.* ◆ Compare **freestone** (sense 2).

clinic ('klɪnɪk) NOUN [1] a place in which outpatients are given medical treatment or advice, often connected to a hospital. [2] a similar place staffed by physicians or surgeons specializing in one or more specific areas: *eye clinic.* [3] *Brit* a private hospital or nursing home. [4] *Obsolete* the teaching of medicine to students at the bedside. [5] *US* a place in which medical lectures are given. [6] *US* a clinical lecture. [7] *Chiefly US and Canadian* a group or centre that offers advice or instruction: *a vocational clinic.*
▷HISTORY C17: from Latin *clīnicus* one on a sickbed, from Greek, from *klinē* bed

clinical ('klɪnɪk^{ə}l) ADJECTIVE [1] of or relating to a clinic. [2] of or relating to the bedside of a patient, the course of his disease, or the observation and treatment of patients directly: *a clinical lecture; clinical medicine.* [3] scientifically detached; strictly objective: *a clinical attitude to life.* [4] plain, simple, and usually unattractive: *clinical furniture.*
▸'**clinically** ADVERB ▸'**clinicalness** NOUN

clinical governance NOUN a systematic approach to raising standards of health care and tackling poor performance in hospitals.

clinical psychology NOUN the branch of psychology that studies and treats mental illness and mental retardation.

clinical thermometer NOUN a finely calibrated thermometer for determining the temperature of the body, usually placed under the tongue, in the armpit, or in the rectum.

clinician (klɪ'nɪʃən) NOUN a physician, psychiatrist, etc., who specializes in clinical work as opposed to one engaged in laboratory or experimental studies.

clink[1] (klɪŋk) VERB [1] to make or cause to make a light and sharply ringing sound. ◆ NOUN [2] a light and sharply ringing sound. [3] *Brit* a pointed steel tool used for breaking up the surface of a road before it is repaired.
▷HISTORY C14: perhaps from Middle Dutch *klinken;* related to Old Low German *chlanch,* German *Klang* sound

clink[2] (klɪŋk) NOUN a slang word for **prison.**
▷HISTORY C16: after *Clink,* name of a prison in Southwark, London

clinker ('klɪŋkə) NOUN [1] the ash and partially fused residues from a coal-fired furnace or fire. [2] Also called: **clinker brick.** a hard brick used as a paving stone. [3] a partially vitrified brick or mass of brick. [4] *Slang, chiefly US* something of poor quality, such as a film. [5] *US and Canadian slang* a mistake or fault, esp a wrong note in music. ◆ VERB [6] (*intr*) to form clinker during burning.
▷HISTORY C17: from Dutch *klinker* a type of brick, from obsolete *klinckaerd,* literally: something that clinks (referring to the sound produced when one was struck), from *klinken* to CLINK[1]

clinker-built *or* **clincher-built** ADJECTIVE (of a boat or ship) having a hull constructed with each plank overlapping that below. Also called: **lapstrake.** Compare **carvel-built.**
▷HISTORY C18 *clinker* a nailing together, probably from CLINCH

clinkstone ('klɪŋkˌstəʊn) NOUN a variety of phonolite that makes a metallic sound when struck.

clino- *or before a vowel* **clin-** COMBINING FORM indicating a slope or inclination: *clinometer.*
▷HISTORY from New Latin, from Greek *klinein* to slant, lean

clinometer (klaɪ'nɒmɪtə) NOUN an instrument used in surveying for measuring an angle of inclination.
▸**clinometric** (ˌklaɪnə'mɛtrɪk) *or* ˌ**clino'metrical** ADJECTIVE ▸**cli'nometry** NOUN

clinopyroxene (ˌklaɪnəʊpaɪ'rɒksiːn) NOUN a member of the pyroxene group of minerals having a monoclinic crystal structure, such as augite, diopside, or jadeite.

clinostat ('klaɪnəʊˌstæt) NOUN an apparatus for studying tropisms in plants, usually a rotating disc to which the plant is attached so that it receives an equal stimulus on all sides.

clinquant ('klɪŋkənt) ADJECTIVE [1] glittering, esp with tinsel. ◆ NOUN [2] tinsel or imitation gold leaf.
▷HISTORY C16: from French, from *clinquer* to clink, from Dutch *klinken,* of imitative origin

clint (klɪnt) NOUN *Physical geography* [1] a section of a limestone pavement separated from adjacent sections by solution fissures. See **grike.** [2] any small surface exposure of hard or flinty rock, as on a hillside or in a stream bed.
▷HISTORY C12: from Danish and Swedish *klint,* from Old Swedish *klinter,* related to Icelandic *klettr* rock

clintonia (klɪn'təʊnɪə) NOUN any temperate liliaceous plant of the genus *Clintonia,* having white, greenish-yellow, or purplish flowers, broad ribbed leaves, and blue berries.
▷HISTORY C19: named after De Witt *Clinton* (1769–1828), US politician and naturalist

Clio ('klaɪəʊ) NOUN *Greek myth* the Muse of history.
▷HISTORY C19: from Latin, from Greek *Kleiō,* from *kleein* to celebrate

cliometrics (ˌklaɪəʊ'mɛtrɪks) NOUN (*functioning as singular*) the study of economic history using statistics and computer analysis.
▷HISTORY C20: CLIO + (ECONO)METRICS
▸ˌ**clio'metric** *or* ˌ**clio'metrical** ADJECTIVE ▸**cliometrician** (ˌklaɪəʊmə'trɪʃən) NOUN

clip[1] (klɪp) VERB **clips, clipping, clipped.** (*mainly tr*) [1] (*also intr*) to cut, snip, or trim with or as if with scissors or shears, esp in order to shorten or remove a part. [2] *Brit* to punch (a hole) in something, esp a ticket. [3] to curtail or cut short. [4] to move a short section from (a film, etc.). [5] to shorten (a word). [6] (*intr*) to trot or move rapidly, esp over a long distance: *a horse clipping along the road.* [7] *Informal* to strike with a sharp, often slanting, blow. [8] *Slang* to obtain (money) by deception or cheating. [9] *US slang* to murder; execute. [10] **clip (someone's) wings. a** to restrict (someone's) freedom. **b** to thwart (someone's) ambition. ◆ NOUN [11] the act or process of clipping. [12] something clipped off. [13] an extract from a film, newspaper, etc. [14] *Informal* a sharp, often slanting, blow. [15] *Informal* speed: *a rapid clip.* [16] *Austral and NZ* the total quantity of wool shorn, as in one place, season, etc. [17] another word for **clipped form.**
▷HISTORY C12: from Old Norse *klippa* to cut; related to Low German *klippen*
▸'**clippable** ADJECTIVE

clip[2] (klɪp) NOUN [1] any of various small implements used to hold loose articles together or to attach one article to another. [2] an article of jewellery that can be clipped onto a dress, hat, etc. [3] short for **paperclip** or **cartridge clip.** [4] the pointed flange on a horseshoe that secures it to the front part of the hoof. ◆ VERB **clips, clipping, clipped.** (*tr*) [5] to hold together tightly, as with a clip. [6] *Archaic or dialect* to embrace.
▷HISTORY Old English *clyppan* to embrace; related to Old Frisian *kleppa,* Lithuanian *glebiu*

clip art NOUN a large collection of simple drawings stored in a computer from which items can be selected for incorporation into documents.

clipboard ('klɪpˌbɔːd) NOUN [1] a portable writing board with a spring clip at the top for holding paper. [2] a temporary storage area in desktop publishing where text or graphics are held after the cut command or the copy command.

clip-clop NOUN the sound made by a horse's hooves.

clip-fed ADJECTIVE (of an automatic firearm) loaded from a cartridge clip.

clip joint NOUN *Slang* a place, such as a nightclub or restaurant, in which customers are overcharged.

clip on VERB 1 (*tr*) to attach by means of a clip. 2 (*intr*) to be attached by means of a clip: *this clips on here.* ◆ ADJECTIVE **clip-on.** 3 designed to be attached by means of a clip: *a clip-on bow tie.* ◆ PLURAL NOUN **clip-ons.** 4 sunglasses designed to be clipped on to a person's spectacles.

clipped (klɪpt) ADJECTIVE (of speech or voice) abrupt and distinct.

clipped form NOUN a shortened form of a word, as for example *doc* for *doctor.*

clipper ('klɪpə) NOUN 1 any fast sailing ship. 2 a person or thing that cuts or clips. 3 something, such as a horse or sled, that moves quickly. 4 *Electronics* another word for **limiter.**

clippers ('klɪpəz) *or* **clips** PLURAL NOUN 1 a hand tool with two cutting blades for clipping fingernails, hedges, etc. 2 a hairdresser's tool, operated either by hand or electrically, with one fixed and one reciprocating set of teeth for cutting short hair.

clippie ('klɪpɪ) NOUN *Brit informal* a bus conductress.

clipping ('klɪpɪŋ) NOUN 1 something cut out or trimmed off, esp an article from a newspaper; cutting. 2 the distortion of an audio or visual signal in which the tops of peaks with a high amplitude are cut off, caused by, for example, overloading of amplifier circuits. ◆ ADJECTIVE 3 (*prenominal*) *Informal* fast: *a clipping pace.*

clipshears ('klɪp,ʃiːrz) *or* **clipshear** ('klɪp,ʃiːr) NOUN a Scot dialect name for an **earwig.**
▷HISTORY from the resemblance of the forceps at the tip of its abdomen to shears

clique (kliːk, klɪk) NOUN a small, exclusive group of friends or associates.
▷HISTORY C18: from French, perhaps from Old French: latch, from *cliquer* to click; suggestive of the necessity to exclude nonmembers
▸**'cliquish** ADJECTIVE ▸**'cliquishly** ADVERB ▸**'cliquishness** NOUN

cliquey *or* **cliquy** ('kliːkɪ, 'klɪkɪ) ADJECTIVE **-ier, -iest.** exclusive, confined to a small group; forming cliques.

clishmaclaver (,klɪʃmə'kleɪvə) NOUN *Scot* idle talk; gossip.
▷HISTORY C16: from *clish-clash,* reduplication of CLASH + CLAVER

clitellum (klɪ'tɛləm) NOUN, *plural* **-la** (-lə). a thickened saddle-like region of epidermis in earthworms and leeches whose secretions bind copulating worms together and later form a cocoon around the eggs.
▷HISTORY C19: from New Latin, from Latin *clītellae* (plural) packsaddle

clitic ('klɪtɪk) ADJECTIVE 1 (of a word) incapable of being stressed, usually pronounced as if part of the word that follows or precedes it: for example, in French, *me, te,* and *le* are clitic pronouns. See also **proclitic, enclitic.** ◆ NOUN 2 a clitic word.
▷HISTORY C20: back formation from ENCLITIC and PROCLITIC

clitoridectomy (,klɪtərɪ'dɛktəmɪ) NOUN, *plural* **-mies.** surgical removal of the clitoris: a form of female circumcision, esp practised as a religious or ethnic rite.

clitoris ('klɪtərɪs, 'klaɪ-) NOUN a part of the female genitalia consisting of a small elongated highly sensitive erectile organ at the front of the vulva: homologous with the penis.
▷HISTORY C17: from New Latin, from Greek *kleitoris;* related to Greek *kleiein* to close
▸**'clitoral** ADJECTIVE

Cliveden ('klɪvdən) NOUN a mansion in Buckinghamshire, on the N bank of the Thames near Maidenhead: formerly the home of Nancy Astor and the scene of gatherings of politicians and others (known as the **Cliveden Set**); now a hotel.

Cllr ABBREVIATION FOR Councillor.

cloaca (kləʊ'eɪkə) NOUN, *plural* **-cae** (-kiː). 1 a cavity in the pelvic region of most vertebrates, except higher mammals, and certain invertebrates, into which the alimentary canal and the genital and urinary ducts open. 2 a sewer.
▷HISTORY C18: from Latin: sewer; related to Greek *kluzein* to wash out
▸**clo'acal** ADJECTIVE

cloacitis (,kləʊə'saɪtɪs) NOUN *Vet science* inflammation of the cloaca in birds, including domestic fowl, and other animals with a common opening of the urinary and gastrointestinal tracts.

cloak (kləʊk) NOUN 1 a wraplike outer garment fastened at the throat and falling straight from the shoulders. 2 something that covers or conceals. ◆ VERB (*tr*) 3 to cover with or as if with a cloak. 4 to hide or disguise.
▷HISTORY C13: from Old French *cloque,* from Medieval Latin *clocca* cloak, bell; referring to the bell-like shape

cloak-and-dagger NOUN (*modifier*) characteristic of or concerned with intrigue and espionage.

cloakroom ('kləʊk,ruːm, -,rʊm) NOUN 1 a room in which hats, coats, luggage, etc., may be temporarily deposited. 2 *Brit* a euphemistic word for **lavatory.**

cloam (kləʊm) *Southwestern English dialect* ◆ ADJECTIVE 1 made of clay or earthenware. ◆ NOUN 2 clay or earthenware pots, dishes, etc., collectively.
▷HISTORY Old English clām mud

clobber[1] ('klɒbə) VERB (*tr*) *Slang* 1 to beat or batter. 2 to defeat utterly. 3 to criticize severely.
▷HISTORY C20: of unknown origin

clobber[2] ('klɒbə) NOUN *Brit slang* personal belongings, such as clothes and accessories.
▷HISTORY C19: of unknown origin

clobber[3] ('klɒbə) VERB (*tr*) to paint over existing decoration on (pottery).
▷HISTORY C19 (originally in the sense: to patch up): of uncertain origin; perhaps related to CLOBBER[2]

clobbering machine NOUN *NZ informal* pressure to conform with accepted standards.

cloche (klɒʃ) NOUN 1 a bell-shaped cover used to protect young plants. 2 a woman's almost brimless close-fitting hat, typical of the 1920s and 1930s.
▷HISTORY C19: from French: bell, from Medieval Latin *clocca*

clock[1] (klɒk) NOUN 1 a timepiece, usually free-standing, hanging, or built into a tower, having mechanically or electrically driven pointers that move constantly over a dial showing the numbers of the hours. Compare **digital clock, watch** (sense 7). 2 any clocklike device for recording or measuring, such as a taximeter or pressure gauge. 3 the downy head of a dandelion that has gone to seed. 4 an electrical circuit that generates pulses at a predetermined rate. 5 *Computing* an electronic pulse generator that transmits streams of regular pulses to which various parts of the computer and its operations are synchronized. 6 short for **time clock.** 7 **around** *or* **round the clock.** all day and all night. 8 (usually preceded by *the*) an informal word for **speedometer** or **mileometer.** 9 *Brit* a slang word for **face.** 10 **against the clock. a** under pressure, as to meet a deadline. **b** (in certain sports, such as show jumping) timed by a stop clock: *the last round will be against the clock.* 11 **put the clock back.** to regress. ◆ VERB 12 (*tr*) *Brit, Austral, and NZ slang* to strike, esp on the face or head. 13 (*tr*) *Brit slang* to see or notice. 14 (*tr*) to record time as with a stopwatch, esp in the calculation of speed. 15 *Electronics* to feed a clock pulse to (a digital device) in order to cause it to switch to a new state. ◆ See also **atomic clock, biological clock, clock off, clock on, clock up.**
▷HISTORY C14: from Middle Dutch *clocke* clock, from Medieval Latin *clocca* bell, ultimately of Celtic origin
▸**'clocker** NOUN ▸**'clock,like** ADJECTIVE

clock[2] (klɒk) NOUN an ornamental design either woven in or embroidered on the side of a stocking.
▷HISTORY C16: from Middle Dutch *clocke,* from Medieval Latin *clocca* bell

clock golf NOUN a putting game played on a circular area on a lawn.

clockmaker ('klɒk,meɪkə) NOUN a person who makes or mends clocks, watches, etc.

clock off *or* **out** VERB (*intr, adverb*) to depart from work, esp when it involves registering the time of departure on a card.

clock on *or* **in** VERB (*intr, adverb*) to arrive at work, esp when it involves registering the time of arrival on a card.

clock up VERB (*tr, adverb*) to record or register: *this car has clocked up 80 000 miles.*

clock-watcher NOUN an employee who checks the time in anticipation of a break or of the end of the working day.

clockwise ('klɒk,waɪz) ADVERB, ADJECTIVE in the direction that the hands of a clock rotate; from top to bottom towards the right when seen from the front.

clockwork ('klɒk,wɜːk) NOUN 1 the mechanism of a clock. 2 any similar mechanism, as in a wind-up toy. 3 **like clockwork.** with complete regularity and precision.

clod (klɒd) NOUN 1 a lump of earth or clay. 2 earth, esp when heavy or in hard lumps. 3 Also called: **clodpole, clod poll, clodpate.** a dull or stupid person. 4 a cut of beef taken from the shoulder.
▷HISTORY Old English *clod-* (occurring in compound words) lump; related to CLOUD
▸**'cloddy** ADJECTIVE ▸**'cloddish** ADJECTIVE ▸**'cloddishly** ADVERB ▸**'cloddishness** NOUN

clodhopper ('klɒd,hɒpə) NOUN *Informal* 1 a clumsy person; lout. 2 (*usually plural*) a large heavy shoe or boot.
▸**'clod,hopping** ADJECTIVE

clog[1] (klɒg) VERB **clogs, clogging, clogged.** 1 to obstruct or become obstructed with thick or sticky matter. 2 (*tr*) to encumber; hinder; impede. 3 (*tr*) to fasten a clog or impediment to (an animal, such as a horse). 4 (*intr*) to adhere or stick in a mass. 5 *Slang* (in soccer) to foul (an opponent). ◆ NOUN 6 **a** any of various wooden or wooden-soled shoes. **b** (*as modifier*): *clog dance.* 7 a heavy block, esp of wood, fastened to the leg of a person or animal to impede motion. 8 something that impedes motion or action; hindrance. 9 **pop one's clogs.** *Slang* to die.
▷HISTORY C14 (in the sense: block of wood): of unknown origin
▸**'cloggy** ADJECTIVE ▸**'clogginess** NOUN

clog[2] (klɒg) VERB **clogs, clogging, clogged.** to use a photo-enabled mobile phone to take a photograph of (someone) and send it to a website without his or her knowledge or consent.
▷HISTORY C21: C(AMERA) + LOG
▸**'clogging** NOUN

cloggy ('klɒgɪ) ADJECTIVE **-gier, -giest.** thick and sticky; causing clogging.

cloisonné (klwɑː'zɒneɪ; *French* klwazɔne) NOUN 1 **a** a design made by filling in with coloured enamel an outline of flattened wire put on edge. **b** the method of doing this. ◆ ADJECTIVE 2 of, relating to, or made by cloisonné.
▷HISTORY C19: from French, from *cloisonner* to divide into compartments, from *cloison* partition, ultimately from Latin *claudere* to close CLOSE[2]

cloister ('klɔɪstə) NOUN 1 a covered walk, usually around a quadrangle in a religious institution, having an open arcade or colonnade on the inside and a wall on the outside. 2 (*sometimes plural*) a place of religious seclusion, such as a monastery. 3 life in a monastery or convent. ◆ VERB 4 (*tr*) to confine or seclude in or as if in a monastery.
▷HISTORY C13: from Old French *cloistre,* from Medieval Latin *claustrum* monastic cell, from Latin: bolt, barrier, from *claudere* to close; influenced in form by Old French *cloison* partition
▸**'cloister-,like** ADJECTIVE

cloistered ('klɔɪstəd) ADJECTIVE 1 secluded or shut up from the world. 2 living in a monastery or nunnery. 3 (of a building, courtyard, etc.) having or provided with a cloister.

cloistral ('klɔɪstrəl) *or* **claustral** ADJECTIVE of, like, or characteristic of a cloister.

clomb (kləʊm) VERB *Archaic* a past tense and past participle of **climb.**

clomiphene ('kləʊmɪ,fiːn) NOUN a drug that stimulates the production of egg cells in the ovary: used to treat infertility in women.

clomp (klɒmp) NOUN, VERB a less common word for **clump** (senses 2, 7).

clone (kləʊn) NOUN 1 a group of organisms or cells of the same genetic constitution that are descended from a common ancestor by asexual reproduction, as by cuttings, grafting, etc., in

plants. 2 Also called: **gene clone.** a segment of DNA that has been isolated and replicated by laboratory manipulation: used to analyse genes and manufacture their products (proteins). 3 *Informal* a person or thing bearing a very close resemblance to another person or thing. 4 *Slang* **a** a mobile phone that has been given the electronic identity of an existing mobile phone, so that calls made on the second phone are charged to the owner of the first phone. **b** any similar object or device, such as a credit card, that has been given the electronic identity of another device usually in order to commit theft. ♦ VERB 5 to produce or cause to produce a clone. 6 *Informal* to produce near copies (of a person or thing). 7 (*tr*) *Slang* to give (a mobile phone, etc.) the electronic identity of an existing mobile phone (or other device), so that calls, purchases, etc. made with the second device are charged to the owner of the first device.
▷**HISTORY** C20: from Greek *klōn* twig, shoot; related to *klan* to break
▸**'clonal** ADJECTIVE ▸**'clonally** ADVERB

clonk (klɒŋk) VERB 1 (*intr*) to make a loud dull thud. 2 (*tr*) *Informal* to hit. ♦ NOUN 3 a loud thudding sound.
▷**HISTORY** C20: of imitative origin

Clonmel (klɒn'mɛl) NOUN the county town of Co. Tipperary, Republic of Ireland; birthplace of Laurence Sterne; meat processing and enamelware. Pop.: 14 500 (1991).

Clontarf (klɒn'tɑ:f) NOUN **Battle of.** a battle fought in 1014, near Dublin, in the Republic of Ireland, in which the Danes were defeated by the Irish but the Irish king, Brian Boru, was killed.

clonus ('kləʊnəs) NOUN a type of convulsion characterized by rapid contraction and relaxation of a muscle.
▷**HISTORY** C19: from New Latin, from Greek *klonos* turmoil
▸**clonic** ('klɒnɪk) ADJECTIVE ▸**clonicity** (klɒ'nɪsɪtɪ) NOUN

clop (klɒp) VERB **clops, clopping, clopped.** 1 (*intr*) to make or move along with a sound as of a horse's hooves striking the ground. ♦ NOUN 2 a sound of this nature.
▷**HISTORY** C20: of imitative origin

cloqué ('klɒkeɪ) NOUN **a** a fabric with an embossed surface. **b** (*as modifier*): *a cloqué dress.*
▷**HISTORY** from French, literally: blistered

close[1] (kləʊs) ADJECTIVE 1 near in space or time; in proximity. 2 having the parts near together; dense: *a close formation.* 3 down or near to the surface; short: *a close haircut.* 4 near in relationship: *a close relative.* 5 intimate or confidential: *a close friend.* 6 almost equal or even: *a close contest.* 7 not deviating or varying greatly from a model or standard: *a close resemblance; a close translation.* 8 careful, strict, or searching: *a close study.* 9 (of a style of play in football, hockey, etc.) characterized by short passes. 10 confined or enclosed. 11 shut or shut tight. 12 oppressive, heavy, or airless: *a close atmosphere.* 13 strictly guarded: *a close prisoner.* 14 neat or tight in fit: *a close cap.* 15 secretive or reticent. 16 miserly; not generous, esp with money. 17 (of money or credit) hard to obtain; scarce. 18 restricted as to public admission or membership. 19 hidden or secluded. 20 Also: **closed.** restricted or prohibited as to the type of game or fish able to be taken. 21 Also: **closed, narrow.** *Phonetics* denoting a vowel pronounced with the lips relatively close together. ♦ ADVERB 22 closely; tightly. 23 near or in proximity. 24 **close to the wind.** *Nautical* sailing as nearly as possible towards the direction from which the wind is blowing. See also **wind[1]** (sense 26).
▷**HISTORY** C13: from Old French *clos* close, enclosed, from Latin *clausus* shut up, from *claudere* to close
▸**'closely** ADVERB ▸**'closeness** NOUN

close[2] (kləʊz) VERB 1 to put or be put in such a position as to cover an opening; shut: *the door closed behind him.* 2 (*tr*) to bar, obstruct, or fill up (an entrance, a hole, etc.): *to close a road.* 3 to bring the parts or edges of (a wound, etc.) together or (of a wound, etc.) to be brought together. 4 (*intr; foll by on, over,* etc.) to take hold: *his hand closed over the money.* 5 to bring or be brought to an end; terminate. 6 to complete (an agreement, a deal, etc.) successfully or (of an agreement, deal, etc.) to be completed successfully. 7 to cease or cause to cease to render service: *the shop closed at six.* 8 (*intr*) *Stock Exchange* to have a value at the end of a day's trading, as specified: *steels closed two points down.* 9 to complete an electrical circuit. 10 (*tr*) *Nautical* to pass near. 11 (*tr*) *Archaic* to enclose or shut in. 12 **close one's eyes. a** *Euphemistic* to die. **b** (often foll by *to*) to ignore. ♦ NOUN 13 the act of closing. 14 the end or conclusion: *the close of the day.* 15 a place of joining or meeting. 16 (kləʊs) *Law* private property, usually enclosed by a fence, hedge, or wall. 17 (kləʊs) *Brit* a courtyard or quadrangle enclosed by buildings or an entry leading to such a courtyard. 18 (kləʊs) *Brit* (*capital when part of a street name*) a small quiet residential road: *Hillside Close.* 19 *Brit* a field. 20 (kləʊs) the precincts of a cathedral or similar building. 21 (kləʊs) *Scot* the entry from the street to a tenement building. 22 *Music* another word for **cadence.** A perfect cadence is called a **full close** an imperfect one a **half close.** 23 *Archaic or rare* an encounter in battle; grapple. ♦ See also **close down, close in, close out, close-up, close with.**
▸**'closer** NOUN

close call (kləʊs) NOUN another expression for **close shave.**

close company (kləʊs) NOUN *Brit* a company under the control of its directors or fewer than five independent participants. Also called: **closed company.**

close corporation (kləʊs) NOUN *South African* a small private limited company. Abbreviation: **c.c.**

closed (kləʊzd) ADJECTIVE 1 blocked against entry; shut. 2 restricted; exclusive. 3 not open to question or debate. 4 (of a hunting season, etc.) close. 5 *Maths* **a** (of a curve or surface) completely enclosing an area or volume. **b** (of a set) having members that can be produced by a specific operation on other members of the same set: *the integers are a closed set under multiplication.* 6 Also: **checked.** *Phonetics* **a** denoting a syllable that ends in a consonant. **b** another word for **close[1]** (sense 21). 7 not open to public entry or membership: *a closed society.*

closed book NOUN 1 something deemed unknown or incapable of being understood. 2 a matter that has been finally concluded and admits of no further consideration.

closed-captioned ADJECTIVE (of a video recording) having subtitles which appear on screen only if the cassette is played through a special decoder.

closed chain NOUN *Chem* another name for **ring[1]** (sense 18).

closed circuit NOUN a complete electrical circuit through which current can flow when a voltage is applied. Compare **open circuit.**

closed-circuit television NOUN a television system in which signals are transmitted from a television camera to the receivers by cables or telephone links forming a closed circuit, as used in security systems, etc.

closed community NOUN *Ecology* a plant community that does not allow for further colonization, all the available niches being occupied.

closed corporation NOUN *US* a corporation the stock of which is owned by a small number of persons and is rarely traded on the open market. Also: **close corporation.**

closed cycle NOUN *Engineering* a heat engine in which the working substance is continuously circulated and does not need replenishment.

closed-door ADJECTIVE private; barred to members of the public: *a closed-door meeting.*

closed game NOUN *Chess* a relatively complex game involving closed ranks and files and permitting only nontactical positional manoeuvring. Compare **open game.**

close down (kləʊz) VERB (*adverb*) 1 to cease or cause to cease operations: *the shop closed down.* 2 (*tr*) *Sport* to mark or move towards (an opposing player) in order to prevent him or her running with the ball or making or receiving a pass. ♦ NOUN **close-down** ('kləʊzˌdaʊn). 3 a closure or stoppage of operations, esp in a factory. 4 *Brit radio, television* the end of a period of broadcasting, esp late at night.

closed interval NOUN *Maths* an interval on the real line including its end points, as [0, 1], the set of reals between and including 0 and 1.

closed primary NOUN *US government* a primary in which only members of a particular party may vote. Compare **open primary.**

closed scholarship NOUN a scholarship for which only certain people, such as those from a particular school or with a particular surname, are eligible.

closed sentence NOUN *Logic* a formula that contains no free occurrence of any variable. Compare **open sentence.**

closed set NOUN *Maths* 1 a set that includes all the values obtained by application of a given operation to its members. 2 (in topological space) a set that includes all its own limit points.

closed shop NOUN (formerly) an industrial establishment in which there exists a contract between a trade union and the employer permitting the employment of the union's members only. Compare **open shop, union shop.**

close-fisted (ˌkləʊs'fɪstɪd) ADJECTIVE very careful with money; mean.
▸**ˌclose-'fistedness** NOUN

close-grained (ˌkləʊs'greɪnd) ADJECTIVE (of wood) dense or compact in texture.

close harmony (kləʊs) NOUN a type of singing in which all the parts except the bass lie close together and are confined to the compass of a tenth.

close-hauled (ˌkləʊs'hɔ:ld) ADJECTIVE *Nautical* with the sails flat, so as to sail as close to the wind as possible.

close in (kləʊz) VERB (*intr, adverb*) 1 (of days) to become shorter with the approach of winter. 2 (foll by *on* or *upon*) to advance (on) so as to encircle or surround.

close-knit (ˌkləʊs'nɪt) ADJECTIVE closely united, esp by social ties.

close-lipped (ˌkləʊs'lɪpt) *or* **close-mouthed** (ˌkləʊs'maʊðd, -'maʊθt) ADJECTIVE not talking or revealing much.

close out (kləʊz) VERB (*adverb*) to terminate (a client's or other account) on which the margin is inadequate or exhausted, usually by sale of securities to realize cash.

close punctuation (kləʊs) NOUN punctuation in which many commas, full stops, etc., are used. Compare **open punctuation.**

close quarters (kləʊs) PLURAL NOUN 1 a narrow cramped space or position. 2 **at close quarters. a** engaged in hand-to-hand combat. **b** in close proximity; very near together.

close season (kləʊs) *or* **closed season** NOUN 1 the period of the year when it is prohibited to kill certain game or fish. 2 *Sport* the period of the year when there is no domestic competition.

close shave (kləʊs) NOUN *Informal* a narrow escape.

close-stool ('kləʊsˌstu:l) NOUN a wooden stool containing a covered chamber pot.

closet ('klɒzɪt) NOUN 1 a small cupboard or recess. 2 a small private room. 3 short for **water closet.** 4 (*modifier*) private or secret. 5 (*modifier*) suited or appropriate for use in private: *closet meditations.* 6 (*modifier*) *US and Canadian* based on or devoted to theory; speculative: *a closet strategist.* ♦ VERB **-ets, -eting, -eted.** 7 (*tr*) to shut up or confine in a small private room, esp for conference or meditation.
▷**HISTORY** C14: from Old French, from *clos* enclosure; see CLOSE[1]

closet drama NOUN *Chiefly US* **a** drama suitable for reading rather than performing. **b** a play of this kind.

closet queen NOUN *Informal* a man who is homosexual but does not admit the fact.

close-up ('kləʊsˌʌp) NOUN 1 a photograph or film or television shot taken at close range. 2 a detailed or intimate view or examination: *a close-up of modern society.* ♦ VERB **close up** (kləʊz). (*adverb*) 3 to shut entirely. 4 (*intr*) to draw together: *the ranks closed up.* 5 (*intr*) (of wounds) to heal completely.

close with (kləʊz) VERB (*intr, preposition*) to engage in battle with (an enemy).

closing time ('kləʊzɪŋ) NOUN the time at which pubs must legally stop selling alcoholic drinks.

clostridium (klɒˈstrɪdɪəm) NOUN, *plural* **-iums** *or* **-ia** (-ɪə). any anaerobic typically rod-shaped bacterium of the genus *Clostridium*, occurring mainly in soil, but also in the intestines of humans and animals: family *Bacillaceae*. The genus includes the species causing botulism and tetanus.
▷HISTORY C20: from New Latin, literally: small spindle, from Greek *klōstēr* spindle, from *klōthein* to spin; see -IUM
▸**closˈtridial** *or* **closˈtridian** ADJECTIVE

closure (ˈkləʊʒə) NOUN [1] the act of closing or the state of being closed. [2] an end or conclusion. [3] something that closes or shuts, such as a cap or seal for a container. [4] (in a deliberative body) a procedure by which debate may be halted and an immediate vote taken. See also **cloture, guillotine, gag rule.** [5] *Chiefly US* **a** the resolution of a significant event or relationship in a person's life. **b** a sense of contentment experienced after such a resolution. [6] *Geology* the vertical distance between the crest of an anticline and the lowest contour that surrounds it. [7] *Phonetics* the obstruction of the breath stream at some point along the vocal tract, such as the complete occlusion preliminary to the articulation of a stop. [8] *Logic* **a** the closed sentence formed from a given open sentence by prefixing universal or existential quantifiers to bind all its free variables. **b** the process of forming such a closed sentence. [9] *Maths* **a** the smallest closed set containing a given set. **b** the operation of forming such a set. [10] *Psychol* the tendency, first noted by Gestalt psychologists, to see an incomplete figure like a circle with a gap in it as more complete than it is. ◆ VERB [11] (*tr*) (in a deliberative body) to end (debate) by closure.
▷HISTORY C14: from Old French, from Late Latin *clausūra* bar, from Latin *claudere* to close

clot (klɒt) NOUN [1] a soft thick lump or mass: *a clot of blood.* [2] *Brit informal* a stupid person; fool. ◆ VERB **clots, clotting, clotted.** [3] to form or cause to form into a soft thick lump or lumps.
▷HISTORY Old English *clott,* of Germanic origin; compare Middle Dutch *klotte* block, lump
▸**ˈclottish** ADJECTIVE

cloth (klɒθ) NOUN, *plural* **cloths** (klɒθs, klɒðz). [1] **a** a fabric formed by weaving, felting or knitting wool, cotton, etc. **b** (*as modifier*): *a cloth bag.* [2] a piece of such fabric used for a particular purpose, as for a dishcloth. [3] (usually preceded by *the*) **a** the clothes worn by a clergyman. **b** the clergy. [4] *Obsolete* clothing. [5] *Nautical* any of the panels of a sail. [6] *Chiefly Brit* a piece of coloured fabric, used on the stage as scenery. [7] *West African* a garment in a traditional non-European style.
▷HISTORY Old English *clāth;* related to Old Frisian *klēth,* Middle High German *kleit* cloth, clothing

clothbound (ˈklɒθˌbaʊnd) ADJECTIVE (of a book) bound in stiff boards covered in cloth.

cloth cap NOUN *Brit* [1] Also called: **flat cap.** a flat woollen cap with a stiff peak. [2] *Informal* **a** a symbol of working-class ethos or origin. **b** (*as modifier*): *cloth-cap attitudes.*

clothe (kləʊð) VERB **clothes, clothing, clothed** *or* **clad.** (*tr*) [1] to dress or attire (a person). [2] to provide with clothing or covering. [3] to conceal or disguise. [4] to endow or invest.
▷HISTORY Old English *clāthian,* from *clāth* CLOTH; related to Old Norse *klætha*

cloth-eared ADJECTIVE *Informal* [1] deaf. [2] insensitive.

clothes (kləʊðz) PLURAL NOUN [1] **a** articles of dress. **b** (*as modifier*): *clothes brush.* Related adjective: **vestiary.** [2] *Chiefly Brit* short for **bedclothes.**
▷HISTORY Old English *clāthas,* plural of *clāth* CLOTH

clotheshorse (ˈkləʊðzˌhɔːs) NOUN [1] a frame on which to hang laundry for drying or airing. [2] *Informal* a dandy.

clothesline (ˈkləʊðzˌlaɪn) NOUN a piece of rope, cord, or wire on which clean washing is hung to dry or air.

clothes moth NOUN any of various tineid moths, esp *Tineola bisselliella,* the larvae of which feed on wool or fur.

clothes peg NOUN a small wooden or plastic clip for attaching washing to a clothesline.

clothes pole NOUN [1] a post to which a clothesline is attached. Also called: **clothes post.** [2] *Scot, US* another term for **clothes prop.**

clothes-press NOUN a piece of furniture for storing clothes, usually containing wide drawers and a cabinet.

clothes prop NOUN a long wooden pole with a forked end, used to raise a line of washing to enable it to catch the breeze.

clothier (ˈkləʊðɪə) NOUN a person who makes, sells, or deals in clothes or cloth.

clothing (ˈkləʊðɪŋ) NOUN [1] garments collectively. [2] something that covers or clothes.

Clotho (ˈkləʊθəʊ) NOUN *Greek myth* one of the three Fates, spinner of the thread of life.
▷HISTORY Latin, from Greek *Klōtho,* one who spins, from *klōthein* to spin

cloth of gold NOUN cloth woven from silk threads interspersed with gold.

clotted cream NOUN *Brit* a thick cream made from scalded milk, esp in SW England. Also called: **Devonshire cream.**

clotting factor NOUN any one of a group of substances, including factor VIII, the presence of which in the blood is essential for blood clotting to occur. Also called: **coagulation factor.**

cloture (ˈkləʊtʃə) NOUN [1] closure in the US Senate. ◆ VERB [2] (*tr*) to end (debate) in the US Senate by cloture.
▷HISTORY C19: from French *clôture,* from Old French CLOSURE

cloud (klaʊd) NOUN [1] a mass of water or ice particles visible in the sky, usually white or grey, from which rain or snow falls when the particles coagulate. See also **cirrus, cumulonimbus, cumulus, stratus.** [2] any collection of particles visible in the air, esp of smoke or dust. [3] a large number of insects or other small animals in flight. [4] something that darkens, threatens, or carries gloom. [5] *Jewellery* a cloudlike blemish in a transparent stone. [6] **in the clouds.** not in contact with reality. [7] **under a cloud. a** under reproach or suspicion. **b** in a state of gloom or bad temper. [8] **on cloud nine.** *Informal* elated; very happy. ◆ VERB [9] (when *intr,* often foll by *over* or *up*) to make or become cloudy, overcast, or indistinct. [10] (*tr*) to make obscure; darken. [11] (*tr*) to confuse or impair: *emotion clouded his judgment.* [12] to make or become gloomy or depressed. [13] (*tr*) to place under or render liable to suspicion or disgrace. [14] to render (liquids) milky or dull or (of liquids) to become milky or dull. [15] to become or render mottled or variegated.
▷HISTORY C13 (in the sense: a mass of vapour): from Old English *clūd* rock, hill; probably related to CLOD
▸**ˈcloudless** ADJECTIVE ▸**ˈcloudlessly** ADVERB
▸**ˈcloudlessness** NOUN ▸**ˈcloudˌlike** ADJECTIVE

cloudberry (ˈklaʊdbərɪ, -brɪ) NOUN, *plural* **-ries.** a creeping Eurasian herbaceous rosaceous plant, *Rubus chamaemorus,* with white flowers and orange berry-like fruits (drupelets).

cloudburst (ˈklaʊdˌbɜːst) NOUN a heavy downpour.

cloud chamber NOUN *Physics* an apparatus for detecting high-energy particles by observing their tracks through a chamber containing a supersaturated vapour. Each particle ionizes molecules along its path and small droplets condense on them to produce a visible track. Also called: **Wilson cloud chamber.**

cloud-cuckoo-land *or* **cloudland** (ˈklaʊdˌlænd) NOUN a realm of fantasy, dreams, or impractical notions.

clouded yellow NOUN See **yellow** (sense 6).

cloudlet (ˈklaʊdlɪt) NOUN a small cloud.

cloud rack NOUN a group of moving clouds.

cloudscape (ˈklaʊdskeɪp) NOUN [1] a picturesque formation of clouds. [2] a picture or photograph of such a formation.

cloudy (ˈklaʊdɪ) ADJECTIVE **cloudier, cloudiest.** [1] covered with cloud or clouds. [2] of or like a cloud or clouds. [3] streaked or mottled like a cloud. [4] opaque or muddy. [5] obscure or unclear. [6] troubled by gloom or depression: *his face had a cloudy expression.*
▸**ˈcloudily** ADVERB ▸**ˈcloudiness** NOUN

clough (klʌf) NOUN *Dialect* a gorge or narrow ravine.
▷HISTORY Old English *clōh*

clout (klaʊt) NOUN [1] *Informal* a blow with the hand or a hard object. [2] power or influence, esp in politics. [3] *Archery* **a** the target used in long-distance shooting. **b** the centre of this target. **c** a shot that hits the centre. [4] Also called: **clout nail.** a short, flat-headed nail used esp for attaching sheet metal to wood. [5] *Brit dialect* **a** a piece of cloth: *a dish clout.* **b** a garment. **c** a patch. ◆ VERB (*tr*) [6] *Informal* to give a hard blow to, esp with the hand. [7] to patch with a piece of cloth or leather.
▷HISTORY Old English *clūt* piece of metal or cloth, *clūtian* to patch (C14: to strike with the hand); related to Dutch *kluit* a lump, and to CLOD
▸**ˈclouter** NOUN

clove¹ (kləʊv) NOUN [1] a tropical evergreen myrtaceous tree, *Syzygium aromaticum,* native to the East Indies but cultivated elsewhere, esp Zanzibar. [2] the dried unopened flower buds of this tree, used as a pungent fragrant spice.
▷HISTORY C14: from Old French *clou de girofle,* literally: nail of clove, *clou* from Latin *clāvus* nail + *girofle* clove tree

clove² (kləʊv) NOUN any of the segments of a compound bulb that arise from the axils of the scales of a large bulb.
▷HISTORY Old English *clufu* bulb; related to Old High German *klovolouh* garlic; see CLEAVE¹

clove³ (kləʊv) VERB a past tense of **cleave¹.**

clove hitch NOUN a knot or hitch used for securing a rope to a spar, post, or larger rope.

Clovelly (kləˈvɛlɪ) NOUN a village in SW England, in Devon on the Bristol Channel: famous for its steep cobbled streets: tourism, fishing. Pop.: 500 (latest est.).

cloven (ˈkləʊvᵊn) VERB [1] a past participle of **cleave¹.** ◆ ADJECTIVE [2] split; cleft; divided.

cloven hoof *or* **foot** NOUN [1] the divided hoof of a pig, goat, cow, deer, or related animal, which consists of the two middle digits of the foot. [2] the mark or symbol of Satan.
▸**ˌcloven-ˈhoofed** *or* **ˌcloven-ˈfooted** ADJECTIVE

clove oil NOUN a volatile pale-yellow aromatic oil obtained from clove flowers, formerly much used in confectionery, dentistry, and microscopy. Also called: **oil of cloves.**

clove pink NOUN another name for **carnation** (sense 1).

clover (ˈkləʊvə) NOUN [1] any plant of the leguminous genus *Trifolium,* having trifoliate leaves and dense flower heads. Many species, such as red clover, white clover, and alsike, are grown as forage plants. [2] any of various similar or related plants. [3] **sweet clover.** another name for **melilot.** [4] **pin clover.** another name for **alfilaria.** [5] **in clover.** *Informal* in a state of ease or luxury.
▷HISTORY Old English *clāfre;* related to Old High German *klēo,* Middle Low German *klēver,* Dutch *klāver*

cloverleaf (ˈkləʊvəˌliːf) NOUN, *plural* **-leaves.** [1] an arrangement of connecting roads, resembling a four-leaf clover in form, that joins two intersecting main roads. [2] (*modifier*) in the shape or pattern of a leaf of clover.

cloverleaf aerial NOUN a type of aerial, having three or four similar coplanar loops arranged symmetrically around an axis, to which in-phase signals are fed.

clovis point (ˈkləʊvɪs) NOUN a concave-based flint projectile dating from the 10th millennium B.C., found throughout most of Central and North America.

clown (klaʊn) NOUN [1] a comic entertainer, usually grotesquely costumed and made up, appearing in the circus. [2] any performer who elicits an amused response. [3] someone who plays jokes or tricks. [4] a person who acts in a comic or buffoon-like manner. [5] a coarse clumsy rude person; boor. [6] *Archaic* a countryman or rustic. ◆ VERB (*intr*) [7] to perform as a clown. [8] to play jokes or tricks. [9] to act foolishly.
▷HISTORY C16: perhaps of Low German origin; compare Frisian *klönne,* Icelandic *klunni* clumsy fellow
▸**ˈclownery** NOUN ▸**ˈclownish** ADJECTIVE ▸**ˈclownishly** ADVERB ▸**ˈclownishness** NOUN

cloxacillin (ˌklɒksəˈsɪlɪn) NOUN a semisynthetic penicillin used to treat staphylococcal infections due to penicillin-resistant organisms.

cloy (klɔɪ) VERB to make weary or cause weariness through an excess of something initially pleasurable or sweet.
▷HISTORY C14 (originally: to nail, hence, to obstruct): from earlier *acloyen,* from Old French *encloer,* from Medieval Latin *inclavāre,* from Latin *clāvāre* to nail, from *clāvus* a nail

cloying ('klɔɪɪŋ) ADJECTIVE initially pleasurable or sweet but wearying in excess.
▸'**cloyingly** ADVERB

cloze test (kləuz) NOUN a test of the ability to comprehend text in which the reader has to supply the missing words that have been removed from the text at regular intervals.
▷HISTORY altered from *close* to complete a pattern (in Gestalt theory)

club (klʌb) NOUN [1] a stout stick, usually with one end thicker than the other, esp one used as a weapon. [2] a stick or bat used to strike the ball in various sports, esp golf. See **golf club** (sense 1). [3] short for **Indian club.** [4] a group or association of people with common aims or interests: *a wine club.* [5] **a** the room, building, or facilities used by such a group. **b** (*in combination*): *clubhouse.* [6] a building in which elected, fee-paying members go to meet, dine, read, etc. [7] a commercial establishment in which people can drink and dance; disco. See also **nightclub.** [8] *Chiefly Brit* an organization, esp in a shop, set up as a means of saving. [9] *Brit* an informal word for **friendly society.** [10] **a** the black trefoil symbol on a playing card. **b** a card with one or more of these symbols or (*when pl.*) the suit of cards so marked. [11] *Nautical* **a** a spar used for extending the clew of a gaff topsail beyond the peak of the gaff. **b** short for **club foot** (sense 3). [12] **in the club.** *Brit slang* pregnant. [13] **on the club.** *Brit slang* away from work due to sickness, esp when receiving sickness benefit. ◆ VERB **clubs, clubbing, clubbed.** [14] (*tr*) to beat with or as if with a club. [15] (often foll by *together*) to gather or become gathered into a group. [16] (often foll by *together*) to unite or combine (resources, efforts, etc.) for a common purpose. [17] (*tr*) to use (a rifle or similar firearm) as a weapon by holding the barrel and hitting with the butt. [18] (*intr*) *Nautical* to drift in a current, reducing speed by dragging anchor.
▷HISTORY C13: from Old Norse *klubba,* related to Middle High German *klumpe* group of trees, CLUMP, Old English *clympre* lump of metal
▸'**clubbing** NOUN

clubbable *or* **clubable** ('klʌbəbᵊl) ADJECTIVE suitable to be a member of a club; sociable.
▸ˌ**clubba'bility** *or* ˌ**cluba'bility** NOUN

clubbed (klʌbd) ADJECTIVE having a thickened end, like a club.

clubber ('klʌbə) NOUN a person who regularly frequents nightclubs and similar establishments.

clubbing ('klʌbɪŋ) NOUN the activity of frequenting nightclubs and similar establishments.

clubby ('klʌbɪ) ADJECTIVE **-bier, -biest.** [1] sociable, esp effusively so. [2] exclusive or cliquish.
▸'**clubbily** ADVERB

club class NOUN [1] a class of air travel which is less luxurious than first class but more luxurious than economy class. ◆ ADJECTIVE [2] **club-class.** of or relating to this class of travel.

club culture NOUN the practice of protecting the reputation of one's workforce in the face of criticism, above all other considerations.

club foot NOUN [1] a congenital deformity of the foot, esp one in which the foot is twisted so that most of the weight rests on the heel. Technical name: **talipes.** [2] a foot so deformed. [3] *Nautical* a boom attached to the foot of a jib.
▸ˌ**club-'footed** ADJECTIVE

club hand NOUN [1] a deformity of the hand, analogous to club foot. [2] a hand so deformed.
▸ˌ**club-'handed** ADJECTIVE

clubhaul ('klʌbˌhɔːl) VERB *Nautical* to force (a sailing vessel) onto a new tack, esp in an emergency, by fastening a lee anchor to the lee quarter, dropping the anchor as the vessel comes about, and hauling in the anchor cable to swing the stern to windward.

clubhouse ('klʌbˌhaus) NOUN the premises of a sports or other club, esp a golf club.

clubland ('klʌbˌlænd) NOUN (in Britain) the area of London around St. James's, which contains most of the famous London clubs.

club line NOUN *Printing* See **orphan** (sense 3).

clubman ('klʌbmən) NOUN, *plural* **-men.** a man who is an enthusiastic member of a club or clubs.

club moss NOUN any mosslike tracheophyte plant of the phylum *Lycopodophyta,* having erect or creeping stems covered with tiny overlapping leaves.

club root NOUN a disease of cabbages and related plants, caused by the fungus *Plasmodiophora brassicae,* in which the roots become thickened and distorted.

club sandwich NOUN a sandwich consisting of three or more slices of toast or bread with a filling.

clubwoman ('klʌbˌwumən) NOUN, *plural* **-women.** a woman who is an enthusiastic member of a club or clubs.

cluck (klʌk) NOUN [1] the low clicking sound made by a hen or any similar sound. ◆ VERB [2] (*intr*) (of a hen) to make a clicking sound. [3] (*tr*) to call or express (a feeling) by making a similar sound.
▷HISTORY C17: of imitative origin

clucky ('klʌkɪ) ADJECTIVE *Austral informal* (of a woman) [1] wishing to have a baby. [2] excessively protective towards her children.

clue (kluː) NOUN [1] something that helps to solve a problem or unravel a mystery. [2] **not to have a clue. a** to be completely baffled. **b** to be completely ignorant or incompetent. ◆ VERB **clues, cluing, clued.** [3] (*tr;* usually foll by *in* or *up*) to provide with helpful information. ◆ NOUN, VERB [4] a variant spelling of **clew.**
▷HISTORY C15: variant of CLEW

clued-up ADJECTIVE *Informal* shrewd; well-informed.

clueless ('kluːlɪs) ADJECTIVE *Slang* helpless; stupid.

Cluj (kluʒ, kluːʒ) NOUN an industrial city in NW Romania, on the Someşul-Mic River: former capital of Transylvania. Pop.: 332 792 (1997 est.). German name: **Klausenburg.** Hungarian name: **Kolozsvár.**

clumber spaniel ('klʌmbə) NOUN a type of thickset spaniel having a broad heavy head. Often shortened to **clumber.**
▷HISTORY C19: named after *Clumber,* stately home of the Dukes of Newcastle where the breed was developed

clump (klʌmp) NOUN [1] a cluster, as of trees or plants. [2] a dull heavy tread or any similar sound. [3] an irregular mass: *a clump of hair or earth.* [4] an inactive mass of microorganisms, esp a mass of bacteria produced as a result of agglutination. [5] an extra sole on a shoe. [6] *Slang* a blow. ◆ VERB [7] (*intr*) to walk or tread heavily. [8] to gather or be gathered into clumps, clusters, clots, etc. [9] to cause (bacteria, blood cells, etc.) to collect together or (of bacteria, etc.) to collect together. [10] (*tr*) *Slang* to punch (someone).
▷HISTORY Old English *clympe;* related to Middle Dutch *klampe* heap of hay, Middle Low German *klampe* CLAMP², Swedish *klimp* small lump
▸'**clumpy** ADJECTIVE ▸'**clumpiness** NOUN

clumsy ('klʌmzɪ) ADJECTIVE **-sier, -siest.** [1] lacking in skill or physical coordination. [2] awkwardly constructed or contrived.
▷HISTORY C16 (in obsolete sense: benumbed with cold; hence, awkward): perhaps from C13 dialect *clumse* to benumb, probably from Scandinavian; compare Swedish dialect *klumsig* numb
▸'**clumsily** ADVERB ▸'**clumsiness** NOUN

clung (klʌŋ) VERB the past tense and past participle of **cling.**

Cluniac ('kluːnɪˌæk) ADJECTIVE of or relating to a reformed Benedictine order founded at the French town of Cluny in 910.

clunk (klʌŋk) NOUN [1] a blow or the sound of a blow. [2] a dull metallic sound. [3] a dull or stupid person. [4] *Chiefly Scot* **a** the gurgling sound of a liquid. **b** the sound of a cork being removed from a bottle. ◆ VERB [5] to make or cause to make such a sound.
▷HISTORY C19: of imitative origin

clunker ('klʌŋkə) NOUN *Informal* [1] *Chiefly US* a dilapidated old car or other machine. [2] something that fails: *the novel's last line is a clunker.*

clunky ('klʌŋkɪ) ADJECTIVE **clunkier, clunkiest.** [1] making a clunking noise. [2] *Informal* ponderously ungraceful or unsophisticated: *clunky boots.* [3] awkward or unsophisticated: *then you guffaw at clunky dialogue.*

Cluny ('kluːnɪ; *French* klyni) NOUN a town in E central France: reformed Benedictine order founded here in 910; important religious and cultural centre in the Middle Ages. Pop.: 4724 (1990).

Cluny lace NOUN a strong heavy silk and cotton bobbin lace made at Cluny or elsewhere.

clupeid ('kluːpɪɪd) NOUN [1] any widely distributed soft-finned teleost fish of the family *Clupeidae,* typically having oily flesh, and including the herrings, sardines, shad, etc. ◆ ADJECTIVE [2] of, relating to, or belonging to the family *Clupeidae.*
▷HISTORY C19: from New Latin *Clupeidae,* from Latin *clupea* small river fish

clupeoid ('kluːpɪˌɔɪd) ADJECTIVE [1] of, relating to, or belonging to the *Isospondyli* (or *Clupeiformes*), a large order of soft-finned fishes, including the herrings, salmon, and tarpon. ◆ NOUN [2] any fish belonging to the order *Isospondyli.*
▷HISTORY C19: from Latin *clupea* small fish + -OID

cluster ('klʌstə) NOUN [1] a number of things growing, fastened, or occurring close together. [2] a number of persons or things grouped together. [3] *US military* a metal insignia worn on a medal ribbon to indicate a second award or a higher class of a decoration or order. [4] *Military* **a** a group of bombs dropped in one stick, esp fragmentation and incendiary bombs. **b** the basic unit of mines used in laying a minefield. [5] *Astronomy* an aggregation of stars or galaxies moving together through space. [6] a group of two or more consecutive vowels or consonants. [7] *Statistics* a naturally occurring subgroup of a population used in stratified sampling. [8] *Chem* **a** a chemical compound or molecule containing groups of metal atoms joined by metal-to-metal bonds. **b** the group of linked metal atoms present. ◆ VERB [9] to gather or be gathered in clusters.
▷HISTORY Old English *clyster;* related to Low German *Kluster;* see CLOD, CLOT
▸'**clustered** ADJECTIVE ▸'**clusteringly** ADVERB ▸'**clustery** ADJECTIVE

cluster area NOUN a place where a concentration of a particular phenomenon is found.

cluster bomb NOUN a bomb that throws out a number of smaller bombs or antipersonnel projectiles when it explodes.

cluster fly NOUN a dipterous fly, *Pollenia rudis,* that tends to gather in large numbers in attics in the autumn: family *Calliphoridae.* The larvae are parasitic in earthworms.

clutch¹ (klʌtʃ) VERB [1] (*tr*) to seize with or as if with hands or claws. [2] (*tr*) to grasp or hold firmly. [3] (*intr;* usually foll by *at*) to attempt to get hold or possession (of). ◆ NOUN [4] a device that enables two revolving shafts to be joined or disconnected as required, esp one that transmits the drive from the engine to the gearbox in a vehicle. [5] a device for holding fast. [6] a firm grasp. [7] a hand, claw, or talon in the act of clutching: *in the clutches of a bear.* [8] (*often plural*) power or control: *in the clutches of the Mafia.* [9] Also called: **clutch bag.** a handbag without handles.
▷HISTORY Old English *clyccan;* related to Old Frisian *kletsie* spear, Swedish *klyka* clasp, fork

clutch² (klʌtʃ) NOUN [1] a hatch of eggs laid by a particular bird or laid in a single nest. [2] a brood of chickens. [3] *Informal* a group, bunch, or cluster. ◆ VERB [4] (*tr*) to hatch (chickens).
▷HISTORY C17 (Northern English dialect) *cletch,* from Old Norse *klekja* to hatch

Clutha ('kluːθə) NOUN a river in New Zealand, the longest river in South Island; rising in the Southern Alps it flows southeast to the Pacific. Length: 338 km (210 miles).

clutter ('klʌtə) VERB [1] (*usually tr;* often foll by *up*) to strew or amass (objects) in a disorderly manner. [2] (*intr*) to move about in a bustling manner. [3] (*intr*) to chatter or babble. ◆ NOUN [4] a disordered heap or mass of objects. [5] a state of disorder. [6] unwanted echoes that confuse the observation of signals on a radar screen.
▷HISTORY C15 *clotter,* from *clotteren* to CLOT

Clwyd ('kluːɪd) NOUN a former county in NE Wales, formed in 1974 from Flintshire, most of Denbighshire, and part of Merionethshire; replaced in 1996 by Flintshire, Denbighshire, Wrexham county borough, and part of Conwy county borough.

Clyde (klaɪd) NOUN [1] **Firth of,** an inlet of the Atlantic in SW Scotland. Length: 103 km (64 miles). [2] a river in S Scotland, rising in South Lanarkshire and flowing northwest to the Firth of Clyde: formerly extensive shipyards. Length: 170 km (106 miles).

Clydebank (ˌklaɪd'bæŋk, 'klaɪdˌbæŋk) NOUN a town in W Scotland, in West Dunbartonshire on the north bank of the River Clyde. Pop.: 29 171 (1991).

Clydesdale ('klaɪdzˌdeɪl) NOUN a heavy powerful breed of carthorse, originally from Scotland.

clype (klaɪp) *Scot* ◆ VERB (*intr*) [1] to tell tales; be an informer. ◆ NOUN [2] a person who tells tales.
▷HISTORY C15: from Old English *clipian, cleopian;* see CLEPE

clypeus ('klɪpɪəs) NOUN, *plural* **clypei** ('klɪpɪˌaɪ). a cuticular plate on the head of some insects between the labrum and the frons.
▷HISTORY C19: from New Latin, from Latin *clipeus* round shield
▸**'clypeal** ADJECTIVE ▸**clypeate** ('klɪpɪˌeɪt) ADJECTIVE

clyster ('klɪstə) NOUN *Med* a former name for an **enema.**
▷HISTORY C14: from Greek *klustēr,* from *kluzein* to rinse

Clytemnestra *or* **Clytaemnestra** (ˌklaɪtɪm'nɛstrə) NOUN *Greek myth* the wife of Agamemnon, whom she killed on his return from the Trojan War.

cm[1] SYMBOL FOR centimetre.

cm[2] THE INTERNET DOMAIN NAME FOR Cameroon.

Cm THE CHEMICAL SYMBOL FOR curium.

CM ABBREVIATION FOR Member of the Order of Canada.

Cmdr *Military* ABBREVIATION FOR Commander.

CMEA ABBREVIATION FOR Council for Mutual Economic Assistance. See **Comecon.**

CMG ABBREVIATION FOR Companion of St. Michael and St. George (a Brit. title).

CMIIW *Text messaging* ABBREVIATION FOR correct me if I'm wrong.

cml ABBREVIATION FOR commercial.

CMOS ('siːmɒs) ADJECTIVE *Computing* ACRONYM FOR complementary metal oxide silicon: *CMOS memory.*

CMV ABBREVIATION FOR cytomegalovirus.

cn THE INTERNET DOMAIN NAME FOR China.

C/N, c/n, *or* **cn** *Commerce* ABBREVIATION FOR credit note.

CNA (in South Africa) ABBREVIATION FOR Central News Agency, a national stationery chain.

CNAA (in Britain) ABBREVIATION FOR the Council for National Academic Awards: a former degree-awarding body separate from the universities.

CNAR ABBREVIATION FOR compound net annual rate.

CND (in Britain) ABBREVIATION FOR Campaign for Nuclear Disarmament.

cnemis ('niːmɪs) NOUN *Anatomy, zoology* the shin or tibia.
▷HISTORY from Greek *knēmē* leg
▸**'cnemial** ADJECTIVE

CNG ABBREVIATION FOR compressed natural gas.

cnidarian (naɪ'dɛərɪən, knaɪ-) NOUN [1] any invertebrate of the phylum *Cnidaria,* which comprises the coelenterates. ◆ ADJECTIVE [2] of, relating to, or belonging to the *Cnidaria.*
▷HISTORY C20: from New Latin *Cnidaria,* from Greek *knidē* nettle

cnidoblast ('naɪdəʊˌblɑːst, 'knaɪ-) NOUN *Zoology* any of the cells of a coelenterate that contain nematocysts.
▷HISTORY C19: from New Latin *cnida,* from Greek *knidē* nettle + -BLAST

Cnidus ('naɪdəs, 'knaɪ-) NOUN an ancient Greek city in SW Asia Minor: famous for its school of medicine.

CNN ABBREVIATION FOR Cable Network News.

Cnossus ('nɒsəs, 'knɒs-) NOUN a variant spelling of **Knossos.**

CNR ABBREVIATION FOR Canadian National Railways.

CNS ABBREVIATION FOR **central nervous system.**

co [1] AN INTERNET DOMAIN NAME FOR a commercial company (used with a country domain name). ◆ [2] THE INTERNET DOMAIN NAME FOR Colombia.

Co THE CHEMICAL SYMBOL FOR cobalt.

CO ABBREVIATION FOR: [1] Commanding Officer. [2] Commonwealth Office. [3] conscientious objector. [4] Colorado. ◆ [5] INTERNATIONAL CAR REGISTRATION FOR Colombia.

Co. *or* **co.** ABBREVIATION FOR: [1] (*esp in names of business organizations*) Company. [2] **and co** (kəʊ). *Informal* and the rest of them: *Harold and co.*

Co. ABBREVIATION FOR County.

co- PREFIX [1] together; joint or jointly; mutual or mutually: *coproduction.* [2] indicating partnership or equality: *cofounder; copilot.* [3] to the same or a similar degree: *coextend.* [4] (in mathematics and astronomy) of the complement of an angle: *cosecant; codeclination.*
▷HISTORY from Latin, reduced form of COM-

c/o ABBREVIATION FOR: [1] care of. [2] *Book-keeping* carried over.

CoA ABBREVIATION FOR coenzyme A.

coacervate (kəʊ'æsəvɪt, -ˌveɪt) NOUN either of two liquid phases that may separate from a hydrophilic sol, each containing a different concentration of a dispersed solid.
▷HISTORY C17: from Latin *coacervāre* to heap up, from *acervus* a heap
▸**coˌacer'vation** NOUN

coach (kəʊtʃ) NOUN [1] a vehicle for several passengers, used for transport over long distances, sightseeing, etc. [2] a large four-wheeled enclosed carriage, usually horse-drawn. [3] a railway carriage carrying passengers. [4] a trainer or instructor: *a drama coach.* [5] a tutor who prepares students for examinations. ◆ VERB [6] to give tuition or instruction to (a pupil). [7] (*tr*) to transport in a bus or coach.
▷HISTORY C16: from French *coche,* from Hungarian *kocsi szekér* wagon of Kocs, village in Hungary where coaches were first made; in the sense: to teach, probably from the idea that the instructor carried his pupils
▸**'coacher** NOUN

coach bolt NOUN a large round-headed bolt used esp to secure wood to masonry. Also called (chiefly US and Canadian): **carriage bolt.**

coach box NOUN the seat of a coachman on a horse-drawn carriage or coach.

coach-built ADJECTIVE (of a vehicle) having specially built bodywork.
▸**'coach-ˌbuilder** NOUN

coach dog NOUN a former name for **Dalmatian.**

coachee (ˌkəʊtʃ'iː) NOUN a person who receives training from a coach, esp in business or office practice.

coach house NOUN [1] a building in which a coach is kept. [2] Also called: **coaching house, coaching inn.** *History* an inn along a coaching route at which horses were changed.

coach line NOUN a decorative line on the bodywork of a motor vehicle. Also called: **carriage line.**

coachman ('kəʊtʃmən) NOUN, *plural* **-men.** [1] the driver of a coach or carriage. [2] a fishing fly with white wings and a brown hackle.

coach screw NOUN a large screw with a square head used in timber work in buildings, etc.

coachwood ('kəʊtʃˌwʊd) NOUN an Australian tree, *Ceratopetalum apetalum,* yielding light aromatic wood used for furniture, turnery, etc.

coachwork ('kəʊtʃˌwɜːk) NOUN [1] the design and manufacture of car bodies. [2] the body of a car.

coaction[1] (kəʊ'ækʃən) NOUN [1] any relationship between organisms within a community. [2] joint action.
▷HISTORY C17: CO- + ACTION
▸**co'active** ADJECTIVE ▸**co'actively** ADVERB ▸**ˌcoac'tivity** NOUN

coaction[2] (kəʊ'ækʃən) NOUN *Obsolete* a force or compulsion, either to compel or restrain.
▷HISTORY C14: from Late Latin *coāctiō,* from Latin *cōgere* to constrain, compel

coadjutant (kəʊ'ædʒətənt) ADJECTIVE [1] cooperating. ◆ NOUN [2] a helper.

coadjutor (kəʊ'ædʒʊtə) NOUN [1] a bishop appointed as assistant to a diocesan bishop. [2] *Rare* an assistant.
▷HISTORY C15: via Old French from Latin *co-* together + *adjūtor* helper, from *adjūtāre* to assist, from *juvāre* to help
▸**co'adjutress** *or* **co'adjutrix** FEMININE NOUN

coadunate (kəʊ'ædjʊnɪt, -ˌneɪt) ADJECTIVE *Biology* another word for **connate** (sense 3).
▷HISTORY C19: from Late Latin *coadūnāre* to join together, from Latin *adūnāre* to join to, from *ūnus* one
▸**coˌadu'nation** NOUN ▸**co'aduˌnative** ADJECTIVE

coagulant (kəʊ'ægjʊlənt) *or* **coagulator** (kəʊ'ægjʊˌleɪtə) NOUN a substance that aids or produces coagulation.

coagulase (kəʊ'ægjʊleɪz) NOUN any enzyme that causes coagulation of blood.

coagulate VERB (kəʊ'ægjʊˌleɪt) [1] to cause (a fluid, such as blood) to change into a soft semisolid mass or (of such a fluid) to change into such a mass; clot; curdle. [2] *Chem* to separate or cause to separate into distinct constituent phases. ◆ NOUN (kəʊ'ægjʊlɪt, -ˌleɪt) [3] the solid or semisolid substance produced by coagulation.
▷HISTORY C16: from Latin *coāgulāre* to make (a liquid) curdle, from *coāgulum* rennet, from *cōgere* to drive together
▸**co'agulable** ADJECTIVE ▸**coˌagula'bility** NOUN ▸**coˌagu'lation** NOUN ▸**coagulative** (kəʊ'ægjʊlətɪv) ADJECTIVE

coagulation factor NOUN *Med* another name for **clotting factor.**

coagulum (kəʊ'ægjʊləm) NOUN, *plural* **-la** (-lə). any coagulated mass; clot; curd.
▷HISTORY C17: from Latin: curdling agent; see COAGULATE

Coahuila (*Spanish* koa'wila) NOUN a state of N Mexico: mainly plateau, crossed by several mountain ranges that contain rich mineral resources. Capital: Saltillo. Pop.: 2 295 808 (2000). Area: 151 571 sq. km (59 112 sq. miles).

coal (kəʊl) NOUN [1] **a** a combustible compact black or dark-brown carbonaceous rock formed from compaction of layers of partially decomposed vegetation: a fuel and a source of coke, coal gas, and coal tar. See also **anthracite, bituminous coal, lignite, peat**[1]. **b** (*as modifier*): *coal cellar; coal merchant; coal mine; coal dust.* [2] one or more lumps of coal. [3] short for **charcoal.** [4] **coals to Newcastle.** something supplied where it is already plentiful. [5] **haul (someone) over the coals.** to reprimand (someone). ◆ VERB [6] to take in, provide with, or turn into coal.
▷HISTORY Old English *col;* related to Old Norse *kol,* Old High German *kolo,* Old Irish *gūal*
▸**'coaly** ADJECTIVE

coaler ('kəʊlə) NOUN [1] a ship, train, etc., used to carry or supply coal. [2] a person who sells or supplies coal.

coalesce (ˌkəʊə'lɛs) VERB (*intr*) to unite or come together in one body or mass; merge; fuse; blend.
▷HISTORY C16: from Latin *coalēscere* from CO- + *alēscere* to increase, from *alere* to nourish
▸**ˌcoa'lescence** NOUN ▸**ˌcoa'lescent** ADJECTIVE

coalface ('kəʊlˌfeɪs) NOUN the exposed seam of coal in a mine.

coalfield ('kəʊlˌfiːld) NOUN an area rich in deposits of coal.

coalfish ('kəʊlˌfɪʃ) NOUN, *plural* **-fish** *or* **-fishes.** a dark-coloured gadoid food fish, *Pollachius virens,* occurring in northern seas. Also called (Brit): **saithe, coley.**

coal gas NOUN a mixture of gases produced by the distillation of bituminous coal and used for heating and lighting: consists mainly of hydrogen, methane, and carbon monoxide.

coal heaver NOUN a workman who moves coal.

coal hole NOUN *Brit informal* a small coal cellar.

coalition (ˌkəʊə'lɪʃən) NOUN [1] **a** an alliance or union between groups, factions, or parties, esp for some temporary and specific reason. **b** (*as modifier*): *a coalition government.* [2] a fusion or merging into one body or mass.
▷HISTORY C17: from Medieval Latin *coalitiō,* from Latin *coalēscere* to COALESCE
▸**ˌcoa'litional** ADJECTIVE ▸**ˌcoa'litionist** *or* **ˌcoa'litioner** NOUN

Coal Measures PLURAL NOUN **the.** a series of coal-bearing rocks formed in the upper Carboniferous period; the uppermost series of the Carboniferous system.

coal miner's lung NOUN an informal name for **anthracosis.**

coal oil NOUN 1 *US and Canadian* petroleum or a refined product from petroleum, esp kerosene. 2 a crude oil produced, together with coal gas, during the distillation of bituminous coal.

Coalport ('kəʊl,pɔːt) NOUN *Antiques* a white translucent bone china having richly coloured moulded patterns, made in the 19th century at Coalport near Shrewsbury.

coal pot NOUN a cooking device using charcoal, consisting of a raised iron bowl and a central grid.

Coal Sack NOUN a dark nebula in the Milky Way close to the Southern Cross.

coal scuttle NOUN a domestic metal container for coal.

coal tar NOUN a black tar, produced by the distillation of bituminous coal, that can be further distilled to yield benzene, toluene, xylene, anthracene, phenol, etc.

coal-tar pitch NOUN a residue left by the distillation of coal tar: a mixture of hydrocarbons and finely divided carbon used as a binder for fuel briquettes, road surfaces, and carbon electrodes.

coal tit NOUN a small European songbird, *Parus ater,* having a black head with a white patch on the nape: family *Paridae* (tits).

coaming ('kəʊmɪŋ) NOUN a raised frame around the cockpit or hatchway of a vessel for keeping out water.
▷HISTORY C17: of unknown origin

coaptation (,kəʊæp'teɪʃən) NOUN the joining or reuniting of two surfaces, esp the ends of a broken bone or the edges of a wound.
▷HISTORY C16: from Late Latin *coaptātiō* a meticulous joining together, from Latin *co-* together + *aptāre* to fit

coarctate (kəʊ'ɑːkteɪt) ADJECTIVE 1 (of a pupa) enclosed in a hard barrel-shaped case (puparium), as in the housefly. 2 crowded or pressed together; constricted. ◆ VERB *(intr)* 3 *Pathol* (esp of the aorta) to become narrower; become constricted.
▷HISTORY C15: from Latin *coarctāre,* to press together, from *artus* tight
▸,**coarc'tation** NOUN

coarse (kɔːs) ADJECTIVE 1 rough in texture, structure, etc.; not fine: *coarse sand.* 2 lacking refinement or taste; indelicate; vulgar: *coarse jokes.* 3 of inferior quality; not pure or choice. 4 (of a metal) not refined. 5 (of a screw) having widely spaced threads.
▷HISTORY C14: of unknown origin
▸'**coarsely** ADVERB ▸'**coarseness** NOUN

coarse fish NOUN a freshwater fish that is not a member of the salmon family. Compare **game fish.**
▸**coarse fishing** NOUN

coarse-grained ADJECTIVE 1 having a large or coarse grain. 2 (of a person) having a coarse nature; gross.

coarsen ('kɔːsᵊn) VERB to make or become coarse.

coast (kəʊst) NOUN 1 **a** the line or zone where the land meets the sea or some other large expanse of water. **b** *(in combination)*: *coastland.* Related adjective: **littoral.** 2 *Brit* the seaside. 3 *US* **a** a slope down which a sledge may slide. **b** the act or an instance of sliding down a slope. 4 *Obsolete* borderland or frontier. 5 **the coast is clear.** *Informal* the obstacles or dangers are gone. ◆ VERB 6 to move or cause to move by momentum or force of gravity. 7 *(intr)* to proceed without great effort: *to coast to victory.* 8 to sail along (a coast).
▷HISTORY C13: from Old French *coste* coast, slope, from Latin *costa* side, rib
▸'**coastal** ADJECTIVE ▸'**coastally** ADVERB

coaster ('kəʊstə) NOUN 1 *Brit* a vessel or trader engaged in coastal commerce. 2 a small tray, sometimes on wheels, for holding a decanter, wine bottle, etc. 3 a person or thing that coasts. 4 a protective disc or mat for glasses or bottles. 5 *US* short for **roller coaster.** 6 *West African* a European resident on the coast.

Coaster ('kəʊstə) NOUN *NZ* a person from the West Coast of the South Island, New Zealand.

coastguard ('kəʊst,gɑːd) NOUN 1 a maritime force which aids shipping, saves lives at sea, prevents smuggling, etc. 2 Also called: **coastguardsman.** a member of such a force.

coastline ('kəʊst,laɪn) NOUN the outline of a coast, esp when seen from the sea, or the land adjacent to it.

Coast Mountains PLURAL NOUN a mountain range in Canada, on the Pacific coast of British Columbia. Highest peak: Mount Waddington, 4043 m (13 266 ft.).

coat (kəʊt) NOUN 1 an outdoor garment with sleeves, covering the body from the shoulder to waist, knee, or foot. 2 any similar garment, esp one forming the top to a suit. 3 a layer that covers or conceals a surface: *a coat of dust.* 4 the hair, wool, or fur of an animal. 5 short for **coat of arms.** 6 **on the coat.** *Austral* in disfavour. ◆ VERB 7 *(tr; often foll by with)* to cover (with) a layer or covering. 8 *(tr)* to provide with a coat.
▷HISTORY C16: from Old French *cote* of Germanic origin; compare Old Saxon *kotta,* Old High German *kozzo*

coat armour NOUN *Heraldry* 1 coat of arms. 2 an emblazoned surcoat.

Coatbridge ('kəʊt,brɪdʒ; *Scot* ,kəʊt'brɪdʒ) NOUN an industrial town in central Scotland, in North Lanarkshire. Pop.: 43 617 (1991).

coat dress NOUN 1 a lightweight button-through garment that can be worn either as a dress or as a coat. 2 formerly, a dress tailored and styled like a coat.

coated ('kəʊtɪd) ADJECTIVE 1 covered with an outer layer, film, etc. 2 (of paper) having a coating of a mineral, esp china clay, to provide a very smooth surface. 3 (of textiles) having been given a plastic or other surface. 4 *Photog, optics* another word for **bloomed.**

coatee (kəʊ'tiː, 'kəʊtiː) NOUN *Chiefly Brit* a short coat, esp for a baby.

coat hanger NOUN a curved piece of wood, wire, plastic, etc., fitted with a hook and used to hang up clothes.

coati (kəʊ'ɑːtɪ), **coati-mondi,** *or* **coati-mundi** (kəʊ,ɑːtɪ'mʌndɪ) NOUN, *plural* **-tis** *or* **-dis.** any omnivorous mammal of the genera *Nasua* and *Nasuella,* of Central and South America: family *Procyonidae,* order *Carnivora* (carnivores). They are related to but larger than the raccoons, having a long flexible snout and a brindled coat.
▷HISTORY C17: from Portuguese *coatì,* from Tupi, literally: belt-nosed, from *cua* belt + *tim* nose

coating ('kəʊtɪŋ) NOUN 1 a layer or film spread over a surface for protection or decoration. 2 a heavy fabric suitable for coats. 3 *Midland English dialect* a severe rebuke; ticking-off.

coat of arms NOUN 1 the heraldic bearings of a person, family, or corporation. 2 a surcoat decorated with family or personal bearings.

coat of mail NOUN a protective garment made of linked metal rings (mail) or of overlapping metal plates; hauberk.

coat-of-mail shell NOUN another name for **chiton** (sense 2).

coat-tail NOUN 1 the long tapering tails at the back of a man's tailed coat. 2 **on someone's coat-tails.** thanks to the popularity or success of someone else.

coauthor (kəʊ'ɔːθə) NOUN 1 a person who shares the writing of a book, article, etc., with another. ◆ VERB 2 *(tr)* to be the joint author of (a book, article, etc.).

coax[1] (kəʊks) VERB 1 to seek to manipulate or persuade (someone) by tenderness, flattery, pleading, etc. 2 *(tr.)* to obtain by persistent coaxing. 3 *(tr)* to work on or tend (something) carefully and patiently so as to make it function as one desires: *he coaxed the engine into starting.* 4 *(tr) Obsolete* to caress. 5 *(tr) Obsolete* to deceive.
▷HISTORY C16: verb formed from obsolete noun *cokes* fool, of unknown origin
▸'**coaxer** NOUN ▸'**coaxingly** ADVERB

coax[2] ('kəʊæks) NOUN short for **coaxial cable.**

coaxial (kəʊ'æksɪəl) *or* **coaxal** (kəʊ'æksᵊl) ADJECTIVE 1 having or being mounted on a common axis. 2 *Geometry* (of a set of circles) having all the centres on a straight line. 3 *Electronics* formed from, using, or connected to a coaxial cable.

coaxial cable NOUN a cable consisting of an inner insulated core of stranded or solid wire surrounded by an outer insulated flexible wire braid, used esp as a transmission line for radio-frequency signals. Often shortened to **coax.**

cob[1] (kɒb) NOUN 1 a male swan. 2 a thickset short-legged type of riding and draught horse. 3 short for **corncob, corncob pipe,** or **cobnut.** 4 *Brit* another name for **hazel** (sense 1). 5 a small rounded lump or heap of coal, ore, etc. 6 *Brit and NZ* a building material consisting of a mixture of clay and chopped straw. 7 Also called: **cob loaf.** *Brit* a round loaf of bread. ◆ VERB **cobs, cobbing, cobbed.** 8 *(tr) Brit informal* to beat, esp on the buttocks.
▷HISTORY C15: of uncertain origin; probably related to Icelandic *kobbi* seal; see CUB

cob[2] *or* **cobb** (kɒb) NOUN an archaic or dialect name for a **gull** esp the greater black-backed gull (*Larus marinus*).
▷HISTORY C16: of Germanic origin; related to Dutch *kob, kobbe*

cobaea (kəʊ'biːə) NOUN any climbing shrub of the tropical American genus *Cobaea,* esp *C. scandens,* grown for its large trumpet-shaped purple or white flowers: family *Polemoniaceae.*
▷HISTORY named after Bernabé *Cobo* (1572–1659), Jesuit missionary and naturalist

cobalt ('kəʊbɔːlt) NOUN a brittle hard silvery-white element that is a ferromagnetic metal: occurs principally in cobaltite and smaltite and is widely used in alloys. The radioisotope **cobalt-60,** with a half-life of 5.3 years, is used in radiotherapy and as a tracer. Symbol: Co; atomic no.: 27; atomic wt.: 58.93320; valency: 2 or 3; relative density: 8.9; melting pt.: 1495°C; boiling pt.: 2928°C.
▷HISTORY C17: German *Kobalt,* from Middle High German *kobolt* goblin; from the miners' belief that malicious goblins placed it in the silver ore

cobalt bloom NOUN another name for **erythrite** (sense 1).

cobalt blue NOUN 1 Also called: **Thénard's blue.** any greenish-blue pigment containing cobalt aluminate, usually made by heating cobaltous sulphate, aluminium oxide, and phosphoric acid together. 2 **a** a deep blue to greenish-blue colour. **b** *(as adjective)*: *a cobalt-blue car.*

cobalt bomb NOUN 1 a cobalt-60 device used in radiotherapy. 2 a nuclear weapon consisting of a hydrogen bomb encased in cobalt, which releases large quantities of radioactive cobalt-60 into the atmosphere.

cobaltic (kəʊ'bɔːltɪk) ADJECTIVE of or containing cobalt, esp in the trivalent state.

cobaltite (kəʊ'bɔːltaɪt, 'kəʊbɔːl,taɪt) *or* **cobaltine** ('kəʊbɔːl,tiːn, -tɪn) NOUN a rare silvery-white mineral consisting of cobalt arsenic sulphide in cubic crystalline form: a major ore of cobalt, used in ceramics. Formula: CoAsS.

cobaltous (kəʊ'bɔːltəs) ADJECTIVE of or containing cobalt in the divalent state.

cobber ('kɒbə) NOUN *Austral and NZ informal* a friend; mate: used as a term of address to males.
▷HISTORY C19: from dialect *cob* to take a liking to someone

cobble[1] ('kɒbᵊl) NOUN 1 short for **cobblestone.** 2 *Geology* a rock fragment, often rounded, with a diameter of 64–256 mm and thus smaller than a boulder but larger than a pebble. ◆ VERB 3 *(tr)* to pave (a road) with cobblestones. ◆ See also **cobbles.**
▷HISTORY C15 (in *cobblestone*): from COB[1]
▸'**cobbled** ADJECTIVE

cobble[2] ('kɒbᵊl) VERB *(tr)* 1 to make or mend (shoes). 2 to put together clumsily.
▷HISTORY C15: back formation from COBBLER[1]

cobbler[1] ('kɒblə) NOUN a person who makes or mends shoes.
▷HISTORY C13 (as surname): of unknown origin

cobbler[2] ('kɒblə) NOUN 1 a sweetened iced drink, usually made from fruit and wine or liqueur. 2 *Chiefly US* a hot dessert made of fruit covered with a rich cakelike crust.
▷HISTORY C19: (for sense 1) perhaps shortened from *cobbler's punch;* (for both senses) compare *cobble* (verb)

cobblers ('kɒbləz) *Brit slang* ◆ PLURAL NOUN 1

rubbish; nonsense: *a load of old cobblers.* [2] another word for **testicles.** ◆ INTERJECTION [3] an exclamation of strong disagreement.
▷HISTORY C20: from rhyming slang *cobblers' awls* balls

> **Language note** The use of *cobblers* meaning "nonsense" is so mild that hardly anyone these days is likely to be offended by it. Most people are probably unaware of its rhyming-slang association with "balls", and therefore take it at its face value as a more colourful synonym for "nonsense". The classic formulation "a load of (old) cobblers" seems to be particularly popular in the tabloid press.

cobbler's pegs (pɛgz) PLURAL NOUN a common Australian weed, *Bidens pilosa*, with spiky peglike awns.

cobbler's wax NOUN a resin used for waxing thread.

cobbles (ˈkɒbᵊlz) PLURAL NOUN [1] coal in small rounded lumps. [2] cobblestones.

cobblestone (ˈkɒbᵊlˌstəʊn) NOUN a rounded stone used for paving. Sometimes shortened to **cobble.** Compare **sett.**

cobelligerent (ˌkəʊbɪˈlɪdʒərənt) NOUN a country fighting in a war on the side of another country.

Cóbh (kəʊv) NOUN a port in S Republic of Ireland, in SE Co. Cork: port of call for Atlantic liners. Pop.: 6200 (1991). Former name (1849–1922): **Queenstown.**

cobia (ˈkəʊbɪə) NOUN a large dark-striped percoid game fish, *Rachycentron canadum*, of tropical and subtropical seas: family *Rachycentridae.*
▷HISTORY of unknown origin

coble (ˈkəʊbᵊl, ˈkɒbᵊl) NOUN *Scot and Northern English* a small single-masted flat-bottomed fishing boat.
▷HISTORY C13: probably of Celtic origin; compare Welsh *ceubal* skiff

Coblenz (*German* ˈkoːblɛnts) NOUN a variant spelling of **Koblenz.**

cob money NOUN crude silver coins issued in the Spanish colonies of the New World from about 1600 until 1820.

cobnut (ˈkɒbˌnʌt) *or* **cob** NOUN other names for a **hazelnut.**
▷HISTORY C16: from earlier *cobylle nut;* see COBBLE[1], NUT

COBOL *or* **Cobol** (ˈkəʊˌbɒl) NOUN a high-level computer programming language designed for general commercial use.
▷HISTORY C20: *co(mmon) b(usiness) o(riented) l(anguage)*

cobra (ˈkəʊbrə) NOUN [1] any highly venomous elapid snake of the genus *Naja,* such as *N. naja* (**Indian cobra**), of tropical Africa and Asia. When alarmed they spread the skin of the neck region into a hood. [2] any related snake, such as the king cobra.
▷HISTORY C19: from Portuguese *cobra (de capello)* snake (with a hood), from Latin *colubra* snake

cobra de capello (diː kəˈpɛləʊ) NOUN, *plural* **cobras de capello.** a cobra, *Naja tripudians,* that has ringlike markings on the body and exists in many varieties in S and SE Asia.

coburg (ˈkəʊˌbɜːg) NOUN (*sometimes capital*) a rounded loaf with a cross cut on the top. Also called: **coburg loaf.**
▷HISTORY C19: apparently named in honour of Prince Albert (of *Saxe-Coburg-Gotha,* name of the British royal family from 1901–17)

Coburg (ˈkəʊbɜːg; *German* ˈkoːbʊrk) NOUN a city in E Germany, in N Bavaria. Pop.: 44 690 (1991).

cobweb (ˈkɒbˌwɛb) NOUN [1] a web spun by certain spiders, esp those of the family *Theridiidae,* often found in the corners of disused rooms. [2] a single thread of such a web. [3] something like a cobweb, as in its flimsiness or ability to trap.
▷HISTORY C14 cob, from *coppe,* from Old English (*ātor*)*coppe* spider; related to Middle Dutch *koppe* spider, Swedish (dialect) *etterkoppa*
▸ˈ**cob,webbed** ADJECTIVE ▸ˈ**cob,webby** ADJECTIVE

cobwebs (ˈkɒbˌwɛbz) PLURAL NOUN [1] mustiness, confusion, or obscurity. [2] *Informal* stickiness of the eyelids experienced upon first awakening.

coca (ˈkəʊkə) NOUN [1] either of two shrubs, *Erythroxylon coca* or *E. truxiuense,* native to the Andes: family *Erythroxylaceae.* [2] the dried leaves of these shrubs and related plants, which contain cocaine and are chewed by the peoples of the Andes for their stimulating effects.
▷HISTORY C17: from Spanish, from Quechuan *kúka*

Coca-Cola (ˌkəʊkəˈkəʊlə) NOUN [1] *Trademark* a carbonated soft drink flavoured with coca leaves, cola nuts, caramel, etc. [2] (*modifier*) denoting the spread of American culture and values to other parts of the world: *Coca-Cola generation.*

cocaine *or* **cocain** (kəˈkeɪn) NOUN an addictive narcotic drug derived from coca leaves or synthesized, used medicinally as a topical anaesthetic. Formula: $C_{17}H_{21}NO_4$.
▷HISTORY C19: from COCA + -INE[1]

cocainize *or* **cocainise** (kəʊˈkeɪˌnaɪz, ˈkəʊkəˌnaɪz) VERB (*tr*) to anaesthetize with cocaine.
▸ˌ**cocainiˈzation** *or* **co,cainiˈsation** NOUN

cocci (ˈkɒksaɪ) NOUN the plural of **coccus.**

coccid (ˈkɒksɪd) NOUN any homopterous insect of the superfamily *Coccoidea,* esp any of the family *Coccidae,* which includes the scale insects.
▷HISTORY C19: from New Latin *Coccidae;* see COCCUS

coccidioidomycosis (kɒkˌsɪdɪˌɔɪdəʊmaɪˈkəʊsɪs) NOUN a disease of the skin or viscera, esp the lungs, caused by infection with the fungus *Coccidioides immitis.*
▷HISTORY C20: from New Latin *Coccidioides* + -O- + MYCOSIS

coccidiosis (kɒkˌsɪdɪˈəʊsɪs) NOUN any disease of domestic and other animals caused by introcellular parasitic protozoa of the order *Coccidia.* One species, *Isospora hominis,* occasionally infects humans.
▷HISTORY C19: from New Latin; see COCCUS, -OSIS

cocciferous (kɒkˈsɪfərəs) ADJECTIVE (of plants) *Obsolete* (of plants) bearing berries.

coccolith (ˈkɒkəlɪθ) NOUN any of the round calcareous plates in chalk formations: formed the outer layer of unicellular plankton.
▷HISTORY C19: New Latin, from Greek *kokkos* berry + *lithos* stone

coccus (ˈkɒkəs) NOUN, *plural* **-ci** (-saɪ). [1] any spherical or nearly spherical bacterium, such as a staphylococcus. Compare **bacillus** (sense 1), **spirillum** (sense 1). [2] the part of a fruit that contains one seed and separates from the whole fruit at maturity. [3] any of the scale insects of the genus *Coccus.*
▷HISTORY C18: from New Latin, from Greek *kokkos* berry, grain
▸ˈ**coccoid,** ˈ**coccal,** *or* **coccic** (ˈkɒksɪk) ADJECTIVE
▸ˈ**coccous** ADJECTIVE

coccyx (ˈkɒksɪks) NOUN, *plural* **coccyges** (kɒkˈsaɪdʒiːz). a small triangular bone at the end of the spinal column in man and some apes, representing a vestigial tail.
▷HISTORY C17: from New Latin, from Greek *kokkux* cuckoo, of imitative origin; from the likeness of the bone to a cuckoo's beak
▸**coccygeal** (kɒkˈsɪdʒɪəl) ADJECTIVE

Cochabamba (*Spanish* kotʃaˈβamba) NOUN a city in central Bolivia. Pop.: 607 129 (2000 est.).

co-channel (ˈkəʊˌtʃænᵊl) ADJECTIVE denoting or relating to a radio transmission that is on the same frequency channel as another: *co-channel interference.*

Cochin (ˈkəʊtʃɪn, ˈkɒtʃ-) NOUN [1] a region and former state of SW India: part of Kerala state since 1956. [2] a port in SW India, on the Malabar Coast: the first European settlement in India, founded by Vasco da Gama in 1502: shipbuilding, engineering. Pop.: 564 589 (1991). [3] a large breed of domestic fowl, with dense plumage and feathered legs, that originated in Cochin China.

Cochin China NOUN a former French colony of Indochina (1862–1948): now the part of Vietnam that lies south of Phan Thiet.

cochineal (ˌkɒtʃɪˈniːl, ˈkɒtʃɪˌniːl) NOUN [1] Also called: **cochineal insect.** a Mexican homopterous insect, *Dactylopius coccus,* that feeds on cacti. [2] a crimson substance obtained from the crushed bodies of these insects, used for colouring food and for dyeing. [3] **a** the colour of this dye. **b** (*as adjective*): *cochineal shoes.*
▷HISTORY C16: from Old Spanish *cochinilla,* from Latin *coccineus* scarlet-coloured, from *coccum* cochineal kermes, from Greek *kokkos* kermes berry

cochlea (ˈkɒklɪə) NOUN, *plural* **-leae** (-lɪˌiː). the spiral tube, shaped like a snail's shell, that forms part of the internal ear, converting sound vibrations into nerve impulses.
▷HISTORY C16: from Latin: snail, spiral, from Greek *kokhlias;* probably related to Greek *konkhē* CONCH
▸ˈ**cochlear** ADJECTIVE

cochlear implant (ˈkɒklɪə) NOUN a device that stimulates the acoustic nerve in the inner ear in order to produce some form of hearing in people who are deaf from inner ear disease.

cochleate (ˈkɒklɪˌeɪt, -lɪɪt) *or* **cochleated** ADJECTIVE *Biology* shaped like a snail's shell; spirally twisted.

cock¹ (kɒk) NOUN [1] the male of the domestic fowl. [2] **a** any other male bird. **b** the male of certain other animals, such as the lobster. **c** (*as modifier*): *a cock sparrow.* [3] short for **stopcock** or **weathercock.** [4] a taboo slang word for **penis.** [5] **a** the hammer of a firearm. **b** its position when the firearm is ready to be discharged. [6] *Brit informal* a friend, mate, or fellow. [7] a jaunty or significant tilting or turning upwards: *a cock of the head.* [8] *Brit informal* nonsense. ◆ VERB [9] (*tr*) to set the firing pin, hammer, or breech block of (a firearm) so that a pull on the trigger will release it and thus fire the weapon. [10] (*tr*) to set the shutter mechanism of (a camera) so that the shutter can be tripped by pressing the shutter-release button. [11] (*tr; sometimes foll by up*) to raise in an alert or jaunty manner. [12] (*intr*) to stick or stand up conspicuously. ◆ See also **cockup.**
▷HISTORY Old English *cocc* (referring to the male fowl; the development of C15 sense spout, tap, and other transferred senses is not clear), ultimately of imitative origin; related to Old Norse *kokkr,* French *coq,* Late Latin *coccus*

cock² (kɒk) NOUN [1] a small, cone-shaped heap of hay, straw, etc. ◆ VERB [2] (*tr*) to stack (hay, straw, etc.) in such heaps.
▷HISTORY C14 (in Old English, *cocc* is attested in place names): perhaps of Scandinavian origin; compare Norwegian *kok,* Danish dialect *kok*

cockabully (ˌkɒkəˈbʊlɪ) NOUN, *plural* **-lies.** any of several small freshwater fish of New Zealand.
▷HISTORY from Maori *kokopu*

cockade (kɒˈkeɪd) NOUN a feather or ribbon worn on military headwear.
▷HISTORY C18: changed from earlier *cockard,* from French *cocarde,* feminine of *cocard* arrogant, strutting, from *coq* COCK[1]
▸**cockˈaded** ADJECTIVE

cock-a-doodle-doo (ˌkɒkəˌduːdᵊlˈduː) INTERJECTION an imitation or representation of a cock crowing.

cock-a-hoop ADJECTIVE (*usually postpositive*) [1] in very high spirits. [2] boastful. [3] askew; confused.
▷HISTORY C16: perhaps from the phrase *to set the cock a hoop* to live prodigally, literally: to put a cock on a *hoop,* a full measure of grain

Cockaigne *or* **Cockayne** (kɒˈkeɪn) NOUN *Medieval legend* an imaginary land of luxury and idleness.
▷HISTORY C14: from Old French *cocaigne,* from Middle Low German *kōkenje* small CAKE (of which the houses in the imaginary land are built); related to Spanish *cucaña,* Italian *cuccagna*

cock-a-leekie (ˌkɒkəˈliːkɪ) NOUN a variant of **cockieleekie.**

cockalorum (ˌkɒkəˈlɔːrəm) NOUN [1] a self-important little man. [2] bragging talk; crowing.
▷HISTORY C18: from COCK[1] + *-alorum,* a variant of Latin genitive plural ending *-orum;* perhaps intended to suggest: the cock of all cocks

cockamamie (ˌkɒkəˈmeɪmɪ) ADJECTIVE *Slang, chiefly US* ridiculous or nonsensical: *a cockamamie story.*
▷HISTORY C20: in an earlier sense: a paper transfer, prob. a variant of DECALCOMANIA

cock-and-bull story NOUN *Informal* an obviously improbable story, esp a boastful one or one used as an excuse.

cockatiel *or* **cockateel** (ˌkɒkəˈtiːl) NOUN a

crested Australian parrot, *Leptolophus hollandicus,* having a greyish-brown and yellow plumage.
▷HISTORY C19: from Dutch *kaketielje,* from Portuguese *cacatilha* a little cockatoo, from *cacatua* COCKATOO

cockatoo (ˌkɒkəˈtuː, ˈkɒkəˌtuː) NOUN, *plural* **-toos.** [1] any of various parrots of the genus *Kakatoe* and related genera, such as *K. galerita* (**sulphur-crested cockatoo**), of Australia and New Guinea. They have an erectile crest and most of them are light-coloured. [2] *Austral and NZ* a small farmer or settler. [3] *Austral informal* a lookout during some illegal activity.
▷HISTORY C17: from Dutch *kaketoe,* from Malay *kakatua*

cockatrice (ˈkɒkətrɪs, -ˌtraɪs) NOUN [1] a legendary monster, part snake and part cock, that could kill with a glance. [2] another name for **basilisk** (sense 1).
▷HISTORY C14: from Old French *cocatris,* from Medieval Latin *cocatrix,* from Late Latin *calcātrix* trampler, tracker (translating Greek *ikhneumon* ICHNEUMON), from Latin *calcāre* to tread, from *calx* heel

Cockayne (kɒˈkeɪn) NOUN a variant spelling of **Cockaigne.**

cockboat (ˈkɒkˌbəʊt) *or* **cockleboat** NOUN any small boat.
▷HISTORY C15 *cokbote,* perhaps ultimately from Late Latin *caudica* dug-out canoe, from Latin *caudex* tree trunk

cockchafer (ˈkɒkˌtʃeɪfə) NOUN any of various Old World scarabaeid beetles, esp *Melolontha melolontha* of Europe, whose larvae feed on crops and grasses. Also called: **May beetle, May bug.**
▷HISTORY C18: from COCK[1] + CHAFER

cockcrow (ˈkɒkˌkrəʊ) *or* **cockcrowing** NOUN daybreak.

cocked hat NOUN [1] a hat with opposing brims turned up and caught together in order to give two points (bicorn) or three points (tricorn). [2] **knock into a cocked hat.** *Slang* to outdo or defeat.

cocker[1] (ˈkɒkə) NOUN [1] a devotee of cockfighting. [2] short for **cocker spaniel.**

cocker[2] (ˈkɒkə) VERB [1] (*tr*) *Rare* to pamper or spoil by indulgence. ◆ NOUN [2] *Brit informal* a mate (esp in the phrase **old cocker**).
▷HISTORY C15: perhaps from COCK[1] with the sense: to make a cock (i.e. pet) of

Cocker (ˈkɒkə) NOUN **according to Cocker.** reliable or reliably; correct or correctly.
▷HISTORY from Edward Cocker (1631–75), English arithmetician

cockerel (ˈkɒkərəl, ˈkɒkrəl) NOUN a young domestic cock, usually less than a year old.
▷HISTORY C15: diminutive of COCK[1]

cocker spaniel NOUN a small compact breed of spaniel having sleek silky fur, a domed head, and long fringed ears.
▷HISTORY C19 *cocker,* from *cocking* hunting woodcocks

cockeye (ˈkɒkˌaɪ) NOUN *Informal* an eye affected with strabismus or one that squints.

cockeye bob *or* **cockeyed bob** NOUN *Austral slang* a sudden storm or cyclone.

cockeyed (ˈkɒkˌaɪd) ADJECTIVE *Informal* [1] afflicted with cross-eye, squint, or any other visible abnormality of the eyes. [2] appearing to be physically or logically abnormal, absurd, etc.; crooked; askew: *cockeyed ideas.* [3] drunk.

cock feather NOUN *Archery* the odd-coloured feather set on the shaft of an arrow at right angles to the nock. Compare **shaft feather.**

cockfight (ˈkɒkˌfaɪt) NOUN a fight between two gamecocks fitted with sharp metal spurs.
▸ **ˈcockˌfighting** NOUN

cockhorse (ˌkɒkˈhɔːs) NOUN another name for **rocking horse** or **hobbyhorse.**

cockieleekie, cockyleeky, *or* **cock-a-leekie** (ˈkɒkəˈliːkɪ) NOUN *Scot* a soup made from a fowl boiled with leeks.

cockiness (ˈkɒkɪnɪs) NOUN conceited self-assurance.

cockle[1] (ˈkɒkəl) NOUN [1] any sand-burrowing bivalve mollusc of the family *Cardiidae,* esp *Cardium edule* (**edible cockle**) of Europe, typically having a rounded shell with radiating ribs. [2] any of certain similar or related molluscs. [3] short for **cockleshell** (sense 1). [4] a wrinkle or puckering, as in cloth or paper. [5] a small furnace or stove. [6] **cockles of one's heart.** one's deepest feelings (esp in the phrase **warm the cockles of one's heart**). ◆ VERB [7] to contract or cause to contract into wrinkles.
▷HISTORY C14: from Old French *coquille* shell, from Latin *conchӯlium* shellfish, from Greek *konkhulion,* diminutive of *konkhule* mussel; see CONCH

cockle[2] (ˈkɒkəl) NOUN any of several plants, esp the corn cockle, that grow as weeds in cornfields.

cockleboat (ˈkɒkəlˌbəʊt) NOUN another word for **cockboat.**

cocklebur (ˈkɒkəlˌbɜː) NOUN [1] any coarse weed of the genus *Xanthium,* having spiny burs: family *Asteraceae* (composites). [2] the bur of any of these plants.

cockleert (ˈkɒklɪərt) NOUN a Southwest English dialect variant of **cockcrow.**

cockleshell (ˈkɒkəlˌʃɛl) NOUN [1] the shell of the cockle. [2] any of the valves of the shells of certain other bivalve molluscs, such as the scallop. [3] any small light boat. [4] a badge worn by pilgrims.

cockloft (ˈkɒkˌlɒft) NOUN a small loft, garret, or attic.

cockney (ˈkɒknɪ) NOUN [1] (*often capital*) a native of London, esp of the working class born in the East End, speaking a characteristic dialect of English. Traditionally defined as someone born within the sound of the bells of St. Mary-le-Bow church. [2] the urban dialect of London or its East End. [3] *Austral* a young snapper fish. ◆ ADJECTIVE [4] characteristic of cockneys or their dialect of English.
▷HISTORY C14: from *cokeney,* literally: cock's egg, later applied contemptuously to townsmen, from *cokene,* genitive plural of *cok* COCK[1] + *ey* EGG[1]
▸ **ˈcockneyish** ADJECTIVE

cockney bream NOUN *Austral* a young snapper fish.

cockneyfy *or* **cocknify** (ˈkɒknɪˌfaɪ) VERB **-fies, -fying, -fied.** (*tr*) to cause (one's speech, manners, etc.) to fit the stereotyped idea of a cockney.
▸ **ˌcockneyfiˈcation** *or* **ˌcocknifiˈcation** NOUN

cockneyism (ˈkɒknɪˌɪzəm) NOUN a characteristic of speech or custom peculiar to cockneys.

cock-of-the-rock NOUN either of two tropical South American birds, *Rupicola rupicola* or *R. peruviana,* having an erectile crest and (in the male) a brilliant red or orange plumage: family *Cotingidae* (cotingas).

cock of the walk NOUN *Informal* a person who asserts himself in a strutting pompous way.

cockpit (ˈkɒkˌpɪt) NOUN [1] the compartment in a small aircraft in which the pilot, crew, and sometimes the passengers sit. Compare **flight deck** (sense 1). [2] the driver's compartment in a racing car. [3] *Nautical* **a** an enclosed or recessed area towards the stern of a small vessel from which it is steered. **b** (formerly) an apartment in a warship used as quarters for junior officers and as a first-aid station during combat. [4] the site of numerous battles or campaigns. [5] an enclosure used for cockfights.

cockroach (ˈkɒkˌrəʊtʃ) NOUN any insect of the suborder *Blattodea* (or *Blattaria*), such as *Blatta orientalis* (**oriental cockroach** or **black beetle**): order *Dictyoptera.* They have an oval flattened body with long antennae and biting mouthparts and are common household pests. See also **German cockroach, mantis.**
▷HISTORY C17: from Spanish *cucaracha,* of obscure origin

cock rock NOUN an aggressive style of rock music performed by male bands.

cockscomb *or* **coxcomb** (ˈkɒksˌkəʊm) NOUN [1] the comb of a domestic cock. [2] an amaranthaceous garden or pot plant, *Celosia cristata,* with yellow, crimson, or purple feathery plumelike flowers in a broad spike resembling the comb of a cock. [3] any similar species of *Celosia.* [4] *Informal* a conceited dandy.

cocksfoot (ˈkɒksˌfʊt) NOUN, *plural* **-foots.** a perennial Eurasian grass, *Dactylis glomerata,* cultivated as a pasture grass in North America and South Africa.

cockshot (ˈkɒkˌʃɒt) NOUN another name for **cockshy.**

cockshy (ˈkɒkˌʃaɪ) NOUN, *plural* **-shies.** *Brit* [1] a target aimed at in throwing games. [2] the throw itself. ◆ Often shortened to **shy.**
▷HISTORY C18: from shying (throwing objects at) a cock, which was given as a prize to the person who hit it

cockspur (ˈkɒkˌspɜː) NOUN [1] a spur on the leg of a cock. [2] an annual grass, *Echinochloa crus-galli,* widely distributed in tropical and warm temperate regions. [3] a small thorny North American hawthorn tree, *Crataegus crus-galli.*

cocksure (ˌkɒkˈʃʊə, -ˈʃɔː) ADJECTIVE overconfident; arrogant.
▷HISTORY C16: of uncertain origin
▸ **ˌcockˈsurely** ADVERB ▸ **ˌcockˈsureness** NOUN

cockswain (ˈkɒksən, -ˌsweɪn) NOUN a variant spelling of **coxswain.**

cocktail[1] (ˈkɒkˌteɪl) NOUN [1] **a** any mixed drink with a spirit base, usually drunk before meals. **b** (*as modifier*): *the cocktail hour.* [2] an appetizer of seafood, mixed fruits, etc. [3] any combination of diverse elements, esp one considered potent. [4] (*modifier*) appropriate for formal occasions: *a cocktail dress.*
▷HISTORY C19: of unknown origin

cocktail[2] (ˈkɒkˌteɪl) NOUN [1] a horse with a docked tail. [2] an animal of unknown or mixed breeding. [3] *Archaic* a person of little breeding pretending to be a gentleman.
▷HISTORY C19: originally *cocktailed* (adjective) having a tail like a cock's

cocktail lounge NOUN a room in a hotel, restaurant, etc., where cocktails or other alcoholic drinks are served.

cocktail stick NOUN a small pointed stick used for holding cherries, olives, etc., in cocktails, and for serving snacks, such as small sausages.

cockup (ˈkɒkˌʌp) NOUN [1] *Brit slang* something done badly. ◆ VERB **cock up.** (*tr, adverb*) [2] (of an animal) to raise (its ears), esp in an alert manner. [3] *Brit slang* to botch.

cocky[1] (ˈkɒkɪ) ADJECTIVE **cockier, cockiest.** excessively proud of oneself.
▸ **ˈcockily** ADVERB

cocky[2] (ˈkɒkɪ) NOUN, *plural* **cockies.** *Austral informal* [1] short for **cockatoo** (sense 2). [2] a farmer whose farm is regarded as small or of little account.

cockyleeky (ˈkɒkəˈliːkɪ) NOUN a variant spelling of **cockieleekie.**

cocky's joy NOUN *Austral slang* golden syrup.

coco (ˈkəʊkəʊ) NOUN, *plural* **-cos.** short for **coconut** or **coconut palm.**
▷HISTORY C16: from Portuguese *coco* grimace; from the likeness of the three holes of the nut to a face

cocoa (ˈkəʊkəʊ) *or* **cacao** NOUN [1] a powder made from cocoa beans after they have been roasted, ground, and freed from most of their fatty oil. [2] a hot or cold drink made from cocoa and milk or water. [3] **a** a light to moderate brown colour. **b** (*as adjective*): *cocoa paint.*
▷HISTORY C18: altered from CACAO

cocoa bean NOUN the seed of the cacao.

cocoa butter NOUN a yellowish-white waxy solid that is obtained from cocoa beans and used for confectionery, soap, etc.

coco de mer (də ˈmɛə) NOUN [1] a palm tree, *Lodoicea maldivica,* of the Seychelles, producing a large fruit containing a two-lobed edible nut. [2] the nut of this palm. ◆ Also called: **double coconut.**
▷HISTORY French: coconut of the sea

coconut *or* **cocoanut** (ˈkəʊkəˌnʌt) NOUN [1] the fruit of the coconut palm, consisting of a thick fibrous oval husk inside which is a thin hard shell enclosing edible white meat. The hollow centre is filled with a milky fluid (**coconut milk**). [2] **a** the meat of the coconut, often shredded and used in cakes, curries, etc. **b** (*as modifier*): *coconut cake.*
▷HISTORY C18: see COCO

coconut butter NOUN a solid form of coconut oil.

coconut ice NOUN a sweetmeat made from desiccated coconut and sugar.

coconut matting NOUN a form of coarse

matting made from the fibrous husk of the coconut.

coconut oil NOUN the fatty oil obtained from the meat of the coconut and used for making soap, cosmetics, etc.

coconut palm NOUN a tall palm tree, *Cocos nucifera,* widely planted throughout the tropics, having coconuts as fruits. Also called: **coco palm, coconut tree.**

coconut shy NOUN a fairground stall in which balls are thrown to knock coconuts off stands.

cocoon (kəˈkuːn) NOUN [1] **a** a silky protective envelope secreted by silkworms and certain other insect larvae, in which the pupae develop. **b** a similar covering for the eggs of the spider, earthworm, etc. [2] a protective spray covering used as a seal on machinery. [3] a cosy warm covering. ◆ VERB [4] *(tr)* to wrap in a cocoon.
▷HISTORY C17: from French *cocon,* from Provençal *coucoun* eggshell, from *coco* shell, from Latin *coccum* kermes berry, from Greek *kokkos* grain, seed, berry; compare COCCUS

cocopan (ˈkəʊkəʊˌpæn) NOUN (in South Africa) a small wagon running on narrow-gauge railway lines used in mines. Also called: **hopper.**
▷HISTORY C20: from Zulu *'ngkumbana* short truck

Cocos Islands (ˈkəʊkɒs, ˈkəʊkəs) PLURAL NOUN a group of 27 coral islands in the Indian Ocean, southwest of Java: a Territory of Australia since 1955. Pop.: 593 (1993). Area: 13 sq. km (5 sq. miles). Also called: **Keeling Islands.**

cocotte (kəʊˈkɒt, kə-; *French* kɔkɔt) NOUN [1] a small fireproof dish in which individual portions of food are cooked and served. [2] a prostitute or promiscuous woman.
▷HISTORY C19: from French, from nursery word for a hen, feminine of *coq* COCK[1]

cocoyam (ˈkəʊkəʊˌjæm) NOUN [1] either of two food plants of West Africa, the taro or the yantia, both of which have edible underground stems. [2] the underground stem of either of these plants.
▷HISTORY C20: from COCOA + YAM

cocuswood (ˈkəʊkəsˌwʊd) NOUN [1] wood from the tropical American leguminous tree *Brya ebenus,* used for inlaying, turnery, musical instruments, etc. [2] the source of this wood, an important timber tree in parts of the Caribbean. ◆ Also called: **Jamaican ebony, West Indian ebony.**

cod[1] (kɒd) NOUN, *plural* **cod** *or* **cods.** [1] any of the gadoid food fishes of the genus *Gadus,* esp *G. morhua* (or *G. callarias*), which occurs in the North Atlantic and has a long body with three rounded dorsal fins: family *Gadidae.* They are also a source of cod-liver oil. [2] any other fish of the family *Gadidae* (see **gadid**). [3] *Austral* any of various unrelated Australian fish, such as the Murray cod.
▷HISTORY C13: probably of Germanic origin; compare Old High German *cutte*

cod[2] (kɒd) NOUN [1] *Brit and US dialect* a pod or husk. [2] an obsolete word for **scrotum.** [3] *Obsolete* a bag or envelope.
▷HISTORY Old English *codd* husk, bag; related to Old Norse *koddi,* Danish *kodde*

cod[3] (kɒd) VERB **cods, codding, codded.** *(tr)* [1] *Brit and Irish slang* to make fun of; tease. [2] *Brit and Irish slang* to play a trick on; fool. ◆ NOUN [3] *Brit and Irish slang* a hoax or trick. [4] *Irish slang* a fraud; hoaxer: *he's an old cod.* ◆ ADJECTIVE *(prenominal)* [5] *Brit slang* mock; sham: *cod Latin.*
▷HISTORY C19: perhaps from earlier *cod* a fool, perhaps shortened from CODGER

cod[4] (kɒd) NOUN *Northern English dialect* a fellow; chap: *he's a nice old cod.*
▷HISTORY of unknown origin

Cod NOUN **Cape.** See **Cape Cod.**

COD ABBREVIATION FOR: [1] cash on delivery. [2] (in the US) collect on delivery.

coda (ˈkəʊdə) NOUN [1] *Music* the final, sometimes inessential, part of a musical structure. [2] a concluding part of a literary work, esp a summary at the end of a novel of further developments in the lives of the characters.
▷HISTORY C18: from Italian: tail, from Latin *cauda*

cod-act VERB *(intr) Irish informal* to play tricks; fool.
▷HISTORY from COD[3] + ACT

codder[1] (ˈkɒdə) NOUN a cod fisherman or his boat.

codder[2] (ˈkɒdə) NOUN *Yorkshire dialect* the leader of a team of workers on a press at a steelworks.
▷HISTORY perhaps from COD[4]

coddle (ˈkɒdᵊl) VERB *(tr)* [1] to treat with indulgence. [2] to cook (something, esp eggs) in water just below the boiling point. ◆ NOUN [3] *Irish dialect* stew made from ham and bacon scraps.
▷HISTORY C16: of obscure origin; perhaps related to CAUDLE
▸ˈ**coddler** NOUN

code (kəʊd) NOUN [1] a system of letters or symbols, and rules for their association by means of which information can be represented or communicated for reasons of secrecy, brevity, etc.: *binary code; Morse code.* See also **genetic code.** [2] a message in code. [3] a symbol used in a code. [4] a conventionalized set of principles, rules, or expectations: *a code of behaviour.* [5] a system of letters or digits used for identification or selection purposes. ◆ VERB *(tr)* [6] to translate, transmit, or arrange into a code.
▷HISTORY C14: from French, from Latin *cōdex* book, CODEX

codec (ˈkəʊˌdɛk) NOUN *Electronics* a set of equipment that encodes an analogue speech or video signal into digital form for transmission purposes and at the receiving end decodes the digital signal into a form close to its original.
▷HISTORY C20: from CO(DE) + DEC(ODE)

codeclination (ˌkəʊdɛklɪˈneɪʃən) NOUN another name for **polar distance.**

codeine (ˈkəʊdiːn) NOUN a white crystalline alkaloid prepared mainly from morphine and having a similar but milder action. It is used as an analgesic, an antidiarrhoeal, and to relieve coughing. Formula: $C_{18}H_{21}NO_3$.
▷HISTORY C19: from Greek *kōdeia* head of a poppy, from *kōos* hollow place + -INE[2]

Code Napoléon *French* (kɔd napɔleɔ̃) NOUN the civil code of France, promulgated between 1804 and 1810, comprising the main body of French civil law. English name: **Napoleonic Code.**

cod end NOUN *Sea fishing* the narrow end of a tapered trawl net.
▷HISTORY from COD[2]

co-dependency (ˌkəʊdɪˈpɛndənsɪ) NOUN *Psychol* a state of mutual dependence between two people, esp when one partner relies emotionally on supporting and caring for the other partner.
▸ˌ**co-deˈpendent** ADJECTIVE, NOUN

coder (ˈkəʊdə) NOUN [1] a person or thing that codes. [2] *Electronics* a device for transforming normal signals into a coded form.

Co. Derry ABBREVIATION FOR County Londonderry.

code-sharing NOUN a commercial agreement between two airlines that allows passengers to use a ticket from one airline to travel on another.

codetermination (ˌkəʊdɪtɜːmɪˈneɪʃən) NOUN joint participation of management and employees or employees' trade union representatives in some decisions.

codeword (ˈkəʊdˌwɜːd) NOUN (esp in military use) a word used to identify a classified plan, operation, etc. Also: **codename.**

codex (ˈkəʊdɛks) NOUN, *plural* **codices** (ˈkəʊdɪˌsiːz, ˈkɒdɪ-). [1] a volume, in book form, of manuscripts of an ancient text. [2] *Obsolete* a legal code.
▷HISTORY C16: from Latin: tree trunk, wooden block, book

Codex Juris Canonici (ˈkəʊdɛks ˈdʒʊərɪs kəˈnɒnɪˌsaɪ) NOUN the official code of canon law in force in the Roman Catholic Church; introduced in 1918 and revised in 1983. See also **Corpus Juris Canonici.**
▷HISTORY Latin: book of canon law

codfish (ˈkɒdˌfɪʃ) NOUN, *plural* **-fish** *or* **-fishes.** a cod, esp *Gadus morhua.*

codger (ˈkɒdʒə) NOUN *Informal* a man, esp an old or eccentric one: a term of affection or mild derision (often in the phrase **old codger**).
▷HISTORY C18: probably variant of CADGER

codices (ˈkəʊdɪˌsiːz, ˈkɒdɪ-) NOUN the plural of **codex.**

codicil (ˈkɒdɪsɪl) NOUN [1] *Law* a supplement modifying a will or revoking some provision of it. [2] an additional provision; appendix.
▷HISTORY C15: from Late Latin *cōdicillus,* literally: a little book, diminutive of CODEX
▸**codicillary** (ˌkɒdɪˈsɪlərɪ) ADJECTIVE

codicology (ˌkəʊdɪˈkɒlədʒɪ) NOUN the study of manuscripts.
▷HISTORY C20: via French from Latin *codic-,* CODEX + -LOGY
▸**codicological** (ˌkəʊdɪkəˈlɒdʒɪkᵊl) ADJECTIVE

codification (ˌkəʊdɪfɪˈkeɪʃən, ˌkɒ-) NOUN [1] systematic organization of methods, rules, etc. [2] *Law* the collection into one body of the principles of a system of law.

codify (ˈkəʊdɪˌfaɪ, ˈkɒ-) VERB **-fies, -fying, -fied.** *(tr)* to organize or collect together (laws, rules, procedures, etc.) into a system or code.
▸ˈ**codiˌfier** NOUN

codling[1] (ˈkɒdlɪŋ) *or* **codlin** (ˈkɒdlɪn) NOUN [1] any of several varieties of long tapering apples used for cooking. [2] any unripe apple.
▷HISTORY C15 *querdlyng,* of uncertain origin

codling[2] (ˈkɒdlɪŋ) NOUN a codfish, esp a young one.

codling moth *or* **codlin moth** NOUN a tortricid moth, *Carpocapsa pomonella,* the larvae of which are a pest of apples.

codlins-and-cream NOUN an onagraceous plant, *Epilobium hirsutum,* native to Europe and Asia and introduced into North America, having purplish-red flowers and hairy stems and leaves. Also called: **hairy willowherb.**

cod-liver oil NOUN an oil extracted from the livers of cod and related fish, rich in vitamins A and D and used to treat deficiency of these vitamins.

codology (kɒdˈɒlədʒɪ) NOUN *Irish informal* the art or practice of bluffing or deception.

codomain (ˌkəʊdəʊˈmeɪn) NOUN *Maths* the set of values that a function is allowed to take.

codominant (kəʊˈdɒmɪnənt) ADJECTIVE *Genetics* (of genes) having both alleles expressed equally in the phenotype of the organism.
▸**coˈdominance** NOUN

codon (ˈkəʊdɒn) NOUN *Genetics, biochem* a unit that consists of three adjacent bases on a DNA molecule and that determines the position of a specific amino acid in a protein molecule during protein synthesis.
▷HISTORY C20: from CODE + -ON

codpiece (ˈkɒdˌpiːs) NOUN a bag covering the male genitals, attached to hose or breeches by laces, etc., worn in the 15th and 16th centuries.
▷HISTORY C15: from COD[2] + PIECE

co-driver NOUN one of two drivers who take turns to drive a car, esp in a rally.

codswallop (ˈkɒdzˌwɒləp) NOUN *Brit slang* nonsense.
▷HISTORY C20: of unknown origin

Co. Durham ABBREVIATION FOR County Durham.

cod war NOUN any of three disputes that occurred in 1958, 1972–73, and 1975–76 between Britain and Iceland, concerning Iceland's unilateral extension of her fishing limits.

co-ed (ˌkəʊˈɛd) ADJECTIVE [1] coeducational. ◆ NOUN [2] *US* a female student in a coeducational college or university. [3] *Brit* a school or college providing coeducation.

coedit (kəʊˈɛdɪt) VERB *(tr)* to edit (a book, newspaper, etc.) jointly.
▸**coˈeditor** NOUN

coeducation (ˌkəʊɛdjʊˈkeɪʃən) NOUN instruction in schools, colleges, etc., attended by both sexes.
▸ˌ**coeduˈcational** ADJECTIVE ▸ˌ**coeduˈcationally** ADVERB

coefficient (ˌkəʊɪˈfɪʃənt) NOUN [1] *Maths* **a** a numerical or constant factor in an algebraic term: *the coefficient of the term 3xyz is 3.* **b** the product of all the factors of a term excluding one or more specified variables: *the coefficient of x in 3axyz is 3ayz.* [2] *Physics* a value that relates one physical quantity to another.
▷HISTORY C17: from New Latin *coefficiēns,* from Latin *co-* together + *efficere* to EFFECT

coefficient of expansion NOUN the amount of expansion (or contraction) per unit length of a material resulting from one degree change in temperature. Also called: **expansivity.**

coefficient of friction NOUN *Mechanical*

engineering the force required to move two sliding surfaces over each other, divided by the force holding them together. It is reduced once the motion has started.

coefficient of variation NOUN *Statistics* a measure of the relative variation of distribution independent of the units of measurement; the standard deviation divided by the mean, sometimes expressed as a percentage.

coel- PREFIX indicating a cavity within a body or a hollow organ or part: *coelacanth; coelenterate; coelenteron.*
▷HISTORY New Latin, from Greek *koilos* hollow

coelacanth ('siːlə,kænθ) NOUN a primitive marine bony fish of the genus *Latimeria* (subclass *Crossopterygii*), having fleshy limblike pectoral fins and occurring off the coast of E Africa: thought to be extinct until a living specimen was discovered in 1938.
▷HISTORY C19: from New Latin *coelacanthus,* literally: hollow spine, from COEL- + Greek *akanthos* spine

coelenterate (sɪ'lɛntə,reɪt, -rɪt) NOUN 1 any invertebrate of the phylum *Cnidaria* (formerly *Coelenterata*), having a saclike body with a single opening (mouth), which occurs in polyp and medusa forms. Coelenterates include the hydra, jellyfishes, sea anemones, and corals. ◆ ADJECTIVE 2 (loosely) any invertebrate of the phyla *Cnidaria* or *Ctenophora.* 3 of or relating to coelenterates.
▷HISTORY C19: from New Latin *Coelenterata,* hollow-intestined (creatures); see COEL-, ENTERON
▸**coelenteric** (,siːlɛn'tɛrɪk) ADJECTIVE

coelenteron (sɪ'lɛntə,rɒn) NOUN, *plural* **-tera** (-tərə). the simple saclike body cavity of a coelenterate.

coeliac *or US* **celiac** ('siːlɪ,æk) ADJECTIVE of or relating to the abdomen.
▷HISTORY C17: from Latin *coeliacus,* from Greek *koiliakos,* from *koilia* belly

coeliac disease NOUN a chronic intestinal disorder of young children caused by sensitivity to the protein gliadin contained in the gluten of cereals, characterized by distention of the abdomen and frothy and pale foul-smelling stools.

coelom *or esp US* **celom** ('siːləʊm, -ləm) NOUN the body cavity of many multicellular animals, situated in the mesoderm and containing the digestive tract and other visceral organs.
▷HISTORY C19: from Greek *koilōma* cavity, from *koilos* hollow; see COEL-
▸**coelomic** *or esp US* **celomic** (sɪ'lɒmɪk) ADJECTIVE

coelostat ('siːlə,stæt) NOUN an astronomical instrument consisting of a plane mirror mounted parallel to the earth's axis and rotated about this axis once every two days so that light from a celestial body, esp the sun, is reflected onto a second mirror, which reflects the beam into a telescope. Compare **siderostat.**
▷HISTORY C19 *coelo-,* from Latin *caelum* heaven, sky + -STAT

coelurosaur (sɪ'ljʊərə,sɔː) NOUN any of various small to very large bipedal carnivorous saurischian dinosaurs belonging to the suborder *Theropoda,* active in the Triassic and Cretaceous periods; Tyrannosaurus was a coelurosaur, and birds are thought to have evolved from small coelurosaurs.
▷HISTORY C20: from New Latin, from Greek *koilos* hollow + *ouros* tail + -SAUR

coemption (kəʊ'ɛmpʃən) NOUN the buying up of the complete supply of a commodity.
▷HISTORY C14: from Latin *coemptiōnem* a buying together

coenacle ('sɛnəkᵊl) NOUN a variant spelling of **cenacle.**

coenesthesia, cenesthesia (,siːnɪs'θiːzɪə), **coenesthesis,** *or* **cenesthesis** (,siːnɪs'θiːsɪs) NOUN *Psychol* general awareness of one's own body.
▸**coenesthetic** *or* **cenesthetic** (,siːnɪs'θɛtɪk) ADJECTIVE

coeno- *or before a vowel* **coen-** COMBINING FORM common: *coenocyte.*
▷HISTORY New Latin, from Greek *koinos* common

coenobite *or* **cenobite** ('siːnəʊ,baɪt) NOUN a member of a religious order following a communal rule of life. Compare **eremite.**
▷HISTORY C17: from Old French or ecclesiastical Latin, from Greek *koinobion* convent, from *koinos* common + *bios* life
▸**coenobitic** (,siːnəʊ'bɪtɪk) ▸**,coeno'bitical, ,ceno'bitic,** *or* **,ceno'bitical** ADJECTIVE

coenocyte ('siːnəʊ,saɪt) NOUN *Botany* a mass of protoplasm containing many nuclei and enclosed by a cell wall: occurs in many fungi and some algae.
▸**coenocytic** (,siːnə'sɪtɪk) ADJECTIVE

coenosarc ('siːnəʊ,sɑːk) NOUN a system of protoplasmic branches connecting the polyps of colonial organisms such as corals.
▷HISTORY C19: from COENO- + Greek *sarx* flesh

coenosteum (sɪ'nɒstɪəm) NOUN *Zoology* the calcareous skeleton of a hydrocoral or a coral colony.

coenurus (siː'njʊərəs) NOUN, *plural* **-ri** (-raɪ). an encysted larval form of the tapeworm *Multiceps,* containing many encapsulated heads. In sheep it can cause the gid, and when eaten by dogs it develops into several adult forms.
▷HISTORY C19: from New Latin, from COENO- + Greek *oura* tail, literally: common tail, referring to the single body with its many heads

coenzyme (kəʊ'ɛnzaɪm) NOUN *Biochem* a nonprotein organic molecule that forms a complex with certain enzymes and is essential for their activity. See also **apoenzyme.**

coenzyme A NOUN a constituent of biological cells that functions as the agent of acylation in metabolic reactions. Abbreviation: **CoA.**

coenzyme Q NOUN a quinone derivative, present in biological cells, that functions as an electron carrier in the electron transport chain. Also called: **ubiquinone.**

coequal (kəʊ'iːkwəl) ADJECTIVE 1 of the same size, rank, etc. ◆ NOUN 2 a person or thing equal with another.
▸**coequality** (,kəʊɪ'kwɒlɪtɪ) *or* **co'equalness** NOUN
▸**co'equally** ADVERB

coerce (kəʊ'ɜːs) VERB (*tr*) to compel or restrain by force or authority without regard to individual wishes or desires.
▷HISTORY C17: from Latin *coercēre* to confine, restrain, from *co-* together + *arcēre* to enclose
▸**co'ercer** NOUN ▸**co'ercible** ADJECTIVE

coercimeter (,kəʊɜː'sɪmɪtə) NOUN an instrument used for measurement of coercive force.

coercion (kəʊ'ɜːʃən) NOUN 1 the act or power of coercing. 2 government by force.
▸**co'ercionist** NOUN ▸**coercive** (kəʊ'ɜːsɪv) ADJECTIVE
▸**co'ercively** ADVERB ▸**co'erciveness** NOUN

coercive force NOUN a measure of the magnetization of a ferromagnetic material as expressed by the external magnetic field strength necessary to demagnetize it. Measured in amperes per metre. Compare **coercivity.**

coercivity (,kəʊɜː'sɪvɪtɪ) NOUN the magnetic-field strength necessary to demagnetize a ferromagnetic material that is magnetized to saturation. It is measured in amperes per metre. Compare **coercive force.**

coessential (,kəʊɪ'sɛnʃəl) ADJECTIVE *Christianity* being one in essence or nature: a term applied to the three persons of the Trinity.
▸**coessentiality** (,kəʊɪ,sɛnʃɪ'ælɪtɪ) *or* **,coes'sentialness** NOUN ▸**,coes'sentially** ADVERB

coetaneous (,kəʊɪ'teɪnɪəs) ADJECTIVE *Rare* of the same age or period.
▷HISTORY C17: from Latin *coaetāneus,* from *co-* same + *aetās* age
▸**,coe'taneously** ADVERB ▸**,coe'taneousness** NOUN

coeternal (,kəʊɪ'tɜːnᵊl) ADJECTIVE existing together eternally.
▸**,coe'ternally** ADVERB

coeternity (,kəʊɪ'tɜːnɪtɪ) NOUN existence for, from, or in eternity with another being.

coeval (kəʊ'iːvᵊl) ADJECTIVE 1 of or belonging to the same age or generation. ◆ NOUN 2 a contemporary.
▷HISTORY C17: from Late Latin *coaevus* from Latin *co-* + *aevum* age
▸**coevality** (,kəʊɪ'vælɪtɪ) NOUN ▸**co'evally** ADVERB

coevolution (kəʊ,iːvə'luːʃən) NOUN the evolution of complementary adaptations in two or more species of organisms because of a special relationship that exists between them, as in insect-pollinated plants and their insect pollinators.

coexecutor (,kəʊɪg'zɛkjʊtə) NOUN *Law* a person acting jointly with another or others as executor.
▸**,coex'ecutrix** FEMININE NOUN

coexist (,kəʊɪg'zɪst) VERB (*intr*) 1 to exist together at the same time or in the same place. 2 to exist together in peace.
▸**,coex'istence** NOUN ▸**,coex'istent** ADJECTIVE

coextend (,kəʊɪk'stɛnd) VERB to extend or cause to extend equally in space or time.
▸**,coex'tension** NOUN

coextensive (,kəʊɪk'stɛnsɪv) ADJECTIVE of the same limits or extent.
▸**,coex'tensively** ADVERB

cofactor ('kəʊ,fæktə) NOUN 1 *Maths* a number associated with an element in a square matrix, equal to the determinant of the matrix formed by removing the row and column in which the element appears from the given determinant. See **minor.** 2 *Biochem* a nonprotein substance that forms a complex with certain enzymes and is essential for their activity. It may be a metal ion or a coenzyme.

C of E ABBREVIATION FOR Church of England.

coff (kɒf) VERB **coffs, coffing, coffed** *or* **coft.** *Scot* to buy; purchase.
▷HISTORY C15: from the past participle of obsolete *copen* to buy, of Low German origin; compare German *kaufen* to buy

coffee ('kɒfɪ) NOUN 1 **a** a drink consisting of an infusion of the roasted and ground or crushed seeds of the coffee tree. **b** (*as modifier*): *coffee grounds.* 2 Also called: **coffee beans.** the beanlike seeds of the coffee tree, used to make this beverage. 3 short for **coffee tree.** 4 **a** a medium to dark brown colour. **b** (*as adjective*): *a coffee carpet.* 5 **wake up and smell the coffee.** See **wake**[1] (sense 7).
▷HISTORY C16: from Italian *caffè,* from Turkish *kahve,* from Arabic *qahwah* coffee, wine

coffee bag NOUN a small bag containing ground coffee beans, infused to make coffee.

coffee bar NOUN a café; snack bar.

coffee cup NOUN a cup from which coffee may be drunk, usually smaller than a teacup.

coffee house NOUN a place where coffee is served, esp one that was a fashionable meeting place in 18th-century London.

coffee mill NOUN a machine for grinding roasted coffee beans.

coffee morning NOUN a social event (often held in order to raise money) at which coffee is served.

coffee nut NOUN 1 the fruit of the Kentucky coffee tree. 2 another name for **Kentucky coffee tree.**

coffeepot ('kɒfɪ,pɒt) NOUN a pot in which coffee is brewed or served.

coffee shop NOUN a shop where coffee is sold or drunk.

coffee table NOUN 1 a low table, on which newspapers, etc., may be placed and coffee served. 2 (*modifier*) implying an emphasis on appearance and an underlying lack of seriousness: *coffee-table music.*

coffee-table book NOUN a book designed to be looked at rather than read.

coffee tree NOUN 1 any of several rubiaceous trees of the genus *Coffea,* esp *C. arabica,* the seeds of which are used in the preparation of the beverage coffee. 2 short for **Kentucky coffee tree.**

coffer ('kɒfə) NOUN 1 a chest, esp for storing valuables. 2 (*usually plural*) a store of money. 3 Also called: **caisson, lacuna.** an ornamental sunken panel in a ceiling, dome, etc. 4 a watertight box or chamber. 5 **a** short for **cofferdam. b** a recessed panel in a concrete, metal, or timber soffit. ◆ VERB (*tr*) 6 to store, as in a coffer. 7 to decorate (a ceiling, dome, etc.) with coffers.
▷HISTORY C13: from Old French *coffre,* from Latin *cophinus* basket, from Greek *kophinos*

cofferdam ('kɒfə,dæm) NOUN 1 a watertight structure, usually of sheet piling, that encloses an area under water, pumped dry to enable construction work to be carried out. Below a certain depth a caisson is required. 2 (on a ship) a compartment separating two bulkheads or floors, as for insulation or to serve as a barrier against the escape of gas or oil. ◆ Often shortened to **coffer.**

coffin ('kɒfɪn) NOUN 1 a box in which a corpse is buried or cremated. 2 the part of a horse's foot that contains the coffin bone. ◆ VERB 3 (*tr*) to place

in or as in a coffin. [4] *Engineering* another name for **flask** (sense 6).
▷HISTORY C14: from Old French *cofin,* from Latin *cophinus* basket; see COFFER

coffin bone NOUN the terminal phalangeal bone inside the hoof of the horse and similar animals.

coffin nail NOUN a slang term for **cigarette.**

coffle ('kɒfəl) NOUN (esp formerly) a line of slaves, beasts, etc., fastened together.
▷HISTORY C18: from Arabic *qāfilah* caravan

C of I ABBREVIATION FOR Church of Ireland.

C of S ABBREVIATION FOR: [1] Chief of Staff. [2] Church of Scotland.

cog¹ (kɒg) NOUN [1] any of the teeth or projections on the rim of a gearwheel or sprocket. [2] a gearwheel, esp a small one. [3] a person or thing playing a small part in a large organization or process. ◆ VERB **cogs, cogging, cogged.** [4] (*tr*) *Metallurgy* to roll (cast-steel ingots) to convert them into blooms.
▷HISTORY C13: of Scandinavian origin; compare Danish *kogge,* Swedish *kugge,* Norwegian *kug*

cog² (kɒg) VERB **cogs, cogging, cogged.** *Slang* to cheat (in a game, esp dice), as by loading a dice.
▷HISTORY C16: originally a dice-playing term, of unknown origin

cog³ (kɒg) NOUN [1] a tenon that projects from the end of a timber beam for fitting into a mortise. ◆ VERB **cogs, cogging, cogged.** [2] (*tr*) to join (pieces of wood) with cogs.
▷HISTORY C19: of uncertain origin

cogent ('kəʊdʒənt) ADJECTIVE compelling belief or assent; forcefully convincing.
▷HISTORY C17: from Latin *cōgent-, cōgēns,* driving together, from *cōgere,* from *co-* together + *agere* to drive
▸'**cogency** NOUN ▸'**cogently** ADVERB

coggle ('kɒgəl) VERB (*intr*) *Scot* to wobble or rock; be unsteady.
▷HISTORY of uncertain origin
▸'**coggly** ADJECTIVE

cogitable ('kɒdʒɪtəbəl) ADJECTIVE *Rare* conceivable.

cogitate ('kɒdʒɪˌteɪt) VERB to think deeply about (a problem, possibility, etc.); ponder.
▷HISTORY C16: from Latin *cōgitāre,* from *co-* (intensive) + *agitāre* to turn over, AGITATE
▸'**cogiˌtatingly** ADVERB ▸ˌ**cogi'tation** NOUN ▸'**cogiˌtator** NOUN

cogitative ('kɒdʒɪtətɪv) ADJECTIVE [1] capable of thinking. [2] thoughtful.
▸'**cogitatively** ADVERB ▸'**cogitativeness** NOUN

cogito, ergo sum *Latin* ('kɒgɪˌtəʊ 'ɜːgəʊ 'sʊm) I think, therefore I am; the basis of the philosophy of René Descartes (1596–1650), French philosopher and mathematician.

Cognac ('kɒnjæk; *French* kɔɲak) NOUN [1] a town in SW France: centre of the district famed for its brandy. Pop.: 21 000 (latest est.). [2] (*sometimes not capital*) a high-quality grape brandy.

cognate ('kɒgneɪt) ADJECTIVE [1] akin; related: *cognate languages.* [2] related by blood or descended from a common maternal ancestor. Compare **agnate.** [3] **cognate object.** *Grammar* a noun functioning as the object of a verb to which it is etymologically related, as in *think a thought* or *sing a song.* ◆ NOUN [4] something that is cognate with something else.
▷HISTORY C17: from Latin *cognātus,* from *co-* same + *gnātus* born, variant of *nātus,* past participle of *nāscī* to be born
▸'**cognately** ADVERB ▸'**cognateness** NOUN ▸**cog'nation** NOUN

cognition (kɒg'nɪʃən) NOUN [1] the mental act or process by which knowledge is acquired, including perception, intuition, and reasoning. [2] the knowledge that results from such an act or process.
▷HISTORY C15: from Latin *cognitiō,* from *cognōscere* from *co-* (intensive) + *nōscere* to learn; see KNOW
▸**cog'nitional** ADJECTIVE

cognitive ('kɒgnɪtɪv) ADJECTIVE of or relating to cognition.

cognitive dissonance NOUN *Psychol* an uncomfortable mental state resulting from conflicting cognitions; usually resolved by changing some of the cognitions.

cognitive ethology NOUN a branch of ethology concerned with the influence of conscious awareness and intention on the behaviour of an animal.

cognitive map NOUN *Psychol* a mental map of one's environment.

cognitive psychology NOUN the psychological study of higher mental processes, including thinking and perception.

cognitive science NOUN the scientific study of cognition, including elements of the traditional disciplines of philosophy, psychology, semantics, and linguistics, together with artificial intelligence and computer science.

cognitive therapy NOUN *Psychol* a form of psychotherapy in which the patient is encouraged to change the way he sees the world and himself: used particularly to treat depression.

cognitivism ('kɒgnɪtɪˌvɪzəm) NOUN *Philosophy* the meta-ethical thesis that moral judgments state facts and so are either true or false. Compare **emotivism, prescriptivism.** See also **naturalism** (sense 4), **non-naturalism.**

cognizable *or* **cognisable** ('kɒgnɪzəbəl, 'kɒnɪ-) ADJECTIVE [1] perceptible. [2] *Law* susceptible to the jurisdiction of a court.
▸'**cognizably** *or* '**cognisably** ADVERB

cognizance *or* **cognisance** ('kɒgnɪzəns, 'kɒnɪ-) NOUN [1] knowledge; acknowledgment. [2] **take cognizance of.** to take notice of; acknowledge, esp officially. [3] the range or scope of knowledge or perception. [4] *Law* **a** the right of a court to hear and determine a cause or matter. **b** knowledge of certain facts upon which the court must act without requiring proof. **c** *Chiefly US* confession. [5] *Heraldry* a distinguishing badge or bearing.
▷HISTORY C14: from Old French *conoissance,* from *conoistre* to know, from Latin *cognōscere* to learn; see COGNITION

cognizant *or* **cognisant** ('kɒgnɪzənt, 'kɒnɪ-) ADJECTIVE (usually foll by *of*) aware; having knowledge.

cognize *or* **cognise** ('kɒgnaɪz, kɒg'naɪz) VERB (*tr*) to perceive, become aware of, or know.

cognomen (kɒg'nəʊmɛn) NOUN, *plural* **-nomens** *or* **-nomina** (-'nɒmɪnə, -'nəʊ-). (originally) an ancient Roman's third name or nickname, which later became his family name. See also **agnomen, nomen, praenomen.**
▷HISTORY C19: from Latin: additional name, from *co-* together + *nōmen* name; influenced in form by *cognōscere* to learn
▸**cognominal** (kɒg'nɒmɪnəl, -'nəʊ-) ADJECTIVE
▸**cog'nominally** ADVERB

cognoscenti (ˌkɒnjəʊ'ʃɛntɪ, ˌkɒgnəʊ-) *or* **conoscenti** PLURAL NOUN, *singular* **-te** (-tiː). (*sometimes singular*) people with informed appreciation of a particular field, esp in the fine arts; connoisseurs.
▷HISTORY C18: from obsolete Italian (modern *conoscente*), from Latin *cognōscere* to know, learn about

cogon ('kəʊgəʊn) NOUN any of the coarse tropical grasses of the genus *Imperata,* esp *I. cylindrica* and *I. exaltata* of the Philippines, which are used for thatching.
▷HISTORY from Spanish *cogón,* from Tagalog *kugon*

cog railway *or* **cogway** ('kɒgˌweɪ) NOUN *Chiefly US* other terms for **rack railway.**

cogwheel ('kɒgˌwiːl) NOUN another name for **gearwheel.**

cohabit (kəʊ'hæbɪt) VERB (*intr*) to live together as husband and wife, esp without being married.
▷HISTORY C16: via Late Latin, from Latin *co-* together + *habitāre* to live
▸ˌ**cohabi'tee, co'habitant,** *or* **co'habiter** NOUN

cohabitation (kəʊˌhæbɪ'teɪʃən) NOUN [1] the state or condition of living together as husband and wife without being married. [2] (of political parties) the state or condition of cooperating for specific purposes without forming a coalition.

coheir (kəʊ'ɛə) NOUN a person who inherits jointly with others.
▸**co'heiress** FEMININE NOUN

Cohen (kɒ'hɛn, kɔɪn) NOUN a variant spelling of **Kohen.**

cohere (kəʊ'hɪə) VERB (*intr*) [1] to hold or stick firmly together. [2] to be connected logically; be consistent. [3] *Physics* to be held together by the action of molecular forces.
▷HISTORY C16: from Latin *cohaerēre* from *co-* together + *haerēre* to cling, adhere

coherence (kəʊ'hɪərəns) *or* **coherency** NOUN [1] logical or natural connection or consistency. [2] another word for **cohesion** (sense 1).

coherent (kəʊ'hɪərənt) ADJECTIVE [1] capable of logical and consistent speech, thought, etc. [2] logical; consistent and orderly. [3] cohering or sticking together. [4] *Physics* (of two or more waves) having the same phase or a fixed phase difference: *coherent light.* [5] (of a system of units) consisting only of units the quotient or product of any two of which yield the unit of the resultant quantity.
▸**co'herently** ADVERB

coherer (kəʊ'hɪərə) NOUN *Physics* an electrical component formerly used to detect radio waves, consisting of a tube containing loosely packed metal particles. The waves caused the particles to cohere, thereby changing the current through the circuit.

cohesion (kəʊ'hiːʒən) NOUN [1] the act or state of cohering; tendency to unite. [2] *Physics* the force that holds together the atoms or molecules in a solid or liquid, as distinguished from adhesion. [3] *Botany* the fusion in some plants of flower parts, such as petals, that are usually separate.
▷HISTORY C17: from Latin *cohaesus* stuck together, past participle of *cohaerēre* to COHERE

cohesionless soil (kəʊ'hiːʒənlɪs) NOUN any free-running type of soil, such as sand or gravel, whose strength depends on friction between particles. Also called: **frictional soil.** Compare **cohesive soil.**

cohesive (kəʊ'hiːsɪv) ADJECTIVE [1] characterized by or causing cohesion. [2] tending to cohere or stick together.
▸**co'hesively** ADVERB ▸**co'hesiveness** NOUN

cohesive soil NOUN sticky soil such as clay or clayey silt whose strength depends on the surface tension of capillary water. Compare **cohesionless soil.**

coho ('kəʊhəʊ) NOUN, *plural* **-ho** *or* **-hos.** a Pacific salmon, *Oncorhynchus kisutch.* Also called: **silver salmon.**
▷HISTORY origin unknown; probably from an American Indian language

cohobate ('kəʊhəʊˌbeɪt) VERB (*tr*) *Pharmacol* to redistil (a distillate), esp by allowing it to mingle with the remaining matter.
▷HISTORY C17: from New Latin *cohobāre,* perhaps from Arabic *ka'aba* to repeat an action

cohort ('kəʊhɔːt) NOUN [1] one of the ten units of between 300 and 600 men in an ancient Roman Legion. [2] any band of warriors or associates: *the cohorts of Satan.* [3] *Chiefly US* an associate or follower. [4] *Biology* a taxonomic group that is a subdivision of a subclass (usually of mammals) or subfamily (of plants). [5] *Statistics* a group of people with a statistic in common, esp having been born in the same year.
▷HISTORY C15: from Latin *cohors* yard, company of soldiers; related to *hortus* garden

cohosh ('kəʊhɒʃ, kəʊ'hɒʃ) NOUN any of several North American plants, such as the **blue cohosh** (*Caulophyllum thalictroides:* family *Leonticaceae*) and **black cohosh** (*Cimicifuga racemosa:* family *Ranunculaceae*).
▷HISTORY C18: probably of Algonquian origin

COHSE ('kəʊzɪ) NOUN (formerly, in Britain) ◆ ACRONYM FOR Confederation of Health Service Employees.

cohune (kəʊ'huːn) NOUN a tropical American feather palm, *Attalea* (or *Orbignya*) *cohune,* whose large oily nuts yield an oil similar to coconut oil. Also called: **cohune palm.** See also **coquilla nut.**
▷HISTORY C19: from American Spanish, from South American Indian *ókhún*

COI (in Britain) ABBREVIATION FOR Central Office of Information.

coif (kɔɪf) NOUN [1] a close-fitting cap worn under a veil, worn in the Middle Ages by many women but now only by nuns. [2] any similar cap, such as a leather cap worn under a chain-mail hood. [3] (formerly in England) the white cap worn by a serjeant at law. [4] a base for the elaborate women's headdresses of the 16th century. [5] (kwɑːf) a less

common word for **coiffure** (sense 1). ◆ VERB **coifs, coiffing, coiffed.** (*tr*) 6 to cover with or as if with a coif. 7 (kwɑːf) to arrange (the hair).
▷HISTORY C14: from Old French *coiffe,* from Late Latin *cofea* helmet, cap, of obscure origin

coiffeur (kwɑːˈfɜː; *French* kwafœr) NOUN a hairdresser.
▸**coiffeuse** (kwɑːˈfɜːz; *French* kwaføz) FEMININE NOUN

coiffure (kwɑːˈfjʊə; *French* kwafyr) NOUN 1 a hairstyle. 2 an obsolete word for **headdress.** ◆ VERB 3 (*tr*) to dress or arrange (the hair).

coign *or* **coigne** (kɔɪn) NOUN variant spellings of **quoin.**

coign of vantage NOUN an advantageous position or stance for observation or action.

coil[1] (kɔɪl) VERB 1 to wind or gather (ropes, hair, etc.) into loops or (of rope, hair, etc.) to be formed in such loops. 2 (*intr*) to move in a winding course. ◆ NOUN 3 something wound in a connected series of loops. 4 a single loop of such a series. 5 an arrangement of pipes in a spiral or loop, as in a condenser. 6 an electrical conductor wound into the form of a spiral, sometimes with a soft iron core, to provide inductance or a magnetic field. See also **induction coil.** 7 an intrauterine contraceptive device in the shape of a coil. 8 the transformer in a petrol engine that supplies the high voltage to the sparking plugs.
▷HISTORY C16: from Old French *coillir* to collect together; see CULL
▸ˈ**coiler** NOUN

coil[2] (kɔɪl) NOUN the troubles and activities of the world (in the Shakespearean phrase **this mortal coil**).
▷HISTORY C16: of unknown origin

coil spring NOUN a helical spring formed from wire.

Coimbatore (ˌkɔːɪmbəˈtɔː) NOUN an industrial city in SW India, in W Tamil Nadu. Pop.: 816 321 (1991).

Coimbra (*Portuguese* ˈkuimbrə) NOUN a city in central Portugal: capital of Portugal from 1190 to 1260; seat of the country's oldest university. Pop.: 103 000 (2001).

coin (kɔɪn) NOUN 1 a metal disc or piece used as money. 2 metal currency, as opposed to securities, paper currency, etc. Related adjective: **nummary.** 3 *Architect* a variant spelling of **quoin.** 4 **pay (a person) back in (his) own coin.** to treat (a person) in the way that he has treated others. 5 **the other side of the coin.** the opposite view of a matter. ◆ VERB 6 (*tr*) to make or stamp (coins). 7 (*tr*) to make into a coin. 8 (*tr*) to fabricate or invent (words, etc.). 9 (*tr*) *Informal* to make (money) rapidly (esp in the phrase **coin it in**). 10 **to coin a phrase.** said ironically after one uses a cliché.
▷HISTORY C14: from Old French: stamping die, from Latin *cuneus* wedge
▸ˈ**coinable** ADJECTIVE ▸ˈ**coiner** NOUN

coinage (ˈkɔɪnɪdʒ) NOUN 1 coins collectively. 2 the act of striking coins. 3 the currency of a country. 4 the act of inventing something, esp a word or phrase. 5 a newly invented word, phrase, usage, etc.

coin box NOUN the part of a coin-operated machine into which coins are placed.

coincide (ˌkəʊɪnˈsaɪd) VERB (*intr*) 1 to occur or exist simultaneously. 2 to be identical in nature, character, etc. 3 to agree.
▷HISTORY C18: from Medieval Latin *coincidere,* from Latin *co-* together + *incidere* to occur, befall, from *cadere* to fall

coincidence (kəʊˈɪnsɪdəns) NOUN 1 a chance occurrence of events remarkable either for being simultaneous or for apparently being connected. 2 the fact, condition, or state of coinciding. 3 (*modifier*) *Electronics* of or relating to a circuit that produces an output pulse only when both its input terminals receive pulses within a specified interval: *coincidence gate.* Compare **anticoincidence.**

coincident (kəʊˈɪnsɪdənt) ADJECTIVE 1 having the same position in space or time. 2 (usually *postpositive* and foll by *with*) in exact agreement; consonant.

coincidental (kəʊˌɪnsɪˈdentᵊl) ADJECTIVE of or happening by a coincidence; fortuitous.

coincidentally (kəʊˌɪnsɪˈdɛntəlɪ) ADVERB (*sentence modifier*) by a coincidence; fortuitously.

coin-op (ˈkɔɪnˌɒp) NOUN a launderette or other service installation in which the machines are operated by the insertion of coins.

coinsurance (ˌkəʊɪnˈʃʊərəns, -ˈʃɔː-) NOUN 1 a method of insurance by which property is insured for a certain percentage of its value by a commercial insurance policy while the owner assumes liability for the remainder. 2 joint insurance held by two or more persons.

coinsure (ˌkəʊɪnˈʃʊə, -ˈʃɔː) VERB 1 (*intr*) to take out coinsurance. 2 to insure (property) jointly with another.
▸ˌ**coinˈsurer** NOUN

Cointreau (ˈkwɑːntrəʊ) NOUN *Trademark* a colourless liqueur with orange flavouring.

coir (kɔɪə) NOUN the fibre prepared from the husk of the coconut, used in making rope and matting.
▷HISTORY C16: from Malayalam *kāyar* rope, from *kāyaru* to be twisted

Coire (kwar) NOUN the French name for **Chur.**

coit (kɔɪt) NOUN *Austral slang* buttocks; backside. Also: **quoit.**
▷HISTORY C20: perhaps a variant and special use of QUOIT, referring to roundness

coitus (ˈkəʊɪtəs) *or* **coition** (kəʊˈɪʃən) NOUN technical terms for **sexual intercourse.**
▷HISTORY C18 *coitus:* from Latin: a uniting, from *coīre* to meet, from *īre* to go
▸ˈ**coital** ADJECTIVE

coitus interruptus (ˌɪntəˈrʌptəs) NOUN the deliberate withdrawal of the penis from the vagina before ejaculation.

coitus reservatus (ˌrɛzəˈvɑːtəs) NOUN the deliberate delaying or avoidance of orgasm during intercourse.

cojones *Spanish* (koˈxones) PLURAL NOUN 1 testicles. 2 manly courage.

coke[1] (kəʊk) NOUN 1 a solid-fuel product containing about 80 per cent of carbon produced by distillation of coal to drive off its volatile constituents: used as a fuel and in metallurgy as a reducing agent for converting metal oxides into metals. 2 any similar material, such as the layer formed in the cylinders of a car engine by incomplete combustion of the fuel. ◆ VERB 3 to become or convert into coke.
▷HISTORY C17: probably a variant of C14 Northern English dialect *colk* core, of obscure origin

coke[2] (kəʊk) NOUN *Slang* short for **cocaine.**

Coke (kəʊk) NOUN *Trademark* short for **Coca-Cola.**

coked-up (ˈkəʊkdʌp) ADJECTIVE *Slang* showing the effects of having taken cocaine.

cokuloris (ˌkɒkəˈlɔːrɪs) NOUN *Films* a palette with irregular holes, placed between lighting and camera to prevent glare.
▷HISTORY C20: of unknown origin

col (kɒl; *French* kɔl) NOUN 1 the lowest point of a ridge connecting two mountain peaks, often constituting a pass. 2 *Meteorol* a pressure region between two anticyclones and two depressions, associated with variable weather.
▷HISTORY C19: from French: neck, col, from Latin *collum* neck

col. ABBREVIATION FOR column.

Col. ABBREVIATION FOR: 1 Colombia(n). 2 Colonel. 3 *Bible* Colossians.

col-[1] PREFIX a variant of **com-** before *l*: *collateral.*

col-[2] PREFIX a variant of **colo-** before a vowel: *colectomy.*

cola[1] *or* **kola** (ˈkəʊlə) NOUN 1 either of two tropical sterculiaceous trees, *Cola nitida* or *C. acuminata,* widely cultivated in tropical regions for their seeds (see **cola nut**). 2 a sweet carbonated drink flavoured with cola nuts.
▷HISTORY C18: from *kola,* probably variant of Mandingo *kolo* nut

cola[2] (ˈkəʊlə) NOUN a plural of **colon**[1] (sense 3) or **colon**[2].

colander (ˈkɒləndə, ˈkʌl-) *or* **cullender** NOUN a pan with a perforated bottom for straining or rinsing foods.
▷HISTORY C14 *colyndore,* probably from Old Provençal *colador,* via Medieval Latin, from Late Latin *cōlāre* to filter, from Latin *cōlum* sieve

cola nut NOUN any of the seeds of the cola tree, which contain caffeine and theobromine and are used medicinally and in the manufacture of soft drinks.

colatitude (kəʊˈlætɪˌtjuːd) NOUN *Astronomy, navigation* the complement of the celestial latitude.

Colby (ˈkɒlbɪ) NOUN (*sometimes not capital*) *NZ* a type of mild-tasting hard cheese.

colcannon (kəlˈkænən, ˈkɒlˌkænən) NOUN a dish, originating in Ireland, of potatoes and cabbage or other greens boiled and mashed together.
▷HISTORY C18: from Irish Gaelic *cál ceannann,* literally: white-headed cabbage

Colchester (ˈkəʊltʃɪstə) NOUN a town in E England, in NE Essex; university (1964). Pop.: 96 063 (1991). Latin name: **Camulodunum** (ˌkæmjʊləʊˈdjuːnəm, ˌkæmʊləʊˈduːnəm).

colchicine (ˈkɒltʃɪˌsiːn, -sɪn, ˈkɒlkɪ-) NOUN a pale-yellow crystalline alkaloid extracted from seeds or corms of the autumn crocus. It is used in the treatment of gout and to create polyploid plants by inhibiting chromosome separation during meiosis. Formula: $C_{22}H_{25}NO_6$.
▷HISTORY C19: from COLCHICUM + -INE[2]

colchicum (ˈkɒltʃɪkəm, ˈkɒlkɪ-) NOUN 1 any Eurasian liliaceous plant of the genus *Colchicum,* such as the autumn crocus. 2 the dried seeds or corms of the autumn crocus: a source of colchicine.
▷HISTORY C16: from Latin, from Greek *kolkhikon,* from *kolkhikos* of COLCHIS

Colchis (ˈkɒlkɪs) NOUN an ancient country on the Black Sea south of the Caucasus; the land of Medea and the Golden Fleece in Greek mythology.

colcothar (ˈkɒlkəˌθɑː) NOUN a finely powdered form of ferric oxide produced by heating ferric sulphate and used as a pigment and as jewellers' rouge. Also called: **crocus.**
▷HISTORY C17: from French *colcotar,* from Spanish *colcótar,* from Arabic dialect *qulqutār*

cold (kəʊld) ADJECTIVE 1 having relatively little warmth; of a rather low temperature: *cold weather; cold hands.* 2 without sufficient or proper warmth: *this meal is cold.* 3 lacking in affection, enthusiasm, or warmth of feeling: *a cold manner.* 4 not affected by emotion; objective: *cold logic.* 5 dead. 6 sexually unresponsive or frigid. 7 lacking in freshness: *a cold scent; cold news.* 8 chilling to the spirit; depressing. 9 (of a colour) having violet, blue, or green predominating; giving no sensation of warmth. 10 *Metallurgy* denoting or relating to a process in which work-hardening occurs as a result of the plastic deformation of a metal at too low a temperature for annealing to take place. 11 (of a process) not involving heat, in contrast with traditional methods: *cold typesetting; cold technology.* 12 *Informal* (of a seeker) far from the object of a search. 13 denoting the contacting of potential customers, voters, etc., without previously approaching them in order to establish their interest: *cold mailing.* 14 **cold comfort.** little or no comfort. 15 **cold steel.** the use of bayonets, knives, etc., in combat. 16 **from cold.** without advance notice; without giving preparatory information. 17 **in cold blood.** showing no passion; deliberately; ruthlessly. 18 **leave (someone) cold.** *Informal* to fail to excite (someone): *the performance left me cold.* 19 **throw** (*or* **pour**) **cold water on.** *Informal* to be unenthusiastic about or discourage. ◆ NOUN 20 the absence of heat regarded as a positive force: *the cold took away our breath.* 21 the sensation caused by loss or lack of heat. 22 **(out) in the cold.** *Informal* neglected; ignored. 23 an acute viral infection of the upper respiratory passages characterized by discharge of watery mucus from the nose, sneezing, etc. 24 **catch a cold.** *Slang* to make a loss; lose one's investment. ◆ ADVERB 25 *Informal* without preparation: *he played his part cold.* 26 *Informal, chiefly US and Canadian* thoroughly; absolutely: *she turned him down cold.*
▷HISTORY Old English *ceald;* related to Old Norse *kaldr,* Gothic *kalds,* Old High German *kalt;* see COOL
▸ˈ**coldish** ADJECTIVE ▸ˈ**coldly** ADVERB ▸ˈ**coldness** NOUN

cold-blooded ADJECTIVE 1 having or showing a lack of feeling or pity: *a cold-blooded killing.* 2 *Informal* particularly sensitive to cold. 3 (of all animals except birds and mammals) having a body temperature that varies with that of the surroundings. Technical term: **poikilothermic.**
▸ˌ**cold-ˈbloodedly** ADVERB ▸ˌ**cold-ˈbloodedness** NOUN

cold call NOUN 1 a call made by a salesman on a

potential customer without making an appointment. ◆ VERB **cold-call.** 2 to call on (a potential customer) without making an appointment.
▸**cold caller** NOUN ▸**cold calling** NOUN

cold cathode NOUN *Electronics* a cathode from which electrons are emitted at ambient temperature, due to a high potential gradient at the surface.

cold chisel NOUN a toughened steel chisel.

cold cream NOUN an emulsion of water and fat used cosmetically for softening and cleansing the skin.

cold cuts PLURAL NOUN cooked meats sliced and served cold.

cold-drawn ADJECTIVE (of metal wire, bars, etc.) having been drawn unheated through a die to reduce dimensions, toughen, and improve surface finish.

cold duck NOUN an alcoholic beverage made from equal parts of burgundy and champagne.

cold feet PLURAL NOUN *Informal* loss or lack of courage or confidence.

cold fish NOUN an unemotional and unfriendly person.

cold frame NOUN an unheated wooden frame with a glass top, used to protect young plants from the cold.

cold front NOUN *Meteorol* 1 the boundary line between a warm air mass and the cold air pushing it from beneath and behind as it moves. 2 the line on the earth's surface where the cold front meets it. ◆ Compare **warm front.**

cold-hearted ADJECTIVE lacking in feeling or warmth; unkind.
▸**ˌcold-ˈheartedly** ADVERB ▸**ˌcold-ˈheartedness** NOUN

coldie (ˈkəʊldɪ) NOUN *Austral slang* a cold can or bottle of beer.

Colditz (ˈkəʊldɪts) NOUN a town in E Germany, on the River Mulde: during World War II its castle was used as a top-security camp for Allied prisoners of war; many daring escape attempts, some successful, were made.

cold light NOUN light emitted at low temperatures from a source that is not incandescent, such as fluorescence, phosphorescence, bioluminescence, or triboluminescence.

cold moulding NOUN the production of moulded articles from resins that polymerize chemically.

cold pack NOUN 1 **a** a method of lowering the body temperature by wrapping a person in a sheet soaked in cold water. **b** the sheet so used. 2 a tinning process in which raw food is packed in cans or jars and then heated.

cold-pressed ADJECTIVE (of an unrefined oil such as olive oil) produced by pressing the parent seed, nut, or grain at the lowest possible temperature without any further pressing.

cold-rolled ADJECTIVE (of metal sheets, etc.) having been rolled without heating, producing a smooth surface finish.

cold rubber NOUN synthetic rubber made at low temperatures (about 5°C). It is stronger than that made at higher temperatures and is used for car tyres.

cold shoulder *Informal* ◆ NOUN 1 (often preceded by *the*) a show of indifference; a slight. ◆ VERB **cold-shoulder.** (*tr*) 2 to treat with indifference.

cold snap NOUN a sudden short spell of cold weather.

cold sore NOUN a cluster of blisters at the margin of the lips that sometimes accompanies the common cold, caused by a viral infection. Technical name: **herpes labialis.**

cold spot NOUN an area where house prices are stable and properties are slow to sell.

cold start NOUN *Computing* the reloading of a program or operating system.

cold storage NOUN 1 the storage of things in an artificially cooled place for preservation. 2 *Informal* a state of temporary suspension: *to put an idea into cold storage.*

Coldstream (ˈkəʊldˌstriːm) NOUN a town in SE Scotland, in Scottish Borders on the English border: the Coldstream Guards were formed here (1660). Pop.: 1746 (1991).

cold sweat NOUN *Informal* a bodily reaction to fear or nervousness, characterized by chill and moist skin.

cold turkey NOUN 1 *Slang* a method of curing drug addiction by abrupt withdrawal of all doses. 2 the withdrawal symptoms, esp nausea and shivering, brought on by this method.

cold war NOUN a state of political hostility and military tension between two countries or power blocs, involving propaganda, subversion, threats, economic sanctions, and other measures short of open warfare, esp that between the American and Soviet blocs after World War II (the **Cold War**).

cold warrior NOUN a person who engages in or promotes a cold war.

cold wave NOUN 1 *Meteorol* a sudden spell of low temperatures over a wide area, often following the passage of a cold front. 2 *Hairdressing* a permanent wave made by chemical agents applied at normal temperatures.

cold-weld VERB (*tr*) to join (two metal surfaces) without heat by forcing them together so that the oxide films are broken and adhesion occurs.
▸**cold welding** NOUN

cold work NOUN 1 the craft of shaping metal without heat. ◆ VERB **cold-work.** (*tr*) 2 to shape (metal) in this way.

cole (kəʊl) NOUN any of various plants of the genus *Brassica,* such as the cabbage and rape. Also called: **colewort.**
▷**HISTORY** Old English *cāl,* from Latin *caulis* plant stalk, cabbage

colectomy (kəˈlɛktəmɪ) NOUN, *plural* **-mies.** surgical removal of part or all of the colon.

colemanite (ˈkəʊlməˌnaɪt) NOUN a colourless or white glassy mineral consisting of hydrated calcium borate in monoclinic crystalline form. It occurs with and is a source of borax. Formula: $Ca_2B_6O_{11}.5H_2O$.
▷**HISTORY** C19: named after William T. *Coleman* (1824–93), American pioneer, owner of the mine in which it was discovered

coleopter (ˌkɒlɪˈɒptə) NOUN *Aeronautics, obsolete* an aircraft that has an annular wing with the fuselage and engine on the centre line.

coleopteran (ˌkɒlɪˈɒptərən) NOUN *also* **coleopteron.** 1 any of the insects of the cosmopolitan order *Coleoptera,* in which the forewings are modified to form shell-like protective elytra. The order includes the beetles and weevils. ◆ ADJECTIVE *also* **coleopterous.** 2 of, relating to, or belonging to the order *Coleoptera.*
▷**HISTORY** C18: from New Latin *Coleoptera,* from Greek *koleoptera,* from *koleopteros* sheath-winged, from *koleon* sheath + *pteron* wing

coleoptile (ˌkɒlɪˈɒptaɪl) NOUN a protective sheath around the plumule in grasses.
▷**HISTORY** C19: from New Latin *coleoptilum,* from Greek *koleon* sheath + *ptilon* down, soft plumage

coleorhiza (ˌkɒlɪəˈraɪzə) NOUN, *plural* **-zae** (-ziː). a protective sheath around the radicle in grasses.
▷**HISTORY** C19: from New Latin, from Greek *koleon* sheath + *rhiza* root

Coleraine (ˈkəʊlˈreɪn) NOUN 1 a town in N Northern Ireland, in Coleraine district, Co. Antrim, on the River Bann; light industries; university (1965). Pop.: 20 721 (1991). 2 a district in N Northern Ireland, in Co. Antrim and Co. Londonderry. Pop.: 56 315 (2001). Area: 485 sq. km (187 sq. miles).

coleslaw (ˈkəʊlˌslɔː) NOUN a salad of shredded cabbage, mayonnaise, carrots, onions, etc.
▷**HISTORY** C19: from Dutch *koolsla,* from *koolsalade,* literally: cabbage salad

colestipol (kəˈlɛstɪˌpɒl) NOUN a drug that reduces the concentration of cholesterol in the blood: used, together with dietary restriction of cholesterol, to treat selected patients with hypercholesterolaemia and so prevent atherosclerosis.

coletit (ˈkəʊlˌtɪt) NOUN another name for **coal tit.**

coleus (ˈkəʊlɪəs) NOUN, *plural* **-uses.** any plant of the Old World genus *Coleus:* cultivated for their variegated leaves, typically marked with red, yellow, or white: family *Lamiaceae* (labiates).
▷**HISTORY** C19: from New Latin, from Greek *koleos,* variant of *koleon* sheath; from the way in which the stamens are joined

colewort (ˈkəʊlˌwɜːt) NOUN another name for **cole.**

coley (ˈkəʊlɪ, ˈkɒlɪ) NOUN *Brit* any of various edible fishes, esp the coalfish.

colic (ˈkɒlɪk) NOUN a condition characterized by acute spasmodic abdominal pain, esp that caused by inflammation, distention, etc., of the gastrointestinal tract.
▷**HISTORY** C15: from Old French *colique,* from Late Latin *cōlicus* ill with colic, from Greek *kōlon,* variant of *kolon* COLON[2]

colicky (ˈkɒlɪkɪ) ADJECTIVE relating to or suffering from colic.

colicroot (ˈkɒlɪkˌruːt) NOUN 1 either of two North American liliaceous plants, *Aletris farinosa* or *A. aurea,* having tubular white or yellow flowers and a bitter root formerly used to relieve colic. 2 any of various other plants formerly used to relieve colic.

colicweed (ˈkɒlɪkˌwiːd) NOUN any of several plants of the genera *Dicentra* or *Corydalis,* such as the squirrel corn and Dutchman's-breeches: family *Fumariaceae.*

coliform bacteria (ˈkɒlɪfɔːm) PLURAL NOUN a large group of bacteria inhabiting the intestinal tract of humans and animals that may cause disease and whose presence in water is an indicator of faecal pollution.

Colima (*Spanish* koˈlima) NOUN 1 a state of SW Mexico, on the Pacific coast: mainly a coastal plain, rising to the foothills of the Sierra Madre, with important mineral resources. Capital: Colima. Pop.: 540 679 (2000). Area: 5455 sq. km (2106 sq. miles). 2 a city in SW Mexico, capital of Colima state, on the Colima River. Pop.: 106 967 (1990). 3 **Nevado de.** a volcano in SW Mexico, in Jalisco state. Height: 4339 m (14 235 ft.).

coliseum (ˌkɒlɪˈsɪəm) *or* **colosseum** NOUN a large building, such as a stadium or theatre, used for entertainments, sports, etc.
▷**HISTORY** C18: from Medieval Latin *Colisseum,* variant of COLOSSEUM

colitis (kɒˈlaɪtɪs, kə-) *or* **colonitis** (ˌkɒləˈnaɪtɪs) NOUN inflammation of the colon.
▸**colitic** (kɒˈlɪtɪk) ADJECTIVE

collaborate (kəˈlæbəˌreɪt) VERB (*intr*) 1 (often foll by *on, with,* etc.) to work with another or others on a joint project. 2 to cooperate as a traitor, esp with an enemy occupying one's own country.
▷**HISTORY** C19: from Late Latin *collabōrāre,* from Latin *com-* together + *labōrāre* to work
▸**colˈlaborative** ADJECTIVE ▸**colˈlaboˌrator** NOUN

collaboration (kəˌlæbəˈreɪʃən) NOUN 1 (often foll by *on, with,* etc.) the act of working with another or others on a joint project. 2 something created by working jointly with another or others. 3 the act of cooperating as a traitor, esp with an enemy occupying one's own country.
▸**colˌlaboˈrationist** NOUN

collage (kəˈlɑːʒ, kɒ-; *French* kɔlaʒ) NOUN 1 an art form in which compositions are made out of pieces of paper, cloth, photographs, and other miscellaneous objects, juxtaposed and pasted on a dry ground. 2 a composition made in this way. 3 any work, such as a piece of music, created by combining unrelated styles.
▷**HISTORY** C20: French, from *coller* to stick, from *colle* glue, from Greek *kolla*
▸**colˈlagist** NOUN

collagen (ˈkɒlədʒən) NOUN a fibrous scleroprotein of connective tissue and bones that is rich in glycine and proline and yields gelatine on boiling.
▷**HISTORY** C19: from Greek *kolla* glue + -GEN
▸**collagenic** (ˌkɒləˈdʒɛnɪk) *or* **collagenous** (kəˈlædʒənəs) ADJECTIVE

collagen injection NOUN an injection of collagen into the lip in order to give it a fuller appearance.

collapsar (kɒˈlæpsɑː) NOUN *Astronomy* a collapsed star, either a white dwarf, neutron star, or black hole.

collapse (kəˈlæps) VERB 1 (*intr*) to fall down or cave in suddenly: *the whole building collapsed.* 2 (*intr*) to fail completely: *his story collapsed on investigation.* 3 (*intr*) to break down or fall down from lack of strength. 4 to fold (furniture, etc.) compactly or (of furniture, etc.) to be designed to fold compactly. ◆ NOUN 5 the act or instance of

suddenly falling down, caving in, or crumbling. [6] a sudden failure or breakdown.
▷HISTORY C18: from Latin *collāpsus,* from *collābī* to fall in ruins, from *lābī* to fall
▸**col'lapsible** *or* **col'lapsable** ADJECTIVE ▸**col,lapsi'bility** *or* **col,lapsa'bility** NOUN

collar ('kɒlə) NOUN [1] the part of a garment around the neck and shoulders, often detachable or folded over. [2] any band, necklace, garland, etc., encircling the neck: *a collar of flowers.* [3] a band or chain of leather, rope, or metal placed around an animal's neck to restrain, harness, or identify it. [4] *Biology* a marking or structure resembling a collar, such as that found around the necks of some birds or at the junction of a stem and a root. [5] a section of a shaft or rod having a locally increased diameter to provide a bearing seat or a locating ring. [6] a cut of meat, esp bacon, taken from around the neck of an animal. [7] **hot under the collar.** *Informal* aroused with anger, annoyance, etc. ◆ VERB (*tr*) [8] to put a collar on; furnish with a collar. [9] to seize by the collar. [10] *Informal* to seize; arrest; detain.
▷HISTORY C13: from Latin *collāre* neckband, neck chain, collar, from *collum* neck

collarbone ('kɒlə,bəʊn) NOUN the nontechnical name for **clavicle.**

collar cell NOUN another name for **choanocyte.**

collard ('kɒləd) NOUN [1] a variety of the cabbage, *Brassica oleracea acephala,* having a crown of edible leaves. See also **kale.** [2] the leaves of this plant, eaten as a vegetable.
▷HISTORY C18: variant of COLEWORT

collared dove NOUN a European dove, *Streptopelia decaocto,* having a brownish-grey plumage with a black band on the back of the neck.

collarette (,kɒlə'rɛt) NOUN a woman's fur or lace collar.

collate (kɒ'leɪt, kə-) VERB (*tr*) [1] to examine and compare (texts, statements, etc.) in order to note points of agreement and disagreement. [2] (in library work) to check the number and order of (the pages of a book). [3] *Bookbinding* **a** to check the sequence of (the sections of a book) after gathering. **b** a nontechnical word for **gather** (sense 9). [4] (often foll by *to*) *Christianity* to appoint (an incumbent) to a benefice.
▷HISTORY C16: from Latin *collātus* brought together (past participle of *conferre* to gather), from *com-* together + *lātus,*past participle of *ferre* to bring

collateral (kɒ'lætərəl, kə-) NOUN [1] **a** security pledged for the repayment of a loan. **b** (*as modifier*): *a collateral loan.* [2] a person, animal, or plant descended from the same ancestor as another but through a different line. ◆ ADJECTIVE [3] situated or running side by side. [4] descended from a common ancestor but through different lines. [5] serving to support or corroborate. [6] aside from the main issue. [7] uniting in tendency.
▷HISTORY C14: from Medieval Latin *collaterālis,* from Latin *com-* together + *laterālis* of the side, from *latus* side
▸**col'laterally** ADVERB

collateral damage NOUN *Military* unintentional damage to civil property and civilian casualties, caused by military operations.

collation (kɒ'leɪʃən, kə-) NOUN [1] the act or process of collating. [2] a description of the technical features of a book. [3] *RC Church* a light meal permitted on fast days. [4] any light informal meal. [5] the appointment of a clergyman to a benefice.

collative (kɒ'leɪtɪv, 'kɒlə-) ADJECTIVE [1] involving collation. [2] (of benefices) presented or held by collation.

collator (kɒ'leɪtə, kəʊ-, 'kɒleɪtə, 'kəʊ-) NOUN [1] a person or machine that collates texts or manuscripts. [2] *Computing* a device for matching or checking punched cards in separate files and for merging two or more files sorted into the same ordered sequence.

colleague ('kɒli:g) NOUN a fellow worker or member of a staff, department, profession, etc.
▷HISTORY C16: from French *collègue,* from Latin *collēga* one selected at the same time as another, from *com-* together + *lēgāre* to choose

collect[1] (kə'lɛkt) VERB [1] to gather together or be gathered together. [2] to accumulate (stamps, books, etc.) as a hobby or for study. [3] (*tr*) to call for or receive payment of (taxes, dues, etc.). [4] (*tr*) to regain control of (oneself, one's emotions, etc.) as after a shock or surprise: *he collected his wits.* [5] (*tr*) to fetch: *collect your own post.* [6] (*intr;* sometimes foll by *on*) *Slang* to receive large sums of money, as from an investment: *he really collected when the will was read.* [7] (*tr*) *Austral and NZ informal* to collide with; be hit by. [8] **collect on delivery.** the US term for **cash on delivery.** ◆ ADVERB, ADJECTIVE [9] *US* (of telephone calls) on a reverse-charge basis. ◆ NOUN [10] *Austral informal* a winning bet.
▷HISTORY C16: from Latin *collēctus* collected, from *colligere* to gather together, from *com-* together + *legere* to gather

collect[2] ('kɒlɛkt) NOUN *Christianity* a short Church prayer generally preceding the lesson or epistle in Communion and other services.
▷HISTORY C13: from Medieval Latin *collecta* (from the phrase *ōrātiō ad collēctam* prayer at the (people's) assembly), from Latin *colligere* to COLLECT[1]

collectable *or* **collectible** (kə'lɛktəbᵊl) ADJECTIVE [1] (of antiques, objets d'art, etc.) of interest to a collector. ◆ NOUN [2] any object regarded as being of interest to a collector.

collectanea (,kɒlɛk'teɪnɪə) PLURAL NOUN a collection of excerpts from one or more authors; miscellany; anthology.
▷HISTORY C18: from Latin, from *collectāneus* assembled, from *colligere* to COLLECT[1]

collected (kə'lɛktɪd) ADJECTIVE [1] in full control of one's faculties; composed. [2] assembled in totality or brought together into one volume or a set of volumes: *the collected works of Dickens.* [3] (of a horse or a horse's pace) controlled so that movement is in short restricted steps: *a collected canter.*
▸**col'lectedly** ADVERB ▸**col'lectedness** NOUN

collection (kə'lɛkʃən) NOUN [1] the act or process of collecting. [2] a number of things collected or assembled together. [3] a selection of clothes, esp as presented by a particular designer for a specified season. [4] something gathered into a mass or pile; accumulation: *a collection of rubbish.* [5] a sum of money collected or solicited, as in church. [6] removal, esp regular removal of letters from a postbox. [7] (*often plural*) (at Oxford University) a college examination or an oral report by a tutor.

collective (kə'lɛktɪv) ADJECTIVE [1] formed or assembled by collection. [2] forming a whole or aggregate. [3] of, done by, or characteristic of individuals acting in cooperation. ◆ NOUN [4] **a** a cooperative enterprise or unit, such as a collective farm. **b** the members of such a cooperative. [5] short for **collective noun.**
▸**col'lectively** ADVERB ▸**col'lectiveness** NOUN

collective agreement NOUN a negotiated agreement, which is not enforceable at law, between an employer and employees' representatives, covering rates of pay or terms and conditions of employment, or both.

collective bargaining NOUN negotiation between one or more trade unions and one or more employers or an employers' organization on the incomes and working conditions of the employees.

collective farm NOUN (chiefly in Communist countries) a farm or group of farms managed and owned, through the state, by the community. Russian name: **kolkhoz.**

collective fruit NOUN another name for **multiple fruit.**

collective memory NOUN the shared memories of a group, family, race, etc.

collective noun NOUN a noun that is singular in form but that refers to a group of people or things.

Language note Collective nouns are usually used with singular verbs: *the family is on holiday; General Motors is mounting a big sales campaign.* In British usage, however, plural verbs are sometimes employed in this context, esp when reference is being made to a collection of individual objects or people rather than to the group as a unit: *the family are all on holiday.* Care should be taken that the same collective noun is not treated as both singular and plural in the same sentence: *the family is well and sends its best wishes* or *the family are all well and send their best wishes,* but not *the family is well and send their best wishes.*

collective ownership NOUN ownership by a group for the benefit of members of that group.

collective pitch lever NOUN a lever in a helicopter to change the angle of attack of all the rotor blades simultaneously, causing it to rise or descend. Compare **cyclic pitch lever.**

collective security NOUN a system of maintaining world peace and security by concerted action on the part of the nations of the world.

collective unconscious NOUN *Psychol* (in Jungian psychological theory) a part of the unconscious mind incorporating patterns of memories, instincts, and experiences common to all mankind. These patterns are inherited, may be arranged into archetypes, and are observable through their effects on dreams, behaviour, etc.

collectivism (kə'lɛktɪ,vɪzəm) NOUN [1] the principle of ownership of the means of production, by the state or the people. [2] a social system based on this principle.
▸**col'lectivist** NOUN ▸**col,lectiv'istic** ADJECTIVE

collectivity (,kɒlɛk'tɪvɪtɪ) NOUN, *plural* **-ties.** [1] the quality or state of being collective. [2] a collective whole or aggregate. [3] people regarded as a whole.

collectivize *or* **collectivise** (kə'lɛktɪ,vaɪz) VERB (*tr*) to organize according to the principles of collectivism.
▸**col,lectivi'zation** *or* **col,lectivi'sation** NOUN

collector (kə'lɛktə) NOUN [1] a person or thing that collects. [2] a person employed to collect debts, rents, etc. [3] the head of a district administration in India. [4] a person who collects or amasses objects as a hobby. [5] *Electronics* the region in a transistor into which charge carriers flow from the base.
▸**col'lector,ship** NOUN

collectorate (kə'lɛktərɪt) NOUN the office of a collector in India.

collector's item *or* **piece** NOUN a thing regarded as being exquisite or rare and thus worthy of the interest of one who collects such things.

colleen ('kɒli:n, kɒ'li:n) NOUN [1] an Irish word for **girl.** [2] an Irish girl.
▷HISTORY C19: from Irish Gaelic *cailín* a girl, a young unmarried woman

college ('kɒlɪdʒ) NOUN [1] an institution of higher education; part of a university. [2] a school or an institution providing specialized courses or teaching: *a college of music.* [3] the building or buildings in which a college is housed. [4] the staff and students of a college. [5] an organized body of persons with specific rights and duties: *an electoral college.* See also **Sacred College.** [6] a body of clerics living in community and supported by endowment. [7] *Chiefly Brit* an obsolete slang word for **prison.**
▷HISTORY C14: from Latin *collēgium* company, society, band of associates, from *collēga;* see COLLEAGUE

college of advanced technology NOUN *Brit* (formerly) a college offering degree or equivalent courses in technology, with research facilities. In the mid-1960s these were granted university status. Abbreviation: **CAT.**

college of arms NOUN any of several institutions in the United Kingdom having a royal charter to deal with matters of heraldry, grant armorial bearings, record and trace genealogies, etc. Also called: **herald's college.**

College of Cardinals NOUN *RC Church* the collective body of cardinals having the function of electing and advising the pope.

college of education NOUN *Brit* a professional training college for teachers.

College of Justice NOUN the official name for the Scottish Court of Session; the supreme court of Scotland.

college pudding NOUN *Brit* a baked or steamed suet pudding containing dried fruit and spice.

collegial (kə'li:dʒɪəl) ADJECTIVE [1] of or relating to a college. [2] having authority or power shared among a number of people associated as colleagues.
▸**col'legially** ADVERB ▸**col,legi'ality** NOUN

collegian (kə'li:dʒɪən) NOUN a current member of a college; student.

collegiate (kə'li:dʒɪɪt) ADJECTIVE [1] Also: **collegial.** of or relating to a college or college students. [2] (of a university) composed of various colleges of equal standing. ◆ NOUN [3] *Canadian* short for **collegiate institute.**

collegiate church NOUN [1] *RC Church, Church of England* a church that has an endowed chapter of canons and prebendaries attached to it but that is not a cathedral. [2] *US Protestantism* one of a group of churches presided over by a body of pastors. [3] *Scot Protestantism* a church served by two or more ministers. [4] a large church endowed in the Middle Ages to become a school. [5] a chapel either endowed by or connected with a college.

collegiate institute NOUN *Canadian* (in certain provinces) a large secondary school with an academic, rather than vocational, emphasis.

collegium (kəˈliːdʒɪəm) NOUN, *plural* **-giums** *or* **-gia** (-dʒɪə). [1] (in the former Soviet Union) a board in charge of a department. [2] another term for **College of Cardinals** or **Sacred College.**
▷HISTORY Latin: COLLEGE

col legno (ˈkɒl ˈlegnəʊ, ˈleɪnjəʊ) ADVERB *Music* to be played (on a stringed instrument) by striking the strings with the back of the bow.
▷HISTORY Italian: with the wood

collembolan (kəˈlɛmbələn) NOUN [1] any small primitive wingless insect of the order *Collembola,* which comprises the springtails. ◆ ADJECTIVE [2] of, relating to, or belonging to the *Collembola.*
▷HISTORY C19: from New Latin *Collembola,* from Greek *kolla* glue + *embolon* peg, wedge

collenchyma (kəˈlɛŋkɪmə) NOUN a strengthening and supporting tissue in plants, consisting of elongated living cells whose walls are thickened with cellulose and pectins.
▷HISTORY C19: New Latin, from Greek *kolla* glue + *enkhuma* infusion
▸**collenchymatous** (ˌkɒlənˈkɪmətəs) ADJECTIVE

Colles' fracture (ˈkɒlɪs) NOUN a fracture of the radius just above the wrist, with backward and outward displacement of the hand.
▷HISTORY C19: named after Abraham *Colles* (died 1843), Irish surgeon

collet (ˈkɒlɪt) NOUN [1] (in a jewellery setting) a band or coronet-shaped claw that holds an individual stone. [2] *Mechanical engineering* an externally tapered sleeve made in two or more segments and used to grip a shaft passed through its centre when the sleeve is compressed by being inserted in a tapered hole. [3] *Horology* a small collar that supports the inner end of the hairspring. ◆ VERB [4] *(tr) Jewellery* to mount in a collet.
▷HISTORY C16: from Old French: a little collar, from *col* neckband, neck, from Latin *collum* neck

colleterial gland (ˌkɒlɪˈtɪərɪəl) NOUN *Zoology* a paired accessory reproductive gland, present in most female insects, secreting a sticky substance that forms either the egg cases or the cement that binds the eggs to a surface.
▷HISTORY C19: from New Latin *colleterium* glue-secreting organ, from Greek *kolla* glue + -AL[1]

colliculus (kɒˈlɪkjʊləs) NOUN, *plural* **-li.** *Anatomy* a small elevation, as on the surface of the optic lobe of the brain.
▷HISTORY C19: New Latin

collide (kəˈlaɪd) VERB *(intr)* [1] to crash together with a violent impact. [2] to conflict in attitude, opinion, or desire; clash; disagree.
▷HISTORY C17: from Latin *collīdere* to clash together, from *com-* together + *laedere* to strike, wound

collider (kəˈlaɪdə) NOUN *Physics* a particle accelerator in which beams of particles are made to collide.

collie (ˈkɒlɪ) NOUN any of several silky-coated breeds of dog developed for herding sheep and cattle. See **Border collie, rough collie, bearded collie.**
▷HISTORY C17: Scottish, probably from earlier *colie* black with coal dust, from *cole* COAL

collier (ˈkɒlɪə) NOUN *Chiefly Brit* [1] a coal miner. [2] **a** a ship designed to transport coal. **b** a member of its crew.
▷HISTORY C14: from COAL + -IER

colliery (ˈkɒljərɪ) NOUN, *plural* **-lieries.** *Chiefly Brit* a coal mine.

colligate (ˈkɒlɪˌgeɪt) VERB *(tr)* [1] to connect or link together; tie; join. [2] to relate (isolated facts, observations, etc.) by a general hypothesis.
▷HISTORY C16: from Latin *colligāre* to fasten together, from *com-* together + *ligāre* to bind
▸ˌ**colliˈgation** NOUN

colligative (kəˈlɪgətɪv) ADJECTIVE (of a physical property of a substance) depending on the concentrations of atoms, ions, and molecules that are present rather than on their nature.

collimate (ˈkɒlɪˌmeɪt) VERB *(tr)* [1] to adjust the line of sight of (an optical instrument). [2] to use a collimator on (a beam of radiation or particles). [3] to make parallel or bring into line.
▷HISTORY C17: from New Latin *collimāre,* erroneously for Latin *collīneāre* to aim, from *com-* (intensive) + *līneāre,* from *līnea* line
▸ˌ**colliˈmation** NOUN

collimator (ˈkɒlɪˌmeɪtə) NOUN [1] a small telescope attached to a larger optical instrument as an aid in fixing its line of sight. [2] an optical system of lenses and slits producing a nondivergent beam of light, usually for use in spectroscopes. [3] any device for limiting the size and angle of spread of a beam of radiation or particles.

collinear (kɒˈlɪnɪə) ADJECTIVE [1] lying on the same straight line. [2] having a common line.
▸**collinearity** (ˌkɒlɪnɪˈærɪtɪ) NOUN ▸**colˈlinearly** ADVERB

collins (ˈkɒlɪnz) NOUN a tall fizzy iced drink made with gin, vodka, rum, etc., mixed with fruit juice, soda water, and sugar.
▷HISTORY C20: probably after the proper name *Collins*

collinsia (kəˈlɪnsɪə, -zɪə) NOUN a North American plant of the scrophulariaceous genus *Collinsia,* having blue, white, or purple flowers.
▷HISTORY C19: New Latin, named after Zaccheus *Collins* (1764–1831), American botanist

Collins Street Farmer NOUN *Austral slang* a businessman who invests in farms, land, etc. Also called: **Pitt Street Farmer.**
▷HISTORY C20: after a principal business street in Melbourne

collision (kəˈlɪʒən) NOUN [1] a violent impact of moving objects; crash. [2] the conflict of opposed ideas, wishes, attitudes, etc.: *a collision of interests.* [3] *Physics* an event in which two or more bodies or particles come together with a resulting change of direction and, normally, energy.
▷HISTORY C15: from Late Latin *collīsiō* from Latin *collīdere* to COLLIDE

collocate (ˈkɒləˌkeɪt) VERB *(tr)* to group or place together in some system or order.
▷HISTORY C16: from Latin *collocāre,* from *com-* together + *locāre* to place, from *locus* place

collocation (ˌkɒləˈkeɪʃən) NOUN a grouping together of things in a certain order, as of the words in a sentence.

collocutor (ˈkɒləˌkjuːtə) NOUN a person who talks or engages in conversation with another.

collodion (kəˈləʊdɪən) *or* **collodium** (kəˈləʊdɪəm) NOUN a colourless or yellow syrupy liquid that consists of a solution of pyroxylin in ether and alcohol: used in medicine and in the manufacture of photographic plates, lacquers, etc.
▷HISTORY C19: from New Latin *collōdium,* from Greek *kollōdēs* glutinous, from *kolla* glue

collogue (kɒˈləʊg) VERB **collogues, colloguing, collogued.** *(intr; usually foll by with)* to confer confidentially; intrigue or conspire.
▷HISTORY C16: perhaps from obsolete *colleague* (verb) to be or act as a colleague, conspire, influenced by Latin *colloquī* to talk with; see COLLEAGUE

colloid (ˈkɒlɔɪd) NOUN [1] Also called: **colloidal solution** *or* **suspension.** a mixture having particles of one component, with diameters between 10^{-7} and 10^{-9} metres, suspended in a continuous phase of another component. The mixture has properties between those of a solution and a fine suspension. [2] the solid suspended phase in such a mixture. [3] *Obsolete* a substance that in solution does not penetrate a semipermeable membrane. Compare **crystalloid** (sense 2). [4] *Physiol* a gelatinous substance of the thyroid follicles that holds the hormonal secretions of the thyroid gland. ◆ ADJECTIVE [5] *Pathol* of or relating to the gluelike translucent material found in certain degenerating tissues. [6] of, denoting, or having the character of a colloid.
▷HISTORY C19: from Greek *kolla* glue + -OID

colloidal (ˌkɒˈlɔɪdəl) ADJECTIVE of, denoting, or having the character of a colloid.
▸**colloidality** (ˌkɒlɔɪˈdælɪtɪ) NOUN

collop (ˈkɒləp) NOUN *Dialect* [1] a slice of meat. [2] a small piece of anything.
▷HISTORY C14: of Scandinavian origin; compare Swedish *kalops* meat stew

colloq. ABBREVIATION FOR colloquial(ly).

colloquial (kəˈləʊkwɪəl) ADJECTIVE [1] of or relating to conversation. [2] denoting or characterized by informal or conversational idiom or vocabulary. Compare **informal.**
▸**colˈloquially** ADVERB ▸**colˈloquialness** NOUN

colloquialism (kəˈləʊkwɪəˌlɪzəm) NOUN [1] a word or phrase appropriate to conversation and other informal situations. [2] the use of colloquial words and phrases.

colloquium (kəˈləʊkwɪəm) NOUN, *plural* **-quiums** *or* **-quia** (-kwɪə). [1] an informal gathering for discussion. [2] an academic seminar.
▷HISTORY C17: from Latin: conversation, conference, COLLOQUY

colloquy (ˈkɒləkwɪ) NOUN, *plural* **-quies.** [1] a formal conversation or conference. [2] a literary work in dialogue form. [3] an informal conference on religious or theological matters.
▷HISTORY C16: from Latin *colloquium* from *colloquī* to talk with, from *com-* together + *loquī* to speak
▸ˈ**colloquist** NOUN

collotype (ˈkɒləʊˌtaɪp) NOUN [1] Also called: **photogelatine process.** a method of lithographic printing from a flat surface of hardened gelatine: used mainly for fine-detail reproduction in monochrome or colour. [2] a print made using this process.
▷HISTORY C19: from Greek *kolla* glue + TYPE
▸**collotypic** (ˌkɒləˈtɪpɪk) ADJECTIVE

collude (kəˈluːd) VERB *(intr)* to conspire together, esp in planning a fraud; connive.
▷HISTORY C16: from Latin *collūdere,* literally: to play together, hence, conspire together, from *com-* together + *lūdere* to play
▸**colˈluder** NOUN

collusion (kəˈluːʒən) NOUN [1] secret agreement for a fraudulent purpose; connivance; conspiracy. [2] a secret agreement between opponents at law in order to obtain a judicial decision for some wrongful or improper purpose.
▷HISTORY C14: from Latin *collūsiō,* from *collūdere* to COLLUDE
▸**colˈlusive** ADJECTIVE

colluvium (kəˈluːvɪəm) NOUN, *plural* **-via** (-vɪə) *or* **-viums.** a mixture of rock fragments from the bases of cliffs.
▷HISTORY Latin: collection of filth, from *colluere* to wash thoroughly, from *com-* (intensive) + *luere* to wash
▸**colˈluvial** ADJECTIVE

colly (ˈkɒlɪ) *Archaic or dialect* ◆ NOUN, *plural* **-lies.** [1] soot or grime, such as coal dust. ◆ VERB **collies, collying, collied.** [2] *(tr)* to begrime; besmirch.
▷HISTORY C16: ultimately from Old English *col* COAL

collyrium (kɒˈlɪərɪəm) NOUN, *plural* **-lyria** (-ˈlɪərɪə) *or* **-lyriums.** a technical name for an **eyewash** (sense 1).
▷HISTORY C16: from Latin, from Greek *kollurion* poultice, eye salve

collywobbles (ˈkɒlɪˌwɒbᵊlz) PLURAL NOUN (usually preceded by *the*) *Slang* [1] an upset stomach. [2] acute diarrhoea. [3] an intense feeling of nervousness.
▷HISTORY C19: probably from New Latin *cholera morbus* the disease cholera, influenced through folk etymology by COLIC and WOBBLE

Colmar (*French* kɔlmar) NOUN a city in NE France: annexed to Germany 1871–1919 and 1940–45; textile industry. Pop.: 63 498 (1990). German name: **Kolmar.**

Colo. ABBREVIATION FOR Colorado.

colo- *or before a vowel* **col-** COMBINING FORM indicating the colon: *colostomy; colotomy.*

coloboma (ˌkɒləˈbəʊmə) NOUN a structural defect of the eye, esp in the choroid, retina, or iris.
▷HISTORY C19: New Latin, from Greek *kolobōma* a part taken away in mutilation, from *kolobos* cut short

colobus (ˈkɒləbəs) NOUN any leaf-eating arboreal Old World monkey of the genus *Colobus,* of W and

central Africa, having a slender body, long silky fur, long tail, and reduced or absent thumbs.
▷**HISTORY** C19: New Latin, from Greek *kolobos* cut short; referring to its thumb

colocynth (ˈkɒləsɪnθ) NOUN 1 a cucurbitaceous climbing plant, *Citrullus colocynthis,* of the Mediterranean region and Asia, having bitter-tasting fruit. 2 the dried fruit pulp of this plant, used as a strong purgative. ◆ Also called: **bitter apple.**
▷**HISTORY** C17: from Latin *colocynthis,* from Greek *kolokunthis,* from *kolokunthē* gourd, of obscure origin

cologarithm (kəʊˈlɒgəˌrɪðəm) NOUN the logarithm of the reciprocal of a number; the negative value of the logarithm: *the cologarithm of 4 is log ¼.* Abbreviation: **colog.**

cologne (kəˈləʊn) NOUN a perfumed liquid or solid made of fragrant essential oils and alcohol. Also called: **Cologne water, eau de Cologne.**
▷**HISTORY** C18: *Cologne water,* from COLOGNE, where it was first manufactured (1709)

Cologne (kəˈləʊn) NOUN an industrial city and river port in W Germany, in North Rhine-Westphalia on the Rhine: important commercially since ancient times; university (1388). Pop.: 963 200 (1999 est.). German name: **Köln.**

Colomb-Béchar (*French* kɔlɔ̃beʃar) NOUN the former name of **Béchar.**

Colombes (*French* kɔlɔ̃b) NOUN an industrial and residential suburb of NW Paris. Pop.: 79 060 (1990).

Colombia (kəˈlɒmbɪə) NOUN a republic in NW South America: inhabited by Chibchas and other Indians before Spanish colonization in the 16th century; independence won by Bolívar in 1819; became the Republic of Colombia in 1886; violence and unrest have been endemic since the 1970s. It consists chiefly of a hot swampy coastal plain, separated by ranges of the Andes from the pampas and the equatorial forests of the Amazon basin in the east. Language: Spanish. Religion: Roman Catholic majority. Currency: peso. Capital: Bogotá. Pop.: 43 071 000 (2001 est.). Area: 1 138 908 sq. km (439 735 sq. miles).

Colombian (kəˈlɒmbɪən) ADJECTIVE 1 of or relating to Colombia or its inhabitants. ◆ NOUN 2 a native or inhabitant of Colombia.

Colombo (kəˈlʌmbəʊ) NOUN the capital and chief port of Sri Lanka, on the W coast, with one of the largest artificial harbours in the world. Pop.: 800 982 (1997 est.).

colon¹ (ˈkəʊlən) NOUN 1 (*plural* **-lons**) the punctuation mark :, usually preceding an explanation or an example of what has gone before, a list, or an extended quotation. 2 (*plural* **-lons**) this mark used for certain other purposes, such as expressions of time, as in *2:45 p.m.,* or when a ratio is given in figures, as in *5:3.* 3 (*plural* **-la** (-lə)) (in classical prosody) a part of a rhythmic period with two to six feet and one principal accent or ictus.
▷**HISTORY** C16: from Latin, from Greek *kōlon* limb, hence part of a strophe, clause of a sentence

colon² (ˈkəʊlən) NOUN, *plural* **-lons** *or* **-la** (-lə). the part of the large intestine between the caecum and the rectum.
▷**HISTORY** C16: from Latin: large intestine, from Greek *kolon*

colon³ (kəˈlɒn; *French* kɔlɔ̃) NOUN a colonial farmer or plantation owner, esp in a French colony.
▷**HISTORY** French: colonist, from Latin *colōnus,* from *colere* to till, inhabit

colón (kəʊˈləʊn; *Spanish* koˈlon) NOUN, *plural* **-lons** *or* **-lones** (*Spanish* -ˈlones). 1 the standard monetary unit of Costa Rica, divided into 100 céntimos. 2 the former standard monetary unit of El Salvador, divided into 100 centavos; replaced by the US dollar in 2001.
▷**HISTORY** C19: American Spanish, from Spanish, after Cristóbal *Colón* Christopher Columbus

Colón (kɒˈlɒn; *Spanish* koˈlɔn) NOUN 1 a port in Panama, at the Caribbean entrance to the Panama Canal. Chief Caribbean port. Pop.: 137 825 (1992 est.). Former name: **Aspinwall.** 2 **Archipiélago** (ˌartʃiˈpjelaɣo ðe). the official name of the **Galápagos Islands.**

colonel (ˈkɜːnᵊl) NOUN an officer of land or air forces junior to a brigadier but senior to a lieutenant colonel.
▷**HISTORY** C16: via Old French, from Old Italian *colonnello* column of soldiers, from *colonna* COLUMN
▸ˈ**colonelcy** *or* ˈ**colonel**ˌ**ship** NOUN

Colonel Blimp NOUN See **blimp²**.

colonial (kəˈləʊnɪəl) ADJECTIVE 1 of, characteristic of, relating to, possessing, or inhabiting a colony or colonies. 2 (*often capital*) characteristic of or relating to the 13 British colonies that became the United States of America (1776). 3 (*often capital*) of or relating to the colonies of the British Empire. 4 denoting, relating to, or having the style of Neoclassical architecture used in the British colonies in America in the 17th and 18th centuries. 5 of or relating to the period of Australian history before Federation (1901). 6 (of organisms such as corals and bryozoans) existing as a colony of polyps. 7 (of animals and plants) having become established in a community in a new environment. ◆ NOUN 8 a native of a colony.
▸**co**ˈ**lonially** ADVERB

colonial experience NOUN *Austral history* experience of farming, etc., gained by a young Englishman in colonial Australia.
▸**colonial experiencer** NOUN

colonial goose NOUN *NZ* an old-fashioned name for stuffed roast mutton.

colonialism (kəˈləʊnɪəˌlɪzəm) NOUN the policy and practice of a power in extending control over weaker peoples or areas. Also called: **imperialism.**
▸**co**ˈ**lonialist** NOUN, ADJECTIVE

colonic (kəˈlɒnɪk) ADJECTIVE 1 **a** *Anatomy* of or relating to the colon. **b** *Med* relating to irrigation of the colon for cleansing purposes. ◆ NOUN 2 *Med* irrigation of the colon by injecting large amounts of fluid high into the colon: *a high colonic.*

Colonies (ˈkɒlənɪz) PLURAL NOUN **the.** 1 *Brit* the subject territories formerly in the British Empire. 2 *US history* the 13 states forming the original United States of America when they declared their independence (1776). These were Connecticut, North and South Carolina, Delaware, Georgia, New Hampshire, New York, Maryland, Massachusetts, Pennsylvania, Rhode Island, Virginia, and New Jersey.

colonist (ˈkɒlənɪst) NOUN 1 a person who settles or colonizes an area. 2 an inhabitant or member of a colony.

colonitis (ˌkɒləˈnaɪtɪs) NOUN *Pathol* another word for **colitis.**

colonize *or* **colonise** (ˈkɒləˌnaɪz) VERB 1 to send colonists to or establish a colony in (an area). 2 to settle in (an area) as colonists. 3 (*tr*) to transform (a community) into a colony. 4 (of plants and animals) to become established in (a new environment).
▸ˈ**colo**ˌ**nizable** *or* ˈ**colo**ˌ**nisable** ADJECTIVE ▸ˌ**coloni**ˈ**zation** *or* ˌ**coloni**ˈ**sation** NOUN ▸ˈ**colo**ˌ**nizer** *or* ˈ**colo**ˌ**niser** NOUN

colonnade (ˌkɒləˈneɪd) NOUN 1 a set of evenly-spaced columns. 2 a row of regularly spaced trees.
▷**HISTORY** C18: from French, from *colonne* COLUMN; on the model of Italian *colonnato,* from *colonna* column
▸ˌ**colon**ˈ**naded** ADJECTIVE

colonoscope (kəˈlɒnəˌskəʊp) NOUN an instrument for examining the colon, consisting of a flexible lighted tube that is inserted in the colon to look for abnormalities and to remove them or take tissue samples.
▷**HISTORY** C20: from COLON² + -O- + -SCOPE
▸**colonoscopy** (ˌkɒlənˈɒskəpɪ) NOUN

Colonsay (ˈkɒlənseɪ, -zeɪ) NOUN an island in W Scotland, in the Inner Hebrides. Area: about 41 sq. km (16 sq. miles).

colony (ˈkɒlənɪ) NOUN, *plural* **-nies.** 1 a body of people who settle in a country distant from their homeland but maintain ties with it. 2 the community formed by such settlers. 3 a subject territory occupied by a settlement from the ruling state. 4 **a** a community of people who form a national, racial, or cultural minority: *an artists' colony; the American colony in London.* **b** the area itself. 5 *Zoology* **a** a group of the same type of animal or plant living or growing together, esp in large numbers. **b** an interconnected group of polyps of a colonial organism. 6 *Bacteriol* a group of bacteria, fungi, etc., derived from one or a few spores, esp when grown on a culture medium.
▷**HISTORY** C16: from Latin *colōnia,* from *colere* to cultivate, inhabit

colony-stimulating factor NOUN *Immunol* any of a number of substances, secreted by the bone marrow, that cause stem cells to proliferate and differentiate, forming colonies of specific blood cells. Synthetic forms are being tested for their ability to reduce the toxic effects of chemotherapy. Abbreviation: **CSF.**

colophon (ˈkɒləˌfɒn, -fən) NOUN 1 a publisher's emblem on a book. 2 (formerly) an inscription at the end of a book showing the title, printer, date, etc.
▷**HISTORY** C17: via Late Latin, from Greek *kolophōn* a finishing stroke

colophony (kɒˈlɒfənɪ) NOUN another name for **rosin** (sense 1).
▷**HISTORY** C14: from Latin *Colophōnia rēsina* resin from Colophon

coloquintida (ˌkɒləˈkwɪntɪdə) NOUN another name for **colocynth.**
▷**HISTORY** C14: from Medieval Latin, from *colocynthid-* COLOCYNTH

color (ˈkʌlə) NOUN, VERB the US spelling of **colour.**
▸ˈ**colorable** ADJECTIVE ▸ˈ**colorer** NOUN ▸ˈ**colorful** ADJECTIVE ▸ˈ**coloring** NOUN ▸ˈ**colorist** NOUN ▸ˈ**colorless** ADJECTIVE

Colorado (ˌkɒləˈrɑːdəʊ) NOUN 1 a state of the central US: consists of the Great Plains in the east and the Rockies in the west; drained chiefly by the Colorado, Arkansas, South Platte, and Rio Grande Rivers. Capital: Denver. Pop.: 4 301 261 (2000). Area: 269 998 sq. km (104 247 sq. miles). Abbreviations: **Colo.,** (with zip code) **CO.** 2 a river in SW North America, rising in the Rocky Mountains and flowing southwest to the Gulf of California: famous for the 1600 km (1000 miles) of canyons along its course. Length: about 2320 km (1440 miles). 3 a river in central Texas, flowing southeast to the Gulf of Mexico. Length: about 1450 km (900 miles). 4 a river in central Argentina, flowing southeast to the Atlantic. Length: about 850 km (530 miles).
▷**HISTORY** Spanish, literally: red, from Latin *colōrātus* coloured, tinted red; see COLOUR

Colorado beetle NOUN a black-and-yellow beetle, *Leptinotarsa decemlineata,* that is a serious pest of potatoes, feeding on the leaves: family *Chrysomelidae.* Also called: **potato beetle.**

Colorado Desert NOUN an arid region of SE California and NW Mexico, West of the Colorado River. Area: over 5000 sq. km (2000 sq. miles).

Colorado ruby NOUN a fire-red form of garnet found in Colorado and other parts of North America.

Colorado Springs NOUN a city and resort in central Colorado. Pop.: 360 890 (2000).

Colorado topaz NOUN 1 a tawny-coloured form of topaz found in Colorado. 2 quartz of a similar colour.

colorant (ˈkʌlərənt) NOUN any substance that imparts colour, such as a pigment, dye, or ink; colouring matter.

coloration *or* **colouration** (ˌkʌləˈreɪʃən) NOUN 1 arrangement of colour and tones; colouring. 2 the colouring or markings of insects, birds, etc. See also **apatetic, aposematic, cryptic.** 3 unwanted extraneous variations in the frequency response of a loudspeaker or listening environment.

coloratura (ˌkɒlərəˈtʊərə) *or* **colorature** (ˈkɒlərəˌtjʊə) NOUN *Music* 1 **a** (in 18th- and 19th-century arias) a florid virtuoso passage. **b** (*as modifier*): *a coloratura aria.* 2 Also called: **coloratura soprano.** a lyric soprano who specializes in such music.
▷**HISTORY** C19: from obsolete Italian, literally: colouring, from Latin *colōrāre* to COLOUR

colorectal (ˌkəʊləʊˈrɛktᵊl) ADJECTIVE of or relating to the colon and rectum.

colorific (ˌkʌləˈrɪfɪk) ADJECTIVE producing, imparting, or relating to colour.

colorimeter (ˌkʌləˈrɪmɪtə) NOUN 1 Also called: **tintometer.** an apparatus for determining the concentration of a solution of a coloured substance by comparing the intensity of its colour with that

of a standard solution or with standard colour slides. [2] any apparatus for measuring the quality of a colour by comparison with standard colours or combinations of colours.
▸**colorimetric** (ˌkʌlərɪˈmɛtrɪk) *or* ˌ**coloriˈmetrical** ADJECTIVE ▸ˌ**coloriˈmetrically** ADVERB ▸ˌ**colorˈimetry** NOUN

Colossae (kəˈlɒsiː) NOUN an ancient city in SW Phrygia in Asia Minor: seat of an early Christian Church.

colossal (kəˈlɒsəl) ADJECTIVE [1] of immense size; huge; gigantic. [2] (in figure sculpture) approximately twice life-size. Compare **heroic** (sense 7). [3] Also: **giant.** *Architect* of or relating to the order of columns and pilasters that extend more than one storey in a façade.
▸**coˈlossally** ADVERB

colosseum (ˌkɒləˈsɪəm) NOUN a variant spelling of **coliseum.**

Colosseum (ˌkɒləˈsɪəm) NOUN an amphitheatre in Rome built about 75–80 A.D.

Colossian (kəˈlɒʃən) NOUN [1] a native or inhabitant of Colossae. [2] *New Testament* any of the Christians of Colossae to whom St. Paul's Epistle was addressed.

Colossians (kəˈlɒʃənz) NOUN (*functioning as singular*) a book of the New Testament (in full **The Epistle of Paul the Apostle to the Colossians**).

colossus (kəˈlɒsəs) NOUN, *plural* **-si** (-saɪ) *or* **-suses.** something very large, esp a statue.
▷HISTORY C14: from Latin, from Greek *kolossos*

Colossus of Rhodes NOUN a giant bronze statue of Apollo built on Rhodes in about 292–280 B.C.; destroyed by an earthquake in 225 B.C.; one of the Seven Wonders of the World.

colostomy (kəˈlɒstəmɪ) NOUN, *plural* **-mies.** the surgical formation of an opening from the colon onto the surface of the body, which functions as an anus.

colostrum (kəˈlɒstrəm) NOUN the thin milky secretion from the nipples that precedes and follows true lactation. It consists largely of serum and white blood cells.
▷HISTORY C16: from Latin, of obscure origin
▸**coˈlostral** ADJECTIVE

colotomy (kəˈlɒtəmɪ) NOUN, *plural* **-mies.** a colonic incision.

colour *or US* **color** (ˈkʌlə) NOUN [1] **a** an attribute of things that results from the light they reflect, transmit, or emit in so far as this light causes a visual sensation that depends on its wavelengths. **b** the aspect of visual perception by which an observer recognizes this attribute. **c** the quality of the light producing this aspect of visual perception. **d** (*as modifier*): *colour vision.* [2] Also called: **chromatic colour. a** a colour, such as red or green, that possesses hue, as opposed to achromatic colours such as white or black. **b** (*as modifier*): *a colour television; a colour film.* Compare **black-and-white** (sense 2). [3] a substance, such as a dye, pigment, or paint, that imparts colour to something. [4] **a** the skin complexion of a person, esp as determined by his race. **b** (*as modifier*): *colour prejudice; colour problem.* [5] the use of all the hues in painting as distinct from composition, form, and light and shade. [6] the quantity and quality of ink used in a printing process. [7] the distinctive tone of a musical sound; timbre. [8] vividness, authenticity, or individuality: *period colour.* [9] semblance or pretext (esp in the phrases **take on a different colour, under colour of**). [10] *US* a precious mineral particle, esp gold, found in auriferous gravel. [11] *Physics* one of three characteristics of quarks, designated red, blue, or green, but having no relationship with the physical sensation. ◆ VERB [12] to give or apply colour to (something). [13] (*tr*) to give a convincing or plausible appearance to (something, esp to that which is spoken or recounted): *to colour an alibi.* [14] (*tr*) to influence or distort (something, esp a report or opinion): *anger coloured her judgment.* [15] (*intr*; often foll by *up*) to become red in the face, esp when embarrassed or annoyed. [16] (*intr*) (esp of ripening fruit) to change hue. ◆ See also **colours.**
▷HISTORY C13: from Old French *colour* from Latin *color* tint, hue

colourable (ˈkʌlərəbəl) ADJECTIVE [1] capable of being coloured. [2] appearing to be true; plausible: *a colourable excuse.* [3] pretended; feigned: *colourable affection.*
▸ˌ**colouraˈbility** *or* ˈ**colourableness** NOUN ▸ˈ**colourably** ADVERB

colour bar NOUN discrimination against people of a different race, esp as practised by Whites against Blacks.

colour-blind ADJECTIVE [1] of or relating to any defect in the normal ability to distinguish certain colours. See **deuteranopia, protanopia, tritanopia.** [2] not discriminating on grounds of skin colour or ethnic origin.
▸**colour blindness** NOUN

colour code NOUN a system of easily distinguishable colours, as for the identification of electrical wires or resistors.

colour commentator NOUN a sports celebrity who works as part of a commentary team.

colour contrast NOUN *Psychol* the change in the appearance of a colour surrounded by another colour; for example, grey looks bluish if surrounded by yellow.

coloured (ˈkʌləd) ADJECTIVE [1] possessing colour. [2] having a strong element of fiction or fantasy; distorted (esp in the phrase **highly coloured**).

Coloured (ˈkʌləd) NOUN, *plural* **Coloureds** *or* **Coloured.** [1] an individual who is not a White person, esp a Black person. [2] Also called: **Cape Coloured.** (in South Africa) a person of racially mixed parentage or descent. ◆ ADJECTIVE [3] designating or relating to a Coloured person or Coloured people: *a Coloured gentleman.*

> **Language note** The use of *Coloured* to refer to a person who is not White can be offensive and should be avoided.

colourfast (ˈkʌləˌfɑːst) ADJECTIVE (of a fabric) having a colour that does not run or change when washed or worn.
▸ˈ**colourˌfastness** NOUN

colour filter NOUN *Photog* a thin layer of coloured gelatine, glass, etc., that transmits light of certain colours or wavelengths but considerably reduces the transmission of others.

colourful (ˈkʌləfʊl) ADJECTIVE [1] having intense colour or richly varied colours. [2] vivid, rich, or distinctive in character.
▸ˈ**colourfully** ADVERB ▸ˈ**colourfulness** NOUN

colour guard NOUN a military guard in a parade, ceremony, etc., that carries and escorts the flag or regimental colours.

colour index NOUN [1] *Astronomy* the difference between the apparent magnitude of a star measured in one standard waveband and in a longer standard waveband, indicating its colour and temperature. [2] *Geology* the sum of the dark or coloured minerals of a rock, expressed as a percentage of the total minerals. [3] *Chem, physics* a systematic arrangement of colours according to their hue, saturation, and brightness.

colouring (ˈkʌlərɪŋ) NOUN [1] the process or art of applying colour. [2] anything used to give colour, such as dye, paint, etc. [3] appearance with regard to shade and colour. [4] arrangements of colours and tones, as in the markings of birds and animals. [5] the colour of a person's features or complexion. [6] a false or misleading appearance.

colourist (ˈkʌlərɪst) NOUN [1] a person who uses colour, esp an artist. [2] a person who colours photographs, esp black-and-white ones.
▸ˌ**colourˈistic** ADJECTIVE

colourize, colourise, *or US* **colorize** (ˈkʌləˌraɪz) VERB (*tr*) to add colour electronically to (an old black-and-white film).
▸ˌ**colouriˈzation,** ˌ**colouriˈsation,** *or US* ˌ**coloriˈzation** NOUN

colourless (ˈkʌləlɪs) ADJECTIVE [1] without colour. [2] lacking in interest: *a colourless individual.* [3] grey or pallid in tone or hue. [4] without prejudice; neutral.
▸ˈ**colourlessly** ADVERB ▸ˈ**colourlessness** NOUN

colour line NOUN the social separation of racial groups within a community (esp in the phrase **to cross the colour line**).

colourman (ˈkʌləmən) NOUN, *plural* **-men.** a person who deals in paints.

colour phase NOUN [1] a seasonal change in the coloration of some animals. [2] an abnormal variation in the coloration shown by a group of animals within a species.

colourpoint cat (ˈkʌləˌpɔɪnt) NOUN a cat with increased pigmentation of cooler points of the body, such as ears, feet, tail, nose, and scrotum (in males). US name: **Himalayan cat.**

colour-reversal NOUN (*modifier*) *Photog* (of film or photographic paper) designed to produce a positive image directly from a positive subject.

colours (ˈkʌləz) PLURAL NOUN [1] **a** the flag that indicates nationality. **b** *Military* the ceremony of hoisting or lowering the colours. [2] a pair of silk flags borne by a military unit, esp British, comprising the **Queen's Colour** showing the unit's crest, and the **Regimental Colour** showing the crest and battle honours. [3] true nature or character (esp in the phrase **show one's colours**). [4] a distinguishing badge or flag, as of an academic institution. [5] *Sport Brit* a badge or other symbol denoting membership of a team, esp at a school or college. [6] *Informal* a distinguishing embroidered patch denoting membership of a motorcycle gang. [7] **nail one's colours to the mast. a** to refuse to admit defeat. **b** to declare openly one's opinions or allegiances.

colour scheme NOUN a planned combination or juxtaposition of colours, as in interior decorating.

colour separation NOUN *Printing* the division of a coloured original into cyan, magenta, yellow, and black so that plates may be made for print reproduction. Separation may be achieved by electronic scanning or by photographic techniques using filters to isolate each colour.

colour separation overlay NOUN another term for **chromakey.**

colour sergeant NOUN a sergeant who carries the regimental, battalion, or national colours, as in a colour guard.

colour subcarrier (ˈsʌbˌkærɪə) NOUN a component of a colour television signal on which is modulated the colour or chrominance information.

colour supplement NOUN *Brit* an illustrated magazine accompanying a newspaper, esp a Sunday newspaper.

colour temperature NOUN *Physics* the temperature of a black-body radiator at which it would emit radiation of the same chromaticity as the light under consideration.

colourwash (ˈkʌləˌwɒʃ) NOUN [1] a coloured distemper. ◆ VERB (*tr*) [2] to paint with colourwash.

colourway (ˈkʌləˌweɪ) NOUN one of several different combinations of colours in which a given pattern is printed on fabrics, wallpapers, etc.

coloury *or* **colory** (ˈkʌlərɪ) ADJECTIVE possessing colour.

-colous ADJECTIVE COMBINING FORM inhabiting or living on: *arenicolous.*
▷HISTORY from Latin *-cola* inhabitant + -OUS; related to *colere* to inhabit

colpitis (kɒlˈpaɪtɪs) NOUN *Pathol* another name for **vaginitis.**
▷HISTORY C19: from Greek *kolpos* bosom, womb, vagina + -ITIS

colpo- *or before a vowel* **colp-** COMBINING FORM indicating the vagina: *colpitis; colpotomy.*
▷HISTORY from Greek *kolpos* womb

colporteur (ˈkɒlˌpɔːtə; *French* kɔlpɔrtœr) NOUN a hawker of books, esp bibles.
▷HISTORY C18: from French, from *colporter,* probably from Old French *comporter* to carry (see COMPORT); influenced through folk etymology by *porter à col* to carry on one's neck
▸ˈ**colˌportage** NOUN

colposcope (ˈkɒlpəˌskəʊp) NOUN an instrument for examining the uterine cervix, esp for early signs of cancer.
▷HISTORY C20: from COLPO- + -SCOPE

colpotomy (kɒlˈpɒtəmɪ) NOUN, *plural* **-mies.** a surgical incision into the wall of the vagina.
▷HISTORY C20: from COLPO- + -TOMY

colt (kəʊlt) NOUN [1] a male horse or pony under the age of four. [2] an awkward or inexperienced young person. [3] *Sport* **a** a young and inexperienced player. **b** a member of a junior team.
▷HISTORY Old English *colt* young ass, of obscure origin; compare Swedish dialect *kult* young animal, boy

Colt (kəʊlt) NOUN *Trademark* a type of revolver, pistol, etc.
▷HISTORY C19: named after Samuel *Colt* (1814–62), American inventor

coltan ('kɒlˌtæn) a metallic ore found esp in the E Congo, consisting of columbite and tantulite and used as a source of tantulum.
▷HISTORY C20: from COLUMBITE + TANTULITE

colter ('kəʊltə) NOUN a variant spelling (esp US) of **coulter.**

coltish ('kəʊltɪʃ) ADJECTIVE [1] inexperienced; unruly. [2] playful and lively.
▸'**coltishly** ADVERB ▸'**coltishness** NOUN

coltsfoot ('kəʊltsˌfʊt) NOUN, *plural* **-foots**. a European plant, *Tussilago farfara,* with yellow daisy-like flowers and heart-shaped leaves: a common weed: family *Asteraceae* (composites).

colubrid ('kɒljubrɪd) NOUN [1] any snake of the family *Colubridae,* including many harmless snakes, such as the grass snake and whip snakes, and some venomous types. ◆ ADJECTIVE [2] of, relating to, or belonging to the *Colubridae.*
▷HISTORY C19: from New Latin *Colubridae,* from Latin *coluber* snake

colubrine ('kɒljuˌbraɪn, -brɪn) ADJECTIVE [1] of or resembling a snake. [2] of, relating to, or belonging to the *Colubrinae,* a subfamily of harmless colubrid snakes.
▷HISTORY C16: from Latin *colubrīnus,* from *coluber* snake

colugo (kə'lu:gəʊ) NOUN, *plural* **-gos**. another name for **flying lemur.**
▷HISTORY from a native word in Malaya

Columba (kə'lʌmbə) NOUN, *Latin genitive* **Columbae** (kə'lʌmbi:), as in *Alpha Columbae.* a small constellation in the S hemisphere south of Orion.
▷HISTORY Latin, literally: dove

columbarium (ˌkɒləm'bɛərɪəm) NOUN, *plural* **-ia** (-ɪə). [1] another name for a **dovecote.** [2] a vault having niches for funeral urns. [3] a hole in a wall into which a beam is inserted.
▷HISTORY C18: from Latin, from *columba* dove

Columbia[1] (kə'lʌmbɪə) NOUN [1] a river in NW North America, rising in the Rocky Mountains and flowing through British Columbia, then west to the Pacific. Length: about 1930 km (1200 miles). [2] a city in central South Carolina, on the Congaree River: the state capital. Pop.: 116 278 (2000).

Columbia[2] (kə'lʌmbɪə) NOUN the first test vehicle of the NASA space shuttle fleet to prove the possibility of routine access to space for scientific and commercial ventures.

Columbian (kə'lʌmbɪən) ADJECTIVE [1] of or relating to the United States. [2] relating to Christopher Columbus (Spanish name *Cristóbal Colón,* Italian name *Cristoforo Colombo.*; 1451–1506), Italian navigator and explorer in the service of Spain, who discovered the New World (1492). ◆ NOUN [3] a size of printer's type, approximately equal to 16 point; two-line Brevier.

columbic (kə'lʌmbɪk) ADJECTIVE another word for **niobic.**

columbine[1] ('kɒləmˌbaɪn) NOUN any plant of the ranunculaceous genus *Aquilegia,* having purple, blue, yellow, or red flowers with five spurred petals. Also called: **aquilegia.**
▷HISTORY C13: from Medieval Latin *columbīna herba* dovelike plant, from Latin *columbīnus* dovelike, from the resemblance of the flower to a group of doves

columbine[2] ('kɒləmˌbaɪn) ADJECTIVE of, relating to, or resembling a dove.
▷HISTORY C14: from Old French *colombin,* from Latin *columbīnus* dovelike, from *columba* dove

Columbine ('kɒləmˌbaɪn) NOUN [1] (originally) the character of a servant girl in commedia dell'arte. [2] (later) the sweetheart of Harlequin in English pantomime.

columbite (kə'lʌmbaɪt) NOUN a black mineral consisting of a niobium oxide of iron and manganese in orthorhombic crystalline form: occurs in coarse granite, often with tantalite, and is an ore of niobium Formula: (Fe, Mn)$(Nb)_2O_6$. Also called: **niobite.**
▷HISTORY C19: from COLUMBIUM + -ITE[1]

columbium (kə'lʌmbɪəm) NOUN the former name of **niobium.**
▷HISTORY C19: from New Latin, from *Columbia,* the United States of America

columbous (kə'lʌmbəs) ADJECTIVE another word for **niobous.**

Columbus (kə'lʌmbəs) NOUN [1] a city in central Ohio: the state capital. Pop.: 711 470 (2000). [2] a city in W Georgia, on the Chattahoochee River. Pop.: 185 781 (2000).

Columbus Day NOUN Oct. 12, a legal holiday in most states of the US: the date of Columbus' landing in the West Indies (Caribbean) in 1492.

columella (ˌkɒlju'mɛlə) NOUN, *plural* **-lae** (-li:). [1] *Biology* **a** the central part of the spore-producing body of some fungi and mosses. **b** any similar columnar structure. [2] Also called: **columella auris** ('ɔ:rɪs). a small rodlike bone in the middle ear of frogs, reptiles, and birds that transmits sound to the inner ear: homologous to the mammalian stapes.
▷HISTORY C16: from Latin: diminutive of *columna* COLUMN
▸ˌ**colu'mellar** ADJECTIVE

column ('kɒləm) NOUN [1] an upright post or pillar usually having a cylindrical shaft, a base, and a capital. [2] **a** a form or structure in the shape of a column: *a column of air.* **b** a monument. [3] a row, line, or file, as of people in a queue. [4] *Military* a narrow formation in which individuals or units follow one behind the other. [5] *Journalism* **a** any of two or more vertical sections of type on a printed page, esp on a newspaper page. **b** a regular article or feature in a paper: *the fashion column.* [6] a vertical array of numbers or mathematical terms. [7] *Botany* a long structure in a flower, such as that of an orchid, consisting of the united stamens and style. [8] *Anatomy, zoology* any elongated structure, such as a tract of grey matter in the spinal cord or the stalk of a crinoid.
▷HISTORY C15: from Latin *columna,* from *columen* top, peak; related to Latin *collis* hill
▸**columnar** (kə'lʌmnə) ADJECTIVE ▸'**columned** *or* **columnated** ('kɒləmˌneɪtɪd) ADJECTIVE

columniation (kəˌlʌmnɪ'eɪʃən) NOUN the arrangement of architectural columns.

column inch NOUN a unit of measurement for advertising space, one inch deep and one column wide.

columnist ('kɒləmɪst, -əmnɪst) NOUN a journalist who writes a regular feature in a newspaper: *a gossip columnist.*

colure (kə'lʊə, 'kəʊlʊə) NOUN either of two great circles on the celestial sphere, one of which passes through the celestial poles and the equinoxes and the other through the poles and the solstices.
▷HISTORY C16: from Late Latin *colūrī* (plural), from Greek *kolourai* cut short, dock-tailed, from *kolos* docked + *oura* tail; so called because the view of the lower part is curtailed

Colwyn Bay ('kɒlwɪn) NOUN a town and resort in N Wales, in Conwy county borough. Pop.: 29 883 (1991).

coly ('kəʊlɪ) NOUN, *plural* **-lies**. any of the arboreal birds of the genus *Colius,* family *Coliidae,* and order *Coliiformes,* of southern Africa. They have a soft hairlike plumage, crested head, and very long tail. Also called: **mousebird.**
▷HISTORY C19: from New Latin *colius,* probably from Greek *kolios* woodpecker

colza ('kɒlzə) NOUN another name for **rape**[2].
▷HISTORY C18: via French (Walloon) *kolzat* from Dutch *koolzaad,* from *kool* cabbage, COLE + *zaad* SEED

colza oil NOUN the oil obtained from the seeds of the rape plant and used in making lubricants and synthetic rubber.

com AN INTERNET DOMAIN NAME FOR a commercial company.

COM (kɒm) NOUN **a** a process in which a computer output is converted direct to microfiche or film, esp 35 or 16 millimetre film. **b** (*as modifier*): *a COM machine.*
▷HISTORY (*C*)omputer (*O*)utput on (*M*)icrofilm

Com. ABBREVIATION FOR: [1] Commander. [2] committee. [3] Commodore.

com- *or* **con-** PREFIX together; with; jointly: *commingle.*
▷HISTORY from Latin *com-;* related to *cum* with. In compound words of Latin origin, *com-* becomes *col-* and *cor-* before *l* and *r, co-* before *gn, h,* and most vowels, and *con-* before consonants other than *b, p,* and*m.* Although its sense in compounds of Latin derivation is often obscured, it means: together, with, etc. (*combine, compile*); similar (*conform*); extremely, completely (*consecrate*)

coma[1] ('kəʊmə) NOUN, *plural* **-mas**. a state of unconsciousness from which a person cannot be aroused, caused by injury to the head, rupture of cerebral blood vessels, narcotics, poisons, etc.
▷HISTORY C17: from medical Latin, from Greek *kōma* heavy sleep; related to Greek *koitē* bed, perhaps to Middle Irish *cuma* grief

coma[2] ('kəʊmə) NOUN, *plural* **-mae** (-mi:). [1] *Astronomy* the luminous cloud surrounding the frozen solid nucleus in the head of a comet, formed by vaporization of part of the nucleus when the comet is close to the sun. [2] *Botany* **a** a tuft of hairs attached to the seed coat of some seeds. **b** the terminal crown of leaves of palms and moss stems. [3] *Optics* a type of lens defect characterized by the formation of a diffuse pear-shaped image from a point object.
▷HISTORY C17: from Latin: hair of the head, from Greek *komē*
▸'**comal** ADJECTIVE

Coma Berenices ('kəʊmə ˌbɛrɪ'naɪsi:z) NOUN, *Latin genitive* **Comae Berenices** ('kəʊmi:). a faint constellation in the N hemisphere between Ursa Major and Boötes containing the **Coma Cluster** a cluster of approximately 1000 galaxies, at a mean distance of 300 million light years.
▷HISTORY from Latin, literally: Berenice's hair, named after *Berenice* (died 221 B.C.), consort of Ptolemy III

Comanche (kə'mæntʃɪ) NOUN [1] (*plural* **-ches** *or* **-che**) a member of a North American Indian people, formerly ranging from the River Platte to the Mexican border, now living in Oklahoma. [2] the language of this people, belonging to the Shoshonean subfamily of the Uto-Aztecan family.

Comanchean (kə'mæntʃɪən) (in North America) ◆ ADJECTIVE [1] of or relating to the early part of the Cretaceous system and period. ◆ NOUN [2] the strata and time corresponding to the early Cretaceous.

comate ('kəʊmeɪt) ADJECTIVE *Botany* [1] having tufts of hair. [2] having or relating to a coma.
▷HISTORY C17: from Latin *comātus,* from *coma* hair

comatose ('kəʊməˌtəʊs, -ˌtəʊz) ADJECTIVE [1] in a state of coma. [2] torpid; lethargic.
▸'**comaˌtosely** ADVERB

comatulid (kə'mætjʊlɪd) *or* **comatula** NOUN, *plural* **-lids** *or* **-lae** (-li:). any of a group of crinoid echinoderms, including the feather stars, in which the adults are free-swimming.
▷HISTORY C19: from New Latin *Comatulidae,* from *Comatula* type genus, from Latin *comātus* hairy

comb (kəʊm) NOUN [1] a toothed device of metal, plastic, wood, etc., used for disentangling or arranging hair. [2] a tool or machine that separates, cleans, and straightens wool, cotton, etc. [3] *Austral and NZ* the fixed cutter on a sheep-shearing machine. [4] anything resembling a toothed comb in form or function. [5] the fleshy deeply serrated outgrowth on the top of the heads of certain birds, esp the domestic fowl. [6] anything resembling the comb of a bird. [7] a currycomb. [8] a honeycomb. [9] the row of fused cilia in a ctenophore. [10] **go over** (*or* **through**) **with a fine-tooth**(**ed**) **comb.** to examine very thoroughly. ◆ VERB [11] (*tr*) to use a comb on. [12] (when *tr,* often foll by *through*) to search or inspect with great care: *the police combed the woods.* ◆ See also **comb out.**
▷HISTORY Old English *camb;* related to Old Norse *kambr,* Old High German *camb*

combat NOUN ('kɒmbæt, -bət, 'kʌm-) [1] a fight, conflict, or struggle. [2] **a** an action fought between two military forces. **b** (*as modifier*): *a combat jacket.* [3] **single combat.** a fight between two individuals; duel. [4] **close** *or* **hand-to-hand combat.** fighting at close quarters. ◆ VERB (kəm'bæt, 'kɒmbæt, 'kʌm-) **-bats, -bating, -bated.** [5] (*tr*) to fight or defy. [6] (*intr;* often foll by *with* or *against*) to struggle or strive (against); be in conflict (with): *to combat against disease.*
▷HISTORY C16: from French, from Old French *combattre,* from Vulgar Latin *combattere* (unattested), from Latin *com-* with + *battuere* to beat, hit
▸**com'batable** ADJECTIVE ▸**com'bater** NOUN

combatant ('kɒmbətᵊnt, 'kʌm-) NOUN [1] a person

or group engaged in or prepared for a fight, struggle, or dispute. ◆ ADJECTIVE [2] engaged in or ready for combat.

combat fatigue NOUN another term for **battle fatigue.**

combative ('kɒmbətɪv, 'kʌm-) ADJECTIVE eager or ready to fight, argue, etc.; aggressive.
▶ **'combatively** ADVERB ▶ **'combativeness** NOUN

combat trousers *or* **combats** ('kɒmbæts, -bəts, 'kʌm-) PLURAL NOUN loose casual trousers with large pockets on the legs.

combe *or* **comb** (ku:m) NOUN variant spellings of **coomb.**

comber ('kəʊmə) NOUN [1] a person, tool, or machine that combs wool, flax, etc. [2] a long curling wave; roller.

combination (ˌkɒmbɪ'neɪʃən) NOUN [1] the act of combining or state of being combined. [2] a union of separate parts, qualities, etc. [3] an alliance of people or parties; group having a common purpose. [4] **a** the set of numbers that opens a combination lock. **b** the mechanism of this type of lock. [5] *Brit* a motorcycle with a sidecar attached. [6] *Maths* **a** an arrangement of the numbers, terms, etc., of a set into specified groups without regard to order in the group: *the combinations of a, b, and c, taken two at a time, are ab, bc, ac.* **b** a group formed in this way. The number of combinations of *n* objects taken *r* at a time is $n!/[(n-r)!r!]$. Symbol: $\binom{n}{r}$ or $_nC_r$. Compare **permutation** (sense 1). [7] the chemical reaction of two or more compounds, usually to form one other compound. [8] *Chess* a tactical manoeuvre involving a sequence of moves and more than one piece. ◆ See also **combinations.**
▶ **ˌcombi'national** ADJECTIVE

combination lock NOUN a type of lock that can only be opened when a set of dials releasing the tumblers of the lock are turned to show a specific sequence of numbers.

combination room NOUN *Brit* (at Cambridge University) a common room.

combinations (ˌkɒmbɪ'neɪʃənz) PLURAL NOUN *Brit* a one-piece woollen undergarment with long sleeves and legs. Often shortened to **combs** *or* **coms.** US and Canadian term: **union suit.**

combination tone NOUN another term for **resultant tone.**

combinative ('kɒmbɪˌneɪtɪv, -nətɪv), **combinatorial** (ˌkɒmbɪnə'tɔ:rɪəl), *or* **combinatory** ('kɒmbɪnətərɪ, -trɪ) ADJECTIVE [1] resulting from being, tending to be, or able to be joined or mixed together. [2] *Linguistics* (of a sound change) occurring only in specific contexts or as a result of some other factor, such as change of stress within a word. Compare **isolative** (sense 1).

combinatorial analysis NOUN the branch of mathematics concerned with the theory of enumeration, or combinations and permutations, in order to solve problems about the possibility of constructing arrangements of objects which satisfy specified conditions. Also called: **combinatorics** (ˌkɒmbɪnə'tɔ:rɪks).

combine VERB (kəm'baɪn) [1] to integrate or cause to be integrated; join together. [2] to unite or cause to unite to form a chemical compound. [3] *Agriculture* to harvest (crops) with a combine harvester. ◆ NOUN ('kɒmbaɪn) [4] *Agriculture* short for **combine harvester.** [5] an association of enterprises, esp in order to gain a monopoly of a market. [6] an association of business corporations, political parties, sporting clubs, etc., for a common purpose.
▷**HISTORY** C15: from Late Latin *combīnāre,* from Latin *com-* together + *bīnī* two by two
▶ **com'binable** ADJECTIVE ▶ **comˌbina'bility** NOUN
▶ **com'biner** NOUN

combine harvester ('kɒmbaɪn) NOUN a machine that simultaneously cuts, threshes, and cleans a standing crop of grain.

combings ('kəʊmɪŋz) PLURAL NOUN [1] the loose hair, wool, etc., removed by combing, esp that of animals. [2] the unwanted loose short fibres removed in combing cotton, etc.

combining form NOUN a linguistic element that occurs only as part of a compound word, such as *anthropo-* in *anthropology.*

comb jelly NOUN another name for a **ctenophore.**

combo ('kɒmbəʊ) NOUN, *plural* **-bos.** [1] a small group of musicians, esp of jazz musicians. [2] *Informal* any combination.

comb out VERB *(tr, adverb)* [1] to remove (tangles or knots) from (the hair) with a comb. [2] to isolate and remove for a purpose. [3] to survey carefully; examine systematically. ◆ NOUN **comb-out.** [4] an act of combing out.

comb-over NOUN a hairstyle in which long strands of hair from the side of the head are swept over the scalp to cover a bald patch.

combust (kəm'bʌst) ADJECTIVE [1] *Astrology* (of a star or planet) invisible for a period between 24 and 30 days each year due to its proximity to the sun. ◆ VERB [2] *Chem* to burn.

combustible (kəm'bʌstəbᵊl) ADJECTIVE [1] capable of igniting and burning. [2] easily annoyed; excitable. ◆ NOUN [3] a combustible substance.
▶ **comˌbusti'bility** *or* **com'bustibleness** NOUN
▶ **com'bustibly** ADVERB

combustion (kəm'bʌstʃən) NOUN [1] the process of burning. [2] any process in which a substance reacts with oxygen to produce a significant rise in temperature and the emission of light. [3] a chemical process in which two compounds, such as sodium and chlorine, react together to produce heat and light. [4] a process in which a compound reacts slowly with oxygen to produce little heat and no light.
▷**HISTORY** C15: from Old French, from Latin *combūrere* to burn up, from *com-* (intensive) + *ūrere* to burn
▶ **com'bustive** NOUN, ADJECTIVE

combustion chamber NOUN an enclosed space in which combustion takes place, such as the space above the piston in the cylinder head of an internal-combustion engine or the chambers in a gas turbine or rocket engine in which fuel and oxidant burn.

combustor (kəm'bʌstə) NOUN the combustion system of a jet engine or ramjet, comprising the combustion chamber, the fuel injection apparatus, and the igniter.

comdg *Military* ABBREVIATION FOR commanding.

Comdr *Military* ABBREVIATION FOR Commander.

Comdt *Military* ABBREVIATION FOR Commandant.

come (kʌm) VERB **comes, coming, came, come.** *(mainly intr)* [1] to move towards a specified person or place: *come to my desk.* [2] to arrive by movement or by making progress. [3] to become perceptible: *light came into the sky.* [4] to occur in the course of time: *Christmas comes but once a year.* [5] to exist or occur at a specific point in a series: *your turn comes next.* [6] to happen as a result: *no good will come of this.* [7] to originate or be derived: *good may come of evil.* [8] to occur to the mind: *the truth suddenly came to me.* [9] to extend or reach: *she comes up to my shoulder.* [10] to be produced or offered: *that dress comes in red only.* [11] to arrive at or be brought into a particular state or condition: *you will soon come to grief; the new timetable comes into effect on Monday.* [12] (foll by *from*) to be or have been a resident or native (of): *I come from London.* [13] to become: *your wishes will come true.* [14] *(tr; takes an infinitive)* to be given awareness: *I came to realize its enormous value.* [15] (of grain) to germinate. [16] *Slang* to have an orgasm. [17] *(tr) Brit informal* to play the part of: *don't come the fine gentleman with me.* [18] *(tr) Brit informal* to cause or produce: *don't come that nonsense again.* [19] *(subjunctive use)* when (a specified time or event has arrived or begun): *she'll be sixteen come Sunday; come the revolution, you'll be the first to go.* [20] **as...as they come.** the most characteristic example of a class or type. [21] **come again?** *Informal* what did you say? [22] **come and.** *(imperative or dependent imperative)* to move towards a particular person or thing or accompany a person with some specified purpose: *come and see what I've found.* [23] **come clean.** *Informal* to make a revelation or confession. [24] **come good.** *Informal* to recover and perform well after a bad start or setback. [25] **come it.** *Slang* **a** to pretend; act a part. **b** to exaggerate. **c** (often foll by *over*) to try to impose (upon). **d** to divulge a secret; inform the police. [26] **come to light.** to be revealed. [27] **come to light with.** *Austral and NZ informal* to find or produce. [28] **come to pass.** *Archaic* to take place. [29] **how come?** *Informal* what is the reason that? ◆ INTERJECTION [30] an exclamation expressing annoyance, irritation, etc.: *come now!; come come!* ◆ NOUN [31] *Taboo slang* semen. ◆ See also **come about, come across, come along, come at, come away, comeback, come between, come by, comedown, come forward, come from, come in, come into, come of, come off, come on, come out, come over, come round, come through, come to, come up, come upon.**
▷**HISTORY** Old English *cuman;* related to Old Norse *koma,* Gothic *qiman,* Old High German *queman* to come, Sanskrit *gámati* he goes

come about VERB *(intr, adverb)* [1] to take place; happen. [2] *Nautical* to change tacks.

come across VERB *(intr)* [1] *(preposition)* to meet or find by accident. [2] *(adverb)* (of a person or his words) to communicate the intended meaning or impression. [3] (often foll by *with*) to provide what is expected.

come-all-ye (kə'mɔ:ljə, -ji:) NOUN a street ballad or folk song.
▷**HISTORY** C19: from the common opening words *come all ye (young maidens, loyal heroes, etc.)...*

come along VERB [1] *(intr, adverb)* to progress: *how's your French coming along?* [2] **come along! a** hurry up! **b** make an effort! ◆ NOUN **come-along.** [3] *US and Canadian informal* a hand tool consisting of a ratchet lever, cable, and pulleys, used for moving heavy loads by hand or for tightening wire.

come at VERB *(intr, preposition)* [1] to discover or reach (facts, the truth, etc.). [2] to attack (a person): *he came at me with an axe.* [3] *Austral slang* to agree to do (something). [4] *(usually used with a negative) Austral slang* to stomach, tolerate: *I couldn't come at it.* [5] *Austral slang* to presume; impose: *what are you coming at?*

come-at-able ADJECTIVE an informal expression for **accessible.**

come away VERB *(intr, adverb)* [1] to become detached. [2] (foll by *with*) to leave (with).

comeback ('kʌmˌbæk) NOUN *Informal* [1] a return to a former position, status, etc. [2] a return or response, esp recriminatory. [3] a quick reply; retort. ◆ VERB **come back.** *(intr, adverb)* [4] to return. [5] to become fashionable again. [6] to reply after a period of consideration: *I'll come back to you on that next week.* [7] *US and Canadian* to argue back; retort. [8] **come back to (someone).** (of something forgotten) to return to (someone's) memory.

come between VERB *(intr, preposition)* to cause the estrangement or separation of (two people): *nothing could come between the two lovers.*

come by VERB *(intr, preposition)* to find or obtain (a thing), esp accidentally: *do you ever come by any old books?*

Comecon ('kɒmɪˌkɒn) NOUN (formerly) an association of Soviet-oriented Communist nations, founded in 1949 to coordinate economic development, etc.; it was disbanded in 1991 when free-market policies were adopted by its members. Also: **CMEA.**
▷**HISTORY** C20 *Co(uncil for) M(utual) Econ(omic Assistance)*

comedian (kə'mi:dɪən) NOUN [1] an entertainer who specializes in jokes, comic skits, etc. [2] an actor in comedy. [3] an amusing or entertaining person: sometimes used ironically.

comedic (kə'mi:dɪk) ADJECTIVE of or relating to comedy.

Comédie Française *French* (kɔmedi frɑ̃sɛz) NOUN the French national theatre, founded in Paris in 1680.

comedienne (kəˌmi:dɪ'ɛn) NOUN a female comedian.

comedo ('kɒmɪˌdəʊ) NOUN, *plural* **comedos** *or* **comedones** (ˌkɒmɪ'dəʊni:z). *Pathol* the technical name for **blackhead.**
▷**HISTORY** C19: from New Latin, from Latin: glutton, from *comedere* to eat up, from *com-* (intensive) + *edere* to eat

comedown ('kʌmˌdaʊn) NOUN [1] a decline in position, status, or prosperity. [2] *Informal* a disappointment. [3] *Slang* a depressed or unexcited state. ◆ VERB **come down.** *(intr, adverb)* [4] to come to a place regarded as lower. [5] to lose status, wealth, etc. (esp in the phrase **to come down in the world**). [6] to reach a decision: *the report came down in favour of a pay increase.* [7] (often foll by *to*) to be handed down or acquired by tradition or inheritance. [8] *Brit* to leave college or university. [9] (foll by *with*) to succumb (to illness or disease). [10] (foll by *on*) to rebuke or criticize harshly. [11] (foll by *to*) to amount in essence (to): *it comes down to two choices.* [12] *Slang* to lose the effects of a drug and return to a normal or more normal state. [13] *Austral informal* (of a river) to flow in flood.

comedy ('kɒmɪdɪ) NOUN, *plural* **-dies.** [1] a dramatic or other work of light and amusing character. [2] the genre of drama represented by works of this type. [3] (in classical literature) a play in which the main characters and motive triumph over adversity. [4] the humorous aspect of life or of events. [5] an amusing event or sequence of events. [6] humour or comic style: *the comedy of Chaplin.*
▷HISTORY C14: from Old French *comédie,* from Latin *cōmoedia,* from Greek *kōmōidia,* from *kōmos* village festival + *aeidein* to sing

comedy of manners NOUN [1] a comedy dealing with the way of life and foibles of a social group. [2] the genre represented by works of this type.

come forward VERB (*intr, adverb*) [1] to offer one's services; volunteer. [2] to present oneself.

come from VERB (*intr, preposition*) [1] to be or have been a resident or native (of): *Ernst comes from Geneva.* [2] to originate from or derive from: *chocolate comes from the cacao tree; the word filibuster comes from the Dutch word for pirate.* [3] **where is someone is coming from.** *Informal* the reasons for someone's behaviour, opinions, or comments: *I can understand where you're coming from.*

come-hither ADJECTIVE (*usually prenominal*) *Informal* alluring; seductive: *a come-hither look.*

come in VERB (*intr, mainly adverb*) [1] to enter, used in the imperative when admitting a person. [2] to prove to be: *it came in useful.* [3] to become fashionable or seasonable. [4] *Cricket* to begin an innings. [5] *Sport* to finish a race (in a certain position). [6] (of a politician or political party) to win an election. [7] *Radio, television* to be received: *news is coming in of a big fire in Glasgow.* [8] (of money) to be received as income. [9] to play a role; advance one's interests: *where do I come in?* [10] (foll by *for*) to be the object of: *the Chancellor came in for a lot of criticism in the Commons.*

come into VERB (*intr, preposition*) [1] to enter. [2] to inherit. [3] **come into one's own. a** to become fulfilled: *she really came into her own when she got divorced.* **b** to receive what is due to one.

comely ('kʌmlɪ) ADJECTIVE **-lier, -liest.** good-looking; attractive.
▷HISTORY Old English *cȳmlīc* beautiful; related to Old High German *cūmi* frail, Middle High German *komlīche* suitably
▸ **'comeliness** NOUN

come of VERB (*intr, preposition*) [1] to be descended from. [2] to result from: *nothing came of his experiments.*

come off VERB (*intr, mainly adverb*) [1] (*also preposition*) to fall (from), losing one's balance. [2] to become detached or be capable of being detached. [3] (*preposition*) to be removed from (a price, tax, etc.): *will anything come off income tax in the budget?* [4] (*copula*) to emerge from or as if from a trial or contest: *he came off the winner.* [5] *Informal* to take place or happen. [6] *Informal* to have the intended effect; succeed: *his jokes did not come off.* [7] *Slang* to have an orgasm. [8] **come off it!** *Informal* stop trying to fool me!

come on VERB (*intr, mainly adverb*) [1] (of power, a water supply, etc.) to become available; start running or functioning. [2] to make or show progress; develop: *my plants are coming on nicely.* [3] to advance, esp in battle. [4] to begin: *she felt a cold coming on; a new bowler has come on.* [5] *Theatre* to make an entrance on stage. [6] to be considered, esp in a court of law. [7] (*preposition*) See **come upon.** [8] **come on! a** hurry up! **b** cheer up! pull yourself together! **c** make an effort! **d** don't exaggerate! stick to the facts! [9] to attempt to give a specified impression: *he came on like a hard man.* [10] **come on strong.** to make a forceful or exaggerated impression. [11] **come on to.** *Informal* to make sexual advances to. ◆ NOUN **come-on.** [12] *Informal* anything that serves as a lure or enticement.

come out VERB (*intr, adverb*) [1] to be made public or revealed: *the news of her death came out last week.* [2] to make a debut in society or on stage. [3] **a** Also: **come out of the closet.** to declare openly that one is a homosexual. **b** to reveal or declare any habit or practice formerly concealed. [4] *Chiefly Brit* to go on strike. [5] to declare oneself: *the government came out in favour of scrapping the project.* [6] to be shown visibly or clearly: *you came out very well in the photos.* [7] to yield a satisfactory solution: *these sums just won't come out.* [8] to be published: *the paper comes out on Fridays.* [9] (foll by *in*) to become covered with: *you're coming out in spots.* [10] (foll by *with*) to speak or declare openly: *you can rely on him to come out with the facts.*

come over VERB (*intr*) [1] (*adverb*) (of a person or his words) to communicate the intended meaning or impression: *he came over very well.* [2] (*adverb*) to change allegiances: *some people came over to our side in the war.* [3] *Informal* to undergo or feel a particular sensation: *I came over funny.* ◆ NOUN **comeover.** [4] (in the Isle of Man) a person who has come over from the mainland of Britain to settle.

comer ('kʌmə) NOUN [1] (*in combination*) a person who comes: *all-comers; newcomers.* [2] *Informal* a potential success.

come round *or* **around** VERB (*intr, adverb*) [1] to be restored to life or consciousness. [2] to change or modify one's mind or opinion.

comestible (kə'mɛstɪbᵊl) NOUN [1] (*usually plural*) food. ◆ ADJECTIVE [2] a rare word for **edible.**
▷HISTORY C15: from Late Latin *comestibilis,* from *comedere* to eat up; see COMEDO

comet ('kɒmɪt) NOUN a celestial body that travels around the sun, usually in a highly elliptical orbit: thought to consist of a solid frozen nucleus part of which vaporizes on approaching the sun to form a gaseous luminous coma and a long luminous tail.
▷HISTORY C13: from Old French *comète,* from Latin *comēta,* from Greek *komētēs* long-haired, from *komē* hair
▸ **'cometary** *or* **cometic** (kɒ'mɛtɪk) ADJECTIVE

come through VERB (*intr*) [1] (*adverb*) to emerge successfully. [2] (*preposition*) to survive (an illness, setback, etc.).

come to VERB (*intr*) [1] (*adverb* or *prep. and reflexive*) to regain consciousness or return to one's normal state. [2] (*adverb*) *Nautical* to slow a vessel or bring her to a stop. [3] (*preposition*) to amount to (a sum of money): *your bill comes to four pounds.* [4] (*preposition*) to arrive at (a certain state): *what is the world coming to?*

come up VERB (*intr, adverb*) [1] to come to a place regarded as higher. [2] (of the sun) to rise. [3] to begin: *a wind came up.* [4] to be regurgitated or vomited. [5] to present itself or be discussed: *that question will come up again.* [6] *Brit* to begin a term, esp one's first term, at a college or university. [7] to appear from out of the ground: *my beans have come up early this year.* [8] *Informal* to win: *have your premium bonds ever come up?* [9] **come up against.** to be faced with; come into conflict or competition with. [10] **come up to.** to equal or meet a standard: *that just doesn't come up to scratch.* [11] **come up with.** to produce or find: *she always comes up with the right answer.*

come upon VERB (*intr, preposition*) to meet or encounter unexpectedly: *I came upon an old friend in the street today.*

comeuppance (ˌkʌm'ʌpəns) NOUN *Informal* just retribution.
▷HISTORY C19: from *come up* (in the sense: to appear before a judge or court for judgment)

comfit ('kʌmfɪt, 'kɒm-) NOUN a sugar-coated sweet containing a nut or seed.
▷HISTORY C15: from Old French, from Latin *confectum* something prepared, from *conficere* to produce; see CONFECT

comfort ('kʌmfət) NOUN [1] a state of ease or well-being. [2] relief from affliction, grief, etc. [3] a person, thing, or event that brings solace or ease. [4] *Obsolete* support. [5] (*usually plural*) something that affords physical ease and relaxation. ◆ VERB (*tr*) [6] to ease the pain of; soothe; cheer. [7] to bring physical ease to.
▷HISTORY C13: from Old French *confort,* from Late Latin *confortāre* to strengthen very much, from Latin *con-* (intensive) + *fortis* strong
▸ **'comforting** ADJECTIVE ▸ **'comfortingly** ADVERB
▸ **'comfortless** ADJECTIVE ▸ **'comfortlessly** ADVERB
▸ **'comfortlessness** NOUN

comfortable ('kʌmftəbᵊl, 'kʌmfətəbᵊl) ADJECTIVE [1] giving comfort or physical relief. [2] at ease. [3] free from affliction or pain. [4] (of a person or situation) relaxing. [5] *Informal* having adequate income. [6] *Informal* (of income) adequate to provide comfort.
▸ **'comfortableness** NOUN ▸ **'comfortably** ADVERB

comforter ('kʌmfətə) NOUN [1] a person or thing that comforts. [2] *Chiefly Brit* a woollen scarf. [3] a baby's dummy. [4] *US* a quilted bed covering.

Comforter ('kʌmfətə) NOUN *Christianity* an epithet of the Holy Spirit.
▷HISTORY C14: translation of Latin *consolātor,* representing Greek *paraklētos;* see PARACLETE

comfort station NOUN *US* a public lavatory and rest room.

comfort stop NOUN *Informal* a short break on a journey to allow travellers to go to the toilet.

comfort zone NOUN a situation or position in which a person feels secure, comfortable, or in control: *encouraging people to work outside their comfort zone.*

comfrey ('kʌmfrɪ) NOUN any hairy Eurasian boraginaceous plant of the genus *Symphytum,* having blue, purplish-pink, or white flowers.
▷HISTORY C15: from Old French *cunfirie,* from Latin *conferva* water plant; see CONFERVA

comfy ('kʌmfɪ) ADJECTIVE **-fier, -fiest.** *Informal* short for **comfortable.**

comic ('kɒmɪk) ADJECTIVE [1] of, relating to, characterized by, or characteristic of comedy. [2] (*prenominal*) acting in, writing, or composing comedy: *a comic writer.* [3] humorous; funny. ◆ NOUN [4] a person who is comic, esp a comic actor; comedian. [5] a book or magazine containing comic strips. [6] (*usually plural*) *Chiefly US and Canadian* comic strips in newspapers, etc.
▷HISTORY C16: from Latin *cōmicus,* from Greek *kōmikos* relating to COMEDY

comical ('kɒmɪkᵊl) ADJECTIVE [1] causing laughter. [2] ludicrous; laughable.
▸ **'comically** ADVERB ▸ **'comicalness** NOUN

comic opera NOUN a play largely set to music, employing comic effects or situations. See also **opéra bouffe, opera buffa.**

comic strip NOUN a sequence of drawings in a newspaper, magazine, etc., relating a humorous story or an adventure. Also called: **strip cartoon.**

Cominform ('kɒmɪnˌfɔːm) NOUN short for **Communist Information Bureau**: established 1947 to exchange information among nine European Communist parties and coordinate their activities; dissolved in 1956.

coming ('kʌmɪŋ) ADJECTIVE [1] (*prenominal*) (of time, events, etc.) approaching or next: *this coming Thursday.* [2] promising (esp in the phrase **up and coming**). [3] of future importance: *this is the coming thing.* [4] **coming up!** *Informal* an expression used to announce that a meal is about to be served. [5] **have it coming to one.** *Informal* to deserve what one is about to suffer. [6] **not know whether one is coming or going.** to be totally confused. ◆ NOUN [7] arrival or approach. [8] (*often capital*) the return of Christ in glory. See also **Second Coming.**

Comintern *or* **Komintern** ('kɒmɪnˌtɜːn) NOUN short for **Communist International**: an international Communist organization founded by Lenin in Moscow in 1919 and dissolved in 1943; it degenerated under Stalin into an instrument of Soviet politics. Also called: **Third International.**

comitia (kə'mɪʃɪə) NOUN an ancient Roman assembly that elected officials and exercised judicial and legislative authority.
▷HISTORY C17: from Latin *comitium* assembly, from *com-* together + *īre* to go
▸ **comitial** (kə'mɪʃəl) ADJECTIVE

comity ('kɒmɪtɪ) NOUN, *plural* **-ties.** [1] mutual civility; courtesy. [2] short for **comity of nations.** [3] the policy whereby one religious denomination refrains from proselytizing the members of another.
▷HISTORY C16: from Latin *cōmitās,* from *cōmis* affable, obliging, of uncertain origin

comity of nations NOUN the friendly recognition accorded by one nation to the laws and usages of another.

comma ('kɒmə) NOUN [1] the punctuation mark, indicating a slight pause in the spoken sentence and used where there is a listing of items or to

separate a nonrestrictive clause or phrase from a main clause. [2] *Music* a minute interval. [3] short for **comma butterfly**.
▷HISTORY C16: from Latin, from Greek *komma* clause, from *koptein*to cut

comma bacillus NOUN a comma-shaped bacterium, *Vibrio comma,* that causes cholera in man: family *Spirillaceae.*

comma butterfly NOUN an orange-brown European vanessid butterfly, *Polygonia c-album,* with a white comma-shaped mark on the underside of each hind wing.

command (kə'mɑ:nd) VERB [1] (when *tr, may take a clause as object or an infinitive*) to order, require, or compel. [2] to have or be in control or authority over (a person, situation, etc.). [3] (*tr*) to have knowledge or use of: *he commands the language.* [4] (*tr*) to receive as due or because of merit: *his nature commands respect.* [5] to dominate (a view, etc.) as from a height. ◆ NOUN [6] an order; mandate. [7] the act of commanding. [8] the power or right to command. [9] the exercise of the power to command. [10] ability or knowledge; control: *a command of French.* [11] *Chiefly military* the jurisdiction of a commander. [12] a military unit or units commanding a specific area or function, as in the RAF. [13] *Brit* **a** an invitation from the monarch. **b** (*as modifier*): *a command performance.* [14] *Computing* a word or phrase that can be selected from a menu or typed after a prompt in order to carry out an action.
▷HISTORY C13: from Old French *commander,* from Latin *com-* (intensive) + *mandāre* to entrust, enjoin, command

Command (kə'mɑ:nd) NOUN any of the three main branches of the Canadian military forces.

commandant ('kɒmən,dænt, -,dɑ:nt) NOUN an officer commanding a place, group, or establishment.

command economy NOUN an economy in which business activities and the allocation of resources are determined by government order rather than market forces. Also called: **planned economy.**

commandeer (,kɒmən'dɪə) VERB (*tr*) [1] to seize for public or military use. [2] to seize arbitrarily.
▷HISTORY C19: from Afrikaans *kommandeer,* from French *commander* to COMMAND

commander (kə'mɑ:ndə) NOUN [1] an officer in command of a military formation or operation. [2] a naval commissioned rank junior to captain but senior to lieutenant commander. [3] the second in command of larger British warships. [4] someone who holds authority. [5] a high-ranking member of some knightly or fraternal orders. [6] an officer responsible for a district of the Metropolitan Police in London. [7] *History* the administrator of a house, priory, or landed estate of a medieval religious order.
▸**com'mander,ship** NOUN

commander in chief NOUN, *plural* **commanders in chief.** [1] the officer holding supreme command of the forces in an area or operation. [2] the officer holding command of a major subdivision of one military service.

command guidance NOUN a method of controlling a missile during flight by transmitting information to it.

commanding (kə'mɑ:ndɪŋ) ADJECTIVE (*usually prenominal*) [1] being in command. [2] having the air of authority: *a commanding voice.* [3] (of a position, situation, etc.) exerting control. [4] (of a height, viewpoint, etc.) overlooking; advantageous.
▸**com'mandingly** ADVERB

commanding officer NOUN an officer in command of a military unit.

command language NOUN *Computing* the language used to access a computer system.

commandment (kə'mɑ:ndmənt) NOUN [1] a divine command, esp one of the Ten Commandments of the Old Testament. [2] *Literary* any command.

command module NOUN the cone-shaped module used as the living quarters in an Apollo spacecraft and functioning as the splashdown vehicle.

commando (kə'mɑ:ndəʊ) NOUN, *plural* **-dos** *or* **-does.** [1] **a** an amphibious military unit trained for raiding. **b** a member of such a unit. [2] the basic unit of the Royal Marine Corps. [3] (originally) an armed force raised by Boers during the Boer War. [4] (*modifier*) denoting or relating to a commando or force of commandos: *a commando raid; a commando unit.*
▷HISTORY C19: from Afrikaans *kommando,* from Dutch *commando* command, from French *commander* to COMMAND

commando operation NOUN *Surgery* a major operation for treatment of cancer of the head and neck, involving removal of many facial structures and subsequent surgical reconstruction.

command paper NOUN (in Britain) a government document that is presented to Parliament, in theory by royal command. See also **green paper, white paper.**

command performance NOUN a performance of a play, opera, etc., at the request of a ruler or of royalty.

command post NOUN *Military* the position from which a unit commander and his staff exercise command.

commeasure (kə'mɛʒə) VERB (*tr*) to coincide with in degree, extent, quality, etc.
▸**com'measurable** ADJECTIVE

commedia dell'arte (*Italian* kom'me:dia del'larte) NOUN a form of popular comedy developed in Italy during the 16th to 18th centuries, with stock characters such as Punchinello, Harlequin, and Columbine, in situations improvised from a plot outline.
▷HISTORY Italian, literally: comedy of art

comme il faut *French* (kɔm il fo) correct or correctly.

commemorate (kə'mɛmə,reɪt) VERB (*tr*) to honour or keep alive the memory of.
▷HISTORY C16: from Latin *commemorāre* be mindful of, from *com-* (intensive) + *memorāre* to remind, from *memor* mindful
▸**com'memorative** *or* **com'memoratory** ADJECTIVE
▸**com'memoratively** ADVERB ▸**com'memo,rator** NOUN

commemoration (kə,mɛmə'reɪʃən) NOUN [1] the act or an instance of commemorating. [2] a ceremony or service in memory of a person or event.
▸**com,memo'rational** ADJECTIVE

commence (kə'mɛns) VERB to start or begin; come or cause to come into being, operation, etc.
▷HISTORY C14: from Old French *comencer,* from Vulgar Latin *cominitiāre* (unattested), from Latin *com-* (intensive) + *initiāre* to begin, from *initium* a beginning
▸**com'mencer** NOUN

commencement (kə'mɛnsmənt) NOUN [1] the beginning; start. [2] **a** *US and Canadian* a ceremony for the presentation of awards at secondary schools. **b** *US* a ceremony for the conferment of academic degrees.

commend (kə'mɛnd) VERB (*tr*) [1] to present or represent as being worthy of regard, confidence, kindness, etc.; recommend. [2] to give in charge; entrust. [3] to express a good opinion of; praise. [4] to give the regards of: *commend me to your aunt.*
▷HISTORY C14: from Latin *commendāre* to commit to someone's care, from *com-* (intensive) + *mandāre* to entrust
▸**com'mendable** ADJECTIVE ▸**com'mendableness** NOUN
▸**com'mendably** ADVERB ▸**com'mendatory** ADJECTIVE

commendam (kə'mɛndæm) NOUN [1] the temporary holding of an ecclesiastical benefice. [2] a benefice so held.
▷HISTORY C16: from Medieval Latin phrase *dare in commendam* to give in trust, from *commenda* trust, back formation from Latin *commendāre* to entrust, COMMEND

commendation (,kɒmɛn'deɪʃən) NOUN [1] the act or an instance of commending; praise. [2] an award.

commensal (kə'mɛnsəl) ADJECTIVE [1] (of two different species of plant or animal) living in close association, such that one species benefits without harming the other. [2] *Rare* of or relating to eating together, esp at the same table: *commensal pleasures.* ◆ NOUN [3] a commensal plant or animal. [4] *Rare* a companion at table.
▷HISTORY C14: from Medieval Latin *commensālis,* from Latin *com-* together + *mensa* table
▸**com'mensalism** NOUN ▸**commensality** (,kɒmɛn'sælɪtɪ) NOUN ▸**com'mensally** ADVERB

commensurable (kə'mɛnsərəbəl, -ʃə-) ADJECTIVE [1] *Maths* **a** having a common factor. **b** having units of the same dimensions and being related by whole numbers: *hours and minutes are commensurable.* [2] well-proportioned; proportionate.
▸**com,mensura'bility** NOUN ▸**com'mensurably** ADVERB

commensurate (kə'mɛnsərɪt, -ʃə-) ADJECTIVE [1] having the same extent or duration. [2] corresponding in degree, amount, or size; proportionate. [3] able to be measured by a common standard; commensurable.
▷HISTORY C17: from Late Latin *commēnsūrātus,* from Latin *com-* same + *mēnsūrāre* to MEASURE
▸**com'mensurately** ADVERB ▸**com'mensurateness** NOUN
▸**commensuration** (kə,mɛnsə'reɪʃən, -ʃə-) NOUN

comment ('kɒmɛnt) NOUN [1] a remark, criticism, or observation. [2] talk or gossip. [3] a note explaining or criticizing a passage in a text. [4] explanatory or critical matter added to a text. ◆ VERB [5] (when *intr,* often foll by *on;* when *tr,* takes a clause as object) to remark or express an opinion. [6] (*intr*) to write notes explaining or criticizing a text.
▷HISTORY C15: from Latin *commentum* invention, from *comminiscī* to contrive, related to *mens* mind
▸**'commenter** NOUN

commentariat (,kɒmən'tɛərɪæt) NOUN the journalists and broadcasters who analyse and comment on current affairs.
▷HISTORY C20: from COMMENTATOR + PROLETARIAT

commentary ('kɒməntərɪ, -trɪ) NOUN, *plural* **-taries.** [1] an explanatory series of notes or comments. [2] a spoken accompaniment to a broadcast, film, etc., esp of a sporting event. [3] an explanatory essay or treatise on a text. [4] (*usually plural*) a personal record of events or facts: *the commentaries of Caesar.*
▸**commentarial** (,kɒmən'tɛərɪəl) ADJECTIVE

commentate ('kɒmən,teɪt) VERB [1] (*intr*) to serve as a commentator. [2] (*tr*) *US* to make a commentary on (a text, event, etc.).

> **Language note** The verb *commentate,* derived from *commentator,* is sometimes used as a synonym for *comment on* or *provide a commentary for.* It is not yet fully accepted as standard, though widespread in sports reporting and journalism.

commentator ('kɒmən,teɪtə) NOUN [1] a person who provides a spoken commentary for a broadcast, film, etc., esp of a sporting event. [2] a person who writes notes on a text, event, etc.

commerce ('kɒmɜ:s) NOUN [1] the activity embracing all forms of the purchase and sale of goods and services. [2] social relations and exchange, esp of opinions, attitudes, etc.
▷HISTORY C16: from Latin *commercium* trade, from *commercārī,* from *mercārī* to trade, from *merx* merchandise

commercial (kə'mɜ:ʃəl) ADJECTIVE [1] of, connected with, or engaged in commerce; mercantile. [2] sponsored or paid for by an advertiser: *commercial television.* [3] having profit as the main aim: *commercial music.* [4] (of goods, chemicals, etc.) of unrefined quality or presentation and produced in bulk for use in industry. ◆ NOUN [5] a commercially sponsored advertisement on radio or television.
▸**commerciality** (kə,mɜ:ʃɪ'ælɪtɪ) NOUN ▸**com'mercially** ADVERB

commercial art NOUN graphic art for commercial uses such as advertising, packaging, etc.
▸**commercial artist** NOUN

commercial bank NOUN a bank primarily engaged in making short-term loans from funds deposited in current accounts.

commercial break NOUN an interruption in a radio or television programme for the broadcasting of advertisements.

commercial college NOUN a college providing tuition in commercial skills, such as shorthand and book-keeping.

commercialism (kə'mɜ:ʃə,lɪzəm) NOUN [1] the spirit, principles, or procedure of commerce. [2] exclusive or inappropriate emphasis on profit.

▶**com'mercialist** NOUN ▶**com,mercial'istic** ADJECTIVE

commercialize *or* **commercialise** (kə'mɜːʃə,laɪz) VERB *(tr)* [1] to make commercial in aim, methods, or character. [2] to exploit for profit, esp at the expense of quality.
▶**com,commerciali'zation** *or* **com,merciali'sation** NOUN

commercial paper NOUN a short-term negotiable document, such as a bill of exchange, promissory note, etc., calling for the transference of a specified sum of money at a designated date.

commercial traveller NOUN another name for a **travelling salesman.**

commercial vehicle NOUN a vehicle for carrying goods or (less commonly) passengers.

commère ('kɒmɛə; *French* kɔmɛr) NOUN a female compere.
▷HISTORY French, literally: godmother, from COM- + *mère* mother; see COMPERE

commie *or* **commy** ('kɒmɪ) NOUN, *plural* **-mies,** ADJECTIVE *Informal and derogatory* short for **communist.**

commination (,kɒmɪ'neɪʃən) NOUN [1] the act or an instance of threatening punishment or vengeance. [2] *Church of England* a recital of prayers, including a list of God's judgments against sinners, in the office for Ash Wednesday.
▷HISTORY C15: from Latin *comminātiō,* from *comminārī* to menace, from *com-* (intensive) + *minārī* to threaten
▶**comminatory** ('kɒmɪnətərɪ, -trɪ) ADJECTIVE

commingle (kɒ'mɪŋgᵊl) VERB to mix or be mixed; blend.

comminute ('kɒmɪ,njuːt) VERB [1] to break (a bone) into several small fragments. [2] to divide (property) into small lots. [3] *(tr)* to pulverize.
▷HISTORY C17: from Latin *comminuere,* from *com-* (intensive) + *minuere* to reduce; related to MINOR
▶**,commi'nution** NOUN

comminuted fracture NOUN a fracture in which the bone is splintered or fragmented.

commis ('kɒmɪs, 'kɒmɪ) NOUN, *plural* **-mis.** [1] an agent or deputy. ◆ ADJECTIVE [2] (of a waiter or chef) apprentice.
▷HISTORY C16 (meaning: deputy): from French, from *commettre* to employ, COMMIT

commiserate (kə'mɪzə,reɪt) VERB (when *intr,* usually foll by *with*) to feel or express sympathy or compassion (for).
▷HISTORY C17: from Latin *commiserārī,* from *com-* together + *miserārī* to bewail, pity, from *miser* wretched
▶**com'miserable** ADJECTIVE ▶**com,miser'ation** NOUN
▶**com'miserative** ADJECTIVE ▶**com'miseratively** ADVERB
▶**com'miser,ator** NOUN

commissaire (,kɒmɪ'sɛə) NOUN (in professional cycle racing) a referee who travels in an open-topped car with the riders to witness any infringement of the rules.
▷HISTORY from French: see COMMISSARY

commissar ('kɒmɪ,sɑː, ,kɒmɪ'sɑː) NOUN (in the former Soviet Union) [1] Also called: **political commissar.** an official of the Communist Party responsible for political education, esp in a military unit. [2] Also called: **People's Commissar.** (before 1946) the head of a government department. Now called: **minister.**
▷HISTORY C20: from Russian *kommissar,* from German, from Medieval Latin *commissārius* COMMISSARY

commissariat (,kɒmɪ'sɛərɪət) NOUN [1] (in the former Soviet Union) a government department before 1946. Now called: **ministry.** [2] **a** a military department in charge of food supplies, equipment, etc. **b** the offices of such a department. [3] food supplies.
▷HISTORY C17: from New Latin *commissāriātus,* from Medieval Latin *commissārius* COMMISSARY

commissary ('kɒmɪsərɪ) NOUN, *plural* **-saries.** [1] *US* a shop supplying food or equipment, as in a military camp. [2] *US army* an officer responsible for supplies and food. [3] *US* a snack bar or restaurant in a film studio. [4] a representative or deputy, esp an official representative of a bishop.
▷HISTORY C14: from Medieval Latin *commissārius* official in charge, from Latin *committere* to entrust, COMMIT
▶**commissarial** (,kɒmɪ'sɛərɪəl) ADJECTIVE
▶**'commissary,ship** NOUN

commission (kə'mɪʃən) NOUN [1] a duty or task committed to a person or group to perform. [2] authority to undertake or perform certain duties or functions. [3] a document granting such authority. [4] *Military* **a** a document conferring a rank on an officer. **b** the rank or authority thereby granted. [5] a group of people charged with certain duties: *a commission of inquiry.* [6] a government agency or board empowered to exercise administrative, judicial, or legislative authority. See also **Royal Commission.** [7] **a** the authority given to a person or organization to act as an agent to a principal in commercial transactions. **b** the fee allotted to an agent for services rendered. [8] the state of being charged with specific duties or responsibilities. [9] the act of committing a sin, crime, etc. [10] something, esp a sin, crime, etc., that is committed. [11] good working condition or (esp of a ship) active service (esp in the phrases **in** *or* **into commission, out of commission**). [12] *US* the head of a department of municipal government. ◆ VERB [13] *(tr)* to grant authority to; charge with a duty or task. [14] *(tr) Military* to confer a rank on or authorize an action by. [15] *(tr)* to equip and test (a ship) for active service. [16] to make or become operative or operable: *the plant is due to commission next year.* [17] *(tr)* to place an order for (something): *to commission a portrait.*
▷HISTORY C14: from Old French, from Latin *commissiō* a bringing together, from *committere* to COMMIT
▶**com'missional** *or* **com'missionary** ADJECTIVE

commissionaire (kə,mɪʃə'nɛə) NOUN *Chiefly Brit* a uniformed doorman at a hotel, theatre, etc.
▷HISTORY C18: from French, from COMMISSION

commissioned officer NOUN a military officer holding a commission, such as Second Lieutenant in the British Army, Acting Sub-Lieutenant in the Royal Navy, Pilot Officer in the Royal Air Force, and officers of all ranks senior to these.

commissioner (kə'mɪʃənə) NOUN [1] a person authorized to perform certain tasks or endowed with certain powers. [2] *Government* **a** any of several types of civil servant. **b** an ombudsman. ◆ See also **Health Service Commissioner, Parliamentary Commissioner.** [3] a member of a commission.
▶**com'missioner,ship** NOUN

Commissioner for Local Administration NOUN (in Britain) the official name for a local ombudsman who investigates personal complaints of maladministration by police, water, or local authorities, referred through a local-government councillor, and who can require the offending authority to state its intention to make redress.

commissioner for oaths NOUN a solicitor authorized to authenticate oaths on sworn statements.

Commission for Racial Equality NOUN (in Britain) a body of fourteen members appointed by the Home Secretary under the Race Relations Act 1976 to enforce the provisions of that Act. Abbreviation: **CRE.**

commission plan NOUN (in the US) a system of municipal government that combines legislative and executive authority in a commission of five or six elected members.

commissure ('kɒmɪ,sjʊə) NOUN [1] a band of tissue linking two parts or organs, such as the nervous tissue connecting the right and left sides of the brain in vertebrates. [2] any of various joints between parts, as between the carpels, leaf lobes, etc., of a plant.
▷HISTORY C15: from Latin *commissūra* a joining together, from *committere* COMMIT
▶**commissural** (kə'mɪsjʊrəl, ,kɒmɪ'sjʊərəl) ADJECTIVE

commit (kə'mɪt) VERB **-mits, -mitting, -mitted.** *(tr)* [1] to hand over, as for safekeeping; charge; entrust: *to commit a child to the care of its aunt.* [2] **commit to memory.** to learn by heart; memorize. [3] to confine officially or take into custody: *to commit someone to prison.* [4] *(usually passive)* to pledge or align (oneself), as to a particular cause, action, or attitude: *a committed radical.* [5] to order (forces) into action. [6] to perform (a crime, error, etc.); do; perpetrate. [7] to surrender, esp for destruction: *she committed the letter to the fire.* [8] to refer (a bill, etc.) to a committee of a legislature.
▷HISTORY C14: from Latin *committere* to join, from *com-* together + *mittere* to put, send
▶**com'mittable** ADJECTIVE ▶**com'mitter** NOUN

commitment (kə'mɪtmənt) NOUN [1] the act of committing or pledging. [2] the state of being committed or pledged. [3] an obligation, promise, etc. that restricts one's freedom of action. [4] the referral of a bill to a committee or legislature. [5] Also called (esp formerly): **mittimus.** *Law* a written order of a court directing that a person be imprisoned. [6] the official consignment of a person to a mental hospital or prison. [7] commission or perpetration, esp of a crime. [8] a future financial obligation or contingent liability. ◆ Also called (esp for senses 5, 6): **committal** (kə'mɪtᵊl).

commitment fee NOUN a charge made by a bank, in addition to interest, to make a loan available to a potential borrower.

committed facility NOUN an agreement by a bank to provide a customer with funds up to a specified limit at a specified rate of interest.

committee NOUN [1] (kə'mɪtɪ) a group of people chosen or appointed to perform a specified service or function. [2] (,kɒmɪ'tiː) (formerly) a person to whom the care of a mentally incompetent person or his property was entrusted by a court. See also **receiver** (sense 2).
▷HISTORY C15: from *committen* to entrust + -EE

committeeman (kə'mɪtɪmən, -,mæn) NOUN, *plural* **-men.** *Chiefly US* a member of one or more committees.
▶**com'mittee,woman** FEMININE NOUN

Committee of the Whole House NOUN (in Britain) an informal sitting of the House of Commons to discuss and amend a bill.

commix (kɒ'mɪks) VERB a rare word for **mix.**
▷HISTORY C15: back formation from *commixt* mixed together; see MIX
▶**com'mixture** NOUN

commo ('kɒməʊ) NOUN, *plural* **-mos,** ADJECTIVE *Austral slang* short for **communist.**

commode (kə'məʊd) NOUN [1] a piece of furniture, usually highly ornamented, containing drawers or shelves. [2] a bedside table with a cabinet below for a chamber pot or washbasin. [3] a movable piece of furniture, sometimes in the form of a chair, with a hinged flap concealing a chamber pot. [4] a woman's high-tiered headdress of lace, worn in the late 17th century.
▷HISTORY C17: from French, from Latin *commodus* COMMODIOUS

commodification (kə,mɒdɪfɪ'keɪʃən) NOUN the inappropriate treatment of something as if it can be acquired or marketed like other commodities: *the commodification of human life.*

commodious (kə'məʊdɪəs) ADJECTIVE [1] (of buildings, rooms, etc.) large and roomy; spacious. [2] *Archaic* suitable; convenient.
▷HISTORY C15: from Medieval Latin *commodiōsus,* from Latin *commodus* convenient, from *com-* with + *modus* measure
▶**com'modiously** ADVERB ▶**com'modiousness** NOUN

commodity (kə'mɒdɪtɪ) NOUN, *plural* **-ties.** [1] an article of commerce. [2] something of use, advantage, or profit. [3] *Economics* an exchangeable unit of economic wealth, esp a primary product or raw material. [4] *Obsolete* **a** a quantity of goods. **b** convenience or expediency.
▷HISTORY C14: from Old French *commodité,* from Latin *commoditās* suitability, benefit; see COMMODIOUS

commodore ('kɒmə,dɔː) NOUN [1] *Brit* a naval rank junior to rear admiral and senior to captain. [2] the senior captain of a shipping line. [3] the officer in command of a convoy of merchant ships. [4] the senior flag office of a yacht or boat club.
▷HISTORY C17: probably from Dutch *commandeur,* from French, from Old French *commander* to COMMAND

common ('kɒmən) ADJECTIVE [1] belonging to or shared by two or more people: *common property.* [2] belonging to or shared by members of one or more nations or communities; public: *a common culture.* [3] of ordinary standard; average: *common decency.* [4] prevailing; widespread: *common opinion.* [5] widely known or frequently encountered; ordinary: *a common brand of soap.* [6] widely known and notorious: *a common nuisance.* [7] *Derogatory* considered by the speaker to be low-class, vulgar, or coarse: *a common accent.* [8] *(prenominal)* having no

special distinction, rank, or status: *the common man.* **9** *Maths* **a** having a specified relationship with a group of numbers or quantities: *common denominator.* **b** (of a tangent) tangential to two or more circles. **10** *Prosody* (of a syllable) able to be long or short, or (in nonquantitative verse) stressed or unstressed. **11** *Grammar* (in certain languages) denoting or belonging to a gender of nouns, esp one that includes both masculine and feminine referents: *Latin* sacerdos *is common.* **12** *Anatomy* **a** having branches: *the common carotid artery.* **b** serving more than one function: *the common bile duct.* **13** *Christianity* of or relating to the common of the Mass or divine office. **14** **common or garden.** *Informal* ordinary; unexceptional. ◆ NOUN **15** *(sometimes plural)* a tract of open public land, esp one now used as a recreation area. **16** *Law* the right to go onto someone else's property and remove natural products, as by pasturing cattle or fishing (esp in the phrase **right of common**). **17** *Christianity* **a** a form of the proper of the Mass used on festivals that have no special proper of their own. **b** the ordinary of the Mass. **18** *Archaic* the ordinary people; the public, esp those undistinguished by rank or title. **19** **in common.** mutually held or used with another or others. ◆ See also **commons.**
▷HISTORY C13: from Old French *commun,* from Latin *commūnis* general, universal
▸**'commonness** NOUN

commonable ('kɒmənəbᵊl) ADJECTIVE **1** (of land) held in common. **2** *English history* (esp of sheep and cattle) entitled to be pastured on common land.

commonage ('kɒmənɪdʒ) NOUN **1** *Chiefly law* **a** the use of something, esp a pasture, in common with others. **b** the right to such use. **2** the state of being held in common. **3** something held in common, such as land. **4** another word for **commonalty** (sense 1).

Common Agricultural Policy NOUN the full name for **CAP.**

commonality (ˌkɒmə'nælɪtɪ) NOUN, *plural* **-ties. 1** the fact of being common to more than one individual; commonness. **2** another word for **commonalty** (sense 1).

commonalty ('kɒmənəltɪ) NOUN, *plural* **-ties. 1** the ordinary people as distinct from those with authority, rank, or title, esp when considered as a political and social unit or estate of the realm. Compare **third estate. 2** the members of an incorporated society.
▷HISTORY C13: from Old French *comunalte,* from *comunal* communal

common carrier NOUN a person or firm engaged in the business of transporting goods or passengers.

common chord NOUN *Music* a chord consisting of the keynote, a major or minor third, and a perfect fifth: *the notes G, B, and D form the common chord of G major.*

common cold NOUN a mild viral infection of the upper respiratory tract, characterized by sneezing, coughing, watery eyes, nasal congestion, etc.

common denominator NOUN **1** an integer exactly divisible by each denominator of a group of fractions: 1/3, 1/4, and 1/6 have a common denominator of 12. **2** a belief, attribute, etc., held in common by members of a class or group.

common divisor NOUN another name for **common factor.**

Common Entrance NOUN (in Britain) an entrance examination for a public school, usually taken at the age of 13.

commoner ('kɒmənə) NOUN **1** a person who does not belong to the nobility. **2** a person who has a right in or over common land jointly with another or others. **3** *Brit* a student at a university or other institution who is not on a scholarship.

Common Era NOUN another name for **Christian Era.**

common factor NOUN a number or quantity that is a factor of each member of a group of numbers or quantities: *5 is a common factor of 15 and 20.* Also called: **common divisor.**

common fee NOUN (in Australia) the agreed usual charge for any medical service, which determines the amount of reimbursement under the federal health scheme.

common fraction NOUN another name for **simple fraction.**

common good NOUN the part of the property of a Scottish burgh, in the form of land or funds, that is at the disposal of the community.

common ground NOUN an agreed basis, accepted by both or all parties, for identifying issues in an argument.

commonhold ('kɒmənˌhəʊld) NOUN a form of property tenure in which each flat in a multi-occupancy building is individually wholly owned and common areas are jointly owned.

common knowledge NOUN something widely or generally known.

common law NOUN **1** the body of law based on judicial decisions and custom, as distinct from statute law. **2** the law of a state that is of general application, as distinct from regional customs. **3** **common-law.** *(modifier)* denoting a marriage deemed to exist after a couple have cohabited for several years: *common-law marriage; common-law wife.*

common logarithm NOUN a logarithm to the base ten. Usually written log or $\log_{10}$. Compare **natural logarithm.**

commonly ('kɒmənlɪ) ADVERB **1** usually; ordinarily: *he was commonly known as Joe.* **2** *Derogatory* in a coarse or vulgar way: *she dresses commonly.*

Common Market NOUN **the.** an informal name for the **European Economic Community** (now the European Community, part of the wider European Community) and its politics of greater economic cooperation between member states.

common measure NOUN **1** another term for **common time. 2** the usual stanza form of a ballad, consisting of four iambic lines rhyming a b c b or a b a b.

common metre NOUN a stanza form, used esp for hymns, consisting of four lines, two of eight syllables alternating with two of six.

common multiple NOUN an integer or polynomial that is a multiple of each integer or polynomial in a group: *20 is a common multiple of 2, 4, 5, 10.*

common noun NOUN *Grammar* a noun that refers to each member of a whole class sharing the features connoted by the noun, as for example *planet, orange,* and *drum.* Compare **proper noun.**

commonplace ('kɒmənˌpleɪs) ADJECTIVE **1** ordinary; everyday: *commonplace duties.* **2** dull and obvious; trite: *commonplace prose.* ◆ NOUN **3** something dull and trite, esp a remark; platitude; truism. **4** a passage in a book marked for inclusion in a commonplace book, etc. **5** an ordinary or common thing.
▷HISTORY C16: translation of Latin *locus commūnis* argument of wide application, translation of Greek *koinos topos*
▸**'commonˌplaceness** NOUN

commonplace book NOUN a notebook in which quotations, poems, remarks, etc., that catch the owner's attention are entered.

common pleas NOUN short for **Court of Common Pleas.**

common prayer NOUN the liturgy of public services of the Church of England, esp Morning and Evening Prayer.

common room NOUN *Chiefly Brit* a sitting room in schools, colleges, etc., for the relaxation of students or staff.

commons ('kɒmənz) NOUN **1** *(functioning as plural)* people not of noble birth viewed as forming a political order. **2** *(functioning as plural)* the lower classes as contrasted to the ruling classes of society; the commonalty. **3** *(functioning as singular) Brit* a building or hall for dining, recreation, etc., usually attached to a college. **4** *(usually functioning as plural) Brit* food or rations (esp in the phrase **short commons**).

Commons ('kɒmənz) NOUN **the.** See **House of Commons.**

common seal NOUN the official seal of a corporate body.

common sense NOUN **1** plain ordinary good judgment; sound practical sense. ◆ ADJECTIVE **common-sense;** *also* **common-sensical. 2** inspired by or displaying sound practical sense.

common stock NOUN the US name for **ordinary shares.**

common time NOUN *Music* a time signature indicating four crotchet beats to the bar; four-four time. Symbol: C.

commonweal ('kɒmənˌwiːl) NOUN *Archaic* **1** the good of the community. **2** another name for **commonwealth.**

commonwealth ('kɒmənˌwelθ) NOUN **1** the people of a state or nation viewed politically; body politic. **2** a state or nation in which the people possess sovereignty; republic. **3** the body politic organized for the general good. **4** a group of persons united by some common interest. **5** *Obsolete* the general good; public welfare.

Commonwealth ('kɒmənˌwelθ) NOUN **the. 1** Official name: **the Commonwealth of Nations.** an association of sovereign states, most of which are or at some time were ruled by Britain. All member states recognize the reigning British sovereign as **Head of the Commonwealth. 2** **a** the republic that existed in Britain from 1649 to 1660. **b** the part of this period up to 1653, when Cromwell became Protector. **3** the official designation of Australia, four states of the US (Kentucky, Massachusetts, Pennsylvania, and Virginia), and Puerto Rico.

Commonwealth Day NOUN the anniversary of Queen Victoria's birth, May 24, celebrated (now on the second Monday in March) as a holiday in many parts of the Commonwealth. Former name: **Empire Day.**

commonwealth of Independent States NOUN a loose organization of former Soviet republics, excluding the Baltic States, formed in 1991. Abbreviation: **CIS.**

commotion (kə'məʊʃən) NOUN **1** violent disturbance; upheaval. **2** political insurrection; disorder. **3** a confused noise; din.
▷HISTORY C15: from Latin *commōtiō,* from *commovēre* to throw into disorder, from *com-* (intensive) + *movēre* to MOVE
▸**com'motional** ADJECTIVE

commove (kə'muːv) VERB *(tr) Rare* **1** to disturb; stir up. **2** to agitate or excite emotionally.

comms (kɒmz) PLURAL NOUN *Informal* communications.

communal ('kɒmjʊnᵊl) ADJECTIVE **1** belonging or relating to a community as a whole. **2** relating to different groups within a society: *communal strife.* **3** of or relating to a commune or a religious community.
▸**communality** (ˌkɒmjʊ'nælɪtɪ) NOUN ▸**'communally** ADVERB

communal aerial *or* **antenna** NOUN a television or radio receiving aerial from which received signals are distributed by cable to several outlets.

communalism ('kɒmjʊnəˌlɪzəm) NOUN **1** a system or theory of government in which the state is seen as a loose federation of self-governing communities. **2** an electoral system in which ethnic groups vote separately for their own representatives. **3** loyalty to the interests of one's own ethnic group rather than to society as a whole. **4** the practice or advocacy of communal living or ownership.
▸**'communalist** NOUN ▸**ˌcommunal'istic** ADJECTIVE

communalize *or* **communalise** ('kɒmjʊnəˌlaɪz) VERB *(tr)* to render (something) the property of a commune or community.
▸**ˌcommunali'zation** *or* **ˌcommunali'sation** NOUN
▸**'communalˌizer** *or* **'communalˌiser** NOUN

communard ('kɒmjʊˌnɑːd) NOUN a member of a commune.

Communard ('kɒmjʊˌnɑːd) NOUN any person who participated in or supported the Paris Commune formed after the Franco-Prussian War in 1871.
▷HISTORY C19: from French

communautaire *French* (kɔmynotɛr) ADJECTIVE supporting the principles of the European Community (now the European Union).
▷HISTORY literally: community (as modifier)

commune¹ VERB (kə'mjuːn) *(intr; usually foll by with)* **1** to talk or converse intimately. **2** to experience strong emotion or spiritual feelings

(for): *to commune with nature.* ◆ NOUN ('kɒmju:n) [3] intimate conversation; exchange of thoughts; communion.
▷HISTORY C13: from Old French *comuner* to hold in common, from *comun* COMMON

commune[2] (kə'mju:n) VERB (*intr*) *Christianity chiefly US* to partake of Communion.
▷HISTORY C16: back formation from COMMUNION

commune[3] ('kɒmju:n) NOUN [1] a group of families or individuals living together and sharing possessions and responsibilities. [2] any small group of people having common interests or responsibilities. [3] the smallest administrative unit in Belgium, France, Italy, and Switzerland, governed by a mayor and council. [4] the government or inhabitants of a commune. [5] a medieval town enjoying a large degree of autonomy.
▷HISTORY C18: from French, from Medieval Latin *commūnia,* from Latin: things held in common, from *commūnis* COMMON

Commune ('kɒmju:n) NOUN *French history* [1] See **Paris Commune.** [2] a committee that governed Paris during the French Revolution and played a leading role in the Reign of Terror: suppressed 1794.

communicable (kə'mju:nɪkəbᵊl) ADJECTIVE [1] capable of being communicated. [2] (of a disease or its causative agent) capable of being passed on readily.
▸**com,munica'bility** *or* **com'municableness** NOUN
▸**com'municably** ADVERB

communicant (kə'mju:nɪkənt) NOUN [1] *Christianity* a person who receives Communion. [2] a person who communicates or informs. ◆ ADJECTIVE [3] communicating.

communicate (kə'mju:nɪ,keɪt) VERB [1] to impart (knowledge) or exchange (thoughts, feelings, or ideas) by speech, writing, gestures, etc. [2] (*tr;* usually foll by *to*) to allow (a feeling, emotion, etc.) to be sensed (by), willingly or unwillingly; transmit (to): *the dog communicated his fear to the other animals.* [3] (*intr*) to have a sympathetic mutual understanding. [4] (*intr;* usually foll by *with*) to make or have a connecting passage or route; connect. [5] (*tr*) to transmit (a disease); infect. [6] (*intr*) *Christianity* to receive or administer Communion.
▷HISTORY C16: from Latin *commūnicāre* to share, from *commūnis* COMMON
▸**com'muni,cator** NOUN ▸**com'municatory** ADJECTIVE

communicating (kə'mju:nɪ,keɪtɪŋ) ADJECTIVE making or having a direct connection from one room to another: *the suite is made up of three communicating rooms.*

communication (kə,mju:nɪ'keɪʃən) NOUN [1] the act or an instance of communicating; the imparting or exchange of information, ideas, or feelings. [2] something communicated, such as a message, letter, or telephone call. [3] **a** (*usually plural; sometimes functioning as singular*) the study of ways in which human beings communicate, including speech, gesture, telecommunication systems, publishing and broadcasting media, etc. **b** (*as modifier*): *communication theory.* [4] a connecting route, passage, or link. [5] (*plural*) *Military* the system of routes and facilities by which forces, supplies, etc., are moved up to or within an area of operations.

communication cord NOUN *Brit* a cord or chain in a train which may be pulled by a passenger to stop the train in an emergency.

communication interface NOUN an electronic circuit, usually designed to a specific standard, that enables one machine to telecommunicate with another machine.

communications satellite NOUN an artificial satellite used to relay radio, television, and telephone signals around the earth, usually in geostationary orbit.

communicative (kə'mju:nɪkətɪv) ADJECTIVE [1] inclined or able to communicate readily; talkative. [2] of or relating to communication.
▸**com'municatively** ADVERB ▸**com'municativeness** NOUN

communion (kə'mju:njən) NOUN [1] an exchange of thoughts, emotions, etc. [2] possession or sharing in common; participation. [3] (foll by *with*) strong emotional or spiritual feelings (for): *communion with nature.* [4] a religious group or denomination having a common body of beliefs, doctrines, and practices. [5] the spiritual union held by Christians to exist between individual Christians and Christ, their Church, or their fellow Christians.
▷HISTORY C14: from Latin *commūniō* general participation, from *commūnis* COMMON
▸**com'munional** ADJECTIVE ▸**com'munionally** ADVERB

Communion (kə'mju:njən) NOUN *Christianity* [1] the act of participating in the Eucharist. [2] the celebration of the Eucharist, esp the part of the service during which the consecrated elements are received. [3] **a** the consecrated elements of the Eucharist. **b** (*as modifier*): *Communion cup.* ◆ Also called: **Holy Communion.**

communion of saints NOUN *Christianity* the spiritual fellowship of all true Christians, living and dead.

communiqué (kə'mju:nɪ,keɪ) NOUN an official communication or announcement, esp to the press or public.
▷HISTORY C19: from French, from *communiquer* to COMMUNICATE

communism ('kɒmjʊ,nɪzəm) NOUN [1] advocacy of a classless society in which private ownership has been abolished and the means of production and subsistence belong to the community. [2] any social, economic, or political movement or doctrine aimed at achieving such a society. [3] (*usually capital*) a political movement based upon the writings of Karl Marx, the German political philosopher (1818–83), that considers history in terms of class conflict and revolutionary struggle, resulting eventually in the victory of the proletariat and the establishment of a socialist order based on public ownership of the means of production. See also **Marxism, Marxism-Leninism, socialism.** [4] (*usually capital*) a social order or system of government established by a ruling Communist Party, esp in the former Soviet Union. [5] (*often capital*) *Chiefly US* any leftist political activity or thought, esp when considered to be subversive. [6] communal living; communalism.
▷HISTORY C19: from French *communisme,* from *commun* COMMON

communist ('kɒmjʊnɪst) NOUN [1] a supporter of any form of communism. [2] (*often capital*) a supporter of Communism or a Communist movement or state. [3] (*often capital*) a member of a Communist party. [4] a person who practises communal living; communalist. [5] another name for **Communard.** ◆ ADJECTIVE [6] of, characterized by, favouring, or relating to communism; communistic.

Communist China NOUN another name for (the People's Republic of) **China.**

communistic (,kɒmjʊ'nɪstɪk) ADJECTIVE of, characteristic of, or relating to communism.
▸**,commu'nistically** ADVERB

Communist Manifesto NOUN a political pamphlet written by Marx and Engels in 1848: a fundamental statement of Marxist principles.

Communist Party NOUN [1] (in non-Communist countries) a political party advocating Communism. [2] (in Communist countries) the single official party of the state, composed of those who officially espouse Communism.

communitarian (kə,mju:nɪ'tɛərɪən) NOUN [1] a member of a communist community. [2] an advocate of communalism.

community (kə'mju:nɪtɪ) NOUN, *plural* **-ties.** [1] **a** the people living in one locality. **b** the locality in which they live. **c** (*as modifier*): *community spirit.* [2] a group of people having cultural, religious, ethnic, or other characteristics in common: *the Protestant community.* [3] a group of nations having certain interests in common. [4] the public in general; society. [5] common ownership or participation. [6] similarity or agreement: *community of interests.* [7] (in Wales since 1974 and Scotland since 1975) the smallest unit of local government; a subdivision of a district. [8] *Ecology* a group of interdependent plants and animals inhabiting the same region and interacting with each other through food and other relationships.
▷HISTORY C14: from Latin *commūnitās,* from *commūnis* COMMON

community association NOUN (in Britain) an organization of people and groups working for the common good of a neighbourhood, usually operating under a written constitution registered with the Charity Commissioners.

community care NOUN *Social welfare* [1] help available to persons living in their own homes, rather than services provided in residential institutions. [2] the policy of transferring responsibility for people in need from large, often isolated, state institutions to their relatives and local welfare agencies.

community centre NOUN a building used by members of a community for social gatherings, educational activities, etc.

community charge NOUN (formerly in Britain) a flat-rate charge paid by each adult in a community to their local authority in place of rates. Also called: **poll tax.**

community chest NOUN *US* a fund raised by voluntary contribution for local welfare activities.

community college NOUN [1] *Brit* another term for **village college.** [2] *Chiefly US and Canadian* a nonresidential college offering two-year courses of study. [3] *NZ* an adult education college with trade classes.

community council NOUN (in Scotland and Wales) an independent voluntary local body set up to attend to local interests and organize community activities.

community education NOUN the provision of a wide range of educational and special interest courses and activities by a local authority.

community home NOUN (in Britain) [1] a home provided by a local authority for children who cannot remain with parents or relatives, or be placed with foster parents. [2] a boarding school for young offenders. Former name: **approved school.** Formal name: **community home with education on the premises.** Abbreviation: **CHE.**

Community of Sovereign Republics NOUN a political and economic union formed in 1996 by Russia and Belarus.

community policing NOUN the assigning of the same one or two policemen to a particular area so that they become familiar with the residents and the residents with them, as a way of reducing crime.

Community Programme NOUN (in Britain) a former government scheme to provide temporary work for people unemployed for over a year. Abbreviation: **CP.**

community relations PLURAL NOUN [1] the particular state of affairs in an area where potentially conflicting ethnic, religious, cultural, political, or linguistic groups live together: *community relations in this neighbourhood were strained before the riots.* [2] **a** social engineering or mediating work with conflicting groups: *he spent ten years in community relations.* **b** (*as modifier*): *a community-relations officer.*

community school NOUN *Brit* a school offering some nonacademic activities related to life in a particular community and often serving as a community centre.

community service NOUN [1] voluntary work, intended to be for the common good, usually done as part of an organized scheme. [2] See **community-service order.**

community-service order NOUN (in Britain) a court order requiring an offender over seventeen years old to do unpaid socially beneficial work under supervision instead of going to prison.

community singing NOUN singing, esp of hymns, by a large gathering of people.

communize *or* **communise** ('kɒmjʊ,naɪz) VERB (*tr; sometimes capital*) [1] to make (property) public; nationalize. [2] to make (a person or country) communist.
▸**,communi'zation** *or* **,communi'sation** NOUN

commutable (kə'mju:təbᵊl) ADJECTIVE [1] *Law* (of a punishment) capable of being reduced in severity. [2] able to be exchanged.
▸**com,muta'bility** *or* **com'mutableness** NOUN

commutate ('kɒmjʊ,teɪt) VERB (*tr*) [1] to reverse the direction of (an electric current). [2] to convert (an alternating current) into a direct current.

commutation (,kɒmjʊ'teɪʃən) NOUN [1] a substitution or exchange. [2] **a** the replacement of one method of payment by another. **b** the payment substituted. [3] the reduction in severity of a penalty imposed by law. [4] the process of commutating an electric current. [5] *US* the travelling done by a commuter.

commutation ticket NOUN a US name for **season ticket.**

commutative (kəˈmjuːtətɪv, ˈkɒmjʊˌteɪtɪv) ADJECTIVE [1] relating to or involving substitution. [2] *Maths, logic* **a** (of an operator) giving the same result irrespective of the order of the arguments; thus disjunction and addition are commutative but implication and subtraction are not. **b** relating to this property: *the commutative law of addition.*
▸**comˈmutatively** ADVERB

commutator (ˈkɒmjʊˌteɪtə) NOUN [1] a device used to reverse the direction of flow of an electric current. [2] the segmented metal cylinder or disc mounted on the armature shaft of an electric motor, generator, etc., used to make electrical contact with the rotating coils and ensure unidirectional current flow.

commute (kəˈmjuːt) VERB [1] (*intr*) to travel some distance regularly between one's home and one's place of work. [2] (*tr*) to substitute; exchange. [3] (*tr*) *Law* to reduce (a sentence) to one less severe. [4] to pay (an annuity) at one time, esp with a discount, instead of in instalments. [5] (*tr*) to transform; change: *to commute base metal into gold.* [6] (*intr*) to act as or be a substitute. [7] (*intr*) to make a substitution; change. ◆ NOUN [8] a journey made by commuting.
▷HISTORY C17: from Latin *commūtāre* to replace, from *com-* mutually + *mūtāre* to change
▸**comˈmutable** ADJECTIVE ▸**comˈmutableness** *or* **comˌmutaˈbility** NOUN

commuter (kəˈmjuːtə) NOUN **a** a person who travels to work over an appreciable distance, usually from the suburbs to the centre of a city. **b** (*as modifier*): *the commuter belt.*

Comnenus (kɒmˈniːnəs) NOUN an important Byzantine family from which the imperial dynasties of Constantinople (1057–59; 1081–1185) and Trebizond (1204–1461) derived.

Como (ˈkəʊməʊ; *Italian* ˈkɔːmo) NOUN a city in N Italy, in Lombardy at the SW end of **Lake Como**: tourist centre. Pop.: 96 900 (1995 est.). Latin name: **Comum** (ˈkəʊmʊm).

comodo *or* **commodo** (kəˈməʊdəʊ) ADJECTIVE, ADVERB *Music* (to be performed) at a convenient relaxed speed.
▷HISTORY Italian: comfortable, from Latin *commodus,* convenient; see COMMODIOUS

Comorin (ˈkɒmərɪn) NOUN **Cape.** a headland at the southernmost point of India, in Tamil Nadu state.

Comoros (ˈkɒməˌrəʊz, kəˈmɔːrəʊz) PLURAL NOUN a republic consisting of three volcanic islands in the Indian Ocean, off the NW coast of Madagascar; a French territory from 1947; became independent in 1976 except for Mayotte, the fourth island in the group, which chose to remain French. Official languages: Comorian, French, and Arabic; Swahili is used commercially. Religion: Muslim. Currency: franc. Capital: Moroni. Pop.: 566 000 (2001 est.). Area: 1862 sq. km (719 sq. miles). Official name: **Federal Islamic Republic of the Comoros.**

comose (ˈkəʊməʊs, kəʊˈməʊs) ADJECTIVE *Botany* another word for **comate.**
▷HISTORY C18: from Latin *comōsus* hairy, from *coma* long hair; see COMA[2]

Comox (ˈkəʊmɒks) NOUN a member of a Salishan Native Canadian people living on Vancouver Island.

comp (kɒmp) *Informal* ◆ NOUN [1] a compositor. [2] an accompanist. [3] an accompaniment. [4] a competition. ◆ VERB [5] (*intr*) to work as a compositor in the printing industry. [6] to play an accompaniment (to).

compact[1] ADJECTIVE (kəmˈpækt, ˈkɒmpækt) [1] closely packed together; dense. [2] neatly fitted into a restricted space. [3] concise; brief. [4] well constructed; solid; firm. [5] (foll by *of*) composed or made up (of). [6] *Logic* (of a relation) having the property that for any pair of elements such that *a* is related to *b,* there is some element *c* such that *a* is related to *c* and *c* to *b,* as *less than* on the rational numbers. [7] *US and Canadian* (of a car) small and economical. ◆ VERB (kəmˈpækt) (*tr*) [8] to pack or join closely together; compress; condense. [9] (foll by *of*) to create or form by pressing together: *sediment compacted of three types of clay.* [10] *Metallurgy* to compress (a metal powder) to form a stable product suitable for sintering. ◆ NOUN (ˈkɒmpækt) [11] a small flat case containing a mirror, face powder, etc., designed to be carried in a woman's handbag. [12] *US and Canadian* a comparatively small and economical car. [13] *Metallurgy* a mass of metal prepared for sintering by cold-pressing a metal powder.
▷HISTORY C16: from Latin *compactus,* from *compingere* to put together, from *com-* together + *pangere* to fasten
▸**comˈpacter** NOUN ▸**comˈpaction** NOUN ▸**comˈpactly** ADVERB ▸**comˈpactness** NOUN

compact[2] (ˈkɒmpækt) NOUN an official contract or agreement.
▷HISTORY C16: from Latin *compactum,* from *compacīscī* to agree, from *com-* together + *pacīscī* to contract; see PACT

compact camera (ˈkɒmpækt) NOUN a simple 35 mm snapshot camera not having interchangeable lenses or through-the-lens focusing but sometimes having automatic focusing, exposure, and winding. Sometimes shortened to **compact.**

compact disc (ˈkɒmpækt) NOUN a small digital audio disc on which sound is recorded as a series of metallic pits enclosed in PVC; the disc is spun by the compact disc player and read by an optical laser system. Also called: **compact audio disc.** Abbreviations: **CD, CAD.**

compact disc erasable NOUN the full name for **CDE.**

compact disc player NOUN a machine for playing compact discs.

compact disc recordable NOUN the full name for **CDR.**

compactify (kəmˈpæktɪˌfaɪ) VERB **-fies, -fying, -fied.** to make or become compact; esp of higher dimensions in space-time, to become tightly curved so as to be unobservable under normal circumstances.
▸**comˌpactifiˈcation** NOUN

compact video disc NOUN a compact laser disc that plays both pictures and sound. Abbreviation: **CDV.**

compadre (kɒmˈpɑːdreɪ, kəm-) NOUN *Southwestern US* a masculine friend.
▷HISTORY from Spanish: godfather, from Medieval Latin *compater,* from Latin *com-* with + *pater* father

compages (kəmˈpeɪdʒiːz) NOUN (*functioning as singular*) a structure or framework.
▷HISTORY C17: from Latin, from *com-* together + *pag-,* from *pangere* to fasten

compander (kəmˈpændə) NOUN a system for improving the signal-to-noise ratio of a signal at a transmitter or recorder by first compressing the volume range of the signal and then restoring it to its original amplitude level at the receiving or reproducing apparatus.
▷HISTORY C20: from COM(PRESSOR) + (EX)PANDER

companion[1] (kəmˈpænjən) NOUN [1] a person who is an associate of another or others; comrade. [2] (esp formerly) an employee, usually a woman, who provides company for an employer, esp an elderly woman. [3] **a** one of a pair; match. **b** (*as modifier*): *a companion volume.* [4] a guidebook or handbook. [5] a member of the lowest rank of any of certain orders of knighthood. [6] *Astronomy* the fainter of the two components of a double star. ◆ VERB [7] (*tr*) to accompany or be a companion to.
▷HISTORY C13: from Late Latin *compāniō,* literally: one who eats bread with another, from Latin *com-* with + *pānis* bread
▸**comˈpanionless** ADJECTIVE

companion[2] (kəmˈpænjən) NOUN *Nautical* **a** a raised frame on an upper deck with windows to give light to the deck below. **b** (*as modifier*): *a companion ladder.*
▷HISTORY C18: from Dutch *kompanje* quarterdeck, from Old French *compagne,* from Old Italian *compagna* pantry, perhaps ultimately from Latin *pānis* bread

companionable (kəmˈpænjənəbᵊl) ADJECTIVE suited to be a companion; sociable.
▸**comˈpanionableness** *or* **comˌpanionaˈbility** NOUN
▸**comˈpanionably** ADVERB

companion animal NOUN an animal kept as a pet.

companionate (kəmˈpænjənɪt) ADJECTIVE [1] resembling, appropriate to, or acting as a companion. [2] harmoniously suited.

companion set NOUN a set of fire irons on a stand.

companionship (kəmˈpænjənˌʃɪp) NOUN the relationship of friends or companions; fellowship.

companionway (kəmˈpænjənˌweɪ) NOUN a stairway or ladder leading from one deck to another in a boat or ship.

company (ˈkʌmpənɪ) NOUN, *plural* **-nies.** [1] a number of people gathered together; assembly. [2] the fact of being with someone; companionship: *I enjoy her company.* [3] a social visitor or visitors; guest or guests. [4] a business enterprise. [5] the members of an enterprise not specifically mentioned in the enterprise's title. Abbreviations: **Co., co.** [6] a group of actors, usually including business and technical personnel. [7] a unit of around 100 troops, usually comprising two or more platoons. [8] the officers and crew of a ship. [9] a unit of Girl Guides. [10] *English history* a medieval guild. [11] **keep** *or* **bear company. a** to accompany (someone). **b** (esp of lovers) to associate with each other; spend time together. [12] **part company. a** to end a friendship or association, esp as a result of a quarrel; separate. **b** (foll by *with*) to leave; go away (from); be separated (from). ◆ VERB **-nies, -nying, -nied.** [13] *Archaic* to keep company or associate (with someone).
▷HISTORY C13: from Old French *compaignie,* from *compain* companion, fellow, from Late Latin *compāniō*; see COMPANION[1]

company doctor NOUN [1] a businessman or accountant who specializes in turning ailing companies into profitable enterprises. [2] a physician employed by a company to look after its staff and to advise on health matters.

company man NOUN an employee who puts allegiance to the company for which he works above personal opinion or friendship.

company secretary NOUN *Brit* an officer of an incorporated company who has certain legal obligations.

company sergeant major NOUN *Military* the senior Warrant Officer II in a British or Commonwealth regiment or battalion, responsible under the company second in command for all aspects of duty and discipline of the NCOs and men in that subunit. Abbreviation: **CSM.** Compare **regimental sergeant major.** See also **warrant officer.**

company town NOUN *US and Canadian* a town built by a company for its employees.

company union NOUN *Chiefly US and Canadian* an unaffiliated union of workers usually restricted to a single business enterprise.

comparable (ˈkɒmpərəbᵊl) ADJECTIVE [1] worthy of comparison. [2] able to be compared (with).
▸**ˌcomparaˈbility** *or* **ˈcomparableness** NOUN ▸**ˈcomparably** ADVERB

comparative (kəmˈpærətɪv) ADJECTIVE [1] denoting or involving comparison: *comparative literature.* [2] judged by comparison; relative: *a comparative loss of prestige.* [3] *Grammar* denoting the form of an adjective that indicates that the quality denoted is possessed to a greater extent. In English the comparative form of an adjective is usually marked by the suffix *-er* or the word *more.* Compare **positive** (sense 10), **superlative** (sense 2). ◆ NOUN [4] the comparative form of an adjective.
▸**comˈparatively** ADVERB ▸**comˈparativeness** NOUN

comparative advertising NOUN a form of advertising in which a product is compared favourably with similar products on the market.

comparative judgment NOUN *Psychol* any judgment about whether there is a difference between two or more stimuli. Compare **absolute judgment.**

comparative psychology NOUN the study of the similarities and differences in the behaviour of different species.

comparator (kəmˈpærətə) NOUN [1] any instrument used to measure a property of a system by comparing it with a standard system. [2] an electric circuit that compares two signals and gives an indication of the extent of their dissimilarity.

compare (kəmˈpɛə) VERB 1 (*tr;* usually foll by *to*) to regard or represent as analogous or similar; liken: *the general has been compared to Napoleon.* 2 (*tr;* usually foll by *with*) to examine in order to observe resemblances or differences: *to compare rum with gin.* 3 (*intr;* usually foll by *with*) to be of the same or similar quality or value: *gin compares with rum in alcoholic content.* 4 (*intr*) to bear a specified relation of quality or value when examined: *this car compares badly with the other.* 5 (*intr;* usually foll by *with*) to correspond to: *profits were £3.2 million. This compares with £2.6 million last year.* 6 (*tr*) *Grammar* to give the positive, comparative, and superlative forms of (an adjective). 7 (*intr*) *Archaic* to compete or vie. 8 **compare notes.** to exchange opinions. ♦ NOUN 9 comparison or analogy (esp in the phrase **beyond compare**).
▷HISTORY C15: from Old French *comparer,* from Latin *comparāre* to couple together, match, from *compar* equal to one another, from *com-* together + *par* equal; see PAR
▸**comˈparer** NOUN

comparison (kəmˈpærɪsᵊn) NOUN 1 the act or process of comparing. 2 the state of being compared. 3 comparable quality or qualities; likeness: *there was no comparison between them.* 4 a rhetorical device involving comparison, such as a simile. 5 Also called: **degrees of comparison.** *Grammar* the listing of the positive, comparative, and superlative forms of an adjective or adverb. 6 **bear** *or* **stand comparison (with).** to be sufficiently similar in class or range to be compared with (something else), esp favourably.

compartment (kəmˈpɑːtmənt) NOUN 1 one of the sections into which an area, esp an enclosed space, is divided or partitioned. 2 any separate part or section: *a compartment of the mind.* 3 a small storage space; locker.
▷HISTORY C16: from French *compartiment,* ultimately from Late Latin *compartīrī* to share, from Latin *com-* with + *partīrī* to apportion, from *pars* PART
▸**compartmental** (ˌkɒmpɑːtˈmɛntᵊl) ADJECTIVE
▸**ˌcompartˈmentally** ADVERB

compartmentalize *or* **compartmentalise** (ˌkɒmpɑːtˈmɛntᵊˌlaɪz) VERB (*usually tr*) to put or divide into (compartments, categories, etc.), esp to an excessive degree.
▸**ˌcompartˌmentaliˈzation** *or* **ˌcompartˌmentaliˈsation** NOUN

compass (ˈkʌmpəs) NOUN 1 an instrument for finding direction, usually having a magnetized needle which points to magnetic north swinging freely on a pivot. 2 (*often plural*) Also called: **pair of compasses.** an instrument used for drawing circles, measuring distances, etc., that consists of two arms, joined at one end, one arm of which serves as a pivot or stationary reference point, while the other is extended or describes a circle. 3 limits or range: *within the compass of education.* 4 *Music* the interval between the lowest and highest note attainable by a voice or musical instrument. 5 *Archaic* a circular course. ♦ VERB (*tr*) 6 to encircle or surround; hem in. 7 to comprehend or grasp mentally. 8 to achieve; attain; accomplish. 9 *Obsolete* to plot.
▷HISTORY C13: from Old French *compas,* from *compasser* to measure, from Vulgar Latin *compassāre* (unattested) to pace out, ultimately from Latin *passus* step
▸**ˈcompassable** ADJECTIVE

compass card NOUN a compass in the form of a card that rotates so that "0°" or "North" points to magnetic north.

compassion (kəmˈpæʃən) NOUN a feeling of distress and pity for the suffering or misfortune of another, often including the desire to alleviate it.
▷HISTORY C14: from Old French, from Late Latin *compassiō* fellow feeling, from *compatī* to suffer with, from Latin *com-* with + *patī* to bear, suffer

compassionate (kəmˈpæʃənət) ADJECTIVE 1 showing or having compassion. 2 **compassionate leave.** leave granted, esp to a serviceman, on the grounds of bereavement, family illness, etc.
▸**comˈpassionately** ADVERB ▸**comˈpassionateness** NOUN

compassion fatigue NOUN the inability to react sympathetically to a crisis, disaster, etc., because of overexposure to previous crises, disasters, etc.

compass plant NOUN 1 Also called: **rosinweed.** a tall plant, *Silphium laciniatum,* of central North America, that has yellow flowers and lower leaves that tend to align themselves at right angles to the strongest light, esp in a north-south plane: family *Asteraceae* (composites). 2 any of several similar plants.

compass rose NOUN a circle or decorative device printed on a map or chart showing the points of the compass measured from true north and usually magnetic north.

compass saw NOUN a hand saw with a narrow tapered blade for making a curved cut.

compass window NOUN *Architect* a bay window having a semicircular shape.

compatible (kəmˈpætəbᵊl) ADJECTIVE 1 (usually foll by *with*) able to exist together harmoniously. 2 (usually foll by *with*) consistent or congruous: *her deeds were not compatible with her ideology.* 3 (of plants) **a** capable of forming successful grafts. **b** capable of successful self-fertilization. ♦ See **self-compatible, self-incompatible.** 4 (of pieces of machinery, computer equipment, etc.) capable of being used together without special modification or adaptation: *a PC-compatible disc.*
▷HISTORY C15: from Medieval Latin *compatibilis,* from Late Latin *compatī* to be in sympathy with; see COMPASSION
▸**comˌpatiˈbility** *or* **comˈpatibleness** NOUN ▸**comˈpatibly** ADVERB

compatriot (kəmˈpætrɪət) NOUN a fellow countryman.
▷HISTORY C17: from French *compatriote,* from Late Latin *compatriōta;* see PATRIOT
▸**comˌpatriˈotic** ADJECTIVE ▸**comˈpatriotism** NOUN

compeer (ˈkɒmpɪə) NOUN 1 a person of equal rank, status, or ability; peer. 2 a companion or comrade.
▷HISTORY C13: from Old French *comper,* from Medieval Latin *compater* godfather; see COMPADRE

compel (kəmˈpɛl) VERB **-pels, -pelling, -pelled.** (*tr*) 1 to cause (someone) by force (to be or do something). 2 to obtain by force; exact: *to compel obedience.* 3 to overpower or subdue. 4 *Archaic* to herd or drive together.
▷HISTORY C14: from Latin *compellere* to drive together, from *com-* together + *pellere* to drive
▸**comˈpellable** ADJECTIVE ▸**comˈpellably** ADVERB
▸**comˈpeller** NOUN

compellation (ˌkɒmpɛˈleɪʃən) NOUN a rare word for **appellation.**
▷HISTORY C17: from Latin *compellātiō,* from *compellāre*to accost, from *appellāre* to call

compelling (kəmˈpɛlɪŋ) ADJECTIVE 1 arousing or denoting strong interest, esp admiring interest. 2 (of an argument, evidence, etc.) convincing.

compendious (kəmˈpɛndɪəs) ADJECTIVE containing or stating the essentials of a subject in a concise form; succinct.
▸**comˈpendiously** ADVERB ▸**comˈpendiousness** NOUN

compendium (kəmˈpɛndɪəm) NOUN, *plural* **-diums** *or* **-dia** (-dɪə). 1 *Brit* a book containing a collection of useful hints. 2 *Brit* a selection, esp of different games or other objects in one container. 3 a concise but comprehensive summary of a larger work.
▷HISTORY C16: from Latin: a saving, literally: something weighed, from *pendere* to weigh

compensable (kəmˈpɛnsəbᵊl) ADJECTIVE *Chiefly US* entitled to compensation or capable of being compensated.

compensate (ˈkɒmpɛnˌseɪt) VERB 1 to make amends to (someone), esp for loss or injury. 2 (*tr*) to serve as compensation or damages for (injury, loss, etc.). 3 to offset or counterbalance the effects of (a force, weight, movement, etc.) so as to nullify the effects of an undesirable influence and produce equilibrium. 4 (*intr*) to attempt to conceal or offset one's shortcomings by the exaggerated exhibition of qualities regarded as desirable.
▷HISTORY C17: from Latin *compēnsāre,* from *pensāre,* from *pendere* to weigh
▸**compensatory** (ˈkɒmpɛnˌseɪtərɪ, kəmˈpɛnsətərɪ, -trɪ) *or* **compensative** (ˈkɒmpɛnˌseɪtɪv, kəmˈpɛnsə-) ADJECTIVE ▸**ˈcompenˌsator** NOUN

compensated semiconductor NOUN *Physics* a semiconductor in which donors and acceptors are related in such a way that their opposing electrical effects are partially cancelled.

compensation (ˌkɒmpɛnˈseɪʃən) NOUN 1 the act or process of making amends for something. 2 something given as reparation for loss, injury, etc.; indemnity. 3 the automatic movements made by the body to maintain balance. 4 the attempt to conceal or offset one's shortcomings by the exaggerated exhibition of qualities regarded as desirable. 5 *Biology* abnormal growth and increase in size in one organ in response to the removal or inactivation of another.
▸**ˌcompenˈsational** ADJECTIVE

compensation order NOUN (in Britain) the requirement of a court that an offender pay compensation for injury, loss, or damage resulting from an offence, either in preference to or as well as a fine.

compensation point NOUN *Botany* the concentration of atmospheric carbon dioxide at which the rate of carbon dioxide uptake by a photosynthesizing plant is exactly balanced by its rate of carbon dioxide release in respiration and photorespiration.

compensatory finance NOUN another name for **deficit financing.**

comper (ˈkɒmpə) NOUN *Informal* a person who regularly enters competitions in newspapers, magazines, etc., esp competitions offering consumer goods as prizes.
▷HISTORY C20: COMP(ETITION) + -ER[1]
▸**ˈcomping** NOUN

compere (ˈkɒmpɛə) *Brit* ♦ NOUN 1 a master of ceremonies who introduces cabaret, television acts, etc. ♦ VERB 2 to act as a compere (for).
▷HISTORY C20: from French, literally: godfather; see COMPEER, COMPADRE

compete (kəmˈpiːt) VERB (*intr;* often foll by *with*) to contend (against) for profit, an award, athletic supremacy, etc.; engage in a contest (with).
▷HISTORY C17: from Late Latin *competere* to strive together, from Latin: to meet, come together, agree, from *com-* together + *petere* to seek

competence (ˈkɒmpɪtəns) NOUN 1 the condition of being capable; ability. 2 a sufficient income to live on. 3 the state of being legally competent or qualified. 4 *Embryol* the ability of embryonic tissues to react to external conditions in a way that influences subsequent development. 5 *Linguistics* (in transformational grammar) the form of the human language faculty, independent of its psychological embodiment in actual human beings. Compare **performance** (sense 7), **langue, parole** (sense 5).

competency (ˈkɒmpɪtənsɪ) NOUN, *plural* **-cies.** 1 *Law* capacity to testify in a court of law; eligibility to be sworn. 2 a less common word for **competence** (senses 1, 2).

competent (ˈkɒmpɪtənt) ADJECTIVE 1 having sufficient skill, knowledge, etc.; capable. 2 suitable or sufficient for the purpose: *a competent answer.* 3 *Law* (of a witness) having legal capacity; qualified to testify, etc. 4 (*postpositive;* foll by *to*) belonging as a right; appropriate.
▷HISTORY C14: from Latin *competēns,* from *competere* to be competent; see COMPETE
▸**ˈcompetently** ADVERB ▸**ˈcompetentness** NOUN

competition (ˌkɒmpɪˈtɪʃən) NOUN 1 the act of competing; rivalry. 2 a contest in which a winner is selected from among two or more entrants. 3 a series of games, sports events, etc. 4 the opposition offered by a competitor or competitors. 5 a competitor or competitors offering opposition. 6 *Ecology* the struggle between individuals of the same or different species for food, space, light, etc., when these are inadequate to supply the needs of all.

competitive (kəmˈpɛtɪtɪv) ADJECTIVE 1 involving or determined by rivalry: *competitive sports.* 2 sufficiently low in price or high in quality to be successful against commercial rivals. 3 relating to or characterized by an urge to compete: *a competitive personality.*
▸**comˈpetitively** ADVERB ▸**comˈpetitiveness** NOUN

competitive exclusion NOUN *Ecology* the dominance of one species over another when both are competing for the same resources, etc.

competitor (kəmˈpɛtɪtə) NOUN a person, group, team, firm, etc., that vies or competes; rival.

Compiègne (*French* kõpjɛɲ) NOUN a city in N France, on the Oise River: scene of the armistice at the end of World War I (1918) and of the Franco-German armistice of 1940. Pop.: 44 703 (1990).

compilation (ˌkɒmpɪˈleɪʃən) NOUN 1 something collected or compiled, such as a list, report, etc. 2 the act or process of collecting or compiling.

compilation film NOUN film from an archive used in a film or documentary to give a feeling of the relevant period.

compile (kəmˈpaɪl) VERB (*tr*) 1 to make or compose from other materials or sources: *to compile a list of names.* 2 to collect or gather for a book, hobby, etc. 3 *Computing* to create (a set of machine instructions) from a high-level programming language, using a compiler.
▷HISTORY C14: from Latin *compīlāre* to pile together, plunder, from *com-* together + *pīlāre* to thrust down, pack

compiler (kəmˈpaɪlə) NOUN 1 a person who collects or compiles something. 2 a computer program by which a high-level programming language, such as COBOL or FORTRAN, is converted into machine language that can be acted upon by a computer. Compare **assembler.**

complacency (kəmˈpleɪsənsɪ) *or* **complacence** NOUN, *plural* **-cencies** *or* **-cences.** 1 a feeling of satisfaction, esp extreme self-satisfaction; smugness. 2 an obsolete word for **complaisance.**

complacent (kəmˈpleɪsᵊnt) ADJECTIVE 1 pleased or satisfied, esp extremely self-satisfied. 2 an obsolete word for **complaisant.**
▷HISTORY C17: from Latin *complacēns* very pleasing, from *complacēre* to be most agreeable to, from *com-* (intensive) + *placēre* to please
▸**comˈplacently** ADVERB

complain (kəmˈpleɪn) VERB (*intr*) 1 to express resentment, displeasure, etc., esp habitually; grumble. 2 (foll by *of*) to state the presence of pain, illness, etc., esp in the hope of sympathy: *she complained of a headache.*
▷HISTORY C14: from Old French *complaindre,* from Vulgar Latin *complangere* (unattested), from Latin *com-* (intensive) + *plangere* to bewail
▸**comˈplainer** NOUN ▸**comˈplainingly** ADVERB

complainant (kəmˈpleɪnənt) NOUN *Law* a person who makes a complaint, usually before justices; plaintiff.

complaint (kəmˈpleɪnt) NOUN 1 the act of complaining; an expression of grievance. 2 a cause for complaining; grievance. 3 a mild ailment. 4 *English law* a statement by which a civil proceeding in a magistrates' court is commenced.

complaisance (kəmˈpleɪzəns) NOUN 1 deference to the wishes of others; willing compliance. 2 an act of willing compliance.

complaisant (kəmˈpleɪzᵊnt) ADJECTIVE showing a desire to comply or oblige; polite.
▷HISTORY C17: from French *complaire,* from Latin *complacēre* to please greatly; compare COMPLACENT
▸**comˈplaisantly** ADVERB

complanate (kəmˈpleɪneɪt) ADJECTIVE *Botany* having a flattened or compressed aspect.

compleat (kəmˈpliːt) ADJECTIVE an archaic spelling of **complete**, used in the titles of handbooks, in imitation of *The Compleat Angler* by Izaak Walton

complect (kəmˈplɛkt) VERB (*tr*) *Archaic* to interweave or entwine.
▷HISTORY C16: from Latin *complectī;* see COMPLEX

complected (kəmˈplɛktɪd) ADJECTIVE (*in combination*) a US dialect word for **complexioned.**

complement NOUN (ˈkɒmplɪmənt) 1 a person or thing that completes something. 2 one of two parts that make up a whole or complete each other. 3 a complete amount, number, etc. (often in the phrase **full complement**). 4 the officers and crew needed to man a ship. 5 *Grammar* **a** a noun phrase that follows a copula or similar verb, as for example *an idiot* in the sentence *He is an idiot.* **b** a clause that serves as the subject or direct object of a verb or the direct object of a preposition, as for example *that he would be early* in the sentence *I hoped that he would be early.* 6 *Maths* the angle that when added to a specified angle produces a right angle. 7 *Logic, maths* the class of all things, or of all members of a given universe of discourse, that are not members of a given set. 8 *Music* the inverted form of an interval that, when added to the interval, completes the octave: *the sixth is the complement of the third.* 9 *Immunol* a group of proteins in the blood serum that, when activated by antibodies, causes destruction of alien cells, such as bacteria. ◆ VERB (ˈkɒmplɪˌmɛnt) 10 (*tr*) to add to, make complete, or form a complement to.
▷HISTORY C14: from Latin *complēmentum,* from *complēre* to fill up, from *com-* (intensive) + *plēre* to fill

> **Language note** Avoid confusion with **compliment.**

complementarity (ˌkɒmplɪmənˈtærɪtɪ) NOUN, *plural* **-ties.** 1 a state or system that involves complementary components. 2 *Physics* the principle that the complete description of a phenomenon in microphysics requires the use of two distinct theories that are complementary to each other. See also **duality** (sense 2).

complementary (ˌkɒmplɪˈmɛntərɪ, -trɪ) *or* **complemental** ADJECTIVE 1 acting as or forming a complement; completing. 2 forming a satisfactory or balanced whole. 3 forming a mathematical complement: *sine and cosine are complementary functions.* 4 *Maths, logic* (of a pair of sets, etc.) mutually exclusive and exhaustive, each being the complement of the other. 5 (of genes) producing an effect in association with other genes. 6 involving or using the treatments and techniques of complementary medicine.
▸ˌ**compleˈmentarily** *or* ˌ**compleˈmentally** ADVERB
▸ˌ**compleˈmentariness** NOUN

complementary angle NOUN either of two angles whose sum is 90°. Compare **supplementary angle.**

complementary colour NOUN one of any pair of colours, such as yellow and blue, that give white or grey when mixed in the correct proportions.

complementary DNA NOUN a form of DNA artificially synthesized from a messenger RNA template and used in genetic engineering to produce gene clones. Abbreviation: **cDNA.**

complementary gene NOUN one of a pair of genes, each from different loci, that together are required for the expression of a certain characteristic.

complementary medicine NOUN the treatment, alleviation, or prevention of disease by such techniques as osteopathy, homeopathy, aromatherapy, and acupuncture, allied with attention to such factors as diet and emotional stability, which can affect a person's wellbeing. Also called: **alternative medicine.** See also **holism** (sense 2).

complementary wavelength NOUN *Physics* the wavelength of monochromatic light that could be mixed in suitable proportions with a given coloured light so as to produce some specified achromatic light.

complementation (ˌkɒmplɪmɛnˈteɪʃən) NOUN 1 the act or process of forming a complement. 2 *Genetics* the combination of two homologous chromosomes, each with a different recessive mutant gene, in a single cell to produce a normal phenotype. The deficiency of one homologue is supplied by the normal allele of the other.

complement fixation test NOUN *Med* a serological test for detecting the presence of a specific antibody or antigen, used in the diagnosis of syphilis, etc.

complementizer (ˈkɒmplɪmənˌtaɪzə) NOUN *Generative grammar* a word or morpheme that serves to introduce a complement clause or a reduced form of such a clause, as *that* in *I wish that he would leave.*

complete (kəmˈpliːt) ADJECTIVE 1 having every necessary part or element; entire. 2 ended; finished. 3 (*prenominal*) thorough; absolute: *he is a complete rogue.* 4 perfect in quality or kind: *he is a complete scholar.* 5 (of a logical system) constituted such that a contradiction arises on the addition of any proposition that cannot be deduced from the axioms of the system. Compare **consistent** (sense 5). 6 (of flowers) having sepals, petals, stamens, and carpels. 7 *Archaic* expert or skilled; accomplished. ◆ VERB (*tr*) 8 to make whole or perfect. 9 to end; finish. 10 (in land law) to pay any outstanding balance on a contract for the conveyance of land in exchange for the title deeds, so that the ownership of the land changes hands. 11 *American football* (of a quarterback) to make a forward pass successfully.
▷HISTORY C14: from Latin *complētus,* past participle of *complēre* to fill up; see COMPLEMENT
▸**comˈpletely** ADVERB ▸**comˈpleteness** NOUN ▸**comˈpleter** NOUN ▸**comˈpletion** NOUN ▸**comˈpletive** ADJECTIVE

completist (kəmˈpliːtɪst) NOUN a person who collects objects or memorabilia obsessively: *ardent John Wayne completists.*

complex (ˈkɒmplɛks) ADJECTIVE 1 made up of various interconnected parts; composite. 2 (of thoughts, writing, etc.) intricate or involved. 3 *Grammar* **a** (of a word) containing at least one bound form. **b** (of a noun phrase) containing both a lexical noun and an embedded clause, as for example the italicized parts of the following sentence: I didn't know *the man who served me.* **c** (of a sentence) formed by subordination of one clause to another. 4 *Maths* of or involving one or more complex numbers. ◆ NOUN 5 a whole made up of interconnected or related parts: *a building complex.* 6 *Psychoanal* a group of emotional ideas or impulses that have been banished from the conscious mind but that continue to influence a person's behaviour. 7 *Informal* an obsession or excessive fear: *he's got a complex about cats.* 8 Also called: **coordination compound.** a chemical compound in which molecules, groups, or ions are attached to a central metal atom, esp a transition metal atom, by coordinate bonds. 9 any chemical compound in which one molecule is linked to another by a coordinate bond.
▷HISTORY C17: from Latin *complexus,* from *complectī* to entwine, from *com-* together + *plectere* to braid
▸ˈ**complexly** ADVERB ▸ˈ**complexness** NOUN

> **Language note** *Complex* is sometimes wrongly used where *complicated* is meant. *Complex* is properly used to say only that something consists of several parts. It should not be used to say that, because something consists of many parts, it is difficult to understand or analyse.

complex conjugate NOUN *Maths* the complex number whose imaginary part is the negative of that of a given complex number, the real parts of both numbers being equal: *a* – i*b is the complex conjugate of a* + i*b.*

complex fraction NOUN *Maths* a fraction in which the numerator or denominator or both contain fractions. Also called: **compound fraction.**

complexion (kəmˈplɛkʃən) NOUN 1 the colour and general appearance of a person's skin, esp of the face. 2 aspect, character, or nature: *the general complexion of a nation's finances.* 3 *Obsolete* **a** the temperament of a person. **b** the temperature and general appearance of the body.
▷HISTORY C14: from medical Latin *complexiō* one's bodily characteristics, from Latin: a combination, from *complectī* to embrace; see COMPLEX
▸**comˈplexional** ADJECTIVE

complexioned (kəmˈplɛkʃənd) ADJECTIVE (*in combination*) of a specified complexion: *light-complexioned.*

complexity (kəmˈplɛksɪtɪ) NOUN, *plural* **-ties.** 1 the state or quality of being intricate or complex. 2 something intricate or complex; complication.

complex number NOUN any number of the form $a + ib$, where a and b are real numbers and $i = \sqrt{-1}$. See **number** (sense 1).

complexometric titration (kəmˌplɛksəʊˈmɛtrɪk) NOUN *Chem* a titration in which a coloured complex is formed, usually by the use of a chelating agent, such as EDTA, the end point being marked by a sharp decrease in the concentration of free metal ions.

complexone (kəmˈplɛksəʊn) NOUN *Chem* any chelating agent, such as EDTA, used for the analytical determination of metals.

complex salt NOUN a salt that contains one or more complex ions. Compare **double salt.**

complex sentence NOUN *Grammar* a sentence containing at least one main clause and one subordinate clause.

complex wave NOUN *Physics* a waveform consisting of a fundamental frequency with superimposed harmonics.

compliance (kəm'plaɪəns) *or* **compliancy** NOUN [1] the act of complying; acquiescence. [2] a disposition to yield to or comply with others. [3] a measure of the ability of a mechanical system to respond to an applied vibrating force, expressed as the reciprocal of the system's stiffness. Symbol: *C*.

compliance officer NOUN a specialist, usually a lawyer, employed by a financial group operating in a variety of fields and for multiple clients to ensure that no conflict of interest arises and that all obligations and regulations are complied with.

compliant (kəm'plaɪənt) *or* **compliable** ADJECTIVE complying, obliging, or yielding. ▸**com'pliantly** *or* **com'pliably** ADVERB ▸**com'pliantness** *or* **com'pliableness** NOUN

complicacy ('kɒmplɪkəsɪ) NOUN, *plural* **-cies**. a less common word for **complexity**.

complicate VERB ('kɒmplɪˌkeɪt) [1] to make or become complex. ◆ ADJECTIVE ('kɒmplɪkɪt) [2] *Biology* folded on itself: *a complicate leaf*. [3] a less common word for **complicated**.
▷HISTORY C17: from Latin *complicāre* to fold together, from *plicāre* to fold

complicated ('kɒmplɪˌkeɪtɪd) ADJECTIVE made up of intricate parts or aspects that are difficult to understand or analyse.
▸**'compliˌcatedly** ADVERB ▸**'compliˌcatedness** NOUN

complication (ˌkɒmplɪ'keɪʃən) NOUN [1] a condition, event, etc., that is complex or confused. [2] the act or process of complicating. [3] a situation, event, or condition that complicates or frustrates: *her coming was a serious complication*. [4] a disease or disorder arising as a consequence of another disease.

complice ('kɒmplɪs, 'kʌm-) NOUN *Obsolete* an associate or accomplice.
▷HISTORY C15: from Old French, from Late Latin *complex* partner, associate, from Latin *complicāre* to fold together; see COMPLICATE

complicity (kəm'plɪsɪtɪ) NOUN, *plural* **-ties**. [1] the fact or condition of being an accomplice, esp in a criminal act. [2] a less common word for **complexity**.

compliment NOUN ('kɒmplɪmənt) [1] a remark or act expressing respect, admiration, etc. [2] (*usually plural*) a greeting of respect or regard. ◆ VERB ('kɒmplɪˌmɛnt) (*tr*) [3] to express admiration of; congratulate or commend. [4] to express or show respect or regard for, esp by a gift.
▷HISTORY C17: from French, from Italian *complimento*, from Spanish *cumplimiento*, from *cumplir* to complete, do what is fitting, be polite

Language note Avoid confusion with **complement**.

complimentary (ˌkɒmplɪ'mɛntərɪ, -trɪ) ADJECTIVE [1] conveying, containing, or resembling a compliment. [2] expressing praise; flattering. [3] given free, esp as a courtesy or for publicity purposes.
▸**ˌcompli'mentarily** ADVERB

compline ('kɒmplɪn, -plaɪn) *or* **complin** ('kɒmplɪn) NOUN *RC Church* the last of the seven canonical hours of the divine office.
▷HISTORY C13: from Old French *complie*, from Medieval Latin *hōra complēta*, literally: the completed hour, from Latin *complēre* to fill up, COMPLETE

complot *Archaic* ◆ NOUN ('kɒmplɒt) [1] a plot or conspiracy. ◆ VERB (kəm'plɒt) **-plots, -plotting, -plotted**. [2] to plot together; conspire.
▷HISTORY C16: from Old French, of unknown origin
▸**com'plotter** NOUN

comply (kəm'plaɪ) VERB **-plies, -plying, -plied**. (*intr*) [1] (usually foll by *with*) to act in accordance with rules, wishes, etc.; be obedient (to). [2] *Obsolete* to be obedient or complaisant.
▷HISTORY C17: from Italian *complire*, from Spanish *cumplir* to complete; see COMPLIMENT
▸**com'plier** NOUN

compo ('kɒmpəʊ) NOUN, *plural* **-pos**. [1] a mixture of materials, such as mortar, plaster, etc. [2] *Austral and NZ informal* compensation, esp for injury or loss of work. ◆ ADJECTIVE [3] *Military* intended to last for several days: *compo rations; a compo pack*.
▷HISTORY short for *composition, compensation, composite*

component (kəm'pəʊnənt) NOUN [1] a constituent part or aspect of something more complex: *a component of a car*. [2] Also called: **element**. any electrical device, such as a resistor, that has distinct electrical characteristics and that may be connected to other electrical devices to form a circuit. [3] *Maths* **a** one of a set of two or more vectors whose resultant is a given vector. **b** the projection of this given vector onto a specified line. [4] one of the minimum number of chemically distinct constituents necessary to describe fully the composition of each phase in a system. See **phase rule**. ◆ ADJECTIVE [5] forming or functioning as a part or aspect; constituent.
▷HISTORY C17: from Latin *compōnere* to put together, from *pōnere* to place, put
▸**componential** (ˌkɒmpə'nɛnʃəl) ADJECTIVE

compony (kəm'pəʊnɪ) *or* **componé** (kəm'pəʊneɪ) ADJECTIVE (*usually postpositive*) *Heraldry* made up of alternating metal and colour, colour and fur, or fur and metal.
▷HISTORY C16: from Old French *componé*, from *copon* piece, COUPON

comport (kəm'pɔːt) VERB [1] (*tr*) to conduct or bear (oneself) in a specified way. [2] (*intr; foll by with*) to agree (with); correspond (to).
▷HISTORY C16: from Latin *comportāre* to bear, collect, from *com-* together + *portāre* to carry

comportment (kəm'pɔːtmənt) NOUN conduct; bearing.

compose (kəm'pəʊz) VERB (*mainly tr*) [1] to put together or make up by combining; put in proper order. [2] to be the component elements of. [3] to produce or create (a musical or literary work). [4] (*intr*) to write music. [5] to calm (someone, esp oneself); make quiet. [6] to adjust or settle (a quarrel, etc.). [7] to order the elements of (a painting, sculpture, etc.); design. [8] *Printing* to set up (type).
▷HISTORY C15: from Old French *composer*, from Latin *compōnere* to put in place; see COMPONENT

composed (kəm'pəʊzd) ADJECTIVE (of people) calm; tranquil; serene.
▸**composedly** (kəm'pəʊzɪdlɪ) ADVERB ▸**com'posedness** NOUN

composer (kəm'pəʊzə) NOUN [1] a person who composes music. [2] a person or machine that composes anything, esp type for printing.

composing room NOUN the room in a printing establishment in which type is set.

composing stick NOUN *Printing* a metal holder of adjustable width in which a compositor sets a line of type at a time by hand; now rarely used.

composite ('kɒmpəzɪt) ADJECTIVE [1] composed of separate parts; compound. [2] of, relating to, or belonging to the plant family *Asteraceae*. [3] *Maths* capable of being factorized or decomposed: *a composite function*. [4] (*sometimes capital*) denoting or relating to one of the five classical orders of architecture: characterized by a combination of the Ionic and Corinthian styles. See also **Doric, Tuscan**. ◆ NOUN [5] something composed of separate parts; compound. [6] any plant of the family *Asteraceae* (formerly *Compositae*), typically having flower heads composed of ray flowers (e.g. dandelion), disc flowers (e.g. thistle), or both (e.g. daisy). [7] a material, such as reinforced concrete, made of two or more distinct materials. [8] a proposal that has been composited. ◆ VERB ('kɒmpəˌzaɪt) [9] (*tr*) to merge related motions from local branches of (a political party, trade union, etc.) so as to produce a manageable number of proposals for discussion at national level.
▷HISTORY C16: from Latin *compositus* well arranged, from *compōnere* to collect, arrange; see COMPONENT
▸**'compositely** ADVERB ▸**'compositeness** NOUN

composite colour signal NOUN a colour television signal in which luminance and two chrominance components are encoded into a single signal.

composite number NOUN a positive integer that can be factorized into two or more other positive integers. Compare **prime number**.

composite photograph NOUN a photograph formed by superimposing two or more separate photographs.

composite school NOUN *Eastern Canadian* a secondary school offering both academic and nonacademic courses.

composition (ˌkɒmpə'zɪʃən) NOUN [1] the act of putting together or making up by combining parts or ingredients. [2] something formed in this manner or the resulting state or quality; a mixture. [3] the parts of which something is composed or made up; constitution. [4] a work of music, art, or literature. [5] the harmonious arrangement of the parts of a work of art in relation to each other and to the whole. [6] a piece of writing undertaken as an academic exercise in grammatically acceptable writing; an essay. [7] *Printing* the act or technique of setting up type. [8] *Linguistics* the formation of compound words. [9] *Logic* the fallacy of inferring that the properties of the part are also true of the whole, as *every member of the team has won a prize, so the team will win a prize*. [10] **a** a settlement by mutual consent, esp a legal agreement whereby the creditors agree to accept partial payment of a debt in full settlement. **b** the sum so agreed. [11] *Chem* the nature and proportions of the elements comprising a chemical compound.
▷HISTORY C14: from Old French, from Latin *compositus*; see COMPOSITE, -ION
▸**ˌcompo'sitional** ADJECTIVE

composition of forces NOUN the combination, by vector algebra, of two or more forces into a single equivalent force (the resultant).

compositor (kəm'pɒzɪtə) NOUN *Printing* a person who sets and corrects type and generally assembles text and illustrations for printing. Sometimes shortened to **comp**.
▸**compositorial** (kəmˌpɒzɪ'tɔːrɪəl) ADJECTIVE

compos mentis *Latin* ('kɒmpəs 'mɛntɪs) ADJECTIVE (*postpositive*) of sound mind; sane.

compossible (kɒm'pɒsɪbᵊl) ADJECTIVE *Rare* possible in coexistence with something else.

compost ('kɒmpɒst) NOUN [1] a mixture of organic residues such as decomposed vegetation, manure, etc., used as a fertilizer. [2] a mixture, normally of plant remains, peat, charcoal, etc., in which plants are grown, esp in pots. [3] *Rare* a compound or mixture. ◆ VERB (*tr*) [4] to make (vegetable matter) into compost. [5] to fertilize with compost.
▷HISTORY C14: from Old French *compost*, from Latin *compositus* put together; see COMPOSITE

compostable (kɒm'pɒstəbᵊl) ADJECTIVE capable of being used as compost: *compostable waste*.

Compostela (*Spanish* kɔmpɔs'tela) NOUN See **Santiago de Compostela**.

composure (kəm'pəʊʒə) NOUN calmness, esp of the mind; tranquillity; serenity.

compotation (ˌkɒmpə'teɪʃən) NOUN *Rare* the act of drinking together in a company.
▷HISTORY C16: from Latin *compōtātiō*, translation of Greek SYMPOSIUM
▸**'compoˌtator** NOUN

compote ('kɒmpəʊt; *French* kɔ̃pɔt) NOUN a dish of fruit stewed with sugar or in a syrup and served hot or cold.
▷HISTORY C17: from French *composte*, from Latin *composita*, feminine of *compositus* put in place; see COMPOSITE

compound[1] NOUN ('kɒmpaʊnd) [1] a substance that contains atoms of two or more chemical elements held together by chemical bonds. [2] any combination of two or more parts, aspects, etc. [3] a word formed from two existing words or combining forms. ◆ VERB (kəm'paʊnd) (*mainly tr*) [4] to mix or combine so as to create a compound or other product. [5] to make by combining parts, elements, aspects, etc.: *to compound a new plastic*. [6] to intensify by an added element: *his anxiety was compounded by her crying*. [7] *Finance* to calculate or pay (interest) on both the principal and its accrued interest. [8] (*also intr*) to come to an agreement in (a quarrel, dispute, etc.). [9] (*also intr*) to settle (a debt, promise, etc.) for less than what is owed; compromise. [10] *Law* to agree not to prosecute in return for a consideration: *to compound a crime*. [11] *Electrical engineering* to place duplex windings on the field coil of (a motor or generator), one acting as a shunt, the other being in series with the main

circuit, thus making the machine self-regulating. ◆ ADJECTIVE ('kɒmpaʊnd) 12 composed of or created by the combination of two or more parts, elements, etc. 13 (of a word) consisting of elements that are also words or productive combining forms. 14 (of a sentence) formed by coordination of two or more sentences. 15 (of a verb or the tense, mood, etc., of a verb) formed by using an auxiliary verb in addition to the main verb: *the future in English is a compound tense involving the use of such auxiliary verbs as "shall" and "will"*. 16 *Music* **a** denoting a time in which the number of beats per bar is a multiple of three: *six-four is an example of compound time*. **b** (of an interval) greater than an octave. 17 *Zoology* another word for **colonial** (sense 6). 18 (of a steam engine, turbine, etc.) having multiple stages in which the steam or working fluid from one stage is used in a subsequent stage. 19 (of a piston engine) having a turbocharger powered by a turbine in the exhaust stream.
▷HISTORY C14: from earlier *compounen*, from Old French *compondre* to collect, set in order, from Latin *compōnere*
▸**com'poundable** ADJECTIVE ▸**com'pounder** NOUN

compound[2] ('kɒmpaʊnd) NOUN 1 (esp formerly in South Africa) an enclosure, esp on the mines, containing the living quarters for Black workers. 2 any similar enclosure, such as a camp for prisoners of war. 3 (formerly in India, China, etc.) the enclosure in which a European's house or factory stood.
▷HISTORY C17: by folk etymology (influenced by COMPOUND[1]) from Malay *kampong* village

compound annual return NOUN the total return available from an investment, deposit, etc., when the interest earned is used to augment the capital. Abbreviation: **CAR**.

compound engine NOUN 1 a steam engine in which the steam is expanded in more than one stage, first in a high-pressure cylinder and then in one or more low-pressure cylinders. 2 a reciprocating engine in which the exhaust gases are expanded in a turbine to drive a turbocharger.

compound eye NOUN the convex eye of insects and some crustaceans, consisting of numerous separate light-sensitive units (ommatidia). See also **ocellus**.

compound fault NOUN *Geology* a series of closely spaced faults.

compound flower NOUN a flower head made up of many small flowers appearing as a single bloom, as in the daisy.

compound fraction NOUN another name for **complex fraction**.

compound fracture NOUN a fracture in which the broken bone either pierces the skin or communicates with an open wound.

compound interest NOUN interest calculated on both the principal and its accrued interest. Compare **simple interest**.

compound leaf NOUN a leaf consisting of two or more leaflets borne on the same leafstalk.

compound lens NOUN a lens consisting of more than one component lens.

compound microscope NOUN an instrument for magnifying small objects, consisting of a lens of short focal length for forming an image that is further magnified by a second lens of longer focal length. Compare **simple microscope**.

compound number NOUN a quantity expressed in two or more different but related units: *3 hours 10 seconds is a compound number*.

compound sentence NOUN a sentence containing at least two coordinate clauses.

compound time NOUN See **compound** (sense 16).

comprador *or* **compradore** (ˌkɒmprəˈdɔː) NOUN (formerly in China and some other Asian countries) a native agent of a foreign enterprise.
▷HISTORY C17: from Portuguese: buyer, from Late Latin *comparātor*, from Latin *comparāre* to purchase, from *parāre* to prepare

comprehend (ˌkɒmprɪˈhɛnd) VERB 1 to perceive or understand. 2 (*tr*) to comprise or embrace; include.
▷HISTORY C14: from Latin *comprehendere*, from *prehendere* to seize

comprehensible (ˌkɒmprɪˈhɛnsəbᵊl) ADJECTIVE capable of being comprehended.
▸**ˌcompreˌhensiˈbility** *or* **ˌcompreˈhensibleness** NOUN
▸**ˌcompreˈhensibly** ADVERB

comprehension (ˌkɒmprɪˈhɛnʃən) NOUN 1 the act or capacity of understanding. 2 the state of including or comprising something; comprehensiveness. 3 *Education* an exercise consisting of a previously unseen passage of text with related questions, designed to test a student's understanding esp of a foreign language. 4 *Logic, obsolete* the attributes implied by a given concept or term; connotation.

comprehensive (ˌkɒmprɪˈhɛnsɪv) ADJECTIVE 1 of broad scope or content; including all or much. 2 (of a car insurance policy) providing protection against most risks, including third-party liability, fire, theft, and damage. 3 having the ability to understand. 4 of, relating to, or being a comprehensive school. ◆ NOUN 5 short for **comprehensive school**.
▸**ˌcompreˈhensively** ADVERB ▸**ˌcompreˈhensiveness** NOUN

comprehensive school NOUN 1 *Chiefly Brit* a secondary school for children of all abilities from the same district. 2 *Eastern Canadian* another name for **composite school**.

compress VERB (kəmˈprɛs) 1 (*tr*) to squeeze together or compact into less space; condense. ◆ NOUN (ˈkɒmprɛs) 2 a wet or dry cloth or gauze pad with or without medication, applied firmly to some part of the body to relieve discomfort, reduce fever, drain a wound, etc. 3 a machine for packing material, esp cotton, under pressure.
▷HISTORY C14: from Late Latin *compressāre*, from Latin *comprimere*, from *premere* to press
▸**comˈpressible** ADJECTIVE ▸**comˈpressibleness** NOUN
▸**comˈpressibly** ADVERB

compressed (kəmˈprɛst) ADJECTIVE 1 squeezed together or condensed. 2 (of the form of flatfishes, certain plant parts, etc.) flattened laterally along the whole length.

compressed air NOUN air at a higher pressure than atmospheric pressure: used esp as a source of power for machines.

compressibility (kəmˌprɛsɪˈbɪlɪtɪ) NOUN 1 the ability to be compressed. 2 *Physics* the reciprocal of the bulk modulus; the ratio of volume strain to stress at constant temperature. Symbol: *k*.

compression (kəmˈprɛʃən) NOUN 1 Also called: **compressure** (kəmˈprɛʃə). the act of compressing or the condition of being compressed. 2 an increase in pressure of the charge in an engine or compressor obtained by reducing its volume.

compression-ignition engine NOUN a type of internal-combustion engine, such as a diesel, in which ignition occurs as a result of the rise in temperature caused by compression of the mixture in the cylinder.

compression ratio NOUN the ratio of the volume enclosed by the cylinder of an internal-combustion engine at the beginning of the compression stroke to the volume enclosed at the end of it.

compressive (kəmˈprɛsɪv) ADJECTIVE compressing or having the power or capacity to compress.
▸**comˈpressively** ADVERB

compressor (kəmˈprɛsə) NOUN 1 any reciprocating or rotating device that compresses a gas. 2 the part of a gas turbine that compresses the air before it enters the combustion chambers. 3 any muscle that causes compression of any part or structure. 4 a medical instrument for holding down a part of the body. 5 an electronic device for reducing the variation in signal amplitude in a transmission system. Compare **expander, compander**.

comprise (kəmˈpraɪz) VERB (*tr*) 1 to include; contain. 2 to constitute the whole of; consist of: *her singing comprised the entertainment*.
▷HISTORY C15: from French *compris* included, understood, from *comprendre* to COMPREHEND
▸**comˈprisable** ADJECTIVE ▸**comˈprisal** NOUN

> **Language note** The use of *of* after *comprise* should be avoided: *the library comprises* (not *comprises of*) *500 000 books and manuscripts*.

compromise (ˈkɒmprəˌmaɪz) NOUN 1 settlement of a dispute by concessions on both or all sides. 2 the terms of such a settlement. 3 something midway between two or more different things. 4 an exposure of one's good name, reputation, etc., to injury. ◆ VERB 5 to settle (a dispute) by making concessions. 6 (*tr*) to expose (a person or persons) to disrepute. 7 (*tr*) to prejudice unfavourably; weaken: *his behaviour compromised his chances*. 8 (*tr*) *Obsolete* to pledge mutually.
▷HISTORY C15: from Old French *compromis*, from Latin *comprōmissum* mutual agreement to accept the decision of an arbiter, from *comprōmittere*, from *prōmittere* to promise
▸**ˈcomproˌmiser** NOUN ▸**ˈcomproˌmisingly** ADVERB

compte rendu *French* (kɔ̃t rɑ̃dy) NOUN, *plural* ***comptes rendus*** (kɔ̃t rɑ̃dy). 1 a short review or notice, esp of a book. 2 a statement of account.
▷HISTORY literally: account rendered

Comptometer (kɒmpˈtɒmɪtə) NOUN *Trademark* a high-speed calculating machine: superseded by electronic calculators.

Compton effect (ˈkɒmptən) NOUN a phenomenon in which a collision between a photon and a particle results in an increase in the kinetic energy of the particle and a corresponding increase in the wavelength of the photon.
▷HISTORY C20: named after Arthur Holly *Compton* (1892–1962), US physicist

comptroller (kənˈtrəʊlə) NOUN a variant spelling of **controller** (sense 2), esp as a title of any of various financial executives
▸**compˈtrollerˌship** NOUN

compulsion (kəmˈpʌlʃən) NOUN 1 the act of compelling or the state of being compelled. 2 something that compels. 3 *Psychiatry* an inner drive that causes a person to perform actions, often of a trivial and repetitive nature, against his or her will. See also **obsession**.
▷HISTORY C15: from Old French, from Latin *compellere* to COMPEL

compulsive (kəmˈpʌlsɪv) ADJECTIVE 1 relating to or involving compulsion. ◆ NOUN 2 *Psychiatry* an individual who is subject to a psychological compulsion.
▸**comˈpulsively** ADVERB ▸**comˈpulsiveness** NOUN

compulsory (kəmˈpʌlsərɪ) ADJECTIVE 1 required by regulations or laws; obligatory: *compulsory education*. 2 involving or employing compulsion; compelling; necessary; essential.
▸**comˈpulsorily** ADVERB ▸**comˈpulsoriness** NOUN

compulsory purchase NOUN purchase of a house or other property by a local authority or government department for public use or to make way for development, regardless of whether or not the owner wishes to sell.

compunction (kəmˈpʌŋkʃən) NOUN a feeling of remorse, guilt, or regret.
▷HISTORY C14: from Church Latin *compunctiō*, from Latin *compungere* to sting, from *com-* (intensive) + *pungere* to puncture; see POINT
▸**comˈpunctious** ADJECTIVE ▸**comˈpunctiously** ADVERB

compurgation (ˌkɒmpɜːˈgeɪʃən) NOUN *Law* (formerly) a method of trial whereby a defendant might be acquitted if a sufficient number of persons swore to his innocence.
▷HISTORY C17: from Medieval Latin *compurgātiō*, from Latin *compurgāre* to purify entirely, from *com-* (intensive) + *purgāre* to PURGE
▸**ˈcompurˌgator** NOUN ▸**comˈpurgatory** *or* **comˌpurgaˈtorial** ADJECTIVE

computation (ˌkɒmpjʊˈteɪʃən) NOUN a calculation involving numbers or quantities.
▸**ˌcompuˈtational** ADJECTIVE

computational fluid dynamics NOUN (*functioning as singular*) the prediction of the behaviour of fluids and of the effects of fluid motion past objects by numerical methods rather than model experiments.

compute (kəmˈpjuːt) VERB 1 to calculate (an answer, result, etc.), often with the aid of a computer. ◆ NOUN 2 calculation; computation (esp in the phrase **beyond compute**).
▷HISTORY C17: from Latin *computāre*, from *putāre* to think
▸**comˈputable** ADJECTIVE ▸**comˌputaˈbility** NOUN

computed tomography NOUN *Med* another name (esp US) for **computerized tomography**.

computer (kəmˈpjuːtə) NOUN 1 **a** a device,

usually electronic, that processes data according to a set of instructions. The **digital computer** stores data in discrete units and performs arithmetical and logical operations at very high speed. The **analog computer** has no memory and is slower than the digital computer but has a continuous rather than a discrete input. The **hybrid computer** combines some of the advantages of digital and analog computers. **b** (*as modifier*): *computer technology*. Related prefix: **cyber-**. 2 a person who computes or calculates.

computer-aided design NOUN the use of computer techniques in designing products, esp involving the use of computer graphics. Abbreviation: **CAD**.

computer-aided engineering NOUN the use of computers to automate manufacturing processes. Abbreviation: **CAE**.

computer architecture NOUN the structure, behaviour, and design of computers.

computerate (kəm'pju:tərɪt) ADJECTIVE able to use computers.
▷HISTORY C20: COMPUTER + -ATE[1], by analogy with *literate*

computer conferencing NOUN the conduct of meetings by the use of computer-based telecommunications.

computer dating NOUN the use of computers by dating agencies to match their clients.

computer game NOUN any of various games, recorded on cassette or disc for use in a home computer, that are played by manipulating a mouse, joystick, or the keys on the keyboard of a computer in response to the graphics on the screen.

computer graphics NOUN (*functioning as singular*) the use of a computer to produce and manipulate pictorial images on a video screen, as in animation techniques or the production of audiovisual aids.

computerize *or* **computerise** (kəm'pju:təˌraɪz) VERB 1 (*tr*) to cause (certain operations) to be performed by a computer, esp as a replacement for human labour. 2 (*intr*) to install a computer. 3 (*tr*) to control or perform (operations within a system) by means of a computer. 4 (*tr*) to process or store (information) by means of or in a computer.
▸**comˌputeri'zation** *or* **comˌputeri'sation** NOUN

computerized tomography NOUN *Med* a radiological technique that produces images of cross sections through a patient's body using low levels of radiation. Also called (esp US): **computed tomography**. Abbreviation: **CT**. See also **CT scanner**.

computer language NOUN another term for **programming language**.

computer literate ADJECTIVE able to use computers.
▸**computer literacy** NOUN

computer science NOUN the study of computers and their application.

computer typesetting NOUN a system for the high-speed composition of type by a device driven by punched paper tape or magnetic tape that has been processed by a computer.

computing (kəm'pju:tɪŋ) NOUN 1 the activity of using computers and writing programs for them. 2 the study of computers and their implications. ◆ ADJECTIVE 3 of or relating to computers: *computing skills*.

Comr ABBREVIATION FOR Commissioner.

comrade ('kɒmreɪd, -rɪd) NOUN 1 an associate or companion. 2 a fellow member of a political party, esp a fellow Communist or socialist.
▷HISTORY C16: from French *camarade*, from Spanish *camarada* group of soldiers sharing a billet, from *cámara* room, from Latin; see CAMERA, CHAMBER
▸**'comradely** ADJECTIVE ▸**'comradeˌship** NOUN

Comrades Marathon NOUN **the.** *South African* an annual long-distance race run each June from Durban to Pietermaritzburg, a distance of approximately 90 kilometres (56 miles). Often shortened to **the Comrades**.
▷HISTORY C20: first run after WWI by returning servicemen to commemorate their fallen comrades

Comsat ('kɒmsæt) NOUN *Trademark* short for **communications satellite**.

comstockery ('kʌmˌstɒkərɪ, 'kɒm-) NOUN *US* immoderate censorship on grounds of immorality.
▷HISTORY C20: coined by G. B. Shaw (1905) after Anthony *Comstock* (1844–1915), US moral crusader, who founded the Society for the Suppression of Vice

Comstock Lode ('kʌmˌstɒk, 'kɒm-) NOUN an extensive gold and silver vein in W Nevada, near Virginia City.
▷HISTORY C19: named after T. P. *Comstock* (1820–70), American prospector

Comus ('kəʊməs) NOUN (in late Roman mythology) a god of revelry.
▷HISTORY C17: from Latin, from Greek *kōmos* a revel

Com. Ver. ABBREVIATION FOR Common Version (of the Bible).

con[1] (kɒn) *Informal* ◆ NOUN 1 **a** short for **confidence trick. b** (*as modifier*): *con man*. ◆ VERB **cons, conning, conned.** 2 (*tr*) to swindle or defraud.
▷HISTORY C19: from CONFIDENCE

con[2] (kɒn) NOUN (*usually plural*) 1 an argument or vote against a proposal, motion, etc. 2 a person who argues or votes against a proposal, motion, etc. ◆ Compare **pro**[1]. See also **pros and cons**.
▷HISTORY from Latin *contrā* against, opposed to

con[3] (kɒn) NOUN *Slang* short for **convict**.

con[4] *or esp US* **conn** (kɒn) *Nautical* ◆ VERB **cons** *or* **conns, conning, conned.** 1 (*tr*) to direct the steering of (a vessel). ◆ NOUN 2 the place where a person who cons a vessel is stationed.
▷HISTORY C17 *cun*, from earlier *condien* to guide, from Old French *conduire*, from Latin *condūcere;* see CONDUCT

con[5] (kɒn) VERB **cons, conning, conned.** (*tr*) *Archaic* to study attentively or learn (esp in the phrase **con by rote**).
▷HISTORY C15: variant of CAN[1] in the sense: to come to know

con[6] (kɒn) PREPOSITION *Music* with.
▷HISTORY Italian

Con. ABBREVIATION FOR Conservative.

con- PREFIX a variant of **com-**.

conacre (kʌ'ne:kər) NOUN *Irish* farming land let for a season or for eleven months.
▷HISTORY C19: from CORN[1] + ACRE

Conakry *or* **Konakri** (*French* kɔnakri) NOUN the capital of Guinea, a port on the island of Tombo. Pop.: 1 764 000 (1999 est.).

con amore (kɒn æ'mɔ:rɪ) ADJECTIVE, ADVERB *Music* (to be performed) lovingly.
▷HISTORY C19: from Italian: with love

conation (kəʊ'neɪʃən) NOUN the element in psychological processes that tends towards activity or change and appears as desire, volition, and striving.
▷HISTORY C19: from Latin *cōnātiō* an attempting, from *cōnārī* to try
▸**co'national** ADJECTIVE

conative ('kɒnətɪv, 'kəʊ-) ADJECTIVE 1 *Grammar* denoting an aspect of verbs in some languages used to indicate the effort of the agent in performing the activity described by the verb. 2 of or relating to conation.

conatus (kəʊ'neɪtəs) NOUN, *plural* **-tus.** 1 an effort or striving of natural impulse. 2 (esp in the philosophy of Spinoza) the tendency of all things to persist in their own being.
▷HISTORY C17: from Latin: effort, from *cōnārī* to try

con brio (kɒn 'bri:əʊ) ADJECTIVE, ADVERB *Music* (to be performed) with liveliness or spirit, as in the phrase **allegro con brio**.
▷HISTORY Italian: with energy

conc. concentrated.

concatenate (kɒn'kætɪˌneɪt) VERB 1 (*tr*) to link or join together, esp in a chain or series. ◆ ADJECTIVE 2 linked or joined together.
▷HISTORY C16: from Late Latin *concatēnāre* from Latin *com-* together + *catēna* CHAIN

concatenation (kɒnˌkætɪ'neɪʃən) NOUN 1 a series of interconnected events, concepts, etc. 2 the act of linking together or the state of being joined. 3 *Logic* a function that forms a single string of symbols from two given strings by placing the second after the first.

concave ('kɒnkeɪv, kɒn'keɪv) ADJECTIVE 1 curving inwards. 2 *Physics* having one or two surfaces curved or ground in the shape of a section of the interior of a sphere, paraboloid, etc.: *a concave lens*. 3 *Maths* (of a polygon) containing an interior angle greater than 180°. 4 an obsolete word for **hollow.** ◆ VERB 5 (*tr*) to make concave. ◆ Compare **convex.**
▷HISTORY C15: from Latin *concavus* arched, from *cavus* hollow
▸**'concavely** ADVERB ▸**'concaveness** NOUN

concavity (kɒn'kævɪtɪ) NOUN, *plural* **-ties.** 1 the state or quality of being concave. 2 a concave surface or thing; cavity.

concavo-concave (kɒnˌkeɪvəʊkɒn'keɪv) ADJECTIVE (esp of a lens) having both sides concave; biconcave.

concavo-convex ADJECTIVE 1 having one side concave and the other side convex. 2 (of a lens) having a concave face with greater curvature than the convex face. Compare **convexo-concave** (sense 2).

conceal (kən'si:l) VERB (*tr*) 1 to keep from discovery; hide. 2 to keep secret.
▷HISTORY C14: from Old French *conceler*, from Latin *concēlāre*, from *com-* (intensive) + *cēlāre* to hide
▸**con'cealable** ADJECTIVE ▸**con'cealer** NOUN
▸**con'cealment** NOUN

concede (kən'si:d) VERB 1 (when *tr, may take a clause as object*) to admit or acknowledge (something) as true or correct. 2 to yield or allow (something, such as a right). 3 (*tr*) to admit as certain in outcome: *to concede an election*.
▷HISTORY C17: from Latin *concēdere*, from *cēdere* to give way, CEDE
▸**con'cededly** ADVERB ▸**con'ceder** NOUN

conceit (kən'si:t) NOUN 1 a high, often exaggerated, opinion of oneself or one's accomplishments; vanity. 2 *Literary* an elaborate image or far-fetched comparison, esp as used by the English Metaphysical poets. 3 *Archaic* **a** a witty expression. **b** fancy; imagination. **c** an idea. 4 *Obsolete* a small ornament. ◆ VERB (*tr*) 5 *Northern English dialect* to like or be able to bear (something, such as food or drink). 6 *Obsolete* to think or imagine.
▷HISTORY C14: from CONCEIVE

conceited (kən'si:tɪd) ADJECTIVE 1 having a high or exaggerated opinion of oneself or one's accomplishments. 2 *Archaic* fanciful. 3 *Obsolete* witty or intelligent.
▸**con'ceitedly** ADVERB ▸**con'ceitedness** NOUN

conceivable (kən'si:vəb^{ə}l) ADJECTIVE capable of being understood, believed, or imagined; possible.
▸**conˌceiva'bility** *or* **con'ceivableness** NOUN
▸**con'ceivably** ADVERB

conceive (kən'si:v) VERB 1 (when *intr*, foll by *of;* when *tr, often takes a clause as object*) to have an idea (of); imagine; think. 2 (*tr; takes a clause as object or an infinitive*) to hold as an opinion; believe. 3 (*tr*) to develop or form, esp in the mind: *she conceived a passion for music*. 4 to become pregnant with (young). 5 (*tr*) *Rare* to express in words.
▷HISTORY C13: from Old French *conceivre*, from Latin *concipere* to take in, from *capere* to take
▸**con'ceiver** NOUN

concelebrate (kən'sɛlɪˌbreɪt) VERB *Christianity* to celebrate (the Eucharist or Mass) jointly with one or more other priests.
▷HISTORY C16: from Latin *concelebrāre*
▸**conˌcele'bration** NOUN

concent (kən'sɛnt) NOUN *Archaic* a concord, as of sounds, voices, etc.
▷HISTORY C16: from Latin *concentus* harmonious sounds, from *concinere* to sing together, from *canere* to sing

concentrate ('kɒnsənˌtreɪt) VERB 1 to come or cause to come to a single purpose or aim: *to concentrate one's hopes on winning*. 2 to make or become denser or purer by the removal of certain elements, esp the solvent of a solution. 3 (*tr*) to remove rock or sand from (an ore) to make it purer. 4 (*intr;* often foll by *on*) to bring one's faculties to bear (on); think intensely (about). ◆ NOUN 5 a concentrated material or solution: *tomato concentrate*.
▷HISTORY C17: back formation from CONCENTRATION, ultimately from Latin *com-* same + *centrum* CENTRE
▸**'concenˌtrator** NOUN

concentration (ˌkɒnsən'treɪʃən) NOUN 1 intense mental application; complete attention. 2 the act or process of concentrating. 3 something that is concentrated. 4 the strength of a solution, esp the amount of dissolved substance in a given volume of solvent, usually expressed in moles per cubic metre or cubic decimetre (litre). Symbol: *c*. 5 the process of increasing the concentration of a solution. 6 *Military* **a** the act of bringing together military forces. **b** the application of fire from a number of weapons against a target. 7 *Economics* the degree to which the output or employment in an industry is accounted for by only a few firms. 8 another name (esp US) for **Pelmanism.**

concentration camp NOUN a guarded prison camp in which nonmilitary prisoners are held, esp one of those in Nazi Germany in which millions were exterminated.

concentrative ('kɒnsənˌtreɪtɪv) ADJECTIVE tending to concentrate; characterized by concentration.
▸**'concenˌtratively** ADVERB ▸**'concenˌtrativeness** NOUN

concentre *or US* **concenter** (kɒn'sɛntə) VERB to converge or cause to converge on a common centre; concentrate.
▷HISTORY C16: from French *concentrer;* see CONCENTRATE

concentric (kən'sɛntrɪk) ADJECTIVE having a common centre: *concentric circles*. Compare **eccentric** (sense 3).
▷HISTORY C14: from Medieval Latin *concentricus,* from Latin *com-* same + *centrum* CENTRE
▸**con'centrically** ADVERB ▸**concentricity** (ˌkɒnsən'trɪsɪtɪ) NOUN

Concepción (*Spanish* konθep'θjon) NOUN an industrial city in S central Chile. Pop.: 362 589 (1999 est.).

concept ('kɒnsɛpt) NOUN 1 an idea, esp an abstract idea: *the concepts of biology*. 2 *Philosophy* a general idea or notion that corresponds to some class of entities and that consists of the characteristic or essential features of the class. 3 *Philosophy* **a** the conjunction of all the characteristic features of something. **b** a theoretical construct within some theory. **c** a directly intuited object of thought. **d** the meaning of a predicate. 4 (*modifier*) (of a product, esp a car) created as an exercise to demonstrate the technical skills and imagination of the designers, and not intended for mass production or sale.
▷HISTORY C16: from Latin *conceptum* something received or conceived, from *concipere* to take in, CONCEIVE

conceptacle (kən'sɛptək^{ə}l) NOUN a flask-shaped cavity containing the reproductive organs in some algae and fungi.
▷HISTORY C17: from Latin *conceptāculum* receptacle, from *concipere* to receive, CONCEIVE

conception (kən'sɛpʃən) NOUN 1 something conceived; notion, idea, design, or plan. 2 the description under which someone considers something: *her conception of freedom is wrong*. 3 the fertilization of an ovum by a sperm in the Fallopian tube followed by implantation in the womb. 4 origin or beginning: *from its conception the plan was a failure*. 5 the act or power of forming notions; invention.
▷HISTORY C13: from Latin *conceptiō,* from *concipere* to CONCEIVE
▸**con'ceptional** *or* **con'ceptive** ADJECTIVE

conception rate NOUN *Vet science* the success rate of artificial insemination in agricultural animals, usually expressed as a percentage.

conceptual (kən'sɛptjʊəl) ADJECTIVE 1 relating to or concerned with concepts; abstract. 2 concerned with the definitions or relations of the concepts of some field of enquiry rather than with the facts.
▸**con'ceptually** ADVERB

conceptual art NOUN art in which the idea behind a particular work, and the means of producing it, are more important than the finished work.

conceptualism (kən'sɛptjʊəˌlɪzəm) NOUN 1 the philosophical theory that the application of general words to a variety of objects reflects the existence of some mental entity through which the application is mediated and which constitutes the meaning of the term. Compare **nominalism, realism, Platonism.** 2 the philosophical view that there is no reality independent of our conception of it, or (as in the philosophy of Immanuel Kant, the German philosopher (1724–1804)) that the intellect is not a merely passive recipient of experience but rather imposes a structure on it.
▸**con'ceptualist** NOUN ▸**conˌceptual'istic** ADJECTIVE

conceptualize *or* **conceptualise** (kən'sɛptjʊəˌlaɪz) VERB to form (a concept or concepts) out of observations, experience, data, etc.
▸**conˌceptuali'zation** *or* **conˌceptuali'sation** NOUN

concern (kən'sɜːn) VERB (*tr*) 1 to relate to; be of importance or interest to; affect. 2 (usually foll by *with* or *in*) to involve or interest (oneself): *he concerns himself with other people's affairs*. ◆ NOUN 3 something that affects or is of importance to a person; affair; business. 4 regard for or interest in a person or a thing: *he felt a strong concern for her*. 5 anxiety, worry, or solicitude. 6 important bearing or relation: *his news has great concern for us*. 7 a commercial company or enterprise. 8 *Informal* a material thing, esp one of which one has a low opinion.
▷HISTORY C15: from Late Latin *concernere* to mingle together, from Latin *com-* together + *cernere* to sift, distinguish

concerned (kən'sɜːnd) ADJECTIVE 1 (*postpositive*) interested, guilty, involved, or appropriate: *I shall find the boy concerned and punish him*. 2 worried, troubled, or solicitous.
▸**concernedly** (kən'sɜːnɪdlɪ) ADVERB ▸**con'cernedness** NOUN

concerning (kən'sɜːnɪŋ) PREPOSITION 1 about; regarding; on the subject of. ◆ ADJECTIVE 2 worrying or troublesome.

concernment (kən'sɜːnmənt) NOUN 1 *Rare* affair or business; concern. 2 *Archaic* a matter of importance.

concert NOUN ('kɒnsɜːt, -sət) 1 **a** a performance of music by players or singers that does not involve theatrical staging. Compare **recital** (sense 1). **b** (*as modifier*): *a concert version of an opera*. 2 agreement in design, plan, or action. 3 **in concert. a** acting in a co-ordinated fashion with a common purpose. **b** (of musicians, esp rock musicians) performing live. ◆ VERB (kən'sɜːt) 4 to arrange or contrive (a plan) by mutual agreement.
▷HISTORY C16: from French *concerter* to bring into agreement, from Italian *concertare,* from Late Latin *concertāre* to work together, from Latin: to dispute, debate, from *certāre* to contend

concertante (ˌkɒntʃə'tæntɪ) *Music* ◆ ADJECTIVE 1 characterized by contrasting alternating tutti and solo passages. ◆ NOUN, *plural* **-ti** (-tɪ). 2 a composition characterized by such contrasts.
▷HISTORY C18: from Italian, from *concertare* to perform a concert, from *concerto* CONCERT

concerted (kən'sɜːtɪd) ADJECTIVE 1 mutually contrived, planned, or arranged; combined (esp in the phrases **concerted action, concerted effort**). 2 *Music* arranged in parts for a group of singers or players.
▸**con'certedly** ADVERB

Concertgebouw (*Dutch* kɔn'sɛrtxəbɔu) NOUN a concert hall in Amsterdam, inaugurated in 1888: the **Concertgebouw Orchestra** established in 1888, has been independent of the hall since World War II.

concertgoer ('kɒnsɜːtˌgəʊə) NOUN a person who attends concerts of music.

concert grand NOUN a full-size grand piano, usually around 7 feet in length. Compare **baby grand, boudoir grand.**

concertina (ˌkɒnsə'tiːnə) NOUN 1 a small hexagonal musical instrument of the reed organ family in which metallic reeds are vibrated by air from a set of bellows operated by the player's hands. Notes are produced by pressing buttons. ◆ VERB **-nas, -naing, -naed.** 2 (*intr*) to collapse or fold up like a concertina.
▷HISTORY C19: CONCERT + *-ina*
▸**ˌconcer'tinist** NOUN

concertino (ˌkɒntʃə'tiːnəʊ) NOUN, *plural* **-ni** (-nɪ). 1 the small group of soloists in a concerto grosso. Compare **ripieno.** 2 a short concerto.
▷HISTORY C19: from Italian: a little CONCERTO

concertize *or* **concertise** ('kɒnsəˌtaɪz) VERB (*intr*) (esp of a soloist or conductor) to give concerts.

concertmaster ('kɒnsətˌmɑːstə) NOUN a US and Canadian word for **leader** (of an orchestra).

concerto (kən'tʃɛətəʊ) NOUN, *plural* **-tos** *or* **-ti** (-tɪ). 1 a composition for an orchestra and one or more soloists. The classical concerto usually consisted of several movements, and often a cadenza. See also **sonata** (sense 1), **symphony** (sense 1). 2 another word for **ripieno.**
▷HISTORY C18: from Italian: CONCERT

concerto grosso ('grɒsəʊ) NOUN, *plural* **concerti grossi** ('grɒsɪ) *or* **concerto grossos.** a composition for an orchestra and a group of soloists, chiefly of the baroque period.
▷HISTORY Italian, literally: big concerto

concert overture NOUN See **overture** (sense 1c).

concert party NOUN 1 a musical entertainment popular in the early 20th century, esp one at a British seaside resort. 2 *Stock Exchange, informal* a group of individuals or companies who secretly agree to purchase shares separately in a particular company, which they plan to amalgamate later into a single holding: a malpractice that is illegal in some countries.

concert pitch NOUN 1 the frequency of 440 hertz assigned to the A above middle C. See **pitch**[1] (sense 28b), **international pitch.** 2 *Informal* a state of extreme readiness.

concertstück (kən'sɜːtˌʃtuːk) NOUN *Music* 1 a composition in concerto style but shorter than a full concerto. 2 (loosely) a piece suitable for concert performance.
▷HISTORY from German *Konzertstück* a concertino

concert tuning NOUN *Music* the standard tuning for a guitar: E A D G B E.

concession (kən'sɛʃən) NOUN 1 the act of yielding or conceding, as to a demand or argument. 2 something conceded. 3 *Brit* a reduction in the usual price of a ticket granted to a special group of customers: *a student concession*. 4 any grant of rights, land, or property by a government, local authority, corporation, or individual. 5 the right, esp an exclusive right, to market a particular product in a given area. 6 *US and Canadian* **a** the right to maintain a subsidiary business on a lessor's premises. **b** the premises so granted or the business so maintained. **c** a free rental period for such premises. 7 *Canadian* (chiefly in Ontario and Quebec) **a** a land subdivision in a township survey. **b** another name for a **concession road.**
▷HISTORY C16: from Latin *concessiō* an allowing, from *concēdere* to CONCEDE
▸**con'cessible** ADJECTIVE

concessionaire (kənˌsɛʃə'nɛə), **concessioner** (kən'sɛʃənə), *or* **concessionary** NOUN someone who holds or operates a concession.

concessionary (kən'sɛʃənərɪ) ADJECTIVE 1 of, granted, or obtained by a concession. ◆ NOUN, *plural* **-aries.** 2 another word for **concessionaire.**

concession road NOUN *Canadian* (esp in Ontario) one of a series of roads separating concessions in a township.

concessive (kən'sɛsɪv) ADJECTIVE 1 implying or involving concession; tending to concede. 2 *Grammar* a conjunction, preposition, phrase, or clause describing a state of affairs that might have been expected to rule out what is described in the main clause but in fact does not: *"Although" in the sentence "Although they had been warned, they refused to take care" is a concessive conjunction.*
▷HISTORY C18: from Late Latin *concēssīvus,* from Latin *concēdere* to CONCEDE

conch (kɒŋk, kɒntʃ) NOUN, *plural* **conchs** (kɒŋks) *or* **conches** ('kɒntʃɪz). 1 any of various tropical marine gastropod molluscs of the genus *Strombus* and related genera, esp *S. gigas* (giant conch), characterized by a large brightly coloured spiral shell. 2 the shell of such a mollusc, used as a trumpet. 3 *Architect* another name for **concha** (sense 2).
▷HISTORY C16: from Latin *concha,* from Greek *konkhē* shellfish

concha ('kɒŋkə) NOUN, *plural* **-chae** (-kiː). 1 any bodily organ or part resembling a shell in shape, such as the external ear. 2 Also called: **conch.** *Architect* the half dome of an apse.
▸**'conchal** ADJECTIVE

conchie *or* **conchy** ('kɒntʃɪ) NOUN, *plural* **-chies.** *Informal* short for **conscientious objector.**

conchiferous (kɒŋ'kɪfərəs) ADJECTIVE 1 (esp of molluscs) having or producing a shell. 2 (of rocks) containing shells.

conchiglie (kɒn'kiːljeɪ) NOUN pasta in the form of shells.
▷HISTORY C20: Italian, literally: little shells, from Latin *concha* shell; see CONCH

conchiolin (kɒŋ'kaɪəlɪn) NOUN a fibrous insoluble protein that forms the basic structure of the shells of molluscs. Formula: $C_{30}H_{48}O_{11}N_9$.
▷HISTORY C19: from CONCH; see -IN

Conchobar ('kɒŋkəuwə, 'kɒnuə) NOUN (in Irish legend) a king of Ulster at about the beginning of the Christian era. See also **Deirdre.**

conchoid ('kɒŋkɔɪd) NOUN *Geometry* a plane curve consisting of two branches situated about a line to which they are asymptotic, so that a line from a fixed point (the pole) intersecting both branches is of constant length between asymptote and either branch. Equation: $(x - a)^2(x^2 + y^2) = b^2x^2$ where *a* is the distance between the pole and a vertical asymptote and *b* is the length of the constant segment.

conchoidal (kɒŋ'kɔɪdᵊl) ADJECTIVE 1 (of the fracture of minerals and rocks) having smooth shell-shaped convex and concave surfaces. 2 (of minerals and rocks, such as flint) having such a fracture.
▸**con'choidally** ADVERB

conchology (kɒŋ'kɒlədʒɪ) NOUN the study and collection of mollusc shells.
▸**conchological** (ˌkɒŋkə'lɒdʒɪkᵊl) ADJECTIVE
▸**con'chologist** NOUN

concierge (ˌkɒnsɪ'ɛəʒ; *French* kɔ̃sjɛrʒ) NOUN (esp in France) a caretaker of a block of flats, hotel, etc., esp one who lives on the premises.
▷HISTORY C17: from French, ultimately from Latin *conservus,* from *servus* slave

conciliar (kən'sɪlɪə) ADJECTIVE of, from, or by means of a council, esp an ecclesiastical one.
▸**con'ciliarly** ADVERB

conciliate (kən'sɪlɪˌeɪt) VERB (*tr*) 1 to overcome the hostility of; placate; win over. 2 to win or gain (favour, regard, etc.), esp by making friendly overtures. 3 *Archaic* to make compatible; reconcile.
▷HISTORY C16: from Latin *conciliāre* to bring together, from *concilium* COUNCIL
▸**con'ciliable** ADJECTIVE ▸**con'ciliˌator** NOUN

conciliation (kənˌsɪlɪ'eɪʃən) NOUN 1 the act or process of conciliating. 2 a method of helping the parties in a dispute to reach agreement, esp divorcing or separating couples to part amicably.

conciliatory (kən'sɪljətərɪ, -trɪ) *or* **conciliative** (kən'sɪljətɪv) ADJECTIVE intended to placate or reconcile.
▸**con'ciliatorily** ADVERB ▸**con'ciliatoriness** NOUN

concinnity (kən'sɪnɪtɪ) NOUN, *plural* **-ties.** a harmonious arrangement of parts, esp in literary works, speeches, etc.
▷HISTORY C16: from Latin *concinnitās* a skilful combining of various things, from *concinnāre* to adjust, of obscure origin
▸**con'cinnous** ADJECTIVE

concise (kən'saɪs) ADJECTIVE expressing much in few words; brief and to the point.
▷HISTORY C16: from Latin *concīsus* cut up, cut short, from *concīdere* to cut to pieces, from *caedere* to cut, strike down
▸**con'cisely** ADVERB ▸**con'ciseness** NOUN

concision (kən'sɪʒən) NOUN the quality of being concise; brevity; terseness.

conclave ('kɒnkleɪv, 'kɒŋ-) NOUN 1 a confidential or secret meeting. 2 *RC Church* **a** the closed apartments where the college of cardinals elects a new pope. **b** a meeting of the college of cardinals for this purpose.
▷HISTORY C14: from Medieval Latin *conclāve,* from Latin: cage, place that may be locked, from *clāvis* key
▸**'conclavist** NOUN

conclude (kən'kluːd) VERB (*mainly tr*) 1 (*also intr*) to come or cause to come to an end or conclusion. 2 (*takes a clause as object*) to decide by reasoning; deduce: *the judge concluded that the witness had told the truth.* 3 to arrange finally; settle: *to conclude a treaty; it was concluded that he should go.* 4 *Obsolete* to confine.
▷HISTORY C14: from Latin *conclūdere* to enclose, end, from *claudere* to close
▸**con'cluder** NOUN

conclusion (kən'kluːʒən) NOUN 1 end or termination. 2 the last main division of a speech, lecture, essay, etc. 3 the outcome or result of an act, process, event, etc. (esp in the phrase **a foregone conclusion**). 4 a final decision or judgment; resolution (esp in the phrase **come to a conclusion**). 5 *Logic* **a** a statement that purports to follow from another or others (the **premises**) by means of an argument. **b** a statement that does validly follow from given premises. 6 *Law* **a** an admission or statement binding on the party making it; estoppel. **b** the close of a pleading or of a conveyance. 7 **in conclusion.** lastly; to sum up. 8 **jump to conclusions.** to come to a conclusion prematurely, without sufficient thought or on incomplete evidence.
▷HISTORY C14: via Old French from Latin; see CONCLUDE, -ION

conclusive (kən'kluːsɪv) ADJECTIVE 1 putting an end to doubt; decisive; final. 2 approaching or involving an end or conclusion.
▸**con'clusively** ADVERB ▸**con'clusiveness** NOUN

concoct (kən'kɒkt) VERB (*tr*) 1 to make by combining different ingredients. 2 to invent; make up; contrive.
▷HISTORY C16: from Latin *concoctus* cooked together, from *concoquere,* from *coquere* to cook
▸**con'cocter** *or* **con'coctor** NOUN ▸**con'coctive** ADJECTIVE

concoction (kən'kɒkʃən) NOUN 1 the act or process of concocting. 2 something concocted. 3 an untruth; lie.

concomitance (kən'kɒmɪtəns) NOUN 1 existence or occurrence together or in connection with another. 2 a thing that exists in connection with another. 3 *Christian theol* the doctrine that the body and blood of Christ are present in the Eucharist.

concomitant (kən'kɒmɪtənt) ADJECTIVE 1 existing or occurring together; associative. ◆ NOUN 2 a concomitant act, person, etc.
▷HISTORY C17: from Late Latin *concomitārī* to accompany, from *com-* with + *comes* companion, fellow
▸**con'comitantly** ADVERB

concord ('kɒnkɔːd, 'kɒŋ-) NOUN 1 agreement or harmony between people or nations; amity. 2 a treaty establishing peaceful relations between nations. 3 agreement or harmony between things, ideas, etc. 4 *Music* a combination of musical notes, esp one containing a series of consonant intervals. Compare **discord** (sense 3). 5 *Grammar* another word for **agreement** (sense 6).
▷HISTORY C13: from Old French *concorde,* from Latin *concordia,* from *concors* of the same mind, harmonious, from *com-* same + *cor* heart

Concord ('kɒŋkəd) NOUN 1 a town in NE Massachusetts: scene of one of the opening military actions (1775) of the War of American Independence. Pop.: 17 080 (1990). 2 a city in New Hampshire, the state capital: printing, publishing. Pop.: 36 364 (1992).

concordance (kən'kɔːdᵊns) NOUN 1 a state or condition of agreement or harmony. 2 a book that indexes the principal words in a literary work, often with the immediate context and an account of the meaning. 3 an index produced by computer or machine, alphabetically listing every word in a text. 4 an alphabetical list of subjects or topics.

concordant (kən'kɔːdᵊnt) ADJECTIVE being in agreement: harmonious.
▸**con'cordantly** ADVERB

concordat (kɒn'kɔːdæt) NOUN a pact or treaty, esp one between the Vatican and another state concerning the interests of religion in that state.
▷HISTORY C17: via French, from Medieval Latin *concordātum,* from Latin: something agreed, from *concordāre* to be of one mind; see CONCORD

Concorde ('kɒnkɔːd, 'kɒŋ-) NOUN the first commercial supersonic airliner. Of Anglo-French construction, it is capable of cruising at over 2160 km per hr (1200 mph).

Concord grape ('kɒŋkəd, 'kɒnkɔːd) NOUN a variety of grape with purple-black fruit covered with a bluish bloom.
▷HISTORY C19: discovered at CONCORD, Mass.

concours d'élégance *French* (kɔ̃kur delegɑ̃s) NOUN a parade of cars or other vehicles, prizes being awarded to the most elegant, best designed, or best turned-out.

concourse ('kɒnkɔːs, 'kɒŋ-) NOUN 1 a crowd; throng. 2 a coming together; confluence: *a concourse of events.* 3 a large open space for the gathering of people in a public place. 4 *Chiefly US* a ground for sports, racing, athletics, etc.
▷HISTORY C14: from Old French *concours,* ultimately from Latin *concurrere* to run together, from *currere* to run

concrescence (kən'krɛsəns) NOUN *Biology* a growing together of initially separate parts or organs.
▷HISTORY C17: from Latin *concrēscentia,* from *concrēscere* to grow together, from *crēscere* to grow; see CRESCENT
▸**con'crescent** ADJECTIVE

concrete ('kɒnkriːt) NOUN 1 **a** a construction material made of a mixture of cement, sand, stone, and water that hardens to a stonelike mass. **b** (*as modifier*): *a concrete slab.* 2 *Physics* a rigid mass formed by the coalescence of separate particles. ◆ ADJECTIVE 3 relating to a particular instance or object; specific as opposed to general: *a concrete example.* 4 **a** relating to or characteristic of things capable of being perceived by the senses, as opposed to abstractions. **b** (*as noun*): *the concrete.* 5 formed by the coalescence of particles; condensed; solid. ◆ VERB 6 (*tr*) to construct in or cover with concrete. 7 (kən'kriːt) to become or cause to become solid; coalesce.
▷HISTORY C14: from Latin *concrētus* grown together, hardened, from *concrēscere;* see CONCRESCENCE
▸**'concretely** ADVERB ▸**'concreteness** NOUN ▸**con'cretive** ADJECTIVE ▸**con'cretively** ADVERB

concrete music NOUN music consisting of an electronically modified montage of tape-recorded sounds.

concrete noun NOUN a noun that refers to a material object, as for example *horse.* Compare **abstract noun.**

concrete number NOUN a number referring to a particular object or objects, as in *three dogs, ten men.*

concrete poetry NOUN poetry in which the visual form of the poem is used to convey meaning.

concretion (kən'kriːʃən) NOUN 1 the act or process of coming or growing together; coalescence. 2 a solid or solidified mass. 3 something made real, tangible, or specific. 4 any of various rounded or irregular mineral masses formed by chemical precipitation around a nucleus, such as a bone or shell, that is different in composition from the sedimentary rock that surrounds it. 5 *Pathol* another word for **calculus.**
▸**con'cretionary** ADJECTIVE

concretize *or* **concretise** ('kɒnkrɪˌtaɪz, 'kɒŋ-) VERB (*tr*) to render concrete; make real or specific; give tangible form to.
▸**ˌconcreti'zation** *or* **ˌconcreti'sation** NOUN

concubinage (kɒn'kjuːbɪnɪdʒ) NOUN 1 cohabitation without legal marriage. 2 the state of living as a concubine.

concubine ('kɒŋkjuˌbaɪn, 'kɒn-) NOUN 1 (in polygamous societies) a secondary wife, usually of lower social rank. 2 a woman who cohabits with a man.
▷HISTORY C13: from Old French, from Latin *concubīna,* from *concumbere* to lie together, from *cubare* to lie
▸**concubinary** (kɒŋ'kjubɪnərɪ) NOUN, ADJECTIVE

concupiscence (kən'kjuːpɪsəns) NOUN strong desire, esp sexual desire.
▷HISTORY C14: from Church Latin *concupiscentia,* from Latin *concupiscere* to covet ardently, from *cupere* to wish, desire
▸**con'cupiscent** ADJECTIVE

concur (kən'kɜː) VERB **-curs, -curring, -curred.** (*intr*) 1 to agree; be of the same mind; be in accord. 2 to combine, act together, or cooperate. 3 to occur simultaneously; coincide. 4 *Rare* to converge.
▷HISTORY C15: from Latin *concurrere* to run together, from *currere* to run
▸**con'curringly** ADVERB

concurrence (kən'kʌrəns) NOUN 1 the act of concurring. 2 agreement in opinion; accord; assent. 3 cooperation or combination. 4 simultaneous occurrence; coincidence. 5 *Geometry* a point at which three or more lines intersect. ◆ Also (for senses 1–4): **concurrency.**

concurrent (kən'kʌrənt) ADJECTIVE 1 taking place

at the same time or in the same location. 2 cooperating. 3 meeting at, approaching, or having a common point: *concurrent lines*. 4 having equal authority or jurisdiction. 5 in accordance or agreement; harmonious. ◆ NOUN 6 something joint or contributory; a concurrent circumstance or cause.
▸**con'currently** ADVERB

concurrent engineering NOUN a method of designing and marketing new products in which development stages are run in parallel rather than in series, to reduce lead times and costs. Also called: **interactive engineering.**

concurrent processing NOUN the ability of a computer to process two or more programs in parallel.

concuss (kən'kʌs) VERB (*tr*) 1 to injure (the brain) by a violent blow, fall, etc. 2 to shake violently; agitate; disturb.
▷HISTORY C16: from Latin *concussus* violently shaken, from *concutere* to disturb greatly, from *quatere* to shake

concussion (kən'kʌʃən) NOUN 1 a jarring of the brain, caused by a blow or a fall, usually resulting in loss of consciousness. 2 any violent shaking; jarring.
▸**con'cussive** ADJECTIVE

condemn (kən'dɛm) VERB (*tr*) 1 to express strong disapproval of; censure. 2 to pronounce judicial sentence on. 3 to demonstrate the guilt of: *his secretive behaviour condemned him*. 4 to judge or pronounce unfit for use: *that food has been condemned*. 5 to compel or force into a particular state or activity: *his disposition condemned him to boredom*.
▷HISTORY C13: from Old French *condempner*, from Latin *condemnāre*, from *damnāre* to condemn; see DAMN
▸**condemnable** (kən'dɛməbᵊl) ADJECTIVE ▸**con'demnably** ADVERB ▸**ˌcondem'nation** NOUN ▸**con'demner** NOUN ▸**con'demningly** ADVERB

condemnatory (ˌkɒndɛm'neɪtərɪ, kən'dɛmnətərɪ, -trɪ) ADJECTIVE expressing strong disapproval or censure.

condemned cell NOUN a prison cell in which a person condemned to death awaits execution.

condensate (kən'dɛnseɪt) NOUN a substance formed by condensation, such as a liquid from a vapour.

condensation (ˌkɒndɛn'seɪʃən) NOUN 1 the act or process of condensing, or the state of being condensed. 2 anything that has condensed from a vapour, esp on a window. 3 *Chem* a type of reaction in which two organic molecules combine to form a larger molecule as well as a simple molecule such as water, methanol, etc. 4 anything that has been shortened, esp an abridged version of a book. 5 *Psychoanal* **a** the fusion of two or more ideas, etc., into one symbol, occurring esp in dreams. **b** the reduction of many experiences into one word or action, as in a phobia.
▸**ˌconden'sational** ADJECTIVE

condensation trail NOUN another name for **vapour trail.**

condense (kən'dɛns) VERB 1 (*tr*) to increase the density of; compress. 2 to reduce or be reduced in volume or size; make or become more compact. 3 to change or cause to change from a gaseous to a liquid or solid state. 4 *Chem* to undergo or cause to undergo condensation.
▷HISTORY C15: from Latin *condēnsāre*, from *dēnsāre* to make thick, from *dēnsus* DENSE
▸**con'densable** *or* **con'densible** ADJECTIVE ▸**conˌdensa'bility** *or* **conˌdensi'bility** NOUN

condensed (kən'dɛnst) ADJECTIVE 1 (of printers' type) narrower than usual for a particular height. Compare **expanded** (sense 1). 2 *Botany* designating an inflorescence in which the flowers are crowded together and are almost or completely sessile. 3 *Chem* designating a polycyclic ring system in a molecule in which two rings share two or more common atoms, as in naphthalene. Also: **fused.**

condensed matter NOUN *Physics* **a** crystalline and amorphous solids and liquids, including liquid crystals, glasses, polymers, and gels. **b** (*as modifier*): *condensed-matter physics*.

condensed milk NOUN milk reduced by evaporation to a thick concentration, with sugar added. Compare **evaporated milk.**

condenser (kən'dɛnsə) NOUN 1 **a** an apparatus for reducing gases to their liquid or solid form by the abstraction of heat. **b** a device for abstracting heat, as in a refrigeration unit. 2 a lens that concentrates light into a small area. 3 another name for **capacitor.** 4 a person or device that condenses.

condescend (ˌkɒndɪ'sɛnd) VERB (*intr*) 1 to act graciously towards another or others regarded as being on a lower level; behave patronizingly. 2 to do something that one regards as below one's dignity.
▷HISTORY C14: from Church Latin *condēscendere* to stoop, condescend, from Latin *dēscendere* to DESCEND

condescendence (ˌkɒndɪ'sɛndəns) NOUN 1 *Scots Law* a statement of facts presented by the plaintiff in a cause. 2 a less common word for **condescension.**

condescending (ˌkɒndɪ'sɛndɪŋ) ADJECTIVE showing or implying condescension by stooping to the level of one's inferiors, esp in a patronizing way.
▸**ˌconde'scendingly** ADVERB

condescension (ˌkɒndɪ'sɛnʃən) NOUN the act or an instance of behaving in a patronizing way.

condign (kən'daɪn) ADJECTIVE (esp of a punishment) fitting; deserved.
▷HISTORY C15: from Old French *condigne*, from Latin *condignus*, from *dignus* worthy
▸**con'dignly** ADVERB

condiment ('kɒndɪmənt) NOUN any spice or sauce such as salt, pepper, mustard, etc.
▷HISTORY C15: from Latin *condīmentum* seasoning, from *condīre* to pickle

condition (kən'dɪʃən) NOUN 1 a particular state of being or existence; situation with respect to circumstances: *the human condition*. 2 something that limits or restricts something else; a qualification: *you may enter only under certain conditions*. 3 (*plural*) external or existing circumstances: *conditions were right for a takeover*. 4 state of health or physical fitness, esp good health (esp in the phrases **in condition, out of condition**). 5 an ailment or physical disability: *a heart condition*. 6 something indispensable to the existence of something else: *your happiness is a condition of mine*. 7 something required as part of an agreement or pact; terms: *the conditions of the lease are set out*. 8 *Law* **a** a declaration or provision in a will, contract, etc., that makes some right or liability contingent upon the happening of some event. **b** the event itself. 9 *Logic* a statement whose truth is either required for the truth of a given statement (a **necessary condition**) or sufficient to guarantee the truth of the given statement (a **sufficient condition**). See **sufficient** (sense 2), **necessary** (sense 3e). 10 *Maths, logic* a presupposition, esp a restriction on the domain of quantification, indispensable to the proof of a theorem and stated as part of it. 11 *Statistics* short for **experimental condition.** 12 rank, status, or position in life. 13 **on** (*or* **upon**) **condition that.** (*conjunction*) provided that. ◆ VERB (*mainly tr*) 14 *Psychol* **a** to alter the response of (a person or animal) to a particular stimulus or situation. **b** to establish a conditioned response in (a person or animal). 15 to put into a fit condition or state. 16 to improve the condition of (one's hair) by use of special cosmetics. 17 to accustom or inure. 18 to subject to a condition. 19 (*intr*) *Archaic* to make conditions.
▷HISTORY C14: from Latin *conditiō*, from *condīcere* to discuss, agree together, from *con-* together + *dīcere* to say

conditional (kən'dɪʃənᵊl) ADJECTIVE 1 depending on other factors; not certain. 2 *Grammar* (of a clause, conjunction, form of a verb, or whole sentence) expressing a condition on which something else is contingent: *"If he comes" is a conditional clause in the sentence "If he comes I shall go"*. 3 **a** (of an equation or inequality) true for only certain values of the variable: $x^2 - 1 = x + 1$ is a conditional equation, only true for $x = 2$ or -1. **b** (of an infinite series) divergent when the absolute values of the terms are considered. 4 Also: **hypothetical.** *Logic* (of a proposition) consisting of two component propositions associated by the words *if…then* so that the proposition is false only when the antecedent is true and the consequent false. Usually written: $p \to q$ or $p \supset q$, where p is the antecedent, q the consequent, and $\to$ or $\supset$ symbolizes *implies*. ◆ NOUN 5 *Grammar* **a** a conditional form of a verb. **b** a conditional clause or sentence. 6 *Logic* a conditional proposition.
▸**conˌdition'ality** NOUN ▸**con'ditionally** ADVERB

conditional access NOUN the encryption of television programme transmissions so that only authorized subscribers with suitable decoding apparatus may have access to them.

conditionalization *or* **conditionalisation** (kənˌdɪʃənᵊlaɪ'zeɪʃən) NOUN *Logic* the derivation from an argument of a conditional statement with the conjunction of the premises as antecedent and the conclusion as consequent. If the argument is valid conditionalization yields a truth.

conditional probability NOUN *Statistics* the probability of one event, *A*, occurring given that another, *B*, is already known to have occurred: written $P(A|B)$ and equal to $P(A \text{ and } B)/P(B)$.

condition code register NOUN *Computing* a hardware register used for storing the current values of the condition codes.

condition codes PLURAL NOUN a set of single bits that indicate specific conditions within a computer. The values of the condition codes are often determined by the outcome of a prior software operation and their principal use is to govern choices between alternative instruction sequences.

conditioned (kən'dɪʃənd) ADJECTIVE 1 *Psychol* of or denoting a response that has been learned. Compare **unconditioned.** 2 (foll by *to*) accustomed; inured; prepared by training.

conditioned response NOUN *Psychol* a response that is transferred from the second to the first of a pair of stimuli. See **classical conditioning.** A well-known Pavlovian example is salivation by a dog when it hears a bell ring, because food has always been presented when the bell has been rung previously. Also called (esp formerly): **conditioned reflex.** See also **unconditioned response.**

conditioned stimulus NOUN *Psychol* a stimulus to which an organism has learned to make a response by classical conditioning. Compare **unconditioned stimulus.**

conditioned suppression NOUN *Psychol* the reduction in the frequency of a learned response, e.g. pressing a bar for water, that occurs when a stimulus previously associated with pain is present.

conditioner (kən'dɪʃənə) NOUN 1 a person or thing that conditions. 2 a substance, esp a cosmetic, applied to something to improve its condition: *hair conditioner*.

conditioning (kən'dɪʃənɪŋ) NOUN 1 *Psychol* the learning process by which the behaviour of an organism becomes dependent on an event occurring in its environment. See also **classical conditioning, instrumental learning.** ◆ ADJECTIVE 2 (of a shampoo, cosmetic, etc.) intended to improve the condition of something: *a conditioning rinse*.

condo ('kɒndəʊ) NOUN, *plural* **-dos.** a condominium building or apartment.

condole (kən'dəʊl) VERB (*intr*; foll by *with*) to express sympathy with someone in grief, pain, etc.
▷HISTORY C16: from Church Latin *condolēre* to suffer pain (with another), from Latin *com-* together + *dolēre* to grieve, feel pain
▸**con'dolatory** ADJECTIVE ▸**con'doler** NOUN ▸**con'dolingly** ADVERB

condolence (kən'dəʊləns) *or* **condolement** NOUN (*often plural*) an expression of sympathy with someone in grief, etc.

con dolore (kɒn dɒ'lɔːrɪ) ADJECTIVE, ADVERB *Music* (to be performed) in a sad manner.
▷HISTORY Italian: with sorrow

condom ('kɒndɒm, 'kɒndəm) NOUN a sheathlike covering of thin rubber worn on the penis or in the vagina during sexual intercourse to prevent conception or infection.
▷HISTORY C18: of unknown origin

condominium (ˌkɒndə'mɪnɪəm) NOUN, *plural* **-ums.** 1 joint rule or sovereignty. 2 a country ruled by two or more foreign powers. 3 *US and Canadian* **a** an apartment building in which each apartment is individually wholly owned and the common areas are jointly owned. **b** the title under

which an apartment in such a building is owned. Sometimes shortened to **condo**. Compare **cooperative** (sense 5).
▷HISTORY C18: from New Latin, from Latin *com-* together + *dominium* ownership; see DOMINION

condone (kən'dəʊn) VERB (*tr*) [1] to overlook or forgive (an offence). [2] *Law* (esp of a spouse) to pardon or overlook (an offence, usually adultery).
▷HISTORY C19: from Latin *condōnāre* to remit a debt, from *com-* (intensive) + *dōnāre* to DONATE
▸**con'donable** ADJECTIVE ▸**condonation** (ˌkɒndəʊ'neɪʃən) NOUN ▸**con'doner** NOUN

condor ('kɒndɔː) NOUN either of two very large rare New World vultures, *Vultur gryphus* (**Andean condor**), which has black plumage with white around the neck, and *Gymnogyps californianus* (**California condor**), which is similar but nearly extinct.
▷HISTORY C17: from Spanish *cóndor,* from Quechuan *kuntur*

condottiere (ˌkɒndɒ'tjɛərɪ) NOUN, *plural* **-ri** (-riː). a commander or soldier in a professional mercenary company in Europe from the 13th to the 16th centuries.
▷HISTORY C18: from Italian, from *condotto* leadership, from *condurre* to lead, from Latin *condūcere;* see CONDUCT

conduce (kən'djuːs) VERB (*intr;* foll by *to*) to lead or contribute (to a result).
▷HISTORY C15: from Latin *condūcere* to lead together, from *com-* together + *dūcere* to lead
▸**con'ducer** NOUN ▸**con'ducible** ADJECTIVE ▸**con'ducingly** ADVERB

conducive (kən'djuːsɪv) ADJECTIVE (when *postpositive,* foll by *to*) contributing, leading, or tending.
▸**con'duciveness** NOUN

conduct NOUN ('kɒndʌkt) [1] the manner in which a person behaves; behaviour. [2] the way of managing a business, affair, etc.; handling. [3] *Rare* the act of guiding or leading. [4] *Rare* a guide or leader. ◆ VERB (kən'dʌkt) [5] (*tr*) to accompany and guide (people, a party, etc.) (esp in the phrase **conducted tour**). [6] (*tr*) to lead or direct (affairs, business, etc.); control. [7] (*tr*) to do or carry out: *conduct a survey.* [8] (*tr*) to behave or manage (oneself): *the child conducted himself well.* [9] Also (esp US): **direct.** to control or guide (an orchestra, choir, etc.) by the movements of the hands or a baton. [10] to transmit (heat, electricity, etc.): *metals conduct heat.*
▷HISTORY C15: from Medieval Latin *conductus* escorted, from Latin: drawn together, from *condūcere* to CONDUCE
▸**con'ductible** ADJECTIVE ▸**conˌducti'bility** NOUN

conductance (kən'dʌktəns) NOUN the ability of a system to conduct electricity, measured by the ratio of the current flowing through the system to the potential difference across it; the reciprocal of resistance. It is measured in reciprocal ohms, mhos, or siemens. Symbol: G.

conducting tissue NOUN *Botany* another name for **vascular tissue.**

conductiometric titration (kənˌdʌktɪəʊ'metrɪk) NOUN *Chem* a titration technique in which the end-point is determined by measuring the conductance of the solution.

conduction (kən'dʌkʃən) NOUN [1] the transfer of energy by a medium without bulk movement of the medium itself: *heat conduction,; electrical conduction,; sound conduction.* Compare **convection** (sense 1). [2] the transmission of an electrical or chemical impulse along a nerve fibre. [3] the act of conveying or conducting, as through a pipe. [4] *Physics* another name for **conductivity** (sense 1).
▸**con'ductional** ADJECTIVE

conduction band NOUN See **energy band.**

conductive (kən'dʌktɪv) ADJECTIVE of, denoting, or having the property of conduction.
▸**con'ductively** ADVERB

conductive education NOUN an educational system, developed in Hungary by András Petö, in which teachers (**conductors**) teach children and adults with motor disorders to function independently, by guiding them to attain their own goals in their own way.

conductivity (ˌkɒndʌk'tɪvɪtɪ) NOUN, *plural* **-ties.** [1] Also called: **conduction.** the property of transmitting heat, electricity, or sound. [2] **a** a measure of the ability of a substance to conduct electricity; the reciprocal of resistivity. **b** in the case of a solution, the electrolytic conductivity is the current density divided by the electric field strength, measured in siemens per metre. Symbol: κ. Formerly called: **specific conductance.** [3] See **thermal conductivity.**

conductivity water NOUN water that has a conductivity of less than 0.043×10^{-6} S cm^{-1}.

conductor (kən'dʌktə) NOUN [1] an official on a bus who collects fares, checks tickets, etc. [2] Also called (esp US): **director.** a person who conducts an orchestra, choir, etc. [3] a person who leads or guides. [4] *US and Canadian* a railway official in charge of a train. [5] a substance, body, or system that conducts electricity, heat, etc. [6] See **lightning conductor.**
▸**con'ductorˌship** NOUN ▸**conductress** (kən'dʌktrɪs) FEMININE NOUN

conduit ('kɒndɪt, -djʊɪt) NOUN [1] a pipe or channel for carrying a fluid. [2] a rigid tube or duct for carrying and protecting electrical wires or cables. [3] an agency or means of access, communication, etc. [4] *Botany* a water-transporting element in a plant; a xylem vessel or a tracheid. [5] a rare word for **fountain.**
▷HISTORY C14: from Old French, from Medieval Latin *conductus* channel, aqueduct, from Latin *condūcere* to lead, CONDUCE

conduplicate (kɒn'djuːplɪkɪt) ADJECTIVE *Botany* folded lengthways on itself: *conduplicate leaves in the bud.*
▷HISTORY C18: from Latin *conduplicāre* to double; see DUPLICATE
▸**conˌdupli'cation** NOUN

condyle ('kɒndɪl) NOUN the rounded projection on the articulating end of a bone, such as the ball portion of a ball-and-socket joint.
▷HISTORY C17: from Latin *condylus* knuckle, joint, from Greek *kondulos*
▸**'condylar** ADJECTIVE

condyloid ('kɒndɪˌlɔɪd) ADJECTIVE of or resembling a condyle.

condyloma (ˌkɒndɪ'ləʊmə) NOUN, *plural* **-mas** *or* **-mata** (-mətə). a skin tumour near the anus or genital organs, esp as a result of syphilis.
▷HISTORY C17: from New Latin, from Greek *kondulōma,* from *kondulos* CONDYLE + -OMA
▸**condylomatous** (ˌkɒndɪ'lɒmətəs, -'ləʊ-) ADJECTIVE

cone (kəʊn) NOUN [1] **a** a geometric solid consisting of a plane base bounded by a closed curve, often a circle or an ellipse, every point of which is joined to a fixed point, the vertex, lying outside the plane of the base. A **right circular cone** has a vertex perpendicularly above or below the centre of a circular base. Volume of a cone: $⅓\pi r^2 h$, where r is the radius of the base and h is the height of the cone. **b** a geometric surface formed by a line rotating about the vertex and connecting the peripheries of two closed plane bases, usually circular or elliptical, above and below the vertex. See also **conic section.** [2] anything that tapers from a circular section to a point, such as a wafer shell used to contain ice cream. [3] **a** the reproductive body of conifers and related plants, made up of overlapping scales, esp the mature **female cone**, whose scales each bear a seed. **b** a similar structure in horsetails, club mosses, etc. Technical name: **strobilus.** [4] a small cone-shaped bollard used as a temporary traffic marker on roads. [5] Also called: **retinal cone.** any one of the cone-shaped cells in the retina of the eye, sensitive to colour and bright light. ◆ VERB [6] (*tr*) to shape like a cone or part of a cone.
▷HISTORY C16: from Latin *cōnus,* from Greek *kōnus* pine cone, geometrical cone

coneflower ('kəʊnˌflaʊə) NOUN any North American plant of the genera *Rudbeckia, Ratibida,* and *Echinacea,* which have rayed flowers with a conelike centre: family *Asteraceae* (composites). See also **black-eyed Susan.**

cone off VERB (*tr, adverb*) *Brit* to close (one carriageway of a motorway) by placing warning cones across it.

cone penetration test NOUN a method of testing soils by pressing a cone of standard dimensions into the soil under a known load and measuring the penetration.

cone shell NOUN any of various tropical marine gastropod molluscs of the genus *Conus* and related genera, having a smooth conical shell. Sometimes shortened to **cone.**

con espressione (*Italian* kɔn ˌespres'sjone) ADJECTIVE, ADVERB *Music* (to be performed) with feeling; expressively.
▷HISTORY Italian, literally: with expression

Conestoga wagon (ˌkɒnɪ'stəʊgə) NOUN *US and Canadian* a large heavy horse-drawn covered wagon used in the 19th century.
▷HISTORY C19: after *Conestoga,* Pennsylvania, where it was first made

coney ('kəʊnɪ) NOUN a variant spelling of **cony.**

Coney Island ('kəʊnɪ) NOUN an island off the S shore of Long Island, New York: site of a large amusement park.

confab ('kɒnfæb) *Informal* ◆ NOUN [1] a conversation or chat. ◆ VERB **-fabs, -fabbing, -fabbed.** [2] (*intr*) to converse.

confabulate (kən'fæbjʊˌleɪt) VERB (*intr*) [1] to talk together; converse; chat. [2] *Psychiatry* to replace the gaps left by a disorder of the memory with imaginary remembered experiences consistently believed to be true. See also **paramnesia.**
▷HISTORY C17: from Latin *confābulārī,* from *fābulārī* to talk, from *fābula* a story; see FABLE
▸**conˌfabu'lation** NOUN ▸**con'fabuˌlator** NOUN
▸**con'fabulatory** ADJECTIVE

confect (kən'fɛkt) VERB (*tr*) [1] to prepare by combining ingredients. [2] to make; construct.
▷HISTORY C16: from Latin *confectus* prepared, from *conficere* to accomplish, from *com-* (intensive) + *facere* to make

confection (kən'fɛkʃən) NOUN [1] the act or process of compounding or mixing. [2] any sweet preparation of fruit, nuts, etc., such as a preserve or a sweet. [3] *Old-fashioned* an elaborate article of clothing, esp for women. [4] *Informal* anything regarded as overelaborate or frivolous: *the play was merely an ingenious confection.* [5] a medicinal drug sweetened with sugar, honey, etc.
▷HISTORY C14: from Old French, from Latin *confectiō* a preparing, from *conficere* to produce; see CONFECT

confectionary (kən'fɛkʃənərɪ) NOUN, *plural* **-aries.** [1] a place where confections are kept or made. [2] a rare word for **confection.** ◆ ADJECTIVE [3] of or characteristic of confections.

confectioner (kən'fɛkʃənə) NOUN a person who makes or sells sweets or confections.

confectioners' sugar NOUN the US term for **icing sugar.**

confectionery (kən'fɛkʃənərɪ) NOUN, *plural* **-eries.** [1] sweets and other confections collectively. [2] the art or business of a confectioner.

Confed. ABBREVIATION FOR: [1] Confederate. [2] Confederation.

confederacy (kən'fɛdərəsɪ, -'fɛdrəsɪ) NOUN, *plural* **-cies.** [1] a union or combination of peoples, states, etc.; alliance; league. [2] a combination of groups or individuals for unlawful purposes.
▷HISTORY C14: from Anglo-French *confederacie,* from Late Latin *confoederātiō* agreement, CONFEDERATION
▸**con'federal** ADJECTIVE

Confederacy (kən'fɛdərəsɪ, -'fɛdrəsɪ) NOUN **the.** another name for the **Confederate States of America.**

confederate NOUN (kən'fɛdərɪt, -'fɛdrɪt) [1] a nation, state, or individual that is part of a confederacy. [2] someone who is part of a conspiracy; accomplice. ◆ ADJECTIVE (kən'fɛdərɪt, -'fɛdrɪt) [3] united in a confederacy; allied. ◆ VERB (kən'fɛdəˌreɪt) [4] to form into or become part of a confederacy.
▷HISTORY C14: from Late Latin *confoederātus,* from *confoederāre* to unite by a league, from Latin *com-* together + *foedus* treaty

Confederate (kən'fɛdərɪt, -'fɛdrɪt) ADJECTIVE [1] of, supporting, or relating to the Confederate States of America. ◆ NOUN [2] a supporter of the Confederate States of America.

Confederate States of America PLURAL NOUN *US history* the 11 Southern states (Alabama, Arkansas, Florida, Georgia, North Carolina, South Carolina, Texas, Virginia, Tennessee, Louisiana, and Mississippi) that seceded from the Union in 1861, precipitating a civil war with the North. The Confederacy was defeated in 1865 and the South reincorporated into the US.

confederation (kən,fɛdəˈreɪʃən) NOUN 1 the act or process of confederating or the state of being confederated. 2 a loose alliance of political units. The union of the Swiss cantons is the oldest surviving confederation. Compare **federation.** 3 (esp in Canada) another name for a **federation.**
▸**con,federˈation,ism** NOUN ▸**con,federˈationist** NOUN
▸**conˈfederative** ADJECTIVE

Confederation (kən,fɛdəˈreɪʃən) NOUN 1 **the.** *US history* the original 13 states of the United States of America constituted under the Articles of Confederation and superseded by the more formal union established in 1789. 2 the federation of Canada, formed with four original provinces in 1867 and since joined by eight more.

confer (kənˈfɜː) VERB **-fers, -ferring, -ferred.** 1 (*tr; foll by on or upon*) to grant or bestow (an honour, gift, etc.). 2 (*intr*) to hold or take part in a conference or consult together. 3 (*tr*) an obsolete word for **compare.**
▷HISTORY C16: from Latin *conferre* to gather together, compare, from *com-* together + *ferre* to bring
▸**conˈferment** *or* **conˈferral** NOUN ▸**conˈferrable** ADJECTIVE
▸**conˈferrer** NOUN

conferee *or* **conferree** (,kɒnfɜːˈriː) NOUN 1 a person who takes part in a conference. 2 a person on whom an honour or gift is conferred.

conference (ˈkɒnfərəns, -frəns) NOUN 1 a meeting for consultation, exchange of information, or discussion, esp one with a formal agenda. 2 a formal meeting of two or more states, political groups, etc., esp to discuss differences or formulate common policy. 3 an assembly of the clergy or of clergy and laity of any of certain Protestant Christian Churches acting as representatives of their denomination: *the Methodist conference.* 4 *Sport* a league or division of clubs or teams. 5 *Rare* an act of bestowal.
▷HISTORY C16: from Medieval Latin *conferentia,* from Latin *conferre* to bring together; see CONFER
▸**conferential** (,kɒnfəˈrɛnʃəl) ADJECTIVE

conference call NOUN a special telephone facility by which three or more people using conventional or cellular phones can be linked up to speak to one another.

Conference pear (ˈkɒnfərəns, -frəns) NOUN a variety of pear that has sweet and juicy fruit.

conferva (kɒnˈfɜːvə) NOUN, *plural* **-vae** (-viː) *or* **-vas.** any of various threadlike green algae, esp any of the genus *Tribonema,* typically occurring in fresh water.
▷HISTORY C18: from Latin: a water plant, from *confervēre* to grow together, heal, literally: to seethe, from *fervēre* to boil; named with reference to its reputed healing properties
▸**conˈferval** ADJECTIVE ▸**conˈfervoid** NOUN, ADJECTIVE

confess (kənˈfɛs) VERB (*when tr, may take a clause as object*) 1 (*when intr, often foll by to*) to make an acknowledgment or admission (of faults, misdeeds, crimes, etc.). 2 (*tr*) to admit or grant to be true; concede. 3 *Christianity, chiefly RC Church* to declare (one's sins) to God or to a priest as his representative, so as to obtain pardon and absolution.
▷HISTORY C14: from Old French *confesser,* from Late Latin *confessāre,* from Latin *confessus* confessed, from *confitērī* to admit, from *fatērī* to acknowledge; related to Latin *fārī* to speak
▸**conˈfessable** ADJECTIVE

confessant (kənˈfɛsᵊnt) NOUN *Christianity, chiefly RC Church* a person who makes a confession.

confessedly (kənˈfɛsɪdlɪ) ADVERB (*sentence modifier*) by admission or confession; avowedly.

confession (kənˈfɛʃən) NOUN 1 the act of confessing. 2 something confessed. 3 an acknowledgment or declaration, esp of one's faults, misdeeds, or crimes. 4 *Christianity, chiefly RC Church* the act of a penitent accusing himself of his sins. 5 **confession of faith.** a formal public avowal of religious beliefs. 6 a religious denomination or sect united by a common system of beliefs.
▸**conˈfessionary** ADJECTIVE

confessional (kənˈfɛʃənᵊl) ADJECTIVE 1 of, like, or suited to a confession. ◆ NOUN 2 *Christianity, chiefly RC Church* a small stall, usually enclosed and divided by a screen or curtain, where a priest hears confessions. 3 a book of penitential prayers.

confessional television NOUN television programmes, esp talk shows, in which members of the public reveal their private lives, personal problems, etc.

confessor (kənˈfɛsə) NOUN 1 *Christianity, chiefly RC Church* a priest who hears confessions and sometimes acts as a spiritual counsellor. 2 *History* a person who bears witness to his Christian religious faith by the holiness of his life, esp in resisting threats or danger, but does not suffer martyrdom. 3 a person who makes a confession.

confetti (kənˈfɛtɪ) NOUN small pieces of coloured paper thrown on festive occasions, esp at the bride and groom at weddings.
▷HISTORY C19: from Italian, plural of *confetto,* originally, a bonbon; see COMFIT

confidant (,kɒnfɪˈdænt, ˈkɒnfɪ,dænt) NOUN a person, esp a man, to whom private matters are confided.
▷HISTORY C17: from French *confident,* from Italian *confidente,* noun use of adjective: trustworthy, from Latin *confīdens* CONFIDENT

confidante (,kɒnfɪˈdænt, ˈkɒnfɪ,dænt) NOUN a person, esp a woman, to whom private matters are confided.

confide (kənˈfaɪd) VERB 1 (usually foll by *in;* when *tr, may take a clause as object*) to disclose (secret or personal matters) in confidence (to); reveal in private (to). 2 (*intr; foll by in*) to have complete trust. 3 (*tr*) to entrust into another's keeping.
▷HISTORY C15: from Latin *confīdere,* from *fīdere* to trust; related to Latin *foedus* treaty
▸**conˈfider** NOUN

confidence (ˈkɒnfɪdəns) NOUN 1 a feeling of trust in a person or thing: *I have confidence in his abilities.* 2 belief in one's own abilities; self-assurance. 3 trust or a trustful relationship: *take me into your confidence.* 4 something confided or entrusted; secret. 5 **in confidence.** as a secret.

confidence interval NOUN *Statistics* an interval of values bounded by **confidence limits** within which the true value of a population parameter is stated to lie with a specified probability.

confidence level NOUN *Statistics* a measure of the reliability of a result. A confidence level of 95 per cent or 0.95 means that there is a probability of at least 95 per cent that the result is reliable. Compare **significance** (sense 4).

confidence man *or* **trickster** NOUN another name for **con man.**

confidence trick *or US and Canadian* **confidence game** NOUN a swindle involving money, goods, etc., in which the victim's trust is won by the swindler. Informal shortened forms: **con trick,** (US and Canadian) **con game.**

confident (ˈkɒnfɪdənt) ADJECTIVE 1 (*postpositive; foll by of*) having or showing confidence or certainty; sure: *confident of success.* 2 sure of oneself; bold. 3 presumptuous; excessively bold.
▷HISTORY C16: from Latin *confīdens* trusting, having self-confidence, from *confīdere* to have complete trust in; see CONFIDE
▸**ˈconfidently** ADVERB

confidential (,kɒnfɪˈdɛnʃəl) ADJECTIVE 1 spoken, written, or given in confidence; secret; private. 2 entrusted with another's confidence or secret affairs: *a confidential secretary.* 3 suggestive of or denoting intimacy: *a confidential approach.*
▸**,confi,dentiˈality** *or* **,confiˈdentialness** NOUN
▸**,confiˈdentially** ADVERB

confiding (kənˈfaɪdɪŋ) ADJECTIVE unsuspicious; trustful.
▸**conˈfidingly** ADVERB ▸**conˈfidingness** NOUN

configuration (kən,fɪgjʊˈreɪʃən) NOUN 1 the arrangement of the parts of something. 2 the external form or outline achieved by such an arrangement. 3 *Physics, chem* **a** Also called: **conformation.** the shape of a molecule as determined by the arrangement of its atoms. **b** the structure of an atom or molecule as determined by the arrangement of its electrons and nucleons. 4 *Psychol* the unit or pattern in perception studied by Gestalt psychologists. 5 *Computing* the particular choice of hardware items and their interconnection that make up a particular computer system.
▷HISTORY C16: from Late Latin *configūrātiō* a similar formation, from *configūrāre* to model on something, from *figūrāre* to shape, fashion
▸**con,figuˈrational** *or* **conˈfigurative** ADJECTIVE
▸**con,figuˈrationally** ADVERB

confine VERB (kənˈfaɪn) (*tr*) 1 to keep or close within bounds; limit; restrict. 2 to keep shut in; restrict the free movement of: *arthritis confined him to bed.* ◆ NOUN (ˈkɒnfaɪn) 3 (*often plural*) a limit; boundary.
▷HISTORY C16: from Medieval Latin *confīnāre* from Latin *confīnis* adjacent, from *fīnis* end, boundary
▸**conˈfinable** *or* **conˈfineable** ADJECTIVE ▸**ˈconfineless** ADJECTIVE ▸**conˈfiner** NOUN

confined (kənˈfaɪnd) ADJECTIVE 1 enclosed or restricted; limited. 2 in childbed; undergoing childbirth.
▸**confinedly** (kənˈfaɪnɪdlɪ) ADVERB ▸**conˈfinedness** NOUN

confinement (kənˈfaɪnmənt) NOUN 1 the act of confining or the state of being confined. 2 the period from the onset of labour to the birth of a child. 3 *Physics* another name for **containment** (sense 3).

confirm (kənˈfɜːm) VERB (*tr*) 1 (*may take a clause as object*) to prove to be true or valid; corroborate; verify. 2 (*may take a clause as object*) to assert for a second or further time, so as to make more definite: *he confirmed that he would appear in court.* 3 to strengthen or make more firm: *his story confirmed my doubts.* 4 to make valid by a formal act or agreement; ratify. 5 to administer the rite of confirmation to.
▷HISTORY C13: from Old French *confermer,* from Latin *confirmāre,* from *firmus* FIRM[1]
▸**conˈfirmable** ADJECTIVE ▸**conˈfirmatory** *or* **conˈfirmative** ADJECTIVE ▸**conˈfirmer** NOUN

confirmand (ˈkɒnfə,mænd) NOUN a candidate for confirmation.

confirmation (,kɒnfəˈmeɪʃən) NOUN 1 the act of confirming. 2 something that confirms; verification. 3 a rite in several Christian churches that confirms a baptized person in his faith and admits him to full participation in the church. 4 (in the philosophy of science) the relationship between an observation and the theory which it supposedly renders more probable. Compare **hypothetico-deductive.**

confirmed (kənˈfɜːmd) ADJECTIVE 1 (*prenominal*) long-established in a habit, way of life, etc.: *a confirmed bachelor.* 2 having received the rite of confirmation. 3 (of a disease) another word for **chronic.**
▸**confirmedly** (kənˈfɜːmɪdlɪ) ADVERB ▸**confirmedness** (kənˈfɜːmɪdnɪs, -ˈfɜːmd-) NOUN

confiscable (kənˈfɪskəbᵊl) ADJECTIVE subject or liable to confiscation or seizure.

confiscate (ˈkɒnfɪ,skeɪt) VERB (*tr*) 1 to seize (property), esp for public use and esp by way of a penalty. ◆ ADJECTIVE 2 seized or confiscated; forfeit. 3 having lost or been deprived of property through confiscation.
▷HISTORY C16: from Latin *confiscāre* to seize for the public treasury, from *fiscus* basket, treasury
▸**,confisˈcation** NOUN ▸**ˈconfis,cator** NOUN

confiscatory (kənˈfɪskətərɪ, -trɪ) ADJECTIVE involving confiscation.

confit *French* (kɔ̃fi) NOUN *Cookery* a preserve: *a confit of duck.*
▷HISTORY literally: preserve

Confiteor (kənˈfɪtɪ,ɔː) NOUN *RC Church* a prayer consisting of a general confession of sinfulness and an entreaty for forgiveness.
▷HISTORY C13: from Latin: I confess; from the beginning of the Latin prayer of confession

confiture (ˈkɒnfɪ,tjʊə) NOUN a confection, preserve of fruit, etc.
▷HISTORY C19: from French, from Old French *confire* to prepare, from Latin *conficere* to produce; see CONFECT

conflagrant (kənˈfleɪgrənt) ADJECTIVE *Rare* burning fiercely.

conflagration (,kɒnfləˈgreɪʃən) NOUN a large destructive fire.
▷HISTORY C16: from Latin *conflagrātiō,* from *conflagrāre* to be burnt up, from *com-* (intensive) + *flagrāre* to burn; related to Latin *fulgur* lightning
▸**ˈconfla,grative** ADJECTIVE

conflate (kən'fleɪt) VERB *(tr)* to combine or blend (two things, esp two versions of a text) so as to form a whole.
▷**HISTORY** C16: from Latin *conflāre* to blow together, from *flāre* to blow
▸**con'flation** NOUN

conflict NOUN ('kɒnflɪkt) [1] a struggle or clash between opposing forces; battle. [2] a state of opposition between ideas, interests, etc.; disagreement or controversy. [3] a clash, as between two appointments made for the same time. [4] *Psychol* opposition between two simultaneous but incompatible wishes or drives, sometimes leading to a state of emotional tension and thought to be responsible for neuroses. ◆ VERB (kən'flɪkt) *(intr)* [5] to come into opposition; clash. [6] to fight.
▷**HISTORY** C15: from Latin *conflictus,* from *conflīgere* to combat, from *flīgere* to strike
▸**con'fliction** NOUN ▸**con'flictive** *or* **con'flictory** ADJECTIVE

conflicting (kən'flɪktɪŋ) ADJECTIVE clashing; contradictory: *conflicting rumours.*
▸**con'flictingly** ADVERB

confluence ('kɒnfluəns) *or* **conflux** ('kɒnflʌks) NOUN [1] a merging or flowing together, esp of rivers. [2] a gathering together, esp of people.

confluent ('kɒnfluənt) ADJECTIVE [1] flowing together or merging. ◆ NOUN [2] a stream that flows into another, usually of approximately equal size.
▷**HISTORY** C17: from Latin *confluēns,* from *confluere* to flow together, from *fluere* to flow

confocal (kɒn'fəʊkᵊl) ADJECTIVE having a common focus or common foci: *confocal ellipses.*

confocal microscope NOUN a light microscope with an optical system designed to reject background from matter outside the focal plane and therefore allowing images of different sections of a specimen to be obtained.

conform (kən'fɔːm) VERB [1] *(intr; usually foll by to)* to comply in actions, behaviour, etc., with accepted standards or norms. [2] *(intr; usually foll by with)* to be in accordance; fit in: *he conforms with my idea of a teacher.* [3] to make or become similar in character or form. [4] *(intr)* to comply with the practices of an established church, esp the Church of England. [5] *(tr)* to bring (oneself, ideas, etc.) into harmony or agreement.
▷**HISTORY** C14: from Old French *conformer,* from Latin *confirmāre* to establish, strengthen, from *firmāre* to make firm, from *firmus* FIRM[1]
▸**con'former** NOUN ▸**con'formingly** ADVERB

conformable (kən'fɔːməbᵊl) ADJECTIVE [1] corresponding in character; similar. [2] obedient; submissive. [3] (foll by *to*) in agreement or harmony (with); consistent (with). [4] (of rock strata) lying in a parallel arrangement so that their original relative positions have remained undisturbed. [5] *Maths* (of two matrices) related so that the number of columns in one is equal to the number of rows in the other.
▸**con,forma'bility** *or* **con'formableness** NOUN
▸**con'formably** ADVERB

conformal (kən'fɔːməl) ADJECTIVE [1] *Maths* **a** (of a transformation) preserving the angles of the depicted surface. **b** (of a parameter) relating to such a transformation. [2] Also called: **orthomorphic.** (of a map projection) maintaining true shape over a small area and scale in every direction.
▷**HISTORY** C17: from Late Latin *conformālis* having the same shape, from Latin *com-* same + *forma* shape

conformation (ˌkɒnfɔː'meɪʃən) NOUN [1] the general shape or outline of an object; configuration. [2] the arrangement of the parts of an object. [3] the act or state of conforming. [4] *Chem* **a** another name for **configuration** (sense 3a). **b** one of the configurations of a molecule that can easily change its shape and can consequently exist in equilibrium with molecules of different configuration.
▸ˌ**confor'mational** ADJECTIVE

conformational analysis NOUN *Chem* the study of the spatial arrangement of atoms or groups of atoms in a molecule and the way in which this influences chemical behaviour.

conformist (kən'fɔːmɪst) NOUN [1] a person who adopts the attitudes, behaviour, dress, etc. of the group to which he belongs. [2] a person who complies with the practices of an established church, esp the Church of England. ◆ ADJECTIVE [3] of a conforming nature or character.

conformity (kən'fɔːmɪtɪ) *or* **conformance** NOUN, *plural* **-ities** *or* **-ances.** [1] compliance in actions, behaviour, etc., with certain accepted standards or norms. [2] correspondence or likeness in form or appearance; congruity; agreement. [3] compliance with the practices of an established church.

confound (kən'faʊnd) VERB *(tr)* [1] to astound or perplex; bewilder. [2] to mix up; confuse. [3] to treat mistakenly as similar to or identical with (one or more other things). [4] (kɒn'faʊnd) to curse or damn (usually as an expletive in the phrase **confound it!**). [5] to contradict or refute (an argument, etc.). [6] to rout or defeat (an enemy). [7] *Obsolete* to waste.
▷**HISTORY** C13: from Old French *confondre,* from Latin *confundere* to mingle, pour together, from *fundere* to pour
▸**con'foundable** ADJECTIVE ▸**con'founder** NOUN

confounded (kən'faʊndɪd) ADJECTIVE [1] bewildered; confused. [2] *(prenominal) Informal* execrable; damned.
▸**con'foundedly** ADVERB ▸**con'foundedness** NOUN

confraternity (ˌkɒnfrə'tɜːnɪtɪ) NOUN, *plural* **-ties.** a group of men united for some particular purpose, esp Christian laymen organized for religious or charitable service; brotherhood.
▷**HISTORY** C15: from Medieval Latin *confrāternitās;* see CONFRÈRE, FRATERNITY
▸ˌ**confra'ternal** ADJECTIVE

confrère ('kɒnfreə) NOUN a fellow member of a profession, fraternity, etc.
▷**HISTORY** C15: from Old French, from Medieval Latin *confrāter* fellow member, from Latin *frāter* brother

confront (kən'frʌnt) VERB *(tr)* [1] (usually foll by *with*) to present or face (with something), esp in order to accuse or criticize. [2] to face boldly; oppose in hostility. [3] to be face to face with; be in front of. [4] to bring together for comparison.
▷**HISTORY** C16: from Medieval Latin *confrontārī* to stand face to face with, from *frons* forehead
▸**con'fronter** NOUN

confrontation (ˌkɒnfrʌn'teɪʃən) *or archaic* **confrontment** (kɒn'frʌntmənt) NOUN [1] the act or an instance of confronting. [2] a situation of mutual hostility between two powers or nations without open warfare. [3] a state of conflict between two antagonistic forces, creeds, or ideas etc.
▸ˌ**confron'tational** ADJECTIVE

Confucian (kən'fjuːʃən) ADJECTIVE [1] of or relating to the doctrines of Confucius (Chinese name *Kong Zi* or *K'ung Fu-tse.*; 551–479 B.C.), the Chinese philosopher and teacher of ethics. ◆ NOUN [2] a follower of Confucius.

Confucianism (kən'fjuːʃəˌnɪzəm) NOUN the ethical system of Confucius, the Chinese philosopher and teacher of ethics (551–479 B.C.), emphasizing moral order, the humanity and virtue of China's ancient rulers, and gentlemanly education.
▸**Con'fucianist** NOUN

con fuoco (kɒn fuː'əʊkəʊ) ADJECTIVE, ADVERB *Music* (to be performed) in a fiery manner.
▷**HISTORY** Italian: with fire

confuse (kən'fjuːz) VERB *(tr)* [1] to bewilder; perplex. [2] to mix up (things, ideas, etc.); jumble. [3] to make unclear: *he confused his talk with irrelevant details.* [4] to fail to recognize the difference between; mistake (one thing) for another. [5] to disconcert; embarrass. [6] to cause to become disordered: *the enemy ranks were confused by gas.*
▷**HISTORY** C18: back formation from *confused,* from Latin *confūsus* mingled together, from *confundere* to pour together; see CONFOUND
▸**con'fusable** ADJECTIVE ▸**con,fusa'bility** NOUN

confused (kən'fjuːzd) ADJECTIVE [1] feeling or exhibiting an inability to understand; bewildered; perplexed. [2] in a disordered state; mixed up; jumbled. [3] lacking sufficient mental abilities for independent living, esp through old age.
▸**confusedly** (kən'fjuːzɪdlɪ, -'fjuːzd-) ADVERB
▸**con'fusedness** NOUN

confused elderly ADJECTIVE *Social welfare* **a** old and no longer having mental abilities sufficient for independent living. **b** *(as collective noun;* preceded by *the): the confused elderly.*

confusing (kən'fjuːzɪŋ) ADJECTIVE causing bewilderment; difficult to follow; puzzling.
▸**con'fusingly** ADVERB

confusion (kən'fjuːʒən) NOUN [1] the act of confusing or the state of being confused. [2] disorder; jumble. [3] bewilderment; perplexity. [4] lack of clarity; indistinctness. [5] embarrassment; abashment.
▸**con'fusional** ADJECTIVE

confute (kən'fjuːt) VERB *(tr)* [1] to prove (a person or thing) wrong, invalid, or mistaken; disprove. [2] *Obsolete* to put an end to.
▷**HISTORY** C16: from Latin *confūtāre* to check, silence
▸**con'futable** ADJECTIVE ▸**confutation** (ˌkɒnfjʊ'teɪʃən) NOUN ▸**con'futative** ADJECTIVE ▸**con'futer** NOUN

cong. ABBREVIATION FOR: [1] *Pharmacol, obsolete* congius. [2] congregation.
▷**HISTORY** (for sense 1) Latin: gallon

Cong. ABBREVIATION FOR: [1] Congregational. [2] Congress. [3] Congressional.

conga ('kɒŋgə) NOUN [1] a Latin American dance of three steps and a kick to each bar, usually performed by a number of people in single file. [2] Also called: **conga drum.** a large tubular bass drum, used chiefly in Latin American and funk music and played with the hands. ◆ VERB **-gas, -gaing, -gaed.** [3] *(intr)* to dance the conga.
▷**HISTORY** C20: from American Spanish, feminine of *congo* belonging to the CONGO

congé ('kɒnʒeɪ) NOUN [1] permission to depart or dismissal, esp when formal. [2] a farewell. [3] *Architect* a concave moulding. See also **cavetto.**
▷**HISTORY** C16: from Old French *congié,* from Latin *commeātus* leave of absence, from *meātus* movement, from *meāre* to go, pass

congeal (kən'dʒiːl) VERB [1] to change or cause to change from a soft or fluid state to a firm or solid state. [2] to form or cause to form into a coagulated mass; curdle; jell. [3] *(intr)* (of ideas) to take shape or become fixed in form.
▷**HISTORY** C14: from Old French *congeler,* from Latin *congelāre,* from *com-* together + *gelāre* to freeze
▸**con'gealable** ADJECTIVE ▸**con'gealer** NOUN
▸**con'gealment** NOUN

congelation (ˌkɒndʒɪ'leɪʃən) NOUN [1] the process of congealing. [2] something formed by this process.

congener (kən'dʒiːnə, 'kɒndʒɪnə) NOUN [1] a member of a class, group, or other category, esp any animal of a specified genus. [2] a by-product formed in alcoholic drinks during the fermentation process, which largely determines the flavour and colour of the drink.
▷**HISTORY** C18: from Latin, from *com-* same + *genus* kind

congeneric (ˌkɒndʒɪ'nɛrɪk) *or* **congenerous** (kɒn'dʒɛnərəs) ADJECTIVE belonging to the same group, esp (of animals or plants) belonging to the same genus.

congenial (kən'dʒiːnjəl, -nɪəl) ADJECTIVE [1] friendly, pleasant, or agreeable: *a congenial atmosphere to work in.* [2] having a similar disposition, tastes, etc.; compatible; sympathetic.
▷**HISTORY** C17: from CON- (same) + GENIAL[1]
▸**congeniality** (kənˌdʒiːnɪ'ælɪtɪ) *or* **con'genialness** NOUN
▸**con'genially** ADVERB

congenic (kən'dʒɛnɪk) ADJECTIVE *Genetics* (of inbred animal cells) genetically identical except for a single gene locus.

congenital (kən'dʒɛnɪtᵊl) ADJECTIVE [1] denoting or relating to any nonhereditary condition, esp an abnormal condition, existing at birth: *congenital blindness.* [2] *Informal* complete, as if from birth: *a congenital idiot.*
▷**HISTORY** C18: from Latin *congenitus* born together with, from *genitus* born, from *gignere* to bear, beget
▸**con'genitally** ADVERB ▸**con'genitalness** NOUN

conger ('kɒŋgə) NOUN any large marine eel of the family *Congridae,* esp *Conger conger,* occurring in temperate and tropical coastal waters.
▷**HISTORY** C14: from Old French *congre,* from Latin *conger,* from Greek *gongros* sea eel

congeries (kɒn'dʒɪəriːz) NOUN *(functioning as*

singular or plural) a collection of objects or ideas; mass; heap.
▷HISTORY C17: from Latin, from *congerere* to pile up, from *gerere* to carry

congest (kən'dʒest) VERB [1] to crowd or become crowded to excess; overfill. [2] to overload or clog (an organ or part) with blood or (of an organ or part) to become overloaded or clogged with blood. [3] (*tr; usually passive*) to block (the nose) with mucus.
▷HISTORY C16: from Latin *congestus* pressed together, from *congerere* to assemble; see CONGERIES
▸**con'gestible** ADJECTIVE ▸**con'gestive** ADJECTIVE ▸**con'gestion** NOUN

congested (kən'dʒestɪd) ADJECTIVE [1] crowded to excess; overfull. [2] (of an organ or part) loaded or clogged with blood. [3] (of the nose) blocked with mucus.

congestion charging NOUN the practice of charging motorists for the right to drive on busy roads, esp at busy times.
▸**congestion charge** NOUN

congius ('kɒndʒɪəs) NOUN, *plural* **-gii** (-dʒɪˌaɪ). [1] *Pharmacol* a unit of liquid measure equal to 1 Imperial gallon. [2] an ancient Roman unit of liquid measure equal to about 0.7 Imperial gallon or 0.84 US gallon.
▷HISTORY C14: from Latin, probably from Greek *konkhos* liquid measure, CONCH

conglobate ('kɒnglәʊˌbeɪt) VERB [1] to form into a globe or ball. ◆ ADJECTIVE [2] a rare word for **globular.**
▷HISTORY C17: from Latin *conglobāre* to gather into a ball, from *globāre* to make round, from *globus* a sphere
▸ˌ**conglo'bation** NOUN

conglomerate NOUN (kən'glɒmərɪt) [1] a thing composed of heterogeneous elements; mass. [2] any coarse-grained sedimentary rock consisting of rounded fragments of rock embedded in a finer matrix. Compare **agglomerate** (sense 3). [3] a large corporation consisting of a group of companies dealing in widely diversified goods, services, etc. ◆ VERB (kən'glɒməˌreɪt) [4] to form into a cluster or mass. ◆ ADJECTIVE (kən'glɒmərɪt) [5] made up of heterogeneous elements; massed. [6] (of sedimentary rocks) consisting of rounded fragments within a finer matrix.
▷HISTORY C16: from Latin *conglomerāre* to roll up, from *glomerāre* to wind into a ball, from *glomus* ball of thread

conglomeration (kənˌglɒmə'reɪʃən) NOUN [1] a conglomerate mass. [2] a mass of miscellaneous things. [3] the act of conglomerating or the state of being conglomerated.

conglutinant (kən'glu:tɪnənt) ADJECTIVE *Obsolete* (of the edges of a wound or fracture) promoting union; adhesive.

conglutinate (kən'glu:tɪˌneɪt) VERB [1] *Obsolete* to cause (the edges of a wound or fracture) to join during the process of healing or (of the edges of a wound or fracture) to join during this process. [2] to stick or become stuck together.
▷HISTORY C16: from Latin *conglūtināre* to glue together, from *glūtināre* to glue, from *glūten* GLUE
▸**conˌgluti'nation** NOUN ▸**con'glutinative** ADJECTIVE

Congo ('kɒŋgəʊ) NOUN [1] **Democratic Republic of.** a republic in S central Africa, with a narrow strip of land along the Congo estuary leading to the Atlantic in the west: Congo Free State established in 1885, with Leopold II of Belgium as absolute monarch; became the Belgian Congo colony in 1908; gained independence in 1960, followed by civil war and the secession of Katanga (until 1963); President Mobutu Sese Seko seized power in 1965; declared a one-party state in 1978, and was overthrown by rebels in 1997. The country consists chiefly of the Congo basin, with large areas of dense tropical forest and marshes, and the Mitumba highlands reaching over 5000 m (16 000 ft.) in the east. Official language: French. Religion: Christian majority, animist minority. Currency: Congolese franc. Capital: Kinshasa. Pop.: 53 625 000 (2001 est.). Area: 2 344 116 sq. km (905 063 sq. miles). Former names: **Congo Free State** (1885–1908), **Belgian Congo** (1908–60), **Congo-Kinshasa** (1960–71), **Zaïre** (1971–97). [2] **Republic of.** a former name (1960–99) of Congo-Brazzaville. [3] the second longest river in Africa, rising as the Lualaba on the Katanga plateau in the Democratic Republic of Congo and flowing in a wide northerly curve to the Atlantic: forms the border between Congo-Brazzaville and the Democratic Republic of Congo Length: about 4800 km (3000 miles). Area of basin: about 3 000 000 sq. km (1 425 000 sq. miles). Former Zaïrese name (1971–97): **Zaïre.** [4] a variant spelling of **Kongo** (the people and language).

Congo-Brazzaville NOUN a republic in W Central Africa: formerly the French colony of Middle Congo, part of French Equatorial Africa, it became independent in 1960; consists mostly of equatorial forest, with savanna and extensive swamps; drained chiefly by the Rivers Congo and Ubangi. Official language: French. Religion: Christian majority. Currency: franc. Capital: Brazzaville. Pop.: 2 894 000 (2001 est.). Area: 342 000 sq. km (132 018 sq. miles). Former names: **Middle Congo** (until 1958), **Republic of Congo** (1960–99).

congo eel *or* **snake** NOUN an aquatic salamander, *Amphiuma means,* having an eel-like body with gill slits and rudimentary limbs and inhabiting still muddy waters in the southern US: family *Amphiumidae.*

Congo Free State NOUN a former name (1885–1908) of (**Democratic Republic of**) **Congo** (sense 2).

Congolese (ˌkɒŋgə'li:z) ADJECTIVE [1] of or relating to the People's Republic of the Congo or the Democratic Republic of Congo or their inhabitants. ◆ NOUN [2] a native or inhabitant of the People's Republic of the Congo or the Democratic Republic of Congo.

Congo red NOUN a brownish-red soluble powder, used as a dye, a diagnostic indicator, a biological stain, and a chemical indicator. Formula: $C_{32}H_{22}N_6O_6S_2Na_2$.

congou ('kɒŋgu:) *or* **congo** ('kɒŋgəʊ) NOUN a kind of black tea from China.
▷HISTORY C18: from Chinese (Amoy) *kong hu tē* tea prepared with care

congrats (kən'græts) *or chiefly Brit* **congratters** (kən'grætəz) PLURAL NOUN, SENTENCE SUBSTITUTE informal shortened forms of **congratulations.**

congratulate (kən'grætjʊˌleɪt) VERB (*tr*) [1] (usually foll by *on*) to communicate pleasure, approval, or praise to (a person or persons); compliment. [2] (often foll by *on*) to consider (oneself) clever or fortunate (as a result of): *she congratulated herself on her tact.* [3] *Obsolete* to greet.
▷HISTORY C16: from Latin *congrātulārī,* from *grātulārī* to rejoice, from *grātus* pleasing
▸**conˌgratu'lation** NOUN ▸**con'gratuˌlator** NOUN ▸**con'gratulatory** *or* **con'gratulative** ADJECTIVE

congratulations (kənˌgrætjʊ'leɪʃənz) PLURAL NOUN, SENTENCE SUBSTITUTE expressions of pleasure or joy; felicitations.

congregant ('kɒŋgrɪgənt) NOUN a member of a congregation, esp a Jewish congregation.

congregate VERB ('kɒŋgrɪˌgeɪt) [1] to collect together in a body or crowd; assemble. ◆ ADJECTIVE ('kɒŋgrɪgɪt, -ˌgeɪt) [2] collected together; assembled. [3] relating to collecting; collective.
▷HISTORY C15: from Latin *congregāre* to collect into a flock, from *grex* flock
▸'**congreˌgative** ADJECTIVE ▸'**congreˌgativeness** NOUN ▸'**congreˌgator** NOUN

congregation (ˌkɒŋgrɪ'geɪʃən) NOUN [1] a group of persons gathered for worship, prayer, etc., esp in a church or chapel. [2] the act of congregating or collecting together. [3] a group of people, objects, etc., collected together; assemblage. [4] the group of persons habitually attending a given church, chapel, etc. [5] *RC Church* **a** a society of persons who follow a common rule of life but who are bound only by simple vows. **b** an administrative subdivision of the papal curia. **c** an administrative committee of bishops for arranging the business of a general council. [6] *Chiefly Brit* an assembly of senior members of a university.

congregational (ˌkɒŋgrɪ'geɪʃənᵊl) ADJECTIVE [1] of or relating to a congregation. [2] (*usually capital*) of, relating to, or denoting the Congregational Church, its members, or its beliefs.
▸ˌ**congre'gationally** ADVERB

Congregational Church NOUN any evangelical Protestant Christian Church that is governed according to the principles of Congregationalism. In 1972 the majority of churches in the Congregational Church in England and Wales voted to become part of the United Reformed Church.

Congregationalism (ˌkɒŋgrɪ'geɪʃənəˌlɪzəm) NOUN a system of Christian doctrines and ecclesiastical government in which each congregation is self-governing and maintains bonds of faith with other similar local congregations.
▸ˌ**Congre'gationalist** ADJECTIVE, NOUN

congress ('kɒŋgres) NOUN [1] a meeting or conference, esp of representatives of a number of sovereign states. [2] a national legislative assembly. [3] a society or association. [4] sexual intercourse.
▷HISTORY C16: from Latin *congressus* from *congredī* to meet with, from *com-* together + *gradī* to walk, step

Congress ('kɒŋgres) NOUN [1] the bicameral federal legislature of the US, consisting of the House of Representatives and the Senate. [2] this body during any two-year term. [3] Also called: **Congress Party.** (in India) a major political party, which controlled the Union government from 1947 to 1977. Official name: **Indian National Congress.**
▸**Con'gressional** ADJECTIVE

congressional (kən'greʃənᵊl) ADJECTIVE of or relating to a congress.
▸**con'gressionalist** NOUN ▸**con'gressionally** ADVERB

Congressional district NOUN (in the US) an electoral division of a state, entitled to send one member to the US House of Representatives.

Congressional Medal of Honor NOUN See **Medal of Honor.**

Congressional Record NOUN (in the US) the government journal that publishes all proceedings of Congress.

Congressman ('kɒŋgresmən) NOUN, *plural* **-men.** (in the US) a male member of Congress, esp of the House of Representatives.

Congress of Industrial Organizations NOUN (in the US) a federation of industrial unions formed in 1935. It united with the AFL in 1955 to form the AFL-CIO. Abbreviation: **CIO.**

Congress of Vienna NOUN the European conference held at Vienna from 1814–15 to settle the territorial problems left by the Napoleonic Wars.

Congresswoman ('kɒŋgreswʊmən) NOUN, *plural* **-women.** (in the US) a female member of Congress, esp of the House of Representatives.

congruence ('kɒŋgrʊəns) *or* **congruency** NOUN [1] the quality or state of corresponding, agreeing, or being congruent. [2] *Maths* the relationship between two integers, *x* and *y,* such that their difference, with respect to another positive integer called the modulus, *n,* is a multiple of the modulus. Usually written $x \equiv y \pmod{n}$, as in $25 \equiv 11 \pmod{7}$.

congruent ('kɒŋgrʊənt) ADJECTIVE [1] agreeing; corresponding; congruous. [2] having identical shapes so that all parts correspond: *congruent triangles.* Compare **similar** (sense 2). [3] of or concerning two integers related by a congruence.
▷HISTORY C15: from Latin *congruere* to meet together, agree
▸'**congruently** ADVERB

congruous ('kɒŋgrʊəs) ADJECTIVE [1] corresponding or agreeing. [2] suitable; appropriate.
▷HISTORY C16: from Latin *congruus* suitable, harmonious; see CONGRUENT
▸**congruity** (kən'gru:ɪtɪ) *or* '**congruousness** NOUN
▸'**congruously** ADVERB

conic ('kɒnɪk) ADJECTIVE *also* **conical.** [1] **a** having the shape of a cone. **b** of or relating to a cone. ◆ NOUN [2] another name for **conic section.** ◆ See also **conics.**
▷HISTORY C16: from New Latin, from Greek *kōnikos,* from *kōnos* CONE
▸'**conically** ADVERB

conic projection *or* **conical projection** NOUN a map projection on which the earth is shown as projected onto a cone with its apex over one of the poles and with parallels of latitude radiating from this apex.

conics ('kɒnɪks) NOUN (*functioning as singular*) the branch of geometry concerned with the parabola, ellipse, and hyperbola.

conic section NOUN one of a group of curves

formed by the intersection of a plane and a right circular cone. It is either a circle, ellipse, parabola, or hyperbola, depending on the eccentricity, *e*, which is constant for a particular curve $e = 0$ for a circle; $e<1$ for an ellipse; $e = 1$ for a parabola; $e>1$ for a hyperbola. Often shortened to **conic.**

conidiophore (kəʊˈnɪdɪəˌfɔː) NOUN a simple or branched hypha that bears spores (conidia) in such fungi as *Penicillium*.
▷HISTORY C19: from CONIDIUM + -PHORE
▸**conidiophorous** (kəʊˌnɪdɪˈɒfərəs, kə-) ADJECTIVE

conidium (kəʊˈnɪdɪəm) NOUN, *plural* **-nidia** (-ˈnɪdɪə). an asexual spore formed at the tip of a specialized hypha (conidiophore) in fungi such as *Penicillium*.
▷HISTORY C19: from New Latin, from Greek *konis* dust + IUM
▸**coˈnidial** *or* **coˈnidian** ADJECTIVE

conifer (ˈkəʊnɪfə, ˈkɒn-) NOUN any gymnosperm tree or shrub of the phylum *Coniferophyta*, typically bearing cones and evergreen leaves. The group includes the pines, spruces, firs, larches, yews, junipers, cedars, cypresses, and sequoias.
▷HISTORY C19: from Latin, from *cōnus* CONE + *ferre* to bear

coniferous (kəˈnɪfərəs, kɒ-) ADJECTIVE of, relating to, or belonging to the plant phylum *Coniferophyta*. See **conifer.**

coniine (ˈkəʊnɪˌiːn, -nɪɪn, -niːn), **conin** (ˈkəʊnɪn), *or* **conine** (ˈkəʊniːn, -nɪn) NOUN a colourless poisonous soluble liquid alkaloid found in hemlock; 2-propylpiperidine. Formula: $C_5H_{10}NC_3H_7$. Also called: **cicutine** (ˈsɪkjʊtiːn), **conicine** (ˈkəʊnɪsiːn).
▷HISTORY C19: from CONIUM + INE[2]

coniology (ˌkəʊnɪˈɒlədʒɪ) NOUN a variant spelling of **koniology.**

Coniston Water (ˈkɒnɪstən) NOUN a lake in NW England, in Cumbria: scene of the establishment of world water speed records by Sir Malcolm Campbell (1939) and his son Donald Campbell (1959). Length: 8 km (5 miles).

conium (ˈkəʊnɪəm) NOUN [1] either of the two N temperate plants of the umbelliferous genus *Conium*, esp hemlock. [2] an extract of either of these plants, formerly used to treat spasmodic disorders.
▷HISTORY C19: from Late Latin: hemlock, from Greek *kōneion;* perhaps related to Greek *kōnos* CONE

conj. *Grammar* ABBREVIATION FOR conjugation, conjunction, *or* conjunctive.

conjectural (kənˈdʒɛktʃərəl) ADJECTIVE involving or inclined to conjecture.
▸**conˈjecturally** ADVERB

conjecture (kənˈdʒɛktʃə) NOUN [1] the formation of conclusions from incomplete evidence; guess. [2] the inference or conclusion so formed. [3] *Obsolete* interpretation of occult signs. ◆ VERB [4] to infer or arrive at (an opinion, conclusion, etc.) from incomplete evidence.
▷HISTORY C14: from Latin *conjectūra* an assembling of facts, from *conjicere* to throw together, from *jacere* to throw
▸**conˈjecturable** ADJECTIVE ▸**conˈjecturably** ADVERB
▸**conˈjecturer** NOUN

conjoin (kənˈdʒɔɪn) VERB to join or become joined.
▷HISTORY C14: from Old French *conjoindre,* from Latin *conjungere,* from *jungere* to JOIN
▸**conˈjoiner** NOUN

conjoined twins PLURAL NOUN twin babies born joined together at some point, such as at the hips. Some have lived for many years without being surgically separated. Non-technical name: **Siamese twins.**

conjoint (kənˈdʒɔɪnt) ADJECTIVE united, joint, or associated.
▸**conˈjointly** ADVERB

conjugal (ˈkɒndʒʊgᵊl) ADJECTIVE of or relating to marriage or the relationship between husband and wife: *conjugal rights.*
▷HISTORY C16: from Latin *conjugālis,* from *conjunx* wife or husband, from *conjungere* to unite; see CONJOIN
▸**conjugality** (ˌkɒndʒʊˈgælɪtɪ) NOUN ▸**ˈconjugally** ADVERB

conjugant (ˈkɒndʒʊgənt) NOUN either of a pair of organisms or gametes undergoing conjugation.

conjugate VERB (ˈkɒndʒʊˌgeɪt) [1] *(tr) Grammar* to inflect (a verb) systematically; state or set out the conjugation of (a verb). [2] *(intr)* (of a verb) to undergo inflection according to a specific set of rules. [3] *(tr)* to join (two or more substances) together, esp in such a way that the resulting substance may easily be turned back into its original components. [4] *(intr) Biology* to undergo conjugation. [5] *(tr) Obsolete* to join together, esp in marriage. ◆ ADJECTIVE (ˈkɒndʒʊgɪt, -ˌgeɪt) [6] joined together in pairs; coupled. [7] *Maths* **a** (of two angles) having a sum of 360°. **b** (of two complex numbers) differing only in the sign of the imaginary part as 4 + 3i and 4 – 3i. **c** (of two algebraic numbers) being roots of the same irreducible algebraic equation with rational coefficients: *$3 \pm 2\sqrt{2}$ are conjugate algebraic numbers, being roots of $x^2 - 6x + 1$.* **d** (of two elements of a square matrix) interchanged when the rows and columns are interchanged. **e** (of two arcs) forming a complete circle or other closed curved figure. [8] *Chem* of, denoting, or concerning the state of equilibrium in which two liquids can exist as two separate phases that are both solutions. The liquid that is the solute in one phase is the solvent in the other. [9] another word for **conjugated.** [10] *Chem* (of acids and bases) related by loss or gain of a proton: *Cl^- is the conjugate base of HCl. HCl is the conjugate acid of Cl^-.* [11] *Physics* **a** joined by a reciprocal relationship, such as in the case of two quantities, points, etc., that are interchangeable with respect to the properties of each of them. **b** (of points connected with a lens) having the property that an object placed at one point will produce an image at the other point. [12] (of a compound leaf) having one pair of leaflets. [13] (of words) cognate; related in origin. ◆ NOUN (ˈkɒndʒʊgɪt) [14] one of a pair or set of conjugate substances, values, quantities, words, etc.
▷HISTORY C15: from Latin *conjugāre* to join together, from *com-* together + *jugāre* to marry, connect, from *jugum* a yoke
▸**ˈconjugable** ADJECTIVE ▸**ˈconjugately** ADVERB
▸**ˈconjugateness** NOUN ▸**ˈconjuˌgative** ADJECTIVE
▸**ˈconjuˌgator** NOUN

conjugated (ˈkɒndʒʊˌgeɪtɪd) ADJECTIVE [1] *Chem* **a** (of a molecule, compound, or substance) containing two or more double bonds alternating with single bonds. **b** (of a double bond) separated from another double bond by one single bond. [2] *Chem* formed by the union of two compounds: *a conjugated protein.* ◆ Also: **conjugate.**

conjugated protein NOUN a biochemical compound consisting of a sequence of amino acids making up a simple protein to which another nonprotein group (a prosthetic group), such as a carbohydrate or lipid group, is attached.

conjugation (ˌkɒndʒʊˈgeɪʃən) NOUN [1] *Grammar* **a** inflection of a verb for person, number, tense, voice, mood, etc. **b** the complete set of the inflections of a given verb. [2] a joining, union, or conjunction. [3] a type of sexual reproduction in ciliate protozoans involving the temporary union of two individuals and the subsequent migration and fusion of the gametic nuclei. [4] (in bacteria) the direct transfer of DNA between two cells that are temporarily joined. [5] the union of gametes, esp isogametes, as in some algae and fungi. [6] the pairing of chromosomes in the early phase of a meiotic division. [7] *Chem* the existence of alternating double or triple bonds in a chemical compound, with consequent electron delocalization over part of the molecule.
▸**ˌconjuˈgational** ADJECTIVE ▸**ˌconjuˈgationally** ADVERB

conjunct (kənˈdʒʌŋkt, ˈkɒndʒʌŋkt) ADJECTIVE [1] joined; united. [2] *Music* relating to or denoting two adjacent degrees of a scale. ◆ NOUN [3] *Logic* one of the propositions or formulas in a conjunction.
▷HISTORY C15: from Latin *conjunctus,* from *conjugere* to unite; see CONJOIN
▸**conˈjunctly** ADVERB

conjunction (kənˈdʒʌŋkʃən) NOUN [1] the act of joining together; combination; union. [2] simultaneous occurrence of events; coincidence. [3] any word or group of words, other than a relative pronoun, that connects words, phrases, or clauses; for example *and* and *while.* Abbreviation: **conj.** See also **coordinating conjunction, subordinating conjunction.** [4] *Astronomy* **a** the position of any two bodies that appear to meet, such as two celestial bodies on the celestial sphere. **b** Also called: **solar conjunction.** the position of a planet or the moon when it is in line with the sun as seen from the earth. The inner planets are in **inferior conjunction** when the planet is between the earth and the sun and in **superior conjunction** when the sun lies between the earth and the planet. Compare **opposition** (sense 8a). [5] *Astrology* an exact aspect of 0° between two planets, etc., an orb of 8° being allowed. Compare **opposition** (sense 9), **square** (sense 10). [6] *Logic* **a** the operator that forms a compound sentence from two given sentences, and corresponds to the English *and.* **b** a sentence so formed. Usually written *p&q, p∧q,* or *p.q.,* where *p,q* are the component sentences, it is true only when both these are true. **c** the relation between such sentences.
▸**conˈjunctional** ADJECTIVE ▸**conˈjunctionally** ADVERB

conjunction-reduction NOUN *Transformational grammar* a rule that reduces coordinate sentences, applied, for example, to convert *John lives in Ireland and Brian lives in Ireland* into *John and Brian live in Ireland.*

conjunctiva (ˌkɒndʒʌŋkˈtaɪvə) NOUN, *plural* **-vas** *or* **-vae** (-viː). the delicate mucous membrane that covers the eyeball and the under surface of the eyelid.
▷HISTORY C16: from New Latin *membrāna conjunctīva* the conjunctive membrane, from Late Latin *conjunctīvus* CONJUNCTIVE
▸**ˌconjuncˈtival** ADJECTIVE

conjunctive (kənˈdʒʌŋktɪv) ADJECTIVE [1] joining; connective. [2] joined. [3] of or relating to conjunctions or their use. [4] *Logic* relating to, characterized by, or containing a conjunction. ◆ NOUN [5] a less common word for **conjunction** (sense 3).
▷HISTORY C15: from Late Latin *conjunctīvus,* from Latin *conjungere* to CONJOIN
▸**conˈjunctively** ADVERB

conjunctive eye movement NOUN any movement of both eyes in the same direction.

conjunctivitis (kənˌdʒʌŋktɪˈvaɪtɪs) NOUN inflammation of the conjunctiva.

conjuncture (kənˈdʒʌŋktʃə) NOUN [1] a combination of events, esp a critical one. [2] *Rare* a union; conjunction.
▸**conˈjunctural** ADJECTIVE

conjuration (ˌkɒndʒʊˈreɪʃən) NOUN [1] a magic spell; incantation. [2] a less common word for **conjuring.** [3] *Archaic* supplication; entreaty.

conjure (ˈkʌndʒə) VERB [1] *(intr)* to practise conjuring or be a conjuror. [2] *(intr)* to call upon supposed supernatural forces by spells and incantations. [3] (kənˈdʒʊə) *(tr)* to appeal earnestly or strongly to: *I conjure you to help me.* [4] **a name to conjure with. a** a person thought to have great power or influence. **b** any name that excites the imagination.
▷HISTORY C13: from Old French *conjurer* to plot, from Latin *conjūrāre* to swear together, form a conspiracy, from *jūrāre* to swear

conjure up VERB *(tr, adverb)* [1] to present to the mind; evoke or imagine: *he conjured up a picture of his childhood.* [2] to call up or command (a spirit or devil) by an incantation.

conjuring (ˈkʌndʒərɪŋ) NOUN [1] the performance of tricks that appear to defy natural laws. ◆ ADJECTIVE [2] denoting or relating to such tricks or entertainment.

conjuror *or* **conjurer** (ˈkʌndʒərə) NOUN [1] a person who practises conjuring, esp for people's entertainment. [2] a person who practises magic; sorcerer.

conk (kɒŋk) *Slang* ◆ VERB [1] to strike (someone) a blow, esp on the head or nose. ◆ NOUN [2] a punch or blow, esp on the head or nose. [3] the head or (esp Brit and NZ) the nose.
▷HISTORY C19: probably changed from CONCH

conker (ˈkɒŋkə) NOUN an informal name for **horse chestnut** (sense 2).

conkers (ˈkɒŋkəz) NOUN *(functioning as singular) Brit* a game in which a player swings a horse chestnut (conker), threaded onto a string, against that of another player to try to break it.
▷HISTORY C19: from dialect *conker* snail shell, originally used in the game

conk out VERB *(intr, adverb) Informal* [1] (of machines, cars, etc.) to fail suddenly. [2] to tire suddenly or collapse, as from exhaustion.
▷HISTORY C20: of uncertain origin

con man NOUN *Informal* [1] a person who swindles another by means of a confidence trick. [2] a plausible character. ◆ More formal term: **confidence man.**

con moto (kɒn 'məʊtəʊ) ADJECTIVE, ADVERB *Music* (to be performed) in a brisk or lively manner.
▷HISTORY Italian, literally: with movement

conn (kɒn) VERB, NOUN a variant spelling (esp US) of **con**[4].

Conn. ABBREVIATION FOR Connecticut.

Connacht ('kɒnət) NOUN a province and ancient kingdom of NW Republic of Ireland: consists of the counties of Galway, Leitrim, Mayo, Roscommon, and Sligo. Pop.: 433 231 (1996). Area: 17 122 sq. km (6611 sq. miles). Former name: **Connaught.**

connate ('kɒneɪt) ADJECTIVE [1] existing in a person or thing from birth; congenital or innate. [2] allied or associated in nature or origin; cognate: *connate qualities.* [3] Also called: **coadunate.** *Biology* (of similar parts or organs) closely joined or united together by growth. [4] *Geology* (of fluids) produced or originating at the same time as the rocks surrounding them: *connate water.*
▷HISTORY C17: from Late Latin *connātus* born at the same time, from Latin *nātus,* from *nāscī* to be born
▸**'connately** ADVERB ▸**'connateness** NOUN

connatural (kə'nætʃərəl) ADJECTIVE [1] having a similar nature or origin. [2] congenital or innate; connate.
▸**con'naturally** ADVERB

Connaught ('kɒnɔ:t) NOUN the former name of **Connacht.**

connect (kə'nɛkt) VERB [1] to link or be linked together; join; fasten. [2] (*tr*) to relate or associate: *I connect him with my childhood.* [3] (*tr*) to establish telephone communications with or between. [4] (*intr*) to be meaningful or meaningfully related. [5] (*intr*) (of two public vehicles, such as trains or buses) to have the arrival of one timed to occur just before the departure of the other, for the convenient transfer of passengers. [6] (*intr*) *Informal* to hit, punch, kick, etc., solidly. [7] (*intr*) *US and Canadian informal* to be successful. [8] (*intr*) *Slang* to find a source of drugs, esp illegal drugs.
▷HISTORY C17: from Latin *connectere* to bind together, from *nectere* to bind, tie
▸**con'nectible** *or* **con'nectable** ADJECTIVE ▸**con'nector** *or* **con'necter** NOUN

connected (kə'nɛktɪd) ADJECTIVE [1] joined or linked together. [2] (of speech) coherent and intelligible. [3] *Logic, maths* (of a relation) such that either it or its converse holds between any two members of its domain.
▸**con'nectedly** ADVERB

Connecticut (kə'nɛtɪkət) NOUN [1] a state of the northeastern US, in New England. Capital: Hartford Pop.: 3 405 565 (1997 est.). Area: 12 973 sq. km (5009 sq. miles). Abbreviations: **Conn.,** (with zip code) **CT.** [2] a river in the northeastern US, rising in N New Hampshire and flowing south to Long Island Sound. Length: 651 km (407 miles).

connecting rod NOUN [1] a rod or bar for transmitting motion, esp one that connects a rotating part to a reciprocating part. [2] such a rod that connects the piston to the crankshaft in an internal-combustion engine or reciprocating pump. See also **big end, little end.** [3] a similar rod that connects the crosshead of a steam engine to the crank. ◆ Often shortened to **con rod.**

connection *or* **connexion** (kə'nɛkʃən) NOUN [1] the act or state of connecting; union. [2] something that connects, joins, or relates; link or bond. [3] a relationship or association. [4] logical sequence in thought or expression; coherence. [5] the relation of a word or phrase to its context: *in this connection the word has no political significance.* [6] (*often plural*) an acquaintance, esp one who is influential or has prestige. [7] a relative, esp if distant and related by marriage. [8] **a** an opportunity to transfer from one train, bus, aircraft, ship, etc., to another. **b** the vehicle, aircraft, etc., scheduled to provide such an opportunity. [9] (*plural*) *NZ* the persons owning or controlling a racehorse. [10] a link, usually a wire or metallic strip, between two components in an electric circuit or system. [11] a communications link between two points, esp by telephone. [12] *Slang* a supplier of illegal drugs, such as heroin. [13] *Rare* sexual intercourse. [14] *Rare* a small sect or religious group united by a body of distinct beliefs or practices.
▸**con'nectional** *or* **con'nexional** ADJECTIVE

connectionism (kə'nɛkʃənɪzəm) NOUN *Psychol* the theory that the connections between brain cells mediate thought and govern behaviour.

connective (kə'nɛktɪv) ADJECTIVE [1] serving to connect or capable of connecting. ◆ NOUN [2] a thing that connects. [3] *Grammar, logic* **a** a less common word for **conjunction** (sense 3). **b** any word that connects phrases, clauses, or individual words. **c** a symbol used in a formal language in the construction of compound sentences from simpler sentences, corresponding to terms such as *or, and, not,* etc., in ordinary speech. [4] *Botany* the tissue of a stamen that connects the two lobes of the anther. [5] *Anatomy* a nerve-fibre bundle connecting two nerve centres.
▸**con'nectively** ADVERB ▸**connectivity** (ˌkɒnɛk'tɪvɪtɪ) NOUN

connective tissue NOUN an animal tissue developed from the embryonic mesoderm that consists of collagen or elastic fibres, fibroblasts, fatty cells, etc., within a jelly-like matrix. It supports organs, fills the spaces between them, and forms tendons and ligaments.

Connemara (ˌkɒnɪ'mɑ:rə) NOUN a barren coastal region of W Republic of Ireland, in Co. Galway: consists of quartzite mountains, peat bogs, and many lakes noted for its breed of pony originating from the hilly regions.

conning tower ('kɒnɪŋ) NOUN [1] Also called: **sail.** a superstructure of a submarine, used as the bridge when the vessel is on the surface. [2] the armoured pilot house of a warship.
▷HISTORY C19: see CON[4]

conniption (kə'nɪpʃən) NOUN (*often plural*) *US and Canadian slang* a fit of rage or tantrums.
▷HISTORY C19: arbitrary pseudo-Latin coinage

connivance (kə'naɪvəns) NOUN [1] the act or fact of conniving. [2] *Law* the tacit encouragement of or assent to another's wrongdoing, esp (formerly) of the petitioner in a divorce suit to the respondent's adultery.

connive (kə'naɪv) VERB (*intr*) [1] to plot together, esp secretly; conspire. [2] (foll by *at*) *Law* to give assent or encouragement (to the commission of a wrong).
▷HISTORY C17: from French *conniver,* from Latin *connīvēre* to blink, hence, leave uncensured; *-nīvēre* related to *nictāre* to wink
▸**con'niver** NOUN ▸**con'nivingly** ADVERB

connivent (kə'naɪvənt) ADJECTIVE (of parts of plants and animals) touching without being fused, as some petals, insect wings, etc.
▷HISTORY C17: from Latin *connīvēns,* from *connīvēre* to shut the eyes, CONNIVE
▸**con'nivently** ADVERB

connoisseur (ˌkɒnɪ'sɜ:) NOUN a person with special knowledge or appreciation of a field, esp in the arts.
▷HISTORY C18: from French, from Old French *conoiseor,* from *connoistre* to know, from Latin *cognōscere*
▸ˌ**connois'seurship** NOUN

connotation (ˌkɒnə'teɪʃən) NOUN [1] an association or idea suggested by a word or phrase; implication. [2] the act or fact of connoting. [3] *Logic* another name for **intension** (sense 1).
▸**connotative** ('kɒnəˌteɪtɪv, kə'nəʊtə-) *or* **con'notive** ADJECTIVE ▸**'connoˌtatively** *or* **con'notively** ADVERB

connote (kɒ'nəʊt) VERB (*tr; often takes a clause as object*) [1] (of a word, phrase, etc.) to imply or suggest (associations or ideas) other than the literal meaning: *the word "maiden" connotes modesty.* [2] to involve as a consequence or condition.
▷HISTORY C17: from Medieval Latin *connotāre,* from *notāre* to mark, make a note, from *nota* mark, sign, note

connubial (kə'nju:bɪəl) ADJECTIVE of or relating to marriage; conjugal: *connubial bliss.*
▷HISTORY C17: from Latin *cōnūbiālis* from *cōnūbium* marriage, from *com-* together + *nūbere* to marry
▸**conˌnubi'ality** NOUN ▸**con'nubially** ADVERB

conodont ('kəʊnədɒnt, 'kɒn-) NOUN any of various small Palaeozoic toothlike fossils derived from an extinct eel-like marine animal.
▷HISTORY C19: from Greek *kōnos* CONE + ODONT

conoid ('kəʊnɔɪd) NOUN [1] a geometric surface formed by rotating a parabola, ellipse, or hyperbola about one axis. ◆ ADJECTIVE *also* **conoidal** (kəʊ'nɔɪdᵊl). [2] conical, cone-shaped.
▷HISTORY C17: from Greek *kōnoeidēs,* from *kōnos* CONE
▸**co'noidally** ADVERB

conoscenti (ˌkɒnəʊ'ʃɛntɪ) PLURAL NOUN, *singular* **-te** (-ti:). a variant spelling of **cognoscenti.**

conquer ('kɒŋkə) VERB [1] to overcome (an enemy, army, etc.); defeat. [2] to overcome (an obstacle, feeling, desire, etc.); surmount. [3] (*tr*) to gain possession or control of by or as if by force or war; win. [4] (*tr*) to gain the love, sympathy, etc., of (someone) by seduction or force of personality.
▷HISTORY C13: from Old French *conquerre,* from Vulgar Latin *conquērere* (unattested) to obtain, from Latin *conquīrere* to search for, collect, from *quaerere* to seek
▸**'conquerable** ADJECTIVE ▸**'conquerableness** NOUN ▸**'conquering** ADJECTIVE ▸**'conqueror** NOUN

conquest ('kɒnkwɛst, 'kɒŋ-) NOUN [1] the act or an instance of conquering or the state of having been conquered; victory. [2] a person, thing, etc., that has been conquered or won. [3] the act or art of gaining a person's compliance, love, etc., by seduction or force of personality. [4] a person, whose compliance, love, etc., has been won over by seduction or force of personality.
▷HISTORY C13: from Old French *conqueste,* from Vulgar Latin *conquēsta* (unattested), from Latin *conquīsīta,* feminine past participle of *conquīrere* to seek out, procure; see CONQUER

Conquest ('kɒnkwɛst, 'kɒŋ-) NOUN [1] **the.** See **Norman Conquest.** [2] **the.** *Canadian* the conquest by the United Kingdom of French North America, ending in 1763.

conquian ('kɒŋkɪən) NOUN another word for **cooncan.**

conquistador (kɒn'kwɪstəˌdɔ:; *Spanish* konkista'ðor) NOUN, *plural* **-dors** *or* **-dores** (*Spanish* -'ðores). an adventurer or conqueror, esp one of the Spanish conquerors of the New World in the 16th century.
▷HISTORY C19: from Spanish, from *conquistar* to conquer; see CONQUEST

con rod NOUN short for **connecting rod.**

Cons. *or* **cons.** ABBREVIATION FOR: [1] Conservative. [2] Constitution. [3] Consul.

consanguinity (ˌkɒnsæŋ'gwɪnɪtɪ) NOUN [1] relationship by blood; kinship. [2] close affinity or connection. [3] *Geology* (of igneous rocks) similarity of origin, as shown by common mineral and chemical compositions and often texture.
▷HISTORY C14: see CON-, SANGUINE
▸ˌ**consan'guineous** *or* **con'sanguine** ADJECTIVE ▸ˌ**consan'guineously** ADVERB

conscience ('kɒnʃəns) NOUN [1] **a** the sense of right and wrong that governs a person's thoughts and actions. **b** regulation of one's actions in conformity to this sense. **c** a supposed universal faculty of moral insight. [2] conscientiousness; diligence. [3] a feeling of guilt or anxiety: *he has a conscience about his unkind action.* [4] *Obsolete* consciousness. [5] **in (all) conscience. a** with regard to truth and justice. **b** certainly. [6] **on one's conscience.** causing feelings of guilt or remorse.
▷HISTORY C13: from Old French, from Latin *conscientia* knowledge, consciousness, from *conscīre* to know; see CONSCIOUS
▸**'conscienceless** ADJECTIVE

conscience clause NOUN a clause in a law or contract exempting persons with moral scruples.

conscience money NOUN money paid voluntarily to compensate for dishonesty, esp money paid voluntarily for taxes formerly evaded.

conscience-stricken ADJECTIVE feeling anxious or guilty. Also: **conscience-smitten.**

conscientious (ˌkɒnʃɪ'ɛnʃəs) ADJECTIVE [1] involving or taking great care; painstaking; diligent. [2] governed by or done according to conscience.
▸ˌ**consci'entiously** ADVERB ▸ˌ**consci'entiousness** NOUN

conscientious objector NOUN a person who refuses to serve in the armed forces on the grounds of conscience.

conscionable ('kɒnʃənəbᵊl) ADJECTIVE *Obsolete* acceptable to one's conscience.

▷**HISTORY** C16: from *conscions,* obsolete form of CONSCIENCE
▸ **'conscionableness** NOUN ▸ **'conscionably** ADVERB

conscious ('kɒnʃəs) ADJECTIVE [1] **a** alert and awake; not sleeping or comatose. **b** aware of one's surroundings, one's own thoughts and motivations, etc. [2] **a** aware of and giving value or emphasis to a particular fact or phenomenon: *I am conscious of your great kindness to me.* **b** (*in combination*): *clothes-conscious.* [3] done with full awareness; deliberate: *a conscious effort; conscious rudeness.* [4] **a** denoting or relating to a part of the human mind that is aware of a person's self, environment, and mental activity and that to a certain extent determines his choices of action. **b** (*as noun*): *the conscious is only a small part of the mind.* ◆ Compare **unconscious.**
▷**HISTORY** C17: from Latin *conscius* sharing knowledge, from *com-* with + *scīre* to know
▸ **'consciously** ADVERB ▸ **'consciousness** NOUN

consciousness raising NOUN **a** the process of developing awareness in a person or group of a situation regarded as wrong or unjust, with the aim of producing active participation in changing it. **b** (*as modifier*): *a consciousness-raising group.*

conscript NOUN ('kɒnskrɪpt) [1] **a** a person who is enrolled for compulsory military service. **b** (*as modifier*): *a conscript army.* ◆ VERB (kən'skrɪpt) [2] (*tr*) to enrol (youths, civilians, etc.) for compulsory military service.
▷**HISTORY** C15: from Latin *conscrīptus,* past participle of *conscrībere* to write together in a list, enrol, from *scrībere* to write

conscript fathers PLURAL NOUN *Literary* august legislators, esp Roman senators.

conscription (kən'skrɪpʃən) NOUN compulsory military service.

consecrate ('kɒnsɪˌkreɪt) VERB (*tr*) [1] to make or declare sacred or holy; sanctify. [2] to dedicate (one's life, time, etc.) to a specific purpose. [3] to ordain (a bishop). [4] *Christianity* to sanctify (bread and wine) for the Eucharist to be received as the body and blood of Christ. [5] to cause to be respected or revered; venerate: *time has consecrated this custom.* ◆ ADJECTIVE [6] *Archaic* consecrated.
▷**HISTORY** C15: from Latin *consecrāre,* from *com-* (intensive) + *sacrāre* to devote, from *sacer* sacred
▸ **ˌconse'cration** NOUN ▸ **'conseˌcrator** NOUN
▸ **consecratory** (ˌkɒnsɪ'kreɪtərɪ) *or* **'conseˌcrative** ADJECTIVE

Consecration (ˌkɒnsɪ'kreɪʃən) NOUN *RC Church* the part of the Mass after the sermon during which the bread and wine are believed to change into the Body and Blood of Christ.

consecution (ˌkɒnsɪ'kjuːʃən) NOUN [1] a sequence or succession of events or things. [2] a logical sequence of deductions; inference.
▷**HISTORY** C16: from Latin *consecūtiō,* from *consequī* to follow up, pursue

consecutive (kən'sɛkjʊtɪv) ADJECTIVE [1] (of a narrative, account, etc.) following chronological sequence. [2] following one another without interruption; successive. [3] characterized by logical sequence. [4] *Music* another word for **parallel** (sense 3). [5] *Grammar* expressing consequence or result: *consecutive clauses.*
▷**HISTORY** C17: from French *consécutif,* from Latin *consecūtus* having followed, from *consequī* to pursue
▸ **con'secutively** ADVERB ▸ **con'secutiveness** NOUN

consensual (kən'sɛnsjʊəl) ADJECTIVE [1] *Law* (of a contract, agreement, etc.) existing by consent. [2] *Law* (of a sexual activity) performed with the consent of all parties involved. [3] (of certain reflex actions of a part of the body) responding to stimulation of another part.
▸ **con'sensually** ADVERB
▷**HISTORY** from CONSENSUS + -AL[1]

consensus (kən'sɛnsəs) NOUN general or widespread agreement (esp in the phrase **consensus of opinion**).
▷**HISTORY** C19: from Latin, from *consentīre* to feel together, agree; see CONSENT

> **Language note** Since *consensus* refers to a collective opinion, the words *of opinion* in the phrase *consensus of opinion* are redundant and should therefore be avoided.

consensus sequence NOUN *Biochem* a DNA sequence common to different organisms and having a similar function in each.

consent (kən'sɛnt) VERB [1] to give assent or permission (to do something); agree; accede. [2] (*intr*) *Obsolete* to be in accord; agree in opinion, feelings, etc. ◆ NOUN [3] acquiescence to or acceptance of something done or planned by another; permission. [4] accordance or harmony in opinion; agreement (esp in the phrase **with one consent**). [5] **age of consent.** the lowest age at which the law recognizes the right of a person to consent to sexual intercourse.
▷**HISTORY** C13: from Old French *consentir,* from Latin *consentīre* to feel together, agree, from *sentīre* to feel
▸ **con'senter** NOUN ▸ **con'senting** ADJECTIVE

consentaneous (ˌkɒnsɛn'teɪnɪəs) ADJECTIVE *Rare* [1] (foll by *to*) accordant or consistent (with). [2] done by general consent.
▷**HISTORY** C17: from Latin *consentāneus,* from *consentīre* to CONSENT
▸ **ˌconsen'taneously** ADVERB ▸ **consentaneity** (kənˌsɛntə'niːɪtɪ) *or* **ˌconsen'taneousness** NOUN

consentient (kən'sɛnʃənt) ADJECTIVE being in agreement; united in opinion.
▸ **con'sentience** NOUN

consenting adult NOUN *Brit* a male person over the age of sixteen, who may legally engage in homosexual behaviour in private.

consequence ('kɒnsɪkwəns) NOUN [1] a result or effect of some previous occurrence. [2] an unpleasant result (esp in the phrase **take the consequences**). [3] significance or importance: *it's of no consequence; a man of consequence.* [4] *Logic* **a** a conclusion reached by reasoning. **b** the conclusion of an argument. **c** the relations between the conclusion and the premises of a valid argument. [5] the relation between an effect and its cause. [6] **in consequence.** as a result.

consequences ('kɒnsɪkwənsɪz) PLURAL NOUN (*functioning as singular*) *Brit* a game in which each player writes down a part of a story, folds over the paper, and passes it on to another player who continues the story. After several stages, the resulting (nonsensical) stories are read out.

consequent ('kɒnsɪkwənt) ADJECTIVE [1] following as an effect or result. [2] following as a logical conclusion or by rational argument. [3] (of a river) flowing in the direction of the original slope of the land or dip of the strata. ◆ NOUN [4] something that follows something else, esp as a result. [5] *Logic* the resultant clause in a conditional sentence. [6] **affirming the consequent.** *Logic* the fallacy of inferring the antecedent of a conditional sentence, given the truth of the conditional and its consequent, as *if John is six feet tall, he's more than five feet: he's more than five feet so he's six feet.* [7] an obsolete term for **denominator** (sense 1).
▷**HISTORY** C15: from Latin *consequēns* following closely, from *consequī* to pursue

> **Language note** See at **consequential.**

consequential (ˌkɒnsɪ'kwɛnʃəl) ADJECTIVE [1] important or significant. [2] self-important; conceited. [3] following as a consequence; resultant, esp indirectly: *consequential loss.*
▸ **ˌconseˌquenti'ality** *or* **ˌconse'quentialness** NOUN
▸ **ˌconse'quentially** ADVERB

> **Language note** Although both *consequential* and *consequent* can refer to something which happens as the result of something else, *consequent* is more common in this sense in modern English: *the new measures were put into effect, and the consequent protest led to the dismissal of those responsible.*

consequentialism (ˌkɒnsɪ'kwɛnʃəˌlɪzəm) NOUN *Ethics* the doctrine that an action is right or wrong according as its consequences are good or bad.

consequently ('kɒnsɪkwəntlɪ) ADVERB, SENTENCE CONNECTOR as a result or effect; therefore; hence.

conservancy (kən'sɜːvənsɪ) NOUN, *plural* **-cies.** [1] (in Britain) a court or commission with jurisdiction over a river, port, area of countryside, etc. [2] another word for **conservation** (sense 2).

conservation (ˌkɒnsə'veɪʃən) NOUN [1] the act or an instance of conserving or keeping from change, loss, injury, etc. [2] **a** protection, preservation, and careful management of natural resources and of the environment. **b** (*as modifier*): *a conservation area.*
▸ **ˌconser'vational** ADJECTIVE

conservationist (ˌkɒnsə'veɪʃənɪst) NOUN a person who advocates or strongly promotes preservation and careful management of natural resources and of the environment.

conservation of charge NOUN the principle that the total charge of any isolated system is constant and independent of changes that take place within the system.

conservation of energy NOUN the principle that the total energy of any isolated system is constant and independent of any changes occurring within the system.

conservation of mass NOUN the principle that the total mass of any isolated system is constant and is independent of any chemical and physical changes taking place within the system.

conservation of momentum NOUN the principle that the total linear or angular momentum in any isolated system is constant, provided that no external force is applied.

conservation of parity NOUN the principle that the parity of the total wave function describing a system of elementary particles is conserved. In fact it is not conserved in weak interactions.

conservatism (kən'sɜːvəˌtɪzəm) NOUN [1] opposition to change and innovation. [2] a political philosophy advocating the preservation of the best of the established order in society and opposing radical change.

Conservatism (kən'sɜːvəˌtɪzəm) NOUN (in Britain, Canada, etc.) [1] the form of conservatism advocated by the Conservative Party. [2] the policies, doctrines, or practices of the Conservative Party.

conservative (kən'sɜːvətɪv) ADJECTIVE [1] favouring the preservation of established customs, values, etc., and opposing innovation. [2] of, characteristic of, or relating to conservatism. [3] tending to be moderate or cautious: *a conservative estimate.* [4] conventional in style or type: *a conservative suit.* [5] *Med* (of treatment) designed to alleviate symptoms. Compare **radical** (sense 4). [6] *Physics* a field of force, system, etc., in which the work done moving a body from one point to another is independent of the path taken between them: *electrostatic fields of force are conservative.* ◆ NOUN [7] a person who is reluctant to change or consider new ideas; conformist. [8] a supporter or advocate of conservatism. ◆ ADJECTIVE, NOUN [9] a less common word for **preservative.**
▸ **con'servatively** ADVERB ▸ **con'servativeness** NOUN

Conservative (kən'sɜːvətɪv) ADJECTIVE (in Britain, Canada, and elsewhere) [1] of, supporting, or relating to a Conservative Party. [2] of, relating to, or characterizing Conservative Judaism. ◆ NOUN [3] a supporter or member of a Conservative Party.

Conservative Judaism NOUN a movement reacting against the radicalism of Reform Judaism, rejecting extreme change and advocating moderate relaxations of traditional Jewish law, by an extension of the process by which its adherents claim traditional orthodox Judaism evolved. Compare **Orthodox Judaism, Reform Judaism.**

Conservative Party NOUN [1] (in Britain) the major right-wing party, which developed from the Tories in the 1830s. It advocates a mixed economy, and encourages property owning and free enterprise. In full: **Conservative and Unionist Party.** [2] (in Canada) short for **Progressive Conservative Party.** [3] (in other countries) any of various political parties generally opposing change.

conservatoire (kən'sɜːvəˌtwɑː) NOUN an institution or school for instruction in music. Also called: **conservatory.**
▷**HISTORY** C18: from French: CONSERVATORY

conservator ('kɒnsəˌveɪtə, kən'sɜːvə-) NOUN a person who conserves or keeps safe; custodian, guardian, or protector.

conservatorium (kənˌsɜːvə'tɔːrɪəm) NOUN *Austral* the usual term for **conservatoire.**

conservatory (kən'sɜːvətrɪ) NOUN, *plural* **-tories.** [1] a greenhouse, esp one attached to a house. [2]

another word for **conservatoire.** ◆ ADJECTIVE [3] preservative.

conserve VERB (kən'sɜːv) (*tr*) [1] to keep or protect from harm, decay, loss, etc. [2] to preserve (a foodstuff, esp fruit) with sugar. ◆ NOUN ('kɒnsɜːv, kən'sɜːv) [3] a preparation of fruit in sugar, similar to jam but usually containing whole pieces of fruit.
▷HISTORY (verb) C14: from Latin *conservāre* to keep safe, from *servāre* to save, protect; (noun) C14: from Medieval Latin *conserva,* from Latin *conservāre*
▸**con'servable** ADJECTIVE ▸**con'server** NOUN

Consett ('kɒnsɪt) NOUN a town in N England, in N Durham. Pop.: 21 153 (1991).

consider (kən'sɪdə) VERB (*mainly tr*) [1] (*also intr*) to think carefully about or ponder on (a problem, decision, etc.); contemplate. [2] (*may take a clause as object*) to judge, deem, or have as an opinion: *I consider him a fool.* [3] to have regard for; respect: *consider your mother's feelings.* [4] to look at; regard: *he considered her face.* [5] (*may take a clause as object*) to bear in mind as possible or acceptable: *when buying a car consider this make.* [6] to describe or discuss: *in this programme we consider the traffic problem.* [7] (*may take a clause as object*) to keep in mind and make allowances (for): *consider his childhood.*
▷HISTORY C14: from Latin *consīderāre* to inspect closely, literally: to observe the stars, from *sīdus* star
▸**con'siderer** NOUN

considerable (kən'sɪdərəbᵊl) ADJECTIVE [1] large enough to reckon with: *a considerable quantity.* [2] a lot of; much: *he had considerable courage.* [3] worthy of respect: *a considerable man in the scientific world.*
▸**con'siderably** ADVERB

considerate (kən'sɪdərɪt) ADJECTIVE [1] thoughtful towards other people; kind. [2] *Rare* carefully thought out; considered.
▸**con'siderately** ADVERB ▸**con'siderateness** NOUN

consideration (kənˌsɪdə'reɪʃən) NOUN [1] the act or an instance of considering; deliberation; contemplation. [2] **take into consideration.** to bear in mind; consider. [3] **under consideration.** being currently discussed or deliberated. [4] a fact or circumstance to be taken into account when making a judgment or decision. [5] **on no consideration.** for no reason whatsoever; never. [6] thoughtfulness for other people; kindness. [7] payment for a service; recompense; fee. [8] thought resulting from deliberation; opinion. [9] *Law* the promise, object, etc., given by one party to persuade another to enter into a contract. [10] estimation; esteem. [11] **in consideration of. a** because of. **b** in return for.

considered (kən'sɪdəd) ADJECTIVE [1] presented or thought out with care: *a considered opinion.* [2] (*qualified by a preceding adverb*) esteemed: *highly considered.*

considering (kən'sɪdərɪŋ) PREPOSITION [1] in view of. ◆ ADVERB [2] *Informal* all in all; taking into account the circumstances: *it's not bad considering.* ◆ CONJUNCTION [3] (*subordinating*) in view of the fact that.

consign (kən'saɪn) VERB (*mainly tr*) [1] to hand over or give into the care or charge of another; entrust. [2] to commit irrevocably: *he consigned the papers to the flames.* [3] to commit for admittance: *to consign someone to jail.* [4] to address or deliver (goods) for sale, disposal, etc.: *it was consigned to his London address.* [5] (*intr*) *Obsolete* to assent; agree.
▷HISTORY C15: from Old French *consigner,* from Latin *consignāre* to put one's seal to, sign, from *signum* mark, SIGN
▸**con'signable** ADJECTIVE ▸**ˌconsign'ation** NOUN

consignee (ˌkɒnsaɪ'niː) NOUN a person, agent, organization, etc., to which merchandise is consigned.

consignment (kən'saɪnmənt) NOUN [1] the act of consigning; commitment. [2] a shipment of goods consigned. [3] **on consignment.** for payment by the consignee after sale: *he made the last shipment on consignment.*

consignor (kən'saɪnə, ˌkɒnsaɪ'nɔː) *or* **consigner** (kən'saɪnə) NOUN a person, enterprise, etc., that consigns goods.

consist (kən'sɪst) VERB (*intr*) [1] (foll by *of*) to be composed (of); be formed (of): *syrup consists of sugar and water.* [2] (foll by *in* or *of*) to have its existence (in); lie (in); be expressed (by): *his religion consists only in going to church.* [3] to be compatible or consistent; accord.
▷HISTORY C16: from Latin *consistere* to halt, stand firm, from *sistere* to stand, cause to stand; related to *stāre* to STAND

consistency (kən'sɪstənsɪ) *or* **consistence** NOUN, *plural* **-encies** *or* **-ences.** [1] agreement or accordance with facts, form, or characteristics previously shown or stated. [2] agreement or harmony between parts of something complex; compatibility. [3] degree of viscosity or firmness. [4] the state or quality of holding or sticking together and retaining shape. [5] conformity with previous attitudes, behaviour, practice, etc.

consistent (kən'sɪstənt) ADJECTIVE [1] showing consistency; not self-contradictory. [2] (*postpositive;* foll by *with*) in agreement or harmony; accordant. [3] steady; even: *consistent growth.* [4] *Maths* (of two or more equations) satisfied by at least one common set of values of the variables: $x + y = 4$ *and* $x - y = 2$ *are consistent.* [5] *Logic* **a** (of a set of statements) capable of all being true at the same time or under the same interpretation. **b** (of a formal system) not permitting the deduction of a contradiction from the axioms. Compare **complete** (sense 5). [6] *Obsolete* stuck together; cohering.
▸**con'sistently** ADVERB

consistory (kən'sɪstərɪ) NOUN, *plural* **-ries.** [1] *Church of England* **a** the court of a diocese (other than Canterbury) administering ecclesiastical law. **b** the area in a church where the consistory meets. [2] *RC Church* an assembly of the cardinals and the pope. [3] (in certain Reformed Churches) the governing body of a local congregation or church. [4] *Archaic* a council or assembly.
▷HISTORY C14: from Old French *consistorie,* from Medieval Latin *consistōrium* ecclesiastical tribunal, ultimately from Latin *consistere* to stand still
▸**consistorial** (ˌkɒnsɪ'stɔːrɪəl) *or* **ˌconsis'torian** ADJECTIVE

consociate VERB (kən'səʊʃɪˌeɪt) [1] to enter into or bring into friendly association. ◆ ADJECTIVE (kən'səʊʃɪɪt, -ˌeɪt) [2] associated or united. ◆ NOUN (kən'səʊʃɪɪt, -ˌeɪt) [3] an associate or partner.
▷HISTORY C16: from Latin *consociāre,* from *socius* partner
▸**conˌsoci'ation** NOUN

consocies (kən'səʊʃiːz) NOUN, *plural* **-cies.** *Ecology* a natural community with a single dominant species.
▷HISTORY C20: from CONSOCIATE + SPECIES

consolation (ˌkɒnsə'leɪʃən) NOUN [1] the act of consoling or state of being consoled; solace. [2] a person or thing that is a source of comfort in a time of suffering, grief, disappointment, etc.
▸**consolatory** (kən'sɒlətərɪ, -trɪ) ADJECTIVE

consolation prize NOUN a prize given to console a loser of a game.

console¹ (kən'səʊl) VERB to serve as a source of comfort to (someone) in disappointment, loss, sadness, etc.
▷HISTORY C17: from Latin *consōlārī,* from *sōlārī* to comfort; see SOLACE
▸**con'solable** ADJECTIVE ▸**con'soler** NOUN ▸**con'solingly** ADVERB

console² ('kɒnsəʊl) NOUN [1] an ornamental bracket, esp one used to support a wall fixture, bust, etc. [2] the part of an organ comprising the manuals, pedals, stops, etc. [3] a unit on which the controls of an electronic system are mounted. [4] an electronic device used in playing computer games on the screen of a television to which it is connected. [5] a cabinet for a television, gramophone, etc., designed to stand on the floor. [6] See **console table.**
▷HISTORY C18: from French, shortened from Old French *consolateur* one that provides support, hence, supporting bracket, from Latin *consōlātor* a comforter; see CONSOLE¹

console table ('kɒnsəʊl) NOUN a table with one or more curved legs of bracket-like construction, designed to stand against a wall.

consolidate (kən'sɒlɪˌdeɪt) VERB [1] to form or cause to form into a solid mass or whole; unite or be united. [2] to make or become stronger or more stable. [3] *Military* to strengthen or improve one's control over (a situation, force, newly captured area, etc.).
▷HISTORY C16: from Latin *consolidāre* to make firm, from *solidus* strong, SOLID

Consolidated Fund NOUN *Brit* a fund into which tax revenue is paid in order to meet standing charges, esp interest payments on the national debt.

consolidation (kənˌsɒlɪ'deɪʃən) NOUN [1] the act of consolidating or state of being consolidated. [2] something that is consolidated or integrated. [3] *Law* **a** the combining of two or more actions at law. **b** the combination of a number of Acts of Parliament into one codifying statute. [4] *Geology* the process, including compression and cementation, by which a loose deposit is transformed into a hard rock. [5] *Psychol* the process in the brain that makes the memory for an event enduring; the process is thought to continue for some time after the event.
▸**con'soliˌdative** ADJECTIVE

consolidation loan NOUN a single loan which is taken out to pay off several separate existing loans.

consolidator (kən'sɒlɪˌdeɪtə) NOUN [1] a person or thing that consolidates. [2] a company that offers flight tickets for a variety of different airlines, usually at a reduced price.

consols ('kɒnsɒlz, kən'sɒlz) PLURAL NOUN irredeemable British government securities carrying annual interest rates of two and a half or four per cent. Also called: **bank annuities.**
▷HISTORY short for *consolidated stock*

consolute ('kɒnsəˌluːt) ADJECTIVE [1] (of two or more liquids) mutually soluble in all proportions. [2] (of a substance) soluble in each of two conjugate liquids. [3] of or concerned with the particular state in which two partially miscible liquids become totally miscible.
▷HISTORY C20: from Late Latin *consolūtus,* from Latin *con-* together + *solvere* to dissolve

consommé (kən'sɒmeɪ, 'kɒnsɒˌmeɪ; *French* kɔ̃sɔme) NOUN a clear soup made from meat or chicken stock.
▷HISTORY C19: from French, from *consommer* to finish, use up, from Latin *consummāre;* so called because all the goodness of the meat goes into the liquid

consonance ('kɒnsənəns) *or* **consonancy** NOUN, *plural* **-nances** *or* **-nancies.** [1] agreement, harmony, or accord. [2] *Prosody* similarity between consonants, but not between vowels, as between the *s* and *t* sounds in *sweet silent thought.* Compare **assonance** (sense 1). [3] *Music* **a** an aesthetically pleasing sensation or perception associated with the interval of the octave, the perfect fourth and fifth, the major and minor third and sixth, and chords based on these intervals. Compare **dissonance** (sense 3). **b** an interval or chord producing this sensation.

consonant ('kɒnsənənt) NOUN [1] a speech sound or letter of the alphabet other than a vowel; a stop, fricative, or continuant. ◆ ADJECTIVE [2] (*postpositive;* foll by *with* or *to*) consistent; in agreement. [3] harmonious in tone or sound. [4] *Music* characterized by the presence of a consonance. [5] being or relating to a consonant.
▷HISTORY C14: from Latin *consonāns,* from *consonāre* to sound at the same time, be in harmony, from *sonāre* to sound
▸**'consonantly** ADVERB

consonantal (ˌkɒnsə'næntᵊl) ADJECTIVE [1] relating to, functioning as, or constituting a consonant, such as the semivowel *w* in English *work.* [2] consisting of or characterized by consonants: *a consonantal cluster.*
▸**ˌconso'nantally** ADVERB

con sordino ADVERB *Music* See **sordino** (sense 3).

consort VERB (kən'sɔːt) [1] (*intr;* usually foll by *with*) to keep company (with undesirable people); associate. [2] (*intr*) to agree or harmonize. [3] (*tr*) *Rare* to combine or unite. ◆ NOUN ('kɒnsɔːt) [4] (esp formerly) **a** a small group of instruments, either of the same type, such as viols, (a **whole consort**) or of different types (a **broken consort**). **b** (*as modifier*): *consort music.* [5] the husband or wife of a reigning monarch. [6] a partner or companion, esp a husband or wife. [7] a ship that escorts another. [8] *Obsolete* **a** companionship or association. **b** agreement or accord.
▷HISTORY C15: from Old French, from Latin *consors* sharer, partner, from *sors* lot, fate, portion
▸**con'sortable** ADJECTIVE ▸**con'sorter** NOUN

consortium (kən'sɔːtɪəm) NOUN, *plural* **-tia** (-tɪə). 1 an association of financiers, companies, etc., esp one formed for a particular purpose. 2 *Law* the right of husband or wife to the company, assistance, and affection of the other.
▷HISTORY C19: from Latin: community of goods, partnership; see CONSORT
▸**con'sortial** ADJECTIVE

conspecific (ˌkɒnspɪ'sɪfɪk) ADJECTIVE (of animals or plants) belonging to the same species.

conspectus (kən'spɛktəs) NOUN 1 an overall view; survey. 2 a summary; résumé.
▷HISTORY C19: from Latin: a viewing, from *conspicere* to observe, from *specere* to look

conspicuous (kən'spɪkjʊəs) ADJECTIVE 1 clearly visible; obvious or showy. 2 attracting attention because of a striking quality or feature: *conspicuous stupidity*.
▷HISTORY C16: from Latin *conspicuus*, from *conspicere* to perceive; see CONSPECTUS
▸**con'spicuously** ADVERB ▸**con'spicuousness** NOUN

conspicuous consumption NOUN spending in a lavish or ostentatious way, esp to impress others with one's wealth.

conspiracy (kən'spɪrəsɪ) NOUN, *plural* **-cies**. 1 a secret plan or agreement to carry out an illegal or harmful act, esp with political motivation; plot. 2 the act of making such plans in secret.
▸**con'spirator** NOUN ▸**conspiratorial** (kənˌspɪrə'tɔːrɪəl) *or* **con'spiratory** ADJECTIVE ▸**conˌspira'torially** ADVERB

conspiracy theory NOUN the belief that the government or a covert organization is responsible for an event that is unusual or unexplained, esp when any such involvement is denied.

conspire (kən'spaɪə) VERB (when *intr*, sometimes foll by *against*) 1 to plan or agree on (a crime or harmful act) together in secret. 2 (*intr*) to act together towards some end as if by design: *the elements conspired to spoil our picnic*.
▷HISTORY C14: from Old French *conspirer*, from Latin *conspīrāre* to plot together, literally: to breathe together, from *spīrāre* to breathe
▸**con'spirer** NOUN ▸**con'spiringly** ADVERB

con spirito (kɒn 'spɪrɪtəʊ) ADJECTIVE, ADVERB *Music* (to be performed) in a spirited or lively manner (also in the phrases **allegro con spirito, presto con spirito**).
▷HISTORY Italian: with spirit

const. ABBREVIATION FOR constant.

constable ('kʌnstəbᵊl, 'kɒn-) NOUN 1 (in Britain, Australia, Canada, New Zealand, etc.) a police officer of the lowest rank. 2 any of various officers of the peace, esp one who arrests offenders, serves writs, etc. 3 the keeper or governor of a royal castle or fortress. 4 (in medieval Europe) the chief military officer and functionary of a royal household, esp in France and England. 5 an officer of a hundred in medieval England, originally responsible for raising the military levy but later assigned other administrative duties.
▷HISTORY C13: from Old French, from Late Latin *comes stabulī* officer in charge of the stable, from Latin *comes* comrade + *stabulum* dwelling, stable; see also COUNT[2]
▸**'constableˌship** NOUN

constabulary (kən'stæbjʊlərɪ) *Chiefly Brit* ◆ NOUN, *plural* **-laries**. 1 the police force of a town or district. ◆ ADJECTIVE 2 of or relating to constables, constabularies, or their duties.

Constance ('kɒnstəns) NOUN 1 a city in S Germany, in Baden-Württemberg on Lake Constance: tourist centre. Pop.: 72 860 (latest est.). German name: **Konstanz**. 2 **Lake.** a lake in W Europe, bounded by S Germany, W Austria, and N Switzerland, through which the Rhine flows. Area: 536 sq. km. (207 sq. miles). German name: **Bodensee.**

constancy ('kɒnstənsɪ) NOUN 1 the quality of having a resolute mind, purpose, or affection; steadfastness. 2 freedom from change or variation; stability. 3 *Psychol* the perceptual phenomenon in which attributes of an object appear to remain the same in a variety of different presentations, e.g., a given object looks roughly the same size regardless of its distance from the observer. 4 *Ecology* the frequency of occurrence of a particular species in sample plots from a plant community.

constant ('kɒnstənt) ADJECTIVE 1 fixed and invariable; unchanging. 2 continual or continuous; incessant: *constant interruptions*. 3 resolute in mind, purpose, or affection; loyal. ◆ NOUN 4 something that is permanent or unchanging. 5 a specific quantity that is always invariable: *the velocity of light is a constant*. 6 **a** *Maths* a symbol representing an unspecified number that remains invariable throughout a particular series of operations. **b** *Physics* a theoretical or experimental quantity or property that is considered invariable throughout a particular series of calculations or experiments. 7 See **logical constant.**
▷HISTORY C14: from Old French, from Latin *constāns* standing firm, from *constāre* to be steadfast, from *stāre* to stand
▸**'constantly** ADVERB

Constanța (*Romanian* kon'stantsa) NOUN a port and resort in SE Romania, on the Black Sea: founded by the Greeks in the 6th century B.C. and rebuilt by Constantine the Great (4th century); exports petroleum. Pop.: 344 876 (1997 est.).

constantan ('kɒnstənˌtæn) NOUN an alloy of copper (60 per cent) and nickel (40 per cent). It has a high resistivity that does not vary significantly with temperature and is used in resistors and, with copper, in thermocouples.
▷HISTORY C20: formed from CONSTANT

Constantia (kɒn'stænʃə) NOUN *South African* 1 a region of the Cape Peninsula. 2 any of several red or white wines produced around Constantia.

Constantine ('kɒnstənˌtaɪn; *French* kɔ̃stɑ̃tin) NOUN a walled city in NE Algeria: built on an isolated rock; military and trading centre. Pop.: 462 187 (1998).

Constantinople (ˌkɒnstæntɪ'nəʊpᵊl) NOUN the former name (330–1926) of **Istanbul.**

constatation (ˌkɒnstə'teɪʃən) NOUN 1 the process of verification. 2 a statement or assertion.
▷HISTORY C20: from French, from *constater* to verify, from Latin *constat* it is certain; see CONSTANT

constellate ('kɒnstɪˌleɪt) VERB to form into clusters in or as if in constellations.

constellation (ˌkɒnstɪ'leɪʃən) NOUN 1 **a** any of the 88 groups of stars as seen from the earth and the solar system, many of which were named by the ancient Greeks after animals, objects, or mythological persons. **b** an area on the celestial sphere containing such a group. 2 a gathering of brilliant or famous people or things. 3 *Psychoanal* a group of ideas felt to be related.
▷HISTORY C14: from Late Latin *constellātiō*, from Latin *com-* together + *stella* star
▸**ˌconstel'lational** ADJECTIVE ▸**constellatory** (kən'stɛlətərɪ, -trɪ) ADJECTIVE

consternate ('kɒnstəˌneɪt) VERB (*tr; usually passive*) to fill with anxiety, dismay, dread, or confusion.
▷HISTORY C17: from Latin *consternāre*, from *sternere* to lay low, spread out

consternation (ˌkɒnstə'neɪʃən) NOUN a feeling of anxiety, dismay, dread, or confusion.

constipate ('kɒnstɪˌpeɪt) VERB (*tr*) to cause constipation in.
▷HISTORY C16: from Latin *constīpāre* to press closely together, from *stīpāre* to crowd together

constipated ('kɒnstɪˌpeɪtɪd) ADJECTIVE 1 suffering from constipation. 2 subject to restriction or blockage in a flow of productive activity or creativity.

constipation (ˌkɒnstɪ'peɪʃən) NOUN infrequent or difficult evacuation of the bowels, with hard faeces, caused by functional or organic disorders or improper diet.

constituency (kən'stɪtjʊənsɪ) NOUN, *plural* **-cies**. 1 the whole body of voters who elect one representative to a legislature or all the residents represented by one deputy. 2 **a** a district that sends one representative to a legislature. **b** (*as modifier*): *constituency organization*.

constituent (kən'stɪtjʊənt) ADJECTIVE (*prenominal*) 1 forming part of a whole; component. 2 having the power to frame a constitution or to constitute a government (esp in the phrases **constituent assembly, constituent power**). 3 *Becoming rare* electing or having the power to elect. ◆ NOUN 4 a component part; ingredient. 5 a resident of a constituency, esp one entitled to vote. 6 *Chiefly law* a person who appoints another to act for him, as by power of attorney. 7 *Linguistics* a word, phrase, or clause forming a part of a larger construction. Compare **immediate constituent, ultimate constituent.**
▷HISTORY C17: from Latin *constituēns* setting up, from *constituere* to establish, CONSTITUTE
▸**con'stituently** ADVERB

constitute ('kɒnstɪˌtjuːt) VERB (*tr*) 1 to make up; form; compose: *the people who constitute a jury*. 2 to appoint to an office or function: *a legally constituted officer*. 3 to set up (a school or other institution) formally; found. 4 *Law* to give legal form to (a court, assembly, etc.). 5 *Law, obsolete* to set up or enact (a law).
▷HISTORY C15: from Latin *constituere*, from *com-* (intensive) + *statuere* to place
▸**'constiˌtuter** *or* **'constiˌtutor** NOUN

constitution (ˌkɒnstɪ'tjuːʃən) NOUN 1 the act of constituting or state of being constituted. 2 the way in which a thing is composed; physical make-up; structure. 3 the fundamental political principles on which a state is governed, esp when considered as embodying the rights of the subjects of that state. 4 (*often capital*) (in certain countries, esp Australia and the US) a statute embodying such principles. 5 a person's state of health. 6 a person's disposition of mind; temperament.

constitutional (ˌkɒnstɪ'tjuːʃənᵊl) ADJECTIVE 1 denoting, characteristic of, or relating to a constitution. 2 authorized by or subject to a constitution. 3 of or inherent in the physical make-up or basic nature of a person or thing: *a constitutional weakness*. 4 beneficial to one's general physical wellbeing. ◆ NOUN 5 a regular walk taken for the benefit of one's health.
▸**ˌconsti'tutionally** ADVERB

constitutionalism (ˌkɒnstɪ'tjuːʃənəˌlɪzəm) NOUN 1 the principles, spirit, or system of government in accord with a constitution, esp a written constitution. 2 adherence to or advocacy of such a system or such principles.
▸**ˌconsti'tutionalist** NOUN

constitutionality (ˌkɒnstɪˌtjuːʃə'nælɪtɪ) NOUN the quality or state of being in accord with a constitution.

constitutional monarchy NOUN a monarchy governed according to a constitution that limits and defines the powers of the sovereign. Also called: **limited monarchy.**

constitutional psychology NOUN a school of thought postulating that the personality of an individual is dependent on the type of his physique (somatotype).

constitutional strike NOUN a stoppage of work by the workforce of an organization, with the approval of the trade union concerned, in accordance with the dispute procedure laid down in a collective agreement between the parties.

constitutive ('kɒnstɪˌtjuːtɪv) ADJECTIVE 1 having power to enact, appoint, or establish. 2 *Chem* (of a physical property) determined by the arrangement of atoms in a molecule rather than by their nature. 3 *Biochem* (of an enzyme) formed continuously, irrespective of the cell's needs. 4 another word for **constituent** (sense 1).
▸**'constiˌtutively** ADVERB

constrain (kən'streɪn) VERB (*tr*) 1 to compel or force, esp by persuasion, circumstances, etc.; oblige. 2 to restrain by or as if by force; confine.
▷HISTORY C14: from Old French *constreindre*, from Latin *constringere* to bind together, from *stringere* to bind
▸**con'strainer** NOUN

constrained (kən'streɪnd) ADJECTIVE embarrassed, unnatural, or forced: *a constrained smile*.
▸**constrainedly** (kən'streɪnɪdlɪ) ADVERB

constraint (kən'streɪnt) NOUN 1 compulsion, force, or restraint. 2 repression or control of natural feelings or impulses. 3 a forced unnatural manner; inhibition. 4 something that serves to constrain; restrictive condition: *social constraints kept him silent*. 5 *Linguistics* any very general restriction on a sentence formation rule.

constrict (kən'strɪkt) VERB (*tr*) 1 to make smaller or narrower, esp by contracting at one place. 2 to hold in or inhibit; limit.
▷HISTORY C18: from Latin *constrictus* compressed, from *constringere* to tie up together; see CONSTRAIN

constriction (kən'strɪkʃən) NOUN 1 a feeling of tightness in some part of the body, such as the

chest. 2 the act of constricting or condition of being constricted. 3 something that is constricted. 4 *Genetics* a localized narrow region of a chromosome, esp at the centromere.
▸**con'strictive** ADJECTIVE ▸**con'strictively** ADVERB ▸**con'strictiveness** NOUN

constrictor (kən'strɪktə) NOUN 1 any of various nonvenomous snakes, such as the pythons, boas, and anaconda, that coil around and squeeze their prey to kill it. 2 any muscle that constricts or narrows a canal or passage; sphincter. 3 a person or thing that constricts.

constringe (kən'strɪndʒ) VERB (*tr*) *Rare* to shrink or contract.
▷HISTORY C17: from Latin *constringere* to bind together; see CONSTRAIN
▸**con'stringency** NOUN ▸**con'stringent** ADJECTIVE

constringence (kən'strɪndʒəns) NOUN *Physics* inverse of the dispersive power of a medium.

construct VERB (kən'strʌkt) (*tr*) 1 to put together substances or parts, esp systematically, in order to make or build (a building, bridge, etc.); assemble. 2 to compose or frame mentally (an argument, sentence, etc.). 3 *Geometry* to draw (a line, angle, or figure) so that certain requirements are satisfied. ◆ NOUN ('kɒnstrʌkt) 4 something formulated or built systematically. 5 a complex idea resulting from a synthesis of simpler ideas. 6 *Psychol* a model devised on the basis of observation, designed to relate what is observed to some theoretical framework.
▷HISTORY C17: from Latin *constructus* piled up, from *construere* to heap together, build, from *struere* to arrange, erect
▸**con'structible** ADJECTIVE ▸**con'structor** *or* **con'structer** NOUN

construction (kən'strʌkʃən) NOUN 1 the process or act of constructing or manner in which a thing is constructed. 2 the thing constructed; a structure. 3 **a** the business or work of building dwellings, offices, etc. **b** (*as modifier*): *a construction site*. 4 an interpretation or explanation of a law, text, action, etc.: *they put a sympathetic construction on her behaviour*. 5 *Grammar* a group of words that together make up one of the constituents into which a sentence may be analysed; a phrase or clause. 6 *Geometry* a drawing of a line, angle, or figure satisfying certain conditions, used in solving a problem or proving a theorem. 7 an abstract work of art in three dimensions or relief. See also **constructivism** (sense 1).
▸**con'structional** ADJECTIVE ▸**con'structionally** ADVERB

constructionist (kən'strʌkʃənɪst) NOUN *US* a person who interprets constitutional law in a certain way, esp strictly.

constructive (kən'strʌktɪv) ADJECTIVE 1 serving to build or improve; positive: *constructive criticism*. 2 *Law* deduced by inference or construction; not expressed but inferred. 3 *Law* having a deemed legal effect: *constructive notice*. 4 another word for **structural.**
▸**con'structively** ADVERB ▸**con'structiveness** NOUN

constructive dismissal NOUN a course of action taken by an employer that is detrimental to an employee and designed to leave the employee with no option but to resign.

constructivism (kən'strʌktɪˌvɪzəm) NOUN 1 a movement in abstract art evolved in Russia after World War I, primarily by Naum Gabo, the Russian-born US sculptor (1890–1977), which explored the use of movement and machine-age materials in sculpture and had considerable influence on modern art and architecture. 2 *Philosophy* the theory that mathematical entities do not exist independently of our construction of them. Compare **intuitionism** (sense 4), **finitism.**
▸**con'structivist** ADJECTIVE, NOUN

construe (kən'struː) VERB **-strues, -struing, -strued.** (*mainly tr*) 1 to interpret the meaning of (something): *you can construe that in different ways*. 2 (*may take a clause as object*) to discover by inference; deduce. 3 to analyse the grammatical structure of; parse (esp a Latin or Greek text as a preliminary to translation). 4 to combine (words) syntactically. 5 (*also intr*) *Old-fashioned* to translate literally, esp aloud as an academic exercise. ◆ NOUN 6 *Old-fashioned* something that is construed, such as a piece of translation.
▷HISTORY C14: from Latin *construere* to pile up; see CONSTRUCT
▸**con'struable** ADJECTIVE ▸**conˌstrua'bility** NOUN ▸**con'struer** NOUN

consubstantial (ˌkɒnsəb'stænʃəl) ADJECTIVE *Christian theol* (esp of the three persons of the Trinity) regarded as identical in substance or essence though different in aspect.
▷HISTORY C15: from Church Latin *consubstantiālis*, from Latin COM- + *substantia* SUBSTANCE
▸ˌ**consubˌstanti'ality** NOUN ▸ˌ**consub'stantially** ADVERB

consubstantiate (ˌkɒnsəb'stænʃɪˌeɪt) VERB (*intr*) *Christian theol* (of the Eucharistic bread and wine and Christ's body and blood) to undergo consubstantiation.

consubstantiation (ˌkɒnsəbˌstænʃɪ'eɪʃən) NOUN *Christian theol* (in the belief of High-Church Anglicans) 1 the doctrine that after the consecration of the Eucharist the substance of the body and blood of Christ coexists within the substance of the consecrated bread and wine. 2 the mystical process by which this is believed to take place during consecration. ◆ Compare **transubstantiation.**

consuetude ('kɒnswɪˌtjuːd) NOUN an established custom or usage, esp one having legal force.
▷HISTORY C14: from Latin *consuētūdō*, from *consuēscere* to accustom, from CON- + *suēscere* to be wont
▸ˌ**consue'tudinary** ADJECTIVE

consul ('kɒns^{ə}l) NOUN 1 an official appointed by a sovereign state to protect its commercial interests and aid its citizens in a foreign city. 2 (in ancient Rome) either of two annually elected magistrates who jointly exercised the highest authority in the republic. 3 (in France from 1799 to 1804) any of the three chief magistrates of the First Republic.
▷HISTORY C14: from Latin, from *consulere* to CONSULT
▸**consular** ('kɒnsjʊlə) ADJECTIVE ▸'**consulˌship** NOUN

consular agent NOUN a consul of one of the lower grades.

consulate ('kɒnsjʊlɪt) NOUN 1 the business premises or residence of a consul. 2 government by consuls. 3 the office or period of office of a consul or consuls. 4 (*often capital*) **a** the government of France by the three consuls from 1799 to 1804. **b** this period of French history. 5 (*often capital*) **a** the consular government of the Roman republic. **b** the office or rank of a Roman consul.

consul general NOUN, *plural* **consuls general.** a consul of the highest grade, usually stationed in a city of considerable commercial importance.

consult (kən'sʌlt) VERB 1 (when *intr*, often foll by *with*) to ask advice from (someone); confer with (someone). 2 (*tr*) to refer to for information: *to consult a map*. 3 (*tr*) to have regard for (a person's feelings, interests, etc.) in making decisions or plans; consider. 4 (*intr*) to make oneself available to give professional advice, esp at scheduled times and for a fee.
▷HISTORY C17: from French *consulter*, from Latin *consultāre* to reflect, take counsel, from *consulere* to consult
▸**con'sultable** ADJECTIVE ▸**con'sulter** *or* **con'sultor** NOUN

consultant (kən'sʌlt^{ə}nt) NOUN 1 **a** a senior physician, esp a specialist, who is asked to confirm a diagnosis or treatment or to provide an opinion. **b** a physician or surgeon holding the highest appointment in a particular branch of medicine or surgery in a hospital. 2 a specialist who gives expert advice or information. 3 a person who asks advice in a consultation.
▸**con'sultancy** NOUN

consultant nurse NOUN (in Britain) another name for **supernurse.**

consultation (ˌkɒns^{ə}l'teɪʃən) NOUN 1 the act or procedure of consulting. 2 a conference for discussion or the seeking of advice, esp from doctors or lawyers.

consultative (kən'sʌltətɪv), **consultatory** (kən'sʌltətərɪ, -trɪ), *or* **consultive** ADJECTIVE available for, relating to, or involving consultation; advisory.
▸**con'sultatively** ADVERB

consulting (kən'sʌltɪŋ) ADJECTIVE (*prenominal*) acting in an advisory capacity on professional matters: *a consulting engineer*.

consulting room NOUN a room in which a doctor, esp a general practitioner, sees his patients.

consumable (kən'sjuːməb^{ə}l) ADJECTIVE 1 capable of being consumed. ◆ NOUN 2 (*usually plural*) goods intended to be bought and used; consumer goods.

consume (kən'sjuːm) VERB 1 (*tr*) to eat or drink. 2 (*tr; often passive*) to engross or obsess. 3 (*tr*) to use up; expend: *my car consumes little oil*. 4 to destroy or be destroyed by burning, decomposition, etc.: *fire consumed the forest*. 5 (*tr*) to waste or squander: *the time consumed on that project was excessive*. 6 (*passive*) to waste away.
▷HISTORY C14: from Latin *consūmere* to devour, from *com-* (intensive) + *sūmere* to take up, from *emere* to take, purchase
▸**con'suming** ADJECTIVE ▸**con'sumingly** ADVERB

consumedly (kən'sjuːmɪdlɪ) ADVERB *Old-fashioned* (intensifier): *a consumedly fascinating performance*.

consumer (kən'sjuːmə) NOUN 1 a person who acquires goods and services for his or her own personal needs. Compare **producer** (sense 6). 2 a person or thing that consumes. 3 (*usually plural*) *Ecology* an organism, esp an animal, within a community that feeds upon plants or other animals. See also **decomposer, producer** (sense 8).

consumer durable NOUN a manufactured product that has a relatively long useful life, such as a car or a television.

consumer goods PLURAL NOUN goods that satisfy personal needs rather than those required for the production of other goods or services. Compare **capital goods.**

consumerism (kən'sjuːməˌrɪzəm) NOUN 1 protection of the interests of consumers. 2 advocacy of a high rate of consumption and spending as a basis for a sound economy.
▸**con'sumerist** NOUN, ADJECTIVE

consumer terrorism NOUN the practice of introducing dangerous substances to foodstuffs or other consumer products, esp to extort money from the manufacturers.

consummate VERB ('kɒnsəˌmeɪt) (*tr*) 1 to bring to completion or perfection; fulfil. 2 to complete (a marriage) legally by sexual intercourse. ◆ ADJECTIVE (kən'sʌmɪt, 'kɒnsəmɪt) 3 accomplished or supremely skilled: *a consummate artist*. 4 (*prenominal*) (intensifier): *a consummate fool*.
▷HISTORY C15: from Latin *consummāre* to complete, from *summus* highest, utmost
▸**con'summately** ADVERB ▸ˌ**consum'mation** NOUN
▸'**consumˌmative** *or* **con'summatory** ADJECTIVE
▸'**consumˌmator** NOUN

consummatory behaviour (kən'sʌmətərɪ) NOUN *Psychol* any behaviour that leads directly to the satisfaction of an innate drive, e.g. eating or drinking.

consumption (kən'sʌmpʃən) NOUN 1 the act of consuming or the state of being consumed, esp by eating, burning, etc. 2 *Economics* expenditure on goods and services for final personal use. 3 the quantity consumed. 4 *Pathol* a condition characterized by a wasting away of the tissues of the body, esp as seen in tuberculosis of the lungs.
▷HISTORY C14: from Latin *consumptiō* a wasting, from *consūmere* to CONSUME

consumptive (kən'sʌmptɪv) ADJECTIVE 1 causing consumption; wasteful; destructive. 2 *Pathol* relating to or affected with consumption, esp tuberculosis of the lungs. ◆ NOUN 3 *Pathol* a person who suffers from consumption.
▸**con'sumptively** ADVERB ▸**con'sumptiveness** NOUN

contact NOUN ('kɒntækt) 1 the act or state of touching physically. 2 the state or fact of close association or communication (esp in the phrases **in contact, make contact**). 3 **a** a junction of two or more electrical conductors. **b** the part of the conductors that makes the junction. **c** the part of an electrical device to which such connections are made. 4 an acquaintance, esp one who might be useful in business, as a means of introduction, etc. 5 any person who has been exposed to a contagious disease. 6 *Photog* See **contact print.** 7 (*usually plural*) an informal name for **contact lens.** 8 (*modifier*) of or relating to irritation or inflammation of the skin caused by touching the causative agent: *contact dermatitis*. 9 (*modifier*) denoting an insecticide or

herbicide that kills on contact, rather than after ingestion or absorption. [10] (*modifier*) of or maintaining contact. [11] (*modifier*) requiring or involving (physical) contact: *the contact sport of boxing.* ◆ VERB ('kɒntækt, kən'tækt) [12] (when *intr*, often foll by *with*) to put, come, or be in association, touch, or communication. ◆ INTERJECTION [13] *Aeronautics* (formerly) a call made by the pilot to indicate that an aircraft's ignition is switched on and that the engine is ready for starting by swinging the propeller.
▷HISTORY C17: from Latin *contactus,* from *contingere* to touch on all sides, pollute, from *tangere* to touch
▸**contactual** (kɒn'tæktjʊəl) ADJECTIVE ▸**con'tactually** ADVERB

contactable (kɒn'tæktəbᵊl) ADJECTIVE able to be communicated with: *the manager is not contactable at the moment.*

contact centre NOUN another name for **call centre.**

contact flight NOUN [1] a flight in which the pilot remains in sight of land or water. [2] air navigation by observation of prominent landmarks, beacons, etc.

contact high NOUN a state of altered consciousness caused by inhaling the drugs other people are smoking.

contact lens NOUN a thin convex lens, usually of plastic, which floats on the layer of tears in front of the cornea to correct defects of vision.

contact magazine NOUN a magazine in which to place adverts to make contacts, esp sexual ones.

contact man NOUN an intermediary or go-between.

contactor (kɒn'tæktə) NOUN a type of switch for repeatedly opening and closing an electric circuit. Its operation can be mechanical, electromagnetic, or pneumatic.

contact print NOUN a photographic print made by exposing the printing paper through a negative placed directly onto it.

contagion (kən'teɪdʒən) NOUN [1] the transmission of disease from one person to another by direct or indirect contact. [2] a contagious disease. [3] another name for **contagium.** [4] a corrupting or harmful influence that tends to spread; pollutant. [5] the spreading of an emotional or mental state among a number of people: *the contagion of mirth.*
▷HISTORY C14: from Latin *contāgiō* a touching, infection, from *contingere;* see CONTACT

contagious (kən'teɪdʒəs) ADJECTIVE [1] (of a disease) capable of being passed on by direct contact with a diseased individual or by handling clothing, etc., contaminated with the causative agent. Compare **infectious.** [2] (of an organism) harbouring or spreading the causative agent of a transmissible disease. [3] causing or likely to cause the same reaction or emotion in several people; catching; infectious: *her laughter was contagious.*
▸**con'tagiously** ADVERB ▸**con'tagiousness** NOUN

contagious abortion NOUN another name for **brucellosis.**

contagious ecthyma NOUN the technical name for **orf.**

contagious stomatitis NOUN another name for **foot and mouth disease.**

contagium (kən'teɪdʒɪəm) NOUN, *plural* **-gia** (-dʒɪə). *Pathol* the specific virus or other direct cause of any infectious disease.
▷HISTORY C17: from Latin, variant of *contāgiō* CONTAGION

contain (kən'teɪn) VERB (*tr*) [1] to hold or be capable of holding or including within a fixed limit or area: *this contains five pints.* [2] to keep (one's feelings, behaviour, etc.) within bounds; restrain. [3] to consist of; comprise: *the book contains three different sections.* [4] *Military* to prevent (enemy forces) from operating beyond a certain level or area. [5] *Maths* **a** to be a multiple of, leaving no remainder: *6 contains 2 and 3.* **b** to have as a subset.
▷HISTORY C13: from Old French *contenir,* from Latin *continēre,* from *com-* together + *tenēre* to hold
▸**con'tainable** ADJECTIVE

container (kən'teɪnə) NOUN [1] an object used for or capable of holding, esp for transport or storage, such as a carton, box, etc. [2] **a** a large cargo-carrying standard-sized container that can be loaded from one mode of transport to another. **b** (*as modifier*): *a container port; a container ship.*

containerize *or* **containerise** (kən'teɪnəˌraɪz) VERB (*tr*) [1] to convey (cargo) in standard-sized containers. [2] to adapt (a port or transportation system) to the use of standard-sized containers.
▸**conˌtaineri'zation** *or* **conˌtaineri'sation** NOUN

containment (kən'teɪnmənt) NOUN [1] the act or condition of containing, esp of restraining the ideological or political power of a hostile country or the operations of a hostile military force. [2] (from 1947 to the mid-1970s) a principle of US foreign policy that sought to prevent the expansion of Communist power. [3] Also called: **confinement.** *Physics* the process of preventing the plasma in a controlled thermonuclear reactor from reaching the walls of the reaction vessel, usually by confining it within a configuration of magnetic fields. See **magnetic bottle.**

contaminate VERB (kən'tæmɪˌneɪt) (*tr*) [1] to make impure, esp by touching or mixing; pollute. [2] to make radioactive by the addition of radioactive material. ◆ ADJECTIVE (kən'tæmɪnɪt, -ˌneɪt) [3] *Archaic* contaminated.
▷HISTORY C15: from Latin *contamināre* to defile; related to Latin *contingere* to touch
▸**con'taminable** ADJECTIVE ▸**con'taminant** NOUN
▸**con'taminative** ADJECTIVE ▸**con'tamiˌnator** NOUN

contamination (kənˌtæmɪ'neɪʃən) NOUN [1] the act or process of contaminating or the state of being contaminated. [2] something that contaminates. [3] *Linguistics* the process by which one word or phrase is altered because of mistaken associations with another word or phrase; for example, the substitution of *irregardless* for *regardless* by association with such words as *irrespective.*

contango (kən'tæŋgəʊ) NOUN, *plural* **-gos.** [1] (formerly, on the London Stock Exchange) postponement of payment for and delivery of stock from one account day to the next. [2] the fee paid for such a postponement. ◆ Also called: **carry-over, continuation.** Compare **backwardation.** ◆ VERB **-goes, -going, -goed.** [3] (*tr*) to arrange such a postponement of payment (for): *my brokers will contango these shares.*
▷HISTORY C19: apparently an arbitrary coinage based on CONTINUE

contd ABBREVIATION FOR continued.

conte *French* (kɔ̃t) NOUN a tale or short story, esp of adventure.

Conté ('kɒnteɪ; *French* kɔ̃te) NOUN *Trademark* a hard crayon used by artists, etc., made of clay and graphite and often coloured a reddish-brown. Also called: **conté-crayon.**
▷HISTORY C19: named after N.J. *Conté,* 18th-century French chemist

contemn (kən'tɛm) VERB (*tr*) *Formal* to treat or regard with contempt; scorn.
▷HISTORY C15: from Latin *contemnere,* from *temnere* to slight
▸**contemner** (kən'tɛmnə, -'tɛmə) NOUN ▸**contemnible** (kən'tɛmnɪbᵊl) ADJECTIVE ▸**con'temnibly** ADVERB

contemplate ('kɒntɛmˌpleɪt, -təm-) VERB (*mainly tr*) [1] to think about intently and at length; consider calmly. [2] (*intr*) to think intently and at length, esp for spiritual reasons; meditate. [3] to look at thoughtfully; observe pensively. [4] to have in mind as a possibility: *to contemplate changing jobs.*
▷HISTORY C16: from Latin *contemplāre,* from *templum* TEMPLE[1]
▸**'contemˌplator** NOUN

contemplation (ˌkɒntɛm'pleɪʃən, -təm-) NOUN [1] thoughtful or long consideration or observation. [2] spiritual meditation esp (in Christian religious practice) concentration of the mind and soul upon God. Compare **meditation.** [3] purpose or intention.

contemplative ('kɒntɛmˌpleɪtɪv, -təm-, kən'tɛmplə-) ADJECTIVE [1] denoting, concerned with, or inclined to contemplation; meditative. ◆ NOUN [2] a person dedicated to religious contemplation or to a way of life conducive to this.
▸**'contemˌplatively** ADVERB ▸**'contemˌplativeness** NOUN

contemporaneous (kənˌtɛmpə'reɪnɪəs) ADJECTIVE existing, beginning, or occurring in the same period of time.
▸**contemporaneity** (kənˌtɛmpərə'niːɪtɪ) *or* **conˌtempo'raneousness** NOUN ▸**conˌtempo'raneously** ADVERB

contemporary (kən'tɛmprərɪ) ADJECTIVE [1] belonging to the same age; living or occurring in the same period of time. [2] existing or occurring at the present time. [3] conforming to modern or current ideas in style, fashion, design, etc. [4] having approximately the same age as one another. ◆ NOUN, *plural* **-raries.** [5] a person living at the same time or of approximately the same age as another. [6] something that is contemporary. [7] *Journalism* a rival newspaper.
▷HISTORY C17: from Medieval Latin *contemporārius,* from Latin *com-* together + *temporārius* relating to time, from *tempus* time
▸**con'temporarily** ADVERB ▸**con'temporariness** NOUN

> **Language note** Since *contemporary* can mean either of the same period or of the present period, it is best to avoid this word where ambiguity might arise, as in *a production of* Othello *in contemporary dress. Modern dress* or *Elizabethan dress* should be used in this example to avoid ambiguity.

contemporize *or* **contemporise** (kən'tɛmpəˌraɪz) VERB to be or make contemporary; synchronize.

contempt (kən'tɛmpt) NOUN [1] the attitude or feeling of a person towards a person or thing that he considers worthless or despicable; scorn. [2] the state of being scorned; disgrace (esp in the phrase **hold in contempt**). [3] wilful disregard of or disrespect for the authority of a court of law or legislative body: *contempt of court.*
▷HISTORY C14: from Latin *contemptus* a despising, from *contemnere* to CONTEMN

contemptible (kən'tɛmptəbᵊl) ADJECTIVE deserving or worthy of contempt; despicable.
▸**conˌtempti'bility** *or* **con'temptibleness** NOUN
▸**con'temptibly** ADVERB

contemptuous (kən'tɛmptjʊəs) ADJECTIVE (when *predicative,* often foll by *of*) showing or feeling contempt; disdainful.
▸**con'temptuously** ADVERB ▸**con'temptuousness** NOUN

contend (kən'tɛnd) VERB [1] (*intr;* often foll by *with*) to struggle in rivalry, battle, etc.; vie. [2] to argue earnestly; debate. [3] (*tr; may take a clause as object*) to assert or maintain.
▷HISTORY C15: from Latin *contendere* to strive, from *com-* with + *tendere* to stretch, aim
▸**con'tender** NOUN ▸**con'tendingly** ADVERB

content[1] ('kɒntɛnt) NOUN [1] (*often plural*) everything that is inside a container: *the contents of a box.* [2] (*usually plural*) **a** the chapters or divisions of a book. **b** a list, printed at the front of a book, of chapters or divisions together with the number of the first page of each. [3] the meaning or significance of a poem, painting, or other work of art, as distinguished from its style or form. [4] all that is contained or dealt with in a discussion, piece of writing, etc.; substance. [5] the capacity or size of a thing. [6] the proportion of a substance contained in an alloy, mixture, etc.: *the lead content of petrol.*
▷HISTORY C15: from Latin *contentus* contained, from *continēre* to CONTAIN

content[2] (kən'tɛnt) ADJECTIVE (*postpositive*) [1] mentally or emotionally satisfied with things as they are. [2] assenting to or willing to accept circumstances, a proposed course of action, etc. ◆ VERB [3] (*tr*) to make (oneself or another person) content or satisfied: *to content oneself with property.* ◆ NOUN [4] peace of mind; mental or emotional satisfaction. ◆ INTERJECTION [5] *Brit* (in the House of Lords) a formal expression of assent, as opposed to the expression **not content.**
▷HISTORY C14: from Old French, from Latin *contentus* contented, that is, having restrained desires, from *continēre* to restrain
▸**con'tently** ADVERB ▸**con'tentment** NOUN

content-addressable storage NOUN *Computing* another name for **associative storage.**

contented (kən'tɛntɪd) ADJECTIVE accepting one's situation or life with equanimity and satisfaction.
▸**con'tentedly** ADVERB ▸**con'tentedness** NOUN

contention (kən'tɛnʃən) NOUN [1] a struggling between opponents; competition. [2] dispute in an

argument (esp in the phrase **bone of contention**). [3] a point asserted in argument.
▷HISTORY C14: from Latin *contentiō* exertion, from *contendere* to CONTEND

contentious (kən'tɛnʃəs) ADJECTIVE [1] tending to argue or quarrel. [2] causing or characterized by dispute; controversial. [3] *Law* relating to a cause or legal business that is contested, esp a probate matter.
▸**con'tentiously** ADVERB ▸**con'tentiousness** NOUN

content word ('kɒntɛnt) NOUN a word to which an independent meaning can be given by reference to a world outside any sentence in which the word may occur. Compare **function word, lexical meaning.**

conterminous (kən'tɜːmɪnəs), **conterminal,** *or* **coterminous** (kəʊ'tɜːmɪnəs) ADJECTIVE [1] enclosed within a common boundary. [2] meeting at the ends; without a break or interruption.
▷HISTORY C17: from Latin *conterminus,* from CON- + *terminus* end, boundary
▸**con'terminously, con'terminally,** *or* **co'terminously** ADVERB

contest NOUN ('kɒntɛst) [1] a formal game or match in which two or more people, teams, etc., compete and attempt to win. [2] a struggle for victory between opposing forces or interests. ◆ VERB (kən'tɛst) [3] (*tr*) to try to disprove; call in question. [4] (when *intr,* foll by *with* or *against*) to fight, dispute, or contend (with): *contest an election.*
▷HISTORY C16: from Latin *contestārī* to introduce a lawsuit, from *testis* witness
▸**con'testable** ADJECTIVE ▸**con'testableness** *or* **con,testa'bility** NOUN ▸**con'testably** ADVERB ▸**,contes'tation** NOUN ▸**con'tester** NOUN ▸**con'testingly** ADVERB

contestant (kən'tɛstənt) NOUN a person who takes part in a contest; competitor.

context ('kɒntɛkst) NOUN [1] the parts of a piece of writing, speech, etc., that precede and follow a word or passage and contribute to its full meaning: *it is unfair to quote out of context.* [2] the conditions and circumstances that are relevant to an event, fact, etc.
▷HISTORY C15: from Latin *contextus* a putting together, from *contexere* to interweave, from *com-* together + *texere* to weave, braid

contextual (kən'tɛkstjʊəl) ADJECTIVE relating to, dependent on, or using context: *contextual criticism of a book.*
▸**con'textually** ADVERB

contextualize *or* **contextualise** (kən'tɛkstjʊə,laɪz) VERB (*tr*) to state the social, grammatical, or other context of; put into context.

contexture (kən'tɛkstʃə) NOUN [1] the fact, process, or manner of weaving or of being woven together. [2] the arrangement of assembled parts; structure. [3] an interwoven structure; fabric.
▸**con'textural** ADJECTIVE

contiguous (kən'tɪgjʊəs) ADJECTIVE [1] touching along the side or boundary; in contact. [2] physically adjacent; neighbouring. [3] preceding or following in time.
▷HISTORY C17: from Latin *contiguus,* from *contingere* to touch; see CONTACT
▸**contiguity** (,kɒntɪ'gjuːɪtɪ) *or* **con'tiguousness** NOUN
▸**con'tiguously** ADVERB

continent[1] ('kɒntɪnənt) NOUN [1] one of the earth's large land masses (Asia, Australia, Africa, Europe, North and South America, and Antarctica). [2] that part of the earth's crust that rises above the oceans and is composed of sialic rocks. Including the continental shelves, the continents occupy 30 per cent of the earth's surface. [3] *Obsolete* **a** mainland as opposed to islands. **b** a continuous extent of land.
▷HISTORY C16: from the Latin phrase *terra continens* continuous land, from *continēre;* see CONTAIN
▸**continental** (,kɒntɪ'nɛntᵊl) ADJECTIVE ▸**,conti'nentally** ADVERB

continent[2] ('kɒntɪnənt) ADJECTIVE [1] able to control urination and defecation. [2] exercising self-restraint, esp from sexual activity; chaste.
▷HISTORY C14: from Latin *continent-,* present participle of *continēre;* see CONTAIN
▸**'continence** *or* **'continency** NOUN ▸**'continently** ADVERB

Continent ('kɒntɪnənt) NOUN **the.** the mainland of Europe as distinguished from the British Isles.

Continental (,kɒntɪ'nɛntᵊl) ADJECTIVE [1] of or characteristic of Europe, excluding the British Isles. [2] of or relating to the 13 original British North American colonies during and immediately after the War of American Independence. ◆ NOUN [3] (*sometimes not capital*) an inhabitant of Europe, excluding the British Isles. [4] a regular soldier of the rebel army during the War of American Independence. [5] *US history* a currency note issued by the Continental Congress.
▸**,Conti'nental,ism** NOUN ▸**,Conti'nentalist** NOUN

continental breakfast NOUN a light breakfast of coffee and rolls.

continental climate NOUN a climate characterized by hot summers, cold winters, and little rainfall, typical of the interior of a continent.

Continental Congress NOUN the assembly of delegates from the North American rebel colonies held during and after the War of American Independence. It issued the Declaration of Independence (1776) and framed the Articles of Confederation (1777).

continental crust NOUN *Geology* that part of the earth's crust that underlies the continents and continental shelves.

continental divide NOUN the watershed of a continent, esp (*often caps.*) the principal watershed of North America, formed by the Rocky Mountains.

continental drift NOUN *Geology* the theory that the earth's continents move gradually over the surface of the planet on a substratum of magma. The present-day configuration of the continents is thought to be the result of the fragmentation of a single landmass, Pangaea, that existed 200 million years ago. See also **plate tectonics.**

continental quilt NOUN *Brit* a quilt, stuffed with down or a synthetic material and containing pockets of air, used as a bed cover in place of the top sheet and blankets. Also called: **duvet,** (Austral) **doona.**

continental shelf NOUN the sea bed surrounding a continent at depths of up to about 200 metres (100 fathoms), at the edge of which the **continental slope** drops steeply to the ocean floor.

Continental System NOUN **the.** Napoleon's plan in 1806 to blockade Britain by excluding her ships from ports on the mainland of Europe.

contingence (kən'tɪndʒəns) NOUN [1] the state of touching or being in contact. [2] another word for **contingency.**

contingency (kən'tɪndʒənsɪ) NOUN, *plural* **-cies.** [1] **a** a possible but not very likely future event or condition; eventuality. **b** (*as modifier*): *a contingency plan.* [2] something dependent on a possible future event. [3] a fact, event, etc., incidental to or dependent on something else. [4] (in systemic grammar) **a** modification of the meaning of a main clause by use of a bound clause introduced by a binder such as *if, when, though,* or *since.* Compare **adding** (sense 3). **b** (*as modifier*): *a contingency clause.* [5] *Logic* **a** the state of being contingent. **b** a contingent statement. [6] dependence on chance; uncertainty. [7] *Statistics* **a** the degree of association between theoretical and observed common frequencies of two graded or classified variables. It is measured by the chi-square test. **b** (*as modifier*): *a contingency table; the contingency coefficient.*

contingency fee NOUN a lawyer's fee that only becomes payable if the case is successful.

contingency table NOUN *Statistics* an array having the frequency of occurrence of certain events in each of a number of samples.

contingent (kən'tɪndʒənt) ADJECTIVE [1] (when *postpositive,* often foll by *on* or *upon*) dependent on events, conditions, etc., not yet known; conditional. [2] *Logic* (of a proposition) true under certain conditions, false under others; not necessary. [3] (in systemic grammar) denoting contingency (sense 4). [4] *Metaphysics* (of some being) existing only as a matter of fact; not necessarily existing. [5] happening by chance or without known cause; accidental. [6] that may or may not happen; uncertain. ◆ NOUN [7] a part of a military force, parade, etc. [8] a representative group distinguished by common origin, interests, etc., that is part of a larger group or gathering. [9] a possible or chance occurrence.
▷HISTORY C14: from Latin *contingere* to touch, fall to one's lot, befall; see also CONTACT
▸**con'tingently** ADVERB

continual (kən'tɪnjʊəl) ADJECTIVE [1] recurring frequently, esp at regular intervals. [2] occurring without interruption; continuous in time.
▷HISTORY C14: from Old French *continuel,* from Latin *continuus* uninterrupted, from *continēre* to hold together, CONTAIN
▸**con,tinu'ality** *or* **con'tinualness** NOUN ▸**con'tinually** ADVERB

Language note See at **continuous.**

continuance (kən'tɪnjʊəns) NOUN [1] the act or state of continuing. [2] the duration of an action, condition, etc. [3] *US* the postponement or adjournment of a legal proceeding.

continuant (kən'tɪnjʊənt) *Phonetics* ◆ NOUN [1] a speech sound, such as (l), (r), (f), or (s), in which the closure of the vocal tract is incomplete, allowing the continuous passage of the breath. ◆ ADJECTIVE [2] relating to or denoting a continuant.

continuation (kən,tɪnjʊ'eɪʃən) NOUN [1] a part or thing added, esp to a book or play, that serves to continue or extend; sequel. [2] a renewal of an interrupted action, process, etc.; resumption. [3] the act or fact of continuing without interruption; prolongation. [4] another word for **contango** (senses 1, 2).

continuative (kən'tɪnjʊətɪv) ADJECTIVE [1] serving or tending to continue. [2] *Grammar* **a** (of any word, phrase, or clause) expressing continuation. **b** (of verbs) another word for **progressive** (sense 8). ◆ NOUN [3] a continuative word, phrase, or clause.
▸**con'tinuatively** ADVERB

continuator (kən'tɪnjʊ,eɪtə) NOUN a person who continues something, esp the work of someone else.

continue (kən'tɪnjuː) VERB **-ues, -uing, -ued.** [1] (when *tr, may take an infinitive*) to remain or cause to remain in a particular condition, capacity, or place. [2] (when *tr, may take an infinitive*) to carry on uninterruptedly (a course of action); persist in (something): *he continued running.* [3] (when *tr, may take an infinitive*) to resume after an interruption: *we'll continue after lunch.* [4] to draw out or be drawn out; prolong or be prolonged: *continue the chord until it meets the tangent.* [5] (*tr*) *Law, chiefly Scot* to postpone or adjourn (legal proceedings).
▷HISTORY C14: from Old French *continuer,* from Latin *continuāre* to join together, from *continuus* CONTINUOUS
▸**con'tinuable** ADJECTIVE ▸**con'tinuer** NOUN ▸**con'tinuingly** ADVERB

continued fraction NOUN a number plus a fraction whose denominator contains a number and a fraction whose denominator contains a number and a fraction, and so on.

continuity (,kɒntɪ'njuːɪtɪ) NOUN, *plural* **-ties.** [1] logical sequence, cohesion, or connection. [2] a continuous or connected whole. [3] the comprehensive script or scenario of detail and movement in a film or broadcast. [4] the continuous projection of a film, using automatic rewind.

continuity announcer NOUN a person who makes linking announcements betweeen programmes to give continuity to a television or radio broadcast channel.

continuity girl *or* **man** NOUN a girl or man whose job is to ensure continuity and consistency, esp in matters of dress, make-up, etc., in successive shots of a film, esp when these shots are filmed on different days.

continuo (kən'tɪnjʊ,əʊ) NOUN, *plural* **-os.** [1] *Music* **a** a shortened form of **basso continuo** (see **thorough bass**). **b** (*as modifier*): *a continuo accompaniment.* [2] the thorough-bass part as played on a keyboard instrument, often supported by a cello, bassoon, etc.
▷HISTORY Italian, literally: continuous

continuous (kən'tɪnjʊəs) ADJECTIVE [1] prolonged without interruption; unceasing: *a continuous noise.* [2] in an unbroken series or pattern. [3] *Maths* (of a function or curve) changing gradually in value as the variable changes in value. A function f is continuous if at every value *a* of the independent variable the difference between f(*x*) and f(*a*) approaches zero as *x* approaches *a.* Compare

discontinuous (sense 2). See also **limit** (sense 5). [4] *Statistics* (of a variable) having a continuum of possible values so that its distribution requires integration rather than summation to determine its cumulative probability. Compare **discrete** (sense 3). [5] *Grammar* another word for **progressive** (sense 8).
▷HISTORY C17: from Latin *continuus,* from *continēre* to hold together, CONTAIN
▸**con'tinuously** ADVERB ▸**con'tinuousness** NOUN

> **Language note** Both *continual* and *continuous* can be used to say that something continues without interruption, but only *continual* can correctly be used to say that something keeps happening repeatedly.

continuous assessment NOUN the assessment of a pupil's progress throughout a course of study rather than exclusively by examination at the end of it.

continuous creation NOUN [1] the theory that matter is being created continuously in the universe. See **steady-state theory.** [2] the theory that animate matter is being continuously created from inanimate matter.

continuous processing NOUN the systems in a plant or factory for the manufacturing of products, treating of materials, etc., that have been designed to run continuously and are often computer-controlled. Compare **batch processing.**

continuous spectrum NOUN a spectrum that contains or appears to contain all wavelengths but not spectrum lines over a wide portion of its range. The emission spectrum of incandescent solids is continuous; bremsstrahlung spectra consisting of a large number of lines may appear continuous.

continuous stationery NOUN *Computing* paper that is perforated between pages and folded concertina fashion, used in dot-matrix, line, and daisywheel printers.

continuous waves PLURAL NOUN radio waves generated as a continuous train of oscillations having a constant frequency and amplitude. Abbreviation: **CW.**

continuum (kən'tɪnjʊəm) NOUN, *plural* **-tinua** (-'tɪnjʊə) *or* **-tinuums.** a continuous series or whole, no part of which is perceptibly different from the adjacent parts.
▷HISTORY C17: from Latin, neuter of *continuus* CONTINUOUS

continuum hypothesis NOUN *Maths* the assertion that there is no set whose cardinality is greater than that of the integers and smaller than that of the reals.

conto ('kɒntəʊ; *Portuguese* 'kõːtu) NOUN, *plural* **-tos** (-təʊz; *Portuguese* -tuʃ). [1] a former Portuguese monetary unit worth 1000 escudos. [2] an unofficial Brazilian monetary unit worth 1000 cruzeiros (now replaced by the real).
▷HISTORY C17: from Portuguese, from Late Latin *computus* calculation, from *computāre* to reckon, COMPUTE; see COUNT[1]

contort (kən'tɔːt) VERB to twist or bend severely out of place or shape, esp in a strained manner.
▷HISTORY C15: from Latin *contortus* intricate, obscure, from *contorquēre* to whirl around, from *torquēre* to twist, wrench
▸**con'tortive** ADJECTIVE

contorted (kən'tɔːtɪd) ADJECTIVE [1] twisted out of shape. [2] (esp of petals and sepals in a bud) twisted so that they overlap on one side.
▸**con'tortedly** ADVERB ▸**con'tortedness** NOUN

contortion (kən'tɔːʃən) NOUN [1] the act or process of contorting or the state of being contorted. [2] a twisted shape or position. [3] something twisted or out of the ordinary in character, meaning, etc: *mental contortions.*
▸**con'tortional** ADJECTIVE ▸**con'tortioned** ADJECTIVE

contortionist (kən'tɔːʃənɪst) NOUN [1] a performer who contorts his body for the entertainment of others. [2] a person who twists or warps meaning or thoughts: *a verbal contortionist.*
▸**con,tortion'istic** ADJECTIVE

contour ('kɒntʊə) NOUN [1] the outline of a mass of land, figure, or body; a defining line. [2] **a** See **contour line. b** (*as modifier*): *a contour map.* [3] (*often plural*) the shape or surface, esp of a curving form: *the contours of her body were full and round.* [4] (*modifier*) shaped to fit the form of something: *a contour chair.* [5] a rising and falling variation pattern, as in music and intonation. ◆ VERB (*tr*) [6] to shape so as to form the contour of something. [7] to mark contour lines on. [8] to construct (a road, railway, etc.) to follow the outline of the land.
▷HISTORY C17: from French, from Italian *contorno,* from *contornare* to sketch, from *tornare* to TURN

contour feather NOUN any of the feathers that cover the body of an adult bird, apart from the wings and tail, and determine its shape.

contour interval NOUN the difference in altitude represented by the space between two contour lines on a map.

contour line NOUN a line on a map or chart joining points of equal height or depth. Often shortened to **contour.**

contour ploughing NOUN ploughing following the contours of the land, to minimize the effects of erosion.

contra- PREFIX [1] against; contrary; opposing; contrasting: *contraceptive; contradistinction.* [2] (in music) pitched below: *contrabass.*
▷HISTORY from Latin, from *contrā* against

contraband ('kɒntrə,bænd) NOUN [1] **a** goods that are prohibited by law from being exported or imported. **b** illegally imported or exported goods. [2] illegal traffic in such goods; smuggling. [3] Also called: **contraband of war.** *International law* goods that a neutral country may not supply to a belligerent. [4] (during the American Civil War) a Black slave captured by the Union forces or one who escaped to the Union lines. ◆ ADJECTIVE [5] (of goods) **a** forbidden by law from being imported or exported. **b** illegally imported or exported.
▷HISTORY C16: from Spanish *contrabanda,* from Italian *contrabando* (modern *contrabbando*), from Medieval Latin *contrabannum,* from CONTRA- + *bannum* ban, of Germanic origin
▸**'contra,bandist** NOUN

contrabass (,kɒntrə'beɪs) NOUN [1] a member of any of various families of musical instruments that is lower in pitch than the bass. [2] another name for **double bass.** ◆ ADJECTIVE [3] of or denoting the instrument of a family that is lower than the bass.
▸**contrabassist** (,kɒntrə'beɪsɪst, -'bæs-) NOUN

contrabassoon (,kɒntrəbə'suːn) NOUN the largest instrument in the oboe family, pitched an octave below the bassoon; double bassoon.
▸**,contrabas'soonist** NOUN

contraception (,kɒntrə'sɛpʃən) NOUN the intentional prevention of conception by artificial or natural means. Artificial methods in common use include preventing the sperm from reaching the ovum (using condoms, diaphragms, etc.), inhibiting ovulation (using oral contraceptive pills), preventing implantation (using intrauterine devices), killing the sperm (using spermicides), and preventing the sperm from entering the seminal fluid (by vasectomy). Natural methods include the rhythm method and coitus interruptus. Compare **birth control, family planning.**
▷HISTORY C19: from CONTRA- + CONCEPTION

contraceptive (,kɒntrə'sɛptɪv) ADJECTIVE [1] relating to or used for contraception; able or tending to prevent impregnation. ◆ NOUN [2] any device that prevents or tends to prevent conception.

contract VERB (kən'trækt) [1] to make or become smaller, narrower, shorter, etc.: *metals contract as the temperature is reduced.* [2] ('kɒntrækt) (when *intr,* sometimes foll by *for;* when *tr, may take an infinitive*) to enter into an agreement with (a person, company, etc.) to deliver (goods or services) or to do (something) on mutually agreed and binding terms, often in writing. [3] to draw or be drawn together; coalesce or cause to coalesce. [4] (*tr*) to acquire, incur, or become affected by (a disease, liability, debt, etc.). [5] (*tr*) to shorten (a word or phrase) by the omission of letters or syllables, usually indicated in writing by an apostrophe. [6] *Phonetics* to unite (two vowels) or (of two vowels) to be united within a word or at a word boundary so that a new long vowel or diphthong is formed. [7] (*tr*) to wrinkle or draw together (the brow or a muscle). [8] (*tr*) to arrange (a marriage) for; betroth. ◆ NOUN ('kɒntrækt) [9] a formal agreement between two or more parties. [10] a document that states the terms of such an agreement. [11] the branch of law treating of contracts. [12] marriage considered as a formal agreement. [13] See **contract bridge.** [14] *Bridge* **a** (in the bidding sequence before play) the highest bid, which determines trumps and the number of tricks one side must try to make. **b** the number and suit of these tricks. [15] *Slang* **a** a criminal agreement to kill a particular person in return for an agreed sum of money. **b** (*as modifier*): *a contract killing.*
▷HISTORY C16: from Latin contractus agreement, something drawn up, from *contrahere* to draw together, from *trahere* to draw
▸**con'tractible** ADJECTIVE ▸**con'tractibly** ADVERB

contract bridge ('kɒntrækt) NOUN the most common variety of bridge, in which the declarer receives points counting towards game and rubber only for tricks he bids as well as makes, any overtricks receiving bonus points. Compare **auction bridge.**

contractile (kən'træktaɪl) ADJECTIVE having the power to contract or to cause contraction.
▸**contractility** (,kɒntræk'tɪlɪtɪ) NOUN

contraction (kən'trækʃən) NOUN [1] an instance of contracting or the state of being contracted. [2] *Physiol* any normal shortening or tensing of an organ or part, esp of a muscle, e.g. during childbirth. [3] *Pathol* any abnormal tightening or shrinking of an organ or part. [4] a shortening of a word or group of words, often marked in written English by an apostrophe: *I've come* for *I have come.*
▸**con'tractive** ADJECTIVE ▸**con'tractively** ADVERB
▸**con'tractiveness** NOUN

contract of employment NOUN a written agreement between an employer and an employee, that, taken together with the rights of each under statute and common law, determines the employment relations between them.

contractor ('kɒntræktə, kən'træk-) NOUN [1] a person or firm that contracts to supply materials or labour, esp for building. [2] something that contracts, esp a muscle. [3] *Law* a person who is a party to a contract. [4] the declarer in bridge.

contract out VERB (*intr, adverb*) *Brit* to agree not to participate in something, esp the state pension scheme.

contractual (kən'træktjʊəl) ADJECTIVE of the nature of or assured by a contract.
▸**con'tractually** ADVERB

contracture (kən'træktə) NOUN a disorder in which a skeletal muscle is permanently tightened (contracted), most often caused by spasm or paralysis of the antagonist muscle that maintains normal muscle tension.

contradance ('kɒntrə,dɑːns) NOUN a variant spelling of **contredanse.**

contradict (,kɒntrə'dɪkt) VERB [1] (*tr*) to affirm the opposite of (a proposition, statement, etc.). [2] (*tr*) to declare (a proposition, statement, etc.) to be false or incorrect; deny. [3] (*intr*) to be argumentative or contrary. [4] (*tr*) to be inconsistent with (a proposition, theory, etc.): *the facts contradicted his theory.* [5] (*intr*) (of two or more facts, principles, etc.) to be at variance; be in contradiction.
▷HISTORY C16: from Latin *contrādīcere,* from CONTRA- + *dīcere* to speak, say
▸**,contra'dictable** ADJECTIVE ▸**,contra'dicter** *or* **,contra'dictor** NOUN ▸**,contra'dictive** *or* **,contra'dictious** ADJECTIVE ▸**,contra'dictively** *or* **,contra'dictiously** ADVERB
▸**,contra'dictiveness** *or* **,contra'dictiousness** NOUN

contradiction (,kɒntrə'dɪkʃən) NOUN [1] the act of going against; opposition; denial. [2] a declaration of the opposite or contrary. [3] a statement that is at variance with itself (often in the phrase **a contradiction in terms**). [4] conflict or inconsistency, as between events, qualities, etc. [5] a person or thing containing conflicting qualities. [6] *Logic* a statement that is false under all circumstances; necessary falsehood.

contradictory (,kɒntrə'dɪktərɪ) ADJECTIVE [1] inconsistent; incompatible. [2] given to argument and contention: *a contradictory person.* [3] *Logic* (of a pair of statements) unable both to be true or both to be false under the same circumstances. Compare **contrary** (sense 5), **subcontrary** (sense 1). ◆ NOUN, *plural* **-ries.** [4] *Logic* a statement that cannot be true when a given statement is true or false when it is false.
▸**,contra'dictorily** ADVERB ▸**,contra'dictoriness** NOUN

contradistinction (ˌkɒntrədɪˈstɪŋkʃən) NOUN a distinction made by contrasting different qualities. ▸ˌ**contradisˈtinctive** ADJECTIVE ▸ˌ**contradisˈtinctively** ADVERB

contradistinguish (ˌkɒntrədɪˈstɪŋgwɪʃ) VERB (*tr*) to differentiate by means of contrasting or opposing qualities.

contraflow (ˈkɒntrəˌfləʊ) NOUN *Brit* two-way traffic on one carriageway of a motorway, esp to allow maintenance work to be carried out or an accident to be cleared.

contrail (ˈkɒntreɪl) NOUN another name for **vapour trail.**
▷HISTORY C20: from CON(DENSATION) + TRAIL

contraindicate (ˌkɒntrəˈɪndɪˌkeɪt) VERB (*tr; usually passive*) *Med* to advise against or indicate the possible danger of (a drug, treatment, etc.). ▸ˌ**contraˈindicant** NOUN ▸ˌ**contraˌindiˈcation** NOUN

contralateral (ˌkɒntrəˈlætərəl) ADJECTIVE *Anatomy, zoology* relating to or denoting the opposite side of a body, structure, etc.

contralto (kənˈtræltəʊ, -ˈtrɑːl-) NOUN, *plural* **-tos** *or* **-ti** (-tɪ). [1] the lowest female voice, usually having a range of approximately from F a fifth below middle C to D a ninth above it. In the context of a choir often shortened to **alto.** [2] a singer with such a voice. ◆ ADJECTIVE [3] of or denoting a contralto: *the contralto part.*
▷HISTORY C18: from Italian; see CONTRA-, ALTO

contraposition (ˌkɒntrəpəˈzɪʃən) NOUN [1] the act of placing opposite or against, esp in contrast or antithesis. [2] *Logic* the derivation of the contrapositive of a given categorial proposition.

contrapositive (ˌkɒntrəˈpɒzɪtɪv) ADJECTIVE [1] placed opposite or against. ◆ NOUN [2] *Logic* **a** a conditional statement derived from another by negating and interchanging antecedent and consequent. **b** a categorial proposition obtained from another, esp validly, by any of a number of operations including negation, transferring the terms, changing their quality, and also possibly weakening from universal to particular.

contrapposto (ˌkɒntrəˈpɒstəʊ) NOUN, *plural* **-tos.** (in the visual arts) a curving or asymmetrical arrangement of the human figure with the shoulders, hips, and legs in different planes.
▷HISTORY C20: from Italian, from the past participle of *contrapporre,* from Latin *contra* CONTRA- + *pōnere* to place

contraption (kənˈtræpʃən) NOUN *Informal, often facetious or derogatory* a device or contrivance, esp one considered strange, unnecessarily intricate, or improvised.
▷HISTORY C19: perhaps from CON(TRIVANCE) + TRAP[1] + (INVEN)TION

contrapuntal (ˌkɒntrəˈpʌntᵊl) ADJECTIVE *Music* characterized by counterpoint.
▷HISTORY C19: from Italian *contrappunto* COUNTERPOINT + AL[1]
▸ˌ**contraˈpuntally** ADVERB

contrapuntist (ˌkɒntrəˈpʌntɪst) *or* **contrapuntalist** NOUN *Music* a composer skilled in counterpoint.

contrarian (kənˈtrɛərɪən) NOUN a contrary or obstinate person.

contrariety (ˌkɒntrəˈraɪətɪ) NOUN, *plural* **-ties.** [1] opposition between one thing and another; disagreement. [2] an instance of such opposition; inconsistency; discrepancy. [3] *Logic* the relationship between two contraries.

contrarily ADVERB [1] (kənˈtrɛərɪlɪ) in a perverse or obstinate manner. [2] (ˈkɒntrərɪlɪ) on the other hand; from the opposite point of view. [3] (ˈkɒntrərɪlɪ) in an opposite, adverse, or unexpected way.

contrarious (kənˈtrɛərɪəs) ADJECTIVE *Rare* [1] (of people or animals) perverse or obstinate. [2] (of conditions) unfavourable.
▸**conˈtrariously** ADVERB ▸**conˈtrariousness** NOUN

contrariwise (ˈkɒntrərɪˌwaɪz) ADVERB [1] from a contrasting point of view; on the other hand. [2] in the reverse way or direction. [3] (kənˈtrɛərɪˌwaɪz) in a contrary manner.

contrary (ˈkɒntrərɪ) ADJECTIVE [1] opposed in nature, position, etc.: *contrary ideas.* [2] (kənˈtrɛərɪ) perverse; obstinate. [3] (esp of wind) adverse; unfavourable. [4] (of plant parts) situated at right angles to each other. [5] *Logic* (of a pair of propositions) related so that they cannot both be true at once, although they may both be false together. Compare **subcontrary** (sense 1), **contradictory** (sense 3). ◆ NOUN, *plural* **-ries.** [6] the exact opposite (esp in the phrase **to the contrary**). [7] **on the contrary.** quite the reverse; not at all. [8] either of two exactly opposite objects, facts, or qualities. [9] *Logic* a statement that cannot be true when a given statement is true. ◆ ADVERB (usually foll by *to*) [10] in an opposite or unexpected way: *contrary to usual belief.* [11] in conflict (with) or contravention (of): *contrary to nature.*
▷HISTORY C14: from Latin *contrārius* opposite, from *contrā* against
▸**conˈtrariness** NOUN

contrast VERB (kənˈtrɑːst) [1] (often foll by *with*) to distinguish or be distinguished by comparison of unlike or opposite qualities. ◆ NOUN (ˈkɒntrɑːst) [2] distinction or emphasis of difference by comparison of opposite or dissimilar things, qualities, etc. (esp in the phrases **by contrast, in contrast to** *or* **with**). [3] a person or thing showing notable differences when compared with another. [4] (in painting) the effect of the juxtaposition of different colours, tones, etc. [5] **a** (of a photographic emulsion) the degree of density measured against exposure used. **b** the extent to which adjacent areas of an optical image, esp on a television screen or in a photographic negative or print, differ in brightness. [6] *Psychol* the phenomenon that when two different but related stimuli are presented close together in space and/or time they are perceived as being more different than they really are.
▷HISTORY C16: (noun): via French from Italian, from *contrastare* (verb), from Latin *contra-* against + *stare* to stand
▸**conˈtrastable** ADJECTIVE ▸**conˈtrastably** ADVERB ▸**conˈtrasting** ADJECTIVE ▸**conˈtrastive** ADJECTIVE ▸**conˈtrastively** ADVERB

contrast medium NOUN *Med* a radiopaque substance, such as barium sulphate, used to increase the contrast of an image in radiography.

contrasty (kənˈtrɑːstɪ) ADJECTIVE (of a photograph or subject) having sharp gradations in tone, esp between light and dark areas.

contrasuggestible (ˌkɒntrəsəˈdʒɛstɪbᵊl) ADJECTIVE *Psychol* responding or tending to respond to a suggestion by doing or believing the opposite. ▸ˌ**contrasugˌgestiˈbility** NOUN ▸ˌ**contrasugˈgestion** NOUN

contravallation (ˌkɒntrəvəˈleɪʃən) NOUN fortifications built by besiegers around the place besieged.
▷HISTORY C17: from CONTRA- + Latin *vallātiō* entrenchment; compare French *contrevallation*

contravene (ˌkɒntrəˈviːn) VERB (*tr*) [1] to come into conflict with or infringe (rules, laws, etc.). [2] to dispute or contradict (a statement, proposition, etc.).
▷HISTORY C16: from Late Latin *contrāvenīre,* from Latin CONTRA- + *venīre* to come
▸ˌ**contraˈvener** NOUN ▸**contravention** (ˌkɒntrəˈvɛnʃən) NOUN

contrayerva (ˌkɒntrəˈjɜːvə) NOUN the root of any of several tropical American moraceous plants of the genus *Dorstenia,* esp *D. contrayerva,* used as a stimulant and tonic.
▷HISTORY C17: from Spanish *contrayerba,* from CONTRA- + *yerba* grass, (poisonous) plant, from Latin *herba;* referring to the belief that it was an antidote to poisons

contredanse *or* **contradance** (ˈkɒntrəˌdɑːns) NOUN [1] a courtly Continental version of the English country dance, similar to the quadrille. [2] music written for or in the rhythm of this dance.
▷HISTORY C19: from French, changed from English *country dance; country* altered to French *contre* (opposite) by folk etymology (because the dancers face each other)

contre-jour (ˈkɒntrəˌʒʊə) NOUN *Photog* **a** the technique of taking photographs into the light, with the light source behind the subject. **b** (*as modifier*): *a contre-jour shot.*
▷HISTORY C20: from French, literally: against day(light)

contretemps (ˈkɒntrəˌtɑːn; *French* kɔ̃trətɑ̃) NOUN, *plural* **-temps.** [1] an awkward or difficult situation or mishap. [2] *Fencing* a feint made with the purpose of producing a counterthrust from one's opponent. [3] a small disagreement that is rather embarrassing.
▷HISTORY C17: from French, from *contre* against + *temps* time, from Latin *tempus*

contrib. ABBREVIATION FOR contributor.

contribute (kənˈtrɪbjuːt) VERB (often foll by *to*) [1] to give (support, money, etc.) for a common purpose or fund. [2] to supply (ideas, opinions, etc.) as part of a debate or discussion. [3] (*intr*) to be partly instrumental (in) or responsible (for): *drink contributed to the accident.* [4] to write (articles) for a publication.
▷HISTORY C16: from Latin *contribuere* to collect, from *tribuere* to grant, bestow
▸**conˈtributable** ADJECTIVE ▸**conˈtributive** ADJECTIVE ▸**conˈtributively** ADVERB ▸**conˈtributiveness** NOUN

contribution (ˌkɒntrɪˈbjuːʃən) NOUN [1] the act of contributing. [2] something contributed, such as money or ideas. [3] an article, story, etc., contributed to a newspaper or other publication. [4] *Insurance* a portion of the total liability incumbent on each of two or more companies for a risk with respect to which all of them have issued policies. [5] *Archaic* a levy, esp towards the cost of a war.

contributor (kənˈtrɪbjʊtə) NOUN [1] a person who contributes, esp one who writes for a newspaper or one who makes a donation to a cause, etc. [2] something that is a factor in or is partly responsible for something: *alcohol was a contributor to his death.*

contributory (kənˈtrɪbjʊtərɪ, -trɪ) ADJECTIVE [1] (often foll by *to*) sharing in or being partly responsible (for the cause of something): *a contributory factor.* [2] giving or donating to a common purpose or fund. [3] of, relating to, or designating an insurance or pension scheme in which the premiums are paid partly by the employer and partly by the employees who benefit from it. [4] liable or subject to a tax or levy. ◆ NOUN, *plural* **-ries.** [5] a person or thing that contributes. [6] *Company law* a member or former member of a company liable to contribute to the assets on the winding-up of the company.

contributory negligence NOUN *Law* failure by an injured person to have taken proper precautions to prevent an accident.

con trick NOUN *Informal* a shortened form of **confidence trick.**

contrite (kənˈtraɪt, ˈkɒntraɪt) ADJECTIVE [1] full of guilt or regret; remorseful. [2] arising from a sense of shame or guilt: *contrite promises.* [3] *Theol* remorseful for past sin and resolved to avoid future sin.
▷HISTORY C14: from Latin *contrītus* worn out, from *conterere* to bruise, from *terere* to grind
▸**conˈtritely** ADVERB ▸**conˈtriteness** NOUN

contrition (kənˈtrɪʃən) NOUN [1] deeply felt remorse; penitence. [2] *Christianity* detestation of past sins and a resolve to make amends, either from love of God (**perfect contrition**) or from hope of heaven (**imperfect contrition**).

contrivance (kənˈtraɪvəns) NOUN [1] something contrived, esp an ingenious device; contraption. [2] the act or faculty of devising or adapting; inventive skill or ability. [3] an artificial rather than natural selection or arrangement of details, parts, etc. [4] an elaborate or deceitful plan or expedient; stratagem.

contrive (kənˈtraɪv) VERB [1] (*tr*) to manage (something or to do something), esp by means of a trick; engineer: *he contrived to make them meet.* [2] (*tr*) to think up or adapt ingeniously or elaborately: *he contrived a new mast for the boat.* [3] to plot or scheme (treachery, evil, etc.).
▷HISTORY C14: from Old French *controver,* from Late Latin *contropāre* to represent by figures of speech, compare, from Latin *com-* together + *tropus* figure of speech, TROPE
▸**conˈtrivable** ADJECTIVE ▸**conˈtriver** NOUN

contrived (kənˈtraɪvd) ADJECTIVE obviously planned, artificial, or lacking in spontaneity; forced; unnatural.

control (kənˈtrəʊl) VERB **-trols, -trolling, -trolled.** (*tr*) [1] to command, direct, or rule: *to control a country.* [2] to check, limit, curb, or regulate; restrain: *to control one's emotions; to control a fire.* [3] to regulate or operate (a machine). [4] to verify (a scientific experiment) by conducting a parallel experiment in which the variable being investigated is held constant or is compared with a standard. [5] **a** to

regulate (financial affairs). **b** to examine and verify (financial accounts). 6 to restrict or regulate the authorized supply of (certain substances, such as drugs). ◆ NOUN 7 power to direct or determine: *under control; out of control.* 8 a means of regulation or restraint; curb; check: *a frontier control.* 9 (*often plural*) a device or mechanism for operating a car, aircraft, etc. 10 a standard of comparison used in a statistical analysis or scientific experiment. 11 **a** a device that regulates the operation of a machine. A **dynamic control** is one that incorporates a governor so that it responds to the output of the machine it regulates. **b** (*as modifier*): *control panel; control room.* 12 *Spiritualism* an agency believed to assist the medium in a séance. 13 Also called: **control mark.** a letter, or letter and number, printed on a sheet of postage stamps, indicating authenticity, date, and series of issue. 14 one of a number of checkpoints on a car rally, orienteering course, etc., where competitors check in and their time, performance, etc., is recorded.
▷HISTORY C15: from Old French *conteroller* to regulate, from *contrerolle* duplicate register, system of checking, from *contre-* COUNTER- + *rolle* ROLL
▸**con'trollable** ADJECTIVE ▸**con,trolla'bility** *or* **con'trollableness** NOUN ▸**con'trollably** ADVERB

control account NOUN *Accounting* an account to which are posted the debit and credit totals of other accounts, usually in preparation of financial statements.

control chart NOUN *Statistics* a chart on which observed values of a variable are plotted, usually against the expected value of the variable and its allowable deviation, so that excessive variations in the quality, quantity, etc., of the variable can be detected.

control column NOUN a lever or pillar, usually fitted with a handwheel, used to control the movements of an aircraft. Also called: **control stick, joy stick.**

control commands PLURAL NOUN keyed instructions conveyed to a computer by using the control key in conjunction with the standard keys.

control experiment NOUN an experiment designed to check or correct the results of another experiment by removing the variable or variables operating in that other experiment. The comparison obtained is an indication or measurement of the effect of the variables concerned.

control freak NOUN a person with an obsessive need to be in control of what is happening.

control freakery NOUN an obsessive need to be in control of what is happening.

control grid NOUN *Electronics* another name for **grid** (sense 6), in a tetrode, pentode and similar devices

control group NOUN any group used as a control in a statistical experiment, esp a group of patients who receive either a placebo or a standard drug during an investigation of the effects of another drug on other patients.

control key NOUN a key on the keyboard of a computer that is used in conjunction with the standard keys in order to initiate a specific function, such as editing.

controller (kən'trəʊlə) NOUN 1 a person who directs, regulates, or restrains. 2 Also called: **comptroller.** a business executive or government officer who is responsible for financial planning, control, etc. 3 the equipment concerned with controlling the operation of an electrical device.
▸**con'troller,ship** NOUN

controlling interest NOUN a quantity of shares in a business that is sufficient to ensure control over its direction.

control rod NOUN one of a number of rods or tubes containing a neutron absorber, such as boron, that can be inserted into or retracted from the core of a nuclear reactor in order to control its rate of reaction.

control stick NOUN the lever by which a pilot controls the lateral and longitudinal movements of an aircraft. Also called: **control column, joy stick.**

control surface NOUN a movable surface, such as a rudder, elevator, aileron, etc., that controls an aircraft or rocket.

control tower NOUN a tower at an airport from which air traffic is controlled.

controversy ('kɒntrə,vɜːsɪ, kən'trɒvəsɪ) NOUN, *plural* **-sies.** dispute, argument, or debate, esp one concerning a matter about which there is strong disagreement and esp one carried on in public or in the press.
▷HISTORY C14: from Latin *contrōversia,* from *contrōversus* turned in an opposite direction, from CONTRA- + *vertere* to turn
▸**controversial** (,kɒntrə'vɜːʃəl) ADJECTIVE
▸**,contro'versial,ism** NOUN ▸**,contro'versialist** NOUN
▸**,contro'versially** ADVERB

controvert ('kɒntrə,vɜːt, ,kɒntrə'vɜːt) VERB (*tr*) 1 to deny, refute, or oppose (some argument or opinion). 2 to argue or wrangle about.
▷HISTORY C17: from Latin *contrōversus;* see CONTROVERSY
▸**'contro,verter** NOUN ▸**,contro'vertible** ADJECTIVE
▸**,contro'vertibly** ADVERB

contumacious (,kɒntjʊ'meɪʃəs) ADJECTIVE stubbornly resistant to authority; wilfully obstinate.
▸**,contu'maciously** ADVERB ▸**,contu'maciousness** NOUN

contumacy ('kɒntjʊməsɪ) NOUN, *plural* **-cies.** 1 obstinate and wilful rebelliousness or resistance to authority; insubordination; disobedience. 2 the wilful refusal of a person to appear before a court or to comply with a court order.
▷HISTORY C14: from Latin *contumācia,* from *contumāx* obstinate; related to *tumēre* to swell, be proud

contumely ('kɒntjʊmɪlɪ) NOUN, *plural* **-lies.** 1 scornful or insulting language or behaviour. 2 a humiliating or scornful insult.
▷HISTORY C14: from Latin *contumēlia* invective, from *tumēre* to swell, as with wrath
▸**contumelious** (,kɒntjʊ'miːlɪəs) ADJECTIVE
▸**,contu'meliously** ADVERB ▸**,contu'meliousness** NOUN

contuse (kən'tjuːz) VERB (*tr*) to injure (the body) without breaking the skin; bruise.
▷HISTORY C15: from Latin *contūsus* bruised, from *contundere* to grind, from *tundere* to beat, batter
▸**con'tusive** ADJECTIVE

contusion (kən'tjuːʒən) NOUN an injury in which the skin is not broken; bruise.
▸**con'tusioned** ADJECTIVE

conundrum (kə'nʌndrəm) NOUN 1 a riddle, esp one whose answer makes a play on words. 2 a puzzling question or problem.
▷HISTORY C16: of unknown origin

conurbation (,kɒnɜː'beɪʃən) NOUN a large densely populated urban sprawl formed by the growth and coalescence of individual towns or cities.
▷HISTORY C20: from CON- + *-urbation,* from Latin *urbs* city; see URBAN

conure ('kɒnjʊə) NOUN any of various small American parrots of the genus *Aratinga* and related genera.
▷HISTORY C19: from New Latin *conurus,* from Greek *kōnos* CONE + *oura* tail

conus ('kəʊnəs) NOUN, *plural* **-ni.** *Anatomy, zoology* any of several cone-shaped structures, such as the conus medullaris, the lower end of the spinal cord.

convalesce (,kɒnvə'lɛs) VERB (*intr*) to recover from illness, injury, or the aftereffects of a surgical operation, esp by resting.
▷HISTORY C15: from Latin *convalēscere,* from *com-* (intensive) + *valēscere* to grow strong, from *valēre* to be strong

convalescence (,kɒnvə'lɛsəns) NOUN 1 gradual return to health after illness, injury, or an operation, esp through rest. 2 the period during which such recovery occurs.
▸**,conva'lescent** NOUN, ADJECTIVE ▸**,conva'lescently** ADVERB

convection (kən'vɛkʃən) NOUN 1 a process of heat transfer through a gas or liquid by bulk motion of hotter material into a cooler region. Compare **conduction** (sense 1). 2 *Meteorol* the process by which masses of relatively warm air are raised into the atmosphere, often cooling and forming clouds, with compensatory downward movements of cooler air. 3 *Geology* the slow circulation of subcrustal material, thought to be the mechanism by which tectonic plates are moved.
▷HISTORY C19: from Late Latin *convectiō* a bringing together, from Latin *convehere* to bring together, gather, from *vehere* to bear, carry
▸**con'vectional** ADJECTIVE ▸**con'vective** ADJECTIVE

convector (kən'vɛktə) NOUN a space-heating device from which heat is transferred to the surrounding air by convection.

convenance *French* (kɔ̃vnɑ̃s) NOUN suitable behaviour; propriety.
▷HISTORY from *convenir* to be suitable, from Latin *convenīre;* see CONVENIENT

convene (kən'viːn) VERB 1 to gather, call together, or summon, esp for a formal meeting. 2 (*tr*) to order to appear before a court of law, judge, tribunal, etc.
▷HISTORY C15: from Latin *convenīre* to assemble, from *venīre* to come

convener *or* **convenor** (kən'viːnə) NOUN 1 a person who convenes or chairs a meeting, committee, etc., esp one who is specifically elected to do so: *a convener of shop stewards.* 2 the chairman and civic head of certain Scottish councils. Compare **provost** (sense 3).
▸**con'venership** *or* **con'venorship** NOUN

convenience (kən'viːnɪəns) NOUN 1 the state or quality of being suitable or opportune: *the convenience of the hour.* 2 a convenient time or situation. 3 **at your convenience.** at a time suitable to you. 4 **at your earliest convenience.** *Formal* as soon as possible. 5 usefulness, comfort, or facility. 6 an object that is particularly useful, esp a labour-saving device. 7 *Euphemistic, chiefly Brit* a lavatory, esp a public one. 8 **make a convenience of.** to take advantage of; impose upon.

convenience food NOUN food that needs little preparation, especially food that has been pre-prepared and preserved for long-term storage.

convenience store NOUN a shop that has long opening hours, caters to local tastes, and is conveniently situated.

convenient (kən'viːnɪənt) ADJECTIVE 1 suitable for one's purpose or needs; opportune. 2 easy to use. 3 close by or easily accessible; handy.
▷HISTORY C14: from Latin *conveniēns* appropriate, fitting, from *convenīre* to come together, be in accord with, from *venīre* to come
▸**con'veniently** ADVERB

convent ('kɒnvənt) NOUN 1 a building inhabited by a religious community, usually of nuns. 2 the religious community inhabiting such a building. 3 Also called: **convent school.** a school in which the teachers are nuns.
▷HISTORY C13: from Old French *covent,* from Latin *conventus* meeting, from *convenīre* to come together; see CONVENE

conventicle (kən'vɛntɪk^{ə}l) NOUN 1 a secret or unauthorized assembly for worship. 2 a small meeting house or chapel for a religious assembly, esp of Nonconformists or Dissenters.
▷HISTORY C14: from Latin *conventiculum* a meeting, from *conventus;* see CONVENT
▸**con'venticler** NOUN

convention (kən'vɛnʃən) NOUN 1 **a** a large formal assembly of a group with common interests, such as a political party or trade union. **b** the persons attending such an assembly. 2 *US politics* an assembly of delegates of one party to select candidates for office. 3 *Diplomacy* an international agreement second only to a treaty in formality: *a telecommunications convention.* 4 any agreement, compact, or contract. 5 the most widely accepted or established view of what is thought to be proper behaviour, good taste, etc. 6 an accepted rule, usage, etc.: *a convention used by printers.* 7 *Bridge* Also called: **conventional.** a bid or play not to be taken at its face value, which one's partner can interpret according to a prearranged bidding system.
▷HISTORY C15: from Latin *conventiō* an assembling, agreeing

conventional (kən'vɛnʃən^{ə}l) ADJECTIVE 1 following the accepted customs and proprieties, esp in a way that lacks originality: *conventional habits.* 2 established by accepted usage or general agreement. 3 of or relating to a convention or assembly. 4 *Law* based upon the agreement or consent of parties. 5 *Arts* represented in a simplified or generalized way; conventionalized. 6 (of weapons, warfare, etc.) not nuclear. ◆ NOUN 7 *Bridge* another word for **convention** (sense 7).
▸**con'ventionally** ADVERB

conventionalism (kənˈvɛnʃənəˌlɪzəm) NOUN [1] advocacy of or conformity to that which is established. [2] something conventional. [3] *Philosophy* a theory that moral principles are not enshrined in the nature of things but merely reflect customary practice. [4] *Philosophy* the theory that meaning is a matter of convention and thus that scientific laws merely reflect such general linguistic agreement.
▸**conˈventionalist** NOUN

conventionality (kənˌvɛnʃəˈnælɪtɪ) NOUN, *plural* **-ties.** [1] the quality or characteristic of being conventional, esp in behaviour, thinking, etc. [2] (*often plural*) something conventional, esp a normal or accepted rule of behaviour; propriety.

conventionalize *or* **conventionalise** (kənˈvɛnʃənəˌlaɪz) VERB (*tr*) [1] to make conventional. [2] to simplify or stylize (a design, decorative device, etc.).
▸**conˌventionaliˈzation** *or* **conˌventionaliˈsation** NOUN

conventual (kənˈvɛntjʊəl) ADJECTIVE [1] of, belonging to, or characteristic of a convent. ◆ NOUN [2] a member of a convent.
▸**conˈventually** ADVERB

converge (kənˈvɜːdʒ) VERB [1] to move or cause to move towards the same point. [2] to meet or cause to meet; join. [3] (*intr*) (of opinions, effects, etc.) to tend towards a common conclusion or result. [4] (*intr*) *Maths* (of an infinite series or sequence) to approach a finite limit as the number of terms increases. [5] (*intr*) (of animals and plants during evolutionary development) to undergo convergence.
▷**HISTORY** C17: from Late Latin *convergere,* from Latin *com-* together + *vergere* to incline

convergence (kənˈvɜːdʒəns) NOUN [1] Also called: **convergency.** the act, degree, or a point of converging. [2] concurrence of opinions, results, etc. [3] *Maths* the property or manner of approaching a finite limit, esp of an infinite series: *conditional convergence.* [4] the combining of different forms of electronic technology, such as data processing and word processing converging into information processing. [5] Also called: **convergent evolution.** the evolutionary development of a superficial resemblance between unrelated animals that occupy a similar environment, as in the evolution of wings in birds and bats. [6] *Meteorol* an accumulation of air in a region that has a greater inflow than outflow of air, often giving rise to vertical air currents. See also **Intertropical Convergence Zone.** [7] the turning of the eyes inwards in order to fixate an object nearer than that previously being fixated. Compare **divergence** (sense 6).

convergence zone NOUN *Geology* a zone where tectonic plates collide, typified by earthquakes, mountain formation, and volcanic activity.

convergent (kənˈvɜːdʒənt) ADJECTIVE [1] (of two or more lines, paths, etc.) moving towards or meeting at some common point. [2] (of forces, ideas, etc.) tending towards the same result; merging. [3] *Maths* (of an infinite series) having a finite limit.

convergent thinking NOUN *Psychol* analytical, usually deductive, thinking in which ideas are examined for their logical validity or in which a set of rules is followed, e.g. in arithmetic.

conversable (kənˈvɜːsəbᵊl) ADJECTIVE [1] easy or pleasant to talk to. [2] able or inclined to talk.
▸**conˈversableness** NOUN ▸**conˈversably** ADVERB

conversant (kənˈvɜːsᵊnt) ADJECTIVE (*usually postpositive* and foll by *with*) experienced (in), familiar (with), or acquainted (with).
▸**conˈversance** *or* **conˈversancy** NOUN ▸**conˈversantly** ADVERB

conversation (ˌkɒnvəˈseɪʃən) NOUN [1] the interchange through speech of information, ideas, etc.; spoken communication. [2] **make conversation.** to talk in an artificial way. Related adjective: **colloquial.**

conversational (ˌkɒnvəˈseɪʃənᵊl) ADJECTIVE [1] of, using, or in the manner of conversation. [2] inclined to or skilled in conversation; conversable.
▸**ˌconverˈsationally** ADVERB

conversational implicature NOUN *Logic, philosophy* another term for **implicature.**

conversationalist (ˌkɒnvəˈseɪʃənəlɪst) *or* **conversationist** NOUN a person who enjoys or excels in conversation.

conversation piece NOUN [1] something, esp an unusual object, that provokes conversation. [2] (esp in 18th-century Britain) a group portrait in a landscape or domestic setting. [3] a play emphasizing dialogue.

conversazione *Italian* (konversatˈtsjone; *English* ˌkɒnvəˌsætsɪˈəʊnɪ) NOUN, *plural* ***-zioni*** (*Italian* -ˈtsjoni) *or* ***-ziones*** (*English* -tsɪˈəʊniːz). a social gathering for discussion of the arts, literature, etc.
▷**HISTORY** C18: literally: conversation

converse[1] VERB (kənˈvɜːs) (*intr; often foll by with*) [1] to engage in conversation (with). [2] to commune spiritually (with). [3] *Obsolete* **a** to associate; consort. **b** to have sexual intercourse. ◆ NOUN (ˈkɒnvɜːs) [4] conversation (often in the phrase **hold converse with**). [5] *Obsolete* **a** fellowship or acquaintance. **b** sexual intercourse.
▷**HISTORY** C16: from Old French *converser,* from Latin *conversārī* to keep company with, from *conversāre* to turn constantly, from *vertere* to turn
▸**conˈverser** NOUN

converse[2] (ˈkɒnvɜːs) ADJECTIVE [1] (*prenominal*) reversed; opposite; contrary. ◆ NOUN [2] something that is opposite or contrary. [3] *Logic* **a** a categorical proposition obtained from another by the transposition of subject and predicate, as *no bad man is bald* from *no bald man is bad.* **b** a proposition so derived, possibly by weakening a universal proposition to the corresponding particular, as *some socialists are rich* from *all rich men are socialists.* [4] *Logic, maths* a relation that holds between two relata only when a given relation holds between them in reverse order: thus *father of* is the converse of *son of.*
▷**HISTORY** C16: from Latin *conversus* turned around; see CONVERSE[1]

conversely (ˈkɒnvɜːslɪ) ADVERB (*sentence modifier*) in a contrary or opposite way; on the other hand.

conversion (kənˈvɜːʃən) NOUN [1] **a** a change or adaptation in form, character, or function. **b** something changed in one of these respects. [2] a change to another attitude or belief, as in a change of religion. [3] *Maths* a change in the units or form of a number or expression: *the conversion of miles to kilometres involves multiplying by 1.61.* [4] *Logic* a form of inference by which one proposition is obtained as the converse of another proposition. [5] *Law* **a** unauthorized dealing with or the assumption of rights of ownership to another's personal property. **b** the changing of real property into personalty or personalty into realty. [6] *Rugby* a score made after a try by kicking the ball over the crossbar from a place kick. [7] *Physics* a change of fertile material to fissile material in a reactor. [8] **a** an alteration to a car engine to improve its performance. **b** (*as modifier*): *a conversion kit.* [9] material alteration to the structure or fittings of a building undergoing a change in function or legal status. [10] *NZ* the unauthorized appropriation of a motor vehicle.
▷**HISTORY** C14: from Latin *conversiō* a turning around; see CONVERT
▸**conˈversional** *or* **conˈversionary** ADJECTIVE

conversion disorder NOUN a psychological disorder in which severe physical symptoms like blindness or paralysis appear with no apparent physical cause.

convert VERB (kənˈvɜːt) (*mainly tr*) [1] to change or adapt the form, character, or function of; transform. [2] to cause (someone) to change in opinion, belief, etc. [3] to change (a person or his way of life, etc.) for the better. [4] (*intr*) to admit of being changed (into): *the table converts into a tray.* [5] (*also intr*) to change or be changed into another chemical compound or physical state: *to convert water into ice.* [6] *Law* **a** to assume unlawful proprietary rights over (personal property). **b** to change (property) from realty into personalty or vice versa. [7] (*also intr*) *Rugby* to make a conversion after (a try). [8] *Logic* to transpose the subject and predicate of (a proposition) by conversion. [9] to change (a value or measurement) from one system of units to another. [10] to exchange (a security or bond) for something of equivalent value. ◆ NOUN (ˈkɒnvɜːt) [11] a person who has been converted to another belief, religion, etc.
▷**HISTORY** C13: from Old French *convertir,* from Latin *convertere* to turn around, alter, transform, from *vertere* to turn
▸**conˈvertive** ADJECTIVE

converter *or* **convertor** (kənˈvɜːtə) NOUN [1] a person or thing that converts. [2] *Physics* **a** a device for converting alternating current to direct current or vice versa. **b** a device for converting a signal from one frequency to another or from analogue to digital forms. [3] a vessel in which molten metal is refined, using a blast of air or oxygen. See also **Bessemer converter, L-D converter.** [4] short for **converter reactor.** [5] *Computing* a device for converting one form of coded information to another, such as an analogue-to-digital converter.

converter reactor NOUN a nuclear reactor for converting one fuel into another, esp one that transforms fertile material into fissionable material. Compare **breeder reactor.**

convertible (kənˈvɜːtəbᵊl) ADJECTIVE [1] capable of being converted. [2] (of a car) having a folding or removable roof. [3] *Finance* **a** a bond or debenture that can be converted to ordinary or preference shares on a fixed date at a fixed price. **b** (of a paper currency) exchangeable on demand for precious metal to an equivalent value. ◆ NOUN [4] a car with a folding or removable roof.
▸**conˌvertiˈbility** *or* **conˈvertibleness** NOUN ▸**conˈvertibly** ADVERB

convertiplane, convertaplane, *or* **convertoplane** (kənˈvɜːtəˌpleɪn) NOUN an aircraft that can land and take off vertically by temporarily directing its propulsive thrust downwards.

convertite (ˈkɒnvəˌtaɪt) NOUN *Archaic* a convert, esp a reformed prostitute.

convex (ˈkɒnvɛks, kɒnˈvɛks) ADJECTIVE [1] curving or bulging outwards. [2] *Physics* having one or two surfaces curved or ground in the shape of a section of the exterior of a sphere, paraboloid, ellipsoid, etc.: *a convex lens.* [3] *Maths* (of a polygon) containing no interior angle greater than 180°. ◆ VERB [4] (*tr*) to make convex. ◆ Compare **concave.**
▷**HISTORY** C16: from Latin *convexus* vaulted, rounded
▸**ˈconvexly** ADVERB

convexity (kənˈvɛksɪtɪ) NOUN, *plural* **-ties.** [1] the state or quality of being convex. [2] a convex surface, object, etc.; bulge.

convexo-concave (kənˌvɛksəʊkɒnˈkeɪv) ADJECTIVE [1] having one side convex and the other side concave. [2] (of a lens) having a convex face with greater curvature than the concave face. Compare **concavo-convex** (sense 2).

convexo-convex ADJECTIVE (esp of a lens) having both sides convex; biconvex.

convex sole NOUN another name for **dropped sole.**

convey (kənˈveɪ) VERB (*tr*) [1] to take, carry, or transport from one place to another. [2] to communicate (a message, information, etc.). [3] (of a channel, path, etc.) to conduct, transmit, or transfer. [4] *Law* to transmit or transfer (the title to property). [5] *Archaic* to steal.
▷**HISTORY** C13: from Old French *conveier,* from Medieval Latin *conviāre* to escort, from Latin *com-* with + *via* way
▸**conˈveyable** ADJECTIVE

conveyance (kənˈveɪəns) NOUN [1] the act of conveying. [2] a means of transport. [3] *Law* **a** a transfer of the legal title to property. **b** the document effecting such a transfer.
▸**conˈveyancer** NOUN

conveyancing (kənˈveɪənsɪŋ) NOUN the branch of law dealing with the transfer of ownership of property.

conveyor *or* **conveyer** (kənˈveɪə) NOUN [1] a person or thing that conveys. [2] short for **conveyor belt.**

conveyor belt NOUN a flexible endless strip of fabric or linked plates driven by rollers and used to transport objects, esp in a factory.

convict VERB (kənˈvɪkt) (*tr*) [1] to pronounce (someone) guilty of an offence. ◆ NOUN (ˈkɒnvɪkt) [2] a person found guilty of an offence against the law, esp one who is sentenced to imprisonment. [3] a person serving a prison sentence. ◆ ADJECTIVE (kənˈvɪkt) [4] *Obsolete* convicted.
▷**HISTORY** C14: from Latin *convictus* convicted of crime, from *convincere* to prove guilty, CONVINCE
▸**conˈvictable** *or* **conˈvictible** ADJECTIVE

conviction (kənˈvɪkʃən) NOUN [1] the state or appearance of being convinced. [2] a fixed or firmly held belief, opinion, etc. [3] the act of convincing.

[4] the act or an instance of convicting or the state of being convicted. [5] **carry conviction.** to be convincing.
▸**con'victional** ADJECTIVE

convictive (kən'vɪktɪv) ADJECTIVE able or serving to convince or convict.
▸**con'victively** ADVERB

convince (kən'vɪns) VERB *(tr)* [1] *(may take a clause as object)* to make (someone) agree, understand, or realize the truth or validity of something; persuade. [2] *Chiefly US* to persuade (someone) to do something. [3] *Obsolete* **a** to overcome. **b** to prove guilty.
▷**HISTORY** C16: from Latin *convincere* to demonstrate incontrovertibly, from *com-* (intensive) + *vincere* to overcome, conquer
▸**con'vincement** NOUN ▸**con'vincer** NOUN ▸**con'vincible** ADJECTIVE

> **Language note** The use of *convince* to talk about persuading someone to do something is considered by many British speakers to be wrong or unacceptable.

convincing (kən'vɪnsɪŋ) ADJECTIVE [1] credible or plausible. [2] *Chiefly law* persuading by evidence or argument.
▸**con'vincingly** ADVERB ▸**con'vincingness** NOUN

convivial (kən'vɪvɪəl) ADJECTIVE sociable; jovial or festive: *a convivial atmosphere.*
▷**HISTORY** C17: from Late Latin *convīviālis* pertaining to a feast, from Latin *convīvium,* a living together, banquet, from *vīvere* to live
▸**con'vivialist** NOUN ▸**con,vivi'ality** NOUN ▸**con'vivially** ADVERB

convocation (ˌkɒnvə'keɪʃən) NOUN [1] a large formal assembly, esp one specifically convened. [2] the act of convoking or state of being convoked. [3] *Church of England* either of the synods of the provinces of Canterbury or York. [4] *Episcopal Church* **a** an assembly of the clergy and part of the laity of a diocese. **b** a district represented at such an assembly. [5] *(sometimes capital)* (in some British universities) a legislative assembly composed mainly of graduates. [6] (in India) a degree-awarding ceremony. [7] (in Australia and New Zealand) the graduate membership of a university.
▸ˌ**convo'cational** ADJECTIVE ▸'**convo,cator** NOUN

convoke (kən'vəʊk) VERB *(tr)* to call (a meeting, assembly, etc.) together; summon.
▷**HISTORY** C16: from Latin *convocāre,* from *vocāre* to call
▸**convocative** (kən'vɒkətɪv) ADJECTIVE ▸**con'voker** NOUN

convolute ('kɒnvəˌluːt) VERB *(tr)* [1] to form into a twisted, coiled, or rolled shape. ◆ ADJECTIVE [2] *Botany* rolled longitudinally upon itself: *a convolute petal.* [3] another word for **convoluted** (sense 2).
▷**HISTORY** C18: from Latin *convolūtus* rolled up, from *convolvere* to roll together, from *volvere* to turn
▸'**convo,lutely** ADVERB

convoluted ('kɒnvəˌluːtɪd) ADJECTIVE [1] (esp of meaning, style, etc.) difficult to comprehend; involved. [2] wound together; coiled.
▸'**convo,lutedly** ADVERB ▸'**convo,lutedness** NOUN

convolution (ˌkɒnvə'luːʃən) NOUN [1] a twisting together; a turn, twist, or coil. [2] an intricate, involved, or confused matter or condition. [3] Also called: **gyrus.** any of the numerous convex folds or ridges of the surface of the brain.
▸ˌ**convo'lutional** or ˌ**convo'lutionary** ADJECTIVE

convolve (kən'vɒlv) VERB to wind or roll together; coil; twist.
▷**HISTORY** C16: from Latin *convolvere;* see CONVOLUTE

convolvulaceous (kənˌvɒlvjʊ'leɪʃəs) ADJECTIVE of, relating to, or belonging to the *Convolvulaceae,* a family of plants having trumpet-shaped flowers and typically a climbing, twining, or prostrate habit: includes bindweed, morning-glory, and sweet potato.

convolvulus (kən'vɒlvjʊləs) NOUN, *plural* **-luses** or **-li** (-ˌlaɪ). any typically twining herbaceous convolvulaceous plant of the genus *Convolvulus,* having funnel-shaped flowers and triangular leaves. See also **bindweed.**
▷**HISTORY** C16: from Latin: bindweed; see CONVOLUTE

convoy ('kɒnvɔɪ) NOUN [1] a group of merchant ships with an escort of warships. [2] a group of land vehicles assembled to travel together. [3] the act of travelling or escorting by convoy (esp in the phrase **in convoy**). ◆ VERB [4] *(tr)* to escort while in transit.
▷**HISTORY** C14: from Old French *convoier* to CONVEY

convulsant (kən'vʌlsənt) ADJECTIVE [1] producing convulsions. ◆ NOUN [2] a drug that produces convulsions.
▷**HISTORY** C19: from French, from *convulser* to CONVULSE

convulse (kən'vʌls) VERB [1] *(tr)* to shake or agitate violently. [2] *(tr)* to cause (muscles) to undergo violent spasms or contractions. [3] *(intr; often foll by with) Informal* to shake or be overcome (with violent emotion, esp laughter). [4] *(tr)* to disrupt the normal running of (a country, etc.): *student riots have convulsed India.*
▷**HISTORY** C17: from Latin *convulsus,* from *convellere* to tear up, from *vellere* to pluck, pull
▸**con'vulsive** ADJECTIVE ▸**con'vulsively** ADVERB
▸**con'vulsiveness** NOUN

convulsion (kən'vʌlʃən) NOUN [1] a violent involuntary contraction of a muscle or muscles. [2] a violent upheaval, disturbance, or agitation, esp a social one. [3] *(usually plural) Informal* uncontrollable laughter: *I was in convulsions.*
▸**con'vulsionary** ADJECTIVE

Conwy ('kɒnwɪ) NOUN [1] a market town and resort in N Wales, in Conwy county borough on the estuary of the River Conwy: medieval town walls, 13th-century castle. Pop.: 13 627 (1991). Former name: **Conway.** [2] a county borough in N Wales, created in 1996 from parts of Gwynedd and Clwyd. Pop.: 109 597 (2001 est.). Area: 1130 sq. km (436 sq. miles).

cony or **coney** ('kəʊnɪ) NOUN, *plural* **-nies** or **-neys.** [1] a rabbit or fur made from the skin of a rabbit. [2] (in the Bible) another name for the **hyrax,** esp the Syrian rock hyrax [3] another name for the **pika.** [4] *Archaic* a fool or dupe.
▷**HISTORY** C13: back formation from *conies,* from Old French *conis,* plural of *conil,* from Latin *cunīculus* rabbit

coo (kuː) VERB **coos, cooing, cooed.** [1] *(intr)* (of doves, pigeons, etc.) to make a characteristic soft throaty call. [2] *(tr)* to speak in a soft murmur. [3] *(intr)* to murmur lovingly (esp in the phrase **bill and coo**). ◆ NOUN [4] the sound of cooing. ◆ INTERJECTION [5] *Brit slang* an exclamation of surprise, awe, etc.
▸'**cooer** NOUN ▸'**cooingly** ADVERB

CoO ABBREVIATION FOR cost of ownership.

COO ABBREVIATION FOR chief operating officer.

Cooch Behar or **Kuch Bihar** (kuːtʃ bɪ'hɑː) NOUN [1] a former state of NE India: part of West Bengal since 1950. [2] a city in India, in NE West Bengal: capital of the former state of Cooch Behar. Pop.: 62 500 (latest est.).

cooee or **cooey** ('kuːiː) INTERJECTION [1] a call used to attract attention, esp (originally) a long loud high-pitched call on two notes used in the Australian bush. ◆ VERB **cooees, cooeeing, cooeed** or **cooeys, cooeying, cooeyed.** [2] *(intr)* to utter this call. ◆ NOUN [3] *Austral and NZ informal* calling distance (esp in the phrase **within (a) cooee (of)**).
▷**HISTORY** C19: from a native Australian language

cook (kʊk) VERB [1] to prepare (food) by the action of heat, as by boiling, baking, etc., or (of food) to become ready for eating through such a process. Related adjective: **culinary.** [2] to subject or be subjected to the action of intense heat: *the town cooked in the sun.* [3] *(tr) Slang* to alter or falsify (something, esp figures, accounts, etc.): *to cook the books.* [4] *(tr) Slang* to spoil or ruin (something). [5] *(intr) Slang* to happen (esp in the phrase **what's cooking?**). [6] *(tr) Slang* to prepare (any of several drugs) by heating. [7] *(intr) Music, slang* to play vigorously: *the band was cooking.* [8] **cook someone's goose.** *Informal* **a** to spoil a person's plans. **b** to bring about someone's ruin, downfall, etc. ◆ NOUN [9] a person who prepares food for eating, esp as an occupation. ◆ See also **cook up.**
▷**HISTORY** Old English *cōc* (noun), from Latin *coquus* a cook, from *coquere* to cook
▸'**cookable** ADJECTIVE

Cook (kʊk) NOUN **Mount.** [1] Official name: **Aorangi-Mount Cook.** a mountain in New Zealand, in the South Island, in the Southern Alps: the highest peak in New Zealand. Height: 3764 m (12 349 ft.). [2] a mountain in SE Alaska, in the St. Elias Mountains. Height: 4194 m (13 760 ft.).

cook-chill NOUN a method of food preparation used by caterers, in which cooked dishes are chilled rapidly and reheated as required.

cooker ('kʊkə) NOUN [1] an apparatus, usually of metal and heated by gas, electricity, oil, or solid fuel, for cooking food; stove. [2] *Brit* any large sour apple used in cooking.

cookery ('kʊkərɪ) NOUN [1] the art, study, or practice of cooking. [2] *US* a place for cooking. [3] *Canadian* a cookhouse at a mining or lumber camp.

cookery book or **cookbook** ('kʊkˌbʊk) NOUN a book containing recipes and instructions for cooking.

cook-general NOUN, *plural* **cooks-general.** *Brit* (formerly, esp in the 1920s and '30s) a domestic servant who did cooking and housework.

cookhouse ('kʊkˌhaʊs) NOUN a place for cooking, esp a camp kitchen.

cookie or **cooky** ('kʊkɪ) NOUN, *plural* **-ies.** [1] the US and Canadian word for **biscuit.** [2] a Scot word for **bun.** [3] *Informal* a person: *smart cookie.* [4] *Computing* a piece of data downloaded to a computer by a website, containing details of the preferences of that computer's user which identify the user when revisiting that website. [5] **that's the way the cookie crumbles.** *Informal* matters are inevitably or unalterably so.
▷**HISTORY** C18: from Dutch *koekje,* diminutive of *koek* cake

cookie-cutter NOUN [1] a shape with a sharp edge for cutting individual biscuits from a sheet of dough. ◆ ADJECTIVE [2] resembling many others of the same kind: *a row of cookie-cutter houses.*

Cook Inlet NOUN an inlet of the Pacific on the coast of S Alaska: part of the Gulf of Alaska.

Cook Island Maori NOUN *NZ* a dialect of Maori spoken in the Cook Islands.

Cook Islands PLURAL NOUN a group of islands in the SW Pacific, an overseas territory of New Zealand: consists of the **Lower Cooks** and the **Northern Cooks** Capital: Avarua, on Rarotonga. Pop.: 18 500 (1994). Area: 234 sq. km (90 sq. miles).

cookout ('kʊkˌaʊt) NOUN *US and Canadian* a party where a meal is cooked and eaten out of doors.

cook shop NOUN [1] *Brit* a shop that sells cookery equipment. [2] *US* a restaurant.

Cook's tour NOUN *Informal* a rapid but extensive tour or survey of anything.
▷**HISTORY** C19: after Thomas Cook (1808–92), British travel agent

Cookstown ('kʊkstaʊn) NOUN a district of central Northern Ireland, in Co. Tyrone. Pop.: 32 581 (2001). Area: 622 sq. km (240 sq. miles).

Cook Strait NOUN the strait between North and South Islands, New Zealand. Width: 26 km (16 miles).

cooktop ('kʊkˌtɒp) NOUN *US* a flat unit for cooking in saucepans or the top part of a stove.

Cooktown orchid ('kʊktaʊn) NOUN a purple Australian orchid, *Dendrobium bigibbum,* found in Queensland, of which it is the floral emblem.
▷**HISTORY** named after *Cooktown,* a coastal town in NE Queensland

cook up VERB *(tr, adverb)* [1] *Informal* to concoct or invent (a story, alibi, etc.). [2] to prepare (a meal), esp quickly. [3] *Slang* to prepare (a drug) for use by heating, as by dissolving heroin in a spoon. ◆ NOUN **cook-up.** [4] (in the Caribbean) a dish consisting of mixed meats, rice, shrimps, and sometimes vegetables.

cool (kuːl) ADJECTIVE [1] moderately cold: *a cool day.* [2] comfortably free of heat: *a cool room.* [3] producing a pleasant feeling of coldness: *a cool shirt.* [4] able to conceal emotion; calm: *a cool head.* [5] lacking in enthusiasm, affection, cordiality, etc.: *a cool welcome.* [6] calmly audacious or impudent. [7] *Informal* (esp of numbers, sums of money, etc.) without exaggeration; actual: *a cool ten thousand.* [8] (of a colour) having violet, blue, or green predominating; cold. [9] (of jazz) characteristic of the late 1940s and early 1950s, economical and rhythmically relaxed. [10] *Informal* sophisticated or elegant, esp in an unruffled way. [11] *Informal* excellent; marvellous. ◆ ADVERB [12] *Not standard* in a

cool manner; coolly. ◆ NOUN [13] coolness: *the cool of the evening.* [14] *Slang* calmness; composure (esp in the phrases **keep** *or* **lose one's cool**). [15] *Slang* unruffled elegance or sophistication. ◆ VERB [16] (usually foll by *down* or *off*) to make or become cooler. [17] (usually foll by *down* or *off*) to lessen the intensity of (anger or excitement) or (of anger or excitement) to become less intense; calm down. [18] **cool it.** (*usually imperative*) *Slang* to calm down; take it easy. [19] **cool one's heels.** to wait or be kept waiting. ◆ See also **cool out.**
▷HISTORY Old English *cōl;* related to Old Norse *kōlna,* Old High German *kuoli;* see COLD, CHILL
▸ˈ**coolingly** ADVERB ▸ˈ**coolingness** NOUN ▸ˈ**coolish** ADJECTIVE ▸ˈ**coolly** ADVERB ▸ˈ**coolness** NOUN

coolabah *or* **coolibah** (ˈkuːləˌbɑː) NOUN an Australian myrtaceous tree, *Eucalyptus microtheca,* that grows along rivers and has smooth bark and long narrow leaves.
▷HISTORY from a native Australian language

coolamon (ˈkuːləmɒn) NOUN *Austral* a shallow dish of wood or bark, used for carrying water.
▷HISTORY C19: from a native Australian language

coolant (ˈkuːlənt) NOUN [1] a fluid used to cool a system or to transfer heat from one part of it to another. [2] a liquid, such as an emulsion of oil, water, and soft soap, used to lubricate and cool the workpiece and cutting tool during machining.

cool bag *or* **box** NOUN an insulated container used to keep food cool on picnics, to carry frozen food, etc.

cool drink NOUN *South African* any soft drink.

cooler (ˈkuːlə) NOUN [1] a container, vessel, or apparatus for cooling, such as a heat exchanger. [2] a slang word for **prison.** [3] a drink consisting of wine, fruit juice, and carbonated water.

Cooley's anaemia (ˈkuːlɪz) NOUN another name for **thalassaemia.**
▷HISTORY named after Thomas B. *Cooley* (1871–1945), US paediatrician who reported on it in children in the Mediterranean area

Coolgardie safe (kuːlˈgɑːdɪ) NOUN a cupboard with wetted hessian walls for keeping food cool: used esp in Australia. Sometimes shortened to **Coolgardie.**
▷HISTORY named after *Coolgardie,* Western Australia, perhaps because of resemblance to COOL and GUARD

cool hunter NOUN *Informal* a person who is employed to identify future trends, esp in fashion or the media.

coolie *or* **cooly** (ˈkuːlɪ) NOUN, *plural* **-ies.** [1] a cheaply hired unskilled Oriental labourer. [2] *Derogatory* an Indian living in South Africa.
▷HISTORY C17: from Hindi *kulī,* probably of Dravidian origin; related to Tamil *kūli* hire, hireling

cooling-off period NOUN [1] a period during which the contending sides to a dispute reconsider their options before taking further action. [2] a statutory period, often 14 days, that begins when a sale contract or life-assurance policy is received by a member of the public, during which the contract or policy can be cancelled without loss.

cooling tower NOUN a tall hollow structure in which steam is condensed or water that is used as a coolant in some industrial process is allowed to cool for reuse by trickling down a surface.

cool out VERB (*intr, adverb*) *Caribbean* to relax and cool down.

cool school NOUN *NZ* a school where the students resolve conflict without the involvement of teachers.

coolth (kuːlθ) NOUN coolness.
▷HISTORY C16: originally dialect, from COOL + -TH[1]

coom *or* **coomb** (kuːm) NOUN *Dialect, chiefly Scot and Northern English* waste material, such as dust from coal, grease from axles, etc.
▷HISTORY C16 (meaning: soot): probably a variant of CULM[1]

coomb, combe, coombe, *or* **comb** (kuːm) NOUN [1] *Chiefly Southern English* a short valley or deep hollow, esp in chalk areas. [2] *Chiefly Northern English* another name for a **cirque.**
▷HISTORY Old English *cumb* (in place names), probably of Celtic origin; compare Old French *combe* small valley and Welsh *cwm* valley

coon (kuːn) NOUN [1] *Informal* short for **raccoon.** [2] *Offensive slang* a Black or a native Australian. [3] *South African offensive* a person of mixed race.

cooncan (ˈkuːnˌkæn) *or* **conquian** NOUN a card game for two players, similar to rummy.
▷HISTORY C19: from (Mexican) Spanish *con quién* with whom?, apparently with reference to the forming and declaring of sequences and sets of cards

coonhound (ˈkuːnˌhaʊnd) NOUN another name for **raccoon dog** (sense 2).

coon's age NOUN *US slang* a long time.

coonskin (ˈkuːnˌskɪn) NOUN [1] the pelt of a raccoon. [2] a raccoon cap with the tail hanging at the back. [3] *US* an overcoat made of raccoon.

coontie (ˈkuːntɪ) NOUN [1] an evergreen plant, *Zamia floridana* of S Florida, related to the cycads and having large dark green leathery leaves: family *Zamiaceae.* [2] a starch derived from the underground stems of this plant.
▷HISTORY C19: from Seminole *kunti* flour from this plant

coop[1] (kuːp) NOUN [1] a cage or small enclosure for poultry or small animals. [2] a small narrow place of confinement, esp a prison cell. [3] a wicker basket for catching fish. ◆ VERB [4] (*tr;* often foll by *up* or *in*) to confine in a restricted area.
▷HISTORY C15: probably from Middle Low German *kūpe* basket, tub; related to Latin *cūpa* cask, vat

coop[2] *or* **co-op** (ˈkəʊˌɒp) NOUN a cooperative, cooperative society, or shop run by a cooperative society.

coop[3] AN INTERNET DOMAIN NAME FOR a cooperative.

coop. *or* **co-op.** ABBREVIATION FOR cooperative.

cooper (ˈkuːpə) NOUN [1] Also called: **hooper.** a person skilled in making and repairing barrels, casks, etc. ◆ VERB [2] (*tr*) to make or mend (barrels, casks, etc.). [3] (*intr*) to work as a cooper.
▷HISTORY C13: from Middle Dutch *cūper* or Middle Low German *kūper;* see COOP[1]

cooperage (ˈkuːpərɪdʒ) NOUN [1] Also called: **coopery.** the craft, place of work, or products of a cooper. [2] the labour fee charged by a cooper.

cooperate *or* **co-operate** (kəʊˈɒpəˌreɪt) VERB (*intr*) [1] to work or act together. [2] to be of assistance or be willing to assist. [3] *Economics* (of firms, workers, consumers, etc.) to engage in economic cooperation.
▷HISTORY C17: from Late Latin *cooperārī* to work with, combine, from Latin *operārī* to work
▸**coˈoperˌator** *or* **co-ˈoperˌator** NOUN

cooperation *or* **co-operation** (kəʊˌɒpəˈreɪʃən) NOUN [1] joint operation or action. [2] assistance or willingness to assist. [3] *Economics* the combination of consumers, workers, farmers, etc., in activities usually embracing production, distribution, or trade. [4] *Ecology* beneficial but inessential interaction between two species in a community.
▸**coˌoperˈationist** *or* **co-ˌoperˈationist** NOUN

cooperative *or* **co-operative** (kəʊˈɒpərətɪv, -ˈɒprə-) ADJECTIVE [1] willing to cooperate; helpful. [2] acting in conjunction with others; cooperating. [3] **a** (of an enterprise, farm, etc.) owned collectively and managed for joint economic benefit. **b** (of an economy or economic activity) based on collective ownership and cooperative use of the means of production and distribution. ◆ NOUN [4] a cooperative organization. [5] Also called: **cooperative apartment.** *US* a block of flats belonging to a corporation in which shares are owned in proportion to the relative value of the flat occupied. Sometimes shortened to **coop.** Compare **condominium** (sense 3).
▸**coˈoperatively** *or* **co-ˈoperatively** ADVERB
▸**coˈoperativeness** *or* **co-ˈoperativeness** NOUN

cooperative bank NOUN a US name for **building society.**

cooperative farm NOUN [1] a farm that is run in cooperation with others in the purchasing and using of machinery, stock, etc., and in the marketing of produce through its own institutions (**farmers' cooperatives**). [2] a farm that is owned by a cooperative society. [3] a farm run on a communal basis, such as a kibbutz. [4] another name for **collective farm.**

Cooperative Party NOUN (in Great Britain) a political party supporting the cooperative movement and linked with the Labour Party: founded in 1917.

cooperative society NOUN a commercial enterprise owned and managed by and for the benefit of customers or workers. Often shortened to **coop, co-op.**

cooperativity (kəʊˌɒpərəˈtɪvɪtɪ) NOUN *Biochem, chem* an interaction between structural units within a molecule or between molecules in an assemblage that enables the system to respond more sharply to an external change than would isolated units.

Cooper Creek (ˈkuːpə) NOUN an intermittent river in E central Australia, in the Channel Country: rises in central Queensland and flows generally southwest, reaching Lake Eyre only during wet-year floods; scene of the death of the explorers Burke and Wills in 1861; the surrounding basin provides cattle pastures after the floods subside. Total length: 1420 km (880 miles).

Cooper pair NOUN *Physics* a pair of weakly bound electrons responsible for the transfer of charge in a superconducting material.
▷HISTORY C20: named after Leon Neil Cooper (born 1930), US physicist

Cooper's hawk NOUN a small North American hawk, *Accipiter cooperii,* having a bluish-grey back and wings and a reddish-brown breast.
▷HISTORY C19: named after William *Cooper* (died 1864), American naturalist

coopery (ˈkuːpərɪ) NOUN, *plural* **-eries.** another word for **cooperage** (sense 1).

co-opetition (ˌkəʊɒpəˈtɪʃən) NOUN cooperation between competitors in business, esp in the computer industry.

coopt *or* **co-opt** (kəʊˈɒpt) VERB (*tr*) [1] to add (someone) to a committee, board, etc., by the agreement of the existing members. [2] to appoint summarily; commandeer.
▷HISTORY C17: from Latin *cooptāre* to elect, from *optāre* to choose
▸**coˈoption, co-ˈoption, ˌcoopˈtation,** *or* **ˌco-opˈtation** NOUN
▸**coˈoptative** *or* **co-ˈoptative** ADJECTIVE

Coopworth (ˈkuːpˌwɜːθ) NOUN a New Zealand and Australian breed of sheep derived from the Romney Marsh.

coordinal *or* **co-ordinal** (kəʊˈɔːdɪnᵊl) ADJECTIVE (of animals or plants) belonging to the same order.

coordinate *or* **co-ordinate** VERB (kəʊˈɔːdɪˌneɪt) [1] (*tr*) to organize or integrate (diverse elements) in a harmonious operation. [2] to place (things) in the same class or order, or (of things) to be placed in the same class or order. [3] (*intr*) to work together, esp harmoniously. [4] (*intr*) to take or be in the form of a harmonious order. [5] *Chem* to form or cause to form a coordinate bond. ◆ NOUN (kəʊˈɔːdɪnɪt, -ˌneɪt) [6] *Maths* any of a set of numbers that defines the location of a point in space. See **Cartesian coordinates, polar coordinates.** [7] a person or thing equal in rank, type, etc. ◆ ADJECTIVE (kəʊˈɔːdɪnɪt, -ˌneɪt) [8] of, concerned with, or involving coordination. [9] of the same rank, type, etc. [10] of or involving the use of coordinates: *coordinate geometry.* ◆ See also **coordinates.**
▸**coˈordinately** *or* **co-ˈordinately** ADVERB ▸**coˈordinateness** *or* **co-ˈordinateness** NOUN ▸**coˈordinative** *or* **co-ˈordinative** ADJECTIVE ▸**coˈordiˌnator** *or* **co-ˈordiˌnator** NOUN

coordinate bond NOUN a type of covalent chemical bond in which both the shared electrons are provided by one of the atoms. Also called: **dative bond, semipolar bond.**

coordinate clause NOUN one of two or more clauses in a sentence having the same status and introduced by coordinating conjunctions. Compare **subordinate clause.**

coordinate geometry NOUN another term for **analytical geometry.**

coordinates (kəʊˈɔːdɪnɪts, -ˌneɪts) PLURAL NOUN clothes of matching or harmonious colours and design, suitable for wearing together. Compare **separates.**

coordinating conjunction NOUN a conjunction that introduces coordinate clauses, such as *and, but,* and *or.* Compare **subordinating conjunction.**

coordination *or* **co-ordination** (kəʊˌɔːdɪˈneɪʃən) NOUN balanced and effective interaction of movement, actions, etc.

▷**HISTORY** C17: from Late Latin *coordinātiō*, from Latin *ordinātiō* an arranging; see ORDINATE

coordination compound NOUN another name for **complex** (sense 8).

coordination number NOUN *Chem* the number of coordinated species surrounding the central atom in a complex or crystal.

Coorg (kʊəg) NOUN a former province of SW India: since 1956 part of Karnataka state.

coorie ('ku:rɪ) VERB (*intr*) *Scot* a variant spelling of **courie**.

coot (ku:t) NOUN [1] any aquatic bird of the genus *Fulica*, esp *F. atra* of Europe and Asia, having lobed toes, dark plumage, and a white bill with a frontal shield: family *Rallidae* (rails, crakes, etc.). [2] a foolish person, esp an old man (often in the phrase **old coot**).
▷**HISTORY** C14: probably from Low German; compare Dutch *koet*

cootch *or* **cwtch** (kʊtʃ) *South Wales dialect* ◆ NOUN [1] a hiding place. [2] a room, shed, etc., used for storage: *a coal cootch*. ◆ VERB [3] (*tr*) to hide. [4] (often foll by *up*) to cuddle or be cuddled. [5] (*tr*) to clasp (someone or something) to oneself.
▷**HISTORY** from French *couche* COUCH, probably influenced by Welsh *cwt* hut

cootie ('ku:tɪ) NOUN *US and NZ* a slang name for the **body louse**. See **louse** (sense 1). Also called (NZ): **kutu**.
▷**HISTORY** C20: perhaps from Malay or Maori *kutu* louse

cop[1] (kɒp) *Slang* ◆ NOUN [1] another name for **policeman**. [2] *Brit* an arrest (esp in the phrase **a fair cop**). [3] an instance of plagiarism. ◆ VERB **cops, copping, copped**. (*tr*) [4] to seize or catch. [5] to steal. [6] to buy, steal, or otherwise obtain (illegal drugs). Compare **score** (sense 26). [7] Also: **cop it**. to suffer (a punishment): *you'll cop a clout if you do that!* [8] **cop it sweet**. *Austral slang* **a** to accept a penalty without complaint. **b** to have good fortune. ◆ See also **cop off, cop out**.
▷**HISTORY** C18: (verb) perhaps from obsolete *cap* to arrest, from Old French *caper* to seize; sense 1, back formation from COPPER[2]

cop[2] (kɒp) NOUN [1] a conical roll of thread wound on a spindle. [2] *Now chiefly dialect* the top or crest, as of a hill.
▷**HISTORY** Old English *cop, copp* top, summit, of uncertain origin; perhaps related to Old English *copp* CUP

cop[3] (kɒp) NOUN *Brit slang* (*usually used with a negative*) worth or value: *that work is not much cop*.
▷**HISTORY** C19: noun use of COP[1] (in the sense: to catch, hence something caught, something of value)

COP (in New Zealand) ABBREVIATION FOR Certificate of Proficiency: a pass in a university subject.

copacetic, copasetic, copesetic, *or* **copesettic** (ˌkəʊpə'sɛtɪk) ADJECTIVE *US and Canadian slang* very good; excellent; completely satisfactory.
▷**HISTORY** C20: of unknown origin

copaiba (kəʊ'paɪbə) *or* **copaiva** (kəʊ'paɪvə) NOUN a transparent yellowish viscous oleoresin obtained from certain tropical South American trees of the leguminous genus *Copaifera*: used in varnishes and ointments. Also called: **copaiba balsam, copaiba resin**.
▷**HISTORY** C18: via Spanish via Portuguese from Tupi

copal ('kəʊpᵊl, -pæl) NOUN a hard aromatic resin, yellow, orange, or red in colour, obtained from various tropical trees and used in making varnishes and lacquers.
▷**HISTORY** C16: from Spanish, from Nahuatl *copalli* resin

copalm ('kəʊˌpɑ:m) NOUN [1] the aromatic brown resin obtained from the sweet gum tree. [2] another name for the **sweet gum**.
▷**HISTORY** C19: from Louisiana French, from Mexican Spanish *copalme;* see COPAL, PALMATE

Copán (*Spanish* ko'pan) NOUN a town in W Honduras: site of a ruined Mayan city. Pop.: 21 200 (1991).

coparcenary (kəʊ'pɑ:sənərɪ) *or* **coparceny** (kəʊ'pɑ:sɪnɪ) NOUN *Law* a form of joint ownership of property, esp joint heirship. Also called: **parcenary**.

coparcener (kəʊ'pɑ:sɪnə) NOUN *Law* a person who inherits an estate as coheir with others. Also called: **parcener**.

copartner (kəʊ'pɑ:tnə) NOUN a partner or associate, esp an equal partner in business.

copartnership (kəʊ'pɑ:tnəʃɪp) NOUN [1] a partnership or association between two equals, esp in a business enterprise. [2] a form of industrial democracy in which the employees of an organization are partners in the company and share in part of its profits.

cope[1] (kəʊp) VERB [1] (*intr;* foll by *with*) to contend (against). [2] (*intr*) to deal successfully with or handle a situation; manage: *she coped well with the problem*. [3] (*tr*) *Archaic* **a** to deal with. **b** to meet in battle.
▷**HISTORY** C14: from Old French *coper* to strike, cut, from *coup* blow; see COUP[1]

cope[2] (kəʊp) NOUN [1] a large ceremonial cloak worn at solemn liturgical functions by priests of certain Christian sects. [2] any covering shaped like a cope. ◆ VERB [3] (*tr*) to dress (someone) in a cope.
▷**HISTORY** Old English *cāp*, from Medieval Latin *cāpa*, from Late Latin *cappa* hooded cloak; see CAP

cope[3] (kəʊp) VERB (*tr*) [1] to provide (a wall) with a coping. [2] to join (two moulded timber members). ◆ NOUN [3] another name for **coping**.
▷**HISTORY** C17: probably from French *couper* to cut; see COPE[1]

copeck ('kəʊpɛk) NOUN a variant spelling of **kopeck**.

Copenhagen (ˌkəʊpən'heɪgən, -'hɑ:-, 'kəʊpənˌheɪ-, -ˌhɑ:-) NOUN the capital of Denmark, a port on Zealand and Amager Islands on a site inhabited for some 6000 years: exports chiefly agricultural products; iron and steel works; university (1479). Pop.: 485 699 (2000 est.). Danish name: **København**.

Copenhagen blue NOUN **a** a greyish-blue colour. **b** (*as adjective*): *Copenhagen-blue markings*.

Copenhagen interpretation NOUN an interpretation of quantum mechanics developed by Niels Bohr and his colleagues at the University of Copenhagen, based on the concept of wave–particle duality and the idea that the observation influences the result of an experiment.

copepod ('kəʊpɪˌpɒd) NOUN [1] any minute free-living or parasitic crustacean of the subclass *Copepoda* of marine and fresh waters: an important constituent of plankton. ◆ ADJECTIVE [2] of, relating to, or belonging to the *Copepoda*.
▷**HISTORY** C19: from New Latin *Copepoda*, from Greek *kōpē* oar + *pous* foot

coper ('kəʊpə) NOUN a horse-dealer.
▷**HISTORY** C17 (a dealer, chapman): from dialect *cope* to buy, barter, from Low German; related to Dutch *koopen* to buy

Copernican (kə'pɜ:nɪkən) ADJECTIVE of or relating to Nicolaus Copernicus, the Polish astronomer (1473–1543).

Copernican system NOUN the theory published in 1543 by Copernicus (1473–1543) which stated that the earth and the planets rotated around the sun and which opposed the Ptolemaic system.

Copernicus (kə'pɜ:nɪkəs) NOUN a conspicuous crater on the moon, over 4000 metres deep and 90 kilometres in diameter, from which a system of rays emanates.

copestone ('kəʊpˌstəʊn) NOUN [1] Also called: **coping stone**. a stone used to form a coping. [2] Also called: **capstone**. the stone at the top of a building, wall, etc.

copier ('kɒpɪə) NOUN [1] a person or device that copies. [2] another word for **copyist**.

copilot ('kəʊˌpaɪlət) NOUN a second or relief pilot of an aircraft.

coping ('kəʊpɪŋ) NOUN the sloping top course of a wall, usually made of masonry or brick. Also called: **cope**.

coping saw NOUN a handsaw with a U-shaped frame used for cutting curves in a material too thick for a fret saw.

coping stone NOUN another word for **copestone** (sense 1).

copious ('kəʊpɪəs) ADJECTIVE [1] abundant; extensive in quantity. [2] having or providing an abundant supply. [3] full of words, ideas, etc.; profuse.
▷**HISTORY** C14: from Latin *cōpiōsus* well supplied, from *cōpia* abundance, from *ops* wealth
▸ **'copiously** ADVERB ▸ **'copiousness** NOUN

copita (*Spanish* ko'pita; *English* kə'pi:tə) NOUN [1] a tulip-shaped sherry glass. [2] a glass of sherry.
▷**HISTORY** diminutive of *copa* cup

coplanar (kəʊ'pleɪnə) ADJECTIVE lying in the same plane: *coplanar lines*.
▸ **ˌcopla'narity** NOUN

cop off VERB (*intr, adverb*) **cop off with**. *Brit informal* to establish an amorous or sexual relationship with.

copolymer (kəʊ'pɒlɪmə) NOUN a chemical compound of high molecular weight formed by uniting the molecules of two or more different compounds (monomers). Compare **polymer, oligomer**.

copolymerize *or* **copolymerise** (kəʊ'pɒlɪməˌraɪz) VERB to react (two compounds) together to produce a copolymer.
▸ **coˌpolymeri'zation** *or* **coˌpolymeri'sation** NOUN

cop out *Slang* ◆ VERB [1] (*intr, adverb*) to fail to assume responsibility or to commit oneself. ◆ NOUN **cop-out**. [2] an instance of avoiding responsibility or commitment. [3] a person who acts in this way.
▷**HISTORY** C20: probably from COP[1]

copper[1] ('kɒpə) NOUN [1] **a** a malleable ductile reddish metallic element occurring as the free metal, copper glance, and copper pyrites: used as an electrical and thermal conductor and in such alloys as brass and bronze. Symbol: Cu; atomic no.: 29; atomic wt.: 63.546; valency: 1 or 2; relative density: 8.96; melting pt.: 1084.87±+0.2°C; boiling pt.: 2563°C. Related adjectives: **cupric, cuprous**. Related prefix: **cupro-**. **b** (*as modifier*): *a copper coin*. [2] **a** the reddish-brown colour of copper. **b** (*as adjective*): *copper hair*. [3] *Informal* any copper or bronze coin. [4] *Chiefly Brit* a large vessel, formerly of copper, used for boiling or washing. [5] any of various small widely distributed butterflies of the genera *Lycaena, Heodes*, etc., typically having reddish-brown wings: family *Lycaenidae*. ◆ VERB [6] (*tr*) to coat or cover with copper.
▷**HISTORY** Old English *coper*, from Latin *Cyprium aes* Cyprian metal, from Greek *Kupris* Cyprus
▸ **'coppery** ADJECTIVE

copper[2] ('kɒpə) NOUN a slang word for **policeman**. Often shortened to **cop**.
▷**HISTORY** C19: from COP[1] (verb) + -ER[1]

copperas ('kɒpərəs) NOUN a less common name for **ferrous sulphate**.
▷**HISTORY** C14: *coperose*, via Old French from Medieval Latin *cuperosa*, perhaps originally in the phrase *aqua cuprosa* copper water

copper beech NOUN a cultivated variety of European beech that has dark purple leaves.

Copper Belt NOUN a region of Central Africa, along the border between Zambia and the Democratic Republic of Congo: rich deposits of copper.

copper-bottomed ADJECTIVE reliable, esp financially reliable.
▷**HISTORY** from the former practice of coating the bottoms of ships with copper to prevent the timbers rotting

copper-fasten VERB (*tr*) *Irish* to make (a bargain or agreement) binding.

copperhead ('kɒpəˌhɛd) NOUN [1] a venomous reddish-brown snake, *Agkistrodon contortrix*, of the eastern US: family *Crotalidae* (pit vipers). [2] a venomous reddish-brown Australian elapid snake, *Denisonia superba*. [3] *US informal* a Yankee supporter of the South during the Civil War.

copperplate ('kɒpəˌpleɪt) NOUN [1] a polished copper plate on which a design has been etched or engraved. [2] a print taken from such a plate. [3] a fine handwriting based upon that used on copperplate engravings.

copper pyrites ('paɪraɪts) NOUN (*functioning as singular*) another name for **chalcopyrite**.

coppersmith ('kɒpəˌsmɪθ) NOUN [1] a person who works copper or copper alloys. [2] an Asian barbet (a bird), *Megalaima haemacephala*, the call of which has a ringing metallic note.

copper sulphate NOUN a copper salt found naturally as chalcanthite and made by the action of sulphuric acid on copper oxide. It usually exists as blue crystals of the pentahydrate that form a white anhydrous powder when heated: used as a mordant, in electroplating, and in plant sprays. Formula: $CuSO_4$.

coppice ('kɒpɪs) NOUN 1 a thicket or dense growth of small trees or bushes, esp one regularly trimmed back to stumps so that a continual supply of small poles and firewood is obtained. ◆ VERB 2 (*tr*) to trim back (trees or bushes) to form a coppice. 3 (*intr*) to form a coppice.
▷HISTORY C14: from Old French *copeiz,* from *couper* to cut
▸'**coppiced** ADJECTIVE ▸'**coppicing** NOUN

copra ('kɒprə) NOUN the dried, oil-yielding kernel of the coconut.
▷HISTORY C16: from Portuguese, from Malayalam *koppara,* probably from Hindi *khoprā* coconut

copro- *or before a vowel* **copr-** COMBINING FORM indicating dung or obscenity: *coprology.*
▷HISTORY from Greek *kopros* dung

coprocessor (ˌkəʊ'prəʊsɛsə) NOUN *Computing* a microprocessor circuit that operates alongside and supplements the capabilities of the main processor, providing, for example, high-speed arithmetic.

coprolalia (ˌkɒprə'leɪlɪə) NOUN obsessive use of obscene or foul language.

coprolite ('kɒprəˌlaɪt) NOUN any of various rounded stony nodules thought to be the fossilized faeces of Palaeozic-Cenozoic vertebrates.
▸**coprolitic** (ˌkɒprə'lɪtɪk) ADJECTIVE

coprology (kɒp'rɒlədʒɪ) NOUN preoccupation with excrement. Also called: **scatology.**

coprophagous (kɒ'prɒfəgəs) ADJECTIVE (esp of certain beetles) feeding on dung.
▸**cop'rophagy** NOUN

coprophilia (ˌkɒprəʊ'fɪlɪə) NOUN an abnormal interest in faeces and their evacuation.

coprophilous (kə'prɒfɪləs) *or* **coprophilic** (ˌkɒprəʊ'fɪlɪk) ADJECTIVE growing in or on dung.

coprosma (kə'prɒzmə) NOUN any shrub of the Australasian rubiaceous genus *Coprosma:* sometimes planted for ornament.
▷HISTORY C19: New Latin, from Greek *kopros* excrement + *osmē* smell

coprozoic (ˌkɒprəʊ'zəʊɪk) ADJECTIVE (of animals) living in dung.

copse (kɒps) NOUN another word for **coppice** (sense 1).
▷HISTORY C16: by shortening from COPPICE

cop shop NOUN *Slang* a police station.

Copt (kɒpt) NOUN 1 a member of the Coptic Church. 2 an Egyptian descended from the ancient Egyptians.
▷HISTORY C17: from Arabic *qubt* Copts, from Coptic *kyptios* Egyptian, from Greek *Aiguptios,* from *Aiguptos* Egypt

copter *or* **'copter** ('kɒptə) NOUN *Informal* short for **helicopter.**

Coptic ('kɒptɪk) NOUN 1 an Afro-Asiatic language, written in the Greek alphabet but descended from ancient Egyptian. It was extinct as a spoken language by about 1600 A.D. but survives in the Coptic Church. ◆ ADJECTIVE 2 of or relating to this language. 3 of or relating to the Copts.

Coptic Church NOUN the ancient Christian Church of Egypt.

copula ('kɒpjʊlə) NOUN, *plural* **-las** *or* **-lae** (-ˌliː). 1 a verb, such as *be, seem,* or *taste,* that is used merely to identify or link the subject with the complement of a sentence. Copulas may serve to link nouns (or pronouns), as in *he became king,* nouns (or pronouns) and adjectival complements, as in *sugar tastes sweet,* or nouns (or pronouns) and adverbial complements, as in *John is in jail.* 2 anything that serves as a link. 3 *Logic* the often unexpressed link between the subject and predicate terms of a categorial proposition, as *are* in *all men are mortal.*
▷HISTORY C17: from Latin: bond, connection, from *co-* together + *apere* to fasten
▸'**copular** ADJECTIVE

copulate ('kɒpjʊˌleɪt) VERB (*intr*) to perform sexual intercourse.
▷HISTORY C17: from Latin *copulāre* to join together; see COPULA
▸ˌ**copu'lation** NOUN ▸'**copulatory** ADJECTIVE

copulative ('kɒpjʊlətɪv) ADJECTIVE 1 serving to join or unite. 2 of or characteristic of copulation. 3 *Grammar* (of a verb) having the nature of a copula.
▸'**copulatively** ADVERB

copy ('kɒpɪ) NOUN, *plural* **copies.** 1 an imitation or reproduction of an original. 2 a single specimen of something that occurs in a multiple edition, such as a book, article, etc. 3 **a** a matter to be reproduced in print. **b** written matter or text as distinct from graphic material in books, newspapers, etc. 4 the words used to present a promotional message in an advertisement. 5 *Journalism, informal* suitable material for an article or story: *disasters are always good copy.* 6 *Archaic* a model to be copied, esp an example of penmanship. ◆ VERB **copies, copying, copied.** 7 (when *tr,* often foll by *out*) to make a copy or reproduction of (an original). 8 (*tr*) to imitate as a model. 9 (*intr*) to imitate unfairly.
▷HISTORY C14: from Medieval Latin *cōpia* an imitation, something copied, from Latin: abundance, riches; see COPIOUS

copybook ('kɒpɪˌbʊk) NOUN 1 a book of specimens, esp of penmanship, for imitation. 2 *Chiefly US* a book for or containing documents. 3 **blot one's copybook.** *Informal* to spoil one's reputation by making a mistake, offending against social customs, etc. 4 (*modifier*) trite or unoriginal: *copybook sentiments.*

copycat ('kɒpɪˌkæt) NOUN *Informal* **a** a person, esp a child, who imitates or copies another. **b** (*as modifier*): *copycat murders.*

copy desk NOUN *Journalism* a desk where copy is edited.

copy-edit VERB *Journalism* to prepare (copy) for printing by styling, correcting, etc.
▸**copy editor** NOUN

copygraph ('kɒpɪˌgrɑːf, -ˌgræf) NOUN another name for **hectograph.**

copyhold ('kɒpɪˌhəʊld) NOUN *Law* (formerly) **a** a tenure less than freehold of land in England evidenced by a copy of the Court roll. **b** land held in this way.

copyholder ('kɒpɪˌhəʊldə) NOUN 1 *Printing* one who reads aloud from the copy as the proof corrector follows the reading in the proof. 2 *Printing* a device that holds copy in place for the compositor. 3 *Law* (formerly) a person who held land by copyhold tenure.

copyist ('kɒpɪɪst) NOUN 1 a person who makes written copies; transcriber. 2 a person who imitates or copies.

copyread ('kɒpɪˌriːd) VERB **-reads, -reading, -read.** *US* to subedit.

copyreader ('kɒpɪˌriːdə) NOUN *US* a person who edits and prepares newspaper copy for publication; subeditor.

copyright ('kɒpɪˌraɪt) NOUN 1 the exclusive right to produce copies and to control an original literary, musical, or artistic work, granted by law for a specified number of years (in Britain, usually 70 years from the death of the author, composer, etc., or from the date of publication if later). Symbol: ©. ◆ ADJECTIVE 2 (of a work, etc.) subject to or controlled by copyright. ◆ VERB 3 (*tr*) to take out a copyright on.
▸'**copyˌrightable** ADJECTIVE ▸'**copyˌrighter** NOUN

copyright deposit library NOUN one of six libraries legally entitled to receive a gratis copy of every book published in the United Kingdom: the British Library, Bodleian, Cambridge University, Trinity College in Dublin, Scottish National Library, and National Library of Wales.

copytaker ('kɒpɪˌteɪkə) NOUN (esp in a newspaper office) a person employed to type reports as journalists dictate them over the telephone.

copy taster NOUN a person who selects or approves text for publication, esp in a periodical.

copy typist NOUN a typist whose job is to type from written or typed drafts rather than dictation.

copywriter ('kɒpɪˌraɪtə) NOUN a person employed to write advertising copy.
▸'**copyˌwriting** NOUN

coq au vin *French* (kɔk o vɛ̃) NOUN chicken stewed with red wine, onions, etc.
▷HISTORY literally: cock with wine

coquelicot ('kəʊklɪˌkəʊ) NOUN another name for **corn poppy.**
▷HISTORY C18: from French: crow of a cock, from its resemblance to a cock's comb

coquet (kəʊ'kɛt, kɒ-) VERB **-quets, -quetting, -quetted.** (*intr*) 1 to behave flirtatiously. 2 to dally or trifle.
▷HISTORY C17: from French: a gallant, literally: a little cock, from *coq* cock

coquetry ('kəʊkɪtrɪ, 'kɒk-) NOUN, *plural* **-ries.** flirtation.

coquette (kəʊ'kɛt, kɒ'kɛt) NOUN 1 a woman who flirts. 2 any hummingbird of the genus *Lophornis,* esp the crested Brazilian species *L. magnifica.*
▷HISTORY C17: from French, feminine of COQUET
▸**co'quettish** ADJECTIVE ▸**co'quettishly** ADVERB
▸**co'quettishness** NOUN

coquilla nut (kɒ'kiːljə) NOUN the nut of a South American palm tree, *Attalea funifera,* having a hard brown shell used for carving. See also **cohune.**
▷HISTORY C19: from Portuguese *coquilho,* diminutive of *côco* coconut; see COCO

coquille (*French* kɔkij) NOUN 1 any dish, esp seafood, served in a scallop shell: *Coquilles St. Jacques.* 2 a scallop shell, or dish resembling a shell. 3 *Fencing* a bell-shaped hand guard on a foil.
▷HISTORY French, literally: shell, from Latin *conchȳlium* mussel; see COCKLE[1]

coquimbite (kɒ'kɪmbaɪt) NOUN *Mineralogy* hydrated ferric sulphate found in certain rocks and in volcanic fumaroles.
▷HISTORY C19: from *Coquimbo,* Chilean province where it was originally found, + -ITE[1]

coquina (kɒ'kiːnə) NOUN a soft limestone consisting of shells, corals, etc., that occurs in parts of the US.
▷HISTORY C19: from Spanish: shellfish, probably from *concha* shell, CONCH

coquito (kɒ'kiːtəʊ) NOUN, *plural* **-tos.** a Chilean palm tree, *Jubaea spectabilis,* yielding edible nuts and a syrup.
▷HISTORY C19: from Spanish: a little coco palm, from *coco* coco palm

cor (kɔː) INTERJECTION *Brit slang* an exclamation of surprise, amazement, or admiration.
▷HISTORY C20: corruption of *God*

Cor. *Bible* ABBREVIATION FOR Corinthians.

coraciiform (ˌkɒrə'saɪɪˌfɔːm) ADJECTIVE of, relating to, or belonging to the *Coraciiformes,* an order of birds including the kingfishers, bee-eaters, hoopoes, and hornbills.
▷HISTORY C20: from New Latin *Coracias* name of genus, from Greek *korakias* a chough + -I- + -FORM; related to Greek *korax* raven

coracle ('kɒrək[ə]l) NOUN a small roundish boat made of waterproofed hides stretched over a wicker frame.
▷HISTORY C16: from Welsh *corwgl;* related to Irish *curach* boat

coracoid ('kɒrəˌkɔɪd) NOUN a paired ventral bone of the pectoral girdle in vertebrates. In mammals it is reduced to a peg (the **coracoid process**) on the scapula.
▷HISTORY C18: from New Latin *coracoīdēs,* from Greek *korakoeidēs* like a raven, curved like a raven's beak, from *korax* raven

coral ('kɒrəl) NOUN 1 any marine mostly colonial coelenterate of the class *Anthozoa* having a calcareous, horny, or soft skeleton. See also **stony coral, sea fan.** 2 **a** the calcareous or horny material forming the skeleton of certain of these animals. **b** (*as modifier*): *a coral reef.* See also **red coral.** 3 **a** a rocklike aggregation of certain of these animals or their skeletons, forming an island or reef. **b** (*as modifier*): *a coral island.* 4 **a** an object made of coral, esp a piece of jewellery. **b** (*as modifier*): *a coral necklace.* 5 **a** a deep-pink to yellowish-pink colour. **b** (*as adjective*): *coral lipstick.* 6 the roe of a lobster or crab, which becomes pink when cooked.
▷HISTORY C14: from Old French, from Latin *corāllium,* from Greek *korallion,* probably of Semitic origin

coral fern NOUN *Austral* a scrambling fern of the genus *Gleichenia,* having repeatedly forked fronds.

coralline ('kɒrəˌlaɪn) ADJECTIVE 1 Also: **coralloid.** of, relating to, or resembling coral. 2 of the colour of coral. ◆ NOUN 3 any of various red algae impregnated with calcium carbonate, esp any of the genus *Corallina.* 4 any of various animals that resemble coral, such as certain sponges.

▷**HISTORY** C16: from Late Latin *corallīnus* coral red, from Latin *corāllium* CORAL

corallite ('kɒrəlaɪt) NOUN the skeleton of a coral polyp.

coralloid ('kɒrəlɔɪd) ADJECTIVE of or resembling coral.

coral reef NOUN a marine ridge or reef consisting of coral and other organic material consolidated into limestone.

coralroot ('kɒrəl,ru:t) NOUN any N temperate leafless orchid of the genus *Corallorhiza*, with small yellow-green or purple flowers and branched roots resembling coral.

Coral Sea NOUN the SW arm of the Pacific, between Australia, New Guinea, and Vanuatu.

coral snake NOUN [1] any venomous elapid snake of the genus *Micrurus* and related genera, of tropical and subtropical America, marked with red, black, yellow, and white transverse bands. [2] any of various other brightly coloured elapid snakes of Africa and SE Asia.

coral tree NOUN *Austral* any of various thorny trees of the leguminous genus *Erythrina*, having bright red flowers and reddish shiny seeds.

coral trout NOUN an Australian fish, *Plectropomus maculatus*, of the Great Barrier Reef which is an important food fish.

coram populo *Latin* ('kɔ:ræm 'pɒpʊ,ləʊ) ADVERB in the presence of the people; publicly.

cor anglais ('kɔ:r 'ɑ:ŋgleɪ) NOUN, *plural* **cors anglais** ('kɔ:z 'ɑ:ŋgleɪ). *Music* a woodwind instrument, the alto of the oboe family. It is a transposing instrument in F. Range: two and a half octaves upwards from E on the third space of the bass staff. Also called: **English horn.**

▷**HISTORY** C19: from French: English horn

Corantijn ('kɔran,tɛjn) NOUN the Dutch name of **Courantyne.**

coranto (kɒ'ræntəʊ) NOUN, *plural* **-tos.** a variant of **courante.**

corban ('kɔ:bᵊn; *Hebrew* kɔr'ban) NOUN [1] *Old Testament* a gift to God. [2] *New Testament, Judaism* the Temple treasury or a consecration or gift to it (Matthew 27:6; Mark 7:11).

▷**HISTORY** C14: from Late Latin, from Greek *korban*, from Hebrew *qorbān* offering, literally: a drawing near

corbeil *or* **corbeille** ('kɔ:bᵊl; *French* kɔrbɛj) NOUN *Architect* a carved ornament in the form of a basket of fruit, flowers, etc.

▷**HISTORY** C18: from French *corbeille* basket, from Late Latin *corbicula* a little basket, from Latin *corbis* basket

corbel ('kɔ:bᵊl) *Architect* ◆ NOUN [1] Also called: **truss.** a bracket, usually of stone or brick. ◆ VERB **-bels, -belling, -belled** *or US* **-bels, -beling, -beled.** [2] *(tr)* to lay (a stone or brick) so that it forms a corbel.

▷**HISTORY** C15: from Old French, literally: a little raven, from Medieval Latin *corvellus*, from Latin *corvus* raven

corbelling *or US* **corbeling** ('kɔ:bəlɪŋ) NOUN a set of corbels stepped outwards, one above another.

corbel out *or* **off** VERB *(tr, adverb)* to support on corbels.

Corbett ('kɔ:bət) NOUN *Mountaineering* any separate mountain peak between 2500 feet and 3000 feet high: originally used of Scotland only, but now sometimes extended to other parts of the British Isles.

corbicula (kɔ:'bɪkjʊlə) NOUN, *plural* **-lae** (-,li:). the technical name for **pollen basket.**

▷**HISTORY** C19: from Late Latin, diminutive of Latin *corbis* basket

corbie ('kɔ:bɪ; *Scot* 'kɔ:rbɪ) NOUN a Scot name for **raven**[1] or **crow**[1].

▷**HISTORY** C15: from Old French *corbin*, from Latin *corvīnus* CORVINE

corbie gable NOUN *Architect* a gable having corbie-steps.

corbie-step *or* **corbel step** NOUN *Architect* any of a set of steps on the top of a gable. Also called: **crow step.**

cor blimey ('kɔ: 'blaɪmɪ) *or* **gorblimey** INTERJECTION *Brit slang* an exclamation of surprise or annoyance.

▷**HISTORY** C20: corruption of *God blind me*

Corby ('kɔ:bɪ) NOUN a town in central England, in N Northamptonshire: designated a new town in 1950. Pop.: 49 053 (1991).

Corcovado NOUN [1] (*Spanish* korko'βaðo) a volcano in S Chile, in the Andes. Height: 2300 m (7546 ft.). [2] (*Portuguese* korku'vɑ:du) a mountain in SE Brazil, in SW Rio de Janeiro city. Height: 704 m (2310 ft.).

Corcyra (kɔ:'saɪərə) NOUN the ancient name for **Corfu.**

cord (kɔ:d) NOUN [1] string or thin rope made of several twisted strands. [2] a length of woven or twisted strands of silk, etc., sewn on clothing or used as a belt. [3] a ribbed fabric, esp corduroy. [4] any influence that binds or restrains. [5] the US and Canadian name for **flex** (sense 1). [6] *Anatomy* any part resembling a string or rope: *the spinal cord.* [7] a unit of volume for measuring cut wood, equal to 128 cubic feet. ◆ VERB *(tr)* [8] to bind or furnish with a cord or cords. [9] to stack (wood) in cords.

▷**HISTORY** C13: from Old French *corde*, from Latin *chorda* cord, from Greek *khordē*; see CHORD[1]

▸**'corder** NOUN ▸**'cord,like** ADJECTIVE

cordage ('kɔ:dɪdʒ) NOUN [1] *Nautical* the lines and rigging of a vessel. [2] an amount of wood measured in cords.

cordate ('kɔ:deɪt) ADJECTIVE heart-shaped: *a cordate leaf; cordate shells.*

▸**'cordately** ADVERB

corded ('kɔ:dɪd) ADJECTIVE [1] bound or fastened with cord. [2] (of a fabric) ribbed. [3] (of muscles) standing out like cords.

Cordelier (,kɔ:dɪ'lɪə) NOUN *RC Church* a Franciscan friar of the order of the Friars Minor.

▷**HISTORY** C19: from Old French *cordelle*, literally: a little cord, from the knotted cord girdles that they wear

Cordeliers (,kɔ:dɪ'lɪəz) NOUN **the.** a political club founded in 1790 and meeting at an old Cordelier convent in Paris.

cord grass NOUN a coarse perennial grass of the genus *Spartina*, characteristically growing in mud or marsh. Also called: **rice grass.**

cordial ('kɔ:dɪəl) ADJECTIVE [1] warm and friendly: *a cordial greeting.* [2] giving heart; stimulating. ◆ NOUN [3] a drink with a fruit base, usually sold in concentrated form and diluted with water before being drunk: *lime cordial.* [4] another word for **liqueur.**

▷**HISTORY** C14: from Medieval Latin *cordiālis*, from Latin *cor* heart

▸**'cordially** ADVERB ▸**'cordialness** NOUN

cordiality (,kɔ:dɪ'ælɪtɪ) NOUN, *plural* **-ties.** warmth of feeling.

cordierite ('kɔ:dɪə,raɪt) NOUN a grey or violet-blue dichroic mineral that consists of magnesium aluminium iron silicate in orthorhombic crystalline form and is found in metamorphic rocks. Formula: $(Mg,Fe)_2AL_4Si_5O_{18}.nH_2O$. Also called: **dichroite, iolite.**

▷**HISTORY** C19: named after Pierre L. A. Cordier (1777–1861), French geologist who described it

cordiform ('kɔ:dɪ,fɔ:m) ADJECTIVE heart-shaped.

▷**HISTORY** C19: from Latin *cor* heart

cordillera (,kɔ:dɪl'jɛərə) NOUN a series of parallel ranges of mountains, esp in the northwestern US.

▷**HISTORY** C18: from Spanish, from *cordilla*, literally: a little cord, from *cuerda* mountain range, CORD

▸**,cordil'leran** ADJECTIVE

Cordilleras (,kɔ:dɪl'jɛərəz; *Spanish* korði'ʎeras) PLURAL NOUN **the.** the complex of mountain ranges on the W side of the Americas, extending from Alaska to Cape Horn and including the Andes and the Rocky Mountains.

cordite ('kɔ:daɪt) NOUN any of various explosive materials used for propelling bullets, shells, etc., containing cellulose nitrate, sometimes mixed with nitroglycerine, plasticizers, and stabilizers.

▷**HISTORY** C19: from CORD + -ITE[1], referring to its stringy appearance

cordless ('kɔ:dlɪs) ADJECTIVE (of an electrical device) operated by an internal battery so that no connection to mains supply or other apparatus is needed.

cordless telephone NOUN a portable battery-powered telephone with a short-range radio link to a fixed base unit.

córdoba ('kɔ:dəbə) NOUN the standard monetary unit of Nicaragua, divided into 100 centavos.

▷**HISTORY** named in honour of Francisco Fernández de *Córdoba* (died 1518), Spanish explorer

Córdoba (*Spanish* 'kɔrðoβa) NOUN [1] a city in central Argentina: university (1613). Pop.: 1 208 713 (1991). [2] a city in S Spain, on the Guadalquivir River: centre of Moorish Spain (711–1236). Pop.: 309 961 (1998 est.). English name: **Cordova.**

cordon ('kɔ:dᵊn) NOUN [1] a chain of police, soldiers, ships, etc., stationed around an area. [2] a ribbon worn as insignia of honour or rank. [3] a cord or ribbon worn as an ornament or fastening. [4] Also called: **string course, belt course, table.** *Architect* an ornamental projecting band or continuous moulding along a wall. [5] *Horticulture* a form of fruit tree consisting of a single stem bearing fruiting spurs, produced by cutting back all lateral branches. ◆ VERB [6] *(tr; often foll by off)* to put or form a cordon (around); close (off).

▷**HISTORY** C16: from Old French, literally: a little cord, from *corde* string, CORD

cordon bleu (*French* kɔrdɔ̃ blø) NOUN [1] *French history* **a** the sky-blue ribbon worn by members of the highest order of knighthood under the Bourbon monarchy. **b** a knight entitled to wear the cordon bleu. [2] any very high distinction. ◆ ADJECTIVE [3] of or denoting food prepared to a very high standard.

▷**HISTORY** French, literally: blue ribbon

cordon sanitaire *French* (kɔrdɔ̃ sanitɛr) NOUN [1] a guarded line serving to cut off an infected area. [2] a line of buffer states, esp when protecting a nation from infiltration or attack.

▷**HISTORY** C19: literally: sanitary line

Cordova ('kɔ:dəvə) NOUN the English name for **Córdoba** (sense 2).

cordovan ('kɔ:dəvᵊn) NOUN a fine leather now made principally from horsehide, isolated from the skin layers above and below it and tanned.

▷**HISTORY** C16: from Spanish *cordobán* (noun), from *cordobán* (adjective) of CÓRDOBA

Cordovan ('kɔ:dəvᵊn) NOUN [1] a native or inhabitant of Córdoba, Spain. ◆ ADJECTIVE [2] of or relating to Córdoba, Spain.

cords (kɔ:dz) PLURAL NOUN trousers, esp jeans, made of corduroy.

corduroy ('kɔ:də,rɔɪ, ,kɔ:də'rɔɪ) NOUN **a** a heavy cotton pile fabric with lengthways ribs. **b** *(as modifier)*: *a corduroy coat.* ◆ See also **corduroys.**

▷**HISTORY** C18: perhaps from the proper name *Corderoy*

corduroy road NOUN a road across swampy ground, made of logs laid transversely.

corduroys (,kɔ:də'rɔɪz, 'kɔ:də,rɔɪz) PLURAL NOUN trousers or breeches of corduroy.

cordwain ('kɔ:d,weɪn) NOUN an archaic name for **cordovan.**

▷**HISTORY** C12 *cordewan*, from Old French *cordoan*, from Old Spanish *cordovan* CORDOVAN

cordwainer ('kɔ:d,weɪnə) NOUN *Archaic* a shoemaker or worker in cordovan leather.

▸**'cord,wainery** NOUN

cordwood ('kɔ:d,wʊd) NOUN wood that has been cut into lengths of four feet so that it can be stacked in cords.

core (kɔ:) NOUN [1] the central part of certain fleshy fruits, such as the apple or pear, consisting of the seeds and supporting parts. [2] **a** the central, innermost, or most essential part of something: *the core of the argument.* **b** *(as modifier)*: *the core meaning.* [3] a piece of magnetic material, such as soft iron, placed inside the windings of an electromagnet or transformer to intensify and direct the magnetic field. [4] *Geology* the central part of the earth, beneath the mantle, consisting mainly of iron and nickel, which has an inner solid part surrounded by an outer liquid part. [5] a cylindrical sample of rock, soil, etc., obtained by the use of a hollow drill. [6] shaped body of material (in metal casting usually of sand) supported inside a mould to form a cavity of predetermined shape in the finished casting. [7] *Physics* the region of a nuclear reactor in which the reaction takes place. [8] a layer of wood serving as a backing for a veneer. [9] *Computing* **a** a ferrite ring formerly used in a computer memory to store one bit of information. **b** short for **core store. c** *(as modifier)*: *core memory.* [10] *Archaeol* a lump of stone

or flint from which flakes or blades have been removed. [11] *Physics* the nucleus together with all complete electron shells of an atom. ◆ VERB [12] *(tr)* to remove the core from (fruit).
▷HISTORY C14: of uncertain origin
▸'**coreless** ADJECTIVE

CORE (kɔː) NOUN (in the US) ACRONYM FOR Congress of Racial Equality.

-core NOUN COMBINING FORM indicating a type of popular music: *dancecore.*

coreferential (ˌkəʊrɛfəˈrɛnʃəl) ADJECTIVE *Philosophy* (of more than one linguistic expression) designating the same individual or class.

coreligionist (ˌkəʊrɪˈlɪdʒənɪst) NOUN an adherent of the same religion as another.

corella (kəˈrɛlə) NOUN any of certain white Australian cockatoos of the genus *Kakatoe.*
▷HISTORY C19: probably from native Australian *carall*

coreopsis (ˌkɒrɪˈɒpsɪs) NOUN any plant of the genus *Coreopsis,* of America and tropical Africa, cultivated for their yellow, brown, or yellow-and-red daisy-like flowers: family *Asteraceae* (composites). Also called: **calliopsis.** Compare **caryopsis.**
▷HISTORY C18: from New Latin, from Greek *koris* bedbug + -OPSIS; so called from the appearance of the seed

co-respondent (ˌkəʊrɪˈspɒndənt) NOUN *Law* a person cited in divorce proceedings, who is alleged to have committed adultery with the respondent.
▸ˌ**co-reˈspondency** NOUN

co-respondent shoes PLURAL NOUN men's two-coloured shoes, usually black and white or brown and white. Also called: **co-respondents.**

core store NOUN an obsolete type of computer memory made up of a matrix of cores.

core subjects PLURAL NOUN *Brit education* three foundation subjects (English, mathematics, and science) that are compulsory throughout each key stage in the National Curriculum.

core time NOUN See **flexitime.**

corf (kɔːf) NOUN, *plural* **corves.** *Brit* a wagon or basket used formerly in mines.
▷HISTORY C14: from Middle Dutch *corf* or Middle Low German *korf,* probably from Latin *corbis* basket

Corfam (ˈkɔːfæm) NOUN *Trademark* a synthetic water-repellent material used as a substitute for shoe leather.

Corfu (kɔːˈfuː) NOUN [1] an island in the Ionian Sea, in the Ionian Islands: forms, with neighbouring islands, a department of Greece. Pop.: 107 592 (1991). Area: 641 sq. km (247 sq. miles). [2] a port on E Corfu island. Pop.: 105 000 (1995 est.). Modern Greek name: **Kérkyra.** Ancient name: **Corcyra.**

corgi (ˈkɔːgɪ) NOUN either of two long-bodied short-legged sturdy breeds of dog, the Cardigan and the Pembroke. Also called: **Welsh corgi.**
▷HISTORY C20: from Welsh, from *cor* dwarf + *ci* dog

coriaceous (ˌkɒrɪˈeɪʃəs) *or* **corious** ADJECTIVE of or resembling leather.
▷HISTORY C17: from Late Latin *coriāceus* from *corium* leather

coriander (ˌkɒrɪˈændə) NOUN a European umbelliferous plant, *Coriandrum sativum,* widely cultivated for its aromatic seeds and leaves, used in flavouring food, etc. US and Canadian name: **cilantro.**
▷HISTORY C14: from Old French *coriandre,* from Latin *coriandrum,* from Greek *koriannon,* of uncertain origin

Corinth (ˈkɒrɪnθ) NOUN [1] a port in S Greece, in the NE Peloponnese: the modern town is near the site of the ancient city, the largest and richest of the city-states after Athens. Pop.: 29 600 (1995 est.). Modern Greek name: **Kórinthos.** [2] a region of ancient Greece, occupying most of the Isthmus of Corinth and part of the NE Peloponnese. [3] **Gulf of.** Also called: Gulf of **Lepanto.** an inlet of the Ionian Sea between the Peloponnese and central Greece. [4] **Isthmus of.** a narrow strip of land between the Gulf of Corinth and the Saronic Gulf: crossed by the **Corinth Canal** making navigation possible between the gulfs.

Corinthian (kəˈrɪnθɪən) ADJECTIVE [1] of, characteristic of, or relating to Corinth. [2] of, denoting, or relating to one of the five classical orders of architecture: characterized by a bell-shaped capital having carved ornaments based on acanthus leaves. See also **Ionic, Doric, Composite, Tuscan.** [3] given to luxury; dissolute. [4] ornate and elaborate. ◆ NOUN [5] a native or inhabitant of Corinth. [6] an amateur sportsman. [7] *Rare* a man about town, esp one who is dissolute.

Corinthians (kəˈrɪnθɪənz) NOUN *(functioning as singular)* either of two books of the New Testament (in full **The First and Second Epistles of Paul the Apostle to the Corinthians**).

Coriolis force (ˌkɒrɪˈəʊlɪs) NOUN a fictitious force used to explain a deflection in the path of a body moving in latitude relative to the earth when observed from the earth. The deflection (**Coriolis effect**) is due to the earth's rotation and is to the east when the motion is towards a pole.
▷HISTORY C19: named after Gaspard G. *Coriolis* (1792–1843), French civil engineer

corious (ˈkɔːrɪəs) ADJECTIVE a variant of **coriaceous.**

corium (ˈkɔːrɪəm) NOUN, *plural* **-ria** (-rɪə). [1] Also called: **derma, dermis.** the deep inner layer of the skin, beneath the epidermis, containing connective tissue, blood vessels, and fat. [2] *Entomol* the leathery basal part of the forewing of hemipterous insects.
▷HISTORY C19: from Latin: rind, skin, leather

corixid (kəˈrɪksɪd) NOUN [1] any heteropterous water bug of the vegetarian family *Corixidae,* typified by *Corixa punctata,* common in sluggish waters. The forelegs have become modified and are used in stridulation, as by the **water singer** (*Micronecta poweri*). See also **water boatman.** ◆ ADJECTIVE [2] of or relating to the Corixidae.
▷HISTORY from New Latin *corixa,* from Greek *koris* bedbug

cork (kɔːk) NOUN [1] the thick light porous outer bark of the cork oak, used widely as an insulator and for stoppers for bottles, casks, etc. [2] a piece of cork or other material used as a stopper. [3] an angling float. [4] Also called: **phellem.** *Botany* a protective layer of dead impermeable cells on the outside of the stems and roots of woody plants, produced by the outer layer of the cork cambium. ◆ ADJECTIVE [5] made of cork. Related adjective: **suberose.** ◆ VERB *(tr)* [6] to stop up (a bottle, cask, etc.) with or as if with a cork; fit with a cork. [7] (often foll by *up*) to restrain: *to cork up the emotions.* [8] to black (the face, hands, etc.) with burnt cork.
▷HISTORY C14: probably from Arabic *qurq,* from Latin *cortex* bark, especially of the cork oak
▸ˈ**corkˌlike** ADJECTIVE

Cork (kɔːk) NOUN [1] a county of SW Republic of Ireland, in Munster province: crossed by ridges of low mountains; scenic coastline. County town: Cork. Pop.: 420 510 (1996). Area: 7459 sq. km (2880 sq. miles). [2] a city and port in S Republic of Ireland, county town of Co. Cork, at the mouth of the River Lee: seat of the University College of Cork (1849). Pop.: 127 092 (1996). Gaelic name: **Corcaigh.**

corkage (ˈkɔːkɪdʒ) NOUN a charge made at a restaurant for serving wine, etc., bought off the premises.

corkboard (ˈkɔːkˌbɔːd) NOUN a thin slab made of granules of cork, used as a floor or wall finish and as an insulator.

cork cambium NOUN a layer of meristematic cells in the cortex of the stems and roots of woody plants, the outside of which gives rise to cork cells and the inside to secondary cortical cells (phelloderm). Also called: **phellogen.**

corked (kɔːkt) ADJECTIVE [1] Also: **corky.** (of a wine) tainted through having a cork containing excess tannin. [2] *(postpositive) Brit* a slang word for **drunk.**

corker (ˈkɔːkə) NOUN [1] *Slang* **a** something or somebody striking or outstanding: *that was a corker of a joke.* **b** an irrefutable remark that puts an end to discussion. [2] a person or machine that inserts corks.

corking (ˈkɔːkɪŋ) ADJECTIVE *(prenominal) Brit slang* excellent.

cork oak NOUN an evergreen Mediterranean oak tree, *Quercus suber,* with a porous outer bark from which cork is obtained. Also called: **cork tree.**

Corkonian (kɔːˈkəʊnɪən, kəˈkɔːnɪən) NOUN a native or inhabitant of the city of Cork.

corkscrew (ˈkɔːkˌskruː) NOUN [1] a device for drawing corks from bottles, typically consisting of a pointed metal spiral attached to a handle or screw mechanism. [2] *Boxing, slang* a blow that ends with a twist of the fist, esp one intended to cut the opponent. [3] *(modifier)* resembling a corkscrew in shape. ◆ VERB [4] to move or cause to move in a spiral or zigzag course.

cork-tipped (ˈkɔːkˌtɪpt) ADJECTIVE (of a cigarette) having a filter of cork or some material resembling cork.

corkwing (ˈkɔːkˌwɪŋ) NOUN a greenish or bluish European fish of the wrasse family, *Ctenolabrus melops.*
▷HISTORY of uncertain origin

corkwood (ˈkɔːkˌwʊd) NOUN [1] a small tree, *Leitneria floridana,* of the southeastern US, having very lightweight porous wood: family *Leitneriaceae.* [2] any other tree with light porous wood. [3] the wood of any of these trees.

corm (kɔːm) NOUN an organ of vegetative reproduction in plants such as the crocus, consisting of a globular stem base swollen with food and surrounded by papery scale leaves. Compare **bulb** (sense 1).
▷HISTORY C19: from New Latin *cormus,* from Greek *kormos* tree trunk from which the branches have been lopped
▸ˈ**cormous** ADJECTIVE

cormel (ˈkɔːməl) NOUN a new small corm arising from the base of a fully developed one.

cormophyte (ˈkɔːməˌfaɪt) NOUN any of the *Cormophyta,* a major division (now obsolete) of plants having a stem, root, and leaves: includes the mosses, ferns, and seed plants.
▷HISTORY C19: from Greek *kormos* tree trunk + -PHYTE
▸**cormophytic** (ˌkɔːməˈfɪtɪk) ADJECTIVE

cormorant (ˈkɔːmərənt) NOUN any aquatic bird of the family *Phalacrocoracidae,* of coastal and inland waters, having a dark plumage, a long neck and body, and a slender hooked beak: order *Pelecaniformes* (pelicans, etc.).
▷HISTORY C13: from Old French *cormareng,* from *corp* raven, from Latin *corvus* + *-mareng* of the sea, from Latin *mare* sea

corn[1] (kɔːn) NOUN [1] *Brit* **a** any of various cereal plants, esp the predominant crop of a region, such as wheat in England and oats in Scotland and Ireland. **b** the seeds of such plants, esp after harvesting. **c** a single seed of such plants; a grain. [2] the usual US, Canadian, Austral, and NZ name for **maize.** See also **sweet corn** (sense 1), **popcorn** (sense 1). [3] **a** the plants producing these kinds of grain considered as a growing crop: *spring corn.* **b** *(in combination)*: *a cornfield.* [4] short for **corn whisky.** [5] *Slang* an idea, song, etc., regarded as banal or sentimental. [6] *Archaic or dialect* any hard particle or grain. ◆ VERB *(tr)* [7] to feed (animals) with corn, esp oats. [8] **a** to preserve in brine. **b** to salt. [9] to plant corn on.
▷HISTORY Old English *corn;* related to Old Norse, Old High German *corn,* Gothic *kaúrn,* Latin *grānum,* Sanskrit *jīrṇá* fragile

corn[2] (kɔːn) NOUN [1] a hardening or thickening of the skin around a central point in the foot, caused by pressure or friction. [2] **tread on (someone's) corns.** *Brit informal* to offend or hurt (someone) by touching on a sensitive subject or encroaching on his privileges.
▷HISTORY C15: from Old French *corne* horn, from Latin *cornū*

cornaceous (kɔːˈneɪʃəs) ADJECTIVE of, relating to, or belonging to the *Cornaceae,* a family of temperate plants, mostly trees and shrubs, including dogwood, cornel, and spotted laurel (see **laurel**(sense 5)).
▷HISTORY C19: from New Latin *Cornaceae,* from *Cornus* genus name, from Latin: CORNEL

cornball (ˈkɔːnˌbɔːl) *Chiefly US* ◆ NOUN [1] a person given to mawkish or unsophisticated behaviour. ◆ ADJECTIVE [2] another word for **corny.**
▷HISTORY C20: from *corn ball* a sweet consisting of a ball of popcorn and molasses

corn borer NOUN the larva of the pyralid moth *Pyrausta nubilalis,* native to S and Central Europe: in E North America a serious pest of maize.

corn bread NOUN a kind of bread made from maize meal. Also called: **Indian bread.**

corn bunting NOUN a heavily built European songbird, *Emberiza calandra,* with a streaked brown plumage: family *Emberizidae* (buntings).

corn circle NOUN another name for **crop circle.**

corncob ('kɔːnˌkɒb) NOUN 1 the core of an ear of maize, to which kernels are attached. 2 short for **corncob pipe.**

corncob pipe NOUN a pipe made from a dried corncob.

corncockle ('kɔːnˌkɒkᵊl) NOUN a European caryophyllaceous plant, *Agrostemma githago,* that has reddish-purple flowers and grows in cornfields and by roadsides.

corncrake ('kɔːnˌkreɪk) NOUN a common Eurasian rail, *Crex crex,* of fields and meadows, with a buff speckled plumage and reddish wings.

corncrib ('kɔːnˌkrɪb) NOUN *Chiefly US and Canadian* a ventilated building for the storage of unhusked maize.

corn dolly NOUN a decorative figure made by plaiting straw.

cornea ('kɔːnɪə) NOUN, *plural* **-neas** (-nɪəz) *or* **-neae** (-nɪˌiː). the convex transparent membrane that forms the anterior covering of the eyeball and is continuous with the sclera.
▷HISTORY C14: from Medieval Latin *cornea tēla* horny web, from Latin *cornū* HORN
▸ **'corneal** ADJECTIVE

corn earworm NOUN *US* the larva of the noctuid moth *Heliothis armigera,* which feeds on maize and many other crop plants. See also **bollworm.**

corned (kɔːnd) ADJECTIVE (esp of beef) cooked and then preserved or pickled in salt or brine, now often canned.

cornel ('kɔːnᵊl) NOUN any cornaceous plant of the genus *Cornus,* such as the dogwood and dwarf cornel.
▷HISTORY C16: probably from Middle Low German *kornelle,* from Old French *cornelle,* from Vulgar Latin *cornicula* (unattested), from Latin *cornum* cornel cherry, from *cornus* cornel tree

cornelian (kɔː'niːlɪən) NOUN a variant spelling of **carnelian.**

corneous ('kɔːnɪəs) ADJECTIVE horny; hornlike.
▷HISTORY C17: from Latin *corneus* horny, from *cornū* HORN

corner ('kɔːnə) NOUN 1 the place, position, or angle formed by the meeting of two converging lines or surfaces. 2 a projecting angle of a solid object or figure. 3 the place where two streets meet. 4 any small, secluded, secret, or private place. 5 a dangerous or awkward position, esp from which escape is difficult: *a tight corner.* 6 any part, region or place, esp a remote place. 7 something used to protect or mark a corner, as of the hard cover of a book. 8 *Commerce* a monopoly over the supply of a commodity so that its market price can be controlled. 9 *Soccer, hockey* a free kick or shot from the corner of the field, taken against a defending team when the ball goes out of play over their goal line after last touching one of their players. 10 either of two opposite angles of a boxing ring in which the opponents take their rests. 11 *Mountaineering* a junction between two rock faces forming an angle of between 60° and 120°. US name: **dihedral.** 12 **cut corners.** to do something in the easiest and shortest way, esp at the expense of high standards. 13 **(just) round the corner.** close at hand. 14 **turn the corner.** to pass the critical point (in an illness, etc.). 15 *(modifier)* located on a corner: *a corner shop.* 16 *(modifier)* suitable or designed for a corner: *a corner table.* 17 *Logic* either of a pair of symbols used in the same way as ordinary quotation marks to indicate quasi quotation. See **quasi-quotation.** ◆ VERB 18 *(tr)* to manoeuvre (a person or animal) into a position from which escape is difficult or impossible: *finally they cornered the fox.* 19 *(tr)* to furnish or provide with corners. 20 *(tr)* to place in or move into a corner. 21 *(tr)* **a** to acquire enough of (a commodity) to attain control of the market. **b** Also: **engross.** to attain control of (a market) in such a manner. Compare **forestall** (sense 3). 22 *(intr)* (of vehicles, etc.) to turn a corner. 23 *(intr) US* to be situated on a corner. 24 *(intr)* (in soccer, etc.) to take a corner.
▷HISTORY C13: from Old French *corniere,* from Latin *cornū* point, extremity, HORN

Corner NOUN **the.** *Informal* an area in central Australia, at the junction of the borders of Queensland and South Australia.

cornerback ('kɔːnəˌbæk) NOUN *American football* a defensive back.

cornerstone ('kɔːnəˌstəʊn) NOUN 1 a stone at the corner of a wall, uniting two intersecting walls; quoin. 2 a stone placed at the corner of a building during a ceremony to mark the start of construction. 3 a person or thing of prime importance; basis: *the cornerstone of the whole argument.*

cornerwise ('kɔːnəˌwaɪz) *or* **cornerways** ('kɔːnəˌweɪz) ADVERB, ADJECTIVE with a corner in front; diagonally.

cornet ('kɔːnɪt) NOUN 1 Also called: **cornet à pistons** ('kɔːnɪt ə 'pɪstənz; *French* kɔrnɛ a pistɔ̃). a three-valved brass instrument of the trumpet family. Written range: about two and a half octaves upwards from E below middle C. It is a transposing instrument in B flat or A. 2 a person who plays the cornet. 3 a variant spelling of **cornett.** 4 a cone-shaped paper container for sweets, etc. 5 *Brit* a cone-shaped wafer container for ice cream. 6 (formerly) the lowest rank of commissioned cavalry officer in the British army. 7 *South African* short for **field cornet.** 8 a starched and wired muslin or lace cap worn by women from the 12th to the 15th centuries. 9 the large white headdress of some nuns.
▷HISTORY C14: from Old French, from *corn,* from Latin *cornū* HORN

cornetcy ('kɔːnɪtsɪ) NOUN, *plural* **-cies.** *Obsolete* the commission or rank of a cornet.

cornetist *or* **cornettist** (kɔː'nɛtɪst) NOUN a person who plays the cornet.

cornett (kɔː'nɛt) *or* **cornet** NOUN a musical instrument consisting of a straight or curved tube of wood or ivory having finger holes like a recorder and a cup-shaped mouthpiece like a trumpet.
▷HISTORY from Old French *cornet* a little horn, from *corn* horn, from Latin *cornū*

corn exchange NOUN a building where corn is bought and sold.

corn factor NOUN a person who deals in corn.

cornfield ('kɔːnˌfiːld) NOUN a field planted with cereal crops.

cornflakes ('kɔːnˌfleɪks) PLURAL NOUN a breakfast cereal made from toasted maize, eaten with milk, sugar, etc.

cornflour ('kɔːnˌflaʊə) NOUN 1 a fine starchy maize flour, used esp for thickening sauces. US and Canadian name: **cornstarch.** 2 *NZ* a fine wheat flour.

cornflower ('kɔːnˌflaʊə) NOUN a Eurasian herbaceous plant, *Centaurea cyanus,* with blue, purple, pink, or white flowers, formerly a common weed in cornfields: family *Asteraceae* (composites). Also called: **bluebottle.** See also **bachelor's-buttons.**

cornhusk ('kɔːnˌhʌsk) NOUN *US and Canadian* the outer protective covering of an ear of maize; the chaff.

cornice ('kɔːnɪs) NOUN 1 *Architect* **a** the top projecting mouldings of an entablature. **b** a continuous horizontal projecting course or moulding at the top of a wall, building, etc. 2 an overhanging ledge of snow formed by the wind on the edge of a mountain ridge, cliff, or corrie. ◆ VERB 3 *(tr) Architect* to furnish or decorate with or as if with a cornice.
▷HISTORY C16: from Old French, from Italian, perhaps from Latin *cornix* crow, but influenced also by Latin *corōnis* decorative flourish used by scribes, from Greek *korōnis,* from *korōnē* curved object, CROWN

corniche ('kɔːnɪʃ) NOUN a coastal road, esp one built into the face of a cliff.
▷HISTORY C19: from *corniche road,* originally the coastal road between Nice and Monte Carlo; see CORNICE

cornichon ('kɔːnɪˌʃɒn) NOUN a type of small gherkin.
▷HISTORY French: gherkin

corniculate (kɔː'nɪkjʊˌleɪt, -lɪt) ADJECTIVE 1 having horns or hornlike projections. 2 relating to or resembling a horn.
▷HISTORY C17: from Latin *corniculātus* horned, from *corniculum* a little horn, from *cornū* HORN

Cornish ('kɔːnɪʃ) ADJECTIVE 1 of, relating to, or characteristic of Cornwall, its inhabitants, their former language, or their present-day dialect of English. ◆ NOUN 2 a former language of Cornwall, belonging to the S Celtic branch of the Indo-European family and closely related to Breton: extinct by 1800. 3 **the.** *(functioning as plural)* the natives or inhabitants of Cornwall.

Cornishman ('kɔːnɪʃmən) NOUN, *plural* **-men.** a man who is a native or inhabitant of Cornwall.

Cornish pasty ('pæstɪ) NOUN *Cookery* a pastry case with a filling of meat and vegetables.

Cornish Rex NOUN a breed of cat with a very soft wavy coat, a small head, large eyes, and very large ears.

Cornish split NOUN another term for **Devonshire split.**

Corn Laws PLURAL NOUN the laws introduced in Britain in 1804 to protect domestic farmers against foreign competition by the imposition of a heavy duty on foreign corn: repealed in 1846. See also **Anti-Corn Law League.**

corn lily NOUN any of several South African iridaceous plants of the genus *Ixia,* which have coloured lily-like flowers.

corn marigold NOUN an annual plant, *Chrysanthemum segetum,* with yellow daisy-like flower heads: a common weed of cultivated land: family *Asteraceae* (composites).

corn meal NOUN meal made from maize. Also called: **Indian meal.**

Corno (*Italian* 'kɔrno) NOUN **Monte** ('monte). a mountain in central Italy: the highest peak in the Apennines. Height: 2912 m (9554 ft.).

corn oil NOUN an oil prepared from maize, used in cooking and in making soaps, lubricants, etc.

corn on the cob NOUN a cob of maize, boiled and eaten as a vegetable.

corn-picker NOUN *Chiefly US and Canadian* a machine for removing ears of maize from the standing stalks, often also equipped to separate the corn from the husk and shell.

corn pone NOUN *Southern US* corn bread, esp a plain type made with water. Sometimes shortened to **pone.**

corn poppy NOUN a poppy, *Papaver rhoeas,* that has bright red flowers and grows in cornfields. Since World War I it has been the symbol of fallen soldiers. Also called: **coquelicot, Flanders poppy, field poppy.**

corn rose NOUN *Brit archaic* any of several red-flowered weeds of cornfields, such as the corn poppy.

corn row (rəʊ) NOUN a Black, originally African, hair-style in which the hair is plaited in close parallel rows, resembling furrows in a ploughed field.

corn salad NOUN any valerianaceous plant of the genus *Valerianella,* esp the European species *V. locusta,* which often grows in cornfields and whose leaves are sometimes used in salads. Also called: **lamb's lettuce.**

corn shock NOUN a stack or bundle of bound or unbound corn piled upright for curing or drying.

corn shuck NOUN *US and Canadian* the husk of an ear of maize.

corn silk NOUN *US and Canadian* the silky tuft of styles and stigmas at the tip of an ear of maize, formerly used as a diuretic.

corn smut NOUN 1 an ascomycetous parasitic fungus, *Ustilago zeae,* that causes gall-like deformations on maize grain. 2 the condition produced by this fungus.

corn snow NOUN *Skiing US and Canadian* granular snow formed by alternate freezing and thawing.

cornstalk ('kɔːnˌstɔːk) NOUN 1 a stalk or stem of corn. 2 *Austral slang* a tall thin man.

cornstarch ('kɔːnˌstɑːtʃ) NOUN the US and Canadian name for **cornflour.**

cornstone ('kɔːnˌstəʊn) NOUN a mottled green and red limestone.

corn syrup NOUN syrup prepared from maize.

cornu ('kɔːnjuː) NOUN, *plural* **-nua** (-njuə). *Anatomy* a part or structure resembling a horn or having a hornlike pattern, such as a cross section of the grey matter of the spinal cord.
▷HISTORY C17: from Latin: a horn
▸ 'cornual ADJECTIVE

cornucopia (ˌkɔːnjʊ'kəʊpɪə) NOUN 1 *Greek myth* the horn of Amalthea, the goat that suckled Zeus. 2 a representation of such a horn in painting, sculpture, etc., overflowing with fruit, vegetables, etc.; horn of plenty. 3 a great abundance; overflowing supply. 4 a horn-shaped container.
▷HISTORY C16: from Late Latin, from Latin *cornūcōpiae* horn of plenty
▸ ˌcornu'copian ADJECTIVE

cornute (kɔː'njuːt) *or* **cornuted** ADJECTIVE *Biology* having or resembling cornua; hornlike: *the cornute process of a bone.*
▷HISTORY C17: from Latin *cornūtus* horned, from *cornū* HORN

Cornwall ('kɔːnˌwɔːl, -wəl) NOUN a county of SW England: hilly, with a deeply indented coastline. Administrative centre: Truro. Pop.: 499 114 (2001). Area: 3564 sq. km (1376 sq. miles).

corn whisky NOUN whisky made from maize.

corny ('kɔːnɪ) ADJECTIVE **cornier, corniest.** *Slang* 1 trite or banal. 2 sentimental or mawkish. 3 abounding in corn.
▷HISTORY C16 (C20 in the sense rustic, banal): from CORN[1] + -Y[1]

corody *or* **corrody** ('kɒrədɪ) NOUN, *plural* **-dies.** *History* 1 (originally) the right of a lord to receive free quarters from his vassal. 2 an allowance for maintenance.
▷HISTORY C15: from Medieval Latin *corrōdium* something provided, from Old French *corroyer* to provide, of Germanic origin

corolla (kə'rɒlə) NOUN the petals of a flower collectively, forming an inner floral envelope. Compare **calyx.**

corollaceous (ˌkɒrə'leɪʃəs) ADJECTIVE of, relating to, resembling, or having a corolla.

corollary (kə'rɒlərɪ) NOUN, *plural* **-laries.** 1 a proposition that follows directly from the proof of another proposition. 2 an obvious deduction. 3 a natural consequence or result. ◆ ADJECTIVE 4 consequent or resultant.
▷HISTORY C14: from Latin *corollārium* money paid for a garland, from Latin *corolla* garland, from *corōna* CROWN

Coromandel Coast (ˌkɒrə'mændᵊl) NOUN the SE coast of India, along the Bay of Bengal, extending from Point Calimere to the mouth of the Krishna River.

corona (kə'rəʊnə) NOUN, *plural* **-nas** *or* **-nae** (-niː). 1 a circle of light around a luminous body, usually the moon. 2 Also called: **aureole.** the outermost region of the sun's atmosphere, visible as a faint halo during a solar eclipse. 3 *Architect* the flat vertical face of a cornice just above the soffit. 4 something resembling a corona or halo. 5 a circular chandelier suspended from the roof of a church. 6 *Botany* **a** the trumpet-shaped part of the corolla of daffodils and similar plants; the crown. **b** a crown of leafy outgrowths from inside the petals of some flowers. 7 *Anatomy* a crownlike structure, such as the top of the head. 8 *Zoology* the head or upper surface of an animal, such as the body of an echinoid or the disc and arms of a crinoid. 9 a long cigar with blunt ends. 10 *Physics* short for **corona discharge.**
▷HISTORY C16: from Latin: crown, from Greek *korōnē* anything curved; related to Greek *korōnis* wreath, *korax* crow, Latin *curvus* curved

Corona Australis (ɒ'streɪlɪs) NOUN, *Latin genitive* **Coronae Australis** (kə'rəʊniː). a small faint constellation in the S hemisphere between Ara and Pavo.
▷HISTORY literally: Southern crown

Corona Borealis (ˌbɔːrɪ'eɪlɪs) NOUN, *Latin genitive* **Coronae Borealis** (kə'rəʊniː). a small compact constellation in the N hemisphere lying between Boötes and Hercules.
▷HISTORY literally: Northern crown

coronach ('kɒrənəx, -nək) NOUN *Scot or Irish* a dirge or lamentation for the dead.
▷HISTORY C16: from Scottish Gaelic *corranach;* related to Irish *rānadh* a crying

corona discharge NOUN an electrical discharge appearing on and around the surface of a charged conductor, caused by ionization of the surrounding gas. Also called: **corona.** See also **Saint Elmo's fire.**

coronagraph *or* **coronograph** (kə'rəʊnəˌgrɑːf, -ˌgræf) NOUN an optical instrument used to simulate an eclipse of the sun so that the faint solar corona can be studied.

coronal NOUN ('kɒrənᵊl) 1 *Poetic* a circlet for the head; crown. 2 a wreath or garland. 3 *Anatomy* short for **coronal suture.** ◆ ADJECTIVE (kə'rəʊnᵊl) 4 of or relating to a corona or coronal. 5 *Phonetics* a less common word for **retroflex.**
▷HISTORY C16: from Late Latin *corōnālis* belonging to a CROWN

coronal suture NOUN the serrated line across the skull between the frontal bone and the parietal bones.

coronary ('kɒrənərɪ) ADJECTIVE 1 *Anatomy* designating blood vessels, nerves, ligaments, etc., that encircle a part or structure. ◆ NOUN, *plural* **-naries.** 2 short for **coronary thrombosis.**
▷HISTORY C17: from Latin *corōnārius* belonging to a wreath or crown; see CORONA

coronary artery NOUN either of two arteries branching from the aorta and supplying blood to the heart.

coronary bypass NOUN the surgical bypass of a narrowed or blocked coronary artery by grafting a section of a healthy blood vessel taken from another part of the patient's body.

coronary heart disease NOUN any heart disorder caused by disease of the coronary arteries.

coronary insufficiency NOUN inadequate circulation of blood through the coronary arteries, characterized by attacks of angina pectoris.

coronary thrombosis NOUN a condition of interrupted blood flow to the heart due to a blood clot in a coronary artery, usually as a consequence of atherosclerosis: characterized by intense pain. Sometimes shortened to **coronary.** Compare **myocardial infarction.**

coronation (ˌkɒrə'neɪʃən) NOUN the act or ceremony of crowning a monarch.
▷HISTORY C14: from Old French, from *coroner* to crown, from Latin *corōnāre*

coronation chicken NOUN (*sometimes capitals*) a dish of cold cooked chicken in a mild creamy curry sauce.
▷HISTORY C20: so-called because it was served at the coronation lunch of Elizabeth II (born 1926), queen of Great Britain and Northern Ireland from 1952

coroner ('kɒrənə) NOUN a public official responsible for the investigation of violent, sudden, or suspicious deaths and inquiries into treasure trove. The investigation (**coroner's inquest**) is held in the presence of a jury (**coroner's jury**). See also **procurator fiscal.** Compare **medical examiner.**
▷HISTORY C14: from Anglo-French *corouner* officer in charge of the pleas of the Crown, from Old French *corone* CROWN
▸ 'coronerˌship NOUN

coronet ('kɒrənɪt) NOUN 1 any small crown, esp one worn by princes or peers as a mark of rank. 2 a woman's jewelled circlet for the head. 3 the margin between the skin of a horse's pastern and the horn of the hoof. 4 the knob at the base of a deer's antler. 5 *Heraldry* a support for a crest shaped like a crown.
▷HISTORY C15: from Old French *coronete* a little crown, from *corone* CROWN

coroneted (ˌkɒrə'netɪd) ADJECTIVE 1 wearing a coronet. 2 belonging to the peerage.

co-routine ('kəʊruːˌtiːn) NOUN *Computing* a section of a computer program similar to but differing from a subroutine in that it can be left and re-entered at any point.

corozo (kə'rəʊzəʊ) NOUN, *plural* **-zos.** a tropical American palm, *Corozo oleifera,* whose seeds yield a useful oil.
▷HISTORY C18: via Spanish from an Indian name

corp. ABBREVIATION FOR: 1 corporation. 2 corporal.

corpora ('kɔːpərə) NOUN the plural of **corpus.**

corporal[1] ('kɔːpərəl, -prəl) ADJECTIVE 1 of or relating to the body; bodily. 2 an obsolete word for **corporeal.**
▷HISTORY C14: from Latin *corporālis* of the body, from *corpus* body
▸ ˌcorpo'rality NOUN ▸ 'corporally ADVERB

corporal[2] ('kɔːpərəl, -prəl) NOUN 1 a noncommissioned officer junior to a sergeant in the army, air force, or marines. 2 (in the Royal Navy) a petty officer who assists the master-at-arms.
▷HISTORY C16: from Old French, via Italian, from Latin *caput* head; perhaps also influenced in Old French by *corps* body (of men)
▸ 'corporalˌship NOUN

corporal[3] ('kɔːpərəl, -prəl) *or* **corporale** (ˌkɔːpə'reɪlɪ) NOUN a white linen cloth on which the bread and wine are placed during the Eucharist.
▷HISTORY C14: from Medieval Latin *corporāle pallium* eucharistic altar cloth, from Latin *corporālis* belonging to the body, from *corpus* body (of Christ)

Corporal of Horse NOUN a noncommissioned rank in the British Household Cavalry above that of sergeant and below that of staff sergeant.

corporal punishment NOUN punishment of a physical nature, such as caning, flogging, or beating.

corporate ('kɔːpərɪt, -prɪt) ADJECTIVE 1 forming a corporation; incorporated. 2 of or belonging to a corporation or corporations: *corporate finance.* 3 of or belonging to a united group; joint.
▷HISTORY C15: from Latin *corporātus* made into a body, from *corporāre,* from *corpus* body
▸ 'corporately ADVERB

corporate anorexia NOUN a malaise of a business organization resulting from making too many creative people redundant in a cost-cutting exercise.

corporate culture NOUN the distinctive ethos of an organization that influences the level of formality, loyalty, and general behaviour of its employees.

corporate identity *or* **image** NOUN the way an organization is presented to or perceived by its members and the public.

corporate raider NOUN *Finance* a person or organization that acquires a substantial holding of the shares of a company in order to take it over or to force its management to act in a desired way.

corporate restructuring NOUN a change in the business strategy of an organization resulting in diversification, closing parts of the business, etc., to increase its long-term profitability.

corporate venturing NOUN *Finance* the provision of venture capital by one company for another in order to obtain information about the company requiring capital or as a step towards acquiring it.

corporate village NOUN an area close to the workplace where many everyday facilities are provided for a company's workers.

corporation (ˌkɔːpə'reɪʃən) NOUN 1 a group of people authorized by law to act as a legal personality and having its own powers, duties, and liabilities. 2 Also called: **municipal corporation.** the municipal authorities of a city or town. 3 a group of people acting as one body. 4 See **public corporation.** 5 *Informal* a large paunch or belly.

corporation tax NOUN a British tax on the profits of a company or other incorporated body.

corporatism ('kɔːpərɪtɪzəm, -prɪtɪzəm) NOUN the organization of a state on a corporative basis.
▸ 'corporatist NOUN, ADJECTIVE

corporative ('kɔːpərətɪv, -prətɪv) ADJECTIVE 1 of or characteristic of a corporation. 2 (of a state) organized into and governed by corporations of individuals involved in any given profession, industry, etc.

corporatize *or* **corporatise** ('kɔːpərətaɪz, -prə-) VERB 1 (*tr*) to convert (a government-controlled industry or enterprise) into an independent company. 2 (*intr*) to be influenced by or take on the features of a large commercial business, esp in being bureaucratic and uncaring.

corporator ('kɔːpəˌreɪtə) NOUN a member of a corporation.

corporeal (kɔː'pɔːrɪəl) ADJECTIVE 1 of the nature

of the physical body; not spiritual. [2] of a material nature; physical.
▷**HISTORY** C17: from Latin *corporeus,* from *corpus* body
▸**cor,pore'ality** *or* **cor'porealness** NOUN ▸**cor'poreally** ADVERB

corporeity (ˌkɔːpəˈriːɪtɪ) NOUN bodily or material nature or substance; physical existence; corporeality.

corposant (ˈkɔːpəˌzænt) NOUN another name for **Saint Elmo's fire.**
▷**HISTORY** C17: from Portuguese *corpo-santo,* literally: holy body, from Latin *corpus sanctum*

corps (kɔː) NOUN, *plural* **corps** (kɔːz). [1] a military formation that comprises two or more divisions and additional support arms. [2] a military body with a specific function: *intelligence corps; medical corps.* [3] a body of people associated together: *the diplomatic corps.*
▷**HISTORY** C18: from French, from Latin *corpus* body

corps de ballet (ˈkɔː də ˈbæleɪ; *French* kɔr də balɛ) NOUN the members of a ballet company who dance together in a group.

corps diplomatique (ˌdɪpləʊmæˈtiːk) NOUN another name for **diplomatic corps.** Abbreviation: **CD.**

corpse (kɔːps) NOUN [1] a dead body, esp of a human being; cadaver. ◆ VERB [2] *Theatre, slang* to laugh or cause to laugh involuntarily or inopportunely while on stage.
▷**HISTORY** C14: from Old French *corps* body, from Latin *corpus* body

corpsman (ˈkɔːmən) NOUN, *plural* **-men.** *US military* a medical orderly or stretcher-bearer.

corpulent (ˈkɔːpjʊlənt) ADJECTIVE physically bulky; fat.
▷**HISTORY** C14: from Latin *corpulentus* fleshy
▸**'corpulence** *or* **'corpulency** NOUN ▸**'corpulently** ADVERB

cor pulmonale (kɔː pʌlməˈnɑːlɪ) NOUN pulmonary heart disease: a serious heart condition in which there is enlargement and failure of the right ventricle resulting from lung disease.
▷**HISTORY** New Latin

corpus (ˈkɔːpəs) NOUN, *plural* **-pora** (-pərə). [1] a collection or body of writings, esp by a single author or on a specific topic: *the corpus of Dickens' works.* [2] the main body, section, or substance of something. [3] *Anatomy* **a** any distinct mass or body. **b** the main part of an organ or structure. [4] the inner layer or layers of cells of the meristem at a shoot tip, which produces the vascular tissue and pith. ◆ Compare **tunica** (sense 2). [5] *Linguistics* a body of data, esp the finite collection of grammatical sentences of a language that a linguistic theory seeks to describe by means of an algorithm. [6] a capital or principal sum, as contrasted with a derived income. [7] *Obsolete* a human or animal body, esp a dead one.
▷**HISTORY** C14: from Latin: body

corpus callosum (kəˈləʊsəm) NOUN, *plural* **corpora callosa** (kəˈləʊsə). the band of white fibres that connects the cerebral hemispheres in mammals.
▷**HISTORY** New Latin, literally: callous body

corpus cavernosum (ˌkævəˈnəʊsəm) NOUN, *plural* **corpora cavernosa.** either of two masses of erectile tissue in the penis of mammals.
▷**HISTORY** New Latin, literally: cavernous body

Corpus Christi[1] (ˈkrɪstɪ) NOUN *Chiefly RC Church* a festival in honour of the Eucharist, observed on the Thursday after Trinity Sunday.
▷**HISTORY** C14: from Latin: body of Christ

Corpus Christi[2] (ˈkrɪstɪ) NOUN a port in S Texas, on **Corpus Christi Bay,** an inlet of the Gulf of Mexico. Pop.: 277 454 (2000).

corpuscle (ˈkɔːpʌsᵊl) NOUN [1] any cell or similar minute body that is suspended in a fluid, esp any of the **red blood corpuscles** (see **erythrocyte**) or **white blood corpuscles** (see **leucocyte**). [2] *Anatomy* the encapsulated ending of a sensory nerve. [3] *Physics* a discrete particle such as an electron, photon, ion, or atom. [4] Also called: **corpuscule** (kɔːˈpʌskjuːl). any minute particle.
▷**HISTORY** C17: from Latin *corpusculum* a little body, from *corpus* body
▸**corpuscular** (kɔːˈpʌskjʊlə) ADJECTIVE

corpuscular theory NOUN the theory, originally proposed by Newton, and revived with the development of the quantum theory, that light consists of a stream of particles. See **photon.** Compare **wave theory.**

corpus delicti (dɪˈlɪktaɪ) NOUN *Law* the body of facts that constitute an offence.
▷**HISTORY** New Latin, literally: the body of the crime

corpus juris (ˈdʒʊərɪs) NOUN a body of law, esp the laws of a nation or state.
▷**HISTORY** from Late Latin, literally: a body of law

Corpus Juris Canonici (kəˈnɒnɪˌsaɪ) NOUN *RC Church* the official compilation of canon law published by authority of Gregory XIII in 1582, superseded by the Codex Juris Canonici in 1918. See also **Clementines, Decretals, Decretum, Extravagantes, Sext.**
▷**HISTORY** Medieval Latin, literally: body of canon law

Corpus Juris Civilis (sɪˈvaɪlɪs) NOUN *Law* the body of Roman or civil law consolidated by Justinian in the 6th century A.D. It consists of four parts, the Institutes, Digest, Code, and Novels.
▷**HISTORY** New Latin, literally: body of civil law

corpus luteum (ˈluːtɪəm) NOUN, *plural* **corpora lutea** (ˈluːtɪə). a yellow glandular mass of tissue that forms in a Graafian follicle following release of an ovum. It secretes progesterone, a hormone necessary to maintain pregnancy.
▷**HISTORY** New Latin, literally: yellow body

corpus luteum hormone NOUN another name for **progesterone.**

corpus spongiosum (ˌspʌndʒɪˈəʊsəm) NOUN a mass of tissue that, with the corpora cavernosa, forms the erectile tissue of the penis of mammals.
▷**HISTORY** New Latin, literally: spongy body

corpus striatum (straɪˈeɪtəm) NOUN, *plural* **corpora striata** (straɪˈeɪtə). a striped mass of white and grey matter situated in front of the thalamus in each cerebral hemisphere.
▷**HISTORY** New Latin, literally: striated body

corpus vile *Latin* (ˈkɔːpəs ˈvaɪlɪ) NOUN, *plural* ***corpora vilia*** (ˈkɔːpərə ˈvɪlɪə). a person or thing fit only to be the object of an experiment.
▷**HISTORY** literally: worthless body

corrade (kɒˈreɪd) VERB (of rivers, streams, etc.) to erode (land) by the abrasive action of rock particles.
▷**HISTORY** C17: from Latin *corrādere* to scrape together, from *rādere* to scrape

corral (kɒˈrɑːl) NOUN [1] *Chiefly US and Canadian* an enclosure for confining cattle or horses. [2] *Chiefly US* (formerly) a defensive enclosure formed by a ring of covered wagons. ◆ VERB **-rals, -ralling, -ralled.** (*tr*) *US and Canadian* [3] to drive into and confine in or as in a corral. [4] *Informal* to capture.
▷**HISTORY** C16: from Spanish, from Vulgar Latin *currāle* (unattested) area for vehicles, from Latin *currus* wagon, from *currere* to run

corrasion (kəˈreɪʒən) NOUN erosion of a rock surface by rock fragments transported over it by water, wind, or ice. Compare **abrasion** (sense 3), **attrition** (sense 4).
▸**corrasive** (kəˈreɪsɪv) ADJECTIVE

correa (ˈkɒrɪə, kəˈriːə) NOUN an Australian evergreen shrub of the genus *Correa,* with large showy tubular flowers.
▷**HISTORY** C19: after Jose Francesco *Correa* da Serra (1750–1823), Portuguese botanist

correct (kəˈrɛkt) VERB (*tr*) [1] to make free from errors. [2] to indicate the errors in. [3] to rebuke or punish in order to set right or improve: *to correct a child; to stand corrected.* [4] to counteract or rectify (a malfunction, ailment, etc.): *these glasses will correct your sight.* [5] to adjust or make conform, esp to a standard. ◆ ADJECTIVE [6] free from error; true; accurate: *the correct version.* [7] in conformity with accepted standards: *correct behaviour.*
▷**HISTORY** C14: from Latin *corrigere* to make straight, put in order, from *com-* (intensive) + *regere* to rule
▸**cor'rectable** *or* **cor'rectible** ADJECTIVE ▸**cor'rectly** ADVERB ▸**cor'rectness** NOUN ▸**cor'rector** NOUN

correction (kəˈrɛkʃən) NOUN [1] the act or process of correcting. [2] something offered or substituted for an error; an improvement. [3] the act or process of punishing; reproof. [4] a number or quantity added to or subtracted from a scientific or mathematical calculation or observation to increase its accuracy.

correctional (kəˈrɛkʃənəl) ADJECTIVE *Chiefly US* of or relating to the punishment and rehabilitation of criminals: *a correctional facility.*

correctitude (kəˈrɛktɪˌtjuːd) NOUN the quality of correctness, esp conscious correctness in behaviour.

corrective (kəˈrɛktɪv) ADJECTIVE [1] tending or intended to correct. ◆ NOUN [2] something that tends or is intended to correct.
▸**cor'rectively** ADVERB

Corregidor (kəˈrɛgɪˌdɔː) NOUN an island at the entrance to Manila Bay, in the Philippines: site of the defeat of American forces by the Japanese (1942) in World War II.

correlate (ˈkɒrɪˌleɪt) VERB [1] to place or be placed in a mutual, complementary, or reciprocal relationship. [2] (*tr*) to establish or show a correlation. ◆ ADJECTIVE [3] having a mutual, complementary, or reciprocal relationship. ◆ NOUN [4] either of two things mutually or reciprocally related.
▸**'corre,latable** ADJECTIVE

correlation (ˌkɒrɪˈleɪʃən) NOUN [1] a mutual or reciprocal relationship between two or more things. [2] the act or process of correlating or the state of being correlated. [3] *Statistics* the extent of correspondence between the ordering of two variables. Correlation is positive or direct when two variables move in the same direction and negative or inverse when they move in opposite directions.
▷**HISTORY** C16: from Medieval Latin *correlātiō,* from *com-* together + *relātiō,* RELATION
▸**,corre'lational** ADJECTIVE

correlation coefficient NOUN *Statistics* a statistic measuring the degree of correlation between two variables as by dividing their covariance by the square root of the product of their variances. The closer the correlation coefficient is to 1 or –1 the greater the correlation; if it is random, the coefficient is zero. See also **Pearson's correlation coefficient, Spearman's rank-order coefficient.**

correlative (kɒˈrɛlətɪv) ADJECTIVE [1] in mutual, complementary, or reciprocal relationship; corresponding. [2] denoting words, usually conjunctions, occurring together though not adjacently in certain grammatical constructions, as for example *neither* and *nor* in such sentences as *he neither ate nor drank.* ◆ NOUN [3] either of two things that are correlative. [4] a correlative word.
▸**cor'relatively** ADVERB ▸**cor'relativeness** *or* **cor,rela'tivity** NOUN

correspond (ˌkɒrɪˈspɒnd) VERB (*intr*) [1] (usually foll by *with* or *to*) to conform, be in agreement, or be consistent or compatible (with); tally (with). [2] (usually foll by *to*) to be similar or analogous in character or function. [3] (usually foll by *with*) to communicate by letter.
▷**HISTORY** C16: from Medieval Latin *corrēspondēre,* from Latin *respondēre* to RESPOND
▸**,corre'spondingly** ADVERB

correspondence (ˌkɒrɪˈspɒndəns) NOUN [1] the act or condition of agreeing or corresponding. [2] similarity or analogy. [3] agreement or conformity. [4] **a** communication by the exchange of letters. **b** the letters so exchanged.

correspondence column NOUN a section of a newspaper or magazine in which are printed readers' letters to the editor.

correspondence school NOUN an educational institution that offers tuition (**correspondence courses**) by post.

correspondent (ˌkɒrɪˈspɒndənt) NOUN [1] a person who communicates by letter or by letters. [2] a person employed by a newspaper, etc., to report on a special subject or to send reports from a foreign country. [3] a person or firm that has regular business relations with another, esp one in a different part of the country or abroad. [4] something that corresponds to another. ◆ ADJECTIVE [5] similar or analogous.

Corrèze (*French* kɔrɛz) NOUN a department of central France, in Limousin region. Capital: Tulle. Pop.: 232 576 (1999). Area: 5888 sq. km (2296 sq. miles).

corrida (koˈrriða) NOUN the Spanish word for **bullfight.**
▷**HISTORY** Spanish, from the phrase *corrida de toros,*

literally: a running of bulls, from *correr* to run, from Latin *currere*

corridor (ˈkɒrɪˌdɔː) NOUN [1] a hallway or passage connecting parts of a building. [2] a strip of land or airspace along the route of a road or river: *the M1 corridor.* [3] a strip of land or airspace that affords access, either from a landlocked country to the sea (such as the **Polish corridor**, 1919-39, which divided Germany) or from a state to an exclave (such as the **Berlin corridor**, 1945–90, which passed through the former East Germany). [4] a passageway connecting the compartments of a railway coach. [5] **corridors of power.** the higher echelons of government, the Civil Service, etc., considered as the location of power and influence. [6] a flight path that affords safe access for intruding aircraft. [7] the path that a spacecraft must follow when re-entering the atmosphere, above which lift is insufficient and below which heating effects are excessive.
▷HISTORY C16: from Old French, from Old Italian *corridore,* literally: place for running, from *correre* to run, from Latin *currere*

corrie (ˈkɒrɪ) NOUN *Geology* another name for **cirque** (sense 1).
▷HISTORY C18: from Gaelic *coire* cauldron, kettle

Corriedale (ˈkɒrɪˌdeɪl) NOUN a breed of sheep reared for both wool and meat, originally developed in New Zealand and Australia.

corrie-fisted (ˌkɒrɪˈfɪstɪd) ADJECTIVE *Scot dialect* left-handed.
▷HISTORY C20: from earlier *car, ker* left hand or side, from Gaelic *cearr* left or wrong hand

Corrientes (*Spanish* koˈrrjentes) NOUN a port in NE Argentina, on the Paraná River. Pop.: 325 628 (1999 est.).

corrigendum (ˌkɒrɪˈdʒɛndəm) NOUN, *plural* **-da** (-də). [1] an error to be corrected. [2] (*sometimes plural*) Also called: **erratum.** a slip of paper inserted into a book after printing, listing errors and corrections.
▷HISTORY C19: from Latin: that which is to be corrected, from *corrigere* to CORRECT

corrigible (ˈkɒrɪdʒɪbəl) ADJECTIVE [1] capable of being corrected. [2] submissive or submitting to correction.
▷HISTORY C15: from Old French, from Medieval Latin *corrigibilis,* from Latin *corrigere* to set right, CORRECT
▸**ˌcorrigiˈbility** NOUN ▸**ˈcorrigibly** ADVERB

corrival (kəˈraɪvəl) NOUN, VERB a rare word for **rival.**
▷HISTORY C16: from Old French, from Late Latin *corrīvālis,* from Latin *com-* together, mutually + *rīvālis* RIVAL
▸**corˈrivalry** NOUN

corroborant (kəˈrɒbərənt) ADJECTIVE *Archaic* [1] serving to corroborate. [2] strengthening.

corroborate VERB (kəˈrɒbəˌreɪt) [1] (*tr*) to confirm or support (facts, opinions, etc.), esp by providing fresh evidence: *the witness corroborated the accused's statement.* ◆ ADJECTIVE (kəˈrɒbərɪt) *Archaic* [2] serving to corroborate a fact, an opinion, etc. [3] (of a fact) corroborated.
▷HISTORY C16: from Latin *corrōborāre* to invigorate, from *rōborāre* to make strong, from *rōbur* strength, literally: oak
▸**corˌroboˈration** NOUN ▸**corroborative** (kəˈrɒbərətɪv) *or* **corˈroboratory** ADJECTIVE ▸**corˈroboratively** ADVERB ▸**corˈroboˌrator** NOUN

corroboree (kəˈrɒbərɪ) NOUN *Austral* [1] a native assembly of sacred, festive, or warlike character. [2] *Informal* any noisy gathering.
▷HISTORY C19: from a native Australian language

corrode (kəˈrəʊd) VERB [1] to eat away or be eaten away, esp by chemical action as in the oxidation or rusting of a metal. [2] (*tr*) to destroy gradually; consume: *his jealousy corroded his happiness.*
▷HISTORY C14: from Latin *corrōdere* to gnaw to pieces, from *rōdere* to gnaw; see RODENT, RAT
▸**corˈrodant** *or* **corˈrodent** NOUN ▸**corˈroder** NOUN ▸**corˈrodible** ADJECTIVE ▸**corˌrodiˈbility** NOUN

corrody (ˈkɒrədɪ) NOUN, *plural* **-dies.** a variant spelling of **corody.**

corrosion (kəˈrəʊʒən) NOUN [1] a process in which a solid, esp a metal, is eaten away and changed by a chemical action, as in the oxidation of iron in the presence of water by an electrolytic process. [2] slow deterioration by being eaten or worn away. [3] the condition produced by or the product of corrosion.

corrosive (kəˈrəʊsɪv) ADJECTIVE [1] (esp of acids or alkalis) capable of destroying solid materials. [2] tending to eat away or consume. [3] cutting; sarcastic: *a corrosive remark.* ◆ NOUN [4] a corrosive substance, such as a strong acid or alkali.
▸**corˈrosively** ADVERB ▸**corˈrosiveness** NOUN

corrosive sublimate NOUN another name for **mercuric chloride.**

corrugate VERB (ˈkɒrʊˌgeɪt) [1] (*usually tr*) to fold or be folded into alternate furrows and ridges. ◆ ADJECTIVE (ˈkɒrʊgɪt, -ˌgeɪt) [2] folded into furrows and ridges; wrinkled.
▷HISTORY C18: from Latin *corrūgāre,* from *rūga* a wrinkle
▸**ˌcorruˈgation** NOUN

corrugated iron NOUN a thin structural sheet made of iron or steel, formed with alternating ridges and troughs.

corrugated paper NOUN a packaging material made from layers of heavy paper, the top layer of which is grooved and ridged.

corrugator (ˈkɒrʊˌgeɪtə) NOUN a muscle whose contraction causes wrinkling of the brow.

corrupt (kəˈrʌpt) ADJECTIVE [1] lacking in integrity; open to or involving bribery or other dishonest practices: *a corrupt official; corrupt practices in an election.* [2] morally depraved. [3] putrid or rotten. [4] contaminated; unclean. [5] (of a text or manuscript) made meaningless or different in meaning from the original by scribal errors or alterations. [6] (of computer programs or data) containing errors. ◆ VERB [7] to become or cause to become dishonest or disloyal. [8] to debase or become debased morally; deprave. [9] (*tr*) to infect or contaminate; taint. [10] (*tr*) to cause to become rotten. [11] (*tr*) to alter (a text, manuscript, etc.) from the original. [12] (*tr*) *Computing* to introduce errors into (data or a program).
▷HISTORY C14: from Latin *corruptus* spoiled, from *corrumpere* to ruin, literally: break to pieces, from *rumpere* to break
▸**corˈrupter** *or* **corˈruptor** NOUN ▸**corˈruptive** ADJECTIVE ▸**corˈruptively** ADVERB ▸**corˈruptly** ADVERB ▸**corˈruptness** NOUN

corruptible (kəˈrʌptəbəl) ADJECTIVE susceptible to corruption; capable of being corrupted.
▸**corˌruptiˈbility** *or* **corˈruptibleness** NOUN ▸**corˈruptibly** ADVERB

corruption (kəˈrʌpʃən) NOUN [1] the act of corrupting or state of being corrupt. [2] moral perversion; depravity. [3] dishonesty, esp bribery. [4] putrefaction or decay. [5] alteration, as of a manuscript. [6] an altered form of a word.
▸**corˈruptionist** NOUN

corsac (ˈkɔːsæk) NOUN a fox, *Vulpes corsac,* of central Asia.
▷HISTORY C19: from a Turkic language

corsage (kɔːˈsɑːʒ) NOUN [1] a flower or small bunch of flowers worn pinned to the lapel, bosom, etc., or sometimes carried by women. [2] the bodice of a dress.
▷HISTORY C15: from Old French, from *cors* body, from Latin *corpus*

corsair (ˈkɔːsɛə) NOUN [1] a pirate. [2] a privateer, esp of the Barbary Coast.
▷HISTORY C15: from Old French *corsaire* pirate, from Medieval Latin *cursārius,* from Latin *cursus* a running, COURSE

corse (kɔːs) NOUN an archaic word for **corpse.**

Corse (kɔrs) NOUN the French name for **Corsica.**

corselet (ˈkɔːslɪt) NOUN [1] Also spelt: **corslet.** a piece of armour for the top part of the body. [2] a one-piece foundation garment, usually combining a brassiere and a corset.
▷HISTORY C15: from Old French, from *cors* bodice of a garment, from Latin *corpus* body

corset (ˈkɔːsɪt) NOUN [1] **a** a stiffened, elasticated, or laced foundation garment, worn esp by women, that usually extends from below the chest to the hips, providing support for the spine and stomach and shaping the figure. **b** a similar garment worn because of injury, weakness, etc., by either sex. [2] *Informal* a restriction or limitation, esp government control of bank lending. [3] a stiffened outer bodice worn by either sex, esp in the 16th century. ◆ VERB [4] (*tr*) to dress or enclose in, or as in, a corset.
▷HISTORY C14: from Old French, literally: a little bodice; see CORSELET

corsetier (ˌkɔːsɪˈtɪə) NOUN a man who makes and fits corsets.

corsetière (ˌkɔːsɛtɪˈɛə, kɔːˌsɛt-) NOUN a woman who makes and fits corsets.

corsetry (ˈkɔːsɪtrɪ) NOUN [1] the making of or dealing in corsets. [2] corsets considered collectively.

corsey (ˈkɔːsɪ) NOUN *Northern English dialect* a pavement or pathway.

Corsica (ˈkɔːsɪkə) NOUN an island in the Mediterranean, west of N Italy: forms, with 43 islets, a region of France; mountainous; settled by Greeks in about 560 B.C.; sold by Genoa to France in 1768. Capital: Ajaccio. Pop.: 260 196 (1999). Area: 8682 sq. km (3367 sq. miles). French name: **Corse.**

Corsican (ˈkɔːsɪkən) ADJECTIVE [1] of or relating to Corsica or its inhabitants. ◆ NOUN [2] a native or inhabitant of Corsica.

CORSO (ˈkɔːsəʊ) NOUN (in New Zealand) ACRONYM FOR Council of Organizations for Relief Services Overseas.

cortege *or* **cortège** (kɔːˈteɪʒ) NOUN [1] a formal procession, esp a funeral procession. [2] a train of attendants; retinue.
▷HISTORY C17: from French, from Italian *corteggio,* from *corteggiare* to attend, from *corte* COURT

Cortes (ˈkɔːtɛz; *Spanish* ˈkortes) NOUN the national assembly of Spain and (until 1910) Portugal.
▷HISTORY C17: from Spanish, literally: courts, plural of *corte* court, from Latin *cohors* COHORT

cortex (ˈkɔːtɛks) NOUN, *plural* **-tices** (-tɪˌsiːz). [1] *Anatomy* the outer layer of any organ or part, such as the grey matter in the brain that covers the cerebrum (**cerebral cortex**) or the outer part of the kidney (**renal cortex**). [2] *Botany* **a** the unspecialized tissue in plant stems and roots between the vascular bundles and the epidermis. **b** the outer layer of a part such as the bark of a stem.
▷HISTORY C17: from Latin: bark, outer layer
▸**cortical** (ˈkɔːtɪkəl) ADJECTIVE ▸**ˈcortically** ADVERB

corticate (ˈkɔːtɪkɪt, -ˌkeɪt) *or* **corticated** ADJECTIVE (of plants, seeds, etc.) having a bark, husk, or rind.
▷HISTORY C19: from Latin *corticātus* covered with bark
▸**ˌcortiˈcation** NOUN

cortico- *or before a vowel* **cortic-** COMBINING FORM indicating the cortex: *corticotrophin.*

corticolous (kɔːˈtɪkələs) ADJECTIVE *Biology* living or growing on the surface of bark.

corticosteroid (ˌkɔːtɪkəʊˈstɪərɔɪd) *or* **corticoid** NOUN [1] any steroid hormone produced by the adrenal cortex that affects carbohydrate, protein, and electrolyte metabolism, gonad function, and immune response. [2] any similar synthetic substance, used in treating inflammatory and allergic diseases. ◆ See also **glucocorticoid, mineralocorticoid.**

corticosterone (ˌkɔːtɪˈkɒstəˌrəʊn) NOUN a glucocorticoid hormone secreted by the adrenal cortex. Formula: $C_{21}H_{30}O_4$. See also **corticosteroid.**
▷HISTORY C20: from CORTICO- + STER(OL) + -ONE

corticotrophic (ˌkɔːtɪkəʊˈtrəʊfɪk) *or* **corticotropic** (ˌkɔːtɪkəʊˈtrɒpɪk) ADJECTIVE stimulating the adrenal cortex; adrenocorticotrophic.

corticotrophin (ˌkɔːtɪkəʊˈtrəʊfɪn) NOUN another name for **adrenocorticotrophic hormone.** See **ACTH.**

cortisol (ˈkɔːtɪˌsɒl) NOUN another name for **hydrocortisone.**
▷HISTORY C20: from CORTIS(ONE) + -OL[2]

cortisone (ˈkɔːtɪˌsəʊn, -ˌzəʊn) NOUN a glucocorticoid hormone, the synthetic form of which has been used in treating rheumatoid arthritis, allergic and skin diseases, leukaemia, etc.; 17-hydroxy-11-dehydrocorticosterone. Formula: $C_{21}H_{28}O_5$.
▷HISTORY C20: shortened from CORTICOSTERONE

Cortona (kɔːˈtəʊnə; *Italian* korˈtona) NOUN a town in central Italy, in Tuscany: Roman and Etruscan remains, 15th-century cathedral. Pop.: 22 700 (latest est.).

corundum (kəˈrʌndəm) NOUN a white, grey, blue, green, red, yellow, or brown mineral, found in metamorphosed shales and limestones, in veins, and in some igneous rocks. It is used as an abrasive and as gemstone; the red variety is ruby, the blue is

sapphire. Composition: aluminium oxide. Formula: Al_2O_3. Crystal structure: hexagonal (rhombohedral).
▷**HISTORY** C18: from Tamil *kuruntam;* related to Sanskrit *kuruvinda* ruby

Corunna (kəˈrʌnə) NOUN the English name for **La Coruña.**

coruscate (ˈkɒrəˌskeɪt) VERB (*intr*) to emit flashes of light; sparkle.
▷**HISTORY** C18: from Latin *coruscāre* to flash, vibrate

coruscation (ˌkɒrəˈskeɪʃən) NOUN 1 a gleam or flash of light. 2 a sudden or striking display of brilliance, wit, etc.

corvée (ˈkɔːveɪ) NOUN 1 *European history* a day's unpaid labour owed by a feudal vassal to his lord. 2 the practice or an instance of forced labour.
▷**HISTORY** C14: from Old French, from Late Latin *corrogāta* contribution, from Latin *corrogāre* to collect, from *rogāre* to ask

corves (kɔːvz) NOUN the plural of **corf.**

corvette (kɔːˈvɛt) NOUN a lightly armed escort warship.
▷**HISTORY** C17: from Old French, perhaps from Middle Dutch *corf* basket, small ship, from Latin *corbis* basket

corvine (ˈkɔːvaɪn) ADJECTIVE 1 of, relating to, or resembling a crow. 2 of, relating to, or belonging to the passerine bird family *Corvidae,* which includes the crows, raven, rook, jackdaw, magpies, and jays.
▷**HISTORY** C17: from Latin *corvīnus* raven-like, from *corvus* a raven

Corvus (ˈkɔːvəs) NOUN, *Latin genitive* **Corvi** (ˈkɔːvaɪ). a small quadrilateral-shaped constellation in the S hemisphere, lying between Virgo and Hydra.
▷**HISTORY** Latin: raven

Corybant (ˈkɒrɪˌbænt) NOUN, *plural* **Corybants** *or* **Corybantes** (ˌkɒrɪˈbæntiːz). *Classical myth* a wild attendant of the goddess Cybele.
▷**HISTORY** C14: from Latin *Corybās,* from Greek *Korubas,* probably of Phrygian origin
▸**ˌCoryˈbantian, ˌCoryˈbantic,** *or* **ˌCoryˈbantine** ADJECTIVE

corydalis (kəˈrɪdəlɪs) NOUN any erect or climbing plant of the N temperate genus *Corydalis,* having finely-lobed leaves and spurred yellow or pinkish flowers: family *Fumariaceae.* Also called: **fumitory.**
▷**HISTORY** C19: from New Latin, from Greek *korudallis* variant of *korudos* crested lark, from *korus* helmet, crest; alluding to the appearance of the flowers

Corydon (ˈkɒrɪdᵊn, -ˌdɒn) NOUN (in pastoral literature) a shepherd or rustic.

corymb (ˈkɒrɪmb, -rɪm) NOUN an inflorescence in the form of a flat-topped flower cluster with the oldest flowers at the periphery. This type of raceme occurs in the candytuft.
▷**HISTORY** C18: from Latin *corymbus,* from Greek *korumbos* cluster
▸**ˈcorymbed** ADJECTIVE ▸**coˈrymbose** *or* **coˈrymbous** ADJECTIVE ▸**coˈrymbosely** ADVERB

coryphaeus (ˌkɒrɪˈfiːəs) NOUN, *plural* **-phaei** (-ˈfiːaɪ). 1 (in ancient Greek drama) the leader of the chorus. 2 *Archaic or literary* a leader of a group.
▷**HISTORY** C17: from Latin, from Greek *koruphaios* leader, from *koruphē* summit

coryphée (ˌkɒrɪˈfeɪ) NOUN a leading dancer of a corps de ballet.
▷**HISTORY** C19: from French, from Latin *coryphaeus* CORYPHAEUS

coryza (kəˈraɪzə) NOUN acute inflammation of the mucous membrane of the nose, with discharge of mucus; a head cold.
▷**HISTORY** C17: from Late Latin: catarrh, from Greek *koruza*

cos[1] *or* **cos lettuce** (kɒs) NOUN a variety of lettuce with a long slender head and crisp leaves. Compare **cabbage lettuce.** Usual US and Canadian name: **romaine.**
▷**HISTORY** C17: named after *Kos,* the Aegean island of its origin

cos[2] (kɒz) ABBREVIATION FOR cosine.

Cos (kɒs) NOUN a variant spelling of **Kos.**

COS ABBREVIATION FOR Chief of Staff.

Cosa Nostra (ˈkəʊsə ˈnɒstrə) NOUN the branch of the Mafia that operates in the US.
▷**HISTORY** Italian, literally: our thing

COSAS (ˈkəʊˌzæs) NOUN ACRONYM FOR Congress of South African Students.

COSATU (ˌkəʊˈzɑːtuː) NOUN ACRONYM FOR Congress of South Africa Trade Unions.

cosec (ˈkəʊsɛk) ABBREVIATION FOR cosecant.

cosecant (kəʊˈsiːkənt) NOUN (of an angle) a trigonometric function that in a right-angled triangle is the ratio of the length of the hypotenuse to that of the opposite side; the reciprocal of sine. Abbreviation: **cosec.**

cosech (ˈkəʊsɛtʃ, -sɛk) NOUN hyperbolic cosecant; a hyperbolic function that is the reciprocal of sinh.

coseismal (kəʊˈsaɪzməl) *or* **coseismic** ADJECTIVE 1 of or designating points at which earthquake waves are felt at the same time. 2 (of a line on a map) connecting such points. ◆ NOUN 3 such a line on a map.

Cosenza (*Italian* koˈzɛntsa) NOUN a city in S Italy, in Calabria. Pop.: 104 480 (1990).

cosh[1] (kɒʃ) *Brit* ◆ NOUN 1 a blunt weapon, often made of hard rubber; bludgeon. 2 an attack with such a weapon. ◆ VERB (*tr*) 3 to hit with such a weapon, esp on the head.
▷**HISTORY** C19: from Romany *kosh,* from *koshter* skewer, stick

cosh[2] (kɒʃ, ˈkɒsˈeɪtʃ) NOUN hyperbolic cosine; a hyperbolic function, $\cosh z = \frac{1}{2}(e^z + e^{-z})$, related to cosine by the expression $\cosh iz = \cos z$, where $i = \sqrt{-1}$.
▷**HISTORY** C19: from COS(INE) + H(YPERBOLIC)

cosher (ˈkɒʃə) VERB *Irish* 1 (*tr*) to pamper or coddle. 2 (*intr*) to live or be entertained at the expense of another.

cosignatory (kəʊˈsɪɡnətərɪ, -trɪ) NOUN, *plural* **-ries.** 1 a person, country, etc., that signs a document jointly with others. ◆ ADJECTIVE 2 signing jointly with another or others.

cosine (ˈkəʊˌsaɪn) NOUN (of an angle) a trigonometric function that in a right-angled triangle is the ratio of the length of the adjacent side to that of the hypotenuse; the sine of the complement. Abbreviation: **cos.**
▷**HISTORY** C17: from New Latin *cosinus;* see CO-, SINE[1]

COSLA (ˈkɒzlə) NOUN ACRONYM FOR Convention of Scottish Local Authorities.

cosmetic (kɒzˈmɛtɪk) NOUN 1 any preparation applied to the body, esp the face, with the intention of beautifying it. ◆ ADJECTIVE 2 serving or designed to beautify the body, esp the face. 3 having no other function than to beautify: *cosmetic illustrations in a book.* 4 *Slightly derogatory* designed to cover up a greater flaw or deficiency; superficial: *their resignation is a cosmetic exercise.*
▷**HISTORY** C17: from Greek *kosmētikos,* from *kosmein* to arrange, from *kosmos* order
▸**cosˈmetically** ADVERB ▸**cosˌmetiˈcology** NOUN

cosmetician (ˌkɒzmɪˈtɪʃən) NOUN a person who makes, sells, or applies cosmetics.

cosmetic surgery NOUN surgery performed to improve the appearance, rather than for medical reasons.

cosmic (ˈkɒzmɪk) ADJECTIVE 1 of or relating to the whole universe: *cosmic laws.* 2 occurring or originating in outer space, esp as opposed to the vicinity of the earth, the solar system, or the local galaxy: *cosmic rays.* 3 immeasurably extended in space or time; vast. 4 *Rare* harmonious.
▸**ˈcosmically** ADVERB

cosmic dust NOUN fine particles of solid matter occurring throughout interstellar space and often collecting into clouds of extremely low density. See also **nebula** (sense 1).

cosmic rays PLURAL NOUN radiation consisting of particles, esp protons, of very high energy that reach the earth from outer space. Also called: **cosmic radiation.**

cosmic string NOUN a one-dimensional defect in space-time postulated in certain theories of cosmology to exist in the universe as a consequence of the big bang.

cosmine (ˈkɒzmiːn) *or* **cosmin** NOUN *Zoology* a substance resembling dentine, forming the outer layer of cosmoid scales.
▷**HISTORY** C20: from Greek *kosmos* arrangement + -INE[1]

cosmo- *or before a vowel* **cosm-** COMBINING FORM indicating the world or universe: *cosmology; cosmonaut; cosmography.*
▷**HISTORY** from Greek: COSMOS

cosmodrome (ˈkɒzməˌdrəʊm) NOUN a site, esp one in the former Soviet Union, from which spacecraft are launched.

cosmogony (kɒzˈmɒɡənɪ) NOUN, *plural* **-nies.** 1 the study of the origin and development of the universe or of a particular system in the universe, such as the solar system. 2 a theory of such an origin or evolution.
▷**HISTORY** C17: from Greek *kosmogonia,* from COSMO- + *gonos* creation
▸**cosˈmogonal** ADJECTIVE ▸**cosmogonic** (ˌkɒzməˈɡɒnɪk) *or* **ˌcosmoˈgonical** ADJECTIVE ▸**cosˈmogonist** NOUN

cosmography (kɒzˈmɒɡrəfɪ) NOUN 1 a representation of the world or the universe. 2 the science dealing with the whole order of nature.
▸**cosˈmographer** *or* **cosˈmographist** NOUN ▸**cosmographic** (ˌkɒzməˈɡræfɪk) *or* **ˌcosmoˈgraphical** ADJECTIVE ▸**ˌcosmoˈgraphically** ADVERB

cosmoid (ˈkɒzmɔɪd) ADJECTIVE (of the scales of coelacanths and lungfish) consisting of two inner bony layers and an outer layer of cosmine.
▷**HISTORY** C20: from COSM(INE) + -OID

cosmological argument NOUN *Philosophy* one of the arguments that purport to prove the existence of God from empirical facts about the universe, esp the argument to the existence of a first cause. Compare **ontological argument** (sense 1), **teleological argument.**

cosmological principle NOUN *Astronomy* the theory that the universe is uniform, homogenous, and isotropic, and therefore appears the same from any position.

cosmology (kɒzˈmɒlədʒɪ) NOUN 1 the philosophical study of the origin and nature of the universe. 2 the branch of astronomy concerned with the evolution and structure of the universe. 3 a particular account of the origin or structure of the universe: *Ptolemaic cosmology.*
▸**cosmological** (ˌkɒzməˈlɒdʒɪkᵊl) *or* **ˌcosmoˈlogic** ADJECTIVE ▸**ˌcosmoˈlogically** ADVERB ▸**cosˈmologist** NOUN

cosmonaut (ˈkɒzməˌnɔːt) NOUN an astronaut, esp in the former Soviet Union.
▷**HISTORY** C20: from Russian *kosmonavt,* from COSMO- + Greek *nautēs* sailor; compare ARGONAUT

cosmopolis (kɒzˈmɒpəlɪs) NOUN an international city.
▷**HISTORY** C19: see COSMO-, POLIS[1]

cosmopolitan (ˌkɒzməˈpɒlɪtᵊn) NOUN 1 a person who has lived and travelled in many countries, esp one who is free of national prejudices. ◆ ADJECTIVE 2 having interest in or familiar with many parts of the world. 3 sophisticated or urbane. 4 composed of people or elements from all parts of the world or from many different spheres. 5 (of plants or animals) widely distributed.
▷**HISTORY** C17: from French, ultimately from Greek *kosmopolitēs,* from *kosmo-* COSMO- + *politēs* citizen
▸**ˌcosmoˈpolitanism** NOUN

cosmopolite (kɒzˈmɒpəˌlaɪt) NOUN 1 a less common word for **cosmopolitan** (sense 1). 2 an animal or plant that occurs in most parts of the world.
▸**cosˈmopolitˌism** NOUN

cosmos (ˈkɒzmɒs) NOUN 1 the world or universe considered as an ordered system. 2 any ordered system. 3 harmony; order. 4 (*plural* **-mos** *or* **-moses**) any tropical American plant of the genus *Cosmos,* cultivated as garden plants for their brightly coloured flowers: family *Asteraceae* (composites).
▷**HISTORY** C17: from Greek *kosmos* order, world, universe

Cosmos (ˈkɒzmɒs) NOUN *Astronautics* any of various types of Soviet satellite, including Cosmos 1 (launched 1962) and nearly 2000 subsequent satellites.

Cosmotron (ˈkɒzməˌtrɒn) NOUN a large synchrotron which was used for accelerating protons to high energies (of the order of 1 GeV).
▷**HISTORY** C20: from COSM(IC RAY) + -TRON

coss (kɒs) NOUN another name for **kos.**

Cossack (ˈkɒsæk) NOUN 1 (formerly) any of the free warrior-peasants of chiefly East Slavonic descent who lived in communes, esp in the Ukraine, and served as cavalry under the tsars. ◆

ADJECTIVE [2] of, relating to, or characteristic of the Cossacks: *a Cossack dance*.
▷HISTORY C16: from Russian *kazak* vagabond, of Turkic origin

cossack hat NOUN a warm brimless hat of fur or sheepskin.

cosset ('kɒsɪt) VERB (*tr*) **-sets, -seting, -seted** [1] to pamper; coddle; pet. ◆ NOUN [2] any pet animal, esp a lamb.
▷HISTORY C16: of unknown origin

cossie ('kɒzɪ) NOUN an informal name for a swimming costume.

cost (kɒst) NOUN [1] the price paid or required for acquiring, producing, or maintaining something, usually measured in money, time, or energy; expense or expenditure; outlay. [2] suffering or sacrifice; loss; penalty: *count the cost to your health; I know to my cost*. [3] **a** the amount paid for a commodity by its seller: *to sell at cost*. **b** (*as modifier*): *the cost price*. [4] (*plural*) *Law* the expenses of judicial proceedings. [5] **at any cost** *or* **at all costs.** regardless of cost or sacrifice involved. [6] **at the cost of.** at the expense of losing. ◆ VERB **costs, costing, cost.** [7] (*tr*) to be obtained or obtainable in exchange for (money or something equivalent); be priced at: *the ride cost one pound*. [8] to cause or require the expenditure, loss, or sacrifice (of): *the accident cost him dearly*. [9] to estimate the cost of (a product, process, etc.) for the purposes of pricing, budgeting, control, etc.
▷HISTORY C13: from Old French (noun), from *coster* to cost, from Latin *constāre* to stand at, cost, from *stāre* to stand
▸'**costless** ADJECTIVE

costa ('kɒstə) NOUN, *plural* **-tae** (-ti:). [1] the technical name for **rib**[1] (sense 1). [2] a riblike part, such as the midrib of a plant leaf.
▷HISTORY C19: from Latin: rib, side, wall
▸'**costal** ADJECTIVE

Costa Brava ('kɒstə 'brɑ:və) NOUN a coastal region of NE Spain along the Mediterranean, extending from Barcelona to the French border: many resorts.

cost accounting NOUN the recording and controlling of all the expenditures of an enterprise in order to facilitate control of separate activities. Also called: **management accounting.**
▸**cost accountant** NOUN

co-star NOUN [1] an actor who shares star billing with another. ◆ VERB **-stars, -starring, -starred.** [2] (*intr*; often foll by *with*) to share star billing (with another actor). [3] (*tr*) to present as sharing top billing: *the film co-starred Mae West and W. C. Fields*.

costard ('kʌstəd) NOUN [1] an English variety of apple tree. [2] the large ribbed apple of this tree. [3] *Archaic, humorous* a slang word for **head.**
▷HISTORY C14: from Anglo-Norman, from Old French *coste* rib

Costa Rica ('kɒstə 'ri:kə) NOUN a republic in Central America: gained independence from Spain in 1821; mostly mountainous and volcanic, with extensive forests. Official language: Spanish. Official religion: Roman Catholic. Currency: colón. Capital: San José. Pop.: 3 936 000 (2001 est.). Area: 50 900 sq. km (19 652 sq. miles).

Costa Rican ('kɒstə 'ri:kən) ADJECTIVE [1] of or relating to Costa Rica or its inhabitants. ◆ NOUN [2] a native or inhabitant of Costa Rica.

costate ('kɒsteɪt) ADJECTIVE [1] *Anatomy* having ribs. [2] (of leaves) having veins or ridges, esp parallel ones.
▷HISTORY C19: from Late Latin *costātus*, from Latin *costa* rib

cost-benefit ADJECTIVE denoting or relating to a method of assessing a project that takes into account its costs and its benefits to society as well as the revenue it generates: *a cost-benefit analysis; the project was assessed on a cost-benefit basis*.

cost centre NOUN a unit, such as a department of a company, to which costs may be allocated for cost accounting purposes.

cost-effective ADJECTIVE providing adequate financial return in relation to outlay.
▸**cost-effectiveness** NOUN

Costermansville ('kɒstəmənz,vɪl) NOUN the former name (until 1966) of **Bukavu.**

costermonger ('kɒstə,mʌŋgə) *or* **coster** NOUN *Brit rare* a person who sells fruit, vegetables, etc., from a barrow.
▷HISTORY C16: *coster-*, from COSTARD + MONGER

costive ('kɒstɪv) ADJECTIVE [1] having constipation; constipated. [2] sluggish. [3] niggardly.
▷HISTORY C14: from Old French *costivé*, from Latin *constipātus*; see CONSTIPATE
▸'**costively** ADVERB ▸'**costiveness** NOUN

costly ('kɒstlɪ) ADJECTIVE **-lier, -liest.** [1] of great price or value; expensive. [2] entailing great loss or sacrifice: *a costly victory*. [3] splendid; lavish.
▸'**costliness** NOUN

costmary ('kɒst,mɛərɪ) NOUN, *plural* **-maries.** a herbaceous plant, *Chrysanthemum balsamita*, native to Asia. Its fragrant leaves were used as a seasoning and to flavour ale: family *Asteraceae* (composites). Also called: **alecost.**
▷HISTORY C15 *costmarie*, from Latin *costum* aromatic plant + *Marie* (the Virgin) Mary

cost of living NOUN [1] **a** the basic cost of the food, clothing, shelter, and fuel necessary to maintain life, esp at a standard regarded as basic or minimal. **b** (*as modifier*): *the cost-of-living index*. [2] the average expenditure of a person or family in a given period.

costotomy (kɒ'stɒtəmɪ) NOUN, *plural* **-mies.** surgical incision into a rib.

cost-plus NOUN **a** a method of establishing a selling price in which an agreed percentage is added to the cost price to cover profit. **b** (*as modifier*): *cost-plus pricing*.

cost-push inflation NOUN See **inflation.**

costrel ('kɒstrəl) NOUN *Obsolete* a flask, usually of earthenware or leather.
▷HISTORY C14: from Old French *costerel*, from *coste* side, rib, from Latin *costa*

cost rent NOUN (in Britain) the rent of a dwelling calculated on the cost of providing and maintaining the property without allowing for a profit.

costume ('kɒstju:m) NOUN [1] a complete style of dressing, including all the clothes, accessories, etc., worn at one time, as in a particular country or period; dress: *national costume*. [2] *Old-fashioned* a woman's suit. [3] a set of clothes, esp unusual or period clothes, worn in a play by an actor or at a fancy dress ball: *a jester's costume*. [4] short for **swimming costume.** ◆ VERB (*tr*) [5] to furnish the costumes for (a show, film, etc.). [6] to dress (someone) in a costume.
▷HISTORY C18: from French, from Italian: dress, habit, CUSTOM

costume jewellery NOUN jewellery that is decorative but has little intrinsic value.

costume piece NOUN any theatrical production, film, television presentation, etc., in which the performers wear the costumes of a former age. Also called: **costume drama.**

costumier (kɒ'stju:mɪə) *or* **costumer** (kɒ'stju:mə) NOUN a person or firm that makes or supplies theatrical or fancy costumes.

cosy *or US* **cozy** ('kəʊzɪ) ADJECTIVE **-sier, -siest** *or US* **-zier, -ziest.** [1] warm and snug. [2] intimate; friendly. [3] convenient, esp for devious purposes: *a cosy deal*. ◆ NOUN, *plural* **-sies** *or US* **-zies.** [4] a cover for keeping things warm: *egg cosy*.
▷HISTORY C18: from Scots, of unknown origin
▸'**cosily** *or US* '**cozily** ADVERB ▸'**cosiness** *or US* '**coziness** NOUN

cosy along VERB **-sies, -sying, -sied.** (*tr, adverb*) to reassure (someone), esp with false assurances.

cosy up *or US* **cozy up** VERB (*intr*, often foll by *to*) *Chiefly US and Canadian* [1] to seek to become intimate or to ingratiate oneself (with someone). [2] to draw close to (somebody or something) for warmth or for affection; snuggle up.

cot[1] (kɒt) NOUN [1] a child's boxlike bed, usually incorporating vertical bars. [2] a collapsible or portable bed. [3] a light bedstead. [4] *Nautical* a hammock-like bed with a stiff frame.
▷HISTORY C17: from Hindi *khāt* bedstead, from Sanskrit *khátvā*, of Dravidian origin; related to Tamil *kattil* bedstead

cot[2] (kɒt) NOUN [1] *Literary or archaic* a small cottage. [2] Also called: **cote. a** a small shelter, esp one for pigeons, sheep, etc. **b** (*in combination*): *dovecot*. [3] another name for **fingerstall.**
▷HISTORY Old English *cot*; related to Old Norse *kot* little hut, Middle Low German *cot*

cot[3] (kɒt) ABBREVIATION FOR cotangent.

cot[4] (kɒt) VERB **cots, cotting, cotted.** *Midland English dialect* to entangle or become entangled.

cotan ('kəʊ,tæn) ABBREVIATION FOR cotangent.

cotangent (kəʊ'tændʒənt) NOUN (of an angle) a trigonometric function that in a right-angled triangle is the ratio of the length of the adjacent side to that of the opposite side; the reciprocal of tangent. Abbreviations: **cot, cotan, ctn.**
▸**cotangential** (,kəʊtæn'dʒɛnʃəl) ADJECTIVE

cot case NOUN *Austral and NZ* [1] a person confined to bed through illness. [2] *Humorous* a person who is incapacitated by drink.

cot death NOUN the unexplained sudden death of an infant during sleep. Technical name: **sudden infant death syndrome.** Also called (US and Canadian): **crib death.**

cote[1] (kəʊt) *or* **cot** NOUN [1] **a** a small shelter for pigeons, sheep, etc. **b** (*in combination*): *dovecote*. [2] *Dialect, chiefly Brit* a small cottage.
▷HISTORY Old English *cote*; related to Low German *Kote*; see COT[2]

cote[2] (kəʊt) VERB (*tr*) *Archaic* to pass by, outstrip, or surpass.
▷HISTORY C16: perhaps from Old French *costoier* to run alongside, from *coste* side; see COAST

Côte d'Azur (*French* kot dazyr) NOUN the Mediterranean coast of France, including the French Riviera: forms an administrative region with Provence.

Côte d'Ivoire (*French* kot divwar) NOUN a republic in West Africa, on the Gulf of Guinea: Portuguese trading for ivory and slaves began in the 16th century; made a French protectorate in 1842 and became independent in 1960; major producer of coffee and cocoa. Official language: French. Religion: Muslim majority, with animist, atheist, and Roman Catholic minorities. Currency: franc. Capital: Yamoussoukro (administrative); Abidjan (legislative). Pop.: 16 393 000 (2001 est.). Area: 319 820 sq. km (123 483 sq. miles). Former name (until 1986): **the Ivory Coast.**

Côte-d'Or (*French* kotdɔr) NOUN a department of E central France, in NE Burgundy. Capital: Dijon. Pop.: 506 755 (1999). Area: 8787 sq. km (3427 sq. miles).

cotemporary (kəʊ'tɛmpərərɪ) ADJECTIVE a variant of **contemporary.**

cotenant (kəʊ'tɛnənt) NOUN a person who holds property jointly or in common with others.
▸**co'tenancy** NOUN

coterie ('kəʊtərɪ) NOUN a small exclusive group of friends or people with common interests; clique.
▷HISTORY C18: from French, from Old French: association of tenants, from *cotier* (unattested) cottager, from Medieval Latin *cotārius* COTTER[2]; see COT[2]

coterminous (kəʊ'tɜ:mɪnəs) *or* **conterminous** ADJECTIVE [1] having a common boundary; bordering; contiguous. [2] coextensive or coincident in range, time, scope, etc.

Côtes-d'Armor (*French* kotdarmɔr) NOUN a department of W France, on the N coast of Brittany. Capital: St Brieuc. Pop.: 542 373 (1999). Area: 6878 sq. km (2656 sq. miles). Former name: **Côtes-du-Nord.**

Côtes-du-Nord (*French* kotdynɔr) NOUN the former name of **Côtes-d'Armor.**

coth (kɒθ) NOUN hyperbolic cotangent; a hyperbolic function that is the ratio of cosh to sinh, being the reciprocal of tanh.
▷HISTORY C20: from COT(ANGENT) + H(YPERBOLIC)

cothurnus (kəʊ'θɜ:nəs) *or* **cothurn** ('kəʊθɜ:n, kəʊ'θɜ:n) NOUN, *plural* **-thurni** (-'θɜ:naɪ) *or* **-thurns.** the buskin worn in ancient Greek tragedy.
▷HISTORY C18: from Latin, from Greek *kothornos*

cotidal (kəʊ'taɪdᵊl) ADJECTIVE (of a line on a tidal chart) joining points at which high tide occurs simultaneously.

cotillion *or* **cotillon** (kə'tɪljən, kəʊ-) NOUN [1] a French formation dance of the 18th century. [2] *US* a quadrille. [3] *US* a complicated dance with frequent changes of partners. [4] *US and Canadian* a

formal ball, esp one at which debutantes are presented.
▷HISTORY C18: from French *cotillon* dance, from Old French: petticoat, from *cote* COAT

cotinga (kə'tɪŋgə) NOUN any tropical American passerine bird of the family *Cotingidae*, such as the umbrella bird and the cock-of-the-rock, having a broad slightly hooked bill. Also called: **chatterer.**

cotoneaster (kə,təʊnɪ'æstə) NOUN any Old World shrub of the rosaceous genus *Cotoneaster:* cultivated for their small ornamental white or pinkish flowers and red or black berries.
▷HISTORY C18: from New Latin, from Latin *cotōneum* QUINCE

Cotonou (,kəʊtə'nu:) NOUN the chief port and official capital of Benin, on the Bight of Benin. Pop.: 750 000 (1994 est.).

Cotopaxi (*Spanish* koto'paksi) NOUN a volcano in central Ecuador, in the Andes: the world's highest active volcano. Height: 5896 m (19 344 ft.).

cotquean ('kɒt,kwi:n) NOUN *Archaic* [1] a coarse woman. [2] a man who does housework.
▷HISTORY C16: see COT[2], QUEAN

cotransport (kəʊ'træns,pɔ:t) NOUN *Biochem* the transport of one solute across a membrane from a region of low concentration of another solute to a region of high concentration of that solute. See **active transport.**

co-trimoxazole (,kəʊtrɪ'mɒksəzəʊl) NOUN an antibiotic consisting of a mixture of trimethoprim and sulfamethoxazole (a sulfa drug): used esp to treat infections of the urinary tract and lungs (as in AIDS).

Cotswold ('kɒts,wəʊld, -wəld) NOUN a breed of sheep with long wool that originated in the Cotswolds. It is believed to be one of the oldest breeds in the world.

Cotswolds ('kɒts,wəʊldz, -wəldz) PLURAL NOUN a range of low hills in SW England, mainly in Gloucestershire: formerly a centre of the wool industry.

cotta ('kɒtə) NOUN *RC Church* a short form of surplice.
▷HISTORY C19: from Italian: tunic, from Medieval Latin; see COAT

cottage ('kɒtɪdʒ) NOUN [1] a small simple house, esp in a rural area. [2] *US and Canadian* a small house in the country or at a resort, used for holiday purposes. [3] *US* one of several housing units, as at a hospital, for accommodating people in groups. [4] *Slang* a public lavatory.
▷HISTORY C14: from COT[2]

cottage cheese NOUN a mild loose soft white cheese made from skimmed milk curds.

cottage country NOUN *Canadian* any lakeside region where many country cottages are located.

cottage flat NOUN *Brit* any of the flats in a two-storey house that is divided into four flats, two on each floor.

cottage hospital NOUN *Brit* a small rural hospital.

cottage industry NOUN an industry in which employees work in their own homes, often using their own equipment.

cottage loaf NOUN *Brit* a loaf consisting of two round pieces, the smaller of which sits on top of the larger.

cottage piano NOUN a small upright piano.

cottage pie NOUN *Brit* another term for **shepherd's pie.**

cottager ('kɒtɪdʒə) NOUN [1] a person who lives in a cottage. [2] a rural labourer. [3] *Chiefly Canadian* a person holidaying in a cottage, esp an owner and seasonal resident of a cottage in a resort area. [4] *History* another name for **cotter**[2].

cottaging ('kɒtɪdʒɪŋ) NOUN *Brit* homosexual activity between men in a public lavatory.
▷HISTORY C20: from COTTAGE (sense 4)

Cottbus (*German* 'kɔtbʊs) NOUN an industrial city in E Germany, in Brandenburg on the Spree River. Pop.: 112 200 (1999 est.).

cotter[1] ('kɒtə) *Machinery* ◆ NOUN [1] any part, such as a pin, wedge, key, etc., that is used to secure two other parts so that relative motion between them is prevented. [2] short for **cotter pin.** ◆ VERB [3] (*tr*) to secure (two parts) with a cotter.
▷HISTORY C14: shortened from *cotterel,* of unknown origin

cotter[2] ('kɒtə) NOUN [1] Also called: **cottier.** *English history* a villein in late Anglo-Saxon and early Norman times occupying a cottage and land in return for labour. [2] Also called: **cottar.** a peasant occupying a cottage and land in the Scottish Highlands under the same tenure as an Irish cottier. ◆ See also **cottier** (sense 2), **cottager** (sense 1).
▷HISTORY C14: from Medieval Latin *cotārius,* from Middle English *cote* COT[2]

cotter pin NOUN *Machinery* [1] a split pin secured, after passing through holes in the parts to be attached, by spreading the ends. [2] a tapered pin threaded at the smaller end and secured by a nut after insertion.

Cottian Alps ('kɒtɪən) PLURAL NOUN a mountain range in SW Europe, between NW Italy and SE France: part of the Alps. Highest peak: Monte Viso, 3841 m (12 600 ft.).

cottid ('kɒtɪd) NOUN any fish of the scorpaenoid family *Cottidae,* typically possessing a large head, tapering body, and spiny fins, including the pogge, sea scorpion, bullhead, father lasher, and cottus.
▷HISTORY from New Latin *Cottidae,* from *cottus,* from Greek *kottos,* the name of an unidentified river fish

cottier ('kɒtɪə) NOUN [1] another name for **cotter**[2] (sense 1). [2] (in Ireland) a peasant farming a smallholding under **cottier tenure** (the holding of not more than half an acre at a rent of not more than five pounds a year). [3] another name for **cottager** (sense 1).
▷HISTORY C14: from Old French *cotier;* see COTE[1], COTERIE

cotton ('kɒtᵊn) NOUN [1] any of various herbaceous plants and shrubs of the malvaceous genus *Gossypium,* such as **sea-island cotton**, cultivated in warm climates for the fibre surrounding the seeds and the oil within the seeds. [2] the soft white downy fibre of these plants: used to manufacture textiles. [3] cotton plants collectively, as a cultivated crop. [4] **a** a cloth or thread made from cotton fibres. **b** (*as modifier*): *a cotton dress.* [5] any substance, such as kapok (**silk cotton**), resembling cotton but obtained from other plants. ◆ See also **cotton on, cotton to.**
▷HISTORY C14: from Old French *coton,* from Arabic dialect *qutun,* from Arabic *qutn*
▸**'cottony** ADJECTIVE

cottonade (,kɒtᵊ'neɪd) NOUN a coarse fabric of cotton or mixed fibres, used for work clothes, etc.
▷HISTORY C19: from French *cotonnade,* from *coton* COTTON + -ADE

cotton belt NOUN a belt of land in the southeastern US that specializes in the production of cotton.

cotton bush NOUN *Austral* any of various downy chenopodiaceous shrubs, esp *Kochia aphylla,* which is used to feed livestock.

cotton cake NOUN cottonseed meal compressed into nuts or cubes of various sizes for feeding to animals.

cotton candy NOUN the US and Canadian name for **candyfloss.**

cotton flannel NOUN a plain-weave or twill-weave fabric with nap on one side only. Also called: **Canton flannel.**

cotton grass NOUN any of various N temperate and arctic grasslike bog plants of the cyperaceous genus *Eriophorum,* whose clusters of long silky hairs resemble cotton tufts. Also called: **bog cotton.**

cottonmouth ('kɒtᵊn,maʊθ) NOUN another name for the **water moccasin.**

cotton on VERB (*intr, adverb;* often foll by *to*) *Informal* [1] to perceive the meaning (of). [2] to make use (of).

cotton picker NOUN [1] a machine for harvesting cotton fibre. [2] a person who picks ripe cotton fibre from the plants.

cotton-picking ADJECTIVE *US and Canadian slang* (intensifier qualifying something undesirable): *you cotton-picking layabout!*

cotton sedge NOUN *Canadian* another name for **cotton grass.**

cottonseed ('kɒtᵊn,si:d) NOUN, *plural* **-seeds** *or* **-seed.** the seed of the cotton plant: a source of oil and fodder.

cottonseed meal NOUN the residue of cottonseed kernels from which oil has been extracted, used as fodder or fertilizer.

cottonseed oil NOUN a yellowish or dark red oil with a nutlike smell, extracted or expelled from cottonseed, used in cooking and in the manufacture of paints, soaps, etc.

cotton stainer NOUN any of various heteropterous insects of the genus *Dysdercus:* serious pests of cotton, piercing and staining the cotton bolls: family *Pyrrhocoridae.*

cottontail ('kɒtᵊn,teɪl) NOUN any of several common rabbits of the genus *Sylvilagus,* such as *S. floridanus* (**eastern cottontail**), of American woodlands.

cotton to VERB (*intr, preposition*) *US and Canadian informal* [1] to become friendly with. [2] to approve of.

cotton waste NOUN refuse cotton yarn, esp when used as a cleaning material.

cottonweed ('kɒtᵊn,wi:d) NOUN [1] a downy perennial plant, *Otanthus maritimus,* of European coastal regions, having small yellow flowers surrounded by large hairy bracts: family *Asteraceae* (composites). [2] any of various similar plants.

cottonwood ('kɒtᵊn,wʊd) NOUN any of several North American poplars, esp *Populus deltoides,* whose seeds are covered with cottony hairs.

cotton wool NOUN [1] Also called: **purified cotton.** *Chiefly Brit* bleached and sterilized cotton from which the gross impurities, such as the seeds and waxy matter, have been removed: used for surgical dressings, tampons, etc. Usual US term: **absorbent cotton.** [2] cotton in the natural state. [3] *Brit informal* **a** a state of pampered comfort and protection. **b** (*as modifier*): *a cotton-wool existence.*

cottony-cushion scale NOUN a small scale insect, *Icerya purchasi,* that is a pest of citrus trees in California: it is controlled by introducing an Australian ladybird, *Rodolia cardinalis,* into affected areas.

cottus ('kɒtəs) NOUN a scorpaenoid fish of the family *Cottidae;* the type genus, having four yellowish knobs on its head. See also **cottid.**

cotyledon (,kɒtɪ'li:dᵊn) NOUN [1] a simple embryonic leaf in seed-bearing plants, which, in some species, forms the first green leaf after germination. [2] a tuft of villi on the mammalian placenta.
▷HISTORY C16: from Latin: a plant, navelwort, from Greek *kotulēdōn,* from *kotulē* cup, hollow
▸**,coty'ledonous** *or* **,coty'ledo,noid** ADJECTIVE
▸**,coty'ledonal** ADJECTIVE ▸**,coty'ledonary** ADJECTIVE

cotyloid ('kɒtɪ,lɔɪd) *or* **cotyloidal** *Anatomy* ◆ ADJECTIVE [1] **a** shaped like a cup. **b** of or relating to the acetabulum. ◆ NOUN [2] a small bone forming part of the acetabular cavity in some mammals.
▷HISTORY C18: from Greek *kotuloeidēs* cup-shaped, from *kotulē* a cup

cotype ('kəʊ,taɪp) NOUN *Biology* an additional type specimen from the same brood as the original type specimen.

coucal ('ku:kæl, -kᵊl) NOUN any ground-living bird of the genus *Centropus,* of Africa, S Asia, and Australia, having long strong legs: family *Cuculidae* (cuckoos).
▷HISTORY C19: from French, perhaps from *couc(ou)* cuckoo + *al(ouette)* lark

couch (kaʊtʃ) NOUN [1] a piece of upholstered furniture, usually having a back and armrests, for seating more than one person. [2] a bed, esp one used in the daytime by the patients of a doctor or a psychoanalyst. [3] a frame upon which barley is malted. [4] a priming layer of paint or varnish, esp in a painting. [5] *Papermaking* **a** a board on which sheets of handmade paper are dried by pressing. **b** a felt blanket onto which sheets of partly dried paper are transferred for further drying. **c** a roll on a papermaking machine from which the wet web of paper on the wire is transferred to the next section. [6] *Archaic* the lair of a wild animal. ◆ VERB [7] (*tr*) to express in a particular style of language: *couched in an archaic style.* [8] (when *tr, usually reflexive or passive*) to lie down or cause to lie down for or as for sleep. [9] (*intr*) *Archaic* to lie in ambush; lurk. [10] (*tr*)

to spread (barley) on a frame for malting. 11 (*intr*) (of decomposing leaves) to lie in a heap or bed. 12 (*tr*) to embroider or depict by couching. 13 (*tr*) to lift (sheets of handmade paper) onto the board on which they will be dried. 14 (*tr*) *Surgery* to remove (a cataract) by downward displacement of the lens of the eye. 15 (*tr*) *Archaic* to lower (a lance) into a horizontal position.
▷HISTORY C14: from Old French *couche* a bed, lair, from *coucher* to lay down, from Latin *collocāre* to arrange, from *locāre* to place; see LOCATE
▸'**coucher** NOUN

couchant ('kaʊtʃənt) ADJECTIVE (*usually postpositive*) *Heraldry* in a lying position: *a lion couchant.*
▷HISTORY C15: from French: lying, from Old French *coucher* to lay down; see COUCH

couchette (kuː'ʃɛt) NOUN a bed in a railway carriage, esp one converted from seats.
▷HISTORY C20: from French, diminutive of *couche* bed

couch grass (kaʊtʃ, kuːtʃ) NOUN a grass, *Agropyron repens,* with a yellowish-white creeping underground stem by which it spreads quickly: a troublesome weed. Sometimes shortened to **couch.** Also called: **scutch grass, twitch grass, quitch grass.**

couching ('kaʊtʃɪŋ) NOUN **a** a method of embroidery in which the thread is caught down at intervals by another thread passed through the material from beneath. **b** a pattern or work done by this method.

couch potato NOUN *Slang* a lazy person whose recreation consists chiefly of watching television and videos.

cou-cou ('kuːkuː, 'kʊkuː) NOUN a preparation of boiled corn meal and okras stirred to a stiff consistency with a **cou-cou stick** eaten in the Caribbean.
▷HISTORY of uncertain origin

coudé (kuː'deɪ) ADJECTIVE (of a reflecting telescope) having plane mirrors positioned to reflect light from the primary mirror along the axis onto a detector.
▷HISTORY French, literally: bent in the shape of an elbow, from *coude* an elbow

cougan ('kuːgən) NOUN *Austral slang* a rowdy person, esp one who drinks large quantities of alcohol.

cougar ('kuːgə) NOUN another name for **puma.**
▷HISTORY C18: from French *couguar,* from Portuguese *cuguardo,* from Tupi *suasuarana,* literally: deerlike, from *suasú* deer + *rana* similar to

cough (kɒf) VERB 1 (*intr*) to expel air or solid matter from the lungs abruptly and explosively through the partially closed vocal chords. 2 (*intr*) to make a sound similar to this. 3 (*tr*) to utter or express with a cough or coughs. 4 (*intr*) *Slang* to confess to a crime. ◆ NOUN 5 an act, instance, or sound of coughing. 6 a condition of the lungs or throat that causes frequent coughing.
▷HISTORY Old English *cohhetten;* related to Middle Dutch *kochen,* Middle High German *kūchen* to wheeze; probably of imitative origin
▸'**cougher** NOUN

cough drop NOUN a lozenge to relieve a cough.

cough mixture NOUN any medicine that relieves coughing.

cough up VERB (*adverb*) 1 *Informal* to surrender (money, information, etc.), esp reluctantly. 2 (*tr*) to bring into the mouth or eject (phlegm, food, etc.) by coughing.

could (kʊd) VERB (takes an infinitive without *to* or an implied infinitive) used as an auxiliary. 1 to make the past tense of **can**[1]. 2 to make the subjunctive mood of **can**[1], esp used in polite requests or in conditional sentences: *could I see you tonight?; she'd telephone if she could.* 3 to indicate suggestion of a course of action: *you could take the car tomorrow if it's raining.* 4 (often foll by *well*) to indicate a possibility: *he could well be a spy.*
▷HISTORY Old English *cūthe;* influenced by WOULD, should; see CAN[1]

couldn't ('kʊdᵊnt) CONTRACTION OF could not.

couldst (kʊdst) VERB *Archaic* the form of **could** used with the pronoun *thou* or its relative form.

coulee ('kuːleɪ, -lɪ) NOUN 1 **a** a flow of molten lava. **b** such lava when solidified. 2 *Western US and Canadian* a dry stream valley, especially a long steep-sided gorge or ravine that once carried melt water from a glacier. 3 a small intermittent stream in such a ravine.
▷HISTORY C19: from Canadian French *coulée* a flow, from French, from *couler* to flow, from Latin *cōlāre* to sift, purify; see COLANDER

coulibiaca (ˌkuːlɪ'bjɑːkə) NOUN a variant spelling of **koulibiaca.**

coulis ('kuːliː) NOUN a thin purée of vegetables, fruit, etc., usually served as a sauce surrounding a dish.
▷HISTORY C20: French, literally: purée

coulisse (kuː'liːs) NOUN 1 Also called: **cullis.** a timber member grooved to take a sliding panel, such as a sluicegate, portcullis, or stage flat. 2 **a** a flat piece of scenery situated in the wings of a theatre; wing flat. **b** a space between wing flats. 3 part of the Paris Bourse where unofficial securities are traded. Compare **parquet** (sense 4).
▷HISTORY C19: from French: groove, from Old French *couleïce* PORTCULLIS

couloir ('kuːlwɑː; *French* kulwar) NOUN a deep gully on a mountain side, esp in the French Alps.
▷HISTORY C19: from French: corridor, from *couler* to pour; see COULEE

coulomb ('kuːlɒm) NOUN the derived SI unit of electric charge; the quantity of electricity transported in one second by a current of 1 ampere. Symbol: C.
▷HISTORY C19: named after Charles Augustin de Coulomb (1736–1806), French physicist

Coulomb field NOUN the electrostatic field around an electrically charged body or particle.

Coulomb's law NOUN the principle that the force of attraction or repulsion between two point electric charges is directly proportional to the product of the charges and inversely proportional to the square of the distance between them. A similar law holds for particles with mass.

coulometer (kuː'lɒmɪtə) *or* **coulombmeter** ('kuːlɒmˌmiːtə) NOUN an electrolytic cell for measuring the magnitude of an electric charge by determining the total amount of decomposition resulting from the passage of the charge through the cell. Also called: **voltameter.**
▷HISTORY C19: from COULOMB + METER[3]
▸**coulometric** (ˌkuːlə'mɛtrɪk) ADJECTIVE ▸**cou'lometry** NOUN

coulter ('kəʊltə) NOUN a blade or sharp-edged disc attached to a plough so that it cuts through the soil vertically in advance of the ploughshare. Also (esp US): **colter.**
▷HISTORY Old English *culter,* from Latin: ploughshare, knife

coumarin *or* **cumarin** ('kuːmərɪn) NOUN a white vanilla-scented crystalline ester, used in perfumes and flavourings and as an anticoagulant. Formula: $C_9H_6O_2$.
▷HISTORY C19: from French *coumarine,* from *coumarou* tonka-bean tree, from Spanish *cumarú,* from Tupi
▸'**coumaric** *or* '**cumaric** ADJECTIVE

coumarone ('kuːməˌrəʊn) NOUN another name for **benzofuran.**
▷HISTORY C19: from COUMAR(IN) + -ONE

council ('kaʊnsəl) NOUN 1 an assembly of people meeting for discussion, consultation, etc.: *an emergency council.* 2 a body of people elected or appointed to serve in an administrative, legislative, or advisory capacity: *a student council.* 3 *Brit* (*sometimes capital;* often preceded by *the*) the local governing authority of a town, county, etc. 4 a meeting or the deliberation of a council. 5 (*modifier*) of, relating to, provided for, or used by a local council: *a council chamber; council offices.* 6 (*modifier*) *Brit* provided by a local council, esp (of housing) at a subsidized rent: *a council house; a council estate.* 7 *Austral* an administrative or legislative assembly, esp the upper house of a state parliament in Australia. 8 *Christianity* an assembly of bishops, theologians, and other representatives of several churches or dioceses, convened for regulating matters of doctrine or discipline.
▷HISTORY C12: from Old French *concile,* from Latin *concilium* assembly, from *com-* together + *calāre* to call; influenced also by Latin *consilium* advice, COUNSEL

Language note Avoid confusion with **counsel.**

council area NOUN any of the 32 unitary authorities into which Scotland has been divided for administrative purposes since April 1996.

councillor *or US* **councilor** ('kaʊnsələ) NOUN a member of a council.
▸'**councillor,ship** *or US* '**councilor,ship** NOUN

Language note Avoid confusion with **counsellor.**

councilman ('kaʊnsəlmən) NOUN, *plural* **-men.** *Chiefly US* a member of a council, esp of a town or city; councillor.

council-manager plan NOUN (in the US) a system of local government with an elected legislative council and an appointed administrative manager. See also **city manager.**

Council of Europe NOUN an association of European states, established in 1949 to promote unity between its members, defend human rights, and increase social and economic progress.

Council of States NOUN another name for **Rajya Sabha.**

Council of Trent NOUN the council of the Roman Catholic Church that met between 1545 and 1563 at Trent in S Tyrol. Reacting against the Protestants, it reaffirmed traditional Catholic beliefs and formulated the ideals of the Counter-Reformation.

council of war NOUN 1 an assembly of military leaders in wartime. 2 an emergency meeting to formulate a plan.

councilor ('kaʊnsələ) NOUN 1 a variant US spelling of **councillor.** 2 an archaic spelling of **counsellor.**
▸'**councilor,ship** NOUN

council school NOUN *Brit* (esp formerly) any school maintained by the state.

council tax NOUN (in Britain) a tax, based on the relative value of property, levied to fund local council services.

counsel ('kaʊnsəl) NOUN 1 advice or guidance on conduct, behaviour, etc. 2 discussion, esp on future procedure; consultation: *to take counsel with a friend.* 3 a person whose advice or guidance is or has been sought. 4 a barrister or group of barristers engaged in conducting cases in court and advising on legal matters: *counsel for the prosecution.* 5 a policy or plan. 6 *Christianity* any of the **counsels of perfection** or **evangelical counsels,** namely poverty, chastity, and obedience. 7 **counsel of perfection.** excellent but unrealizable advice. 8 private opinions or plans (esp in the phrase **keep one's own counsel**). 9 *Archaic* wisdom; prudence. ◆ VERB **-sels, -selling, -selled** *or US* **-sels, -seling, -seled.** 10 (*tr*) to give advice or guidance to. 11 (*tr; often takes a clause as object*) to recommend the acceptance of (a plan, idea, etc.); urge. 12 (*intr*) *Archaic* to take counsel; consult.
▷HISTORY C13: from Old French *counseil,* from Latin *consilium* deliberating body; related to CONSUL, CONSULT
▸'**counsellable** *or US* '**counselable** ADJECTIVE

Language note Avoid confusion with **council.**

counselling *or US* **counseling** ('kaʊnsəlɪŋ) NOUN guidance offered by social workers, doctors, etc., to help a person resolve social or personal problems.

counsellor *or US* **counselor** ('kaʊnsələ) NOUN 1 a person who gives counsel; adviser. 2 a person, such as a social worker, who is involved in counselling. 3 Also called: **counselor-at-law.** *US* a lawyer, esp one who conducts cases in court; attorney. 4 a senior British diplomatic officer. 5 a US diplomatic officer ranking just below an ambassador or minister. 6 a person who advises students or others on personal problems or academic and occupational choice.
▸'**counsellor,ship** *or US* '**counselor,ship** NOUN

Language note Avoid confusion with **councillor.**

count[1] (kaʊnt) VERB 1 to add up or check (each unit in a collection) in order to ascertain the sum;

enumerate: *count your change.* [2] (*tr*) to recite numbers in ascending order up to and including. [3] (*tr; often foll by in*) to take into account or include: *we must count him in.* [4] **not counting.** excluding. [5] (*tr*) to believe to be; consider; think; deem: *count yourself lucky.* [6] (*intr*) to recite or list numbers in ascending order either in units or groups: *to count in tens.* [7] (*intr*) to have value, importance, or influence: *this picture counts as a rarity.* [8] (*intr; often foll by for*) to have a certain specified value or importance: *the job counts for a lot.* [9] (*intr*) *Music* to keep time by counting beats. ◆ NOUN [10] the act of counting or reckoning. [11] the number reached by counting; sum. [12] *Law* a paragraph in an indictment containing a distinct and separate charge. [13] *Physics* the total number of photons or ionized particles detected by a counter. [14] **keep count.** to keep a record of items, events, etc. [15] **lose count.** to fail to keep an accurate record of items, events, etc. [16] *Boxing, wrestling* the act of telling off a number of seconds by the referee, as when a boxer has been knocked down or a wrestler pinned by his opponent. [17] **out for the count.** *Boxing* knocked out and unable to continue after a count of ten by the referee. [18] **take the count.** *Boxing* to be unable to continue after a count of ten. [19] *Archaic* notice; regard; account. ◆ See also **count against, countdown, count on, count out.**
▷HISTORY C14: from Anglo-French *counter,* from Old French *conter,* from Latin *computāre* to calculate, COMPUTE

count[2] (kaʊnt) NOUN [1] a nobleman in any of various European countries having a rank corresponding to that of a British earl. [2] any of various officials in the late Roman Empire and under various Germanic kings in the early Middle Ages. [3] a man who has received an honour (**papal knighthood**) from the Pope in recognition of good deeds, achievements, etc.
▷HISTORY C16: from Old French *conte,* from Late Latin *comes* occupant of a state office, from Latin: overseer, associate, literally: one who goes with, from COM- with + *īre* to go
▸ˈ**count,ship** NOUN

countable (ˈkaʊntəbᵊl) ADJECTIVE [1] capable of being counted. [2] *Maths, logic* able to be counted using the natural numbers; finite or denumerable. [3] *Linguistics* denoting a count noun.

count against VERB (*intr, preposition*) to have influence to the disadvantage of: *your bad timekeeping will count against you.*

countback (ˈkaʊnt,bæk) NOUN a system of deciding the winner of a tied competition by comparing earlier points or scores.

countdown (ˈkaʊnt,daʊn) NOUN [1] the act of counting backwards to time a critical operation exactly, such as the launching of a rocket or the detonation of explosives. ◆ VERB **count down.** (*intr, adverb*) [2] to count numbers backwards towards zero, esp in timing such a critical operation.

countenance (ˈkaʊntɪnəns) NOUN [1] the face, esp when considered as expressing a person's character or mood: *a pleasant countenance.* [2] support or encouragement; sanction. [3] composure; self-control (esp in the phrases **keep** *or* **lose one's countenance; out of countenance**). ◆ VERB (*tr*) [4] to support or encourage; sanction. [5] to tolerate; endure.
▷HISTORY C13: from Old French *contenance* mien, behaviour, from Latin *continentia* restraint, control; see CONTAIN
▸ˈ**countenancer** NOUN

counter[1] (ˈkaʊntə) NOUN [1] a horizontal surface, as in a shop or bank, over which business is transacted. [2] (in some cafeterias) a long table on which food is served to customers. [3] **a** a small flat disc of wood, metal, or plastic, used in various board games. **b** a similar disc or token used as an imitation coin. [4] a person or thing that may be used or manipulated. [5] a skating figure consisting of three circles. [6] **under the counter.** (**under-the-counter** *when prenominal*) (of the sale of goods, esp goods in short supply) clandestine, surreptitious, or illegal; not in an open manner. [7] **over the counter.** (**over-the-counter** *when prenominal*) (of security transactions) through a broker rather than on a stock exchange.
▷HISTORY C14: from Old French *comptouer,* ultimately from Latin *computāre* to COMPUTE

counter[2] (ˈkaʊntə) NOUN [1] a person who counts. [2] an apparatus that records the number of occurrences of events. [3] any instrument for detecting or counting ionizing particles or photons. See **Geiger counter, scintillation counter, crystal counter.** [4] *Electronics* another name for **scaler** (sense 2).
▷HISTORY C14: from Old French *conteor,* from Latin *computātor;* see COUNT[1]

counter[3] (ˈkaʊntə) ADVERB [1] in a contrary direction or manner. [2] in a wrong or reverse direction. [3] **run counter to.** to have a contrary effect or action to. ◆ ADJECTIVE [4] opposing; opposite; contrary. ◆ NOUN [5] something that is contrary or opposite to some other thing. [6] an act, effect, or force that opposes another. [7] a return attack, such as a blow in boxing. [8] *Fencing* a parry in which the foils move in a circular fashion. [9] the portion of the stern of a boat or ship that overhangs the water aft of the rudder. [10] Also called: **void.** *Printing* the inside area of a typeface that is not type high, such as the centre of an "o", and therefore does not print. [11] the part of a horse's breast under the neck and between the shoulders. [12] a piece of leather forming the back of a shoe. ◆ VERB [13] to say or do (something) in retaliation or response. [14] (*tr*) to move, act, or perform in a manner or direction opposite to (a person or thing). [15] to return the attack of (an opponent).
▷HISTORY C15: from Old French *contre,* from Latin *contrā* against

counter- PREFIX [1] against; opposite; contrary: *counterattack.* [2] complementary; corresponding: *counterfoil.* [3] duplicate or substitute: *counterfeit.*
▷HISTORY via Norman French from Latin *contrā* against, opposite; see CONTRA-

counteract (,kaʊntərˈækt) VERB (*tr*) to oppose, neutralize, or mitigate the effects of by contrary action; check.
▸,**counterˈaction** NOUN ▸,**counterˈactive** ADJECTIVE ▸,**counterˈactively** ADVERB

counterattack (ˈkaʊntərə,tæk) NOUN [1] an attack in response to an attack. ◆ VERB [2] to make a counterattack (against).

counterattraction (ˈkaʊntərə,trækʃən) NOUN a rival attraction.

counterbalance NOUN (ˈkaʊntə,bæləns) [1] a weight or force that balances or offsets another. ◆ VERB (,kaʊntəˈbæləns) (*tr*) [2] to act as a counterbalance. ◆ Also: **counterpoise.**

counterblast (ˈkaʊntə,blɑːst) NOUN [1] an aggressive response to a verbal attack. [2] a blast that counteracts another.

counterchange (,kaʊntəˈtʃeɪndʒ) VERB (*tr*) [1] to change parts, qualities, etc. [2] *Poetic* to chequer, as with contrasting colours.

countercharge (ˈkaʊntə,tʃɑːdʒ) NOUN [1] a charge brought by an accused person against the accuser. [2] *Military* a retaliatory charge. ◆ VERB [3] (*tr*) to make a countercharge against.

countercheck NOUN (ˈkaʊntə,tʃɛk) [1] a check or restraint, esp one that acts in opposition to another. [2] a restraint that reinforces another restraint. [3] a double check, as for accuracy. ◆ VERB (,kaʊntəˈtʃɛk) (*tr*) [4] to oppose by counteraction. [5] to control or restrain by a second check. [6] to double-check.

counterclaim (ˈkaʊntə,kleɪm) *Chiefly law* ◆ NOUN [1] a claim set up in opposition to another, esp by the defendant in a civil action against the plaintiff. ◆ VERB [2] to set up (a claim) in opposition to another claim.
▸,**counterˈclaimant** NOUN

counterclockwise (,kaʊntəˈklɒk,waɪz) *or* **contraclockwise** ADVERB, ADJECTIVE the US and Canadian equivalent of **anticlockwise.**

counterconditioning (,kaʊntəkənˈdɪʃənɪŋ) NOUN *Psychol* the conditioning of a response that is incompatible with some previously learned response; for example, in psychotherapy an anxious person might be taught relaxation, which is incompatible with anxiety.

counterculture (ˈkaʊntə,kʌltʃə) NOUN an alternative culture, deliberately at variance with the social norm.

counterespionage (,kaʊntərˈɛspɪə,nɑːʒ) NOUN activities designed to detect and counteract enemy espionage.

counterexample (ˈkaʊntərɪg,zɑːmpᵊl) NOUN an example or fact that is inconsistent with a hypothesis and may be used in argument against it.

counterfactual (,kaʊntəˈfæktʃʊəl) *Logic* ◆ ADJECTIVE [1] expressing what has not happened but could, would, or might under differing conditions. ◆ NOUN [2] a conditional statement in which the first clause is a past tense subjunctive statement expressing something contrary to fact, as in: *if she had hurried she would have caught the bus.*

counterfeit (ˈkaʊntəfɪt) ADJECTIVE [1] made in imitation of something genuine with the intent to deceive or defraud; forged. [2] simulated; sham: *counterfeit affection.* ◆ NOUN [3] an imitation designed to deceive or defraud. [4] *Archaic* an impostor; cheat. ◆ VERB [5] (*tr*) to make a fraudulent imitation of. [6] (*intr*) to make counterfeits. [7] to feign; simulate. [8] (*tr*) to imitate; copy.
▷HISTORY C13: from Old French *contrefait,* from *contrefaire* to copy, from *contre-* COUNTER- + *faire* to make, from Latin *facere*
▸ˈ**counterfeiter** NOUN

counterfoil (ˈkaʊntə,fɔɪl) NOUN *Brit* the part of a cheque, postal order, receipt, etc., detached and retained as a record of the transaction. Also called (esp US and Canadian): **stub.**

counterfort (ˈkaʊntə,fɔːt) NOUN *Civil engineering* a strengthening buttress at right angles to a retaining wall, bonded to it to prevent overturning or to increase its bending strength.
▷HISTORY from a partial translation of French *contrefort,* from *contre* counter + *fort* strength; see FORT

counterglow (ˈkaʊntə,gləʊ) NOUN another name for **gegenschein.**

counterinsurgency (,kaʊntərɪnˈsɜːdʒənsɪ) NOUN action taken by a government to counter the activities of rebels, guerrillas, etc.

counterintelligence (,kaʊntərɪnˈtɛlɪdʒəns) NOUN [1] activities designed to frustrate enemy espionage. [2] intelligence collected about enemy espionage.

counterirritant (,kaʊntərˈɪrɪtᵊnt) NOUN [1] an agent that causes a superficial irritation of the skin and thereby relieves inflammation of deep structures. ◆ ADJECTIVE [2] producing a counterirritation.
▸,**counter,irriˈtation** NOUN

counter jumper NOUN *Old-fashioned derogatory* a sales assistant in a shop.

countermand VERB (,kaʊntəˈmɑːnd) (*tr*) [1] to revoke or cancel (a command, order, etc.). [2] to order (forces, etc.) to return or retreat; recall. ◆ NOUN (ˈkaʊntə,mɑːnd) [3] a command revoking another.
▷HISTORY C15: from Old French *contremander,* from *contre-* COUNTER- + *mander* to command, from Latin *mandāre;* see MANDATE

countermarch (ˈkaʊntə,mɑːtʃ) VERB [1] *Chiefly military* **a** to march or cause to march back along the same route. **b** to change the order of soldiers during a march. ◆ NOUN [2] the act or instance of countermarching. [3] a reversal of method, conduct, etc.

countermeasure (ˈkaʊntə,mɛʒə) NOUN action taken to oppose, neutralize, or retaliate against some other action.

countermine NOUN (ˈkaʊntə,maɪn) [1] *Military* a tunnel dug to defeat similar activities by an enemy. [2] a plot to frustrate another plot. ◆ VERB (,kaʊntəˈmaɪn) [3] to frustrate by countermeasures. [4] *Military* to take measures to defeat the underground operations of (an enemy). [5] *Military* to destroy enemy mines in (an area) with mines of one's own.

countermove (ˈkaʊntə,muːv) NOUN [1] an opposing move. ◆ VERB [2] to make or do (something) as an opposing move.
▸ˈ**counter,movement** NOUN

counteroffensive (ˈkaʊntərə,fɛnsɪv) NOUN a series of attacks by a defending force against an attacking enemy.

counteroffer (ˈkaʊntər,ɒfə) NOUN a response to a bid in which a seller amends his original offer, making it more favourable to the buyer.

counterpane (ˈkaʊntə,peɪn) NOUN another word for **bedspread.**

▷HISTORY C17: from obsolete *counterpoint* (influenced by *pane* coverlet), changed from Old French *coutepointe* quilt, from Medieval Latin *culcita puncta* quilted mattress

counterpart ('kaʊntəˌpɑːt) NOUN 1 a person or thing identical to or closely resembling another. 2 one of two parts that complement or correspond to each other. 3 a person acting opposite another in a play. 4 a duplicate, esp of a legal document; copy.

counterparty ('kaʊntəˌpɑːtɪ) NOUN, *plural* **-parties.** a person who is a party to a contract.

counterparty risk NOUN the risk that a person who is a party to a contract will default on their obligations under that contract.

counterplot ('kaʊntəˌplɒt) NOUN 1 a plot designed to frustrate another plot. ◆ VERB **-plots, -plotting, -plotted.** 2 (*tr*) to oppose with a counterplot. 3 (*intr*) to devise or carry out a counterplot.

counterpoint ('kaʊntəˌpɔɪnt) NOUN 1 the technique involving the simultaneous sounding of two or more parts or melodies. 2 a melody or part combined with another melody or part. See also **descant** (sense 1). 3 the musical texture resulting from the simultaneous sounding of two or more melodies or parts. 4 **strict counterpoint.** the application of the rules of counterpoint as an academic exercise. 5 a contrasting or interacting element, theme, or item; foil. 6 *Prosody* the use of a stress or stresses at variance with the regular metrical stress. ◆ VERB 7 (*tr*) to set in contrast. ◆ Related adjective: **contrapuntal.**

▷HISTORY C15: from Old French *contrepoint,* from *contre-* COUNTER- + *point* dot, note in musical notation, that is, an accompaniment set against the notes of a melody

counterpoise ('kaʊntəˌpɔɪz) NOUN 1 a force, influence, etc., that counterbalances another. 2 a state of balance; equilibrium. 3 a weight that balances another. 4 a radial array of metallic wires, rods, or tubes arranged horizontally around the base of a vertical aerial to increase its transmitting efficiency. ◆ VERB (*tr*) 5 to oppose with something of equal effect, weight, or force; offset. 6 to bring into equilibrium. 7 *Archaic* to consider (one thing) carefully in relation to another.

counterpoise bridge NOUN another name for **bascule bridge** (see **bascule** (sense 1)).

counterproductive (ˌkaʊntəprəˈdʌktɪv) ADJECTIVE tending to hinder or act against the achievement of an aim.

counterproof ('kaʊntəˌpruːf) NOUN *Printing* a reverse impression of a newly printed proof of an engraving made by laying it while wet upon plain paper and passing it through the press.

counterproposal ('kaʊntəprəˌpəʊzᵊl) NOUN a proposal offered as an alternative to a previous proposal.

counterpunch ('kaʊntəˌpʌntʃ) *Boxing* ◆ VERB (*intr*) 1 to punch an attacking opponent; return an attack. ◆ NOUN 2 a return punch.

Counter-Reformation (ˌkaʊntəˌrɛfəˈmeɪʃən) NOUN the reform movement of the Roman Catholic Church in the 16th and early 17th centuries considered as a reaction to the Protestant Reformation.

counter-revolution (ˌkaʊntəˌrɛvəˈluːʃən) NOUN a revolution opposed to a previous revolution and aimed at reversing its effects.
▸ˌ**counter-ˌrevoˈlutionist** NOUN

counter-revolutionary (ˌkaʊntəˌrɛvəˈluːʃənərɪ, -nrɪ) NOUN, *plural* **-aries.** 1 a person opposed to revolution. 2 a person who opposes a specific revolution or revolutionary government. ◆ ADJECTIVE 3 characterized by opposition to a revolution or revolutions in general.

counterscarp ('kaʊntəˌskɑːp) NOUN *Fortifications* the outer side of the ditch of a fort. Compare **escarp** (sense 1).

countershading (ˌkaʊntəˈʃeɪdɪŋ) NOUN (in the coloration of certain animals) a pattern, serving as camouflage, in which dark colours occur on parts of the body exposed to the light and pale colours on parts in the shade.

countershaft ('kaʊntəˌʃɑːft) NOUN an intermediate shaft that is driven by, but rotates in the opposite direction to, a main shaft, esp in a gear train.

countersign VERB ('kaʊntəˌsaɪn, ˌkaʊntəˈsaɪn) 1 (*tr*) to sign (a document already signed by another). ◆ NOUN ('kaʊntəˌsaɪn) 2 Also called: **countersignature.** the signature so written. 3 a secret sign given in response to another sign. 4 *Chiefly military* a password.

countersink ('kaʊntəˌsɪŋk) VERB **-sinks, -sinking, -sank, -sunk.** (*tr*) 1 to enlarge the upper part of (a hole) in timber, metal, etc., so that the head of a bolt or screw can be sunk below the surface. 2 to drive (a screw) or sink (a bolt) into such an enlarged hole. ◆ NOUN 3 Also called: **countersink bit.** a tool for countersinking. 4 a countersunk depression or hole.

counterspy ('kaʊntəˌspaɪ) NOUN, *plural* **-spies.** a spy working against or investigating enemy espionage.

counterstain ('kaʊntəˌsteɪn) VERB *Microscopy* 1 to apply two or more stains in sequence to (a specimen to be examined), each of which colours a different tissue. 2 (*tr; usually passive*) to apply (one of a series of stains) to a specimen to be examined: *haematoxylin is counterstained with eosin.*

countersubject ('kaʊntəˌsʌbdʒɪkt) NOUN *Music* (in a fugue) the theme in one voice that accompanies the statement of the subject in another.

countertenor (ˌkaʊntəˈtɛnə) NOUN 1 an adult male voice with an alto range. 2 a singer with such a voice.

counterterrorism (ˌkaʊntəˈtɛrəˌrɪzəm) NOUN an act or acts of terrorism committed in revenge or retaliation for a previous terrorist act.
▸ˌ**counterˈterrorist** ADJECTIVE

countertrade ('kaʊntəˌtreɪd) NOUN 1 international trade in which payment is made in goods rather than currency. ◆ VERB (*tr*) 2 to buy or sell goods by countertrade: *countertrading weapons for coffee beans.*

countertype ('kaʊntəˌtaɪp) NOUN 1 an opposite type. 2 a corresponding type.

countervail (ˌkaʊntəˈveɪl, ˈkaʊntəˌveɪl) VERB 1 (when *intr,* usually foll by *against*) to act or act against with equal power or force. 2 (*tr*) to make up for; compensate; offset.

▷HISTORY C14: from Old French *contrevaloir,* from Latin *contrā valēre,* from *contrā* against + *valēre* to be strong

countervailing duty NOUN an extra import duty imposed by a country on certain imports, esp to prevent dumping or to counteract subsidies in the exporting country.

counterweigh (ˌkaʊntəˈweɪ) VERB another word for **counterbalance.**

counterweight ('kaʊntəˌweɪt) NOUN a counterbalancing weight, influence, or force.
▸ˈ**counterˌweighted** ADJECTIVE

counterword ('kaʊntəˌwɜːd) NOUN a word widely used in a sense much looser than its original meaning, such as *tremendous* or *awful.*

counterwork ('kaʊntəˌwɜːk) NOUN 1 work done in opposition to other work. 2 defensive fortifications put up against attack.
▸ˈ**counterˌworker** NOUN

countess ('kaʊntɪs) NOUN 1 the wife or widow of a count or earl. 2 a woman of the rank of count or earl.

counting house NOUN *Rare, chiefly Brit* a room or building used by the accountants of a business.

countless ('kaʊntlɪs) ADJECTIVE innumerable; myriad.

count noun NOUN *Linguistics, logic* a noun that can be qualified by the indefinite article, and may be used in the plural, as *telephone* and *thing* but not *airs and graces* or *bravery.* Compare **mass noun, sortal.**

count on VERB (*intr, preposition*) to rely or depend on.

count out VERB (*tr, adverb*) 1 *Informal* to leave out; exclude: *count me out!* 2 (of a boxing referee) to judge (a floored boxer) to have failed to recover within the specified time. See **count¹** (sense 16). 3 to count (something) aloud.

count palatine NOUN, *plural* **counts palatine.** *History* 1 (in the Holy Roman Empire) **a** originally an official who administered the king's domains or his justice. **b** later, a count who exercised royal authority in his own domains. 2 (in England and Ireland) an earl or other lord of a county palatine. 3 (in the late Roman Empire) a palace official who exercised judicial authority.

countrified *or* **countryfied** ('kʌntrɪˌfaɪd) ADJECTIVE in the style, manners, etc., of the country; rural.

country ('kʌntrɪ) NOUN, *plural* **-tries.** 1 a territory distinguished by its people, culture, language, geography, etc. 2 an area of land distinguished by its political autonomy; state. 3 the people of a territory or state: *the whole country rebelled.* 4 an area associated with a particular person: *Burns country.* 5 **a** the part of the land that is away from cities or industrial areas; rural districts. **b** (*as modifier*): *country cottage.* **c** (*in combination*): *a countryman.* Related adjectives: **pastoral, rural.** 6 short for **country music.** 7 *Archaic* a particular locality or district. 8 **up country.** away from the coast or the capital. 9 one's native land or nation of citizenship. 10 (usually preceded by *the*) *Brit informal* the outlying area or area furthest from the finish of a sports ground or racecourse. 11 (*modifier*) rough; uncouth; rustic: *country manners.* 12 **across country.** not keeping to roads, etc. 13 **go** *or* **appeal to the country.** *Chiefly Brit* to dissolve Parliament and hold an election. 14 **unknown country.** an unfamiliar topic, place, matter, etc.

▷HISTORY C13: from Old French *contrée,* from Medieval Latin *contrāta,* literally: that which lies opposite, from Latin *contrā* opposite

country and western NOUN 1 another name for **country music.** 2 a fusion of cowboy songs and Appalachian music. 3 (*as modifier*): *country-and-western music.* Abbreviation: **C & W.**

country blues NOUN (*sometimes functioning as singular*) acoustic folk blues with a guitar accompaniment. Compare **urban blues.**

country club NOUN a club in the country, having sporting and social facilities.

country code NOUN (in Britain) a code of good practice recommended to those who use the countryside for recreational purposes.

country cousin NOUN an unsophisticated person from the country, esp one regarded as an object of amusement.

country dance NOUN a type of folk dance in which couples are arranged in sets and perform a series of movements, esp facing one another in a line.
▸**country dancing** NOUN

country gentleman NOUN a rich man with an estate in the country.

country house NOUN a large house in the country, esp a mansion belonging to a wealthy family.

countryman ('kʌntrɪmən) NOUN, *plural* **-men.** 1 a person who lives in the country. 2 a person from a particular country or from one's own country (esp in the phrase **fellow countryman**).
▸ˈ**countryˌwoman** FEMININE NOUN

country music NOUN a type of 20th-century popular music based on White folk music of the southeastern US. Sometimes shortened to **country.**

country park NOUN *Brit* an area of countryside, usually not less than 10 hectares, set aside for public recreation: often funded by a Countryside Commission grant.

country rock¹ NOUN the rock surrounding a mineral vein or igneous intrusion.

country rock² NOUN a style of rock music influenced by country and western.

country seat NOUN a large estate or property in the country.

countryside ('kʌntrɪˌsaɪd) NOUN a rural area or its population.

Countryside Agency NOUN (in England) a government agency that promotes the conservation and enjoyment of the countryside and aims to stimulate employment in rural areas.

county ('kaʊntɪ) NOUN, *plural* **-ties.** 1 **a** any of the administrative or geographic subdivisions of certain states, esp any of the major units into which England and Wales are or have been divided for purposes of local government. **b** (*as modifier*): *county*

cricket. [2] *NZ* an electoral division in a rural area. [3] *Obsolete* the lands under the jurisdiction of a count or earl. ◆ ADJECTIVE [4] *Brit informal* having the characteristics and habits of the inhabitants of country houses and estates, esp an upper-class accent and an interest in horses, dogs, etc.
▷HISTORY C14: from Old French *conté* land belonging to a count, from Late Latin *comitātus* office of a count, from *comes* COUNT²

county borough NOUN [1] (in England and Wales from 1888 to 1974 and in Wales from 1996) a borough administered independently of any higher tier of local government. [2] (in the Republic of Ireland) any of the four largest boroughs, governed independently of the administrative county around it by an elected council that constitutes an all-purpose authority.

county court NOUN (in England) a local court exercising limited jurisdiction in civil matters.

county palatine NOUN, *plural* **counties palatine.** [1] the lands of a count palatine. [2] (in England and Ireland) a county in which the earl or other lord exercised many royal powers, esp judicial authority.

county seat NOUN *Chiefly US* another term for **county town.**

county town NOUN the town in which a county's affairs are or were administered.

coup¹ (kuː) NOUN [1] a brilliant and successful stroke or action. [2] short for **coup d'état.**
▷HISTORY C18: from French: blow, from Latin *colaphus* blow with the fist, from Greek *kolaphos*

coup² *or* **cowp** (kaʊp) *Scot* ◆ VERB [1] to turn or fall over. ◆ NOUN [2] a rubbish tip.
▷HISTORY C15: perhaps identical with obsolete *cope* to strike; see COPE¹

coup³ (kaʊp) VERB *Scot* to barter; traffic; deal.
▷HISTORY C14: from Old Norse *kaupa* to buy

coup de foudre *French* (ku də fudrə) NOUN, *plural* ***coups de foudre*** (ku də fudrə). a sudden and amazing action or event.
▷HISTORY literally: lightning flash

coup de grâce *French* (ku də grɑs) NOUN, *plural* ***coups de grâce*** (ku də grɑs). [1] a mortal or finishing blow, esp one delivered as an act of mercy to a sufferer. [2] a final or decisive stroke.
▷HISTORY literally: blow of mercy

coup de main *French* (ku də mɛ̃) NOUN, *plural* ***coups de main*** (ku də mɛ̃). *Chiefly military* an attack that achieves complete surprise.
▷HISTORY literally: blow with the hand

coup d'état (ˈkuː deɪˈtɑː; *French* ku deta) NOUN, *plural* **coups d'état** (ˈkuːz deɪˈtɑː; *French* ku deta). a sudden violent or illegal seizure of government.
▷HISTORY French, literally: stroke of state

coup de théâtre *French* (ku də teɑtrə) NOUN, *plural* ***coups de théâtre*** (ku də teɑtrə). [1] a dramatic turn of events, esp in a play. [2] a sensational device of stagecraft. [3] a stage success.
▷HISTORY literally: stroke of the theatre

coup d'oeil *French* (ku dœj) NOUN, *plural* ***coups d'oeil*** (ku dœj). a quick glance.
▷HISTORY literally: stroke of the eye

coupe (kuːp) NOUN [1] a dessert of fruit and ice cream, usually served in a glass goblet. [2] a dish or stemmed glass bowl designed for this dessert.
▷HISTORY C19: from French: goblet, CUP

coupé (ˈkuːpeɪ) NOUN [1] Also called: **fixed-head coupé.** a four-seater car with a fixed roof, a sloping back, and usually two doors. Compare **drophead coupé.** [2] a four-wheeled horse-drawn carriage with two seats inside and one outside for the driver. [3] an end compartment in a European railway carriage with seats on one side only.
▷HISTORY C19: from French, short for *carosse coupé,* literally: cut-off carriage, from *couper* to cut, from *coup* blow, stroke

couple (ˈkʌpᵊl) NOUN [1] two people who regularly associate with each other or live together: *an engaged couple.* [2] (*functioning as singular or plural*) two people considered as a pair, for or as if for dancing, games, etc. [3] *Chiefly hunting or coursing* **a** a pair of collars joined by a leash, used to attach hounds to one another. **b** two hounds joined in this way. **c** the unit of reckoning for hounds in a pack: *twenty and a half couple.* [4] a pair of equal and opposite parallel forces that have a tendency to produce rotation with a torque or turning moment equal to the product of either force and the perpendicular distance between them. [5] *Physics* **a** two dissimilar metals, alloys, or semiconductors in electrical contact, across which a voltage develops. See **thermocouple. b** Also called: **galvanic couple.** two dissimilar metals or alloys in electrical contact that when immersed in an electrolyte act as the electrodes of an electrolytic cell. [6] a connector or link between two members, such as a tie connecting a pair of rafters in a roof. [7] **a couple of.** (*functioning as singular or plural*) **a** a combination of two; a pair of: *a couple of men.* **b** *Informal* a small number of; a few: *a couple of days.* ◆ PRONOUN [8] (usually preceded by *a; functioning as singular or plural*) two; a pair: *give him a couple.* ◆ VERB [9] (*tr*) to connect (two things) together or to connect (one thing) to (another): *to couple railway carriages.* [10] (*tr*) to do (two things) simultaneously or alternately: *he couples studying with teaching.* [11] to form or be formed into a pair or pairs. [12] to associate, put, or connect together: *history is coupled with sociology.* [13] to link (two circuits) by electromagnetic induction. [14] (*intr*) to have sexual intercourse. [15] to join or be joined in marriage; marry. [16] (*tr*) to attach (two hounds to each other).
▷HISTORY C13: from Old French: a pair, from Latin *cōpula* a bond; see COPULA

coupled (ˈkʌpᵊld) ADJECTIVE being one of the partners in a permanent sexual relationship.

coupledom (ˈkʌpᵊldəm) NOUN the state of living as a couple, esp when regarded as being interested in each other to the exclusion of the outside world.

coupler (ˈkʌplə) NOUN [1] a link or rod transmitting power between two rotating mechanisms or a rotating part and a reciprocating part. [2] *Music* a device on an organ or harpsichord connecting two keys, two manuals, etc., so that both may be played at once. [3] *Electronics* a device, such as a transformer, used to couple two or more electrical circuits. [4] a US and Canadian word for **coupling** (sense 2).

couplet (ˈkʌplɪt) NOUN two successive lines of verse, usually rhymed and of the same metre.
▷HISTORY C16: from French, literally: a little pair; see COUPLE

coupling (ˈkʌplɪŋ) NOUN [1] a mechanical device that connects two things. [2] a device for connecting railway cars or trucks together. [3] the part of the body of a horse, dog, or other quadruped that lies between the forequarters and the hindquarters. [4] *Electronics* the act or process of linking two or more circuits so that power can be transferred between them usually by mutual induction, as in a transformer, or by means of a capacitor or inductor common to both circuits. See also **direct coupling.** [5] *Physics* an interaction between different properties of a system, such as a group of atoms or nuclei, or between two or more systems. [6] *Genetics* the occurrence of two specified nonallelic genes from the same parent on the same chromosome.

coupon (ˈkuːpɒn) NOUN [1] **a** a detachable part of a ticket or advertisement entitling the holder to a discount, free gift, etc. **b** a detachable slip usable as a commercial order form. **c** a voucher given away with certain goods, a certain number of which are exchangeable for goods offered by the manufacturers. [2] one of a number of detachable certificates attached to a bond, esp a bearer bond, the surrender of which entitles the bearer to receive interest payments. [3] one of several detachable cards used for making hire-purchase payments. [4] a ticket issued to facilitate rationing. [5] *Brit* a detachable entry form for any of certain competitions, esp football pools.
▷HISTORY C19: from French, from Old French *colpon* piece cut off, from *colper* to cut, variant of *couper;* see COPE¹

courage (ˈkʌrɪdʒ) NOUN [1] the power or quality of dealing with or facing danger, fear, pain, etc. [2] **the courage of one's convictions.** the confidence to act in accordance with one's beliefs. [3] **take one's courage in both hands.** to nerve oneself to perform an action. [4] *Obsolete* mind; disposition; spirit.
▷HISTORY C13: from Old French *corage,* from *cuer* heart, from Latin *cor*

courageous (kəˈreɪdʒəs) ADJECTIVE possessing or expressing courage.
▸**couˈrageously** ADVERB ▸**couˈrageousness** NOUN

courante (kʊˈrɑːnt) NOUN *Music* [1] an old dance in quick triple time. [2] a movement of a (mostly) 16th- to 18th-century suite based on this. ◆ Also called (esp for the dance): **coranto.**
▷HISTORY C16: from French, literally: running, feminine of *courant,* present participle of *courir* to run, from Latin *currere*

Courantyne (ˈkɜːrənˌtaɪn) NOUN a river in N South America, rising in S Guyana and flowing north to the Atlantic, forming the boundary between Guyana and Surinam. Length: 765 km (475 miles). Dutch name: **Corantijn.**

courbaril (ˈkʊəbərɪl) NOUN a tropical American leguminous tree, *Hymenaea courbaril.* Its wood is a useful timber and its gum is a source of copal. Also called: **West Indian locust.**
▷HISTORY C18: from a native American name

Courbevoie (*French* kurbəvwa) NOUN an industrial suburb of Paris, on the Seine. Pop.: 54 500 (latest est.).

coureur de bois (*French* kurœr də bwa) NOUN, *plural* **coureurs de bois** (kurœr də bwa). *Canadian history* a French Canadian woodsman or Métis who traded with Indians for furs.
▷HISTORY Canadian French: trapper (literally: wood-runner)

courgette (kʊəˈʒɛt) NOUN a small variety of vegetable marrow, cooked and eaten as a vegetable. US, Canadian, and Austral name: **zucchini.**
▷HISTORY from French, diminutive of *courge* marrow, gourd

courie *or* **coorie** (ˈkuːrɪ) VERB (*intr*) *Scot* (often foll by *doun*) to nestle or snuggle.
▷HISTORY C19: from *coor* a Scot word for COWER

courier (ˈkʊərɪə) NOUN [1] a special messenger, esp one carrying diplomatic correspondence. [2] a person who makes arrangements for or accompanies a group of travellers on a journey or tour. ◆ VERB [3] (*tr*) to send (a parcel, letter, etc.) by courier.
▷HISTORY C16: from Old French *courrier,* from Old Latin *corriere,* from *correre* to run, from Latin *currere*

courlan (ˈkʊələn) NOUN another name for **limpkin.**
▷HISTORY C19: from French, variant of *courliri,* from Galibi *kurliri*

Courland *or* **Kurland** (ˈkʊələnd) NOUN a region of Latvia, between the Gulf of Riga and the Lithuanian border. Latvian name: **Kurzeme.**

course (kɔːs) NOUN [1] a continuous progression from one point to the next in time or space; onward movement: *the course of his life.* [2] a route or direction followed: *they kept on a southerly course.* [3] **a** the path or channel along which something moves: *the course of a river.* **b** (*in combination*): *a watercourse.* [4] an area or stretch of land or water on which a sport is played or a race is run: *a golf course.* [5] a period of time; duration: *in the course of the next hour.* [6] the usual order of and time required for a sequence of events; regular procedure: *the illness ran its course.* [7] a mode of conduct or action: *if you follow that course, you will fail.* [8] a connected series of events, actions, etc. [9] **a** a prescribed number of lessons, lectures, etc., in an educational curriculum. **b** the material covered in such a curriculum. [10] a prescribed regimen to be followed for a specific period of time: *a course of treatment.* [11] a part of a meal served at one time: *the fish course.* [12] a continuous, usually horizontal, layer of building material, such as a row of bricks, tiles, etc. [13] *Nautical* any of the sails on the lowest yards of a square-rigged ship. [14] *Knitting* the horizontal rows of stitches. Compare **wale¹** (sense 2b). [15] (in medieval Europe) a charge by knights in a tournament. [16] **a** a hunt by hounds relying on sight rather than scent. **b** a match in which two greyhounds compete in chasing a hare. [17] the part or function assigned to an individual bell in a set of changes. [18] *Archaic* a running race. [19] **as a matter of course.** as a natural or normal consequence, mode of action, or event. [20] **the course of nature.** the ordinary course of events. [21] **in course of.** in the process of: *the ship was in course of construction.* [22] **in due course.** at some future time, esp the natural or appropriate time. [23] **of course. a** (*adverb*) as expected; naturally. **b** (*sentence substitute*) certainly; definitely. [24] **run** (*or* **take**) **its course.** (of something) to complete its development or action. ◆ VERB [25] (*intr*) to run, race, or flow, esp swiftly and without interruption. [26] to cause (hounds) to hunt by

sight rather than scent or (of hounds) to hunt (a quarry) thus. 27 (*tr*) to run through or over; traverse. 28 (*intr*) to take a direction; proceed on a course. ◆ See also **courses.**
▷HISTORY C13: from Old French *cours,* from Latin *cursus* a running, from *currere* to run

courser[1] ('kɔːsə) NOUN 1 a person who courses hounds or dogs, esp. greyhounds. 2 a hound or dog trained for coursing.

courser[2] ('kɔːsə) NOUN *Literary* a swift horse; steed.
▷HISTORY C13: from Old French *coursier,* from *cours* COURSE

courser[3] ('kɔːsə) NOUN a terrestrial plover-like shore bird, such as *Cursorius cursor* (cream-coloured courser), of the subfamily *Cursoriinae* of desert and semidesert regions of the Old World: family *Glareolidae,* order *Charadriiformes.*
▷HISTORY C18: from Latin *cursōrius* suited for running, from *cursus* COURSE

courses ('kɔːsɪz) PLURAL NOUN (*sometimes singular*) *Physiol* another word for **menses.**

coursework ('kɔːsˌwɜːk) NOUN written or oral work completed by a student within a given period, which is assessed as an integral part of an educational course.

coursing ('kɔːsɪŋ) NOUN 1 hunting with hounds or dogs that follow their quarry by sight. 2 a sport in which hounds are matched against one another in pairs for the hunting of hares by sight.

court (kɔːt) NOUN 1 an area of ground wholly or partly surrounded by walls or buildings. 2 *Brit* (*capital when part of a name*) **a** a block of flats: *Selwyn Court.* **b** a mansion or country house. **c** a short street, sometimes closed at one end. 3 a space inside a building, sometimes surrounded with galleries. 4 **a** the residence, retinues, or household of a sovereign or nobleman. **b** (*as modifier*): *a court ball.* 5 a sovereign or prince and his retinue, advisers, etc. 6 any formal assembly, reception, etc., held by a sovereign or nobleman with his courtiers. 7 homage, flattering attention, or amorous approaches (esp in the phrase **pay court to someone**). 8 *Law* **a** an authority having power to adjudicate in civil, criminal, military, or ecclesiastical matters. **b** the regular sitting of such a judicial authority. **c** the room or building in which such a tribunal sits. 9 **a** a marked outdoor or enclosed area used for any of various ball games, such as tennis, squash, etc. **b** a marked section of such an area: *the service court.* 10 **a** the board of directors or council of a corporation, company, etc. **b** *Chiefly Brit* the supreme council of some universities. 11 a branch of any of several friendly societies. 12 **go to court.** to take legal action. 13 **hold court.** to preside over admirers, attendants, etc. 14 **out of court. a** without a trial or legal case: *the case was settled out of court.* **b** too unimportant for consideration. **c** *Brit* so as to ridicule completely (in the phrase **laugh out of court**). 15 **the ball is in your court.** you are obliged to make the next move. ◆ VERB 16 to attempt to gain the love of (someone); woo. 17 (*tr*) to pay attention to (someone) in order to gain favour. 18 (*tr*) to try to obtain (fame, honour, etc.). 19 (*tr*) to invite, usually foolishly, as by taking risks: *to court disaster.* 20 *Old-fashioned* to be conducting a serious emotional relationship usually leading to marriage.
▷HISTORY C12: from Old French, from Latin *cohors* COHORT

court-bouillon ('kʊətˈbuːjɒn; *French* kurbujɔ̃) NOUN a stock made from root vegetables, water, and wine or vinegar, used primarily for poaching fish.
▷HISTORY from French, from *court* short, from Latin *curtus* + *bouillon* broth, from *bouillir* to BOIL[1]

court card NOUN (in a pack of playing cards) a king, queen, or jack of any suit. US equivalent: **face card.**
▷HISTORY C17: altered from earlier *coat-card,* from the decorative coats worn by the figures depicted

court circular NOUN (in countries having a monarchy) a daily report of the activities, engagements, etc., of the sovereign, published in a national newspaper.

court cupboard NOUN a wooden stand with two or three tiers, used in the 16th and 17th centuries to display pewter, silver, etc.

court dress NOUN the formal clothing worn at court.

Courtelle (kɔːˈtɛl) NOUN *Trademark* a synthetic acrylic fibre resembling wool.

courteous ('kɜːtɪəs) ADJECTIVE polite and considerate in manner.
▷HISTORY C13 *corteis,* literally: with courtly manners, from Old French; see COURT
▸'**courteously** ADVERB ▸'**courteousness** NOUN

courtesan *or* **courtezan** (ˌkɔːtɪˈzæn) NOUN (esp formerly) a prostitute, or the mistress of a man of rank.
▷HISTORY C16: from Old French *courtisane,* from Italian *cortigiana* female courtier, from *cortigiano* courtier, from *corte* COURT

courtesy ('kɜːtɪsɪ) NOUN, *plural* **-sies.** 1 politeness; good manners. 2 a courteous gesture or remark. 3 favour or consent (esp in the phrase **by courtesy of**). 4 common consent as opposed to right (esp in the phrase **by courtesy**). See also **courtesy title.** 5 ('kɜːtsɪ) an archaic spelling of **curtsy.**
▷HISTORY C13 *curteisie,* from Old French, from *corteis* COURTEOUS

courtesy light NOUN the interior light in a motor vehicle.

courtesy title NOUN any of several titles having no legal significance, such as those borne by the children of peers.

court hand NOUN a style of handwriting formerly used in English law courts.

courthouse ('kɔːtˌhaʊs) NOUN a public building in which courts of law are held.

courtier ('kɔːtɪə) NOUN 1 an attendant at a court. 2 a person who seeks favour in an ingratiating manner.
▷HISTORY C13: from Anglo-French *courteour* (unattested), from Old French *corteier* to attend at court

court-leet NOUN the full name for **leet**[1] (sense 1).

courtly ('kɔːtlɪ) ADJECTIVE **-lier, -liest.** 1 of or suitable for a royal court. 2 refined in manner. 3 ingratiating.
▸'**courtliness** NOUN

courtly love NOUN a tradition represented in Western European literature between the 12th and the 14th centuries, idealizing love between a knight and a revered (usually married) lady.

court martial NOUN, *plural* **court martials** *or* **courts martial.** 1 a military court that tries persons subject to military law. ◆ VERB **court-martial, -tials, -tialling, -tialled** *or US* **-tials, -tialing, -tialed.** 2 (*tr*) to try by court martial.

Court of Appeal NOUN a branch of the Supreme Court of Judicature that hears appeals from the High Court in both criminal and civil matters and from the county and crown courts.

Court of Common Pleas NOUN 1 *English law* (formerly) a superior court exercising jurisdiction in civil actions between private citizens. 2 *US law* (in some states) a court exercising original and general jurisdiction.

Court of Exchequer NOUN (formerly) an English civil court where Crown revenue cases were tried. Also called: **Exchequer.**

court of first instance NOUN a court in which legal proceedings are begun or first heard.

court of honour NOUN a military court that is instituted to investigate matters involving personal honour.

court of inquiry NOUN 1 *Brit* a group of people appointed to investigate the causes of a disaster, accident, etc. 2 a military court set up to inquire into a military matter such as a failure of equipment or procedure.

Court of Justiciary NOUN short for **High Court of Justiciary.**

Court of Session NOUN the supreme civil court in Scotland.

Court of St James's NOUN the official name of the royal court of Britain.

court plaster NOUN a plaster, composed of isinglass on silk, formerly used to cover superficial wounds.
▷HISTORY C18: so called because formerly used by court ladies for beauty spots

Courtrai (*French* kurtrɛ) NOUN a town in W Belgium, in West Flanders on the Lys River: the largest producer of linen in W Europe. Pop.: 76 040 (1995 est.). Flemish name: **Kortrijk.**

court roll NOUN *History* the register of land holdings, etc., of a manorial court.

courtroom ('kɔːtˌruːm, -ˌrʊm) NOUN a room in which the sittings of a law court are held.

courtship ('kɔːtʃɪp) NOUN 1 the act, period, or art of seeking the love of someone with intent to marry. 2 the seeking or soliciting of favours. 3 *Obsolete* courtly behaviour.

court shoe NOUN a low-cut shoe for women, having no laces or straps.

court tennis NOUN the US term for **real tennis.**

courtyard ('kɔːtˌjɑːd) NOUN an open area of ground surrounded by walls or buildings; court.

couscous ('kuːskuːs) NOUN 1 a type of semolina originating from North Africa, consisting of granules of crushed durum wheat. 2 a spicy North African dish consisting of steamed semolina with meat, vegetables, or fruit C17: via French from Arabic *kouskous,* from *kaskasa* to pound until fine.

cousin ('kʌzᵊn) NOUN 1 Also called: **first cousin, cousin-german, full cousin.** the child of one's aunt or uncle. 2 a relative who has descended from one of one's common ancestors. A person's **second cousin** is the child of one of his parents' first cousins. A person's **third cousin** is the child of one of his parents' second cousins. A **first cousin once removed** (or loosely **second cousin**) is the child of one's first cousin. 3 a member of a group related by race, ancestry, interests, etc.: *our Australian cousins.* 4 a title used by a sovereign when addressing another sovereign or a nobleman.
▷HISTORY C13: from Old French *cosin,* from Latin *consōbrīnus* cousin, from *sōbrīnus* cousin on the mother's side; related to *soror* sister
▸'**cousinˌhood** *or* '**cousinˌship** NOUN ▸'**cousinly** ADJECTIVE, ADVERB

couteau (kuːˈtəʊ) NOUN, *plural* **-teaux** (-ˈtəʊz). a large two-edged knife used formerly as a weapon.
▷HISTORY C17: from Old French *coutel,* from Latin *cultellus* a little knife, from *culter* knife, ploughshare

couth (kuːθ) ADJECTIVE 1 *Facetious* refined. 2 *Archaic* familiar; known.
▷HISTORY Old English *cūth* known, past participle of *cunnan* to know; sense 1, back formation from UNCOUTH

couthie *or* **couthy** ('kuːθɪ) ADJECTIVE *Scot* 1 sociable; friendly; congenial. 2 comfortable; snug. 3 plain; homely; unsophisticated: *a couthie saying.*
▷HISTORY C13: see COUTH, UNCOUTH

couture (kuːˈtʊə; *French* kutyr) NOUN **a** high-fashion designing and dressmaking. **b** (*as modifier*): *couture clothes.*
▷HISTORY from French: sewing, dressmaking, from Old French *cousture* seam, from Latin *consuere* to stitch together, from *suere* to sew

couturier (kuːˈtʊərɪˌeɪ; *French* kutyrje) NOUN a person who designs, makes, and sells fashion clothes for women.
▷HISTORY from French: dressmaker; see COUTURE
▸**couturière** (kuːˌtuːrɪˈɛə; *French* kutyrjɛr) FEMININE NOUN

couvade (kuːˈvɑːd; *French* kuvad) NOUN *Anthropol* a custom in certain cultures of treating the husband of a woman giving birth as if he were bearing the child.
▷HISTORY C19: from French, from *couver* to hatch, from Latin *cubāre* to lie down

couvert (kʊˈvɛə) NOUN another word for **cover** (sense 32).
▷HISTORY C18: from French

COV ABBREVIATION FOR: 1 *Statistics* covariance. 2 *Genetics* **crossover value.**

covalency (kəʊˈveɪlənsɪ) *or US* **covalence** NOUN 1 the formation and nature of covalent bonds. 2 the number of covalent bonds that a particular atom can make with other atoms in forming a molecule.
▸**coˈvalent** ADJECTIVE ▸**coˈvalently** ADVERB

covalent bond NOUN a type of chemical bond involving the sharing of electrons between atoms in a molecule, esp the sharing of a pair of electrons by two adjacent atoms.

covariance (kəʊˈvɛərɪəns) NOUN *Statistics* a measure of the association between two random variables, equal to the expected value of the product of the deviations from the mean of the two variables, and estimated by the sum of products of deviations from the sample mean for associated values of the two variables, divided by the number of sample points. Written as *Cov (X, Y)*.

cove[1] (kəʊv) NOUN [1] a small bay or inlet, usually between rocky headlands. [2] a narrow cavern formed in the sides of cliffs, mountains, etc., usually by erosion. [3] a sheltered place. [4] Also called: **coving.** *Architect* a concave curved surface between the wall and ceiling of a room. ◆ VERB [5] (*tr*) to form an architectural cove in.
▷HISTORY Old English *cofa;* related to Old Norse *kofi,* Old High German *kubisi* tent

cove[2] (kəʊv) NOUN [1] *Old-fashioned slang, Brit and Austral* a fellow; chap. [2] *Austral history* an overseer of convict labourers.
▷HISTORY C16: probably from Romany *kova* thing, person

coven (ˈkʌvᵊn) NOUN [1] a meeting of witches. [2] a company of 13 witches.
▷HISTORY C16: probably from Old French *covin* group, ultimately from Latin *convenīre* to come together; compare CONVENT

covenant (ˈkʌvənənt) NOUN [1] a binding agreement; contract. [2] *Law* **a** an agreement in writing under seal, as to pay a stated annual sum to a charity. **b** a particular clause in such an agreement, esp in a lease. [3] (in early English law) an action in which damages were sought for breach of a sealed agreement. [4] *Bible* God's promise to the Israelites and their commitment to worship him alone. ◆ VERB [5] to agree to a covenant (concerning).
▷HISTORY C13: from Old French, from *covenir* to agree, from Latin *convenīre* to come together, make an agreement; see CONVENE
▸**covenantal** (ˌkʌvəˈnæntᵊl) ADJECTIVE ▸ˌ**coveˈnantally** ADVERB

Covenant (ˈkʌvənənt) NOUN *Scot history* any of the bonds entered into by Scottish Presbyterians to defend their religion, esp one in 1638 (**National Covenant**) and one of 1643 (**Solemn League and Covenant**).

covenantee (ˌkʌvənənˈtiː) NOUN the person to whom the promise in a covenant is made.

Covenanter (ˈkʌvənəntə, ˌkʌvəˈnæntə) NOUN a person upholding the National Covenant of 1638 or the Solemn League and Covenant of 1643 between Scotland and England to establish and defend Presbyterianism.

covenantor *or* **covenanter** (ˈkʌvənəntə) NOUN a party who makes a promise and who is to perform the obligation expressed in a covenant.

Covent Garden (ˈkɒvənt, ˈkʌv-) NOUN [1] a district of central London: famous for its former fruit, vegetable, and flower market, now a shopping precinct. [2] the Royal Opera House (built 1858) in Covent Garden.

Coventry (ˈkɒvəntrɪ) NOUN [1] a city in central England, in Coventry unitary authority, West Midlands: devastated in World War II; modern cathedral (1954–62); industrial centre, esp for motor vehicles; two universities (1965, 1992). Pop.: 299 316 (1991). [2] a unitary authority in central England, in West Midlands. Pop.: 300 844 (2001). Area: 97 sq. km (37 sq. miles). [3] **send to Coventry.** to ostracize or ignore.

cover (ˈkʌvə) VERB (*mainly tr*) [1] to place or spread something over so as to protect or conceal. [2] to provide with a covering; clothe. [3] to put a garment, esp a hat, on (the body or head). [4] to extend over or lie thickly on the surface of; spread: *snow covered the fields.* [5] to bring upon (oneself); invest (oneself) as if with a covering: *covered with shame.* [6] (sometimes foll by *up*) to act as a screen or concealment for; hide from view. [7] *Military* to protect (an individual, formation, or place) by taking up a position from which fire may be returned if those being protected are fired upon. [8] (*also intr,* often foll by *for*) to assume responsibility for (a person or thing): *to cover for a colleague in his absence.* [9] (*intr;* foll by *for* or *up for*) to provide an alibi (for). [10] to have as one's territory: *this salesman covers your area.* [11] to travel over: *to cover three miles a day.* [12] (*tr*) to have or place in the aim and within the range of (a firearm). [13] to include or deal with: *his talk covered all aspects of the subject.* [14] (of an asset or income) to be sufficient to meet (a liability or expense). [15] **a** to insure against loss, risk, etc. **b** to provide for (loss, risk, etc.) by insurance. [16] (*also intr*) *Finance* to purchase (securities, etc.) in order to meet contracts, esp short sales. [17] to deposit (an equivalent stake) in a bet or wager. [18] (*also intr*) to play a card higher in rank than (one played beforehand by another player). [19] to act as reporter or photographer on (a news event, etc.) for a newspaper or magazine: *to cover sports events.* [20] *Sport* to guard or protect (an opponent, team-mate, or area). [21] *Music* to record a cover version of. [22] (of a male animal, esp a horse) to copulate with (a female animal). [23] (of a bird) to brood (eggs). ◆ NOUN [24] anything that covers, spreads over, protects, or conceals. [25] woods or bushes providing shelter or a habitat for wild creatures. [26] **a** a blanket used on a bed for warmth. **b** another word for **bedspread.** [27] *Finance* liquid assets, reserves, or guaranteed income sufficient to discharge a liability or meet an expenditure, etc. [28] a pretext, disguise, or false identity: *the thief sold brushes as a cover.* [29] *Insurance* another word for **coverage** (sense 3). [30] an envelope or package for sending through the post: *under plain cover.* [31] *Philately* **a** an entire envelope that has been postmarked. **b on cover.** (of a postage stamp) kept in this form by collectors. [32] an individual table setting, esp in a restaurant. [33] *Sport* the guarding or protection of an opponent, team-mate, or area. [34] Also called: **cover version.** a version by a different artist of a previously recorded musical item. [35] *Cricket* **a** (*often plural*) the area more or less at right angles to the pitch on the off side and usually about halfway to the boundary: *to field in the covers.* **b** (*as modifier*): *a cover drive by a batsman.* **c** Also called: **cover point.** a fielder in such a position. [36] *Ecology* the percentage of the ground surface covered by a given species of plant. [37] **break cover.** (esp of game animals) to come out from a shelter or hiding place. [38] **take cover.** to make for a place of safety or shelter. [39] **under cover.** protected, concealed, or in secret: *under cover of night.* ◆ See also **cover-up.**
▷HISTORY C13: from Old French *covrir,* from Latin *cooperīre* to cover completely, from *operīre* to cover over
▸ˈ**coverable** ADJECTIVE ▸ˈ**coverer** NOUN ▸ˈ**coverless** ADJECTIVE

coverage (ˈkʌvərɪdʒ) NOUN [1] the amount or extent to which something is covered. [2] *Journalism* the amount and quality of reporting or analysis given to a particular subject or event. [3] the extent of the protection provided by insurance. [4] *Finance* **a** the value of liquid assets reserved to meet liabilities. **b** the ratio of liquid assets to specific liabilities. **c** the ratio of total net profit to distributed profit in a company. [5] the section of the public reached by a medium of communication.

coverall (ˈkʌvərˌɔːl) NOUN [1] a thing that covers something entirely. [2] (*usually plural*) protective outer garments for the body.

cover charge NOUN a sum of money charged in a restaurant for each individual customer in addition to the cost of food and drink.

cover crop NOUN a crop planted between main crops to prevent leaching or soil erosion or to provide green manure.

covered wagon NOUN *US and Canadian* a large wagon with an arched canvas top, used formerly for prairie travel.

cover girl NOUN a girl, esp a glamorous one, whose picture appears on the cover of a newspaper or magazine.

cover glass NOUN a thin square of mounted glass used to protect a photographic slide.

covering (ˈkʌvərɪŋ) NOUN another word for **cover** (sense 24).

covering fire NOUN *Military* firing intended to protect an individual or formation making a movement by forcing the enemy to take cover.

covering letter NOUN an accompanying letter sent as an explanation, introduction, or record.

coverlet (ˈkʌvəlɪt) NOUN another word for **bedspread.**

Coverley (ˈkʌvəlɪ) NOUN See **Sir Roger de Coverley.**

covermount (ˈkʌvəˌmaʊnt) *Marketing* ◆ NOUN [1] an item attached to the front of a magazine as a gift. ◆ VERB [2] (*tr*) to attach (an item) to the front of a magazine as a gift.

cover note NOUN *Brit* a certificate issued by an insurance company stating that a policy is operative: used as a temporary measure between the commencement of cover and the issue of the policy.

cover point NOUN *Cricket* **a** a fielding position in the covers. **b** a fielder in this position.

covers (ˈkəʊvɜːs) ABBREVIATION FOR coversed sine.

coversed sine (ˈkəʊvɜːst) NOUN *Obsolete* a trigonometric function equal to one minus the sine of the specified angle. Abbreviation: **covers.**

cover-shoulder NOUN a type of blouse worn in Ghana.

cover slip NOUN a very thin piece of glass placed over a specimen on a glass slide that is to be examined under a microscope.

covert (ˈkʌvət) ADJECTIVE [1] concealed or secret: *covert jealousy.* [2] *Law* See **feme covert.** Compare **discovert.** ◆ NOUN [3] a shelter or disguise. [4] a thicket or woodland providing shelter for game. [5] short for **covert cloth.** [6] *Ornithol* any of the small feathers on the wings and tail of a bird that surround the bases of the larger feathers. [7] a flock of coots.
▷HISTORY C14: from Old French: covered, from *covrir* to COVER
▸ˈ**covertly** ADVERB ▸ˈ**covertness** NOUN

covert cloth NOUN a twill-weave cotton or worsted suiting fabric. Sometimes shortened to **covert.**

covert coat NOUN *Brit* a short topcoat worn for hunting.

coverture (ˈkʌvətʃə) NOUN [1] *Law* the condition or status of a married woman considered as being under the protection and influence of her husband. [2] *Rare* shelter, concealment, or disguise.
▷HISTORY C13: from Old French, from *covert* covered; see COVERT

cover-up NOUN [1] concealment or attempted concealment of a mistake, crime, etc. ◆ VERB **cover up.** (*adverb*) [2] (*tr*) to cover completely. [3] (when *intr,* often foll by *for*) to attempt to conceal (a mistake or crime): *she tried to cover up for her friend.* [4] (*intr*) *Boxing* to defend the body and head with the arms.

cover version NOUN another name for **cover** (sense 34).

cove stripe NOUN *Nautical* a decorative stripe painted along the sheer strake of a vessel, esp of a sailing boat.

covet (ˈkʌvɪt) VERB (*tr*) **-vets, -veting, -veted** to wish, long, or crave for (something, esp the property of another person).
▷HISTORY C13: from Old French *coveitier,* from *coveitié* eager desire, ultimately from Latin *cupiditā* CUPIDITY
▸ˈ**covetable** ADJECTIVE ▸ˈ**coveter** NOUN

covetous (ˈkʌvɪtəs) ADJECTIVE (*usually postpositive* and foll by *of*) jealously eager for the possession of something (esp the property of another person).
▸ˈ**covetously** ADVERB ▸ˈ**covetousness** NOUN

covey (ˈkʌvɪ) NOUN [1] a small flock of grouse or partridge. [2] a small group, as of people.
▷HISTORY C14: from Old French *covee,* from *cover* to sit on, hatch; see COUVADE

covin (ˈkʌvɪn) NOUN *Law* a conspiracy between two or more persons to act to the detriment or injury of another.
▷HISTORY C14: from Old French; see COVEN, CONVENE

cow[1] (kaʊ) NOUN [1] the mature female of any species of cattle, esp domesticated cattle. [2] the mature female of various other mammals, such as the elephant, whale, and seal. [3] (*not in technical use*) any domestic species of cattle. [4] *Informal* a disagreeable woman. [5] *Austral and NZ slang* something objectionable (esp in the phrase **a fair cow**). [6] **till the cows come home.** *Informal* for a very long time; effectively for ever.
▷HISTORY Old English *cū;* related to Old Norse *kýr,* Old High German *kuo,* Latin *bōs,* Greek *boūs,* Sanskrit *gāūs*

cow[2] (kaʊ) VERB (*tr*) to frighten or overawe, as with threats.

▷HISTORY C17: from Old Norse *kūga* to oppress, related to Norwegian *kue,* Swedish *kuva*

cowage *or* **cowhage** ('kaʊɪdʒ) NOUN 1 a tropical climbing leguminous plant, *Stizolobium* (or *Mucuna*) *pruriens,* whose bristly pods cause severe itching and stinging. 2 the pods of this plant or the stinging hairs covering them.
▷HISTORY C17: from Hindi *kavāch,* of obscure origin

cowal ('kaʊəl) NOUN *Austral* a shallow lake or swampy depression supporting vegetation.
▷HISTORY from a native Australian language

coward ('kaʊəd) NOUN a person who shrinks from or avoids danger, pain, or difficulty.
▷HISTORY C13: from Old French *cuard,* from *coue* tail, from Latin *cauda;* perhaps suggestive of a frightened animal with its tail between its legs

cowardice ('kaʊədɪs) NOUN lack of courage in facing danger, pain, or difficulty.

cowardly ('kaʊədlɪ) ADJECTIVE of or characteristic of a coward; lacking courage.
▸ **'cowardliness** NOUN

cow bail NOUN See **bail**[3] (sense 3).

cowbane ('kaʊˌbeɪn) NOUN 1 Also called: **water hemlock.** any of several N temperate poisonous umbelliferous marsh plants of the genus *Cicuta,* esp *C. virosa,* having clusters of small white flowers. 2 a similar and related plant, *Oxypolis rigidior* of the southeastern and central US. 3 any umbelliferous plant reputed to be poisonous to cattle.

cowbell ('kaʊˌbɛl) NOUN 1 a bell hung around a cow's neck so that the cow can be easily located. 2 a metal percussion instrument usually mounted on the bass drum or hand-held and struck with a drumstick. 3 *US* another name for **bladder campion.**

cowberry ('kaʊbərɪ, -brɪ) NOUN, *plural* **-ries.** 1 a creeping ericaceous evergreen shrub, *Vaccinium vitis-idaea,* of N temperate and arctic regions, with pink or red flowers and edible slightly acid berries. 2 the berry of this plant. ◆ Also called: **red whortleberry.**

cowbind ('kaʊˌbaɪnd) NOUN any of various bryony plants, esp the white bryony.

cowbird ('kaʊˌbɜːd) NOUN any of various American orioles of the genera *Molothrus, Tangavius,* etc., esp *M. ater* (common or brown-headed cowbird). They have a dark plumage and short bill.

cowboy ('kaʊˌbɔɪ) NOUN 1 Also called: **cowhand.** a hired man who herds and tends cattle, usually on horseback, esp in the western US. 2 a conventional character of Wild West folklore, films, etc., esp one involved in fighting Indians. 3 *Informal* **a** a person who is an irresponsible or unscrupulous operator in business. **b** (*as modifier*): *cowboy contractors; cowboy shop steward.* 4 *Austral* a man or boy who tends cattle.
▸ **'cowˌgirl** FEMININE NOUN

cowcatcher ('kaʊˌkætʃə) NOUN *US and Canadian* a metal frame on the front of a locomotive to clear the track of animals or other obstructions.

cow cocky NOUN, *plural* **cow cockies.** *Austral and NZ* a one-man dairy farmer.

cower ('kaʊə) VERB (*intr*) to crouch or cringe, as in fear.
▷HISTORY C13: from Middle Low German *kūren* to lie in wait; related to Swedish *kura* to lie in wait, Danish *kure* to squat

Cowes (kaʊz) NOUN a town in S England, on the Isle of Wight: famous for its annual regatta. Pop.: 16 335 (1991).

cowfeteria (ˌkaʊfɪ'tɪərɪə) NOUN *NZ informal* a calf feeder with multiple teats.
▷HISTORY from a blend of *cow* and *cafeteria*

cowfish ('kaʊˌfɪʃ) NOUN, *plural* **-fish** *or* **-fishes.** 1 any trunkfish, such as *Lactophrys quadricornis,* having hornlike spines over the eyes. 2 (loosely) any of various large aquatic animals, such as a sea cow.

cowflop ('kaʊˌflɒp) NOUN *Southwest English dialect* a foxglove.

Cow Gum NOUN *Trademark* a colourless adhesive based on a natural rubber solution.

cowherb ('kaʊˌhɜːb) NOUN a European caryophyllaceous plant, *Saponaria vaccaria,* having clusters of pink flowers: a weed in the US. See also **soapwort.**

cowherd ('kaʊˌhɜːd) NOUN a person employed to tend cattle.

cowhide ('kaʊˌhaɪd) NOUN 1 the hide of a cow. 2 the leather made from such a hide. ◆ Also called: **cowskin.**

Cowichan sweater ('kaʊɪtʃən) NOUN *Canadian* a heavy sweater of grey, unbleached wool with distinctive designs that were originally black-and-white but are now sometimes coloured: knitted originally by Cowichan Indians in British Columbia. Also called: **Cowichan Indian sweater, siwash, siwash sweater.**

cowitch ('kaʊɪtʃ) NOUN another name for **cowage.**
▷HISTORY C17: alteration of COWAGE by folk etymology

cowk (kaʊk) VERB (*intr*) *Northeast Scot dialect* to retch or feel nauseated.
▷HISTORY of obscure origin

cowl (kaʊl) NOUN 1 a hood, esp a loose one. 2 the hooded habit of a monk. 3 a cover fitted to a chimney to increase ventilation and prevent draughts. 4 the part of a car body that supports the windscreen and the bonnet. 5 *Aeronautics* another word for **cowling.** ◆ VERB (*tr*) 6 to cover or provide with a cowl. 7 to make a monk of.
▷HISTORY Old English *cugele,* from Late Latin *cuculla* cowl, from Latin *cucullus* covering, cap, hood

cowlick ('kaʊˌlɪk) NOUN a tuft of hair over the forehead.

cowling ('kaʊlɪŋ) NOUN a streamlined metal covering, esp one fitted around an aircraft engine. Also called: **cowl.** Compare **fairing**[1].

cowl neckline NOUN a neckline of women's clothes loosely folded over and sometimes resembling a folded hood.

cowman ('kaʊmən) NOUN, *plural* **-men.** 1 *Brit* another name for **cowherd.** 2 *US and Canadian* a man who owns cattle; rancher.

co-worker NOUN a fellow worker; associate.

cow parsley NOUN a common Eurasian umbelliferous hedgerow plant, *Anthriscus sylvestris,* having umbrella-shaped clusters of white flowers. Also called: **keck, Queen Anne's lace.**

cow parsnip NOUN any tall coarse umbelliferous plant of the genus *Heracleum,* such as *H. sphondylium* of Europe and Asia, having thick stems and flattened clusters of white or purple flowers. Also called: **hogweed, keck.**

cowpat ('kaʊˌpæt) NOUN a single dropping of cow dung.

cowpea ('kaʊˌpiː) NOUN 1 a leguminous tropical climbing plant, *Vigna sinensis,* producing long pods containing edible pealike seeds: grown for animal fodder and sometimes as human food. 2 Also called: **black-eyed pea.** the seed of this plant.

Cowper's glands ('kuːpəz) PLURAL NOUN two small yellowish glands near the prostate that secrete a mucous substance into the urethra during sexual stimulation in males. Compare **Bartholin's glands.**
▷HISTORY C18: named after William *Cowper* (1666–1709), English anatomist who discovered them

cow pillow NOUN (in India) a large cylindrical pillow stuffed with cotton and used for reclining rather than sleeping.

cow pony NOUN a horse used by cowboys when herding.

cowpox ('kaʊˌpɒks) NOUN a contagious viral disease of cows characterized by vesicles on the skin, esp on the teats and udder. Inoculation of humans with this virus provides temporary immunity to smallpox. It can be transmitted to other species, esp cats.

cowpuncher ('kaʊˌpʌntʃə) *or* **cowpoke** ('kaʊˌpəʊk) NOUN *US and Canadian* informal words for **cowboy.**

cowrie *or* **cowry** ('kaʊrɪ) NOUN, *plural* **-ries.** 1 any marine gastropod mollusc of the mostly tropical family *Cypraeidae,* having a glossy brightly marked shell with an elongated opening. 2 the shell of any of these molluscs, esp the shell of *Cypraea moneta* (**money cowry**), used as money in parts of Africa and S Asia.
▷HISTORY C17: from Hindi *kaurī,* from Sanskrit *kaparda,* of Dravidian origin; related to Tamil *kōtu* shell

cow shark NOUN any large primitive shark, esp *Hexanchus griseum,* of the family *Hexanchidae* of warm and temperate waters. Also called: **six-gilled shark.**

cowskin ('kaʊˌskɪn) NOUN another word for **cowhide.**

cowslip ('kaʊˌslɪp) NOUN 1 Also called: **paigle.** a primrose, *Primula veris,* native to temperate regions of the Old World, having fragrant yellow flowers. 2 *US and Canadian* another name for **marsh marigold.**
▷HISTORY Old English *cūslyppe;* see COW[1], SLIP[3]

cow tree NOUN a South American moraceous tree, *Brosimum galactodendron,* producing latex used as a substitute for milk.

cox (kɒks) NOUN 1 a coxswain, esp of a racing eight or four. ◆ VERB 2 to act as coxswain of (a boat).
▸ **'coxless** ADJECTIVE

coxa ('kɒksə) NOUN, *plural* **coxae** ('kɒksiː). 1 a technical name for the hipbone or hip joint. 2 the basal segment of the leg of an insect.
▷HISTORY C18: from Latin: hip
▸ **'coxal** ADJECTIVE

coxalgia (kɒk'sældʒɪə) NOUN 1 pain in the hip joint. 2 disease of the hip joint causing pain.
▷HISTORY C19: from COXA + -ALGIA
▸ **cox'algic** ADJECTIVE

coxcomb ('kɒksˌkəʊm) NOUN 1 a variant spelling of **cockscomb.** 2 *Archaic* a foppish man. 3 *Obsolete* the cap, resembling a cock's comb, worn by a jester.

coxcombry ('kɒksˌkəʊmrɪ) NOUN, *plural* **-ries.** conceited arrogance or foppishness.

Coxsackie virus (kʊk'sɑːkɪ) NOUN any of various viruses that occur in the intestinal tract of man and cause diseases, some of which resemble poliomyelitis.
▷HISTORY C20: after *Coxsackie,* a town in New York state, where the virus was first found

Cox's Orange Pippin ('kɒksɪz) NOUN a variety of eating apple with sweet flesh and a red-tinged green skin. Often shortened to **Cox.**
▷HISTORY C19: named after R. *Cox,* its English propagator

coxswain ('kɒksən, -ˌsweɪn) NOUN the helmsman of a lifeboat, racing shell, etc. Also called: **cockswain.**
▷HISTORY C15: from *cock* a ship's boat + SWAIN

coy (kɔɪ) ADJECTIVE 1 (usually of a woman) affectedly demure, esp in a playful or provocative manner. 2 shy; modest. 3 evasive, esp in an annoying way.
▷HISTORY C14: from Old French *coi* reserved, from Latin *quiētus* QUIET
▸ **'coyish** ADJECTIVE ▸ **'coyly** ADVERB ▸ **'coyness** NOUN

Coy. *Military* ABBREVIATION FOR company.

coyote ('kɔɪəʊt, kɔɪ'əʊt, kɔɪ'əʊtɪ) NOUN, *plural* **-otes** *or* **-ote.** 1 Also called: **prairie wolf.** a predatory canine mammal, *Canis latrans,* related to but smaller than the wolf, roaming the deserts and prairies of North America. 2 (in American Indian legends of the West) a trickster and culture hero represented as a man or as an animal.
▷HISTORY C19: from Mexican Spanish, from Nahuatl *coyotl*

coyotillo (ˌkəʊjəʊ'tiːljəʊ) NOUN, *plural* **-los.** a thorny poisonous rhamnaceous shrub, *Karwinskia humboldtiana* of Mexico and the southwestern US, the berries of which cause paralysis.
▷HISTORY Mexican Spanish, literally: a little COYOTE

coypu ('kɔɪpuː) NOUN, *plural* **-pus** *or* **-pu.** 1 an aquatic South American hystricomorph rodent, *Myocastor coypus,* introduced into Europe: family *Capromyidae.* It resembles a small beaver with a ratlike tail and is bred in captivity for its soft grey underfur. 2 the fur of this animal. ◆ Also called: **nutria.**
▷HISTORY C18: from American Spanish *coipú,* from Araucanian *kóypu*

coz (kʌz) NOUN an archaic word for **cousin:** used chiefly as a term of address.

cozen ('kʌzᵊn) VERB to cheat or trick (someone).
▷HISTORY C16: cant term perhaps related to COUSIN
▸ **'cozenage** NOUN ▸ **'cozener** NOUN

cozy ('kəʊzɪ) ADJECTIVE **-zier, -ziest,** NOUN, *plural* **-zies.** the usual US spelling of **cosy.**
▸ **'cozily** ADVERB ▸ **'coziness** NOUN

cp ABBREVIATION FOR: 1 candlepower. 2 chemically pure.

CP ABBREVIATION FOR: 1 Canadian Press. 2 *Military* Command Post. 3 Common Prayer. 4 Communist Party. 5 (formerly in Britain) **Community Programme.** 6 Court of Probate.

cp. ABBREVIATION FOR compare.

CPA (in the US) ABBREVIATION FOR certified public accountant.

CPAG (in Britain) ABBREVIATION FOR Child Poverty Action Group.

cpd *Zoology, botany, chem* ABBREVIATION FOR compound.

CPD ABBREVIATION FOR continuing professional development.

cpi ABBREVIATION FOR characters per inch.

CPI ABBREVIATION FOR consumer price index.

Cpl ABBREVIATION FOR Corporal.

CP/M NOUN an operating system widely used on microcomputers to enable a wide range of software from many suppliers to be run on them.

CPO ABBREVIATION FOR Chief Petty Officer.

CPR ABBREVIATION FOR **cardiopulmonary resuscitation.**

CPRE ABBREVIATION FOR Council for the Protection of Rural England.

cps ABBREVIATION FOR: 1 *Physics* cycles per second. 2 *Computing* characters per second.

CPS (in England and Wales) ABBREVIATION FOR **Crown Prosecution Service.**

CPSA (in Britain) ABBREVIATION FOR Civil and Public Services Association.

CPSU ABBREVIATION FOR (formerly) Communist Party of the Soviet Union.

CPU *Computing* ABBREVIATION FOR **central processing unit.**

CPVE (in Britain) ABBREVIATION FOR Certificate of Pre-vocational Education: a certificate awarded for completion of a broad-based course of study offered as a less advanced alternative to traditional school-leaving qualifications.

CQ NOUN 1 *Telegraphy, telephony* a symbol transmitted by an amateur radio operator requesting two-way communication with any other amateur radio operator listening. ◆ 2 *Military* ABBREVIATION FOR **charge of quarters.**

CQB *Military* ABBREVIATION FOR close-quarter battle.

CQSW (in Britain) ABBREVIATION FOR Certificate of Qualification in Social Work.

cr THE INTERNET DOMAIN NAME FOR Costa Rica.

Cr 1 ABBREVIATION FOR Councillor. ◆ 2 THE CHEMICAL SYMBOL FOR chromium.

CR ABBREVIATION FOR: 1 Community of the Resurrection. 2 Costa Rica. ◆ 3 INTERNATIONAL CAR REGISTRATION FOR Costa Rica.

cr. ABBREVIATION FOR: 1 credit. 2 creditor.

crab[1] (kræb) NOUN 1 any chiefly marine decapod crustacean of the genus *Cancer* and related genera (section *Brachyura*), having a broad flattened carapace covering the cephalothorax, beneath which is folded the abdomen. The first pair of limbs are modified as pincers. See also **fiddler crab, soft-shell crab, pea crab, oyster crab.** Related adjective: **cancroid.** 2 any of various similar or related arthropods, such as the hermit crab and horseshoe crab. 3 short for **crab louse.** 4 a manoeuvre in which an aircraft flies slightly into the crosswind to compensate for drift. 5 a mechanical lifting device, esp the travelling hoist of a gantry crane. 6 *Wrestling* See **Boston crab.** 7 **catch a crab.** *Rowing* to make a stroke in which the oar either misses the water or digs too deeply, causing the rower to fall backwards. ◆ VERB **crabs, crabbing, crabbed.** 8 *(intr)* to hunt or catch crabs. 9 *(tr)* to fly (an aircraft) slightly into a crosswind to compensate for drift. 10 *(intr) Nautical* to move forwards with a slight sideways motion, as to overcome an offsetting current. 11 *(intr)* to move sideways. ◆ See also **crabs.**
▹**HISTORY** Old English *crabba;* related to Old Norse *krabbi,* Old High German *krebiz* crab, Dutch *krabben* to scratch

crab[2] (kræb) *Informal* ◆ VERB **crabs, crabbing, crabbed.** 1 *(intr)* to find fault; grumble. 2 *(tr) Chiefly US* to spoil (esp in the phrase **crab someone's act**). ◆ NOUN 3 an irritable person. 4 **draw the crabs.** *Austral* to attract unwelcome attention.
▹**HISTORY** C16: probably back formation from CRABBED

crab[3] (kræb) NOUN short for **crab apple.**
▹**HISTORY** C15: perhaps of Scandinavian origin; compare Swedish *skrabbe* crab apple

Crab (kræb) NOUN **the.** the constellation Cancer, the fourth sign of the zodiac.

crab apple NOUN 1 any of several rosaceous trees of the genus *Malus* that have white, pink, or red flowers and small sour apple-like fruits. 2 the fruit of any of these trees, used to make jam.

crabbed (ˈkræbɪd) ADJECTIVE 1 surly; irritable; perverse. 2 (esp of handwriting) cramped and hard to decipher.
▹**HISTORY** C13: probably from CRAB[1] (from its wayward gait), influenced by CRAB(APPLE) (from its tartness)
▸ **ˈcrabbedly** ADVERB ▸ **ˈcrabbedness** NOUN

crabber (ˈkræbə) NOUN 1 a crab fisherman. 2 a boat used for crab-fishing.

crabby (ˈkræbɪ) ADJECTIVE **-bier, -biest.** bad-tempered.

crab canon NOUN *Music* a canon in which the imitating voice repeats the notes of the theme in reverse order. Also called: **retrograde canon, canon cancrizans.**
▹**HISTORY** from the mistaken medieval notion that crabs move backwards

crab grass NOUN any of several coarse weedy grasses of the genus *Digitaria,* which grow in warm regions and tend to displace other grasses in lawns.

crab louse NOUN a parasitic louse, *Pthirus* (or *Phthirus*) *pubis,* that infests the pubic region in man.

Crab Nebula NOUN the expanding remnant of the supernova observed in 1054 A.D., lying in the constellation Taurus at an approximate distance of 6500 light years.

crabs (kræbz) NOUN *(sometimes functioning as singular)* the lowest throw in a game of chance, esp two aces in dice.
▹**HISTORY** plural of CRAB[1]

crabstick (ˈkræbˌstɪk) NOUN 1 a stick, cane, or cudgel made of crab-apple wood. 2 *Informal* a bad-tempered person.

crabwise (ˈkræbˌwaɪz) ADJECTIVE, ADVERB (of motion) sideways; like a crab.

crabwood (ˈkræbˌwʊd) NOUN 1 a tropical American meliaceous tree, *Carapa guianensis.* 2 the wood of this tree, used for construction.

CRAC ABBREVIATION FOR Careers Research and Advisory Centre.

crack (kræk) VERB 1 to break or cause to break without complete separation of the parts: *the vase was cracked but unbroken.* 2 to break or cause to break with a sudden sharp sound; snap: *to crack a nut.* 3 to make or cause to make a sudden sharp sound: *to crack a whip.* 4 to cause (the voice) to change tone or become harsh or (of the voice) to change tone, esp to a higher register; break. 5 *Informal* to fail or cause to fail. 6 to yield or cause to yield: *to crack under torture.* 7 *(tr)* to hit with a forceful or resounding blow. 8 *(tr)* to break into or force open: *to crack a safe.* 9 *(tr)* to solve or decipher (a code, problem, etc.). 10 *(tr) Informal* to tell (a joke, etc.). 11 to break (a molecule) into smaller molecules or radicals by the action of heat, as in the distillation of petroleum. 12 *(tr)* to open (esp a bottle) for drinking: *let's crack another bottle.* 13 *(intr) Scot, Northern English dialect* to chat; gossip. 14 *(tr) Informal* to achieve (esp in the phrase **crack it**). 15 *(tr) Austral informal* to find or catch: *to crack a wave in surfing.* 16 **crack a smile.** *Informal* to break into a smile. 17 **crack hardy** *or* **hearty.** *Austral and NZ informal* to disguise one's discomfort, etc.; put on a bold front. ◆ NOUN 18 a sudden sharp noise. 19 a break or fracture without complete separation of the two parts: *a crack in the window.* 20 a narrow opening or fissure. 21 *Informal* a resounding blow. 22 a physical or mental defect; flaw. 23 a moment or specific instant: *the crack of day.* 24 a broken or cracked tone of voice, as a boy's during puberty. 25 (often foll by *at*) *Informal* an attempt; opportunity to try: *he had a crack at the problem.* 26 *Slang* a gibe; wisecrack; joke. 27 *Slang* a person that excels. 28 *Scot, Northern English dialect* a talk; chat. 29 *Slang* a processed form of cocaine hydrochloride used as a stimulant. It is highly addictive. 30 Also: **craic.** *Informal, chiefly Irish* fun; informal entertainment;: *the crack was great in here last night.* 31 *Obsolete slang* a burglar or burglary. 32 **crack of dawn. a** the very instant that the sun rises. **b** very early in the morning. 33 **a fair crack of the whip.** *Informal* a fair chance or opportunity. 34 **crack of doom.** doomsday; the end of the world; the Day of Judgment. ◆ ADJECTIVE 35 *(prenominal) Slang* first-class; excellent: *a crack shot.* ◆ See also **crack down, crack on, crack up.**
▹**HISTORY** Old English *cracian;* related to Old High German *krahhōn,* Dutch *kraken,* Sanskrit *gárjati* he roars

crackbrain (ˈkrækˌbreɪn) NOUN a person who is insane.

crackbrained (ˈkrækˌbreɪnd) ADJECTIVE insane, idiotic, or crazy.

crack down VERB *(intr, adverb;* often foll by *on)* 1 to take severe measures (against); become stricter (with). ◆ NOUN **crackdown.** 2 severe or repressive measures.

cracked (krækt) ADJECTIVE 1 damaged by cracking. 2 *Informal* crazy.

cracked heels PLURAL NOUN another name for **scratches.**

cracked wheat NOUN whole wheat cracked between rollers so that it will cook more quickly.

cracker (ˈkrækə) NOUN 1 a decorated cardboard tube that emits a bang when pulled apart, releasing a toy, a joke, or a paper hat. 2 short for **firecracker.** 3 a thin crisp biscuit, usually unsweetened. 4 a person or thing that cracks. 5 *US* another word for **poor White.** 6 *Brit slang* a thing or person of notable qualities or abilities. 7 **not worth a cracker.** *Austral and NZ informal* worthless; useless.

cracker-barrel ADJECTIVE *US* rural; rustic; homespun: *a cracker-barrel philosopher.*

crackerjack (ˈkrækəˌdʒæk) *Informal* ◆ ADJECTIVE 1 excellent. ◆ NOUN 2 a person or thing of exceptional quality or ability.
▹**HISTORY** C20: changed from CRACK (first-class) + JACK[1] (man)

crackers (ˈkrækəz) ADJECTIVE *(postpositive) Brit* a slang word for **insane.**

cracket (ˈkrækɪt) NOUN *Dialect* 1 a low stool, often one with three legs. 2 a box for a miner to kneel on when working a low seam.
▹**HISTORY** variant of CRICKET[3]

crackhead (ˈkrækˌhɛd) NOUN *Slang* a person addicted to the drug crack.

cracking (ˈkrækɪŋ) ADJECTIVE 1 *(prenominal) Informal* fast; vigorous (esp in the phrase **a cracking pace**). 2 **get cracking.** *Informal* to start doing something quickly or do something with increased speed. ◆ ADVERB, ADJECTIVE 3 *Brit informal* first-class; excellent: *a cracking good match.* ◆ NOUN 4 the process in which molecules are cracked, esp the oil-refining process in which heavy oils are broken down into hydrocarbons of lower molecular weight by heat or catalysis. See also **catalytic cracker.**

crackjaw (ˈkrækˌdʒɔː) *Informal* ◆ ADJECTIVE 1 difficult to pronounce. ◆ NOUN 2 a word or phrase that is difficult to pronounce.

crackle (ˈkræk[ə]l) VERB 1 to make or cause to make a series of slight sharp noises, as of paper being crushed or of a wood fire burning. 2 *(tr)* to decorate (porcelain or pottery) by causing a fine network of cracks to appear in the glaze. 3 *(intr)* to abound in vivacity or energy. ◆ NOUN 4 the act or sound of crackling. 5 intentional crazing in the glaze of a piece of porcelain or pottery. 6 Also called: **crackleware.** porcelain or pottery so decorated.

crackling (ˈkræklɪŋ) NOUN the crisp browned skin of roast pork.

cracknel (ˈkrækn[ə]l) NOUN 1 a type of hard plain biscuit. 2 *(often plural) US and Canadian* crisply fried bits of fat pork.
▹**HISTORY** C15: perhaps from Old French *craquelin,* from Middle Dutch *krākelinc,* from *krāken* to CRACK

crack on VERB *(intr;* often foll by *with) Informal* to continue to do something as quickly as possible.

crackpot (ˈkrækˌpɒt) *Informal* ◆ NOUN 1 an eccentric person; crank. ◆ ADJECTIVE 2 *(usually prenominal)* eccentric; crazy.

cracksman (ˈkræksmən) NOUN, *plural* **-men.** *Slang* a burglar, esp a safe-breaker.

crack up VERB *(adverb)* 1 *(intr)* to break into pieces. 2 *(intr) Informal* to undergo a physical or mental breakdown. 3 *(tr) Informal* to present or report, esp in glowing terms: *it's not all it's cracked up to be*. 4 *Informal, chiefly US and Canadian* to laugh or cause to laugh uproariously or uncontrollably. ◆ NOUN **crackup.** 5 *Informal* a physical or mental breakdown.

crack willow NOUN 1 a species of commonly grown willow, *Salix fragilis*, with branches that snap easily. 2 any of various related willows.

Cracow ('krækaʊ, -əʊ, -ɒf) NOUN an industrial city in S Poland, on the River Vistula: former capital of the country (1320–1609); university (1364). Pop.: 740 000 (1999 est.). Polish name: **Kraków.** German name: **Krakau.**

-cracy NOUN COMBINING FORM indicating a type of government or rule: *plutocracy; mobocracy*. See also **-crat.**
▷HISTORY from Greek *-kratia*, from *kratos* power

cradle ('kreɪdᵊl) NOUN 1 a baby's bed with enclosed sides, often with a hood and rockers. 2 a place where something originates or is nurtured during its early life: *the cradle of civilization*. 3 the earliest period of life: *they knew each other from the cradle*. 4 a frame, rest, or trolley made to support or transport a piece of equipment, aircraft, ship, etc. 5 a platform, cage, or trolley, in which workmen are suspended on the side of a building or ship. 6 the part of a telephone on which the handset rests when not in use. 7 a holder connected to a computer allowing data to be transferred from a PDA, digital camera, etc. 8 another name for **creeper** (sense 5). 9 *Agriculture* **a** a framework of several wooden fingers attached to a scythe to gather the grain into bunches as it is cut. **b** a scythe equipped with such a cradle; cradle scythe. **c** a collar of wooden fingers that prevents a horse or cow from turning its head and biting itself. 10 Also called: **rocker.** a boxlike apparatus for washing rocks, sand, etc., containing gold or gem stones. 11 *Engraving* a tool that produces the pitted surface of a copper mezzotint plate before the design is engraved upon it. 12 a framework used to prevent the bedclothes from touching a sensitive part of an injured person. 13 **from the cradle to the grave.** throughout life. ◆ VERB 14 *(tr)* to rock or place in or as if in a cradle; hold tenderly. 15 *(tr)* to nurture in or bring up from infancy. 16 *(tr)* to replace (the handset of a telephone) on the cradle. 17 to reap (grain) with a cradle scythe. 18 *(tr)* to wash (soil bearing gold, etc.) in a cradle. 19 *Lacrosse* to keep (the ball) in the net of the stick, esp while running with it.
▷HISTORY Old English *cradol;* related to Old High German *kratto* basket
►'**cradler** NOUN

cradle cap NOUN a form of seborrhoea of the scalp common in young babies. Technical name: **crusta lactea.**

cradle snatcher NOUN *Informal* someone who marries or has an affair with a much younger person.

cradlesong ('kreɪdᵊl,sɒŋ) NOUN another word for **lullaby.**

cradling ('kreɪdlɪŋ) NOUN *Architect* a framework of iron or wood, esp as used in the construction of a ceiling.

craft (krɑːft) NOUN 1 skill or ability, esp in handiwork. 2 skill in deception and trickery; guile; cunning. 3 an occupation or trade requiring special skill, esp manual dexterity. 4 **a** the members of such a trade, regarded collectively. **b** *(as modifier): a craft guild*. 5 a single vessel, aircraft, or spacecraft. 6 *(functioning as plural)* ships, boats, aircraft, or spacecraft collectively. ◆ VERB 7 *(tr)* to make or fashion with skill, esp by hand.
▷HISTORY Old English *cræft* skill, strength; related to Old Norse *kraptr* power, skill, Old High German *kraft*

craft apprenticeship NOUN a period of training for a skilled trade in industry, such as for a plumber or electrician.

craftsman ('krɑːftsmən) NOUN, *plural* **-men.** 1 a member of a skilled trade; someone who practises a craft; artisan. 2 Also called: *(feminine)* **craftswoman.** an artist skilled in the techniques of an art or craft.
►'**craftsmanly** ADJECTIVE ►'**craftsman,ship** NOUN

craft union NOUN a labour organization membership of which is restricted to workers in a specified trade or craft. Compare **industrial union.**

crafty ('krɑːftɪ) ADJECTIVE **craftier, craftiest.** 1 skilled in deception; shrewd; cunning. 2 *Archaic* skilful.
►'**craftily** ADVERB ►'**craftiness** NOUN

crag (kræg) NOUN a steep rugged rock or peak.
▷HISTORY C13: of Celtic origin; related to Old Welsh *creik* rock

Crag (kræg) NOUN a formation of shelly sandstone in E England, deposited during the Pliocene and Pleistocene epochs.

craggy ('krægɪ) *or US* **cragged** ('krægɪd) ADJECTIVE **-gier, -giest.** 1 having many crags. 2 (of the face) rugged; rocklike.
►'**craggily** ADVERB ►'**cragginess** NOUN

cragsman ('krægzmən) NOUN, *plural* **-men.** a rock climber.

craic (kræk) NOUN an Irish spelling of **crack** (sense 30).

craig (kreg, kreɪg) NOUN a Scot word for **crag.**

Craigavon (,kreɪg'ævᵊn) NOUN a district in central Northern Ireland, in Co. Armagh. Pop.: 80 671 (2001). Area: 279 sq. km (108 sq. miles).

Craiova (*Romanian* kra'jova) NOUN a city in SW Romania, on the Jiul River. Pop.: 312 891 (1997 est.).

crake (kreɪk) NOUN *Zoology* any of several rails that occur in the Old World, such as the corncrake and the spotted crake.
▷HISTORY C14: from Old Norse *krāka* crow or *krākr* raven, of imitative origin

cram (kræm) VERB **crams, cramming, crammed.** 1 *(tr)* to force (people, material, etc.) into (a room, container, etc.) with more than it can hold; stuff. 2 to eat or cause to eat more than necessary. 3 *Informal* to study or cause to study (facts, etc.), esp for an examination, by hastily memorizing. ◆ NOUN 4 the act or condition of cramming. 5 a crush.
▷HISTORY Old English *crammian;* related to Old Norse *kremja* to press

crambo ('kræmbəʊ) NOUN a word game in which one team says a rhyme or rhyming line for a word or line given by the other team.
▷HISTORY C17: from earlier *crambe*, probably from Latin *crambē repetīta* cabbage repeated, hence an old story, a rhyming game, from Greek *krambē*

cram-full ADJECTIVE stuffed full.

crammer ('kræmə) NOUN a person or school that prepares pupils for an examination, esp pupils who have already failed that examination.

cramoisy *or* **cramoisie** ('kræmɔɪzɪ, -əzɪ) *Archaic* ◆ ADJECTIVE 1 of a crimson colour. ◆ NOUN 2 crimson cloth.
▷HISTORY C15: from Old French *cramoisi*, from Arabic *qirmizī* red obtained from kermes; see CRIMSON, KERMES

cramp[1] (kræmp) NOUN 1 a painful involuntary contraction of a muscle, typically caused by overexertion, heat, or chill. 2 temporary partial paralysis of a muscle group: *writer's cramp*. 3 *(usually plural in the US and Canada)* severe abdominal pain. ◆ VERB 4 *(tr)* to affect with or as if with a cramp.
▷HISTORY C14: from Old French *crampe*, of Germanic origin; compare Old High German *krampho*

cramp[2] (kræmp) NOUN 1 Also called: **cramp iron.** a strip of metal with its ends bent at right angles, used to bind masonry. 2 a device for holding pieces of wood while they are glued; clamp. 3 something that confines or restricts. 4 a confined state or position. ◆ VERB *(tr)* 5 to secure or hold with a cramp. 6 to confine, hamper, or restrict. 7 **cramp (someone's) style.** *Informal* to prevent (a person) from using his abilities or acting freely and confidently.
▷HISTORY C15: from Middle Dutch *crampe* cramp, hook, of Germanic origin; compare Old High German *khramph* bent; see CRAMP[1]

cramp ball NOUN a hard round blackish ascomycetous fungus, *Daldinia concentrica*, characteristically found on the bark of ash trees and formerly carried to ward off cramp. The specific name refers to the concentric rings revealed if the fungus is sliced.

cramped (kræmpt) ADJECTIVE 1 closed in; restricted. 2 (esp of handwriting) small and irregular; difficult to read.

cramper ('kræmpə) NOUN *Curling* a spiked metal plate used as a brace for the feet in throwing the stone.

crampon ('kræmpən) NOUN 1 one of a pair of pivoted steel levers used to lift heavy objects; grappling iron. 2 *(often plural)* one of a pair of frames each with 10 or 12 metal spikes, strapped to boots for climbing or walking on ice or snow. ◆ VERB 3 to climb using crampons.
▷HISTORY C15: from French, from Middle Dutch *crampe* hook; see CRAMP[2]

cran (kræn) NOUN a unit of capacity used for measuring fresh herring, equal to 37.5 gallons.
▷HISTORY C18: of uncertain origin

cranage ('kreɪnɪdʒ) NOUN 1 the use of a crane. 2 a fee charged for such use.

cranberry ('krænbərɪ, -brɪ) NOUN, *plural* **-ries.** 1 any of several trailing ericaceous shrubs of the genus *Vaccinium*, such as the European *V. oxycoccus*, that bear sour edible red berries. 2 the berry of this plant, used to make sauce or jelly.
▷HISTORY C17: from Low German *kraanbere*, from *kraan* CRANE + *bere* BERRY

cranberry bush *or* **tree** NOUN a North American caprifoliaceous shrub or small tree, *Viburnum trilobum*, producing acid red fruit.

Cranborne money ('krænbɔːn) NOUN (in Britain) the annual payment made to Opposition parties in the House of Lords to help them pay for certain services necessary to the carrying out of their parliamentary duties; established in 1996. Compare **Short money.**
▷HISTORY named after Viscount Cranborne, Leader of the House of Lords in 1996

crane (kreɪn) NOUN 1 any large long-necked long-legged wading bird of the family *Gruidae*, inhabiting marshes and plains in most parts of the world except South America, New Zealand, and Indonesia: order *Gruiformes*. See also **demoiselle** (sense 1), **whooping crane.** 2 *(not in ornithological use)* any similar bird, such as a heron. 3 a device for lifting and moving heavy objects, typically consisting of a moving boom, beam, or gantry from which lifting gear is suspended. See also **gantry.** 4 *Films* a large trolley carrying a boom, on the end of which is mounted a camera. ◆ VERB 5 *(tr)* to lift or move (an object) by or as if by a crane. 6 to stretch out (esp the neck), as to see over other people's heads. 7 *(intr)* (of a horse) to pull up short before a jump.
▷HISTORY Old English *cran;* related to Middle High German *krane*, Latin *grūs*, Greek *géranos*

crane fly NOUN any dipterous fly of the family *Tipulidae*, having long legs, slender wings, and a narrow body. Also called (Brit): **daddy-longlegs.**

cranesbill ('kreɪnz,bɪl) NOUN any of various plants of the genus *Geranium*, having pink or purple flowers and long slender beaked fruits: family *Geraniaceae*. See also **herb Robert, storksbill.**

cranial ('kreɪnɪəl) ADJECTIVE of or relating to the skull.
►'**cranially** ADVERB

cranial index NOUN the ratio of the greatest length to the greatest width of the cranium, multiplied by 100: used in comparative anthropology. Compare **cephalic index.**

cranial nerve NOUN any of the 12 paired nerves that have their origin in the brain and reach the periphery through natural openings in the skull.

craniate ('kreɪnɪɪt, -,eɪt) ADJECTIVE 1 having a skull or cranium. ◆ ADJECTIVE, NOUN 2 another word for **vertebrate.**

cranio- *or before a vowel* **crani-** COMBINING FORM indicating the cranium or cranial: *craniotomy*.

craniology (,kreɪnɪ'ɒlədʒɪ) NOUN the branch of science concerned with the shape and size of the human skull, esp with reference to variations between different races.
►**craniological** (,kreɪnɪə'lɒdʒɪkᵊl) ADJECTIVE ►,**cranio'logically** ADVERB ►,**crani'ologist** NOUN

craniometer (,kreɪnɪ'ɒmɪtə) NOUN an instrument for measuring the cranium or skull.

craniometry (,kreɪnɪ'ɒmɪtrɪ) NOUN the study and measurement of skulls.
►**craniometric** (,kreɪnɪə'mɛtrɪk) *or* ,**cranio'metrical** ADJECTIVE ►,**cranio'metrically** ADVERB ►,**crani'ometrist** NOUN

craniopagus (ˌkreɪnɪ'ɒpəgəs) NOUN the condition of Siamese twins joined at the head.

craniotomy (ˌkreɪnɪ'ɒtəmɪ) NOUN, *plural* **-mies.** 1 surgical incision into the skull, esp to expose the brain for neurosurgery. 2 surgical crushing of a fetal skull to extract a dead fetus.

cranium ('kreɪnɪəm) NOUN, *plural* **-niums** *or* **-nia** (-nɪə). 1 the skull of a vertebrate. 2 the part of the skull that encloses the brain. Nontechnical name: **brainpan.**
▷HISTORY C16: from Medieval Latin *crānium* skull, from Greek *kranion*

crank[1] (kræŋk) NOUN 1 a device for communicating motion or for converting reciprocating motion into rotary motion or vice versa. It consists of an arm projecting from a shaft, often with a second member attached to it parallel to the shaft. 2 Also called: **crank handle, starting handle.** a handle incorporating a crank, used to start an engine or motor. 3 *Informal* **a** an eccentric or odd person, esp someone who stubbornly maintains unusual views. **b** *US and Canadian* a bad-tempered person. ◆ VERB 4 (*tr*) to rotate (a shaft) by means of a crank. 5 (*tr*) to start (an engine, motor, etc.) by means of a crank handle. 6 (*tr*) to bend, twist, or make into the shape of a crank. 7 (*intr*) *Obsolete* to twist or wind. ◆ See also **crank up.**
▷HISTORY Old English *cranc;* related to Middle Low German *krunke* wrinkle, Dutch *krinkel* CRINKLE

crank[2] (kræŋk) *or* **cranky** ADJECTIVE (of a sailing vessel) easily keeled over by the wind; tender.
▷HISTORY C17: of uncertain origin; perhaps related to CRANK[1]

crankcase ('kræŋkˌkeɪs) NOUN the metal housing that encloses the crankshaft, connecting rods, etc., in an internal-combustion engine, reciprocating pump, etc.

crankpin ('kræŋkˌpɪn) NOUN a short cylindrical bearing surface fitted between two arms of a crank and set parallel to the main shaft of the crankshaft.

crankshaft ('kræŋkˌʃɑːft) NOUN a shaft having one or more cranks, esp the main shaft of an internal-combustion engine to which the connecting rods are attached.

crank up VERB (*tr*) *Slang* 1 to increase (loudness, output, etc.): *he cranked up his pace.* 2 to set in motion or invigorate: *news editors have to crank up tired reporters.* 3 (*intr, adverb*) to inject a narcotic drug.

cranky[1] ('kræŋkɪ) ADJECTIVE **crankier, crankiest.** 1 *Informal* eccentric. 2 *Chiefly US, Canadian, and Irish informal* fussy and bad-tempered. 3 shaky; out of order. 4 full of bends and turns. 5 *Dialect* unwell.
▸ **'crankily** ADVERB ▸ **'crankiness** NOUN

cranky[2] ('kræŋkɪ) ADJECTIVE **crankier, crankiest.** *Nautical* another word for **crank**[2].

crannog ('krænəg) *or* **crannoge** ('krænədʒ) NOUN an ancient Celtic lake or bog dwelling dating from the late Bronze Age to the 16th century A.D., often fortified and used as a refuge.
▷HISTORY C19: from Irish Gaelic *crannóg,* from Old Irish *crann* tree

cranny ('krænɪ) NOUN, *plural* **-nies.** a narrow opening, as in a wall or rock face; chink; crevice (esp in the phrase **every nook and cranny**).
▷HISTORY C15: from Old French *cran* notch, fissure; compare CRENEL
▸ **'crannied** ADJECTIVE

Cranwell ('krænwəl) NOUN a village in E England, in Lincolnshire: Royal Air Force College (1920).

crap[1] (kræp) NOUN 1 a losing throw in the game of craps. 2 another name for **craps.**
▷HISTORY C20: back formation from CRAPS

crap[2] (kræp) *Slang* ◆ NOUN 1 nonsense. 2 rubbish. 3 another word for **faeces.** ◆ VERB **craps, crapping, crapped.** 4 (*intr*) another word for **defecate.**
▷HISTORY C15 *crappe* chaff, from Middle Dutch, probably from *crappen* to break off

> **Language note** This word was formerly considered to be taboo, and it was labelled as such in previous editions of *Collins English Dictionary*. However, it has now become acceptable in speech, although some older or more conservative people may object to its use.

crapaud ('kræpəʊ, 'krɑː-) NOUN *Caribbean* a frog or toad.
▷HISTORY from French: toad

crape (kreɪp) NOUN 1 a variant spelling of **crepe.** 2 crepe, esp when used for mourning clothes. 3 a band of black crepe worn in mourning.
▸ **'crapy** ADJECTIVE

crape myrtle *or* **crepe myrtle** NOUN an oriental lythraceous shrub, *Lagerstroemia indica,* cultivated in warm climates for its pink, red, or white flowers.

crapola (kræ'pəʊlə) NOUN *Informal* rubbish; nonsense.

crap out VERB (*intr, adverb*) 1 *US slang* to make a losing throw in craps. 2 *US slang* to fail; withdraw. 3 *US slang* to rest. 4 *Slang* to fail to do or attempt something through fear.

crappie ('kræpɪ) NOUN either of two North American freshwater percoid food and game fishes, *Pomoxis nigromaculatus* (**black crappie**) or *P. annularis* (**white crappie**): family *Centrarchidae* (sunfishes, etc.).
▷HISTORY C19: from Canadian French *crapet*

craps (kræps) NOUN (*usually functioning as singular*) 1 a gambling game using two dice, in which a player wins the bet if 7 or 11 is thrown first, and loses if 2, 3, or 12 is thrown. 2 **shoot craps.** to play this game.
▷HISTORY C19: probably from *crabs* lowest throw at dice, plural of CRAB[1]

crapshooter ('kræpˌʃuːtə) NOUN *US* a person who plays the game of craps.

crapulent ('kræpjʊlənt) *or* **crapulous** ('kræpjʊləs) ADJECTIVE 1 given to or resulting from intemperance. 2 suffering from intemperance; drunken.
▷HISTORY C18: from Late Latin *crāpulentus* drunk, from Latin *crāpula,* from Greek *kraipalē* drunkenness, headache resulting therefrom
▸ **'crapulence** NOUN ▸ **'crapulently** *or* **'crapulously** ADVERB
▸ **'crapulousness** NOUN

craquelure ('krækəlʊə) NOUN a network of fine cracks on old paintings caused by the deterioration of pigment or varnish.
▷HISTORY C20: from French, from *craqueler* to crackle, from *craquer* to crack, of imitative origin

crash[1] (kræʃ) VERB 1 to make or cause to make a loud noise as of solid objects smashing or clattering. 2 to fall or cause to fall with force, breaking in pieces with a loud noise as of solid objects smashing. 3 (*intr*) to break or smash in pieces with a loud noise. 4 (*intr*) to collapse or fail suddenly: *this business is sure to crash.* 5 to cause (an aircraft) to hit land or water violently resulting in severe damage or (of an aircraft) to hit land or water in this way. 6 to cause (a car, etc.) to collide with another car or other object or (of two or more cars) to be involved in a collision. 7 to move or cause to move violently or noisily: *to crash through a barrier.* 8 *Brit informal* short for **gate-crash.** 9 (*intr*) (of a computer system or program) to fail suddenly and completely because of a malfunction. 10 (*intr*) *Slang* another term for **crash out.** 11 **crash and burn.** *Informal* to fail; be unsuccessful. ◆ NOUN 12 an act or instance of breaking and falling to pieces. 13 a sudden loud noise: *the crash of thunder.* 14 a collision, as between vehicles. 15 a sudden descent of an aircraft as a result of which it hits land or water. 16 the sudden collapse of a business, stock exchange, etc., esp one causing further financial failure. 17 (*modifier*) **a** requiring or using intensive effort and all possible resources in order to accomplish something quickly: *a crash programme.* **b** sudden or vigorous: *a crash halt; a crash tackle.* 18 **crash-and-burn.** *Informal* a complete failure. ◆ See also **crash out.**
▷HISTORY C14: probably from *crasen* to smash, shatter + *dasshen* to strike violently, DASH[1]; see CRAZE
▸ **'crasher** NOUN

crash[2] (kræʃ) NOUN a coarse cotton or linen cloth used for towelling, curtains, etc.
▷HISTORY C19: from Russian *krashenina* coloured linen

crash barrier NOUN a barrier erected along the centre of a motorway, around a racetrack, etc., for safety purposes.

crash dive NOUN 1 a sudden steep dive from the surface by a submarine. ◆ VERB **crash-dive.** 2 (usually of an aircraft) to descend steeply and rapidly, before hitting the ground. 3 to perform or cause to perform a crash dive.

crash helmet NOUN a padded helmet worn for motorcycling, flying, bobsleighing, etc., to protect the head in a crash.

crashing ('kræʃɪŋ) ADJECTIVE (*prenominal*) *Informal* (intensifier) (esp in the phrase **a crashing bore**).

crash-land VERB to land (an aircraft) in an emergency causing damage or (of an aircraft) to land in this way.
▸ **'crash-ˌlanding** NOUN

crash out VERB (*intr, adverb*) *Slang* 1 **a** to go to sleep. **b** to spend the night (in a place): *we crashed out at John's place.* 2 to pass out.

crash pad NOUN *Slang* a place to sleep or live temporarily.

crash team NOUN a medical team with special equipment able to be mobilized quickly to treat cardiac arrest.

crash-test VERB (*tr*) to test (a new product) for safety and reliability by finding out its breaking point under pressure, heat, etc.

crashworthiness ('kræʃˌwɜːðɪnɪs) NOUN the ability of a vehicle structure to withstand a crash.
▸ **'crashˌworthy** ADJECTIVE

crasis ('kreɪsɪs) NOUN, *plural* **-ses** (-siːz). the fusion or contraction of two adjacent vowels into one. Also called: **syneresis.**
▷HISTORY C17: from Greek *krasis* a mingling, from *kerannunai* to mix

crass (kræs) ADJECTIVE stupid; gross.
▷HISTORY C16: from Latin *crassus* thick, dense, gross
▸ **'crassly** ADVERB ▸ **'crassness** *or* **'crassiˌtude** NOUN

crassulacean acid metabolism (ˌkræsjʊ'leɪʃən) NOUN the full name for **CAM** (sense 2).

crassulaceous (ˌkræsjʊ'leɪʃəs) ADJECTIVE of, relating to, or belonging to the *Crassulaceae,* a family of herbaceous or shrubby flowering plants with fleshy succulent leaves, including the houseleeks and stonecrops.
▷HISTORY C19: from New Latin *Crassula* name of genus, from Medieval Latin: stonecrop, from Latin *crassus* thick

-crat NOUN COMBINING FORM indicating a person who takes part in or is a member of a form of government or class: *democrat; technocrat.* See also **-cracy.**
▷HISTORY from Greek *-kratēs,* from *-kratia* -CRACY
▸ **-cratic** *or* **-cratical** ADJECTIVE COMBINING FORM

cratch (krætʃ) NOUN a rack for holding fodder for cattle, etc.
▷HISTORY C14: from Old French: CRÈCHE

crate (kreɪt) NOUN 1 a fairly large container, usually made of wooden slats or wickerwork, used for packing, storing, or transporting goods. 2 *Slang* an old car, aeroplane, etc. ◆ VERB 3 (*tr*) to pack or place in a crate.
▷HISTORY C16: from Latin *crātis* wickerwork, hurdle
▸ **'crater** NOUN ▸ **'crateful** NOUN

crater ('kreɪtə) NOUN 1 the bowl-shaped opening at the top or side of a volcano or top of a geyser through which lava and gases are emitted. 2 a similarly shaped depression formed by the impact of a meteorite or exploding bomb. 3 any of the circular or polygonal walled formations covering the surface of the moon and some other planets, formed probably either by volcanic action or by the impact of meteorites. They can have a diameter of up to 240 kilometres (150 miles) and a depth of 8900 metres (29 000 feet). 4 a pit in an otherwise smooth surface. 5 a large open bowl with two handles, used for mixing wines, esp in ancient Greece. ◆ VERB 6 to make or form craters in (a surface, such as the ground). 7 *Slang* to fail; collapse; crash.
▷HISTORY C17: from Latin: mixing bowl, crater, from Greek *kratēr,* from *kerannunai* to mix
▸ **'cratered** ADJECTIVE ▸ **'craterless** ADJECTIVE ▸ **'crater-ˌlike** ADJECTIVE

Crater ('kreɪtə) NOUN, *Latin genitive* **Crateris** ('kreɪtərɪs). a small faint constellation in the S hemisphere lying between Virgo and Hydra.

C rations *or* **C-rations** PLURAL NOUN tinned food formerly issued in packs to US soldiers.
▷HISTORY C20: *C(ombat) rations*

craton (ˈkreɪtᵊn) NOUN *Geology* a stable part of the earth's continental crust or lithosphere that has not been deformed significantly for many millions, even hundreds of millions, of years. See **shield** (sense 7).
▷HISTORY C20: from Greek *kratos* strength
▸**cratonic** (krəˈtɒnɪk) ADJECTIVE

cratur (ˈkretər) NOUN *Irish and Scot* 1 **the.** whisky or whiskey: *a drop of the cratur.* 2 a person.
▷HISTORY from CREATURE

craunch (krɔːntʃ) VERB a dialect word for **crunch.**
▸ˈ**craunchable** ADJECTIVE ▸ˈ**craunchy** ADJECTIVE
▸ˈ**craunchiness** NOUN

cravat (krəˈvæt) NOUN a scarf of silk or fine wool, worn round the neck, esp by men.
▷HISTORY C17: from French *cravate,* from Serbo-Croat *Hrvat* Croat; so called because worn by Croats in the French army during the Thirty Years' War

crave (kreɪv) VERB 1 (when *intr,* foll by *for* or *after*) to desire intensely; long (for). 2 (*tr*) to need greatly or urgently. 3 (*tr*) to beg or plead for.
▷HISTORY Old English *crafian;* related to Old Norse *krefja* to demand, *kræfr* strong; see CRAFT
▸ˈ**craver** NOUN

craven (ˈkreɪvᵊn) ADJECTIVE 1 cowardly; mean-spirited. ◆ NOUN 2 a coward.
▷HISTORY C13 *cravant,* probably from Old French *crevant* bursting, from *crever* to burst, die, from Latin *crepāre* to burst, crack
▸ˈ**cravenly** ADVERB ▸ˈ**cravenness** NOUN

craving (ˈkreɪvɪŋ) NOUN an intense desire or longing.

craw (krɔː) NOUN 1 a less common word for **crop** (sense 6). 2 the stomach of an animal. 3 **stick in one's craw** *or* **throat.** *Informal* to be difficult, or against one's conscience, for one to accept, utter, or believe.
▷HISTORY C14: related to Middle High German *krage,* Middle Dutch *crāghe* neck, Icelandic *kragi* collar

crawfish (ˈkrɔːˌfɪʃ) NOUN, *plural* **-fish** *or* **-fishes.** a variant (esp US) of **crayfish** (esp sense 2).

crawl[1] (krɔːl) VERB (*intr*) 1 to move slowly, either by dragging the body along the ground or on the hands and knees. 2 to proceed or move along very slowly or laboriously: *the traffic crawled along the road.* 3 to act or behave in a servile manner; fawn; cringe. 4 to be or feel as if overrun by something unpleasant, esp crawling creatures: *the pile of refuse crawled with insects.* 5 (of insects, worms, snakes, etc.) to move with the body close to the ground. 6 to swim the crawl. ◆ NOUN 7 a slow creeping pace or motion. 8 Also called: **Australian crawl, front crawl.** *Swimming* a stroke in which the feet are kicked like paddles while the arms reach forward and pull back through the water.
▷HISTORY C14: probably from Old Norse *krafla* to creep; compare Swedish *kravla,* Middle Low German *krabbelen* to crawl, Old Norse *krabbi* CRAB[1]
▸ˈ**crawlingly** ADVERB

crawl[2] (krɔːl) NOUN an enclosure in shallow, coastal water for fish, lobsters, etc.
▷HISTORY C17: from Dutch *kraal* KRAAL

crawler (ˈkrɔːlə) NOUN 1 *Slang* a servile flatterer. 2 a person or animal that crawls. 3 *US* an informal name for an **earthworm.** 4 a computer program that is capable of performing recursive searches on the World Wide Web. 5 (*plural*) a baby's overalls; rompers.

crawler lane NOUN a lane on an uphill section of a motorway reserved for slow vehicles.

crawler track NOUN 1 another name for **crawler lane.** 2 another name for **caterpillar** (sense 2).

Crawley (ˈkrɔːlɪ) NOUN a town in S England, in NE West Sussex: designated a new town in 1956. Pop.: 88 203 (1991).

crawling (ˈkrɔːlɪŋ) NOUN a defect in freshly applied paint or varnish characterized by bare patches and ridging.

crawling peg NOUN a method of stabilizing exchange rates, prices, etc., by maintaining a fixed level for a specified period or until the level has persisted at an upper or lower limit for a specified period and then permitting a predetermined incremental rise or fall.

crawly (ˈkrɔːlɪ) ADJECTIVE **crawlier, crawliest.** *Informal* feeling or causing a sensation like creatures crawling on one's skin.

craw-thumper NOUN *Irish informal* an ostentatiously pious person.
▷HISTORY C18: in the sense: breast-beater, from CRAW

cray (kreɪ) NOUN *Austral and NZ informal* a crayfish.

crayfish (ˈkreɪˌfɪʃ) *or esp US* **crawfish** NOUN, *plural* **-fish** *or* **-fishes.** 1 any freshwater decapod crustacean of the genera *Astacus* and *Cambarus,* resembling a small lobster. 2 any of various similar crustaceans, esp the spiny lobster.
▷HISTORY C14: *cray,* by folk etymology, from Old French *crevice* crab, from Old High German *krebiz* + FISH

crayon (ˈkreɪən, -ɒn) NOUN 1 a small stick or pencil of charcoal, wax, clay, or chalk mixed with coloured pigment. 2 a drawing made with crayons. ◆ VERB 3 to draw or colour with crayons.
▷HISTORY C17: from French, from *craie,* from Latin *crēta* chalk
▸ˈ**crayonist** NOUN

craythur NOUN *Irish* 1 (ˈkreːθər) **the.** a variant of **cratur** (sense 1). 2 (ˈkreːtʃər) a variant of **cratur** (sense 2).
▷HISTORY from Irish Gaelic *Créatur* creature

craze (kreɪz) NOUN 1 a short-lived current fashion. 2 a wild or exaggerated enthusiasm: *a craze for chestnuts.* 3 mental disturbance; insanity. ◆ VERB 4 to make or become mad. 5 *Ceramics, metallurgy* to develop or cause to develop a fine network of cracks. 6 (*tr*) *Brit dialect or obsolete* to break. 7 (*tr*) *Archaic* to weaken.
▷HISTORY C14 (in the sense: to break, shatter): probably of Scandinavian origin; compare Swedish *krasa* to shatter, ultimately of imitative origin

crazed (kreɪzd) ADJECTIVE 1 driven insane. 2 (of porcelain or pottery) having a fine network of cracks in the glaze.

crazy (ˈkreɪzɪ) ADJECTIVE **-zier, -ziest.** 1 *Informal* insane. 2 fantastic; strange; ridiculous: *a crazy dream.* 3 (*postpositive;* foll by *about* or *over*) *Informal* extremely fond (of). 4 *Slang* very good or excellent.
▸ˈ**crazily** ADVERB ▸ˈ**craziness** NOUN

crazy bone NOUN a US name for **funny bone.**

crazy golf NOUN a putting game in which the ball has to be played via various obstacles.

crazy paving NOUN *Brit* a form of paving, as for a path, made of slabs of stone of irregular shape fitted together.

crazy quilt NOUN a patchwork quilt made from assorted pieces of material of irregular shape, size, and colour.

CRE (in Britain) ABBREVIATION FOR **Commission for Racial Equality.**

creak (kriːk) VERB 1 to make or cause to make a harsh squeaking sound. 2 (*intr*) to make such sounds while moving: *the old car creaked along.* ◆ NOUN 3 a harsh squeaking sound.
▷HISTORY C14: variant of CROAK, of imitative origin
▸ˈ**creaky** ADJECTIVE ▸ˈ**creakily** ADVERB ▸ˈ**creakiness** NOUN
▸ˈ**creakingly** ADVERB

cream (kriːm) NOUN 1 **a** the fatty part of milk, which rises to the top if the milk is allowed to stand. **b** (*as modifier*): *cream buns.* 2 anything resembling cream in consistency: *shoe cream; beauty cream.* 3 the best one or most essential part of something; pick: *the cream of the bunch; the cream of the joke.* 4 a soup containing cream or milk: *cream of chicken soup.* 5 any of various dishes, cakes, biscuits, etc., resembling or containing cream. 6 a confection made of fondant or soft fudge, often covered in chocolate. 7 **cream sherry.** a full-bodied sweet sherry. 8 **a** a yellowish-white colour. **b** (*as adjective*): *cream wallpaper.* ◆ VERB 9 (*tr*) to skim or otherwise separate the cream from (milk). 10 (*tr*) to beat (foodstuffs, esp butter and sugar) to a light creamy consistency. 11 (*intr*) to form cream. 12 (*tr*) to add or apply cream or any creamlike substance to: *to cream one's face; to cream coffee.* 13 (*tr;* sometimes foll by *off*) to take away the best part of. 14 (*tr*) to prepare or cook (vegetables, chicken, etc.) with cream or milk. 15 to allow (milk) to form a layer of cream on its surface or (of milk) to form such a layer. 16 (*tr*) *Slang, chiefly US, Canadian, and Austral* to beat thoroughly. 17 (*intr*) *Slang* (of a man) to ejaculate during orgasm.
▷HISTORY C14: from Old French *cresme,* from Late Latin *crāmum* cream, of Celtic origin; influenced by Church Latin *chrisma* unction, CHRISM
▸ˈ**creamˌlike** ADJECTIVE

cream cheese NOUN a smooth soft white cheese made from soured cream or milk.

cream cracker NOUN *Brit* a crisp unsweetened biscuit, often eaten with cheese.

cream-crackered ADJECTIVE *Brit slang* exhausted.
▷HISTORY C20: rhyming slang for *knackered*

creamcups (ˈkriːmˌkʌps) NOUN (*functioning as singular or plural*) a Californian papaveraceous plant, *Platystemon californicus,* with small cream-coloured or yellow flowers on long flower stalks.

creamer (ˈkriːmə) NOUN 1 a vessel or device for separating cream from milk. 2 a powdered substitute for cream, used in coffee. 3 *Chiefly US and Canadian* a small jug or pitcher for serving cream.

creamery (ˈkriːmərɪ) NOUN, *plural* **-eries.** 1 an establishment where milk and cream are made into butter and cheese. 2 a place where dairy products are sold. 3 a place where milk is left to stand until the cream rises to the top.

creamlaid (ˈkriːmˌleɪd) ADJECTIVE (of laid paper) cream-coloured and of a ribbed appearance.

cream of tartar NOUN another name for **potassium hydrogen tartrate,** esp when used in baking powders

cream puff NOUN 1 a shell of light pastry with a custard or cream filling. 2 *Informal* an effeminate man.

cream sauce NOUN a white sauce made from cream, butter, etc.

cream soda NOUN a carbonated soft drink flavoured with vanilla.

cream tea NOUN afternoon tea including bread or scones served with clotted cream and jam.

creamware (ˈkriːmˌwɛə) NOUN a type of earthenware with a deep cream body developed about 1720 and widely produced. See also **Queensware.**

creamwove (ˈkriːmˌwəʊv) ADJECTIVE (of wove paper) cream-coloured and even-surfaced.

creamy (ˈkriːmɪ) ADJECTIVE **creamier, creamiest.** 1 resembling cream in colour, taste, or consistency. 2 containing cream.
▸ˈ**creamily** ADVERB ▸ˈ**creaminess** NOUN

crease[1] (kriːs) NOUN 1 a line or mark produced by folding, pressing, or wrinkling. 2 a wrinkle or furrow, esp on the face. 3 *Cricket* any three lines near each wicket marking positions for the bowler or batsman. See also **bowling crease, popping crease, return crease.** 4 *Ice hockey* the small rectangular area in front of each goal cage. 5 Also called: **goal crease.** *Lacrosse* the circular area surrounding the goal. ◆ VERB 6 to make or become wrinkled or furrowed. 7 (*tr*) to graze with a bullet, causing superficial injury. 8 (often foll by *up*) *Slang* to be or cause to be greatly amused.
▷HISTORY C15: from earlier *crēst;* probably related to Old French *cresté* wrinkled
▸ˈ**creaseless** ADJECTIVE ▸ˈ**creaser** NOUN ▸ˈ**creasy** ADJECTIVE

crease[2] (kriːs) NOUN a rare spelling of **kris.**

crease-resistant ADJECTIVE (of a fabric, garment, etc.) designed to remain uncreased when subjected to wear or use.

create (kriːˈeɪt) VERB 1 (*tr*) to cause to come into existence. 2 (*tr*) to invest with a new honour, office, or title; appoint. 3 (*tr*) to be the cause of: *these circumstances created the revolution.* 4 (*tr*) to act (a role) in the first production of a play. 5 (*intr*) to be engaged in creative work. 6 (*intr*) *Brit slang* to make a fuss or uproar.
▷HISTORY C14 *creat* created, from Latin *creātus,* from *creāre* to produce, make
▸creˈ**atable** ADJECTIVE

creatine (ˈkriːəˌtiːn, -tɪn) *or* **creatin** (ˈkriːətɪn) NOUN an important metabolite involved in many biochemical reactions and present in many types of living cells.
▷HISTORY C19: *creat-* from Greek *kreas* flesh + -INE[2]

creatinine (kriːˈætəˌniːn) NOUN an anhydride of creatine that is abundant in muscle and excreted in the urine.

▷HISTORY C19: from German *Kreatinin,* from *Kreatin* CREATINE + *-in* -INE[2]

creation (kriːˈeɪʃən) NOUN [1] the act or process of creating. [2] the fact of being created or produced. [3] something that has been brought into existence or created, esp a product of human intelligence or imagination. [4] the whole universe, including the world and all the things in it. [5] an unusual or striking garment or hat.
▸**creˈational** ADJECTIVE

Creation (kriːˈeɪʃən) NOUN *Theol* [1] (often preceded by *the*) God's act of bringing the universe into being. [2] the universe as thus brought into being by God.

creationism (kriːˈeɪʃəˌnɪzəm) NOUN [1] the belief that God brings individual human souls into existence at conception or birth. Compare **traducianism.** [2] the doctrine that ascribes the origins of all things to God's acts of creation rather than to evolution.
▸**creˈationist** NOUN ▸**creˌationˈistic** ADJECTIVE

creative (kriːˈeɪtɪv) ADJECTIVE [1] having the ability to create. [2] characterized by originality of thought; having or showing imagination: *a creative mind.* [3] designed to or tending to stimulate the imagination: *creative toys.* [4] characterized by sophisticated bending of the rules or conventions: *creative accounting.* ◆ NOUN [5] a creative person, esp one who devises advertising campaigns.
▸**creˈatively** ADVERB ▸**creˈativeness** NOUN ▸**ˌcreaˈtivity** NOUN

creative tension NOUN a situation where disagreement or discord ultimately gives rise to better ideas or outcomes.

creator (kriːˈeɪtə) NOUN a person or thing that creates; originator.
▸**creˈatorˌship** NOUN ▸**creˈatress** *or* **creˈatrix** FEMININE NOUN

Creator (kriːˈeɪtə) NOUN (usually preceded by *the*) an epithet of God.

creature (ˈkriːtʃə) NOUN [1] a living being, esp an animal. [2] something that has been created, whether animate or inanimate: *a creature of the imagination.* [3] a human being; person: used as a term of scorn, pity, or endearment. [4] a person who is dependent upon another; tool or puppet.
▷HISTORY C13: from Church Latin *creātūra,* from Latin *creāre* to create
▸**ˈcreatural** *or* **ˈcreaturely** ADJECTIVE ▸**ˈcreatureliness** NOUN

creature comforts PLURAL NOUN material things or luxuries that help to provide for one's bodily comfort.

creature feature NOUN a horror film featuring a monster.

crèche (krɛʃ, kreɪʃ; *French* krɛʃ) NOUN [1] *Chiefly Brit* **a** a day nursery for very young children. **b** a supervised play area provided for young children for short periods. [2] a tableau of Christ's Nativity. [3] a foundling home or hospital.
▷HISTORY C19: from Old French: manger, crib, ultimately of Germanic origin; compare Old High German *krippa* crib

Crécy (ˈkrɛsɪ; *French* kresi) NOUN a village in N France: scene of the first decisive battle of the Hundred Years' War when the English defeated the French (1346). Official name: **Crécy-en-Ponthieu** (-ɑ̃pɔ̃tjø). English name: **Cressy.**

cred (krɛd) NOUN *Slang* short for **credibility** (esp in the phrase **street cred**).

credence (ˈkriːdᵊns) NOUN [1] acceptance or belief, esp with regard to the truth of the evidence of others: *I cannot give credence to his account.* [2] something supporting a claim to belief; recommendation; credential (esp in the phrase **letters of credence**). [3] short for **credence table.**
▷HISTORY C14: from Medieval Latin *crēdentia* trust, credit, from Latin *crēdere* to believe

credence table NOUN [1] a small sideboard, originally one at which food was tasted for poison before serving. [2] *Christianity* a small table or ledge on which the bread, wine, etc., are placed before being consecrated in the Eucharist.

credendum (krɪˈdɛndəm) NOUN, *plural* **-da** (-də). (*often plural*) *Christianity* an article of faith.
▷HISTORY Latin: a thing to be believed, from *crēdere* to believe

credent (ˈkriːdᵊnt) ADJECTIVE *Obsolete* believing or believable.
▷HISTORY C17: from Latin *crēdēns* believing

credential (krɪˈdɛnʃəl) NOUN [1] something that entitles a person to confidence, authority, etc. [2] (*plural*) a letter or certificate giving evidence of the bearer's identity or competence. ◆ ADJECTIVE [3] entitling one to confidence, authority, etc.
▷HISTORY C16: from Medieval Latin *crēdentia* credit, trust; see CREDENCE
▸**creˈdentialed** ADJECTIVE

credenza (krɪˈdɛnzə) NOUN another name for **credence table.**
▷HISTORY Italian: see CREDENCE

credibility (ˌkrɛdɪˈbɪlɪtɪ) NOUN the quality of being believed or trusted.

credibility gap NOUN a disparity between claims or statements made and the evident facts of the situation or circumstances to which they relate.

credible (ˈkrɛdɪbᵊl) ADJECTIVE [1] capable of being believed. [2] trustworthy or reliable: *the latest claim is the only one to involve a credible witness.*
▷HISTORY C14: from Latin *crēdibilis,* from Latin *crēdere* to believe
▸**ˈcredibleness** NOUN ▸**ˈcredibly** ADVERB

credit (ˈkrɛdɪt) NOUN [1] commendation or approval, as for an act or quality: *she was given credit for her work.* [2] a person or thing serving as a source of good influence, repute, ability, etc.: *a credit to the team.* [3] the quality of being believable or trustworthy: *that statement had credit.* [4] influence or reputation coming from the approval or good opinion of others: *he acquired credit within the community.* [5] belief in the truth, reliability, quality, etc., of someone or something: *I would give credit to that philosophy.* [6] a sum of money or equivalent purchasing power, as at a shop, available for a person's use. [7] **a** the positive balance in a person's bank account. **b** the sum of money that a bank makes available to a client in excess of any deposit. [8] **a** the practice of permitting a buyer to receive goods or services before payment. **b** the time permitted for paying for such goods or services. [9] reputation for solvency and commercial or financial probity, inducing confidence among creditors. [10] *Accounting* **a** acknowledgment of an income, liability, or capital item by entry on the right-hand side of an account. **b** the right-hand side of an account. **c** an entry on this side. **d** the total of such entries. **e** (*as modifier*): *credit entries.* Compare **debit** (sense 1). [11] short for **tax credit.** [12] *Education* **a** a distinction awarded to an examination candidate obtaining good marks. **b** a section of an examination syllabus satisfactorily completed, as in higher and professional education. [13] **letter of credit.** an order authorizing a named person to draw money from correspondents of the issuer. [14] **on credit.** with payment to be made at a future date. ◆ VERB (*tr*) **-dits, -diting, -dited** [15] (foll by *with*) to ascribe (to); give credit (for): *they credited him with the discovery.* [16] to accept as true; believe. [17] to do credit to. [18] *Accounting* **a** to enter (an item) as a credit in an account. **b** to acknowledge (a payer) by making such an entry. Compare **debit** (sense 2). [19] to award a credit to (a student). ◆ See also **credits.**
▷HISTORY C16: from Old French *crédit,* from Italian *credito,* from Latin *crēditum* loan, from *crēdere* to believe
▸**ˈcreditless** ADJECTIVE

creditable (ˈkrɛdɪtəbᵊl) ADJECTIVE [1] deserving credit, honour, etc.; praiseworthy. [2] *Obsolete* credible.
▸**ˈcreditableness** *or* **ˌcreditaˈbility** NOUN ▸**ˈcreditably** ADVERB

credit account NOUN *Brit* a credit system by means of which customers may obtain goods and services before payment. Also called: **charge account.**

credit card NOUN a card issued by banks, businesses, etc., enabling the holder to obtain goods and services on credit.

credit line NOUN [1] an acknowledgment of origin or authorship, as in a newspaper or film. [2] Also called: **line of credit.** *US and Canadian* the maximum credit that a customer is allowed.

creditor (ˈkrɛdɪtə) NOUN a person or commercial enterprise to whom money is owed. Compare **debtor.**

credit rating NOUN an evaluation of the creditworthiness of an individual or business enterprise.

credit-reference agency NOUN an agency, other than a bank, that specializes in providing credit ratings of people or organizations.

credits (ˈkrɛdɪts) PLURAL NOUN a list of those responsible for the production of a film or television programme.

credit squeeze NOUN the control of credit facilities as an instrument of economic policy, associated with restrictions on bank loans and overdrafts, raised interest rates, etc.

credit standing NOUN reputation for discharging financial obligations.

credit transfer NOUN a method of settling a debt by transferring money through a bank or post office, esp for those who do not have cheque accounts.

credit union NOUN a cooperative association whose members can obtain low-interest loans out of their combined savings.

creditworthy (ˈkrɛdɪtˌwɜːðɪ) ADJECTIVE (of an individual or business enterprise) adjudged as meriting credit on the basis of such factors as earning power, previous record of debt repayment, etc.
▸**ˈcreditˌworthiness** NOUN

credo (ˈkriːdəʊ, ˈkreɪ-) NOUN, *plural* **-dos.** any formal or authorized statement of beliefs, principles, or opinions.

Credo (ˈkriːdəʊ, ˈkreɪ-) NOUN, *plural* **-dos.** [1] the Apostles' Creed or the Nicene Creed. [2] a musical setting of the Creed.
▷HISTORY C12: from Latin, literally: I believe; first word of the Apostles' and Nicene Creeds

credulity (krɪˈdjuːlɪtɪ) NOUN disposition to believe something on little evidence; gullibility.

credulous (ˈkrɛdjʊləs) ADJECTIVE [1] tending to believe something on little evidence. [2] arising from or characterized by credulity: *credulous beliefs.*
▷HISTORY C16: from Latin *crēdulus,* from *crēdere* to believe
▸**ˈcredulously** ADVERB ▸**ˈcredulousness** NOUN

cree (kriː) NOUN *South Wales and southwest English dialect* temporary immunity from the rules of a game: said by children.
▷HISTORY of unknown origin

Cree (kriː) NOUN [1] (*plural* **Cree** *or* **Crees**) a member of a North American Indian people living in Ontario, Saskatchewan, and Manitoba. [2] the language of this people, belonging to the Algonquian family. [3] a syllabic writing system of this and certain other languages.
▷HISTORY from first syllable of Canadian French *Christianaux,* probably based on Ojibwa *Kenistenoag* (tribal name)

creed (kriːd) NOUN [1] a concise, formal statement of the essential articles of Christian belief, such as the Apostles' Creed or the Nicene Creed. [2] any statement or system of beliefs or principles.
▷HISTORY Old English *crēda,* from Latin *crēdo* I believe
▸**ˈcreedal** *or* **ˈcredal** ADJECTIVE

creek (kriːk) NOUN [1] *Chiefly Brit* a narrow inlet or bay, esp of the sea. [2] *US, Canadian, Austral, and NZ* a small stream or tributary. [3] **up the creek.** *Slang* in trouble; in a difficult position.
▷HISTORY C13: from Old Norse *kriki* nook; related to Middle Dutch *krēke* creek, inlet

Creek (kriːk) NOUN [1] (*plural* **Creek** *or* **Creeks**) a member of a confederacy of North American Indian peoples formerly living in Georgia and Alabama, now chiefly in Oklahoma. [2] any of the languages of these peoples, belonging to the Muskhogean family.

creel (kriːl) NOUN [1] a wickerwork basket, esp one used to hold fish. [2] a wickerwork trap for catching lobsters, etc. [3] the framework on a spinning machine that holds the bobbins. [4] *West Yorkshire dialect* a wooden frame suspended from a ceiling, used for drying clothes.
▷HISTORY C15: from Scottish, of obscure origin

creep (kriːp) VERB **creeps, creeping, crept.** (*intr*) [1] to crawl with the body near to or touching the ground. [2] to move slowly, quietly, or cautiously. [3] to act in a servile way; fawn; cringe. [4] to move or slip out of place, as from pressure or wear. [5] (of

plants) to grow along the ground or over rocks, producing roots, suckers, or tendrils at intervals. 6 (of a body or substance) to become permanently deformed as a result of an applied stress, often when combined with heating. 7 to develop gradually: *creeping unrest.* 8 to have the sensation of something crawling over the skin. 9 (of metals) to undergo slow plastic deformation. ◆ NOUN 10 the act of creeping or a creeping movement. 11 *Slang* a person considered to be obnoxious or servile. 12 the continuous permanent deformation of a body or substance as a result of stress or heat. 13 *Geology* the gradual downwards movement of loose rock material, soil, etc., on a slope. 14 a slow relative movement of two adjacent parts, structural components, etc. 15 slow plastic deformation of metals. ◆ See also **creeps.**
▷HISTORY Old English *crēopan;* related to Old Frisian *kriāpa,* Old Norse *krjūpa,* Middle Low German *krūpen*

creeper (ˈkriːpə) NOUN 1 a person or animal that creeps. 2 a plant, such as the ivy or periwinkle, that grows by creeping. 3 the US and Canadian name for the **tree creeper.** 4 a hooked instrument for dragging deep water. 5 Also called: **cradle.** a flat board or framework mounted on casters, used to lie on when working under cars. 6 Also called: **daisycutter.** *Cricket* a bowled ball that keeps low or travels along the ground. 7 either of a pair of low iron supports for logs in a hearth. 8 *Informal* a shoe with a soft sole.

creep-feeding NOUN the practice of feeding young farm animals (esp piglets, calves, and lambs) in a sectioned-off part of their indoor environment, in order to prevent the mother from gaining access to the food.

creep-grazing NOUN a method of pasture management that allows young farm animals (esp lambs) to graze part of the pasture before the adults in the group.

creepie (ˈkriːpɪ, ˈkrɪp-) NOUN *Chiefly Scot* a low stool.

creeping bent grass NOUN a grass, *Agrostis stolonifera,* grown as a pasture grass in Europe and North America: roots readily from the stem.

creeping Jennie (ˈdʒɛnɪ) *or US and Canadian* **creeping Charlie** NOUN other names for **moneywort.**

creeping Jesus NOUN *Derogatory slang* 1 an obsequious or servile person. 2 a hypocritically religious person.

creeping thistle NOUN a weedy Eurasian thistle, *Cirsium arvense,* common as a fast-spreading weed in the US. US and Canadian name: **Canada thistle.**

creeps (kriːps) PLURAL NOUN (preceded by *the*) *Informal* a feeling of fear, repulsion, disgust, etc.

creepy (ˈkriːpɪ) ADJECTIVE **creepier, creepiest.** 1 *Informal* having or causing a sensation of repulsion, horror, or fear, as of creatures crawling on the skin. 2 creeping; slow-moving.
▸ **ˈcreepily** ADVERB ▸ **ˈcreepiness** NOUN

creepy-crawly *Brit informal* ◆ NOUN, *plural* **-crawlies.** 1 a small crawling creature. ◆ ADJECTIVE 2 feeling or causing a sensation as of creatures crawling on one's skin.

creese (kriːs) NOUN a rare spelling of **kris.**

crem (krɛm) NOUN *Informal* short for **crematorium.**

cremate (krɪˈmeɪt) VERB (*tr*) to burn up (something, esp a corpse) and reduce to ash.
▷HISTORY C19: from Latin *cremāre*
▸ **creˈmation** NOUN ▸ **creˈmationism** NOUN ▸ **creˈmationist** NOUN

cremator (krɪˈmeɪtə) NOUN 1 Also called (esp US): **cinerator.** *Brit* a furnace for cremating corpses. 2 a person who operates such a furnace.

crematorium (ˌkrɛməˈtɔːrɪəm) NOUN, *plural* **-riums** *or* **-ria** (-rɪə). *Brit* a building in which corpses are cremated.

crematory (ˈkrɛmətərɪ, -trɪ) ADJECTIVE 1 of or relating to cremation or crematoriums. ◆ NOUN, *plural* **-ries.** 2 another word (esp US) for **crematorium.**

crème (krɛm, kriːm, kreɪm) NOUN 1 cream. 2 any of various sweet liqueurs: *crème de moka.* ◆ ADJECTIVE 3 (of a liqueur) rich and sweet.

crème brûlée *French* (krɛm bryle) NOUN a cream or custard dessert covered with caramelized sugar.
▷HISTORY literally, burnt cream

crème caramel NOUN a dessert made of eggs, sugar, milk, etc., topped with caramel. Also called: **caramel cream.**

crème de cacao (ˈkrɛm də kɑːˈkɑːəʊ, ˈkəʊkəʊ; ˈkriːm, ˈkreɪm) NOUN a sweet liqueur with a chocolate flavour.
▷HISTORY French, literally: cream of cacao

crème de la crème *French* (krɛm də la krɛm) NOUN the very best.
▷HISTORY literally: cream of the cream

crème de menthe (ˈkrɛm də ˈmɛnθ, ˈmɪnt; ˈkriːm, ˈkreɪm) NOUN a liqueur flavoured with peppermint, usually bright green in colour.
▷HISTORY French, literally: cream of mint

crème fraîche (ˈkrɛm ˈfrɛʃ) NOUN thickened and slightly fermented cream.
▷HISTORY French, literally: fresh cream

Cremona (*Italian* kreˈmoːna) NOUN a city in N Italy, in Lombardy on the River Po: noted for the manufacture of fine violins in the 16th–18th centuries. Pop.: 75 160 (1990).

crenate (ˈkriːneɪt) *or* **crenated** ADJECTIVE having a scalloped margin, as certain leaves.
▷HISTORY C18: from New Latin *crēnātus,* from Medieval Latin, probably from Late Latin *crēna* a notch
▸ **ˈcrenately** ADVERB

crenation (krɪˈneɪʃən) *or* **crenature** (ˈkrɛnəˌtjʊə, ˈkriː-) NOUN 1 any of the rounded teeth or the notches between them on a crenate structure. 2 a crenate formation or condition.

crenel (ˈkrɛnᵊl) *or* **crenelle** (krɪˈnɛl) NOUN 1 any of a set of openings formed in the top of a wall or parapet and having slanting sides, as in a battlement. 2 another name for **crenation.**
▷HISTORY C15: from Old French, literally: a little notch, from *cren* notch, from Late Latin *crēna*

crenellate *or US* **crenelate** (ˈkrɛnɪˌleɪt) VERB (*tr*) 1 to supply with battlements. 2 to form square indentations in (a moulding, etc.).
▷HISTORY C19: from Old French *creneler,* from CRENEL
▸ **ˌcrenelˈlation** *or US* **ˌcrenelˈation** NOUN

crenellated *or US* **crenelated** (ˈkrɛnɪˌleɪtɪd) ADJECTIVE 1 having battlements. 2 (of a moulding, etc.) having square indentations.

crenulate (ˈkrɛnjʊˌleɪt, -lɪt) *or* **crenulated** ADJECTIVE having a margin very finely notched with rounded projections, as certain leaves.
▷HISTORY C18: from New Latin *crēnulātus,* from *crēnula,* literally: a little notch; see CRENEL

crenulation (ˌkrɛnjʊˈleɪʃən) NOUN 1 any of the teeth or notches of a crenulate structure. 2 a crenulate formation.

creodont (ˈkriːəˌdɒnt) NOUN any of a group of extinct Tertiary mammals some of which are thought to have been the ancestors of modern carnivores: order *Carnivora.*
▷HISTORY C19: from New Latin *Creodonta,* from Greek *kreas* flesh + *odōn* tooth

creole (ˈkriːəʊl) NOUN 1 a language that has its origin in extended contact between two language communities, one of which is generally European. It incorporates features from each and constitutes the mother tongue of a community. Compare **pidgin.** ◆ ADJECTIVE 2 denoting, relating to, or characteristic of creole. 3 (of a sauce or dish) containing or cooked with tomatoes, green peppers, onions, etc.
▷HISTORY C17: via French and Spanish probably from Portuguese *crioulo* slave born in one's household, person of European ancestry born in the colonies, probably from *criar* to bring up, from Latin *creāre* to CREATE

Creole (ˈkriːəʊl) NOUN 1 (*sometimes not capital*) (in the Caribbean and Latin America) **a** a native-born person of European, esp Spanish, ancestry. **b** a native-born person of mixed European and African ancestry who speaks a French or Spanish creole. **c** a native-born Black person as distinguished from one brought from Africa. 2 (in Louisiana and other Gulf States of the US) a native-born person of French ancestry. 3 the creolized French spoken in Louisiana, esp in New Orleans. ◆ ADJECTIVE 4 of, relating to, or characteristic of any of these peoples.

creolized *or* **creolised** (ˈkriːəˌlaɪzd) ADJECTIVE (of a language) incorporating a considerable range of features from one or more unrelated languages, as the result of contact between language communities.

Creon (ˈkriːɒn) NOUN *Greek myth* the successor to Oedipus as king of Thebes; the brother of Jocasta. See also **Antigone.**

creophagous (krɪˈɒfəgəs) ADJECTIVE flesh-eating or carnivorous.
▷HISTORY C19: from Greek *kreophagos,* from *kreas* flesh + *-phagein* to consume
▸ **creophagy** (krɪˈɒfədʒɪ) NOUN

creosol (ˈkriːəˌsɒl) NOUN a colourless or pale yellow insoluble oily liquid with a smoky odour and a burning taste; 2-methoxy-4-methylphenol: an active principle of creosote. Formula: $CH_3O(CH_3)C_6H_3OH$.
▷HISTORY C19: from CREOS(OTE) + -OL[1]

creosote (ˈkrɪəˌsəʊt) NOUN 1 a colourless or pale yellow liquid mixture with a burning taste and penetrating odour distilled from wood tar, esp from beechwood, contains creosol and other phenols, and is used as an antiseptic. 2 Also called: **coal-tar creosote.** a thick dark liquid mixture prepared from coal tar, containing phenols: used as a preservative for wood. ◆ VERB 3 to treat (wood) with creosote.
▷HISTORY C19: from Greek *kreas* flesh + *sōtēr* preserver, from *sōzein* to keep safe
▸ **creosotic** (ˌkrɪəˈsɒtɪk) ADJECTIVE

creosote bush NOUN a shrub, *Larrea* (or *Covillea*) *tridentata* of the western US and Mexico, that has resinous leaves with an odour resembling creosote: family *Zygophyllaceae.* Also called: **greasewood.**

crepe *or* **crape** (kreɪp) NOUN 1 **a** a light cotton, silk, or other fabric with a fine ridged or crinkled surface. **b** (*as modifier*): *a crepe dress.* 2 a black armband originally made of this, worn as a sign of mourning. 3 a very thin pancake, often rolled or folded around a filling. 4 short for **crepe paper** or **crepe rubber.** ◆ VERB 5 (*tr*) to cover or drape with crepe.
▷HISTORY C19: from French *crêpe,* from Latin *crispus* curled, uneven, wrinkled

crepe de Chine (kreɪp də ˈʃiːn) NOUN **a** a very thin crepe of silk or a similar light fabric. **b** (*as modifier*): *a crepe-de-Chine blouse.*
▷HISTORY C19: from French: Chinese crepe

crepe hair NOUN artificial hair, usually plaited and made of wool or vegetable fibre, used in theatrical make-up.

crepe paper NOUN thin crinkled coloured paper, resembling crepe and used for decorations.

creperie (ˈkrɛpərɪ, ˈkreɪp-) NOUN an eating establishment that specializes in pancakes; pancake house.

crepe rubber NOUN 1 a type of crude natural rubber in the form of colourless or pale yellow crinkled sheets, prepared by pressing bleached coagulated latex through corrugated rollers: used for the soles of shoes and in making certain surgical and medical goods. Sometimes shortened to **crepe.** Compare **smoked rubber.** 2 a similar synthetic rubber.

crêpe suzette (kreɪp suːˈzɛt) NOUN, *plural* **crêpes suzettes.** (*sometimes plural*) an orange-flavoured pancake flambéed in a liqueur or brandy.

crepitate (ˈkrɛpɪˌteɪt) VERB (*intr*) to make a rattling or crackling sound; rattle or crackle.
▷HISTORY C17: from Latin *crepitāre*
▸ **ˈcrepitant** ADJECTIVE

crepitation (ˌkrɛpɪˈteɪʃən) NOUN 1 the act of crepitating. 2 *Zoology* the sudden expulsion of an acrid fluid by some beetles as a means of self-defence. 3 another name for **crepitus.**

crepitus (ˈkrɛpɪtəs) NOUN 1 a crackling chest sound heard in pneumonia and other lung diseases. 2 the grating sound of two ends of a broken bone rubbing together. ◆ Also called: **crepitation.**
▷HISTORY C19: from Latin, from *crepāre* to crack, creak

crept (krɛpt) VERB the past tense and past participle of **creep.**

crepuscular (krɪˈpʌskjʊlə) ADJECTIVE 1 of or like twilight; dim. 2 (of certain insects, birds, and other animals) active at twilight or just before dawn.
▷HISTORY C17: from Latin *crepusculum* dusk, from *creper* dark

crepy *or* **crepey** (ˈkreɪpɪ) ADJECTIVE (esp of the skin) having a dry wrinkled appearance like crepe.

Cres. ABBREVIATION FOR Crescent.

crescendo (krɪˈʃɛndəʊ) NOUN, *plural* **-dos** *or* **-di** (-dɪ). [1] *Music* **a** a gradual increase in loudness or the musical direction or symbol indicating this. Abbreviation: **cresc.** Symbol: < (written over the music affected). **b** (*as modifier*): *a crescendo passage.* [2] a gradual increase in loudness or intensity: *the rising crescendo of a song.* [3] a peak of noise or intensity: *the cheers reached a crescendo.* ◆ VERB **-does, -doing, -doed.** [4] (*intr*) to increase in loudness or force. ◆ ADVERB [5] with a crescendo.
▷HISTORY C18: from Italian, literally: increasing, from *crescere* to grow, from Latin

crescent (ˈkrɛsᵊnt, -zᵊnt) NOUN [1] the biconcave shape of the moon in its first or last quarters. [2] any shape or object resembling this. [3] *Chiefly Brit* **a** a crescent-shaped street, often lined with houses of the same style. **b** (*capital when part of a name*): *Pelham Crescent.* [4] *Heraldry* a crescent moon, used as the cadency mark of a second son. [5] (*often capital* and preceded by *the*) **a** the emblem of Islam or Turkey. **b** Islamic or Turkish power. ◆ ADJECTIVE [6] *Archaic or poetic* increasing or growing.
▷HISTORY C14: from Latin *crescēns* increasing, from *crescere* to grow
▸**crescentic** (krəˈsɛntɪk) ADJECTIVE

cresol (ˈkriːsɒl) NOUN an aromatic compound derived from phenol, existing in three isomeric forms: found in coal tar and creosote and used in making synthetic resins and as an antiseptic and disinfectant; hydroxytoluene. Formula: $C_6H_4(CH_3)OH$. Also called: **cresylic acid.** Systematic name: **methylphenol.**

cress (krɛs) NOUN any of various plants of the genera *Lepidium, Cardamine, Arabis*, etc., having pungent-tasting leaves often used in salads and as a garnish: family *Brassicaceae* (crucifers). See also **watercress, garden cress.**
▷HISTORY Old English *cressa;* related to Old High German *cresso* cress, *kresan* to crawl

cresset (ˈkrɛsɪt) NOUN *History* a metal basket mounted on a pole in which oil or pitch was burned for illumination.
▷HISTORY C14: from Old French *craisset,* from *craisse* GREASE

Cressida (ˈkrɛsɪdə), **Criseyde,** *or* **Cressid** NOUN (in medieval adaptations of the story of Troy) a lady who deserts her Trojan lover Troilus for the Greek Diomedes.

Cressy (ˈkrɛsɪ) NOUN *Rare* the English name for **Crécy.**

crest (krɛst) NOUN [1] a tuft or growth of feathers, fur, or skin along the top of the heads of some birds, reptiles, and other animals. [2] something resembling or suggesting this. [3] the top, highest point, or highest stage of something. [4] a ridge on the neck of a horse, dog, lion, etc. [5] the mane or hair growing from this ridge. [6] an ornamental piece, such as a plume, on top of a helmet. [7] *Heraldry* a symbol of a family or office, usually representing a beast or bird, borne in addition to a coat of arms and used in medieval times to decorate the helmet. [8] a ridge along the top of a roof, wall, etc. [9] a ridge along the surface of a bone. [10] Also called: **cresting.** *Archery* identifying rings painted around an arrow shaft. ◆ VERB [11] (*intr*) to come or rise to a high point. [12] (*tr*) to lie at the top of; cap. [13] (*tr*) to go to or reach the top of (a hill, wave, etc.).
▷HISTORY C14: from Old French *creste,* from Latin *crista*
▸ˈ**crested** ADJECTIVE ▸ˈ**crestless** ADJECTIVE

CREST (krɛst) NOUN an electronic share-settlement system, created by the Bank of England and owned by 69 firms, that began operations in 1996.
▷HISTORY C20: from *CrestCo,* the name of the operating company

cresta run (ˈkrɛstə) NOUN **a** an activity involving travelling at high speed in a toboggan down a steep narrow passage of compacted snow and ice. **b** the passage itself.

crested dog's-tail NOUN a common wiry perennial grass, *Cynosurus cristatus,* of meadows and pasture.
▷HISTORY C19: named from the fancied resemblance between its one-sided flower spike and a dog's feathery tail

crested tit NOUN a small European songbird, *Parus cristatus,* that has a greyish-brown plumage with a prominent speckled black-and-white crest: family *Paridae* (tits).

crestfallen (ˈkrɛstˌfɔːlən) ADJECTIVE dejected, depressed, or disheartened.
▸ˈ**crestˌfallenly** ADVERB

cresting (ˈkrɛstɪŋ) NOUN [1] an ornamental ridge along the top of a roof, wall, etc. [2] *Furniture* a shaped decorative toprail or horizontal carved ornament surmounting a chair, mirror, etc.

cresylic (krɪˈsɪlɪk) ADJECTIVE of, concerned with, or containing creosote or cresol.
▷HISTORY C19: from CRE(O)S(OTE) + -YL+ -IC

cretaceous (krɪˈteɪʃəs) ADJECTIVE consisting of or resembling chalk.
▷HISTORY C17: from Latin *crētāceus,* from *crēta,* literally: Cretan earth, that is, chalk
▸**creˈtaceously** ADVERB

Cretaceous (krɪˈteɪʃəs) ADJECTIVE [1] of, denoting, or formed in the last period of the Mesozoic era, between the Jurassic and Tertiary periods, lasting 80 million years during which chalk deposits were formed and flowering plants first appeared. ◆ NOUN [2] **the.** the Cretaceous period or rock system.

Cretan (ˈkriːtən) ADJECTIVE [1] of or relating to Crete or its inhabitants. ◆ NOUN [2] a native or inhabitant of Crete.

Crete (kriːt) NOUN a mountainous island in the E Mediterranean, the largest island of Greece: of archaeological importance for the ruins of Minoan civilization. Pop.: 601 159 (2001). Area: 8331 sq. km (3216 sq. miles). Modern Greek name: **Kríti.**

cretic (ˈkriːtɪk) NOUN *Prosody* a metrical foot consisting of three syllables, the first long, the second short, and the third long (–⏑–). Also called: **amphimacer.** Compare **amphibrach.**
▷HISTORY C16: from Latin *crēticus* consisting of the amphimacer, literally: Cretan, from Greek *krētikos,* from *Krētē* CRETE

cretin (ˈkrɛtɪn) NOUN [1] a person afflicted with cretinism: a mentally retarded dwarf with wide-set eyes, a broad flat nose, and protruding tongue. [2] a person considered to be extremely stupid.
▷HISTORY C18: from French *crétin,* from Swiss French *crestin,* from Latin *Chrīstiānus* CHRISTIAN, alluding to the humanity of such people, despite their handicaps
▸ˈ**cretinˌoid** ADJECTIVE ▸ˈ**cretinous** ADJECTIVE

cretinism (ˈkrɛtɪˌnɪzəm) NOUN a condition arising from a deficiency of thyroid hormone, present from birth, characterized by dwarfism and mental retardation. See also **myxoedema.**

cretonne (krɛˈtɒn, ˈkrɛtɒn) NOUN **a** a heavy cotton or linen fabric with a printed design, used for furnishing. **b** (*as modifier*): *cretonne chair covers.*
▷HISTORY C19: from French, from *Creton* Norman village where it originated

Creuse (*French* krøz) NOUN a department of central France, in Limousin region. Capital: Guéret. Pop.: 124 470 (1999). Area: 5606 sq. km (2186 sq. miles).

Creutzfeldt-Jakob disease (ˈkrɔɪtsfɛltˈjaːkɒp) NOUN *Pathol* a fatal slow-developing disease that affects the central nervous system, characterized by mental deterioration and loss of coordination of the limbs. It is thought to be caused by an abnormal prion protein in the brain.
▷HISTORY C20: named after Hans G. *Creutzfeldt* (1885–1964) and Alfons *Jakob* (1884–1931), German physicians

crevasse (krɪˈvæs) NOUN [1] a deep crack or fissure, esp in the ice of a glacier. [2] *US* a break in a river embankment. ◆ VERB [3] (*tr*) *US* to make a break or fissure in (a dyke, wall, etc.).
▷HISTORY C19: from French: CREVICE

crevice (ˈkrɛvɪs) NOUN a narrow fissure or crack; split; cleft.
▷HISTORY C14: from Old French *crevace,* from *crever* to burst, from Latin *crepāre* to crack

crew¹ (kruː) NOUN (*sometimes functioning as plural*) [1] the men who man a ship, boat, aircraft, etc. [2] *Nautical* a group of people assigned to a particular job or type of work. [3] *Informal* a gang, company, or crowd. ◆ VERB [4] to serve on (a ship) as a member of the crew.
▷HISTORY C15 *crue* (military) reinforcement, from Old French *creue* augmentation, from Old French *creistre* to increase, from Latin *crescere*

crew² (kruː) VERB a past tense of **crow².**

crew cut NOUN a closely cropped haircut for men, originating in the US.
▷HISTORY C20: from the style of haircut worn by the boat crews at Harvard and Yale Universities

Crewe (kruː) NOUN a town in NW England, in Cheshire: major railway junction. Pop.: 63 351 (1991).

crewel (ˈkruːɪl) NOUN a loosely twisted worsted yarn, used in fancy work and embroidery.
▷HISTORY C15: of unknown origin
▸ˈ**crewelist** NOUN ▸ˈ**crewelˌwork** NOUN

crewmate (ˈkruːˌmeɪt) NOUN a colleague on the crew of a boat or ship.

crew neck NOUN a plain round neckline in sweaters.
▸ˈ**crew-ˌneck** *or* ˈ**crew-ˌnecked** ADJECTIVE

CRI (in New Zealand) ABBREVIATION FOR Crown Research Institutes.

crib (krɪb) NOUN [1] a child's bed with slatted wooden sides; cot. [2] a cattle stall or pen. [3] a fodder rack or manger. [4] a bin or granary for storing grain, etc. [5] a small crude cottage or room. [6] *US informal* a house or residence. [7] *NZ* a weekend cottage: term is South Island usage only. [8] any small confined space. [9] *Informal* a brothel. [10] a wicker basket. [11] a representation of the manger in which the infant Jesus was laid at birth. [12] *Informal* a theft, esp of another's writing or thoughts. [13] Also called (esp US): **pony.** *Informal, chiefly Brit* a translation of a foreign text or a list of answers used by students, often illicitly, as an aid in lessons, examinations, etc. [14] short for **cribbage.** [15] *Cribbage* the discard pile. [16] Also called: **cribwork.** a framework of heavy timbers laid in layers at right angles to one another, used in the construction of foundations, mines, etc. [17] a storage area for floating logs contained by booms. [18] *Austral and NZ* a packed lunch taken to work. ◆ VERB **cribs, cribbing, cribbed.** [19] (*tr*) to put or enclose in or as if in a crib; furnish with a crib. [20] (*tr*) *Informal* to steal (another's writings or thoughts). [21] (*intr*) *Informal* to copy either from a crib or from someone else during a lesson or examination. [22] (*tr*) to line (a construction hole) with timber beams, logs, or planks. [23] (*intr*) *Informal* to grumble.
▷HISTORY Old English *cribb;* related to Old Saxon *kribbia,* Old High German *krippa;* compare Middle High German *krēbe* basket
▸ˈ**cribber** NOUN

cribbage (ˈkrɪbɪdʒ) NOUN a game of cards for two to four, in which players try to win a set number of points before their opponents. Often shortened to **crib.**
▷HISTORY C17: of uncertain origin

cribbage board NOUN a board, with pegs and holes, used for scoring at cribbage.

crib-biting NOUN a harmful habit of horses in which the animal leans on the manger or seizes it with the teeth and swallows a gulp of air.
▸ˈ**crib-ˌbiter** NOUN

crib death NOUN the US and Canadian term for **cot death.**

cribellum (krɪˈbɛləm) NOUN, *plural* **-la** (-lə). a sievelike spinning organ in certain spiders that occurs between the spinnerets.
▷HISTORY C19: New Latin, from Late Latin *cribellum,* diminutive of Latin *cribrum* a sieve

cribriform (ˈkrɪbrɪˌfɔːm), **cribrous** (ˈkrɪbrəs), *or* **cribrose** (ˈkraɪˌbrəʊs) ADJECTIVE pierced with holes; sievelike.
▷HISTORY C18: from New Latin *crībriformis,* from Latin *crībrum* a sieve + -FORM

crib-wall NOUN *NZ* a supporting wall constructed by laying cribs at right angles to each other, as in cribwork.

cribwork (ˈkrɪbˌwɜːk) NOUN another name for **crib** (sense 16).

crick¹ (krɪk) *Informal* ◆ NOUN [1] a painful muscle spasm or cramp, esp in the neck or back. ◆ VERB [2] (*tr*) to cause a crick in (the neck, back, etc.).
▷HISTORY C15: of uncertain origin

crick² (krɪk) NOUN *US and Canadian* a dialect word for **creek** (sense 2).

cricket[1] ('krɪkɪt) NOUN 1 any insect of the orthopterous family *Gryllidae,* having long antennae and, in the males, the ability to produce a chirping sound (stridulation) by rubbing together the leathery forewings. 2 any of various related insects, such as the mole cricket.
▷HISTORY C14: from Old French *criquet,* from *criquer* to creak, of imitative origin

cricket[2] ('krɪkɪt) NOUN 1 **a** a game played by two teams of eleven players on a field with a wicket at either end of a 22-yard pitch, the object being for one side to score runs by hitting a hard leather-covered ball with a bat while the other side tries to dismiss them by bowling, catching, running them out, etc. **b** (*as modifier*): *a cricket bat.* 2 **not cricket.** *Informal* not fair play. ◆ VERB (*intr*) 3 to play cricket.
▷HISTORY C16: from Old French *criquet* goalpost, wicket, of uncertain origin
▸ **'cricketer** NOUN

cricket[3] ('krɪkɪt) NOUN a small low stool.
▷HISTORY C17: of unknown origin

cricoid ('kraɪkɔɪd) ADJECTIVE 1 of or relating to the ring-shaped lowermost cartilage of the larynx. ◆ NOUN 2 this cartilage.
▷HISTORY C18: from New Latin *cricoīdes,* from Greek *krikoeidēs* ring-shaped, from *krikos* ring

cri de coeur (ˌkriː də 'kɜː) NOUN, *plural* **cris de coeur.** a cry from the heart; heartfelt or sincere appeal.
▷HISTORY C20: altered from French *cri du coeur*

crier ('kraɪə) NOUN 1 a person or animal that cries. 2 (formerly) an official who made public announcements, esp in a town or court. 3 a person who shouts advertisements about the goods he is selling.

crikey ('kraɪkɪ) INTERJECTION *Slang* an expression of surprise.
▷HISTORY C19: euphemistic for *Christ!*

crim (krɪm) NOUN, ADJECTIVE *Slang* short for **criminal.**

crim. ABBREVIATION FOR criminal.

crime (kraɪm) NOUN 1 an act or omission prohibited and punished by law. 2 **a** unlawful acts in general: *a wave of crime.* **b** (*as modifier*): *crime wave.* 3 an evil act. 4 *Informal* something to be regretted: *it is a crime that he died young.*
▷HISTORY C14: from Old French, from Latin *crīmen* verdict, accusation, crime

Crimea (kraɪ'mɪə) NOUN a peninsula and autonomous region in the Ukraine between the Black Sea and the Sea of Azov: a former autonomous republic of the Soviet Union (1921–45), part of the Ukrainian SSR from 1945 until 1991. Russian name: **Krym.**

Crimean (kraɪ'mɪən) ADJECTIVE 1 of or relating to the Crimea or its inhabitants. ◆ NOUN 2 a native or inhabitant of the Crimea.

Crimean War NOUN the war fought mainly in the Crimea between Russia on one side and Turkey, France, Sardinia, and Britain on the other (1853-56).

crimen injuria ('kraɪmən ɪn'dʒʊərɪə) NOUN *South African law* an action that injures the dignity of another person, esp use of racially offensive language.

crime passionnel (*French* krim pɑsjɔnɛl) NOUN, *plural* **crimes passionnels.** a crime committed from passion, esp sexual passion. Also called: **crime of passion.**
▷HISTORY from French

crime sheet NOUN *Military* a record of an individual's offences against regulations.

crimewave ('kraɪmˌweɪv) NOUN a period of increased criminal activity.

criminal ('krɪmɪnᵊl) NOUN 1 a person charged with and convicted of crime. 2 a person who commits crimes for a living. ◆ ADJECTIVE 3 of, involving, or guilty of crime. 4 (*prenominal*) of or relating to crime or its punishment: *criminal court; criminal lawyer.* 5 *Informal* senseless or deplorable: *a criminal waste of money.*
▷HISTORY C15: from Late Latin *crīminālis;* see CRIME, -AL[1]
▸ **'criminally** ADVERB

criminal conversation NOUN 1 (formerly) a common law action brought by a husband by which he claimed damages against an adulterer. 2 another term for **adultery.**

Criminal Investigation Department NOUN the full name for **CID.**

criminality (ˌkrɪmɪ'nælɪtɪ) NOUN, *plural* **-ties.** 1 the state or quality of being criminal. 2 (*often plural*) *Now rare* a criminal act or practice.

criminalize *or* **criminalise** ('krɪmɪnəˌlaɪz) VERB (*tr*) 1 to make (an action or activity) criminal. 2 to treat (a person) as a criminal.
▸ **ˌcriminali'zation** *or* **ˌcriminali'sation** NOUN

criminal law NOUN the body of law dealing with the constitution of offences and the punishment of offenders.

criminate ('krɪmɪˌneɪt) VERB (*tr*) *Rare* 1 to charge with a crime; accuse. 2 to condemn or censure (an action, event, etc.). 3 short for **incriminate.**
▷HISTORY C17: from Latin *crīmināri* to accuse
▸ **ˌcrimi'nation** NOUN ▸ **'criminative** *or* **criminatory** ('krɪmɪnətərɪ, -trɪ) ADJECTIVE ▸ **'crimiˌnator** NOUN

criminology (ˌkrɪmɪ'nɒlədʒɪ) NOUN the scientific study of crime, criminal behaviour, law enforcement, etc. See also **penology.**
▷HISTORY C19: from Latin *crimin-* CRIME, -LOGY
▸ **criminological** (ˌkrɪmɪnə'lɒdʒɪkᵊl) *or* **ˌcrimino'logic** ADJECTIVE ▸ **ˌcrimino'logically** ADVERB ▸ **ˌcrimi'nologist** NOUN

crimmer ('krɪmə) NOUN a variant spelling of **krimmer.**

crimp[1] (krɪmp) VERB (*tr*) 1 to fold or press into ridges. 2 to fold and pinch together (something, such as the edges of two pieces of metal). 3 to curl or wave (the hair) tightly, esp with curling tongs. 4 to decorate (the edge of pastry) by pinching with the fingers to give a fluted effect. 5 to gash (fish or meat) with a knife to make the flesh firmer and crisper when cooked. 6 to bend or mould (leather) into shape, as for shoes. 7 *Metallurgy* to bend the edges of (a metal plate) before forming into a cylinder. 8 *Informal, chiefly US* to hinder. ◆ NOUN 9 the act or result of folding or pressing together or into ridges. 10 a tight wave or curl in the hair. 11 a crease or fold in a metal sheet. 12 the natural wave of wool fibres.
▷HISTORY Old English *crympan;* related to *crump* bent, Old Norse *kreppa* to contract, Old High German *crumpf,* Old Swedish *crumb* crooked; see CRAMP[1]
▸ **'crimper** NOUN ▸ **'crimpy** ADJECTIVE

crimp[2] (krɪmp) NOUN 1 (formerly) a person who swindled or pressganged men into naval or military service. ◆ VERB 2 to recruit by coercion or under false pretences.
▷HISTORY C17: of unknown origin

crimple ('krɪmpᵊl) VERB to crumple, wrinkle, or curl.

Crimplene ('krɪmpliːn) NOUN *Trademark* a synthetic material similar to Terylene, characterized by its crease-resistance.

crimson ('krɪmzən) NOUN 1 **a** a deep or vivid red colour. **b** (*as adjective*): *a crimson rose.* ◆ VERB 2 to make or become crimson. 3 (*intr*) to blush.
▷HISTORY C14: from Old Spanish *cremesin,* from Arabic *qirmizi* red of the kermes, from *qirmiz* KERMES
▸ **'crimsonness** NOUN

cringe (krɪndʒ) VERB (*intr*) 1 to shrink or flinch, esp in fear or servility. 2 to behave in a servile or timid way. 3 *Informal* **a** to wince in embarrassment or distaste. **b** to experience a sudden feeling of embarrassment or distaste. ◆ NOUN 4 the act of cringing. 5 **the cultural cringe.** *Austral* subservience to overseas cultural standards.
▷HISTORY Old English *cringan* to yield in battle; related to Old Norse *krangr* weak, Middle High German *krenken* to weaken
▸ **'cringer** NOUN ▸ **'cringingly** ADVERB

cringe-making *or* **cringeworthy** ('krɪndʒˌwɜːðɪ) ADJECTIVE *Brit informal* causing feelings of acute embarrassment or distaste.

cringle ('krɪŋgᵊl) NOUN an eye at the edge of a sail, usually formed from a thimble or grommet.
▷HISTORY C17: from Low German *Kringel* small RING[1]; see CRANK[1], CRINKLE

crinite[1] ('kraɪnaɪt) ADJECTIVE *Biology* covered with soft hairs or tufts.
▷HISTORY C16: from Latin *crīnītus* hairy, from *crīnis* hair

crinite[2] ('kraɪnaɪt, 'krɪn-) NOUN short for **encrinite.**
▷HISTORY C19: from Greek *krinon* lily + -ITE[1]

crinkle ('krɪŋkᵊl) VERB 1 to form or cause to form wrinkles, twists, or folds. 2 to make or cause to make a rustling noise. ◆ NOUN 3 a wrinkle, twist, or fold. 4 a rustling noise.
▷HISTORY Old English *crincan* to bend, give way; related to Middle Dutch *krinkelen* to crinkle, Middle High German *krank* weak, ill, *krenken* to weaken

crinkleroot ('krɪŋkᵊlˌruːt) NOUN any of several species of the toothwort *Dentaria,* esp *D. diphylla* of E North America, which has a fleshy pungent rhizome and clusters of white or pinkish flowers: family *Brassicaceae* (crucifers).

crinkly ('krɪŋklɪ) ADJECTIVE 1 wrinkled; crinkled. ◆ NOUN, *plural* **-lies.** 2 *Slang* an old person.

crinkum-crankum ('krɪŋkəm'kræŋkəm) NOUN a fanciful name for any object that is full of twists and turns.
▷HISTORY C18: coinage based on CRANK[1]

crinoid ('kraɪnɔɪd, 'krɪn-) NOUN 1 any primitive echinoderm of the class *Crinoidea,* having delicate feathery arms radiating from a central disc. The group includes the free-swimming feather stars, the sessile sea lilies, and many stemmed fossil forms. ◆ ADJECTIVE 2 of, relating to, or belonging to the *Crinoidea.* 3 shaped like a lily.
▷HISTORY C19: from Greek *krinoeidēs* lily-like
▸ **cri'noidal** ADJECTIVE

crinoline ('krɪnᵊlɪn) NOUN 1 a stiff fabric, originally of horsehair and linen used in lining garments. 2 a petticoat stiffened with this, worn to distend skirts, esp in the mid-19th century. 3 a framework of steel hoops worn for the same purpose.
▷HISTORY C19: from French, from Italian *crinolino,* from *crino* horsehair, from Latin *crīnis* hair + *lino* flax, from Latin *līnum*

crinum ('kraɪnəm) NOUN any plant of the mostly tropical amaryllidaceous genus *Crinum,* having straplike leaves and clusters of lily-like flowers. Also called: **crinum lily.**
▷HISTORY Latin: lily, from Greek *krinon*

criollo (kriː'əʊləʊ; *Spanish* 'krjoʎo) NOUN, *plural* **-los** (-ləʊz; *Spanish* -ʎos). 1 a native or inhabitant of Latin America of European descent, esp of Spanish descent. 2 **a** any of various South American breeds of domestic animal. **b** (*as modifier*): *a criollo pony.* 3 a high-quality variety of cocoa. ◆ ADJECTIVE 4 of, relating to, or characteristic of a criollo or criollos.
▷HISTORY Spanish: native; see CREOLE

crios (krɪs) NOUN *Irish* a multicoloured woven woollen belt traditionally worn by men in the Aran Islands.
▷HISTORY Irish Gaelic

cripes (kraɪps) INTERJECTION *Old-fashioned slang* an expression of surprise.
▷HISTORY C20: euphemistic for *Christ!*

cripple ('krɪpᵊl) NOUN 1 *Offensive* a person who is lame. 2 *Offensive* a person who is or seems disabled or deficient in some way: *a mental cripple.* 3 *US dialect* a dense thicket, usually in marshy land. ◆ VERB 4 (*tr*) to make a cripple of; disable.
▷HISTORY Old English *crypel;* related to *crēopan* to CREEP, Old Frisian *kreppel* a cripple, Middle Low German *kröpel*
▸ **'crippler** NOUN

Cripple Creek NOUN a village in central Colorado: gold-mining centre since 1891, once the richest in the world.

crippling ('krɪplɪŋ) ADJECTIVE damaging or injurious.
▸ **'cripplingly** ADVERB

Criseyde (krɪ'seɪdə) NOUN a variant of **Cressida.**

crisis ('kraɪsɪs) NOUN, *plural* **-ses** (-siːz). 1 a crucial stage or turning point in the course of something, esp in a sequence of events or a disease. 2 an unstable period, esp one of extreme trouble or danger in politics, economics, etc. 3 *Pathol* a sudden change, for better or worse, in the course of a disease.
▷HISTORY C15: from Latin: decision, from Greek *krisis,* from *krinein* to decide

crisp (krɪsp) ADJECTIVE 1 dry and brittle. 2 fresh and firm: *crisp lettuce.* 3 invigorating or bracing: *a crisp breeze.* 4 clear; sharp: *crisp reasoning.* 5 lively or stimulating: *crisp conversation.* 6 clean and

orderly; neat: *a crisp appearance.* 7 concise and pithy; terse: *a crisp reply.* 8 wrinkled or curly: *crisp hair.* ◆ VERB 9 to make or become crisp. ◆ NOUN 10 *Brit* a very thin slice of potato fried and eaten cold as a snack. 11 something that is crisp.
▷HISTORY Old English, from Latin *crispus* curled, uneven, wrinkled
▸'**crisply** ADVERB ▸'**crispness** NOUN

crispate ('krɪspeɪt, -pɪt), **crispated,** *or* **crisped** ADJECTIVE having a curled or waved appearance.
▷HISTORY C19: from Latin *crispāre* to curl

crispation (krɪ'speɪʃən) NOUN 1 the act of curling or state of being curled. 2 any slight muscular spasm or contraction that gives a creeping sensation. 3 a slight undulation, such as a ripple on the surface of water.

crispbread ('krɪsp,brɛd) NOUN a thin dry biscuit made of wheat or rye.

crisper ('krɪspə) NOUN a compartment in a refrigerator for storing salads, vegetables, etc., in order to keep them fresh.

crispy ('krɪspɪ) ADJECTIVE **crispier, crispiest.** 1 crisp. 2 having waves or curls.
▸'**crispily** ADVERB ▸'**crispiness** NOUN

crisscross ('krɪs,krɒs) VERB 1 to move or cause to move in a crosswise pattern. 2 to mark with or consist of a pattern of crossing lines. ◆ ADJECTIVE 3 (esp of a number of lines) crossing one another in different directions. ◆ NOUN 4 a pattern made of crossing lines. 5 a US term for **noughts and crosses.** ◆ ADVERB 6 in a crosswise manner or pattern.

crissum ('krɪsəm) NOUN, *plural* **-sa** (-sə). the area or feathers surrounding the cloaca of a bird.
▷HISTORY C19: from New Latin, from Latin *crissāre* to move the haunches
▸'**crissal** ADJECTIVE

crista ('krɪstə) NOUN, *plural* **-tae** (-tiː). *Biology* a structure resembling a ridge or crest, such as that formed by folding of the inner membrane of a mitochondrion.
▷HISTORY C20: from Latin: CREST

cristate ('krɪsteɪt) *or* **cristated** ADJECTIVE 1 having a crest. 2 forming a crest.
▷HISTORY C17: from Latin *cristātus,* from *crista* CREST

cristobalite (krɪs'təʊbə,laɪt) NOUN a white microcrystalline mineral consisting of silica and occurring in volcanic rocks. Formula: SiO_2.
▷HISTORY C19: from German, named after Cerro San *Cristóbal,* Mexico, where it was discovered

crit. ABBREVIATION FOR: 1 critic. 2 criticism.

criterion (kraɪ'tɪərɪən) NOUN, *plural* **-ria** (-rɪə) *or* **-rions.** 1 a standard by which something can be judged or decided. 2 *Philosophy* a defining characteristic of something.
▷HISTORY C17: from Greek *kritērion* from *kritēs* judge, from *krinein* to decide

> **Language note** *Criteria,* the plural of *criterion,* is not acceptable as a singular noun: *this criterion is not valid; these criteria are not valid.*

critic ('krɪtɪk) NOUN 1 a person who judges something. 2 a professional judge of art, music, literature, etc. 3 a person who often finds fault and criticizes.
▷HISTORY C16: from Latin *criticus,* from Greek *kritikos* capable of judging, from *kritēs* judge; see CRITERION

critical ('krɪtɪkᵊl) ADJECTIVE 1 containing or making severe or negative judgments. 2 containing careful or analytical evaluations: *a critical dissertation.* 3 of or involving a critic or criticism. 4 of or forming a crisis; crucial; decisive: *a critical operation.* 5 urgently needed: *critical medical supplies.* 6 *Informal* so seriously injured or ill as to be in danger of dying. 7 *Physics* of, denoting, or concerned with a state in which the properties of a system undergo an abrupt change: *a critical temperature.* 8 **go critical.** (of a nuclear power station or reactor) to reach a state in which a nuclear-fission chain reaction becomes self-sustaining.
▸'**critically** ADVERB ▸'**criticalness** NOUN

critical angle NOUN 1 the smallest possible angle of incidence for which light rays are totally reflected at an interface between substances of different refractive index. 2 another name for **stalling angle.**

critical apparatus NOUN the variant readings, footnotes, etc. found in a scholarly work or a critical edition of a text. Also called: **apparatus criticus.**

critical constants PLURAL NOUN the physical constants that express the properties of a substance in its critical state. See **critical pressure, critical temperature.**

critical damping NOUN *Physics* the minimum amount of viscous damping that results in a displaced system returning to its original position without oscillation. Symbol: C_c.

criticality (,krɪtɪ'kælɪtɪ) NOUN 1 the state of being critical. 2 *Physics* the condition in a nuclear reactor when the fissionable material can sustain a chain reaction by itself.

critical mass NOUN 1 the minimum mass of fissionable material that can sustain a nuclear chain reaction. 2 the minimum amount of money or number of people required to start or sustain an operation, business, process, etc.: *the critical mass for a subscription digital sports channel.*

critical path analysis NOUN a technique for planning complex projects by analysing alternative systems with reference to the critical path, which is the sequence of stages requiring the longest time. Compare **programme evaluation and review technique.**

critical period NOUN *Psychol* a period in a lifetime during which a specific stage of development usually occurs. If it fails to do so, it cannot readily occur afterwards.

critical point NOUN 1 *Physics* **a** the point on a phase diagram that represents the critical state of a substance. **b** another name for **critical state.** 2 *Maths* the US name for **stationary point.**

critical pressure NOUN the pressure of a gas or the saturated vapour pressure of a substance in its critical state.

critical region NOUN that part of a statistical distribution in which the probability of a given hypothesis is less than the chosen significance level, so that the hypothesis would be rejected.

critical state NOUN the state of a substance in which two of its phases have the same temperature, pressure, and volume. Also called: **critical point.**

critical temperature NOUN the temperature of a substance in its critical state. A gas can only be liquefied by pressure alone at temperatures below its critical temperature.

critical volume NOUN the volume occupied by one mole or unit mass of a substance in its critical state.

criticism ('krɪtɪ,sɪzəm) NOUN 1 the act or an instance of making an unfavourable or severe judgment, comment, etc. 2 the analysis or evaluation of a work of art, literature, etc. 3 the occupation of a critic. 4 a work that sets out to evaluate or analyse. 5 Also called: **textual criticism.** the investigation of a particular text, with related material, in order to establish an authentic text.

criticize *or* **criticise** ('krɪtɪ,saɪz) VERB 1 to judge (something) with disapproval; censure. 2 to evaluate or analyse (something).
▸'**criti,cizable** *or* '**criti,cisable** ADJECTIVE ▸'**criti,cizer** *or* '**criti,ciser** NOUN ▸'**criti,cizingly** *or* '**criti,cisingly** ADVERB

critique (krɪ'tiːk) NOUN 1 a critical essay or commentary, esp on artistic work. 2 the act or art of criticizing.
▷HISTORY C17: from French, from Greek *kritikē,* from *kritikos* able to discern

critter ('krɪtə) NOUN *US and Canadian* a dialect word for **creature.**

CRM ABBREVIATION FOR customer relationship management.

CRO ABBREVIATION FOR: 1 cathode-ray oscilloscope. 2 (in Britain) Community Relations Officer. 3 Criminal Records Office.

Croagh Patrick (kroːx) NOUN a mountain in NW Republic of Ireland, in Mayo: a place of pilgrimage as Saint Patrick is said to have prayed and fasted there. Height: 765 m (2510 ft.).

croak (krəʊk) VERB 1 *(intr)* (of frogs, crows, etc.) to make a low, hoarse cry. 2 to utter (something) in this manner: *he croaked out the news.* 3 *(intr)* to grumble or be pessimistic. 4 *Slang* **a** *(intr)* to die. **b** *(tr)* to kill. ◆ NOUN 5 a low hoarse utterance or sound.
▷HISTORY Old English *crăcettan;* related to Old Norse *krāka* a crow; see CREAK
▸'**croaky** ADJECTIVE ▸'**croakily** ADVERB ▸'**croakiness** NOUN

croaker ('krəʊkə) NOUN 1 an animal, bird, etc., that croaks. 2 any of various mainly tropical marine sciaenid fishes, such as *Umbrina roncador* (**yellowfin croaker**), that utter croaking noises. 3 a grumbling person.

Croat ('krəʊæt) NOUN 1 **a** a native or inhabitant of Croatia. **b** a speaker of Croatian. ◆ NOUN, ADJECTIVE 2 another word for **Croatian.**

Croatia (krəʊ'eɪʃə) NOUN a republic in SE Europe: settled by Croats in the 7th century; belonged successively to Hungary, Turkey, and Austria; formed part of Yugoslavia (1918–91); became independent in 1991 but was invaded by Serbia and fighting continued until 1995; involved in the civil war in Bosnia-Herzegovina (1991–95). Language: Croatian. Religion: Roman Catholic majority. Currency: kuna. Capital: Zagreb. Pop.: 4 393 000 (2001 est.). Area: 55 322 sq. km (21 359 sq. miles). Croatian name: **Hrvatska.**

Croatian (krəʊ'eɪʃən) ADJECTIVE 1 of, relating to, or characteristic of Croatia, its people, or their language. ◆ NOUN 2 the language that is spoken in Croatia, a dialect of Serbo-Croat (Croato-Serb). 3 **a** a native or inhabitant of Croatia. **b** a speaker of Croatian.

Croato-Serb (krəʊ,eɪtəʊ'sɜːb) NOUN, ADJECTIVE another name for **Serbo-Croat.**

croc (krɒk) NOUN short for **crocodile** (senses 1–3).

crocein ('krəʊsɪɪn) NOUN any one of a group of red or orange acid azo dyes.
▷HISTORY C20: from Latin *croceus* yellow + -IN

crochet ('krəʊʃeɪ, -ʃɪ) VERB **-chets** (-ʃeɪz, -ʃɪz), **-cheting** (-ʃeɪɪŋ, -ʃɪɪŋ), **-cheted** (-ʃeɪd, -ʃɪd). 1 to make (a piece of needlework, a garment, etc.) by looping and intertwining thread with a hooked needle (**crochet hook**). ◆ NOUN 2 work made by crocheting. 3 *Architect* another name for **crocket.** 4 *Zoology* a hooklike structure of insect larvae that aids locomotion.
▷HISTORY C19: from French *crochet,* diminutive of *croc* hook, probably of Scandinavian origin
▸'**crocheter** NOUN

crocidolite (krəʊ'sɪdə,laɪt) NOUN a blue fibrous amphibole mineral consisting of sodium iron silicate: a variety of asbestos used in cement products and pressure piping.
▷HISTORY C19: from Greek *krokis* nap on woollen cloth + -LITE

crock[1] (krɒk) NOUN 1 an earthen pot, jar, etc. 2 a piece of broken earthenware. 3 Also: **crock of shit.** *US and Canadian informal* a quantity or source of lies or nonsense.
▷HISTORY Old English *crocc* pot; related to Old Norse *krukka* jug, Middle Low German *krūke* pot

crock[2] (krɒk) NOUN 1 *Slang, chiefly Brit* a person or thing, such as a car, that is old or decrepit (esp in the phrase **old crock**). 2 an old broken-down horse or ewe. ◆ VERB 3 *Slang, chiefly Brit* to become or cause to become weak or disabled.
▷HISTORY C15: originally Scottish; related to Norwegian *krake* unhealthy animal, Dutch *kraak* decrepit person or animal

crock[3] (krɒk) NOUN 1 *Dialect, chiefly Brit* soot or smut. 2 colour that rubs off fabric. ◆ VERB 3 *(tr) Dialect, chiefly Brit* to soil with or as if with soot. 4 *(intr)* (of a dyed fabric) to release colour when rubbed, as a result of imperfect dyeing.
▷HISTORY C17: probably from CROCK[1]

crocked (krɒkt) ADJECTIVE *Slang* 1 *Brit* injured. 2 *US and Canadian* drunk.

crockery ('krɒkərɪ) NOUN china dishes, earthen vessels, etc., collectively.

crocket ('krɒkɪt) NOUN a carved ornament in the form of a curled leaf or cusp, used in Gothic architecture. Also called: **crochet.**
▷HISTORY C17: from Anglo-French *croket* a little hook, from *croc* hook, of Scandinavian origin

Crockford ('krɒkfəd) NOUN short for *Crockford's Clerical Directory,* the standard directory of living Anglican clergy.
▷HISTORY C19: named after John *Crockford* (1823–

65), clerk to Edward William Cox (1809–79), a lawyer who devised the directory

crocodile ('krɒkə,daɪl) NOUN [1] any large tropical reptile, such as *C. niloticus* (**African crocodile**), of the family *Crocodylidae:* order *Crocodilia* (crocodilians). They have a broad head, tapering snout, massive jaws, and a thick outer covering of bony plates. [2] any other reptile of the order *Crocodilia;* a crocodilian. [3] **a** leather made from the skin of any of these animals. **b** (*as modifier*): *crocodile shoes.* [4] *Brit informal* a line of people, esp schoolchildren, walking two by two.
▷HISTORY C13: via Old French, from Latin *crocodīlus,* from Greek *krokodeilos* lizard, ultimately from *krokē* pebble + *drilos* worm; referring to its fondness for basking on shingle

crocodile bird NOUN an African courser, *Pluvianus aegyptius,* that lives close to rivers and is thought to feed on insects parasitic on crocodiles.

crocodile clip NOUN a clasp with serrated interlocking edges used for making electrical connections.

Crocodile River NOUN [1] a river in N South Africa, rising north of Johannesburg and flowing north-westerly into the Marico River on the Botswanan border; a tributary of the Limpopo. [2] a river that rises in NE South Africa, in the Kruger National Park and flows south-easterly into Mozambique.

crocodile tears PLURAL NOUN an insincere show of grief; false tears.
▷HISTORY from the belief that crocodiles wept over their prey to allure further victims

crocodilian (,krɒkə'dɪlɪən) NOUN [1] any large predatory reptile of the order *Crocodilia,* which includes the crocodiles, alligators, and caymans. They live in or near water and have a long broad snout, powerful jaws, a four-chambered heart, and socketed teeth. ◆ ADJECTIVE [2] of, relating to, or belonging to the *Crocodilia.* [3] of, relating to, or resembling a crocodile.

crocoite ('krəʊkəʊ,aɪt) *or* **crocoisite** (krəʊ'kəʊɪ,saɪt, 'krəʊkwə,saɪt) NOUN a rare orange secondary mineral consisting of lead chromate in monoclinic crystalline form. Formula: $PbCrO_4$. Also called: **red-lead ore.**
▷HISTORY C19: from Greek *krokoeis* saffron-coloured, golden + -ITE[1]

crocosmia (krə'kɒzmɪə) NOUN any plant of the cormous S. African genus *Crocosmia,* including the plant known to gardeners as montbretia: family *Iridaceae.*
▷HISTORY New Latin, from Greek *krokos* saffron + *osmē* smell, from the odour of the dried flowers when wetted

crocus ('krəʊkəs) NOUN, *plural* **-cuses.** [1] any plant of the iridaceous genus *Crocus,* widely cultivated in gardens, having white, yellow, or purple flowers. See also **autumn crocus.** [2] another name for **jeweller's rouge.** ◆ ADJECTIVE [3] of a saffron yellow colour.
▷HISTORY C17: from New Latin, from Latin *crocus,* from Greek *krokos* saffron, of Semitic origin

Croesus ('kri:səs) NOUN any very rich man.
▷HISTORY from Croesus, the last king of Lydia (560–546), noted for his great wealth

croft (krɒft) NOUN *Brit* [1] a small enclosed plot of land, adjoining a house, worked by the occupier and his family, esp in Scotland. [2] *Lancashire dialect* a patch of wasteland, formerly one used for bleaching fabric in the sun.
▷HISTORY Old English *croft;* related to Middle Dutch *krocht* hill, field, Old English *creopan* to CREEP

crofter ('krɒftə) NOUN *Brit* an owner or tenant of a small farm, esp in Scotland or northern England.

crofting ('krɒftɪŋ) NOUN *Brit* the system or occupation of working land in crofts.

crog (krɒg) VERB (*intr*) *Northern and Midland English dialect* to ride on a bicycle as a passenger.

croggy ('krɒgɪ) NOUN, *plural* **croggies.** *Northern and Midland English dialect* a ride on a bicycle as a passenger: *give us a croggy!*

Crohn's disease (krəʊnz) NOUN inflammation, thickening, and ulceration of any of various parts of the intestine, esp the ileum. Also called: **regional enteritis.** See also **Johne's disease.**
▷HISTORY C20: named after B. B. *Crohn* (1884–1983), US physician

croissant ('krwʌsɒŋ; *French* krwasɑ̃) NOUN a flaky crescent-shaped bread roll made of a yeast dough similar to puff pastry.
▷HISTORY French, literally: crescent

Croix de Guerre *French* (krwa də ger) NOUN a French military decoration awarded for gallantry in battle: established 1915.
▷HISTORY literally: cross of war

Cro-Magnon man ('krəʊ'mænjɒn, -'mægnɒn) NOUN an early type of modern man, *Homo sapiens,* who lived in Europe during late Palaeolithic times, having tall stature, long head, and a relatively large cranial capacity.
▷HISTORY C19: named after the cave (Cro-Magnon), Dordogne, France, where the remains were first found

crombec ('krɒmbɛk) NOUN any African Old World warbler of the genus *Sylvietta,* having colourful plumage.
▷HISTORY C19: via French from Dutch *krom* crooked + *bek* BEAK[1]

Cromer ('krəʊmə) NOUN a resort in E England, on the Norfolk coast: fishing. Pop.: 7267 (1991).

cromlech ('krɒmlɛk) NOUN [1] a circle of prehistoric standing stones. [2] (no longer in technical usage) a megalithic chamber tomb or dolmen.
▷HISTORY C17: from Welsh, from *crom,* feminine of *crwm* bent, arched + *llech* flat stone

Cromwell Current ('krɒmwɛl, -wəl) NOUN an equatorial Pacific current, flowing eastward from the Hawaiian Islands to the Galápagos Islands.
▷HISTORY C20: named after T. *Cromwell* (1922–58), US oceanographer

crone (krəʊn) NOUN a witchlike old woman.
▷HISTORY C14: from Old Northern French *carogne* carrion, ultimately from Latin *caro* flesh

cronk (krɒŋk) ADJECTIVE *Austral* unfit; unsound.
▷HISTORY C19: compare CRANK[2]

Cronus ('krəʊnəs), **Cronos,** *or* **Kronos** ('krəʊnɒs) NOUN *Greek myth* a Titan, son of Uranus (sky) and Gaea (earth), who ruled the world until his son Zeus dethroned him. Roman counterpart: **Saturn.**

crony ('krəʊnɪ) NOUN, *plural* **-nies.** a friend or companion.
▷HISTORY C17: student slang (Cambridge), from Greek *khronios* of long duration, from *khronos* time

cronyism ('krəʊnɪ,ɪzəm) NOUN the practice of appointing friends to high-level, esp political, posts regardless of their suitability.

crook (krʊk) NOUN [1] a curved or hooked thing. [2] a staff with a hooked end, such as a bishop's crosier or shepherd's staff. [3] a turn or curve; bend. [4] *Informal* a dishonest person, esp a swindler or thief. [5] the act or an instance of crooking or bending. [6] Also called: **shank.** a piece of tubing added to a brass instrument in order to obtain a lower harmonic series. ◆ VERB [7] to bend or curve or cause to bend or curve. ◆ ADJECTIVE [8] *Austral and NZ informal* **a** ill. **b** of poor quality. **c** unpleasant; bad. [9] **go (off) crook.** *Austral and NZ informal* to lose one's temper. [10] **go crook at** *or* **on.** *Austral and NZ informal* to rebuke or upbraid.
▷HISTORY C12: from Old Norse *krokr* hook; related to Swedish *krok,* Danish *krog* hook, Old High German *krācho* hooked tool

crookback ('krʊk,bæk) NOUN a rare word for **hunchback.**
▸'**crook,backed** ADJECTIVE

crooked ('krʊkɪd) ADJECTIVE [1] bent, angled or winding. [2] set at an angle; not straight. [3] deformed or contorted. [4] *Informal* dishonest or illegal. [5] **crooked on** (*also* krʊkt). *Austral informal* hostile or averse to.
▸'**crookedly** ADVERB ▸'**crookedness** NOUN

Crookes lens (krʊks) NOUN a type of lens, used in sunglasses, that is made from glass containing cerium. It reduces the transmission of ultraviolet radiation.

Crookes radiometer NOUN *Physics* a type of radiometer consisting of an evacuated glass bulb containing a set of lightweight vanes, each blackened on one side. The vanes are mounted on a vertical axis and revolve when light, or other radiant energy, falls on them.

Crookes space NOUN a dark region near the cathode in some low-pressure gas-discharge tubes. Also called: **Crookes dark space.**

Crookes tube NOUN a type of cathode-ray tube in which the electrons are produced by a glow discharge in a low-pressure gas.

crool (kru:l) VERB *Austral slang* [1] (*tr*) to spoil: *don't crool your chances.* [2] **crool someone's pitch.** to spoil an opportunity for someone.

croon (kru:n) VERB [1] to sing or speak in a soft low tone. ◆ NOUN [2] a soft low singing or humming.
▷HISTORY C14: via Middle Dutch *crōnen* to groan; compare Old High German *chrōnan* to chatter, Latin *gingrīre* to cackle (of geese)
▸'**crooner** NOUN

crop (krɒp) NOUN [1] the produce of cultivated plants, esp cereals, vegetables, and fruit. [2] **a** the amount of such produce in any particular season. **b** the yield of some other farm produce: *the lamb crop.* [3] a group of products, thoughts, people, etc., appearing at one time or in one season: *a crop of new publications.* [4] the stock of a thonged whip. [5] short for **riding crop.** [6] **a** a pouchlike expanded part of the oesophagus of birds, in which food is stored or partially digested before passing on to the gizzard. **b** a similar structure in insects, earthworms, and other invertebrates. [7] the entire tanned hide of an animal. [8] a short cropped hairstyle. See also **Eton crop.** [9] a notch in or a piece cut out of the ear of an animal. [10] the act of cropping. ◆ VERB **crops, cropping, cropped.** (*mainly tr*) [11] to cut (hair, grass, etc.) very short. [12] to cut and collect (mature produce) from the land or plant on which it has been grown. [13] to clip part of (the ear or ears) of (an animal), esp as a means of identification. [14] (*also intr*) to cause (land) to bear or (of land) to bear or yield a crop: *the land cropped well.* [15] (of herbivorous animals) to graze on (grass or similar vegetation). [16] *Photog* to cut off or mask unwanted edges or areas of (a negative or print). ◆ See also **crop out, crop up.**
▷HISTORY Old English *cropp;* related to Old Norse *kroppr* rump, body, Old High German *kropf* goitre, Norwegian *kröypa* to bend

crop circle NOUN any of various patterns, usually wholly or partly consisting of ring shapes, formed by the unexplained flattening of cereals growing in a field.

crop-dusting NOUN the spreading of fungicide, etc. on crops in the form of dust, often from an aircraft.

crop-eared ADJECTIVE having the ears or hair cut short.

crop out VERB (*intr, adverb*) (of a formation of rock strata) to appear or be exposed at the surface of the ground; outcrop.

cropper ('krɒpə) NOUN [1] a person who cultivates or harvests a crop. [2] **a** a cutting machine for removing the heads from castings and ingots. **b** a guillotine for cutting lengths of bar or strip. [3] a machine for shearing the nap from cloth. [4] a plant or breed of plant that will produce a certain kind of crop under specified conditions: *a poor cropper on light land.* [5] (*often capital*) a variety of domestic pigeon with a puffed-out crop. [6] **come a cropper.** *Informal* **a** to fall heavily. **b** to fail completely.

crop rotation NOUN the system of growing a sequence of different crops on the same ground so as to maintain or increase its fertility.

crop top NOUN a short T-shirt or vest that reveals the wearer's midriff.

crop up VERB (*intr, adverb*) *Informal* to occur or appear, esp unexpectedly.

croquet ('krəʊkeɪ, -kɪ) NOUN [1] a game for two to four players who hit a wooden ball through iron hoops with mallets in order to hit a peg. [2] the act of croqueting. ◆ VERB **-quets** (-keɪz, -kɪz), **-queting** (-keɪɪŋ, -kɪɪŋ), **-queted** (-keɪd, -kɪd). [3] to drive away (another player's ball) by hitting one's own ball when the two are in contact.
▷HISTORY C19: perhaps from French dialect, variant of CROCHET (little hook)

croquette (krəʊ'kɛt, krɒ-) NOUN a savoury cake of minced meat, fish, etc., fried in breadcrumbs.

▷HISTORY C18: from French, from *croquer* to crunch, of imitative origin

crore (krɔː) NOUN (in Indian English) ten million. ▷HISTORY C17: from Hindi *karōr,* from Prakrit *krodi*

Crosby (ˈkrɒzbɪ) NOUN a town in NW England, in Sefton unitary authority, Merseyside. Pop.: 52 869 (1991).

crosier *or* **crozier** (ˈkrəʊʒə) NOUN [1] a staff surmounted by a crook or cross, carried by bishops as a symbol of pastoral office. [2] the tip of a young plant, esp a fern frond, that is coiled into a hook. ▷HISTORY C14: from Old French *crossier* staff bearer, from *crosse* pastoral staff, literally: hooked stick, of Germanic origin

cross (krɒs) NOUN [1] a structure or symbol consisting essentially of two intersecting lines or pieces at right angles to one another. [2] a wooden structure used as a means of execution, consisting of an upright post with a transverse piece to which people were nailed or tied. [3] a representation of the Cross used as an emblem of Christianity or as a reminder of Christ's death. [4] any mark or shape consisting of two intersecting lines, esp such a symbol (×) used as a signature, point of intersection, error mark, etc. [5] a sign representing the Cross made either by tracing a figure in the air or by touching the forehead, breast, and either shoulder in turn. [6] any conventional variation of the Christian symbol, used emblematically, decoratively, or heraldically, such as a Maltese, tau, or Greek cross. [7] *Heraldry* any of several charges in which one line crosses or joins another at right angles. [8] a cruciform emblem awarded to indicate membership of an order or as a decoration for distinguished service. [9] (*sometimes capital*) Christianity or Christendom, esp as contrasted with non-Christian religions: *Cross and Crescent.* [10] the place in a town or village where a cross has been set up. [11] a pipe fitting, in the form of a cross, for connecting four pipes. [12] *Biology* **a** the process of crossing; hybridization. **b** an individual produced as a result of this process. [13] a mixture of two qualities or types: *he's a cross between a dictator and a saint.* [14] an opposition, hindrance, or misfortune; affliction (esp in the phrase **bear one's cross**). [15] *Slang* a match or game in which the outcome has been rigged. [16] *Slang* a fraud or swindle. [17] *Boxing* a straight punch delivered from the side, esp with the right hand. [18] *Football* the act or an instance of kicking or passing the ball from a wing to the middle of the field. [19] **on the cross. a** diagonally. **b** *Slang* dishonestly. ◆ VERB [20] (sometimes foll by *over*) to move or go across (something); traverse or intersect: *we crossed the road.* [21] **a** to meet and pass: *the two trains crossed.* **b** (of each of two letters in the post) to be dispatched before receipt of the other. [22] (*tr;* usually foll by *out, off,* or *through*) to cancel with a cross or with lines; delete. [23] (*tr*) to place or put in a form resembling a cross: *to cross one's legs.* [24] (*tr*) to mark with a cross or crosses. [25] (*tr*) *Brit* to draw two parallel lines across the face of (a cheque) and so make it payable only into a bank account. [26] (*tr*) **a** to trace the form of the Cross, usually with the thumb or index finger upon (someone or something) in token of blessing. **b** to make the sign of the Cross upon (oneself). [27] (*intr*) (of telephone lines) to interfere with each other so that three or perhaps four callers are connected together at one time. [28] to cause fertilization between (plants or animals of different breeds, races, varieties, etc.). [29] (*tr*) to oppose the wishes or plans of; thwart: *his opponent crosses him at every turn.* [30] *Football* to kick or pass (the ball) from a wing to the middle of the field. [31] (*tr*) *Nautical* to set (the yard of a square sail) athwartships. [32] **cross a bridge when one comes to it.** to deal with matters, problems, etc., as they arise; not to anticipate difficulties. [33] **cross one's fingers.** to fold one finger across another in the hope of bringing good luck: *keep your fingers crossed.* [34] **cross one's heart.** to promise or pledge, esp by making the sign of a cross over one's heart. [35] **cross one's mind.** to occur to one briefly or suddenly. [36] **cross someone's palm.** to give someone money. [37] **cross the path (of).** to meet or thwart (someone). [38] **cross swords.** to argue or fight. ◆ ADJECTIVE [39] angry; ill-humoured; vexed. [40] lying or placed across; transverse: *a cross timber.* [41] involving interchange; reciprocal. [42] contrary or unfavourable. [43] another word for **crossbred** (sense 1). [44] a Brit slang word for **dishonest.**

▷HISTORY Old English *cros,* from Old Irish *cross* (unattested), from Latin *crux;* see CRUX ▶ˈ**crosser** NOUN ▶ˈ**crossly** ADVERB ▶ˈ**crossness** NOUN

Cross (krɒs) NOUN **the.** [1] the cross on which Jesus Christ was crucified. [2] the Crucifixion of Jesus.

cross- COMBINING FORM [1] indicating action from one individual, group, etc., to another: *cross-cultural; cross-fertilize; cross-refer.* [2] indicating movement, position, etc., across something (sometimes implying interference, opposition, or contrary action): *crosscurrent; crosstalk.* [3] indicating a crosslike figure or intersection: *crossbones.* ▷HISTORY from CROSS (in various senses)

crossandra (krɒˈsɑːndrə) NOUN any shrub of the free-flowering mostly African genus *Crossandra,* grown in greenhouses for their large yellow, lilac, or orange flowers: family *Acanthaceae.* ▷HISTORY New Latin, from Greek *krossos* fringed + *andros,* genitive of *anēr* man, male (from the fringed anthers)

cross assembler NOUN an assembler that runs on a computer other than the one for which it assembles programs.

crossbar (ˈkrɒsˌbɑː) NOUN [1] a horizontal bar, line, stripe, etc. [2] a horizontal beam across a pair of goalposts. [3] a horizontal bar mounted on vertical posts used in athletics or show-jumping. [4] the horizontal bar on a man's bicycle that joins the handlebar and saddle supports.

crossbeam (ˈkrɒsˌbiːm) NOUN a beam that spans from one support to another.

cross bedding NOUN *Geology* layering within one or more beds in a series of rock strata that does not run parallel to the plane of stratification. Also called: **false bedding.**

cross-bench NOUN (*usually plural*) *Brit* a seat in Parliament occupied by a neutral or independent member. ▶ˈ**cross-ˌbencher** NOUN

crossbill (ˈkrɒsˌbɪl) NOUN any of various widely distributed finches of the genus *Loxia,* such as *L. curvirostra,* that occur in coniferous woods and have a bill with crossed mandible tips for feeding on conifer seeds.

crossbones (ˈkrɒsˌbəʊnz) PLURAL NOUN See **skull and crossbones.**

crossbow (ˈkrɒsˌbəʊ) NOUN a type of medieval bow fixed transversely on a wooden stock grooved to direct a square-headed arrow (quarrel). ▶ˈ**crossˌbowman** NOUN

crossbred (ˈkrɒsˌbrɛd) ADJECTIVE [1] (of plants or animals) produced as a result of crossbreeding. ◆ NOUN [2] a crossbred plant or animal, esp an animal resulting from a cross between two pure breeds. Compare **grade** (sense 9), **purebred** (sense 2).

crossbreed (ˈkrɒsˌbriːd) VERB **-breeds, -breeding, -bred.** [1] Also: **interbreed.** to breed (animals or plants) using parents of different races, varieties, breeds, etc. ◆ NOUN [2] the offspring produced by such a breeding.

cross-buttock NOUN a wrestling throw in which the hips are used as a fulcrum to throw an opponent.

crosscheck (ˌkrɒsˈtʃɛk) VERB [1] to verify (a fact, report, etc.) by considering conflicting opinions or consulting other sources. [2] (in ice hockey) to check illegally, as by chopping at an opponent's arms or stick. ◆ NOUN [3] the act or an instance of crosschecking.

cross colour NOUN distortion in a colour television receiver in which high-frequency luminance detail is interpreted as colour information and reproduced as flashes of spurious colour.

cross-correlation NOUN *Statistics* the correlation between two sequences of random variables in a time series.

cross-country ADJECTIVE, ADVERB [1] by way of fields, woods, etc., as opposed to roads: *cross-country running.* [2] across a country: *a cross-country railway.* ◆ NOUN [3] a long race held over open ground.

cross-cultural ADJECTIVE involving or bridging the differences between cultures.

crosscurrent (ˈkrɒsˌkʌrənt) NOUN [1] a current in a river or sea flowing across another current. [2] a conflicting tendency moving counter to the usual trend.

cross-curricular ADJECTIVE *Brit education* denoting or relating to an approach to a topic that includes contributions from several different disciplines and viewpoints.

crosscut (ˈkrɒsˌkʌt) ADJECTIVE [1] cut at right angles or obliquely to the major axis. ◆ NOUN [2] a transverse cut or course. [3] a less common word for **short cut.** [4] *Mining* a tunnel through a vein of ore or from the shaft to a vein. ◆ VERB **-cuts, -cutting, -cut.** [5] to cut across. [6] Also: **intercut.** *Films* to link (two sequences or two shots) so that they appear to be taking place at the same time.

crosscut file NOUN a file having two intersecting rows of teeth.

crosscut saw NOUN a saw for cutting timber across the grain.

cross-cutting ADJECTIVE linking traditionally separate or independent parties or interests: *a multi-agency, cross-cutting approach on drugs.*

cross-dating NOUN *Archaeol* a method of dating objects, remains, etc., by comparison and correlation with other sites and levels.

cross-dressing NOUN [1] transvestism. See **transvestite.** [2] the wearing of clothes normally associated with the opposite sex. ▶ˌ**cross-ˈdresser** NOUN

crosse (krɒs) NOUN a light staff with a triangular frame to which a network is attached, used in playing lacrosse. ▷HISTORY French, from Old French *croce* CROSIER

cross-examine VERB (*tr*) [1] *Law* to examine (a witness for the opposing side), as in attempting to discredit his testimony. Compare **examine-in-chief.** [2] to examine closely or relentlessly. ▶ˈ**cross-exˌamiˈnation** NOUN ▶ˌ**cross-exˈaminer** NOUN

cross-eye NOUN a turning inwards towards the nose of one or both eyes, caused by abnormal alignment. See also **strabismus.**

cross-eyed ADJECTIVE having one or both eyes turning inwards towards the nose.

cross-fade VERB *Radio, television* to fade in (one sound or picture source) as another is being faded out.

cross-fertilization NOUN fertilization by the fusion of male and female gametes from different individuals of the same species. Compare **self-fertilization.** ▶ˌ**cross-ˈfertile** ADJECTIVE

cross-fertilize VERB to subject or be subjected to cross-fertilization.

crossfire (ˈkrɒsˌfaɪə) NOUN [1] *Military* converging fire from one or more positions. [2] a lively exchange of ideas, opinions, etc.

cross-garnet NOUN a hinge with a long horizontal strap fixed to the face of a door and a short vertical leaf fixed to the door frame.

cross-grained ADJECTIVE [1] (of timber) having the fibres arranged irregularly or in a direction that deviates from the axis of the piece. [2] perverse, cantankerous, or stubborn.

cross hairs PLURAL NOUN two fine mutually perpendicular lines or wires that cross in the focal plane of a theodolite, gunsight, or other optical instrument and are used to define the line of sight. Also called: **cross wires.**

crosshatch (ˈkrɒsˌhætʃ) VERB *Drawing* to shade or hatch (forms, figures, etc.) with two or more sets of parallel lines that cross one another. ▶ˈ**crossˌhatching** NOUN

crosshead (ˈkrɒsˌhɛd) NOUN [1] *Printing* a subsection or paragraph heading printed within the body of the text. [2] a block or beam, usually restrained by sliding bearings in a reciprocating mechanism, esp the junction piece between the piston rod and connecting rod of an engine. [3] *Nautical* a bar fixed across the top of the rudder post to which the tiller is attached. [4] a block, rod, or beam fixed at the head of any part of a mechanism.

cross-index NOUN [1] a note or notes referring the reader to other material. ◆ VERB [2] (*intr*) (of a note in a book) to refer to related material. [3] to provide or be provided with cross-indexes.

crossing (ˈkrɒsɪŋ) NOUN [1] the place where one thing crosses another. [2] a place, often shown by markings, lights, or poles, where a street, railway, etc., may be crossed. [3] the intersection of the nave and transept in a church. [4] the act or instance of travelling across something, esp the sea. [5] the act or process of crossbreeding.

crossing over NOUN *Biology* the interchange of sections between pairing homologous chromosomes during the diplotene stage of meiosis. It results in the rearrangement of genes and produces variation in the inherited characteristics of the offspring. See also **linkage** (sense 4).

crossjack ('krɒsˌdʒæk; *Nautical* 'krɔːdʒɪk, 'krɒdʒ-) NOUN *Nautical* a square sail on a ship's mizzenmast.

cross-legged ('krɒs'lɛgɪd, -'lɛgd) ADJECTIVE [1] sitting with the legs bent and the knees pointing outwards. [2] standing or sitting with one leg crossed over the other.

crosslet *or* **cross crosslet** ('krɒslɪt) NOUN *Heraldry* a cross having a smaller cross near the end of each arm.
▷HISTORY C16 *croslet* a little CROSS

cross-link *or* **cross-linkage** NOUN a chemical bond, atom, or group of atoms that connects two adjacent chains of atoms in a large molecule such as a polymer or protein.

cross-match VERB *Immunol* to test the compatibility of (a donor's and recipient's blood) by checking that the red cells of each do not agglutinate in the other's serum.

cross-nodal ADJECTIVE having to do with interaction between the senses.

cross of Lorraine NOUN a cross with two horizontal bars above and below the midpoint of the vertical bar, the lower longer than the upper.

Cross of Valour NOUN the highest Canadian award for bravery. Abbreviation: **CV**.

crossopterygian (krɒˌsɒptəˈrɪdʒɪən) NOUN [1] any bony fish of the subclass *Crossopterygii*, having fleshy limblike pectoral fins. The group, now mostly extinct, contains the ancestors of the amphibians. See also **coelacanth.** ◆ ADJECTIVE [2] of, relating to, or belonging to the *Crossopterygii*.
▷HISTORY C19: from New Latin *Crossopterygiī*, from Greek *krossoi* fringe, tassels + *pterugion* a little wing, from *pterux* wing

crossover ('krɒsˌəʊvə) NOUN [1] a place at which a crossing is made. [2] *Genetics* **a** another term for **crossing over. b** a chromosomal structure or character resulting from crossing over. [3] *Railways* a point of transfer between two main lines. [4] short for **crossover network.** [5] a recording, book, or other product that becomes popular in a genre other than its own. ◆ ADJECTIVE [6] (of music, fashion, art, etc.) combining two distinct styles. [7] (of a performer, writer, recording, book, etc.) having become popular in more than one genre.

crossover network NOUN an electronic network in a loudspeaker system that separates the signal into two or more frequency bands, the lower frequencies being fed to a woofer, the higher frequencies to a tweeter.

crossover value NOUN *Genetics* the percentage of offspring showing recombination among the total offspring of a given cross. It indicates the amount of crossing over that has occurred and therefore the relative positions of the genes on the chromosomes. Abbreviation: **COV.**

crosspatch ('krɒsˌpætʃ) NOUN *Informal* a peevish bad-tempered person.
▷HISTORY C18: from CROSS + obsolete *patch* fool

crosspiece ('krɒsˌpiːs) NOUN a transverse beam, joist, etc.

cross-ply ADJECTIVE (of a motor tyre) having the fabric cords in the outer casing running diagonally to stiffen the sidewalls. Compare **radial-ply.**

cross-pollinate VERB to subject or be subjected to cross-pollination.

cross-pollination NOUN the transfer of pollen from the anthers of one flower to the stigma of another flower by the action of wind, insects, etc. Compare **self-pollination.**

cross press NOUN a fall in wrestling using the weight of the body to pin an opponent's shoulders to the floor.

cross product NOUN *Maths* [1] another name for **vector product.** [2] another name for **Cartesian product.**

cross protection NOUN *Botany* the protection against a viral infection given to a plant by its prior inoculation with a related but milder virus.

cross-purpose NOUN [1] a contrary aim or purpose. [2] **at cross-purposes.** conflicting; opposed; disagreeing.

cross-question VERB (*tr*) [1] to cross-examine. ◆ NOUN [2] a question asked in cross-examination.
▸'**cross-'questioning** NOUN

cross-refer VERB to refer from one part of something, esp a book, to another.

cross-reference NOUN [1] a reference within a text to another part of the text. ◆ VERB [2] to cross-refer.

cross relation NOUN another term (esp US) for **false relation.**

Cross River NOUN a state of SE Nigeria, on the Gulf of Guinea. Capital: Calabar. Pop.: 2 085 926 (1995 est.). Area: 20 156 sq. km (7782 sq. miles). Former name (until 1976): **South-Eastern State.**

crossroad ('krɒsˌrəʊd) NOUN *US and Canadian* [1] a road that crosses another road. [2] Also called: **crossway.** a road that crosses from one main road to another.

crossroads ('krɒsˌrəʊdz) NOUN (*functioning as singular*) [1] an area or the point at which two or more roads cross each other. [2] the point at which an important choice has to be made (esp in the phrase **at the crossroads**).

Crossroads care attendant scheme NOUN *Social welfare* (in Britain) a service providing paid attendants for disabled people who need continuous supervision.
▷HISTORY so named because the idea arose out of criticism of the plight of a disabled character in the TV serial *Crossroads*

crossruff ('krɒsˌrʌf) *Bridge, whist* ◆ NOUN [1] the alternate trumping of each other's leads by two partners, or by declarer and dummy. ◆ VERB [2] (*intr*) to trump alternately in two hands of a partnership.

cross section NOUN [1] *Maths* a plane surface formed by cutting across a solid, esp perpendicular to its longest axis. [2] a section cut off in this way. [3] the act of cutting anything in this way. [4] a random selection or sample, esp one regarded as representative: *a cross section of the public.* [5] *Surveying* a vertical section of a line of ground at right angles to a survey line. [6] *Physics* a measure of the probability that a collision process will result in a particular reaction. It is expressed by the effective area that one participant presents as a target for the other.
▸ˌ**cross-'sectional** ADJECTIVE

cross-slide NOUN the part of a lathe or planing machine on which the tool post is mounted and across which it slides at right angles to the bed of the lathe.

cross-stitch NOUN [1] an embroidery stitch made by two stitches forming a cross. [2] embroidery worked with this stitch. ◆ VERB [3] to embroider (a piece of needlework) with cross-stitch.

crosstalk ('krɒsˌtɔːk) NOUN [1] unwanted signals in one channel of a communications system as a result of a transfer of energy from one or more other channels. [2] *Brit* rapid or witty talk or conversation.

cross-town ADJECTIVE *US and Canadian* going across or following a route across a town: *a cross-town bus.*

cross training NOUN training in two or more sports to improve performance, esp on one's main sport.

crosstree ('krɒsˌtriː) NOUN *Nautical* either of a pair of wooden or metal braces on the head of a mast to support the topmast, etc.

cross vine NOUN a woody bignoniaceous vine, *Bignonia capreolata*, of the southeastern US, having large trumpet-shaped reddish flowers.

crosswalk ('krɒsˌwɔːk) NOUN the US and Canadian name for **pedestrian crossing.**

crosswind ('krɒsˌwɪnd) NOUN a wind that blows at right angles to the direction of travel.

cross wires PLURAL NOUN another name for **cross hairs.**

crosswise ('krɒsˌwaɪz) *or* **crossways** ('krɒsˌweɪz) ADJECTIVE, ADVERB [1] across; transversely. [2] in the shape of a cross.

crossword puzzle ('krɒsˌwɜːd) NOUN a puzzle in which the solver deduces words suggested by numbered clues and writes them into corresponding boxes in a grid to form a vertical and horizontal pattern. Sometimes shortened to **crossword.**

crosswort ('krɒsˌwɜːt) NOUN a herbaceous perennial Eurasian rubiaceous plant, *Galium cruciata*, with pale yellow flowers and whorls of hairy leaves. Also called: **mugwort.**

crostini (krɒ'stiːniː) PLURAL NOUN pieces of toasted bread served with a savoury topping.
▷HISTORY Italian: literally, little crusts

crotal *or* **crottle** ('krɒtᵊl) NOUN *Scot* any of various lichens used in dyeing wool, esp for the manufacture of tweeds.
▷HISTORY Gaelic *crotal*

crotch (krɒtʃ) NOUN [1] Also called (Brit): **crutch. a** the angle formed by the inner sides of the legs where they join the human trunk. **b** the human external genitals or the genital area. **c** the corresponding part of a pair of trousers, pants, etc. [2] a forked region formed by the junction of two members. [3] a forked pole or stick.
▷HISTORY C16: probably variant of CRUTCH
▸**crotched** ADJECTIVE

crotchet ('krɒtʃɪt) NOUN [1] *Music* a note having the time value of a quarter of a semibreve. Usual US and Canadian name: **quarter note.** [2] a small hook or hooklike device. [3] a perverse notion. [4] *Zoology* a small notched or hooked process, as in an insect.
▷HISTORY C14: from Old French *crochet*, literally: little hook, from *croche* hook; see CROCKET

crotchety ('krɒtʃɪtɪ) ADJECTIVE [1] *Informal* cross; irritable; contrary. [2] full of crotchets.
▸'**crotchetiness** NOUN

croton ('krəʊtᵊn) NOUN [1] any shrub or tree of the chiefly tropical euphorbiaceous genus *Croton*, esp *C. tiglium*, the seeds of which yield croton oil. [2] any of various tropical plants of the related genus *Codiaeum*, esp *C. variegatum pictum*, a house plant with variegated foliage.
▷HISTORY C18: from New Latin, from Greek *krotōn* tick, castor-oil plant (whose berries resemble ticks)

Croton bug NOUN *US* another name for the **German cockroach.**
▷HISTORY C19: named after the *Croton* river, whose water was piped to New York City in 1842

Crotone (*Italian* kro'toːne) NOUN a town in S Italy, on the coast of Calabria: founded in about 700 B.C. by the Achaeans; chemical works and zinc-smelting. Pop.: 61 326 (latest est.).

crotonic acid (krəʊ'tɒnɪk) NOUN a colourless crystalline insoluble unsaturated carboxylic acid produced by oxidation of crotonaldehyde and used in organic synthesis; *trans*-2-butenoic acid. Formula: $CH_3CH{:}CHCOOH$.

croton oil NOUN a yellowish-brown oil obtained from the plant *Croton tiglium*, formerly used as a drastic purgative. See also **croton** (sense 1).

crottle ('krɒtᵊl) NOUN a variant spelling of **crotal.**

crouch (kraʊtʃ) VERB [1] (*intr*) to bend low with the limbs pulled up close together, esp (of an animal) in readiness to pounce. [2] (*intr*) to cringe, as in humility or fear. [3] (*tr*) to bend (parts of the body), as in humility or fear. ◆ NOUN [4] the act of stooping or bending.
▷HISTORY C14: perhaps from Old French *crochir* to become bent like a hook, from *croche* hook

croup¹ (kruːp) NOUN a throat condition, occurring usually in children, characterized by a hoarse cough and laboured breathing, resulting from inflammation and partial obstruction of the larynx.
▷HISTORY C16 *croup* to cry hoarsely, probably of imitative origin
▸'**croupous** *or* '**croupy** ADJECTIVE

croup² *or* **croupe** (kruːp) NOUN the hindquarters of a quadruped, esp a horse.
▷HISTORY C13: from Old French *croupe*; related to German *Kruppe*

croupier ('kruːpɪə; *French* krupje) NOUN a person who deals cards, collects bets, etc., at a gaming table.
▷HISTORY C18: literally: one who rides behind another, from French *croupe* CROUP²

crouse (kru:s) ADJECTIVE *Scot and Northern English dialect* lively, confident, or saucy.
▷**HISTORY** C14 (Scottish and Northern) English: from Middle Low German *krūs* twisted, curled, confused

croute (kru:t) NOUN a small round of toasted bread on which a savoury mixture is served.
▷**HISTORY** from French *croûte* CRUST

crouton ('kru:tɒn) NOUN a small piece of fried or toasted bread, usually served in soup.
▷**HISTORY** French: diminutive of *croûte* CRUST

crow¹ (krəʊ) NOUN [1] any large gregarious songbird of the genus *Corvus*, esp *C. corone* (**carrion crow**) of Europe and Asia: family *Corvidae*. Other species are the raven, rook, and jackdaw and all have a heavy bill, glossy black plumage, and rounded wings. Related adjective: **corvine.** [2] any of various other corvine birds, such as the jay, magpie, and nutcracker. [3] any of various similar birds of other families. [4] short for **crowbar.** [5] **as the crow flies.** as directly as possible. [6] **eat crow.** *US and Canadian informal* to be forced to do something humiliating. [7] **stone the crows.** (*interjection*) *Brit and Austral slang* an expression of surprise, dismay, etc.
▷**HISTORY** Old English *crāwa;* related to Old Norse *krāka*, Old High German *krāia*, Dutch *kraai*

crow² (krəʊ) VERB (*intr*) [1] (past tense **crowed** or **crew**) to utter a shrill squawking sound, as a cock. [2] (often foll by *over*) to boast one's superiority. [3] (esp of babies) to utter cries of pleasure. ◆ NOUN [4] the act or an instance of crowing.
▷**HISTORY** Old English *crāwan;* related to Old High German *krāen*, Dutch *kraaien*
▸ **'crower** NOUN ▸ **'crowingly** ADVERB

Crow (krəʊ) NOUN [1] (*plural* **Crows** *or* **Crow**) a member of a North American Indian people living in E Montana. [2] the language of this people, belonging to the Siouan family.

crowbar ('krəʊ,bɑ:) NOUN a heavy iron lever with one pointed end, and one forged into a wedge shape.

crowberry ('krəʊbərɪ, -brɪ) NOUN, *plural* **-ries.** [1] a low-growing N temperate evergreen shrub, *Empetrum nigrum*, with small purplish flowers and black berry-like fruit: family *Empetraceae*. [2] any of several similar or related plants. [3] the fruit of any of these plants.

crow-bill NOUN a type of forceps used to extract bullets, etc., from wounds.

crow blackbird NOUN another name for **grackle.**

crowboot ('krəʊ,bu:t) NOUN a type of Eskimo boot made of fur and leather.

crowd¹ (kraʊd) NOUN [1] a large number of things or people gathered or considered together. [2] a particular group of people, esp considered as a social or business set: *the crowd from the office*. [3] **a** (preceded by *the*) the common people; the masses. **b** (*as modifier*): *crowd ideas*. [4] **follow the crowd.** to conform with the majority. ◆ VERB [5] (*intr*) to gather together in large numbers; throng. [6] (*tr*) to press together into a confined space. [7] (*tr*) to fill to excess; fill by pushing into. [8] (*tr*) *Informal* to urge or harass by urging. [9] **crowd on sail.** *Nautical* to hoist as much sail as possible.
▷**HISTORY** Old English *crūdan;* related to Middle Low German *krūden* to molest, Middle Dutch *crūden* to push, Norwegian *kryda* to swarm
▸ **'crowded** ADJECTIVE ▸ **'crowdedly** ADVERB
▸ **'crowdedness** NOUN ▸ **'crowder** NOUN

crowd² (kraʊd) NOUN *Music* an ancient bowed stringed instrument; crwth.
▷**HISTORY** C13: from Welsh *crwth*

crowdie ('kraʊdɪ) NOUN *Scot* [1] a porridge of meal and water; brose. [2] a cheese-like dish made by straining the whey from soured milk and beating up the remaining curd with salt.
▷**HISTORY** C17: of unknown origin

crowd puller NOUN *Informal* a person, object, event, etc., that attracts a large audience.

crowea ('krəʊɪə) NOUN an Australian shrub of the genus *Crowea*, having pink flowers.
▷**HISTORY** named after James *Crowe* (1750–1807), British surgeon and botanist

crowfoot ('krəʊ,fʊt) NOUN, *plural* **-foots.** [1] any of several plants of the genus *Ranunculus*, such as *R. sceleratus* and *R. aquatilis* (**water crowfoot**) that have yellow or white flowers and divided leaves resembling the foot of a crow. See also **buttercup.** [2] any of various other plants that have leaves or other parts resembling a bird's foot. [3] (*plural* **-feet**) *Nautical* a bridle-like arrangement of lines rove through a wooden block or attached to a ring for supporting an awning from above. [4] (*plural* **-feet**) *Military* another name for **caltrop.**

crown (kraʊn) NOUN [1] an ornamental headdress denoting sovereignty, usually made of gold embedded with precious stones. [2] a wreath or garland for the head, awarded as a sign of victory, success, honour, etc. [3] (*sometimes capital*) monarchy or kingship. [4] an award, distinction, or title, given as an honour to reward merit, victory, etc. [5] anything resembling or symbolizing a crown, such as a sergeant major's badge or a heraldic bearing. [6] **a** *History* a coin worth 25 pence (five shillings). **b** any of several continental coins, such as the krona or krone, with a name meaning *crown*. [7] the top or summit of something, esp of a rounded object: *crown of a hill; crown of the head*. [8] the centre part of a road, esp when it is cambered. [9] *Botany* **a** the leaves and upper branches of a tree. **b** the junction of root and stem, usually at the level of the ground. **c** another name for **corona** (sense 6). [10] *Zoology* **a** the cup and arms of a crinoid, as distinct from the stem. **b** the crest of a bird. [11] the outstanding quality, achievement, state, etc.: *the crown of his achievements*. [12] **a** the enamel-covered part of a tooth above the gum. **b artificial crown.** a substitute crown, usually of gold, porcelain, or acrylic resin, fitted over a decayed or broken tooth. [13] the part of a cut gem above the girdle. [14] *Horology* a knurled knob for winding a watch. [15] the part of an anchor where the arms are joined to the shank. [16] the highest part of an arch or vault. [17] a standard size of printing paper, 15 by 20 inches. ◆ VERB (*tr*) [18] to put a crown on the head of, symbolically vesting with royal title, powers, etc. [19] to place a crown, wreath, garland, etc., on the head of. [20] to place something on or over the head or top of: *he crowned the pie with cream*. [21] to confer a title, dignity, or reward upon: *he crowned her best cook*. [22] to form the summit or topmost part of: *the steeple crowned the tower*. [23] to cap or put the finishing touch to a series of events: *to crown it all it rained, too*. [24] *Draughts* to promote (a draught) to a king by placing another draught on top of it, as after reaching the end of the board. [25] to attach a crown to (a tooth). [26] *Slang* to hit over the head.
▷**HISTORY** C12: from Old French *corone*, from Latin *corōna* wreath, crown, from Greek *korōnē* crown, something curved
▸ **'crownless** ADJECTIVE

Crown (kraʊn) NOUN (*sometimes not capital;* usually preceded by *the*) [1] the sovereignty or realm of a monarch. [2] **a** the government of a constitutional monarchy. **b** (*as modifier*): *Crown property*.

Crown Agent NOUN [1] a member of a board appointed by the Minister for Overseas Development to provide financial, commercial, and professional services for a number of overseas governments and international bodies. [2] *Scot* (*not capitals*) a solicitor dealing with criminal prosecutions.

crown and anchor NOUN a game played with dice marked with crowns and anchors.

Crown attorney NOUN *Canadian* a lawyer who acts for the Crown, esp as prosecutor in a criminal court.

crown cap NOUN *Brit* an airtight metal seal crimped on the top of most bottled beers, ciders, mineral waters, etc.

crown colony NOUN a British colony whose administration and legislature is controlled by the Crown.

crown court NOUN *English law* a court of criminal jurisdiction holding sessions in towns throughout England and Wales at which circuit judges hear and determine cases.

Crown Derby NOUN a type of porcelain manufactured at Derby from 1784–1848.

crowned head NOUN a monarch: *the crowned heads of Europe*.

crowner ('kraʊnə) NOUN a promotional label consisting of a shaped printed piece of card or paper attached to a product on display.

crown ether NOUN *Chem* a type of cyclic ether consisting of a ring of carbon and oxygen atoms, with two or more carbon atoms between each oxygen atom.

crown glass NOUN [1] another name for **optical crown.** [2] an old form of window glass made by blowing a globe and spinning it until it formed a flat disc.

crown graft NOUN *Horticulture* a type of graft in which the scion is inserted at the crown of the stock.

crown green NOUN a type of bowling green in which the sides are lower than the middle.

crown imperial NOUN a liliaceous garden plant, *Fritillaria imperialis*, with a cluster of leaves and orange bell-shaped flowers at the top of the stem.

crowning ('kraʊnɪŋ) NOUN *Obstetrics* the stage of labour when the infant's head is passing through the vaginal opening.

crown-jewel option NOUN *Informal* an option given by a company subjected to an unwelcome takeover bid to a friendly firm, allowing this firm to buy one or more of its best businesses if the bid succeeds.

crown jewels PLURAL NOUN the jewellery, including the regalia, used by a sovereign on a state occasion.

crownland ('kraʊn,lænd) NOUN a large administrative division of the former empire of Austria-Hungary.

crown land NOUN [1] (in the United Kingdom) land belonging to the Crown. [2] public land in some dominions of the Commonwealth.

crown lens NOUN a lens made of optical crown, esp the optical-crown part of a compound achromatic lens.

Crown Office NOUN (in England) an office of the Queen's Bench Division of the High Court that is responsible for administration and where actions are entered for trial.

crown-of-thorns NOUN [1] a starfish, *Acanthaster planci*, that has a spiny test and feeds on living coral in coral reefs. [2] Also called: **Christ's thorn.** a thorny euphorbiaceous Madagascan shrub, *Euphorbia milii* var. *splendens*, cultivated as a hedging shrub or pot plant, having flowers with scarlet bracts.

crownpiece ('kraʊn,pi:s) NOUN [1] the piece forming or fitting the top of something. [2] the strap of a bridle that goes over a horse's head behind the ears.

crown prince NOUN the male heir to a sovereign throne.

crown princess NOUN [1] the wife of a crown prince. [2] the female heir to a sovereign throne.

Crown Prosecution Service NOUN (in England and Wales) an independent prosecuting body, established in 1986, that decides whether cases brought by the police should go to the courts: headed by the Director of Public Prosecutions. Compare **procurator fiscal.** Abbreviation: **CPS.**

Crown prosecutor NOUN *Canadian* another name for **Crown attorney.**

crown roast NOUN a roast consisting of ribs of lamb or pork arranged in a crown shape.

crown saw NOUN a hollow cylinder with cutting teeth forming a rotary saw for trepanning.

crown vetch NOUN a trailing leguminous European plant, *Coronilla varia*, with clusters of white or pink flowers: cultivated in North America as a border plant. Also called (US): **axseed** ('æksi:d).

crown wheel NOUN [1] *Horology* the wheel next to the winding knob that has one set of teeth at right angles to the other. [2] the larger of the two gears in a bevel gear.

crownwork ('kraʊn,wɜ:k) NOUN [1] **a** the manufacture of artificial crowns for teeth. **b** such an artificial crown or crowns. [2] *Fortifications* a covering or protective outwork.

crow's-foot NOUN, *plural* **-feet.** [1] (*often plural*) a wrinkle at the outer corner of the eye. [2] an embroidery stitch with three points, used esp as a finishing at the end of a seam. [3] a system of diverging short ropes to distribute the pull of a single rope, used esp in balloon and airship riggings.

crow's-nest NOUN a lookout platform high up on a ship's mast.

crow step NOUN another term for **corbie-step**.

Croydon ('krɔɪdᵊn) NOUN a borough in S Greater London (since 1965): formerly important for its airport (1915–59). Pop.: 330 688 (2001). Area: 87 sq. km (33 sq. miles).

croze (krəʊz) NOUN [1] the recess cut at the end of a barrel or cask to receive the head. [2] a tool for cutting this recess.
▷HISTORY C17: probably from Old French *crues* a hollow

crozier ('krəʊʒə) NOUN a variant spelling of **crosier**.

crozzled ('krɒzᵊld) ADJECTIVE *Northern English dialect* blackened or burnt at the edges: *that bacon is crozzled*.

CRP (in India) ABBREVIATION FOR Central Reserve Police.

CRT ABBREVIATION FOR: [1] **cathode-ray tube**. [2] (in Britain) composite rate tax: a system of paying interest to savers by which a rate of tax for a period, such as one financial year, is determined in advance, and interest is paid net of tax which is deducted at source.

cru (kru:; *French* kry) NOUN *Winemaking* (in France) a vineyard, group of vineyards, or wine-producing region.
▷HISTORY from French: production, from *crû*, past participle of *croître* to grow

cruces ('kru:si:z) NOUN a plural of **crux**.

crucial ('kru:ʃəl) ADJECTIVE [1] involving a final or supremely important decision or event; decisive; critical. [2] *Informal* very important. [3] *Slang* very good.
▷HISTORY C18: from French, from Latin *crux* CROSS
▸'**crucially** ADVERB

crucian ('kru:ʃən) NOUN a European cyprinid fish, *Carassius carassius*, with a dark-green back, a golden-yellow undersurface, and reddish dorsal and tail fins: an aquarium fish.
▷HISTORY C18: from Low German *Karusse*

cruciate ('kru:ʃɪɪt, -ˌeɪt) ADJECTIVE shaped or arranged like a cross: *cruciate petals*.
▷HISTORY C17: from New Latin *cruciātus*, from Latin *crux* cross
▸'**cruciately** ADVERB

crucible ('kru:sɪbᵊl) NOUN [1] a vessel in which substances are heated to high temperatures. [2] the hearth at the bottom of a metallurgical furnace in which the metal collects. [3] a severe trial or test.
▷HISTORY C15 *corusible*, from Medieval Latin *crūcibulum* night lamp, crucible, of uncertain origin

Crucible ('kru:sɪbᵊl) NOUN **the**. a Sheffield theatre, venue of the annual world professional snooker championship.

crucible steel NOUN a high-quality steel made by melting wrought iron, charcoal, and other additives in a crucible.

crucifer ('kru:sɪfə) NOUN [1] any plant of the family *Brassicaceae* (formerly *Cruciferae*), having a corolla of four petals arranged like a cross and a fruit called a siliqua. The family includes the brassicas, mustard, cress, and wallflower. [2] a person who carries a cross.
▷HISTORY C16: from Late Latin, from Latin *crux* cross + *ferre* to carry
▸**cruciferous** (kru:'sɪfərəs) ADJECTIVE

crucifix ('kru:sɪfɪks) NOUN a cross or image of a cross with a figure of Christ upon it.
▷HISTORY C13: from Church Latin *crucifixus* the crucified Christ, from *crucifigere* to CRUCIFY

crucifixion (ˌkru:sɪ'fɪkʃən) NOUN a method of putting to death by nailing or binding to a cross, normally by the hands and feet, which was widespread in the ancient world.

Crucifixion (ˌkru:sɪ'fɪkʃən) NOUN [1] (usually preceded by *the*) the crucifying of Christ at Calvary, regarded by Christians as the culminating redemptive act of his ministry. [2] a picture or representation of this.

cruciform ('kru:sɪˌfɔ:m) ADJECTIVE [1] shaped like a cross. ◆ NOUN [2] a geometric curve, shaped like a cross, that has four similar branches asymptotic to two mutually perpendicular pairs of lines. Equation: $x^2y^2 - a^2x^2 - a^2y^2 = 0$, where $x = y = \pm a$ are the four lines.
▷HISTORY C17: from Latin *crux* cross + -FORM
▸'**cruciˌformly** ADVERB

crucify ('kru:sɪˌfaɪ) VERB **-fies, -fying, -fied**. (*tr*) [1] to put to death by crucifixion. [2] *Slang* to defeat, ridicule, etc., totally: *the critics crucified his performance*. [3] to treat very cruelly; torment. [4] to subdue (passion, lust, etc.); mortify.
▷HISTORY C13: from Old French *crucifier*, from Late Latin *crucifigere* to crucify, to fasten to a cross, from Latin *crux* cross + *figere* to fasten
▸'**cruciˌfier** NOUN

cruciverbalist (ˌkru:sɪ'vɜ:bəlɪst) NOUN a crossword puzzle enthusiast.
▷HISTORY C20: from Latin *crux* cross + *verbum* word

cruck (krʌk) NOUN one of a pair of curved wooden timbers supporting the end of the roof in certain types of building.
▷HISTORY C19: variant of CROOK (noun)

crud (krʌd) *Slang* ◆ NOUN [1] a sticky substance, esp when dirty and encrusted. [2] an undesirable residue from a process, esp one inside a nuclear reactor. [3] something or someone that is worthless, disgusting, or contemptible. [4] (sometimes preceded by *the*) a disease; rot. ◆ INTERJECTION [5] an expression of disgust, disappointment, etc.
▷HISTORY C14: earlier form of CURD

cruddy ('krʌdɪ) ADJECTIVE **cruddier, cruddiest** *Slang* [1] dirty or unpleasant. [2] of poor quality; contemptible.

crude (kru:d) ADJECTIVE [1] lacking taste, tact, or refinement; vulgar: *a crude joke*. [2] in a natural or unrefined state. [3] lacking care, knowledge, or skill: *a crude sketch*. [4] (*prenominal*) stark; blunt: *the crude facts*. [5] (of statistical data) unclassified or unanalysed. [6] *Archaic* unripe. ◆ NOUN [7] short for **crude oil**.
▷HISTORY C14: from Latin *crūdus* bloody, raw; related to Latin *cruor* blood
▸'**crudely** ADVERB ▸'**crudity** *or* '**crudeness** NOUN

crude oil NOUN petroleum before it has been refined.

crudités (ˌkru:dɪ'teɪ) PLURAL NOUN a selection of raw vegetables, usually cut into strips or small chunks and served, with a dip, as an hors d'oeuvre.
▷HISTORY C20: from French, plural of *crudité*, literally: rawness

cruel ('kru:əl) ADJECTIVE [1] causing or inflicting pain without pity: *a cruel teacher*. [2] causing pain or suffering: *a cruel accident*.
▷HISTORY C13: from Old French, from Latin *crūdēlis*, from *crūdus* raw, bloody
▸'**cruelly** ADVERB ▸'**cruelness** NOUN

cruels NOUN another name for **Actinobacillosis** (in sheep).

cruelty ('kru:əltɪ) NOUN, *plural* **-ties**. [1] deliberate infliction of pain or suffering. [2] the quality or characteristic of being cruel. [3] a cruel action. [4] *Law* conduct that causes danger to life or limb or a threat to bodily or mental health, on proof of which a decree of divorce may be granted.

cruelty-free ADJECTIVE (of a cosmetic or other product) developed without being tested on animals.

cruet ('kru:ɪt) NOUN [1] a small container for holding pepper, salt, vinegar, oil, etc., at table. [2] a set of such containers, esp on a stand. [3] *Christianity* either of a pair of small containers for the wine and water used in the Eucharist. [4] *Austral* a slang word for **head** (sense 1). [5] **do one's cruet**. *Austral slang* to be extremely angry; go into a rage. ◆ PLURAL NOUN [6] *Austral slang* the testicles.
▷HISTORY C13: from Anglo-French, diminutive of Old French *crue* flask, of Germanic origin; compare Old Saxon *krūka*, Old English *crūce* pot

cruise (kru:z) VERB [1] (*intr*) to make a trip by sea in a liner for pleasure, usually calling at a number of ports. [2] to sail or travel over (a body of water) for pleasure in a yacht, cruiser, etc. [3] (*intr*) to search for enemy vessels in a warship. [4] (*intr*) (of a vehicle, aircraft, or vessel) to travel at a moderate and efficient speed. [5] (*intr*) *Informal* to search the streets or other public places for a sexual partner. ◆ NOUN [6] an act or instance of cruising, esp a trip by sea.
▷HISTORY C17: from Dutch *kruisen* to cross, from *cruis* CROSS; related to French *croiser* to cross, cruise, Spanish *cruzar*, German *kreuzen*

cruise control NOUN a system in a road vehicle that automatically maintains a selected speed until cancelled.

cruise missile NOUN an air-breathing low-flying subsonic missile that is continuously powered and guided throughout its flight and carries a warhead.

cruiser ('kru:zə) NOUN [1] a high-speed, long-range warship of medium displacement, armed with medium calibre weapons or missiles. [2] Also called: **cabin cruiser**. a pleasure boat, esp one that is power-driven and has a cabin. [3] any person or thing that cruises. [4] *Boxing* short for **cruiserweight** (see **light heavyweight**).

cruiserweight ('kru:zəˌweɪt) NOUN *Boxing* another term (esp Brit) for **light heavyweight**.

cruiseway ('kru:zˌweɪ) NOUN a canal used for recreational purposes.

cruizie, cruzie, *or* **crusie** ('kru:zɪ) NOUN *Scot* an oil lamp.
▷HISTORY C18: perhaps from *cruset* crucible, from French *creuset*

cruller *or* **kruller** ('krʌlə) NOUN *US and Canadian* a light sweet ring-shaped cake, fried in deep fat.
▷HISTORY C19: from Dutch *krulle*, from *krullen* to CURL

crumb (krʌm) NOUN [1] a small fragment of bread, cake, or other baked foods. [2] a small piece or bit: *crumbs of information*. [3] the soft inner part of bread. [4] *Slang* a contemptible person. ◆ VERB [5] (*tr*) to prepare or cover (food) with breadcrumbs. [6] to break into small fragments. ◆ ADJECTIVE [7] (esp of pie crusts) made with a mixture of biscuit crumbs, sugar, etc.
▷HISTORY Old English *cruma*; related to Middle Dutch *krome*, Middle High German *krūme*, Latin *grūmus* heap of earth
▸'**crumber** NOUN

crumble ('krʌmbᵊl) VERB [1] to break or be broken into crumbs or fragments. [2] (*intr*) to fall apart or away: *his resolution crumbled*. ◆ NOUN [3] *Brit* a baked pudding consisting of a crumbly mixture of flour, fat, and sugar over stewed fruit: *apple crumble*.
▷HISTORY C16: variant of *crimble*, of Germanic origin; compare Low German *krömeln*, Dutch *kruimelen*

crumbly ('krʌmblɪ) ADJECTIVE **-blier, -bliest**. easily crumbled or crumbling.
▸'**crumbliness** NOUN

crumbs (krʌmz) INTERJECTION *Slang* an expression of dismay or surprise.
▷HISTORY C20: euphemistic for *Christ!*

crumby ('krʌmɪ) ADJECTIVE **crumbier, crumbiest**. [1] full of or littered with crumbs. [2] soft, like the inside of bread. [3] a variant spelling of **crummy**[1].

crumhorn *or* **krummhorn** ('krʌmˌhɔ:n) NOUN a medieval woodwind instrument of bass pitch, consisting of an almost cylindrical tube curving upwards and blown through a double reed covered by a pierced cap.
▷HISTORY C17 *cromorne*, *krumhorn*, from German *Krummhorn* curved horn

Crummock Water ('krʌmək) NOUN a lake in NW England, in Cumbria in the Lake District. Length: 4 km (2.5 miles).

crummy[1] ('krʌmɪ) ADJECTIVE **-mier, -miest**. *Slang* [1] of little value; inferior; contemptible. [2] unwell or depressed: *to feel crummy*.
▷HISTORY C19: variant spelling of CRUMBY

crummy[2] ('krʌmɪ) NOUN, *plural* **-mies**. *Canadian* a lorry that carries loggers to work from their camp.
▷HISTORY probably originally meaning: makeshift camp, from CRUMMY[1]

crump (krʌmp) VERB [1] (*intr*) to thud or explode with a loud dull sound. [2] (*tr*) to bombard with heavy shells. ◆ NOUN [3] a crunching, thudding, or exploding noise.
▷HISTORY C17: of imitative origin

crumpet ('krʌmpɪt) NOUN *Chiefly Brit* [1] a light soft yeast cake full of small holes on the top side, eaten toasted and buttered. [2] (in Scotland) a large flat sweetened cake made of batter. [3] *Slang* women collectively. [4] **a piece of crumpet**. *Slang* a sexually desirable woman. [5] **not worth a crumpet**. *Austral slang* utterly worthless.
▷HISTORY C17: of uncertain origin

crumple ('krʌmpᵊl) VERB [1] (when *intr*, often foll by *up*) to collapse or cause to collapse: *his courage crumpled*. [2] (when *tr*, often foll by *up*) to crush or cause to be crushed so as to form wrinkles or creases. [3] (*intr*) to shrink; shrivel. ◆ NOUN [4] a loose crease or wrinkle.

▷**HISTORY** C16: from obsolete *crump* to bend; related to Old High German *krimpfan* to wrinkle, Old Norse *kreppa* to contract
▸ˈ**crumply** ADJECTIVE

crumple zones PLURAL NOUN parts of a motor vehicle, at the front and the rear, that are designed to crumple in a collision, thereby absorbing the impact.

crunch (krʌntʃ) VERB [1] to bite or chew (crisp foods) with a crushing or crackling sound. [2] to make or cause to make a crisp or brittle sound: *the snow crunched beneath his feet.* ◆ NOUN [3] the sound or act of crunching. [4] **the crunch.** *Informal* the critical moment or situation. ◆ ADJECTIVE [5] *Informal* critical; decisive: *crunch time.* ◆ Also: **craunch.**
▷**HISTORY** C19: changed (through influence of MUNCH) from earlier *craunch,* of imitative origin
▸ˈ**crunchable** ADJECTIVE ▸ˈ**crunchy** ADJECTIVE ▸ˈ**crunchily** ADVERB ▸ˈ**crunchiness** NOUN

crunchie (ˈkrʌntʃɪ) NOUN *South African derogatory slang* another name for an **Afrikaner.**

crunode (ˈkruːnəʊd) NOUN a point at which two branches of a curve intersect, each branch having a distinct tangent; node.
▷**HISTORY** C19: *cru-* from Latin *crux* cross + NODE

cruor (ˈkruɔː) NOUN, *plural* **cruores** (ˈkruɔːriːz). *Med* a blood clot.

crupper (ˈkrʌpə) NOUN [1] a strap from the back of a saddle that passes under the horse's tail to prevent the saddle from slipping forwards. [2] the part of the horse's rump behind the saddle.
▷**HISTORY** C13: from Old French *crupiere,* from *crupe* CROUP[2]

crura (ˈkrʊərə) NOUN the plural of **crus.**

crural (ˈkrʊərəl) ADJECTIVE of or relating to the leg or thigh.
▷**HISTORY** C16: from Latin *crūrālis,* from *crūs* leg, shin

crus (krʌs) NOUN, *plural* **crura** (ˈkrʊərə). [1] *Anatomy* the leg, esp from the knee to the foot. [2] (*usually plural*) leglike parts or structures.
▷**HISTORY** C17: from Latin: leg

crusade (kruːˈseɪd) NOUN [1] (*often capital*) any of the military expeditions undertaken in the 11th, 12th, and 13th centuries by the Christian powers of Europe to recapture the Holy Land from the Muslims. [2] (formerly) any holy war undertaken on behalf of a religious cause. [3] a vigorous and dedicated action or movement in favour of a cause. ◆ VERB (*intr*) [4] to campaign vigorously for something. [5] to go on a crusade.
▷**HISTORY** C16: from earlier *croisade,* from Old French *crois* cross, from Latin *crux;* influenced also by Spanish *cruzada,* from *cruzar* to take up the cross
▸**cruˈsader** NOUN

crusado (kruːˈseɪdəʊ) *or* **cruzado** (kruːˈzeɪdəʊ; *Portuguese* kruˈzɑːdu) NOUN, *plural* **-does** *or* **-dos** (-dəʊz; *Portuguese* -duʃ). a former gold or silver coin of Portugal bearing on its reverse the figure of a cross.
▷**HISTORY** C16: literally, marked with a cross, from *cruzar* to bear a cross; see CRUSADE

cruse (kruːz) NOUN a small earthenware container used, esp formerly, for liquids.
▷**HISTORY** Old English *crūse;* related to Middle High German *krūse,* Dutch *kroes* jug

crush[1] (krʌʃ) VERB (*mainly tr*) [1] to press, mash, or squeeze so as to injure, break, crease, etc. [2] to break or grind (rock, ore, etc.) into small particles. [3] to put down or subdue, esp by force: *to crush a rebellion.* [4] to extract (juice, water, etc.) by pressing: *to crush the juice from a lemon.* [5] to oppress harshly. [6] to hug or clasp tightly: *he crushed her to him.* [7] to defeat or humiliate utterly, as in argument or by a cruel remark. [8] (*intr*) to crowd; throng. [9] (*intr*) to become injured, broken, or distorted by pressure. ◆ NOUN [10] a dense crowd, esp at a social occasion. [11] the act of crushing; pressure. [12] a drink or pulp prepared by or as if by crushing fruit: *orange crush.* [13] *Informal* **a** an infatuation: *she had a crush on him.* **b** the person with whom one is infatuated.
▷**HISTORY** C14: from Old French *croissir,* of Germanic origin; compare Gothic *kriustan* to gnash; see CRUNCH
▸ˈ**crushable** ADJECTIVE ▸ˌ**crushaˈbility** NOUN ▸ˈ**crusher** NOUN

crush[2] (krʌʃ) NOUN *Vet science* a construction designed to confine and limit the movement of an animal, esp a large or dangerous animal, for examination or to perform a procedure on it.

crush bar NOUN a bar at a theatre for serving drinks during the intervals of a play.

crush barrier NOUN a barrier erected to separate sections of large crowds in order to prevent crushing.

crush-resistant ADJECTIVE not being easily creased.

crusie (ˈkruːzɪ) NOUN a variant spelling of **cruizie.**

Crusoe (ˈkruːsəʊ, -zəʊ) NOUN **Robinson.** See **Robinson Crusoe.**

crust (krʌst) NOUN [1] **a** the hard outer part of bread. **b** a piece of bread consisting mainly of this. [2] the baked shell of a pie, tart, etc. [3] any hard or stiff outer covering or surface: *a crust of ice.* [4] the solid outer shell of the earth, with an average thickness of 30–35 km in continental regions and 5 km beneath the oceans, forming the upper part of the lithosphere and lying immediately above the mantle, from which it is separated by the Mohorovičić discontinuity. See also **sial, sima.** [5] the dry covering of a skin sore or lesion; scab. [6] a layer of acid potassium tartrate deposited by some wine, esp port, on the inside of the bottle. [7] the hard outer layer of such organisms as lichens and crustaceans. [8] *Slang* impertinence. [9] *Brit, Austral, and NZ slang* a living (esp in the phrase **earn a crust**). ◆ VERB [10] to cover with or acquire a crust. [11] to form or be formed into a crust.
▷**HISTORY** C14: from Latin *crūsta* hard surface, rind, shell

crustacean (krʌˈsteɪʃən) NOUN [1] any arthropod of the mainly aquatic class *Crustacea,* typically having a carapace hardened with lime and including the lobsters, crabs, shrimps, woodlice, barnacles, copepods, and water fleas. ◆ ADJECTIVE *also* **crustaceous.** [2] of, relating to, or belonging to the *Crustacea.*
▷**HISTORY** C19: from New Latin *crūstāceus* hard-shelled, from Latin *crūsta* shell, CRUST

crustaceous (krʌˈsteɪʃəs) ADJECTIVE [1] forming, resembling, or possessing a surrounding crust or shell. [2] *Zoology* another word for **crustacean** (sense 2).

crustal (ˈkrʌstᵊl) ADJECTIVE of or relating to the earth's crust.

crustose (ˈkrʌstəʊs) ADJECTIVE *Biology* having a crustlike appearance: *crustose lichens.*

crusty (ˈkrʌstɪ) ADJECTIVE **crustier, crustiest.** [1] having or characterized by a crust, esp having a thick crust. [2] having a rude or harsh character or exterior; surly; curt: *a crusty remark.* ◆ NOUN, *plural* **crusties.** [3] *Slang* a dirty type of punk or hippy whose lifestyle involves travelling and squatting.
▸ˈ**crustily** ADVERB ▸ˈ**crustiness** NOUN

crutch (krʌtʃ) NOUN [1] a long staff of wood or metal having a rest for the armpit, for supporting the weight of the body. [2] something that supports or sustains: *a crutch to the economy.* [3] *Brit* another word for **crotch** (sense 1). [4] *Nautical* **a** a forked support for a boom or oar, etc. **b** a brace for reinforcing the frames at the stern of a wooden vessel. ◆ VERB [5] (*tr*) to support or sustain (a person or thing) as with a crutch. [6] *Austral and NZ slang* to clip (wool) from the hindquarters of a sheep.
▷**HISTORY** Old English *crycc;* related to Old High German *krucka,* Old Norse *krykkja;* see CROSIER, CROOK

Crutched Friar (krʌtʃt, ˈkrʌtʃɪd) NOUN a member of a mendicant order, suppressed in 1656.
▷**HISTORY** C16: *crutched,* variant of *crouched,* literally: crossed, referring to the cross worn on their habits

crutchings (ˈkrʌtʃɪŋz) PLURAL NOUN *Austral and NZ* the wool clipped from a sheep's hindquarters.

crux (krʌks) NOUN, *plural* **cruxes** *or* **cruces** (ˈkruːsiːz). [1] a vital or decisive stage, point, etc. (often in the phrase **the crux of the matter**). [2] a baffling problem or difficulty. [3] *Mountaineering* the most difficult and often decisive part of a climb or pitch. [4] a rare word for **cross.**
▷**HISTORY** C18: from Latin: cross

Crux (krʌks) NOUN, *Latin genitive* **Crucis** (ˈkruːsɪs). the more formal name for the **Southern Cross.**

crux ansata (ænˈseɪtə) NOUN, *plural* **cruces ansatae** (ænˈseɪtiː). another term for **ankh.**
▷**HISTORY** New Latin, literally: cross with a handle

cruzado (kruːˈzeɪdəʊ; *Portuguese* kruˈzɑːdu) NOUN, *plural* **-does** *or* **-dos** (-dəʊz; *Portuguese* -duʃ). [1] a former standard monetary unit of Brazil, replaced by the cruzeiro. [2] another name for **crusado.**
▷**HISTORY** C16: literally marked with a cross, from *cruzar* to bear a cross; see CRUSADE

cruzeiro (kruːˈzɛərəʊ; *Portuguese* kruˈzeiru) NOUN, *plural* **-ros** (-rəʊz; *Portuguese* -ruʃ). a former monetary unit of Brazil, replaced by the cruzeiro real.
▷**HISTORY** Portuguese: from *cruz* CROSS

cruzeiro real NOUN a former monetary unit of Brazil, replaced by the **real[3]** (sense 1).

cruzie (ˈkruːzɪ) NOUN a variant spelling of **cruizie.**

crwth (kruːθ) NOUN an ancient stringed instrument of Celtic origin similar to the cithara but bowed in later types.
▷**HISTORY** Welsh; compare Middle Irish *crott* harp

cry (kraɪ) VERB **cries, crying, cried.** [1] (*intr*) to utter inarticulate sounds, esp when weeping; sob. [2] (*intr*) to shed tears; weep. [3] (*intr;* usually foll by *out*) to scream or shout in pain, terror, etc. [4] (*tr;* often foll by *out*) to utter or shout (words of appeal, exclamation, fear, etc.). [5] (*intr;* often foll by *out*) (of animals, birds, etc.) to utter loud characteristic sounds. [6] (*tr*) to hawk or sell by public announcement: *to cry newspapers.* [7] to announce (something) publicly or in the streets. [8] (*intr;* foll by *for*) to clamour or beg. [9] *Scot* to call. [10] **cry for the moon.** to desire the unattainable. [11] **cry one's eyes** *or* **heart out.** to weep bitterly. [12] **cry quits** *or* **mercy.** to give up a task, fight, etc. ◆ NOUN, *plural* **cries.** [13] the act or sound of crying; a shout, exclamation, scream, or wail. [14] the characteristic utterance of an animal or bird: *the cry of gulls.* [15] *Scot* a call. [16] *Archaic* an oral announcement, esp one made by town criers. [17] a fit of weeping. [18] *Hunting* the baying of a pack of hounds hunting their quarry by scent. [19] a pack of hounds. [20] **a far cry. a** a long way. **b** something very different. [21] **in full cry.** (esp of a pack of hounds) in hot pursuit of a quarry. ◆ See also **cry down, cry off, cry out, cry up.**
▷**HISTORY** C13: from Old French *crier,* from Latin *quirītāre* to call for help

crybaby (ˈkraɪˌbeɪbɪ) NOUN, *plural* **-bies.** a person, esp a child, given to frequent crying or complaint.

cry down VERB (*tr, adverb*) [1] to belittle; disparage. [2] to silence by making a greater noise: *to cry down opposition.*

crying (ˈkraɪɪŋ) ADJECTIVE (*prenominal*) notorious; lamentable (esp in the phrase **crying shame**).

cryo- COMBINING FORM indicating low temperature; frost, cold, or freezing: *cryogenics; cryosurgery.*
▷**HISTORY** from Greek *kruos* icy cold, frost

cryobiology (ˌkraɪəʊbaɪˈɒlədʒɪ) NOUN the branch of biology concerned with the study of the effects of very low temperatures on organisms.
▸ˌ**cryobiˈologist** NOUN

cryocable (ˌkraɪəʊˈkeɪbᵊl) NOUN a highly conducting electrical cable cooled with a refrigerant such as liquid nitrogen.

cry off VERB (*intr*) *Informal* to withdraw from or cancel (an agreement or arrangement).

cryogen (ˈkraɪədʒən) NOUN a substance used to produce low temperatures; a freezing mixture.

cryogenics (ˌkraɪəˈdʒɛnɪks) NOUN (*functioning as singular*) the branch of physics concerned with the production of very low temperatures and the phenomena occurring at these temperatures.
▸ˌ**cryoˈgenic** ADJECTIVE

cryoglobulin (ˌkraɪəʊˈglɒbjʊlɪn) NOUN *Med* an abnormal immunoglobulin, present in the blood in certain diseases, that precipitates below about 10°C, obstructing small blood vessels in the fingers and toes.

cryohydrate (ˌkraɪəʊˈhaɪdreɪt) NOUN a crystalline substance containing water and a salt in definite proportions at low temperatures: a eutectic crystallizing below the freezing point of water.

cryolite (ˈkraɪəˌlaɪt) NOUN a white or colourless mineral consisting of a fluoride of sodium and aluminium in monoclinic crystalline form: used in the production of aluminium, glass, and enamel. Formula: Na_3AlF_6.

cryometer (kraɪˈɒmɪtə) NOUN a thermometer for measuring low temperatures.
▸**cryˈometry** NOUN

cryonics (kraɪˈɒnɪks) NOUN (*functioning as singular*)

the practice of freezing a human corpse in the hope of restoring it to life in the future.

cryophilic (ˌkraɪəˈfɪlɪk) ADJECTIVE *Biology* able to thrive at low temperatures.

cryophyte (ˈkraɪəˌfaɪt) NOUN an organism, esp an alga or moss, that grows on snow or ice.

cryoplankton (ˌkraɪəʊˈplæŋktən) NOUN minute organisms, esp algae, living in ice, snow, or icy water.

cryoprecipitate (ˌkraɪəʊprɪˈsɪpɪteɪt) NOUN a precipitate obtained by controlled thawing of a previously frozen substance. Factor VIII, for treating haemophilia, is often obtained as a cryoprecipitate from frozen blood.

cryoscope (ˈkraɪəˌskəʊp) NOUN any instrument used to determine the freezing point of a substance.

cryoscopy (kraɪˈɒskəpɪ) NOUN, *plural* **-pies**. the determination of freezing points, esp for the determination of molecular weights by measuring the lowering of the freezing point of a solvent when a known quantity of solute is added.
▸ **cryoscopic** (ˌkraɪəˈskɒpɪk) ADJECTIVE

cryostat (ˈkraɪəˌstæt) NOUN an apparatus for maintaining a constant low temperature or a vessel in which a substance is stored at a low temperature.

cryosurgery (ˌkraɪəʊˈsɜːdʒərɪ) NOUN surgery involving the local destruction of tissues by quick freezing for therapeutic benefit.

cryotherapy (ˌkraɪəʊˈθɛrəpɪ) *or* **crymotherapy** (ˌkraɪməʊˈθɛrəpɪ) NOUN medical treatment in which all or part of the body is subjected to cold temperatures, as by means of ice packs.

cryotron (ˈkraɪəˌtrɒn) NOUN a miniature switch working at the temperature of liquid helium and depending for its action on the production and destruction of superconducting properties in the conductor.

cry out VERB (*intr, adverb*) 1 to scream or shout aloud, esp in pain, terror, etc. 2 (often foll by *for*) *Informal* to demand in an obvious manner: *our inner cities are crying out for redevelopment.* 3 **for crying out loud.** *Informal* an exclamation of anger or dismay.

crypt (krɪpt) NOUN 1 a cellar, vault, or underground chamber, esp beneath a church, where it is often used as a chapel, burial place, etc. 2 *Anatomy* any pitlike recess or depression.
▷ HISTORY C18: from Latin *crypta,* from Greek *kruptē* vault, secret place, from *kruptos* hidden, from *kruptein* to hide
▸ **ˈcryptal** ADJECTIVE

cryptaesthesia *or US* **cryptesthesia** (ˌkrɪptəsˈθiːzɪə) NOUN *Psychol* another term for **extrasensory perception.**

cryptanalysis (ˌkrɪptəˈnælɪsɪs) NOUN the study of codes and ciphers; cryptography.
▷ HISTORY C20: from CRYPTOGRAPH + ANALYSIS
▸ **cryptanalytic** (ˌkrɪptænəˈlɪtɪk) ADJECTIVE ▸ **cryptˈanalyst** NOUN

cryptic (ˈkrɪptɪk) *or* **cryptical** ADJECTIVE 1 hidden; secret; occult. 2 (esp of comments, sayings, etc.) obscure in meaning. 3 (of the coloration of animals) tending to conceal by disguising or camouflaging the shape.
▷ HISTORY C17: from Late Latin *crypticus,* from Greek *kruptikos,* from *kruptos* concealed; see CRYPT
▸ **ˈcryptically** ADVERB

crypto- *or before a vowel* **crypt-** COMBINING FORM secret, hidden, or concealed: *cryptography; crypto-fascist.*
▷ HISTORY New Latin, from Greek *kruptos* hidden, from *kruptein* to hide

cryptobiont (ˌkrɪptəʊˈbaɪɒnt) NOUN any organism that exhibits cryptobiosis.

cryptobiosis (ˌkrɪptəʊbaɪˈəʊsɪs) NOUN *Zoology* a temporary state in an organism in which metabolic activity is absent or undetectable.

cryptoclastic (ˌkrɪptəʊˈklæstɪk) ADJECTIVE (of minerals and rocks) composed of microscopic fragments.

cryptocrystalline (ˌkrɪptəʊˈkrɪstəlaɪn) ADJECTIVE (of rocks) composed of crystals that can be distinguished individually only by the use of a polarizing microscope.

cryptogam (ˈkrɪptəʊˌgæm) NOUN (in former plant classification schemes) any organism that does not produce seeds, including algae, fungi, mosses, and ferns. Compare **phanerogam.**
▷ HISTORY C19: from New Latin *Cryptogamia,* from CRYPTO- + Greek *gamos* marriage
▸ **ˌcryptoˈgamic** *or* **cryptogamous** (krɪpˈtɒgəməs) ADJECTIVE

cryptogenic (ˌkrɪptəʊˈdʒɛnɪk) ADJECTIVE (esp of diseases) of unknown or obscure origin.

cryptograph (ˈkrɪptəʊˌgræf, -ˌgrɑːf) NOUN 1 something written in code or cipher. 2 a code using secret symbols (**cryptograms**). 3 a device for translating text into cipher, or vice versa.

cryptography (krɪpˈtɒgrəfɪ) *or* **cryptology** (krɪpˈtɒlədʒɪ) NOUN the science or study of analysing and deciphering codes, ciphers, etc.; cryptanalysis.
▸ **crypˈtographer, crypˈtographist,** *or* **crypˈtologist** NOUN
▸ **cryptographic** (ˌkrɪptəˈgræfɪk) *or* **ˌcryptoˈgraphical** ADJECTIVE ▸ **ˌcryptoˈgraphically** ADVERB

cryptomeria (ˌkrɪptəʊˈmɪərɪə) NOUN a coniferous tree, *Cryptomeria japonica,* of China and Japan, with curved needle-like leaves and small round cones: family *Taxodiaceae.*
▷ HISTORY C19: from New Latin, from CRYPTO- + Greek *meros* part; so called because the seeds are hidden by scales

cryptometer (krɪpˈtɒmɪtə) NOUN an instrument used to determine the opacity of pigments and paints.

cryptophyte (ˈkrɪptəˌfaɪt) NOUN any perennial plant that bears its buds below the soil or water surface.
▸ **cryptophytic** (ˌkrɪptəˈfɪtɪk) ADJECTIVE

cryptorchid (krɪpˈtɔːkɪd) NOUN 1 an animal or human in which the testes fail to descend into the scrotum. ◆ ADJECTIVE 2 denoting or relating to such an individual.
▷ HISTORY from CRYPTO- + *orchid,* from Greek *orkhis* testicle
▸ **crypˈtorchidˌism** NOUN

cryptosporidium (ˌkrɪptəʊspɔːˈrɪdɪəm) NOUN any parasitic sporozoan protozoan of the genus *Cryptosporidium,* species of which are parasites of birds and animals and can be transmitted to humans, causing severe abdominal pain and diarrhoea (**cryptosporidiosis**).

cryptozoic (ˌkrɪptəʊˈzəʊɪk) ADJECTIVE (of animals) living in dark places, such as holes, caves, and beneath stones.

Cryptozoic (ˌkrɪptəʊˈzəʊɪk) ADJECTIVE 1 of or relating to that part of geological time represented by rocks in which the evidence of life is slight and the life forms are primitive; pre-Phanerozoic. ◆ NOUN 2 **the.** the Cryptozoic era. ◆ See also **Precambrian.** Compare **Phanerozoic.**

cryptozoite (ˌkrɪptəʊˈzəʊaɪt) NOUN a malarial parasite at the stage of development in its host before it enters the red blood cells.

cryptozoology (ˌkrɪptəʊzəʊˈɒlədʒɪ, -zuː-) NOUN the study of creatures, such as the Loch Ness monster, whose existence has not been scientifically proved.

cryst. ABBREVIATION FOR: 1 crystalline. 2 Also: **crystall.** crystallography.

crystal (ˈkrɪstᵊl) NOUN 1 a piece of solid substance, such as quartz, with a regular shape in which plane faces intersect at definite angles, due to the regular internal structure of its atoms, ions, or molecules. 2 a single grain of a crystalline substance. 3 anything resembling a crystal, such as a piece of cut glass. 4 **a** a highly transparent and brilliant type of glass, often used in cut-glass tableware, ornaments, etc. **b** (*as modifier*): *a crystal chandelier.* 5 something made of or resembling crystal. 6 crystal glass articles collectively. 7 *Electronics* **a** a crystalline element used in certain electronic devices as a detector, oscillator, transducer, etc. **b** (*as modifier*): *crystal pick-up; crystal detector.* 8 a transparent cover for the face of a watch, usually of glass or plastic. 9 (*modifier*) of or relating to a crystal or the regular atomic arrangement of crystals: *crystal structure; crystal lattice.* ◆ ADJECTIVE 10 resembling crystal; transparent: *crystal water.*
▷ HISTORY Old English *cristalla,* from Latin *crystallum,* from Greek *krustallos* ice, crystal, from *krustainein* to freeze

crystal ball NOUN the glass globe used in crystal gazing.

crystal class NOUN *Crystallog* any of 32 possible types of crystals, classified according to their rotational symmetry about axes through a point. Also called: **point group.**

crystal counter NOUN an instrument for detecting and measuring the intensity of high-energy radiation, in which particles collide with a crystal and momentarily increase its conductivity.

crystal detector NOUN *Electronics* a demodulator, used esp in microwave circuits and in early radio receivers, consisting of a thin metal wire in point contact with a semiconductor crystal.

crystal form NOUN *Crystallog* a symmetrical set of planes in space, associated with a crystal, having the same symmetry as the crystal class. Compare **crystal habit.**

crystal gazing NOUN 1 the act of staring into a crystal globe (**crystal ball**) supposedly in order to arouse visual perceptions of the future, etc. 2 the act of trying to predict something.
▸ **crystal gazer** NOUN

crystal habit NOUN *Crystallog* the external shape of a crystal. Compare **crystal form.**

crystal healing NOUN (in alternative therapy) the use of the supposed power of crystals to affect the human energy field.

crystal lattice NOUN the regular array of points about which the atoms, ions, or molecules composing a crystal are centred.

crystalline (ˈkrɪstəˌlaɪn) ADJECTIVE 1 having the characteristics or structure of crystals. 2 consisting of or containing crystals. 3 made of or like crystal; transparent; clear.
▸ **crystallinity** (ˌkrɪstəˈlɪnɪtɪ) NOUN

crystalline lens NOUN a biconvex transparent elastic structure in the eye situated behind the iris, serving to focus images on the retina.

crystallite (ˈkrɪstəˌlaɪt) NOUN any of the minute rudimentary or imperfect crystals occurring in many glassy rocks.
▸ **crystallitic** (ˌkrɪstəˈlɪtɪk) ADJECTIVE

crystallize, crystalize, crystallise, *or* **crystalise** (ˈkrɪstəˌlaɪz) VERB 1 to form or cause to form crystals; assume or cause to assume a crystalline form or structure. 2 to coat or become coated with sugar: *crystallized fruit.* 3 to give a definite form or expression to (an idea, argument, etc.) or (of an idea, argument, etc.) to assume a recognizable or definite form.
▸ **ˈcrystalˌlizable, ˈcrystalˌizable, ˈcrystalˌlisable,** *or* **ˈcrystalˌisable** ADJECTIVE ▸ **ˌcrystalˌlizaˈbility, ˌcrystalˌizaˈbility, ˌcrystalˌlisaˈbility,** *or* **ˌcrystalˌisaˈbility** NOUN ▸ **ˌcrystalliˈzation, ˌcrystaliˈzation, ˌcrystalliˈsation,** *or* **ˌcrystaliˈsation** NOUN ▸ **ˈcrystalˌlizer, ˈcrystalˌizer, ˈcrystalˌliser,** *or* **ˈcrystalˌiser** NOUN

crystallo- *or before a vowel* **crystall-** COMBINING FORM crystal: *crystallography.*

crystallography (ˌkrɪstəˈlɒgrəfɪ) NOUN the science concerned with the formation, properties, and structure of crystals.
▸ **ˌcrystalˈlographer** NOUN ▸ **crystallographic** (ˌkrɪstələʊˈgræfɪk) ADJECTIVE ▸ **ˌcrystalloˈgraphically** ADVERB

crystalloid (ˈkrɪstəˌlɔɪd) ADJECTIVE 1 resembling or having the appearance or properties of a crystal or crystalloid. ◆ NOUN 2 a substance that in solution can pass through a semipermeable membrane. Compare **colloid** (sense 3). 3 *Botany* any of numerous crystals of protein occurring in certain seeds and other storage organs.
▸ **ˌcrystalˈloidal** ADJECTIVE

crystal microphone NOUN a microphone that uses a piezoelectric crystal to convert sound energy into electrical energy.

crystal nucleus NOUN *Chem* the tiny crystal that forms at the onset of crystallization.

Crystal Palace NOUN a building of glass and iron designed by Joseph Paxton to house the Great Exhibition of 1851. Erected in Hyde Park, London, it was moved to Sydenham (1852–53): destroyed by fire in 1936.

crystal pick-up NOUN a record-player pick-up in which the current is generated by the deformation of a piezoelectric crystal caused by the movements of the stylus.

crystal set NOUN an early form of radio receiver

having a crystal detector to demodulate the radio signals but no amplifier, therefore requiring earphones.

crystal system NOUN *Crystallog* any of six, or sometimes seven, classifications of crystals depending on their symmetry. The classes are cubic, tetragonal, hexagonal, orthorhombic, monoclinic, and triclinic. Sometimes an additional system, trigonal, is distinguished, although this is usually included in the hexagonal system. See also **crystal class.**

crystal violet NOUN another name for **gentian violet.**

cry up VERB (*tr, adverb*) to praise highly; extol.

Cs THE CHEMICAL SYMBOL FOR caesium.

CS ABBREVIATION FOR: [1] Also: **cs. capital stock.** [2] chartered surveyor. [3] Christian Science. [4] Christian Scientist. [5] Civil Service. [6] Also: **cs. Court of Session.** ◆ [7] (formerly) INTERNATIONAL CAR REGISTRATION FOR Czechoslovakia.

CSA (in Britain) ABBREVIATION FOR Child Support Agency.

CSB ABBREVIATION FOR chemical stimulation of the brain.

csc ABBREVIATION FOR cosecant.

CSC ABBREVIATION FOR Civil Service Commission.

CSCE ABBREVIATION FOR (formerly) Conference for Security and Cooperation in Europe.

csch NOUN a US form of **cosech.**

CSE (in Britain, formerly) ABBREVIATION FOR Certificate of Secondary Education.

CSF ABBREVIATION FOR: [1] *Physiol* **cerebrospinal fluid.** [2] *Immunol* **colony-stimulating factor.**

CS gas NOUN a gas causing tears, salivation, and painful breathing, used in civil disturbances; *ortho*-chlorobenzal malononitrile. Formula: $C_6H_4ClCH{:}C(CN)_2$.
▷HISTORY C20: from the surname initials of its US inventors, Ben Carson and Roger Staughton

CSIRO (in Australia) ABBREVIATION FOR Commonwealth Scientific and Industrial Research Organization.

CSM (in Britain) ABBREVIATION FOR **company sergeant-major.**

C-spanner NOUN a sickle-shaped spanner having a projection at the end of the curve, used for turning large narrow nuts that have an indentation into which the projection on the spanner fits.

CSR (in Australia) ABBREVIATION FOR Colonial Sugar Refining Company.

CSS (in Britain) ABBREVIATION FOR Certificate in Social Service.

CST ABBREVIATION FOR **Central Standard Time.**

CSV ABBREVIATION FOR Community Service Volunteer.

CSYS (in Scotland) ABBREVIATION FOR Certificate of Sixth Year Studies.

ct ABBREVIATION FOR: [1] cent. [2] court.

CT ABBREVIATION FOR: [1] central time. [2] Connecticut. [3] computerized tomography (see also **CT scanner**).

CTC (in Britain) ABBREVIATION FOR **city technology college.**

ctenidium (tɪˈnɪdɪəm) NOUN, *plural* **-ia** (-ɪə). one of the comblike respiratory gills of molluscs.
▷HISTORY C19: New Latin, from Greek *ktenidion*, diminutive of *kteis* comb

ctenoid (ˈtiːnɔɪd, ˈtɛn-) ADJECTIVE *Biology* toothed like a comb, as the scales of perches.
▷HISTORY C19: from Greek *ktenoeidēs*, from *kteis* comb + *-oeidēs* -OID

ctenophore (ˈtɛnəˌfɔː, ˈtiːnə-) NOUN any marine invertebrate of the phylum *Ctenophora*, including the sea gooseberry and Venus's-girdle, whose body bears eight rows of fused cilia, for locomotion. Also called: **comb jelly.**
▷HISTORY C19: from New Latin *ctenophorus*, from Greek *kteno-*, *kteis* comb + -PHORE
▸**ctenophoran** (tɪˈnɒfərən) ADJECTIVE, NOUN

Ctesiphon (ˈtɛsɪˌfɒn) NOUN an ancient city on the River Tigris about 100 km (60 miles) above Babylon. First mentioned in 221 B.C., it was destroyed in the 7th and 8th centuries A.D.

ctn ABBREVIATION FOR cotangent.

CTO *Philately* ABBREVIATION FOR cancelled to order (of postage stamps); postmarked in sheets for private sale.

CTR ABBREVIATION FOR Control Traffic Zone: an area established around an airport to afford protection to aircraft entering or leaving the terminal area.

cts ABBREVIATION FOR cents.

CT scanner NOUN computerized tomography scanner: an X-ray machine that can produce stereographic images. Former name: **CAT scanner.**

CTU (in New Zealand) ABBREVIATION FOR Conference of Trade Unions.

CTV ABBREVIATION FOR Canadian Television Network Limited.

cu THE INTERNET DOMAIN NAME FOR Cuba.

Cu THE CHEMICAL SYMBOL FOR copper.
▷HISTORY from Late Latin *cuprum*

CU[1] *Text messaging* ABBREVIATION FOR see you.

CU[2] INTERNATIONAL CAR REGISTRATION FOR Cuba.

cu. ABBREVIATION FOR cubic.

cub (kʌb) NOUN [1] the young of certain animals, such as the lion, bear, etc. [2] a young or inexperienced person. ◆ VERB **cubs, cubbing, cubbed.** [3] to give birth to (cubs).
▷HISTORY C16: perhaps from Old Norse *kubbi* young seal; see COB[1]
▸ˈ**cubbish** ADJECTIVE ▸ˈ**cubbishly** ADVERB

Cub (kʌb) NOUN short for **Cub Scout.**

Cuba (ˈkjuːbə) NOUN a republic and the largest island in the Caribbean, at the entrance to the Gulf of Mexico: became a Spanish colony after its discovery by Columbus in 1492; gained independence after the Spanish-American War of 1898 but remained subject to US influence until declared a people's republic under Castro in 1960; subject of an international crisis in 1962, when the US blockaded the island in order to compel the Soviet Union to dismantle its nuclear missile base. Sugar comprises about 80 per cent of total exports; the economy has been devastated by loss of trade following the collapse of the Soviet Union and by the continuing US trade embargo. Language: Spanish. Religion: nonreligious majority. Currency: peso. Capital: Havana. Pop.: 11 190 000 (2001 est.). Area: 110 922 sq. km (42 827 sq. miles).

cubage (ˈkjuːbɪdʒ) NOUN another word for **cubature** (sense 2).

Cuba libre (ˈkjuːbə ˈliːbrə) NOUN *Chiefly US* a drink of rum, cola, lime juice, and ice.
▷HISTORY Spanish, literally: free Cuba, a toast during the Cuban War of Independence

Cuban (ˈkjuːbən) ADJECTIVE [1] of or relating to Cuba or its inhabitants. ◆ NOUN [2] a native or inhabitant of Cuba.

cubane (ˈkjuːbeɪn) NOUN **a** a rare octahedral hydrocarbon formed by eight CH groups, each of which is situated at the corner of a cube. Formula: C_8H_8. **b** (*as modifier*): *cubane chemistry.*
▷HISTORY C20: from CUBE[1] + -ANE

Cuban heel NOUN a moderately high heel for a shoe or boot.

cubature (ˈkjuːbətʃə) NOUN [1] the determination of the cubic contents of something. [2] Also called: **cubage.** cubic contents.
▷HISTORY C17: from CUBE[1] + *-ature*, on the model of *quadrature*

cubby (ˈkʌbɪ) ADJECTIVE *Midland English dialect* short and plump; squat.

cubbyhole (ˈkʌbɪˌhəʊl) NOUN [1] a small enclosed space or room. [2] any small compartment, such as a pigeonhole. Often shortened to **cubby** (ˈkʌbɪ).
▷HISTORY C19: from dialect *cub* cattle pen; see COVE[1]

cube[1] (kjuːb) NOUN [1] a solid having six plane square faces in which the angle between two adjacent sides is a right angle. [2] the product of three equal factors: the cube of 2 is 2 × 2 × 2 (usually written 2^3). [3] something in the form of a cube: *a bath cube.* ◆ VERB [4] to raise (a number or quantity) to the third power. [5] (*tr*) to measure the cubic contents of. [6] (*tr*) to make, shape, or cut (something, esp food) into cubes. [7] (*tr*) *US and Canadian* to tenderize (meat) by scoring into squares or by pounding with a device which has a surface of metal cubes.
▷HISTORY C16: from Latin *cubus* die, cube, from Greek *kubos*
▸ˈ**cuber** NOUN

cube[2] (ˈkjuːbeɪ) NOUN [1] any of various tropical American plants, esp any of the leguminous genus *Lonchocarpus*, the roots of which yield rotenone. [2] an extract from the roots of these plants: a fish poison and insecticide.
▷HISTORY American Spanish *cubé*, of unknown origin

cubeb (ˈkjuːbɛb) NOUN [1] a SE Asian treelike piperaceous woody climbing plant, *Piper cubeba*, with brownish berries. [2] the unripe spicy fruit of this plant, dried and used as a stimulant and diuretic and sometimes smoked in cigarettes.
▷HISTORY C14: from Old French *cubebe*, from Medieval Latin *cubēba*, from Arabic *kubābah*

cube root NOUN the number or quantity whose cube is a given number or quantity: 2 is the cube root of 8 (usually written $\sqrt[3]{8}$ or $8^{1/3}$).

cubic (ˈkjuːbɪk) ADJECTIVE [1] having the shape of a cube. [2] **a** having three dimensions. **b** denoting or relating to a linear measure that is raised to the third power: *a cubic metre*. Abbreviations: **cu., c.** [3] *Maths* of, relating to, or containing a variable to the third power or a term in which the sum of the exponents of the variables is three. [4] Also: **isometric, regular.** *Crystallog* relating to or belonging to the crystal system characterized by three equal perpendicular axes. The unit cell of cubic crystals is a cube with a lattice point at each corner (**simple cubic**) and one in the cube's centre (**body-centred cubic**), or a lattice point at each corner and one at the centre of each face (**face-centred cubic**). ◆ NOUN [5] *Maths* **a** a cubic equation, such as $x^3 + x + 2 = 0$. **b** a cubic term or expression.

cubical (ˈkjuːbɪkəl) ADJECTIVE [1] of or related to volume: *cubical expansion.* [2] shaped like a cube. [3] of or involving the third power.
▸ˈ**cubically** ADVERB ▸ˈ**cubicalness** NOUN

cubicle (ˈkjuːbɪkəl) NOUN [1] a partially or totally enclosed section of a room, as in a dormitory. [2] an indoor construction designed to house individual cattle while allowing them free access to silage.
▷HISTORY C15: from Latin *cubiculum*, from *cubāre* to lie down, lie asleep

cubic measure NOUN a system of units for the measurement of volumes, based on the cubic inch, the cubic centimetre, etc.

cubiculum (kjuːˈbɪkjʊləm) NOUN, *plural* **-la** (-lə). an underground burial chamber in Imperial Rome, such as those found in the catacombs.
▷HISTORY C19: from Latin: CUBICLE

cubiform (ˈkjuːbɪˌfɔːm) ADJECTIVE having the shape of a cube.

cubism (ˈkjuːbɪzəm) NOUN (*often capital*) a French school of painting, collage, relief, and sculpture initiated in 1907 by Pablo Picasso, the Spanish painter and sculptor (1881–1973) and Georges Braque, the French painter (1882–1963), which amalgamated viewpoints of natural forms into a multifaceted surface of geometrical planes.
▸ˈ**cubist** ADJECTIVE, NOUN ▸**cuˈbistic** ADJECTIVE ▸**cuˈbistically** ADVERB

cubit (ˈkjuːbɪt) NOUN an ancient measure of length based on the length of the forearm.
▷HISTORY C14: from Latin *cubitum* elbow, cubit

cubital (ˈkjuːbɪtəl) ADJECTIVE of or relating to the forearm.

cuboid (ˈkjuːbɔɪd) ADJECTIVE *also* **cuboidal** (kjuːˈbɔɪdəl). [1] shaped like a cube; cubic. [2] of or denoting the cuboid bone. ◆ NOUN [3] the cubelike bone of the foot; the outer distal bone of the tarsus. [4] *Maths* a geometric solid whose six faces are rectangles; rectangular parallelepiped.

Cu-bop (ˈkjuːˌbɒp) NOUN *Jazz* music of the 1940s in which Cuban rhythms are combined with bop. Compare **Afro-Cuban.**

cub reporter NOUN a trainee reporter on a newspaper.

Cub Scout *or* **Cub** NOUN a member of a junior branch (for those aged 8–11 years) of the Scout Association.

Cuchulain, Cuchulainn, *or* **Cuchullain** (kuːˈkʌlɪn, kʊˈxʊlɪn) NOUN *Celtic myth* a legendary hero of Ulster.

cucking stool (ˈkʌkɪŋ) NOUN *History* a stool to

which suspected witches, scolds, etc., were tied and pelted or ducked into water as a punishment. Compare **ducking stool.**
▷HISTORY C13 *cucking stol,* literally: defecating chair, from *cukken* to defecate; compare Old Norse *kúkr* excrement

cuckold ('kʌkəld) NOUN [1] a man whose wife has committed adultery, often regarded as an object of scorn. ◆ VERB [2] (*tr*) to make a cuckold of.
▷HISTORY C13 *cukeweld,* from Old French *cucuault,* from *cucu* CUCKOO; perhaps an allusion to the parasitic cuckoos that lay their eggs in the nests of other birds
▸'**cuckoldry** NOUN

cuckoo ('kʊku:) NOUN, *plural* **-oos.** [1] any bird of the family *Cuculidae,* having pointed wings, a long tail, and zygodactyl feet: order *Cuculiformes.* Many species, including the **European cuckoo** (*Cuculus canorus*), lay their eggs in the nests of other birds and have a two-note call. [2] *Informal* an insane or foolish person. ◆ ADJECTIVE [3] *Informal* insane or foolish. ◆ INTERJECTION [4] an imitation or representation of the call of a cuckoo. ◆ VERB **-oos, -ooing, -ooed.** [5] (*tr*) to repeat over and over. [6] (*intr*) to make the sound imitated by the word *cuckoo.*
▷HISTORY C13: from Old French *cucu,* of imitative origin; related to German *kuckuck,* Latin *cucūlus,* Greek *kokkux*

cuckoo bee NOUN any of several species of parasitic or inquiline bee the queen of which lays her eggs in the nest of the bumblebee or other species, sometimes killing the host queen, leaving her eggs to be raised by the workers of the nest.

cuckoo clock NOUN a clock in which a mechanical cuckoo pops out with a sound like a cuckoo's call when the clock strikes.

cuckooflower ('kʊku:ˌflaʊə) NOUN another name for **lady's-smock** and **ragged robin.**

cuckoopint ('kʊku:ˌpaɪnt) NOUN a European aroid plant, *Arum maculatum,* with arrow-shaped leaves, a spathe marked with purple, a pale purple spadix, and scarlet berries. Also called: **lords-and-ladies,** (chiefly US) **wake-robin.**

cuckoo shrike NOUN any Old World tropical songbird of the family *Campephagidae,* typically having a strong notched bill, long rounded tail, and pointed wings. See also **minivet.**

cuckoo spit NOUN a white frothy mass on the stems and leaves of many plants, produced by froghopper larvae (**cuckoo spit insects**) which feed on the plant juices. Also called: **frog spit.**

cuculiform (kju'kju:lɪˌfɔ:m) ADJECTIVE of, relating to, or belonging to the order *Cuculiformes,* which includes the cuckoos.
▷HISTORY from Latin *cucūlus* cuckoo + -FORM

cucullate ('kju:kəˌleɪt, -lɪt) ADJECTIVE shaped like a hood or having a hoodlike part: *cucullate sepals.*
▷HISTORY C18: from Late Latin *cucullātus,* from Latin *cucullus* hood, cap
▸'**cucul,lately** ADVERB

cucumber ('kju:ˌkʌmbə) NOUN [1] a creeping cucurbitaceous plant, *Cucumis sativus,* cultivated in many forms for its edible fruit. Compare **squirting cucumber.** [2] the cylindrical fruit of this plant, which has hard thin green rind and white crisp flesh. [3] any of various similar or related plants or their fruits. [4] **cool as a cucumber.** very calm; self-possessed.
▷HISTORY C14: from Latin *cucumis,* of unknown origin

cucumber tree NOUN [1] any of several American trees or shrubs of the genus *Magnolia,* esp *M. acuminata,* of E and central North America, having cup-shaped greenish flowers and cucumber-shaped fruits. [2] an E Asian tree, *Averrhoa bilimbi,* with edible fruits resembling small cucumbers: family *Averrhoaceae.* See also **carambola.**

cucurbit (kju:'kɜ:bɪt) NOUN any creeping flowering plant of the mainly tropical and subtropical family *Cucurbitaceae,* which includes the pumpkin, cucumber, squashes, and gourds.
▷HISTORY C14: from Old French, from Latin *cucurbita* gourd, cup
▸**cu,curbi'taceous** ADJECTIVE

Cúcuta (*Spanish* 'kukuta) NOUN a city in E Colombia: commercial centre of a coffee-producing region. Pop.: 606 932 (1999 est.). Official name: **San José de Cúcuta** (san xo'se ðe).

cud (kʌd) NOUN [1] partially digested food regurgitated from the first stomach of cattle and other ruminants to the mouth for a second chewing. [2] **chew the cud.** to reflect or think over something.
▷HISTORY Old English *cudu,* from *cwidu* what has been chewed; related to Old Norse *kvātha* resin (for chewing), Old High German *quiti* glue, Sanskrit *jatu* rubber

cudbear ('kʌdˌbɛə) NOUN another name for **orchil.**
▷HISTORY C18: whimsical alteration of *Cuthbert,* the Christian name of Dr Gordon, 18th-century Scot who patented the dye. See CUDDY[2]

cuddle ('kʌdᵊl) VERB [1] to hold (another person or thing) close or (of two people, etc.) to hold each other close, as for affection, comfort, or warmth; embrace; hug. [2] (*intr;* foll by *up*) to curl or snuggle up into a comfortable or warm position. ◆ NOUN [3] a close embrace, esp when prolonged.
▷HISTORY C18: of uncertain origin
▸'**cuddlesome** ADJECTIVE ▸'**cuddly** ADJECTIVE

cuddy[1] ('kʌdɪ) NOUN, *plural* **-dies.** [1] a small cabin in a boat. [2] a small room, cupboard, etc.
▷HISTORY C17: perhaps from Dutch *kajute;* compare Old French *cahute*

cuddy[2] *or* **cuddie** ('kʌdɪ) NOUN, *plural* **-dies.** *dialect, chiefly Scot* a donkey or horse.
▷HISTORY C18: probably from *Cuddy,* nickname for *Cuthbert*

cuddy[3] ('kʌdɪ) NOUN, *plural* **-dies.** a young coalfish.
▷HISTORY C18: of unknown origin

cudgel ('kʌdʒəl) NOUN [1] a short stout stick used as a weapon. [2] **take up the cudgels.** (often foll by *for* or *on behalf of*) to join in a dispute, esp to defend oneself or another. ◆ VERB **-els, -elling, -elled** *or US* **-els, -eling, -eled.** [3] (*tr*) to strike with a cudgel or similar weapon. [4] **cudgel one's brains.** to think hard about a problem.
▷HISTORY Old English *cycgel;* related to Middle Dutch *koghele* stick with knob
▸'**cudgeller** NOUN

cudgerie ('kʌdʒərɪ) NOUN *Austral* [1] a large tropical rutaceous tree, *Flindersia schottina,* having light-coloured wood. [2] Also called: **pink poplar.** an anacardiaceous rainforest tree, *Euroschinus falcatus.*

cudweed ('kʌdˌwi:d) NOUN [1] any of various temperate woolly plants of the genus *Gnaphalium,* having clusters of whitish or yellow button-like flowers: family *Asteraceae* (composites). [2] any of several similar and related plants of the genus *Filago,* esp *F. germanica.*

cue[1] (kju:) NOUN [1] **a** (in the theatre, films, music, etc.) anything spoken or done that serves as a signal to an actor, musician, etc., to follow with specific lines or action. **b on cue.** at the right moment. [2] a signal or reminder to do something. [3] *Psychol* the part of any sensory pattern that is identified as the signal for a response. [4] the part, function, or action assigned to or expected of a person. ◆ VERB **cues, cueing, cued.** [5] (*tr*) to give a cue or cues to (an actor). [6] (usually foll by *in* or *into*) to signal (to something or somebody) at a specific moment in a musical or dramatic performance: *to cue in a flourish of trumpets.* [7] (*tr*) to give information or a reminder to (someone). [8] (*intr*) to signal the commencement of filming, as with the word "Action!".
▷HISTORY C16: probably from name of the letter *q,* used in an actor's script to represent Latin *quando* when

cue[2] (kju:) NOUN [1] *Billiards, snooker* a long tapered shaft with a leather tip, used to drive the balls. [2] hair caught at the back forming a tail or braid. [3] *US* a variant spelling of **queue.** ◆ VERB **cues, cueing, cued.** [4] to drive (a ball) with a cue. [5] (*tr*) to twist or tie (the hair) into a cue.
▷HISTORY C18: variant of QUEUE

cue ball NOUN *Billiards, snooker* the ball struck by the cue, as distinguished from the object balls.

cue bid NOUN *Contract bridge* a bid in a suit made to show an ace or a void in that suit.

cueing ('kju:ɪŋ) NOUN another name for **foldback.**

Cuenca (*Spanish* 'kweŋka) NOUN [1] a city in SW Ecuador: university (1868). Pop.: 255 028 (1997 est.). [2] a town in central Spain: prosperous in the Middle Ages for its silver and textile industries. Pop.: 45 800 (1991).

Cuernavaca (*Spanish* kwerna'βaka) NOUN a city in S central Mexico, capital of Morelos state: resort with nearby Cacahuamilpa Caverns. Pop.: 330 000 (2000 est.).

cuesta ('kwɛstə) NOUN a long low ridge with a steep scarp slope and a gentle back slope, formed by the differential erosion of strata of differing hardness.
▷HISTORY Spanish: shoulder, from Latin *costa* side, rib

cuff[1] (kʌf) NOUN [1] the part of a sleeve nearest the hand, sometimes turned back and decorative. [2] the part of a gauntlet or glove that extends past the wrist. [3] the US, Canadian, and Austral name for **turn-up** (sense 5). [4] **off the cuff.** *Informal* improvised; extemporary. ◆ See also **cuffs.**
▷HISTORY C14 *cuffe* glove, of obscure origin

cuff[2] (kʌf) VERB [1] (*tr*) to strike with an open hand. ◆ NOUN [2] a blow of this kind.
▷HISTORY C16: of obscure origin

cuff link NOUN one of a pair of linked buttons, used to join the buttonholes on the cuffs of a shirt.

cuffs (kʌfs) PLURAL NOUN *Informal* short for **handcuffs.**

Cufic ('ku:fɪk, 'kju:-) NOUN, ADJECTIVE a variant spelling of **Kufic.**

Cuiabá *or* **Cuyabá** (*Portuguese* kuia'ba) NOUN [1] a port in W Brazil, capital of Mato Grosso state, on the Cuibá River. Pop. (urban area): 475 632 (2000). [2] a river in SW Brazil, rising on the Mato Grosso plateau and flowing southwest into the São Lourenço River. Length: 483 km (300 miles).

cui bono *Latin* (kwi: 'bəʊnəʊ) for whose benefit? for what purpose?

cuirass (kwɪ'ræs) NOUN [1] a piece of armour, of leather or metal covering the chest and back. [2] a hard outer protective covering of some animals, consisting of shell, plate, or scales. [3] any similar protective covering, as on a ship. ◆ VERB [4] (*tr*) to equip with a cuirass.
▷HISTORY C15: from French *cuirasse,* from Late Latin *coriacea,* from *coriaceus* made of leather, from Latin *corium* leather

cuirassier (ˌkwɪərə'sɪə) NOUN a mounted soldier, esp of the 16th century, who wore a cuirass.

cuir-bouilli (ˌkwɪəbu:'ji:) NOUN a type of leather hardened by soaking in wax, used for armour before the 14th century.
▷HISTORY French, literally: boiled leather

Cuisenaire rod (ˌkwɪzə'nɛə) NOUN *Trademark* one of a set of rods of various colours and lengths representing different numbers, used to teach arithmetic to young children.
▷HISTORY C20: named after Emil-Georges *Cuisenaire* (?1891–1976), Belgian educationalist

cuisine (kwɪ'zi:n) NOUN [1] a style or manner of cooking: *French cuisine.* [2] the food prepared by a restaurant, household, etc.
▷HISTORY C18: from French, literally: kitchen, from Late Latin *coquīna,* from Latin *coquere* to cook

cuisine minceur *French* (kɥizin mɛ̃sœr) NOUN a style of cooking, originating in France, that limits the use of starch, sugar, butter, and cream traditionally used in French cookery.
▷HISTORY literally: slimness cooking

cuisse (kwɪs) *or* **cuish** (kwɪʃ) NOUN a piece of armour for the thigh.
▷HISTORY C15: back formation from *cuisses* (plural), from Old French *cuisseaux* thigh guards, from *cuisse* thigh, from Latin *coxa* hipbone

culch *or* **cultch** (kʌltʃ) NOUN [1] a mass of broken stones, shells, and gravel that forms the basis of an oyster bed. [2] the oyster spawn attached to such a structure. [3] *Dialect* refuse; rubbish.
▷HISTORY C17: perhaps ultimately from Old French *culche* bed, COUCH

culchie ('kʌltʃi:) NOUN *Irish informal* a rough or unsophisticated country-dweller from outside Dublin.
▷HISTORY from a local pronunciation of the Mayo town of Kiltimagh

cul-de-sac ('kʌldəˌsæk, 'kʊl-) NOUN, *plural* **culs-de-sac** *or* **cul-de-sacs.** [1] a road with one end blocked off; dead end. [2] an inescapable position. [3] any tube-shaped bodily cavity or pouch closed at one end, such as the caecum.
▷HISTORY C18: from French, literally: bottom of the bag

-cule SUFFIX FORMING NOUNS indicating smallness: *animalcule*.
▷HISTORY from Latin *-culus*, diminutive suffix; compare -CLE

Culebra Cut (ku:ˈlɛbrə) NOUN the former name of the **Gaillard Cut**.

culet (ˈkju:lɪt) NOUN 1 *Jewellery* the flat face at the bottom of a gem. 2 either of the plates of armour worn at the small of the back.
▷HISTORY C17: from obsolete French, diminutive of *cul*, from Latin *cūlus* bottom

culex (ˈkju:lɛks) NOUN, *plural* **-lices** (-lɪˌsi:z). any mosquito of the genus *Culex*, such as *C. pipiens*, the common mosquito.
▷HISTORY C15: from Latin: midge, gnat; related to Old Irish *cuil* gnat

Culham (ˈkʌləm) NOUN a village in S central England, in Oxfordshire: site of the UK centre for thermonuclear reactor research and of the Joint European Torus (JET) programme.

Culiacán (*Spanish* kuljaˈkan) NOUN a city in NW Mexico, capital of Sinaloa state. Pop.: 536 942 (2000 est.).

culicid (kju:ˈlɪsɪd) NOUN 1 any dipterous insect of the family *Culicidae*, which comprises the mosquitos. ◆ ADJECTIVE 2 of, relating to, or belonging to the *Culicidae*.
▷HISTORY C19: from New Latin *Culicidae*, from Latin *culex* gnat, CULEX

culinary (ˈkʌlɪnərɪ) ADJECTIVE of, relating to, or used in the kitchen or in cookery.
▷HISTORY C17: from Latin *culīnārius*, from *culīna* kitchen
▸ˈ**culinarily** ADVERB

cull (kʌl) VERB (*tr*) 1 to choose or gather the best or required examples. 2 to take out (an animal, esp an inferior one) from a herd. 3 to reduce the size of (a herd or flock) by killing a proportion of its members. 4 to gather (flowers, fruit, etc.). 5 to cease to employ; get rid of. ◆ NOUN 6 the act or product of culling. 7 an inferior animal taken from a herd or group.
▷HISTORY C15: from Old French *coillir* to pick, from Latin *colligere*; see COLLECT[1]

cullender (ˈkʌlɪndə) NOUN a variant of **colander**.

culler (ˈkʌlə) NOUN 1 a person employed to cull animals. 2 *Austral and NZ* an animal, esp a sheep, designated for culling.

cullet (ˈkʌlɪt) NOUN waste glass for melting down to be reused.
▷HISTORY C17: perhaps variant of COLLET (literally: little neck, referring to the glass neck of newly blown bottles, etc.)

cullis (ˈkʌlɪs) NOUN 1 a gutter in or at the eaves of a roof. 2 another word for **coulisse** (sense 1).
▷HISTORY C19: from French *coulisse* channel, groove; see COULISSE

Culloden (kəˈlɒdᵊn) NOUN a moor near Inverness in N Scotland: site of a battle in 1746 in which government troops under the Duke of Cumberland defeated the Jacobites under Prince Charles Edward Stuart.

cully (ˈkʌlɪ) NOUN, *plural* **-lies**. *Slang* pal; mate.
▷HISTORY C17: of unknown origin

culm[1] (kʌlm) NOUN *Mining* 1 coal-mine waste. 2 inferior anthracite.
▷HISTORY C14: probably related to COAL

culm[2] (kʌlm) NOUN the hollow jointed stem of a grass or sedge.
▷HISTORY C17: from Latin *culmus* stalk; see HAULM

Culm *or* **Culm Measures** NOUN a formation consisting mainly of shales and sandstone deposited during the Carboniferous period in parts of Europe.
▷HISTORY C19: from CULM[1]

culmiferous (kʌlˈmɪfərəs) ADJECTIVE (of grasses) having a hollow jointed stem.

culminant (ˈkʌlmɪnənt) ADJECTIVE highest or culminating.

culminate (ˈkʌlmɪˌneɪt) VERB 1 (when *intr*, usually foll by *in*) to end or cause to end, esp to reach or bring to a final or climactic stage. 2 (*intr*) (of a celestial body) to cross the meridian of the observer.
▷HISTORY C17: from Late Latin *culmināre* to reach the highest point, from Latin *culmen* top

culmination (ˌkʌlmɪˈneɪʃən) NOUN 1 the final, highest, or decisive point. 2 the act of culminating. 3 *Astronomy* the highest or lowest altitude attained by a heavenly body as it crosses the meridian.

culottes (kju:ˈlɒts) PLURAL NOUN women's flared trousers cut to look like a skirt.
▷HISTORY C20: from French, literally: breeches, from *cul* bottom; see CULET

culpa (ˈkʊlpɑ:) NOUN, *plural* **-pae** (-pi:). 1 *Civil law* an act of neglect. 2 a fault; sin; guilt.
▷HISTORY Latin: fault

culpable (ˈkʌlpəbᵊl) ADJECTIVE deserving censure; blameworthy.
▷HISTORY C14: from Old French *coupable*, from Latin *culpābilis*, from *culpāre* to blame, from *culpa* fault
▸ˌ**culpaˈbility** *or* ˈ**culpableness** NOUN ▸ˈ**culpably** ADVERB

culpable homicide NOUN *Scots Law* manslaughter.

culprit (ˈkʌlprɪt) NOUN 1 *Law* a person awaiting trial, esp one who has pleaded not guilty. 2 the person responsible for a particular offence, misdeed, etc.
▷HISTORY C17: from Anglo-French *cul-*, short for *culpable* guilty + *prit* ready, indicating that the prosecution was ready to prove the guilt of the one charged

CUL8R *Text messaging* ABBREVIATION FOR see you later.

cult (kʌlt) NOUN 1 a specific system of religious worship, esp with reference to its rites and deity. 2 a sect devoted to such a system. 3 a quasi-religious organization using devious psychological techniques to gain and control adherents. 4 *Sociol* a group having an exclusive ideology and ritual practices centred on sacred symbols, esp one characterized by lack of organizational structure. 5 intense interest in and devotion to a person, idea, or activity: *the cult of yoga*. 6 the person, idea, etc., arousing such devotion. 7 **a** something regarded as fashionable or significant by a particular group. **b** (*as modifier*): *a cult show*. 8 (*modifier*) of, relating to, or characteristic of a cult or cults: *a cult figure*.
▷HISTORY C17: from Latin *cultus* cultivation, refinement, from *colere* to till
▸ˈ**cultism** NOUN ▸ˈ**cultist** NOUN

cultch (kʌltʃ) NOUN a variant spelling of **culch**.

cultic (ˈkʌltɪk) ADJECTIVE of or relating to a religious cult.

cultigen (ˈkʌltɪdʒən) NOUN a species of plant that is known only as a cultivated form and did not originate from a wild type.
▷HISTORY C20: from CULTI(VATED) + -GEN

cultish (ˈkʌltɪʃ) *or* **culty** (ˈkʌltɪ) ADJECTIVE intended to appeal to a small group of fashionable people.
▸ˈ**cultishly** ADVERB

cultivable (ˈkʌltɪvəbᵊl) *or* **cultivatable** (ˈkʌltɪˌveɪtəbᵊl) ADJECTIVE (of land) capable of being cultivated.
▷HISTORY C17: from French, from Old French *cultiver* to CULTIVATE
▸ˌ**cultivaˈbility** NOUN

cultivar (ˈkʌltɪˌvɑ:) NOUN a variety of a plant that was produced from a natural species and is maintained by cultivation.
▷HISTORY C20: from CULTI(VATED) + VAR(IETY)

cultivate (ˈkʌltɪˌveɪt) VERB (*tr*) 1 to till and prepare (land or soil) for the growth of crops. 2 to plant, tend, harvest, or improve (plants) by labour and skill. 3 to break up (land or soil) with a cultivator or hoe. 4 to improve or foster (the mind, body, etc.) as by study, education, or labour. 5 to give special attention to: *to cultivate a friendship; to cultivate a hobby*. 6 to give or bring culture to (a person, society, etc.); civilize.
▷HISTORY C17: from Medieval Latin *cultivāre* to till, from Old French *cultiver*, from Medieval Latin *cultīvus* cultivable, from Latin *cultus* cultivated, from *colere* to till, toil over

cultivated (ˈkʌltɪˌveɪtɪd) ADJECTIVE 1 cultured, refined, or educated. 2 (of land or soil) **a** subjected to tillage or cultivation. **b** tilled and broken up. 3 (of plants) specially bred or improved by cultivation.

cultivation (ˌkʌltɪˈveɪʃən) NOUN 1 *Agriculture* **a** the planting, tending, improving, or harvesting of crops or plants. **b** the preparation of ground to promote their growth. 2 development, esp through education, training, etc. 3 culture or sophistication, esp social refinement.

cultivator (ˈkʌltɪˌveɪtə) NOUN 1 a farm implement equipped with shovels, blades, etc., used to break up soil and remove weeds. 2 a person or thing that cultivates. 3 a person who grows, tends, or improves plants or crops.

cultrate (ˈkʌltreɪt) *or* **cultrated** ADJECTIVE shaped like a knife blade: *cultrate leaves*.
▷HISTORY C19: from Latin *cultrātus*, from *culter* knife

cultural (ˈkʌltʃərəl) ADJECTIVE 1 of or relating to artistic or social pursuits or events considered to be valuable or enlightened. 2 of or relating to a culture or civilization. 3 (of certain varieties of plant) obtained by specialized breeding.
▸ˈ**culturally** ADVERB

cultural anthropology NOUN the branch of anthropology dealing with cultural as opposed to biological and racial features.
▸**cultural anthropologist** NOUN

cultural lag *or* **culture lag** NOUN the difference in the rate of change between two parts of a culture.

Cultural Revolution NOUN (in China) a mass movement (1965–68), in which the youthful Red Guard played a prominent part. It was initiated by Mao Tse-tung to destroy the power of the bureaucrats and to revolutionize the attitudes and behaviour of the people. Also called: **Great Proletarian Cultural Revolution.**

culture (ˈkʌltʃə) NOUN 1 the total of the inherited ideas, beliefs, values, and knowledge, which constitute the shared bases of social action. 2 the total range of activities and ideas of a group of people with shared traditions, which are transmitted and reinforced by members of the group: *the Mayan culture*. 3 a particular civilization at a particular period. 4 the artistic and social pursuits, expression, and tastes valued by a society or class, as in the arts, manners, dress, etc. 5 the enlightenment or refinement resulting from these pursuits. 6 the attitudes, feelings, values, and behaviour that characterize and inform society as a whole or any social group within it: *yob culture*. 7 the cultivation of plants, esp by scientific methods designed to improve stock or to produce new ones. 8 *Stockbreeding* the rearing and breeding of animals, esp with a view to improving the strain. 9 the act or practice of tilling or cultivating the soil. 10 *Biology* **a** the experimental growth of microorganisms, such as bacteria and fungi, in a nutrient substance (see **culture medium**), usually under controlled conditions. **b** a group of microorganisms grown in this way. ◆ VERB (*tr*) 11 to cultivate (plants or animals). 12 to grow (microorganisms) in a culture medium.
▷HISTORY C15: from Old French, from Latin *cultūra* a cultivating, from *colere* to till; see CULT
▸ˈ**culturist** NOUN ▸ˈ**cultureless** ADJECTIVE

cultured (ˈkʌltʃəd) ADJECTIVE 1 showing or having good taste, manners, upbringing, and education. 2 artificially grown or synthesized: *cultured pearls*.

cultured pearl NOUN a pearl induced to grow in the shell of an oyster or clam, by the insertion of a small object around which layers of nacre are deposited.

culture-free test NOUN a test (usually for intelligence) that does not put anyone taking it at a disadvantage, for instance, as regards material or cultural background.

culture jamming NOUN a form of political and social activism which, by means of fake adverts, hoax news stories, pastiches of company logos and product labels, computer hacking, etc., draws attention to and at the same time subverts the power of the media, governments, and large corporations to control and distort the information that they give to the public in order to promote consumerism, militarism, etc.

culture medium NOUN a nutritive substance, such as an agar gel or liquid medium, in which cultures of bacteria, fungi, animal cells, or plant cells are grown.

culture shock NOUN *Sociol* the feelings of

isolation, rejection, etc., experienced when one culture is brought into sudden contact with another, as when a primitive tribe is confronted by modern civilization.

culture vulture NOUN *Informal* a person considered to be excessively, and often pretentiously, interested in the arts.

cultus ('kʌltəs) NOUN, *plural* **-tuses** *or* **-ti** (-taɪ). *Chiefly RC Church* another word for **cult** (sense 1).
▷HISTORY C17: from Latin: a toiling over something, refinement, CULT

culver ('kʌlvə) NOUN an archaic or poetic name for **pigeon**[1] or **dove**[1].
▷HISTORY Old English *culfre,* from Latin *columbula* a little dove, from *columba* dove

culverin ('kʌlvərɪn) NOUN 1 a long-range medium to heavy cannon used during the 15th, 16th, and 17th centuries. 2 a medieval musket.
▷HISTORY C15: from Old French *coulevrine,* from *couleuvre,* from Latin *coluber* serpent

Culver's root *or* **physic** ('kʌlvəz) NOUN 1 a tall North American scrophulariaceous plant, *Veronicastrum virginicum,* having spikes of small white or purple flowers. 2 the dried roots of this plant, formerly used as a cathartic and emetic.
▷HISTORY C19: named after a Dr *Culver,* 18th-century American physician

culvert ('kʌlvət) NOUN 1 a drain or covered channel that crosses under a road, railway, etc. 2 a channel for an electric cable. 3 a tunnel through which water is pumped into or out of a dry dock.
▷HISTORY C18: of unknown origin

Culzean Castle (kə'leɪn) NOUN a Gothic Revival castle near Ayr in South Ayrshire, in SW Scotland: designed by Robert Adam (1772–92); includes a room dedicated to General Eisenhower.

cum (kʌm) PREPOSITION used between two nouns to designate an object of a combined nature: *a kitchen-cum-dining room.*
▷HISTORY Latin: with, together with, along with

cumacean (kju'meɪʃ[ə]n) NOUN 1 any small malacostracan marine crustacean of the *Cumacea* family, mostly dwelling on the sea bed but sometimes found among the plankton. ◆ ADJECTIVE 2 of, relating to, or belonging to the *Cumacea.*
▷HISTORY C19: from New Latin *cuma,* from Greek *kuma* (see CYMA) + -EAN

Cumae ('kju:mi:) NOUN the oldest Greek colony in Italy, founded about 750 B.C. near Naples.
▸**Cu'maean** ADJECTIVE

Cumaná (*Spanish* kuma'na) NOUN a city in NE Venezuela: founded in 1523; the oldest European settlement in South America. Pop.: 269 428 (2000 est.).

cumber ('kʌmbə) VERB (*tr*) 1 to obstruct or hinder. 2 *Obsolete* to inconvenience. ◆ NOUN 3 a hindrance or burden.
▷HISTORY C13: probably from Old French *combrer* to impede, prevent, from *combre* barrier; see ENCUMBER
▸**'cumberer** NOUN

Cumberland ('kʌmbələnd) NOUN (until 1974) a county of NW England, now part of Cumbria.

Cumbernauld (ˌkʌmbə'nɔ:ld) NOUN a town in central Scotland, in North Lanarkshire, northeast of Glasgow: developed as a new town since 1956. Pop.: 48 762 (1991).

cumbersome ('kʌmbəsəm) *or* **cumbrous** ('kʌmbrəs) ADJECTIVE 1 awkward because of size, weight, or shape: *cumbersome baggage.* 2 difficult because of extent or complexity: *cumbersome accounts.*
▷HISTORY C14: *cumber,* short for ENCUMBER + -SOME[1]
▸**'cumbersomely** *or* **'cumbrously** ADVERB
▸**'cumbersomeness** *or* **'cumbrousness** NOUN

cumbrance ('kʌmbrəns) NOUN 1 a burden, obstacle, or hindrance. 2 trouble or bother.

Cumbria ('kʌmbrɪə) NOUN (since 1974) a county of NW England comprising the former counties of Westmorland and Cumberland together with N Lancashire: includes the Lake District mountain area and surrounding coastal lowlands with the Pennine uplands in the extreme east. Administrative centre: Carlisle. Pop.: 487 607 (2001). Area: 6810 sq. km (2629 sq. miles).

Cumbrian ('kʌmbrɪən) ADJECTIVE 1 of or relating to Cumbria or its inhabitants. ◆ NOUN 2 a native or inhabitant of Cumbria.

Cumbrian Mountains ('kʌmbrɪən) PLURAL NOUN a mountain range in NW England, in Cumbria. Highest peak: Scafell Pike, 978 m (3210 ft.).

cumbungi (kʌm'bʌŋgɪ) NOUN any of various tall Australian marsh plants of the genus *Typha.*
▷HISTORY from a native Australian language

cum dividend ADVERB (of shares, etc.) with the right to current dividend. Compare **ex dividend.**
▷HISTORY *cum,* from Latin: with

cum grano salis *Latin* (kʊm 'grɑ:nəʊ 'sɑ:lɪs) ADVERB with a grain of salt; not too literally.

cumin *or* **cummin** ('kʌmɪn) NOUN 1 an umbelliferous Mediterranean plant, *Cuminum cyminum,* with finely divided leaves and small white or pink flowers. 2 the aromatic seeds (collectively) of this plant, used as a condiment and a flavouring.
▷HISTORY C12: from Old French, from Latin *cumīnum,* from Greek *kuminon,* of Semitic origin; compare Hebrew *kammōn*

cum laude (kʌm 'lɔ:dɪ, kʊm 'laʊdeɪ) ADVERB *Chiefly US* with praise: the lowest of three designations for above-average achievement in examinations. Compare **magna cum laude, summa cum laude.**
▷HISTORY Latin

cummerbund *or* **kummerbund** ('kʌməˌbʌnd) NOUN a wide sash, worn with a dinner jacket.
▷HISTORY C17: from Hindi *kamarband,* from Persian, from *kamar* loins, waist + *band* band

cum new ADVERB, ADJECTIVE (of shares, etc.) with the right to take up any scrip issue or rights issue. Compare **ex new.**

cumquat ('kʌmkwɒt) NOUN a variant spelling of **kumquat.**

cumshaw ('kʌmʃɔ:) NOUN (used, esp formerly, by beggars in Chinese ports) a present or tip.
▷HISTORY C19: from pidgin English, from Chinese (Amoy) *kam siā,* from Mandarin *kan hsieh* grateful thanks

cumulate VERB ('kju:mjʊˌleɪt) 1 to accumulate. 2 (*tr*) to combine (two or more sequences) into one. ◆ ADJECTIVE ('kju:mjʊlɪt, -ˌleɪt) 3 heaped up.
▷HISTORY C16: from Latin *cumulāre* from *cumulus* heap
▸**'cumulately** ADVERB ▸**ˌcumu'lation** NOUN

cumulative ('kju:mjʊlətɪv) ADJECTIVE 1 growing in quantity, strength, or effect by successive additions or gradual steps: *cumulative pollution.* 2 gained by or resulting from a gradual building up: *cumulative benefits.* 3 *Finance* **a** (of preference shares) entitling the holder to receive any arrears of dividend before any dividend is distributed to ordinary shareholders. **b** (of dividends or interest) intended to be accumulated if not paid when due. 4 *Statistics* **a** (of a frequency) including all values of a variable either below or above a specified value. **b** (of error) tending to increase as the sample size is increased.
▸**'cumulatively** ADVERB ▸**'cumulativeness** NOUN

cumulative distribution function NOUN *Statistics* a function defined on the sample space of a distribution and taking as its value at each point the probability that the random variable has that value or less. The function $F(x) = P(X \leq x)$ where X is the random variable, which is the sum or integral of the probability density function of the distribution. Sometimes shortened to **distribution function.**

cumulative evidence NOUN *Law* additional evidence reinforcing testimony previously given.

cumulative voting NOUN a system of voting in which each elector has as many votes as there are candidates in his constituency. Votes may all be cast for one candidate or distributed among several.

cumulet ('kju:mjʊlɪt) NOUN (*sometimes capital*) a variety of domestic fancy pigeon, pure white or white with light red markings.
▷HISTORY C19: from CUMULUS

cumuliform ('kju:mjʊlɪˌfɔ:m) ADJECTIVE resembling a cumulus cloud.

cumulonimbus (ˌkju:mjʊləʊ'nɪmbəs) NOUN, *plural* **-bi** (-baɪ) *or* **-buses.** *Meteorol* a cumulus cloud of great vertical extent, the top often forming an anvil shape and the bottom being dark coloured, indicating rain or hail: associated with thunderstorms.

cumulostratus (ˌkju:mjʊləʊ'streɪtəs) NOUN, *plural* **-ti** (-taɪ). *Meteorol* another name for **stratocumulus.**

cumulous ('kju:mjʊləs) ADJECTIVE resembling or consisting of cumulus clouds.

cumulus ('kju:mjʊləs) NOUN, *plural* **-li** (-ˌlaɪ). 1 a bulbous or billowing white or dark grey cloud associated with rising air currents. Compare **cirrus** (sense 1), **stratus.** 2 *Histology* the mass of cells surrounding a recently ovulated egg cell in a Graafian follicle.
▷HISTORY C17: from Latin: mass

Cunaxa (kju:'næksə) NOUN the site near the lower Euphrates where Artaxerxes II defeated Cyrus the Younger in 401 B.C.

cunctation (kʌŋk'teɪʃən) NOUN *Rare* delay.
▷HISTORY C16: from Latin *cunctātiō* a hesitation, from *cunctārī* to delay
▸**cunctative** ('kʌŋktətɪv) ADJECTIVE ▸**cunc'tator** NOUN

cuneal ('kju:nɪəl) ADJECTIVE wedge-shaped; cuneiform.
▷HISTORY C16: from New Latin *cuneālis,* from *cuneus* wedge

cuneate ('kju:nɪɪt, -ˌeɪt) ADJECTIVE wedge-shaped: cuneate leaves are attached at the narrow end.
▷HISTORY C19: from Latin *cuneāre* to make wedge-shaped, from *cuneus* a wedge
▸**'cuneately** ADVERB

cuneiform ('kju:nɪˌfɔ:m) ADJECTIVE 1 Also: **cuneal.** wedge-shaped. 2 of, relating to, or denoting the wedge-shaped characters employed in the writing of several ancient languages of Mesopotamia and Persia, esp Sumerian, Babylonian, etc. 3 of or relating to a tablet in which this script is employed. 4 of or relating to any of the three tarsal bones. ◆ NOUN 5 cuneiform characters or writing. 6 any one of the three tarsal bones.
▷HISTORY C17: probably from Old French *cunéiforme,* from Latin *cuneus* wedge

Cuneo (*Italian* 'ku:neo) NOUN a city in NW Italy, in Piedmont. Pop.: 55 840 (1990).

cuneus ('kju:nɪəs) NOUN a small wedge-shaped area of the cerebral cortex.
▷HISTORY C19: from Latin *cuneus* wedge

cunjevoi ('kʌndʒɪˌvɔɪ) NOUN *Austral* 1 an aroid plant, *Alocasia macrorrhiza,* of tropical Asia and Australia, cultivated for its edible rhizome. 2 a sea squirt.
▷HISTORY C19: from a native Australian language

cunnilingus (ˌkʌnɪ'lɪŋgəs) *or* **cunnilinctus** (ˌkʌnɪ'lɪŋktəs) NOUN a sexual activity in which the female genitalia are stimulated by the partner's lips and tongue. Compare **fellatio.**
▷HISTORY C19: from New Latin, from Latin *cunnus* vulva + *lingere* to lick

cunning ('kʌnɪŋ) ADJECTIVE 1 crafty and shrewd, esp in deception; sly: *cunning as a fox.* 2 made with or showing skill or cleverness; ingenious. ◆ NOUN 3 craftiness, esp in deceiving; slyness. 4 cleverness, skill, or ingenuity.
▷HISTORY Old English *cunnende;* related to *cunnan* to know (see CAN[1]), *cunnian* to test, experience, Old Norse *kunna* to know
▸**'cunningly** ADVERB ▸**'cunningness** NOUN

cunt (kʌnt) NOUN *Taboo* 1 the female genitals. 2 *Offensive slang* a woman considered sexually. 3 *Offensive slang* a mean or obnoxious person.
▷HISTORY C13: of Germanic origin; related to Old Norse *kunta,* Middle Low German *kunte*

> **Language note** Although there has been some relaxation of the taboo against using words such as *fuck* in conversation and print, the use of *cunt* is still not considered acceptable by most people outside very limited social contexts. Though originally a racily descriptive word in Middle English, it has been taboo for many centuries and continues to be so.

cup (kʌp) NOUN 1 a small open container, usually having one handle, used for drinking from. 2 the contents of such a container: *that cup was too sweet.* 3 Also called: **teacup, cupful.** a unit of capacity used in cooking equal to approximately half a pint, 8 fluid ounces, or about one quarter of a litre. 4 something resembling a cup in shape or function,

such as the flower base of some plants of the rose family or a cuplike bodily organ. 5 either of two cup-shaped parts of a brassiere, designed to support the breasts. 6 a cup-shaped trophy awarded as a prize. 7 *Brit* **a** a sporting contest in which a cup is awarded to the winner. **b** (*as modifier*): *a cup competition.* 8 a mixed drink with one ingredient as a base, usually served from a bowl: *claret cup.* 9 *Golf* the hole or metal container in the hole on a green. 10 the chalice or the consecrated wine used in the Eucharist. 11 one's lot in life. 12 **in one's cups.** drunk. 13 **one's cup of tea.** *Informal* one's chosen or preferred thing, task, company, etc.: *she's not my cup of tea.* ◆ VERB **cups, cupping, cupped.** (*tr*) 14 to form (something, such as the hands) into the shape of a cup. 15 to put into or as if into a cup. 16 *Archaic* to draw blood to the surface of the body of (a person) by using a cupping glass.
▷HISTORY Old English *cuppe*, from Late Latin *cuppa* cup, alteration of Latin *cūpa* cask
▸ **'cup,like** ADJECTIVE

cupbearer ('kʌp,bɛərə) NOUN an attendant who fills and serves wine cups, as in a royal household.

cupboard ('kʌbəd) NOUN a piece of furniture or a recessed area of a room, with a door concealing storage space.

cupboard love NOUN a show of love inspired only by some selfish or greedy motive.

cupcake ('kʌp,keɪk) NOUN a small cake baked in a cup-shaped foil or paper case.

CUPE ('kjuːpɪ) NOUN ACRONYM FOR Canadian Union of Public Employees.

cupel ('kjuːpᵊl, kjʊ'pɛl) NOUN 1 a refractory pot in which gold or silver is refined. 2 a small porous bowl made of bone ash in which gold and silver are recovered from a lead button during assaying. ◆ VERB **-pels, -pelling, -pelled** *or US* **-pels, -peling, -peled.** 3 (*tr*) to refine (gold or silver) by means of cupellation.
▷HISTORY C17: from French *coupelle*, diminutive of *coupe* CUP
▸ **'cupeller** NOUN

cupellation (,kjuːpɪ'leɪʃən) NOUN 1 the process of recovering precious metals from lead by melting the alloy in a cupel and oxidizing the lead by means of an air blast. 2 the manufacture of lead oxide by melting and oxidizing lead.

Cup Final NOUN 1 (often preceded by *the*) the annual final of the FA Cup soccer competition, played at Wembley, or the Scottish Cup, played at Hampden Park. 2 (*often not capitals*) the final of any cup competition.

cup-holder NOUN 1 a device for holding a cup upright, esp in a motor vehicle. 2 the reigning champion or champions in a cup competition.

Cupid ('kjuːpɪd) NOUN 1 the Roman god of love, represented as a winged boy with a bow and arrow. Greek counterpart: **Eros.** 2 (*not capital*) any similar figure, esp as represented in Baroque art.
▷HISTORY C14: from Latin *Cupīdō*, from *cupīdō* desire, from *cupidus* desirous; see CUPIDITY

cupidity (kjuː'pɪdɪtɪ) NOUN strong desire, esp for possessions or money; greed.
▷HISTORY C15: from Latin *cupiditās*, from *cupidus* eagerly desiring, from *cupere* to long for

Cupid's bow NOUN a shape of the upper lip considered to resemble Cupid's double-curved bow.

cupid's dart NOUN another name for **catananche.**

cupola ('kjuːpələ) NOUN 1 a roof or ceiling in the form of a dome. 2 a small structure, usually domed, on the top of a roof or dome. 3 a protective dome for a gun on a warship. 4 a vertical air-blown coke-fired cylindrical furnace in which iron is remelted for casting.
▷HISTORY C16: from Italian, from Late Latin *cūpula* a small cask, from Latin *cūpa* tub
▸ **cupolated** ('kjuːpə,leɪtɪd) ADJECTIVE

cuppa *or* **cupper** ('kʌpə) NOUN *Brit informal* a cup of tea.

cupped (kʌpt) ADJECTIVE hollowed like a cup; concave.

cupping ('kʌpɪŋ) NOUN *Med Archaic* the process of applying a cupping glass to the skin.

cupping glass NOUN *Med, archaic* a glass vessel from which air can be removed by suction or heat to create a partial vacuum: formerly used in drawing blood to the surface of the skin for slow bloodletting. Also called: **artificial leech.**

cupreous ('kjuːprɪəs) ADJECTIVE 1 of, consisting of, containing, or resembling copper; coppery. 2 of the reddish-brown colour of copper.
▷HISTORY C17: from Late Latin *cupreus*, from *cuprum* COPPER¹

cupressus (kjʊ'prɛsəs) NOUN any tree of the genus *Cupressus*. See **cypress¹.**

cupric ('kjuːprɪk) ADJECTIVE of or containing copper in the divalent state.
▷HISTORY C18: from Late Latin *cuprum* copper

cupriferous (kjuː'prɪfərəs) ADJECTIVE (of a substance such as an ore) containing or yielding copper.

cuprite ('kjuːpraɪt) NOUN a red secondary mineral consisting of cuprous oxide in cubic crystalline form: a source of copper. Formula: Cu_2O.

cupro-, cupri-, *or before a vowel* **cupr-** COMBINING FORM indicating copper: *cupronickel; cuprite.*
▷HISTORY from Latin *cuprum*

cupronickel (,kjuːprəʊ'nɪkᵊl) NOUN any ductile corrosion-resistant copper alloy containing up to 40 per cent nickel: used in coins, condenser tubes, turbine blades, etc.

cuprous ('kjuːprəs) ADJECTIVE of or containing copper in the monovalent state.

cuprum ('kjuːprəm) NOUN an obsolete name for **copper.**
▷HISTORY Latin: COPPER¹

cup tie NOUN *Sport* an eliminating match or round between two teams in a cup competition.

cup-tied ADJECTIVE *Sport* 1 (of a team) unable to play another fixture because of involvement in a cup tie. 2 (of a player) unable to play in a cup tie because of some disallowance.

cupula ('kʌpjʊlə) NOUN, *plural* **-lae** (-liː). *Anatomy, zoology* a dome-shaped structure, esp the sensory structure within the semicircular canals of the ear.

cupulate ('kjuːpjʊ,leɪt) *or* **cupular** ('kjuːpjʊlə) ADJECTIVE 1 shaped like a small cup. 2 (of plants or animals) having cupules.

cupule ('kjuːpjuːl) NOUN *Biology* a cup-shaped part or structure, such as the cup around the base of an acorn.
▷HISTORY C19: from Late Latin *cūpula;* see CUPOLA

cur (kɜː) NOUN 1 any vicious dog, esp a mongrel. 2 a despicable or cowardly person.
▷HISTORY C13: shortened from *kurdogge;* probably related to Old Norse *kurra* to growl

curable ('kjʊərəbᵊl) ADJECTIVE capable of being cured.
▸ **,cura'bility** *or* **'curableness** NOUN ▸ **'curably** ADVERB

Curaçao (,kjʊərə'səʊ) NOUN 1 an island in the Caribbean, the largest in the Netherlands Antilles. Capital: Willemstad. Pop.: 143 387 (2000 est.). Area: 444 sq. km (171 sq. miles). 2 an orange-flavoured liqueur originally made there.

curacy ('kjʊərəsɪ) NOUN, *plural* **-cies.** the office or position of curate.

Cur. adv. vult ABBREVIATION See **CAV.**

curagh *Gaelic* ('kʌrəx, 'kʌrə) NOUN a variant spelling of **currach.**

curare *or* **curari** (kjʊ'rɑːrɪ) NOUN 1 black resin obtained from certain tropical South American trees, esp *Chondrodendron tomentosum*, acting on the motor nerves to cause muscular paralysis: used medicinally as a muscle relaxant and by South American Indians as an arrow poison. 2 any of various trees of the genera *Chondrodendron* (family *Menispermaceae*) and *Strychnos* (family *Loganiaceae*) from which this resin is obtained.
▷HISTORY C18: from Portuguese and Spanish, from Carib *kurari*

curarize *or* **curarise** ('kjʊərə,raɪz) VERB (*tr*) to paralyse or treat with curare.
▸ **,curari'zation** *or* **,curari'sation** NOUN

curassow ('kjʊərə,səʊ) NOUN any gallinaceous ground-nesting bird of the family *Cracidae*, of S North, Central, and South America. Curassows have long legs and tails and, typically, a distinctive crest of curled feathers. See also **guan.**
▷HISTORY C17: anglicized variant of CURAÇAO (island)

curate¹ ('kjʊərɪt) NOUN 1 a clergyman appointed to assist a parish priest. 2 a clergyman who has the charge of a parish (**curate-in-charge**). 3 *Irish* an assistant barman.
▷HISTORY C14: from Medieval Latin *cūrātus*, from *cūra* spiritual oversight, CURE

curate² (kjʊə'reɪt) VERB (*tr*) to be in charge of (an art exhibition or museum).
▷HISTORY C20: back formation from CURATOR

curate's egg NOUN something that has both good and bad parts.
▷HISTORY C20: derived from a cartoon in *Punch* (November, 1895) in which a timid curate, who has been served a bad egg while breakfasting with his bishop, says that parts of the egg are excellent

curative ('kjʊərətɪv) ADJECTIVE 1 able or tending to cure. ◆ NOUN 2 anything able to heal or cure.
▸ **'curatively** ADVERB ▸ **'curativeness** NOUN

curator (kjʊə'reɪtə) NOUN 1 the administrative head of a museum, art gallery, or similar institution. 2 *Law, chiefly Scot* a guardian of a minor, mentally ill person, etc.
▷HISTORY C14: from Latin: one who cares, from *cūrāre* to care for, from *cūra* care
▸ **curatorial** (,kjʊərə'tɔːrɪəl) ADJECTIVE ▸ **cu'rator,ship** NOUN

curb¹ (kɜːb) NOUN 1 something that restrains or holds back. 2 any enclosing framework, such as a wall of stones around the top of a well. 3 **a** Also called: **curb bit.** a horse's bit with an attached chain or strap, which checks the horse. **b** Also called: **curb chain.** the chain or strap itself. 4 a hard swelling on the hock of a horse. ◆ VERB (*tr*) 5 to control with or as if with a curb; restrain. ◆ See also **kerb.**
▷HISTORY C15: from Old French *courbe* curved piece of wood or metal, from Latin *curvus* curved

curb² NOUN *Vet science* a swelling on the leg of a horse, below the point of the hock, usually caused by a sprain.

curbing ('kɜːbɪŋ) NOUN the US spelling of **kerbing.**

curb roof NOUN a roof having two or more slopes on each side of the ridge. See also **mansard** (sense 1), **gambrel roof** (sense 2).

curbstone ('kɜːb,stəʊn) NOUN the US spelling of **kerbstone.**

curch (kɜːtʃ) NOUN a woman's plain cap or kerchief. Also called: **curchef.**
▷HISTORY C15: probably back formation from *courcheis* (plural), from Old French *couvrechies*, plural of *couvrechef* KERCHIEF

curculio (kɜː'kjuːlɪ,əʊ) NOUN, *plural* **-lios.** any of various American weevils, esp *Conotrachelus nenuphar* (**plum curculio**), a pest of fruit trees.
▷HISTORY C18: from Latin: grain weevil

curcuma ('kɜːkjʊmə) NOUN any tropical Asian tuberous plant of the genus *Curcuma*, such as *C. longa*, which is the source of turmeric, and *C. zedoaria*, which is the source of zedoary: family *Zingiberaceae*.
▷HISTORY C17: from New Latin, from Arabic *kurkum* turmeric

curd (kɜːd) NOUN 1 (*often plural*) a substance formed from the coagulation of milk by acid or rennet, used in making cheese or eaten as a food. 2 something similar in consistency. ◆ VERB 3 to turn into or become curd.
▷HISTORY C15: from earlier *crud*, of unknown origin
▸ **'curdy** ADJECTIVE ▸ **'curdiness** NOUN

curd cheese NOUN a mild white cheese made from skimmed milk curds, smoother and fattier than cottage cheese.

curdle ('kɜːdᵊl) VERB 1 to turn or cause to turn into curd. 2 **curdle someone's blood.** to fill someone with fear.
▷HISTORY C16 (*crudled*, past participle): from CURD
▸ **'curdler** NOUN

cure (kjʊə) VERB 1 (*tr*) to get rid of (an ailment, fault, or problem); heal. 2 (*tr*) to restore to health or good condition. 3 (*intr*) to bring about a cure. 4 (*tr*) to preserve (meat, fish, etc.) by salting, smoking, etc. 5 (*tr*) **a** to treat or finish (a substance) by chemical or physical means. **b** to vulcanize (rubber). **c** to allow (a polymer) to set often using heat or pressure. 6 (*tr*) to assist the hardening of (concrete, mortar, etc.) by keeping it moist. ◆ NOUN 7 a return to health, esp after specific treatment. 8 any course of medical therapy, esp one proved effective in combating a disease. 9 a means of restoring health or

improving a condition, situation, etc. [10] the spiritual and pastoral charge of a parish: *the cure of souls.* [11] a process or method of preserving meat, fish, etc., by salting, pickling, or smoking.
▷HISTORY (noun) C13: from Old French, from Latin *cūra* care; in ecclesiastical sense, from Medieval Latin *cūra* spiritual charge; (verb) C14: from Old French *curer,* from Latin *cūrāre* to attend to, heal, from *cūra* care
▸ **'cureless** ADJECTIVE ▸ **'curer** NOUN

curé ('kjʊəreɪ) NOUN a parish priest in France.
▷HISTORY French, from Medieval Latin *cūrātus;* see CURATE[1]

cure-all NOUN something reputed to cure all ailments.

curettage (ˌkjʊərɪ'tɑːʒ, kjʊə'rɛtɪdʒ) *or* **curettement** (kjʊə'rɛtmənt) NOUN the process of using a curette. See also **D and C.**

curette *or* **curet** (kjʊə'rɛt) NOUN [1] a surgical instrument for removing dead tissue, growths, etc., from the walls of certain body cavities. ◆ VERB **-rettes** *or* **-rets, -retting, -retted.** [2] (*tr*) to scrape or clean with such an instrument.
▷HISTORY C18: from French, from *curer* to heal, make clean; see CURE

curfew ('kɜːfjuː) NOUN [1] an official regulation setting restrictions on movement, esp after a specific time at night. [2] the time set as a deadline by such a regulation. [3] (in medieval Europe) **a** the ringing of a bell to prompt people to extinguish fires and lights. **b** the time at which the curfew bell was rung. **c** the bell itself.
▷HISTORY C13: from Old French *cuevrefeu,* literally: cover the fire

curia ('kjʊərɪə) NOUN, *plural* **-riae** (-rɪˌiː). [1] (*sometimes capital*) the papal court and government of the Roman Catholic Church. [2] (in ancient Rome) **a** any of the ten subdivisions of the Latin, Sabine, or Etruscan tribes. **b** a meeting place of such a subdivision. **c** the senate house of Rome. **d** the senate of an Italian town under Roman administration. [3] (in the Middle Ages) a court held in the king's name. See also **Curia Regis.**
▷HISTORY C16: from Latin, from Old Latin *coviria*(unattested), from CO- + *vir* man
▸ **'curial** ADJECTIVE

Curia Regis ('riːdʒɪs) NOUN, *plural* **Curiae Regis.** (in Norman England) the king's court, which performed all functions of government.
▷HISTORY Latin, literally: council of the king

curie ('kjʊərɪ, -riː) NOUN a unit of radioactivity that is equal to 3.7×10^{10} disintegrations per second. Symbol: Ci.
▷HISTORY C20: named after Pierre Curie (1859–1906), French physicist and chemist

Curie point *or* **temperature** NOUN the temperature above which a ferromagnetic substance loses its ferromagnetism and becomes paramagnetic.
▷HISTORY C20: named after Pierre Curie (1859–1906), French physicist and chemist

Curie's law NOUN the principle that the magnetic susceptibility of a paramagnetic substance is inversely proportional to its thermodynamic temperature. See also **Curie-Weiss law.**

Curie-Weiss law ('kjʊərɪ'waɪs, -'vaɪs) NOUN the principle that the magnetic susceptibility of a paramagnetic substance is inversely proportional to the difference between its temperature and its Curie point.
▷HISTORY C20: named after Pierre Curie (1859–1906), French physicist and chemist and Pierre-Ernest *Weiss* (died 1940), French physicist

curio ('kjʊərɪˌəʊ) NOUN, *plural* **-rios.** a small article valued as a collector's item, esp something fascinating or unusual.
▷HISTORY C19: shortened from CURIOSITY

curiosa (ˌkjʊərɪ'əʊsə) NOUN (*functioning as plural*) [1] curiosities. [2] books on strange subjects, esp erotica.
▷HISTORY New Latin: from Latin *cūriōsus* CURIOUS

curiosity (ˌkjʊərɪ'ɒsɪtɪ) NOUN, *plural* **-ties.** [1] an eager desire to know; inquisitiveness. [2] **a** the quality of being curious; strangeness. **b** (*as modifier*): *the ring had curiosity value only.* [3] something strange or fascinating. [4] a rare or strange object; curio. [5] *Obsolete* fastidiousness.

curious ('kjʊərɪəs) ADJECTIVE [1] eager to learn; inquisitive. [2] over inquisitive; prying. [3] interesting because of oddness or novelty; strange; unexpected. [4] *Rare* (of workmanship, etc.) highly detailed, intricate, or subtle. [5] *Obsolete* fastidious or hard to please.
▷HISTORY C14: from Latin *cūriōsus* taking pains over something, from *cūra* care
▸ **'curiously** ADVERB ▸ **'curiousness** NOUN

Curitiba (ˌkʊərɪ'tiːbə) NOUN a city in SE Brazil, capital of Paraná state: seat of the University of Paraná (1946). Pop. (urban area): 1 586 898 (2000).

curium ('kjʊərɪəm) NOUN a silvery-white metallic transuranic element artificially produced from plutonium. Symbol: Cm; atomic no.: 96; half-life of most stable isotope, ^{247}Cm: 1.6×10^7 years; valency: 3 and 4; relative density: 13.51 (calculated); melting pt.: 1345±400°C.
▷HISTORY C20: New Latin, named after Pierre Curie (1859–1906), French physicist and chemist, and his wife Marie Curie (1867–1934), Polish-born French physicist and chemist

curl (kɜːl) VERB [1] (*intr*) (esp of hair) to grow into curves or ringlets. [2] (*tr; sometimes foll by up*) to twist or roll (something, esp hair) into coils or ringlets. [3] (often foll by *up*) to become or cause to become spiral-shaped or curved; coil: *the heat made the leaves curl up.* [4] (*intr*) to move in a curving or twisting manner. [5] (*intr*) to play the game of curling. [6] **curl one's lip.** to show contempt, as by raising a corner of the lip. ◆ NOUN [7] a curve or coil of hair. [8] a curved or spiral shape or mark, as in wood. [9] the act of curling or state of being curled. [10] any of various plant diseases characterized by curling of the leaves. [11] Also called: **rot, rotation.** *Maths* a vector quantity associated with a vector field that is the vector product of the operator ∇ and a vector function ***A***, where $\nabla = \boldsymbol{i}\partial/\partial x + \boldsymbol{j}\partial/\partial y + \boldsymbol{k}\partial/\partial z$, ***i, j,*** and ***k*** being unit vectors. Usually written curl ***A***, rot ***A***. Compare **divergence** (sense 4), **gradient** (sense 4). ◆ See also **curl up.**
▷HISTORY C14: probably from Middle Dutch *crullen* to curl; related to Middle High German *krol* curly, Middle Low German *krūs* curly

curled paperwork NOUN another name for **rolled paperwork.**

curler ('kɜːlə) NOUN [1] any of various pins, clasps, or rollers used to curl or wave hair. [2] a person or thing that curls. [3] a person who plays curling.

curlew ('kɜːljuː) NOUN any large shore bird of the genus *Numenius,* such as *N. arquata* of Europe and Asia: family *Scolopacidae* (sandpipers, etc.), order *Charadriiformes.* They have a long downward-curving bill and occur in northern and arctic regions. Compare **stone curlew.**
▷HISTORY C14: from Old French *corlieu,* perhaps of imitative origin

curlew sandpiper NOUN a common Eurasian sandpiper, *Calidris ferruginea,* having a brick-red breeding plumage and a greyish winter plumage.

curli ('kɜːlɪ) PLURAL NOUN *Bacteriol* curled hairlike processes on the surface of the bacterium *Escherichia coli* by means of which the bacterium adheres to and infects wounds.
▷HISTORY C20: from *curl(ed)* (PIL)I

curlicue ('kɜːlɪˌkjuː) NOUN an intricate ornamental curl or twist.
▷HISTORY C19: from CURLY + CUE[2]

curling ('kɜːlɪŋ) NOUN a game played on ice, esp in Scotland and Canada, in which heavy stones with handles (**curling stones**) are slid towards a target (**tee**).

curling tongs PLURAL NOUN a metal scissor-like device that is heated, so that strands of hair may be twined around it in order to form curls. Also called: **curling iron, curling irons, curling pins.**

curlpaper ('kɜːlˌpeɪpə) NOUN a strip of paper used to roll up and set a section of hair, usually wetted, into a curl.

curl up VERB (*adverb*) [1] (*intr*) to adopt a reclining position with the legs close to the body and the back rounded. [2] to become or cause to become spiral-shaped or curved. [3] (*intr*) to retire to a quiet cosy setting: *to curl up with a good novel.* [4] *Brit informal* to be or cause to be embarrassed or disgusted (esp in the phrase **curl up and die**).

curly ('kɜːlɪ) ADJECTIVE **curlier, curliest.** [1] tending to curl; curling. [2] having curls. [3] (of timber) having irregular curves or waves in the grain. [4] *Austral and NZ* difficult to counter or answer: *a curly question.*
▸ **'curliness** NOUN

curly-coated retriever NOUN a strongly built variety of retriever with a tightly curled black or liver-coloured coat.

curmudgeon (kɜː'mʌdʒən) NOUN a surly or miserly person.
▷HISTORY C16: of unknown origin
▸ **cur'mudgeonly** ADJECTIVE

currach, curagh, *or* ***curragh*** *Gaelic* ('kʌrəx, 'kʌrə) NOUN a Scot or Irish name for **coracle.**
▷HISTORY C15: from Irish Gaelic *currach;* compare CORACLE

currajong ('kʌrəˌdʒɒŋ) NOUN a variant spelling of **kurrajong.**

currant ('kʌrənt) NOUN [1] a small dried seedless grape of the Mediterranean region, used in cooking. [2] any of several mainly N temperate shrubs of the genus *Ribes,* esp *R. rubrum* (redcurrant) and *R. nigrum* (blackcurrant): family *Grossulariaceae.* See also **gooseberry** (sense 1). [3] the small acid fruit of any of these plants.
▷HISTORY C16: shortened from *rayson of Corannte* raisin of Corinth

currant bun NOUN [1] *Brit* a sweet bun containing currants. [2] *Scot* another name for **black bun.** [3] *Cockney rhyming slang* son.

currawong ('kʌrəˌwɒŋ) NOUN any Australian crowlike songbird of the genus *Strepera,* having black, grey, and white plumage: family *Cracticidae.* Also called: **bell magpie.**
▷HISTORY from a native Australian name

currency ('kʌrənsɪ) NOUN, *plural* **-cies.** [1] a metal or paper medium of exchange that is in current use in a particular country. [2] general acceptance or circulation; prevalence: *the currency of ideas.* [3] the period of time during which something is valid, accepted, or in force. [4] the act of being passed from person to person. [5] *Austral* (formerly) the local medium of exchange, esp in the colonies, as distinct from sterling. [6] *Austral slang* (formerly) the native-born Australians, as distinct from the British immigrants.
▷HISTORY C17: from Medieval Latin *currentia,* literally: a flowing, from Latin *currere* to run, flow

currency bar NOUN [1] a long narrow iron bar, often sword-like or spear-like in shape, dating from the pre-Roman and Roman period in Britain; the purpose of currency bars is not certain, and while they may have been used in trade, they may have had a ritual significance. [2] a metal bar of any of various shapes, used as a form of currency.

currency note NOUN another name for **treasury note** (sense b).

current ('kʌrənt) ADJECTIVE [1] of the immediate present; in progress: *current events.* [2] most recent; up-to-date. [3] commonly known, practised, or accepted; widespread: *a current rumour.* [4] circulating and valid at present: *current coins.* ◆ NOUN [5] (esp of water or air) a steady usually natural flow. [6] a mass of air, body of water, etc., that has a steady flow in a particular direction. [7] the rate of flow of such a mass. [8] Also called: **electric current.** *Physics* **a** a flow of electric charge through a conductor. **b** the rate of flow of this charge. It is measured in amperes. Symbol: I. [9] a general trend or drift: *currents of opinion.*
▷HISTORY C13: from Old French *corant,* literally: running, from *corre* to run, from Latin *currere*
▸ **'currently** ADVERB ▸ **'currentness** NOUN

current account NOUN [1] an account at a bank or building society against which cheques may be drawn at any time. US name: **checking account.** Canadian name: **chequing account.** [2] *Economics* that part of the balance of payments composed of the balance of trade and the invisible balance. Compare **capital account** (sense 1).

current assets PLURAL NOUN cash and operating assets that are convertible into cash within a year. Also called: **floating assets.** Compare **fixed assets.**

current-cost accounting NOUN a method of accounting that values assets at their current replacement cost rather than their original cost. Compare **historical-cost accounting.**

current density NOUN the ratio of the electric current flowing at a particular point in a conductor to the cross-sectional area of the conductor taken perpendicular to the current flow at that point. It is measured in amperes per square metre. Symbol: J.

current efficiency NOUN *Physics* the ratio of the actual mass of a substance liberated from an electrolyte by the passage of current to the theoretical mass liberated according to Faraday's law.

current expenses PLURAL NOUN noncapital and usually recurrent expenditures necessary for the operation of a business.

current liabilities PLURAL NOUN business liabilities maturing within a year.

curricle ('kʌrɪkᵊl) NOUN a two-wheeled open carriage drawn by two horses side by side.
▷HISTORY C18: from Latin *curriculum* from *currus* chariot, from *currere* to run

curriculum (kəˈrɪkjʊləm) NOUN, *plural* **-la** (-lə) *or* **-lums.** [1] a course of study in one subject at a school or college. [2] a list of all the courses of study offered by a school or college. [3] any programme or plan of activities.
▷HISTORY C19: from Latin: course, from *currere* to run
▸**cur'ricular** ADJECTIVE

curriculum vitae ('viːtaɪ, 'vaɪtiː) NOUN, *plural* **curricula vitae.** an outline of a person's educational and professional history, usually prepared for job applications. Abbreviation: **CV.**
▷HISTORY Latin, literally: the course of one's life

currier ('kʌrɪə) NOUN a person who curries leather.
▷HISTORY C14: from Old French *corier,* from Latin *coriārius* a tanner, from *corium* leather

curriery ('kʌrɪərɪ) NOUN, *plural* **-eries.** the trade, work, or place of occupation of a currier.

currish ('kɜːrɪʃ) ADJECTIVE of or like a cur; rude or bad-tempered.
▸**'currishly** ADVERB ▸**'currishness** NOUN

curry¹ ('kʌrɪ) NOUN, *plural* **-ries.** [1] a spicy dish of oriental, esp Indian, origin that is made in many ways but usually consists of meat or fish prepared in a hot piquant sauce. [2] curry seasoning or sauce. [3] **give someone curry.** *Austral slang* to assault (a person) verbally or physically. ◆ VERB **-ries, -rying, -ried.** [4] (*tr*) to prepare (food) with curry powder or sauce.
▷HISTORY C16: from Tamil *kari* sauce, relish

curry² ('kʌrɪ) VERB **-ries, -rying, -ried.** (*tr*) [1] to beat vigorously, as in order to clean. [2] to dress and finish (leather) after it has been tanned to make it strong, flexible, and waterproof. [3] to groom (a horse). [4] **curry favour.** to ingratiate oneself, esp with superiors.
▷HISTORY C13: from Old French *correer* to make ready, from Vulgar Latin *conrēdāre* (unattested), from *rēdāre* (unattested) to provide, of Germanic origin

currycomb ('kʌrɪˌkəʊm) NOUN a square comb consisting of rows of small teeth, used for grooming horses.

curry powder NOUN a mixture of finely ground pungent spices, such as turmeric, cumin, coriander, ginger, etc., used in making curries.

curry puff NOUN (in eastern cookery) a type of pie or pasty consisting of a pastry case containing curried meat and vegetables.

curse (kɜːs) NOUN [1] a profane or obscene expression of anger, disgust, surprise, etc.; oath. [2] an appeal to a supernatural power for harm to come to a specific person, group, etc. [3] harm resulting from an appeal to a supernatural power: *to be under a curse.* [4] something that brings or causes great trouble or harm. [5] a saying, charm, effigy, etc., used to invoke a curse. [6] an ecclesiastical censure of excommunication. [7] (preceded by *the*) *Informal* menstruation or a menstrual period. ◆ VERB **curses, cursing, cursed** *or archaic* **curst.** [8] (*intr*) to utter obscenities or oaths. [9] (*tr*) to abuse (someone) with obscenities or oaths. [10] (*tr*) to invoke supernatural powers to bring harm to (someone or something). [11] (*tr*) to bring harm upon. [12] (*tr*) another word for **excommunicate.**
▷HISTORY Old English *cursian* to curse, from *curs* a curse
▸**'curser** NOUN

cursed ('kɜːsɪd, kɜːst) *or* **curst** ADJECTIVE [1] under a curse. [2] deserving to be cursed; detestable; hateful.
▸**'cursedly** ADVERB ▸**'cursedness** NOUN

curses ('kɜːsɪz) INTERJECTION *Often facetious* an expression of disappointment or dismay.

cursive ('kɜːsɪv) ADJECTIVE [1] of or relating to handwriting in which letters are formed and joined in a rapid flowing style. [2] *Printing* of or relating to typefaces that resemble handwriting. ◆ NOUN [3] a cursive letter or printing type. [4] a manuscript written in cursive letters.
▷HISTORY C18: from Medieval Latin *cursīvus* running, ultimately from Latin *currere* to run
▸**'cursively** ADVERB

cursor ('kɜːsə) NOUN [1] the sliding part of a measuring instrument, esp a transparent sliding square on a slide rule. [2] any of various means, typically a flashing bar or underline, of identifying a particular position on a computer screen, such as the insertion point for text.

cursorial (kɜːˈsɔːrɪəl) ADJECTIVE *Zoology* adapted for running: *a cursorial skeleton; cursorial birds.*

cursory ('kɜːsərɪ) ADJECTIVE hasty and usually superficial; quick: *a cursory check.*
▷HISTORY C17: from Late Latin *cursōrius* of running, from Latin *cursus* a course, from *currere* to run
▸**'cursorily** ADVERB ▸**'cursoriness** NOUN

curst (kɜːst) VERB [1] *Archaic* a past tense and past participle of **curse.** ◆ ADJECTIVE [2] a variant of **cursed.**

curt (kɜːt) ADJECTIVE [1] rudely blunt and brief; abrupt: *a curt reply.* [2] short or concise.
▷HISTORY C17: from Latin *curtus* cut short, mutilated
▸**'curtly** ADVERB ▸**'curtness** NOUN

curtail (kɜːˈteɪl) VERB (*tr*) to cut short; abridge.
▷HISTORY C16: changed (through influence of TAIL¹) from obsolete *curtal* to dock; see CURTAL
▸**cur'tailer** NOUN ▸**cur'tailment** NOUN

curtail step ('kɜːteɪl) NOUN the step or steps at the foot of a flight of stairs, widened at one or both ends and terminated with a scroll.

curtain ('kɜːtᵊn) NOUN [1] a piece of material that can be drawn across an opening or window, to shut out light or to provide privacy. [2] a barrier to vision, access, or communication: *a curtain of secrecy.* [3] a hanging cloth or similar barrier for concealing all or part of a theatre stage from the audience. [4] (often preceded by *the*) the end of a scene of a play, opera, etc., marked by the fall or closing of the curtain. [5] the rise or opening of the curtain at the start of a performance. ◆ VERB [6] (*tr;* sometimes foll by *off*) to shut off or conceal with or as if with a curtain. [7] (*tr*) to provide (a window, etc.) with curtains. ◆ See also **curtains.**
▷HISTORY C13: from Old French *courtine,* from Late Latin *cortīna* enclosed place, curtain, probably from Latin *cohors* courtyard

curtain call NOUN the appearance of performers at the end of a theatrical performance to acknowledge applause.

curtain lecture NOUN a scolding or rebuke given in private, esp by a wife to her husband.
▷HISTORY alluding to the curtained beds where such rebukes were once given

curtain-raiser NOUN [1] *Theatre* a short dramatic piece presented before the main play. [2] any preliminary event: *the debate was a curtain-raiser to the election.*

curtains ('kɜːtᵊnz) PLURAL NOUN [1] *Informal* death or ruin; the end: *if the enemy see us it will be curtains for us.* [2] a hairstyle in which the hair is parted in the centre of the forehead and curved out over the temples.

curtain speech NOUN [1] a talk given in front of the curtain after a stage performance, often by the author or an actor. [2] the final speech of an act or a play.

curtain-twitcher NOUN *Informal* a person who likes to watch unobserved what other people are doing.

curtain wall NOUN [1] a non-load-bearing external wall attached to a framed structure, often one that is prefabricated. [2] a low wall outside the outer wall of a castle, serving as a first line of defence.

curtal ('kɜːtᵊl) *Obsolete* ◆ ADJECTIVE [1] cut short. [2] (of friars) wearing a short frock. ◆ NOUN [3] an animal whose tail has been docked. [4] something that is cut short.
▷HISTORY C16: from Old French *courtault* animal whose tail has been docked, from *court* short, from Latin *curtus;* see CURT

curtal axe NOUN an obsolete term for **cutlass.**
▷HISTORY C16: alteration by folk etymology of Old French *coutelas* CUTLASS; see CURTAL

curtana (kɜːˈtɑːnə) NOUN the unpointed sword carried before an English sovereign at a coronation as an emblem of mercy.
▷HISTORY C15: from Anglo-Latin, from Old French *cortain,* the name of Roland's sword, which was broken at the point, ultimately from Latin *curtus* short

curtate ('kɜːteɪt) ADJECTIVE shortened.
▷HISTORY C17: from Late Latin *curtāre* to shorten, from Latin *curtus* cut short; see CURT

curtilage ('kɜːtɪlɪdʒ) NOUN the enclosed area of land adjacent to a dwelling house.
▷HISTORY C14: from Old French *cortillage,* from *cortil* a little yard, from *cort* COURT

curtsy *or* **curtsey** ('kɜːtsɪ) NOUN, *plural* **-sies** *or* **-seys.** [1] a formal gesture of greeting and respect made by women in which the knees are bent, the head slightly bowed, and the skirt held outwards. ◆ VERB **-sies, -sying, -sied** *or* **-seys, -seying, -seyed.** [2] (*intr*) to make a curtsy.
▷HISTORY C16: variant of COURTESY

curule ('kjʊəruːl) ADJECTIVE (in ancient Rome) of the highest rank, esp one entitled to use a curule chair.
▷HISTORY C16: from Latin *curūlis* of a chariot, from *currus* chariot, from *currere* to run

curule chair NOUN an upholstered folding seat with curved legs used by the highest civil officials of ancient Rome.

curvaceous (kɜːˈveɪʃəs) ADJECTIVE *Informal* (esp of a woman) having shapely curves or a well-rounded body.
▸**cur'vaceously** ADVERB

curvature ('kɜːvətʃə) NOUN [1] something curved or a curved part of a thing. [2] any normal or abnormal curving of a bodily part: *curvature of the spine.* [3] *Geometry* the change in inclination of a tangent to a curve over unit length of arc. For a circle or sphere it is the reciprocal of the radius. See also **radius of curvature, centre of curvature.** [4] the act of curving or the state or degree of being curved or bent.

curve (kɜːv) NOUN [1] a continuously bending line that has no straight parts. [2] something that curves or is curved, such as a bend in a road or the contour of a woman's body. [3] the act or extent of curving; curvature. [4] *Maths* **a** a system of points whose coordinates satisfy a given equation; a locus of points. **b** the graph of a function with one independent variable. [5] a line representing data, esp statistical data, on a graph: *an unemployment curve.* [6] short for **French curve.** [7] **behind the curve.** behind schedule; behind the times. ◆ VERB [8] to take or cause to take the shape or path of a curve; bend. ◆ Related adjective: **sinuous.**
▷HISTORY C15: from Latin *curvāre* to bend, from *curvus* crooked
▸**curvedly** ('kɜːvɪdlɪ) ADVERB ▸**'curvedness** NOUN ▸**'curvy** ADJECTIVE

curve ball NOUN [1] *Baseball* a ball pitched in a curving path so as to make it more difficult to hit. [2] *Informal* something deceptive: *his wholesome image was a curve ball thrown to deceive the public.*

curvet (kɜːˈvɛt) NOUN [1] *Dressage* a low leap with all four feet off the ground. ◆ VERB **-vets, -vetting, -vetted** *or* **-vets, -veting, -veted.** [2] *Dressage* to make or cause to make such a leap. [3] (*intr*) to prance or frisk about.
▷HISTORY C16: from Old Italian *corvetta,* from Old French *courbette,* from *courber* to bend, from Latin *curvāre*

curvilinear (ˌkɜːvɪˈlɪnɪə) *or* **curvilineal** ADJECTIVE [1] consisting of, bounded by, or characterized by a curved line. [2] along a curved line: *curvilinear motion.* [3] *Maths* (of a set of coordinates) determined by or determining a system of three orthogonal surfaces.
▸**ˌcurviˌline'arity** NOUN ▸**ˌcurvi'linearly** ADVERB

Cusco (*Spanish* 'kusko) NOUN a variant of **Cuzco.**

cuscus ('kʌskʌs) NOUN, *plural* **-cuses.** any of several large nocturnal phalangers of the genus *Phalanger,* of N Australia, New Guinea, and adjacent islands,

having dense fur, prehensile tails, large eyes, and a yellow nose.
▷**HISTORY** C17: New Latin, probably from a native name in New Guinea

cusec (ˈkjuːsɛk) NOUN a unit of flow equal to 1 cubic foot per second. 1 cusec is equivalent to 0.028 317 cubic metre per second.
▷**HISTORY** C20: from *cu(bic foot per) sec(ond)*

Cush *or* **Kush** (kʌʃ, kʊʃ) NOUN *Old Testament* 1 the son of Ham and brother of Canaan (Genesis 10:6). 2 the country of the supposed descendants of Cush (ancient Ethiopia), comprising approximately Nubia and the modern Sudan, and the territory of southern (or Upper) Egypt.

cushat (ˈkʌʃət) NOUN another name for **wood pigeon.**
▷**HISTORY** Old English *cūscote;* perhaps related to *sceōtan* to shoot

cushie-doo (ˌkʊʃɪˈduː) NOUN a Scot name for a **wood pigeon.** Often shortened to **cushie.**
▷**HISTORY** from CUSHAT + DOO

Cushing's disease *or* **syndrome** (ˈkʊʃɪŋz) NOUN a rare condition caused by excess corticosteroid hormones in the body, characterized chiefly by obesity of the trunk and face, high blood pressure, fatigue, and loss of calcium from the bones.
▷**HISTORY** C20: named after Harvey Williams *Cushing* (1869–1939), US neurosurgeon

cushion (ˈkʊʃən) NOUN 1 a bag made of cloth, leather, plastic, etc., filled with feathers, air, or other yielding substance, used for sitting on, leaning against, etc. 2 something resembling a cushion in function or appearance, esp one to support or pad or to absorb shock. 3 the resilient felt-covered rim of a billiard table. 4 another name for **pillow** (sense 2). 5 short for **air cushion.** 6 a capital, used in Byzantine, Romanesque, and Norman architecture, in the form of a bowl with a square top. ◆ VERB *(tr)* 7 to place on or as on a cushion. 8 to provide with cushions. 9 to protect, esp against hardship or change. 10 **a** to check the motion of (a mechanism) gently, esp by the compression of trapped fluid in a cylinder. **b** to provide with a means of absorbing shock.
▷**HISTORY** from Latin *culcita* mattress
▸ˈ**cushiony** ADJECTIVE

cushion plant NOUN a type of low-growing plant having many closely spaced short upright shoots, typical of alpine and arctic habitats.

Cushitic (kʊˈʃɪtɪk) NOUN 1 a group of languages of Somalia, Ethiopia, NE Kenya, and adjacent regions: a subfamily within the Afro-Asiatic family of languages. ◆ ADJECTIVE 2 denoting, relating to, or belonging to this group of languages.

cushty (ˈkʊʃtɪ) INTERJECTION *Brit informal* an exclamation of pleasure, agreement, approval, etc.

cushy (ˈkʊʃɪ) ADJECTIVE **cushier, cushiest.** *Informal* easy; comfortable: *a cushy job.*
▷**HISTORY** C20: from Hindi *khush* pleasant, from Persian *khōsh*

cusk (kʌsk) NOUN, *plural* **cusks** *or* **cusk.** the usual Eastern US and Canadian name for the **torsk.**
▷**HISTORY** C17: probably alteration of *tusk* of Scandinavian origin; compare Old Norse *thorskr* codfish

CUSO (ˈkjuːsəʊ) NOUN ACRONYM FOR Canadian University Services Overseas; an organization that sends students to work as volunteers in developing countries.

cusp (kʌsp) NOUN 1 any of the small elevations on the grinding or chewing surface of a tooth. 2 any of the triangular flaps of a heart valve. 3 a point or pointed end. 4 Also called: **spinode.** *Geometry* a point at which two arcs of a curve intersect and at which the two tangents are coincident. 5 *Architect* a carving at the meeting place of two arcs. 6 *Astronomy* either of the points of a crescent moon or of a satellite or inferior planet in a similar phase. 7 *Astrology* any division between houses or signs of the zodiac.
▷**HISTORY** C16: from Latin *cuspis* point, pointed end

cuspate (ˈkʌspɪt, -peɪt), **cuspated,** *or* **cusped** (kʌspt) ADJECTIVE 1 having a cusp or cusps. 2 shaped like a cusp; cusplike.

cuspid (ˈkʌspɪd) NOUN a tooth having one point; canine tooth.

cuspidate (ˈkʌspɪˌdeɪt), **cuspidated,** *or* **cuspidal** (ˈkʌspɪdᵊl) ADJECTIVE 1 having a cusp or cusps. 2 (esp of leaves) narrowing to a point.
▷**HISTORY** C17: from Latin *cuspidāre* to make pointed, from *cuspis* a point

cuspidation (ˌkʌspɪˈdeɪʃən) NOUN *Architect* decoration using cusps.

cuspidor (ˈkʌspɪˌdɔː) NOUN another word (esp US) for **spittoon.**
▷**HISTORY** C18: from Portuguese, from *cuspir* to spit, from Latin *conspuere,* from *spuere* to spit

cuss (kʌs) *Informal* ◆ NOUN 1 a curse; oath. 2 a person or animal, esp an annoying one. ◆ VERB 3 another word for **curse** (senses 8, 9).

cussed (ˈkʌsɪd) ADJECTIVE *Informal* 1 another word for **cursed.** 2 obstinate. 3 annoying: *a cussed nuisance.*
▸ˈ**cussedly** ADVERB ▸ˈ**cussedness** NOUN

custard (ˈkʌstəd) NOUN 1 a baked sweetened mixture of eggs and milk. 2 a sauce made of milk and sugar and thickened with cornflour.
▷**HISTORY** C15: alteration of Middle English *crustade* kind of pie, probably from Old Provençal *croustado,* from *crosta* CRUST

custard apple NOUN 1 a West Indian tree, *Annona reticulata:* family *Annonaceae.* 2 the large heart-shaped fruit of this tree, which has a fleshy edible pulp. 3 any of several related trees or fruits, esp the papaw and sweetsop. ◆ Also called (for senses 1, 2): **bullock's heart.**

custard pie NOUN **a** a flat, open pie filled with real or artificial custard, as thrown in slapstick comedy. **b** *(as modifier)*: *custard-pie humour.*

custard powder NOUN a powder containing cornflour, sugar, etc., for thickening milk to make a yellow sauce. See **custard** (sense 2).

custodian (kʌˈstəʊdɪən) NOUN 1 a person who has custody, as of a prisoner, ward, etc. 2 a guardian or keeper, as of an art collection, etc.

custodianship (kʌˈstəʊdɪənʃɪp) NOUN 1 the condition of being a custodian. 2 (in Britain) a legal basis for the care of children under the Children's Act 1975, midway between fostering and adoption, devised for children settled in long-term foster care or living permanently with relatives or a step-parent.

custody (ˈkʌstədɪ) NOUN, *plural* **-dies.** 1 the act of keeping safe or guarding, esp the right of guardianship of a minor. 2 the state of being held by the police; arrest (esp in the phrases **in custody, take into custody**).
▷**HISTORY** C15: from Latin *custōdia,* from *custōs* guard, defender
▸**custodial** (kʌˈstəʊdɪəl) ADJECTIVE

custom (ˈkʌstəm) NOUN 1 a usual or habitual practice; typical mode of behaviour. 2 the long-established habits or traditions of a society collectively; convention: *custom dictates good manners.* 3 **a** a practice which by long-established usage has come to have the force of law. **b** such practices collectively (esp in the phrase **custom and practice**). 4 habitual patronage, esp of a shop or business. 5 the customers of a shop or business collectively. 6 (in feudal Europe) a tribute paid by a vassal to his lord. ◆ ADJECTIVE 7 made to the specifications of an individual customer (often in the combinations **custom-built, custom-made**). 8 specializing in goods so made. ◆ See also **customs.**
▷**HISTORY** C12: from Old French *costume,* from Latin *consuētūdō,* from *consuēscere* to grow accustomed to, from *suēscere* to be used to

customable (ˈkʌstəməbᵊl) ADJECTIVE subject to customs.

customary (ˈkʌstəmərɪ, -təmrɪ) ADJECTIVE 1 in accordance with custom or habitual practice; usual; habitual. 2 *Law* **a** founded upon long continued practices and usage rather than law. **b** (of land, esp a feudal estate) held by custom. ◆ NOUN, *plural* **-aries.** 3 **a** a statement in writing of customary laws and practices. **b** a body of such laws and customs.
▸ˈ**customarily** ADVERB ▸ˈ**customariness** NOUN

custom-built ADJECTIVE (of cars, houses, etc.) made according to the specifications of an individual buyer.

customer (ˈkʌstəmə) NOUN 1 a person who buys. 2 *Informal* a person with whom one has dealings: *a cool customer.*

customer-facing ADJECTIVE interacting or communicating directly with customers: *good customer-facing skills.*

customer relationship management NOUN the practice of building a strong relationship between a business and its customers and potential customers. Abbreviation: **CRM.**

custom house *or* **customs house** NOUN a government office, esp at a port, where customs are collected and ships cleared for entry.

customize *or* **customise** (ˈkʌstəˌmaɪz) VERB *(tr)* to make (something) according to a customer's individual requirements.

custom-made ADJECTIVE (of suits, dresses, etc.) made according to the specifications of an individual buyer.

customs (ˈkʌstəmz) NOUN *(functioning as singular or plural)* 1 duty on imports or exports. 2 the government department responsible for the collection of these duties. 3 the part of a port, airport, frontier station, etc., where baggage and freight are examined for dutiable goods and contraband. 4 the procedure for examining baggage and freight, paying duty, etc. 5 *(as modifier)*: *customs officer.*

customs union NOUN an association of nations which promotes free trade within the union and establishes common tariffs on trade with nonmember nations.

custos (ˈkʌstɒs) NOUN, *plural* **custodes** (kʌˈstəʊdiːz). a superior in the Franciscan religious order. Also called (in England): **guardian.**
▷**HISTORY** C15: from Latin: keeper, guard

custumal (ˈkʌstjuməl) NOUN, ADJECTIVE another word for **customary** (senses 2, 3).
▷**HISTORY** C16: from Medieval Latin *custumālis* relating to CUSTOM

cut (kʌt) VERB **cuts, cutting, cut.** 1 to open up or incise (a person or thing) with a sharp edge or instrument; gash. 2 (of a sharp instrument) to penetrate or incise (a person or thing). 3 to divide or be divided with or as if with a sharp instrument: *cut a slice of bread.* 4 *(intr)* to use a sharp-edged instrument or an instrument that cuts. 5 *(tr)* to trim or prune by or as if by clipping: *to cut hair.* 6 *(tr)* to reap or mow (a crop, grass, etc.). 7 *(tr)* to geld or castrate. 8 *(tr; sometimes foll by out)* to make, form, or shape by cutting: *to cut a suit.* 9 *(tr)* to hollow or dig out; excavate: *to cut a tunnel through the mountain.* 10 to strike (an object) sharply. 11 *(tr) Sport* to hit (a ball) with a downward slicing stroke so as to impart spin or cause it to fall short. 12 *Cricket* to hit (the ball) to the off side, usually between cover and third man, with a roughly horizontal bat. 13 to hurt or wound the feelings of (a person), esp by malicious speech or action. 14 *(tr) Informal* to refuse to recognize; snub. 15 *(tr) Informal* to absent oneself from (an activity, location, etc.), esp without permission or in haste: *to cut class.* 16 *(tr)* to abridge, shorten, or edit by excising a part or parts. 17 *(tr; often foll by down)* to lower, reduce, or curtail: *to cut losses.* 18 *(tr)* to dilute or weaken: *heroin that was cut with nontoxic elements.* 19 *(tr)* to dissolve or break up: *to cut fat.* 20 (when *intr,* foll by *across* or *through*) to cross or traverse: *the footpath cuts through the field.* 21 *(intr)* to make a sharp or sudden change in direction; veer. 22 to grow (teeth) through the gums or (of teeth) to appear through the gums. 23 *(intr) Films* **a** to call a halt to a shooting sequence. **b** (foll by *to*) to move quickly to another scene. 24 *Films* to edit (film). 25 *(tr)* to switch off (a light, car engine, etc.). 26 *(tr)* (of a performer, recording company, etc.) to make (a record or tape of a song, concert, performance, etc.). 27 *Cards* **a** to divide (the pack) at random into two parts after shuffling. **b** *(intr)* to pick cards from a spread pack to decide dealer, partners, etc. 28 *(tr)* to remove (material) from an object by means of a chisel, lathe, etc. 29 *(tr)* (of a tool) to bite into (an object). 30 *(intr)* (of a horse) to injure the leg just above the hoof by a blow from the opposite foot. 31 **cut a caper** *or* **capers. a** to skip or jump playfully. **b** to act or behave playfully; frolic. 32 **cut both ways. a** to have both good and bad effects. **b** to affect both sides of something, as two parties in an argument, etc. 33 **cut a dash.** to behave or dress showily or strikingly; make a stylish impression. 34 **cut (a person) dead.** *Informal* to ignore (a person) completely. 35 **cut a (good, poor,** etc.)

figure. to appear or behave in a specified manner. 36 **cut and run.** *Informal* to make a rapid escape. 37 **cut it.** *Slang* be successful in doing something. 38 **cut it fine.** *Informal* to allow little margin of time, space, etc. 39 **cut corners.** to do something in the easiest or shortest way, esp at the expense of high standards: *we could finish this project early only if we cut corners.* 40 **cut loose.** to free or become freed from restraint, custody, anchorage, etc. 41 **cut no ice.** *Informal* to fail to make an impression. 42 **cut one's losses.** to give up spending time, money, or energy on an unprofitable or unsuccessful activity. 43 **cut one's teeth on.** *Informal* **a** to use at an early age or stage. **b** to practise on. ◆ ADJECTIVE 44 detached, divided, or separated by cutting. 45 *Botany* incised or divided: *cut leaves.* 46 made, shaped, or fashioned by cutting. 47 reduced or diminished by or as if by cutting: *cut prices.* 48 gelded or castrated. 49 weakened or diluted. 50 *Brit* a slang word for **drunk.** 51 hurt; resentful. 52 **cut and dried.** *Informal* settled or arranged in advance. 53 **cut lunch.** *Austral and NZ* a sandwich lunch carried from home to work, school, etc. ◆ NOUN 54 the act of cutting. 55 a stroke or incision made by cutting; gash. 56 a piece or part cut off, esp a section of food cut from the whole: *a cut of meat.* 57 the edge of anything cut or sliced. 58 a passage, channel, path, etc., cut or hollowed out. 59 an omission or deletion, esp in a text, film, or play. 60 a reduction in price, salary, etc. 61 a decrease in government finance in a particular department or area, usually leading to a reduction of services, staff numbers, etc. 62 short for **power cut.** 63 *Chiefly US and Canadian* a quantity of timber cut during a specific time or operation. 64 *Informal* a portion or share. 65 *Informal* a straw, slip of paper, etc., used in drawing lots. 66 the manner or style in which a thing, esp a garment, is cut; fashion. 67 **a** *Irish informal* a person's general appearance: *I didn't like the cut of him.* **b** *Irish derogatory* a dirty or untidy condition: *look at the cut of your shoes.* 68 a direct route; short cut. 69 the US name for **block** (sense 15). 70 *Sport* the spin of a cut ball. 71 *Cricket* a stroke made with the bat in a roughly horizontal position. 72 *Films* an immediate transition from one shot to the next, brought about by splicing the two shots together. 73 *Informal* an individual piece of music on a record; track. 74 words or an action that hurt another person's feelings. 75 a refusal to recognize an acquaintance; snub. 76 *Informal, chiefly US* an unauthorized absence, esp from a school class. 77 *Chem* a fraction obtained in distillation, as in oil refining. 78 the metal removed in a single pass of a machine tool. 79 **a** the shape of the teeth of a file. **b** their coarseness or fineness. 80 *Brit* a stretch of water, esp a canal. 81 **a cut above.** *Informal* superior (to); better (than). ◆ See also **cut across, cut along, cutback, cut down, cut in, cut off, cut out, cut up.**
▷HISTORY C13: probably of Scandinavian origin; compare Norwegian *kutte* to cut, Icelandic *kuti* small knife

cut across VERB (*preposition*) 1 (*intr*) to be contrary to ordinary procedure or limitations: *opinion on European integration still cuts clean across party lines.* 2 to cross or traverse, making a shorter route: *she cut across the field quickly.*

cut along VERB (*intr, adverb*) *Brit informal* to hurry off.

cut-and-cover ADJECTIVE designating a method of constructing a tunnel by excavating a cutting to the required depth and then backfilling the excavation over the tunnel roof.

cut and paste NOUN a technique used in word processing by which a section of text can be moved within a document.

cut and thrust NOUN 1 *Fencing* using both the blade and the point of a sword. 2 (in argument, debate, etc.) a lively and spirited exchange of ideas or opinions.

cutaneous (kjuːˈteɪnɪəs) ADJECTIVE of, relating to, or affecting the skin.
▷HISTORY C16: from New Latin *cutāneus,* from Latin *cutis* skin; see HIDE^2
▸**cuˈtaneously** ADVERB

cutaway (ˈkʌtəˌweɪ) NOUN 1 a man's coat cut diagonally from the front waist to the back of the knees. 2 **a** a drawing or model of a machine, engine, etc., in which part of the casing is omitted to reveal the workings. **b** (*as modifier*): *a cutaway model.* 3 *Films, television* a shot separate from the main action of a scene, to emphasize something or to show simultaneous events.

cutback (ˈkʌtˌbæk) NOUN 1 a decrease or reduction. 2 another word (esp US) for **flashback.** ◆ VERB **cut back.** (*adverb*) 3 (*tr*) to shorten by cutting off the end; prune. 4 (when *intr,* foll by *on*) to reduce or make a reduction (in). 5 (*intr*) *Chiefly US* (in films) to show an event that took place earlier in the narrative; flash back.

cutch (kʌtʃ) NOUN another name for **catechu.**

Cutch (kʌtʃ) NOUN a variant spelling of **Kutch.**

cutcherry *or* **cutchery** (ˈkʌtʃərɪ) NOUN, *plural* **-cherries** *or* **-cheries.** (formerly, in India) government offices and law courts collectively.
▷HISTORY C17: from Hindi *Kachahrī*

cut down VERB (*adverb*) 1 (*tr*) to fell. 2 (when *intr,* often foll by *on*) to reduce or make a reduction (in): *to cut down on drink.* 3 (*tr*) to remake (an old garment) in order to make a smaller one. 4 (*tr*) to kill: *he was cut down in battle.* 5 **cut (a person) down to size.** to reduce in importance or decrease the conceit of.

cute (kjuːt) ADJECTIVE 1 appealing or attractive, esp in a pretty way. 2 *Informal* affecting cleverness or prettiness. 3 clever; shrewd.
▷HISTORY C18 (in the sense: clever): shortened from ACUTE
▸ˈ**cutely** ADVERB ▸ˈ**cuteness** NOUN

cutesy (ˈkjuːtsɪ) ADJECTIVE **cutesier, cutesiest.** *Informal, chiefly US* affectedly cute or coy.

cut glass NOUN 1 **a** glass, esp bowls, vases, etc., decorated by facet-cutting or grinding. **b** (*as modifier*): *a cut-glass vase.* 2 (*modifier*) (of an accent) upper-class; refined.

cuticle (ˈkjuːtɪk^{ə}l) NOUN 1 dead skin, esp that round the base of a fingernail or toenail. 2 another name for **epidermis.** 3 any covering layer or membrane. 4 the protective layer, containing cutin, that covers the epidermis of higher plants. 5 the hard protective layer covering the epidermis of many invertebrates.
▷HISTORY C17: from Latin *cutīcula* diminutive of *cutis* skin
▸**cuticular** (kjuːˈtɪkjʊlə) ADJECTIVE

cuticula (kjuːˈtɪkjʊlə) NOUN, *plural* **-lae** (-liː). *Anatomy* cuticle.
▷HISTORY C18: from Latin; see CUTICLE

cutie *or* **cutey** (ˈkjuːtɪ) NOUN *Slang* a person regarded as appealing or attractive, esp a girl or woman.

cut in VERB (*adverb*) 1 (*intr;* often foll by *on*) Also: **cut into.** to break in or interrupt. 2 (*intr*) to interrupt a dancing couple to dance with one of them. 3 (*intr*) (of a driver, motor vehicle, etc.) to draw in front of another vehicle leaving too little space. 4 (*tr*) *Informal* to allow to have a share. 5 (*intr*) to take the place of a person in a card game. ◆ NOUN **cut-in.** 6 *Films* a separate shot or scene inserted at a relevant point.

cutin (ˈkjuːtɪn) NOUN a waxy waterproof substance, consisting of derivatives of fatty acids, that is the main constituent of the plant cuticle.
▷HISTORY C19: from Latin *cutis* skin + -IN

cutinize *or* **cutinise** (ˈkjuːtɪˌnaɪz) VERB to become or cause to become covered or impregnated with cutin.
▸ˌ**cutiniˈzation** *or* ˌ**cutiniˈsation** NOUN

cutis (ˈkjuːtɪs) NOUN, *plural* **-tes** (-tiːz) *or* **-tises.** *Zoology* a technical name for the **skin.**
▷HISTORY C17: from Latin: skin

cutlass (ˈkʌtləs) NOUN a curved, one-edged sword formerly used by sailors.
▷HISTORY C16: from French *coutelas,* from *coutel* knife, from Latin *cultellus* a small knife, from *culter* knife; see COULTER

cutlass fish NOUN *US* another name for the **hairtail** (the fish).

cutler (ˈkʌtlə) NOUN a person who makes or sells cutlery.
▷HISTORY C14: from French *coutelier,* ultimately from Latin *culter* knife; see CUTLASS

cutlery (ˈkʌtlərɪ) NOUN 1 implements used for eating, such as knives, forks, and spoons. 2 instruments used for cutting. 3 the art or business of a cutler.

cutlet (ˈkʌtlɪt) NOUN 1 a piece of meat taken esp from the best end of neck of lamb, pork, etc. 2 a flat croquette of minced chicken, lobster, etc.
▷HISTORY C18: from Old French *costelette,* literally: a little rib, from *coste* rib, from Latin *costa*

cut off VERB (*tr, adverb*) 1 to remove by cutting. 2 to intercept or interrupt something, esp a telephone conversation. 3 to discontinue the supply of: *to cut off the water.* 4 to bring to an end. 5 to deprive of rights; disinherit: *she was cut off without a penny.* 6 to sever or separate: *she was cut off from her family.* 7 to occupy a position so as to prevent or obstruct (a retreat or escape). ◆ NOUN **cutoff.** 8 **a** the act of cutting off; limit or termination. **b** (*as modifier*): *the cutoff point.* 9 *Chiefly US* a route or way that is shorter than the usual one; short cut. 10 a device to terminate the flow of a fluid in a pipe or duct. 11 the remnant of metal, plastic, etc., left after parts have been machined or trimmed. Also called: **offcut.** 12 *Electronics* **a** the value of voltage, frequency, etc., below or above which an electronic device cannot function efficiently. **b** (*as modifier*): *cutoff voltage.* 13 a channel cutting across the neck of a meander, which leaves an oxbow lake. 14 another name for **oxbow** (the lake).

cut-offs (ˈkʌtɒfs) PLURAL NOUN trousers that have been shortened to calf length or to make shorts.

cut out VERB (*adverb*) 1 (*tr*) to delete or remove. 2 (*tr*) to shape or form by cutting: *to cut out a dress.* 3 (*tr; usually passive*) to suit or equip for: *you're not cut out for this job.* 4 (*intr*) (of an engine, etc.) to cease to operate suddenly. 5 (*tr*) *Printing* to remove the background from a photograph or drawing to make the outline of the subject stand out. 6 (*intr*) (of an electrical device) to switch off, usually automatically. 7 (*tr*) *Informal* to oust and supplant (a rival). 8 (*intr*) (of a person) to be excluded from a card game. 9 (*tr*) *Informal* to cease doing something, esp something undesirable (esp in the phrase **cut it out**). 10 (*tr*) *Soccer* to intercept (a pass). 11 (*tr*) to separate (cattle) from a herd. 12 (*intr*) *Austral and NZ* to end or finish: *the road cuts out at the creek.* 13 **have one's work cut out.** to have as much work as one can manage. ◆ NOUN **cutout.** 14 something that has been or is intended to be cut out from something else. 15 a photograph or drawing from which the background has been cut away. 16 a device that switches off or interrupts an electric circuit, esp a switch acting as a safety device. 17 an impressed stamp cut out from an envelope for collecting purposes. 18 *Austral slang* the end of shearing.

cut-price *or esp US* **cut-rate** ADJECTIVE 1 available at prices or rates below the standard price or rate. 2 (*prenominal*) offering goods or services at prices below the standard price: *a cut-price shop.*

cutpurse (ˈkʌtˌpɜːs) NOUN an archaic word for **pickpocket.**

CUTS (kʌts) NOUN ACRONYM FOR Computer Users' Tape System.

cut sheet feed NOUN *Computing* the automatic movement of single sheets of paper through the platen of the printer.

cut string NOUN another name for **bridgeboard.**

Cuttack (kʌˈtæk) NOUN a city in NE India, in E Orissa near the mouth of the Mahanadi River: former state capital until 1948. Pop.: 403 418 (1991).

cutter (ˈkʌtə) NOUN 1 a person or thing that cuts, esp a person who cuts cloth for clothing. 2 a sailing boat with its mast stepped further aft so as to have a larger foretriangle than that of a sloop. 3 a ship's boat, powered by oars or sail, for carrying passengers or light cargo. 4 a small lightly armed boat, as used in the enforcement of customs regulations. 5 a pig weighing between 68 and 82 kg, from which fillets and larger joints are cut.

cut-throat NOUN 1 a person who cuts throats; murderer. 2 Also called: **cut-throat razor.** *Brit* a razor with a long blade that usually folds into the handle. US name: **straight razor.** ◆ ADJECTIVE 3 bloodthirsty or murderous; cruel. 4 fierce or relentless in competition: *cut-throat prices.* 5 (of some games) played by three people: *cut-throat poker.*

cutting (ˈkʌtɪŋ) NOUN 1 a piece cut off from the main part of something. 2 *Horticulture* **a** a method of vegetative propagation in which a part of a

plant, such as a stem or leaf, is induced to form its own roots. **b** a part separated for this purpose. 3 Also called (esp US and Canadian): **clipping.** an article, photograph, etc., cut from a newspaper or other publication. 4 the editing process by which a film is cut and made. 5 an excavation in a piece of high land for a road, railway, etc., enabling it to remain at approximately the same level. 6 *Irish informal* sharp-wittedness: *there is no cutting in him.* 7 (*modifier*) designed for or adapted to cutting; edged; sharp: *a cutting tool.* ♦ ADJECTIVE 8 keen; piercing: *a cutting wind.* 9 tending to hurt the feelings: *a cutting remark.*
▸ **'cuttingly** ADVERB

cutting compound NOUN *Engineering* a mixture, such as oil, water, and soap, used for cooling drills and other cutting tools.

cutting edge NOUN the leading position in any field; forefront: *on the cutting edge of space technology.*

cutting grass NOUN a W African name for **cane rat** (sense 1).

cutting horse NOUN *US and Canadian* a saddle horse trained for use in separating an individual animal, such as a cow, from a herd.

cuttle ('kʌtᵊl) NOUN 1 short for **cuttlefish** or **cuttlebone.** 2 **little cuttle.** a small cuttlefish, *Sepiola atlantica,* often found on beaches.
▹**HISTORY** Old English *cudele;* related to Old High German *kiot* bag, Norwegian dialect *kaule* cuttle, Old English *codd* bag

cuttlebone ('kʌtᵊl,bəʊn) NOUN the internal calcareous shell of the cuttlefish, used as a mineral supplement to the diet of cage-birds and as a polishing agent.

cuttlefish ('kʌtᵊl,fɪʃ) NOUN, *plural* **-fish** *or* **-fishes.** any cephalopod mollusc of the genus *Sepia* and related genera, which occur near the bottom of inshore waters and have a broad flattened body: order *Decapoda* (decapods). Sometimes shortened to **cuttle.** See also **squid.**

cutty ('kʌtɪ) *Scot and Northern English dialect* ♦ ADJECTIVE 1 short or cut short. ♦ NOUN, *plural* **-ties.** 2 something cut short, such as a spoon or short-stemmed tobacco pipe. 3 an immoral girl or woman (in Scotland used as a general term of abuse for a woman). 4 a short thickset girl.
▹**HISTORY** C18 (Scottish and Northern English): from CUT (verb)

cutty grass NOUN a species of sedge, *Cyperus ustulatus,* of New Zealand with sharp leaves.

Cutty Sark NOUN a three-masted merchant clipper built in 1869: now kept at Greenwich, London.
▹**HISTORY** named after the witch in Robert Burns' poem *Tam O'Shanter,* who wore only a *cutty sark* (short shirt)

cutty stool NOUN (formerly, in Scotland) the church seat on which an unchaste person sat while being harangued by the minister.

cut up VERB (*tr, adverb*) 1 to cut into pieces. 2 to inflict injuries on. 3 (*usually passive*) *Informal* to affect the feelings of deeply. 4 *Informal* to subject to severe criticism. 5 *Informal* (of a driver) to overtake or pull in front of (another driver) in a dangerous manner. 6 **cut up rough.** *Brit informal* to become angry or bad-tempered. ♦ NOUN **cut-up.** 7 *Informal, chiefly US* a joker or prankster.

cut-up technique NOUN a technique of writing involving cutting up lines or pages of prose and rearranging these fragments, popularized by the novelist William Burroughs.

cutwater ('kʌt,wɔ:tə) NOUN the forward part of the stem of a vessel, which cuts through the water.

cutwork ('kʌt,wɜ:k) NOUN openwork embroidery in which the pattern is cut away from the background.

cutworm ('kʌt,wɜ:m) NOUN the caterpillar of various noctuid moths, esp those of the genus *Argrotis,* which is a pest of young crop plants in North America.

cuvée (ku:'veɪ) NOUN an individual batch or blend of wine.
▹**HISTORY** C19: from French, literally: put in a cask, from *cuve* cask

cuvette (kju:'vɛt) NOUN a shallow dish or vessel for holding liquid.
▹**HISTORY** C17: from French, diminutive of *cuve* cask, from Latin *cupa*

Cuxhaven ('kʊks,hɑ:vᵊn; *German* kʊks'ha:fən) NOUN a port in NW Germany, at the mouth of the River Elbe. Pop.: 55 250 (latest est.).

Cuyabá (*Portuguese* kuja'ba) NOUN a variant spelling of **Cuiabá.**

Cuzco (*Spanish* 'kuθko) *or* **Cusco** NOUN a city in S central Peru: former capital of the Inca Empire, with extensive Inca remains; university (1692). Pop.: 278 590 (1998 est.).

cv THE INTERNET DOMAIN NAME FOR Cap Verde.

CV ABBREVIATION FOR: 1 **curriculum vitae.** 2 (in Canada) Cross of Valour.

CVA ABBREVIATION FOR **cerebrovascular accident.**

CVO ABBREVIATION FOR Commander of the Royal Victorian Order.

CVS ABBREVIATION FOR: 1 (in Britain) Council of Voluntary Service. 2 **chorionic villus sampling.**

CW 1 *Radio* ABBREVIATION FOR **continuous waves.** ♦ NOUN 2 **a** an informal term for **Morse code. b** (*as modifier*): *his CW speed is 30 words per minute.* ♦ 3 ABBREVIATION FOR chemical weapons *or* chemical warfare.

CWA (in Australia) ABBREVIATION FOR Country Women's Association.

Cwlth ABBREVIATION FOR Commonwealth.

cwm (ku:m) NOUN 1 (in Wales) a valley. 2 *Geology* another name for **cirque** (sense 1).

Cwmbran (,ku:m'brɑ:n) NOUN a new town in SE Wales, in Torfaen county borough, developed in the 1950s. Pop.: 46 021 (1991).

c.w.o. *or* **CWO** ABBREVIATION FOR cash with order.

c-word NOUN (*sometimes capital;* preceded by *the*) a euphemistic way of referring to the word **cunt.**

CWS ABBREVIATION FOR Cooperative Wholesale Society.

cwt ABBREVIATION FOR hundredweight.
▹**HISTORY** *c,* from the Latin numeral *C* one hundred (*centum*)

CWU (in Britain) ABBREVIATION FOR Communications Workers Union.

cx THE INTERNET DOMAIN NAME FOR Christmas Island.

CY INTERNATIONAL CAR REGISTRATION FOR Cyprus.

-cy SUFFIX 1 (*forming nouns from adjectives ending in -t, -tic, -te, and -nt*) indicating state, quality, or condition: *plutocracy; lunacy; intimacy; infancy.* 2 (*forming abstract nouns from other nouns*) rank or office: *captaincy.*
▹**HISTORY** via Old French from Latin *-cia, -tia,* Greek *-kia, -tia,* abstract noun suffixes

CYA *Text messaging* ABBREVIATION FOR see you: used as a farewell in text messages, emails, etc.
▹**HISTORY** C20

cyan ('saɪæn, 'saɪən) NOUN 1 a highly saturated green-blue that is the complementary colour of red and forms, with magenta and yellow, a set of primary colours. ♦ ADJECTIVE 2 of this colour: *a cyan filter.*
▹**HISTORY** C19: from Greek *kuanos* dark blue

cyan- COMBINING FORM a variant of **cyano-** before a vowel: *cyanamide; cyanide.*

cyanamide (saɪ'ænə,maɪd, -mɪd) *or* **cyanamid** (saɪ'ænəmɪd) NOUN 1 Also called: **cyanogenamide** (,saɪənəʊ'dʒɛnə,maɪd, -mɪd). a white or colourless crystalline soluble weak dibasic acid, which can be hydrolysed to urea. Formula: H_2NCN. 2 a salt or ester of cyanamide. 3 short for **calcium cyanamide.**

cyanate ('saɪə,neɪt) NOUN any salt or ester of cyanic acid, containing the ion ^-OCN or the group –OCN.

cyanic acid (saɪ'ænɪk) NOUN a colourless poisonous volatile liquid acid that hydrolyses readily to ammonia and carbon dioxide. Formula: HOCN. Compare **isocyanic acid, fulminic acid.**

cyanide ('saɪə,naɪd) *or* **cyanid** ('saɪənɪd) NOUN 1 any salt of hydrocyanic acid. Cyanides contain the ion CN^- and are extremely poisonous. 2 another name (not in technical usage) for **nitrile.**
▸ **,cyani'dation** NOUN

cyanide process NOUN a process for recovering gold and silver from ores by treatment with a weak solution of sodium cyanide. Also called: **cyaniding.**

cyanine ('saɪə,ni:n) *or* **cyanin** ('saɪənɪn) NOUN 1 a blue dye used to extend the sensitivity of photographic emulsions to colours other than blue and ultraviolet. 2 any of a class of chemically related dyes, used for the same purpose.

cyanite ('saɪə,naɪt) NOUN a variant spelling of **kyanite.**
▸ **cyanitic** (,saɪə'nɪtɪk) ADJECTIVE

cyano- *or before a vowel* **cyan-** COMBINING FORM 1 blue or dark blue: *cyanotype.* 2 indicating cyanogen: *cyanohydrin.* 3 indicating cyanide.
▹**HISTORY** from Greek *kuanos* (adjective) dark blue, (noun) dark blue enamel, lapis lazuli

cyanobacteria (,saɪənəʊbæk'tɪərɪə) PLURAL NOUN, *singular* **-rium** (-rɪəm). a group of photosynthetic bacteria (phylum *Cyanobacteria*) containing a blue photosynthetic pigment. Former name: **blue-green algae.**

cyanocobalamin (,saɪənəʊkəʊ'bæləmɪn) NOUN a complex red crystalline compound, containing cyanide and cobalt and occurring in liver: lack of it in the tissues leads to pernicious anaemia. Formula: $C_{63}H_{88}O_{14}N_{14}PCo$. Also called: **vitamin B_{12}.**
▹**HISTORY** C20: from CYANO- + COBAL(T) + (VIT)AMIN

cyanogen (saɪ'ænədʒɪn) NOUN an extremely poisonous colourless flammable gas with an almond-like odour: has been used in chemical warfare. Formula: $(CN)_2$.
▹**HISTORY** C19: from French *cyanogène;* see CYANO-, -GEN; so named because it is one of the constituents of Prussian blue

cyanogenesis (,saɪənəʊ'dʒɛnɪsɪs) NOUN *Botany* the release by certain plants, such as cherry laurel, of hydrogen cyanide, esp after wounding or invasion by pathogens.

cyanohydrin (,saɪənəʊ'haɪdrɪn) NOUN any of a class of organic compounds containing a cyanide group and a hydroxyl group bound to the same carbon atom.

cyanophyte (saɪ'ænəfaɪt) NOUN a former name for a cyanobacterium. See **cyanobacteria.**

cyanosis (,saɪə'nəʊsɪs) NOUN *Pathol* a bluish-purple discoloration of skin and mucous membranes usually resulting from a deficiency of oxygen in the blood.
▸ **cyanotic** (,saɪə'nɒtɪk) ADJECTIVE

cyanotype (saɪ'ænə,taɪp) NOUN another name for **blueprint** (sense 1).

Cybele ('sɪbɪlɪ) NOUN *Classical myth* the Phrygian goddess of nature, mother of all living things and consort of Attis; identified with the Greek Rhea or Demeter.

cyber- COMBINING FORM indicating computers: *cyberphobia.*
▹**HISTORY** C20: back formation from CYBERNETICS

cybercafé ('saɪbə,kæfeɪ, -,kæfɪ) NOUN a café with computer equipment that gives public access to the Internet.

cybercrime ('saɪbə,kraɪm) NOUN 1 the illegal use of computers and the Internet. 2 crime committed by means of computers or the Internet.
▸ **,cyber'criminal** NOUN

cybernate ('saɪbə,neɪt) VERB to control (a manufacturing process) with a servomechanism or (of a process) to be controlled by a servomechanism.
▹**HISTORY** C20: from CYBER(NETICS) + -ATE[1]
▸ **,cyber'nation** NOUN

cybernetics (,saɪbə'nɛtɪks) NOUN (*functioning as singular*) the branch of science concerned with control systems in electronic and mechanical devices and the extent to which useful comparisons can be made between man-made and biological systems. See also **feedback** (sense 1).
▹**HISTORY** C20: from Greek *kubernētēs* steersman, from *kubernan* to steer, control
▸ **,cyber'netic** ADJECTIVE ▸ **,cyber'neticist** NOUN

cyberpet ('saɪbə,pɛt) NOUN an electronic toy that simulates the activities of a pet, requiring the owner to feed, discipline, and entertain it.

cyberphobia (,saɪbə'fəʊbɪə) NOUN an irrational fear of computers.
▸ **,cyber'phobic** ADJECTIVE

cyberpunk ('saɪbə,pʌŋk) NOUN 1 a genre of science fiction that features rebellious computer hackers and is set in a dystopian society integrated by computer networks. 2 a writer of cyberpunk.

cybersex ('saɪbə,sɛks) NOUN 1 the exchanging of sexual messages or information via the Internet. 2

sexual activity performed in hyperspace by means of virtual reality equipment.

cyberspace (ˈsaɪbəˌspeɪs) NOUN all of the data stored in a large computer or network represented as a three-dimensional model through which a virtual-reality user can move.

cybersquatting (ˈsaɪbəˌskwɒtɪŋ) NOUN the practice of registering an Internet domain name that is likely to be wanted by another person, business, or organization in the hope that it can be sold to them for a profit.
▸ **ˈcyberˌsquatter** NOUN

cyberterrorism (ˈsaɪbəˌtɛrərɪzəm) NOUN the illegal use of computers and the Internet to achieve some goal.
▸ **ˈcyberˌterrorist** NOUN

cyberwar (ˈsaɪbəˌwɔː) NOUN another term for **information warfare.**

cyborg (ˈsaɪˌbɔːg) NOUN (in science fiction) a living being whose powers are enhanced by computer implants.
▷ HISTORY C20: from *cyb(ernetic) org(anism)*

cycad (ˈsaɪkæd) NOUN any tropical or subtropical gymnosperm plant of the phylum *Cycadophyta,* having an unbranched stem with fernlike leaves crowded at the top. See also **sago palm** (sense 2).
▷ HISTORY C19: from New Latin *Cycas* name of genus, from Greek *kukas,* scribe's error for *koïkas,* from *koïx* a kind of palm, probably of Egyptian origin
▸ **ˌcycaˈdaceous** ADJECTIVE

Cyclades (ˈsɪkləˌdiːz) PLURAL NOUN a group of over 200 islands in the S Aegean Sea, forming a department of Greece. Capital: Hermoupolis (Siros). Pop.: 94 005 (1991). Area: 2572 sq. km (993 sq. miles). Modern Greek name: **Kikládhes.**

Cycladic (sɪˈklædɪk) ADJECTIVE of or relating to the Cyclades or their inhabitants.

cyclamate (ˈsaɪkləˌmeɪt, ˈsɪkləˌmeɪt) NOUN a salt or ester of cyclamic acid. Certain of the salts have a very sweet taste and were formerly used as food additives and sugar substitutes.
▷ HISTORY C20: *cycl(ohexyl-sulph)amate*

cyclamen (ˈsɪkləmən, -ˌmɛn) NOUN [1] any Old World plant of the primulaceous genus *Cyclamen,* having nodding white, pink, or red flowers, with reflexed petals. See also **sowbread.** ◆ ADJECTIVE [2] of a dark reddish-purple colour.
▷ HISTORY C16: from Medieval Latin, from Latin *cyclamīnos,* from Greek *kuklaminos,* probably from *kuklos* circle, referring to the bulb-like roots

cycle (ˈsaɪkᵊl) NOUN [1] a recurring period of time in which certain events or phenomena occur and reach completion or repeat themselves in a regular sequence. [2] a completed series of events that follows or is followed by another series of similar events occurring in the same sequence. [3] the time taken or needed for one such series. [4] a vast period of time; age; aeon. [5] a group of poems or prose narratives forming a continuous story about a central figure or event: *the Arthurian cycle.* [6] a series of miracle plays: *the Chester cycle.* [7] a group or sequence of songs (see **song cycle**). [8] short for **bicycle, tricycle, motorcycle,** etc. [9] *Astronomy* the orbit of a celestial body. [10] a recurrent series of events or processes in plants and animals: *a life cycle; a growth cycle; a metabolic cycle.* [11] *Physics* a continuous change or a sequence of changes in the state of a system that leads to the restoration of the system to its original state after a finite period of time. [12] one of a series of repeated changes in the magnitude of a periodically varying quantity, such as current or voltage. [13] *Computing* **a** a set of operations that can be both treated and repeated as a unit. **b** the time required to complete a set of operations. **c** one oscillation of the regular voltage waveform used to synchronize processes in a digital computer. [14] (in generative grammar) the set of cyclic rules. ◆ VERB [15] *(tr)* to process through a cycle or system. [16] *(intr)* to move in or pass through cycles. [17] to travel by or ride a bicycle or tricycle.
▷ HISTORY C14: from Late Latin *cyclus,* from Greek *kuklos* cycle, circle, ring, wheel; see WHEEL
▸ **ˈcycling** NOUN, ADJECTIVE

cycle of erosion NOUN the hypothetical sequence of modifications to the earth's surface by erosion, from the original uplift of the land to the ultimate low plain, usually divided into the youthful, mature, and old stages.

cyclic (ˈsaɪklɪk, ˈsɪklɪk) *or* **cyclical** (ˈsaɪklɪkᵊl, ˈsɪklɪkᵊl) ADJECTIVE [1] recurring or revolving in cycles. [2] (of an organic compound) containing a closed saturated or unsaturated ring of atoms. See also **heterocyclic** and **homocyclic.** [3] *Botany* **a** arranged in whorls: *cyclic petals.* **b** having parts arranged in this way: *cyclic flowers.* [4] *Music* of or relating to a musical form consisting of several movements sharing thematic material. [5] *Geometry* (of a polygon) having vertices that lie on a circle. [6] (in generative grammar) denoting one of a set of transformational rules all of which must apply to a clause before any one of them applies to any clause in which the first clause is embedded.
▸ **ˈcyclically** ADVERB

cyclical unemployment NOUN unemployment caused by fluctuations in the level of economic activity inherent in trade cycles.

cyclic AMP NOUN cyclic adenosine monophosphate: a constituent of biological cells, responsible for triggering processes that are dependent on hormones.

cyclic pitch lever NOUN a lever in a helicopter to change the angle of attack of individual rotor blades, causing the helicopter to move forwards, backwards, or sideways. Compare **collective pitch lever.**

cycling shorts PLURAL NOUN tight-fitting shorts reaching partway to the knee for cycling, sport, etc.

cyclist (ˈsaɪklɪst) *or US* **cycler** NOUN a person who rides or travels by bicycle, motorcycle, etc.

cyclo- *or before a vowel* **cycl-** COMBINING FORM [1] indicating a circle or ring: *cyclotron.* [2] denoting a cyclic compound: *cyclohexane.*
▷ HISTORY from Greek *kuklos* CYCLE

cycloalkane (ˌsaɪkləʊˈælkeɪn) NOUN any saturated hydrocarbon similar to an alkane but having a cyclic molecular structure and the general formula C_nH_{2n}. Also called: **cycloparaffin.**

cyclo-cross NOUN **a** a form of cycle race held over rough ground. **b** this sport.

cyclogiro (ˈsaɪkləʊˌdʒaɪrəʊ) NOUN *Aeronautics, obsolete* an aircraft lifted and propelled by pivoted blades rotating parallel to roughly horizontal transverse axes.

cyclograph (ˈsaɪkləʊˌgrɑːf, -ˌgræf) NOUN another name for **arcograph.**

cyclohexane (ˌsaɪkləʊˈhɛkseɪn, ˌsɪk-) NOUN a colourless insoluble flammable liquid cycloalkane with a pungent odour, made by hydrogenation of benzene and used as a paint remover and solvent. Formula: C_6H_{12}.

cyclohexanone (ˌsaɪkləʊˈhɛksəˌnəʊn) NOUN a colourless liquid used as a solvent for cellulose lacquers. Formula: $C_6H_{10}O$.

cycloid (ˈsaɪklɔɪd) ADJECTIVE [1] resembling a circle. [2] (of fish scales) rounded, thin, and smooth-edged, as those of the salmon. [3] *Psychiatry* (of a type of personality) characterized by exaggerated swings of mood between elation and depression. See also **cyclothymia.** ◆ NOUN [4] *Geometry* the curve described by a point on the circumference of a circle as the circle rolls along a straight line. Compare **trochoid** (sense 1). [5] a fish that has cycloid scales.
▸ **cyˈcloidal** ADJECTIVE ▸ **cyˈcloidally** ADVERB

cyclometer (saɪˈklɒmɪtə) NOUN a device that records the number of revolutions made by a wheel and hence the distance travelled.
▸ **cyˈclometry** NOUN

cyclone (ˈsaɪkləʊn) NOUN [1] another name for **depression** (sense 6). [2] a violent tropical storm; hurricane.
▷ HISTORY C19: from Greek *kuklōn* a turning around, from *kukloein* to revolve, from *kuklos* wheel
▸ **cyclonic** (saɪˈklɒnɪk) ▸ **cyˈclonical** *or* **ˈcyclonal** ADJECTIVE ▸ **cyˈclonically** ADVERB

Cyclone (ˈsaɪkləʊn) ADJECTIVE *Trademark, Austral and NZ* (of fencing) made of interlaced wire and metal.

cyclonite (ˈsaɪkləˌnaɪt) NOUN a white crystalline insoluble explosive prepared by the action of nitric acid on hexamethylenetetramine; cyclotrimethylenetrinitramine: used in bombs and shells. Formula: $C_3H_6N_6O_6$.

▷ HISTORY C20: from CYCLO- + *(trimethylene-tri)nit(ramin)e*

cycloparaffin (ˌsaɪkləʊˈpærəfɪn, ˌsɪk-) NOUN another name for **cycloalkane.**

Cyclopean (ˌsaɪkləʊˈpiːən, saɪˈkləʊpɪən) ADJECTIVE [1] of, relating to, or resembling the Cyclops. [2] denoting, relating to, or having the kind of masonry used in preclassical Greek architecture, characterized by large dry undressed blocks of stone.

cyclopedia *or* **cyclopaedia** (ˌsaɪkləʊˈpiːdɪə) NOUN a less common word for **encyclopedia.**
▸ **ˌcycloˈpedic** *or* **ˌcycloˈpaedic** ADJECTIVE ▸ **ˌcycloˈpedist** *or* **ˌcycloˈpaedist** NOUN

cyclopentadiene (ˌsaɪkləʊˌpɛntəˈdaɪiːn) NOUN a colourless liquid unsaturated cyclic hydrocarbon obtained in the cracking of petroleum hydrocarbons and the distillation of coal tar: used in the manufacture of plastics and insecticides. Formula: C_5H_6.

cyclopentane (ˌsaɪkləʊˈpɛnteɪn, ˌsɪk-) NOUN a colourless insoluble cycloalkane found in petroleum and used mainly as a solvent. Formula: C_5H_{10}.

cyclophosphamide (ˌsaɪkləʊˈfɒsfəˌmaɪd) NOUN an alkylating agent used in the treatment of leukaemia and lymphomas.
▷ HISTORY C20: from CYCLO- + PHOSPH(ORUS) + AMIDE

cycloplegia (ˌsaɪkləʊˈpliːdʒɪə, ˌsɪk-) NOUN paralysis of the muscles that adjust the shape of the lens of the eye, resulting in loss of ability to focus.
▸ **ˌcycloˈplegic** ADJECTIVE

cyclopropane (ˌsaɪkləʊˈprəʊpeɪn, ˌsɪk-) NOUN a colourless flammable gaseous hydrocarbon, used in medicine as an anaesthetic; trimethylene. It is a cycloalkane with molecules containing rings of three carbon atoms. Formula: C_3H_6; boiling pt.: –34°C.

cyclops (ˈsaɪklɒps) NOUN, *plural* **cyclops** *or* **cyclopes** (saɪˈkləʊpiːz). any copepod of the genus *Cyclops,* characterized by having one eye.

Cyclops (ˈsaɪklɒps) NOUN, *plural* **Cyclopes** (saɪˈkləʊpiːz) *or* **Cyclopses.** *Classical myth* one of a race of giants having a single eye in the middle of the forehead, encountered by Odysseus in the *Odyssey.* See also **Polyphemus.**
▷ HISTORY C15: from Latin *Cyclōps,* from Greek *Kuklōps,* literally: round eye, from *kuklos* circle + *ōps* eye

cyclorama (ˌsaɪkləʊˈrɑːmə) NOUN [1] Also called: **panorama.** a large picture, such as a battle scene, on the interior wall of a cylindrical room, designed to appear in natural perspective to a spectator in the centre. [2] *Theatre* **a** a curtain or wall curving along the back of a stage, usually painted to represent the sky and serving to enhance certain lighting effects. **b** any set of curtains that enclose the back and sides of a stage setting.
▷ HISTORY C19: CYCLO- + Greek *horama* view, sight, on the model of *panorama*
▸ **cycloramic** (ˌsaɪkləʊˈræmɪk) ADJECTIVE

cyclosis (saɪˈkləʊsɪs) NOUN, *plural* **-ses** (-siːz). *Biology* the circulation of cytoplasm or cell organelles, such as food vacuoles in some protozoans.
▷ HISTORY C19: from Greek *kuklōsis* an encircling, from *kukloun* to surround, from *kuklos* circle

cyclosporin (ˌsaɪkləʊˈspɔːrɪn) NOUN a variant spelling of **ciclosporin.**

cyclostome (ˈsaɪkləˌstəʊm, ˈsɪk-) NOUN [1] any primitive aquatic jawless vertebrate of the class *Cyclostomata,* such as the lamprey and hagfish, having a round sucking mouth and pouchlike gills. ◆ ADJECTIVE [2] of, relating to, or belonging to the class *Cyclostomata.* ◆ Also: **marsipobranch.**
▸ **cyclostomate** (saɪˈklɒstəmɪt, -ˌmeɪt) *or* **cyclostomatous** (ˌsaɪkləʊˈstɒmətəs, -ˈstəʊmə-, ˌsɪk-) ADJECTIVE

cyclostyle (ˈsaɪkləˌstaɪl) NOUN [1] a kind of pen with a small toothed wheel, used for cutting minute holes in a specially prepared stencil. Copies of the design so formed can be printed on a duplicator by forcing ink through the holes. [2] an office duplicator using a stencil prepared in this way. ◆ VERB [3] *(tr)* to print on a duplicator using such a stencil.
▸ **ˈcycloˌstyled** ADJECTIVE

cyclothymia (ˌsaɪkləʊˈθaɪmɪə, ˌsɪk-) NOUN

Psychiatry a condition characterized by periodical swings of mood between excitement and depression, activity and inactivity. See also **manic-depressive.**
▸ **ˌcycloˈthymic** *or* **ˌcycloˈthymiˌac** ADJECTIVE, NOUN

cyclotron (ˈsaɪkləˌtrɒn) NOUN a type of particle accelerator in which the particles spiral inside two D-shaped hollow metal electrodes placed facing each other under the effect of a strong vertical magnetic field, gaining energy by a high-frequency voltage applied between these electrodes.

cyder (ˈsaɪdə) NOUN a variant spelling (esp Brit) of **cider.**

Cydnus (ˈsɪdnəs) NOUN the ancient name for the (River) **Tarsus.**

cyesis (saɪˈiːsɪs) NOUN, *plural* **-ses** (-siːz). *Med* the technical name for **pregnancy.**
▹HISTORY from Greek *kuēsis*

CYF (in New Zealand) ABBREVIATION FOR Child, Youth, and Family: a section of the Ministry of Social Development.

cygnet (ˈsɪgnɪt) NOUN a young swan.
▹HISTORY C15 *sygnett,* from Old French *cygne* swan, from Latin *cygnus,* from Greek *kuknos*

Cygnus (ˈsɪgnəs) NOUN, *Latin genitive* **Cygni** (ˈsɪgnaɪ). a constellation in the N hemisphere lying between Pegasus and Draco in the Milky Way. The constellation contains the **Cygnus Loop** supernova remnant, the intense radio galaxy Cygnus A, and the intense galactic X-ray source Cygnus X–1, which is probably a black hole.
▹HISTORY Latin: swan; see CYGNET

cylinder (ˈsɪlɪndə) NOUN [1] a solid consisting of two parallel planes bounded by identical closed curves, usually circles, that are interconnected at every point by a set of parallel lines, usually perpendicular to the planes. Volume *base area* × *length.* [2] a surface formed by a line moving round a closed plane curve at a fixed angle to it. [3] any object shaped like a cylinder. [4] the chamber in a reciprocating internal-combustion engine, pump, or compressor within which the piston moves. See also **cylinder block.** [5] the rotating mechanism of a revolver, situated behind the barrel and containing cartridge chambers. [6] *Printing* any of the rotating drums on a printing press. [7] Also called: **cylinder seal.** a cylindrical seal of stone, clay, or precious stone decorated with linear designs, found in the Middle East and Balkans: dating from about 6000 B.C. [8] Also called: **hot-water cylinder.** *Brit* a vertical cylindrical tank for storing hot water, esp an insulated one made of copper used in a domestic hot-water system. [9] **firing on all cylinders.** working or performing at full capability. ◆ VERB [10] (*tr*) to provide (a system) with cylinders.
▹HISTORY C16: from Latin *cylindrus,* from Greek *kulindros* a roller, from *kulindein* to roll
▸ **ˈcylinder-ˌlike** ADJECTIVE

cylinder barrel NOUN *Engineering* the metal casting containing a cylinder of a reciprocating internal-combustion engine.

cylinder block NOUN the metal casting containing the cylinders and cooling channels or fins of a reciprocating internal-combustion engine. Sometimes shortened to **block.**

cylinder head NOUN the detachable metal casting that fits onto the top of a cylinder block. In an engine it contains part of the combustion chamber and in an overhead-valve four-stroke engine it houses the valves and their operating mechanisms. Sometimes shortened to **head.**

cylinder press NOUN *Printing* another name for **flat-bed press.**

cylindrical (sɪˈlɪndrɪkᵊl) *or* **cylindric** ADJECTIVE of, shaped like, or characteristic of a cylinder.
▸ **cyˌlindriˈcality** *or* **cyˈlindricalness** NOUN ▸ **cyˈlindrically** ADVERB

cylindrical coordinates PLURAL NOUN three coordinates defining the location of a point in three-dimensional space in terms of its polar coordinates (r, θ) in one plane, usually the (x, y) plane, and its perpendicular distance, z, measured from this plane.

cylindroid (ˈsɪlɪnˌdrɔɪd) NOUN [1] a cylinder with an elliptical cross section. ◆ ADJECTIVE [2] resembling a cylinder.

cylix (ˈsaɪlɪks, ˈsɪl-) NOUN, *plural* **-lices** (-lɪˌsiːz). a variant of **kylix.**

cyma (ˈsaɪmə) NOUN, *plural* **-mae** (-miː) *or* **-mas.** [1] either of two mouldings having a double curve, part concave and part convex. **Cyma recta** has the convex part nearer the wall and **cyma reversa** has the concave part nearer the wall. [2] *Botany* a rare variant of **cyme.**
▹HISTORY C16: from New Latin, from Greek *kuma* something swollen, from *kuein* to be pregnant

cymar (sɪˈmɑː) NOUN a woman's short fur-trimmed jacket, popular in the 17th and 18th centuries.
▹HISTORY C17: variant of *simar,* from French *simarre,* perhaps ultimately from Basque *zamar* sheepskin

cymatium (sɪˈmeɪtɪəm, -ʃɪəm) NOUN, *plural* **-tia** (-tɪə, -ʃɪə). *Architect* the top moulding of a classical cornice or entablature.
▹HISTORY C16: see CYMA

cymbal (ˈsɪmbᵊl) NOUN a percussion instrument of indefinite pitch consisting of a thin circular piece of brass, which vibrates when clashed together with another cymbal or struck with a stick.
▹HISTORY Old English *cymbala,* from Medieval Latin, from Latin *cymbalum,* from Greek *kumbalon,* from *kumbē* something hollow
▸ **ˈcymbaler, ˌcymbalˈeer,** *or* **ˈcymbalist** NOUN
▸ **ˈcymbal-ˌlike** ADJECTIVE

cymbalo (ˈsɪmbəˌləʊ) NOUN, *plural* **-los.** another name for **dulcimer.**
▹HISTORY from Italian; see CYMBAL

cyme (saɪm) NOUN an inflorescence in which the first flower is the terminal bud of the main stem and subsequent flowers develop as terminal buds of lateral stems.
▹HISTORY C18: from Latin *cȳma* cabbage sprout, from Greek *kuma* anything swollen; see CYMA
▸ **cymiferous** (saɪˈmɪfərəs) ADJECTIVE

cymene (ˈsaɪmiːn) NOUN a colourless insoluble liquid with an aromatic odour that exists in three isomeric forms; methylpropylbenzene: used as solvents and for making synthetic resins. The *para*-isomer is present in several essential oils. Formula: $CH_3C_6H_4CH(CH_3)_2$.
▹HISTORY C19: *cym-* from Greek *kuminon* CUMIN + -ENE

cymogene (ˈsaɪməˌdʒiːn) NOUN *US* a mixture of volatile flammable hydrocarbons, mainly butane, obtained in the distillation of petroleum.
▹HISTORY C19: from CYMENE + -GENE

cymograph (ˈsaɪməˌgrɑːf, -ˌgræf) NOUN [1] a variant of **kymograph.** [2] an instrument for tracing the outline of an architectural moulding.
▸ **cymographic** (ˌsaɪməˈgræfɪk) ADJECTIVE

cymoid (ˈsaɪmɔɪd) ADJECTIVE *Architect, botany* resembling a cyme or cyma.

cymophane (ˈsaɪməˌfeɪn) NOUN a yellow or green opalescent variety of chrysoberyl.
▹HISTORY C19: from Greek *kuma* wave, undulation + -PHANE

cymose (ˈsaɪməʊs, -məʊz, saɪˈməʊs) ADJECTIVE having the characteristics of a cyme.
▸ **ˈcymosely** ADVERB

Cymric *or* **Kymric** (ˈkɪmrɪk) NOUN [1] the Welsh language. [2] the Brythonic group of Celtic languages. [3] a breed of medium-sized cat with soft semi-long hair. ◆ ADJECTIVE [4] of or relating to the Cymry, any of their languages, Wales, or the Welsh.

Cymru (*Welsh* kumˈri) NOUN the Welsh name for **Wales.**

Cymry *or* **Kymry** (ˈkɪmrɪ) NOUN **the.** (*functioning as plural*) [1] the Brythonic branch of the Celtic people, comprising the present-day Welsh, Cornish, and Bretons. See **Brythonic.** [2] the Welsh people.
▹HISTORY Welsh: the Welsh

cynghanedd (kʌŋˈhaneð) NOUN a complex system of rhyme and alliteration used in Welsh verse.
▹HISTORY from Welsh

cynic (ˈsɪnɪk) NOUN [1] a person who believes the worst about people or the outcome of events. ◆ ADJECTIVE [2] a less common word for **cynical.** [3] *Astronomy* of or relating to Sirius, the Dog Star.
▹HISTORY C16: via Latin from Greek *Kunikos,* from *kuōn* dog

Cynic (ˈsɪnɪk) NOUN a member of a sect founded by Antisthenes that scorned worldly things and held that self-control was the key to the only good.

cynical (ˈsɪnɪkᵊl) ADJECTIVE [1] distrustful or contemptuous of virtue, esp selflessness in others; believing the worst of others, esp that all acts are selfish. [2] sarcastic; mocking. [3] showing contempt for accepted standards of behaviour, esp of honesty or morality: *the politician betrayed his promises in a cynical way.*
▸ **ˈcynically** ADVERB ▸ **ˈcynicalness** NOUN

cynicism (ˈsɪnɪˌsɪzəm) NOUN [1] the attitude or beliefs of a cynic. [2] a cynical action, remark, idea, etc.

Cynicism (ˈsɪnɪˌsɪzəm) NOUN the doctrines of the Cynics.

cyno- COMBINING FORM indicating a dog: *cynopodous; cynophobia.*
▹HISTORY from Greek *kuōn* dog

cynodont (ˈsaɪnəˌdɒnt) NOUN a carnivorous mammal-like reptile of the late Permian and Triassic perods, whose specialized teeth were well developed.

cynophobia (ˌsaɪnəˈfəʊbɪə) NOUN an irrational fear of dogs.

cynopodous (saɪˈnɒpədəs) ADJECTIVE (of some mammals, such as dogs) having claws that do not retract.
▹HISTORY from New Latin, from CYNO- + -PODOUS

cynosure (ˈsɪnəˌzjʊə, -ʃʊə) NOUN [1] a person or thing that attracts notice, esp because of its brilliance or beauty. [2] something that serves as a guide.
▹HISTORY C16: from Latin *Cynosūra* the constellation of Ursa Minor, from Greek *Kunosoura,* from CYNO- + *oura* tail
▸ **ˌcynoˈsural** ADJECTIVE

Cynthia (ˈsɪnθɪə) NOUN another name for **Artemis** (Diana).

cyperaceous (ˌsaɪpəˈreɪʃəs) ADJECTIVE of, relating to, or belonging to the *Cyperaceae,* a family of grasslike flowering plants with solid triangular stems, including the sedges, bulrush, cotton grass, and certain rushes. Some are grown as water plants or as ornamental grasses; and *Cyperus papyrus* is the papyrus plant. Compare **juncaceous.**
▹HISTORY C19: from New Latin *Cypērus* type genus, from Latin *cypēros* a kind of rush, from Greek *kupeiros* marsh plant, probably of Semitic origin

cypher (ˈsaɪfə) NOUN, VERB a variant spelling of **cipher.**

cy pres (siː ˈpreɪ) NOUN *Law* the doctrine that the intention of a donor or testator should be carried out as closely as practicable when literal compliance is impossible.
▹HISTORY C15: from Anglo-French, literally: as near (as possible, etc.)

cypress[1] (ˈsaɪprəs) NOUN [1] any coniferous tree of the N temperate genus *Cupressus,* having dark green scalelike leaves and rounded cones: family *Cupressaceae.* See also **Leyland cypress.** [2] any of several similar and related trees, such as the widely cultivated *Chamaecyparis lawsoniana* (**Lawson's cypress**), of the western US. [3] any of various other coniferous trees, esp the swamp cypress. [4] the wood of any of these trees.
▹HISTORY Old English *cypresse,* from Latin *cyparissus,* from Greek *kuparissos;* related to Latin *cupressus*

cypress[2] *or* **cyprus** (ˈsaɪprəs) NOUN a fabric, esp a fine silk, lawn, or crepelike material, often black and worn as mourning.
▹HISTORY C14 *cyprus* from the island of CYPRUS

cypress pine NOUN any coniferous tree of the Australian genus *Callitrus,* having leaves in whorls and yielding valuable timber: family *Cupressaceae.*

cypress vine NOUN a tropical American convolvulaceous climbing plant, *Ipomoea pennata,* having finely divided compound leaves and scarlet or white tubular flowers.

Cyprian (ˈsɪprɪən) ADJECTIVE [1] of or relating to Cyprus. [2] of or resembling the ancient orgiastic worship of Aphrodite on Cyprus. ◆ NOUN [3] (*often not capital*) *Obsolete* a licentious person, esp a prostitute or dancer. ◆ NOUN, ADJECTIVE [4] another word for **Cypriot.**

cyprinid (sɪˈpraɪnɪd, ˈsɪprɪnɪd) NOUN [1] any teleost fish of the mainly freshwater family *Cyprinidae,*

typically having toothless jaws and cycloid scales and including such food and game fishes as the carp, tench, roach, rudd, and dace. ◆ ADJECTIVE [2] of, relating to, or belonging to the *Cyprinidae.* [3] resembling a carp; cyprinoid.
▷**HISTORY** C19: from New Latin *Cyprīnidae,* from Latin *cyprīnus* carp, from Greek *kuprinos*

cyprinodont (sɪˈprɪnəˌdɒnt, sɪˈpraɪ-) NOUN [1] any small tropical or subtropical soft-finned fish of the mostly marine family *Cyprinodontidae,* resembling carp but having toothed jaws. The group includes the guppy, killifish, swordtail, and topminnow. ◆ ADJECTIVE [2] of, relating to, or belonging to the *Cyprinodontidae.*
▷**HISTORY** C19: from Latin *cyprīnus* carp (see CYPRINID) + -ODONT

cyprinoid (ˈsɪprɪˌnɔɪd, sɪˈpraɪnɔɪd) ADJECTIVE [1] of, relating to, or belonging to the *Cyprinoidea,* a large suborder of teleost fishes including the cyprinids, characins, electric eels, and loaches. [2] of, relating to, or resembling the carp. ◆ NOUN [3] any fish belonging to the *Cyprinoidea.*
▷**HISTORY** C19: from Latin *cyprīnus* carp

Cypriot (ˈsɪprɪət) *or* **Cypriote** (ˈsɪprɪˌəʊt) NOUN [1] a native, citizen, or inhabitant of Cyprus. [2] the dialect of Ancient or Modern Greek spoken in Cyprus. ◆ ADJECTIVE [3] denoting or relating to Cyprus, its inhabitants, or dialects.

cypripedium (ˌsɪprɪˈpiːdɪəm) NOUN [1] any orchid of the genus *Cypripedium,* having large flowers with an inflated pouchlike lip. See also **lady's-slipper.** [2] any cultivated tropical orchid of the genus *Paphiopedilum,* having yellow, green, or brownish-purple waxy flowers.
▷**HISTORY** C18: from New Latin, from Latin *Cypria* the Cyprian, that is, Venus + *pēs* foot (that is, Venus' slipper)

Cyprus (ˈsaɪprəs) NOUN an island in the E Mediterranean: ceded to Britain by Turkey in 1878 and made a colony in 1925; became an independent republic in 1960 as a member of the Commonwealth; invaded by Turkey in 1974 following a Greek-supported military coup, leading to the virtual partition of the island. In 1983 the Turkish-controlled northern sector declared itself to be an independent state as the Turkish Republic of Northern Cyprus but failed to receive international recognition. Attempts by the U.N. to broker a reunification agreement have failed. Languages: Greek and Turkish. Religions: Greek Orthodox and Muslim. Currency: pound and Turkish lira. Capital: Nicosia. Pop. (Greek): 675 000 (2001 est.); (Turkish): 198 000 (2001 est.). Area: 9251 sq. km (3571 sq. miles).

cypsela (ˈsɪpsɪlə) NOUN, *plural* **-lae** (-ˌliː). the dry one-seeded fruit of the daisy and related plants, which resembles an achene but is surrounded by a calyx sheath.
▷**HISTORY** C19: from New Latin, from Greek *kupselē* chest, hollow vessel

Cyrenaic (ˌsaɪrəˈneɪɪk, ˌsɪrə-) ADJECTIVE [1] (in the ancient world) of or relating to the city of Cyrene or the territory of Cyrenaica. [2] of or relating to the philosophical school founded by the Greek philosopher Aristippus (?435–?356 B.C.) in Cyrene that held pleasure to be the highest good. ◆ NOUN [3] an inhabitant of Cyrene or Cyrenaica. [4] a follower of the Cyrenaic school of philosophy.

Cyrenaica *or* **Cirenaica** (ˌsaɪrəˈneɪɪkə, ˌsɪrə-) NOUN a region and former province (1951–63) of E Libya: largely desert; settled by the Greeks in about 630 B.C.; ruled successively by the Egyptians, Romans, Arabs, Turks, and Italians. Area: 855 370 sq. km (330 258 sq. miles).

Cyrene (saɪˈriːnɪ) NOUN an ancient Greek city of N Africa, near the coast of Cyrenaica: famous for its medical school.

Cyrillic (sɪˈrɪlɪk) ADJECTIVE [1] denoting or relating to the alphabet derived from that of the Greeks, supposedly by Saint Cyril, for the writing of Slavonic languages: now used primarily for Russian, Bulgarian, and the Serbian dialect of Serbo-Croat. ◆ NOUN [2] this alphabet.

cyst (sɪst) NOUN [1] *Pathol* any abnormal membranous sac or blisterlike pouch containing fluid or semisolid material. [2] *Anatomy* any normal sac or vesicle in the body. [3] a thick-walled protective membrane enclosing a cell, larva, or organism.
▷**HISTORY** C18: from New Latin *cystis,* from Greek *kustis* pouch, bag, bladder

-cyst NOUN COMBINING FORM indicating a bladder or sac: *otocyst.*
▷**HISTORY** from Greek *kustis* bladder

cystectomy (sɪˈstɛktəmɪ) NOUN, *plural* **-mies.** [1] surgical removal of the gall bladder or of part of the urinary bladder. [2] surgical removal of any abnormal cyst.

cysteine (ˈsɪstɪˌiːn, -ɪn) NOUN a sulphur-containing amino acid, present in proteins, that oxidizes on exposure to air to form cystine. Formula: $HSCH_2CH(NH_2)COOH$.
▷**HISTORY** C19: variant of CYSTINE
▸ˌcysteˈinic ADJECTIVE

cystic (ˈsɪstɪk) ADJECTIVE [1] of, relating to, or resembling a cyst. [2] having or enclosed within a cyst; encysted. [3] relating to the gall bladder or urinary bladder.

cysticercoid (ˌsɪstɪˈsɜːkɔɪd) NOUN the larva of any of certain tapeworms, which resembles a cysticercus but has a smaller bladder.

cysticercus (ˌsɪstɪˈsɜːkəs) NOUN, *plural* **-ci** (-saɪ). an encysted larval form of many tapeworms, consisting of a head (scolex) inverted in a fluid-filled bladder. See also **hydatid** (sense 1), **coenurus.**
▷**HISTORY** C19: from New Latin, from Greek *kustis* pouch, bladder + *kerkos* tail

cystic fibrosis NOUN an inheritable disease of the exocrine glands, controlled by a recessive gene: affected children inherit defective alleles from both parents. It is characterized by chronic infection of the respiratory tract and by pancreatic insufficiency.

cystine (ˈsɪstiːn, -tɪn) NOUN a sulphur-containing amino acid present in proteins: yields two molecules of cysteine on reduction. Formula: $HOOCCH(NH_2)CH_2SSCH_2CH(NH_2)COOH$.
▷**HISTORY** C19: see CYSTO- (bladder), -INE²; named from its being discovered in a type of urinary calculus

cystitis (sɪˈstaɪtɪs) NOUN inflammation of the urinary bladder.

cysto- *or before a vowel* **cyst-** COMBINING FORM indicating a cyst or bladder: *cystocarp; cystoscope.*

cystocarp (ˈsɪstəˌkɑːp) NOUN a reproductive body in red algae, developed after fertilization and consisting of filaments bearing carpospores.
▸ˌcystoˈcarpic ADJECTIVE

cystocele (ˈsɪstəˌsiːl) NOUN *Pathol* a hernia of the urinary bladder, esp one protruding into the vagina.

cystogenous (sɪsˈtɒdʒɪnəs) ADJECTIVE *Biology* forming or secreting cysts.

cystography (sɪsˈtɒgrəfɪ) NOUN radiography of the urinary bladder using a contrast medium.

cystoid (ˈsɪstɔɪd) ADJECTIVE [1] resembling a cyst or bladder. ◆ NOUN [2] a tissue mass, such as a tumour, that resembles a cyst but lacks an outer membrane.

cystolith (ˈsɪstəlɪθ) NOUN [1] a knoblike deposit of calcium carbonate in the epidermal cells of such plants as the stinging nettle. [2] *Pathol* a urinary calculus.

cystoscope (ˈsɪstəˌskəʊp) NOUN a slender tubular medical instrument for examining the interior of the urethra and urinary bladder.
▸**cystoscopic** (ˌsɪstəˈskɒpɪk) ADJECTIVE ▸**cystoscopy** (sɪsˈtɒskəpɪ) NOUN

cystotomy (sɪˈstɒtəmɪ) NOUN, *plural* **-mies.** [1] surgical incision into the gall bladder or urinary bladder. [2] surgical incision into the capsule of the lens of the eye.

-cyte NOUN COMBINING FORM indicating a cell: *spermatocyte.*
▷**HISTORY** from New Latin *-cyta,* from Greek *kutos* container, body, hollow vessel

Cythera (sɪˈθɪərə) NOUN [1] a Greek island off the SE coast of the Peloponnese: in ancient times a centre of the worship of Aphrodite. Pop.: 3500 (latest est.). Area: about 285 sq. km (110 sq. miles). [2] the chief town of this island, on the S coast. Pop.: 300 (latest est.). ◆ Modern Greek name: **Kíthira.**

Cytherea (ˌsɪθəˈriːə) NOUN another name for **Aphrodite** (Venus).
▸ˌCytherˈean ADJECTIVE

cytidine (ˈsɪtɪˌdaɪn) NOUN *Biochem* a nucleoside formed by the condensation of cytosine and ribose.
▷**HISTORY** C20: from CYTO- + -IDE + -INE²

cytidylic acid (ˌsɪtɪˈdɪlɪk) NOUN a nucleotide consisting of cytosine, ribose or deoxyribose, and a phosphate group. It is a constituent of DNA or RNA. Also called: **cytidine monophosphate.**

cyto- COMBINING FORM indicating a cell: *cytolysis; cytoplasm.*
▷**HISTORY** from Greek *kutos* vessel, container; related to *kuein* to contain

cytochemistry (ˌsaɪtəʊˈkɛmɪstrɪ) NOUN the chemistry of living cells.
▸ˌcytoˈchemical ADJECTIVE

cytochrome (ˈsaɪtəʊˌkrəʊm) NOUN any of a group of naturally occurring compounds, consisting of iron, a protein, and a porphyrin, that are important in cell oxidation-reduction reactions.

cytochrome reductase NOUN another name for **flavoprotein.**

cytogenesis (ˌsaɪtəʊˈdʒɛnɪsɪs) *or* **cytogeny** (saɪˈtɒdʒənɪ) NOUN the origin and development of plant and animal cells.

cytogenetics (ˌsaɪtəʊdʒɪˈnɛtɪks) NOUN (*functioning as singular*) the branch of genetics that correlates the structure, number, and behaviour of chromosomes with heredity and variation.
▸ˌcytogeˈnetic ADJECTIVE ▸ˌcytogeˈnetically ADVERB ▸ˌcytogeˈneticist NOUN

cytokine (ˈsaɪtəʊˌkaɪn) NOUN any of various proteins, secreted by cells, that carry signals to neighbouring cells. Cytokines include interferon.

cytokinesis (ˌsaɪtəʊkɪˈniːsɪs, -kaɪ-) NOUN division of the cytoplasm of a cell, occurring at the end of mitosis or meiosis.

cytokinin (ˌsaɪtəʊˈkaɪnɪn) NOUN any of a group of plant hormones that promote cell division and retard ageing in plants. Also called: **kinin.**

cytology (saɪˈtɒlədʒɪ) NOUN [1] the study of plant and animal cells, including their structure, function, and formation. [2] the detailed structure of a tissue, as revealed by microscopic examination.
▸**cytological** (ˌsaɪtəˈlɒdʒɪkᵊl) ADJECTIVE ▸ˌcytoˈlogically ADVERB ▸cyˈtologist NOUN

cytolysin (saɪˈtɒlɪsɪn) NOUN a substance that can partially or completely destroy animal cells.

cytolysis (saɪˈtɒlɪsɪs) NOUN *Cytology* the dissolution of cells, esp by the destruction of their membranes.
▸**cytolytic** (ˌsaɪtəˈlɪtɪk) ADJECTIVE

cytomegalovirus (ˌsaɪtəʊˈmɛgələʊˌvaɪrəs) NOUN a virus of the herpes virus family that may cause serious disease in patients whose immune systems are compromised. Abbreviation: **CMV.**

cytoplasm (ˈsaɪtəʊˌplæzəm) NOUN the protoplasm of a cell contained within the cell membrane but excluding the nucleus: contains organelles, vesicles, and other inclusions.
▸ˌcytoˈplasmic ADJECTIVE

cytosine (ˈsaɪtəsɪn) NOUN a white crystalline pyrimidine occurring in nucleic acids; 6-amino-2-hydroxy pyrimidine. Formula: $C_4H_5N_3O$. See also **DNA, RNA.**

cytoskeleton (ˈsaɪtəʊˌskɛlɪtən) NOUN a network of fibrous proteins that governs the shape and movement of a biological cell.

cytosol (ˈsaɪtəʊˌsɒl) NOUN the solution of proteins and metabolites inside a biological cell, in which the organelles are suspended.

cytotaxis (ˌsaɪtəʊˈtæksɪs) NOUN *Biology* movement of cells due to external stimulation.

cytotaxonomy (ˌsaɪtəʊtækˈsɒnəmɪ) NOUN classification of organisms based on cell structure, esp the number, shape, etc., of the chromosomes.
▸ˌcytoˌtaxoˈnomic ADJECTIVE ▸ˌcytotaxˈonomist NOUN

cytotoxic (ˌsaɪtəʊˈtɒksɪk) ADJECTIVE poisonous to living cells: denoting certain drugs used in the treatment of leukaemia and other cancers.
▸**cytotoxicity** (ˌsaɪtəʊtɒkˈsɪsɪtɪ) NOUN

cytotoxin (ˌsaɪtəʊˈtɒksɪn) NOUN any substance that is poisonous to living cells.

Cyzicus (ˈsɪzɪkəs) NOUN an ancient Greek colony in NW Asia Minor on the S shore of the Sea of

Marmara: site of Alcibiades' naval victory over the Peloponnesians (410 B.C.).

cz THE INTERNET DOMAIN NAME FOR Czech Republic.

CZ INTERNATIONAL CAR REGISTRATION FOR the Czech Republic.

czar (zɑː) NOUN a variant spelling (esp US) of **tsar**.
▸ **'czardom** NOUN

czardas ('tʃɑːdæʃ) NOUN [1] a Hungarian national dance of alternating slow and fast sections. [2] a piece of music composed for or in the rhythm of this dance.
▷HISTORY from Hungarian *csárdás*

czarevitch ('zɑːrɪvɪtʃ) NOUN a variant spelling (esp US) of **tsarevitch**.

czarevna (zɑː'rɛvnə) NOUN a variant spelling (esp US) of **tsarevna**.

czarina (zɑː'riːnə) *or* **czaritza** (zɑː'rɪtsə) NOUN variant spellings (esp US) of **tsarina** or **tsaritsa**.

czarism ('zɑːrɪzəm) NOUN a variant spelling (esp US) of **tsarism**.

czarist ('zɑːrɪst) ADJECTIVE, NOUN a variant spelling (esp US) of **tsarist**.

Czech (tʃɛk) ADJECTIVE [1] **a** of, relating to, or characteristic of the Czech Republic, its people, or its language. **b** of, relating to, or characteristic of Bohemia and Moravia, their people, or their language. **c** (loosely) of, relating to, or characteristic of the former Czechoslovakia or its people. ◆ NOUN [2] the official language of the Czech Republic, belonging to the West Slavonic branch of the Indo-European family; also spoken in Slovakia. Czech and Slovak are closely related and mutually intelligible. [3] **a** a native or inhabitant of the Czech Republic. **b** a native or inhabitant of Bohemia or Moravia. **c** (loosely) a native, inhabitant, or citizen of the former Czechoslovakia.
▷HISTORY C19: from Polish, from Czech *Čech*

Czechoslovak (ˌtʃɛkəʊ'sləʊvæk) ADJECTIVE [1] of, relating to, or characteristic of the former Czechoslovakia, its peoples, or their languages. ◆ NOUN [2] (loosely) either of the two mutually intelligible languages of the former Czechoslovakia; Czech or Slovak.

Czechoslovakia (ˌtʃɛkəʊsləʊ'vækɪə) NOUN a former republic in central Europe: formed after the defeat of Austria-Hungary (1918) as a nation of Czechs in Bohemia and Moravia and Slovaks in Slovakia; occupied by Germany from 1939 until its liberation by the Soviet Union in 1945; became a people's republic under the Communists in 1948; invaded by Warsaw Pact troops in 1968, ending Dubček's attempt to liberalize communism; in 1989 popular unrest led to the resignation of the politburo and the formation of a non-Communist government. It consisted of two federal republics, the **Czech Republic** and the **Slovak Republic**, which became independent in 1993. Czech name: **Československo**.

Czechoslovakian (ˌtʃɛkəʊsləʊ'vækɪən) ADJECTIVE [1] of, relating to, or characteristic of the former republic of Czechoslovakia, its peoples, or their languages. ◆ NOUN [2] a native or inhabitant of the former republic of Czechoslovakia.

Czech Republic NOUN a country in central Europe; formed part of Czechoslovakia until 1993; mostly wooded, with lowlands surrounding the River Morava, rising to the Bohemian plateau in the W and to highlands in the N. Language: Czech. Religion: Christian majority. Currency: koruna. Capital Prague. Pop.: 10 269 000 (2001 est.). Area: 78 864 sq. km (30 450 sq. miles).

Czernowitz ('tʃɛrnovɪts) NOUN the German name for **Chernovtsy**.

Częstochowa (*Polish* tʃɛ̃stɔ'ɔxva) NOUN an industrial city in S Poland, on the River Warta: pilgrimage centre. Pop.: 257 812 (1999 est.).

Dd

d *or* **D** (di:) NOUN, *plural* **d's, D's** *or* **Ds.** [1] the fourth letter and third consonant of the modern English alphabet. [2] a speech sound represented by this letter, usually a voiced alveolar stop, as in *dagger.* [3] the semicircle on a billiards table having a radius of 11½ inches and its straight edge in the middle of the baulk line.

d SYMBOL FOR: [1] *Physics* density or relative density. [2] *Maths* a small increment in a given variable or function: used to indicate a derivative of one variable with respect to another, as in dy/dx. [3] *Chess* See **algebraic notation.**

D SYMBOL FOR: [1] *Music* **a** a note having a frequency of 293.66 hertz (**D above middle C**) or this value multiplied or divided by any power of 2; the second note of the scale of C major. **b** a key, string, or pipe producing this note. **c** the major or minor key having this note as its tonic. [2] *Chem* deuterium. [3] *Maths* the first derivative of a function, as in $D(x^3 + x^2) = 3x^2 + 2x$. [4] *Physics* **a** dispersion. **b** electric displacement. [5] *Aeronautics* drag. [6] **a** a semiskilled or unskilled manual worker, or a trainee or apprentice to a skilled worker. **b** (*as modifier*): *D worker.* See also **occupation groupings.** ◆ ABBREVIATION FOR: [7] *Austral informal* defence: *I'm playing D in the match this afternoon.* [8] *Austral informal* defensive play. ◆ [9] THE ROMAN NUMERAL FOR 500. See **Roman numerals.** ◆ [10] INTERNATIONAL CAR REGISTRATION FOR Germany.
▷HISTORY (for sense 10) from German *Deutschland*

D *or* **D.** ABBREVIATION FOR Deutsch: indicating the serial number in the catalogue (1951) of the musical compositions of Schubert made by Otto Deutsch (1883–1967).

2,4-D NOUN a synthetic auxin widely used as a weedkiller; 2,4-dichlorophenoxyacetic acid.

d. ABBREVIATION FOR: [1] (in animal pedigrees) dam. [2] daughter. [3] *Brit currency before decimalization* penny *or* pennies. [Latin *denarius*] [4] diameter. [5] died. [6] dinar(s). [7] dollar(s). [8] drachma(s).

D. ABBREVIATION FOR: [1] *US politics* Democrat(ic). [2] *Government* Department. [3] dinar(s). [4] Don (a Spanish title). [5] Duchess. [6] Duke. [7] (in the US and Canada) Doctor.

'd CONTRACTION OF would *or* had: *I'd; you'd.*

DA ABBREVIATION FOR: [1] (in the US) District Attorney. [2] Diploma of Art. [3] duck's arse (hairstyle).

D/A *or* **d.a.** ABBREVIATION FOR: [1] deposit account. [2] *Commerce* documents against acceptance.

DAB ABBREVIATION FOR digital audio broadcasting.

dab¹ (dæb) VERB **dabs, dabbing, dabbed.** [1] to touch lightly and quickly. [2] (*tr*) to daub with short tapping strokes: *to dab the wall with paint.* [3] (*tr*) to apply (paint, cream, etc.) with short tapping strokes. ◆ NOUN [4] a small amount, esp of something soft or moist: *a dab of ink.* [5] a small light stroke or tap, as with the hand. [6] (*often plural*) *Chiefly Brit* a slang word for **fingerprint.**
▷HISTORY C14: of imitative origin

dab² (dæb) NOUN [1] a small common European brown flatfish, *Limanda limanda,* covered with rough toothed scales: family *Pleuronectidae:* a food fish. [2] (*often plural*) any of various other small flatfish, esp flounders. ◆ Compare **sand dab.**
▷HISTORY C15: from Anglo-French *dabbe,* of uncertain origin

dab³ (dæb) NOUN *Brit informal* See **dab hand.**
▷HISTORY C17: perhaps from DAB¹ (verb)

dabber ('dæbə) NOUN [1] a pad used by printers for applying ink by hand. [2] a felt-tip pen with a very broad writing point, used especially by bingo players to cancel numbers on their cards.

dabble ('dæbᵊl) VERB [1] to dip, move, or splash (the fingers, feet, etc.) in a liquid. [2] (*intr; usually foll by in, with,* or *at*) to deal (with) or work (at) frivolously or superficially; play (at). [3] (*tr*) to daub, mottle, splash, or smear: *his face was dabbled with paint.*
▷HISTORY C16: probably from Dutch *dabbelen;* see DAB¹
▸'**dabbler** NOUN

dabchick ('dæb,tʃɪk) NOUN any of several small grebes of the genera *Podiceps* and *Podilymbus,* such as *Podiceps ruficollis* of the Old World.
▷HISTORY C16: probably from Old English *dop* to dive + CHICK; see DEEP, DIP

dab hand NOUN *Brit informal* a person who is particularly skilled at something; expert: *a dab hand at chess.*

dabster ('dæbstə) NOUN [1] *Brit* a dialect word for **dab hand.** [2] *US informal* an incompetent or amateurish worker; bungler.
▷HISTORY C18: from DAB¹ + -STER

da capo (dɑː 'kɑːpəʊ) ADJECTIVE, ADVERB *Music* to be repeated (in whole or part) from the beginning. Abbreviation: **DC.** See also **fine³.**
▷HISTORY C18: from Italian, literally: from the head

Dacca ('dækə) NOUN the former name (until 1982) of **Dhaka.**

dace (deɪs) NOUN, *plural* **dace** *or* **daces.** [1] a European freshwater cyprinid fish, *Leuciscus leuciscus,* with a slender bluish-green body. [2] any of various similar fishes.
▷HISTORY C15: from Old French *dars* DART, probably referring to its swiftness

dacha *or* **datcha** ('dætʃə) NOUN a country house or cottage in Russia.
▷HISTORY from Russian: a giving, gift

Dachau (*German* 'daxau) NOUN a town in S Germany, in Bavaria: site of a Nazi concentration camp. Pop.: 33 200 (latest est.).

dachshund ('dæks,hʊnd; *German* 'dakshʊnt) NOUN a long-bodied short-legged breed of dog.
▷HISTORY C19: from German, from *Dachs* badger + *Hund* dog, HOUND¹

Dacia ('deɪsɪə) NOUN an ancient region bounded by the Carpathians, the Tisza, and the Danube, roughly corresponding to modern Romania. United under kings from about 60 B.C., it later contained the Roman province of the same name (about 105 to 270 A.D.).
▸'**Dacian** ADJECTIVE, NOUN

dack (dæk) VERB (*tr*) *Austral informal* to remove the trousers from (someone) by force.

dacks (dæks) PLURAL NOUN *Austral* another word for **daks.**

dacoit (də'kɔɪt) NOUN (in India and Myanmar) a member of a gang of armed robbers.
▷HISTORY C19: from Hindi *dakait,* from *dākā* robbery

dacoity (də'kɔɪtɪ) NOUN, *plural* **-coities.** (in India and Myanmar) robbery by an armed gang.

Dacron ('deɪkrɒn, 'dæk-) NOUN the US name (trademark) for **Terylene.**

dactyl ('dæktɪl) NOUN [1] Also called: **dactylic.** *Prosody* a metrical foot of three syllables, one long followed by two short (–˘˘). Compare **bacchius.** [2] *Zoology* any digit of a vertebrate.
▷HISTORY C14: via Latin from Greek *daktulos* finger, dactyl, comparing the finger's three joints to the three syllables

dactylic (dæk'tɪlɪk) ADJECTIVE [1] of, relating to, or having a dactyl: *dactylic verse.* ◆ NOUN [2] a variant of **dactyl** (sense 1).
▸**dac'tylically** ADVERB

dactylo- *or before a vowel* **dactyl-** COMBINING FORM finger or toe: *dactylogram.*
▷HISTORY from Greek *daktulos* finger

dactylogram (dæk'tɪlə,græm) NOUN *Chiefly US* a technical term for **fingerprint.**

dactylography (,dæktɪ'lɒgrəfɪ) NOUN *Chiefly US* the scientific study of fingerprints for purposes of identification.
▸,**dacty'lographer** NOUN ▸**dactylographic** (dæk,tɪlə'græfɪk) ADJECTIVE

dactylology (,dæktɪ'lɒlədʒɪ) NOUN, *plural* **-gies.** the method of using manual sign language, as in communicating with deaf people.

dad (dæd) NOUN an informal word for **father.**
▷HISTORY C16: childish word; compare Greek *tata,* Sanskrit *tatas*

Dada ('dɑːdɑː) *or* **Dadaism** ('dɑːdɑː,ɪzəm) NOUN a nihilistic artistic movement of the early 20th century in W Europe and the US, founded on principles of irrationality, incongruity, and irreverence towards accepted aesthetic criteria.
▷HISTORY C20: from French, from a children's word for hobbyhorse, the name being arbitrarily chosen
▸'**Dadaist** NOUN, ADJECTIVE ▸,**Dada'istic** ADJECTIVE
▸,**Dada'istically** ADVERB

dadah ('dɑː,dɑː) NOUN *Austral slang* illegal drugs.
▷HISTORY Malay: medicinal herb

Dad and Dave (dæd ən deɪv) NOUN *Austral* stereotypes of the unsophisticated rural dweller before World War II.
▷HISTORY from characters in the stories of Steele Rudd, pen name of Arthur Hoey Davis (1868–1935), Australian author

daddy ('dædɪ) NOUN, *plural* **-dies.** [1] an informal word for **father.** [2] **the daddy.** *Slang, chiefly US, Canadian, and Austral* the supreme or finest example: *the daddy of them all.* [3] *Slang* the dominant male in a group; boss; top man.

daddy-longlegs NOUN [1] *Brit* an informal name for a **crane fly.** [2] *Austral, US, and Canadian* an informal name for **harvestman** (sense 2).

dado ('deɪdəʊ) NOUN, *plural* **-does** *or* **-dos.** [1] the lower part of an interior wall that is decorated differently from the upper part. [2] *Architect* the part of a pedestal between the base and the cornice. ◆ VERB [3] (*tr*) to provide with a dado.
▷HISTORY C17: from Italian: die, die-shaped pedestal, perhaps from Arabic *dad* game

Dadra and Nagar Haveli (də'drɑː 'nʌgə ə'vɛlɪ) NOUN a union territory of W India, on the Gulf of Cambay: until 1961 administratively part of Portuguese Damão. Capital: Silvassa. Pop.: 220 451 (2001). Area: 489 sq. km (191 sq. miles).

Dad rock NOUN *Often disparaging* a type of classic rock music that tends to appeal to adults, often played by middle-aged musicians.

dae (de) VERB a Scot word for **do¹.**

daedal *or* **dedal** ('diːdᵊl) ADJECTIVE *Literary* skilful or intricate.
▷HISTORY C16: via Latin from Greek *daidalos;* see DAEDALUS

Daedalus ('diːdələs) NOUN *Greek myth* an Athenian architect and inventor who built the labyrinth for Minos on Crete and fashioned wings for himself and his son Icarus to flee the island.
▸**Daedalian** *or* **Daedalean** (dɪ'deɪlɪən) *or* **Daedalic** (dɪ'dælɪk) ADJECTIVE

daemon ('diːmən) *or* **daimon** NOUN [1] a demigod. [2] the guardian spirit of a place or person. [3] a variant spelling of **demon** (sense 3).
▸**daemonic** (diː'mɒnɪk) ADJECTIVE

daff¹ (dæf) NOUN *Informal* short for **daffodil.**

daff² (dɑːf) VERB (*intr*) *Chiefly Scot* to frolic; play the fool.
▷HISTORY C16: from obsolete *daff* fool, of uncertain origin

daffodil ('dæfədɪl) NOUN [1] Also called: **Lent lily.** a widely cultivated Eurasian amaryllidaceous plant, *Narcissus pseudonarcissus,* having spring-blooming yellow flowers. [2] any other plant of the genus *Narcissus.* [3] **a** a brilliant yellow colour. **b** (*as adjective*): *daffodil paint.* [4] a daffodil, or a representation of one, as a national emblem of Wales.
▷HISTORY C14: from Dutch *de affodil* the asphodel, from Medieval Latin *affodillus,* variant of Latin *asphodelus* ASPHODEL

daffy ('dæfɪ) ADJECTIVE **daffier, daffiest.** *Informal* another word for **daft** (senses 1, 2).
▷HISTORY C19: from obsolete *daff* fool; see DAFT

daft (dɑːft) ADJECTIVE *Chiefly Brit* 1 *Informal* foolish, simple, or stupid. 2 a slang word for **insane.** 3 *Informal* (*postpositive;* foll by *about*) extremely fond (of). 4 *Slang* frivolous; giddy.
▷HISTORY Old English *gedæfte* gentle, foolish; related to Middle Low German *ondaft* incapable
▸ **'daftly** ADVERB ▸ **'daftness** NOUN

dag[1] (dæg) NOUN 1 short for **daglock.** 2 *NZ informal* an amusing person. 3 **rattle one's dags.** *NZ informal* to hurry up. ◆ VERB **dags, dagging, dagged.** 4 to cut the daglock away from (a sheep).
▷HISTORY C18: of obscure origin
▸ **'dagger** NOUN

dag[2] (dæg) NOUN *Austral and NZ informal* 1 a character; eccentric. 2 a person who is untidily dressed. 3 a person with a good sense of humour.
▷HISTORY back formation from DAGGY

Dagan ('dɑːgən) NOUN an earth god of the Babylonians and Assyrians.

Dagenham ('dægənəm) NOUN part of the Greater London borough of Barking and Dagenham: engineering and chemicals.

Dagestan Republic (ˌdɑːgɪ'stɑːn) NOUN a constituent republic of S Russia, on the Caspian Sea: annexed from Persia in 1813; rich mineral resources. Capital: Makhachkala. Pop.: 2 149 000 (2000 est.). Area: 50 278 sq. km (19 416 sq. miles). Also called: **Dagestan** *or* **Daghestan.**

dagga ('daxə, 'dɑːgə) NOUN *South African informal* a local name for marijuana.
▷HISTORY C19: from Afrikaans, from Khoikhoi *dagab*

dagger ('dægə) NOUN 1 a short stabbing weapon with a pointed blade. 2 Also called: **obelisk.** a character (†) used in printing to indicate a cross reference, esp to a footnote. 3 **at daggers drawn.** in a state of open hostility. 4 **look daggers.** to glare with hostility; scowl. ◆ VERB (*tr*) 5 to mark with a dagger. 6 *Archaic* to stab with a dagger.
▷HISTORY C14: of uncertain origin

daggerboard ('dægəˌbɔːd) NOUN a light bladelike board inserted into the water through a slot in the keel of a boat to reduce keeling and leeway. Compare **centreboard.**

daggy ('dægɪ) *Austral and NZ informal* ADJECTIVE 1 untidy; dishevelled. 2 eccentric.
▷HISTORY from DAG[1]

daglock ('dægˌlɒk) NOUN a dung-caked lock of wool around the hindquarters of a sheep.
▷HISTORY C17: see DAG[1], LOCK[2]

dago ('deɪgəʊ) NOUN, *plural* **-gos** *or* **-goes.** *Derogatory* a member of a Latin race, esp a Spaniard or Portuguese.
▷HISTORY C19: alteration of *Diego,* a common Spanish name

dagoba ('dɑːgəbə) NOUN a dome-shaped shrine containing relics of the Buddha or a Buddhist saint.
▷HISTORY C19: from Sinhalese *dāgoba,* from Sanskrit *dhātugarbha* containing relics

Dagon ('deɪgɒn) NOUN *Bible* a god worshipped by the Philistines, represented as half man and half fish.
▷HISTORY C14: via Latin and Greek from Hebrew *Dāgōn,* literally: little fish

daguerreotype (də'gɛrəʊˌtaɪp) NOUN 1 one of the earliest photographic processes, in which the image was produced on iodine-sensitized silver and developed in mercury vapour. 2 a photograph formed by this process.
▸ **da'guerreoˌtyper** *or* **da'guerreoˌtypist** NOUN
▸ **da'guerreoˌtypy** NOUN

dah (dɑː) NOUN the long sound used in combination with the short sound *dit,* in the spoken representation of Morse and other telegraphic codes. Compare **dash**[1] (sense 14).

dahabeah, dahabeeyah, *or* **dahabiah** (ˌdɑːhə'biːə) NOUN a houseboat used on the Nile.
▷HISTORY from Arabic *dhahabīyah,* literally: the golden one (that is, gilded barge)

dahlia ('deɪljə) NOUN 1 any herbaceous perennial plant of the Mexican genus *Dahlia,* having showy flowers and tuberous roots, esp any horticultural variety derived from *D. pinnata:* family *Asteraceae* (composites). 2 the flower or root of any of these plants.
▷HISTORY C19: named after Anders *Dahl,* 18th-century Swedish botanist; see -IA

Dahna ('dɑːxnɑː) NOUN another name for **Rub' al Khali.**

Dahomey (də'həʊmɪ) NOUN the former name (until 1975) of **Benin.**

daikon ('daɪkɒn) NOUN another name for **mooli.**
▷HISTORY C20: Japanese, from *dai* big + *kon* root

Dáil Éireann ('dɑːl 'eːrɪn) *or* **Dáil** NOUN (in the Republic of Ireland) the lower chamber of parliament. See also **Oireachtas.**
▷HISTORY from Irish *dáil* assembly (from Old Irish *dāl*) + *Éireann* of Eire

dailies ('deɪlɪz) PLURAL NOUN *Films* another word for **rushes.**

daily ('deɪlɪ) ADJECTIVE 1 of or occurring every day or every weekday: *a daily paper.* 2 **earn one's daily bread.** to earn one's living. 3 **the daily round.** the usual activities of one's day. ◆ NOUN, *plural* **-lies.** 4 a daily publication, esp a newspaper. 5 Also called: **daily help.** *Brit* another name for a **charwoman.** ◆ ADVERB 6 every day. 7 constantly; often.
▷HISTORY Old English *dæglīc;* see DAY, -LY[1]

daily double NOUN *Horse racing* a single bet on the winners of two named races in any one day's racing.

Daimoku *or* **daimoku** ('daɪməʊkuː) NOUN **a** (in Nichiren Buddhism) the words *nam myoho renge kyo* ('devotion to the Lotus Sutra') chanted to the Gohonzon. **b** the act of chanting these words.
▷HISTORY from Japanese, literally: title

daimon ('daɪmɒn) NOUN a variant of **daemon** or **demon** (sense 3).
▸ **dai'monic** ADJECTIVE

daimyo *or* **daimio** ('daɪmjəʊ) NOUN, *plural* **-myo, -myos** *or* **-mio, -mios.** (in Japan) one of the territorial magnates who dominated much of the country from about the 11th to the 19th century.
▷HISTORY from Japanese, from Ancient Chinese *d'âi miäng* great name

daimyo bond NOUN a bearer bond issued in Japan and the eurobond market by the World Bank.

dainty ('deɪntɪ) ADJECTIVE **-tier, -tiest.** 1 delicate or elegant: *a dainty teacup.* 2 pleasing to the taste; choice; delicious: *a dainty morsel.* 3 refined, esp excessively genteel; fastidious. ◆ NOUN, *plural* **-ties.** 4 a choice piece of food, esp a small cake or sweet; delicacy.
▷HISTORY C13: from Old French *deintié,* from Latin *dignitās* DIGNITY
▸ **'daintily** ADVERB ▸ **'daintiness** NOUN

daiquiri ('daɪkɪrɪ, 'dæk-) NOUN, *plural* **-ris.** *Chiefly US and Canadian* an iced drink containing rum, lime juice, and syrup or sugar.
▷HISTORY C20: named after *Daiquiri,* rum-producing town in Cuba

Dairen (daɪ'rɛn) NOUN a former name of **Dalian.**

dairy ('dɛərɪ) NOUN, *plural* **dairies.** 1 a company that supplies milk and milk products. 2 **a** a shop that sells provisions, esp milk and milk products. **b** *NZ* a shop that remains open outside normal trading hours. 3 a room or building where milk and cream are stored or made into butter and cheese. 4 **a** (*modifier*) of or relating to the production of milk and milk products: *dairy cattle.* **b** (*in combination*): *a dairymaid; a dairyman.* 5 (*modifier*) containing milk or milk products: *dairy produce.*
▷HISTORY C13 *daierie,* from Old English *dæge* servant girl, one who kneads bread; see DOUGH, LADY

dairy factory NOUN *NZ* a factory making butter, cheese, lactose, etc. from milk collected from surrounding farming areas.

dairying ('dɛərɪɪŋ) NOUN the business of producing, processing, and selling dairy products.

dairymaid ('dɛərɪˌmeɪd) NOUN (esp formerly) a girl or woman who works in a dairy, esp one who milks cows and makes butter and cheese on a farm.

dairyman ('dɛərɪmən) NOUN, *plural* **-men.** a man who works in a dairy or deals in dairy products.

dais ('deɪɪs, deɪs) NOUN a raised platform, usually at one end of a hall, used by speakers, etc.
▷HISTORY C13: from Old French *deis,* from Latin *discus* DISCUS

daisy ('deɪzɪ) NOUN, *plural* **-sies.** 1 a small low-growing European plant, *Bellis perennis,* having a rosette of leaves and flower heads of yellow central disc flowers and pinkish-white outer ray flowers: family *Asteraceae* (composites). 2 Also called: **oxeye daisy, marguerite, moon daisy.** a Eurasian composite plant, *Leucanthemum vulgare* having flower heads with a yellow centre and white outer rays. 3 any of various other composite plants having conspicuous ray flowers, such as the Michaelmas daisy and Shasta daisy. 4 *Slang* an excellent person or thing. 5 **pushing up the daisies.** dead and buried.
▷HISTORY Old English *dægesēge* day's eye
▸ **'daisied** ADJECTIVE

daisy bush NOUN any of various shrubs of the genus *Olearia,* of Australia and New Zealand, with daisy-like flowers: family *Asteraceae* (composites).

daisy chain NOUN a garland made, esp by children, by threading daisies together.

daisy cutter NOUN 1 *Soccer* a powerful shot that moves close to the ground. 2 a powerful bomb with a huge blast effect.

daisywheel ('deɪzɪˌwiːl) NOUN *Computing* a component of a computer printer in the shape of a wheel with many spokes that prints characters using a disk with characters around the circumference as the print element. Also called: **printwheel.**

dak (dɑːk) *or* **dawk** (dɔːk) NOUN (formerly, in India) **a** a system of mail delivery or passenger transport by relays of bearers or horses stationed at intervals along a route. **b** (*as modifier*): *dak bearers.*
▷HISTORY C18: from Hindi *dāk,* from Sanskrit *drāk* quickly

Dak. ABBREVIATION FOR Dakota.

Dakar ('dækə) NOUN the capital and chief port of Senegal, on the SE side of Cape Verde peninsula. Pop.: 1 999 000 (1998 est.).

dak bungalow NOUN (in India, formerly) a house where travellers on a dak route could be accommodated.

Dakin's solution ('deɪkɪnz) NOUN a dilute solution containing sodium hypochlorite and boric acid, used as an antiseptic in the treatment of wounds.
▷HISTORY C20: named after Henry D. *Dakin* (1880–1952), English chemist

Dakota (də'kəʊtə) NOUN a former territory of the US: divided into the states of North Dakota and South Dakota in 1889.

Dakotan (də'kəʊtən) ADJECTIVE 1 of or relating to Dakota or its inhabitants. ◆ NOUN 2 a native or inhabitant of Dakota.

daks *or* **dacks** (dæks) PLURAL NOUN *Austral* an informal name for **trousers.**
▷HISTORY from a brand name

dal[1] (dɑːl) NOUN 1 split grain, a common foodstuff in India; pulse. 2 a variant spelling of **dhal.**

dal[2] SYMBOL FOR decalitre(s).

dalasi (də'lɑːsɪ) NOUN the standard monetary unit of The Gambia, divided into 100 bututs.
▷HISTORY from a Gambian native name

dale (deɪl) NOUN an open valley, usually in an area of low hills.
▷HISTORY Old English *dæl;* related to Old Frisian *del,* Old Norse *dalr,* Old High German *tal* valley

Dalek ('dɑːlɛk) NOUN any of a set of fictional robot-like creations that are aggressive, mobile, and produce rasping staccato speech.
▷HISTORY C20: from a children's television series, *Dr Who*

d'Alembert's principle (*French* dalɑ̃bɛr) NOUN *Physics* the principle that for a moving body the external forces are in equilibrium with the inertial forces; a generalization of Newton's third law of motion.
▷HISTORY C18: named after Jean Le Rond *d'Alembert* (1717–83), French mathematician, physicist, and rationalist philosopher

Dales[1] (deɪlz) PLURAL NOUN (*sometimes not capital*) **the.** short for the **Yorkshire Dales.**

Dales[2] (deɪlz) NOUN a strong working breed of pony, originating from Yorkshire and Durham.

dalesman ('deɪlzmən) NOUN, *plural* **-men**. a person living in a dale, esp in the dales of N England.

daleth *or* **daled** ('dɑːlɪd; *Hebrew* 'dalɛt) NOUN the fourth letter of the Hebrew alphabet (ד), transliterated as *d* or, when final, *dh*.
▷HISTORY Hebrew

dalgyte ('dælgaɪt) NOUN *Austral* another name for **bilby**.

Dalian (dɑːl'jɛn) *or* **Talien** (tɑːl'jɛn) NOUN a city in NE China, at the end of the Liaodong Peninsula: with the adjoining city of Lü-shun comprises the port complex of Lüda. Pop.: 2 000 944 (1999 est.). Former name: **Dairen**.

Dalit ('dɑːlɪt) NOUN another name for **untouchable** (sense 4).
▷HISTORY from Hindi, from Sanskrit *dalita*, literally: oppressed

Dallas ('dæləs) NOUN a city in NE Texas, on the Trinity River: scene of the assassination of President John F. Kennedy (1963). Pop.: 1 188 580 (2000).

dalles ('dæləs, dælz) PLURAL NOUN *Canadian* a stretch of a river between high rock walls, with rapids and dangerous currents.
▷HISTORY from Canadian French, from French (Normandy dialect): sink; compare DALE

dalliance ('dælɪəns) NOUN [1] waste of time in frivolous action or in dawdling. [2] an archaic word for **flirtation**.

dally ('dælɪ) VERB **-lies, -lying, -lied**. (*intr*) [1] to waste time idly; dawdle. [2] (usually foll by *with*) to deal frivolously or lightly with; trifle; toy: *to dally with someone's affections*.
▷HISTORY C14: from Anglo-French *dalier* to gossip, of uncertain origin
▸'**dallier** NOUN

Dalmatia (dæl'meɪʃə) NOUN a region of W Croatia along the Adriatic: mountainous, with many offshore islands.

Dalmatian (dæl'meɪʃən) NOUN [1] Also called (esp formerly): **carriage dog, coach dog**. a large breed of dog having a short smooth white coat with black or (in liver-spotted dalmatians) brown spots. [2] a native or inhabitant of Dalmatia. ◆ ADJECTIVE [3] of or relating to Dalmatia or its inhabitants.

dalmatic (dæl'mætɪk) NOUN [1] a wide-sleeved tunic-like vestment open at the sides, worn by deacons and bishops. [2] a similar robe worn by a king at his coronation.
▷HISTORY C15: from Late Latin *dalmatica* (*vestis*) Dalmatian (robe) (originally made of Dalmatian wool)

Dalriada (dæl'rɪədə) NOUN a former Gaelic kingdom (5th century A.D.–9th century A.D.) comprising Argyll, parts of the Inner Hebrides, and parts of modern Antrim.
▷HISTORY named after the *Dalriada* family, its founders

dal segno ('dæl 'sɛnjəʊ) ADJECTIVE, ADVERB *Music* (of a piece of music) to be repeated from the point marked with a sign to the word *fine*. Abbreviation: **DS**. See also **fine**[3].
▷HISTORY Italian, literally: from the sign

dalton ('dɔːltən) NOUN another name for **atomic mass unit**.
▷HISTORY C20: named after John *Dalton* (1766–1844), English chemist and physicist

daltonism ('dɔːltəˌnɪzəm) NOUN colour blindness, esp the confusion of red and green.
▷HISTORY C19: from French *daltonisme*, after John *Dalton* (1766–1844), English chemist and physicist, who gave the first accurate description of colour blindness, from which he suffered
▸**daltonic** (dɔːl'tɒnɪk) ADJECTIVE

Dalton plan *or* **system** ('dɔːltən) NOUN a system devised to encourage pupils to learn and develop at their own speed, using libraries and other sources to complete long assignments.
▷HISTORY C20: named after *Dalton*, Massachusetts, where the plan was used in schools

Dalton's atomic theory ('dɔːltənz) NOUN *Chem* the theory that matter consists of indivisible particles called atoms and that atoms of a given element are all identical and can neither be created nor destroyed. Compounds are formed by combination of atoms in simple ratios to give compound atoms (molecules). The theory was the basis of modern chemistry.
▷HISTORY C19: named after John *Dalton* (1766–1844), English chemist and physicist

Dalton's law ('dɔːltənz) NOUN the principle that the pressure exerted by a mixture of gases in a fixed volume is equal to the sum of the pressures that each gas would exert if it occupied the whole volume. Also called: **Dalton's law of partial pressures**.
▷HISTORY C19: named after John *Dalton* (1766–1844), English chemist and physicist

dam[1] (dæm) NOUN [1] a barrier of concrete, earth, etc., built across a river to create a body of water for a hydroelectric power station, domestic water supply, etc. [2] a reservoir of water created by such a barrier. [3] something that resembles or functions as a dam. ◆ VERB **dams, damming, dammed**. [4] (*tr; often foll by up*) to obstruct or restrict by or as if by a dam.
▷HISTORY C12: probably from Middle Low German; compare Old Icelandic *damma* to block up

dam[2] (dæm) NOUN the female parent of an animal, esp of domestic livestock.
▷HISTORY C13: variant of DAME

dam[3] (dæm) INTERJECTION, ADVERB, ADJECTIVE a variant spelling of **damn** (senses 1–4); often used in combination, as in **damfool, damme, dammit**.

dam[4] SYMBOL FOR decametre(s).

damage ('dæmɪdʒ) NOUN [1] injury or harm impairing the function or condition of a person or thing. [2] loss of something desirable. [3] *Informal* cost; expense (esp in the phrase **what's the damage?**). ◆ VERB [4] (*tr*) to cause damage to. [5] (*intr*) to suffer damage.
▷HISTORY C14: from Old French, from Latin *damnum* injury, loss, fine
▸'**damageable** ADJECTIVE ▸ˌ**damagea'bility** NOUN
▸'**damager** NOUN ▸'**damaging** ADJECTIVE ▸'**damagingly** ADVERB

damages ('dæmɪdʒɪz) PLURAL NOUN *Law* money to be paid as compensation to a person for injury, loss, etc.

daman ('dæmən) NOUN a rare name for the **hyrax**, esp the Syrian rock hyrax. See also **cony** (sense 2).
▷HISTORY from Arabic *damān Isrā'īl* sheep of Israel

Daman (dɑː'mɑːn) NOUN a coastal town in W India, the chief town of Daman and Diu. Pop.: 26 895 (1991 est.). Portuguese name: **Damão**.

Daman and Diu (dɑː'mɑːn 'diːuː) NOUN a union territory in W India: formerly a district of Portuguese India (1559–1961) then part of the union territory of Goa, Daman, and Diu (1961–87). Area: 112 sq. km (43 sq. miles). Pop.: 158 059 (2001).

Damanhûr (ˌdɑːmən'hʊə) NOUN a city in NE Egypt, in the Nile delta. Pop.: 212 203 (1996).

Damão (də'mɑ̃ʊ) NOUN the Portuguese name for **Daman**, a former Portuguese settlement now in **Daman and Diu**.

damar ('dæmə) NOUN a variant spelling of **dammar**.

Damara (də'mɑːrə) NOUN [1] (*plural* **-ras** *or* **-ra**) Also called: **Bergdama**. a member of a Negroid people of South West Africa. [2] the language of this people, a dialect of Nama.

Damaraland (də'mɑːrəˌlænd) NOUN a plateau region of central Namibia, the traditional homeland of the Damara people.

damascene ('dæməˌsiːn, ˌdæmə'siːn) VERB [1] (*tr*) to ornament (metal, esp steel) by etching or by inlaying, usually with gold or silver. ◆ NOUN [2] a design or article produced by this process. ◆ ADJECTIVE [3] of or relating to this process.
▷HISTORY C14: from Latin *damascēnus* of Damascus

Damascene ('dæməˌsiːn, ˌdæmə'siːn) ADJECTIVE [1] of or relating to Damascus. ◆ NOUN [2] a native or inhabitant of Damascus. [3] a variety of domestic fancy pigeon with silvery plumage.

Damascus (də'mɑːskəs, -'mæs-) NOUN the capital of Syria, in the southwest: reputedly the oldest city in the world, having been inhabited continuously since before 2000 B.C. Pop.: 1 394 322 (1994). Arabic names: **Dimashq, Esh Sham** (ɛʃ ʃæm).

Damascus steel *or* **damask steel** NOUN *History* a hard flexible steel with wavy markings caused by forging the metal in strips: used for sword blades.

damask ('dæməsk) NOUN [1] **a** a reversible fabric, usually silk or linen, with a pattern woven into it. It is used for table linen, curtains, etc. **b** table linen made from this. **c** (*as modifier*): *a damask tablecloth*. [2] short for **Damascus steel**. [3] the wavy markings on such steel. [4] **a** the greyish-pink colour of the damask rose. **b** (*as adjective*): *damask wallpaper*. ◆ VERB [5] (*tr*) another word for **damascene** (sense 1).
▷HISTORY C14: from Medieval Latin *damascus*, from Damascus, where this fabric was originally made

damask rose NOUN a rose, *Rosa damascena*, native to Asia and cultivated for its pink or red fragrant flowers, which are used to make the perfume attar.
▷HISTORY C16: from Medieval Latin *rosa damascēna* rose of Damascus

dame (deɪm) NOUN [1] (formerly) a woman of rank or dignity; lady. [2] a nun who has taken the vows of her order, esp a Benedictine. [3] *Archaic, chiefly Brit* a matronly or elderly woman. [4] *Slang, chiefly US and Canadian* a woman. [5] Also called: **pantomime dame**. *Brit* the role of a comic old woman in a pantomime, usually played by a man.
▷HISTORY C13: from Old French, from Latin *domina* lady, mistress of a household

Dame (deɪm) NOUN (in Britain) [1] the title of a woman who has been awarded the Order of the British Empire or any of certain other orders of chivalry. [2] the legal title of the wife or widow of a knight or baronet, placed before her name: *Dame Judith*. Compare **Lady**.

dame school NOUN (formerly) a small school, often in a village, usually run by an elderly woman in her own home to teach young children to read and write.

dame's violet, dame's rocket, *or* **damewort** ('deɪmˌwɜːt) NOUN a Eurasian hairy perennial plant, *Hesperis matronalis*, cultivated in gardens for its mauve or white fragrant flowers: family *Brassicaceae* (crucifers).

Damietta (ˌdæmɪ'ɛtə) NOUN a town in NE Egypt, in the Nile delta: important medieval commercial centre. Pop.: 113 000 (1991). Arabic name: **Dumyat**.

dammar, damar, *or* **dammer** ('dæmə) NOUN any of various resins obtained from SE Asian trees, esp of the genera *Agathis* (conifers) and *Shorea* (family *Dipterocarpaceae*): used for varnishes, lacquers, bases for oil paints, etc.
▷HISTORY C17: from Malay *damar* resin

dammit ('dæmɪt) INTERJECTION a contracted form of *damn it*.

damn (dæm) INTERJECTION [1] *Slang* an exclamation of annoyance (often in exclamatory phrases such as **damn it! damn you!** etc.). [2] *Informal* an exclamation of surprise or pleasure (esp in the exclamatory phrase **damn me!**). ◆ ADJECTIVE [3] (*prenominal*) *Slang* deserving damnation; detestable. ◆ ADVERB, ADJECTIVE (*prenominal*) [4] *Slang* (intensifier): *damn fool; a damn good pianist*. ◆ ADVERB [5] **damn all**. *Slang* absolutely nothing. ◆ VERB (*mainly tr*) [6] to condemn as bad, worthless, etc. [7] to curse. [8] to condemn to eternal damnation. [9] (*often passive*) to doom to ruin; cause to fail: *the venture was damned from the start*. [10] (*also intr*) to prove (someone) guilty: *damning evidence*. [11] to swear (at) using the word *damn*. [12] **as near as damn it**. *Brit informal* as near as possible; very near. [13] **damn with faint praise**. to praise so unenthusiastically that the effect is condemnation. ◆ NOUN [14] *Slang* something of negligible value; jot (esp in the phrase **not worth a damn**). [15] **not give a damn**. *Informal* to be unconcerned; not care.
▷HISTORY C13: from Old French *dampner*, from Latin *damnāre* to injure, condemn, from *damnum* loss, injury, penalty

damnable ('dæmnəbᵊl) ADJECTIVE [1] execrable; detestable. [2] liable to or deserving damnation.
▸'**damnableness** *or* ˌ**damna'bility** NOUN

damnably ('dæmnəblɪ) ADVERB [1] in a detestable manner. [2] (intensifier): *it was damnably unfair*.

damnation (dæm'neɪʃən) NOUN [1] the act of damning or state of being damned. [2] a cause or instance of being damned. ◆ INTERJECTION [3] an exclamation of anger, disappointment, etc.

damnatory ('dæmnətərɪ, -trɪ) ADJECTIVE threatening or occasioning condemnation.

damned (dæmd) ADJECTIVE [1] **a** condemned to hell. **b** (*as noun*): *the damned*. ◆ ADVERB, ADJECTIVE *Slang* [2] (intensifier): *a damned good try; a damned liar; I should damned well think so!* [3] used to indicate amazement, disavowal, or refusal (in such phrases as **I'll be damned** and **damned if I care**).

damnedest ('dæmdɪst) NOUN *Informal* utmost; best (esp in the phrases **do** or **try one's damnedest**).

damnify ('dæmnɪˌfaɪ) VERB **-fies, -fying, -fied.** (*tr*) *Law* to cause loss or damage to (a person); injure.
▷HISTORY C16: from Old French *damnifier,* ultimately from Latin *damnum* harm, + *facere* to make
▸ˌ**damnifiˈcation** NOUN

Damocles ('dæməˌkliːz) NOUN *Classical legend* a sycophant forced by Dionysius, tyrant of Syracuse, to sit under a sword suspended by a hair to demonstrate that being a king was not the happy state Damocles had said it was. See also **Sword of Damocles.**
▸ˌ**Damoˈclean** ADJECTIVE

Damodar ('dæməˌdɑː) NOUN a river in NE India, rising in Jharkand and flowing east through West Bengal to the Hooghly River: the **Damodar Valley** is an important centre of heavy industry.

damoiselle, damosel, *or* **damozel** (ˌdæmə'zɛl) NOUN archaic variants of **damsel.**

Damon and Pythias ('deɪmən) NOUN *Classical legend* two friends noted for their mutual loyalty. Damon offered himself as a hostage for Pythias, who was to be executed for treason by Dionysius of Syracuse. When Pythias returned to save his friend's life, he was pardoned.

damp (dæmp) ADJECTIVE [1] slightly wet, as from dew, steam, etc. [2] *Archaic* dejected. ◆ NOUN [3] slight wetness; moisture; humidity. [4] rank air or poisonous gas, esp in a mine. See also **firedamp.** [5] a discouragement; damper. [6] *Archaic* dejection. ◆ VERB (*tr*) [7] to make slightly wet. [8] (often foll by *down*) to stifle or deaden: *to damp one's ardour.* [9] (often foll by *down*) to reduce the flow of air to (a fire) to make it burn more slowly or to extinguish it. [10] *Physics* to reduce the amplitude of (an oscillation or wave). [11] *Music* to muffle (the sound of an instrument). ◆ See also **damp off.**
▷HISTORY C14: from Middle Low German *damp* steam; related to Old High German *demphen* to cause to steam
▸ˈ**dampish** ADJECTIVE ▸ˈ**damply** ADVERB ▸ˈ**dampness** NOUN

dampcourse ('dæmpˌkɔːs) NOUN a horizontal layer of impervious material in a brick wall, fairly close to the ground, to stop moisture rising. Also called: **damp-proof course.**

dampen ('dæmpən) VERB [1] to make or become damp. [2] (*tr*) to stifle; deaden.
▸ˈ**dampener** NOUN

damper ('dæmpə) NOUN [1] a person, event, or circumstance that depresses or discourages. [2] **put a damper on.** to produce a depressing or inhibiting effect on. [3] a movable plate to regulate the draught in a stove or furnace flue. [4] a device to reduce electronic, mechanical, acoustic, or aerodynamic oscillations in a system. [5] *Music* the pad in a piano or harpsichord that deadens the vibration of each string as its key is released. [6] *Chiefly Austral and NZ* any of various unleavened loaves and scones, typically cooked on an open fire.

damping ('dæmpɪŋ) NOUN [1] moistening or wetting. [2] stifling, as of spirits. [3] *Electronics* the introduction of resistance into a resonant circuit with the result that the sharpness of response at the peak of a frequency is reduced. [4] *Engineering* any method of dispersing energy in a vibrating system.

damping off NOUN any of various diseases of plants, esp the collapse and death of seedlings caused by the parasitic fungus *Pythium debaryanum* and related fungi in conditions of excessive moisture.

damp off VERB (*intr, adverb*) (of plants, seedlings, shoots, etc.) to be affected by damping off.

damp-proof VERB *Building trades* [1] to protect against the incursion of damp by adding a dampcourse or by coating with a moisture-resistant preparation. ◆ ADJECTIVE [2] protected against damp or causing protection against damp: *a damp-proof course.*

damsel ('dæmzᵊl) NOUN *Archaic or poetic* a young unmarried woman; maiden.
▷HISTORY C13: from Old French *damoisele,* from Vulgar Latin *domnicella* (unattested) young lady, from Latin *domina* mistress; see DAME

damsel bug NOUN any of various bugs of the carnivorous family *Nabiidae,* related to the bedbugs but feeding on other insects. The larvae of some species mimic and associate with ants.

damselfish ('dæmzᵊlˌfɪʃ) NOUN, *plural* **-fish** *or* **-fishes.** any small tropical percoid fish of the family *Pomacentridae,* having a brightly coloured deep compressed body. See also **anemone fish.**

damselfly ('dæmzᵊlˌflaɪ) NOUN, *plural* **-flies.** any insect of the suborder *Zygoptera* similar to but smaller than dragonflies and usually resting with the wings closed over the back: order *Odonata.*

damson ('dæmzən) NOUN [1] a small rosaceous tree, *Prunus domestica institiia* (or *P. institiia*), cultivated for its blue-black edible plumlike fruit and probably derived from the bullace. See also **plum¹** (sense 1). [2] the fruit of this tree.
▷HISTORY C14: from Latin *prūnum Damascēnum* Damascus plum

damson cheese NOUN thick damson jam.

dan¹ (dæn) NOUN a small buoy used as a marker at sea. Also called: **dan buoy.**
▷HISTORY C17: of unknown origin

dan² (dæn) NOUN *Martial Arts* [1] any one of the 10 black-belt grades of proficiency. [2] a competitor entitled to dan grading. ◆ Compare **kyu.**
▷HISTORY Japanese

Dan¹ (dæn) NOUN an archaic title of honour, equivalent to *Master* or *Sir*: *Dan Chaucer.*

Dan² (dæn) NOUN *Old Testament* [1] **a** the fourth son of Jacob (Genesis 30:1–6). **b** the tribe descended from him. [2] a city in the northern territory of Canaan.

Dan. ABBREVIATION FOR: [1] *Bible* Daniel. [2] Danish.

Danaë ('dæneɪˌiː) NOUN *Greek myth* the mother of Perseus by Zeus, who came to her in prison as a shower of gold.

Danaides (də'neɪɪˌdiːz) PLURAL NOUN, *singular* **Danaid.** *Greek myth* the fifty daughters of Danaüs. All but Hypermnestra murdered their bridegrooms and were punished in Hades by having to pour water perpetually into a jar with a hole in the bottom.
▸**Danaidean** (ˌdænɪ'ɪdɪən, ˌdænɪəɪ'diːən) ADJECTIVE

Da Nang ('dɑː 'næŋ) NOUN a port in central Vietnam, on the South China Sea. Pop.: 382 674 (1992 est.). Former name: **Tourane.**

Danaüs ('dænɪəs) NOUN *Greek myth* a king of Argos who told his fifty daughters, the Danaides, to kill their bridegrooms on their wedding night.

dance (dɑːns) VERB [1] (*intr*) to move the feet and body rhythmically, esp in time to music. [2] (*tr*) to perform (a particular dance). [3] (*intr*) to skip or leap, as in joy, etc. [4] to move or cause to move in a light rhythmic way. [5] **dance attendance on (someone).** to attend (someone) solicitously or obsequiously. ◆ NOUN [6] a series of rhythmic steps and movements, usually in time to music. Related adjective: **Terpsichorean.** [7] an act of dancing. [8] **a** a social meeting arranged for dancing; ball. **b** (*as modifier*): *a dance hall.* [9] a piece of music in the rhythm of a particular dance form, such as a waltz. [10] short for **dance music** (sense 2). [11] dancelike movements made by some insects and birds, esp as part of a behaviour pattern. [12] **lead (someone) a dance.** *Brit informal* to cause (someone) continued worry and exasperation; play up.
▷HISTORY C13: from Old French *dancier*
▸ˈ**danceable** ADJECTIVE ▸ˈ**dancer** NOUN ▸ˈ**dancing** NOUN, ADJECTIVE

dancehall ('dɑːnsˌhɔːl) NOUN a style of dance-oriented reggae, originating in the late 1980s.

dance music NOUN [1] music that is suitable for dancing. [2] Also called: **dance.** pop music with a strong electronic rhythm.

dance of death NOUN a pictorial, literary, or musical representation, current esp in the Middle Ages, of a dance in which living people, in order of social precedence, are led off to their graves, by a personification of death. Also called (French): **danse macabre.**

dancette (dɑː'nsɛt) NOUN another name for **chevron** (sense 5).

dancey (ˌdɑːnsɪ) ADJECTIVE **dancier, danciest.** of, relating to, or resembling dance music: *a cool dancey track.*

dancing girl NOUN a professional female dancer who dances to entertain customers at a club, theatre, etc.

D and C NOUN *Med* dilation and curettage; a therapeutic or diagnostic procedure in obstetrics and gynaecology involving dilation of the cervix and curettage of the cavity of the uterus, as for abortion.

dandelion ('dændɪˌlaɪən) NOUN [1] a plant, *Taraxacum officinale,* native to Europe and Asia and naturalized as a weed in North America, having yellow rayed flowers and deeply notched basal leaves, which are used for salad or wine: family *Asteraceae* (composites). [2] any of several similar related plants.
▷HISTORY C15: from Old French *dent de lion,* literally: tooth of a lion, referring to its leaves

dander¹ ('dændə) NOUN [1] small particles or scales of hair or feathers. [2] **get one's** (*or* **someone's**) **dander up.** *Informal* to become or cause to become annoyed or angry.
▷HISTORY C19: changed from DANDRUFF

dander² ('dændə; *Scot* 'dændər) *Scot and northern English dialect* ◆ NOUN [1] a stroll. ◆ VERB [2] (*intr*) to stroll.
▷HISTORY C19: of unknown origin

Dandie Dinmont ('dændɪ 'dɪnmɒnt) NOUN a breed of small terrier with a long coat and drooping ears. Also called: **Dandie Dinmont terrier.**
▷HISTORY C19: named after a character who owned two terriers in *Guy Mannering* (1815), a novel by Sir Walter Scott

dandify ('dændɪˌfaɪ) VERB **-fies, -fying, -fied.** (*tr*) to dress like or cause to resemble a dandy.
▸ˌ**dandifiˈcation** NOUN

dandiprat ('dændɪˌpræt) NOUN [1] a small English coin minted in the 16th century. [2] *Archaic* **a** a small boy. **b** an insignificant person.
▷HISTORY C16: of unknown origin

dandle ('dændᵊl) VERB (*tr*) [1] to move (a young child, etc.) up and down (on the knee or in the arms). [2] to pet; fondle.
▷HISTORY C16: of uncertain origin
▸ˈ**dandler** NOUN

dandruff ('dændrəf) NOUN loose scales of dry dead skin shed from the scalp. Also called (now rarely): **dandriff.**
▷HISTORY C16: *dand-,* of unknown origin + *-ruff,* probably from Middle English *roufe* scab, from Old Norse *hrūfa*
▸ˈ**dandruffy** ADJECTIVE

dandy¹ ('dændɪ) NOUN, *plural* **-dies.** [1] a man greatly concerned with smartness of dress; beau. [2] a yawl or ketch. ◆ ADJECTIVE **-dier, -diest.** [3] *Informal* very good or fine.
▷HISTORY C18: perhaps short for *jack-a-dandy*
▸ˈ**dandily** ADVERB ▸ˈ**dandyish** ADJECTIVE ▸ˈ**dandyism** NOUN

dandy² ('dændɪ) NOUN another name for **dengue.**

dandy-brush NOUN a stiff brush used for grooming a horse.

dandy roll *or* **roller** NOUN a light roller used in the manufacture of certain papers to produce watermarks.

Dane (deɪn) NOUN [1] a native, citizen, or inhabitant of Denmark. [2] any of the Vikings who invaded England from the late 8th to the 11th century A.D.

Danegeld ('deɪnˌgɛld) *or* **Danegelt** ('deɪnˌgɛlt) NOUN the tax first levied in the late 9th century in Anglo-Saxon England to provide protection money for or to finance forces to oppose Viking invaders.
▷HISTORY C11: from *Dan* Dane + *geld* tribute; see YIELD

Danelaw *or* **Danelagh** ('deɪnˌlɔː) NOUN the northern, central and eastern parts of Anglo-Saxon England in which Danish law and custom were observed.
▷HISTORY Old English *Dena lagu* Danes' law; term revived in the 19th century

danewort ('deɪnˌwɜːt) NOUN a caprifoliaceous shrub, *Sambucus ebulus,* native to Europe and Asia and having serrated leaves and white flowers. See also **elder².**

dang (dæŋ) INTERJECTION, ADVERB, ADJECTIVE a euphemistic word for **damn** (senses 1–4).

danger ('deɪndʒə) NOUN [1] the state of being vulnerable to injury, loss, or evil; risk. [2] a person or thing that may cause injury, pain, etc. [3] *Obsolete* power. [4] **in danger of.** liable to. [5] **on the danger list.** critically ill in hospital.

▷HISTORY C13: *daunger* power, hence power to inflict injury, from Old French *dongier* (from Latin *dominium* ownership) blended with Old French *dam* injury, from Latin *damnum*
▸'**dangerless** ADJECTIVE

danger money NOUN extra money paid to compensate for the risks involved in certain dangerous jobs.

dangerous ('deɪndʒərəs) ADJECTIVE causing danger; perilous.
▸'**dangerously** ADVERB ▸'**dangerousness** NOUN

dangle ('dæŋgᵊl) VERB 1 to hang or cause to hang freely: *his legs dangled over the wall.* 2 (*tr*) to display as an enticement: *the hope of a legacy was dangled before her.* ◆ NOUN 3 the act of dangling or something that dangles.
▷HISTORY C16: perhaps from Danish *dangle*, probably of imitative origin
▸'**dangler** NOUN ▸'**danglingly** ADVERB

dangling participle NOUN *Grammar* another name (esp US and Canadian) for **misplaced modifier.**

Dani ('dɑ:nɪ) NOUN 1 (*plural* **Dani** ('dɑ:nɪ)) a member of a New Guinea people living in the central highlands of West Irian. 2 the language of this people, probably related to other languages of New Guinea.

Daniel ('dænjəl) NOUN 1 *Old Testament* **a** a youth who was taken into the household of Nebuchadnezzar, received guidance and apocalyptic visions from God, and was given divine protection when thrown into the lions' den. **b** the book that recounts these experiences and visions (in full **The Book of the Prophet Daniel**). 2 (often preceded by *a*) a wise upright person.
▷HISTORY sense 2: referring to Daniel in the Apocryphal *Book of Susanna*

Daniell cell ('dænjəl) NOUN *Physics* a type of cell having a zinc anode in dilute sulphuric acid separated by a porous barrier from a copper cathode in copper sulphate solution. It has an emf of 1.1 volts.
▷HISTORY C19: named after John *Daniell* (1790–1845), English scientist

danio ('deɪnɪˌəʊ) NOUN, *plural* **-os.** any brightly coloured tropical freshwater cyprinid fish of the genus *Danio* and related genera: popular aquarium fishes.
▷HISTORY C19: from New Latin, of obscure origin

Danish ('deɪnɪʃ) ADJECTIVE 1 of, relating to, or characteristic of Denmark, its people, or their language. ◆ NOUN 2 the official language of Denmark, belonging to the North Germanic branch of the Indo-European family.

Danish blue NOUN a strong-tasting white cheese with blue veins.

Danish loaf NOUN *Brit* a large white loaf with a centre split having the top crust dusted with flour, esp one baked on the sole of the oven.

Danish pastry NOUN a rich puff pastry filled with apple, almond paste, icing, etc.

Danish West Indies PLURAL NOUN the former possession of Denmark in the W Lesser Antilles, sold to the US in 1917 and since then named the **Virgin Islands of the United States.**

dank (dæŋk) ADJECTIVE (esp of cellars, caves, etc.) unpleasantly damp and chilly.
▷HISTORY C14: probably of Scandinavian origin; compare Swedish *dank* marshy spot
▸'**dankly** ADVERB ▸'**dankness** NOUN

Danmark ('danmarg) NOUN the Danish name for **Denmark.**

danny ('dænɪ) *or* **donny** NOUN, *plural* **-nies.** *Dialect* the hand (used esp when addressing children).
▷HISTORY probably from *dandy*, childish pronunciation of HAND

Dano-Norwegian (ˌdeɪnəʊnɔ:'wi:dʒən) NOUN another name for **Bokmål.**

danse macabre *French* (dɑ̃s makɑbrə) NOUN another name for **dance of death.**

danseur *French* (dɑ̃sœr) NOUN a male ballet dancer.

danseuse *French* (dɑ̃søz) NOUN a female ballet dancer.

Dantean ('dæntɪən, dæn'ti:ən) *or* **Dantesque** (dæn'tɛsk) ADJECTIVE of or relating to Dante (Alighieri), the Italian poet (1265–1321), or reminiscent of his allegorical account of a journey through Hell in *La Divina Commedia.*

danthonia (dæn'θəʊnɪə) NOUN any of various grasses of the genus *Danthonia*, of N temperate regions and South America.
▷HISTORY named after E. *Danthoine*, French botanist

Danube ('dænju:b) NOUN a river in central and SE Europe, rising in the Black Forest in Germany and flowing to the Black Sea. Length: 2859 km (1776 miles). German name: **Donau.** Czech name: **Dunaj.** Hungarian name: **Duna.** Serbo-Croat name: **Dunav** ('dunaf). Romanian name: **Dunărea.**

Danubian (dæn'ju:bɪən) ADJECTIVE of or relating to the river Danube.

Danzig ('dænsɪg; *German* 'dantsɪç) NOUN 1 the German name for **Gdańsk.** 2 a rare variety of domestic fancy pigeon originating in this area.

dap[1] (dæp) VERB **daps, dapping, dapped.** 1 *Angling* to fish with a natural or artificial fly on a floss silk line so that the wind makes the fly bob on and off the surface of the water. 2 (*intr*) (as of a bird) to dip lightly into water. 3 to bounce or cause to bounce.
▷HISTORY C17: of imitative origin

dap[2] (dæp) NOUN *Southwest Brit dialect* another word for **plimsoll.**
▷HISTORY C20: probably special use of DAP[1] (in the sense: to bounce, skip)

DAP *Computing* ABBREVIATION FOR **distributed array processor.**

daphne ('dæfnɪ) NOUN any shrub of the Eurasian thymelaeaceous genus *Daphne*, such as the mezereon and spurge laurel: ornamentals with shiny evergreen leaves and clusters of small bell-shaped flowers. See also **laurel** (sense 4).
▷HISTORY via Latin from Greek: laurel

Daphne ('dæfnɪ) NOUN *Greek myth* a nymph who was saved from the amorous attentions of Apollo by being changed into a laurel tree.

daphnia ('dæfnɪə) NOUN any water flea of the genus *Daphnia*, having a rounded body enclosed in a transparent shell and bearing branched swimming antennae.
▷HISTORY C19: from New Latin, probably from DAPHNE

Daphnis ('dæfnɪs) NOUN *Greek myth* a Sicilian shepherd, the son of Hermes and a nymph, who was regarded as the inventor of pastoral poetry.

Daphnis and Chloe NOUN two lovers in pastoral literature, esp in a prose idyll attributed to the Greek writer Longus.

dapper ('dæpə) ADJECTIVE 1 neat and spruce in dress and bearing; trim. 2 small and nimble.
▷HISTORY C15: from Middle Dutch: active, nimble
▸'**dapperly** ADVERB ▸'**dapperness** NOUN

dapple ('dæpᵊl) VERB 1 to mark or become marked with spots or patches of a different colour; mottle. ◆ NOUN 2 mottled or spotted markings. 3 a dappled horse, etc. ◆ ADJECTIVE 4 marked with dapples or spots.
▷HISTORY C14: of unknown origin

dapple-grey NOUN a horse with a grey coat having spots of darker colour.

Dapsang (dʌp'sʌŋ) NOUN another name for **K2.**

dapsone ('dæpˌsəʊn) NOUN an antimicrobial drug used to treat leprosy and certain types of dermatitis. Formula: $C_{12}H_{12}N_2O_2S$.
▷HISTORY C20: from *d(i)a(minodi)p(henyl) s(ulph)one*

DAR ABBREVIATION FOR *Daughters of the American Revolution.*

daraf ('dærəf) NOUN *Physics* a unit of elastance equal to a reciprocal farad.
▷HISTORY C20: reverse spelling of FARAD

darbies ('dɑ:bɪz) PLURAL NOUN *Brit* a slang term for **handcuffs.**
▷HISTORY C16: perhaps from the phrase *Father Derby's* or *Father Darby's bonds*, a rigid agreement between a usurer and his client

Darby and Joan ('dɑ:bɪ) NOUN 1 an ideal elderly married couple living in domestic harmony. 2 **Darby and Joan Club.** a club for elderly people.
▷HISTORY C18: a couple in an 18th-century English ballad

darcy ('dɑ:sɪ) NOUN *Geology* a unit expressing the permeability coefficient of rock. Symbol: D.
▷HISTORY named after Henri-Philibert-Gaspard *Darcy* (1803–58), French hydraulic engineer

Dard (dɑ:d) NOUN a member of any of the Indo-European peoples speaking a Dardic language.

Dardan ('dɑ:dᵊn) *or* **Dardanian** (dɑ:'deɪnɪən) NOUN another name for a **Trojan.**

Dardanelles (ˌdɑ:də'nɛlz) NOUN the strait between the Aegean and the Sea of Marmara, separating European from Asian Turkey. Ancient name: **Hellespont.**

Dardanus ('dɑ:dənəs) NOUN *Classical myth* the son of Zeus and Electra who founded the royal house of Troy.

Dardic ('dɑ:dɪk) ADJECTIVE 1 belonging or relating to a group of languages spoken in Kashmir, N Pakistan, and E Afghanistan, regarded as a subbranch of the Indic branch of the Indo-European family but showing certain Iranian characteristics. ◆ NOUN 2 this group of languages.

dare (dɛə) VERB 1 (*tr*) to challenge (a person to do something) as proof of courage. 2 (can take an infinitive with or without *to*) to be courageous enough to try (to do something): *she dares to dress differently from the others; you wouldn't dare!* 3 (*tr*) *Rare* to oppose without fear; defy. 4 **I dare say.** Also: **I daresay. a** (it is) quite possible (that). **b** probably: used as sentence substitute. ◆ NOUN 5 a challenge to do something as proof of courage. 6 something done in response to such a challenge.
▷HISTORY Old English *durran*; related to Old High German *turran* to venture
▸'**darer** NOUN

> **Language note** When used negatively or interrogatively, *dare* does not usually add *-s: he dare not come; dare she come?* When used negatively in the past tense, however, *dare* usually adds *-d: he dared not come.*

daredevil ('dɛəˌdɛvᵊl) NOUN 1 a recklessly bold person. ◆ ADJECTIVE 2 reckless; daring; bold.
▸'**dareˌdevilry** *or* '**dareˌdeviltry** NOUN

Dar es Salaam ('dɑ:r ɛs sə'lɑ:m) NOUN the chief port of Tanzania, on the Indian Ocean: capital of German East Africa (1891–1916); capital of Tanzania until 1983 when it was replaced by Dodoma; university (1963). Pop.: 1 360 850 (latest est.).

Darfur (dɑ:'fʊə) NOUN a region of the W Sudan; an independent kingdom until conquered by Egypt in 1874.

darg (dɑ:g) NOUN *Scot and northern English dialect* a day's work.
▷HISTORY C15: formed by syncope from *day-work*

dargah *or* **durgah** ('dɜ:gɑ:) NOUN the tomb of a Muslim saint; a Muslim shrine.
▷HISTORY Persian

daric ('dærɪk) NOUN a gold coin of ancient Persia. Compare **siglos.**
▷HISTORY C16: from Greek *Dareikos*, probably after Darius I of Persia

Darien ('dɛərɪən, 'dæ-) NOUN 1 the E part of the Isthmus of Panama, between the **Gulf of Darien** on the Caribbean coast and the Gulf of San Miguel on the Pacific coast; chiefly within the republic of Panama but extending also into Colombia: site of a disastrous attempt to establish a Scottish colony in 1698. 2 **Isthmus of.** the former name of the Isthmus of **Panama.** ◆ Spanish name: **Darién** (da'rjen).

daring ('dɛərɪŋ) ADJECTIVE 1 bold or adventurous; reckless. ◆ NOUN 2 courage in taking risks; boldness.
▸'**daringly** ADVERB

dariole ('dærɪˌəʊl) NOUN 1 Also called: **dariole mould.** a small cup-shaped mould used for making individual sweet or savoury dishes. 2 a dish prepared in such a mould.
▷HISTORY C14: from Old French

Darjeeling (dɑ:'dʒi:lɪŋ) NOUN 1 a town in NE India, in West Bengal in the Himalayas, at an altitude of about 2250 m (7500 ft.). Pop.: 73 090 (1991). 2 a high-quality black tea grown in the mountains around Darjeeling.

dark (dɑ:k) ADJECTIVE 1 having little or no light: *a dark street.* 2 (of a colour) reflecting or transmitting little light: *dark brown.* Compare **light**[1] (sense 29),

medium (sense 2). **3** **a** (of complexion, hair colour, etc.) not fair or blond; swarthy; brunette. **b** (*in combination*): *dark-eyed*. **4** gloomy or dismal. **5** sinister; evil: *a dark purpose*. **6** sullen or angry: *a dark scowl*. **7** ignorant or unenlightened: *a dark period in our history*. **8** secret or mysterious: *keep it dark*. **9** *Phonetics* denoting an (l) pronounced with a velar articulation giving back vowel resonance. In English, *l* is usually dark when final or preconsonantal. Compare **light**[1] (sense 30). ◆ NOUN **10** absence of light; darkness. **11** night or nightfall. **12** a dark place, patch, or shadow. **13** a state of ignorance (esp in the phrase **in the dark**). ◆ VERB **14** an archaic word for **darken.**
▷ HISTORY Old English *deorc*; related to Old High German *terchennen* to hide
▸ **'darkish** ADJECTIVE ▸ **'darkly** ADVERB ▸ **'darkness** NOUN

Dark Ages PLURAL NOUN **the.** *European history* **1** the period from about the late 5th century A.D. to about 1000 A.D., once considered an unenlightened period. **2** (occasionally) the whole medieval period.

Dark Continent NOUN **the.** a term for Africa when it was relatively unexplored.

dark current NOUN the residual current produced by a photoelectric device when not illuminated.

darken ('dɑːkən) VERB **1** to make or become dark or darker. **2** to make or become gloomy, angry, or sad: *his mood darkened*. **3** **darken (someone's) door.** (*usually used with a negative*) to visit someone: *never darken my door again!*
▸ **'darkener** NOUN

dark-field illumination NOUN illumination of the field of a microscope from the side so that the specimen is viewed against a dark background.

dark-field microscope NOUN another name for an **ultramicroscope.**

dark glasses PLURAL NOUN spectacles with lenses tinted to reduce transmitted light.

dark horse NOUN **1** a competitor in a race or contest about whom little is known; an unknown. **2** a person who reveals little about himself or his activities, esp one who has unexpected talents or abilities. **3** *US politics* a candidate who is unexpectedly nominated or elected.

dark lantern NOUN a lantern having a sliding shutter or panel to dim or hide the light.

darkle ('dɑːkᵊl) VERB *Archaic or literary* **1** to grow dark; darken. **2** (*intr*) to appear dark or indistinct.
▷ HISTORY C19: back formation from DARKLING

darkling ('dɑːklɪŋ) *Poetic* ◆ ADVERB, ADJECTIVE **1** in the dark or night. ◆ ADJECTIVE **2** darkening or almost dark; obscure.
▷ HISTORY C15: from DARK + -LING[2]

dark matter NOUN *Astronomy* matter known to make up perhaps 90% of the mass of the universe, but not detectable by its absorption or emission of electromagnetic radiation.

dark nebula NOUN a type of nebula that is observed by its blocking of radiation from other sources. See **nebula.**

dark reaction NOUN *Botany* the stage of photosynthesis involving the reduction of carbon dioxide and the dissociation of water, using chemical energy stored in ATP: does not require the presence of light. Compare **light reaction.**

darkroom ('dɑːkˌruːm, -ˌrʊm) NOUN a room in which photographs are processed in darkness or safe light.

darksome ('dɑːksəm) ADJECTIVE *Literary* dark or darkish.

dark star NOUN an invisible star known to exist only from observation of its radio, infrared, or other spectrum or of its gravitational effect, such as an invisible component of a binary or multiple star.

darky, darkie, *or* **darkey** ('dɑːkɪ) NOUN, *plural* **darkies** *or* **darkeys.** *Informal* **1** an offensive word for a Black. **2** *Austral* an offensive word for a native Australian.

darling ('dɑːlɪŋ) NOUN **1** a person very much loved: often used as a term of address. **2** a favourite: *the teacher's darling*. ◆ ADJECTIVE (*prenominal*) **3** beloved. **4** much admired; pleasing: *a darling hat*.
▷ HISTORY Old English *dēorling*; see DEAR, -LING[1]

Darling Downs PLURAL NOUN a plateau in NE Australia, in SE Queensland: a vast agricultural and stock-raising area.

Darling Range NOUN a ridge in SW Western Australia, parallel to the coast. Highest point: about 582 m (1669 ft.).

Darling River NOUN a river in SE Australia, rising in the Eastern Highlands and flowing southwest to the Murray River. Length: 2740 km (1702 miles).

Darlington ('dɑːlɪŋtən) NOUN **1** an industrial town in NE England in Darlington unitary authority, S Durham: developed mainly with the opening of the Stockton-Darlington railway (1825). Pop.: 86 767 (1991). **2** a unitary authority in NE England, in Durham. Pop.: 97 822 (2001). Area: 198 sq. km (77 sq. miles).

Darmstadt ('dɑːmstæt; *German* 'darmʃtat) NOUN an industrial city in central Germany, in Hesse: former capital of the grand duchy of Hesse-Darmstadt (1567–1945). Pop.: 137 600 (1999 est.).

darn[1] (dɑːn) VERB **1** to mend (a hole or a garment) with a series of crossing or interwoven stitches. ◆ NOUN **2** a patch of darned work on a garment. **3** the process or act of darning.
▷ HISTORY C16: probably from French (Channel Islands dialect) *darner*; compare Welsh, Breton *darn* piece
▸ **'darner** NOUN ▸ **'darning** NOUN

darn[2] (dɑːn) INTERJECTION, ADJECTIVE, ADVERB, NOUN a euphemistic word for **damn** (senses 1–4, 15).

darned (dɑːnd) ADVERB, ADJECTIVE *Slang* **1** (intensifier): *this darned car won't start; a darned good shot*. ◆ ADJECTIVE **2** another word for **damned** (senses 2, 3).

darnedest (ˌdɑːndɪst) NOUN a euphemistic word for **damnedest.**

darnel ('dɑːnᵊl) NOUN any of several grasses of the genus *Lolium*, esp *L. temulentum*, that grow as weeds in grain fields in Europe and Asia.
▷ HISTORY C14: probably related to French (Walloon dialect) *darnelle*, of obscure origin

darning egg *or* **mushroom** NOUN a rounded piece of wood or plastic used in darning to support the fabric around the hole.

darning needle NOUN **1** a long needle with a large eye used for darning. **2** *US and Canadian* a dialect name for a **dragonfly.**

darogha (dɑː'rəʊgɑː) NOUN (in India and Pakistan) **1** a manager. **2** an inspector.
▷ HISTORY Urdu

dart[1] (dɑːt) NOUN **1** a small narrow pointed missile that is thrown or shot, as in the game of darts. **2** a sudden quick movement. **3** *Zoology* a slender pointed structure, as in snails for aiding copulation or in nematodes for penetrating the host's tissues. **4** a tapered tuck made in dressmaking. ◆ VERB **5** to move or throw swiftly and suddenly; shoot: *she darted across the room*. ◆ See also **darts.**
▷ HISTORY C14: from Old French, of Germanic origin; related to Old English *daroth* spear, Old High German *tart* dart
▸ **'darting** ADJECTIVE ▸ **'dartingly** ADVERB

dart[2] (dɑːt) NOUN any of various tropical and semitropical marine fish.
▷ HISTORY from Middle English *darce*, from Late Latin *dardus*, dart, javelin

dartboard ('dɑːtˌbɔːd) NOUN a circular piece of wood, cork, etc., used as the target in the game of darts. It is divided into numbered sectors with central inner and outer bull's-eyes.

darter ('dɑːtə) NOUN **1** Also called: **anhinga, snakebird.** any aquatic bird of the genus *Anhinga* and family *Anhingidae*, of tropical and subtropical inland waters, having a long slender neck and bill: order *Pelecaniformes* (pelicans, cormorants, etc.). **2** any small brightly coloured North American freshwater fish of the genus *Etheostoma* and related genera: family *Percidae* (perches).

Dartford ('dɑːtfəd) NOUN a town in SE England, in NW Kent. Pop.: 59 411 (1991).

Dartmoor ('dɑːtˌmʊə) NOUN **1** a moorland plateau in SW England, in SW Devon: a national park since 1951. Area: 945 sq. km (365 sq. miles). **2** a prison in SW England, on Dartmoor: England's main prison for long-term convicts. **3** a small strong breed of pony, originally from Dartmoor. **4** a hardy coarse-woolled breed of sheep originally from Dartmoor.

Dartmouth ('dɑːtməθ) NOUN **1** a port in SW England, in S Devon: Royal Naval College (1905). Pop.: 5676 (1991). **2** a city in SE Canada, in S Nova Scotia, on Halifax Harbour: oil refineries and shipyards. Pop.: 67 798 (1991).

darts (dɑːts) NOUN (*functioning as singular*) any of various competitive games in which darts are thrown at a dartboard.

Darwin ('dɑːwɪn) NOUN a port in N Australia, capital of the Northern Territory: destroyed by a cyclone in 1974 but rebuilt on the same site. Pop.: 78 100 (1994). Former name (1869–1911): **Palmerston.**

Darwinian (dɑː'wɪnɪən) ADJECTIVE **1** of or relating to Charles Darwin (1809–82), the English naturalist who formulated the theory of evolution by natural selection, or his theory. ◆ NOUN **2** a person who accepts, supports, or uses this theory.

Darwinism ('dɑːwɪˌnɪzəm) *or* **Darwinian theory** NOUN the theory of the origin of animal and plant species by evolution through a process of natural selection. Compare **Lamarckism.** See also **Neo-Darwinism.**
▸ **'Darwinist** *or* **'Darwinite** NOUN, ADJECTIVE ▸ **ˌDarwin'istic** ADJECTIVE

Darwin's finches PLURAL NOUN the finches of the subfamily *Geospizinae* of the Galapagos Islands, showing great variation in bill structure and feeding habits: provided Darwin with evidence to support his theory of evolution.

dash[1] (dæʃ) VERB (*mainly tr*) **1** to hurl; crash: *he dashed the cup to the floor; the waves dashed against the rocks*. **2** to mix: *white paint dashed with blue*. **3** (*intr*) to move hastily or recklessly; rush: *he dashed to her rescue*. **4** (usually foll by *off* or *down*) to write (down) or finish (off) hastily. **5** to destroy; frustrate: *his hopes were dashed*. **6** to daunt (someone); cast down; discourage: *he was dashed by her refusal*. ◆ NOUN **7** a sudden quick movement; dart. **8** a small admixture: *coffee with a dash of cream*. **9** a violent stroke or blow. **10** the sound of splashing or smashing: *the dash of the waves*. **11** panache; style: *he rides with dash*. **12** **cut a dash.** See **cut** (sense 33). **13** the punctuation mark —, used singly in place of a colon, esp to indicate a sudden change of subject or grammatical anacoluthon, or in pairs to enclose a parenthetical remark. **14** the symbol (–) used, in combination with the symbol *dot* (·), in the written representation of Morse and other telegraphic codes. Compare **dah.** **15** *Athletics* another word (esp US and Canadian) for **sprint.** **16** *Informal* short for **dashboard.**
▷ HISTORY Middle English *dasche, dasse*

dash[2] (dæʃ) INTERJECTION *Informal* a euphemistic word for **damn** (senses 1, 2).

dash[3] (dæʃ) *W African* ◆ NOUN **1** a gift, commission, tip, or bribe. ◆ VERB **2** to give (a dash) to someone.
▷ HISTORY C16: perhaps from Fanti

dashboard ('dæʃˌbɔːd) NOUN **1** Also called (Brit): **fascia.** the instrument panel in a car, boat, or aircraft. Sometimes shortened to: **dash.** **2** *Obsolete* a board at the side of a carriage or boat to protect against splashing.

dasheen (dæ'ʃiːn) NOUN another name for **taro.**
▷ HISTORY C19: perhaps changed from French (*chou*) *de Chine* (cabbage) of China

dasher ('dæʃə) NOUN the plunger in a churn, often with paddles attached.

dashi ('daʃɪ) NOUN a clear stock made from dried fish and kelp.
▷ HISTORY C20: Japanese

dashiki (dɑː'ʃiːkɪ) NOUN a large loose-fitting buttonless upper garment worn esp by Blacks in the US, Africa, and the Caribbean.
▷ HISTORY C20: of W African origin

dashing ('dæʃɪŋ) ADJECTIVE **1** spirited; lively: *a dashing young man*. **2** stylish; showy: *a dashing hat*.
▸ **'dashingly** ADVERB

Dashing White Sergeant NOUN a lively Scottish dance for sets of six people.

dashpot ('dæʃˌpɒt) NOUN a device for damping vibrations; the vibrating part is attached to a piston moving in a liquid-filled cylinder.
▷ HISTORY C20: from DASH[1] + POT[1]

Dasht-i-Kavir *or* **Dasht-e-Kavir** (ˌdæʃti:kæ'vɪə) NOUN a salt waste on the central plateau of Iran: a treacherous marsh beneath a salt crust. Also called: **Kavir Desert.**

Dasht-i-Lut *or* **Dasht-e-Lut** (ˌdæʃti:'lʊt) NOUN a desert plateau in central and E central Iran.

Dassehra ('dæsɛræ) NOUN an annual Hindu festival celebrated on the 10th lunar day of Navaratri; images of the goddess Durga are immersed in water.

dassie ('dæsɪ) NOUN another name for a **hyrax**, esp the rock hyrax
▷HISTORY C19: from Afrikaans

dastard ('dæstəd) NOUN *Archaic* a contemptible sneaking coward.
▷HISTORY C15 (in the sense: dullard): probably from Old Norse *dæstr* exhausted, out of breath

dastardly ('dæstədlɪ) ADJECTIVE mean and cowardly.
▸ **'dastardliness** NOUN

dasypaedal (ˌdæsɪ'pi:d^{ə}l) ADJECTIVE (of the young of some species of birds after hatching) having a covering of down.
▷HISTORY from Greek *dasus* shaggy + *pais, paid-* child

dasyure ('dæsɪˌjʊə) NOUN any small carnivorous marsupial, such as *Dasyurus quoll* (**eastern dasyure**), of the subfamily *Dasyurinae,* of Australia, New Guinea, and adjacent islands. See also **Tasmanian devil.**
▷HISTORY C19: from New Latin *Dasyūrus,* from Greek *dasus* shaggy + *oura* tail; see DENSE

DAT ABBREVIATION FOR **digital audio tape.**

dat. ABBREVIATION FOR dative.

data ('deɪtə, 'dɑ:tə) PLURAL NOUN [1] a series of observations, measurements, or facts; information. [2] Also called: **information.** *Computing* the information operated on by a computer program.
▷HISTORY C17: from Latin, literally: (things) given, from *dare* to give

> **Language note** Although now often used as a singular noun, *data* is properly a plural.

data bank NOUN a store of a large amount of information, esp in a form that can be handled by a computer.

database ('deɪtəˌbeɪs) NOUN [1] a systematized collection of data that can be accessed immediately and manipulated by a data-processing system for a specific purpose. [2] *Informal* any large store of information: *a database of knowledge.*

database management NOUN the maintenance of information stored in a computer system.

data capture NOUN any process for converting information into a form that can be handled by a computer.

data dictionary NOUN *Computing* an index of data held in a database and used to assist in the access to data. Also called: **data directory.**

dataflow architecture ('deɪtəˌfləʊ, 'dɑ:tə-) NOUN a means of arranging computer data processing in which operations are governed by the data present and the processing it requires rather than by a prewritten program that awaits data to be processed.

datal ('deɪt^{ə}l) ADJECTIVE *Northern English dialect* slow-witted.

data mining NOUN the gathering of information from pre-existing data stored in a database, such as one held by a supermarket about customers' shopping habits.

data pen NOUN a device for reading or scanning magnetically coded data on labels, packets, etc.

data processing NOUN **a** a sequence of operations performed on data, esp by a computer, in order to extract information, reorder files, etc. **b** (*as modifier*): *a data-processing centre.* See also **automatic data processing.**

data protection NOUN (in Britain) safeguards for individuals relating to personal data stored on a computer.

datary ('deɪtərɪ) NOUN, *plural* **-ries.** *RC Church* the head of the **dataria** (deɪ'tɛərɪə), the papal office that assesses candidates for benefices reserved to the Holy See.
▷HISTORY C16: from Medieval Latin *datārius* official who dated papal letters, from Late Latin *data* DATE[1]

data set NOUN *Computing* another name for **file[1]** (sense 7).

data structure NOUN an organized form, such as an array list or string, in which connected data items are held in a computer.

datcha ('dætʃə) NOUN a variant spelling of **dacha.**

date[1] (deɪt) NOUN [1] a specified day of the month: *today's date is October 27.* [2] the particular day or year of an event: *the date of the Norman Conquest was 1066.* [3] (*plural*) the years of a person's birth and death or of the beginning and end of an event or period. [4] an inscription on a coin, letter, etc., stating when it was made or written. [5] **a** an appointment for a particular time, esp with a person to whom one is sexually or romantically attached: *she has a dinner date.* **b** the person with whom the appointment is made. [6] the present moment; now (esp in the phrases **to date, up to date**). ◆ VERB [7] (*tr*) to mark (a letter, coin, etc.) with the day, month, or year. [8] (*tr*) to assign a date of occurrence or creation to. [9] (*intr; foll by from* or *back to*) to have originated (at a specified time): *his decline dates from last summer.* [10] (*tr*) to reveal the age of: *that dress dates her.* [11] to make or become old-fashioned: *some good films hardly date at all.* [12] *Informal, chiefly US and Canadian* **a** to be a boyfriend or girlfriend of (someone of the opposite sex). **b** to accompany (a member of the opposite sex) on a date.
▷HISTORY C14: from Old French, from Latin *dare* to give, as in the phrase *epistula data Romae* letter handed over at Rome
▸ **'datable** *or* **'dateable** ADJECTIVE ▸ **'dateless** ADJECTIVE

> **Language note** See at **year.**

date[2] (deɪt) NOUN [1] the fruit of the date palm, having sweet edible flesh and a single large woody seed. [2] short for **date palm.**
▷HISTORY C13: from Old French, from Latin, from Greek *daktulos* finger

dated ('deɪtɪd) ADJECTIVE [1] unfashionable; outmoded. [2] (of a security) having a fixed date for redemption.

Datel ('deɪˌtɛl) NOUN *Trademark* a British Telecom service providing for the direct transmission of data from one computer to another.
▷HISTORY C20: from DA(TA) + TEL(EX)

dateless ('deɪtlɪs) ADJECTIVE [1] likely to remain fashionable, relevant, or interesting regardless of age; timeless. [2] having no date or limit.

dateline ('deɪtˌlaɪn) NOUN *Journalism* the date and location of a story, placed at the top of an article.

date line NOUN (*often capitals*) short for **International Date Line.**

date palm NOUN a feather palm, *Phoenix dactylifera,* probably native to N Africa and SW Asia and widely grown in other arid warm temperate and subtropical regions for its edible fruit (dates).

date rape NOUN [1] the act or an instance of a man raping a woman while they are on a date together. [2] an act of sexual intercourse regarded as tantamount to rape, esp if the woman was encouraged to drink excessively or was subjected to undue pressure.

date stamp NOUN [1] an adjustable rubber stamp for recording the date. [2] an inked impression made by this.

dating ('deɪtɪŋ) NOUN any of several techniques, such as radioactive dating, dendrochronology, or varve dating, for establishing the age of rocks, palaeontological or archaeological specimens, etc.

dating agency NOUN an agency that provides introductions to people seeking a companion with similar interests.

dative ('deɪtɪv) *Grammar* ◆ ADJECTIVE [1] denoting a case of nouns, pronouns, and adjectives used to express the indirect object, to identify the recipients, and for other purposes. ◆ NOUN [2] **a** the dative case. **b** a word or speech element in this case.
▷HISTORY C15: from Latin *datīvus,* from *dare* to give; translation of Greek *dotikos*
▸ **datival** (deɪ'taɪv^{ə}l) ADJECTIVE ▸ **'datively** ADVERB

dative bond NOUN *Chem* another name for **coordinate bond.**

dato ('dɑ:təʊ) NOUN, *plural* **-tos.** the chief of any of certain Muslim tribes in the Philippine Islands.
▷HISTORY C19: from Spanish, ultimately from Malay *dato'* grandfather

datolite ('deɪtəˌlaɪt) NOUN a colourless mineral consisting of a hydrated silicate of calcium and boron in monoclinic crystalline form, occurring in cavities in igneous rocks. Formula: $CaBSiO_4(OH)$.
▷HISTORY C19: *dato-* from Greek *dateisthai* to divide + -LITE

Datuk (dæ'tʊk) NOUN (in Malaysia) a title denoting membership of a high order of chivalry.
▷HISTORY from Malay *datu* chief
▸ **Datin** (dæ'ti:n) FEMININE NOUN

datum ('deɪtəm, 'dɑ:təm) NOUN, *plural* **-ta** (-tə). [1] a single piece of information; fact. [2] a proposition taken for granted, often in order to construct some theoretical framework upon it; a given. See also **sense datum.**
▷HISTORY C17: from Latin: something given; see DATA

datum plane, level, *or* **line** NOUN *Surveying* the horizontal plane from which heights and depths are calculated.

datura (də'tjʊərə) NOUN any of various chiefly Indian solanaceous plants of the genus *Datura,* such as the moonflower and thorn apple, having large trumpet-shaped flowers, prickly pods, and narcotic properties.
▷HISTORY C16: from New Latin, from Hindi *dhatūra* jimson weed, from Sanskrit *dhattūra*

DATV ABBREVIATION FOR digitally assisted television: a technique in which special digital signals are transmitted with an analogue picture signal to assist the receiver to display the picture to the best advantage.

daub (dɔ:b) VERB [1] (*tr*) to smear or spread (paint, mud, etc.), esp carelessly. [2] (*tr*) to cover or coat (with paint, plaster, etc.) carelessly. [3] to paint (a picture) clumsily or badly. ◆ NOUN [4] an unskilful or crude painting. [5] something daubed on, esp as a wall covering. See also **wattle and daub.** [6] a smear (of paint, mud, etc.). [7] the act of daubing.
▷HISTORY C14: from Old French *dauber* to paint, whitewash, from Latin *dealbāre,* from *albāre* to whiten, from *albus* white
▸ **'dauber** NOUN ▸ **'dauby** ADJECTIVE

daube (dəʊb) NOUN a braised meat stew.
▷HISTORY from French

daubery ('dɔ:bərɪ) NOUN [1] the act or an instance of daubing. [2] an unskilful painting.

daud (dɔ:d, dɒd) NOUN *Scot* a lump or chunk of something.
▷HISTORY C18: from earlier *dad* to strike, of unknown origin

Daugava ('daʊgaˌva) NOUN the Latvian name for the Western **Dvina.**

Daugavpils (*Latvian* 'daugafˌpils) NOUN a city in SE Latvia on the Western Dvina River: founded in 1274 by Teutonic Knights; ruled by Poland (1559–1772) and Russia (1772–1915); retaken by the Russians in 1940. Pop.: 114 510 (2000 est.). German name (until 1893): **Dünaburg.** Former Russian name (1893–1920): **Dvinsk.**

daughter ('dɔ:tə) NOUN [1] a female offspring; a girl or woman in relation to her parents. [2] a female descendant. [3] a female from a certain country, etc., or one closely connected with a certain environment, etc.: *a daughter of the church.* ◆ Related adjective: **filial.** [4] (*often capital*) *Archaic* a form of address for a girl or woman. ◆ MODIFIER [5] *Biology* denoting a cell or unicellular organism produced by the division of one of its own kind. [6] *Physics* (of a nuclide) formed from another nuclide by radioactive decay.
▷HISTORY Old English *dohtor;* related to Old High German *tohter* daughter, Greek *thugatēr,* Sanskrit *duhitá*
▸ **'daughterhood** NOUN ▸ **'daughterless** ADJECTIVE
▸ **'daughter-ˌlike** ADJECTIVE ▸ **'daughterliness** NOUN
▸ **'daughterly** ADJECTIVE

daughter-in-law NOUN, *plural* **daughters-in-law.** the wife of one's son.

Daughters of the American Revolution NOUN **the.** an organization of women descended from patriots of the period of the War of Independence. Abbreviation: **DAR.**

daunt (dɔ:nt) VERB (*tr; often passive*) [1] to intimidate. [2] to dishearten.
▷HISTORY C13: from Old French *danter,* changed from *donter* to conquer, from Latin *domitāre* to tame
▸'**daunter** NOUN

daunting ('dɔ:ntɪŋ) ADJECTIVE causing fear or discouragement; intimidating.
▸'**dauntingly** ADVERB

dauntless ('dɔ:ntlɪs) ADJECTIVE bold; fearless; intrepid.
▸'**dauntlessly** ADVERB ▸'**dauntlessness** NOUN

dauphin ('dɔ:fɪn, dɔ:'fɪn; *French* dofɛ̃) NOUN (1349–1830) the title of the direct heir to the French throne; the eldest son of the king of France.
▷HISTORY C15: from Old French: originally a family name; adopted as a title by the Counts of Vienne and later by the French crown princes

dauphine ('dɔ:fi:n, dɔ:'fi:n; *French* dofin) *or* **dauphiness** ('dɔ:fɪnɪs) NOUN *French history* the wife of a dauphin.

Dauphiné (*French* dofine) NOUN a former province of SE France: its rulers, the Counts of Vienne, assumed the title of *dauphin;* annexed to France in 1457.

daur (dɔ:r) VERB a Scot word for **dare.**

Davao (da'va:o) NOUN a port in the S Philippines, in SE Mindanao. Pop.: 700 000 (2000 est.).

daven ('dɑvən) VERB (*intr*) *Judaism* [1] to pray. [2] to lead prayers.
▷HISTORY from Yiddish

davenport ('dævən,pɔ:t) NOUN [1] *Chiefly Brit* a tall narrow desk with a slanted writing surface and drawers at the side. [2] *US and Canadian* a large sofa, esp one convertible into a bed.
▷HISTORY C19: sense 1 said to be named after Captain *Davenport* who commissioned the first ones

Daventry ('dævəntrɪ) NOUN a town in central England, in Northamptonshire: light industries, site of an important international radio transmitter. Pop.: 18 099 (1991).

Davis Cup ('deɪvɪs) NOUN [1] an annual international lawn tennis championship for men's teams. [2] the trophy awarded for this.
▷HISTORY C20: after Dwight F. *Davis* (1879–1945), American civic leader who donated the cup

Davis Strait ('deɪvɪs) NOUN a strait between Baffin Island, in Canada, and Greenland.
▷HISTORY named after John *Davis* (??1550–1605), English navigator

davit ('dævɪt, 'deɪ-) NOUN a cranelike device, usually one of a pair, fitted with a tackle for suspending or lowering equipment, esp a lifeboat.
▷HISTORY C14: from Anglo-French *daviot,* diminutive of *Davi* David

Davos ('dævɒs) NOUN a mountain resort in Switzerland: winter sports, site of the Parsenn ski run. Pop.: 10 500 (1990). Height: about 1560 m (5118 ft.). Romansh name: **Tarau.**

Davy Jones ('deɪvɪ) NOUN [1] Also called: **Davy Jones's locker.** the ocean's bottom, esp when regarded as the grave of those lost or buried at sea. [2] the spirit or devil of the sea.
▷HISTORY C18: of unknown origin

Davy lamp NOUN See **safety lamp.**
▷HISTORY C19: named after its inventor Sir Humphry *Davy* (1778–1829), English chemist

daw (dɔ:) NOUN an archaic, dialect, or poetic name for a **jackdaw.**
▷HISTORY C15: related to Old High German *taha*

dawbake ('dɔ:beɪk) NOUN *Southwest English dialect* a foolish or slow-witted person.

dawdle ('dɔ:dᵊl) VERB [1] (*intr*) to be slow or lag behind. [2] (when *tr,* often foll by *away*) to waste (time); trifle.
▷HISTORY C17: of uncertain origin
▸'**dawdler** NOUN ▸'**dawdlingly** ADVERB

dawk[1] (dɔ:k) NOUN a variant spelling of **dak.**

dawk[2] (dɔ:k) NOUN *dialect* a Northern English dialect word for **hand.**

dawn (dɔ:n) NOUN [1] daybreak; sunrise. Related adjective: **auroral.** [2] the sky when light first appears in the morning. [3] the beginning of something. ◆ VERB (*intr*) [4] to begin to grow light after the night. [5] to begin to develop, appear, or expand. [6] (usually foll by *on* or *upon*) to begin to become apparent (to).
▷HISTORY Old English *dagian* to dawn; see DAY
▸'**dawn,like** ADJECTIVE

dawn chorus NOUN the singing of large numbers of birds at dawn.

dawney ('dɑ:ni:) ADJECTIVE *Irish* (of a person) dull or slow; listless.
▷HISTORY of unknown origin

dawn raid NOUN *Stock Exchange* an unexpected attempt to acquire a substantial proportion of a company's shares at the start of a day's trading as a preliminary to a takeover bid.

dawn redwood NOUN a deciduous conifer, *Metasequoia glyptostroboides,* native to China but planted in other regions as an ornamental tree: family *Taxodiaceae.* Until the 1940s it was known only as a fossil.

Dawson ('dɔ:sᵊn) NOUN a town in NW Canada, in the Yukon on the Yukon River: a boom town during the Klondike gold rush (at its height in 1899). Pop.: 1988 (1995 est.).

Dawson Creek NOUN a town in W Canada, in NE British Columbia: SE terminus of the Alaska Highway. Pop.: 10 981 (1991).

day (deɪ) NOUN [1] Also called: **civil day.** the period of time, the **calendar day,** of 24 hours' duration reckoned from one midnight to the next. [2] the period of light between sunrise and sunset, as distinguished from the night. [3] the part of a day occupied with regular activity, esp work: *he took a day off.* [4] (*sometimes plural*) a period or point in time: *he was a good singer in his day; in days gone by; any day now.* [5] the period of time, the **sidereal day** during which the earth makes one complete revolution on its axis relative to a particular star. The **mean sidereal day** lasts 23 hours 56 minutes 4.1 seconds of the mean solar day. [6] the period of time, the **solar day** during which the earth makes one complete revolution on its axis relative to the sun. The **mean solar day** is the average length of the apparent solar day and is some four minutes (3 minutes 56.5 seconds of sidereal time) longer than the sidereal day. [7] the period of time taken by a specified planet to make one complete rotation on its axis: *the Martian day.* [8] (*often capital*) a day designated for a special observance, esp a holiday: *Christmas Day.* [9] **all in a day's work.** part of one's normal activity; no trouble. [10] **at the end of the day.** in the final reckoning. [11] **day of rest.** the Sabbath; Sunday. [12] **end one's days.** to pass the end of one's life. [13] **every dog has his day.** one's luck will come. [14] **in this day and age.** nowadays. [15] **it's early days.** it's too early to tell how things will turn out. [16] **late in the day. a** very late (in a particular situation). **b** too late. [17] **that will be the day. a** I look forward to that. **b** that is most unlikely to happen. [18] a time of success, recognition, power, etc.: *his day will soon come.* [19] a struggle or issue at hand: *the day is lost.* [20] **a** the ground surface over a mine. **b** (*as modifier*): *the day level.* [21] **from day to day.** without thinking of the future. [22] **call it a day.** to stop work or other activity. [23] **day after day.** without respite; relentlessly. [24] **day by day.** gradually or progressively; daily: *he weakened day by day.* [25] **day in, day out.** every day and all day long. [26] **from Day 1** *or* **Day One.** from the very beginning. [27] **one of these days.** at some future time. [28] (*modifier*) of, relating to, or occurring in the day: *the day shift.* ◆ Related adjective: **diurnal.** See also **days.**
▷HISTORY Old English *dæg;* related to Old High German *tag,* Old Norse *dagr*

Dayak ('daɪæk) NOUN, *plural* **-aks** *or* **-ak.** a variant spelling of **Dyak.**

dayan (dɑ'jɑn, 'dɑjən) NOUN *Judaism* a senior rabbi, esp one who sits in a religious court.
▷HISTORY from Hebrew, literally: judge

day bed NOUN a narrow bed, with a head piece and sometimes a foot piece and back, on which to recline during the day.

day blindness NOUN a nontechnical name for **hemeralopia.**

daybook ('deɪ,bʊk) NOUN *Book-keeping* a book in which the transactions of each day are recorded as they occur.

dayboy ('deɪ,bɔɪ) NOUN *Brit* a boy who attends a boarding school daily, but returns home each evening.

daybreak ('deɪ,breɪk) NOUN the time in the morning when light first appears; dawn; sunrise.

daycare ('deɪ,kɛə) NOUN *Social welfare* [1] *Brit* occupation, treatment, or supervision during the working day for people who might be at risk if left on their own, or whose usual carers need daytime relief. [2] *Brit* welfare services provided by a local authority, health service, or voluntary body during the day. Compare **residential care.** [3] *NZ* short for **daycare centre.**

daycare centre NOUN another name (esp US and NZ) for **day nursery.**

daycentre ('deɪ,sɛntə) *or* **day centre** NOUN *Social welfare* (in Britain) [1] a building used for daycare or other welfare services. See also **drop-in centre.** [2] the enterprise itself, including staff, users, and organization.

daych (deɪtʃ) VERB *Southwest English dialect* to thatch.

day-clean NOUN *Caribbean and West African informal* the time after first dawn when the sun begins to shine; clear daybreak.

daydream ('deɪ,dri:m) NOUN [1] a pleasant dreamlike fantasy indulged in while awake; idle reverie. [2] a pleasant scheme or wish that is unlikely to be fulfilled; pipe dream. ◆ VERB [3] (*intr*) to have daydreams; indulge in idle fantasy.
▸'**day,dreamer** NOUN ▸'**day,dreamy** ADJECTIVE

dayflower ('deɪ,flaʊə) NOUN any of various tropical and subtropical plants of the genus *Commelina,* having jointed creeping stems, narrow pointed leaves, and blue or purplish flowers which wilt quickly: family *Commelinaceae.*

dayfly ('deɪ,flaɪ) NOUN, *plural* **-flies.** another name for a **mayfly.**

Day-Glo NOUN *Trademark* **a** a brand of fluorescent colouring materials, as of paint. **b** (*as modifier*): *Day-Glo colours.*

day hospital NOUN *Brit* part of a hospital that offers therapeutic services, where patients usually attend all day but go home or to a hospital ward at night.

day labourer NOUN an unskilled worker hired and paid by the day.

daylight ('deɪ,laɪt) NOUN [1] **a** light from the sun. **b** (*as modifier*): *daylight film.* [2] the period when it is light; daytime. [3] daybreak. [4] **see daylight. a** to understand something previously obscure. **b** to realize that the end of a difficult task is approaching. ◆ See also **daylights.**

daylight lamp NOUN *Physics* a lamp whose light has a range of wavelengths similar to that of natural sunlight.

daylight robbery NOUN *Informal* blatant overcharging.

daylights ('deɪ,laɪts) PLURAL NOUN consciousness or wits (esp in the phrases **scare, knock,** or **beat the (living) daylights out of someone**).

daylight-saving time NOUN time set usually one hour ahead of the local standard time, widely adopted in the summer to provide extra daylight in the evening. Also called (in the US): **daylight time.** See also **British Summer Time.**

day lily NOUN [1] any widely cultivated Eurasian liliaceous plant of the genus *Hemerocallis,* having large yellow, orange, or red lily-like flowers, which typically last for only one day and are immediately succeeded by others. [2] the flower of any of these plants.

daylong ('deɪ,lɒŋ) ADJECTIVE, ADVERB lasting the entire day; all day.

day name NOUN *W African* a name indicating a person's day of birth.

day-neutral ADJECTIVE (of plants) having an ability to mature and bloom that is not affected by day length.

day nursery NOUN *Social welfare, Brit and NZ* an establishment offering daycare to preschool children, enabling their parents to work full time or have extended relief if child care is a problem. Also called (NZ): **daycare centre.**

Day of Atonement NOUN another name for **Yom Kippur.**

Day of Judgment NOUN another name for **Judgment Day.**

day of reckoning NOUN a time when the effects

of one's past mistakes or misdeeds catch up with one.

day release NOUN *Brit* a system whereby workers are released for part-time education without loss of pay.

day return NOUN a reduced fare for a journey (by train, etc.) travelling both ways in one day.

day room NOUN a communal living room in a residential institution such as a hospital.

days (deɪz) ADVERB *Informal* during the day, esp regularly: *he works days.*

day school NOUN 1 a private school taking day students only. Compare **boarding school.** 2 a school giving instruction during the daytime. Compare **night school.**

dayshell (ˈdeɪˌʃɛl) NOUN *Southwest English dialect* a thistle.

day shift NOUN 1 a group of workers who work a shift during the daytime in an industry or occupation where a night shift or a back shift is also worked. 2 the period worked. ◆ See also **back shift.**

Days of Awe PLURAL NOUN *Judaism* another name for **High Holidays.**
▷**HISTORY** a literal translation of YAMIM NORA'IM

days of grace PLURAL NOUN days permitted by custom for payment of a promissory note, bill of exchange, etc., after it falls due.

dayspring (ˈdeɪˌsprɪŋ) NOUN a poetic word for **dawn.**

daystar (ˈdeɪˌstɑː) NOUN 1 a poetic word for the **sun.** 2 another word for the **morning star.**

daytime (ˈdeɪˌtaɪm) NOUN the time between dawn and dusk; the day as distinct from evening or night.

day-to-day ADJECTIVE routine; everyday: *day-to-day chores.*

Dayton (ˈdeɪt^{ə}n) NOUN an industrial city in SW Ohio: aviation research centre. Pop.: 166 179 (2000).

Daytona Beach (deɪˈtəʊnə) NOUN a city in NE Florida, on the Atlantic: a resort with a beach of hard white sand, used since 1903 for motor speed trials. Pop.: 61 921 (1990).

day trading NOUN the practice of buying and selling shares on the same day, often via the Internet, in order to make a quick profit.
▸**day trader** NOUN

day trip NOUN a journey made to and from a place within one day.
▸**ˈday-ˌtripper** NOUN

Da Yunhe (ˈdæ ˈjuːnhə) NOUN the Pinyin transliteration of the Chinese name for the **Grand Canal** (sense 1).

daze (deɪz) VERB (*tr*) 1 to stun or stupefy, esp by a blow or shock. 2 to bewilder, amaze, or dazzle. ◆ NOUN 3 a state of stunned confusion or shock (esp in the phrase **in a daze**).
▷**HISTORY** C14: from Old Norse *dasa-,* as in *dasask* to grow weary
▸**dazedly** (ˈdeɪzɪdlɪ) ADVERB

dazzle (ˈdæz^{ə}l) VERB 1 (*usually tr*) to blind or be blinded partially and temporarily by sudden excessive light. 2 to amaze, as with brilliance: *she was dazzled by his wit; she dazzles in this film.* ◆ NOUN 3 bright light that dazzles. 4 bewilderment caused by glamour, brilliance, etc.: *the dazzle of fame.*
▷**HISTORY** C15: from DAZE

dazzling (ˈdæzlɪŋ) ADJECTIVE 1 so bright as to blind someone temporarily. 2 extremely clever, attractive, or impressive; brilliant; amazing.
▸**ˈdazzlingly** ADVERB

dB *or* **db** SYMBOL FOR decibel *or* decibels.

DB ABBREVIATION FOR **defined-benefit.**

DBE ABBREVIATION FOR Dame (Commander of the Order) of the British Empire (a Brit. title).

Dbh *or* **DBH** *Forestry* ABBREVIATION FOR diameter at breast height.

DBib ABBREVIATION FOR **Douay Bible.**

DBMS ABBREVIATION FOR database management system.

DBS ABBREVIATION FOR: 1 direct broadcasting by satellite. 2 direct broadcasting satellite.

dbx *or* **DBX** NOUN *Trademark, Electronics* a noise-reduction system that works as a compander across the full frequency spectrum.

DC ABBREVIATION FOR: 1 *Music* **da capo.** 2 Detective Constable. 3 direct current. Compare **AC.** 4 district commissioner. 5 Also: **D.C.** District of Columbia. 6 **defined-contribution.**

D.C. (in the US and Canada) ABBREVIATION FOR Doctor of Chiropractic.

DCB ABBREVIATION FOR Dame Commander of the Order of the Bath (a Brit. title).

DCC ABBREVIATION FOR **digital compact cassette.**

DCF *Accounting* ABBREVIATION FOR **discounted cash flow.**

DCL ABBREVIATION FOR Doctor of Civil Law.

DCM *Brit military* ABBREVIATION FOR Distinguished Conduct Medal.

DCMG ABBREVIATION FOR Dame Commander of the Order of St Michael and St George (a Brit. title).

DCMS (in Britain) ABBREVIATION FOR Department for Culture, Media, and Sport.

DCVO ABBREVIATION FOR Dame Commander of the Royal Victorian Order (a Brit. title).

DD ABBREVIATION FOR: 1 Also: **dd.** direct debit. 2 Doctor of Divinity.

D-day NOUN 1 the day, June 6, 1944, on which the Allied invasion of Europe began. 2 the day on which any large-scale operation is planned to start.
▷**HISTORY** C20: from *D(ay)-day;* compare H-HOUR

DDR ABBREVIATION FOR Deutsche Demokratische Republik (the former East Germany; GDR).

DDS ABBREVIATION FOR: 1 **Dewey Decimal System.** 2 Doctor of Dental Surgery.

DDSc ABBREVIATION FOR Doctor of Dental Science.

DDT NOUN dichlorodiphenyltrichloroethane; a colourless odourless substance used as an insecticide. It is toxic to animals and is known to accumulate in the tissues. It is now banned in the UK.

de[1]**, De,** *or before a vowel* **d', D'** (də) of; from: occurring as part of some personal names and originally indicating place of origin: *Simon de Montfort; D'Arcy; de la Mare.*
▷**HISTORY** from Latin *dē;* see DE-

de[2] THE INTERNET DOMAIN NAME FOR Germany.

DE ABBREVIATION FOR: 1 (formerly in Britain) Department of Employment. 2 Delaware.

de- PREFIX FORMING VERBS AND VERBAL DERIVATIVES 1 removal of or from something specified: *deforest; dethrone.* 2 reversal of something: *decode; decompose; desegregate.* 3 departure from: *decamp.*
▷**HISTORY** from Latin, from *dē* (prep) from, away from, out of, etc. In compound words of Latin origin, *de-* also means away, away from (*decease*); down (*degrade*); reversal (*detect*); removal (*defoliate*); and is used intensively (*devote*) and pejoratively (*detest*)

deacon (ˈdiːkən) NOUN *Christianity* 1 (in the Roman Catholic and other episcopal churches) an ordained minister ranking immediately below a priest. 2 (in Protestant churches) a lay official appointed or elected to assist the minister, esp in secular affairs. 3 *Scot* the president of an incorporated trade or body of craftsmen in a burgh. ◆ Related adjective: **diaconal.**
▷**HISTORY** Old English, ultimately from Greek *diakonos* servant
▸**ˈdeaconˌship** NOUN

deaconess (ˈdiːkənɪs) NOUN *Christianity* (in the early church and in some modern Churches) a female member of the laity with duties similar to those of a deacon.

deaconry (ˈdiːkənrɪ) NOUN, *plural* **-ries.** 1 the office or status of a deacon. 2 deacons collectively.

deactivate (diːˈæktɪˌveɪt) VERB 1 (*tr*) to make (a bomb, etc.) harmless or inoperative. 2 (*intr*) to become less radioactive. 3 (*tr*) *US* to end the active status of (a military unit). 4 *Chem* to return or cause to return from an activated state to a normal or ground state.
▸**deˌactiˈvation** NOUN ▸**deˈactiˌvator** NOUN

dead (dɛd) ADJECTIVE 1 **a** no longer alive. **b** (*as noun*): *the dead.* 2 not endowed with life; inanimate. 3 no longer in use, valid, effective, or relevant: *a dead issue; a dead language.* 4 unresponsive or unaware; insensible: *he is dead to my strongest pleas.* 5 lacking in freshness, interest, or vitality: *a dead handshake.* 6 devoid of physical sensation; numb: *his gums were dead from the anaesthetic.* 7 resembling death; deathlike: *a dead sleep.* 8 no longer burning or hot: *dead coals.* 9 (of flowers or foliage) withered; faded. 10 (*prenominal*) (intensifier): *a dead stop; a dead loss.* 11 *Informal* very tired. 12 *Electronics* **a** drained of electric charge; fully discharged: *the battery was dead.* **b** not connected to a source of potential difference or electric charge. 13 lacking acoustic reverberation: *a dead sound; a dead surface.* 14 *Sport* (of a ball, etc.) out of play. 15 unerring; accurate; precise (esp in the phrase **a dead shot**). 16 lacking resilience or bounce: *a dead ball.* 17 *Printing* **a** (of type) set but no longer needed for use. Compare **standing** (sense 7). **b** (of copy) already composed. 18 not yielding a return; idle: *dead capital.* 19 *Informal* certain to suffer a terrible fate; doomed: *you're dead if your mother catches you at that.* 20 (of colours) not glossy or bright; lacklustre. 21 stagnant: *dead air.* 22 *Military* shielded from view, as by a geographic feature or environmental condition: *a dead zone; dead space.* 23 **dead as a doornail.** *Informal* completely dead. 24 **dead from the neck up.** *Informal* stupid or unintelligent. 25 **dead in the water.** *Informal* unsuccessful, and with little hope of future success: *the talks are now dead in the water.* 26 **dead to the world.** *Informal* unaware of one's surroundings, esp fast asleep or very drunk. 27 **leave for dead. a** to abandon. **b** *Informal* to surpass or outdistance by far. 28 **wouldn't be seen dead** (**in, at,** etc.). *Informal* to refuse to wear, to go (to), etc. ◆ NOUN 29 a period during which coldness, darkness, or some other quality associated with death is at its most intense: *the dead of winter.* ◆ ADVERB 30 (intensifier): *dead easy; stop dead; dead level.* 31 **dead on.** exactly right.
▷**HISTORY** Old English *dēad;* related to Old High German *tōt,* Old Norse *dauthr;* see DIE[1]
▸**ˈdeadness** NOUN

dead-and-alive ADJECTIVE *Brit* (of a place, activity, or person) dull; uninteresting.

dead arm NOUN *Informal* temporary loss of sensation in the arm, caused by a blow to a muscle.

dead-ball line NOUN *Rugby* a line not more than 22 metres behind the goal line at each end of the field beyond which the ball is out of play.

deadbeat (ˈdɛdˌbiːt) NOUN 1 *Informal* a lazy or socially undesirable person. 2 *Chiefly US* **a** a person who makes a habit of avoiding or evading his or her responsibilities or debts. **b** (*as modifier*): *a deadbeat dad.* 3 a high grade escapement used in pendulum clocks. 4 (*modifier*) (of a clock escapement) having a beat without any recoil. 5 (*modifier*) *Physics* **a** (of a system) returning to an equilibrium position with little or no oscillation. **b** (of an instrument or indicator) indicating a true reading without oscillation.

dead beat ADJECTIVE *Informal* tired out; exhausted.

deadboy (ˈdɛdˌbɔɪ) NOUN See **deadman** (sense 2).

dead-cat bounce NOUN *Stock Exchange informal* a temporary recovery in prices following a substantial fall as a result of speculators buying stocks they have already sold rather than as a result of a genuine reversal of the downward trend.

dead centre NOUN 1 the exact top (**top dead centre**) or bottom (**bottom dead centre**) of the piston stroke in a reciprocating engine or pump. 2 a pointed rod mounted in the tailstock of a lathe to support a workpiece. ◆ Also called: **dead point.**

dead duck NOUN *Slang* a person or thing doomed to death, failure, etc., esp because of a mistake or misjudgment.

deaden (ˈdɛd^{ə}n) VERB 1 to make or become less sensitive, intense, lively, etc.; damp or be damped down; dull. 2 (*tr*) to make acoustically less resonant: *he deadened the room with heavy curtains.*
▸**ˈdeadener** NOUN ▸**ˈdeadening** ADJECTIVE

dead end NOUN 1 another name for **cul-de-sac.** 2 a situation in which further progress is impossible. 3 (*as modifier*): *a dead-end street; a dead-end job.* **dead-end.** ◆ VERB 4 (*intr*) *Chiefly US and Canadian* to come to a dead end.

deadeye (ˈdɛdˌaɪ) NOUN 1 *Nautical* either of a pair of disclike wooden blocks, supported by straps in grooves around them, between which a line is rove so as to draw them together to tighten a shroud. Compare **bull's-eye** (sense 9). 2 *Informal, chiefly US* an expert marksman.

deadfall ('dɛd,fɔːl) NOUN a type of trap, used esp for catching large animals, in which a heavy weight falls to crush the prey. Also called: **downfall.**

dead fingers NOUN (*functioning as singular*) *Med* a disease of users of pneumatic drills, characterized by anaesthesia of the fingertips and cyanosis.

dead hand NOUN 1 an oppressive or discouraging influence or factor: *the dead hand of centralized control.* 2 *Law* a less common word for **mortmain.**

deadhead ('dɛd,hɛd) NOUN 1 a dull unenterprising person. 2 a person who uses a free ticket, as for a train, the theatre, etc. 3 *US and Canadian* a train, etc., travelling empty. 4 *US and Canadian* a totally or partially submerged log floating in a lake, etc. ◆ VERB 5 (*tr*) to cut off withered flowers from (a plant). 6 (*intr*) *US and Canadian* to drive an empty bus, train, etc.

Dead Heart NOUN (usually preceded by *the*) *Austral* the remote interior of Australia.
▷ HISTORY C20: from the title *The Dead Heart of Australia* (1906) by J. W. Gregory (1864–1932), British geologist

dead heat NOUN **a** a race or contest in which two or more participants tie for first place. **b** a tie between two or more contestants in any position.

dead key NOUN a key on the keyboard of a typewriter which does not automatically advance the carriage when depressed.

dead leg NOUN *Informal* temporary loss of sensation in the leg, caused by a blow to a muscle.

dead letter NOUN 1 a letter that cannot be delivered or returned because it lacks adequate directions. 2 a law or ordinance that is no longer enforced but has not been formally repealed. 3 *Informal* anything considered no longer worthy of consideration.

dead letter box *or* **drop** NOUN a place where messages and other material can be left and collected secretly without the sender and the recipient meeting.

deadlight ('dɛd,laɪt) NOUN 1 *Nautical* **a** a bull's-eye let into the deck or hull of a vessel to admit light to a cabin. **b** a shutter of wood or metal for sealing off a porthole or cabin window. 2 a skylight designed not to be opened.

deadline ('dɛd,laɪn) NOUN a time limit for any activity.

dead load NOUN the intrinsic invariable weight of a structure, such as a bridge. It may also include any permanent loads attached to the structure. Also called: **dead weight.** Compare **live load.**

deadlock ('dɛd,lɒk) NOUN 1 a state of affairs in which further action between two opposing forces is impossible; stalemate. 2 a tie between opposite sides in a contest. 3 a lock having a bolt that can be opened only with a key. ◆ VERB 4 to bring or come to a deadlock.

dead loss NOUN 1 *Informal* a person, thing, or situation that is completely useless or unprofitable. 2 a complete loss for which no compensation is received.

deadly ('dɛdlɪ) ADJECTIVE **-lier, -liest.** 1 likely to cause death: *deadly poison; deadly combat.* 2 *Informal* extremely boring. ◆ ADVERB, ADJECTIVE 3 like death in appearance or certainty: *deadly pale; a deadly sleep.*
▸ **'deadliness** NOUN

deadly nightshade NOUN a poisonous Eurasian solanaceous plant, *Atropa belladonna,* having dull purple bell-shaped flowers and small very poisonous black berries. Also called: **belladonna, dwale.**

deadly sins PLURAL NOUN *Theol* the sins of pride, covetousness, lust, envy, gluttony, anger, and sloth.

deadman ('dɛd,mæn) NOUN, *plural* **-men.** 1 *Civil engineering* a heavy plate, wall, or block buried in the ground that acts as an anchor for a retaining wall, sheet pile, etc., by a tie connecting the two. 2 *Mountaineering* a metal plate with a wire loop attached for thrusting into firm snow to serve as a belay point, a smaller version being known as a **deadboy.**

dead man's fingers NOUN (*functioning as singular*) a soft coral, *Alcyonium digitatum,* with long finger-like polyps.

dead man's handle *or* **pedal** NOUN a safety switch on a piece of machinery, such as a train, that allows operation only while depressed by the operator.

dead march NOUN a piece of solemn funeral music played to accompany a procession, esp at military funerals.

dead-nettle NOUN any Eurasian plant of the genus *Lamium,* such as *L. alba* (white dead-nettle), having leaves resembling nettles but lacking stinging hairs: family *Lamiaceae* (labiates).

deadpan ('dɛd,pæn) ADJECTIVE, ADVERB with a deliberately emotionless face or manner: *deadpan humour.*

dead point NOUN another name for **dead centre.**

dead reckoning NOUN a method of establishing one's position using the distance and direction travelled rather than astronomical observations.

Dead Sea NOUN a lake between Israel and Jordan, 397 m (1302 ft.) below sea level: the lowest lake in the world, with no outlet and very high salinity. Area: 1020 sq. km (394 sq. miles).

Dead Sea Scrolls PLURAL NOUN a collection of manuscripts in Hebrew and Aramaic discovered in caves near the Dead Sea between 1947 and 1956. They are widely held to have been written between about 100 B.C. and 68 A.D. and provide important biblical evidence.

dead set ADVERB 1 absolutely: *he is dead set against going to Spain.* ◆ NOUN 2 the motionless position of a dog when pointing with its muzzle towards game. ◆ ADJECTIVE 3 (of a hunting dog) in this position. ◆ INTERJECTION 4 *Austral slang* an expression of affirmation: *dead set, I worked from dawn to dusk.*

dead-smooth file NOUN *Engineering* the smoothest grade of file commonly used.

dead soldier *or* **marine** NOUN *Informal* an empty beer or spirit bottle.

dead stock NOUN farm equipment. Compare **livestock.**

dead time NOUN *Electronics* the interval of time immediately following a stimulus, during which an electrical device, component, etc., is insensitive to a further stimulus.

dead-tree ADJECTIVE *Informal* printed on paper: *a dead-tree edition of her book.*

dead weight NOUN 1 a heavy weight or load. 2 an oppressive burden; encumbrance. 3 the difference between the loaded and the unloaded weights of a ship. 4 another name for **dead load.** 5 (in shipping) freight chargeable by weight rather than by bulk.

Dead White European Male *or* **Dead White Male** NOUN a man whose importance and talents may have been exaggerated because he belonged to a historically dominant gender and ethnic group.

deadwood ('dɛd,wʊd) NOUN 1 dead trees or branches. 2 *Informal* a useless person; encumbrance. 3 *Nautical* a filler piece between the keel and the stern of a wooden vessel.

deaf (dɛf) ADJECTIVE 1 **a** partially or totally unable to hear. **b** (*as collective noun;* preceded by *the*): *the deaf.* ◆ See also **tone-deaf.** 2 refusing to heed: *deaf to the cries of the hungry.*
▷ HISTORY Old English *dēaf;* related to Old Norse *daufr*
▸ **'deafly** ADVERB ▸ **'deafness** NOUN

Language note See at **disabled.**

deaf aid NOUN another name for **hearing aid.**

deaf-and-dumb *Offensive* ◆ ADJECTIVE 1 unable to hear or speak. ◆ NOUN 2 a deaf-mute person.

deafblind ('dɛf'blaɪnd) ADJECTIVE **a** unable to hear or see. **b** (*as collective noun;* preceded by *the*): *the deafblind.*

deafen ('dɛfᵊn) VERB (*tr*) to make deaf, esp momentarily, as by a loud noise.
▸ **'deafeningly** ADVERB

deaf-mute NOUN 1 a person who is unable to hear or speak. See also **mute**¹ (sense 7), **mutism** (sense 2b). ◆ ADJECTIVE 2 unable to hear or speak.
▷ HISTORY C19: translation of French *sourd-muet*
▸ **'deaf-,muteness** *or* **'deaf-,mutism** NOUN

deaf without speech ADJECTIVE **a** (usually of a prelingually deaf person) able to utter sounds but not speak. **b** (*as collective noun;* preceded by *the*): *the deaf without speech.*

deal¹ (diːl) VERB **deals, dealing, dealt** (dɛlt). 1 (*intr;* foll by *in*) to engage (in) commercially: *to deal in upholstery.* 2 (often foll by *out*) to apportion (something, such as cards) to a number of people; distribute. 3 (*tr*) to give (a blow) to (someone); inflict. 4 (*intr*) *Slang* to sell any illegal drug. ◆ NOUN 5 *Informal* a bargain, transaction, or agreement. 6 a particular type of treatment received, esp as the result of an agreement: *a fair deal.* 7 an indefinite amount, extent, or degree (esp in the phrases **good** *or* **great deal**). 8 *Cards* **a** the process of distributing the cards. **b** a player's turn to do this. **c** a single round in a card game. 9 See **big deal.** 10 **cut a deal.** *Informal, chiefly US* to come to an arrangement; make a deal. ◆ See also **deal with.**
▷ HISTORY Old English *dǣlan,* from *dǣl* a part; compare Old High German *teil* a part, Old Norse *deild* a share

deal² (diːl) NOUN 1 a plank of softwood timber, such as fir or pine, or such planks collectively. 2 the sawn wood of various coniferous trees, such as that from the Scots pine (**red deal**) or from the Norway Spruce (**white deal**). ◆ ADJECTIVE 3 of fir or pine.
▷ HISTORY C14: from Middle Low German *dele* plank; see THILL

Deal (diːl) NOUN a town in SE England, in Kent, on the English Channel: two 16th-century castles: tourism, light industries. Pop.: 28 504 (1991).

dealate ('diːeɪ,leɪt, -lɪt) *or* **dealated** ('diːeɪ,leɪtɪd) ADJECTIVE (of ants and other insects) having lost their wings, esp by biting or rubbing them off after mating.
▷ HISTORY from DE- + ALATE
▸ **,dea'lation** NOUN

dealer ('diːlə) NOUN 1 a person or firm engaged in commercial purchase and sale; trader: *a car dealer.* 2 *Cards* the person who distributes the cards. 3 *Slang* a person who sells illegal drugs.
▸ **'dealer,ship** NOUN

dealfish ('diːl,fɪʃ) NOUN, *plural* **-fish** *or* **-fishes.** any deep-sea teleost fish of the genus *Trachipterus,* esp *T. arcticus,* related to the ribbonfishes and having a very long tapelike body and a fan-shaped tail fin.

dealings ('diːlɪŋz) PLURAL NOUN (*sometimes singular*) transactions or business relations.

dealt (dɛlt) VERB the past tense and past participle of **deal**¹.

deal with VERB (*tr, adverb*) 1 to take action on: *to deal with each problem in turn.* 2 to punish: *the headmaster will deal with the culprit.* 3 to be concerned with: *the book deals with Dutch art.* 4 to conduct oneself (towards others), esp with regard to fairness: *he can be relied on to deal fairly with everyone.* 5 to do business with: *the firm deals with many overseas suppliers.*

deaminate (diː'æmɪ,neɪt), **deaminize,** *or* **deaminise** VERB (*tr*) to remove one or more amino groups from (a molecule).
▸ **de,ami'nation** *or* **de,amini'zation** *or* **de,amini'sation** NOUN

dean (diːn) NOUN 1 the chief administrative official of a college or university faculty. 2 (at Oxford and Cambridge universities) a college fellow with responsibility for undergraduate discipline. 3 *Chiefly Church of England* the head of a chapter of canons and administrator of a cathedral or collegiate church. 4 *RC Church* the cardinal bishop senior by consecration and head of the college of cardinals. ◆ Related adjective: **decanal.** See also **rural dean.**
▷ HISTORY C14: from Old French *deien,* from Late Latin *decānus* one set over ten persons, from Latin *decem* ten
▸ **'dean,ship** NOUN

Dean (diːn) NOUN **Forest of.** a forest in W England, in Gloucestershire, between the Rivers Severn and Wye: formerly a royal hunting ground.

deanery ('diːnərɪ) NOUN, *plural* **-eries.** 1 the office or residence of dean. 2 the group of parishes presided over by a rural dean.

de-anglicization *or* **de-anglicisation** NOUN (in Ireland) the elimination of English influence, language, customs, etc.

Dean of Faculty NOUN the president of the Faculty of Advocates in Scotland.

dean of guild NOUN the titular head of the guild or merchant company in a Scots burgh, who formerly exercised jurisdiction over all building in the burgh in the **Dean of Guild Court**.

dear (dɪə) ADJECTIVE 1 beloved; precious. 2 used in conventional forms of address preceding a title or name, as in *Dear Sir* or *my dear Mr Smith*. 3 (*postpositive;* foll by *to*) important; close: *a wish dear to her heart*. 4 **a** highly priced. **b** charging high prices. 5 appealing or pretty: *what a dear little ring!* 6 **for dear life.** urgently or with extreme vigour or desperation. ◆ INTERJECTION 7 used in exclamations of surprise or dismay, such as *Oh dear!* and *dear me!* ◆ NOUN 8 (*often used in direct address*) someone regarded with affection and tenderness; darling. ◆ ADVERB 9 dearly: *his errors have cost him dear*.
▷HISTORY Old English *dēore;* related to Old Norse *dȳrr*
▸ˈ**dearness** NOUN

Dearborn (ˈdɪəbən, -ˌbɔːn) NOUN a city in SE Michigan, near Detroit: automobile industry. Pop.: 97 775 (2000).

Dear John letter NOUN *Informal* a letter from someone (esp to a man) breaking off a love affair.

dearly (ˈdɪəlɪ) ADVERB 1 very much: *I would dearly like you to go*. 2 affectionately. 3 at a great cost.

dearth (dɜːθ) NOUN an inadequate amount, esp of food; scarcity.
▷HISTORY C13: *derthe*, from *dēr* DEAR

deary *or* **dearie** (ˈdɪərɪ) NOUN 1 (*plural* **dearies**) *Informal* a term of affection: now often sarcastic or facetious. 2 **deary** *or* **dearie me!** an exclamation of surprise or dismay.

deasil (ˈdiːzəl, ˈdiːʃəl) *Scot* ◆ ADVERB 1 in the direction of the apparent course of the sun; clockwise. ◆ NOUN 2 motion in this direction. ◆ Compare **withershins.**
▷HISTORY C18: Scot Gaelic *deiseil*

death (dɛθ) NOUN 1 the permanent end of all functions of life in an organism or some of its cellular components. 2 an instance of this: *his death ended an era*. 3 a murder or killing: *he had five deaths on his conscience*. 4 termination or destruction: *the death of colonialism*. 5 a state of affairs or an experience considered as terrible as death: *your constant nagging will be the death of me*. 6 a cause or source of death. 7 (*usually capital*) a personification of death, usually a skeleton or an old man holding a scythe. 8 **a to death** *or* **to the death.** until dead: *bleed to death; a fight to the death*. **b to death.** excessively: *bored to death*. 9 **at death's door.** likely to die soon. 10 **catch one's death (of cold).** *Informal* to contract a severe cold. 11 **do to death. a** to kill. **b** to overuse (a joke, etc.) so that it no longer has any effect. 12 **in at the death. a** present when an animal that is being hunted is caught and killed. **b** present at the finish or climax. 13 **like death warmed up.** *Informal* very ill. 14 **like grim death.** as if afraid of one's life. 15 **put to death.** to kill deliberately or execute. ◆ Related adjectives: **fatal, lethal, mortal.** ◆ Related prefixes: **necro-, thanato-.**
▷HISTORY Old English *dēath;* related to Old High German *tōd* death, Gothic *dauthus*

death adder NOUN a venomous Australian elapid snake, *Acanthophis antarcticus,* resembling an adder.

deathbed (ˈdɛθˌbɛd) NOUN 1 **a** the bed in which a person is about to die. **b** (*as modifier*): *a deathbed conversion*. 2 **on one's deathbed.** about to die.

deathblow (ˈdɛθˌbləʊ) NOUN a thing or event that destroys life or hope, esp suddenly.

death camp NOUN a concentration camp in which the conditions are so brutal that few prisoners survive, or one to which prisoners are sent for execution.

death cap *or* **angel** NOUN a poisonous woodland saprotrophic basidiomycetous fungus, *Amanita phalloides,* differing from the edible mushroom (*Agaricus*) only in its white gills (pinkish-brown in *Agaricus*) and the presence of a volva. See also **amanita.**

death cell NOUN a prison cell for criminals sentenced to death.

death certificate NOUN a legal document issued by a qualified medical practitioner certifying the death of a person and stating the cause if known.

death-dealing ADJECTIVE fatal; lethal.

death duty NOUN a tax on property inheritances: in Britain, replaced in 1975 by capital transfer tax and since 1986 by inheritance tax. Also called: **estate duty.**

death futures PLURAL NOUN life insurance policies of terminally ill people that are bought speculatively for a lump sum by a company, enabling it to collect the proceeds of the policies when the sufferers die.

death grant NOUN (in the British National Insurance scheme) a grant payable to a relative, executor, etc., after the death of a person.

death knell *or* **bell** NOUN 1 something that heralds death or destruction. 2 a bell rung to announce a death.

deathless (ˈdɛθlɪs) ADJECTIVE immortal, esp because of greatness; everlasting.
▸ˈ**deathlessly** ADVERB ▸ˈ**deathlessness** NOUN

deathly (ˈdɛθlɪ) ADJECTIVE 1 deadly. 2 resembling death: *a deathly quiet*.
▸ˈ**deathliness** NOUN

death mask NOUN a cast of a person's face taken shortly after death. Compare **life mask.**

death metal NOUN **a** a type of heavy-metal music characterized by extreme speed and lyrics dealing with violence, satanism, etc. **b** (*as modifier*): *a death-metal band*.

death penalty NOUN (often preceded by *the*) capital punishment.

death rate NOUN the ratio of deaths in a specified area, group, etc., to the population of that area, group, etc. Also called (esp US): **mortality rate.**

death rattle NOUN a low-pitched gurgling sound sometimes made by a dying person, caused by air passing through an accumulation of mucus in the trachea.

death ray NOUN an imaginary ray capable of killing.

death row *or* **house** NOUN *US* the part of a prison where those sentenced to death are confined.

death seat NOUN *US and Austral slang* the seat beside the driver of a vehicle.

death's-head NOUN a human skull or a representation of one.

death's-head moth NOUN a European hawk moth, *Acherontia atropos,* having markings resembling a human skull on its upper thorax.

death tourist NOUN *Informal* a seriously ill person who seeks to terminate his or her own life by travelling to a country where medically assisted suicide is legal.

death trap NOUN a building, vehicle, etc., that is considered very unsafe.

Death Valley NOUN a desert valley in E California and W Nevada: the lowest, hottest, and driest area of the US. Lowest point: 86 m (282 ft.) below sea level. Area: about 3885 sq. km (1500 sq. miles).

death-valley curve NOUN a curve on a graph showing how the capital of a new company plotted against time declines sharply as the venture capital is used up before income reaches predicted levels.

death warrant NOUN 1 the official authorization for carrying out a sentence of death. 2 **sign one's (own) death warrant.** to cause one's own destruction.

deathwatch (ˈdɛθˌwɒtʃ) NOUN 1 a vigil held beside a dying or dead person. 2 **deathwatch beetle.** a beetle, *Xestobium rufovillosum,* whose woodboring larvae are a serious pest. The adult produces a rapid tapping sound with its head that was once popularly supposed to presage death. See also **anobiid.**

death wish NOUN (in Freudian psychology) the desire for self-annihilation. See also **Thanatos.**

Deauville (ˈdəʊviːl; *French* dovil) NOUN a town and resort in NW France: casino. Pop.: 4770 (latest est.).

deave (diːv) VERB (*tr*) *Scot* 1 to deafen. 2 to bewilder or weary (a person) with noise.
▷HISTORY Old English *dēafian*

deb (dɛb) NOUN *Informal* short for **debutante.**

deb. ABBREVIATION FOR debenture.

debacle (deɪˈbɑːkəl, dɪ-) NOUN 1 a sudden disastrous collapse or defeat, esp one involving a disorderly retreat; rout. 2 the breaking up of ice in a river during spring or summer, often causing flooding. 3 a violent rush of water carrying along debris.
▷HISTORY C19: from French *débâcle,* from Old French *desbacler* to unbolt, ultimately from Latin *baculum* rod, staff

debag (diːˈbæg) VERB **-bags, -bagging, -bagged.** (*tr*) *Brit slang* to remove the trousers from (someone) by force.

debar (dɪˈbɑː) VERB **-bars, -barring, -barred.** (*tr;* usually foll by *from*) to exclude from a place, a right, etc.; bar.
▸**deˈbarment** NOUN

Language note See at **disbar.**

debark^1 (dɪˈbɑːk) VERB a less common word for **disembark.**
▷HISTORY C17: from French *débarquer,* from *dé-* DIS^1 + *barque* BARQUE
▸**debarkation** (ˌdiːbɑːˈkeɪʃən) NOUN

debark^2 (diːˈbɑːk) VERB (*tr*) to remove the bark from (a tree).

debase (dɪˈbeɪs) VERB (*tr*) to lower in quality, character, or value, as by adding cheaper metal to coins; adulterate.
▷HISTORY C16: see DE-, BASE^2
▸**debasedness** (dɪˈbeɪsɪdnɪs) NOUN ▸**deˈbasement** NOUN ▸**deˈbaser** NOUN ▸**deˈbasingly** ADVERB

debatable *or* **debateable** (dɪˈbeɪtəbəl) ADJECTIVE 1 open to question; disputable. 2 *Law* in dispute, as land or territory to which two parties lay claim.

debate (dɪˈbeɪt) NOUN 1 a formal discussion, as in a legislative body, in which opposing arguments are put forward. 2 discussion or dispute. 3 the formal presentation and opposition of a specific motion, followed by a vote. ◆ VERB 4 to discuss (a motion), esp in a formal assembly. 5 to deliberate upon (something): *he debated with himself whether to go*.
▷HISTORY C13: from Old French *debatre* to discuss, argue, from Latin *battuere*
▸**deˈbater** NOUN

debauch (dɪˈbɔːtʃ) VERB 1 (when *tr, usually passive*) to lead into a life of depraved self-indulgence. 2 (*tr*) to seduce (a woman). ◆ NOUN 3 an instance or period of extreme dissipation.
▷HISTORY C16: from Old French *desbaucher* to corrupt, literally: to shape (timber) roughly, from *bauch* beam, of Germanic origin
▸**debauchedly** (dɪˈbɔːtʃɪdlɪ) ADVERB ▸**deˈbauchedness** NOUN ▸**deˈbaucher** NOUN ▸**deˈbauchery** *or* **deˈbauchment** NOUN

debauchee (ˌdɛbɔːˈtʃiː, -ɔːˈʃiː) NOUN a man who leads a life of reckless drinking, promiscuity, and self-indulgence.

debe (ˈdɛbɛ) NOUN *E African* a tin.
▷HISTORY C20: from Swahili

debeak VERB (*tr*) to remove part of the beak of poultry to reduce the risk of such habits as feather-picking or cannibalism.

debenture (dɪˈbɛntʃə) NOUN 1 Also called: **debenture bond.** a long-term bond, bearing fixed interest and usually unsecured, issued by a company or governmental agency. 2 a certificate acknowledging the debt of a stated sum of money to a specified person. 3 a customs certificate providing for a refund of excise or import duty.
▷HISTORY C15: from Latin phrase *dēbentur mihi* there are owed to me, from *dēbēre* to owe
▸**deˈbentured** ADJECTIVE

debilitate (dɪˈbɪlɪˌteɪt) VERB (*tr*) to make feeble; weaken.
▷HISTORY C16: from Latin *dēbilitāre,* from *dēbilis* weak
▸**deˌbiliˈtation** NOUN

debilitating (dɪˈbɪlɪteɪtɪŋ) ADJECTIVE tending to weaken or enfeeble.

debility (dɪˈbɪlɪtɪ) NOUN, *plural* **-ties.** weakness or infirmity.

debit (ˈdɛbɪt) *Accounting* ◆ NOUN 1 **a** acknowledgment of a sum owing by entry on the left side of an account. **b** the left side of an account. **c** an entry on this side. **d** the total of such entries. **e** (*as modifier*): *a debit balance*. Compare **credit** (sense 10). ◆ VERB **-its, -iting, -ited.** 2 (*tr*) **a** to record (an item) as a debit in an account. **b** to charge (a person

or his account) with a debt. Compare **credit** (sense 17).
▷HISTORY C15: from Latin *dēbitum* DEBT

debit card NOUN an embossed plastic card issued by a bank or building society to enable its customers to pay for goods or services by inserting it into a computer-controlled device at the place of sale, which is connected through the telephone network to the bank or building society. It may also function as a cash card, a cheque card, or both.

debonair *or* **debonnaire** (ˌdɛbəˈnɛə) ADJECTIVE (esp of a man or his manner) [1] suave and refined. [2] carefree; light-hearted. [3] courteous and cheerful; affable.
▷HISTORY C13: from Old French *debonaire,* from *de bon aire* having a good disposition
▸ **ˌdeboˈnairly** ADVERB ▸ **ˌdeboˈnairness** NOUN

Deborah (ˈdɛbərə, -brə) NOUN *Old Testament* [1] a prophetess and judge of Israel who fought the Canaanites (Judges 4, 5). [2] Rebecca's nurse (Genesis 35:8).

debouch (dɪˈbaʊtʃ) VERB [1] *(intr)* (esp of troops) to move into a more open space, as from a narrow or concealed place. [2] *(intr)* (of a river, glacier, etc.) to flow from a valley into a larger area or body. ◆ NOUN [3] Also called: **débouché** (*French* debuʃe). *Fortifications* an outlet or passage, as for the exit of troops.
▷HISTORY C18: from French *déboucher,* from *dé-* DIS[1] + *bouche* mouth, from Latin *bucca* cheek

debouchment (dɪˈbaʊtʃmənt) NOUN [1] the act or an instance of debouching. [2] Also called: **debouchure** (ˌdeɪbuːˈʃʊə). an outlet, mouth, or opening.

Debrecen (ˈdɛbrɛtsɛn) NOUN a city in E Hungary: seat of the revolutionary government of 1849. Pop.: 203 648 (2000 est.).

Debrett (dəˈbrɛt) NOUN a list of the British aristocracy. In full: **Debrett's Peerage.**
▷HISTORY C19: after J. *Debrett* (c. 1750–1822), London publisher who first issued it

débridement (dɪˈbriːdmənt, deɪ-) NOUN the surgical removal of dead tissue or cellular debris from the surface of a wound.
▷HISTORY C19: from French, from Old French *desbrider* to unbridle, from *des-* DE- + *bride* BRIDLE

debrief (diːˈbriːf) VERB (of a soldier, astronaut, diplomat, etc.) to make or (of his superiors) to elicit a report after a mission or event. Compare **brief** (sense 13).

debris *or* **débris** (ˈdeɪbrɪ, ˈdɛbrɪ) NOUN [1] fragments or remnants of something destroyed or broken; rubble. [2] a collection of loose material derived from rocks, or an accumulation of animal or vegetable matter.
▷HISTORY C18: from French, from obsolete *debrisier* to break into pieces, from *bruisier* to shatter, of Celtic origin

debris bug NOUN a bug of the family *Cimicidae* found where vegetable debris accumulates and feeding on small arthropods like springtails: related to the bedbugs.

de Broglie waves (də ˈbrəʊglɪ) PLURAL NOUN *Physics* the set of waves that represent the behaviour of an elementary particle, or some atoms and molecules, under certain conditions. The **de Broglie wavelength**, λ, is given by $\lambda = h/mv$, where *h* is the Planck constant, *m* the mass, and *v* the velocity of the particle. Also called: **matter waves.**
▷HISTORY C20: named after Prince Louis Victor *de Broglie* (1892–1987), French physicist

debt (dɛt) NOUN [1] something that is owed, such as money, goods, or services. [2] **bad debt.** a debt that has little or no prospect of being paid. [3] an obligation to pay or perform something; liability. [4] the state of owing something, esp money, or of being under an obligation (esp in the phrases **in debt, in (someone's) debt**).
▷HISTORY C13: from Old French *dette,* from Latin *dēbitum,* from *dēbēre* to owe, from DE- + *habēre* to have; English spelling influenced by the Latin etymon
▸ **ˈdebtless** ADJECTIVE

debt of honour NOUN a debt that is morally but not legally binding, such as one contracted in gambling.

debtor (ˈdɛtə) NOUN a person or commercial enterprise that owes a financial obligation. Compare **creditor.**

debt swap NOUN See **swap** (sense 4).

debud (diːˈbʌd) VERB **-buds, -budding, -budded.** another word for **disbud.**

debug (diːˈbʌg) *Informal* ◆ VERB **-bugs, -bugging, -bugged.** *(tr)* [1] to locate and remove concealed microphones from (a room, etc.). [2] to locate and remove defects in (a device, system, plan, etc.). [3] to remove insects from. ◆ NOUN [4] **a** something, esp a computer program, that locates and removes defects in (a device, system, etc.). **b** (*as modifier*): *a debug program.*
▷HISTORY C20: from DE- + BUG[1]

debunk (diːˈbʌŋk) VERB *(tr) Informal* to expose the pretensions or falseness of, esp by ridicule.
▷HISTORY C20: from DE- + BUNK[2]
▸ **deˈbunker** NOUN

deburr (diːˈbɜː) VERB *(tr)* [1] to remove burrs from (a workpiece). [2] *Textiles* to remove dirt and debris from (raw wool).

debus (diːˈbʌs) VERB **debuses, debusing, debused** *or* **debusses, debussing, debussed.** to unload (goods) or (esp of troops) to alight from a motor vehicle.

debut (ˈdeɪbjuː, ˈdɛbjuː) NOUN [1] **a** the first public appearance of an actor, musician, etc., or the first public presentation of a show. **b** (*as modifier*): *debut album.* [2] the presentation of a debutante. ◆ VERB *(intr)* [3] to make a debut.
▷HISTORY C18: from French *début,* from Old French *desbuter* to play first (hence: make one's first appearance), from *des-* DE- + *but* goal, target; see BUTT[2]

debutant (ˈdɛbjʊˌtɑːnt, -ˌtænt) NOUN a person who is making a first appearance in a particular capacity, such as a sportsperson playing in a first game for a team.

debutante (ˈdɛbjʊˌtɑːnt, -ˌtænt) NOUN [1] a young woman of upper-class background who is presented to society, usually at a formal ball. [2] a girl or young woman regarded as being upper-class, wealthy, and of a frivolous or snobbish social set.
▷HISTORY C19: from French, from *débuter* to lead off in a game, make one's first appearance; see DEBUT

dec. ABBREVIATION FOR: [1] deceased. [2] *Music* decrescendo.

Dec. ABBREVIATION FOR December.

deca-, deka-, *or before a vowel* **dec-, dek-** PREFIX denoting ten: *decagon.* In conjunction with scientific units the symbol **da** is used.
▷HISTORY from Greek *deka*

decade (ˈdɛkeɪd, dɪˈkeɪd) NOUN [1] a period of ten consecutive years. [2] a group or series of ten.
▷HISTORY C15: from Old French, from Late Latin *decad-, decas,* from Greek *dekas,* from *deka* ten
▸ **deˈcadal** ADJECTIVE

decadence (ˈdɛkədəns) *or* **decadency** NOUN [1] deterioration, esp of morality or culture; decay; degeneration. [2] the state reached through such a process.
▷HISTORY C16: from French, from Medieval Latin *dēcadentia,* literally: a falling away; see DECAY

decadent (ˈdɛkədənt) ADJECTIVE [1] characterized by decay or decline, as in being self-indulgent or morally corrupt. [2] belonging to a period of decline in artistic standards. ◆ NOUN [3] a decadent person. [4] *(often capital)* one of a group of French and English writers of the late 19th century whose works were characterized by refinement of style and a tendency toward the artificial and abnormal.
▸ **ˈdecadently** ADVERB

decaf (ˈdiːkæf) *Informal* ◆ NOUN [1] decaffeinated coffee. ◆ ADJECTIVE [2] decaffeinated.

decaffeinate (dɪˈkæfɪˌneɪt) VERB *(tr)* to remove all or part of the caffeine from (coffee, tea, etc.).

decagon (ˈdɛkəˌgɒn) NOUN a polygon having ten sides.
▸ **decagonal** (dɪˈkægən[ə]l) ADJECTIVE ▸ **deˈcagonally** ADVERB

decahedron (ˌdɛkəˈhiːdrən) NOUN a solid figure having ten plane faces. See also **polyhedron.**
▸ **ˌdecaˈhedral** ADJECTIVE

decal (dɪˈkæl, ˈdiːkæl) NOUN [1] short for **decalcomania.** ◆ VERB [2] to transfer (a design) by decalcomania.

decalcify (diːˈkælsɪˌfaɪ) VERB **-fies, -fying, -fied.** *(tr)* to remove calcium or lime from (bones, teeth, etc.).
▸ **decalcification** (diːˌkælsɪfɪˈkeɪʃən) NOUN ▸ **deˈcalciˌfier** NOUN

decalcomania (dɪˌkælkəˈmeɪnɪə) NOUN [1] the art or process of transferring a design from prepared paper onto another surface, such as china, glass or paper. [2] a design so transferred.
▷HISTORY C19: from French *décalcomanie,* from *décalquer* to transfer by tracing, from *dé-* DE- + *calquer* to trace + *-manie* -MANIA

decalescence (ˌdiːkəˈlɛs[ə]ns) NOUN the absorption of heat when a metal is heated through a particular temperature range, caused by a change in internal crystal structure.
▷HISTORY C19: from Late Latin *dēcalescere* to become warm, from Latin DE- + *calescere,* from *calēre* to be warm
▸ **ˌdecaˈlescent** ADJECTIVE

decalitre *or US* **decaliter** (ˈdɛkəˌliːtə) NOUN ten litres. One decalitre is equal to about 2.2 imperial gallons. Symbol: dal.

Decalogue (ˈdɛkəˌlɒg) NOUN another name for the **Ten Commandments.**
▷HISTORY C14: from Church Latin *decalogus,* from Greek, from *deka* ten + *logos* word

decametre *or US* **decameter** (ˈdɛkəˌmiːtə) NOUN ten metres. Symbol: dam.

decamp (dɪˈkæmp) VERB *(intr)* [1] to leave a camp; break camp. [2] to depart secretly or suddenly; abscond.
▸ **deˈcampment** NOUN

decanal (dɪˈkeɪn[ə]l) ADJECTIVE [1] of or relating to a dean or deanery. [2] (of part of a choir) on the same side of a cathedral, etc., as the dean; on the S side of the choir. ◆ Compare **cantorial.**
▷HISTORY C18: from Medieval Latin *decānālis, decānus* DEAN
▸ **deˈcanally** *or* **decanically** (dɪˈkænɪkəlɪ) ADVERB

decane (ˈdɛkeɪn) NOUN a liquid alkane hydrocarbon existing in several isomeric forms. Formula: $C_{10}H_{22}$.
▷HISTORY C19: from DECA- + -ANE

decanedioic acid (ˌdɛkeɪndaɪˈəʊɪk) NOUN a white crystalline carboxylic acid obtained by heating castor oil with sodium hydroxide, used in the manufacture of polyester resins and rubbers and plasticizers. Formula: $HOOC(CH_2)_8COOH$. Also called: **sebacic acid.**

decani (dɪˈkeɪnaɪ) ADJECTIVE, ADVERB *Music* to be sung by the decanal side of a choir. Compare **cantoris.**
▷HISTORY Latin: genitive of *decānus*

decanoic acid (ˌdɛkəˈnəʊɪk) NOUN a white crystalline insoluble carboxylic acid with an unpleasant odour, used in perfumes and for making fruit flavours. Formula: $C_9H_{19}COOH$. Also called: **capric acid.**

decant (dɪˈkænt) VERB [1] to pour (a liquid, such as wine) from one container to another, esp without disturbing any sediment. [2] *(tr)* to rehouse (people) while their homes are being rebuilt or refurbished.
▷HISTORY C17: from Medieval Latin *dēcanthāre,* from *canthus* spout, rim; see CANTHUS

decanter (dɪˈkæntə) NOUN a stoppered bottle, usually of glass, into which a drink, such as wine, is poured for serving.

decapitate (dɪˈkæpɪˌteɪt) VERB *(tr)* to behead.
▷HISTORY C17: from Late Latin *dēcapitāre,* from Latin DE- + *caput* head
▸ **deˌcapiˈtation** NOUN ▸ **deˈcapiˌtator** NOUN

decapod (ˈdɛkəˌpɒd) NOUN [1] any crustacean of the mostly marine order *Decapoda,* having five pairs of walking limbs: includes the crabs, lobsters, shrimps, prawns, and crayfish. [2] any cephalopod mollusc of the order *Decapoda,* having a ring of eight short tentacles and two longer ones: includes the squids and cuttlefish. ◆ ADJECTIVE [3] of, relating to, or belonging to either of these orders. [4] (of any other animal) having ten limbs.
▸ **decapodal** (dɪˈkæpəd[ə]l) *or* **deˈcapodan** *or* **deˈcapodous** ADJECTIVE

Decapolis (dɪˈkæpəlɪs) NOUN a league of ten cities, including Damascus, in the northeast of ancient Palestine: established in 63 B.C. by Pompey and governed by Rome.

decapsulate (diːˈkæpsjʊˌleɪt) VERB *(tr) Med* to

remove a capsule from (a part or organ, esp the kidney).
▸**deˌcapsuˈlation** NOUN

decarbonate (diːˈkɑːbəˌneɪt) VERB *(tr)* to remove carbon dioxide from (a solution, substance, etc.).
▸**deˌcarbonˈation** NOUN ▸**deˈcarbonˌator** NOUN

decarbonize *or* **decarbonise** (diːˈkɑːbəˌnaɪz) VERB *(tr)* to remove carbon from (the walls of the combustion chamber of an internal-combustion engine). Also: **decoke, decarburize.**
▸**deˌcarboniˈzation** *or* **deˌcarboniˈsation** NOUN
▸**deˈcarbonˌizer** *or* **deˈcarbonˌiser** NOUN

decarboxylase (ˌdiːkɑːˈbɒksɪˌleɪs) NOUN an enzyme that catalyses the removal of carbon dioxide from a compound.

decarboxylation (ˌdiːkɑːˌbɒksəˈleɪʃən) NOUN the removal or loss of a carboxyl group from an organic compound.

decarburize *or* **decarburise** (diːˈkɑːbjʊˌraɪz) VERB another word for **decarbonize.**
▸**deˌcarburiˈzation** *or* **deˌcarburiˈsation** *or* **deˌcarbuˈration** NOUN

decare (ˈdɛkɛə, dɛˈkɛə) NOUN ten ares or 1000 square metres.
▷**HISTORY** C19: from French *décare;* see DECA-, ARE[2]

decastyle (ˈdɛkəˌstaɪl) NOUN *Architect* a portico consisting of ten columns.

decasyllable (ˈdɛkəˌsɪləbᵊl) NOUN a word or line of verse consisting of ten syllables.
▸**decasyllabic** (ˌdɛkəsɪˈlæbɪk) ADJECTIVE

decathlon (dɪˈkæθlɒn) NOUN an athletic contest for men in which each athlete competes in ten different events. Compare **pentathlon.**
▷**HISTORY** C20: from DECA- + Greek *athlon* contest, prize; see ATHLETE
▸**deˈcathlete** NOUN

decay (dɪˈkeɪ) VERB [1] to decline or cause to decline gradually in health, prosperity, excellence, etc.; deteriorate; waste away. [2] to rot or cause to rot as a result of bacterial, fungal, or chemical action; decompose. [3] *(intr)* Also*:* **disintegrate,** *Physics.* **a** (of an atomic nucleus) to undergo radioactive disintegration. **b** (of an elementary particle) to transform into two or more different elementary particles. [4] *(intr) Physics* (of a stored charge, magnetic flux, etc.) to decrease gradually when the source of energy has been removed. ◆ NOUN [5] the process of decline, as in health, mentality, beauty, etc. [6] the state brought about by this process. [7] decomposition, as of vegetable matter. [8] rotten or decayed matter: *the dentist drilled out the decay.* [9] *Physics* **a** See **radioactive decay. b** a spontaneous transformation of an elementary particle into two or more different particles. **c** of an excited atom or molecule, losing energy by the spontaneous emission of photons. [10] *Physics* a gradual decrease of a stored charge, magnetic flux, current, etc., when the source of energy has been removed. See also **time constant.** [11] *Music* the fading away of a note.
▷**HISTORY** C15: from Old Northern French *decaïr,* from Late Latin *dēcadere,* literally: to fall away, from Latin *cadere* to fall
▸**deˈcayable** ADJECTIVE

Deccan (ˈdɛkən) NOUN **the.** [1] a plateau in S India, between the Eastern Ghats, the Western Ghats, and the Narmada River. [2] the whole Indian peninsula south of the Narmada River.

decd ABBREVIATION FOR deceased.

decease (dɪˈsiːs) NOUN [1] a more formal word for **death.** ◆ VERB [2] *(intr)* a more formal word for **die**[1].
▷**HISTORY** C14 (n): from Old French *deces,* from Latin *dēcēdere* to depart

deceased (dɪˈsiːst) ADJECTIVE **a** a more formal word for **dead** (sense 1). **b** *(as noun): the deceased.*

decedent (dɪˈsiːdᵊnt) NOUN *Law, chiefly US* a deceased person.
▷**HISTORY** C16: from Latin *dēcēdēns* departing; see DECEASE

deceit (dɪˈsiːt) NOUN [1] the act or practice of deceiving. [2] a statement, act, or device intended to mislead; fraud; trick. [3] a tendency to deceive.
▷**HISTORY** C13: from Old French *deceite,* from *deceivre* to DECEIVE

deceitful (dɪˈsiːtfʊl) ADJECTIVE full of deceit.
▸**deˈceitfully** ADVERB ▸**deˈceitfulness** NOUN

deceive (dɪˈsiːv) VERB *(tr)* [1] to mislead by deliberate misrepresentation or lies. [2] to delude (oneself). [3] to be unfaithful to (one's sexual partner). [4] *Archaic* to disappoint: *his hopes were deceived.*
▷**HISTORY** C13: from Old French *deceivre,* from Latin *dēcipere* to ensnare, cheat, from *capere* to take
▸**deˈceivable** ADJECTIVE ▸**deˈceivably** ADVERB
▸**deˈceivableness** *or* **deˌceivaˈbility** NOUN ▸**deˈceiver** NOUN ▸**deˈceiving** NOUN, ADJECTIVE ▸**deˈceivingly** ADVERB

decelerate (diːˈsɛləˌreɪt) VERB to slow down or cause to slow down.
▷**HISTORY** C19: from DE- + ACCELERATE
▸**deˌcelerˈation** NOUN ▸**deˈcelerˌator** NOUN

decelerometer (dɪˌsɛləˈrɒmɪtə) NOUN an instrument for measuring deceleration.

December (dɪˈsɛmbə) NOUN the twelfth and last month of the year, consisting of 31 days.
▷**HISTORY** C13: from Old French *decembre,* from Latin *december* the tenth month (the Roman year originally began with March), from *decem* ten

Decembrist (dɪˈsɛmbrɪst) NOUN *Russian history* a participant in the unsuccessful revolt against Tsar Nicolas I in Dec. 1825.
▷**HISTORY** C19: translation of Russian *dekabrist*

decemvir (dɪˈsɛmvə) NOUN, *plural* **-virs** *or* **-viri** (-vɪˌriː). [1] (in ancient Rome) a member of a board of ten magistrates, esp either of the two commissions established in 451 and 450 B.C. to revise the laws. [2] a member of any governing body composed of ten men.
▷**HISTORY** C17: from Latin, from *decem* ten + *virī* men
▸**deˈcemviral** ADJECTIVE

decemvirate (dɪˈsɛmvɪrɪt, -ˌreɪt) NOUN [1] a board of decemvirs. [2] the rule or rank of decemvirs.

decenary *or* **decennary** (dɪˈsɛnərɪ) ADJECTIVE *History* of or relating to a tithing.
▷**HISTORY** C13: from Medieval Latin *decēna* a tithing, from *decem* ten

decencies (ˈdiːsᵊnsɪz) PLURAL NOUN [1] **the.** those things that are considered necessary for a decent life. [2] another word for **proprieties.**

decency (ˈdiːsᵊnsɪ) NOUN, *plural* **-cies.** [1] conformity to the prevailing standards of propriety, morality, modesty, etc. [2] the quality of being decent.

decennial (dɪˈsɛnɪəl) ADJECTIVE [1] lasting for ten years. [2] occurring every ten years. ◆ NOUN [3] a tenth anniversary or its celebration.
▸**deˈcennially** ADVERB

decennium (dɪˈsɛnɪəm) *or* **decennary** (dɪˈsɛnərɪ) NOUN, *plural* **-niums, -nia** (-nɪə) *or* **-naries.** a less common word for **decade** (sense 1).
▷**HISTORY** C17: from Latin, from *decem* ten + *annus* year

decent (ˈdiːsᵊnt) ADJECTIVE [1] polite or respectable: *a decent family.* [2] proper and suitable; fitting: *a decent burial.* [3] conforming to conventions of sexual behaviour; not indecent. [4] free of oaths, blasphemy, etc.: *decent language.* [5] good or adequate: *a decent wage.* [6] *Informal* kind; generous: *he was pretty decent to me.* [7] *Informal* sufficiently clothed to be seen by other people: *are you decent?*
▷**HISTORY** C16: from Latin *decēns* suitable, from *decēre* to be fitting
▸**ˈdecently** ADVERB ▸**ˈdecentness** NOUN

decentralize *or* **decentralise** (diːˈsɛntrəˌlaɪz) VERB [1] to reorganize (a government, industry, etc.) into smaller more autonomous units. [2] to disperse (a concentration, as of industry or population).
▸**deˈcentralist** NOUN, ADJECTIVE ▸**deˌcentraliˈzation** *or* **deˌcentraliˈsation** NOUN

decentralized processing NOUN *Computing* the use of word processing or data processing units in stand-alone or localized situations.

deception (dɪˈsɛpʃən) NOUN [1] the act of deceiving or the state of being deceived. [2] something that deceives; trick.

deceptive (dɪˈsɛptɪv) ADJECTIVE [1] likely or designed to deceive; misleading: *appearances can be deceptive.* [2] *Music* (of a cadence) another word for **interrupted** (sense 3).
▸**deˈceptively** ADVERB ▸**deˈceptiveness** NOUN

decerebrate VERB (diːˈsɛrɪˌbreɪt) [1] *(tr)* to remove the brain or a large section of the brain or to cut the spinal cord at the level of the brain stem of (a person or animal). ◆ NOUN (diːˈsɛrɪbrɪt) [2] a decerebrated individual.
▷**HISTORY** C19: from DE- + CEREBRO- + -ATE[1]
▸**deˌcereˈbration** NOUN

decern (dɪˈsɜːn) VERB *(tr)* [1] *Scots law* to decree or adjudge. [2] an archaic spelling of **discern.**
▷**HISTORY** C15: from Old French *decerner,* from Latin *dēcernere* to judge, from *cernere* to discern

decertify (diːˈsɜːtɪfaɪ) VERB **-fies, -fying, -fied.** *(tr)* to withdraw or remove a certificate or certification from (a person, organization, or country).
▸**deˌcertifiˈcation** NOUN

deci- PREFIX denoting one tenth; 10^{-1}: *decimetre.* Symbol: d.
▷**HISTORY** from French *déci-,* from Latin *decimus* tenth

deciare (ˈdɛsɪˌɛə) NOUN one tenth of an are or 10 square metres.
▷**HISTORY** C19: from French *déciare;* see DECI-, ARE[2]

decibel (ˈdɛsɪˌbɛl) NOUN [1] a unit for comparing two currents, voltages, or power levels, equal to one tenth of a bel. [2] a similar unit for measuring the intensity of a sound. It is equal to ten times the logarithm to the base ten of the ratio of the intensity of the sound to be measured to the intensity of some reference sound, usually the lowest audible note of the same frequency. Abbreviation: **dB.** See also **perceived noise decibel.**

decidable (dɪˈsaɪdəbᵊl) ADJECTIVE [1] able to be decided. [2] *Logic* (of a formal theory) having the property that it is possible by a mechanistic procedure to determine whether or not any well-formed formula is a theorem.

decide (dɪˈsaɪd) VERB [1] *(may take a clause or an infinitive as object;* when *intr,* sometimes foll by *on* or *about)* to reach a decision: *decide what you want; he decided to go.* [2] *(tr)* to cause (a person) to reach a decision: *the weather decided me against going.* [3] *(tr)* to determine or settle (a contest or question): *he decided his future plans.* [4] *(tr)* to influence decisively the outcome of (a contest or question): *Borg's stamina decided the match.* [5] *(intr;* foll by *for* or *against)* to pronounce a formal verdict.
▷**HISTORY** C14: from Old French *decider,* from Latin *dēcīdere,* literally: to cut off, from *caedere* to cut

decided (dɪˈsaɪdɪd) ADJECTIVE *(prenominal)* [1] unmistakable: *a decided improvement.* [2] determined; resolute: *a girl of decided character.*
▸**deˈcidedly** ADVERB ▸**deˈcidedness** NOUN

decider (dɪˈsaɪdə) NOUN the point, goal, game, etc., that determines who wins a match or championship.

decidua (dɪˈsɪdjʊə) NOUN, *plural* **-ciduas** *or* **-ciduae** (-ˈsɪdjʊˌiː). the specialized mucous membrane that lines the uterus of some mammals during pregnancy: is shed, with the placenta, at parturition.
▷**HISTORY** C18: from New Latin, from Latin *dēciduus* falling down; see DECIDUOUS
▸**deˈcidual** *or* **deˈciduate** ADJECTIVE

deciduous (dɪˈsɪdjʊəs) ADJECTIVE [1] (of trees and shrubs) shedding all leaves annually at the end of the growing season and then having a dormant period without leaves. Compare **evergreen** (sense 1). [2] (of antlers, wings, teeth, etc.) being shed at the end of a period of growth. [3] *Rare* impermanent; transitory. Compare **evergreen** (sense 2).
▷**HISTORY** C17: from Latin *dēciduus* falling off, from *dēcidere* to fall down, from *cadere* to fall
▸**deˈciduously** ADVERB ▸**deˈciduousness** NOUN

decile (ˈdɛsɪl, -aɪl) NOUN *Statistics* **a** one of nine actual or notional values of a variable dividing its distribution into ten groups with equal frequencies: the ninth decile is the value below which 90% of the population lie. See also **percentile. b** a tenth part of a distribution.
▷**HISTORY** C17: from DECA- + -ILE

decilitre *or US* **deciliter** (ˈdɛsɪˌliːtə) NOUN one tenth of a litre. Symbol: dl.

decillion (dɪˈsɪljən) NOUN [1] (in Britain, France, and Germany) the number represented as one followed by 60 zeros (10^{60}). [2] (in the US and Canada) the number represented as one followed by 33 zeros (10^{33}).
▷**HISTORY** C19: from Latin *decem* ten + *-illion* as in *million*
▸**deˈcillionth** ADJECTIVE

decimal (ˈdɛsɪməl) NOUN [1] Also called: **decimal**

fraction. a fraction that has a denominator of a power of ten, the power depending on or deciding the decimal place. It is indicated by a decimal point to the left of the numerator, the denominator being omitted. Zeros are inserted between the point and the numerator, if necessary, to obtain the correct decimal place. 2 any number used in the decimal system. ◆ ADJECTIVE 3 **a** relating to or using powers of ten. **b** of the base ten. 4 (*prenominal*) expressed as a decimal.
▷HISTORY C17: from Medieval Latin *decimālis* of tithes, from Latin *decima* a tenth, from *decem* ten
▸ **'decimally** ADVERB

decimal classification NOUN another term for **Dewey Decimal System.**

decimal currency NOUN a system of currency in which the monetary units are parts or powers of ten.

decimal fraction NOUN another name for **decimal** (sense 1).

decimalize *or* **decimalise** ('dɛsɪmə,laɪz) VERB to change (a system, number, etc.) to the decimal system: *Britain has decimalized her currency.*
▸ **,decimali'zation** *or* **,decimali'sation** NOUN

decimal place NOUN 1 the position of a digit after the decimal point, each successive position to the right having a denominator of an increased power of ten: *in 0.025, 5 is in the third decimal place.* 2 the number of digits to the right of the decimal point: *3.142 is a number given to three decimal places.* Compare **significant figures** (sense 2).

decimal point NOUN a full stop or a raised full stop placed between the integral and fractional parts of a number in the decimal system.

> **Language note** Conventions relating to the use of the decimal point are confused. The IX General Conference on Weights and Measures resolved in 1948 that the decimal point should be a point on the line or a comma, but not a centre dot. It also resolved that figures could be grouped in threes about the decimal point, but that no point or comma should be used for this purpose. These conventions are adopted in this dictionary. However, the Decimal Currency Board recommended that for sums of money the centre dot should be used as the decimal point and that the comma should be used as the thousand marker. Moreover, in some countries the position is reversed, the comma being used as the decimal point and the dot as the thousand marker.

decimal system NOUN 1 the number system in general use, having a base of ten, in which numbers are expressed by combinations of the ten digits 0 to 9. 2 a system of measurement, such as the metric system, in which the multiple and submultiple units are related to a basic unit by powers of ten.

decimate ('dɛsɪ,meɪt) VERB (*tr*) 1 to destroy or kill a large proportion of: *a plague decimated the population.* 2 (esp in the ancient Roman army) to kill every tenth man of (a mutinous section).
▷HISTORY C17: from Latin *decimāre,* from *decimus* tenth, from *decem* ten
▸ **,deci'mation** NOUN ▸ **'deci,mator** NOUN

> **Language note** One talks about the whole of something being *decimated,* not a part: *disease decimated the population,* not *disease decimated most of the population.*

decimetre *or US* **decimeter** ('dɛsɪ,mi:tə) NOUN one tenth of a metre. Symbol: dm.
▸ **decimetric** (,dɛsɪ'mɛtrɪk) ADJECTIVE

decipher (dɪ'saɪfə) VERB (*tr*) 1 to determine the meaning of (something obscure or illegible). 2 to convert from code into plain text; decode.
▸ **de'cipherable** ADJECTIVE ▸ **de,ciphera'bility** NOUN ▸ **de'cipherer** NOUN ▸ **de'cipherment** NOUN

decision (dɪ'sɪʒən) NOUN 1 a judgment, conclusion, or resolution reached or given; verdict. 2 the act of making up one's mind. 3 firmness of purpose or character; determination.
▷HISTORY C15: from Old French, from Latin *dēcīsiō,* literally: a cutting off; see DECIDE
▸ **de'cisional** ADJECTIVE

decision support system NOUN a system in which one or more computers and computer programs assist in decision-making by providing information.

decision table NOUN a table within a computer program that specifies the actions to be taken when certain conditions arise.

decision theory NOUN *Statistics* the study of strategies for decision making under conditions of uncertainty in such a way as to maximize the expected utility. See also **game theory.**

decision tree NOUN a treelike diagram illustrating the choices available to a decision maker, each possible decision and its estimated outcome being shown as a separate branch of the tree.

decisive (dɪ'saɪsɪv) ADJECTIVE 1 influential; conclusive: *a decisive argument.* 2 characterized by the ability to make decisions, esp quickly; resolute.
▸ **de'cisively** ADVERB ▸ **de'cisiveness** NOUN

deck (dɛk) NOUN 1 *Nautical* any of various platforms built into a vessel: *a promenade deck; the poop deck.* 2 a similar floor or platform, as in a bus. 3 **a** the horizontal platform that supports the turntable and pick-up of a record player. **b** See **tape deck.** 4 *Chiefly US* a pack of playing cards. 5 Also called: **pack.** *Computing, obsolete* a collection of punched cards relevant to a particular program. 6 a raised wooden platform built in a garden to provide a seating area. 7 **clear the decks.** *Informal* to prepare for action, as by removing obstacles from a field of activity or combat. 8 **hit the deck.** *Informal* **a** to fall to the floor or ground, esp in order to avoid injury. **b** to prepare for action. **c** to get out of bed. ◆ VERB (*tr*) 9 (often foll by *out*) to dress or decorate. 10 to build a deck on (a vessel). 11 *Slang* to knock (a person) to the ground. ◆ See also **deck over.**
▷HISTORY C15: from Middle Dutch *dec* a covering; related to THATCH
▸ **'decker** NOUN

deck-access ADJECTIVE (of a block of flats) having a continuous inset balcony at each level onto which the front door of each flat on that level opens.

deck beam NOUN *Nautical* a stiffening deck member supported at its extremities by knee connections to frames or bulkheads.

deck-botherer NOUN *Slang* a disc jockey.

deck bridge NOUN *Civil engineering* a bridge with an upper horizontal beam that carries the roadway. Compare **through bridge.**

deckchair ('dɛk,tʃɛə) NOUN a folding chair for use out of doors, consisting of a wooden frame suspending a length of canvas. 2 **rearranging the deckchairs on the Titanic.** *Humorous* engaged in futile or ineffectual actions.

deck crane NOUN *Nautical* a deck-mounted crane used for loading and unloading cargo.

deck department NOUN the part of a ship's crew, from the captain down, concerned with running the ship but not with heavy machinery or catering.

decked (dɛkt) ADJECTIVE having a wooden deck or platform: *a decked terrace.*

-decker ADJECTIVE (*in combination:*) having a certain specified number of levels or layers: *a double-decker bus.*

deck hand NOUN 1 a seaman assigned various duties, such as mooring and cargo handling, on the deck of a ship. 2 (in Britain) a seaman over 17 years of age who has seen sea duty for at least one year. 3 a helper aboard a yacht.

deckhouse ('dɛk,haus) NOUN a houselike cabin on the deck of a ship.

decking ('dɛkɪŋ) NOUN a wooden deck or platform, esp one in a garden for deckchairs, etc.

deckle *or* **deckel** ('dɛkᵊl) NOUN 1 a frame used to contain pulp on the mould in the making of handmade paper. 2 Also called: **deckle strap.** a strap on each edge of the moving web of paper on a paper-making machine that fixes the width of the paper. 3 See **deckle edge.**
▷HISTORY C19: from German *Deckel* lid, from *decken* to cover

deckle edge NOUN 1 the rough edge of handmade paper, caused by pulp seeping between the mould and the deckle: often left as ornamentation in fine books and writing papers. 2 a trimmed edge imitating this.
▸ **'deckle-'edged** ADJECTIVE

deck officer NOUN a ship's officer who is part of the deck crew.

deck over VERB (*tr*) to complete the construction of the upper deck between the bulwarks of (a vessel).

deck shoe NOUN 1 a rubber-soled leather shoe worn when boating. 2 a casual cloth or soft leather shoe resembling this.

deck tennis NOUN a game played on board ship in which a quoit is tossed to and fro across a high net on a small court resembling a tennis court.

declaim (dɪ'kleɪm) VERB 1 to make (a speech, statement, etc.) loudly and in a rhetorical manner. 2 to speak lines from (a play, poem, etc.) with studied eloquence; recite. 3 (*intr;* foll by *against*) to protest (against) loudly and publicly.
▷HISTORY C14: from Latin *dēclāmāre,* from *clāmāre* to call out
▸ **de'claimer** NOUN

declamation (,dɛklə'meɪʃən) NOUN 1 a rhetorical or emotional speech, made esp in order to protest or condemn; tirade. 2 a speech, verse, etc., that is or can be spoken. 3 the act or art of declaiming. 4 *Music* the artistry or technique involved in singing recitative passages.

declamatory (dɪ'klæmətərɪ, -trɪ) ADJECTIVE 1 relating to or having the characteristics of a declamation. 2 merely rhetorical; empty and bombastic.
▸ **de'clamatorily** ADVERB

declarant (dɪ'klɛərənt) NOUN *Chiefly law* a person who makes a declaration.

declaration (,dɛklə'reɪʃən) NOUN 1 an explicit or emphatic statement. 2 a formal statement or announcement; proclamation. 3 the act of declaring. 4 the ruling of a judge or court on a question of law, esp in the chancery division of the High Court. 5 *Law* an unsworn statement of a witness admissible in evidence under certain conditions. See also **statutory declaration.** 6 *Cricket* the voluntary closure of an innings before all ten wickets have fallen. 7 *Contract bridge* the final contract. 8 a statement or inventory of goods, etc., submitted for tax assessment: *a customs declaration.* 9 *Cards* an announcement of points made after taking a trick, as in bezique.

Declaration of Independence NOUN 1 the proclamation made by the second American Continental Congress on July 4, 1776, which asserted the freedom and independence of the 13 Colonies from Great Britain. 2 the document formally recording this proclamation.

declarative (dɪ'klærətɪv) ADJECTIVE making or having the nature of a declaration.
▸ **de'claratively** ADVERB

declarator (dɪ'klærətə) NOUN *Scots law* an action seeking to have some right, status, etc., judicially ascertained.

declaratory (dɪ'klærətərɪ, -trɪ) ADJECTIVE 1 another word for **declarative.** 2 *Law* **a** (of a statute) stating the existing law on a particular subject; explanatory. **b** (of a decree or judgment) stating the rights of the parties without specifying the action to be taken.
▸ **de'claratorily** ADVERB

declare (dɪ'klɛə) VERB (*mainly tr*) 1 (*may take a clause as object*) to make clearly known or announce officially: *to declare one's interests; war was declared.* 2 to state officially that (a person, fact, etc.) is as specified: *he declared him fit.* 3 (*may take a clause as object*) to state emphatically; assert. 4 to show, reveal, or manifest: *the heavens declare the glory of God.* 5 (*intr;* often foll by *for* or *against*) to make known one's choice or opinion. 6 to make a complete statement of (dutiable goods, etc.). 7 (*also intr*) *Cards* **a** to display (a card or series of) on the table so as to add to one's score. **b** to decide (the trump suit) by making the final bid. 8 (*intr*) *Cricket* to close an innings voluntarily before all ten wickets have fallen. 9 to authorize the payment of (a dividend) from corporate net profit.
▷HISTORY C14: from Latin *dēclārāre* to make clear, from *clārus* bright, clear
▸ **de'clarable** ADJECTIVE

declarer (dɪˈklɛərə) NOUN [1] a person who declares. [2] *Bridge* the player who, as first bidder of the suit of the final contract, plays both hands of the partnership.

declass (diːˈklɑːs) VERB (*tr*) to lower in social status or position; degrade.

déclassé (*French* deklɑse) ADJECTIVE having lost social standing or status.
▷HISTORY C19: from French *déclasser* to DECLASS
▸**déclassée** FEMININE ADJECTIVE

declassify (diːˈklæsɪˌfaɪ) VERB **-fies, -fying, -fied.** (*tr*) to release (a document or information) from the security list.
▸**deˈclassiˌfiable** ADJECTIVE ▸**deˌclassifiˈcation** NOUN

declension (dɪˈklɛnʃən) NOUN [1] *Grammar* **a** inflection of nouns, pronouns, or adjectives for case, number, and gender. **b** the complete set of the inflections of such a word: *"puella" is a first-declension noun in Latin.* [2] a decline or deviation from a standard, belief, etc. [3] a downward slope or bend.
▷HISTORY C15: from Latin *dēclīnātiō*, literally: a bending aside, hence variation, inflection; see DECLINE
▸**deˈclensional** ADJECTIVE ▸**deˈclensionally** ADVERB

declinate (ˈdɛklɪˌneɪt, -nɪt) ADJECTIVE (esp of plant parts) descending from the horizontal in a curve; drooping.

declination (ˌdɛklɪˈneɪʃən) NOUN [1] *Astronomy* the angular distance, esp in degrees, of a star, planet, etc., from the celestial equator measured north (positive) or south (negative) along the great circle passing through the celestial poles and the body. Symbol: δ. Compare **right ascension.** [2] See **magnetic declination.** [3] a refusal, esp a courteous or formal one.
▸**ˌdecliˈnational** ADJECTIVE

decline (dɪˈklaɪn) VERB [1] to refuse to do or accept (something), esp politely. [2] (*intr*) to grow smaller; diminish: *demand has declined over the years.* [3] to slope or cause to slope downwards. [4] (*intr*) to deteriorate gradually, as in quality, health, or character. [5] *Grammar* to state or list the inflections of (a noun, adjective, or pronoun), or (of a noun, adjective, or pronoun) to be inflected for number, case, or gender. Compare **conjugate** (sense 1). ◆ NOUN [6] gradual deterioration or loss. [7] a movement downward or towards something smaller; diminution. [8] a downward slope; declivity. [9] *Archaic* any slowly progressive disease, such as tuberculosis.
▷HISTORY C14: from Old French *decliner* to inflect, turn away, sink, from Latin *dēclīnāre* to bend away, inflect grammatically
▸**deˈclinable** ADJECTIVE ▸**deˈcliner** NOUN

declinometer (ˌdɛklɪˈnɒmɪtə) NOUN an instrument for measuring magnetic declination.

declivity (dɪˈklɪvɪtɪ) NOUN, *plural* **-ties.** a downward slope, esp of the ground. Compare **acclivity.**
▷HISTORY C17: from Latin *dēclīvitās*, from DE- + *clīvus* a slope, hill
▸**deˈclivitous** ADJECTIVE

declutch (dɪˈklʌtʃ) VERB (*intr*) to disengage the clutch of a motor vehicle.

declutter (diːˈklʌtə) VERB to simplify or get rid of mess, disorder, complications, etc.: *it's time to declutter your life.*

decoct (dɪˈkɒkt) VERB to extract (the essence or active principle) from (a medicinal or similar substance) by boiling.
▷HISTORY C15: see DECOCTION

decoction (dɪˈkɒkʃən) NOUN [1] *Pharmacol* the extraction of the water-soluble substances of a drug or medicinal plants by boiling. [2] the essence or liquor resulting from this.
▷HISTORY C14: from Old French, from Late Latin *dēcoctiō*, from *dēcoquere* to boil down, from *coquere* to COOK

decode (diːˈkəʊd) VERB [1] to convert (a message, text, etc.) from code into ordinary language. [2] *Computing* to convert (coded characters) from one form to another, as from binary-coded decimals to decimal numbers. Compare **encode** (sense 2). [3] *Electronics* to convert (a coded electrical signal) into normal analogue components. [4] to analyse and understand the construction of words and phrases, esp in a foreign language.
▸**deˈcoder** NOUN

decoke (diːˈkəʊk) VERB (*tr*) another word for **decarbonize.**

decollate (dɪˈkɒleɪt, ˈdɛkəˌleɪt, ˌdiːkəˈleɪt) VERB [1] to separate (continuous stationery, etc.) into individual forms. [2] an archaic word for **decapitate.**
▷HISTORY C16: from Latin *dēcollāre* to behead, from DE- + *collum* neck
▸**ˌdecolˈlation** NOUN ▸**ˈdecolˌlator** NOUN

décolletage (ˌdeɪkɒlˈtɑːʒ; *French* dekɔltaʒ) NOUN a low-cut neckline or a woman's garment with a low neck.
▷HISTORY C19: from French; see DÉCOLLETÉ

décolleté (deɪˈkɒlteɪ; *French* dekɔlte) ADJECTIVE [1] (of a woman's garment) low-cut. [2] wearing a low-cut garment. ◆ NOUN [3] a low-cut neckline.
▷HISTORY C19: from French *décolleter* to cut out the neck (of a dress), from *collet* collar

decolonize *or* **decolonise** (diːˈkɒləˌnaɪz) VERB (*tr*) to grant independence to (a colony).
▸**deˌcoloniˈzation** *or* **deˌcoloniˈsation** NOUN

decolorant (diːˈkʌlərənt) ADJECTIVE [1] able to decolour or bleach. ◆ NOUN [2] a substance that decolours.

decolour (diːˈkʌlə), **decolorize,** *or* **decolorise** VERB (*tr*) to deprive of colour, as by bleaching.
▸**deˌcolorˈation** NOUN ▸**deˌcoloriˈzation** *or* **deˌcoloriˈsation** NOUN

decommission (ˌdiːkəˈmɪʃən) VERB (*tr*) to dismantle or remove from service (a nuclear reactor, weapon, ship, etc. which is no longer required).

decommit (ˌdikəˈmɪt) VERB **-mits, -mitting, -mitted.** (*intr*) to withdraw from a commitment or agreed course of action.

decompensation (diːˌkɒmpɛnˈseɪʃən) NOUN *Pathol* inability of an organ, esp the heart, to maintain its function due to overload caused by a disease.

decompose (ˌdiːkəmˈpəʊz) VERB [1] to break down (organic matter) or (of organic matter) to be broken down physically and chemically by bacterial or fungal action; rot. [2] *Chem* to break down or cause to break down into simpler chemical compounds. [3] to break up or separate into constituent parts. [4] (*tr*) *Maths* to express in terms of a number of independent simpler components, as a set as a canonical union of disjoint subsets, or a vector into orthogonal components.
▸**ˌdecomˈposable** ADJECTIVE ▸**ˌdecomˌposaˈbility** NOUN
▸**decomposition** (ˌdiːkɒmpəˈzɪʃən) NOUN

decomposer (ˌdiːkəmˈpəʊzə) NOUN *Ecology* any organism in a community, such as a bacterium or fungus, that breaks down dead tissue enabling the constituents to be recycled to the environment. See also **consumer** (sense 3), **producer** (sense 8).

decompound (ˌdiːkəmˈpaʊnd) ADJECTIVE [1] (of a compound leaf) having leaflets consisting of several distinct parts. [2] made up of one or more compounds. ◆ VERB [3] a less common word for **decompose.** [4] *Obsolete* to mix with or form from one or more compounds.

decompress (ˌdiːkəmˈprɛs) VERB [1] to relieve (a substance) of pressure or (of a substance) to be relieved of pressure. [2] to return (a diver, caisson worker, etc.) to a condition of normal atmospheric pressure gradually from a condition of increased pressure or (of a diver, etc.) to be returned to such a condition.
▸**ˌdecomˈpression** NOUN ▸**ˌdecomˈpressive** ADJECTIVE

decompression chamber NOUN a chamber in which the pressure of air can be varied slowly for returning people from abnormal pressures to atmospheric pressure without inducing decompression sickness.

decompression sickness *or* **illness** NOUN a disorder characterized by severe pain in muscles and joints, cramp, and difficulty in breathing, caused by a sudden and sustained decrease in air pressure, resulting in the deposition of nitrogen bubbles in the tissues. Also called: **caisson disease, aeroembolism.** Nontechnical name: **the bends.**

decongestant (ˌdiːkənˈdʒɛstənt) ADJECTIVE [1] relieving congestion, esp nasal congestion. ◆ NOUN [2] a decongestant drug.

deconsecrate (diːˈkɒnsɪˌkreɪt) VERB (*tr*) to transfer (a church) to secular use.
▸**deˌconseˈcration** NOUN

deconstruct (ˌdiːkənˈstrʌkt) VERB (*tr*) [1] to apply the theories of deconstruction to (a text, film, etc.). [2] to expose or dismantle the existing structure in (a system, organization, etc.).

deconstructed (ˌdiːkənˈstrʌktɪd) ADJECTIVE having no formal structure: *a deconstructed jacket.*

deconstruction (ˌdiːkənˈstrʌkʃən) NOUN a technique of literary analysis that regards meaning as resulting from the differences between words rather than their reference to the things they stand for. Different meanings are discovered by taking apart the structure of the language used and exposing the assumption that words have a fixed reference point beyond themselves.

decontaminate (ˌdiːkənˈtæmɪˌneɪt) VERB (*tr*) to render (an area, building, object, etc.) harmless by the removal, distribution, or neutralization of poisons, radioactivity, etc.
▸**ˌdeconˈtaminant** NOUN ▸**ˌdeconˌtamiˈnation** NOUN
▸**ˌdeconˈtaminative** ADJECTIVE ▸**ˌdeconˈtamiˌnator** NOUN

decontrol (ˌdiːkənˈtrəʊl) VERB **-trols, -trolling, -trolled.** (*tr*) to free of restraints or controls, esp government controls: *to decontrol prices.*

décor *or* **decor** (ˈdeɪkɔː) NOUN [1] a style or scheme of interior decoration, furnishings, etc., as in a room or house. [2] stage decoration; scenery.
▷HISTORY C19: from French, from *décorer* to DECORATE

decorate (ˈdɛkəˌreɪt) VERB [1] (*tr*) to make more attractive by adding ornament, colour, etc. [2] to paint or wallpaper (a room, house, etc.). [3] (*tr*) to confer a mark of distinction, esp a military medal, upon. [4] (*tr*) to evaporate a metal film onto (a crystal) in order to display dislocations in structure.
▷HISTORY C16: from Latin *decorāre*, from *decus* adornment; see DECENT

Decorated style *or* **architecture** NOUN a 14th-century style of English architecture characterized by the ogee arch, geometrical tracery, and floral decoration.

decoration (ˌdɛkəˈreɪʃən) NOUN [1] an addition that renders something more attractive or ornate; adornment. [2] the act, process, or art of decorating. [3] a medal, badge, etc., conferred as a mark of honour.

decorative (ˈdɛkərətɪv, ˈdɛkrətɪv) ADJECTIVE serving to decorate or adorn; ornamental.
▸**ˈdecoratively** ADVERB ▸**ˈdecorativeness** NOUN

decorator (ˈdɛkəˌreɪtə) NOUN [1] *Brit* a person whose profession is the painting and wallpapering of buildings. [2] a person who decorates. [3] See **interior decorator** (sense 1).

decorous (ˈdɛkərəs) ADJECTIVE characterized by propriety in manners, conduct, etc.
▷HISTORY C17: from Latin *decōrus*, from *decor* elegance
▸**ˈdecorously** ADVERB ▸**ˈdecorousness** NOUN

decorticate (diːˈkɔːtɪˌkeɪt) VERB [1] (*tr*) to remove the bark or some other outer layer from. [2] *Surgery* to remove the cortex of (an organ or part).
▷HISTORY C17: from Latin *dēcorticāre*, from DE- + *-corticāre*, from *cortex* bark
▸**deˌcortiˈcation** NOUN ▸**deˈcortiˌcator** NOUN

decorum (dɪˈkɔːrəm) NOUN [1] propriety, esp in behaviour or conduct. [2] a requirement of correct behaviour in polite society.
▷HISTORY C16: from Latin: propriety

decoupage (ˌdeɪkuːˈpɑːʒ) NOUN [1] the art or process of decorating a surface with shapes or illustrations cut from paper, card, etc. [2] anything produced by this technique.
▷HISTORY C20: from French, from *découper* to cut out, from DE- + *couper* to cut

decouple (ˌdiːˈkʌpᵊl) VERB (*tr*) to separate (joined or coupled subsystems) thereby enabling them to exist and operate separately.

decoupling (diːˈkʌplɪŋ) NOUN [1] the separation of previously linked systems so that they may operate independently. [2] *Electronics* the reduction or avoidance of undesired distortion or oscillations in a circuit, caused by unwanted common coupling between two or more circuits.

decoy NOUN (ˈdiːkɔɪ, dɪˈkɔɪ) [1] a person or thing used to beguile or lead someone into danger; lure. [2] *Military* something designed to deceive an enemy or divert his attention. [3] a bird or animal,

or an image of one, used to lure game into a trap or within shooting range. [4] an enclosed space or large trap, often with a wide funnelled entrance, into which game can be lured for capture. ◆ VERB (dɪˈkɔɪ) [5] to lure or be lured by or as if by means of a decoy.
▷HISTORY C17: probably from Dutch *de kooi*, literally: the cage, from Latin *cavea* CAGE
▸deˈcoyer NOUN

decrease VERB (dɪˈkriːs) [1] to diminish or cause to diminish in size, number, strength, etc. ◆ NOUN (ˈdiːkriːs, dɪˈkriːs) [2] the act or process of diminishing; reduction. [3] the amount by which something has been diminished.
▷HISTORY C14: from Old French *descreistre*, from Latin *dēcrescere* to grow less, from DE- + *crescere* to grow
▸deˈcreasingly ADVERB

decree (dɪˈkriː) NOUN [1] an edict, law, etc., made by someone in authority. [2] an order or judgment of a court made after hearing a suit, esp in matrimonial proceedings. See **decree nisi, decree absolute.** ◆ VERB **decrees, decreeing, decreed.** [3] to order, adjudge, or ordain by decree.
▷HISTORY C14: from Old French *decre*, from Latin *dēcrētum* ordinance, from *dēcrētus* decided, past participle of *dēcernere* to determine; see DECERN
▸deˈcreeable ADJECTIVE ▸deˈcreer NOUN

decree absolute NOUN the final decree in divorce proceedings, which leaves the parties free to remarry. Compare **decree nisi.**

decree nisi (ˈnaɪsaɪ) NOUN a provisional decree, esp in divorce proceedings, which will later be made absolute unless cause is shown why it should not. Compare **decree absolute.**

decreet (dɪˈkriːt) NOUN *Scots law* the final judgment or sentence of a court.
▷HISTORY C14: *decret*: from Old French, from Latin *dēcrētum* DECREE

decrement (ˈdɛkrɪmənt) NOUN [1] the act of decreasing; diminution. [2] *Maths* a negative increment. [3] *Physics* a measure of the damping of an oscillator, expressed by the ratio of the amplitude of a cycle to its amplitude after one period. [4] of spectra, a sequence of related spectrum lines decaying in intensity, e.g. Balmer decay.
▷HISTORY C17: from Latin *dēcrēmentum*, from *dēcrescere* to DECREASE

decrepit (dɪˈkrɛpɪt) ADJECTIVE [1] enfeebled by old age; infirm. [2] broken down or worn out by hard or long use; dilapidated.
▷HISTORY C15: from Latin *dēcrepitus*, from *crepāre* to creak
▸deˈcrepitly ADVERB ▸deˈcrepiˌtude NOUN

decrepitate (dɪˈkrɛpɪˌteɪt) VERB [1] *(tr)* to heat (a substance, such as a salt) until it emits a crackling sound or until this sound stops. [2] *(intr)* (esp of a salt) to crackle, as while being heated.
▷HISTORY C17: from New Latin *dēcrepitāre*, from Latin *crepitāre* to crackle, from *crepāre* to creak
▸deˌcrepiˈtation NOUN

decresc. *Music* ABBREVIATION FOR decrescendo.

decrescendo (ˌdiːkrɪˈʃɛndəʊ) NOUN, ADJECTIVE another word for **diminuendo.**
▷HISTORY Italian, from *decrescere* to DECREASE

decrescent (dɪˈkrɛsənt) ADJECTIVE (esp of the moon) decreasing; waning.
▷HISTORY C17: from Latin *dēcrescēns* growing less; see DECREASE
▸deˈcrescence NOUN

decretal (dɪˈkriːtᵊl) NOUN [1] *RC Church* a papal edict on doctrine or church law. ◆ ADJECTIVE [2] of or relating to a decretal or a decree.
▷HISTORY C15: from Old French, from Late Latin *dēcrētālis*; see DECREE
▸deˈcretalist NOUN

Decretals (dɪˈkriːtᵊlz) PLURAL NOUN *RC Church* a compilation of decretals, esp the authoritative compilation (**Liber Extra**) of Gregory IX (1234) which forms part of the Corpus Juris Canonici.

Decretum (dɪˈkriːtəm) NOUN *RC Church* the name given to various collections of canon law, esp that made by the monk Gratian in the 12th century, which forms the first part of the Corpus Juris Canonici.

decriminalize *or* **decriminalise** (diːˈkrɪmɪnᵊˌlaɪz) VERB *(tr)* to remove (an action) from the legal category of criminal offence: *to decriminalize the possession of marijuana.*
▸ˌdecriminaliˈzation *or* ˌdecriminaliˈsation NOUN

decry (dɪˈkraɪ) VERB **-cries, -crying, -cried.** *(tr)* [1] to express open disapproval of; disparage. [2] to depreciate by proclamation: *to decry obsolete coinage.*
▷HISTORY C17: from Old French *descrier*, from DES-[1] + *crier* to CRY
▸deˈcrial NOUN ▸deˈcrier NOUN

decrypt (diːˈkrɪpt) VERB *(tr)* [1] to decode (a message) with or without previous knowledge of its key. [2] to make intelligible (a television or other signal) that has been deliberately distorted for transmission.
▷HISTORY C20: from DE- + *crypt*, as in CRYPTIC
▸deˈcrypted ADJECTIVE ▸deˈcryption NOUN

decubitus (dɪˈkjuːbɪtəs) NOUN *Med* the posture adopted when lying down.
▷HISTORY C19: Latin, past participle of *decumbere* to lie down
▸deˈcubital ADJECTIVE

decubitus ulcer NOUN a chronic ulcer of the skin and underlying tissues caused by prolonged pressure on the body surface of bedridden patients. Nontechnical names: **bedsore, pressure sore.**

decumbent (dɪˈkʌmbənt) ADJECTIVE [1] lying down or lying flat. [2] *Botany* (of certain stems) lying flat with the tip growing upwards.
▷HISTORY C17: from Latin *dēcumbēns*, present participle of *dēcumbere* to lie down
▸deˈcumbence *or* deˈcumbency NOUN ▸deˈcumbently ADVERB

decuple (ˈdɛkjʊpᵊl) VERB [1] *(tr)* to increase by ten times. ◆ NOUN [2] an amount ten times as large as a given reference. ◆ ADJECTIVE [3] increasing tenfold.
▷HISTORY C15: from Old French, from Late Latin *decuplus* tenfold, from Latin *decem* ten

decurion (dɪˈkjʊərɪən) NOUN (in the Roman Empire) [1] a local councillor. [2] the commander of a troop of ten cavalrymen.
▷HISTORY C14: from Latin *decuriō*, from *decuria* company of ten, from *decem* ten

decurrent (dɪˈkʌrənt) ADJECTIVE *Botany* extending down the stem, esp (of a leaf) having the base of the blade extending down the stem as two wings.
▷HISTORY C15: from Latin *dēcurrere* to run down, from *currere* to run
▸deˈcurrently ADVERB

decurved (diːˈkɜːvd) ADJECTIVE bent or curved downwards: *a decurved bill; decurved petals.*

decury (ˈdɛkjʊərɪ) NOUN, *plural* **-ries.** (in ancient Rome) a body of ten men.
▷HISTORY C16: from Latin *decuria*; see DECURION

decussate VERB (dɪˈkʌseɪt) [1] to cross or cause to cross in the form of the letter X; intersect. ◆ ADJECTIVE (dɪˈkʌseɪt, dɪˈkʌsɪt) [2] in the form of the letter X; crossed; intersected. [3] *Botany* (esp of leaves) arranged in opposite pairs, with each pair at right angles to the one above and below it.
▷HISTORY C17: from Latin *decussāre*, from *decussis* the number ten, from *decem* ten
▸deˈcussately ADVERB ▸ˌdecusˈsation NOUN

Ded (dɛd) NOUN (in the Russian army) a soldier who has served two or three years.
▷HISTORY Russian *ded* grandfather

dedal (ˈdiːdᵊl) ADJECTIVE a variant spelling (esp US) of **daedal.**

dedans *French* (dədɑ̃) NOUN *Real Tennis* the open gallery at the server's end of the court.
▷HISTORY literally: interior

Dedéagach, Dedeagatch, *or* **Dedeağaç** (ˈdedeɪɑːˈgɑːtʃ) NOUN a former name (until the end of World War I) of **Alexandroúpolis.**

Dedekind cut (*German* ˈdedəˌkɪnt) NOUN a method of according the same status to irrational and rational numbers, devised by Julius Wilhelm *Dedekind* (1831–1916).

dedicate (ˈdɛdɪˌkeɪt) VERB *(tr)* [1] (often foll by *to*) to devote (oneself, one's time, etc.) wholly to a special purpose or cause; commit wholeheartedly or unreservedly. [2] (foll by *to*) to address or inscribe (a book, artistic performance, etc.) to a person, cause, etc. as a token of affection or respect. [3] (foll by *to*) to request or play (a record) on radio for another person as a greeting. [4] to assign or allocate to a particular project, function, etc. [5] to set apart for a deity or for sacred uses; consecrate. ◆ ADJECTIVE [6] an archaic word for **dedicated.**
▷HISTORY C15: from Latin *dēdicāre* to announce, from *dīcāre* to make known, variant of *dīcere* to say
▸ˌdedicaˈtee NOUN ▸ˈdediˌcator NOUN ▸dedicatory (ˈdɛdɪˌkeɪtərɪ, ˈdɛdɪkətərɪ, -trɪ) *or* ˈdediˌcative ADJECTIVE

dedicated (ˈdɛdɪˌkeɪtɪd) ADJECTIVE [1] devoted to a particular purpose or cause: *a dedicated man.* [2] assigned or allocated to a particular project, function, etc.: *a dedicated transmission line; dedicated parking space.* [3] *Computing* designed to fulfil one function: *a dedicated microprocessor.*

dedication (ˌdɛdɪˈkeɪʃən) NOUN [1] the act of dedicating or the state of being dedicated. [2] an inscription or announcement prefixed to a book, piece of music, etc., dedicating it to a person or thing. [3] complete and wholehearted devotion, esp to a career, ideal, etc. [4] a ceremony in which something, such as a church, is dedicated.
▸ˌdediˈcational ADJECTIVE

de dicto *Latin* (ˈdeɪˈdɪktəʊ) ADJECTIVE *Logic, philosophy* relating to the expression of a belief, possibility, etc., rather than to the individuals mentioned, as in *the number of the planets is the number of satellites of the sun*, the truth of which is independent of what number that is. Compare **de re.** See also **Electra paradox.**
▷HISTORY literally: about the saying

dedifferentiation (diːˌdɪfəˌrɛnʃɪˈeɪʃən) NOUN the reversion of the cells of differentiated tissue to a less specialized form.

deduce (dɪˈdjuːs) VERB *(tr)* [1] *(may take a clause as object)* to reach (a conclusion about something) by reasoning; conclude (that); infer. [2] *Archaic* to trace the origin, course, or derivation of.
▷HISTORY C15: from Latin *dēdūcere* to lead away, derive, from DE- + *dūcere* to lead
▸deˈducible ADJECTIVE ▸deˌduciˈbility *or* deˈducibleness NOUN

deduct (dɪˈdʌkt) VERB *(tr)* to take away or subtract (a number, quantity, part, etc.): *income tax is deducted from one's wages.*
▷HISTORY C15: from Latin *dēductus*, past participle of *dēdūcere* to DEDUCE

deductible (dɪˈdʌktɪbᵊl) ADJECTIVE [1] capable of being deducted. [2] *US and Canadian* short for **tax-deductible.** ◆ NOUN [3] *Insurance* the US and Canadian name for **excess** (sense 6).
▸deˌductiˈbility NOUN

deduction (dɪˈdʌkʃən) NOUN [1] the act or process of deducting or subtracting. [2] something, esp a sum of money, that is or may be deducted. [3] **a** the process of reasoning typical of mathematics and logic, whose conclusions follow necessarily from their premises. **b** an argument of this type. **c** the conclusion of such an argument. [4] *Logic* **a** a systematic method of deriving conclusions that cannot be false when the premises are true, esp one amenable to formalization and study by the science of logic. **b** an argument of this type. Compare **induction** (sense 4).

deduction theorem NOUN *Logic* the property of many formal systems that the conditional derived from a valid argument by taking the conjunction of the premises as antecedent and the conclusion as consequent is true.

deductive (dɪˈdʌktɪv) ADJECTIVE of or relating to deduction: *deductive reasoning.*
▸deˈductively ADVERB

dee (diː) VERB a Scot word for **die[1].**

Dee (diː) NOUN [1] a river in N Wales and NW England, rising in S Gwynedd and flowing east and north to the Irish Sea. Length: about 112 km (70 miles). [2] a river in NE Scotland, rising in the Cairngorms and flowing east to the North Sea. Length: about 140 km (87 miles). [3] a river in S Scotland, flowing south to the Solway Firth. Length: about 80 km (50 miles).

deed (diːd) NOUN [1] something that is done or performed; act. [2] a notable achievement; feat; exploit. [3] action or performance, as opposed to words. [4] *Law* a formal legal document signed, witnessed, and delivered to effect a conveyance or transfer of property or to create a legal obligation or contract. ◆ VERB [5] *(tr) US and Canadian* to convey or transfer (property) by deed.
▷HISTORY Old English *dēd*; related to Old High German *tāt*, Gothic *gadeths*; see DO[1]

deed box NOUN a lockable metal box for storing documents.

deed poll NOUN *Law* a deed made by one party only, esp one by which a person changes his name.

deejay ('di:ˌdʒeɪ) NOUN an informal name for **disc jockey**.
▷HISTORY C20: from the initials DJ

deek (di:k) VERB (*tr; imperative*) *Edinburgh and Northumbrian dialect* to look at: *deek that!*
▷HISTORY perhaps of Romany origin

deely boppers ('di:lɪˌbɒpəz) PLURAL NOUN a hairband with two balls on springs attached, resembling antennae.

deem (di:m) VERB (*tr*) to judge or consider: *I do not deem him worthy of this honour.*
▷HISTORY Old English *dēman;* related to Old High German *tuomen* to judge, Gothic *domjan;* see DOOM

de-emphasize *or* **de-emphasise** (di:'ɛmfəˌsaɪz) VERB (*tr*) to remove emphasis from.

deemster ('di:mstə) NOUN the title of one of the two justices in the Isle of Man. Also called: **dempster**.
▸'**deemster**ˌ**ship** NOUN

de-energize *or* **de-energise** (di:'ɛnədʒaɪz) VERB (*tr*) *Electrical engineering* to disconnect (an electrical circuit) from its source.
▸**de-**ˌ**energi'zation** *or* **de-**ˌ**energi'sation** NOUN

deep (di:p) ADJECTIVE [1] extending or situated relatively far down from a surface: *a deep pool.* [2] extending or situated relatively far inwards, backwards, or sideways: *a deep border of trees.* [3] *Cricket* relatively far from the pitch: *the deep field; deep third man.* [4] **a** (*postpositive*) of a specified dimension downwards, inwards, or backwards: *six feet deep.* **b** (*in combination*): *a six-foot-deep trench.* [5] coming from or penetrating to a great depth: *a deep breath.* [6] difficult to understand or penetrate; abstruse. [7] learned or intellectually demanding: *a deep discussion.* [8] of great intensity; extreme: *deep happiness; deep trouble.* [9] (*postpositive; foll by in*) absorbed or enveloped (by); engrossed or immersed (in): *deep in study; deep in debt.* [10] very cunning or crafty; devious: *a deep plot.* [11] mysterious or obscure: *a deep secret.* [12] (of a colour) having an intense or dark hue. [13] low in pitch or tone: *a deep voice.* [14] **go off the deep end.** *Informal* **a** to lose one's temper; react angrily. **b** *Chiefly US* to act rashly. [15] **in deep water.** in a tricky position or in trouble. [16] **throw (someone) in at the deep end.** See **end** (sense 28). ◆ NOUN [17] any deep place on land or under water, esp below 6000 metres (3000 fathoms). [18] **the deep. a** a poetic term for the **ocean. b** *Cricket* the area of the field relatively far from the pitch. [19] the most profound, intense, or central part: *the deep of winter.* [20] a vast extent, as of space or time. [21] *Nautical* one of the intervals on a sounding lead, one fathom apart. ◆ ADVERB [22] far on in time; late: *they worked deep into the night.* [23] profoundly or intensely. [24] **deep down.** *Informal* in reality, esp as opposed to appearance: *she is a very kind person deep down.* [25] **deep in the past.** long ago.
▷HISTORY Old English *dēop;* related to Old High German *tiof* deep, Old Norse *djupr*
▸'**deeply** ADVERB ▸'**deepness** NOUN

deep-discount bond NOUN a fixed-interest security that pays little or no interest but is issued at a substantial discount to its redemption value, thus largely substituting capital gain for income.

deep-dish pie NOUN *Chiefly US and Canadian* a pie baked in a deep dish and having only a top crust.

deep-dyed ADJECTIVE *Usually derogatory* thoroughgoing; absolute; complete.

deepen ('di:pᵊn) VERB to make or become deep, deeper, or more intense.
▸'**deepener** NOUN

deepfreeze (ˌdi:p'fri:z) NOUN [1] a type of refrigerator in which food, etc., is stored for long periods at temperatures below freezing. [2] storage in or as if in a deepfreeze. [3] *Informal* a state of suspended activity. ◆ VERB **deep-freeze, -freezes, -freezing, -froze, -frozen.** [4] (*tr*) to freeze or keep in or as if in a deepfreeze.

deep-fry VERB **-fries, -frying, -fried.** to cook (fish, potatoes, etc.) in sufficient hot fat to cover the food entirely.

deep green NOUN [1] a person, esp a politician, who is in favour of taking extreme measures to tackle environmentalist issues. ◆ ADJECTIVE [2] in favour of or relating to extreme measures to tackle environmentalist issues: *deep green environmentalists.*

deep kiss NOUN another name for **French kiss.**

deep-laid ADJECTIVE (of a plot or plan) carefully worked out and kept secret.

deep-litter NOUN (*modifier*) *Poultry farming* [1] denoting a system in which a number of hens are housed in one covered enclosure, within which they can move about freely, on a layer of straw or wood shavings several centimetres deep: *deep-litter system.* [2] kept in or produced by the deep-litter method: *deep-litter eggs.*

deep-rooted *or* **deep-seated** ADJECTIVE (of ideas, beliefs, prejudices, etc.) firmly fixed, implanted, or held; ingrained.

deep-sea NOUN (*modifier*) of, found in, or characteristic of the deep parts of the sea: *deep-sea fishing.*

deep-set ADJECTIVE (of the eyes) deeply set into the face.

deep-six VERB (*tr*) *US slang* to dispose of (something, such as documents) completely; destroy.
▷HISTORY C20: from *six feet deep,* the traditional depth for a grave

Deep South NOUN the SE part of the US, esp South Carolina, Georgia, Alabama, Mississippi, and Louisiana.

deep space NOUN any region of outer space beyond the system of the earth and moon.

deep structure NOUN *Generative grammar* a representation of a sentence at a level where logical or grammatical relations are made explicit, before transformational rules have been applied. Compare **surface structure.**

deep therapy NOUN radiotherapy with very penetrating short-wave radiation.

deep throat NOUN an anonymous source of secret information.
▷HISTORY C20: from the code name of such a source in the Watergate scandal; a reference to the title of a pornographic film

deep-vein thrombosis NOUN, *plural* **-ses** (-si:z). a blood clot in one of the major veins, usually in the legs or pelvis; can be caused by prolonged sitting in the same position, as on long-haul air flights. Abbreviation: **DVT.**

deer (dɪə) NOUN, *plural* **deer** *or* **deers.** [1] any ruminant artiodactyl mammal of the family *Cervidae,* including reindeer, elk, muntjacs, and roe deer, typically having antlers in the male. Related adjective: **cervine.** [2] (in N Canada) another name for **caribou.**
▷HISTORY Old English *dēor* beast; related to Old High German *tior* wild beast, Old Norse *dȳr*

deergrass ('dɪəˌgrɑ:s) NOUN a perennial cyperaceous plant, *Trichophorum caespitosum,* that grows in dense tufts in peat bogs of temperate regions.

deerhound ('dɪəˌhaʊnd) NOUN a very large rough-coated breed of dog of the greyhound type.

deer lick NOUN a naturally or artificially salty area of ground where deer come to lick the salt.

deer mouse NOUN any of various mice of the genus *Peromyscus,* esp *P. maniculatus,* of North and Central America, having brownish fur with white underparts: family *Cricetidae.* See also **white-footed mouse.**
▷HISTORY so named because of its agility

deerskin ('dɪəˌskɪn) NOUN **a** the hide of a deer. **b** (*as modifier*): *a deerskin jacket.*

deerstalker ('dɪəˌstɔ:kə) NOUN [1] Also called: **stalker.** a person who stalks deer, esp in order to shoot them. [2] a hat, peaked in front and behind, with earflaps usually turned up and tied together on the top.
▸'**deer**ˌ**stalking** ADJECTIVE, NOUN

de-escalate (di:'ɛskəˌleɪt) VERB to reduce the level or intensity of (a crisis, etc.).
▸**de-**ˌ**esca'lation** NOUN

DEET (di:t) NOUN ACRONYM FOR diethyl(meta)toluamide; an insect repellent.

def (dɛf) ADJECTIVE *Slang* very good, esp of hip-hop.
▷HISTORY C20: perhaps from *definitive*

def. ABBREVIATION FOR definition.

deface (dɪ'feɪs) VERB (*tr*) to spoil or mar the surface, legibility, or appearance of; disfigure.
▸**de'faceable** ADJECTIVE ▸**de'facement** NOUN ▸**de'facer** NOUN

de facto (deɪ 'fæktəʊ) ADVERB [1] in fact. ◆ ADJECTIVE [2] existing in fact, whether legally recognized or not: *a de facto regime.* Compare **de jure.** ◆ NOUN, *plural* **-tos.** [3] *Austral and NZ* a de facto husband or wife.
▷HISTORY C17: Latin

defaecate ('dɛfɪˌkeɪt) VERB a variant spelling of **defecate.**

defalcate ('di:fælˌkeɪt) VERB (*intr*) *Law* to misuse or misappropriate property or funds entrusted to one.
▷HISTORY C15: from Medieval Latin *dēfalcāre* to cut off, from Latin DE- + *falx* sickle
▸ˌ**defal'cation** NOUN ▸'**defal**ˌ**cator** NOUN

defamation (ˌdɛfə'meɪʃən) NOUN [1] *Law* the injuring of a person's good name or reputation. Compare **libel, slander.** [2] the act of defaming or state of being defamed.

defamatory (dɪ'fæmətərɪ, -trɪ) ADJECTIVE injurious to someone's name or reputation.
▸**de'famatorily** ADVERB

defame (dɪ'feɪm) VERB (*tr*) [1] to attack the good name or reputation of; slander; libel. [2] *Archaic* to indict or accuse.
▷HISTORY C14: from Old French *defamer,* from Latin *dēfāmāre,* from *diffāmāre* to spread by unfavourable report, from *fāma* FAME
▸**de'famer** NOUN

default (dɪ'fɔ:lt) NOUN [1] a failure to act, esp a failure to meet a financial obligation or to appear in a court of law at a time specified. [2] absence: *he lost the chess game by default.* [3] **in default of.** through or in the lack or absence of. [4] **judgment by default.** *Law* a judgment in the plaintiff's favour when the defendant fails to plead or to appear. [5] lack, want, or need. [6] (*also* 'di:fɔ:lt) *Computing* **a** the preset selection of an option offered by a system, which will always be followed except when explicitly altered. **b** (*as modifier*): *default setting.* ◆ VERB [7] (*intr; often foll by on or in*) to fail to make payment when due. [8] (*intr*) to fail to fulfil or perform an obligation, engagement, etc.: *to default in a sporting contest.* [9] *Law* to lose (a case) by failure to appear in court. [10] (*tr*) to declare that (someone) is in default.
▷HISTORY C13: from Old French *defaute,* from *defaillir* to fail, from Vulgar Latin *dēfallīre* (unattested) to be lacking

defaulter (dɪ'fɔ:ltə) NOUN [1] a person who defaults. [2] *Chiefly Brit* a person, esp a soldier, who has broken the disciplinary code of his service.

defeasance (dɪ'fi:zᵊns) NOUN *Chiefly law* [1] the act or process of rendering null and void; annulment. [2] **a** a condition, the fulfilment of which renders a deed void. **b** the document containing such a condition.
▷HISTORY C14: from Old French, from *desfaire* to DEFEAT

defeasible (dɪ'fi:zəbᵊl) ADJECTIVE [1] *Law* (of an estate or interest in land) capable of being defeated or rendered void. [2] *Philosophy* (of a judgment, opinion, etc.) having a presupposition in its favour but open to revision if countervailing evidence becomes known. Compare **incorrigible** (sense 3).
▸**de'feasibleness** *or* **de**ˌ**feasi'bility** NOUN

defeat (dɪ'fi:t) VERB (*tr*) [1] to overcome in a contest or competition; win a victory over. [2] to thwart or frustrate: *this accident has defeated all his hopes of winning.* [3] *Law* to render null and void; annul. ◆ NOUN [4] the act of defeating or state of being defeated. [5] an instance of defeat. [6] overthrow or destruction. [7] *Law* an annulment.
▷HISTORY C14: from Old French *desfait,* from *desfaire* to undo, ruin, from *des-* DIS-[1] + *faire* to do, from Latin *facere*
▸**de'feater** NOUN

defeatism (dɪ'fi:tɪzəm) NOUN a ready acceptance or expectation of defeat.
▸**de'featist** NOUN, ADJECTIVE

defecate *or* **defaecate** ('dɛfɪˌkeɪt) VERB [1] (*intr*) to discharge waste from the body through the anus. [2] (*tr*) to clarify or remove impurities from (a solution, esp of sugar).
▷HISTORY C16: from Latin *dēfaecāre* to cleanse from dregs, from DE- + *faex* sediment, dregs

▸ˌdefeˈcation *or* ˌdefaeˈcation NOUN ▸ˈdefeˌcator *or* ˈdefaeˌcator NOUN

defect NOUN (dɪˈfɛkt, ˈdiːfɛkt) 1 a lack of something necessary for completeness or perfection; shortcoming; deficiency. 2 an imperfection, failing, or blemish. 3 *Crystallog* a local deviation from regularity in the crystal lattice of a solid. See also **point defect, dislocation** (sense 3). ◆ VERB (dɪˈfɛkt) 4 (*intr*) to desert one's country, cause, allegiance, etc., esp in order to join the opposing forces.
▷HISTORY C15: from Latin *dēfectus,* from *dēficere* to forsake, fail; see DEFICIENT
▸deˈfector NOUN

defection (dɪˈfɛkʃən) NOUN 1 the act or an instance of defecting. 2 abandonment of duty, allegiance, principles, etc.; backsliding. 3 another word for **defect** (senses 1, 2).

defective (dɪˈfɛktɪv) ADJECTIVE 1 having a defect or flaw; imperfect; faulty. 2 (of a person) below the usual standard or level, esp in intelligence. 3 *Grammar* (of a word) lacking the full range of inflections characteristic of its form class, as for example *must,* which has no past tense.
▸deˈfectively ADVERB ▸deˈfectiveness NOUN

defence *or US* **defense** (dɪˈfɛns) NOUN 1 resistance against danger, attack, or harm; protection. 2 a person or thing that provides such resistance. 3 a plea, essay, speech, etc., in support of something; vindication; justification. 4 **a** a country's military measures or resources. **b** (*as modifier*): *defence spending.* 5 *Law* a defendant's denial of the truth of the allegations or charge against him. 6 *Law* the defendant and his legal advisers collectively. Compare **prosecution.** 7 *Sport* **a** the action of protecting oneself, one's goal, or one's allotted part of the playing area against an opponent's attacks. **b** the method of doing this. **c** (usually preceded by *the*) the players in a team whose function is to do this. 8 *American football* (usually preceded by *the*) **a** the team that does not have possession of the ball. **b** the members of a team that play in such circumstances. 9 *Psychoanal* See **defence mechanism.** 10 (*plural*) fortifications.
▷HISTORY C13: from Old French, from Late Latin *dēfensum,* past participle of *dēfendere* to DEFEND
▸deˈfenceless *or US* deˈfenseless ADJECTIVE
▸deˈfencelessly *or US* deˈfenselessly ADVERB
▸deˈfencelessness *or US* deˈfenselessness NOUN

defence in depth NOUN *Military* the act or practice of positioning successive mutually supporting lines of defence in a given area.

defence mechanism NOUN 1 *Psychoanal* a usually unconscious mental process designed to reduce the anxiety, shame, etc., associated with instinctive desires. 2 *Physiol* the protective response of the body against disease organisms.

defend (dɪˈfɛnd) VERB 1 to protect (a person, place, etc.) from harm or danger; ward off an attack on. 2 (*tr*) to support in the face of criticism, esp by argument or evidence. 3 to represent (a defendant) in court in a civil or criminal action. 4 *Sport* to guard or protect (oneself, one's goal, etc.) against attack. 5 (*tr*) to protect (a championship or title) against a challenge.
▷HISTORY C13: from Old French *defendre,* from Latin *dēfendere* to ward off, from DE- + *-fendere* to strike
▸deˈfendable ADJECTIVE ▸deˈfender NOUN

defendant (dɪˈfɛndənt) NOUN 1 a person against whom an action or claim is brought in a court of law. Compare **plaintiff.** ◆ ADJECTIVE 2 making a defence; defending.

Defender of the Faith NOUN the title conferred upon Henry VIII by Pope Leo X in 1521 in recognition of the King's pamphlet attacking Luther's doctrines and retained by subsequent monarchs of England. Latin term: ***Fidei Defensor.***

defenestration (diːˌfɛnɪˈstreɪʃən) NOUN the act of throwing someone out of a window.
▷HISTORY C17: from New Latin *dēfenestrātiō,* from Latin DE- + *fenestra* window

defensible (dɪˈfɛnsɪbᵊl) ADJECTIVE capable of being defended, as in war, an argument, etc.
▸deˌfensiˈbility *or* deˈfensibleness NOUN ▸deˈfensibly ADVERB

defensive (dɪˈfɛnsɪv) ADJECTIVE 1 intended, suitable, or done for defence, as opposed to offence. 2 rejecting criticisms of oneself or covering up one's failings. ◆ NOUN 3 a position of defence. 4 **on the defensive.** in an attitude or position of defence, as in being ready to reject criticism.
▸deˈfensively ADVERB ▸deˈfensiveness NOUN

defensive medicine NOUN the practice by a doctor of ordering extensive, often unnecessary tests in order to minimize liability if accused of negligence.

defer[1] (dɪˈfɜː) VERB **-fers, -ferring, -ferred.** (*tr*) to delay or cause to be delayed until a future time; postpone.
▷HISTORY C14: from Old French *differer* to be different, postpone; see DIFFER
▸deˈferrable *or* deˈferable ADJECTIVE ▸deˈferrer NOUN

defer[2] (dɪˈfɜː) VERB **-fers, -ferring, -ferred.** (*intr;* foll by *to*) to yield (to) or comply (with) the wishes or judgments of another.
▷HISTORY C15: from Latin *dēferre,* literally: to bear down, from DE- + *ferre* to bear

deference (ˈdɛfərəns) NOUN 1 submission to or compliance with the will, wishes, etc., of another. 2 courteous regard; respect.
▷HISTORY C17: from French *déférence;* see DEFER[2]

deferent[1] (ˈdɛfərənt) ADJECTIVE another word for **deferential.**

deferent[2] (ˈdɛfərənt) ADJECTIVE 1 (esp of a bodily nerve, vessel, or duct) conveying an impulse, fluid, etc., outwards, down, or away; efferent. ◆ NOUN 2 *Astronomy* (in the Ptolemaic system) a circle centred on the earth around which the centre of the epicycle was thought to move.
▷HISTORY C17: from Latin *dēferre;* see DEFER[2]

deferential (ˌdɛfəˈrɛnʃəl) ADJECTIVE marked by or showing deference or respect; respectful.
▸ˌdeferˈentially ADVERB

deferment (dɪˈfɜːmənt) *or* **deferral** (dɪˈfɜːrəl) NOUN the act of deferring or putting off until another time; postponement.

deferred (dɪˈfɜːd) ADJECTIVE 1 withheld over a certain period; postponed: *a deferred payment.* 2 (of shares) ranking behind other types of shares for dividend.

deferred annuity NOUN an annuity that commences not less than one year after the final purchase premium. Compare **immediate annuity.**

deferred sentence NOUN *Law* a sentence that is postponed for a specific period to allow a court to examine the conduct of the offender during the deferment. Compare **suspended sentence.**

defervescence (ˌdɛfəˈvɛsəns) NOUN *Med* 1 the abatement of a fever. 2 the period during which this occurs.

deffo (ˈdɛfəʊ) INTERJECTION *Brit informal* definitely: an expression of agreement or consent.

defiance (dɪˈfaɪəns) NOUN 1 open or bold resistance to or disregard for authority, opposition, or power. 2 a challenging attitude or behaviour; challenge.

defiant (dɪˈfaɪənt) ADJECTIVE marked by resistance or bold opposition, as to authority; challenging.
▸deˈfiantly ADVERB

defibrillation (dɪˌfaɪbrɪˈleɪʃən, -fɪb-) NOUN *Med* the application of an electric current to the heart to restore normal rhythmic contractions after the onset of atrial or ventricular fibrillation.

defibrillator (dɪˈfaɪbrɪˌleɪtə, -ˈfɪb-) NOUN *Med* an apparatus for stopping fibrillation of the heart by application of an electric current to the chest wall or directly to the heart.

deficiency (dɪˈfɪʃənsɪ) NOUN, *plural* **-cies.** 1 the state or quality of being deficient. 2 a lack or insufficiency; shortage. 3 another word for **deficit.** 4 *Biology* the absence of a gene or a region of a chromosome normally present.

deficiency disease NOUN 1 *Med* any condition, such as pellagra, beriberi, or scurvy, produced by a lack of vitamins or other essential substances. Compare **avitaminosis.** 2 *Botany* any disease caused by lack of essential minerals.

deficient (dɪˈfɪʃənt) ADJECTIVE 1 lacking some essential; incomplete; defective. 2 inadequate in quantity or supply; insufficient.
▷HISTORY C16: from Latin *dēficiēns* lacking, from *dēficere* to fall short; see DEFECT
▸deˈficiently ADVERB

deficit (ˈdɛfɪsɪt, dɪˈfɪsɪt) NOUN 1 the amount by which an actual sum is lower than that expected or required. 2 **a** an excess of liabilities over assets. **b** an excess of expenditures over revenues during a certain period. **c** an excess of payments over receipts on the balance of payments.
▷HISTORY C18: from Latin, literally: there is lacking, from *dēficere* to be lacking

deficit financing NOUN government spending in excess of revenues so that a budget deficit is incurred, which is financed by borrowing: recommended by Keynesian economists in order to increase economic activity and reduce unemployment. Also called: **compensatory finance, pump priming.**

de fide *Latin* (diː ˈfaɪdɪ) ADJECTIVE *RC Church* (of a doctrine) belonging to the essentials of the faith, esp by virtue of a papal ruling.
▷HISTORY literally: from faith

defilade (ˌdɛfɪˈleɪd) *Military* ◆ NOUN 1 protection provided by obstacles against enemy crossfire from the rear, or observation. 2 the disposition of defensive fortifications to produce this protection. ◆ VERB (*tr*) 3 to provide protection for by defilade.
▷HISTORY C19: see DE-, ENFILADE

defile[1] (dɪˈfaɪl) VERB (*tr*) 1 to make foul or dirty; pollute. 2 to tarnish or sully the brightness of; taint; corrupt. 3 to damage or sully (someone's good name, reputation, etc.). 4 to make unfit for ceremonial use; desecrate. 5 to violate the chastity of.
▷HISTORY C14: from earlier *defoilen* (influenced by *filen* to FILE[3]), from Old French *defouler* to trample underfoot, abuse, from DE- + *fouler* to tread upon; see FULL[2]
▸deˈfilement NOUN ▸deˈfiler NOUN

defile[2] (ˈdiːfaɪl, dɪˈfaɪl) NOUN 1 a narrow pass or gorge, esp one between two mountains. 2 a single file of soldiers, etc. ◆ VERB 3 *Chiefly military* to march or cause to march in single file.
▷HISTORY C17: from French *défilé,* from *défiler* to file off, from *filer* to march in a column, from Old French: to spin, from *fil* thread, from Latin *fīlum*

define (dɪˈfaɪn) VERB (*tr*) 1 to state precisely the meaning of (words, terms, etc.). 2 to describe the nature, properties, or essential qualities of. 3 to determine the boundary or extent of. 4 (*often passive*) to delineate the form or outline of: *the shape of the tree was clearly defined by the light behind it.* 5 to fix with precision; specify.
▷HISTORY C14: from Old French *definer* to determine, from Latin *dēfīnīre* to set bounds to, from *fīnīre* to FINISH
▸deˈfinable ADJECTIVE ▸deˌfinaˈbility NOUN ▸deˈfinably ADVERB ▸deˈfiner NOUN

defined-benefit ADJECTIVE denoting an occupational pension scheme that guarantees a specified payout, usually based on an employee's final salary and years of service. Abbreviation: **DB.** Also called: **final-salary.**

definiendum (dɪˌfɪnɪˈɛndəm) NOUN, *plural* **-da** (-də). something to be defined, esp the term or phrase to be accounted for in a dictionary entry. Compare **definiens.**
▷HISTORY Latin

definiens (dɪˈfɪnɪənz) NOUN, *plural* **definientia** (dɪˌfɪnɪˈɛnʃə). the word or words used to define or give an account of the meaning of another word, as in a dictionary entry. Compare **definiendum.**
▷HISTORY Latin: defining

definite (ˈdɛfɪnɪt) ADJECTIVE 1 clearly defined; exact; explicit. 2 having precise limits or boundaries. 3 known for certain; sure: *it is definite that they have won.* 4 *Botany* **a** denoting a type of growth in which the main stem ends in a flower, as in a cymose inflorescence; determinate. **b** (esp of flower parts) limited or fixed in number in a given species.
▷HISTORY C15: from Latin *dēfīnītus* limited, distinct; see DEFINE
▸ˈdefiniteness NOUN ▸definitude (dɪˈfɪnɪˌtjuːd) NOUN

definite article NOUN *Grammar* a determiner that expresses specificity of reference, such as *the* in English. Compare **indefinite article.**

definite description NOUN 1 a description that is modified by the definite article or a possessive, such as *the woman in white* or *Rosemary's* *baby*. 2 a similar plural expression, such as *the kings of Scotland*.

definite integral NOUN *Maths* **a** the evaluation of the indefinite integral between two limits, representing the area between the given function and the *x*-axis between these two values of *x*. **b** the expression for that function, $\int^b_a f(x)dx$, where $f(x)$ is the given function and $x = a$ and $x = b$ are the limits of integration. Where $F(x) = \int f(x)dx$, the indefinite integral, $\int^b_a f(x)dx = F(b)–F(a)$.

definitely (ˈdɛfɪnɪtlɪ) ADVERB 1 in a definite manner. 2 (*sentence modifier*) certainly: *he said he was coming, definitely*. ◆ SENTENCE SUBSTITUTE 3 unquestionably: used to confirm an assumption by a questioner.

definition (ˌdɛfɪˈnɪʃən) NOUN 1 a formal and concise statement of the meaning of a word, phrase, etc. 2 the act of defining a word, phrase, etc. 3 specification of the essential properties of something, or of the criteria which uniquely identify it. 4 the act of making clear or definite. 5 the state or condition of being clearly defined or definite. 6 a measure of the clarity of an optical, photographic, or television image as characterized by its sharpness and contrast.
▸ **ˌdefiˈnitional** ADJECTIVE

definitive (dɪˈfɪnɪtɪv) ADJECTIVE 1 serving to decide or settle finally; conclusive. 2 most reliable, complete, or authoritative: *the definitive reading of a text*. 3 serving to define or outline. 4 *Zoology* fully developed; complete: *the definitive form of a parasite*. 5 **a** (of postage stamps) permanently on sale. **b** (*as noun*) a definitive postage stamp. ◆ NOUN 6 *Grammar* a word indicating specificity of reference, such as the definite article or a demonstrative adjective or pronoun.
▸ **deˈfinitively** ADVERB ▸ **deˈfinitiveness** NOUN

deflagrate (ˈdɛfləˌgreɪt, ˈdiː-) VERB to burn or cause to burn with great heat and light.
▷ HISTORY C18: from Latin *dēflagrāre,* from DE- + *flagrāre* to burn
▸ **ˌdeflaˈgration** NOUN

deflate (dɪˈfleɪt) VERB 1 to collapse or cause to collapse through the release of gas. 2 (*tr*) to take away the self-esteem or conceit from. 3 *Economics* to cause deflation of (an economy, the money supply, etc.).
▷ HISTORY C19: from DE- + (IN)FLATE
▸ **deˈflator** NOUN

deflation (dɪˈfleɪʃən) NOUN 1 the act of deflating or state of being deflated. 2 *Economics* a reduction in the level of total spending and economic activity resulting in lower levels of output, employment, investment, trade, profits, and prices. Compare **disinflation.** 3 *Geology* the removal of loose rock material, sand, and dust by the wind.
▸ **deˈflationary** ADJECTIVE ▸ **deˈflationist** NOUN, ADJECTIVE

deflationary gap NOUN *Economics* a situation in which total spending in an economy is insufficient to buy all the output that can be produced with full employment.

deflect (dɪˈflɛkt) VERB to turn or cause to turn aside from a course; swerve.
▷ HISTORY C17: from Latin *dēflectere,* from *flectere* to bend
▸ **deˈflector** NOUN

deflection *or* **deflexion** (dɪˈflɛkʃən) NOUN 1 the act of deflecting or the state of being deflected. 2 the amount of deviation. 3 the change in direction of a light beam as it crosses a boundary between two media with different refractive indexes. 4 a deviation of the indicator of a measuring instrument from its zero position. 5 the movement of a structure or structural member when subjected to a load.
▸ **deˈflective** ADJECTIVE

deflexed (dɪˈflɛkst, ˈdiːflɛkst) ADJECTIVE (of leaves, petals, etc.) bent sharply outwards and downwards.

deflocculate (dɪˈflɒkjʊˌleɪt) VERB (*tr*) 1 to disperse, forming a colloid or suspension. 2 to prevent flocculation of (a colloid or suspension).
▸ **deˌflocculˈlation** NOUN ▸ **deˈfloccuˌlant** NOUN

defloration (ˌdiːflɔːˈreɪʃən) NOUN the act of deflowering.
▷ HISTORY C15: from Late Latin *dēflōrātiō*; see DE-, FLOWER

deflower (diːˈflaʊə) VERB (*tr*) 1 to deprive of virginity, esp by rupturing the hymen through sexual intercourse. 2 to despoil of beauty, innocence, etc.; mar; violate. 3 to rob or despoil of flowers.
▸ **deˈflowerer** NOUN

defoliant (diːˈfəʊlɪənt) NOUN a chemical sprayed or dusted onto trees to cause their leaves to fall, esp to remove cover from an enemy in warfare.

defoliate VERB (diːˈfəʊlɪˌeɪt) 1 to deprive (a plant) of its leaves, as by the use of a herbicide, or (of a plant) to shed its leaves. ◆ ADJECTIVE (diːˈfəʊlɪɪt) 2 (of a plant) having shed its leaves.
▷ HISTORY C18: from Medieval Latin *dēfoliāre,* from Latin DE- + *folium* leaf
▸ **deˌfoliˈation** NOUN ▸ **deˈfoliˌator** NOUN

deforce (dɪˈfɔːs) VERB (*tr*) *Property law* 1 to withhold (property, esp land) wrongfully or by force from the rightful owner. 2 to eject or keep forcibly from possession of property.
▷ HISTORY C13: from Anglo-French, from *deforcer*
▸ **deˈforcement** NOUN

deforest (diːˈfɒrɪst) VERB (*tr*) to clear of trees. Also: **disforest.**
▸ **deˌforesˈtation** NOUN ▸ **deˈforester** NOUN

deform (dɪˈfɔːm) VERB 1 to make or become misshapen or distorted. 2 (*tr*) to mar the beauty of; disfigure. 3 (*tr*) to subject or be subjected to a stress that causes a change of dimensions.
▷ HISTORY C15: from Latin *dēformāre,* from DE- + *forma* shape, beauty
▸ **deˈformable** ADJECTIVE ▸ **deˌformaˈbility** NOUN ▸ **deˈformer** NOUN

deformation (ˌdiːfɔːˈmeɪʃən) NOUN 1 the act of deforming; distortion. 2 the result of deforming; a change in form, esp for the worse. 3 a change in the dimensions of an object resulting from a stress.

deformed (dɪˈfɔːmd) ADJECTIVE 1 disfigured or misshapen. 2 morally perverted; warped.
▸ **deformedly** (dɪˈfɔːmɪdlɪ) ADVERB ▸ **deˈformedness** NOUN

deformity (dɪˈfɔːmɪtɪ) NOUN, *plural* **-ties.** 1 a deformed condition; disfigurement. 2 *Pathol* an acquired or congenital distortion of an organ or part. 3 a deformed person or thing. 4 a defect, esp of the mind or morals; depravity.

Defra (ˈdɛfrə) (in Britain) NOUN ACRONYM FOR Department for Environment, Food and Rural Affairs.

defraud (dɪˈfrɔːd) VERB (*tr*) to take away or withhold money, rights, property, etc., from (a person) by fraud; cheat; swindle.
▸ **defraudation** (ˌdiːfrɔːˈdeɪʃən) *or* **deˈfraudment** NOUN
▸ **deˈfrauder** NOUN

defray (dɪˈfreɪ) VERB (*tr*) to furnish or provide money for (costs, expenses, etc.); pay.
▷ HISTORY C16: from Old French *deffroier* to pay expenses, from *de-* DIS-[1] + *frai* expenditure, originally: cost incurred through breaking something, from Latin *frangere* to break
▸ **deˈfrayable** ADJECTIVE ▸ **deˈfrayal** *or* **deˈfrayment** NOUN
▸ **deˈfrayer** NOUN

defrock (diːˈfrɒk) VERB (*tr*) to deprive (a person in holy orders) of ecclesiastical status; unfrock.

defrost (diːˈfrɒst) VERB 1 to make or become free of frost or ice. 2 to thaw, esp through removal from a refrigerator.

defroster (diːˈfrɒstə) NOUN a device by which the de-icing process of a refrigerator is accelerated, usually by circulating the refrigerant without the expansion process.

deft (dɛft) ADJECTIVE quick and neat in movement; nimble; dexterous.
▷ HISTORY C13 (in the sense: gentle): see DAFT
▸ **ˈdeftly** ADVERB ▸ **ˈdeftness** NOUN

defunct (dɪˈfʌŋkt) ADJECTIVE 1 no longer living; dead or extinct. 2 no longer operative or valid.
▷ HISTORY C16: from Latin *dēfungī* to discharge (one's obligations), die; see DE-, FUNCTION
▸ **deˈfunctive** ADJECTIVE ▸ **deˈfunctness** NOUN

defuse *or sometimes US* **defuze** (diːˈfjuːz) VERB (*tr*) 1 to remove the triggering device of (a bomb, etc.). 2 to remove the cause of tension from (a crisis, etc.).

> **Language note** Avoid confusion with **diffuse.**

defy (dɪˈfaɪ) VERB **-fies, -fying, -fied.** (*tr*) 1 to resist (a powerful person, authority, etc.) openly and boldly. 2 to elude, esp in a baffling way: *his actions defy explanation*. 3 *Formal* to challenge or provoke (someone to do something judged to be impossible); dare: *I defy you to climb that cliff*. 4 *Archaic* to invite to do battle or combat.
▷ HISTORY C14: from Old French *desfier,* from *des-* DE- + *fier* to trust, from Latin *fīdere*
▸ **deˈfier** NOUN

deg (dɛg) VERB **degs, degging, degged.** (*tr*) *Northern English dialect* to water (a plant, etc.).

deg. ABBREVIATION FOR degree.

dégagé *French* (degaʒe) ADJECTIVE 1 unconstrained in manner; casual; relaxed. 2 uninvolved; detached.

degas (diːˈgæs) VERB **-gases** *or* **-gasses, -gassing, -gassed.** 1 (*tr*) to remove gas from (a container, vacuum tube, liquid, adsorbent, etc.). 2 (*intr*) to lose adsorbed or absorbed gas by desorption.
▸ **deˈgasser** NOUN

degauss (diːˈgaʊs, -ˈgɔːs) VERB (*tr*) 1 to neutralize the magnetic field of a ship's hull (as a protection against magnetic mines) using equipment producing an opposing magnetic field. 2 another word for **demagnetize.**

degearing (diːˈgɪərɪŋ) NOUN *Finance* the process in which a company replaces some or all of its fixed-interest loan stock with ordinary shares.

degeneracy (dɪˈdʒɛnərəsɪ) NOUN, *plural* **-cies.** 1 the act or state of being degenerate. 2 the process of becoming degenerate. 3 *Physics* the number of degenerate quantum states of a particular orbital, degree of freedom, energy level, etc.

degenerate VERB (dɪˈdʒɛnəˌreɪt) (*intr*) 1 to become degenerate. 2 *Biology* (of organisms or their parts) to become less specialized or functionally useless. ◆ ADJECTIVE (dɪˈdʒɛnərɪt) 3 having declined or deteriorated to a lower mental, moral, or physical level; debased; degraded; corrupt. 4 *Physics* **a** (of the constituents of a system) having the same energy but different wave functions. **b** (of a semiconductor) containing a similar number of electrons in the conduction band to the number of electrons in the conduction band of metals. **c** (of a resonant device) having two or more modes of equal frequency. 5 (of a code) containing symbols that represent more than one letter, figure, etc. 6 (of a plant or animal) having undergone degeneration. ◆ NOUN (dɪˈdʒɛnərɪt) 7 a degenerate person.
▷ HISTORY C15: from Latin *dēgenerāre,* from *dēgener* departing from its kind, ignoble, from DE- + *genus* origin, race
▸ **deˈgenerately** ADVERB ▸ **deˈgenerateness** NOUN

degenerate matter NOUN *Astronomy* the highly compressed state of matter, esp in white dwarfs and neutron stars, supported against gravitational collapse by quantum mechanical effects.

degeneration (dɪˌdʒɛnəˈreɪʃən) NOUN 1 the process of degenerating. 2 the state of being degenerate. 3 *Biology* the loss of specialization, function, or structure by organisms and their parts, as in the development of vestigial organs. 4 **a** impairment or loss of the function and structure of cells or tissues, as by disease or injury, often leading to death (necrosis) of the involved part. **b** the resulting condition. 5 *Electronics* negative feedback of a signal.

degenerative (dɪˈdʒɛnəˌreɪtɪv) ADJECTIVE (of a disease or condition) getting steadily worse.

degenerative joint disease NOUN another name for **osteoarthritis.**

deglaze (diːˈgleɪz) VERB (*tr*) to dilute meat sediments in (a pan) in order to make a sauce or gravy.

deglutinate (diːˈgluːtɪˌneɪt) VERB (*tr*) to extract the gluten from (a cereal, esp wheat).
▷ HISTORY C17: from Latin *dēglūtināre* to unglue, from DE- + *glūtināre,* from *glūten* GLUE
▸ **deˌglutiˈnation** NOUN

deglutition (ˌdiːgluˈtɪʃən) NOUN the act of swallowing.
▷ HISTORY C17: from French *déglutition,* from Late Latin *dēglūtīre* to swallow down, from DE- + *glūtīre* to swallow

degradable (dɪˈgreɪdəb[ə]l) ADJECTIVE 1 (of waste products, packaging materials, etc.) capable of

being decomposed chemically or biologically. See also **biodegradable.** [2] capable of being degraded.
▸**de͵grada'bility** NOUN

degradation (͵degrə'deɪʃən) NOUN [1] the act of degrading or the state of being degraded. [2] a state of degeneration, squalor, or poverty. [3] some act, constraint, etc., that is degrading. [4] the wearing down of the surface of rocks, cliffs, etc., by erosion, weathering, or some other process. [5] *Chem* a breakdown of a molecule into atoms or smaller molecules. [6] *Physics* an irreversible process in which the energy available to do work is decreased. [7] *RC Church* the permanent unfrocking of a priest.

degrade (dɪ'greɪd) VERB [1] (*tr*) to reduce in worth, character, etc.; disgrace; dishonour. [2] (diː'greɪd) (*tr*) to reduce in rank, status, or degree; remove from office; demote. [3] (*tr*) to reduce in strength, quality, intensity, etc. [4] to reduce or be reduced by erosion or down-cutting, as a land surface or bed of a river. Compare **aggrade.** [5] *Chem* to decompose or be decomposed into atoms or smaller molecules.
▷HISTORY C14: from Late Latin *dēgradāre,* from Latin DE- + *gradus* rank, degree
▸**de'grader** NOUN

degrading (dɪ'greɪdɪŋ) ADJECTIVE causing humiliation; debasing.
▸**de'gradingly** ADVERB ▸**de'gradingness** NOUN

degrease (diː'griːs) VERB (*tr*) to remove grease from.

degree (dɪ'griː) NOUN [1] a stage in a scale of relative amount or intensity: *a high degree of competence.* [2] an academic award conferred by a university or college on successful completion of a course or as an honorary distinction (**honorary degree**). [3] any of three categories of seriousness of a burn. See **burn**[1] (sense 22). [4] (in the US) any of the categories into which a crime is divided according to its seriousness: *first-degree murder.* [5] *Genealogy* a step in a line of descent, used as a measure of the closeness of a blood relationship. [6] *Grammar* any of the forms of an adjective used to indicate relative amount or intensity: in English they are *positive, comparative,* and *superlative.* [7] *Music* any note of a diatonic scale relative to the other notes in that scale: *D is the second degree of the scale of C major.* [8] a unit of temperature on a specified scale: *the normal body temperature of man is 36.8 degrees Celsius.* Symbol: °. See also **Celsius scale, Fahrenheit scale.** [9] a measure of angle equal to one three-hundred-and-sixtieth of the angle traced by one complete revolution of a line about one of its ends. Symbol: °. See also **minute**[1] (sense 2), **second**[2] (sense 2). Compare **radian.** [10] **a** a unit of latitude or longitude, divided into 60 minutes, used to define points on the earth's surface or on the celestial sphere. **b** a point or line defined by units of latitude and/or longitude. Symbol: °. [11] a unit on any of several scales of measurement, as for alcohol content or specific gravity. Symbol: °. [12] *Maths* **a** the highest power or the sum of the powers of any term in a polynomial or by itself: $x^4 + x + 3$ *and* xyz^2 *are of the fourth degree.* **b** the greatest power of the highest order derivative in a differential equation. [13] *Obsolete* a step; rung. [14] *Archaic* a stage in social status or rank. [15] **by degrees.** little by little; gradually. [16] **to a degree.** somewhat; rather. [17] **degrees of frost.** See **frost** (sense 3).
▷HISTORY C13: from Old French *degre,* from Latin DE- + *gradus* step, GRADE
▸**de'greeless** ADJECTIVE

degree day NOUN a day on which university degrees are conferred.

degree-day NOUN a unit used in estimating fuel requirements in heating buildings. It is equal to a fall of temperature of 1 degree below the mean outside temperature (usually taken as 18°C) for one day.

degree of freedom NOUN [1] *Physics* one of the minimum number of parameters necessary to describe a state or property of a system. [2] one of the independent components of motion (translation, vibration, and rotation) of an atom or molecule. [3] *Chem* one of a number of intensive properties that can be independently varied without changing the number of phases in a system. See also **phase rule.** [4] *Statistics* one of the independent unrestricted random variables constituting a statistic.

degression (dɪ'greʃən) NOUN [1] a decrease by stages. [2] a gradual decrease in the tax rate on amounts below a specified sum.
▷HISTORY C15: from Medieval Latin *dēgressiō* descent, from Latin *dēgredī* to go down, from DE- + *gradī* to take steps, go

degust (dɪ'gʌst) *or* **degustate** (dɪ'gʌsteɪt) VERB (*tr*) *Rare* to taste, esp with care or relish; savour.
▷HISTORY C17: from Latin *dēgustāre,* from *gustāre,* from *gustus* a tasting, taste
▸**degustation** (͵diːgʌ'steɪʃən) NOUN

dehisce (dɪ'hɪs) VERB (*intr*) (of fruits, anthers, etc.) to burst open spontaneously, releasing seeds, pollen, etc.
▷HISTORY C17: from Latin *dēhiscere* to split open, from DE- + *hiscere* to yawn, gape

dehiscent (dɪ'hɪsənt) ADJECTIVE (of fruits, anthers, etc.) opening spontaneously to release seeds or pollen.
▸**de'hiscence** NOUN

dehorn (diː'hɔːn) VERB (*tr*) [1] to remove or prevent the growth of the horns of (cattle, sheep, or goats). [2] to cut back (the larger limbs of a tree) drastically.
▸**de'horner** NOUN

Dehra Dun ('deərə 'duːn) NOUN a city in N India, the capital of Uttaranchal: Indian military academy (1932). Pop.: 270 159 (1991).

dehumanize *or* **dehumanise** (diː'hjuːmə͵naɪz) VERB (*tr*) [1] to deprive of human qualities. [2] to render mechanical, artificial, or routine.
▸**de͵humani'zation** *or* **de͵humani'sation** NOUN

dehumidifier (͵diːhjuː'mɪdɪ͵faɪə) NOUN a device for reducing the moisture content of the atmosphere.

dehumidify (͵diːhjuː'mɪdɪ͵faɪ) VERB **-fies, -fying, -fied.** (*tr*) to remove water from (something, esp the air).
▸**͵dehu͵midifi'cation** NOUN

dehydrate (diː'haɪdreɪt, ͵diːhaɪ'dreɪt) VERB [1] to lose or cause to lose water; make or become anhydrous. [2] to lose or cause to lose hydrogen atoms and oxygen atoms in the proportions in which they occur in water, as in a chemical reaction. [3] to lose or deprive of water, as the body or tissues.
▸**͵dehy'dration** NOUN ▸**de'hydrator** NOUN

dehydrogenase (diː'haɪdrədʒə͵neɪz) NOUN an enzyme, such as any of the respiratory enzymes, that activates oxidation-reduction reactions by transferring hydrogen from substrate to acceptor.

dehydrogenate (diː'haɪdrədʒə͵neɪt), **dehydrogenize,** *or* **dehydrogenise** (diː'haɪdrədʒə͵naɪz) VERB (*tr*) to remove hydrogen from.
▸**de͵hydroge'nation** *or* **de͵hydrogeni'zation** *or* **de͵hydrogeni'sation** NOUN

dehydroretinol (diː͵haɪdrəʊ'retɪnɒl) NOUN another name for **vitamin** A_2.

dehypnotize *or* **dehypnotise** (diː'hɪpnə͵taɪz) VERB (*tr*) to bring out of the hypnotic state.
▸**de͵hypnoti'zation** *or* **de͵hypnoti'sation** NOUN

Deianira (͵diːə'naɪərə, ͵deɪə-) NOUN *Greek myth* a sister of Meleager and wife of Hercules. She unintentionally killed Hercules by dipping his tunic in the poisonous blood of the Centaur Nessus, thinking it to be a love charm.

de-ice (diː'aɪs) VERB to free or be freed of ice.

de-icer (diː'aɪsə) NOUN [1] a mechanical or thermal device designed to melt or stop the formation of ice on an aircraft, usually fitted to the aerofoil surfaces. Compare **anti-icer.** [2] a chemical or other substance used for this purpose, esp an aerosol that can be sprayed on car windscreens to remove ice or frost.

deicide ('diːɪ͵saɪd) NOUN [1] the act of killing a god. [2] a person who kills a god.
▷HISTORY C17: from ecclesiastical Latin *deicida,* from Latin *deus* god; see -CIDE
▸**͵dei'cidal** ADJECTIVE

deictic ('daɪktɪk) ADJECTIVE [1] *Logic* proving by direct argument. Compare **elenctic.** ◆ NOUN [2] another word for **indexical** (sense 2).
▷HISTORY C17: from Greek *deiktikos* concerning proof, from *deiknunai* to show
▸**'deictically** ADVERB

deid (diːd) ADJECTIVE a Scot word for **dead.**

deif (diːf) ADJECTIVE a Scot word for **deaf.**

deific (diː'ɪfɪk, deɪ-) ADJECTIVE [1] making divine or exalting to the position of a god. [2] divine or godlike.

deification (͵diːɪfɪ'keɪʃən, ͵deɪ-) NOUN [1] the act or process of exalting to the position of a god. [2] the state or condition of being deified.

deiform ('diːɪ͵fɔːm) ADJECTIVE having the form or appearance of a god; sacred or divine.

deify ('diːɪ͵faɪ, 'deɪɪ-) VERB **-fies, -fying, -fied.** (*tr*) [1] to exalt to the position of a god or personify as a god. [2] to accord divine honour or worship to. [3] to exalt in an extreme way; idealize.
▷HISTORY C14: from Old French *deifier,* from Late Latin *deificāre,* from Latin *deus* god + *facere* to make
▸**'dei͵fier** NOUN

deign (deɪn) VERB [1] (*intr*) to think it fit or worthy of oneself (to do something); condescend: *he will not deign to speak to us.* [2] (*tr*) *Archaic* to vouchsafe: *he deigned no reply.*
▷HISTORY C13: from Old French *deignier,* from Latin *dignārī* to consider worthy, from *dignus* worthy

Dei gratia *Latin* ('diːɪ 'greɪʃɪə, 'deɪɪ 'grɑːtɪə) ADVERB by the grace of God.

deil (diːl) NOUN a Scot word for **devil.**

Deimos ('deɪmɒs) NOUN the smaller of the two satellites of Mars and the more distant from the planet. Approximate diameter: 13 km. Compare **Phobos.**

deindex (diː'ɪndeks) VERB (*tr*) to cause to become no longer index-linked.

deindividuation (diː͵ɪndɪvɪdjʊ'eɪʃən) NOUN *Psychol* the loss of a person's sense of individuality and personal responsibility.

deindustrialization *or* **deindustrialisation** (͵diːɪn͵dʌstrɪəlaɪ'zeɪʃən) NOUN the decline in importance of manufacturing industry in the economy of a nation or area.

deindustrialize *or* **deindustrialise** (͵diːɪn'dʌstrɪəl͵aɪ'z) VERB [1] (*tr*) to reduce the importance of manufacturing industry in the economy of (a nation or area). [2] (*intr*) (of a nation or area) to undergo reduction in the importance of manufacturing industry in the economy.

de-ionize *or* **de-ionise** (diː'aɪə͵naɪz) VERB (*tr*) to remove ions from (water, etc.), esp by ion exchange.
▸**de͵ioni'zation** *or* **de͵ioni'sation** NOUN

deipnosophist (daɪp'nɒsəfɪst) NOUN *Rare* a person who is a master of dinner-table conversation.
▷HISTORY C17: from Greek *deipnosophistai,* title of a Greek work by Athenaeus (3rd century), describing learned discussions at a banquet, from *deipnon* meal + *sophistai* wise men; see SOPHIST

Deirdre ('dɪədrɪ) NOUN *Irish myth* a beautiful girl who was raised by Conchobar to be his wife but eloped with Naoise. When Conchobar treacherously killed Naoise she took her own life: often used to symbolize Ireland. See also **Naoise.**

deism ('diːɪzəm, 'deɪ-) NOUN belief in the existence of God based solely on natural reason, without reference to revelation. Compare **theism.**
▷HISTORY C17: from French *déisme,* from Latin *deus* god
▸**'deist** NOUN, ADJECTIVE ▸**de'istic** *or* **de'istical** ADJECTIVE
▸**de'istically** ADVERB

deity ('deɪtɪ, 'diːɪ-) NOUN, *plural* **-ties.** [1] a god or goddess. [2] the state of being divine; godhead. [3] the rank, status, or position of a god. [4] the nature or character of God.
▷HISTORY C14: from Old French, from Late Latin *deitās,* from Latin *deus* god

Deity ('deɪtɪ, 'diːɪ-) NOUN **the.** the Supreme Being; God.

deixis ('daɪksɪs) NOUN *Grammar* the use or reference of a deictic word.
▷HISTORY C20: from Greek, from *deiknunai* to show

déjà vu ('deɪʒæ 'vuː; *French* deʒa vy) NOUN the experience of perceiving a new situation as if it had occurred before. It is sometimes associated with exhaustion or certain types of mental disorder.
▷HISTORY from French, literally: already seen

deject (dɪ'dʒekt) VERB [1] (*tr*) to have a depressing effect on; dispirit; dishearten. ◆ ADJECTIVE [2] *Archaic* downcast; dejected.
▷HISTORY C15: from Latin *dēicere* to cast down, from DE- + *iacere* to throw

dejecta (dɪˈdʒɛktə) PLURAL NOUN waste products excreted through the anus; faeces.
▷**HISTORY** C19: New Latin: things cast down; see DEJECT

dejected (dɪˈdʒɛktɪd) ADJECTIVE miserable; despondent; downhearted.
▸**deˈjectedly** ADVERB ▸**deˈjectedness** NOUN

dejection (dɪˈdʒɛkʃən) NOUN 1 lowness of spirits; depression; melancholy. 2 **a** faecal matter evacuated from the bowels; excrement. **b** the act of defecating; defecation.

de jure (deɪ ˈdʒʊəreɪ) ADVERB according to law; by right; legally. Compare **de facto.**
▷**HISTORY** Latin

deka- *or* **dek-** COMBINING FORM variants of **deca-.**

deke (di:k) *US and Canadian* ◆ NOUN 1 *Sport* (esp in ice hockey) the act or an instance of feinting. ◆ VERB 2 *Sport* (esp in ice hockey) to deceive (an opponent) by carrying out a feint.
▷**HISTORY** C20: shortened from DECOY

dekko (ˈdɛkəʊ) NOUN, *plural* **-kos.** *Brit slang* a look; glance; view (esp in the phrase **take a dekko (at)**).
▷**HISTORY** C19: from Hindi *dekho!* look! from *dekhnā* to see

del (dɛl) NOUN *Maths* the differential operator $\boldsymbol{i}(\partial/\partial x) + \boldsymbol{j}(\partial/\partial y) + \boldsymbol{k}(\partial/\partial z)$, where ***i, j,*** and ***k*** are unit vectors in the *x*, *y*, and *z* directions. Symbol: ∇. Also called: **nabla.**

del. ABBREVIATION FOR delegate.

Del. ABBREVIATION FOR Delaware.

Delagoa Bay (ˌdɛləˈgəʊə) NOUN an inlet of the Indian Ocean, in S Mozambique. Official name: **Baía de Lourenço Marques.**

delaine (dəˈleɪn) NOUN a sheer wool or wool and cotton fabric.
▷**HISTORY** C19: from French *mousseline de laine* muslin of wool

delaminate (di:ˈlæmɪˌneɪt) VERB to divide or cause to divide into thin layers.
▸**deˌlamiˈnation** NOUN

delate (dɪˈleɪt) VERB *(tr)* 1 (formerly) to bring a charge against; denounce; impeach. 2 *Rare* to report (an offence, etc.). 3 *Obsolete* to make known or public.
▷**HISTORY** C16: from Latin *dēlātus*, from *dēferre* to bring down, report, indict, from DE- + *ferre* to bear
▸**deˈlation** NOUN ▸**deˈlator** NOUN

Delaware[1] (ˈdɛləˌwɛə) NOUN 1 *(plural* **-wares** *or* **-ware)** a member of a North American Indian people formerly living near the Delaware River. 2 the language of this people, belonging to the Algonquian family.

Delaware[2] (ˈdɛləˌwɛə) NOUN 1 a state of the northeastern US, on the Delmarva Peninsula: mostly flat and low-lying, with hills in the extreme north and cypress swamps in the extreme south. Capital: Dover. Pop.: 783 600 (2000). Area: 5004 sq. km (1932 sq. miles). Abbreviations: **Del,** (with zip code) **DE.** 2 a river in the northeastern US, rising in the Catskill Mountains and flowing south into **Delaware Bay**, an inlet of the Atlantic. Length 660 km (410 miles).

Delaware[3] (ˈdɛləˌwɛə) NOUN an American variety of grape that has sweet light red fruit.

Delawarean (ˌdɛləˈwɛərɪən) ADJECTIVE 1 of or relating to the state of Delaware or its inhabitants. 2 of or relating to the Delaware river.

delay (dɪˈleɪ) VERB 1 *(tr)* to put off to a later time; defer. 2 *(tr)* to slow up, hinder, or cause to be late; detain. 3 *(intr)* to be irresolute or put off doing something; procrastinate. 4 *(intr)* to linger; dawdle. ◆ NOUN 5 the act or an instance of delaying or being delayed. 6 the interval between one event and another; lull; interlude.
▷**HISTORY** C13: from Old French *delaier*, from *des-* off + *laier*, variant of *laissier* to leave, from Latin *laxāre* to loosen, from *laxus* slack, LAX
▸**deˈlayer** NOUN

delayed action *or* **delay action** NOUN **a** a device for operating a mechanism, such as a camera shutter, a short time after setting. **b** *(as modifier)*: *a delayed-action fuse.*

delayed drop NOUN *Aeronautics* a parachute descent with the opening of the parachute delayed, usually for a predetermined period.

delayed neutron NOUN a neutron produced in a nuclear reactor by the breakdown of a fission product and released a short time after neutrons produced in the primary process.

delayed opening NOUN *Aeronautics* the automatic opening of a parachute after a predetermined delay to allow the parachutist to reach a particular height.

delayer (di:ˈleɪə) VERB *(tr)* to prune the administrative structure of (a large organization) by reducing the number of tiers in its hierarchy.

delayering (di:ˈleɪərɪŋ) NOUN the process of pruning the administrative structure of a large organization by reducing the number of tiers in its hierarchy.

delaying action NOUN a measure or measures taken to gain time, as when weaker military forces harass the advance of a superior enemy without coming to a pitched battle.

delay line NOUN a device in which a known delay time is introduced in the transmission of a signal. An **acoustic delay line** delays a sound wave by circulating it through a liquid or solid medium.

dele (ˈdi:lɪ) NOUN, *plural* **deles.** 1 a sign (δ) indicating that typeset matter is to be deleted. Compare **stet.** ◆ VERB **deles, deleing, deled.** 2 *(tr)* to mark (matter to be deleted) with a dele.
▷**HISTORY** C18: from Latin: delete (imperative), from *dēlēre* to destroy, obliterate; see DELETE

delectable (dɪˈlɛktəbᵊl) ADJECTIVE highly enjoyable, esp pleasing to the taste; delightful.
▷**HISTORY** C14: from Latin *dēlectābilis*, from *dēlectāre* to DELIGHT
▸**deˈlectableness** *or* **deˌlectaˈbility** NOUN ▸**deˈlectably** ADVERB

delectation (ˌdi:lɛkˈteɪʃən) NOUN pleasure; enjoyment.

delegacy (ˈdɛlɪgəsɪ) NOUN, *plural* **-cies.** 1 a less common word for **delegation** (senses 1, 2). 2 **a** an elected standing committee at some British universities. **b** a department or institute of a university: *a delegacy of Education.*

delegate NOUN (ˈdɛlɪˌgeɪt, -gɪt) 1 a person chosen or elected to act for or represent another or others, esp at a conference or meeting. 2 *US government* a representative of a territory in the US House of Representatives. ◆ VERB (ˈdɛlɪˌgeɪt) 3 to give or commit (duties, powers, etc.) to another as agent or representative; depute. 4 *(tr)* to send, authorize, or elect (a person) as agent or representative. 5 *(tr) Chiefly US* to assign (a person owing a debt to oneself) to one's creditor in substitution for oneself.
▷**HISTORY** C14: from Latin *dēlēgāre* to send on a mission, from *lēgāre* to send, depute; see LEGATE
▸**delegable** (ˈdɛlɪgəbᵊl) ADJECTIVE

delegation (ˌdɛlɪˈgeɪʃən) NOUN 1 a person or group chosen to represent another or others. 2 the act of delegating or state of being delegated. 3 *US politics* all the members of Congress from one state.

delegitimize *or* **delegitimise** (ˌdi:lɪˈdʒɪtɪmaɪz) VERB *(tr)* to make invalid, illegal, or unacceptable: *crushing and delegitimizing all dissent in Central Asia.*
▸**ˌdelegitimiˈzation** *or* **ˌdelegitimiˈsation** NOUN

delete (dɪˈli:t) VERB *(tr)* to remove (something printed or written); erase; cancel; strike out.
▷**HISTORY** C17: from Latin *dēlēre* to destroy, obliterate

deleterious (ˌdɛlɪˈtɪərɪəs) ADJECTIVE harmful; injurious; hurtful.
▷**HISTORY** C17: from New Latin *dēlētērius*, from Greek *dēlētērios* injurious, destructive, from *dēleisthai* to hurt
▸**ˌdeleˈteriously** ADVERB ▸**ˌdeleˈteriousness** NOUN

deletion (dɪˈli:ʃən) NOUN 1 the act of deleting or fact of being deleted. 2 a deleted passage, word, etc., in text. 3 the loss or absence of a section of a chromosome.

Delft (dɛlft) NOUN 1 a town in the SW Netherlands, in South Holland province. Pop.: 91 941 (1994). 2 Also called: **delftware.** tin-glazed earthenware made in Delft since the 17th century, typically having blue decoration on a white ground. 3 a similar earthenware made in England.

Delgado (dɛlˈgɑ:dəʊ) NOUN **Cape.** a headland on the NE coast of Mozambique.

Delhi (ˈdɛlɪ) NOUN 1 the capital of India, in the N central part, on the Jumna river: consists of **Old Delhi** (a walled city reconstructed in 1639 on the site of former cities of Delhi, which date from the 15th century B.C.) and **New Delhi** to the south, chosen as the capital in 1912, replacing Calcutta; university (1922). Pop.: (total) 9 882 000 (1995). 2 an administrative division (National Capital Territory) of N India, formerly a Union Territory. Capital: Delhi. Area: 1483 sq. km (572 sq. miles). Pop.: 13 782 976 (2001).

deli (ˈdɛlɪ) NOUN, *plural* **delis.** an informal word for **delicatessen.**

Delia (ˈdi:lɪə) NOUN **a** the recipes or style of cooking of British cookery writer Delia Smith (born 1941). **b** *(as modifier)*: *a Delia dish.*

Delian (ˈdi:lɪən) NOUN 1 a native or inhabitant of Delos. ◆ ADJECTIVE 2 of or relating to Delos. 3 of or relating to Delius.

Delian League *or* **Confederacy** NOUN an alliance of ancient Greek states formed in 478–77 B.C. to fight Persia.

deliberate ADJECTIVE (dɪˈlɪbərɪt) 1 carefully thought out in advance; planned; studied; intentional: *a deliberate insult.* 2 careful or unhurried in speech or action: *a deliberate pace.* ◆ VERB (dɪˈlɪbəˌreɪt) 3 to consider (something) deeply; ponder; think over.
▷**HISTORY** C15: from Latin *dēlīberāre* to consider well, from *lībrāre* to weigh, from *lībra* scales
▸**deˈliberately** ADVERB ▸**deˈliberateness** NOUN
▸**deˈliberˌator** NOUN

deliberation (dɪˌlɪbəˈreɪʃən) NOUN 1 thoughtful, careful, or lengthy consideration. 2 *(often plural)* formal discussion and debate, as of a committee, jury, etc. 3 care, thoughtfulness, or absence of hurry, esp in movement or speech.

deliberative (dɪˈlɪbərətɪv) ADJECTIVE 1 involved in, organized for, or having the function of deliberating: *a deliberative assembly.* 2 characterized by or resulting from deliberation: *a deliberative conclusion.*
▸**deˈliberatively** ADVERB ▸**deˈliberativeness** NOUN

delicacy (ˈdɛlɪkəsɪ) NOUN, *plural* **-cies.** 1 fine or subtle quality, character, construction, etc.: *delicacy of craftsmanship.* 2 fragile, soft, or graceful beauty. 3 something that is considered choice to eat, such as caviar. 4 fragile construction or constitution; frailty. 5 refinement of feeling, manner, or appreciation: *the delicacy of the orchestra's playing.* 6 fussy or squeamish refinement, esp in matters of taste, propriety, etc. 7 need for tactful or sensitive handling. 8 accuracy or sensitivity of response or operation, as of an instrument. 9 (in systemic grammar) the level of detail at which a linguistic description is made; the degree of fine distinction in a linguistic description. 10 *Obsolete* gratification, luxury, or voluptuousness.

delicate (ˈdɛlɪkɪt) ADJECTIVE 1 exquisite, fine, or subtle in quality, character, construction, etc. 2 having a soft or fragile beauty. 3 (of colour, tone, taste, etc.) pleasantly subtle, soft, or faint. 4 easily damaged or injured; lacking robustness, esp in health; fragile. 5 precise, skilled, or sensitive in action or operation: *a delicate mechanism.* 6 requiring tact and diplomacy. 7 sensitive in feeling or manner; showing regard for the feelings of others. 8 excessively refined; squeamish. ◆ NOUN 9 *Archaic* a delicacy; dainty.
▷**HISTORY** C14: from Latin *dēlicātus* affording pleasure, from *dēliciae* (pl) delight, pleasure; see DELICIOUS
▸**ˈdelicately** ADVERB ▸**ˈdelicateness** NOUN

delicatessen (ˌdɛlɪkəˈtɛsᵊn) NOUN 1 a shop selling various foods, esp unusual or imported foods, already cooked or prepared. 2 such foods.
▷**HISTORY** C19: from German *Delikatessen*, literally: delicacies, plural of *Delikatesse* a delicacy, from French *délicatesse*

delicious (dɪˈlɪʃəs) ADJECTIVE 1 very appealing to the senses, esp to the taste or smell. 2 extremely enjoyable or entertaining: *a delicious joke.*
▷**HISTORY** C13: from Old French, from Late Latin *dēliciōsus*, from Latin *dēliciae* delights, charms, from *dēlicere* to entice; see DELIGHT
▸**deˈliciously** ADVERB ▸**deˈliciousness** NOUN

delict (dɪˈlɪkt, ˈdi:lɪkt) NOUN 1 *Law, chiefly Scots* a wrongful act for which the person injured has the right to a civil remedy. See also **tort.** 2 *Roman law* a civil wrong redressable by compensation or punitive damages.

▷HISTORY C16: from Latin *dēlictum* a fault, crime, from *dēlinquere* to fail, do wrong; see DELINQUENCY

delight (dɪˈlaɪt) VERB 1 (*tr*) to please greatly. 2 (*intr; foll by in*) to take great pleasure (in). ◆ NOUN 3 extreme pleasure or satisfaction; joy. 4 something that causes this: *music was always his delight.*
▷HISTORY C13: from Old French *delit,* from *deleitier* to please, from Latin *dēlectāre,* from *dēlicere* to allure, from DE- + *lacere* to entice; see DELICIOUS; English spelling influenced by *light*
▸**deˈlighter** NOUN

delighted (dɪˈlaɪtɪd) ADJECTIVE 1 (often foll by an infinitive) extremely pleased (to do something): *I'm delighted to hear it!* ◆ SENTENCE SUBSTITUTE 2 I should be delighted to!
▸**deˈlightedly** ADVERB ▸**deˈlightedness** NOUN

delightful (dɪˈlaɪtfʊl) ADJECTIVE giving great delight; very pleasing, beautiful, charming, etc.
▸**deˈlightfully** ADVERB ▸**deˈlightfulness** NOUN

Delilah (dɪˈlaɪlə) NOUN 1 Samson's Philistine mistress, who deprived him of his strength by cutting off his hair (Judges 16:4–22). 2 a voluptuous and treacherous woman; temptress.

delimit (diːˈlɪmɪt) *or* **delimitate** VERB (*tr*) to mark or prescribe the limits or boundaries of; demarcate.
▸**de,limiˈtation** NOUN ▸**deˈlimitative** ADJECTIVE

delineate (dɪˈlɪnɪ,eɪt) VERB (*tr*) 1 to trace the shape or outline of; sketch. 2 to represent pictorially, as by making a chart or diagram; depict. 3 to portray in words, esp with detail and precision; describe.
▷HISTORY C16: from Latin *dēlīneāre* to sketch out, from *līnea* LINE[1]
▸**deˈlineable** ADJECTIVE ▸**de,lineˈation** NOUN ▸**deˈlineative** ADJECTIVE

delineator (dɪˈlɪnɪ,eɪtə) NOUN a tailor's pattern, adjustable for different sizes.

delinquency (dɪˈlɪŋkwənsɪ) NOUN, *plural* **-cies.** 1 an offence or misdeed, usually of a minor nature, esp one committed by a young person. See **juvenile delinquency.** 2 failure or negligence in duty or obligation; dereliction. 3 a delinquent nature or delinquent behaviour.
▷HISTORY C17: from Late Latin *dēlinquentia* a fault, offence, from Latin *dēlinquere* to transgress, from DE- + *linquere* to forsake

delinquent (dɪˈlɪŋkwənt) NOUN 1 someone, esp a young person, guilty of delinquency. See **juvenile delinquent.** 2 *Archaic* a person who fails in an obligation or duty. ◆ ADJECTIVE 3 guilty of an offence or misdeed, esp one of a minor nature. 4 failing in or neglectful of duty or obligation.
▷HISTORY C17: from Latin *dēlinquēns* offending; see DELINQUENCY
▸**deˈlinquently** ADVERB

deliquesce (,delɪˈkwes) VERB (*intr*) 1 (esp of certain salts) to dissolve gradually in water absorbed from the air. 2 (esp of certain fungi) to dissolve into liquid, usually at maturity. 3 (of a plant stem) to form many branches.
▷HISTORY C18: from Latin *dēliquēscere* to melt away, become liquid, from DE- + *liquēscere* to melt, from *liquēre* to be liquid

deliquescence (,delɪˈkwesᵊns) NOUN 1 the process of deliquescing. 2 a solution formed when a solid or liquid deliquesces.
▸**,deliˈquescent** ADJECTIVE

delirious (dɪˈlɪrɪəs) ADJECTIVE 1 affected with delirium. 2 wildly excited, esp with joy or enthusiasm.
▸**deˈliriously** ADVERB ▸**deˈliriousness** NOUN

delirium (dɪˈlɪrɪəm) NOUN, *plural* **-liriums, -liria** (-ˈlɪrɪə). 1 a state of excitement and mental confusion, often accompanied by hallucinations, caused by high fever, poisoning, brain injury, etc. 2 violent excitement or emotion; frenzy.
▷HISTORY C16: from Latin: madness, from *dēlīrāre,* literally: to swerve from a furrow, hence be crazy, from DE- + *līra* ridge, furrow
▸**deˈliriant** ADJECTIVE

delirium tremens (ˈtremenz, ˈtriː-) NOUN a severe psychotic condition occurring in some persons with chronic alcoholism, characterized by delirium, tremor, anxiety, and vivid hallucinations. Abbreviations: **dt,** (informal) **DT's.**
▷HISTORY C19: New Latin, literally: trembling delirium

delist (,diːˈlɪst) VERB (*tr*) 1 to remove from a list. 2 *Stock Exchange* to remove (a security) from the register of those that may be traded on the recognized market.

delitescence (,delɪˈtesᵊns) NOUN the sudden disappearance of a lesion or of the signs and symptoms of a disease.
▷HISTORY C18: from Latin *dēlitēscens,* present participle of *dēlitēscere* to lurk, from *latēscere* to become hidden, from *latēre* to be hidden; see LATENT
▸**,deliˈtescent** ADJECTIVE

deliver (dɪˈlɪvə) VERB (*mainly tr*) 1 to carry (goods, etc.) to a destination, esp to carry and distribute (goods, mail, etc.) to several places: *to deliver letters; our local butcher delivers.* 2 (often foll by *over* or *up*) to hand over, transfer, or surrender. 3 (often foll by *from*) to release or rescue (from captivity, harm, corruption, etc.). 4 (*also intr*) **a** to aid in the birth of (offspring). **b** to give birth to (offspring). **c** (usually foll by *of*) to aid or assist (a female) in the birth (of offspring). **d** (*passive;* foll by *of*) to give birth (to offspring). 5 to utter or present (a speech, oration, idea, etc.). 6 short for **deliver the goods**: see sense 11, below. 7 to utter (an exclamation, noise, etc.): *to deliver a cry of exultation.* 8 to discharge or release (something, such as a blow or shot) suddenly. 9 *Chiefly US* to cause (voters, constituencies, etc.) to support a given candidate, cause, etc.: *can you deliver the Bronx?* 10 **deliver oneself of.** to speak with deliberation or at length: *to deliver oneself of a speech.* 11 **deliver the goods.** *Informal* to produce or perform something promised or expected.
▷HISTORY C13: from Old French *delivrer,* from Late Latin *dēlīberāre* to set free, from Latin DE- + *līberāre* to free
▸**deˈliverable** ADJECTIVE ▸**de,liveraˈbility** NOUN ▸**deˈliverer** NOUN

deliverance (dɪˈlɪvərəns) NOUN 1 a formal pronouncement or expression of opinion. 2 rescue from moral corruption or evil; salvation. 3 another word for **delivery** (senses 3–5).

delivery (dɪˈlɪvərɪ) NOUN, *plural* **-eries.** 1 **a** the act of delivering or distributing goods, mail, etc. **b** something that is delivered. **c** (*as modifier*): *a delivery service.* 2 the act of giving birth to a child: *she had an easy delivery.* 3 manner or style of utterance, esp in public speaking or recitation: *the chairman had a clear delivery.* 4 the act of giving or transferring or the state of being given or transferred. 5 the act of rescuing or state of being rescued; liberation. 6 *Sport* **a** the act or manner of bowling or throwing a ball. **b** the ball so delivered: *a fast delivery.* 7 an actual or symbolic handing over of property, a deed, etc. 8 the discharge rate of a compressor or pump. 9 (in South Africa) the supply of basic services to communities deprived under apartheid.

delivery van NOUN a small van used esp for delivery rounds. US and Canadian name: **panel truck.**

dell (del) NOUN a small, esp wooded hollow.
▷HISTORY Old English; related to Middle Low German *delle* valley; compare DALE

Delmarva Peninsula (delˈmɑːvə) NOUN a peninsula of the northeast US, between Chesapeake Bay and the Atlantic.

delo (ˈdeləʊ) NOUN *Austral* an informal word for **delegate.**

delocalize *or* **delocalise** (diːˈləʊkᵊ,laɪz) VERB (*tr*) 1 to remove from the usual locality. 2 to free from local influences.
▸**de,localiˈzation** *or* **de,localiˈsation** NOUN

Delors plan (dəlɔː) NOUN a plan for closer European union, originated by Jacques *Delors,* President of the European Commission (1985–94).

Delos (ˈdiːlɒs) NOUN a Greek island in the SW Aegean Sea, in the Cyclades: a commercial centre in ancient times; the legendary birthplace of Apollo and Artemis. Area: about 5 sq. km (2 sq. miles). Modern Greek name: **Dhílos.**

delouse (diːˈlaʊs, -ˈlaʊz) VERB (*tr*) to rid (a person or animal) of lice as a sanitary measure.

Delphi (ˈdelfɪ) NOUN an ancient Greek city on the S slopes of Mount Parnassus: site of the most famous oracle of Apollo.

Delphic (ˈdelfɪk) *or* **Delphian** ADJECTIVE 1 of or relating to Delphi or its oracle or temple. 2 obscure or ambiguous.

Delphic oracle NOUN the oracle of Apollo at Delphi that gave answers held by the ancient Greeks to be of great authority but also noted for their ambiguity. Related word: **Pythian.**

delphinium (delˈfɪnɪəm) NOUN, *plural* **-iums** *or* **-ia** (-ɪə). any ranunculaceous plant of the genus *Delphinium:* many varieties are cultivated as garden plants for their spikes of blue, pink, or white spurred flowers. See also **larkspur.**
▷HISTORY C17: New Latin, from Greek *delphinion* larkspur, from *delphis* DOLPHIN, referring to the shape of the nectary

Delphinus (delˈfaɪnəs) NOUN, *Latin genitive* **Delphini** (delˈfaɪnaɪ). a small constellation in the N hemisphere, between Pegasus and Sagitta.
▷HISTORY C17: from Latin: DOLPHIN

Delphi technique NOUN a forecasting or decision-making technique that makes use of written questionnaires to eliminate the influence of personal relationships and the domination of committees by strong personalities.

Delsarte system (ˈdelsɑːt) NOUN a method of teaching drama and dancing based on the exercises of Alexandre Delsarte (1811–71), famous teacher at the Paris Conservatoire.

delta (ˈdeltə) NOUN 1 the fourth letter in the Greek alphabet (Δ or δ), a consonant transliterated as *d.* 2 an object resembling a capital delta in shape. 3 (*capital when part of name*) the flat alluvial area at the mouth of some rivers where the mainstream splits up into several distributaries: *the Mississippi Delta.* 4 *Maths* a finite increment in a variable.
▷HISTORY C16: via Latin from Greek, of Semitic origin; compare Hebrew *dāleth*
▸**deltaic** (delˈteɪɪk) *or* **ˈdeltic** ADJECTIVE

Delta (ˈdeltə) NOUN 1 (*foll by the genitive case of a specified constellation*) usually the fourth brightest star in a constellation. 2 any of a group of US launch vehicles used to put unmanned satellites into orbit. 3 *Communications* a code word for the letter *d.*

delta connection NOUN a connection used in a three-phase electrical system in which three elements in series form a triangle, the supply being input and output at the three junctions. Compare **star connection.**

delta iron NOUN an allotrope of iron that exists between 1400°C and the melting point of iron and has the same structure as alpha iron.

delta particle NOUN *Physics* a very short-lived hyperon.

delta ray NOUN a particle, esp an electron, ejected from matter by ionizing radiation.

delta rhythm *or* **wave** NOUN *Physiol* the normal electrical activity of the cerebral cortex during deep sleep, occurring at a frequency of 1 to 4 hertz and detectable with an electroencephalograph. See also **brain wave.**

delta stock NOUN any of the fourth rank of active securities on the Stock Exchange. Market makers need not display prices of these securities continuously and any prices displayed are taken only as an indication rather than an offer to buy or sell.

delta wing NOUN a triangular sweptback aircraft wing.

deltiology (,deltɪˈɒlədʒɪ) NOUN the collection and study of picture postcards.
▷HISTORY C20: from Greek *deltion,* diminutive of *deltos* a writing tablet + -LOGY
▸**,deltiˈologist** NOUN

deltoid (ˈdeltɔɪd) NOUN 1 the thick muscle forming the rounded contour of the outer edge of the shoulder and acting to raise the arm. ◆ ADJECTIVE 2 shaped like a Greek capital delta, Δ; triangular.
▷HISTORY C18: from Greek *deltoeidēs* triangular, from DELTA

delude (dɪˈluːd) VERB (*tr*) 1 to deceive the mind or judgment of; mislead; beguile. 2 *Rare* to frustrate (hopes, expectations, etc.).
▷HISTORY C15: from Latin *dēlūdere* to mock, play false, from DE- + *lūdere* to play
▸**deˈludable** ADJECTIVE ▸**deˈluder** NOUN ▸**deˈludingly** ADVERB

deluge (ˈdeljuːdʒ) NOUN 1 a great flood of water. 2 torrential rain; downpour. 3 an overwhelming rush or number: *a deluge of requests.* ◆ VERB (*tr*) 4 to

flood, as with water; soak, swamp, or drown. [5] to overwhelm or overrun; inundate.
▷HISTORY C14: from Old French, from Latin *dīluvium* a washing away, flood, from *dīluere* to wash away, drench, from *di-* DIS-[1] + *-luere,* from *lavere* to wash

Deluge ('dɛlju:dʒ) NOUN **the.** another name for the **Flood.**

delusion (dɪ'lu:ʒən) NOUN [1] a mistaken or misleading opinion, idea, belief, etc.: *he has delusions of grandeur.* [2] *Psychiatry* a belief held in the face of evidence to the contrary, that is resistant to all reason. See also **illusion, hallucination.** [3] the act of deluding or state of being deluded.
▸**de'lusional** ADJECTIVE ▸**de'lusive** ADJECTIVE ▸**de'lusively** ADVERB ▸**de'lusiveness** NOUN ▸**delusory** (dɪ'lu:sərɪ) ADJECTIVE

de luxe (də 'lʌks, 'lʊks) ADJECTIVE [1] (esp of products, articles for sale, etc.) rich, elegant, or sumptuous; superior in quality, number of accessories, etc.: *the de luxe model of a car.* ◆ ADVERB [2] *Chiefly US* in a luxurious manner.
▷HISTORY C19: from French, literally: of luxury

delve (dɛlv) VERB *(mainly intr;* often foll by *in* or *into)* [1] to inquire or research deeply or intensively (for information, etc.): *he delved in the Bible for quotations.* [2] to search or rummage (in a drawer, the pockets, etc.). [3] (esp of an animal) to dig or burrow deeply (into the ground, etc.). [4] *(also tr) Archaic or dialect* to dig or turn up (earth, a garden, etc.), as with a spade.
▷HISTORY Old English *delfan;* related to Old High German *telban* to dig, Russian *dolbit* to hollow out with a chisel
▸**'delver** NOUN

Dem. *US* ABBREVIATION FOR Democrat(ic).

demagnetize *or* **demagnetise** (di:'mægnə,taɪz) VERB to lose magnetic properties or remove magnetic properties from. Also: **degauss.**
▸**de,magneti'zation** *or* **de,magneti'sation** NOUN
▸**de'magnet,izer** *or* **de'magnet,iser** NOUN

demagogic (,dɛmə'gɒgɪk) *or* **demagogical** ADJECTIVE of, characteristic of, relating to, or resembling a demagogue.
▸**,dema'gogically** ADVERB

demagogue *or sometimes US* **demagog** ('dɛmə,gɒg) NOUN [1] a political agitator who appeals with crude oratory to the prejudice and passions of the mob. [2] (esp in the ancient world) any popular political leader or orator.
▷HISTORY C17: from Greek *dēmagōgos* people's leader, from *dēmos* people + *agein* to lead

demagoguery (,dɛmə'gɒgərɪ) *or* **demagoguism** ('dɛmə,gɒgɪzəm) NOUN the methods, practices, or rhetoric of a demagogue.

demagogy ('dɛmə,gɒgɪ) NOUN, *plural* **-gogies.** [1] demagoguery. [2] rule by a demagogue or by demagogues. [3] a group of demagogues.

de-man VERB *(tr)* **-mans, -manning, -manned** *Brit* to reduce the workforce of (a plant, industry, etc.).

demand (dɪ'mɑ:nd) VERB *(tr; may take a clause as object or an infinitive)* [1] to request peremptorily or urgently. [2] to require or need as just, urgent, etc.: *the situation demands attention.* [3] to claim as a right; exact: *his parents demanded obedience of him.* [4] *Law* to make a formal legal claim to (property, esp realty). ◆ NOUN [5] an urgent or peremptory requirement or request. [6] something that requires special effort or sacrifice: *a demand on one's time.* [7] the act of demanding something or the thing demanded: *the kidnappers' demand was a million pounds.* [8] an insistent question or query. [9] *Economics* **a** willingness and ability to purchase goods and services. **b** the amount of a commodity that consumers are willing and able to purchase at a specified price. Compare **supply**[1] (sense 9). [10] *Law* a formal legal claim, esp to real property. [11] **in demand.** sought after; popular. [12] **on demand.** as soon as requested: *a draft payable on demand.*
▷HISTORY C13: from Anglo-French *demaunder,* from Medieval Latin *dēmandāre,* from Latin: to commit to, from DE- + *mandāre* to command, entrust; see MANDATE
▸**de'mandable** ADJECTIVE ▸**de'mander** NOUN

demandant (dɪ'mɑ:ndənt) NOUN *Law* (formerly) the plaintiff in an action relating to real property.
▷HISTORY C14: from Old French, from *demander* to DEMAND

demand bill *or* **draft** NOUN a bill of exchange that is payable on demand. Also called: **sight bill.**

demand deposit NOUN a bank deposit from which withdrawals may be made without notice. Compare **time deposit.**

demand feeding NOUN the practice of feeding a baby whenever it seems to be hungry, rather than at set intervals.

demanding (dɪ'mɑ:ndɪŋ) ADJECTIVE requiring great patience, skill, etc.: *a demanding job.*
▸**de'mandingly** ADVERB

demand loan NOUN another name for **call loan.**

demand management NOUN *Economics* the regulation of total spending in an economy to required levels, attempted by a government esp in order to avoid unemployment or inflation: a measure advocated by Keynesian economists.

demand note NOUN a promissory note payable on demand.

demand-pull inflation NOUN See **inflation** (sense 2).

demantoid (dɪ'mæntɔɪd) NOUN a bright green variety of andradite garnet.
▷HISTORY C19: from German, from obsolete *Demant* diamond, from Old French *diamant* + -OID

demarcate ('di:mɑ:,keɪt) VERB *(tr)* [1] to mark, fix, or draw the boundaries, limits, etc., of. [2] to separate or distinguish between (areas with unclear boundaries).
▸**'demar,cator** NOUN

demarcation *or* **demarkation** (,di:mɑ:'keɪʃən) NOUN [1] the act of establishing limits or boundaries. [2] a limit or boundary. [3] **a** a strict separation of the kinds of work performed by members of different trade unions. **b** *(as modifier): demarcation dispute.* [4] separation or distinction (often in the phrase **line of demarcation**).
▷HISTORY C18: Latinized version of Spanish *demarcación,* from *demarcar* to appoint the boundaries of, from *marcar* to mark, from Italian *marcare,* of Germanic origin; see MARK[1]

démarche *French* (demarʃ) NOUN [1] a move, step, or manoeuvre, esp in diplomatic affairs. [2] a representation or statement of views, complaints, etc., to a public authority.
▷HISTORY C17: literally: walk, gait, from Old French *demarcher* to tread, trample; see DE-, MARCH[1]

demarket (di:'mɑ:kɪt) VERB to discourage consumers from buying (a particular product), either because it is faulty or because it could jeopardize the seller's reputation.

dematerialize *or* **dematerialise** (di:mə'tɪərɪə,laɪz) VERB *(intr)* [1] to cease to have material existence, as in science fiction or spiritualism. [2] to disappear without trace; vanish.
▸**dema,teriali'zation** *or* **dema,teriali'sation** NOUN

Demavend ('dɛməvɛnd) NOUN **Mount.** a volcanic peak in N Iran, in the Elburz Mountains. Height: 5601 m (18 376 ft.).

deme (di:m) NOUN [1] **a** (in preclassical Greece) the territory inhabited by a tribe. **b** (in ancient Attica) a geographical unit of local government. [2] *Biology* a group of individuals within a species that possess particular characteristics of cytology, genetics, etc.
▷HISTORY C19: from Greek *dēmos* district in local government, the populace

demean[1] (dɪ'mi:n) VERB *(tr)* to lower (oneself) in dignity, status, or character; humble; debase.
▷HISTORY C17: see DE-, MEAN[2]; on the model of *debase*

demean[2] (dɪ'mi:n) VERB *(tr) Rare* to behave or conduct (oneself) in a specified way.
▷HISTORY C13: from Old French *demener,* from DE- + *mener* to lead, drive, from Latin *mināre* to drive (animals), from *minārī* to use threats

demeanour *or US* **demeanor** (dɪ'mi:nə) NOUN [1] the way a person behaves towards others; conduct. [2] bearing, appearance, or mien.
▷HISTORY C15: see DEMEAN[2]

dement (dɪ'mɛnt) VERB [1] *(intr)* to deteriorate mentally, esp because of old age. [2] *(tr) Rare* to drive mad; make insane.
▷HISTORY C16: from Late Latin *dēmentāre* to drive mad, from Latin DE- + *mēns* mind

demented (dɪ'mɛntɪd) ADJECTIVE mad; insane.
▸**de'mentedly** ADVERB ▸**de'mentedness** NOUN

dementia (dɪ'mɛnʃə, -ʃɪə) NOUN a state of serious emotional and mental deterioration, of organic or functional origin.
▷HISTORY C19: from Latin: madness; see DEMENT

dementia praecox ('pri:kɒks) NOUN a former name for **schizophrenia.**
▷HISTORY C19: New Latin, literally: premature dementia

demerara (,dɛmə'rɛərə, -'rɑ:rə) NOUN [1] brown crystallized cane sugar from the Caribbean and nearby countries. [2] a highly flavoured rum used mainly for blending purposes.
▷HISTORY C19: named after *Demerara,* a region of Guyana

Demerara (,dɛmə'rɛərə, -'rɑ:rə) NOUN **the.** a river in Guyana, rising in the central forest area and flowing north to the Atlantic at Georgetown. Length: 346 km (215 miles).

demerge (di:'mɜ:dʒ) VERB [1] *(tr)* to separate a company from another with which it was previously merged. [2] *(intr)* to carry out the separation of a company from another with which it was previously merged.

demerger (di:'mɜ:dʒə) NOUN the separation of two or more companies which have previously been merged.

demerit (di:'mɛrɪt, 'di:,mɛrɪt) NOUN [1] something, esp conduct, that deserves censure. [2] *US and Canadian* a mark given against a person for failure or misconduct, esp in schools or the armed forces. [3] a fault or disadvantage.
▷HISTORY C14 (originally: worth, later specialized to mean: something worthy of blame): from Latin *dēmerērī* to deserve
▸**de,meri'torious** ADJECTIVE ▸**de,meri'toriously** ADVERB

demersal (dɪ'mɜ:sᵊl) ADJECTIVE living or occurring on the bottom of a sea or a lake: *demersal fish.*
▷HISTORY C19: from Latin *dēmersus* submerged (from *dēmergere* to plunge into, from *mergere* to dip) + -AL[1]

demesne (dɪ'meɪn, -'mi:n) NOUN [1] land, esp surrounding a house or manor, retained by the owner for his own use. [2] *Property law* the possession and use of one's own property or land. [3] the territory ruled by a state or a sovereign; realm; domain. [4] a region or district; domain.
▷HISTORY C14: from Old French *demeine;* see DOMAIN

Demeter (dɪ'mi:tə) NOUN *Greek myth* the goddess of agricultural fertility and protector of marriage and women. Roman counterpart: **Ceres.**

demi- PREFIX [1] half: *demirelief.* Compare **hemi-, semi-** (sense 1). [2] of less than full size, status, or rank: *demigod.*
▷HISTORY via French from Medieval Latin *dīmedius,* from Latin *dīmidius* half, from *dis-* apart + *medius* middle

demibastion (,dɛmɪ'bæstɪən) NOUN *Fortifications* half a bastion, having only one flank, at right angles to the wall.

demicanton (,dɛmɪ'kæntɒn, -kæn'tɒn) NOUN either of the two parts of certain Swiss cantons.

demigod ('dɛmɪ,gɒd) NOUN [1] **a** a mythological being who is part mortal, part god. **b** a lesser deity. [2] a person with outstanding or godlike attributes.
▷HISTORY C16: translation of Latin *sēmideus*
▸**'demi,goddess** FEMININE NOUN

demijohn ('dɛmɪ,dʒɒn) NOUN a large bottle with a short narrow neck, often with small handles at the neck and encased in wickerwork.
▷HISTORY C18: probably by folk etymology from French *dame-jeanne,* from *dame* lady + *Jeanne* Jane

demilitarize *or* **demilitarise** (di:'mɪlɪtə,raɪz) VERB *(tr)* [1] to remove any military presence or function in (an area): *demilitarized zone.* [2] to free of military character, purpose, etc.: *11 regiments were demilitarized.*
▸**de,militari'zation** *or* **de,militari'sation** NOUN

demilune ('dɛmɪ,lu:n, -,lju:n) NOUN [1] *Fortifications* an outwork in front of a fort, shaped like a crescent moon. [2] a crescent-shaped object or formation; half-moon.
▷HISTORY C18: from French, literally: half-moon

demimondaine (,dɛmɪ'mɒndeɪn; *French* dəmimɔ̃dɛn) NOUN a woman of the demimonde.
▷HISTORY C19: from French

demimonde (,dɛmɪ'mɒnd; *French* dəmimɔ̃d)

NOUN [1] (esp in the 19th century) those women considered to be outside respectable society, esp on account of sexual promiscuity. [2] any social group considered to be not wholly respectable.
▷HISTORY C19: from French, literally: half-world

demineralize *or* **demineralise** (diːˈmɪnərəˌlaɪz) VERB (*tr*) to remove dissolved salts from (a liquid, esp water).
▸**deˌmineraliˈzation** *or* **deˌmineraliˈsation** NOUN

demi-pension *French* (dəmipɑ̃sjɔ̃) NOUN another name for **half board.**

demirelief (ˌdɛmɪrɪˈliːf) NOUN a less common term for **mezzo-relievo.**

demirep (ˈdɛmɪˌrɛp) NOUN *Rare* a woman of bad repute, esp a prostitute.
▷HISTORY C18: from DEMI- + REP(UTATION)

demise (dɪˈmaɪz) NOUN [1] failure or termination: *the demise of one's hopes.* [2] a euphemistic or formal word for **death.** [3] *Property law* **a** a transfer of an estate by lease. **b** the passing or transfer of an estate on the death of the owner. [4] the immediate transfer of sovereignty to a successor upon the death, abdication, etc., of a ruler (esp in the phrase **demise of the crown**). ◆ VERB [5] to transfer or be transferred by inheritance, will, or succession. [6] (*tr*) *Property law* to transfer (an estate, etc.) for a limited period; lease. [7] (*tr*) to transfer (sovereignty, a title, etc.) by or as if by the death, deposition, etc., of a ruler.
▷HISTORY C16: from Old French, feminine of *demis* dismissed, from *demettre* to send away, from Latin *dīmittere;* see DISMISS
▸**deˈmisable** ADJECTIVE

demi-sec (ˌdɛmɪˈsɛk) ADJECTIVE (of wine, esp champagne) medium-sweet.
▷HISTORY C20: from French, from *demi* half + *sec* dry

demisemiquaver (ˈdɛmɪˌsɛmɪˌkweɪvə) NOUN *Music* a note having the time value of one thirty-second of a semibreve. Usual US and Canadian name: **thirty-second note.**

demission (dɪˈmɪʃən) NOUN *Rare* relinquishment of or abdication from an office, responsibility, etc.
▷HISTORY C16: from Anglo-French *dimissioun,* from Latin *dīmissiō* a dismissing; see DISMISS

demist (diːˈmɪst) VERB to free or become free of condensation through evaporation produced by a heater and/or blower.

demister (diːˈmɪstə) NOUN a device incorporating a heater and/or blower used in a motor vehicle to free the windscreen of condensation.

demit (dɪˈmɪt) VERB **-mits, -mitting, -mitted.** *Scot* [1] to resign (an office, position, etc.). [2] (*tr*) to dismiss.
▷HISTORY C16: from Latin *dīmittere* to send forth, discharge, renounce, from DI-^{2} + *mittere* to send

demitasse (ˈdɛmɪˌtæs; *French* dəmitɑs) NOUN a small cup used to serve coffee, esp after a meal.
▷HISTORY C19: French, literally: half-cup

demiurge (ˈdɛmɪˌɜːdʒ, ˈdiː-) NOUN [1] **a** (in the philosophy of Plato) the creator of the universe. **b** (in Gnostic and some other philosophies) the creator of the universe, supernatural but subordinate to the Supreme Being. [2] (in ancient Greece) a magistrate with varying powers found in any of several states.
▷HISTORY C17: from Church Latin *dēmiūrgus,* from Greek *dēmiourgos* skilled workman, literally: one who works for the people, from *dēmos* people + *ergon* work
▸**ˌdemiˈurgeous** *or* **ˌdemiˈurgic** *or* **ˌdemiˈurgical** ADJECTIVE
▸**ˌdemiˈurgically** ADVERB

demiveg (ˈdɛmɪˌvɛdʒ) *Informal* ◆ NOUN [1] a person who eats poultry and fish, but no red meat. ◆ ADJECTIVE [2] denoting a person who eats poultry and fish, but no red meat.
▷HISTORY C20: from DEMI- + VEG(ETARIAN)

demivierge (ˈdɛmɪˌvjɛəʒ) NOUN a woman who engages in promiscuous sexual activity but retains her virginity.
▷HISTORY C20: French, literally: half-virgin

demivolt *or* **demivolte** (ˈdɛmɪˌvɒlt) NOUN *Dressage* a half turn on the hind legs.

demo (ˈdɛməʊ) NOUN, *plural* **-os.** *Informal* [1] short for **demonstration** (sense 4). [2] **a** a demonstration record or tape, used for audition purposes. **b** a demonstration of a prototype system. [3] *US* short for **demonstrator** (sense 3).

demo- *or before a vowel* **dem-** COMBINING FORM indicating people or population: *demography.*
▷HISTORY from Greek *dēmos*

demob (diːˈmɒb) *Brit informal* ◆ VERB **-mobs, -mobbing, -mobbed.** [1] short for **demobilize.** ◆ NOUN [2] **a** short for **demobilization. b** (*as modifier*): *a demob suit.* [3] a soldier who has been demobilized.

demobilize *or* **demobilise** (diːˈməʊbɪˌlaɪz) VERB to disband, as troops, etc.
▸**deˌmobiliˈzation** *or* **deˌmobiliˈsation** NOUN

demob suit NOUN *Brit informal* a suit of civilian clothes issued to a demobilized soldier, esp at the end of World War II.

democracy (dɪˈmɒkrəsɪ) NOUN, *plural* **-cies.** [1] government by the people or their elected representatives. [2] a political or social unit governed ultimately by all its members. [3] the practice or spirit of social equality. [4] a social condition of classlessness and equality. [5] the common people, esp as a political force.
▷HISTORY C16: from French *démocratie,* from Late Latin *dēmocratia,* from Greek *dēmokratia* government by the people; see DEMO-, -CRACY

democrat (ˈdɛməˌkræt) NOUN [1] an advocate of democracy; adherent of democratic principles. [2] a member or supporter of a democratic party or movement.

Democrat (ˈdɛməˌkræt) NOUN (in the US) a member or supporter of the Democratic Party.
▸**ˌDemoˈcratic** ADJECTIVE

democratic (ˌdɛməˈkrætɪk) ADJECTIVE [1] of, characterized by, derived from, or relating to the principles of democracy. [2] upholding or favouring democracy or the interests of the common people. [3] popular with or for the benefit of all: *democratic sports.*
▸**ˌdemoˈcratically** ADVERB

democratic centralism NOUN the Leninist principle that policy should be decided centrally by officials, who are nominally democratically elected.

democratic deficit NOUN any situation in which there is believed to be a lack of democratic accountability and control over the decision-making process.

Democratic Party NOUN [1] (in the US) the older and more liberal of the two major political parties, so named since 1840. Compare **Republican Party.** [2] (in South Africa) a multiracial political party of the centre-left, now the main opposition to the African National Congress. Abbrev.: DP.

Democratic-Republican Party NOUN *US history* the antifederalist party originally led by Thomas Jefferson, which developed into the modern Democratic Party.

Democratic Republic of Congo NOUN **the.** See **Congo** (sense 2).

democratize *or* **democratise** (dɪˈmɒkrəˌtaɪz) VERB (*tr*) to make democratic.
▸**deˌmocratiˈzation** *or* **deˌmocratiˈsation** NOUN

démodé *French* (demɔde) ADJECTIVE out of fashion; outmoded.
▷HISTORY French, from *dé-* out of + *mode* style, fashion

demodulate (diːˈmɒdjʊˌleɪt) VERB to carry out demodulation on (a wave or signal).
▸**deˈmoduˌlator** NOUN

demodulation (ˌdiːmɒdjʊˈleɪʃən) NOUN *Electronics* the act or process by which an output wave or signal is obtained having the characteristics of the original modulating wave or signal; the reverse of modulation.

Demogorgon (ˌdiːməʊˈgɔːgən) NOUN a mysterious and awesome god in ancient mythology, often represented as ruling in the underworld.
▷HISTORY C16: via Late Latin from Greek

demographic (ˌdɛməˈgræfɪk, ˌdiːmə-) ADJECTIVE of or relating to demography.
▸**ˌdemoˈgraphical** ADJECTIVE ▸**ˌdemoˈgraphically** ADVERB

demographics (ˌdɛməˈgræfɪks, ˌdiːmə-) PLURAL NOUN data resulting from the science of demography; population statistics.

demographic timebomb NOUN *Chiefly Brit* a predicted shortage of school-leavers and consequently of available workers, caused by an earlier drop in the birth rate, resulting in an older workforce.

demography (dɪˈmɒgrəfɪ) NOUN the scientific study of human populations, esp with reference to their size, structure, and distribution.
▷HISTORY C19: from French *démographie,* from Greek *dēmos* the populace; see -GRAPHY
▸**deˈmographer** *or* **deˈmographist** NOUN -

demoiselle (dəmwɑːˈzɛl) NOUN [1] Also called: **demoiselle crane, Numidian crane.** a small crane, *Anthropoides virgo,* of central Asia, N Africa, and SE Europe, having grey plumage with long black breast feathers and white ear tufts. [2] a less common name for a **damselfly.** [3] another name for **damselfish.** [4] a literary word for **damsel.**
▷HISTORY C16: from French: young woman; see DAMSEL

demolish (dɪˈmɒlɪʃ) VERB (*tr*) [1] to tear down or break up (buildings, etc.). [2] to destroy; put an end to (an argument, etc.). [3] *Facetious* to eat up: *she demolished the whole cake!*
▷HISTORY C16: from French *démolir,* from Latin *dēmōlīrī* to throw down, destroy, from DE- + *mōlīrī* to strive, toil, construct, from *mōles* mass, bulk
▸**deˈmolisher** NOUN ▸**deˈmolishment** NOUN

demolition (ˌdɛməˈlɪʃən, ˌdiː-) NOUN [1] the act of demolishing or state of being demolished. [2] *Chiefly military* **a** destruction by explosives. **b** (*as modifier*): *a demolition charge.*
▸**ˌdemoˈlitionist** NOUN, ADJECTIVE

demolition derby NOUN *Chiefly US and Canadian* a competition in which contestants drive old cars into each other until there is only one car left running.

demolitions (ˌdɛməˈlɪʃənz, ˌdiː-) PLURAL NOUN *Chiefly military* [1] **a** explosives, as when used to blow up bridges, etc. **b** (*as modifier*): *a demolitions expert.* [2] targets prepared for destruction by explosives.

demon (ˈdiːmən) NOUN [1] an evil spirit or devil. [2] a person, habit, obsession, etc., thought of as evil, cruel, or persistently tormenting. [3] Also called: **daemon, daimon.** an attendant or ministering spirit; genius: *the demon of inspiration.* [4] **a** a person who is extremely skilful in, energetic at, or devoted to a given activity, esp a sport: *a demon at cycling.* **b** (*as modifier*): *a demon cyclist.* [5] a variant spelling of **daemon** (sense 1). [6] *Austral and NZ informal, archaic* a detective or policeman.
▷HISTORY C15: from Latin *daemōn* evil spirit, spirit, from Greek *daimōn* spirit, deity, fate; see DAEMON

demonetarize *or* **demonetarise** (diːˈmʌnətəraɪz) VERB (*tr*) another word for **demonetize** (sense 1).
▸**deˌmonetariˈzation** *or* **deˌmonetariˈsation** NOUN

demonetize *or* **demonetise** (diːˈmʌnɪˌtaɪz) VERB (*tr*) [1] to deprive (a metal) of its capacity as a monetary standard. [2] to withdraw from use as currency.
▸**deˌmonetiˈzation** *or* **deˌmonetiˈsation** NOUN

demoniac (dɪˈməʊnɪˌæk) ADJECTIVE *also* **demoniacal** (ˌdiːməˈnaɪəkᵊl). [1] of, like, or suggestive of a demon; demonic. [2] suggesting inner possession or inspiration: *the demoniac fire of genius.* [3] frantic; frenzied; feverish: *demoniac activity.* ◆ NOUN [4] a person possessed by an evil spirit or demon.
▸**ˌdemoˈniacally** ADVERB

demonic (dɪˈmɒnɪk) ADJECTIVE [1] of, relating to, or characteristic of a demon; fiendish. [2] inspired or possessed by a demon, or seemingly so: *demonic laughter.*
▸**deˈmonically** ADVERB

demonism (ˈdiːməˌnɪzəm) NOUN [1] **a** belief in the existence and power of demons. **b** worship of demons. [2] another word for **demonology.**
▸**ˈdemonist** NOUN

demonize *or* **demonise** (ˈdiːməˌnaɪz) VERB (*tr*) [1] to make into or like a demon. [2] to subject to demonic influence. [3] to mark out or describe as evil or culpable: *the technique of demonizing the enemy in the run-up to war.*

demonolater (ˌdiːməˈnɒlətə) NOUN a person who worships demons.
▷HISTORY C19: back formation from DEMONOLATRY

demonolatry (ˌdiːməˈnɒlətrɪ) NOUN the worship of demons.
▷HISTORY C17: see DEMON, -LATRY

demonology (ˌdiːməˈnɒlədʒɪ) NOUN [1] the study of demons or demonic beliefs. Also called: **demonism.** [2] a set of people or things that are

disliked or held in low esteem: *the place occupied by Hitler in contemporary demonology.*
▸**demonological** (ˌdiːmənəˈlɒdʒɪkəl) ADJECTIVE
▸**ˌdemonˈologist** NOUN

demonstrable (ˈdɛmənstrəbəl, dɪˈmɒn-) ADJECTIVE able to be demonstrated or proved.
▸**ˌdemonstraˈbility** *or* **ˈdemonstrableness** NOUN
▸**demonstrably** (ˈdɛmənstrəblɪ, dɪˈmɒn-) ADVERB

demonstrate (ˈdɛmənˌstreɪt) VERB [1] (*tr*) to show, manifest, or prove, esp by reasoning, evidence, etc.: *it is easy to demonstrate the truth of this proposition.* [2] (*tr*) to evince; reveal the existence of: *the scheme later demonstrated a fatal flaw.* [3] (*tr*) to explain or illustrate by experiment, example, etc. [4] (*tr*) to display, operate, and explain the workings of (a machine, product, etc.). [5] (*intr*) to manifest support, protest, etc., by public parades or rallies. [6] (*intr*) to be employed as a demonstrator of machinery, etc. [7] (*intr*) *Military* to make a show of force, esp in order to deceive one's enemy.
▹HISTORY C16: from Latin *dēmonstrāre* to point out, from *monstrāre* to show

demonstration (ˌdɛmənˈstreɪʃən) NOUN [1] the act of demonstrating. [2] proof or evidence leading to proof. [3] an explanation, display, illustration, or experiment showing how something works. [4] a manifestation of grievances, support, or protest by public rallies, parades, etc. [5] a manifestation of emotion. [6] a show of military force or preparedness. [7] *Maths* a logical presentation of the assumptions and equations used in solving a problem or proving a theorem.
▸**ˌdemonˈstrational** ADJECTIVE ▸**ˌdemonˈstrationist** NOUN

demonstration model NOUN a nearly new product, such as a car or washing machine, that has been used only to demonstrate its performance by a dealer and is offered for sale at a discount.

demonstrative (dɪˈmɒnstrətɪv) ADJECTIVE [1] tending to manifest or express one's feelings easily or unreservedly. [2] (*postpositive; foll by of*) serving as proof; indicative. [3] involving or characterized by demonstration: *a demonstrative lecture.* [4] conclusive; indubitable: *demonstrative arguments.* [5] *Grammar* denoting or belonging to a class of determiners used to point out the individual referent or referents intended, such as *this, that, these,* and *those.* Compare **interrogative, relative.** ◆ NOUN [6] *Grammar* a demonstrative word or construction.
▸**deˈmonstratively** ADVERB ▸**deˈmonstrativeness** NOUN

demonstrator (ˈdɛmənˌstreɪtə) NOUN [1] a person who demonstrates equipment, machines, products, etc. [2] a person who takes part in a public demonstration. [3] a piece of merchandise, such as a car that one test-drives, used to display merits or performance to prospective buyers.

demoralize *or* **demoralise** (dɪˈmɒrəˌlaɪz) VERB (*tr*) [1] to undermine the morale of; dishearten: *he was demoralized by his defeat.* [2] to debase morally; corrupt. [3] to throw into confusion.
▸**deˌmoraliˈzation** *or* **deˌmoraliˈsation** NOUN ▸**deˈmoralˌizer** *or* **deˈmoralˌiser** NOUN

De Morgan's laws PLURAL NOUN (in formal logic and set theory) the principles that conjunction and disjunction, or union and intersection, are dual. Thus the negation of *P* & *Q* is equivalent to *not-P* or *not-Q*.
▹HISTORY named after Augustus *De Morgan* (1806–71), British mathematician

demos (ˈdiːmɒs) NOUN [1] the people of a nation regarded as a political unit. [2] *Rare* the common people; masses.
▹HISTORY C19: from Greek: the populace; see DEME

demote (dɪˈməʊt) VERB (*tr*) to lower in rank or position; relegate.
▹HISTORY C19: from DE- + (PRO)MOTE
▸**deˈmotion** NOUN

demotic (dɪˈmɒtɪk) ADJECTIVE [1] of or relating to the common people; popular. [2] of or relating to a simplified form of hieroglyphics used in ancient Egypt by the ordinary literate class outside the priesthood. Compare **hieratic.** ◆ NOUN [3] the demotic script of ancient Egypt.
▹HISTORY C19: from Greek *dēmotikos* of the people, from *dēmotēs* a man of the people, commoner; see DEMOS
▸**deˈmotist** NOUN

Demotic (dɪˈmɒtɪk) NOUN [1] the spoken form of Modern Greek, now increasingly used in literature. Compare **Katharevusa.** ◆ ADJECTIVE [2] denoting or relating to this.

demount (diːˈmaʊnt) VERB (*tr*) to remove (a motor, gun, etc.) from its mounting or setting.
▸**deˈmountable** ADJECTIVE

dempster (ˈdɛmpstə) NOUN a variant spelling of **deemster.**

demulcent (dɪˈmʌlsənt) ADJECTIVE [1] soothing; mollifying. ◆ NOUN [2] a drug or agent that soothes the irritation of inflamed or injured skin surfaces.
▹HISTORY C18: from Latin *dēmulcēre* to caress soothingly, from DE- + *mulcēre* to stroke

demulsify (diːˈmʌlsɪˌfaɪ) VERB **-fies, -fying, -fied.** to undergo or cause to undergo a process in which an emulsion is permanently broken down into its constituents.
▹HISTORY C20: from DE- + EMULSIFY
▸**deˌmulsifiˈcation** NOUN ▸**deˈmulsiˌfier** NOUN

demur (dɪˈmɜː) VERB **-murs, -murring, -murred.** (*intr*) [1] to raise objections or show reluctance; object. [2] *Law* to raise an objection by entering a demurrer. [3] *Archaic* to hesitate; delay. ◆ NOUN *also* **demurral** (dɪˈmʌrəl). [4] the act of demurring. [5] an objection raised. [6] *Archaic* hesitation.
▹HISTORY C13: from Old French *demorer,* from Latin *dēmorārī* to loiter, linger, from *morārī* to delay, from *mora* a delay
▸**deˈmurrable** ADJECTIVE

demure (dɪˈmjʊə) ADJECTIVE [1] sedate; decorous; reserved. [2] affectedly modest or prim; coy.
▹HISTORY C14: perhaps from Old French *demorer* to delay, linger; perhaps influenced by *meur* ripe, MATURE
▸**deˈmurely** ADVERB ▸**deˈmureness** NOUN

demurrage (dɪˈmʌrɪdʒ) NOUN [1] the delaying of a ship, railway wagon, etc., caused by the charterer's failure to load, unload, etc., before the time of scheduled departure. [2] the extra charge required as compensation for such delay. [3] a fee charged by the Bank of England for changing bullion into notes.
▹HISTORY C17: from Old French *demorage, demourage;* see DEMUR

demurrer (dɪˈmʌrə) NOUN [1] *Law* a pleading that admits an opponent's point but denies that it is a relevant or valid argument. [2] any objection raised.

demutualize *or* **demutualise** (diːˈmjuːtʃʊəˌlaɪz) VERB to convert (a mutual society, such as a building society) to a public limited company or (of such a society) to be converted.
▸**ˌdemutualiˈzation** *or* **ˌdemutualiˈsation** NOUN

demy (dɪˈmaɪ) NOUN, *plural* **-mies.** [1] **a** a size of printing paper, 17½ by 22½ inches (444.5 × 571.5 mm). **b** a size of writing paper, 15½ by 20 inches (Brit.) (393.7 × 508 mm) or 16 by 21 inches (US) (406.4 × 533.4 mm). [2] either one of two book sizes, 8½ by 5½ inches (**demy octavo**) or (chiefly Brit.) 11¼ by 8⅝ inches (**demy quarto**).
▹HISTORY C16: see DEMI-

demystify (diːˈmɪstɪˌfaɪ) VERB **-fies, -fying, -fied.** (*tr*) to remove the mystery from; make clear.
▸**deˌmystifiˈcation** NOUN

demythologize *or* **demythologise** (ˌdiːmɪˈθɒləˌdʒaɪz) VERB (*tr*) [1] to eliminate all mythical elements from (a piece of writing, esp the Bible) so as to arrive at an essential meaning. [2] to restate (a message, esp a religious one) in rational terms.
▸**ˌdemyˌthologiˈzation** *or* **ˌdemyˌthologiˈsation** NOUN

den (dɛn) NOUN [1] the habitat or retreat of a lion or similar wild animal; lair. [2] a small or secluded room in a home, often used for carrying on a hobby. [3] a squalid or wretched room or retreat. [4] a site or haunt: *a den of vice.* [5] *Scot* a small wooded valley; dingle. [6] *Scot and northern English dialect* a place of sanctuary in certain catching games; home or base. ◆ VERB **dens, denning, denned.** [7] (*intr*) to live in or as if in a den.
▹HISTORY Old English *denn;* related to Old High German *tenni* threshing floor, early Dutch *denne* low ground, den, cave

Den. ABBREVIATION FOR Denmark.

denar (ˈdiːnə) NOUN the standard monetary unit of Macedonia, divided into 100 deni.

denarius (dɪˈnɛərɪəs) NOUN, *plural* **-narii** (-ˈnɛərɪˌaɪ). [1] a silver coin of ancient Rome, often called a penny in translation. [2] a gold coin worth 25 silver denarii.
▹HISTORY C16: from Latin: coin originally equal to ten asses, from *dēnārius* (adjective) containing ten, from *dēnī* ten each, from *decem* ten

denary (ˈdiːnərɪ) ADJECTIVE [1] calculated by tens; based on ten; decimal. [2] containing ten parts; tenfold.
▹HISTORY C16: from Latin *dēnārius* containing ten; see DENARIUS

denationalize *or* **denationalise** (diːˈnæʃənəˌlaɪz) VERB [1] to return or transfer (an industry, etc.) from public to private ownership. [2] to deprive (an individual, people, institution, etc.) of national character or nationality.
▸**deˌnationaliˈzation** *or* **deˌnationaliˈsation** NOUN

denaturalize *or* **denaturalise** (diːˈnætʃrəˌlaɪz) VERB (*tr*) [1] to deprive of nationality. [2] to make unnatural.
▸**deˌnaturaliˈzation** *or* **deˌnaturaliˈsation** NOUN

denature (diːˈneɪtʃə), **denaturize,** *or* **denaturise** (diːˈneɪtʃəˌraɪz) VERB (*tr*) [1] to change the nature of. [2] to change (a protein) by chemical or physical means, such as the action of acid or heat, to cause loss of solubility, biological activity, etc. [3] to render (something, such as ethanol) unfit for consumption by adding nauseous substances. [4] to render (fissile material) unfit for use in nuclear weapons by addition of an isotope.
▸**deˈnaturant** NOUN ▸**deˌnaturˈation** NOUN

denatured alcohol NOUN *Chem* ethanol rendered unfit for human consumption by the addition of a noxious substance, as in methylated spirits.

denazify (diːˈnɑːtsɪˌfaɪ) VERB **-fies, -fying, -fied.** (*tr*) to free or declare (people, institutions, etc.) freed from Nazi influence or ideology.
▸**deˌnazifiˈcation** NOUN

Denbighshire (ˈdɛnbɪˌʃɪə, -ʃə) NOUN a county of N Wales: split between Clwyd and Gwynedd in 1974; reinstated with different boundaries in 1996: borders the Irish Sea, with the Cambrian Mountains in the south: chiefly agricultural. Administrative centre: Ruthin. Pop.: 93 092 (2001). Area: 844 sq. km (327 sq. miles).

Den Bosch (dən bɒs) NOUN another name for **'s Hertogenbosch.**

dendriform (ˈdɛndrɪˌfɔːm) ADJECTIVE branching or treelike in appearance.

dendrite (ˈdɛndraɪt) NOUN [1] Also called: **dendron.** any of the short branched threadlike extensions of a nerve cell, which conduct impulses towards the cell body. [2] a branching mosslike crystalline structure in some rocks and minerals. [3] a crystal that has branched during growth and has a treelike form.
▹HISTORY C18: from Greek *dendritēs* relating to a tree
▸**dendritic** (dɛnˈdrɪtɪk) *or* **denˈdritical** ADJECTIVE
▸**denˈdritically** ADVERB

dendro-, dendri-, *or before a vowel* **dendr-** COMBINING FORM tree: *dendrochronology; dendrite.*
▹HISTORY New Latin, from Greek, from *dendron* tree

dendrochronology (ˌdɛndrəʊkrəˈnɒlədʒɪ) NOUN the study of the annual rings of trees, used esp to date past events.
▸**dendrochronological** (ˌdɛndrəʊˌkrɒnəˈlɒdʒɪkəl) ADJECTIVE ▸**ˌdendrochroˈnologist** NOUN

dendrogram (ˈdɛndrəʊˌgræm) NOUN any branching diagram, such as a cladogram, showing the interconnections between treelike organisms.

dendroid (ˈdɛndrɔɪd) *or* **dendroidal** (dɛnˈdrɔɪdəl) ADJECTIVE [1] freely branching; arborescent; treelike. [2] (esp of tree ferns) having a tall trunklike stem.
▹HISTORY C19: from Greek *dendroeidēs* like a tree

dendrology (dɛnˈdrɒlədʒɪ) NOUN the branch of botany that is concerned with the natural history of trees and shrubs.
▸**dendrological** (ˌdɛndrəˈlɒdʒɪkəl) *or* **ˌdendroˈlogic** *or* **denˈdrologous** ADJECTIVE ▸**denˈdrologist** NOUN

dendron (ˈdɛndrɒn) NOUN another name for **dendrite** (sense 1).

dene[1] *or* **dean** (diːn) NOUN *Brit* a valley, esp one that is narrow and wooded.
▹HISTORY Old English *denu* valley; see DEN

dene[2] *or* **dean** (diːn) NOUN *Dialect, chiefly southern English* a sandy stretch of land or dune near the sea.
▷HISTORY C13: probably related to Old English *dūn* hill; see DOWN[3]

Dene (ˈdɛnɪ, ˈdɛneɪ) PLURAL NOUN the North American Indian peoples of Nunavut and the Northwest Territories in Canada. The official body representing them is called the Dene Nation.
▷HISTORY via French *déné,* from Athapascan *dene* people

Deneb (ˈdɛnɛb) NOUN the brightest star in the constellation Cygnus and one of the brightest but remotest stars in the night sky. Visual magnitude: 1.25; spectral type: A2I.
▷HISTORY C19: from Arabic *dhanab* a tail

Denebola (dɪˈnɛbələ) NOUN the second brightest star in the constellation Leo. Visual magnitude: 2.14; spectral type: A3V.
▷HISTORY from Arabic *dhanab al-(asad)* tail of the (lion)

denegation (ˌdɛnɪˈgeɪʃən) NOUN a denial, contradiction, or refusal.
▷HISTORY C17: from Late Latin *dēnegātiō,* from Latin *dēnegāre* to deny, refuse, from *negāre* to deny

dene hole NOUN a hole or shaft excavated in the chalk of southern England or northern France, of uncertain origin and purpose.
▷HISTORY of uncertain origin: perhaps from DENE[1]

denervate (ˈdɛnəˌveɪt) VERB *(tr)* to deprive (a tissue or organ) of its nerve supply.
▸ˌ**denerˈvation** NOUN

DEng. ABBREVIATION FOR Doctor of Engineering.

Denglish (ˈdɛŋglɪʃ) NOUN a variety of German containing a high proportion of English words.
▷HISTORY C20: from a blend of German *Deutsch* German + ENGLISH

dengue (ˈdɛŋgɪ) *or* **dandy** (ˈdændɪ) NOUN an acute viral disease transmitted by mosquitoes, characterized by headache, fever, pains in the joints, and skin rash. Also called: **breakbone fever.**
▷HISTORY C19: from Spanish, probably of African origin; compare Swahili *kidinga*

Den Haag (dɛn ˈhaːx) NOUN the Dutch name for (The) **Hague.**

Den Helder (*Dutch* dɛn ˈhɛldər) NOUN a port in the W Netherlands, in North Holland province: fortified by Napoleon in 1811; naval station. Pop.: 61 024 (1994).

deni (dɪˈnɪ) NOUN a monetary unit of the Former Yugoslav Republic of Macedonia, worth one hundredth of a denar.

deniable (dɪˈnaɪəbᵊl) ADJECTIVE able to be denied; questionable.
▸**deˈniably** ADVERB

denial (dɪˈnaɪəl) NOUN [1] a refusal to agree or comply with a statement; contradiction. [2] the rejection of the truth of a proposition, doctrine, etc.: *a denial of God's existence.* [3] a negative reply; rejection of a request. [4] a refusal to acknowledge; renunciation; disavowal: *a denial of one's leader.* [5] a psychological process by which painful truths are not admitted into an individual's consciousness. See also **defence mechanism.** [6] abstinence; self-denial.

denier[1] NOUN [1] (ˈdɛnɪˌeɪ, ˈdɛnjə) a unit of weight used to measure the fineness of silk and man-made fibres, esp when woven into women's tights, etc. It is equal to 1 gram per 9000 metres. [2] (dəˈnjeɪ, -ˈnɪə) any of several former European coins of various denominations.
▷HISTORY C15: from Old French: coin, from Latin *dēnārius* DENARIUS

denier[2] (dɪˈnaɪə) NOUN a person who denies.

denigrate (ˈdɛnɪˌgreɪt) VERB [1] *(tr)* to belittle or disparage the character of; defame. [2] a rare word for **blacken.**
▷HISTORY C16: from Latin *dēnigrāre* to make very black, defame, from *nigrāre* to blacken, from *niger* black
▸ˌ**deniˈgration** NOUN ▸ˈ**deniˌgrator** NOUN

denim (ˈdɛnɪm) NOUN *Textiles* [1] **a** a hard-wearing twill-weave cotton fabric used for trousers, work clothes, etc. **b** *(as modifier)*: *a denim jacket.* [2] **a** a similar lighter fabric used in upholstery. **b** *(as modifier)*: *denim cushion covers.*
▷HISTORY C17: from French *(serge) de Nîmes* (serge) of NÎMES

denims (ˈdɛnɪmz) PLURAL NOUN jeans or overalls made of denim.

denitrate (diːˈnaɪtreɪt) VERB to undergo or cause to undergo a process in which a compound loses a nitro or nitrate group, nitrogen dioxide, or nitric acid.
▸ˌ**deniˈtration** NOUN

denitrify (diːˈnaɪtrɪˌfaɪ) VERB **-fies, -fying, -fied.** to undergo or cause to undergo loss or removal of nitrogen compounds or nitrogen.
▸**deˌnitrifiˈcation** NOUN

denizen (ˈdɛnɪzən) NOUN [1] an inhabitant; occupant; resident. [2] *Brit* an individual permanently resident in a foreign country where he enjoys certain rights of citizenship. [3] a plant or animal established in a place to which it is not native. [4] a naturalized foreign word. ◆ VERB [5] *(tr)* to make a denizen.
▷HISTORY C15: from Anglo-French *denisein,* from Old French *denzein,* from *denz* within, from Latin *de intus* from within

Denmark (ˈdɛnmɑːk) NOUN a kingdom in N Europe, between the Baltic and the North Sea: consists of the mainland of Jutland and about 100 inhabited islands (chiefly Zealand, Lolland, Funen, Falster, Langeland, and Bornholm); extended its territory throughout the Middle Ages, ruling Sweden until 1523 and Norway until 1814, and incorporating Greenland as a province from 1953 to 1979; joined the Common Market (now the EU) in 1973; an important exporter of dairy produce. Language: Danish. Religion: Christian, Lutheran majority. Currency: krone. Capital: Copenhagen. Pop.: 5 358 000 (2001 est). Area: 43 031 sq. km (16 614 sq. miles). Danish name: **Danmark.** Related adjective: **Danish.**

Denmark Strait NOUN a channel between SE Greenland and Iceland, linking the Arctic Ocean with the Atlantic.

denom. ABBREVIATION FOR (religious) denomination.

denominate VERB (dɪˈnɒmɪˌneɪt) [1] *(tr)* to give a specific name to; designate. ◆ ADJECTIVE (dɪˈnɒmɪnɪt, -ˌneɪt) [2] *Maths* (of a number) representing a multiple of a unit of measurement: *4 is the denominate number in 4 miles.*
▷HISTORY C16: from DE- + Latin *nōmināre* to call by name; see NOMINATE
▸**deˈnominable** ADJECTIVE

denomination (dɪˌnɒmɪˈneɪʃən) NOUN [1] a group having a distinctive interpretation of a religious faith and usually its own organization. [2] a grade or unit in a series of designations of value, weight, measure, etc.: *coins of this denomination are being withdrawn.* [3] a name given to a class or group; classification. [4] the act of giving a name. [5] a name; designation.
▷HISTORY C15: from Latin *dēnōminātiō* a calling by name; see DENOMINATE
▸**deˌnomiˈnational** ADJECTIVE ▸**deˌnomiˈnationally** ADVERB

denominationalism (dɪˌnɒmɪˈneɪʃənᵊˌlɪzəm) NOUN [1] adherence to particular principles, esp to the tenets of a religious denomination; sectarianism. [2] the tendency to divide or cause to divide into sects or denominations. [3] division into denominations.
▸**deˌnomiˈnationalist** NOUN, ADJECTIVE

denominative (dɪˈnɒmɪnətɪv) ADJECTIVE [1] giving or constituting a name; naming. [2] *Grammar* **a** (of a word other than a noun) formed from or having the same form as a noun. **b** *(as noun)*: *the verb "to mushroom" is a denominative.*
▸**deˈnominatively** ADVERB

denominator (dɪˈnɒmɪˌneɪtə) NOUN [1] the divisor of a fraction, as 8 in ⅞. Compare **numerator** (sense 1). [2] *Archaic* a person or thing that denominates or designates.

denotation (ˌdiːnəʊˈteɪʃən) NOUN [1] the act or process of denoting; indication. [2] a particular meaning, esp one given explicitly rather than by suggestion. [3] **a** something designated or referred to. See **referent.** Compare **connotation. b** another name for **extension** (sense 11).

denotative (dɪˈnəʊtətɪv) ADJECTIVE [1] able to denote; designative. [2] explicit; overt.
▸**deˈnotatively** ADVERB

denote (dɪˈnəʊt) VERB *(tr; may take a clause as object)* [1] to be a sign, symbol, or symptom of; indicate or designate. [2] (of words, phrases, expressions, etc.) to have as a literal or obvious meaning.
▷HISTORY C16: from Latin *dēnotāre* to mark, from *notāre* to mark, NOTE
▸**deˈnotable** ADJECTIVE ▸**deˈnotement** NOUN

denouement (deɪˈnuːmɒn) *or* **dénouement** (*French* denumɑ̃) NOUN [1] **a** the final clarification or resolution of a plot in a play or other work. **b** the point at which this occurs. [2] final outcome; solution.
▷HISTORY C18: from French, literally: an untying, from *dénouer* to untie, from Old French *desnoer,* from *des-* DE- + *noer* to tie, knot, from Latin *nōdāre,* from *nōdus* a knot; see NODE

denounce (dɪˈnaʊns) VERB *(tr)* [1] to deplore or condemn openly or vehemently. [2] to give information against; accuse. [3] to announce formally the termination of (a treaty, etc.). [4] *Obsolete* **a** to announce (something evil). **b** to portend.
▷HISTORY C13: from Old French *denoncier* to proclaim, from Latin *dēnuntiāre* to make an official proclamation, threaten, from DE- + *nuntiāre* to announce
▸**deˈnouncement** NOUN ▸**deˈnouncer** NOUN

de novo *Latin* (diː ˈnəʊvəʊ) ADVERB from the beginning; anew.

dense (dɛns) ADJECTIVE [1] thickly crowded or closely set: *a dense crowd.* [2] thick; impenetrable: *a dense fog.* [3] *Physics* having a high density. [4] stupid; dull; obtuse. [5] (of a photographic negative) having many dark or exposed areas. [6] (of an optical glass, colour, etc.) transmitting little or no light.
▷HISTORY C15: from Latin *densus* thick; related to Greek *dasus* thickly covered with hair or leaves
▸ˈ**densely** ADVERB ▸ˈ**denseness** NOUN

densimeter (dɛnˈsɪmɪtə) NOUN *Physics* any instrument for measuring density.
▸**densimetric** (ˌdɛnsɪˈmɛtrɪk) ADJECTIVE ▸**denˈsimetry** NOUN

densitometer (ˌdɛnsɪˈtɒmɪtə) NOUN an instrument for measuring the optical density of a material by directing a beam of light onto the specimen and measuring its transmission or reflection.
▸**densitometric** (ˌdɛnsɪtəˈmɛtrɪk) ADJECTIVE
▸ˌ**densiˈtometry** NOUN

density (ˈdɛnsɪtɪ) NOUN, *plural* **-ties.** [1] the degree to which something is filled, crowded, or occupied: *high density of building in towns.* [2] obtuseness; stupidity. [3] a measure of the compactness of a substance, expressed as its mass per unit volume. It is measured in kilograms per cubic metre or pounds per cubic foot. Symbol: ρ. See also **relative density.** [4] a measure of a physical quantity per unit of length, area, or volume. See **charge density, current density.** [5] *Physics, photog* See **transmission density, reflection density.**

density function NOUN *Statistics* short for **probability density function.**

dent[1] (dɛnt) NOUN [1] a hollow or dip in a surface, as one made by pressure or a blow. [2] an appreciable effect, esp of lessening: *a dent in our resources.* ◆ VERB [3] to impress or be impressed with a dent or dents.
▷HISTORY C13 (in the sense: a stroke, blow): variant of DINT

dent[2] (dɛnt) NOUN [1] a toothlike protuberance, esp the tooth of a sprocket or gearwheel. [2] *Textiles* the space between two wires in a loom through which a warp thread is drawn.
▷HISTORY C16: from French: tooth

dent. ABBREVIATION FOR: [1] dental. [2] dentistry.

dental (ˈdɛntᵊl) ADJECTIVE [1] of or relating to the teeth. [2] of or relating to dentistry. [3] *Phonetics* **a** pronounced or articulated with the tip of the tongue touching the backs of the upper teeth, as for *t* in French *tout.* **b** (esp in the phonology of some languages, such as English) another word for **alveolar.** ◆ NOUN [4] *Phonetics* a dental consonant.
▷HISTORY C16: from Medieval Latin *dentālis,* from Latin *dens* tooth

dental clinic NOUN *NZ* a school clinic in which minor dental work is carried out by dental nurses.

dental floss NOUN a soft usually flattened often waxed thread for cleaning the teeth and the spaces between them.

dental hygiene NOUN the maintenance of the teeth and gums in healthy condition, esp by proper brushing, the removal of plaque, etc. Also called: **oral hygiene.**

dental hygienist NOUN a dentist's assistant skilled in dental hygiene. Also called: **oral hygienist.**

dentalium (dɛn'teɪlɪəm) NOUN, *plural* **-liums** *or* **-lia** (-lɪə). any scaphopod mollusc of the genus *Dentalium*. See **tusk shell.**
▷HISTORY C19: New Latin, from Medieval Latin *dentālis* DENTAL

dental nurse NOUN [1] a dentist's assistant, esp one who passes instruments, mixes fillings, etc. [2] *NZ* a nurse trained to do fillings and carry out other minor dental work on schoolchildren.

dental plaque NOUN a filmy deposit on the surface of a tooth consisting of a mixture of mucus, bacteria, food, etc. Also called: **bacterial plaque.**

dental surgeon NOUN another name for **dentist.**

dentate ('dɛnteɪt) ADJECTIVE [1] having teeth or toothlike processes. [2] (of leaves) having a toothed margin.
▷HISTORY C19: from Latin *dentātus*
▸**'dentately** ADVERB

dentation (dɛn'teɪʃən) NOUN [1] the state or condition of being dentate. [2] an angular projection or series of projections, as on the margin of a leaf.

dentex ('dɛntɛks) NOUN a large active predatory sparid fish, *Dentex dentex*, of Mediterranean and E Atlantic waters, having long sharp teeth and powerful jaws.
▷HISTORY C19: from Latin *dentix, dentex* from *dens* tooth

denti- *or before a vowel* **dent-** COMBINING FORM indicating a tooth: *dentiform; dentine.*
▷HISTORY from Latin *dēns, dent-*

denticle ('dɛntɪkᵊl) NOUN a small tooth or toothlike part, such as any of the placoid scales of sharks.
▷HISTORY C14: from Latin *denticulus*

denticulate (dɛn'tɪkjʊlɪt, -ˌleɪt) ADJECTIVE [1] *Biology* very finely toothed: *denticulate leaves.* [2] having denticles. [3] *Architect* having dentils.
▷HISTORY C17: from Latin *denticulātus* having small teeth
▸**den'ticulately** ADVERB

denticulation (dɛnˌtɪkjʊ'leɪʃən) NOUN [1] a denticulate structure. [2] a less common word for **denticle.**

dentiform ('dɛntɪˌfɔːm) ADJECTIVE shaped like a tooth.

dentifrice ('dɛntɪfrɪs) NOUN any substance, esp paste or powder, for use in cleaning the teeth.
▷HISTORY C16: from Latin *dentifricium* tooth powder, from *dent-, dens* tooth + *fricāre* to rub

dentil ('dɛntɪl) NOUN one of a set of small square or rectangular blocks evenly spaced to form an ornamental row, usually under a classical cornice on a building, piece of furniture, etc.
▷HISTORY C17: from French, from obsolete *dentille* a little tooth, from *dent* tooth

dentilabial (ˌdɛntɪ'leɪbɪəl) ADJECTIVE another word for **labiodental.**

dentilingual (ˌdɛntɪ'lɪŋgwəl) ADJECTIVE [1] *Phonetics* pronounced or articulated with the tongue touching the upper teeth. ◆ NOUN [2] a consonant so pronounced.

dentine ('dɛntiːn) *or* **dentin** ('dɛntɪn) NOUN the calcified tissue surrounding the pulp cavity of a tooth and comprising the bulk of the tooth.
▷HISTORY C19: from DENTI- + -IN
▸**'dentinal** ADJECTIVE

dentist ('dɛntɪst) NOUN a person qualified to practise dentistry.
▷HISTORY C18: from French *dentiste,* from *dent* tooth

dentistry ('dɛntɪstrɪ) NOUN the branch of medical science concerned with the diagnosis and treatment of diseases and disorders of the teeth and gums.

dentition (dɛn'tɪʃən) NOUN [1] the arrangement, type, and number of the teeth in a particular species. Man has a **primary dentition** of deciduous teeth and a **secondary dentition** of permanent teeth. [2] teething or the time or process of teething.
▷HISTORY C17: from Latin *dentītiō* a teething

dentoid ('dɛntɔɪd) ADJECTIVE resembling a tooth.

Denton ('dɛntᵊn) NOUN a town in NW England, in Tameside unitary authority, Greater Manchester. Pop.: 37 785 (1991).

denture ('dɛntʃə) NOUN (*usually plural*) [1] Also called: **dental plate, false teeth.** a partial or full set of artificial teeth. [2] *Rare* a set of natural teeth.
▷HISTORY C19: from French, from *dent* tooth + -URE

denuclearize *or* **denuclearise** (diː'njuːklɪəˌraɪz) VERB (*tr*) to deprive (a country, state, etc.) of nuclear weapons.
▸**deˌnucleari'zation** *or* **deˌnucleari'sation** NOUN

denudate ('dɛnjʊˌdeɪt, dɪ'njuːdeɪt) VERB [1] a less common word for **denude.** ◆ ADJECTIVE [2] denuded; bare.

denude (dɪ'njuːd) VERB (*tr*) [1] to divest of covering; make bare; uncover; strip. [2] to expose (rock) by the erosion of the layers above.
▷HISTORY C16: from Latin *dēnūdāre;* see NUDE
▸**denudation** (ˌdɛnjʊ'deɪʃən, ˌdiː-) NOUN ▸**de'nuder** NOUN

denumerable (dɪ'njuːmərəbᵊl) ADJECTIVE *Maths* capable of being put into a one-to-one correspondence with the positive integers; countable.
▸**de'numerably** ADVERB

denunciate (dɪ'nʌnsɪˌeɪt) VERB (*tr*) to condemn; denounce.
▷HISTORY C16: from Latin *dēnuntiāre;* see DENOUNCE
▸**de'nunciˌator** NOUN ▸**de'nunciatory** ADJECTIVE

denunciation (dɪˌnʌnsɪ'eɪʃən) NOUN [1] open condemnation; censure; denouncing. [2] *Law, obsolete* a charge or accusation of crime made by an individual before a public prosecutor or tribunal. [3] a formal announcement of the termination of a treaty. [4] *Archaic* an announcement in the form of an impending threat or warning.

Denver ('dɛnvə) NOUN a city in central Colorado: the state capital. Pop.: 554 636 (2000).

Denver boot NOUN a slang name for **wheel clamp.**
▷HISTORY C20: from DENVER, Colorado, where the device was first used

deny (dɪ'naɪ) VERB **-nies, -nying, -nied.** (*tr*) [1] to declare (an assertion, statement, etc.) to be untrue: *he denied that he had killed her.* [2] to reject as false; refuse to accept or believe. [3] to withhold; refuse to give. [4] to refuse to fulfil the requests or expectations of: *it is hard to deny a child.* [5] to refuse to acknowledge or recognize; disown; disavow: *the baron denied his wicked son.* [6] to refuse (oneself) things desired.
▷HISTORY C13: from Old French *denier,* from Latin *dēnegāre,* from *negāre*

deoch-an-doruis ('djɒxən'dɒrɪs, dɒx-) NOUN *Scot* a parting drink or stirrup cup. Also: **doch-an-doris.**
▷HISTORY Scottish Gaelic: drink at the door

deodand ('diːəʊˌdænd) NOUN *English law* (formerly) a thing that had caused a person's death and was forfeited to the crown for a charitable purpose: abolished 1862.
▷HISTORY C16: from Anglo-French *deodande,* from Medieval Latin *deōdandum,* from Latin *Deō dandum* (something) to be given to God, from *deus* god + *dare* to give

deodar ('diːəʊˌdɑː) NOUN [1] a Himalayan cedar, *Cedrus deodara,* with drooping branches. [2] the durable fragrant highly valued wood of this tree.
▷HISTORY C19: from Hindi *deodār,* from Sanskrit *devadāru,* literally: wood of the gods, from *deva* god + *dāru* wood

deodorant (diː'əʊdərənt) NOUN [1] **a** a substance applied to the body to suppress or mask the odour of perspiration or other body odours. **b** (*as modifier*): *a deodorant spray.* Compare **antiperspirant.** [2] any substance for destroying or masking odours, such as liquid sprayed into the air.

deodorize *or* **deodorise** (diː'əʊdəˌraɪz) VERB (*tr*) to remove, disguise, or absorb the odour of, esp when unpleasant.
▸**deˌodori'zation** *or* **deˌodori'sation** NOUN ▸**de'odorˌizer** *or* **de'odorˌiser** NOUN

Deo gratias *Latin* ('deɪəʊ 'grɑːtɪəs) thanks be to God. Abbreviation: **DG.**

deontic (diː'ɒntɪk) ADJECTIVE *Logic* **a** of or relating to such ethical concepts as obligation and permissibility. **b** designating the branch of modal logic that deals with the formalization of these concepts.
▷HISTORY C19: from Greek *deon* duty, from impersonal *dei* it behoves, it is binding

deontological (dɪˌɒntə'lɒdʒɪkᵊl) ADJECTIVE *Philosophy* (of an ethical theory) regarding obligation as deriving from reason or as residing primarily in certain specific rules of conduct rather than in the maximization of some good.

deontology (ˌdiːɒn'tɒlədʒɪ) NOUN the branch of ethics dealing with duty, moral obligation, and moral commitment.
▷HISTORY C19: from Greek *deon* duty (see DEONTIC) + -LOGY
▸**ˌdeon'tologist** NOUN

Deo volente *Latin* ('deɪəʊ vɒ'lɛntɪ) God willing. Abbreviation: **DV.**

deoxidize *or* **deoxidise** (diː'ɒksɪˌdaɪz) VERB [1] (*tr*) **a** to remove oxygen atoms from (a compound, molecule, etc.). **b** another word for **deoxygenate.** [2] another word for **reduce** (sense 12).
▸**deˌoxidi'zation** *or* **deˌoxidi'sation** NOUN ▸**de'oxiˌdizer** *or* **de'oxiˌdiser** NOUN

deoxy- *or* **desoxy-** COMBINING FORM indicating the presence of less oxygen than in a specified related compound: *deoxyribonucleic acid.*

deoxycorticosterone (diːˌɒksɪˌkɔːtɪkəʊ'stɪərəʊn) *or* **deoxycortone** (diːˌɒksɪ'kɔːtəʊn) NOUN a corticosteroid hormone important in maintaining sodium and water balance in the body.

deoxygenate (diː'ɒksɪdʒɪˌneɪt), **deoxygenize,** *or* **deoxygenise** (diː'ɒksɪdʒɪˌnaɪz) VERB (*tr*) to remove oxygen from (water, air, etc.).
▸**deˌoxygen'ation** NOUN

deoxyribonuclease (diːˌɒksɪˌraɪbəʊ'njuːklɪeɪz) NOUN the full name for **DNAase.**

deoxyribonucleic acid (diːˌɒksɪˌraɪbəʊnjuː'kleɪɪk) *or* **desoxyribonucleic acid** NOUN the full name for **DNA.**

deoxyribose (diːˌɒksɪ'raɪbəʊs, -bəʊz) *or* **desoxyribose** (dɛsˌɒksɪ'raɪbəʊs, -bəʊz) NOUN a pentose sugar obtained by the hydrolysis of DNA. Formula: $C_5H_{10}O_4$.

dep. ABBREVIATION FOR: [1] departs. [2] departure. [3] deposit. [4] depot. [5] deputy.

dépanneur (ˌdɛpə'nɜː) NOUN *Canadian* (in Quebec) a convenience store.
▷HISTORY from Canadian French

depart (dɪ'pɑːt) VERB (*mainly intr*) [1] to go away; leave. [2] to start out; set forth. [3] (usually foll by *from*) to deviate; differ; vary: *to depart from normal procedure.* [4] (*tr*) to quit (archaic, except in the phrase **depart this life**).
▷HISTORY C13: from Old French *departir,* from DE- + *partir* to go away, divide, from Latin *partīrī* to divide, distribute, from *pars* a part

departed (dɪ'pɑːtɪd) ADJECTIVE *Euphemistic* **a** dead; deceased. **b** (*as singular or collective noun;* preceded by *the*): *the departed.*

department (dɪ'pɑːtmənt) NOUN [1] a specialized division of a large concern, such as a business, store, or university: *the geography department.* [2] a major subdivision or branch of the administration of a government. [3] a branch or subdivision of learning: *physics is a department of science.* [4] a territorial and administrative division in several countries, such as France. [5] *Informal* a specialized sphere of knowledge, skill, or activity: *wine-making is my wife's department.*
▷HISTORY C18: from French *département,* from *départir* to divide; see DEPART
▸**departmental** (ˌdiːpɑːt'mɛntᵊl) ADJECTIVE
▸**ˌdepart'mentally** ADVERB

département (*French* departəmɑ̃) NOUN (in France) a major subdivision or branch of the administration of the government.
▷HISTORY C18: from *départir* to divide; see DEPART

departmentalism (ˌdiːpɑːt'mɛntᵊˌlɪzəm) NOUN division into departments, esp when resulting in impaired efficiency.

departmentalize *or* **departmentalise** (ˌdiːpɑːt'mɛntᵊˌlaɪz) VERB (*tr*) to organize into departments, esp excessively.
▸**ˌdepartˌmentali'zation** *or* **ˌdepartˌmentali'sation** NOUN

department store NOUN a large shop divided

into departments selling a great many kinds of goods.

departure (dɪˈpɑːtʃə) NOUN [1] the act or an instance of departing. [2] a deviation or variation from previous custom; divergence. [3] a project, course of action, venture, etc.: *selling is a new departure for him.* [4] *Nautical* **a** the net distance travelled due east or west by a vessel. **b** Also called: **point of departure.** the latitude and longitude of the point from which a vessel calculates dead reckoning. [5] a euphemistic word for **death.**

depasture (diːˈpɑːstʃə) VERB [1] to graze or denude by grazing (a pasture, esp a meadow specially grown for the purpose). [2] (*tr*) to pasture (cattle or sheep).

depend (dɪˈpɛnd) VERB (*intr*) [1] (foll by *on* or *upon*) to put trust (in); rely (on); be sure (of). [2] (usually foll by *on* or *upon;* often with *it* as subject) to be influenced or determined (by); be resultant (from): *whether you come or not depends on what father says; it all depends on you.* [3] (foll by *on* or *upon*) to rely (on) for income, support, etc. [4] (foll by *from*) *Rare* to hang down; be suspended. [5] to be undecided or pending.
▷HISTORY C15: from Old French *dependre,* from Latin *dēpendēre* to hang from, from DE- + *pendēre* to hang

dependable (dɪˈpɛndəbᵊl) ADJECTIVE able to be depended on; reliable; trustworthy.
▸**deˌpendaˈbility** *or* **deˈpendableness** NOUN ▸**deˈpendably** ADVERB

dependant (dɪˈpɛndənt) NOUN a person who depends on another person, organization, etc., for support, aid, or sustenance, esp financial support.

> **Language note** Avoid confusion with **dependent.**

dependence *or sometimes US* **dependance** (dɪˈpɛndəns) NOUN [1] the state or fact of being dependent, esp for support or help. [2] reliance; trust; confidence. [3] *Rare* an object or person relied upon.

dependency *or sometimes US* **dependancy** (dɪˈpɛndənsɪ) NOUN, *plural* **-cies.** [1] a territory subject to a state on which it does not border. [2] a dependent or subordinate person or thing. [3] *Psychol* overreliance by a person on another person or on a drug, etc. [4] another word for **dependence.**

dependent *or sometimes US* **dependant** (dɪˈpɛndənt) ADJECTIVE [1] depending on a person or thing for aid, support, life, etc. [2] (*postpositive;* foll by *on* or *upon*) influenced or conditioned (by); contingent (on). [3] subordinate; subject: *a dependent prince.* [4] *Obsolete* hanging down. [5] *Maths* **a** (of a variable) having a value depending on that assumed by a related independent variable. **b** (of a linear equation) having every solution as a solution of one or more given linear equations. ◆ NOUN [6] *Grammar* an element in a phrase or clause that is not the governor. [7] a variant spelling (esp US) of **dependant.**
▸**deˈpendently** ADVERB

> **Language note** Avoid confusion with **dependant.**

dependent clause NOUN *Grammar* another term for **subordinate clause.**

dependent variable NOUN [1] a variable in a mathematical equation or statement whose value depends on that taken on by the independent variable: *in "y = f(x)", "y" is the dependent variable.* [2] *Psychol, statistics* the variable measured by the experimenter. It is controlled by the value of the independent variable, of which it is an index.

depersonalization *or* **depersonalisation** (dɪˌpɜːsnᵊlaɪˈzeɪʃən) NOUN [1] the act or an instance of depersonalizing. [2] *Psychiatry* an abnormal state of consciousness in which the subject feels unreal and detached from himself and the world.

depersonalize *or* **depersonalise** (dɪˈpɜːsnᵊˌlaɪz) VERB (*tr*) [1] to deprive (a person, organization, system, etc.) of individual or personal qualities; render impersonal. [2] to cause (someone) to lose his sense of personal identity.
▷HISTORY C19: from DE- + PERSONAL + -IZE

depict (dɪˈpɪkt) VERB (*tr*) [1] to represent by or as by drawing, sculpture, painting, etc.; delineate; portray. [2] to represent in words; describe.
▷HISTORY C17: from Latin *dēpingere,* from *pingere* to paint
▸**deˈpicter** *or* **deˈpictor** NOUN ▸**deˈpiction** NOUN ▸**deˈpictive** ADJECTIVE

depicture (dɪˈpɪktʃə) VERB a less common word for **depict.**

depilate (ˈdɛpɪˌleɪt) VERB (*tr*) to remove the hair from.
▷HISTORY C16: from Latin *dēpilāre,* from *pilāre* to make bald, from *pilus* hair
▸ˌ**depiˈlation** NOUN ▸ˈ**depiˌlator** NOUN

depilatory (dɪˈpɪlətərɪ, -trɪ) ADJECTIVE [1] able or serving to remove hair. ◆ NOUN, *plural* **-ries.** [2] a chemical that is used to remove hair from the body.

deplane (diːˈpleɪn) VERB (*intr*) *Chiefly US and Canadian* to disembark from an aeroplane.
▷HISTORY C20: from DE- + PLANE[1]

deplete (dɪˈpliːt) VERB (*tr*) [1] to use up (supplies, money, energy, etc.); reduce or exhaust. [2] to empty entirely or partially. [3] *Med* to empty or reduce the fluid contents of (an organ or vessel).
▷HISTORY C19: from Latin *dēplēre* to empty out, from DE- + *plēre* to fill
▸**deˈpletable** ADJECTIVE ▸**deˈpletion** NOUN ▸**deˈpletive** *or* **deˈpletory** ADJECTIVE

depleted uranium NOUN *Chem* uranium containing a smaller proportion of the isotope uranium–235 than is present in the natural form of uranium; used in anti-tank weapons and other armaments.

depletion layer NOUN *Electronics* a region at the interface between dissimilar zones of conductivity in a semiconductor, in which there are few charge carriers.

deplorable (dɪˈplɔːrəbᵊl) ADJECTIVE [1] lamentable: *a deplorable lack of taste.* [2] worthy of censure or reproach; very bad: *deplorable behaviour.*
▸**deˈplorableness** *or* **deˌploraˈbility** NOUN ▸**deˈplorably** ADVERB

deplore (dɪˈplɔː) VERB (*tr*) [1] to express or feel sorrow about; lament; regret. [2] to express or feel strong disapproval of; censure.
▷HISTORY C16: from Old French *deplorer,* from Latin *dēplōrāre* to weep bitterly, from *plōrāre* to weep, lament
▸**deˈplorer** NOUN ▸**deˈploringly** ADVERB

deploy (dɪˈplɔɪ) VERB *Chiefly military* [1] to adopt or cause to adopt a battle formation, esp from a narrow front formation. [2] (*tr*) to redistribute (forces) to or within a given area.
▷HISTORY C18: from French *déployer,* from Latin *displicāre* to unfold; see DISPLAY
▸**deˈployment** NOUN

deplume (diːˈpluːm) VERB (*tr*) [1] to deprive of feathers; pluck. [2] to deprive of honour, position, wealth, etc.
▸ˌ**depluˈmation** NOUN

depolarize *or* **depolarise** (diːˈpəʊləˌraɪz) VERB to undergo or cause to undergo a loss of polarity or polarization.
▸**deˌpolariˈzation** *or* **deˌpolariˈsation** NOUN ▸**deˈpolarˌizer** *or* **deˈpolarˌiser** NOUN

depoliticize *or* **depoliticise** (ˌdiːpəˈlɪtɪˌsaɪz) VERB (*tr*) to deprive of a political nature; render apolitical: *two years on the committee totally depoliticized him.*

depolymerize *or* **depolymerise** (diːˈpɒlɪməˌraɪz) VERB to break (a polymer) into constituent monomers or (of a polymer) to decompose in this way.
▸**deˌpolymeriˈzation** *or* **deˌpolymeriˈsation** NOUN

depone (dɪˈpəʊn) VERB *Law, chiefly Scots* to declare (something) under oath; testify; depose.
▷HISTORY C16: from Latin *dēpōnere* to put down, from DE- + *pōnere* to put, place

deponent (dɪˈpəʊnənt) ADJECTIVE [1] *Grammar* (of a verb, esp in Latin) having the inflectional endings of a passive verb but the meaning of an active verb. ◆ NOUN [2] *Grammar* a deponent verb. [3] *Law* **a** a person who makes an affidavit. **b** a person, esp a witness, who makes a deposition.
▷HISTORY C16: from Latin *dēpōnēns* putting aside, putting down, from *dēpōnere* to put down, DEPONE

depopulate (dɪˈpɒpjʊˌleɪt) VERB to be or cause to be reduced in population.
▸**deˌpopuˈlation** NOUN

deport (dɪˈpɔːt) VERB (*tr*) [1] to remove (an alien) forcibly from a country; expel. [2] to carry (an inhabitant) forcibly away from his homeland; transport; exile; banish. [3] to conduct, hold, or behave (oneself) in a specified manner.
▷HISTORY C15: from French *déporter,* from Latin *dēportāre* to carry away, banish, from DE- + *portāre* to carry
▸**deˈportable** ADJECTIVE

deportation (ˌdiːpɔːˈteɪʃən) NOUN [1] the act of expelling an alien from a country; expulsion. [2] the act of transporting someone from his country; banishment.

deportee (ˌdiːpɔːˈtiː) NOUN a person deported or awaiting deportation.

deportment (dɪˈpɔːtmənt) NOUN the manner in which a person behaves, esp in physical bearing: *military deportment.*
▷HISTORY C17: from French *déportement,* from Old French *deporter* to conduct (oneself); see DEPORT

deposal (dɪˈpəʊzᵊl) NOUN another word for **deposition** (sense 2).

depose (dɪˈpəʊz) VERB [1] (*tr*) to remove from an office or position, esp one of power or rank. [2] *Law* to testify or give (evidence, etc.) on oath, esp when taken down in writing; make a deposition.
▷HISTORY C13: from Old French *deposer* to put away, put down, from Late Latin *dēpōnere* to depose from office, from Latin: to put aside; see DEPONE
▸**deˈposable** ADJECTIVE ▸**deˈposer** NOUN

deposit (dɪˈpɒzɪt) VERB (*tr*) [1] to put or set down, esp carefully or in a proper place; place. [2] to entrust for safekeeping; consign. [3] to place (money) in a bank or similar institution in order to earn interest or for safekeeping. [4] to give (money) in part payment or as security. [5] to lay down naturally; cause to settle: *the river deposits silt.* ◆ NOUN [6] **a** an instance of entrusting money or valuables to a bank or similar institution. **b** the money or valuables so entrusted. [7] money given in part payment or as security, as when goods are bought on hire-purchase. See also **down payment.** [8] a consideration, esp money, given temporarily as security against loss of or damage to something borrowed or hired. [9] an accumulation of sediments, mineral ores, coal, etc. [10] any deposited material, such as a sediment or a precipitate that has settled out of solution. [11] a coating produced on a surface, esp a layer of metal formed by electrolysis. [12] a depository or storehouse. [13] **on deposit.** payable as the first instalment, as when buying on hire-purchase.
▷HISTORY C17: from Medieval Latin *dēpositāre,* from Latin *dēpositus* put down

deposit account NOUN *Brit* a bank account that earns interest and usually requires notice of withdrawal.

depositary (dɪˈpɒzɪtərɪ, -trɪ) NOUN, *plural* **-taries.** [1] a person or group to whom something is entrusted for safety or preservation. [2] a variant spelling of **depository** (sense 1).

deposition (ˌdɛpəˈzɪʃən, ˌdiːpə-) NOUN [1] *Law* **a** the giving of testimony on oath. **b** the testimony so given. **c** the sworn statement of a witness used in court in his absence. [2] the act or instance of deposing. [3] the act or an instance of depositing. [4] something that is deposited; deposit.
▷HISTORY C14: from Late Latin *dēpositiō* a laying down, disposal, burying, testimony

Deposition (ˌdɛpəˈzɪʃən, ˌdiːpə-) NOUN the taking down of Christ's body from the Cross or a representation of this.

depositor (dɪˈpɒzɪtə) NOUN a person who places or has money on deposit in a bank or similar organization.

depository (dɪˈpɒzɪtərɪ, -trɪ) NOUN, *plural* **-ries.** [1] a store, such as a warehouse, for furniture, valuables, etc.; repository. [2] a variant spelling of **depositary** (sense 1).
▷HISTORY C17 (in the sense: place of a deposit): from Medieval Latin *dēpositōrium;* C18 (in the sense: depositary): see DEPOSIT, -ORY[1]

depot (ˈdɛpəʊ; *US and Canadian* ˈdiːpəʊ) NOUN [1] a storehouse or warehouse. [2] *Military* **a** a store for supplies. **b** a training and holding centre for recruits and replacements. [3] *Chiefly Brit* a building used for the storage and servicing of buses or railway

engines. [4] *US and Canadian* **a** a bus or railway station. **b** (*as modifier*): *a depot manager*. ◆ ADJECTIVE [5] (of a drug or drug dose) designed for gradual release from the site of an injection so as to act over a long period.
▷HISTORY C18: from French *dépôt*, from Latin *dēpositum* a deposit, trust

deprave (dɪ'preɪv) VERB (*tr*) [1] to make morally bad; corrupt; vitiate. [2] *Obsolete* to defame; slander.
▷HISTORY C14: from Latin *dēprāvāre* to distort, corrupt, from DE- + *prāvus* crooked
▸**depravation** (ˌdɛprə'veɪʃən) NOUN ▸**de'praver** NOUN

depraved (dɪ'preɪvd) ADJECTIVE morally bad or debased; corrupt; perverted.
▸**depravedness** (dɪ'preɪvɪdnɪs) NOUN

depravity (dɪ'prævɪtɪ) NOUN, *plural* **-ties**. the state or an instance of moral corruption.

deprecate ('dɛprɪˌkeɪt) VERB (*tr*) [1] to express disapproval of; protest against. [2] to depreciate (a person, someone's character, etc.); belittle. [3] *Archaic* to try to ward off by prayer.
▷HISTORY C17: from Latin *dēprecārī* to avert, ward off by entreaty, from DE- + *precārī* to PRAY
▸**'depreˌcating** ADJECTIVE ▸**'depreˌcatingly** ADVERB ▸**ˌdepre'cation** NOUN ▸**'deprecative** ADJECTIVE ▸**'deprecatively** ADVERB ▸**'depreˌcator** NOUN

Language note Avoid confusion with **depreciate**.

deprecatory ('dɛprɪkətərɪ) ADJECTIVE [1] expressing disapproval; protesting. [2] expressing apology; apologetic.
▸**'deprecatorily** ADVERB

depreciable (dɪ'priːʃəb^{ə}l) ADJECTIVE [1] *US* able to be depreciated for tax deduction. [2] liable to depreciation.

depreciate (dɪ'priːʃɪˌeɪt) VERB [1] to reduce or decline in value or price. [2] (*tr*) to lessen the value of by derision, criticism, etc.; disparage.
▷HISTORY C15: from Late Latin *dēpretiāre* to lower the price of, from Latin DE- + *pretium* PRICE
▸**de'preciˌatingly** ADVERB ▸**de'preciˌator** NOUN ▸**depreciatory** (dɪ'priːʃɪətərɪ, -trɪ) *or* **de'preciative** ADJECTIVE

Language note Avoid confusion with **deprecate**.

depreciation (dɪˌpriːʃɪ'eɪʃən) NOUN [1] *Accounting* **a** the reduction in value of a fixed asset due to use, obsolescence, etc. **b** the amount deducted from gross profit to allow for such reduction in value. [2] *Accounting* a modified amount permitted for purposes of tax deduction. [3] the act or an instance of depreciating or belittling; disparagement. [4] a decrease in the exchange value of currency against gold or other currencies brought about by excess supply of that currency under conditions of fluctuating exchange rates. Compare **devaluation** (sense 1).

depredate ('dɛprɪˌdeɪt) VERB (*tr*) *Rare* to plunder or destroy; pillage.
▷HISTORY C17: from Late Latin *dēpraedārī* to ravage, from Latin DE- + *praeda* booty; see PREY
▸**'depreˌdator** NOUN ▸**depredatory** ('dɛprɪˌdeɪtərɪ, dɪ'prɛdɪtərɪ, -trɪ) ADJECTIVE

depredation (ˌdɛprɪ'deɪʃən) NOUN the act or an instance of plundering; robbery; pillage.

depress (dɪ'prɛs) VERB (*tr*) [1] to lower in spirits; make gloomy; deject. [2] to weaken or lower the force, vigour, or energy of. [3] to lower prices of (securities or a security market). [4] to press or push down. [5] to lower the pitch of (a musical sound). [6] *Obsolete* to suppress or subjugate.
▷HISTORY C14: from Old French *depresser*, from Latin *dēprimere* from DE- + *premere* to PRESS[1]
▸**de'pressible** ADJECTIVE

depressant (dɪ'prɛs^{ə}nt) ADJECTIVE [1] *Med* able to diminish or reduce nervous or functional activity. [2] causing gloom or dejection; depressing. ◆ NOUN [3] a depressant drug.

depressed (dɪ'prɛst) ADJECTIVE [1] low in spirits; downcast; despondent. [2] lower than the surrounding surface. [3] pressed down or flattened. [4] Also: **distressed.** characterized by relative economic hardship, such as unemployment: *a depressed area*. [5] lowered in force, intensity, or amount. [6] (of plant parts) flattened as though pressed from above. [7] *Zoology* flattened from top to bottom: *the depressed bill of the spoonbill*.

depressing (dɪ'prɛsɪŋ) ADJECTIVE causing a feeling of dejection or low spirits.
▸**de'pressingly** ADVERB

depression (dɪ'prɛʃən) NOUN [1] the act of depressing or state of being depressed. [2] a depressed or sunken place or area. [3] a mental disorder characterized by extreme gloom, feelings of inadequacy, and inability to concentrate. [4] *Pathol* an abnormal lowering of the rate of any physiological activity or function, such as respiration. [5] an economic condition characterized by substantial and protracted unemployment, low output and investment, etc.; slump. [6] Also called: **cyclone, low.** *Meteorol* a large body of rotating and rising air below normal atmospheric pressure, which often brings rain. [7] (esp in surveying and astronomy) the angular distance of an object, celestial body, etc., below the horizontal plane through the point of observation. Compare **elevation** (sense 11).

Depression (dɪ'prɛʃən) NOUN (usually preceded by *the*) the worldwide economic depression of the early 1930s, when there was mass unemployment. Also called: **the Great Depression, the Slump.**

depressive (dɪ'prɛsɪv) ADJECTIVE [1] tending to depress; causing depression. [2] *Psychol* tending to be subject to periods of depression. See also **manic-depressive.**
▸**de'pressively** ADVERB ▸**de'pressiveness** NOUN

depressomotor (dɪˌprɛsəʊ'məʊtə) ADJECTIVE [1] *Physiol* retarding motor activity. ◆ NOUN [2] a depressomotor drug.

depressor (dɪ'prɛsə) NOUN [1] a person or thing that depresses. [2] any muscle that draws down a part. [3] *Med* an instrument used to press down or aside an organ or part: *a tongue depressor*. [4] Also called: **depressor nerve.** any nerve that when stimulated produces a fall in blood pressure by dilating the arteries or lowering the heartbeat.

depressurize *or* **depressurise** (dɪ'prɛʃəˌraɪz) VERB (*tr*) to reduce the pressure of a gas inside (a container or enclosed space), as in an aircraft cabin.
▸**deˌpressuri'zation** *or* **deˌpressuri'sation** NOUN

deprivation (ˌdɛprɪ'veɪʃən) NOUN [1] an act or instance of depriving. [2] the state of being deprived: *social deprivation; a cycle of deprivation and violence*.

deprive (dɪ'praɪv) VERB (*tr*) [1] (foll by *of*) to prevent from possessing or enjoying; dispossess (of). [2] *Archaic* to remove from rank or office; depose; demote.
▷HISTORY C14: from Old French *depriver*, from Medieval Latin *dēprīvāre*, from Latin DE- + *prīvāre* to deprive of, rob; see PRIVATE
▸**de'privable** ADJECTIVE ▸**de'prival** NOUN ▸**de'priver** NOUN

deprived (dɪ'praɪvd) ADJECTIVE lacking adequate food, shelter, education, etc.: *deprived inner-city areas*.

de profundis *Latin* (deɪ prɒ'fʊndɪs) ADVERB out of the depths of misery or dejection.
▷HISTORY from the first words of Psalm 130

deprogramme *or* **deprogram** (diː'prəʊgræm) VERB to free (someone) from the effects of indoctrination, esp by a religious cult or political group.

depside ('dɛpsaɪd, -sɪd) NOUN any ester formed by the condensation of the carboxyl group of one phenolic carboxylic acid with the hydroxyl group of another, found in plant cells.
▷HISTORY C20: *deps-*, from Greek *depsein* to knead + -IDE

dept ABBREVIATION FOR department.

Deptford ('dɛtfəd) NOUN a district in the Greater London borough of Lewisham, on the S bank of the River Thames: formerly the site of the Royal Naval dockyard.

depth (dɛpθ) NOUN [1] the extent, measurement, or distance downwards, backwards, or inwards. [2] the quality of being deep; deepness. [3] intensity or profundity of emotion or feeling. [4] profundity of moral character; penetration; sagacity; integrity. [5] complexity or abstruseness, as of thought or objects of thought. [6] intensity, as of silence, colour, etc. [7] lowness of pitch. [8] *Nautical* the distance from the top of a ship's keel to the top of a particular deck. [9] (*often plural*) a deep, far, inner, or remote part, such as an inaccessible region of a country. [10] (*often plural*) the deepest, most intense, or most severe part: *the depths of winter*. [11] (*usually plural*) a low moral state; demoralization: *how could you sink to such depths?* [12] (*often plural*) a vast space or abyss. [13] **beyond** *or* **out of one's depth. a** in water deeper than one is tall. **b** beyond the range of one's competence or understanding. [14] **in depth.** thoroughly or comprehensively. See also **in-depth.**
▷HISTORY C14: from *dep* DEEP + -TH[1]

depth charge *or* **bomb** NOUN a bomb used to attack submarines that explodes at a pre-set depth of water.

depth gauge NOUN a device attached to a drill bit to prevent the hole from exceeding a predetermined depth.

depth of field NOUN the range of distance in front of and behind an object focused by an optical instrument, such as a camera or microscope, within which other objects will also appear clear and sharply defined in the resulting image. Compare **depth of focus.**

depth of focus NOUN the amount by which the distance between the camera lens and the film can be altered without the resulting image appearing blurred. Compare **depth of field.**

depth psychology NOUN *Psychol* the study of unconscious motives and attitudes.

depurate ('dɛpjʊˌreɪt) VERB [1] to cleanse or purify or to be cleansed or purified. [2] *Obsolete* to promote the elimination of waste products from (the body).
▷HISTORY C17: from Medieval Latin *dēpūrāre*, from Latin DE- + *pūrāre* to purify; see PURE
▸**ˌdepu'ration** NOUN ▸**'depuˌrator** NOUN

depurative ('dɛpjʊˌreɪtɪv, -rətɪv) ADJECTIVE [1] used for or capable of depurating; purifying; purgative. ◆ NOUN [2] a depurative substance or agent.

deputation (ˌdɛpjʊ'teɪʃən) NOUN [1] the act of appointing a person or body of people to represent or act on behalf of others. [2] a person or, more often, a body of people so appointed; delegation.

depute VERB (dɪ'pjuːt) (*tr*) [1] to appoint as an agent, substitute, or representative. [2] to assign or transfer (authority, duties, etc.) to a deputy; delegate. ◆ NOUN ('dɛpjuːt) [3] *Scot* **a** a deputy. **b** (*as modifier; usually postpositive*): *sheriff depute*.
▷HISTORY C15: from Old French *deputer*, from Late Latin *dēputāre* to assign, allot, from Latin DE- + *putāre* to think, consider

deputize *or* **deputise** ('dɛpjʊˌtaɪz) VERB to appoint or act as deputy.

deputy ('dɛpjʊtɪ) NOUN, *plural* **-ties.** [1] **a** a person appointed to act on behalf of or represent another. **b** (*as modifier*): *the deputy chairman*. [2] a member of the legislative assembly or of the lower chamber of the legislature in various countries, such as France. [3] *Brit mining* another word for **fireman** (sense 4).
▷HISTORY C16: from Old French *depute*, from *deputer* to appoint; see DEPUTE

deputy minister NOUN (in Canada) the senior civil servant in a government department.

deracinate (dɪ'ræsɪˌneɪt) VERB (*tr*) [1] to pull up by or as if by the roots; uproot; extirpate. [2] to remove, as from a natural environment.
▷HISTORY C16: from Old French *desraciner*, from *des-* DIS-[1] + *racine* root, from Late Latin *rādīcīna* a little root, from Latin *rādīx* a root
▸**deˌraci'nation** NOUN

deraign *or* **darraign** (də'reɪn) VERB (*tr*) *Obsolete* [1] *Law* to contest (a claim, suit, etc.). [2] to arrange (soldiers) for battle.
▷HISTORY C13: from Old French *deraisnier* to defend, from Vulgar Latin *ratiōnāre* (unattested) to REASON
▸**de'raignment** *or* **dar'raignment** NOUN

derail (dɪ'reɪl) VERB [1] to go or cause to go off the rails, as a train, tram, etc. ◆ NOUN [2] Also called: **derailer.** *Chiefly US* a device designed to make rolling stock or locomotives leave the rails to avoid a collision or accident.
▸**de'railment** NOUN

derailleur (də'reɪljə) NOUN a mechanism for changing gear on bicycles, consisting of a device that lifts the driving chain from one sprocket wheel to another of different size.

▷HISTORY French *dérailleur* derailer

derange (dɪˈreɪndʒ) VERB (*tr*) 1 to disturb the order or arrangement of; throw into disorder; disarrange. 2 to disturb the action or operation of. 3 to make insane; drive mad.
▷HISTORY C18: from Old French *desrengier,* from *des-* DIS-¹ + *reng* row, order

derangement (dɪˈreɪndʒmənt) NOUN 1 the act of deranging or state of being deranged. 2 disorder or confusion. 3 *Psychiatry* a mental disorder or serious mental disturbance.

derate (diːˈreɪt) VERB (*tr*) *Brit* to assess the value of (some types of property, such as agricultural land) at a lower rate than others for local taxation.
▸**deˈrating** NOUN

deration (diːˈræʃən) VERB (*tr*) to end rationing of (food, petrol, etc.).

derby (ˈdɜːrbɪ) NOUN, *plural* **-bies.** the US and Canadian name for **bowler²**.

Derby¹ (ˈdɑːbɪ; *US* ˈdɜːrbɪ) NOUN 1 **the.** an annual horse race run at Epsom Downs, Surrey, since 1780: one of the English flat-racing classics. 2 any of various other horse races. 3 **local Derby.** a football match between two teams from the same area.
▷HISTORY C18: named after the twelfth Earl of *Derby* (died 1834), who founded the horse race at Epsom Downs in 1780

Derby² (ˈdɑːbɪ) NOUN 1 a city in central England, in Derby unitary authority, Derbyshire: engineering industries (esp aircraft engines and railway rolling stock); university (1991). Pop.: 223 836 (1991). 2 a unitary authority in central England, in Derbyshire. Pop.: 221 716 (2001 est.). Area: 78 sq. km (30 sq. miles). 3 a firm-textured pale-coloured type of cheese. 4 **sage Derby.** a green-and-white Derby cheese flavoured with sage.

Derbyshire (ˈdɑːbɪˌʃɪə, -ʃə) NOUN a county of N central England: contains the Peak District and several resorts with mineral springs: the geographical and ceremonial county includes the city of Derby, which became an independent unitary authority in 1997. Administrative centre: Matlock. Pop. (excluding Derby city): 734 581 (2001). Area (excluding Derby city): 2551 sq. km (985 sq. miles).

de re *Latin* (ˈdeɪ ˈreɪ) ADJECTIVE *Logic, philosophy* (of a belief, possibility, etc.) relating to the individual rather than to an expression, as the necessity of *the number of wonders of the world is prime* since that number, seven, is necessarily prime. Compare **de dicto.**
▷HISTORY literally: about the thing

derecognize *or* **derecognise** (diːˈrɛkəgˌnaɪz) VERB (*tr*) 1 to cease to recognize a trade union as having special negotiating rights within a company or industry. 2 to advise (a trade union) of such action.
▸ˌ**derecogˈnition** NOUN

deregister (diːˈrɛdʒɪstə) VERB to remove (oneself, a car, etc.) from a register.
▸ˌ**deregisˈtration** NOUN

deregulate (diːˈrɛgjʊˌleɪt) VERB (*tr*) to remove regulations or controls from.
▸**deˌreguˈlation** NOUN ▸**deˈregulator** NOUN ▸**deˈregulatory** ADJECTIVE

derelict (ˈdɛrɪlɪkt) ADJECTIVE 1 deserted or abandoned, as by an owner, occupant, etc. 2 falling into ruins; neglected; dilapidated. 3 neglectful of duty or obligation; remiss. ♦ NOUN 4 a person abandoned or neglected by society; a social outcast or vagrant. 5 property deserted or abandoned by an owner, occupant, etc. 6 a vessel abandoned at sea. 7 a person who is neglectful of duty or obligation.
▷HISTORY C17: from Latin *dērelictus* forsaken, from *dērelinquere* to abandon, from DE- + *relinquere* to leave

dereliction (ˌdɛrɪˈlɪkʃən) NOUN 1 deliberate, conscious, or wilful neglect (esp in the phrase **dereliction of duty**). 2 the act of abandoning or deserting or the state of being abandoned or deserted. 3 *Law* **a** accretion of dry land gained by the gradual receding of the sea or by a river changing its course. **b** the land thus left.

derequisition (diːˌrɛkwɪˈzɪʃən) VERB (*tr*) to release from military to civilian use.

derestrict (ˌdiːrɪˈstrɪkt) VERB (*tr*) to render or leave free from restriction, esp a road from speed limits.
▸ˌ**dereˈstriction** NOUN

Dergue (dɜːg) NOUN **the.** the socialist ruling body of Ethiopia, established in 1974.
▷HISTORY C20: from Amharic, literally, committee

deride (dɪˈraɪd) VERB (*tr*) to speak of or treat with contempt, mockery, or ridicule; scoff or jeer at.
▷HISTORY C16: from Latin *dērīdēre* to laugh to scorn, from DE- + *rīdēre* to laugh, smile
▸**deˈrider** NOUN ▸**deˈridingly** ADVERB

de rigueur *French* (də rigœr; *English* də rɪˈgɜː) ADJECTIVE required by etiquette or fashion.
▷HISTORY literally: of strictness

derisible (dɪˈrɪzɪbᵊl) ADJECTIVE subject to or deserving of derision; ridiculous.

derision (dɪˈrɪʒən) NOUN 1 the act of deriding; mockery; scorn. 2 an object of mockery or scorn.
▷HISTORY C15: from Late Latin *dērīsiō,* from Latin *dērīsus;* see DERIDE

derisive (dɪˈraɪsɪv, -zɪv) ADJECTIVE showing or characterized by derision; mocking; scornful.
▸**deˈrisively** ADVERB ▸**deˈrisiveness** NOUN

derisory (dɪˈraɪsərɪ, -zərɪ) ADJECTIVE 1 subject to or worthy of derision, esp because of being ridiculously small or inadequate. 2 another word for **derisive.**

derivation (ˌdɛrɪˈveɪʃən) NOUN 1 the act of deriving or state of being derived. 2 the source, origin, or descent of something, such as a word. 3 something derived; a derivative. 4 **a** the process of deducing a mathematical theorem, formula, etc., as a necessary consequence of a set of accepted statements. **b** this sequence of statements. **c** the operation of finding a derivative.
▸ˌ**deriˈvational** ADJECTIVE

derivative (dɪˈrɪvətɪv) ADJECTIVE 1 resulting from derivation; derived. 2 based on or making use of other sources; not original or primary. 3 copied from others, esp slavishly; plagiaristic. ♦ NOUN 4 a term, idea, etc., that is based on or derived from another in the same class. 5 a word derived from another word. 6 *Chem* a compound that is formed from, or can be regarded as formed from, a structurally related compound: *chloroform is a derivative of methane.* 7 *Maths* **a** Also called: **differential coefficient, first derivative.** the change of a function, f(x), with respect to an infinitesimally small change in the independent variable, x; the limit of $[f(a + \Delta x)-f(a)]/\Delta x$, at $x = a$, as the increment, Δx, tends to 0. Symbols: $df(x)/dx$, $f'(x)$, $Df(x)$: *the derivative of* x^n *is* nx^{n-1}. **b** the rate of change of one quantity with respect to another: *velocity is the derivative of distance with respect to time.* 8 *Finance* a financial instrument, such as a futures contract or option, the price of which is largely determined by the commodity, currency, share price, interest rate, etc., to which it is linked. 9 *Psychoanal* an activity that represents the expression of hidden impulses and desires by channelling them into socially acceptable forms.
▸**deˈrivatively** ADVERB

derive (dɪˈraɪv) VERB 1 (usually foll by *from*) to draw or be drawn (from) in source or origin; trace or be traced. 2 (*tr*) to obtain by reasoning; deduce; infer. 3 (*tr*) to trace the source or development of. 4 (usually foll by *from*) to produce or be produced (from) by a chemical reaction. 5 *Maths* to obtain (a function) by differentiation.
▷HISTORY C14: from Old French *deriver* to spring from, from Latin *dērīvāre* to draw off, from DE- + *rīvus* a stream
▸**deˈrivable** ADJECTIVE ▸**deˈriver** NOUN

derived fossil NOUN another name for **reworked fossil.**

derived unit NOUN a unit of measurement obtained by multiplication or division of the base units of a system without the introduction of numerical factors.

-derm NOUN COMBINING FORM indicating skin: *endoderm.*
▷HISTORY via French from Greek *derma* skin

derma¹ (ˈdɜːmə) NOUN another name for **corium.** Also: **derm** (dɜːm).
▷HISTORY C18: New Latin, from Greek: skin, from *derein* to skin

derma² (ˈdɜːmə) NOUN beef or fowl intestine used as a casing for certain dishes, esp kishke.
▷HISTORY from Yiddish *derme,* plural of *darm* intestine, from Old High German *daram;* related to Old English *thearm* gut, Old Norse *tharmr*

dermabrasion (ˌdɜːməˈbreɪʒən) NOUN a procedure in cosmetic surgery in which rough facial skin is removed by scrubbing.
▷HISTORY C20: from Greek *derma* skin + ABRASION

dermal (ˈdɜːməl) ADJECTIVE of or relating to the skin.

dermapteran (dɜːˈmæptərən) NOUN 1 any insect of the order *Dermaptera,* the earwigs. ♦ ADJECTIVE 2 of, relating to, or belonging to this order.
▷HISTORY C19: from Greek *derma* (see DERMA¹) + *pteron* wing

dermatitis (ˌdɜːməˈtaɪtɪs) NOUN inflammation of the skin.

dermato-, derma-, *or before a vowel* **dermat-, derm-** COMBINING FORM indicating skin: *dermatology; dermatome; dermal; dermatitis.*
▷HISTORY from Greek *derma* skin

dermatogen (dəˈmætədʒən, ˈdɜːməˌtəudʒən) NOUN *Botany* a meristem at the apex of stems and roots that gives rise to the epidermis.

dermatoglyphics (ˌdɜːmətəʊˈglɪfɪks) PLURAL NOUN 1 the lines forming a skin pattern, esp on the palms of the hands and soles of the feet. 2 (*functioning as singular*) the study of such skin patterns.
▷HISTORY C20: from DERMATO- + Greek *gluphē* a carving; see GLYPH

dermatoid (ˈdɜːməˌtɔɪd) ADJECTIVE resembling skin.

dermatology (ˌdɜːməˈtɒlədʒɪ) NOUN the branch of medicine concerned with the skin and its diseases.
▸**dermatological** (ˌdɜːmətəˈlɒdʒɪkᵊl) ADJECTIVE
▸ˌ**dermaˈtologist** NOUN

dermatome (ˈdɜːməˌtəʊm) NOUN 1 a surgical instrument for cutting thin slices of skin, esp for grafting. 2 the area of skin supplied by nerve fibres from a single posterior spinal root. 3 *Embryol* the part of a somite in a vertebrate embryo that gives rise to the dermis.
▸**dermatomic** (ˌdɜːməˈtɒmɪk) ADJECTIVE

dermatophyte (ˈdɜːmətəʊˌfaɪt) NOUN any parasitic fungus that affects the skin.
▸**dermatophytic** (ˌdɜːmətəʊˈfɪtɪk) ADJECTIVE

dermatophytosis (ˌdɜːmətəʊfaɪˈtəʊsɪs) NOUN a fungal infection of the skin, esp the feet. See **athlete's foot.**

dermatoplasty (ˈdɜːmətəʊˌplæstɪ) NOUN any surgical operation on the skin, esp skin grafting.
▸ˌ**dermatoˈplastic** ADJECTIVE

dermatosis (ˌdɜːməˈtəʊsɪs) NOUN, *plural* **-toses** (-ˈtəʊsiːz). any skin disease.

dermestid (ˌdɜːˈmɛstɪd) NOUN any beetle of the family *Dermestidae,* whose members are destructive at both larval and adult stages to a wide range of stored organic materials such as wool, fur, feathers, and meat. They include the bacon (*or* larder), cabinet, carpet, leather, and museum beetles.
▷HISTORY C19: from New Latin *dermestida,* from Greek *dermēstēs,* from *derma* skin + *esthiein* to eat

dermis (ˈdɜːmɪs) NOUN another name for **corium.**
▷HISTORY C19: New Latin, from EPIDERMIS
▸ˈ**dermic** ADJECTIVE

dermoid (ˈdɜːmɔɪd) ADJECTIVE 1 of or resembling skin. ♦ NOUN 2 a congenital cystic tumour whose walls are lined with epithelium.

dernier cri *French* (dɛrnje kri) NOUN **le** (lə). the latest fashion; the last word.
▷HISTORY literally: last cry

dero (ˈdɛrəʊ) NOUN, *plural* **deros.** a tramp or derelict.
▷HISTORY C20: shortened from DERELICT

derogate VERB (ˈdɛrəˌgeɪt) 1 (*intr;* foll by *from*) to cause to seem inferior or be in disrepute; detract. 2 (*intr;* foll by *from*) to deviate in standard or quality; degenerate. 3 (*tr*) to cause to seem inferior, etc.; disparage. 4 (*tr*) to curtail the application of (a law or regulation). ♦ ADJECTIVE (ˈdɛrəgɪt, -ˌgeɪt) 5 *Archaic* debased or degraded.
▷HISTORY C15: from Latin *dērogāre* to repeal some part of a law, modify it, from DE- + *rogāre* to ask, propose a law
▸ˈ**derogately** ADVERB ▸ˌ**deroˈgation** NOUN ▸**derogative** (dɪˈrɒgətɪv) ADJECTIVE ▸**deˈrogatively** ADVERB

derogatory (dɪˈrɒgətərɪ, -trɪ) ADJECTIVE tending or

intended to detract, disparage, or belittle; intentionally offensive.
▸**de'rogatorily** ADVERB ▸**de'rogatoriness** NOUN

derrick ('dɛrɪk) NOUN [1] a simple crane having lifting tackle slung from a boom. [2] the framework erected over an oil well to enable drill tubes to be raised and lowered. ◆ VERB [3] to raise or lower the jib of (a crane).
▹HISTORY C17 (in the sense: gallows): from *Derrick*, name of a celebrated hangman at Tyburn

derrière (ˌdɛrɪ'ɛə; *French* dɛrjɛr) NOUN a euphemistic word for **buttocks**.
▹HISTORY C18: literally: behind (prep), from Old French *deriere*, from Latin *dē retrō* from the back

derring-do ('dɛrɪŋ'duː) NOUN *Archaic or literary* a daring spirit or deed; boldness or bold action.
▹HISTORY C16: from Middle English *durring don* daring to do, from *durren* to dare + *don* to do

derringer *or* **deringer** ('dɛrɪndʒə) NOUN a short-barrelled pocket pistol of large calibre.
▹HISTORY C19: named after Henry *Deringer*, American gunsmith who invented it

derris ('dɛrɪs) NOUN any East Indian leguminous woody climbing plant of the genus *Derris*, esp *D. elliptica*, whose roots yield the compound rotenone.
▹HISTORY C19: New Latin, from Greek: covering, leather, from *deros* skin, hide, from *derein* to skin

derro ('dɛrəʊ) NOUN, *plural* **derros**. *Austral slang* a vagrant.
▹HISTORY from DERELICT

derry[1] ('dɛrɪ) NOUN, *plural* **-ries**. *Austral and NZ* **have a derry on.** to have a prejudice or grudge against.
▹HISTORY C19: probably from *derry down*, a refrain in some folk songs, alluding to the phrase *have a down on*; see DOWN[1]

derry[2] ('dɛrɪ) NOUN, *plural* **-ries**. *Slang* a derelict house, esp one used by tramps, drug addicts, etc.
▹HISTORY C20: shortened from DERELICT

Derry ('dɛrɪ) NOUN [1] a district in NW Northern Ireland, in Co. Londonderry. Pop.: 106 066 (2001). Area: 387 sq. km (149 sq. miles). [2] another name for **Londonderry**.

derv (dɜːv) NOUN a Brit name for **diesel oil** when used for road transport.
▹HISTORY C20: from *d(iesel) e(ngine) r(oad) v(ehicle)*

dervish ('dɜːvɪʃ) NOUN a member of any of various Muslim orders of ascetics, some of which (**whirling dervishes**) are noted for a frenzied, ecstatic, whirling dance.
▹HISTORY C16: from Turkish: beggar, from Persian *darvīsh* mendicant monk
▸**'dervish-ˌlike** ADJECTIVE

Derwent ('dɜːwənt) NOUN [1] a river in S Australia, in S Tasmania, flowing southeast to the Tasman Sea. Length: 172 km (107 miles). [2] a river in N central England, in N Derbyshire, flowing southeast to the River Trent. Length: 96 km (60 miles). [3] a river in N England, in Yorkshire, rising on the North York Moors and flowing south to the River Ouse. Length: 92 km (57 miles). [4] a river in NW England, in Cumbria, rising on the Borrowdale Fells and flowing north and west to the Irish Sea. Length: 54 km (34 miles).

Derwentwater ('dɜːwəntˌwɔːtə) NOUN a lake in NW England, in Cumbria in the Lake District. Area: about 8 sq. km (3 sq. miles).

DES (in Britain) ABBREVIATION FOR (former) Department of Education and Science.

desalinate (diː'sælɪˌneɪt), **desalinize,** *or* **desalinise** VERB (*tr*) to remove the salt from (esp from sea water). Also: **desalt** (diː'sɔːlt).

desalination (diːˌsælɪ'neɪʃən), **desalinization,** *or* **desalinisation** NOUN the process of removing salt, esp from sea water so that it can be used for drinking or irrigation.

desaturation (diːˌsætʃə'reɪʃən) NOUN *Physics* the addition of white light to a pure colour to produce a paler less saturated colour.

descale (ˌdiː'skeɪl) VERB (*tr*) to remove the hard deposit formed by chemicals in water from (a kettle, pipe, etc.).

descant NOUN ('dɛskænt, 'dɪs-) [1] Also called: **discant.** a decorative counterpoint added above a basic melody. [2] a comment, criticism, or discourse. ◆ ADJECTIVE ('dɛskænt, 'dɪs-) [3] Also: **discant.** of or pertaining to the highest member in common use of a family of musical instruments: *a descant recorder*. ◆ VERB (dɛs'kænt, dɪs-) (*intr*) [4] Also: **discant.** (often foll by *on* or *upon*) to compose or perform a descant (for a piece of music). [5] (often foll by *on* or *upon*) to discourse at length or make varied comments.
▹HISTORY C14: from Old Northern French, from Medieval Latin *discantus*, from Latin DIS-[1] + *cantus* song; see CHANT
▸**des'canter** NOUN

descend (dɪ'sɛnd) VERB (*mainly intr*) [1] (*also tr*) to move, pass, or go down (a hill, slope, staircase, etc.). [2] (of a hill, slope, or path) to lead or extend down; slope; incline. [3] to move to a lower level, pitch, etc.; fall. [4] (often foll by *from*) to be connected by a blood relationship (to a dead or extinct individual, race, species, etc.). [5] to be passed on by parents or ancestors; be inherited. [6] to sink or come down in morals or behaviour; lower oneself. [7] (often foll by *on* or *upon*) to arrive or attack in a sudden or overwhelming way: *their relatives descended upon them last week*. [8] (of the sun, moon, etc.) to move towards the horizon.
▹HISTORY C13: from Old French *descendre*, from Latin *dēscendere*, from DE- + *scandere* to climb; see SCAN
▸**des'cendable** ADJECTIVE

descendant (dɪ'sɛndənt) NOUN [1] a person, animal, or plant when described as descended from an individual, race, species, etc. [2] something that derives or is descended from an earlier form. ◆ ADJECTIVE [3] a variant spelling of **descendent**.

Descendant (dɪ'sɛndənt) NOUN *Astrology* the point on the ecliptic lying directly opposite the Ascendant.

descendent (dɪ'sɛndənt) ADJECTIVE [1] coming or going downwards; descending. [2] deriving by descent, as from an ancestor.

descender (dɪ'sɛndə) NOUN [1] a person or thing that descends. [2] *Printing* the portion of a letter, such as j, p, or y, below the level of the base of an x or n.

descendeur (*French* desɑ̃dœr) NOUN *Mountaineering* a shaped metal piece through which the rope can be fed: used to control the rate of descent in abseiling. Also called: **descender.**
▹HISTORY C20

descendible *or* **descendable** (dɪ'sɛndəbᵊl) ADJECTIVE *Law* capable of being inherited.

descent (dɪ'sɛnt) NOUN [1] the act of descending. [2] a downward slope or inclination. [3] a passage, path, or way leading downwards. [4] derivation from an ancestor or ancestral group; lineage. [5] (in genealogy) a generation in a particular lineage. [6] a decline or degeneration. [7] a movement or passage in degree or state from higher to lower. [8] (often foll by *on*) a sudden and overwhelming arrival or attack. [9] *Property law* (formerly) the transmission of real property to the heir on an intestacy.

deschool (ˌdiː'skuːl) VERB (*tr*) to separate education from the institution of school and operate through the pupil's life experience as opposed to a set curriculum.

descramble (diː'skræmbᵊl) VERB to restore (a scrambled signal) to an intelligible form, esp automatically by the use of electronic devices.
▸**ˌde'scrambler** NOUN

describe (dɪ'skraɪb) VERB (*tr*) [1] to give an account or representation of in words. [2] to pronounce or label: *he has been described as a genius*. [3] to draw a line or figure, such as a circle.
▹HISTORY C15: from Latin *dēscrībere* to copy off, write out, delineate, from DE- + *scrībere* to write
▸**de'scribable** ADJECTIVE ▸**de'scriber** NOUN

description (dɪ'skrɪpʃən) NOUN [1] a statement or account that describes; representation in words. [2] the act, process, or technique of describing. [3] sort, kind, or variety: *reptiles of every description*. [4] *Geometry* the act of drawing a line or figure, such as an arc. [5] *Philosophy* a noun phrase containing a predicate that may replace a name as the subject of a sentence.

descriptive (dɪ'skrɪptɪv) ADJECTIVE [1] characterized by or containing description; serving to describe. [2] *Grammar* (of an adjective) serving to describe the referent of the noun modified, as for example the adjective *brown* as contrasted with *my* and *former*. [3] relating to or based upon description or classification rather than explanation or prescription: *descriptive linguistics*.
▸**de'scriptively** ADVERB ▸**de'scriptiveness** NOUN

descriptive geometry NOUN the study of the projection of three-dimensional figures onto a plane surface.

descriptive linguistics NOUN (*functioning as singular*) the study of the description of the internal phonological, grammatical, and semantic structures of languages at given points in time without reference to their histories or to one another. Also called: **synchronic linguistics.** Compare **historical linguistics.**

descriptive metaphysics NOUN (*functioning as singular*) the philosophical study of the structure of how we think about the world.

descriptive notation NOUN *Chess* a method of denoting the squares on the chessboard in which each player names the files from the pieces that stand on them at the opening and numbers the ranks away from himself. Compare **algebraic notation.**

descriptive statistics NOUN (*functioning as singular*) the use of statistics to describe a set of known data in a clear and concise manner, as in terms of its mean and variance, or diagramatically, as by a histogram. Compare **statistical inference.**

descriptivism (dɪ'skrɪptɪˌvɪzəm) NOUN *Ethics* the theory that moral utterances have a truth value. Compare **prescriptivism, emotivism.**
▸**de'scriptiˌvist** ADJECTIVE

descry (dɪ'skraɪ) VERB **-scries, -scrying, -scried.** (*tr*) [1] to discern or make out; catch sight of. [2] to discover by looking carefully; detect.
▹HISTORY C14: from Old French *descrier* to proclaim, DECRY
▸**de'scrier** NOUN

desecrate ('dɛsɪˌkreɪt) VERB (*tr*) [1] to violate or outrage the sacred character of (an object or place) by destructive, blasphemous, or sacrilegious action. [2] to remove the consecration from (a person, object, building, etc.); deconsecrate.
▹HISTORY C17: from DE- + CONSECRATE
▸**'deseˌcrator** *or* **'deseˌcrater** NOUN ▸**ˌdese'cration** NOUN

desegregate (diː'sɛgrɪˌgeɪt) VERB to end racial segregation in (a school or other public institution).
▸**ˌdesegre'gation** NOUN ▸**ˌdesegre'gationist** NOUN, ADJECTIVE

deselect (ˌdiːsɪ'lɛkt) VERB (*tr*) [1] *Brit politics* (of a constituency organization) to refuse to select (an existing MP) for re-election. [2] *US* to discharge (a trainee) during the period of training.
▸**ˌdese'lection** NOUN

desensitize *or* **desensitise** (diː'sɛnsɪˌtaɪz) VERB (*tr*) [1] to render insensitive or less sensitive: *the patient was desensitized to the allergen; to desensitize photographic film*. [2] *Psychol* to decrease the abnormal fear in (a person) of a situation or object, by exposing him to it either in reality or in his imagination.
▸**deˌsensiti'zation** *or* **deˌsensiti'sation** NOUN ▸**de'sensiˌtizer** *or* **de'sensiˌtiser** NOUN

desert[1] ('dɛzət) NOUN [1] a region that is devoid or almost devoid of vegetation, esp because of low rainfall. [2] an uncultivated uninhabited region. [3] a place which lacks some desirable feature or quality: *a cultural desert*. [4] (*modifier*) of, relating to, or like a desert; infertile or desolate.
▹HISTORY C13: from Old French, from Church Latin *dēsertum*, from Latin *dēserere* to abandon, literally: to sever one's links with, from DE- + *serere* to bind together

desert[2] (dɪ'zɜːt) VERB [1] (*tr*) to leave or abandon (a person, place, etc.) without intending to return, esp in violation of a duty, promise, or obligation. [2] *Military* to abscond from (a post or duty) with no intention of returning. [3] (*tr*) to fail (someone) in time of need: *his good humour temporarily deserted him*. [4] (*tr*) *Scots law* to give up or postpone (a case or charge).
▹HISTORY C15: from French *déserter*, from Late Latin *dēsertāre*, from Latin *dēserere* to forsake; see DESERT[1]
▸**de'serter** NOUN ▸**de'serted** ADJECTIVE

desert[3] (dɪ'zɜːt) NOUN [1] (*often plural*) something that is deserved or merited; just reward or punishment. [2] the state of deserving a reward or punishment. [3] virtue or merit.

▷HISTORY C13: from Old French *deserte,* from *deservir* to DESERVE

desert boots PLURAL NOUN ankle-high suede boots with laces and soft soles, worn informally by men and women.

desert cooler NOUN (in India) a cooling device in which air is driven by an electric fan through wet grass.

desertification (dɪˌzɜːtɪfɪˈkeɪʃən) NOUN a process by which fertile land turns into barren land or desert.

desertion (dɪˈzɜːʃən) NOUN 1 the act of deserting or abandoning or the state of being deserted or abandoned. 2 *Law* wilful abandonment, esp of one's spouse or children, without consent and in breach of obligations.

desert island NOUN a small remote tropical island.

desert lynx NOUN another name for **caracal.**

desert oak NOUN a tree, *Casuarina decaisneana,* of Central and NW Australia, the timber of which is resistant to termite attack.

desert pea NOUN an Australian trailing leguminous plant, *Clianthus formosus,* with scarlet flowers.

desert rat NOUN 1 a jerboa, *Jaculus orientalis,* inhabiting the deserts of N Africa. 2 *Brit informal* a soldier who served in North Africa with the British 7th Armoured Division in 1941–42.

desert rock NOUN a type of heavy-metal music that has strong country-rock and folk influences.

desert soil NOUN a type of soil developed in arid climates, characterized by a lack of leaching and small humus content.

deserve (dɪˈzɜːv) VERB 1 (*tr*) to be entitled to or worthy of; merit. 2 (*intr;* foll by *of*) *Obsolete* to be worthy.
▷HISTORY C13: from Old French *deservir,* from Latin *dēservīre* to serve devotedly, from DE- + *servīre* to SERVE
▸**deˈserved** ADJECTIVE ▸**deservedness** (dɪˈzɜːvɪdnɪs) NOUN ▸**deˈserver** NOUN

deservedly (dɪˈzɜːvɪdlɪ) ADVERB according to merit; justly.

deserving (dɪˈzɜːvɪŋ) ADJECTIVE 1 (often *postpositive* and foll by *of*) worthy, esp of praise or reward. ◆ NOUN 2 *Rare* a merit or demerit; desert.
▸**deˈservingly** ADVERB ▸**deˈservingness** NOUN

desexualize *or* **desexualise** (diːˈsɛksjʊəˌlaɪz) VERB (*tr*) to deprive of sexual characteristics by the surgical removal of the testicles or ovaries; castrate or spay. Often shortened to: **desex** (diːˈsɛks).
▸**deˌsexualiˈzation** *or* **deˌsexualiˈsation** NOUN

deshabille (ˌdeɪzæˈbiːl) *or* **dishabille** NOUN 1 the state of being partly or carelessly dressed. 2 *Archaic* clothes worn in such a state.
▷HISTORY C17: from French *déshabillé* undressed, from *dés-* DIS-[1] + *habiller* to dress; see HABILIMENT

desiccant (ˈdɛsɪkənt) ADJECTIVE 1 desiccating or drying. ◆ NOUN 2 a substance, such as calcium oxide, that absorbs water and is used to remove moisture; a drying agent.
▷HISTORY C17: from Latin *dēsiccāns* drying up; see DESICCATE

desiccate (ˈdɛsɪˌkeɪt) VERB 1 (*tr*) to remove most of the water from (a substance or material); dehydrate. 2 (*tr*) to preserve (food) by removing moisture; dry. 3 (*intr*) to become dried up.
▷HISTORY C16: from Latin *dēsiccāre* to dry up, from DE- + *siccāre* to dry, from *siccus* dry
▸**ˌdesicˈcation** NOUN ▸**ˈdesiccative** ADJECTIVE

desiccated (ˈdɛsɪˌkeɪtɪd) ADJECTIVE 1 dehydrated and powdered: *desiccated coconut.* 2 lacking in spirit or animation.

desiccator (ˈdɛsɪˌkeɪtə) NOUN 1 any apparatus for drying milk, fruit, etc. 2 an airtight box or jar containing a desiccant, used to dry chemicals and protect them from the water vapour in the atmosphere.

desiderata (dɪˌzɪdəˈrɑːtə) NOUN the plural of **desideratum.**

desiderate (dɪˈzɪdəˌreɪt) VERB (*tr*) to feel the lack of or need for; long for; miss.
▷HISTORY C17: from Latin *dēsīderāre,* from DE- + *sīdus* star; see DESIRE
▸**deˌsiderˈation** NOUN

desiderative (dɪˈzɪdərətɪv) ADJECTIVE 1 feeling or expressing desire. 2 (in certain languages, of a verb) related in form to another verb and expressing the subject's desire or intention to perform the act denoted by the other verb. ◆ NOUN 3 a desiderative verb.

desideratum (dɪˌzɪdəˈrɑːtəm) NOUN, *plural* **-ta** (-tə). something lacked and wanted.
▷HISTORY C17: from Latin; see DESIDERATE

design (dɪˈzaɪn) VERB 1 to work out the structure or form of (something), as by making a sketch, outline, pattern, or plans. 2 to plan and make (something) artistically or skilfully. 3 (*tr*) to form or conceive in the mind; invent. 4 (*tr*) to intend, as for a specific purpose; plan. 5 (*tr*) *Obsolete* to mark out or designate. ◆ NOUN 6 a plan, sketch, or preliminary drawing. 7 the arrangement or pattern of elements or features of an artistic or decorative work: *the design of the desk is Chippendale.* 8 a finished artistic or decorative creation. 9 the art of designing. 10 a plan, scheme, or project. 11 an end aimed at or planned for; intention; purpose. 12 (*often plural;* often foll by *on* or *against*) a plot or hostile scheme, often to gain possession of (something) by illegitimate means. 13 a coherent or purposeful pattern, as opposed to chaos: *God's design appears in nature.* 14 **argument from design.** *Philosophy* another name for **teleological argument.**
▷HISTORY C16: from Latin *dēsignāre* to mark out, describe, from DE- + *signāre* to mark, from *signum* a mark, SIGN
▸**deˈsignable** ADJECTIVE

designate VERB (ˈdɛzɪɡˌneɪt) (*tr*) 1 to indicate or specify. 2 to give a name to; style; entitle. 3 to select or name for an office or duty; appoint. ◆ ADJECTIVE (ˈdɛzɪɡnɪt, -ˌneɪt) 4 (*immediately postpositive*) appointed, but not yet in office: *a minister designate.*
▷HISTORY C15: from Latin *dēsignātus* marked out, defined; see DESIGN
▸**ˈdesigˌnative** *or* **designatory** (ˌdɛzɪɡˈneɪtərɪ) ADJECTIVE
▸**ˈdesigˌnator** NOUN

designated ADJECTIVE *Logic* (of a truth value) corresponding to truth in a two-valued logic, or having one of the analogous values in a many-valued logic.

designated driver NOUN a person who volunteers not to drink alcohol on a social occasion, so that he or she can safely drive other people who have been drinking.

designated employment NOUN (in Britain) any of certain kinds of jobs reserved for handicapped workers under the Disabled Persons (Employment) Act 1944.

designation (ˌdɛzɪɡˈneɪʃən) NOUN 1 something that designates, such as a name or distinctive mark. 2 the act of designating or the fact of being designated.

designedly (dɪˈzaɪnɪdlɪ) ADVERB by intention or design; on purpose.

designer (dɪˈzaɪnə) NOUN 1 a person who devises and executes designs, as for works of art, clothes, machines, etc. 2 (*modifier*) designed by and bearing the label or signature of a well-known fashion designer: *designer jeans.* 3 (*modifier*) (of things, ideas, etc.) having an appearance of fashionable trendiness: *designer pop songs; designer stubble.* 4 (*modifier*) (of cells, chemicals, etc.) designed (or produced) to perform a specific function or combat a specific problem: *designer insecticide.* 5 a person who devises plots or schemes; intriguer.

designer baby NOUN *Informal* a baby that is the product of genetic engineering.

designer drug NOUN 1 any of various narcotic or hallucinogenic substances manufactured illegally from a range of chemicals. 2 *Med* a drug designed to act on a specific molecular target.

designing (dɪˈzaɪnɪŋ) ADJECTIVE artful and scheming; conniving; crafty.
▸**deˈsigningly** ADVERB

desinence (ˈdɛsɪnəns) NOUN *Grammar* an ending or termination, esp an inflectional ending of a word.
▷HISTORY C16: from French *désinence,* from Latin *dēsinēns* ending, from *dēsinere* to leave off, from DE- + *sinere* to leave, permit
▸**ˈdesinent** *or* **desinential** (ˌdɛsɪˈnɛnʃəl) ADJECTIVE

desirable (dɪˈzaɪərəbᵊl) ADJECTIVE 1 worthy of desire or recommendation: *a desirable residence.* 2 arousing desire, esp sexual desire; attractive. ◆ NOUN 3 a person or thing that is the object of desire.
▸**deˌsiraˈbility** *or* **deˈsirableness** NOUN ▸**deˈsirably** ADVERB

desire (dɪˈzaɪə) VERB (*tr*) 1 to wish or long for; crave; want. 2 to express a wish or make a request for; ask for. ◆ NOUN 3 a wish or longing; craving. 4 an expressed wish; request. 5 sexual appetite; lust. 6 a person or thing that is desired. Related adjective: **orectic.**
▷HISTORY C13: from Old French *desirer,* from Latin *dēsīderāre* to desire earnestly; see DESIDERATE
▸**deˈsirer** NOUN

desirous (dɪˈzaɪərəs) ADJECTIVE (usually *postpositive* and foll by *of*) having or expressing desire (for); having a wish or longing (for).
▸**deˈsirously** ADVERB ▸**deˈsirousness** NOUN

desist (dɪˈzɪst) VERB (*intr;* often foll by *from*) to cease, as from an action; stop or abstain.
▷HISTORY C15: from Old French *desister,* from Latin *dēsistere* to leave off, stand apart, from DE- + *sistere* to stand, halt
▸**deˈsistance** *or* **deˈsistence** NOUN

desk (dɛsk) NOUN 1 a piece of furniture with a writing surface and usually drawers or other compartments. 2 a service counter or table in a public building, such as a hotel: *information desk.* 3 a support, lectern, or book rest for the book from which services are read in a church. 4 the editorial section of a newspaper, etc., responsible for a particular subject: *the news desk.* 5 **a** a music stand shared by two orchestral players. **b** these two players. 6 (*modifier*) **a** made for use at a desk: *a desk calendar.* **b** done at a desk: *a desk job.*
▷HISTORY C14: from Medieval Latin *desca* table, from Latin *discus* disc, dish

desk-bound ADJECTIVE engaged in or involving sedentary work, as at an office desk.

desk clerk NOUN *US and Canadian* a hotel receptionist. Also called: **clerk.**

deskfast (ˈdɛskfəst) NOUN breakfast eaten at one's desk at work.
▷HISTORY C20: from DESK + (BREAK)FAST

deskill (diːˈskɪl) VERB (*tr*) 1 to mechanize or computerize (a job or process) to such an extent that little human skill is required to do it. 2 to cause (skilled persons or a labour force) to work at a job that does not utilize their skills.
▸**deˈskilling** NOUN

desktop (ˈdɛskˌtɒp) NOUN (*modifier*) denoting a computer system, esp for word processing, that is small enough to use at a desk.

desktop publishing NOUN a means of publishing reports, advertising, etc., to typeset quality using a desktop computer. Abbreviation: **DTP.**

desman (ˈdɛsmən) NOUN, *plural* **-mans.** either of two molelike amphibious mammals *Desmana moschata* (**Russian desman**) or *Galemys pyrenaicus* (**Pyrenean desman**), having dense fur and webbed feet: family *Talpidae,* order *Insectivora* (insectivores).
▷HISTORY C18: from Swedish *desmansråtta,* from *desman* musk (of Germanic origin) + *råtta* rat

desmid (ˈdɛsmɪd) NOUN any freshwater green alga of the mainly unicellular family *Desmidioideae,* typically constricted into two symmetrical halves.
▷HISTORY C19: from New Latin *Desmidium* (genus name), from Greek *desmos* bond, from *dein* to bind
▸**desˈmidian** ADJECTIVE

desmoid (ˈdɛsmɔɪd) ADJECTIVE 1 *Anatomy* resembling a tendon or ligament. ◆ NOUN 2 *Pathol* a very firm tumour of connective tissue.
▷HISTORY C19: from Greek *desmos* band + -OID; see DESMID

Des Moines (də ˈmɔɪn, ˈmɔɪnz) NOUN 1 a city in S central Iowa: state capital. Pop.: 198 682 (2000). 2 a river in the N central US, rising in SW Minnesota and flowing southeast to join the Mississippi. Length: 861 km (535 miles).

Desmond Tutu (ˌdɛzmənd ˈtuːtuː) NOUN *Brit informal* a university degree graded 2:2 (second class lower bracket). Often shortened to: **Desmond.**
▷HISTORY C20: from rhyming slang, after Desmond *Tutu* (born 1931), South African clergyman and anti-apartheid campaigner

desmosome (ˈdɛsməˌsəʊm) NOUN *Cytology* a

structure in the cell membranes of adjacent cells that binds them together.

desnood (diːˈsnuːd) VERB (*tr*) to remove the snood of a turkey poult to reduce the risk of cannibalism.

desolate ADJECTIVE (ˈdɛsəlɪt) 1 uninhabited; deserted. 2 made uninhabitable; laid waste; devastated. 3 without friends, hope, or encouragement; forlorn, wretched, or abandoned. 4 gloomy or dismal; depressing. ◆ VERB (ˈdɛsəˌleɪt) (*tr*) 5 to deprive of inhabitants; depopulate. 6 to make barren or lay waste; devastate. 7 to make wretched or forlorn. 8 to forsake or abandon.
▷HISTORY C14: from Latin *dēsōlāre* to leave alone, from DE- + *sōlāre* to make lonely, lay waste, from *sōlus* alone
▸ˈ**desoˌlater** *or* ˈ**desoˌlator** NOUN ▸ˈ**desolately** ADVERB
▸ˈ**desolateness** NOUN

desolation (ˌdɛsəˈleɪʃən) NOUN 1 the act of desolating or the state of being desolated; ruin or devastation. 2 solitary misery; wretchedness. 3 a desolate region; barren waste.

desorb (dɪˈsɔːb, -ˈzɔːb) VERB *Chem* to change from an adsorbed state on a surface to a gaseous or liquid state.

desorption (dɪˈsɔːpʃən, -ˈzɔːp-) NOUN the action or process of desorbing.

desoxy- COMBINING FORM a variant of **deoxy-**.

despair (dɪˈspɛə) VERB 1 (*intr;* often foll by *of*) to lose or give up hope: *I despair of his coming.* 2 (*tr*) *Obsolete* to give up hope of; lose hope in. ◆ NOUN 3 total loss of hope. 4 a person or thing that causes hopelessness or for which there is no hope.
▷HISTORY C14: from Old French *despoir* hopelessness, from *desperer* to despair, from Latin *dēspērāre,* from DE- + *spērāre* to hope

despairing (dɪˈspɛərɪŋ) ADJECTIVE marked by or resulting from despair; hopeless or desperate.
▸**desˈpairingly** ADVERB

despatch (dɪˈspætʃ) VERB (*tr*) a less common spelling of **dispatch.**
▸**desˈpatcher** NOUN

desperado (ˌdɛspəˈrɑːdəʊ) NOUN, *plural* **-does** *or* **-dos.** a reckless or desperate person, esp one ready to commit any violent illegal act.
▷HISTORY C17: probably pseudo-Spanish variant of obsolete *desperate* (noun) a reckless character

desperate (ˈdɛspərɪt, -prɪt) ADJECTIVE 1 careless of danger, as from despair; utterly reckless. 2 (of an act) reckless; risky. 3 used or undertaken in desperation or as a last resort: *desperate measures.* 4 critical; very grave: *in desperate need.* 5 (often *postpositive* and foll by *for*) in distress and having a great need or desire. 6 moved by or showing despair or hopelessness; despairing.
▷HISTORY C15: from Latin *dēspērāre* to have no hope; see DESPAIR
▸ˈ**desperately** ADVERB ▸ˈ**desperateness** NOUN

desperation (ˌdɛspəˈreɪʃən) NOUN 1 desperate recklessness. 2 the act of despairing or the state of being desperate.

despicable (dɪˈspɪkəbᵊl, ˈdɛspɪk-) ADJECTIVE worthy of being despised; contemptible; mean.
▷HISTORY C16: from Late Latin *dēspicābilis,* from *dēspicārī* to disdain; compare DESPISE
▸**deˌspicaˈbility** *or* **deˈspicableness** NOUN ▸**deˈspicably** ADVERB

despise (dɪˈspaɪz) VERB (*tr*) to look down on with contempt; scorn: *he despises flattery.*
▷HISTORY C13: from Old French *despire,* from Latin *dēspicere* to look down, from DE- + *specere* to look
▸**deˈspiser** NOUN

despite (dɪˈspaɪt) PREPOSITION 1 in spite of; undeterred by. ◆ NOUN 2 *Archaic* contempt; insult. 3 **in despite of.** (*preposition*) *Rare* in spite of. ◆ VERB 4 (*tr*) an archaic word for **spite.**
▷HISTORY C13: from Old French *despit,* from Latin *dēspectus* contempt; see DESPISE

despiteful (dɪˈspaɪtfʊl) *or* **despiteous** (dɪˈspɪtɪəs) ADJECTIVE an archaic word for **spiteful.**
▸**deˈspitefully** ADVERB ▸**deˈspitefulness** NOUN

despoil (dɪˈspɔɪl) VERB (*tr*) to strip or deprive by force; plunder; rob; loot.
▷HISTORY C13: from Old French *despoillier,* from Latin *dēspoliāre,* from DE- + *spoliāre* to rob (esp of clothing); see SPOIL
▸**deˈspoiler** NOUN ▸**deˈspoilment** NOUN

despoliation (dɪˌspəʊlɪˈeɪʃən) NOUN 1 the act of despoiling; plunder or pillage. 2 the state of being despoiled.

despond VERB (dɪˈspɒnd) 1 (*intr*) to lose heart or hope; become disheartened; despair. ◆ NOUN (ˈdɛspɒnd, dɪˈspɒnd) 2 an archaic word for **despondency.**
▷HISTORY C17: from Latin *dēspondēre* to promise, make over to, yield, lose heart, from DE- + *spondēre* to promise
▸**deˈspondingly** ADVERB

despondent (dɪˈspɒndənt) ADJECTIVE downcast or disheartened; lacking hope or courage; dejected.
▸**deˈspondence** NOUN ▸**deˈspondency** NOUN
▸**deˈspondently** ADVERB

despot (ˈdɛspɒt) NOUN 1 an absolute or tyrannical ruler; autocrat or tyrant. 2 any person in power who acts tyrannically. 3 a title borne by numerous persons of rank in the later Roman, Byzantine, and Ottoman Empires: *the despot of Servia.*
▷HISTORY C16: from Medieval Latin *despota,* from Greek *despotēs* lord, master; related to Latin *domus* house
▸**despotic** (dɛsˈpɒtɪk) *or* **desˈpotical** ADJECTIVE
▸**desˈpotically** ADVERB

despotism (ˈdɛspəˌtɪzəm) NOUN 1 the rule of a despot; arbitrary, absolute, or tyrannical government. 2 arbitrary or tyrannical authority or behaviour.

despumate (dɪˈspjuːmeɪt, ˈdɛspjʊˌmeɪt) VERB 1 (*tr*) to clarify or purify (a liquid) by skimming a scum from its surface. 2 (*intr*) (of a liquid) to form a scum or froth.
▷HISTORY C17: from Latin *dēspūmāre* to skim off, from DE- + *spūma* foam, froth
▸ˌ**despuˈmation** NOUN

desquamate (ˈdɛskwəˌmeɪt) VERB (*intr*) (esp of the skin in certain diseases) to peel or come off in scales.
▷HISTORY C18: from Latin *dēsquāmāre* to scale off, from DE- + *squāma* a scale
▸ˌ**desquaˈmation** NOUN

des res (dɛz rɛz) NOUN (in estate agents' jargon) a desirable residence.

Dessau (*German* ˈdɛsau) NOUN an industrial city in E Germany, in Saxony-Anhalt: capital of Anhalt state from 1340 to 1918. Pop.: 95 100 (1991).

dessert (dɪˈzɜːt) NOUN 1 the sweet, usually last course of a meal. 2 *Chiefly Brit* (esp formerly) fruit, dates, nuts, etc., served at the end of a meal.
▷HISTORY C17: from French, from *desservir* to clear a table, from *des-* DIS-[1] + *servir* to SERVE

dessertspoon (dɪˈzɜːtˌspuːn) NOUN a spoon intermediate in size between a tablespoon and a teaspoon.

dessiatine (ˈdɛsjəˌtiːn) NOUN a Russian unit of area equal to approximately 2.7 acres or 10 800 square metres.
▷HISTORY C18: from Russian *desyatina,* literally: tithe, from *desyat* ten

destabilize *or* **destabilise** (diːˈsteɪbɪˌlaɪz) VERB (*tr*) to undermine or subvert (a government, economy, etc.) so as to cause unrest or collapse.
▸ˌ**destabiliˈzation** *or* ˌ**destabiliˈsation** NOUN

de-Stalinization *or* **de-Stalinisation** (diːˌstɑːlɪnaɪˈzeɪʃən) NOUN the elimination of the influence of Stalin.

De Stijl (də staɪl) NOUN a group of artists and architects in the Netherlands in the 1920s, including Mondrian and van Doesburg, devoted to neoplasticism and then dada.
▷HISTORY Dutch, literally: the style, title of this group's own magazine

destination (ˌdɛstɪˈneɪʃən) NOUN 1 the predetermined end of a journey or voyage. 2 the ultimate end or purpose for which something is created or a person is destined.

destine (ˈdɛstɪn) VERB (*tr*) to set apart or appoint (for a certain purpose or person, or to do something); intend; design.
▷HISTORY C14: from Old French *destiner,* from Latin *dēstināre* to appoint, from DE- + *-stināre,* from *stāre* to stand

destined (ˈdɛstɪnd) ADJECTIVE (*postpositive*) 1 foreordained or certain; meant: *he is destined to be famous.* 2 (usually foll by *for*) heading (towards a specific destination); directed: *a letter destined for Europe.*

destiny (ˈdɛstɪnɪ) NOUN, *plural* **-nies.** 1 the future destined for a person or thing; fate; fortune; lot. 2 the predetermined or inevitable course of events. 3 the ultimate power or agency that predetermines the course of events.
▷HISTORY C14: from Old French *destinee,* from *destiner* to DESTINE

Destiny (ˈdɛstɪnɪ) NOUN, *plural* **-nies.** the power that predetermines events, personified as a goddess.

destitute (ˈdɛstɪˌtjuːt) ADJECTIVE 1 lacking the means of subsistence; totally impoverished. 2 (*postpositive;* foll by *of*) completely lacking; deprived or bereft (of): *destitute of words.* 3 *Obsolete* abandoned or deserted.
▷HISTORY C14: from Latin *dēstitūtus* forsaken, from *dēstituere* to leave alone, from *statuere* to place
▸ˈ**destiˌtuteness** NOUN

destitution (ˌdɛstɪˈtjuːʃən) NOUN 1 the state of being destitute; utter poverty. 2 *Rare* lack or deficiency.

destock (diːˈstɒk) VERB (of a retailer) to reduce the amount of stock held or cease to stock certain products.

de-stress VERB to become or cause to become less stressed or anxious.

destrier (ˈdɛstrɪə) NOUN an archaic word for **warhorse** (sense 1).
▷HISTORY C13: from Old French, from *destre* right hand, from Latin *dextra;* from the fact that a squire led a knight's horse with his right hand

destroy (dɪˈstrɔɪ) VERB (*mainly tr*) 1 to ruin; spoil; render useless. 2 to tear down or demolish; break up; raze. 3 to put an end to; do away with; extinguish. 4 to kill or annihilate. 5 to crush, subdue, or defeat. 6 (*intr*) to be destructive or cause destruction.
▷HISTORY C13: from Old French *destruire,* from Latin *dēstruere* to pull down, from DE- + *struere* to pile up, build
▸**deˈstroyable** ADJECTIVE

destroyer (dɪˈstrɔɪə) NOUN 1 a small fast lightly armoured but heavily armed warship. 2 a person or thing that destroys.

destroyer escort NOUN a lightly armed warship smaller than a destroyer, designed to escort fleets or convoys.

destroying angel NOUN a white slender very poisonous basidiomycetous toadstool, *Amanita virosa,* having a pronounced volva, frilled, shaggy stalk, and sickly smell.

destruct (dɪˈstrʌkt) VERB 1 to destroy (one's own missile or rocket) for safety. 2 (*intr*) (of a missile or rocket) to be destroyed, for safety, by those controlling it; self-destruct. ◆ NOUN 3 the act of destructing. ◆ ADJECTIVE 4 designed to be capable of destroying itself or the object, system, or installation containing it: *destruct mechanism.*

destructible (dɪˈstrʌktəbᵊl) ADJECTIVE capable of being or liable to be destroyed.
▸**deˌstructiˈbility** NOUN

destruction (dɪˈstrʌkʃən) NOUN 1 the act of destroying or state of being destroyed; demolition. 2 a cause of ruin or means of destroying.
▷HISTORY C14: from Latin *dēstructiō* a pulling down; see DESTROY

destructionist (dɪˈstrʌkʃənɪst) NOUN a person who believes in destruction, esp of social institutions.

destructive (dɪˈstrʌktɪv) ADJECTIVE 1 (often *postpositive* and foll by *of* or *to*) causing or tending to cause the destruction (of). 2 intended to disprove or discredit, esp without positive suggestions or help; negative: *destructive criticism.* Compare **constructive** (sense 1).
▸**deˈstructively** ADVERB ▸**deˈstructiveness** *or* **destructivity** (ˌdiːstrʌkˈtɪvɪtɪ) NOUN

destructive distillation NOUN the decomposition of a complex substance, such as wood or coal, by heating it in the absence of air and collecting the volatile products.

destructo (dɪˈstrʌktəʊ) NOUN, *plural* **-ctos.** *Austral informal* a person who causes havoc or destruction.

destructor (dɪˈstrʌktə) NOUN 1 a furnace or incinerator for the disposal of refuse, esp one that uses the resulting heat to generate power. 2 a device used to blow up a dangerously defective missile or rocket after launching.

desuetude (dɪˈsjuːɪˌtjuːd, ˈdɛswɪtjuːd) NOUN *Formal* the condition of not being in use or practice; disuse: *those ceremonies had fallen into desuetude.*
▷HISTORY C15: from Latin *dēsuētūdō*, from *dēsuescere* to lay aside a habit, from DE- + *suescere* to grow accustomed

desulphurize *or* **desulphurise** (diːˈsʌlfjʊˌraɪz) VERB to free or become free from sulphur.
▸**deˌsulphuriˈzation** *or* **deˌsulphuriˈsation** NOUN
▸**deˈsulphurˌizer** *or* **deˈsulphurˌiser** NOUN

desultory (ˈdɛsəltərɪ, -trɪ) ADJECTIVE 1 passing or jumping from one thing to another, esp in a fitful way; unmethodical; disconnected. 2 occurring in a random or incidental way; haphazard: *a desultory thought.*
▷HISTORY C16: from Latin *dēsultōrius*, relating to one who vaults or jumps, hence superficial, from *dēsilīre* to jump down, from DE- + *salīre* to jump
▸**ˈdesultorily** ADVERB ▸**ˈdesultoriness** NOUN

DET ABBREVIATION FOR diethyltryptamine, a hallucinogenic drug.

detach (dɪˈtætʃ) VERB (*tr*) 1 to disengage and separate or remove, as by pulling; unfasten; disconnect. 2 *Military* to separate (a small unit) from a larger, esp for a special assignment.
▷HISTORY C17: from Old French *destachier*, from *des-* DIS-[1] + *attachier* to ATTACH
▸**deˈtachable** ADJECTIVE ▸**deˌtachaˈbility** NOUN ▸**deˈtacher** NOUN

detached (dɪˈtætʃt) ADJECTIVE 1 disconnected or standing apart; not attached: *a detached house.* 2 having or showing no bias or emotional involvement; disinterested. 3 *Social welfare* working at the clients' normal location rather than from an office; not dependent on premises for providing a service: *a detached youth worker.* Compare **outreach** (sense 7). 4 *Ophthalmol* (of the retina) separated from the choroid layer of the eyeball to which it is normally attached, resulting in loss of vision in the affected part.

detachment (dɪˈtætʃmənt) NOUN 1 indifference to other people or to one's surroundings; aloofness. 2 freedom from self-interest or bias; disinterest. 3 the act of disengaging or separating something. 4 the condition of being disengaged or separated; disconnection. 5 *Military* **a** the separation of a small unit from its main body, esp of ships or troops. **b** the unit so detached. 6 *Logic* the rule whereby the consequent of a true conditional statement, given the truth of its antecedent, may be asserted on its own. See also **modus ponens.**

detail (ˈdiːteɪl) NOUN 1 an item or smaller part that is considered separately; particular. 2 an item or circumstance that is insignificant or unimportant: *passengers' comfort was regarded as a detail.* 3 treatment of or attention to items or particulars: *this essay includes too much detail.* 4 items collectively; particulars. 5 a small or accessory section or element in a painting, building, statue, etc., esp when considered in isolation. 6 *Military* **a** the act of assigning personnel for a specific duty, esp a fatigue. **b** the personnel selected. **c** the duty or assignment. 7 **go into detail.** to include all or most particulars. 8 **in detail.** including all or most particulars or items thoroughly. ◆ VERB (*tr*) 9 to list or relate fully. 10 *Military* to select (personnel) for a specific duty. 11 to decorate or elaborate (carving, etc.) with fine delicate drawing or designs.
▷HISTORY C17: from French *détail*, from Old French *detailler* to cut in pieces, from *de-* DIS-[1] + *tailler* to cut; see TAILOR

detail drawing NOUN a separate large-scale drawing of a small part or section of a building, machine, etc.

detailed (ˈdiːteɪld) ADJECTIVE having many details or giving careful attention to details.

detain (dɪˈteɪn) VERB (*tr*) 1 to delay; hold back; stop. 2 to confine or hold in custody; restrain. 3 *Archaic* to retain or withhold.
▷HISTORY C15: from Old French *detenir*, from Latin *dētinēre* to hold off, keep back, from DE- + *tenēre* to hold
▸**deˈtainable** ADJECTIVE ▸**detainee** (ˌdiːteɪˈniː) NOUN
▸**deˈtainment** NOUN

detainer (dɪˈteɪnə) NOUN *Law* 1 the wrongful withholding of the property of another person. 2 **a** the detention of a person in custody. **b** a writ authorizing the further detention of a person already in custody.
▷HISTORY C17: from Anglo-French *detener* (noun), from *detener* to DETAIN

detect (dɪˈtɛkt) VERB (*tr*) 1 to perceive or notice: *to detect a note of sarcasm.* 2 to discover the existence or presence of (esp something likely to elude observation): *to detect alcohol in the blood.* 3 to extract information from (an electromagnetic wave). 4 *Obsolete* to reveal or expose (a crime, criminal, etc.).
▷HISTORY C15: from Latin *dētectus* uncovered, from *dētegere* to uncover, from DE- + *tegere* to cover
▸**deˈtectable** *or* **deˈtectible** ADJECTIVE ▸**deˈtecter** NOUN

detection (dɪˈtɛkʃən) NOUN 1 the act of discovering or the fact of being discovered: *detection of crime.* 2 the act or process of extracting information, esp at audio or video frequencies, from an electromagnetic wave. See also **demodulation.**

detective (dɪˈtɛktɪv) NOUN 1 **a** a police officer who investigates crimes. **b** See **private detective.** **c** (*as modifier*): *a detective story.* ◆ ADJECTIVE 2 used in or serving for detection. 3 serving to detect.

detector (dɪˈtɛktə) NOUN 1 a person or thing that detects. 2 any mechanical sensing device. 3 *Electronics* a device used in the detection of radio signals.

detectorist (dɪˈtɛktərɪst) NOUN *Informal* a person whose hobby is using a metal detector.

detent (dɪˈtɛnt) NOUN the locking piece of a mechanism, often spring-loaded to check the movement of a wheel in one direction only. See also **pawl.**
▷HISTORY C17: from Old French *destente*, a loosening, trigger: see DÉTENTE

détente (deɪˈtɑːnt; *French* detɑ̃t) NOUN the relaxing or easing of tension, esp between nations.
▷HISTORY French, literally: a loosening, from Old French *destendre* to release, from *tendre* to stretch

detention (dɪˈtɛnʃən) NOUN 1 the act of detaining or state of being detained. 2 **a** custody or confinement, esp of a suspect awaiting trial. **b** (*as modifier*): *a detention order.* 3 a form of punishment in which a pupil is detained after school. 4 the withholding of something belonging to or claimed by another.
▷HISTORY C16: from Latin *dētentiō* a keeping back; see DETAIN

detention centre NOUN a place where young persons may be detained for short periods by order of a court.

deter (dɪˈtɜː) VERB **-ters, -terring, -terred.** (*tr*) to discourage (from acting) or prevent (from occurring), usually by instilling fear, doubt, or anxiety.
▷HISTORY C16: from Latin *dēterrēre*, from DE- + *terrēre* to frighten
▸**deˈterment** NOUN

deterge (dɪˈtɜːdʒ) VERB (*tr*) to wash or wipe away; cleanse: *to deterge a wound.*
▷HISTORY C17: from Latin *dētergēre* to wipe away, from DE- + *tergēre* to wipe

detergency (dɪˈtɜːdʒənsɪ) *or* **detergence** NOUN cleansing power.

detergent (dɪˈtɜːdʒənt) NOUN 1 a cleansing agent, esp a surface-active chemical such as an alkyl sulphonate, widely used in industry, laundering, shampoos, etc. ◆ ADJECTIVE *also* **detersive** (dɪˈtɜːsɪv) 2 having cleansing power.
▷HISTORY C17: from Latin *dētergēns* wiping off; see DETERGE

deteriorate (dɪˈtɪərɪəˌreɪt) VERB 1 to make or become worse or lower in quality, value, character, etc.; depreciate. 2 (*intr*) to wear away or disintegrate.
▷HISTORY C16: from Late Latin *dēteriōrāre*, from Latin *dēterior* worse
▸**deˌterioˈration** NOUN ▸**deˈteriorative** ADJECTIVE

determinable (dɪˈtɜːmɪnəbᵊl) ADJECTIVE 1 able to be decided, fixed, or found out. 2 *Law* liable to termination under certain conditions; terminable.
▸**deˈterminably** ADVERB

determinant (dɪˈtɜːmɪnənt) ADJECTIVE 1 serving to determine or affect. ◆ NOUN 2 a factor, circumstance, etc., that influences or determines. 3 *Maths* a square array of elements that represents the sum of certain products of these elements, used to solve simultaneous equations, in vector studies, etc. Compare **matrix** (sense 9).

determinate (dɪˈtɜːmɪnɪt) ADJECTIVE 1 definitely limited, defined, or fixed; distinct. 2 a less common word for **determined.** 3 **a** able to be predicted or deduced. **b** (of an effect) obeying the law of causality. 4 *Botany* (of an inflorescence) having the main and branch stems ending in flowers and unable to grow further; cymose. 5 (of a structure, stress, etc.) able to be fully analysed or determined.
▸**deˈterminately** ADVERB ▸**deˈterminateness** NOUN

determination (dɪˌtɜːmɪˈneɪʃən) NOUN 1 the act or an instance of making a decision. 2 the condition of being determined; resoluteness. 3 the act or an instance of ending an argument by the opinion or decision of an authority. 4 the act or an instance of fixing or settling the quality, limit, position, etc., of something. 5 a decision or opinion reached, rendered, or settled upon. 6 a resolute movement towards some object or end. 7 *Law* the termination of an estate or interest. 8 *Law* the decision reached by a court of justice on a disputed matter. 9 *Logic* **a** the process of qualifying or limiting a proposition or concept. **b** the qualifications or limitations used in this process. 10 the condition of embryonic tissues of being able to develop into only one particular tissue or organ in the adult.

determinative (dɪˈtɜːmɪnətɪv) ADJECTIVE 1 able to or serving to settle or determine; deciding. ◆ NOUN 2 a factor, circumstance, etc., that settles or determines. 3 *Grammar* a less common word for **determiner.** 4 (in a logographic writing system) a logogram that bears a separate meaning, from which compounds and inflected forms are built up.
▸**deˈterminatively** ADVERB ▸**deˈterminativeness** NOUN

determine (dɪˈtɜːmɪn) VERB 1 to settle or decide (an argument, question, etc.) conclusively, as by referring to an authority. 2 (*tr*) to ascertain or conclude, esp after observation or consideration. 3 (*tr*) to shape or influence; give direction to: *experience often determines ability.* 4 (*tr*) to fix in scope, extent, variety, etc.: *the river determined the edge of the property.* 5 to make or cause to make a decision: *he determined never to marry.* 6 (*tr*) *Logic* to define or limit (a notion) by adding or requiring certain features or characteristics. 7 (*tr*) *Geometry* to fix or specify the position, form, or configuration of: *two points determine a line.* 8 *Chiefly law* to come or bring to an end, as an estate or interest in land. 9 (*tr*) to decide (a legal action or dispute).
▷HISTORY C14: from Old French *determiner*, from Latin *dētermināre* to set boundaries to, from DE- + *termināre* to limit; see TERMINATE

determined (dɪˈtɜːmɪnd) ADJECTIVE of unwavering mind; resolute; firm.
▸**deˈterminedly** ADVERB ▸**deˈterminedness** NOUN

determiner (dɪˈtɜːmɪnə) NOUN 1 a word, such as a number, article, personal pronoun, that determines (limits) the meaning of a noun phrase, e.g. *their* in 'their black cat'. 2 a person or thing that determines.

determinism (dɪˈtɜːmɪˌnɪzəm) NOUN 1 the philosophical doctrine that all events including human actions and choices are fully determined by preceding events and states of affairs, and so that freedom of choice is illusory. Also called: **necessitarianism.** Compare **free will** (sense 1b). 2 the scientific doctrine that all occurrences in nature take place in accordance with natural laws. 3 the principle in classical mechanics that the values of dynamic variables of a system and of the forces acting on the system at a given time, completely determine the values of the variables at any later time.
▸**deˈterminist** NOUN, ADJECTIVE ▸**deˌterminˈistic** ADJECTIVE

deterrent (dɪˈtɛrənt) NOUN 1 something that deters. 2 a weapon or combination of weapons, esp nuclear, held by one state, etc., to deter attack by another. ◆ ADJECTIVE 3 tending or used to deter; restraining.
▷HISTORY C19: from Latin *dēterrēns* hindering; see DETER
▸**deˈterrence** NOUN

detest (dɪˈtɛst) VERB (*tr*) to dislike intensely; loathe.

▷HISTORY C16: from Latin *dētestārī* to curse (while invoking a god as witness), from DE- + *testārī* to bear witness, from *testis* a witness
▸**deˈtester** NOUN

detestable (dɪˈtɛstəb^{ə}l) ADJECTIVE being or deserving to be abhorred or detested; abominable; odious.
▸**deˌtestaˈbility** *or* **deˈtestableness** NOUN ▸**deˈtestably** ADVERB

detestation (ˌdiːtɛsˈteɪʃən) NOUN **1** intense hatred; abhorrence. **2** a person or thing that is detested.

dethrone (dɪˈθrəʊn) VERB (*tr*) to remove from a throne or deprive of any high position or title; depose: *the champion was dethroned by a young boxer.*
▸**deˈthronement** NOUN ▸**deˈthroner** NOUN

detinue (ˈdɛtɪˌnjuː) NOUN *Law* an action brought by a plaintiff to recover goods wrongfully detained.
▷HISTORY C15: from Old French *detenue,* from *detenir* to DETAIN

detonate (ˈdɛtəˌneɪt) VERB to cause (a bomb, mine, etc.) to explode or (of a bomb, mine, etc.) to explode; set off or be set off.
▷HISTORY C18: from Latin *dētonāre* to thunder down, from DE- + *tonāre* to THUNDER

detonation (ˌdɛtəˈneɪʃən) NOUN **1** an explosion or the act of exploding. **2** the spontaneous combustion in an internal-combustion engine of part of the mixture before it has been reached by the flame front, causing the engine to knock. **3** *Physics* rapid combustion, esp that occurring within a shock wave.
▸**ˈdetoˌnative** ADJECTIVE

detonator (ˈdɛtəˌneɪtə) NOUN **1** a small amount of explosive, as in a percussion cap, used to initiate a larger explosion. **2** a device, such as an electrical generator, used to set off an explosion from a distance. **3** a substance or object that explodes or is capable of exploding.

detour (ˈdiːtʊə) NOUN **1** a deviation from a direct, usually shorter route or course of action. ◆ VERB **2** to deviate or cause to deviate from a direct route or course of action.
▷HISTORY C18: from French *détour,* from Old French *destorner* to divert, turn away, from *des-* DE- + *torner* to TURN

detox (ˈdiːˌtɒks) *Informal* ◆ NOUN **1** treatment designed to rid the body of poisonous substances, esp alcohol and drugs. ◆ VERB **2** to undergo treatment to rid the body of poisonous substances, esp alcohol and drugs.
▷HISTORY C20: from (for sense 1) DETOXIFICATION or (for sense 2) DETOXICATE

detoxicate (diːˈtɒksɪˌkeɪt) VERB (*tr*) **1** to rid (a patient) of a poison or its effects. **2** to counteract (a poison).
▷HISTORY C19: DE- + *-toxicate,* from Latin *toxicum* poison; see TOXIC
▸**deˈtoxicant** ADJECTIVE, NOUN ▸**deˌtoxiˈcation** NOUN

detoxification centre NOUN a place that specializes in the treatment of alcoholism or drug addiction.

detoxify (diːˈtɒksɪˌfaɪ) VERB **-fies, -fying, -fied.** (*tr*) to remove poison from; detoxicate.
▸**deˌtoxifiˈcation** NOUN

DETR (in Britain) ABBREVIATION FOR Department of the Environment, Transport, and the Regions.

detract (dɪˈtrækt) VERB **1** (when *intr,* usually foll by *from*) to take away a part (of); diminish: *her anger detracts from her beauty.* **2** (*tr*) to distract or divert. **3** (*tr*) *Obsolete* to belittle or disparage.
▷HISTORY C15: from Latin *dētractus* drawn away, from *dētrahere* to pull away, disparage, from DE- + *trahere* to drag
▸**deˈtractingly** ADVERB ▸**deˈtractive** *or* **deˈtractory** ADJECTIVE ▸**deˈtractively** ADVERB ▸**deˈtractor** NOUN

> **Language note** *Detract* is sometimes wrongly used where *distract* is meant: *a noise distracted* (not *detracted) my attention.*

detraction (dɪˈtrækʃən) NOUN **1** a person, thing, circumstance, etc., that detracts. **2** the act of discrediting or detracting from another's reputation, esp by slander; disparagement.

detrain (diːˈtreɪn) VERB to leave or cause to leave a railway train, as passengers, etc.
▸**deˈtrainment** NOUN

detribalize *or* **detribalise** (diːˈtraɪbəˌlaɪz) VERB (*tr*) **1** to cause members of a tribe to lose their characteristic customs or social, religious, or other organizational features. **2** to cause tribal people to adopt urban ways of life.
▸**deˌtribaliˈzation** *or* **deˌtribaliˈsation** NOUN

detriment (ˈdɛtrɪmənt) NOUN **1** disadvantage or damage; harm; loss. **2** a cause of disadvantage or damage.
▷HISTORY C15: from Latin *dētrīmentum,* a rubbing off, hence damage, from *dēterere* to rub away, from DE- + *terere* to rub

detrimental (ˌdɛtrɪˈmɛnt^{ə}l) ADJECTIVE (when *postpositive,* foll by *to*) harmful; injurious; prejudicial: *smoking can be detrimental to health.*
▸**ˌdetriˈmentally** ADVERB

detrition (dɪˈtrɪʃən) NOUN the act of rubbing or wearing away by friction.
▷HISTORY C17: from Medieval Latin *dētrītiō,* from Latin *dētrītus* worn away; see DETRIMENT

detritovore (dɪˈtraɪtəˌvɔː) NOUN *Ecology* any organism that feeds on detritus.

detritus (dɪˈtraɪtəs) NOUN **1** a loose mass of stones, silt, etc., worn away from rocks. **2** an accumulation of disintegrated material or debris. **3** the organic debris formed from the decay of organisms.
▷HISTORY C18: from French *détritus,* from Latin *dētrītus* a rubbing away; see DETRIMENT
▸**deˈtrital** ADJECTIVE

Detroit (dɪˈtrɔɪt) NOUN **1** a city in SE Michigan, on the Detroit River: a major Great Lakes port; largest car-manufacturing centre in the world. Pop.: 951 270 (2000). **2** a river in central North America, flowing along the US-Canadian border from Lake St Clair to Lake Erie.

de trop *French* (də tro) ADJECTIVE (*postpositive*) not wanted; in the way; superfluous.
▷HISTORY literally: of too much

detrude (dɪˈtruːd) VERB (*tr*) to force down or thrust away or out.
▷HISTORY C16: from Latin *dētrūdere* to push away, from DE- + *trūdere* to thrust
▸**detrusion** (dɪˈtruːʒən) NOUN

detruncate (diːˈtrʌŋkeɪt) VERB (*tr*) another word for **truncate.**
▸**ˌdetrunˈcation** NOUN

detumescence (ˌdiːtjʊˈmɛsəns) NOUN the subsidence of a swelling, esp the return of a swollen organ, such as the penis, to the flaccid state.
▷HISTORY C17: from Latin *dētumescere* to cease swelling, from DE- + *tumescere,* from *tumēre* to swell

Deucalion (djuːˈkeɪlɪən) NOUN the son of Prometheus and, with his wife Pyrrha, the only survivor on earth of a flood sent by Zeus (**Deucalion's flood**). Together, they were allowed to repopulate the world by throwing stones over their shoulders, which became men and women.

deuce^{1} (djuːs) NOUN **1** **a** a playing card or dice with two pips or spots; two. **b** a throw of two in dice. **2** *Tennis* a tied score (in tennis 40-all) that requires one player to gain two successive points to win the game.
▷HISTORY C15: from Old French *deus* two, from Latin *duos,* accusative masculine of *duo* two

deuce^{2} (djuːs) *Informal* ◆ INTERJECTION **1** an expression of annoyance or frustration. ◆ NOUN **2** **the deuce.** (intensifier): used in such phrases as **what the deuce, where the deuce,** etc.
▷HISTORY C17: probably special use of DEUCE^{1} (in the sense: lowest throw at dice)

deuced (ˈdjuːsɪd, djuːst) *Brit informal* ◆ ADJECTIVE **1** (intensifier, usually qualifying something undesirable) damned; confounded: *he's a deuced idiot.* ◆ ADVERB **2** (intensifier): *deuced good luck.*
▸**ˈdeucedly** ADVERB

Deurne (*Flemish* ˈdøːrnə) NOUN a town in N Belgium, a suburb of E Antwerp: site of Antwerp airport. Pop.: 80 000 (latest est.).

Deus *Latin* (ˈdeɪʊs) NOUN God.
▷HISTORY related to Greek *Zeus*

deus ex machina *Latin* (ˈdeɪʊs ɛks ˈmækɪnə) NOUN **1** (in ancient Greek and Roman drama) a god introduced into a play to resolve the plot. **2** any unlikely or artificial device serving this purpose.
▷HISTORY literally: god out of a machine, translating Greek *theos ek mēkhanēs*

Deut. *Bible* ABBREVIATION FOR Deuteronomy.

deuteragonist (ˌdjuːtəˈrægənɪst) NOUN (in ancient Greek drama) the character next in importance to the protagonist, esp the antagonist.
▷HISTORY C19: from Greek *deuteragōnistēs,* from DEUTERO- + *agōnistēs* contestant, actor

deuteranopia (ˌdjuːtərəˈnəʊpɪə) NOUN a form of colour blindness in which there is a tendency to confuse blues and greens, and greens and reds, and in which sensitivity to green is reduced.
▷HISTORY C20: New Latin, from DEUTERO- (referring to the theory in which green is the second primary colour) + AN- + Greek *-ops* eye
▸**deuteranopic** (ˌdjuːtərəˈnɒpɪk) ADJECTIVE

deuterate (ˈdjuːtəˌreɪt) VERB to treat or combine with deuterium.

deuteride (ˈdjuːtəˌraɪd) NOUN a compound of deuterium with some other element. It is analogous to a hydride.

deuterium (djuːˈtɪərɪəm) NOUN a stable isotope of hydrogen, occurring in natural hydrogen (156 parts per million) and in heavy water: used as a tracer in chemistry and biology. Symbol: D or ^{2}H; atomic no.: 1; atomic wt.: 2.014; boiling pt.: –249.7°C.
▷HISTORY C20: New Latin; see DEUTERO-, -IUM; from the fact that it is the second heaviest hydrogen isotope

deuterium oxide NOUN another name for **heavy water.**

deutero-, deuto-, *or before a vowel* **deuter-, deut-** COMBINING FORM **1** second or secondary: *deuterogamy; deuterium.* **2** (in chemistry) indicating the presence of deuterium.
▷HISTORY from Greek *deuteros* second

deuterogamy (ˌdjuːtəˈrɒgəmɪ) NOUN another word for **digamy.**
▸**ˌdeuterˈogamist** NOUN

deuteron (ˈdjuːtəˌrɒn) NOUN the nucleus of a deuterium atom, consisting of one proton and one neutron.

Deuteronomist (ˌdjuːtəˈrɒnəmɪst) NOUN one of the writers of Deuteronomy.

Deuteronomy (ˌdjuːtəˈrɒnəmɪ) NOUN the fifth book of the Old Testament, containing a second statement of the Mosaic Law.
▷HISTORY from Late Latin *Deuteronomium,* from Greek *Deuteronomion;* see DEUTERO-, -NOMY
▸**Deuteronomic** (ˌdjuːtərəˈnɒmɪk) ADJECTIVE

deuterotoky (ˌdjuːtəˈrɒtəkɪ) NOUN *Biology* parthenogenesis in which both males and females are produced.
▷HISTORY from DEUTERO- + *-toky* from Greek *tokos* bringing forth

deutoplasm (ˈdjuːtəˌplæzəm) *or* **deuteroplasm** (ˈdjuːtərəʊˌplæzəm) NOUN *Now rare* nutritive material in a cell, esp the yolk in a developing ovum.
▸**ˌdeutoˈplasmic** *or* **ˌdeutoˈplastic** ADJECTIVE

Deutschland (ˈdɔytʃlant) NOUN the German name for **Germany.**

Deutschmark (ˈdɔɪtʃˌmɑːk) *or* **Deutsche Mark** (ˈdɔɪtʃə) NOUN the former standard monetary unit of Germany, divided into 100 pfennigs; replaced by the euro in 2002: until 1990 the standard monetary unit of West Germany. Abbreviation: **DM.**

deutzia (ˈdjuːtsɪə) NOUN any saxifragaceous shrub of the genus *Deutzia:* cultivated for their clusters of white or pink spring-blooming flowers.
▷HISTORY C19: New Latin, named after Jean *Deutz,* 18th-century Dutch patron of botany

Deux-Sèvres (*French* døsɛvrə) NOUN a department of W France, in Poitou-Charentes region. Capital: Niort. Pop.: 344 392 (1999). Area: 6054 sq. km (2337 sq. miles).

deva (ˈdeɪvə) NOUN (in Hinduism and Buddhism) a divine being or god.
▷HISTORY C19: from Sanskrit: god

devaluation (diːˌvæljuːˈeɪʃən) NOUN **1** a decrease in the exchange value of a currency against gold or other currencies, brought about by a government. Compare **depreciation** (sense 4). **2** a reduction in value, status, importance, etc.

devalue (diːˈvæljuː) *or* **devaluate** (diːˈvæljuːˌeɪt) VERB **-values, -valuing, -valued** *or* **-valuates, -valuating, -valuated.** **1** to reduce (a currency) or (of a currency) be reduced in exchange value. 2 (*tr*) to reduce the value or worth of (something).

Devanagari (ˌdeɪvəˈnɑːgərɪ) NOUN a syllabic script in which Sanskrit, Hindi, and other modern languages of India are written.
▷HISTORY C18: from Sanskrit: alphabet of the gods, from *deva* god + *nagari* an Indian alphabet

devastate (ˈdɛvəˌsteɪt) VERB (*tr*) 1 to lay waste or make desolate; ravage; destroy. 2 to confound or overwhelm, as with grief or shock.
▷HISTORY C17: from Latin *dēvastāre,* from DE- + *vastāre* to ravage; related to *vastus* waste, empty
▸ˌ**devasˈtation** NOUN ▸ˈ**devasˌtative** ADJECTIVE
▸ˈ**devasˌtator** NOUN

devastating (ˈdɛvəˌsteɪtɪŋ) ADJECTIVE extremely effective in a destructive way: *a devastating war; a devastating report on urban deprivation.*
▸ˈ**devasˌtatingly** ADVERB

develop (dɪˈvɛləp) VERB 1 to come or bring to a later or more advanced or expanded stage; grow or cause to grow gradually. 2 (*tr*) to elaborate or work out in detail. 3 to disclose or unfold (thoughts, a plot, etc.) gradually or (of thoughts, etc.) to be gradually disclosed or unfolded. 4 to come or bring into existence; generate or be generated: *he developed a new faith in God.* 5 (*intr; often foll by from*) to follow as a result (of); ensue (from): *a row developed following the chairman's remarks.* 6 (*tr*) to contract (a disease or illness). 7 (*tr*) to improve the value or change the use of (land), as by building. 8 (*tr*) to exploit or make available the natural resources of (a country or region). 9 (*tr*) *Photog* **a** to treat (film, plate, or paper previously exposed to light, or the latent image in such material) with chemical solutions in order to produce a visible image. **b** to process (photographic material) in order to produce negatives and prints. 10 *Biology* to progress or cause to progress from simple to complex stages in the growth of an individual or the evolution of a species. 11 (*tr*) to elaborate upon (a musical theme) by varying the melody, key, etc. 12 (*tr*) *Maths* to expand (a function or expression) in the form of a series. 13 (*tr*) *Geometry* to project or roll out (a surface) onto a plane without stretching or shrinking any element. 14 *Chess* to bring (a piece) into play from its initial position on the back rank. 15 (*tr*) *Obsolete* to disclose or reveal.
▷HISTORY C19: from Old French *desveloper* to unwrap, from *des-* DIS-[1] + *veloper* to wrap; see ENVELOP
▸**deˈvelopable** ADJECTIVE

developer (dɪˈvɛləpə) NOUN 1 a person or thing that develops something, esp a person who develops property. 2 *Photog* a solution of a chemical reducing agent that converts the latent image recorded in the emulsion of a film or paper into a visible image.

developing agent NOUN another name for **developer** (sense 2).

developing country NOUN a nonindustrialized poor country that is seeking to develop its resources by industrialization.

developing world NOUN another name for **Third World.**

development (dɪˈvɛləpmənt) NOUN 1 the act or process of growing, progressing, or developing. 2 the product or result of developing. 3 a fact, event, or happening, esp one that changes a situation. 4 an area or tract of land that has been developed. 5 Also called: **development section.** the section of a movement, usually in sonata form, in which the basic musical themes are developed. 6 *Chess* **a** the process of developing pieces. **b** the manner in which they are developed. **c** the position of the pieces in the early part of a game with reference to their attacking potential or defensive efficiency.
▸**deˌvelopˈmental** ADJECTIVE ▸**deˌvelopˈmentally** ADVERB

developmental disorder NOUN *Psychiatry* any condition, such as autism or dyslexia, that appears in childhood and is characterized by delay in the development of one or more psychological functions, such as language skill.

development area NOUN (in Britain) an area suffering from high unemployment and economic depression, because of the decline of its main industries, that is given government help to establish new industries.

development education NOUN *Brit* an area of study that aims to give pupils an understanding of their involvement in world affairs.

development system NOUN a computer system, including hardware and software, that is specifically designed to aid in the development of software and interfaces.

development well NOUN (in the oil industry) a well drilled for the production of oil or gas from a field already proven by appraisal drilling to be suitable for exploitation.

devest (dɪˈvɛst) VERB (*tr*) a rare variant spelling of **divest.**

Devi (ˈdeɪviː) NOUN a Hindu goddess and embodiment of the female energy of Siva.
▷HISTORY Sanskrit: goddess; see DEVA

deviance (ˈdiːvɪəns) NOUN 1 Also called: **deviancy.** the act or state of being deviant. 2 *Statistics* a measure of the degree of fit of a statistical model compared to that of a more complete model.

deviant (ˈdiːvɪənt) ADJECTIVE 1 deviating, as from what is considered acceptable behaviour. ◆ NOUN 2 a person whose behaviour, esp sexual behaviour, deviates from what is considered to be acceptable.

deviate VERB (ˈdiːvɪˌeɪt) 1 (*usually intr*) to differ or diverge or cause to differ or diverge, as in belief or thought. 2 (*usually intr*) to turn aside or cause to turn aside; diverge or cause to diverge. 3 (*intr*) *Psychol* to depart from an accepted standard or convention. ◆ NOUN, ADJECTIVE (ˈdiːvɪɪt) 4 another word for **deviant.**
▷HISTORY C17: from Late Latin *dēviāre* to turn aside from the direct road, from DE- + *via* road
▸ˈ**deviˌator** NOUN ▸ˈ**deviatory** ADJECTIVE

deviation (ˌdiːvɪˈeɪʃən) NOUN 1 an act or result of deviating. 2 *Statistics* the difference between an observed value in a series of such values and their arithmetic mean. 3 the error of a compass due to local magnetic disturbances.

deviationism (ˌdiːvɪˈeɪʃəˌnɪzəm) NOUN ideological deviation (esp from orthodox Communism).
▸ˌ**deviˈationist** NOUN, ADJECTIVE

device (dɪˈvaɪs) NOUN 1 a machine or tool used for a specific task; contrivance. 2 *Euphemistic* a bomb. 3 a plan or plot, esp a clever or evil one; scheme; trick. 4 any ornamental pattern or picture, as in embroidery. 5 computer hardware that is designed for a specific function. 6 a written, printed, or painted design or figure, used as a heraldic sign, emblem, trademark, etc. 7 a particular pattern of words, figures of speech, etc., used in literature to produce an effect on the reader. 8 *Archaic* the act or process of planning or devising. 9 **leave (someone) to his own devices.** to leave (someone) alone to do as he wishes.
▷HISTORY C13: from Old French *devis* purpose, contrivance and *devise* difference, intention, from *deviser* to divide, control; see DEVISE

devil (ˈdɛvᵊl) NOUN 1 *Theol* (*often capital*) the chief spirit of evil and enemy of God, often represented as the ruler of hell and often depicted as a human figure with horns, cloven hoofs, and tail. 2 *Theol* one of the subordinate evil spirits of traditional Jewish and Christian belief. 3 a person or animal regarded as cruel, wicked, or ill-natured. 4 a person or animal regarded as unfortunate or wretched: *that poor devil was ill for months.* 5 a person or animal regarded as clever, daring, mischievous, or energetic. 6 *Informal* something difficult or annoying. 7 *Christian Science* the opposite of truth; an error, lie, or false belief in sin, sickness, and death. 8 (in Malaysia) a ghost. 9 a portable furnace or brazier, esp one used in road-making or one used by plumbers. Compare **salamander** (sense 7). 10 any of various mechanical devices, usually with teeth, such as a machine for making wooden screws or a rag-tearing machine. 11 See **printer's devil.** 12 *Law* (in England) a junior barrister who does work for another in order to gain experience, usually for a half fee. 13 *Meteorol* a small whirlwind in arid areas that raises dust or sand in a column. 14 **between the devil and the deep blue sea.** between equally undesirable alternatives. 15 **devil of.** *Informal* (intensifier): *a devil of a fine horse.* 16 **give the devil his due.** to acknowledge the talent or the success of an opponent or unpleasant person. 17 **go to the devil. a** to fail or become dissipated. **b** (*interjection*) used to express annoyance with the person causing it. 18 **like the devil.** with great speed, determination, etc. 19 **play the devil with.** *Informal* to make much worse; upset considerably: *the damp plays the devil with my rheumatism.* 20 **raise the devil. a** to cause a commotion. **b** to make a great protest. 21 **talk** (*or* **speak**) **of the devil!** (*interjection*) used when an absent person who has been the subject of conversation appears. 22 **the devil!** (intensifier): **a** used in such phrases as **what the devil, where the devil,** etc. **b** an exclamation of anger, surprise, disgust, etc. 23 **the devil's own.** a very difficult or problematic (thing). 24 **(let) the devil take the hindmost.** look after oneself and leave others to their fate. 25 **the devil to pay.** problems or trouble to be faced as a consequence of an action. 26 **the very devil.** something very difficult or awkward. ◆ VERB **-ils, -illing, -illed** *or US* **-ils, -iling, -iled.** 27 (*tr*) to prepare (esp meat, poultry, or fish) by coating with a highly flavoured spiced paste or mixture of condiments before cooking. 28 (*tr*) to tear (rags) with a devil. 29 (*intr*) to serve as a printer's devil. 30 (*intr*) *Chiefly Brit* to do hackwork, esp for a lawyer or author; perform arduous tasks, often without pay or recognition of one's services. 31 (*tr*) *US informal* to harass, vex, torment, etc.
▷HISTORY Old English *dēofol,* from Latin *diabolus,* from Greek *diabolos* enemy, accuser, slanderer, from *diaballein,* literally: to throw across, hence, to slander

devilfish (ˈdɛvᵊlˌfɪʃ) NOUN, *plural* **-fish** *or* **-fishes.** 1 Also called: **devil ray.** another name for **manta** (the fish). 2 another name for **octopus.**

devilish (ˈdɛvəlɪʃ, ˈdɛvlɪʃ) ADJECTIVE 1 of, resembling, or befitting a devil; diabolic; fiendish. ◆ ADVERB, ADJECTIVE *Informal* 2 (intensifier): *devilish good food; this devilish heat.*
▸ˈ**devilishly** ADVERB ▸ˈ**devilishness** NOUN

devil-may-care ADJECTIVE careless or reckless; happy-go-lucky: *a devil-may-care attitude.*

devilment (ˈdɛvᵊlmənt) NOUN devilish or mischievous conduct.

devilry (ˈdɛvᵊlrɪ) *or* **deviltry** NOUN, *plural* **-ries** *or* **-tries.** 1 reckless or malicious fun or mischief. 2 wickedness or cruelty. 3 black magic or other forms of diabolism.
▷HISTORY C18: from French *diablerie,* from *diable* DEVIL

devil's advocate NOUN 1 a person who advocates an opposing or unpopular view, often for the sake of argument. 2 *RC Church* the official appointed to put the case against the beatification or canonization of a candidate. Technical name: **promotor fidei** (prəʊˈməʊtɔː fɪˈdeɪiː).
▷HISTORY translation of New Latin *advocātus diabolī*

devil's bit NOUN short for **devil's bit scabious** (see **scabious**[2] (sense 3)).

devil's coach-horse NOUN a large black rove beetle, *Ocypus olens,* with large jaws and ferocious habits.

devil's darning needle NOUN a popular name for a **dragonfly.**

devil's food cake NOUN *Chiefly US and Canadian* a rich chocolate cake.

Devil's Island NOUN one of the three Safety Islands, off the coast of French Guiana: formerly a leper colony, then a French penal colony from 1895 until 1938. Area: less than 2 sq. km (1 sq. mile). French name: **Île du Diable.**

devils-on-horseback NOUN (*functioning as singular or plural*) a savoury of prunes wrapped in bacon slices and served on toast.

devious (ˈdiːvɪəs) ADJECTIVE 1 not sincere or candid; deceitful; underhand. 2 (of a route or course of action) rambling; indirect; roundabout. 3 going astray from a proper or accepted way; erring.
▷HISTORY C16: from Latin *dēvius* lying to one side of the road, from DE- + *via* road
▸ˈ**deviously** ADVERB ▸ˈ**deviousness** NOUN

devisable (dɪˈvaɪzəbᵊl) ADJECTIVE 1 *Law* (of property, esp realty) capable of being transferred by will. 2 able to be invented, contrived, or devised.

devisal (dɪˈvaɪzᵊl) NOUN the act of inventing, contriving, or devising; contrivance.

devise (dɪˈvaɪz) VERB 1 to work out, contrive, or plan (something) in one's mind. 2 (*tr*) *Law* to dispose of (property, esp real property) by will. 3 (*tr*) *Obsolete* to imagine or guess. ◆ NOUN *Law* 4 **a** a disposition of property by will. **b** the property so

transmitted. Compare **bequeath** (sense 1). 5 a will or clause in a will disposing of real property. Compare **bequest** (sense 2).
▷HISTORY C15: from Old French *deviser* to divide, apportion, intend, from Latin *dīvidere* to DIVIDE
▸**de'viser** NOUN

devisee (dɪvaɪ'zi:, ˌdɛvɪ-) NOUN *Property law* a person to whom property, esp realty, is devised by will. Compare **legatee.**

devisor (dɪ'vaɪzə) NOUN *Property law* a person who devises property, esp realty, by will.

devitalize *or* **devitalise** (di:'vaɪtəˌlaɪz) VERB *(tr)* to lower or destroy the vitality of; make weak or lifeless: *the war devitalized the economy.*
▸**deˌvitali'zation** *or* **deˌvitali'sation** NOUN

devitrify (di:'vɪtrɪˌfaɪ) VERB **-fies, -fying, -fied.** 1 to change from a vitreous state to a crystalline state. 2 to lose or cause to lose the properties of a glass and become brittle and opaque.
▸**deˌvitrifi'cation** NOUN

Devizes (də'vaɪzəz) NOUN a market town in S England, in Wiltshire: agricultural and dairy products. Pop.: 13 205 (1991).

devoice (di:'vɔɪs), **devocalize,** *or* **devocalise** (di:'vəʊkəˌlaɪz) VERB *(tr) Phonetics* to make (a voiced speech sound) voiceless.

devoid (dɪ'vɔɪd) ADJECTIVE *(postpositive;* foll by *of)* destitute or void (of); free (from).
▷HISTORY C15: originally past participle of *devoid (vb)* to remove, from Old French *devoidier,* from *de-* DE- + *voider* to VOID

devoirs (də'vwɑ:; *French* dəvwar) PLURAL NOUN *(sometimes singular)* compliments or respects; courteous attentions.
▷HISTORY C13: from Old French: duty, from *devoir* to be obliged to, owe, from Latin *dēbēre;* see DEBT

devolution (ˌdi:və'lu:ʃən) NOUN 1 the act, fact, or result of devolving. 2 a passing onwards or downwards from one stage to another. 3 another word for **degeneration** (sense 3). 4 a transfer or allocation of authority, esp from a central government to regional governments or particular interests.
▷HISTORY C16: from Medieval Latin *dēvolūtiō* a rolling down, from Latin *dēvolvere* to roll down, sink into; see DEVOLVE
▸**ˌdevo'lutionary** ADJECTIVE ▸**ˌdevo'lutionist** NOUN, ADJECTIVE

devolve (dɪ'vɒlv) VERB 1 (foll by *on, upon, to,* etc.) to pass or cause to pass to a successor or substitute, as duties, power, etc. 2 *(intr;* foll by *on* or *upon) Law* (of an estate, etc.) to pass to another by operation of law, esp on intestacy or bankruptcy. 3 *(intr;* foll by *on* or *upon)* to depend (on): *your argument devolves on how you interpret this clause.* 4 *Archaic* to roll down or cause to roll down.
▷HISTORY C15: from Latin *dēvolvere* to roll down, fall into, from DE- + *volvere* to roll
▸**de'volvement** NOUN

devon ('dɛvən) NOUN *Austral* a bland processed meat in sausage form, eaten cold in slices.
▷HISTORY named after DEVON

Devon ('dɛvᵊn) NOUN 1 Also called: **Devonshire.** a county of SW England, between the Bristol Channel and the English Channel, including the island of Lundy: the geographic and ceremonial county includes Plymouth and Torbay, which became independent unitary authorities in 1998; hilly, rising to the uplands of Exmoor and Dartmoor, with wooded river valleys and a rugged coastline. Administrative centre: Exeter. Pop. (excluding unitary authorities): 704 499 (2001). Area (excluding unitary authorities): 6569 sq. km (2536 sq. miles). 2 a breed of large red beef cattle originally from Devon.

Devonian (də'vəʊnɪən) ADJECTIVE 1 of, denoting, or formed in the fourth period of the Palaeozoic era, between the Silurian and Carboniferous periods, lasting 60–70 million years during which amphibians first appeared. 2 of or relating to Devon. ◆ NOUN 3 **the.** the Devonian period or rock system.

Devon minnow NOUN *Angling* a spinning lure intended to imitate the swimming motion of a minnow. Often shortened to: **Devon.**

Devon Rex NOUN a breed of medium-sized curly-haired cat with large eyes and very large ears.

Devonshire cream NOUN another name for **clotted cream.**

Devonshire split NOUN a kind of yeast bun split open and served with whipped cream or butter and jam. Also called: **Cornish split, split.**

devoré (də'vɔ:reɪ) NOUN a velvet fabric with a raised pattern created by disintegrating some of the pile with chemicals.
▷HISTORY from French, past participle of *dévorer* to devour

devote (dɪ'vəʊt) VERB *(tr)* 1 to apply or dedicate (oneself, time, money, etc.) to some pursuit, cause, etc. 2 *Obsolete* to curse or doom.
▷HISTORY C16: from Latin *dēvōtus* devoted, solemnly promised, from *dēvovēre* to vow; see DE-, VOW
▸**de'votement** NOUN

devoted (dɪ'vəʊtɪd) ADJECTIVE 1 feeling or demonstrating loyalty or devotion; ardent; devout. 2 *(postpositive;* foll by *to)* set apart, dedicated, or consecrated.
▸**de'votedly** ADVERB ▸**de'votedness** NOUN

devotee (ˌdɛvə'ti:) NOUN 1 a person ardently enthusiastic about or devoted to something, such as a sport or pastime. 2 a zealous follower of a religion.

devotion (dɪ'vəʊʃən) NOUN 1 (often foll by *to*) strong attachment (to) or affection (for a cause, person, etc.) marked by dedicated loyalty. 2 religious zeal; piety. 3 *(often plural)* religious observance or prayers.

devotional (dɪ'vəʊʃənᵊl) ADJECTIVE 1 relating to, characterized by, or conducive to devotion. ◆ NOUN 2 *(often plural)* a short religious or prayer service.
▸**deˌvotion'ality** *or* **de'votionalness** NOUN ▸**de'votionally** ADVERB

devour (dɪ'vaʊə) VERB *(tr)* 1 to swallow or eat up greedily or voraciously. 2 to waste or destroy; consume: *the flames devoured the curtains.* 3 to consume greedily or avidly with the senses or mind: *he devoured the manuscripts.* 4 to engulf or absorb: *the flood devoured the land.*
▷HISTORY C14: from Old French *devourer,* from Latin *dēvorāre* to gulp down, from DE- + *vorāre* to consume greedily; see VORACIOUS
▸**de'vourer** NOUN ▸**de'vouring** ADJECTIVE ▸**de'vouringly** ADVERB

devout (dɪ'vaʊt) ADJECTIVE 1 deeply religious; reverent. 2 sincere; earnest; heartfelt: *a devout confession.*
▷HISTORY C13: from Old French *devot,* from Late Latin *dēvōtus,* from Latin: faithful; see DEVOTE
▸**de'voutly** ADVERB ▸**de'voutness** NOUN

dew (dju:) NOUN 1 **a** drops of water condensed on a cool surface, esp at night, from vapour in the air. **b** *(in combination): dewdrop.* 2 something like or suggestive of this, esp in freshness: *the dew of youth.* 3 small drops of moisture, such as tears. ◆ VERB 4 *(tr) Poetic* to moisten with or as with dew.
▷HISTORY Old English *dēaw;* related to Old High German *tou* dew, Old Norse *dögg*

dewan *or* **diwan** (dɪ'wɑ:n) NOUN (formerly in India) the chief minister or finance minister of a state ruled by an Indian prince.
▷HISTORY C17: from Hindi *dīwān,* from Persian *dēvan* register, book of accounts; see DIVAN

Dewar flask ('dju:ə) NOUN a type of vacuum flask, esp one used in scientific experiments to keep liquid air, helium, etc.; Thermos.
▷HISTORY C20: named after Sir James *Dewar* (1842–1923), Scottish chemist and physicist

dewberry ('dju:bərɪ, -brɪ) NOUN, *plural* **-ries.** 1 any trailing bramble, such as *Rubus hispidus* of North America and *R. caesius* of Europe and NW Asia, having blue-black fruits. 2 the fruit of any such plant.

dewclaw ('dju:ˌklɔ:) NOUN 1 a nonfunctional claw in dogs; the rudimentary first digit. 2 an analogous rudimentary hoof in deer, goats, etc.
▸**'dewˌclawed** ADJECTIVE

dewdrop ('dju:ˌdrɒp) NOUN 1 a drop of dew. 2 *Brit euphemistic* a drop of mucus on the end of one's nose.

Dewey Decimal System ('dju:ɪ) NOUN a frequently used system of library book classification and arrangement with ten main subject classes. Also called: **decimal classification.** Abbreviation: **DDS.**
▷HISTORY C19: named after Melvil *Dewey* (1851–1931), US educator who invented the system

dewlap ('dju:ˌlæp) NOUN 1 a loose fold of skin hanging from beneath the throat in cattle, dogs, etc. 2 loose skin on an elderly person's throat.
▷HISTORY C14 *dewlappe,* from DEW (probably changed by folk etymology from an earlier form of different meaning) + LAP[1] (from Old English *læppa* hanging flap), perhaps of Scandinavian origin; compare Danish *doglæp*
▸**'dewˌlapped** ADJECTIVE

DEW line (dju:) NOUN ACRONYM FOR distant early warning line, a network of radar stations situated mainly in Arctic regions to give early warning of aircraft or missile attack on North America.

dew point NOUN the temperature at which water vapour in the air becomes saturated and water droplets begin to form.

dew pond NOUN a shallow pond, usually man-made, that is kept supplied with water by dew and condensation.

Dewsbury ('dju:zbərɪ, -brɪ) NOUN a town in N England, in Kirklees unitary authority, West Yorkshire: formerly a centre of the woollen industry. Pop.: 50 168 (1991).

dew snail NOUN *Southwest English dialect* a slug.

dew-worm NOUN any large earthworm that is found on the ground at night and is used as fishing bait.

dewy ('dju:ɪ) ADJECTIVE **dewier, dewiest.** 1 moist with or as with dew: *a dewy complexion.* 2 of or resembling dew. 3 *Poetic* suggesting, falling, or refreshing like dew: *dewy sleep.*
▸**'dewily** ADVERB ▸**'dewiness** NOUN

dewy-eyed ADJECTIVE naive, innocent, or trusting, esp in a romantic or childlike way.

Dexedrine ('dɛksɪˌdri:n) NOUN a trademark for **dextroamphetamine.**

dexiotropic (ˌdɛksɪəʊ'trɒpɪk) ADJECTIVE *Embryol* (of cleavage) spiral; twisting in a spiral fashion from left to right.
▷HISTORY C19: from Greek *dexios* right + -TROPIC

dexter[1] ('dɛkstə) ADJECTIVE 1 *Archaic* of or located on the right side. 2 *(usually postpositive) Heraldry* of, on, or starting from the right side of a shield from the bearer's point of view and therefore on the spectator's left. ◆ Compare **sinister.**
▷HISTORY C16: from Latin; compare Greek *dexios* on the right hand

dexter[2] ('dɛkstə) NOUN a small breed of red or black beef cattle, originally from Ireland.
▷HISTORY C19: perhaps from the surname of the original breeder

dexterity (dɛk'stɛrɪtɪ) NOUN 1 physical, esp manual, skill or nimbleness. 2 mental skill or adroitness: cleverness. 3 *Rare* the characteristic of being right-handed.
▷HISTORY C16: from Latin *dexteritās* aptness, readiness, prosperity; see DEXTER[1]

dexterous *or* **dextrous** ('dɛkstrəs) ADJECTIVE 1 possessing or done with dexterity. 2 a rare word for **right-handed.**
▸**'dexterously** *or* **'dextrously** ADVERB ▸**'dexterousness** *or* **'dextrousness** NOUN

dextral ('dɛkstrəl) ADJECTIVE 1 of, relating to, or located on the right side, esp of the body; right-hand. 2 of or relating to a person who prefers to use his right foot, hand, or eye; right-handed. 3 (of the shells of certain gastropod molluscs) coiling in an anticlockwise direction from the apex; dextrorse. ◆ Compare **sinistral.**
▸**dextrality** (dɛk'strælɪtɪ) NOUN ▸**'dextrally** ADVERB

dextran ('dɛkstrən) NOUN *Biochem* a polysaccharide produced by the action of bacteria on sucrose: used as a substitute for plasma in blood transfusions.
▷HISTORY C19: from DEXTRO- + -AN

dextrin ('dɛkstrɪn) *or* **dextrine** ('dɛkstrɪn, -tri:n) NOUN any of a group of sticky substances that are intermediate products in the conversion of starch to maltose: used as thickening agents in foods and as gums.
▷HISTORY C19: from French *dextrine;* see DEXTRO-, -IN

dextro ('dɛkstrəʊ) ADJECTIVE short for **dextrorotatory.**

dextro- *or before a vowel* **dextr-** COMBINING FORM 1 on or towards the right: *dextrorotation.* 2 (in chemistry) indicating a dextrorotatory compound: *dextroglucose.*

▷HISTORY from Latin, from *dexter* on the right side

dextroamphetamine (ˌdɛkstrəʊæmˈfɛtəˌmiːn, -mɪn) NOUN a dextrorotatory amphetamine, used to suppress appetite.

dextrocardia (ˌdɛkstrəʊˈkɑːdɪə) NOUN *Med* the abnormal location of the heart in the right side of the chest.

dextroglucose (ˌdɛkstrəʊˈgluːkəʊz, -kəʊs) NOUN another name for **dextrose**.

dextrogyrate (ˌdɛkstrəʊˈdʒaɪrɪt, -ˌreɪt) *or* **dextrogyre** (ˈdɛkstrəʊˌdʒaɪə) ADJECTIVE having dextrorotation.

dextrorotation (ˌdɛkstrəʊrəʊˈteɪʃən) NOUN a rotation to the right; clockwise rotation, esp of the plane of polarization of plane-polarized light passing through a crystal, liquid, or solution, as seen by an observer facing the oncoming light. Compare **laevorotation**.
▸**dextrorotatory** (ˌdɛkstrəʊˈrəʊtətərɪ, -trɪ) *or* ˌ**dextroˈrotary** ADJECTIVE

dextrorse (ˈdɛkstrɔːs, dɛkˈstrɔːs) *or* **dextrorsal** (dɛkˈstrɔːsᵊl) ADJECTIVE (of some climbing plants) growing upwards in a helix from left to right or anticlockwise. Compare **sinistrorse**.
▷HISTORY C19: from Latin *dextrorsum* towards the right, from DEXTRO- + *vorsus* turned, variant of *versus,* from *vertere* to turn
▸ˈ**dextrorsely** ADVERB

dextrose (ˈdɛkstrəʊz, -trəʊs) NOUN a white soluble sweet-tasting crystalline solid that is the dextrorotatory isomer of glucose, occurring widely in fruit, honey, and in the blood and tissue of animals. Formula: $C_6H_{12}O_6$. Also called: **grape sugar, dextroglucose**.

dextrous (ˈdɛkstrəs) ADJECTIVE a variant spelling of **dexterous**.
▸ˈ**dextrously** ADVERB ▸ˈ**dextrousness** NOUN

dey (deɪ) NOUN [1] the title given to commanders or (from 1710) governors of the Janissaries of Algiers (1671–1830). [2] a title applied by Western writers to various other Ottoman governors, such as the bey of Tunis.
▷HISTORY C17: from French, from Turkish *dayi,* literally: maternal uncle, hence title given to an older person

Dezhnev (*Russian* dɪʒˈnjɔf) NOUN **Cape.** a cape in NE Russia at the E end of Chukotski Peninsula: the northeasternmost point of Asia. Former name: **East Cape**.

DF ABBREVIATION FOR **Defender of the Faith**.

D/F *or* **DF** *Telecomm* ABBREVIATION FOR: [1] direction finder. [2] direction finding.

DFC ABBREVIATION FOR Distinguished Flying Cross.

DfEE (in Britain) ABBREVIATION FOR Department for Education and Employment.

DFID (in Britain) ABBREVIATION FOR Department for International Development.

DFM ABBREVIATION FOR Distinguished Flying Medal.

dg *or* **dg.** ABBREVIATION FOR decigram.

DG ABBREVIATION FOR: [1] Deo gratias. [2] director-general.

DHA (in Britain) ABBREVIATION FOR District Health Authority.

dhak (dɑːk, dɔːk) NOUN a tropical Asian leguminous tree, *Butea frondosa,* that has bright red flowers and yields a red resin, used as an astringent.
▷HISTORY C19: from Hindi

Dhaka *or* **Dacca** (ˈdækə) NOUN the capital of Bangladesh, in the E central part: capital of Bengal (1608–39; 1660–1704) and of East Pakistan (1949–71); jute and cotton mills; university (1921). Pop.: 3 839 000 (1991).

dhal, dal, *or* **dholl** (dɑːl) NOUN [1] a tropical African and Asian leguminous shrub, *Cajanus cajan,* cultivated in tropical regions for its nutritious pealike seeds. [2] the seed of this shrub. ◆ Also called: **pigeon pea.** [3] a curry made from lentils or other pulses.
▷HISTORY C17: from Hindi *dāl* split pulse, from Sanskrit *dal* to split

dhamma (ˈdɑːmə, ˈdʌmə) NOUN a variant of **dharma**.
▷HISTORY from Pali, from Sanskrit: see DHARMA

dhansak (ˈdænzæk) NOUN any of a variety of Indian dishes consisting of meat or vegetables braised with water or stock and lentils.
▷HISTORY C20: from Urdu

dharma (ˈdɑːmə) NOUN [1] *Hinduism* social custom regarded as a religious and moral duty. [2] *Hinduism* **a** the essential principle of the cosmos; natural law. **b** conduct that conforms with this. [3] *Buddhism* ideal truth as set forth in the teaching of Buddha.
▷HISTORY Sanskrit: habit, usage, law, from *dhārayati* he holds

dharna *or* **dhurna** (ˈdʌnə, ˈdɑː-) NOUN (in India) a method of obtaining justice, as the payment of a debt, by sitting, fasting, at the door of the person from whom reparation is sought.
▷HISTORY C18: from Hindi, literally: a placing

DHB (in New Zealand) ABBREVIATION FOR District Health Board.

Dhílos (ˈðilɔs) NOUN transliteration of the Modern Greek name for **Delos**.

dhobi (ˈdəʊbɪ) NOUN, *plural* **-bis.** (in India, Malaya, East Africa, etc., esp formerly) a washerman.
▷HISTORY C19: from Hindi, from *dhōb* washing; related to Sanskrit *dhāvaka* washerman

dhobi itch NOUN a fungal disease of the skin: a type of ringworm chiefly affecting the groin. Also called: **tinea cruris**.

Dhodhekánisos (ðɔðɛˈkanisɔs) NOUN a transliteration of the modern Greek name for the **Dodecanese**.

dhole (dəʊl) NOUN a fierce canine mammal, *Cuon alpinus,* of the forests of central and SE Asia, having a reddish-brown coat and rounded ears: hunts in packs.
▷HISTORY C19: of uncertain origin

dholl (dɑːl) NOUN a variant spelling of **dhal**.

dhoti (ˈdəʊtɪ), **dhooti, dhootie,** *or* **dhuti** (ˈduːtɪ) NOUN, *plural* **-tis.** a long loincloth worn by men in India.
▷HISTORY C17: from Hindi

dhow (daʊ) NOUN a lateen-rigged coastal Arab sailing vessel with one or two masts.
▷HISTORY C19: from Arabic *dāwa*

DHS (in Canada) ABBREVIATION FOR district high school.

DHSS (formerly, in Britain) ABBREVIATION FOR Department of Health and Social Security.

Di THE CHEMICAL SYMBOL FOR didymium.

DI ABBREVIATION FOR: [1] Defence Intelligence. [2] Detective Inspector. [3] Donor Insemination.

di-¹ PREFIX [1] twice; two; double: *dicotyledon.* [2] **a** containing two specified atoms or groups of atoms: *dimethyl ether; carbon dioxide.* **b** a nontechnical equivalent of **bi-¹** (sense 5c).
▷HISTORY via Latin from Greek, from *dis* twice, double, related to *duo* two. Compare BI-¹

di-² COMBINING FORM variant of **dia-** before a vowel: *diopter.*

dia- *or* **di-** PREFIX [1] through, throughout, or during: *diachronic.* [2] across: *diactinic.* [3] apart: *diacritic.* [4] (in botany) at right angles: *diatropism.* [5] in opposite or different directions: *diamagnetism.*
▷HISTORY from Greek *dia* through, between, across, by

diabase (ˈdaɪəˌbeɪs) NOUN [1] *Brit* an altered dolerite. [2] *US* another name for **dolerite**.
▷HISTORY C19: from French, from Greek *diabasis* a crossing over, from *diabainein* to cross over, from DIA- + *bainein* to go
▸ˌ**diaˈbasic** ADJECTIVE

diabetes (ˌdaɪəˈbiːtɪs, -tiːz) NOUN any of various disorders, esp diabetes mellitus, characterized by excretion of an abnormally large amount of urine.
▷HISTORY C16: from Latin: siphon, from Greek, literally: a passing through (referring to the excessive urination), from *diabainein* to pass through, cross over; see DIABASE

diabetes insipidus (ɪnˈsɪpɪdəs) NOUN a disorder of the pituitary gland causing excessive thirst and excretion of large quantities of dilute urine.
▷HISTORY C18: New Latin, literally: insipid diabetes

diabetes mellitus (məˈlaɪtəs) NOUN a disorder of carbohydrate metabolism characterized by excessive thirst and excretion of abnormally large quantities of urine containing an excess of sugar, caused by a deficiency of insulin. ◆ See also **IDDM, NIDDM**.
▷HISTORY C18: New Latin, literally: honey-sweet diabetes

diabetic (ˌdaɪəˈbɛtɪk) ADJECTIVE [1] of, relating to, or having diabetes. [2] for the use of diabetics: *diabetic chocolate.* ◆ NOUN [3] a person who has diabetes.

diablerie (dɪˈɑːblərɪ; *French* djɑbləri) NOUN [1] magic or witchcraft connected with devils. [2] demonic lore or esoteric knowledge of devils. [3] the domain of devils. [4] devilry; mischief.
▷HISTORY C18: from Old French, from *diable* devil, from Latin *diabolus;* see DEVIL

diabolic (ˌdaɪəˈbɒlɪk) ADJECTIVE [1] of, relating to, or proceeding from the devil; satanic. [2] befitting a devil; extremely cruel or wicked; fiendish. [3] very difficult or unpleasant.
▷HISTORY C14: from Late Latin *diabolicus,* from Greek *diabolikos,* from *diabolos* DEVIL
▸ˌ**diaˈbolically** ADVERB ▸ˌ**diaˈbolicalness** NOUN

diabolical (ˌdaɪəˈbɒlɪkᵊl) ADJECTIVE *Informal* [1] excruciatingly bad; outrageous. [2] (intensifier): *a diabolical liberty.*
▸ˌ**diaˈbolically** ADVERB ▸ˌ**diaˈbolicalness** NOUN

diabolism (daɪˈæbəˌlɪzəm) NOUN [1] **a** activities designed to enlist the aid of devils, esp in witchcraft or sorcery. **b** worship of devils or beliefs and teachings concerning them. **c** the nature of devils. [2] character or conduct that is devilish or fiendish; devilry.
▸**diˈabolist** NOUN

diabolize *or* **diabolise** (daɪˈæbəˌlaɪz) VERB (*tr*) [1] **a** to make (someone or something) diabolical. **b** to subject to the influence of devils. [2] to portray as diabolical.

diabolo (dɪˈæbəˌləʊ) NOUN, *plural* **-los.** [1] a game in which one throws and catches a spinning top on a cord fastened to two sticks held in the hands. [2] the top used in this game.

diacaustic (ˌdaɪəˈkɔːstɪk, -ˈkɒs-) ADJECTIVE [1] (of a caustic curve or surface) formed by refracted light rays. ◆ NOUN [2] a diacaustic curve or surface. ◆ Compare **catacaustic**.

diacetylmorphine (daɪˌæsətɪlˈmɔːfiːn) NOUN another name for **heroin**.

diachronic (ˌdaɪəˈkrɒnɪk) ADJECTIVE of, relating to, or studying the development of a phenomenon through time; historical: *diachronic linguistics.* Compare **synchronic**.
▷HISTORY C19: from DIA- + Greek *khronos* time

diachronism (daɪˈækrəˌnɪzəm) NOUN *Geology* the passage of a geological formation across time planes, as occurs when a marine sediment laid down by an advancing sea is noticeably younger in the direction of advancement.
▸**diˈachronous** ADJECTIVE

diacid (daɪˈæsɪd) ADJECTIVE [1] another word for **diacidic.** [2] (of a salt or acid) containing two acidic hydrogen atoms: *NaH_2PO_4 is a diacid salt of phosphoric acid.* ◆ NOUN [3] an acid or salt that contains two acidic hydrogen atoms.

diacidic (ˌdaɪəˈsɪdɪk) ADJECTIVE (of a base, such as calcium hydroxide $Ca(OH)_2$) capable of neutralizing two protons with one of its molecules. Also: **diacid.** Compare **dibasic**.

diaconal (daɪˈækənᵊl) ADJECTIVE of or associated with a deacon or the diaconate.
▷HISTORY C17: from Late Latin *diāconālis,* from *diāconus* DEACON

diaconate (daɪˈækənɪt, -ˌneɪt) NOUN the office, sacramental status, or period of office of a deacon.
▷HISTORY C17: from Late Latin *diāconātus;* see DEACON

diacritic (ˌdaɪəˈkrɪtɪk) NOUN [1] Also called: **diacritical mark.** a sign placed above or below a character or letter to indicate that it has a different phonetic value, is stressed, or for some other reason. ◆ ADJECTIVE [2] another word for **diacritical**.
▷HISTORY C17: from Greek *diakritikos* serving to distinguish, from *diakrinein,* from DIA- + *krinein* to separate

diacritical (ˌdaɪəˈkrɪtɪkᵊl) ADJECTIVE [1] of or relating to a diacritic. [2] showing up a distinction.
▸ˌ**diaˈcritically** ADVERB

diactinic (ˌdaɪækˈtɪnɪk) ADJECTIVE *Physics* able to transmit photochemically active radiation.
▸**diˈactinism** NOUN

diadelphous (ˌdaɪəˈdɛlfəs) ADJECTIVE [1] (of stamens) having united filaments so that they are

arranged in two groups. [2] (of flowers) having diadelphous stamens.
▷HISTORY C19: from DI-[1] + Greek *adelphos* brother

diadem ('daɪəˌdɛm) NOUN [1] a royal crown, esp a light jewelled circlet. [2] royal dignity or power. ◆ VERB [3] (*tr*) to adorn or crown with or as with a diadem.
▷HISTORY C13: from Latin *diadēma,* from Greek: fillet, royal headdress, from *diadein* to bind around, from DIA- + *dein* to bind

diadem spider NOUN a common Eurasian spider, *Araneus diadematus,* that constructs orb webs: family *Argiopidae.*

diadochy (daɪ'ædəʊkɪ) NOUN *Geology* the replacement of one element in a crystal by another.
▷HISTORY C20: from Greek *diadochē* succession

diadromous (daɪ'ædrəməs) ADJECTIVE [1] *Botany* of or possessing a leaf venation in the shape of a fan. [2] (of some fishes) migrating between fresh and salt water. See also **anadromous, catadromous.**

diaeresis *or* **dieresis** (daɪ'ɛrɪsɪs) NOUN, *plural* **-ses** (-ˌsiːz). [1] the mark ¨, in writing placed over the second of two adjacent vowels to indicate that it is to be pronounced separately rather than forming a diphthong with the first, as in some spellings of *coöperate, naïve,* etc. [2] this mark used for any other purpose, such as to indicate that a special pronunciation is appropriate to a particular vowel. Compare **umlaut.** [3] a pause in a line of verse occurring when the end of a foot coincides with the end of a word.
▷HISTORY C17: from Latin *diarēsis,* from Greek *diairesis* a division, from *diairein,* from DIA- + *hairein* to take; compare HERESY
▸**diaeretic** *or* **dieretic** (ˌdaɪə'rɛtɪk) ADJECTIVE

diag. ABBREVIATION FOR diagram.

diagenesis (ˌdaɪə'dʒɛnɪsɪs) NOUN [1] the sum of the physical, chemical, and biological changes that take place in sediments as they become consolidated into rocks, including compaction and cementation, but excluding weathering and metamorphic changes. [2] *Chem* recrystallization of a solid to form large crystal grains from smaller ones.
▸**diagenetic** (ˌdaɪədʒə'nɛtɪk) ADJECTIVE

diageotropism (ˌdaɪədʒɪ'ɒtrəˌpɪzəm) NOUN a diatropic response of plant parts, such as rhizomes, to the stimulus of gravity.
▸**diageotropic** (ˌdaɪəˌdʒiːəʊ'trɒpɪk) ADJECTIVE

diagnose ('daɪəgˌnəʊz) VERB [1] to determine or distinguish by diagnosis. [2] (*tr*) to examine (a person or thing), as for a disease.
▸ˌ**diag'nosable** ADJECTIVE

diagnosis (ˌdaɪəg'nəʊsɪs) NOUN, *plural* **-ses** (-siːz). [1] **a** the identification of diseases by the examination of symptoms and signs and by other investigations. **b** an opinion or conclusion so reached. [2] **a** thorough analysis of facts or problems in order to gain understanding and aid future planning. **b** an opinion or conclusion reached through such analysis. [3] a detailed description of an organism, esp a plant, for the purpose of classification.
▷HISTORY C17: New Latin, from Greek: a distinguishing, from *diagignōskein* to distinguish, from *gignōskein* to perceive, KNOW

diagnostic (ˌdaɪəg'nɒstɪk) ADJECTIVE [1] of, relating to, or of value in diagnosis. ◆ NOUN [2] *Med* any symptom that provides evidence for making a specific diagnosis. [3] a diagnosis.
▸ˌ**diag'nostically** ADVERB

diagnostician (ˌdaɪəgnɒs'tɪʃən) NOUN a specialist or expert in making diagnoses.

diagnostics (ˌdaɪəg'nɒstɪks) NOUN (*functioning as singular*) the art or practice of diagnosis, esp of diseases.

diagonal (daɪ'ægənᵊl) ADJECTIVE [1] *Maths* connecting any two vertices that in a polygon are not adjacent and in a polyhedron are not in the same face. [2] slanting; oblique. [3] marked with slanting lines or patterns. ◆ NOUN [4] *Maths* a diagonal line or plane. [5] *Chess* any oblique row of squares of the same colour. [6] cloth marked or woven with slanting lines or patterns. [7] something put, set, or drawn obliquely. [8] another name for **solidus** (sense 1). [9] one front leg and the hind leg on the opposite side of a horse, which are on the ground together when the horse is trotting.
▷HISTORY C16: from Latin *diagōnālis,* from Greek *diagōnios,* from DIA- + *gōnia* angle
▸**di'agonally** ADVERB

diagonal process NOUN *Maths, logic* a form of argument in which a new member of a set is constructed from a list of its known members by making the *n*th term of the new member differ from the *n*th term of the *n*th member. The new member is thus different from every member of the list.

diagram ('daɪəˌgræm) NOUN [1] a sketch, outline, or plan demonstrating the form or workings of something. [2] *Maths* a pictorial representation of a quantity or of a relationship: *a Venn diagram.* ◆ VERB **-grams, -gramming, -grammed** *or US* **-grams, -graming, -gramed.** [3] to show in or as if in a diagram.
▷HISTORY C17: from Latin *diagramma,* from Greek, from *diagraphein,* from *graphein* to write
▸**diagrammatic** (ˌdaɪəgrə'mætɪk) ADJECTIVE
▸ˌ**diagram'matically** ADVERB

diagraph ('daɪəˌgrɑːf, -ˌgræf) NOUN [1] a device for enlarging or reducing maps, plans, etc. [2] a protractor and scale used in drawing.
▷HISTORY C19: from French *diagraphe,* from Greek *diagraphein* to represent with lines; see DIAGRAM

diakinesis (ˌdaɪəkɪ'niːsɪs, -kaɪ-) NOUN the final stage of the prophase of meiosis, during which homologous chromosomes start to separate after crossing over.
▷HISTORY C20: from DIA- + Greek *kinēsis* movement

dial ('daɪəl, daɪl) NOUN [1] the face of a watch, clock, chronometer, sundial, etc., marked with divisions representing units of time. [2] the circular graduated disc of various measuring instruments. [3] **a** the control on a radio or television set used to change the station or channel. **b** the panel on a radio on which the frequency, wavelength, or station is indicated by means of a pointer. [4] a numbered disc on a telephone that is rotated a set distance for each digit of a number being called. [5] a miner's compass for surveying in a mine. [6] *Brit* a slang word for **face** (sense 1). ◆ VERB **dials, dialling, dialled** *or US* **dials, dialing, dialed.** [7] to establish or try to establish a telephone connection with (a subscriber or his number) by operating the dial on a telephone. [8] (*tr*) to indicate, measure, or operate with a dial.
▷HISTORY C14: from Medieval Latin *diālis* daily, from Latin *diēs* day
▸'**dialler** NOUN

dial. ABBREVIATION FOR dialect(al).

dialect ('daɪəˌlɛkt) NOUN **a** a form of a language spoken in a particular geographical area or by members of a particular social class or occupational group, distinguished by its vocabulary, grammar, and pronunciation. **b** a form of a language that is considered inferior: *the farmer spoke dialect and was despised by the merchants.* **c** (*as modifier*): *a dialect word.*
▷HISTORY C16: from Latin *dialectus,* from Greek *dialektos* speech, dialect, discourse, from *dialegesthai* to converse, from *legein* to talk, speak
▸ˌ**dia'lectal** ADJECTIVE

dialect atlas NOUN another term for **linguistic atlas.**

dialect geography NOUN another term for **linguistic geography.**
▸**dialect geographer** NOUN

dialectic (ˌdaɪə'lɛktɪk) NOUN [1] disputation or debate, esp intended to resolve differences between two views rather than to establish one of them as true. [2] *Philosophy* **a** the conversational Socratic method of argument. **b** (in Plato) the highest study, that of the Forms. [3] (in the writings of Kant) the exposure of the contradictions implicit in applying empirical concepts beyond the limits of experience. [4] *Philosophy* the process of reconciliation of contradiction either of beliefs or in historical processes. See also **Hegelian dialectic, dialectical materialism.** ◆ ADJECTIVE [5] of or relating to logical disputation.
▷HISTORY C17: from Latin *dialectica,* from Greek *dialektikē* (*tekhnē*) (the art) of argument; see DIALECT
▸ˌ**dialec'tician** NOUN

dialectical (ˌdaɪə'lɛktɪkᵊl) ADJECTIVE of or relating to dialectic or dialectics.
▸ˌ**dia'lectically** ADVERB

dialectical materialism NOUN the economic, political, and philosophical system of Karl Marx (1818-83) and Friedrich Engels (1820–95), the German political philosophers, that combines traditional materialism and Hegelian dialectic.
▸**dialectical materialist** NOUN

dialectics (ˌdaɪə'lɛktɪks) NOUN (*functioning as plural or* (*sometimes*) *singular*) [1] the study of reasoning or of argumentative methodology. [2] a particular methodology or system; a logic. [3] the application of the Hegelian dialectic or the rationale of dialectical materialism.

dialectology (ˌdaɪəlɛk'tɒlədʒɪ) NOUN the study of dialects and dialectal variations.
▸**dialectological** (ˌdaɪəˌlɛktə'lɒdʒɪkᵊl) ADJECTIVE
▸ˌ**diaˌlecto'logically** ADVERB ▸ˌ**dialec'tologist** NOUN

dial gauge NOUN another name for an **indicator** (sense 6).

diallage ('daɪəlɪdʒ) NOUN a green or brownish-black variety of the mineral augite in the form of layers of platelike crystals.
▷HISTORY C19: from Greek *diallagē* interchange

dialling code NOUN a sequence of numbers which are dialled for connection with another exchange before an individual subscriber's telephone number is dialled.

dialling tone *or US and Canadian* **dial tone** NOUN a continuous sound, either purring or high-pitched, heard over a telephone indicating that a number can be dialled. Compare **ringing tone, engaged tone.**

dialogism (daɪ'æləˌdʒɪzəm) NOUN [1] *Logic* a deduction with one premise and a disjunctive conclusion. [2] *Rhetoric* a discussion in an imaginary dialogue or discourse.

dialogist (daɪ'ælədʒɪst) NOUN a person who writes or takes part in a dialogue.
▸ˌ**dialo'gistic** *or* ˌ**dialo'gistical** ADJECTIVE

dialogize *or* **dialogise** (daɪ'æləˌdʒaɪz) VERB (*intr*) to carry on a dialogue.

dialogue *or often US* **dialog** ('daɪəˌlɒg) NOUN [1] conversation between two or more people. [2] an exchange of opinions on a particular subject; discussion. [3] the lines spoken by characters in drama or fiction. [4] a particular passage of conversation in a literary or dramatic work. [5] a literary composition in the form of a dialogue. [6] a political discussion between representatives of two nations or groups. ◆ VERB *Rare* [7] (*tr*) to put into the form of a dialogue. [8] (*intr*) to take part in a dialogue; converse.
▷HISTORY C13: from Old French *dialoge,* from Latin *dialogus,* from Greek *dialogos,* from *dialegesthai* to converse; see DIALECT
▸**dialogic** (ˌdaɪə'lɒdʒɪk) ADJECTIVE ▸'**diaˌloguer** NOUN

dialogue *or* **dialog box** NOUN *Computing* a window that may appear on a VDU display to prompt the user to enter further information or select an option.

dialyse *or US* **dialyze** ('daɪəˌlaɪz) VERB (*tr*) to separate by dialysis.
▸'**diaˌlysable** *or US* '**diaˌlyzable** ADJECTIVE ▸ˌ**diaˌlysa'bility** *or US* ˌ**diaˌlyza'bility** NOUN ▸ˌ**dialy'sation** *or US* ˌ**dialy'zation** NOUN

dialyser *or US* **dialyzer** ('daɪəˌlaɪzə) NOUN a machine that performs dialysis, esp one that removes impurities from the blood of patients with malfunctioning kidneys; kidney machine.

dialysis (daɪ'ælɪsɪs) NOUN, *plural* **-ses** (-ˌsiːz). [1] the separation of small molecules from large molecules and colloids in a solution by the selective diffusion of the small molecules through a semipermeable membrane. [2] *Med* See **haemodialysis, peritoneal dialysis.**
▷HISTORY C16: from Late Latin: a separation, from Greek *dialusis* a dissolution, from *dialuein* to tear apart, dissolve, from *luein* to loosen
▸**dialytic** (ˌdaɪə'lɪtɪk) ADJECTIVE ▸ˌ**dia'lytically** ADVERB

diam. ABBREVIATION FOR diameter.

diamagnet ('daɪəˌmægnɪt) NOUN a substance exhibiting diamagnetism.

diamagnetic (ˌdaɪəmæg'nɛtɪk) ADJECTIVE of, exhibiting, or concerned with diamagnetism.
▸ˌ**diamag'netically** ADVERB

diamagnetism (ˌdaɪə'mægnɪˌtɪzəm) NOUN the phenomenon exhibited by substances that have a relative permeability less than unity and a negative susceptibility. It is caused by the orbital motion of electrons in the atoms of the material and is unaffected by temperature. Compare **ferromagnetism, paramagnetism.**

diamanté (ˌdaɪəˈmæntɪ, ˌdɪə-) ADJECTIVE 1 decorated with glittering ornaments, such as artificial jewels or sequins. ◆ NOUN 2 a fabric so covered.
▷HISTORY C20: from French, from *diamanter* to adorn with diamonds, from *diamant* DIAMOND

diamantine (ˌdaɪəˈmæntaɪn) ADJECTIVE of or resembling diamonds.
▷HISTORY C17: from French *diamantin,* from *diamant* DIAMOND

diameter (daɪˈæmɪtə) NOUN 1 **a** a straight line connecting the centre of a geometric figure, esp a circle or sphere, with two points on the perimeter or surface. **b** the length of such a line. 2 the thickness of something, esp with circular cross section.
▷HISTORY C14: from Medieval Latin *diametrus,* variant of Latin *diametros,* from Greek: diameter, diagonal, from DIA- + *metron* measure

diametral (daɪˈæmɪtrəl) ADJECTIVE 1 located on or forming a diameter: *diametral plane.* 2 a less common word for **diametric.**
▸**diˈametrally** ADVERB

diametric (ˌdaɪəˈmɛtrɪk) *or* **diametrical** ADJECTIVE 1 Also: **diametral.** of, related to, or along a diameter. 2 completely opposed.

diametrically (ˌdaɪəˈmɛtrɪkəlɪ) ADVERB completely; utterly (esp in the phrase **diametrically opposed**).

diamine (ˈdaɪəˌmiːn, -mɪn, ˌdaɪəˈmiːn) NOUN any chemical compound containing two amino groups in its molecules.

diamond (ˈdaɪəmənd) NOUN 1 **a** a colourless exceptionally hard mineral (but often tinted yellow, orange, blue, brown, or black by impurities), found in certain igneous rocks (esp the kimberlites of South Africa). It is used as a gemstone, as an abrasive, and on the working edges of cutting tools. Composition: carbon. Formula: C. Crystal structure: cubic. **b** (*as modifier*): *a diamond ring.* Related adjective: **diamantine.** 2 *Geometry* **a** a figure having four sides of equal length forming two acute angles and two obtuse angles; rhombus. **b** (*modifier*) rhombic. 3 **a** a red lozenge-shaped symbol on a playing card. **b** a card with one or more of these symbols or (*when plural*) the suit of cards so marked. 4 *Baseball* **a** the whole playing field. **b** the square formed by the four bases. 5 (formerly) a size of printer's type approximately equal to 4½ point. 6 **black diamond.** a figurative name for **coal.** 7 **rough diamond. a** an unpolished diamond. **b** a person of fine character who lacks refinement and polish. ◆ VERB 8 (*tr*) to decorate with or as with diamonds.
▷HISTORY C13: from Old French *diamant,* from Medieval Latin *diamas,* modification of Latin *adamas* the hardest iron or steel, diamond; see ADAMANT
▸**ˈdiamond-ˌlike** ADJECTIVE

diamond anniversary NOUN a 60th, or occasionally 75th, anniversary.

diamondback (ˈdaɪəmәndˌbæk) NOUN 1 Also called: **diamondback terrapin** *or* **turtle.** any edible North American terrapin of the genus *Malaclemys,* esp *M. terrapin,* occurring in brackish and tidal waters and having diamond-shaped markings on the shell: family *Emydidae.* 2 a large North American rattlesnake, *Crotalus adamanteus,* having cream-and-grey diamond-shaped markings.

diamond bird NOUN any small insectivorous Australian songbird of the genus *Pardalotus,* having a diamond-patterned plumage. Also called: **pardalote.**

diamond jubilee NOUN the celebration of a 60th, or occasionally 75th, anniversary.

diamond point NOUN a diamond-tipped engraving tool.

diamond snake NOUN a python, *Morelia argus,* of Australia and New Guinea, with yellow diamond-shaped markings.

diamond wedding NOUN the 60th, or occasionally the 75th, anniversary of a marriage.

diamond willow NOUN *Canadian* wood that may come from any species of willow and has a diamond pattern in the grain, used for making walking sticks, table lamps, etc.

diamorphine (ˌdaɪəˈmɔːfiːn) NOUN a technical name for **heroin.**

diandrous (daɪˈændrəs) ADJECTIVE (of some flowers or flowering plants) having two stamens.

dianoetic (ˌdaɪənəʊˈɛtɪk) ADJECTIVE of or relating to thought, esp to discursive reasoning rather than intuition. Compare **discursive** (sense 2).
▷HISTORY C17: from Greek *dianoētikos,* from *dianoia* the thinking process, an opinion, from DIA- + *noein* to think

dianoia (ˌdaɪəˈnɔɪə) NOUN *Philosophy* 1 perception and experience regarded as lower modes of knowledge. Compare **noesis.** 2 the faculty of discursive reasoning.
▷HISTORY from Greek; see DIANOETIC

dianthus (daɪˈænθəs) NOUN, *plural* **-thuses.** any Eurasian caryophyllaceous plant of the widely cultivated genus *Dianthus,* such as the carnation, pink, and sweet william.
▷HISTORY C19: New Latin, from Greek DI-¹ + *anthos* flower

diapason (ˌdaɪəˈpeɪzᵊn, -ˈpeɪsᵊn) NOUN *Music* 1 either of two stops (**open** and **stopped diapason**) usually found throughout the compass of a pipe organ that give it its characteristic tone colour. 2 the compass of an instrument or voice. 3 (chiefly in French usage) **a** a standard pitch used for tuning, esp the now largely obsolete one of A above middle C = 435 hertz, known as **diapason normal** (*French* djapazɔ̃ nɔrmal). **b** a tuning fork or pitch pipe. 4 (in classical Greece) an octave.
▷HISTORY C14: from Latin: the whole octave, from Greek: (*hē*) *dia pasōn* (*khordōn sumphōnia*) (concord) through all (the notes), from *dia* through + *pas* all
▸**diaˈpasonal** *or* **diapasonic** (ˌdaɪəpeɪˈzɒnɪk, -ˈsɒn-) ADJECTIVE

diapause (ˈdaɪəˌpɔːz) NOUN a period of suspended development and growth accompanied by decreased metabolism in insects and some other animals. It is correlated with seasonal changes.
▷HISTORY C19: from Greek *diapausis* pause, from *diapauein* to pause, bring to an end, from DIA- + *pauein* to stop

diapedesis (ˌdaɪəpəˈdiːsɪs) NOUN the passage of blood cells through the unruptured wall of a blood vessel into the surrounding tissues.
▷HISTORY C17: New Latin, from Greek: a leaping through, from *diapēdan* to spring through, from DIA- + *pēdan* to leap
▸**diapedetic** (ˌdaɪəpəˈdɛtɪk) ADJECTIVE

diapente (ˌdaɪəˈpɛntɪ) NOUN *Music* (in classical Greece) the interval of a perfect fifth.
▷HISTORY C14: from Latin, from Greek *dia pente khordōn sumphōnia* concord through five notes, from *dia* through + *pente* five

diaper (ˈdaɪəpə) NOUN 1 the US and Canadian word for **nappy¹.** 2 **a** a woven pattern on fabric consisting of a small repeating design, esp diamonds. **b** fabric having such a pattern. **c** such a pattern, used as decoration. ◆ VERB 3 (*tr*) to decorate with such a pattern.
▷HISTORY C14: from Old French *diaspre,* from Medieval Latin *diasprus* made of diaper, from Medieval Greek *diaspros* pure white, from DIA- + *aspros* white, shining

diaphanous (daɪˈæfənəs) ADJECTIVE (usually of fabrics such as silk) fine and translucent.
▷HISTORY C17: from Medieval Latin *diaphanus,* from Greek *diaphanēs* transparent, from *diaphainein* to show through, from DIA- + *phainein* to show
▸**diˈaphanously** ADVERB ▸**diˈaphanousness** *or* **diaphaneity** (ˌdaɪəfəˈniːɪtɪ) NOUN

diaphone (ˈdaɪəˌfəʊn) NOUN 1 **a** the set of all realizations of a given phoneme in a language. **b** one of any number of corresponding sounds in different dialects of a language. 2 a foghorn that emits a two-toned signal.
▷HISTORY C20: from DIA(LECT) + PHONE²

diaphony (daɪˈæfənɪ) NOUN *Music* 1 a style of two-part polyphonic singing; organum or a freer form resembling it. 2 (in classical Greece) another word for **dissonance** (sense 3). Compare **symphony** (sense 5a).
▷HISTORY C17: from Late Latin *diaphōnia,* from Greek, from *diaphōnos* discordant, from DIA- + *phōnē* sound
▸**diaphonic** (ˌdaɪəˈfɒnɪk) ADJECTIVE

diaphoresis (ˌdaɪəfəˈriːsɪs) NOUN 1 a technical name for **sweating.** 2 perceptible and excessive sweating; sweat.
▷HISTORY C17: via Late Latin from Greek, from *diaphorein* to disperse by perspiration, from DIA- + *phorein* to carry, variant of *pherein*

diaphoretic (ˌdaɪəfəˈrɛtɪk) ADJECTIVE 1 relating to or causing sweat. ◆ NOUN 2 a diaphoretic drug or agent.

diaphototropism (ˌdaɪəfəʊtəʊˈtrəʊpɪzəm) NOUN growth of a plant or plant part in a direction transverse to that of the light.
▷HISTORY C20: from Greek, from DIA- + PHOTOTROPIC
▸**diaphototropic** (ˌdaɪəfəʊtəʊˈtrɒpɪk) ADJECTIVE

diaphragm (ˈdaɪəˌfræm) NOUN 1 *Anatomy* any separating membrane, esp the dome-shaped muscular partition that separates the abdominal and thoracic cavities in mammals. Related adjective: **phrenic.** 2 a circular rubber or plastic contraceptive membrane placed over the mouth of the uterine cervix before copulation to prevent entrance of sperm. 3 any thin dividing membrane. 4 Also called: **stop.** a disc with a fixed or adjustable aperture to control the amount of light or other radiation entering an optical instrument, such as a camera. 5 a thin disc that vibrates when receiving or producing sound waves, used to convert sound signals to electrical signals or vice versa in telephones, etc. 6 *Chem* **a** a porous plate or cylinder dividing an electrolytic cell, used to permit the passage of ions and prevent the mixing of products formed at the electrodes. **b** a semipermeable membrane used to separate two solutions in osmosis. 7 *Botany* a transverse plate of cells that occurs in the stems of certain aquatic plants.
▷HISTORY C17: from Late Latin *diaphragma,* from Greek, from DIA- + *phragma* fence
▸**diaphragmatic** (ˌdaɪəfrægˈmætɪk) ADJECTIVE
▸**ˌdiaphragˈmatically** ADVERB

diaphysis (daɪˈæfɪsɪs) NOUN, *plural* **-ses** (-ˌsiːz). the shaft of a long bone. Compare **epiphysis.**
▷HISTORY C19: New Latin, from Greek *diaphusis,* from *diaphuesthai* to grow between, from DIA- + *phuein* to produce
▸**diaphysial** (ˌdaɪəˈfɪzɪəl) ADJECTIVE

diapir (ˈdaɪəˌpɪə) NOUN *Geology* an anticlinal fold in which the brittle overlying rock has been pierced by material, such as salt, from beneath.
▷HISTORY C20: from Greek *diapeirainein* to make holes through, pierce

diapophysis (ˌdaɪəˈpɒfɪsɪs) NOUN, *plural* **-ses** (-ˌsiːz). *Anatomy* the upper or articular surface of a transverse vertebral process.
▷HISTORY C19: New Latin, from DI-² + APOPHYSIS
▸**diapophysial** (ˌdaɪæpəˈfɪzɪəl) ADJECTIVE

diapositive (ˌdaɪəˈpɒzɪtɪv) NOUN a positive transparency; slide.

diarch (ˈdaɪɑːk) ADJECTIVE *Botany* (of a vascular bundle) having two strands of xylem.
▷HISTORY C19: from Greek DI-¹ + *archē* beginning, origin

diarchy *or* **dyarchy** (ˈdaɪɑːkɪ) NOUN, *plural* **-chies.** government by two states, individuals, etc.
▸**diˈarchic** *or* **diˈarchical** *or* **diˈarchal** *or* **dyˈarchic** *or* **dyˈarchical** *or* **dyˈarchal** ADJECTIVE

diarist (ˈdaɪərɪst) NOUN a person who keeps or writes a diary, esp one that is subsequently published.

diarrhoea *or esp US* **diarrhea** (ˌdaɪəˈrɪə) NOUN frequent and copious discharge of abnormally liquid faeces.
▷HISTORY C16: from Late Latin, from Greek *diarrhoia,* from *diarrhein* to flow through, from DIA- + *rhein* to flow
▸**ˌdiarˈrhoeal** *or* **ˌdiarˈrhoeic** *or* (*esp US*) **ˌdiarˈrheal** *or* **ˌdiarˈrheic** ADJECTIVE

diarthrosis (ˌdaɪɑːˈθrəʊsɪs) NOUN, *plural* **-ses** (-siːz). *Anatomy* any freely movable joint, such as the shoulder and hip joints.
▷HISTORY C16: New Latin, from DI-² + Greek *arthrōsis,* from *arthroun* to fasten by a joint, from *arthron* joint
▸**ˌdiarˈthrodial** ADJECTIVE

diary (ˈdaɪərɪ) NOUN, *plural* **-ries.** 1 a personal record of daily events, appointments, observations, etc. 2 a book for keeping such a record.

▷HISTORY C16: from Latin *diārium* daily allocation of food or money, journal, from *diēs* day

diascope ('daɪəˌskəʊp) NOUN an optical projector used to display transparencies.

Diaspora (daɪ'æspərə) NOUN 1 **a** the dispersion of the Jews after the Babylonian and Roman conquests of Palestine. **b** the Jewish communities outside Israel. **c** the Jews living outside Israel. **d** the extent of Jewish settlement outside Israel. 2 (in the New Testament) the body of Christians living outside Palestine. 3 (*often not capital*) a dispersion or spreading, as of people originally belonging to one nation or having a common culture.
▷HISTORY C19: from Greek: a scattering, from *diaspeirein* to disperse, from DIA- + *speirein* to scatter, sow; see SPORE

diaspore ('daɪəˌspɔː) NOUN 1 a white, yellowish, or grey mineral consisting of hydrated aluminium oxide in orthorhombic crystalline form, found in bauxite and corundum. Formula: AlO(OH). 2 any propagative part of a plant, esp one that is easily dispersed, such as a spore.
▷HISTORY C19: from Greek *diaspora* a scattering, dispersion; see DIASPORA: so named from its dispersion and crackling when highly heated

diastalsis (ˌdaɪə'stælsɪs) NOUN, *plural* **-ses** (-siːz). *Physiol* a downward wave of contraction occurring in the intestine during digestion. See also **peristalsis.**
▷HISTORY C20: New Latin, from DIA- + (PERI)STALSIS
▸ˌ**dia'staltic** ADJECTIVE

diastase ('daɪəˌsteɪs, -ˌsteɪz) NOUN any of a group of enzymes that hydrolyse starch to maltose. They are present in germinated barley and in the pancreas. See also **amylase.**
▷HISTORY C19: from French, from Greek *diastasis* a separation; see DIASTASIS
▸ˌ**dia'stasic** ADJECTIVE

diastasis (daɪ'æstəsɪs) NOUN, *plural* **-ses** (-ˌsiːz). 1 *Pathol* **a** the separation of an epiphysis from the long bone to which it is normally attached without fracture of the bone. **b** the separation of any two parts normally joined. 2 *Physiol* the last part of the diastolic phase of the heartbeat.
▷HISTORY C18: New Latin, from Greek: a separation, from *diistanai* to separate, from DIA- + *histanai* to place, make stand
▸**diastatic** (ˌdaɪə'stætɪk) ADJECTIVE

diastema (ˌdaɪə'stiːmə) NOUN, *plural* **-mata** (-mətə). 1 an abnormal space, fissure, or cleft in a bodily organ or part. 2 a gap between the teeth.
▷HISTORY C19: New Latin, from Greek: gap, from *diistanai* to separate; see DIASTASIS

diaster (daɪ'æstə) NOUN *Cytology, now rare* the stage in cell division at which the chromosomes are in two groups at the poles of the spindle before forming daughter nuclei.
▷HISTORY C19: from DI-[1] + Greek *astēr* star
▸**di'astral** ADJECTIVE

diastereoisomer (ˌdaɪəˌstɛrɪəʊ'aɪsəmə) NOUN *Chem* a type of isomer that differs in the spatial arrangement of atoms in the molecule, but is not a mirror image; a stereoisomer that is not an enantiomer.

diastole (daɪ'æstəlɪ) NOUN the dilatation of the chambers of the heart that follows each contraction, during which they refill with blood. Compare **systole.**
▷HISTORY C16: via Late Latin from Greek: an expansion, from *diastellein* to expand, from DIA- + *stellein* to place, bring together, make ready
▸**diastolic** (ˌdaɪə'stɒlɪk) ADJECTIVE

diastrophism (daɪ'æstrəˌfɪzəm) NOUN the process of movement and deformation of the earth's crust that gives rise to large-scale features such as continents, ocean basins, and mountains. See also **orogeny, epeirogeny.**
▷HISTORY C19: from Greek *diastrophē* a twisting; see DIA-, STROPHE
▸**diastrophic** (ˌdaɪə'strɒfɪk) ADJECTIVE

diastyle ('daɪəˌstaɪl) *Architect* ◆ ADJECTIVE 1 having columns about three diameters apart. ◆ NOUN 2 a diastyle building.
▷HISTORY C16: via Latin from Greek *diastylos* having spaced pillars

diatessaron (ˌdaɪə'tɛsəˌrɒn) NOUN 1 *Music* (in classical Greece) the interval of a perfect fourth. 2 a conflation of the four Gospels into a single continuous narrative.
▷HISTORY C14: from Late Latin, from Greek *dia tessarōn khordōn sumphōnia* concord through four notes, from *dia* through + *tessares* four

diathermancy (ˌdaɪə'θɜːmənsɪ) NOUN, *plural* **-cies.** the property of transmitting infrared radiation.
▷HISTORY C19: from French *diathermansie,* from DIA- + Greek *thermansis* heating, from *thermainein* to heat, from *thermos* hot
▸ˌ**dia'thermanous** ADJECTIVE

diathermic (ˌdaɪə'θɜːmɪk) ADJECTIVE 1 of or relating to diathermy. 2 able to conduct heat; passing heat freely.

diathermy ('daɪəˌθɜːmɪ) *or* **diathermia** (ˌdaɪə'θɜːmɪə) NOUN local heating of the body tissues with an electric current for medical or surgical purposes.
▷HISTORY C20: from New Latin *diathermia,* from DIA- + Greek *thermē* heat

diathesis (daɪ'æθɪsɪs) NOUN, *plural* **-ses** (-ˌsiːz). a hereditary or acquired susceptibility of the body to one or more diseases.
▷HISTORY C17: New Latin, from Greek: propensity, from *diatithenai* to dispose, from DIA- + *tithenai* to place
▸**diathetic** (ˌdaɪə'θɛtɪk) ADJECTIVE

diatom ('daɪətəm, -ˌtɒm) NOUN any microscopic unicellular alga of the phylum *Bacillariophyta,* occurring in marine or fresh water singly or in colonies, each cell having a cell wall made of two halves and impregnated with silica. See also **diatomite.**
▷HISTORY C19: from New Latin *Diatoma* (genus name), from Greek *diatomos* cut in two, from *diatemnein* to cut through, from DIA- + *temnein* to cut

diatomaceous (ˌdaɪətə'meɪʃəs) ADJECTIVE of, relating to, consisting of, or containing diatoms or their fossil remains.

diatomaceous earth NOUN an unconsolidated form of diatomite. Also called: **kieselguhr.**

diatomic (ˌdaɪə'tɒmɪk) ADJECTIVE (of a compound or molecule). **a** containing two atoms. **b** containing two characteristic groups or atoms: *ethylene glycol is a diatomic alcohol.*
▸**diatomicity** (ˌdaɪætə'mɪsɪtɪ) NOUN

diatomite (daɪ'ætəˌmaɪt) NOUN a soft very fine-grained whitish rock consisting of the siliceous remains of diatoms deposited in the ocean or in ponds or lakes. It is used as an absorbent, filtering medium, insulator, filler, etc. See also **diatomaceous earth.**

diatonic (ˌdaɪə'tɒnɪk) ADJECTIVE 1 of, relating to, or based upon any scale of five tones and two semitones produced by playing the white keys of a keyboard instrument, esp the natural major or minor scales forming the basis of the key system in Western music. Compare **chromatic** (sense 2). 2 not involving the sharpening or flattening of the notes of the major or minor scale nor the use of such notes as modified by accidentals.
▷HISTORY C16: from Late Latin *diatonicus,* from Greek *diatonikos,* from *diatonos* extending, from *diateinein* to stretch out, from DIA- + *teinein* to stretch
▸ˌ**dia'tonically** ADVERB ▸**diatonicism** (ˌdaɪə'tɒnɪˌsɪzəm) NOUN

diatribe ('daɪəˌtraɪb) NOUN a bitter or violent criticism or attack; denunciation.
▷HISTORY C16: from Latin *diatriba* learned debate, from Greek *diatribē* discourse, pastime, from *diatribein* to while away, from DIA- + *tribein* to rub

diatropism (daɪ'ætrəˌpɪzəm) NOUN a response of plants or parts of plants to an external stimulus by growing at right angles to the direction of the stimulus.
▸**diatropic** (ˌdaɪə'trɒpɪk) ADJECTIVE

diazepam (daɪ'æzəˌpæm) NOUN a chemical compound used as a minor tranquillizer and muscle relaxant and to treat acute epilepsy. Formula: $C_{16}H_{13}ClN_2O$.
▷HISTORY C20: from DI-[1] + AZO- + EP(OXIDE) + *-am*

diazine ('daɪəˌziːn, daɪ'æziːn, -ɪn) *or* **diazin** ('daɪəzɪn, daɪ'æzɪn) NOUN any organic compound whose molecules contain a hexagonal ring of four carbon atoms and two nitrogen atoms, esp any of three isomers with the formula $C_4N_2H_4$. See also **pyrimidine.**

diazo (daɪ'eɪzəʊ) ADJECTIVE 1 of, consisting of, or containing the divalent group, =N:N, or the divalent group, -N:N-: *diazo compound.* See also **azo.** 2 Also: **dyeline.** of or relating to the reproduction of documents using the bleaching action of ultraviolet radiation on diazonium salts. ◆ NOUN, *plural* **-os** *or* **-oes.** 3 a document produced by this method.

diazole (daɪ'eɪzəʊl) NOUN any organic compound whose molecules contain a pentagonal ring of three carbon atoms and two nitrogen atoms, esp imidazole (**1,3-diazole**) or pyrazole (**1,1–diazole**).

diazomethane (daɪˌeɪzəʊ'miːθeɪn) NOUN a yellow odourless explosive gas, used as a methylating agent. Formula: CH_2:N:N.

diazonium (ˌdaɪə'zəʊnɪəm) NOUN (*modifier*) of, consisting of, or containing the group, Ar-N:N-, where Ar is an aryl group: *diazonium group or radical; a diazonium compound.*
▷HISTORY C19: DIAZO + (AMM)ONIUM

diazonium salt NOUN any of a class of compounds with the general formula $ArN:N^-M^+$, where Ar is an aryl group and M is a metal atom; made by the action of nitrous acid on aromatic amines and used in dyeing.

diazotize *or* **diazotise** (daɪ'eɪzəˌtaɪz) VERB (*tr*) to cause (an aryl amine) to react with nitrous acid to produce a diazonium salt.
▸**diˌazoti'zation** *or* **diˌazoti'sation** NOUN

dib (dɪb) VERB **dibs, dibbing, dibbed.** (*intr*) to fish by allowing the bait to bob and dip on the surface.
▷HISTORY C17: perhaps alteration of DAB[1]

dibasic (daɪ'beɪsɪk) ADJECTIVE 1 (of an acid, such as sulphuric acid, H_2SO_4) containing two acidic hydrogen atoms. Compare **diacidic.** 2 (of a salt) derived by replacing two acidic hydrogen atoms: *dibasic sodium phosphate,* Na_2HPO_4.
▸**dibasicity** (ˌdaɪbeɪ'sɪsɪtɪ) NOUN

dibble[1] ('dɪbᵊl) NOUN 1 Also called (esp Brit): **dibber** ('dɪbə). a small hand tool used to make holes in the ground for planting or transplanting bulbs, seeds, or roots. ◆ VERB 2 to make a hole in (the ground) with a dibble. 3 to plant (bulbs, seeds, etc.) with a dibble.
▷HISTORY C15: of obscure origin
▸**'dibbler** NOUN

dibble[2] ('dɪbᵊl) VERB (*intr*) 1 a variant of **dib.** 2 a less common word for **dabble.**

dibble[3] ('dɪbᵊl) NOUN *Brit slang* a policeman.
▷HISTORY C20: allusion to the police officer of that name in the childrens' animated cartoon *Top Cat*

dibbuk ('dɪbək; *Hebrew* di'buk) NOUN, *plural* **-buks** *or* **-bukkim** (*Hebrew* -bu'kim). a variant spelling of **dybbuk.**

dibranchiate (daɪ'bræŋkɪɪt, -ˌeɪt) ADJECTIVE 1 of, relating to, or belonging to the *Dibranchiata,* a group or former order of cephalopod molluscs, including the octopuses, squids, and cuttlefish, having two gills. ◆ NOUN 2 any dibranchiate mollusc.

dibromide (daɪ'brəʊmaɪd) NOUN a chemical compound that contains two bromine atoms per molecule.

dibs (dɪbz) PLURAL NOUN 1 another word for **jacks.** 2 a slang word for **money.** 3 (foll by *on*) *Informal* rights (to) or claims (on): used mainly by children.
▷HISTORY C18: shortened from *dibstones* children's game played with knucklebones or pebbles, probably from *dib* to tap, dip, variant of DAB[1]

dicarboxylic acid (daɪˌkɑːbɒk'sɪlɪk) NOUN any carboxylic acid that contains two carboxyl groups per molecule.

dicast ('dɪkæst) NOUN (in ancient Athens) a juror in the popular courts chosen by lot from a list of citizens.
▷HISTORY C19: from Greek *dikastēs,* from *dikazein* to judge, from *dikē* right, judgment, order
▸**di'castic** ADJECTIVE

dicastery (dɪ'kæstərɪ) NOUN, *plural* **-ries.** *RC Church* another word for **congregation** (sense 5b).
▷HISTORY C19: from DICAST

dice (daɪs) PLURAL NOUN 1 cubes of wood, plastic, etc., each of whose sides has a different number of spots (1 to 6), used in games of chance and in gambling to give random numbers. 2 (*functioning as singular*) Also called: **die.** one of these cubes. 3 small cubes as of vegetables, chopped meat, etc. 4 **no dice.** *Slang, chiefly US and Canadian* an expression of refusal or rejection. ◆ VERB 5 to cut (food, etc.) into small cubes. 6 (*intr*) to gamble with or play at a game involving dice. 7 (*intr*) to take a chance or

risk (esp in the phrase **dice with death**). [8] (*tr*) *Austral informal* to abandon or reject. [9] (*tr*) to decorate or mark with dicelike shapes.
▷HISTORY C14: plural of DIE[2]
▸'**dicer** NOUN

dicentra (daɪ'sɛntrə) NOUN any Asian or North American plant of the genus *Dicentra,* such as bleeding heart and Dutchman's-breeches, having finely divided leaves and ornamental clusters of drooping flowers: family *Fumariaceae.*
▷HISTORY C19: New Latin, from Greek *dikentros* having two sharp points, from DI-[1] + *kentron* sharp point, from *kentein* to prick; see CENTRE

dicephalous (daɪ'sɛfələs) ADJECTIVE having two heads.
▸di'**cephalism** NOUN

dicey ('daɪsɪ) ADJECTIVE **dicier, diciest.** *Informal, chiefly Brit* difficult or dangerous; risky; tricky.

dichasium (daɪ'keɪzɪəm) NOUN, *plural* **-sia** (-zɪə). a cymose inflorescence in which each branch bearing a flower gives rise to two other flowering branches, as in the stitchwort. Compare **monochasium.**
▷HISTORY C19: New Latin, from Greek *dikhasis* a dividing, from *dikhazein* to divide in two, from *dikha* in two
▸di'**chasial** ADJECTIVE ▸di'**chasially** ADVERB

dichlamydeous (ˌdaɪklə'mɪdɪəs) ADJECTIVE (of a flower) having a corolla and calyx.
▷HISTORY C19: from Greek, from DI-[1] + *khlamus* a cloak + -EOUS

dichloride (daɪ'klɔːraɪd) NOUN a compound in which two atoms of chlorine are combined with another atom or group. Also called: **bichloride.**

dichlorodifluoromethane (daɪˌklɔːrəʊdaɪˌflʊərəʊ'miːθeɪn) NOUN a colourless nonflammable gas easily liquefied by pressure: used as a propellant in aerosols and fire extinguishers and as a refrigerant. Formula: CCl_2F_2. See also **Freon.**

dichlorodiphenyltrichloroethane (daɪˌklɔːrəʊdaɪˌfiːnaɪltraɪˌklɔːrəʊ'iːθeɪn, -nɪl-, -ˌfɛn-) NOUN the full name for **DDT.**

dichloromethane (dɑɪˌklɔːrəʊ'miːθeɪn) NOUN a noxious colourless liquid widely used as a solvent, e.g. in paint strippers. Formula: CH_2Cl_2. Traditional name: **methylene dichloride.**

dicho- *or before a vowel* **dich-** COMBINING FORM in two parts; in pairs: *dichotomy.*
▷HISTORY from Greek *dikho-,* from *dikha* in two

dichogamy (daɪ'kɒgəmɪ) NOUN the maturation of male and female parts of a flower at different times, preventing automatic self-pollination. Compare **homogamy** (sense 2).
▸di'**chogamous** *or* **dichogamic** (ˌdaɪkəʊ'gæmɪk) ADJECTIVE

dichoptic (daɪ'kɒptɪk) ADJECTIVE *Zoology* having the eyes distinctly separate.

dichotic (daɪ'kɒtɪk) ADJECTIVE relating to or involving the stimulation of each ear simultaneously by different sounds.
▷HISTORY DICHO- + -IC

dichotomize *or* **dichotomise** (daɪ'kɒtəˌmaɪz) VERB to divide or become divided into two parts or classifications.
▸di'**chotomist** NOUN ▸di**ˌchotomi'zation** *or* **diˌchotomi'sation** NOUN

dichotomous key NOUN a key used to identify a plant or animal in which each stage presents descriptions of two distinguishing characters, with a direction to another stage in the key, until the species is identified.

dichotomous question NOUN a question to which there can only be one of two answers, often "yes" or "no".

dichotomy (daɪ'kɒtəmɪ) NOUN, *plural* **-mies.** [1] division into two parts or classifications, esp when they are sharply distinguished or opposed: *the dichotomy between eastern and western cultures.* [2] *Logic* the division of a class into two mutually exclusive subclasses: *the dichotomy of married and single people.* [3] *Botany* a simple method of branching by repeated division into two equal parts. [4] the phase of the moon, Venus, or Mercury when half of the disc is visible.
ISTORY C17: from Greek *dichotomia;* see DICHO-, Y
hotomous *or* **dichotomic** (ˌdaɪkəʊ'tɒmɪk) ADJECTIVE
otomously ADVERB

> **Language note** *Dichotomy* should always refer to a division of some kind into two groups. It is sometimes used to refer to a puzzling situation which seems to involve a contradiction, but this use is generally thought to be incorrect.

dichroic (daɪ'krəʊɪk) *or* **dichroitic** (ˌdaɪkrəʊ'ɪtɪk) ADJECTIVE [1] (of a solution or uniaxial crystal) exhibiting dichroism. [2] another word for **dichromatic.**
▷HISTORY C19: from Greek *dikhroos* having two colours, from DI[1] + *khrōs* colour

dichroic filter NOUN an optical colour filter operating on the principle of wave interference between closely spaced reflecting surfaces, rather than by colour absorption.

dichroism ('daɪkrəʊˌɪzəm) NOUN [1] Also called: **dichromaticism.** a property of a uniaxial crystal, such as tourmaline, of showing a perceptible difference in colour when viewed along two different axes in transmitted white light. See also **pleochroism.** [2] a property of certain solutions as a result of which the wavelength (colour) of the light transmitted depends on the concentration of the solution and the length of the path of the light within the solution.

dichroite ('daɪkrəʊˌaɪt) NOUN another name for **cordierite.**
▷HISTORY C19: from Greek *dikhroos* two-coloured + -ITE[1]

dichromate (daɪ'krəʊmeɪt) NOUN any salt or ester of dichromic acid. Dichromate salts contain the ion $Cr_2O_7^{2-}$. Also called: **bichromate.**

dichromatic (ˌdaɪkrəʊ'mætɪk) ADJECTIVE [1] Also: **dichroic.** having or consisting of only two colours. [2] (of animal species) having two different colour varieties that are independent of sex and age. [3] able to perceive only two (instead of three) primary colours and the mixes of these colours.
▸**dichromatism** (daɪ'krəʊməˌtɪzəm) NOUN

dichromaticism (ˌdaɪkrəʊ'mætɪˌsɪzəm) NOUN another name for **dichroism** (sense 1).

dichromic (daɪ'krəʊmɪk) ADJECTIVE of or involving only two colours; dichromatic.

dichromic acid NOUN an unstable dibasic oxidizing acid known only in solution and in the form of dichromate salts. Formula: $H_2Cr_2O_7$.

dichroscope ('daɪkrəˌskəʊp) NOUN an instrument for investigating the dichroism of solutions or crystals. Also called: **dichroiscope, dichrooscope.**
▷HISTORY C19: from Greek *dikhroos* two-coloured + -SCOPE
▸**dichroscopic** (ˌdaɪkrə'skɒpɪk) ▸ˌ**dichroi'scopic** *or* ˌ**dichroo'scopic** ADJECTIVE

dick[1] (dɪk) NOUN *Chiefly US* a slang word for **detective.**
▷HISTORY C20: by shortening and alteration from DETECTIVE; probably influenced by proper name *Dick*

dick[2] (dɪk) NOUN *Slang* [1] *Brit* a fellow or person. [2] **clever dick.** *Brit* a person who is obnoxiously opinionated or self-satisfied; know-all. [3] a slang word for **penis.**
▷HISTORY C16 (meaning: fellow): from the name *Dick,* familiar form of *Richard,* applied generally (like *Jack*) to any fellow, lad, etc.; hence, C19: penis

> **Language note** The third sense of this word was formerly considered to be taboo and it was labelled as such in previous editions of *Collins English Dictionary.* However, it has now become acceptable in speech, although some older or more conservative people may object to its use.

dickens ('dɪkɪnz) NOUN *Informal* a euphemistic word for **devil** (used as intensifier in the interrogative phrase **what the dickens**).
▷HISTORY C16: from the name *Dickens*

Dickensian (dɪ'kɛnzɪən) ADJECTIVE [1] of Charles Dickens (1812–70), the English novelist, or his works. [2] resembling or suggestive of conditions described in Dickens' novels, esp **a** squalid and poverty-stricken: *working conditions were truly Dickensian.* **b** characterized by jollity and conviviality: *a Dickensian scene round the Christmas tree.* [3] grotesquely comic, as some of the characters of Dickens.

dicker ('dɪkə) VERB [1] to trade (goods) by bargaining; barter. [2] (*intr*) to negotiate a political deal. ◆ NOUN [3] **a** a petty bargain or barter. **b** the item or items bargained or bartered. [4] a political deal or bargain.
▷HISTORY C12: ultimately from Latin *decuria* DECURY; related to Middle Low German *dēker* lot of ten hides

dickhead ('dɪkˌhɛd) NOUN *Slang* a stupid or despicable man or boy.
▷HISTORY C20: from DICK[2] (in the sense: penis) + HEAD

Dick test (dɪk) NOUN a skin test for determining whether a person is immune or susceptible to scarlet fever.
▷HISTORY C20: named after George F. *Dick* (1881–1967), US physician who devised it

dicky[1] *or* **dickey** ('dɪkɪ) NOUN, *plural* **dickies** *or* **dickeys.** [1] a woman's false blouse front, worn to fill in the neck of a jacket or low-cut dress. [2] a man's false shirt front, esp one worn with full evening dress. [3] Also called: **dicky bow.** *Brit* a bow tie. [4] *Chiefly Brit* an informal name for **donkey,** esp a male one [5] Also called: '**dickyˌbird,** '**dickeyˌbird.** a child's word for a **bird,** esp a small one [6] a folding outside seat at the rear of some early cars. US and Canadian name: **rumble seat.**
▷HISTORY C18 (in the senses: donkey, shirt front): from *Dickey,* diminutive of *Dick* (name); the relationship of the various senses is obscure

dicky[2] *or* **dickey** ('dɪkɪ) ADJECTIVE **dickier, dickiest.** *Brit informal* in bad condition; shaky, unsteady, or unreliable: *I feel a bit dicky today.*
▷HISTORY C18: perhaps from the name *Dick* in the phrase *as queer as Dick's hatband* feeling ill

dickybird *or* **dickeybird** ('dɪkɪˌbɜːd) NOUN [1] See **dicky**[1] (sense 5). [2] **not a dickybird.** *Informal* not a word; nothing: *I haven't heard a dickybird from them.*

diclinous ('daɪklɪnəs, daɪ'klaɪ-) ADJECTIVE [1] (of flowering plants) bearing unisexual flowers. [2] (of flowers) unisexual. Compare **monoclinous.**
▸'**diclinism** NOUN ▸**dicliny** ('daɪklɪnɪ, daɪ'klaɪ-) NOUN

Diconal ('daɪkənæl) NOUN *Trademark* a brand of dipanone, an opiate drug with potent analgesic properties: used to relieve severe pain.

dicotyledon (daɪˌkɒtɪ'liːdᵊn, ˌdaɪkɒt-) NOUN [1] any flowering plant of the class *Dicotyledonae,* normally having two embryonic seed leaves and leaves with netlike veins. The group includes many herbaceous plants and most families of trees and shrubs. [2] **primitive dicotyledon.** any living relative of early angiosperms that branched off before the evolution of monocotyledons and eudicotyledons. The group comprises about 5 per cent of the world's plants. Often shortened to: **dicot.** Compare **monocotyledon.**
▸ˌ**dicoty'ledonous** ADJECTIVE

dicrotic (daɪ'krɒtɪk) *or* **dicrotal** ('daɪkrətᵊl) ADJECTIVE *Physiol* having or relating to a double pulse for each heartbeat.
▷HISTORY C19: from Greek *dikrotos* double-beating, from DI-[1] + *krotein* to beat
▸**dicrotism** ('daɪkrəˌtɪzəm) NOUN

dicta ('dɪktə) NOUN a plural of **dictum.**

Dictaphone ('dɪktəˌfəʊn) NOUN *Trademark* a tape recorder designed for recording dictation and later reproducing it for typing.

dictate VERB (dɪk'teɪt) [1] to say (messages, letters, speeches, etc.) aloud for mechanical recording or verbatim transcription by another person. [2] (*tr*) to prescribe (commands) authoritatively. [3] (*intr*) to act in a tyrannical manner; seek to impose one's will on others. ◆ NOUN ('dɪkteɪt) [4] an authoritative command. [5] a guiding principle or rule: *the dictates of reason.*
▷HISTORY C17: from Latin *dictāre* to say repeatedly, order, from *dīcere* to say

dictation (dɪk'teɪʃən) NOUN [1] the act of dictating material to be recorded or taken down in writing. [2] the material dictated. [3] authoritative commands or the act of giving them.
▸**dic'tational** ADJECTIVE

dictator (dɪk'teɪtə) NOUN [1] **a** a ruler who is not effectively restricted by a constitution, laws, recognized opposition, etc. **b** an absolute, esp tyrannical, ruler. [2] (in ancient Rome) a person appointed during a crisis to exercise supreme authority. [3] a person who makes

pronouncements, as on conduct, fashion, etc., which are regarded as authoritative. [4] a person who behaves in an authoritarian or tyrannical manner.
▸**dictatress** (dɪk'teɪtrɪs) *or* **dictatrix** ('dɪktətrɪks) FEMININE NOUN

dictatorial (ˌdɪktə'tɔːrɪəl) ADJECTIVE [1] of or characteristic of a dictator. [2] tending to dictate; tyrannical; overbearing.
▸ˌ**dicta'torially** ADVERB ▸ˌ**dicta'torialness** NOUN

dictatorship (dɪk'teɪtəˌʃɪp) NOUN [1] the rank, office, or period of rule of a dictator. [2] government by a dictator or dictators. [3] a country ruled by a dictator or dictators. [4] absolute or supreme power or authority.

diction ('dɪkʃən) NOUN [1] the choice and use of words in writing or speech. [2] the manner of uttering or enunciating words and sounds; elocution.
▷HISTORY C15: from Latin *dictiō* a saying, mode of expression, from *dīcere* to speak, say

dictionary ('dɪkʃənərɪ, -ʃənrɪ) NOUN, *plural* **-aries**. [1] **a** a reference book that consists of an alphabetical list of words with their meanings and parts of speech, and often a guide to accepted pronunciation and syllabification, irregular inflections of words, derived words of different parts of speech, and etymologies. **b** a similar reference book giving equivalent words in two or more languages. Such dictionaries often consist of two or more parts, in each of which the alphabetical list is given in a different language: *a German-English dictionary*. **c** (*as modifier*): *a dictionary definition*. See also **glossary, lexicon, thesaurus.** [2] a reference book listing words or terms of a particular subject or activity, giving information about their meanings and other attributes: *a dictionary of gardening*. [3] a collection of information or examples with the entries alphabetically arranged: *a dictionary of quotations*.
▷HISTORY C16: from Medieval Latin *dictiōnārium* collection of words, from Late Latin *dictiō* word; see DICTION

dictionary catalogue NOUN a catalogue of the authors, titles and subjects of books in one alphabetical sequence.

Dictograph ('dɪktəˌgrɑːf, -ˌgræf) NOUN *Trademark* a telephonic instrument for secretly monitoring or recording conversations by means of a small, sensitive, and often concealed microphone.

dictum ('dɪktəm) NOUN, *plural* **-tums** *or* **-ta** (-tə). [1] a formal or authoritative statement or assertion; pronouncement. [2] a popular saying or maxim. [3] *Law* See **obiter dictum.**
▷HISTORY C16: from Latin, from *dīcere* to say

dictyopteran (ˌdɪktɪ'ɒptərən) NOUN any insect of the order *Dictyoptera*, which comprises the cockroaches and mantises.
▷HISTORY New Latin, from Greek *diktuon* a net, from *dikein* to cast + *pteron* a wing

dicyclic (daɪ'saɪklɪk) ADJECTIVE [1] *Botany* having the perianth arranged in two whorls; having separate petals and sepals. [2] *Chem* (of a molecule) containing only two rings of atoms.

dicynodont (daɪ'sɪnəˌdɒnt) NOUN any of various extinct Triassic mammal-like reptiles having a single pair of tusklike teeth.
▷HISTORY C19: from Greek, from DI-[1] + *kuōn* dog + -ODONT

did (dɪd) VERB the past tense of **do**[1].

Didache ('dɪdəˌkiː) NOUN a treatise, perhaps of the 1st or early 2nd century A.D., on Christian morality and practices. Also called: **the Teaching of the Twelve Apostles.**
▷HISTORY C19: from Greek, literally: a teaching, from *didaskein* to teach

didactic (dɪ'dæktɪk) ADJECTIVE [1] intended to instruct, esp excessively. [2] morally instructive; improving. [3] (of works of art or literature) containing a political or moral message to which aesthetic considerations are subordinated.
▷HISTORY C17: from Greek *didaktikos* skilled in teaching, from *didaskein* to teach
▸**di'dactically** ADVERB ▸**di'dacticism** NOUN

didactics (dɪ'dæktɪks) NOUN (*functioning as singular*) the art or science of teaching.

didactyl (daɪ'dæktɪl) ADJECTIVE (esp of many marsupials) having the hind toes separate.
▸**di'dactylism** NOUN

diddle[1] ('dɪdᵊl) VERB *Informal* [1] (*tr*) to cheat or swindle. [2] (*intr*) an obsolete word for **dawdle.**
▷HISTORY C19: back formation from Jeremy *Diddler*, a scrounger in J. Kenney's farce *Raising the Wind* (1803)
▸'**diddler** NOUN

diddle[2] ('dɪdᵊl) VERB *Dialect* to jerk (an object) up and down or back and forth; shake rapidly.
▷HISTORY C17: probably variant of *doderen* to tremble, totter; see DODDER[1]

diddly-squat ('dɪdlɪˌskwɒt) PRONOUN *US and Canadian informal* (*usually used with a negative*) anything: *that doesn't mean diddly-squat.*

diddy ('dɪdɪ) NOUN, *plural* **-dies**. *Dialect* a female breast or nipple.
▷HISTORY C18: from *titty*, diminutive of TIT[2]

didgeridoo (ˌdɪdʒərɪ'duː) NOUN *Music* a deep-toned native Australian wind instrument made from a long hollowed-out piece of wood.
▷HISTORY C20: imitative of its sound

didicoy, diddicoy ('dɪdɪˌkɔɪ), *or* **didakai** ('dɪdəˌkaɪ) NOUN, *plural* **-coys** *or* **-kais**. (in Britain) one of a group of caravan-dwelling roadside people who live like Gypsies but are not true Romanies.
▷HISTORY C19: from Romany

didn't ('dɪdᵊnt) CONTRACTION OF did not.

dido ('daɪdəʊ) NOUN, *plural* **-dos** *or* **-does**. (*usually plural*) *Informal* an antic; prank; trick.
▷HISTORY C19: originally US: of uncertain origin

Dido ('daɪdəʊ) NOUN *Classical myth* a princess of Tyre who founded Carthage and became its queen. Virgil tells of her suicide when abandoned by her lover Aeneas.

didst (dɪdst) VERB *Archaic* (used with the pronoun *thou* or its relative equivalent) a form of the past tense of **do**[1].

didymium (daɪ'dɪmɪəm, dɪ-) NOUN [1] a mixture of the metallic rare earths neodymium and praseodymium, once thought to be an element. [2] a mixture of rare earths and their oxides used in colouring glass.
▷HISTORY C19: from New Latin, from Greek *didumos* twin + -IUM

didymous ('dɪdɪməs) ADJECTIVE *Biology* in pairs or in two parts.
▷HISTORY C18: from Greek *didumos* twin, from *duo* two

didynamous (daɪ'dɪnəməs) ADJECTIVE (of plants) having four stamens arranged in two pairs of unequal length, as in the foxglove.
▷HISTORY C18: from New Latin *Didynamia* name of former class, from DI-[1] + Greek *dunamis* power, referring to the greater strength of the two long stamens

die[1] (daɪ) VERB **dies, dying, died.** (*mainly intr*) [1] (of an organism or its cells, organs, etc.) to cease all biological activity permanently: *she died of pneumonia.* [2] (of something inanimate) to cease to exist; come to an end: *the memory of her will never die.* [3] (often foll by *away, down,* or *out*) to lose strength, power, or energy, esp by degrees. [4] (often foll by *away* or *down*) to become calm or quiet; subside: *the noise slowly died down.* [5] to stop functioning: *the engine died.* [6] to languish or pine, as with love, longing, etc. [7] (usually foll by *of*) *Informal* to be nearly overcome (with laughter, boredom, etc.). [8] *Theol* to lack spiritual life within the soul, thus separating it from God and leading to eternal punishment. [9] (*tr*) to undergo or suffer (a death of a specified kind) (esp in phrases such as **die a saintly death**). [10] (foll by *to*) to become indifferent or apathetic (to): *to die to the world.* [11] **never say die.** *Informal* never give up. [12] **die hard.** to cease to exist after resistance or a struggle: *old habits die hard.* [13] **die in harness.** to die while still working or active, prior to retirement. [14] **be dying.** (foll by *for* or an infinitive) to be eager or desperate (for something or to do something): *I'm dying to see the new house.* [15] **to die for.** *Informal* highly desirable: *a salary to die for.* ◆ See also **dieback, die down, die out.**
▷HISTORY Old English *dīegan*, probably of Scandinavian origin; compare Old Norse *deyja*, Old High German *touwen*

> **Language note** It was formerly considered incorrect to use the preposition *from* after *die*, but *of* and *from* are now both acceptable: *he died of/from his injuries.*

die[2] (daɪ) NOUN [1] **a** a shaped block of metal or other hard material used to cut or form metal in a drop forge, press, or similar device. **b** a tool of metal, silicon carbide, or other hard material with a conical hole through which wires, rods, or tubes are drawn to reduce their diameter. [2] an internally-threaded tool for cutting external threads. Compare **tap**[2] (sense 6). [3] a casting mould giving accurate dimensions and a good surface to the object cast. See also **die-cast.** [4] *Architect* the dado of a pedestal, usually cubic. [5] another name for **dice** (sense 2). [6] **as straight as a die.** perfectly honest. [7] **the die is cast.** the decision that commits a person irrevocably to an action has been taken.
▷HISTORY C13 *dee*, from Old French *de*, perhaps from Vulgar Latin *datum* (unattested) a piece in games, noun use of past participle of Latin *dare* to play

dieback ('daɪˌbæk) NOUN [1] a disease of trees and shrubs characterized by death of the young shoots, which spreads to the larger branches: caused by injury to the roots or attack by bacteria or fungi. [2] any similar condition of herbaceous plants. ◆ VERB **die back.** [3] (*intr, adverb*) (of plants) to suffer from dieback.

die-cast VERB **-casts, -casting, -cast.** (*tr*) to shape or form (a metal or plastic object) by introducing molten metal or plastic into a reusable mould, esp under pressure, by gravity, or by centrifugal force.
▸'**die-ˌcasting** NOUN

diecious (daɪ'iːʃəs) ADJECTIVE a variant spelling of **dioecious.**
▸**di'eciously** ADVERB

die-cutting ADVERB, NOUN *Printing* the cutting by machine of paper or card into shapes with sharp steel knives, such as in the manufacture of cardboard boxes.

die down VERB (*intr, adverb*) [1] (of some perennial plants) to wither and die above ground, leaving only the root alive during the winter. [2] to lose strength or power, esp by degrees. [3] to become calm or quiet.

dièdre (*French* djɛdrə) NOUN *Mountaineering* a large shallow groove or corner in a rock face.
▷HISTORY C20: dihedral

dieffenbachia (ˌdiːfᵊn'bækɪə) NOUN any plant of the tropical American evergreen perennial genus *Dieffenbachia*, some species of which are grown as pot plants for their handsome variegated foliage. The plants are poisonous and the sap is extremely acrid: family *Araceae*.
▷HISTORY named after Ernst *Dieffenbach* (died 1855), German horticulturist

Diégo-Suarez (*French* djegosɥarɛs) NOUN the former name of **Antseranana.**

die-hard NOUN [1] a person who resists change or who holds onto an untenable position or outdated attitude. [2] (*modifier*) obstinately resistant to change.
▸'**die-ˌhardism** NOUN

dieldrin ('diːldrɪn) NOUN a crystalline insoluble substance, consisting of a chlorinated derivative of naphthalene: a contact insecticide the use of which is now restricted as it accumulates in the tissues of animals. Formula: $C_{12}H_8OCl_6$.
▷HISTORY C20: from DIEL(S-AL)D(E)R (REACTION) + -IN

dielectric (ˌdaɪɪ'lɛktrɪk) NOUN [1] a substance or medium that can sustain a static electric field within it. [2] a substance or body of very low electrical conductivity; insulator. ◆ ADJECTIVE [3] of, concerned with, or having the properties of a dielectric.
▷HISTORY from DIA- + ELECTRIC
▸ˌ**die'lectrically** ADVERB

dielectric constant NOUN another name for **relative permittivity.**

dielectric heating NOUN a technique in which an insulator is heated by the application of a high-frequency electric field.

dielectric lens NOUN *Physics* a lens constructed of a material that converges or diverges a beam of electromagnetic radiation of radio frequency.

Diels-Alder reaction ('diːlz'ɔːldə) NOUN *Chem* a type of chemical reaction in which one organic compound containing conjugated double bonds adds to another containing an ethylenic bond to form a product containing a ring.

▷HISTORY C20: named after Otto *Diels* (1876–1954) and Kurt *Alder* (1902–58), German chemists

Dien Bien Phu (ˌdjɛn bjɛn 'fuː) NOUN a village in NW Vietnam: French military post during the Indochina War; scene of a major defeat of French forces by the Vietminh (1954).

diencephalon (ˌdaɪɛn'sɛfəˌlɒn) NOUN the part of the brain that includes the basal ganglia, thalamus, hypothalamus, and associated areas.
▸**diencephalic** (ˌdaɪɛnsɪ'fælɪk) ADJECTIVE

diene ('daɪiːn) NOUN *Chem* a hydrocarbon that contains two carbon-to-carbon double bonds in its molecules.

-diene NOUN COMBINING FORM denoting an organic compound containing two double bonds between carbon atoms: *butadiene*.
▷HISTORY from DI-[1] + -ENE

die out *or* **off** VERB (*intr, adverb*) [1] (of a family, race, etc.) to die one after another until few or none are left. [2] to become extinct, esp after a period of gradual decline.

Dieppe (dɪ'ɛp; *French* djɛp) NOUN a port and resort in N France, on the English Channel. Pop.: 36 600 (1990).

dieresis (daɪ'ɛrɪsɪs) NOUN, *plural* **-ses** (-ˌsiːz). a variant spelling of **diaeresis.**
▸**dieretic** (ˌdaɪə'rɛtɪk) ADJECTIVE

diesel ('diːzᵊl) NOUN [1] See **diesel engine.** [2] a ship, locomotive, lorry, etc., driven by a diesel engine. [3] *Informal* short for **diesel oil** (*or* **fuel**).

diesel cycle NOUN a four-stroke cycle in which combustion takes place at constant pressure and heat is rejected at constant volume. Compare **Otto cycle.**

diesel-electric NOUN [1] a locomotive fitted with a diesel engine driving an electric generator that feeds electric traction motors. ◆ ADJECTIVE [2] of or relating to such a locomotive or system.

diesel engine *or* **motor** NOUN a type of internal-combustion engine in which atomized fuel oil is sprayed into the cylinder and ignited by compression alone.

diesel-hydraulic NOUN [1] a locomotive driven by a diesel engine through hydraulic transmission and torque converters. ◆ ADJECTIVE [2] of or relating to such a locomotive or system.

diesel oil *or* **fuel** NOUN a fuel obtained from petroleum distillation that is used in diesel engines. It has a relatively low ignition temperature (540°C) and is ignited by the heat of compression. Also called (Brit): **derv.** See also **cetane number.**

Dies Irae *Latin* ('diːeɪz 'ɪəraɪ) NOUN [1] *Christianity* a famous Latin hymn of the 13th century, describing the Last Judgment. It is used in the Mass for the dead. [2] a musical setting of this hymn, usually part of a setting of the Requiem.
▷HISTORY literally: day of wrath

diesis ('daɪɪsɪs) NOUN, *plural* **-ses** (-ˌsiːz). [1] *Printing* another name for **double dagger.** [2] *Music* **a** (in ancient Greek theory) any interval smaller than a whole tone, esp a semitone in the Pythagorean scale. **b** (in modern theory) the discrepancy of pitch in just intonation between an octave and either a succession of four ascending minor thirds (**great diesis**), or a succession of three ascending major thirds (**minor diesis**).
▷HISTORY C16: via Latin from Greek: a quarter tone, literally: a sending through, from *diienai;* the double dagger was originally used in musical notation

dies non ('daɪiːz nɒn) NOUN *Law* a day on which no legal business may be transacted. Also called: **dies non juridicus** (dʒʊ'rɪdɪkəs). Compare **juridical days.**
▷HISTORY C19: shortened from Latin phrase *diēs nōn jūridicus* literally: day which is not juridical, that is, not reserved for legal affairs

die stamping NOUN *Printing* the production of words or decoration on a surface by using a steel die so that the printed images stand in relief.

diestock ('daɪˌstɒk) NOUN the device holding the dies used to cut an external screw thread.

diestrus (daɪ'iːstrəs) NOUN the US spelling of **dioestrus.**

diet[1] ('daɪət) NOUN [1] **a** a specific allowance or selection of food, esp prescribed to control weight or in disorders in which certain foods are contraindicated: *a salt-free diet; a 900-calorie diet.* **b** (*as modifier*): *a diet bread.* [2] the food and drink that a person or animal regularly consumes: *a diet of nuts and water.* [3] regular activities or occupations. ◆ VERB [4] (*usually intr*) to follow or cause to follow a dietary regimen.
▷HISTORY C13: from Old French *diete,* from Latin *diaeta,* from Greek *diaita* mode of living, from *diaitan* to direct one's own life
▸'**dieter** NOUN

diet[2] ('daɪət) NOUN [1] (*sometimes capital*) a legislative assembly in various countries, such as Japan. [2] (*sometimes capital*) Also called: **Reichstag.** the assembly of the estates of the Holy Roman Empire. [3] *Scots law* **a** the date fixed by a court for hearing a case. **b** a single session of a court.
▷HISTORY C15: from Medieval Latin *diēta* public meeting, probably from Latin *diaeta* DIET[1] but associated with Latin *diēs* day

dietary ('daɪətərɪ, -trɪ) ADJECTIVE [1] of or relating to a diet. ◆ NOUN, *plural* **-taries.** [2] a regulated diet. [3] a system of dieting.

dietary fibre NOUN fibrous substances in fruits and vegetables, such as the structural polymers of cell walls, consumption of which aids digestion and is believed to help prevent certain diseases. Also called: **roughage.**

dietetic (ˌdaɪɪ'tɛtɪk) *or* **dietetical** ADJECTIVE [1] denoting or relating to diet or the regulation of food intake. [2] prepared for special dietary requirements.
▸ˌ**die'tetically** ADVERB

dietetics (ˌdaɪɪ'tɛtɪks) NOUN (*functioning as singular*) the scientific study and regulation of food intake and preparation.

diethylene glycol (daɪ'ɛθɪˌliːn 'glaɪkɒl) NOUN a colourless soluble liquid used as an antifreeze and solvent. Formula: $(C_2H_4OH)_2O$.

diethyl ether (daɪ'ɛθɪl) NOUN a formal name for **ether** (sense 1).

diethylstilbestrol *or* **diethylstilboestrol** (daɪˌɛθɪlstɪl'bestrɒl, -ˌiːθaɪl-) NOUN a synthetic hormone with oestrogenic properties, used to relieve menopausal symptoms. Formula: $OHC_6H_4CH{:}CHC_6H_4OH$. Also called: **stilbestrol, stilboestrol.**

dietician *or* **dietitian** (ˌdaɪɪ'tɪʃən) NOUN a person who specializes in dietetics.

Dieu et mon droit *French* (djø e mɔ̃ drwa) God and my right: motto of the Royal Arms of Great Britain.

differ ('dɪfə) VERB (*intr*) [1] (often foll by *from*) to be dissimilar in quality, nature, or degree (to); vary (from). [2] (often foll by *from* or *with*) to be at variance (with); disagree (with). [3] *Dialect* to quarrel or dispute. [4] **agree to differ.** to end an argument amicably while maintaining differences of opinion.
▷HISTORY C14: from Latin *differre,* literally: to bear off in different directions, hence scatter, put off, be different, from *dis-* apart + *ferre* to bear

difference ('dɪfərəns, 'dɪfrəns) NOUN [1] the state or quality of being unlike. [2] a specific instance of being unlike. [3] a distinguishing mark or feature. [4] a significant change in a situation: *the difference in her is amazing.* [5] a disagreement or argument: *he had a difference with his wife.* [6] a degree of distinctness, as between two people or things. [7] **a** the result of the subtraction of one number, quantity, etc., from another. **b** the single number that when added to the subtrahend gives the minuend; remainder. [8] *Logic* another name for **differentia.** [9] *Maths* (of two sets) **a** the set of members of the first that are not members of the second. Symbol: A – B. **b symmetric difference.** the set of members of one but not both of the given sets. Often symbolized: **A + B.** [10] *Heraldry* an addition to the arms of a family to represent a younger branch. [11] **make a difference. a** to have an effect. **b** to treat differently. [12] **split the difference. a** to settle a dispute by a compromise. **b** to divide a remainder equally. [13] **with a difference.** with some peculiarly distinguishing quality, good or bad. ◆ VERB (*tr*) [14] *Rare* to distinguish. [15] *Heraldry* to add a charge to (arms) to differentiate a branch of a family.

difference threshold NOUN *Psychol* the minimum difference between two stimuli that is just detectable by a person.

different ('dɪfərənt, 'dɪfrənt) ADJECTIVE [1] partly or completely unlike. [2] not identical or the same; other: *he always wears a different tie.* [3] out of the ordinary; unusual.
▸'**differently** ADVERB ▸'**differentness** NOUN

> **Language note** The constructions *different from, different to,* and *different than* are all found in the works of writers of English during the past. Nowadays, however, the most widely acceptable preposition to use after *different* is *from. Different to* is common in British English, but is considered by some people to be incorrect, or less acceptable. *Different than* is a standard construction in American English, and has the advantage of conciseness when a clause or phrase follows, as in *this result is only slightly different than in the US.* As, however, this idiom is not regarded as totally acceptable in British usage, it is preferable either to use *different from: this result is only slightly different from that obtained in the US* or to rephrase the sentence: *this result differs only slightly from that in the US.*

differentia (ˌdɪfə'rɛnʃɪə) NOUN, *plural* **-tiae** (-ʃɪˌiː). *Logic* a feature by which two subclasses of the same class of named objects can be distinguished. Also called: **difference.**
▷HISTORY C19: from Latin: diversity, DIFFERENCE

differentiable (ˌdɪfə'rɛnʃɪəbᵊl) ADJECTIVE [1] capable of being differentiated. [2] *Maths* possessing a derivative.
▸ˌ**differˌentia'bility** NOUN

differential (ˌdɪfə'rɛnʃəl) ADJECTIVE [1] of, relating to, or using a difference. [2] constituting a difference; distinguishing. [3] *Maths* of, containing, or involving one or more derivatives or differentials. [4] *Physics, engineering* relating to, operating on, or based on the difference between two effects, motions, forces, etc.: *differential amplifier.* ◆ NOUN [5] a factor that differentiates between two comparable things. [6] *Maths* **a** an increment in a given function, expressed as the product of the derivative of that function and the corresponding increment in the independent variable. **b** an increment in a given function of two or more variables, $f(x_1, x_2, \ldots x_n)$, expressed as the sum of the products of each partial derivative and the increment in the corresponding variable. [7] an epicyclic gear train that permits two shafts to rotate at different speeds while being driven by a third shaft. See also **differential gear.** [8] *Chiefly Brit* the difference between rates of pay for different types of labour, esp when forming a pay structure within an industry. [9] (in commerce) a difference in rates, esp between comparable labour services or transportation routes.
▸ˌ**differ'entially** ADVERB

differential calculus NOUN the branch of calculus concerned with the study, evaluation, and use of derivatives and differentials. Compare **integral calculus.**

differential coefficient NOUN *Maths* another name for **derivative.**

differential equation NOUN an equation containing differentials or derivatives of a function of one independent variable. A **partial differential equation** results from a function of more than one variable.

differential gear NOUN the epicyclic gear mounted in the driving axle of a road vehicle that permits one driving wheel to rotate faster than the other, as when cornering.

differential geometry NOUN the application of differential calculus to geometrical problems; the study of objects that remain unchanged by transformations that preserve derivatives.

differential operator NOUN any operator involving differentiation, such as the mathematical operator del ∇, used in vector analysis, where $\nabla = \mathbf{i}\partial/\partial x + \mathbf{j}\partial/\partial y + \mathbf{k}\partial/\partial z$, **i**, **j**, and **k** being unit vectors and $\partial/\partial x$, $\partial/\partial y$, and $\partial/\partial z$ the partial derivatives of a function in *x*, *y*, and *z*.

differential windlass NOUN a windlass employing the velocity ratio incurred in unwinding from a small drum while winding onto a larger drum rotating at a common speed. Also called: **Chinese windlass.**

differentiate (ˌdɪfəˈrɛnʃɪˌeɪt) VERB [1] (*tr*) to serve to distinguish between. [2] (when *intr,* often foll by *between*) to perceive, show, or make a difference (in or between); discriminate. [3] (*intr*) to become dissimilar or distinct. [4] *Maths* to perform a differentiation on (a quantity, expression, etc.). [5] (*intr*) (of unspecialized cells, etc.) to change during development to more specialized forms.
▸ **ˌdifferˈentiˌator** NOUN

differentiation (ˌdɪfəˌrɛnʃɪˈeɪʃən) NOUN [1] the act, process, or result of differentiating. [2] *Maths* an operation used in calculus in which the derivative of a function or variable is determined; the inverse of **integration** (sense 6). [3] any process in which a mixture of materials separates out partially or completely into its constituent parts, as in the cooling and solidification of a magma into two or more different rock types or in the gradual separation of an originally homogeneous earth into crust, mantle, and core.

difficult (ˈdɪfɪkᵊlt) ADJECTIVE [1] not easy to do; requiring effort: *a difficult job.* [2] not easy to understand or solve; intricate: *a difficult problem.* [3] hard to deal with; troublesome: *a difficult child.* [4] not easily convinced, pleased, or satisfied. [5] full of hardships or trials: *difficult times ahead.*
▷ **HISTORY** C14: back formation from DIFFICULTY
▸ **ˈdifficultly** ADVERB

difficulty (ˈdɪfɪkᵊltɪ) NOUN, *plural* **-ties.** [1] the state or quality of being difficult. [2] a task, problem, etc., that is hard to deal with. [3] (*often plural*) a troublesome or embarrassing situation, esp a financial one. [4] a dispute or disagreement. [5] (*often plural*) an objection or obstacle: *he always makes difficulties.* [6] a trouble or source of trouble; worry. [7] lack of ease; awkwardness: *he could run only with difficulty.*
▷ **HISTORY** C14: from Latin *difficultās,* from *difficilis* difficult, from *dis-* not + *facilis* easy, FACILE

diffident (ˈdɪfɪdənt) ADJECTIVE lacking self-confidence; timid; shy.
▷ **HISTORY** C15: from Latin *diffīdere* to distrust, from *dis-* not + *fīdere* to trust
▸ **ˈdiffidence** NOUN ▸ **ˈdiffidently** ADVERB

diffract (dɪˈfrækt) VERB to undergo or cause to undergo diffraction: *to diffract light; the light diffracts at a slit.*
▸ **difˈfractive** ADJECTIVE ▸ **difˈfractively** ADVERB ▸ **difˈfractiveness** NOUN

diffraction (dɪˈfrækʃən) NOUN [1] *Physics* a deviation in the direction of a wave at the edge of an obstacle in its path. [2] any phenomenon caused by diffraction and interference of light, such as the formation of light and dark fringes by the passage of light through a small aperture. [3] deflection of sound waves caused by an obstacle or by nonhomogeneity of a medium.
▷ **HISTORY** C17: from New Latin *diffractiō* a breaking to pieces, from Latin *diffringere* to shatter, from *dis-* apart + *frangere* to break

diffraction grating NOUN a glass plate or a mirror with a large number of equidistant parallel lines or grooves on its surface. It causes diffraction of transmitted or reflected light, ultraviolet radiation, or X-rays.

diffraction pattern NOUN *Physics* the distinctive pattern of light and dark fringes, rings, etc., formed by diffraction.

diffractometer (ˌdɪfrækˈtɒmɪtə) NOUN *Physics* an instrument used in studying diffraction, as in the determination of crystal structure by diffraction of X-rays.

diffuse VERB (dɪˈfjuːz) [1] to spread or cause to spread in all directions. [2] to undergo or cause to undergo diffusion. [3] to scatter or cause to scatter; disseminate; disperse. ◆ ADJECTIVE (dɪˈfjuːs) [4] spread out over a wide area. [5] lacking conciseness. [6] (esp of some creeping stems) spreading loosely over a large area. [7] characterized by or exhibiting diffusion: *diffuse light; diffuse reflection.* [8] *Botany* (of plant growth) occurring throughout a tissue.
▷ **HISTORY** C15: from Latin *diffūsus* spread abroad, from *diffundere* to pour forth, from *dis-* away + *fundere* to pour
▸ **diffusely** (dɪˈfjuːslɪ) ADVERB ▸ **difˈfuseness** NOUN ▸ **diffusible** (dɪˈfjuːzəbᵊl) ADJECTIVE ▸ **difˌfusiˈbility** *or* **difˈfusibleness** NOUN

Language note Avoid confusion with **defuse.**

diffused junction NOUN a semiconductor junction formed by diffusing acceptor or donor impurity atoms into semiconductor material to form regions of p-type or n-type conductivity. See also **photolithography** (sense 2). Compare **alloyed junction.**

diffuser *or* **diffusor** (dɪˈfjuːzə) NOUN [1] a person or thing that diffuses. [2] a part of a lighting fixture consisting of a translucent or frosted covering or of a rough reflector: used to scatter the light and prevent glare. [3] a cone, wedge, or baffle placed in front of the diaphragm of a loudspeaker to diffuse the sound waves. [4] a duct, esp in a wind tunnel or jet engine, that widens gradually in the direction of flow to reduce the speed and increase the pressure of the air or fluid. [5] *Photog* a light-scattering medium, such as a screen of fine fabric, placed in the path of a source of light to reduce the sharpness of shadows and thus soften the lighting. [6] a perforated plate or similar device for distributing compressed air in the aeration of sewage. [7] a device, attached to a hairdryer, which diffuses the warm air as it comes out.

diffusion (dɪˈfjuːʒən) NOUN [1] the act or process of diffusing or being diffused; dispersion. [2] verbosity. [3] *Physics* **a** the random thermal motion of atoms, molecules, clusters of atoms, etc., in gases, liquids, and some solids. **b** the transfer of atoms or molecules by their random motion from one part of a medium to another. [4] *Physics* the transmission or reflection of electromagnetic radiation, esp light, in which the radiation is scattered in many directions and not directly reflected or refracted; scattering. [5] Also called: **diffusivity.** *Physics* the degree to which the directions of propagation of reverberant sound waves differ from point to point in an enclosure. [6] *Anthropol* the transmission of social institutions, skills, and myths from one culture to another.

diffusion coefficient *or* **constant** NOUN the rate at which a diffusing substance is transported between opposite faces of a unit cube of a system when there is unit concentration difference between them. Symbol: *D.* Also called: **diffusivity.**

diffusion line NOUN a range of clothes made by a top fashion designer for a high-street retailer.

diffusive (dɪˈfjuːsɪv) ADJECTIVE characterized by diffusion.
▸ **difˈfusively** ADVERB ▸ **difˈfusiveness** NOUN

diffusivity (ˌdɪfjuːˈsɪvɪtɪ) NOUN [1] a measure of the ability of a substance to transmit a difference in temperature; expressed as the thermal conductivity divided by the product of specific heat capacity and density. [2] *Physics* **a** the ability of a substance to permit or undergo diffusion. **b** another name for **diffusion coefficient.** [3] another name for **diffusion** (sense 5).

difunctional (daɪˈfʌŋkʃənᵊl) *Chem* ◆ ADJECTIVE [1] (of a compound) having two sites in the molecule that are highly reactive. ◆ NOUN [2] a compound having two sites in the molecule that are highly reactive.

dig (dɪg) VERB **digs, digging, dug.** [1] (when *tr,* often foll by *up*) to cut into, break up, and turn over or remove (earth, soil, etc.), esp with a spade. [2] to form or excavate (a hole, tunnel, passage, etc.) by digging, usually with an implement or (of animals) with feet, claws, etc.: *to dig a tunnel.* [3] (often foll by *through*) to make or force (one's way), esp by removing obstructions: *he dug his way through the crowd.* [4] (*tr;* often foll by *out* or *up*) to obtain by digging: *to dig potatoes; to dig up treasure.* [5] (*tr;* often foll by *out* or *up*) to find or discover by effort or searching: *to dig out unexpected facts.* [6] (*tr;* foll by *in* or *into*) to thrust or jab (a sharp instrument, weapon, etc.); poke: *he dug his spurs into the horse's side.* [7] (*tr;* foll by *in* or *into*) to mix (compost, etc.) with soil by digging. [8] (*tr*) *Informal* to like, understand, or appreciate. [9] (*intr*) *US slang* to work hard, esp for an examination. [10] (*intr*) *Brit informal* to have lodgings: *I dig in South London.* ◆ NOUN [11] the act of digging. [12] a thrust or poke, esp in the ribs. [13] a cutting or sarcastic remark. [14] *Informal* an archaeological excavation. ◆ See also **dig in, digs.**
▷ **HISTORY** C13 *diggen,* of uncertain origin

Dig (dɪg) NOUN *NZ informal* short for **Digger** (sense 1).

digamma (daɪˈgæmə) NOUN a letter of the Greek alphabet (*F*) that became obsolete before the classical period of the language. It represented a semivowel like English *W* and was used as a numeral in later stages of written Greek, and passed into the Roman alphabet as *F.*
▷ **HISTORY** C17: via Latin from Greek, from DI-¹ + GAMMA; from its shape, which suggests one gamma upon another

digamy (ˈdɪgəmɪ) NOUN, *plural* **-mies.** a second marriage contracted after the termination of the first by death or divorce. Also called: **deuterogamy.** Compare **bigamy.**
▷ **HISTORY** C17: from Late Latin *digamia,* from Greek, from DI¹ + *gamos* marriage
▸ **ˈdigamist** NOUN ▸ **ˈdigamous** ADJECTIVE

digastric (daɪˈgæstrɪk) ADJECTIVE [1] (of certain muscles) having two fleshy portions joined by a tendon. ◆ NOUN [2] a muscle of the mandible that assists in lowering the lower jaw.
▷ **HISTORY** C17: from New Latin *digastricus* (with two bellies), from DI-¹ + *gastricus* gastric, from Greek *gastēr* belly

Digby chicken *or* **chick** (ˈdɪgbɪ) NOUN *Canadian informal* dried herring.
▷ **HISTORY** after *Digby,* a town in Nova Scotia, Canada

digenesis (daɪˈdʒɛnɪsɪs) NOUN *Zoology* another name for **alternation of generations.**

digenetic (ˌdaɪdʒɪˈnɛtɪk) ADJECTIVE *Zoology* [1] of or relating to digenesis. [2] (of parasites) having two hosts.

digerati (ˌdɪdʒəˈrɑːtɪ) PLURAL NOUN the people who earn large amounts of money through Internet-related business.

digest VERB (dɪˈdʒɛst, daɪ-) [1] to subject (food) to a process of digestion. [2] (*tr*) to assimilate mentally. [3] *Chem* to soften or disintegrate or be softened or disintegrated by the action of heat, moisture, or chemicals; decompose. [4] (*tr*) to arrange in a methodical or systematic order; classify. [5] (*tr*) to reduce to a summary. [6] (*tr*) *Archaic* to tolerate. ◆ NOUN (ˈdaɪdʒɛst) [7] a comprehensive and systematic compilation of information or material, often condensed. [8] a magazine, periodical, etc., that summarizes news of current events. [9] a compilation of rules of law based on decided cases.
▷ **HISTORY** C14: from Late Latin *dīgesta* writings grouped under various heads, from Latin *dīgerere* to divide, from *di-* apart + *gerere* to bear

Digest (ˈdaɪdʒɛst) NOUN *Roman law* an arrangement of excerpts from the writings and opinions of eminent lawyers, contained in 50 books compiled by order of Justinian in the sixth century A.D.

digestant (dɪˈdʒɛstənt, daɪ-) NOUN a substance, such as hydrochloric acid or a bile salt, that promotes or aids digestion.

digester (dɪˈdʒɛstə, daɪ-) NOUN [1] *Chem* an apparatus or vessel, such as an autoclave, in which digestion is carried out. [2] a less common word for **digestant.** [3] a person or thing that digests.

digestible (dɪˈdʒɛstəbᵊl, daɪ-) ADJECTIVE capable of being digested or easy to digest.
▸ **diˌgestiˈbility** *or* **diˈgestibleness** NOUN ▸ **diˈgestibly** ADVERB

digestif *French* (diʒɛstif) NOUN something, esp a drink, taken as an aid to digestion, either before or after a meal.

digestion (dɪˈdʒɛstʃən, daɪ-) NOUN [1] the act or process in living organisms of breaking down ingested food material into easily absorbed and assimilated substances by the action of enzymes and other agents. Related adjective: **peptic.** [2] mental assimilation, esp of ideas. [3] *Bacteriol* the decomposition of sewage by the action of bacteria. [4] *Chem* the treatment of material with heat, solvents, chemicals, etc., to cause softening or decomposition.
▷ **HISTORY** C14: from Old French, from Latin *digestiō* a dissolving, digestion
▸ **diˈgestional** ADJECTIVE

digestive (dɪˈdʒɛstɪv, daɪ-) *or* **digestant** (daɪˈdʒɛstənt) ADJECTIVE [1] relating to, aiding, or subjecting to digestion: *a digestive enzyme.* ◆ NOUN [2]

a less common word for **digestant.** [3] short for **digestive biscuit.**
▸**di'gestively** ADVERB

digestive biscuit NOUN a round semisweet biscuit made from wholemeal flour.

digged (dɪgd) VERB *Archaic* a past tense of **dig.**

digger ('dɪgə) NOUN [1] a person, animal, or machine that digs. [2] a miner, esp one who digs for gold. [3] a tool or part of a machine used for excavation, esp a mechanical digger fitted with a head for digging trenches.

Digger ('dɪgə) NOUN [1] (*sometimes not capital*) *Archaic slang* **a** an Australian or New Zealander, esp a soldier: often used as a term of address. **b** (*as modifier*): *a Digger accent.* [2] one of a number of tribes of America whose diet was largely composed of roots dug out of the ground.

Diggers ('dɪgəz) PLURAL NOUN **the.** a radical English Puritan group, led by Gerrard Winstanley, which advocated communal ownership of land (1649–50).

digger wasp NOUN any solitary wasp of the families *Sphecidae* and *Pamphilidae* that digs nest holes in the ground, rotten wood, or a hollow stem and stocks them with live insects for the larvae.

diggings ('dɪgɪŋz) PLURAL NOUN [1] (*functioning as plural*) material that has been dug out. [2] (*functioning as singular or plural*) a place where mining, esp gold mining, has taken place. [3] (*functioning as plural*) *Brit informal* a less common name for **digs.**

dight (daɪt) VERB **dights, dighting, dight** *or* **dighted.** (*tr*) *Archaic* to adorn or equip, as for battle.
▹HISTORY Old English *dihtan* to compose, from Latin *dictāre* to DICTATE

Digibox ('dɪdʒɪbɒks) NOUN *Trademark* a device which converts the signals from a digital television broadcast into a form which can be viewed on a standard television set.
▹HISTORY C20: from DIGI(tal) (sense 3) + BOX[1]

dig in VERB (*adverb*) [1] *Military* to create (a defensive position) by digging foxholes, trenches, etc. [2] *Informal* to entrench (oneself) firmly. [3] (*intr*) *Informal* to defend or maintain a position firmly, as in an argument. [4] (*intr*) *Informal* to begin vigorously to eat: *don't wait, just dig in.* [5] **dig one's heels in.** *Informal* to refuse stubbornly to move or be persuaded.

digit ('dɪdʒɪt) NOUN [1] a finger or toe. [2] Also called: **figure.** any of the ten Arabic numerals from 0 to 9. [3] another name for **finger** (sense 4). [4] *Astronomy* one twelfth of the diameter of the sun or moon, used to express the magnitude of an eclipse.
▹HISTORY C15: from Latin *digitus* toe, finger

digital ('dɪdʒɪtᵊl) ADJECTIVE [1] of, relating to, resembling, or possessing a digit or digits. [2] performed with the fingers. [3] representing data as a series of numerical values. [4] displaying information as numbers rather than by a pointer moving over a dial: *a digital voltmeter; digital read-out.* [5] *Electronics* responding to discrete values of input voltage and producing discrete output voltage levels, as in a logic circuit: *digital circuit.* [6] a less common word for **digitate.** ◆ NOUN [7] *Music* one of the keys on the manuals of an organ or on a piano, harpsichord, etc.
▸**'digitally** ADVERB

digital audio tape NOUN magnetic tape on which sound is recorded digitally, giving high-fidelity reproduction. Abbreviation: **DAT.**

digital camera NOUN a camera that produces digital images that can be stored in a computer, displayed on a screen and printed.

digital clock *or* **watch** NOUN a clock or watch in which the hours, minutes, and sometimes seconds are indicated by digits, rather than by hands on a dial. Compare **analogue clock.**

digital compact cassette NOUN a magnetic tape cassette on which sound can be recorded in a digital format. Abbreviation: **DCC.**

digital computer NOUN an electronic computer in which the input is discrete rather than continuous, consisting of combinations of numbers, letters, and other characters written in an appropriate programming language and represented internally in binary notation. Compare **analog computer.**

digital divide NOUN *Informal* the gap between those people who have Internet access and those who do not.

digital fount NOUN a typeface of which the letter-shapes have been converted into digital form so that they can be used in computer-aided typesetting.

digitalin (ˌdɪdʒɪ'teɪlɪn) NOUN a poisonous amorphous crystalline mixture of glycosides extracted from digitalis leaves and formerly used in treating heart disease.
▹HISTORY C19: from DIGITAL(IS) + -IN

digitalis (ˌdɪdʒɪ'teɪlɪs) NOUN [1] any Eurasian scrophulariaceous plant of the genus *Digitalis,* such as the foxglove, having bell-shaped flowers and a basal rosette of leaves. [2] **a** a drug prepared from the dried leaves or seeds of the foxglove: a mixture of glycosides used medicinally to treat heart failure and some abnormal heart rhythms. **b** any cardiac glycoside, whatever its origin.
▹HISTORY C17: from New Latin, from Latin: relating to a finger (referring to the corollas of the flower); based on German *Fingerhut* foxglove, literally: finger-hat or thimble

digitalism ('dɪdʒɪtəˌlɪzəm) NOUN a serious condition resulting from digitalis poisoning, characterized by nausea, vomiting, and a disturbance in heart rhythm or rate.

digitalize *or* **digitalise** ('dɪdʒɪtəˌlaɪz) VERB (*tr*) to administer digitoxin or digoxin to (a patient) for the treatment of certain heart disorders.
▸**ˌdigitali'zation** *or* **ˌdigitali'sation** NOUN

digital mapping NOUN a method of preparing maps in which the data is stored in a computer for ease of access and updating.
▸**digital map** NOUN

digital radio NOUN [1] radio in which the audio information is transmitted in digital form and decoded at the radio receiver. [2] a radio that can receive and decode digital audio information.

digital recording NOUN a sound recording process that converts audio or analogue signals into a series of pulses that correspond to the voltage level. These can be stored on tape or on any other memory system.

digital television NOUN [1] television in which the picture information is transmitted in digital form and decoded at the television receiver. [2] a television set that can decode digital picture information and convert it into visible images.

digital versatile disk *or* **digital video disk** See **DVD.**

digital video NOUN video output based on digital rather than analogue signals.

digitate ('dɪdʒɪˌteɪt) *or* **digitated** ADJECTIVE [1] (of compound leaves) having the leaflets in the form of a spread hand. [2] (of animals) having digits or corresponding parts.
▸**'digiˌtately** ADVERB ▸**ˌdigi'tation** NOUN

digitiform ('dɪdʒɪtɪˌfɔːm) ADJECTIVE shaped like a finger.

digitigrade ('dɪdʒɪtɪˌgreɪd) ADJECTIVE [1] (of dogs, cats, horses, etc.) walking so that only the toes touch the ground. ◆ NOUN [2] a digitigrade animal.

digitize *or* **digitise** ('dɪdʒɪˌtaɪz) VERB (*tr*) to transcribe (data) into a digital form so that it can be directly processed by a computer.
▸**ˌdigiti'zation** *or* **ˌdigiti'sation** NOUN ▸**'digiˌtizer** *or* **'digiˌtiser** NOUN

digitoxin (ˌdɪdʒɪ'tɒksɪn) NOUN a white toxic bitter-tasting glycoside, extracted from the leaves of the purple foxglove (*Digitalis purpurea*) and used in the treatment of heart failure and some abnormal heart rhythms. Formula: $C_{41}H_{64}O_{13}$.
▹HISTORY from DIGI(TALIS) + TOXIN

digitron ('dɪdʒɪˌtrɒn) NOUN *Electronics* a type of tube, for displaying information, having a common anode and several cathodes shaped in the form of characters, which can be lit by a glow discharge. Also called: **Nixie tube.**
▹HISTORY C20: from DIGIT + -TRON

digitule ('dɪdʒɪtjuːl) NOUN *Zoology* any small finger-like process.

diglossia (daɪ'glɒsɪə) NOUN *Linguistics* the existence in a language of a high, or socially prestigious, and a low, or everyday, form, as German and Swiss German in Switzerland.
▹HISTORY C20: New Latin, via French, from Greek *diglōssos* speaking two languages: see DIGLOT

diglot ('daɪglɒt) ADJECTIVE [1] a less common word for **bilingual.** ◆ NOUN [2] a bilingual book.
▹HISTORY C19: from Greek (Attic) *diglōttos,* from DI-[1] + *glōtta* tongue
▸**di'glottic** ADJECTIVE

dignified ('dɪgnɪˌfaɪd) ADJECTIVE characterized by dignity of manner or appearance; stately.
▸**'digniˌfiedly** ADVERB ▸**'digniˌfiedness** NOUN

dignify ('dɪgnɪˌfaɪ) VERB **-fies, -fying, -fied.** (*tr*) [1] to invest with honour or dignity; ennoble. [2] to add distinction to: *the meeting was dignified by the minister.* [3] to add a semblance of dignity to, esp by the use of a pretentious name or title: *she dignifies every plant with its Latin name.*
▹HISTORY C15: from Old French *dignifier,* from Late Latin *dignificāre,* from Latin *dignus* worthy + *facere* to make

dignitary ('dɪgnɪtərɪ, -trɪ) NOUN, *plural* **-taries.** a person of high official position or rank, esp in government or the church.

dignity ('dɪgnɪtɪ) NOUN, *plural* **-ties.** [1] a formal, stately, or grave bearing: *he entered with dignity.* [2] the state or quality of being worthy of honour: *the dignity of manual labour.* [3] relative importance; rank: *he is next in dignity to the mayor.* [4] sense of self-importance (often in the phrases **stand** (or **be**) **on one's dignity, beneath one's dignity**). [5] high rank, esp in government or the church. [6] a person of high rank or such persons collectively.
▹HISTORY C13: from Old French *dignite,* from Latin *dignitās* merit, from *dignus* worthy

digonal (daɪ'gəʊnəl) ADJECTIVE *Maths* of or relating to a symmetry operation in which the original figure is reconstructed after a 180° turn about an axis.

digoneutic (ˌdaɪgə'njuːtɪk) ADJECTIVE *Zoology* producing offspring twice yearly.
▹HISTORY C19: from DI-[1] + Greek *gonein* to beget
▸**ˌdigo'neutism** NOUN

digoxin (daɪ'dʒɒksɪn) NOUN a glycoside extracted from the leaves of the woolly foxglove (*Digitalis lanata*) and used in the treatment of heart failure. Formula: $C_{41}H_{64}O_{14}$.

digraph ('daɪgrɑːf, -græf) NOUN a combination of two letters or characters used to represent a single speech sound such as *gh* in English *tough.* Compare **ligature** (sense 5), **diphthong.**
▸**digraphic** (daɪ'græfɪk) ADJECTIVE

digress (daɪ'grɛs) VERB (*intr*) [1] to depart from the main subject in speech or writing. [2] to wander from one's path or main direction.
▹HISTORY C16: from Latin *dīgressus* turned aside, from *dīgredī,* from *dis-* apart + *gradī* to go
▸**di'gresser** NOUN

digression (daɪ'grɛʃən) NOUN an act or instance of digressing from a main subject in speech or writing.
▸**di'gressional** ADJECTIVE

digressive (daɪ'grɛsɪv) ADJECTIVE characterized by digression or tending to digress.
▸**di'gressively** ADVERB ▸**di'gressiveness** NOUN

digs (dɪgz) PLURAL NOUN *Brit informal* lodgings.
▹HISTORY C19: shortened from DIGGINGS, perhaps referring to where one *digs* or works, but see also DIG IN

dihedral (daɪ'hiːdrəl) ADJECTIVE [1] having or formed by two intersecting planes; two-sided: *a dihedral angle.* ◆ NOUN [2] Also called: **dihedron, dihedral angle.** the figure formed by two intersecting planes. [3] the US name for **corner** (sense 11). [4] the upward inclination of an aircraft wing in relation to the lateral axis. Compare **anhedral.**

dihedron (daɪ'hiːdrən) NOUN another name for **dihedral** (sense 2).

dihybrid (daɪ'haɪbrɪd) NOUN *Genetics* the offspring of two individuals that differ with respect to two pairs of genes; an individual heterozygous for two pairs of genes.
▸**di'hybridism** NOUN

dihydric (daɪ'haɪdrɪk) ADJECTIVE (of an alcohol) containing two hydroxyl groups per molecule.

Dijon (*French* diʒɔ̃) NOUN a city in E France: capital of the former duchy of Burgundy. Pop.: 149 867 (1999).

dik-dik ('dɪkˌdɪk) NOUN any small antelope of the genus *Madoqua,* inhabiting semiarid regions of

Africa, having an elongated muzzle and, in the male, small stout horns.
▷HISTORY C19: an East African name, probably of imitative origin

dike (daɪk) NOUN, VERB a variant spelling of **dyke.**

dikkop ('dɪkəp) NOUN a South African name for **stone curlew.**
▷HISTORY from Afrikaans, from *dik* thick + *kop* head

diktat ('dɪktɑ:t) NOUN [1] decree or settlement imposed, esp by a ruler or a victorious nation. [2] a dogmatic statement.
▷HISTORY German: dictation, from Latin *dictātum,* from *dictāre* to DICTATE

dilapidate (dɪ'læpɪˌdeɪt) VERB to fall or cause to fall into ruin or decay.
▷HISTORY C16: from Latin *dīlapidāre* to scatter, waste, from *dis-* apart + *lapidāre* to stone, throw stones, from *lapis* stone

dilapidated (dɪ'læpɪˌdeɪtɪd) ADJECTIVE falling to pieces or in a state of disrepair; shabby.

dilapidation (dɪˌlæpɪ'deɪʃən) NOUN [1] the state of being or becoming dilapidated. [2] (*often plural*) *Property law* **a** the state of disrepair of premises at the end of a tenancy due to neglect. **b** the extent of repairs necessary to such premises.
▸**di'lapiˌdator** NOUN

dilatancy (daɪ'leɪtənsɪ, dɪ-) NOUN a phenomenon caused by the nature of the stacking or fitting together of particles or granules in a heterogeneous system, such as the solidification of certain sols under pressure, and the thixotropy of certain gels.

dilatant (daɪ'leɪtᵊnt, dɪ-) ADJECTIVE [1] tending to dilate; dilating. [2] *Physics* of, concerned with, or exhibiting dilatancy. ◆ NOUN [3] something, such as a catheter, that causes dilation.

dilate (daɪ'leɪt, dɪ-) VERB [1] to expand or cause to expand; make or become wider or larger: *the pupil of the eye dilates in the dark.* [2] (*intr;* often foll by *on* or *upon*) to speak or write at length; expand or enlarge.
▷HISTORY C14: from Latin *dīlātāre* to spread out, amplify, from *dis-* apart + *lātus* wide
▸**di'latable** ADJECTIVE ▸**diˌlata'bility** *or* **di'latableness** NOUN ▸**di'lation** *or* **dilatation** (ˌdaɪlə'teɪʃən, ˌdɪ-) NOUN ▸**ˌdila'tational** ADJECTIVE ▸**dilative** (daɪ'leɪtɪv, dɪ-) ADJECTIVE

dilatometer (ˌdɪlə'tɒmɪtə) NOUN any instrument for measuring changes in dimension: often a glass bulb fitted with a long stopper through which a capillary tube runs, used for measuring volume changes of liquids.
▸**dilatometric** (ˌdɪlətə'mɛtrɪk) ADJECTIVE
▸**ˌdilato'metrically** ADVERB ▸**ˌdila'tometry** NOUN

dilator, dilater (daɪ'leɪtə, dɪ-), *or* **dilatator** (ˌdaɪlə'teɪtə, ˌdɪ-) NOUN [1] something that dilates an object, esp a surgical instrument for dilating a bodily cavity. [2] a muscle that expands an orifice or dilates an organ.

dilatory ('dɪlətərɪ, -trɪ) ADJECTIVE [1] tending or inclined to delay or waste time. [2] intended or designed to waste time or defer action.
▷HISTORY C15: from Late Latin *dīlātōrius* inclined to delay, from *differre* to postpone; see DIFFER
▸**'dilatorily** ADVERB ▸**'dilatoriness** NOUN

dildo *or* **dildoe** ('dɪldəʊ) NOUN, *plural* **-dos** *or* **-does.** an object used as a substitute for an erect penis.
▷HISTORY C16: of unknown origin

dilemma (dɪ'lɛmə, daɪ-) NOUN [1] a situation necessitating a choice between two equal, esp equally undesirable, alternatives. [2] a problem that seems incapable of a solution. [3] *Logic* a form of argument one of whose premises is the conjunction of two conditional statements and the other of which affirms the disjunction of their antecedents, and whose conclusion is the disjunction of their consequents. Its form is *if p then q and if r then s; either p or r so either q or s.* [4] **on the horns of a dilemma. a** faced with the choice between two equally unpalatable alternatives. **b** in an awkward situation.
▷HISTORY C16: via Latin from Greek, from DI-[1] + *lēmma* assumption, proposition, from *lambanein* to take, grasp
▸**dilemmatic** (ˌdɪlɪ'mætɪk, ˌdaɪlɪ-) *or* **dil'emmic** ADJECTIVE

Language note The use of *dilemma* to refer to a problem that seems incapable of a solution is considered by some people to be incorrect.

dilettante (ˌdɪlɪ'tɑ:ntɪ) NOUN, *plural* **-tantes** *or* **-tanti** (-'tɑ:ntɪ). [1] a person whose interest in a subject is superficial rather than professional. [2] a person who loves the arts. ◆ ADJECTIVE [3] of or characteristic of a dilettante.
▷HISTORY C18: from Italian, from *dilettare* to delight, from Latin *dēlectāre*
▸**ˌdilet'tantish** *or* **ˌdilet'tanteish** ADJECTIVE ▸**ˌdilet'tantism** *or* **ˌdilet'tanteism** NOUN

Díli *or* **Dilli** ('di:li:) NOUN the capital (from 2002) of independent East Timor: the former capital (until 1976) of Portuguese Timor. Pop.: 65 000 (1999 est.).

diligence[1] ('dɪlɪdʒəns) NOUN [1] steady and careful application. [2] proper attention or care. [3] *Law* the degree of care required in a given situation.
▷HISTORY C14: from Latin *dīligentia* care, attentiveness

diligence[2] ('dɪlɪdʒəns; *French* diliʒɑ̃s) NOUN *History* a stagecoach.
▷HISTORY C18: from French, shortened from *carosse de diligence,* literally: coach of speed

diligent ('dɪlɪdʒənt) ADJECTIVE [1] careful and persevering in carrying out tasks or duties. [2] carried out with care and perseverance: *diligent work.*
▷HISTORY C14: from Old French, from Latin *dīligere* to value, from *dis-* apart + *legere* to read
▸**'diligently** ADVERB

dill (dɪl) NOUN [1] an umbelliferous aromatic Eurasian plant, *Anethum graveolens,* with finely dissected leaves and umbrella-shaped clusters of yellow flowers. [2] the leaves or seedlike fruits of this plant, used for flavouring in pickles, soups, etc., and in medicine. [3] *Informal, chiefly Austral and NZ* a fool; idiot.
▷HISTORY Old English *dile;* related to Old High German *tilli*
▸**'dilly** ADJECTIVE

dill pickle NOUN a pickled cucumber flavoured with dill.

dilly ('dɪlɪ) NOUN, *plural* **-lies.** *Slang, chiefly US and Canadian* a person or thing that is remarkable.
▷HISTORY C20: perhaps from girl's proper name *Dilly*

dilly bag NOUN *Austral* a small bag, esp one made of plaited grass, etc., often used for carrying food. Sometimes shortened to: **dilly.**
▷HISTORY from native Australian *dilly* small bag or basket

dilly-dally (ˌdɪlɪ'dælɪ) VERB **-lies, -lying, -lied.** (*intr*) *Informal* to loiter or vacillate.
▷HISTORY C17: by reduplication from DALLY

diluent ('dɪljʊənt) ADJECTIVE [1] causing dilution or serving to dilute. ◆ NOUN [2] a substance used for or causing dilution.
▷HISTORY C18: from Latin *dīluēns* dissolving; see DILUTE

dilute (daɪ'lu:t) VERB [1] to make or become less concentrated, esp by adding water or a thinner. [2] to make or become weaker in force, effect, etc.: *he diluted his story.* ◆ ADJECTIVE [3] *Chem* **a** (of a solution, suspension, mixture, etc.) having a low concentration or a concentration that has been reduced by admixture. **b** (of a substance) present in solution, esp a weak solution in water: *dilute acetic acid.*
▷HISTORY C16: from Latin *dīluere,* from *dis-* apart + *-luere,* from *lavāre* to wash
▸**ˌdilu'tee** NOUN ▸**di'luter** NOUN

dilution (daɪ'lu:ʃən) NOUN [1] the act of diluting or state of being diluted. [2] a diluted solution.

diluvial (daɪ'lu:vɪəl, dɪ-) *or* **diluvian** ADJECTIVE [1] of or connected with a deluge, esp with the great Flood described in Genesis. [2] of or relating to diluvium.
▷HISTORY C17: from Late Latin *dīluviālis;* see DILUVIUM

diluvialism (daɪ'lu:vɪəlɪzm) NOUN the theory, generally abandoned in the mid-19th century, that the earth's surface was shaped by the biblical flood.

diluvium (daɪ'lu:vɪəm, dɪ-) NOUN, *plural* **-via** (-vɪə). *Geology* a former name for **glacial drift** (sense 12).
▷HISTORY C19: from Latin: flood, from *dīluere* to wash away; see DILUTE

dim (dɪm) ADJECTIVE **dimmer, dimmest.** [1] badly illuminated: *a dim room.* [2] not clearly seen; indistinct; faint: *a dim shape.* [3] having weak or indistinct vision: *eyes dim with tears.* [4] lacking in understanding; mentally dull. [5] not clear in the mind; obscure: *a dim memory.* [6] lacking in brilliance, brightness, or lustre: *a dim colour.* [7] tending to be unfavourable; gloomy or disapproving (esp in the phrase **take a dim view**). ◆ VERB **dims, dimming, dimmed.** [8] to become or cause to become dim. [9] (*tr*) to cause to seem less bright, as by comparison. [10] the US and Canadian word for **dip** (sense 5).
▷HISTORY Old English *dimm;* related to Old Norse *dimmr* gloomy, dark
▸**'dimly** ADVERB ▸**'dimness** NOUN

dim. *or* **dimin** *Music* ABBREVIATION FOR diminuendo.

Dimashq (di:'mæʃk) NOUN an Arabic name for **Damascus.**

dim bulb NOUN *Informal* a slow-witted unintelligent person.

dime (daɪm) NOUN [1] a coin of the US and Canada, worth one tenth of a dollar or ten cents. [2] **a dime a dozen.** very cheap or common.
▷HISTORY C14: from Old French *disme,* from Latin *decimus* tenth, from *decem* ten

dimenhydrinate (ˌdaɪmɛn'haɪdrɪˌneɪt) NOUN a white slightly soluble bitter-tasting crystalline substance: an antihistamine used in the prevention of nausea, esp in travel sickness. Formula: $C_{24}H_{28}ClN_5O_3$.
▷HISTORY from *dime(thyl* + AMI)N(E) + (*diphen)hydr(am)in(e)* + -ATE[1]

dime novel NOUN *US* (formerly) a cheap melodramatic novel, usually in paperback. Also called (esp Brit): **penny-dreadful.**

dimension (dɪ'mɛnʃən) NOUN [1] (*often plural*) a measurement of the size of something in a particular direction, such as the length, width, height, or diameter. [2] (*often plural*) scope; size; extent: *a problem of enormous dimensions.* [3] aspect: *a new dimension to politics.* [4] *Maths* the number of coordinates required to locate a point in space. [5] *Physics* **a** the product or the quotient of the fundamental physical quantities (such as mass, length, or time) raised to the appropriate power in a derived physical quantity: *the dimensions of velocity are length divided by time.* **b** the power to which such a fundamental quantity has to be raised in a derived quantity. ◆ VERB [6] (*tr*) *Chiefly US* **a** to shape or cut to specified dimensions. **b** to mark with specified dimensions.
▷HISTORY C14: from Old French, from Latin *dīmensiō* an extent, from *dīmētīrī* to measure out, from *mētīrī*
▸**di'mensional** ADJECTIVE ▸**diˌmension'ality** NOUN
▸**di'mensionally** ADVERB ▸**di'mensionless** ADJECTIVE

dimer ('daɪmə) NOUN *Chem* **a** a molecule composed of two identical simpler molecules (monomers). **b** a compound consisting of dimers.

dimercaprol (ˌdaɪmə'kæprɒl) NOUN a colourless oily liquid with an offensive smell, used as an antidote to lewisite and similar toxic substances. Formula: $CH_2(SH)CH(SH)CH_2OH$. Also called: **BAL.**
▷HISTORY C20: by shortening and altering from *dimercaptopropanol*

dimerize *or* **dimerise** ('daɪməˌraɪz) VERB to react or cause to react to form a dimer.
▸**ˌdimeri'zation** *or* **ˌdimeri'sation** NOUN

dimerous ('dɪmərəs) ADJECTIVE [1] consisting of or divided into two segments, as the tarsi of some insects. [2] (of flowers) having their floral parts arranged in whorls of two.
▷HISTORY C19: from New Latin *dimerus,* from Greek *dimerēs,* from DI-[1] + *meros* part
▸**'dimerism** NOUN

dimeter ('dɪmɪtə) NOUN *Prosody* a line of verse consisting of two metrical feet or a verse written in this metre.

dimethylformamide (daɪˌmi:θaɪl'fɔ:məˌmaɪd, -ˌmɛθɪ-) NOUN a colourless liquid widely used as a solvent and sometimes as a catalyst. Formula: $(CH_3)_2NCHO$. Abbreviation: **DMF.**

dimethylsulphoxide *or* **dimethylsulfoxide** (daɪˌmi:θaɪlsʌl'fɒksaɪd, -ˌmɛθɪl-) NOUN a colourless odourless liquid substance used as a solvent and in medicine as an agent to improve the penetration of drugs applied to the skin. Formula: $(CH_3)_2SO$. Abbreviation: **DMSO.**

Language note See at **sulphur.**

dimetric (daɪˈmetrɪk) ADJECTIVE *Crystallog* another word for **tetragonal.**

dimidiate ADJECTIVE (dɪˈmɪdɪɪt) [1] divided in halves. [2] *Biology, now rare* having one of two sides or parts less developed than the other: *dimidiate antlers.* ◆ VERB (dɪˈmɪdɪˌeɪt) [3] *(tr) Heraldry* to halve (two bearings) so that they can be represented on the same shield.
▷HISTORY C17: from Latin *dīmidiāre* to halve, from *dīmidius* half, from *dis-* apart + *medius* middle
▶**diˌmidiˈation** NOUN

diminish (dɪˈmɪnɪʃ) VERB [1] to make or become smaller, fewer, or less. [2] *(tr) Architect* to cause (a column, etc.) to taper. [3] *(tr) Music* to decrease (a minor or perfect interval) by a semitone. [4] to belittle or be belittled; reduce in authority, status, etc.; depreciate.
▷HISTORY C15: blend of *diminuen* to lessen (from Latin *dēminuere* to make smaller, from *minuere* to reduce) + archaic *minish* to lessen
▶**diˈminishable** ADJECTIVE ▶**diˈminishingly** ADVERB
▶**diˈminishment** NOUN

diminished (dɪˈmɪnɪʃt) ADJECTIVE [1] reduced or lessened; made smaller. [2] *Music* denoting any minor or perfect interval reduced by a semitone. [3] *Music* denoting a triad consisting of the root plus a minor third and a diminished fifth. [4] *Music (postpositive)* (esp in jazz or pop music) denoting a diminished seventh chord having as its root the note specified: *B diminished.*

diminished responsibility NOUN *Law* a plea under which proof of an impairing abnormality of mind is submitted as demonstrating lack of premeditation and therefore criminal responsibility.

diminished seventh chord NOUN a chord often used in an enharmonic modulation and very common in modern music, esp jazz and pop music, consisting of a diminished triad with an added diminished seventh above the root. Often shortened to: **diminished seventh.**

diminishing returns PLURAL NOUN *Economics* [1] progressively smaller rises in output resulting from the increased application of a variable input, such as labour, to a fixed quantity, as of capital or land. [2] the increase in the average cost of production that may arise beyond a certain point as a result of increasing the overall scale of production.

diminuendo (dɪˌmɪnjuˈendəʊ) *Music* ◆ NOUN, *plural* **-dos.** [1] **a** a gradual decrease in loudness or the musical direction indicating this. Abbreviation: **dim.** Symbol: > (written over the music affected). **b** a musical passage affected by a diminuendo. ◆ ADJECTIVE [2] gradually decreasing in loudness. [3] with a diminuendo. ◆ Also: **decrescendo.**
▷HISTORY C18: from Italian, from *diminuire* to DIMINISH

diminution (ˌdɪmɪˈnjuːʃən) NOUN [1] reduction; decrease. [2] *Music* the presentation of the subject of a fugue, etc., in which the note values are reduced in length. Compare **augmentation** (sense 3).
▷HISTORY C14: from Latin *dēminūtiō;* see DIMINISH

diminutive (dɪˈmɪnjʊtɪv) ADJECTIVE [1] very small; tiny. [2] *Grammar* **a** denoting an affix added to a word to convey the meaning *small* or *unimportant* or to express affection, as for example, the suffix *-ette* in French. **b** denoting a word formed by the addition of a diminutive affix. ◆ NOUN [3] *Grammar* a diminutive word or affix. [4] a tiny person or thing. ◆ Compare (for senses 2, 3) **augmentative.**
▶**diminutival** (dɪˌmɪnjʊˈtaɪvᵊl) ADJECTIVE ▶**diˈminutively** ADVERB ▶**diˈminutiveness** NOUN

dimissory (dɪˈmɪsərɪ) ADJECTIVE [1] granting permission to be ordained: *a bishop's dimissory letter.* [2] granting permission to depart.

Dimitrovo (*Bulgarian* diˈmitrovo) NOUN the former name (1949–62) of **Pernik.**

dimity (ˈdɪmɪtɪ) NOUN, *plural* **-ties. a** a light strong cotton fabric with woven stripes or squares. **b** (*as modifier*): *a dimity bonnet.*
▷HISTORY C15: from Medieval Latin *dimitum,* from Greek *dimiton,* from DI-[1] + *mitos* thread of the warp

dimmer (ˈdɪmə) NOUN [1] a device, such as a rheostat, for varying the current through an electric light and thus changing the illumination. [2] *(often plural) US* **a** a dipped headlight on a road vehicle. **b** a parking light on a car.

dimorph (ˈdaɪmɔːf) NOUN either of two forms of a substance that exhibits dimorphism.

dimorphism (daɪˈmɔːfɪzəm) NOUN [1] the occurrence within a plant of two distinct forms of any part, such as the leaves of some aquatic plants. [2] the occurrence in an animal or plant species of two distinct types of individual. [3] a property of certain substances that enables them to exist in two distinct crystalline forms.
▶**diˈmorphic** *or* **diˈmorphous** ADJECTIVE

dimp (dɪmp) NOUN *Northern English dialect* a cigarette butt.

dimple (ˈdɪmpᵊl) NOUN [1] a small natural dent or crease in the flesh, esp on the cheeks or chin. [2] any slight depression in a surface. [3] a bubble or dent in glass. ◆ VERB [4] to make or become dimpled. [5] *(intr)* to produce dimples by smiling.
▷HISTORY C13 *dympull;* compare Old English *dyppan* to dip, German *Tümpel* pool
▶**ˈdimply** ADJECTIVE

dimpsy (ˈdɪmpsɪ) NOUN *Southwest English dialect* twilight.

dim sum (ˈdɪm ˈsʌm) NOUN a Chinese appetizer of steamed dumplings containing various fillings.
▷HISTORY Cantonese

dimwit (ˈdɪmˌwɪt) NOUN *Informal* a stupid or silly person.
▶**ˌdim-ˈwitted** ADJECTIVE ▶**ˌdim-ˈwittedly** ADVERB
▶**ˌdim-ˈwittedness** NOUN

din[1] (dɪn) NOUN [1] a loud discordant confused noise. ◆ VERB **dins, dinning, dinned.** [2] *(tr; usually foll by into)* to instil (into a person) by constant repetition. [3] *(tr)* to subject to a din. [4] *(intr)* to make a din.
▷HISTORY Old English *dynn;* compare Old Norse *dynr,* Old High German *tuni*

din[2] (dɪn) NOUN *Judaism* [1] a particular religious law; the halacha about something. [2] the ruling of a Beth Din or religious court.
▷HISTORY from Hebrew, literally: judgment

din[3] (diːn) NOUN *Islam* religion in general, esp the beliefs and obligations of Islam.
▷HISTORY Arabic, related to *dain* debt

DIN (dɪn) NOUN [1] a formerly used logarithmic expression of the speed of a photographic film, plate, etc., given as $-10\log_{10}E$, where E is the exposure of a point 0.1 density units above the fog level; high-speed films have high numbers. Compare **ISO rating.** [2] a system of standard plugs, sockets, and cables formerly used for interconnecting domestic audio and video equipment.
▷HISTORY C20: from German *D(eutsche) I(ndustrie) N(orm)* German Industry Standard

Din. ABBREVIATION FOR dinar.

Dinah (ˈdaɪnə) NOUN the daughter of Jacob and Leah (Genesis 30:21; 34).

Dinan (*French* dinɑ̃) NOUN a town in NW France, in Brittany, on the estuary of the River Rance: medieval buildings, including town walls and castle: tourism, hosiery, cider: Pop.: 14 200 (latest est.).

Dinant (*French* dinɑ̃) NOUN a town in S Belgium, on the River Meuse below steep limestone cliffs: 11th-century citadel: famous in the Middle Ages for fine brassware, known as *dinanderie*: tourism, metalwork, biscuits. Pop.: 12 200 (1991).

dinar (ˈdiːnɑː) NOUN [1] the standard monetary unit of the following countries or territories. Algeria: divided into 100 centimes. Bahrain: divided into 1000 fils. Iraq: divided into 1000 fils. Jordan: divided into 1000 fils. Kuwait: divided into 1000 fils. Libya: divided into 1000 dirhams. Serbia: divided into 100 paras (formerly the standard monetary unit of Yugoslavia). Sudan, Tunisia: divided into 1000 millimes. Abbreviation: **Din, D, d.** [2] a monetary unit of the United Arab Emirates worth one tenth of a dirham. [3] a coin, esp one of gold, formerly used in the Middle East.
▷HISTORY C17: from Arabic, from Late Greek *dēnarion,* from Latin *dēnārius* DENARIUS

dine (daɪn) VERB [1] *(intr)* to eat dinner. [2] *(intr;* often foll by *on, off,* or *upon)* to make one's meal (of): *the guests dined upon roast beef.* [3] *(tr) Informal* to entertain to dinner (esp in the phrase **to wine and dine someone**).
▷HISTORY C13: from Old French *disner,* contracted from Vulgar Latin *disjējūnāre* (unattested) to cease fasting, from *dis-* not + Late Latin *jējūnāre* to fast; see JEJUNE

dine out VERB *(intr, adverb)* [1] to dine away from home, esp in a restaurant. [2] (foll by *on*) to have dinner at the expense of someone else mainly for the sake of one's knowledge or conversation about (a subject or story).

diner (ˈdaɪnə) NOUN [1] a person eating a meal, esp in a restaurant. [2] *Chiefly US and Canadian* a small restaurant, often at the roadside. [3] a fashionable bar, or a section of one, where food is served.

dineric (dɪˈnerɪk) ADJECTIVE of or concerned with the interface between immiscible liquids.
▷HISTORY C20: from DI-[1] + Late Greek *nēron* water + -IC

dinette (daɪˈnet) NOUN an alcove or small area for use as a dining room.

ding[1] (dɪŋ) VERB [1] to ring or cause to ring, esp with tedious repetition. [2] *(tr)* another word for **din**[1] (sense 2). ◆ NOUN [3] an imitation or representation of the sound of a bell. [4] *Austral informal* a party or social event.
▷HISTORY C13: probably of imitative origin, but influenced by DIN[1] + RING[2]; compare Old Swedish *diunga* to beat

ding[2] (dɪŋ) VERB *Scot* [1] to strike; dash down. [2] to surpass.
▷HISTORY Middle English *dingen*

Ding an sich (dɪŋ æn sɪk; *German* dɪŋ an zɪç) NOUN *Philosophy* the thing in itself.

dingbat (ˈdɪŋˌbæt) NOUN *US slang* [1] any unnamed object, esp one used as a missile. [2] a crazy or stupid person.
▷HISTORY C19: of unknown origin

dingbats (ˈdɪŋˌbæts) *Austral and NZ* ◆ PLURAL NOUN [1] **the.** *Slang* delirium tremens. [2] **give someone the dingbats.** *Informal* to make someone nervous. ◆ ADJECTIVE [3] *Informal* crazy or stupid.

ding-dong NOUN [1] the sound of a bell or bells, esp two bells tuned a fourth or fifth apart. [2] an imitation or representation of the sound of a bell. [3] **a** a violent exchange of blows or words. **b** (*as modifier*): *a ding-dong battle.* ◆ ADJECTIVE [4] sounding or ringing repeatedly.
▷HISTORY C16: of imitative origin; see DING[1]

dinge[1] (dɪndʒ) NOUN dinginess.
▷HISTORY C19: back formation from DINGY

dinge[2] (dɪndʒ) *US derogatory slang* ◆ NOUN [1] a Black person. ◆ ADJECTIVE [2] of or relating to Black people.

dinge[3] (dɪndʒ) *Dialect* ◆ VERB *(tr)* [1] to make a dent in (something). ◆ NOUN [2] a dent.
▷HISTORY of unknown origin

dinger (ˈdɪŋə) NOUN *US* an informal word for **home run.**

dinges (ˈdɪŋəs) NOUN *South African informal* a jocular word for something whose name is unknown or forgotten; thingumabob.
▷HISTORY from Afrikaans, from *ding* thing

dinghy (ˈdɪŋɪ) NOUN, *plural* **-ghies.** any small boat, powered by sail, oars, or outboard motor. Also (esp formerly): **dingy, dingey.**
▷HISTORY C19: from Hindi or Bengali *dingi* a little boat, from *dingā* boat

dingle (ˈdɪŋgᵊl) NOUN a small wooded dell.
▷HISTORY C13: of uncertain origin

dingo (ˈdɪŋgəʊ) NOUN, *plural* **-goes.** [1] a wild dog, *Canis dingo,* of Australia, having a yellowish-brown coat and resembling a wolf. [2] *Austral slang* a cheat or coward. ◆ VERB **-goes, -going, -goed.** *(intr) Austral slang* [3] **a** to act in a cowardly manner. **b** to drop out of something. [4] (foll by *on*) to let (someone) down.
▷HISTORY C18: native Australian name

dingy (ˈdɪndʒɪ) ADJECTIVE **-gier, -giest.** [1] lacking light or brightness; drab. [2] dirty; discoloured.
▷HISTORY C18: perhaps from an earlier dialect word related to Old English *dynge* dung
▶**ˈdingily** ADVERB ▶**ˈdinginess** NOUN

dining car NOUN a railway coach in which meals are served at tables. Also called: **restaurant car.**

dining room NOUN a room where meals are eaten.

dinitrobenzene (daɪˌnaɪtrəʊˈbɛnziːn, -bɛnˈziːn) NOUN a yellow crystalline compound existing in three isomeric forms, obtained by reaction of benzene with nitric and sulphuric acids. The *meta-* form is used in the manufacture of dyes and plastics. Formula: $C_6H_4(NO_2)_2$.

dinitrogen tetroxide (daɪˈnaɪtrədʒən) NOUN a colourless gaseous substance that exists in equilibrium with nitrogen dioxide. As the temperature is reduced the proportion of the tetroxide increases. Formula: N_2O_4.

dink[1] (dɪŋk) ADJECTIVE [1] *Scot and northern English dialect* neat or neatly dressed. ◆ VERB [2] *Austral and NZ chiefly children's slang* **a** (*tr*) to carry (a second person) on a horse, bicycle, etc. **b** (*intr*) (of two people) to travel together on a horse, bicycle, etc.
▷HISTORY C16: of unknown origin

dink[2] (dɪŋk) NOUN *Sport* [1] a ball struck delicately. ◆ VERB [2] to hit or kick (a ball) delicately.
▷HISTORY C20: imitative of a delicate strike

Dinka (ˈdɪŋkə) NOUN [1] (*plural* **-kas** *or* **-ka**) a member of a Nilotic people of the S Sudan, noted for their height, which often reaches seven feet tall: chiefly herdsmen. [2] the language of this people, belonging to the Nilotic group of the Nilo-Saharan family.
▷HISTORY from Dinka *jieng* people

dinkie (ˈdɪŋkɪ) NOUN [1] an affluent married childless person. ◆ ADJECTIVE [2] designed for or appealing to dinkies.
▷HISTORY C20: from *d(ouble) i(ncome) n(o) k(ids)* + -IE

dinkum (ˈdɪŋkəm) ADJECTIVE *Austral and NZ informal* [1] Also: **dinky-di.** genuine or right (usually preceded by *fair* and used esp as an interjection): *a fair dinkum offer.* [2] **dinkum oil.** *Archaic* the truth.
▷HISTORY C19: from English dialect: work, of unknown origin

dinky (ˈdɪŋkɪ) ADJECTIVE **dinkier, dinkiest.** *Informal* [1] *Brit* small and neat; dainty. [2] *US* inconsequential; insignificant.
▷HISTORY C18 (in the sense: dainty): from DINK

dinna (ˈdɪnə) VERB *Scot* do not.

dinner (ˈdɪnə) NOUN [1] a meal taken in the evening. [2] a meal taken at midday, esp when it is the main meal of the day; lunch. [3] **a** a formal evening meal, as of a club, society, etc. **b** a public banquet in honour of someone or something. [4] a complete meal at a fixed price in a restaurant; table d'hôte. [5] (*modifier*) of, relating to, or used at dinner: *dinner plate; dinner table; dinner hour.* [6] **do like a dinner.** (*usually passive*) *Austral informal* to do for, overpower, or outdo.
▷HISTORY C13: from Old French *disner;* see DINE

dinner-dance NOUN a formal dinner followed by dancing.

dinner jacket NOUN a man's semiformal evening jacket without tails, usually black with a silk facing over the collar and lapels. Abbreviations: **DJ, dj.** US and Canadian name: **tuxedo.**

dinner lady NOUN *Brit* a female cook or canteen worker in a school.

dinner service NOUN a set of matching plates, dishes, etc., suitable for serving a meal to a certain number of people.

dinoceras (daɪˈnɒsərəs) NOUN another name for a **uintathere.**
▷HISTORY C19: New Latin, from Greek *deinos* fearful + *keras* horn

dinoflagellate (ˌdaɪnəʊˈflædʒɪlɪt, -ˌleɪt) NOUN [1] any of a group of unicellular biflagellate aquatic organisms forming a constituent of plankton: now usually classified as a phylum of protoctists (*Dinoflagellata*). ◆ ADJECTIVE [2] of or relating to dinoflagellates.
▷HISTORY C19: from New Latin *Dinoflagellata,* from Greek *dinos* whirling + FLAGELLUM + -ATE[1]

dinosaur (ˈdaɪnəˌsɔː) NOUN [1] any extinct terrestrial reptile of the orders *Saurischia* and *Ornithischia,* many of which were of gigantic size and abundant in the Mesozoic era. See also **saurischian, ornithischian.** Compare **pterosaur, plesiosaur.** [2] a person or thing that is considered to be out of date.
▷HISTORY C19: from New Latin *dinosaurus,* from Greek *deinos* fearful + *sauros* lizard

▸ˌ**dinoˈsaurian** ADJECTIVE

dinothere (ˈdaɪnəˌθɪə) NOUN any extinct late Tertiary elephant-like mammal of the genus *Dinotherium* (or *Deinotherium*), having a down-turned jaw with tusks curving downwards and backwards.
▷HISTORY C19: from New Latin *dinotherium,* from Greek *deinos* fearful + *thērion,* diminutive of *thēr* beast

dint (dɪnt) NOUN [1] **by dint of.** by means or use of: *by dint of hard work.* [2] *Archaic* a blow or a mark made by a blow. ◆ VERB [3] (*tr*) to mark with dints. ◆ NOUN, VERB [4] a variant of **dent**[1].
▷HISTORY Old English *dynt;* related to Old Norse *dyttr* blow
▸ˈ**dintless** ADJECTIVE

diocesan (daɪˈɒsɪsᵊn) ADJECTIVE [1] of or relating to a diocese. ◆ NOUN [2] the bishop of a diocese.

diocese (ˈdaɪəsɪs) NOUN the district under the jurisdiction of a bishop.
▷HISTORY C14: from Old French, from Late Latin *diocēsis,* from Greek *dioikēsis* administration, from *dioikein* to manage a household, from *oikos* house

diode (ˈdaɪəʊd) NOUN [1] a semiconductor device containing one p-n junction, used in circuits for converting alternating current to direct current. More formal name: **semiconductor diode.** [2] the earliest and simplest type of electronic valve having two electrodes, an anode and a cathode, between which a current can flow only in one direction. It was formerly widely used as a rectifier and detector but has now been replaced in most electrical circuits by the more efficient and reliable semiconductor diode.
▷HISTORY C20: from DI-[1] + -ODE[2]

dioecious, diecious (daɪˈiːʃəs), *or* **dioicous** (daɪˈɔɪkəs) ADJECTIVE (of some plants) having the male and female reproductive organs in separate flowers on separate plants. Compare **monoecious.**
▷HISTORY C18: from New Latin *Dioecia* name of class, from DI[1] + Greek *oikia* house, dwelling
▸**diˈoeciously** *or* **diˈeciously** *or* **diˈoicously** ADVERB
▸**diˈoeciousness** *or* **diˈeciousness** *or* **diˈoicousness** NOUN

dioestrus *or US* **diestrus** (daɪˈiːstrəs) NOUN a period of sexual inactivity between periods of oestrus in animals that have several oestrous cycles in one breeding season.

diol (ˈdaɪɒl) NOUN *Chem* any of a class of alcohols that have two hydroxyl groups in each molecule. Also called: **glycol, dihydric alcohol.**
▷HISTORY from DI-[1] + (ALCOH)OL

Diomede Islands (ˈdaɪəˌmiːd) PLURAL NOUN two small islands in the Bering Strait, separated by the international date line and by the boundary line between the US and Russia.

Diomedes (ˌdaɪəˈmiːdiːz), **Diomede,** *or* **Diomed** (ˈdaɪəˌmɛd) NOUN *Greek myth* [1] a king of Argos, and suitor of Helen, who fought with the Greeks at Troy. [2] a king of the Bistones in Thrace whose savage horses ate strangers.

Dione[1] (daɪˈəʊnɪ) NOUN *Greek myth* a Titaness; the earliest consort of Zeus and mother of Aphrodite.

Dione[2] (daɪˈəʊnɪ) NOUN one of the larger satellites of the planet Saturn.

Dionysia (ˌdaɪəˈnɪzɪə) PLURAL NOUN (in ancient Greece) festivals of the god Dionysus: a source of Athenian drama.

Dionysiac (ˌdaɪəˈnɪzɪˌæk) ADJECTIVE [1] of or relating to Dionysus or his worship. [2] a less common word for **Dionysian.**

Dionysian (ˌdaɪəˈnɪzɪən) ADJECTIVE [1] of or relating to Dionysus. [2] (*sometimes not capital*) (in the philosophy of Nietzsche) of or relating to the set of creative qualities that encompasses spontaneity, irrationality, the rejection of discipline, etc. [3] (*often not capital*) wild or orgiastic. [4] of or relating to any of the historical characters named Dionysius. ◆ Compare (for senses 2, 3) **Apollonian.**

Dionysus *or* **Dionysos** (ˌdaɪəˈnaɪsəs) NOUN the Greek god of wine, fruitfulness, and vegetation, worshipped in orgiastic rites. He was also known as the bestower of ecstasy and god of the drama, and identified with Bacchus.

Diophantine equation (ˌdaɪəʊˈfæntaɪn) NOUN (in number theory) an equation in more than one variable and with integral coefficients, for which integral solutions are sought.
▷HISTORY C18: after *Diophantus,* Greek mathematician of the 3rd century A.D.

diopside (daɪˈɒpsaɪd, -sɪd) NOUN a colourless or pale-green pyroxene mineral consisting of calcium magnesium silicate in monoclinic crystalline form: used as a gemstone. Formula: $CaMgSi_2O_6$.
▷HISTORY C19: from DI-[2] + Greek *opsis* sight, appearance + -IDE

dioptase (daɪˈɒpteɪs, -teɪz) NOUN a green glassy mineral consisting of hydrated copper silicate in hexagonal crystalline form. Formula: $Cu_6Si_6O_{18}.6H_2O$.
▷HISTORY C19: from French, from Greek *dia-* through + *optos* visible

dioptometer (ˌdaɪɒpˈtɒmɪtə) NOUN an instrument for measuring ocular refraction.
▷HISTORY from DI-[2] + OPT(IC) + METER
▸ˌ**diopˈtometry** NOUN

dioptre *or US* **diopter** (daɪˈɒptə) NOUN a unit for measuring the refractive power of a lens: the reciprocal of the focal length of the lens expressed in metres.
▷HISTORY C16: from Latin *dioptra* optical instrument, from Greek, from *dia-* through + *opsesthai* to see
▸**diˈoptral** ADJECTIVE

dioptric (daɪˈɒptrɪk) *or* **dioptrical** ADJECTIVE [1] of or concerned with dioptrics. [2] of or denoting refraction or refracted light.
▸**diˈoptrically** ADVERB

dioptrics (daɪˈɒptrɪks) NOUN (*functioning as singular*) the branch of geometrical optics concerned with the formation of images by lenses.
▷HISTORY C20: from DIOPTRE + -ICS

diorama (ˌdaɪəˈrɑːmə) NOUN [1] a miniature three-dimensional scene, in which models of figures are seen against a background. [2] a picture made up of illuminated translucent curtains, viewed through an aperture. [3] a museum display, as of an animal, of a specimen in its natural setting. [4] *Films* a scene produced by the rearrangement of lighting effects.
▷HISTORY C19: from French, from Greek *dia-* through + Greek *horama* view, from *horan* to see
▸**dioramic** (ˌdaɪəˈræmɪk) ADJECTIVE

diorite (ˈdaɪəˌraɪt) NOUN a dark coarse-grained igneous plutonic rock consisting of plagioclase feldspar and ferromagnesian minerals such as hornblende.
▷HISTORY C19: from French, from Greek *diorizein* to distinguish (from *dia-* apart + *horizein* to define) + -ITE[1]
▸**dioritic** (ˌdaɪəˈrɪtɪk) ADJECTIVE

Dioscuri (ˌdaɪɒsˈkjʊərɪ) PLURAL NOUN the Greek name for **Castor and Pollux,** when considered together

dioxan (daɪˈɒksən) *or* **dioxane** (daɪˈɒkseɪn) NOUN a colourless insoluble toxic liquid made by heating ethanediol with sulphuric acid; 1,4-diethylene dioxide: used as a solvent, esp for waxes and cellulose acetate resins. Formula: $(CH_2)_2O(CH_2)_2O$.

dioxide (daɪˈɒksaɪd) NOUN [1] any oxide containing two oxygen atoms per molecule, both of which are bonded to an atom of another element. [2] another name for a **peroxide** (sense 4).

dioxin (daɪˈɒksɪn) NOUN any of a number of mostly poisonous chemical by-products of the manufacture of certain herbicides and bactericides, esp the extremely toxic 2,3,7,8-tetrachlorodibenzo-para-dioxin.

dip (dɪp) VERB **dips, dipping, dipped.** [1] to plunge or be plunged quickly or briefly into a liquid, esp to wet or coat. [2] (*intr*) to undergo a slight decline, esp temporarily: *sales dipped in November.* [3] (*intr*) to slope downwards: *the land dips towards the river.* [4] (*intr*) to sink or appear to sink quickly: *the sun dipped below the horizon.* [5] (*tr*) to switch (car headlights) from the main to the lower beam. US and Canadian word: **dim.** [6] (*tr*) **a** to immerse (poultry, sheep, etc.) briefly in a liquid chemical to rid them of or prevent infestation by insects, etc. **b** to immerse (grain, vegetables, or wood) in a preservative liquid. [7] (*tr*) to stain or dye by immersing in a liquid. [8] (*tr*) to baptize (someone) by immersion. [9] (*tr*) to plate or galvanize (a metal, etc.) by immersion in an electrolyte or electrolytic cell. [10] (*tr*) to scoop

up a liquid or something from a liquid in the hands or in a container. [11] to lower or be lowered briefly: *she dipped her knee in a curtsy.* [12] (*tr*) to make (a candle) by plunging the wick into melted wax. [13] (*intr*) to plunge a container, the hands, etc., into something, esp to obtain or retrieve an object: *he dipped in his pocket for money.* [14] (*intr;* foll by *in* or *into*) to dabble (in); play (at): *he dipped into black magic.* [15] (*intr*) (of an aircraft) to drop suddenly and then regain height. [16] (*intr*) (of a rock stratum or mineral vein) to slope downwards from the horizontal. [17] (*intr;* often foll by *for*) (in children's games) to select (a leader, etc.) by reciting any of various rhymes. [18] (*tr*) *Slang* to pick (a person's) pocket. ◆ NOUN [19] the act of dipping or state of being dipped. [20] a brief swim in water. [21] **a** any liquid chemical preparation in which poultry, sheep, etc. are dipped. **b** any liquid preservative into which objects, esp of wood, are dipped. [22] a preparation of dyeing agents into which fabric is immersed. [23] a depression, esp in a landscape. [24] something taken up by dipping. [25] a container used for dipping; dipper. [26] a momentary sinking down. [27] the angle of slope of rock strata, fault planes, etc., from the horizontal plane. [28] Also called: **angle of dip, magnetic dip, inclination.** the angle between the direction of the earth's magnetic field and the plane of the horizon; the angle that a magnetic needle free to swing in a vertical plane makes with the horizontal. [29] a creamy mixture into which pieces of food are dipped before being eaten. [30] *Surveying* the angular distance of the horizon below the plane of observation. [31] a candle made by plunging a wick repeatedly into wax. [32] a momentary loss of altitude when flying. [33] (in gymnastics) a chinning exercise on the parallel bars. [34] a slang word for **pickpocket.** ◆ See also **dip into, dip out.**
▷HISTORY Old English *dyppan;* related to Old High German *tupfen* to wash, German *taufen* to baptize; see DEEP

dip. *or* **Dip.** ABBREVIATION FOR diploma.

DipAD (in Britain) ABBREVIATION FOR Diploma in Art and Design.

dip-and-scarp ADJECTIVE (of topography) characterized by alternating steeper scarp slopes and gentler dip slopes.

DipChemEng ABBREVIATION FOR Diploma in Chemical Engineering.

dip circle NOUN an instrument for measuring dip, consisting of a dip needle with a vertical circular scale of angles. Also called: **inclinometer.**

DipCom ABBREVIATION FOR Diploma of Commerce.

DipEd (in Britain) ABBREVIATION FOR Diploma in Education.

dipeptide (daɪˈpɛptaɪd) NOUN a compound consisting of two linked amino acids. See **peptide.**

dipetalous (daɪˈpɛtələs) ADJECTIVE another word for **bipetalous.**

dip fault NOUN *Geology* a fault that runs perpendicular to the strike of the affected rocks (i.e. parallel to the plane of the angle of dip of the rocks).

diphase (ˈdaɪˌfeɪz) *or* **diphasic** ADJECTIVE *Physics* of, having, or concerned with two phases.

diphasic (daɪˈfeɪzɪk) ADJECTIVE [1] *Zoology* (of parasites) having a free active stage in the life cycle. [2] *Physics* another word for **diphase.**

diphenyl (daɪˈfiːnaɪl, -nɪl, -ˈfɛnɪl) NOUN another name for **biphenyl.**

diphenylamine (daɪˌfiːnaɪləˈmiːn, -ˈæmɪn, -nɪl-, -ˌfɛn-) NOUN a colourless insoluble crystalline derivative of benzene, used in the manufacture of dyes, as a stabilizer in plastics, etc. Formula: $(C_6H_5)_2NH$.

diphenylhydantoin sodium (daɪˌfiːnaɪlhaɪˈdæntəʊɪn, -nɪl-, -ˌfɛn-) NOUN another name for **phenytoin.**

diphosgene (daɪˈfɒzdʒiːn) NOUN an oily liquid with an extremely poisonous vapour, made by treating methanol with phosgene and chlorinating the product: has been used in chemical warfare. Formula: $ClCOOCCl_3$.

diphtheria (dɪpˈθɪərɪə, dɪf-) NOUN an acute contagious disease caused by the bacillus *Corynebacterium diphtheriae,* producing fever, severe prostration, and difficulty in breathing and swallowing as the result of swelling of the throat and formation of a false membrane.
▷HISTORY C19: New Latin, from French *diphthérie,* from Greek *diphthera* leather; from the nature of the membrane
▸**diphˈtherial** *or* **diphtheritic** (ˌdɪpθəˈrɪtɪk, dɪf-) *or* **diphtheric** (dɪpˈθɛrɪk, dɪf-) ADJECTIVE ▸**ˈdiphtheˌroid** ADJECTIVE

diphthong (ˈdɪfθɒŋ, ˈdɪp-) NOUN [1] a vowel sound, occupying a single syllable, during the articulation of which the tongue moves from one position to another, causing a continual change in vowel quality, as in the pronunciation of *a* in English *late,* during which the tongue moves from the position of (e) towards (ɪ). [2] a digraph or ligature representing a composite vowel such as this, as *ae* in *Caesar.*
▷HISTORY C15: from Late Latin *diphthongus,* from Greek *diphthongos,* from DI-[1] + *phthongos* sound
▸**diphˈthongal** ADJECTIVE

diphthongize *or* **diphthongise** (ˈdɪfθɒŋˌaɪz, -ˌgaɪz, ˈdɪp-) VERB (*often passive*) to make (a simple vowel) into a diphthong.
▸**ˌdiphthongiˈzation** *or* **ˌdiphthongiˈsation** NOUN

diphycercal (ˌdɪfɪˈsɜːkəl) ADJECTIVE *Ichthyol* of or possessing a symmetrical or pointed tail with the vertebral column extending to the tip, as in primitive fishes.
▷HISTORY C19: from Greek *diphuēs* twofold (from DI[1] + *phuē* growth) + *kerkos* tail

diphyletic (ˌdaɪfaɪˈlɛtɪk) ADJECTIVE relating to or characterized by descent from two ancestral groups of animals or plants.

diphyllous (daɪˈfɪləs) ADJECTIVE (of certain plants) having two leaves.

diphyodont (ˈdɪfɪəʊˌdɒnt) ADJECTIVE having two successive sets of teeth, as mammals (including man). Compare **polyphyodont.**
▷HISTORY C19: from Greek *diphuēs* double (see DIPHYCERCAL) + -ODONT

dip into VERB (*intr, preposition*) [1] to draw (upon): *he dipped into his savings.* [2] to read (passages) at random or cursorily in (a book, newspaper, etc.).

diplegia (daɪˈpliːdʒə) NOUN paralysis of corresponding parts on both sides of the body; bilateral paralysis.
▸**diˈplegic** ADJECTIVE

diplo- *or before a vowel* **dipl-** COMBINING FORM double: *diplococcus.*
▷HISTORY from Greek, from *diploos,* from DI-[1] + *-ploos* -fold

diplobiont (ˌdɪpləʊˈbaɪɒnt) NOUN *Biology* an organism that has both haploid and diploid individuals in its life cycle.
▸**ˌdiplobiˈontic** ADJECTIVE

diploblastic (ˌdɪpləʊˈblæstɪk) ADJECTIVE (of jellyfish, corals, and other coelenterates) having a body developed from only two germ layers (ectoderm and endoderm). Compare **triploblastic.**

diplocardiac (ˌdɪpləʊˈkɑːdɪˌæk) ADJECTIVE (of birds and mammals) having a four-chambered heart, which enables two separate circulations and prevents mixing of the arterial and venous blood.

Diplock court (ˈdɪplɒk) NOUN in Northern Ireland, a court of law designed to try cases linked with terrorism. In order to prevent the intimidation of jurors, the court consists of a single judge and no jury.
▷HISTORY C20: named after Lord *Diplock,* who introduced the courts in 1972

diplococcus (ˌdɪpləʊˈkɒkəs) NOUN, *plural* **-cocci** (-ˈkɒksaɪ). any of various spherical Gram-positive bacteria that occur in pairs, esp any of the genus *Diplococcus,* such as *D. pneumoniae,* which causes pneumonia: family *Lactobacillaceae.*
▸**ˌdiploˈcoccal** *or* **diplococcic** (ˌdɪpləʊˈkɒksɪk, -ˈkɒkɪk) ADJECTIVE

diplodocus (dɪˈplɒdəkəs, ˌdɪpləʊˈdəʊkəs) NOUN, *plural* **-cuses.** any herbivorous quadrupedal late Jurassic dinosaur of the genus *Diplodocus,* characterized by a very long neck and tail and a total body length of 27 metres: suborder *Sauropoda* (sauropods).
▷HISTORY C19: from New Latin, from DIPLO- + Greek *dokos* beam

diploë (ˈdɪpləʊˌiː) NOUN *Anatomy* the spongy bone separating the two layers of compact bone of the skull.
▷HISTORY C17: via New Latin, from Greek: a fold, from *diploos* double

diploid (ˈdɪplɔɪd) ADJECTIVE [1] *Biology* (of cells or organisms) having pairs of homologous chromosomes so that twice the haploid number is present. [2] double or twofold. ◆ NOUN [3] *Biology* a diploid cell or organism.
▸**dipˈloidic** ADJECTIVE ▸**ˈdiploidy** NOUN

diploma (dɪˈpləʊmə) NOUN [1] a document conferring a qualification, recording success in examinations or successful completion of a course of study. [2] an official document that confers an honour or privilege.
▷HISTORY C17: from Latin: official letter or document, literally: letter folded double, from Greek; see DIPLO-

diplomacy (dɪˈpləʊməsɪ) NOUN, *plural* **-cies.** [1] the conduct of the relations of one state with another by peaceful means. [2] skill in the management of international relations. [3] tact, skill, or cunning in dealing with people.
▷HISTORY C18: from French *diplomatie,* from *diplomatique* DIPLOMATIC

diplomat (ˈdɪpləˌmæt) NOUN [1] an official, such as an ambassador or first secretary, engaged in diplomacy. [2] a person who deals with people tactfully or skilfully.

diplomate (ˈdɪpləˌmeɪt) NOUN any person who has been granted a diploma, esp a physician certified as a specialist.

diplomatic (ˌdɪpləˈmætɪk) ADJECTIVE [1] of or relating to diplomacy or diplomats. [2] skilled in negotiating, esp between states or people. [3] tactful in dealing with people. [4] of or relating to diplomatics.
▷HISTORY C18: from French *diplomatique* concerning the documents of diplomacy, from New Latin *diplōmaticus;* see DIPLOMA
▸**ˌdiploˈmatically** ADVERB

diplomatic bag NOUN a container or bag in which official mail is sent, free from customs inspection, to and from an embassy or consulate.

diplomatic corps *or* **body** NOUN the entire body of diplomats accredited to a given state.

diplomatic immunity NOUN the immunity from local jurisdiction and exemption from taxation in the country to which they are accredited afforded to diplomats.

diplomatics (ˌdɪpləˈmætɪks) NOUN (*functioning as singular*) [1] the critical study of historical documents. [2] a less common word for **diplomacy.**

Diplomatic Service NOUN [1] (in Britain) the division of the Civil Service which provides diplomats to represent the UK abroad. [2] (*not capitals*) the equivalent institution of any other country.

diplomatist (dɪˈpləʊmətɪst) NOUN a less common word for **diplomat.**

diplonema (ˌdɪpləʊˈniːmə) NOUN *Biology* a less common name for **diplotene.**

diplont (ˈdɪplɒnt) NOUN an animal or plant that has the diploid number of chromosomes in its somatic cells.
▷HISTORY C20: DIPLO- + Greek *ōn* being, from *einai* to be
▸**dipˈlontic** ADJECTIVE

diplopia (dɪˈpləʊpɪə) NOUN a visual defect in which a single object is seen in duplicate; double vision. It can be caused by incorrect fixation or by an abnormality in the visual system.
▷HISTORY C19: New Latin, from DIPLO- + Greek *ōps* eye
▸**diplopic** (dɪˈplɒpɪk) ADJECTIVE

diplopod (ˈdɪpləˌpɒd) NOUN any arthropod of the class *Diplopoda,* which includes the millipedes.

diplosis (dɪˈpləʊsɪs) NOUN *Biology* the doubling of the haploid number of chromosomes that occurs during fusion of gametes to form a diploid zygote.
▷HISTORY C20: from Greek *diplōsis* doubling, from *diploun* to double, from *diploos* double

diplostemonous (ˌdɪpləʊˈstiːmənəs, -ˈstɛm-) ADJECTIVE (of plants) having twice as many stamens as petals, esp with the stamens arranged in two whorls.
▷HISTORY C19: from New Latin *diplostemonus*

(unattested), from DIPLO- + *-stemonus* relating to a STAMEN

diplotene ('dɪpləʊˌti:n) NOUN the fourth stage of the prophase of meiosis, during which the paired homologous chromosomes separate except at the places where genetic exchange has occurred. See also **chiasma** (sense 1), **crossing over.**
▷HISTORY C20: from DIPLO- + Greek *tainia* band

diplozoic (ˌdɪplə'zəʊɪk) ADJECTIVE (of certain animals) bilaterally symmetrical.

DipMet ABBREVIATION FOR Diploma in Metallurgy.

dip needle NOUN a magnetized needle pivoted through its centre of gravity able to rotate freely in a vertical plane, used to determine the inclination of the earth's magnetic field. See also **dip circle.**

dipnoan (dɪp'nəʊən) ADJECTIVE 1 of, relating to, or belonging to the *Dipnoi*, a subclass of bony fishes comprising the lungfishes. ◆ NOUN 2 any lungfish.
▷HISTORY C19: from New Latin *Dipnoi,* from Greek *dipnoos,* double-breathing, from DI-[1] + *pnoē* breathing, air, from *pnein* to breathe

dipody ('dɪpədɪ) NOUN, *plural* **-dies.** *Prosody* a metrical unit consisting of two feet.
▷HISTORY C19: from Late Latin *dipodia,* from Greek DI-[1] + *pous* foot

dipole ('daɪˌpəʊl) NOUN 1 two electric charges or magnetic poles that have equal magnitudes but opposite signs and are separated by a small distance. 2 a molecule in which the centre of positive charge does not coincide with the centre of negative charge. 3 Also called: **dipole aerial.** a directional radio or television aerial consisting of two equal lengths of metal wire or rods, with a connecting wire fixed between them in the form of a T.
▸**di'polar** ADJECTIVE

dipole moment NOUN *Chem* a measure of the polarity in a chemical bond or molecule, equal to the product of one charge and the distance between the charges. Symbol: μ.

dip out VERB *(intr, adverb) Austral and NZ informal* (often foll by *on*) to miss out on or fail to participate in something: *he dipped out on the examination.*

dipper ('dɪpə) NOUN 1 a ladle used for dipping. 2 Also called: **water ouzel.** any aquatic songbird of the genus *Cinclus* and family *Cinclidae,* esp *C. cinclus.* They inhabit fast-flowing streams and resemble large wrens. 3 a slang word for **pickpocket.** 4 a person or thing that dips, such as the mechanism for directing car headlights downwards. 5 a small metal cup clipped onto a painter's palette for holding diluent or medium. 6 *Archaic* an Anabaptist. ◆ See also **big dipper.**

dippy ('dɪpɪ) ADJECTIVE **-pier, -piest.** *Slang* odd, eccentric, or crazy.
▷HISTORY C20: of unknown origin

dipropellant (ˌdaɪprə'pelənt) NOUN another name for **bipropellant.**

diprotodon (daɪ'prəʊtəʊˌdɒn) NOUN a large extinct marsupial of the Australian genus *Diprotodon.*
▷HISTORY C19: from Greek from DI-[1] + PROTO- + -ODONT, from its two prominent lower incisors

diprotodont (daɪ'prəʊtəʊˌdɒnt) NOUN any marsupial of the group or suborder *Diprotodontia,* including kangaroos, phalangers, and wombats, having fewer than three upper incisor teeth on each side of the jaw. Compare **polyprotodont.**
▷HISTORY C19: from Greek from DI-[1] + PROTO- + -ODONT

dip-slip fault NOUN *Geology* a fault on which the movement is in the direction of the dip of the fault.

dipsomania (ˌdɪpsəʊ'meɪnɪə) NOUN a compulsive desire to drink alcoholic beverages.
▷HISTORY C19: New Latin, from Greek *dipsa* thirst + -MANIA

dipsomaniac (ˌdɪpsəʊ'meɪnɪˌæk) NOUN 1 any person who has an uncontrollable and recurring urge to drink alcohol. Shortened form: **dipso.** ◆ ADJECTIVE 2 relating to or affected with dipsomania.
▸**dipsomaniacal** (ˌdɪpsəʊmə'naɪəkəl) ADJECTIVE

dipstick ('dɪpˌstɪk) NOUN a graduated rod or strip dipped into a container to indicate the fluid level.

dip switch NOUN a device for dipping car headlights.

dipteral ('dɪptərəl) ADJECTIVE *Architect* having a double row of columns.

dipteran ('dɪptərən) *or* **dipteron** ('dɪptəˌrɒn) NOUN 1 any dipterous insect. ◆ ADJECTIVE 2 another word for **dipterous** (sense 1).

dipterocarpaceous (ˌdɪptərəʊkɑ:'peɪʃəs) ADJECTIVE of, relating to, or belonging to the *Dipterocarpaceae,* a family of trees chiefly native to tropical SE Asia, having two-winged fruits. Many species yield useful timber and resins.
▷HISTORY C19: via New Latin from Greek *dipteros* two-winged + *karpos* fruit

dipterous ('dɪptərəs) ADJECTIVE 1 Also: **dipteran.** of, relating to, or belonging to the *Diptera,* a large order of insects having a single pair of wings and sucking or piercing mouthparts. The group includes flies, mosquitoes, craneflies, and midges. 2 *Botany* having two winglike parts: *a dipterous seed.*
▷HISTORY C18: from New Latin, from Greek *dipteros,* from *di-* two + *pteros* wing

diptych ('dɪptɪk) NOUN 1 a pair of hinged wooden tablets with waxed surfaces for writing. 2 a painting or carving on two panels, usually hinged like a book.
▷HISTORY C17: from Greek *diptukhos* folded together, from DI[1] + *ptukhos* fold; compare TRIPTYCH

dir. ABBREVIATION FOR director.

Dirac constant (dɪ'ræk) NOUN a constant used in quantum mechanics, equal to the Planck constant divided by 2π. It has a value of $1.054571596 \pm 0.000000078 \times 10^{-34}$ joule seconds. Symbol: $\hbar$ or $\underline{h}$. Also called: **crossed-h, h-bar.**
▷HISTORY C20: named after Paul Adrien Maurice *Dirac* (1902–84), English physicist

dire (daɪə) ADJECTIVE *(usually prenominal)* 1 Also: **direful.** disastrous; fearful. 2 desperate; urgent: *a dire need.* 3 foreboding disaster; ominous: *a dire warning.*
▷HISTORY C16: from Latin *dīrus* ominous, fearful; related to Greek *deos* fear
▸**'direly** ADVERB ▸**'direness** NOUN

direct (dɪ'rekt, daɪ-) VERB *(mainly tr)* 1 to regulate, conduct, or control the affairs of. 2 *(also intr)* to give commands or orders with authority to (a person or group): *he directed them to go away.* 3 to tell or show (someone) the way to a place. 4 to aim, point, or cause to move towards a goal. 5 to address (a letter, parcel, etc.). 6 to address (remarks, words, etc.): *to direct comments at someone.* 7 *(also intr)* to provide guidance to (actors, cameramen, etc.) in the rehearsal of a play or the filming of a motion picture. 8 *(also intr)* **a** to conduct (a piece of music or musicians), usually while performing oneself. **b** another word (esp US) for **conduct** (sense 9). ◆ ADJECTIVE 9 without delay or evasion; straightforward: *a direct approach.* 10 without turning aside; uninterrupted; shortest; straight: *a direct route.* 11 without intervening persons or agencies; immediate: *a direct link.* 12 honest; frank; candid: *a direct answer.* 13 *(usually prenominal)* precise; exact: *a direct quotation.* 14 diametrical: *the direct opposite.* 15 in an unbroken line of descent, as from father to son over succeeding generations: *a direct descendant.* 16 (of government, decisions, etc.) by or from the electorate rather than through representatives. 17 *Logic, maths* (of a proof) progressing from the premises to the conclusion, rather than eliminating the possibility of the falsehood of the conclusion. Compare **indirect proof.** 18 *Astronomy* moving from west to east on the celestial sphere. Compare **retrograde** (sense 4a). 19 **a** of or relating to direct current. **b** (of a secondary induced current) having the same direction as the primary current. 20 *Music* **a** (of motion) in the same direction. See **motion** (sense 9). **b** (of an interval or chord) in root position; not inverted. ◆ ADVERB 21 directly; straight: *he went direct to the office.*
▷HISTORY C14: from Latin *dīrectus;* from *dīrigere* to guide, from *dis-* apart + *regere* to rule
▸**di'rectness** NOUN

direct access NOUN a method of reading data from a computer file without reading through the file from the beginning as on a disk or drum. Also called: **random access.** Compare **sequential access.**

direct action NOUN action such as strikes or civil disobedience, employed by organized labour or other groups to obtain demands from an employer, government, etc.

direct coupling NOUN *Electronics* conductive coupling between electronic circuits, as opposed to inductive or capacitative coupling. See also **coupling** (sense 4).
▸**direct coupled** ADJECTIVE

direct current NOUN a continuous electric current that flows in one direction only, without substantial variation in magnitude. Abbreviation: **DC.** Compare **alternating current.**

direct debit NOUN an order given to a bank or building society by a holder of an account, instructing it to pay to a specified person or organization any sum demanded by that person or organization. Compare **standing order.**

direct distance dialing NOUN the US and Canadian equivalent of **subscriber trunk dialling.**

direct dye NOUN any of a number of dyes that can be applied without the use of a mordant. They are usually azo dyes applied to cotton or rayon from a liquid bath containing an electrolyte such as sodium sulphate.

directed (dɪ'rektɪd, daɪ-) ADJECTIVE *Maths* (of a number, line, or angle) having either a positive or negative sign to distinguish measurement in one direction or orientation from that in the opposite direction or orientation.

direct evidence NOUN *Law* evidence, usually the testimony of a witness, directly relating to the fact in dispute. Compare **circumstantial evidence.**

direct-grant school NOUN (in Britain, formerly) a school financed by endowment, fees, and a state grant conditional upon admittance of a percentage of nonpaying pupils nominated by the local education authority.

direct injection NOUN See **solid injection.**

direct input NOUN a device, such as a keyboard, used to insert data directly into a computerized system.

direction (dɪ'rekʃən, daɪ-) NOUN 1 the act of directing or the state of being directed. 2 management, control, or guidance. 3 the work of a stage or film director. 4 the course or line along which a person or thing moves, points, or lies. 5 the course along which a ship, aircraft, etc., is travelling, expressed as the angle between true or magnetic north and an imaginary line through the main fore-and-aft axis of the vessel. 6 the place towards which a person or thing is directed. 7 a line of action; course. 8 the name and address on a letter, parcel, etc. 9 *Music* the process of conducting an orchestra, choir, etc. 10 *Music* an instruction in the form of a word or symbol heading or occurring in the body of a passage, movement, or piece to indicate tempo, dynamics, mood, etc. 11 *(modifier) Maths* **a** (of an angle) being any one of the three angles that a line in space makes with the three positive directions of the coordinate axes. Usually given as α, β, and γ with respect to the *x-, y-,* and *z-* axes. **b** (of a cosine) being the cosine of any of the direction angles. ◆ See also **directions.**

directional (dɪ'rekʃənəl, daɪ-) ADJECTIVE 1 of or relating to a spatial direction. 2 *Electronics* **a** having or relating to an increased sensitivity to radio waves, sound waves, nuclear particles, etc., coming from a particular direction. **b** (of an aerial) transmitting or receiving radio waves more effectively in some directions than in others. 3 *Physics, electronics* **a** concentrated in, following, or producing motion in a particular direction. **b** indicating direction. 4 indicating the direction something, such as a fashion trend, might take: *directional fashion looks.*
▸**diˌrection'ality** NOUN

directional drilling NOUN a method of drilling for oil in which the well is not drilled vertically, as when a number of wells are to be drilled from a single platform to reach different areas of an oil field. Also called: **deviated drilling.**

direction finder NOUN a highly directional aerial system that can be used to determine the direction of incoming radio signals, used esp as a navigation aid. Abbreviations: **D/F** *or* **DF.**
▸**direction finding** NOUN

directions (dɪ'rekʃənz, daɪ-) PLURAL NOUN *(sometimes singular)* instructions for doing something or for reaching a place.

directive (dɪ'rektɪv, daɪ-) NOUN 1 an instruction;

order. ◆ ADJECTIVE [2] tending to direct; directing. [3] indicating direction.

direct labour NOUN *Commerce* [1] work that is an essential part of a production process or the provision of a service. Compare **indirect labour.** [2] *Brit* workers who are part of an employer's own labour force rather than hired through a contractor, such as building workers employed by a local authority.

direct lighting NOUN *Electrical engineering* a lighting system in which a large proportion (at least 90 per cent) of the light is directed downwards.

directly (dɪˈrɛktlɪ, daɪ-) ADVERB [1] in a direct manner. [2] at once; without delay. [3] (foll by *before* or *after*) immediately; just. ◆ CONJUNCTION [4] (*subordinating*) as soon as: *we left directly the money arrived.*

direct-mail shot NOUN *Marketing* the posting of unsolicited sales literature to potential customers' homes or business addresses.

direct marketing NOUN selling goods directly to consumers rather than through retailers, usually by mail order, direct-mail shot, newspaper advertising, door-to-door selling, telephone selling, the Internet, or television home-shopping channels. Also called: **direct selling.**

direct memory access NOUN a process in which data may be moved directly to or from the main memory of a computer system by operations not under the control of the central processing unit. Abbreviation: **DMA.**

direct method NOUN a method of teaching a foreign language with minimal use of the pupil's native language and of formal grammar.

direct object NOUN *Grammar* a noun, pronoun, or noun phrase whose referent receives the direct action of a verb. For example, *a book* is the direct object in the sentence *They bought Anne a book.* Compare **indirect object.**

Directoire *French* (dirɛktwar) NOUN [1] *History* the French Directory. See **Directory.** ◆ ADJECTIVE [2] of, in, or relating to a decorative style of the end of the 18th century in France; a form of neoclassicism. [3] characteristic of women's dress during the French Directory, typically an almost transparent dress with the waistline under the bust.

director (dɪˈrɛktə, daɪ-) NOUN [1] a person or thing that directs, controls, or regulates. [2] a member of the governing board of a business concern who may or may not have an executive function. [3] a person who directs the affairs of an institution, trust, educational programme, etc. [4] the person responsible for the artistic and technical aspects of making a film or television programme. Compare **producer** (sense 4). [5] *Music* another word (esp US) for **conductor** (sense 2).
▸ **ˌdirecˈtorial** ADJECTIVE ▸ **ˌdirecˈtorially** ADVERB
▸ **diˈrectorˌship** NOUN ▸ **diˈrectress** FEMININE NOUN

directorate (dɪˈrɛktərɪt, daɪ-) NOUN [1] a board of directors. [2] Also: **directorship.** the position of director.

director-general NOUN, *plural* **directors-general.** the head of a large organization such as the CBI or BBC.

Director of Education NOUN *Brit* another term for **Chief Education Officer.**

Director of Public Prosecutions NOUN (in Britain) an official who, as head of the Crown Prosecution Service, is responsible for conducting all criminal prosecutions initiated by the police. Abbreviation: **DPP.**

director's chair NOUN a light wooden folding chair with arm rests and a canvas seat and back.

director's cut NOUN *Films* a version of a film which realizes the artistic aims of the director more fully than the original version.

directory (dɪˈrɛktərɪ, -trɪ, daɪ-) NOUN, *plural* **-ries.** [1] a book, arranged alphabetically or classified by trade listing names, addresses, telephone numbers, etc., of individuals or firms. [2] a book or manual giving directions. [3] a book containing the rules to be observed in the forms of worship used in churches. [4] a less common word for **directorate** (sense 2). [5] *Computing* an area of a disk, Winchester disk, or floppy disk that contains the names and locations of files currently held on that disk. ◆ ADJECTIVE [6] directing.

Directory (dɪˈrɛktərɪ, -trɪ, daɪ-) NOUN **the.** *History* the body of five directors in power in France from 1795 until their overthrow by Napoleon in 1799. Also called: **French Directory.**

direct primary NOUN *US government* a primary in which voters directly select the candidates who will run for office.

direct question NOUN a question asked in direct speech, such as *Why did you come?* Compare **indirect question.**

direct-reading ADJECTIVE (of an instrument) calibrated so that a given quantity to be measured can be read directly off the scale without the need of a multiplying constant.

directrix (dɪˈrɛktrɪks, daɪ-) NOUN [1] *Geometry* a fixed reference line, situated on the convex side of a conic section, that is used when defining or calculating its eccentricity. [2] a directress.
▷ HISTORY C17: New Latin, feminine of DIRECTOR

direct selling NOUN another name for **direct marketing.**

direct speech *or esp US* **direct discourse** NOUN the reporting of what someone has said or written by quoting his exact words.

direct tax NOUN a tax paid by the person or organization on which it is levied. Compare **indirect tax.**
▸ **direct taxation** NOUN

dirge (dɜːdʒ) NOUN [1] a chant of lamentation for the dead. [2] the funeral service in its solemn or sung forms. [3] any mourning song or melody.
▷ HISTORY C13: changed from Latin *dīrigē* direct (imperative), opening word of the Latin antiphon used in the office of the dead
▸ **ˈdirgeful** ADJECTIVE

dirham (ˈdɪəræm) NOUN [1] the standard monetary unit of Morocco, divided into 100 centimes. [2] the standard monetary unit of the United Arab Emirates, divided into 10 dinars and 100 fils. [3] **a** a Kuwaiti monetary unit worth one tenth of a dinar and 100 fils. **b** a Tunisian monetary unit worth one tenth of a dinar and 100 millimes. **c** a Qatari monetary unit worth one hundredth of a riyal. **d** a Libyan monetary unit worth one thousandth of a dinar. [4] any of various silver coins minted in North African countries at different periods.
▷ HISTORY C18: from Arabic, from Latin: DRACHMA

dirigible (dɪˈrɪdʒɪbᵊl) ADJECTIVE [1] able to be steered or directed. ◆ NOUN [2] another name for **airship.**
▷ HISTORY C16: from Latin *dīrigere* to DIRECT
▸ **ˌdirigiˈbility** NOUN

dirigisme (diːriːˈʒiːzəm) NOUN control by the state of economic and social matters.
▷ HISTORY C20: from French
▸ **dirigˈiste** ADJECTIVE

diriment (ˈdɪrɪmənt) ADJECTIVE [1] (of an impediment to marriage in canon law) totally invalidating. [2] *Rare* nullifying.
▷ HISTORY C19: from Latin *dirimēns* separating, from Latin *dirimere* to part, from DIS-[1] + *emere* to obtain

dirk (dɜːk) NOUN [1] a dagger esp as formerly worn by Scottish Highlanders. ◆ VERB (*tr*) [2] to stab with a dirk.
▷ HISTORY C16: from Scottish *durk,* perhaps from German *Dolch* dagger

dirndl (ˈdɜːndᵊl) NOUN [1] a woman's dress with a full gathered skirt and fitted bodice; originating from Tyrolean peasant wear. [2] a gathered skirt of this kind.
▷ HISTORY German (Bavarian and Austrian): shortened from *Dirndlkleid,* from *Dirndl* little girl + *Kleid* dress

dirt (dɜːt) NOUN [1] any unclean substance, such as mud, dust, excrement, etc.; filth. [2] loose earth; soil. [3] **a** packed earth, gravel, cinders, etc., used to make a racetrack. **b** (*as modifier*): *a dirt track.* [4] *Mining* the gravel or soil from which minerals are extracted. [5] a person or thing regarded as worthless. [6] obscene or indecent speech or writing. [7] *Slang* gossip; scandalous information. [8] moral corruption. [9] **do (someone) dirt.** *Slang* to do something vicious to (someone). [10] **dish the dirt.** *Informal* to spread malicious gossip. [11] **eat dirt.** *Slang* to accept insult without complaining. [12] **treat someone like dirt.** to have no respect or consideration for someone.
▷ HISTORY C13: from Old Norse *drit* excrement; related to Middle Dutch *drēte*

dirt bike NOUN a type of motorbike designed for use over rough ground.

dirt-cheap ADJECTIVE, ADVERB *Informal* at an extremely low price.

dirt-poor ADJECTIVE *Chiefly US* extremely poor.

dirt road NOUN an unsealed country road.

dirty (ˈdɜːtɪ) ADJECTIVE **dirtier, dirtiest.** [1] covered or marked with dirt; filthy. [2] **a** obscene; salacious: *dirty books.* **b** sexually clandestine: *a dirty weekend.* [3] causing one to become grimy: *a dirty job.* [4] (of a colour) not clear and bright; impure. [5] unfair; dishonest; unscrupulous; unsporting. [6] mean; nasty: *a dirty cheat.* [7] scandalous; unkind: *a dirty rumour.* [8] revealing dislike or anger: *a dirty look.* [9] (of weather) rainy or squally; stormy. [10] (of an aircraft) having projections into the airstream, such as lowered flaps. [11] (of a nuclear weapon) producing a large quantity of radioactive fallout or contamination. Compare **clean** (sense 5). [12] **be dirty on.** *Austral slang* to be offended by or be hostile towards. [13] **dirty dog.** a despicable person. [14] **dirty linen.** *Informal* intimate secrets, esp those that might give rise to gossip. [15] **dirty word. a** an obscene word. **b** something that is regarded with disapproval: *federalism is a dirty word.* [16] **dirty work.** unpleasant or illicit activity. [17] **do the dirty on.** *Brit informal* to behave meanly or unkindly towards. ◆ VERB **dirties, dirtying, dirtied.** [18] to make or become dirty; stain; soil.
▸ **ˈdirtily** ADVERB ▸ **ˈdirtiness** NOUN

dirty bomb NOUN *Informal* a bomb made from nuclear waste combined with conventional explosives that is capable of spreading radioactive material over a very wide area.

dirty realism NOUN a style of writing, originating in the US in the 1980s, which depicts in great detail the seamier or more mundane aspects of ordinary life.
▸ **dirty realist** NOUN

dirty trick NOUN [1] a malicious and contemptible action. [2] (*plural*) **a** underhand activity and machinations in political or governmental affairs. **b** (*as modifier*): *dirty-tricks operation.*

dis (dɪs) VERB a variant spelling of **diss.**

Dis (dɪs) NOUN [1] Also called: **Orcus, Pluto.** the Roman god of the underworld. [2] the abode of the dead; underworld. ◆ Greek equivalent: **Hades.**

dis-[1] PREFIX [1] indicating reversal: *disconnect; disembark.* [2] indicating negation, lack, or deprivation: *dissimilar; distrust; disgrace.* [3] indicating removal or release: *disembowel; disburden.* [4] expressing intensive force: *dissever.*
▷ HISTORY from Latin *dis-* apart; in some cases, via Old French *des-*. In compound words of Latin origin, *dis-* becomes *dif-* before *f* and *di-* before some consonants

dis-[2] COMBINING FORM variant of **di-**[1] before *s*: *dissyllable.*

disability (ˌdɪsəˈbɪlɪtɪ) NOUN, *plural* **-ties.** [1] the condition of being unable to perform a task or function because of a physical or mental impairment. [2] something that disables; handicap. [3] lack of necessary intelligence, strength, etc. [4] an incapacity in the eyes of the law to enter into certain transactions.

disability clause NOUN (in life assurance policies) a clause enabling a policyholder to cease payment of premiums without loss of coverage and often to receive a pension or indemnity if he becomes permanently disabled.

Disability Rights Commission NOUN (in Britain) a body appointed by the Government to enforce anti-discrimination law affecting people with disabilities.

disable (dɪsˈeɪbᵊl) VERB (*tr*) [1] to make ineffective, unfit, or incapable, as by crippling. [2] to make or pronounce legally incapable. [3] to switch off (an electronic device).
▸ **disˈablement** NOUN

disabled (dɪˈseɪbᵊld) ADJECTIVE **a** lacking one or more physical powers, such as the ability to walk or to coordinate one's movements, as from the effects of a disease or accident, or through mental impairment. **b** (*as collective noun; preceded by the*): *the disabled.*

> **Language note** The use of *the disabled, the blind,* etc. can be offensive and should be avoided. Instead one should talk about *disabled people, blind people,* etc.

disablement benefit NOUN (in Britain) a noncontributory benefit payable to a person disabled through injury or disease caused by their work.

disabuse (ˌdɪsəˈbjuːz) VERB (*tr;* usually foll by *of*) to rid (oneself, another person, etc.) of a mistaken or misguided idea; set right.
▸**ˌdisaˈbusal** NOUN

disaccharide (daɪˈsækəˌraɪd, -rɪd) *or* **disaccharid** NOUN any of a class of sugars, such as maltose, lactose, and sucrose, having two linked monosaccharide units per molecule.

disaccord (ˌdɪsəˈkɔːd) NOUN **1** lack of agreement or harmony. ◆ VERB **2** (*intr*) to be out of agreement; disagree.

disaccredit (ˌdɪsəˈkrɛdɪt) VERB (*tr*) to take away the authorization or credentials of.

disaccustom (ˌdɪsəˈkʌstəm) VERB (*tr;* usually foll by *to*) to cause to lose a habit.

disadvantage (ˌdɪsədˈvɑːntɪdʒ) NOUN **1** an unfavourable circumstance, state of affairs, thing, person, etc. **2** injury, loss, or detriment. **3** an unfavourable condition or situation (esp in the phrase **at a disadvantage**). ◆ VERB **4** (*tr*) to put at a disadvantage; handicap.

disadvantaged (ˌdɪsədˈvɑːntɪdʒd) ADJECTIVE socially or economically deprived or discriminated against.

disadvantageous (dɪsˌædvənˈteɪdʒəs, ˌdɪsæd-) ADJECTIVE unfavourable; detrimental.
▸**disˌadvanˈtageously** ADVERB ▸**disˌadvanˈtageousness** NOUN

disaffect (ˌdɪsəˈfɛkt) VERB (*tr; often passive*) to cause to lose loyalty or affection; alienate.
▸**ˌdisafˈfectedly** ADVERB ▸**ˌdisafˈfectedness** NOUN
▸**ˌdisafˈfection** NOUN

disaffiliate (ˌdɪsəˈfɪlɪˌeɪt) VERB to sever an affiliation (with); dissociate.
▸**ˌdisafˌfiliˈation** NOUN

disaffirm (ˌdɪsəˈfɜːm) VERB (*tr*) **1** to deny or contradict (a statement). **2** *Law* **a** to annul or reverse (a decision). **b** to repudiate obligations.
▸**ˌdisafˈfirmance** *or* **disaffirmation** (ˌdɪsæfəˈmeɪʃən) NOUN

disafforest (ˌdɪsəˈfɒrɪst) VERB (*tr*) **1** *English law* to reduce (land) from the status of a forest to the state of ordinary ground. **2** to remove forests from (land).
▸**ˌdisafˌforesˈtation** *or* **ˌdisafˈforestment** NOUN

disaggregate (dɪsˈægrɪˌgeɪt) VERB **1** to separate from a group or mass. **2** to divide into parts.
▸**ˌdisaggreˈgation** NOUN

disagree (ˌdɪsəˈgriː) VERB **-grees, -greeing, -greed.** (*intr;* often foll by *with*) **1** to dissent in opinion (from another person) or dispute (about an idea, fact, etc.). **2** to fail to correspond; conflict. **3** to be unacceptable (to) or unfavourable (for); be incompatible (with): *curry disagrees with me.* **4** to be opposed (to) in principle.

disagreeable (ˌdɪsəˈgriːəbəl) ADJECTIVE **1** not likable, esp bad-tempered, offensive, or disobliging: *disagreeable remarks.* **2** not to one's liking; unpleasant: *a disagreeable task.*
▸**ˌdisaˈgreeableness** *or* **ˌdisaˌgreeaˈbility** NOUN
▸**ˌdisaˈgreeably** ADVERB

disagreement (ˌdɪsəˈgriːmənt) NOUN **1** refusal or failure to agree. **2** a failure to correspond. **3** an argument or dispute.

disallow (ˌdɪsəˈlaʊ) VERB (*tr*) **1** to reject as untrue or invalid. **2** to cancel.
▸**ˌdisalˈlowable** ADJECTIVE ▸**ˌdisalˈlowance** NOUN

disambiguate (ˌdɪsæmˈbɪgjʊˌeɪt) VERB (*tr*) to make (an ambiguous expression) unambiguous.
▸**ˌdisamˌbiguˈation** NOUN

disannul (ˌdɪsəˈnʌl) VERB **-nuls, -nulling, -nulled.** (*tr*) *Chiefly law* to cancel; make void.
▸**ˌdisanˈnulment** NOUN

disappear (ˌdɪsəˈpɪə) VERB **1** (*intr*) to cease to be visible; vanish. **2** (*intr*) to go away or become lost, esp secretly or without explanation. **3** (*intr*) to cease to exist, have effect, or be known; become extinct or lost: *the pain has disappeared.* **4** (*tr*) (esp in South and Central America) to arrest secretly and presumably imprison or kill (a member of an opposing political group).
▸**ˌdisapˈpearance** NOUN

disapplication (ˌdɪsæplɪˈkeɪʃən) NOUN *Brit education* a provision for exempting schools or individuals from the requirements of the National Curriculum in special circumstances.

disappoint (ˌdɪsəˈpɔɪnt) VERB (*tr*) **1** to fail to meet the expectations, hopes, desires, or standards of; let down. **2** to prevent the fulfilment of (a plan, intention, etc.); frustrate; thwart.
▷**HISTORY** C15 (originally meaning: to remove from office): from Old French *desapointier;* see DIS-[1], APPOINT

disappointed (ˌdɪsəˈpɔɪntɪd) ADJECTIVE saddened by the failure of an expectation, etc.
▸**ˌdisapˈpointedly** ADVERB

disappointing (ˌdɪsəˈpɔɪntɪŋ) ADJECTIVE failing to meet one's expectations, hopes, desires, or standards.
▸**ˌdisapˈpointingly** ADVERB

disappointment (ˌdɪsəˈpɔɪntmənt) NOUN **1** the act of disappointing or the state of being disappointed. **2** a person, thing, or state of affairs that disappoints.

disapprobation (ˌdɪsæprəʊˈbeɪʃən) NOUN moral or social disapproval.

disapproval (ˌdɪsəˈpruːvəl) NOUN the act or a state or feeling of disapproving; censure; condemnation.

disapprove (ˌdɪsəˈpruːv) VERB **1** (*intr;* often foll by *of*) to consider wrong, bad, etc. **2** (*tr*) to withhold approval from.
▸**ˌdisapˈproving** ADJECTIVE ▸**ˌdisapˈprovingly** ADVERB

disarm (dɪsˈɑːm) VERB **1** (*tr*) to remove defensive or offensive capability from (a country, army, etc.). **2** (*tr*) to deprive of weapons. **3** (*tr*) to remove the triggering device of (a bomb, shell, etc.). **4** (*tr*) to win the confidence or affection of. **5** (*intr*) (of a nation, etc.) to decrease the size and capability of one's armed forces. **6** (*intr*) to lay down weapons.
▸**disˈarmer** NOUN

disarmament (dɪsˈɑːməmənt) NOUN **1** the reduction of offensive or defensive fighting capability, as by a nation. **2** the act of disarming or state of being disarmed.

disarming (dɪsˈɑːmɪŋ) ADJECTIVE tending to neutralize or counteract hostility, suspicion, etc.
▸**disˈarmingly** ADVERB

disarrange (ˌdɪsəˈreɪndʒ) VERB (*tr*) to throw into disorder.
▸**ˌdisarˈrangement** NOUN

disarray (ˌdɪsəˈreɪ) NOUN **1** confusion, dismay, and lack of discipline. **2** (esp of clothing) disorderliness; untidiness. ◆ VERB (*tr*) **3** to throw into confusion. **4** *Archaic* to undress.

disarticulate (ˌdɪsɑːˈtɪkjʊˌleɪt) VERB to separate or cause to separate at the joints, esp those of bones.
▸**ˌdisarˌticuˈlation** NOUN ▸**ˌdisarˈticuˌlator** NOUN

disassemble (ˌdɪsəˈsɛmbəl) VERB (*tr*) to take apart (a piece of machinery, etc.); dismantle.
▸**ˌdisasˈsembly** NOUN

disassembler (ˌdɪsəˈsɛmblə) NOUN *Computing* a computer program that translates machine code into assembly language.

disassociate (ˌdɪsəˈsəʊʃɪˌeɪt) VERB a less common word for **dissociate.**
▸**ˌdisasˌsociˈation** NOUN

disaster (dɪˈzɑːstə) NOUN **1** an occurrence that causes great distress or destruction. **2** a thing, project, etc., that fails or has been ruined.
▷**HISTORY** C16 (originally in the sense: malevolent astral influence): from Italian *disastro,* from *dis-* (pejorative) + *astro* star, from Latin *astrum,* from Greek *astron*
▸**disˈastrous** ADJECTIVE

disavow (ˌdɪsəˈvaʊ) VERB (*tr*) to deny knowledge of, connection with, or responsibility for.
▸**ˌdisaˈvowal** NOUN ▸**ˌdisaˈvowedly** ADVERB ▸**ˌdisaˈvower** NOUN

disband (dɪsˈbænd) VERB to cease to function or cause to stop functioning, as a unit, group, etc.
▸**disˈbandment** NOUN

disbar (dɪsˈbɑː) VERB **-bars, -barring, -barred.** (*tr*) *Law* to deprive of the status of barrister; expel from the Bar.
▸**disˈbarment** NOUN

> **Language note** *Disbar* is sometimes wrongly used where *debar* is meant: *he was debarred* (not *disbarred*) *from attending meetings.*

disbelief (ˌdɪsbɪˈliːf) NOUN refusal or reluctance to believe.

disbelieve (ˌdɪsbɪˈliːv) VERB **1** (*tr*) to reject as false or lying; refuse to accept as true or truthful. **2** (*intr;* usually foll by *in*) to have no faith (in): *disbelieve in God.*
▸**ˌdisbeˈliever** NOUN ▸**ˌdisbeˈlieving** ADJECTIVE
▸**ˌdisbeˈlievingly** ADVERB

disbranch (dɪsˈbrɑːntʃ) VERB (*tr*) to remove or cut a branch or branches from (a tree).

disbud (dɪsˈbʌd) *or* **debud** (diːˈbʌd) VERB **-buds, -budding, -budded.** **1** to remove superfluous buds, flowers, or shoots from (a plant, esp a fruit tree). **2** *Vet science* to remove the horn buds of (calves, lambs, and kids) to prevent horns growing.

disburden (dɪsˈbɜːdən) VERB **1** to remove a load from (a person or animal). **2** (*tr*) to relieve (oneself, one's mind, etc.) of a distressing worry or oppressive thought.
▸**disˈburdenment** NOUN

disburse (dɪsˈbɜːs) VERB (*tr*) to pay out.
▷**HISTORY** C16: from Old French *desborser,* from *des-* DIS-[1] + *borser* to obtain money, from *borse* bag, from Late Latin *bursa*
▸**disˈbursable** ADJECTIVE ▸**disˈbursement** NOUN
▸**disˈburser** NOUN

> **Language note** *Disburse* is sometimes wrongly used where *disperse* is meant: *the police used a water cannon to disperse* (not *disburse*) *the crowd.*

disc *or now esp US* **disk** (dɪsk) NOUN **1** a flat circular plate. **2** something resembling or appearing to resemble this: *the sun's disc.* **3** another word for (gramophone) **record. 4** *Anatomy* any approximately circular flat structure in the body, esp an intervertebral disc. **5** **a** the flat receptacle of composite flowers, such as the daisy. **b** (*as modifier*): *a disc floret.* **6** the middle part of the lip of an orchid. **7** **a** Also called: **parking disc.** a marker or device for display in a parked vehicle showing the time of arrival or the latest permitted time of departure or both. **b** (*as modifier*): *a disc zone; disc parking.* **8** *Computing* a variant spelling of **disk** (sense 2). ◆ VERB **9** to work (land) with a disc harrow.
▷**HISTORY** C18: from Latin *discus,* from Greek *diskos* quoit

discal (ˈdɪskəl) ADJECTIVE *Biology, zoology* relating to or resembling a disc; disclike: *discal cells.*

discalced (dɪsˈkælst) ADJECTIVE barefooted: used to denote friars and nuns who wear sandals.
▷**HISTORY** C17: from Latin *discalceātus,* from DIS-[1] + *calceātus* shod, from *calceāre* to provide with shoes, from *calceus* shoe, from *calx* heel

discant NOUN (ˈdɪskænt), VERB (dɪsˈkænt) a variant of **descant** (senses 1, 3, 4).
▸**disˈcanter** NOUN

discard VERB (dɪsˈkɑːd) **1** (*tr*) to get rid of as useless or undesirable. **2** *Cards* to throw out (a card or cards) from one's hand. **3** *Cards* to play (a card not of the suit led nor a trump) when unable to follow suit. ◆ NOUN (ˈdɪskɑːd) **4** a person or thing that has been cast aside. **5** *Cards* a discarded card. **6** the act of discarding.
▸**disˈcarder** NOUN

disc brake NOUN a type of brake in which two calliper-operated pads rub against a flat disc attached to the wheel hub when the brake is applied.

discern (dɪˈsɜːn) VERB **1** (*tr*) to recognize or perceive clearly. **2** to recognize or perceive (differences).
▷**HISTORY** C14: from Old French *discerner,* from

Latin *discernere* to divide, from DIS-[1] (apart) + *cernere* to separate
▸**dis'cerner** NOUN

discernible *or rarely* **discernable** (dɪˈsɜːnəbᵊl) ADJECTIVE able to be discerned; perceptible.
▸**dis'cernibly** *or* (*rarely*) **dis'cernably** ADVERB

discerning (dɪˈsɜːnɪŋ) ADJECTIVE having or showing good taste or judgment; discriminating.
▸**dis'cerningly** ADVERB

discernment (dɪˈsɜːnmənt) NOUN keen perception or judgment.

disc floret *or* **flower** NOUN any of the small tubular flowers at the centre of the flower head of certain composite plants, such as the daisy. Compare **ray floret.**

discharge VERB (dɪsˈtʃɑːdʒ) [1] (*tr*) to release or allow to go: *the hospital discharged the patient.* [2] (*tr*) to dismiss from or relieve of duty, office, employment, etc. [3] to fire or be fired, as a gun. [4] to pour forth or cause to pour forth: *the boil discharges pus.* [5] (*tr*) to remove (the cargo) from (a boat, etc.); unload. [6] (*tr*) to perform (the duties of) or meet (the demands of an office, obligation, etc.): *he discharged his responsibilities as mayor.* [7] (*tr*) to relieve oneself of (a responsibility, debt, etc.). [8] (*intr*) *Physics* **a** to lose or remove electric charge. **b** to form an arc, spark, or corona in a gas. **c** to take or supply electrical current from a cell or battery. [9] (*tr*) *Law* to release (a prisoner from custody, etc.). [10] (*tr*) to remove dye from (a fabric), as by bleaching. [11] (*intr*) (of a dye or colour) to blur or run. [12] (*tr*) *Architect* **a** to spread (weight) evenly over a supporting member. **b** to relieve a member of (excess weight) by distribution of pressure. ◆ NOUN (ˈdɪstʃɑːdʒ, dɪsˈtʃɑːdʒ) [13] a person or thing that is discharged. [14] **a** a dismissal or release from an office, job, institution, etc. **b** the document certifying such release. [15] the fulfilment of an obligation or release from a responsibility or liability: *honourable discharge.* [16] the act of removing a load, as of cargo. [17] a pouring forth of a fluid; emission. [18] **a** the act of firing a projectile. **b** the volley, bullet, missile, etc., fired. [19] *Law* **a** a release, as of a person held under legal restraint. **b** an annulment, as of a court order. [20] *Physics* **a** the act or process of removing or losing charge or of equalizing a potential difference. **b** a transient or continuous conduction of electricity through a gas by the formation and movement of electrons and ions in an applied electric field. [21] **a** the volume of fluid flowing along a pipe or a channel in unit time. **b** the output rate of a plant or piece of machinery, such as a pump.
▸**dis'chargeable** ADJECTIVE ▸**dis'charger** NOUN

discharge tube NOUN *Electronics* an electrical device in which current flow is by electrons and ions in an ionized gas, as in a fluorescent light or neon tube.

disc harrow NOUN a harrow with sharp-edged slightly concave discs mounted on horizontal shafts and used to cut clods or debris on the surface of the soil or to cover seed after planting.

disciple (dɪˈsaɪpᵊl) NOUN [1] a follower of the doctrines of a teacher or a school of thought. [2] one of the personal followers of Christ (including his 12 apostles) during his earthly life.
▹HISTORY Old English *discipul,* from Latin *discipulus* pupil, from *discere* to learn
▸**dis'ciple,ship** NOUN ▸**discipular** (dɪˈsɪpjʊlə) ADJECTIVE

Disciples of Christ PLURAL NOUN a Christian denomination founded in the US in 1809 by Thomas and Alexander Campbell.

disciplinant (ˈdɪsɪˌplɪnənt) NOUN (*often capital*) *RC Church* a person belonging to a former order of flagellants in Spain.

disciplinarian (ˌdɪsɪplɪˈnɛərɪən) NOUN [1] a person who imposes or advocates discipline. ◆ ADJECTIVE [2] a less common word for **disciplinary.**

disciplinary (ˈdɪsɪˌplɪnərɪ) *or* **disciplinarian** ADJECTIVE [1] of, promoting, or used for discipline; corrective. [2] relating to a branch of learning: *criticism that crosses disciplinary boundaries.*

discipline (ˈdɪsɪplɪn) NOUN [1] training or conditions imposed for the improvement of physical powers, self-control, etc. [2] systematic training in obedience to regulations and authority. [3] the state of improved behaviour, etc., resulting from such training or conditions. [4] punishment or chastisement. [5] a system of rules for behaviour, methods of practice, etc. [6] a branch of learning or instruction. [7] the laws governing members of a Church. [8] a scourge of knotted cords. ◆ VERB (*tr*) [9] to improve or attempt to improve the behaviour, orderliness, etc., of by training, conditions, or rules. [10] to punish or correct.
▹HISTORY C13: from Latin *disciplīna* teaching, from *discipulus* DISCIPLE
▸**'disci,plinable** ADJECTIVE ▸**disciplinal** (ˌdɪsɪˈplaɪnᵊl, ˈdɪsɪplɪnᵊl) ADJECTIVE ▸**'disci,pliner** NOUN

discission (dɪsˈsɪʒən) NOUN *Med* surgical incision, esp of a cataract.

disc jockey NOUN a person who announces and plays recorded music, esp pop music, on a radio programme, etc. Abbreviations: **DJ, dj.**

disclaim (dɪsˈkleɪm) VERB [1] (*tr*) to deny or renounce (any claim, connection, etc.). [2] (*tr*) to deny the validity or authority of. [3] *Law* to renounce or repudiate (a legal claim or right).
▸**disclamation** (ˌdɪskləˈmeɪʃən) NOUN

disclaimer (dɪsˈkleɪmə) NOUN a repudiation or denial.

disclimax (dɪsˈklaɪmæks) NOUN *Ecology* a climax community resulting from the activities of man or domestic animals in climatic and other conditions that would otherwise support a different type of community.

disclose (dɪsˈkləʊz) VERB (*tr*) [1] to make (information) known. [2] to allow to be seen; lay bare.
▸**dis'closer** NOUN

disclosing agent NOUN *Dentistry* a vegetable dye, administered as a liquid or in tablet form (**disclosing tablet**), that stains plaque, making it readily apparent on the teeth.

disclosure (dɪsˈkləʊʒə) NOUN [1] something that is disclosed. [2] the act of disclosing; revelation.

Discman (ˈdɪskmən) NOUN *Trademark* a small portable CD player with light headphones.

disco (ˈdɪskəʊ) NOUN, *plural* **-cos.** [1] **a** an occasion at which typically young people dance to amplified pop records, usually compered by a disc jockey and featuring special lighting effects. **b** (*as modifier*): *disco dancing.* [2] a nightclub or other public place where such dances take place. [3] mobile equipment, usually accompanied by a disc jockey who operates it, for providing music for a disco. [4] **a** a type of dance music designed to be played in discos, with a solid thump on each beat. **b** (*as modifier*): *a disco record.*
▹HISTORY C20: shortened from DISCOTHEQUE

discobolus *or* **discobolos** (dɪsˈkɒbələs) NOUN, *plural* **-li** (-ˌlaɪ). [1] (in classical Greece) a discus thrower. [2] a statue of a discus thrower.
▹HISTORY C18: from Latin, from Greek *diskobolos,* from *diskos* DISCUS + *-bolos,* from *ballein* to throw

discography (dɪsˈkɒɡrəfɪ) NOUN [1] a classified reference list of gramophone records. [2] another word for **discology.**
▸**dis'cographer** NOUN

discoid (ˈdɪskɔɪd) ADJECTIVE *also* **discoidal** (dɪsˈkɔɪdᵊl). [1] like a disc. [2] (of a composite flower such as the tansy) consisting of disc florets only. ◆ NOUN [3] a disclike object.

discology (dɪsˈkɒlədʒɪ) NOUN the study of gramophone records.
▸**dis'cologist** NOUN

discolour *or US* **discolor** (dɪsˈkʌlə) VERB to change or cause to change in colour; fade or stain.
▸**dis,color'ation** *or* **dis,colour'ation** NOUN ▸**dis'colourment** *or US* **dis'colorment** NOUN

discombobulate (ˌdɪskəmˈbɒbjʊˌleɪt) VERB (*tr*) *Informal, chiefly US and Canadian* to throw into confusion.
▹HISTORY C20: probably a whimsical alteration of DISCOMPOSE or DISCOMFIT

discomfit (dɪsˈkʌmfɪt) VERB (*tr*) [1] to make uneasy, confused, or embarrassed. [2] to frustrate the plans or purpose of. [3] *Archaic* to defeat in battle.
▹HISTORY C14: from Old French *desconfire* to destroy, from *des-* (indicating reversal) + *confire* to make, from Latin *conficere* to produce; see CONFECT
▸**dis'comfiter** NOUN ▸**dis'comfiture** NOUN

discomfort (dɪsˈkʌmfət) NOUN [1] an inconvenience, distress, or mild pain. [2] something that disturbs or deprives of ease. ◆ VERB [3] (*tr*) to make uncomfortable or uneasy.

discomfortable (dɪsˈkʌmfətəbᵊl, -ˈkʌmftə-) ADJECTIVE *Archaic* tending to deprive of mental or physical ease or comfort.

discommend (ˌdɪskəˈmɛnd) VERB (*tr*) [1] *Rare* to express disapproval of. [2] *Obsolete* to bring into disfavour.
▸**,discom'mendable** ADJECTIVE ▸**dis,commen'dation** NOUN

discommode (ˌdɪskəˈməʊd) VERB (*tr*) to cause inconvenience or annoyance to; disturb.
▸**,discom'modious** ADJECTIVE ▸**,discom'modiously** ADVERB

discommodity (ˌdɪskəˈmɒdɪtɪ) NOUN, *plural* **-ties.** [1] *Economics* a commodity without utility. [2] *Archaic* the state or a source of inconvenience.

discommon (dɪsˈkɒmən) VERB (*tr*) *Law* to deprive (land) of the character and status of common, as by enclosure.

discompose (ˌdɪskəmˈpəʊz) VERB (*tr*) [1] to disturb the composure of; disconcert. [2] *Now rare* to disarrange.
▸**,discom'posedly** ADVERB ▸**,discom'posingly** ADVERB ▸**,discom'posure** NOUN

disconcert (ˌdɪskənˈsɜːt) VERB (*tr*) [1] to disturb the composure of. [2] to frustrate or upset.
▸**,discon'certion** *or* **,discon'certment** NOUN

disconcerted (ˌdɪskənˈsɜːtɪd) ADJECTIVE perturbed, embarrassed, or confused.
▸**,discon'certedly** ADVERB ▸**,discon'certedness** NOUN

disconcerting (ˌdɪskənˈsɜːtɪŋ) ADJECTIVE causing a feeling of disturbance, embarrassment, or confusion; perturbing; worrying.
▸**,discon'certingly** ADVERB

disconfirm (ˌdɪskənˈfɜːm) VERB (*tr*) (of a fact or argument) to suggest that a hypothesis is wrong or ill-formulated.
▸**,disconfir'mation** NOUN

disconformity (ˌdɪskənˈfɔːmɪtɪ) NOUN, *plural* **-ties.** [1] lack of conformity; discrepancy. [2] the junction between two parallel series of stratified rocks, representing a considerable period of erosion of the much older underlying rocks before the more recent ones were deposited.

disconnect (ˌdɪskəˈnɛkt) VERB (*tr*) to undo or break the connection of or between (something, such as a plug and a socket).
▸**,discon'necter** NOUN ▸**,discon'nection** *or* **,discon'nexion** NOUN ▸**,discon'nective** ADJECTIVE

disconnected (ˌdɪskəˈnɛktɪd) ADJECTIVE [1] not rationally connected; confused or incoherent. [2] not connected or joined.
▸**,discon'nectedly** ADVERB ▸**,discon'nectedness** NOUN

disconsolate (dɪsˈkɒnsəlɪt) ADJECTIVE [1] sad beyond comfort; inconsolable. [2] disappointed; dejected.
▹HISTORY C14: from Medieval Latin *disconsōlātus,* from DIS-[1] + *consōlātus* comforted; see CONSOLE[1]
▸**dis'consolately** ADVERB ▸**dis'consolateness** *or* **dis,conso'lation** NOUN

discontent (ˌdɪskənˈtɛnt) NOUN [1] Also called: **discontentment.** lack of contentment, as with one's condition or lot in life. [2] a discontented person. ◆ ADJECTIVE [3] dissatisfied. ◆ VERB [4] (*tr*) to make dissatisfied.
▸**,discon'tented** ADJECTIVE ▸**,discon'tentedly** ADVERB ▸**,discon'tentedness** NOUN

discontinue (ˌdɪskənˈtɪnjuː) VERB **-ues, -uing, -ued.** [1] to come or bring to an end; interrupt or be interrupted; stop. [2] (*tr*) *Law* to terminate or abandon (an action, suit, etc.).
▸**,discon'tinuance** NOUN ▸**,discon,tinu'ation** NOUN ▸**,discon'tinuer** NOUN

discontinuity (dɪsˌkɒntɪˈnjuːɪtɪ) NOUN, *plural* **-ties.** [1] lack of rational connection or cohesion. [2] a break or interruption. [3] *Maths* **a** the property of being discontinuous. **b** the point or the value of the variable at which a curve or function becomes discontinuous. [4] *Geology* **a** a zone within the earth where a sudden change in physical properties, such as the velocity of earthquake waves, occurs. Such a zone marks the boundary between the different layers of the earth, as between the core and mantle. See also **Mohorovičić discontinuity. b** a surface separating rocks that are not continuous with each other.

discontinuous (ˌdɪskənˈtɪnjʊəs) ADJECTIVE [1]

characterized by interruptions or breaks; intermittent. 2 *Maths* (of a function or curve) changing suddenly in value for one or more values of the variable or at one or more points. Compare **continuous** (sense 3).
▸ **ˌdisconˈtinuously** ADVERB ▸ **ˌdisconˈtinuousness** NOUN

discord NOUN (ˈdɪskɔːd) 1 lack of agreement of harmony; strife. 2 harsh confused mingling of sounds. 3 a combination of musical notes containing one or more dissonant intervals. See **dissonance** (sense 3), **concord** (sense 4). ◆ VERB (dɪsˈkɔːd) 4 (*intr*) to disagree; clash.
▷HISTORY C13: from Old French *descort*, from *descorder* to disagree, from Latin *discordāre*, from *discors* at variance, from DIS-[1] + *cor* heart

discordance (dɪsˈkɔːdᵊns) *or* **discordancy** NOUN 1 *Geology* an arrangement of rock strata in which the older underlying ones dip at a different angle from the younger overlying ones; unconformity. 2 lack of agreement or consonance. 3 variants of **discord**.

discordant (dɪsˈkɔːdᵊnt) ADJECTIVE 1 at variance; disagreeing. 2 harsh in sound; inharmonious.
▸ **disˈcordantly** ADVERB

discotheque (ˈdɪskəˌtɛk) NOUN the full name of **disco**.
▷HISTORY C20: from French *discothèque*, from Greek *diskos* disc + -O- + Greek *thēkē* case

discount VERB (dɪsˈkaʊnt, ˈdɪskaʊnt) (*mainly tr*) 1 to leave out of account as being unreliable, prejudiced, or irrelevant. 2 to anticipate and make allowance for, often so as to diminish the effect of. 3 **a** to deduct (a specified amount or percentage) from the usual price, cost, etc. **b** to reduce (the regular price, cost, etc.) by a stated percentage or amount. 4 to sell or offer for sale at a reduced price. 5 to buy or sell (a bill of exchange, etc.) before maturity, with a deduction for interest determined by the time to maturity and also by risk. 6 (*also intr*) to loan money on (a negotiable instrument that is not immediately payable) with a deduction for interest determined by risk and time to maturity. ◆ NOUN (ˈdɪskaʊnt) 7 a deduction from the full amount of a price or debt, as in return for prompt payment or to a special group of customers. See also **cash discount, trade discount.** 8 Also called: **discount rate. a** the amount of interest deducted in the purchase or sale of or the loan of money on unmatured negotiable instruments. **b** the rate of interest deducted. 9 **a** (in the issue of shares) a percentage deducted from the par value to give a reduced amount payable by subscribers. **b** the amount by which the par value of something, esp shares, exceeds its market value. Compare **premium** (sense 3). 10 the act or an instance of discounting a negotiable instrument. 11 **at a discount. a** below the regular price. **b** (of share values) below par. **c** held in low regard; not sought after or valued. 12 (*modifier*) offering or selling at reduced prices: *a discount shop*.
▸ **disˈcountable** ADJECTIVE ▸ **ˈdiscounter** NOUN

discounted cash flow NOUN *Accounting* a technique for appraising an investment that takes into account the different values of future returns according to when they will be received. Abbreviation: **DCF.**

discountenance (dɪsˈkaʊntɪnəns) VERB (*tr*) 1 to make ashamed or confused. 2 to disapprove of. ◆ NOUN 3 disapproval.

discount house NOUN 1 *Chiefly Brit* a financial organization engaged in discounting bills of exchange, etc. on a large scale primarily by borrowing call money from commercial banks. 2 *Chiefly US* another name for **discount store.**

discount market NOUN the part of the money market consisting of banks, discount houses, and brokers on which bills are discounted.

discount store NOUN a shop where goods are sold at a low price.

discourage (dɪsˈkʌrɪdʒ) VERB (*tr*) 1 to deprive of the will to persist in something. 2 to inhibit; prevent: *this solution discourages rust.* 3 to oppose by expressing disapproval.
▸ **disˈcouragement** NOUN ▸ **disˈcourager** NOUN
▸ **disˈcouragingly** ADVERB

discourse NOUN (ˈdɪskɔːs, dɪsˈkɔːs) 1 verbal communication; talk; conversation. 2 a formal treatment of a subject in speech or writing, such as a sermon or dissertation. 3 a unit of text used by linguists for the analysis of linguistic phenomena that range over more than one sentence. 4 *Archaic* the ability to reason or the reasoning process. ◆ VERB (dɪsˈkɔːs) 5 (*intr; often foll by on or upon*) to speak or write (about) formally and extensively. 6 (*intr*) to hold a discussion. 7 (*tr*) *Archaic* to give forth (music).
▷HISTORY C14: from Medieval Latin *discursus* argument, from Latin: a running to and fro, from *discurrere* to run different ways, from DIS-[1] + *currere* to run
▸ **disˈcourser** NOUN

discourteous (dɪsˈkɜːtɪəs) ADJECTIVE showing bad manners; impolite; rude.
▸ **disˈcourteously** ADVERB ▸ **disˈcourteousness** NOUN

discourtesy (dɪsˈkɜːtɪsɪ) NOUN, *plural* **-sies.** 1 bad manners; rudeness. 2 a rude remark or act.

discover (dɪˈskʌvə) VERB (*tr; may take a clause as object*) 1 to be the first to find or find out about: *Fleming discovered penicillin.* 2 to learn about or encounter for the first time; realize: *she discovered the pleasures of wine.* 3 to find after study or search: *I discovered a leak in the tank.* 4 to reveal or make known.
▸ **disˈcoverable** ADJECTIVE ▸ **disˈcoverer** NOUN

discovered check NOUN *Chess* check given by moving a man that has been masking a potential check from a bishop, rook, or queen.

discovert (dɪsˈkʌvət) ADJECTIVE *Law* (of a woman) not under the protection of a husband; being a widow, spinster, or divorcée.
▷HISTORY C14: from Old French *descovert*, past participle of *descouvrir* to DISCOVER
▸ **disˈcoverture** NOUN

discovery (dɪˈskʌvərɪ) NOUN, *plural* **-eries.** 1 the act, process, or an instance of discovering. 2 a person, place, or thing that has been discovered. 3 *Law* the compulsory disclosure by a party to an action of relevant documents in his possession.

Discovery Bay NOUN an inlet of the Indian Ocean in SE Australia.

disc plough NOUN a plough that cuts by means of revolving steel discs.

discredit (dɪsˈkrɛdɪt) VERB (*tr*) 1 to damage the reputation of. 2 to cause to be disbelieved or distrusted. 3 to reject as untrue or of questionable accuracy. ◆ NOUN 4 a person, thing, or state of affairs that causes disgrace. 5 damage to a reputation. 6 lack of belief or confidence.

discreditable (dɪsˈkrɛdɪtəbᵊl) ADJECTIVE tending to bring discredit; shameful or unworthy.
▸ **disˈcreditably** ADVERB

discreet (dɪˈskriːt) ADJECTIVE careful to avoid social embarrassment or distress, esp by keeping confidences secret; tactful.
▷HISTORY C14: from Old French *discret*, from Medieval Latin *discrētus*, from Latin *discernere* to DISCERN
▸ **disˈcreetly** ADVERB ▸ **disˈcreetness** NOUN

> **Language note** Avoid confusion with **discrete**.

discrepancy (dɪˈskrɛpənsɪ) NOUN, *plural* **-cies.** a conflict or variation, as between facts, figures, or claims.

> **Language note** *Discrepancy* is sometimes wrongly used where *disparity* is meant. A *discrepancy* exists between things which ought to be the same; it can be small but is usually significant. A *disparity* is a large difference between measurable things such as age, rank, or wages.

discrepant (dɪˈskrɛpənt) ADJECTIVE inconsistent; conflicting; at variance.
▷HISTORY C15: from Latin *discrepāns*, from *discrepāre* to differ in sound, from DIS-[1] + *crepāre* to be noisy
▸ **disˈcrepantly** ADVERB

discrete (dɪsˈkriːt) ADJECTIVE 1 separate or distinct in form or concept. 2 consisting of distinct or separate parts. 3 *Statistics* **a** (of a variable) having consecutive values that are not infinitesimally close, so that its analysis requires summation rather than integration. **b** (of a distribution) relating to a discrete variable. Compare **continuous** (sense 4).
▷HISTORY C14: from Latin *discrētus* separated, set apart; see DISCREET
▸ **disˈcretely** ADVERB ▸ **disˈcreteness** NOUN

> **Language note** Avoid confusion with **discreet.**

discretion (dɪˈskrɛʃən) NOUN 1 the quality of behaving or speaking in such a way as to avoid social embarrassment or distress. 2 freedom or authority to make judgments and to act as one sees fit (esp in the phrases **at one's own discretion, at the discretion of**). 3 **age** *or* **years of discretion.** the age at which a person is considered to be able to manage his own affairs.

discretionary (dɪˈskrɛʃənərɪ, -ənrɪ) *or* **discretional** ADJECTIVE having or using the ability to decide at one's own discretion: *discretionary powers.*
▸ **disˈcretionarily** *or* **disˈcretionally** ADVERB

discretionary trust NOUN a trust in which the beneficiaries' shares are not fixed in the trust deed but are left to the discretion of other persons, often the trustees.

discriminant (dɪˈskrɪmɪnənt) NOUN an algebraic expression related to the coefficients of a polynomial equation whose value gives information about the roots of the polynomial: $b^2 - 4ac$ *is the discriminant of* $ax^2 + bx + c = 0$.

discriminate VERB (dɪˈskrɪmɪˌneɪt) 1 (*intr; usually foll by in favour of or against*) to single out a particular person, group, etc., for special favour or, esp, disfavour, often because of a characteristic such as race, colour, sex, intelligence, etc. 2 (when *intr*, foll by *between* or *among*) to recognize or understand the difference (between); distinguish: *to discriminate right and wrong; to discriminate between right and wrong.* 3 (*intr*) to constitute or mark a difference. 4 (*intr*) to be discerning in matters of taste. ◆ ADJECTIVE (dɪˈskrɪmɪnɪt) 5 showing or marked by discrimination.
▷HISTORY C17: from Latin *discrīmināre* to divide, from *discrīmen* a separation, from *discernere* to DISCERN
▸ **disˈcriminately** ADVERB ▸ **disˈcrimiˌnator** NOUN

discriminating (dɪˈskrɪmɪˌneɪtɪŋ) ADJECTIVE 1 able to see fine distinctions and differences. 2 discerning in matters of taste. 3 (of a tariff, import duty, etc.) levied at differential rates in order to favour or discourage imports or exports.
▸ **disˈcrimiˌnatingly** ADVERB

discrimination (dɪˌskrɪmɪˈneɪʃən) NOUN 1 unfair treatment of a person, racial group, minority, etc.; action based on prejudice. 2 subtle appreciation in matters of taste. 3 the ability to see fine distinctions and differences. 4 *Electronics* the selection of a signal having a particular frequency, amplitude, phase, etc., effected by the elimination of other signals by means of a discriminator.
▸ **disˌcrimiˈnational** ADJECTIVE

discrimination learning NOUN *Psychol* a learning process in which an organism learns to react differently to different stimuli. Compare **generalization** (sense 3).

discriminator (dɪˈskrɪmɪˌneɪtə) NOUN 1 an electronic circuit that converts a frequency or phase modulation into an amplitude modulation for subsequent demodulation. 2 an electronic circuit that has an output voltage only when the amplitude of the input pulses exceeds a predetermined value.

discriminatory (dɪˈskrɪmɪnətərɪ, -trɪ) *or* **discriminative** (dɪˈskrɪmɪnətɪv) ADJECTIVE 1 based on or showing prejudice; biased. 2 capable of making fine distinctions. 3 (of a statistical test) unbiased.
▸ **disˈcriminatorily** *or* **disˈcriminatively** ADVERB

discursive (dɪˈskɜːsɪv) ADJECTIVE 1 passing from one topic to another, usually in an unmethodical way; digressive. 2 *Philosophy* of or relating to knowledge obtained by reason and argument rather than intuition. Compare **dianoetic.**
▷HISTORY C16: from Medieval Latin *discursīvus*, from Late Latin *discursus* DISCOURSE
▸ **disˈcursively** ADVERB ▸ **disˈcursiveness** NOUN

discus (ˈdɪskəs) NOUN, *plural* **discuses** *or* **disci** (ˈdɪskaɪ). 1 (originally) a circular stone or plate used in throwing competitions by the ancient

Greeks. [2] *Athletics* **a** a similar disc-shaped object with a heavy middle thrown by athletes. **b** (*as modifier*): *a discus thrower.* [3] (preceded by *the*) the event or sport of throwing the discus. [4] a South American cichlid fish, *Symphysodon discus,* that has a compressed coloured body and is a popular aquarium fish.
▷HISTORY C17: from Latin, from Greek *diskos* from *dikein* to throw

discuss (dɪ'skʌs) VERB (*tr*) [1] to have a conversation about; consider by talking over; debate. [2] to treat (a subject) in speech or writing: *the first three volumes discuss basic principles.* [3] *Facetious, rare* to eat or drink with enthusiasm.
▷HISTORY C14: from Late Latin *discussus* examined, from *discutere* to investigate, from Latin: to dash to pieces, from DIS-[1] + *quatere* to shake, strike
▸**dis'cussant** *or* **dis'cusser** NOUN ▸**dis'cussible** *or* **dis'cussable** ADJECTIVE

discussion (dɪ'skʌʃən) NOUN the examination or consideration of a matter in speech or writing.
▸**dis'cussional** ADJECTIVE

disc wheel NOUN a road wheel of a motor vehicle that has a round pressed disc in place of spokes. Compare **wire wheel.**

disdain (dɪs'deɪn) NOUN [1] a feeling or show of superiority and dislike; contempt; scorn. ◆ VERB [2] (*tr; may take an infinitive*) to refuse or reject with disdain.
▷HISTORY C13 *dedeyne,* from Old French *desdeign,* from *desdeigner* to reject as unworthy, from Latin *dēdignārī;* see DIS-[1], DEIGN

disdainful (dɪs'deɪnfʊl) ADJECTIVE showing or feeling disdain.
▸**dis'dainfully** ADVERB ▸**dis'dainfulness** NOUN

disease (dɪ'zi:z) NOUN [1] any impairment of normal physiological function affecting all or part of an organism, esp a specific pathological change caused by infection, stress, etc., producing characteristic symptoms; illness or sickness in general. [2] a corresponding condition in plants. [3] any situation or condition likened to this: *the disease of materialism.* Related adjective: **pathological.**
▷HISTORY C14: from Old French *desaise;* see DIS-[1], EASE

diseased (dɪ'zi:zd) ADJECTIVE having or affected with disease.

diseconomy (ˌdɪsɪ'kɒnəmɪ) NOUN, *plural* **-mies.** *Economics* disadvantage, such as lower efficiency or higher average costs, resulting from the scale on which an enterprise produces goods or services.

disembark (ˌdɪsɪm'bɑ:k) VERB to land or cause to land from a ship, aircraft, etc.: *several passengers disembarked; we will disembark the passengers.*
▸**disembarkation** (dɪsˌɛmbɑ:'keɪʃən) *or* ˌ**disem'barkment** NOUN

disembarrass (ˌdɪsɪm'bærəs) VERB (*tr*) [1] to free from embarrassment, entanglement, etc. [2] to relieve or rid of something burdensome.
▸ˌ**disem'barrassment** NOUN

disembodied (ˌdɪsɪm'bɒdɪd) ADJECTIVE [1] lacking a body or freed from the body; incorporeal. [2] lacking in substance, solidity, or any firm relation to reality.

disembody (ˌdɪsɪm'bɒdɪ) VERB **-bodies, -bodying, -bodied.** (*tr*) to free from the body or from physical form.
▸ˌ**disem'bodiment** NOUN

disembogue (ˌdɪsɪm'bəʊg) VERB **-bogues, -boguing, -bogued.** [1] (of a river, stream, etc.) to discharge (water) at the mouth. [2] (*intr*) to flow out.
▷HISTORY C16: from Spanish *desembocar,* from *des-* DIS-[1] + *embocar* put into the mouth, from *em-* in + *boca* mouth, from Latin *bucca* cheek
▸ˌ**disem'boguement** NOUN

disembowel (ˌdɪsɪm'baʊəl) VERB **-els, -elling, -elled** *or US* **-els, -eling, -eled.** (*tr*) to remove the entrails of.
▸ˌ**disem'bowelment** NOUN

disembroil (ˌdɪsɪm'brɔɪl) VERB (*tr*) to free from entanglement or a confused situation.

disempower (ˌdɪsɪm'paʊə) VERB (*tr*) to deprive (a person) of power or authority.
▸ˌ**disem'powerment** NOUN

disenable (ˌdɪsɪ'neɪbəl) VERB (*tr*) to cause to become incapable; prevent.
▸ˌ**disen'ablement** NOUN

disenchant (ˌdɪsɪn'tʃɑ:nt) VERB (*tr; when passive,* foll by *with* or *by*) to make disappointed or disillusioned: *she is disenchanted with the marriage.*
▸ˌ**disen'chantment** NOUN

disenchanted (ˌdɪsɪn'tʃɑ:ntɪd) ADJECTIVE disappointed or disillusioned.

disencumber (ˌdɪsɪn'kʌmbə) VERB (*tr*) to free from encumbrances.
▸ˌ**disen'cumberment** NOUN

disendow (ˌdɪsɪn'daʊ) VERB (*tr*) to take away an endowment from.
▸ˌ**disen'dower** NOUN ▸ˌ**disen'dowment** NOUN

disenfranchise (ˌdɪsɪn'fræntʃaɪz) *or* **disfranchise** VERB (*tr*) [1] to deprive (a person) of the right to vote or other rights of citizenship. [2] to deprive (a place) of the right to send representatives to an elected body. [3] to deprive (a business concern, etc.) of some privilege or right. [4] to deprive (a person, place, etc.) of any franchise or right.
▸**disenfranchisement** (ˌdɪsɪn'fræntʃɪzmənt) *or* **dis'franchisement** NOUN

disengage (ˌdɪsɪn'geɪdʒ) VERB [1] to release or become released from a connection, obligation, etc.: *press the clutch to disengage the gears.* [2] *Military* to withdraw (forces) from close action. [3] *Fencing* to move (one's blade) from one side of an opponent's blade to another in a circular motion to bring the blade into an open line of attack.

disengagement (ˌdɪsɪn'geɪdʒmənt) NOUN [1] the act or process of disengaging or the state of being disengaged. [2] leisure; ease.
▸ˌ**disen'gaged** ADJECTIVE

disentail (ˌdɪsɪn'teɪl) *Property law* ◆ VERB [1] to free (an estate) from entail. ◆ NOUN [2] the act of disentailing; disentailment.
▸ˌ**disen'tailment** NOUN

disentangle (ˌdɪsɪn'tæŋgəl) VERB [1] to release or become free from entanglement or confusion. [2] (*tr*) to unravel or work out.
▸ˌ**disen'tanglement** NOUN

disenthral *or US* **disenthrall** (ˌdɪsɪn'θrɔ:l) VERB **-thrals, -thralling, -thralled** *or US* **-thralls, -thralling, -thralled.** (*tr*) to set free.
▸ˌ**disen'thralment** *or US* ˌ**disen'thrallment** NOUN

disentitle (ˌdɪsɪn'taɪtəl) VERB (*tr*) to deprive of a title, right, or claim.

disentomb (ˌdɪsɪn'tu:m) VERB (*tr*) to disinter; unearth.

disentwine (ˌdɪsɪn'twaɪn) VERB to become or cause to become untwined; unwind.

disepalous (daɪ'sɛpələs) ADJECTIVE (of flowers or plants) having two sepals.

disequilibrium (ˌdɪsi:kwɪ'lɪbrɪəm) NOUN a loss or absence of equilibrium, esp in an economy.

disestablish (ˌdɪsɪ'stæblɪʃ) VERB (*tr*) to deprive (a church, custom, institution, etc.) of established status.
▸ˌ**dises'tablishment** NOUN

disesteem (ˌdɪsɪ'sti:m) VERB [1] (*tr*) to think little of. ◆ NOUN [2] lack of esteem.

diseuse (*French* dizøz) NOUN (esp formerly) an actress who presents dramatic recitals, usually sung accompanied by music. Male counterpart: **diseur** (*French* dizœr).
▷HISTORY C19: from French, feminine of *diseur* speaker, from *dire* to speak, from Latin *dīcere*

disfavour *or US* **disfavor** (dɪs'feɪvə) NOUN [1] disapproval or dislike. [2] the state of being disapproved of or disliked. [3] an unkind act. [4] a damaging or disadvantageous effect; detriment. ◆ VERB [5] (*tr*) to regard or treat with disapproval or dislike.

disfeature (dɪs'fi:tʃə) VERB (*tr*) to mar the features or appearance of; deface.
▸**dis'featurement** NOUN

disfellowship (ˌdɪs'fɛləʊʃɪp) VERB **-ships, -shipping, -shipped** *or US* **-ships, -shiping, -shiped.** (*tr*) to excommunicate.

disfigure (dɪs'fɪgə) VERB (*tr*) [1] to spoil the appearance or shape of; deface. [2] to mar the effect or quality of.
▸**dis'figurer** NOUN

disfigurement (dɪs'fɪgəmənt) *or* **disfiguration** (ˌdɪsfɪgə'reɪʃən) NOUN [1] something that disfigures. [2] the act of disfiguring or the state of being disfigured.

disforest (dɪs'fɒrɪst) VERB (*tr*) [1] another word for **deforest.** [2] *English law* a less common word for **disafforest.**
▸**disˌfores'tation** NOUN

disfranchise (dɪs'fræntʃaɪz) VERB another word for **disenfranchise.**

disfrock (dɪs'frɒk) VERB another word for **unfrock.**

disgorge (dɪs'gɔ:dʒ) VERB [1] to throw out (swallowed food, etc.) from the throat or stomach; vomit. [2] to discharge or empty of (contents). [3] (*tr*) to yield up unwillingly or under pressure. [4] (*tr*) *Angling* to remove (a hook) from the mouth or throat of (a fish).
▸**dis'gorgement** NOUN

disgorger (dɪs'gɔ:dʒə) NOUN *Angling* a thin notched metal implement for removing hooks from a fish.

disgrace (dɪs'greɪs) NOUN [1] a condition of shame, loss of reputation, or dishonour. [2] a shameful person, thing, or state of affairs. [3] exclusion from confidence or trust: *he is in disgrace with his father.* ◆ VERB (*tr*) [4] to bring shame upon; be a discredit to. [5] to treat or cause to be treated with disfavour.
▸**dis'gracer** NOUN

disgraceful (dɪs'greɪsfʊl) ADJECTIVE shameful; scandalous.
▸**dis'gracefully** ADVERB ▸**dis'gracefulness** NOUN

disgruntle (dɪs'grʌntəl) VERB (*tr; usually passive*) to make sulky or discontented.
▷HISTORY C17: DIS-[1] + obsolete *gruntle* to complain; see GRUNT
▸**dis'gruntlement** NOUN

disgruntled (dɪs'grʌntəld) ADJECTIVE feeling or expressing discontent or anger.

disguise (dɪs'gaɪz) VERB [1] to modify the appearance or manner in order to conceal the identity of (oneself, someone, or something). [2] (*tr*) to misrepresent in order to obscure the actual nature or meaning: *to disguise the facts.* ◆ NOUN [3] a mask, costume, or manner that disguises. [4] the act of disguising or the state of being disguised.
▷HISTORY C14: from Old French *desguisier,* from *des-* DIS-[1] + *guise* manner; see GUISE
▸**dis'guisable** ADJECTIVE ▸**dis'guised** ADJECTIVE
▸**disguisedly** (dɪs'gaɪzɪdlɪ) ADVERB ▸**dis'guiser** NOUN

disgust (dɪs'gʌst) VERB (*tr*) [1] to sicken or fill with loathing. [2] to offend the moral sense, principles, or taste of. ◆ NOUN [3] a great loathing or distaste aroused by someone or something. [4] **in disgust.** as a result of disgust.
▷HISTORY C16: from Old French *desgouster,* from *des-* DIS-[1] + *gouster* to taste, from *goust* taste, from Latin *gustus*
▸**dis'gustedly** ADVERB ▸**dis'gustedness** NOUN

disgusting (dɪs'gʌstɪŋ) ADJECTIVE loathsome; repugnant. Also (rare): **disgustful.**
▸**dis'gustingly** ADVERB

dish (dɪʃ) NOUN [1] a container used for holding or serving food, esp an open shallow container of pottery, glass, etc. [2] the food that is served or contained in a dish. [3] a particular article or preparation of food: *a local fish dish.* [4] Also called: **dishful.** the amount contained in a dish. [5] something resembling a dish, esp in shape. [6] a concavity or depression. [7] short for **dish aerial** or **satellite dish aerial.** [8] *Informal* an attractive person. [9] *Informal* something that one particularly enjoys or excels in. ◆ VERB (*tr*) [10] to put into a dish. [11] to make hollow or concave. [12] *Brit informal* to ruin or spoil: *he dished his chances of getting the job.* ◆ See also **dish out, dish up.**
▷HISTORY Old English *disc,* from Latin *discus* quoit, see DISC
▸'**dishˌlike** ADJECTIVE

dishabille (ˌdɪsæ'bi:l) NOUN a variant of **deshabille.**

dish aerial NOUN [1] a microwave aerial, used esp in radar, radio telescopes, and satellite broadcasting, consisting of a parabolic reflector. Formal name: **parabolic aerial.** Often shortened to: **dish.** [2] short for **satellite dish aerial.** ◆ Also called: **dish antenna.**

disharmony (dɪs'hɑ:mənɪ) NOUN, *plural* **-nies.** [1] lack of accord or harmony. [2] a situation, circumstance, etc., that is inharmonious.
▸**disharmonious** (ˌdɪshɑ:'məʊnɪəs) ADJECTIVE
▸ˌ**dishar'moniously** ADVERB

dishcloth ('dɪʃˌklɒθ) NOUN a cloth or rag for washing or drying dishes. Also called (dialect): **dishclout** ('dɪʃˌkluːt).

dishcloth gourd NOUN 1 any of several tropical climbing plants of the cucurbitaceous genus *Luffa,* esp *L. cylindrica,* which is cultivated for ornament and for the fibrous interior of its fruits (see **loofah**). 2 the fruit of any of these plants. ◆ Also called: **vegetable sponge.**

dishearten (dɪsˈhɑːtᵊn) VERB (tr) to weaken or destroy the hope, courage, enthusiasm, etc., of.
▸**disˈhearteningly** ADVERB ▸**disˈheartenment** NOUN

dished (dɪʃt) ADJECTIVE 1 shaped like a dish; concave. 2 (of a pair of road wheels) arranged so that they are closer to one another at the bottom than at the top. 3 *Informal* exhausted or defeated.

dishevel (dɪˈʃɛvᵊl) VERB **-els, -elling, -elled** *or US* **-els, -eling, -eled.** to disarrange (the hair or clothes) of (someone).
▷HISTORY C15: back formation from DISHEVELLED
▸**diˈshevelment** NOUN

dishevelled (dɪˈʃɛvᵊld) ADJECTIVE 1 (esp of hair) hanging loosely. 2 (of general appearance) unkempt; untidy.
▷HISTORY C15 *dischevelee,* from Old French *deschevelé,* from *des-* DIS-[1] + *chevel* hair, from Latin *capillus*

dishonest (dɪsˈɒnɪst) ADJECTIVE not honest or fair; deceiving or fraudulent.
▸**disˈhonestly** ADVERB

dishonesty (dɪsˈɒnɪstɪ) NOUN, *plural* **-ties.** 1 lack of honesty or fairness; deceit. 2 a deceiving act or statement; fraud.

dishonour *or US* **dishonor** (dɪsˈɒnə) VERB (tr) 1 to treat with disrespect. 2 to fail or refuse to pay (a cheque, bill of exchange, etc.). 3 to cause the disgrace of (a woman) by seduction or rape. ◆ NOUN 4 a lack of honour or respect. 5 a state of shame or disgrace. 6 a person or thing that causes a loss of honour: *he was a dishonour to his family.* 7 an insult; affront: *we did him a dishonour by not including him.* 8 refusal or failure to accept or pay a commercial paper.
▸**disˈhonourer** *or US* **disˈhonorer** NOUN

dishonourable *or US* **dishonorable** (dɪsˈɒnərəbᵊl, -ˈɒnrəbᵊl) ADJECTIVE 1 characterized by or causing dishonour or discredit. 2 having little or no integrity; unprincipled.
▸**disˈhonourableness** *or US* **disˈhonorableness** NOUN
▸**disˈhonourably** *or US* **disˈhonorably** ADVERB

dish out VERB *Informal* 1 (*tr, adverb*) to distribute. 2 **dish it out.** to inflict punishment: *he can't take it, but he can sure dish it out.*

dishpan (ˈdɪʃˌpæn) NOUN *Chiefly US and Canadian* a large pan for washing dishes, pots, etc.

dishtowel (ˈdɪʃˌtaʊəl) NOUN another name (esp US and Canadian) for a **tea towel.**

dish up VERB (*adverb*) 1 to serve (a meal, food, etc.). 2 (*tr*) *Informal* to prepare or present, esp in an attractive manner.

dishwasher (ˈdɪʃˌwɒʃə) NOUN 1 an electrically operated machine for washing, rinsing, and drying dishes, cutlery, etc. 2 a person who washes dishes, etc.

dishwater (ˈdɪʃˌwɔːtə) NOUN 1 water in which dishes and kitchen utensils are or have been washed. 2 something resembling this: *that was dishwater, not coffee.*

dishy (ˈdɪʃɪ) ADJECTIVE **dishier, dishiest.** *Informal, chiefly Brit* good-looking or attractive.

disillusion (ˌdɪsɪˈluːʒən) VERB 1 (*tr*) to destroy the ideals, illusions, or false ideas of. ◆ NOUN *also* **disillusionment.** 2 the act of disillusioning or the state of being disillusioned.

disillusioned (ˌdɪsɪˈluːʒənd) ADJECTIVE having lost one's ideals, illusions, or false ideas about someone or something; disenchanted.

disincentive (ˌdɪsɪnˈsɛntɪv) NOUN 1 something that acts as a deterrent. ◆ ADJECTIVE 2 acting as a deterrent: *a disincentive effect on productivity.*

disincline (ˌdɪsɪnˈklaɪn) VERB to make or be unwilling, reluctant, or averse.
▸**disinclination** (ˌdɪsɪnklɪˈneɪʃən) NOUN

disinfect (ˌdɪsɪnˈfɛkt) VERB (*tr*) to rid of microorganisms potentially harmful to man, esp by chemical means.
▸ˌ**disinˈfection** NOUN ▸ˌ**disinˈfector** NOUN

disinfectant (ˌdɪsɪnˈfɛktənt) NOUN an agent that destroys or inhibits the activity of microorganisms that cause disease.

disinfest (ˌdɪsɪnˈfɛst) VERB (*tr*) to rid of vermin.
▸**disˌinfesˈtation** NOUN

disinflation (ˌdɪsɪnˈfleɪʃən) NOUN *Economics* a reduction or stabilization of the general price level intended to improve the balance of payments without incurring reductions in output, employment, and investment. Compare **deflation** (sense 2).

disinformation (ˌdɪsɪnfəˈmeɪʃən) NOUN false information intended to deceive or mislead.

disingenuous (ˌdɪsɪnˈdʒɛnjʊəs) ADJECTIVE not sincere; lacking candour.
▸ˌ**disinˈgenuously** ADVERB ▸ˌ**disinˈgenuousness** NOUN

disinherit (ˌdɪsɪnˈhɛrɪt) VERB (*tr*) 1 *Law* to deprive (an heir or next of kin) of inheritance or right to inherit. 2 to deprive of a right or heritage.
▸ˌ**disinˈheritance** NOUN

disinhibition (ˌdɪsɪnɪˈbɪʃən, -ɪnhɪ-) NOUN *Psychol* a temporary loss of inhibition, caused by an outside stimulus such as alcohol or a drug.

disintegrate (dɪsˈɪntɪˌgreɪt) VERB 1 to break or be broken into fragments or constituent parts; shatter. 2 to lose or cause to lose cohesion or unity. 3 (*intr*) to lose judgment or control; deteriorate. 4 *Physics* **a** to induce or undergo nuclear fission, as by bombardment with fast particles. **b** another word for **decay** (sense 3).
▸**disˈintegrable** ADJECTIVE ▸**disˌinteˈgration** NOUN
▸**disˈintegrative** ADJECTIVE ▸**disˈinteˌgrator** NOUN

disinter (ˌdɪsɪnˈtɜː) VERB **-ters, -terring, -terred.** (*tr*) 1 to remove or dig up; exhume. 2 to bring (a secret, hidden facts, etc.) to light; expose.
▸ˌ**disinˈterment** NOUN

disinterest (dɪsˈɪntrɪst, -tərɪst) NOUN 1 freedom from bias or involvement. 2 lack of interest; indifference. ◆ VERB 3 (*tr*) to free from concern for personal interests.

disinterested (dɪsˈɪntrɪstɪd, -tərɪs-) ADJECTIVE 1 free from bias or partiality; objective. 2 not interested.
▸**disˈinterestedly** ADVERB ▸**disˈinterestedness** NOUN

> **Language note** Many people consider that the use of *disinterested* to mean not interested is incorrect and that *uninterested* should be used.

disintermediation (dɪsˌɪntəˌmiːdɪˈeɪʃən) NOUN *Finance* the elimination of such financial intermediaries as banks and brokers in transactions between principals, often as a result of deregulation and the use of computers.

disinvest (dɪsɪnˈvɛst) VERB *Economics* 1 (usually foll by *in*) to remove investment (from). 2 (*intr*) to reduce the capital stock of an economy or enterprise, as by not replacing obsolete machinery.
▸ˌ**disinˈvestment** NOUN

disject (dɪsˈdʒɛkt) VERB (*tr*) to break apart; scatter.
▷HISTORY C16: from Latin *disjectus,* from *disjicere* to scatter, from DIS-[1] + *jacere* to throw

disjecta membra *Latin* (dɪsˈdʒɛktə ˈmɛmbrə) PLURAL NOUN scattered fragments, esp parts taken from a writing or writings.

disjoin (dɪsˈdʒɔɪn) VERB to disconnect or become disconnected; separate.
▸**disˈjoinable** ADJECTIVE

disjoint (dɪsˈdʒɔɪnt) VERB 1 to take apart or come apart at the joints. 2 (*tr*) to disunite or disjoin. 3 to dislocate or become dislocated. 4 (*tr; usually passive*) to end the unity, sequence, or coherence of. ◆ ADJECTIVE 5 *Maths* (of two sets) having no members in common. 6 *Obsolete* disjointed.

disjointed (dɪsˈdʒɔɪntɪd) ADJECTIVE 1 having no coherence; disconnected. 2 separated at the joint. 3 dislocated.
▸**disˈjointedly** ADVERB ▸**disˈjointedness** NOUN

disjunct ADJECTIVE (dɪsˈdʒʌŋkt) 1 not united or joined. 2 (of certain insects) having deep constrictions between the head, thorax, and abdomen. 3 *Music* denoting two notes the interval between which is greater than a second. ◆ NOUN (ˈdɪsdʒʌŋkt) 4 *Logic* one of the propositions or formulas in a disjunction.

disjunction (dɪsˈdʒʌŋkʃən) NOUN 1 Also called: **disjuncture.** the act of disconnecting or the state of being disconnected; separation. 2 *Cytology* the separation of the chromosomes of each homologous pair during the anaphase of meiosis. 3 *Logic* **a** the operator that forms a compound sentence from two given sentences and corresponds to the English *or.* **b** a sentence so formed. Usually written $p \vee q$ where *p, q* are the component sentences, it is true (inclusive sense) whenever either or both of the latter are true; the exclusive disjunction, for which there is no symbol, is true when either but not both disjuncts is. **c** the relation between such sentences.

disjunctive (dɪsˈdʒʌŋktɪv) ADJECTIVE 1 serving to disconnect or separate. 2 *Grammar* **a** denoting a word, esp a conjunction, that serves to express opposition or contrast: *but* in the sentence *She was poor but she was honest.* **b** denoting an inflection of pronouns in some languages that is used alone or after a preposition, such as *moi* in French. 3 Also: **alternative.** *Logic* relating to, characterized by, or containing disjunction. ◆ NOUN 4 *Grammar* **a** a disjunctive word, esp a conjunction. **b** a disjunctive pronoun. 5 *Logic* a disjunctive proposition; disjunction.
▸**disˈjunctively** ADVERB

disk (dɪsk) NOUN 1 a variant spelling (esp US and Canadian) of **disc.** 2 Also called: **magnetic disk, hard disk.** *Computing* a direct-access storage device consisting of a stack of plates coated with a magnetic layer, the whole assembly rotating rapidly as a single unit. Each surface has a read-write head that can move radially to read or write data on concentric tracks. Compare **drum**[1] (sense 9). See also **floppy disk.**

disk crash NOUN *Computing* the failure of a disk storage system, usually resulting from the read/write head touching the moving disk surface and causing mechanical damage.

disk drive NOUN *Computing* the controller and mechanism for reading and writing data on computer disks. See also **disk** (sense 2).

diskette (dɪsˈkɛt) NOUN *Computing* another name for **floppy disk.**

disk operating system NOUN an operating system used on a computer system with one or more disk drives. Often shortened to: **DOS.**

dislike (dɪsˈlaɪk) VERB 1 (*tr*) to consider unpleasant or disagreeable. ◆ NOUN 2 a feeling of aversion or antipathy.
▸**disˈlikable** *or* **disˈlikeable** ADJECTIVE

dislimn (dɪsˈlɪm) VERB (*tr*) *Poetic* to efface.

dislocate (ˈdɪsləˌkeɪt) VERB (*tr*) 1 to disrupt or shift out of place or position. 2 to displace (an organ or part) from its normal position, esp a bone from its joint.

dislocation (ˌdɪsləˈkeɪʃən) NOUN 1 the act of displacing or the state of being displaced; disruption. 2 (esp of the bones in a joint) the state or condition of being dislocated. 3 a line, plane, or region in which there is a discontinuity in the regularity of a crystal lattice. 4 *Geology* a less common word for **fault** (sense 6).

dislodge (dɪsˈlɒdʒ) VERB to remove from or leave a lodging place, hiding place, or previously fixed position.
▸**disˈlodgment** *or* **disˈlodgement** NOUN

disloyal (dɪsˈlɔɪəl) ADJECTIVE not loyal or faithful; deserting one's allegiance or duty.
▸**disˈloyally** ADVERB

disloyalty (dɪsˈlɔɪəltɪ) NOUN, *plural* **-ties.** the condition or an instance of being unfaithful or disloyal.

dismal (ˈdɪzməl) ADJECTIVE 1 causing gloom or depression. 2 causing dismay or terror.
▷HISTORY C13: from *dismal* (noun) list of 24 unlucky days in the year, from Medieval Latin *diēs malī* bad days, from Latin *diēs* day + *malus* bad
▸ˈ**dismally** ADVERB ▸ˈ**dismalness** NOUN

dismal science NOUN **the.** a name for economics coined by Thomas Carlyle, the Scottish essayist and historian (1795–1881).

Dismal Swamp *or* **Great Dismal Swamp** NOUN a coastal marshland in SE Virginia and NE North Carolina: partly reclaimed. Area: about 1940 sq. km (750 sq. miles). Area before reclamation: 5200 sq. km (2000 sq. miles).

dismantle (dɪsˈmæntᵊl) VERB (tr) 1 to take apart. 2 to demolish or raze. 3 to strip of covering.
▷HISTORY C17: from Old French *desmanteler* to remove a cloak from; see MANTLE
▸**disˈmantlement** NOUN ▸**disˈmantler** NOUN

dismast (dɪsˈmɑːst) VERB (tr) to break off the mast or masts of (a sailing vessel).
▸**disˈmastment** NOUN

dismay (dɪsˈmeɪ) VERB (tr) 1 to fill with apprehension or alarm. 2 to fill with depression or discouragement. ◆ NOUN 3 consternation or agitation.
▷HISTORY C13: from Old French *desmaiier* (unattested), from *des-* DIS-[1] + *esmayer* to frighten, ultimately of Germanic origin; see MAY[1]
▸**disˈmaying** ADJECTIVE

dismember (dɪsˈmɛmbə) VERB (tr) 1 to remove the limbs or members of. 2 to cut to pieces. 3 to divide or partition (something, such as an empire).
▸**disˈmemberer** NOUN ▸**disˈmemberment** NOUN

dismiss (dɪsˈmɪs) VERB (tr) 1 to remove or discharge from employment or service. 2 to send away or allow to go or disperse. 3 to dispel from one's mind; discard; reject. 4 to cease to consider (a subject): *they dismissed the problem.* to decline further hearing to (a claim or action): *the judge dismissed the case.* 6 *Cricket* to bowl out a side for a particular number of runs. ◆ SENTENCE SUBSTITUTE 7 *Military* an order to end an activity or give permission to disperse.
▷HISTORY C15: from Medieval Latin *dismissus* sent away, variant of Latin *dīmissus,* from *dīmittere,* from *dī-* DIS-[1] + *mittere* to send
▸**disˈmissible** ADJECTIVE ▸**disˈmissive** ADJECTIVE

dismissal (dɪsˈmɪsᵊl) NOUN 1 an official notice of discharge from employment or service. 2 the act of dismissing or the condition of being dismissed.

dismount (dɪsˈmaʊnt) VERB 1 to get off a horse, bicycle, etc. 2 (tr) to disassemble or remove from a mounting. ◆ NOUN 3 the act of dismounting.
▸**disˈmountable** ADJECTIVE

Disneyesque (ˌdɪznɪˈɛsk) ADJECTIVE reminiscent of the animated cartoons produced by Walt(er Elias) Disney, the US film producer (1901–66) or his studio.

Disneyfy (ˈdɪznɪˌfaɪ) VERB **-fies, -fying, -fied.** (tr) to transform (historical places, local customs, etc.) into trivial entertainment for tourists.
▷HISTORY C20: from DISNEYLAND
▸**ˌDisneyfiˈcation** NOUN

Disneyland (ˈdɪznɪˌlænd) NOUN an amusement park in Anaheim, California, founded by Walt Disney and opened in 1955. **Walt Disney World**, a second amusement park, opened in 1971 near Orlando, Florida. Further parks have opened in Tokyo and near Paris.

disobedience (ˌdɪsəˈbiːdɪəns) NOUN lack of obedience.

disobedient (ˌdɪsəˈbiːdɪənt) ADJECTIVE not obedient; neglecting or refusing to obey.
▸**ˌdisoˈbediently** ADVERB

disobey (ˌdɪsəˈbeɪ) VERB to neglect or refuse to obey (someone, an order, etc.).
▸**ˌdisoˈbeyer** NOUN

disoblige (ˌdɪsəˈblaɪdʒ) VERB (tr) 1 to disregard the desires of. 2 to slight; insult. 3 *Informal* to cause trouble or inconvenience to.
▸**ˌdisoˈbliging** ADJECTIVE ▸**ˌdisoˈbligingly** ADVERB
▸**ˌdisoˈbligingness** NOUN

disomic (daɪˈsəʊmɪk) ADJECTIVE *Genetics* having an extra chromosome in the haploid state that is homologous to an existing chromosome in this set.
▸**diˈsomy** NOUN

disoperation (dɪsˌɒpəˈreɪʃən) NOUN *Ecology* a relationship between two organisms in a community that is harmful to both.

disorder (dɪsˈɔːdə) NOUN 1 a lack of order; disarray; confusion. 2 a disturbance of public order or peace. 3 an upset of health; ailment. 4 a deviation from the normal system or order. ◆ VERB (tr) 5 to upset the order of; disarrange; muddle. 6 to disturb the health or mind of.

disorderly (dɪsˈɔːdəlɪ) ADJECTIVE 1 untidy; irregular. 2 uncontrolled; unruly. 3 *Law* violating public peace or order. ◆ ADVERB 4 in an irregular or confused manner.
▸**disˈorderliness** NOUN

disorderly conduct NOUN *Law* any of various minor offences tending to cause a disturbance of the peace.

disorderly house NOUN *Law* an establishment in which unruly behaviour habitually occurs, esp a brothel or a gaming house.

disorganize *or* **disorganise** (dɪsˈɔːgəˌnaɪz) VERB (tr) to disrupt or destroy the arrangement, system, or unity of.
▸**disˌorganiˈzation** *or* **disˌorganiˈsation** NOUN
▸**disˈorganˌizer** *or* **disˈorganˌiser** NOUN

disorientate (dɪsˈɔːrɪɛnˌteɪt) *or* **disorient** VERB (tr) 1 to cause (someone) to lose his bearings. 2 to perplex; confuse.
▸**disˌorienˈtation** NOUN

disown (dɪsˈəʊn) VERB (tr) to deny any connection with; refuse to acknowledge.
▸**disˈowner** NOUN ▸**disˈownment** NOUN

disparage (dɪˈspærɪdʒ) VERB (tr) 1 to speak contemptuously of; belittle. 2 to damage the reputation of.
▷HISTORY C14: from Old French *desparagier,* from *des-* DIS-[1] + *parage* equality, from Latin *par* equal
▸**disˈparagement** NOUN ▸**disˈparager** NOUN ▸**disˈparaging** ADJECTIVE ▸**disˈparagingly** ADVERB

disparate (ˈdɪspərɪt) ADJECTIVE 1 utterly different or distinct in kind. ◆ NOUN 2 (*plural*) unlike things or people.
▷HISTORY C16: from Latin *disparāre* to divide, from DIS-[1] + *parāre* to prepare; also influenced by Latin *dispar* unequal
▸**ˈdisparately** ADVERB ▸**ˈdisparateness** NOUN

disparity (dɪˈspærɪtɪ) NOUN, *plural* **-ties.** 1 inequality or difference, as in age, rank, wages, etc. 2 dissimilarity.

> **Language note** See at **discrepancy**.

dispassion (dɪsˈpæʃən) NOUN detachment; objectivity.

dispassionate (dɪsˈpæʃənɪt) ADJECTIVE devoid of or uninfluenced by emotion or prejudice; objective; impartial.
▸**disˈpassionately** ADVERB ▸**disˈpassionateness** NOUN

dispatch *or* **despatch** (dɪˈspætʃ) VERB (tr) 1 to send off promptly, as to a destination or to perform a task. 2 to discharge or complete (a task, duty, etc.) promptly. 3 *Informal* to eat up quickly. 4 to murder or execute. ◆ NOUN 5 the act of sending off a letter, messenger, etc. 6 prompt action or speed (often in the phrase **with dispatch**). 7 an official communication or report, sent in haste. 8 *Journalism* a report sent to a newspaper, etc., by a correspondent. 9 murder or execution.
▷HISTORY C16: from Italian *dispacciare,* from Provençal *despachar,* from Old French *despeechier* to set free, from *des-* DIS-[1] + *-peechier,* ultimately from Latin *pedica* a fetter
▸**disˈpatcher** NOUN

dispatch box NOUN a case or box used to hold valuables or documents, esp official state documents.

dispatch case NOUN a case used for carrying papers, documents, books, etc., usually flat and stiff.

dispatch rider NOUN a horseman or motorcyclist who carries dispatches.

dispel (dɪˈspɛl) VERB **-pels, -pelling, -pelled.** (tr) to disperse or drive away.
▷HISTORY C17: from Latin *dispellere,* from DIS-[1] + *pellere* to drive
▸**disˈpeller** NOUN

dispend (dɪˈspɛnd) VERB (tr) *Obsolete* to spend.
▷HISTORY C14: from Old French *despendre,* from Latin *dispendere* to distribute; see DISPENSE

dispensable (dɪˈspɛnsəbᵊl) ADJECTIVE 1 not essential; expendable. 2 capable of being distributed. 3 (of a law, vow, etc.) able to be relaxed.
▸**disˌpensaˈbility** *or* **disˈpensableness** NOUN

dispensary (dɪˈspɛnsərɪ, -srɪ) NOUN, *plural* **-ries.** a place where medicine and medical supplies are dispensed.

dispensation (ˌdɪspɛnˈseɪʃən) NOUN 1 the act of distributing or dispensing. 2 something distributed or dispensed. 3 a system or plan of administering or dispensing. 4 *Chiefly RC Church* **a** permission to dispense with an obligation of church law. **b** the document authorizing such permission. 5 any exemption from a rule or obligation. 6 *Christianity* **a** the ordering of life and events by God. **b** a divine decree affecting an individual or group. **c** a religious system or code of prescriptions for life and conduct regarded as of divine origin.
▸**ˌdispenˈsational** ADJECTIVE

dispensatory (dɪˈspɛnsətərɪ, -trɪ) NOUN, *plural* **-ries.** 1 a book listing the composition, preparation, and application of various drugs. ◆ ADJECTIVE 2 of or involving dispensation.

dispense (dɪˈspɛns) VERB 1 (tr) to give out or issue in portions. 2 (tr) to prepare and distribute (medicine), esp on prescription. 3 (tr) to administer (the law, etc.). 4 (intr; foll by *with*) to do away (with) or manage (without). 5 to grant a dispensation to (someone) from (some obligation of church law). 6 to exempt or excuse from a rule or obligation.
▷HISTORY C14: from Medieval Latin *dispensāre* to pardon, from Latin *dispendere* to weigh out, from DIS-[1] + *pendere* to weigh

> **Language note** *Dispense with* is sometimes wrongly used where *dispose of* is meant: *this task can be disposed of* (not *dispensed with*) *quickly and easily.*

dispenser (dɪˈspɛnsə) NOUN 1 a device, such as a vending machine, that automatically dispenses a single item or a measured quantity. 2 a person or thing that dispenses.

dispensing optician NOUN See **optician.**

dispermous (daɪˈspɜːməs) ADJECTIVE (of flowering plants) producing or having two seeds.
▷HISTORY C18: from DI-[1] + Greek *sperma* seed

dispersal (dɪˈspɜːsᵊl) NOUN 1 the act of dispersing or the condition of being dispersed. 2 the spread of animals, plants, or seeds to new areas.

dispersal prison NOUN a prison organized and equipped to accommodate a proportion of the most dangerous and highest security risk prisoners.

dispersant (dɪsˈpɜːsənt) NOUN a liquid or gas used to disperse small particles or droplets, as in an aerosol.

disperse (dɪˈspɜːs) VERB 1 to scatter; distribute over a wide area. 2 to dissipate or cause to dissipate. 3 to leave or cause to leave a gathering, often in a random manner. 4 to separate or be separated by dispersion. 5 (tr) to diffuse or spread (news, information, etc.). 6 to separate (particles) throughout a solid, liquid, or gas, as in the formation of a suspension or colloid. ◆ ADJECTIVE 7 of or consisting of the particles in a colloid or suspension: *disperse phase.*
▷HISTORY C14: from Latin *dispersus* scattered, from *dispergere* to scatter widely, from DI-[2] + *spargere* to strew
▸**dispersedly** (dɪˈspɜːsɪdlɪ) ADVERB ▸**disˈperser** NOUN

> **Language note** See at **disburse**.

dispersion (dɪˈspɜːʃən) NOUN 1 another word for **dispersal.** 2 *Physics* **a** the separation of electromagnetic radiation into constituents of different wavelengths. **b** a measure of the ability of a substance to separate by refraction, expressed by the first differential of the refractive index with respect to wavelength at a given value of wavelength. Symbol: *D.* 3 *Statistics* the degree to which values of a frequency distribution are scattered around some central point, usually the arithmetic mean or median. 4 *Chem* a system containing particles dispersed in a solid, liquid, or gas. 5 *Military* the pattern of fire from a weapon system. 6 **a** the range of speeds of such objects as the stars in a galaxy. **b** the frequency-dependent retardation of radio waves as they pass through the interstellar medium. **c** the deviation of a rocket from its prescribed path. 7 *Ecology* the distribution pattern of an animal or a plant population.

Dispersion (dɪ'spɜːʃən) NOUN **the.** another name for the **Diaspora.**

dispersion hardening NOUN the strengthening of an alloy as a result of the presence of fine particles in the lattice.

dispersion relation NOUN *Physics* the relationship between the angular frequency (ω) of a wave and the magnitude of its wave vector (*k*). Thus the wave's speed is ω/*k*.

dispersive (dɪ'spɜːsɪv) ADJECTIVE tending or serving to disperse.
▸**dis'persively** ADVERB ▸**dis'persiveness** NOUN

dispersive medium NOUN *Physics* a substance in which waves of different frequencies travel at different speeds.

dispersoid (dɪ'spɜːsɔɪd) NOUN *Chem* a system, such as a colloid or suspension, in which one phase is dispersed in another.

dispirit (dɪ'spɪrɪt) VERB *(tr)* to lower the spirit or enthusiasm of; make downhearted or depressed; discourage.

dispirited (dɪ'spɪrɪtɪd) ADJECTIVE low in spirit or enthusiasm; downhearted or depressed; discouraged.
▸**dis'piritedly** ADVERB ▸**dis'piritedness** NOUN

dispiriting (dɪ'spɪrɪtɪŋ) ADJECTIVE tending to lower the spirit or enthusiasm; depressing; discouraging.
▸**dis'piritingly** ADVERB

displace (dɪs'pleɪs) VERB *(tr)* [1] to move from the usual or correct location. [2] to remove from office or employment. [3] to occupy the place of; replace; supplant. [4] to force (someone) to leave home or country, as during a war. [5] *Chem* to replace (an atom or group in a chemical compound) by another atom or group. [6] *Physics* to cause a displacement of (a quantity of liquid, usually water of a specified type and density).
▸**dis'placeable** ADJECTIVE ▸**dis'placer** NOUN

displaced person NOUN a person forced from his home or country, esp by war or revolution. Abbreviation: **DP.**

displacement (dɪs'pleɪsmənt) NOUN [1] the act of displacing or the condition of being displaced. [2] the weight or volume displaced by a floating or submerged body in a fluid. [3] *Chem* another name for **substitution.** [4] the volume displaced by the piston of a reciprocating pump or engine. [5] *Psychoanal* the transferring of emotional feelings from their original object to one that disguises their real nature. [6] *Geology* the distance any point on one side of a fault plane has moved in relation to a corresponding point on the opposite side. [7] *Astronomy* an apparent change in position of a body, such as a star. [8] *Maths* the distance measured in a particular direction from a reference point. Symbol: *s.*

displacement activity NOUN [1] *Psychol* behaviour that occurs typically when there is a conflict between motives and that has no relevance to either motive: e.g. head scratching. [2] *Zoology* the substitution of a pattern of animal behaviour that is different from behaviour relevant to the situation: e.g. preening at an apparently inappropriate time.

displacement ton NOUN the full name for **ton**^{1} (sense 6).

displant (dɪs'plɑːnt) VERB *(tr) Obsolete* [1] to displace. [2] to transplant (a plant).

display (dɪ'spleɪ) VERB [1] *(tr)* to show or make visible. [2] *(tr)* to disclose or make evident; reveal: *to display anger.* [3] *(tr)* to flaunt in an ostentatious way: *to display military might.* [4] *(tr)* to spread or open out; unfurl or unfold. [5] *(tr)* to give prominence to (headings, captions, etc.) by the use of certain typefaces. [6] *(intr) Zoology* to engage in a display. ◆ NOUN [7] the act of exhibiting or displaying; show: *a display of fear.* [8] something exhibited or displayed. [9] an ostentatious or pretentious exhibition: *a display of his accomplishments.* [10] **a** an arrangement of certain typefaces to give prominence to headings, captions, advertisements, etc. **b** printed matter that is eye-catching. [11] *Electronics* **a** a device capable of representing information visually, as on a cathode-ray tube screen. **b** the information so presented. [12] *Zoology* a pattern of behaviour in birds, fishes, etc., by which the animal attracts attention while it is courting the female, defending its territory, etc. [13] *(modifier)* relating to or using typefaces that give prominence to the words they are used to set.
▷**HISTORY** C14: from Anglo-French *despleier* to unfold, from Late Latin *displicāre* to scatter, from DIS-^{1} + *plicāre* to fold
▸**dis'player** NOUN

display advertisement *or* **display ad** NOUN an advertisement designed to attract attention by using devices such as conspicuous or elegant typefaces, graphics, etc. See **small advertisement.**

displease (dɪs'pliːz) VERB to annoy, offend, or cause displeasure to (someone).
▸**dis'pleasing** ADJECTIVE ▸**dis'pleasingly** ADVERB

displeasure (dɪs'plɛʒə) NOUN [1] the condition of being displeased. [2] *Archaic* **a** pain. **b** an act or cause of offence. ◆ VERB [3] an archaic word for **displease.**

displode (dɪs'pləʊd) VERB an obsolete word for **explode.**
▷**HISTORY** C17: from Latin *displōdere* from DIS-^{1} + *plaudere* to clap

disport (dɪ'spɔːt) VERB [1] *(tr)* to indulge (oneself) in pleasure. [2] *(intr)* to frolic or gambol. ◆ NOUN [3] *Archaic* amusement.
▷**HISTORY** C14: from Anglo-French *desporter,* from *des-* DIS-^{1} + *porter* to carry

disposable (dɪ'spəʊzəb^{ə}l) ADJECTIVE [1] designed for disposal after use: *disposable cups.* [2] available for use if needed: *disposable assets.* ◆ NOUN [3] something, such as a baby's nappy, that is designed for disposal. [4] *(plural)* short for **disposable goods.**
▸**dis,posa'bility** *or* **dis'posableness** NOUN

disposable goods PLURAL NOUN consumer goods that are used up a short time after purchase, including perishables, newspapers, clothes, etc. Compare **durable goods.** Also called: **disposables.**

disposable income NOUN [1] the money a person has available to spend after paying taxes, pension contributions, etc. [2] the total amount of money that the individuals in a community, country, etc., have available to buy consumer goods.

disposal (dɪ'spəʊz^{ə}l) NOUN [1] the act or means of getting rid of something. [2] placement or arrangement in a particular order. [3] a specific method of tending to matters, as in business. [4] the act or process of transferring something to or providing something for another. [5] the power or opportunity to make use of someone or something (esp in the phrase **at one's disposal**). [6] a means of destroying waste products, as by grinding into particles. ◆ Also (for senses 2–5): **disposition.**

dispose (dɪ'spəʊz) VERB [1] *(intr; foll by of)* **a** to deal with or settle. **b** to give, sell, or transfer to another. **c** to throw out or away. **d** to consume, esp hurriedly. **e** to kill. [2] to arrange or settle (matters) by placing into correct or final condition: *man proposes, God disposes.* [3] *(tr)* to make willing or receptive. [4] *(tr)* to adjust or place in a certain order or position. [5] *(tr; often foll by to)* to accustom or condition. ◆ NOUN [6] an obsolete word for **disposal** or **disposition.**
▷**HISTORY** C14: from Old French *disposer,* from Latin *dispōnere* to set in different places, arrange, from DIS-^{1} + *pōnere* to place
▸**dis'poser** NOUN

disposed (dɪ'spəʊzd) ADJECTIVE **a** having an inclination as specified (towards something). **b** *(in combination)*: *well-disposed.*

disposition (ˌdɪspə'zɪʃən) NOUN [1] a person's usual temperament or frame of mind. [2] a natural or acquired tendency, inclination, or habit in a person or thing. [3] another word for **disposal** (senses 2–5). [4] *Philosophy, logic* a property that consists not in the present state of an object, but in its propensity to change in a certain way under certain conditions, as brittleness which consists in the propensity to break when struck. Compare **occurrent.** [5] *Archaic* manner of placing or arranging.
▸**ˌdispo'sitional** ADJECTIVE

dispossess (ˌdɪspə'zɛs) VERB *(tr)* to take away possession of something, esp property; expel.
▸**ˌdispos'session** NOUN ▸**ˌdispos'sessor** NOUN
▸**ˌdispos'sessory** ADJECTIVE

disposure (dɪ'spəʊʒə) NOUN a rare word for **disposal** or **disposition.**

dispraise (dɪs'preɪz) VERB [1] *(tr)* to express disapproval or condemnation of. ◆ NOUN [2] the disapproval, etc., expressed.
▸**dis'praiser** NOUN ▸**dis'praisingly** ADVERB

disprize (dɪs'praɪz) VERB *(tr) Archaic* to scorn; disdain.

disproof (dɪs'pruːf) NOUN [1] facts that disprove something. [2] the act of disproving.

disproportion (ˌdɪsprə'pɔːʃən) NOUN [1] lack of proportion or equality. [2] an instance of disparity or inequality. ◆ VERB [3] *(tr)* to cause to become exaggerated or unequal.
▸**ˌdispro'portionable** ADJECTIVE ▸**ˌdispro'portionableness** NOUN ▸**ˌdispro'portionably** ADVERB

disproportionate ADJECTIVE (ˌdɪsprə'pɔːʃənɪt) [1] out of proportion; unequal. ◆ VERB (ˌdɪsprə'pɔːʃəˌneɪt) [2] *Chem* to undergo or cause to undergo disproportionation.
▸**ˌdispro'portionately** ADVERB ▸**ˌdispro'portionateness** NOUN

disproportionation (ˌdɪsprəˌpɔːʃə'neɪʃən) NOUN a reaction between two identical molecules in which one is reduced and the other oxidized.

disprove (dɪs'pruːv) VERB *(tr)* to show (an assertion, claim, etc.) to be incorrect.
▸**dis'provable** ADJECTIVE ▸**dis'proval** NOUN

disputable (dɪ'spjuːtəb^{ə}l, 'dɪspjʊtə-) ADJECTIVE capable of being argued; debatable.
▸**disˌputa'bility** *or* **dis'putableness** NOUN ▸**dis'putably** ADVERB

disputant (dɪ'spjuːt^{ə}nt, 'dɪspjʊtənt) NOUN [1] a person who argues; contestant. ◆ ADJECTIVE [2] engaged in argument.

disputation (ˌdɪspjʊ'teɪʃən) NOUN [1] the act or an instance of arguing. [2] a formal academic debate on a thesis. [3] an obsolete word for **conversation.**

disputatious (ˌdɪspjʊ'teɪʃəs) *or* **disputative** (dɪ'spjuːtətɪv) ADJECTIVE inclined to argument.
▸**ˌdispu'tatiously** *or* **dis'putatively** ADVERB
▸**ˌdispu'tatiousness** *or* **dis'putativeness** NOUN

dispute VERB (dɪ'spjuːt) [1] to argue, debate, or quarrel about (something). [2] *(tr; may take a clause as object)* to doubt the validity, etc., of. [3] *(tr)* to seek to win; contest for. [4] *(tr)* to struggle against; resist. ◆ NOUN (dɪ'spjuːt, 'dɪspjuːt) [5] an argument or quarrel.
▷**HISTORY** C13: from Late Latin *disputāre* to contend verbally, from Latin: to discuss, from DIS-^{1} + *putāre* to think
▸**dis'puter** NOUN

disqualify (dɪs'kwɒlɪˌfaɪ) VERB **-fies, -fying, -fied.** *(tr)* [1] to make unfit or unqualified. [2] to make ineligible, as for entry to an examination. [3] to debar (a player or team) from a sporting contest. [4] to divest or deprive of rights, powers, or privileges: *disqualified from driving.*
▸**dis'qualiˌfiable** ADJECTIVE ▸**disˌqualifi'cation** NOUN
▸**dis'qualiˌfier** NOUN

disquiet (dɪs'kwaɪət) NOUN [1] a feeling or condition of anxiety or uneasiness. ◆ VERB [2] *(tr)* to make anxious or upset. ◆ ADJECTIVE [3] *Archaic* uneasy or anxious.
▸**dis'quietedly** *or* **dis'quietly** ADVERB ▸**dis'quietedness** *or* **dis'quietness** NOUN ▸**dis'quieting** ADJECTIVE
▸**dis'quietingly** ADVERB

disquietude (dɪs'kwaɪɪˌtjuːd) NOUN a feeling or state of anxiety or uneasiness.

disquisition (ˌdɪskwɪ'zɪʃən) NOUN a formal written or oral examination of a subject.
▷**HISTORY** C17: from Latin *disquīsītiō,* from *disquīrere* to make an investigation, from DIS-^{1} + *quaerere* to seek
▸**ˌdisqui'sitional** ADJECTIVE

disrate (dɪs'reɪt) VERB *(tr) Naval* to punish (an officer) by lowering him in rank.

disregard (ˌdɪsrɪ'gɑːd) VERB *(tr)* [1] to give little or no attention to; ignore. [2] to treat as unworthy of consideration or respect. ◆ NOUN [3] lack of attention or respect. [4] *(often plural) Social welfare* capital or income which is not counted in calculating the amount payable to a claimant for a means-tested benefit.
▸**ˌdisre'garder** NOUN ▸**ˌdisre'gardful** ADJECTIVE
▸**ˌdisre'gardfully** ADVERB ▸**ˌdisre'gardfulness** NOUN

disrelish (dɪs'rɛlɪʃ) VERB [1] *(tr)* to have a feeling of aversion for; dislike. ◆ NOUN [2] such a feeling.

disremember (ˌdɪsrɪ'mɛmbə) VERB *Informal, chiefly US* to fail to recall (someone or something).

disrepair (ˌdɪsrɪˈpɛə) NOUN the condition of being worn out or in poor working order; a condition requiring repairs.

disreputable (dɪsˈrɛpjʊtəbᵊl) ADJECTIVE [1] having or causing a lack of repute. [2] disordered in appearance.
▸ **disˌreputaˈbility** *or* **disˈreputableness** NOUN
▸ **disˈreputably** ADVERB

disrepute (ˌdɪsrɪˈpjuːt) NOUN a loss or lack of credit or repute.

disrespect (ˌdɪsrɪˈspɛkt) NOUN [1] contempt; rudeness. ◆ VERB [2] (*tr*) to show lack of respect for.
▸ **ˌdisreˈspectful** ADJECTIVE ▸ **ˌdisreˈspectfully** ADVERB
▸ **ˌdisreˈspectfulness** NOUN

disrespectable (ˌdɪsrɪˈspɛktəbᵊl) ADJECTIVE unworthy of respect; not respectable.
▸ **ˌdisreˌspectaˈbility** NOUN

disrobe (dɪsˈrəʊb) VERB [1] to remove the clothing of (a person) or (of a person) to undress. [2] (*tr*) to divest of authority, etc.
▸ **disˈrobement** NOUN ▸ **disˈrober** NOUN

disrupt (dɪsˈrʌpt) VERB [1] (*tr*) to throw into turmoil or disorder. [2] (*tr*) to interrupt the progress of (a movement, meeting, etc.). [3] to break or split (something) apart.
▷ HISTORY C17: from Latin *disruptus* burst asunder, from *dīrumpere* to dash to pieces, from DIS-[1] + *rumpere* to burst
▸ **disˈrupter** *or* **disˈruptor** NOUN ▸ **disˈruption** NOUN

disruptive (dɪsˈrʌptɪv) ADJECTIVE involving, causing, or tending to cause disruption.
▸ **disˈruptively** ADVERB

disruptive discharge NOUN a sudden large increase in current through an insulating medium resulting from failure of the medium to withstand an applied electric field.

diss *or* **dis** (dɪs) VERB *Slang, chiefly US* to treat (someone) with contempt.
▷ HISTORY C20: originally Black rap slang, short for DISRESPECT

dissatisfied (dɪsˈsætɪsˌfaɪd) ADJECTIVE having or showing dissatisfaction; discontented.
▸ **disˈsatisˌfiedly** ADVERB

dissatisfy (dɪsˈsætɪsˌfaɪ) VERB **-fies, -fying, -fied.** (*tr*) to fail to satisfy; disappoint.
▸ **ˌdissatisˈfaction** NOUN ▸ **ˌdissatisˈfactory** ADJECTIVE

dissect (dɪˈsɛkt, daɪ-) VERB [1] to cut open and examine the structure of (a dead animal or plant). [2] (*tr*) to examine critically and minutely.
▷ HISTORY C17: from Latin *dissecāre*, from DIS-[1] + *secāre* to cut
▸ **disˈsectible** ADJECTIVE ▸ **disˈsection** NOUN ▸ **disˈsector** NOUN

dissected (dɪˈsɛktɪd, daɪ-) ADJECTIVE [1] *Botany* in the form of narrow lobes or segments: *dissected leaves.* [2] *Geology* (of plains) cut by erosion into hills and valleys, esp following tectonic movements.

disseise *or* **disseize** (dɪsˈsiːz) VERB (*tr*) *Property law* to deprive of seisin; wrongfully dispossess of a freehold interest in land.
▷ HISTORY C14: from Anglo-Norman *desseisir*, from DIS-[1] + SEIZE
▸ **disˈseisor** *or* **disˈseizor** NOUN

disseisin *or* **disseizin** (dɪsˈsiːzɪn) NOUN the act of disseising or state of being disseised.
▷ HISTORY C14: from Old French *dessaisine;* see DIS-[1], SEISIN

disselboom (ˈdɪsəlˌbʊəm) NOUN *South African* the main haulage shaft of a wagon or cart.
▷ HISTORY from Afrikaans *dissel* shaft + *boom* beam

dissemble (dɪˈsɛmbᵊl) VERB [1] to conceal (one's real motives, emotions, etc.) by pretence. [2] (*tr*) to pretend; simulate. [3] *Obsolete* to ignore.
▷ HISTORY C15: from earlier *dissimulen*, from Latin *dissimulāre;* probably influenced by obsolete *semble* to resemble
▸ **disˈsemblance** NOUN ▸ **disˈsembler** NOUN ▸ **disˈsembling** NOUN, ADJECTIVE ▸ **disˈsemblingly** ADVERB

disseminate (dɪˈsɛmɪˌneɪt) VERB (*tr*) to distribute or scatter about; diffuse.
▷ HISTORY C17: from Latin *dissēmināre*, from DIS-[1] + *sēmināre* to sow, from *sēmen* seed
▸ **disˌsemiˈnation** NOUN ▸ **disˈseminative** ADJECTIVE
▸ **disˈsemiˌnator** NOUN

disseminated sclerosis NOUN another name for **multiple sclerosis.**

disseminule (dɪˈsɛmɪˌnjuːl) NOUN any propagative part of a plant, such as a seed or spore, that helps to spread the species.
▷ HISTORY C20: from DISSEMINATE + -ULE

dissension (dɪˈsɛnʃən) NOUN disagreement, esp when leading to a quarrel.
▷ HISTORY C13: from Latin *dissēnsiō*, from *dissentīre* to dissent

dissent (dɪˈsɛnt) VERB (*intr*) [1] to have a disagreement or withhold assent. [2] *Christianity* to refuse to conform to the doctrines, beliefs, or practices of an established church, and to adhere to a different system of beliefs and practices. ◆ NOUN [3] a difference of opinion. [4] *Christianity* separation from an established church; Nonconformism. [5] the voicing of a minority opinion in announcing the decision on a case at law; dissenting judgment.
▷ HISTORY C16: from Latin *dissentīre* to disagree, from DIS-[1] + *sentīre* to perceive, feel
▸ **disˈsenter** NOUN ▸ **disˈsenting** ADJECTIVE ▸ **disˈsentingly** ADVERB

Dissenter (dɪˈsɛntə) NOUN *Christianity chiefly Brit* a Nonconformist or a person who refuses to conform to the established church.

dissentient (dɪˈsɛnʃənt) ADJECTIVE [1] dissenting, esp from the opinion of the majority. ◆ NOUN [2] a dissenter.
▸ **disˈsentience** *or* **disˈsentiency** NOUN ▸ **disˈsentiently** ADVERB

dissentious (dɪˈsɛnʃəs) ADJECTIVE argumentative.

dissepiment (dɪˈsɛpɪmənt) NOUN *Biology* a dividing partition or membrane, such as that between the chambers of a syncarpous ovary.
▷ HISTORY C18: from Late Latin *dissaepīmentum*, from DIS-[1] + *saepīmentum* hedge, from *saepīre* to enclose
▸ **disˌsepiˈmental** ADJECTIVE

dissertate (ˈdɪsəˌteɪt) VERB (*intr*) *Rare* to give or make a dissertation.
▷ HISTORY C18: from Latin *dissertāre* to debate, from *disserere* to examine, from DIS-[1] + *serere* to arrange
▸ **ˈdisserˌtator** NOUN

dissertation (ˌdɪsəˈteɪʃən) NOUN [1] a written thesis, often based on original research, usually required for a higher degree. [2] a formal discourse.
▸ **ˌdisserˈtational** ADJECTIVE ▸ **ˌdisserˈtationist** NOUN

disserve (dɪsˈsɜːv) VERB (*tr*) *Archaic* to do a disservice to.

disservice (dɪsˈsɜːvɪs) NOUN an ill turn; wrong; injury, esp when trying to help.
▸ **disˈserviceable** ADJECTIVE

dissever (dɪˈsɛvə) VERB [1] to break off or become broken off. [2] (*tr*) to divide up into parts.
▷ HISTORY C13: from Old French *dessevrer*, from Late Latin DIS-[1] + *sēparāre* to SEPARATE
▸ **disˈseverance** *or* **disˈseverment** *or* **disˌseverˈation** NOUN

dissident (ˈdɪsɪdənt) ADJECTIVE [1] disagreeing; dissenting. ◆ NOUN [2] a person who disagrees, esp one who disagrees with the government.
▷ HISTORY C16: from Latin *dissidēre* to be remote from, from DIS-[1] + *sedēre* to sit
▸ **ˈdissidence** NOUN ▸ **ˈdissidently** ADVERB

dissimilar (dɪˈsɪmɪlə) ADJECTIVE not alike; not similar; different.
▸ **disˈsimilarly** ADVERB

dissimilarity (ˌdɪsɪmɪˈlærɪtɪ) NOUN, *plural* **-ties.** [1] difference; unlikeness. [2] a point or instance of difference.

dissimilate (dɪˈsɪmɪˌleɪt) VERB [1] to make or become dissimilar. [2] (usually foll by *to*) *Phonetics* to change or displace (a consonant) or (of a consonant) to be changed to or displaced by (another consonant) so that its manner of articulation becomes less similar to a speech sound in the same word. Thus (r) in the final syllable of French *marbre* is dissimilated to (l) in its English form *marble.*
▷ HISTORY C19: from DIS-[1] + ASSIMILATE
▸ **disˈsimilative** ADJECTIVE ▸ **disˈsimilatory** ADJECTIVE

dissimilation (ˌdɪsɪmɪˈleɪʃən) NOUN [1] the act or an instance of making dissimilar. [2] *Phonetics* the alteration or omission of a consonant as a result of being dissimilated. [3] *Biology* a less common word for **catabolism.**

dissimilitude (ˌdɪsɪˈmɪlɪˌtjuːd) NOUN [1] dissimilarity; difference. [2] a point of difference.

dissimulate (dɪˈsɪmjʊˌleɪt) VERB to conceal (one's real feelings) by pretence.
▸ **disˌsimuˈlation** NOUN ▸ **disˈsimulative** ADJECTIVE
▸ **disˈsimuˌlator** NOUN

dissipate (ˈdɪsɪˌpeɪt) VERB [1] to exhaust or be exhausted by dispersion. [2] (*tr*) to scatter or break up. [3] (*intr*) to indulge in the pursuit of pleasure.
▷ HISTORY C15: from Latin *dissipāre* to disperse, from DIS-[1] + *supāre* to throw
▸ **ˈdissiˌpater** *or* **ˈdissiˌpator** NOUN ▸ **ˈdissiˌpative** ADJECTIVE

dissipated (ˈdɪsɪˌpeɪtɪd) ADJECTIVE [1] indulging without restraint in the pursuit of pleasure; debauched. [2] wasted, scattered, or exhausted.
▸ **ˈdissiˌpatedly** ADVERB ▸ **ˈdissiˌpatedness** NOUN

dissipation (ˌdɪsɪˈpeɪʃən) NOUN [1] the act of dissipating or condition of being dissipated. [2] unrestrained indulgence in physical pleasures, esp alcohol. [3] excessive expenditure; wastefulness. [4] amusement; diversion.

dissociable (dɪˈsəʊʃɪəbᵊl, -ʃə-) ADJECTIVE [1] able to be dissociated; distinguishable. [2] incongruous; irreconcilable. [3] (dɪˈsəʊʃəbᵊl) Also: **dissocial.** a less common word for **unsociable.**
▸ **disˌsociaˈbility** *or* **disˈsociableness** NOUN ▸ **disˈsociably** ADVERB

dissociate (dɪˈsəʊʃɪˌeɪt, -sɪ-) VERB [1] to break or cause to break the association between (people, organizations, etc.). [2] (*tr*) to regard or treat as separate or unconnected. [3] to undergo or subject to dissociation.
▸ **disˈsociative** ADJECTIVE

dissociation (dɪˌsəʊsɪˈeɪʃən, -ʃɪ-) NOUN [1] the act of dissociating or the state of being dissociated. [2] *Chem* **a** a reversible chemical change of the molecules of a single compound into two or more other molecules, atoms, ions, or radicals. **b** any decomposition of the molecules of a single compound into two or more other compounds, atoms, ions, or radicals. [3] separation of molecules or atoms that occurs when a liquid or solid changes to a gas. [4] *Psychiatry* the separation of a group of mental processes or ideas from the rest of the personality, so that they lead an independent existence, as in cases of multiple personality.

dissociative disorder NOUN *Psychol* an emotional disorder characterized by fugue states or multiple personality.

dissoluble (dɪˈsɒljʊbᵊl) ADJECTIVE a less common word for **soluble.**
▷ HISTORY C16: from Latin *dissolūbilis*, from *dissolvere* to DISSOLVE
▸ **disˌsoluˈbility** *or* **disˈsolubleness** NOUN

dissolute (ˈdɪsəˌluːt) ADJECTIVE given to dissipation; debauched.
▷ HISTORY C14: from Latin *dissolūtus* loose, from *dissolvere* to DISSOLVE
▸ **ˈdissoˌlutely** ADVERB ▸ **ˈdissoˌluteness** NOUN

dissolution (ˌdɪsəˈluːʃən) NOUN [1] the resolution or separation into component parts; disintegration. [2] destruction by breaking up and dispersing. [3] the termination of a meeting or assembly, such as Parliament. [4] the termination of a formal or legal relationship, such as a business enterprise, marriage, etc. [5] the state of being dissolute; dissipation. [6] the act or process of dissolving.
▸ **ˈdissoˌlutive** ADJECTIVE

dissolve (dɪˈzɒlv) VERB [1] to go or cause to go into solution: *salt dissolves in water; water dissolves sugar.* [2] to become or cause to become liquid; melt. [3] to disintegrate or disperse. [4] to come or bring to an end. [5] to dismiss (a meeting, parliament, etc.) or (of a meeting, etc.) to be dismissed. [6] to collapse or cause to collapse emotionally: *to dissolve into tears.* [7] to lose or cause to lose distinctness or clarity. [8] (*tr*) to terminate legally, as a marriage, etc. [9] (*intr*) *Films, television* to fade out one scene and replace with another to make two scenes merge imperceptibly (**fast dissolve**) or slowly overlap (**slow dissolve**) over a period of about three or four seconds. ◆ NOUN [10] *Films, television* a scene filmed or televised by dissolving.
▷ HISTORY C14: from Latin *dissolvere* to make loose, from DIS-[1] + *solvere* to release
▸ **disˈsolvable** ADJECTIVE ▸ **disˌsolvaˈbility** *or* **disˈsolvableness** NOUN ▸ **disˈsolver** NOUN

dissolvent (dɪˈzɒlvənt) NOUN [1] a rare word for **solvent** (sense 3). ◆ ADJECTIVE [2] able to dissolve.

dissonance (ˈdɪsənəns) *or* **dissonancy** NOUN [1]

a discordant combination of sounds. [2] lack of agreement or consistency. [3] *Music* **a** a sensation commonly associated with all intervals of the second and seventh, all diminished and augmented intervals, and all chords based on these intervals. Compare **consonance** (sense 3). **b** an interval or chord of this kind.

dissonant ('dɪsənənt) ADJECTIVE [1] discordant; cacophonous. [2] incongruous or discrepant. [3] *Music* characterized by dissonance.
▷HISTORY C15: from Latin *dissonāre* to be discordant, from DIS-[1] + *sonāre* to sound
▸'**dissonantly** ADVERB

dissuade (dɪ'sweɪd) VERB (*tr*) [1] (often foll by *from*) to deter (someone) by persuasion from a course of action, policy, etc. [2] to advise against (an action, etc.).
▷HISTORY C15: from Latin *dissuādēre*, from DIS-[1] + *suādēre* to persuade
▸**dis'suadable** ADJECTIVE ▸**dis'suader** NOUN ▸**dis'suasion** NOUN ▸**dis'suasive** ADJECTIVE ▸**dis'suasively** ADVERB ▸**dis'suasiveness** NOUN

dissyllable (dɪ'sɪləbᵊl, 'dɪsˌsɪl-, 'daɪsɪl-) *or* **disyllable** ('daɪsɪləbᵊl, dɪ'sɪl-) NOUN *Grammar* a word of two syllables.
▸**dissyllabic** (ˌdɪsɪ'læbɪk, ˌdɪssɪ-, ˌdaɪ-) *or* **disyllabic** (ˌdaɪsɪ'læbɪk, ˌdɪ-) ADJECTIVE

dissymmetry (dɪ'sɪmɪtrɪ, dɪs'sɪm-) NOUN, *plural* **-tries.** [1] lack of symmetry. [2] the relationship between two objects when one is the mirror image of the other. See also **chirality.** [3] another name for **chirality.**
▸**dissymmetric** (ˌdɪsɪ'mɛtrɪk, ˌdɪssɪ-) *or* ˌ**dissym'metrical** ADJECTIVE ▸ˌ**dissym'metrically** ADVERB

distaff ('dɪstɑːf) NOUN [1] the rod on which flax is wound preparatory to spinning. [2] *Figurative* women's work.
▷HISTORY Old English *distæf*, from *dis-* bunch of flax + *stæf* STAFF[1]; see DIZEN

distaff side NOUN the female side or branch of a family. Compare **spear side.**

distal ('dɪstᵊl) ADJECTIVE *Anatomy* (of a muscle, bone, limb, etc.) situated farthest from the centre, median line, or point of attachment or origin. Compare **proximal.**
▷HISTORY C19: from DISTANT + -AL[1]
▸'**distally** ADVERB

distance ('dɪstəns) NOUN [1] the intervening space between two points or things. [2] the length of this gap. [3] the state of being apart in space; remoteness. [4] an interval between two points in time. [5] the extent of progress; advance. [6] a distant place or time: *he lives at a distance from his work.* [7] a separation or remoteness in relationship; disparity. [8] **keep one's distance.** to maintain a proper or discreet reserve in respect of another person. [9] *Geometry* **a** the length of the shortest line segment joining two points. **b** the length along a straight line or curve. [10] (preceded by *the*) the most distant or a faraway part of the visible scene or landscape. [11] *Horse racing* **a** *Brit* a point on a racecourse 240 yards from the winning post. **b** *Brit* any interval of more than 20 lengths between any two finishers in a race. **c** *US* the part of a racecourse that a horse must reach in any heat before the winner passes the finishing line in order to qualify for later heats. [12] **go the distance. a** *Boxing* to complete a bout without being knocked out. **b** to be able to complete an assigned task or responsibility. [13] the distant parts of a picture, such as a landscape. [14] **middle distance. a** (in a picture) halfway between the foreground and the horizon. **b** (in a natural situation) halfway between the observer and the horizon. [15] (*modifier*) *Athletics* relating to or denoting the longer races, usually those longer than a mile: *a distance runner.* ◆ VERB (*tr*) [16] to hold or place at a distance. [17] to separate (oneself) mentally or emotionally from something. [18] to outdo; outstrip.

distance learning NOUN a teaching system consisting of video, audio, and written material designed for a person to use in studying a subject at home.

distance modulus NOUN *Astronomy* a measure of the distance, *r*, of a celestial object too far away to show measurable parallax. It is given by $m–M = 5 \log(r/10)$, where *m* is its apparent magnitude (corrected for interstellar absorption) and *M* is its absolute magnitude.

distant ('dɪstənt) ADJECTIVE [1] far away or apart in space or time. [2] (*postpositive*) separated in space or time by a specified distance. [3] apart in relevance, association, or relationship: *a distant cousin.* [4] coming from or going to a faraway place: *a distant journey.* [5] remote in manner; aloof. [6] abstracted; absent: *a distant look.*
▷HISTORY C14: from Latin *distāre* to be distant, from DIS-[1] + *stāre* to stand
▸'**distantly** ADVERB ▸'**distantness** NOUN

distant early warning NOUN a US radar detection system to warn of missile attack. See also **DEW line.**

distaste (dɪs'teɪst) NOUN [1] (often foll by *for*) an absence of pleasure (in); dislike (of); aversion (to): *to look at someone with distaste.* ◆ VERB [2] (*tr*) an archaic word for **dislike.**

distasteful (dɪs'teɪstfʊl) ADJECTIVE unpleasant or offensive.
▸**dis'tastefully** ADVERB ▸**dis'tastefulness** NOUN

distemper[1] (dɪs'tɛmpə) NOUN [1] any of various infectious diseases of animals, esp **canine distemper**, a highly contagious viral disease of dogs, characterized initially by high fever and a discharge from the nose and eyes. See also **hard pad, strangles.** [2] *Archaic* **a** a disease or disorder. **b** disturbance. **c** discontent. ◆ VERB [3] (*tr*) *Archaic* to disturb.
▷HISTORY C14: from Late Latin *distemperāre* to derange the health of, from Latin DIS-[1] + *temperāre* to mix in correct proportions

distemper[2] (dɪs'tɛmpə) NOUN [1] a technique of painting in which the pigments are mixed with water, glue, size, etc., used for poster, mural, and scene painting. [2] the paint used in this technique or any of various water-based paints, including, in Britain, whitewash. ◆ VERB [3] (*tr*) to mix (pigments) with water and size. [4] to paint (something) with distemper.
▷HISTORY C14: from Medieval Latin *distemperāre* to soak, from Latin DIS-[1] + *temperāre* to mingle

distend (dɪ'stɛnd) VERB [1] to expand or be expanded by or as if by pressure from within; swell; inflate. [2] (*tr*) to stretch out or extend. [3] (*tr*) to magnify in importance; exaggerate.
▷HISTORY C14: from Latin *distendere*, from DIS-[1] + *tendere* to stretch
▸**dis'tender** NOUN ▸**dis'tensible** ADJECTIVE ▸**disˌtensi'bility** NOUN ▸**dis'tension** *or* **dis'tention** NOUN

distich ('dɪstɪk) NOUN *Prosody* a unit of two verse lines, usually a couplet.
▷HISTORY C16: from Greek *distikhos* having two lines, from DI-[1] + *stikhos* STICH
▸'**distichal** ADJECTIVE

distichous ('dɪstɪkəs) ADJECTIVE (of leaves) arranged in two vertical rows on opposite sides of the stem.
▸'**distichously** ADVERB

distil *or US* **distill** (dɪs'tɪl) VERB **-tils** *or* **-tills, -tilling, -tilled.** [1] to subject to or undergo distillation. See also **rectify** (sense 2). [2] (sometimes foll by *out* or *off*) to purify, separate, or concentrate, or be purified, separated, or concentrated by distillation. [3] to obtain or be obtained by distillation: *to distil whisky.* [4] to exude or give off (a substance) in drops or small quantities. [5] (*tr*) to extract the essence of as if by distillation.
▷HISTORY C14: from Latin *dēstillāre* to distil, from DE- + *stillāre* to drip
▸**dis'tillable** ADJECTIVE

distillate ('dɪstɪlɪt, -ˌleɪt) NOUN [1] Also called: **distillation.** the product of distillation. [2] a concentrated essence.

distillation (ˌdɪstɪ'leɪʃən) NOUN [1] the act, process, or product of distilling. [2] the process of evaporating or boiling a liquid and condensing its vapour. [3] purification or separation of mixture by using different evaporation rates or boiling points of their components. See also **fractional distillation.** [4] the process of obtaining the essence or an extract of a substance, usually by heating it in a solvent. [5] another name for **distillate** (sense 1). [6] a concentrated essence.
▸**dis'tillatory** ADJECTIVE

distiller (dɪ'stɪlə) NOUN a person or organization that distils, esp a company that makes spirits.

distiller's grain NOUN a by-product of the distillation process for making whisky, used as an animal foodstuff.

distillery (dɪ'stɪlərɪ) NOUN, *plural* **-eries.** a place where alcoholic drinks, etc., are made by distillation.

distinct (dɪ'stɪŋkt) ADJECTIVE [1] easily sensed or understood; clear; precise. [2] (when postpositive, foll by *from*) not the same (as); separate (from); distinguished (from). [3] not alike; different. [4] sharp; clear. [5] recognizable; definite: *a distinct improvement.* [6] explicit; unequivocal. [7] *Maths, logic* (of a pair of entities) not identical. [8] *Botany* (of parts of a plant) not joined together; separate.
▷HISTORY C14: from Latin *distinctus*, from *distinguere* to DISTINGUISH
▸**dis'tinctly** ADVERB ▸**dis'tinctness** NOUN

distinction (dɪ'stɪŋkʃən) NOUN [1] the act or an instance of distinguishing or differentiating. [2] a distinguishing feature. [3] the state of being different or distinguishable. [4] special honour, recognition, or fame. [5] excellence of character; distinctive qualities: *a man of distinction.* [6] distinguished appearance. [7] a symbol of honour or rank.

distinctive (dɪ'stɪŋktɪv) ADJECTIVE [1] serving or tending to distinguish. [2] denoting one of a set of minimal features of a phoneme in a given language that serve to distinguish it from other phonemes. The distinctive features of /p/ in English are that it is voiceless, bilabial, non-nasal, and plosive; /b/ is voiced, bilabial, non-nasal, and plosive: the two differ by the distinctive feature of voice.
▸**dis'tinctively** ADVERB ▸**dis'tinctiveness** NOUN

distinctiveness ratio NOUN *Statistics* the ratio of the relative frequency of some event in a given sample to that in the general population or another relevant sample.

distingué *French* (distɛ̃ge) ADJECTIVE distinguished or noble.

distinguish (dɪ'stɪŋgwɪʃ) VERB (*mainly tr*) [1] (when *intr*, foll by *between* or *among*) to make, show, or recognize a difference or differences (between or among); differentiate (between). [2] to be a distinctive feature of; characterize. [3] to make out; perceive. [4] to mark for a special honour or title. [5] to make (oneself) noteworthy: *he distinguished himself by his cowardice.* [6] to classify; categorize: *we distinguished three species.*
▷HISTORY C16: from Latin *distinguere* to separate, discriminate
▸**dis'tinguishable** ADJECTIVE ▸**dis'tinguishably** ADVERB ▸**dis'tinguisher** NOUN ▸**dis'tinguishing** ADJECTIVE ▸**dis'tinguishingly** ADVERB

distinguished (dɪ'stɪŋgwɪʃt) ADJECTIVE [1] noble or dignified in appearance or behaviour. [2] eminent; famous; celebrated.

distort (dɪ'stɔːt) VERB (*tr*) [1] (*often passive*) to twist or pull out of shape; make bent or misshapen; contort; deform. [2] to alter or misrepresent (facts, motives, etc.). [3] *Electronics* to reproduce or amplify (a signal) inaccurately, changing the shape of the waveform.
▷HISTORY C16: from Latin *distortus* misshapen, from *distorquēre* to turn different ways, from DIS-[1] + *torquēre* to twist
▸**dis'torted** ADJECTIVE ▸**dis'tortedly** ADVERB ▸**dis'tortedness** NOUN ▸**dis'torter** NOUN ▸**dis'tortive** ADJECTIVE

distortion (dɪ'stɔːʃən) NOUN [1] the act or an instance of distorting or the state of being distorted. [2] something that is distorted. [3] an aberration of a lens or optical system in which the magnification varies with the lateral distance from the axis. [4] *Electronics* **a** an undesired change in the shape of an electromagnetic wave or signal. **b** the result of such a change in waveform, esp a loss of clarity in radio reception or sound reproduction. [5] *Psychol* a change in perception so that it does not correspond to reality. [6] *Psychoanal* the disguising of the meaning of unconscious thoughts so that they may appear in consciousness, e.g. in dreams.
▸**dis'tortional** ADJECTIVE

distract (dɪ'strækt) VERB (*tr*) [1] (*often passive*) to draw the attention of (a person) away from something. [2] to divide or confuse the attention of (a person). [3] to amuse or entertain. [4] to trouble greatly. [5] to make mad.
▷HISTORY C14: from Latin *distractus* perplexed, from *distrahere* to pull in different directions, from DIS-[1] + *trahere* to drag
▸**dis'tracter** NOUN ▸**dis'tractible** ADJECTIVE

▸dis,tracti'bility NOUN ▸dis'tracting ADJECTIVE ▸dis'tractingly ADVERB ▸dis'tractive ADJECTIVE ▸dis'tractively ADVERB

distracted (dɪ'stræktɪd) ADJECTIVE [1] bewildered; confused. [2] mad.
▸dis'tractedly ADVERB ▸dis'tractedness NOUN

distraction (dɪ'strækʃən) NOUN [1] the act or an instance of distracting or the state of being distracted. [2] something that serves as a diversion or entertainment. [3] an interruption; an obstacle to concentration. [4] mental turmoil or madness.

distrain (dɪ'streɪn) VERB *Law* to seize (personal property) by way of distress.
▷HISTORY C13: from Old French *destreindre,* from Latin *distringere* to impede, from DIS-[1] + *stringere* to draw tight
▸dis'trainable ADJECTIVE ▸dis'trainment NOUN ▸dis'trainor *or* dis'trainer NOUN

distrainee (,dɪstreɪ'niː) NOUN *Law* a person whose property has been seized by way of distraint.

distraint (dɪ'streɪnt) NOUN *Law* the act or process of distraining; distress.

distrait (dɪ'streɪ; *French* distrɛ) ADJECTIVE absent-minded; abstracted.
▷HISTORY C18: from French, from *distraire* to DISTRACT

distraught (dɪ'strɔːt) ADJECTIVE [1] distracted or agitated. [2] *Rare* mad.
▷HISTORY C14: changed from obsolete *distract* through influence of obsolete *straught,* past participle of STRETCH

distress (dɪ'strɛs) VERB (*tr*) [1] to cause mental pain to; upset badly. [2] (*usually passive*) to subject to financial or other trouble. [3] to damage (esp furniture), as by scratching or denting it, in order to make it appear older than it is. [4] *Law* a less common word for **distrain.** [5] *Archaic* to compel. ◆ NOUN [6] mental pain; anguish. [7] the act of distressing or the state of being distressed. [8] physical or financial trouble. [9] **in distress.** (of a ship, aircraft, etc.) in dire need of help. [10] *Law* **a** the seizure and holding of property as security for payment of or in satisfaction of a debt, claim, etc.; distraint. **b** the property thus seized. **c** *US* (*as modifier*): *distress merchandise.*
▷HISTORY C13: from Old French *destresse* distress, via Vulgar Latin, from Latin *districtus* divided in mind; see DISTRAIN
▸dis'tressful ADJECTIVE ▸dis'tressfully ADVERB ▸dis'tressfulness NOUN ▸dis'tressing ADJECTIVE, NOUN ▸dis'tressingly ADVERB

distressed (dɪ'strɛst) ADJECTIVE [1] much troubled; upset; afflicted. [2] in financial straits; poor. [3] (of furniture, fabric, etc.) having signs of ageing artificially applied. [4] *Economics* another word for **depressed** (sense 4).

distress merchandise NOUN *US* goods sold at reduced prices in order to pay overdue debts, etc.

distress signal NOUN a signal by radio, Very light, etc. from a ship or other vessel in need of immediate assistance.

distributary (dɪ'strɪbjutərɪ, -trɪ) NOUN, *plural* **-taries.** one of several outlet streams draining a river, esp on a delta.

distribute (dɪ'strɪbjuːt) VERB (*tr*) [1] to give out in shares; dispense. [2] to hand out or deliver: *to distribute handbills.* [3] (*often passive*) to spread throughout a space or area: *gulls are distributed along the west coast.* [4] (*often passive*) to divide into classes or categories; classify: *these books are distributed in four main categories.* [5] *Printing* to return (used type) to the correct positions in the type case. [6] *Logic* to incorporate in a distributed term of a categorial proposition. [7] *Maths, logic* to expand an expression containing two operators in such a way that the precedence of the operators is changed; for example, distributing multiplication over addition in $a(b + c)$ yields $ab + ac$. [8] *Obsolete* to dispense (justice).
▷HISTORY C15: from Latin *distribuere* from DIS-[1] + *tribuere* to give
▸dis'tributable ADJECTIVE

distributed array processor NOUN a type of computer system that uses a coordinated array of separate processors applied to a single problem. Abbreviation: **DAP.**

distributed logic NOUN a computer system in which remote terminals and electronic devices, distributed throughout the system, supplement the main computer by doing some of the computing or decision making.

distributed practice NOUN *Psychol* learning with reasonably long intervals between separate occasions of learning. Compare **massed practice.**

distributed systems PLURAL NOUN two or more computers linked by telecommunication, each of which can perform independently.

distributed term NOUN *Logic* a term applying equally to every member of the class it designates, as *doctors* in *no doctors are overworked.*

distributee (dɪ,strɪbju'tiː) NOUN *Law chiefly US* a person entitled to share in the estate of an intestate.

distribution (,dɪstrɪ'bjuːʃən) NOUN [1] the act of distributing or the state or manner of being distributed. [2] a thing or portion distributed. [3] arrangement or location. [4] *Commerce* the process of physically satisfying the demand for goods and services. [5] *Economics* the division of the total income of a community among its members, esp between labour incomes (wages and salaries) and property incomes (rents, interest, and dividends). [6] *Statistics* the set of possible values of a random variable, or points in a sample space, considered in terms of new theoretical or observed frequency: *a normal distribution.* [7] *Law* the apportioning of the estate of a deceased intestate among the persons entitled to share in it. [8] *Law* the lawful division of the assets of a bankrupt among his creditors. [9] *Finance* **a** the division of part of a company's profit as a dividend to its shareholders. **b** the amount paid by dividend in a particular distribution. [10] *Engineering* the way in which the fuel-air mixture is supplied to each cylinder of a multicylinder internal-combustion engine.
▸,distri'butional ADJECTIVE

distribution channel NOUN *Marketing* the network of organizations, including manufacturers, wholesalers, and retailers, that distributes goods or services to consumers.

distribution function NOUN short for **cumulative distribution function.**

distributive (dɪ'strɪbjutɪv) ADJECTIVE [1] characterized by or relating to distribution. [2] *Grammar* referring separately to the individual people or items in a group, as the words *each* and *every.* ◆ NOUN [3] *Grammar* a distributive word. [4] *Maths* able to be distributed: *multiplication is distributive over addition.*
▸dis'tributively ADVERB ▸dis'tributiveness NOUN

distributive bargaining NOUN *Industrial relations* a negotiation process aimed at reaching a compromise agreement over how resources may be allocated between the parties.

distributive law NOUN *Maths, logic* a theorem asserting that one operator can validly be distributed over another. See **distribute** (sense 7).

distributor *or* **distributer** (dɪ'strɪbjutə) NOUN [1] a person or thing that distributes. [2] a wholesaler or middleman engaged in the distribution of a category of goods, esp to retailers in a specific area. [3] the device in a petrol engine that distributes the high-tension voltage to the sparking plugs in the sequence of the firing order.

district ('dɪstrɪkt) NOUN [1] **a** an area of land marked off for administrative or other purposes. **b** (*as modifier*): *district nurse.* [2] a locality separated by geographical attributes; region. [3] any subdivision of any territory, region, etc. [4] (in England from 1974 and in Wales 1974–96) any of the subdivisions of the nonmetropolitan counties that elects a council responsible for local planning, housing, rates, etc. See also **metropolitan district.** [5] (in Scotland until 1975) a landward division of a county. [6] (in Scotland 1975–96) any of the subdivisions of the regions that elected a council responsible for environmental health services, housing, etc. [7] any of the 26 areas into which Northern Ireland has been divided since 1973. Elected district councils are responsible for environmental health services, etc. ◆ VERB [8] (*tr*) to divide into districts.
▷HISTORY C17: from Medieval Latin *districtus* area of jurisdiction, from Latin *distringere* to stretch out; see DISTRAIN

district attorney NOUN (in the US) the state prosecuting officer in a specified judicial district.

district court NOUN [1] (in Scotland) a court of summary jurisdiction held by a stipendiary magistrate or one or more justices of the peace to deal with minor criminal offences. [2] (in the US) **a** a federal trial court serving a federal judicial district. **b** (in some states) a court having general jurisdiction in a state judicial district. [3] (in Australia and New Zealand) a court lower than a high court. Former name: **magistrates' court.**

district court judge NOUN *Austral and NZ* a judge presiding over a lower court. Former name: **magistrate.**

district high school NOUN *NZ* a school in a rural area that includes primary and post-primary classes.

district nurse NOUN (in Britain) a nurse employed within the National Health Service to attend patients in a particular area, usually by visiting them in their own homes.

District of Columbia NOUN a federal district of the eastern US, coextensive with the federal capital, Washington. Pop.: 572 059 (2000). Area: 178 sq. km (69 sq. miles). Abbreviations: **D.C.,** (with zip code) **DC.**

District Six NOUN an area of Cape Town that was inhabited by a racially mixed community until it was forcibly removed in 1966.

distringas (dɪs'trɪŋgæs) NOUN *Law* (formerly) a writ directing a sheriff to distrain.
▷HISTORY from Latin: you shall distrain (the opening word of the writ)

Distrito Federal (*Portuguese* dis'tritu fede'ral) NOUN a district in S central Brazil, containing Brasília: detached from Goiás state in 1960. Pop.: 2 043 169 (2000). Area: 5815 sq. km (2245 sq. miles).

distrix ('dɪstrɪks) NOUN *Med* the splitting of the ends of hairs.
▷HISTORY from Greek DIS-[2] + *thrix* hair

distrust (dɪs'trʌst) VERB [1] to regard as untrustworthy or dishonest. ◆ NOUN [2] suspicion; doubt.
▸dis'truster NOUN ▸dis'trustful ADJECTIVE ▸dis'trustfully ADVERB ▸dis'trustfulness NOUN

disturb (dɪ'stɜːb) VERB (*tr*) [1] to intrude on; interrupt. [2] to destroy or interrupt the quietness or peace of. [3] to disarrange; muddle. [4] (*often passive*) to upset or agitate; trouble: *I am disturbed at your bad news.* [5] to inconvenience; put out: *don't disturb yourself on my account.*
▷HISTORY C13: from Latin *disturbāre,* from DIS-[1] + *turbāre* to confuse
▸dis'turber NOUN

disturbance (dɪ'stɜːbəns) NOUN [1] the act of disturbing or the state of being disturbed. [2] an interruption or intrusion. [3] an unruly outburst or tumult. [4] *Law* an interference with another's rights. [5] *Geology* **a** a minor movement of the earth causing a small earthquake. **b** a minor mountain-building event. [6] *Meteorol* a small depression. [7] *Psychiatry* a mental or emotional disorder.

disturbed (dɪ'stɜːbd) ADJECTIVE *Psychiatry* emotionally upset, troubled, or maladjusted.

disturbing (dɪ'stɜːbɪŋ) ADJECTIVE tending to upset or agitate; troubling; worrying.
▸dis'turbingly ADVERB

disulfiram (,daɪsʌl'fɪərəm) NOUN a drug used in the treatment of alcoholism that acts by inducing nausea and other unpleasant effects following ingestion of alcohol.
▷HISTORY C20: from tetraethylthiu*ram disulf*ide

disulphate (daɪ'sʌlfeɪt) NOUN another name for **pyrosulphate.**

disulphide (daɪ'sʌlfaɪd) NOUN any chemical compound containing two sulphur atoms per molecule. Also called (not in technical usage): **bisulphide.**

disulphuric acid (,daɪsʌl'fjuərɪk) NOUN another name for **pyrosulphuric acid.**

disunite (,dɪsju'naɪt) VERB [1] to separate or become separate; disrupt. [2] (*tr*) to set at variance; estrange.
▸dis'union NOUN ▸,disu'niter NOUN

disunity (dɪsˈjuːnɪtɪ) NOUN, *plural* **-ties**. dissension or disagreement.

disuse (dɪsˈjuːs) NOUN the condition of being unused; neglect (often in the phrases **in** *or* **into disuse**).

disused (dɪsˈjuːzd) ADJECTIVE no longer used: *a disused mine.*

disutility (ˌdɪsjuːˈtɪlɪtɪ) NOUN, *plural* **-ties**. *Economics* **a** the shortcomings of a commodity or activity in satisfying human wants. **b** the degree to which a commodity or activity fails to satisfy human wants. ◆ Compare **utility** (sense 4).

disyllable (ˈdaɪsɪləbᵊl, dɪˈsɪl-) NOUN a variant of **dissyllable**.
▸**disyllabic** (ˌdaɪsɪˈlæbɪk, ˌdɪ-) ADJECTIVE

dit (dɪt) NOUN the short sound used, in combination with the long sound *dah,* in the spoken representation of Morse and other telegraphic codes. Compare **dot**[1] (sense 6).

dita (ˈdiːtə) NOUN an apocynaceous shrub, *Alstonia scholaris,* of tropical Africa and Asia, having large shiny whorled leaves and medicinal bark.
▷HISTORY C19: from Tagalog

ditch (dɪtʃ) NOUN 1 a narrow channel dug in the earth, usually used for drainage, irrigation, or as a boundary marker. 2 any small, natural waterway. 3 *Irish* a bank made of earth excavated from and placed alongside a drain or stream. 4 *Informal* either of the gutters at the side of a tenpin bowling lane. 5 **last ditch.** a last resort or place of last defence. ◆ VERB 6 to make a ditch or ditches in (a piece of ground). 7 *(intr)* to edge with a ditch. 8 *Slang* to crash or be crashed, esp deliberately, as to avoid more unpleasant circumstances: *he had to ditch the car.* 9 *(tr) Slang* to abandon or discard: *to ditch a girlfriend.* 10 *Slang* to land (an aircraft) on water in an emergency. 11 *(tr) US slang* to evade: *to ditch the police.*
▷HISTORY Old English *dīc;* related to Old Saxon *dīk,* Old Norse *dīki,* Middle High German *tīch* dyke, pond, Latin *fīgere* to stick, see DYKE[1]
▸ˈ**ditcher** NOUN ▸ˈ**ditchless** ADJECTIVE

ditchwater (ˈdɪtʃˌwɔːtə) NOUN 1 stagnant water. 2 **(as) dull as ditchwater.** extremely uninspiring.

ditheism (ˈdaɪθiːˌɪzəm) NOUN *Theol* 1 the belief in two equal gods. 2 the belief that two equal principles reign over the world, one good and one evil.
▸ˈ**ditheist** NOUN ▸ˌ**ditheˈistic** ADJECTIVE

dither (ˈdɪðə) VERB *(intr)* 1 *Chiefly Brit* to be uncertain or indecisive. 2 *Chiefly US* to be in an agitated state. 3 to tremble, as with cold. ◆ NOUN 4 *Chiefly Brit* a state of indecision. 5 a state of agitation.
▷HISTORY C17: variant of C14 (northern English dialect) *didder,* of uncertain origin
▸ˈ**ditherer** NOUN ▸ˈ**dithery** ADJECTIVE

dithionite (daɪˈθaɪəˌnaɪt) NOUN any salt of dithionous acid. Also called: **hyposulphite, hydrosulphite.**

dithionous acid (daɪˈθaɪənəs) NOUN an unstable dibasic acid known only in solution and in the form of dithionite salts. It is a powerful reducing agent. Formula: $H_2S_2O_4$. Also called: **hyposulphurous acid, hydrosulphurous acid.**
▷HISTORY from DI-[1] + *thion-,* from Greek *theion* sulphur + -OUS

dithyramb (ˈdɪθɪˌræm, -ˌræmb) NOUN 1 (in ancient Greece) a passionate choral hymn in honour of Dionysus; the forerunner of Greek drama. 2 any utterance or a piece of writing that resembles this.
▷HISTORY C17: from Latin *dīthyrambus,* from Greek *dithurambos;* related to *iambos* IAMB

dithyrambic (ˌdɪθɪˈræmbɪk) ADJECTIVE 1 *Prosody* of or relating to a dithyramb. 2 passionately eloquent.
▸ˌ**dithyˈrambically** ADVERB

dittander (dɪˈtændə, ˈdɪtᵊn-) NOUN a plant, *Lepidium latifolium,* of coastal regions of Europe, N Africa, and SW Asia, with clusters of small white flowers: family *Brassicaceae* (crucifers).

dittany (ˈdɪtənɪ) NOUN, *plural* **-nies.** 1 an aromatic Cretan plant, *Origanum dictamnus,* with pink drooping flowers: formerly credited with great medicinal properties: family *Lamiaceae* (labiates). 2 Also called: **stone mint.** a North American labiate plant, *Cunila origanoides,* with clusters of purplish flowers. 3 another name for **gas plant.**
▷HISTORY C14: from Old French *ditan,* from Latin *dictamnus,* from Greek *diktamnon,* perhaps from *Diktē,* mountain in Crete

ditto (ˈdɪtəʊ) NOUN, *plural* **-tos.** 1 the aforementioned; the above; the same. Used in accounts, lists, etc., to avoid repetition and symbolized by two small marks (") known as **ditto marks,** placed under the thing repeated. Abbreviation: **do.** 2 *Informal* **a** a duplicate. **b** (*as modifier*): *a ditto copy.* ◆ ADVERB 3 in the same way. ◆ 4 SENTENCE SUBSTITUTE *Informal* used to avoid repeating or to confirm agreement with an immediately preceding sentence. ◆ VERB **-tos, -toing, -toed.** 5 *(tr)* to copy; repeat.
▷HISTORY C17: from Italian (Tuscan dialect), variant of *detto* said, from *dicere* to say, from Latin

dittography (dɪˈtɒgrəfɪ) NOUN, *plural* **-phies.** 1 the unintentional repetition of letters or words. 2 a passage of manuscript demonstrating dittography.
▸**dittographic** (ˌdɪtəˈgræfɪk) ADJECTIVE

ditty (ˈdɪtɪ) NOUN, *plural* **-ties.** a short simple song or poem.
▷HISTORY C13: from Old French *ditie* poem, from *ditier* to compose, from Latin *dictāre* DICTATE

ditty bag NOUN a sailor's cloth bag for personal belongings or tools. A box used for these purposes is termed a **ditty box.**
▷HISTORY C19: perhaps from obsolete *dutty* calico, from Hindi *dhōtī* loincloth, DHOTI

ditz (dɪts) NOUN *Slang, chiefly US* a silly scatterbrained person.
▷HISTORY C20: back-formation from DITZY

ditzy *or* **ditsy** (ˈdɪtzɪ) ADJECTIVE **-zier, -ziest** *or* **-sier, -siest.** *Slang* silly and scatterbrained.
▷HISTORY C20: perhaps from DOTTY + DIZZY

Diu (ˈdiːuː) NOUN a small island off the NW coast of India: together with a mainland area, it formed a district of Portuguese India (1535–1961); formerly part of the Indian Union Territory of Goa, Daman, and Diu (1962–87).

diuresis (ˌdaɪjʊˈriːsɪs) NOUN excretion of an unusually large quantity of urine.
▷HISTORY C17: from New Latin, from Greek *diourein* to urinate

diuretic (ˌdaɪjʊˈrɛtɪk) ADJECTIVE 1 acting to increase the flow of urine. ◆ NOUN 2 a drug or agent that increases the flow of urine.
▸ˌ**diuˈretically** ADVERB ▸ˌ**diuˈreticalness** NOUN

diurnal (daɪˈɜːnᵊl) ADJECTIVE 1 happening during the day or daily. 2 (of flowers) open during the day and closed at night. 3 (of animals) active during the day. ◆ Compare **nocturnal.** ◆ NOUN 4 a service book containing all the canonical hours except matins.
▷HISTORY C15: from Late Latin *diurnālis,* from Latin *diurnus,* from *diēs* day
▸**diˈurnally** ADVERB

diurnal motion NOUN motion that occurs during the day or daily, such as the diurnal rotation of the celestial sphere.

diurnal parallax NOUN See **parallax** (sense 2).

div[1] (dɪv) NOUN *Maths* short for **divergence** (sense 4).

div[2] (dɪv) NOUN *Prison slang* a stupid or foolish person.
▷HISTORY C20: probably shortened and changed from DEVIANT

diva (ˈdiːvə) NOUN, *plural* **-vas** *or* **-ve** (-vɪ). a highly distinguished female singer; prima donna.
▷HISTORY C19: via Italian from Latin: a goddess, from *dīvus* DIVINE

divagate (ˈdaɪvəˌgeɪt) VERB *(intr) Rare* to digress or wander.
▷HISTORY C16: from Latin DI-[2] + *vagārī* to wander
▸ˌ**divaˈgation** NOUN

divalent (daɪˈveɪlənt, ˈdaɪˌveɪ-) ADJECTIVE *Chem* 1 having a valency of two. 2 having two valencies. ◆ Also: **bivalent.**
▸**diˈvalency** NOUN

divan (dɪˈvæn) NOUN 1 **a** a backless sofa or couch, designed to be set against a wall. **b** a bed resembling such a couch. 2 (esp formerly) a room for smoking and drinking, as in a coffee shop. 3 **a** a Muslim law court, council chamber, or counting house. **b** a Muslim council of state. 4 a collection of poems. 5 (in Muslim law) an account book. ◆ Also called (for senses 2–5): **diwan.**
▷HISTORY C16: from Turkish *dīvān,* from Persian *dīwān*

divaricate VERB (daɪˈværɪˌkeɪt) 1 *(intr)* (esp of branches) to diverge at a wide angle. ◆ ADJECTIVE (daɪˈværɪkɪt, -ˌkeɪt) 2 branching widely; forked.
▷HISTORY C17: from Latin *dīvāricāre* to stretch apart, from DI-[2] + *vāricāre* to stand astride
▸**diˈvaricately** ADVERB ▸**diˈvariˌcatingly** ADVERB
▸**diˌvariˈcation** NOUN

divaricator (daɪˈværɪˌkeɪtə) NOUN *Zoology* a muscle in brachiopods that controls the opening of the shell.

dive (daɪv) VERB **dives, diving, dived** *or US* **dove, dived.** *(mainly intr)* 1 to plunge headfirst into water. 2 (of a submarine, swimmer, etc.) to submerge under water. 3 *(also tr)* to fly (an aircraft) in a steep nose-down descending path, or (of an aircraft) to fly in such a path. 4 to rush, go, or reach quickly, as in a headlong plunge: *he dived for the ball.* 5 *(also tr;* foll by *in* or *into)* to dip or put (one's hand) quickly or forcefully (into): *to dive into one's pocket.* 6 (usually foll by *in* or *into*) to involve oneself (in something), as in eating food. 7 *Soccer, slang* (of a footballer) to pretend to have been tripped or impeded by an opposing player in order to win a free kick or penalty. ◆ NOUN 8 a headlong plunge into water, esp one of several formalized movements executed as a sport. 9 an act or instance of diving. 10 a steep nose-down descent of an aircraft. 11 *Slang* a disreputable or seedy bar or club. 12 *Boxing, slang* the act of a boxer pretending to be knocked down or out: *he took a dive in the fourth round.* 13 *Soccer, slang* the act of a player pretending to have been tripped or impeded.
▷HISTORY Old English *dȳfan;* related to Old Norse *dȳfa* to dip, Frisian *dīvi;* see DEEP, DIP

dive-bomb VERB *(tr)* to bomb (a target) using or in the manner of a dive bomber.

dive bomber NOUN a military aircraft designed to release its bombs on a target during a steep dive.

dive brake NOUN 1 a flap or spoiler extended from the wings of a ground-attack aircraft for controlling a dive. 2 another name for **air brake.**

Divehi (ˈdɪveɪ) NOUN the language of the Maldive Islands, belonging to the Indic branch of the Indo-European family.

diver (ˈdaɪvə) NOUN 1 a person or thing that dives. 2 a person who works or explores underwater. 3 any aquatic bird of the genus *Gavia,* family *Gaviidae,* and order *Gaviiformes* of northern oceans, having a straight pointed bill, small wings, and a long body: noted for swiftness and skill in swimming and diving. US and Canadian name: **loon.** 4 any of various other diving birds. 5 *Soccer, slang* a player who pretends to have been tripped or impeded by an opposing player in order to win a free kick or penalty.

diverge (daɪˈvɜːdʒ) VERB 1 to separate or cause to separate and go in different directions from a point. 2 *(intr)* to be at variance; differ: *our opinions diverge.* 3 *(intr)* to deviate from a prescribed course. 4 *(intr) Maths* (of a series or sequence) to have no limit.
▷HISTORY C17: from Medieval Latin *dīvergere,* from Latin DI-[2] + *vergere* to turn

divergence (daɪˈvɜːdʒəns) NOUN 1 the act or result of diverging or the amount by which something diverges. 2 the condition of being divergent. 3 *Meteorol* the outflowing of airstreams from a particular area, caused by expanding air. 4 *Maths* **a** the scalar product of the operator, ∇, and a vector function, $\boldsymbol{A}$, where $\nabla = \boldsymbol{i}\partial/\partial x + \boldsymbol{j}\partial/\partial y + \boldsymbol{k}\partial/\partial z$, and $\boldsymbol{i}$, $\boldsymbol{j}$, and $\boldsymbol{k}$ are unit vectors. Usually written: div **A**, $\nabla\boldsymbol{A}$, or $\nabla\cdot\mathbf{A}$. Compare **curl** (sense 11), **gradient** (sense 4). **b** the property of being divergent. 5 the spreading of a stream of electrons as a result of their mutual electrostatic repulsion. 6 the turning of the eyes outwards in order to fixate an object farther away than that previously being fixated. Compare **convergence** (sense 7). 7 Also called: **divergent evolution.** the evolutionary development of structures or organisms that differ from each other in form and function but have evolved from the same basic structure or organism. Compare **convergence** (sense 5). ◆ Also called (for senses 1, 2): **divergency.**

divergent (daɪˈvɜːdʒənt) ADJECTIVE [1] diverging or causing divergence. [2] (of opinions, interests, etc.) different. [3] *Maths* (of a series) having no limit; not convergent. [4] *Botany* (of plant organs) farther apart at their tops than at their bases.
▸**diˈvergently** ADVERB

> **Language note** The use of *divergent* to mean *different* as in *they hold widely divergent views* is considered by some people to be incorrect.

divergent thinking NOUN *Psychol* thinking in an unusual and unstereotyped way, e.g. to generate several possible solutions to a problem. Compare **convergent thinking.**

divers (ˈdaɪvəz) DETERMINER *Archaic or literary* **a** various; sundry; some. **b** (*as pronoun; functioning as plural*): *divers of them.*
▷HISTORY C13: from Old French, from Latin *dīversus* turned in different directions; see DIVERT

diverse (daɪˈvɜːs, ˈdaɪvɜːs) ADJECTIVE [1] having variety; assorted. [2] distinct in kind.
▷HISTORY C13: from Latin *dīversus;* see DIVERS
▸**diˈversely** ADVERB ▸**diˈverseness** NOUN

diversification (daɪˌvɜːsɪfɪˈkeɪʃən) NOUN [1] *Commerce* the practice of varying products, operations, etc., in order to spread risk, expand, exploit spare capacity, etc. [2] (in regional planning policies) the attempt to provide regions with an adequate variety of industries. [3] the act of diversifying.

diversiform (daɪˈvɜːsɪˌfɔːm) ADJECTIVE having various forms.

diversify (daɪˈvɜːsɪˌfaɪ) VERB **-fies, -fying, -fied.** [1] (*tr*) to create different forms of; variegate; vary. [2] (of an enterprise) to vary (products, operations, etc.) in order to spread risk, expand, etc. [3] to distribute (investments) among several securities in order to spread risk.
▷HISTORY C15: from Old French *diversifier,* from Medieval Latin *dīversificāre,* from Latin *dīversus* DIVERSE + *facere* to make
▸**diˈversiˌfiable** ADJECTIVE ▸**diˌversiˌfiaˈbility** NOUN
▸**diˈversiˌfier** NOUN

diversion (daɪˈvɜːʃən) NOUN [1] the act of diverting from a specified course. [2] *Chiefly Brit* an official detour used by traffic when a main route is closed. [3] something that distracts from business, etc.; amusement. [4] *Military* a feint attack designed to draw an enemy away from the main attack.
▸**diˈversional** *or* **diˈversionary** ADJECTIVE

diversity (daɪˈvɜːsɪtɪ) NOUN [1] the state or quality of being different or varied. [2] a point of difference. [3] *Logic* the relation that holds between two entities when and only when they are not identical; the property of being numerically distinct.

divert (daɪˈvɜːt) VERB [1] to turn (a person or thing) aside from a course; deflect. [2] (*tr*) to entertain; amuse. [3] (*tr*) to distract the attention of.
▷HISTORY C15: from French *divertir,* from Latin *dīvertere* to turn aside, from DI-[2] + *vertere* to turn
▸**diˈverter** NOUN ▸**diˈvertible** ADJECTIVE ▸**diˈverting** ADJECTIVE ▸**diˈvertingly** ADVERB ▸**diˈvertive** ADJECTIVE

diverticulitis (ˌdaɪvəˌtɪkjʊˈlaɪtɪs) NOUN inflammation of one or more diverticula, esp of the colon.

diverticulosis (ˌdaɪvəˌtɪkjʊˈləʊsɪs) NOUN *Pathol* the presence of several diverticula, esp in the intestines.
▷HISTORY from New Latin, from DIVERTICULUM + -OSIS

diverticulum (ˌdaɪvəˈtɪkjʊləm) NOUN, *plural* **-la** (-lə). any sac or pouch formed by herniation of the wall of a tubular organ or part, esp the intestines.
▷HISTORY C16: from New Latin, from Latin *dēverticulum* by-path, from *dēvertere* to turn aside, from *vertere* to turn
▸**ˌdiverˈticular** ADJECTIVE

divertimento (dɪˌvɜːtɪˈmɛntəʊ) NOUN, *plural* **-ti** (-tɪ). [1] a piece of entertaining music in several movements, often scored for a mixed ensemble and having no fixed form. [2] an episode in a fugue. ◆ See also **divertissement.**
▷HISTORY C18: from Italian

divertissement (dɪˈvɜːtɪsmənt; *French* divɛrtismɑ̃) NOUN [1] a brief entertainment or diversion, usually between the acts of a play. [2] *Music* **a** a fantasia on popular melodies; potpourri. **b** a piece or pieces written to be played during the intervals in a play, opera, etc. **c** another word for **divertimento.**
▷HISTORY C18: from French: entertainment

Dives (ˈdaɪviːz) NOUN [1] a rich man in the parable in Luke 16:19–31. [2] a very rich man.

divest (daɪˈvɛst) VERB (*tr;* usually foll by *of*) [1] to strip (of clothes): *to divest oneself of one's coat.* [2] to deprive or dispossess. [3] *Property law* to take away an estate or interest in property vested (in a person).
▷HISTORY C17: changed from earlier DEVEST
▸**diˈvestible** ADJECTIVE ▸**divestiture** (daɪˈvɛstɪtʃə) *or* **divesture** (daɪˈvɛstʃə) *or* **diˈvestment** NOUN

divi (ˈdɪvɪ) NOUN an alternative spelling of **divvy**[1].

divide (dɪˈvaɪd) VERB [1] to separate or be separated into parts or groups; split up; part. [2] to share or be shared out in parts; distribute. [3] to diverge or cause to diverge in opinion or aim: *the issue divided the management.* [4] (*tr*) to keep apart or be a boundary between: *the Rio Grande divides Mexico from the United States.* [5] (*intr*) (in Parliament and similar legislatures) to vote by separating into two groups. [6] to categorize; classify. [7] to calculate the quotient of (one number or quantity) and (another number or quantity) by division: *to divide 50 by 10; to divide 10 into 50; to divide by 10.* [8] (*intr*) to diverge: *the roads divide.* [9] (*tr*) to mark increments of (length, angle, etc.) as by use of an engraving machine. ◆ NOUN [10] *Chiefly US and Canadian* an area of relatively high ground separating drainage basins; watershed. See also **continental divide.** [11] a division; split.
▷HISTORY C14: from Latin *dīvidere* to force apart, from DI-[2] + *vid-* separate, from the source of *viduus* bereaved, *vidua* WIDOW
▸**diˈvidable** ADJECTIVE

divided (dɪˈvaɪdɪd) ADJECTIVE [1] *Botany* another word for **dissected** (sense 1). [2] split; not united.
▸**diˈvidedly** ADVERB ▸**diˈvidedness** NOUN

divided highway NOUN the US and Canadian term for **dual carriageway.**

dividend (ˈdɪvɪˌdɛnd) NOUN [1] *Finance* **a** a distribution from the net profits of a company to its shareholders. **b** a pro-rata portion of this distribution received by a shareholder. [2] the share of a cooperative society's surplus allocated at the end of a period to members. [3] *Insurance* a sum of money distributed from a company's net profits to the holders of certain policies. [4] something extra; bonus. [5] a number or quantity to be divided by another number or quantity. Compare **divisor.** [6] *Law* the proportion of an insolvent estate payable to the creditors.
▷HISTORY C15: from Latin *dīvidendum* what is to be divided; see DIVIDE

dividend cover NOUN the number of times that a company's dividends to shareholders could be paid out of its annual profits after tax, used as an indication of the probability that dividends will be maintained in subsequent years.

divider (dɪˈvaɪdə) NOUN [1] Also called: **room divider.** a screen or piece of furniture placed so as to divide a room into separate areas. [2] a person or thing that divides. [3] *Electronics* an electrical circuit with an output that is a well-defined fraction of the given input: *a voltage divider.*

dividers (dɪˈvaɪdəz) PLURAL NOUN a type of compass with two pointed arms, used for measuring lines or dividing them.

divi-divi (ˌdɪvɪˈdɪvɪ) NOUN, *plural* **-divis** *or* **-divi.** [1] a tropical American leguminous tree, *Caesalpinia coriaria.* [2] the pods of this plant, which yield a substance used in tanning leather.
▷HISTORY C19: from Spanish, of Cariban origin

divination (ˌdɪvɪˈneɪʃən) NOUN [1] the art, practice, or gift of discerning or discovering future events or unknown things, as though by supernatural powers. [2] a prophecy. [3] a presentiment or guess.
▸**divinatory** (dɪˈvɪnətərɪ, -trɪ) ADJECTIVE

divine (dɪˈvaɪn) ADJECTIVE [1] of, relating to, or characterizing God or a deity. [2] godlike. [3] of, relating to, or associated with religion or worship: *the divine liturgy.* [4] of supreme excellence or worth. [5] *Informal* splendid; perfect. ◆ NOUN [6] (*often capital;* preceded by *the*) another term for **God.** [7] a priest, esp one learned in theology. ◆ VERB [8] to perceive or understand (something) by intuition or insight. [9] to conjecture (something); guess. [10] to discern (a hidden or future reality) as though by supernatural power. [11] (*tr*) to search for (underground supplies of water, metal, etc.) using a divining rod.
▷HISTORY C14: from Latin *dīvīnus,* from *dīvus* a god; related to *deus* a god
▸**diˈvinable** ADJECTIVE ▸**diˈvinely** ADVERB ▸**diˈvineness** NOUN ▸**diˈviner** NOUN

divine office NOUN (*sometimes capitals*) the canonical prayers (in the Roman Catholic Church those of the breviary) recited daily by priests, those in religious orders, etc.

divine right of kings NOUN *History* the concept that the right to rule derives from God and that kings are answerable for their actions to God alone.

divine service NOUN a service of the Christian church, esp one at which no sacrament is given.

diving beetle NOUN any of the aquatic predatory beetles of the widely distributed family *Dytiscidae,* characterized by flattened hindlegs adapted for swimming and diving.

diving bell NOUN an early diving submersible having an open bottom and being supplied with compressed air.

diving board NOUN a platform or springboard from which swimmers may dive.

diving duck NOUN any of various ducks, such as the pochard, scaup, redhead, and canvasback, that inhabit bays, estuaries, lakes, etc., and can dive and swim beneath the surface of the water.

diving suit *or* **dress** NOUN a waterproof suit used by divers, having a heavy detachable helmet and an air supply.

divining rod NOUN a rod, usually a forked hazel twig, said to move or dip when held over ground in which water, metal, etc., is to be found. Also called: **dowsing rod.**

divinity (dɪˈvɪnɪtɪ) NOUN, *plural* **-ties.** [1] the nature of a deity or the state of being divine. [2] a god or other divine being. [3] (*often capital;* preceded by *the*) another term for **God.** [4] another word for **theology.**

divinize *or* **divinise** (ˈdɪvɪˌnaɪz) VERB (*tr*) to make divine; deify.
▸**ˌdiviniˈzation** *or* **ˌdiviniˈsation** NOUN

divisibility (dɪˌvɪzɪˈbɪlɪtɪ) NOUN the capacity of a dividend to be exactly divided by a given number.

divisible (dɪˈvɪzəbᵊl) ADJECTIVE capable of being divided, usually with no remainder.
▸**diˈvisibleness** NOUN ▸**diˈvisibly** ADVERB

division (dɪˈvɪʒən) NOUN [1] the act of dividing or state of being divided. [2] the act of sharing out; distribution. [3] something that divides or keeps apart, such as a boundary. [4] one of the parts, groups, etc., into which something is divided. [5] a part of a government, business, country, etc., that has been made into a unit for administrative, political, or other reasons. [6] a formal vote in Parliament or a similar legislative body. [7] a difference of opinion, esp one that causes separation. [8] (in sports) a section, category, or class organized according to age, weight, skill, etc. [9] a mathematical operation, the inverse of multiplication, in which the quotient of two numbers or quantities is calculated. Usually written: $a \div b$, $\frac{a}{b}$, a/b. [10] **a** *Army* a major formation, larger than a regiment or brigade but smaller than a corps, containing the necessary arms to sustain independent combat. **b** *Navy* a group of ships of similar type or a tactical unit of naval aircraft. **c** *Air Force* an organization normally comprising two or more wings with required support units. [11] (*plural*) *Navy* the assembly of all crew members for the captain's inspection. [12] *Biology* (in traditional classification systems) a major category of the plant kingdom that contains one or more related classes. Compare **phylum** (sense 1). [13] *Horticulture* any type of propagation in plants in which a new plant grows from a separated part of the original. [14] *Logic* the fallacy of inferring that the properties of the whole are also true of the parts, as *Britain is in debt, so John Smith is in debt.* [15] (esp in 17th-century English music) the art of breaking up a melody into quick phrases, esp over a ground bass.
▷HISTORY C14: from Latin *dīvīsiō,* from *dīvidere* to DIVIDE

▸**di'visional** *or* **di'visionary** ADJECTIVE ▸**di'visionally** ADVERB

divisionism (dɪ'vɪʒəˌnɪzəm) NOUN the pointillism of Georges Seurat, the French neoimpressionist painter (1859–91), and his followers. ▸**di'visionist** NOUN, ADJECTIVE

division of labour NOUN a system of organizing the manufacture of an article in a series of separate specialized operations, each of which is carried out by a different worker or group of workers.

division sign NOUN the symbol ÷, placed between the dividend and the divisor to indicate division, as in 12 ÷ 6 = 2.

divisive (dɪ'vaɪsɪv) ADJECTIVE 1 causing or tending to cause disagreement or dissension. 2 *Archaic* having the quality of distinguishing. ▸**di'visively** ADVERB ▸**di'visiveness** NOUN

divisor (dɪ'vaɪzə) NOUN 1 a number or quantity to be divided into another number or quantity (the dividend). 2 a number that is a factor of another number.

divorce (dɪ'vɔːs) NOUN 1 the dissolution of a marriage by judgment of a court or by accepted custom. 2 a judicial decree declaring a marriage to be dissolved. 3 a separation, esp one that is total or complete. ◆ VERB 4 to separate or be separated by divorce; give or obtain a divorce (to a couple or from one's spouse). 5 (*tr*) to remove or separate, esp completely.
▹HISTORY C14: from Old French, from Latin *dīvortium* from *dīvertere* to separate; see DIVERT
▸**di'vorceable** ADJECTIVE ▸**di'vorcer** NOUN ▸**di'vorcive** ADJECTIVE

divorcé (dɪ'vɔːseɪ) NOUN a man who has been divorced.

divorcée (dɪvɔː'siː) NOUN a person, esp a woman, who has been divorced.

divorcement (dɪ'vɔːsmənt) NOUN a less common word for **divorce.**

divot ('dɪvət) NOUN a piece of turf dug out of a grass surface, esp by a golf club or by horses' hooves.
▹HISTORY C16: from Scottish, of obscure origin

divulgate (dɪ'vʌlgeɪt) VERB (*tr*) *Archaic* to make publicly known.
▹HISTORY C16: from Latin *dīvulgāre;* see DIVULGE
▸**di'vulgator** *or* **di'vulgater** NOUN ▸ˌ**divul'gation** NOUN

divulge (daɪ'vʌldʒ) VERB (*tr; may take a clause as object*) to make known (something private or secret); disclose.
▹HISTORY C15: from Latin *dīvulgāre,* from DI-[2] + *vulgāre* to spread among the people, from *vulgus* the common people
▸**di'vulgence** *or* **di'vulgement** NOUN ▸**di'vulger** NOUN

divulsion (daɪ'vʌlʃən) NOUN a tearing or pulling apart.
▹HISTORY C17: from Latin *dīvulsiō,* from *dīvulsus* torn apart, from *dīvellere* to rend, from DI-[2] + *vellere* to pull
▸**di'vulsive** ADJECTIVE

divvy[1] ('dɪvɪ) *Informal* ◆ NOUN, *plural* **-vies.** 1 *Brit* short for **dividend,** esp (formerly) one paid by a cooperative society 2 *US and Canadian* a share; portion. ◆ VERB **-vies, -vying, -vied.** 3 (*tr;* usually foll by *up*) to divide and share.

divvy[2] ('dɪvɪ) NOUN, *plural* **-vies.** *Dialect* a stupid or foolish person.

Diwali (dɪ'wɑːlɪ) NOUN a major Hindu religious festival, honouring Lakshmi, the goddess of wealth. Held over the New Year according to the Vikrama calendar, it is marked by feasting, gifts, and the lighting of lamps.

diwan (dɪ'wɑːn) NOUN a variant of **dewan** or **divan** (senses 2–5).

dixie[1] ('dɪksɪ) NOUN 1 *Chiefly military* a large metal pot for cooking, brewing tea, etc. 2 a mess tin.
▹HISTORY C19: from Hindi *degcī,* diminutive of *degcā* pot

dixie[2] ('dɪksɪ) NOUN *Northern English dialect* a lookout.

Dixie ('dɪksɪ) NOUN 1 Also called: **Dixieland.** the southern states of the US; the states that joined the Confederacy during the Civil War. 2 a song adopted as a marching tune by the Confederate states during the American Civil War. ◆ ADJECTIVE 3 of, relating to, or characteristic of the southern states of the US.
▹HISTORY C19: perhaps from the nickname of New Orleans, from *dixie* a ten-dollar bill printed there, from French *dix* ten

Dixieland ('dɪksɪˌlænd) NOUN 1 a form of jazz that originated in New Orleans, becoming popular esp with White musicians in the second decade of the 20th century. 2 a revival of this style in the 1950s. 3 See **Dixie** (sense 1).

DIY *or* **d.i.y.** (in Britain and Canada) ABBREVIATION FOR do-it-yourself.

Diyarbakir *or* **Diyarbekir** (diː'jɑːbɛkɪə) NOUN a city in SE Turkey, on the River Tigris: ancient black basalt walls. Pop.: 511 640 (1997). Ancient name: **Amida** (ə'miːdə).

dizen ('daɪzᵊn) VERB an archaic word for **bedizen.**
▹HISTORY C16: from Middle Dutch *dīsen* to dress a distaff with flax; see DISTAFF
▸'**dizenment** NOUN

dizzy ('dɪzɪ) ADJECTIVE **-zier, -ziest.** 1 affected with a whirling or reeling sensation; giddy. 2 mentally confused or bewildered. 3 causing or tending to cause vertigo or bewilderment. 4 *Informal* foolish or flighty. ◆ VERB **-zies, -zying, -zied.** 5 (*tr*) to make dizzy.
▹HISTORY Old English *dysig* silly; related to Old High German *tusīg* weak, Old Norse *dos* quiet
▸'**dizzily** ADVERB ▸'**dizziness** NOUN

dj THE INTERNET DOMAIN NAME FOR Djibouti.

DJ *or* **dj** ABBREVIATION FOR: 1 disc jockey. 2 dinner jacket.

Djailolo *or* **Jilolo** (dʒaɪ'ləʊləʊ) NOUN the Dutch name for **Halmahera.**

Djaja ('dʒɑːdʒə) NOUN a variant spelling of (Mount) **Jaya.**

Djajapura (ˌdʒɑːdʒɑː'pʊərə) NOUN a variant spelling of **Jayapura.**

Djakarta (dʒə'kɑːtə) NOUN a variant spelling of **Jakarta.**

Djambi ('dʒæmbɪ) NOUN a variant spelling of **Jambi.**

djebel ('dʒɛbᵊl) NOUN a variant spelling of **jebel.**

djellaba, djellabah, jellaba, *or* **jellabah** ('dʒɛləbə) NOUN a kind of loose cloak with a hood, worn by men esp in North Africa and the Middle East.
▹HISTORY from Arabic *jallabah*

djembe ('dʒɛmbe) NOUN a W African drum played by beating with the hand.

Djerba *or* **Jerba** ('dʒɜːbə) NOUN an island off the SE coast of Tunisia, in the Gulf of Gabès: traditionally Homer's land of the lotus-eaters. Pop.: 92 269 (latest est.). Area: 510 sq. km (197 sq. miles). Ancient name: **Meninx** ('menɪŋks).

Djibouti *or* **Jibouti** (dʒɪ'buːtɪ) NOUN 1 a republic in E Africa, on the Gulf of Aden: a French overseas territory (1946–77); became independent in 1977; mainly desert. Official languages: Arabic and French. Religion: Muslim majority. Currency: Djibouti franc. Capital: Djibouti. Pop.: 461 000 (2001 est.). Area: 23 200 sq. km (8950 sq. miles). Former name (until 1977): (Territory of the) **Afars and the Issas.** 2 the capital of Djibouti, a port on the Gulf of Aden: an outlet for Ethiopian goods. Pop.: 383 000 (1995).

djinni *or* **djinny** (dʒɪ'niː, 'dʒɪnɪ) NOUN, *plural* **djinn** (dʒɪn). variant spellings of **jinni.**

dk THE INTERNET DOMAIN NAME FOR Denmark.

DK INTERNATIONAL CAR REGISTRATION FOR Denmark.

dl SYMBOL FOR decilitre(s).

DLitt *or* **DLit** ABBREVIATION FOR: 1 Doctor of Letters. 2 Doctor of Literature.
▹HISTORY Latin *Doctor Litterarum*

DLL ABBREVIATION FOR Dynamic Linked Library.

dlr ABBREVIATION FOR dealer.

DLR (in Britain) ABBREVIATION FOR Docklands Light Railway (in E London).

dm[1] SYMBOL FOR decimetre.

dm[2] THE INTERNET DOMAIN NAME FOR Dominica.

DM ABBREVIATION FOR: 1 (in Canada) deputy minister. 2 (the former) **Deutschmark.**

DMA *Computing* ABBREVIATION FOR **direct memory access.**

DMAC ABBREVIATION FOR duobinary multiplexed analogue component: a transmission coding system using duobinary techniques for the digital sound and data components of colour television using satellite broadcasting.

D-mark *or* **D-Mark** NOUN short for (the former) **Deutschmark.**

DMD ABBREVIATION FOR Duchenne muscular dystrophy.

DMF ABBREVIATION FOR dimethylformamide.

DMK (in India) ABBREVIATION FOR Dravida Munnetra Kazgham: a political party in the state of Tamil Nadu.

DMs ABBREVIATION FOR **Doc Martens.**

DMS (in Britain) ABBREVIATION FOR Diploma in Management Studies.

DMSO ABBREVIATION FOR dimethylsulphoxide.

DMT ABBREVIATION FOR dimethyltryptamine, a hallucinogenic drug.

DMus ABBREVIATION FOR Doctor of Music.

DMZ ABBREVIATION FOR demilitarized zone.

DNA NOUN deoxyribonucleic acid; a nucleic acid that is the main constituent of the chromosomes of all organisms (except some viruses). The DNA molecule consists of two polynucleotide chains in the form of a double helix, containing phosphate and the sugar deoxyribose and linked by hydrogen bonds between the complementary bases adenine and thymine or cytosine and guanine. DNA is self-replicating, plays a central role in protein synthesis, and is responsible for the transmission of hereditary characteristics from parents to offspring. See also **genetic code.**

DNAase (ˌdiːɛn'eɪeɪz) *or* **DNase** (ˌdiːɛn'eɪz) NOUN deoxyribonuclease; any of a number of enzymes that hydrolyse DNA. See **endonuclease, exonuclease.**

DNA fingerprinting *or* **profiling** NOUN another name for **genetic fingerprinting.**

Dneprodzerzhinsk (*Russian* dnɪprədzɪr'ʒinsk) NOUN an industrial city in the E Ukraine on the Dnieper River. Pop.: 275 000 (1998 est.).

Dnepropetrovsk (*Russian* dnɪprəpɪ'trɔfsk) NOUN a city in the E central Ukraine on the Dnieper River: a major centre of the metallurgical industry. Pop.: 1 122 400 (1998 est.). Former name (1787–1796, 1802–1926): **Yekaterinoslav.**

Dnieper ('dniːpə) NOUN a river in NE Europe, rising in Russia, in the Valdai Hills NE of Smolensk and flowing south to the Black Sea: the third longest river in Europe; a major navigable waterway. Length: 2200 km (1370 miles). Russian name: **Dnepr** ('dnjɛpə).

D-notice NOUN *Brit* an official notice sent to newspapers, prohibiting the publication of certain security information.
▹HISTORY C20: from their administrative classification letter

DNR ABBREVIATION FOR do not resuscitate.

DNS ABBREVIATION FOR: 1 (formerly in Britain) Department for National Savings. 2 *Computing* domain name system.

do[1] (duː; *unstressed* dʊ, də) VERB **does, doing, did, done.** 1 to perform or complete (a deed or action): *to do a portrait; the work is done.* 2 (often *intr;* foll by *for*) to serve the needs of; be suitable for (a person, situation, etc.); suffice: *there isn't much food, but it'll do for the two of us.* 3 (*tr*) to arrange or fix: *you should do the garden now.* 4 (*tr*) to prepare or provide; serve: *this restaurant doesn't do lunch on Sundays.* 5 (*tr*) to make tidy, elegant, ready, etc., as by arranging or adorning: *to do one's hair.* 6 (*tr*) to improve (esp in the phrase **do something to** *or* **for**). 7 (*tr*) to find an answer to (a problem or puzzle). 8 (*tr*) to translate or adapt the form or language of: *the book was done into a play.* 9 (*intr*) to conduct oneself: *do as you please.* 10 (*intr*) to fare or manage: *how are you doing these days?* 11 (*tr*) to cause or produce: *complaints do nothing to help.* 12 (*tr*) to give or render: *your portrait doesn't do you justice; do me a favour.* 13 (*tr*) to work at, esp as a course of study or a profession: *he is doing chemistry; what do you do for a living?* 14 (*tr*) to perform (a play, etc.); act: *they are doing "Hamlet" next week.* 15 (*tr*) to travel at a specified speed, esp as a maximum: *this car will do 120 mph.* 16 (*tr*) to travel or traverse (a distance): *we did 15 miles on our walk.* 17 (takes an infinitive without *to*) used as an auxiliary before the subject of an interrogative sentence as a way of forming a question: *do you agree?; when did John go out?* 18 (takes an infinitive without *to*) used as an auxiliary

to intensify positive statements and commands: *I do like your new house; do hurry!* 19 (takes an infinitive without *to*) used as an auxiliary before a negative adverb to form negative statements or commands: *he does not like cheese; do not leave me here alone!* 20 (takes an infinitive without *to*) used as an auxiliary in inverted constructions: *little did he realize that; only rarely does he come in before ten o'clock.* 21 used as an auxiliary to replace an earlier verb or verb phrase to avoid repetition: *he likes you as much as I do.* 22 (*tr*) *Informal* to visit or explore as a sightseer or tourist: *to do Westminster Abbey.* 23 (*tr*) to wear out; exhaust. 24 (*intr*) to happen (esp in the phrase **nothing doing**). 25 (*tr*) *Slang* to serve (a period of time) as a prison sentence: *he's doing three years for burglary; he's doing time.* 26 (*tr*) *Informal* to cheat or swindle. 27 (*tr*) *Slang* to rob: *they did three shops last night.* 28 (*tr*) *Slang* **a** to arrest. **b** to convict of a crime. 29 (*tr*) *Austral informal* to lose or spend (money) completely. 30 (*tr*) *Slang, chiefly Brit* to treat violently; assault. 31 (*tr*) *Slang* to take or use (a drug). 32 (*tr*) *Taboo slang* (of a male) to have sexual intercourse with. 33 (*tr*) to partake in (a meal): *let's do lunch.* 34 **do (a).** *Informal* to act like; imitate: *he's a good mimic — he can do all his friends well.* 35 **do or die.** to make a final or supreme effort. 36 **how do you do?** a conventional formula when being introduced. 37 **make do.** to manage with whatever is available. ◆ NOUN, *plural* **dos** *or* **do's.** 38 *Slang* an act or instance of cheating or swindling. 39 *Informal, chiefly Brit and NZ* a formal or festive gathering; party. 40 **do's and don'ts.** *Informal* those things that should or should not be done; rules. ◆ See also **do away with, do by, do down, do for, do in, done, do out, do over, do up, do with, do without.**
▷HISTORY Old English *dōn;* related to Old Frisian *duān,* Old High German *tuon,* Latin *abdere* to put away, Greek *tithenai* to place; see DEED, DOOM

do² (dəʊ) NOUN, *plural* **dos.** a variant spelling of **doh.**

do³ THE INTERNET DOMAIN NAME FOR Dominican Republic.

DO ABBREVIATION FOR: 1 Doctor of Optometry. 2 Doctor of Osteopathy.

do. ABBREVIATION FOR ditto.

D/O *or* **d.o.** *Commerce* ABBREVIATION FOR delivery order.

DOA ABBREVIATION FOR dead on arrival.

doab ('dəʊɑːb) NOUN the alluvial land between two converging rivers, esp the area between the Ganges and Jumna in N India.
▷HISTORY C20: from Persian *dōāb,* from *dō* two + *āb* water

doable ('duːəbᵊl) ADJECTIVE capable of being done; practical.

doat (dəʊt) VERB (*intr*) a variant (now rare) spelling of **dote.**

do away with VERB (*intr, adverb + preposition*) 1 to kill or destroy. 2 to discard or abolish.

dobber-in (ˌdɒbər'ɪn) NOUN *Austral slang* an informant or traitor. Sometimes shortened to: **dobber.**

dobbin ('dɒbɪn) NOUN 1 a name for a horse, esp a workhorse, often used in children's tales, etc. 2 *NZ* a trolley for moving loose wool in a woolshed or shearing shed.
▷HISTORY C16: from *Robin,* pet form of *Robert*

dobby ('dɒbɪ) NOUN, *plural* **-bies.** an attachment to a loom, used in weaving small figures.
▷HISTORY C17: perhaps from *Dobby,* pet form of *Robert*

Dobell's solution ('dəʊbəlz) NOUN a solution of sodium borate, sodium bicarbonate, phenol, and glycerol, used as an astringent or antiseptic wash for the throat and nose.
▷HISTORY C19: named after Horace B. *Dobell* (1828–1917), British physician

Doberman pinscher ('dəʊbəmən 'pɪnʃə) *or* **Doberman** NOUN a fairly large slender but muscular breed of dog, originally from Germany, with a glossy black-and-tan coat, a short tail, and erect ears. Also spelt: **Dobermann.**
▷HISTORY C19: probably named after L. *Dobermann,* 19th-century German dog breeder who bred it + *Pinscher,* a type of terrier, perhaps after *Pinzgau,* district in Austria

dob in VERB **dobs, dobbing, dobbed.** (*adverb*) *Austral and NZ informal* 1 (*tr*) to inform against or report, esp to the police. 2 to contribute to a fund for a specific purpose.

dobla ('dəʊblɑː) NOUN a medieval Spanish gold coin, probably worth 20 maravedis.
▷HISTORY Spanish, from Latin *dupla,* feminine of *duplus* twofold, DOUBLE

doblón (də'bləʊn; *Spanish* do'βlon) NOUN a variant spelling of **doubloon.**
▷HISTORY Spanish; see DOUBLOON

dobra ('dəʊbrə) NOUN the standard monetary unit of São Tomé e Principe, divided into 100 cêntimos.

Dobro ('dəʊbrəʊ) NOUN, *plural* **-bros.** *Trademark* an acoustic guitar having a metal resonator built into the body.

Dobruja (*Bulgarian* 'dɔbrudʒa) NOUN a region of E Europe, between the River Danube and the Black Sea: the north passed to Romania and the south to Bulgaria after the Berlin Congress (1878). Romanian name: **Dobrogea** (do'brodʒea).

dobsonfly ('dɒbsᵊnˌflaɪ) NOUN, *plural* **-flies.** *US and Canadian* a large North American neuropterous insect, *Corydalis cornutus:* the male has elongated horn-like mouthparts and the larva (a **hellgrammite** or **dobson**) is used as bait by anglers: suborder *Megaloptera.*
▷HISTORY C20: origin uncertain, perhaps after the surname *Dobson*

do by VERB (*intr, preposition*) to treat in the manner specified: *employers do well by hard working employees.*

doc (dɒk) NOUN *Informal* short for **doctor,** esp a medical doctor: often used as a term of address

DOC ABBREVIATION FOR: 1 Denominazione di Origine Controllata: used of wines. [Italian, literally: name of origin controlled] 2 (in New Zealand) Department of Conservation.

doc. ABBREVIATION FOR document.

docent ('dəʊsᵊnt) NOUN 1 a voluntary worker who acts as a guide in a museum, art gallery, etc. 2 (dəʊ'sɛnt; *German* do'tsɛnt) (in the US) a lecturer in some colleges or universities.
▷HISTORY C19: from German *Dozent,* from Latin *docēns* from *docēre* to teach
▸ **'docentˌship** NOUN

Docetism ('dəʊsɪˌtɪzəm) NOUN (in the early Christian Church) a heresy that the humanity of Christ, his sufferings, and his death were apparent rather than real.
▷HISTORY C19: from Medieval Latin *Docētae,* from Greek *Dokētai,* from *dokein* to seem

DOCG ABBREVIATION FOR Denominazione di Origine Controllata Garantita: used of wines.
▷HISTORY Italian, literally: name of origin guaranteed controlled

doch-an-doris ('dɒxən'dɒrɪs) NOUN a variant spelling of **deoch-an-doruis.**

docile ('dəʊsaɪl) ADJECTIVE 1 easy to manage, control, or discipline; submissive. 2 *Rare* ready to learn; easy to teach.
▷HISTORY C15: from Latin *docilis* easily taught, from *docēre* to teach
▸ **'docilely** ADVERB ▸ **docility** (dəʊ'sɪlɪtɪ) NOUN

dock¹ (dɒk) NOUN 1 a wharf or pier. 2 a space between two wharves or piers for the mooring of ships. 3 an area of water that can accommodate a ship and can be closed off to allow regulation of the water level. 4 short for **dry dock.** 5 short for **scene dock.** 6 *Chiefly US and Canadian* a platform from which lorries, goods trains, etc., are loaded and unloaded. ◆ VERB 7 to moor (a vessel) at a dock or (of a vessel) to be moored at a dock. 8 to put (a vessel) into a dry dock for repairs or (of a vessel) to come into a dry dock. 9 (of two spacecraft) to link together in space or link together (two spacecraft) in space.
▷HISTORY C14: from Middle Dutch *docke;* perhaps related to Latin *ducere* to lead

dock² (dɒk) NOUN 1 the bony part of the tail of an animal, esp a dog or sheep. 2 the part of an animal's tail left after the major part of it has been cut off. ◆ VERB (*tr*) 3 to remove (the tail or part of the tail) of (an animal) by cutting through the bone: *to dock a tail; to dock a horse.* 4 to deduct (an amount) from (a person's wages, pension, etc.): *they docked a third of his wages.*
▷HISTORY C14: *dok,* of uncertain origin

dock³ (dɒk) NOUN an enclosed space in a court of law where the accused sits or stands during his trial.
▷HISTORY C16: from Flemish *dok* sty

dock⁴ (dɒk) NOUN 1 any of various temperate weedy plants of the polygonaceous genus *Rumex,* having greenish or reddish flowers and typically broad leaves. 2 any of several similar or related plants.
▷HISTORY Old English *docce;* related to Middle Dutch, Old Danish *docke,* Gaelic *dogha*

dockage¹ ('dɒkɪdʒ) NOUN 1 a charge levied upon a vessel for using a dock. 2 facilities for docking vessels. 3 the practice of docking vessels.

dockage² ('dɒkɪdʒ) NOUN 1 a deduction, as from a price or wages. 2 *Agriculture* the seeds of weeds and other waste material in commercial seeds, removable by normal cleaning methods.

docken ('dɒkᵊn) NOUN *Chiefly Scot* 1 another name for **dock⁴.** 2 something of no value or importance: *not worth a docken.*
▷HISTORY C14 *doken,* from Old English *doccan,* pl of *docce* DOCK⁴

docker¹ ('dɒkə) NOUN *Brit* a man employed in the loading or unloading of ships. US and Canadian equivalent: **longshoreman.** See also **stevedore.**

docker² ('dɒkə) NOUN a person or thing that docks something, such as the tail of a horse.

docket ('dɒkɪt) NOUN 1 *Chiefly Brit* a piece of paper accompanying or referring to a package or other delivery, stating contents, delivery instructions, etc., sometimes serving as a receipt. 2 *Law* **a** an official summary of the proceedings in a court of justice. **b** a register containing such a summary. 3 *Brit* **a** a customs certificate declaring that duty has been paid. **b** a certificate giving particulars of a shipment and allowing its holder to obtain a delivery order. 4 a summary of contents, as in a document. 5 *US* a list of things to be done. 6 *US law* **a** a list of cases awaiting trial. **b** the names of the parties to pending litigation. ◆ VERB (*tr*) 7 to fix a docket to (a package, etc.). 8 *Law* **a** to make a summary of (a document, judgment, etc.). **b** to abstract and enter in a book or register. 9 to endorse (a document, etc.) with a summary.
▷HISTORY C15: of unknown origin

dockland ('dɒkˌlænd) NOUN the area around the docks.

dockyard ('dɒkˌjɑːd) NOUN a naval establishment with docks, workshops, etc., for the building, fitting out, and repair of vessels.

Doc Martens (dɒk 'mɑːtənz) PLURAL NOUN *Trademark* a brand of lace-up boots with thick lightweight resistant soles. In full: **Doctor Martens.** Abbreviation: **DMs.**

doco ('dɒkəʊ) NOUN, *plural* **docos.** *Austral informal* short for **documentary.**

doctor ('dɒktə) NOUN 1 a person licensed to practise medicine. 2 a person who has been awarded a higher academic degree in any field of knowledge. 3 *Chiefly US and Canadian* a person licensed to practise dentistry or veterinary medicine. 4 (*often capital*) Also called: **Doctor of the Church.** a title given to any of several of the leading Fathers or theologians in the history of the Christian Church down to the late Middle Ages whose teachings have greatly influenced orthodox Christian thought. 5 *Angling* any of various gaudy artificial flies. 6 *Informal* a person who mends or repairs things. 7 *Slang* a cook on a ship or at a camp. 8 *Archaic* a man, esp a teacher, of learning. 9 a device used for local repair of electroplated surfaces, consisting of an anode of the plating material embedded in an absorbent material containing the solution. 10 (in a paper-making machine) a blade that is set to scrape the roller in order to regulate the thickness of pulp or ink on it. 11 **go for the doctor.** *Austral slang* to make a great effort or move very fast, esp in a horse race. 12 **what the doctor ordered.** something needed or desired. ◆ VERB 13 (*tr*) **a** to give medical treatment to. **b** to prescribe for (a disease or disorder). 14 (*intr*) *Informal* to practise medicine: *he doctored in Easter Island for six years.* 15 (*tr*) to repair or mend, esp in a makeshift manner. 16 (*tr*) to make different in order to deceive, tamper with, falsify, or adulterate. 17 (*tr*) to adapt for a desired end, effect, etc. 18 (*tr*) to castrate (a cat, dog, etc.).
▷HISTORY C14: from Latin: teacher, from *docēre* to teach
▸ **'doctoral** *or* **doctorial** (dɒk'tɔːrɪəl) ADJECTIVE

doctorate (ˈdɒktərɪt, -trɪt) NOUN the highest academic degree in any field of knowledge. Also called: **doctor's degree.**

Doctor of Philosophy NOUN a doctorate awarded for original research in any subject except law, medicine, or theology. Abbreviations: **PhD, DPhil.**

Doctor's Commons NOUN *Informal* the London building of the College of Advocates and Doctors of Law between 1572 and 1867, in which the ecclesiastical and Admiralty courts were housed.

doctrinaire (ˌdɒktrɪˈnɛə) ADJECTIVE [1] stubbornly insistent on the observation of the niceties of a theory, esp without regard to practicality, suitability, etc. [2] theoretical; impractical. ◆ NOUN [3] a person who stubbornly attempts to apply a theory without regard to practical difficulties. ▸ **ˌdoctriˈnairism** *or* **ˌdoctriˈnarism** NOUN ▸ **ˌdoctriˈnarian** NOUN

doctrine (ˈdɒktrɪn) NOUN [1] a creed or body of teachings of a religious, political, or philosophical group presented for acceptance or belief; dogma. [2] a principle or body of principles that is taught or advocated.
▷HISTORY C14: from Old French, from Latin *doctrīna* teaching, from *doctor* see DOCTOR
▸ **doctrinal** (dɒkˈtraɪnᵊl) ADJECTIVE ▸ **doctrinality** (ˌdɒktrɪˈnælɪtɪ) NOUN ▸ **docˈtrinally** ADVERB ▸ **ˈdoctrinism** NOUN ▸ **ˈdoctrinist** NOUN

doctrine of descent NOUN the theory that animals and plants arose by descent from previously existing organisms; theory of evolution.

docudrama (ˈdɒkjuˌdrɑːmə) NOUN a film or television programme based on true events, presented in a dramatized form.

document NOUN (ˈdɒkjumənt) [1] a piece of paper, booklet, etc., providing information, esp of an official or legal nature. [2] a piece of text or text and graphics stored in a computer as a file for manipulation by document processing software. [3] *Archaic* evidence; proof. ◆ VERB (ˈdɒkjuˌmɛnt) *(tr)* [4] to record or report in detail, as in the press, on television, etc.: *the trial was well documented by the media.* [5] to support (statements in a book) with citations, references, etc. [6] to support (a claim, etc.) with evidence or proof. [7] to furnish (a vessel) with official documents specifying its ownership, registration, weight, dimensions, and function.
▷HISTORY C15: from Latin *documentum* a lesson, from *docēre* to teach

documentary (ˌdɒkjuˈmɛntərɪ, -trɪ) ADJECTIVE [1] Also: **documental.** consisting of, derived from, or relating to documents. [2] presenting factual material with little or no fictional additions: *the book gives a documentary account of the war.* ◆ NOUN, *plural* **-ries.** [3] a factual film or television programme about an event, person, etc., presenting the facts with little or no fiction.
▸ **ˌdocuˈmentarily** ADVERB

documentation (ˌdɒkjumɛnˈteɪʃən) NOUN [1] the act of supplying with or using documents or references. [2] the documents or references supplied. [3] the furnishing and use of documentary evidence, as in a court of law. [4] *Computing* the written comments, graphical illustrations, flowcharts, manuals, etc., supplied with a program or software system.

document reader NOUN *Computing* a device that reads and inputs into a computer marks and characters on a special form, as by optical or magnetic character recognition.

docu-soap (ˈdɒkjuˌsəup) NOUN a television documentary series in which the lives of the people filmed are presented as entertainment or drama.
▷HISTORY C20: from DOCU(MENTARY) + SOAP (OPERA)

DOD (in the US) ABBREVIATION FOR Department of Defense.

dodder¹ (ˈdɒdə) VERB *(intr)* [1] to move unsteadily; totter. [2] to shake or tremble, as from age.
▷HISTORY C17: variant of earlier *dadder;* related to Norwegian *dudra* to tremble
▸ **ˈdodderer** NOUN ▸ **ˈdoddery** ADJECTIVE

dodder² (ˈdɒdə) NOUN any rootless parasitic plant of the convolvulaceous genus *Cuscuta,* lacking chlorophyll and having slender twining stems with suckers for drawing nourishment from the host plant, scalelike leaves, and whitish flowers.
▷HISTORY C13: of Germanic origin; related to Middle Dutch, Middle Low German *dodder,* Middle High German *toter*

doddering (ˈdɒdərɪŋ) ADJECTIVE shaky, feeble, or infirm, esp from old age.

doddle (ˈdɒdᵊl) NOUN *Brit informal* something easily accomplished.

dodeca- NOUN COMBINING FORM indicating twelve: *dodecagon; dodecahedron; dodecaphonic.*
▷HISTORY from Greek *dōdeka* twelve

dodecagon (dəuˈdɛkəˌgɒn) NOUN a polygon having twelve sides.
▸ **dodecagonal** (ˌdəudɛˈkægənᵊl) ADJECTIVE

dodecahedron (ˌdəudɛkəˈhiːdrən) NOUN a solid figure having twelve plane faces. A **regular dodecahedron** has regular pentagons as faces. See also **polyhedron.**
▸ **ˌdodecaˈhedral** ADJECTIVE

Dodecanese (ˌdəudɪkəˈniːz) PLURAL NOUN a group of islands in the SE Aegean Sea, forming a department of Greece: part of the Southern Sporades. Capital: Rhodes. Pop.: 162 439 (1991). Area: 2663 sq. km (1028 sq. miles). Modern Greek name: **Dhodhekánisos.**

dodecanoic acid (ˌdəudɛkəˈnəuɪk) NOUN a crystalline fatty acid found as glycerides in many vegetable oils: used in making soaps, insecticides, and synthetic resins. Formula: $CH_3(CH_2)_{10}COOH$. Also called: **lauric acid.**
▷HISTORY C20: from *dodecane* (see DODECA-, -ANE)

dodecaphonic (ˌdəudɛkəˈfɒnɪk) ADJECTIVE of or relating to the twelve-tone system of serial music.
▸ **ˌdodecaˈphonism** NOUN ▸ **ˌdodecaˈphony** NOUN

dodecasyllable (ˌdəudɛkəˈsɪləbᵊl) NOUN *Prosody* a line of twelve syllables.

dodge (dɒdʒ) VERB [1] to avoid or attempt to avoid (a blow, discovery, etc.), as by moving suddenly. [2] to evade (questions, etc.) by cleverness or trickery. [3] *(intr) Bell-ringing* to make a bell change places with its neighbour when sounding in successive changes. [4] *(tr) Photog* to lighten or darken (selected areas on a print) by manipulating the light from an enlarger. ◆ NOUN [5] a plan or expedient contrived to deceive. [6] a sudden evasive or hiding movement. [7] a clever contrivance. [8] *Bell-ringing* the act of dodging.
▷HISTORY C16: of unknown origin

dodge ball NOUN a game in which the players form a circle and try to hit opponents in the circle with a large ball.

Dodge City NOUN a city in SW Kansas, on the Arkansas River: famous as a frontier town on the Santa Fe Trail. Pop.: 21 130 (1990).

Dodgem (ˈdɒdʒəm) NOUN *Trademark* another name for **bumper car.**

dodger (ˈdɒdʒə) NOUN [1] a person who evades or shirks. [2] a shifty dishonest person. [3] a canvas shelter, mounted on a ship's bridge or over the companionway of a sailing yacht to protect the helmsman from bad weather. [4] *Archaic, US and Austral* a handbill. [5] *Austral informal* food, esp bread.

dodgy (ˈdɒdʒɪ) ADJECTIVE **dodgier, dodgiest.** *Brit, Austral, and NZ informal* [1] risky, difficult, or dangerous. [2] uncertain or unreliable; tricky.

dodo (ˈdəudəu) NOUN, *plural* **dodos** *or* **dodoes.** [1] any flightless bird, esp *Raphus cucullatus,* of the recently extinct family *Raphidae* of Mauritius and adjacent islands: order *Columbiformes* (pigeons, etc.). They had a hooked bill, short stout legs, and greyish plumage. See also **ratite.** [2] *Informal* an intensely conservative or reactionary person who is unaware of changing fashions, ideas, etc. [3] **(as) dead as a dodo.** (of a person or thing) irretrievably defunct or out of date.
▷HISTORY C17: from Portuguese *doudo,* from *doudo* stupid
▸ **ˈdodoism** NOUN

Dodoma (ˈdəudəmə) NOUN a city in central Tanzania, the legislative capital of the country. Pop.: 203 833 (latest est.).

Dodona (dəuˈdəunə) NOUN an ancient Greek town in Epirus: seat of an ancient sanctuary and oracle of Zeus and later the religious centre of Pyrrhus' kingdom.
▸ **Dodonaean** *or* **Dodonean** (ˌdəudəuˈniːən) ADJECTIVE

do down VERB *(tr, adverb)* [1] to belittle or humiliate. [2] to deceive or cheat.

doe (dəu) NOUN, *plural* **does** *or* **doe.** the female of the deer, hare, rabbit, and certain other animals.
▷HISTORY Old English *dā;* related to Old English *dēon* to suck, Sanskrit *dhēnā* cow

Doe (dəu) NOUN [1] *Law* (formerly) the plaintiff in a fictitious action, Doe versus Roe, to test a point of law. See also **Roe.** [2] **John** *or* **Jane.** *US* an unknown or unidentified male or female person.

DOE *or* **DoE** ABBREVIATION FOR: [1] (in Canada and, formerly, in Britain) Department of the Environment. [2] (in the US) Department of Energy.

doek (dʊk) NOUN *South African informal* a square of cloth worn mainly by African women to cover the head, esp to indicate married status.
▷HISTORY C18: from Afrikaans: cloth

doer (ˈduːə) NOUN [1] a person or thing that does something or acts in a specified manner: *a doer of good.* [2] an active or energetic person. [3] a thriving animal, esp a horse.

does¹ (dʌz) VERB (used with a singular noun or the pronouns *he, she,* or *it*) a form of the present tense (indicative mood) of **do¹.**

does² (dʊəs) NOUN *South African taboo slang* a foolish or despicable person.
▷HISTORY Afrikaans

doeskin (ˈdəuˌskɪn) NOUN [1] the skin of a deer, lamb, or sheep. [2] a very supple leather made from this skin and used esp for gloves. [3] a heavy smooth satin-weave or twill-weave cloth. [4] *(modifier)* made of doeskin.

doff (dɒf) VERB *(tr)* [1] to take off or lift (one's hat) in salutation. [2] to remove (clothing).
▷HISTORY Old English *dōn of;* see DO¹, OFF; compare DON¹
▸ **ˈdoffer** NOUN

do for VERB *(preposition) Informal* [1] *(tr)* to convict of a crime or offence: *they did him for manslaughter.* [2] *(intr)* to cause the ruin, death, or defeat of: *the last punch did for him.* [3] *(intr)* to do housework for. [4] **do well for oneself.** to thrive or succeed.

dog (dɒg) NOUN [1] **a** a domesticated canine mammal, *Canis familiaris,* occurring in many breeds that show a great variety in size and form. **b** *(as modifier): dog biscuit.* [2] **a** any other carnivore of the family *Canidae,* such as the dingo and coyote. **b** *(as modifier): the dog family.* Related adjective: **canine.** [3] **a** the male of animals of the dog family. **b** *(as modifier): a dog fox.* [4] *(modifier)* **a** spurious, inferior, or useless: *dog Latin.* **b** *(in combination): dogberry.* [5] a mechanical device for gripping or holding, esp one of the axial slots by which gear wheels or shafts are engaged to transmit torque. [6] *Informal* a fellow; chap: *you lucky dog.* [7] *Informal* a man or boy regarded as unpleasant, contemptible, or wretched. [8] *Slang* an unattractive or boring girl or woman. [9] *US and Canadian informal* something unsatisfactory or inferior. [10] short for **firedog.** [11] any of various atmospheric phenomena. See **fogdog, seadog, sundog.** [12] **a dog's chance.** no chance at all. [13] **a dog's dinner** *or* **breakfast.** *Informal* something that is messy or bungled. [14] **a dog's life.** a wretched existence. [15] **dog eat dog.** ruthless competition or self-interest. [16] **like a dog's dinner.** *Informal* dressed smartly or ostentatiously. [17] **put on the dog.** *US and Canadian informal* to behave or dress in an ostentatious or showy manner. ◆ VERB **dogs, dogging, dogged.** *(tr)* [18] to pursue or follow after like a dog. [19] to trouble; plague: *to be dogged by ill health.* [20] to chase with a dog or dogs. [21] to grip, hold, or secure by a mechanical device. ◆ ADVERB [22] (usually in combination) thoroughly; utterly: *dog-tired.* ◆ See also **dogs.**
▷HISTORY Old English *docga,* of obscure origin
▸ **ˈdogˌlike** ADJECTIVE

dog and bone NOUN *Cockney rhyming slang* a telephone.

dogbane (ˈdɒgˌbeɪn) NOUN any of several North American apocynaceous plants of the genus *Apocynum,* esp *A. androsaemifolium,* having bell-shaped white or pink flowers: thought to be poisonous to dogs.

dogberry¹ (ˈdɒgˌbɛrɪ, -bərɪ, -brɪ) NOUN, *plural* **-ries.** [1] any of certain plants that have berry-like fruits, such as the European dogwood or the bearberry. [2] the fruit of any of these plants.

dogberry² (ˈdɒgˌbɛrɪ, -bərɪ, -brɪ) NOUN, *plural* **-ries.** *(sometimes capital)* a foolish, meddling, and usually old official.

▷HISTORY after *Dogberry,* character in Shakespeare's *Much Ado about Nothing* (1598)
▸ 'dogberry,ism NOUN

dog biscuit NOUN a hard biscuit for dogs.

dog box NOUN [1] *Austral informal* a compartment in a railway carriage with no corridor. [2] *NZ informal* disgrace; disfavour (in the phrase **in the dog box**).

dogcart ('dɒg,kɑːt) NOUN a light horse-drawn two-wheeled vehicle: originally, one containing a box or section for transporting gun dogs.

dog-catcher NOUN *Now chiefly US and Canadian* a local official whose job is to catch and impound stray dogs, cats, etc.

dog collar NOUN [1] a collar for a dog. [2] an informal name for a **clerical collar.** [3] *Informal* a tight-fitting necklace.

dog days PLURAL NOUN [1] the hot period of the summer reckoned in ancient times from the heliacal rising of Sirius (the Dog Star). [2] a period marked by inactivity.
▷HISTORY C16: translation of Late Latin *diēs caniculārēs,* translation of Greek *hēmerai kunades*

doge (dəʊdʒ) NOUN (formerly) the chief magistrate in the republics of Venice (until 1797) and Genoa (until 1805).
▷HISTORY C16: via French from Italian (Venetian dialect), from Latin *dux* leader
▸ 'dogeship NOUN

dog-ear VERB [1] *(tr)* to fold down the corner of (a page). [2] *Computing* to bookmark (a website). ◆ NOUN *also* **dog's-ear.** [3] a folded-down corner of a page. [4] *Computing* a bookmark.

dog-eared ADJECTIVE [1] having dog-ears. [2] shabby or worn.

dog-end NOUN an informal name for **cigarette end.**

dog fennel NOUN [1] another name for **mayweed.** [2] a weedy plant, *Eupatorium capillifolium,* of the southeastern US, having divided leaves and greenish rayless flower heads: family *Asteraceae* (composites).

dogfight ('dɒg,faɪt) NOUN [1] close quarters combat between fighter aircraft. [2] any rough violent fight.

dogfish ('dɒg,fɪʃ) NOUN, *plural* **-fish** *or* **-fishes.** [1] any of several small spotted European sharks, esp *Scyliorhinus caniculus* (**lesser spotted dogfish**): family *Scyliorhinidae.* [2] any small shark of the family *Squalidae,* esp *Squalus acanthias* (**spiny dogfish**), typically having a spine on each dorsal fin. [3] any small smooth-skinned shark of the family *Triakidae,* esp *Mustelus canis* (**smooth dogfish** or **smooth hound**). [4] a less common name for the **bowfin.**

dogged ('dɒgɪd) ADJECTIVE obstinately determined; wilful or tenacious.
▸ 'doggedly ADVERB ▸ 'doggedness NOUN

dogger[1] ('dɒgə) NOUN a Dutch fishing vessel with two masts.
▷HISTORY C14: probably from Middle Dutch *dogge* trawler

dogger[2] ('dɒgə) NOUN a large concretion of consolidated material occurring in certain sedimentary rocks.
▷HISTORY C17: of uncertain origin

dogger[3] ('dɒgə) NOUN *Austral* a hunter of dingoes.
▷HISTORY C20: from DOG (see sense 2a) + -ER[1]

Dogger ('dɒgə) NOUN *Geology* a formation of mid-Jurassic rocks in N England.

Dogger Bank ('dɒgə) NOUN an extensive submerged sandbank in the North Sea between N England and Denmark: fishing ground.

doggerel ('dɒgərəl) *or* **dogrel** ('dɒgrəl) NOUN [1] **a** comic verse, usually irregular in measure. **b** (*as modifier*): *a doggerel rhythm.* [2] nonsense; drivel.
▷HISTORY C14 *dogerel* worthless, perhaps from *dogge* DOG

doggery ('dɒgərɪ) NOUN, *plural* **-geries.** [1] surly behaviour. [2] dogs collectively. [3] a mob.

Doggett's Coat and Badge race ('dɒgɪts) NOUN an annual rowing race held on the River Thames to commemorate the accession of George I: the winner is presented with a coat bearing an embroidered badge.
▷HISTORY C18: after Thomas Doggett (1670–1721), British actor who initiated it

doggish ('dɒgɪʃ) ADJECTIVE [1] of or like a dog. [2] surly; snappish.
▸ 'doggishly ADVERB ▸ 'doggishness NOUN

doggo ('dɒgəʊ) ADVERB *Brit informal* in hiding and keeping quiet (esp in the phrase **lie doggo**).
▷HISTORY C19: probably from DOG

doggone ('dɒgɒn) *US and Canadian informal* ◆ INTERJECTION [1] an exclamation of annoyance, disappointment, etc. ◆ ADJECTIVE (*prenominal*), ADVERB [2] Also: **doggoned.** another word for **damn** (senses 3, 4).
▷HISTORY C19: euphemism for *God damn*

doggy *or* **doggie** ('dɒgɪ) NOUN, *plural* **-gies.** [1] a children's word for a dog. ◆ ADJECTIVE [2] of, like, or relating to a dog. [3] fond of dogs.

doggy bag NOUN a bag into which leftovers from a meal may be put and taken away, supposedly for the diner's dog.

doggy paddle *or* **doggie paddle** NOUN [1] a swimming stroke in which the swimmer lies on his front, paddles his hands in imitation of a swimming dog, and beats his legs up and down. ◆ VERB **doggy-paddle, doggie-paddle.** [2] *(intr)* to swim using the doggy paddle. Also called: **dog paddle.**

dog handler NOUN a member of the police force, security organization, etc., who works in collaboration with a specially trained dog.

doghouse ('dɒg,haʊs) NOUN [1] the US and Canadian name for **kennel**[1]. [2] *Informal* disfavour (in the phrase **in the doghouse**).

dogie, dogy, *or* **dogey** ('dəʊgɪ) NOUN, *plural* **-gies** *or* **-geys.** *Western US and Canadian* a motherless calf.
▷HISTORY C19: from *dough-guts,* because they were fed on flour and water paste

dog in the manger NOUN **a** a person who prevents others from using something he has no use for. **b** (*as modifier*): *a dog-in-the-manger attitude.*

dog Latin NOUN spurious or incorrect Latin.

dogleg ('dɒg,lɛg) NOUN [1] **a** a sharp bend or angle. **b** something with a sharp bend. ◆ VERB **-legs, -legging, -legged.** [2] *(intr)* to go off at an angle. ◆ ADJECTIVE [3] of or with the shape of a dogleg.
▸ doglegged (,dɒg'lɛgɪd, 'dɒg,lɛgd) ADJECTIVE

dogleg fence NOUN *Austral* a fence made of sloping poles supported by forked uprights.

dogma ('dɒgmə) NOUN, *plural* **-mas** *or* **-mata** (-mətə). [1] a religious doctrine or system of doctrines proclaimed by ecclesiastical authority as true. [2] a belief, principle, or doctrine or a code of beliefs, principles, or doctrines: *Marxist dogma.*
▷HISTORY C17: via Latin from Greek: opinion, belief, from *dokein* to seem good

dogman ('dɒgmən) NOUN, *plural* **-men.** *Austral* a person who directs the operation of a crane whilst riding on an object being lifted by it.

dogmatic (dɒg'mætɪk) *or* **dogmatical** ADJECTIVE [1] **a** (of a statement, opinion, etc.) forcibly asserted as if authoritative and unchallengeable. **b** (of a person) prone to making such statements. [2] of, relating to, or constituting dogma: *dogmatic writings.* [3] based on assumption rather than empirical observation.
▸ dog'matically ADVERB

dogmatics (dɒg'mætɪks) NOUN (*functioning as singular*) the study of religious dogmas and doctrines. Also called: **dogmatic** (*or* **doctrinal**) **theology.**

dogmatist ('dɒgmətɪst) NOUN [1] a dogmatic person. [2] a person who formulates dogmas.

dogmatize *or* **dogmatise** ('dɒgmə,taɪz) VERB to say or state (something) in a dogmatic manner.
▸ 'dogmatism NOUN ▸ ,dogmati'zation *or* ,dogmati'sation NOUN ▸ 'dogma,tizer *or* 'dogma,tiser NOUN

Dogme ('dɒgmɪ) NOUN a group of Danish film-makers, formed by Lars von Trier and Thomas Vinterberg, who have a set of strict rules, such as not using artificial lighting, always filming on location, and always using a hand-held camera.
▷HISTORY Danish: literally, dogma

dognap ('dɒgnæp) VERB **-naps, -napping, -napped** *or US* **-naps, -naping, -naped** *(tr)* to carry off and hold (a dog), usually for ransom.
▷HISTORY C20:from DOG + KIDNAP
▸ 'dognapper NOUN ▸ 'dognapping *or US* 'dognaping NOUN

do-gooder NOUN *Informal, usually disparaging* a well-intentioned person, esp a naive or impractical one.
▸ ,do-'goodery NOUN ▸ ,do-'gooding NOUN, ADJECTIVE

dog paddle NOUN another name for **doggy paddle.**

Dogrib ('dɒg,rɪb) NOUN [1] a member of a Dene Native Canadian people of northern Canada. [2] the Athapascan language of this people.
▷HISTORY from Dogrib *Thlingchadinne,* dog's flank, referring to the people's belief that they are descended from a dog

dog rose NOUN a prickly wild rose, *Rosa canina,* that is native to Europe and has pink or white delicate scentless flowers.
▷HISTORY translation of the Latin name, from Greek; from the belief that its root was effective against the bite of a mad dog

dogs (dɒgz) PLURAL NOUN [1] **the.** *Brit informal* greyhound racing. [2] *Slang* the feet. [3] *Marketing informal* goods with a low market share, which are unlikely to yield substantial profits. [4] **go to the dogs.** *Informal* to go to ruin physically or morally. [5] **let sleeping dogs lie.** to leave things undisturbed. [6] **throw (someone) to the dogs.** to abandon (someone) to criticism or attack.

Dogs (dɒgz) NOUN **Isle of.** a district in the East End of London, bounded on three sides by the River Thames.

dogsbody ('dɒgz,bɒdɪ) NOUN, *plural* **-bodies.** [1] *Informal* a person who carries out menial tasks for others; drudge. ◆ VERB **-bodies, -bodying, -bodied.** [2] *(intr)* to act as a dogsbody.

dog-sitter NOUN a person who looks after a dog while its owner is away.

dogsled ('dɒg,slɛd) NOUN *Chiefly US and Canadian* a sleigh drawn by dogs. Also called: (Brit) **dog sledge, dog sleigh.**

dog's mercury NOUN a hairy somewhat poisonous euphorbiaceous perennial, *Mercurialis perennis,* having broad lanceolate toothed leaves and small greenish male and female flowers, the males borne in catkins. It often carpets shady woodlands.

dog's-tail NOUN any of several grasses of the genus *Cynosurus,* esp *C. cristatus* (crested dog's-tail), that are native to Europe and have flowers clustered in a dense narrow spike.

Dog Star NOUN **the.** another name for **Sirius.**

dog's-tongue NOUN another name for **hound's-tongue.**

dog's-tooth check *or* **dog-tooth check** NOUN other names for **hound's-tooth check.**

dog tag NOUN *US slang* a military personal-identification disc.

dog-tired ADJECTIVE (*usually postpositive*) *Informal* exhausted.

dogtooth ('dɒg,tuːθ) NOUN, *plural* **-teeth.** [1] another name for a **canine** (sense 3). [2] *Architect* a carved ornament in the form of four leaflike projections radiating from a raised centre, used in England in the 13th century.

dogtooth violet NOUN a name for various plants of the liliaceous genus *Erythronium,* esp the North American *E. americanum,* with yellow nodding flowers, or the European *E. dens-canis,* with purple flowers. Also called: **adders-tongue, fawn lily.**

dog train NOUN *Canadian* a sleigh drawn by a team of dogs.

dogtrot ('dɒg,trɒt) NOUN a gently paced trot.

dog tucker NOUN *NZ* the meat of a sheep killed on a farm and used as dog food.

dogvane ('dɒg,veɪn) NOUN *Nautical* a light windvane consisting of a feather or a piece of cloth or yarn mounted on the side of a vessel. Also called: **telltale.**

dog violet NOUN a violet, *Viola canina,* that grows in Europe and N Asia and has blue yellow-spurred flowers.

dogwatch ('dɒg,wɒtʃ) NOUN [1] either of two two-hour watches aboard ship, from four to six p.m. or from six to eight p.m. [2] *NZ* a shift from midnight to six a.m. in a mine.

dogwood ('dɒg,wʊd) NOUN any of various cornaceous trees or shrubs of the genus *Cornus,* esp *C. sanguinea,* a European shrub with clusters of small white flowers and black berries: the shoots are red in winter.

dogy ('dəʊgɪ) NOUN, *plural* **-gies.** a variant spelling of **dogie.**

doh[1] (dəʊ) NOUN, *plural* **dohs.** [1] *Music* (in tonic sol-fa) the first degree of any major scale. [2] **up to high doh.** *Informal, chiefly Scot* extremely excited or keyed up.
▷HISTORY C18: from Italian; see GAMUT

doh[2] (dəʊ) INTERJECTION *Informal* an exclamation of annoyance when something goes wrong.

DoH (in Britain) ABBREVIATION FOR Department of Health.

Doha ('dəʊhɑː, 'dəʊə) NOUN the capital and chief port of Qatar, on the E coast of the peninsula. Pop.: 264 009 (1997). Former name: **Bida, El Beda.**

doily, doyley, *or* **doyly** ('dɔɪlɪ) NOUN, *plural* **-lies** *or* **-leys.** a decorative mat of lace or lacelike paper, etc., laid on or under plates.
▷HISTORY C18: named after *Doily,* a London draper

do in VERB *(tr, adverb) Slang* [1] to murder or kill. [2] to exhaust.

doing ('duːɪŋ) NOUN [1] an action or the performance of an action: *whose doing is this?* [2] *Informal* a beating or castigation.

doings ('duːɪŋz) PLURAL NOUN [1] deeds, actions or events. [2] *Brit and NZ informal* anything of which the name is not known, or euphemistically left unsaid, etc.: *have you got the doings for starting the car?*

doit (dɔɪt) NOUN [1] a former small copper coin of the Netherlands. [2] a trifle.
▷HISTORY C16: from Middle Dutch *duit*

doited ('dɔɪtɪd) *or* **doitit** ('dɔɪtɪt) ADJECTIVE *Scot* foolish or childish, as from senility.
▷HISTORY C15: probably from *doten* to DOTE

do-it-yourself NOUN **a** the hobby or process of constructing and repairing things oneself. **b** *(as modifier): a do-it-yourself kit.*

dojo ('dəʊdʒəʊ) NOUN, *plural* **-jos.** a room or hall for the practice of martial arts.
▷HISTORY C20: from Japanese *dōjō* Buddhist seminary, from Sanskrit *bodhi-manda* seat of wisdom

dol (dɒl) NOUN a unit of pain intensity, as measured by dolorimetry.
▷HISTORY C20: by shortening, from Latin *dolor* pain

dol. ABBREVIATION FOR: [1] *Music* dolce. [2] *(plural* **dols)** dollar.

dolabriform (dəʊ'læbrɪˌfɔːm) *or* **dolabrate** (dəʊ'læbreɪt) ADJECTIVE *Biology* shaped like a hatchet or axe head.
▷HISTORY C18: from Latin *dolābra* pickaxe

Dolby ('dɒlbɪ) NOUN *Trademark* any of various specialized electronic circuits, esp those used for noise reduction in tape recorders by functioning as companders on high-frequency signals.
▷HISTORY named after R. *Dolby* (born 1933), its US inventor

dolce ('dɒltʃɪ; *Italian* 'doltʃe) ADJECTIVE, ADVERB *Music* (to be performed) gently and sweetly.
▷HISTORY Italian: sweet

dolce far niente *Italian* ('doltʃe far 'njente) NOUN pleasant idleness.
▷HISTORY literally: sweet doing nothing

Dolcelatte (ˌdɒltʃiː'lɑːtɪ) NOUN a soft creamy blue-veined cheese made in Italy.
▷HISTORY Italian, literally: sweet milk

dolce vita ('dɒltʃɪ 'viːtə; *Italian* 'doltʃe 'vita) NOUN a life of luxury.
▷HISTORY Italian, literally: sweet life

doldrums ('dɒldrəmz) NOUN **the.** [1] a depressed or bored state of mind. [2] a state of inactivity or stagnation. [3] **a** a belt of light winds or calms along the equator. **b** the weather conditions experienced in this belt, formerly a hazard to sailing vessels.
▷HISTORY C19: probably from Old English *dol* DULL, influenced by TANTRUM

dole[1] (dəʊl) NOUN [1] a small portion or share, as of money or food, given to a poor person. [2] the act of giving or distributing such portions. [3] (usually preceded by *the) Brit informal* money received from the state while out of work. [4] **on the dole.** *Brit informal* receiving such money. [5] *Archaic* fate. ◆ VERB [6] *(tr; usually foll by out)* to distribute, esp in small portions.
▷HISTORY Old English *dāl* share; related to Old Saxon *dēl,* Old Norse *deild,* Gothic *dails,* Old High German *teil;* see DEAL[1]

dole[2] (dəʊl) NOUN *Archaic* grief or mourning.
▷HISTORY C13: from Old French, from Late Latin *dolus,* from Latin *dolēre* to lament

dole bludger NOUN *Austral slang, offensive* a person who draws unemployment benefit without making any attempt to find work.

doleful ('dəʊlfʊl) ADJECTIVE dreary; mournful. Archaic word: **dolesome** ('dəʊlsəm).
▸'**dolefully** ADVERB ▸'**dolefulness** NOUN

dolente (dɒ'lɛntɪ) ADJECTIVE, ADVERB *Music* (to be performed) in a sorrowful manner.

dolerite ('dɒləˌraɪt) NOUN [1] a dark basic intrusive igneous rock consisting of plagioclase feldspar and a pyroxene, such as augite; often emplaced in dykes. [2] any dark igneous rock whose composition cannot be determined with the naked eye.
▷HISTORY C19: from French *dolérite,* from Greek *doleros* deceitful; so called because of the difficulty of determining its composition
▸**doleritic** (ˌdɒlə'rɪtɪk) ADJECTIVE

Dolgellau (dɒl'geθlaɪ; *Welsh* dɒl'gɛhlaɪ) NOUN a market town and tourist centre in NW Wales, in Gwynedd. Pop.: 2396 (1991).

dolichocephalic (ˌdɒlɪkəʊsɪ'fælɪk) *or* **dolichocephalous** (ˌdɒlɪkəʊ'sɛfələs) ADJECTIVE [1] having a head much longer than it is broad, esp one with a cephalic index under 75. ◆ NOUN [2] an individual with such a head. ◆ Compare **brachycephalic, mesocephalic, scaphocephalic.**
▸ˌ**dolicho'cephalism** *or* ˌ**dolicho'cephaly** NOUN

dolichosaurus (ˌdɒlɪkəʊ'sɔːrəs) NOUN any of various extinct Cretaceous aquatic reptiles that had long necks and bodies and well-developed limbs.
▷HISTORY C20: from Greek, from *dolikhos* long + -SAUR

doline *or* **dolina** (də'liːnə) NOUN a shallow usually funnel-shaped depression of the ground surface formed by solution in limestone regions.
▷HISTORY C20: from Russian *dolina,* valley, plain; related to DALE

doll (dɒl) NOUN [1] a small model or dummy of a human being, used as a toy. [2] *Slang* a pretty girl or woman of little intelligence: sometimes used as a term of address.
▷HISTORY C16: probably from *Doll,* pet name for *Dorothy*
▸'**dollish** ADJECTIVE ▸'**dollishly** ADVERB ▸'**dollishness** NOUN

dollar ('dɒlə) NOUN [1] the standard monetary unit of the US and its dependencies, divided into 100 cents. [2] the standard monetary unit, comprising 100 cents, of the following countries or territories: Antigua and Barbuda, Australia, the Bahamas, Barbados, Belize, Bermuda, the British Virgin Islands, Brunei, Canada, the Cayman Islands, Dominica, East Timor, Ecuador, El Salvador, Fiji, Grenada, Guatemala, Guyana, Hong Kong, Jamaica, Kiribati, Liberia, Malaysia, the Marshall Islands, Micronesia, Namibia, Nauru, New Zealand, Saint Kitts and Nevis, Saint Lucia, Saint Vincent and the Grenadines, Singapore, Solomon Islands, Taiwan, Trinidad and Tobago, Tuvalu, and Zimbabwe. [3] *Brit informal* (formerly) five shillings or a coin of this value. [4] **look** *or* **feel (like) a million dollars.** *Informal* to look *or* feel extremely well.
▷HISTORY C16: from Low German *daler,* from German *Taler, Thaler,* short for *Joachimsthaler* coin made from metal mined in *Joachimsthal* Jachymov, town now in the Czech Republic

dollarbird ('dɒləˌbɜːd) NOUN a bird, *Eurystomus orientalis,* of S and SE Asia and Australia, with a round white spot on each wing: family *Coraciidae* (rollers), order *Coraciiformes.*

dollar diplomacy NOUN *Chiefly US* [1] a foreign policy that encourages and protects capital investment and commercial and financial involvement abroad. [2] use of financial power as a diplomatic weapon.

dollarfish ('dɒləˌfɪʃ) NOUN, *plural* **-fish** *or* **-fishes.** any of various fishes that have a rounded compressed silvery body, esp the moonfishes or the American butterfish.

dollarization *or* **dollarisation** (ˌdɒləraɪ'zeɪʃən) NOUN the process of converting a country's currency to US dollars.

dollop ('dɒləp) *Informal* ◆ NOUN [1] a semisolid lump. [2] a large serving, esp of food. ◆ VERB [3] *(tr; foll by out)* to serve out (food).
▷HISTORY C16: of unknown origin

doll up VERB *(tr, adverb) Slang* to adorn or dress (oneself or another, esp a child) in a stylish or showy manner.

dolly ('dɒlɪ) NOUN, *plural* **-lies.** [1] a child's word for a **doll.** [2] *Films, television* a wheeled support on which a camera may be mounted. [3] a cup-shaped anvil held against the head of a rivet while the other end is being hammered. [4] a shaped block of lead used to hammer dents out of sheet metal. [5] a distance piece placed between the head of a pile and the pile-driver to form an extension to the length of the pile. [6] *Cricket* a simple catch. [7] Also called: **dolly bird.** *Slang, chiefly Brit* an attractive and fashionable girl, esp one who is considered to be unintelligent. ◆ VERB **-lies, -lying, -lied.** [8] *Films, television* to wheel (a camera) backwards or forwards on a dolly.

dolly-posh ADJECTIVE *Northern English dialect* left-handed.

Dolly Varden ('dɒlɪ 'vɑːdᵊn) NOUN [1] a woman's large-brimmed hat trimmed with flowers. [2] a red-spotted trout, *Salvelinus malma,* occurring in lakes in W North America.
▷HISTORY C19: from the name of a character in Dickens' *Barnaby Rudge* (1841)

dolma ('dɒlmə, -mɑː) NOUN, *plural* **dolmas, dolmades** (dɒl'mɑːdiːz). a vine leaf stuffed with a filling of meat and rice.
▷HISTORY C19: Turkish *dolma* literally something filled

dolman ('dɒlmən) NOUN, *plural* **-mans.** [1] a long Turkish outer robe. [2] Also called: **dolman jacket.** a hussar's jacket worn slung over the shoulder. [3] a woman's cloak with voluminous capelike sleeves.
▷HISTORY C16: via French from German *Dolman,* from Turkish *dolaman* a winding round, from *dolamak* to wind

dolman sleeve NOUN a sleeve that is very wide at the armhole and tapers to a tight wrist.

dolmen ('dɒlmɛn) NOUN [1] (in British archaeology) a Neolithic stone formation, consisting of a horizontal stone supported by several vertical stones, and thought to be a tomb. [2] (in French archaeology) any megalithic tomb.
▷HISTORY C19: from French, probably from Old Breton *tol* table, from Latin *tabula* board + Breton *mēn* stone, of Celtic origin; see TABLE

dolomite ('dɒləˌmaɪt) NOUN [1] a white mineral often tinted by impurities, found in sedimentary rocks and veins. It is used in the manufacture of cement and as a building stone (marble). Composition: calcium magnesium carbonate. Formula: $CaMg(CO_3)_2$. Crystal structure: hexagonal (rhombohedral). [2] a sedimentary rock resembling limestone but consisting principally of the mineral dolomite. It is an important source of magnesium and its compounds, and is used as a building material and refractory.
▷HISTORY C18: named after Déodat de *Dolomieu* (1750–1801), French mineralogist
▸**dolomitic** (ˌdɒlə'mɪtɪk) ADJECTIVE

Dolomites ('dɒləˌmaɪts) PLURAL NOUN a mountain range in NE Italy: part of the Alps; formed of dolomitic limestone. Highest peak: Marmolada, 3342 m (10 965 ft.).

dolorimetry (ˌdɒlə'rɪmətrɪ) NOUN a technique for measuring the level of pain perception by applying heat to the skin.

doloroso (ˌdɒlə'rəʊsəʊ) ADJECTIVE, ADVERB *Music* (to be performed) in a sorrowful manner.
▷HISTORY Italian: dolorous

dolorous ('dɒlərəs) ADJECTIVE causing or involving pain or sorrow.
▸'**dolorously** ADVERB ▸'**dolorousness** NOUN

dolos ('dɒlɒs) NOUN, *plural* **-osse.** *South African* a knucklebone of a sheep, buck, etc., used esp by diviners.
▷HISTORY from Afrikaans, possibly from *dollen* play + *os* ox or from *dobbel* dice + *os* ox

dolostone ('dɒləˌstəʊn) NOUN rock composed of the mineral dolomite.

dolour *or US* **dolor** ('dɒlə) NOUN *Poetic* grief or sorrow.
▷HISTORY C14: from Latin, from *dolēre* to grieve

dolphin ('dɒlfɪn) NOUN [1] any of various marine cetacean mammals of the family *Delphinidae,* esp *Delphinus delphis,* that are typically smaller than whales and larger than porpoises and have a

beaklike snout. 2 **river dolphin.** any freshwater cetacean of the family *Platanistidae,* inhabiting rivers of North and South America and S Asia. They are smaller than marine dolphins and have a longer narrower snout. 3 Also called: **dorado.** either of two large marine percoid fishes, *Coryphaena hippurus* or *C. equisetis,* that resemble the cetacean dolphins and have an iridescent coloration. 4 *Nautical* a post or buoy for mooring a vessel.
▷HISTORY C13: from Old French *dauphin,* via Latin, from Greek *delphin-, delphis*

dolphinarium (ˌdɒlfɪˈnɛərɪəm) NOUN a pool or aquarium for dolphins, esp one in which they give public displays.

dolphin striker NOUN *Nautical* a short vertical strut between the bowsprit and a rope or cable (martingale) from the end of the jib boom to the stem or bows, used for maintaining tension and preventing upward movement of the jib boom. Also called: **martingale boom, martingale.**

dolt (dəʊlt) NOUN a slow-witted or stupid person.
▷HISTORY C16: probably related to Old English *dol* stupid; see DULL
▸ˈ**doltish** ADJECTIVE ▸ˈ**doltishly** ADVERB ▸ˈ**doltishness** NOUN

dom (dɒm) NOUN 1 (*sometimes capital*) *RC Church* a title given to Benedictine, Carthusian, and Cistercian monks and to certain of the canons regular. 2 (formerly in Portugal and Brazil) a title borne by royalty, princes of the Church, and nobles.
▷HISTORY C18 (monastic title): from Latin *dominus* lord

DOM ABBREVIATION FOR: 1 Deo Optimo Maximo. [Latin: to God, the best, the Greatest] 2 *Informal* Dirty Old Man. ◆ 3 INTERNATIONAL CAR REGISTRATION FOR Dominican Republic.

Dom. *RC Church* ABBREVIATION FOR Dominican.

-dom SUFFIX FORMING NOUNS 1 state or condition: *freedom; martyrdom.* 2 rank or office: *earldom.* 3 domain: *kingdom; Christendom.* 4 a collection of persons: *officialdom.*
▷HISTORY Old English *-dōm*

domain (dəˈmeɪn) NOUN 1 land governed by a ruler or government. 2 land owned by one person or family. 3 a field or scope of knowledge or activity. 4 a region having specific characteristics or containing certain types of plants or animals. 5 *Austral and NZ* a park or recreation reserve maintained by a public authority, often the government. 6 *Law* the absolute ownership and right to dispose of land. See also **demesne, eminent domain.** 7 *Maths* **a** the set of values of the independent variable of a function for which the functional value exists: *the domain of sin x is all real numbers.* Compare **range** (sense 8a). **b** any open set containing at least one point. 8 *Logic* another term for **universe of discourse** (esp in the phrase **domain of quantification**). 9 *Philosophy* range of significance (esp in the phrase **domain of definition**). 10 Also called: **magnetic domain.** *Physics* one of the regions in a ferromagnetic solid in which all the atoms have their magnetic moments aligned in the same direction. 11 *Computing* a group of computers that have the same suffix (**domain name**) in their names on the Internet, specifying the country, type of institution, etc. where they are located. 12 Also called: **superkingdom.** *Biology* the highest level of classification of living organisms. Three domains are recognized: *Archaea* (see **archaean**), *Bacteria* (see **bacteria**), and *Eukarya* (see **eukaryote**). 13 *Biochem* a structurally compact portion of a protein molecule.
▷HISTORY C17: from French *domaine,* from Latin *dominium* property, from *dominus* lord

domain name NOUN *Computing* the suffix in a computer's Internet name, specifying the country, type of institution, etc., where it is located.

domatium (dɒˈmeɪʃɪəm) NOUN, *plural* **-tia.** *Botany* a plant cavity inhabited by commensal insects or mites or, occasionally, microorganisms.

dome (dəʊm) NOUN 1 a hemispherical roof or vault or a structure of similar form. 2 something shaped like this. 3 *Crystallog* a crystal form in which two planes intersect along an edge parallel to a lateral axis. 4 a slang word for the **head.** 5 *Geology* **a** a structure in which rock layers slope away in all directions from a central point. **b** another name for **pericline** (sense 2). ◆ VERB (*tr*) 6 to cover with or as if with a dome. 7 to shape like a dome.
▷HISTORY C16: from French, from Italian *duomo* cathedral, from Latin *domus* house
▸ˈ**dome,like** ADJECTIVE ▸**domical** (ˈdəʊmɪkᵊl, ˈdɒm-) ADJECTIVE

dome fastener NOUN the usual Canadian name for **press stud.**

Dome of the Rock NOUN the mosque in Jerusalem, Israel, built in 691 A.D. by caliph 'Abd al-Malik: the third most holy place of Islam; stands on the Temple Mount alongside the **al-Aqsa** mosque. Also called (not in Muslim usage): **Mosque of Omar.**

domesday (ˈduːmzˌdeɪ) NOUN a variant spelling of **doomsday.**

Domesday Book *or* **Doomsday Book** NOUN *History* the record of a survey of the land of England carried out by the commissioners of William I in 1086.

domestic (dəˈmɛstɪk) ADJECTIVE 1 of or involving the home or family. 2 enjoying or accustomed to home or family life. 3 (of an animal) bred or kept by man as a pet or for purposes such as the supply of food. 4 of, produced in, or involving one's own country or a specific country: *domestic and foreign affairs.* ◆ NOUN 5 a household servant. 6 *Informal* (esp in police use) an incident of violence in the home, esp between a man and a woman.
▷HISTORY C16: from Old French *domestique,* from Latin *domesticus* belonging to the house, from *domus* house
▸**doˈmestically** ADVERB

domesticate (dəˈmɛstɪˌkeɪt) *or sometimes US* **domesticize** (dəˈmɛstɪˌsaɪz) VERB (*tr*) 1 to bring or keep (wild animals or plants) under control or cultivation. 2 to accustom to home life. 3 to adapt to an environment: *to domesticate foreign trees.*
▸**doˈmesticable** ADJECTIVE ▸**doˌmestiˈcation** NOUN ▸**doˈmesticative** ADJECTIVE ▸**doˈmestiˌcator** NOUN

domestic court NOUN (in England) a magistrates' court for domestic proceedings, such as matrimonial, guardianship, custodianship, affiliation, or adoption disputes.

domestic fowl NOUN a domesticated gallinaceous bird thought to be descended from the red jungle fowl (*Gallus gallus*) and occurring in many varieties. Often shortened to: **fowl.**

domesticity (ˌdəʊmɛˈstɪsɪtɪ) NOUN, *plural* **-ties.** 1 home life. 2 devotion to or familiarity with home life. 3 (*usually plural*) a domestic duty, matter, or condition.

domestic science NOUN the study of cooking, needlework, and other subjects concerned with household skills.

domicile (ˈdɒmɪˌsaɪl) *or* **domicil** (ˈdɒmɪsɪl) *Formal* ◆ NOUN 1 a dwelling place. 2 a permanent legal residence. 3 *Commerce, Brit* the place where a bill of exchange is to be paid. ◆ VERB *also* **domiciliate** (ˌdɒmɪˈsɪlɪˌeɪt). 4 to establish or be established in a dwelling place.
▷HISTORY C15: from Latin *domicilium,* from *domus* house

domiciliary (ˌdɒmɪˈsɪlɪərɪ) ADJECTIVE of, involving, or taking place in the home.

domiciliary care *or* **services** NOUN *Social welfare* services, such as meals-on-wheels, health visiting, and home help, provided by a welfare agency for people in their own homes.

dominance (ˈdɒmɪnəns) NOUN control; ascendancy.

dominant (ˈdɒmɪnənt) ADJECTIVE 1 having primary control, authority, or influence; governing; ruling. 2 predominant or primary: *the dominant topic of the day.* 3 occupying a commanding position. 4 *Genetics* **a** (of an allele) producing the same phenotype in the organism irrespective of whether the allele of the same gene is identical or dissimilar. **b** (of a character) controlled by such a gene. Compare **recessive** (sense 2). 5 *Music* of or relating to the fifth degree of a scale. 6 *Ecology* (of a plant or animal species within a community) more prevalent than any other species and determining the appearance and composition of the community. ◆ NOUN 7 *Genetics* **a** a dominant allele or character. **b** an organism having such an allele or character. 8 *Music* **a** the fifth degree of a scale and the second in importance after the tonic. **b** a key or chord based on this. 9 *Ecology* a dominant plant or animal in a community.
▸ˈ**dominantly** ADVERB

dominant hemisphere NOUN See **cerebral dominance.**

dominant seventh chord NOUN a chord consisting of the dominant and the major third, perfect fifth, and minor seventh above it. Its most natural resolution is to a chord on the tonic.

dominant tenement NOUN *Property law* the land or tenement with the benefit of an easement over land belonging to another. Compare **servient tenement.**

dominant wavelength NOUN *Physics* the wavelength of monochromatic light that would give the same visual sensation if combined in a suitable proportion with an achromatic light. See also **complementary wavelength.**

dominate (ˈdɒmɪˌneɪt) VERB 1 to control, rule, or govern (someone or something). 2 to tower above (surroundings, etc.); overlook. 3 (*tr; usually passive*) to predominate in (something or someone).
▷HISTORY C17: from Latin *dominārī* to be lord over, from *dominus* lord
▸ˈ**domiˌnating** ADJECTIVE ▸ˈ**domiˌnatingly** ADVERB ▸ˈ**dominative** ADJECTIVE ▸ˈ**domiˌnator** NOUN

domination (ˌdɒmɪˈneɪʃən) NOUN 1 the act of dominating or state of being dominated. 2 authority; rule; control.

dominations (ˌdɒmɪˈneɪʃənz) PLURAL NOUN (*sometimes capital*) the fourth order of medieval angelology. Also called: **dominions.**

dominatrix (ˌdɒmɪˈneɪtrɪks) NOUN, *plural* **dominatrices** (ˌdɒmɪnəˈtraɪsiːz). 1 a woman who is the dominant sexual partner in a sadomasochistic relationship. 2 a dominant woman.
▷HISTORY C16: from Latin, fem of *dominātor,* from *dominārī* to be lord over

dominee (ˈduːmɪnɪ, ˈdʊə-) NOUN (in South Africa) a minister in any of the Afrikaner Churches. Also called: **predikant.**
▷HISTORY from Afrikaans, from Dutch; compare DOMINIE

domineer (ˌdɒmɪˈnɪə) VERB (*intr;* often foll by *over*) to act with arrogance or tyranny; behave imperiously.
▷HISTORY C16: from Dutch *domineren,* from French *dominer* to DOMINATE

domineering (ˌdɒmɪˈnɪərɪŋ) ADJECTIVE acting with or showing arrogance or tyranny; imperious.
▸ˌ**domiˈneeringly** ADVERB ▸ˌ**domiˈneeringness** NOUN

Dominica (ˌdɒmɪˈniːkə, dəˈmɪnɪkə) NOUN a republic in the E Caribbean, comprising a volcanic island in the Windward Islands group; a former British colony; became independent as a member of the Commonwealth in 1978. Official language: English. Religion: Roman Catholic majority. Currency: East Caribbean dollar. Capital: Roseau. Pop.: 71 700 (2001 est.). Area: 751 sq. km (290 sq. miles). Official name: **Commonwealth of Dominica.**

dominical (dəˈmɪnɪkᵊl) ADJECTIVE 1 of, relating to, or emanating from Jesus Christ as Lord. 2 of or relating to Sunday as the Lord's Day.
▷HISTORY C15: from Late Latin *dominicālis,* from Latin *dominus* lord

dominical letter NOUN *Christianity* any one of the letters A to G as used to denote Sundays in a given year in order to determine the church calendar.

Dominican[1] (dəˈmɪnɪkən) NOUN 1 **a** a member of an order of preaching friars founded by Saint Dominic (original name *Domingo de Guzman;* ?1170–1221), the Spanish priest, in 1215; a Blackfriar. **b** a nun of one of the orders founded under the patronage of Saint Dominic. ◆ ADJECTIVE 2 of or relating to Saint Dominic or the Dominican order.

Dominican[2] (dəˈmɪnɪkən) ADJECTIVE 1 of or relating to the Dominican Republic or Dominica. ◆ NOUN 2 a native or inhabitant of the Dominican Republic or Dominica.

Dominican Republic NOUN a republic in the Caribbean, occupying the eastern half of the island of Hispaniola: colonized by the Spanish after its discovery by Columbus in 1492; gained independence from Spain in 1821. It is generally mountainous, dominated by the Cordillera Central, which rises over 3000 m (10 000 ft.), with fertile lowlands. Language: Spanish. Religion: Roman Catholic majority. Currency: peso. Capital: Santo Domingo. Pop.: 8 693 000 (2001 est.). Area: 48 441 sq. km (18 703 sq. miles). Former name (until 1844): **Santo Domingo**.

dominie ('dɒmɪnɪ) NOUN [1] a Scot word for **schoolmaster.** [2] a minister or clergyman: also used as a term of address.
▷HISTORY C17: from Latin *dominē,* vocative case of *dominus* lord

dominion (də'mɪnjən) NOUN [1] rule; authority. [2] the land governed by one ruler or government. [3] sphere of influence; area of control. [4] a name formerly applied to self-governing divisions of the British Empire. [5] (*capital*) **the.** New Zealand. [6] *Law* a less common word for **dominium.**
▷HISTORY C15: from Old French, from Latin *dominium* ownership, from *dominus* master

Dominion Day NOUN the former name for **Canada Day.**

dominions (də'mɪnjənz) PLURAL NOUN (*often capital*) another term for **dominations.**

dominium (də'mɪnɪəm) *or rarely* **dominion** NOUN *Property law* the ownership or right to possession of property, esp realty.
▷HISTORY C19: from Latin: property, ownership; see DOMINION

domino¹ ('dɒmɪˌnəʊ) NOUN, *plural* **-noes.** [1] a small rectangular block used in dominoes, divided on one side into two equal areas, each of which is either blank or marked with from one to six dots. [2] (*modifier*) exhibiting the domino effect: *a domino pattern of takeovers.* ◆ See also **dominoes.**
▷HISTORY C19: from French, from Italian, perhaps from *domino!* master, said by the winner

domino² ('dɒmɪˌnəʊ) NOUN, *plural* **-noes** *or* **-nos.** [1] a large hooded cloak worn with an eye mask at a masquerade. [2] the eye mask worn with such a cloak.
▷HISTORY C18: from French or Italian, probably from Latin *dominus* lord, master

domino effect NOUN a series of similar or related events occurring as a direct and inevitable result of one initial event.
▷HISTORY C20: alluding to a row of dominoes, each standing on end, all of which fall when one is pushed: originally used with reference to possible Communist takeovers of countries in SE Asia

dominoes ('dɒmɪˌnəʊz) NOUN (*functioning as singular*) any of several games in which matching halves of dominoes are laid together.

Dominus *Latin* ('dɒmɪnʊs) NOUN God or Christ.

Domrémy-la-Pucelle (*French* dɔ̃remilapysɛl) *or* **Domrémy** NOUN a village in NE France, in the Vosges: birthplace of Joan of Arc.

don¹ (dɒn) VERB **dons, donning, donned.** (*tr*) to put on (clothing).
▷HISTORY C14: from DO¹ + ON; compare DOFF

don² (dɒn) NOUN [1] *Brit* a member of the teaching staff at a university or college, esp at Oxford or Cambridge. [2] a Spanish gentleman or nobleman. [3] (in the Mafia) the head of a family.
▷HISTORY C17: ultimately from Latin *dominus* lord

Don¹ (dɒn; *Spanish* don) NOUN a Spanish title equivalent to *Mr:* placed before a name to indicate respect.
▷HISTORY C16: via Spanish, from Latin *dominus* lord; see DON²

Don² (dɒn) NOUN [1] a river rising in W Russia, southeast of Tula and flowing generally south, to the Sea of Azov: linked by canal to the River Volga. Length: 1870 km (1162 miles). [2] a river in NE Scotland, rising in the Cairngorm Mountains and flowing east to the North Sea. Length: 100 km (62 miles). [3] a river in N central England, rising in S Yorkshire and flowing northeast to the Humber. Length: about 96 km (60 miles).

Dona (*Portuguese* 'dõnə) NOUN a Portuguese title of address equivalent to *Mrs* or *Madam*: placed before a name to indicate respect.
▷HISTORY C19: from Latin *domina* lady, feminine of *dominus* master

Doña ('dɒnjə; *Spanish* 'doɲa) NOUN a Spanish title of address equivalent to *Mrs* or *Madam*: placed before a name to indicate respect.
▷HISTORY C17: via Spanish, from Latin *domina;* see DONA

Donar ('dəʊnɑː; *German* 'doːnar) NOUN the Germanic god of thunder, corresponding to Thor in Norse mythology.

donate (dəʊ'neɪt) VERB to give (money, time, etc.), esp to a charity.
▸**do'nator** NOUN

donation (dəʊ'neɪʃən) NOUN [1] the act of giving, esp to a charity. [2] a contribution.
▷HISTORY C15: from Latin *dōnātiō* a presenting, from *dōnāre* to give, from *dōnum* gift

Donatist ('dəʊnətɪst) NOUN a member of a schismatic heretical Christian sect originating in N Africa in 311 A.D., that maintained that it alone constituted the true church.
▷HISTORY C15: from Late Latin *Dōnātista* a follower of *Dōnātus,* bishop of Carthage
▸**'Dona,tism** NOUN

donative ('dəʊnətɪv) NOUN [1] a gift or donation. [2] a benefice capable of being conferred as a gift. ◆ ADJECTIVE [3] of or like a donation. [4] being or relating to a benefice.
▷HISTORY C15: from Latin *dōnātīvum* donation made to soldiers by a Roman emperor, from *dōnāre* to present

Donau ('doːnau) NOUN the German name for the **Danube.**

Donbass *or* **Donbas** (dɒn'bɑːs) NOUN an industrial region in the E Ukraine in the plain of the Rivers Donets and lower Dnieper: the site of a major coalfield. Also called: **Donets Basin.**

Doncaster ('dɒŋkəstə) NOUN [1] an industrial town in N England, in Doncaster unitary authority, South Yorkshire, on the River Don. Pop.: 71 595 (1991). [2] a unitary authority in N England, in South Yorkshire. Pop.: 286 865 (2001). Area: 582 sq. km (225 sq. miles).

donder ('dɒndə) *South African slang* ◆ VERB (*tr*) [1] to beat (someone) up. ◆ NOUN [2] a wretch; swine.
▷HISTORY C19: Afrikaans, from Dutch *donderen* to swear, bully

done (dʌn) VERB [1] the past participle of **do¹.** [2] **be** *or* **have done with.** to end relations with. [3] **have done.** to be completely finished: *have you done?* [4] **that's done it. a** an exclamation of frustration when something is ruined. **b** an exclamation when something is completed. ◆ INTERJECTION [5] an expression of agreement, as on the settlement of a bargain between two parties. ◆ ADJECTIVE [6] completed; finished. [7] cooked enough: *done to a turn.* [8] used up: *they had to surrender when the ammunition was done.* [9] socially proper or acceptable: *that isn't done in higher circles.* [10] *Informal* cheated; tricked. [11] **done for.** *Informal* **a** dead or almost dead. **b** in serious difficulty. [12] **done in** *or* **up.** *Informal* physically exhausted.

donee (dəʊ'niː) NOUN *Law* [1] a person who receives a gift. [2] a person to whom a power of appointment is given.
▷HISTORY C16: from DON(OR) + -EE

Donegal ('dɒnɪˌgɔːl, ˌdɒnɪ'gɔːl) NOUN a county in NW Republic of Ireland, on the Atlantic: mountainous, with a rugged coastline and many offshore islands. County town: Lifford. Pop.: 129 994 (1996). Area: 4830 sq. km (1865 sq. miles).

doner kebab ('dɒnə) NOUN a fast-food dish comprising grilled meat and salad served in pitta bread with chilli sauce.
▷HISTORY from Turkish *döner* rotating + KEBAB

Donets (*Russian* da'njɛts) NOUN a river rising in SW Russia, in the Kursk steppe and flowing southeast, through the Ukraine, to the Don River. Length: about 1078 km (670 miles).

Donets Basin (də'nɛts) NOUN another name for the **Donbass.**

Donetsk (*Russian* da'njɛtsk) NOUN a city in the E Ukraine: the chief industrial centre of the Donbass; first ironworks founded by a Welshman, John Hughes (1872), after whom the town was named **Yuzovka** (Hughesovka). Pop.: 1 065 400 (1998 est.). Former names (from 1924 until 1961): **Stalin** *or* **Stalino.**

dong (dɒŋ) NOUN [1] the deep reverberating sound of a large bell. [2] *Austral and NZ informal* a heavy blow. [3] a slang word for **penis.** ◆ VERB [4] (*intr*) (of a bell) to make a deep reverberating sound. [5] (*tr*) *Austral and NZ informal* to strike or punch.
▷HISTORY C16: of imitative origin

dông (dɒŋ) NOUN the standard monetary unit of Vietnam, divided into 10 hào or 100 xu.
▷HISTORY from Vietnamese

donga¹ ('dɒŋgə) NOUN *South African, Austral, and NZ* a steep-sided gully created by soil erosion.
▷HISTORY C19: Afrikaans, from Nguni *donga* washed out gully

donga² ('dɒŋgə) NOUN (in Papua New Guinea) a house or shelter.

dongle ('dɒŋgᵊl) NOUN *Computing* an electronic device that accompanies a software item to prevent the unauthorized copying of programs.

Dongting ('dʊŋ'tɪŋ), **Tungting,** *or* **Tung-t'ing** NOUN a lake in S China, in NE Hunan province: main outlet flows to the Yangtze; rice-growing in winter. Area: (in winter) 3900 sq. km (1500 sq. miles).

donjon ('dʌndʒən, 'dɒn-) NOUN the heavily fortified central tower or keep of a medieval castle. Also called: **dungeon.**
▷HISTORY C14: archaic variant of *dungeon*

Don Juan ('dɒn 'dʒuːən; *Spanish* don xwan) NOUN [1] a legendary Spanish nobleman and philanderer: hero of many poems, plays, and operas, including treatments by de Molina, Molière, Goldoni, Mozart, Byron, and Shaw. [2] a successful seducer of women.

donkey ('dɒŋkɪ) NOUN [1] Also called: **ass.** a long-eared domesticated member of the horse family (*Equidae*), descended from the African wild ass (*Equus asinus*). [2] a stupid or stubborn person. [3] *Brit slang, derogatory* a footballer known for his or her lack of skill: *the players are a bunch of overpriced and overrated donkeys.* [4] **talk the hind leg(s) off a donkey.** to talk endlessly.
▷HISTORY C18: perhaps from *dun* dark + *-key,* as in *monkey*

donkey derby NOUN a race in which contestants ride donkeys, esp at a rural fête.

donkey engine NOUN a small auxiliary engine, such as one used for pumping water into the boilers of a steamship.

donkey jacket NOUN a hip-length jacket usually made of a thick navy fabric with a waterproof panel across the shoulders.

donkey-lick VERB *Austral slang* to defeat decisively.

donkey's years NOUN *Informal* a long time.

donkey vote NOUN *Austral* a vote on a preferential ballot on which the voter's order of preference follows the order in which the candidates are listed.

donkey-work NOUN [1] groundwork. [2] drudgery. US equivalent: **draft-mule work.**

donko ('dɒŋkəʊ) NOUN, *plural* **-kos.** *NZ informal* a tearoom or cafeteria in a factory, wharf area, etc.
▷HISTORY origin unknown

Donna ('dɒnə; *Italian* 'dɔnna) NOUN an Italian title of address equivalent to *Madam,* indicating respect.
▷HISTORY C17: from Italian, from Latin *domina* lady, feminine of *dominus* lord, master

donnée *or* ***donné*** *French* (dɔne) NOUN [1] a subject or theme. [2] a basic assumption or fact.
▷HISTORY literally: (a) given

donnert ('dɒnərt), **donnard,** *or* **donnered** ('dɒnərd) ADJECTIVE *Scot* stunned.
▷HISTORY C18: from Scottish dialect *donner* to astound, perhaps from Dutch *donderen* to thunder, from Middle Dutch *donder* thunder

donnish ('dɒnɪʃ) ADJECTIVE of or resembling a university don.
▸**'donnishly** ADVERB ▸**'donnishness** NOUN

donny ('dɒnɪ) NOUN a variant of **danny.**

donnybrook ('dɒnɪˌbrʊk) NOUN a rowdy brawl.
▷HISTORY C19: after *Donnybrook Fair,* an annual event until 1855 near Dublin

donor ('dəʊnə) NOUN [1] a person who makes a donation. [2] *Med* any person who voluntarily gives blood, skin, a kidney etc., for use in the treatment of another person. [3] *Law* **a** a person who makes a gift of property. **b** a person who bestows upon another a power of appointment over property. [4] the atom supplying both electrons in a coordinate

bond. 5 an impurity, such as antimony or arsenic, that is added to a semiconductor material in order to increase its n-type conductivity by contributing free electrons. Compare **acceptor** (sense 2).
▷HISTORY C15: from Old French *doneur,* from Latin *dōnātor,* from *dōnāre* to give
▸'**donor,ship** NOUN

donor card NOUN a card carried by a person to show that the bodily organs specified on it may be used for transplants after the person's death.

Don Quixote ('dɒn kiː'həʊtiː, 'kwɪksət; *Spanish* don ki'xote) NOUN an impractical idealist.
▷HISTORY after the hero of Cervantes' *Don Quixote de la Mancha*

don't (dəʊnt) CONTRACTION OF do not.

don't know NOUN a person who has not reached a definite opinion on a subject, esp as a response to a questionnaire.

donut ('dəʊnʌt) NOUN a variant spelling (esp US) of **doughnut.**

doo (duː) NOUN a Scot word for **dove**[1] or **pigeon**[1].

doob (duːb) NOUN *US slang* a cannabis cigarette.
▷HISTORY C20: origin unknown

doodah ('duːdɑː) *or US and Canadian* **doodad** ('duːdæd) NOUN *Informal* 1 an unnamed thing, esp an object the name of which is unknown or forgotten. 2 **all of a doodah.** excited; agitated.
▷HISTORY C20: of uncertain origin

doodle ('duːdᵊl) *Informal* ◆ VERB 1 to scribble or draw aimlessly. 2 to play or improvise idly. 3 (*intr; often foll by away*) *US* to dawdle or waste time. ◆ NOUN 4 a shape, picture, etc., drawn aimlessly.
▷HISTORY C20: perhaps from C17 *doodle* a foolish person, but influenced in meaning by DAWDLE; compare Low German *dudeltopf* simpleton
▸'**doodler** NOUN

doodlebug ('duːdᵊl,bʌg) NOUN 1 another name for the **V-1.** 2 a diviner's rod. 3 a US name for an **antlion** (the larva). 4 *US* any of certain insect larvae that resemble the antlion.
▷HISTORY C20: probably from DOODLE + BUG[1]

doo-doo ('duː,duː) NOUN *US and Canadian informal* a child's word for **excrement.**

doofus ('duːfəs) NOUN *Informal, chiefly US* a slow-witted or stupid person.
▷HISTORY C20: from Black slang

doohickey ('duː,hɪkɪ) NOUN *US and Canadian informal* another name for **doodah** (sense 1).

dook[1] *or* **douk**[1] (dʊk) NOUN *Scot* a wooden plug driven into a wall to hold a nail, screw, etc.
▷HISTORY of unknown origin

dook[2] *or* **douk**[2] (dʊk) *Scot* ◆ VERB 1 to dip or plunge. 2 to bathe. ◆ NOUN 3 an instance of dipping, plunging, or bathing.
▷HISTORY a Scot form of DUCK[2]

dooket ('duːkɪt, 'dʊkɪt) NOUN *Scot* 1 a dovecote. 2 a small closet or cupboard.

doolally (duː'lælɪ) ADJECTIVE *Slang* out of one's mind; crazy. In full: **doolally tap.**
▷HISTORY C19: originally military slang, from *Deolali,* a town near Bombay, the location of a military sanatorium + Hindustani *tap* fever

doolan ('duːlən) NOUN *NZ informal* a Roman Catholic.
▷HISTORY probably from the Irish surname *Doolan*

doom (duːm) NOUN 1 death or a terrible fate. 2 a judgment or decision. 3 (*sometimes capital*) another term for the **Last Judgment.** ◆ VERB 4 (*tr*) to destine or condemn to death or a terrible fate.
▷HISTORY Old English *dōm;* related to Old Norse *dōmr* judgment, Gothic *dōms* sentence, Old High German *tuom* condition, Greek *thomos* crowd, Sanskrit *dhāman* custom; see DO[1], DEEM, DEED, -DOM

doom-laden ADJECTIVE conveying a sense of disaster and tragedy.

doom palm NOUN a variant spelling of **doum palm.**

doomsday *or* **domesday** ('duːmz,deɪ) NOUN 1 (*sometimes capital*) the day on which the Last Judgment will occur. 2 any day of reckoning. 3 (*modifier*) characterized by predictions of disaster: *doomsday scenario.*
▷HISTORY Old English *dōmes dæg* Judgment Day; related to Old Norse *domsdagr*

Doomsday Book NOUN a variant spelling of **Domesday Book.**

doomster ('duːmstə) NOUN *Informal* 1 a person habitually given to predictions of impending disaster or doom. 2 *Archaic* a judge.

doomwatch ('duːm,wɒtʃ) NOUN 1 surveillance of the environment to warn of and prevent harm to it from human factors such as pollution or overpopulation. 2 a watching for or prediction of impending disaster.
▸'**doomwatcher** NOUN

doomy ('duːmɪ) ADJECTIVE *Informal* 1 despondent or pessimistic. 2 depressing, frightening, or chilling.
▸'**doomily** ADVERB

doon *or* **doun** (duːn) PREPOSITION, ADVERB, ADJECTIVE a Scot word for **down**[1].

doona ('duːnə) NOUN the Austral name for **continental quilt.**
▷HISTORY from a trademark

door (dɔː) NOUN 1 **a** a hinged or sliding panel for closing the entrance to a room, cupboard, etc. **b** (*in combination*): *doorbell; doorknob.* 2 a doorway or entrance to a room or building. 3 a means of access or escape: *a door to success.* 4 **lay at someone's door.** to lay (the blame or responsibility) on someone. 5 **out of doors.** in or into the open air. 6 **show someone the door.** to order someone to leave. ◆ See also **next door.**
▷HISTORY Old English *duru;* related to Old Frisian *dure,* Old Norse *dyrr,* Old High German *turi,* Latin *forēs,* Greek *thura*

do-or-die ADJECTIVE (*prenominal*) of or involving a determined and sometimes reckless effort to succeed.

doorframe ('dɔː,freɪm) NOUN a frame that supports a door. Also called: **doorcase.**

door furniture NOUN locks, handles, etc., designed for use on doors.

doorjamb ('dɔː,dʒæm) NOUN one of the two vertical members forming the sides of a doorframe. Also called: **doorpost.**

doorkeeper ('dɔː,kiːpə) NOUN 1 a person attending or guarding a door or gateway. 2 *RC Church* (formerly) the lowest grade of holy orders.

doorknock ('dɔːnɒk) NOUN *Austral* a fund-raising campaign for charity conducted by seeking donations from door to door.

doorman ('dɔː,mæn, -mən) NOUN, *plural* **-men.** a man employed to attend the doors of certain buildings.

doormat ('dɔː,mæt) NOUN 1 a mat, placed at the entrance to a building, for wiping dirt from shoes. 2 *Informal* a person who offers little resistance to ill-treatment by others.

Doorn (*Dutch* doːrn) NOUN a town in the central Netherlands, in Utrecht province: residence of Kaiser William II of Germany from his abdication (1919) until his death (1941).

doornail ('dɔː,neɪl) NOUN (**as**) **dead as a doornail.** dead beyond any doubt.

Doornik ('doːrnɪk) NOUN the Flemish name for **Tournai.**

doorpost ('dɔː,pəʊst) NOUN another name for **doorjamb.**

doorsill ('dɔː,sɪl) NOUN a horizontal member of wood, stone, etc., forming the bottom of a doorframe.

doorstep ('dɔː,stɛp) NOUN 1 a step in front of a door. 2 **on one's doorstep.** very close or accessible. 3 *Informal* a thick slice of bread. ◆ VERB **-steps, -stepping, -stepped.** (*tr*) 4 to canvass (a district) or interview (a member of the public) by or in the course of door-to-door visiting.

doorstop ('dɔː,stɒp) NOUN 1 a heavy object, wedge, or other device which prevents an open door from moving. 2 a projecting piece of rubber, etc., fixed to the floor to stop a door from striking a wall. 3 *Informal* a very thick book.

door to door ADJECTIVE (**door-to-door** when prenominal), ADVERB 1 (of selling, canvassing, etc.) from one house to the next. 2 (of journeys, deliveries, etc.) direct.

doorway ('dɔː,weɪ) NOUN 1 an opening into a building, room, etc., esp one that has a door. 2 a means of access or escape: *a doorway to freedom.*

dooryard ('dɔː,jɑːd) NOUN *US and Canadian* a yard in front of the front or back door of a house.

do out VERB (*tr, adverb*) *Informal* 1 to make tidy or clean; redecorate. 2 (foll by *of*) to deprive (a person) of by swindling or cheating.

do over VERB (*tr, adverb*) 1 *Informal* to renovate or redecorate. 2 *Brit, Austral, and NZ slang* to beat up; thrash.

doo-wop ('duː,wɒp) NOUN rhythm-and-blues harmony vocalizing developed by unaccompanied street-corner groups in the US in the 1950s.
▷HISTORY C20: of imitative origin

doozy ('duːzɪ) NOUN, *plural* **-zies.** *Slang* something excellent: *the plot's a doozy.*

dop (dɒp) NOUN *South African informal* a tot or small drink, usually alcoholic.
▷HISTORY Afrikaans

dopa ('dəʊpə) NOUN See **L-dopa.**

dopamine ('dɒpəmɪn) NOUN a chemical found in the brain that acts as a neurotransmitter and is an intermediate compound in the synthesis of noradrenaline. Formula: $(HO)_2C_6(CH_2)_2NH_2$.
▷HISTORY from *d(ihydr)o(xy)p(henylethyl)amine*

dopant ('dəʊpənt) NOUN an element or compound used to dope a semiconductor.
▷HISTORY C20: see DOPE, -ANT

dope (dəʊp) NOUN 1 any of a number of preparations made by dissolving cellulose derivatives in a volatile solvent, applied to fabric in order to improve strength, tautness, etc. 2 an additive used to improve the properties of something, such as an antiknock compound added to petrol. 3 a thick liquid, such as a lubricant, applied to a surface. 4 a combustible absorbent material, such as sawdust or wood pulp, used to hold the nitroglycerine in dynamite. 5 *Slang* **a** any illegal drug, usually cannabis. **b** (*as modifier*): *a dope fiend.* 6 a drug administered to a racehorse or greyhound to affect its performance. 7 *Informal* a person considered to be stupid or slow-witted. 8 *Informal* news or facts, esp confidential information. 9 *US and Canadian informal* a photographic developing solution. ◆ VERB (*tr*) 10 *Electronics* to add impurities to (a semiconductor) in order to produce or modify its properties. 11 to apply or add a dopant to. 12 to administer a drug to (oneself or another). 13 (*intr*) to take dope. ◆ ADJECTIVE 14 *Slang, chiefly US* excellent.
▷HISTORY C19: from Dutch *doop* sauce, from *doopen* to DIP

dope out VERB (*tr, adverb*) *US slang* to devise, solve, or contrive: *to dope out a floor plan.*

dope sheet NOUN *Horse racing, slang* a publication giving information on horses running in races.

dopester ('dəʊpstə) NOUN *US and Canadian slang* a person who makes predictions, esp in sport or politics.

dopey *or* **dopy** ('dəʊpɪ) ADJECTIVE **dopier, dopiest.** 1 *Slang* silly. 2 *Informal* half-asleep or in a state of semiconsciousness, as when under the influence of a drug.
▸'**dopily** ADVERB ▸'**dopiness** NOUN

doppelgänger ('dɒpᵊl,gɛŋə; *German* 'dɔpəl,gɛŋər) NOUN *Legend* a ghostly duplicate of a living person.
▷HISTORY from German *Doppelgänger,* literally: double-goer

Dopper ('dɒpə) NOUN (in South Africa) a member of the most conservative Afrikaner Church, which practises a strict Calvinism.
▷HISTORY C19: from Afrikaans, of unknown origin

doppio ('dɒpɪəʊ) NOUN a double measure, esp of espresso coffee.
▷HISTORY C20: from Italian, literally: double

Doppler effect ('dɒplə) NOUN a phenomenon, observed for sound waves and electromagnetic radiation, characterized by a change in the apparent frequency of a wave as a result of relative motion between the observer and the source. Also called: **Doppler shift.**
▷HISTORY C19: named after C. J. *Doppler* (1803–53), Austrian physicist

dor (dɔː) NOUN any European dung beetle of the genus *Geotrupes* and related genera, esp *G. stercorarius,* having a droning flight.
▷HISTORY Old English *dora* bumblebee; related to Middle Low German *dorte* DRONE[1]

dorado (də'rɑːdəʊ) NOUN 1 another name for **dolphin** (sense 3). 2 a South American river fish of the genus *Salminus* that resembles a salmon.

Dorado (də'rɑːdəʊ) NOUN, *Latin genitive* **Doradus**

(də'rɑːdəs). a constellation in the S hemisphere lying between Reticulum and Pictor and containing part of the Large Magellanic cloud.
▷HISTORY C17: from Spanish, from *dorar* to gild, from Latin DE- + *-aurāre,* from *aurum* gold

dorba ('dɔːbə) NOUN *Austral slang* a stupid, inept, or clumsy person. Also called: **dorb.**

Dorcas ('dɔːkəs) NOUN a charitable woman of Joppa (Acts 9:36–42).

Dorcas society NOUN a Christian charitable society for women with the aim of providing clothes for the poor.

Dorchester ('dɔːtʃɪstə) NOUN a town in S England, administrative centre of Dorset: associated with Thomas Hardy, esp as the Casterbridge of his novels. Pop.: 15 037 (1991). Latin name: **Durnovaria** (ˌdjʊrnəʊ'veɪrɪə).

Dordogne (*French* dɔrdɔɲ) NOUN 1 a river in SW France, rising in the Auvergne Mountains and flowing southwest and west to join the Garonne river and form the Gironde estuary. Length: 472 km (293 miles). 2 a department of SW France, in Aquitaine region. Capital: Périgueux. Pop.: 388 293 (1999). Area: 9224 sq. km (3597 sq. miles).

Dordrecht (*Dutch* 'dɔrdrɛxt) NOUN a port in the SW Netherlands, in South Holland province: chief port of the Netherlands until the 17th century. Pop.: 119 462 (1999 est.). Also called: **Dort.**

doré ('dɔreɪ, -riː) NOUN another name for **walleye** (the fish).
▷HISTORY C18: from French, gilded; see DORY

do-re-mi NOUN *US slang* money.
▷HISTORY C20: pun on DOUGH (SENSE 3)

Dorian ('dɔːrɪən) NOUN 1 a member of a Hellenic people who invaded Greece around 1100 B.C., overthrew the Mycenaean civilization, and settled chiefly in the Peloponnese. ◆ ADJECTIVE 2 of or relating to this people or their dialect of Ancient Greek; Doric. 3 *Music* of or relating to a mode represented by the ascending natural diatonic scale from D to D. See also **Hypo-.**

Doric ('dɒrɪk) ADJECTIVE 1 of or relating to the Dorians, esp the Spartans, or their dialect of Ancient Greek. 2 of, denoting, or relating to one of the five classical orders of architecture: characterized by a column having no base, a heavy fluted shaft, and a capital consisting of an ovolo moulding beneath a square abacus. See also **Ionic, composite** (sense 4), **Corinthian, Tuscan.** 3 (*sometimes not capital*) rustic. ◆ NOUN 4 one of four chief dialects of Ancient Greek, spoken chiefly in the Peloponnese. Compare **Aeolic, Arcadic, Ionic.** See also **Attic** (sense 3). 5 any rural dialect, esp that spoken in the northeast of Scotland.

doris ('dɒrɪs) NOUN *Slang* a woman.
▷HISTORY C20: from the girl's name *Doris*

Doris[1] ('dɒrɪs) NOUN (in ancient Greece) 1 a small landlocked area north of the Gulf of Corinth. Traditionally regarded as the home of the Dorians, it was perhaps settled by some of them during their southward migration. 2 the coastal area of Caria in SW Asia Minor, settled by Dorians.

Doris[2] ('dɒrɪs) NOUN *Greek myth* a sea nymph.

dork (dɔːk) NOUN *Slang* 1 a stupid or incompetent person. 2 *US* a penis.
▷HISTORY C20: of unknown origin
▸'**dorky** ADJECTIVE

Dorking ('dɔːkɪŋ) NOUN a heavy breed of domestic fowl.
▷HISTORY C19: after *Dorking,* town in Surrey

Dorkland ('dɔːklənd) NOUN *NZ informal* an offensive name for Auckland.
▸'**Dorklander** NOUN

dorm (dɔːm) NOUN *Informal* short for **dormitory.**

dormant ('dɔːmənt) ADJECTIVE 1 quiet and inactive, as during sleep. 2 latent or inoperative. 3 (of a volcano) neither extinct nor erupting. 4 *Biology* alive but in a resting torpid condition with suspended growth and reduced metabolism. 5 (*usually postpositive*) *Heraldry* (of a beast) in a sleeping position. ◆ Compare **active, passive.**
▷HISTORY C14: from Old French *dormant,* from *dormir* to sleep, from Latin *dormīre*
▸'**dormancy** NOUN

dormer ('dɔːmə) NOUN a construction with a gable roof and a window at its outer end that projects from a sloping roof. Also called: **dormer window.**
▷HISTORY C16: from Old French *dormoir,* from Latin *dormītōrium* DORMITORY

dormie *or* **dormy** ('dɔːmɪ) ADJECTIVE *Golf* (of a player or side) as many holes ahead of an opponent as there are still to play: *dormie three.*
▷HISTORY C19: of unknown origin

Dormition of the Blessed Virgin (dɔː'mɪʃᵊn) NOUN another name for **Feast of the Assumption**: see **Assumption.**

dormitory ('dɔːmɪtərɪ, -trɪ) NOUN, *plural* **-ries.** 1 a large room, esp at a school or institution, containing several beds. 2 *US* a building, esp at a college or camp, providing living and sleeping accommodation. 3 (*modifier*) *Brit* denoting or relating to an area from which most of the residents commute to work (esp in the phrase **dormitory suburb**). ◆ Often (for senses 1, 2) shortened to: **dorm.**
▷HISTORY C15: from Latin *dormītōrium,* from *dormīre* to sleep

Dormobile ('dɔːməʊˌbiːl) NOUN *Trademark* a vanlike vehicle specially equipped for living in while travelling.

dormouse ('dɔːˌmaʊs) NOUN, *plural* **-mice.** any small Old World rodent of the family *Gliridae,* esp the Eurasian *Muscardinus avellanarius,* resembling a mouse with a furry tail.
▷HISTORY C15: *dor-,* perhaps from Old French *dormir* to sleep, from Latin *dormīre* + MOUSE

dornick[1] ('dɔːnɪk) *or* **dorneck** NOUN a heavy damask cloth, formerly used for vestments, curtains, etc.
▷HISTORY C15: from *Doornik* Tournai in Belgium where it was first manufactured

dornick[2] ('dɔːnɪk) NOUN *US* a small stone or pebble.
▷HISTORY C15: probably from Irish Gaelic *dornōg,* from *dorn* hand

doronicum (də'rɒnɪkəm) NOUN any plant of the Eurasian and N African genus *Doronicum,* such as leopard's-bane, having yellow daisy-like flower heads: family *Asteraceae* (composites).
▷HISTORY C17: New Latin, from Arabic *dorūnaj*

Dorothy Dixer (ˌdɒrəθɪ 'dɪksə) NOUN *Austral informal* a parliamentary question asked by a member of the government so that the minister may give a prepared answer.
▷HISTORY from pen name *Dorothy Dix* of US journalist Elizabeth Meriwether (1870–1951), who wrote a column replying to correspondents' problems

dorp (dɔːp) NOUN *Archaic except in South Africa* a small town or village.
▷HISTORY C16: from Dutch: village; related to THORP

Dorpat ('dɔrpat) NOUN the German name for **Tartu.**

dorsad ('dɔːsæd) ADJECTIVE *Anatomy* towards the back or dorsal aspect.
▷HISTORY C19: from Latin *dorsum* back + *ad* to, towards

dorsal ('dɔːsᵊl) ADJECTIVE 1 *Anatomy, zoology* relating to the back or spinal part of the body. Compare **ventral** (sense 1). 2 *Botany* of, relating to, or situated on the side of an organ that is directed away from the axis. 3 articulated with the back of the tongue, as the (k) sound in English *coot.*
▷HISTORY C15: from Medieval Latin *dorsālis,* from Latin *dorsum* back
▸'**dorsally** ADVERB

dorsal fin NOUN any unpaired median fin on the backs of fishes and some other aquatic vertebrates: maintains balance during locomotion.

Dorset ('dɔːsɪt) NOUN a county in SW England, on the English Channel: mainly hilly but low-lying in the east: the geographical and ceremonial county includes Bournemouth and Poole, which became independent unitary authorities in 1997. Administrative centre: Dorchester. Pop. (excluding unitary authorities): 390 986 (2001 est.). Area (excluding unitary authorities): 2544 sq. km (982 sq. miles).

Dorset Down NOUN a breed of stocky hornless sheep having a broad head, dark face, and a dense fleece: kept for lamb production.

Dorset Horn NOUN a breed of horned sheep with dense fine-textured wool.

dorsiferous (dɔː'sɪfərəs) ADJECTIVE *Botany, zoology, rare* bearing or carrying (young, spores, etc.) on the back or dorsal surface.

dorsiflexion (ˌdɔːsɪ'flɛkʃən) NOUN *Med* the bending back of a part, esp the hand or foot or their digits.

dorsigrade ('dɔːsɪˌgreɪd) ADJECTIVE (of animals such as certain armadillos) walking on the backs of the toes.
▷HISTORY C19: from Latin, from *dorsum* back + -GRADE

dorsiventral (ˌdɔːsɪ'vɛntrəl) ADJECTIVE 1 (of leaves and similar flat parts) having distinct upper and lower faces. 2 a variant spelling of **dorsoventral.**
▸**dorsiventrality** (ˌdɔːsɪvɛn'trælɪtɪ) NOUN
▸ˌ**dorsi'ventrally** ADVERB

dorso-, dorsi-, *or before a vowel* **dors-** COMBINING FORM indicating dorsum or dorsal: *dorsoventral.*

dorsoventral (ˌdɔːsəʊ'vɛntrəl) ADJECTIVE 1 relating to both the dorsal and ventral sides; extending from the back to the belly. 2 *Botany* a variant spelling of **dorsiventral.**
▸ˌ**dorso'ventrally** ADVERB

dorsum ('dɔːsəm) NOUN, *plural* **-sa** (-sə). *Anatomy* 1 a technical name for the **back.** 2 any analogous surface: *the dorsum of the hand.*
▷HISTORY C18: from Latin: back

Dort (*Dutch* dɔrt) NOUN another name for **Dordrecht.**

Dortmund ('dɔːtmənd; *German* 'dɔrtmʊnt) NOUN an industrial city in W Germany, in North Rhine-Westphalia at the head of the **Dortmund–Ems Canal**: university (1966). Pop.: 590 300 (1999 est.).

dorty ('dɔːtɪ) ADJECTIVE **dortier, dortiest.** *Scot* haughty, or sullen.
▷HISTORY C17: from Scottish *dort* peevishness
▸'**dortiness** NOUN

dory[1] ('dɔːrɪ) NOUN, *plural* **-ries.** 1 any spiny-finned marine teleost food fish of the family *Zeidae,* esp the John Dory, having a deep compressed body. 2 another name for **walleye** (the fish).
▷HISTORY C14: from French *dorée* gilded, from *dorer* to gild, from Late Latin *deaurāre,* ultimately from Latin *aurum* gold

dory[2] ('dɔːrɪ) NOUN, *plural* **-ries.** *US and Canadian* a flat-bottomed rowing boat with a high bow, stern, and sides.
▷HISTORY C18: from Mosquito (an American Indian language of Honduras and Nicaragua) *dóri* dugout

DOS (dɒs) NOUN *Trademark, Computing* ACRONYM FOR disk-operating system, often prefixed, as in MS-DOS and PC-DOS; a computer operating system.

dos-à-dos (ˌdəʊsɪ'dəʊ; *French* dozado) NOUN 1 a seat on which the users sit back to back. 2 an alternative spelling of **do-si-do.**
▷HISTORY literally: back to back

dosage ('dəʊsɪdʒ) NOUN 1 the administration of a drug or agent in prescribed amounts and at prescribed intervals. 2 the optimum therapeutic dose and optimum interval between doses. 3 another name for **dose** (senses 3, 4).

dose (dəʊs) NOUN 1 *Med* a specific quantity of a therapeutic drug or agent taken at any one time or at specified intervals. 2 *Informal* something unpleasant to experience: *a dose of influenza.* 3 Also called: **dosage.** the total energy of ionizing radiation absorbed by unit mass of material, esp of living tissue; usually measured in grays (SI unit) or rads. 4 Also called: **dosage.** a small amount of syrup added to wine, esp sparkling wine, when the sediment is removed and the bottle is corked. 5 *Slang* a venereal infection, esp gonorrhoea. 6 **like a dose of salts.** very quickly indeed. ◆ VERB (*tr*) 7 to administer a dose or doses to (someone). 8 *Med* to give (a therapeutic drug or agent) in appropriate quantities. 9 (often foll by *up*) to give (someone, esp oneself) drugs, medicine, etc., esp in large quantities. 10 to add syrup to (wine) during bottling.
▷HISTORY C15: from French, from Late Latin *dosis,* from Greek: a giving, from *didonai* to give
▸'**doser** NOUN

dose equivalent NOUN a quantity that expresses the probability that exposure to ionizing radiation will cause biological effects. It is usually obtained by multiplying the dose by the quality factor of the radiation, but other factors may be considered. It is measured in sieverts (SI unit) or rems.

dosh (dɒʃ) NOUN *Brit* a slang word for **money**.
▷HISTORY C20: of unknown origin

do-si-do (ˌdəʊsɪˈdəʊ) NOUN 1 a square-dance figure in which dancers pass each other with right shoulders close or touching and circle back to back. ◆ SENTENCE SUBSTITUTE 2 a call instructing dancers to perform such a figure. ◆ Also: **dos-à-dos**.
▷HISTORY C20: from DOS-À-DOS

dosimeter (dəʊˈsɪmiːtə) *or* **dosemeter** (ˈdəʊsˌmiːtə) NOUN an instrument for measuring the dose of X-rays or other radiation absorbed by matter or the intensity of a source of radiation.
▸**dosimetric** (ˌdəʊsɪˈmɛtrɪk) ADJECTIVE ▸**dosimetrician** (ˌdəʊsɪməˈtrɪʃən) *or* **doˈsimetrist** NOUN ▸**doˈsimetry** NOUN

dosing strip NOUN (in New Zealand) an area set aside for treating dogs suspected of having hydatid disease.

doss (dɒs) *Brit slang* ◆ VERB 1 (*intr*; often foll by *down*) to sleep, esp in a dosshouse. 2 (*intr*; often foll by *around*) to pass time aimlessly. ◆ NOUN 3 a bed, esp in a dosshouse. 4 a slang word for **sleep**. 5 short for **dosshouse**. 6 a task or pastime requiring little effort: *making a film is a bit of a doss*.
▷HISTORY C18: of uncertain origin

dossal *or* **dossel** (ˈdɒsᵊl) NOUN an ornamental hanging, placed at the back of an altar or at the sides of a chancel.
▷HISTORY C17: from Medieval Latin *dossāle*, neuter of *dossālis*, variant of *dorsālis* DORSAL

dosser[1] (ˈdɒsə) NOUN *Rare* a bag or basket for carrying objects on the back.
▷HISTORY C14: from Old French *dossier*, from Medieval Latin *dorsārium*, from Latin *dorsum* back

dosser[2] (ˈdɒsə) NOUN 1 *Brit slang* a person who sleeps in dosshouses. 2 *Brit slang* another word for **dosshouse**. 3 *Slang* a lazy person; idler.

dosshouse (ˈdɒsˌhaʊs) NOUN *Brit slang* a cheap lodging house, esp one used by tramps. US name: **flophouse**.

dossier (ˈdɒsɪˌeɪ, -sɪə; *French* dosje) NOUN a collection of papers containing information on a particular subject or person.
▷HISTORY C19: from French: a file with a label on the back, from *dos* back, from Latin *dorsum*

dost (dʌst) VERB *Archaic or dialect* (used with the pronoun *thou* or its relative equivalent) a singular form of the present tense (indicative mood) of **do**[1].

dot[1] (dɒt) NOUN 1 a small round mark made with or as with a pen, etc.; spot; speck; point. 2 anything resembling a dot; a small amount: *a dot of paint*. 3 the mark (˙) that appears above the main stem of the letters *i, j*. 4 *Music* **a** the symbol (.) placed after a note or rest to increase its time value by half. **b** this symbol written above or below a note indicating that it must be played or sung staccato. 5 *Maths, logic* **a** the symbol (.) indicating multiplication or logical conjunction. **b** a decimal point. 6 the symbol (·) used, in combination with the symbol for *dash* (—), in the written representation of Morse and other telegraphic codes. Compare **dit**. 7 **the year dot**. *Informal* as long ago as can be remembered. 8 **on the dot**. at exactly the arranged time. ◆ VERB **dots, dotting, dotted**. 9 (*tr*) to mark or form with a dot: *to dot a letter; a dotted crotchet*. 10 (*tr*) to scatter or intersperse (with dots or something resembling dots): *bushes dotting the plain*. 11 (*intr*) to make a dot or dots. 12 **dot one's i's and cross one's t's**. to pay meticulous attention to detail.
▷HISTORY Old English *dott* head of a boil; related to Old High German *tutta* nipple, Norwegian *dott*, Dutch *dott* lump
▸**ˈdotter** NOUN

dot[2] (dɒt) NOUN *Civil law* a woman's dowry.
▷HISTORY C19: from French, from Latin *dōs*; related to *dōtāre* to endow, *dāre* to give
▸**dotal** (ˈdəʊtᵊl) ADJECTIVE

dotage (ˈdəʊtɪdʒ) NOUN 1 feebleness of mind, esp as a result of old age. 2 foolish infatuation.
▷HISTORY C14: from DOTE + -AGE

dotard (ˈdəʊtəd) NOUN a person who is weak-minded, esp through senility.
▷HISTORY C14: from DOTE + -ARD
▸**ˈdotardly** ADJECTIVE

dotation (dəʊˈteɪʃən) NOUN *Law* the act of giving a dowry; endowment.
▷HISTORY C14: from Latin *dōtātiō*, from *dōtāre* to endow

dot ball NOUN *Cricket* a ball from which a run is not scored.
▷HISTORY when no run is scored, the scorer places a dot in his or her record book

dotcom *or* **dot.com** (ˌdɒtˈkɒm) NOUN **a** a company that conducts most of its business on the Internet. **b** (*as modifier*): *dotcom stocks*.
▷HISTORY C20: from *.com*, the domain name suffix of businesses trading on the Internet

dotcommer (dɒtˈkɒmə) NOUN a person who carries out business on the Internet.

dote *or now rarely* **doat** (dəʊt) VERB (*intr*) 1 (foll by *on* or *upon*) to love to an excessive or foolish degree. 2 to be foolish or weak-minded, esp as a result of old age.
▷HISTORY C13: related to Middle Dutch *doten* to be silly, Norwegian *dudra* to shake
▸**ˈdoter** *or* (*now rarely*) **ˈdoater** NOUN

doth (dʌθ) VERB *Archaic or dialect* (used with the pronouns *he, she*, or *it* or with a noun) a singular form of the present tense of **do**[1].

dot-matrix printer NOUN *Computing* a printer in which each character is produced as an array of dots by a printhead.

dot product NOUN another name for **scalar product**.

dotted (ˈdɒtɪd) ADJECTIVE 1 having dots, esp having a pattern of dots. 2 *Music* **a** (of a note) increased to one and a half times its original time value. See **dot**[1] (sense 4). **b** (of a musical rhythm) characterized by dotted notes. Compare **double-dotted**. See also **notes inégales**.

dotted line NOUN 1 a line of dots or dashes on a form or document. 2 **sign on the dotted line**. to agree formally, esp by signing one's name on a document.

dotterel *or* **dottrel** (ˈdɒtrəl) NOUN 1 a rare Eurasian plover, *Eudromias morinellus*, with reddish-brown underparts and white bands around the head and neck. 2 *Austral* any similar and related bird, esp of the genus *Charadrius*. 3 *Dialect* a person who is foolish or easily duped.
▷HISTORY C15 *dotrelle*; see DOTE

dottle *or* **dottel** (ˈdɒtᵊl) NOUN the plug of tobacco left in a pipe after smoking.
▷HISTORY C15: diminutive of *dot* lump; see DOT[1]

dotty (ˈdɒtɪ) ADJECTIVE **-tier, -tiest**. 1 *Slang, chiefly Brit* feeble-minded; slightly crazy. 2 *Brit slang* (foll by *about*) extremely fond (of). 3 marked with dots.
▷HISTORY C19: from DOT[1]: sense development of 1 from meaning of "unsteady on one's feet"
▸**ˈdottily** ADVERB ▸**ˈdottiness** NOUN

Douai (ˈduːeɪ; *French* dwɛ) NOUN an industrial city in N France: the political and religious centre of exiled English Roman Catholics in the 16th and 17th centuries. Pop.: 199 562 (1990).

Douala *or* **Duala** (duˈɑːlə) NOUN the chief port and largest city in W Cameroon, on the Bight of Bonny: capital of the German colony of Kamerun (1901–16). Pop.: 1 200 000 (1992 est.).

Douay Bible *or* **Version** (ˈduːeɪ) NOUN an English translation of the Bible from the Latin Vulgate text completed by Roman Catholic scholars at Douai in 1610.

double (ˈdʌbᵊl) ADJECTIVE (*usually prenominal*) 1 as much again in size, strength, number, etc.: *a double portion*. 2 composed of two equal or similar parts; in a pair; twofold: *a double egg cup*. 3 designed for two users: *a double room*. 4 folded in two; composed of two layers: *double paper*. 5 stooping; bent over. 6 having two aspects or existing in two different ways; ambiguous: *a double meaning*. 7 false, deceitful, or hypocritical: *a double life*. 8 (of flowers) having more than the normal number of petals. 9 *Maths* **a** (of a root) being one of two equal roots of a polynomial equation. **b** (of an integral) having an integrand containing two independent variables requiring two integrations, in each of which one variable is kept constant. 10 *Music* **a** (of an instrument) sounding an octave lower than the pitch indicated by the notation: *a double bass*. **b** (of time) duple, usually accompanied by the direction *alla breve*. ◆ ADVERB 11 twice over; twofold. 12 two together; two at a time (esp in the phrase **see double**). ◆ NOUN 13 twice the number, amount, size, etc. 14 a double measure of spirits, such as whisky or brandy. 15 a duplicate or counterpart, esp a person who closely resembles another; understudy. 16 a wraith or ghostly apparition that is the exact counterpart of a living person; doppelgänger. 17 a sharp turn, esp a return on one's own tracks. 18 an evasive shift or artifice; trick. 19 an actor who plays two parts in one play. 20 *Bridge* a call that increases certain scoring points if the last preceding bid becomes the contract. 21 *Billiards, snooker* a strike in which the object ball is struck so as to make it rebound against the cushion to an opposite pocket. 22 a bet on two horses in different races in which any winnings from the horse in the first race are placed on the horse in the later race. 23 (*often capital*) *Chiefly RC Church* one of the higher-ranking feasts on which the antiphons are recited both before and after the psalms. 24 *Music* an ornamented variation in 16th and 17th century music. 25 Also called: **double time**. a pace of twice the normal marching speed. 26 *Tennis* See **double fault**. 27 **a** the narrow outermost ring on a dartboard. **b** a hit on this ring. 28 **at** *or* **on the double**. **a** at twice normal marching speed. **b** quickly or immediately. ◆ VERB 29 to make or become twice as much. 30 to bend or fold (material, a bandage, etc.). 31 (*tr*; sometimes foll by *up*) to clench (a fist). 32 (*tr*; often foll by *together* or *up*) to join or couple: *he doubled up the team*. 33 (*tr*) to repeat exactly; copy. 34 (*intr*) to play two parts or serve two roles. 35 (*intr*) to turn sharply; follow a winding course. 36 *Nautical* to sail around (a headland or other point). 37 *Music* **a** to duplicate (a voice or instrumental part) either in unison or at the octave above or below it. **b** (*intr*; usually foll by *on*) to be capable of performing (upon an instrument additional to one's normal one): *the third trumpeter doubles on cornet*. 38 *Bridge* to make a call that will double certain scoring points if the preceding bid becomes the contract. 39 *Billiards, snooker* to cause (a ball) to rebound or (of a ball) to rebound from a cushion across or up or down the table. 40 *Chess* **a** to cause two pawns of the same colour to be on the same file. **b** to place both rooks of the same colour on the same rank or the same file. 41 (*intr*; foll by *for*) to act as substitute (for an actor or actress). 42 (*intr*) to go or march at twice the normal speed. ◆ See also **double back, doubles, double up**.
▷HISTORY C13: from Old French, from Latin *duplus* twofold, from *duo* two + *-plus* -FOLD
▸**ˈdoubleness** NOUN ▸**ˈdoubler** NOUN

double-acting ADJECTIVE 1 (of a reciprocating engine or pump) having a piston or pistons that are pressurized alternately on opposite sides. Compare **single-acting**. 2 (of a hinge, door, etc.) having complementary actions in opposed directions.

double agent NOUN a spy employed by two mutually antagonistic countries, companies, etc.

double-aspect theory NOUN *Philosophy* a monistic theory that holds that mind and body are not distinct substances but merely different aspects of a single substance.

double back VERB (*intr, adverb*) to go back in the opposite direction (esp in the phrase **to double back on one's tracks**).

double-bank VERB *Austral and NZ informal* to carry a second person on (a horse, bicycle, etc.). Also: **dub**.

double bar NOUN *Music* a symbol, consisting of two ordinary bar lines or a single heavy one, that marks the end of a composition or a section within it.

double-barrelled *or US* **double-barreled** ADJECTIVE 1 (of a gun) having two barrels. 2 extremely forceful or vehement. 3 *Brit* (of a surname) having hyphenated parts. 4 serving two purposes; ambiguous: *a double-barrelled remark*.

double bass (beɪs) NOUN 1 Also called (US): **bass viol**. a stringed instrument, the largest and lowest member of the violin family. Range: almost three octaves upwards from E in the space between the fourth and fifth leger lines below the bass staff. It is normally bowed in classical music, but it is very common in a jazz or dance band, where it is practically always played pizzicato. Informal name: **bass fiddle**. ◆ ADJECTIVE **double-bass**. 2 of or relating to an instrument whose pitch lies below that regarded as the bass; contrabass.

double bassoon NOUN *Music* the lowest and largest instrument in the oboe class; contrabassoon.

double bill NOUN a programme or event with two main items.

double bind NOUN a situation of conflict from which there is no escape; unresolvable dilemma.

double-blind ADJECTIVE of or relating to an experiment to discover reactions to certain commodities, drugs, etc., in which neither the experimenters nor the subjects know the particulars of the test items during the experiments. Compare **single-blind**.

double boiler NOUN the US and Canadian name for **double saucepan**.

double bond NOUN a type of chemical bond consisting of two covalent bonds linking two atoms in a molecule.

double-breasted ADJECTIVE (of a garment) having overlapping fronts such as to give a double thickness of cloth.

double bridle NOUN a bridle with four reins coming from a bit with two rings on each side.

double-check VERB [1] to check twice or again; verify. ♦ NOUN **double check.** [2] a second examination or verification. [3] *Chess* a simultaneous check from two pieces brought about by moving one piece to give check and thereby revealing a second check from another piece.

double chin NOUN a fold of fat under the chin.
▸ **ˌdouble-ˈchinned** ADJECTIVE

double concerto NOUN a concerto for two solo instruments.

double cream NOUN thick cream with a high fat-content.

double cross NOUN a technique for producing hybrid stock, esp seed for cereal crops, by crossing the hybrids between two different pairs of inbred lines.

double-cross VERB [1] (*tr*) to cheat or betray. ♦ NOUN [2] the act or an instance of double-crossing; betrayal.
▸ **ˈdouble-ˈcrosser** NOUN

double dagger NOUN a character (‡) used in printing to indicate a cross reference, esp to a footnote. Also called: **diesis, double obelisk.**

double-dealing NOUN **a** action characterized by treachery or deceit. **b** (*as modifier*): *double-dealing treachery.*
▸ **ˈdouble-ˈdealer** NOUN

double-decker NOUN [1] *Chiefly Brit* a bus with two passenger decks. [2] *Informal* **a** a thing or structure having two decks, layers, etc. **b** (*as modifier*): *a double-decker sandwich.*

double-declutch VERB (*intr*) *Brit* to change to a lower gear in a motor vehicle by first placing the gear lever into the neutral position before engaging the desired gear, at the same time releasing the clutch pedal and increasing the engine speed. US term: **double-clutch.**

double decomposition NOUN a chemical reaction between two compounds that results in the interchange of one part of each to form two different compounds, as in $AgNO_3 + KI \rightarrow AgI + KNO_3$. Also called: **metathesis.**

double density *Computing* ♦ NOUN a disk with more than the normal capacity for storage.

double digging NOUN *Brit* a method of digging ground in a series of trenches two spits deep, mixing the soil of the bottom spit with manure, and then transferring the soil from the top spit of one trench to the top spit of the preceding one.

double dip NOUN *Economics* **a** a recession in which a brief recovery in output is followed by another fall, because demand remains low. **b** (*as modifier*): *a double-dip recession.*

double-dotted ADJECTIVE *Music* [1] (of a note) increased to one and three quarters of its original time value by the addition of two dots. [2] (of a rhythm) characterized by pairs of notes in which the first one, lengthened by two dots, makes up seven eighths of the time value of the pair.

double drummer NOUN *Austral informal* a type of cicada.

double-dumped ADJECTIVE *NZ* (of a wool bale) compressed, with two bales occupying the volume-equivalent of one ordinary bale.

double Dutch NOUN *Brit informal* incomprehensible talk; gibberish.

double-dyed ADJECTIVE [1] confirmed; inveterate: *a double-dyed villain.* [2] dyed twice.

double eagle NOUN a former US gold coin, having a nominal value of 20 dollars.

double-edged ADJECTIVE [1] acting in two ways; having a dual effect: *a double-edged law.* [2] (of a remark, argument, etc.) having two possible interpretations, esp applicable both for and against or being really malicious though apparently innocuous. [3] (of a sword, knife, etc.) having a cutting edge on either side of the blade.

double entendre (ˈdʌbᵊl ɑːnˈtɑːndrə, -ˈtɑːnd; *French* dubl ɑ̃tɑ̃drə) NOUN [1] a word, phrase, etc., that can be interpreted in two ways, esp one having one meaning that is indelicate. [2] the type of humour that depends upon such ambiguity.
▹**HISTORY** C17: from obsolete French: double meaning

double entry NOUN **a** a book-keeping system in which any commercial transaction is entered as a debit in one account and as a credit in another. Compare **single entry. b** (*as modifier*): *double-entry book-keeping.*

double exposure NOUN [1] the act or process of recording two superimposed images on a photographic medium, usually done intentionally to produce a special effect. [2] the photograph resulting from such an act.

double-faced ADJECTIVE [1] (of textiles) having a finished nap on each side; reversible. [2] insincere or deceitful.

double fault *Tennis* ♦ NOUN [1] the serving of two faults in succession, thereby losing a point. ♦ VERB **double-fault.** [2] (*intr*) to serve a double fault.

double feature NOUN *Films* a programme showing two full-length films. Informal name (US): **twin bill.**

double first NOUN *Brit* a first-class honours degree in two subjects.

double flat NOUN [1] *Music* **a** an accidental that lowers the pitch of the following note two semitones. Usual symbol: 𝄫. **b** a note affected by this accidental. ♦ ADJECTIVE **double-flat.** [2] (*postpositive*) denoting a note of a given letter name lowered in pitch by two semitones.

double glazing NOUN [1] two panes of glass in a window, fitted to reduce the transmission of heat, sound, etc. [2] the fitting of glass in such a manner.

double Gloucester NOUN a type of smooth orange-red cheese of mild flavour.

double-header NOUN [1] a train drawn by two locomotives coupled together to provide extra power. [2] Also called: **twin bill.** *Sport, US and Canadian* two games played consecutively by the same teams or by two different teams. [3] *Austral and NZ informal* a coin with the impression of a head on each side. [4] *Austral informal* a double ice-cream cone.

double-helical gear NOUN another name for **herringbone gear.**

double helix NOUN *Biochem* the form of the molecular structure of DNA, consisting of two helical polynucleotide chains linked by hydrogen bonds and coiled around the same axis.

double-hung ADJECTIVE (of a window) having two vertical sashes, the upper one sliding in grooves outside those of the lower.

double indemnity NOUN *US and Canadian* (in life assurance policies) a clause providing for the payment of double the policy's face value in the event of the policyholder's accidental death.

double jeopardy NOUN the act of prosecuting a defendant a second time for an offence for which he has already been tried.

double-jointed ADJECTIVE having unusually flexible joints permitting an abnormal degree of motion of the parts.

double knit NOUN **a** a knitted material made on two sets of needles that produce a double thickness joined with interlocking stitches. **b** (*as modifier*): *a double-knit fabric.*

double knitting NOUN **a** a widely used medium thickness of knitting wool. **b** (*as modifier*): *double-knitting wool.*

double-minded ADJECTIVE *Rare* undecided; vacillating.
▸ **ˌdouble-ˈmindedness** NOUN

double negation NOUN *Logic* the principle that a statement is equivalent to the denial of its negation, as *it is not the case that John is not here* meaning *John is here.*

double negative NOUN a syntactic construction, often considered ungrammatical in standard Modern English, in which two negatives are used where one is needed, as in *I wouldn't never have believed it.*

> **Language note** There are two contexts where double negatives are used. An adjective with negative force is often used with a negative in order to express a nuance of meaning somewhere between the positive and the negative: *he was a not infrequent visitor; it is a not uncommon sight.* Two negatives are also found together where they reinforce each other rather than conflict: *he never went back, not even to collect his belongings.* These two uses of what is technically a double negative are acceptaable. A third case, illustrated by *I shouldn't wonder if it didn't rain today*, has the force of a weak positive statement (*I expect it to rain today*) and is common in informal English.

double obelisk NOUN another name for **double dagger.**

double or quits NOUN a game, throw, toss, etc., to decide whether the stake due is to be doubled or cancelled.

double-park VERB to park (a car or other vehicle) alongside or directly opposite another already parked by the roadside, thereby causing an obstruction.

double play NOUN *Baseball* a play in which two runners are put out.

double pneumonia NOUN pneumonia affecting both lungs.

double printing NOUN *Photog* the exposure of the same positive photographic emulsion to two or more negatives, resulting in the superimposition of multiple images after development.

double-quick ADJECTIVE [1] very quick; rapid. ♦ ADVERB [2] in a very quick or rapid manner.

double-reed ADJECTIVE relating to or denoting a wind instrument in which the sounds are produced by air passing over two reeds that vibrate against each other.

double refraction NOUN the splitting of a ray of unpolarized light into two unequally refracted rays polarized in mutually perpendicular planes. Also called: **birefringence.**

doubles (ˈdʌbᵊlz) NOUN (*functioning as plural*) **a** a game between two pairs of players, as in tennis, badminton, etc. **b** (*as modifier*): *a doubles player.*

double salt NOUN a solid solution of two simple salts formed by crystallizing a solution of the two salts. Compare **complex salt.**

double saucepan NOUN *Brit* a cooking utensil consisting of two saucepans, one fitting inside the other. The bottom saucepan contains water that, while boiling, gently heats food in the upper pan. US and Canadian name: **double boiler.**

double scull NOUN *Rowing* a racing shell in which two scullers sit one behind the other and pull two oars each. Compare **pair-oar.**

double sharp NOUN [1] *Music* **a** an accidental that raises the pitch of the following note by two semitones. Usual symbol: 𝄪. **b** a note affected by this accidental. ♦ ADJECTIVE [2] (*immediately postpositive*) denoting a note of a given letter name raised in pitch by two semitones.

double-space VERB to type (copy) with a full space between lines.

double spread NOUN *Printing* two facing pages of a publication treated as a single unit.

double standard NOUN a set of principles that allows greater freedom to one person or group than to another.

double star NOUN two stars, appearing close together when viewed through a telescope; either physically associated (see **binary star**) or not associated (**optical double star**).

double-stop VERB **-stops, -stopping, -stopped**. to play (two notes or parts) simultaneously on a violin or related instrument by drawing the bow over two strings.

double-system sound recording NOUN *Films* a system in which picture and sound are taken simultaneously and the sound is recorded separately on magnetic tape.

doublet ('dʌblɪt) NOUN 1 (formerly) a man's close-fitting jacket, with or without sleeves (esp in the phrase **doublet and hose.**). 2 **a** a pair of similar things, esp two words deriving ultimately from the same source, for example *reason* and *ratio* or *fragile* and *frail*. **b** one of such a pair. 3 *Jewellery* a false gem made by welding a thin layer of a gemstone onto a coloured glass base or by fusing two small stones together to make a larger one. 4 *Physics* **a** a multiplet that has two members. **b** a closely spaced pair of related spectral lines. 5 *(plural)* two dice each showing the same number of spots on one throw. 6 *Physics* two simple lenses designed to be used together, the optical distortion in one being balanced by that in the other.
▷HISTORY C14: from Old French, from DOUBLE

double tackle NOUN a lifting or pulling tackle in which a rope is passed around the twin pulleys of a pair of pulley blocks in sequence.

double take NOUN (esp in comedy) a delayed reaction by a person to a remark, situation, etc.

double talk NOUN 1 rapid speech with a mixture of nonsense syllables and real words; gibberish. 2 empty, deceptive, or ambiguous talk, esp by politicians.

doublethink ('dʌbᵊlˌθɪŋk) NOUN deliberate, perverse, or unconscious acceptance or promulgation of conflicting facts, principles, etc.

double time NOUN 1 a doubled wage rate, paid for working on public holidays, etc. 2 *Music* **a** a time twice as fast as an earlier section. **b** two beats per bar. 3 a slow running pace, keeping in step. 4 *US army* a fast march of 180 paces to the minute. ◆ VERB **double-time.** 5 to move or cause to move in double time.

doubleton ('dʌbᵊltən) NOUN *Bridge* an original holding of two cards only in a suit.

double-tongue VERB **-tongues, -tonguing, -tongued.** *Music* to play (fast staccato passages) on a wind instrument by rapid obstruction and uncovering of the air passage through the lips with the tongue. Compare **single-tongue, triple-tongue.**
▸**double tonguing** NOUN

double-tongued ADJECTIVE deceitful or hypocritical in speech.

double top NOUN *Darts* a score of double 20.

doubletree ('dʌbᵊlˌtri:) NOUN a horizontal pivoted bar on a vehicle to the ends of which swingletrees are attached for harnessing two horses side by side.

double up VERB *(adverb)* 1 to bend or cause to bend in two: *he doubled up with the pain.* 2 *(intr)* to share a room or bed designed for one person, family, etc. 3 *(intr) Brit* to use the winnings from one bet as the stake for another. US and Canadian term: **parlay.**

doubloon (dʌ'blu:n) *or* **doblón** NOUN 1 a former Spanish gold coin. 2 *(plural) Slang* money.
▷HISTORY C17: from Spanish *doblón,* from DOBLA

doublure (də'bluə; *French* dublyr) NOUN a decorative lining of vellum or leather, etc., on the inside of a book cover.
▷HISTORY C19: from French: lining, from Old French *doubler* to make double

doubly ('dʌblɪ) ADVERB 1 to or in a double degree, quantity, or measure: *doubly careful.* 2 in two ways: *doubly wrong.*

Doubs (*French* du) NOUN 1 a department of E France, in Franche-Comté region. Capital: Besançon. Pop.: 499 062 (1999). Area: 5258 sq. km (2030 sq. miles). 2 a river in E France, rising in the Jura Mountains, becoming part of the border between France and Switzerland and flowing generally southwest to the Saône River. Length: 430 km (267 miles).

doubt (daʊt) NOUN 1 uncertainty about the truth, fact, or existence of something (esp in the phrases **in doubt, without doubt, beyond a shadow of doubt,** etc.). 2 *(often plural)* lack of belief in or conviction about something: *all his doubts about the project disappeared.* 3 an unresolved difficulty, point, etc. 4 *Philosophy* the methodical device, esp in the philosophy of Descartes, of identifying certain knowledge as the residue after rejecting any proposition which might, however improbably, be false. 5 *Obsolete* fear. 6 **give (someone) the benefit of the doubt.** to presume (someone suspected of guilt) innocent; judge leniently. 7 **no doubt.** almost certainly. ◆ VERB 8 *(tr; may take a clause as object)* to be inclined to disbelieve: *I doubt we are late.* 9 *(tr)* to distrust or be suspicious of: *he doubted their motives.* 10 *(intr)* to feel uncertainty or be undecided. 11 *(tr; may take a clause as object) Scot* to be inclined to believe. 12 *(tr) Archaic* to fear. 13 **I wouldn't doubt (someone).** *Irish* I would expect nothing else from (someone).
▷HISTORY C13: from Old French *douter,* from Latin *dubitāre*
▸'**doubtable** ADJECTIVE ▸'**doubtably** ADVERB ▸'**doubter** NOUN ▸'**doubtingly** ADVERB

> **Language note** Where a clause follows *doubt* in a positive sentence, it was formerly considered correct to use *whether: (I doubt whether he will come),* but now *if* and *that* are also acceptable. In negative statements, *doubt* is followed by *that: I do not doubt that he is telling the truth.* In such sentences, *but (I do not doubt but that he is telling the truth)* is redundant.

doubtful ('daʊtfʊl) ADJECTIVE 1 unlikely; improbable. 2 characterized by or causing doubt; uncertain: *a doubtful answer.* 3 unsettled; unresolved. 4 of questionable reputation or morality. 5 having reservations or misgivings. 6 (of a sportsperson) not likely to be fit enough to play or take part. ◆ NOUN 7 a person who is undecided or uncertain about an issue. 8 a sportsperson who is not likely to be fit enough to play or take part.
▸'**doubtfully** ADVERB ▸'**doubtfulness** NOUN

doubting Thomas NOUN a person who insists on proof before he will believe anything; sceptic.
▷HISTORY after THOMAS (the apostle), who did not believe that Jesus had been resurrected until he had proof

doubtless ('daʊtlɪs) ADVERB *also* **doubtlessly.** *(sentence substitute or sentence modifier)* 1 certainly. 2 probably. ◆ ADJECTIVE 3 certain; assured.
▸'**doubtlessness** NOUN

douc (du:k) NOUN an Old World monkey, *Pygathrix nemaeus,* of SE Asia, with a bright yellow face surrounded by tufts of reddish-brown fur, a white tail, and white hindquarters: one of the langurs.
▷HISTORY C18: from French, from the native name

douce (du:s) ADJECTIVE *Scot and northern English dialect* quiet; sober; sedate.
▷HISTORY C14: from Old French, feminine of *dous,* from Latin *dulcis* sweet
▸'**doucely** ADVERB

douceur (du:'sɜ:; *French* dusœr) NOUN 1 a gratuity, tip, or bribe. 2 sweetness.
▷HISTORY C17: from French, from Late Latin *dulcor,* from Latin *dulcis* sweet

douche (du:ʃ) NOUN 1 a stream of water or air directed onto the body surface or into a body cavity, for cleansing or medical purposes. 2 the application of such a stream of water or air. 3 an instrument, such as a special syringe, for applying a douche. ◆ VERB 4 to cleanse or treat or be cleansed or treated by means of a douche.
▷HISTORY C18: from French, from Italian *doccia,* pipe; related to Latin *ductus* DUCT

douche bag NOUN 1 the bag forming part of a douche. 2 *Slang* a contemptible person.

dough (dəʊ) NOUN 1 a thick mixture of flour or meal and water or milk, used for making bread, pastry, etc. 2 any similar pasty mass. 3 a slang word for **money.**
▷HISTORY Old English *dāg;* related to Old Norse *deig,* Gothic *daigs,* Old High German *teig* dough, Sanskrit *degdhi* he daubs; see DAIRY, DUFF¹, LADY

doughboy ('dəʊˌbɔɪ) NOUN 1 *US informal* an infantryman, esp in World War I. 2 dough that is boiled or steamed as a dumpling.

> **Language note** It was formerly considered correct to use *whether* after *doubtful (it is doubtful whether he will come),* but now *if* and *that* are also acceptable.

doughnut *or esp US* **donut** ('dəʊnʌt) NOUN 1 a small cake of sweetened dough, often ring-shaped or spherical with a jam or cream filling, cooked in hot fat. 2 anything shaped like a ring, such as the reaction vessel of a thermonuclear reactor. ◆ VERB **-nuts, -nutting, -nutted.** 3 *(tr) Informal* (of Members of Parliament) to surround (a speaker) during the televising of Parliament to give the impression that the chamber is crowded or the speaker is well supported.

doughty ('daʊtɪ) ADJECTIVE **-tier, -tiest.** hardy; resolute.
▷HISTORY Old English *dohtig;* related to Old High German *toht* worth, Middle Dutch *duchtich* strong, Greek *tukhē* luck
▸'**doughtily** ADVERB ▸'**doughtiness** NOUN

doughy ('dəʊɪ) ADJECTIVE **doughier, doughiest.** resembling dough in consistency, colour, etc.; soft, pallid, or flabby.

Douglas ('dʌgləs) NOUN a town and resort on the Isle of Man, capital of the island, on the E coast. Pop.: 23 487 (1996).

Douglas fir, spruce, *or* **hemlock** NOUN a North American pyramidal coniferous tree, *Pseudotsuga menziesii,* widely planted for ornament and for timber, having needle-like leaves and hanging cones: family *Pinaceae*. Also called: **Oregon fir, Oregon pine.**
▷HISTORY C19: named after David *Douglas* (1798–1834), Scottish botanist

Douglas Hurd (ˌdʌgləs 'hɜ:d) NOUN *Brit informal* a third-class university degree. Often shortened to: **Douglas.**
▷HISTORY C20: from rhyming slang, after *Douglas Hurd* (born 1930), British Conservative politician

Douglas scale NOUN an international scale of sea disturbance and swell ranging from 0 to 9 with one figure for disturbance and one for swell.
▷HISTORY C20: named after Sir Henry *Douglas* (1876–1939), former director of the British Naval Meteorological Service

douk (dʊk) NOUN a variant spelling of **dook¹, dook².**

Doukhobor *or* **Dukhobor** ('du:kəʊˌbɔ:) NOUN a member of a Russian sect of Christians that originated in the 18th century. In the late 19th century a large minority emigrated to W Canada, where most Doukhobors now live.
▷HISTORY from Russian *dukhoborcy* spirit wrestler, from *dukh* spirit + *borcy* wrestler

doula ('du:lə) NOUN a woman who is trained to provide support to women and their families during pregnancy, childbirth, and the period of time following the birth.
▷HISTORY C20: from Greek *doule* female slave

douma *Russian* ('du:mə) NOUN a variant spelling of **duma.**

doum palm *or* **doom palm** (du:m) NOUN an Egyptian palm tree, *Hyphaene thebaica,* with a divided trunk and edible apple-sized fruits.
▷HISTORY C19 *doum,* via French from Arabic *dawm*

doun (du:n) PREPOSITION, ADVERB, ADJECTIVE a variant spelling of **doon.**

Dounreay (du:n'reɪ) NOUN the site in N Scotland of a nuclear power station, which contained the world's first fast-breeder reactor (1962–77). A prototype fast-breeder operated from 1974 until 1994: a nuclear fuel re-processing plant has also operated at the site.

do up VERB *(adverb; mainly tr)* 1 to wrap and make into a bundle: *to do up a parcel.* 2 to cause the downfall of (a person). 3 to beautify or adorn. 4 *(also intr)* to fasten or be fastened: *this skirt does up at the back.* 5 *Informal* to renovate or redecorate. 6 *Slang* to assault.

dour (dʊə, 'daʊə) ADJECTIVE 1 sullen. 2 hard or obstinate.
▷HISTORY C14: probably from Latin *dūrus* hard
▸'**dourly** ADVERB ▸'**dourness** NOUN

doura ('dʊərə) NOUN a variant of **durra.**

dourine ('dʊəri:n) NOUN an infectious venereal disease of horses characterized by swollen glands, inflamed genitals, and paralysis of the hindquarters, caused by the protozoan *Trypanosoma equiperdum* contracted during copulation.

▷**HISTORY** C19: from French, from Arabic *darina* to be dirty, scabby

Douro ('dʊərəʊ; *Portuguese* 'doru) NOUN a river in SW Europe, rising in N central Spain and flowing west to NE Portugal, then south as part of the border between the two countries and finally west to the Atlantic. Length: 895 km (556 miles). Spanish name: **Duero.**

douroucouli (ˌduːruːˈkuːlɪ) NOUN a nocturnal omnivorous New World monkey, *Aotus trivirgatus,* of Central and South America, with large eyes, thick fur, and a round head with pale and dark markings.
▷**HISTORY** from a South American Indian name

douse[1] *or* **dowse** (daʊs) VERB [1] to plunge or be plunged into water or some other liquid; duck. [2] (*tr*) to drench with water, esp in order to wash or clean. [3] (*tr*) to put out (a light, candle, etc.). ◆ NOUN [4] an immersion.
▷**HISTORY** C16: perhaps related to obsolete *douse* to strike, of obscure origin
▸ **'douser** *or* **'dowser** NOUN

douse[2] (daʊs) VERB (*tr*) [1] *Nautical* to lower (sail) quickly. [2] *Archaic* to strike or beat. ◆ NOUN [3] *Archaic* a blow.
▷**HISTORY** C16: of uncertain origin; perhaps related to DOUSE[1]

D out VERB (*adverb*) *Austral slang* (in sport) to prevent an opponent from attacking by using successful defence techniques.

douzepers ('duːzˌpeəz) PLURAL NOUN *French history* the 12 great peers of the realm, seen as the symbolic heirs of Charlemagne's 12 chosen peers.
▷**HISTORY** C13: from Old French *douze pers;* see DOZEN, PEER[1]

DOVAP ('dəʊˌvæp) NOUN a tracking system for determining the position and velocity of spacecraft, missiles, etc., based on the Doppler effect.
▷**HISTORY** C20: from *Do(ppler) v(elocity) a(nd) p(osition)*

dove[1] (dʌv) NOUN [1] any of various birds of the family *Columbidae,* having a heavy body, small head, short legs, and long pointed wings: order *Columbiformes.* They are typically smaller than pigeons. Related adjective: **columbine.** [2] *Politics* a person opposed to war. Compare **hawk**[1] (sense 3). [3] a gentle or innocent person: used as a term of endearment. [4] **a** a greyish-brown colour. **b** (*as adjective*): *dove walls.*
▷**HISTORY** Old English *dūfe* (unattested except as a feminine proper name); related to Old Saxon *dūbva,* Old High German *tūba*
▸ **'doveˌlike** ADJECTIVE ▸ **'dovish** ADJECTIVE

dove[2] (dəʊv) VERB *Chiefly US* a past tense of **dive.**

Dove (dʌv) NOUN *Christianity* **the.** a manifestation of the Holy Spirit (John 1:32).

dovecote ('dʌvˌkəʊt) *or* **dovecot** ('dʌvˌkɒt) NOUN a structure for housing pigeons, often raised on a pole or set on a wall, containing compartments for the birds to roost and lay eggs.

dovekie *or* **dovekey** ('dʌvkɪ) NOUN another name for the **little auk** (see **auk**).
▷**HISTORY** C19: Scottish diminutive of DOVE[1]

dove prion NOUN a common petrel, *Pachyptila desolata,* of the southern seas, having a bluish back and white underparts. Also called: **Antarctic prion,** (NZ informal) **blue billy.**

Dover ('dəʊvə) NOUN [1] a port in SE England, in E Kent on the Strait of Dover: the only one of the Cinque Ports that is still important; a stronghold since ancient times and Caesar's first point of attack in the invasion of Britain (55 B.C.). Pop.: 34 179 (1991). [2] **Strait of.** a strait between SE England and N France, linking the English Channel with the North Sea. Width: about 32 km (20 miles). French name: **Pas de Calais.** [3] a city in the US, the capital of Delaware, founded in 1683: 18th-century buildings. Pop.: 27 630 (1990).

Dover's powder NOUN a preparation of opium and ipecacuanha, formerly used to relieve pain, induce sweating, and check spasms.
▷**HISTORY** C19: named after Thomas *Dover* (1660–1742), English physician

dovetail ('dʌvˌteɪl) NOUN [1] a wedge-shaped tenon. [2] Also called: **dovetail joint.** a joint containing such tenons. ◆ VERB [3] (*tr*) to join by means of dovetails. [4] to fit or cause to fit together closely or neatly: *he dovetailed his arguments to the desired conclusion.*

dovetail saw NOUN *Building trades* a saw similar to a tenon saw but of smaller size.

dowable ('daʊəbᵊl) ADJECTIVE *Law* [1] capable of being endowed. [2] (of a person, esp a widow) entitled to dower.

dowager ('daʊədʒə) NOUN [1] **a** a widow possessing property or a title obtained from her husband. **b** (*as modifier*): *the dowager duchess.* [2] a wealthy or dignified elderly woman.
▷**HISTORY** C16: from Old French *douagiere,* from *douage* DOWER

dowdy ('daʊdɪ) ADJECTIVE **-dier, -diest.** [1] (esp of a woman's dress) drab, unflattering, and old-fashioned. ◆ NOUN, *plural* **-dies.** [2] a dowdy woman.
▷**HISTORY** C14: *dowd* slut, of unknown origin
▸ **'dowdily** ADVERB ▸ **'dowdiness** NOUN ▸ **'dowdyish** ADJECTIVE

dowel ('daʊəl) NOUN a wooden or metal peg that fits into two corresponding holes to join two adjacent parts. Also called: **dowel pin.**
▷**HISTORY** C14: from Middle Low German *dövel* plug, from Old High German *tubili;* related to Greek *thuphos* wedge

doweling *or* **dowelling** ('daʊlɪŋ, -əlɪŋ) NOUN *Carpentry, cabinetmaking* [1] the joining of two pieces of wood using dowels. [2] wood or other material in a long thin rod for cutting up into dowels.

dower ('daʊə) NOUN [1] the life interest in a part of her husband's estate allotted to a widow by law. [2] an archaic word for **dowry** (sense 1). [3] a natural gift or talent. ◆ VERB [4] (*tr*) to endow.
▷**HISTORY** C14: from Old French *douaire,* from Medieval Latin *dōtārium,* from Latin *dōs* gift
▸ **'dowerless** ADJECTIVE

dower house NOUN a house set apart for the use of a widow, often on her deceased husband's estate.

dowitcher ('daʊɪtʃə) NOUN either of two snipelike shore birds, *Limnodromus griseus* or *L. scolopaceus,* of arctic and subarctic North America: family *Scolopacidae* (sandpipers, etc.), order *Charadriiformes.*
▷**HISTORY** C19: of Iroquoian origin

do with VERB [1] **could** *or* **can do with.** to find useful; benefit from: *she could do with a night's sleep.* [2] **have to do with.** to be involved in or connected with: *his illness has a lot to do with his failing the exam.* [3] **to do with.** concerning; related to. [4] **what…do with. a** to put or place: *what did you do with my coat?* **b** to handle or treat: *what are we going to do with these hooligans?* **c** to fill one's time usefully: *she didn't know what to do with herself when term ended.*

do without VERB (*intr, preposition*) [1] to forgo; manage without: *I can't do without cigarettes.* [2] not to require (uncalled-for comments or advice): *we can do without your criticisms thank you.*

Dow-Jones average ('daʊ'dʒəʊnz) NOUN *US* a daily index of stock-exchange prices based on the average price of a selected number of securities.
▷**HISTORY** C20: named after Charles H. *Dow* (died 1902) and Edward D. *Jones* (died 1920), American financial statisticians

dowly ('daʊlɪ) ADJECTIVE *Northern English dialect* dull; low-spirited; dismal.
▷**HISTORY** perhaps from Old English *dol* dull

down[1] (daʊn) PREPOSITION [1] used to indicate movement from a higher to a lower position: *they went down the mountain.* [2] at a lower or further level or position on, in, or along: *he ran down the street.* ◆ ADVERB [3] downwards; at or to a lower level or position: *don't fall down.* [4] (*particle*) used with many verbs when the result of the verb's action is to lower or destroy its object: *pull down; knock down; bring down.* [5] (*particle*) used with several verbs to indicate intensity or completion: *calm down.* [6] immediately: *cash down.* [7] on paper: *write this down.* [8] arranged; scheduled: *the meeting is down for next week.* [9] in a helpless position: *they had him down on the ground.* [10] **a** away from a more important place: *down from London.* **b** away from a more northerly place: *down from Scotland.* **c** (of a member of some British universities) away from the university; on vacation. **d** in a particular part of a country: *down south.* [11] *Nautical* (of a helm) having the rudder to windward. [12] reduced to a state of lack or want: *down to the last pound.* [13] lacking a specified amount: *at the end of the day the cashier was ten pounds down.* [14] lower in price: *bacon is down.* [15] including all intermediate terms, grades, people, etc.: *from managing director down to tea-lady.* [16] from an earlier to a later time: *the heirloom was handed down.* [17] to a finer or more concentrated state: *to grind down; boil down.* [18] *Sport* being a specified number of points, goals, etc. behind another competitor, team, etc.: *six goals down.* [19] (of a person) being inactive, owing to illness: *down with flu.* [20] (*functioning as imperative*) (to dogs): *down Rover!* [21] (*functioning as imperative*) **down with.** wanting the end of somebody or something: *down with the king!* [22] **get down on something.** *Austral and NZ* to procure something, esp in advance of needs or in anticipation of someone else. ◆ ADJECTIVE [23] (*postpositive*) depressed or miserable. [24] (*prenominal*) of or relating to a train or trains from a more important place or one regarded as higher: *the down line.* [25] (*postpositive*) (of a device, machine, etc., esp a computer) temporarily out of action. [26] made in cash: *a down payment.* [27] **down to.** the responsibility or fault of: *this defeat was down to me.* ◆ VERB [28] (*tr*) to knock, push or pull down. [29] (*intr*) to go or come down. [30] (*tr*) *Informal* to drink, esp quickly: *he downed three gins.* [31] (*tr*) to bring (someone) down, esp by tackling. ◆ NOUN [32] *American football* one of a maximum of four consecutive attempts by one team to advance the ball a total of at least ten yards. [33] a descent; downward movement. [34] a lowering or a poor period (esp in the phrase **ups and downs**). [35] **have a down on.** *Informal* to bear ill will towards (someone or something).
▷**HISTORY** Old English *dūne,* short for *adūne,* variant of *of dūne,* literally: from the hill, from *of,* OFF + *dūn* hill; see DOWN[3]

down[2] (daʊn) NOUN [1] the soft fine feathers with free barbs that cover the body of a bird and prevent loss of heat. In the adult they lie beneath and between the contour feathers. [2] another name for **eiderdown** (sense 1). [3] *Botany* a fine coating of soft hairs, as on certain leaves, fruits, and seeds. [4] any growth or coating of soft fine hair, such as that on the human face.
▷**HISTORY** C14: of Scandinavian origin; related to Old Norse *dūnn*

down[3] (daʊn) NOUN *Archaic* a hill, esp a sand dune. ◆ See also **downs** (sense 1), **Downs** (sense 1).
▷**HISTORY** Old English *dūn;* related to Old Frisian *dūne,* Old Saxon *dūna* hill, Old Irish *dūn* fortress, Greek *this* sandbank; see DUNE, TOWN

Down[1] (daʊn) NOUN [1] a district of SE Northern Ireland, in Co. Down. Pop.: 63 828 (2001). Area: 649 sq. km (250 sq. miles). [2] a historical county of SE Northern Ireland, on the Irish Sea: generally hilly, rising to the Mountains of Mourne: in 1973 it was replaced for administrative purposes by the districts of Ards, Banbridge, Castlereagh, Down, Newry and Mourne, North Down, and part of Lisburn. Area: 2466 sq. km (952 sq. miles).

Down[2] (daʊn) NOUN [1] any of various lowland breeds of sheep, typically of stocky build and having dense close wool, originating from various parts of southern England, such as Oxford, Hampshire, etc. See also **Dorset Down.** [2] another name for **Hampshire Down.**

down and dirty ADJECTIVE (**down-and-dirty** when prenominal) *Informal, chiefly US* [1] ruthlessly competitive or underhand: *if Bush gets down and dirty the Governor will give as good as he gets.* [2] uninhibited; frank.

down-and-out ADJECTIVE [1] without any means of livelihood; impoverished and, often, socially outcast. ◆ NOUN [2] a person who is destitute and, often, homeless; a social outcast or derelict.

downbeat ('daʊnˌbiːt) NOUN [1] *Music* the first beat of a bar or the downward gesture of a conductor's baton indicating this. Compare **upbeat.** ◆ ADJECTIVE [2] *Informal* depressed; gloomy. [3] *Informal* relaxed; unemphatic.

down-bow ('daʊnˌbəʊ) NOUN a downward stroke of the bow from its nut to its tip across a stringed instrument. Compare **up-bow.**

downburst ('daʊnˌbɜːst) NOUN a very high-speed downward movement of turbulent air in a limited area for a short time. Near the ground it spreads out from its centre with high horizontal velocities. Also called: **microburst.**

downcast ('daʊnˌkɑːst) ADJECTIVE [1] dejected. [2] (esp of the eyes) directed downwards. ◆ NOUN [3]

Mining a ventilation shaft. [4] *Geology* another word for **downthrow.**

downcome ('daʊnˌkʌm) NOUN [1] *Archaic* downfall. [2] another name for **downcomer.**

downcomer ('daʊnˌkʌmə) NOUN a pipe that connects a cistern to a WC, wash basin, etc. Also called: **downcome.**

downdraught ('daʊnˌdrɑːft) NOUN the large-scale downward movement of air in the lee of large objects, mountains, etc.

downer ('daʊnə) NOUN *Slang* [1] Also called: **down.** a barbiturate, tranquillizer, or narcotic. Compare **upper.** [2] a depressing experience. [3] a state of depression: *he's on a downer today.*

downfall ('daʊnˌfɔːl) NOUN [1] a sudden loss of position, health, or reputation. [2] a fall of rain, snow, etc., esp a sudden heavy one. [3] another word for **deadfall.**

downfallen ('daʊnˌfɔːlən) ADJECTIVE [1] (of a building, etc.) decrepit. [2] *Chiefly US* (of a person) ruined; fallen.

downforce ('daʊnˌfɔːs) NOUN a force produced by air resistance plus gravity that increases the stability of an aircraft or motor vehicle by pressing it downwards.

downgrade ('daʊnˌgreɪd) VERB (*tr*) [1] to reduce in importance, esteem, or value, esp to demote (a person) to a poorer job. [2] to speak of disparagingly. ◆ NOUN [3] *Chiefly US and Canadian* a downward slope, esp in a road. [4] **on the downgrade.** waning in importance, popularity, health, etc.

downhaul ('daʊnˌhɔːl) NOUN *Nautical* a line for hauling down a sail or for increasing the tension at its luff.

downhearted (ˌdaʊn'hɑːtɪd) ADJECTIVE discouraged; dejected.
▸ **ˌdown'heartedly** ADVERB ▸ **ˌdown'heartedness** NOUN

downhill ('daʊn'hɪl) ADJECTIVE [1] going or sloping down. ◆ ADVERB [2] towards the bottom of a hill; downwards. [3] **go downhill.** *Informal* to decline; deteriorate. ◆ NOUN [4] the downward slope of a hill; descent. [5] a competitive event in which skiers are timed in a downhill run.

downhole ('daʊnˌhəʊl) ADJECTIVE (in the oil industry) denoting any piece of equipment that is used in the well itself.

down-home ADJECTIVE *Slang, chiefly US* of, relating to, or reminiscent of rural life, esp in the southern US; unsophisticated.

Downing Street ('daʊnɪŋ) NOUN [1] a street in W central London, in Westminster: official residences of the British prime minister and the chancellor of the exchequer. [2] *Informal* the prime minister or the British Government.
▹HISTORY named after Sir George *Downing* (1623–84), English statesman

downlifting ('daʊnˌlɪftɪŋ) ADJECTIVE tending to lower the spirits; depressing.
▹HISTORY C20: a humorous coinage based on *uplifting*

download ('daʊnˌləʊd) VERB (*tr*) [1] to copy or transfer (data or a program) into the memory of one's own computer from another computer. [2] to broadcast specialist programmes, for such groups as doctors, outside normal broadcasting hours. They are often recorded on video tapes and viewed later. Compare **upload.** [3] to delegate or assign (work) to someone else; off-load.

down-market ADJECTIVE relating to commercial products, services, etc., that are cheap, have little prestige, or are poor in quality.

Downpatrick (ˌdaʊn'pætrɪk) NOUN a market town in Northern Ireland: reputedly the burial place of Saint Patrick. Pop.: 10 257 (1991).

down payment NOUN the deposit paid on an item purchased on hire-purchase, mortgage, etc.

downpipe ('daʊnˌpaɪp) NOUN *Brit and NZ* a pipe for carrying rainwater from a roof gutter to the ground or to a drain. Also called: **rainwater pipe, drainpipe.** Usual US and Canadian name: **downspout.**

downplay ('daʊnˌpleɪ) VERB (*tr*) to play down; make little of.

downpour ('daʊnˌpɔː) NOUN a heavy continuous fall of rain.

downrange ('daʊn'reɪndʒ) ADJECTIVE, ADVERB in the direction of the intended flight path of a rocket or missile.

downright ('daʊnˌraɪt) ADJECTIVE [1] frank or straightforward; blunt: *downright speech.* [2] *Archaic* directed or pointing straight down. ◆ ADVERB, ADJECTIVE (*prenominal*) [3] (intensifier): *a downright certainty; downright rude.*
▸ **'downˌrightly** ADVERB ▸ **'downˌrightness** NOUN

downs (daʊnz) PLURAL NOUN [1] Also called: **downland.** rolling upland, esp in the chalk areas of S Britain, characterized by lack of trees and used mainly as pasture. [2] *Austral and NZ* a flat grassy area, not necessarily of uplands.

Downs (daʊnz) NOUN **the.** [1] any of various ranges of low chalk hills in S England, esp the **South Downs** in Sussex. [2] a roadstead off the SE coast of Kent, protected by the Goodwin Sands.

downshifting ('daʊnˌʃɪftɪŋ) NOUN the practice of simplifying one's lifestyle and becoming less materialistic.
▸ **'downˌshifter** NOUN

downside ('daʊnˌsaɪd) NOUN the disadvantageous aspect of a situation: *the downside of twentieth-century living.*

downsize ('daʊnˌsaɪz) VERB **-sizes, -sizing, -sized.** (*tr*) [1] to reduce the operating costs of a company by reducing the number of people it employs. [2] to reduce the size of or produce a smaller version of (something). [3] to upgrade (a computer system) by replacing a mainframe or minicomputer with a network of microcomputers. Compare **rightsize.**

downspout ('daʊnˌspaʊt) NOUN a US and Canadian name for **downpipe.**

Down's syndrome NOUN **a** *Pathol* a chromosomal abnormality resulting in a flat face and nose, short stubby fingers, a vertical fold of skin at the inner edge of the eye, and mental retardation. Former name: **mongolism. b** (*as modifier*): *a Down's syndrome baby.*
▹HISTORY C19: after John *Langdon-Down* (1828–96), English physician

downstage ('daʊn'steɪdʒ) *Theatre* ◆ ADVERB [1] at or towards the front of the stage. ◆ ADJECTIVE [2] of or relating to the front of the stage. ◆ NOUN [3] the front half of the stage.

downstairs ('daʊn'stɛəz) ADVERB [1] down the stairs; to or on a lower floor. ◆ NOUN [2] **a** a lower or ground floor. **b** (*as modifier*): *a downstairs room.* [3] *Brit informal, old-fashioned* the servants of a household collectively. Compare **upstairs** (sense 6).

downstate ('daʊnˌsteɪt) *US* ◆ ADJECTIVE [1] in, or relating to the part of the state away from large cities, esp the southern part. ◆ ADVERB [2] towards the southern part of a state. ◆ NOUN [3] the southern part of a state.

downstream ('daʊn'striːm) ADVERB, ADJECTIVE [1] in or towards the lower part of a stream; with the current. [2] (in the oil industry) of or for the refining, distribution, or marketing of oil or its derived products. Compare **upstream** (sense 2).

downswing ('daʊnˌswɪŋ) NOUN [1] a statistical downward trend in business activity, the death rate, etc. [2] *Golf* the downward movement or line of a club when striking the ball.

downthrow ('daʊnˌθrəʊ) NOUN [1] the state of throwing down or being thrown down. [2] *Geology* the sinking of rocks on one side of a fault plane.

downtime ('daʊnˌtaɪm) NOUN [1] *Commerce* time during which a machine or plant is not working because it is incapable of production, as when under repair: the term is sometimes used to include all nonproductive time. Compare **idle time.** [2] *Informal* time spent not working; spare time.

down-to-earth ADJECTIVE sensible; practical; realistic.

downtown ('daʊn'taʊn) *US, Canadian, and NZ* ◆ NOUN [1] the central or lower part of a city, esp the main commercial area. ◆ ADVERB [2] towards, to, or into this area. ◆ ADJECTIVE [3] of, relating to, or situated in the downtown area: *downtown Manhattan.*
▸ **'down'towner** NOUN

downtrodden ('daʊnˌtrɒdᵊn) *or* **downtrod** ADJECTIVE [1] subjugated; oppressed. [2] trodden down; trampled.

downturn ('daʊnˌtɜːn) NOUN a drop or reduction in the success of a business or economy.

down under *Informal* ◆ NOUN [1] Australia or New Zealand. ◆ ADVERB [2] in or to Australia or New Zealand.

downward ('daʊnwəd) ADJECTIVE [1] descending from a higher to a lower level, condition, position, etc. [2] descending from a beginning. ◆ ADVERB [3] a variant of **downwards.**
▸ **'downwardly** ADVERB ▸ **'downwardness** NOUN

downward mobility NOUN *Sociol* the movement of an individual, social group, or class to a lower status. Compare **upward mobility.** See also **horizontal mobility, vertical mobility.**

downwards ('daʊnwədz) *or* **downward** ADVERB [1] from a higher to a lower place, level, etc. [2] from an earlier time or source to a later: *from the Tudors downwards.*

downwash ('daʊnˌwɒʃ) NOUN the downward deflection of an airflow, esp one caused by an aircraft wing.

downwind ('daʊn'wɪnd) ADVERB, ADJECTIVE [1] in the same direction towards which the wind is blowing; with the wind from behind. [2] towards or on the side away from the wind; leeward.

downy ('daʊnɪ) ADJECTIVE **downier, downiest.** [1] covered with soft fine hair or feathers. [2] light, soft, and fluffy. [3] made from or filled with down. [4] resembling downs; undulating. [5] *Brit slang* sharp-witted; knowing.
▸ **'downiness** NOUN

downy mildew NOUN [1] a serious plant disease, characterized by yellowish patches on the undersurface of the leaves, caused by the parasitic fungi of the family *Peronosporaceae,* such as *Peronospora destructor:* affects onions, cauliflower, lettuce, etc. [2] any of the fungi causing this disease. ◆ Compare **powdery mildew.**

dowry ('daʊərɪ) NOUN, *plural* **-ries.** [1] the money or property brought by a woman to her husband at marriage. [2] (esp formerly) a gift made by a man to his bride or her parents. [3] *Christianity* a sum of money required on entering certain orders of nuns. [4] a natural talent or gift. [5] *Obsolete* a widow's dower.
▹HISTORY C14: from Anglo-French *douarie,* from Medieval Latin *dōtārium;* see DOWER

dowsabel ('duːsəˌbɛl, 'daʊs-) NOUN an obsolete word for **sweetheart.**
▹HISTORY C16: from Latin *Dulcibella* feminine given name, from *dulcis* sweet + *bellus* beautiful

dowse[1] (daʊs) VERB, NOUN a variant spelling of **douse**[1].
▸ **'dowser** NOUN

dowse[2] (daʊz) VERB (*intr*) to search for underground water, minerals, etc., using a divining rod; divine.
▹HISTORY C17: of unknown origin
▸ **'dowser** NOUN

dowsing rod ('daʊzɪŋ) NOUN another name for **divining rod.**

doxastic (dɒks'æstɪk) ADJECTIVE *Logic* [1] of or relating to belief. [2] denoting the branch of modal logic that studies the concept of belief.
▹HISTORY C18: from Greek *doxastikos* having an opinion, ultimately from *doxazein* to conjecture

doxographer (ˌdɒks'ɒgrəfə) NOUN *Rare* a person who collects the opinions and conjectures of ancient Greek philosophers.
▹HISTORY C19: from New Latin *doxographus,* from Greek *doxa* opinion, conjecture + *graphos* writer
▸ **ˌdoxo'graphic** ADJECTIVE ▸ **ˌdox'ography** NOUN

doxology (dɒk'sɒlədʒɪ) NOUN, *plural* **-gies.** a hymn, verse, or form of words in Christian liturgy glorifying God.
▹HISTORY C17: from Medieval Latin *doxologia,* from Greek, from *doxologos* uttering praise, from *doxa* praise; see -LOGY
▸ **doxological** (ˌdɒksə'lɒdʒɪkᵊl) ADJECTIVE
▸ **ˌdoxo'logically** ADVERB

doxy[1] *or* **doxie** ('dɒksɪ) NOUN, *plural* **doxies.** opinion or doctrine, esp concerning religious matters.
▹HISTORY C18: independent use of *-doxy* as in *orthodoxy, heterodoxy*

doxy[2] ('dɒksɪ) NOUN, *plural* **doxies.** *Archaic slang* a prostitute or mistress.
▹HISTORY C16: probably from Middle Flemish *docke* doll; compare Middle Dutch *docke* doll

doxycycline (ˌdɒksɪˈsaɪklɪn) NOUN a tetracycline antibiotic used to treat conditions caused by a wide range of bacteria, including anthrax.

doy (ˈdɔɪ) NOUN *Northern English dialect* a beloved person: used esp as an endearment.

doyen (ˈdɔɪən; *French* dwayɛ̃) NOUN the senior member of a group, profession, or society.
▷HISTORY C17: from French, from Late Latin *decānus* leader of a group of ten; see DEAN
▸**doyenne** (dɔɪˈɛn; *French* dwajɛn) FEMININE NOUN

doyley (ˈdɔɪlɪ) NOUN a variant spelling of **doily**.

doz. ABBREVIATION FOR dozen.

doze (dəʊz) VERB (*intr*) [1] to sleep lightly or intermittently. [2] (often foll by *off*) to fall into a light sleep. ◆ NOUN [3] a short sleep.
▷HISTORY C17: probably from Old Norse *dūs* lull; related to Danish *döse* to drowse, Swedish dialect *dusa* slumber
▸ˈ**dozer** NOUN

dozed (dozd, dəʊzd) ADJECTIVE *Chiefly Irish* (of timber or rubber) rotten or decayed.
▷HISTORY C18: probably from DOZE

dozen (ˈdʌzᵊn) DETERMINER [1] (preceded by *a* or a numeral) **a** twelve or a group of twelve: *a dozen eggs; two dozen oranges.* **b** (*as pronoun; functioning as singular or plural*): *give me a dozen; there are at least a dozen who haven't arrived yet.* ◆ NOUN, *plural* **dozens** *or* **dozen**. [2] **by the dozen.** in large quantities. [3] See **baker's dozen**. [4] **talk nineteen to the dozen.** to talk without stopping. ◆ See also **dozens**.
▷HISTORY C13: from Old French *douzaine,* from *douze* twelve, from Latin *duodecim,* from *duo* two + *decem* ten
▸ˈ**dozenth** ADJECTIVE

dozens (ˈdʌzᵊnz) PLURAL NOUN (usually foll by *of*) *Informal* a lot: *I've got dozens of things to do.*

dozer (ˈdəʊzə) NOUN *Chiefly US* short for **bulldozer**.

dozy (ˈdəʊzɪ) ADJECTIVE **dozier, doziest.** [1] drowsy. [2] *Brit informal* stupid.
▸ˈ**dozily** ADVERB ▸ˈ**doziness** NOUN

DP ABBREVIATION FOR: [1] data processing. [2] displaced person. [3] (in South Africa) Democratic Party.

D/P *Commerce* ABBREVIATION FOR documents against presentation.

DPB (in New Zealand) ABBREVIATION FOR domestic purposes benefit: an allowance paid to solo parents.

DPH ABBREVIATION FOR Diploma in Public Health.

DPhil *or* **DPh** ABBREVIATION FOR Doctor of Philosophy. Also: **PhD**.

dpi ABBREVIATION FOR dots per inch: a measure of the resolution of a typesetting machine, computer screen, etc.

DPM ABBREVIATION FOR Diploma in Psychological Medicine.

DPN NOUN *Biochem* diphosphopyridine nucleotide; the former name for **NAD**.

DPNH NOUN *Biochem* the reduced form of DPN; the former name for **NADH**.

DPP (in Britain) ABBREVIATION FOR **Director of Public Prosecutions**.

dpt ABBREVIATION FOR department.

DPW (in Britain, formerly) ABBREVIATION FOR Department of Public Works.

dr ABBREVIATION FOR: [1] debtor. [2] Also: **dr.** dram. [3] drawer.

Dr ABBREVIATION FOR: [1] Doctor. [2] (in street names) Drive.

DR ABBREVIATION FOR **dry riser**.

dr. ABBREVIATION FOR: [1] debit. [2] Also: **dr.** dram. [3] (the former) drachma.

drab[1] (dræb) ADJECTIVE **drabber, drabbest.** [1] dull; dingy; shabby. [2] cheerless; dreary: *a drab evening.* [3] of the colour drab. ◆ NOUN [4] a light olive-brown colour. [5] a fabric of a dull grey or brown colour.
▷HISTORY C16: from Old French *drap* cloth, from Late Latin *drappus,* perhaps of Celtic origin
▸ˈ**drably** ADVERB ▸ˈ**drabness** NOUN

drab[2] (dræb) *Archaic* ◆ NOUN [1] a slatternly woman. [2] a whore. ◆ VERB **drabs, drabbing, drabbed.** [3] (*intr*) to consort with prostitutes.
▷HISTORY C16: of Celtic origin; compare Scottish Gaelic *drabag*

drabbet (ˈdræbɪt) NOUN *Brit* a yellowish-brown fabric of coarse linen.
▷HISTORY C19: see DRAB[1]

drabble (ˈdræbᵊl) VERB to make or become wet or dirty.
▷HISTORY C14: from Low German *drabbelen* to paddle in mud; related to DRAB[2]

dracaena (drəˈsiːnə) NOUN [1] any tropical plant of the genus *Dracaena*: some species are cultivated as house plants for their decorative foliage: family *Agavaceae*. See also **dragon's blood, dragon tree.** [2] any of several similar plants of the related genus *Cordyline*.
▷HISTORY C19: from New Latin, from Latin: she-dragon, from Greek *drakaina,* feminine of *drakōn* DRAGON

drachm (dræm) NOUN [1] Also called: **fluid dram.** *Brit* one eighth of a fluid ounce. [2] *US* another name for **dram** (sense 2). [3] another name for **drachma.**
▷HISTORY C14: learned variant of DRAM

drachma (ˈdrækmə) NOUN, *plural* **-mas** *or* **-mae** (-miː). [1] the former standard monetary unit of Greece, divided into 100 lepta; replaced by the euro in 2002. [2] *US* another name for **dram** (sense 2). [3] a silver coin of ancient Greece. [4] a unit of weight in ancient Greece.
▷HISTORY C16: from Latin, from Greek *drakhmē* a handful, from *drassesthai* to seize

drack *or* **drac** (dræk) ADJECTIVE *Austral slang* (esp of a woman) unattractive.
▷HISTORY perhaps from *Dracula's* Daughter

Draco (ˈdreɪkəʊ) NOUN, *Latin genitive* **Draconis** (dreɪˈkəʊnɪs). a faint extensive constellation twisting around the N celestial pole and lying between Ursa Major and Cepheus.
▷HISTORY from Latin, from Greek *drakōn* DRAGON

draco lizard (ˈdreɪkəʊ) NOUN another name for **flying lizard.**

dracone (ˈdrækəʊn) NOUN a large flexible cylindrical container towed by a ship, used for transporting liquids.
▷HISTORY C20: from Latin: DRAGON

draconic (dreɪˈkɒnɪk) ADJECTIVE of, like, or relating to a dragon.
▷HISTORY C17: from Latin *dracō* DRAGON
▸**draˈconically** ADVERB

draconic month NOUN *Astronomy* the mean time taken by the moon between successive passages through the ascending node of its orbit. It is about 2.5 hours shorter than the sidereal month. Also called: **nodical month.**

draff (dræf) NOUN the residue of husks after fermentation of the grain used in brewing, used as a food for cattle.
▷HISTORY C13: from Old Norse *draf;* related to Old High German *trebir,* Russian *drob* fragment; see DRIVEL
▸ˈ**draffy** ADJECTIVE

draft (drɑːft) NOUN [1] a plan, sketch, or drawing of something. [2] a preliminary outline of a book, speech, etc. [3] another word for **bill of exchange.** [4] a demand or drain on something. [5] the divergent duct leading from a water turbine to its tailrace. [6] *US* selection for compulsory military service. [7] detachment of military personnel from one unit to another. [8] *Commerce* an allowance on merchandise sold by weight. [9] a line or narrow border that is chiselled on the surface of a stone to serve as a guide for levelling it. [10] *Austral and NZ* a group of livestock separated from the rest of the herd or flock. ◆ VERB (*tr*) [11] to draw up an outline or sketch for something: *to draft a speech.* [12] to prepare a plan or design of. [13] to detach (military personnel) from one unit to another. [14] *Chiefly US* to select for compulsory military service. [15] to chisel a draft on (stone, etc.). [16] *Austral and NZ* **a** to select (cattle or sheep) from a herd or flock. **b** to select (farm stock) for sale. ◆ NOUN, VERB [17] the usual US spelling of **draught** (senses 1–8, 11).
▷HISTORY C16: variant of DRAUGHT
▸ˈ**drafter** NOUN

draft board NOUN *US* a tribunal responsible for the selection of personnel liable for compulsory military service.

draft dodger NOUN *US* one who evades compulsory military service.

draftee (drɑːfˈtiː) NOUN *US* a conscript.

draft-mule work NOUN the US and Canadian word for **donkey-work.**

draft-quality printing NOUN *Computing* low-quality, high-speed output in printed form from a printer linked to a word processor. Compare **letter-quality printing.**

draftsman (ˈdrɑːftsmən) NOUN, *plural* **-men.** the usual US spelling of **draughtsman** (senses 1, 2).
▸ˈ**draftsmanship** NOUN

drafty (ˈdrɑːftɪ) ADJECTIVE **draftier, draftiest.** the usual US spelling of **draughty.**
▸ˈ**draftily** ADVERB ▸ˈ**draftiness** NOUN

drag (dræg) VERB **drags, dragging, dragged.** [1] to pull or be pulled with force, esp along the ground or other surface. [2] (*tr; often foll by away or from*) to persuade to come away (from something attractive or interesting): *he couldn't drag himself away from the shop.* [3] to trail or cause to trail on the ground. [4] (*tr*) to move (oneself, one's feet, etc.) with effort or difficulty: *he drags himself out of bed at dawn.* [5] to linger behind. [6] (often foll by *on* or *out*) to prolong or be prolonged tediously or unnecessarily: *his talk dragged on for hours.* [7] (*tr;* foll by *out*) to pass (time) in discomfort, poverty, unhappiness, etc.: *he dragged out his few remaining years.* [8] (when *intr,* usually foll by *for*) to search (the bed of a river, canal, etc.) with a dragnet or hook: *they dragged the river for the body.* [9] (*tr* foll by *out* or *from*) to crush (clods) or level (a soil surface) by use of a drag. [10] (of hounds) to follow (a fox or its trail) to the place where it has been lying. [11] (*intr*) *Slang* to draw (on a cigarette, pipe, etc.). [12] *Computing* to move (data) from one place to another on the screen by manipulating a mouse with its button held down. [13] **drag anchor.** (of a vessel) to move away from its mooring because the anchor has failed to hold. [14] **drag one's feet** *or* **heels.** *Informal* to act with deliberate slowness. [15] **drag (someone's) name in the mud.** to disgrace or defame (someone). ◆ NOUN [16] the act of dragging or the state of being dragged. [17] an implement, such as a dragnet, dredge, etc., used for dragging. [18] Also called: **drag harrow.** a type of harrow consisting of heavy beams, often with spikes inserted, used to crush clods, level soil, or prepare seedbeds. [19] a sporting coach with seats inside and out, usually drawn by four horses. [20] a braking or retarding device, such as a metal piece fitted to the underside of the wheel of a horse-drawn vehicle. [21] a person or thing that slows up progress. [22] slow progress or movement. [23] *Aeronautics* the resistance to the motion of a body passing through a fluid, esp through air: applied to an aircraft in flight, it is the component of the resultant aerodynamic force measured parallel to the direction of air flow. [24] the trail of scent left by a fox or other animal hunted with hounds. [25] an artificial trail of a strong-smelling substance, sometimes including aniseed, drawn over the ground for hounds to follow. [26] See **drag hunt.** [27] *Angling* unnatural movement imparted to a fly, esp a dry fly, by tension on the angler's line. [28] *Informal* a person or thing that is very tedious; bore: *exams are a drag.* [29] *Slang* a car. [30] short for **drag race.** [31] *Slang* **a** women's clothes worn by a man, usually by a transvestite (esp in the phrase **in drag**). **b** (*as modifier*): *a drag club; drag show.* **c** clothes collectively. [32] *Informal* a draw on a cigarette, pipe, etc. [33] *US slang* influence or persuasive power. [34] *Chiefly US slang* a street or road. ◆ See also **drag down, drag in, drag out of, drag up.**
▷HISTORY Old English *dragan* to DRAW; related to Swedish *dragga*

drag down VERB (*tr, adverb*) to depress or demoralize: *the flu really dragged her down.*

dragée (dræˈʒeɪ) NOUN [1] a sweet made of a nut, fruit, etc., coated with a hard sugar icing. [2] a tiny beadlike sweet used for decorating cakes, etc. [3] a medicinal formulation coated with sugar to disguise the taste.
▷HISTORY C19: from French; see DREDGE[2]

dragging (ˈdrægɪŋ) NOUN a decorating technique in which paint is applied with a specially modified brush to create a marbled or grainy effect.

draggle (ˈdrægᵊl) VERB [1] to make or become wet or dirty by trailing on the ground; bedraggle. [2] (*intr*) to lag; dawdle.
▷HISTORY C16: probably frequentative of DRAG

draggletailed (ˈdrægᵊlˌteɪld) ADJECTIVE *Archaic* (esp of a woman) bedraggled; besmirched.

draggy (ˈdræɡɪ) ADJECTIVE **-gier, -giest.** *Slang* [1] slow or boring: *a draggy party.* [2] dull and listless.

draghound (ˈdræɡˌhaʊnd) NOUN a hound used to follow an artificial trail of scent in a drag hunt.

drag hunt NOUN [1] a hunt in which hounds follow an artificial trail of scent. [2] a club that organizes such hunts. ◆ VERB **drag-hunt.** [3] to follow draghounds, esp on horseback, or cause (draghounds) to follow an artificial trail of scent.

drag in VERB (*tr, adverb*) to introduce or mention (a topic, name, etc.) with slight or no pretext.

dragline (ˈdræɡˌlaɪn) NOUN [1] another word for **dragrope** (sense 2). [2] Also called: **dragline crane, dragline excavator.** a power shovel that operates by being dragged by cables at the end of an arm or jib: used for quarrying, opencast mining, etc.

drag link NOUN a link for conveying motion between cranks on parallel shafts that are slightly offset. It is used in cars to connect the steering gear to the steering arm.

dragnet (ˈdræɡˌnɛt) NOUN [1] a heavy or weighted net used to scour the bottom of a pond, river, etc., as when searching for something. [2] any system of coordinated efforts by police forces to track down wanted persons.

dragoman (ˈdræɡəʊmən) NOUN, *plural* **-mans** *or* **-men.** (in some Middle Eastern countries, esp formerly) a professional interpreter or guide.
▷HISTORY C14: from French, from Italian *dragomano,* from Medieval Greek *dragoumanos,* from Arabic *targumān* an interpreter, from Aramaic *tūrgemānā,* of Akkadian origin

dragon (ˈdræɡən) NOUN [1] a mythical monster usually represented as breathing fire and having a scaly reptilian body, wings, claws, and a long tail. [2] *Informal* a fierce or intractable person, esp a woman. [3] any of various very large lizards, esp the Komodo dragon. [4] any of various North American aroid plants, esp the green dragon. [5] *Christianity* a manifestation of Satan or an attendant devil. [6] a yacht of the International Dragon Class, 8.88m long (29.2 feet), used in racing. [7] **chase the dragon.** *Slang* to smoke opium or heroin.
▷HISTORY C13: from Old French, from Latin *dracō,* from Greek *drakōn;* related to *drakos* eye
▸ˈ**dragoness** FEMININE NOUN ▸ˈ**dragonish** ADJECTIVE

dragonet (ˈdræɡənɪt) NOUN any small spiny-finned fish of the family *Callionymidae,* having a flat head and a slender tapering brightly coloured body and living at the bottom of shallow seas.
▷HISTORY C14 (meaning: small dragon): from French; applied to fish C18

dragonfly (ˈdræɡənˌflaɪ) NOUN, *plural* **-flies.** [1] any predatory insect of the suborder *Anisoptera,* having a large head and eyes, a long slender body, two pairs of iridescent wings that are outspread at rest, and aquatic larvae: order *Odonata.* See also **damselfly.** [2] any other insect of the order *Odonata.*

dragonhead (ˈdræɡənˌhɛd) *or* **dragon's-head** NOUN [1] any plant of the genus *Dracocephalum,* of Europe, Asia, and North America, having dense spikes of white or bluish flowers: family *Lamiaceae* (labiates). [2] any North American plant of the related genus *Physostegia,* having pink or purplish flowers.

dragon market NOUN *Informal* any of the emerging markets of the Pacific rim, esp Indonesia, Malaysia, Thailand, and the Philippines. Compare **tiger market.**

dragonnade (ˌdræɡəˈneɪd) NOUN [1] *History* the persecution of French Huguenots during the reign of Louis XIV by dragoons quartered in their villages and homes. [2] subjection by military force. ◆ VERB [3] (*tr*) to subject to persecution by military troops.
▷HISTORY C18: from French, from *dragon* DRAGOON

dragonroot (ˈdræɡənˌruːt) NOUN [1] a North American aroid plant, *Arisaema dracontium,* having a greenish spathe and a long pointed spadix. [2] the tuberous root of this plant, formerly used in medicine as an expectorant and diaphoretic.

dragon's blood NOUN [1] a red resinous substance obtained from the fruit of a Malaysian palm, *Daemonorops* (or *Calamus*) *draco:* formerly used medicinally and now used in varnishes and lacquers. [2] any of several similar resins obtained from other trees, esp from the dragon tree and a related species, *Dracaena cinnabari* (Socotra dragon's blood dracaena).

dragon's teeth PLURAL NOUN [1] *Informal* conical or wedge-shaped concrete antitank obstacles protruding from the ground in rows: used in World War II. [2] **sow dragon's teeth.** to take some action that is intended to prevent strife or trouble but that actually brings it about.
▷HISTORY sense 2 from the story of CADMUS

dragon tree NOUN a tree, *Dracaena draco,* of the Canary Islands, having clusters of sword-shaped leaves at the tips of its branches: family *Agavaceae.* It is a source of dragon's blood.

dragoon (drəˈɡuːn) NOUN [1] (originally) a mounted infantryman armed with a carbine. [2] (*sometimes capital*) a domestic fancy pigeon. [3] **a** a type of cavalryman. **b** (*plural; capital when part of a name*): *the Royal Dragoons.* ◆ VERB (*tr*) [4] to coerce; force: *he was dragooned into admitting it.* [5] to persecute by military force.
▷HISTORY C17: from French *dragon* (special use of DRAGON), soldier armed with a carbine, perhaps suggesting that a carbine, like a dragon, breathed forth fire
▸**draˈgoonage** NOUN

drag out of VERB (*tr, adverb + prep*) to obtain or extract (a confession, statement, etc.), esp by force: *we dragged the name out of him.* Also: **drag from.**

drag race NOUN a type of motor race in which specially built or modified cars or motorcycles are timed over a measured course.
▸**drag racer** NOUN ▸**drag racing** NOUN

dragrope (ˈdræɡˌrəʊp) NOUN [1] a rope used to drag military equipment, esp artillery. [2] Also called: **dragline, guide rope.** a rope trailing from a balloon or airship for mooring or braking purposes.

drag sail NOUN another term for **sea anchor.**

dragster (ˈdræɡstə) NOUN a car specially built or modified for drag racing.

drag up VERB (*tr, adverb*) *Informal* [1] to rear (a child) poorly and in an undisciplined manner. [2] to introduce or revive (an unpleasant fact or story).

drail (dreɪl) *Angling* ◆ NOUN [1] a weighted hook used in trolling. ◆ VERB [2] (*intr*) to fish with a drail.
▷HISTORY C16: apparently from TRAIL, influenced by DRAW

drain (dreɪn) NOUN [1] a pipe or channel that carries off water, sewage, etc. [2] an instance or cause of continuous diminution in resources or energy; depletion. [3] *Surgery* a device, such as a tube, for insertion into a wound, incision, or bodily cavity to drain off pus, etc. [4] *Electronics* the electrode region in a field-effect transistor into which majority carriers flow from the interelectrode conductivity channel. [5] **down the drain.** wasted. ◆ VERB [6] (*tr; often foll by off*) to draw off or remove (liquid) from: *to drain water from vegetables; to drain vegetables.* [7] (*intr; often foll by away*) to flow (away) or filter (off). [8] (*intr*) to dry or be emptied as a result of liquid running off or flowing away: *leave the dishes to drain.* [9] (*tr*) to drink the entire contents of (a glass, cup, etc.). [10] (*tr*) to consume or make constant demands on (resources, energy, etc.); exhaust; sap. [11] (*intr*) to disappear or leave, esp gradually: *the colour drained from his face.* [12] (*tr*) (of a river, etc.) to carry off the surface water from (an area). [13] (*intr*) (of an area) to discharge its surface water into rivers, streams, etc.
▷HISTORY Old English *drēahnian;* related to Old Norse *drangr* dry wood; see DRY
▸ˈ**drainable** ADJECTIVE

drainage (ˈdreɪnɪdʒ) NOUN [1] the process or a method of draining. [2] a system of watercourses or drains. [3] liquid, sewage, etc., that is drained away.

drainage basin *or* **area** NOUN another name for **catchment area.**

drainer (ˈdreɪnə) NOUN [1] a person or thing that drains. [2] another name for **draining board.** [3] a rack near a sink on which washed dishes, etc. are placed to drain.

draining board NOUN a sloping grooved surface at the side of a sink, used for draining washed dishes, etc. Also called: **drainer.**

drainlayer (ˈdreɪnˌleɪə) NOUN *NZ* a person trained to build or repair drains.

drainpipe (ˈdreɪnˌpaɪp) NOUN a pipe for carrying off rainwater, sewage, etc.; downpipe.

drainpipes (ˈdreɪnˌpaɪps) PLURAL NOUN trousers with very narrow legs.

drain rod NOUN one of a series of flexible rods with threaded ends that screw together and can be pushed to and fro in a drain to clear a blockage.

drake[1] (dreɪk) NOUN the male of any duck.
▷HISTORY C13: perhaps from Low German; compare Middle Dutch *andrake,* Old High German *antrahho*

drake[2] (dreɪk) NOUN [1] *Angling* an artificial fly resembling a mayfly. [2] *History* a small cannon. [3] an obsolete word for **dragon.**
▷HISTORY Old English *draca,* ultimately from Latin *dracō* DRAGON

Drakensberg (ˈdrɑːkənzˌbɜːɡ) NOUN a mountain range in southern Africa, extending through Lesotho, E South Africa, and Swaziland. Highest peak: Thabana Ntlenyana, 3482 m (11 425 ft.). Sotho name: **Quathlamba.**

Drake Passage NOUN a strait between S South America and the South Shetland Islands, connecting the Atlantic and Pacific Oceans.

Dralon (ˈdreɪlɒn) NOUN *Trademark* an acrylic fibre fabric used esp for upholstery.

dram (dræm) NOUN [1] one sixteenth of an ounce (avoirdupois). 1 dram is equivalent to 0.0018 kilogram. [2] Also called: **drachm, drachma.** *US* one eighth of an apothecaries' ounce; 60 grains. 1 dram is equivalent to 0.0039 kilogram. [3] a small amount of an alcoholic drink, esp a spirit; tot. [4] the standard monetary unit of Armenia, divided into 100 lumas.
▷HISTORY C15: from Old French *dragme,* from Late Latin *dragma,* from Greek *drakhmē;* see DRACHMA

DRAM *or* **D-RAM** (ˈdiːræm) ACRONYM FOR dynamic random access memory: **a** a widely used type of random access memory. See **RAM**[1]. **b** a chip containing such a memory.

drama (ˈdrɑːmə) NOUN [1] a work to be performed by actors on stage, radio, or television; play. [2] the genre of literature represented by works intended for the stage. [3] the art of the writing and production of plays. [4] a situation or sequence of events that is highly emotional, tragic, or turbulent.
▷HISTORY C17: from Late Latin: a play, from Greek: something performed, from *drān* to do

Dramamine (ˈdræməˌmiːn) NOUN a trademark for **dimenhydrinate.**

drama queen NOUN *Informal* a person who tends to react to every situation in an overdramatic or exaggerated manner.

dramatic (drəˈmætɪk) ADJECTIVE [1] of or relating to drama. [2] like a drama in suddenness, emotional impact, etc. [3] striking; effective. [4] acting or performed in a flamboyant way. [5] *Music* (of a voice) powerful and marked by histrionic quality.
▸**draˈmatically** ADVERB

dramatic irony NOUN *Theatre* the irony occurring when the implications of a situation, speech, etc., are understood by the audience but not by the characters in the play.

dramatics (drəˈmætɪks) NOUN [1] (*functioning as singular or plural*) **a** the art of acting or producing plays. **b** dramatic productions. [2] (*usually functioning as plural*) histrionic behaviour.

dramatis personae (ˈdrɑːmətɪs pəˈsəʊnaɪ) PLURAL NOUN (*often functioning as singular*) [1] the characters or a list of characters in a play or story. [2] the main personalities in any situation or event.
▷HISTORY C18: from New Latin

dramatist (ˈdræmətɪst) NOUN a writer of plays; playwright.

dramatization *or* **dramatisation** (ˌdræmətaɪˈzeɪʃən) NOUN [1] the reconstruction of an event, novel, story, etc. in a form suitable for dramatic presentation. [2] the art or act of dramatizing.

dramatize *or* **dramatise** (ˈdræməˌtaɪz) VERB [1] (*tr*) to put into dramatic form. [2] to express or represent (something) in a dramatic or exaggerated way: *he dramatizes his illness.*
▸ˈ**dramaˌtizable** *or* ˈ**dramaˌtisable** ADJECTIVE ▸ˈ**dramaˌtizer** *or* ˈ**dramaˌtiser** NOUN

dramaturge (ˈdræməˌtɜːdʒ) NOUN [1] Also called:

dramaturgist. a dramatist, esp one associated with a particular company or theatre. 2 Also called: **dramaturg.** a literary adviser on the staff of a theatre, film corporation, etc., whose responsibilities may include selection and editing of texts, liaison with authors, preparation of printed programmes, and public relations work.
▷HISTORY C19: probably from French, from Greek *dramatourgos* playwright, from DRAMA + *ergon* work

dramaturgy ('dræmə,tɜːdʒɪ) NOUN the art and technique of the theatre; dramatics.
▸ **,drama'turgic** *or* **,drama'turgical** ADJECTIVE
▸ **,drama'turgically** ADVERB

Drambuie (dræm'bjuːɪ) NOUN *Trademark* a liqueur based on Scotch whisky and made exclusively in Scotland from a recipe dating from the 18th century.

dramedy ('drɑːmɪdɪ) NOUN, *plural* **-dies.** a television or film drama in which there are important elements of comedy.
▷HISTORY C20: from DRAM(A) + (COM)EDY

Drancy (*French* drɑ̃si) NOUN a residential suburb of NE Paris. Pop.: 64 363 (latest est.).

drangway ('dræŋ,weɪ) NOUN *Southwest English dialect* a narrow lane; passageway.

drank (dræŋk) VERB the past tense of **drink.**

drap (dræp) NOUN, VERB a Scot word for **drop.**

drape (dreɪp) VERB 1 (*tr*) to hang or cover with flexible material or fabric, usually in folds; adorn. 2 to hang or arrange or be hung or arranged, esp in folds. 3 (*tr*) to place casually and loosely; hang: *she draped her arm over the back of the chair.* ◆ NOUN 4 (*often plural*) a cloth or hanging that covers something in folds; drapery. 5 the way in which fabric hangs. ◆ See also **drapes.**
▷HISTORY C15: from Old French *draper,* from *drap* piece of cloth; see DRAB[1]
▸ **'drapable** *or* **'drapeable** ADJECTIVE

draper ('dreɪpə) NOUN *Brit* a dealer in fabrics and sewing materials.

drapery ('dreɪpərɪ) NOUN, *plural* **-peries.** 1 fabric or clothing arranged and draped. 2 (*often plural*) curtains or hangings that drape. 3 *Brit* the occupation or shop of a draper. 4 fabrics and cloth collectively.
▸ **'draperied** ADJECTIVE

drapes (dreɪps) *or* **draperies** ('dreɪpərɪz) PLURAL NOUN *Chiefly US and Canadian* curtains, esp ones of heavy fabric.

drappie ('dræpɪ) NOUN *Scot* a little drop, esp a small amount of spirits.

drastic ('dræstɪk) ADJECTIVE extreme or forceful; severe.
▷HISTORY C17: from Greek *drastikos,* from *dran* to do, act
▸ **'drastically** ADVERB

drat (dræt) INTERJECTION *Slang* an exclamation of annoyance (also in the phrases **drat it! drat you!** etc.).
▷HISTORY C19: probably alteration of *God rot*

dratted ('drætɪd) ADJECTIVE (*prenominal*) *Informal* wretched; annoying.

draught *or US* **draft** (drɑːft) NOUN 1 a current of air, esp one intruding into an enclosed space. 2 **a** the act of pulling a load, as by a vehicle or animal. **b** (*as modifier*): *a draught horse.* 3 the load or quantity drawn. 4 a portion of liquid to be drunk, esp a dose of medicine. 5 the act or an instance of drinking; a gulp or swallow. 6 the act or process of drawing air, smoke, etc., into the lungs. 7 the amount of air, smoke, etc., inhaled in one breath. 8 **a** beer, wine, etc., stored in bulk, esp in a cask, as opposed to being bottled. **b** (*as modifier*): *draught beer.* **c on draught.** drawn from a cask or keg. 9 Also called: **draughtsman.** any one of the 12 flat thick discs used by each player in the game of draughts. US and Canadian equivalent: **checker.** 10 the depth of a loaded vessel in the water, taken from the level of the waterline to the lowest point of the hull. 11 **feel the draught.** to be short of money. ◆ See also **draughts.**
▷HISTORY C14: probably from Old Norse *drahtr,* of Germanic origin; related to DRAW
▸ **'draughter** *or US* **'drafter** NOUN

draughtboard ('drɑːft,bɔːd) NOUN a square board divided into 64 squares of alternating colours, used for playing draughts or chess.

draughts (drɑːfts) NOUN (*functioning as singular*) a game for two players using a draughtboard and 12 draughtsmen each. The object is to jump over and capture the opponent's pieces. US and Canadian name: **checkers.**
▷HISTORY C14: plural of DRAUGHT (in obsolete sense: a chess move)

draughtsman *or US* **draftsman** ('drɑːftsmən) NOUN, *plural* **-men.** 1 Also called (feminine): **draughtswoman.** a person who practises or is qualified in mechanical drawing, employed to prepare detailed scale drawings of machinery, buildings, devices, etc. 2 Also called (feminine): **draughtswoman.** a person skilled in drawing. 3 *Brit* any of the 12 flat thick discs used by each player in the game of draughts. US and Canadian equivalent: **checker.**
▸ **'draughtsman,ship** *or US* **'draftsman,ship** NOUN

draughty *or US* **drafty** ('drɑːftɪ) ADJECTIVE **draughtier, draughtiest** *or US* **draftier, draftiest.** characterized by or exposed to draughts of air.
▸ **'draughtily** *or US* **'draftily** ADVERB ▸ **'draughtiness** *or US* **'draftiness** NOUN

Drava *or* **Drave** ('drɑːvə) NOUN a river in S central Europe, rising in N Italy and flowing east through Austria, then southeast along the southern Hungarian border to join the River Danube. Length: 725 km (450 miles). German name: **Drau** (drau).

Dravidian (drə'vɪdɪən) NOUN 1 a family of languages spoken in S and central India and Sri Lanka, including Tamil, Malayalam, Telugu, Kannada, and Gondi. 2 a member of one of the aboriginal races of India, pushed south by the Indo-Europeans and now mixed with them. ◆ ADJECTIVE 3 denoting, belonging to, or relating to this family of languages or these peoples.

draw (drɔː) VERB **draws, drawing, drew, drawn.** 1 to cause (a person or thing) to move towards or away by pulling. 2 to bring, take, or pull (something) out, as from a drawer, holster, etc. 3 (*tr*) to extract or pull or take out: *to draw teeth; to draw a card from a pack.* 4 (*tr; often foll by off*) to take (liquid) out of a cask, keg, tank, etc., by means of a tap. 5 (*intr*) to move, go, or proceed, esp in a specified direction: *to draw alongside.* 6 (*tr*) to attract or elicit: *to draw a crowd; draw attention.* 7 (*tr*) to cause to flow: *to draw blood.* 8 to depict or sketch (a form, figure, picture, etc.) in lines, as with a pencil or pen, esp without the use of colour; delineate. 9 (*tr*) to make, formulate, or derive: *to draw conclusions, comparisons, parallels.* 10 (*tr*) to write (a legal document) in proper form. 11 (*tr; sometimes foll by in*) to suck or take in (air, liquid, etc.): *to draw a breath.* 12 (*intr*) to induce or allow a draught to carry off air, smoke, etc.: *the flue draws well.* 13 (*tr*) to take or receive from a source: *to draw money from the bank.* 14 (*tr*) to earn: *draw interest.* 15 (*tr*) *Finance* to write out (a bill of exchange or promissory note): *to draw a cheque.* 16 (*tr*) to choose at random: *to draw lots.* 17 (*tr*) to reduce the diameter of (a wire or metal rod) by pulling it through a die. 18 (*tr*) to shape (a sheet of metal or glass) by rolling, by pulling it through a die or by stretching. 19 *Archery* to bend (a bow) by pulling the string. 20 to steep (tea) or (of tea) to steep in boiling water. 21 (*tr*) to disembowel: *draw a chicken.* 22 (*tr*) to cause (pus, blood, etc.) to discharge from an abscess or wound. 23 (*intr*) (of two teams, contestants, etc.) to finish a game with an equal number of points, goals, etc.; tie. 24 (*tr*) *Bridge, whist* to keep leading a suit in order to force out (all outstanding cards). 25 **draw trumps.** *Bridge, whist* to play the trump suit until the opponents have none left. 26 (*tr*) *Billiards* to cause (the cue ball) to spin back after a direct impact with another ball by applying backspin when making the stroke. 27 (*tr*) to search (a place) in order to find wild animals, game, etc., for hunting. 28 *Golf* to cause (a golf ball) to move with a controlled right-to-left trajectory or (of a golf ball) to veer gradually from right to left. 29 (*tr*) *Curling* to deliver (the stone) gently. 30 (*tr*) *Nautical* (of a vessel) to require (a certain depth) in which to float. 31 **draw (a) blank.** to get no results from something. 32 **draw and quarter.** to disembowel and dismember (a person) after hanging. 33 **draw stumps.** *Cricket* to close play, as by pulling out the stumps. 34 **draw the line (at).** See **line**[1] (sense 51). 35 **draw the short straw.** See **short straw.** 36 **draw the shot.** *Bowls* to deliver the bowl in such a way that it approaches the jack. ◆ NOUN 37 the act of drawing. 38 *US* a sum of money advanced to finance anticipated expenses. 39 an event, occasion, act, etc., that attracts a large audience. 40 a raffle or lottery. 41 something taken or chosen at random, as a ticket in a raffle or lottery. 42 a contest or game ending in a tie. 43 *US and Canadian* a small natural drainage way or gully. 44 a defect found in metal castings due to the contraction of the metal on solidification. ◆ See also **drawback, draw in, draw off, draw on, draw out, draw up.**
▷HISTORY Old English *dragan;* related to Old Norse *draga;* Old Frisian *draga,* Old Saxon *dragan,* Old High German *tragan* to carry
▸ **'drawable** ADJECTIVE

drawback ('drɔː,bæk) NOUN 1 a disadvantage or hindrance. 2 a refund of customs or excise duty paid on goods that are being exported or used in the production of manufactured exports. ◆ VERB **draw back.** (*intr, adverb; often foll by from*) 3 to retreat; move backwards. 4 to turn aside from an undertaking.

drawbar ('drɔː,bɑː) NOUN a strong metal bar on a tractor, locomotive, etc., bearing a hook or link and pin to attach a trailer, wagon, etc.

drawbridge ('drɔː,brɪdʒ) NOUN a bridge that may be raised to prevent access or to enable vessels to pass.

drawee (drɔː'iː) NOUN the person or organization on which a cheque or other order for payment is drawn.

drawer ('drɔːə) NOUN 1 a person or thing that draws, esp a draughtsman. 2 a person who draws a cheque. See **draw** (sense 15). 3 a person who draws up a commercial paper. 4 *Archaic* a person who draws beer, etc., in a bar. 5 (drɔː) a boxlike container in a chest, table, etc., made for sliding in and out.

drawers (drɔːz) PLURAL NOUN a legged undergarment for either sex, worn below the waist. Also called: **underdrawers.**

draw-gate NOUN the valve that controls a sluice.

draw gear NOUN *Brit* an apparatus for coupling railway cars.

draw in VERB (*intr, adverb*) 1 (of hours of daylight) to become shorter. 2 (of a train) to arrive at a station.

drawing ('drɔːɪŋ) NOUN 1 a picture or plan made by means of lines on a surface, esp one made with a pencil or pen without the use of colour. 2 a sketch, plan, or outline. 3 the art of making drawings; draughtsmanship.

drawing account NOUN *US* an account out of which an employee, partner, or salesman may make withdrawals to meet expenses or as advances against expected income.

drawing board NOUN 1 a smooth flat rectangular board on which paper, canvas, etc., is placed for making drawings. 2 **back to the drawing board.** return to an earlier stage in an enterprise because a planned undertaking has failed.

drawing card NOUN *US and Canadian theatre* a performer, act, etc., certain to attract a large audience.

drawing pin NOUN *Brit* a short tack with a broad smooth head for fastening papers to a drawing board, etc. US and Canadian name: **thumbtack.**

drawing room NOUN 1 a room where visitors are received and entertained; living room; sitting room. 2 *Archaic* a ceremonial or formal reception, esp at court.

drawknife ('drɔː,naɪf) *or* **drawshave** NOUN, *plural* **-knives** *or* **-shaves.** a woodcutting tool with two handles at right angles to the blade, used to shave wood. US name: **spokeshave.**

drawl (drɔːl) VERB 1 to speak or utter (words) slowly, esp prolonging the vowel sounds. ◆ NOUN 2 the way of speech of someone who drawls.
▷HISTORY C16: probably frequentative of DRAW
▸ **'drawler** NOUN ▸ **'drawling** ADJECTIVE ▸ **'drawly** ADJECTIVE

drawn (drɔːn) ADJECTIVE haggard, tired, or tense in appearance.

drawn butter NOUN melted butter often with seasonings.

drawn work NOUN ornamental needlework done by drawing threads out of the fabric and using the remaining threads to form lacelike patterns. Also called: **drawn-thread work.**

draw off VERB *(adverb)* 1 *(tr)* to cause (a liquid) to flow from something. 2 to withdraw (troops).

draw on VERB 1 *(intr, preposition)* to use or exploit (a source, fund, etc.): *to draw on one's experience.* 2 *(intr, adverb)* to come near: *the time for his interview drew on.* 3 *(tr, preposition)* to withdraw (money) from (an account). 4 *(tr, adverb)* to put on (clothes). 5 *(tr, adverb)* to lead further; entice or encourage: *the prospect of nearing his goal drew him on.*

draw out VERB *(adverb)* 1 to extend or cause to be extended: *he drew out his stay.* 2 *(tr)* to cause (a person) to talk freely: *she's been quiet all evening — see if you can draw her out.* 3 *(tr;* foll by *of)* Also: **draw from.** to elicit (information) (from): *he managed to draw out of his son where he had been.* 4 *(tr)* to withdraw (money) as from a bank account or a business. 5 *(intr)* (of hours of daylight) to become longer. 6 *(intr)* (of a train) to leave a station. 7 *(tr)* to extend (troops) in line; lead from camp. 8 *(intr)* (of troops) to proceed from camp.

drawplate ('drɔːˌpleɪt) NOUN a plate used to reduce the diameter of wire by drawing it through conical holes.

drawstring ('drɔːˌstrɪŋ) NOUN **a** a cord, ribbon, etc., run through a hem around an opening, as on the bottom of a sleeve or at the mouth of a bag, so that when it is pulled tighter, the opening closes. **b** *(as modifier)*: *a drawstring neckline.*

drawtube ('drɔːˌtjuːb) NOUN a tube, such as one of the component tubes of a telescope, fitting coaxially within another tube through which it can slide.

draw up VERB *(adverb)* 1 to come or cause to come to a halt. 2 *(tr)* **a** to prepare a draft of (a legal document). **b** to formulate and write out in appropriate form: *to draw up a contract.* 3 *(used reflexively)* to straighten oneself. 4 to form or arrange (a body of soldiers, etc.) in order or formation.

dray[1] (dreɪ) NOUN 1 **a** a low cart without fixed sides, used for carrying heavy loads. **b** *(in combination)*: *a drayman.* 2 any other vehicle or sledge used to carry a heavy load.
▷HISTORY Old English *dræge* dragnet; related to Old Norse *draga* load of timber carried on horseback and trailing on the ground; see DRAW

dray[2] (dreɪ) NOUN a variant spelling of **drey.**

drayage ('dreɪɪdʒ) NOUN *US* **a** the act of transporting something a short distance by lorry or other vehicle. **b** the charge made for such a transport.

drayhorse ('dreɪˌhɔːs) NOUN a large powerful horse used for drawing a dray.

dread (drɛd) VERB *(tr)* 1 to anticipate with apprehension or terror. 2 to fear greatly. 3 *Archaic* to be in awe of. ◆ NOUN 4 great fear; horror. 5 an object of terror. 6 *Slang* a Rastafarian. 7 *Archaic* deep reverence. ◆ ADJECTIVE 8 *Literary* awesome; awe-inspiring.
▷HISTORY Old English *ondrǣdan;* related to Old Saxon *antdrādan,* Old High German *intrātan*

dreadful ('drɛdfʊl) ADJECTIVE 1 extremely disagreeable, shocking, or bad: *what a dreadful play.* 2 (intensifier): *this is a dreadful waste of time.* 3 causing dread; terrifying. 4 *Archaic* inspiring awe.
▸ '**dreadfulness** NOUN

dreadfully ('drɛdfʊlɪ) ADVERB 1 in a shocking, or disagreeable manner. 2 (intensifier): *you're dreadfully kind.*

dreadlocks ('drɛdˌlɒks) PLURAL NOUN hair worn in the Rastafarian style of long matted or tightly curled strands.

dreadnought *or* **dreadnaught** ('drɛdˌnɔːt) NOUN 1 a battleship armed with heavy guns of uniform calibre. 2 an overcoat made of heavy cloth. 3 *Slang* a heavyweight boxer. 4 a person who fears nothing.

dream (driːm) NOUN 1 **a** a mental activity, usually in the form of an imagined series of events, occurring during certain phases of sleep. **b** *(as modifier)*: *a dream sequence.* **c** *(in combination)*: *dreamland.* Related adjective: **oneiric.** 2 **a** a sequence of imaginative thoughts indulged in while awake; daydream; fantasy. **b** *(as modifier)*: *a dream world.* 3 a person or thing seen or occurring in a dream. 4 a cherished hope; ambition; aspiration. 5 a vain hope. 6 a person or thing that is as pleasant, or seemingly unreal as a dream. 7 **go like a dream.** to move, develop, or work very well. ◆ VERB **dreams, dreaming, dreamed** *or* **dreamt** (drɛmt). 8 *(may take a clause as object)* to undergo or experience (a dream or dreams). 9 *(intr)* to indulge in daydreams. 10 *(intr)* to suffer delusions; be unrealistic: *you're dreaming if you think you can win.* 11 (when *intr,* foll by *of* or *about)* to have an image (of) or fantasy (about) in or as if in a dream. 12 *(intr;* foll by *of)* to consider the possibility (of): *I wouldn't dream of troubling you.* ◆ See also **dream up.** ◆ ADJECTIVE 13 too good to be true; ideal: *dream kitchen.*
▷HISTORY Old English *drēam* song; related to Old High German *troum,* Old Norse *draumr,* Greek *thrulos* noise
▸ '**dreamful** ADJECTIVE ▸ '**dreamfully** ADVERB ▸ '**dreaming** NOUN, ADJECTIVE ▸ '**dreamingly** ADVERB ▸ '**dreamless** ADJECTIVE ▸ '**dreamlessly** ADVERB ▸ '**dreamlessness** NOUN ▸ '**dreamˌlike** ADJECTIVE

dreamboat ('driːmˌbəʊt) NOUN *Old-fashioned slang* an exceptionally attractive person or thing, esp a person of the opposite sex.

dreamer ('driːmə) NOUN 1 a person who dreams habitually. 2 a person who lives in or escapes to a world of fantasy or illusion; escapist. 3 *Archaic* a prophet; visionary.

dreamland ('driːmlænd) NOUN an ideal land existing in dreams or in the imagination.

dreamt (drɛmt) VERB a past tense and past participle of **dream.**

dream team NOUN *Informal* a group of people regarded as having the prefect combination of talents.

dream ticket NOUN a combination of two people, usu. candidates in an election, that is considered to be ideal.

Dreamtime ('driːmtaɪm) NOUN 1 (in the mythology of Australian Aboriginal peoples) a mythical Golden Age of the past. Also called: **alchera** ('æltʃərə), **alcheringa.** 2 *Austral informal* any remote period, out of touch with the actualities of the present.

dream up VERB *(tr, adverb)* to invent by ingenuity and imagination: *to dream up an excuse for leaving.*

dreamy ('driːmɪ) ADJECTIVE **dreamier, dreamiest.** 1 vague or impractical. 2 resembling a dream in quality. 3 relaxing; gentle: *dreamy music.* 4 *Informal* wonderful. 5 having dreams, esp daydreams.
▸ '**dreamily** ADVERB ▸ '**dreaminess** NOUN

dreary ('drɪərɪ) ADJECTIVE **drearier, dreariest.** 1 sad or dull; dismal. 2 wearying; boring. 3 *Archaic* miserable. ◆ Also (literary): **drear.**
▷HISTORY Old English *drēorig* gory; related to Old High German *trūreg* sad
▸ '**drearily** ADVERB ▸ '**dreariness** NOUN

dreck (drɛk) NOUN *Slang, chiefly US* rubbish; trash.
▷HISTORY from Yiddish *drek* filth, dregs
▸ '**drecky** ADJECTIVE

drecksill ('drɛkˌsɪl) NOUN *Southwest English dialect* a doorstep.

dredge[1] (drɛdʒ) NOUN 1 Also called: **dredger.** a machine, in the form of a bucket ladder, grab, or suction device, used to remove material from a riverbed, channel, etc. 2 another name for **dredger**[1] (sense 1). ◆ VERB 3 to remove (material) from a riverbed, channel, etc., by means of a dredge. 4 *(tr)* to search for (a submerged object) with or as if with a dredge; drag.
▷HISTORY C16: perhaps ultimately from Old English *dragan* to DRAW; see DRAG

dredge[2] (drɛdʒ) VERB to sprinkle or coat (food) with flour, sugar, etc.
▷HISTORY C16: from Old French *dragie,* perhaps from Latin *tragēmata* spices, from Greek

dredger[1] ('drɛdʒə) NOUN 1 Also called: **dredge.** a vessel used for dredging, often bargelike and sometimes equipped with retractable steel piles that are driven into the bottom for stability. 2 another name for **dredge**[1] (sense 1).

dredger[2] ('drɛdʒə) NOUN a container with a perforated top for sprinkling flour, sugar, etc.

dredge up VERB *(tr, adverb)* 1 to bring to notice, esp with considerable effort and from an obscure, remote, or unlikely source: *to dredge up worthless ideas.* 2 to raise with or as if with a dredge: *they dredged up the corpse from the lake.*

dree (driː) *Scot literary* ◆ VERB **drees, dreeing, dreed.** 1 *(tr)* to endure. 2 **dree one's weird.** to endure one's fate. ◆ ADJECTIVE 3 another word for **dreich.**
▷HISTORY Old English *drēogan;* related to Old Norse *drȳgja* to perpetrate

dreg (drɛg) NOUN a small quantity: *not a dreg of pity.* See also **dregs.**
▷HISTORY see DREGS

dreggy ('drɛgɪ) ADJECTIVE **-gier, -giest.** like or full of dregs.

D region *or* **layer** NOUN the lowest region of the ionosphere, extending from a height of about 60 kilometres to about 90 kilometres: contains a low concentration of free electrons and reflects low-frequency radio waves. See also **ionosphere.**

dregs (drɛgz) PLURAL NOUN 1 solid particles that tend to settle at the bottom of some liquids, such as wine or coffee. 2 residue or remains. 3 *Brit slang* a despicable person.
▷HISTORY C14 *dreg,* from Old Norse *dregg;* compare Icelandic *dreggjar* dregs, Latin *fracēs* oil dregs

Dreibund *German* ('draibʊnt) NOUN a triple alliance, esp that formed between Germany, Austria-Hungary, and Italy (1882–1915).
▷HISTORY from *drei* THREE + *Bund* union, alliance

dreich *or* **dreigh** (driːx) ADJECTIVE *Scot dialect* dreary.
▷HISTORY Middle English *dreig, drih* enduring, from Old English *drēog* (unattested); see DREE

dreikanter ('draɪkæntə) NOUN a pebble, common in desert areas, typically having three curved faces shaped by wind-blown sand.
▷HISTORY C20: from German: three-edged thing

drench (drɛntʃ) VERB *(tr)* 1 to make completely wet; soak. 2 to give liquid medicine to (an animal), esp by force. ◆ NOUN 3 the act or an instance of drenching. 4 a dose of liquid medicine given to an animal.
▷HISTORY Old English *drencan* to cause to drink; related to Old High German *trenken*
▸ '**drencher** NOUN ▸ '**drenching** NOUN, ADJECTIVE

Drenthe *(Dutch* 'drɛntə) NOUN a province of the NE Netherlands: a low plateau, with many raised bogs, partially reclaimed; agricultural, with oil deposits. Capital: Assen. Pop.: 469 800 (2000 est.). Area: 2647 sq. km (1032 sq. miles).

drepanid ('drɛpənɪd) NOUN any moth of the superfamily *Drepanoidae* (family *Drepanidae*): it comprises the hook-tip moths.

Dresden ('drɛzdᵊn) NOUN 1 an industrial city in SE Germany, the capital of Saxony on the River Elbe: it was severely damaged in the Seven Years' War (1760); the baroque city was almost totally destroyed in World War II by Allied bombing (1945). Pop.: 477 700 (1999 est.). ◆ ADJECTIVE 2 relating to, designating, or made of Dresden china.

Dresden china NOUN porcelain ware, esp delicate and elegantly decorative objects and figures of high quality, made at Meissen, near Dresden, since 1710.

dress (drɛs) VERB 1 to put clothes on (oneself or another); attire. 2 *(intr)* **a** to change one's clothes. **b** to wear formal or evening clothes. 3 *(tr)* to provide (someone) with clothing; clothe. 4 *(tr)* to arrange merchandise in (a shop window) for effective display. 5 *(tr)* to comb out or arrange (the hair) into position. 6 *(tr)* to apply protective or therapeutic covering to (a wound, sore, etc.). 7 *(tr)* to prepare (food, esp fowl and fish) for cooking or serving by cleaning, trimming, gutting, etc. 8 *(tr)* to put a finish on (the surface of stone, metal, etc.). 9 *(tr)* to till and cultivate (land), esp by applying manure, compost, or fertilizer. 10 *(tr)* to prune and trim (trees, bushes, etc.). 11 *(tr)* to groom (an animal, esp a horse). 12 *(tr)* to convert (tanned hides) into leather. 13 *(tr) Archaic* to spay or neuter (an animal). 14 *Angling* to tie (a fly). 15 *Military* to bring (troops) into line or (of troops) to come into line (esp in the phrase **dress ranks**). 16 **dress ship.** *Nautical* to decorate a vessel by displaying all signal flags on lines run from the bow to the stern over the mast trucks. ◆ NOUN 17 a one-piece garment for a woman, consisting of a skirt and bodice. 18 complete style of clothing; costume: *formal dress; military dress.* 19 *(modifier)* suitable or required for a formal occasion: *a dress shirt.* 20 the outer covering

or appearance, esp of living things: *trees in their spring dress of leaves.* ◆ See also **dress down, dress up.**
▷HISTORY C14: from Old French *drecier,* ultimately from Latin *dīrigere* to DIRECT

dressage ('drɛsɑːʒ) NOUN 1 the method of training a horse to perform manoeuvres in response to the rider's body signals. 2 the manoeuvres performed by a horse trained in this method.
▷HISTORY French: preparation, from Old French *dresser* to prepare; see DRESS

dress circle NOUN a tier of seats in a theatre or other auditorium, usually the first gallery above the ground floor.

dress coat NOUN a man's formal tailcoat with a cutaway skirt.

dress code NOUN a set of rules or guidelines regarding the manner of dress acceptable in an office, restaurant, etc.

dress down VERB (*adverb*) 1 (*tr*) *Informal* to reprimand severely or scold (a person). 2 (*intr*) to dress in a casual or informal manner, esp at work. ◆ NOUN **dress-down.** 3 (*modifier*) of or relating to a policy adopted by some business organizations of promoting a relaxed atmosphere by wearing informal clothing on certain days, usually Fridays: *dress-down Friday.*

dresser[1] ('drɛsə) NOUN 1 a set of shelves, usually also with cupboards or drawers, for storing or displaying dishes, etc. 2 *US* a chest of drawers for storing clothing in a bedroom or dressing room, often having a mirror on the top.
▷HISTORY C14 *dressour,* from Old French *dreceore,* from *drecier* to arrange; see DRESS

dresser[2] ('drɛsə) NOUN 1 a person who dresses in a specified way: *a fashionable dresser.* 2 *Theatre* a person employed to assist actors in putting on and taking off their costumes. 3 a tool used for dressing stone or other materials. 4 *Brit* a person who assists a surgeon during operations. 5 *Brit* See **window-dresser.**

dress form NOUN an adjustable dummy used in dressmaking that can be made to conform to a person's figure.

dressing ('drɛsɪŋ) NOUN 1 a sauce for food, esp for salad. 2 the US and Canadian name for **stuffing** (sense 2). 3 a covering for a wound, sore, etc. 4 manure or artificial fertilizer spread on land. 5 size used for stiffening textiles. 6 the processes in the conversion of certain rough tanned hides into leather ready for use. ◆ See also **dressings.**

dressing case NOUN (esp formerly) a box or case fitted with all the toilet articles necessary for dressing oneself, arranging one's hair, etc.

dressing-down NOUN *Informal* a severe scolding or thrashing.

dressing gown NOUN a full robe worn before dressing or for lounging.

dressing room NOUN 1 *Theatre* a room backstage for an actor to change clothing and to make up. 2 any room used for changing clothes, such as one at a sports ground or off a bedroom.

dressings ('drɛsɪŋz) PLURAL NOUN dressed stonework, mouldings, and carved ornaments used to form quoins, keystones, sills, and similar features.

dressing station NOUN *Military* a first-aid post close to a combat area.

dressing table NOUN a piece of bedroom furniture with a mirror and a set of drawers for clothes, cosmetics, etc.

dressmaker ('drɛsˌmeɪkə) NOUN a person whose occupation is making clothes, esp for women.
▸ **'dressˌmaking** NOUN

dress parade NOUN *Military* a formal parade of sufficient ceremonial importance for the wearing of dress uniform.

dress rehearsal NOUN 1 the last complete rehearsal of a play or other work, using costumes, scenery, lighting, etc., as for the first night. 2 any full-scale practice.

dress shield NOUN a fabric pad worn under the armpits or attached to the armhole of a garment to prevent sweat from showing on or staining the clothing.

dress shirt NOUN a man's shirt, usually white, worn as part of formal evening dress, usually having a stiffened or decorative front.

dress suit NOUN a man's evening suit, esp tails.

dress uniform NOUN *Military* formal ceremonial uniform.

dress up VERB (*adverb*) 1 to attire (oneself or another) in one's best clothes. 2 to put fancy dress, disguise, etc., on (oneself or another), as in children's games: *let's dress up as ghosts!* 3 (*tr*) to improve the appearance or impression of: *it's no good trying to dress up the facts.*

dressy ('drɛsɪ) ADJECTIVE **dressier, dressiest.** 1 (of clothes) elegant. 2 (of persons) dressing stylishly. 3 over-elegant.
▸ **'dressily** ADVERB ▸ **'dressiness** NOUN

dressy casual ADJECTIVE (of clothes) informal yet expensive, smart, or stylish.

drew (druː) VERB the past tense of **draw.**

drey *or* **dray** (dreɪ) NOUN a squirrel's nest.
▷HISTORY C17: of unknown origin

dribble ('drɪbᵊl) VERB 1 (*usually intr*) to flow or allow to flow in a thin stream or drops; trickle. 2 (*intr*) to allow saliva to trickle from the mouth. 3 (in soccer, basketball, hockey, etc.) to propel (the ball) by repeatedly tapping it with the hand, foot, or stick. ◆ NOUN 4 a small quantity of liquid falling in drops or flowing in a thin stream. 5 a small quantity or supply. 6 an act or instance of dribbling.
▷HISTORY C16: frequentative of *drib,* variant of DRIP
▸ **'dribbler** NOUN ▸ **'dribbly** ADJECTIVE

driblet *or* **dribblet** ('drɪblɪt) NOUN a small quantity or amount, as of liquid.
▷HISTORY C17: from obsolete *drib* to fall bit by bit + -LET

dribs and drabs (drɪbz) PLURAL NOUN small sporadic amounts.

dried (draɪd) VERB the past tense and past participle of **dry.**

drier[1] ('draɪə) ADJECTIVE a comparative of **dry.**

drier[2] ('draɪə) NOUN a variant spelling of **dryer**[1].

driest ('draɪɪst) ADJECTIVE a superlative of **dry.**

drift (drɪft) VERB (*mainly intr*) 1 (*also tr*) to be carried along by or as if by currents of air or water or (of a current) to carry (a vessel, etc.) along. 2 to move aimlessly from place to place or from one activity to another. 3 to wander or move gradually away from a fixed course or point; stray. 4 (*also tr*) (of snow, sand, etc.) to accumulate in heaps or banks or to drive (snow, sand, etc.) into heaps or banks. ◆ NOUN 5 something piled up by the wind or current, such as a snowdrift. 6 tendency, trend, meaning, or purport: *the drift of the argument.* 7 a state of indecision or inaction. 8 the extent to which a vessel, aircraft, projectile, etc. is driven off its course by adverse winds, tide, or current. 9 a general tendency of surface ocean water to flow in the direction of the prevailing winds: *North Atlantic Drift.* 10 a driving movement, force, or influence; impulse. 11 a controlled four-wheel skid, used by racing drivers to take bends at high speed. 12 a loose unstratified deposit of sand, gravel, etc., esp one transported and deposited by a glacier or ice sheet. 13 a horizontal passage in a mine that follows the mineral vein. 14 something, esp a group of animals, driven along by human or natural agencies: *a drift of cattle.* 15 Also called: **driftpin.** a tapering steel tool driven into holes to enlarge or align them before bolting or riveting. 16 an uncontrolled slow change in some operating characteristic of a piece of equipment, esp an electronic circuit or component. 17 *Linguistics* gradual change in a language, esp in so far as this is influenced by the internal structure of the language rather than by contact with other languages. 18 *South African* a ford. 19 *Engineering* a copper or brass bar used as a punch.
▷HISTORY C13: from Old Norse: snowdrift; related to Old High German *trift* pasturage
▸ **'drifty** ADJECTIVE

driftage ('drɪftɪdʒ) NOUN 1 the act of drifting. 2 matter carried along or deposited by drifting. 3 the amount by which an aircraft or vessel has drifted from its intended course.

drift anchor NOUN another term for **sea anchor.**

drifter ('drɪftə) NOUN 1 a person or thing that drifts. 2 a person who moves aimlessly from place to place, usually without a regular job. 3 a boat used for drift-net fishing. 4 *Nautical* a large jib of thin material used in light breezes.

drift ice NOUN masses of ice floating in the open sea.

drift net NOUN a large fishing net supported by floats or attached to a drifter that is allowed to drift with the tide or current.

drift transistor NOUN a transistor in which the impurity concentration in the base increases from the collector-base junction to the emitter-base junction, producing a resistivity gradient that greatly increases its high-frequency response.

drift tube NOUN *Physics* a hollow cylindrical electrode to which a radio-frequency voltage is applied in a linear accelerator.

driftwood ('drɪftˌwʊd) NOUN wood floating on or washed ashore by the sea or other body of water.

drill[1] (drɪl) NOUN 1 a rotating tool that is inserted into a drilling machine or tool for boring cylindrical holes. 2 a hand tool, either manually or electrically operated, for drilling holes. 3 *Military* **a** training in procedures or movements, as for ceremonial parades or the use of weapons. **b** (*as modifier*): *drill hall.* 4 strict and often repetitious training or exercises used as a method of teaching. 5 *Informal* correct procedure or routine. 6 a marine gastropod mollusc, *Urosalpinx cinera,* closely related to the whelk, that preys on oysters. ◆ VERB 7 to pierce, bore, or cut (a hole) in (material) with or as if with a drill: *to drill a hole; to drill metal.* 8 to instruct or be instructed in military procedures or movements. 9 (*tr*) to teach by rigorous exercises or training. 10 (*tr*) *Informal* to hit (a ball) in a straight line at great speed. 11 (*tr*) *Informal* to riddle with bullets. ◆ See also **drill down.**
▷HISTORY C17: from Middle Dutch *drillen;* related to Old High German *drāen* to turn
▸ **'drillable** ADJECTIVE ▸ **'driller** NOUN

drill[2] (drɪl) NOUN 1 a machine for planting seeds in rows or depositing fertilizer. 2 a small furrow in which seeds are sown. 3 a row of seeds planted using a drill. ◆ VERB 4 to plant (seeds) by means of a drill.
▷HISTORY C18: of uncertain origin; compare German *Rille* furrow
▸ **'driller** NOUN

drill[3] (drɪl) *or* **drilling** NOUN a hard-wearing twill-weave cotton cloth, used for uniforms, etc.
▷HISTORY C18: variant of German *Drillich,* from Latin *trilīx,* from TRI- + *līcium* thread

drill[4] (drɪl) NOUN an Old World monkey, *Mandrillus leucophaeus,* of W Africa, related to the mandrill but smaller and less brightly coloured.
▷HISTORY C17: from a West African word; compare MANDRILL

drill down VERB (*intr, adverb*) to look at or examine something in depth: *to drill down through financial data.*

drilling mud NOUN a mixture of clays, water, and chemicals pumped down the drill string while an oil well is being drilled to lubricate the mechanism, carry away rock cuttings, and maintain pressure so that oil or gas does not escape.

drilling platform NOUN a structure, either fixed to the sea bed or mobile, which supports the machinery and equipment (**drilling rig**), together with the stores, required for digging an offshore oil well.

drilling rig NOUN 1 the full name for **rig** (sense 6). 2 a mobile drilling platform used for exploratory offshore drilling.

drillmaster ('drɪlˌmɑːstə) NOUN 1 *Obsolete* Also called: **drill sergeant.** a military drill instructor. 2 a person who instructs in a strict manner.

drill press NOUN a machine tool for boring holes, having a stand and work table with facilities for lowering the tool to the workpiece.

drillstock ('drɪlˌstɒk) NOUN the part of a machine tool that holds the shank of a drill or bit; chuck.

drill string *or* **pipe** NOUN (in the oil industry) a pipe made of lengths of steel tubing that is attached to the drilling tool and rotates during drilling to form a bore.

drily *or* **dryly** ('draɪlɪ) ADVERB in a dry manner.

drink (drɪŋk) VERB **drinks, drinking, drank** (dræŋk), **drunk** (drʌŋk). 1 to swallow (a liquid); imbibe. 2

(*tr*) to take in or soak up (liquid); absorb: *this plant drinks a lot of water*. [3] (*tr*; usually foll by *in*) to pay close attention (to); be fascinated (by): *he drank in the speaker's every word*. [4] (*tr*) to bring (oneself into a certain condition) by consuming alcohol. [5] (*tr*; often foll by *away*) to dispose of or ruin by excessive expenditure on alcohol: *he drank away his fortune*. [6] (*intr*) to consume alcohol, esp to excess. [7] (when *intr*, foll by *to*) to drink (a toast) in celebration, honour, or hope (of). [8] **drink (someone) under the table.** to be able to drink more intoxicating beverage than (someone). [9] **drink the health of.** to salute or celebrate with a toast. [10] **drink with the flies.** *Austral informal* to drink alone. ◆ NOUN [11] liquid suitable for drinking; any beverage. [12] alcohol or its habitual or excessive consumption. [13] a portion of liquid for drinking; draught. [14] **the drink.** *Informal* the sea.
▷HISTORY Old English *drincan*; related to Old Frisian *drinka*, Gothic *drigkan*, Old High German *trinkan*
▸ˈ**drinkable** ADJECTIVE

drink-driving NOUN (*modifier*) of or relating to driving a car after drinking alcohol: *drink-driving offences; drink-driving campaign*.

drinker (ˈdrɪŋkə) NOUN [1] a person who drinks, esp a person who drinks alcohol habitually. [2] short for **drinker moth.**

drinker moth NOUN a large yellowish-brown bombycid eggar moth, *Philudoria potatoria*, having a stout hairy body, the larvae of which drink dew and feed on grasses. Also called: **drinker.**

drinking fountain NOUN a device for providing a flow or jet of drinking water, usually in public places.

drinking-up time NOUN (in Britain) a short time allowed for finishing drinks before closing time in a public house.

drinking water NOUN water reserved or suitable for drinking.

drip (drɪp) VERB **drips, dripping, dripped.** [1] to fall or let fall in drops. ◆ NOUN [2] the formation and falling of drops of liquid. [3] the sound made by falling drops. [4] *Architect* a projection at the front lower edge of a sill or cornice designed to throw water clear of the wall below. [5] *Informal* an inane, insipid person. [6] *Med* **a** the usually intravenous drop-by-drop administration of a therapeutic solution, as of salt or sugar. **b** the solution administered. **c** the equipment used to administer a solution in this way.
▷HISTORY Old English *dryppan*, from *dropa* DROP

drip-dry ADJECTIVE [1] designating clothing or a fabric that will dry relatively free of creases if hung up when wet. ◆ VERB **-dries, -drying, -dried.** [2] to dry or become dry thus.

drip-feed NOUN [1] another name for **drip** (sense 6). ◆ VERB (*tr*) **drip feed.** [2] to administer a solution (to someone) by means of a drip-feed. [3] *Informal* to fund (a new company) in stages rather than by injecting a large sum at its inception.

dripping (ˈdrɪpɪŋ) NOUN [1] the fat exuded by roasting meat. [2] (*often plural*) liquid that falls in drops. ◆ ADVERB [3] (intensifier): *dripping wet*.

dripping pan *or* **drip pan** NOUN a shallow pan placed under roasting meat to catch the dripping.

drippy (ˈdrɪpɪ) ADJECTIVE **-pier, -piest.** [1] *Informal* mawkish, insipid, or inane. [2] tending to drip.

dripstone (ˈdrɪpˌstəʊn) NOUN [1] the form of calcium carbonate existing in stalactites or stalagmites. [2] Also called: **label, hood mould.** *Architect* a drip made of stone.

drisheen (drɪˈʃiːn) NOUN *Irish* a pudding made of sheep's intestines filled with meal and sheep's blood.
▷HISTORY C20: from Irish Gaelic *drisín* an animal's intestines

drive (draɪv) VERB **drives, driving, drove** (drəʊv), **driven** (ˈdrɪvᵊn). [1] to push, propel, or be pushed or propelled. [2] to control and guide the movement of (a vehicle, draught animal, etc.): *to drive a car*. [3] (*tr*) to compel or urge to work or act, esp excessively. [4] (*tr*) to goad or force into a specified attitude or state: *work drove him to despair*. [5] (*tr*) to cause (an object) to make or form (a hole, crack, etc.): *his blow drove a hole in the wall*. [6] to move or cause to move rapidly by striking or throwing with force. [7] *Sport* to hit (a ball) very hard and straight, as (in cricket) with the bat swinging more or less vertically. [8] *Golf* to strike (the ball) with a driver, as in teeing off. [9] (*tr*) **a** to chase (game) from cover into more open ground. **b** to search (an area) for game. [10] to transport or be transported in a driven vehicle. [11] (*intr*) to rush or dash violently, esp against an obstacle or solid object: *the waves drove against the rock*. [12] (*tr*) to carry through or transact with vigour (esp in the phrase **drive a hard bargain**). [13] (*tr*) to force (a component) into or out of its location by means of blows or a press. [14] (*tr*) *Mining* to excavate horizontally. [15] (*tr*) *NZ* to fell (a tree or trees) by the impact of another felled tree. [16] **drive home. a** to cause to penetrate to the fullest extent. **b** to make clear by special emphasis. ◆ NOUN [17] the act of driving. [18] a trip or journey in a driven vehicle. [19] **a** a road for vehicles, esp a private road leading to a house. **b** (*capital when part of a street name*): *Woodland Drive*. [20] vigorous or urgent pressure, as in business. [21] a united effort, esp directed towards a common goal: *a charity drive*. [22] *Brit* a large gathering of persons to play cards, etc. See **beetle drive, whist drive.** [23] energy, ambition, or initiative. [24] *Psychol* a motive or interest, such as sex, hunger, or ambition, that actuates an organism to attain a goal. [25] a sustained and powerful military offensive. [26] **a** the means by which force, torque, motion, or power is transmitted in a mechanism: *fluid drive*. **b** (*as modifier*): *a drive shaft*. [27] *Sport* a hard straight shot or stroke. [28] a search for and chasing of game towards waiting guns. [29] *Electronics* the signal applied to the input of an amplifier.
▷HISTORY Old English *drīfan*; related to Old Frisian *drīva*, Old Norse *drīfa*, Gothic *dreiban*, Old High German *trīban*
▸ˈ**drivable** *or* ˈ**driveable** ADJECTIVE ▸ˌ**drivaˈbility** *or* ˌ**driveaˈbility** NOUN

drive at VERB (*intr, preposition*) *Informal* to intend or mean: *what are you driving at?*

drive-by shooting NOUN an incident in which a person, building, or vehicle is shot at by someone in a moving vehicle. Sometimes shortened to: **drive-by.**

drive-in NOUN *Chiefly US and Canadian* **a** a cinema designed to be used by patrons seated in their cars. **b** (*modifier*) a public facility or service designed for use in such a manner: *a drive-in restaurant; a drive-in bank*.

drivel (ˈdrɪvᵊl) VERB **-els, -elling, -elled** *or US* **-els, -eling, -eled.** [1] to allow (saliva) to flow from the mouth; dribble. [2] (*intr*) to speak foolishly or childishly. ◆ NOUN [3] foolish or senseless talk. [4] saliva flowing from the mouth; slaver.
▷HISTORY Old English *dreflian* to slaver; see DRAFF
▸ˈ**driveller** NOUN

driven (ˈdrɪvᵊn) VERB the past participle of **drive.**

drive-off NOUN *Informal* **a** the act or an instance of leaving a filling station without paying for one's fuel. **b** (*as modifier*): *a drive-off theft*.

driver (ˈdraɪvə) NOUN [1] a person who drives a vehicle. [2] **in the driver's seat.** in a position of control. [3] a person who drives animals. [4] a mechanical component that exerts a force on another to produce motion. [5] *Golf* a club, a No. 1 wood, with a large head and deep face for tee shots. [6] *Electronics* a circuit whose output provides the input of another circuit. [7] *Computing* a computer program that controls a device. [8] something that creates and fuels activity, or gives force or impetus.
▸ˈ**driverless** ADJECTIVE

driver ant NOUN any of various tropical African predatory ants of the subfamily *Dorylinae*, which live in temporary nests and travel in vast hordes preying on other animals. See also **army ant.**

drive shaft NOUN another name for **propeller shaft.**

drive-thru NOUN **a** a takeaway restaurant, bank, etc. designed so that customers can use it without leaving their cars. **b** (*as modifier*): *a drive-thru restaurant*.

drive-time NOUN **a** the time of day when many people are driving to or from work, regarded as a broadcasting slot. **b** (*as modifier*): *the daily drive-time show*.

driveway (ˈdraɪvˌweɪ) NOUN a private road for vehicles, often connecting a house or garage with a public road; drive.

driving (ˈdraɪvɪŋ) ADJECTIVE [1] having or moving with force and violence: *driving rain*. [2] forceful or energetic. [3] relating to the controlling of a motor vehicle in motion: *driving test*.

driving chain NOUN *Engineering* a roller chain that transmits power from one toothed wheel to another. Also called: **drive chain.**

driving licence NOUN an official document or certificate authorizing a person to drive a motor vehicle.

driving wheel NOUN [1] a wheel, esp a gear wheel, that causes other wheels to rotate. [2] any wheel of a vehicle that transforms torque into a tractive force.

drizzle (ˈdrɪzᵊl) NOUN [1] very light rain, specifically consisting of droplets less than 0.5 mm in diameter. ◆ VERB [2] (*intr*) to rain lightly. [3] (*tr*) to moisten with tiny droplets.
▷HISTORY Old English *drēosan* to fall; related to Old Saxon *driosan*, Gothic *driusan*, Norwegian *drjōsa*
▸ˈ**drizzly** ADJECTIVE

drizzle cake NOUN a sponge cake that has syrup drizzled over it immediately after baking.

Drogheda (ˈdrɔɪɪdə) NOUN a port in NE Republic of Ireland, in Co. Louth near the mouth of the River Boyne: captured by Cromwell in 1649 and its inhabitants massacred. Pop.: 23 800 (1991).

drogue (drəʊg) NOUN [1] any funnel-like device, esp one of canvas, used as a sea anchor. [2] **a** a small parachute released behind a jet aircraft to reduce its landing speed. **b** a small parachute released before a heavier main parachute during the landing of a spacecraft. [3] a device towed behind an aircraft as a target for firing practice. [4] a funnel-shaped device on the end of the refuelling hose of a tanker aircraft, to assist stability and the location of the probe of the receiving aircraft. [5] another name for **windsock.**
▷HISTORY C18: probably based ultimately on Old English *dragan* to DRAW

droit (drɔɪt; *French* drwa) NOUN, *plural* **droits** (drɔɪts; *French* drwa). a legal or moral right or claim; due.
▷HISTORY C15: from French: legal right, from Medieval Latin *dīrēctum* law, from Latin: a straight line; see DIRECT

droit de suite (*French* drwad sɥit) NOUN a right recognized by the legislation of several member countries of the European Union whereby an artist, or his or her heirs, is entitled to a share of the price of a work of art if it is resold during the artist's lifetime or for 70 years after his or her death.
▷HISTORY from French, literally: the right of following

droit du seigneur (*French* drwa dy sɛɲœr) NOUN in feudal times, the right of a lord to have sexual intercourse with a vassal's bride on her wedding night.
▷HISTORY from French, literally: the right of the lord

droll (drəʊl) ADJECTIVE amusing in a quaint or odd manner; comical.
▷HISTORY C17: from French *drôle* scamp, from Middle Dutch: imp
▸ˈ**drollness** NOUN ▸ˈ**drolly** ADVERB

drollery (ˈdrəʊlərɪ) NOUN, *plural* **-eries.** [1] humour; comedy. [2] *Rare* a droll act, story, or remark.

Drôme (*French* drom) NOUN a department of SE France, in Rhône-Alpes region. Capital: Valence. Pop.: 437 778 (1999). Area: 6561 sq. km (2559 sq. miles).

-drome NOUN COMBINING FORM [1] a course, racecourse: *hippodrome*. [2] a large place for a special purpose: *aerodrome*.
▷HISTORY via Latin from Greek *dromos* race, course

dromedary (ˈdrʌmədərɪ, -drɪ, ˈdrɒm-) NOUN, *plural* **-daries.** [1] a type of Arabian camel bred for racing and riding, having a single hump and long slender legs. [2] another name for **Arabian camel.**
▷HISTORY C14: from Late Latin *dromedārius* (*camēlus*), from Greek *dromas* running

dromond (ˈdrɒmənd, ˈdrʌm-) *or* **dromon** (ˈdrɒmən, ˈdrʌm-) NOUN a large swift sailing vessel of the 12th to 15th centuries.
▷HISTORY C13: from Anglo-French *dromund*, ultimately from Late Greek *dromōn* light swift ship, from *dromos* a running

-dromous ADJECTIVE COMBINING FORM moving or running: *anadromous; catadromous*.

▷**HISTORY** via New Latin from Greek *-dromos,* from *dromos* a running

drone[1] (drəʊn) NOUN [1] a male bee in a colony of social bees, whose sole function is to mate with the queen. [2] *Brit* a person who lives off the work of others. [3] a pilotless radio-controlled aircraft.
▷**HISTORY** Old English *drān;* related to Old High German *treno* drone, Gothic *drunjus* noise, Greek *tenthrēnē* wasp; see DRONE[2]
▸'**dronish** ADJECTIVE

drone[2] (drəʊn) VERB [1] *(intr)* to make a monotonous low dull sound; buzz or hum. [2] (when *intr,* often foll by *on*) to utter (words) in a monotonous tone, esp to talk without stopping. ◆ NOUN [3] a monotonous low dull sound. [4] *Music* **a** a sustained bass note or chord of unvarying pitch accompanying a melody. **b** *(as modifier)*: *a drone bass.* [5] *Music* one of the single-reed pipes in a set of bagpipes, used for accompanying the melody played on the chanter. [6] a person who speaks in a low monotonous tone.
▷**HISTORY** C16: related to DRONE[1] and Middle Dutch *drōnen,* German *dröhnen*
▸'**droning** ADJECTIVE ▸'**droningly** ADVERB

drongo ('drɒŋgəʊ) NOUN, *plural* **-gos.** [1] Also called: **drongo shrike.** any insectivorous songbird of the family *Dicruridae,* of the Old World tropics, having a glossy black plumage, a forked tail, and a stout bill. [2] *Austral and NZ slang* a slow-witted person. [3] *Austral informal* a new recruit in the Royal Australian Air Force.
▷**HISTORY** C19: from Malagasy

droob (druːb) NOUN *Austral archaic slang* a pathetic person.
▷**HISTORY** C20: of unknown origin

drook (drʊk) VERB *(tr) Scot* a variant spelling of **drouk.**

drookit ('drʊkɪt) ADJECTIVE *Scot* a variant spelling of **droukit.**

drool (druːl) VERB [1] *(intr;* often foll by *over)* to show excessive enthusiasm (for) or pleasure (in); gloat (over). ◆ VERB, NOUN [2] another word for **drivel** (senses 1, 2, 4).
▷**HISTORY** C19: probably alteration of DRIVEL

droop (druːp) VERB [1] to sag or allow to sag, as from weakness or exhaustion; hang down; sink. [2] *(intr)* to be overcome by weariness; languish; flag. [3] *(intr)* to lose courage; become dejected. ◆ NOUN [4] the act or state of drooping.
▷**HISTORY** C13: from Old Norse *drūpa;* see DROP
▸'**drooping** ADJECTIVE ▸'**droopingly** ADVERB

droopy ('druːpɪ) ADJECTIVE hanging or sagging downwards: *a droopy moustache.*
▸'**droopily** ADVERB ▸'**droopiness** NOUN

drop (drɒp) NOUN [1] a small quantity of liquid that forms or falls in a spherical or pear-shaped mass; globule. [2] a very small quantity of liquid. [3] a very small quantity of anything. [4] something resembling a drop in shape or size, such as a decorative pendant or small sweet. [5] the act or an instance of falling; descent. [6] a decrease in amount or value; slump: *a drop in prices.* [7] the vertical distance that anything may fall. [8] a steep or sheer incline or slope. [9] short for **fruit drop.** [10] the act of unloading troops, equipment, or supplies by parachute. [11] (in cable television) a short spur from a trunk cable that feeds signals to an individual house. [12] *Theatre* See **drop curtain.** [13] another word for **trap door** or **gallows.** [14] *Chiefly US and Canadian* a slot or aperture through which an object can be dropped to fall into a receptacle. [15] *Nautical* the midships height of a sail bent to a fixed yard. Compare **hoist** (sense 6a). [16] *Austral cricket slang* a fall of the wicket: *he came in at first drop.* [17] See **drop shot.** [18] **a drop in the bucket** (*or* **in the ocean**). an amount very small in relation to what is needed or desired. [19] **at the drop of a hat.** without hesitation or delay. [20] **have had a drop too much.** to be drunk. [21] **have the drop on (someone).** *US and NZ* to have the advantage over (someone). ◆ VERB **drops, dropping, dropped.** [22] (of liquids) to fall or allow to fall in globules. [23] to fall or allow to fall vertically. [24] *(tr)* to allow to fall by letting go of. [25] to sink or fall or cause to sink or fall to the ground, as from a blow, wound, shot, weariness, etc. [26] *(intr;* foll by *back, behind,* etc.) to fall, move, or go in a specified manner, direction, etc. [27] *(intr;* foll by *in, by,* etc.) *Informal* to pay a casual visit (to). [28] to decrease or cause to decrease in amount or value: *the cost of living never drops.* [29] to sink or cause to sink to a lower position, as on a scale. [30] to make or become less in strength, volume, etc. [31] *(intr)* to sink or decline in health or condition. [32] *(intr;* sometimes foll by *into)* to pass easily into a state or condition: *to drop into a habit.* [33] *(intr)* to move along gently as with a current of water or air. [34] *(tr)* to allow to pass casually in conversation: *to drop a hint.* [35] *(tr)* to leave out (a word or letter). [36] *(tr)* to set down or unload (passengers or goods). [37] *(tr)* to send or post: *drop me a line.* [38] *(tr)* to discontinue; terminate: *let's drop the matter.* [39] *(tr)* to cease to associate or have to do with. [40] *(tr) Slang, chiefly US* to cease to employ: *he was dropped from his job.* [41] *(tr;* sometimes foll by *in, off,* etc.) *Informal* to leave or deposit, esp at a specified place. [42] (of animals) to give birth to (offspring). [43] *Slang, chiefly US and Canadian* to lose (money), esp when gambling. [44] *(tr)* to lengthen (a hem, etc.). [45] *(tr)* to unload (troops, equipment, or supplies) by parachute. [46] *(tr) Nautical* to leave behind; sail out of sight of. [47] *(tr) Sport* to omit (a player) from a team. [48] *(tr)* to lose (a score, game, or contest): *the champion dropped his first service game.* [49] *(tr) Sport* to hit or throw (a ball) into a goal: *he dropped a 30 foot putt.* [50] *(tr)* to hit (a ball) with a drop shot. [51] **drop astern.** *Nautical* to fall back to the stern (of another vessel). [52] *(tr) Motor racing, slang* to spin (the car) and (usually) crash out of the race. [53] *(tr) Slang* to swallow (a drug, esp a barbiturate or LSD). [54] **drop dead!** *Slang* an exclamation of contempt. ◆ NOUN, VERB [55] *Rugby* short for **drop kick** or **drop-kick.** ◆ See also **drop away, drop in, drop off, dropout, drops.**
▷**HISTORY** Old English *dropian;* related to Old High German *triofan* to DRIP

drop away VERB *(intr, adverb)* to fall or go away gradually.

drop cannon NOUN *Billiards* a shot in which the first object ball joins or gathers with the cue ball and the other object ball, esp at the top of the table.

drop curtain NOUN *Theatre* a curtain that is suspended from the flies and can be raised and lowered onto the stage. Also called: **drop cloth, drop.**

drop-dead ADVERB *Informal* outstandingly or exceptionally: *drop-dead gorgeous.*

drop-dead fee NOUN a fee paid to an organization lending money to a company that is hoping to use it to finance a takeover bid. The fee is only paid if the bid fails and interest charges are only incurred if the money is needed.

drop-down menu NOUN a menu that appears on a computer screen when its title is selected and remains on display until dismissed.

drop forge NOUN [1] Also called: **drop hammer.** a device for forging metal between two dies, one of which is fixed, the other acting by gravity or by steam or hydraulic pressure. ◆ VERB **drop-forge.** *(tr)* [2] to forge (metal) into (a component) by the use of a drop forge.

drop goal NOUN *Rugby* a goal scored with a drop kick during the run of play.

drop hammer NOUN another name for **drop forge.**

drophead coupé NOUN *Brit* a two-door four-seater car with a folding roof and a sloping back.

drop in VERB *(intr, adverb) Surfing* to intrude on a wave that another surfer is already riding.

drop-in centre NOUN *Social welfare* (in Britain) a daycentre run by the social services or a charity that clients may attend on an informal basis.

drop kick NOUN [1] a kick in certain sports such as rugby, in which the ball is dropped and kicked as it bounces from the ground. Compare **punt**[2], **place kick.** [2] a wrestling attack, illegal in amateur wrestling, in which a wrestler leaps in the air and kicks his opponent in the face or body with both feet. ◆ VERB **drop-kick.** [3] to kick (a ball, etc.) using a drop kick. [4] to kick (an opponent in wrestling) by the use of a drop kick.

drop leaf NOUN **a** a hinged flap on a table that can be raised and supported by a bracket or additional pivoted leg to extend the surface. **b** *(as modifier)*: *a drop-leaf table.*

droplet ('drɒplɪt) NOUN a tiny drop.

droplight ('drɒp,laɪt) NOUN an electric light that may be raised or lowered by means of a pulley or other mechanism.

drop lock NOUN *Finance* a variable-rate bank loan used on international markets that is automatically replaced by a fixed-rate long-term bond if the long-term interest rates fall to a specified level; it thus combines the advantages of a bank loan with those of a bond.

drop off VERB *(adverb)* [1] *(intr)* to grow smaller or less; decline. [2] *(tr)* to allow to alight; set down. [3] *(intr) Informal* to fall asleep. ◆ NOUN **drop-off.** [4] a steep or vertical descent. [5] a sharp decrease.

dropout ('drɒp,aʊt) NOUN [1] a student who fails to complete a school or college course. [2] a person who rejects conventional society. [3] **drop-out** *Rugby* a drop kick taken by the defending team to restart play, as after a touchdown. [4] **drop-out** *Electronics* a momentary loss of signal in a magnetic recording medium as a result of an imperfection in its magnetic coating. ◆ VERB **drop out.** *(intr, adverb;* often foll by *of)* [5] to abandon or withdraw from (a school, social group, job, etc.).

dropped sole NOUN *Vet science* a condition in which the foot of a horse is convex instead of concave. Also called: **convex sole.**

dropper ('drɒpə) NOUN [1] a small tube having a rubber bulb at one end for drawing up and dispensing drops of liquid. [2] a person or thing that drops. [3] *Angling* a short length of monofilament by which a fly is attached to the main trace or leader above the tail fly. [4] *Austral and NZ* a batten attached to the top wire of a fence to keep the wires apart.

droppings ('drɒpɪŋz) PLURAL NOUN the dung of certain animals, such as rabbits, sheep, and birds.

drops (drɒps) PLURAL NOUN any liquid medication applied by means of a dropper.

drop scone NOUN a flat spongy cake made by dropping a spoonful of batter on a griddle. Also called: **girdlecake, griddlecake, Scotch pancake,** (Scot) **pancake.**

drop shipment NOUN a consignment invoiced to a wholesaler or other middleman but sent directly to the retailer by a manufacturer.

drop shot NOUN [1] **a** *Tennis* a softly-played return that drops abruptly after clearing the net, intended to give an opponent no chance of reaching the ball and usually achieved by imparting backspin. **b** *Squash* a similar shot that stops abruptly after hitting the front wall of the court. [2] a type of shot made by permitting molten metal to percolate through a sieve and then dropping it into a tank of water.

dropsonde ('drɒpsɒnd) NOUN *Meteorol* a radiosonde dropped by parachute.
▷**HISTORY** C20: DROP + (RADIO)SONDE

dropsy ('drɒpsɪ) NOUN [1] *Pathol* a condition characterized by an accumulation of watery fluid in the tissues or in a body cavity. [2] *Slang* a tip or bribe.
▷**HISTORY** C13: shortened from *ydropesie,* from Latin *hydrōpisis,* from Greek *hudrōps,* from *hudōr* water
▸**dropsical** ('drɒpsɪkᵊl) *or* '**dropsied** ADJECTIVE
▸'**dropsically** ADVERB

drop tank NOUN an external aircraft tank, usually containing fuel, that can be detached and dropped in flight.

dropwort ('drɒp,wɜːt) NOUN [1] a Eurasian rosaceous plant, *Filipendula vulgaris,* with finely divided leaves and clusters of white or reddish flowers. See also **meadowsweet** (sense 1). [2] **water dropwort.** any of several umbelliferous marsh plants of the genus *Oenanthe,* with umbrella-shaped clusters of white flowers.

droshky ('drɒʃkɪ) *or* **drosky** ('drɒskɪ) NOUN, *plural* **-kies.** an open four-wheeled horse-drawn passenger carriage, formerly used in Russia.
▷**HISTORY** C19: from Russian *drozhki,* diminutive of *drogi* a wagon, from *droga* shaft

drosometer (drɒ'sɒmɪtə) NOUN an instrument that measures the amount of dew deposited.
▷**HISTORY** C19: from Greek *drosos* dew + -METER

drosophila (drɒ'sɒfɪlə) NOUN, *plural* **-las** *or* **-lae** (-,liː). any small dipterous fly of the genus *Drosophila,* esp *D. melanogaster,* a species widely used in laboratory genetics studies: family *Drosophilidae.*

They feed on plant sap, decaying fruit, etc. Also called: **fruit fly, vinegar fly.**
▷HISTORY C19: New Latin, from Greek *drosos* dew, water + *-phila;* see -PHILE

dross (drɒs) NOUN 1 the scum formed, usually by oxidation, on the surfaces of molten metals. 2 worthless matter; waste.
▷HISTORY Old English *drōs* dregs; related to Old High German *truosana*
▸'**drossy** ADJECTIVE ▸'**drossiness** NOUN

drought (draʊt) NOUN 1 a prolonged period of scanty rainfall. 2 a prolonged shortage. 3 an archaic or dialect word for **thirst.** Archaic and Scot form: **drouth** (dru:θ).
▷HISTORY Old English *drūgoth;* related to Dutch *droogte;* see DRY
▸'**droughty** ADJECTIVE

drouk *or* **drook** (drʊk) VERB (*tr*) *Scot* to drench; soak.
▷HISTORY C16: of uncertain origin; compare Old Norse *drukna* to be drowned

droukit *or* **drookit** ('drʊkɪt) ADJECTIVE *Scot* drenched; soaked.
▷HISTORY from DROUK

drouthy ('drʊθɪ) ADJECTIVE *Scot* thirsty or dry.

drove[1] (drəʊv) VERB the past tense of **drive.**

drove[2] (drəʊv) NOUN 1 a herd of livestock being driven together. 2 (*often plural*) a moving crowd of people. 3 a narrow irrigation channel. 4 Also called: **drove chisel.** a chisel with a broad edge used for dressing stone. ◆ VERB 5 **a** (*tr*) to drive (a group of livestock), usually for a considerable distance. **b** (*intr*) to be employed as a drover. 6 to work (a stone surface) with a drove.
▷HISTORY Old English *drāf* herd; related to Middle Low German *drēfwech* cattle pasture; see DRIVE, DRIFT

drover ('drəʊvə) NOUN a person whose occupation is the driving of sheep or cattle, esp to and from market.

drown (draʊn) VERB 1 to die or kill by immersion in liquid. 2 (*tr*) to destroy or get rid of as if by submerging: *he drowned his sorrows in drink.* 3 (*tr*) to drench thoroughly; inundate; flood. 4 (*tr; sometimes foll by out*) to render (a sound) inaudible by making a loud noise.
▷HISTORY C13: probably from Old English *druncnian;* related to Old Norse *drukna* to be drowned
▸'**drowner** NOUN

drowse (draʊz) VERB 1 to be or cause to be sleepy, dull, or sluggish. ◆ NOUN 2 the state of being drowsy.
▷HISTORY C16: probably from Old English *drūsian* to sink; related to *drēosan* to fall

drowsy ('draʊzɪ) ADJECTIVE **drowsier, drowsiest.** 1 heavy with sleepiness; sleepy. 2 inducing sleep; soporific. 3 sluggish or lethargic; dull.
▸'**drowsily** ADVERB ▸'**drowsiness** NOUN

drub (drʌb) VERB **drubs, drubbing, drubbed.** (*tr*) 1 to beat as with a stick; cudgel; club. 2 to defeat utterly, as in a contest. 3 to drum or stamp (the feet). 4 to instil with force or repetition: *the master drubbed Latin into the boys.* ◆ NOUN 5 a blow, as from a stick.
▷HISTORY C17: probably from Arabic *dáraba* to beat

drubbing ('drʌbɪŋ) NOUN 1 a beating, as with a stick, cudgel, etc. 2 a comprehensive or heavy defeat.

drudge (drʌdʒ) NOUN 1 a person, such as a servant, who works hard at wearisome menial tasks. ◆ VERB 2 (*intr*) to toil at such tasks.
▷HISTORY C16: perhaps from *druggen* to toil
▸'**drudger** NOUN ▸'**drudgingly** ADVERB

drudgery ('drʌdʒərɪ) NOUN, *plural* **-eries.** hard, menial, and monotonous work.

drug (drʌg) NOUN 1 any synthetic, semisynthetic, or natural chemical substance used in the treatment, prevention, or diagnosis of disease, or for other medical reasons. Related adjective: **pharmaceutical.** 2 a chemical substance, esp a narcotic, taken for the pleasant effects it produces. 3 **drug on the market.** a commodity available in excess of the demands of the market. ◆ VERB **drugs, drugging, drugged.** (*tr*) 4 to mix a drug with (food, drink, etc.). 5 to administer a drug to. 6 to stupefy or poison with or as if with a drug. Related prefix: **pharmaco-.**
▷HISTORY C14: from Old French *drogue,* probably of Germanic origin
▸'**druggy** ADJECTIVE

drug addict NOUN any person who is abnormally dependent on narcotic drugs. See **addiction.**

drug baron NOUN the head of an organization that deals in illegal drugs.

drugget ('drʌgɪt) NOUN a coarse fabric used as a protective floor-covering, etc.
▷HISTORY C16: from French *droguet* useless fabric, from *drogue* trash

druggie ('drʌgɪ) NOUN *Informal* a drug addict.

druggist ('drʌgɪst) NOUN a US and Canadian term for a **pharmacist.**

druglord ('drʌgɪˌlɔ:d) NOUN a criminal who controls the distribution and sale of large quantities of illegal drugs.

drugstore ('drʌgˌstɔ:) NOUN *US and Canadian* a shop where medical prescriptions are made up and a wide variety of goods and sometimes light meals are sold.

druid ('dru:ɪd) NOUN (*sometimes capital*) 1 a member of an ancient order of priests in Gaul, Britain, and Ireland in the pre-Christian era. 2 a member of any of several modern movements attempting to revive druidism.
▷HISTORY C16: from Latin *druides,* of Gaulish origin; compare Old Irish *druid* wizards
▸**druidess** ('dru:ɪdɪs) FEMININE NOUN ▸**dru'idic** *or* **dru'idical** ADJECTIVE ▸'**druidˌism** NOUN

drum[1] (drʌm) NOUN 1 *Music* a percussion instrument sounded by striking a membrane stretched across the opening of a hollow cylinder or hemisphere. 2 **beat the drum for.** *Informal* to attempt to arouse interest in. 3 the sound produced by a drum or any similar sound. 4 an object that resembles a drum in shape, such as a large spool or a cylindrical container. 5 *Architect* **a** one of a number of cylindrical blocks of stone used to construct the shaft of a column. **b** the wall or structure supporting a dome or cupola. 6 short for **eardrum.** 7 Also called: **drumfish.** any of various North American marine and freshwater sciaenid fishes, such as *Equetus pulcher* (**striped drum**), that utter a drumming sound. 8 a type of hollow rotor for steam turbines or axial compressors. 9 *Computing* a rotating cylindrical device on which data may be stored for later retrieval: now mostly superseded by disks. See **disk** (sense 2). 10 *Archaic* a drummer. 11 **the drum.** *Austral informal* the necessary information (esp in the phrase **give (someone) the drum**). ◆ VERB **drums, drumming, drummed.** 12 to play (music) on or as if on a drum. 13 to beat or tap (the fingers) rhythmically or regularly. 14 (*intr*) (of birds) to produce a rhythmic sound, as by beating the bill against a tree, branch, etc. 15 (*tr; sometimes foll by up*) to summon or call by drumming. 16 (*tr*) to instil by constant repetition: *to drum an idea into someone's head.* ◆ See also **drum out, drum up.**
▷HISTORY C16: probably from Middle Dutch *tromme,* of imitative origin

drum[2] (drʌm) NOUN *Scot, Irish* a narrow ridge or hill.
▷HISTORY C18: from Scottish Gaelic *druim*

drumbeat ('drʌmˌbi:t) NOUN the sound made by beating a drum.

drum brake NOUN a type of brake used on the wheels of vehicles, consisting of two pivoted shoes that rub against the inside walls of the brake drum when the brake is applied.

drumfire ('drʌmˌfaɪə) NOUN heavy, rapid, and continuous gunfire, the sound of which resembles rapid drumbeats.

drumfish ('drʌmˌfɪʃ) NOUN, *plural* **-fish** *or* **-fishes.** another name for **drum**[1] (sense 7).

drumhead ('drʌmˌhɛd) NOUN 1 *Music* the part of a drum that is actually struck with a stick or the hand. 2 the head of a capstan, pierced with holes for the capstan bars. 3 another name for **eardrum.**

drumhead court-martial NOUN a military court convened to hear urgent charges of offences committed in action.
▷HISTORY C19: from the use of a drumhead as a table around which the court-martial was held

drumhead service NOUN a religious service attended by members of a military unit while in the field.

drumlin ('drʌmlɪn) NOUN a streamlined mound of glacial drift, rounded or elongated in the direction of the original flow of ice.
▷HISTORY C19: from Irish Gaelic *druim* ridge + *-lin* -LING[1]

drum machine NOUN a synthesizer specially programmed to reproduce the sound of drums and other percussion instruments in variable rhythms and combinations selected by the musician; the resulting beat is produced continually until stopped or changed.

drum major NOUN the noncommissioned officer, usually of warrant officer's rank, who is appointed to command the corps of drums of a military band and who is in command of both the drums and the band when paraded together.

drum majorette NOUN a girl who marches at the head of a procession, twirling a baton.

drummer ('drʌmə) NOUN 1 a person who plays a drum or set of drums. 2 *Chiefly US* a salesman, esp a travelling salesman. 3 *Austral and NZ slang* the slowest shearer in a team.

drummy ('drʌmɪ) NOUN, *plural* **-mies.** (in South Africa) short for **drum majorette.**

drum'n'bass *or* **drum and bass** NOUN **a** a type of electronic dance music using mainly bass guitar and drum sounds. **b** (*as modifier*): *a drum'n'bass backing.*

drum out VERB (*tr, adverb; usually foll by of*) **a** to expel from a club, association, etc. **b** (formerly) to dismiss from military service to the beat of a drum.

drumstick ('drʌmˌstɪk) NOUN 1 a stick used for playing a drum. 2 the lower joint of the leg of a cooked fowl.

drum up VERB (*tr, adverb*) to evoke or obtain (support, business, etc.) by solicitation or canvassing.

drunk (drʌŋk) ADJECTIVE 1 intoxicated with alcohol to the extent of losing control over normal physical and mental functions. 2 overwhelmed by strong influence or emotion: *drunk with power.* ◆ NOUN 3 a person who is drunk or drinks habitually to excess. 4 *Informal* a drinking bout.
▷HISTORY Old English *druncen,* past participle of *drincan* to drink; see DRINK

drunkard ('drʌŋkəd) NOUN a person who is frequently or habitually drunk.

drunkathon ('drʌŋkəˌθɒn) NOUN *Informal* a session in which excessive quantities of alcohol are consumed.

drunken ('drʌŋkən) ADJECTIVE 1 intoxicated with or as if with alcohol. 2 frequently or habitually drunk. 3 (*prenominal*) caused by or relating to alcoholic intoxication: *a drunken brawl.*
▸'**drunkenly** ADVERB ▸'**drunkenness** NOUN

drupe (dru:p) NOUN an indehiscent fruit consisting of outer epicarp, fleshy or fibrous mesocarp, and stony endocarp enclosing a single seed, as in the peach, plum, and cherry.
▷HISTORY C18: from Latin *druppa* wrinkled overripe olive, from Greek: olive
▸**drupaceous** (dru:'peɪʃəs) ADJECTIVE

drupelet ('dru:plɪt) *or* **drupel** ('dru:pᵊl) NOUN a small drupe, usually one of a number forming a compound fruit.

Drury Lane ('drʊərɪ) NOUN a street in the West End of London, formerly famous for its theatres.

druse (dru:z) NOUN 1 an aggregate of small crystals within a cavity, esp those lining a cavity in a rock or mineral. 2 *Botany* a globular mass of calcium oxalate crystals formed around an organic core, found in some plant cells.
▷HISTORY C19: from German, from Old High German *druos* bump

Druse *or* **Druze** (dru:z) NOUN, *plural* **Druse** *or* **Druze.** **a** a member of a religious sect, mainly living in Syria, Lebanon, and Israel, having certain characteristics in common with Muslims. **b** (*as modifier*): *Druse beliefs.*
▷HISTORY C18: from Arabic *Durūz* the Druses, after *Ismail al-Darazi* Ismail the tailor, 11th-century Muslim leader who founded the sect
▸'**Drusean** *or* '**Drusian** *or* '**Druzean** *or* '**Druzian** ADJECTIVE

dry (draɪ) ADJECTIVE **drier, driest** *or* **dryer, dryest.** 1 lacking moisture; not damp or wet. 2 having little or no rainfall. [3] not in or under water: *dry land.* [4] having the water drained away or evaporated: *a dry river.* [5] not providing milk: *a dry cow.* [6] (of the eyes) free from tears. [7] **a** *Informal* in need of a drink; thirsty. **b** causing thirst: *dry work.* [8] eaten without butter, jam, etc.: *dry toast.* [9] (of a wine, cider, etc.) not sweet. [10] *Pathol* not accompanied by or producing a mucous or watery discharge: *a dry cough.* [11] consisting of solid as opposed to liquid substances or commodities. [12] without adornment; plain: *dry facts.* [13] lacking interest or stimulation: *a dry book.* [14] lacking warmth or emotion; cold: *a dry greeting.* [15] (of wit or humour) shrewd and keen in an impersonal, sarcastic, or laconic way. [16] opposed to or prohibiting the sale of alcoholic liquor for human consumption: *a dry area.* [17] *NZ* (of a ewe) without a lamb after the mating season. [18] *Electronics* (of a soldered electrical joint) imperfect because the solder has not adhered to the metal, thus reducing conductance. ◆ VERB **dries, drying, dried.** [19] (when *intr,* often foll by *off*) to make or become dry or free from moisture. [20] (*tr*) to preserve (meat, vegetables, fruit, etc.) by removing the moisture. ◆ NOUN, *plural* **drys** *or* **dries.** [21] *Brit informal* a Conservative politician who is considered to be a hard-liner. Compare **wet** (sense 10). [22] **the dry.** *Austral informal* the dry season. [23] *US and Canadian* an informal word for **prohibitionist.** ◆ See also **dry out, dry up.**

▷**HISTORY** Old English *drȳge;* related to Old High German *truckan,* Old Norse *draugr* dry wood

▸**ˈdryable** ADJECTIVE ▸**ˈdryness** NOUN

dryad (ˈdraɪəd, -æd) NOUN, *plural* **-ads** *or* **-ades** (-əˌdiːz). *Greek myth* a nymph or divinity of the woods.

▷**HISTORY** C14: from Latin *Dryas,* from Greek *Druas,* from *drus* tree

▸**dryadic** (draɪˈædɪk) ADJECTIVE

dry battery NOUN an electric battery consisting of two or more dry cells.

dry-bone ore NOUN a mining term for **smithsonite.**

dry-bulb thermometer NOUN an ordinary thermometer used alongside a wet-bulb thermometer to obtain relative humidity. See also **psychrometer.**

dry cell NOUN a primary cell in which the electrolyte is in the form of a paste or is treated in some way to prevent it from spilling. Compare **wet cell.**

dry-clean VERB (*tr*) to clean (clothing, fabrics, etc.) with a solvent other than water, such as trichloroethylene.

▸**ˌdry-ˈcleaner** NOUN ▸**ˌdry-ˈcleaning** NOUN

dry distillation NOUN another name for **destructive distillation.**

dry dock NOUN [1] a basin-like structure that is large enough to admit a ship and that can be pumped dry for work on the ship's bottom. ◆ VERB **dry-dock.** [2] to put (a ship) into a dry dock, or (of a ship) to go into a dry dock.

dry drunk NOUN an alcoholic who is not currently drinking alcohol but is still following an irregular undisciplined lifestyle like that of a drunkard.

dryer[1] (ˈdraɪə) NOUN [1] a person or thing that dries. [2] an apparatus for removing moisture by forced draught, heating, or centrifuging. [3] any of certain chemicals added to oils such as linseed oil to accelerate their drying when used as bases in paints, etc.

dryer[2] (ˈdraɪə) ADJECTIVE a variant spelling of **drier**[1].

dry farming NOUN a system of growing crops in arid or semiarid regions without artificial irrigation, by reducing evaporation and by special methods of tillage.

▸**dry farmer** NOUN

dry fly NOUN *Angling* **a** an artificial fly designed and prepared to be floated or skimmed on the surface of the water. **b** (*as modifier*): *dry-fly fishing.* ◆ Compare **wet fly.**

dry hole NOUN (in the oil industry) a well that is drilled but does not produce oil or gas in commercially worthwhile amounts.

dry ice NOUN solid carbon dioxide, which sublimes at –78.5°C: used as a refrigerant, and to create billows of smoke in stage shows. Also called: **carbon dioxide snow.**

drying (ˈdraɪɪŋ) NOUN [1] the action or process of making or becoming dry. [2] Also called (not now in technical usage): **seasoning.** the processing of timber until it has a moisture content suitable for the purposes for which it is to be used. ◆ ADJECTIVE [3] causing dryness: *a drying wind.*

drying oil NOUN one of a number of animal or vegetable oils, such as linseed oil, that harden by oxidation on exposure to air: used as a base for some paints and varnishes.

dry kiln NOUN an oven in which cut timber is dried and seasoned.

dry law NOUN *Chiefly US* a law prohibiting the sale of alcoholic beverages.

dry lightning NOUN *US* lightning produced by a thunderstorm that is unaccompanied by rain.

dryly (ˈdraɪlɪ) ADVERB a variant spelling of **drily.**

dry martini NOUN a cocktail of between four and ten parts gin to one part dry vermouth.

dry measure NOUN a unit or a system of units for measuring dry goods, such as fruit, grains, etc.

dry nurse NOUN [1] a nurse who cares for a child without suckling it. Compare **wet nurse.** ◆ VERB **dry-nurse.** [2] to care for (a baby or young child) without suckling.

dryopithecine (ˌdraɪəʊˈpɪθəˌsiːn) NOUN any extinct Old World ape of the genus *Dryopithecus,* common in Miocene and Pliocene times: thought to be the ancestors of modern apes.

▷**HISTORY** C20: from New Latin *Dryopithēcus,* from Greek *drus* tree + *pithēkos* ape

dry out VERB (*adverb*) [1] to make or become dry. [2] to undergo or cause to undergo treatment for alcoholism or drug addiction.

dry point NOUN [1] a technique of intaglio engraving with a hard steel needle, without acid, on a copper plate. [2] the sharp steel needle used in this process. [3] an engraving or print produced by this method.

dry riser NOUN a vertical pipe, not containing water, having connections on different floors of a building for a fireman's hose to be attached. A fire tender can be connected at the lowest level to make water rise under pressure within the pipe. Abbreviation: **DR.**

dry rot NOUN [1] crumbling and drying of timber, bulbs, potatoes, or fruit, caused by saprotrophic basidiomycetous fungi. [2] any fungus causing this decay, esp of the genus *Merulius.* [3] moral degeneration or corrupt practices, esp when previously unsuspected.

dry run NOUN [1] *Military* practice in weapon firing, a drill, or a manoeuvre without using live ammunition. [2] *Informal* a trial or practice, esp in simulated conditions; rehearsal.

dry-salt VERB to preserve (food) by salting and removing moisture.

drysalter (ˈdraɪˌsɔːltə) NOUN *Obsolete* a dealer in certain chemical products, such as dyestuffs and gums, and in dried, tinned, or salted foods and edible oils.

Drysdale (ˈdraɪzdeɪl) NOUN a New Zealand breed of sheep with hair growing among its wool: bred for its coat which is used in making carpets.

dry slope NOUN an artifical ski slope used for tuition and practice. Also called: **dry-ski slope.**

dry steam NOUN steam that does not contain droplets of water.

dry-stone ADJECTIVE (of a wall) made without mortar.

Dry Tortugas (tɔːˈtuːgəz) NOUN a group of eight coral islands at the entrance to the Gulf of Mexico: part of Florida.

dry up VERB (*adverb*) [1] (*intr*) to become barren or unproductive; fail: *in middle age his inspiration dried up.* [2] to dry (dishes, cutlery, etc.) with a tea towel after they have been washed. [3] (*intr*) *Informal* to stop talking or speaking: *when I got on the stage I just dried up; dry up!*

dry valley NOUN a valley originally produced by running water but now waterless.

DS ABBREVIATION FOR: [1] Also: **ds.** *Music* **dal segno.** [2] Detective Sergeant.

DSc ABBREVIATION FOR Doctor of Science.

DSC *Military* ABBREVIATION FOR Distinguished Service Cross.

DSM *Military* ABBREVIATION FOR Distinguished Service Medal.

DSO *Brit military* ABBREVIATION FOR Distinguished Service Order.

dsp ABBREVIATION FOR decessit sine prole.

▷**HISTORY** Latin: died without issue

DSS (in Britain) ABBREVIATION FOR: [1] Director of Social Services. [2] Department of Social Security.

DST ABBREVIATION FOR Daylight Saving Time.

DTI (in Britain) ABBREVIATION FOR Department of Trade and Industry.

DTL *Electronics* ABBREVIATION FOR diode transistor logic: a stage in the development of electronic logic circuits.

DTLR (in Britain) ABBREVIATION FOR Department of Transport, Local Government, and the Regions.

DTP ABBREVIATION FOR **desktop publishing.**

DT's *Informal* ABBREVIATION FOR **delirium tremens.**

DTT ABBREVIATION FOR digital terrestrial television.

DU ABBREVIATION FOR depleted uranium.

Du. ABBREVIATION FOR: [1] Duke. [2] Dutch.

duad (ˈdjuːæd) NOUN a rare word for **pair**[1].

▷**HISTORY** C17: from Greek *duas* two, a pair

dual (ˈdjuːəl) ADJECTIVE [1] relating to or denoting two. [2] twofold; double. [3] (in the grammar of Old English, Ancient Greek, and certain other languages) denoting a form of a word indicating that exactly two referents are being referred to. [4] *Maths, logic* (of structures or expressions) having the property that the interchange of certain pairs of terms, and usually the distribution of negation, yields equivalent structures or expressions. ◆ NOUN [5] *Grammar* **a** the dual number. **b** a dual form of a word. ◆ VERB **duals, dualling, dualled.** [6] (*tr*) *Brit* to make (a road) into a dual carriageway.

▷**HISTORY** C17: from Latin *duālis* concerning two, from *duo* two

▸**ˈdually** ADVERB

Duala (dʊˈɑːlə, -lɑː) NOUN [1] (*plural* **-la** *or* **-las**) a member of a Negroid people of W Africa living chiefly in Cameroon. [2] the language of this people, belonging to the Bantu group of the Niger-Congo family.

Dual Alliance NOUN [1] the alliance between France and Russia (1893–1917). [2] the secret Austro-German alliance against Russia (1879) later expanded to the Triple Alliance.

dual carriageway NOUN *Brit* a road on which traffic travelling in opposite directions is separated by a central strip of turf, etc. US and Canadian name: **divided highway.**

dualism (ˈdjuːəˌlɪzəm) NOUN [1] the state of being twofold or double. [2] *Philosophy* the doctrine, as opposed to idealism and materialism, that reality consists of two basic types of substance usually taken to be mind and matter or two basic types of entity, mental and physical. Compare **monism.** [3] **a** the theory that the universe has been ruled from its origins by two conflicting powers, one good and one evil, both existing as equally ultimate first causes. **b** the theory that there are two personalities, one human and one divine, in Christ.

▸**ˈdualist** NOUN ▸**ˌdualˈistic** ADJECTIVE ▸**ˌdualˈistically** ADVERB

duality (djuːˈælɪtɪ) NOUN, *plural* **-ties.** [1] the state or quality of being two or in two parts; dichotomy. [2] *Physics* the principle that a wave-particle duality exists in microphysics in which wave theory and corpuscular theory are complementary. The propagation of electromagnetic radiation is analysed using wave theory but its interaction with matter is described in terms of photons. The condition of particles such as electrons, neutrons, and atoms is described in terms of de Broglie waves. [3] *Geometry* the interchangeability of the roles of the point and the plane in statements and theorems in projective geometry.

Dual Monarchy NOUN the monarchy of Austria-Hungary from 1867 to 1918.

dual-purpose ADJECTIVE having or serving two functions.

duathlon (djuːˈæθlɒn) NOUN an athletic contest in which each athlete competes in running and cycling events.

▷HISTORY C20: from DUO- + Greek *athlon* contest

dub¹ (dʌb) VERB **dubs, dubbing, dubbed.** 1 (*tr*) to invest (a person) with knighthood by the ritual of tapping on the shoulder with a sword. 2 (*tr*) to invest with a title, name, or nickname. 3 (*tr*) to dress (leather) by rubbing. 4 *Angling* to dress (a fly). ◆ NOUN 5 the sound of a drum.
▷HISTORY Old English *dubbian;* related to Old Norse *dubba* to dub a knight, Old High German *tubili* plug, peg

dub² (dʌb) VERB **dubs, dubbing, dubbed.** *Films, television* 1 to alter the soundtrack of (an old recording, film, etc.). 2 (*tr*) to substitute for the soundtrack of (a film) a new soundtrack, esp in a different language. 3 (*tr*) to provide (a film or tape) with a soundtrack. 4 (*tr*) to alter (a taped soundtrack) by removing some parts and exaggerating others. ◆ NOUN 5 *Films* the new sounds added. 6 **a** *Music* a style of record production associated with reggae, involving the removal or exaggeration of instrumental parts, extensive use of echo, etc. **b** (*as modifier*): *a dub mix.*
▷HISTORY C20: shortened from DOUBLE

dub³ (dʌb) VERB **dubs, dubbing, dubbed.** *Austral and NZ informal* short for **double-bank.**

dub⁴ (dʌb) *US and Canadian informal* ◆ NOUN 1 a clumsy or awkward person or player. ◆ VERB **dubs, dubbing, dubbed.** 2 to bungle (a shot), as in golf.
▷HISTORY C19: of uncertain origin

dub⁵ (dʌb) NOUN *Scot and northern English dialect* a pool of water; puddle.
▷HISTORY C16: Scottish dialect *dubbe;* related to Middle Low German *dobbe*

dub⁶ (dʌb) VERB **dubs, dubbing, dubbed.** (*intr;* foll by *in, up,* or *out*) *Slang* to contribute to the cost of (something); pay.
▷HISTORY C19: of obscure origin

Dubai (du:ˈbaɪ) NOUN a sheikhdom in the NE United Arab Emirates, consisting principally of the port of Dubai, on the Persian Gulf: oilfields. Pop.: 913 000 (2001 est.).

dubbin (ˈdʌbɪn) *or* **dubbing** NOUN *Brit* a greasy mixture of tallow and oil applied to leather to soften it and make it waterproof.
▷HISTORY C18: from *dub* to dress leather; see DUB¹

dubbing¹ (ˈdʌbɪŋ) NOUN *Films* 1 the replacement of a soundtrack in one language by one in another language. 2 the combination of several soundtracks into a single track. 3 the addition of a soundtrack to a film or broadcast.

dubbing² (ˈdʌbɪŋ) NOUN 1 *Angling* hair or fur spun on waxed silk and added to the body of an artificial fly to give it shape. 2 a variant of **dubbin.**

dubbo (ˈdʌbəʊ) *Austral slang* ◆ ADJECTIVE 1 stupid. ◆ NOUN, *plural* **-bos.** 2 a stupid person.
▷HISTORY from *Dubbo,* a town in New South Wales, Australia

dubiety (dju:ˈbaɪɪtɪ) *or* **dubiosity** (ˌdju:bɪˈɒsɪtɪ) NOUN, *plural* **-ties.** 1 the state of being doubtful. 2 a doubtful matter.
▷HISTORY C18: from Late Latin *dubietās,* from Latin *dubius* DUBIOUS

dubious (ˈdju:bɪəs) ADJECTIVE 1 marked by or causing doubt: *a dubious reply.* 2 unsettled in mind; uncertain; doubtful. 3 of doubtful quality; untrustworthy: *a dubious reputation.* 4 not certain in outcome.
▷HISTORY C16: from Latin *dubius* wavering
▸ˈ**dubiously** ADVERB ▸ˈ**dubiousness** NOUN

dubitable (ˈdju:bɪtəbᵊl) ADJECTIVE open to doubt.
▷HISTORY C17: from Latin *dubitāre* to DOUBT
▸ˈ**dubitably** ADVERB

dubitation (ˌdju:bɪˈteɪʃən) NOUN another word for **doubt.**

Dublin (ˈdʌblɪn) NOUN 1 the capital of the Republic of Ireland, on **Dublin Bay**: under English rule from 1171 until 1922; commercial and cultural centre; contains one of the world's largest breweries and exports whiskey, stout, and agricultural produce. Pop.: 480 996 (1996). Gaelic name: **Baile Átha Cliath.** 2 a county in E Republic of Ireland, in Leinster on the Irish Sea: mountainous in the south but low-lying in the north and centre. County seat: Dublin. Pop.: 1 058 264 (1996). Area: 922 sq. km (356 sq. miles).

Dublin Bay prawn NOUN a large prawn usually used in a dish of scampi.

Dubliner (ˈdʌblɪnə) NOUN a native or inhabitant of Dublin.

Dubna (ˈdʌbnə) NOUN a new town in W Russia, founded in 1956: site of the United Institute of Nuclear Research. Pop.: 66 000 (1990 est.).

dubnium (ˈdʌbnɪəm) NOUN a synthetic transactinide element produced in minute quantities by bombarding plutonium with high-energy neon ions. Symbol: Du; atomic no. 105.
▷HISTORY C20: after DUBNA in Russia, where it was first reported

dubonnet (dju:ˈbɒneɪ) NOUN **a** a dark purplish-red colour. **b** (*as adjective*): *a dubonnet coat.*
▷HISTORY from DUBONNET

Dubonnet (dju:ˈbɒneɪ) NOUN *Trademark* a sweet usually red apéritif wine flavoured with quinine and cinchona.

Dubrovnik (dʊˈbrɒvnɪk) NOUN a port in W Croatia, on the Dalmatian coast: an important commercial centre in the Middle Ages; damaged in 1991 when it was shelled by Serbian artillery. Pop.: 49 730 (1991). Former Italian name (until 1918): **Ragusa.**

ducal (ˈdju:kᵊl) ADJECTIVE of or relating to a duke or duchy.
▷HISTORY C16: from French, from Late Latin *ducālis* of a leader, from *dux* leader
▸ˈ**ducally** ADVERB

ducat (ˈdʌkət) NOUN 1 any of various former European gold or silver coins, esp those used in Italy or the Netherlands. 2 (*often plural*) any coin or money.
▷HISTORY C14: from Old French, from Old Italian *ducato* coin stamped with the doge's image, from *duca* doge, from Latin *dux* leader

duce (ˈdu:tʃɪ; *Italian* ˈdu:tʃe) NOUN leader.
▷HISTORY C20: from Italian, from Latin *dux*

Duce (*Italian* ˈdu:tʃe) NOUN **Il** (il). the title assumed by Benito Mussolini as leader of Fascist Italy (1922–43).

Duchenne dystrophy (du:ˈʃɛn) *or* **Duchenne muscular dystrophy** NOUN the most common form of muscular dystrophy, usually affecting only boys. Abbreviation: **DMD.**
▷HISTORY named after Guillaume *Duchenne* (1806–75), French neurologist

duchess (ˈdʌtʃɪs) NOUN 1 the wife or widow of a duke. 2 a woman who holds the rank of duke in her own right. ◆ VERB 3 *Austral informal* to overwhelm with flattering attention.
▷HISTORY C14: from Old French *duchesse,* feminine of *duc* DUKE

duchy (ˈdʌtʃɪ) NOUN, *plural* **duchies.** the territory of a duke or duchess; dukedom.
▷HISTORY C14: from Old French *duche,* from *duc* DUKE

duck¹ (dʌk) NOUN, *plural* **ducks** *or* **duck.** 1 any of various small aquatic birds of the family *Anatidae,* typically having short legs, webbed feet, and a broad blunt bill: order *Anseriformes.* 2 the flesh of this bird, used as food. 3 the female of such a bird, as opposed to the male (drake). 4 any other bird of the family *Anatidae,* including geese, and swans. 5 Also: **ducks.** *Brit informal* dear or darling: used as a term of endearment or of general address. See also **ducky.** 6 *Informal* a person, esp one regarded as odd or endearing. 7 *Cricket* a score of nothing by a batsman. 8 **like water off a duck's back.** *Informal* without effect. 9 **take to something like a duck to water.** *Informal* to become adept at or attracted to something very quickly.
▷HISTORY Old English *dūce* duck, diver; related to DUCK²

duck² (dʌk) VERB 1 to move (the head or body) quickly downwards or away, esp so as to escape observation or evade a blow. 2 to submerge or plunge suddenly and often briefly under water. 3 (when *intr,* often foll by *out*) *Informal* to dodge or escape (a person, duty, etc.). 4 (*intr*) *Bridge* to play a low card when possessing a higher one rather than try to win a trick. ◆ NOUN 5 the act or an instance of ducking.
▷HISTORY C14: related to Old High German *tūhhan* to dive, Middle Dutch *dūken*
▸ˈ**ducker** NOUN

duck³ (dʌk) NOUN a heavy cotton fabric of plain weave, used for clothing, tents, etc. See also **ducks.**
▷HISTORY C17: from Middle Dutch *doek;* related to Old High German *tuoh* cloth

duck⁴ (dʌk) NOUN an amphibious vehicle used in World War II.
▷HISTORY C20: from code name DUKW

duck-billed dinosaur NOUN another name for **hadrosaur.**

duck-billed platypus NOUN an amphibious egg-laying mammal, *Ornithorhynchus anatinus,* of E Australia, having dense fur, a broad bill and tail, and webbed feet: family *Ornithorhynchidae.* Sometimes shortened to: **duckbill, platypus.** See also **monotreme.**

duckboard (ˈdʌkˌbɔ:d) NOUN a board or boards laid so as to form a floor or path over wet or muddy ground.

duck-egg blue NOUN **a** a pale greenish-blue colour. **b** (*as adjective*): *duck-egg blue walls.*

duckfoot quote (ˈdʌkfʊt) NOUN *Printing* a chevron-shaped quotation mark (≪ or ≫) used in Europe. Also called: **guillemet.**

duck hawk NOUN a variety of peregrine falcon, *Falco peregrinus anatum,* occurring in North America.

ducking stool NOUN *History* a chair or stool used for the punishment of offenders by plunging them into water.

duckling (ˈdʌklɪŋ) NOUN a young duck.

ducks (dʌks) PLURAL NOUN clothing made of duck, esp white trousers for sports.

ducks and drakes NOUN (*functioning as singular*) 1 a game in which a flat stone is bounced across the surface of water. 2 **make ducks and drakes of** *or* **play (at) ducks and drakes with.** to use recklessly; squander or waste.

duck's arse NOUN a hairstyle in which the hair is swept back to a point at the nape of the neck, resembling a duck's tail. Also called: **DA.**

duck shove VERB *Austral and NZ informal* to evade responsibility.
▸**duck shover** NOUN ▸**duck shoving** NOUN

duck soup NOUN *US slang* something that is easy to do.

duckweed (ˈdʌkˌwi:d) NOUN any of various small stemless aquatic plants of the family *Lemnaceae,* esp any of the genus *Lemna,* that have rounded leaves and occur floating on still water in temperate regions.

ducky *or* **duckie** (ˈdʌkɪ) *Informal* ◆ NOUN, *plural* **duckies.** 1 *Brit* darling or dear: used as a term of endearment among women, but now often used in imitation of the supposed usage of homosexual men. ◆ ADJECTIVE 2 delightful; fine.

duct (dʌkt) NOUN 1 a tube, pipe, or canal by means of which a substance, esp a fluid or gas, is conveyed. 2 any bodily passage, esp one conveying secretions or excretions. 3 a narrow tubular cavity in plants, often containing resin or some other substance. 4 Also called: **conduit.** a channel or pipe carrying electric cable or wires. 5 a passage through which air can flow, as in air conditioning. 6 the ink reservoir in a printing press.
▷HISTORY C17: from Latin *ductus* a leading (in Medieval Latin: aqueduct), from *dūcere* to lead
▸ˈ**ductless** ADJECTIVE

ductile (ˈdʌktaɪl) ADJECTIVE 1 (of a metal, such as gold or copper) able to be drawn out into wire. 2 able to be moulded; pliant; plastic. 3 easily led or influenced; tractable.
▷HISTORY C14: from Old French, from Latin *ductilis,* from *dūcere* to lead
▸ˈ**ductilely** ADVERB ▸**ductility** (dʌkˈtɪlɪtɪ) *or* ˈ**ductileness** NOUN

ductless gland NOUN *Anatomy* See **endocrine gland.**

duct tape NOUN a type of strong waterproof adhesive silver-coloured cloth tape used for repairs by plumbers, electricians, etc.

ductule (ˈdʌktju:l) NOUN *Anatomy, zoology* a small duct.

dud (dʌd) *Informal* ◆ NOUN 1 a person or thing that proves ineffectual or a failure. 2 a shell, etc., that fails to explode. 3 (*plural*) *Old-fashioned* clothes or other personal belongings. ◆ ADJECTIVE 4 failing in its purpose or function: *a dud cheque.*

▷HISTORY C15 (in the sense: an article of clothing, a thing, used disparagingly): of unknown origin

dude (du:d, dju:d) NOUN *Informal* [1] *Western US and Canadian* a city dweller, esp one holidaying on a ranch. [2] *Chiefly US and Canadian* a dandy. [3] *US and Canadian* a person: often used to any male in direct address.
▷HISTORY C19: of unknown origin
▸ˈ**dudish** ADJECTIVE ▸ˈ**dudishly** ADVERB

dudeen (du:ˈdi:n) NOUN a clay pipe with a short stem.
▷HISTORY C19: from Irish *dúidín* a little pipe, from *dúd* pipe

dude ranch NOUN *US and Canadian* a ranch used as a holiday resort offering activities such as riding and camping.

dudgeon^{1} (ˈdʌdʒən) NOUN anger or resentment (archaic, except in the phrase **in high dudgeon**).
▷HISTORY C16: of unknown origin

dudgeon^{2} (ˈdʌdʒən) NOUN [1] *Obsolete* a wood used in making the handles of knives, daggers, etc. [2] *Archaic* a dagger, knife, etc., with a dudgeon hilt.
▷HISTORY C15: from Anglo-Norman *digeon,* of obscure origin

Dudley (ˈdʌdlɪ) NOUN [1] a town in W central England, in Dudley unitary authority, West Midlands: wrought-iron industry. Pop.: 192 171 (1991). [2] a unitary authority in W central England, in West Midlands. Pop.: 305 164 (2001). Area: 98 sq. km (38 sq. miles).

due (dju:) ADJECTIVE [1] (*postpositive*) immediately payable. [2] (*postpositive*) owed as a debt, irrespective of any date for payment. [3] requisite; fitting; proper. [4] (*prenominal*) adequate or sufficient; enough. [5] (*postpositive*) expected or appointed to be present or arrive: *the train is now due.* [6] **due to.** attributable to or caused by. ◆ NOUN [7] something that is owed, required, or due. [8] **give (a person) his due.** to give or allow what is deserved or right. ◆ ADVERB [9] directly or exactly; straight: *a course due west.* ◆ See also **dues.**
▷HISTORY C13: from Old French *deu,* from *devoir* to owe, from Latin *debēre;* see DEBT, DEBIT

> **Language note** The use of *due to* as a compound preposition *(the performance has been cancelled due to bad weather)* was formerly considered incorrect, but is now acceptable.

due bill NOUN *Chiefly US* a document acknowledging indebtedness, exchangeable for goods or services.

duel (ˈdju:əl) NOUN [1] a prearranged combat with deadly weapons between two people following a formal procedure in the presence of seconds and traditionally fought until one party was wounded or killed, usually to settle a quarrel involving a point of honour. [2] a contest or conflict between two persons or parties. ◆ VERB **duels, duelling, duelled** *or US* **duels, dueling, dueled.** (*intr*) [3] to fight in a duel. [4] to contest closely.
▷HISTORY C15: from Medieval Latin *duellum,* from Latin, poetical variant of *bellum* war; associated by folk etymology with Latin *duo* two
▸ˈ**dueller** *or* ˈ**duellist** NOUN

duello (dju:ˈɛləʊ) NOUN, *plural* **-los.** [1] the art of duelling. [2] the code of rules for duelling.
▷HISTORY C16: from Italian; see DUEL

duenna (dju:ˈɛnə) NOUN (in Spain and Portugal, etc.) an elderly woman retained by a family to act as governess and chaperon to young girls.
▷HISTORY C17: from Spanish *dueña,* from Latin *domina* lady, feminine of *dominus* master

due process of law NOUN the administration of justice in accordance with established rules and principles.

Duero (ˈduero) NOUN the Spanish name for the **Douro.**

dues (dju:z) PLURAL NOUN (*sometimes singular*) charges, as for membership of a club or organization; fees: *trade-union dues.*

duet (dju:ˈɛt) NOUN [1] Also called (esp for instrumental compositions): **duo.** a musical composition for two performers or voices. [2] an action or activity performed by a pair of closely connected individuals. ◆ VERB **duets, duetting, duetted.** [3] (*intr*) to perform a duet.
▷HISTORY C18: from Italian *duetto* a little duet, from *duo* duet, from Latin: two
▸**duˈettist** NOUN

duff^{1} (dʌf) NOUN [1] a thick flour pudding, often flavoured with currants, citron, etc., and boiled in a cloth bag: *plum duff.* [2] **up the duff.** *Slang* pregnant.
▷HISTORY C19: Northern English variant of DOUGH

duff^{2} (dʌf) VERB (*tr*) [1] *Slang* to change the appearance of or give a false appearance to (old or stolen goods); fake. [2] *Austral slang* to steal (cattle), altering the brand. [3] Also: **sclaff.** *Golf informal* to bungle (a shot) by hitting the ground behind the ball. ◆ ADJECTIVE [4] *Brit informal* bad or useless, as by not working out or operating correctly; dud: *a duff idea; a duff engine.* ◆ See also **duff up.**
▷HISTORY C19: probably back formation from DUFFER

duff^{3} (dʌf) NOUN *Slang* the rump or buttocks.
▷HISTORY C20: special use of DUFF^{1}

duffel *or* **duffle** (ˈdʌfᵊl) NOUN [1] a heavy woollen cloth with a thick nap. [2] *Chiefly US and Canadian* equipment or supplies, esp those of a camper.
▷HISTORY C17: after *Duffel,* Belgian town

duffel bag NOUN a cylindrical drawstring canvas bag, originally used esp by sailors for carrying personal articles.

duffel coat NOUN a knee-length or short wool coat, usually with a hood and fastened with toggles.

duffer (ˈdʌfə) NOUN [1] *Informal* a dull or incompetent person. [2] *Slang* something worthless. [3] *Dialect* a peddler or hawker. [4] *Austral slang* **a** a mine that proves unproductive. **b** a person who steals cattle.
▷HISTORY C19: of uncertain origin

duff up VERB (*tr, adverb*) *Brit slang* to beat or thrash (a person) severely.

dug^{1} (dʌg) VERB the past tense and past participle of **dig.**

dug^{2} (dʌg) NOUN [1] the nipple, teat, udder, or breast of a female mammal. [2] a human breast, esp when old and withered.
▷HISTORY C16: of Scandinavian origin; compare Danish *dægge* to coddle, Gothic *daddjan* to give suck

dug^{3} (dʌg) NOUN a Scot word for **dog.**

dugite (ˈdu:gaɪt) NOUN a medium-sized venomous snake, *Pseudonaja affinis,* of Central and W Australia, having a small head and slender olive-coloured body with black specks.

dugong (ˈdu:gɒŋ) NOUN a whalelike sirenian mammal, *Dugong dugon,* occurring in shallow tropical waters from E Africa to Australia: family *Dugongidae.*
▷HISTORY C19: from Malay *duyong*

dugout (ˈdʌgˌaʊt) NOUN [1] a canoe made by hollowing out a log. [2] *Military* a covered excavation dug to provide shelter. [3] *Slang* a retired officer, former civil servant, etc., recalled to employment. [4] (at a sports ground) the covered bench where managers, trainers, etc. sit and players wait when not on the field.

duh (dɜ:) INTERJECTION *Slang* an ironic response to a question or statement, implying that the speaker is stupid or that the reply is obvious: *how did you get in here? – through the door, duh.*

duiker *or* **duyker** (ˈdaɪkə) NOUN, *plural* **-kers** *or* **-ker.** [1] Also called: **duikerbok** (ˈdaɪkəbɒk). any small antelope of the genera *Cephalophus* and *Sylvicapra,* occurring throughout Africa south of the Sahara, having short straight backward-pointing horns, pointed hooves, and an arched back. [2] *South African* any of several cormorants, esp the long-tailed shag (*Phalacrocorax africanus*).
▷HISTORY C18: via Afrikaans from Dutch *duiker* diver, from *duiken* to dive; see DUCK^{2}

Duisburg (*German* ˈdy:sbʊrk) NOUN an industrial city in NW Germany, in North Rhine-Westphalia at the confluence of the Rivers Rhine and Ruhr: one of the world's largest and busiest inland ports; university (1972). Pop.: 521 300 (1999 est.).

du jour (du: ˈʒɔ:; *French* dy ʒur) NOUN (*postpositive*) *Informal* currently very fashionable or popular: *the young writer du jour.*
▷HISTORY C20: from French, literally: of the day (as used on restaurant menus of items that change daily)

duka (ˈdu:ka) NOUN *E African* a shop; store.
▷HISTORY C20: from Swahili

duke (dju:k) NOUN [1] a nobleman of high rank: in the British Isles standing above the other grades of the nobility. [2] the prince or ruler of a small principality or duchy. Related adjective: **ducal.**
▷HISTORY C12: from Old French *duc,* from Latin *dux* leader

dukedom (ˈdju:kdəm) NOUN [1] another name for a **duchy.** [2] the title, rank, or position of a duke.

dukes (dju:ks) PLURAL NOUN *Slang* the fists.
▷HISTORY C19: from *Duke of Yorks* rhyming slang for *forks* (fingers)

Dukhobor (ˈdu:kəʊˌbɔ:) PLURAL NOUN a variant spelling of **Doukhobor.**

dukka *or* **dukkah** (ˈdʊkə) NOUN a mix of ground roast nuts and spices, originating in Egypt, and used for sprinkling on meat or as a dip.

dukkha (ˈdukə) NOUN (in Theravada Buddhism) the belief that all things are suffering, due to the desire to seek permanence or recognise the self when neither exist: one of the three basic characteristics of existence. Sanskrit word: **duhkha.** Compare **anatta, anicca.**
▷HISTORY Pali, literally: suffering, illness

dulcet (ˈdʌlsɪt) ADJECTIVE (of a sound) soothing or pleasant; sweet.
▷HISTORY C14: from Latin *dulcis* sweet
▸ˈ**dulcetly** ADVERB ▸ˈ**dulcetness** NOUN

dulciana (ˌdʌlsɪˈɑ:nə) NOUN a sweet-toned organ stop, controlling metal pipes of narrow scale.
▷HISTORY C18: from Latin *dulcis* sweet

dulcify (ˈdʌlsɪˌfaɪ) VERB **-fies, -fying, -fied.** (*tr*) [1] *Rare* to make pleasant or agreeable. [2] a rare word for **sweeten.**
▷HISTORY C16: from Late Latin *dulcificāre,* from Latin *dulcis* sweet + *facere* to make
▸ˌ**dulcifiˈcation** NOUN

dulcimer (ˈdʌlsɪmə) NOUN *Music* [1] a tuned percussion instrument consisting of a set of strings of graduated length stretched over a sounding board and struck with a pair of hammers. [2] an instrument used in US folk music, consisting of an elliptical body, a fretted fingerboard, and usually three strings plucked with a goose quill.
▷HISTORY C15: from Old French *doulcemer,* from Old Italian *dolcimelo,* from *dolce* sweet, from Latin *dulcis* + *-melo,* perhaps from Greek *melos* song

dulcinea (ˌdʌlsɪˈnɪə) NOUN a man's sweetheart.
▷HISTORY C18: from the name of Don Quixote's mistress Dulcinea del Toboso in Cervantes' novel; from Spanish *dulce* sweet

dulia (ˈdju:lɪə) NOUN the veneration accorded to saints in the Roman Catholic and Eastern Churches, as contrasted with hyperdulia and latria.
▷HISTORY C17: from Medieval Latin: service, from Greek *douleia* slavery, from *doulos* slave

dull (dʌl) ADJECTIVE [1] slow to think or understand; stupid. [2] lacking in interest. [3] lacking in perception or the ability to respond; insensitive. [4] lacking sharpness; blunt. [5] not acute, intense, or piercing. [6] (of weather) not bright or clear; cloudy. [7] not active, busy, or brisk. [8] lacking in spirit or animation; listless. [9] (of colour) lacking brilliance or brightness; sombre. [10] not loud or clear; muffled. [11] *Med* (of sound elicited by percussion, esp of the chest) not resonant. ◆ VERB [12] to make or become dull.
▷HISTORY Old English *dol;* related to Old Norse *dul* conceit, Old High German *tol* foolish, Greek *tholeros* confused
▸ˈ**dullish** ADJECTIVE ▸ˈ**dullness** *or* ˈ**dulness** NOUN ▸ˈ**dully** ADVERB

dullard (ˈdʌləd) NOUN a dull or stupid person.

dullsville (ˈdʌlzvɪl) NOUN *Slang* [1] a thing, place, or activity that is boring or dull. [2] the state of being bored.

dulosis (dju:ˈləʊsɪs) NOUN a practice of some ants, in which one species forces members of a different species to do the work of the colony. Also called: **helotism.**
▷HISTORY C20: from Greek: enslavement, from *doulos* slave
▸**dulotic** (dju:ˈlɒtɪk) ADJECTIVE

dulse (dʌls) NOUN any of several seaweeds, esp *Rhodymenia palmata,* that occur on rocks and have large red edible fronds.
▷HISTORY C17: from Old Irish *duilesc* seaweed

Duluth (də'lu:θ) NOUN a port in E Minnesota, at the W end of Lake Superior. Pop.: 86 918 (2000).

Dulwich ('dʌlɪtʃ) NOUN a residential district in the Greater London borough of Southwark: site of an art gallery and the public school, Dulwich College.

duly ('dju:lɪ) ADVERB 1 in a proper or fitting manner. 2 at the proper time; punctually.
▷HISTORY C14: see DUE, -LY²

duma *or* ***douma*** *Russian* ('du:mə) NOUN *Russian history* 1 (*usually capital*) the elective legislative assembly established by Tsar Nicholas II in 1905: overthrown by the Bolsheviks in 1917. 2 (before 1917) any official assembly or council. 3 short for **State Duma**, the lower chamber of the Russian parliament
▷HISTORY C20: from *duma* thought, of Germanic origin; related to Gothic *dōms* judgment

dumb (dʌm) ADJECTIVE 1 lacking the power to speak, either because of defects in the vocal organs or because of hereditary deafness; mute. 2 lacking the power of human speech: *dumb animals*. 3 temporarily lacking or bereft of the power to speak: *struck dumb*. 4 refraining from speech; uncommunicative. 5 producing no sound; silent: *a dumb piano*. 6 made, done, or performed without speech. 7 *Informal* **a** slow to understand; dim-witted. **b** foolish; stupid. See also **dumb down**. 8 (of a projectile or bomb) not guided to its target.
▷HISTORY Old English; related to Old Norse *dumbr*, Gothic *dumbs*, Old High German *tump*
▸'**dumbly** ADVERB ▸'**dumbness** NOUN

dumb ague NOUN an irregular form of malarial fever (ague) lacking the typically symptomatic chill.

Dumbarton (dʌm'bɑ:tᵊn) NOUN a town in W Scotland, in West Dunbartonshire near the confluence of the Rivers Leven and Clyde: centred around the **Rock of Dumbarton**, an important stronghold since ancient times; engineering and distilling. Pop.: 21 962 (1991).

Dumbarton Oaks ('dʌm,bɑ:tᵊn) NOUN an estate in the District of Columbia in the US: scene of conferences in 1944 concerned with creating the United Nations.

dumb-ass *Slang* ◆ NOUN 1 a stupid person. ◆ ADJECTIVE 2 extremely stupid.

dumbbell ('dʌm,bɛl) NOUN 1 *Gymnastics, weightlifting* an exercising weight consisting of a single bar with a heavy ball or disc at either end. 2 a small wooden object shaped like this used in dog training for the dog to retrieve. 3 *Slang, chiefly US and Canadian* a fool.

dumb-cane NOUN a West Indian aroid plant, *Dieffenbachia seguine*, chewing the stem of which induces speechlessness by paralysing the throat muscles.

dumb down VERB (*tr*) to make or become less intellectually demanding or sophisticated: *attempts to dumb down news coverage*.

dumbfound *or* **dumfound** (dʌm'faʊnd) VERB (*tr*) to strike dumb with astonishment; amaze.
▷HISTORY C17: from DUMB + (CON)FOUND

dumbledore ('dʌmbᵊl,dɔ:) NOUN *English dialect* a bumblebee. Also (Southwest English): **drumbledrane.**
▷HISTORY Old English *dumble*, variant of *drumble* to move sluggishly + *dor* humming insect

dumbo ('dʌmbəʊ) NOUN, *plural* **-bos**. *Slang* a slow-witted unintelligent person.
▷HISTORY C20: after the flying elephant in *Dumbo*, the Walt Disney cartoon released in 1941

dumb show NOUN 1 a part of a play acted in pantomime, popular in early English drama. 2 meaningful gestures; mime.

dumbstruck ('dʌm,strʌk) *or* **dumbstricken** ('dʌm,strɪkᵊn) ADJECTIVE temporarily deprived of speech through shock or surprise.

dumbwaiter ('dʌm,weɪtə) NOUN 1 *Brit* **a** a stand placed near a dining table to hold food. **b** a revolving circular tray placed on a table to hold food. US and Canadian name: **lazy Susan.** 2 a lift for carrying food, rubbish, etc., between floors.

dumdum ('dʌm,dʌm) NOUN a soft-nosed or hollow-nosed small-arms bullet that expands on impact and inflicts extensive laceration. Also called: **dumdum bullet.**
▷HISTORY C19: named after *Dum-Dum*, town near Calcutta where these bullets were made

dumela (dumɛla) SENTENCE SUBSTITUTE *South African* hello; good morning.
▷HISTORY Sotho

Dumfries (dʌm'fri:s) NOUN a town in S Scotland on the River Nith, administrative centre of Dumfries and Galloway. Pop.: 32 136 (1991).

Dumfries and Galloway NOUN a council area in SW Scotland: created in 1975 from the counties of Dumfries, Kirkcudbright, and Wigtown; became a unitary authority in 1996; chiefly agricultural. Administrative centre: Dumfries. Pop.: 147 765 (2001). Area: 6439 sq. km (2486 sq. miles).

Dumfriesshire (dʌm'fri:s,ʃɪə, -ʃə) NOUN (until 1975) a county in S Scotland, on the Solway Firth, now part of Dumfries and Galloway.

dummelhead ('dʌməl,hɛd) NOUN *Northern English dialect* a stupid or slow-witted person.

dummy ('dʌmɪ) NOUN, *plural* **-mies**. 1 a figure representing the human form, used for displaying clothes, in a ventriloquist's act, as a target, etc. 2 **a** a copy or imitation of an object, often lacking some essential feature of the original. **b** (*as modifier*): *a dummy drawer*. 3 *Slang* a stupid person; fool. 4 *Derogatory, slang* a person without the power of speech; mute. 5 *Informal* a person who says or does nothing. 6 **a** a person who appears to act for himself while acting on behalf of another. **b** (*as modifier*): *a dummy buyer*. 7 *Military* a weighted round without explosives, used in drill and training. 8 *Bridge* **a** the hand exposed on the table by the declarer's partner and played by the declarer. **b** the declarer's partner. 9 **a** a prototype of a proposed book, indicating the general appearance and dimensions of the finished product. **b** a designer's layout of a page indicating the positions for illustrations, etc. 10 a feigned pass or move in a sport such as football or rugby. 11 *Brit* a rubber teat for babies to suck or bite on. US and Canadian equivalent: **pacifier.** 12 (*modifier*) counterfeit; sham. 13 (*modifier*) (of a card game) played with one hand exposed or unplayed. ◆ VERB **-mies, -mying, -mied.** 14 to prepare a dummy of (a proposed book, page, etc.). 15 Also: **sell (someone) a dummy.** *Sport* to use a dummy pass in order to trick (an opponent).
▷HISTORY C16: see DUMB, -Y³

dummy head NOUN a model of the human head with a microphone in each ear intended to receive sound in binaural and surround sound reproduction and transmission.

dummy load NOUN a resistive component that absorbs all the output power of an electrical generator or radio transmitter in order to simulate working conditions for test purposes.

dummy run NOUN a practice or rehearsal; trial run.

dummy variable NOUN a variable appearing in a mathematical expression that can be replaced by any arbitrary variable, not occurring in the expression, without affecting the value of the whole.

dumortierite (dju:'mɔ:tɪə,raɪt) NOUN a hard fibrous blue or green mineral consisting of hydrated aluminium borosilicate. Formula: $Al_7O_3BO_3(SiO_4)_3$.
▷HISTORY C19: named after Eugène *Dumortier*, 19th-century French palaeontologist who discovered it

dump¹ (dʌmp) VERB 1 to drop, fall, or let fall heavily or in a mass. 2 (*tr*) to empty (objects or material) out of a container. 3 to unload, empty, or make empty (a container), as by tilting or overturning. 4 (*tr*) *Informal* to dispose of. 5 (*tr*) to dispose of (waste, esp radioactive nuclear waste) in the sea or on land. 6 *Commerce* **a** to market (goods) in bulk and at low prices. **b** to offer for sale large quantities of (goods) on foreign markets at low prices in order to maintain a high price in the home market and obtain a share of the foreign markets. 7 (*tr*) to store (supplies, arms, etc.) temporarily. 8 (*intr*) *Slang, chiefly US* to defecate. 9 (*tr*) *Surfing* (of a wave) to hurl a swimmer or surfer down. 10 (*tr*) *Austral and NZ* to compact (bales of wool) by hydraulic pressure. 11 (*tr*) *Computing* to record (the contents of part or all of the memory) on a storage device, such as magnetic tape, at a series of points during a computer run. ◆ NOUN 12 **a** a place or area where waste materials are dumped. **b** (*in combination*): *rubbish dump*. 13 a pile or accumulation of rubbish. 14 the act of dumping. 15 *Informal* a dirty or unkempt place. 16 *Military* a place where weapons, supplies, etc., are stored. 17 *Slang, chiefly US* an act of defecation. ◆ See also **dump on.**
▷HISTORY C14: probably of Scandinavian origin; compare Norwegian *dumpa* to fall suddenly, Middle Low German *dumpeln* to duck
▸'**dumper** NOUN

dump² (dʌmp) NOUN *Obsolete* a mournful song; lament.
▷HISTORY C16: see DAMP

dump bin NOUN 1 a free-standing unit in a bookshop in which the books of a particular publisher are displayed. 2 a container in a shop in which goods are heaped, often in a disorderly fashion.

dumpling ('dʌmplɪŋ) NOUN 1 a small ball of dough cooked and served with stew. 2 a pudding consisting of a round pastry case filled with fruit: *apple dumpling*. 3 *Informal* a short plump person.
▷HISTORY C16: *dump-*, perhaps variant of LUMP¹ + -LING¹

dump on VERB (*intr, preposition*) *Informal, chiefly US* to abuse or criticize.

dump orbit NOUN an earth orbit into which communications satellites may be moved at the end of their operational lives, where there is no risk of their interference or collision with working satellites in the normal orbits. Also called: **graveyard orbit.**

dumps (dʌmps) PLURAL NOUN *Informal* a state of melancholy or depression (esp in the phrase **down in the dumps**).
▷HISTORY C16: probably from Middle Dutch *domp* haze, mist; see DAMP

dump truck *or* **dumper-truck** NOUN a small truck used on building sites, having a load-bearing container at the front that can be tipped up to unload the contents.

dumpy¹ ('dʌmpɪ) ADJECTIVE **dumpier, dumpiest.** short and plump; squat.
▷HISTORY C18: perhaps related to DUMPLING
▸'**dumpily** ADVERB ▸'**dumpiness** NOUN

dumpy² ('dʌmpɪ) *or* **dumpish** ('dʌmpɪʃ) ADJECTIVE *Rare* in low spirits; depressed; morose.
▷HISTORY C17: from C16 *dump*; see DUMPS

dumpy level NOUN *Surveying* a levelling instrument consisting of a horizontal telescope with various rotational arrangements and a spirit level.

Dumyat (dum'jæt) NOUN the Arabic name for **Damietta.**

dun¹ (dʌn) VERB **duns, dunning, dunned.** 1 (*tr*) to press or importune (a debtor) for the payment of a debt. ◆ NOUN 2 a person, esp a hired agent, who importunes another for the payment of a debt. 3 a demand for payment, esp one in writing.
▷HISTORY C17: of unknown origin

dun² (dʌn) NOUN 1 a brownish-grey colour. 2 a horse of this colour. 3 *Angling* **a** an immature adult mayfly (the subimago), esp one of the genus *Ephemera*. **b** an artificial fly imitating this or a similar fly. ◆ ADJECTIVE **dunner, dunnest.** 4 of a dun colour. 5 dark and gloomy.
▷HISTORY Old English *dunn*; related to Old Norse *dunna* wild duck, Middle Irish *donn* dark; see DUSK

Duna ('dunɔ) NOUN the Hungarian name for the **Danube.**

Dünaburg ('dy:naburk) NOUN the German name (until 1893) for **Daugavpils.**

Dunaj ('dunaj) NOUN the Czech name for the **Danube.**

Dunărea ('dunərja) NOUN the Romanian name for the **Danube.**

Dunbar (dʌn'bɑ:) NOUN a port and resort in SE Scotland, in East Lothian: scene of Cromwell's defeat of the Scots (1650). Pop.: 6518 (1991).

Dunbartonshire (dʌn'bɑ:tᵊnʃɪə, -ʃə) NOUN a historical county of W Scotland: became part of Strathclyde region in 1975; administered since 1996 by the council areas of East Dunbartonshire and West Dunbartonshire.

Duncan Phyfe *or* **Fife** (faɪf) NOUN (*modifier*) *US furniture* of or in the manner of Duncan Phyfe (?1768–1854), Scottish-born US cabinetmaker, esp in that which followed the Sheraton and Directoire styles.

dunce (dʌns) NOUN a person who is stupid or slow to learn.
▷HISTORY C16: from *Dunses* or *Dunsmen*, term of ridicule applied to the followers of John *Duns* Scotus (?1265–1308), Scottish scholastic theologian and Franciscan priest, especially by 16th-century humanists
▸'**dunce,like** ADJECTIVE

dunce cap *or* **dunce's cap** NOUN a conical paper hat, formerly placed on the head of a dull child at school.

Dundalk (dʌn'dɔ:k) NOUN a town in NE Republic of Ireland, on **Dundalk Bay**: county town of Co. Louth. Pop.: 25 800 (1991).

Dundee (dʌn'di:) NOUN 1 a port in E Scotland, in City of Dundee council area, on the Firth of Tay: centre of the former British jute industry; university (1967). Pop.: 158 981 (1991). 2 **City of.** a council area in E Scotland. Pop.: 145 663 (1996 est.). Area: 65 sq. km (25 sq. miles).

Dundee cake NOUN *Chiefly Brit* a fairly rich fruit cake decorated with almonds.

dunderhead ('dʌndə,hɛd) NOUN a stupid or slow-witted person; dunce. Also called: **dunderpate.**
▷HISTORY C17: probably from Dutch *donder* thunder + HEAD; compare BLOCKHEAD
▸'**dunder,headed** ADJECTIVE ▸'**dunder,headedness** NOUN

Dundonian (dʌn'dəʊnɪən) NOUN 1 a native or inhabitant of Dundee. ◆ ADJECTIVE 2 of or relating to Dundee or its inhabitants.

dune (dju:n) NOUN a mound or ridge of drifted sand, occurring on the sea coast and in deserts.
▷HISTORY C18: via Old French from Middle Dutch *dūne;* see DOWN³

Dunedin (dʌn'i:dɪn) NOUN a port in New Zealand, on SE South Island: founded (1848) by Scottish settlers. Pop. (urban area): 119 600 (1999 est.).

Dunfermline (dʌn'fɜ:mlɪn) NOUN a city in E Scotland, in SW Fife: ruined palace, a former residence of Scottish kings. Pop.: 55 083 (1991).

dung (dʌŋ) NOUN 1 **a** excrement, esp of animals; manure. **b** (*as modifier*): *dung cart.* 2 something filthy. ◆ VERB 3 (*tr*) to cover (ground) with manure.
▷HISTORY Old English: prison; related to Old High German *tunc* cellar roofed with dung, Old Norse *dyngja* manure heap
▸'**dungy** ADJECTIVE

Dungannon (dʌn'gænən) NOUN a district of S Northern Ireland, in Co. Tyrone. Pop.: 47 735 (2001). Area: 783 sq. km (302 sq. miles).

dungaree (,dʌŋgə'ri:) NOUN 1 a coarse cotton fabric used chiefly for work clothes, etc. 2 (*plural*) **a** a suit of workman's overalls made of this material consisting of trousers with a bib attached. **b** a casual garment resembling this, usually worn by women or children. 3 *US* trousers.
▷HISTORY C17: from Hindi *dungrī*, after *Dungrī*, district of Bombay, where this fabric originated

dung beetle *or* **chafer** NOUN any of the various beetles of the family *Scarabaeidae* and related families that feed on or breed in dung.

Dungeness (,dʌndʒə'nɛs) NOUN a low shingle headland on the S coast of England, in Kent: two nuclear power stations: automatic lighthouse.

dungeon ('dʌndʒən) NOUN 1 a close prison cell, often underground. 2 a variant of **donjon.**
▷HISTORY C14: from Old French *donjon;* related to Latin *dominus* master

dunger ('dʌŋə) *NZ informal* NOUN 1 an old decrepit car. 2 any old worn-out machine.

dung fly NOUN any of various muscid flies of the subfamily *Cordilurinae,* such as the predatory **yellow dung fly** (*Scatophaga stercoraria*), that frequents cowpats to feed and lay its eggs.

dunghill ('dʌŋ,hɪl) NOUN 1 a heap of dung. 2 a foul place, condition, or person.

dunite ('dʌnaɪt) NOUN an ultrabasic igneous rock consisting mainly of olivine.
▷HISTORY C19: named after Dun Mountain, a mountain in New Zealand where it is abundant

duniwassal ('du:nɪ,wɑ:sᵊl) NOUN (in Scotland) a minor nobleman.
▷HISTORY C16: from Gaelic *duine* man + *uasal* noble

dunk (dʌŋk) VERB 1 to dip (bread, etc.) in tea, soup, etc., before eating. 2 to submerge or be submerged in liquid.
▷HISTORY C20: from Pennsylvania Dutch, from Middle High German *dunken,* from Old High German *dunkōn;* see DUCK², TINGE
▸'**dunker** NOUN

Dunker ('dʌŋkə) *or* **Dunkard** ('dʌŋkəd) NOUN a member of the German Baptist Brethren.
▷HISTORY C18: from German *Tunker* ducker

Dunkerque (*French* dœ̃kɛrk) NOUN a port in N France, on the Strait of Dover: scene of the evacuation of British and other Allied troops after the fall of France in 1940; industrial centre with an oil refinery and naval shipbuilding yards. Pop.: 190 879 (1990). English name: **Dunkirk** (dʌn'kɜ:k).

Dún Laoghaire (du:n 'lɪərɪ) NOUN a port in E Republic of Ireland, on Dublin Bay. Pop.: 189 999 (1996). Former names: **Dunleary** (until 1821), **Kingstown** (1821–1921).

dunlin ('dʌnlɪn) NOUN a small sandpiper, *Calidris* (or *Erolia*) *alpina,* of northern and arctic regions, having a brown back and black breast in summer. Also called: **red-backed sandpiper.**
▷HISTORY C16: DUN² + -LING¹

dunnage ('dʌnɪdʒ) NOUN loose material used for packing cargo.
▷HISTORY C14: of uncertain origin

dunnakin ('dʌnəkɪn) NOUN *Dialect* a lavatory. Also called: **dunny.**
▷HISTORY of obscure origin; but perhaps related to DUNG

dunnart ('dʌnɑ:t) NOUN a mouselike insectivorous marsupial of the genus *Sminthopsis* of Australia and New Guinea.
▷HISTORY C20: from a native Australian language

dunnite ('dʌnaɪt) NOUN an explosive containing ammonium picrate.
▷HISTORY C20: named after Colonel B. W. *Dunn* (1860–1936), American army officer who invented it

dunno (dʌ'nəʊ, dʊ-, də-) *Slang* CONTRACTION OF (I) do not know.

dunnock ('dʌnək) NOUN another name for **hedge sparrow.**
▷HISTORY C15: from DUN² + -OCK

dunny ('dʌnɪ) NOUN, *plural* **-nies.** 1 *Scot dialect* a cellar or basement. 2 *Dialect* another word for **dunnakin.** 3 *Austral and NZ informal* **a** an outside lavatory. **b** (*as modifier*): *a dunny roll; a dunny seat.*
▷HISTORY C20: of obscure origin; but see DUNNAKIN

Dunoon (də'nu:n) NOUN a town and resort in W Scotland, in Argyll and Bute, on the Firth of Clyde. Pop.: 9038 (1991).

Dunsinane (dʌn'sɪnən) NOUN a hill in central Scotland, in the Sidlaw Hills: the ruined fort at its summit is regarded as Macbeth's castle. Height: 308 m (1012 ft.).

> **Language note** The pronunciation ('dʌnsɪ,neɪn) is used in Shakespeare's *Macbeth* for the purposes of rhyme.

Dunstable ('dʌnstəbᵊl) NOUN an industrial town in SE central England, in Bedfordshire. Pop.: 49 666 (1991).

dunt (dʌnt, dʊnt) *Scot and northern English dialect* ◆ NOUN 1 a blow; thump. 2 the injury caused by such a blow. ◆ VERB 3 to strike or hit.
▷HISTORY C15: perhaps variant of DINT

Duntroon (dʌn'tru:n) NOUN a suburb of Canberra: seat of the Royal Military College of Australia.

duo ('dju:əʊ) NOUN, *plural* **duos** *or* **dui** ('dju:i:). 1 *Music* **a** a pair of performers. **b** another word for **duet.** 2 a pair of actors, entertainers, etc. 3 *Informal* a pair of closely connected individuals.
▷HISTORY C16: via Italian from Latin: two

duo- COMBINING FORM indicating two: *duotone.*
▷HISTORY from Latin

duobinary (,dju:əʊ'baɪnərɪ) ADJECTIVE denoting a communications system for coding digital data in which three data bands are used, 0, +1, –1. Compare **binary notation.**

duodecimal (,dju:əʊ'dɛsɪməl) ADJECTIVE 1 relating to twelve or twelfths. ◆ NOUN 2 a twelfth. 3 one of the numbers used in a duodecimal number system.
▸,**duo'decimally** ADVERB

duodecimo (,dju:əʊ'dɛsɪ,məʊ) NOUN, *plural* **-mos.** 1 a book size resulting from folding a sheet of paper into twelve leaves. Also called: **twelvemo.** Often written: **12mo, 12°.** 2 a book of this size.
▷HISTORY C17: from Latin phrase *in duodecimō* in twelfth, from *duodecim* twelve

duodenary (,dju:ə'di:nərɪ) ADJECTIVE of or relating to the number 12; duodecimal.
▷HISTORY C17: from Latin *duodēnārius* containing twelve

duodenitis (,dju:əʊdɪ'naɪtɪs) NOUN inflammation of the duodenum.

duodenum (,dju:əʊ'di:nəm) NOUN, *plural* **-na** (-nə) *or* **-nums.** the first part of the small intestine, between the stomach and the jejunum.
▷HISTORY C14: from Medieval Latin, shortened from *intestinum duodenum digitorum* intestine of twelve fingers' length, from Latin *duodēnī* twelve each
▸,**duo'denal** ADJECTIVE

duologue *or sometimes US* **duolog** ('dju:ə,lɒg) NOUN 1 a part or all of a play in which the speaking roles are limited to two actors. 2 a less common word for **dialogue.**

duopoly (dju'ɒpəlɪ) NOUN a situation in which control of a commodity or service in a particular market is vested in just two producers or suppliers.
▸**duopolistic** (djuɒ,pə'lɪstɪk) ADJECTIVE

Duo-Tang ('dju:ə,tæŋ) NOUN *Trademark, Canadian* a type of folder with flexible metal fasteners.

duotone ('dju:ə,təʊn) NOUN *Printing* 1 a process for producing halftone illustrations using two shades of a single colour or black and a colour. 2 a picture produced by this process.

dup (dʌp) VERB **dups, dupping, dupped.** (*tr*) *Archaic or dialect* to open.
▷HISTORY C16: contraction of DO¹ + UP

D up VERB (*adverb*) *Austral sport* **a** to set up a defence. **b** to mark an opponent.

dupatta (du'pʌtə) NOUN a scarf worn in India.

dupe (dju:p) NOUN 1 a person who is easily deceived. 2 a person who unwittingly serves as the tool of another person or power. ◆ VERB 3 (*tr*) to deceive, esp by trickery; make a dupe or tool of; cheat; fool.
▷HISTORY C17: from French, from Old French *duppe,* contraction of *de huppe* of (a) hoopoe (from Latin *upupa*); from the bird's reputation for extreme stupidity
▸'**dupable** ADJECTIVE ▸,**dupa'bility** NOUN ▸'**duper** NOUN
▸'**dupery** NOUN

dupion ('dju:pɪən, -'pi:ɒn) NOUN a silk fabric made from the threads of double cocoons.
▷HISTORY C19: from French *doupion,* from Italian *doppione* double

duple ('dju:pᵊl) ADJECTIVE 1 a less common word for **double.** 2 *Music* (of time or music) having two beats in a bar.
▷HISTORY C16: from Latin *duplus* twofold, double

duplet ('dju:plɪt) NOUN 1 a pair of electrons shared between two atoms in a covalent bond. 2 *Music* a group of two notes played in the time of three.

duple time NOUN musical time with two beats in each bar.

duplex ('dju:plɛks) NOUN 1 *US and Canadian* a duplex apartment or house. 2 a double-stranded region in a nucleic acid molecule. ◆ ADJECTIVE 3 having two parts. 4 *Machinery* having pairs of components of independent but identical function. 5 permitting the transmission of simultaneous signals in both directions in a radio, telecommunications, or computer channel.
▷HISTORY C19: from Latin: twofold, from *duo* two + *-plex* -FOLD
▸**du'plexity** NOUN

duplex apartment NOUN *US and Canadian* an apartment on two floors.

duplex chain NOUN *Engineering* a roller chain having two sets of rollers linked together, used for heavy-duty applications.

duplex house NOUN *US and Canadian* a house divided into two separate dwellings. Also called (US): **semidetached.**

duplicate ADJECTIVE ('dju:plɪkɪt) 1 copied exactly from an original. 2 identical. 3 existing as a pair or in pairs; twofold. ◆ NOUN ('dju:plɪkɪt) 4 an exact

copy; double. 5 something additional or supplementary of the same kind. 6 two exact copies (esp in the phrase **in duplicate**). ◆ VERB ('dju:plɪˌkeɪt) 7 (*tr*) to make a replica of. 8 (*tr*) to do or make again. 9 (*tr*) to make in a pair; make double. 10 (*intr*) *Biology* to reproduce by dividing into two identical parts: *the chromosomes duplicated in mitosis.*
▷HISTORY C15: from Latin *duplicāre* to double, from *duo* two + *plicāre* to fold
▸**duplicable** ('dju:plɪkəbᵊl) ADJECTIVE ▸ˌ**duplica'bility** NOUN ▸'**duplicately** ADVERB ▸'**duplicative** ADJECTIVE

duplicate bridge NOUN a form of contract bridge, esp at clubs and in competitions, in which the hands are kept as dealt and played by different players. The partners with the highest average score are the winners. Also called: **board bridge.** Compare **rubber bridge.**

duplication (ˌdju:plɪ'keɪʃən) NOUN 1 the act of duplicating or the state of being duplicated. 2 a copy; duplicate. 3 *Genetics* a mutation in which there are two or more copies of a gene or of a segment of a chromosome.

duplicator ('dju:plɪˌkeɪtə) NOUN an apparatus for making replicas of an original, such as a machine using a stencil wrapped on an ink-loaded drum.

duplicident (dju:'plɪsɪdənt) ADJECTIVE (of certain animals, such as rabbits) having two pairs of incisors in the upper jaw.

duplicity (dju:'plɪsɪtɪ) NOUN, *plural* **-ties**. deception; double-dealing.
▷HISTORY C15: from Old French *duplicite,* from Late Latin *duplicitās* a being double, from Latin DUPLEX
▸**du'plicitous** ADJECTIVE

dupondius (dju:'pɒndɪəs) NOUN, *plural* **-dii** (-dɪˌaɪ). a brass coin of ancient Rome worth half a sesterce.
▷HISTORY from Latin, from *duo* two + *pondus* weight

duppy ('dʌpɪ) NOUN, *plural* **-pies**. *Caribbean* a spirit or ghost.
▷HISTORY C18: probably of African origin

Dur. ABBREVIATION FOR Durham.

durable ('djʊərəbᵊl) ADJECTIVE long-lasting; enduring: *a durable fabric.*
▷HISTORY C14: from Old French, from Latin *dūrābilis,* from *dūrāre* to last; see ENDURE
▸ˌ**dura'bility** *or* '**durableness** NOUN ▸'**durably** ADVERB

durable goods PLURAL NOUN goods, such as most producer goods and some consumer goods, that require infrequent replacement. Compare **disposable goods, perishables.** Also called: **durables.**

durable press NOUN **a** another term for **permanent press. b** (*as modifier*): *durable-press skirts.*

dural ('djʊərəl) ADJECTIVE relating to or affecting the dura mater.

Duralumin (djʊ'ræljʊmɪn) NOUN *Trademark* a light strong aluminium alloy containing 3.5–4.5 per cent of copper with small quantities of silicon, magnesium, and manganese; used in aircraft manufacture.

dura mater ('djʊərə 'meɪtə) NOUN the outermost and toughest of the three membranes (see **meninges**) covering the brain and spinal cord. Often shortened to: **dura.**
▷HISTORY C15: from Medieval Latin, hard mother

duramen (djʊ'reɪmɛn) NOUN another name for **heartwood.**
▷HISTORY C19: from Latin: hardness, from *dūrāre* to harden

durance ('djʊərəns) NOUN *Archaic or literary* 1 imprisonment. 2 duration.
▷HISTORY C15: from Old French, from *durer* to last, from Latin *dūrāre*

Durance (*French* dyrɑ̃s) NOUN a river in S France, rising in the Alps and flowing generally southwest into the Rhône. Length: 304 km (189 miles).

Durango (djʊ'ræŋgəʊ; *Spanish* du'raŋgo) NOUN 1 a state in N central Mexico: high plateau, with the Sierra Madre Occidental in the west; irrigated agriculture (esp cotton) and rich mineral resources. Capital: Durango. Pop.: 1 445 922 (1995 est.). Area: 119 648 sq. km (46 662 sq. miles). 2 a city in NW central Mexico, capital of Durango state: mining centre. Pop.: 430 000 (2000 est.). Official name: **Victoria de Durango.**

duration (djʊ'reɪʃən) NOUN the length of time that something lasts or continues.
▷HISTORY C14: from Medieval Latin *dūrātiō,* from Latin *dūrāre* to last
▸**du'rational** ADJECTIVE

durative ('djʊərətɪv) *Grammar* ◆ ADJECTIVE 1 denoting an aspect of verbs that includes the imperfective and the progressive. ◆ NOUN 2 **a** the durative aspect of a verb. **b** a verb in this aspect.

Durazzo (du'rattso) NOUN the Italian name for **Durrës.**

Durban ('dɜ:bᵊn) NOUN a port in E South Africa, in E KwaZulu/Natal province on the Indian Ocean: University of Natal (1909); resort and industrial centre, with oil refineries, shipbuilding yards, etc. Pop. (urban area): 2 117 650 (1996).

Durban poison NOUN *South African slang* a particularly potent variety of cannabis grown in Natal.

durbar ('dɜ:bɑ:, ˌdɜ:'bɑ:) NOUN **a** (formerly) the court of a native ruler or a governor in India and British Colonial West Africa. **b** a levee at such a court.
▷HISTORY C17: from Hindi *darbār* court, from Persian, from *dar* door + *bār* entry, audience

Düren (*German* 'dy:rən) NOUN a city in W Germany, in North Rhine-Westphalia. Pop.: 83 150 (latest est.).

duress (djʊ'rɛs, djʊə-) NOUN 1 compulsion by use of force or threat; constraint; coercion (often in the phrase **under duress**). 2 *Law* the illegal exercise of coercion. 3 confinement; imprisonment.
▷HISTORY C14: from Old French *duresse,* from Latin *dūritia* hardness, from *dūrus* hard

Durex ('djʊərɛks) NOUN, *plural* **-rex**. *Trademark* 1 a brand of condom. 2 *Austral* a brand of adhesive tape.

Durga ('dʊəgæ) NOUN *Hinduism* the goddess Parvati portrayed as a warrior: renowned for slaying the buffalo demon, Mahisha.
▷HISTORY from Sanskrit: the inaccessible one

durgah ('dɜ:gɑ:) NOUN a variant spelling of **dargah.**

Durga Puja (ˌdʊəgæ 'pu:dʒə) NOUN another name for **Navaratri.**
▷HISTORY from Sanskrit DURGA + *puja* worship

Durgapur ('dɜ:gəˌpʊə) NOUN a city in NE India, in West Bengal: heavy industry, including steelworks. Pop.: 425 836 (1991).

Durham ('dʌrəm) NOUN 1 a county of NE England, on the North Sea: rises to the N Pennines in the west: the geographical and ceremonial county includes the unitary authorities of Hartlepool and Stockton-on-Tees (both part of Cleveland until 1996) and Darlington (created in 1997). Administrative centre: Durham. Pop. (excluding unitary authorities): 493 470 (1994 est.). Area (excluding unitary authorities): 2434 sq. km (940 sq. miles). Abbreviation: **Dur.** 2 a city in NE England, administrative centre of Co. Durham, on the River Wear: Norman cathedral; 11th-century castle (founded by William the Conqueror), now occupied by the University of Durham (1832). Pop.: 36 937 (1991). 3 a rare variety of shorthorn cattle. See **shorthorn.**

durian *or* **durion** ('djʊərɪən) NOUN 1 a SE Asian bombacaceous tree, *Durio zibethinus,* having very large oval fruits with a hard spiny rind containing seeds surrounded by edible evil-smelling aril. 2 the fruit of this tree, which has an offensive smell but a pleasant taste: supposedly an aphrodisiac.
▷HISTORY C16: from Malay, from *duri* thorn

duricrust ('djʊərɪˌkrʌst) NOUN another name for **caliche** (sense 2).

during ('djʊərɪŋ) PREPOSITION 1 concurrently with (some other activity): *kindly don't sleep during my lectures!* 2 within the limit of (a period of time): *during the day.*
▷HISTORY C14: from *duren* to last, ultimately from Latin *dūrāre* to last

durmast *or* **durmast oak** ('dɜ:ˌmɑ:st) NOUN 1 Also called: **sessile oak.** a large Eurasian oak tree, *Quercus petraea,* with lobed leaves and sessile acorns. Compare **pedunculate oak.** 2 the heavy elastic wood of this tree, used in building and cabinetwork.
▷HISTORY C18: probably alteration of *dun mast;* see DUN², MAST²

durn (dɜ:n) INTERJECTION, ADJECTIVE, ADVERB, NOUN a US variant of **darn²**.

duro ('dʊərəʊ) NOUN, *plural* **-ros**. the silver peso of Spain or Spanish America.
▷HISTORY from Spanish, shortened from *peso duro* hard peso, ultimately from Latin *dūrus* hard

Duroc ('djʊərɒk) NOUN an American breed of red lard pig.
▷HISTORY C19: from *Duroc,* name of a stallion owned by the man who developed this breed

durra ('dʌrə), **doura,** *or* **dourah** ('dʊərə) NOUN an Old World variety of sorghum, *Sorghum vulgare durra,* with erect hairy flower spikes and round seeds: cultivated for grain and fodder. Also called: **Guinea corn, Indian millet.**
▷HISTORY C18: from Arabic *dhurah* grain

Durrës ('durrəs) NOUN a port in W Albania, on the Adriatic. Pop.: 86 900 (1991 est.). Ancient names: **Epidamnus** (ɛpɪ'dæmnəs), **Dyrrachium** (də'reɪkɪəm). Italian name: **Durazzo.**

durrie ('dʌrɪ) NOUN a cotton carpet made in India, often in rectangular pieces fringed at the ends: sometimes used as a sofa cover, wall hanging, etc.
▷HISTORY from Hindi *darī*

durry ('dʌrɪ) NOUN, *plural* **-ries**. *Austral slang* a cigarette.
▷HISTORY from DURRIE

durst (dɜ:st) VERB a past tense of **dare.**

durum *or* **durum wheat** ('djʊərəm) NOUN a variety of wheat, *Triticum durum,* with a high gluten content, cultivated mainly in the Mediterranean region, and used chiefly to make pastas.
▷HISTORY C20: short for New Latin *trīticum dūrum,* literally: hard wheat

durzi ('dɜ:zɪ) NOUN an Indian tailor.
▷HISTORY C19: from Hindi, from Persian *darzi* from *darz* sewing

Dushanbe (du:'ʃɑ:nbɪ) NOUN the capital of Tajikistan; a cultural centre. Pop.: 513 000 (1998 est.). Former name (1929–61): **Stalinabad.**

dusk (dʌsk) NOUN 1 twilight or the darker part of twilight. 2 *Poetic* gloom; shade. ◆ ADJECTIVE 3 *Poetic* shady; gloomy. ◆ VERB 4 *Poetic* to make or become dark.
▷HISTORY Old English *dox;* related to Old Saxon *dosan* brown, Old High German *tusin* yellow, Norwegian *dusmen* misty, Latin *fuscus* dark brown

dusky ('dʌskɪ) ADJECTIVE **duskier, duskiest.** 1 dark in colour; swarthy or dark-skinned. 2 dim.
▸'**duskily** ADVERB ▸'**duskiness** NOUN

Düsseldorf ('dʊsəlˌdɔ:f; *German* 'dysəldɔrf) NOUN an industrial city in W Germany, capital of North Rhine-Westphalia, on the Rhine: commercial centre of the Rhine-Ruhr industrial area. Pop.: 568 500 (1999 est.).

dust (dʌst) NOUN 1 dry fine powdery material, such as particles of dirt, earth or pollen. 2 a cloud of such fine particles. 3 the powdery particles to which something is thought to be reduced by death, decay, or disintegration. 4 **a** the mortal body of man. **b** the corpse of a dead person. 5 the earth; ground. 6 *Informal* a disturbance; fuss (esp in the phrases **kick up a dust, raise a dust**). 7 something of little or no worth. 8 *Informal* (in mining parlance) silicosis or any similar respiratory disease. 9 short for **gold dust.** 10 ashes or household refuse. 11 **bite the dust. a** to fail completely or cease to exist. **b** to fall down dead. 12 **dust and ashes.** something that is very disappointing. 13 **leave (someone** *or* **something) in the dust.** to outdo comprehensively or with ease: *leaving their competitors in the dust.* 14 **shake the dust off one's feet.** to depart angrily or contemptuously. 15 **throw dust in the eyes of.** to confuse or mislead. ◆ VERB 16 (*tr*) to sprinkle or cover (something) with (dust or some other powdery substance): *to dust a cake with sugar; to dust sugar onto a cake.* 17 to remove dust by wiping, sweeping, or brushing. 18 *Archaic* to make or become dirty with dust. ◆ See also **dust down, dust-up.**
▷HISTORY Old English *dūst;* related to Danish *dyst* flour dust, Middle Dutch *dūst* dust, meal dust, Old High German *tunst* storm
▸'**dustless** ADJECTIVE

dust-bath NOUN the action of a bird of driving dust into its feathers, which may dislodge parasites.

dustbin ('dʌstˌbɪn) NOUN a large, usually cylindrical container for rubbish, esp one used by a household. US and Canadian names: **garbage can, trash can.**

dust bowl NOUN a semiarid area in which the surface soil is exposed to wind erosion and dust storms occur.

Dust Bowl NOUN **the.** the area of the south central US that became denuded of topsoil by wind erosion during the droughts of the mid-1930s.

dust bunny NOUN a small mass of fluff and dust.

dustcart ('dʌstˌkɑ:t) NOUN a road vehicle for collecting domestic refuse. US and Canadian name: **garbage truck.**

dust coat NOUN *Brit* a loose lightweight coat worn for early open motor-car riding. US name: **duster.**

dust cover NOUN [1] another name for **dustsheet.** [2] another name for **dust jacket.** [3] a perspex cover for the turntable of a record player.

dust devil NOUN a strong miniature whirlwind that whips up dust, litter, leaves, etc. into the air.

dust down VERB *(tr, adverb)* [1] to remove dust from by brushing or wiping. [2] to reprimand severely.
▸**dusting down** NOUN

duster ('dʌstə) NOUN [1] a cloth used for dusting furniture, etc. US name: **dust cloth.** [2] a machine for blowing out dust over trees or crops. [3] a person or thing that dusts.

duster coat NOUN a woman's loose summer coat with wide sleeves and no buttons, popular in the mid-20th century.

dust explosion NOUN an explosion caused by the ignition of an inflammable dust, such as flour or sawdust, in the air.

dusting-powder NOUN fine powder (such as talcum powder) used to absorb moisture, etc.

dust jacket *or* **cover** NOUN a removable paper cover used to protect a bound book. Also called: **book jacket, jacket.**

dustman ('dʌstmən) NOUN, *plural* **-men.** *Brit* a man whose job is to collect domestic refuse.

dustpan ('dʌstˌpæn) NOUN a short-handled hooded shovel into which dust is swept from floors, etc.

dustsheet ('dʌstˌʃi:t) NOUN *Brit* a large cloth or sheet used for covering furniture to protect it from dust. Also called: **dust cover.**

dust shot NOUN the smallest size of shot for a shotgun.

dust storm NOUN a windstorm that whips up clouds of dust.

dust-up *Informal* ◆ NOUN [1] a quarrel, fight, or argument. ◆ VERB **dust up.** [2] *(tr, adverb)* to attack or assault (someone).

dusty ('dʌstɪ) ADJECTIVE **dustier, dustiest.** [1] covered with or involving dust. [2] like dust in appearance or colour. [3] (of a colour) tinged with grey; pale: *dusty pink.* [4] **a dusty answer.** an unhelpful or bad-tempered reply. [5] **not so dusty.** *Informal* not too bad; fairly well: often in response to the greeting *how are you?*
▸'**dustily** ADVERB ▸'**dustiness** NOUN

dusty miller NOUN [1] Also called: **snow-in-summer.** a caryophyllaceous plant, *Cerastium tomentosum,* of SE Europe and Asia, having white flowers and downy stems and leaves: cultivated as a rock plant. [2] a plant, *Artemisia stelleriana,* of NE Asia and E North America, having small yellow flower heads and downy stems and leaves: family *Asteraceae* (composites). [3] any of various other downy plants, such as the rose campion.

dutch (dʌtʃ) NOUN *Cockney slang* wife.
▷**HISTORY** C19: short for *duchess*

Dutch (dʌtʃ) NOUN [1] the language of the Netherlands, belonging to the West Germanic branch of the Indo-European family and quite closely related to German and English. See also **Flemish, Afrikaans.** [2] **the Dutch.** *(functioning as plural)* the natives, citizens, or inhabitants of the Netherlands. [3] See **Pennsylvania Dutch.** [4] See **double Dutch.** [5] **in Dutch.** *Slang* in trouble. ◆ ADJECTIVE [6] of, relating to, or characteristic of the Netherlands, its inhabitants, or their language. ◆ ADVERB [7] **go Dutch.** *Informal* to share expenses equally.

Dutch auction NOUN an auction in which the price is lowered by stages until a buyer is found.

Dutch barn NOUN *Brit* a farm building consisting of a steel frame and a curved roof.

Dutch cap NOUN [1] a woman's lace cap with triangular flaps, characteristic of Dutch national dress. [2] a contraceptive device for women. See **diaphragm** (sense 2).

Dutch courage NOUN [1] false courage gained from drinking alcohol. [2] alcoholic drink.

Dutch disease NOUN the deindustrialization of an economy as a result of the discovery of a natural resource, as that which occurred in Holland with the exploitation of North Sea Oil, which raised the value of the Dutch currency, making its exports uncompetitive and causing its industry to decline.

Dutch doll NOUN a jointed wooden doll.

Dutch door NOUN the US and Canadian name for **stable door.**

Dutch East Indies NOUN **the.** a former name (1798–1945) of **Indonesia.** Also called: **Netherlands East Indies.**

Dutch elm NOUN a widely planted hybrid elm tree, *Ulmus hollandica,* with spreading branches and a short trunk.

Dutch elm disease NOUN a disease of elm trees caused by the fungus *Ceratocystis ulmi* and characterized by withering of the foliage and stems and eventual death of the parts of the tree above ground.

Dutch gold NOUN another name for **Dutch metal.**

Dutch Guiana *or* **Netherlands Guiana** NOUN the former name of **Surinam.**

Dutch guinea pig NOUN a breed of two-tone short-haired guinea pig.

Dutch hoe NOUN a type of hoe in which the head consists of a two-edged cross-blade attached to two prongs or of a single pressing of this shape.

Dutchman ('dʌtʃmən) NOUN, *plural* **-men.** [1] a native, citizen, or inhabitant of the Netherlands. [2] a piece of wood, metal, etc., used to repair or patch faulty workmanship. [3] *South African often derogatory* an Afrikaaner.

Dutchman's-breeches NOUN *(functioning as singular)* a North American plant, *Dicentra cucullaria,* with finely divided basal leaves and pink flowers: family *Fumariaceae.* Also called: **colicweed.**

Dutchman's-pipe NOUN a woody climbing plant, *Aristolochia sipho,* of the eastern US, cultivated for its greenish-brown mottled flowers, which are shaped like a curved pipe: family *Aristolochiaceae.*

Dutch mattress NOUN another name for **mattress** (sense 2).

Dutch medicine NOUN *South African* patent medicine, esp made of herbs.

Dutch metal *or* **gold** NOUN a substitute for gold leaf, consisting of thin sheets of copper that have been turned yellow by exposure to the fumes of molten zinc.

Dutch New Guinea NOUN a former name (until 1963) of **Irian Jaya.**

Dutch oven NOUN [1] an iron or earthenware container with a cover used for stews, etc. [2] a metal box, open in front, for cooking in front of an open fire.

Dutch Reformed Church NOUN any of the three Calvinist Churches to which most Afrikaans-speaking South Africans belong.

Dutch rise NOUN *NZ* an increase in wages that is of no benefit to the recipient.

Dutch rush NOUN *(sometimes not capital)* a horsetail, *Equisetum hyemale,* whose siliceous stems have been used for polishing and scouring pots and pans. Also called: **scouring rush.**

Dutch treat NOUN *Informal* an entertainment, meal, etc., where each person pays for himself.

Dutch uncle NOUN *Informal* a person who criticizes or reproves frankly and severely.

Dutch West Indies PLURAL NOUN **the.** a former name of the **Netherlands Antilles.**

Dutch wife NOUN a long hard bolster used, esp in the tropics, to support one's uppermost knee when sleeping on one's side.

duteous ('dju:tɪəs) ADJECTIVE *Formal or archaic* dutiful; obedient.
▸'**duteously** ADVERB ▸'**duteousness** NOUN

dutiable ('dju:tɪəbᵊl) ADJECTIVE (of goods) liable to duty.
▸ˌ**dutia'bility** NOUN

dutiful ('dju:tɪful) ADJECTIVE [1] exhibiting or having a sense of duty. [2] characterized by or resulting from a sense of duty: *a dutiful answer.*
▸'**dutifully** ADVERB ▸'**dutifulness** NOUN

duty ('dju:tɪ) NOUN, *plural* **-ties.** [1] a task or action that a person is bound to perform for moral or legal reasons. [2] respect or obedience due to a superior, older persons, etc.: *filial duty.* [3] the force that binds one morally or legally to one's obligations. [4] a government tax, esp on imports. [5] *Brit* **a** the quantity or intensity of work for which a machine is designed. **b** a measure of the efficiency of a machine. [6] the quantity of water necessary to irrigate an area of land to grow a particular crop. [7] **a** a job or service allocated. **b** *(as modifier)*: *duty rota.* [8] **do duty for.** to act as a substitute for. [9] **on** *(or* **off***)* **duty.** at *(or* not at*)* work.
▷**HISTORY** C13: from Anglo-French *dueté,* from Old French *deu* DUE

duty-bound ADJECTIVE morally obliged as a matter of duty.

duty-free ADJECTIVE, ADVERB [1] with exemption from customs or excise duties. ◆ NOUN [2] goods sold in a duty-free shop.

duty-free shop NOUN a shop, esp one at an airport or on board a ship, that sells perfume, tobacco, etc., at duty-free prices.

duty officer NOUN an officer (in the armed forces, police, etc.) on duty at a particular time.

duumvir (dju:'ʌmvə) NOUN, *plural* **-virs** *or* **-viri** (-vɪˌri:). [1] *Roman history* one of two coequal magistrates or officers. [2] either of two men who exercise a joint authority.
▷**HISTORY** C16: from Latin, from *duo* two + *vir* man

duumvirate (dju:'ʌmvɪrɪt) NOUN the office of or government by duumvirs.

duvet ('du:veɪ) NOUN [1] another name for **continental quilt.** [2] Also called: **duvet jacket.** a down-filled jacket used esp by mountaineers.
▷**HISTORY** C18: from French, from earlier *dumet,* from Old French *dum* DOWN²

duvet day NOUN *Informal* a day of leave from work that an employee is allowed to take at short notice.
▷**HISTORY** C20: from the idea of staying in bed rather than going to work

duvetyn, duvetine, *or* **duvetyne** ('dju:vəˌti:n) NOUN a soft napped velvety fabric of cotton, silk, wool, or rayon.
▷**HISTORY** C20: from French *duvetine,* from *duvet* down + -INE¹

dux (dʌks) NOUN (in Scottish and certain other schools) the top pupil in a class or school.
▷**HISTORY** Latin: leader

duyker ('daɪkə) NOUN a variant spelling of **duiker.**

DV ABBREVIATION FOR: [1] Deo volente. [Latin: God willing] [2] Douay Version (of the Bible). [3] digital video.

dvandva ('dvɑ:ndvɑ:) NOUN [1] a class of compound words consisting of two elements having a coordinate relationship as if connected by *and.* [2] a compound word of this type, such as *Austro-Hungarian, tragicomic.*
▷**HISTORY** from Sanskrit *dvamdva* a pair, from the reduplication of *dva* TWO

DVD ABBREVIATION FOR digital versatile *or* digital video disk: an optical disk used to store audio, video, or computer data, esp feature films for home viewing.

Dvina (*Russian* dvi'na) NOUN [1] **Northern.** a river in NW Russia, formed by the confluence of the Sukhona and Yug Rivers and flowing northwest to *Dvina Bay* in the White Sea. Length: 750 km (466 miles). Russian name: **Severnaya Dvina.** [2] **Western.** a river rising in W Russia, in the Valdai Hills and flowing south and southwest then northwest to the Gulf of Riga. Length: 1021 km (634 miles). Russian name: **Zapadnaya Dvina** ('zapədnəjə). Latvian name: **Daugava.**

Dvina Bay *or* **Dvina Gulf** NOUN an inlet of the White Sea, off the coast of NW Russia.

Dvinsk (dvinsk) NOUN transliteration of the former Russian name for **Daugavpils.**

DVLA (in Britain) ABBREVIATION FOR Driver and Vehicle Licensing Agency.

DVM ABBREVIATION FOR Doctor of Veterinary Medicine.

DVT ABBREVIATION FOR **deep vein thrombosis.**

D/W ABBREVIATION FOR dock warrant.

dwaal (dwɑːl) NOUN *South African* a state of befuddlement.
▷HISTORY Afrikaans

dwale (dweɪl) NOUN another name for **deadly nightshade.**
▷HISTORY C14: perhaps of Scandinavian origin

dwam (dwɑːm) *or* **dwaum** (dwɔːm) *Scot* ◆ NOUN [1] a stupor or daydream (esp in the phrase **in a dwam**). ◆ VERB [2] (*intr*) to faint or fall ill.
▷HISTORY Old English *dwolma* confusion

dwang (dwæŋ) NOUN *Scot and NZ* another name for **nogging** (sense 1).
▷HISTORY C19: Scot; compare Dutch *dwang* force, Middle Low German *dwanc*

dwarf (dwɔːf) NOUN, *plural* **dwarfs** *or* **dwarves** (dwɔːvz). [1] an abnormally undersized person, esp one with a large head and short arms and legs. Compare **midget.** [2] **a** an animal or plant much below the average height for the species. **b** (*as modifier*): *a dwarf tree.* [3] (in folklore) a small ugly manlike creature, often possessing magical powers. [4] *Astronomy* short for **dwarf star.** ◆ VERB [5] to become or cause to become comparatively small in size, importance, etc. [6] (*tr*) to stunt the growth of.
▷HISTORY Old English *dweorg;* related to Old Norse *dvergr,* Old High German *twerc*
▸'**dwarfish** ADJECTIVE ▸'**dwarfishly** ADVERB
▸'**dwarfishness** NOUN

dwarf bean NOUN another name for **French bean.**

dwarf chestnut NOUN [1] the edible nut of the chinquapin tree. [2] another name for **chinquapin** (sense 1).

dwarf cornel NOUN an arctic and subarctic cornaceous plant *Cornus suecica,* having small purple flowers surrounded by white petal-like bracts.

dwarfism ('dwɔːfɪzəm) NOUN the condition of being a dwarf.

dwarf male NOUN a male animal that is much smaller, and often internally simpler, than its female counterpart. Dwarf males are commonly carried by the female, as in species of angler fish.

dwarf mallow NOUN a European malvaceous plant, *Malva neglecta* (or *M. rotundifolia*), having rounded leaves and small pinkish-white flowers.

dwarf star NOUN any luminosity class V star, such as the sun, lying in the main sequence of the Hertzsprung-Russell diagram. Also called: **main-sequence star.** See also **red dwarf, white dwarf.**

dweeb (dwiːb) NOUN *Slang, chiefly US* a stupid or uninteresting person.
▷HISTORY C20: of unknown origin

dweeby ('dwiːbɪ) ADJECTIVE **dweebier, dweebiest.** *Slang, chiefly US* like or typical of a dweeb.

dwell (dwɛl) VERB **dwells, dwelling, dwelt** (dwɛlt) *or* **dwelled.** (*intr*) [1] *Formal, literary* to live as a permanent resident. [2] to live (in a specified state): *to dwell in poverty.* ◆ NOUN [3] a regular pause in the operation of a machine. [4] a flat or constant-radius portion on a linear or rotary cam enabling the cam follower to remain static for a brief time.
▷HISTORY Old English *dwellan* to seduce, get lost; related to Old Saxon *bidwellian* to prevent, Old Norse *dvelja,* Old High German *twellen* to prevent
▸'**dweller** NOUN

dwelling ('dwɛlɪŋ) NOUN *Formal, literary* a place of residence.

dwell on *or* **upon** VERB (*intr, preposition*) to think, speak, or write at length: *he dwells on his misfortunes.*

dwelt (dwɛlt) VERB a past tense of **dwell.**

Dwem (dwɛm) NOUN ACRONYM FOR Dead White European Male.

dwindle ('dwɪndᵊl) VERB to grow or cause to grow less in size, intensity, or number; diminish or shrink gradually.
▷HISTORY C16: from Old English *dwīnan* to waste away; related to Old Norse *dvīna* to pine away

DWP (in Britain) ABBREVIATION FOR Department for Work and Pensions.

dwt ABBREVIATION FOR: [1] deadweight tonnage. [2] Also: **dwt.** *Obsolete* pennyweight.
▷HISTORY *d,* from Latin *denarius* penny

DX *Telegraphy, telephony* [1] SYMBOL FOR long distance. [2] (of a radio station) indicating that it is far away.

DX code NOUN *Photog* a code on a film cassette that automatically adjusts the film-speed setting on a suitably equipped camera to the correct ISO rating.
▷HISTORY C20: from *d(aylight) (e)x(posure)*

Dy THE CHEMICAL SYMBOL FOR dysprosium.

DY INTERNATIONAL CAR REGISTRATION FOR Benin.
▷HISTORY from *Dahomey*

dyad ('daɪæd) NOUN [1] *Maths* an operator that is the unspecified product of two vectors. It can operate on a vector to produce either a scalar or vector product. [2] an atom or group that has a valency of two. [3] a group of two; couple.
▷HISTORY C17: from Late Latin *dyas,* from Greek *duas* two, a pair

dyadic (daɪ'ædɪk) ADJECTIVE [1] of or relating to a dyad. [2] relating to or based on two; twofold. [3] *Logic, maths* (of a relation, predicate, etc.) relating two terms; binary. Compare **monadic, polyadic.**

Dyak *or* **Dayak** ('daɪæk) NOUN, *plural* **-aks** *or* **-ak.** a member of a Malaysian people of the interior of Borneo: noted for their long houses.
▷HISTORY from Malay *Dayak* upcountry, from *darat* land

dyarchy ('daɪɑːkɪ) NOUN, *plural* **-chies.** a variant spelling of **diarchy.**
▸**dy'archic** *or* **dy'archical** *or* **dy'archal** ADJECTIVE

dybbuk ('dɪbək; *Hebrew* di'buk) NOUN, *plural* **-buks** *or* **-bukkim** (*Hebrew* -bu'kim). *Judaism* (in the folklore of the cabala) the soul of a dead sinner that has transmigrated into the body of a living person.
▷HISTORY from Yiddish *dibbūk* devil, from Hebrew *dibbūq;* related to *dābhaq* to hang on, cling

dye (daɪ) NOUN [1] a staining or colouring substance, such as a natural or synthetic pigment. [2] a liquid that contains a colouring material and can be used to stain fabrics, skins, etc. [3] the colour or shade produced by dyeing. ◆ VERB **dyes, dyeing, dyed.** [4] (*tr*) to impart a colour or stain to (something, such as fabric or hair) by or as if by the application of a dye.
▷HISTORY Old English *dēagian,* from *dēag* a dye; related to Old High German *tugōn* to change, Lettish *dūkans* dark
▸'**dyable** *or* '**dyeable** ADJECTIVE ▸'**dyer** NOUN

dyed-in-the-wool ADJECTIVE [1] extreme or unchanging in attitude, opinion, etc. [2] (of a fabric) made of dyed yarn.

dyeing ('daɪɪŋ) NOUN the process or industry of colouring yarns, fabric, etc.

dyeline ('daɪˌlaɪn) ADJECTIVE another word for **diazo** (sense 2).

dyer's-greenweed *or esp US* **dyer's-broom** NOUN a small Eurasian leguminous shrub, *Genista tinctoria,* whose yellow flowers yield a yellow dye, formerly mixed with woad to produce the colour Kendal green. Also called: **woadwaxen, woodwaxen.**

dyer's rocket NOUN a Eurasian resedaceous plant, *Reseda luteola,* with a spike of yellowish-green flowers and long narrow leaves: formerly cultivated as the source of a yellow dye, used with woad to make Lincoln green. Also called: **weld.**

dyer's-weed NOUN any of several plants that yield a dye, such as woad, dyer's rocket, and dyer's-greenweed.

dyestuff ('daɪˌstʌf) NOUN a substance that can be used as a dye or from which a dye can be obtained.

dyewood ('daɪˌwʊd) NOUN any wood, such as brazil, from which dyes and pigments can be obtained.

Dyfed ('dʌvɛd) NOUN a former county in SW Wales: created in 1974 from Cardiganshire, Pembrokeshire, and Carmarthenshire; in 1996 it was replaced by Pembrokeshire, Carmarthenshire, and Ceredigion.

dying ('daɪɪŋ) VERB [1] the present participle of **die**[1]. ◆ ADJECTIVE [2] relating to or occurring at the moment of death: *a dying wish.*

dyke[1] *or* **dike** (daɪk) NOUN [1] an embankment constructed to prevent flooding, keep out the sea, etc. [2] a ditch or watercourse. [3] a bank made of earth excavated for and placed alongside a ditch. [4] *Scot* a wall, esp a dry-stone wall. [5] a barrier or obstruction. [6] a vertical or near-vertical wall-like body of igneous rock intruded into cracks in older rock. [7] *Austral and NZ informal* **a** a lavatory. **b** (*as modifier*): *a dyke roll.* ◆ VERB [8] *Civil engineering* an embankment or wall built to confine a river to a particular course. [9] (*tr*) to protect, enclose, or drain (land) with a dyke.
▷HISTORY C13: modification of Old English *dic* ditch; compare Old Norse *dīki* ditch

dyke[2] *or* **dike** (daɪk) NOUN *Slang* a lesbian.
▷HISTORY C20: of unknown origin

dynameter (daɪ'næmɪtə) NOUN an instrument for determining the magnifying power of telescopes.

dynamic (daɪ'næmɪk) ADJECTIVE [1] of or concerned with energy or forces that produce motion, as opposed to *static.* [2] of or concerned with dynamics. [3] Also: **dynamical.** characterized by force of personality, ambition, energy, new ideas, etc. [4] *Music* of, relating to, or indicating dynamics: *dynamic marks.* [5] *Computing* (of a memory) needing its contents refreshed periodically. Compare **static** (sense 8).
▷HISTORY C19: from French *dynamique,* from Greek *dunamikos* powerful, from *dunamis* power, from *dunasthai* to be able
▸**dy'namically** ADVERB

dynamic pricing NOUN *Commerce* offering goods at a price that changes according to the level of demand, the type of customer, or the state of the weather.

dynamic psychology NOUN *Psychol* any system of psychology that emphasizes the interaction between different motives, emotions, and drives.

dynamic range NOUN the range of signal amplitudes over which an electronic communications channel can operate within acceptable limits of distortion. The range is determined by system noise at the lower end and by the onset of overload at the upper end.

dynamics (daɪ'næmɪks) NOUN [1] (*functioning as singular*) the branch of mechanics concerned with the forces that change or produce the motions of bodies. Compare **statics, kinematics.** [2] (*functioning as singular*) the branch of mechanics that includes statics and kinetics. See **statics, kinetics.** [3] (*functioning as singular*) the branch of any science concerned with forces. [4] those forces that produce change in any field or system. [5] *Music* **a** the various degrees of loudness called for in performance. **b** Also called: **dynamic marks, dynamic markings.** directions and symbols used to indicate degrees of loudness.

dynamism ('daɪnəˌmɪzəm) NOUN [1] *Philosophy* any of several theories that attempt to explain phenomena in terms of an immanent force or energy. Compare **mechanism** (sense 5), **vitalism.** [2] the forcefulness of an energetic personality.
▸'**dynamist** NOUN ▸ˌ**dyna'mistic** ADJECTIVE

dynamite ('daɪnəˌmaɪt) NOUN [1] an explosive consisting of nitroglycerine or ammonium nitrate mixed with kieselguhr, sawdust, or wood pulp. [2] *Informal* a spectacular or potentially dangerous person or thing. ◆ VERB [3] (*tr*) to mine or blow up with dynamite.
▷HISTORY C19 (coined by Alfred Nobel): from DYNAMO- + -ITE[1]
▸'**dynaˌmiter** NOUN

dynamo ('daɪnəˌməʊ) NOUN, *plural* **-mos.** [1] a device for converting mechanical energy into electrical energy, esp one that produces direct current. Compare **generator** (sense 1). [2] *Informal* an energetic hard-working person.
▷HISTORY C19: short for *dynamoelectric machine*

dynamo- *or sometimes before a vowel* **dynam-** COMBINING FORM indicating power: *dynamoelectric; dynamite.*
▷HISTORY from Greek, from *dunamis* power

dynamoelectric (ˌdaɪnəməʊɪ'lɛktrɪk) *or* **dynamoelectrical** ADJECTIVE of or concerned with the interconversion of mechanical and electrical energy.

dynamometer (ˌdaɪnə'mɒmɪtə) NOUN any of a number of instruments for measuring power or force.

dynamometry (ˌdaɪnə'mɒmɪtrɪ) NOUN [1] the science of power measurement. [2] the manufacture and use of dynamometers.
▸**dynamometric** (ˌdaɪnəməʊ'mɛtrɪk) *or* ˌ**dynamo'metrical** ADJECTIVE

dynamotor ('daɪnəˌməʊtə) NOUN an electrical

machine having a single magnetic field and two independent armature windings of which one acts as a motor and the other a generator: used to convert direct current from a battery into alternating current.

dynast ('dɪnəst, -æst) NOUN a ruler, esp a hereditary one.
▷HISTORY C17: from Latin *dynastēs,* from Greek *dunastēs,* from *dunasthai* to be powerful

dynasty ('dɪnəstɪ) NOUN, *plural* **-ties.** [1] a sequence of hereditary rulers: *an Egyptian dynasty.* [2] any sequence of powerful leaders of the same family: *the Kennedy dynasty.*
▷HISTORY C15: via Late Latin from Greek *dunasteia,* from *dunastēs* DYNAST
▸**dynastic** (dɪ'næstɪk) *or* **dy'nastical** ADJECTIVE
▸**dy'nastically** ADVERB

dynatron oscillator ('daɪnəˌtrɒn) NOUN *Electronics* an oscillator containing a tetrode in which the screen grid is more positive than the anode, causing the anode current to decrease as its voltage increases.
▷HISTORY C20: from DYNA(MO-) + -TRON

dyne (daɪn) NOUN the cgs unit of force; the force that imparts an acceleration of 1 centimetre per second per second to a mass of 1 gram. 1 dyne is equivalent to 10^{-5} newton or 7.233×10^{-5} poundal.
▷HISTORY C19: from French, from Greek *dunamis* power, force

dynode ('daɪnəʊd) NOUN an electrode onto which a beam of electrons can fall, causing the emission of a greater number of electrons by secondary emission. They are used in photomultipliers to amplify the signal.

dys- PREFIX [1] diseased, abnormal, or faulty: *dysentery; dyslexia.* [2] difficult or painful: *dysuria.* [3] unfavourable or bad: *dyslogistic.*
▷HISTORY via Latin from Greek *dus-*

dysarthria (dɪs'ɑːθrɪə) NOUN imperfect articulation of speech caused by damage to the nervous system.
▷HISTORY from DYS- + *arthria* from Greek *arthron* articulation

dyscalculia (ˌdɪskæl'kjuːlɪə) NOUN severe difficulty in making simple mathematical calculations, due to cerebral disease or injury.
▷HISTORY C20: from DYS- + Latin *calculare* to calculate

dyscrasia (dɪs'kreɪzɪə) NOUN *Obsolete* any abnormal physiological condition, esp of the blood.
▷HISTORY C19: New Latin, from Medieval Latin: an imbalance of humours, from Greek, from DYS- + *-krasia,* from *krasis* a mixing

dysentery ('dɪsᵊntrɪ) NOUN infection of the intestine with bacteria or amoebae, marked chiefly by severe diarrhoea with the passage of mucus and blood.
▷HISTORY C14: via Latin from Greek *dusenteria,* from *dusentera,* literally: bad bowels, from DYS- + *enteron* intestine
▸**dysenteric** (ˌdɪsᵊn'tɛrɪk) ADJECTIVE

dysfunction (dɪs'fʌŋkʃən) NOUN [1] *Med* any disturbance or abnormality in the function of an organ or part. [2] (esp of a family) failure to show the characteristics or fulfil the purposes accepted as normal or beneficial.

dysfunctional (dɪs'fʌŋkʃənᵊl) ADJECTIVE [1] *Med* (of an organ or part) not functioning normally. [2] (esp of a family) characterized by a breakdown of normal or beneficial relationships between members of the group.

dysgenic (dɪs'dʒɛnɪk) ADJECTIVE [1] of, relating to, or contributing to a degeneration or deterioration in the fitness and quality of a race or strain. [2] of or relating to dysgenics.

dysgenics (dɪs'dʒɛnɪks) NOUN (*functioning as singular*) the study of factors capable of reducing the quality of a race or strain, esp the human race. Also called: **cacogenics.**

dysgraphia (dɪs'græfɪə) NOUN inability to write correctly, caused by disease of part of the brain.

dyskinesia (dɪskɪ'niːzɪə) NOUN involuntary repetitive movements, such as those occurring in chorea.
▷HISTORY DYS- + *-kinesia* from Greek *kinesis* movement

dyslalia (dɪs'leɪlɪə) NOUN defective speech characteristic of those affected by aphasia.

dyslexia (dɪs'lɛksɪə) NOUN a developmental disorder which can cause learning difficulty in one or more of the areas of reading, writing, and numeracy. Nontechnical name: **word blindness.**
▷HISTORY from DYS- + *-lexia* from Greek *lexis* word
▸**dyslectic** (dɪs'lɛktɪk) ADJECTIVE, NOUN ▸**dys'lexic** ADJECTIVE

dyslogistic (ˌdɪslə'dʒɪstɪk) ADJECTIVE *Rare* disapproving.
▷HISTORY C19: from DYS- + *-logistic,* as in *eulogistic*
▸ˌ**dyslo'gistically** ADVERB

dysmenorrhoea *or esp US* **dysmenorrhea** (ˌdɪsmɛnə'rɪə, dɪsˌmɛn-) NOUN abnormally difficult or painful menstruation.
▸ˌ**dysmenor'rhoeal** *or (esp US)* ˌ**dysmenor'rheal** ADJECTIVE

dysmorphophobia (dɪsˌmɔːfəʊ'fəʊbɪə) NOUN an obsessive fear that one's body, or any part of it, is repulsive or may become so.

dyspepsia (dɪs'pɛpsɪə) *or* **dyspepsy** (dɪs'pɛpsɪ) NOUN indigestion or upset stomach.
▷HISTORY C18: from Latin, from Greek *duspepsia,* from DYS- + *pepsis* digestion

dyspeptic (dɪs'pɛptɪk) ADJECTIVE *also* **dyspeptical.** [1] relating to or suffering from dyspepsia. [2] irritable. ◆ NOUN [3] a person suffering from dyspepsia.
▸**dys'peptically** ADVERB

dysphagia (dɪs'feɪdʒɪə) NOUN difficulty in swallowing, caused by obstruction or spasm of the oesophagus.
▷HISTORY C18: New Latin, from DYS- + Greek *-phagos;* see PHAGO-
▸**dysphagic** (dɪs'fædʒɪk) ADJECTIVE

dysphasia (dɪs'feɪzɪə) NOUN a disorder of language caused by a brain lesion.
▷HISTORY see DYS- + -PHASIA
▸**dys'phasic** ADJECTIVE, NOUN

dysphemism ('dɪsfɪˌmɪzəm) NOUN [1] substitution of a derogatory or offensive word or phrase for an innocuous one. [2] the word or phrase so substituted.
▷HISTORY C19: DYS- + EUPHEMISM
▸ˌ**dysphe'mistic** ADJECTIVE

dysphonia (dɪs'fəʊnɪə) NOUN any impairment in the ability to speak normally, as from spasm or strain of the vocal cords.
▷HISTORY C18: New Latin, from Greek: harshness of sound, from DYS- + *-phōnia* -PHONY
▸**dysphonic** (dɪs'fɒnɪk) ADJECTIVE

dysphoria (dɪs'fɔːrɪə) NOUN a feeling of being ill at ease.
▷HISTORY C20: New Latin, from Greek DYS- + *-phoria,* from *pherein* to bear
▸**dysphoric** (dɪs'fɒrɪk) ADJECTIVE

dysplasia (dɪs'pleɪzɪə) NOUN abnormal development of an organ or part of the body, including congenital absence.
▷HISTORY C20: New Latin, from DYS- + *-plasia,* from Greek *plasis* a moulding
▸**dysplastic** (dɪs'plæstɪk) ADJECTIVE

dyspnoea *or US* **dyspnea** (dɪsp'niːə) NOUN difficulty in breathing or in catching the breath. Compare **eupnoea.**
▷HISTORY C17: via Latin from Greek *duspnoia,* from DYS- + *pnoē* breath, from *pnein* to breathe
▸**dysp'noeal** *or* **dysp'noeic,** *or US* **dysp'neal** *or* **dysp'neic** ADJECTIVE

dyspraxia (dɪs'præksɪə) NOUN *Pathol* an impairment in the control of the motor system; it may be developmental or acquired, resulting from a cerebral lesion.
▷HISTORY DYS- + PRAX(IS) + -IA

dysprosium (dɪs'prəʊsɪəm) NOUN a soft silvery-white metallic element of the lanthanide series: used in laser materials and as a neutron absorber in nuclear control rods. Symbol: Dy; atomic no.: 66; atomic wt.: 162.50; valency: 3; relative density: 8.551; melting pt.: 1412°C; boiling pt.: 2567°C.
▷HISTORY C20: New Latin, from Greek *dusprositos* difficult to get near + -IUM

dyssynergia (dɪsɪ'nɜːdʒɪə) NOUN muscular incoordination caused by a brain disorder.
▷HISTORY from DYS- + Greek *synergia* cooperation

dystaxia (dɪs'tæksɪə) NOUN *Pathol* lack of muscular coordination resulting in shaky limb movements and unsteady gait.
▷HISTORY from DYS- + Greek *-taxia,* from *tassein* to put in order

dysteleology (ˌdɪstɛlɪ'ɒlədʒɪ, -tiːlɪ-) NOUN *Philosophy* the denial of purpose in life. Compare **teleology.**
▸**dysˌteleo'logical** ADJECTIVE ▸ˌ**dystele'ologist** NOUN

dysthymia (dɪs'θaɪmɪə) NOUN *Psychiatry* [1] the characteristics of the neurotic and introverted, including anxiety, depression, and compulsive behaviour. [2] *Obsolete* a relatively mild depression.
▷HISTORY C19: New Latin, from Greek *dusthumia,* from DYS- + *thumos* mind
▸**dys'thymic** ADJECTIVE

dysthymic disorder NOUN a psychiatric disorder characterized by generalized depression that lasts for at least a year.

dystocia (dɪs'təʊʃə) NOUN *Med* abnormal, slow, or difficult childbirth, usually because of disordered or ineffective contractions of the uterus.
▷HISTORY New Latin, from Greek, from *dus-* (see DYS-) + *tokos* childbirth + -IA
▸**dys'tocial** ADJECTIVE

dystonia (dɪs'təʊnɪə) NOUN a neurological disorder, caused by disease of the basal ganglia, in which the muscles of the trunk, shoulders, and neck go into spasm, so that the head and limbs are held in unnatural positions.
▷HISTORY from DYS- + *-tonia* from Greek *tonos* tension, from *teinen* to stretch

dystopia (dɪs'təʊpɪə) NOUN an imaginary place where everything is as bad as it can be.
▷HISTORY C19 (coined by John Stuart Mill (1806–73), English philosopher and economist): from DYS- + UTOPIA
▸**dys'topian** ADJECTIVE, NOUN

dystrophin ('dɪstrəfɪn) NOUN a protein, the absence of which is believed to cause muscular dystrophy.

dystrophy ('dɪstrəfɪ) *or* **dystrophia** (dɪ'strəʊfɪə) NOUN [1] any of various bodily disorders, characterized by wasting of tissues. See also **muscular dystrophy.** [2] *Ecology* a condition of lake water when it is too acidic and poor in oxygen to support life, resulting from excessive humus content.
▷HISTORY C19: New Latin *dystrophia,* from DYS- + Greek *trophē* food
▸**dystrophic** (dɪs'trɒfɪk) ADJECTIVE

dysuria (dɪs'jʊərɪə) NOUN difficult or painful urination.
▷HISTORY C14: via Latin from Greek *dusouria,* from DYS- + -URIA
▸**dys'uric** ADJECTIVE

dytiscid (dɪ'tɪsɪd, daɪ-) NOUN [1] any carnivorous aquatic beetle of the family *Dytiscidae,* having large flattened back legs used for swimming. ◆ ADJECTIVE [2] of, relating to, or belonging to the *Dytiscidae.*
▷HISTORY C19: from New Latin *Dytiscus* genus name, changed from Greek *dutikos* able to dive, from *duein* to dive

Dyula (diː'uːlə, 'djuːlə) NOUN [1] (*plural* **-la** *or* **-las**) a member of a negroid people of W Africa, living chiefly in the rain forests of the Ivory Coast, where they farm rice, etc. [2] the language of this people, belonging to the Mande branch of the Niger-Congo family.

dz THE INTERNET DOMAIN NAME FOR Algeria.

DZ INTERNATIONAL CAR REGISTRATION FOR Algeria.
▷HISTORY from Arabic *Djazir*

Dzaudzhikau (dzaudʒi'kau) NOUN the former name (1944–54) of **Ordzhonikidze.**

Dzhambul (*Russian* dʒam'bul) NOUN the former name (1938–91) of **Auliye-Ata.**

dziggetai ('dʒɪgɪˌtaɪ) NOUN a variant of **chigetai.**

dzo (zəʊ) NOUN, *plural* **dzos** *or* **dzo.** a variant spelling of **zo.**

Dzongka *or* **Dzongkha** ('zɒŋkə) NOUN the official language of Bhutan: a dialect of Tibetan.

Dzungaria (dzʊŋ'gɛərɪə, zʊŋ-) NOUN a variant transliteration of the Chinese name for **Junggar Pendi.**

Ee

e *or* **E** (iː) NOUN, *plural* **e's** *or* **E's,** *or* **Es.** [1] the fifth letter and second vowel of the modern English alphabet. [2] any of several speech sounds represented by this letter, in English as in *he, bet,* or *below.*

e SYMBOL FOR: [1] *Maths* a transcendental number, fundamental to mathematics, that is the limit of $(1 + 1/n)^n$ as *n* increases to infinity: used as the base of natural logarithms. Approximate value: 2.718 282...; relation to π: $e^{\pi i} = -1$, where $i = \sqrt{-1}$. [2] electron. [3] *Chess* See **algebraic notation.**

E SYMBOL FOR: [1] earth. [2] East. [3] English. [4] Egypt(ian). [5] exa-. [6] *Music* **a** a note having a frequency of 329.63 hertz (**E above middle C**) or this value multiplied or divided by any power of 2; the third note of the scale of C major. **b** a key, string, or pipe producing this note. **c** the major or minor key having this note as its tonic. [7] *Physics* **a** energy. **b** electric field strength. **c** electromotive force. **d** Young's modulus (of elasticity). [8] *Logic* a universal negative categorical proposition, such as *no pigs can fly:* often symbolized as **SeP**. Compare **A, I², O¹**. [from Latin *(n)e(go)* I deny] [9] **a** a person without a regular income, or who is dependent on the state on a long-term basis because of unemployment, sickness, old age, etc. **b** (*as modifier*): *E worker.* ◆ See also **occupation groupings.** ◆ [10] INTERNATIONAL CAR REGISTRATION FOR Spain.
▷**HISTORY** (for sense 10) from Spanish *España*

E. ABBREVIATION FOR Earl.

e-^{1} PREFIX FORMING VERBS AND VERBAL DERIVATIVES [1] out: *eviscerate; egest.* [2] away: *elapse; elongate.* [3] outside: *evaginate.* [4] completely: *evaporate.* [5] without: *ebracteate.*
▷**HISTORY** from Latin *ē* away; related to EX-^{1}

e-^{2} PREFIX electronic, indicating the involvement of the Internet: *e-business; e-money.*

E- PREFIX used with numbers indicating a standardized system within the European Union, as of recognized food additives or standard pack sizes. See also **E number.**

ea. ABBREVIATION FOR each.

each (iːtʃ) DETERMINER [1] **a** every (one) of two or more considered individually: *each day; each person.* **b** (*as pronoun*): *each gave according to his ability.* ◆ ADVERB [2] for, to, or from each one; apiece: *four apples each.*
▷**HISTORY** Old English *ǣlc;* related to Old High German *ēogilīh,* Old Frisian *ellik,* Dutch *elk*

> **Language note** *Each* is a singular pronoun and should be used with a singular form of a verb: *each of the candidates was* (not *were*) *interviewed separately.* See also at **either.**

each other PRONOUN used when the action, attribution, etc., is reciprocal: *furious with each other.*

> **Language note** *Each other* and *one another* are interchangeable in modern British usage.

each way ADJECTIVE, ADVERB *Horse racing, chiefly Brit* (of a bet) made on the same runner or contestant to win or come second or third in a race. Also: **both ways.** US term: **across-the-board.**

EACSO (iːˈɑːksəʊ) NOUN ACRONYM FOR East African Common Services Organization.

e-address NOUN an e-mail address.

eager^1 (ˈiːgə) ADJECTIVE [1] (*postpositive;* often foll by *to* or *for*) impatiently desirous (of); anxious or avid (for): *he was eager to see her departure.* [2] characterized by or feeling expectancy or great desire: *an eager look.* [3] *Archaic* tart or biting; sharp.
▷**HISTORY** C13: from Old French *egre,* from Latin *acer* sharp, keen
► **ˈeagerly** ADVERB ► **ˈeagerness** NOUN

eager^2 (ˈeɪgə) NOUN a variant spelling of **eagre.**

eager beaver NOUN *Informal* a person who displays conspicuous diligence, esp one who volunteers for extra work.

eagle (ˈiːgᵊl) NOUN [1] any of various birds of prey of the genera *Aquila, Harpia,* etc. (see **golden eagle, harpy eagle**), having large broad wings and strong soaring flight: family *Accipitridae* (hawks, etc.). See also **sea eagle.** Related adjective: **aquiline.** [2] a representation of an eagle used as an emblem, etc., esp representing power: *the Roman eagle.* [3] a standard, seal, etc., bearing the figure of an eagle. [4] *Golf* a score of two strokes under par for a hole. [5] a former US gold coin worth ten dollars: withdrawn from circulation in 1934. [6] the shoulder insignia worn by a US full colonel or equivalent rank. ◆ VERB [7] *Golf* to score two strokes under par for a hole.
▷**HISTORY** C14: from Old French *aigle,* from Old Provençal *aigla,* from Latin *aquila,* perhaps from *aquilus* dark

eagle-eyed ADJECTIVE having keen or piercing eyesight.

eagle-hawk NOUN a large aggressive Australian eagle, *Aquila audax.* Also called: **wedge-tailed eagle.**

eagle owl NOUN a large owl, *Bubo bubo,* of Europe and Asia. It has brownish speckled plumage and large ear tufts.

eagle ray NOUN any of various rays of the family *Myliobatidae,* related to the stingrays but having narrower pectoral fins and a projecting snout with heavily browed eyes.

eaglestone (ˈiːgᵊlˌstəʊn) NOUN a hollow oval nodule of clay ironstone, formerly thought to have magical properties.

eaglet (ˈiːglɪt) NOUN a young eagle.

eaglewood (ˈiːgᵊlˌwʊd) NOUN [1] an Asian thymelaeaceous tree, *Aquilaria agallocha,* having fragrant wood that yields a resin used as a perfume. [2] the wood of this tree. ◆ Also called: **aloes, aloes wood, agalloch, lignaloes.**

eagre *or* **eager** (ˈeɪgə) NOUN a tidal bore, esp of the Humber or Severn estuaries.
▷**HISTORY** C17: perhaps from Old English *ēagor* flood; compare Old English *ēa* river, water

EAK INTERNATIONAL CAR REGISTRATION FOR (East Africa) Kenya.

ealdorman (ˈɔːldəmən) NOUN, *plural* **-men.** an official of Anglo-Saxon England, appointed by the king, who was responsible for law, order, and justice in his shire and for leading his local fyrd in battle.
▷**HISTORY** Old English *ealdor* lord + MAN

Ealing (ˈiːlɪŋ) NOUN a borough of W Greater London, formed in 1965 from Acton, Ealing, and Southall. Pop.: 300 947 (2001). Area: 55 sq. km (21 sq. miles).

EAM NOUN (in World War II) the leftist resistance in German-occupied Greece.
▷**HISTORY** C20: from Modern Greek *Ethniko Apeleutherotiko Metopo* National Liberation Front

-ean SUFFIX FORMING ADJECTIVES a variant of **-an**: *Caesarean.*

E & OE ABBREVIATION FOR errors and omissions excepted.

ear^1 (ɪə) NOUN [1] the organ of hearing and balance in higher vertebrates and of balance only in fishes. In man and other mammals it consists of three parts (see **external ear, middle ear, internal ear**). Related adjectives: **aural, otic.** [2] the outermost cartilaginous part of the ear (pinna) in mammals, esp man. [3] the sense of hearing. [4] sensitivity to musical sounds, poetic diction, etc.: *he has an ear for music.* [5] attention, esp favourable attention; consideration; heed (esp in the phrases **give ear to, lend an ear**). [6] an object resembling the external ear in shape or position, such as a handle on a jug. [7] Also called (esp Brit): **earpiece.** a display box at the head of a newspaper page, esp the front page, for advertisements, etc. [8] **all ears.** very attentive; listening carefully. [9] **by ear.** without reading from written music. [10] **chew someone's ear.** *Slang* to reprimand severely. [11] **fall on deaf ears.** to be ignored or pass unnoticed. [12] **have hard ears.** *Caribbean* to be stubbornly disobedient. [13] **a flea in one's ear.** *Informal* a sharp rebuke. [14] **have the ear of.** to be in a position to influence: *he has the ear of the president.* [15] **in one ear and out the other.** heard but unheeded. [16] **keep** (*or* **have**) **one's ear to the ground.** to be or try to be well informed about current trends and opinions. [17] **make a pig's ear of.** *Informal* to ruin disastrously. [18] **one's ears are burning.** one is aware of being the topic of another's conversation. [19] **out on one's ear.** *Informal* dismissed unceremoniously. [20] **play by ear. a** to act according to the demands of a situation rather than to a plan; improvise. **b** to perform a musical piece on an instrument without written music. [21] **prick up one's ears.** to start to listen attentively; become interested. [22] **set by the ears.** to cause disagreement or commotion. [23] **a thick ear.** *Informal* a blow on the ear delivered as punishment, in anger, etc. [24] **turn a deaf ear.** to be deliberately unresponsive. [25] **up to one's ears.** *Informal* deeply involved, as in work or debt. [26] **wet behind the ears.** *Informal* inexperienced; naive; immature.
▷**HISTORY** Old English *ēare;* related to Old Norse *eyra,* Old High German *ōra,* Gothic *ausō,* Greek *ous,* Latin *auris*
► **ˈearless** ADJECTIVE ► **ˈearˌlike** ADJECTIVE

ear^2 (ɪə) NOUN [1] the part of a cereal plant, such as wheat or barley, that contains the seeds, grains, or kernels. ◆ VERB [2] (*intr*) (of cereal plants) to develop such parts.
▷**HISTORY** Old English *ēar;* related to Old High German *ahar,* Old Norse *ax,* Gothic *ahs* ear, Latin *acus* chaff, Greek *akros* pointed

earache (ˈɪərˌeɪk) NOUN pain in the middle or inner ear. Technical name: **otalgia.** Compare **otitis.**

earball (ˈɪərˌbɒl) NOUN (in acupressure) a small ball kept in position in the ear and pressed when needed to relieve stress.

earbash (ˈɪəˌbæʃ) VERB (*intr*) *Austral and NZ slang* to talk incessantly.
► **ˈearˌbasher** NOUN ► **ˈearˌbashing** NOUN

eardrop (ˈɪəˌdrɒp) NOUN a pendant earring.

eardrops (ˈɪəˌdrɒps) PLURAL NOUN liquid medication for inserting into the external ear.

eardrum (ˈɪəˌdrʌm) NOUN the nontechnical name for **tympanic membrane.**

eared (ɪəd) ADJECTIVE **a** having an ear or ears. **b** (*in combination*): *long-eared; two-eared.*

eared seal NOUN any seal of the pinniped family *Otariidae,* typically having visible earflaps and conspicuous hind limbs that can be used for locomotion on land. Compare **earless seal.**

earflap (ˈɪəˌflæp) NOUN [1] Also called: **earlap.** either of two pieces of fabric or fur attached to a cap, which can be let down to keep the ears warm. [2] *Zoology* a small flap of skin forming the pinna of such animals as seals.

earful (ˈɪəfʊl) NOUN *Informal* [1] something heard or overheard. [2] a rebuke or scolding, esp a lengthy or severe one.

ear-grabbing ADJECTIVE *Informal* (of music) immediately capturing and holding the attention of listeners.

earing (ˈɪərɪŋ) NOUN *Nautical* a line fastened to a corner of a sail for reefing.
▷**HISTORY** C17: from EAR^1 + -ING^1 or perhaps RING^1

earl (ɜːl) NOUN [1] (in the British Isles) a nobleman ranking below a marquess and above a viscount. Female equivalent: **countess.** [2] (in Anglo-Saxon England) a royal governor of any of the large divisions of the kingdom, such as Wessex.
▷**HISTORY** Old English *eorl;* related to Old Norse *jarl* chieftain, Old Saxon *erl* man

earlap ('ɪəˌlæp) NOUN 1 another word for **earflap** (sense 1). 2 *Rare* **a** the external ear. **b** the ear lobe.
▷HISTORY C16: from EAR[1] + LAP[1]

earldom ('ɜːldəm) NOUN 1 the rank, title, or dignity of an earl or countess. 2 the lands of an earl or countess.

earless seal NOUN any seal of the pinniped family *Phocidae,* typically having rudimentary hind limbs, no external earflaps, and a body covering of hair with no underfur. Also called: **hair seal.** Compare **eared seal.**

Earl Grey NOUN a variety of China tea flavoured with oil of bergamot.

Earl Marshal NOUN an officer of the English peerage who presides over the College of Heralds and organizes royal processions and other important ceremonies.

ear lobe NOUN the fleshy lower part of the external ear.

early ('ɜːlɪ) ADJECTIVE **-lier, -liest**, ADVERB 1 before the expected or usual time. 2 occurring in or characteristic of the first part of a period or sequence. 3 occurring in or characteristic of a period far back in time. 4 occurring in the near future. 5 **at the earliest.** not before the time or date mentioned. 6 **early days.** too soon to tell how things will turn out.
▷HISTORY Old English *ǣrlīce,* from *ǣr* ERE + *-līce* -LY[2]; related to Old Norse *arliga*
▸ 'earliness NOUN

early bird NOUN *Informal* a person who rises early or arrives in good time.

Early Bird NOUN one of a number of communications satellites, the first of which was launched in 1965 into a stationary orbit and provided telephone channels between Europe and the US. See also **Intelsat.**

Early Christian ADJECTIVE denoting or relating to the style of architecture that started in Italy in the 3rd century A.D. and spread through the Roman empire until the 5th century.

early closing NOUN *Brit* 1 **a** the shutting of most of the shops in a town one afternoon each week. **b** (*as adjective*): *early-closing day.* 2 the day on which this happens: *Thursday is early closing in Aylesbury.*

Early English NOUN a style of architecture used in England in the 12th and 13th centuries, characterized by lancet arches, narrow openings, and plate tracery.

early music NOUN 1 music of the Middle Ages and Renaissance, sometimes also including music of the baroque and early classical periods. ◆ MODIFIER **early-music.** 2 of or denoting an approach to musical performance emphasizing the use of period instruments and historically researched scores and playing techniques: *the early-music movement.*

early purple orchid NOUN a Eurasian orchid, *Orchis mascula,* with purplish-crimson flowers and stems marked with blackish-purple spots.

Early Renaissance NOUN **the.** the period from about 1400 to 1500 in European, esp Italian, painting, sculpture, and architecture, when naturalistic styles and humanist theories were evolved from the study of classical sources, notably by Donatello, Masaccio, and Alberti.

early-type star NOUN *Astronomy* any massive hot star of spectral type O, B, or A. Compare: **late-type star.**
▷HISTORY C20: from the mistaken belief that hot and old stars evolved into cool young stars

early warning NOUN advance notice of some impending event or development.

early warning system NOUN 1 a network of radar and communications units intended to detect at the earliest possible moment an attack by enemy aircraft or missiles. 2 anything that gives advance notice of something.

earmark ('ɪəˌmɑːk) VERB (*tr*) 1 to set aside or mark out for a specific purpose. 2 to make an identification mark on the ear of (a domestic animal). ◆ NOUN 3 a mark of identification on the ear of a domestic animal. 4 any distinguishing mark or characteristic.

earmuff ('ɪəˌmʌf) NOUN one of a pair of pads of fur or cloth, joined by a headband, for keeping the ears warm.

earn (ɜːn) VERB 1 to gain or be paid (money or other payment) in return for work or service. 2 (*tr*) to acquire, merit, or deserve through behaviour or action: *he has earned a name for duplicity.* 3 (*tr*) (of securities, investments, etc.) to gain (interest, return, profit, etc.).
▷HISTORY Old English *earnian;* related to Old High German *arnēn* to reap, Old Saxon *asna* salary, tithe
▸ 'earner NOUN

earned income NOUN income derived from paid employment and comprising mainly wages and salaries.

earnest[1] ('ɜːnɪst) ADJECTIVE 1 serious in mind or intention: *an earnest student.* 2 showing or characterized by sincerity of intention: *an earnest promise.* 3 demanding or receiving serious attention. ◆ NOUN 4 with serious or sincere intentions.
▷HISTORY Old English *eornost;* related to Old High German *ernust* seriousness, Old Norse *ern* energetic, efficient, Gothic *arniba* secure
▸ 'earnestly ADVERB ▸ 'earnestness NOUN

earnest[2] ('ɜːnɪst) NOUN 1 a part or portion of something given in advance as a guarantee of the remainder. 2 Also called: **earnest money.** *Contract law* something given, usually a nominal sum of money, to confirm a contract. 3 any token of something to follow; pledge; assurance.
▷HISTORY C13: from Old French *erres* pledges, plural of *erre* earnest money, from Latin *arrha,* shortened from *arrabō* pledge, from Greek *arrabon,* from Hebrew *'ērābhōn* pledge, from *'ārabh* he pledged

earnings ('ɜːnɪŋz) PLURAL NOUN 1 money or other payment earned. 2 the profits of an enterprise.

Earnings Related Supplement *or* **Benefit** NOUN (formerly, in the British National Insurance scheme) a payment based on earnings in the previous tax year, payable (in addition to unemployment or sickness benefit) for about six months to a sick or unemployed person. Abbreviation: **ERS.**

EAROM ('ɪərɒm) NOUN *Computing* ◆ ACRONYM FOR electrically alterable read-only memory.

earphone ('ɪəˌfəʊn) NOUN a device for converting electric currents into sound waves, held close to or inserted into the ear.

earpiece ('ɪəˌpiːs) NOUN the earphone in a telephone receiver.

ear piercing NOUN 1 the making of a hole in the lobe of an ear, using a sterilized needle, so that an earring may be worn fastened in the hole. ◆ ADJECTIVE **ear-piercing.** 2 so loud or shrill as to hurt the ears.

earplug ('ɪəˌplʌg) NOUN a small piece of soft material, such as wax, placed in the ear to keep out noise or water.

earring ('ɪəˌrɪŋ) NOUN an ornament for the ear, usually clipped onto the lobe or fastened through a hole pierced in the lobe.

ear shell NOUN another name for the **abalone.**

earshot ('ɪəˌʃɒt) NOUN the range or distance within which sound may be heard (esp in the phrases **within earshot, out of earshot**).

ear-splitting ADJECTIVE so loud or shrill as to hurt the ears.

earth (ɜːθ) NOUN 1 (*sometimes capital*) the third planet from the sun, the only planet on which life is known to exist. It is not quite spherical, being flattened at the poles, and consists of three geological zones, the core, mantle, and thin outer crust. The surface, covered with large areas of water, is enveloped by an atmosphere principally of nitrogen (78 per cent), oxygen (21 per cent), and some water vapour. The age is estimated at over four thousand million years. Distance from sun: 149.6 million km; equatorial diameter: 12 756 km; mass: 5.976×10^{24} kg; sidereal period of axial rotation: 23 hours 56 minutes 4 seconds; sidereal period of revolution about sun: 365.256 days. Related adjectives: **terrestrial, tellurian, telluric, terrene.** 2 the inhabitants of this planet: *the whole earth rejoiced.* 3 the dry surface of this planet as distinguished from sea or sky; land; ground. 4 the loose soft material that makes up a large part of the surface of the ground and consists of disintegrated rock particles, mould, clay, etc.; soil. 5 worldly or temporal matters as opposed to the concerns of the spirit. 6 the hole in which some species of burrowing animals, esp foxes, live. 7 *Chem* See **rare earth, alkaline earth.** 8 **a** a connection between an electrical circuit or device and the earth, which is at zero potential. **b** a terminal to which this connection is made. US and Canadian equivalent: **ground.** 9 Also called: **earth colour.** any of various brown pigments composed chiefly of iron oxides. 10 (*modifier*) *Astrology* of or relating to a group of three signs of the zodiac, Taurus, Virgo, and Capricorn. Compare **air** (sense 20), **fire** (sense 24), **water** (sense 12). 11 **cost the earth.** *Informal* to be very expensive. 12 **come back** *or* **down to earth.** to return to reality from a fantasy or daydream. 13 **on earth.** used as an intensifier in such phrases as **what on earth, who on earth,** etc. 14 **run to earth. a** to hunt (an animal, esp a fox) to its earth and trap it there. **b** to find (someone) after searching. ◆ VERB 15 (*intr*) (of a hunted fox) to go to ground. 16 (*tr*) to connect (a circuit, device, etc.) to earth. ◆ See also **earth up.**
▷HISTORY Old English *eorthe;* related to Old Norse *jorth,* Old High German *ertha,* Gothic *airtha,* Greek *erā*

earthborn ('ɜːθˌbɔːn) ADJECTIVE *Chiefly poetic* 1 of earthly origin. 2 human; mortal.

earthbound ('ɜːθˌbaʊnd) ADJECTIVE 1 confined to the earth. 2 lacking in imagination; pedestrian or dull. 3 moving or heading towards the earth.

earth closet NOUN a type of lavatory in which earth is used to cover excreta.

earthen ('ɜːθən) ADJECTIVE (*prenominal*) 1 made of baked clay: *an earthen pot.* 2 made of earth.

earthenware ('ɜːθənˌwɛə) NOUN **a** vessels, etc., made of baked clay. **b** (*as adjective*): *an earthenware pot.*

earth-grazer NOUN an asteroid in an orbit that takes it close to the earth. Also called: **near-earth asteroid.**

earth inductor compass NOUN a compass that depends on the current induced in a coil revolving in the earth's magnetic field. Also called: **inductor compass.**

earthlight ('ɜːθˌlaɪt) NOUN another name for **earthshine.**

earthling ('ɜːθlɪŋ) NOUN (esp in poetry or science fiction) an inhabitant of the earth; human being.
▷HISTORY C16: from EARTH + LING[1]

earthly ('ɜːθlɪ) ADJECTIVE **-lier, -liest.** 1 of or characteristic of the earth as opposed to heaven; material or materialistic; worldly. 2 (*usually used with a negative*) *Informal* conceivable or possible; feasible (in such phrases as **not an earthly** (**chance**), etc.).
▸ 'earthliness NOUN

earthman ('ɜːθˌmæn) NOUN, *plural* **-men.** (esp in science fiction) an inhabitant or native of the earth.

earth mother NOUN 1 (in various mythologies) **a** a female goddess considered as the source of fertility and life. **b** the earth personified. 2 *Informal* a sensual or fecund woman.

earth mover NOUN a machine, such as a bulldozer, that is used for excavating and moving large quantities of earth.

earthnut ('ɜːθˌnʌt) NOUN 1 Also called: **pignut.** a perennial umbelliferous plant, *Conopodium majus,* of Europe and Asia, having edible dark brown tubers. 2 any of various plants having an edible root, tuber, underground pod, or similar part, such as the peanut or truffle.

earth pillar NOUN a landform consisting of a column of clay or earth capped and protected from erosion by a boulder.

earthquake ('ɜːθˌkweɪk) NOUN a sudden release of energy in the earth's crust or upper mantle, usually caused by movement along a fault plane or by volcanic activity and resulting in the generation of seismic waves which can be destructive. Related adjective: **seismic.**

earth return NOUN the return path for an electrical circuit made by connections to earth at each end.

earthrise ('ɜːθˌraɪz) NOUN the rising of the earth above the lunar horizon, as seen from a spacecraft emerging from the lunar farside.

earth science NOUN any of various sciences, such as geology, geography, and geomorphology, that are concerned with the structure, age, and other aspects of the earth.

Earthshaker (ˈɜːθˌʃeɪkə) NOUN **the.** *Classical myth* Poseidon (or Neptune) in his capacity as the bringer of earthquakes.

earthshaking (ˈɜːθˌʃeɪkɪŋ) ADJECTIVE *Informal* of enormous importance or consequence; momentous.

earthshine (ˈɜːθˌʃaɪn) *or* **earthlight** NOUN the ashen light reflected from the earth, which illuminates the new moon when it is not receiving light directly from the sun.

earthstar (ˈɜːθˌstɑː) NOUN any of various basidiomycetous saprotrophic woodland fungi of the genus *Geastrum,* whose brown onion-shaped reproductive body splits into a star shape to release the spores.

earth up VERB (*tr, adverb*) to cover (part of a plant, esp the stem) with soil in order to protect from frost, light, etc.

earthward (ˈɜːθwəd) ADJECTIVE 1 directed towards the earth. ◆ ADVERB 2 a variant of **earthwards.**

earthwards (ˈɜːθwədz) *or* **earthward** ADVERB towards the earth.

earth wax NOUN another name for **ozocerite.**

earthwork (ˈɜːθˌwɜːk) NOUN 1 excavation of earth, as in engineering construction. 2 a fortification made of earth.

earthworm (ˈɜːθˌwɜːm) NOUN any of numerous oligochaete worms of the genera *Lumbricus, Allolobophora, Eisenia,* etc., which burrow in the soil and help aerate and break up the ground. Related adjective: **lumbricoid.**

earthy (ˈɜːθɪ) ADJECTIVE **earthier, earthiest.** 1 of, composed of, or characteristic of earth. 2 robust, lusty, or uninhibited. 3 unrefined, coarse, or crude. 4 an archaic word for **worldly** (sense 1). 5 *Electrical engineering* on the earthed side of an electrical circuit, but not necessarily with a direct current connection to earth.
▸ ˈ**earthily** ADVERB ▸ ˈ**earthiness** NOUN

ear trumpet NOUN a trumpet-shaped instrument that amplifies sounds and is held to the ear: an old form of hearing aid.

earwax (ˈɪəˌwæks) NOUN the nontechnical name for **cerumen.**

earwig (ˈɪəˌwɪɡ) NOUN 1 any of various insects of the order *Dermaptera,* esp *Forficula auricularia* (**common European earwig**), which typically have an elongated body with small leathery forewings, semicircular membranous hindwings, and curved forceps at the tip of the abdomen. ◆ VERB **-wigs, -wigging, -wigged.** 2 *Informal* to eavesdrop. 3 (*tr*) *Archaic* to attempt to influence (a person) by private insinuation.
▷ **HISTORY** Old English *ēarwicga,* from *ēare* EAR[1] + *wicga* beetle, insect; probably from a superstition that the insect crept into human ears

earwigging (ˈɪəˌwɪɡɪŋ) NOUN *Informal* a scolding or harangue: *I'll give him an earwigging about that.*

earworm (ˈɪəˌwɜːm) NOUN *Informal* an irritatingly catchy tune.
▷ **HISTORY** C20: from German *Ohrwurm* earwig

EAS *Aeronautics* ABBREVIATION FOR **equivalent air speed.**

ease (iːz) NOUN 1 freedom from discomfort, worry, or anxiety. 2 lack of difficulty, labour, or awkwardness; facility. 3 rest, leisure, or relaxation. 4 freedom from poverty or financial embarrassment; affluence: *a life of ease.* 5 lack of restraint, embarrassment, or stiffness: *his ease of manner disarmed us.* 6 *Military* **at ease. a** (of a standing soldier, etc.) in a relaxed position with the feet apart and hands linked behind the back. **b** a command to adopt such a position. **c** in a relaxed attitude or frame of mind. ◆ VERB 7 to make or become less burdensome. 8 (*tr*) to relieve (a person) of worry or care; comfort. 9 (*tr*) to make comfortable or give rest to. 10 (*tr*) to make less difficult; facilitate. 11 to move or cause to move into, out of, etc., with careful manipulation: *to ease a car into a narrow space.* 12 (when *intr,* often foll by *off* or *up*) to lessen or cause to lessen in severity, pressure, tension, or strain; slacken, loosen, or abate. 13 **ease oneself** *or* **ease nature.** *Archaic, euphemistic* to urinate or defecate. 14 **ease the helm.** *Nautical* to relieve the pressure on the rudder of a vessel, esp by bringing the bow into the wind.
▷ **HISTORY** C13: from Old French *aise* ease, opportunity, from Latin *adjacēns* neighbouring (area); see ADJACENT
▸ ˈ**easer** NOUN

easeful (ˈiːzfʊl) ADJECTIVE characterized by or bringing ease; peaceful; tranquil.
▸ ˈ**easefully** ADVERB ▸ ˈ**easefulness** NOUN

easel (ˈiːzəl) NOUN a frame, usually in the form of an upright tripod, used for supporting or displaying an artist's canvas, blackboard, etc.
▷ **HISTORY** C17: from Dutch *ezel* ASS[1]; related to Gothic *asilus,* German *Esel,* Latin *asinus* ass

easement (ˈiːzmənt) NOUN 1 *Property law* the right enjoyed by a landowner of making limited use of his neighbour's land, as by crossing it to reach his own property. 2 the act of easing or something that brings ease.

easily (ˈiːzɪlɪ) ADVERB 1 with ease; without difficulty or exertion. 2 by far; beyond question; undoubtedly: *he is easily the best in the contest.* 3 probably; almost certainly: *he may easily come first.*

Language note See at **easy.**

easiness (ˈiːzɪnɪs) NOUN 1 the quality or condition of being easy to accomplish, do, obtain, etc. 2 ease or relaxation of manner; nonchalance.

east (iːst) NOUN 1 one of the four cardinal points of the compass, 90° clockwise from north and 180° from west. 2 the direction along a parallel towards the sunrise, at 90° to north; the direction of the earth's rotation. 3 **the east.** (*often capital*) any area lying in or towards the east. Related adjective: **oriental.** 4 *Cards* (*usually capital*) the player or position at the table corresponding to east on the compass. ◆ ADJECTIVE 5 situated in, moving towards, or facing the east. 6 (esp of the wind) from the east. ◆ ADVERB 7 in, to, or towards the east. 8 *Archaic* (of the wind) from the east. ◆ Symbol: E.
▷ **HISTORY** Old English *ēast;* related to Old High German *ōstar* to the east, Old Norse *austr,* Latin *aurora* dawn, Greek *eōs,* Sanskrit *usās* dawn, morning

East (iːst) NOUN **the.** 1 the continent of Asia regarded as culturally distinct from Europe and the West; the Orient. 2 the countries under Communist rule and formerly under Communist rule, lying mainly in the E hemisphere. Compare **West**[1] (sense 2). 3 (in the US) **a** the area north of the Ohio and east of the Mississippi. **b** the area north of Maryland and east of the Alleghenies. ◆ ADJECTIVE 4 **a** of or denoting the eastern part of a specified country, area, etc. **b** (*as part of a name*): *East Sussex.*
▸ ˈ**Eastern** ADJECTIVE

East Africa NOUN a region of Africa comprising Kenya, Uganda, and Tanzania.

East African ADJECTIVE 1 of or relating to East Africa or its inhabitants. ◆ NOUN 2 a native or inhabitant of East Africa.

East African Community NOUN an association established in 1967 by Kenya, Uganda, and Tanzania to promote closer economic and social ties between member states: dissolved in 1977.

East Anglia NOUN 1 a region of E England south of the Wash: consists of Norfolk and Suffolk, and parts of Essex and Cambridgeshire. 2 an Anglo-Saxon kingdom that consisted of Norfolk and Suffolk in the 6th century A.D.; became a dependency of Mercia in the 8th century.

East Anglian ADJECTIVE 1 of or relating to East Anglia or its inhabitants. ◆ NOUN 2 a native or inhabitant of East Anglia.

East Ayrshire NOUN a council area of SW Scotland, comprising the E part of the historical county of Ayrshire: part of Strathclyde region from 1975 to 1996: chiefly agricultural. Administrative centre: Kilmarnock. Pop.: 120 235 (2001). Area: 1252 sq. km (483 sq. miles).

East Bengal NOUN the part of the former Indian province of Bengal assigned to Pakistan in 1947 (now Bangladesh).

East Bengali ADJECTIVE 1 of or relating to East Bengal (now Bangladesh) or its inhabitants. ◆ NOUN 2 a native or inhabitant of East Bengal.

East Berlin NOUN (formerly) the part of Berlin under East German control.

East Berliner NOUN a native or inhabitant of the former East Berlin.

eastbound (ˈiːstˌbaʊnd) ADJECTIVE going or leading towards the east.

Eastbourne (ˈiːstˌbɔːn) NOUN a resort in SE England, in East Sussex on the English Channel. Pop.: 83 200 (1991 est.).

east by north NOUN 1 one point on the compass north of east, 78° 45′ clockwise from north. ◆ ADJECTIVE, ADVERB 2 in, from, or towards this direction.

east by south NOUN 1 one point on the compass south of east, 101° 15′ clockwise from north. ◆ ADJECTIVE, ADVERB 2 in, from, or towards this direction.

East Cape NOUN 1 the easternmost point of New Guinea, on Milne Bay. 2 the easternmost point of New Zealand, on North Island. 3 the former name for Cape **Dezhnev.**

East China Sea NOUN part of the N Pacific, between the E coast of China and the Ryukyu Islands.

east coast fever NOUN a disease of cattle, endemic in east and central Africa, caused by a parasite, *Theileria parva,* that is carried by ticks.

East Dunbartonshire NOUN a council area of central Scotland to the N of Glasgow: part of Strathclyde region from 1975 until 1996: mainly agricultural and residential. Administrative centre: Kirkintilloch. Pop.: 108 243 (2001). Area: 172 sq. km (66 sq. miles).

East End NOUN **the.** a densely populated part of E London containing former industrial and dock areas.

East Ender NOUN a native or inhabitant of the East End of London.

Easter (ˈiːstə) NOUN 1 the most important festival of the Christian Church, commemorating the Resurrection of Christ: falls on the Sunday following the first full moon after the vernal equinox. 2 Also called: **Easter Sunday, Easter Day.** the day on which this festival is celebrated. 3 the period between Good Friday and Easter Monday. Related adjective: **Paschal.**
▷ **HISTORY** Old English *ēastre,* after a Germanic goddess *Eostre;* related to Old High German *ōstarūn* Easter, Old Norse *austr* to the EAST, Old Slavonic *ustru* like summer

Easter cactus NOUN a Brazilian cactus, *Rhipsalidopsis gaertneri,* widely cultivated as an ornamental for its showy red flowers.

Easter egg NOUN 1 an egg given to children at Easter, usually a chocolate egg or a hen's egg with its shell painted. 2 a bonus or extra feature hidden inside a website, computer game, or DVD, that is only revealed after repeated or lengthy viewing or playing.

Easter Island NOUN an isolated volcanic island in the Pacific, 3700 km (2300 miles) west of Chile, of which it is a dependency: discovered on Easter Sunday, 1722; annexed by Chile in 1888; noted for the remains of an aboriginal culture, which includes gigantic stone figures. Pop.: 2000 (latest est.). Area: 166 sq. km (64 sq. miles). Also called: **Rapa Nui.**

Easter Islander NOUN a native or inhabitant of Easter Island.

Easter-ledges NOUN 1 (*functioning as singular*) another name for **bistort** (sense 1). 2 *Northern English dialect* a pudding made from the young leaves of the bistort.

Easter lily NOUN any of various lilies, esp *Lilium longiflorum,* that have large showy white flowers.

easterly (ˈiːstəlɪ) ADJECTIVE 1 of, relating to, or situated in the east. ◆ ADVERB, ADJECTIVE 2 towards or in the direction of the east. 3 from the east: *an easterly wind.* ◆ NOUN, *plural* **-lies.** 4 a wind from the east.

eastern (ˈiːstən) ADJECTIVE 1 situated in or towards the east. 2 facing or moving towards the east.

Eastern Cape NOUN a province of S South Africa; formed in 1994 from the E part of the former Cape Province: service industries, agriculture, and mining. Capital: Bisho. Pop.: 6 658 670 (1999 est.). Area: 169 600 sq. km (65 483 sq. miles). Also called: **Eastern Province.**

Eastern Church NOUN [1] any of the Christian Churches of the former Byzantine Empire. [2] any Church owing allegiance to the Orthodox Church and in communion with the Greek patriarchal see of Constantinople. [3] any Church, including Uniat Churches, having Eastern forms of liturgy and institutions.

Easterner ('iːstənə) NOUN (*sometimes not capital*) a native or inhabitant of the east of any specified region, esp of the Orient or of the eastern states of the US.

Eastern Ghats PLURAL NOUN a mountain range in S India, parallel to the Bay of Bengal: united with the Western Ghats by the Nilgiri Hills; forms the E margin of the Deccan plateau.

eastern hemisphere NOUN (*often capitals*) [1] that half of the globe containing Europe, Asia, Africa, and Australia, lying east of the Greenwich meridian. [2] the lands in this, esp Asia.

easternmost ('iːstənˌməʊst) ADJECTIVE situated or occurring farthest east.

Eastern Orthodox Church NOUN another name for the **Orthodox Church.**

Eastern Province NOUN another name for **Eastern Cape.**

Eastern rite NOUN the rite and liturgy of an Eastern Church or of a Uniat Church.

Eastern Roman Empire NOUN the eastern of the two empires created by the division of the Roman Empire in 395 A.D. See also **Byzantine Empire.**

Eastern Standard Time [1] NOUN one of the standard times used in North America, five hours behind Greenwich Mean Time. [2] one of the standard times used in Australia. ◆ Abbreviation: **EST.**

Eastern Townships NOUN an area of central Canada, in S Quebec: consists of 11 townships south of the St Lawrence.

Eastern tradition NOUN any of the philosophies and teachings that derive from Hinduism, Buddhism, Taoism, and other spiritual traditions of the East.

Easter Rising NOUN an armed insurrection in Dublin in 1916 against British rule in Ireland: the insurgents proclaimed the establishment of an independent Irish republic before surrendering, sixteen of the leaders later being executed.

Easter term NOUN the term at the Inns of Court following the Hilary term.

Eastertide ('iːstəˌtaɪd) NOUN the Easter season.

East Flanders NOUN a province of W Belgium: low-lying, with reclaimed land in the northeast: textile industries. Capital: Ghent. Pop.: 1 361 623 (2000 est.). Area: 2979 sq. km (1150 sq. miles).

East German ADJECTIVE [1] of or relating to the former republic of East Germany or its inhabitants. ◆ NOUN [2] a native or inhabitant of the former East Germany.

East Germanic NOUN a subbranch of the Germanic languages: now extinct. The only member of which records survive is Gothic.

East Germany NOUN a former republic in N central Europe: established in 1949 and declared a sovereign state by the Soviet Union in 1954; Communist regime replaced by a multiparty democracy in 1989; reunited with West Germany in 1990. Official name: **German Democratic Republic.** Abbreviations: **DDR, GDR.** See also **Germany.**

East India Company NOUN [1] the company chartered in 1600 by the British government to trade in the East Indies: after being driven out by the Dutch it developed trade with India until the Indian Mutiny (1857), when the Crown took over the administration: the company was dissolved in 1874. [2] any similar trading company, such as any of those founded by the Dutch, French, and Danes in the 17th and 18th centuries.

East Indian NOUN [1] *Caribbean* an immigrant to the countries of the Caribbean (West Indies) who is of Indian origin; an Asian West Indian. ◆ ADJECTIVE [2] *US and Canadian* of, relating to, or originating in the East Indies.

East Indies PLURAL NOUN **the.** [1] the Malay Archipelago, including or excluding the Philippines. [2] SE Asia in general.

easting ('iːstɪŋ) NOUN [1] *Nautical* the net distance eastwards made by a vessel moving towards the east. [2] *Cartography* **a** the distance eastwards of a point from a given meridian indicated by the first half of a map grid reference. **b** a longitudinal grid line. Compare **northing** (sense 3).

East Kilbride (kɪl'braɪd) NOUN a town in W Scotland, in South Lanarkshire near Glasgow: designated a new town in 1947. Pop.: 70 422 (1991).

Eastleigh ('iːstˌliː) NOUN a town in S England, in S Hampshire: railway engineering industry. Pop.: 49 934 (1991).

East London NOUN a port in S South Africa, in S Eastern Cape province. Pop.: 102 325 (1991).

East Lothian NOUN a council area and historical county of E central Scotland, on the Firth of Forth and the North Sea: part of Lothian region from 1975 to 1996: chiefly agricultural. Administrative centre: Haddington. Pop.: 90 088 (2001). Area: 678 sq. km (262 sq. miles).

east-northeast NOUN [1] the point on the compass or the direction midway between northeast and east, 67° 30′ clockwise from north. ◆ ADJECTIVE, ADVERB [2] in, from, or towards this direction. ◆ Symbol: ENE.

East Pakistan NOUN the former name (until 1971) of **Bangladesh.**

East Pakistani ADJECTIVE [1] of or relating to East Pakistan (now Bangladesh) or its inhabitants. ◆ NOUN [2] a native or inhabitant of the former East Pakistan.

East Prussia NOUN a former province of NE Germany on the Baltic Sea: separated in 1919 from the rest of Germany by the Polish Corridor and Danzig: in 1945 Poland received the south part, the Soviet Union the north. German name: **Ostpreussen** (ost'prɔysən).

East Prussian ADJECTIVE [1] of or relating to the former German province of East Prussia or its inhabitants. ◆ NOUN [2] a native or inhabitant of the former East Prussia.

East Renfrewshire NOUN a council area of W central Scotland, comprising part of the historical county of Renfrewshire; part of Strathclyde region from 1975 to 1996: chiefly agricultural and residential. Administrative centre: Giffnock. Pop.: 89 311 (2001). Area: 173 sq. km (67 sq. miles).

East Riding of Yorkshire NOUN a county of NE England, a historical division of Yorkshire on the North Sea and the Humber estuary: became part of Humberside in 1974; reinstated as an independent unitary authority in 1996, with a separate authority for Kingston upon Hull: chiefly agricultural and low-lying, with various industries in Hull. Administrative centre: Beverley. Pop. (excluding Hull): 314 076 (2001). Area (excluding Hull): 748 sq. km (675 sq. miles).

east-southeast NOUN [1] the point on the compass or the direction midway between east and southeast, 112° 30′ clockwise from north. ◆ ADJECTIVE, ADVERB [2] in, from, or towards this direction. ◆ Symbol: ESE.

East Sussex NOUN a county of SE England comprising part of the former county of Sussex: mainly undulating agricultural land, with the South Downs and seaside resorts in the south: Brighton and Hove became an independent unitary authority in 1997 but is part of the geographical and ceremonial county. Administrative centre: Lewes. Pop. (excluding Brighton and Hove): 492 324 (2001). Area (excluding Brighton and Hove): 1795 sq. km (693 sq. miles).

East Timor NOUN a small country in SE Asia, comprising part of the island of Timor: colonized by Portugal in the 19th century; declared independence in 1975 but immediately invaded by Indonesia; under UN administration from 1999 and an independent state from 2002. It is mountainous with a monsoon climate; subsistence agriculture is the main occupation. Languages: Portuguese, Tetun (a lingua franca), and Bahasa Indonesia. Religion: Roman Catholic majority. Currency: US dollar. Capital: Dilli. Pop.: 750 000 (2002 est.). Area: 14 874 sq. km (5743 sq. miles).

East Timorese ADJECTIVE [1] of or relating to East Timor or its inhabitants. ◆ NOUN [2] a native or inhabitant of East Timor.

eastward ('iːstwəd) ADJECTIVE [1] situated or directed towards the east. ◆ ADVERB [2] a variant of **eastwards.** ◆ NOUN [3] the eastward part, direction, etc.

▸ **'eastwardly** ADVERB, ADJECTIVE

eastwards *or* **eastward** ('iːstwədz) ADVERB towards the east.

easy ('iːzɪ) ADJECTIVE **easier, easiest.** [1] not requiring much labour or effort; not difficult; simple: *an easy job.* [2] free from pain, care, or anxiety: *easy in one's mind.* [3] not harsh or restricting; lenient: *easy laws.* [4] tolerant and undemanding; easy-going: *an easy disposition.* [5] readily influenced or persuaded; pliant: *she was an easy victim of his wiles.* [6] not tight or constricting; loose: *an easy fit.* [7] not strained or extreme; moderate; gentle: *an easy pace; an easy ascent.* [8] *Economics* **a** readily obtainable. **b** (of a market) characterized by low demand or excess supply with prices tending to fall. Compare **tight** (sense 10). [9] *Informal* ready to fall in with any suggestion made; not predisposed: *he is easy about what to do.* [10] *Slang* sexually available. [11] **easy on the eye.** *Informal* pleasant to look at; attractive, esp sexually. [12] **woman of easy virtue.** a sexually available woman, esp a prostitute. ◆ ADVERB [13] *Informal* in an easy or relaxed manner. [14] *Informal* **easy does it.** go slowly and carefully; be careful. [15] **go easy on. a** to use in moderation. **b** to treat leniently. [16] **stand easy.** *Military* a command to soldiers standing at ease that they may relax further. [17] **take it easy. a** to avoid stress or undue hurry. **b** to remain calm; not become agitated or angry. ◆ VERB **easies, easying, easied.** [18] (*usually imperative*) Also: **easy-oar.** to stop rowing.

▹ **HISTORY** C12: from Old French *aisié,* past participle of *aisier* to relieve, EASE

> **Language note** *Easy* is not used as an adverb by careful speakers and writers except in certain set phrases: *to take it easy; easy does it.* Where a fixed expression is not involved, the usual adverbial form of *easily* is preferred: *this polish goes on more easily* (not *easier*) *than the other.*

easy-care ADJECTIVE (esp of a fabric or garment) hardwearing, practical, and requiring no special treatment during washing, cleaning, etc.

easy chair NOUN a comfortable upholstered armchair.

easy game *or* **easy mark** NOUN *Informal* a person who is easily deceived or taken advantage of.

easy-going ('iːzɪ'gəʊɪŋ) ADJECTIVE [1] relaxed in manner or attitude; inclined to be excessively tolerant. [2] moving at a comfortable pace: *an easy-going horse.*

easy meat NOUN *Informal* [1] someone easily seduced or deceived. [2] something easy to get or do.

easy money NOUN [1] money made with little effort, sometimes dishonestly. [2] *Commerce* money that can be borrowed at a low interest rate.

Easy Street NOUN (*sometimes not capitals*) *Informal* a state of financial security.

eat (iːt) VERB **eats, eating, ate, eaten.** [1] to take into the mouth and swallow (food, etc.), esp after biting and chewing. [2] (*tr; often foll by* away *or* up) to destroy as if by eating: *the damp had eaten away the woodwork.* [3] (often foll by *into*) to use up or waste: *taxes ate into his inheritance.* [4] (often foll by *into* or *through*) to make (a hole, passage, etc.) by eating or gnawing: *rats ate through the floor.* [5] to take or have (a meal or meals): *we always eat at six.* [6] (*tr*) to include as part of one's diet: *he doesn't eat fish.* [7] (*tr*) *Informal* to cause to worry; make anxious: *what's eating you?* [8] (*tr*) *Slang* to perform cunnilingus or fellatio upon. [9] **I'll eat my hat if.** *Informal* to be greatly surprised if (something happens that proves one wrong). [10] **eat one's heart out.** to brood or pine with grief or longing. [11] **eat one's words.** to take back something said; recant; retract. [12] **eat out of (someone's) hand.** to be entirely obedient to (someone). [13] **eat (someone) out of house and home.** to

ruin (someone, esp one's parent or one's host) by consuming all his food. See also **eat out, eats, eat up.**
▷HISTORY Old English *etan;* related to Gothic *itan,* Old High German *ezzan,* Latin *edere,* Greek *edein,* Sanskrit *admi*
▸ **'eater** NOUN

EAT *or* **EAZ** INTERNATIONAL CAR REGISTRATION FOR Tanzania.
▷HISTORY from E(ast) A(frica) T(anganyika) or E(ast) A(frica) Z(anzibar)

eatable ('i:təbəl) ADJECTIVE fit or suitable for eating; edible.

eatables ('i:təbəlz) PLURAL NOUN (*sometimes singular*) food.

eatage ('i:tɪdʒ) NOUN *Northern English dialect* grazing rights.

eaten ('i:tən) VERB the past participle of **eat.**

eatery ('i:tərɪ) *or* **eaterie** NOUN, *plural* **-eries** (-ərɪz). *Informal* a restaurant or eating house.

eating ('i:tɪŋ) NOUN [1] food, esp in relation to its quality or taste: *this fruit makes excellent eating.* ♦ ADJECTIVE [2] relating to or suitable for eating, esp uncooked: *eating pears.* [3] relating to or for eating: *an eating house.*

eat out VERB (*intr, adverb*) to eat away from home, esp in a restaurant.

eats (i:ts) PLURAL NOUN *Informal* articles of food; provisions.

eat up VERB (*adverb, mainly tr*) [1] (*also intr*) to eat or consume entirely: often used as an exhortation to children. [2] *Informal* to listen to with enthusiasm or appreciation: *the audience ate up the speaker's every word.* [3] (*often passive*) *Informal* to affect grossly: *she was eaten up by jealousy.* [4] *Informal* to travel (a distance) quickly: *we just ate up the miles.*

EAU INTERNATIONAL CAR REGISTRATION FOR (East Africa) Uganda.

eau de Cologne (əʊ də kə'ləʊn) NOUN See **cologne.**
▷HISTORY French, literally: water of Cologne

eau de Javelle (əʊ də ʒæ'vɛl, ʒə-; *French* od ʒavɛl) NOUN another name for **Javel water.**

eau de nil (əʊ də ni:l) NOUN, ADJECTIVE **a** a pale yellowish-green colour. **b** (*as adjective*): *eau-de-nil walls.*
▷HISTORY French, literally: water of (the) Nile

eau de vie (əʊ də vi:; *French* od vi) NOUN brandy or other spirits.
▷HISTORY French, literally: water of life

eaves (i:vz) PLURAL NOUN the edge of a roof that projects beyond the wall.
▷HISTORY Old English *efes;* related to Gothic *ubizwa* porch, Greek *hupsos* height

eavesdrop ('i:vz,drɒp) VERB **-drops, -dropping, -dropped.** (*intr*) to listen secretly to the private conversation of others.
▷HISTORY C17: back formation from earlier *evesdropper,* from Old English *yfesdrype* water dripping from the eaves; see EAVES, DROP; compare Old Norse *upsardropi*
▸ **'eaves,dropper** NOUN

ebb (ɛb) VERB (*intr*) [1] (of tide water) to flow back or recede. Compare **flow** (sense 9). [2] to fall away or decline. ♦ NOUN [3] **a** the flowing back of the tide from high to low water or the period in which this takes place. **b** (*as modifier*): *the ebb tide.* Compare **flood** (sense 3). [4] **at a low ebb.** in a state or period of weakness, lack of vigour, or decline.
▷HISTORY Old English *ebba;* related to Old Norse *efja* river bend, Gothic *ibuks* moving backwards, Old High German *ippihōn* to roll backwards, Middle Dutch *ebbe* ebb

Ebbw Vale ('ɛbu: veɪl) NOUN a town in S Wales, in Blaenau Gwent county borough: a former coal mining centre. Pop.: 19 484 (1991).

EBCDIC ('ɛbsɪ,dɪk) NOUN ACRONYM FOR extended binary-coded decimal-interchange code: a computer code for representing alphanumeric characters.

EBITDA ABBREVIATION FOR earnings before interest, tax, depreciation, and amortization.

Eblis ('ɛblɪs) NOUN the chief evil jinni in Islamic mythology.
▷HISTORY Arabic *Iblīs,* from Greek *diabolos* slanderer, DEVIL

E-boat NOUN (in World War II) a fast German boat carrying guns and torpedoes.
▷HISTORY C20: from *enemy* boat

Ebola virus disease (i:'bəʊlə) NOUN a severe infectious disease characterized by fever, vomiting, and internal bleeding. Compare **Marburg disease.**
▷HISTORY C20: named after the *Ebola* river, N Democratic Republic of Congo (formerly Zaïre), where an outbreak occurred in 1976

ebon ('ɛbən) NOUN, ADJECTIVE a poetic word for **ebony.**
▷HISTORY C14: from Latin *hebenus;* see EBONY

ebonite ('ɛbə,naɪt) NOUN another name for **vulcanite.**

ebonize *or* **ebonise** ('ɛbə,naɪz) VERB (*tr*) to stain or otherwise finish in imitation of ebony.

ebony ('ɛbənɪ) NOUN, *plural* **-onies.** [1] any of various tropical and subtropical trees of the genus *Diospyros,* esp *D. ebenum* of S India, that have hard dark wood: family *Ebenaceae.* See also **persimmon.** [2] the wood of such a tree, much used for cabinetwork. [3] **a** a black colour, sometimes with a dark olive tinge. **b** (*as adjective*): *an ebony skin.*
▷HISTORY C16 *hebeny,* from Late Latin *ebeninus* from Greek *ebeninos,* from *ebenos* ebony, of Egyptian origin

e-book NOUN a book in electronic form.
▷HISTORY C20: *e*lectronic *book*

Ebor. ('i:bɔ:) ABBREVIATION FOR Eboracensis.
▷HISTORY Latin: (Archbishop) of York

Eboracum (i:'bɒrəkəm, ,i:bɔ:'rɑ:kəm) NOUN the Roman name for **York** (sense 1).

ebracteate (ɪ'bræktɪ,eɪt, -tɪɪt) ADJECTIVE (of plants) having no bracts.
▷HISTORY C19: from New Latin *ebracteātus;* see E-[1], BRACTEATE

EBRD ABBREVIATION FOR European Bank for Reconstruction and Development.

Ebro ('i:brəʊ; *Spanish* 'eβro) NOUN the second largest river in Spain, rising in the Cantabrian Mountains and flowing southeast to the Mediterranean. Length: 910 km (565 miles).

EBS ABBREVIATION FOR electronic braking system.

EBU ABBREVIATION FOR European Broadcasting Union.

ebullient (ɪ'bʌljənt, ɪ'bʊl-) ADJECTIVE [1] overflowing with enthusiasm or excitement; exuberant. [2] boiling.
▷HISTORY C16: from Latin *ēbullīre* to bubble forth, be boisterous, from *bullīre* to BOIL[1]
▸ **e'bullience** *or* **e'bulliency** NOUN ▸ **e'bulliently** ADVERB

ebulliometer (ɪ,bʌlɪ'ɒmɪtə) NOUN *Physics* a device used to determine the boiling point of a solution.
▸ **e,bulli'ometry** NOUN

ebullioscopy (ɪ,bʌlɪ'ɒskəpɪ, ɪ,bʊl-) NOUN *Chem* a technique for finding molecular weights of substances by measuring the extent to which they change the boiling point of a solvent.
▷HISTORY C19: from *ebullioscope,* from Latin *ebullire* to boil over + -SCOPE
▸ **ebullioscopic** (ɪ,bʌlɪə'skɒpɪk, ɪ,bʊl-) ADJECTIVE
▸ **e,bullio'scopically** ADVERB

ebullition (,ɛbə'lɪʃən) NOUN [1] the process of boiling. [2] a sudden outburst, as of intense emotion.
▷HISTORY C16: from Late Latin *ēbullītiō;* see EBULLIENT

eburnation (,i:bə'neɪʃən, ,ɛb-) NOUN a degenerative condition of bone or cartilage characterized by unusual hardness and a polished appearance.
▷HISTORY C19: from Latin *eburnus* of ivory, from *ebur* ivory

EBV ABBREVIATION FOR **Epstein-Barr virus.**

ec THE INTERNET DOMAIN NAME FOR Ecuador.

EC ABBREVIATION FOR: [1] European Community (now subsumed within the European Union). [2] (in London postal code) East Central. ♦ [3] INTERNATIONAL CAR REGISTRATION FOR Ecuador.

ec- COMBINING FORM out from; away from: *ecbolic; eccentric; ecdysis.*
▷HISTORY from Greek *ek* (before a vowel *ex*) out of, away from; see EX-[1]

ecad ('i:kæd) NOUN an organism whose form has been affected by its environment.
▷HISTORY C20: from EC(OLOGY) + -AD[1]

e-car NOUN a car powered by electricity.
▷HISTORY C20: *e*lectric *car*

ecarinate (i:'kærɪnɪt) ADJECTIVE *Biology* having no carina or keel.
▷HISTORY E-[1] + CARINATE

écarté (eɪ'kɑ:teɪ; *French* ekarte) NOUN [1] a card game for two, played with 32 cards and king high. [2] *Ballet* **a** a body position in which one arm and the same leg are extended at the side of the body. **b** (*as adjective*): *the écarté position.*
▷HISTORY C19: from French, from *écarter* to discard, from *carte* CARD[1]

ECB ABBREVIATION FOR **European Central Bank.**

Ecbatana (ɛk'bætənə) NOUN an ancient city in Iran, on the site of modern Hamadān; capital of Media and royal residence of the Persians and Parthians.

ecbolic (ɛk'bɒlɪk) ADJECTIVE [1] hastening labour or abortion. ♦ NOUN [2] a drug or agent that hastens labour or abortion.
▷HISTORY C18: from Greek *ekbolē* a throwing out, from *ekballein* to throw out, from *ballein* to throw

Ecce Homo ('ɛkeɪ 'həʊməʊ, 'ɛksɪ) NOUN a picture or sculpture of Christ crowned with thorns.
▷HISTORY Latin: behold the man, the words of Pontius Pilate to his accusers (John 19:5)

eccentric (ɪk'sɛntrɪk) ADJECTIVE [1] deviating or departing from convention, esp in a bizarre manner; irregular or odd. [2] situated away from the centre or the axis. [3] not having a common centre: *eccentric circles.* Compare **concentric.** [4] not precisely circular. ♦ NOUN [5] a person who deviates from normal forms of behaviour esp in a bizarre manner. [6] a device for converting rotary motion to reciprocating motion.
▷HISTORY C16: from Medieval Latin *eccentricus,* from Greek *ekkentros* out of centre, from *ek-* EX-[1] + *kentron* centre
▸ **ec'centrically** ADVERB

eccentricity (,ɛksɛn'trɪsɪtɪ) NOUN, *plural* **-ties.** [1] unconventional or irregular behaviour. [2] deviation from a circular path or orbit. [3] a measure of the noncircularity of an elliptical orbit, the distance between the foci divided by the length of the major axis. [4] *Geometry* a number that expresses the shape of a conic section: the ratio of the distance of a point on the curve from a fixed point (the focus) to the distance of the point from a fixed line (the directrix). [5] the degree of displacement of the geometric centre of a rotating part from the true centre, esp of the axis of rotation of a wheel or shaft.

ecchymosis (,ɛkɪ'məʊsɪs) NOUN, *plural* **-ses** (-si:z). discoloration of the skin through bruising.
▷HISTORY C16: from New Latin, from Greek *ekkhumōsis,* from *ekkhumousthai* to pour out, from *khumos* juice
▸ **ecchymosed** ('ɛkɪ,məʊzd, -,məʊst) *or* **ecchymotic** (,ɛkɪ'mɒtɪk) ADJECTIVE

eccl. *or* **eccles.** ABBREVIATION FOR ecclesiastic(al).

Eccles ('ɛkəlz) NOUN a town in NW England, in Salford unitary authority, Greater Manchester. Pop.: 36 000 (1991).

Eccles. *or* **Eccl.** *Bible* ABBREVIATION FOR Ecclesiastes.

Eccles cake NOUN *Brit* a pastry with a filling of dried fruit.

ecclesia (ɪ'kli:zɪə) NOUN, *plural* **-siae** (-zɪ,i:). [1] (in formal Church usage) a congregation. [2] the assembly of citizens of an ancient Greek state.
▷HISTORY C16: from Medieval Latin, from Late Greek *ekklēsia* assembly, from *ekklētos* called, from *ekkalein* to call out, from *kalein* to call

Ecclesiastes (ɪ,kli:zɪ'æsti:z) NOUN (*functioning as singular*) a book of the Old Testament, probably written about 250 B.C.
▷HISTORY via Late Latin, from Greek *ekklēsiastēs* member of the assembly; see ECCLESIA

ecclesiastic (ɪ,kli:zɪ'æstɪk) NOUN [1] a clergyman or other person in holy orders. ♦ ADJECTIVE [2] of or associated with the Christian Church or clergy.

ecclesiastical (ɪ,kli:zɪ'æstɪkəl) ADJECTIVE of or relating to the Christian Church.
▸ **ec,clesi'astically** ADVERB

Ecclesiastical Commissioners PLURAL NOUN the administrators of the properties of the Church of England from 1836 to 1948, when they were combined with Queen Anne's Bounty to form the Church Commissioners.

ecclesiasticism (ɪˌkliːzɪˈæstɪˌsɪzəm) NOUN exaggerated attachment to the practices or principles of the Christian Church.

Ecclesiasticus (ɪˌkliːzɪˈæstɪkəs) NOUN one of the books of the Apocrypha, written around 180 B.C. and also called **the Wisdom of Jesus, the son of Sirach**.

ecclesiolatry (ɪˌkliːzɪˈɒlətrɪ) NOUN obsessional devotion to ecclesiastical traditions.
▸**ecˌclesiˈolater** NOUN

ecclesiology (ɪˌkliːzɪˈɒlədʒɪ) NOUN [1] the study of the Christian Church. [2] the study of Church architecture and decoration.
▸**ecclesiological** (ɪˌkliːzɪəˈlɒdʒɪkᵊl) ADJECTIVE
▸**ecˌclesioˈlogically** ADVERB ▸**ecˌclesiˈologist** NOUN

Ecclus. *Bible* ABBREVIATION FOR Ecclesiasticus.

eccremocarpus (ˌɛkrəməˈkɑːpəs) NOUN any plant of the evergreen climbing genus *Eccremocarpus,* esp *E. scaber,* grown for its decorative pinnate foliage and bright orange-red bell flowers: family *Bignoniaceae.*
▷**HISTORY** New Latin, from Greek *ekkremēs* suspended + *karpos* fruit

eccrine (ˈɛkrɪn) ADJECTIVE of or denoting glands that secrete externally, esp the numerous sweat glands on the human body. Compare **apocrine**.
▷**HISTORY** from Greek *ekkrinein* to secrete, from *ek-* EC- + *krinein* to separate

eccrinology (ˌɛkrɪˈnɒlədʒɪ) NOUN the branch of medical science concerned with secretions of the eccrine glands.

ecdemic (ɛkˈdɛmɪk) ADJECTIVE not indigenous or endemic; foreign: *an ecdemic disease.*

ecdysiast (ɛkˈdɪzɪˌæst) NOUN a facetious word for **stripper** (sense 1).
▷**HISTORY** C20: (coined by H. L. Mencken) from ECDYSIS + *-ast,* variant of -IST

ecdysis (ˈɛkdɪsɪs) NOUN, *plural* **-ses** (-ˌsiːz). the periodic shedding of the cuticle in insects and other arthropods or the outer epidermal layer in reptiles. See also **ecdysone**.
▷**HISTORY** C19: New Latin, from Greek *ekdusis,* from *ekduein* to strip, from *ek-* EX-[1] + *duein* to put on
▸**ecˈdysial** ADJECTIVE

ecdysone (ɛkˈdaɪˌsəʊn) NOUN a hormone secreted by the prothoracic gland of insects that controls ecdysis and stimulates metamorphosis.
▷**HISTORY** C20: from German *ecdyson,* from Greek *ekdusis;* see ECDYSIS

ecesis (ɪˈsiːsɪs) NOUN the establishment of a plant in a new environment.
▷**HISTORY** C20: from Greek *oikēsis* a dwelling in, from *oikein* to inhabit; related to *oikos* a house

ECG ABBREVIATION FOR: [1] electrocardiogram. [2] electrocardiograph.

echard (ˈɛkɑːd) NOUN water that is present in the soil but cannot be absorbed or otherwise utilized by plants.
▷**HISTORY** C20: from Greek *ekhein* to hold back + *ardein* to water

echelon (ˈɛʃəˌlɒn) NOUN [1] a level of command, responsibility, etc. (esp in the phrase **the upper echelons**). [2] *Military* **a** a formation in which units follow one another but are offset sufficiently to allow each unit a line of fire ahead. **b** a group formed in this way. [3] *Physics* a type of diffraction grating used in spectroscopy consisting of a series of plates of equal thickness arranged stepwise with a constant offset. ◆ VERB [4] to assemble in echelon.
▷**HISTORY** C18: from French *échelon,* literally: rung of a ladder, from Old French *eschiele* ladder, from Latin *scāla;* see SCALE[3]

echeveria (ˌɛtʃɪˈvɪərɪə) NOUN any of various tropical American crassulaceous plants of the genus *Echeveria,* cultivated for their colourful foliage.
▷**HISTORY** named after M. *Echeveri,* 19th-century Mexican botanical artist

echidna (ɪˈkɪdnə) NOUN, *plural* **-nas** *or* **-nae** (-niː). any of the spine-covered monotreme mammals of the genera *Tachyglossus* of Australia and *Zaglossus* of New Guinea: family *Tachyglossidae.* They have a long snout and claws for hunting ants and termites. Also called: **spiny anteater.**
▷**HISTORY** C19: from New Latin, from Latin: viper, from Greek *ekhidna*

echinacea (ˌɛkɪˈneɪʃɪə) NOUN [1] either of the two N American plants of the genus *Echinacea,* having flower heads with purple rays and black centres: family *Compositae* (composites). Also called: **purple coneflower.** See **coneflower.** [2] the powdered root of either of these plants, used to stimulate the immune system.
▷**HISTORY** from New Latin, from Latin *echīnātus* prickly, from *echīnus* hedgehog

echinate (ˈɛkɪˌneɪt) *or* **echinated** ADJECTIVE *Biology* covered with spines, bristles, or bristle-like outgrowths.

echino- *or before a vowel* **echin-** COMBINING FORM indicating spiny or prickly: *echinoderm.*
▷**HISTORY** from New Latin, via Latin from Greek *ekhinos* sea urchin, hedgehog

echinococcus (ɪˌkaɪnəˈkɒkəs) NOUN any of the tapeworms constituting the genus *Echinococcus,* the larvae of which are parasitic in man and domestic animals.

echinoderm (ɪˈkaɪnəʊˌdɜːm) NOUN any of the marine invertebrate animals constituting the phylum *Echinodermata,* characterized by tube feet, a calcite body-covering (test), and a five-part symmetrical body. The group includes the starfish, sea urchins, and sea cucumbers.
▸**eˌchinoˈdermal** *or* **eˌchinoˈdermatous** ADJECTIVE

echinoid (ɪˈkaɪnɔɪd, ˈɛkə-) NOUN [1] any of the echinoderms constituting the class *Echinoidea,* typically having a rigid ovoid body. The class includes the sea urchins and sand dollars. ◆ ADJECTIVE [2] of or belonging to this class.

echinus (ɪˈkaɪnəs) NOUN, *plural* **-ni** (-naɪ). [1] *Architect* an ovolo moulding between the shaft and the abacus of a Doric column. [2] any of the sea urchins of the genus *Echinus,* such as *E. esculentus* (**edible sea urchin**) of the Mediterranean.
▷**HISTORY** C14: from Latin, from Greek *ekhinos*

echium (ˈɛkɪəm) NOUN any plant of the Eurasian and African genus *Echium* with bell-shaped flowers sometimes borne on single-sided spikes in a wide variety of colours; *E. vulgare* is viper's bugloss: family *Boraginaceae.*
▷**HISTORY** New Latin, from Greek *echion,* from *echis* viper, from its use as an antidote to a viper bite

echo (ˈɛkəʊ) NOUN, *plural* **-oes.** [1] **a** the reflection of sound or other radiation by a reflecting medium, esp a solid object. **b** the sound so reflected. [2] a repetition or imitation, esp an unoriginal reproduction of another's opinions. [3] something that evokes memories, esp of a particular style or era. [4] (*sometimes plural*) an effect that continues after the original cause has disappeared; repercussion: *the echoes of the French Revolution.* [5] a person who copies another, esp one who obsequiously agrees with another's opinions. [6] **a** the signal reflected by a radar target. **b** the trace produced by such a signal on a radar screen. [7] the repetition of certain sounds or syllables in a verse line. [8] the quiet repetition of a musical phrase. [9] Also called: **echo organ** *or* **echo stop.** a manual or stop on an organ that controls a set of quiet pipes that give the illusion of sounding at a distance. [10] an electronic effect in recorded music that adds vibration or resonance. ◆ VERB **-oes, -oing, -oed.** [11] to resound or cause to resound with an echo: *the cave echoed their shouts.* [12] (*intr*) (of sounds) to repeat or resound by echoes; reverberate. [13] (*tr*) (of persons) to repeat (words, opinions, etc.), in imitation, agreement, or flattery. [14] (*tr*) (of things) to resemble or imitate (another style, earlier model, etc.). [15] (*tr*) (of a computer) to display (a character) on the screen of a visual display unit as a response to receiving that character from a keyboard entry.
▷**HISTORY** C14: via Latin from Greek *ēkhō;* related to Greek *ēkhē* sound
▸**ˈechoing** ADJECTIVE ▸**ˈecholess** ADJECTIVE ▸**ˈecho-ˌlike** ADJECTIVE

Echo[1] (ˈɛkəʊ) NOUN either of two US passive communications satellites, the first of which was launched in 1960.

Echo[2] (ˈɛkəʊ) NOUN *Greek myth* a nymph who, spurned by Narcissus, pined away until only her voice remained.

Echo[3] (ˈɛkəʊ) NOUN *Communications* code word for the letter *e.*

echocardiography (ˌɛkəʊkɑːdɪˈɒgrəfɪ) NOUN examination of the heart using ultrasound techniques.

echo chamber NOUN a room with walls that reflect sound. It is used to make acoustic measurements and as a source of reverberant sound to be mixed with direct sound for recording or broadcasting. Also called: **reverberation chamber.**

echography (ɛˈkɒgrəfɪ) NOUN medical examination of the internal structures of the body by means of ultrasound.

echoic (ɛˈkəʊɪk) ADJECTIVE [1] characteristic of or resembling an echo. [2] onomatopoeic; imitative.

echoic memory NOUN *Psychol* the ability to recapture the exact impression of a sound shortly after the sound has finished. Compare **iconic memory.**

echoism (ˈɛkəʊˌɪzəm) NOUN [1] onomatopoeia as a source of word formation. [2] phonetic assimilation of one vowel to the vowel in the preceding syllable.

echolalia (ˌɛkəʊˈleɪlɪə) NOUN *Psychiatry* the tendency to repeat mechanically words just spoken by another person: can occur in cases of brain damage, mental retardation, and schizophrenia.
▷**HISTORY** C19: from New Latin, from ECHO + Greek *lalia* talk, chatter, from *lalein* to chatter
▸**echolalic** (ˌɛkəʊˈlælɪk) ADJECTIVE

echolocation (ˌɛkəʊləʊˈkeɪʃən) NOUN determination of the position of an object by measuring the time taken for an echo to return from it and its direction.

echo plate NOUN (in sound recording or broadcasting) an electromechanical device for producing echo and reverbation effects.

echopraxia (ˌɛkəʊˈpræksɪə) *or* **echopraxis** NOUN the involuntary imitation of the actions of others.

echo sounder NOUN a navigation and position-finding device that determines depth by measuring the time taken for a pulse of high-frequency sound to reach the sea bed or a submerged object and for the echo to return.
▸**echo sounding** NOUN

echovirus (ˈɛkəʊˌvaɪrəs) *or* **ECHO virus** NOUN any of a group of viruses that can cause symptoms of mild meningitis, the common cold, or infections of the intestinal and respiratory tracts.
▷**HISTORY** C20: from the initials of *Enteric Cytopathic Human Orphan* ("orphan" because originally believed to be unrelated to any disease) + VIRUS

echt *German* (ɛçt; *English* ɛkt) ADJECTIVE real; genuine; authentic.

éclair (eɪˈklɛə, ɪˈklɛə) NOUN a finger-shaped cake of choux pastry, usually filled with cream and covered with chocolate.
▷**HISTORY** C19: from French, literally: lightning (probably so called because it does not last long), from *éclairer,* from Latin *clārāre* to make bright, from *clārus* bright

eclampsia (ɪˈklæmpsɪə) NOUN [1] *Pathol* a toxic condition of unknown cause that sometimes develops in the last three months of pregnancy, characterized by high blood pressure, abnormal weight gain and convulsions. Compare **pre-eclampsia.** [2] another name for **milk fever** (in cattle).
▷**HISTORY** C19: from New Latin, from Greek *eklampsis* a shining forth, from *eklampein,* from *lampein* to shine
▸**ecˈlamptic** ADJECTIVE

éclat (eɪˈklɑː; *French* ekla) NOUN [1] brilliant or conspicuous success, effect, etc. [2] showy display; ostentation. [3] social distinction. [4] approval; acclaim; applause.
▷**HISTORY** C17: from French, from *éclater* to burst; related to Old French *esclater* to splinter, perhaps of Germanic origin; compare SLIT

eclectic (ɪˈklɛktɪk, ɛˈklɛk-) ADJECTIVE [1] (in art, philosophy, etc.) selecting what seems best from various styles, doctrines, ideas, methods, etc. [2] composed of elements drawn from a variety of sources, styles, etc. ◆ NOUN [3] a person who favours an eclectic approach, esp in art or philosophy.
▷**HISTORY** C17: from Greek *eklektikos,* from *eklegein* to select, from *legein* to gather
▸**ecˈlectically** ADVERB

eclecticism (ɪˈklɛktɪˌsɪzəm, ɛˈklɛk-) NOUN [1] an eclectic system or method. [2] the use or advocacy of such a system.

eclipse (ɪˈklɪps) NOUN [1] the total or partial

obscuring of one celestial body by another. A **solar eclipse** occurs when the moon passes between the sun and the earth; a **lunar eclipse** when the earth passes between the sun and the moon. See also **total eclipse, partial eclipse, annular eclipse.** Compare **occultation.** 2 the period of time during which such a phenomenon occurs. 3 any dimming or obstruction of light. 4 a loss of importance, power, fame, etc., esp through overshadowing by another. ♦ VERB (*tr*) 5 to cause an eclipse of. 6 to cast a shadow upon; darken; obscure. 7 to overshadow or surpass in importance, power, etc.
▷HISTORY C13: back formation from Old English *eclypsis,* from Latin *eclīpsis,* from Greek *ekleipsis* a forsaking, from *ekleipein* to abandon, from *leipein* to leave
▸**e'clipser** NOUN

eclipse plumage NOUN seasonal plumage that occurs in certain birds after the breeding plumage and before the winter plumage: is characterized by dull coloration.

eclipsing binary *or* **variable** NOUN a binary star whose orbital plane lies in or near the line of sight so that one component is regularly eclipsed by its companion. See also **variable star.**

eclipsis (ɪ'klɪpsɪs) NOUN *Linguistics* 1 a rare word for **ellipsis** (sense 1). 2 (in Gaelic) phonetic change of an initial consonant under the influence of a preceding word. Unvoiced plosives become voiced, while voiced plosives are changed to nasals.

ecliptic (ɪ'klɪptɪk) NOUN 1 *Astronomy* **a** the great circle on the celestial sphere representing the apparent annual path of the sun relative to the stars. It is inclined at 23.45° to the celestial equator. The **poles of the ecliptic** lie on the celestial sphere due north and south of the plane of the ecliptic. **b** (*as modifier*): *the ecliptic plane.* 2 an equivalent great circle, opposite points of which pass through the Tropics of Cancer and Capricorn, on the terrestrial globe. ♦ ADJECTIVE 3 of or relating to an eclipse.
▸**e'cliptically** ADVERB

ecliptic latitude NOUN *Astronomy* another name for **celestial latitude.**

ecliptic longitude NOUN *Astronomy* another name for **celestial longitude.**

eclogite ('ɛklə,dʒaɪt) NOUN a rare coarse-grained basic rock consisting principally of garnet and pyroxene. Quartz, feldspar, etc., may also be present. It is thought to originate by metamorphism or igneous crystallization at extremely high pressure.
▷HISTORY C19: from Greek *eklogē* a selection

eclogue ('ɛklɒg) NOUN a pastoral or idyllic poem, usually in the form of a conversation or soliloquy.
▷HISTORY C15: from Latin *ecloga* short poem, collection of extracts, from Greek *eklogē* selection, from *eklegein* to select; see ECLECTIC

eclosion (ɪ'kləʊʒən) NOUN the emergence of an insect larva from the egg or an adult from the pupal case.
▷HISTORY C19: from French *éclosion,* from *éclore* to hatch, ultimately from Latin *exclūdere* to shut out, EXCLUDE

eco ('i:kəʊ) NOUN **a** short for **ecology. b** (*as modifier*): *an eco group.*

eco- COMBINING FORM denoting ecology or ecological: *ecocide; ecosphere.*

ecocentric (,i:kəʊ'sentrɪk) ADJECTIVE having a serious concern for environmental issues: *ecocentric management.*

ecocide ('i:kə,saɪd, 'ɛkə-) NOUN total destruction of an area of the natural environment, esp by human agency.

ecofriendly ('i:kəʊ,frɛndlɪ) ADJECTIVE having a beneficial effect on the environment or at least not causing environmental damage.

ecol. ABBREVIATION FOR: 1 ecological. 2 ecology.

E. coli (i:'kəʊlaɪ) NOUN short for *Escherichia coli*; see ***Escherichia.***

ecological (,i:kə'lɒdʒɪkᵊl) ADJECTIVE 1 of or relating to ecology. 2 (of a practice, policy, product, etc.) tending to benefit or cause minimal damage to the environment.
▸**,eco'logically** ADVERB

ecological footprint NOUN the amount of productive land appropriated on average by each person (in the world, a country, etc.) for food, water, transport, housing, waste management, and other purposes.

ecology (ɪ'kɒlədʒɪ) NOUN 1 the study of the relationships between living organisms and their environment. 2 the set of relationships of a particular organism with its environment. 3 the study of the relationships between human groups and their physical environment. ♦ Also called (for senses 1, 2): **bionomics.**
▷HISTORY C19: from German *Ökologie,* from Greek *oikos* house (hence, environment)
▸**e'cologist** NOUN

e-commerce *or* **ecommerce** ('i:kɒmɜ:s) NOUN business transactions conducted on the Internet.
▷HISTORY C20: from E-² + COMMERCE

econ. ABBREVIATION FOR: 1 economical. 2 economics. 3 economy.

econometrics (ɪ,kɒnə'mɛtrɪks) NOUN (*functioning as singular*) the application of mathematical and statistical techniques to economic problems and theories.
▸**e,cono'metric** *or* **e,cono'metrical** ADJECTIVE
▸**econometrician** (ɪ,kɒnəmə'trɪʃən) *or* **e,cono'metrist** NOUN

economic (,i:kə'nɒmɪk, ,ɛkə-) ADJECTIVE 1 of or relating to an economy, economics, or finance: *economic development; economic theories.* 2 *Brit* capable of being produced, operated, etc., for profit; profitable: *the firm is barely economic.* 3 concerning or affecting material resources or welfare: *economic pests.* 4 concerned with or relating to the necessities of life; utilitarian. 5 a variant of **economical.** 6 *Informal* inexpensive; cheap.

economical (,i:kə'nɒmɪkᵊl, ,ɛkə-) ADJECTIVE 1 using the minimum required; not wasteful of time, effort, resources, etc.: *an economical car; an economical style.* 2 frugal; thrifty: *she was economical by nature.* 3 a variant of **economic** (senses 1–4). 4 *Euphemistic* deliberately withholding information (esp in the phrase **economical with the truth**).

economically (,i:kə'nɒmɪkəlɪ, ,ɛkə-) ADVERB 1 with economy or thrift; without waste. 2 with regard to the economy of a person, country, etc.

economic determinism NOUN a doctrine that states that all cultural, social, political, and intellectual activities are a product of the economic organization of society.

economic geography NOUN the study of the geographical distribution of economic resources and their use.

economic geology NOUN the study of how geological deposits can be used as economic resources.

economic indicator NOUN a statistical measure representing an economic variable: *the retail price index is an economic indicator of the actual level of prices.*

economic rent NOUN 1 *Economics* a payment to a factor of production (land, labour, or capital) in excess of that needed to keep it in its present use. 2 (in Britain) the rent of a dwelling based on recouping the costs of providing it plus a profit sufficient to motivate the landlord to let it.

economics (,i:kə'nɒmɪks, ,ɛkə-) NOUN 1 (*functioning as singular*) the social science concerned with the production and consumption of goods and services and the analysis of the commercial activities of a society. See also **macroeconomics, microeconomics.** 2 (*plural*) financial aspects: *the economics of the project are very doubtful.*

economic sanctions PLURAL NOUN any actions taken by one nation or group of nations to harm the economy of another nation or group, often to force a political change.

economic zone NOUN another term for **exclusive economic zone.**

economism (ɪ'kɒnə,mɪzəm) NOUN 1 **a** a political theory that regards economics as the main factor in society, ignoring or reducing to simplistic economic terms other factors such as culture, nationality, etc. **b** the belief that the main aim of a political group, trade union, etc., is to improve the material living standards of its members. 2 (*often capital*) (in Tsarist Russia) a political belief that the sole concern of the working classes should be with improving their living conditions and not with political reforms.

economist (ɪ'kɒnəmɪst) NOUN 1 a specialist in economics. 2 *Archaic* a person who advocates or practises frugality.

economistic (ɪ,kɒnə'mɪstɪk) ADJECTIVE of or relating to economics or finances: *economistic issues.*

economize *or* **economise** (ɪ'kɒnə,maɪz) VERB (often foll by *on*) to limit or reduce (expense, waste, etc.).
▸**e,conomi'zation** *or* **e,conomi'sation** NOUN

economizer *or* **economiser** (ɪ'kɒnə,maɪzə) NOUN 1 a device that uses the waste heat from a boiler flue to preheat the feed water. 2 a person or thing that economizes.

Economo's disease (ɪ'kɒnəməʊz) NOUN *Pathol* another name for **sleeping sickness** (sense 2).
▷HISTORY C20: named after K. von *Economo* (1876–1931), Austrian neurologist

economy (ɪ'kɒnəmɪ) NOUN, *plural* **-mies.** 1 careful management of resources to avoid unnecessary expenditure or waste; thrift. 2 a means or instance of this; saving. 3 sparing, restrained, or efficient use, esp to achieve the maximum effect for the minimum effort: *economy of language.* 4 **a** the complex of human activities concerned with the production, distribution, and consumption of goods and services. **b** a particular type or branch of such production, distribution, and consumption: *a socialist economy; an agricultural economy.* 5 the management of the resources, finances, income, and expenditure of a community, business enterprise, etc. 6 **a** a class of travel in aircraft, providing less luxurious accommodation than first class at a lower fare. **b** (*as modifier*): *economy class.* 7 (*modifier*) offering or purporting to offer a larger quantity for a lower price: *economy pack.* 8 the orderly interplay between the parts of a system or structure: *the economy of nature.* 9 *Philosophy* the principle that, of two competing theories, the one with less ontological presupposition is to be preferred. 10 *Archaic* the management of household affairs; domestic economy.
▷HISTORY C16: via Latin from Greek *oikonomia* domestic management, from *oikos* house + *-nomia,* from *nemein* to manage

economy-class syndrome NOUN (not in technical usage) the development of a deep-vein thrombosis in the legs or pelvis of a person travelling for a long period of time in cramped conditions.
▷HISTORY C20: reference to the restricted legroom of cheaper seats on passenger aircraft

economy of scale NOUN *Economics* a fall in average costs resulting from an increase in the scale of production.

ecophysiology (,i:kəʊ,fɪzɪ'ɒlədʒɪ) NOUN the study of the physiology of organisms with respect to their adaptation to the environment.

écorché (,eɪkɔ:'ʃeɪ) NOUN an anatomical figure without the skin, so that the muscular structure is visible.
▷HISTORY C19: French, literally: skinned

ecoregion ('i:kəʊ,ri:dʒən) NOUN an area defined by its environmental conditions, esp climate, landforms, and soil characteristics.

ecospecies ('i:kəʊ,spi:ʃi:z, -,spi:si:z, 'ɛkəʊ-) NOUN *Ecology* a species of plant or animal that can be divided into several ecotypes.
▷HISTORY C20: from ECO(LOGY) + SPECIES
▸**ecospecific** (,i:kəʊspɪ'sɪfɪk, ,ɛkəʊ-) ADJECTIVE

ecosphere ('i:kəʊ,sfɪə, 'ɛkəʊ-) NOUN the planetary ecosystem, consisting of all living organisms and their environment.

écossaise (,eɪkɒ'seɪz; *French* ekɔsɛz) NOUN 1 a lively dance in two-four time. 2 the tune for such a dance.
▷HISTORY C19: French, literally: Scottish (dance)

ecosystem ('i:kəʊ,sɪstəm, 'ɛkəʊ-) NOUN *Ecology* a system involving the interactions between a community of living organisms in a particular area and its nonliving environment.
▷HISTORY C20: from ECO(LOGY) + SYSTEM

ecosystem services NOUN the important benefits for human beings that arise from healthily functioning ecosystems, notably production of oxygen, soil genesis, and water detoxification.

ecoterrorist (ˈi:kəʊˌtɛrərɪst) NOUN a person who uses violence in order to achieve environmentalist aims.
▷HISTORY C20: from ECO- + TERRORIST

ecotone (ˈi:kəˌtəʊn, ˈɛkə-) NOUN the zone between two major ecological communities.
▷HISTORY C20: from ECO(LOGY) + *-tone*, from Greek *tonos* tension, TONE
▸ˈ**ecoˌtonal** ADJECTIVE

ecotourism ADJECTIVE (ˈi:kəʊˌtʊərɪzəm), NOUN tourism which is designed to contribute to the protection of the environment or at least minimize damage to it, often involving travel to areas of natural interest in developing countries or participation in environmental projects.
▸ˈ**ecoˌtourist** NOUN

ecotype (ˈi:kəˌtaɪp, ˈɛkə-) NOUN *Ecology* a group of organisms within a species that is adapted to particular environmental conditions and therefore exhibits behavioural, structural, or physiological differences from other members of the species.
▸**ecotypic** (ˌi:kəˈtɪpɪk, ˌɛkə-) ADJECTIVE ▸ˌ**ecoˈtypically** ADVERB

eco-warrior NOUN *Informal* a person who zealously pursues environmentalist aims.
▷HISTORY C20: from ECO- + WARRIOR

ECOWAS (ɛˈkəʊəs) NOUN ACRONYM FOR Economic Community of West African States; an economic association established in 1975 among Benin, Burkina-Faso (then called Upper Volta), The Gambia, Ghana, Guinea, Guinea-Bissau, Ivory Coast, Liberia, Mali, Mauritania, Niger, Nigeria, Senegal, Sierra Leone, and Togo.

ECR ABBREVIATION FOR efficient consumer response: the use of point-of-sale data to initiate the reordering of stock from a supplier.

écraseur (ˌeɪkrɑ:ˈzɜ:) NOUN a surgical device consisting of a heavy wire loop placed around a part to be removed and tightened until it cuts through.
▷HISTORY C19: from French, from *écraser* to crush

e-CRM NOUN customer relationship management carried out on the Internet.

ecru (ˈɛkru:, ˈeɪkru:) NOUN 1 a greyish-yellow to a light greyish colour; the colour of unbleached linen. ◆ ADJECTIVE 2 of the colour ecru.
▷HISTORY C19: from French, from *é-* (intensive) + *cru* raw, from Latin *crūdus*; see CRUDE

ECS ABBREVIATION FOR European Communications Satellite.

ECSC ABBREVIATION FOR European Coal and Steel Community.

ecstasy (ˈɛkstəsɪ) NOUN, *plural* **-sies**. 1 (*often plural*) a state of exalted delight, joy, etc.; rapture. 2 intense emotion of any kind: *an ecstasy of rage*. 3 *Psychol* overpowering emotion characterized by loss of self-control and sometimes a temporary loss of consciousness: often associated with orgasm, religious mysticism, and the use of certain drugs. 4 *Archaic* a state of prophetic inspiration, esp of poetic rapture. 5 *Slang* 3,4-methylenedioxymethamphetamine; MDMA: a powerful drug that acts as a stimulant and can produce hallucinations.
▷HISTORY C14: from Old French *extasie*, via Medieval Latin from Greek *ekstasis* displacement, trance, from *existanai* to displace, from *ex-* out + *histanai* to cause to stand

ecstatic (ɛkˈstætɪk) ADJECTIVE 1 in a trancelike state of great rapture or delight. 2 showing or feeling great enthusiasm: *ecstatic applause*. ◆ NOUN 3 a person who has periods of intense trancelike joy.
▸**ecˈstatically** ADVERB

ecstatics (ɛkˈstætɪks) PLURAL NOUN fits of delight or rapture.

ECT ABBREVIATION FOR **electroconvulsive therapy**.

ectasia (ɛkˈteɪzɪə) *or* **ectasis** (ɛkˈteɪsɪs) NOUN *Pathol* the distension or dilation of a duct, vessel, or hollow viscus.
▸**ecˈtatic** ADJECTIVE

ecthyma (ˈɛkθɪmə) NOUN *Pathol* a local inflammation of the skin characterized by flat ulcerating pustules.
▷HISTORY C19: from New Latin, from Greek *ekthuma* pustule, from *ekthuein* to break out, from *ek-* out + *thuein* to seethe

ecto- COMBINING FORM indicating outer, outside, external: *ectoplasm*.
▷HISTORY from Greek *ektos* outside, from *ek*, *ex* out

ectoblast (ˈɛktəʊˌblæst) NOUN another name for **ectoderm** or **epiblast**.
▸ˌ**ectoˈblastic** ADJECTIVE

ectocrine (ˈɛktəʊˌkri:n, -krɪn) NOUN a substance that is released by an organism into the external environment and influences the development, behaviour, etc., of members of the same or different species.
▷HISTORY C20: from ECTO- + *-crine*, as in *endocrine*

ectoderm (ˈɛktəʊˌdɜ:m) *or* **exoderm** NOUN the outer germ layer of an animal embryo, which gives rise to epidermis and nervous tissue. See also **mesoderm, endoderm**.
▸ˌ**ectoˈdermal** *or* ˌ**ectoˈdermic** ADJECTIVE

ectoenzyme (ˌɛktəʊˈɛnzaɪm) NOUN any of a group of enzymes secreted from the cells in which they are produced into the surrounding medium; extracellular enzyme. Also called: **exoenzyme**.

ectogenesis (ˌɛktəʊˈdʒɛnəsɪs) NOUN the growth of an organism outside the body in which it would normally be found, such as the growth of an embryo outside the mother's body or the growth of bacteria outside the body of a host.
▸ˌ**ectogeˈnetic** *or* ˌ**ectoˈgenic** *or* **ectogenous** (ɛkˈtɒdʒɪnəs) ADJECTIVE ▸ˌ**ectoˈgenically** ADVERB

ectomere (ˈɛktəʊˌmɪə) NOUN *Embryol* any of the blastomeres that later develop into ectoderm.
▸**ectomeric** (ˌɛktəʊˈmɛrɪk) ADJECTIVE

ectomorph (ˈɛktəʊˌmɔ:f) NOUN a person with a thin body build: said to be correlated with cerebrotonia. Compare **endomorph, mesomorph**.
▸ˌ**ectoˈmorphic** ADJECTIVE ▸ˈ**ectoˌmorphy** NOUN

-ectomy NOUN COMBINING FORM indicating surgical excision of a part: *appendectomy*.
▷HISTORY from New Latin *-ectomia*, from Greek *ek-* out + -TOMY

ectomycorrhiza (ˌɛktəʊˌmaɪkəˈraɪzə) NOUN another name for **ectotrophic mycorrhiza**.

ectoparasite (ˌɛktəʊˈpærəˌsaɪt) NOUN a parasite, such as the flea, that lives on the outer surface of its host. Also called: **exoparasite**.
▸**ectoparasitic** (ˌɛktəʊˌpærəˈsɪtɪk) ADJECTIVE

ectophyte (ˈɛktəʊˌfaɪt) NOUN a parasitic plant that lives on the surface of its host.
▸**ectophytic** (ˌɛktəʊˈfɪtɪk) ADJECTIVE

ectopia (ɛkˈtəʊpɪə) NOUN *Med* congenital displacement or abnormal positioning of an organ or part.
▷HISTORY C19: from New Latin, from Greek *ektopos* out of position, from *ek-* out of + *topos* place
▸**ectopic** (ɛkˈtɒpɪk) ADJECTIVE

ectopic pregnancy NOUN *Pathol* the abnormal development of a fertilized egg outside the cavity of the uterus, usually within a Fallopian tube.

ectoplasm (ˈɛktəʊˌplæzəm) NOUN 1 *Cytology* the outer layer of cytoplasm in some cells, esp protozoa, which differs from the inner cytoplasm (see **endoplasm**) in being a clear gel. 2 *Spiritualism* the substance supposedly emanating from the body of a medium during trances.
▸ˌ**ectoˈplasmic** ADJECTIVE

ectoproct (ˈɛktəʊˌprɒkt) NOUN, ADJECTIVE another word for **bryozoan**.
▷HISTORY from ECTO- + *-proct*, from Greek *prōktos* rectum

ectosarc (ˈɛktəʊˌsɑ:k) NOUN *Zoology* the ectoplasm of an amoeba or any other protozoan.
▷HISTORY C19: ECTO- + *-sarc*, from Greek *sarx* flesh
▸ˌ**ectoˈsarcous** ADJECTIVE

ectotrophic mycorrhiza (ˌɛktəʊˈtrɒfɪk) NOUN *Botany* a type of mycorrhiza, typical of temperate and Boreal trees, in which the fungus forms a layer on the outside of the roots of the plant. Also called: **ectomycorrhiza**. Compare **endotrophic mycorrhiza**.

ectype (ˈɛkˌtaɪp) NOUN 1 a copy as distinguished from a prototype. 2 *Architect* a cast embossed or in relief.
▷HISTORY C17: from Greek *ektupos* worked in relief, from *ek-* out of + *tupos* mould; see TYPE
▸**ectypal** (ˈɛktɪpᵊl) ADJECTIVE

écu (eɪˈkju:; *French* eky) NOUN 1 any of various former French gold or silver coins. 2 a small shield.
▷HISTORY C18: from Old French *escu*, from Latin *scūtum* shield

ECU (ˈeɪkju:; *sometimes* ˈi:ˈsi:ˈju:) NOUN ACRONYM FOR European Currency Unit: a former unit of currency based on the composite value of several different currencies in the European Union and functioning both as the reserve asset and accounting unit of the European Monetary System; replaced by the euro in 1999.

Ecua. ABBREVIATION FOR Ecuador.

Ecuador (ˈɛkwəˌdɔ:) NOUN a republic in South America, on the Pacific: under the Incas when Spanish colonization began in 1532; gained independence in 1822; declared a republic in 1830. It consists chiefly of a coastal plain in the west, separated from the densely forested upper Amazon basin (Oriente) by ranges and plateaus of the Andes. Official language: Spanish; Quechua is also widely spoken. Religion: Roman Catholic majority. Currency: US dollar. Capital: Quito. Pop.: 12 879 000 (2001 est.). Area: 283 560 sq. km (109 483 sq. miles).

Ecuadorean (ˌɛkwəˈdɔ:rɪən) ADJECTIVE 1 of or relating to Ecuador or its inhabitants. ◆ NOUN 2 a native or inhabitant of Ecuador.

ecumenical, oecumenical (ˌi:kjʊˈmɛnɪkᵊl, ˌɛk-), **ecumenic,** *or* **oecumenic** ADJECTIVE 1 of or relating to the Christian Church throughout the world, esp with regard to its unity. 2 **a** tending to promote unity among Churches. **b** of or relating to the international movement initiated among non-Catholic Churches in 1910 aimed at Christian unity: embodied, since 1937, in the World Council of Churches. 3 *Rare* universal; general; worldwide.
▷HISTORY C16: via Late Latin from Greek *oikoumenikos*, from *oikein* to inhabit, from *oikos* house
▸ˌ**ecuˈmenically** *or* ˌ**oecuˈmenically** ADVERB

ecumenical council NOUN an assembly of bishops and other ecclesiastics representative of the Christian Church throughout the world. Roman Catholic canon law states that an ecumenical council must be convened by the pope.

ecumenism (ɪˈkju:məˌnɪzəm, ˈɛkjʊm-), **ecumenicism** (ˌi:kjʊˈmɛnɪˌsɪzəm, ˌɛk-), *or* **ecumenicalism** NOUN the aim of unity among all Christian churches throughout the world.

écurie (*French* ekyri) NOUN a team of motor-racing cars.
▷HISTORY C20: French, literally: a stable

eczema (ˈɛksɪmə, ɪgˈzi:mə) NOUN *Pathol* a skin inflammation with lesions that scale, crust, or ooze a serous fluid, often accompanied by intense itching or burning.
▷HISTORY C18: from New Latin, from Greek *ekzema*, from *ek-* out + *zein* to boil; see YEAST
▸**eczematous** (ɛkˈsɛmətəs) ADJECTIVE

ed. ABBREVIATION FOR: 1 edited. 2 (*plural* **eds**) edition. 3 (*plural* **eds**) editor.

-ed[1] SUFFIX forming the past tense of most English verbs.
▷HISTORY Old English *-de, -ede, -ode, -ade*

-ed[2] SUFFIX forming the past participle of most English verbs.
▷HISTORY Old English *-ed, -od, -ad*

-ed[3] SUFFIX FORMING ADJECTIVES FROM NOUNS possessing or having the characteristics of: *salaried*; *red-blooded*.
▷HISTORY Old English *-ede*

edacious (ɪˈdeɪʃəs) ADJECTIVE *Chiefly humorous* devoted to eating; voracious; greedy.
▷HISTORY C19: from Latin *edāx* voracious, from *edere* to eat
▸**eˈdaciously** ADVERB ▸**edacity** (ɪˈdæsɪtɪ) *or* **eˈdaciousness** NOUN

Edam (ˈi:dæm) NOUN 1 a town in the NW Netherlands, in North Holland province, on the IJsselmeer: cheese, light manufacturing. Pop.: 24 572 (latest est.). 2 a hard round mild-tasting Dutch cheese, yellow in colour with a red outside covering.

edaphic (ɪˈdæfɪk) ADJECTIVE of or relating to the physical and chemical conditions of the soil, esp in relation to the plant and animal life it supports. Compare **biotic** (sense 2).
▷HISTORY C20: from Greek *edaphos* bottom, soil
▸**eˈdaphically** ADVERB

EDC ABBREVIATION FOR European Defence Community.

Edda ('ɛdə) NOUN 1 Also called: **Elder Edda, Poetic Edda.** a collection of mythological Old Norse poems made in the 12th century. 2 Also called: **Younger Edda, Prose Edda.** a treatise on versification together with a collection of Scandinavian myths, legends, and poems compiled by Snorri Sturluson (1179–1241), the Icelandic historian and poet.
▷HISTORY C18: Old Norse
▸**Eddaic** (ɛ'deɪɪk) ADJECTIVE

Eddington limit NOUN *Astronomy* the theoretical upper limit of luminosity that a star of a given mass can reach; occurs when the outward force of the radiation just balances the inward gravitational force.
▷HISTORY C20: named after A. S. *Eddington* (1882–1944), English astronomer and physicist

eddo *or* **Chinese eddo** ('ɛdəʊ) NOUN, *plural* **eddoes**. other names for **taro**.

eddy ('ɛdɪ) NOUN, *plural* **-dies**. 1 a movement in a stream of air, water, or other fluid in which the current doubles back on itself causing a miniature whirlwind or whirlpool. 2 a deviation from or disturbance in the main trend of thought, life, etc., esp one that is relatively unimportant. ◆ VERB **-dies, -dying, -died**. 3 to move or cause to move against the main current.
▷HISTORY C15: probably of Scandinavian origin; compare Old Norse *itha;* related to Old English *ed-* again, back, Old High German *it-*

eddy current NOUN an electric current induced in a massive conductor, such as the core of an electromagnet, transformer, etc., by an alternating magnetic field. Also called: **Foucault current.**

Eddystone Rocks ('ɛdɪstən) NOUN a dangerous group of rocks at the W end of the English Channel, southwest of Plymouth: lighthouse.

Ede ('eɪdə) NOUN a city in the central Netherlands, in Gelderland province. Pop.: 101 542 (1999 est.).

edelweiss ('eɪdᵊl,vaɪs) NOUN a small alpine flowering plant, *Leontopodium alpinum,* having white woolly oblong leaves and a tuft of attractive floral leaves surrounding the flowers: family *Asteraceae* (composites).
▷HISTORY C19: German, literally: noble white

edema (ɪ'diːmə) NOUN, *plural* **-mata** (-mətə). the usual US spelling of **oedema.**
▸**edematous** (ɪ'dɛmətəs) *or* **e'dema,tose** ADJECTIVE

Eden ('iːdᵊn) NOUN 1 Also called: **Garden of Eden.** *Old Testament* the garden in which Adam and Eve were placed at the Creation. 2 a delightful place, region, dwelling, etc.; paradise. 3 a state of great delight, happiness, or contentment; bliss.
▷HISTORY C14: from Late Latin, from Hebrew *'ēdhen* place of pleasure
▸**Edenic** (iː'dɛnɪk) ADJECTIVE

edentate (iː'dɛnteɪt) NOUN 1 any of the placental mammals that constitute the order *Edentata,* which inhabit tropical regions of Central and South America. The order includes anteaters, sloths, and armadillos. ◆ ADJECTIVE 2 of, relating to, or belonging to the order *Edentata.*
▷HISTORY C19: from Latin *ēdentātus* lacking teeth, from *ēdentāre* to render toothless, from *e-* out + *dēns* tooth

edentulous (iː'dɛntʃʊləs) *or* **edentulate** (iː'dɛntʃʊlɪt) ADJECTIVE having no teeth.

Edessa (ɪ'dɛsə) NOUN 1 an ancient city on the N edge of the Syrian plateau, founded as a Macedonian colony by Seleucus I: a centre of early Christianity. Modern name: **Urfa.** 2 a market town in Greece: ancient capital of Macedonia. Pop.: 15 980 (latest est.). Ancient name: **Aegae** ('iːgiː). Modern Greek name: **Édhessa.**

edge (ɛdʒ) NOUN 1 the border, brim, or margin of a surface, object, etc. 2 a brink or verge: *the edge of a cliff; the edge of a breakthrough.* 3 *Maths* **a** a line along which two faces or surfaces of a solid meet. **b** a line joining two vertices of a graph. 4 the sharp cutting side of a blade. 5 keenness, sharpness, or urgency: *the walk gave an edge to his appetite.* 6 force, effectiveness, or incisiveness: *the performance lacked edge.* 7 *Dialect* **a** a cliff, ridge, or hillside. **b** (*capital*) (in place names): *Hade Edge.* 8 **have the edge on** *or* **over.** to have a slight advantage or superiority (over). 9 **on edge. a** nervously irritable; tense. **b** nervously excited or eager. 10 **set (someone's) teeth on edge.** to make (someone) acutely irritated or uncomfortable. ◆ VERB 11 (*tr*) to provide an edge or border for. 12 (*tr*) to shape or trim (the edge or border of something), as with a knife or scissors: *to edge a pie.* 13 to push (one's way, someone, something, etc.) gradually, esp edgeways. 14 (*tr*) *Cricket* to hit (a bowled ball) with the edge of the bat. 15 (*tr*) to tilt (a ski) sideways so that one edge digs into the snow. 16 (*tr*) to sharpen (a knife, etc.).
▷HISTORY Old English *ecg;* related to Old Norse *egg,* Old High German *ecka* edge, Latin *aciēs* sharpness, Greek *akis* point
▸**'edgeless** ADJECTIVE ▸**'edger** NOUN

Edgehill (,ɛdʒ'hɪl) NOUN a ridge in S Warwickshire: site of the indecisive first battle between Charles I and the Parliamentarians (1642) in the Civil War.

edge tool NOUN a tool with one or more cutting edges.

edgeways ('ɛdʒ,weɪz) *or esp US and Canadian* **edgewise** ('ɛdʒ,waɪz) ADVERB 1 with the edge forwards or uppermost: *they carried the piano in edgeways.* 2 on, by, with, or towards the edge: *he held it edgeways.* 3 **get a word in edgeways.** (*usually used with a negative*) to succeed in interrupting a conversation in which someone else is talking incessantly.

edging ('ɛdʒɪŋ) NOUN 1 anything placed along an edge to finish it, esp as an ornament, fringe, or border on clothing or along a path in a garden. 2 the act of making an edge. ◆ ADJECTIVE 3 relating to or used for making an edge: *edging shears.*

edgy ('ɛdʒɪ) ADJECTIVE **-ier, -iest.** 1 (*usually postpositive*) nervous, irritable, tense, or anxious. 2 (of paintings, drawings, etc.) excessively defined. 3 innovative, or at the cutting edge, with the concomitant qualities of intensity and excitement.
▸**'edgily** ADVERB ▸**'edginess** NOUN

edh (ɛð) *or* **eth** NOUN a character of the runic alphabet (ð) used to represent the voiced dental fricative as in *then, mother, bathe.* It is used in modern phonetic transcription for the same purpose. Compare **theta** (sense 2), **thorn** (sense 5).

Édhessa (*Greek* 'ɛðɛsa) NOUN transliteration of the Modern Greek name for **Edessa.**

EDI ABBREVIATION FOR electronic data interchange: an interactive electronic system that enables a supplier and a customer to communicate efficiently.

edible ('ɛdɪbᵊl) ADJECTIVE fit to be eaten; eatable.
▷HISTORY C17: from Late Latin *edibilis,* from Latin *edere* to eat
▸**,edi'bility** *or* **'edibleness** NOUN

edibles ('ɛdɪbᵊlz) PLURAL NOUN articles fit to eat; food.

edict ('iːdɪkt) NOUN 1 a decree, order, or ordinance issued by a sovereign, state, or any other holder of authority. 2 any formal or authoritative command, proclamation, etc.
▷HISTORY C15: from Latin *ēdictum,* from *ēdīcere* to declare
▸**e'dictal** ADJECTIVE ▸**e'dictally** ADVERB

Edict of Nantes NOUN the law granting religious and civil liberties to the French Protestants, promulgated by Henry IV in 1598 and revoked by Louis XIV in 1685.

edification (,ɛdɪfɪ'keɪʃən) NOUN 1 improvement, instruction, or enlightenment, esp when morally or spiritually uplifting. 2 the act of edifying or state of being edified.
▸**,edifi'catory** ADJECTIVE

edifice ('ɛdɪfɪs) NOUN 1 a building, esp a large or imposing one. 2 a complex or elaborate institution or organization.
▷HISTORY C14: from Old French, from Latin *aedificium,* from *aedificāre* to build; see EDIFY
▸**edificial** (,ɛdɪ'fɪʃəl) ADJECTIVE

edify ('ɛdɪ,faɪ) VERB **-fies, -fying, -fied.** (*tr*) to improve the morality, intellect, etc., of, esp by instruction.
▷HISTORY C14: from Old French *edifier,* from Latin *aedificāre* to construct, from *aedēs* a dwelling, temple + *facere* to make
▸**'edi,fier** NOUN ▸**'edi,fying** ADJECTIVE ▸**'edi,fyingly** ADVERB

edile ('iːdaɪl) NOUN a variant spelling of **aedile.**

Edinburgh ('ɛdɪnbərə, -brə) NOUN 1 the capital of Scotland and seat of the Scottish Parliament (from 1999), in City of Edinburgh council area on the S side of the Firth of Forth: became the capital in the 15th century; castle; universities (1583, 1966); commercial and cultural centre, noted for its annual festival. Pop.: 401 910 (1991). 2 **City of.** a council area in central Scotland, created from part of Lothian region in 1996. Pop.: 448 624 (2001). Area: 262 sq. km (101 sq. miles).

Edirne (ɛ'dirnɛ) NOUN a city in NW Turkey: a Thracian town, rebuilt and renamed by the Roman emperor Hadrian. Pop.: 115 083 (1997). Former name: **Adrianople.**

edit ('ɛdɪt) VERB (*tr*) 1 to prepare (text) for publication by checking and improving its accuracy, clarity, etc. 2 to be in charge of (a publication, esp a periodical): *he edits the local newspaper.* 3 to prepare (a film, tape, etc.) by rearrangement, selection, or rejection of previously filmed or taped material. 4 (*tr*) to modify (a computer file) by, for example, deleting, inserting, moving, or copying text. 5 (often foll by *out*) to remove (incorrect or unwanted matter), as from a manuscript or film. ◆ NOUN 6 *Informal* an act of editing: *give the book a final edit.*
▷HISTORY C18: back formation from EDITOR

edition (ɪ'dɪʃən) NOUN 1 *Printing* **a** the entire number of copies of a book, newspaper, or other publication printed at one time from a single setting of type. **b** a single copy from this number: *a first edition; the evening edition.* 2 one of a number of printings of a book or other publication, issued at separate times with alterations, amendments, etc. Compare **impression** (sense 6). 3 **a** an issue of a work identified by its format: *a leather-bound edition of Shakespeare.* **b** an issue of a work identified by its editor or publisher: *the Oxford edition of Shakespeare.* ◆ VERB 4 (*tr*) to produce multiple copies of (an original work of art).
▷HISTORY C16: from Latin *ēditiō* a bringing forth, publishing, from *ēdere* to give out; see EDITOR

editio princeps *Latin* (ɪ'dɪʃɪəʊ 'prɪnsɛps) NOUN, *plural* ***editiones principes*** (ɪ,dɪʃɪ'əʊniːz 'prɪnsɪ,piːz). the first printed edition of a work.

editor ('ɛdɪtə) NOUN 1 a person who edits written material for publication. 2 a person in overall charge of the editing and often the policy of a newspaper or periodical. 3 a person in charge of one section of a newspaper or periodical: *the sports editor.* 4 *Films* **a** a person who makes a selection and arrangement of individual shots in order to construct the flowing sequence of images for a film. **b** a device for editing film, including a viewer and a splicer. 5 *Television, radio* a person in overall control of a programme that consists of various items, such as a news or magazine style programme. 6 a computer program that facilitates the deletion or insertion of data within information already stored in a computer.
▷HISTORY C17: from Late Latin: producer, exhibitor, from *ēdere* to give out, publish, from *ē-* out + *dāre* to give
▸**'editor,ship** NOUN

editorial (,ɛdɪ'tɔːrɪəl) ADJECTIVE 1 of or relating to editing or editors. 2 of, relating to, or expressed in an editorial. 3 of or relating to the content of a publication rather than its commercial aspects. ◆ NOUN 4 an article in a newspaper, etc., expressing the opinion of the editor or the publishers.
▸**,edi'torialist** NOUN ▸**,edi'torially** ADVERB

editorialize *or* **editorialise** (,ɛdɪ'tɔːrɪə,laɪz) VERB (*intr*) 1 to express an opinion in or as in an editorial. 2 to insert one's personal opinions into an otherwise objective account.
▸**,edi,toriali'zation** *or* **,edi,toriali'sation** NOUN
▸**,edi'torial,izer** *or* **,edi'torial,iser** NOUN

editor in chief NOUN the controlling editor of a publication.

EDM *Surveying* ABBREVIATION FOR electronic distance measurement.

Edmonton ('ɛdməntən) NOUN a city in W Canada, capital of Alberta: oil industry. Pop.: 616 306 (1991).

Edo ('ɛdəʊ) NOUN 1 (*plural* **Edo** *or* **Edos**) a member of a Negroid people of SW Nigeria around Benin, noted for their 16th-century bronze sculptures. 2 Also called: **Bini.** the language of this people, belonging to the Kwa branch of the Niger-Congo family.

Edom (ˈiːdəm) NOUN 1 a nomadic people descended from Esau. 2 the son of Esau who was the supposed ancestor of this nation. 3 the ancient kingdom of this people, situated between the Dead Sea and the Gulf of Aqaba.

Edomite (ˈiːdəˌmaɪt) NOUN 1 an inhabitant of the ancient kingdom of Edom, whose people were hostile to the Israelites in Old Testament times. 2 the ancient Semitic language of this people, closely related to Hebrew.
▸ **ˈEdomˌitish** *or* **Edomitic** (ˌiːdəˈmɪtɪk) ADJECTIVE

EDT (in the US and Canada) ABBREVIATION FOR Eastern Daylight Time.

EDTA NOUN ethylenediaminetetra-acetic acid; a colourless crystalline slightly soluble organic compound used in inorganic chemistry and biochemistry. It is a powerful chelating agent used to stabilize bleach in detergents. Formula: $[(HOOCCH_2)_2NCH_2]_2$.

edu AN INTERNET DOMAIN NAME FOR an educational establishment.

educable (ˈɛdjʊkəbᵊl) *or* **educatable** (ˈɛdjʊˌkeɪtəbᵊl) ADJECTIVE capable of being trained or educated; able to learn.
▸ **ˌeducaˈbility** *or* **ˌeduˌcataˈbility** NOUN

educate (ˈɛdjʊˌkeɪt) VERB (*mainly tr*) 1 (*also intr*) to impart knowledge by formal instruction to (a pupil); teach. 2 to provide schooling for (children): *I have educated my children at the best schools.* 3 to improve or develop (a person, judgment, taste, skills, etc.). 4 to train for some particular purpose or occupation.
▷ HISTORY C15: from Latin *ēducāre* to rear, educate, from *dūcere* to lead

educated (ˈɛdjʊˌkeɪtɪd) ADJECTIVE 1 having an education, esp a good one. 2 displaying culture, taste, and knowledge; cultivated. 3 (*prenominal*) based on experience or information (esp in the phrase **an educated guess**).

education (ˌɛdjʊˈkeɪʃən) NOUN 1 the act or process of acquiring knowledge, esp systematically during childhood and adolescence. 2 the knowledge or training acquired by this process: *his education has been invaluable to him.* 3 the act or process of imparting knowledge, esp at a school, college, or university: *education is my profession.* 4 the theory of teaching and learning: *a course in education.* 5 a particular kind of instruction or training: *a university education; consumer education.*

educational (ˌɛdjʊˈkeɪʃənᵊl) ADJECTIVE 1 providing knowledge; instructive or informative: *an educational toy.* 2 of or relating to education.
▸ **ˌeduˈcationally** ADVERB

educationalist (ˌɛdjʊˈkeɪʃənəlɪst) *or* **educationist** NOUN a specialist in educational theory or administration.

educational psychology NOUN the study of methods of training and teaching and their effectiveness, and of the problems experienced in learning formal material; in particular, the study of how to help people, esp school children, with learning problems to overcome their difficulties.

Educational Welfare Officer NOUN (in Britain) a local education authority worker whose job it is to find out whether difficulties outside school are contributing to a child's classroom problems or irregular attendance and who may intervene to help the child to benefit more from schooling. Former names: **school attendance officer, truancy officer.**

educative (ˈɛdjʊkətɪv) ADJECTIVE producing or resulting in education: *an educative experience.*

educator (ˈɛdjʊˌkeɪtə) NOUN 1 a person who educates; teacher. 2 a specialist in education; educationalist.

educatory (ˈɛdjʊkətərɪ, -trɪ, ˌɛdjʊˈkeɪtərɪ, -trɪ) ADJECTIVE educative or educational: *an educatory procedure.*

educe (ɪˈdjuːs) VERB (*tr*) *Rare* 1 to evolve or develop, esp from a latent or potential state. 2 to draw out or elicit (information, solutions, etc.).
▷ HISTORY C15: from Latin *ēdūcere* to draw out, from *ē-* out + *dūcere* to lead
▸ **eˈducible** ADJECTIVE ▸ **eductive** (ɪˈdʌktɪv) ADJECTIVE

educt (ˈiːdʌkt) NOUN a substance separated from another substance without chemical change. Compare **product** (sense 4).
▷ HISTORY C18: from Latin *ēductus;* see EDUCE

eduction (ɪˈdʌkʃən) NOUN 1 something educed. 2 the act or process of educing. 3 the exhaust stroke of a steam or internal-combustion engine. Compare **induction.**
▷ HISTORY C17: from Latin *ēductiō,* from *ēdūcere* to EDUCE

edulcorate (ɪˈdʌlkəˌreɪt) VERB (*tr*) to free from soluble impurities by washing.
▷ HISTORY C17: from Medieval Latin *ēdulcorāre,* from Late Latin *dulcor* sweetness
▸ **eˌdulcoˈration** NOUN

edutainment NOUN (ˌɛdjʊˈteɪnmənt), NOUN the presentation of informative or educational material in an entertaining style.
▷ HISTORY C20: from EDU(CATION) + (ENTER)TAINMENT

Edward (ˈɛdwəd) NOUN **Lake.** a lake in central Africa, between Uganda and the Democratic Republic of Congo (formerly Zaïre) in the Great Rift Valley: empties through the Semliki River into Lake Albert. Area: about 2150 sq. km (830 sq. miles). Former official name: **Lake Amin.**

Edwardian (ɛdˈwɔːdɪən) ADJECTIVE 1 denoting, relating to, or having the style of life, architecture, dress, etc., current in Britain during the reign (1901–10) of Edward VII (1841–1910). ◆ NOUN 2 a person who lived during the reign of Edward VII.
▸ **Edˈwardianism** NOUN

ee (iː) NOUN, *plural* **een** (iːn). a Scot word for **eye**[1].

ee THE INTERNET DOMAIN NAME FOR Estonia.

EE ABBREVIATION FOR: 1 **Early English.** 2 electrical engineer(ing). 3 (in New Zealand) **ewe equivalent.**

e.e. ABBREVIATION FOR errors excepted.

-ee SUFFIX FORMING NOUNS 1 indicating a person who is the recipient of an action (as opposed, esp in legal terminology, to the agent, indicated by *-or* or *-er*): *assignee; grantee; lessee.* 2 indicating a person in a specified state or condition: *absentee; employee.* 3 indicating a diminutive form of something: *bootee.*
▷ HISTORY via Old French *-e, -ee,* past participial endings, from Latin *-ātus, -āta* -ATE[1]

EEA ABBREVIATION FOR **European Economic Area.**

EE & MP ABBREVIATION FOR Envoy Extraordinary and Minister Plenipotentiary.

EEC ABBREVIATION FOR European Economic Community (now subsumed within the European Union).

EEG ABBREVIATION FOR: 1 electroencephalogram. 2 electroencephalograph.

eejit (ˈiːdʒɪt) NOUN a Scot and Irish word for **idiot** (sense 2).

eel (iːl) NOUN 1 any teleost fish of the order *Apodes* (or *Anguilliformes*), such as the European freshwater species *Anguilla anguilla,* having a long snakelike body, a smooth slimy skin, and reduced fins. 2 any of various other animals with a long body and smooth skin, such as the mud eel and the electric eel. 3 an evasive or untrustworthy person.
▷ HISTORY Old English *ǣl;* related to Old Frisian *ēl,* Old Norse *āll,* Old High German *āl*
▸ **ˈeel-ˌlike** ADJECTIVE ▸ **ˈeely** ADJECTIVE

eelgrass (ˈiːlˌgrɑːs) NOUN 1 any of several perennial submerged marine plants of the genus *Zostera,* esp *Z. marina,* having grasslike leaves: family *Zosteraceae.* 2 another name for **tape grass.**

eelpout (ˈiːlˌpaʊt) NOUN 1 any marine eel-like blennioid fish of the family *Zoarcidae,* such as *Zoarces viviparus* (**viviparous eelpout** or blenny). 2 another name for **burbot.**
▷ HISTORY Old English *ǣlepūte;* related to Middle Dutch *aalpuit*

eelworm (ˈiːlˌwɜːm) NOUN any of various nematode worms, esp the wheatworm and the vinegar eel.

e'en (iːn) ADVERB, NOUN *Poetic or archaic* a contraction of **even**[2] and **evening.**

e'er (ɛə) ADVERB *Poetic or archaic* a contraction of **ever.**

-eer *or* **-ier** SUFFIX 1 (*forming nouns*) indicating a person who is concerned with or who does something specified: *auctioneer; engineer; profiteer; mutineer.* 2 (*forming verbs*) to be concerned with something specified: *electioneer.*
▷ HISTORY from Old French *-ier,* from Latin *-arius* -ARY

eerie (ˈɪərɪ) ADJECTIVE **eerier, eeriest.** (esp of places, an atmosphere, etc.) mysteriously or uncannily frightening or disturbing; weird; ghostly.
▷ HISTORY C13: originally Scottish and Northern English, probably from Old English *earg* cowardly, miserable
▸ **ˈeerily** ADVERB ▸ **ˈeeriness** NOUN

EFA ABBREVIATION FOR: 1 **essential fatty acid.** ◆ NOUN 2 European Fighter Aircraft.

eff (ɛf) VERB 1 euphemism for **fuck** (esp in the phrase **eff off**). 2 **eff and blind.** *Slang* to use obscene language.
▸ **ˈeffing** NOUN, ADJECTIVE

effable (ˈɛfəbᵊl) ADJECTIVE *Archaic* capable of being expressed in words.
▷ HISTORY C17: from Old French, from Late Latin *effābilis,* from Latin *effārī,* from *ex-* out + *fārī* to speak

efface (ɪˈfeɪs) VERB (*tr*) 1 to obliterate or make dim: *to efface a memory.* 2 to make (oneself) inconspicuous or humble through modesty, cowardice, or obsequiousness. 3 to rub out (a line, drawing, etc.); erase.
▷ HISTORY C15: from French *effacer,* literally: to obliterate the face; see FACE
▸ **efˈfaceable** ADJECTIVE ▸ **efˈfacement** NOUN ▸ **efˈfacer** NOUN

effect (ɪˈfɛkt) NOUN 1 something that is produced by a cause or agent; result. 2 power or ability to influence or produce a result; efficacy: *with no effect.* 3 the condition of being operative (esp in the phrases **in** or **into effect**): *the law comes into effect at midnight.* 4 **take effect.** to become operative or begin to produce results. 5 basic meaning or purpose (esp in the phrase **to that effect**). 6 an impression, usually one that is artificial or contrived (esp in the phrase **for effect**). 7 a scientific phenomenon: *the Doppler effect.* 8 **in effect. a** in fact; actually. **b** for all practical purposes. 9 the overall impression or result: *the effect of a painting.* ◆ VERB 10 (*tr*) to cause to occur; bring about; accomplish. ◆ See also **effects.**
▷ HISTORY C14: from Latin *effectus* a performing, tendency, from *efficere* to accomplish, from *facere* to do
▸ **efˈfecter** NOUN ▸ **efˈfectible** ADJECTIVE

effective (ɪˈfɛktɪv) ADJECTIVE 1 productive of or capable of producing a result. 2 in effect; operative: *effective from midnight.* 3 producing a striking impression; impressive: *an effective entrance.* 4 (*prenominal*) actual rather than theoretical; real: *the effective income after deductions.* 5 (of a military force, etc.) equipped and prepared for action. 6 *Physics* (of an alternating quantity) having a value that is the square root of the mean of the squares of the magnitude measured at each instant over a defined period of time, usually one cycle. See also **root mean square.** ◆ NOUN 7 a serviceman who is equipped and prepared for action.
▸ **efˈfectively** ADVERB ▸ **efˈfectiveness** NOUN

effector *or* **effecter** (ɪˈfɛktə) NOUN *Physiol* a nerve ending that terminates in a muscle or gland and provides neural stimulation causing contraction or secretion.

effects (ɪˈfɛkts) PLURAL NOUN 1 Also called: **personal effects.** personal property or belongings. 2 lighting, sounds, etc., to accompany and enhance a stage, film, or broadcast production.

effectual (ɪˈfɛktjʊəl) ADJECTIVE 1 capable of or successful in producing an intended result; effective. 2 (of documents, agreements, etc.) having legal force.
▸ **efˌfectuˈality** *or* **efˈfectualness** NOUN

effectually (ɪˈfɛktjʊəlɪ) ADVERB 1 with the intended effect; thoroughly. 2 to all practical purposes; in effect.

effectuate (ɪˈfɛktjʊˌeɪt) VERB (*tr*) to cause to happen; effect; accomplish.
▸ **efˌfectuˈation** NOUN

effeminate (ɪˈfɛmɪnɪt) ADJECTIVE 1 (of a man or boy) displaying characteristics regarded as typical of a woman; not manly. 2 lacking firmness or vigour: *an effeminate piece of writing.*
▷ HISTORY C14: from Latin *effēmināre* to make into a woman, from *fēmina* woman
▸ **efˈfeminacy** *or* **efˈfeminateness** NOUN ▸ **efˈfeminately** ADVERB

effendi (ɛˈfɛndɪ) NOUN, *plural* **-dis.** 1 (in the Ottoman Empire) a title of respect used to address

men of learning or social standing. [2] (in Turkey since 1934) the oral title of address equivalent to *Mr.*
▷**HISTORY** C17: from Turkish *efendi* master, from Modern Greek *aphentēs,* from Greek *authentēs* lord, doer; see AUTHENTIC

efferent (ˈɛfərənt) ADJECTIVE carrying or conducting outwards from a part or an organ of the body, esp from the brain or spinal cord. Compare **afferent.**
▷**HISTORY** C19: from Latin *efferre* to bear off, from *ferre* to bear
▸ˈ**efference** NOUN ▸ˈ**efferently** ADVERB

effervesce (ˌɛfəˈvɛs) VERB (*intr*) [1] (of a liquid) to give off bubbles of gas. [2] (of a gas) to issue in bubbles from a liquid. [3] to exhibit great excitement, vivacity, etc.
▷**HISTORY** C18: from Latin *effervescere* to foam up, from *fervescere* to begin to boil, from *fervēre* to boil, ferment
▸ˌ**efferˈvescible** ADJECTIVE ▸ˌ**efferˈvescingly** ADVERB

effervescent (ˌɛfəˈvɛsᵊnt) ADJECTIVE [1] (of a liquid) giving off bubbles of gas; bubbling. [2] high-spirited; vivacious.
▸ˌ**efferˈvescence** NOUN ▸ˌ**efferˈvescently** ADVERB

effete (ɪˈfiːt) ADJECTIVE [1] weak, ineffectual, or decadent as a result of overrefinement: *an effete academic.* [2] exhausted of vitality or strength; worn out; spent. [3] (of animals or plants) no longer capable of reproduction.
▷**HISTORY** C17: from Latin *effētus* having produced young, hence, exhausted by bearing, from *fētus* having brought forth; see FETUS
▸**efˈfetely** ADVERB ▸**efˈfeteness** NOUN

efficacious (ˌɛfɪˈkeɪʃəs) ADJECTIVE capable of or successful in producing an intended result; effective as a means, remedy, etc.
▷**HISTORY** C16: from Latin *efficāx* powerful, efficient, from *efficere* to achieve; see EFFECT
▸ˌ**effiˈcaciously** ADVERB *or* ˌ**effiˈcaciousness** ◆ NOUN

efficacy (ˈɛfɪkəsɪ) NOUN the quality of being successful in producing an intended result; effectiveness.

efficiency (ɪˈfɪʃənsɪ) NOUN, *plural* **-cies.** [1] the quality or state of being efficient; competence; effectiveness. [2] the ratio of the useful work done by a machine, engine, device, etc., to the energy supplied to it, often expressed as a percentage. See also **thermal efficiency.**

efficiency apartment NOUN *US* a small flat or bedsit.

efficient (ɪˈfɪʃənt) ADJECTIVE [1] functioning or producing effectively and with the least waste of effort; competent. [2] *Philosophy* producing a direct effect; causative.
▷**HISTORY** C14: from Latin *efficiēns* effecting
▸**efˈficiently** ADVERB

efficient cause NOUN *Philosophy* that which produces an effect by a causal process. Compare **final cause.** See also **cause** (sense 7).

effigy (ˈɛfɪdʒɪ) NOUN, *plural* **-gies.** [1] a portrait of a person, esp as a monument or architectural decoration. [2] a crude representation of someone, used as a focus for contempt or ridicule and often hung up or burnt in public (often in the phrases **burn** or **hang in effigy**).
▷**HISTORY** C18: from Latin *effigiēs,* from *effingere* to form, portray, from *fingere* to shape
▸**effigial** (ɪˈfɪdʒɪəl) ADJECTIVE

effleurage (ˌɛflɜːˈrɑːʒ) NOUN [1] a light stroking technique used in massage. ◆ VERB [2] (*intr*) to massage using this movement.
▷**HISTORY** C19: from French *effleurer* to stroke lightly

effloresce (ˌɛflɔːˈrɛs) VERB (*intr*) [1] to burst forth into or as if into flower; bloom. [2] to become powdery by loss of water or crystallization. [3] to become encrusted with powder or crystals as a result of chemical change or the evaporation of a solution.
▷**HISTORY** C18: from Latin *efflōrēscere* to blossom, from *flōrēscere,* from *flōs* flower

efflorescence (ˌɛflɔːˈrɛsᵊns) NOUN [1] a bursting forth or flowering. [2] *Chem, geology* **a** the process of efflorescing. **b** the powdery substance formed as a result of this process, esp on the surface of rocks. [3] any skin rash or eruption.
▸ˌ**effloˈrescent** ADJECTIVE

effluence (ˈɛfluəns) *or* **efflux** (ˈɛflʌks) NOUN [1] the act or process of flowing out. [2] something that flows out.

effluent (ˈɛfluənt) NOUN [1] liquid discharged as waste, as from an industrial plant or sewage works. [2] radioactive waste released from a nuclear power station. [3] a stream that flows out of another body of water. [4] something that flows out or forth. ◆ ADJECTIVE [5] flowing out or forth.
▷**HISTORY** C18: from Latin *effluere* to run forth, from *fluere* to flow

effluvium (ɛˈfluːvɪəm) NOUN, *plural* **-via** (-vɪə) *or* **-viums.** an unpleasant smell or exhalation, as of gaseous waste or decaying matter.
▷**HISTORY** C17: from Latin: a flowing out; see EFFLUENT
▸**efˈfluvial** ADJECTIVE

effort (ˈɛfət) NOUN [1] physical or mental exertion, usually considerable when unqualified: *the rock was moved with effort.* [2] a determined attempt: *our effort to save him failed.* [3] achievement; creation: *a great literary effort.* [4] *Physics* an applied force acting against inertia.
▷**HISTORY** C15: from Old French *esfort,* from *esforcier* to force, ultimately from Latin *fortis* strong; see FORCE[1]
▸ˈ**effortful** ADJECTIVE

effort bargain NOUN a bargain in which the reward to an employee is based on the effort that the employee puts in.

effortless (ˈɛfətlɪs) ADJECTIVE [1] requiring or involving little effort; easy. [2] *Archaic* making little effort; passive.
▸ˈ**effortlessly** ADVERB ▸ˈ**effortlessness** NOUN

effrontery (ɪˈfrʌntərɪ) NOUN, *plural* **-ies.** shameless or insolent boldness; impudent presumption; audacity; temerity.
▷**HISTORY** C18: from French *effronterie,* from Old French *esfront* barefaced, shameless, from Late Latin *effrons,* literally: putting forth one's forehead; see FRONT

effulgent (ɪˈfʌldʒənt) ADJECTIVE radiant; brilliant.
▷**HISTORY** C18: from Latin *effulgēre* to shine forth, from *fulgēre* to shine
▸**efˈfulgence** NOUN ▸**efˈfulgently** ADVERB

effuse VERB (ɪˈfjuːz) [1] to pour or flow out. [2] to spread out; diffuse. [3] (*intr*) to talk profusely, esp in an excited manner. [4] to cause (a gas) to flow or (of a gas) to flow under pressure. ◆ ADJECTIVE (ɪˈfjuːs) [5] *Botany* (esp of an inflorescence) spreading out loosely.
▷**HISTORY** C16: from Latin *effūsus* poured out, from *effundere* to shed, from *fundere* to pour

effusiometer (ɪˌfjuːzɪˈɒmɪtə) NOUN *Physics* an apparatus for determining rates of effusion of gases, usually used for measuring molecular weights.

effusion (ɪˈfjuːʒən) NOUN [1] an unrestrained outpouring in speech or words. [2] the act or process of being poured out. [3] something that is poured out. [4] the flow of a gas through a small aperture under pressure, esp when the density is such that the mean distance between molecules is large compared to the diameter of the aperture. [5] *Med* **a** the escape of blood or other fluid into a body cavity or tissue. **b** the fluid that has escaped.

effusive (ɪˈfjuːsɪv) ADJECTIVE [1] extravagantly demonstrative of emotion; gushing. [2] (of rock) formed by the solidification of magma.
▸**efˈfusively** ADVERB ▸**efˈfusiveness** NOUN

Efik (ˈɛfɪk) NOUN [1] (*plural* **Efiks** *or* **Efik**) a member of a subgroup of the Ibibio people of SE Nigeria. [2] the language spoken by this people, variously classified as belonging to the Benue-Congo or Kwa divisions of the Niger-Congo family.

EFIS *Aeronautics* ABBREVIATION FOR **electronic flight information systems.**

E-FIT (ˈiːfɪt) NOUN *Trademark* [1] a technique which uses psychological principles and computer technology to generate a likeness of a face: used by the police to trace suspects from witnesses' descriptions. [2] an image generated by this technique.
▷**HISTORY** C20: from *E*lectronic *F*acial *I*dentification *T*echnique

EFL ABBREVIATION FOR English as a Foreign Language.

eft[1] (ɛft) NOUN [1] a dialect or archaic name for a **newt.** [2] any of certain terrestrial newts, such as *Diemictylus viridescens* (**red eft**) of eastern North America.
▷**HISTORY** Old English *efeta*

eft[2] (ɛft) ADVERB *Archaic* **a** again. **b** afterwards.
▷**HISTORY** Old English; see AFT, AFTER

EFTA (ˈɛftə) NOUN ACRONYM FOR European Free Trade Association; established in 1960 to eliminate trade tariffs on industrial products; now comprises Norway, Switzerland, Iceland, and Liechtenstein. Free trade was established between EFTA and the EC (now EU) in 1984. In 1994 EFTA (excluding Switzerland) and the EU together created the European Economic Area (EEA).

EFTPOS (ˈɛftpɒs) ACRONYM FOR **electronic funds transfer at point of sale.**

EFTS *Computing* ABBREVIATION FOR electronic funds transfer system.

eftsoons (ɛftˈsuːnz) ADVERB *Archaic* [1] soon afterwards. [2] repeatedly.
▷**HISTORY** Old English *eft sōna,* literally: afterwards soon

eg THE INTERNET DOMAIN NAME FOR Egypt.

Eg. ABBREVIATION FOR: [1] Egypt(ian). [2] Egyptology.

e.g., eg, *or* **eg.** ABBREVIATIONS FOR exempli gratia.
▷**HISTORY** Latin: for example

egad (ɪˈgæd, iːˈgæd) INTERJECTION *Archaic* a mild oath or expression of surprise.
▷**HISTORY** C17: probably variant of *Ah God!*

egalitarian (ɪˌgælɪˈtɛərɪən) ADJECTIVE [1] of, relating to, or upholding the doctrine of the equality of mankind and the desirability of political, social, and economic equality. ◆ NOUN [2] an adherent of egalitarian principles.
▷**HISTORY** C19: alteration of *equalitarian,* through influence of French *égal* EQUAL
▸**eˌgaliˈtarianˌism** NOUN

Eger NOUN [1] (*Hungarian* ˈɛgɛr) a city in N central Hungary. Pop.: 60 000 (1995 est.). [2] (ˈeːgər) the German name for **Cheb.**

Egeria (ɪˈdʒɪərɪə) NOUN a female adviser.
▷**HISTORY** C17: name of the mythical adviser of Numa Pompilius, king of Rome

egest (iːˈdʒɛst) VERB (*tr*) to excrete (waste material).
▷**HISTORY** C17: from Latin *ēgerere* to carry out, from *gerere* to carry
▸**eˈgestion** NOUN ▸**eˈgestive** ADJECTIVE

egesta (iːˈdʒɛstə) PLURAL NOUN anything egested, as waste material from the body; excrement.
▷**HISTORY** C18: from Latin, literally: (things) carried out; see EGEST

egg[1] (ɛg) NOUN [1] the oval or round reproductive body laid by the females of birds, reptiles, fishes, insects, and some other animals, consisting of a developing embryo, its food store, and sometimes jelly or albumen, all surrounded by an outer shell or membrane. [2] Also called: **egg cell.** any female gamete; ovum. [3] the egg of the domestic hen used as food. [4] something resembling an egg, esp in shape or in being in an early stage of development. [5] **good** (*or* **bad**) **egg.** *Old-fashioned informal* **a** a good (or bad) person. **b** an exclamation of delight (or dismay). [6] **lay an egg.** *Slang, chiefly US and Canadian* **a** to make a joke or give a performance, etc., that fails completely. **b** (of a joke, performance, etc.) to fail completely; flop. [7] **put** *or* **have all one's eggs in one basket.** to stake everything on a single venture. [8] **teach one's grandmother to suck eggs.** to presume to teach someone something that he knows already. [9] **with egg on one's face.** *Informal* made to look ridiculous. ◆ VERB (*tr*) [10] to dip (food) in beaten egg before cooking. [11] *US informal* to throw eggs at.
▷**HISTORY** C14: from Old Norse *egg;* related to Old English *ǣg,* Old High German *ei*

egg[2] (ɛg) VERB (*tr;* usually foll by *on*) to urge or incite, esp to daring or foolish acts.
▷**HISTORY** Old English *eggian,* from Old Norse *eggja* to urge; related to Old English *ecg* EDGE, Middle Low German *eggen* to harrow

egg and dart, egg and tongue, *or* **egg and anchor** NOUN (in architecture and cabinetwork) **a** an ornamental moulding in which a half egg shape alternates with a dart, tongue, or anchor shape. **b** (*as modifier*): *egg-and-dart moulding.*

egg-and-spoon race NOUN a race in which runners carry an egg balanced in a spoon.

eggbeater (ˈɛgˌbiːtə) NOUN [1] Also called: **eggwhisk.** a kitchen utensil for beating eggs, whipping cream, etc.; whisk. 2 *Chiefly US and Canadian* an informal name for **helicopter.**

egg-binding NOUN a condition with a variety of causes, such as lack of sunlight and a cold damp environment, that causes a female bird to be unable to lay an egg that she is carrying.

egg-bound ADJECTIVE describing egg-bearing animals and birds that have difficulty passing their eggs.

egg cup NOUN a small cuplike container, used for holding a boiled egg while it is being eaten.

egger *or* **eggar** ('ɛɡə) NOUN any of various widely distributed moths of the family *Lasiocampidae,* such as *Lasiocampa quercus* (**oak egger**) of Europe, having brown bodies and wings.
▷HISTORY C18: from EGG[1], from the egg-shaped cocoon

egghead ('ɛɡˌhɛd) NOUN *Informal* an intellectual; highbrow.

eggler ('ɛɡlə) NOUN *Archaic or dialect* an egg dealer: sometimes itinerant.

eggnog (ˌɛɡ'nɒɡ) NOUN a drink that can be served hot or cold, made of eggs, milk, sugar, spice, and brandy, rum, or other spirit. Also called: **egg flip.**
▷HISTORY C19: from EGG[1] + NOG[1]

eggplant ('ɛɡˌplɑːnt) NOUN another name (esp US, Canadian, and Austral) for **aubergine** (sense 1).

egg roll NOUN a Chinese-American dish consisting of egg dough filled with a minced mixture of pork, bamboo shoots, onions, etc., and browned in deep fat.

eggs Benedict NOUN a dish consisting of toast, covered with a slice of ham, poached egg, and hollandaise sauce.

eggshell ('ɛɡˌʃɛl) NOUN 1 the hard porous protective outer layer of a bird's egg, consisting of calcite and protein. 2 a yellowish-white colour. 3 a type of paper with a slightly rough finish. 4 (*modifier*) (of paint) having a very slight sheen. 5 **walk on eggshells.** to be very cautious or diplomatic for fear of upsetting someone. ◆ ADJECTIVE 6 of a yellowish-white colour.

eggshell porcelain *or* **china** NOUN a type of very thin translucent porcelain originally made in China.

egg slice NOUN a spatula for removing omelettes, fried eggs, etc., from a pan.

egg spoon NOUN a small spoon for eating a boiled egg.

egg timer NOUN a device, typically a miniature hourglass, for timing the boiling of an egg.

egg tooth NOUN (in embryo birds and reptiles) a temporary tooth or (in birds) projection of the beak used for piercing the eggshell.

egg white NOUN the white of an egg; albumen.

Egham ('ɛɡəm) NOUN a town in S England, in N Surrey on the River Thames. Pop.: 23 816 (1991).

egis ('iːdʒɪs) NOUN a rare spelling of **aegis.**

eglandular (iː'ɡlændjʊlə) ADJECTIVE having no glands.
▷HISTORY E-[1] + GLANDULAR

eglantine ('ɛɡlənˌtaɪn) NOUN another name for **sweetbrier.**
▷HISTORY C14: from Old French *aiglent,* ultimately from Latin *acus* needle, from *acer* sharp, keen

EGM ABBREVIATION FOR **extraordinary general meeting.**

Egmont ('ɛɡmɒnt) NOUN an extinct volcano in New Zealand, in W central North Island in the **Egmont National Park:** an almost perfect cone. Height: 2518 m (8261 ft.).

ego ('iːɡəʊ, 'ɛɡəʊ) NOUN, *plural* **egos.** 1 the self of an individual person; the conscious subject. 2 *Psychoanal* the conscious mind, based on perception of the environment from birth onwards: responsible for modifying the antisocial instincts of the id and itself modified by the conscience (superego). 3 one's image of oneself; morale: *to boost one's ego.* 4 egotism; conceit.
▷HISTORY C19: from Latin: I

ego boost NOUN something such as praise, success, etc., that makes one feel better about oneself or raises one's morale.

egocentric (ˌiːɡəʊ'sɛntrɪk, ˌɛɡ-) ADJECTIVE 1 regarding everything only in relation to oneself; self-centred; selfish. 2 *Philosophy* pertaining to a theory in which everything is considered in relation to the self: *an egocentric universe.* ◆ NOUN 3 a self-centred person; egotist.
▸ **ˌegocen'tricity** NOUN

egocentrism (ˌiːɡəʊ'sɛntrɪzəm, ˌɛɡəʊ-) NOUN 1 the condition or fact of being egocentric. 2 *Psychol* a stage in a child's development characterized by lack of awareness that other people's points of view differ from his own.

ego ideal NOUN *Psychoanal* an internal ideal of personal perfection that represents what one wants to be rather than what one ought to be and is derived from one's early relationship with one's parents. See also **superego.**

egoism ('iːɡəʊˌɪzəm, 'ɛɡ-) NOUN 1 concern for one's own interests and welfare. 2 *Ethics* the theory that the pursuit of one's own welfare is the highest good. Compare **altruism.** 3 self-centredness; egotism.

egoist ('iːɡəʊɪst, 'ɛɡ-) NOUN 1 a person who is preoccupied with his own interests; a selfish person. 2 a conceited person; egotist. 3 *Ethics* a person who lives by the values of egoism.
▸ **ˌego'istic** *or* **ˌego'istical** ADJECTIVE ▸ **ˌego'istically** ADVERB

Egoli (ɛ'ɡəʊlɪ) an informal name for **Johannesburg.**
▷HISTORY from Zulu *eGoli* place of gold

egomania (ˌiːɡəʊ'meɪnɪə, ˌɛɡ-) NOUN *Psychiatry* 1 obsessive love for oneself and regard for one's own needs. 2 any action dictated by this point of view.
▸ **ˌego'maniˌac** NOUN ▸ **egomaniacal** (ˌiːɡəʊmə'naɪɪkᵊl, ˌɛɡ-) ADJECTIVE

egotism ('iːɡəˌtɪzəm, 'ɛɡə-) NOUN 1 an inflated sense of self-importance or superiority; self-centredness. 2 excessive reference to oneself.
▷HISTORY C18: from Latin *ego* I + -ISM

egotist ('iːɡətɪst, 'ɛɡ-) NOUN 1 a conceited boastful person. 2 a self-interested person; egoist.
▸ **ˌego'tistic** *or* **ˌego'tistical** ADJECTIVE ▸ **ˌego'tistically** ADVERB

ego trip *Informal* ◆ NOUN 1 something undertaken to boost or draw attention to a person's own image or appraisal of himself. ◆ VERB **ego-trip, -trips, -tripping, -tripped.** (*intr*) 2 to act in this way.

e-government NOUN the provision of government information and services by means of the Internet and other computer resources.
▷HISTORY C20: *e*lectronic *government*

egregious (ɪ'ɡriːdʒəs, -dʒɪəs) ADJECTIVE 1 outstandingly bad; flagrant: *an egregious lie.* 2 *Archaic* distinguished; eminent.
▷HISTORY C16: from Latin *ēgregius* outstanding (literally: standing out from the herd), from *ē-* out + *grex* flock, herd
▸ **e'gregiously** ADVERB ▸ **e'gregiousness** NOUN

egress NOUN ('iːɡrɛs) 1 Also called: **egression.** the act of going or coming out; emergence. 2 a way out, such as a path; exit. 3 the right or permission to go out or depart. 4 *Astronomy* another name for **emersion** (sense 2). ◆ VERB (ɪ'ɡrɛs) (*intr*) 5 to go forth; issue.
▷HISTORY C16: from Latin *ēgredī* to come forth, depart, from *gradī* to move, step

egret ('iːɡrɪt) NOUN any of various wading birds of the genera *Egretta, Hydranassa,* etc., that are similar to herons but usually have a white plumage and, in the breeding season, long feathery plumes (see **aigrette**): family *Ardeidae,* order *Ciconiiformes.*
▷HISTORY C15: from Old French *aigrette,* from Old Provençal *aigreta,* from *aigron* heron, of Germanic origin; compare Old High German *heigaro* HERON

Egypt ('iːdʒɪpt) NOUN a republic in NE Africa, on the Mediterranean and Red Sea: its history dates back about 5000 years. Occupied by the British from 1882, it became an independent kingdom in 1922 and a republic in 1953. Over 96 per cent of the total area is desert, with the chief areas of habitation and cultivation in the Nile delta and valley. Cotton is the main export. Official language: Arabic. Official religion: Muslim; Sunni majority. Currency: pound. Capital: Cairo. Pop.: 65 239 000 (2001 est). Area: 997 739 sq. km (385 229 sq. miles). Official name: **Arab Republic of Egypt.** Former official name (1958–71): **United Arab Republic.**

Egyptian (ɪ'dʒɪpʃən) ADJECTIVE 1 of, relating to, or characteristic of Egypt, its inhabitants, or their dialect of Arabic. 2 of, relating to, or characteristic of the ancient Egyptians, their language, or culture. 3 (of type) having square slab serifs. 4 *Archaic* of or relating to the Gypsies. ◆ NOUN 5 a native or inhabitant of Egypt. 6 a member of an indigenous non-Semitic people who established an advanced civilization in Egypt that flourished from the late fourth millennium B.C. 7 the extinct language of the ancient Egyptians, belonging to the Afro-Asiatic family of languages. It is recorded in hieroglyphic inscriptions, the earliest of which date from before 3000 B.C. It was extinct by the fourth century A.D. See also **Coptic.** 8 a large size of drawing paper. 9 an archaic name for a **Gypsy.**

Egyptian jasper NOUN a type of jasper, generally with zones of colour, found in desert regions of Egypt.

Egyptian Mau (maʊ) NOUN a breed of medium-sized cat with a spotted coat of medium length.
▷HISTORY Arabic *mau* cat

Egyptology (ˌiːdʒɪp'tɒlədʒɪ) NOUN the study of the archaeology and language of ancient Egypt.
▸ **Egyptological** (ɪˌdʒɪptə'lɒdʒɪkᵊl) ADJECTIVE
▸ **ˌEgyp'tologist** NOUN

eh[1] (eɪ) INTERJECTION an exclamation used to express questioning surprise or to seek the repetition or confirmation of a statement or question: *Eh? What did you say?*

eh[2] THE INTERNET DOMAIN NAME FOR Western Sahara.

EHF ABBREVIATION FOR **extremely high frequency.**

EHO (in Britain) ABBREVIATION FOR **Environmental Health Officer.**

EHV ABBREVIATION FOR equine herpesvirus.

EI ABBREVIATION FOR: 1 East Indian. 2 East Indies. 3 *Social psychol* emotional intelligence. 4 (in Canada) Employment Insurance.

EIA ABBREVIATION FOR equine infectious anaemia.

EIB ABBREVIATION FOR European Investment Bank.

eider *or* **eider duck** ('aɪdə) NOUN any of several sea ducks of the genus *Somateria,* esp *S. mollissima,* and related genera, which occur in the N hemisphere. The male has black and white plumage, and the female is the source of eiderdown.
▷HISTORY C18: from Old Norse *æthr;* related to Swedish *ejder,* Dutch, German *Eider*

eiderdown ('aɪdəˌdaʊn) NOUN 1 the breast down of the female eider duck, with which it lines the nest, used for stuffing pillows, quilts, etc. 2 a thick warm cover for a bed, made of two layers of material enclosing a soft filling. 3 *US* a warm cotton fabric having a woollen nap.

eidetic (aɪ'dɛtɪk) ADJECTIVE *Psychol* 1 (of visual, or sometimes auditory, images) exceptionally vivid and allowing detailed recall of something previously perceived: thought to be common in children. 2 relating to or subject to such imagery.
▷HISTORY C20: from Greek *eidētikos,* from *eidos* shape, form
▸ **ei'detically** ADVERB

eidolon (aɪ'dəʊlɒn) NOUN, *plural* **-la** (-lə) *or* **-lons.** 1 an unsubstantial image; apparition; phantom. 2 an ideal or idealized figure.
▷HISTORY C19: from Greek: phantom, IDOL

Eid-ul-Adha ('iːdʊlˌɑːdə) NOUN an annual Muslim festival marking the end of the pilgrimage to Mecca. Animals are sacrificed and their meat shared among the poor.
▷HISTORY from Arabic *id ul adha* festival of sacrifice

Eid-ul-Fitr ('iːdʊlˌfiːtə) NOUN an annual Muslim festival marking the end of Ramadan, involving the exchange of gifts and a festive meal.
▷HISTORY from Arabic *id ul fitr* festival of fast-breaking

Eifel ('aɪfəl; *German* 'aifəl) NOUN a plateau region in W Germany, between the River Moselle and the Belgian frontier: quarrying.

Eiffel Tower ('aɪfᵊl) NOUN a tower in Paris: designed by A. G. Eiffel; erected for the 1889 Paris Exposition. Height: 300 m (984 ft.), raised in 1959 to 321 m (1052 ft.).

eigen NOUN COMBINING FORM characteristic; proper: *eigenvalue.*
▷HISTORY from German, literally: own

eigenfrequency ('aɪɡənˌfriːkwənsɪ) NOUN, *plural* **-cies.** *Physics* a resonance frequency of a system.

eigenfunction ('aɪɡənˌfʌŋkʃən) NOUN *Maths,*

physics a function satisfying a differential equation, esp an allowed function for a system in wave mechanics.

eigentone (ˈaɪɡənˌtəʊn) NOUN a characteristic acoustic resonance frequency of a system.

eigenvalue (ˈaɪɡənˌvælju:) NOUN *Maths, physics* one of the particular values of a certain parameter for which a differential equation or matrix equation has an eigenfunction. In wave mechanics an eigenvalue is equivalent to the energy of a quantum state of a system.

eigenvector (ˈaɪɡənˌvɛktə) NOUN *Maths, physics* a vector $\boldsymbol{x}$ satisfying an equation $A\boldsymbol{x} = \lambda\boldsymbol{x}$, where A is a square matrix and λ is a constant.

Eiger (*German* ˈaiɡər) NOUN a mountain in central Switzerland, in the Bernese Alps. Height: 3970 m (13 025 ft.).

eight (eɪt) NOUN 1 the cardinal number that is the sum of one and seven and the product of two and four. See also **number** (sense 1). 2 a numeral, 8, VIII, etc., representing this number. 3 *Music* the numeral 8 used as the lower figure in a time signature to indicate that the beat is measured in quavers. 4 the amount or quantity that is one greater than seven. 5 something representing, represented by, or consisting of eight units, such as a playing card with eight symbols on it. 6 *Rowing* **a** a racing shell propelled by eight oarsmen. **b** the crew of such a shell. 7 Also called: **eight o'clock.** eight hours after noon or midnight. 8 **have one over the eight.** *Slang* to be drunk. 9 See **figure of eight.** ◆ DETERMINER 10 **a** amounting to eight. **b** (*as pronoun*): *I could only find eight.* ◆ Related prefixes **octa-, octo-.**
▷HISTORY Old English *eahta;* related to Old High German *ahto,* Old Norse *ātta,* Old Irish *ocht,* Latin *octō,* Greek *okto,* Sanskrit *astau*

eight ball NOUN *US and Canadian* 1 (in pool) the black ball, marked with the number eight. 2 **behind the eight ball.** in a difficult situation; snookered.

eighteen (ˈeɪˈti:n) NOUN 1 the cardinal number that is the sum of ten and eight and the product of two and nine. See also **number** (sense 1). 2 a numeral, 18, XVIII, etc., representing this number. 3 the amount or quantity that is eight more than ten. 4 something represented by, representing, or consisting of 18 units. 5 (*functioning as singular or plural*) a team of 18 players in Australian Rules football. ◆ DETERMINER 6 **a** amounting to eighteen: *eighteen weeks.* **b** (*as pronoun*): *eighteen of them knew.*
▷HISTORY Old English *eahtatēne;* related to Old Norse *attjan,* Old High German *ahtozehan*

eighteenmo (ˈeɪˈti:nməʊ) NOUN, *plural* **-mos.** 1 Also called: **octodecimo.** a book size resulting from folding a sheet of paper into 18 leaves or 36 pages. Often written: **18mo, 18°.** 2 a book of this size.

eighteenth (ˈeɪˈti:nθ) ADJECTIVE 1 (*usually prenominal*) **a** coming after the seventeenth in numbering or counting order, position, time, etc.; being the ordinal number of *eighteen:* often written 18th. **b** (*as noun*): *come on the eighteenth.* ◆ NOUN 2 **a** one of 18 approximately equal parts of something. **b** (*as modifier*): *an eighteenth part.* 3 the fraction that is equal to one divided by 18 (1/18).

eightfold (ˈeɪtˌfəʊld) ADJECTIVE 1 equal to or having eight times as many or as much. 2 composed of eight parts. ◆ ADVERB 3 by or up to eight times as much.

eighth (eɪtθ) ADJECTIVE 1 (*usually prenominal*) **a** coming after the seventh and before the ninth in numbering or counting order, position, time, etc.; being the ordinal number of *eight:* often written 8th. **b** (*as noun*): *the eighth in line.* ◆ NOUN 2 **a** one of eight equal or nearly equal parts of an object, quantity, measurement, etc. **b** (*as modifier*): *an eighth part.* 3 the fraction equal to one divided by eight (1/8). 4 another word for **octave.** ◆ ADVERB 5 Also: **eighthly.** after the seventh person, position, event, etc.

eighth note NOUN the usual US and Canadian name for **quaver** (sense 4).

eightieth (ˈeɪtɪɪθ) ADJECTIVE 1 (*usually prenominal*) **a** being the ordinal number of *eighty* in numbering or counting order, position, time, etc.: often written 80th. **b** (*as noun*): *the eightieth in succession.* ◆ NOUN 2 **a** one of 80 approximately equal parts of something. **b** (*as modifier*): *an eightieth part.* 3 the fraction equal to one divided by 80 (1/80).

eightsome reel (ˈeɪtsəm) NOUN a Scottish dance for eight people.

eightvo (ˈeɪtvəʊ) NOUN, *plural* **-vos.** *Bookbinding* another word for **octavo.**

eighty (ˈeɪtɪ) NOUN, *plural* **-ies.** 1 the cardinal number that is the product of ten and eight. See also **number** (sense 1). 2 a numeral, 80, LXXX, etc., representing this number. 3 (*plural*) the numbers 80-89, esp a person's age or the year of a particular century. 4 the amount or quantity that is eight times as big as ten. 5 something represented by, representing, or consisting of 80 units. ◆ DETERMINER 6 **a** amounting to eighty: *eighty pages of nonsense.* **b** (*as pronoun*): *eighty are expected.*
▷HISTORY Old English *eahtatig;* related to Old Frisian *achtig,* Old High German *ahtozug*

eighty-seven NOUN *Cricket* a score traditionally regarded as being unlucky.
▷HISTORY possibly because 13 less than a century

eikon (ˈaɪkɒn) NOUN a variant spelling of **icon.**

Eilat, Elat, *or* **Elath** (eɪˈlɑ:t) NOUN a port in S Israel, on the Gulf of Aqaba: Israel's only outlet to the Red Sea. Pop.: 26 010 (latest est.).

Eilean Donan Castle (ˈeɪlən ˈdɒnən) NOUN a castle near the Kyle of Lochalsh in Highland, Scotland: built in the 13th century; famous for its picturesque setting.

Eilean Siar (ˈeɪlən ˈsɪə) NOUN the Scottish Gaelic name for **Western Isles.**

eina (ˈeɪˌnɑ:) INTERJECTION *South African* an exclamation of sudden pain.
▷HISTORY C19: Afrikaans, from Khoi

Eindhoven (*Dutch* ˈaɪntˌhəʊvᵊn, ˈeintho:və) NOUN a city in the SE Netherlands, in North Brabant province: radio and electrical industry. Pop.: 199 877 (1999 est.)

einkorn (ˈaɪnˌkɔ:n) NOUN a variety of wheat, *Triticum monococcum,* of Greece and SW Asia, having pale red kernels, and cultivated in hilly regions as grain for horses.
▷HISTORY C20: from German, literally: one kernel

einsteinium (aɪnˈstaɪnɪəm) NOUN a metallic transuranic element artificially produced from plutonium. Symbol: Es; atomic no.: 99; half-life of most stable isotope, ^{252}Es: 276 days.
▷HISTORY C20: New Latin, named after Albert *Einstein* (1879–1955), German-born US physicist and mathematician

Einstein shift NOUN *Astronomy* a small displacement towards the red in the spectra, caused by the interaction between the radiation and the gravitational field of a massive body, such as the sun.

Einstein's mass-energy law NOUN the principle that mass (m) and energy (E) are equivalent according to the equation $E = mc^2$, where c is the velocity of light.

Einstein's photoelectric law NOUN the principle that the maximum energy of a photoelectron is $h\nu - \Phi$, where ν is the frequency of the incident radiation, h is the Planck constant, and Φ is the work function.

Eire (ˈɛərə) NOUN 1 the Irish Gaelic name for **Ireland**¹: often used to mean the **Republic of Ireland.** 2 a former name for the **Republic of Ireland** (1937–49).

eirenic (aɪˈri:nɪk) ADJECTIVE a variant spelling of **irenic.**

eirenicon *or* **irenicon** (aɪˈri:nɪˌkɒn) NOUN a proposition that attempts to harmonize conflicting viewpoints.
▷HISTORY C19: from Greek, from *eirēnikos* of or concerning peace, from *eirēnē* peace

eisegesis (ˌaɪsəˈdʒi:sɪs) NOUN, *plural* **-ses** (-si:z). the interpretation of a text, esp. a biblical text, using one's own ideas. Compare **exegesis.**
▷HISTORY C19: from Greek *eis* into, in + *-egesis,* as in EXEGESIS

Eisenach (*German* ˈaizənax) NOUN a city in central Germany, in Thuringia: birthplace of Johann Sebastian Bach. Pop.: 48 361 (latest est.).

Eisenstadt (*German* ˈaizənʃtat) NOUN a town in E Austria, capital of Burgenland province: Hungarian until 1921. Pop.: 10 506 (1991).

Eisk *or* **Eysk** (*Russian* jejsk) NOUN variant transliterations of the Russian name for **Yeisk.**

eisteddfod (aɪˈstedfəd; *Welsh* aɪˈsteðvɔd) NOUN, *plural* **-fods** *or* **-fodau** (*Welsh* aɪˌsteðˈvɒdaɪ). any of a number of annual festivals in Wales, esp. the **Royal National Eisteddfod,** in which competitions are held in music, poetry, drama, and the fine arts.
▷HISTORY C19: from Welsh, literally: session, from *eistedd* to sit (from *sedd* seat) + *-fod,* from *bod* to be
▸**ˌeisteddˈfodic** ADJECTIVE

either (ˈaɪðə, ˈi:ðə) DETERMINER 1 **a** one or the other (of two): *either coat will do.* **b** (*as pronoun*): *either is acceptable.* 2 both one and the other: *there were ladies at either end of the table.* 3 (*coordinating*) used preceding two or more possibilities joined by *"or"*: *you may have either cheese or a sweet.* ◆ ADVERB (*sentence modifier*) 4 (*used with a negative*) used to indicate that the clause immediately preceding is a partial reiteration of a previous clause: *John isn't a liar, but he isn't exactly honest either.*
▷HISTORY Old English *ǣgther,* short for *ǣghwæther* each of two; related to Old Frisian *ēider,* Old High German *ēogihweder;* see EACH, WHETHER

> **Language note** *Either* is followed by a singular verb in good usage: *either is good; either of these books is useful.* Care should be taken to avoid ambiguity when using *either* to mean *both* or *each,* as in the following sentence: *a ship could be moored on either side of the channel.* Agreement between the verb and its subject in *either...or...* constructions follows the pattern given for *neither...nor...* See at **neither.**

either-or ADJECTIVE presenting an unavoidable need to choose between two alternatives: *an either-or situation.*

ejaculate VERB (ɪˈdʒækjʊˌleɪt) 1 to eject or discharge (semen) in orgasm. 2 (*tr*) to utter abruptly; blurt out. ◆ NOUN (ɪˈdʒækjʊlɪt) 3 another word for **semen.**
▷HISTORY C16: from Latin *ējaculārī* to hurl out, from *jaculum* javelin, from *jacere* to throw
▸**eˈjacuˌlator** NOUN

ejaculation (ɪˌdʒækjʊˈleɪʃən) NOUN 1 an abrupt emphatic utterance or exclamation. 2 a discharge of semen.
▸**eˈjaculatory** *or* **eˈjaculative** ADJECTIVE

ejaculatio praecox (ɪˌdʒækjʊˈleɪʃɪəʊ ˈpri:kɒks) NOUN premature ejaculation during sexual intercourse.
▷HISTORY Latin

eject (ɪˈdʒɛkt) VERB 1 (*tr*) to drive or force out; expel or emit. 2 (*tr*) to compel (a person) to leave; evict; dispossess. 3 (*tr*) to dismiss, as from office. 4 (*intr*) to leave an aircraft rapidly, using an ejection seat or capsule. 5 (*tr*) *Psychiatry* to attribute (one's own motivations and characteristics) to others.
▷HISTORY C15: from Latin *ejicere,* from *jacere* to throw
▸**eˈjection** NOUN

ejecta (ɪˈdʒɛktə) PLURAL NOUN matter thrown out of a crater by an erupting volcano or during a meteorite impact.
▷HISTORY C19: Latin, literally: (things) ejected; see EJECT

ejection seat *or* **ejector seat** NOUN a seat, esp as fitted to military aircraft, that is fired by a cartridge or rocket to eject the occupant from the aircraft in an emergency.

ejective (ɪˈdʒɛktɪv) ADJECTIVE 1 relating to or causing ejection. 2 *Phonetics* (of a plosive or fricative consonant, as in some African languages) pronounced with a glottal stop. ◆ NOUN 3 *Phonetics* an ejective consonant.
▸**eˈjectively** ADVERB

ejectment (ɪˈdʒɛktmənt) NOUN 1 *Property law* (formerly) an action brought by a wrongfully dispossessed owner seeking to recover possession of his land. 2 the act of ejecting or state of being ejected; dispossession.

ejector (ɪˈdʒɛktə) NOUN 1 a person or thing that ejects. 2 the mechanism in a firearm that ejects the empty cartridge or shell after firing.

Ekaterinburg (*Russian* jɪkətɪrinˈburk) NOUN a variant transliteration of the Russian name for **Yekaterinburg.**

Ekaterinodar (*Russian* jɪkətɪrina'dar) NOUN the former name (until 1920) of **Krasnodar**.

Ekaterinoslav (*Russian* jɪkətɪrina'slaf) NOUN the former name (1787–96, 1802–1926) of **Dnepropetrovsk**.

eke[1] (i:k) VERB (*tr*) *Archaic* to increase, enlarge, or lengthen.
▷HISTORY Old English *eacan;* related to Old Norse *auka* to increase, Latin *augēre* to increase

eke[2] (i:k) SENTENCE CONNECTOR *Archaic* also; moreover.
▷HISTORY Old English *eac;* related to Old Norse, Gothic *auk* also, Old High German *ouh,* Latin *autem* but, *aut* or

eke out VERB (*tr, adverb*) 1 to make (a supply) last, esp by frugal use: *they eked out what little food was left.* 2 to support (existence) with difficulty and effort. 3 to add to (something insufficient), esp with effort: *to eke out an income with evening work.*

EKG (in the US and Canada) ABBREVIATION FOR: 1 electrocardiogram. 2 electrocardiograph.

ekistics (ɪ'kɪstɪks) NOUN (*functioning as singular*) the science or study of human settlements.
▷HISTORY C20: from Greek *oikistikos* of or concerning settlements, from *oikizein* to settle (a colony), from *oikos* a house
▸**e'kistic** *or* **e'kistical** ADJECTIVE ▸**ˌekis'tician** NOUN

Ekman layer (*Swedish* 'ekman) NOUN the thin top layer of the sea that flows at 90° to the wind direction, discovered by Vagn Walfrid Ekman (1874–1954), Swedish oceanographer.

Ekman Spiral NOUN a complex interaction on the surface of the sea between wind, rotation of the earth, and friction forces, discovered by Vagn Walfrid Ekman (1874–1954).

ekpwele (ɛk'pweɪleɪ) *or* **ekuele** (eɪ'kweɪleɪ) NOUN, *plural* **-le** (-leɪ). a former monetary unit of Equatorial Guinea.
▷HISTORY from the native name in Equatorial Guinea

el (ɛl) NOUN *US informal* a shortened form of **elevated railway** or **railroad**.

El Aaiún (ɛl aɪ'ju:n) NOUN a city in Morocco, in Western Sahara: the capital of the former Spanish Sahara; port facilities begun in 1967 at **Playa de El Aaiún** 20 km (12 miles) away, following the discovery of rich phosphate deposits. Pop. (urban area): 164 000 (1998 est.).

elaborate ADJECTIVE (ɪ'læbərɪt) 1 planned or executed with care and exactness; detailed. 2 marked by complexity, ornateness, or detail. ◆ VERB (ɪ'læbəˌreɪt) 3 (*intr;* usually foll by *on* or *upon*) to add information or detail (to an account); expand (upon). 4 (*tr*) to work out in detail; develop. 5 (*tr*) to make more complicated or ornate. 6 (*tr*) to produce by careful labour; create. 7 (*tr*) *Physiol* to change (food or simple substances) into more complex substances for use in the body.
▷HISTORY C16: from Latin *ēlabōrāre* to take pains, from *labōrāre* to toil
▸**e'laborately** ADVERB ▸**e'laborateness** NOUN ▸**eˌlabo'ration** NOUN ▸**elaborative** (ɪ'læbərətɪv) ADJECTIVE ▸**e'laboˌrator** NOUN

elaeoptene (ˌɛlɪ'ɒpti:n) NOUN a variant spelling of **eleoptene**.

elaiosome (ɪ'leɪəsəʊm) NOUN an oil-rich body on seeds or fruits that attracts ants, which act as dispersal agents.
▷HISTORY from Greek *elaion* oil + -SOME[3]

El Alamein *or* **Alamein** (ɛl 'æləˌmeɪn) NOUN a village on the N coast of Egypt, about 112 km (70 miles) west of Alexandria: scene of a decisive Allied victory over the Axis forces (1942).

Elam ('i:ləm) NOUN an ancient kingdom east of the River Tigris: established before 4000 B.C.; probably inhabited by a non-Semitic people.

Elamite ('i:ləˌmaɪt) NOUN 1 an inhabitant of the ancient kingdom of Elam. 2 Also called: **Elamitic, Susian.** the extinct language of this people, of no known relationship, recorded in cuneiform inscriptions dating from the 25th to the 4th centuries B.C. ◆ ADJECTIVE 3 of or relating to Elam, its people, or their language.

élan (eɪ'lɑ:n, eɪ'læn; *French* elɑ̃) NOUN a combination of style and vigour: *he performed the concerto with élan.*
▷HISTORY C19: from French, from *élancer* to throw forth, ultimately from Latin *lancea* LANCE

eland ('i:lənd) NOUN 1 a large spiral-horned antelope, *Taurotragus oryx,* inhabiting bushland in eastern and southern Africa. It has a dewlap and a hump on the shoulders and is light brown with vertical white stripes. 2 **giant eland.** a similar but larger animal, *T. derbianus,* living in wooded areas of central and W Africa.
▷HISTORY C18: via Afrikaans from Dutch *eland* elk; related to Old Slavonic *jeleni* stag, Greek *ellos* fawn

élan vital *French* (elɑ̃ vital) NOUN a creative principle held by Henri Bergson to be present in all organisms and responsible for evolution. Compare **Bergsonism.**
▷HISTORY literally: vital impetus

elapid ('ɛləpɪd) NOUN 1 any venomous snake of the mostly tropical family *Elapidae,* having fixed poison fangs at the front of the upper jaw and including the cobras, coral snakes, and mambas. ◆ ADJECTIVE 2 of, relating to, or belonging to the *Elapidae.*
▷HISTORY C19: from New Latin *Elapidae,* from Medieval Greek *elaps, elops* a fish, sea serpent; perhaps related to Greek *lepis* scale

elapse (ɪ'læps) VERB (*intr*) (of time) to pass by.
▷HISTORY C17: from Latin *ēlābī* to slip away, from *lābī* to slip, glide

Elara (ɛ'lærə) NOUN *Astronomy* a small satellite of Jupiter in an intermediate orbit.

elasmobranch (ɪ'læsməˌbræŋk, ɪ'læz-) NOUN 1 any cartilaginous fish of the subclass *Elasmobranchii* (or *Selachii*), which includes the sharks, rays, dogfish, and skates. ◆ ADJECTIVE 2 of, relating to, or belonging to the *Elasmobranchii.* ◆ Also called: **selachian.**
▷HISTORY C19: from New Latin *elasmobranchii,* from Greek *elasmos* metal plate + *brankhia* gills

elasmosaur (ɪ'læzməˌsɔ:) NOUN a very long-necked extinct marine reptile: a type of plesiosaur.
▷HISTORY C19: from Greek *elasmos* metal plate + *sauros* lizard

elastance (ɪ'læstəns) NOUN *Physics* the reciprocal of capacitance. It is measured in reciprocal farads (darafs).
▷HISTORY C19: from ELASTIC + -ANCE

elastane (ɪ'læsteɪn) NOUN a synthetic fibre characterized by its ability to revert to its original shape after being stretched.

elastase (ɪ'læsteɪs) NOUN an enzyme that digests elastin.

elastic (ɪ'læstɪk) ADJECTIVE 1 (of a body or material) capable of returning to its original shape after compression, expansion, stretching, or other deformation. 2 capable of adapting to change: *an elastic schedule.* 3 quick to recover from fatigue, dejection, etc.; buoyant. 4 springy or resilient: *an elastic walk.* 5 (of gases) capable of expanding spontaneously. 6 *Physics* (of collisions) involving no overall change in translational kinetic energy. 7 made of elastic. ◆ NOUN 8 tape, cord, or fabric containing interwoven strands of flexible rubber or similar substance allowing it to stretch and return to its original shape. 9 *Chiefly US and Canadian* something made of elastic, such as a rubber band or a garter.
▷HISTORY C17: from New Latin *elasticus* impulsive, from Greek *elastikos,* from *elaunein* to beat, drive
▸**e'lastically** ADVERB

elasticate (ɪ'læstɪˌkeɪt) VERB (*tr*) to insert elastic sections or thread into (a fabric or garment): *an elasticated waistband.*
▸**eˌlasti'cation** NOUN

elastic band NOUN another name for **rubber band.**

elasticity (ɪlæ'stɪsɪtɪ, ˌi:læ-) NOUN 1 the property of a body or substance that enables it to resume its original shape or size when a distorting force is removed. See also **elastic limit.** 2 the state or quality of being elastic; flexibility or buoyancy. 3 a measure of the sensitivity of demand for goods or services to changes in price or other marketing variables, such as advertising.

elasticize *or* **elasticise** (ɪ'læstɪˌsaɪz) VERB (*tr*) 1 to make elastic. 2 another word for **elasticate.**

elastic limit NOUN the greatest stress that can be applied to a material without causing permanent deformation.

elastic modulus NOUN another name for **modulus of elasticity.**

elastic rebound NOUN *Geology* a theory of earthquakes that envisages gradual deformation of the fault zone without fault slippage until friction is overcome, when the fault suddenly slips to produce the earthquake.

elastin (ɪ'læstɪn) NOUN *Biochem* a fibrous scleroprotein constituting the major part of elastic tissue, such as the walls of arteries.
▷HISTORY C19: from ELASTIC + -IN

elastomer (ɪ'læstəmə) NOUN any material, such as natural or synthetic rubber, that is able to resume its original shape when a deforming force is removed.
▷HISTORY C20: from ELASTIC + -MER
▸**elastomeric** (ɪˌlæstə'mɛrɪk) ADJECTIVE

Elastoplast (ɪ'læstəˌplɑ:st) NOUN *Trademark* a gauze surgical dressing backed by adhesive tape.

Elat *or* **Elath** (eɪ'lɑ:t) NOUN variant spellings of **Eilat.**

elate (ɪ'leɪt) VERB (*tr*) to fill with high spirits, exhilaration, pride or optimism.
▷HISTORY C16: from Latin *ēlāt-* stem of past participle of *efferre* to bear away, from *ferre* to carry

elated (ɪ'leɪtɪd) ADJECTIVE full of high spirits, exhilaration, pride or optimism; very happy.
▸**e'lated** ADJECTIVE ▸**e'latedly** ADVERB ▸**e'latedness** NOUN

elater ('ɛlətə) NOUN 1 an elaterid beetle. 2 *Botany* a spirally thickened filament, occurring in liverwort capsules and horsetails, thought to aid dispersal of spores.
▷HISTORY C17: via New Latin from Greek: driver, from *elaunein* to beat, drive; compare ELASTIC

elaterid (ɪ'lætərɪd) NOUN 1 any of the beetles constituting the widely distributed family *Elateridae* (click beetles). The group includes the wireworms and certain fireflies. ◆ ADJECTIVE 2 of, relating to, or belonging to the family *Elateridae.*
▷HISTORY C19: from New Latin *Elateridae,* from ELATER

elaterin (ɪ'lætərɪn) NOUN a white crystalline substance found in elaterium, used as a purgative.
▷HISTORY C19: from ELATERIUM + -IN

elaterite (ɪ'lætəˌraɪt) NOUN a dark brown naturally occurring bitumen resembling rubber.
▷HISTORY C19: from ELATER + -ITE[1]

elaterium (ˌɛlə'tɪərɪəm) NOUN a greenish sediment prepared from the juice of the squirting cucumber, used as a purgative.
▷HISTORY C16: from Latin, from Greek *elatērion* squirting cucumber, from *elatērios* purgative, from *elaunein* to drive

elation (ɪ'leɪʃən) NOUN joyfulness or exaltation of spirit, as from success, pleasure, or relief; high spirits.

elative ('i:lətɪv) ADJECTIVE 1 (in the grammar of Finnish and other languages) denoting a case of nouns expressing a relation of motion or direction, usually translated by the English prepositions *out of* or *away from.* Compare **illative** (sense 3). ◆ NOUN 2 **a** the elative case. **b** an elative word or speech element.
▷HISTORY C19: from Latin *ēlātus,* past participle of *efferre* to carry out; see ELATE

E layer NOUN another name for **E region.**

Elba ('ɛlbə) NOUN a mountainous island off the W coast of Italy, in the Mediterranean: Napoleon Bonaparte's first place of exile (1814–15). Pop.: 27 722 (1991 est.). Area: 223 sq. km (86 sq. miles).

Elbe (ɛlb; *German* 'ɛlbə) NOUN a river in central Europe, rising in the N Czech Republic and flowing generally northwest through Germany to the North Sea at Hamburg. Length: 1165 km (724 miles). Czech name: **Labe.**

Elbert ('ɛlbət) NOUN **Mount.** a mountain in central Colorado, in the Sawatch range. Height: 4399 m (14 431 ft.).

Elbląg (*Polish* 'ɛlblɔŋk) NOUN a port in N Poland: metallurgical industries. Pop.: 129 782 (1999 est.). German name: **Elbing** ('ɛlbɪŋ).

elbow ('ɛlbəʊ) NOUN 1 the joint between the upper arm and the forearm, formed by the junction of the radius and ulna with the humerus. 2 the

corresponding joint or bone of birds or mammals. [3] the part of a garment that covers the elbow. [4] something resembling an elbow, such as a sharp bend in a road or river. [5] **at one's elbow.** within easy reach. [6] **out at elbow(s).** ragged or impoverished. [7] **up to the elbows with** *or* **in.** busily occupied with; deeply immersed in. [8] to reject; dismiss (esp in the phrases **give** *or* **get the elbow**). [9] to make (one's way) by shoving, jostling, etc. [10] (*tr*) to knock or shove with or as if with the elbow.
▷**HISTORY** Old English *elnboga;* see ELL², BOW²; related to Old Norse *olbogi,* Old High German *elinbogo*

elbow grease NOUN *Facetious* vigorous physical labour, esp hard rubbing.

elbowroom (ˈɛlbəʊˌruːm, -ˌrʊm) NOUN sufficient scope to move or function.

Elbrus (ɪlˈbruːs) NOUN a mountain in SW Russia, on the border with Georgia, in the Caucasus Mountains, with two extinct volcanic peaks: the highest mountain in Europe. Height: 5642 m (18 510 ft.).

Elburz Mountains (ɛlˈbʊəz) PLURAL NOUN a mountain range in N Iran, parallel to the SW and S shores of the Caspian Sea. Highest peak: Mount Demavend, 5601 m (18 376 ft.).

El Capitan (ɛl ˌkæpɪˈtæn) NOUN a mountain in E central California, in the Sierra Nevada: a monolith with a precipice rising over 1100 m (3600 ft.) above the floor of the Yosemite Valley. Height: 2306 m (7564 ft.).

Elche (*Spanish* ˈɛltʃe) NOUN a town in S Spain, in Valencia: noted for Iberian and Roman archaeological finds and the medieval religious drama performed there annually: fruit growing, esp dates, pomegranates, figs. Pop.: 191 713 (1998 est.).

eld (ɛld) NOUN *Archaic* [1] old age. [2] olden days; antiquity.
▷**HISTORY** Old English *eldu;* related to Old Norse *elli;* see OLD

elder¹ (ˈɛldə) ADJECTIVE [1] born earlier; senior. Compare **older.** [2] (in piquet and similar card games) denoting or relating to the nondealer (the **elder hand**), who has certain advantages in the play. [3] *Archaic* **a** prior in rank, position, or office. **b** of a previous time; former. ◆ NOUN [4] an older person; one's senior. [5] *Anthropol* a senior member of a tribe who has influence or authority. [6] (in certain Protestant Churches) a lay office having teaching, pastoral, or administrative functions. [7] another word for **presbyter.**
▷**HISTORY** Old English *eldra,* comparative of *eald* OLD; related to Old Norse *ellri,* Old High German *altiro,* Gothic *althiza*
▸ **ˈelderˌship** NOUN

elder² (ˈɛldə) NOUN [1] Also called: **elderberry.** any of various caprifoliaceous shrubs or small trees of the genus *Sambucus,* having clusters of small white flowers and red, purple, or black berry-like fruits. [2] any of various unrelated plants, such as box elder and marsh elder. ◆ Compare **alder.**
▷**HISTORY** Old English *ellern;* related to Old Norse *elrir,* Old High German *erlīn,* Old Slavonic *jelĭcha,* Latin *alnus*

elderberry (ˈɛldəˌbɛrɪ) NOUN, *plural* **-ries.** [1] the berry-like fruit of the elder, used for making wines, jellies, etc. [2] another name for **elder¹** (sense 1).

Elder Brethren PLURAL NOUN the senior members of the governing body of Trinity House.

elderly (ˈɛldəlɪ) ADJECTIVE (of people) **a** quite old; past middle age. **b** (*as collective noun;* preceded by *the*): *the elderly.* Related adjective: **geriatric.**
▸ **ˈelderliness** NOUN

elder statesman NOUN an old, experienced, and eminent person, esp a politician, whose advice is often sought.

eldest (ˈɛldɪst) ADJECTIVE being the oldest, esp the oldest surviving child of the same parents.
▷**HISTORY** Old English *eldesta,* superlative of *eald* OLD

ELDO (ˈɛldəʊ) NOUN ACRONYM FOR European Launcher Development Organization.

El Dorado (ɛl dɒˈrɑːdəʊ; *Spanish* ɛl doˈraðo) NOUN [1] a fabled city in South America, rich in treasure and sought by Spanish explorers in the 16th century. [2] Also: **eldorado.** any place of great riches or fabulous opportunity.
▷**HISTORY** C16: from Spanish, literally: the gilded (place)

eldritch *or* **eldrich** (ˈɛldrɪtʃ) ADJECTIVE *Poetic, Scot* unearthly; weird.
▷**HISTORY** C16: perhaps from Old English *ælf* ELF + *rīce* realm; see RICH

Elea (ˈiːlɪə) NOUN (in ancient Italy) a Greek colony on the Tyrrhenian coast of Lucana.

Eleanor Cross (ˈɛlɪnə, -ˌnɔː) NOUN any of the crosses erected at each place where the body of Eleanor of Castile (1246–90, Edward I's Spanish wife) rested between Nottingham (where she died) and London (where she is buried).

e-learning NOUN an Internet-based teaching system.
▷**HISTORY** C20: *e*lectronic *learning*

Eleatic (ˌɛlɪˈætɪk) ADJECTIVE [1] denoting or relating to a school of philosophy founded in Elea in Greece in the 6th century B.C. by Xenophanes, Parmenides, and Zeno. It held that one pure immutable Being is the only object of knowledge and that information obtained by the senses is illusory. ◆ NOUN [2] a follower of this school.
▸ **Eleaticism** (ˌɛlɪˈætɪˌsɪzəm) NOUN

elecampane (ˌɛlɪkæmˈpeɪn) NOUN a perennial flowering plant, *Inula helenium,* of Europe, Asia, and North America having large hairy leaves and narrow yellow petals: family *Asteraceae* (composites).
▷**HISTORY** C16: from Medieval Latin *enula campāna,* from *enula* (from Greek *helenion*) + *campānus* of the field

elect (ɪˈlɛkt) VERB [1] (*tr*) to choose (someone) to be (a representative or a public official) by voting: *they elected him Mayor.* [2] to select; choose: *to elect to die rather than surrender.* [3] (*tr*) (of God) to select or predestine for the grace of salvation. ◆ ADJECTIVE [4] (*immediately postpositive*) voted into office but not yet installed: *the president elect.* [5] **a** chosen or choice; selected or elite. **b** (*as collective noun;* preceded by *the*): *the elect.* [6] *Christianity* **a** selected or predestined by God to receive salvation; chosen. **b** (*as collective noun;* preceded by *the*): *the elect.*
▷**HISTORY** C15: from Latin *ēligere* to select, from *legere* to choose
▸ **eˈlectable** ADJECTIVE

election (ɪˈlɛkʃən) NOUN [1] the selection by vote of a person or persons from among candidates for a position, esp a political office. [2] a public vote on an official proposition. [3] the act or an instance of choosing. [4] *Christianity* **a** the doctrine of Calvin that God chooses certain individuals for salvation without reference to their faith or works. **b** the doctrine of Arminius and others that God chooses for salvation those who, by grace, persevere in faith and works.

electioneer (ɪˌlɛkʃəˈnɪə) VERB (*intr*) [1] to be active in a political election or campaign. ◆ NOUN [2] a person who engages in this activity.
▸ **eˌlectionˈeering** NOUN, ADJECTIVE

elective (ɪˈlɛktɪv) ADJECTIVE [1] of or based on selection by vote: *elective procedure.* [2] selected by vote: *an elective official.* [3] having the power to elect. [4] open to choice; optional: *an elective course of study.* ◆ NOUN [5] an optional course or hospital placement undertaken by a medical student.
▸ **eˈlectively** ADVERB ▸ **electivity** (ˌiːlɛkˈtɪvɪtɪ) *or* **eˈlectiveness** NOUN

elector (ɪˈlɛktə) NOUN [1] someone who is eligible to vote in the election of a government. [2] (*often capital*) a member of the US electoral college. [3] (*often capital*) (in the Holy Roman Empire) any of the German princes entitled to take part in the election of a new emperor.
▸ **eˈlectorˌship** NOUN

electoral (ɪˈlɛktərəl) ADJECTIVE relating to or consisting of electors.
▸ **eˈlectorally** ADVERB

electoral college NOUN [1] (*often capitals*) *US* a body of electors chosen by the voters who formally elect the president and vice president. [2] any body of electors with similar functions.

electorate (ɪˈlɛktərɪt) NOUN [1] the body of all qualified voters. [2] the rank, position, or territory of an elector of the Holy Roman Empire. [3] *Austral and NZ* the area represented by a Member of Parliament. [4] *Austral and NZ* the voters in a constituency.

Electra (ɪˈlɛktrə) NOUN *Greek myth* the daughter of Agamemnon and Clytemnestra. She persuaded her brother Orestes to avenge their father by killing his murderess Clytemnestra and her lover Aegisthus.

Electra complex NOUN *Psychoanal* the sexual attachment of a female child to her father. See also **penis envy.**

Electra paradox NOUN *Logic* the supposed paradox that one may know something to be true of an object under one description but not another, as when Electra knew that Orestes was her brother but not that the man before her was her brother although he was Orestes. This shows the predicate "knows" to be intensional, that Electra's knowledge here is de dicto, and that the statement of it yields an opaque context. See also **de dicto.**

electret (ɪˈlɛktrət) NOUN a permanently polarized dielectric material; its electric field is similar to the magnetic field of a permanent magnet.
▷**HISTORY** C20: from *electr(icity* + *magn)et*

electric (ɪˈlɛktrɪk) ADJECTIVE [1] of, derived from, produced by, producing, transmitting, or powered by electricity: *electric current; an electric cord; an electric blanket; an electric fence; an electric fire.* [2] (of a musical instrument) amplified electronically: *an electric guitar; an electric mandolin.* [3] very tense or exciting; emotionally charged: *an electric atmosphere.* ◆ NOUN [4] *Informal* an electric train, car, etc. [5] *Brit informal* electricity or electrical power. [6] (*plural*) an electric circuit or electric appliances.
▷**HISTORY** C17: from New Latin *electricus* amber-like (because friction causes amber to become charged), from Latin *ēlectrum* amber, from Greek *ēlektron,* of obscure origin

> **Language note** See at **electronic.**

electrical (ɪˈlɛktrɪkᵊl) ADJECTIVE of, relating to, or concerned with electricity.
▸ **eˈlectrically** ADVERB

> **Language note** See at **electronic.**

electrical engineering NOUN the branch of engineering concerned with the practical applications of electricity.
▸ **electrical engineer** NOUN

electric-arc furnace NOUN another name for **arc furnace.**

electric-arc welding NOUN another name for **arc welding.**

electric blanket NOUN a blanket that contains an electric heating element, used to warm a bed.

electric blue NOUN, ADJECTIVE **a** a strong metallic blue colour. **b** (*as adjective*): *an electric-blue evening dress.*

electric chair NOUN (in the US) **a** an electrified chair for executing criminals. **b** (usually preceded by *the*) execution by this method.

electric charge NOUN another name for **charge** (sense 25).

electric circuit NOUN *Physics* another name for **circuit** (sense 3a).

electric constant NOUN the permittivity of free space, which has the value $8.854\ 187 \times 10^{-12}$ farad per metre. Symbol: ε_0. Also called: **absolute permittivity.**

electric current NOUN another name for **current** (sense 8).

electric discharge NOUN *Physics* another name for **discharge** (sense 20b).

electric-discharge lamp NOUN another name for **fluorescent lamp.**

electric displacement NOUN *Physics* the electric flux density when an electric field exists in free space into which a dielectric is introduced. Symbol: *D.* Also called: **electric flux density.**

electric eel NOUN an eel-like freshwater cyprinoid fish, *Electrophorus electricus,* of N South America, having electric organs in the body: family *Electrophoridae.*

electric eye NOUN another name for **photocell.**

electric field NOUN a field of force surrounding a charged particle within which another charged particle experiences a force. Compare **magnetic field.**

electric field strength NOUN the strength or

intensity of an electric field at any point, usually measured in volts per metre. Symbol: *E*.

electric fire NOUN a device that provides heat for a room from an incandescent electric element.

electric flux NOUN the product of the electric displacement and the area across which it is displaced in an electric field. Symbol: Ψ.

electric flux density NOUN another name for **electric displacement.**

electric furnace NOUN any furnace in which the heat is provided by an electric current.

electric guitar NOUN an electrically amplified guitar, used mainly in pop music. Compare **acoustic guitar.**

electric hare NOUN (in greyhound racing) a model of a hare, mounted on an electrified rail, which the dogs chase.

electrician (ɪlɛk'trɪʃən, ˌiːlɛk-) NOUN a person whose occupation is the installation, maintenance, and repair of electrical devices.

electricity (ɪlɛk'trɪsɪtɪ, ˌiːlɛk-) NOUN 1 any phenomenon associated with stationary or moving electrons, ions, or other charged particles. 2 the science concerned with electricity. 3 an electric current or charge: *a motor powered by electricity*. 4 emotional tension or excitement, esp between or among people.

electric motor NOUN a device that converts electrical energy to mechanical torque.

electric needle NOUN a surgical instrument for cutting tissue by the application of a high-frequency current.

electric organ NOUN 1 *Music* **a** a pipe organ operated by electrical means. **b** another name for **electronic organ.** 2 *Zoology* a small group of modified muscle cells on the body of certain fishes, such as the electric eel, that gives an electric shock to any animal touching them.

electric potential NOUN **a** the work required to transfer a unit positive electric charge from an infinite distance to a given point against an electric field. **b** the potential difference between the point and some other reference point. Symbol: *V or* ϕ. Sometimes shortened to: **potential.**

electric ray NOUN any ray of the order *Torpediniformes,* of tropical and temperate seas, having a flat rounded body with an electric organ in each of the fins, close to the head.

electric shock NOUN the physiological reaction, characterized by pain and muscular spasm, to the passage of an electric current through the body. It can affect the respiratory system and heart rhythm. Sometimes shortened to: **shock.**

electric storm NOUN a violent atmospheric disturbance in which the air is highly charged with static electricity, causing a storm. Compare **thunderstorm.**

electric strength NOUN the maximum voltage sustainable by an insulating material, after which it loses its insulating properties.

electric susceptibility NOUN another name for **susceptibility** (sense 4a).

electrify (ɪ'lɛktrɪˌfaɪ) VERB **-fies, -fying, -fied.** *(tr)* 1 to adapt or equip (a system, device, etc.) for operation by electrical power. 2 to charge with or subject to electricity. 3 to startle or excite intensely; shock or thrill.
▸**e'lectriˌfiable** ADJECTIVE ▸**eˌlectrifi'cation** NOUN
▸**e'lectriˌfier** NOUN

electro (ɪ'lɛktrəʊ) NOUN, *plural* **-tros.** short for **electroplate** or **electrotype.**

electro- *or sometimes before a vowel* **electr-** COMBINING FORM 1 electric or electrically: *electrocardiograph; electrocute.* 2 electrolytic: *electroanalysis.*
▷**HISTORY** from New Latin, from Latin *ēlectrum* amber, from Greek *ēlektron*

electroacoustic (ɪˌlɛktrəʊə'kuːstɪk) ADJECTIVE another word for **acoustoelectronic.**

electroanalysis (ɪˌlɛktrəʊə'nælɪsɪs) NOUN chemical analysis by electrolysis or electrodeposition.
▸**electroanalytic** (ɪˌlɛktrəʊˌænə'lɪtɪk) *or* **eˌlectroˌana'lytical** ADJECTIVE

electrocardiogram (ɪˌlɛktrəʊ'kɑːdɪəʊˌgræm) NOUN a tracing of the electric currents that initiate the heartbeat, used to diagnose possible heart disorders. Abbreviation: **ECG.**

electrocardiograph (ɪˌlɛktrəʊ'kɑːdɪəʊˌgrɑːf, -ˌgræf) NOUN an instrument for recording the electrical activity of the heart. Abbreviation: **ECG.**
▸**eˌlectroˌcardio'graphic** ADJECTIVE
▸**eˌlectroˌcardio'graphically** ADVERB ▸**electrocardiography** (ɪˌlɛktrəʊˌkɑːdɪ'ɒgrəfɪ) NOUN

electrocautery (ɪˌlɛktrəʊ'kɔːtərɪ) NOUN *Vet science* the use of an electrically heated metal instrument for cautery.

electrochemical (ɪˌlɛktrəʊ'kɛmɪk^{ə}l) ADJECTIVE of or relating to electrochemistry.
▸**eˌlectro'chemically** ADVERB

electrochemical equivalent NOUN the mass of an element liberated from its ions or converted into them by one coulomb of electric charge.

electrochemical series NOUN another name for **electromotive series.**

electrochemistry (ɪˌlɛktrəʊ'kɛmɪstrɪ) NOUN the branch of chemistry concerned with the study of electric cells and electrolysis.
▸**eˌlectro'chemist** NOUN

electrochromatography (ɪˌlɛktrəʊkrəʊmə'tɒgrəfɪ) NOUN chromatography effected by the influence of an applied electric field.
▸**eˌlectrochro'matic** ADJECTIVE

electroclash (ɪˌlɛktrəʊ'klæʃ) NOUN **a** a type of electronic music, originating in the first decade of the 21st century, that combines modern techno with synthesizer music characteristic of the 1980s. **b** *(as modifier)*: *the electroclash scene.*

electroconvulsive therapy (ɪˌlɛktrəʊkən'vʌlsɪv) NOUN *Med* the treatment of certain psychotic conditions by passing an electric current through the brain to induce coma or convulsions. Abbreviation: **ECT.** Also called: **electroshock therapy.** See also **shock therapy.**

electrocorticogram (ɪˌlɛktrəʊ'kɔːtɪkəʊˌgræm) NOUN a record of brain waves obtained by placing electrodes directly on the surface of the exposed cerebral cortex. Compare **electroencephalogram, electroencephalograph.**

electrocute (ɪ'lɛktrəˌkjuːt) VERB *(tr)* 1 to kill as a result of an electric shock. 2 *US* to execute in the electric chair.
▷**HISTORY** C19: from ELECTRO- + (exe)cute
▸**eˌlectro'cution** NOUN

electrocyte (ɪ'lɛktrəʊˌsaɪt) NOUN *Zoology* a specialized muscle or nerve cell that generates electricity, as found in an electric organ.

electrode (ɪ'lɛktrəʊd) NOUN 1 a conductor through which an electric current enters or leaves an electrolyte, an electric arc, or an electronic valve or tube. 2 an element in a semiconducting device that emits, collects, or controls the movement of electrons or holes.

electrode efficiency NOUN *Chem* the ratio of the amount of metal deposited in an electrolytic cell to that theoretically deposited according to Faraday's laws.

electrodeposit (ɪˌlɛktrəʊdɪ'pɒzɪt) VERB 1 *(tr)* to deposit (a metal) by electrolysis. ◆ NOUN 2 the deposit so formed.
▸**electrodeposition** (ɪˌlɛktrəʊˌdɛpə'zɪʃən) NOUN

electrode potential NOUN *Chem* the potential difference developed when an electrode of an element is placed in a solution containing ions of that element.

electrodialysis (ɪˌlɛktrəʊdaɪ'ælɪsɪs) NOUN dialysis in which electrolytes are removed from a colloidal solution by a potential difference between two electrodes separated by one or more membranes.

electrodynamic (ɪˌlɛktrəʊdaɪ'næmɪk) ADJECTIVE 1 operated by an electromotive force between current-carrying coils: *an electrodynamic wattmeter.* 2 of or relating to electrodynamics.

electrodynamics (ɪˌlɛktrəʊdaɪ'næmɪks) NOUN *(functioning as singular)* the branch of physics concerned with the interactions between electrical and mechanical forces.

electrodynamometer (ɪˌlɛktrəʊˌdaɪnə'mɒmɪtə) NOUN an instrument that uses the interaction of the magnetic fields of two coils to measure electric current, voltage, or power.

electroencephalogram (ɪˌlɛktrəʊɛn'sɛfələˌgræm) NOUN *Med* the tracing obtained from an electroencephalograph. Abbreviation: **EEG.**

electroencephalograph (ɪˌlɛktrəʊɛn'sɛfələˌgrɑːf, -ˌgræf) NOUN an instrument for recording the electrical activity of the brain, usually by means of electrodes placed on the scalp: used to diagnose tumours of the brain, to study brain waves, etc. Abbreviation: **EEG.** See also **brain wave.**
▸**eˌlectroenˌcephalo'graphic** ADJECTIVE
▸**eˌlectroenˌcephalo'graphically** ADVERB
▸**electroencephalography** (ɪˌlɛktrəʊɛnˌsɛfə'lɒgrəfɪ) NOUN

electroendosmosis (ɪˌlɛktrəʊˌɛndɒz'məʊsɪs, -dɒs-) NOUN another name for **electro-osmosis.**

electrofluor (ɪ'lɛktrəʊˌfluːɔː) NOUN *Physics* a transparent material that stores electrical energy and subsequently releases it as light.
▷**HISTORY** C20: from ELECTRO- + FLUOR(ESCENCE)

electroform (ɪ'lɛktrəˌfɔːm) VERB to form (a metallic object) by electrolytic deposition on a mould or matrix.

electrogen (ɪ'lɛktrəʊˌdʒɛn) NOUN a molecule that emits electrons when it is illuminated.
▸**eˌlectro'genic** ADJECTIVE

electrograph (ɪ'lɛktrəʊˌgrɑːf, -ˌgræf) NOUN 1 an apparatus for engraving metal printing cylinders, esp in gravure printing. 2 the equipment used for the electrical transmission of pictures. 3 **a** a recording electrometer. **b** a graph produced by this instrument. 4 a visual record of the surface composition of a metal, obtained by placing an electrolyte-soaked paper over the metal and passing a current through the paper to an electrode on the other side.
▸**electrographic** (ɪˌlɛktrəʊ'græfɪk) ADJECTIVE
▸**eˌlectro'graphically** ADVERB ▸**electrography** (ɪlɛk'trɒgrəfɪ, ˌiːlɛk-) NOUN

electrojet (ɪ'lɛktrəʊˌdʒɛt) NOUN a narrow belt of fast-moving ions in the ionosphere, under the influence of the earth's magnetic field, causing auroral displays.

electrokinetic (ɪˌlɛktrəʊkɪ'nɛtɪk, -kaɪ-) ADJECTIVE of or relating to the motion of charged particles and its effects.

electrokinetics (ɪˌlɛktrəʊkɪ'nɛtɪks, -kaɪ-) NOUN *(functioning as singular)* the branch of physics concerned with the motion of charged particles.

electroluminescence (ɪˌlɛktrəʊˌluːmɪ'nɛs^{ə}ns) NOUN *Physics* **a** the emission of light by a phosphor when activated by an alternating field or by a gas when activated by an electric discharge. **b** the light emitted by this process.
▸**eˌlectroˌlumi'nescent** ADJECTIVE

electrolyse *or US* **electrolyze** (ɪ'lɛktrəʊˌlaɪz) VERB *(tr)* 1 to decompose (a chemical compound) by electrolysis. 2 to destroy (living tissue, such as hair roots) by electrolysis.
▷**HISTORY** C19: back formation from ELECTROLYSIS on pattern of *analyse*
▸**eˌlectroly'sation** *or US* **eˌlectroly'zation** NOUN
▸**e'lectroˌlyser** *or US* **e'lectroˌlyzer** NOUN

electrolysis (ɪlɛk'trɒlɪsɪs) NOUN 1 the conduction of electricity by a solution or melt, esp the use of this process to induce chemical changes. 2 the destruction of living tissue, such as hair roots, by an electric current, usually for cosmetic reasons.
▷**HISTORY** C19: from ELECTRO- + -LYSIS

electrolyte (ɪ'lɛktrəʊˌlaɪt) NOUN 1 a solution or molten substance that conducts electricity. 2 **a** a chemical compound that dissociates in solution into ions. **b** any of the ions themselves.

electrolytic (ɪˌlɛktrəʊ'lɪtɪk) ADJECTIVE 1 *Physics* **a** of, concerned with, or produced by electrolysis or electrodeposition. **b** of, relating to, or containing an electrolyte. ◆ NOUN 2 *Electronics* Also called: **electrolytic capacitor.** a small capacitor consisting of two electrodes separated by an electrolyte.
▸**eˌlectro'lytically** ADVERB

electrolytic cell NOUN any device in which electrolysis occurs. Sometimes shortened to: **cell.**

electrolytic gas NOUN a mixture of two parts of hydrogen and one part of oxygen by volume, formed by the electrolysis of water.

electromagnet (ɪˌlɛktrəʊ'mægnɪt) NOUN a

magnet consisting of an iron or steel core wound with a coil of wire, through which a current is passed.

electromagnetic (ɪˌlɛktrəʊmæɡˈnɛtɪk) ADJECTIVE 1 of, containing, or operated by an electromagnet: *an electromagnetic pump.* 2 of, relating to, or consisting of electromagnetism: *electromagnetic moment.* 3 of or relating to electromagnetic radiation: *the electromagnetic spectrum.*
▸**eˌlectromagˈnetically** ADVERB

electromagnetic field NOUN a field of force associated with a moving electric charge equivalent to an electric field and a magnetic field at right angles to each other and to the direction of propagation.

electromagnetic interaction *or* **force** NOUN *Physics* an interaction between charged particles arising from their electric and magnetic fields; its strength is about 100 times weaker than the strong interaction. See **interaction** (sense 2), **electroweak interaction.**

electromagnetic moment NOUN a measure of the magnetic strength of a magnet or current-carrying coil, expressed as the torque produced when the magnet or coil is set with its axis perpendicular to unit magnetic flux density. It is measured in ampere metres squared. Symbol: m. Also called: **magnetic moment.** Compare **magnetic dipole moment.**

electromagnetic pump NOUN a device for pumping liquid metals by placing a pipe between the poles of an electromagnet and passing a current through the liquid metal.

electromagnetic radiation NOUN radiation consisting of self-sustaining oscillating electric and magnetic fields at right angles to each other and to the direction of propagation. It does not require a supporting medium and travels through empty space at the speed of light. See also **photon.**

electromagnetics (ɪˌlɛktrəʊmæɡˈnɛtɪks) NOUN (*functioning as singular*) *Physics* another name for **electromagnetism** (sense 2).

electromagnetic spectrum NOUN the complete range of electromagnetic radiation from the longest radio waves (wavelength 10^5 metres) to the shortest gamma radiation (wavelength 10^{-13} metre).

electromagnetic unit NOUN any unit that belongs to a system of electrical cgs units in which the magnetic constant is given the value of unity and is taken as a pure number. Abbreviations: **EMU, e.m.u.** Compare **electrostatic unit.**

electromagnetic wave NOUN a wave of energy propagated in an electromagnetic field. See also **electromagnetic radiation.**

electromagnetism (ɪˌlɛktrəʊˈmæɡnɪˌtɪzəm) NOUN 1 magnetism produced by an electric current. 2 Also called: **electromagnetics.** the branch of physics concerned with magnetism produced by electric currents and with the interaction of electric and magnetic fields.

electromechanical (ɪˌlɛktrəʊmɪˈkænɪkᵊl) ADJECTIVE of, relating to, or concerning an electrically operated mechanical device.
▸**eˌlectromeˈchanically** ADVERB

electromerism (ɪˌlɛktrəʊˈmɛrɪzəm) NOUN *Chem* a type of tautomerism in which the isomers (**electromers**) differ in the distribution of charge in their molecules.
▹**HISTORY** C20: from ELECTRO- + (iso)merism

electrometallurgy (ɪˌlɛktrəʊmɪˈtælədʒɪ, -ˈmɛtəˌlɜːdʒɪ) NOUN metallurgy involving the use of electric-arc furnaces, electrolysis, and other electrical operations.
▸**eˌlectroˌmetalˈlurgical** ADJECTIVE ▸**eˌlectrometˈallurgist** NOUN

electrometer (ɪlɛkˈtrɒmɪtə, ˌiːlɛk-) NOUN an instrument for detecting or determining the magnitude of a potential difference or charge by the electrostatic forces between charged bodies.
▸**electrometric** (ɪˌlɛktrəʊˈmɛtrɪk) *or* **eˌlectroˈmetrical** ADJECTIVE ▸**eˌlectroˈmetrically** ADVERB ▸**elecˈtrometry** NOUN

electromotive (ɪˌlɛktrəʊˈməʊtɪv) ADJECTIVE of, concerned with, producing, or tending to produce an electric current.

electromotive force NOUN *Physics* **a** a source of energy that can cause a current to flow in an electrical circuit or device. **b** the rate at which energy is drawn from this source when unit current flows through the circuit or device, measured in volts. Abbreviations: **emf, EMF.** Symbol: *E.* Compare **potential difference.**

electromotive series NOUN *Chem* a series of the metals, together with hydrogen, ranged in the order of their electrode potentials.

electromyography (ɪˌlɛktrəʊmaɪˈɒɡrəfɪ) NOUN *Med* a technique for recording the electrical activity of muscles: used in the diagnosis of nerve and muscle disorders.

electron (ɪˈlɛktrɒn) NOUN a stable elementary particle present in all atoms, orbiting the nucleus in numbers equal to the atomic number of the element in the neutral atom; a lepton with a negative charge of 1.602 176 462 × 10^{-19} coulomb, a rest mass of 9.109 381 88 × 10^{-31} kilogram, a radius of 2.817 940 285 × 10^{-15} metre, and a spin of ½.
▹**HISTORY** C19: from ELECTRO- + -ON

electron affinity NOUN a measure of the ability of an atom or molecule to form a negative ion, expressed as the energy released when an electron is attached. Symbol: *A.*

electron capture NOUN 1 *Physics* the transformation of an atomic nucleus in which an electron from the atom is spontaneously absorbed into the nucleus. A proton is changed into a neutron, thereby reducing the atomic number by one. A neutrino is emitted. The process may be detected by the consequent emission of the characteristic X-rays of the resultant element. Former name: **K-capture.** 2 the spontaneous or induced recombination of free electrons with ions or by transfer from other atoms or ions.

electronegative (ɪˌlɛktrəʊˈnɛɡətɪv) ADJECTIVE 1 having a negative electric charge. 2 (of an atom, group, molecule, etc.) tending to gain or attract electrons and form negative ions or polarized bonds. Compare **electropositive.**

electronegativity (ɪˌlɛktrəʊˌnɛɡəˈtɪvɪtɪ) NOUN 1 the state of being electronegative. 2 a measure of the ability of a specified atom to attract electrons in a molecule.

electron gun NOUN a heated cathode with an associated system of electrodes and coils for producing and focusing a beam of electrons, used esp in cathode-ray tubes.

electronic (ɪlɛkˈtrɒnɪk, ˌiːlɛk-) ADJECTIVE 1 of, concerned with, using, or operated by devices in which electrons are conducted through a semiconductor, free space, or gas. 2 of or concerned with electronics. 3 of or concerned with electrons or an electron: *an electronic energy level in a molecule.* 4 involving or concerned with the representation, storage, or transmission of information by electronic systems: *electronic mail; electronic shopping.*
▸**elecˈtronically** ADVERB

> **Language note** *Electronic* is used to refer to equipment, such as television sets, computers, etc., in which the current is controlled by transistors, valves, and similar components and also to the components themselves. *Electrical* is used in a more general sense, often to refer to the use of electricity as a whole as opposed to other forms of energy: *electrical engineering; an electrical appliance. Electric,* in many cases used interchangeably with *electrical,* is often restricted to the description of particular devices or to concepts relating to the flow of current: *electric fire; electric charge.*

electronica (ɪlɛkˈtrɒnɪkə, ˌiːlɛk-) PLURAL NOUN electronic equipment, systems, music, etc., collectively.

electronic configuration NOUN *Chem* the arrangement of electrons in the orbitals of an atom or molecule.

electronic countermeasures NOUN *Military* (in electronic warfare) actions intended to interfere with an enemy's use of electromagnetic radiation equipment.

electronic editing NOUN *Radio, television* editing of a sound or vision tape recording by electronic rerecording rather than by physical cutting.

electronic file cabinet NOUN *Computing* a device, controlled by software, for the storage and retrieval of information.

electronic flash NOUN *Photog* an electronic device for producing a very bright flash of light by means of an electric discharge in a gas-filled tube.

electronic flight information systems PLURAL NOUN (in an aircraft) the computer-operated visual displays on the flight deck, showing information about the aircraft's state and performance in flight.

electronic funds transfer at point of sale NOUN a system for debiting a retail sale direct to the customer's bank, building-society, or credit-card account by means of a computer link using the telephone network. Acronym: **EFTPOS.**

electronic game NOUN any of various small hand-held computerized games, usually battery operated, having a small screen on which graphics are displayed and buttons to operate the game.

electronic graphics PLURAL NOUN (on television) the production of graphic designs and text by electronic means.

electronic ignition NOUN any system that uses an electronic circuit to supply the voltage to the sparking plugs of an internal-combustion engine.

electronic keyboard NOUN 1 a typewriter keyboard used to operate an electronic device such as a computer, word processor, etc. 2 the full name for **keyboard** (sense 2).

electronic mail NOUN the transmission and distribution of messages, information, facsimiles of documents, etc., from one computer terminal to another. Abbreviations: **E-mail, e-mail, email.**

electronic mailbox NOUN a device used to store electronic mail.

electronic music NOUN a form of music consisting of sounds produced by oscillating electric currents either controlled from an instrument panel or keyboard or prerecorded on magnetic tape.

electronic office NOUN integrated computer systems designed to handle office work.

electronic organ NOUN *Music* an electrophonic instrument played by means of a keyboard, in which sounds are produced and amplified by any of various electronic or electrical means. See also **synthesizer.**

electronic organizer NOUN See **personal organizer** (sense 2).

electronic point of sale NOUN a computerized system for recording sales in retail shops, using a laser scanner at the cash till to read bar codes on the packages of the items sold. Acronym: **EPOS.**

electronic programme guide NOUN an on-screen guide that enables viewers of digital television to select programmes using a hand-held device. Abbreviation: **EPG.**

electronic publishing NOUN the publication of information on magnetic tape, disks, etc., so that it can be accessed by a computer.

electronics (ɪlɛkˈtrɒnɪks, ˌiːlɛk-) NOUN 1 (*functioning as singular*) the science and technology concerned with the development, behaviour, and applications of electronic devices and circuits. 2 (*functioning as plural*) the circuits and devices of a piece of electronic equipment: *the electronics of a television set.*

electronic surveillance NOUN 1 the use of such electronic devices as television monitors, video cameras, etc., to prevent burglary, shop lifting, break-ins, etc. 2 monitoring events, conversations, etc., at a distance by electronic means, esp by such covert means as wiretapping or bugging.

electronic tag NOUN another name for **tag**[1] (sense 2).

electronic transfer of funds NOUN the transfer of money from one bank or building-society account to another by means of a computer link using the telephone network. Abbreviation: **ETF.**

electronic warfare NOUN the military use of electronics to prevent or reduce an enemy's effective use and to protect friendly use of electromagnetic radiation equipment.

electron lens NOUN a system, such as an arrangement of electrodes or magnets, that produces a field for focusing a beam of electrons.

electron micrograph NOUN a photograph or image of a specimen taken using an electron microscope.

electron microscope NOUN a powerful type of microscope that uses electrons, rather than light, and electron lenses to produce a magnified image.

electron multiplier NOUN *Physics* a device for amplifying and measuring a flux of electrons. Each electron hits an anode surface and releases secondary electrons that are accelerated to a second surface; after several such stages a measurable pulse of current is obtained.

electron optics NOUN (*functioning as singular*) the study and use of beams of electrons and of their deflection and focusing by electric and magnetic fields.

electron paramagnetic resonance NOUN *Physics* another name for **electron spin resonance.** Abbreviation: **EPR.**

electron probe microanalysis NOUN a technique for the analysis of a very small amount of material by bombarding it with a narrow beam of electrons and examining the resulting X-ray emission spectrum.

electron spin resonance NOUN a technique for investigating paramagnetic substances by subjecting them to high-frequency radiation in a strong magnetic field. Changes in the spin of unpaired electrons cause radiation to be absorbed at certain frequencies. Abbreviation: **ESR.** See also **nuclear magnetic resonance.**

electron telescope NOUN an astronomical telescope with an attachment for converting the infrared radiation emitted from the surface of planets into a visible image.

electron transport NOUN *Biochem* the metabolic process in mitochondria or chloroplasts, in which electrons are transferred in stages from energy-rich compounds to molecular oxygen with liberation of energy.

electron tube NOUN an electrical device, such as a valve, in which a flow of electrons between electrodes takes place. Also called: **vacuum tube.** Sometimes shortened to: **tube.**

electronvolt (ɪˌlɛktrɒnˈvəʊlt) NOUN a unit of energy equal to the work done on an electron accelerated through a potential difference of 1 volt. 1 electronvolt is equivalent to 1.602×10^{-19} joule. Symbol: **eV.**

electro-osmosis NOUN movement of liquid through a capillary tube or membrane under the influence of an electric field: used in controlling rising damp. Also called: **electroendosmosis.**

electropalatography (ɪˌlɛktrəʊˌpæləˈtɒgrəfɪ) NOUN the study of the movements of the tongue during speech using touch-sensitive electrodes in the mouth linked to a computer.

electrophilic (ɪˌlɛktrəʊˈfɪlɪk) ADJECTIVE *Chem* having or involving an affinity for negative charge. Electrophilic reagents (**electrophiles**) are atoms, molecules, and ions that behave as electron acceptors. Compare **nucleophilic.**
▸**electrophile** (ɪˈlɛktrəʊˌfaɪl) NOUN

electrophone (ɪˈlɛktrəˌfəʊn) NOUN *Music* any instrument whose sound is produced by the oscillation of an electric current, such as an electronic organ, synthesizer, etc.
▸**electrophonic** (ɪˌlɛktrəˈfɒnɪk) ADJECTIVE

electrophoresis (ɪˌlɛktrəʊfəˈriːsɪs) NOUN the motion of charged particles in a colloid under the influence of an applied electric field. Also called: **cataphoresis.**
▸**electrophoretic** (ɪˌlɛktrəʊfəˈrɛtɪk) ADJECTIVE

electrophorus (ɪlɛkˈtrɒfərəs, ˌiːlɛk-) NOUN an apparatus for generating static electricity. It consists of an insulating plate charged by friction and used to charge a metal plate by induction.
▹**HISTORY** C18: from ELECTRO- + *-phorus,* from Greek *-phoros* bearing, from *pherein* to bear

electrophotography (ɪˌlɛktrəʊˌfəˈtɒgrəfɪ) NOUN photography in which an image is transferred onto paper by means of electrical rather than chemical processes.
▸**eˌlectroˌphotoˈgraphic** ADJECTIVE

electrophysiology (ɪˌlɛktrəʊˌfɪzɪˈɒlədʒɪ) NOUN the branch of medical science concerned with the electrical activity associated with bodily processes.
▸**eˌlectroˌphysioˈlogical** ADJECTIVE ▸**eˌlectroˌphysiˈologist** NOUN

electroplate (ɪˈlɛktrəʊˌpleɪt) VERB [1] (*tr*) to plate (an object) by electrolysis. ◆ NOUN [2] electroplated articles collectively, esp when plated with silver. ◆ ADJECTIVE [3] coated with metal by electrolysis; electroplated.
▸**eˈlectroˌplater** NOUN

electropositive (ɪˌlɛktrəʊˈpɒzɪtɪv) ADJECTIVE [1] having a positive electric charge. [2] (of an atom, group, molecule, etc.) tending to release electrons and form positive ions or polarized bonds. Compare **electronegative.**

electroreceptor (ɪˈlɛktrəʊrɪˌsɛptə) NOUN *Zoology* an organ, present in some fishes, that detects electrical discharges.

electrorheology (ɪˌlɛktrəʊrɪˈɒlədʒɪ) NOUN [1] the study of the flow of fluids under the influence of electric fields. [2] the way in which fluid flow is influenced by an electric field.
▸**eˌlectrorheoˈlogical** ADJECTIVE

electroscope (ɪˈlɛktrəʊˌskəʊp) NOUN an apparatus for detecting an electric charge, typically consisting of a rod holding two gold foils that separate when a charge is applied.
▸**electroscopic** (ɪˌlɛktrəʊˈskɒpɪk) ADJECTIVE

electroshock therapy (ɪˈlɛktrəʊˌʃɒk) NOUN another name for **electroconvulsive therapy.**

electrostatic (ɪˌlɛktrəʊˈstætɪk) ADJECTIVE [1] of, concerned with, producing, or caused by static electricity. [2] concerned with electrostatics.
▸**eˌlectroˈstatically** ADVERB

electrostatic field NOUN an electric field associated with static electric charges.

electrostatic generator NOUN any device for producing a high voltage by building up a charge of static electricity.

electrostatic lens NOUN an electron lens consisting of a system of metal electrodes, the electrostatic field of which focuses the charged particles.

electrostatic precipitation NOUN *Chem* the removal of suspended solid particles from a gas by giving them an electric charge and attracting them to charged plates.

electrostatics (ɪˌlɛktrəʊˈstætɪks) NOUN (*functioning as singular*) the branch of physics concerned with static charges and the electrostatic field.

electrostatic unit NOUN any unit that belongs to a system of electrical cgs units in which the electric constant is given the value of unity and is taken as a pure number. Abbreviations: **ESU, e.s.u.** Compare **electromagnetic unit.**

electrostriction (ɪˌlɛktrəʊˈstrɪkʃən) NOUN the change in dimensions of a dielectric occurring as an elastic strain when an electric field is applied.

electrosurgery (ɪˌlɛktrəʊˈsɜːdʒərɪ) NOUN the surgical use of electricity, as in cauterization.
▸**eˌlectroˈsurgical** ADJECTIVE

electrotechnics (ɪˌlɛktrəʊˈtɛknɪks) NOUN (*functioning as singular*) another name for **electrotechnology.**
▸**eˌlectroˈtechnical** ADJECTIVE ▸**eˌlectrotechˈnician** NOUN

electrotechnology (ɪˌlɛktrəʊtɛkˈnɒlədʒɪ) NOUN the technological use of electric power.

electrotherapeutics (ɪˌlɛktrəʊˌθɛrəˈpjuːtɪks) NOUN (*functioning as singular*) the branch of medical science concerned with the use of electrotherapy.
▸**eˌlectroˌtheraˈpeutic** *or* **eˌlectroˌtheraˈpeutical** ADJECTIVE

electrotherapy (ɪˌlɛktrəʊˈθɛrəpɪ) NOUN treatment in which electric currents are passed through the tissues to stimulate muscle function in paralysed patients.
▸**eˌlectroˈtherapist** NOUN

electrothermal (ɪˌlɛktrəʊˈθɜːməl) *or* **electrothermic** (ɪˌlɛktrəʊˈθɜːmɪk) ADJECTIVE concerned with both electricity and heat, esp the production of electricity by heat.

electrothermal printer (ɪˌlɛktrəʊˈθɜːməl) NOUN *Computing* a printer that produces characters by burning the image on specially coated paper. Also called: **thermal printer.**

electrotint (ɪˈlɛktrəʊˌtɪnt) NOUN a printing block made by drawing on a metal plate with varnish and electrolytically depositing a layer of metal on the nonvarnished areas of the plate.

electrotonus (ɪlɛkˈtrɒtənəs, ˌiːlɛk-) NOUN *Physiol* the change in the state of irritability and conductivity of a nerve or muscle caused by the passage of an electric current.
▹**HISTORY** C19: from New Latin, from ELECTRO- + Latin *tonus* TONE
▸**electrotonic** (ɪˌlɛktrəʊˈtɒnɪk) ADJECTIVE

electrotype (ɪˈlɛktrəʊˌtaɪp) NOUN [1] a duplicate printing plate made by electrolytically depositing a layer of copper or nickel onto a mould of the original. Sometimes shortened to: **electro.** ◆ VERB [2] (*tr*) to make an electrotype of (printed matter, illustrations, etc.).
▸**eˈlectroˌtyper** NOUN

electrovalency (ɪˌlɛktrəʊˈveɪlənsɪ) *or* **electrovalence** NOUN *Chem* the valency of a substance in forming ions, equal to the number of electrons gained or lost.
▸**eˌlectroˈvalent** ADJECTIVE ▸**eˌlectroˈvalently** ADVERB

electrovalent bond NOUN a type of chemical bond in which one atom loses an electron to form a positive ion and the other atom gains the electron to form a negative ion. The resulting ions are held together by electrostatic attraction. Also called: **ionic bond.** Compare **covalent bond.**

electroweak interaction (ɪˌlɛktrəʊˈwiːk) NOUN *Physics* a type of fundamental interaction combining both the electromagnetic interaction and the weak interaction. See also **electromagnetic interaction, weak interaction.**

electrum (ɪˈlɛktrəm) NOUN an alloy of gold (55–88 per cent) and silver used for jewellery and ornaments.
▹**HISTORY** C14: from Latin, from Greek *ēlektron* amber

electuary (ɪˈlɛktjʊərɪ) NOUN, *plural* **-aries.** *Archaic* a paste taken orally, containing a drug mixed with syrup or honey.
▹**HISTORY** C14: from Late Latin *ēlēctuārium,* probably from Greek *ekleikton* electuary, from *ekleikhein* to lick out, from *leikhein* to lick

eleemosynary (ˌɛlɪiːˈmɒsɪnərɪ) ADJECTIVE [1] of, concerned with, or dependent on charity. [2] given as an act of charity.
▹**HISTORY** C17: from Church Latin *eleēmosyna* ALMS

elegance (ˈɛlɪgəns) *or* **elegancy** NOUN, *plural* **-gances** *or* **-gancies.** [1] dignified grace in appearance, movement, or behaviour. [2] good taste in design, style, arrangement, etc. [3] something elegant; a refinement.

elegant (ˈɛlɪgənt) ADJECTIVE [1] tasteful in dress, style, or design. [2] dignified and graceful in appearance, behaviour, etc. [3] cleverly simple; ingenious: *an elegant solution to a problem.*
▹**HISTORY** C16: from Latin *ēlegāns* tasteful, related to *ēligere* to select; see ELECT
▸**ˈelegantly** ADVERB

elegiac (ˌɛlɪˈdʒaɪək) ADJECTIVE [1] resembling, characteristic of, relating to, or appropriate to an elegy. [2] lamenting; mournful; plaintive. [3] denoting or written in elegiac couplets or elegiac stanzas. ◆ NOUN [4] (*often plural*) an elegiac couplet or stanza.
▸**ˌeleˈgiacally** ADVERB

elegiac couplet NOUN *Classical prosody* a couplet composed of a dactylic hexameter followed by a dactylic pentameter.

elegiac stanza NOUN *Prosody* a quatrain in iambic pentameters with alternate lines rhyming.

elegize *or* **elegise** (ˈɛlɪˌdʒaɪz) VERB [1] to compose an elegy or elegies (in memory of). [2] (*intr*) to write elegiacally.
▸**ˈelegist** NOUN

elegy (ˈɛlɪdʒɪ) NOUN, *plural* **-gies.** [1] a mournful or plaintive poem or song, esp a lament for the dead. [2] poetry or a poem written in elegiac couplets or stanzas.

▷HISTORY C16: via French and Latin from Greek *elegeia,* from *elegos* lament sung to flute accompaniment

> Language note Avoid confusion with **eulogy**.

Eleia ('iːlɪə) NOUN a variant spelling of **Elia**.

element ('ɛlɪmənt) NOUN [1] any of the 118 known substances (of which 93 occur naturally) that consist of atoms with the same number of protons in their nuclei. Compare **compound**[1] (sense 1). [2] one of the fundamental or irreducible components making up a whole. [3] a cause that contributes to a result; factor. [4] any group that is part of a larger unit, such as a military formation. [5] a small amount; hint: *an element of sarcasm in her voice.* [6] a distinguishable section of a social group: *he belonged to the stable element in the expedition.* [7] the most favourable environment for an animal or plant. [8] the situation in which a person is happiest or most effective (esp in the phrases **in** or **out of one's element**). [9] the resistance wire and its former that constitute the electrical heater in a cooker, heater, etc. [10] *Electronics* another name for **component** (sense 2). [11] one of the four substances thought in ancient and medieval cosmology to constitute the universe (earth, air, water, or fire). [12] *(plural)* atmospheric conditions or forces, esp wind, rain, and cold: *exposed to the elements.* [13] *(plural)* the first principles of a subject. [14] *Geometry* a point, line, plane, or part of a geometric figure. [15] *Maths* **a** any of the terms in a determinant or matrix. **b** one of the infinitesimally small quantities summed by an integral, often represented by the expression following the integral sign: *in* $\int_a^b f(x)dx$, $f(x)dx$ *is an element of area.* [16] *Maths, logic* one of the objects or numbers that together constitute a set. [17] *Christianity* the bread or wine consecrated in the Eucharist. [18] *Astronomy* any of the numerical quantities, such as the major axis or eccentricity, used in describing the orbit of a planet, satellite, etc. [19] one of the vertical or horizontal rods forming a television or VHF radio receiving aerial. [20] *Physics* a component of a compound lens.
▷HISTORY C13: from Latin *elementum* a first principle, alphabet, element, of uncertain origin

elemental (ˌɛlɪ'mɛntᵊl) ADJECTIVE [1] fundamental; basic; primal: *the elemental needs of man.* [2] motivated by or symbolic of primitive and powerful natural forces or passions: *elemental rites of worship.* [3] of or relating to earth, air, water, and fire considered as elements. [4] of or relating to atmospheric forces, esp wind, rain, and cold. [5] of, relating to, or denoting a chemical element. ◆ NOUN [6] *Rare* a spirit or force that is said to appear in physical form.
▸ˌele'mentally ADVERB ▸ˌele'mentalˌism NOUN

elementary (ˌɛlɪ'mɛntərɪ, -trɪ) ADJECTIVE [1] not difficult; simple; rudimentary. [2] of or concerned with the first principles of a subject; introductory or fundamental. [3] *Maths* (of a function) having the form of an algebraic, exponential, trigonometric, or a logarithmic function, or any combination of these. [4] *Chem* another word for **elemental** (sense 5).
▸ˌele'mentarily ADVERB ▸ˌele'mentariness NOUN

elementary particle NOUN any of several entities, such as electrons, neutrons, or protons, that are less complex than atoms and are regarded as the constituents of all matter. Also called: **fundamental particle.**

elementary school NOUN [1] *Brit* a former name for **primary school.** [2] Also called (in the US): **grade school, grammar school.** *US and Canadian* a state school in which instruction is given for the first six to eight years of a child's education.

elemi ('ɛlɪmɪ) NOUN, *plural* **-mis.** any of various fragrant resins obtained from tropical trees, esp trees of the family *Burseraceae:* used in making varnishes, ointments, inks, etc.
▷HISTORY C16: via Spanish from Arabic *al-lāmī* the elemi

elenchus (ɪ'lɛŋkəs) NOUN, *plural* **-chi** (-kaɪ). *Logic* [1] refutation of an argument by proving the contrary of its conclusion, esp syllogistically. [2] **Socratic elenchus.** the drawing out of the consequences of a position in order to show them to be contrary to some accepted position.
▷HISTORY C17: from Latin, from Greek *elenkhos* refutation, from *elenkhein* to put to shame, refute

elenctic (ɪ'lɛŋktɪk) ADJECTIVE *Logic* refuting an argument by proving the falsehood of its conclusion. Compare **deictic** (sense 1).

eleoptene *or* **elaeoptene** (ˌɛlɪ'ɒptiːn) NOUN the liquid part of a volatile oil.
▷HISTORY C20: from Greek *elaion* oil + *ptēnos* having wings, volatile; related to Greek *petesthai* to fly

elephant ('ɛlɪfənt) NOUN, *plural* **-phants** *or* **-phant.** [1] either of the two proboscidean mammals of the family *Elephantidae.* The **African elephant** (*Loxodonta africana*) is the larger species, with large flapping ears and a less humped back than the **Indian elephant** (*Elephas maximus*), of S and SE Asia. [2] *Chiefly Brit* a size of writing paper, 23 by 28 inches.
▷HISTORY C13: from Latin *elephantus,* from Greek *elephas* elephant, ivory, of uncertain origin
▸'elephanˌtoid ADJECTIVE

elephant bird NOUN another name for **aepyornis.**

elephant grass NOUN any of various stout tropical grasses or grasslike plants, esp *Pennisetum purpureum,* and *Typha elephantina,* a type of reed mace.

elephant gun NOUN [1] a gun used in the hunting of elephants. [2] *Austral slang* a surfboard for riding large waves.

elephantiasis (ˌɛlɪfən'taɪəsɪs) NOUN *Pathol* a complication of chronic filariasis, in which nematode worms block the lymphatic vessels, usually in the legs or scrotum, causing extreme enlargement of the affected area. See also **filariasis.**
▷HISTORY C16: via Latin from Greek, from *elephas* ELEPHANT + -IASIS
▸**elephantiasic** (ˌɛlɪˌfæntɪ'æsɪk, -fən'taɪəsɪk) ADJECTIVE

elephantine (ˌɛlɪ'fæntaɪn) ADJECTIVE [1] denoting, relating to, or characteristic of an elephant or elephants. [2] huge, clumsy, or ponderous.

elephants ('ɛlɪfənts) ADJECTIVE *Austral slang* drunk; intoxicated.
▷HISTORY C20: shortened from *elephant's trunk,* rhyming slang for DRUNK

elephant seal NOUN either of two large earless seals, *Mirounga leonina* of southern oceans or *M. angustirostris* of the N Atlantic, the males of which have a long trunklike snout.

elephant's-ear NOUN [1] any aroid plant of the genus *Colocasia,* of tropical Asia and Polynesia, having very large heart-shaped leaves: grown for ornament and for their edible tubers. See also **taro.** [2] any of various cultivated begonias with large showy leaves.

elephant's-foot *or* **elephant foot** NOUN a monocotyledonous plant, *Testudinaria elephantipes,* of southern Africa, with a very large starchy tuberous stem, covered in corky scales: family *Dioscoreaceae.*

elephant shrew NOUN any small active African mammal of the family *Macroscelididae* and order *Macroscelidea,* having an elongated nose, large ears, and long hind legs.

Eleusinian mysteries PLURAL NOUN a mystical religious festival, held in September at Eleusis in classical times, in which initiates celebrated Persephone, Demeter, and Dionysus.

Eleusis (ɪ'luːsɪs) NOUN a town in Greece, in Attica about 23 km (14 miles) west of Athens, of which it is now an industrial suburb. Modern Greek name: **Elevsís.**
▸**Eleusinian** (ˌɛlju'sɪnɪən) NOUN, ADJECTIVE

elevate ('ɛlɪˌveɪt) VERB *(tr)* [1] to move to a higher place. [2] to raise in rank or status; promote. [3] to put in a cheerful mood; elate. [4] to put on a higher cultural plane; uplift: *to elevate the tone of a conversation.* [5] to raise the axis of a gun. [6] to raise the intensity or pitch of (the voice). [7] *RC Church* to lift up (the Host) at Mass for adoration.
▷HISTORY C15: from Latin *ēlevāre* from *levāre* to raise, from *levis* (adj) light
▸ˌele'vatory ADJECTIVE

elevated ('ɛlɪˌveɪtɪd) ADJECTIVE [1] raised to or being at a higher level. [2] inflated or lofty; exalted: *an elevated opinion of oneself.* [3] in a cheerful mood; elated. [4] *Informal* slightly drunk. ◆ NOUN [5] *US* short for **elevated railway** or **railroad.**

elevated railway *or* **railroad** NOUN *US* an urban railway track built on supports above a road.

elevation (ˌɛlɪ'veɪʃən) NOUN [1] the act of elevating or the state of being elevated. [2] the height of something above a given or implied place, esp above sea level. [3] a raised area; height. [4] nobleness or grandeur; loftiness: *elevation of thought.* [5] a drawing to scale of the external face of a building or structure. Compare **plan** (sense 3), **ground plan** (sense 1). [6] the external face of a building or structure. [7] a ballet dancer's ability to leap high. [8] *RC Church* the lifting up of the Host at Mass for adoration. [9] *Astronomy* another name for **altitude** (sense 3). [10] the angle formed between the muzzle of a gun and the horizontal. [11] *Surveying* the angular distance between the plane through a point of observation and an object above it. Compare **depression** (sense 7). [12] *Linguistics* another term for **amelioration.**
▸ˌele'vational ADJECTIVE

elevator ('ɛlɪˌveɪtə) NOUN [1] a person or thing that elevates. [2] *Chiefly US* a mechanical hoist for raising something, esp grain or coal, often consisting of a chain of scoops linked together on a conveyor belt. [3] the US and Canadian name for **lift**[1] (sense 17a). [4] *Chiefly US and Canadian* a large granary equipped with an elevator and, usually, facilities for cleaning and grading the grain. [5] any muscle that raises a part of the body. [6] a surgical instrument for lifting a part of the body. [7] a control surface on the tailplane of an aircraft, for making it climb or descend.

eleven (ɪ'lɛvᵊn) NOUN [1] the cardinal number that is the sum of ten and one. [2] a numeral 11, XI, etc., representing this number. [3] something representing, represented by, or consisting of 11 units. [4] *(functioning as singular or plural)* a team of 11 players in football, cricket, hockey, etc. [5] Also called: **eleven o'clock.** eleven hours after noon or midnight. ◆ DETERMINER [6] **a** amounting to eleven: *eleven chances.* **b** *(as pronoun): have another eleven today.*
▷HISTORY Old English *endleofan;* related to Old Norse *ellefo,* Gothic *ainlif,* Old Frisian *andlova,* Old High German *einlif*

eleven-plus NOUN (esp formerly) an examination, taken by children aged 11 or 12, that determines the type of secondary education a child will be given.

elevenses (ɪ'lɛvᵊnzɪz) PLURAL NOUN *(sometimes functioning as singular) Brit informal* a light snack, usually with tea or coffee, taken in mid-morning.

eleventh (ɪ'lɛvᵊnθ) ADJECTIVE [1] *(usually prenominal)* **a** coming after the tenth in numbering or counting order, position, time, etc.; being the ordinal number of *eleven:* often written 11th. **b** *(as pronoun): the eleventh in succession.* ◆ NOUN [2] **a** one of 11 equal or nearly equal parts of an object, quantity, measurement, etc. **b** *(as modifier): an eleventh part.* [3] the fraction equal to one divided by 11 (1/11). [4] *Music* **a** an interval of one octave plus one fourth. **b** See **eleventh chord.**

eleventh chord NOUN a chord much used in jazz, consisting of a major or minor triad upon which are superimposed the seventh, ninth, and eleventh above the root.

eleventh hour NOUN **a** the latest possible time; last minute. **b** *(as modifier): an eleventh-hour decision.*

elevon ('ɛlɪˌvɒn) NOUN an aircraft control surface that combines the functions of an elevator and aileron, usually fitted to tailless or delta-wing aircraft.
▷HISTORY C20: from ELEV(ATOR) + (AILER)ON

Elevsís (ˌɛlɛf'sis) NOUN transliteration of the Modern Greek name for **Eleusis.**

elf (ɛlf) NOUN, *plural* **elves** (ɛlvz). [1] (in folklore) one of a kind of legendary beings, usually characterized as small, manlike, and mischievous. [2] a mischievous or whimsical child.
▷HISTORY Old English *ælf;* related to Old Norse *elfr* elf, Middle Low German *alf* incubus, Latin *albus* white
▸'elfˌlike ADJECTIVE

ELF ABBREVIATION FOR **extremely low frequency.**

El Faiyûm (ɛl faɪ'juːm) *or* **Al Faiyûm** (æl faɪ'juːm) NOUN a city in N Egypt: a site of towns going back at least to the 12th dynasty. Pop.: 260 964 (1996).

elf-cup NOUN any of various cup-shaped ascomycetous fungi of the order *Pezizales,* often strikingly coloured, such as the **orange-peel elf-cup** (*Aleuria aurantia*), that is bright orange inside and dirty white outside, and the **scarlet elf-cup** (*Sarcoscypha coccinea*).

El Ferrol (*Spanish* ɛl fe'rrɔl) NOUN a port in NW Spain, on the Atlantic: fortified naval base, with a deep natural harbour. Pop.: 82 371 (1991). Official name (since 1939): **El Ferrol del Caudillo** (dɛl kau'ðiʎo).

elfin ('ɛlfɪn) ADJECTIVE 1 of, relating to, or like an elf or elves. 2 small, delicate, and charming.

elfin forest *or* **woodland** NOUN the zone of stunted wind-blown trees growing at high altitudes just above the timber line on tropical mountains. Also called: **krummholz.**

elfish ('ɛlfɪʃ) *or* **elvish** ADJECTIVE 1 of, relating to, or like an elf or elves; charmingly mischievous or sprightly; impish. ◆ NOUN 2 the supposed language of elves.
▸**'elfishly** *or* **'elvishly** ADVERB ▸**'elfishness** *or* **'elvishness** NOUN

elfland ('ɛlf,lænd) NOUN another name for **fairyland.**

elflock ('ɛlf,lɒk) NOUN a lock of hair, fancifully regarded as having been tangled by the elves.

Elgin ('ɛlgɪn) NOUN a market town in NE Scotland, the administrative centre of Moray, on the River Lossie: ruined 13th-century cathedral: distilling, engineering. Pop.: 19 027 (1991).

Elgin marbles PLURAL NOUN a group of 5th-century B.C. Greek sculptures originally decorating the Parthenon in Athens, brought to England by Thomas Bruce, seventh Earl of Elgin (1766–1841), and now at the British Museum.

El Gîza (ɛl 'gi:zə) NOUN a city in NE Egypt, on the W bank of the Nile opposite Cairo: nearby are the Great Pyramid of Cheops (Khufu) and the Sphinx. Pop.: 2 221 868 (1996).

Elgon ('ɛlgɒn) NOUN **Mount.** an extinct volcano in E Africa, on the Kenya-Uganda border. Height: 4321m (14 178 ft.).

Eli ('i:laɪ) NOUN *Old Testament* the highest priest at Shiloh and teacher of Samuel (I Samuel 1–3).

Elia *or* **Eleia** ('i:lɪə) NOUN a department of SW Greece, in the W Peloponnese: in ancient times most of the region formed the state of Elis. Pop.: 179 429 (1991). Area: 2681 sq. km (1035 sq. miles). Modern Greek name: **Ilía.**

Elias (ɪ'laɪəs) NOUN *Bible* the Douay spelling of **Elijah.**

eliche (*Italian* elike) NOUN pasta in the form of spirals.
▷HISTORY Italian: literally, propellers

elicit (ɪ'lɪsɪt) VERB (*tr*) 1 to give rise to; evoke: *to elicit a sharp retort.* 2 to bring to light: *to elicit the truth.*
▷HISTORY C17: from Latin *ēlicere* to lure forth, from *licere* to entice
▸**e'licitable** ADJECTIVE ▸**e,lici'tation** NOUN ▸**e'licitor** NOUN

elide (ɪ'laɪd) VERB *Phonetics* to undergo or cause to undergo elision.
▷HISTORY C16: from Latin *ēlīdere* to knock, from *laedere* to hit, wound
▸**e'lidible** ADJECTIVE

eligible ('ɛlɪdʒəbᵊl) ADJECTIVE 1 fit, worthy, or qualified, as for an office or function. 2 desirable and worthy of being chosen, esp as a spouse: *an eligible young man.*
▷HISTORY C15: from Late Latin *ēligibilis* able to be chosen, from *ēligere* to ELECT
▸**,eligi'bility** NOUN ▸**'eligibly** ADVERB

Elijah (ɪ'laɪdʒə) NOUN *Old Testament* a Hebrew prophet of the 9th century B.C., who was persecuted for denouncing Ahab and Jezebel. (I Kings 17–21: 21; II Kings 1–2:18).

Elikón (ɛli'kɔn) NOUN transliteration of the Modern Greek name for **Helicon.**

eliminate (ɪ'lɪmɪ,neɪt) VERB (*tr*) 1 to remove or take out; get rid of. 2 to reject as trivial or irrelevant; omit from consideration. 3 to remove (a competitor, team, etc.) from a contest, usually by defeat. 4 *Slang* to murder in a cold-blooded manner. 5 *Physiol* to expel (waste matter) from the body. 6 *Maths* to remove (an unknown variable) from two or more simultaneous equations.
▷HISTORY C16: from Latin *ēlīmināre* to turn out of the house, from *e-* out + *līmen* threshold
▸**e'liminable** ADJECTIVE ▸**e,limina'bility** NOUN ▸**e'liminant** NOUN ▸**e'liminative** *or* **e'liminatory** ADJECTIVE ▸**e'limi,nator** NOUN

> **Language note** *Eliminate* is sometimes wrongly used to talk about avoiding the repetition of something undesirable: *we must prevent* (not *eliminate*) *further mistakes of this kind.*

elimination (ɪ,lɪmɪ'neɪʃən) NOUN 1 the act of eliminating or the state of being eliminated. 2 *Logic* (qualified by the name of an operation) a syntactic rule specifying the conditions under which a formula or statement containing the specified operation may permit the derivation of others that do not contain it: *conjunction-elimination; universal elimination.* 3 *Chem* a type of chemical reaction involving the loss of a simple molecule, such as water or carbon dioxide.

Elis ('i:lɪs) NOUN an ancient city-state of SW Greece, in the NW Peloponnese: site of the ancient Olympic games.

ELISA (ɪ'laɪzə) NOUN ACRONYM FOR enzyme-linked immunosorbent assay: an immunological technique for accurately measuring the amount of a substance, for example in a blood sample.

Élisabethville (ɪ'lɪzəbəθ,vɪl) NOUN the former name (until 1966) of **Lubumbashi.**

Elisavetgrad (*Russian* jɪliza'vjɛtgrət) NOUN a former name (until 1924) of **Kirovograd.**

Elisavetpol (*Russian* jɪliza'vjɛtpəlj) NOUN a former name (until 1920) of **Kirovabad.**

Elisha (ɪ'laɪʃə) NOUN *Old Testament* a Hebrew prophet of the 9th century B.C.: successor of Elijah (II Kings 3–9).

elision (ɪ'lɪʒən) NOUN 1 the omission of a syllable or vowel at the beginning or end of a word, esp when a word ending with a vowel is next to one beginning with a vowel. 2 any omission of a part or parts.
▷HISTORY C16: from Latin *ēlīsiō,* from *ēlīdere* to ELIDE

elite *or* **élite** (ɪ'li:t, eɪ-) NOUN 1 (*sometimes functioning as plural*) the most powerful, rich, gifted, or educated members of a group, community, etc. 2 Also called: **twelve pitch.** a typewriter typesize having 12 characters to the inch. ◆ ADJECTIVE 3 of, relating to, or suitable for an elite; exclusive.
▷HISTORY C18: from French, from Old French *eslit* chosen, from *eslire* to choose, from Latin *ēligere* to ELECT

elitism (ɪ'li:tɪzəm, eɪ-) NOUN 1 **a** the belief that society should be governed by a select group of gifted and highly educated individuals. **b** such government. 2 pride in or awareness of being one of an elite group.
▸**e'litist** ADJECTIVE, NOUN

elixir (ɪ'lɪksə) NOUN 1 an alchemical preparation supposed to be capable of prolonging life indefinitely (**elixir of life**) or of transmuting base metals into gold. 2 anything that purports to be a sovereign remedy; panacea. 3 an underlying principle; quintessence. 4 a liquid containing a medicinal drug with syrup, glycerine, or alcohol added to mask its unpleasant taste.
▷HISTORY C14: from Medieval Latin, from Arabic *al iksīr* the elixir, probably from Greek *xērion* powder used for drying wounds, from *xēros* dry

Elizabeth (ɪ'lɪzəbəθ) NOUN 1 a city in NE New Jersey, on Newark Bay. Pop.: 120 568 (2000). 2 a town in SE South Australia, near Adelaide. Pop.: 34 000 (latest est.).

Elizabethan (ɪ,lɪzə'bi:θən) ADJECTIVE 1 of, characteristic of, or relating to England or its culture in the age of Elizabeth I (1533–1603; reigned 1558–1603) or to the United Kingdom or its culture in the age of Elizabeth II (born 1926; queen from 1952). 2 of, relating to, or designating a style of architecture used in England during the reign of Elizabeth I, characterized by moulded and sculptured ornament based on German and Flemish models. ◆ NOUN 3 a person who lived in England during the reign of Elizabeth I.

Elizabethan sonnet NOUN another term for **Shakespearean sonnet.**

elk (ɛlk) NOUN, *plural* **elks** *or* **elk.** 1 a large deer, *Alces alces,* of N Europe and Asia, having large flattened palmate antlers: also occurs in North America, where it is called a moose. 2 **American elk.** another name for **wapiti.** 3 a stout pliable waterproof leather made from calfskin or horsehide.
▷HISTORY Old English *eolh;* related to Old Norse *elgr,* Old High German *elaho,* Latin *alcēs,* Greek *alkē, elaphos* deer

El Khalil (ɛl xɒ'li:l) NOUN transliteration of the Arabic name for **Hebron.**

elkhound ('ɛlk,haʊnd) NOUN a powerful breed of dog of the spitz type with a thick grey coat and tightly curled tail. Also called: **Norwegian elkhound.**

ell[1] (ɛl) NOUN an obsolete unit of length equal to approximately 45 inches.
▷HISTORY Old English *eln* the forearm (the measure originally being from the elbow to the fingertips); related to Old High German *elina,* Latin *ulna,* Greek *ōlenē*

ell[2] (ɛl) NOUN 1 an extension to a building, usually at right angles and located at one end. 2 a pipe fitting, pipe, or tube with a sharp right-angle bend.
▷HISTORY C20: a spelling of *L,* indicating a right angle

Ellás (ɛ'las) NOUN transliteration of the Modern Greek name for **Greece.**

Ellesmere Island ('ɛlzmɪə) NOUN a Canadian island in the Arctic Ocean: part of Nunavut; mountainous, with many glaciers. Area: 212 688 sq. km (82 119 sq. miles).

Ellesmere Port NOUN a port in NW England, in NW Cheshire on the Mersey estuary and Manchester Ship Canal. Pop.: 64 504 (1991).

Ellice Islands ('ɛlɪs) PLURAL NOUN the former name (until 1975) of **Tuvalu.**

ellipse (ɪ'lɪps) NOUN a closed conic section shaped like a flattened circle and formed by an inclined plane that does not cut the base of the cone. Standard equation $x^2/a^2 + y^2/b^2 = 1$, where $2a$ and $2b$ are the lengths of the major and minor axes. Area: πab.
▷HISTORY C18: back formation from ELLIPSIS

ellipsis (ɪ'lɪpsɪs) NOUN, *plural* **-ses** (-si:z). 1 Also called: **eclipsis.** omission of parts of a word or sentence. 2 *Printing* a sequence of three dots (...) indicating an omission in text.
▷HISTORY C16: from Latin, from Greek *elleipsis* omission, from *elleipein* to leave out, from *leipein* to leave

ellipsoid (ɪ'lɪpsɔɪd) NOUN **a** a geometric surface, symmetrical about the three coordinate axes, whose plane sections are ellipses or circles. Standard equation: $x^2/a^2 + y^2/b^2 + z^2/c^2 = 1$, where $\pm a$, $\pm b$, $\pm c$ are the intercepts on the *x-, y-,* and *z-* axes. **b** a solid having this shape: *the earth is an ellipsoid.*
▸**ellipsoidal** (ɪlɪp'sɔɪdᵊl, ,ɛl-) ADJECTIVE

ellipsoid of revolution NOUN a geometric surface produced by rotating an ellipse about one of its two axes and having circular plane surfaces perpendicular to the axis of revolution. Also called: **spheroid.**

elliptical (ɪ'lɪptɪkᵊl) ADJECTIVE 1 relating to or having the shape of an ellipse. 2 relating to or resulting from ellipsis. 3 (of speech, literary style, etc.) **a** very condensed or concise, often so as to be obscure or ambiguous. **b** circumlocutory or long-winded. ◆ Also (for senses 1, 2): **elliptic.**
▸**el'liptically** ADVERB ▸**el'lipticalness** NOUN

> **Language note** The use of *elliptical* to mean *circumlocutory* should be avoided as it may be interpreted wrongly as meaning *condensed* or *concise.*

elliptic geometry NOUN another name for **Riemannian geometry.**

ellipticity (ɪlɪp'tɪsɪtɪ, ,ɛl-) NOUN the degree of deviation from a circle or sphere of an elliptical or ellipsoidal shape or path, measured as the ratio of the major to the minor axes.

elm (ɛlm) NOUN 1 any ulmaceous tree of the genus *Ulmus,* occurring in the N hemisphere, having serrated leaves and winged fruits (samaras): cultivated for shade, ornament, and timber. 2 the hard heavy wood of this tree. ◆ See also **slippery elm, wahoo**[1]**, wych-elm.**
▷HISTORY Old English *elm;* related to Old Norse *almr,* Old High German *elm,* Latin *ulmus*

El Mansûra (ɛl mæn'sʊərə) *or* **Al Mansûrah** NOUN a city in NE Egypt: scene of a battle (1250) in which the Crusaders were defeated by the Mamelukes and Louis IX of France was captured; cotton-manufacturing centre. Pop.: 369 621 (1996).

El Minya (ɛl 'mɪnjə) NOUN a river port in central Egypt on the Nile. Pop.: 201 360 (1996).

El Misti (ɛl 'miːstiː) NOUN a volcano in S Peru, in the Andes. Height: 5852 m (19 199 ft.).

El Niño (ɛl 'niːnjəʊ) NOUN *Meteorol* a warming of the eastern tropical Pacific occurring every few years, which alters the weather pattern of the tropics.
▷HISTORY C20: from Spanish: The Child, i.e. Christ, referring to its original occurrence at Christmas time

El Obeid (ɛl əʊ'beɪd) NOUN a city in the central Sudan, in Kordofan province: scene of the defeat of a British and Egyptian army by the Mahdi (1883). Pop.: 228 096 (1993).

elocute ('ɛləˌkjuːt) VERB (*intr*) *Facetious* to speak as if practising elocution; declaim.
▷HISTORY C19: back formation from ELOCUTION

elocution (ˌɛlə'kjuːʃən) NOUN the art of public speaking, esp of voice production, delivery, and gesture.
▷HISTORY C15: from Latin *ēlocūtiō* a speaking out, from *ēloquī,* from *loquī* to speak
▸**ˌelo'cutionary** ADJECTIVE ▸**ˌelo'cutionist** NOUN

Elohim (ɛ'ləʊhɪm, ˌɛləʊ'hiːm) NOUN *Old Testament* a Hebrew word for God or gods.
▷HISTORY C17: from Hebrew *'Ělōhīm,* plural (used to indicate uniqueness) of *'Elōah* God; probably related to *'El* God

Elohist (ɛ'ləʊhɪst) NOUN *Old Testament* the supposed author or authors of one of the four main strands of text of the Pentateuch, identified chiefly by the use of the word *Elohim* for God instead of *YHVH* (Jehovah).

eloign *or* **eloin** (ɪ'lɔɪn) VERB (*tr*) *Archaic* to remove (oneself, one's property, etc.) to a distant place.
▷HISTORY C16: from Anglo-French *esloigner* to go far away; related to Latin *longē* (adv) far; compare ELONGATE
▸**e'loigner** *or* **e'loiner** NOUN ▸**e'loignment** *or* **e'loinment** NOUN

elongate ('iːlɒŋgeɪt) VERB 1 to make or become longer; stretch. ◆ ADJECTIVE 2 long and narrow; slender: *elongate leaves.* 3 lengthened or tapered.
▷HISTORY C16: from Late Latin *ēlongāre* to keep at a distance, from *ē-* away + Latin *longē* (adv) far, but also later: to lengthen, as if from *ē-* + Latin *longus* (adjective) long

elongation (ˌiːlɒŋ'geɪʃən) NOUN 1 the act of elongating or state of being elongated; lengthening. 2 something that is elongated. 3 *Astronomy* the difference between the celestial longitude of the sun and that of a planet or the moon.

elope (ɪ'ləʊp) VERB (*intr*) to run away secretly with a lover, esp in order to marry.
▷HISTORY C16: from Anglo-French *aloper,* perhaps from Middle Dutch *lōpen* to run; see LOPE
▸**e'lopement** NOUN ▸**e'loper** NOUN

eloquence ('ɛləkwəns) NOUN 1 ease in using language to best effect. 2 powerful and effective language. 3 the quality of being persuasive or moving.

eloquent ('ɛləkwənt) ADJECTIVE 1 (of speech, writing, etc.) characterized by fluency and persuasiveness. 2 visibly or vividly expressive, as of an emotion: *an eloquent yawn.*
▷HISTORY C14: from Latin *ēloquēns,* from *ēloquī* to speak out, from *loquī* to speak
▸**'eloquently** ADVERB

El Paso (ɛl 'pæsəʊ) NOUN a city in W Texas, on the Rio Grande opposite Ciudad Juárez, Mexico. Pop.: 599 865 (1996 est.).

El Salvador (ɛl 'sælvəˌdɔː) NOUN a republic in Central America, on the Pacific: colonized by the Spanish from 1524; declared independence in 1841, becoming a republic in 1856. It consists of coastal lowlands rising to a central plateau. Coffee constitutes over a third of the total exports. Official language: Spanish. Religion: Roman Catholic majority. Currency: US dollar. Capital: San Salvador. Pop.: 6 238 000 (2001 est). Area: 21 393 sq. km (8236 sq. miles).
▸**ˌSalva'doran** *or* **ˌSalva'dorean** *or* **ˌSalva'dorian** ADJECTIVE, NOUN

Elsan ('ɛlsæn) NOUN *Trademark* a type of portable lavatory in which chemicals are used to kill bacteria and deodorize the sludge.
▷HISTORY C20: from the initials of *E. L.* Jackson, the manufacturer + SAN(ITATION)

Elsass ('ɛlzas) NOUN the German name for **Alsace.**

Elsass-Lothringen ('ɛlzas'loːtrɪŋən) NOUN the German name for **Alsace-Lorraine.**

else (ɛls) DETERMINER (*postpositive; used after an indefinite pronoun or an interrogative*) 1 in addition; more: *there is nobody else here.* 2 other; different: *where else could he be?* ◆ ADVERB 3 **or else. a** if not, then: *go away or else I won't finish my work today.* **b** or something terrible will result: used as a threat: *sit down, or else!*
▷HISTORY Old English *elles,* genitive of *el-* strange, foreign; related to Old High German *eli-* other, Gothic *alja,* Latin *alius,* Greek *allos*

elsewhere (ˌɛls'wɛə) ADVERB in or to another place; somewhere else.
▷HISTORY Old English *elles hwǣr;* see ELSE, WHERE

Elsinore ('ɛlsɪˌnɔː, ˌɛlsɪ'nɔː) NOUN the English name for **Helsingør.**

ELT ABBREVIATION FOR English Language Teaching: the teaching of English specifically to students whose native language is not English.

eluate ('ɛljuːˌeɪt) NOUN a solution of adsorbed material in the eluent obtained during the process of elution.

elucidate (ɪ'luːsɪˌdeɪt) VERB to make clear (something obscure or difficult); clarify.
▷HISTORY C16: from Late Latin *ēlūcidāre* to enlighten; see LUCID
▸**eˌluci'dation** NOUN ▸**e'luciˌdative** *or* **e'luciˌdatory** ADJECTIVE ▸**e'luciˌdator** NOUN

elude (ɪ'luːd) VERB (*tr*) 1 to escape or avoid (capture, one's pursuers, etc.), esp by cunning. 2 to avoid fulfilment of (a responsibility, obligation, etc.); evade. 3 to escape discovery, or understanding by; baffle: *the solution eluded her.*
▷HISTORY C16: from Latin *ēlūdere* to deceive, from *lūdere* to play
▸**e'luder** NOUN ▸**elusion** (ɪ'luːʒən) NOUN

> **Language note** *Elude* is sometimes wrongly used where *allude* is meant: *he was alluding* (not *eluding*) *to his previous visit to the city.*

eluent *or* **eluant** ('ɛljuːənt) NOUN a solvent used for eluting.

Elul (ɛ'luːl) NOUN (in the Jewish calendar) the sixth month of the year according to biblical reckoning and the twelfth month of the civil year, usually falling within August and September.
▷HISTORY from Hebrew

elusive (ɪ'luːsɪv) ADJECTIVE 1 difficult to catch: *an elusive thief.* 2 preferring or living in solitude and anonymity. 3 difficult to remember: *an elusive thought.*
▸**e'lusively** ADVERB ▸**e'lusiveness** NOUN

> **Language note** See at **illusory.**

elusory (ɪ'luːsərɪ) ADJECTIVE 1 avoiding the issue; evasive: *elusory arguments.* 2 difficult to grasp mentally; elusive: *elusory ideas.*

elute (iː'luːt, ɪ'luːt) VERB (*tr*) to wash out (a substance) by the action of a solvent, as in chromatography.
▷HISTORY C18: from Latin *ēlūtus* rinsed out, from *ēluere* to wash clean, from *luere* to wash, LAVE
▸**e'lution** NOUN

elutriate (ɪ'luːtrɪˌeɪt) VERB (*tr*) to purify or separate (a substance or mixture) by washing and straining or decanting.
▷HISTORY C18: from Latin *ēlūtriāre* to wash out, from *ēluere,* from *ē-* out + *lavere* to wash
▸**eˌlutri'ation** NOUN ▸**e'lutriˌator** NOUN

eluviation (ɪˌluːvɪ'eɪʃən) NOUN the process by which material suspended in water is removed from one layer of soil to another by the action of rainfall or chemical decomposition.
▷HISTORY C20: from ELUVIUM

eluvium (ɪ'luːvɪəm) NOUN, *plural* **-via** (-vɪə). a mass of sand, silt, etc.: a product of the erosion of rocks that has remained in its place of origin.
▷HISTORY C19: New Latin, from Latin *ēluere* to wash out
▸**e'luvial** ADJECTIVE

elver ('ɛlvə) NOUN a young eel, esp one migrating up a river from the sea. See also **leptocephalus.**
▷HISTORY C17: variant of *eelfare* migration of young eels, literally: eel-journey; see EEL, FARE

elves (ɛlvz) NOUN the plural of **elf.**

elvish ('ɛlvɪʃ) ADJECTIVE a variant of **elfish.**

Ely ('iːlɪ) NOUN 1 a cathedral city in E England, in E Cambridgeshire on the River Ouse. Pop.: 10 329 (1991). 2 a former county of E England, part of Cambridgeshire since 1965.

Elysée (eɪ'liːzeɪ) NOUN a palace in Paris, in the Champs Elysées: official residence of the president of France.

Elysian (ɪ'lɪzɪən) ADJECTIVE 1 of or relating to Elysium. 2 *Literary* delightful; glorious; blissful.

Elysium (ɪ'lɪzɪəm) NOUN 1 Also called: **Elysian fields.** *Greek myth* the dwelling place of the blessed after death. See also **Islands of the Blessed.** 2 a state or place of perfect bliss.
▷HISTORY C16: from Latin, from Greek *Ēlusion pedion* Elysian (that is, blessed) fields

elytron ('ɛlɪˌtrɒn) *or* **elytrum** ('ɛlɪtrəm) NOUN, *plural* **-tra** (-trə). either of the horny front wings of beetles and some other insects, which cover and protect the hind wings.
▷HISTORY C18: from Greek *elutron* sheath, covering
▸**'elyˌtroid** *or* **'elytrous** ADJECTIVE

em (ɛm) NOUN *Printing* 1 Also called: **mutton, mut.** the square of a body of any size of type, used as a unit of measurement. 2 Also called: **pica em, pica.** a unit of measurement used in printing, equal to one sixth of an inch.
▷HISTORY C19: from the name of the letter *M*

em- PREFIX a variant of **en-**[1] and **en-**[2] before *b, m,* and *p.*

'em (əm) PRONOUN an informal variant of **them.**

emaciate (ɪ'meɪsɪˌeɪt) VERB (*usually tr*) to become or cause to become abnormally thin.
▷HISTORY C17: from Latin *ēmaciāre* to make lean, from *macer* thin
▸**eˌmaci'ation** NOUN

emaciated (ɪ'meɪsɪˌeɪtɪd) ADJECTIVE abnormally thin.

E-mail, Email, e-mail, *or* **email** ('iːmeɪl) NOUN 1 short for **electronic mail.** ◆ VERB (*tr*) 2 to contact (a person) by electronic mail. 3 to send (a message, document, etc.) by electronic mail.

emalangeni (ˌɛmɒːlɒːŋ'geɪnɪ) NOUN the plural of **lilangeni.**

emanate ('ɛməˌneɪt) VERB 1 (*intr; often foll by from*) to issue or proceed from or as from a source. 2 (*tr*) to send forth; emit.
▷HISTORY C18: from Latin *ēmānāre* to flow out, from *mānāre* to flow
▸**emanative** ('ɛmənətɪv) ADJECTIVE ▸**'emaˌnator** NOUN
▸**emanatory** ('ɛməˌneɪtərɪ, -trɪ) ADJECTIVE

emanation (ˌɛmə'neɪʃən) NOUN 1 an act or instance of emanating. 2 something that emanates or is produced; effusion. 3 a gaseous product of radioactive decay, such as radon.
▸**ˌema'national** ADJECTIVE

emancipate (ɪ'mænsɪˌpeɪt) VERB (*tr*) 1 to free from restriction or restraint, esp social or legal restraint. 2 (*often passive*) to free from the inhibitions imposed by conventional morality. 3 to liberate (a slave) from bondage.
▷HISTORY C17: from Latin *ēmancipāre* to give independence (to a son), from *mancipāre* to transfer property, from *manceps* a purchaser; see MANCIPLE
▸**e'manciˌpated** ADJECTIVE ▸**e'manciˌpative** ADJECTIVE
▸**e'mancipist** *or* **e'manciˌpator** NOUN ▸**emancipatory** (ɪ'mænsɪpətərɪ, -trɪ) ADJECTIVE

emancipation (ɪˌmænsɪ'peɪʃən) NOUN 1 the act of freeing or state of being freed; liberation. 2 *Informal* freedom from inhibition and convention.
▸**eˌmanci'pationist** NOUN

emarginate (ɪ'mɑːdʒɪˌneɪt) *or* **emarginated** ADJECTIVE having a notched tip or edge: *emarginate leaves.*
▷HISTORY C17: from Latin *ēmargināre* to deprive of its edge, from *margō* MARGIN

▸e'margi,nately ADVERB ▸e,margi'nation NOUN

e-marketing NOUN the practice of marketing by means of the Internet.
▷HISTORY C20: electronic *marketing*

emasculate VERB (ɪ'mæskjʊ,leɪt) (*tr*) 1 to remove the testicles of; castrate; geld. 2 to deprive of vigour, effectiveness, etc. 3 *Botany* to remove the stamens from (a flower) to prevent self-pollination for the purposes of plant breeding. ◆ ADJECTIVE (ɪ'mæskjʊlɪt, -,leɪt) 4 castrated; gelded. 5 deprived of strength, effectiveness, etc.
▷HISTORY C17: from Latin *ēmasculāre,* from *masculus* male; see MASCULINE
▸e,mascu'lation NOUN ▸e'masculative *or* e'masculatory ADJECTIVE ▸e'mascu,lator NOUN

embalm (ɪm'bɑːm) VERB (*tr*) 1 to treat (a dead body) with preservatives, as by injecting formaldehyde into the blood vessels, to retard putrefaction. 2 to preserve or cherish the memory of. 3 *Poetic* to give a sweet fragrance to.
▷HISTORY C13: from Old French *embaumer;* see BALM
▸em'balmer NOUN ▸em'balmment NOUN

embank (ɪm'bæŋk) VERB (*tr*) to protect, enclose, or confine (a waterway, road, etc.) with an embankment.

embankment (ɪm'bæŋkmənt) NOUN a man-made ridge of earth or stone that carries a road or railway or confines a waterway. See also **levee.**

embargo (ɛm'bɑːɡəʊ) NOUN, *plural* **-goes.** 1 a government order prohibiting the departure or arrival of merchant ships in its ports. 2 any legal stoppage of commerce: *an embargo on arms shipments.* 3 a restraint, hindrance, or prohibition. ◆ VERB **-goes, -going, -goed.** (*tr*) 4 to lay an embargo upon. 5 to seize for use by the state.
▷HISTORY C16: from Spanish, from *embargar,* from Latin IM- + *barra* BAR[1]

embark (ɛm'bɑːk) VERB 1 to board (a ship or aircraft). 2 (*intr;* usually foll by *on* or *upon*) to commence or engage (in) a new project, venture, etc.
▷HISTORY C16: via French from Old Provençal *embarcar,* from EM- + *barca* boat, BARQUE
▸,embar'kation NOUN ▸em'barkment NOUN

embarras de richesses *French* (ɑ̃bara də riʃɛs) NOUN a superfluous abundance of options, from which one finds it difficult to select. Also called: ***embarras de choix*** (də ʃwa).
▷HISTORY C18: literally: embarrassment of riches

embarrass (ɪm'bærəs) VERB (*mainly tr*) 1 (*also intr*) to feel or cause to feel confusion or self-consciousness; disconcert; fluster. 2 (*usually passive*) to involve in financial difficulties. 3 *Archaic* to make difficult; complicate. 4 *Archaic* to impede; obstruct; hamper.
▷HISTORY C17 (in the sense: to impede): via French and Spanish from Italian *imbarrazzare,* from *imbarrare* to confine within bars; see EN-[1], BAR[1]
▸em'barrassed ADJECTIVE ▸em'barrassedly ADVERB

embarrassing (ɪm'bærəsɪŋ) ADJECTIVE causing one to feel confusion or self-consciousness; disconcerting.
▸em'barrassingly ADVERB

embarrassment (ɪm'bærəsmənt) NOUN 1 the state of being embarrassed. 2 something that embarrasses. 3 a financial predicament. 4 an excessive amount; superfluity.

embassy ('ɛmbəsɪ) NOUN, *plural* **-sies.** 1 the residence or place of official business of an ambassador. 2 an ambassador and his entourage collectively. 3 the position, business, or mission of an ambassador. 4 any important or official mission, duty, etc., esp one undertaken by an agent.
▷HISTORY C16: from Old French *ambassee,* from Old Italian *ambasciata,* from Old Provençal *ambaisada,* ultimately of Germanic origin; see AMBASSADOR

embattle (ɪm'bæt°l) VERB (*tr*) 1 to deploy (troops) for battle. 2 to strengthen or fortify (a position, town, etc.). 3 to provide (a building) with battlements.
▷HISTORY C14: from Old French *embataillier;* see EN-[1], BATTLE

embattled (ɪm'bæt°ld) ADJECTIVE 1 prepared for or engaged in conflict, controversy, or battle. 2 *Heraldry* having an indented edge resembling battlements.

embay (ɪm'beɪ) VERB (*tr; usually passive*) 1 to form into a bay. 2 to enclose in or as if in a bay. 3 (esp of the wind) to force (a ship, esp a sailing ship) into a bay.

embayment (ɪm'beɪmənt) NOUN a shape resembling a bay.

Embden-Meyerhof pathway ('ɛmdən'maɪə,hɒf) NOUN the metabolic reaction sequence in glycolysis by which glucose is converted to pyruvic acid with production of ATP.
▷HISTORY C20: named after Gustav *Embden* (1874–1933) and Otto *Meyerhof* (1884–1951), German biochemists

embed (ɪm'bɛd) VERB **-beds, -bedding, -bedded.** 1 (usually foll by *in*) to fix or become fixed firmly and deeply in a surrounding solid mass: *to embed a nail in wood.* 2 (*tr*) to surround closely: *hard rock embeds the roots.* 3 (*tr*) to fix or retain (a thought, idea, etc.) in the mind. 4 (*tr*) *Grammar* to insert (a subordinate clause) into a sentence. ◆ Also: **imbed.**
▸em'bedment NOUN

embellish (ɪm'bɛlɪʃ) VERB (*tr*) 1 to improve or beautify by adding detail or ornament; adorn. 2 to make (a story) more interesting by adding detail. 3 to provide (a melody, part, etc.) with ornaments. See **ornament** (sense 5).
▷HISTORY C14: from Old French *embelir,* from *bel* beautiful, from Latin *bellus*
▸em'bellisher NOUN ▸em'bellishment NOUN

ember ('ɛmbə) NOUN 1 a glowing or smouldering piece of coal or wood, as in a dying fire. 2 the fading remains of a past emotion: *the embers of his love.*
▷HISTORY Old English *ǣmyrge;* related to Old Norse *eimyrja* ember, *eimr* smoke, Old High German *eimuria* ember

Ember days PLURAL NOUN *RC and Anglican Church* any of four groups of three days (always Wednesday, Friday, and Saturday) of prayer and fasting, the groups occurring after Pentecost, after the first Sunday of Lent, after the feast of St Lucy (Dec. 13), and after the feast of the Holy Cross (Sept. 14).
▷HISTORY Old English *ymbrendæg,* from *ymbren,* perhaps from *ymbryne* a (recurring) period, from *ymb* around + *ryne* a course + *dæg* day

ember goose NOUN (*not in ornithological use*) another name for the **great northern diver.**
▷HISTORY C18: from Norwegian *emmer-gaas*

Ember week NOUN a week in which Ember days fall.

embezzle (ɪm'bɛz°l) VERB to convert (money or property entrusted to one) fraudulently to one's own use.
▷HISTORY C15: from Anglo-French *embeseiller* to destroy, from Old French *beseiller* to make away with, of uncertain origin
▸em'bezzlement NOUN ▸em'bezzler NOUN

embitter (ɪm'bɪtə) VERB (*tr*) 1 to make (a person) resentful or bitter. 2 to aggravate (an already hostile feeling, difficult situation, etc.).
▸em'bittered ADJECTIVE ▸em'bitterer NOUN ▸em'bitterment NOUN

emblaze (ɪm'bleɪz) VERB (*tr*) *Archaic* 1 to cause to light up; illuminate. 2 to set fire to.

emblazon (ɪm'bleɪz°n) VERB (*tr*) 1 to describe, portray, or colour (arms) according to the conventions of heraldry. 2 to portray heraldic arms on (a shield, one's notepaper, etc.). 3 to make bright or splendid, as with colours, flowers, etc. 4 to glorify, praise, or extol, often so as to attract great publicity: *his feat was emblazoned on the front page.*
▸em'blazonment NOUN

emblazonry (ɪm'bleɪz°nrɪ) NOUN another name for **blazonry.**

emblem ('ɛmbləm) NOUN 1 a visible object or representation that symbolizes a quality, type, group, etc., esp the concrete symbol of an abstract idea: *the dove is an emblem of peace.* 2 an allegorical picture containing a moral lesson, often with an explanatory motto or verses, esp one printed in an **emblem book.**
▷HISTORY C15: from Latin *emblēma* raised decoration, mosaic, from Greek, literally: something inserted, from *emballein* to insert, from *ballein* to throw
▸,emblem'atic *or* ,emblem'atical ADJECTIVE ▸,emblem'atically ADVERB

emblematize (ɛm'blɛmə,taɪz), **emblemize** ('ɛmblə,maɪz), **emblematise,** *or* **emblemise** VERB (*tr*) 1 to function as an emblem of; symbolize. 2 to represent by or as by an emblem.

emblements ('ɛmbləmənts) PLURAL NOUN *Law* 1 annual crops and vegetable products cultivated by man's labour. 2 the profits from such crops.
▷HISTORY C15: from Old French *emblaement,* from *emblaer* to sow with grain, from Medieval Latin *imblādāre,* from *blāda* grain, of Germanic origin; compare Old English *blǣd* grain

embody (ɪm'bɒdɪ) VERB **-bodies, -bodying, -bodied.** (*tr*) 1 to give a tangible, bodily, or concrete form to (an abstract concept). 2 to be an example of or express (an idea, principle, etc.), esp in action: *his gentleness embodies a Christian ideal.* 3 (often foll by *in*) to collect or unite in a comprehensive whole, system, etc.; comprise; include: *all the different essays were embodied in one long article.* 4 to invest (a spiritual entity) with a body or with bodily form; render incarnate.
▸em'bodiment NOUN

embolden (ɪm'bəʊld°n) VERB (*tr*) to encourage; make bold.

embolectomy (,ɛmbə'lɛktəmɪ) NOUN, *plural* **-mies.** the surgical removal of an embolus that is blocking a blood vessel.

embolic (ɛm'bɒlɪk) ADJECTIVE 1 of or relating to an embolus or embolism. 2 *Embryol* of, relating to, or resulting from invagination.

embolism ('ɛmbə,lɪzəm) NOUN 1 the occlusion of a blood vessel by an embolus. 2 *Botany* the blocking of a xylem vessel by an air bubble. 3 the insertion of one or more days into a calendar, esp the Jewish calendar; intercalation. 4 *RC Church* a prayer inserted in the canon of the Mass between the Lord's Prayer and the breaking of the bread. 5 another name (not in technical use) for **embolus.**
▷HISTORY C14: from Medieval Latin *embolismus,* from Late Greek *embolismos* intercalary; see EMBOLUS
▸,embo'lismic ADJECTIVE

embolize *or* **embolise** ('ɛmbə,laɪz) VERB (*tr*) to cause embolism in (a blood vessel).
▸,emboli'zation *or* ,emboli'sation NOUN

embolus ('ɛmbələs) NOUN, *plural* **-li** (-,laɪ). material, such as part of a blood clot or an air bubble, that is transported by the blood stream until it becomes lodged within a small vessel and impedes the circulation. Compare **thrombus.**
▷HISTORY C17: via Latin from Greek *embolos* stopper, from *emballein* to insert, from *ballein* to throw; see EMBLEM

emboly ('ɛmbəlɪ) NOUN, *plural* **-lies.** another name for **invagination** (sense 3).
▷HISTORY C19: from Greek *embolē* an insertion, from *emballein* to throw in; see EMBLEM

embonpoint *French* (ɑ̃bɔ̃pwɛ̃) NOUN 1 plumpness or stoutness. ◆ ADJECTIVE 2 plump; stout.
▷HISTORY C18: from phrase *en bon point* in good condition

embosom (ɪm'bʊzəm) VERB (*tr*) *Archaic* 1 to enclose or envelop, esp protectively. 2 to clasp to the bosom; hug. 3 to cherish.

emboss (ɪm'bɒs) VERB 1 to mould or carve (a decoration or design) on (a surface) so that it is raised above the surface in low relief. 2 to cause to bulge; make protrude.
▷HISTORY C14: from Old French *embocer,* from EM- + *boce* BOSS[2]
▸em'bosser NOUN ▸em'bossment NOUN

embossed (ɪm'bɒsd) ADJECTIVE having a moulded or carved decoration or design on the surface so that it is raised above the surface in low relief.

embothrium (ɪm'bɒθrɪəm) NOUN any evergreen shrub of the genus *Embothrium,* esp *E. coccineum,* native to South America but widely cultivated as an ornamental for its scarlet flowers: family *Proteaceae.* Also called: **Chilean firebush.**
▷HISTORY C19: from EM- + Greek *bothrion* small pit (referring to its anthers)

embouchure (,ɒmbʊ'ʃʊə) NOUN 1 the mouth of a river or valley. 2 *Music* **a** the correct application of the lips and tongue in playing a wind instrument. **b** the mouthpiece of a wind instrument.
▷HISTORY C18: from French, from Old French *emboucher* to put to one's mouth, from *bouche* mouth, from Latin *bucca* cheek

embourgeoisement (*French* ɑ̃burʒwazˈmɑ̃) NOUN the process of becoming middle class; the assimilation into the middle class of traditionally working-class people.
▷HISTORY from French, from EN-[1] + BOURGEOIS[1]

embow (ɪmˈbəʊ) VERB (*tr*) to design or create (a structure) in the form of an arch or vault.
▸**emˈbowed** ADJECTIVE ▸**emˈbowment** NOUN

embowel (ɪmˈbaʊəl) VERB *Obsolete* 1 to bury or embed deeply. 2 another word for **disembowel.**

embower (ɪmˈbaʊə) VERB (*tr*) *Archaic* to enclose in or as in a bower.

embrace[1] (ɪmˈbreɪs) VERB (*mainly tr*) 1 (*also intr*) (of a person) to take or clasp (another person) in the arms, or (of two people) to clasp each other, as in affection, greeting, etc.; hug. 2 to accept (an opportunity, challenge, etc.) willingly or eagerly. 3 to take up (a new idea, faith, etc.); adopt: *to embrace Judaism.* 4 to comprise or include as an integral part: *geology embraces the science of mineralogy.* 5 to encircle or enclose. ◆ NOUN 6 the act of embracing. 7 (*often plural*) *Euphemistic* sexual intercourse.
▷HISTORY C14: from Old French *embracier,* from EM- + *brace* a pair of arms, from Latin *bracchia* arms
▸**emˈbraceable** ADJECTIVE ▸**emˈbracement** NOUN
▸**emˈbracer** NOUN

embrace[2] (ɪmˈbreɪs) VERB (*tr*) *Criminal law* to commit or attempt to commit embracery against (a jury, etc.).
▷HISTORY C15: back formation from EMBRACEOR

embraceor *or* **embracer** (ɪmˈbreɪsə) NOUN *Criminal law* a person guilty of embracery.
▷HISTORY C15: from Old French *embraseor,* from *embraser* to instigate, literally: to set on fire, from *braser* to burn, from *brese* live coals

embracery (ɪmˈbreɪsərɪ) NOUN *Criminal law* the offence of attempting by corrupt means to influence a jury or juror, as by bribery or threats.

embranchment (ɪmˈbrɑːntʃmənt) NOUN 1 the process of branching out, esp by a river. 2 a branching out or ramification, as of a river or mountain range.

embrangle (ɪmˈbræŋgəl) VERB (*tr*) *Rare* to confuse or entangle.
▷HISTORY C17: from EM- + obsolete *brangle* to wrangle, perhaps a blend of BRAWL[1] + WRANGLE
▸**emˈbranglement** NOUN

embrasure (ɪmˈbreɪʒə) NOUN 1 *Fortifications* an opening or indentation, as in a battlement, for shooting through. 2 an opening forming a door or window, having splayed sides that increase the width of the opening in the interior.
▷HISTORY C18: from French, from obsolete *embraser* to widen, of uncertain origin
▸**emˈbrasured** ADJECTIVE

embrocate (ˈɛmbrəʊˌkeɪt) VERB (*tr*) to apply a liniment or lotion to (a part of the body).
▷HISTORY C17: from Medieval Latin *embrocāre,* from *embrocha* poultice, from Greek *embrokhē* lotion, infusion, from *brokhē* a moistening

embrocation (ˌɛmbrəʊˈkeɪʃən) NOUN a drug or agent for rubbing into the skin; liniment.

embroider (ɪmˈbrɔɪdə) VERB 1 to do decorative needlework (upon). 2 to add fictitious or fanciful detail to (a story). 3 to add exaggerated or improbable details to (an account of an event, etc.).
▷HISTORY C15: from Old French *embroder; see em-* EN-[1], BROIDER
▸**emˈbroiderer** NOUN

embroidery (ɪmˈbrɔɪdərɪ) NOUN, *plural* **-deries.** 1 decorative needlework done usually on loosely woven cloth or canvas, often being a picture or pattern. 2 elaboration or exaggeration, esp in writing or reporting; embellishment.

embroil (ɪmˈbrɔɪl) VERB (*tr*) 1 to involve (a person, oneself, etc.) in trouble, conflict, or argument. 2 to throw (affairs) into a state of confusion or disorder; complicate; entangle.
▷HISTORY C17: from French *embrouiller,* from *brouiller* to mingle, confuse
▸**emˈbroiler** NOUN ▸**emˈbroilment** NOUN

embrue (ɪmˈbruː) VERB **-brues, -bruing, -brued.** a variant spelling of **imbrue.**
▸**emˈbruement** NOUN

embryectomy (ˌɛmbrɪˈɛktəmɪ) NOUN, *plural* **-mies.** the surgical removal of an embryo.

embryo (ˈɛmbrɪˌəʊ) NOUN, *plural* **-bryos.** 1 an animal in the early stages of development following cleavage of the zygote and ending at birth or hatching. 2 the human product of conception up to approximately the end of the second month of pregnancy. Compare **fetus.** 3 a plant in the early stages of development: in higher plants, the plumule, cotyledons, and radicle within the seed. 4 an undeveloped or rudimentary state (esp in the phrase **in embryo**). 5 something in an early stage of development: *an embryo of an idea.*
▷HISTORY C16: from Late Latin, from Greek *embruon,* from *bruein* to swell
▸**ˈembryˌoid** ADJECTIVE

embryogeny (ˌɛmbrɪˈɒdʒɪnɪ) NOUN 1 Also called: **embryogenesis** (ˌɛmbrɪəʊˈdʒɛnəsɪs). the formation and development of an embryo. 2 the study of these processes.
▸**embryogenic** (ˌɛmbrɪəʊˈdʒɛnɪk) ADJECTIVE

embryol. ABBREVIATION FOR embryology.

embryology (ˌɛmbrɪˈɒlədʒɪ) NOUN 1 the branch of science concerned with the study of embryos. 2 the structure and development of the embryo of a particular organism.
▸**embryological** (ˌɛmbrɪəˈlɒdʒɪkəl) *or* ˌ**embryoˈlogic** ADJECTIVE ▸ˌ**embryoˈlogically** ADVERB ▸ˌ**embryˈologist** NOUN

embryonic (ˌɛmbrɪˈɒnɪk) *or* **embryonal** (ˈɛmbrɪənəl) ADJECTIVE 1 of or relating to an embryo. 2 in an early stage; rudimentary; undeveloped.
▸ˌ**embryˈonically** ADVERB

embryo sac NOUN the structure within a plant ovule that contains the egg cell: develops from the megaspore and contains the embryo plant and endosperm after fertilization.

embus (ɪmˈbʌs) VERB **-buses, -busing, -bused** *or* **-busses, -bussing, -bussed.** *Military* to cause (troops) to board or (of troops) to board a transport vehicle.

embusqué *French* (ɑ̃byske) NOUN, *plural* ***-qués*** (-ke). a man who avoids military conscription by obtaining a government job.
▷HISTORY C20: from *embusquer* to lie in ambush, shirk

emcee (ˌɛmˈsiː) *Informal* ◆ NOUN 1 a master of ceremonies. ◆ VERB **-cees, -ceeing, -ceed.** 2 to act as master of ceremonies (for or at).
▷HISTORY C20: from the abbreviation MC

em dash *or* **rule** NOUN *Printing* a dash (—) one em long.

Emden (*German* ˈɛmdən) NOUN a port in NW Germany, in Lower Saxony at the mouth of the River Ems. Pop.: 51 100 (1991).

-eme SUFFIX FORMING NOUNS *Linguistics* indicating a minimal distinctive unit of a specified type in a language: *morpheme; phoneme.*
▷HISTORY C20: via French, abstracted from PHONEME

emend (ɪˈmɛnd) VERB (*tr*) to make corrections or improvements in (a text) by critical editing.
▷HISTORY C15: from Latin *ēmendāre* to correct, from *ē-* out + *mendum* a mistake
▸**eˈmendable** ADJECTIVE

emendation (ˌiːmɛnˈdeɪʃən) NOUN 1 a correction or improvement in a text. 2 the act or process of emending.
▸**ˈemenˌdator** NOUN ▸**emendatory** (ɪˈmɛndətərɪ, -trɪ) ADJECTIVE

emerald (ˈɛmərəld, ˈɛmrəld) NOUN 1 a green transparent variety of beryl: highly valued as a gem. 2 **a** the clear green colour of an emerald. **b** (*as adjective*): *an emerald carpet.* 3 (formerly) a size of printer's type approximately equal to 6½ point. 4 short for **emerald moth.**
▷HISTORY C13: from Old French *esmeraude,* from Latin *smaragdus,* from Greek *smaragdos;* related to Sanskrit *marakata* emerald

Emerald Isle NOUN a poetic name for **Ireland.**

emerald moth NOUN any of various green geometrid moths, esp the **large emerald** (*Geometra papilionaria*) a handsome pale green moth with white wavy markings.

emerge (ɪˈmɜːdʒ) VERB (*intr;* often foll by *from*) 1 to come up to the surface of or rise from water or other liquid. 2 to come into view, as from concealment or obscurity: *he emerged from the cave.* 3 (foll by *from*) to come out (of) or live (through a difficult experience): *he emerged from his ordeal with dignity.* 4 to become apparent: *several interesting things emerged from the report.*
▷HISTORY C17: from Latin *ēmergere* to rise up from, from *mergere* to dip
▸**eˈmerging** ADJECTIVE

emergence (ɪˈmɜːdʒəns) NOUN 1 the act or process of emerging. 2 an outgrowth, such as a prickle, that contains no vascular tissue and does not develop into stem, leaf, etc.

emergency (ɪˈmɜːdʒənsɪ) NOUN, *plural* **-cies.** 1 **a** an unforeseen or sudden occurrence, esp of a danger demanding immediate remedy or action. **b** (*as modifier*): *an emergency exit.* 2 **a** a patient requiring urgent treatment. **b** (*as modifier*): *an emergency ward.* 3 **state of emergency.** a condition, declared by a government, in which martial law applies, usually because of civil unrest or natural disaster. 4 *NZ* a player selected to stand by to replace an injured member of a team; reserve.

emergent (ɪˈmɜːdʒənt) ADJECTIVE 1 coming into being or notice: *an emergent political structure.* 2 (of a nation) recently independent. ◆ NOUN 3 an aquatic plant with stem and leaves above the water.
▸**eˈmergently** ADVERB

emergent evolution NOUN *Philosophy* the doctrine that, in the course of evolution, some entirely new properties, such as life and consciousness, appear at certain critical points, usually because of an unpredictable rearrangement of the already existing entities.

emerging market NOUN a financial or consumer market in a newly developing country or former communist country.

emeritus (ɪˈmɛrɪtəs) ADJECTIVE (*usually postpositive*) retired or honourably discharged from full-time work, but retaining one's title on an honorary basis: *a professor emeritus.*
▷HISTORY C19: from Latin, from *merēre* to deserve; see MERIT

emersed (ɪˈmɜːst) ADJECTIVE (of the leaves or stems of aquatic plants) protruding above the surface of the water.

emersion (ɪˈmɜːʃən) NOUN 1 the act or an instance of emerging. 2 Also called: **egress.** *Astronomy* the reappearance of a celestial body after an eclipse or occultation.
▷HISTORY C17: from Latin *ēmersus,* from *ēmergere;* see EMERGE

emery (ˈɛmərɪ) NOUN **a** a hard greyish-black mineral consisting of corundum with either magnetite or haematite: used as an abrasive and polishing agent, esp as a coating on paper, cloth, etc. Formula: Al_2O_3. **b** (*as modifier*): *emery paper.*
▷HISTORY C15: from Old French *esmeril,* ultimately from Greek *smuris* powder for rubbing

emery board NOUN a strip of cardboard or wood with a rough surface of crushed emery, for filing one's nails.

emery wheel NOUN a grinding or polishing wheel consisting of, or the surface of which is coated with, abrasive emery particles.

emesis (ˈɛmɪsɪs) NOUN the technical name for **vomiting.**
▷HISTORY C19: via New Latin from Greek, from *emein* to vomit

emetic (ɪˈmɛtɪk) ADJECTIVE 1 causing vomiting. ◆ NOUN 2 an emetic agent or drug.
▷HISTORY C17: from Late Latin *ēmeticus,* from Greek *emetikos,* from *emein* to vomit
▸**eˈmetically** ADVERB

emetine (ˈɛməˌtiːn, -tɪn) *or* **emetin** (ˈɛmətɪn) NOUN a white bitter poisonous alkaloid obtained from ipecacuanha: the hydrochloride is used to treat amoebic infections. Formula: $C_{29}H_{40}O_4N_2$.
▷HISTORY C19: from French *émétine;* see EMETIC, -INE[2]

emf *or* **EMF** ABBREVIATION FOR electromotive force.

-emia NOUN COMBINING FORM a US variant of **-aemia.**

emigrant (ˈɛmɪgrənt) NOUN **a** a person who leaves one place or country, esp a native country, to settle in another. Compare **immigrant. b** (*as modifier*): *an emigrant worker.*

emigrate (ˈɛmɪˌgreɪt) VERB (*intr*) to leave one place or country, esp one's native country, in order to settle in another. Compare **immigrate.**
▷HISTORY C18: from Latin *ēmīgrāre,* from *mīgrāre* to depart, MIGRATE
▸**ˈemiˌgratory** ADJECTIVE

emigration (ˌɛmɪˈɡreɪʃən) NOUN 1 the act or an instance of emigrating. 2 emigrants considered collectively.

émigré (ˈɛmɪˌɡreɪ; *French* emigre) NOUN an emigrant, esp one forced to leave his native country for political reasons.
▷HISTORY C18: from French, from *émigrer* to EMIGRATE

Emilia-Romagna (ɪˈmiːlɪərəʊˈmɑːnjə; *Italian* eˈmiːlia-roˈmaɲɲa) NOUN a region of N central Italy, on the Adriatic: rises from the plains of the Po valley in the north to the Apennines in the south. Capital: Bologna. Pop.: 3 981 146 (2000 est.). Area: 22 123 sq. km (8628 sq. miles).

eminence (ˈɛmɪnəns) NOUN, *plural* **-nences.** 1 a position of superiority, distinction, high rank, or fame. 2 a high or raised piece of ground. 3 *Anatomy* a projection of an organ or part. ◆ Also: **eminency.**
▷HISTORY C17: from French, from Latin *ēminentia* a standing out; see EMINENT

Eminence (ˈɛmɪnəns) *or* **Eminency** NOUN, *plural* **-nences** *or* **-nencies.** (preceded by *Your* or *His*) a title used to address or refer to a cardinal.

éminence grise *French* (eminɑ̃s ɡriz) NOUN, *plural* ***éminences grises*** (eminɑ̃s ɡriz). a person who wields power and influence unofficially or behind the scenes.
▷HISTORY C19: literally: grey eminence, originally applied to Père Joseph (François Le Clerc du Tremblay; died 1638), French monk, secretary of Cardinal Richelieu

eminent (ˈɛmɪnənt) ADJECTIVE 1 above others in rank, merit, or reputation; distinguished: *an eminent scientist.* 2 (*prenominal*) noteworthy, conspicuous, or outstanding: *eminent good sense.* 3 projecting or protruding; prominent.
▷HISTORY C15: from Latin *ēminēre* to project, stand out, from *minēre* to stand
▸ˈ**eminently** ADVERB

eminent domain NOUN *Law* the right of a state to confiscate private property for public use, payment usually being made to the owners in compensation.

eminently (ˈɛmɪnəntlɪ) ADVERB extremely: *eminently sensible.*

emir (ɛˈmɪə) NOUN (in the Islamic world) 1 an independent ruler or chieftain. 2 a military commander or governor. 3 a descendant of Mohammed. ◆ Also spelt: **amir.**
▷HISTORY C17: via French from Spanish *emir,* from Arabic *ʼamīr* commander

emirate (ɛˈmɪərɪt, ˈɛmɪrɪt) NOUN 1 the rank or office of an emir. 2 the government, jurisdiction, or territory of an emir.

Emiscan (ˌɛmɪˈskæn) NOUN *Trademark* a computerized radiological technique for examining the soft tissues of the body, esp the brain, to detect the presence of tumours, abscesses, etc.

emissary (ˈɛmɪsərɪ, -ɪsrɪ) NOUN, *plural* **-saries.** 1 **a** an agent or messenger sent on a mission, esp one who represents a government or head of state. **b** (*as modifier*): *an emissary delegation.* 2 an agent sent on a secret mission, as a spy. ◆ ADJECTIVE 3 (of veins) draining blood from sinuses in the dura mater to veins outside the skull.
▷HISTORY C17: from Latin *ēmissārius* emissary, spy, from *ēmittere* to send out; see EMIT

emission (ɪˈmɪʃən) NOUN 1 the act of emitting or sending forth. 2 energy, in the form of heat, light, radio waves, etc., emitted from a source. 3 a substance, fluid, etc., that is emitted; discharge. 4 a measure of the number of electrons emitted by a cathode or electron gun: *at 1000°C the emission is 3 mA.* See also **secondary emission, thermionic emission.** 5 *Physiol* any bodily discharge, esp an involuntary release of semen during sleep. 6 an issue, as of currency.
▷HISTORY C17: from Latin *ēmissiō,* from *ēmittere* to send forth, EMIT
▸**eˈmissive** ADJECTIVE

emission nebula NOUN a type of nebula that emits visible radiation. See **nebula.**

emission spectrum NOUN the continuous spectrum or pattern of bright lines or bands seen when the electromagnetic radiation emitted by a substance is passed into a spectrometer. The spectrum is characteristic of the emitting substance and the type of excitation to which it is subjected. Compare **absorption spectrum.**

emissivity (ɪmɪˈsɪvɪtɪ, ˌɛm-) NOUN a measure of the ability of a surface to radiate energy; the ratio of the radiant flux emitted per unit area to that emitted by a black body at the same temperature. Symbol: ε.

emit (ɪˈmɪt) VERB **emits, emitting, emitted.** (*tr*) 1 to give or send forth; discharge: *the pipe emitted a stream of water.* 2 to give voice to; utter: *she emitted a shrill scream.* 3 *Physics* to give off (radiation or particles). 4 to put (currency) into circulation.
▷HISTORY C17: from Latin *ēmittere* to send out, from *mittere* to send

emitter (ɪˈmɪtə) NOUN 1 a person or thing that emits. 2 a radioactive substance that emits radiation: *a beta emitter.* 3 the region in a transistor in which the charge-carrying holes or electrons originate.

Emmanuel (ɪˈmænjʊəl) NOUN a variant spelling of **Immanuel.**

Emmen (ˈɛmən; *Dutch* ˈɛmə) NOUN a city in the NE Netherlands, in Drenthe province: a new town developed since World War II. Pop.: 105 497 (1999 est.).

emmenagogue (ɪˈmɛnəˌɡɒɡ, -ˈmiː-) NOUN 1 a drug or agent that increases menstrual flow. ◆ ADJECTIVE *also* **emmenagogic** (ɪˌmɛnəˈɡɒdʒɪk). 2 inducing or increasing menstrual flow.
▷HISTORY C18: from Greek *emmēna* menses, (from *mēn* month) + -AGOGUE

Emmenthal, Emmental (ˈɛmənˌtɑːl), **Emmenthaler,** *or* **Emmentaler** NOUN a hard Swiss cheese with holes in it, similar to Gruyère.
▷HISTORY C20: named after *Emmenthal,* a valley in Switzerland

emmer (ˈɛmə) NOUN a variety of wheat, *Triticum dicoccum,* grown in mountainous parts of Europe as a cereal crop and for livestock food: thought to be an ancestor of many other varieties of wheat.
▷HISTORY C20: from German; related to Old High German *amari* spelt

emmet (ˈɛmɪt) NOUN 1 *Brit* an archaic or dialect word for **ant.** 2 *Cornish dialect* a tourist or holiday-maker.
▷HISTORY Old English *ǣmette* ANT; related to Old Norse *meita,* Old High German *āmeiza,* Gothic *maitan*

emmetropia (ˌɛmɪˈtrəʊpɪə) NOUN the normal condition of perfect vision, in which parallel light rays are focused on the retina without the need for accommodation.
▷HISTORY C19: from New Latin, from Greek *emmetros* in due measure + -OPIA
▸**emmetropic** (ˌɛmɪˈtrɒpɪk) ADJECTIVE

Emmy (ˈɛmɪ) NOUN, *plural* **-mys** *or* **-mies.** (in the US) one of the gold-plated statuettes awarded annually for outstanding television performances and productions.
▷HISTORY C20: alteration of *Immy,* short for *image orthicon tube*

emo (ˈiːməʊ) NOUN **a** a type of music combining traditional hard rock with personal and emotional lyrics. **b** (*as modifier*): *emo bands.*
▷HISTORY C20: short for *emotional rock*

emollient (ɪˈmɒljənt) ADJECTIVE 1 softening or soothing, esp to the skin. 2 helping to avoid confrontation; calming. ◆ NOUN 3 any preparation or substance that has a softening or soothing effect, esp when applied to the skin.
▷HISTORY C17: from Latin *ēmollīre* to soften, from *mollis* soft
▸**eˈmollience** NOUN

emolument (ɪˈmɒljʊmənt) NOUN the profit arising from an office or employment, usually in the form of fees or wages.
▷HISTORY C15: from Latin *ēmolumentum* benefit; originally, fee paid to a miller, from *ēmolere,* from *molere* to grind

emote (ɪˈməʊt) VERB (*intr*) to display exaggerated emotion, as in acting; behave theatrically.
▷HISTORY C20: back formation from EMOTION
▸**eˈmoter** NOUN

emoticon (ɪˈməʊtɪˌkɒn) NOUN any of several combinations of symbols used in electronic mail and text messaging to indicate the state of mind of the writer, such as :-) to express happiness.
▷HISTORY C20: from EMOT(ION) + ICON

emotion (ɪˈməʊʃən) NOUN any strong feeling, as of joy, sorrow, or fear.
▷HISTORY C16: from French, from Old French *esmovoir* to excite, from Latin *ēmovēre* to disturb, from *movēre* to MOVE
▸**eˈmotionless** ADJECTIVE

emotional (ɪˈməʊʃənᵊl) ADJECTIVE 1 of, characteristic of, or expressive of emotion. 2 readily or excessively affected by emotion. 3 appealing to or arousing emotion: *an emotional piece of music.* 4 caused, determined, or actuated by emotion rather than reason: *an emotional argument.*
▸**eˌmotionˈality** NOUN ▸**eˈmotionally** ADVERB

emotional correctness NOUN pressure on an individual to be seen to feel the same emotion as others.

emotional intelligence NOUN awareness of one's own emotions and moods and those of others, esp in managing people.

emotionalism (ɪˈməʊʃənəˌlɪzəm) NOUN 1 emotional nature, character, or quality. 2 a tendency to yield readily to the emotions. 3 an appeal to the emotions, esp an excessive appeal, as to an audience. 4 a doctrine stressing the value of deeply felt responses in ethics and the arts.
▸**eˈmotionalist** NOUN ▸**eˌmotionalˈistic** ADJECTIVE

emotionalize *or* **emotionalise** (ɪˈməʊʃənəˌlaɪz) VERB (*tr*) to make emotional; subject to emotional treatment.
▸**eˌmotionaliˈzation** *or* **eˌmotionaliˈsation** NOUN

emotional literacy NOUN the ability to deal with one's emotions and recognize their causes.

emotive (ɪˈməʊtɪv) ADJECTIVE 1 tending or designed to arouse emotion. 2 of or characterized by emotion.
▸**eˈmotively** ADVERB ▸**eˈmotiveness** *or* ˌ**emoˈtivity** NOUN

> **Language note** *Emotional* is preferred to *emotive* when describing a display of emotion: *he was given an emotional* (not *emotive*) *welcome.*

emotivism (ɪˈməʊtɪˌvɪzəm) NOUN *Ethics* the theory that moral utterances do not have a truth value but express the feelings of the speaker, so that *murder is wrong* is equivalent to *down with murder.* Also called: **boo-hurrah theory.** Compare **prescriptivism, descriptivism.**

empale (ɪmˈpeɪl) VERB a less common spelling of **impale.**
▸**emˈpalement** NOUN ▸**emˈpaler** NOUN

empanel *or* **impanel** (ɪmˈpænᵊl) VERB **-els, -elling, -elled** *or US* **-els, -eling, -eled.** (*tr*) *Law* 1 to enter on a list (names of persons to be summoned for jury service). 2 to select (a jury) from the names on such a list.
▸**emˈpanelment** *or* **imˈpanelment** NOUN

empathic (ɛmˈpæθɪk) *or* **empathetic** (ˌɛmpəˈθɛtɪk) ADJECTIVE of or relating to empathy.
▸**emˈpathically** *or* ˌ**empaˈthetically** ADVERB

empathize *or* **empathise** (ˈɛmpəˌθaɪz) VERB (*intr*) to engage in or feel empathy.

empathy (ˈɛmpəθɪ) NOUN 1 the power of understanding and imaginatively entering into another person's feelings. See also **identification** (sense 3b). 2 the attribution to an object, such as a work of art, of one's own emotional or intellectual feelings about it.
▷HISTORY C20: from Greek *empatheia* affection, passion, intended as a rendering of German *Einfühlung,* literally: a feeling in; see EN-², -PATHY
▸ˈ**empathist** NOUN

empennage (ɛmˈpɛnɪdʒ; *French* ɑ̃pɛnaʒ) NOUN the rear part of an aircraft, comprising the fin, rudder, and tailplane.
▷HISTORY C20: from French: feathering, from *empenner* to feather an arrow, from *penne* feather, from Latin *pinna*

emperor (ˈɛmpərə) NOUN 1 a monarch who rules or reigns over an empire. 2 Also called: **emperor moth.** any of several large saturniid moths with eyelike markings on each wing, esp *Saturnia pavonia* of Europe. See also **giant peacock moth.** 3 See **purple emperor.**
▷HISTORY C13: from Old French *empereor,* from

Latin *imperātor* commander-in-chief, from *imperāre* to command, from IM- + *parāre* to make ready
▸ **'emperor,ship** NOUN

emperor penguin NOUN an Antarctic penguin, *Aptenodytes forsteri,* with orange-yellow patches on the neck: the largest penguin, reaching a height of 1.3 m (4 ft.).

empery ('ɛmpərɪ) NOUN, *plural* **-peries.** *Archaic* dominion or power; empire.
▷ HISTORY C13 (in the sense: the status of an emperor): from Anglo-French *emperie,* from Latin *imperium* power; see EMPIRE

emphasis ('ɛmfəsɪs) NOUN, *plural* **-ses** (-si:z). 1 special importance or significance. 2 an object, idea, etc., that is given special importance or significance. 3 stress made to fall on a particular syllable, word, or phrase in speaking. 4 force or intensity of expression: *he spoke with special emphasis on the subject of civil rights.* 5 sharpness or clarity of form or outline: *the sunlight gave emphasis to the shape of the mountain.*
▷ HISTORY C16: via Latin from Greek: meaning, (in rhetoric) significant stress; see EMPHATIC

emphasize *or* **emphasise** ('ɛmfə,saɪz) VERB (*tr*) to give emphasis or prominence to; stress.

emphatic (ɪm'fætɪk) ADJECTIVE 1 expressed, spoken, or done with emphasis. 2 forceful and positive; definite; direct: *an emphatic personality.* 3 sharp or clear in form, contour, or outline. 4 important or significant; stressed: *the emphatic points in an argument.* 5 *Phonetics* denoting certain dental consonants of Arabic that are pronounced with accompanying pharyngeal constriction. ◆ NOUN 6 *Phonetics* an emphatic consonant, as used in Arabic.
▷ HISTORY C18: from Greek *emphatikos* expressive, forceful, from *emphainein* to exhibit, display, from *phainein* to show

emphatically (ɪm'fætɪkəlɪ, -klɪ) ADVERB 1 with emphasis or force. 2 definitely or unquestionably.

emphysema (,ɛmfɪ'si:mə) NOUN *Pathol* 1 Also called: **pulmonary emphysema.** a condition in which the air sacs of the lungs are grossly enlarged, causing breathlessness and wheezing. 2 the abnormal presence of air in a tissue or part.
▷ HISTORY C17: from New Latin, from Greek *emphusēma,* a swelling up, from *emphusan* to inflate, from *phusan* to blow
▸ **emphysematous** (,ɛmfɪ'sɛmətəs, -'si:-) ADJECTIVE

empire ('ɛmpaɪə) NOUN 1 an aggregate of peoples and territories, often of great extent, under the rule of a single person, oligarchy, or sovereign state. 2 any monarchy that for reasons of history, prestige, etc., has an emperor rather than a king as head of state. 3 the period during which a particular empire exists. 4 supreme power; sovereignty. Related adjective: **imperial.** 5 a large industrial organization with many ramifications, esp a multinational corporation.
▷ HISTORY C13: from Old French, from Latin *imperium* rule, from *imperāre* to command, from *parāre* to prepare

Empire ('ɛmpaɪə) NOUN **the.** 1 See **British Empire.** 2 *French history* **a** the period of imperial rule in France from 1804 to 1815 under Napoleon Bonaparte (1769–1821). **b** Also called: **Second Empire.** the period from 1852 to 1870 when Napoleon III (1808–73) ruled as emperor. ◆ ADJECTIVE 3 denoting, characteristic of, or relating to the British Empire. 4 denoting, characteristic of, or relating to either French Empire, esp the first: in particular, denoting the neoclassical style of architecture and furniture and the high-waisted style of women's dresses characteristic of the period.

empire-builder NOUN *Informal* a person who seeks extra power for its own sake, esp by increasing the number of his subordinates or staff.
▸ **'empire-,building** NOUN, ADJECTIVE

Empire Day NOUN the former name of **Commonwealth Day.**

Empire State NOUN nickname of **New York** (state).

empiric (ɛm'pɪrɪk) NOUN 1 a person who relies on empirical methods. 2 a medical quack; charlatan. ◆ ADJECTIVE 3 a variant of **empirical.**
▷ HISTORY C16: from Latin *empīricus,* from Greek *empeirikos* practised, from *peiran* to attempt

empirical (ɛm'pɪrɪk^{ə}l) ADJECTIVE 1 derived from or relating to experiment and observation rather than theory. 2 (of medical treatment) based on practical experience rather than scientific proof. 3 *Philosophy* **a** (of knowledge) derived from experience rather than by logic from first principles. Compare **a priori, a posteriori. b** (of a proposition) subject, at least theoretically, to verification. Compare **analytic** (sense 4), **synthetic** (sense 4). 4 of or relating to medical quackery. ◆ NOUN 5 *Statistics* the posterior probability of an event derived on the basis of its observed frequency in a sample. Compare **mathematical probability.** See also **posterior probability.**
▸ **em'pirically** ADVERB ▸ **em'piricalness** NOUN

empirical formula NOUN 1 a chemical formula indicating the proportion of each element present in a molecule: *$C_6H_{12}O_6$ is the molecular formula of sucrose whereas CH_2O is its empirical formula.* Compare **molecular formula, structural formula.** 2 a formula or expression obtained from experimental data rather than theory.

empiricism (ɛm'pɪrɪ,sɪzəm) NOUN 1 *Philosophy* the doctrine that all knowledge of matters of fact derives from experience and that the mind is not furnished with a set of concepts in advance of experience. Compare **intuitionism, rationalism.** 2 the use of empirical methods. 3 medical quackery; charlatanism.
▸ **em'piricist** NOUN, ADJECTIVE

emplace (ɪm'pleɪs) VERB (*tr*) to put in place or position.

emplacement (ɪm'pleɪsmənt) NOUN 1 a prepared position for the siting of a gun or other weapon. 2 the act of putting or state of being put in place.
▷ HISTORY C19: from French, from obsolete *emplacer* to put in position, from PLACE

emplane (ɪm'pleɪn) VERB to board or put on board an aeroplane.

employ (ɪm'plɔɪ) VERB (*tr*) 1 to engage or make use of the services of (a person) in return for money; hire. 2 to provide work or occupation for; keep busy; occupy: *collecting stamps employs a lot of his time.* 3 to use as a means: *to employ secret measures to get one's ends.* ◆ NOUN 4 the state of being employed (esp in the phrase **in someone's employ**).
▷ HISTORY C15: from Old French *emploier,* from Latin *implicāre* to entangle, engage, from *plicāre* to fold

employee (ɛm'plɔɪi:, ,ɛmplɔɪ'i:) *or sometimes US* **employe** NOUN a person who is hired to work for another or for a business, firm, etc., in return for payment. Also called (esp formerly): **employé.**

employee association NOUN an organization, other than a trade union, whose members comprise employees of a single employing organization. The aims of the association may be social, recreational, or professional.

employer (ɪm'plɔɪə) NOUN 1 a person, business, firm, etc., that employs workers. 2 a person who employs; user.

employers' association NOUN a body of employers, usually from the same sector of the economy, associated to further the interests of member companies by conducting negotiations with trade unions, providing advice, making representations to other bodies, etc.

employment (ɪm'plɔɪmənt) NOUN 1 the act of employing or state of being employed. 2 the work or occupation in which a person is employed. 3 the purpose for which something is used.

employment agency NOUN a private firm whose business is placing people in jobs.

employment exchange NOUN *Brit* a former name for **employment office.**

employment office NOUN *Brit* any of a number of government offices established to collect and supply to the unemployed information about job vacancies and to employers information about availability of prospective workers. Former names: **employment exchange, labour exchange.** See also **Jobcentre.**

employment tribunal NOUN (in England, Scotland, and Wales) a tribunal that rules on disputes between employers and employees regarding unfair dismissal, redundancy, etc. See also: **industrial tribunal.**

empoison (ɪm'pɔɪz^{ə}n) VERB (*tr*) 1 *Rare* to embitter or corrupt. 2 an archaic word for **poison** (senses 6–9).
▸ **em'poisonment** NOUN

empolder (ɪm'pəʊldə) VERB a variant spelling of **impolder.**

emporium (ɛm'pɔ:rɪəm) NOUN, *plural* **-riums, -ria** (-rɪə). a large and often ostentatious retail shop offering for sale a wide variety of merchandise.
▷ HISTORY C16: from Latin, from Greek *emporion,* from *emporos* merchant, from *poros* a journey

empoverish (ɪm'pɒvərɪʃ) VERB an obsolete spelling of **impoverish.**
▸ **em'poverisher** NOUN ▸ **em'poverishment** NOUN

empower (ɪm'paʊə) VERB (*tr*) 1 to give or delegate power or authority to; authorize. 2 to give ability to; enable or permit.

empowerment (ɪm'paʊəmənt) NOUN 1 the giving or delegation of power or authority; authorization. 2 the giving of an ability; enablement or permission. 3 (in South Africa) a policy of providing special opportunities in employment, training, etc. for Blacks and others disadvantaged under apartheid.

empress ('ɛmprɪs) NOUN 1 the wife or widow of an emperor. 2 a woman who holds the rank of emperor in her own right. 3 a woman of great power and influence.
▷ HISTORY C12: from Old French *empereriz,* from Latin *imperātrix* feminine of *imperātor* EMPEROR

emprise (ɛm'praɪz) NOUN *Archaic* 1 a chivalrous or daring enterprise; adventure. 2 chivalrous daring or prowess.
▷ HISTORY C13: from Old French, from *emprendre* to undertake; see ENTERPRISE

empt (ɛmpt, ɛmt) VERB (*tr*) *Dialect* to empty.
▷ HISTORY from Old English *ǣmtian* to be without duties; compare EMPTY

empty ('ɛmptɪ) ADJECTIVE **-tier, -tiest.** 1 containing nothing. 2 without inhabitants; vacant or unoccupied. 3 carrying no load, passengers, etc. 4 without purpose, substance, or value: *an empty life.* 5 insincere or trivial: *empty words.* 6 not expressive or vital; vacant: *she has an empty look.* 7 *Informal* hungry. 8 (*postpositive,* foll by *of*) devoid; destitute: *a life empty of happiness.* 9 *Informal* drained of energy or emotion: *after the violent argument he felt very empty.* 10 *Maths, logic* (of a set or class) containing no members. 11 *Philosophy, logic* (of a name or description) having no reference. ◆ VERB **-ties, -tying, -tied.** 12 to make or become empty. 13 (when *intr,* foll by *into*) to discharge (contents). 14 (*tr;* often foll by *of*) to unburden or rid (oneself): *to empty oneself of emotion.* ◆ NOUN, *plural* **-ties.** 15 an empty container, esp a bottle.
▷ HISTORY Old English *ǣmtig,* from *ǣmetta* free time, from *ǣ-* without + *-metta,* from *mōtan* to be obliged to; see MUST[1]
▸ **'emptiable** ADJECTIVE ▸ **'emptier** NOUN ▸ **'emptily** ADVERB
▸ **'emptiness** NOUN

empty cow NOUN a cow that does not produce calves during the breeding season.

empty-handed ADJECTIVE 1 carrying nothing in the hands. 2 having gained nothing: *they returned from the negotiations empty-handed.*

empty-headed ADJECTIVE lacking intelligence or sense; frivolous.

empty-nester NOUN *Informal* a married person whose children have grown up and left home.

empty-nest syndrome NOUN *Informal* a condition, often involving depression, loneliness, etc., experienced by parents living in a home from which the children have grown up and left.

Empty Quarter NOUN another name for **Rub' al Khali.**

empyema (,ɛmpaɪ'i:mə) NOUN, *plural* **-emata** (-'i:mətə) *or* **-emas.** a collection of pus in a body cavity, esp in the chest.
▷ HISTORY C17: from Medieval Latin, from Greek *empuēma* abscess, from *empuein* to suppurate, from *puon* pus
▸ **,empy'emic** ADJECTIVE

empyrean (,ɛmpaɪ'ri:ən) NOUN 1 *Archaic* the highest part of the (supposedly spherical) heavens, thought in ancient times to contain the pure element of fire and by early Christians to be the abode of God and the angels. 2 *Poetic* the heavens or sky. ◆ ADJECTIVE *also* **empyreal.** 3 of or relating to

the sky, the heavens, or the empyrean. 4 heavenly or sublime. 5 *Archaic* composed of fire.
▷HISTORY C17: from Medieval Latin *empyreus*, from Greek *empuros* fiery, from *pur* fire

empyreuma (ˌɛmpɪˈruːmə) NOUN, *plural* **-mata** (-mətə). the smell and taste associated with burning vegetable and animal matter.
▷HISTORY C17: from Greek, from *empureuein* to set on fire

Ems (ɛmz) NOUN 1 a town in W Germany, in the Rhineland-Palatinate: famous for the **Ems Telegram** (1870), Bismarck's dispatch that led to the outbreak of the Franco-Prussian War. Pop.: 10 241 (latest est.). 2 a river in West Germany, rising in the Teutoburger Wald and flowing generally north to the North Sea. Length: about 370 km (230 miles).

EMS ABBREVIATION FOR **European Monetary System.**

emu (ˈiːmjuː) NOUN a large Australian flightless bird, *Dromaius novaehollandiae*, similar to the ostrich but with three-toed feet and grey or brown plumage: order *Casuariiformes*. See also **ratite.**
▷HISTORY C17: changed from Portuguese *ema* ostrich, from Arabic *Na-ʻamah* ostrich

EMU 1 ABBREVIATION FOR European Monetary Union. 2 See **e.m.u.**

e.m.u. *or* **EMU** ABBREVIATION FOR electromagnetic unit.

emu-bob *Austral informal* ◆ VERB **-bobs, -bobbing, -bobbed.** 1 (*intr*) to bend over to collect litter or small pieces of wood. ◆ NOUN 2 Also called: **emu parade.** a parade of soldiers or schoolchildren for litter collection.
▸ˈ**emu-bobbing** NOUN

emu bush NOUN any of various Australian shrubs, esp those of the genus *Eremophila* (family Myoporaceae), whose fruits are eaten by emus.

emulate (ˈɛmjʊˌleɪt) VERB (*tr*) 1 to attempt to equal or surpass, esp by imitation. 2 to rival or compete with. 3 to make one computer behave like (another different type of computer) so that the imitating system can operate on the same data and execute the same programs as the imitated system.
▷HISTORY C16: from Latin *aemulārī*, from *aemulus* competing with; probably related to *imitārī* to IMITATE
▸ˈ**emulative** ADJECTIVE ▸ˈ**emulatively** ADVERB ▸ˈ**emuˌlator** NOUN

emulation (ˌɛmjʊˈleɪʃən) NOUN 1 the act of emulating or imitating. 2 the effort or desire to equal or surpass another or others. 3 *Archaic* jealous rivalry.

emulous (ˈɛmjʊləs) ADJECTIVE 1 desiring or aiming to equal or surpass another; competitive. 2 characterized by or arising from emulation or imitation. 3 *Archaic* envious or jealous.
▷HISTORY C14: from Latin *aemulus* rivalling; see EMULATE
▸ˈ**emulously** ADVERB ▸ˈ**emulousness** NOUN

emulsifier (ɪˈmʌlsɪˌfaɪə) NOUN an agent that forms or preserves an emulsion, esp any food additive, such as lecithin, that prevents separation of sauces or other processed foods.

emulsify (ɪˈmʌlsɪˌfaɪ) VERB **-fies, -fying, -fied.** to make or form into an emulsion.
▸**eˌmulsiˈfiable** *or* **eˈmulsible** ADJECTIVE ▸**eˌmulsifiˈcation** NOUN

emulsion (ɪˈmʌlʃən) NOUN 1 *Photog* a light-sensitive coating on a base, such as paper or film, consisting of fine grains of silver bromide suspended in gelatine. 2 *Chem* a colloid in which both phases are liquids: *an oil-in-water emulsion*. 3 Also called: **emulsion paint.** a type of paint in which the pigment is suspended in a vehicle, usually a synthetic resin, that is dispersed in water as an emulsion. It usually gives a mat finish. 4 *Pharmacol* a mixture in which an oily medicine is dispersed in another liquid. 5 any liquid resembling milk.
▷HISTORY C17: from New Latin *ēmulsiō*, from Latin *ēmulsus* milked out, from *ēmulgēre* to milk out, drain out, from *mulgēre* to milk
▸**eˈmulsive** ADJECTIVE

emulsoid (ɪˈmʌlsɔɪd) NOUN *Chem* a sol with a liquid disperse phase.

emunctory (ɪˈmʌŋktərɪ) ADJECTIVE 1 of or relating to a bodily organ or duct having an excretory function. ◆ NOUN, *plural* **-ries.** 2 an excretory organ or duct, such as a skin pore.
▷HISTORY C16: from New Latin *ēmunctōrium*, from Latin *ēmungere* to wipe clean, from *mungere* to wipe

emu parade NOUN 1 *Austral* an army exercise devoted to emu-bobbing. 2 Also called: **emu walk.** an organized session of combing an area for clues, esp by the police.

emu-wren NOUN any Australian wren of the genus *Stipiturus*, having long plumy tail feathers.

EMV ABBREVIATION FOR expected monetary value: the product of the monetary outcome of a particular decision in a decision tree and the probability of this outcome happening.

en (ɛn) NOUN *Printing* a unit of measurement, half the width of an em. Also called: **nut.** See also **ennage.**

EN (in Britain) ABBREVIATION FOR: 1 enrolled nurse. 2 English Nature.

en-[1] *or* **em-** PREFIX FORMING VERBS 1 (*from nouns*) **a** put in or on: *entomb*; *enthrone*. **b** go on or into: *enplane*. **c** surround or cover with: *enmesh*. **d** furnish with: *empower*. 2 (*from adjectives and nouns*) cause to be in a certain condition: *enable*; *encourage*; *enrich*; *enslave*.
▷HISTORY via Old French from Latin *in-* IN-[2]

en-[2] *or* **em-** PREFIX FORMING NOUNS AND ADJECTIVES in; into; inside: *endemic*.
▷HISTORY from Greek (often via Latin); compare IN-[1], IN-[2]

-en[1] SUFFIX FORMING VERBS FROM ADJECTIVES AND NOUNS cause to be; become; cause to have: *blacken*; *heighten*.
▷HISTORY Old English *-n-*, as in *fæst-n-ian* to fasten, of common Germanic origin; compare Icelandic *fastna*

-en[2] SUFFIX FORMING ADJECTIVES FROM NOUNS of; made of; resembling: *ashen*; *earthen*; *wooden*.
▷HISTORY Old English *-en*; related to Gothic *-eins*, Latin *-īnus* -INE[1]

enable (ɪnˈeɪbᵊl) VERB (*tr*) 1 to provide (someone) with adequate power, means, opportunity, or authority (to do something). 2 to make possible. 3 to put (a digital electronic circuit element) into an operative condition by supplying a suitable input pulse.
▸**enˈablement** NOUN ▸**enˈabler** NOUN

enabling act NOUN a legislative act conferring certain specified powers on a person or organization.

enact (ɪnˈækt) VERB (*tr*) 1 to make into an act or statute. 2 to establish by law; ordain or decree. 3 to represent or perform in or as if in a play; to act out.
▸**enˈactable** ADJECTIVE ▸**enˈactive** *or* **enˈactory** ADJECTIVE ▸**enˈactment** *or* **enˈaction** NOUN ▸**enˈactor** NOUN

enalapril (ɪˈnæləprɪl) NOUN an ACE inhibitor used to treat high blood pressure and congestive heart failure.

enamel (ɪˈnæməl) NOUN 1 a coloured glassy substance, translucent or opaque, fused to the surface of articles made of metal, glass, etc., for ornament or protection. 2 an article or articles ornamented with enamel. 3 an enamel-like paint or varnish. 4 any smooth glossy coating resembling enamel. 5 another word for **nail polish.** 6 the hard white calcified substance that covers the crown of each tooth. 7 (*modifier*) **a** decorated or covered with enamel: *an enamel ring*. **b** made with enamel: *enamel paste*. ◆ VERB **-els, -elling, -elled** *or US* **-els, -eling, -eled.** (*tr*) 8 to inlay, coat, or otherwise decorate with enamel. 9 to ornament with glossy variegated colours, as if with enamel. 10 to portray in enamel.
▷HISTORY C15: from Old French *esmail*, of Germanic origin; compare Old High German *smalz* lard; see SMELT[1]
▸**eˈnameller** *or* **eˈnamellist** *or US* **eˈnameler** *or* **eˈnamelist** NOUN ▸**eˈnamelˌwork** NOUN

enamour *or US* **enamor** (ɪnˈæmə) VERB (*tr*; *usually passive* and foll by *of*) to inspire with love; captivate; charm.
▷HISTORY C14: from Old French *enamourer*, from *amour* love, from Latin *amor*

enamoured *or US* **enamored** (ɪnˈæməd) ADJECTIVE in love; captivated; charmed.

enantiomer (ɛnˈæntɪəmə) NOUN *Chem* a molecule that exhibits stereoisomerism because of the presence of one or more chiral centres.

enantiomorph (ɛnˈæntɪəˌmɔːf) NOUN either of the two crystal forms of a substance that are mirror images of each other.
▷HISTORY C19: from Greek *enantios* opposite + -MORPH
▸**enˌantioˈmorphic** ADJECTIVE ▸**enˌantioˈmorphism** NOUN

enarthrosis (ˌɛnɑːˈθrəʊsɪs) NOUN, *plural* **-ses** (-siːz). *Anatomy* a ball-and-socket joint, such as that of the hip.
▷HISTORY C17: via New Latin from Greek, from *arthrōsis*, from *arthron* a joint + -OSIS
▸ˌ**enarˈthrodial** ADJECTIVE

enate (ˈiːneɪt) ADJECTIVE *also* **enatic** (iːˈnætɪk). 1 *Biology* growing out or outwards. 2 related on the side of the mother. ◆ NOUN 3 a relative on the mother's side.
▷HISTORY C17: from Latin *ēnātus*, from *ēnāscī* to be born from, from *nāscī* to be born

en attendant *French* (ɑ̃n atɑ̃dɑ̃) ADVERB in the mean time; while waiting.

en bloc *French* (ɑ̃ blɔk) ADVERB in a lump or block; as a body or whole; all together.

en brochette *French* (ɑ̃ brɔʃɛt) ADJECTIVE, ADVERB (esp of meat) roasted or grilled on a skewer.
▷HISTORY literally: on a skewer

en brosse *French* (ɑ̃ brɔs) ADJECTIVE, ADVERB (of the hair) cut very short so that the hair stands up stiffly.
▷HISTORY literally: in the style of a brush

enc. ABBREVIATION FOR: 1 enclosed. 2 enclosure.

encaenia (ɛnˈsiːnɪə) NOUN *Rare* a festival of dedication or commemoration.
▷HISTORY C14: via Late Latin from Greek *enkainia*, from *kainos* new

encage (ɪnˈkeɪdʒ) VERB (*tr*) to confine in or as in a cage.

encamp (ɪnˈkæmp) VERB to lodge or cause to lodge in a camp.

encampment (ɪnˈkæmpmənt) NOUN 1 the act of setting up a camp. 2 the place where a camp, esp a military camp, is set up.

encapsulate *or* **incapsulate** (ɪnˈkæpsjʊˌleɪt) VERB 1 to enclose or be enclosed in or as if in a capsule. 2 (*tr*) to sum up in a short or concise form; condense; abridge.
▸**enˌcapsuˈlation** *or* **inˌcapsuˈlation** NOUN

encarnalize *or* **encarnalise** (ɪnˈkɑːnəˌlaɪz) VERB (*tr*) *Rare* 1 to provide with a bodily form; incarnate. 2 to make carnal, gross, or sensual.

encase *or* **incase** (ɪnˈkeɪs) VERB (*tr*) to place or enclose in or as if in a case.
▸**enˈcasement** *or* **inˈcasement** NOUN

encash (ɪnˈkæʃ) VERB (*tr*) *Brit formal* to exchange (a cheque) for cash.
▸**enˈcashable** ADJECTIVE ▸**enˈcashment** NOUN

encastré (ɛnˈkɑːstreɪ) ADJECTIVE *Civil engineering* (of a beam) fixed at the ends; built into its supports.
▷HISTORY from French, past participle of *encastrer*, from Latin *incastrare* to cut in; see CASTRATE

encaustic (ɪnˈkɒstɪk) *Ceramics* ◆ ADJECTIVE 1 decorated by any process involving burning in colours, esp by inlaying coloured clays and baking or by fusing wax colours to the surface. ◆ NOUN 2 the process of burning in colours. 3 a product of such a process.
▷HISTORY C17: from Latin *encausticus*, from Greek *enkaustikos*, from *enkaiein* to burn in, from *kaiein* to burn
▸**enˈcaustically** ADVERB

-ence *or* **-ency** SUFFIX FORMING NOUNS indicating an action, state, condition, or quality: *benevolence*; *residence*; *patience*.
▷HISTORY via Old French from Latin *-entia*, from *-ēns*, present participial ending

enceinte[1] (ɒnˈsænt; *French* ɑ̃sɛ̃t) ADJECTIVE another word for **pregnant.**
▷HISTORY C17: from French, from Latin *inciēns* pregnant; related to Greek *enkuos*, from *kuein* to be pregnant

enceinte[2] (ɒnˈsænt; *French* ɑ̃sɛ̃t) NOUN 1 a boundary wall enclosing a defended area. 2 the area enclosed.
▷HISTORY C18: from French: enclosure, from

enceindre to encompass, from Latin *incingere,* from *cingere* to gird

Enceladus[1] (ɛn'sɛlədəs) NOUN *Greek myth* a giant who was punished for his rebellion against the gods by a fatal blow from a stone cast by Athena. He was believed to be buried under Mount Etna in Sicily.

Enceladus[2] NOUN a very bright satellite of Saturn.

encephalalgia (ɛn,sɛfə'lældʒɪə) NOUN *Med* pain in the head; headache.

encephalic (,ɛnsɪ'fælɪk, ,ɛnkɪ-) ADJECTIVE of or relating to the brain.

encephalin (ɛn'sɛfəlɪn) NOUN a variant of **enkephalin.**

encephalitis (,ɛnsɛfə'laɪtɪs, ,ɛnkɛf-) NOUN inflammation of the brain.
▸**encephalitic** (,ɛnsɛfə'lɪtɪk) ADJECTIVE

encephalitis lethargica (lɪ'θɑ:dʒɪkə) NOUN *Pathol* a technical name for **sleeping sickness** (sense 2).

encephalo- *or before a vowel* **encephal-** COMBINING FORM indicating the brain: *encephalogram; encephalitis.*
▷**HISTORY** from New Latin, from Greek *enkephalos,* from *en-* in + *kephalē* head

encephalogram (ɛn'sɛfələ,græm) NOUN [1] an X-ray photograph of the brain, esp one (a **pneumoencephalogram**) taken after replacing some of the cerebrospinal fluid with air or oxygen so that the brain cavities show clearly. [2] short for **electroencephalogram.**

encephalograph (ɛn'sɛfələ,grɑ:f, -,græf) NOUN [1] short for **electroencephalograph.** [2] any other apparatus used to produce an encephalogram.

encephalography (,ɛnsɛfə'lɒgrəfɪ) NOUN [1] the branch of medical science concerned with taking and analysing X-ray photographs of the brain. [2] another name for **electroencephalography.**
▸**encephalographic** (ɛn,sɛfələ'græfɪk) ADJECTIVE
▸**en,cephalo'graphically** ADVERB

encephaloma (,ɛnsɛfə'ləʊmə) NOUN, *plural* **-mas** *or* **-mata** (-mətə). a brain tumour.

encephalomyelitis (ɛn,sɛfələʊ,maɪə'laɪtɪs) NOUN acute inflammation of the brain and spinal cord.
▸**encephalomyelitic** (ɛn,sɛfələʊ,maɪə'lɪtɪk) ADJECTIVE

encephalon (ɛn'sɛfə,lɒn) NOUN, *plural* **-la** (-lə). a technical name for **brain.**
▷**HISTORY** C18: from New Latin, from Greek *enkephalos* brain (literally: that which is in the head), from EN-[2] + *kephalē* head
▸**en'cephalous** ADJECTIVE

encephalopathy (ɛn,sɛfə'lɒpəθɪ) NOUN any degenerative disease of the brain, often associated with toxic conditions. See also **BSE.**

enchain (ɪn'tʃeɪn) VERB *(tr)* [1] to bind with chains. [2] to hold fast or captivate (the attention, etc.).
▸**en'chainment** NOUN

enchant (ɪn'tʃɑ:nt) VERB *(tr)* [1] to cast a spell on; bewitch. [2] to delight or captivate utterly; fascinate; charm.
▷**HISTORY** C14: from Old French *enchanter,* from Latin *incantāre* to chant a spell, from *cantāre* to chant, from *canere* to sing
▸**en'chanter** NOUN ▸**en'chantress** FEMININE NOUN

enchanted (ɪn'tʃɑ:ntɪd) ADJECTIVE [1] under a spell; bewitched; magical. [2] utterly delighted or captivated; fascinated; charmed.

enchanter's nightshade NOUN any of several onagraceous plants of the genus *Circaea,* esp *C. lutetiana,* having small white flowers and bristly fruits.

enchanting (ɪn'tʃɑ:ntɪŋ) ADJECTIVE pleasant; delightful.
▸**en'chantingly** ADVERB

enchantment (ɪn'tʃɑ:ntmənt) NOUN [1] the act of enchanting or state of being enchanted. [2] a magic spell or act of witchcraft. [3] great charm or fascination.

enchase (ɪn'tʃeɪs) VERB *(tr)* a less common word for **chase** (sense 3).
▷**HISTORY** C15: from Old French *enchasser* to enclose, set, from EN-[1] + *casse* CASE[2]
▸**en'chaser** NOUN

enchilada (,ɛntʃɪ'lɑ:də) NOUN a Mexican dish consisting of a tortilla fried in hot fat, filled with meat, and served with a chilli sauce.
▷**HISTORY** C19: American Spanish, feminine of *enchilado* seasoned with chilli, from *enchilar* to spice with chilli, from *chile* CHILLI

enchiridion (,ɛnkaɪ'rɪdɪən) NOUN, *plural* **-ions** *or* **-ia** (-ɪə). *Rare* a handbook or manual.
▷**HISTORY** C16: from Late Latin, from Greek *enkheiridion,* from EN-[2] + *kheir* hand

enchondroma (,ɛnkən'drəʊmə) NOUN, *plural* **-mas** *or* **-mata** (-mətə). *Pathol* a benign cartilaginous tumour, most commonly in the bones of the hands or feet.
▷**HISTORY** C19: New Latin from Greek, from EN-[2] + *khondros* cartilage
▸**,enchon'dromatous** ADJECTIVE

enchorial (ɛn'kɔ:rɪəl) *or* **enchoric** ADJECTIVE of or used in a particular country: used esp of the popular (demotic) writing of the ancient Egyptians.
▷**HISTORY** C19: via Late Latin from Greek *enkhōrios,* from EN-[2] + *khōra* country

-enchyma COMBINING FORM denoting cellular tissue: *aerenchyma.*
▷**HISTORY** C20: abstracted from PARENCHYMA

encipher (ɪn'saɪfə) VERB *(tr)* to convert (a message, document, etc.) from plain text into code or cipher; encode.
▸**en'cipherer** NOUN ▸**en'cipherment** NOUN

encircle (ɪn'sɜ:kᵊl) VERB *(tr)* to form a circle around; enclose within a circle; surround.
▸**en'circlement** NOUN ▸**en'circling** ADJECTIVE

encl. ABBREVIATION FOR: [1] enclosed. [2] enclosure.

en clair *French* (ɑ̃ klɛr) ADVERB, ADJECTIVE in ordinary language; not in cipher.
▷**HISTORY** literally: in clear

enclasp (ɪn'klɑ:sp) VERB *(tr)* to clasp; embrace.

enclave ('ɛnkleɪv) NOUN a part of a country entirely surrounded by foreign territory: viewed from the position of the surrounding territories. Compare **exclave.**
▷**HISTORY** C19: from French, from Old French *enclaver* to enclose, from Vulgar Latin *inclāvāre* (unattested) to lock up, from Latin IN-[2] + *clavis* key

enclitic (ɪn'klɪtɪk) ADJECTIVE [1] **a** denoting or relating to a monosyllabic word or form that is treated as a suffix of the preceding word, as Latin *-que* in *populusque.* **b** (in classical Greek) denoting or relating to a word that throws an accent back onto the preceding word. ◆ NOUN [2] an enclitic word or linguistic form. ◆ Compare **proclitic.**
▷**HISTORY** C17: from Late Latin *encliticus,* from Greek *enklitikos,* from *enklinein* to cause to lean, from EN-[2] + *klinein* to lean
▸**en'clitically** ADVERB

enclose *or* **inclose** (ɪn'kləʊz) VERB *(tr)* [1] to close; hem in; surround. [2] to surround (land) with or as if with a fence. [3] to put in an envelope or wrapper, esp together with a letter. [4] to contain or hold.
▸**en'closable** *or* **in'closable** ADJECTIVE ▸**en'closer** *or* **in'closer** NOUN

enclosed order NOUN a Christian religious order that does not permit its members to go into the outside world.

enclosure *or* **inclosure** (ɪn'kləʊʒə) NOUN [1] the act of enclosing or state of being enclosed. [2] a region or area enclosed by or as if by a fence. [3] **a** the act of appropriating land, esp common land, by putting a hedge or other barrier around it. **b** *History* such acts as were carried out at various periods in England, esp between the 12th and 14th centuries and finally in the 18th and 19th centuries. [4] a fence, wall, etc., that serves to enclose. [5] something, esp a supporting document, enclosed within an envelope or wrapper, esp together with a letter. [6] *Brit* a section of a sports ground, racecourse, etc., allotted to certain spectators.

encode (ɪn'kəʊd) VERB *(tr)* [1] to convert (a message) from plain text into code. [2] *Computing* to convert (characters and symbols) into a digital form as a series of impulses. Compare **decode** (sense 2). [3] to convert (an electrical signal) into a form suitable for transmission. [4] to convert (a nerve signal) into a form that can be received by the brain. [5] to use (a word, phrase, etc., esp of a foreign language) in the construction appropriate to it in that language.
▸**en'codement** NOUN ▸**en'coder** NOUN

encomiast (ɛn'kəʊmɪ,æst) NOUN a person who speaks or writes an encomium.
▷**HISTORY** C17: from Greek *enkōmiastēs,* from *enkōmiazein* to utter an ENCOMIUM
▸**en,comi'astic** *or* **en,comi'astical** ADJECTIVE
▸**en,comi'astically** ADVERB

encomium (ɛn'kəʊmɪəm) NOUN, *plural* **-miums** *or* **-mia** (-mɪə). a formal expression of praise; eulogy; panegyric.
▷**HISTORY** C16: from Latin, from Greek *enkōmion,* from EN-[2] + *kōmos* festivity

encompass (ɪn'kʌmpəs) VERB *(tr)* [1] to enclose within a circle; surround. [2] to bring about; cause to happen; contrive: *he encompassed the enemy's ruin.* [3] to include entirely or comprehensively: *this book encompasses the whole range of knowledge.*
▸**en'compassment** NOUN

encopresis (,ɛnkəʊ'pri:sɪs) NOUN involuntary discharge of faeces, esp when associated with psychiatric disturbance.
▷**HISTORY** C20: from New Latin, from Greek EN-[2] + COPR(O)-, + *-esis* as in ENURESIS
▸**encopretic** (,ɛnkəʊ'prɛtɪk) ADJECTIVE

encore ('ɒŋkɔ:) INTERJECTION [1] again; once more: used by an audience to demand an extra or repeated performance. ◆ NOUN [2] an extra or repeated performance given in response to enthusiastic demand. ◆ VERB [3] *(tr)* to demand an extra or repeated performance of (a work, piece of music, etc.) by (a performer).
▷**HISTORY** C18: from French: still, again, perhaps from Latin *in hanc hōram* until this hour

encounter (ɪn'kaʊntə) VERB [1] to come upon or meet casually or unexpectedly. [2] to come into conflict with (an enemy, army, etc.) in battle or contest. [3] *(tr)* to be faced with; contend with: *he encounters many obstacles in his work.* ◆ NOUN [4] a meeting with a person or thing, esp when casual or unexpected. [5] a hostile meeting; contest or conflict.
▷**HISTORY** C13: from Old French *encontrer,* from Vulgar Latin *incontrāre* (unattested), from Latin IN-[2] + *contrā* against, opposite
▸**en'counterer** NOUN

encounter group NOUN a group of people who meet in order to develop self-awareness and mutual understanding by openly expressing their feelings, by confrontation, physical contact, etc.

encourage (ɪn'kʌrɪdʒ) VERB *(tr)* [1] to inspire (someone) with the courage or confidence (to do something). [2] to stimulate (something or someone to do something) by approval or help; support.
▸**en'couragement** NOUN ▸**en'courager** NOUN
▸**en'couraging** ADJECTIVE ▸**en'couragingly** ADVERB

encrinite ('ɛnkrɪ,naɪt) NOUN (in the US) a sedimentary rock formed almost exclusively from the skeletal plates of crinoids. Sometimes shortened to: **crinite.**
▷**HISTORY** C19: from New Latin *encrinus* (from Greek EN-[2] + *krinon* lily) + -ITE[1]

encroach (ɪn'krəʊtʃ) VERB *(intr)* [1] (often foll by *on* or *upon*) to intrude gradually, stealthily, or insidiously upon the rights, property, etc., of another. [2] to advance beyond the usual or proper limits.
▷**HISTORY** C14: from Old French *encrochier* to seize, literally: fasten upon with hooks, from EN-[1] + *croc* hook, of Germanic origin; see CROOK
▸**en'croacher** NOUN ▸**en'croachingly** ADVERB
▸**en'croachment** NOUN

encrust *or* **incrust** (ɪn'krʌst) VERB [1] *(tr)* to cover or overlay with or as with a crust or hard coating. [2] to form or cause to form a crust or hard coating. [3] *(tr)* to decorate lavishly, as with jewels.
▸**,encrus'tation** *or* **,incrus'tation** NOUN

encrypt (ɪn'krɪpt) VERB *(tr)* [1] to put (a message) into code. [2] to put (computer data) into a coded form. [3] to distort (a television or other signal) so that it cannot be understood without the appropriate decryption equipment.
▷**HISTORY** C20: from EN-[1] + *crypt,* as in CRYPTO-
▸**en'crypted** ADJECTIVE ▸**en'cryption** NOUN

enculturation (ɛn,kʌltʃʊ'reɪʃən) NOUN another word for **socialization.**
▸**enculturative** (ɛn'kʌltʃʊrətɪv) ADJECTIVE

encumber *or* **incumber** (ɪn'kʌmbə) VERB *(tr)* [1] to hinder or impede; make difficult; hamper: *encumbered with parcels after going shopping at Christmas; his stupidity encumbers his efforts to learn.* [2]

to fill with superfluous or useless matter. [3] to burden with debts, obligations, etc.
▷**HISTORY** C14: from Old French *encombrer,* from EN-[1] + *combre* a barrier, from Late Latin *combrus,* of uncertain origin
▸**en'cumberingly** *or* **in'cumberingly** ADVERB

encumbrance *or* **incumbrance** (ɪn'kʌmbrəns) NOUN [1] a thing that impedes or is burdensome; hindrance. [2] *Law* a burden or charge upon property, such as a mortgage or lien. [3] *Rare* a dependent person, esp a child.

encumbrancer (ɪn'kʌmbrənsə) NOUN *Law* a person who holds an encumbrance on property belonging to another.

-ency SUFFIX FORMING NOUNS a variant of **-ence**: *fluency; permanency.*

encyclical (ɛn'sɪklɪkᵊl) NOUN [1] a letter sent by the pope to all Roman Catholic bishops throughout the world. ◆ ADJECTIVE *also* **encyclic.** [2] (of letters) intended for general or wide circulation.
▷**HISTORY** C17: from Late Latin *encyclicus,* from Greek *enkuklios* general, from *kuklos* circle

encyclopedia *or* **encyclopaedia** (ɛnˌsaɪkləʊ'piːdɪə) NOUN a book, often in many volumes, containing articles on various topics, often arranged in alphabetical order, dealing either with the whole range of human knowledge or with one particular subject: *a medical encyclopedia.*
▷**HISTORY** C16: from New Latin *encyclopaedia,* erroneously for Greek *enkuklios paideia* general education, from *enkuklios* general (see ENCYCLICAL), + *paideia* education, from *pais* child

encyclopedic *or* **encyclopaedic** (ɛnˌsaɪkləʊ'piːdɪk) ADJECTIVE [1] of, characteristic of, or relating to an encyclopedia. [2] covering a wide range of knowledge; comprehensive.
▸**enˌcyclo'pedically** *or* **enˌcyclo'paedically** ADVERB

encyclopedist *or* **encyclopaedist** (ɛnˌsaɪkləʊ'piːdɪst) NOUN a person who compiles or contributes to an encyclopedia.
▸**enˌcyclo'pedism** *or* **enˌcyclo'paedism** NOUN

encyst (ɛn'sɪst) VERB *Biology* to enclose or become enclosed by a cyst, thick membrane, or shell.
▸**en'cysted** ADJECTIVE ▸**en'cystment** *or* **ˌencys'tation** NOUN

end[1] (ɛnd) NOUN [1] the extremity of the length of something, such as a road, line, etc. [2] the surface at either extremity of a three-dimensional object. [3] the extreme extent, limit, or degree of something. [4] the most distant place or time that can be imagined: *the ends of the earth.* [5] the time at which something is concluded. [6] **a** the last section or part. **b** (*as modifier*): *the end office.* Related adjectives: **final, terminal, ultimate.** [7] a share or part: *his end of the bargain.* [8] (*often plural*) a remnant or fragment (esp in the phrase **odds and ends**). [9] a final state, esp death; destruction. [10] the purpose of an action or existence. [11] *Sport* either of the two defended areas of a playing field, rink, etc. [12] *Bowls, curling* a section of play from one side of the rink to the other. [13] *American football* a player at the extremity of the playing line; wing. [14] **all ends up.** totally or completely. [15] **a sticky end.** *Informal* an unpleasant death. [16] **at a loose end** *or* (*US and Canadian*) **at loose ends.** without purpose or occupation. [17] **at an end.** exhausted or completed. [18] **at the end of the day.** See **day** (sense 10). [19] **come to an end.** to become completed or exhausted. [20] **end on. a** with the end pointing towards one. **b** with the end adjacent to the end of another object. [21] **go off the deep end.** *Informal* to lose one's temper; react angrily. [22] **in the end.** finally. [23] **make** (**both**) **ends meet.** to spend no more than the money one has. [24] **no end** (**of**). *Informal* (intensifier): *I had no end of work.* [25] **on end. a** upright. **b** without pause or interruption. [26] **the end.** *Informal* **a** the worst, esp something that goes beyond the limits of endurance. **b** *Chiefly US* the best in quality. [27] **the end of the road.** the point beyond which survival or continuation is impossible. [28] **throw** (**someone**) **in at the deep end.** to put (someone) into a new situation, job, etc., without preparation or introduction. ◆ VERB [29] to bring or come to a finish; conclude. [30] to die or cause to die. [31] (*tr*) surpass; outdo: *a novel to end all novels.* [32] **end it all.** *Informal* to commit suicide. ◆ See also **end up.**
▷**HISTORY** Old English *ende;* related to Old Norse *endir,* Gothic *andeis,* Old High German *endi,* Latin *antiae* forelocks, Sanskrit *antya* last
▸**'ender** NOUN

end[2] (ɛnd) VERB (*tr*) *Brit* to put (hay or grain) into a barn or stack.
▷**HISTORY** Old English *innian;* related to Old High German *innōn;* see INN

end- COMBINING FORM a variant of **endo-** before a vowel.

-end SUFFIX FORMING NOUNS See **-and.**

end-all NOUN short for **be-all and end-all.**

endamage (ɛn'dæmɪdʒ) VERB (*tr*) to cause injury to; damage.
▸**en'damagement** NOUN

endamoeba *or US* **endameba** (ˌɛndə'miːbə) NOUN, *plural* **-bae** (-biː) *or* **-bas.** variants of **entamoeba.**

endanger (ɪn'deɪndʒə) VERB (*tr*) to put in danger or peril; imperil.
▸**en'dangerment** NOUN

endangered (ɪn'deɪndʒəd) ADJECTIVE in danger: used esp of animals in danger of extinction: *the giant panda is an endangered species.*

endarch ('ɛndˌɑːk) ADJECTIVE *Botany* (of a xylem strand) having the first-formed xylem internal to that formed later. Compare **exarch.**
▷**HISTORY** C20: from ENDO- + Greek *arkhē* beginning

en dash *or* **rule** NOUN *Printing* a dash (–) one en long.

end-blown ADJECTIVE *Music* (of a recorder) held downwards and blown through one end.

endbrain ('ɛndˌbreɪn) NOUN *Anatomy* another name for **telencephalon.**

endear (ɪn'dɪə) VERB (*tr*) to cause to be beloved or esteemed.

endearing (ɪn'dɪərɪŋ) ADJECTIVE giving rise to love or esteem; charming.
▸**en'dearingly** ADVERB

endearment (ɪn'dɪəmənt) NOUN [1] something that endears, such as an affectionate utterance. [2] the act or process of endearing or the condition of being endeared.

endeavour *or US* **endeavor** (ɪn'dɛvə) VERB [1] to try (to do something). ◆ NOUN [2] an effort to do or attain something.
▷**HISTORY** C14: *endeveren,* from EN-[1] + *-deveren* from *dever* duty, from Old French *deveir;* see DEVOIRS
▸**en'deavourer** *or US* **en'deavorer** NOUN

endemic (ɛn'dɛmɪk) ADJECTIVE *also* **endemial** (ɛn'diːmɪəl), **endemical.** [1] present within a localized area or peculiar to persons in such an area. ◆ NOUN [2] an endemic disease or plant.
▷**HISTORY** C18: from New Latin *endēmicus,* from Greek *endēmos* native, from EN-[2] + *dēmos* the people
▸**en'demically** ADVERB ▸**'endemism** *or* **ˌende'micity** NOUN

Enderby Land ('ɛndəbɪ) NOUN part of the coastal region of Antarctica, between Kempland and Queen Maud Land: the westernmost part of the Australian Antarctic Territory; discovered in 1831.

endergonic (ˌɛndə'gɒnɪk) ADJECTIVE (of a biochemical reaction) requiring energy to proceed. Compare **exergonic.**
▷**HISTORY** C20: from END(O-) + Greek *ergon* work + -IC

endermic (ɛn'dɜːmɪk) ADJECTIVE (of a medicine) acting by absorption through the skin.
▷**HISTORY** C19: from EN-[2] + Greek *derma* skin

endgame ('ɛndˌgeɪm) NOUN [1] Also called: **ending.** the closing stage of a game of chess, in which only a few pieces are left on the board. [2] the closing stage of any of certain other games.

ending ('ɛndɪŋ) NOUN [1] the act of bringing to or reaching an end. [2] the last part of something, as a book, film, etc. [3] the final part of a word, esp a suffix. [4] *Chess* another word for **endgame.**

endive ('ɛndaɪv) NOUN a plant, *Cichorium endivia,* cultivated for its crisp curly leaves, which are used in salads: family *Asteraceae* (composites). Compare **chicory.**
▷**HISTORY** C15: from Old French, from Medieval Latin *endīvia,* variant of Latin *intubus, entubus,* of uncertain origin

endless ('ɛndlɪs) ADJECTIVE [1] having or seeming to have no end; eternal or infinite. [2] continuing too long or continually recurring. [3] formed with the ends joined: *an endless belt.*
▸**'endlessly** ADVERB ▸**'endlessness** NOUN

endlong ('ɛndˌlɒŋ) ADVERB *Archaic* lengthways or on end.

end matter NOUN another name for **back matter.**

endmost ('ɛndˌməʊst) ADJECTIVE nearest the end; most distant.

endo- *or before a vowel* **end-** COMBINING FORM inside; within: *endocrine.*
▷**HISTORY** from Greek, from *endon* within

endobiotic (ˌɛndəʊbaɪ'ɒtɪk) formed within a host cell.

endoblast ('ɛndəʊˌblæst) NOUN [1] *Embryol* a less common name for **endoderm.** [2] another name for **hypoblast** (sense 1).
▸**ˌendo'blastic** ADJECTIVE

endocardial (ˌɛndəʊ'kɑːdɪəl) *or* **endocardiac** ADJECTIVE [1] of or relating to the endocardium. [2] within the heart.

endocarditis (ˌɛndəʊkɑː'daɪtɪs) NOUN inflammation of the endocardium.
▸**endocarditic** (ˌɛndəʊkɑː'dɪtɪk) ADJECTIVE

endocardium (ˌɛndəʊ'kɑːdɪəm) NOUN, *plural* **-dia** (-dɪə). the membrane that lines the cavities of the heart and forms part of the valves.
▷**HISTORY** C19: from New Latin, from ENDO- + Greek *kardia* heart

endocarp ('ɛndəˌkɑːp) NOUN the inner, usually woody, layer of the pericarp of a fruit, such as the stone of a peach or cherry.
▸**ˌendo'carpal** *or* **ˌendo'carpic** ADJECTIVE

endocentric (ˌɛndəʊ'sɛntrɪk) ADJECTIVE *Grammar* (of a construction) fulfilling the grammatical role of one of its constituents; as in *three blind mice,* where the whole noun phrase fulfills the same role as its head noun *mice.* Compare **exocentric.**

endocranial cast (ˌɛndəʊ'kreɪnɪəl) NOUN a cast made of the inside of a cranial cavity to show the size and shape of the brain: used esp in anthropology. Sometimes shortened to: **endocast.**

endocranium (ˌɛndəʊ'kreɪnɪəm) NOUN, *plural* **-nia** (-nɪə). *Anatomy* the thick fibrous membrane that lines the cranial cavity and forms the outermost layer of the dura mater.

endocrine ('ɛndəʊˌkraɪn, -krɪn) ADJECTIVE *also* **endocrinal** (ˌɛndəʊ'kraɪnᵊl), **endocrinic** (ˌɛndəʊ'krɪnɪk) **endocrinous** (ɛn'dɒkrɪnəs). [1] of or denoting endocrine glands or their secretions: *endocrine disorders.* ◆ NOUN [2] an endocrine gland. ◆ Compare **exocrine.**
▷**HISTORY** C20: from ENDO- + *-crine,* from Greek *krinein* to separate

endocrine gland NOUN any of the glands that secrete hormones directly into the bloodstream, including the pituitary, pineal, thyroid, parathyroid, adrenal, testes, ovaries, and the pancreatic islets of Langerhans. Also called: **ductless gland.**

endocrinology (ˌɛndəʊkraɪ'nɒlədʒɪ, -krɪ-) NOUN the branch of medical science concerned with the endocrine glands and their secretions.
▸**endocrinologic** (ˌɛndəʊˌkrɪnə'lɒdʒɪk) *or* **ˌendoˌcrino'logical** ADJECTIVE ▸**ˌendocri'nologist** NOUN

endocrinopathy (ˌɛndəʊkrɪ'nɒpəθɪ) NOUN any disease due to disorder of the endocrine system.
▸**endocrinopathic** (ˌɛndəʊˌkrɪnəʊ'pæθɪk) ADJECTIVE

endocuticle ('ɛndəʊˌkjuːtɪkᵊl) NOUN the inner layer of the cuticle of an insect.

endocytosis (ˌɛndəʊsaɪ'təʊsɪs) NOUN the process by which a living cell takes up molecules bound to its surface.

endoderm ('ɛndəʊˌdɜːm) *or* **entoderm** NOUN the inner germ layer of an animal embryo, which gives rise to the lining of the digestive and respiratory tracts. See also **ectoderm, mesoderm.**
▸**ˌendo'dermal** *or* **ˌendo'dermic** *or* **ˌento'dermal** *or* **ˌento'dermic** ADJECTIVE

endodermis (ˌɛndəʊ'dɜːmɪs) NOUN *Botany* the specialized innermost layer of cortex in roots and some stems, which controls the passage of water and dissolved substances between the cortex and stele.
▷**HISTORY** C19: from New Latin, from ENDO- + Greek *derma* skin

endodontics (ˌɛndəʊ'dɒntɪks) NOUN (*functioning as singular*) the branch of dentistry concerned with diseases of the dental pulp.
▷**HISTORY** C19: from New Latin *endodontia,* from ENDO- + Greek *odōn* tooth
▸**ˌendo'dontal** *or* **ˌendo'dontic** ADJECTIVE ▸**ˌendo'dontist** NOUN

endoenzyme (ˌɛndəʊ'ɛnzaɪm) NOUN any of a

group of enzymes, esp endopeptidases, that act upon inner chemical bonds in a chain of molecules. Compare **exoenzyme** (sense 1).

endoergic (ˌɛndəʊ'ɜ:dʒɪk) ADJECTIVE (of a nuclear reaction) occurring with absorption of energy, as opposed to *exoergic*. Compare **endothermic.**
▷HISTORY from ENDO- + *-ergic* from Greek *ergon* work

end of steel NOUN *Canadian* 1 a point up to which railway tracks have been laid. 2 a town located at such a point.

endogamy (ɛn'dɒgəmɪ) NOUN 1 *Anthropol* marriage within one's own tribe or similar unit. Compare **exogamy** (sense 1). 2 pollination between two flowers on the same plant.
▸**en'dogamous** *or* **endogamic** (ˌɛndəʊ'gæmɪk) ADJECTIVE

endogen ('ɛndəʊˌdʒɛn) NOUN a former name for **monocotyledon.**

endogenous (ɛn'dɒdʒɪnəs) ADJECTIVE 1 *Biology* developing or originating within an organism or part of an organism: *endogenous rhythms.* 2 having no apparent external cause: *endogenous depression.*
▸**en'dogenously** ADVERB ▸**en'dogeny** NOUN

endolithic (ˌɛndəʊ'lɪθɪk) ADJECTIVE (of organisms, such as algae) growing inside rock.

endolymph ('ɛndəʊˌlɪmf) NOUN the fluid that fills the membranous labyrinth of the internal ear.
▸**endolymphatic** (ˌɛndəʊlɪm'fætɪk) ADJECTIVE

endometriosis (ˌɛndəʊˌmi:trɪ'əʊsɪs) NOUN *Pathol* the presence of endometrium in areas other than the lining of the uterus, as on the ovaries, resulting in premenstrual pain.

endometritis (ˌɛndəʊmɪ'traɪtɪs) NOUN inflammation of the endometrium, which is caused by infection, as by bacteria, foreign bodies, etc.

endometrium (ˌɛndəʊ'mi:trɪəm) NOUN, *plural* **-tria** (-trɪə). the mucous membrane that lines the uterus.
▷HISTORY C19: New Latin, from ENDO- + Greek *mētra* uterus
▸**ˌendo'metrial** ADJECTIVE

endomitosis (ˌɛndəʊmaɪ'təʊsɪs) NOUN *Biology* the division of chromosomes but not of the cell nucleus, resulting in a polyploid cell.

endomorph ('ɛndəʊˌmɔ:f) NOUN 1 a person with a fat and heavy body build: said to be correlated with viscerotonia. Compare **ectomorph, mesomorph.** 2 a mineral that naturally occurs enclosed within another mineral, as within quartz.
▸**ˌendo'morphic** ADJECTIVE ▸**'endoˌmorphy** NOUN

endomorphism (ˌɛndəʊ'mɔ:ˌfɪzəm) NOUN *Geology* changes in a cooling body of igneous rock brought about by assimilation of fragments of, or chemical reaction with, the surrounding country rock.

endoneurium (ˌɛndəʊ'njʊərɪəm) NOUN the delicate connective tissue surrounding nerve fibres within a bundle.
▷HISTORY New Latin, from ENDO- + NEURO- + -IUM

endonuclease (ˌɛndəʊ'nju:klɪˌeɪz) NOUN an enzyme that is responsible for scission of a nucleic acid chain, the action of which is not confined to the terminal nucleotide. Compare **exonuclease.**

endoparasite (ˌɛndəʊ'pærəˌsaɪt) NOUN a parasite, such as the tapeworm, that lives within the body of its host.
▸**endoparasitic** (ˌɛndəʊˌpærə'sɪtɪk) ADJECTIVE

endopeptidase (ˌɛndəʊ'pɛptɪˌdeɪz) NOUN any proteolytic enzyme, such as pepsin, that splits a protein into smaller peptide fragments. Also called: **proteinase.** Compare **exopeptidase.**

endophyte ('ɛndəʊˌfaɪt) NOUN a fungus, or occasionally an alga or other organism, that lives within a plant.
▸**endophytic** (ˌɛndəʊ'fɪtɪk) ADJECTIVE ▸**ˌendo'phytically** ADVERB

endoplasm ('ɛndəʊˌplæzəm) NOUN *Cytology* the inner cytoplasm in some cells, esp protozoa, which is more granular and fluid than the outer cytoplasm (see **ectoplasm** (sense 1)).
▸**ˌendo'plasmic** ADJECTIVE

endoplasmic reticulum NOUN an extensive intracellular membrane system whose functions include synthesis and transport of lipids and, in regions where ribosomes are attached, of proteins.

end organ NOUN *Anatomy* the expanded end of a peripheral motor or sensory nerve.

endorphin (ɛn'dɔ:fɪn) NOUN any of a class of polypeptides, including enkephalin, occurring naturally in the brain, that bind to pain receptors and so block pain sensation.
▷HISTORY C20: from ENDO- + MORPHINE

endorse *or* **indorse** (ɪn'dɔ:s) VERB (*tr*) 1 to give approval or sanction to. 2 to sign (one's name) on the back of (a cheque, etc.) to specify oneself as payee. 3 *Commerce* **a** to sign the back of (a negotiable document) to transfer ownership of the rights to a specified payee. **b** to specify (a designated sum) as transferable to another as payee. 4 to write (a qualifying comment, recommendation, etc.) on the back of a document. 5 to sign (a document), as when confirming receipt of payment. 6 *Chiefly Brit* to record (a conviction) on (a driving licence).
▷HISTORY C16: from Old French *endosser* to put on the back, from EN-[1] + *dos* back, from Latin *dorsum*
▸**en'dorsable** *or* **in'dorsable** ADJECTIVE ▸**en'dorser** *or* **en'dorsor** *or* **in'dorser** *or* **in'dorsor** NOUN

endorsee (ɪnˌdɔ:'si:, ˌɛndɔ:-) *or* **indorsee** NOUN the person in whose favour a negotiable instrument is endorsed.

endorsement *or* **indorsement** (ɪn'dɔ:smənt) NOUN 1 the act or an instance of endorsing. 2 something that endorses, such as a signature or qualifying comment. 3 approval or support. 4 a record of a motoring offence on a driving licence. 5 *Insurance* a clause in or amendment to an insurance policy allowing for alteration of coverage.

endoscope ('ɛndəʊˌskəʊp) NOUN a long slender medical instrument used for examining the interior of hollow organs including the lung, stomach, bladder and bowel.
▸**endoscopic** (ˌɛndəʊ'skɒpɪk) ADJECTIVE ▸**endoscopist** (ɛn'dɒskəpɪst) NOUN ▸**en'doscopy** NOUN

endoskeleton (ˌɛndəʊ'skɛlɪtᵊn) NOUN the internal skeleton of an animal, esp the bony or cartilaginous skeleton of vertebrates. Compare **exoskeleton.**
▸**ˌendo'skeletal** ADJECTIVE

endosmosis (ˌɛndɒs'məʊsɪs, -dɒz-) NOUN *Biology* osmosis in which water enters a cell or organism from the surrounding solution. Compare **exosmosis.**
▸**endosmotic** (ˌɛndɒs'mɒtɪk, -dɒz-) ADJECTIVE ▸**ˌendos'motically** ADVERB

endosperm ('ɛndəʊˌspɜ:m) NOUN the tissue within the seed of a flowering plant that surrounds and nourishes the developing embryo.
▸**ˌendo'spermic** ADJECTIVE

endospore ('ɛndəʊˌspɔ:) NOUN 1 a small asexual spore produced by some bacteria and algae. 2 the innermost wall of a spore or pollen grain.
▸**endosporous** (ɛn'dɒspərəs, ˌɛndəʊ'spɔ:rəs) ADJECTIVE

endosteum (ɛn'dɒstɪəm) NOUN, *plural* **-tea** (-tɪə). a highly vascular membrane lining the marrow cavity of long bones, such as the femur and humerus.
▷HISTORY C19: New Latin, from ENDO- + Greek *osteon* bone
▸**en'dosteal** ADJECTIVE

endostosis (ˌɛndɒs'təʊsɪs) NOUN, *plural* **-ses** (-si:z). the conversion of cartilage into bone.

endosymbiosis (ˌɛndəʊˌsɪmbɪ'əʊsɪs) NOUN a type of symbiosis in which one organism lives inside the other, the two typically behaving as a single organism. It is believed to be the means by which such organelles as mitochondria and chloroplasts arose within eukaryotic cells.
▸**ˌendoˌsymbi'otic** ADJECTIVE

endothecium (ˌɛndəʊ'θi:ʃɪəm, -sɪəm) NOUN, *plural* **-cia** (-ʃɪə, -sɪə). *Botany* 1 the inner mass of cells of the developing capsule in mosses. 2 the fibrous tissue of the inner wall of an anther.
▷HISTORY C19: New Latin, from ENDO- + Greek *thēkion* case; see THECA
▸**ˌendo'thecial** ADJECTIVE

endothelioma (ˌɛndəʊˌθi:lɪ'əʊmə) NOUN, *plural* **-mata** (-mətə). *Pathol* a tumour originating in endothelial tissue, such as the lining of blood vessels.

endothelium (ˌɛndəʊ'θi:lɪəm) NOUN, *plural* **-lia** (-lɪə). a tissue consisting of a single layer of cells that lines the blood and lymph vessels, heart, and some other cavities.
▷HISTORY C19: New Latin, from ENDO- + *-thelium,* from Greek *thēlē* nipple
▸**ˌendo'thelial** ADJECTIVE ▸**ˌendo'theliˌoid** ADJECTIVE

endothermic (ˌɛndəʊ'θɜ:mɪk) *or* **endothermal** ADJECTIVE (of a chemical reaction or compound) occurring or formed with the absorption of heat. Compare **exothermic, endoergic.**
▸**ˌendo'thermically** ADVERB ▸**ˌendo'thermism** NOUN

endotoxin (ˌɛndəʊ'tɒksɪn) NOUN a toxin contained within the protoplasm of an organism, esp a bacterium, and liberated only at death.
▸**ˌendo'toxic** ADJECTIVE

endotracheal anaesthesia (ˌɛndəʊ'trækɪəl) NOUN a method of administering gaseous anaesthetics to animals through a tube inserted into the trachea.

endotrophic mycorrhiza (ˌɛndəʊ'trɒfɪk) NOUN *Botany* the most widespread and common type of mycorrhiza, in which the fungus lives within the cells of the roots of the plant. Also called: **endomycorrhiza, arbuscular mycorrhiza.** Compare **ectotrophic mycorrhiza.**

endow (ɪn'daʊ) VERB (*tr*) 1 to provide with or bequeath a source of permanent income. 2 (usually foll by *with*) to provide (with qualities, characteristics, etc.). 3 *Obsolete* to provide with a dower.
▷HISTORY C14: from Old French *endouer,* from EN-[1] + *douer,* from Latin *dōtāre,* from *dōs* dowry
▸**en'dower** NOUN

endowment (ɪn'daʊmənt) NOUN 1 **a** the source of income with which an institution, etc., is endowed. **b** the income itself. 2 the act or process of endowing. 3 (*usually plural*) natural talents or qualities.

endowment assurance *or* **insurance** NOUN a form of life insurance that provides for the payment of a specified sum directly to the policyholder at a designated date or to his beneficiary should he die before this date.

endowment mortgage NOUN an arrangement whereby a person takes out a mortgage and pays the capital repayment instalments into a life assurance policy and only the interest to the mortgagee during the term of the policy. The loan is repaid by the policy either when it matures or on the prior death of the policyholder.

endozoic (ˌɛndəʊ'zəʊɪk) ADJECTIVE *Botany* 1 (of a plant) living within an animal. 2 denoting seed dispersal in which the seeds are swallowed by an animal and subsequently pass out in the faeces.

endpaper ('ɛndˌpeɪpə) NOUN either of two leaves at the front and back of a book pasted to the inside of the board covers and the first leaf of the book to secure the binding.

end pin NOUN *Music* the adjustable metal spike attached to the bottom of a cello, double bass, etc., that supports it while it is being played.

endplate ('ɛndˌpleɪt) NOUN 1 any usually flat platelike structure at the end of something. 2 *Physiol* the flattened end of a motor nerve fibre, which transmits impulses to muscle.

endplay ('ɛndˌpleɪ) *Bridge* ◆ NOUN 1 a way of playing the last few tricks in a hand so that an opponent is forced to make a particular lead. ◆ VERB (*tr*) 2 to force (an opponent) to make a particular lead near the end of a hand: *declarer endplayed West for the jack of spades.*

end point NOUN 1 *Chem* the point at which a titration is complete, usually marked by a change in colour of an indicator. 2 the point at which anything is complete.

end product NOUN the final result or outcome of a process, series, endeavour, etc., esp in manufacturing.

end-stopped ADJECTIVE (of verse) having a pause at the end of each line.

endue *or* **indue** (ɪn'dju:) VERB **-dues, -duing, -dued.** (*tr*) 1 (usually foll by *with*) to invest or provide, as with some quality or trait. 2 *Rare* (foll by *with*) to clothe or dress (in).
▷HISTORY C15: from Old French *enduire,* from Latin *indūcere,* from *dūcere* to lead

end up VERB (*adverb*) 1 (*copula*) to become eventually; turn out to be: *he ended up a thief.* 2 (*intr*) to arrive, esp by a circuitous or lengthy route or process: *to end up in prison.*

endurance (ɪn'djʊərəns) NOUN 1 the capacity, state, or an instance of enduring. 2 something endured; a hardship, strain, or privation.

endure (ɪn'djʊə) VERB 1 to undergo (hardship, strain, privation, etc.) without yielding; bear. 2 (*tr*) to permit or tolerate. 3 (*intr*) to last or continue to exist.

▷HISTORY C14: from Old French *endurer*, from Latin *indūrāre* to harden, from *dūrus* hard
▸**en'durable** ADJECTIVE ▸**en,dura'bility** *or* **en'durableness** NOUN ▸**en'durably** ADVERB

enduring (ɪn'djʊərɪŋ) ADJECTIVE 1 permanent; lasting. 2 having forbearance; long-suffering.
▸**en'duringly** ADVERB ▸**en'duringness** NOUN

end user NOUN 1 **a** (in international trading) the person, organization, or nation that will be the ultimate recipient of goods, esp such as arms or advanced technology. **b** (*as modifier*): *an end-user certificate*. 2 *Computing* the ultimate destination, such as a program or operator, of information that is being transferred within a system.

endways ('ɛnd,weɪz) *or esp US and Canadian* **endwise** ('ɛnd,waɪz) ADVERB 1 having the end forwards or upwards. ◆ ADJECTIVE 2 vertical or upright. 3 lengthways. 4 standing or lying end to end.

Endymion (ɛn'dɪmɪən) NOUN *Greek myth* a handsome youth who was visited every night by the moon goddess Selene, who loved him.

endysis (ɛn'daɪsɪs) NOUN *Zoology* the formation of new layers of integument after ecdysis.

end zone NOUN *American football* the area behind the goals at each end of the field that the ball must cross for a touchdown to be awarded.

ENE SYMBOL FOR east-northeast.

-ene NOUN COMBINING FORM (in chemistry) indicating an unsaturated compound containing double bonds: *benzene; ethylene*.
▷HISTORY from Greek *-ēnē*, feminine patronymic suffix

ENEA ABBREVIATION FOR European Nuclear Energy Agency: the European body responsible for the development of nuclear-generated electric power.

enema ('ɛnɪmə) NOUN, *plural* **-mas** *or* **-mata** (-mətə). *Med* 1 the introduction of liquid into the rectum to evacuate the bowels, medicate, or nourish. 2 the liquid so introduced.
▷HISTORY C15: from New Latin, from Greek: injection, from *enienai* to send in, from *hienai* to send

enemy ('ɛnəmɪ) NOUN, *plural* **-mies**. 1 a person hostile or opposed to a policy, cause, person, or group, esp one who actively tries to do damage; opponent. 2 **a** an armed adversary; opposing military force. **b** (*as modifier*): *enemy aircraft*. 3 **a** a hostile nation or people. **b** (*as modifier*): *an enemy alien*. 4 something that harms or opposes; adversary: *courage is the enemy of failure*. ◆ Related adjective **inimical**.
▷HISTORY C13: from Old French *enemi*, from Latin *inimīcus* hostile, from IN-[1] + *amīcus* friend

energetic (,ɛnə'dʒɛtɪk) ADJECTIVE having or showing much energy or force; vigorous.
▸**,ener'getically** ADVERB

energetics (,ɛnə'dʒɛtɪks) NOUN (*functioning as singular*) the branch of science concerned with energy and its transformations.

energid ('ɛnədʒɪd) NOUN *Biology* a nucleus and the cytoplasm associated with it in a syncytium.
▷HISTORY C19: adapted from German, from ENERGY + -ID[1]

energize *or* **energise** ('ɛnə,dʒaɪz) VERB 1 to have or cause to have energy; invigorate. 2 (*tr*) to apply a source of electric current or electromotive force to (a circuit, field winding, etc.).
▸**'ener,gizer** *or* **'ener,giser** NOUN

energumen (,ɛnə'gjuːmɛn) NOUN 1 a person thought to be possessed by an evil spirit. 2 a fanatic or zealot.
▷HISTORY C18: via Late Latin from Greek *energoumenos* having been worked on, from *energein* to be in action, from *energos* effective; see ENERGY

energy ('ɛnədʒɪ) NOUN, *plural* **-gies**. 1 intensity or vitality of action or expression; forcefulness. 2 capacity or tendency for intense activity; vigour. 3 vigorous or intense action; exertion. 4 *Physics* **a** the capacity of a body or system to do work. **b** a measure of this capacity, expressed as the work that it does in changing to some specified reference state. It is measured in joules (SI units). Symbol: *E*. See also **kinetic energy, potential energy.**
▷HISTORY C16: from Late Latin *energīa*, from Greek *energeia* activity, from *energos* effective, from EN-[2] + *ergon* work

energy band NOUN *Physics* a range of energies associated with the quantum states of electrons in a crystalline solid. In a semiconductor or an insulator there is a **valence band** containing many states, most of which are occupied. Above this is a **forbidden band** with only a few isolated states caused by impurities. Above this is a **conduction band** containing many states most of which are empty. In a metal there is a continuous **valence-conduction band**. See also **energy gap.**

energy conversion NOUN the process of changing one form of energy into another, such as nuclear energy into heat or solar energy into electrical energy.

energy crop NOUN a crop that is grown because it can be used as fuel.

energy drink NOUN a soft drink containing ingredients designed to boost the drinker's energy, esp after exercise.

energy gap NOUN *Physics* the difference of energy between the bottom of the conduction band and the top of the valence band of the electrons in a crystalline solid. For values below about 2eV the substance is considered to be a semiconductor whilst for higher values it is considered to be an insulator.

energy level NOUN *Physics* 1 a constant value of energy in the distribution of energies among a number of atomic particles. 2 the energy of a quantum state of a system. The terms **energy level** and **energy state** are often used loosely to mean **quantum state**. This is avoided in precise communication.

energy-smart ADJECTIVE using electrical power in an efficient or economical way.

enervate VERB ('ɛnə,veɪt) 1 (*tr*) to deprive of strength or vitality; weaken physically or mentally; debilitate. ◆ ADJECTIVE (ɪ'nɜːvɪt) 2 deprived of strength or vitality; weakened.
▷HISTORY C17: from Latin *ēnervāre* to remove the nerves from, from *nervus* nerve, sinew
▸**,ener'vation** NOUN ▸**'ener,vative** ADJECTIVE ▸**'ener,vator** NOUN

enervating ('ɛnə,veɪtɪŋ) ADJECTIVE tending to deprive of strength or vitality; physically or mentally weakening; debilitating.

enface (ɪn'feɪs) VERB (*tr*) to write, print, or stamp (something) on the face of (a document).
▸**en'facement** NOUN

en face *French* (ɑ̃ fas) ADJECTIVE 1 facing forwards. 2 opposite; facing.

en famille *French* (ɑ̃ famij) ADVERB 1 with one's family; at home. 2 in a casual way; informally.

enfant sauvage (*French* ɑ̃fɑ̃ sovaʒ) NOUN, *plural* ***enfants sauvages*** (ɑ̃fɑ̃ sovaʒ). a person given to naive, undisciplined, or unpredictable behaviour, largely because of youth and inexperience.
▷HISTORY C20: literally: wild child

enfant terrible *French* (ɑ̃fɑ̃ tɛriblə) NOUN, *plural* ***enfants terribles*** (ɑ̃fɑ̃ tɛriblə). a person given to unconventional conduct or indiscreet remarks.
▷HISTORY C19: literally: terrible child

enfeeble (ɪn'fiːbᵊl) VERB (*tr*) to make weak; deprive of strength.
▸**en'feeblement** NOUN ▸**en'feebler** NOUN

enfeoff (ɪn'fiːf) VERB (*tr*) 1 *Property law* to invest (a person) with possession of a freehold estate in land. 2 (in feudal society) to take (someone) into vassalage by giving a fee or fief in return for certain services.
▷HISTORY C14: from Anglo-French *enfeoffer*; see FIEF
▸**en'feoffment** NOUN

en fête *French* (ɑ̃ fɛt) ADVERB 1 dressed for a festivity. 2 engaged in a festivity.
▷HISTORY C19: literally: in festival

Enfield ('ɛnfiːld) NOUN a borough of Greater London: a N residential suburb. Pop.: 273 563 (2001 est.). Area: 55 sq. km (31 sq. miles).

Enfield rifle NOUN 1 a breech-loading bolt-action magazine rifle, usually .303 calibre, used by the British army until World War II and by other countries. 2 a nineteenth-century muzzle-loading musket used by the British army.
▷HISTORY C19: from ENFIELD, where it was first made

enfilade (,ɛnfɪ'leɪd) *Military* ◆ NOUN 1 a position or formation subject to fire from a flank along the length of its front. ◆ VERB (*tr*) 2 to subject (a position or formation) to fire from a flank. 3 to position (troops or guns) so as to be able to fire at a flank.
▷HISTORY C18: from French: suite, from *enfiler* to thread on string, from *fil* thread

enfleurage *French* (ɑ̃flœraʒ) NOUN the process of exposing odourless oils to the scent of fresh flowers, used in perfume-making.
▷HISTORY C19: literally: inflowering

enfold *or* **infold** (ɪn'fəʊld) VERB (*tr*) 1 to cover by enclosing. 2 to embrace. 3 to form with or as with folds.
▸**en'folder** *or* **in'folder** NOUN ▸**en'foldment** *or* **in'foldment** NOUN

enforce (ɪn'fɔːs) VERB (*tr*) 1 to ensure observance of or obedience to (a law, decision, etc.). 2 to impose (obedience, loyalty, etc.) by or as by force. 3 to emphasize or reinforce (an argument, demand, etc.).
▸**en'forceable** ADJECTIVE ▸**en,forcea'bility** NOUN
▸**enforcedly** (ɪn'fɔːsɪdlɪ) ADVERB ▸**en'forcement** NOUN
▸**en'forcer** NOUN

enfranchise (ɪn'fræntʃaɪz) VERB (*tr*) 1 to grant the power of voting to, esp as a right of citizenship. 2 to liberate, as from servitude. 3 (in England) to invest (a town, city, etc.) with the right to be represented in Parliament. 4 *English law* to convert (leasehold) to freehold.
▸**en'franchisement** NOUN ▸**en'franchiser** NOUN

eng (ɛŋ) NOUN *Phonetics* another name for **agma.**

ENG ABBREVIATION FOR electronic news gathering: TV news obtained at the point of action by means of modern video equipment.

eng. 1 engineer. 2 engineering.

Eng. ABBREVIATION FOR: 1 England. 2 English.

Engadine ('ɛŋgə,diːn) NOUN the upper part of the valley of the River Inn in Switzerland, in Graubünden canton: tourist and winter sports centre.

engage (ɪn'geɪdʒ) VERB (*mainly tr*) 1 to secure the services of; employ. 2 to secure for use; reserve: *engage a room*. 3 to involve (a person or his attention) intensely; engross; occupy. 4 to attract (the affection) of (a person): *her innocence engaged him*. 5 to draw (somebody) into conversation. 6 (*intr*) to take part; participate: *he engages in many sports*. 7 to promise (to do something). 8 (*also intr*) *Military* to begin an action with (an enemy). 9 to bring (a mechanism) into operation: *he engaged the clutch*. 10 (*also intr*) to undergo or cause to undergo interlocking, as of the components of a driving mechanism, such as a gear train. 11 *Machinery* to locate (a locking device) in its operative position or to advance (a tool) into a workpiece to commence cutting.
▷HISTORY C15: from Old French *engagier*, from EN-[1] + *gage* a pledge, see GAGE[1]
▸**en'gager** NOUN

engagé *French* (ɑ̃gaʒe) ADJECTIVE (of a writer or artist, esp a man) morally or politically committed to some ideology.

engaged (ɪn'geɪdʒd) ADJECTIVE 1 pledged to be married; betrothed. 2 employed, occupied, or busy. 3 *Architect* built against or attached to a wall or similar structure: *an engaged column*. 4 (of a telephone line) already in use.
▸**engagedly** (ɪn'geɪdʒɪdlɪ) ADVERB

engaged tone NOUN *Brit* a repeated single note heard on a telephone when the number called is already in use. US and Canadian equivalent: **busy signal.** Compare **ringing tone, dialling tone.**

engagée *French* (ɑ̃gaʒe) ADJECTIVE (of a female writer or artist) morally or politically committed to some ideology.

engagement (ɪn'geɪdʒmənt) NOUN 1 a pledge of marriage; betrothal. 2 an appointment or arrangement, esp for business or social purposes. 3 the act of engaging or condition of being engaged. 4 a promise, obligation, or other condition that binds. 5 a period of employment, esp a limited period. 6 an action; battle. 7 (*plural*) financial obligations.

engagement ring NOUN a ring given by a man to a woman as a token of their betrothal.

engaging (ɪn'geɪdʒɪŋ) ADJECTIVE pleasing, charming, or winning.

▸**en'gagingly** ADVERB ▸**en'gagingness** NOUN

en garde *French* (ɑ̃ gard) INTERJECTION 1 on guard; a call to a fencer to adopt a defensive stance in readiness for an attack or bout. ◆ ADJECTIVE 2 (of a fencer) in such a stance.

engender (ɪnˈdʒɛndə) VERB 1 (*tr*) to bring about or give rise to; produce or cause. 2 to be born or cause to be born; bring or come into being.
▹HISTORY C14: from Old French *engendrer,* from Latin *ingenerāre,* from *generāre* to beget
▸**en'genderer** NOUN ▸**en'genderment** NOUN

engine (ˈɛndʒɪn) NOUN 1 any machine designed to convert energy, esp heat energy, into mechanical work: *a steam engine; a petrol engine.* 2 **a** a railway locomotive. **b** (*as modifier*): *the engine cab.* 3 *Military* any of various pieces of equipment formerly used in warfare, such as a battering ram or gun. 4 *Obsolete* any instrument or device: *engines of torture.*
▹HISTORY C13: from Old French *engin,* from Latin *ingenium* nature, talent, ingenious contrivance, from IN-[2] + *-genium,* related to *gignere* to beget, produce

engine driver NOUN *Chiefly Brit* a man who drives a railway locomotive; train driver.

engineer (ˌɛndʒɪˈnɪə) NOUN 1 a person trained in any branch of the profession of engineering. 2 the originator or manager of a situation, system, etc. 3 a mechanic; one who repairs or services machines. 4 *US and Canadian* the driver of a railway locomotive. 5 an officer responsible for a ship's engines. 6 Informal name: **sapper.** a member of the armed forces, esp the army, trained in engineering and construction work. ◆ VERB (*tr*) 7 to originate, cause, or plan in a clever or devious manner: *he engineered the minister's downfall.* 8 to design, plan, or construct as a professional engineer.
▹HISTORY C14: *enginer,* from Old French *engigneor,* from *engignier* to contrive, ultimately from Latin *ingenium* skill, talent; see ENGINE

engineering (ˌɛndʒɪˈnɪərɪŋ) NOUN the profession of applying scientific principles to the design, construction, and maintenance of engines, cars, machines, etc. (**mechanical engineering**), buildings, bridges, roads, etc. (**civil engineering**), electrical machines and communication systems (**electrical engineering**), chemical plant and machinery (**chemical engineering**), or aircraft (**aeronautical engineering**). See also **military engineering.**

engineer officer NOUN a ship's officer who is qualified to be in charge of the vessel's propulsion and other machinery.

engine pod NOUN *Aeronautics* an aircraft turbojet unit comprising the engine and its cowling suspended by a pylon, often below the wing.

engine room NOUN a place where engines are housed, esp on a ship.

enginery (ˈɛndʒɪnrɪ) NOUN, *plural* **-ries.** 1 a collection or assembly of engines; machinery. 2 engines employed in warfare. 3 *Rare* skilful manoeuvring or contrivance.

englacial (ɪnˈgleɪsɪəl) ADJECTIVE embedded in, carried by, or running through a glacier: *englacial drift; an englacial river.*
▸**en'glacially** ADVERB

England (ˈɪŋglənd) NOUN the largest division of Great Britain, bordering on Scotland and Wales: unified in the mid-tenth century and conquered by the Normans in 1066; united with Wales in 1536 and Scotland in 1707; monarchy overthrown in 1649 but restored in 1660. Capital: London. Pop.: 49 138 831 (2001). Area: 130 439 sq. km (50 352 sq. miles). See **United Kingdom, Great Britain.**

Engler degrees (ˈɛŋlə) NOUN (*functioning as singular*) a scale of measurement of viscosity based on the ratio of the time taken by a particular liquid to flow through a standard orifice to the time taken by water to flow through the same orifice.
▹HISTORY named after C. *Engler* (1842–1925), German chemist, who proposed it

English (ˈɪŋglɪʃ) NOUN 1 the official language of Britain, the US, most parts of the Commonwealth, and certain other countries. It is the native language of over 280 million people and is acquired as a second language by many more. It is an Indo-European language belonging to the West Germanic branch. See also **Middle English, Old English, Modern English.** 2 **the English.** (*functioning as plural*) the natives or inhabitants of England collectively. 3 (formerly) a size of printer's type approximately equal to 14 point. 4 an old style of black-letter typeface. 5 (*often not capital*) the usual US and Canadian term for **side** (in billiards). ◆ ADJECTIVE 6 denoting, using, or relating to the English language. 7 relating to or characteristic of England or the English. ◆ VERB (*tr*) 8 *Archaic* to translate or adapt into English. ◆ Related prefix **Anglo-.**
▸**'Englishness** NOUN

English bond NOUN a bond used in brickwork that has a course of headers alternating with a course of stretchers.

English Canadian NOUN a Canadian citizen whose first language is English, esp one of English descent.

English Channel NOUN an arm of the Atlantic Ocean between S England and N France, linked with the North Sea by the Strait of Dover. Length: about 560 km (350 miles). Width: between 32 km (20 miles) and 161 km (100 miles).

English flute NOUN *Music* another name for **recorder** (sense 4).

English Heritage NOUN an organization, partly funded by government aid, that looks after ancient monuments and historic buildings in England. Official name: **The Historic Buildings and Monuments Commission for England.**

English horn NOUN *Music* another name for **cor anglais.**

Englishism (ˈɪŋglɪˌʃɪzəm) NOUN *Chiefly US* 1 an English custom, practice, etc. 2 a word or expression not found in forms of English other than British English; Anglicism. 3 high regard for English customs, institutions, etc.

Englishman (ˈɪŋglɪʃmən) NOUN, *plural* **-men.** a male native or inhabitant of England.

Englishman's tie *or* **knot** NOUN a type of knot for tying together heavy ropes.

Englishry (ˈɪŋglɪʃrɪ) NOUN *Now rare* 1 people of English descent, esp in Ireland. 2 the fact or condition of being an Englishman or Englishwoman, esp by birth.

English self NOUN a breed of short-haired guinea pig that is a single colour throughout.

English setter NOUN a breed of setter having a white coat speckled with liver, brown, or yellowish markings.

English springer spaniel NOUN See **springer spaniel.**

Englishwoman (ˈɪŋglɪʃˌwʊmən) NOUN, *plural* **-women.** a female native or inhabitant of England.

englut (ɪnˈglʌt) VERB **-gluts, -glutting, -glutted.** (*tr*) *Literary* 1 to devour ravenously; swallow eagerly. 2 to glut or sate (oneself); surfeit; satiate.

engorge (ɪnˈgɔːdʒ) VERB (*tr*) 1 *Pathol* to congest with blood. 2 to eat (food) ravenously or greedily. 3 to gorge (oneself); glut; satiate.
▸**en'gorgement** NOUN

engr ABBREVIATION FOR: 1 engineer. 2 engraver.

engraft *or* **ingraft** (ɪnˈgrɑːft) VERB (*tr*) 1 to graft (a shoot, bud, etc.) onto a stock. 2 to incorporate in a firm or permanent way; implant: *they engrafted their principles into the document.*
▸ˌ**engraf'tation** *or* ˌ**ingraf'tation** *or* **en'graftment** *or* **in'graftment** NOUN

engrail (ɪnˈgreɪl) VERB (*tr*) to decorate or mark (the edge of) (a coin) with small carved notches.
▹HISTORY C14: from Old French *engresler,* from EN-[1] + *gresle* slim, from Latin *gracilis* slender, graceful
▸**en'grailment** NOUN

engrain (ɪnˈgreɪn) VERB a variant spelling of **ingrain.**

engram (ˈɛngræm) NOUN *Psychol* the physical basis of an individual memory in the brain. See also **memory trace.**
▹HISTORY C20: from German *Engramm,* from Greek *en-* IN + *gramma* letter
▸**en'grammic** *or* ˌ**engram'matic** ADJECTIVE

engrave (ɪnˈgreɪv) VERB (*tr*) 1 to inscribe (a design, writing, etc.) onto (a block, plate, or other surface used for printing) by carving, etching with acid, or other process. 2 to print (designs or characters) from a printing plate so made. 3 to fix deeply or permanently in the mind.
▹HISTORY C16: from EN-[1] + GRAVE[3], on the model of French *engraver*
▸**en'graver** NOUN

engraving (ɪnˈgreɪvɪŋ) NOUN 1 the art of a person who engraves. 2 a block, plate, or other surface that has been engraved. 3 a print made from such a surface. Related adjective: **glyptic.**

engross (ɪnˈgrəʊs) VERB (*tr*) 1 to occupy one's attention completely; absorb. 2 to write or copy (manuscript) in large legible handwriting. 3 *Law* to write or type out formally (a deed, agreement, or other document) preparatory to execution. 4 another word for **corner** (sense 21b).
▹HISTORY C14 (in the sense: to buy up wholesale): from Old French *en gros* in quantity; C15 (in the sense: to write in large letters): probably from Medieval Latin *ingrossāre;* both from Latin *grossus* thick, GROSS
▸**en'grossed** ADJECTIVE ▸**engrossedly** (ɪnˈgrəʊsɪdlɪ) ADVERB ▸**en'grosser** NOUN

engrossing (ɪnˈgrəʊsɪŋ) ADJECTIVE so interesting as to occupy one's attention completely; absorbing.

engrossment (ɪnˈgrəʊsmənt) NOUN 1 a deed or other document that has been engrossed. 2 the state of being engrossed.

engulf *or* **ingulf** (ɪnˈgʌlf) VERB (*tr*) 1 to immerse, plunge, bury, or swallow up. 2 (*often passive*) to overwhelm: *engulfed by debts.*
▸**en'gulfment** NOUN

enhance (ɪnˈhɑːns) VERB (*tr*) to intensify or increase in quality, value, power, etc.; improve; augment.
▹HISTORY C14: from Old French *enhaucier,* from EN-[1] + *haucier* to raise, from Vulgar Latin *altiāre* (unattested), from Latin *altus* high
▸**en'hancement** NOUN ▸**en'hancer** NOUN ▸**en'hancive** ADJECTIVE

enhanced oil recovery NOUN any of several techniques that make it possible to recover more oil than can be obtained by natural pressure, such as the injection of fluid or gases into an oilfield to force more oil to the surface.

enhanced radiation weapon NOUN a technical name for **neutron bomb.**

enharmonic (ˌɛnhɑːˈmɒnɪk) ADJECTIVE *Music* 1 denoting or relating to a small difference in pitch between two notes such as A flat and G sharp: not present in instruments of equal temperament such as the piano, but significant in the intonation of stringed and wind instruments. 2 denoting or relating to enharmonic modulation.
▹HISTORY C17: from Latin *enharmonicus,* from Greek *enarmonios,* from EN-[2] + *harmonia;* see HARMONY
▸ˌ**enhar'monically** ADVERB

enharmonic modulation NOUN *Music* a change of key achieved by regarding a note in one key as an equivalent note in another. Thus E flat in the key of A flat could be regarded as D sharp in the key of B major.

Enid (ˈiːnɪd) NOUN (in Arthurian legend) the faithful wife of Geraint.

enigma (ɪˈnɪgmə) NOUN a person, thing, or situation that is mysterious, puzzling, or ambiguous.
▹HISTORY C16: from Latin *aenigma,* from Greek *ainigma,* from *ainissesthai* to speak in riddles, from *ainos* fable, story
▸**enigmatic** (ˌɛnɪgˈmætɪk) *or* ˌ**enig'matical** ADJECTIVE ▸ˌ**enig'matically** ADVERB

enigmatize *or* **enigmatise** (ɪˈnɪgməˌtaɪz) VERB (*tr*) to make enigmatic.

enisle (ɪnˈaɪl) VERB (*tr*) *Poetic* to put on or make into an island.

Eniwetok (ˌɛnəˈwiːtɒk, əˈniːwɪˌtɔːk) NOUN an atoll in the W Pacific Ocean, in the NW Marshall Islands: taken by the US from Japan in 1944; became a naval base and later a testing ground for atomic weapons. Pop.: 715 (latest est.).

enjambment *or* **enjambement** (ɪnˈdʒæmmənt; *French* ɑ̃ʒɑ̃bmɑ̃) NOUN *Prosody* the running over of a sentence from one line of verse into the next.
▹HISTORY C19: from French, literally: a straddling, from *enjamber* to straddle, from EN-[1] + *jambe* leg; see JAMB
▸**en'jambed** ADJECTIVE

enjoin (ɪnˈdʒɔɪn) VERB (*tr*) 1 to order (someone) to do (something); urge strongly; command. 2 to impose or prescribe (a condition, mode of behaviour, etc.). 3 *Law* to require (a person) to do

or refrain from doing (some act), esp by issuing an injunction.
▷HISTORY C13: from Old French *enjoindre,* from Latin *injungere* to fasten to, from IN-[2] + *jungere* to JOIN
▸**en'joiner** NOUN ▸**en'joinment** NOUN

enjoy (ɪnˈdʒɔɪ) VERB *(tr)* [1] to receive pleasure from; take joy in. [2] to have the benefit of; use with satisfaction. [3] to have as a condition; experience: *the land enjoyed a summer of rain.* [4] *Archaic* to have sexual intercourse with. [5] **enjoy oneself.** to have a good time.
▷HISTORY C14: from Old French *enjoir,* from EN-[1] + *joir* to find pleasure in, from Latin *gaudēre* to rejoice
▸**en'joyable** ADJECTIVE ▸**en'joyableness** NOUN ▸**en'joyably** ADVERB ▸**en'joyer** NOUN

enjoyment (ɪnˈdʒɔɪmənt) NOUN [1] the act or condition of receiving pleasure from something. [2] the use or possession of something that is satisfying or beneficial. [3] something that provides joy or satisfaction. [4] the possession or exercise of a legal right.

enkephalin (ɛnˈkɛfəlɪn) *or* **encephalin** (ɛnˈsɛfəlɪn) NOUN a chemical occurring in the brain, having effects similar to those of morphine. See also **endorphin.**

enkindle (ɪnˈkɪndəl) VERB *(tr)* [1] to set on fire; kindle. [2] to excite to activity or ardour; arouse.
▸**en'kindler** NOUN

enlace (ɪnˈleɪs) VERB *(tr)* [1] to bind or encircle with or as with laces. [2] to entangle; intertwine.
▸**en'lacement** NOUN

enlarge (ɪnˈlɑːdʒ) VERB [1] to make or grow larger in size, scope, etc.; increase or expand. [2] *(tr)* to make (a photographic print) of a larger size than the negative. [3] *(intr; foll by on or upon)* to speak or write (about) in greater detail; expatiate (on).
▸**en'largeable** ADJECTIVE

enlargement (ɪnˈlɑːdʒmənt) NOUN [1] the act of enlarging or the condition of being enlarged. [2] something that enlarges or is intended to enlarge. [3] a photographic print that is larger than the negative from which it is made.

enlarger (ɪnˈlɑːdʒə) NOUN an optical instrument for making enlarged photographic prints in which a negative is brightly illuminated and its enlarged image is focused onto a sheet of sensitized paper.

enlighten (ɪnˈlaɪtən) VERB *(tr)* [1] to give information or understanding to; instruct; edify. [2] to free from ignorance, prejudice, or superstition. [3] to give spiritual or religious revelation to. [4] *Poetic* to shed light on.
▸**en'lightener** NOUN ▸**en'lightening** ADJECTIVE

enlightened (ɪnˈlaɪtənd) ADJECTIVE [1] factually well-informed, tolerant of alternative opinions, and guided by rational thought: *an enlightened administration; enlightened self-interest.* [2] privy to or claiming a sense of spiritual or religious revelation of truth: *an enlightened spiritual master.*

enlightenment (ɪnˈlaɪtənmənt) NOUN [1] the act or means of enlightening or the state of being enlightened. [2] *Buddhism* the awakening to ultimate truth by which man is freed from the endless cycle of personal reincarnations to which all men are otherwise subject. [3] *Hinduism* a state of transcendent divine experience represented by Vishnu: regarded as a goal of all religion.

Enlightenment (ɪnˈlaɪtənmənt) NOUN **the.** an 18th-century philosophical movement stressing the importance of reason and the critical reappraisal of existing ideas and social institutions.

enlist (ɪnˈlɪst) VERB [1] to enter or persuade to enter into an engagement to serve in the armed forces. [2] *(tr)* to engage or secure (a person, his services, or his support) for a venture, cause, etc. [3] *(intr; foll by in)* to enter into or join an enterprise, cause, etc.
▸**en'lister** NOUN ▸**en'listment** NOUN

enlisted man NOUN *US* a serviceman who holds neither a commission nor a warrant and is not under training for officer rank as a cadet or midshipman.

enliven (ɪnˈlaɪvən) VERB *(tr)* [1] to make active, vivacious, or spirited; invigorate. [2] to make cheerful or bright; gladden or brighten.
▸**en'livener** NOUN ▸**en'livening** ADJECTIVE ▸**en'livenment** NOUN

en masse (*French* ɑ̃ mas) ADVERB in a group, body, or mass; as a whole; all together.
▷HISTORY C19: from French

enmesh, inmesh (ɪnˈmɛʃ), *or* **immesh** VERB *(tr)* to catch or involve in or as if in a net or snare; entangle.
▸**en'meshment** NOUN

enmity (ˈɛnmɪtɪ) NOUN, *plural* **-ties.** a feeling of hostility or ill will, as between enemies; antagonism.
▷HISTORY C13: from Old French *enemistié,* from *enemi* ENEMY

ennage (ˈɛnɪdʒ) NOUN *Printing* the total number of ens in a piece of matter to be set in type.

ennead (ˈɛnɪˌæd) NOUN [1] a group or series of nine. [2] the sum of or number nine.
▷HISTORY C17: from Greek *enneas,* from *ennea* nine
▸ˌ**enne'adic** ADJECTIVE

enneagon (ˈɛnɪəgən) NOUN another name for **nonagon.**

enneahedron (ˌɛnɪəˈhiːdrən) NOUN, *plural* **-drons** *or* **-dra** (-drə). a solid figure having nine plane faces. See also **polyhedron.**
▸ˌ**ennea'hedral** ADJECTIVE

Ennerdale Water (ˈɛnəˌdeɪl) NOUN a lake in NW England, in Cumbria in the Lake District. Length: 4 km (2.5 miles).

Ennis (ˈɛnɪs) NOUN a town in the W Republic of Ireland, county town of Co. Clare. Pop.: 13 750 (1991).

Enniskillen (ˌɛnɪsˈkɪlɪn) *or formerly* **Inniskilling** NOUN a town in SW Northern Ireland, in Fermanagh, on an island in the River Erne: scene of the defeat of James II's forces in 1689. Pop.: 11 436 (1991).

ennoble (ɪˈnəʊbəl) VERB *(tr)* [1] to make noble, honourable, or excellent; dignify; exalt. [2] to raise to a noble rank; confer a title of nobility upon.
▸**en'noblement** NOUN ▸**en'nobler** NOUN ▸**en'nobling** ADJECTIVE

ennog (ˈɛnɒg) NOUN *Northern English dialect* a back alley.

ennui (ˈɒnwiː; *French* ɑ̃nɥi) NOUN a feeling of listlessness and general dissatisfaction resulting from lack of activity or excitement.
▷HISTORY C18: from French: apathy, from Old French *enui* annoyance, vexation; see ANNOY

ennuied, ennuyed (ˈɒnwiːd), *or* **ennuyé** (*French* ɑ̃nɥije) ADJECTIVE affected with ennui; bored.

ENO ABBREVIATION FOR English National Opera.

Enoch (ˈiːnɒk) NOUN *Old Testament* [1] the eldest son of Cain after whom the first city was named (Genesis 4:17). [2] the father of Methuselah: said to have walked with God and to have been taken by God at the end of his earthly life (Genesis 5:24).

enol (ˈiːnɒl) NOUN any organic compound containing the group -CH:CO-, often existing in chemical equilibrium with the corresponding keto form. See **keto-enol tautomerism.**
▷HISTORY C19: from -ENE + -OL[1]
▸**e'nolic** ADJECTIVE

enology (iːˈnɒlədʒɪ) NOUN the usual US spelling of **oenology.**

enormity (ɪˈnɔːmɪtɪ) NOUN, *plural* **-ties.** [1] the quality or character of being outrageous; extreme wickedness. [2] an act of great wickedness; atrocity. [3] *Informal* vastness of size or extent.
▷HISTORY C15: from Old French *enormite,* from Late Latin *ēnormitās* hugeness; see ENORMOUS

> **Language note** In modern English, it is common to talk about the *enormity* of something such as a task or a problem, but one should not talk about the *enormity* of an object or area: *distribution is a problem because of India's enormous size* (not *India's enormity*).

enormous (ɪˈnɔːməs) ADJECTIVE [1] unusually large in size, extent, or degree; immense; vast. [2] *Archaic* extremely wicked; heinous.
▷HISTORY C16: from Latin *ēnormis,* from *ē-* out of, away from + *norma* rule, pattern
▸**e'normously** ADVERB ▸**e'normousness** NOUN

Enos (ˈiːnɒs) NOUN *Old Testament* a son of Seth (Genesis 4:26; 5:6).

enosis (ˈɛnəʊsɪs) NOUN the union of Greece and Cyprus: the aim of a group of Greek Cypriots.
▷HISTORY C20: Modern Greek: from Greek *henoun* to unite, from *heis* one

enough (ɪˈnʌf) DETERMINER [1] **a** sufficient to answer a need, demand, supposition, or requirement; adequate: *enough cake.* **b** *(as pronoun)*: *enough is now known.* [2] **that's enough!** that will do: used to put an end to an action, speech, performance, etc. ◆ ADVERB [3] so as to be adequate or sufficient; as much as necessary: *you have worked hard enough.* [4] *(not used with a negative)* very or quite; rather: *she was pleased enough to see me.* [5] (intensifier): *oddly enough; surprisingly enough.* [6] just adequately; tolerably: *he did it well enough.*
▷HISTORY Old English *genōh;* related to Old Norse *gnōgr,* Gothic *ganōhs,* Old High German *ginuog*

enounce (ɪˈnaʊns) VERB *(tr) Formal* [1] to enunciate. [2] to pronounce.
▷HISTORY C19: from French *énoncer,* from Latin *ēnuntiāre* ENUNCIATE
▸**e'nouncement** NOUN

enow (ɪˈnaʊ) ADJECTIVE, ADVERB an archaic word for **enough.**

en passant (ɒn pæˈsɑːnt; *French* ɑ̃ pasɑ̃) ADVERB in passing: in chess, said of capturing a pawn that has made an initial move of two squares to its fourth rank, bypassing the square where an enemy pawn on its own fifth rank could capture it. The capture is made as if the captured pawn had moved one square instead of two.
▷HISTORY C17: from French

en pension *French* (ɑ̃ pɑ̃sjɔ̃) ADVERB in lodgings with all meals provided.

enphytotic (ˌɛnfaɪˈtɒtɪk) ADJECTIVE (of plant diseases) causing a constant amount of damage each year.
▷HISTORY C20: from EN-[2] + -PHYTE + -OTIC

enplane (ɛnˈpleɪn) VERB *(intr)* to board an aircraft.

en plein (*French* ɑ̃ plɛ̃) ADJECTIVE *(postpositive),* ADVERB (of a gambling bet) placed entirely on a single number, etc.
▷HISTORY from French: in full

enprint (ˈɛnprɪnt) NOUN a standard photographic print (5 × 3.5 in.) produced from a negative.

en prise (*French* ɑ̃ priz) ADJECTIVE *(postpositive),* ADVERB (of a chess piece) exposed to capture.
▷HISTORY C19: from French; see PRIZE[1]

enquire (ɪnˈkwaɪə) VERB a variant of **inquire.**
▸**en'quirer** NOUN ▸**en'quiry** NOUN

enrage (ɪnˈreɪdʒ) VERB *(tr)* to provoke to fury; put into a rage; anger.
▸**en'raged** ADJECTIVE ▸**enragedly** (ɪnˈreɪdʒɪdlɪ) ADVERB
▸**en'ragement** NOUN

en rapport *French* (ɑ̃ rapɔr) ADJECTIVE *(postpositive),* ADVERB in sympathy, harmony, or accord.

enrapture (ɪnˈræptʃə) VERB *(tr)* to fill with delight; enchant.

enrich (ɪnˈrɪtʃ) VERB *(tr)* [1] to increase the wealth of. [2] to endow with fine or desirable qualities: *to enrich one's experience by travelling.* [3] to make more beautiful; adorn; decorate: *a robe enriched with jewels.* [4] to improve in quality, colour, flavour, etc. [5] to increase the food value of by adding nutrients: *to enrich dog biscuits with calcium.* [6] to make (soil) more productive, esp by adding fertilizer. [7] *Physics* to increase the concentration or abundance of one component or isotope in (a solution or mixture); concentrate: *to enrich a solution by evaporation; enrich a nuclear fuel.*
▸**en'riched** ADJECTIVE ▸**en'richer** NOUN ▸**en'richment** NOUN

enrobe (ɪnˈrəʊb) VERB *(tr)* to dress in or as if in a robe; attire.
▸**en'rober** NOUN

enrol *or US* **enroll** (ɪnˈrəʊl) VERB **-rols** *or US* **-rolls, -rolling, -rolled.** *(mainly tr)* [1] to record or note in a roll or list. [2] *(also intr)* to become or cause to become a member; enlist; register. [3] to put on record; record. [4] *Rare* to roll or wrap up.
▸ˌ**enrol'lee** NOUN ▸**en'roller** NOUN

enrolment *or US* **enrollment** (ɪnˈrəʊlmənt) NOUN [1] the act of enrolling or state of being enrolled. [2] a list of people enrolled. [3] the total number of people enrolled.

enroot (ɪnˈruːt) VERB *(tr; usually passive)* [1] to establish (plants) by fixing their roots in the earth. [2] to fix firmly, implant, or embed: *to enroot an idea in the mind.*

en route (ɒn ˈruːt; *French* ɑ̃ rut) ADVERB on or along the way; on the road.
▷HISTORY C18: from French

ens (ɛnz) NOUN, *plural* **entia** (ˈɛnʃɪə). *Metaphysics* 1 being or existence in the most general abstract sense. 2 a real thing, esp as opposed to an attribute; entity.
▷HISTORY C16: from Late Latin, literally: being, from Latin *esse* to be

Ens. ABBREVIATION FOR Ensign.

ENSA (ˈɛnsə) NOUN ACRONYM FOR Entertainments National Service Association: a British organization providing entertainment for the armed forces during World War II.

ensample (ɛnˈsɑːmpᵊl) NOUN an archaic word for **example.**

ensanguine (ɪnˈsæŋgwɪn) VERB (*tr*) *Literary* to cover or stain with or as with blood.

Enschede (*Dutch* ˈɛnsxədeː) NOUN a city in the E Netherlands, in Overijssel province: a major centre of the Dutch cotton industry. Pop.: 148 814 (1999 est.).

ensconce (ɪnˈskɒns) VERB (*tr; often passive*) 1 to establish or settle firmly or comfortably: *ensconced in a chair.* 2 to place in safety; hide.
▷HISTORY C16: see EN-[1], SCONCE[2]

ensemble (ɒnˈsɒmbᵊl; *French* ɑ̃sɑ̃blə) NOUN 1 all the parts of something considered together and in relation to the whole. 2 a person's complete costume; outfit. 3 **a** the cast of a play other than the principals; supporting players. **b** (*as modifier*): *an ensemble role.* 4 *Music* **a** a group of soloists singing or playing together. **b** (*as modifier*): *an ensemble passage.* 5 *Music* the degree of precision and unity exhibited by a group of instrumentalists or singers performing together: *the ensemble of the strings is good.* 6 the general or total effect of something made up of individual parts. 7 *Physics* **a** a set of systems (such as a set of collections of atoms) that are identical in all respects apart from the motions of their constituents. **b** a single system (such as a collection of atoms) in which the properties are determined by the statistical behaviour of its constituents. ◆ ADVERB 8 all together or at once. ◆ ADJECTIVE 9 (of a film or play) involving several separate but often interrelated story lines: *ensemble comedy drama.* 10 involving no individual star but several actors whose roles are of equal importance: *fine ensemble playing.*
▷HISTORY C15: from French: together, from Latin *insimul,* from IN-[2] + *simul* at the same time

enshrine *or* **inshrine** (ɪnˈʃraɪn) VERB (*tr*) 1 to place or enclose in or as if in a shrine. 2 to hold as sacred; cherish; treasure.
▸**enˈshrinement** NOUN

enshroud (ɪnˈʃraʊd) VERB (*tr*) to cover or hide with or as if with a shroud: *the sky was enshrouded in mist.*

ensiform (ˈɛnsɪˌfɔːm) ADJECTIVE *Biology* shaped like a sword blade: *ensiform leaves.*
▷HISTORY C16: from Latin *ensis* sword

ensign (ˈɛnsaɪn) NOUN 1 (*also* ˈɛnsən) a flag flown by a ship, branch of the armed forces, etc., to indicate nationality, allegiance, etc. See also **Red Ensign, White Ensign.** 2 any flag, standard, or banner. 3 a standard-bearer. 4 a symbol, token, or emblem; sign. 5 (in the US Navy) a commissioned officer of the lowest rank. 6 (in the British infantry) a colours bearer. 7 (formerly in the British infantry) a commissioned officer of the lowest rank.
▷HISTORY C14: from Old French *enseigne,* from Latin INSIGNIA
▸**ˈensignˌship** *or* **ˈensigncy** NOUN

ensilage (ˈɛnsɪlɪdʒ) NOUN 1 the process of ensiling green fodder. 2 a less common name for **silage.**

ensile (ɛnˈsaɪl, ˈɛnsaɪl) VERB (*tr*) 1 to store and preserve (green fodder) in an enclosed pit or silo. 2 to turn (green fodder) into silage by causing it to ferment in a closed pit or silo.
▷HISTORY C19: from French *ensiler,* from Spanish *ensilar,* from EN-[1] + *silo* SILO
▸**enˌsilaˈbility** NOUN

enslave (ɪnˈsleɪv) VERB (*tr*) to make a slave of; reduce to slavery; subjugate.
▸**enˈslavement** NOUN ▸**enˈslaver** NOUN

ensnare *or* **insnare** (ɪnˈsnɛə) VERB (*tr*) 1 to catch or trap in a snare. 2 to trap or gain power over someone by dishonest or underhand means.
▸**enˈsnarement** NOUN ▸**enˈsnarer** NOUN

ensoul *or* **insoul** (ɪnˈsəʊl) VERB (*tr*) 1 to endow with a soul. 2 to cherish within the soul.
▸**enˈsoulment** *or* **inˈsoulment** NOUN

ensphere *or* **insphere** (ɪnˈsfɪə) VERB (*tr*) 1 to enclose in or as if in a sphere. 2 to make spherical in form.

enstatite (ˈɛnstəˌtaɪt) NOUN a grey, green, yellow, or brown pyroxene mineral consisting of magnesium silicate in orthorhombic crystalline form. Formula: $Mg_2Si_2O_6$.
▷HISTORY C19: from Greek *enstatēs* adversary (referring to its refractory quality) + -ITE[1]

ensue (ɪnˈsjuː) VERB **-sues, -suing, -sued.** 1 (*intr*) to follow subsequently or in order; come next or afterwards. 2 (*intr*) to follow or occur as a consequence; result. 3 (*tr*) *Obsolete* to pursue.
▷HISTORY C14: from Anglo-French *ensuer,* from Old French *ensuivre,* from EN-[1] + *suivre* to follow, from Latin *sequī*

ensuing (ɪnˈsjuːɪŋ) 1 following subsequently or in order. 2 (*intr*) following or occurring as a consequence; resulting.

en suite *French* (ɑ̃ sɥit) ADVERB as part of a set; forming a unit: *a hotel room with bathroom en suite.*
▷HISTORY C19: literally: in sequence

ensure (ɛnˈʃʊə, -ˈʃɔː) *or esp US* **insure** VERB (*tr*) 1 (*may take a clause as object*) to make certain or sure; guarantee: *this victory will ensure his happiness.* 2 to make safe or secure; protect.
▸**enˈsurer** NOUN

enswathe (ɪnˈsweɪð) VERB (*tr*) to bind or wrap; swathe.
▸**enˈswathement** NOUN

ENT *Med* ABBREVIATION FOR ear, nose, and throat.

-ent SUFFIX FORMING ADJECTIVES AND NOUNS causing or performing an action or existing in a certain condition; the agent that performs an action: *astringent; dependent.*
▷HISTORY from Latin *-ent-, -ens,* present participial ending

entablature (ɛnˈtæblətʃə) NOUN *Architect* 1 the part of a classical temple above the columns, having an architrave, a frieze, and a cornice. 2 any construction of similar form.
▷HISTORY C17: from French, from Italian *intavolatura* something put on a table, hence, something laid flat, from *tavola* table, from Latin *tabula* TABLE

entablement (ɪnˈteɪbᵊlmənt) NOUN the platform of a pedestal, above the dado, that supports a statue.
▷HISTORY C17: from Old French

entail (ɪnˈteɪl) VERB (*tr*) 1 to bring about or impose by necessity; have as a necessary consequence: *this task entails careful thought.* 2 *Property law* to restrict (the descent of an estate) to a designated line of heirs. 3 *Logic* to have as a necessary consequence. ◆ NOUN 4 *Property law* **a** the restriction imposed by entailing an estate. **b** an estate that has been entailed.
▷HISTORY C14: *entaillen,* from EN-[1] + *taille* limitation, TAIL[2]
▸**enˈtailer** NOUN

entailment (ɪnˈteɪlmənt) NOUN 1 the act of entailing or the condition of being entailed. 2 *Philosophy, logic* **a** a relationship between propositions such that one must be true if the others are. **b** a proposition whose truth depends on such a relationship. Usual symbol: —ɜ See **fish-hook** (sense 2).

entamoeba (ˌɛntəˈmiːbə), **endamoeba,** *or US* **entameba, endameba** NOUN, *plural* **-bae** (-biː) *or* **-bas.** any parasitic amoeba of the genus *Entamoeba* (or *Endamoeba*), esp *E. histolytica,* which lives in the intestines of man and causes amoebic dysentery.

entangle (ɪnˈtæŋgᵊl) VERB (*tr*) 1 to catch or involve in or as if in a tangle; ensnare or enmesh. 2 to make tangled or twisted; snarl. 3 to make complicated; confuse. 4 to involve in difficulties; entrap.
▸**enˈtangler** NOUN

entanglement (ɪnˈtæŋgᵊlmənt) NOUN 1 something that entangles or is itself entangled. 2 a sexual relationship regarded as unfortunate, damaging, or compromising.

entasis (ˈɛntəsɪs) NOUN, *plural* **-ses** (-siːz). 1 a slightly convex curve given to the shaft of a column, pier, or similar structure, to correct the illusion of concavity produced by a straight shaft. 2 Also called: **entasia** (ɛnˈteɪzɪə). *Physiol* an involuntary or spasmodic muscular contraction.
▷HISTORY C18: from Greek, from *enteinein* to stretch tight, from *teinein* to stretch

Entebbe (ɛnˈtɛbɪ) NOUN a town in S Uganda, on Lake Victoria: British administrative centre of Uganda (1893–1958); international airport. Pop.: 41 638 (1991).

entelechy (ɛnˈtɛlɪkɪ) NOUN, *plural* **-chies.** *Metaphysics* 1 (in the philosophy of Aristotle) actuality as opposed to potentiality. 2 (in the system of Leibnitz) the soul or principle of perfection of an object or person; a monad or basic constituent. 3 something that contains or realizes a final cause, esp the vital force thought to direct the life of an organism.
▷HISTORY C17: from Late Latin *entelechia,* from Greek *entelekheia,* from EN-[2] + *telos* goal, completion + *ekhein* to have

entellus (ɛnˈtɛləs) NOUN an Old World monkey, *Presbytes entellus,* of S Asia. This langur is regarded as sacred in India. Also called: **hanuman.**
▷HISTORY C19: New Latin, apparently from the name of the aged Sicilian character in Book V of Virgil's *Aeneid*

entente (*French* ɑ̃tɑ̃t) NOUN 1 short for **entente cordiale.** 2 the parties to an entente cordiale collectively.
▷HISTORY C19: French: understanding

entente cordiale (*French* ɑ̃tɑ̃t kɔrdjal) NOUN 1 a friendly understanding between political powers: less formal than an alliance. 2 (*often capitals*) the understanding reached by France and Britain in April 1904, which settled outstanding colonial disputes.
▷HISTORY C19: French: cordial understanding

enter (ˈɛntə) VERB 1 to come or go into (a place, house, etc.). 2 to penetrate or pierce. 3 (*tr*) to introduce or insert. 4 to join (a party, organization, etc.). 5 (when *intr,* foll by *into*) to become involved or take part (in): *to enter a game; to enter into an agreement.* 6 (*tr*) to record (an item such as a commercial transaction) in a journal, account, register, etc. 7 (*tr*) to record (a name, etc.) on a list. 8 (*tr*) to present or submit: *to enter a proposal.* 9 (*intr*) *Theatre* to come on stage: used as a stage direction: *enter Juliet.* 10 (when *intr,* often foll by *into, on,* or *upon*) to begin; start: *to enter upon a new career.* 11 (*intr; often foll by upon*) to come into possession (of). 12 (*tr*) to place (evidence, a plea, etc.) before a court of law or upon the court records. 13 (*tr*) *Law* **a** to go onto and occupy (land). **b** *Chiefly US* to file a claim to (public lands).
▷HISTORY C13: from Old French *entrer,* from Latin *intrāre* to go in, from *intrā* within
▸**ˈenterable** ADJECTIVE ▸**ˈenterer** NOUN

enterectomy (ˌɛntəˈrɛktəmɪ) NOUN surgical excision of part of the intestine.

enteric (ɛnˈtɛrɪk) *or* **enteral** (ˈɛntərəl) ADJECTIVE intestinal.
▷HISTORY C19: from Greek *enterikos,* from *enteron* intestine
▸**ˈenterally** ADVERB

enteric fever NOUN another name for **typhoid fever.**

enter into VERB (*intr, preposition*) 1 to be considered as a necessary part of (one's plans, calculations, etc.). 2 to be in sympathy with: *he enters into his patient's problems.*

enteritis (ˌɛntəˈraɪtɪs) NOUN inflammation of the small intestine.

entero- *or before a vowel* **enter-** COMBINING FORM indicating an intestine: *enterovirus; enteritis.*
▷HISTORY from New Latin, from Greek *enteron* intestine

enterobacterium (ˌɛntərəʊbækˈtɪərɪəm) NOUN any of a class of Gram-negative rodlike bacteria that occur in the gastrointestinal tract.

enterobiasis (ˌɛntərəʊˈbaɪəsɪs) NOUN a disease, common in children, caused by infestation of the large intestine with nematodes of the genus *Enterobius,* esp the pinworm (*E. vermicularis*).

enterocolitis (ˌɛntərəʊkɒˈlaɪtɪs) NOUN inflammation of the small intestine and colon.

enterogastrone (ˌɛntərəʊˈɡæstrəʊn) NOUN a hormone liberated by the upper intestinal mucosa when stimulated by fat: reduces peristalsis and secretion in the stomach.
▷HISTORY C20: from ENTERO- + GASTRO- + (HORM)ONE

enterokinase (ˌɛntərəʊˈkaɪneɪz) NOUN an enzyme in intestinal juice that converts trypsinogen to trypsin.

enteron (ˈɛntəˌrɒn) NOUN, *plural* **-tera** (-tərə). the alimentary canal, esp of an embryo or a coelenterate.
▷HISTORY C19: via New Latin from Greek: intestine; related to Latin *inter* between

enterostomy (ˌɛntəˈrɒstəmɪ) NOUN, *plural* **-mies**. surgical formation of a permanent opening into the intestine through the abdominal wall, used as an artificial anus, for feeding, etc.

enterotomy (ˌɛntəˈrɒtəmɪ) NOUN, *plural* **-mies**. surgical incision into the intestine.

enterovirus (ˌɛntərəʊˈvaɪrəs) NOUN, *plural* **-viruses**. any of a group of viruses that occur in and cause diseases of the gastrointestinal tract.

enterprise (ˈɛntəˌpraɪz) NOUN [1] a project or undertaking, esp one that requires boldness or effort. [2] participation in such projects. [3] readiness to embark on new ventures; boldness and energy. [4] **a** initiative in business. **b** (*as modifier*): *the enterprise culture*. [5] a business unit; a company or firm.
▷HISTORY C15: from Old French *entreprise* (n), from *entreprendre* from *entre-* between (from Latin: INTER-) + *prendre* to take, from Latin *prehendere* to grasp
▸**ˈenterˌpriser** NOUN

Enterprise Allowance Scheme NOUN (in Britain) a scheme to provide a weekly allowance to an unemployed person who wishes to set up a business and is willing to invest a specified amount in it during its first year.

Enterprise Investment Scheme NOUN (in Britain) a scheme to provide tax relief on investments in certain small companies: came into operation in 1994, when it replaced the Business Expansion Scheme.

enterprise zone NOUN a designated zone in a depressed area, esp an inner urban area, where firms are given tax concessions and various planning restrictions are lifted, in order to attract new industry and business to the area: first introduced in Britain in 1981.

enterprising (ˈɛntəˌpraɪzɪŋ) ADJECTIVE ready to embark on new ventures; full of boldness and initiative.
▸**ˈenterˌprisingly** ADVERB

entertain (ˌɛntəˈteɪn) VERB [1] to provide amusement for (a person or audience). [2] to show hospitality to (guests). [3] (*tr*) to hold in the mind: *to entertain an idea*.
▷HISTORY C15: from Old French *entretenir*, from *entre-* mutually + *tenir* to hold, from Latin *tenēre*

entertainer (ˌɛntəˈteɪnə) NOUN [1] a professional singer, comedian, or other performer who takes part in public entertainments. [2] any person who entertains.

entertaining (ˌɛntəˈteɪnɪŋ) ADJECTIVE serving to entertain or give pleasure; diverting; amusing.
▸**ˌenterˈtainingly** ADVERB

entertainment (ˌɛntəˈteɪnmənt) NOUN [1] the act or art of entertaining or state of being entertained. [2] an act, production, etc., that entertains; diversion; amusement.

enthalpy (ˈɛnθəlpɪ, ɛnˈθæl-) NOUN a thermodynamic property of a system equal to the sum of its internal energy and the product of its pressure and volume. Symbol: *H*. Also called: **heat content, total heat.**
▷HISTORY C20: from Greek *enthalpein* to warm in, from EN-[2] + *thalpein* to warm

enthetic (ɛnˈθɛtɪk) ADJECTIVE (esp of infectious diseases) introduced into the body from without.
▷HISTORY C19: from Greek *enthetikos*, from *entithenai* to put in

enthral *or US* **enthrall** (ɪnˈθrɔːl) VERB **-thrals** *or US* **-thralls, -thralling, -thralled.** (*tr*) [1] to hold spellbound; enchant; captivate. [2] *Obsolete* to hold as thrall; enslave.
▷HISTORY C16: from EN-[1] + THRALL
▸**enˈthraller** NOUN ▸**enˈthralment** *or US* **enˈthrallment** NOUN

enthralling (ɪnˈθrɔːlɪŋ) ADJECTIVE holding the attention completely; fascinating; spellbinding.

enthrone (ɛnˈθrəʊn) VERB tr. [1] to place on a throne. [2] to honour or exalt. [3] to assign authority to.
▸**enˈthronement** NOUN

enthuse (ɪnˈθjuːz) VERB to feel or show or cause to feel or show enthusiasm.

enthusiasm (ɪnˈθjuːzɪˌæzəm) NOUN [1] ardent and lively interest or eagerness. [2] an object of keen interest; passion. [3] *Archaic* extravagant or unbalanced religious fervour. [4] *Obsolete* possession or inspiration by a god.
▷HISTORY C17: from Late Latin *enthūsiasmus*, from Greek *enthousiasmos*, from *enthousiazein* to be possessed by a god, from *entheos* inspired, from EN-[2] + *theos* god

enthusiast (ɪnˈθjuːzɪˌæst) NOUN [1] a person filled with or motivated by enthusiasm; fanatic. [2] *Archaic* a religious visionary, esp one whose zeal for religion is extravagant or unbalanced.

enthusiastic (ɪnˌθjuːzɪˈæstɪk) ADJECTIVE filled with or motivated by enthusiasm; fanatical; keen.
▸**enˌthusiˈastically** ADVERB

enthymeme (ˈɛnθɪˌmiːm) NOUN *Logic* [1] an incomplete syllogism, in which one or more premises are unexpressed as their truth is considered to be self-evident. [2] any argument some of whose premises are omitted as obvious.
▷HISTORY C16: via Latin from Greek *enthumēma*, from *enthumeisthai* to infer (literally: to have in the mind), from EN-[2] + *thumos* mind
▸**ˌenthymeˈmatic** *or* **ˌenthymeˈmatical** ADJECTIVE

entice (ɪnˈtaɪs) VERB (*tr*) to attract or draw towards oneself by exciting hope or desire; tempt; allure.
▷HISTORY C13: from Old French *enticier*, from Vulgar Latin *intitiāre* (unattested) to incite, from Latin *titiō* firebrand
▸**enˈticement** NOUN ▸**enˈticer** NOUN ▸**enˈticing** ADJECTIVE ▸**enˈticingly** ADVERB ▸**enˈticingness** NOUN

entire (ɪnˈtaɪə) ADJECTIVE [1] (*prenominal*) whole; complete: *the entire project is going well*. [2] (*prenominal*) without reservation or exception; total: *you have my entire support*. [3] not broken or damaged; intact. [4] consisting of a single piece or section; undivided; continuous. [5] (of leaves, petals, etc.) having a smooth margin not broken up into teeth or lobes. [6] not castrated: *an entire horse*. [7] *Obsolete* of one substance or kind; unmixed; pure. ◆ NOUN [8] a less common word for **entirety.** [9] an uncastrated horse. [10] *Philately* **a** a complete item consisting of an envelope, postcard, or wrapper with stamps affixed. **b on entire.** (of a stamp) placed on an envelope, postcard, etc., and bearing postal directions.
▷HISTORY C14: from Old French *entier*, from Latin *integer* whole, from IN-[1] + *tangere* to touch
▸**enˈtireness** NOUN

entirely (ɪnˈtaɪəlɪ) ADVERB [1] without reservation or exception; wholly; completely. [2] solely or exclusively; only.

entirety (ɪnˈtaɪərɪtɪ) NOUN, *plural* **-ties.** [1] the state of being entire or whole; completeness. [2] a thing, sum, amount, etc., that is entire; whole; total.

entitle (ɪnˈtaɪtᵊl) VERB (*tr*) [1] to give (a person) the right to do or have something; qualify; allow. [2] to give a name or title to. [3] to confer a title of rank or honour upon.
▷HISTORY C14: from Old French *entituler*, from Late Latin *intitulāre*, from Latin *titulus* TITLE
▸**enˈtitlement** NOUN

entity (ˈɛntɪtɪ) NOUN, *plural* **-ties.** [1] something having real or distinct existence; a thing, esp when considered as independent of other things. [2] existence or being. [3] the essence or real nature.
▷HISTORY C16: from Medieval Latin *entitās*, from *ēns* being; see ENS
▸**entitative** (ˈɛntɪtətɪv) ADJECTIVE

ento- COMBINING FORM inside; within: *entoderm*.
▷HISTORY New Latin, from Greek *entos* within

entoblast (ˈɛntəʊˌblæst) NOUN [1] *Embryol* a less common name for **endoderm.** [2] a less common name for **hypoblast.**
▸**entoblastic** (ˌɛntəʊˈblæstɪk) ADJECTIVE

entoderm (ˈɛntəʊˌdɜːm) NOUN *Embryol* another name for **endoderm.**
▸**ˌentoˈdermal** *or* **ˌentoˈdermic** ADJECTIVE

entoil (ɪnˈtɔɪl) VERB (*tr*) an archaic word for **ensnare.**
▸**enˈtoilment** NOUN

entomb (ɪnˈtuːm) VERB (*tr*) [1] to place in or as if in a tomb; bury; inter. [2] to serve as a tomb for.
▸**enˈtombment** NOUN

entomic (ɛnˈtɒmɪk) ADJECTIVE denoting or relating to insects.
▷HISTORY C19: from Greek *entomon* (see ENTOMO-) + -IC

entomo- COMBINING FORM indicating an insect: *entomology*.
▷HISTORY from Greek *entomon* insect (literally: creature cut into sections), from *en-* in + *-tomon*, from *temnein* to cut

entomol. *or* **entom.** ABBREVIATION FOR entomology.

entomologize *or* **entomologise** (ˌɛntəˈmɒləˌdʒaɪz) VERB (*intr*) to collect or study insects.

entomology (ˌɛntəˈmɒlədʒɪ) NOUN the branch of science concerned with the study of insects.
▸**entomological** (ˌɛntəməˈlɒdʒɪkᵊl) *or* **ˌentomoˈlogic** ADJECTIVE ▸**ˌentomoˈlogically** ADVERB ▸**ˌentoˈmologist** NOUN

entomophagous (ˌɛntəˈmɒfəɡəs) ADJECTIVE feeding mainly on insects; insectivorous.

entomophilous (ˌɛntəˈmɒfɪləs) ADJECTIVE (of flowering plants) pollinated by insects. Compare **anemophilous.**
▸**ˌentoˈmophily** NOUN

entomostracan (ˌɛntəˈmɒstrəkən) NOUN [1] any small crustacean of the group (formerly subclass) *Entomostraca*, including the branchiopods, ostracods, and copepods. ◆ ADJECTIVE [2] of, relating to, or belonging to the *Entomostraca*.
▷HISTORY C19: from New Latin ENTOMO- + Greek *ostrakon* shell; see OSTRACIZE
▸**ˌentoˈmostracous** ADJECTIVE

entophyte (ˈɛntəʊˌfaɪt) NOUN *Botany* a variant of **endophyte.**
▸**entophytic** (ˌɛntəʊˈfɪtɪk) ADJECTIVE

entopic (ɛnˈtɒpɪk) ADJECTIVE *Anatomy* situated in its normal place or position. See also **ectopia.**
▷HISTORY from Greek *entopos* in a place, from *topos* place

entoptic (ɛnˈtɒptɪk) ADJECTIVE (of visual sensation) resulting from structures within the eye itself.
▷HISTORY ENTO- + OPTIC

entourage (ɒntʊˈrɑːʒ; *French* ɑ̃turaʒ) NOUN [1] a group of attendants or retainers, esp such as surround an important person; retinue. [2] surroundings or environment.
▷HISTORY C19: from French, from *entourer* to surround, from *entour* around, from *tour* circuit; see TOUR, TURN

entozoic (ˌɛntəʊˈzəʊɪk) ADJECTIVE [1] of or relating to an entozoon. [2] living inside an animal: *entozoic fungi*.

entozoon (ˌɛntəʊˈzəʊɒn) *or* **entozoan** NOUN, *plural* **-zoa** (-ˈzəʊə). any animal, such as a tapeworm, that lives within another animal, usually as a parasite.

entr'acte (ɒnˈtrækt; *French* ɑ̃trakt) NOUN [1] an interval between two acts of a play or opera. [2] (esp formerly) an entertainment during an interval, such as dancing between acts of an opera.
▷HISTORY C19: French, literally: between-act

entrails (ˈɛntreɪlz) PLURAL NOUN [1] the internal organs of a person or animal; intestines; guts. [2] the innermost parts of anything.
▷HISTORY C13: from Old French *entrailles*, from Medieval Latin *intrālia*, changed from Latin *interānea* intestines, ultimately from *inter* between

entrain[1] (ɪnˈtreɪn) VERB to board or put aboard a train.
▸**enˈtrainment** NOUN

entrain[2] (ɪnˈtreɪn) VERB (*tr*) [1] (of a liquid or gas) to carry along (drops of liquid, bubbles, etc.), as in certain distillations. [2] to disperse (air bubbles) through concrete in order to increase its resistance to frost. [3] *Zoology* to adjust (an internal rhythm of an organism) so that it synchronizes with an external cycle, such as that of light and dark.
▸**enˈtrainment** NOUN

entrammel (ɪnˈtræməl) VERB **-mels, -melling, -melled.** (*tr*) to hamper or obstruct by entangling.

entrance[1] (ˈɛntrəns) NOUN [1] the act or an instance of entering; entry. [2] a place for entering, such as a door or gate. [3] **a** the power, liberty, or right of entering; admission. **b** (*as modifier*): *an entrance fee.* [4] the coming of an actor or other performer onto a stage.
▷HISTORY C16: from French, from *entrer* to ENTER

entrance[2] (ɪnˈtrɑːns) VERB (*tr*) [1] to fill with wonder and delight; enchant. [2] to put into a trance; hypnotize.
▸**enˈtrancement** NOUN ▸**enˈtrancing** ADJECTIVE

entrant (ˈɛntrənt) NOUN [1] a person who enters. [2] a new member of a group, society, or association. [3] a person who enters a competition or contest; competitor.
▷HISTORY C17: from French, literally: entering, from *entrer* to ENTER

entrap (ɪnˈtræp) VERB **-traps, -trapping, -trapped.** (*tr*) [1] to catch or snare in or as if in a trap. [2] to lure or trick into danger, difficulty, or embarrassment.
▸**enˈtrapper** NOUN

entrapment (ɪnˈtræpmənt) NOUN the luring, by a police officer, of a person into committing a crime so that he may be prosecuted for it.

entreat *or* **intreat** (ɪnˈtriːt) VERB [1] to ask (a person) earnestly; beg or plead with; implore. [2] to make an earnest request or petition for (something). [3] an archaic word for **treat** (sense 4).
▷HISTORY C15: from Old French *entraiter,* from EN-[1] + *traiter* to TREAT
▸**enˈtreatingly** *or* **inˈtreatingly** ADVERB ▸**enˈtreatment** *or* **inˈtreatment** NOUN

entreaty (ɪnˈtriːtɪ) NOUN, *plural* **-treaties.** an earnest request or petition; supplication; plea.

entrechat (*French* ɑ̃trəʃa) NOUN a leap in ballet during which the dancer repeatedly crosses his feet or beats them together.
▷HISTORY C18: from French, from earlier *entrechase,* changed by folk etymology from Italian *(capriola) intrecciata,* literally: entwined (caper), from *intrecciare* to interlace, from IN-[2] + *treccia* TRESS

entrecôte (*French* ɑ̃trəkot) NOUN a beefsteak cut from between the ribs.
▷HISTORY C19: French *entrecôte,* from *entre-* INTER- + *côte* rib, from Latin *costa*

Entre-Deux-Mers (*French* ɑ̃trədømɛr) NOUN any wine produced in the area of the Gironde between the rivers Dordogne and Garonne in S France.

entrée (ˈɒntreɪ) NOUN [1] a dish served before a main course. [2] *Chiefly US* the main course of a meal. [3] the power or right of entry.
▷HISTORY C18: from French, from *entrer* to ENTER; in cookery, so called because formerly the course was served after an intermediate course called the *relevé* (remove)

entremets (*French* ɑ̃trəmɛ) NOUN, *plural* **-mets** (*French* -mɛ). [1] a dessert. [2] a light dish, formerly served at formal dinners between the main course and the dessert.
▷HISTORY C18: from French, from Old French *entremes,* from *entre-* between, INTER- + *mes* dish, MESS

entrench *or* **intrench** (ɪnˈtrɛntʃ) VERB [1] (*tr*) to construct (a defensive position) by digging trenches around it. [2] (*tr*) to fix or establish firmly, esp so as to prevent removal or change. [3] (*intr; foll by on or upon*) to trespass or encroach; infringe.
▸**enˈtrenched** *or* **inˈtrenched** ADJECTIVE ▸**enˈtrencher** *or* **inˈtrencher** NOUN

entrenchment *or* **intrenchment** (ɪnˈtrɛntʃmənt) NOUN [1] the act of entrenching or state of being entrenched. [2] a position protected by trenches. [3] one of a series of deep trenches constructed as a shelter from gunfire.

entre nous (*French* ɑ̃trə nu) ADVERB between ourselves; in confidence.
▷HISTORY C17: from French

entrepôt (*French* ɑ̃trəpo) NOUN [1] a warehouse for commercial goods. [2] **a** a trading centre or port at a geographically convenient location, at which goods are imported and re-exported without incurring liability for duty. **b** (*as modifier*): *an entrepôt trade.*
▷HISTORY C18: French, from *entreposer* to put in, from *entre-* between, INTER- + *poser* to place (see POSE[1]); formed on the model of DEPOT

entrepreneur (ˌɒntrəprəˈnɜː; *French* ɑ̃trəprənœr) NOUN [1] the owner or manager of a business enterprise who, by risk and initiative, attempts to make profits. [2] a middleman or commercial intermediary.
▷HISTORY C19: from French, from *entreprendre* to undertake; see ENTERPRISE
▸ˌ**entrepreˈneurial** ADJECTIVE ▸ˌ**entrepreˈneurship** NOUN

entresol (ˌɒntrəˈsɒl; *French* ɑ̃trəsɔl) NOUN another name for **mezzanine** (sense 1).
▷HISTORY C18: from French, literally: between floors, from *entre-* INTER- + *sol* floor, ground, from Latin *solum*

entropy (ˈɛntrəpɪ) NOUN, *plural* **-pies.** [1] a thermodynamic quantity that changes in a reversible process by an amount equal to the heat absorbed or emitted divided by the thermodynamic temperature. It is measured in joules per kelvin. Symbol: *S.* See also **law of thermodynamics** (sense 1). [2] a statistical measure of the disorder of a closed system expressed by $S = k \log P + c$ where P is the probability that a particular state of the system exists, k is the Boltzmann constant, and c is another constant. [3] lack of pattern or organization; disorder. [4] a measure of the efficiency of a system, such as a code or language, in transmitting information.
▷HISTORY C19: from EN-[2] + -TROPE

entrust *or* **intrust** (ɪnˈtrʌst) VERB (*tr*) [1] (usually foll by *with*) to invest or charge (with a duty, responsibility, etc.). [2] (often foll by *to*) to put into the care or protection of someone.
▸**enˈtrustment** *or* **inˈtrustment** NOUN

> **Language note** It is usually considered incorrect to talk about *entrusting* someone *to do* something: *the army cannot be trusted* (not *entrusted*) *to carry out orders.*

entry (ˈɛntrɪ) NOUN, *plural* **-tries.** [1] the act or an instance of entering; entrance. [2] a point or place for entering, such as a door, gate, etc. [3] **a** the right or liberty of entering; admission; access. **b** (*as modifier*): *an entry permit.* [4] the act of recording an item, such as a commercial transaction, in a journal, account, register, etc. [5] an item recorded, as in a diary, dictionary, or account. [6] **a** a person, horse, car, etc., entering a competition or contest; competitor. **b** (*as modifier*): *an entry fee.* [7] the competitors entering a contest considered collectively: *a good entry this year for the speed trials.* [8] the people admitted at one time to a school, college, or course of study, etc., considered collectively; intake. [9] the action of an actor in going on stage or his manner of doing this. [10] *Criminal law* the act of unlawfully going onto the premises of another with the intention of committing a crime. [11] *Property law* the act of going upon another person's land with the intention of asserting the right to possession. [12] any point in a piece of music, esp a fugue, at which a performer commences or resumes playing or singing. [13] *Cards* a card that enables one to transfer the lead from one's own hand to that of one's partner or to the dummy hand. [14] *English dialect* a passage between the backs of two rows of terraced houses.
▷HISTORY C13: from Old French *entree,* past participle of *entrer* to ENTER

entryism (ˈɛntrɪɪzəm) NOUN the policy or practice of members of a particular political group joining an existing political party with the intention of changing its principles and policies, instead of forming a new party.
▸ˈ**entryist** NOUN, ADJECTIVE

entry-level ADJECTIVE [1] (of a job or worker) at the most elementary level in a career structure. [2] (of a product) characterized by being at the most appropriate level for use by a beginner: *an entry-level camera.*

entwine *or* **intwine** (ɪnˈtwaɪn) VERB (of two or more things) to twine together or (of one or more things) to twine around (something else).
▸**enˈtwinement** *or* **inˈtwinement** NOUN

enucleate VERB (ɪˈnjuːklɪˌeɪt) (*tr*) [1] *Biology* to remove the nucleus from (a cell). [2] *Surgery* to remove (a tumour or other structure) from its capsule without rupturing it. [3] *Archaic* to explain or disclose. ◆ ADJECTIVE (ɪˈnjuːklɪɪt, -ˌeɪt) [4] (of cells) deprived of their nuclei.
▷HISTORY C16: from Latin *ēnūcleāre* to remove the kernel, from *nūcleus* kernel
▸**eˌnucleˈation** NOUN

Enugu (ɛˈnuːguː) NOUN a city in S Nigeria, capital of Enugu state: capital of the former Eastern region and of the breakaway state of Biafra during the Civil War (1967–70): coal-mining. Pop.: 316 100 (1996 est.).

E number NOUN any of a series of numbers with the prefix E indicating a specific food additive recognized by the European Union and used on labels of processed food.

enumerate (ɪˈnjuːməˌreɪt) VERB [1] (*tr*) to mention separately or in order; name one by one; list. [2] (*tr*) to determine the number of; count. [3] *Canadian* to compile or enter (a name or names) in a voting list for an area.
▷HISTORY C17: from Latin *ēnumerāre,* from *numerāre* to count, reckon; see NUMBER
▸**eˈnumerable** ADJECTIVE ▸**eˌnumerˈation** NOUN
▸**eˈnumerative** ADJECTIVE

enumerator (ɪˈnjuːməˌreɪtə) NOUN [1] a person or thing that enumerates. [2] *Canadian* a person who compiles the voting list for an area. [3] *Brit* a person who issues and retrieves forms during a census of population.

enunciable (ɪˈnʌnsɪəbᵊl) ADJECTIVE capable of being enunciated.

enunciate (ɪˈnʌnsɪˌeɪt) VERB [1] to articulate or pronounce (words), esp clearly and distinctly. [2] (*tr*) to state precisely or formally.
▷HISTORY C17: from Latin *ēnuntiāre* to declare, from *nuntiāre* to announce, from *nuntius* messenger
▸**eˌnunciˈation** NOUN ▸**eˈnunciative** *or* **eˈnunciatory** ADJECTIVE ▸**eˈnunciatively** ADVERB ▸**eˈnunciˌator** NOUN

enure (ɪˈnjʊə) VERB a variant spelling of **inure.**
▸**enˈurement** NOUN

enuresis (ˌɛnjʊˈriːsɪs) NOUN involuntary discharge of urine, esp during sleep.
▷HISTORY C19: from New Latin, from Greek EN-[2] + *ourein* to urinate, from *ouron* urine
▸**enuretic** (ˌɛnjʊˈrɛtɪk) ADJECTIVE, NOUN

envelop (ɪnˈvɛləp) VERB (*tr*) **-lops, -loping, -loped** [1] to wrap or enclose in or as if in a covering. [2] to conceal or obscure, as from sight or understanding: *a plan enveloped in mystery.* [3] to surround or partially surround (an enemy force).
▷HISTORY C14: from Old French *envoluper,* from EN-[1] + *voluper, voloper,* of obscure origin
▸**enˈvelopment** NOUN

envelope (ˈɛnvəˌləʊp, ˈɒn-) NOUN [1] a flat covering of paper, usually rectangular in shape and with a flap that can be folded over and sealed, used to enclose a letter, etc. [2] any covering or wrapper. [3] *Biology* any enclosing structure, such as a membrane, shell, or skin. [4] the bag enclosing the gas in a balloon. [5] *Maths* a curve or surface that is tangent to each one of a group of curves or surfaces. [6] *Electronics* the sealed glass or metal housing of a valve, electric light, etc. [7] *Telecomm* the outer shape of a modulated wave, formed by the peaks of successive cycles of the carrier wave. [8] **push the envelope.** *Informal* to push the boundaries of what is possible.
▷HISTORY C18: from French *enveloppe,* from *envelopper* to wrap around; see ENVELOP; sense 8 from aeronautics jargon, referring to graphs of aircraft performance

envenom (ɪnˈvɛnəm) VERB (*tr*) [1] to fill or impregnate with venom; make poisonous. [2] to fill with bitterness or malice.

enviable (ˈɛnvɪəbᵊl) ADJECTIVE exciting envy; fortunate or privileged.
▸ˈ**enviableness** NOUN ▸ˈ**enviably** ADVERB

envious (ˈɛnvɪəs) ADJECTIVE feeling, showing, or resulting from envy.
▷HISTORY C13: from Anglo-Norman, ultimately from Latin *invidiōsus* full of envy, INVIDIOUS; see ENVY
▸ˈ**enviously** ADVERB ▸ˈ**enviousness** NOUN

enviro (ɪnˈvaɪrəʊ) NOUN, *plural* **enviros.** *Informal* an environmentalist.

environ (ɪnˈvaɪrən) VERB (*tr*) to encircle or surround.
▷HISTORY C14: from Old French *environner* to surround, from *environ* around, from EN-[1] + *viron* a circle, from *virer* to turn, VEER[1]

environment (ɪn'vaɪrənmənt) NOUN 1 external conditions or surroundings, esp those in which people live or work. 2 *Ecology* the external surroundings in which a plant or animal lives, which tend to influence its development and behaviour. 3 the state of being environed; encirclement. 4 *Computing* an operating system, program, or integrated suite of programs that provides all the facilities necessary for a particular application: *a word-processing environment.*
▸**en,viron'mental** ADJECTIVE ▸**en,viron'mentally** ADVERB

environmental audit NOUN the systematic examination of an organization's interaction with the environment, to assess the success of its conservation or antipollution programme.

Environmental Health Officer NOUN (in Britain) an employee of the Environmental Health Service. Former names: **public health inspector, sanitary inspector.**

Environmental Health Service NOUN (in Britain) a service provided by a local authority, which deals with prevention of the spread of communicable diseases, food safety and hygiene, control of infestation by insects or rodents, etc.

environmentalism (ɪn,vaɪrən'mɛntə,lɪzəm) NOUN *Psychol* the belief that a person's behaviour is affected chiefly by his environment. Compare **hereditarianism.**

environmentalist (ɪn,vaɪrən'mɛntəlɪst) NOUN 1 an adherent of environmentalism. 2 a person who is concerned with the maintenance of ecological balance and the conservation of the environment. 3 a person concerned with issues that affect the environment, such as pollution.

environs (ɪn'vaɪrənz) PLURAL NOUN a surrounding area or region, esp the suburbs or outskirts of a town or city; vicinity.

envisage (ɪn'vɪzɪdʒ) VERB (*tr*) 1 to form a mental image of; visualize; contemplate. 2 to conceive of as a possibility in the future; foresee. 3 *Archaic* to look in the face of; confront.
▷**HISTORY** C19: from French *envisager,* from EN-[1] + *visage* face, VISAGE
▸**en'visagement** NOUN

> **Language note** It was formerly considered incorrect to use a clause after *envisage* as in *it is envisaged that the new centre will cost £40 million,* but this use is now acceptable.

envision (ɪn'vɪʒən) VERB (*tr*) to conceive of as a possibility, esp in the future; foresee.

envoy[1] ('ɛnvɔɪ) NOUN 1 Formal name: **envoy extraordinary and minister plenipotentiary.** a diplomat of the second class, ranking between an ambassador and a minister resident. 2 an accredited messenger, agent, or representative.
▷**HISTORY** C17: from French *envoyé,* literally: sent, from *envoyer* to send, from Vulgar Latin *inviāre* (unattested) to send on a journey, from IN-[2] + *via* road
▸**'envoyship** NOUN

envoy[2] *or* **envoi** ('ɛnvɔɪ) NOUN 1 a brief dedicatory or explanatory stanza concluding certain forms of poetry, notably ballades. 2 a postscript in other forms of verse or prose.
▷**HISTORY** C14: from Old French *envoye,* from *envoyer* to send; see ENVOY[1]

envy ('ɛnvɪ) NOUN, *plural* **-vies.** 1 a feeling of grudging or somewhat admiring discontent aroused by the possessions, achievements, or qualities of another. 2 the desire to have for oneself something possessed by another; covetousness. 3 an object of envy. ◆ VERB **-vies, -vying, -vied.** 4 to be envious of (a person or thing).
▷**HISTORY** C13: via Old French from Latin *invidia,* from *invidēre* to eye maliciously, from IN-[2] + *vidēre* to see
▸**'envier** NOUN ▸**'envyingly** ADVERB

enwind (ɪn'waɪnd) VERB **-winds, -winding, -wound.** (*tr*) to wind or coil around; encircle.

enwomb (ɪn'wuːm) VERB (*tr; often passive*) to enclose in or as if in a womb.

enwrap *or* **inwrap** (ɪn'ræp) VERB **-wraps, -wrapping, -wrapped.** (*tr*) 1 to wrap or cover up; envelop. 2 (*usually passive*) to engross or absorb: *enwrapped in thought.*

enwreath (ɪn'riːð) VERB (*tr*) to surround or encircle with or as with a wreath or wreaths.

Enzed ('ɛn'zɛd) NOUN *Austral and NZ informal* 1 New Zealand. 2 Also called: **Enzedder.** a New Zealander.

enzootic (,ɛnzəʊ'ɒtɪk) ADJECTIVE 1 (of diseases) affecting animals within a limited region. ◆ NOUN 2 an enzootic disease. ◆ Compare **epizootic.**
▷**HISTORY** C19: from EN-[2] + Greek *zōion* animal + -OTIC
▸**,enzo'otically** ADVERB

enzyme ('ɛnzaɪm) NOUN any of a group of complex proteins or conjugated proteins that are produced by living cells and act as catalysts in specific biochemical reactions.
▷**HISTORY** C19: from Medieval Greek *enzumos* leavened, from Greek EN-[2] + *zumē* leaven
▸**enzymatic** (,ɛnzaɪ'mætɪk, -zɪ-) *or* **enzymic** (ɛn'zaɪmɪk, -'zɪm-) ADJECTIVE

enzyme-linked immunosorbent assay (,ɪmjunəʊ'sɔːbənt) NOUN the full name for **ELISA.**

enzymology (,ɛnzaɪ'mɒlədʒɪ) NOUN the branch of science concerned with the study of enzymes.
▸**enzymological** (,ɛnzaɪmə'lɒdʒɪkᵊl) ADJECTIVE
▸**,enzy'mologist** NOUN

enzymolysis (,ɛnzaɪ'mɒlɪsɪs) NOUN a biochemical decomposition, such as a fermentation, that is catalysed by an enzyme.
▸**enzymolytic** (,ɛnzaɪmə'lɪtɪk) ADJECTIVE

e.o. ABBREVIATION FOR ex officio.

eo- COMBINING FORM early or primeval: *Eocene; eohippus.*
▷**HISTORY** from Greek, from *ēos* dawn

eobiont (,iːəʊ'baɪənt) NOUN a hypothetical chemical precursor of a living cell.
▷**HISTORY** C20: from EO- + Greek *biōnt* stem of present participle of *biōn* to live, from *bios* life

EOC ABBREVIATION FOR **Equal Opportunities Commission.**

Eocene ('iːəʊ,siːn) ADJECTIVE 1 of, denoting, or formed in the second epoch of the Tertiary period, which lasted for 20 000 000 years, during which hooved mammals appeared. ◆ NOUN 2 **the.** the Eocene epoch or rock series.
▷**HISTORY** C19: from EO- + -CENE

Eogene ('iːəʊ,dʒiːn) ADJECTIVE, NOUN another word for **Palaeogene.**

eohippus (,iːəʊ'hɪpəs) NOUN, *plural* **-puses.** the earliest horse: an extinct Eocene dog-sized animal of the genus with four-toed forelegs, three-toed hindlegs, and teeth specialized for browsing.
▷**HISTORY** C19: New Latin, from EO- + Greek *hippos* horse

Eolian (iː'əʊlɪən) ADJECTIVE, NOUN a variant spelling of **Aeolian.**

Eolic (iː'ɒlɪk, ɪ'əʊlɪk) ADJECTIVE, NOUN a variant spelling of **Aeolic.**

eolipile (iː'ɒlɪ,paɪl) NOUN a variant spelling of **aeolipile.**

eolith ('iːəʊlɪθ) NOUN a stone, usually crudely broken, used as a primitive tool in Eolithic times.

Eolithic (,iːəʊ'lɪθɪk) ADJECTIVE denoting, relating to, or characteristic of the early part of the Stone Age, characterized by the use of crude stone tools.

e.o.m. *Commerce* ABBREVIATION FOR end of the month.

eon ('iːən, 'iːɒn) NOUN 1 the usual US spelling of **aeon.** 2 *Geology* the longest division of geological time, comprising two or more eras.

eonian (iː'əʊnɪən) ADJECTIVE 1 the usual US spelling of **aeonian.** 2 *Geology* of or relating to an eon.

eonism ('iːə,nɪzəm) NOUN *Psychiatry* the adoption of female dress and behaviour by a male. See also **transvestite.**
▷**HISTORY** C19: named after Charles *Éon* de Beaumont (died 1810), French transvestite

Eos ('iːɒs) NOUN *Greek myth* the winged goddess of the dawn, the daughter of Hyperion. Roman counterpart: **Aurora.**

eosin ('iːəʊsɪn) *or* **eosine** ('iːəʊsɪn, -,siːn) NOUN 1 Also called: **bromeosin.** a red crystalline water-insoluble derivative of fluorescein. Its soluble salts are used as dyes. Formula: $C_{20}H_8Br_4O_5$. 2 any of several similar dyes.
▷**HISTORY** C19: from Greek *ēos* dawn + -IN; referring to the colour it gives to silk
▸**,eo'sinic** ADJECTIVE ▸**'eosin-,like** ADJECTIVE

eosinophil (,iːəʊ'sɪnəfɪl) *or* **eosinophile** (,iːəʊ'sɪnə,faɪl) NOUN a leucocyte with a multilobed nucleus and coarse granular cytoplasm that stains readily with acidic dyes such as eosin.
▸**,eo,sino'philic** *or* **eosinophilous** (,iːəʊsɪ'nɒfɪləs) ADJECTIVE

eosinophilia (,iːəʊ,sɪnə'fɪlɪə) NOUN the presence of abnormally large numbers of eosinophils in the blood, occurring in various diseases and in response to certain drugs.

-eous SUFFIX OF ADJECTIVES relating to or having the nature of: *gaseous.* Compare **-ious.**
▷**HISTORY** from Latin *-eus*

Eozoic (,iːəʊ'zəʊɪk) ADJECTIVE *Archaic* of or formed in the part of the Precambrian era during which life first appeared.

ep (ɛp) ABBREVIATION FOR episode.

EP NOUN 1 an extended-play single, one of the formats in which music is sold, usually comprising four or five tracks. ◆ ABBREVIATION FOR: 2 Eastern (Cape) Province.

Ep. ABBREVIATION FOR Epistle.

ep- PREFIX variant of **epi-** before a vowel: *epexegesis.*

EPA ABBREVIATION FOR eicosapentaenoic acid: a fatty acid, found in certain fish oils, that can reduce blood cholesterol.

epact ('iːpækt) NOUN 1 the difference in time, about 11 days, between the solar year and the lunar year. 2 the number of days between the beginning of the calendar year and the new moon immediately preceding this. 3 the difference in time between the calendar month and the synodic month.
▷**HISTORY** C16: via Late Latin from Greek *epaktē,* from *epagein* to bring in, intercalate, from *agein* to lead

epanalepsis (ɪ,pænə'lɛpsɪs) NOUN *Rhetoric* the repetition, after a more or less lengthy passage of subordinate or parenthetic text, of a word or clause that was used before.
▷**HISTORY** C16: from Greek, from EPI- + ANA- + *lēpis* taking, from *lambanein* to take up
▸**,epana'leptic** ADJECTIVE

epanaphora (,ɛpə'næfərə) NOUN *Rhetoric* another word for **anaphora.**
▸**,epanaph'oral** ADJECTIVE

epanorthosis (ɪ,pænɔː'θəʊsɪs) NOUN *Rhetoric* the almost immediate replacement of a preceding word or phrase by a more correct or more emphatic one, as for example in *thousands, nay, millions.*
▷**HISTORY** C16: from Greek: correction, from EPI- + ANA- + *orthos* straight
▸**,epanor'thotic** ADJECTIVE

eparch ('ɛpɑːk) NOUN 1 a bishop or metropolitan in charge of an eparchy (sense 1). 2 a government official in charge of an eparchy (senses 2 or 3).
▷**HISTORY** C17: from Greek *eparkhos,* from *epi-* over, on + -ARCH

eparchy ('ɛpɑːkɪ) *or* **eparchate** ('ɛpɑːkɪt) NOUN, *plural* **-chies** *or* **-chates.** 1 a diocese of the Eastern Christian Church. 2 (in ancient Greece) a province. 3 (in modern Greece) a subdivision of a province.
▸**ep'archial** ADJECTIVE

épatant *French* (epatɑ̃) ADJECTIVE startling or shocking, esp through being unconventional.
▷**HISTORY** C20: from present participle of *épater* to flabbergast

epaulette *or US* **epaulet** ('ɛpə,lɛt, -lɪt) NOUN a piece of ornamental material on the shoulder of a garment, esp a military uniform.
▷**HISTORY** C18: from French *épaulette,* from *épaule* shoulder, from Latin *spatula* shoulder blade; see SPATULA

e-payment NOUN a digital payment for a transaction made on the Internet.

épée ('ɛpeɪ; *French* epe) NOUN a sword similar to the foil but with a larger guard and a heavier blade of triangular cross section.
▷**HISTORY** C19: from French: sword, from Latin *spatha,* from Greek *spathē* blade; see SPADE[1]

épéeist ('ɛpeɪɪst) NOUN *Fencing* one who uses or specializes in using an épée.

epeiric (ɪ'paɪrɪk) ADJECTIVE *Geology* in, of, or relating to a continent: *an epeiric sea.*

▷**HISTORY** C20: from Greek *ēpeiros* continent + -IC

epeirogeny (ˌɛpaɪˈrɒdʒɪnɪ) *or* **epeirogenesis** (ɪˌpaɪrəʊˈdʒɛnɪsɪs) NOUN the formation and submergence of continents by broad relatively slow displacements of the earth's crust. Also called: **epirogeny.**
▷**HISTORY** C19: from Greek *ēpeiros* continent + -GENY
▸**epeirogenic** (ɪˌpaɪrəʊˈdʒɛnɪk) *or* **epeirogenetic** (ɪˌpaɪrəʊdʒɪˈnɛtɪk) ADJECTIVE

epencephalon (ˌɛpɛnˈsɛfəˌlɒn) NOUN, *plural* **-la** (-lə). *Anatomy* [1] the cerebellum and pons Varolii. [2] the part of the embryonic brain that develops into this; metencephalon.
▷**HISTORY** C19: New Latin; see EPI-, ENCEPHALON
▸**ˌencephalic** (ˌɛpɛnsɛˈfælɪk) ADJECTIVE

ependyma (ɪˈpɛndɪmə) NOUN the membrane lining the ventricles of the brain and the central canal of the spinal cord.
▸**eˈpendymal** ADJECTIVE

epenthesis (ɛˈpɛnθɪsɪs) NOUN, *plural* **-ses** (-ˌsiːz). the insertion of a sound or letter into a word.
▷**HISTORY** C17: via Late Latin from Greek, from *epentithenai* to insert, from EPI- + EN-^{2} + *tithenai* to place
▸**epenthetic** (ˌɛpɛnˈθɛtɪk) ADJECTIVE

epergne (ɪˈpɜːn) NOUN an ornamental centrepiece for a table: a stand with holders for sweetmeats, fruit, flowers, etc.
▷**HISTORY** C18: probably from French *épargne* a saving, from *épargner* to economize, of Germanic origin; compare SPARE

epexegesis (ɛˌpɛksɪˈdʒiːsɪs) NOUN, *plural* **-ses** (-ˌsiːz). *Rhetoric* [1] the addition of a phrase, clause, or sentence to a text to provide further explanation. [2] the phrase, clause, or sentence added for this purpose.
▷**HISTORY** C17: from Greek; see EPI-, EXEGESIS
▸**epexegetic** (ɛˌpɛksɪˈdʒɛtɪk) *or* **epˌexeˈgetical** ADJECTIVE
▸**epˌexeˈgetically** ADVERB

EPG ABBREVIATION FOR electronic programme guide.

Eph. *or* **Ephes.** *Bible* ABBREVIATION FOR Ephesians.

eph- PREFIX a variant of **epi-** before an aspirate: *ephedra; ephedrine.*

ephah *or* **epha** (ˈiːfə) NOUN a Hebrew unit of dry measure equal to approximately one bushel or about 33 litres.
▷**HISTORY** C16: from Hebrew *'ephāh,* of Egyptian origin

ephebe (ɪˈfiːb, ˈɛfiːb) NOUN (in ancient Greece) a youth about to enter full citizenship, esp one undergoing military training.
▷**HISTORY** C19: from Latin *ephēbus,* from Greek *ephēbos,* from *hēbē* young manhood
▸**eˈphebic** ADJECTIVE

ephedra (ɪˈfɛdrə) NOUN any gymnosperm shrub of the genus *Ephedra,* of warm regions of America and Eurasia: the source of ephedrine: family *Ephedraceae,* phylum *Gnetophyta.*
▷**HISTORY** C18: New Latin, from Latin, from Greek *ephedros* a sitting upon, from EPI- + *hedra* seat

ephedrine *or* **ephedrin** (ɪˈfɛdrɪn, ˈɛfɪˌdriːn, -drɪn) NOUN a white crystalline alkaloid obtained from plants of the genus *Ephedra:* used for the treatment of asthma and hay fever; l-phenyl-2-methylaminopropanol. Formula: $C_6H_5CH(OH)CH(NHCH_3)CH_3$.
▷**HISTORY** C19: from New Latin EPHEDRA + -INE^{2}

ephemera (ɪˈfɛmərə) NOUN, *plural* **-eras** *or* **-erae** (-əˌriː). [1] a mayfly, esp one of the genus *Ephemera.* [2] something transitory or short-lived. [3] (*functioning as plural*) a class of collectable items not originally intended to last for more than a short time, such as tickets, posters, postcards, or labels. [4] a plural of **ephemeron.**
▷**HISTORY** C16; see EPHEMERAL

ephemeral (ɪˈfɛmərəl) ADJECTIVE [1] lasting for only a short time; transitory; short-lived: *ephemeral pleasure.* ◆ NOUN [2] a short-lived organism, such as the mayfly. [3] a plant that completes its life cycle in less than one year, usually less than six months.
▷**HISTORY** C16: from Greek *ephēmeros* lasting only a day, from *hēmera* day
▸**eˈphemerally** ADVERB ▸**eˌphemerˈality** *or* **eˈphemeralness** NOUN

ephemerid (ɪˈfɛmərɪd) NOUN any insect of the order *Ephemeroptera* (or *Ephemerida*), which comprises the mayflies. Also called: **ephemeropteran.**
▷**HISTORY** C19: from New Latin *Ephēmerida,* from Greek *ephēmeros* short-lived + -ID^{2}

ephemeris (ɪˈfɛmərɪs) NOUN, *plural* **ephemerides** (ˌɛfɪˈmɛrɪˌdiːz). [1] a table giving the future positions of a planet, comet, or satellite. [2] an annual publication giving the positions of the sun, moon, and planets during the course of a year, information concerning eclipses, astronomical constants, etc. [3] *Obsolete* a diary or almanac.
▷**HISTORY** C16: from Latin, from Greek: diary, journal; see EPHEMERAL

ephemeris time NOUN time that is based on the orbit of the earth around the sun rather than the axial rotation of the earth, one **ephemeris second** being 1/31 556 925.9747 of the tropical year 1900. It was used from 1960 to 1983 as an astronomical timescale but has been replaced by terrestrial dynamical time and barycentric dynamic time. See **TDT, TDB.**

ephemeron (ɪˈfɛməˌrɒn) NOUN, *plural* **-era** (-ərə) *or* **-erons.** (*usually plural*) something transitory or short-lived.
▷**HISTORY** C16: see EPHEMERAL

ephemeropteran (iːˌfɛməˈrɒptərən) NOUN [1] another word for **ephemerid.** ◆ ADJECTIVE [2] of or relating to the *Ephemeroptera.*

Ephesian (ɪˈfiːʒən) ADJECTIVE [1] of or relating to Ephesus. ◆ NOUN [2] an inhabitant or native of Ephesus.

Ephesians (ɪˈfiːʒənz) NOUN (*functioning as singular*) a book of the New Testament (in full **The Epistle of Paul the Apostle to the Ephesians**), containing an exposition of the divine plan for the world and the consummation of this in Christ.

Ephesus (ˈɛfɪsəs) NOUN (in ancient Greece) a major trading city on the W coast of Asia Minor: famous for its temple of Artemis (Diana); sacked by the Goths (262 A.D.).

ephod (ˈiːfɒd) NOUN *Old Testament* an embroidered vestment believed to resemble an apron with shoulder straps, worn by priests in ancient Israel.
▷**HISTORY** C14: from Hebrew *ēphōdh*

ephor (ˈɛfɔː) NOUN, *plural* **-ors** *or* **-ori** (-əˌraɪ). (in ancient Greece) one of a board of senior magistrates in any of several Dorian states, esp the five Spartan ephors, who were elected by vote of all full citizens and who wielded effective power.
▷**HISTORY** C16: from Greek *ephoros,* from *ephoran* to supervise, from EPI- + *horan* to look
▸**ˈephoral** ADJECTIVE ▸**ˈephorate** NOUN

Ephraim (ˈiːfreɪɪm) NOUN *Old Testament* [1] **a** the younger son of Joseph, who received the principal blessing of his grandfather Jacob (Genesis 48:8–22). **b** the tribe descended from him. **c** the territory of this tribe, west of the River Jordan. [2] the northern kingdom of Israel after the kingdom of Solomon had been divided into two.

Ephraimite (ˈiːfreɪɪˌmaɪt) NOUN a member of the tribe of Ephraim.

epi-, eph-, *or before a vowel* **ep-** PREFIX [1] on; upon; above; over: *epidermis; epicentre.* [2] in addition to: *epiphenomenon.* [3] after: *epigenesis; epilogue.* [4] near; close to: *epicalyx.*
▷**HISTORY** from Greek, from *epi* (prep)

epibiosis (ˌɛpɪbaɪˈəʊsɪs) NOUN any relationship between two organisms in which one grows on the other but is not parasitic on it. See also **epiphyte, epizoite.**
▸**epibiotic** (ˌɛpɪbaɪˈɒtɪk) ADJECTIVE

epiblast (ˈɛpɪˌblæst) NOUN *Embryol* the outermost layer of an embryo, which becomes the ectoderm at gastrulation. Also called: **ectoblast.**
▸**ˌepiˈblastic** ADJECTIVE

epiblem (ˈɛpɪblɛm) NOUN *Botany* the outermost cell layer of a root; epidermis.

epiboly (ɪˈpɪbəlɪ) NOUN, *plural* **-lies.** *Embryol* a process that occurs during gastrulation in vertebrates, in which cells on one side of the blastula grow over and surround the remaining cells and yolk and eventually form the ectoderm.
▷**HISTORY** C19: from Greek *epibolē* a laying on, from *epiballein* to throw on, from EPI- + *ballein* to throw
▸**epibolic** (ˌɛpɪˈbɒlɪk) ADJECTIVE

epic (ˈɛpɪk) NOUN [1] a long narrative poem recounting in elevated style the deeds of a legendary hero, esp one originating in oral folk tradition. [2] the genre of epic poetry. [3] any work of literature, film, etc., having heroic deeds for its subject matter or having other qualities associated with the epic: *a Hollywood epic.* [4] an episode in the lives of men in which heroic deeds are performed or attempted: *the epic of Scott's expedition to the South Pole.* ◆ ADJECTIVE [5] denoting, relating to, or characteristic of an epic or epics. [6] of heroic or impressive proportions: *an epic voyage.*
▷**HISTORY** C16: from Latin *epicus,* from Greek *epikos,* from *epos* speech, word, song

epicalyx (ˌɛpɪˈkeɪlɪks, -ˈkæl-) NOUN, *plural* **-lyxes** *or* **-lyces** (-lɪˌsiːz). *Botany* a series of small sepal-like bracts forming an outer calyx beneath the true calyx in some flowers.

epicanthus (ˌɛpɪˈkænθəs) NOUN, *plural* **-thi** (-θaɪ). a fold of skin extending vertically over the inner angle of the eye: characteristic of Mongolian peoples and a congenital anomaly among other races. Also called: **epicanthic fold.**
▷**HISTORY** C19: New Latin, from EPI- + Latin *canthus* corner of the eye, from Greek *kanthos*
▸**ˌepiˈcanthic** ADJECTIVE

epicardium (ˌɛpɪˈkɑːdɪəm) NOUN, *plural* **-dia** (-dɪə). *Anatomy* the innermost layer of the pericardium, in direct contact with the heart.
▷**HISTORY** C19: New Latin, from EPI- + Greek *kardia* heart
▸**ˌepiˈcardiac** *or* **ˌepiˈcardial** ADJECTIVE

epicarp (ˈɛpɪˌkɑːp) *or* **exocarp** NOUN the outermost layer of the pericarp of fruits: forms the skin of a peach or grape.
▷**HISTORY** C19: from French *épicarpe,* from EPI- + Greek *karpos* fruit

epicedium (ˌɛpɪˈsiːdɪəm) NOUN, *plural* **-dia** (-dɪə). *Rare* a funeral ode.
▷**HISTORY** C16: Latin, from Greek *epikēdeion,* from EPI- + *kēdos* care

epicene (ˈɛpɪˌsiːn) ADJECTIVE [1] having the characteristics of both sexes; hermaphroditic. [2] of neither sex; sexless. [3] effeminate. [4] *Grammar* **a** denoting a noun that may refer to a male or a female, such as *teacher* as opposed to *businessman* or *shepherd.* **b** (in Latin, Greek, etc.) denoting a noun that retains the same grammatical gender regardless of the sex of the referent. ◆ NOUN [5] an epicene person or creature. [6] an epicene noun.
▷**HISTORY** C15: from Latin *epicoenus* of both genders, from Greek *epikoinos* common to many, from *koinos* common
▸**ˌepiˈcenism** NOUN

epicentre *or* US **epicenter** (ˈɛpɪˌsɛntə) NOUN, *plural* **-tres** *or* US **-ters.** [1] the point on the earth's surface directly above the focus of an earthquake or underground nuclear explosion. Compare **focus** (sense 6). [2] *Informal* the absolute centre of something: *the epicentre of world sprinting.*
▷**HISTORY** C19: from New Latin *epicentrum,* from Greek *epikentros* over the centre, from EPI- + *kentron* needle; see CENTRE
▸**ˌepiˈcentral** ADJECTIVE

epiclesis (ˌɛpɪˈkliːsɪs) NOUN, *plural* **-ses** (-siːz). *Christianity* the invocation of the Holy Spirit to consecrate the bread and wine of the Eucharist.
▷**HISTORY** C19: from Greek, from EPI- + *klēsis* a prayer, from *kalein* to call

epicontinental (ˌɛpɪˌkɒntɪˈnɛntᵊl) ADJECTIVE (esp of a sea) situated on a continental shelf or continent.

epicotyl (ˌɛpɪˈkɒtɪl) NOUN the part of an embryo plant stem above the cotyledons but beneath the terminal bud.
▷**HISTORY** C19: from EPI- + Greek *kotulē;* see COTYLEDON

epicrisis (ˈɛpɪˌkraɪsɪs) NOUN *Pathol* a secondary crisis occurring in the course of a disease.
▷**HISTORY** C20: from EPI- + CRISIS

epicritic (ˌɛpɪˈkrɪtɪk) ADJECTIVE (of certain nerve fibres of the skin) serving to perceive and distinguish fine variations of temperature or touch.
▷**HISTORY** C20: from Greek *epikritikos* decisive, from *epikrinein* to decide, from EPI- + *krinein* to judge

epic simile NOUN an extended simile, as used in the epic poetry of Homer and other writers.

epicure (ˈɛpɪˌkjʊə) NOUN [1] a person who cultivates a discriminating palate for the enjoyment of good food and drink; gourmet. [2] a person devoted to sensual pleasures.

▷HISTORY C16: from Medieval Latin *epicūrus*, after Epicurus; see **Epicurean**
▸**ˈepicurˌism** NOUN

epicurean (ˌɛpɪkjʊˈriːən) ADJECTIVE [1] devoted to sensual pleasures, esp food and drink; hedonistic. [2] suitable for an epicure: *an epicurean feast*. ◆ NOUN [3] an epicure; gourmet.
▸**ˌepicuˈreanism** NOUN

Epicurean (ˌɛpɪkjʊˈriːən) ADJECTIVE [1] of or relating to the philosophy of Epicurus, the Greek philosopher (341–270 B.C.), who held that the highest good is pleasure. ◆ NOUN [2] a follower of the philosophy of Epicurus.
▸**ˌEpicuˈreanism** NOUN

epicuticle (ˈɛpɪˌkjuːtɪkᵊl) NOUN [1] *Botany* a waxy layer on the surface of the cuticle. [2] *Zoology* the outermost lipoprotein layer of the insect cuticle.

epicycle (ˈɛpɪˌsaɪkᵊl) NOUN [1] *Astronomy* (in the Ptolemaic system) a small circle, around which a planet was thought to revolve, whose centre describes a larger circle (the **deferent**) centred on the earth. [2] a circle that rolls around the inside or outside of another circle, so generating an epicycloid or hypocycloid.
▷HISTORY C14: from Late Latin *epicyclus*, from Greek *epikuklos;* see EPI-, CYCLE
▸**epicyclic** (ˌɛpɪˈsaɪklɪk, -ˈsɪklɪk) *or* **ˌepiˈcyclical** ADJECTIVE

epicyclic train NOUN a cluster of gears consisting of a central gearwheel with external teeth (the sun), a coaxial gearwheel of greater diameter with internal teeth (the annulus), and one or more planetary gears engaging with both of them to provide a large gear ratio in a compact space.

epicycloid (ˌɛpɪˈsaɪklɔɪd) NOUN the curve described by a point on the circumference of a circle as this circle rolls around the outside of another fixed circle, the two circles being coplanar. Compare **hypocycloid, cycloid** (sense 4).
▸**ˌepicyˈcloidal** ADJECTIVE

epicycloidal wheel NOUN one of the planetary gears of an epicyclic train.

Epidaurus (ˌɛpɪˈdɔːrəs; *Greek* ɛpiˈðaurɔs) NOUN an ancient port in Greece, in the NE Peloponnese, in Argolis on the Saronic Gulf.

epideictic (ˌɛpɪˈdaɪktɪk) ADJECTIVE designed to display something, esp the skill of the speaker in rhetoric. Also: **epidictic** (ˌɛpɪˈdɪktɪk).
▷HISTORY C18: from Greek *epideiktikos*, from *epideiknunai* to display, show off, from *deiknunai* to show

epidemic (ˌɛpɪˈdɛmɪk) ADJECTIVE [1] (esp of a disease) attacking or affecting many persons simultaneously in a community or area. ◆ NOUN [2] a widespread occurrence of a disease: *an influenza epidemic*. [3] a rapid development, spread, or growth of something, esp something unpleasant: *an epidemic of strikes*.
▷HISTORY C17: from French *épidémique*, via Late Latin from Greek *epidēmia* literally: among the people, from EPI- + *dēmos* people
▸**ˌepiˈdemically** ADVERB

epidemic encephalitis NOUN *Pathol* a technical name for **sleeping sickness** (sense 2).

epidemic meningitis NOUN another name for **cerebrospinal meningitis.**

epidemic parotitis NOUN another name for **mumps.**

epidemiology (ˌɛpɪˌdiːmɪˈɒlədʒɪ) NOUN the branch of medical science concerned with the occurrence, transmission, and control of epidemic diseases.
▸**epidemiological** (ˌɛpɪˌdiːmɪəˈlɒdʒɪkᵊl) ADJECTIVE ▸**ˌepiˌdemioˈlogically** ADVERB ▸**ˌepiˌdemiˈologist** NOUN

epidermis (ˌɛpɪˈdɜːmɪs) NOUN [1] Also called: **cuticle.** the thin protective outer layer of the skin, composed of stratified epithelial tissue. [2] the outer layer of cells of an invertebrate. [3] the outer protective layer of cells of a plant, which may be thickened by a cuticle.
▷HISTORY C17: via Late Latin from Greek, from EPI- + *derma* skin
▸**ˌepiˈdermal** *or* **ˌepiˈdermic** *or* **ˌepiˈdermoid** ADJECTIVE

epidermolysis bullosa (ˌɛpɪdɜːˈmɒlɪsɪs bʊˈləʊzə) NOUN a group of genetic disorders causing blistering of the skin and mucous membranes. In simple cases the blistering is induced by injury, but in serious cases it occurs spontaneously.

epidiascope (ˌɛpɪˈdaɪəˌskəʊp) NOUN an optical device for projecting a magnified image onto a screen. See also **episcope.**

epididymis (ˌɛpɪˈdɪdɪmɪs) NOUN, *plural* **-didymides** (-dɪˈdɪmɪˌdiːz). *Anatomy* a convoluted tube situated along the posterior margin of each testis, in which spermatozoa are stored and conveyed to the vas deferens.
▷HISTORY C17: from Greek *epididumis*, from EPI- + *didumos* twin, testicle; see DIDYMOUS
▸**ˌepiˈdidymal** ADJECTIVE

epidote (ˈɛpɪˌdəʊt) NOUN a green mineral consisting of hydrated calcium iron aluminium silicate in monoclinic crystalline form: common in metamorphic rocks. Formula: $Ca_2(Al,Fe)_3(SiO_4)_3(OH)$.
▷HISTORY C19: from French *épidote*, ultimately from Greek *epididonai* to increase, from *didonai* to give; so called because two sides of its crystal are longer than the other two sides
▸**epidotic** (ˌɛpɪˈdɒtɪk) ADJECTIVE

epidural (ˌɛpɪˈdjʊərəl) ADJECTIVE [1] Also: **extradural.** upon or outside the dura mater. ◆ NOUN [2] Also called: **epidural anaesthesia. a** injection of anaesthetic into the space outside the dura mater enveloping the spinal cord. **b** anaesthesia induced by this method.
▷HISTORY C19: from EPI- + DUR(A MATER) + -AL[1]

epifocal (ˌɛpɪˈfəʊkᵊl) ADJECTIVE *Geology* situated or occurring at an epicentre.

epigamic (ˌɛpɪˈgæmɪk) ADJECTIVE *Zoology* attractive to the opposite sex: *epigamic coloration*.

epigastrium (ˌɛpɪˈgæstrɪəm) NOUN, *plural* **-tria** (-trɪə). the upper middle part of the abdomen, above the navel and below the breast.
▷HISTORY C17: from New Latin, from Greek EPI- + *gastrion*, from *gastēr* stomach
▸**ˌepiˈgastric** *or* **ˌepiˈgastrial** ADJECTIVE

epigeal (ˌɛpɪˈdʒiːəl), **epigean,** *or* **epigeous** ADJECTIVE [1] of or relating to seed germination in which the cotyledons appear above the ground because of the growth of the hypocotyl. [2] living or growing on or close to the surface of the ground.
▷HISTORY C19: from Greek *epigeios* of the earth, from EPI- + *gē* earth

epigene (ˈɛpɪˌdʒiːn) ADJECTIVE formed or taking place at or near the surface of the earth. Compare **hypogene.**
▷HISTORY C19: from French *épigène*, ultimately from Greek *epigignesthai* to be born after, from *gignesthai* to be born

epigenesis (ˌɛpɪˈdʒɛnɪsɪs) NOUN [1] the widely accepted theory that an individual animal or plant develops by the gradual differentiation and elaboration of a fertilized egg cell. Compare **preformation** (sense 2). [2] the formation or alteration of rocks after the surrounding rock has been formed. [3] alteration of the mineral composition of a rock by external agents: a type of metamorphism.
▸**ˌepiˈgenesist** *or* **epigenist** (ɪˈpɪdʒɪnɪst) NOUN

epigenetic (ˌɛpɪdʒɪˈnɛtɪk) ADJECTIVE [1] of or relating to epigenesis. [2] denoting processes by which heritable modifications in gene function occur without a change in the sequence of the DNA.
▸**ˌepigeˈnetically** ADVERB

epigenous (ɪˈpɪdʒɪnəs) ADJECTIVE *Biology* growing on the surface, esp the upper surface, of an organism or part: *an epigenous fungus*.

epigeous (ˌɛpɪˈdʒiːəs) ADJECTIVE a variant of **epigeal.**

epiglottis (ˌɛpɪˈglɒtɪs) NOUN, *plural* **-tises** *or* **-tides** (-tɪˌdiːz). a thin cartilaginous flap that covers the entrance to the larynx during swallowing, preventing food from entering the trachea.
▸**ˌepiˈglottal** *or* **ˌepiˈglottic** ADJECTIVE

epignathous (ˌɛpɪgˈneɪθəs) ADJECTIVE *Zoology* having a protruding upper jaw.

epigone (ˈɛpɪˌgəʊn) *or* **epigon** (ˈɛpɪˌgɒn) NOUN *Rare* an inferior follower or imitator.
▷HISTORY C19: from Greek *epigonos* one born after, from *epigignesthai;* see EPIGENE

Epigoni (ɪˈpɪgəˌnaɪ) PLURAL NOUN, *singular* **-onus** (-ənəs). *Greek myth* the descendants of the Seven against Thebes, who undertook a second expedition against the city and eventually captured and destroyed it.
▷HISTORY C20: from Greek *epigonoi* those born after

epigram (ˈɛpɪˌgræm) NOUN [1] a witty, often paradoxical remark, concisely expressed. [2] a short, pungent, and often satirical poem, esp one having a witty and ingenious ending.
▷HISTORY C15: from Latin *epigramma*, from Greek: inscription, from *epigraphein* to write upon, from *graphein* to write
▸**ˌepigramˈmatic** ADJECTIVE ▸**ˌepigramˈmatically** ADVERB

epigrammatize *or* **epigrammatise** (ˌɛpɪˈgræməˌtaɪz) VERB to make an epigram or epigrams (about).
▸**ˌepiˈgrammatism** NOUN ▸**ˌepiˈgrammatist** NOUN

epigraph (ˈɛpɪˌgrɑːf, -ˌgræf) NOUN [1] a quotation at the beginning of a book, chapter, etc., suggesting its theme. [2] an inscription on a monument or building.
▷HISTORY C17: from Greek *epigraphē;* see EPIGRAM
▸**epigraphic** (ˌɛpɪˈgræfɪk) *or* **ˌepiˈgraphical** ADJECTIVE
▸**ˌepiˈgraphically** ADVERB

epigraphy (ɪˈpɪgrəfɪ) NOUN [1] the study of ancient inscriptions. [2] epigraphs collectively.
▸**eˈpigraphist** *or* **eˈpigrapher** NOUN

epigynous (ɪˈpɪdʒɪnəs) ADJECTIVE (of flowers) having the receptacle enclosing and fused with the gynoecium so that the other floral parts arise above it.
▷HISTORY C19: from EPI- + Greek *gunē* (female organ, pistil) + -OUS
▸**eˈpigyny** NOUN

epilate (ˈɛpɪˌleɪt) VERB (*tr*) *Rare* to remove hair from.
▷HISTORY C19: from French *épiler* (modelled on *dépiler* DEPILATE) + -ATE[1]
▸**ˌepiˈlation** NOUN

epilator (ˈɛpɪˌleɪtə) NOUN an electrical appliance consisting of a metal spiral head that rotates at high speed, plucking unwanted hair.

epilepsy (ˈɛpɪˌlɛpsɪ) NOUN a disorder of the central nervous system characterized by periodic loss of consciousness with or without convulsions. In some cases it is due to brain damage but in others the cause is unknown. See also **grand mal, petit mal.**
▷HISTORY C16: from Late Latin *epilēpsia*, from Greek, from *epilambanein* to attack, seize, from *lambanein* to take

epileptic (ˌɛpɪˈlɛptɪk) ADJECTIVE [1] of, relating to, or having epilepsy. ◆ NOUN [2] a person who has epilepsy.
▸**ˌepiˈleptically** ADVERB

epileptogenic (ˌɛpɪˌlɛptəʊˈdʒɛnɪk) ADJECTIVE causing an epileptic attack.

epileptoid (ˌɛpɪˈlɛptɔɪd) *or* **epileptiform** (ˌɛpɪˈlɛptɪˌfɔːm) ADJECTIVE resembling epilepsy.

epilimnion (ˌɛpɪˈlɪmnɪən) NOUN the upper layer of water in a lake.
▷HISTORY C20: from EPI- + Greek *limnion*, diminutive of *limnē* lake

epilithic (ˌɛpɪˈlɪθɪk) ADJECTIVE (of plants) growing on the surface of rock.

epilogue (ˈɛpɪˌlɒg) NOUN [1] **a** a speech, usually in verse, addressed to the audience by an actor at the end of a play. **b** the actor speaking this. [2] a short postscript to any literary work, such as a brief description of the fates of the characters in a novel. [3] *Brit* (esp formerly) the concluding programme of the day on a radio or television station, often having a religious content.
▷HISTORY C15: from Latin *epilogus*, from Greek *epilogos*, from *logos* word, speech
▸**epilogist** (ɪˈpɪlədʒɪst) NOUN

epimere (ˈɛpɪˌmɪə) NOUN *Embryol* the dorsal part of the mesoderm of a vertebrate embryo, consisting of a series of segments (somites).

epimerism (ɪˈpɪməˌrɪzəm) NOUN optical isomerism in which isomers (**epimers**) can form about asymmetric atoms within the molecule, esp in carbohydrates.
▷HISTORY C20: German *Epimer* (see EPI-, -MER) + -ISM
▸**epimeric** (ˌɛpɪˈmɛrɪk) ADJECTIVE

epimorphosis (ˌɛpɪmɔːˈfəʊsɪs) NOUN a type of development in animals, such as certain insect larvae, in which segmentation of the body is complete before hatching.
▸**ˌepiˈmorphic** ADJECTIVE

epimysium (ˌɛpɪˈmɪzɪəm) NOUN, *plural* **-sia** (-zɪə). *Anatomy* the sheath of connective tissue that encloses a skeletal muscle.
▷HISTORY from New Latin, from EPI- + Greek *mus* mouse, MUSCLE

epinasty (ˈɛpɪˌnæstɪ) NOUN, *plural* **-ties**. increased growth of the upper surface of a plant part, such as a leaf, resulting in a downward bending of the part. Compare **hyponasty**.
▷HISTORY C19: from EPI- + *-nasty,* from Greek *nastos* pressed down, from *nassein* to press
▸ˌ**epiˈnastic** ADJECTIVE

epinephrine (ˌɛpɪˈnɛfrɪn, -riːn) *or* **epinephrin** NOUN a US name for **adrenaline**.
▷HISTORY C19: from EPI- + *nephro-* + -INE[2]

epineurium (ˌɛpɪˈnjʊərɪəm) NOUN a sheath of connective tissue around two or more bundles of nerve fibres.
▷HISTORY C19: from New Latin, from EPI- + Greek *neuron* nerve + -IUM
▸ˌ**epiˈneurial** ADJECTIVE

epipelagic (ˌɛpɪpəˈlædʒɪk) ADJECTIVE of, relating to, or inhabiting the upper zone of the ocean from just below the surface to approximately 100 metres deep.

epipetalous (ˌɛpɪˈpɛtələs) ADJECTIVE *Botany* (of stamens) attached to the petals.

Epiph. ABBREVIATION FOR Epiphany.

epiphany (ɪˈpɪfənɪ) NOUN, *plural* **-nies**. 1 the manifestation of a supernatural or divine reality. 2 any moment of great or sudden revelation.
▷HISTORY C17: via Church Latin from Greek *epiphaneia* an appearing, from EPI- + *phainein* to show
▸**epiphanic** (ˌɛpɪˈfænɪk) ADJECTIVE

Epiphany (ɪˈpɪfənɪ) NOUN, *plural* **-nies**. a Christian festival held on Jan. 6, commemorating, in the Western Church, the manifestation of Christ to the Magi and, in the Eastern Church, the baptism of Christ.

epiphenomenalism (ˌɛpɪfɪˈnɒmɪnəˌlɪzəm) NOUN the dualistic doctrine that consciousness is merely a by-product of physiological processes and has no power to affect them. Compare **interactionism**, **parallelism**.
▸ˌ**epipheˈnomenalist** NOUN, ADJECTIVE

epiphenomenon (ˌɛpɪfɪˈnɒmɪnən) NOUN, *plural* **-na** (-nə). 1 a secondary or additional phenomenon; by-product. 2 *Pathol* an unexpected or atypical symptom or occurrence during the course of a disease.
▸ˌ**epipheˈnomenal** ADJECTIVE ▸ˌ**epipheˈnomenally** ADVERB

epiphragm (ˈɛpɪˌfræm) NOUN a disc of calcium phosphate and mucilage secreted by snails over the aperture of their shells before hibernation.
▷HISTORY C19: via New Latin from Greek *epiphragma* a lid, from *epiphrassein,* from EPI- + *phrassein* to place in an enclosure

epiphyllous (ˌɛpɪˈfɪləs) ADJECTIVE *Botany* (of plants) growing on, or attached to, the leaf of another plant.

epiphysis (ɪˈpɪfɪsɪs) NOUN, *plural* **-ses** (-ˌsiːz). 1 the end of a long bone, initially separated from the shaft (diaphysis) by a section of cartilage that eventually ossifies so that the two portions fuse together. 2 Also called: **epiphysis cerebri** (ˈsɛrɪbraɪ). the technical name for **pineal gland**.
▷HISTORY C17: via New Latin from Greek: a growth upon, from EPI- + *phusis* growth, from *phuein* to bring forth, produce
▸**epiphyseal** *or* **epiphysial** (ˌɛpɪˈfɪzɪəl) ADJECTIVE

epiphyte (ˈɛpɪˌfaɪt) NOUN a plant that grows on another plant but is not parasitic on it.
▸**epiphytic** (ˌɛpɪˈfɪtɪk) *or* ˌ**epiˈphytal** *or* ˌ**epiˈphytical** ADJECTIVE ▸ˌ**epiˈphytically** ADVERB

epiphytotic (ˌɛpɪfaɪˈtɒtɪk) ADJECTIVE (of plant diseases and parasites) affecting plants over a wide geographical region.
▷HISTORY from EPI- + -PHYTE + -OTIC

epirogeny (ˌɛpaɪˈrɒdʒɪnɪ) NOUN a variant spelling of **epeirogeny**.
▸**epirogenic** (ɪˌpaɪrəʊˈdʒɛnɪk) *or* **epirogenetic** (ɪˌpaɪrəʊdʒɪˈnɛtɪk) ADJECTIVE

Epirus (ɪˈpaɪərəs) NOUN 1 a region of NW Greece, part of ancient Epirus ceded to Greece after independence in 1830. 2 (in ancient Greece) a region between the Pindus mountains and the Ionian Sea, straddling the modern border with Albania.

Epis. *Bible* Also: **Epist.** Epistle.

episcopacy (ɪˈpɪskəpəsɪ) NOUN, *plural* **-cies**. 1 government of a Church by bishops. 2 another word for **episcopate**.

episcopal (ɪˈpɪskəpᵊl) ADJECTIVE of, denoting, governed by, or relating to a bishop or bishops.
▷HISTORY C15: from Church Latin *episcopālis,* from *episcopus* BISHOP
▸**eˈpiscopally** ADVERB

Episcopal (ɪˈpɪskəpᵊl) ADJECTIVE belonging to or denoting the Episcopal Church.
▸**Eˈpiscopally** ADVERB

Episcopal Church NOUN an autonomous branch of the Anglican Communion in Scotland and the US.

episcopalian (ɪˌpɪskəˈpeɪlɪən) ADJECTIVE *also* **episcopal**. 1 practising or advocating the principle of Church government by bishops. ◆ NOUN 2 an advocate of such Church government.
▸**eˌpiscoˈpalianism** NOUN

Episcopalian (ɪˌpɪskəˈpeɪlɪən) ADJECTIVE 1 belonging to or denoting the Episcopal Church. ◆ NOUN 2 a member or adherent of this Church.

episcopalism (ɪˈpɪskəpəˌlɪzəm) NOUN the belief that a Church should be governed by bishops.

episcopate (ɪˈpɪskəpɪt, -ˌpeɪt) NOUN 1 the office, status, or term of office of a bishop. 2 bishops collectively.

episcope (ˈɛpɪˌskəʊp) NOUN *Brit* an optical device that projects an enlarged image of an opaque object, such as a printed page or photographic print, onto a screen by means of reflected light. US and Canadian name: **opaque projector**. See also **epidiascope**.

episematic (ˌɛpɪsɪˈmætɪk) ADJECTIVE *Zoology* (esp of coloration) aiding recognition between animals of the same species.

episiotomy (əˌpiːzɪˈɒtəmɪ) NOUN, *plural* **-mies**. surgical incision into the perineum during the late stages of labour to prevent its laceration during childbirth and to make delivery easier.
▷HISTORY C20: from *episio-,* from Greek *epision* pubic region + -TOMY

episode (ˈɛpɪˌsəʊd) NOUN 1 an incident, event, or series of events. 2 any one of the sections into which a serialized novel or radio or television programme is divided. 3 an incident, sequence, or scene that forms part of a narrative but may be a digression from the main story. 4 (in ancient Greek tragedy) a section between two choric songs. 5 *Music* a contrasting section between statements of the subject, as in a fugue or rondo.
▷HISTORY C17: from Greek *epeisodion* something added, from *epi-* (in addition) + *eisodios* coming in, from *eis-* in + *hodos* road

episodic (ˌɛpɪˈsɒdɪk) *or* **episodical** ADJECTIVE 1 resembling or relating to an episode. 2 divided into or composed of episodes. **3.** irregular, occasional, or sporadic.
▸ˌ**epiˈsodically** ADVERB

episome (ˈɛpɪˌsəʊm) NOUN a unit of genetic material (DNA) in bacteria, such as a plasmid, that can either replicate independently or can be integrated into the host chromosome.

epispastic (ˌɛpɪˈspæstɪk) *Med* ◆ ADJECTIVE 1 producing a serous discharge or a blister. ◆ NOUN 2 an epispastic agent.
▷HISTORY C17: from Greek *epispastikos,* from *epispan* to attract, from *span* to draw; alluding to the ancient belief that blisters consisted of humours drawn to the surface of the skin

Epist. *or* **Epis.** *Bible* ABBREVIATION FOR Epistle.

epistasis (ɪˈpɪstəsɪs) NOUN 1 *Obsolete* scum on the surface of a liquid, esp on an old specimen of urine. 2 *Med* the arrest or checking of a bodily discharge, esp bleeding. 3 Also called: **hypostasis**. *Genetics* the suppression by a gene of the effect of another gene that is not its allele.
▷HISTORY C19: from Greek: a stopping, from *ephistanai* to stop, from EPI- + *histanai* to put
▸**epistatic** (ˌɛpɪˈstætɪk) ADJECTIVE

epistaxis (ˌɛpɪˈstæksɪs) NOUN the technical name for **nosebleed**.
▷HISTORY C18: from Greek: a dropping, from *epistazein* to drop on, from *stazein* to drip

epistemic (ˌɛpɪˈstiːmɪk) ADJECTIVE 1 of or relating to knowledge or epistemology. 2 denoting the branch of modal logic that deals with the formalization of certain epistemological concepts, such as knowledge, certainty, and ignorance. See also **doxastic**.
▷HISTORY C20: from Greek *epistēmē* knowledge
▸ˌ**episˈtemically** ADVERB

epistemics (ˌɛpɪˈstiːmɪks, -ˈstɛm-) NOUN (*functioning as singular*) *Chiefly Brit* the interdisciplinary study of knowledge and human information-processing, using the formal techniques of logic, linguistics, philosophy, and psychology. Compare **artificial intelligence**.

epistemological (ɪˌpɪstɪməˈlɒdʒɪkᵊl) ADJECTIVE 1 concerned with or arising from epistemology. 2 (of a philosophical problem) requiring an account of how knowledge of the given subject could be obtained.
▸**eˌpistemoˈlogically** ADVERB

epistemology (ɪˌpɪstɪˈmɒlədʒɪ) NOUN the theory of knowledge, esp the critical study of its validity, methods, and scope.
▷HISTORY C19: from Greek *epistēmē* knowledge
▸**eˌpisteˈmologist** NOUN

episternum (ˌɛpɪˈstɜːnəm) NOUN, *plural* **-na** (-nə). 1 the manubrium of the sternum in mammals. 2 another name for **interclavicle**.
▸ˌ**epiˈsternal** ADJECTIVE

epistle (ɪˈpɪsᵊl) NOUN 1 a letter, esp one that is long, formal, or didactic. 2 a literary work in letter form, esp a dedicatory verse letter of a type originated by Horace.
▷HISTORY Old English *epistol,* via Latin from Greek *epistolē,* from *epistellein* to send to, from *stellein* to prepare, send

Epistle (ɪˈpɪsᵊl) NOUN 1 *New Testament* any of the apostolic letters of Saints Paul, Peter, James, Jude, or John. 2 a reading from one of the Epistles, forming part of the Eucharistic service in many Christian Churches.

epistler (ɪˈpɪslə, ɪˈpɪstlə) *or* **epistoler** (ɪˈpɪstᵊlə) NOUN (*often capital*) 1 a writer of an epistle or epistles. 2 the person who reads the Epistle in a Christian religious service.

epistolary (ɪˈpɪstələrɪ) *or archaic* **epistolatory** ADJECTIVE 1 relating to, denoting, conducted by, or contained in letters. 2 (of a novel or other work) constructed in the form of a series of letters.

epistrophe (ɪˈpɪstrəfɪ) NOUN *Rhetoric* repetition of a word at the end of successive clauses or sentences.
▷HISTORY C17: New Latin, from Greek, from EPI- + *strophē* a turning

epistyle (ˈɛpɪˌstaɪl) NOUN another name for **architrave** (sense 1).
▷HISTORY C17: via Latin *epistȳlium* from Greek *epistulion,* from EPI- + *stulos* column, STYLE

epitaph (ˈɛpɪˌtɑːf, -ˌtæf) NOUN 1 a commemorative inscription on a tombstone or monument. 2 a speech or written passage composed in commemoration of a dead person. 3 a final judgment on a person or thing.
▷HISTORY C14: via Latin from Greek *epitaphion,* from *epitaphios* over a tomb, from EPI- + *taphos* tomb
▸**epitaphic** (ˌɛpɪˈtæfɪk) ADJECTIVE ▸ˈ**epiˌtaphist** NOUN

epitasis (ɪˈpɪtəsɪs) NOUN (in classical drama) the part of a play in which the main action develops. Compare **protasis** (sense 2), **catastrophe** (sense 2).
▷HISTORY C16: from Greek: a stretching, intensification, from *teinein* to stretch

epitaxial transistor (ˌɛpɪˈtæksɪəl) NOUN a transistor made by depositing a thin pure layer of semiconductor material (**epitaxial layer**) onto a crystalline support by epitaxy. The layer acts as one of the electrode regions, usually the collector.

epitaxy (ˈɛpɪˌtæksɪ) *or* **epitaxis** NOUN the growth of a thin layer on the surface of a crystal so that the layer has the same structure as the underlying crystal.
▸**epitaxial** (ˌɛpɪˈtæksɪəl) ADJECTIVE

epithalamium (ˌɛpɪθəˈleɪmɪəm) *or* **epithalamion** NOUN, *plural* **-mia** (-mɪə). a poem or song written to celebrate a marriage; nuptial ode.
▷HISTORY C17: from Latin, from Greek *epithalamion* marriage song, from *thalamos* bridal chamber
▸**epithalamic** (ˌɛpɪθəˈlæmɪk) ADJECTIVE

epitheca (ˌɛpɪˈθiːkə) NOUN, *plural* **-cae** (-siː). the

outer and older layer of the cell wall of a diatom. Compare **hypotheca.**
▷**HISTORY** C19: from EPI- + THECA

epithelioma (ˌɛpɪˌθiːlɪˈəʊmə) NOUN, *plural* **-mas** *or* **-mata** (-mətə). *Pathol* a malignant tumour of epithelial tissue.
▸**epitheliomatous** (ˌɛpɪˌθiːlɪˈɒmətəs) ADJECTIVE

epithelium (ˌɛpɪˈθiːlɪəm) NOUN, *plural* **-liums** *or* **-lia** (-lɪə). an animal tissue consisting of one or more layers of closely packed cells covering the external and internal surfaces of the body. The cells vary in structure according to their function, which may be protective, secretory, or absorptive.
▷**HISTORY** C18: New Latin, from EPI- + Greek *thēlē* nipple
▸ˌ**epiˈthelial** ADJECTIVE

epithet (ˈɛpɪˌθɛt) NOUN a descriptive word or phrase added to or substituted for a person's name: *"Lackland" is an epithet for King John.*
▷**HISTORY** C16: from Latin *epitheton,* from Greek, from *epitithenai* to add, from *tithenai* to put
▸ˌ**epiˈthetic** *or* ˌ**epiˈthetical** ADJECTIVE

epitome (ɪˈpɪtəmɪ) NOUN [1] a typical example of a characteristic or class; embodiment; personification: *he is the epitome of sloth.* [2] a summary of a written work; abstract.
▷**HISTORY** C16: via Latin from Greek *epitomē,* from *epitemnein* to abridge, from EPI- + *temnein* to cut
▸**epitomical** (ˌɛpɪˈtɒmɪkᵊl) *or* ˌ**epiˈtomic** ADJECTIVE

epitomize *or* **epitomise** (ɪˈpɪtəˌmaɪz) VERB *(tr)* [1] to be a personification of; typify. [2] to make an epitome of.
▸**eˈpitomist** NOUN ▸**eˌpitomiˈzation** *or* **eˌpitomiˈsation** NOUN ▸**eˈpitoˌmizer** *or* **eˈpitoˌmiser** NOUN

epitope (ˈɛpɪˌtəʊp) NOUN the site on an antigen at which a specific antibody becomes attached.

epizoic (ˌɛpɪˈzəʊɪk) ADJECTIVE [1] (of an animal or plant) growing or living on the exterior of a living animal. [2] (of plants) having seeds or fruit dispersed by animals.
▸ˌ**epiˈzoism** NOUN

epizoite (ˌɛpɪˈzəʊɪt) NOUN an organism that lives on an animal but is not parasitic on it.

epizoon (ˌɛpɪˈzəʊɒn) NOUN, *plural* **-zoa** (-ˈzəʊə). an animal, such as a parasite, that lives on the body of another animal.
▷**HISTORY** C19: New Latin, from EPI- + Greek *zōion* animal
▸ˌ**epiˈzoan** ADJECTIVE

epizootic (ˌɛpɪzəʊˈɒtɪk) ADJECTIVE [1] (of a disease) suddenly and temporarily affecting a large number of animals over a large area. ◆ NOUN [2] an epizootic disease. Compare **enzootic.**
▸ˌ**epizoˈotically** ADVERB

e pluribus unum *Latin* (eɪ ˈplʊərɪbʊs ˈuːnʊm) one out of many: the motto of the USA.

EPNS ABBREVIATION FOR electroplated nickel silver.

EPO ABBREVIATION FOR erythropoietin.

epoch (ˈiːpɒk) NOUN [1] a point in time beginning a new or distinctive period: *the invention of nuclear weapons marked an epoch in the history of warfare.* [2] a long period of time marked by some predominant or typical characteristic; era. [3] *Astronomy* a precise date to which information, such as coordinates, relating to a celestial body is referred. [4] *Geology* a unit of geological time within a period during which a series of rocks is formed: *the Pleistocene epoch.* [5] *Physics* the displacement of an oscillating or vibrating body at zero time.
▷**HISTORY** C17: from New Latin *epocha,* from Greek *epokhē* cessation; related to *ekhein* to hold, have
▸**epochal** (ˈɛpˌɒkᵊl) ADJECTIVE ▸ˈ**epˌochally** ADVERB

epoch-making ADJECTIVE of great importance; momentous.

epode (ˈɛpəʊd) NOUN *Greek prosody* [1] the part of a lyric ode that follows the strophe and the antistrophe. [2] a type of lyric poem composed of couplets in which a long line is followed by a shorter one, invented by Archilochus.
▷**HISTORY** C16: via Latin from Greek *epōidos* a singing after, from *epaidein* to sing after, from *aidein* to sing

eponym (ˈɛpənɪm) NOUN [1] a name, esp a place name, derived from the name of a real or mythical person, as for example *Constantinople* from *Constantine I.* [2] the name of the person from which such a name is derived: *in the Middle Ages, "Brutus" was thought to be the eponym of "Britain.".*
▷**HISTORY** C19: from Greek *epōnumos* giving a significant name
▸ˌ**epoˈnymic** ADJECTIVE

eponymous ADJECTIVE (ɪˈpɒnɪməs), ADJECTIVE [1] (of a person) being the person after whom a literary work, film, etc., is named: *the eponymous heroine in the film of Jane Eyre.* [2] (of a literary work, film, etc.) named after its central character or creator: *The Stooges' eponymous debut album.*
▸**eˈponymously** ADVERB

eponymy (ɪˈpɒnɪmɪ) NOUN the derivation of names of places, etc., from those of persons.

epopee (ˈɛpəʊˌpiː; *French* epɔpe) *or* **epopoeia** (ˌɛpəˈpiːə) NOUN [1] an epic poem. [2] epic poetry in general.
▷**HISTORY** C17: from French *épopée,* from Greek *epopoiia,* from EPOS + *poiein* to make

epos (ˈɛpɒs) NOUN [1] a body of poetry in which the tradition of a people is conveyed, esp a group of poems concerned with a common epic theme. [2] another word for **epic** (sense 1).
▷**HISTORY** C19: via Latin from Greek: speech, word, epic poem, song; related to Latin *vōx* VOICE

EPOS (ˈiːpɒs) ACRONYM FOR **electronic point of sale.**

epoxide (ɪˈpɒksaɪd) NOUN **a** a compound containing an oxygen atom joined to two different groups that are themselves joined to other groups. **b** *(as modifier)*: *epoxide resin.*
▷**HISTORY** C20: from EPI- + OXIDE

epoxy (ɪˈpɒksɪ) ADJECTIVE *Chem* [1] of, consisting of, or containing an oxygen atom joined to two different groups that are themselves joined to other groups: *epoxy group.* [2] of, relating to, or consisting of an epoxy resin. ◆ NOUN, *plural* **epoxies.** [3] short for **epoxy resin.**
▷**HISTORY** C20: from EPI- + OXY-²

epoxy *or* **epoxide resin** NOUN any of various tough resistant thermosetting synthetic resins containing epoxy groups: used in surface coatings, laminates, and adhesives.

EPP ABBREVIATION FOR executive pension plan.

Epping (ˈɛpɪŋ) NOUN a town in E England, in Essex, on the edge of Epping Forest: a residential centre for London. Pop.: 9922 (1991).

Epping Forest (ˈɛpɪŋ) NOUN a forest in E England, northeast of London: formerly a royal hunting ground.

EPR ABBREVIATION FOR **electron paramagnetic resonance.**

EPROM (ˈiːprɒm) NOUN *Computing* ◆ ACRONYM FOR erasable programmable read-only memory.

eps ABBREVIATION FOR earnings per share.

epsilon (ˈɛpsɪˌlɒn, ɛpˈsaɪlən) NOUN the fifth letter of the Greek alphabet (Ε, ε), a short vowel, transliterated as *e.*
▷**HISTORY** Greek *e psilon,* literally: simple *e*

Epsilon (ˈɛpsɪˌlɒn, ɛpˈsaɪlən) NOUN *(foll by the genitive case of a specified constellation)* the fifth brightest star in a constellation: *Epsilon Aurigae.*

Epsom (ˈɛpsəm) NOUN a town in SE England, in Surrey: famous for its mineral springs and for horse racing. Pop. (with Ewell): 64 405 (1991).

Epsom salts NOUN *(functioning as singular or plural)* a medicinal preparation of hydrated magnesium sulphate, used as a purgative.
▷**HISTORY** C18: named after EPSOM, where they occur naturally in the water

Epstein-Barr virus (ˈɛpstaɪn ˈbɑː) NOUN a virus belonging to the herpes family that causes infectious mononucleosis; it is also implicated in the development of Burkitt's lymphoma and Hodgkin's disease. Abbreviation: **EBV.**
▷**HISTORY** C20: named after Sir M. A. *Epstein* (born 1921), and Yvonne M. *Barr* (born 1932), British pathologists who discovered the virus

epulis (ɛˈpuːlɪs) NOUN [1] *Pathol* a swelling of the gum, usually as a result of fibrous hyperplasia. [2] *Vet science* a benign tumour attached to the jaw of an animal, esp a dog.

epyllion (ɪˈpɪlɪən) NOUN, *plural* **-lia** (-lɪə). a miniature epic.
▷**HISTORY** C19: from Greek, diminutive of EPOS

EPZ ABBREVIATION FOR export processing zone: an industrial area containing many foreign-owned factories.

EQ ABBREVIATION FOR: [1] emotional quotient, a (notional) measure of a person's adequacy in such areas as self-awareness, empathy, and dealing sensitively with other people. [late C20: by analogy with IQ] [2] equalization, the electronic balancing of sound frequencies on audio recording equipment or hi-fi to reduce distortion or achieve a specific effect.

eq. ABBREVIATION FOR: [1] equal. [2] equation. [3] equivalent.

EQC (in New Zealand) ABBREVIATION FOR Earthquake Commission.

equable (ˈɛkwəbᵊl) ADJECTIVE [1] even-tempered; placid. [2] unvarying; uniform: *an equable climate.*
▷**HISTORY** C17: from Latin *aequābilis,* from *aequāre* to make equal
▸ˌ**equaˈbility** *or* ˈ**equableness** NOUN ▸ˈ**equably** ADVERB

equal (ˈiːkwəl) ADJECTIVE [1] (often foll by *to* or *with*) identical in size, quantity, degree, intensity, etc.; the same (as). [2] having identical privileges, rights, status, etc.: *all men are equal before the law.* [3] having uniform effect or application: *equal opportunities.* [4] evenly balanced or proportioned: *the game was equal between the teams.* [5] (usually followed by *to*) having the necessary or adequate strength, ability, means, etc. (for): *to be equal to one's work.* [6] another word for **equivalent** (sense 3a). ◆ NOUN [7] a person or thing equal to another, esp in merit, ability, etc.: *he has no equal when it comes to boxing.* ◆ VERB **equals, equalling, equalled** *or US* **equals, equaling, equaled.** [8] *(tr)* to be equal to; correspond to; match: *my offer equals his.* [9] *(intr;* usually foll by *out)* to become equal or level. [10] *(tr)* to make, perform, or do something equal to: *to equal the world record.* [11] *(tr) Archaic* to make equal.
▷**HISTORY** C14: from Latin *aequālis,* from *aequus* level, of obscure origin
▸ˈ**equally** ADVERB

Language note The use of *more equal* as in *from now on their relationship will be a more equal one* is acceptable in modern English usage. *Equally* is preferred to *equally as* in sentences such as *reassuring the victims is equally important. Just as* is preferred to *equally as* in sentences such as *their surprise was just as great as his.*

equal-area NOUN *(modifier)* (of a map projection) showing area accurately and therefore distorting shape and direction. Also: **homolographic.**

equali (ɪˈkwɑːlɪ) PLURAL NOUN *Music* pieces for a group of instruments of the same kind: *Beethoven's Equali for four trombones.*
▷**HISTORY** Italian: old pl form of *uguale* equal

equalitarian (ɪˌkwɒlɪˈtɛərɪən) ADJECTIVE, NOUN a less common word for **egalitarian.**
▸**eˌqualiˈtarianism** NOUN

equality (ɪˈkwɒlɪtɪ) NOUN, *plural* **-ties.** [1] the state of being equal. [2] *Maths* a statement, usually an equation, indicating that quantities or expressions on either side of an equal sign are equal in value.

equalization payment *or* **grant** NOUN *Canadian* a financial grant made by the federal government to a poorer province in order to facilitate a level of services equal to that of a richer province.

equalize *or* **equalise** (ˈiːkwəˌlaɪz) VERB [1] *(tr)* to make equal or uniform; regularize. [2] *(intr)* (in sports) to reach the same score as one's opponent or opponents.
▸ˌ**equaliˈzation** *or* ˌ**equaliˈsation** NOUN

equalizer *or* **equaliser** (ˈiːkwəˌlaɪzə) NOUN [1] a person or thing that equalizes, esp a device to counterbalance opposing forces. [2] an electronic network introduced into a transmission circuit to alter its response, esp to reduce distortion by equalizing its response over a specified frequency range. [3] *Sport* a goal, point, etc., that levels the score. [4] *US slang* a weapon, esp a gun.

Equal Opportunities Commission NOUN (in Britain) a body appointed by the Government to enforce the provisions of the Equal Pay Act 1970 and the Sex Discrimination Act 1975. Abbreviation: **EOC.**

equal opportunity NOUN **a** the offering of employment, pay, or promotion equally to all, without discrimination as to sex, race, colour, disability, etc. **b** (*as modifier*): *our equal-opportunity policy; an equal-opportunities employer.*

equal pay NOUN the right of a man or woman to receive the same pay as a person of the opposite sex doing the same or similar work for the same or a similar employer.

equal sign *or* **equals sign** NOUN the symbol =, used to indicate a mathematical equality.

equanimity (ˌiːkwəˈnɪmɪtɪ, ˌɛkwə-) NOUN calmness of mind or temper; composure.
▷HISTORY C17: from Latin *aequanimitās,* from *aequus* even, EQUAL + *animus* mind, spirit
▸**equanimous** (ɪˈkwænɪməs) ADJECTIVE ▸**eˈquanimously** ADVERB

equate (ɪˈkweɪt) VERB (*mainly tr*) [1] to make or regard as equivalent or similar, esp in order to compare or balance. [2] *Maths* to indicate the equality of; form an equation from. [3] (*intr*) to be equal; correspond.
▷HISTORY C15: from Latin *aequāre* to make EQUAL
▸**eˈquatable** ADJECTIVE ▸**eˌquataˈbility** NOUN

equation (ɪˈkweɪʒən, -ʃən) NOUN [1] a mathematical statement that two expressions are equal: it is either an **identity** in which the variables can assume any value, or a **conditional equation** in which the variables have only certain values (roots). [2] the act of regarding as equal; equating. [3] the act of making equal or balanced; equalization. [4] a situation, esp one regarded as having a number of conflicting elements: *what you want doesn't come into the equation.* [5] the state of being equal, equivalent, or equally balanced. [6] a situation or problem in which a number of factors need to be considered. [7] See **chemical equation.** [8] *Astronomy* See **personal equation.**
▸**eˈquational** ADJECTIVE ▸**eˈquationally** ADVERB

equation of state NOUN any equation that expresses the relationship between the temperature, pressure, and volume of a substance.

equation of time NOUN the difference between apparent solar time and mean solar time, being at a maximum in February (over 14 minutes) and November (over 16 minutes).

equator (ɪˈkweɪtə) NOUN [1] the great circle of the earth with a latitude of 0°, lying equidistant from the poles; dividing the N and S hemispheres. [2] a circle dividing a sphere or other surface into two equal symmetrical parts. [3] See **magnetic equator.** [4] *Astronomy* See **celestial equator.**
▷HISTORY C14: from Medieval Latin (*circulus*) *aequātor* (*diei et noctis*) (circle) that equalizes (the day and night), from Latin *aequāre* to make EQUAL

equatorial (ˌɛkwəˈtɔːrɪəl) ADJECTIVE [1] of, like, or existing at or near the equator. [2] *Astronautics* lying in the plane of the equator: *an equatorial orbit.* [3] *Astronomy* of or referring to the celestial equator: *equatorial coordinates.* ◆ NOUN [4] an equatorial mounting.
▸**ˌequaˈtorially** ADVERB

Equatorial Guinea NOUN a republic of W Africa, consisting of Río Muni on the mainland and the island of Bioko in the Gulf of Guinea, with four smaller islands: ceded by Portugal to Spain in 1778; gained independence in 1968. Official languages: Spanish and French. Religion: Roman Catholic majority. Currency: franc. Capital: Malabo. Pop.: 486 000 (2001 est). Area: 28 049 sq. km (10 830 sq. miles). Former name (until 1964): **Spanish Guinea.**

equatorial mounting NOUN an astronomical telescope mounting that allows motion of the telescope about two mutually perpendicular axes, one of which is parallel to the earth's axis.

equerry (ˈɛkwərɪ; *at the British court* ɪˈkwɛrɪ) NOUN, *plural* **-ries.** [1] an officer attendant upon the British sovereign. [2] (formerly) an officer in a royal household responsible for the horses.
▷HISTORY C16: alteration (through influence of Latin *equus* horse) of earlier *escuirie,* from Old French: stable, group of squires, from *escuyer* SQUIRE

equestrian (ɪˈkwɛstrɪən) ADJECTIVE [1] of or relating to horses and riding. [2] on horseback; mounted. [3] depicting or representing a person on horseback: *an equestrian statue.* [4] of, relating to, or composed of Roman equites. [5] of, relating to, or composed of knights, esp the imperial free knights of the Holy Roman Empire. ◆ NOUN [6] a person skilled in riding and horsemanship.
▷HISTORY C17: from Latin *equestris,* from *eques* horseman, knight, from *equus* horse
▸**eˈquestrianˌism** NOUN

equestrienne (ɪˌkwɛstrɪˈɛn) NOUN a female rider on horseback, esp one in a circus who performs acrobatics.

equi- COMBINING FORM equal or equally: *equidistant; equilateral.*

equiangular (ˌiːkwɪˈæŋɡjʊlə) ADJECTIVE having all angles equal.

equidistant (ˌiːkwɪˈdɪstənt) ADJECTIVE distant by equal amounts from two or more places.
▸**ˌequiˈdistance** NOUN ▸**ˌequiˈdistantly** ADVERB

equilateral (ˌiːkwɪˈlætərəl) ADJECTIVE [1] having all sides of equal length: *an equilateral triangle.* ◆ NOUN [2] a geometric figure having all its sides of equal length. [3] a side that is equal in length to other sides.
▸**ˌequiˈlaterally** ADVERB

equilibrant (ɪˈkwɪlɪbrənt) NOUN a force capable of balancing another force and producing equilibrium.

equilibrate (ˌiːkwɪˈlaɪbreɪt, ɪˈkwɪlɪˌbreɪt) VERB to bring to or be in equilibrium; balance.
▷HISTORY C17: from Late Latin *aequilībrāre,* from *aequilībris* in balance; see EQUILIBRIUM
▸**equilibration** (ˌiːkwɪlaɪˈbreɪʃən, ɪˌkwɪlɪ-) NOUN
▸**equilibrator** (ɪˈkwɪlɪˌbreɪtə) NOUN

equilibrist (ɪˈkwɪlɪbrɪst) NOUN a person who performs balancing feats, esp on a high wire.
▸**eˌquiliˈbristic** ADJECTIVE

equilibrium (ˌiːkwɪˈlɪbrɪəm) NOUN, *plural* **-riums** *or* **-ria** (-rɪə). [1] a stable condition in which forces cancel one another. [2] a state or feeling of mental balance; composure. [3] any unchanging condition or state of a body, system, etc., resulting from the balance or cancelling out of the influences or processes to which it is subjected. See **thermodynamic equilibrium.** [4] *Physics* a state of rest or uniform motion in which there is no resultant force on a body. [5] *Chem* the condition existing when a chemical reaction and its reverse reaction take place at equal rates. [6] *Physics* the condition of a system that has its total energy distributed among its component parts in the statistically most probable manner. [7] *Physiol* a state of bodily balance, maintained primarily by special receptors in the inner ear. [8] the economic condition in which there is neither excess demand nor excess supply in a market.
▷HISTORY C17: from Latin *aequilībrium,* from *aequi-* EQUI- + *lībra* pound, balance

equimolecular (ˌiːkwɪməˈlɛkjʊlə) ADJECTIVE (of substances, solutions, etc.) containing equal numbers of molecules.

equine (ˈɛkwaɪn) ADJECTIVE [1] of, relating to, or resembling a horse. [2] of, relating to, or belonging to the family *Equidae,* which comprises horses, zebras, and asses.
▷HISTORY C18: from Latin *equīnus,* from *equus* horse
▸**ˈequinely** ADVERB

equine distemper NOUN another name for **strangles.**

equine herpesvirus NOUN *Vet science* a viral disease of horses that may cause respiratory signs, abortion, neonatal death, and paresis. A vaccine is available against this disease. Abbreviation: **EHV.**

equine infectious anaemia NOUN *Vet science* a viral disease of horses, donkeys, and mules characterized by fever, anaemia, jaundice, depression, and weight loss. Abbreviation: **EIA.**

equine influenza NOUN *Vet science* a respiratory disease of horses, caused by the *Orthomyxoviridae type A* virus, characterized by a fever and persistent cough.

equinoctial (ˌiːkwɪˈnɒkʃəl) ADJECTIVE [1] relating to or occurring at either or both equinoxes. [2] (of a plant) having flowers that open and close at specific regular times. [3] *Astronomy* of or relating to the celestial equator. ◆ NOUN [4] a storm or gale at or near an equinox. [5] another name for **celestial equator.**
▷HISTORY C14: from Latin *aequinoctiālis* concerning the EQUINOX

equinoctial circle *or* **line** NOUN another name for **celestial equator.**

equinoctial point NOUN either of the two points at which the celestial equator intersects the ecliptic.

equinox (ˈiːkwɪˌnɒks, ˈɛkwɪˌnɒks) NOUN [1] either of the two occasions, six months apart, when day and night are of equal length. See **vernal equinox, autumnal equinox.** [2] another name for **equinoctial point.**
▷HISTORY C14: from Medieval Latin *equinoxium,* changed from Latin *aequinoctium,* from *aequi-* EQUI- + *nox* night

equinumerous (ˌiːkwɪˈnjuːmərəs) ADJECTIVE *Logic* having the same number of members.

equip (ɪˈkwɪp) VERB **equips, equipping, equipped.** (*tr*) [1] to furnish with (necessary supplies, etc.). [2] (*usually passive*) to provide with abilities, understanding, etc.: *her son was never equipped to be a scholar.* [3] to dress out; attire.
▷HISTORY C16: from Old French *eschiper* to embark, fit out (a ship), of Germanic origin; compare Old Norse *skipa* to put in order, *skip* SHIP
▸**eˈquipper** NOUN

equipage (ˈɛkwɪpɪdʒ) NOUN [1] a horse-drawn carriage, esp one elegantly equipped and attended by liveried footmen. [2] (formerly) the stores and equipment of a military unit. [3] *Archaic* **a** a set of useful articles. **b** a group of attendants; retinue.

equipartition (ˌɛkwɪpɑːˈtɪʃən) NOUN the equal division of the energy of a system in thermal equilibrium between different degrees of freedom. This principle was assumed to be exact in classical physics, but quantum theory shows that it is true only in certain special cases.

équipe (eɪˈkiːp) NOUN (esp in motor racing) a team.
▷HISTORY French

equipment (ɪˈkwɪpmənt) NOUN [1] an act or instance of equipping. [2] the items so provided. [3] a set of tools, devices, kit, etc., assembled for a specific purpose, such as a soldier's kit and weapons.

equipoise (ˈɛkwɪˌpɔɪz) NOUN [1] even balance of weight or other forces; equilibrium. [2] a counterbalance; counterpoise. ◆ VERB [3] (*tr*) to offset or balance in weight or force; balance.

equipollent (ˌiːkwɪˈpɒlənt) ADJECTIVE [1] equal or equivalent in significance, power, or effect. [2] *Logic* (of two propositions) logically deducible from each other; equivalent. [3] *Maths, logic* (of two classes) having the same cardinality. ◆ NOUN [4] something that is equipollent.
▷HISTORY C15: from Latin *aequipollēns* of equal importance, from EQUI- + *pollēre* to be able, be strong
▸**ˌequiˈpollence** *or* **ˌequiˈpollency** NOUN ▸**ˌequiˈpollently** ADVERB

equiponderate (ˌiːkwɪˈpɒndəˌreɪt) VERB (*tr*) to equal or balance in weight, power, force, etc.; offset; counterbalance.
▷HISTORY C17: from Medieval Latin *aequiponderāre,* from Latin EQUI- + *ponderāre* to weigh
▸**ˌequiˈponderance** *or* **ˌequiˈponderancy** NOUN
▸**ˌequiˈponderant** ADJECTIVE

equipotential (ˌiːkwɪpəˈtɛnʃəl) ADJECTIVE [1] having the same electric potential or uniform electric potential. [2] Also: **equipotent** (ˌiːkwɪˈpəʊtᵊnt). equivalent in power or effect. ◆ NOUN [3] an equipotential line or surface.
▸**ˌequipoˌtentiˈality** NOUN

equiprobable (ˌiːkwɪˈprɒbəbᵊl) ADJECTIVE equally probable.
▸**ˌequiˌprobaˈbility** NOUN

equisetum (ˌɛkwɪˈsiːtəm) NOUN, *plural* **-tums** *or* **-ta** (-tə). any tracheophyte plant of the genus *Equisetum,* which comprises the horsetails.
▷HISTORY C19: New Latin, changed from Latin *equisaetum,* from *equus* horse + *saeta* bristle

equitable (ˈɛkwɪtəbᵊl) ADJECTIVE [1] impartial or reasonable; fair; just: *an equitable decision.* [2] *Law* relating to or valid in equity, as distinct from common law or statute law. [3] *Law* (formerly) recognized in a court of equity only, as claims, rights, etc.
▷HISTORY C17: from French *équitable,* from *équité* EQUITY
▸**ˈequitableness** NOUN ▸**ˈequitably** ADVERB

equitant (ˈɛkwɪtᵊnt) ADJECTIVE (of a leaf) having the base folded around the stem so that it overlaps the leaf above and opposite.

▷HISTORY C19: from Latin *equitāns* riding, from *equitāre* to ride, from *equus* horse

equitation (ˌɛkwɪˈteɪʃən) NOUN the study and practice of riding and horsemanship.
▷HISTORY C16: from Latin *equitātiō*, from *equitāre* to ride, from *equus* horse

equites (ˈɛkwɪˌtiːz) PLURAL NOUN (in ancient Rome) 1 the cavalry. 2 members of a social order distinguished by wealth and ranking just below the senators. Also called: **knights.**
▷HISTORY from Latin, plural of *eques* horseman, from *equus* horse

equities (ˈɛkwɪtɪz) PLURAL NOUN another name for **ordinary shares.**

equity (ˈɛkwɪtɪ) NOUN, *plural* **-ties.** 1 the quality of being impartial or reasonable; fairness. 2 an impartial or fair act, decision, etc. 3 *Law* a system of jurisprudence founded on principles of natural justice and fair conduct. It supplements the common law and mitigates its inflexibility, as by providing a remedy where none exists at law. 4 *Law* an equitable right or claim: *equity of redemption.* 5 the interest of ordinary shareholders in a company. 6 the market value of a debtor's property in excess of all debts to which it is liable.
▷HISTORY C14: from Old French *equite*, from Latin *aequitās*, from *aequus* level, EQUAL

Equity (ˈɛkwɪtɪ) NOUN the actors' trade union. Full name: **Actors' Equity Association.**

equity capital NOUN the part of the share capital of a company owned by ordinary shareholders or in certain circumstances by other classes of shareholder.

equity-linked policy NOUN an insurance or assurance policy in which premiums are invested partially or wholly in ordinary shares for the eventual benefit of the beneficiaries of the policy.

equity of redemption NOUN *Property law* the right that a mortgager has in equity to redeem his property on payment of the sum owing, even though the sum is overdue. See also **foreclose.**

equiv. ABBREVIATION FOR equivalent.

equivalence (ɪˈkwɪvələns) *or* **equivalency** NOUN 1 the state of being equivalent or interchangeable. 2 *Maths, logic* **a** the relationship between two statements each of which implies the other. **b** the binary truth-function that takes the value *true* when both component sentences are true or when both are false, corresponding to English *if and only if*. Symbol: ≡ or ↔ , as in $-(p \wedge q) \equiv -p \vee -q$. Also called: **biconditional.**

equivalence relation NOUN *Logic, maths* a relation that is reflexive, symmetric, and transitive: it imposes a partition on its domain of definition so that two elements belong to the same subset if and only if the relation holds between them.

equivalency (ˌɛkwɪˈveɪlənsɪ) *or* **equivalence** NOUN *Chem* the state of having equal valencies.
▸ˌ**equiˈvalent** ADJECTIVE

equivalent (ɪˈkwɪvələnt) ADJECTIVE 1 equal or interchangeable in value, quantity, significance, etc. 2 having the same or a similar effect or meaning. 3 *Maths* **a** having a particular property in common; equal. **b** (of two equations or inequalities) having the same set of solutions. **c** (of two sets) having the same cardinal number. 4 *Maths, logic* (of two propositions) having an equivalence between them. ◆ NOUN 5 something that is equivalent. 6 short for **equivalent weight.**
▷HISTORY C15: from Late Latin *aequivalēns*, from *aequivalēre* to be equally significant, from Latin *aequi-* EQUI- + *valēre* to be worth
▸**eˈquivalently** ADVERB

equivalent air speed NOUN the speed at sea level that would produce the same Pitot-static tube reading as that measured at altitude.

equivalent circuit NOUN an arrangement of simple electrical components that is electrically equivalent to a complex circuit and is used to simplify circuit analysis.

equivalent focal length NOUN *Optics* the ratio of the size of an image of a small distant object near the optical axis to the angular distance of the object in radians.

equivalent weight NOUN the weight of an element or compound that will combine with or displace 8 grams of oxygen or 1.007 97 grams of hydrogen. Also called: **gram equivalent.**

equivocal (ɪˈkwɪvəkᵊl) ADJECTIVE 1 capable of varying interpretations; ambiguous. 2 deliberately misleading or vague; evasive. 3 of doubtful character or sincerity; dubious.
▷HISTORY C17: from Late Latin *aequivocus*, from Latin EQUI- + *vōx* voice
▸**eˈquivocally** ADVERB ▸**eˌquivoˈcality** *or* **eˌquivocalness** NOUN

equivocate (ɪˈkwɪvəˌkeɪt) VERB (*intr*) to use vague or ambiguous language, esp in order to avoid speaking directly or honestly; hedge.
▷HISTORY C15: from Medieval Latin *aequivocāre*, from Late Latin *aequivocus* ambiguous, EQUIVOCAL
▸**eˈquivoˌcatingly** ADVERB ▸**eˈquivoˌcator** NOUN
▸**eˈquivocatory** ADJECTIVE

equivocation (ɪˌkwɪvəˈkeɪʃən) NOUN 1 the act or an instance of equivocating. 2 *Logic* a fallacy based on the use of the same term in different senses, esp as the middle term of a syllogism, as *the badger lives in the bank, and the bank is in the High Street, so the badger lives in the High Street.*

equivoque *or* **equivoke** (ˈɛkwɪˌvəʊk) NOUN 1 a play on words; pun. 2 an ambiguous phrase or expression. 3 double meaning; ambiguity.
▷HISTORY C14: *equivoc* EQUIVOCAL

Equuleus (ɛˈkwʊlɪəs) NOUN, *Latin genitive* **Equulei** (ɛˈkwʊlɪˌaɪ). a small faint constellation in the N hemisphere between Pegasus and Aquarius.
▷HISTORY from Latin: a young horse, from *equus* horse

er¹ (ə, ɜː) INTERJECTION a sound made when hesitating in speech.

er² THE INTERNET DOMAIN NAME FOR Eritrea.

Er THE CHEMICAL SYMBOL FOR erbium.

ER ABBREVIATION FOR: 1 (in the US) Emergency Room (in hospitals). 2 Elizabeth Regina. [Latin: Queen Elizabeth] 3 Eduardus Rex.
▷HISTORY Latin: King Edward

-er¹ SUFFIX FORMING NOUNS 1 a person or thing that performs a specified action: *reader; decanter; lighter.* 2 a person engaged in a profession, occupation, etc.: *writer; baker; bootlegger.* 3 a native or inhabitant of: *islander; Londoner; villager.* 4 a person or thing having a certain characteristic: *newcomer; double-decker; fiver.*
▷HISTORY Old English *-ere*; related to German *-er*, Latin *-ārius*

-er² SUFFIX forming the comparative degree of adjectives (*deeper, freer, sunnier*, etc.) and adverbs (*faster, slower*, etc.).
▷HISTORY Old English *-rd, -re* (adj), *-or* (adv)

era (ˈɪərə) NOUN 1 a period of time considered as being of a distinctive character; epoch. 2 an extended period of time the years of which are numbered from a fixed point or event: *the Christian era.* 3 a point in time, esp one beginning a new or distinctive period: *the discovery of antibiotics marked an era in modern medicine.* 4 *Geology* a major division of geological time, divided into several periods: *the Mesozoic era.*
▷HISTORY C17: from Latin *aera* counters, plural of *aes* brass, pieces of brass money

ERA (ˈiːrə) NOUN, ABBREVIATION OR ACRONYM FOR: 1 (in Britain) Education Reform Act: the 1988 act which established the key elements of the National Curriculum. 2 (in the US) Equal Rights Amendment: a proposed amendment to the US Constitution enshrining equality between the sexes.

eradiate (ɪˈreɪdɪˌeɪt) VERB a less common word for **radiate.** Compare **irradiate.**
▸**eˌradiˈation** NOUN

eradicate (ɪˈrædɪˌkeɪt) VERB (*tr*) 1 to obliterate; stamp out. 2 to pull or tear up by the roots.
▷HISTORY C16: from Latin *ērādīcāre* to uproot, from EX-¹ + *rādīx* root
▸**eˈradicable** ADJECTIVE ▸**eˈradicably** ADVERB
▸**eˌradiˈcation** NOUN ▸**eˈradicative** ADJECTIVE
▸**eˈradiˌcator** NOUN

erase (ɪˈreɪz) VERB 1 to obliterate or rub out (something written, typed, etc.). 2 (*tr*) to destroy all traces of; remove completely: *time erases grief.* 3 to remove (a recording) from (magnetic tape). 4 (*tr*) *Computing* to replace (data) on a storage device with characters representing an absence of data.
▷HISTORY C17: from Latin *ērādere* to scrape off, from EX-¹ + *rādere* to scratch, scrape
▸**eˈrasable** ADJECTIVE

eraser (ɪˈreɪzə) NOUN an object, such as a piece of rubber or felt, used for erasing something written, typed, etc.: *a pencil eraser.*

erasion (ɪˈreɪʒən) NOUN 1 the act of erasing; erasure. 2 the surgical scraping away of tissue, esp of bone.

Erastianism (ɪˈræstɪəˌnɪzəm) NOUN the theory that the state should have authority over the church in ecclesiastical matters.
▷HISTORY C17: named after Thomas *Erastus* (1524–83), Swiss theologian to whom such views were attributed
▸**Eˈrastian** NOUN, ADJECTIVE

erasure (ɪˈreɪʒə) NOUN 1 the act or an instance of erasing. 2 the place or mark, as on a piece of paper, where something has been erased.

Erato (ˈɛrəˌtəʊ) NOUN *Greek myth* the Muse of love poetry.

Erbil, Irbil (ˈɜːbɪl), *or* **Arbil** NOUN a city in N Iraq: important in Assyrian times. Pop.: 485 968 (latest est.). Ancient name: **Arbela.**

erbium (ˈɜːbɪəm) NOUN a soft malleable silvery-white element of the lanthanide series of metals: used in special alloys, room-temperature lasers, and as a pigment. Symbol: Er; atomic no.: 68; atomic wt.: 167.26; valency: 3; relative density: 9.006; melting pt.: 1529°C; boiling pt.: 2868°C.
▷HISTORY C19: from New Latin, from (*Ytt*)*erb*(*y*), Sweden, where it was first found + -IUM

Erciyas Dağı (*Turkish* ˈɛrdʒijɑs dɑːˈi) NOUN an extinct volcano in central Turkey. Height 3916 m (12 848 ft.).

ERCP ABBREVIATION FOR endoscopic retrograde cholangiopancreatography.

ERDF ABBREVIATION FOR European Regional Development Fund: a fund to provide money for specific projects for work on the infrastructure in countries of the European Union.

ere (ɛə) CONJUNCTION, PREPOSITION a poetic word for **before.**
▷HISTORY Old English *ǣr*; related to Old Norse *ār* early, Gothic *airis* earlier, Old High German *ēr* earlier, Greek *eri* early

Erebus¹ (ˈɛrɪbəs) NOUN *Greek myth* 1 the god of darkness, son of Chaos and brother of Night. 2 the darkness below the earth, thought to be the abode of the dead or the region they pass through on their way to Hades.

Erebus² (ˈɛrɪbəs) NOUN **Mount.** a volcano in Antarctica, on Ross Island: discovered by Sir James Ross in 1841 and named after his ship. Height: 3794 m (12 448 ft.).

Erechtheum (ɪˈrɛkθɪəm, ˌɛrəkˈθiːəm) *or* **Erechtheion** (ɪˈrɛkθɪən, ˌɛrəkˈθiːən) NOUN a temple on the Acropolis at Athens, which has a porch of caryatids.

Erechtheus (ɛˈrɛkθjuːs, -θɪəs) NOUN *Greek myth* a king of Athens who sacrificed one of his daughters because the oracle at Delphi said this was the only way to win the war against the Eleusinians.

erect (ɪˈrɛkt) ADJECTIVE 1 upright in posture or position; not bent or leaning: *an erect stance.* 2 (of an optical image) having the same orientation as the object; not inverted. 3 *Physiol* (of the penis, clitoris, or nipples) firm or rigid after swelling with blood, esp as a result of sexual excitement. 4 (of plant parts) growing vertically or at right angles to the parts from which they arise. ◆ VERB (*mainly tr*) 5 to put up; construct; build. 6 to raise to an upright position; lift up: *to erect a flagpole.* 7 to found or form; set up. 8 (*also intr*) *Physiol* to become or cause to become firm or rigid by filling with blood. 9 to hold up as an ideal; exalt. 10 *Optics* to change (an inverted image) to an upright position. 11 to draw or construct (a line, figure, etc.) on a given line or figure, esp at right angles to it.
▷HISTORY C14: from Latin *ērigere* to set up, from *regere* to control, govern
▸**eˈrectable** ADJECTIVE ▸**eˈrectly** ADVERB ▸**eˈrectness** NOUN

erectile (ɪˈrɛktaɪl) ADJECTIVE 1 *Physiol* (of tissues or organs, such as the penis or clitoris) capable of becoming rigid or erect as the result of being filled with blood. 2 capable of being erected.
▸**erectility** (ɪrɛkˈtɪlɪtɪ, ˌiːrɛk-) NOUN

erectile impotence NOUN impotence caused by the inability of the penis to become sufficiently firm to penetrate the vagina.

erection (ɪ'rɛkʃən) NOUN [1] the act of erecting or the state of being erected. [2] something that has been erected; a building or construction. [3] *Physiol* the enlarged state or condition of erectile tissues or organs, esp the penis, when filled with blood. [4] an erect penis.

erector *or* **erecter** (ɪ'rɛktə) NOUN [1] *Anatomy* any muscle that raises a part or makes it erect. [2] a person or thing that erects.

E region *or* **layer** NOUN a region of the ionosphere, extending from a height of 90 to about 150 kilometres. It reflects radio waves of medium wavelength. Also called: **Heaviside layer, Kennelly-Heaviside layer.** See also **ionosphere.**

erelong (ɛə'lɒŋ) ADVERB *Archaic or poetic* before long; soon.

eremite ('ɛrɪˌmaɪt) NOUN a Christian hermit or recluse. Compare **coenobite.**
▷HISTORY C13: see HERMIT
▸**eremitic** (ˌɛrɪ'mɪtɪk) *or* ˌ**ere'mitical** ADJECTIVE
▸**eremitism** ('ɛrɪmaɪˌtɪzəm) NOUN

erepsin (ɪ'rɛpsɪn) NOUN a mixture of proteolytic enzymes secreted by the small intestine.
▷HISTORY C20 *er-*, from Latin *ēripere* to snatch (from *rapere* to seize) + (P)EPSIN

erethism ('ɛrɪˌθɪzəm) NOUN [1] *Physiol* an abnormally high degree of irritability or sensitivity in any part of the body. [2] *Psychiatry* **a** a personality disorder resulting from mercury poisoning. **b** an abnormal tendency to become aroused quickly, esp sexually, as the result of a verbal or psychic stimulus.
▷HISTORY C18: from French *éréthisme*, from Greek *erethismos* irritation, from *erethizein* to excite, irritate
▸ˌ**ere'thismic** *or* ˌ**ere'thistic** *or* ˌ**ere'thitic** ADJECTIVE

Eretria (ɪ'rɛtrɪə) NOUN an ancient city in Greece, on the S coast of Euboea: founded as an Ionian colony; destroyed by the Persians in 490 B.C. following which it never regained its former significance.

Eretz Yisrael *or* ***Eretz Israel*** *Hebrew* ('ɛrets jis'rɑeɪl; *Yiddish* 'ɛrets jisrɑ'eɪl) NOUN *Judaism* [1] the Holy Land; Israel. [2] the concept, favoured by some extreme Zionists, of a Jewish state the territory of which matched the largest expanse of biblical Israel.
▷HISTORY literally: Land of Israel

erev ('ɛrɛv) NOUN (*in combination*) *Judaism* the day before; the eve of: *erev Shabbat* (the Sabbath eve, i.e., Friday); *erev Pesach* (the day before Passover).
▷HISTORY from Hebrew

Erevan (*Russian* jɪrɪ'van) NOUN a variant spelling of **Yerevan.**

erewhile (ɛə'waɪl) *or* **erewhiles** ADVERB *Archaic* a short time ago; a little while before.

erf (ɜːf) NOUN, *plural* **erven** ('ɜːvən). *South African* a plot of land, usually urban, marked off for building purposes.
▷HISTORY Afrikaans

Erf (ɜːf) ABBREVIATION FOR electrorheological fluid: a man-made liquid that thickens or solidifies when an electric current passes through it and returns to a liquid when the current ceases.

erg[1] (ɜːg) NOUN the cgs unit of work or energy. 1 erg is equivalent to 10^{-7} joule.
▷HISTORY C19: from Greek *ergon* work

erg[2] (ɜːg) NOUN, *plural* **ergs** *or* **areg.** an area of shifting sand dunes in a desert, esp the Sahara.
▷HISTORY C19: from Arabic *'irj*

ergative ('ɜːgətɪv) *Linguistics* ◆ ADJECTIVE [1] denoting a type of verb that takes the same noun as either direct object or as subject, with equivalent meaning. Thus, "fuse" is an ergative verb: "He fused the lights" and "The lights fused" have equivalent meaning. [2] denoting a case of nouns in certain languages, for example, Eskimo or Basque, marking a noun used interchangeably as either the direct object of a transitive verb or the subject of an intransitive verb. [3] denoting a language that has ergative verbs or ergative nouns. ◆ NOUN [4] an ergative verb. [5] an ergative noun or case of nouns.
▷HISTORY C20: from Greek *ergatēs* a workman + -IVE

ergatocracy (ˌɜːgə'tɒkrəsɪ) NOUN, *plural* **-cies.** *Rare* government by the workers.
▷HISTORY C20: from Greek *ergatēs* a workman, from *ergon* work, deed + -CRACY

ergo ('ɜːgəʊ) SENTENCE CONNECTOR therefore; hence.
▷HISTORY C14: from Latin: therefore

ergograph ('ɜːgəˌgrɑːf, -ˌgræf) NOUN an instrument that measures and records the amount of work a muscle does during contraction, its rate of fatigue, etc.

ergometer (ɜː'gɒmɪtə) NOUN a dynamometer.
▷HISTORY C20: from Greek *ergon* work + -METER

ergonomic (ˌɜːgə'nɒmɪk) ADJECTIVE [1] of or relating to ergonomics. [2] designed to minimize physical effort and discomfort, and hence maximize efficiency.

ergonomics (ˌɜːgə'nɒmɪks) NOUN (*functioning as singular*) the study of the relationship between workers and their environment, esp the equipment they use. Also called: **biotechnology.**
▷HISTORY C20: from Greek *ergon* work + (ECO)NOMICS
▸**ergonomist** (ɜː'gɒnəmɪst) NOUN

ergosterol (ɜː'gɒstəˌrɒl) NOUN a plant sterol that is converted into vitamin D by the action of ultraviolet radiation. Formula: $C_{28}H_{43}OH$.

ergot ('ɜːgət, -gɒt) NOUN [1] a disease of cereals and other grasses caused by ascomycete fungi of the genus *Claviceps*, esp *C. purpurea*, in which the seeds or grain of the plants are replaced by the spore-containing bodies (sclerotia) of the fungus. [2] any fungus causing this disease. [3] the dried sclerotia of *C. purpurea*, used as the source of certain alkaloids used to treat haemorrhage, facilitate uterine contraction in childbirth, etc.
▷HISTORY C17: from French: spur (of a cock), of unknown origin

ergotism ('ɜːgəˌtɪzəm) NOUN ergot poisoning, producing either burning pains and eventually gangrene in the limbs or itching skin and convulsions. Also called: **Saint Anthony's fire.**

eric *or* **eriach** ('ɛrɪk) NOUN (in old Irish law) a fine paid by a murderer to the family of his victim. Compare **wergild.**
▷HISTORY C16: from Irish *eiric*

erica ('ɛrɪkə) NOUN any shrub of the ericaceous genus *Erica*, including the heaths and some heathers.
▷HISTORY C19: via Latin from Greek *ereikē* heath

ericaceous (ˌɛrɪ'keɪʃəs) ADJECTIVE of, relating to, or belonging to the *Ericaceae*, a family of trees and shrubs with typically bell-shaped flowers: includes heather, rhododendron, azalea, and arbutus.
▷HISTORY C19: from New Latin *Ericăceae*, from Latin *erīca* heath, from Greek *ereikē*

ericoid ('ɛrɪˌkɔɪd) ADJECTIVE *Botany* (of leaves) small and tough, resembling those of heather.

Eridanus (ɛ'rɪdənəs) NOUN, *Latin genitive* **Eridani** (ɛ'rɪdəˌnaɪ). a long twisting constellation in the S hemisphere extending from Orion to Hydrus and containing the first magnitude star Achernar.
▷HISTORY from Greek *Eridanos* river in Italy (sometimes identified with the Po) into which, according to legend, Phaëthon fell

Erie[1] ('ɪərɪ) NOUN [1] (*plural* **Eries** *or* **Erie**) a member of a North American Indian people formerly living south of Lake Erie. [2] the language of this people, possibly belonging to the Iroquoian family.

Erie[2] ('ɪərɪ) NOUN [1] **Lake.** a lake between the US and Canada: the southernmost and the shallowest of the Great Lakes; empties by the Niagara River into Lake Ontario. Area: 25 718 sq. km (9930 sq. miles). [2] a port in NW Pennsylvania, on Lake Erie. Pop.: 103 717 (2000).

Erie Canal NOUN a canal in New York State between Albany and Buffalo, linking the Hudson River with Lake Erie. Length: 579 km (360 miles).

erigeron (ɪ'rɪdʒərən, -'rɪg-) NOUN any plant of the genus *Erigeron*, whose flowers resemble asters but have narrower rays: family *Asteraceae* (composites). See also **fleabane** (sense 1).
▷HISTORY C17: via Latin from Greek, from *ēri* early + *gerōn* old man; from the white down characteristic of some species

Erin ('ɪərɪn, 'ɛərɪn) NOUN an archaic or poetic name for **Ireland**[1].
▷HISTORY from Irish Gaelic *Éirinn*, dative of Ireland

erinaceous (ˌɛrɪ'neɪʃəs) ADJECTIVE of, relating to, or resembling hedgehogs.
▷HISTORY C18: from Latin *ērinăceus* hedgehog

eringo (ɪ'rɪŋgəʊ) NOUN, *plural* **-goes** *or* **-gos.** a variant spelling of **eryngo.**

erinus (ɪ'raɪnəs) NOUN any plant of the scrophulariaceous genus *Erinus*, native to S Africa and S Europe, esp *E. alpinus*, grown as a rock plant for its white, purple, or carmine flowers.
▷HISTORY New Latin, from Greek *erinos*, an unidentified plant

Erinyes (ɪ'rɪnɪˌiːz) PLURAL NOUN, *singular* **Erinys** (ɪ'rɪnɪs, ɪ'raɪ-). *Myth* another name for the **Furies.**

eriostemon (ɛrɪ'ɒstəmən) NOUN *Austral* any rutaceous shrub of the mainly Australian genus *Eriostemon*, having waxy white or pink flowers. Also called: **wax flower.**
▷HISTORY New Latin, from Greek *erion* wool + *stemon* stamen

Eris ('ɛrɪs) NOUN *Greek myth* the goddess of discord, sister of Ares.

Eriskay pony (ˌɛrɪs'keɪ) NOUN a breed of medium-sized pony, typically grey, with a dense waterproof coat. The Eriskay is the only surviving variety of the native ponies of the Western Isles of Scotland.

eristic (ɛ'rɪstɪk) ADJECTIVE *also* **eristical.** [1] of, relating, or given to controversy or logical disputation, esp for its own sake. ◆ NOUN [2] a person who engages in logical disputes; a controversialist. [3] the art or practice of logical disputation, esp if specious.
▷HISTORY C17: from Greek *eristikos*, from *erizein* to wrangle, from *eris* discord

Eritrea (ˌɛrɪ'treɪə) NOUN a small country in NE Africa, on the Red Sea: became an Italian colony in 1890; federated with Ethiopia (1952–93); an independence movement was engaged in war with the Ethiopian government from 1961 until independence was gained in 1993; consists of hot and arid coastal lowlands, rising to the foothills of the Ethiopian highlands. Languages: Arabic, English, Afar, and others. Religions: Muslim and Christian. Currency: nakfa. Capital: Asmara. Pop.: 4 298 000 (2001 est.). Area: 117 400 sq. km (45 300 sq. miles).

Eritrean (ˌɛrɪ'treɪən) ADJECTIVE [1] of or relating to Eritrea or its inhabitants. ◆ NOUN [2] a native or inhabitant of Eritrea.

Erivan (*Russian* jɪrɪ'van) NOUN a variant spelling of **Yerevan.**

erk (ɜːk) NOUN *Brit slang* an aircraftman or naval rating.
▷HISTORY C20: perhaps a corruption of *AC* (aircraftman)

erlang ('ɜːlæŋ) NOUN a unit of traffic intensity in a telephone system equal to the intensity for a specific period when the average number of simultaneous calls is unity. Abbreviation: **e.**
▷HISTORY C20: named after A. K. *Erlang* (1878–1929), Danish mathematician

Erlenmeyer flask ('ɜːlənˌmaɪə) NOUN a flask, for use in a laboratory, with a narrow neck, wide base, and conical shape; conical flask.
▷HISTORY C19: named after Emil *Erlenmeyer* (1825–1909), German chemist

erlking ('ɜːlˌkɪŋ) NOUN *German myth* a malevolent spirit who carries children off to death.
▷HISTORY C18: from German *Erlkönig*, literally: alder king, coined in 1778 by Herder, a mistranslation of Danish *ellerkonge* king of the elves

ERM ABBREVIATION FOR **Exchange Rate Mechanism.**

ermine ('ɜːmɪn) NOUN, *plural* **-mines** *or* **-mine.** [1] the stoat in northern regions, where it has a white winter coat with a black-tipped tail. [2] the fur of this animal. [3] one of the two principal furs used on heraldic shields, conventionally represented by a white field flecked with black ermine tails. Compare **vair.** [4] the dignity or office of a judge, noble, or king. [5] short for **ermine moth.**
▷HISTORY C12: from Old French *hermine*, from Medieval Latin *Armenius* (*mūs*) Armenian (mouse)

ermine moth NOUN [1] Also called: **ermine.** an arctiid moth of the genus *Spilosoma*, characterized by dark spots on the light coloured wings, and producing woolly bear caterpillars. [2] **small ermine.** an unrelated micro, *Yponomeuta padella.*

Ermite ('ɜːmaɪt) NOUN a salty blue cheese made in Quebec, Canada.

▷HISTORY via Canadian French from French *ermite* hermit, the cheese being made originally by monks

erne *or* **ern** (ɜːn) NOUN another name for the (European) **sea eagle.**
▷HISTORY Old English *earn;* related to Old Norse *örn* eagle, Old High German *aro* eagle, Greek *ornis* bird

Erne (ɜːn) NOUN a river in N central Republic of Ireland, rising in County Cavan and flowing north across the border, through **Upper Lough Erne** and **Lower Lough Erne** and then west to Donegal Bay. Length: about 96 km (60 miles).

Ernie (ˈɜːnɪ) NOUN (in Britain) a machine that randomly selects winning numbers of Premium Bonds.
▷HISTORY C20: acronym of *E*lectronic *R*andom *N*umber *I*ndicator *E*quipment

ERO (in New Zealand) ABBREVIATION FOR Education Review Office.

erode (ɪˈrəʊd) VERB 1 to grind or wear down or away or become ground or worn down or away. 2 to deteriorate or cause to deteriorate: *jealousy eroded the relationship.* 3 (*tr; usually passive*) *Pathol* to remove (tissue) by ulceration.
▷HISTORY C17: from Latin *ērōdere,* from EX-[1] + *rōdere* to gnaw
▸**eˈrodent** ADJECTIVE, NOUN ▸**eˈrodible** ADJECTIVE

erogenous (ɪˈrɒdʒɪnəs) *or* **erogenic** (ˌɛrəˈdʒɛnɪk) ADJECTIVE 1 sensitive to sexual stimulation: *erogenous zones of the body.* 2 arousing sexual desire or giving sexual pleasure.
▷HISTORY C19: from Greek *erōs* love, desire + -GENOUS
▸**erogeneity** (ˌɛrədʒɪˈniːɪtɪ) NOUN

Eros (ˈɪərɒs, ˈɛrɒs) NOUN 1 *Greek myth* the god of love, son of Aphrodite. Roman counterpart: **Cupid.** 2 Also called: **life instinct.** (in Freudian theory) the group of instincts, esp sexual, that govern acts of self-preservation and that tend towards uninhibited enjoyment of life. Compare **Thanatos.**
▷HISTORY Greek: desire, sexual love

Eros–433 NOUN an asteroid with an orbital period around the sun of 1.76 years. The NEAR Shoemaker spacecraft made the first asteroid landing on Eros on 12 Feb 2001.

erose (ɪˈrəʊs, -ˈrəʊz) ADJECTIVE jagged or uneven, as though gnawed or bitten: *erose leaves.*
▷HISTORY C18: from Latin *ērōsus* eaten away, from *ērōdere* to ERODE
▸**eˈrosely** ADVERB

erosion (ɪˈrəʊʒən) NOUN 1 the wearing away of rocks and other deposits on the earth's surface by the action of water, ice, wind, etc. 2 the act or process of eroding or the state of being eroded.
▸**eˈrosive** *or* **eˈrosional** ADJECTIVE

erotema (ˌɛrəʊˈtiːmə), **eroteme** (ˈɛrəʊˌtiːm), *or* **erotesis** (ˌɛrəʊˈtiːsɪs) NOUN *Rhetoric* a rhetorical question.
▷HISTORY C16: New Latin, from Greek, from *erōtaein* to ask

erotetic (ˌɛrəʊˈtɛtɪk) ADJECTIVE 1 *Rhetoric* pertaining to a rhetorical question. 2 *Grammar, philosophy* pertaining to questions; interrogative.

erotic (ɪˈrɒtɪk) ADJECTIVE *also* **erotical.** 1 of, concerning, or arousing sexual desire or giving sexual pleasure. 2 marked by strong sexual desire or being especially sensitive to sexual stimulation. ◆ NOUN 3 a person who has strong sexual desires or is especially responsive to sexual stimulation.
▷HISTORY C17: from Greek *erōtikos* of love, from *erōs* love
▸**eˈrotically** ADVERB

erotica (ɪˈrɒtɪkə) PLURAL NOUN explicitly sexual literature or art.
▷HISTORY C19: from Greek *erōtika,* neuter plural of *erōtikos* EROTIC

eroticism (ɪˈrɒtɪˌsɪzəm) *or* **erotism** (ˈɛrəˌtɪzəm) NOUN 1 erotic quality or nature. 2 the use of sexually arousing or pleasing symbolism in literature or art. 3 sexual excitement or desire. 4 a tendency to exalt sex. 5 *Psychol* an overt display of sexual behaviour.

eroticize *or* **eroticise** (ɪˈrɒtɪˌsaɪz) VERB (*tr*) to regard or present in a sexual way.
▸**eˌroticiˈzation** *or* **eˌroticiˈsation** NOUN

eroto- COMBINING FORM denoting erotic desire, excitement, etc.: *erotogenic; erotology.*
▷HISTORY from Greek *erōt-, erōs* love

erotogenic (ɪˌrɒtəˈdʒɛnɪk) ADJECTIVE originating from or causing sexual stimulation; erogenous.

erotology (ˌɛrəˈtɒlədʒɪ) NOUN 1 the study of erotic stimuli and sexual behaviour. 2 a description of such stimuli and behaviour.
▸**erotological** (ˌɛrətəˈlɒdʒɪkᵊl) ADJECTIVE ▸**ˌerotˈologist** NOUN

erotomania (ɪˌrɒtəʊˈmeɪnɪə) NOUN 1 abnormally strong sexual desire. 2 a condition in which a person is obsessed with another person and groundlessly believes that person to be in love with him or her.
▸**eˌrotoˈmaniac** NOUN

err (ɜː) VERB (*intr*) 1 to make a mistake; be incorrect. 2 to stray from the right course or accepted standards; sin. 3 to act with bias, esp favourable bias: *to err on the side of justice.*
▷HISTORY C14: *erren* to wander, stray, from Old French *errer,* from Latin *errāre*

errancy (ˈɛrənsɪ) NOUN, *plural* **-cies.** 1 the state or an instance of erring or a tendency to err. 2 *Christianity* the holding of views at variance with accepted doctrine.

errand (ˈɛrənd) NOUN 1 a short trip undertaken to perform a necessary task or commission (esp in the phrase **run errands**). 2 the purpose or object of such a trip.
▷HISTORY Old English *ǣrende;* related to *ār* messenger, Old Norse *erendi* message, Old High German *ārunti,* Swedish *ärende*

errand boy NOUN (in Britain, esp formerly) a boy employed by a shopkeeper to deliver goods and run other errands.

errant (ˈɛrənt) ADJECTIVE (*often postpositive*) 1 *Archaic or literary* wandering in search of adventure. 2 erring or straying from the right course or accepted standards.
▷HISTORY C14: from Old French: journeying, from Vulgar Latin *iterāre* (unattested), from Latin *iter* journey; influenced by Latin *errāre* to ERR
▸**ˈerrantly** ADVERB

errantry (ˈɛrəntrɪ) NOUN, *plural* **-ries.** the way of life of a knight errant.

errata (ɪˈrɑːtə) NOUN the plural of **erratum.**

erratic (ɪˈrætɪk) ADJECTIVE 1 irregular in performance, behaviour, or attitude; inconsistent and unpredictable. 2 having no fixed or regular course; wandering. ◆ NOUN 3 a piece of rock that differs in composition, shape, etc., from the rock surrounding it, having been transported from its place of origin, esp by glacial action. 4 an erratic person or thing.
▷HISTORY C14: from Latin *errāticus,* from *errāre* to wander, ERR
▸**erˈratically** ADVERB

erratum (ɪˈrɑːtəm) NOUN, *plural* **-ta** (-tə). 1 an error in writing or printing. 2 another name for **corrigendum.**
▷HISTORY C16: from Latin: mistake, from *errāre* to ERR

errhine (ˈɛraɪn, ˈɛrɪn) *Med* ◆ ADJECTIVE 1 *Obsolete* causing nasal secretion. ◆ NOUN 2 *Obsolete* an errhine drug or agent.
▷HISTORY C17: from Greek *errhinos,* from EN-[2] + *rhis* nose

erroneous (ɪˈrəʊnɪəs) ADJECTIVE based on or containing error; mistaken; incorrect.
▷HISTORY C14: (in the sense: deviating from what is right), from Latin *errōneus,* from *errāre* to wander
▸**erˈroneously** ADVERB ▸**erˈroneousness** NOUN

error (ˈɛrə) NOUN 1 a mistake or inaccuracy, as in action or speech: *a typing error.* 2 an incorrect belief or wrong judgment. 3 the condition of deviating from accuracy or correctness, as in belief, action, or speech: *he was in error about the train times.* 4 deviation from a moral standard; wrongdoing: *he saw the error of his ways.* 5 *Maths, statistics* a measure of the difference between some quantity and an approximation to or estimate of it, often expressed as a percentage: *an error of* $\pm 5\%$. 6 *Statistics* See **type I error, type II error.**
▷HISTORY C13: from Latin, from *errāre* to ERR
▸**ˈerror-ˌfree** ADJECTIVE

error correction NOUN *Computing* the automatic correction of errors in data that arise from missing or distorted digital pulses.

error message NOUN a message displayed on a visual display unit, printout, etc., indicating that an incorrect instruction has been given to the computer.

error of closure NOUN *Surveying* the amount by which a computed, plotted, or observed quantity or position differs from the true or established one, esp when plotting a closed traverse. Also called: **closing error.**

ERS ABBREVIATION FOR earnings related supplement.

ersatz (ˈɛəzæts, ˈɜː-) ADJECTIVE 1 made in imitation of some natural or genuine product; artificial. ◆ NOUN 2 an ersatz substance or article.
▷HISTORY C20: German, from *ersetzen* to substitute

Erse (ɜːs) NOUN 1 another name for Irish **Gaelic.** ◆ ADJECTIVE 2 of or relating to the Irish Gaelic language.
▷HISTORY C14: from Lowland Scots *Erisch* Irish; Irish being regarded as the literary form of Gaelic

erst (ɜːst) ADVERB *Archaic* 1 long ago; formerly. 2 at first.
▷HISTORY Old English *ǣrest* earliest, superlative of *ǣr* early; see ERE; related to Old High German *ērist,* Dutch *eerst*

erstwhile (ˈɜːstˌwaɪl) ADJECTIVE 1 former; one-time: *my erstwhile companions.* ◆ ADVERB 2 *Archaic* long ago; formerly.

erubescence (ˌɛrʊˈbɛsᵊns) NOUN the process of growing red or a condition of redness.
▷HISTORY C18: from Latin *ērubescentia* blushing, from *rubēscere* to grow red, from *ruber* red
▸**ˌeruˈbescent** ADJECTIVE

erucic acid ADJECTIVE (ɪˈruːsɪk), NOUN a crystalline fatty acid derived from the oils of rapeseed, mustard seed, and wallflower seed.

eruct (ɪˈrʌkt) *or* **eructate** VERB 1 to raise (gas and often a small quantity of acid) from the stomach; belch. 2 (of a volcano) to pour out (fumes or volcanic matter).
▷HISTORY C17: from Latin *ēructāre,* from *ructāre* to belch
▸**eructation** (ɪˌrʌkˈteɪʃən, ˌiːrʌk-) NOUN ▸**eructative** (ɪˈrʌktətɪv) ADJECTIVE

erudite (ˈɛrʊˌdaɪt) ADJECTIVE having or showing extensive scholarship; learned.
▷HISTORY C15: from Latin *ērudītus,* from *ērudīre* to polish, from EX-[1] + *rudis* unpolished, rough
▸**ˈeruˌditely** ADVERB ▸**erudition** (ˌɛrʊˈdɪʃən) *or* **ˈeruˌditeness** NOUN

erumpent (ɪˈrʌmpənt) ADJECTIVE bursting out or (esp of plant parts) developing as though bursting through an overlying structure.
▷HISTORY C17: from Latin *ērumpere* to burst forth, from *rumpere* to shatter, burst

erupt (ɪˈrʌpt) VERB 1 to eject (steam, water, and volcanic material such as lava and ash) violently or (of volcanic material, etc.) to be so ejected. 2 (*intr*) (of a skin blemish) to appear on the skin; break out. 3 (*intr*) (of a tooth) to emerge through the gum and become visible during the normal process of tooth development. 4 (*intr*) to burst forth suddenly and violently, as from restraint: *to erupt in anger.*
▷HISTORY C17: from Latin *ēruptus* having burst forth, from *ērumpere,* from *rumpere* to burst
▸**eˈruptible** ADJECTIVE ▸**eˈruption** NOUN

eruptive (ɪˈrʌptɪv) ADJECTIVE 1 erupting or tending to erupt. 2 resembling or of the nature of an eruption. 3 (of rocks) formed from such products as ash and lava resulting from volcanic eruptions. 4 (of a disease) characterized by skin eruptions.
▸**eˈruptively** ADVERB ▸**eˌrupˈtivity** *or* **eˈruptiveness** NOUN

eruv NOUN (ˈɛəruːv, ˈɛruːv), NOUN *Judaism* an area, circumscribed by a symbolic line, within which certain activities forbidden to Orthodox Jews on the Sabbath are permitted.
▷HISTORY C20: from Hebrew, literally: mixture, mixing

-ery *or* **-ry** SUFFIX FORMING NOUNS 1 indicating a place of business or some other activity: *bakery; brewery; refinery.* 2 indicating a class or collection of things: *cutlery; greenery.* 3 indicating qualities or actions collectively: *snobbery; trickery.* 4 indicating a practice or occupation: *husbandry.* 5 indicating a state or condition: *slavery.*
▷HISTORY from Old French *-erie;* see -ER[1], -Y[3]

Erymanthian boar (ˌɛrɪˈmænθɪən) NOUN *Greek*

myth a wild boar that ravaged the district around Mount Erymanthus: captured by Hercules as his fourth labour.

Erymanthus (ˌɛrɪˈmænθəs) NOUN **Mount.** a mountain in SW Greece, in the NW Peloponnese. Height: 2224 m (7297 ft.). Modern Greek name: **Erímanthos** (eˈrimanθɔs).

eryngium (ɪˈrɪndʒɪəm) NOUN any plant of the temperate and subtropical perennial umbelliferous genus *Eryngium,* with distinctive spiny foliage, metallic blue flower heads, and bluish stems, several species of which are grown as garden plants. See also **sea holly.**
▷HISTORY New Latin, from Greek *ērynggion* a species of thistle

eryngo (ɪˈrɪŋɡəʊ) NOUN, *plural* **-goes** *or* **-gos.** any umbelliferous plant of the genus *Eryngium,* such as the sea holly, having toothed or lobed leaves. Also called: **eringo.**
▷HISTORY C16: from Latin *ērynqion* variety of thistle, from Greek *ērungion,* diminutive of *ērungos* thistle

erysipelas (ˌɛrɪˈsɪpɪləs) NOUN an acute streptococcal infectious disease of the skin, characterized by fever, headache, vomiting, and purplish raised lesions, esp on the face. Also called: **Saint Anthony's fire.**
▷HISTORY C16: from Latin, from Greek *erusipelas,* from Greek *erusi-* red + *-pelas* skin
▸**erysipelatous** (ˌɛrɪsɪˈpɛlətəs) ADJECTIVE

erysipeloid (ˌɛrɪˈsɪpɪˌlɔɪd) NOUN an infective dermatitis mainly affecting the hands, characterized by inflammation and caused by the microorganism *Erysipelothrix rhusiopathiae* on contaminated meat, poultry, or fish: most prevalent among fishermen and butchers.

erythema (ˌɛrɪˈθiːmə) NOUN *Pathol* redness of the skin, usually occurring in patches, caused by irritation or injury to the tissue.
▷HISTORY C18: from New Latin, from Greek *eruthēma,* from *eruthros* red
▸**erythematic** (ˌɛrɪθɪˈmætɪk) *or* **erythematous** (ˌɛrɪˈθiːmətəs) *or* ˌ**eryˈthemal** ADJECTIVE

erythraemia *or esp US* **erythremia** (ˌɛrɪˈθriːmɪə) NOUN *Med* another name for **polycythaemia vera** (see **polycythaemia**).

erythrism (ɪˈrɪθrɪzəm) NOUN abnormal red coloration, as in plumage or hair.
▸**erythrismal** (ˌɛrɪˈθrɪzməl) ADJECTIVE

erythrite (ɪˈrɪθraɪt) NOUN [1] Also called: **cobalt bloom.** a pink to purple secondary mineral consisting of hydrated cobalt arsenate in monoclinic crystalline form. Formula: $Co_3(AsO_4)_2.8H_2O$. [2] another name for **erythritol.**

erythritol (ɪˈrɪθrɪˌtɒl) *or* **erythrite** NOUN a sweet crystalline compound extracted from certain algae and lichens and used in medicine to dilate the blood vessels of the heart; 1,2,3,4-butanetetrol. Formula: $C_4H_{10}O_4$.

erythro- *or* **erythr-** COMBINING FORM red: *erythrocyte.*
▷HISTORY from Greek *eruthros* red

erythroblast (ɪˈrɪθrəʊˌblæst) NOUN a nucleated cell in bone marrow that develops into an erythrocyte.
▸**eˌrythroˈblastic** ADJECTIVE

erythroblastosis (ɪˌrɪθrəʊblæˈstəʊsɪs) NOUN [1] the abnormal presence of erythroblasts in the circulating blood. [2] Also called: **erythroblastosis fetalis.** an anaemic blood disease of a fetus or newborn child, characterized by erythroblasts in the circulating blood: caused by a blood incompatibility between mother and fetus.

erythrocyte (ɪˈrɪθrəʊˌsaɪt) NOUN a blood cell of vertebrates that transports oxygen and carbon dioxide, combined with the red pigment haemoglobin, to and from the tissues. Also called: **red blood cell.**
▸**erythrocytic** (ɪˌrɪθrəʊˈsɪtɪk) ADJECTIVE

erythrocytometer (ɪˌrɪθrəʊsaɪˈtɒmɪtə) NOUN an instrument for counting the number or measuring the size of red blood cells in a sample of blood.
▸**eˌrythrocyˈtometry** NOUN

erythromelalgia (ɪˌrɪθrəʊmɛlˈældʒə) NOUN a condition resulting from excessive dilation of the blood vessels, usually affecting the extremities, which feel hot and painful.

erythromycin (ɪˌrɪθrəʊˈmaɪsɪn) NOUN an antibiotic used in treating certain infections,sometimes as an alternative to penicillin. It is obtained from the bacterium *Streptomyces erythreus.* Formula: $C_{37}M_{67}NO_{13}$.
▷HISTORY C20: from ERYTHRO- + Greek *mukēs* fungus + -IN

erythronium (ˌɛrɪˈθrəʊnɪəm) NOUN any plant of the bulbous genus *Erythronium,* with decoratively mottled leaves and cyclamen-like yellow, rose, purple, or white flowers: family *Liliaceae.* See also **dogtooth violet.**
▷HISTORY New Latin, from Greek *erythros* red

erythropenia (ɪˌrɪθrəʊˈpiːnɪə) NOUN the presence of decreased numbers of erythrocytes in the blood, as occurs in some forms of anaemia. Also called: **erythrocytopenia.**
▷HISTORY from ERYTHRO- + Greek *penia* poverty

erythropoiesis (ɪˌrɪθrəʊpɔɪˈiːsɪs) NOUN *Physiol* the formation of red blood cells.
▷HISTORY C19: from ERYTHRO- + Greek *poiēsis* a making, from *poiein* to make
▸**eˌrythropoiˈetic** ADJECTIVE

erythropoietin (ɪˌrɪθrəʊpɔɪˈiːtɪn) NOUN a hormone, secreted by the kidney in response to low levels of oxygen in the tissues, that increases the rate of erythropoiesis. It has been used as a performance-enhancing drug for athletes and racehorses. Abbreviation: **EPO.**

erythropsia (ˌɛrɪˈθrɒpsɪə) NOUN *Med* a defect of vision in which objects appear red.

Erzgebirge (*German* ˈeːrtsɡəbɪrɡə) PLURAL NOUN a mountain range on the border between Germany and the Czech Republic: formerly rich in mineral resources. Highest peak: Mount Klínovec (Keilberg), 1244 m (4081 ft.). Czech name: **Krušné Hory.** Also called: **Ore Mountains.**

es THE INTERNET DOMAIN NAME FOR Spain.

Es THE CHEMICAL SYMBOL FOR einsteinium.

ES INTERNATIONAL CAR REGISTRATION FOR El Salvador.

-es SUFFIX [1] a variant of **-s**[1] for nouns ending in *ch, s, sh, z,* postconsonantal *y,* for some nouns ending in a vowel, and nouns in *f* with *v* in the plural: *ashes; heroes; calves.* [2] a variant of **-s**[1] for verbs ending in *ch, s, sh, z,* postconsonantal *y,* or a vowel: *preaches; steadies; echoes.*

ESA ABBREVIATION FOR: [1] Environmentally Sensitive Area: an area which contains a natural feature, such as the habitat of a rare species, and which is protected by government regulations. [2] European Space Agency.

Esaki diode (ɪˈsɑːkɪ) NOUN another name for **tunnel diode.**
▷HISTORY named after L. *Esaki* (born 1925), its Japanese designer

Esau (ˈiːsɔː) NOUN *Bible* son of Isaac and Rebecca and twin brother of Jacob, to whom he sold his birthright (Genesis 25).

ESB ABBREVIATION FOR electrical stimulation of the brain.

escadrille (ˌɛskəˈdrɪl; *French* ɛskadrij) NOUN [1] a French squadron of aircraft, esp in World War I. [2] a small squadron of ships.
▷HISTORY from French: flotilla, from Spanish *escuadrilla,* from *escuadra* SQUADRON

escalade (ˌɛskəˈleɪd) NOUN [1] an assault by the use of ladders, esp on a fortification. ◆ VERB [2] to gain access to (a place) by the use of ladders.
▷HISTORY C16: from French, from Italian *scalata,* from *scalare* to mount, SCALE[3]
▸ˌ**escaˈlader** NOUN

escalate (ˈɛskəˌleɪt) VERB to increase or be increased in extent, intensity, or magnitude: *to escalate a war; prices escalated because of inflation.*
▷HISTORY C20: back formation from ESCALATOR
▸ˌ**escaˈlation** NOUN

escalator (ˈɛskəˌleɪtə) NOUN [1] a moving staircase consisting of stair treads fixed to a conveyor belt, for transporting passengers between levels, esp between the floors of a building. [2] short for **escalator clause.**
▷HISTORY C20: originally a trademark

escalator clause NOUN a clause in a contract stipulating an adjustment in wages, prices, etc., in the event of specified changes in conditions, such as a large rise in the cost of living or price of raw materials.

escallonia (ˌɛskəˈləʊnɪə) NOUN any evergreen shrub of the South American saxifragaceous genus *Escallonia,* with white or red flowers: cultivated for ornament.
▷HISTORY C19: from *Escallon,* 18th-century Spanish traveller who discovered it

escallop (ɛˈskɒləp, ɛˈskæl-) NOUN, VERB another word for **scallop.**

escalope (ˈɛskəˌlɒp) NOUN a thin slice of meat, usually veal, coated with egg and breadcrumbs, fried, and served with a rich sauce.
▷HISTORY C19: from Old French: shell

escapade (ˈɛskəˌpeɪd, ˌɛskəˈpeɪd) NOUN [1] a wild or exciting adventure, esp one that is mischievous or unlawful; scrape. [2] any lighthearted or carefree episode; prank; romp.
▷HISTORY C17: from French, from Old Italian *scappata,* from Vulgar Latin *ex-cappāre* (unattested) to ESCAPE

escape (ɪˈskeɪp) VERB [1] to get away or break free from (confinements, captors, etc.): *the lion escaped from the zoo.* [2] to manage to avoid (imminent danger, punishment, evil, etc.): *to escape death.* [3] (*intr;* usually foll by *from*) (of gases, liquids, etc.) to issue gradually, as from a crack or fissure; seep; leak: *water was escaping from the dam.* [4] (*tr*) to elude; be forgotten by: *the actual figure escapes me.* [5] (*tr*) to be articulated inadvertently or involuntarily: *a roar escaped his lips.* [6] (*intr*) (of cultivated plants) to grow wild. ◆ NOUN [7] the act of escaping or state of having escaped. [8] avoidance of injury, harm, etc.: *a narrow escape.* [9] **a** a means or way of escape. **b** (*as modifier*): *an escape route.* [10] a means of distraction or relief, esp from reality or boredom: *angling provides an escape for many city dwellers.* [11] a gradual outflow; leakage; seepage. [12] Also called: **escape valve, escape cock.** a valve that releases air, steam, etc., above a certain pressure; relief valve or safety valve. [13] a plant that was originally cultivated but is now growing wild.
▷HISTORY C14: from Old Northern French *escaper,* from Vulgar Latin *excappāre* (unattested) to escape (literally: to remove one's cloak, hence free oneself), from EX-[1] + Late Latin *cappa* cloak
▸**esˈcapable** ADJECTIVE ▸**esˈcaper** NOUN

escape clause NOUN a clause in a contract freeing one of the parties from his obligations in certain circumstances.

escapee (ɪˌskeɪˈpiː) NOUN a person who has escaped, esp an escaped prisoner.

escape hatch NOUN a means of escape in an emergency, esp from a submarine.

escape mechanism NOUN *Psychol* any emotional or mental mechanism that enables a person to avoid acknowledging unpleasant or threatening realities. See also **escapism.**

escapement (ɪˈskeɪpmənt) NOUN [1] *Horology* a mechanism consisting of an escape wheel and anchor, used in timepieces to provide periodic impulses to the pendulum or balance. [2] any similar mechanism that regulates movement, usually consisting of toothed wheels engaged by rocking levers. [3] (in a piano) the mechanism that allows the hammer to clear the string after striking, so that the string can vibrate. [4] an overflow channel. [5] *Rare* an act or means of escaping.

escape pipe NOUN a pipe for overflowing water, escaping steam, etc.

escape road NOUN a road, usually ending in a pile of sand, provided on a hill for a driver to drive into if his brakes fail or on a bend if he loses control of the turn.

escape routine NOUN *Computing* a means of leaving a computer-program sequence before its end, in order to commence another sequence.

escape shaft NOUN a shaft in a mine through which miners can escape if the regular shaft is blocked.

escape velocity NOUN the minimum velocity that a body must have in order to escape from the gravitational field of the earth or other celestial body.

escape wheel NOUN *Horology* a toothed wheel that engages intermittently with a balance wheel or pendulum, causing the mechanism to oscillate and thereby moving the hands of a clock or watch. Also called: **scapewheel.**

escapism (ɪˈskeɪpɪzəm) NOUN an inclination to or habit of retreating from unpleasant reality, as through diversion or fantasy.
▸**esˈcapist** NOUN, ADJECTIVE

escapologist (ˌɛskəˈpɒlədʒɪst) NOUN an entertainer who specializes in freeing himself from confinement. Also called: **escape artist.**
▸**ˌescaˈpology** NOUN

escargot *French* (ɛskargo) NOUN a variety of edible snail, usually eaten with a sauce made of melted butter and garlic.

escarole (ˈɛskərəʊl) NOUN *US and Canadian name* a variety of endive with broad leaves, used in salads.
▹HISTORY C20: French from Italian *scar(i)ola,* from Latin *esca* food

escarp (ɪˈskɑːp) NOUN 1 *Fortifications* the inner side of the ditch separating besiegers and besieged. Compare **counterscarp.** ◆ VERB 2 a rare word for **scarp** (sense 3).
▹HISTORY C17: from French *escarpe;* see SCARP

escarpment (ɪˈskɑːpmənt) NOUN 1 **a** the long continuous steep face of a ridge or plateau formed by erosion; scarp. **b** any steep slope, such as one resulting from faulting. 2 a steep artificial slope immediately in front of the rampart of a fortified place.

Escaut (ɛsko) NOUN the French name for the **Scheldt.**

-escent SUFFIX FORMING ADJECTIVES beginning to be, do, show, etc.: *convalescent; luminescent.*
▹HISTORY via Old French from Latin *-ēscent-,* stem of present participial suffix of *-ēscere,* ending of inceptive verbs
▸**-escence** SUFFIX FORMING NOUNS

eschalot (ˈɛʃəˌlɒt, ˌɛʃəˈlɒt) NOUN another name for a **shallot.**
▹HISTORY C18: from Old French *eschalotte* a little SCALLION

eschar (ˈɛskɑː) NOUN a dry scab or slough, esp one following a burn or cauterization of the skin.
▹HISTORY C16: from Late Latin *eschara* scab, from Greek *eskhara* hearth, pan of hot coals (which could inflict burns); see SCAR[1]

escharotic (ˌɛskəˈrɒtɪk) *Med* ◆ ADJECTIVE 1 capable of producing an eschar. ◆ NOUN 2 a caustic or corrosive agent.

eschatology (ˌɛskəˈtɒlədʒɪ) NOUN the branch of theology or biblical exegesis concerned with the end of the world.
▹HISTORY C19: from Greek *eskhatos* last
▸**eschatological** (ˌɛskətəˈlɒdʒɪkᵊl) ADJECTIVE
▸**ˌeschatoˈlogically** ADVERB ▸**ˌeschaˈtologist** NOUN

escheat (ɪsˈtʃiːt) *Law* ◆ NOUN 1 (in England before 1926) the reversion of property to the Crown in the absence of legal heirs. 2 (in feudal times) the reversion of property to the feudal lord in the absence of legal heirs or upon outlawry of the tenant. 3 the property so reverting. ◆ VERB 4 to take (land) by escheat or (of land) to revert by escheat.
▹HISTORY C14: from Old French *eschete,* from *escheoir* to fall to the lot of, from Late Latin *excadere* (unattested), from Latin *cadere* to fall
▸**esˈcheatable** ADJECTIVE ▸**esˈcheatage** NOUN

Escher figure (ˈɛʃə) NOUN another name for **impossible figure.**
▹HISTORY named after M. C. *Escher* (1898–1970), Dutch graphic artist who produced many such drawings

Escherichia (ˌɛʃəˈrɪkɪə) NOUN a genus of Gram-negative rodlike bacteria that are found in the intestines of humans and many animals, esp *E. coli,* which is sometimes pathogenic and is widely used in genetic research.
▹HISTORY C19: named after Theodor *Escherich* (1857–1911), German paediatrician who first described *E. coli*

eschew (ɪsˈtʃuː) VERB *(tr)* to keep clear of or abstain from (something disliked, injurious, etc.); shun; avoid.
▹HISTORY C14: from Old French *eschiver,* of Germanic origin; compare Old High German *skiuhan* to frighten away; see SHY[1], SKEW
▸**esˈchewal** NOUN ▸**esˈchewer** NOUN

eschscholtzia *or* **eschscholzia** (ɛˈʃɒltsɪə) NOUN See **California poppy.**
▹HISTORY named after J. F. von *Eschscholtz* (1743–1831), German naturalist

escolar (ˌɛskəˈlɑː) NOUN, *plural* **-lars** *or* **-lar.** any slender spiny-finned fish of the family *Gempylidae,* of warm and tropical seas: similar and closely related to the scombroid fishes. Also called: **snake mackerel.**
▹HISTORY from Spanish: SCHOLAR; so called from the rings round its eyes, suggestive of spectacles

escort NOUN (ˈɛskɔːt) 1 one or more persons, soldiers, vehicles, etc., accompanying another or others for protection, guidance, restraint, or as a mark of honour. 2 a man or youth who accompanies a woman or girl: *he was her escort for the evening.* 3 **a** a person, esp a young woman, who may be hired to accompany another for entertainment, etc. **b** *(as modifier): an escort agency.* ◆ VERB (ɪsˈkɔːt) 4 *(tr)* to accompany or attend as an escort.
▹HISTORY C16: from French *escorte,* from Italian *scorta,* from *scorgere* to guide, from Latin *corrigere* to straighten; see CORRECT

escribe (ɪˈskraɪb) VERB *(tr)* to draw (a circle) so that it is tangential to one side of a triangle and to the other two sides produced.
▹HISTORY C16 (meaning: to write out): from EX-[1] + Latin *scrībere* to write

escritoire (ˌɛskrɪˈtwɑː) NOUN a writing desk with compartments and drawers, concealed by a hinged flap, on a chest of drawers or plain stand.
▹HISTORY C18: from French, from Medieval Latin *scriptōrium* writing room in a monastery, from Latin *scrībere* to write

escrow (ˈɛskrəʊ, ɛˈskrəʊ) *Law* ◆ NOUN 1 money, goods, or a written document, such as a contract bond, delivered to a third party and held by him pending fulfilment of some condition. 2 the state or condition of being an escrow (esp in the phrase **in escrow**). ◆ VERB *(tr)* 3 to place (money, a document, etc.) in escrow.
▹HISTORY C16: from Old French *escroe,* of Germanic origin; see SCREED, SHRED, SCROLL

escuage (ˈɛskjuɪdʒ) NOUN (in medieval Europe) another word for **scutage.**
▹HISTORY C16: from Old French, from *escu* shield, from Latin *scūtum*

escudo (ɛˈskuːdəʊ; *Portuguese* ɪʃˈkuðu) NOUN, *plural* **-dos** (-dəʊz; *Portuguese* -ðuʃ). 1 the standard monetary unit of Cape Verde, divided into 100 centavos. 2 the former standard monetary unit of Portugal, divided into 100 centavos; replaced by the euro in 2002. 3 a former monetary unit of Chile, divided into 100 centesimos. 4 an old Spanish silver coin worth 10 reals.
▹HISTORY C19: Spanish, literally: shield, from Latin *scūtum*

esculent (ˈɛskjʊlənt) NOUN 1 any edible substance. ◆ ADJECTIVE 2 edible.
▹HISTORY C17: from Latin *ēsculentus* good to eat, from *ēsca* food, from *edere* to eat

Escurial (ɛˌskjʊərɪˈɑːl, ɛˈskjʊərɪəl) NOUN a variant of **Escorial.**

escutcheon (ɪˈskʌtʃən) NOUN 1 a shield, esp a heraldic one that displays a coat of arms. 2 Also called: **escutcheon plate.** a plate or shield that surrounds a keyhole, door handle, light switch, etc., esp an ornamental one protecting a door or wall surface. 3 the place on the stern or transom of a vessel where the name is shown. 4 **blot on one's escutcheon.** a stain on one's honour.
▹HISTORY C15: from Old Northern French *escuchon,* ultimately from Latin *scūtum* shield
▸**esˈcutcheoned** ADJECTIVE

Esd. *Bible* ABBREVIATION FOR Esdras.

ESDA *or* **Esda** (ˈɛzdə) NOUN ACRONYM FOR Electrostatic Deposition Analysis: a technique used to check the sequence in which a statement written in police custody was made. The chronology of the statement is arrived at by the examination of indentations on subsequent pages.

Esdraelon (ˌɛzdreɪˈiːlɒn) NOUN a plain in N Israel, east of Mount Carmel. Also called: (Plain of) **Jezreel.**

Esdras (ˈɛzdræs) NOUN 1 either of two books of the Apocrypha, **I** and **II Esdras** called **III** and **IV Esdras** in the Douay Bible. 2 either of two books of the Douay Bible Old Testament, **I** and **II Esdras** corresponding to the books of Ezra and Nehemiah in the Authorized Version.

ESE SYMBOL FOR east-southeast.

-ese SUFFIX FORMING ADJECTIVES AND NOUNS indicating place of origin, language, or style: *Cantonese; Japanese; journalese.*

esemplastic (ˌɛsɛmˈplæstɪk) ADJECTIVE *Literature* making into one; unifying.
▹HISTORY C19 (first used by Samuel Taylor Coleridge): from Greek *es, eis* into + *em,* from *hen,* neuter of *heis* one + -PLASTIC

eserine (ˈɛsəriːn, -rɪn) NOUN another name for **physostigmine.**
▹HISTORY C19 *eser-,* of African origin + -INE[2]

Esher (ˈiːʃə) NOUN a town in SE England, in NE Surrey near London: racecourse. Pop.: 46 599 (1991).

esker (ˈɛskə) *or* **eskar** (ˈɛskɑː, -kə) NOUN a long winding ridge of gravel, sand, etc., originally deposited by a meltwater stream running under a glacier. Also called: **os.**
▹HISTORY C19: from Old Irish *escir* ridge

Eskimo (ˈɛskɪˌməʊ) NOUN 1 *(plural* **-mos** *or* **-mo)** a member of a group of peoples inhabiting N Canada, Greenland, Alaska, and E Siberia, having a material culture adapted to an extremely cold climate. 2 the language of these peoples. 3 a family of languages that includes Eskimo and Aleut. ◆ ADJECTIVE 4 relating to, denoting, or characteristic of the Eskimos. ◆ Former spelling: **Esquimau.** See also **Inuit, Inuktitut.**
▹HISTORY C18 *Esquimawes:* related to Abnaki *esquimantsic* eaters of raw flesh

> **Language note** *Eskimo* is considered by many people to be offensive, and in North America the term *Inuit* is often used.

Eskimo dog NOUN a large powerful breed of sled dog with a long thick coat and curled tail.

Esky (ˈɛskɪ) NOUN, *plural* **-kies.** *(sometimes not capital) Austral Trademark* a portable insulated container for keeping food and drink cool.
▹HISTORY C20: from ESKIMO, alluding to the Eskimos' cold habitat

ESL ABBREVIATION FOR English as a second language.

ESN ABBREVIATION FOR educationally subnormal; formerly used to designate a person of limited intelligence who needs special schooling.

ESO ABBREVIATION FOR European Southern Observatory.

esophagus (iːˈsɒfəgəs) NOUN, *plural* **-gi** (-ˌdʒaɪ) *or* **-guses.** the US spelling of **oesophagus.**
▸**esophageal** (iːˌsɒfəˈdʒiːəl) ADJECTIVE

esoteric (ˌɛsəʊˈtɛrɪk) ADJECTIVE 1 restricted to or intended for an enlightened or initiated minority, esp because of abstruseness or obscurity: *an esoteric cult.* Compare **exoteric.** 2 difficult to understand; abstruse: *an esoteric statement.* 3 not openly admitted; private: *esoteric aims.*
▹HISTORY C17: from Greek *esōterikos,* from *esōterō* inner
▸**ˌesoˈterically** ADVERB ▸**ˌesoˈteriˌcism** NOUN

ESP ABBREVIATION FOR: 1 English for Specific *(or* Special) Purposes: the technique of teaching English to students who need it for a particular purpose, such as business dealings. 2 **extrasensory perception.**

esp ABBREVIATION FOR especially.

espadrille (ˌɛspəˈdrɪl) NOUN a light shoe with a canvas upper, esp with a braided cord sole.
▹HISTORY C19: from French, from Provençal *espardilho,* diminutive of *espart* ESPARTO; so called from the use of esparto for the soles of such shoes

espalier (ɪˈspæljə) NOUN 1 an ornamental shrub or fruit tree that has been trained to grow flat, as against a wall. 2 the trellis, framework, or arrangement of stakes on which such plants are trained. 3 the method used to produce such plants. ◆ VERB 4 *(tr)* to train (a plant) on an espalier.
▹HISTORY C17: from French: trellis, from Old Italian: shoulder supports, from *spalla* shoulder, from Late Latin SPATULA

España (esˈpaɲa) NOUN the Spanish name for **Spain.**

esparto *or* **esparto grass** (ɛˈspɑːtəʊ) NOUN, *plural* **-tos.** any of various grasses, esp *Stipa*

tenacissima of S Europe and N Africa, that yield a fibre used to make ropes, mats, etc.
▷HISTORY C18: from Spanish, via Latin from Greek *sparton* rope made of rushes, from *spartos* a kind of rush

especial (ɪˈspɛʃəl) ADJECTIVE (*prenominal*) [1] unusual; notable; exceptional: *he paid especial attention to her that evening.* [2] applying to one person or thing in particular; not general; specific; peculiar: *he had an especial dislike of relatives.*
▷HISTORY C14: from Old French, from Latin *speciālis* individual; see SPECIAL

> **Language note** *Especial* and *especially* have a more limited use than *special* and *specially*. *Special* is always used in preference to *especial* when the sense is one of being out of the ordinary: *a special lesson; he has been specially trained*. *Special* is also used when something is referred to as being for a particular purpose: *the word was specially underlined for you*. Where an idea of pre-eminence or individuality is involved, either *especial* or *special* may be used: *he is my especial* (or *special*) *friend; he is especially* (or *specially*) *good at his job*. In informal English, however, *special* is usually preferred in all contexts.

especially (ɪˈspɛʃəlɪ) ADVERB [1] in particular; specifically: *for everyone's sake, especially your children's.* [2] very much: *especially useful for vegans.*

esperance (ˈɛspərəns) NOUN *Archaic* hope or expectation.
▷HISTORY C15: from Old French, from Vulgar Latin *sperantia* (unattested), from Latin *spērāre* to hope, from *spēs* hope

Esperanto (ˌɛspəˈræntəʊ) NOUN an international artificial language based on words common to the chief European languages, invented in 1887.
▷HISTORY C19: literally: the one who hopes, pseudonym of Dr. L. L. Zamenhof (1859–1917), Polish philologist who invented it
▸**ˌEspeˈrantist** NOUN, ADJECTIVE

espial (ɪˈspaɪəl) NOUN *Archaic* [1] the act or fact of being seen or discovered. [2] the act of noticing. [3] the act of spying upon; secret observation.

espionage (ˈɛspɪəˌnɑːʒ, ˌɛspɪəˈnɑːʒ, ˈɛspɪənɪdʒ) NOUN [1] the systematic use of spies to obtain secret information, esp by governments to discover military or political secrets. [2] the act or practice of spying.
▷HISTORY C18: from French *espionnage*, from *espionner* to spy, from *espion* spy, from Old Italian *spione*, of Germanic origin; compare German *spähen* to SPY

Espíritu Santo (ɛsˈpɪrɪtuː ˈsæntəʊ) NOUN an island in the SW Pacific: the largest and westernmost of the Vanuatu islands. Pop.: 25 581 (latest est.). Area: 4856 sq. km (1875 sq. miles).

esplanade (ˌɛspləˈneɪd, -ˈnɑːd) NOUN [1] a long open level stretch of ground for walking along, esp beside the seashore. Compare **promenade** (sense 1). [2] an open area in front of a fortified place, in which attackers are exposed to the defenders' fire.
▷HISTORY C17: from French, from Old Italian *spianata*, from *spianare* to make level, from Latin *explānāre*; see EXPLAIN

espousal (ɪˈspaʊzᵊl) NOUN [1] adoption or support: *an espousal of new beliefs.* [2] (*sometimes plural*) *Archaic* a marriage or betrothal ceremony.

espouse (ɪˈspaʊz) VERB (*tr*) [1] to adopt or give support to (a cause, ideal, etc.): *to espouse socialism.* [2] *Archaic* (esp of a man) to take as spouse; marry.
▷HISTORY C15: from Old French *espouser*, from Latin *spōnsāre* to affiance, espouse
▸**esˈpouser** NOUN

espressivo (ˌɛsprɛˈsiːvəʊ) ADJECTIVE, ADVERB *Music* (to be performed) in an expressive manner.
▷HISTORY Italian

espresso (ɛˈsprɛsəʊ) NOUN, *plural* **-sos.** [1] strong coffee made by forcing steam or boiling water through ground coffee beans. [2] an apparatus for making coffee in this way.
▷HISTORY C20: Italian, short for *caffè espresso*, literally: pressed coffee

esprit (ɛˈspriː) NOUN spirit and liveliness, esp in wit.
▷HISTORY C16: from French, from Latin *spīritus* a breathing, SPIRIT[1]

esprit de corps (ɛˈspriː də ˈkɔː; *French* ɛspri də kɔr) NOUN consciousness of and pride in belonging to a particular group; the sense of shared purpose and fellowship.

espy (ɪˈspaɪ) VERB **-pies, -pying, -pied.** (*tr*) to catch sight of or perceive (something distant or previously unnoticed); detect: *to espy a ship on the horizon.*
▷HISTORY C14: from Old French *espier* to SPY, of Germanic origin
▸**esˈpier** NOUN

Esq. ABBREVIATION FOR esquire: used esp in correspondence.

-esque SUFFIX FORMING ADJECTIVES indicating a specified character, manner, style, or resemblance: *picturesque; Romanesque; statuesque; Chaplinesque.*
▷HISTORY via French from Italian *-esco*, of Germanic origin; compare -ISH

Esquiline (ˈɛskwəˌlaɪn) NOUN one of the seven hills on which ancient Rome was built.

Esquimau (ˈɛskɪˌməʊ) NOUN, *plural* **-maus** *or* **-mau,** ADJECTIVE a former spelling of **Eskimo.**

esquire (ɪˈskwaɪə) NOUN [1] *Chiefly Brit* a title of respect, usually abbreviated *Esq.*, placed after a man's name. [2] (in medieval times) the attendant and shield bearer of a knight, subsequently often knighted himself. [3] *Rare* a male escort.
▷HISTORY C15: from Old French *escuier*, from Late Latin *scūtārius* shield bearer, from Latin *scūtum* shield

ESR ABBREVIATION FOR **electron spin resonance.**

ESRC ABBREVIATION FOR Economic and Social Research Council.

ESRO (ˈɛzrəʊ) NOUN ACRONYM FOR European Space Research Organization.

-ess SUFFIX FORMING NOUNS indicating a female: *waitress; lioness.*
▷HISTORY via Old French from Late Latin *-issa*, from Greek

> **Language note** The suffix *-ess* in such words as *poetess, authoress* is now often regarded as disparaging; a sexually neutral term *poet, author* is preferred.

essay NOUN (ˈɛseɪ; *for senses 2,3 also* ɛˈseɪ) [1] a short literary composition dealing with a subject analytically or speculatively. [2] an attempt or endeavour; effort. [3] a test or trial. ◆ VERB (ɛˈseɪ) (*tr*) [4] to attempt or endeavour; try. [5] to test or try out.
▷HISTORY C15: from Old French *essaier* to attempt, from *essai* an attempt, from Late Latin *exagium* a weighing, from Latin *agere* to do, compel, influenced by *exigere* to investigate

essayist (ˈɛseɪɪst) NOUN a person who writes essays.

esse (ˈɛsɪ) NOUN *Philosophy* [1] existence. [2] essential nature; essence.
▷HISTORY C17: from Latin: to be

Essen (*German* ˈɛsən) NOUN a city in W Germany, in North Rhine-Westphalia: the leading administrative centre of the Ruhr; university. Pop.: 600 700 (1999 est.).

essence (ˈɛsᵊns) NOUN [1] the characteristic or intrinsic feature of a thing, which determines its identity; fundamental nature. [2] the most distinctive element of a thing: *the essence of a problem.* [3] a perfect or complete form of something, esp a person who typifies an abstract quality: *he was the essence of gentility.* [4] *Philosophy* **a** the unchanging and unchangeable nature of something which is necessary to its being the thing it is; its necessary properties. Compare **accident** (sense 4). **b** the properties in virtue of which something is called by its name. **c** the nature of something as distinct from, and logically prior to, its existence. [5] *Theol* an immaterial or spiritual entity. [6] **a** the constituent of a plant, usually an oil, alkaloid, or glycoside, that determines its chemical or pharmacological properties. **b** an alcoholic solution of such a substance. [7] a substance, usually a liquid, containing the properties of a plant or foodstuff in concentrated form: *vanilla essence.* [8] a rare word for **perfume.** [9] **in essence.** essentially; fundamentally. [10] **of the essence.** indispensable; vitally important.
▷HISTORY C14: from Medieval Latin *essentia*, from Latin: the being (of something), from *esse* to be

Essene (ˈɛsiːn, ɛˈsiːn) NOUN *Judaism* a member of an ascetic sect that flourished in Palestine from the second century B.C. to the second century A.D., living in strictly organized communities.
▸**Essenian** (ɛˈsiːnɪən) *or* **Essenic** (ɛˈsɛnɪk) ADJECTIVE

essential (ɪˈsɛnʃəl) ADJECTIVE [1] vitally important; absolutely necessary. [2] basic; fundamental: *the essential feature.* [3] completely realized; absolute; perfect: *essential beauty.* [4] *Biochem* (of an amino acid or a fatty acid) necessary for the normal growth of an organism but not synthesized by the organism and therefore required in the diet. [5] derived from or relating to an extract of a plant, drug, etc.: *an essential oil.* [6] *Logic* (of a property) guaranteed by the identity of the subject; necessary. Thus, if having the atomic number 79 is an essential property of gold, nothing can be gold unless it has that atomic number. [7] *Music* denoting or relating to a note that belongs to the fundamental harmony of a chord or piece. [8] *Pathol* (of a disease) having no obvious external cause: *essential hypertension.* [9] *Geology* (of a mineral constituent of a rock) necessary for defining the classification of a rock. Its absence alters the rock's name and classification. ◆ NOUN [10] something fundamental or indispensable: *a sharp eye is an essential for a printer.* [11] *Music* an essential note.
▸**essentiality** (ɪˌsɛnʃɪˈælɪtɪ) *or* **esˈsentialness** NOUN

essential element NOUN *Biochem* any chemical element required by an organism for healthy growth. It may be required in large amounts (see **macronutrient**) or in very small amounts (see **trace element**).

essential fatty acid NOUN *Biochem* any fatty acid required by the body in manufacturing prostaglandins, found in such foods as oily fish and nuts. Abbreviation: **EFA.**

essentialism (ɪˈsɛnʃəˌlɪzəm) NOUN [1] *Philosophy* one of a number of related doctrines which hold that there are necessary properties of things, that these are logically prior to the existence of the individuals which instantiate them, and that their classification depends upon their satisfaction of sets of necessary conditions. [2] the doctrine that education should concentrate on teaching basic skills and encouraging intellectual self-discipline.
▸**esˈsentialist** NOUN

essentially (ɪˈsɛnʃəlɪ) ADVERB [1] in a fundamental or basic way; in essence.

essential oil NOUN any of various volatile organic oils present in plants, usually containing terpenes and esters and having the odour or flavour of the plant from which they are extracted: used in flavouring and perfumery. Compare **fixed oil.** See also **oleoresin.**

Essex (ˈɛsɪks) NOUN [1] a county of SE England, on the North Sea and the Thames estuary; the geographical and ceremonial county includes Thurrock and Southend-on-Sea, which became independent unitary authorities in 1998. Administrative centre: Chelmsford. Pop. (excluding unitary authorities): 1 310 922 (2001). Area (excluding unitary authorities): 3446 sq. km (1310 sq. miles). [2] an Anglo-Saxon kingdom that in the early 7th century A.D. comprised the modern county of Essex and much of Hertfordshire and Surrey. By the late 8th century, Essex had become a dependency of the kingdom of Mercia.

Essex girl NOUN *Informal, derogatory* a young working-class woman from the Essex area, typically considered as being unintelligent, materialistic, devoid of taste, and sexually promiscuous.

Essex Man NOUN *Informal, derogatory* a working man, typically a Londoner who has moved out to Essex, who flaunts his new-found success and status.

Esslingen (ˈɛsˌlɪŋən) NOUN a town in SW Germany, on the River Neckar: Gothic church, medieval buildings: wines, light industry. Pop.: 91 685 (1991 est.).

essonite (ˈɛsəˌnaɪt) NOUN a variant spelling of **hessonite.**

Essonne (*French* ɛsɔn) NOUN a department of N

France, south of Paris in Île-de-France region: formed in 1964. Capital: Évry. Pop.: 1 134 238 (1999). Area: 1811 sq. km (706 sq. miles).

est (ɛst) NOUN a treatment intended to help people towards psychological growth, in which they spend many hours in large groups, deprived of food and water and hectored by stewards.
▷HISTORY *Erhard Seminars Training*; after Werner Erhard, American businessman, who devised the system

EST ABBREVIATION FOR: [1] **Eastern Standard Time.** ◆ [2] ABBREVIATION FOR electric-shock treatment. ◆ INTERNATIONAL CAR REGISTRATION FOR: [3] Estonia.

est. ABBREVIATION FOR: [1] Also: **estab.** established. [2] estimate(d).

-est¹ SUFFIX forming the superlative degree of adjectives and adverbs: *shortest; fastest.*
▷HISTORY Old English *-est, -ost*

-est² *or* **-st** SUFFIX forming the archaic second person singular present and past indicative tense of verbs: *thou goest; thou hadst.*
▷HISTORY Old English *-est, -ast*

establish (ɪ'stæblɪʃ) VERB (*usually tr*) [1] to make secure or permanent in a certain place, condition, job, etc.: *to establish one's usefulness; to establish a house.* [2] to create or set up (an organization, etc.) on or as if on a permanent basis: *to establish a company.* [3] to prove correct or free from doubt; validate: *to establish a fact.* [4] to cause (a principle, theory, etc.) to be widely or permanently accepted: *to establish a precedent.* [5] to give (a Church) the status of a national institution. [6] (of a person) to become recognized and accepted: *he established himself as a reliable GP.* [7] (in works of imagination) to cause (a character, place, etc.) to be credible and recognized: *the first scene established the period.* [8] *Cards* to make winners of (the remaining cards of a suit) by forcing out opponents' top cards. [9] *Botany* (*also intr*) **a** to cause (a plant) to grow or (of a plant) to grow in a new place: *the birch scrub has established over the past 25 years.* **b** to become or cause to become a sapling or adult plant from a seedling.
▷HISTORY C14: from Old French *establir,* from Latin *stabilīre* to make firm, from *stabilis* STABLE²
▸**es'tablisher** NOUN

Established Church NOUN a Church that is officially recognized as a national institution, esp the Church of England.

establishment (ɪ'stæblɪʃmənt) NOUN [1] the act of establishing or state of being established. [2] **a** a business organization or other large institution. **b** the place where a business is carried on. [3] the staff and equipment of a commercial or other organization. [4] the approved size, composition, and equipment of a military unit, government department, business division, etc., as formally promulgated. [5] any large organization, institution, or system. [6] a household or place of residence. [7] a body of employees or servants. [8] (*modifier*) belonging to or characteristic of the Establishment; orthodox or conservative: *the establishment view of history.*

Establishment (ɪ'stæblɪʃmənt) NOUN **the.** a group or class of people having institutional authority within a society, esp those who control the civil service, the government, the armed forces, and the Church: usually identified with a conservative outlook.

establishmentarian (ɪˌstæblɪʃmən'tɛərɪən) ADJECTIVE [1] denoting or relating to an Established Church, esp the Church of England. [2] denoting or relating to the principle of a Church being officially recognized as a national institution. ◆ NOUN [3] an upholder of this principle, esp as applied to the Church of England.
▸**esˌtablishmen'tarianism** NOUN

estaminet *French* (ɛstaminɛ) NOUN a small café, bar, or bistro, esp a shabby one.
▷HISTORY C19: from French, perhaps from Walloon dialect *staminet* manger

estancia (ɪ'stænsɪə; *Spanish* es'tanθia) NOUN (in Spanish America) a large estate or cattle ranch.
▷HISTORY C18: from American Spanish, from Spanish: dwelling, from Vulgar Latin *stantia* (unattested) a remaining, from Latin *stāre* to stand

estate (ɪ'steɪt) NOUN [1] a large piece of landed property, esp in the country. [2] *Chiefly Brit* a large area of property development, esp of new houses or (**trading estate**) of factories. [3] *Property law* **a** property or possessions. **b** the nature of interest that a person has in land or other property, esp in relation to the right of others. **c** the total extent of the real and personal property of a deceased person or bankrupt. [4] Also called: **estate of the realm.** an order or class of persons in a political community, regarded collectively as a part of the body politic: usually regarded as being the lords temporal (peers), lords spiritual and commons. See also **States General, fourth estate.** [5] state, period, or position in life, esp with regard to wealth or social standing: *youth's estate; a poor man's estate.*
▷HISTORY C13: from Old French *estat,* from Latin *status* condition, STATE

estate agent NOUN [1] *Brit* an agent concerned with the valuation, management, lease, and sale of property. Usual US and Canadian name: **real-estate agent.** [2] the administrator of a large landed property, acting on behalf of its owner; estate manager.

estate car NOUN *Brit* a car with a comparatively long body containing a large carrying space, reached through a rear door: usually the back seats can be folded forward to increase the carrying space. Also called (esp US, Canadian, Austral, and NZ): **station wagon.**

estate duty NOUN another name for **death duty.**

Estates General NOUN See **States General.**

esteem (ɪ'sti:m) VERB (*tr*) [1] to have great respect or high regard for: *to esteem a colleague.* [2] *Formal* to judge or consider; deem: *to esteem an idea improper.* ◆ NOUN [3] high regard or respect; good opinion. [4] *Archaic* judgment; opinion.
▷HISTORY C15: from Old French *estimer,* from Latin *aestimāre* ESTIMATE
▸**es'teemed** ADJECTIVE

ester ('ɛstə) NOUN *Chem* any of a class of compounds produced by reaction between acids and alcohols with the elimination of water. Esters with low molecular weights, such as ethyl acetate, are usually volatile fragrant liquids; fats are solid esters.
▷HISTORY C19: from German, probably a contraction of *Essigäther* acetic ether, from *Essig* vinegar (ultimately from Latin *acētum*) + *Äther* ETHER

esterase ('ɛstəˌreɪs, -ˌreɪz) NOUN any of a group of enzymes that hydrolyse esters into alcohols and acids.

esterify (ɛ'stɛrɪˌfaɪ) VERB **-fies, -fying, -fied.** *Chem* to change or cause to change into an ester.
▸**esˌterifi'cation** NOUN

Esth. *Bible* ABBREVIATION FOR Esther.

Esther ('ɛstə) NOUN *Old Testament* [1] a beautiful Jewish woman who became queen of Persia and saved her people from massacre. [2] the book in which this episode is recounted.

esthesia (i:s'θi:zɪə) NOUN a US spelling of **aesthesia.**

esthete ('i:sθi:t) NOUN a US spelling of **aesthete.**
▸**esthetic** (ɛs'θɛtɪk) *or* **es'thetical** ADJECTIVE ▸**es'thetically** ADVERB ▸**esthetician** (ˌi:sθɪ'tɪʃən) ▸**es'thetiˌcism** NOUN ▸**es'thetics** NOUN

Esthonia (ɛ'stəʊnɪə, ɛ'sθəʊ-) NOUN See **Estonia.**

estimable ('ɛstɪməbᵊl) ADJECTIVE worthy of respect; deserving of admiration: *my estimable companion.*
▸**'estimableness** NOUN ▸**'estimably** ADVERB

estimate VERB ('ɛstɪˌmeɪt) [1] to form an approximate idea of (distance, size, cost, etc.); calculate roughly; gauge. [2] (*tr; may take a clause as object*) to form an opinion about; judge: *to estimate one's chances.* [3] to submit (an approximate price) for (a job) to a prospective client. [4] (*tr*) *Statistics* to assign a value (a **point estimate**) or range of values (an **interval estimate**) to a parameter of a population on the basis of sampling statistics. See **estimator.** ◆ NOUN ('ɛstɪmɪt) [5] an approximate calculation. [6] a statement indicating the likely charge for or cost of certain work. [7] a judgment; appraisal; opinion.
▷HISTORY C16: from Latin *aestimāre* to assess the worth of, of obscure origin
▸**'estimative** ADJECTIVE

estimation (ˌɛstɪ'meɪʃən) NOUN [1] a considered opinion; judgment: *what is your estimation of the situation?* [2] esteem; respect. [3] the act of estimating.

estimator ('ɛstɪˌmeɪtə) NOUN [1] a person or thing that estimates. [2] *Statistics* a derived random variable that generates estimates of a parameter of a given distribution, such as $\bar{X}$, the mean of a number of identically distributed random variables X_i. If $\bar{X}$ is unbiased, $\bar{x}$, the observed value should be close to $E(X_i)$. See also **sampling statistic.**

estipulate (ɪ'stɪpjʊlɪt, -ˌleɪt) ADJECTIVE a variant of **exstipulate.**

estival (i:'staɪvᵊl, 'ɛstɪ-) ADJECTIVE the usual US spelling of **aestival.**

estivate ('i:stɪˌveɪt, 'ɛs-) VERB (*intr*) the usual US spelling of **aestivate.**
▸**'estiˌvator** NOUN

estivation (ˌi:stɪ'veɪʃən, ˌɛs-) NOUN the usual US spelling of **aestivation.**

Estonia *or* **Esthonia** (ɛ'stəʊnɪə, ɛ'sθəʊ-) NOUN a republic in NE Europe, on the Gulf of Finland and the Baltic: low-lying with many lakes and forests, it includes numerous islands in the Baltic Sea. It was under Scandinavian and Teutonic rule from the 13th century to 1721, when it passed to Russia: it was an independent republic from 1920 to 1940, when it was annexed by the Soviet Union; became independent in 1991. Official language: Estonian. Religion: believers are mostly Christian. Currency: kroon. Capital: Tallinn. Pop.: 1 363 000 (2001 est). Area: 45 227 sq. km (17 462 sq. miles).

Estonian *or* **Esthonian** (ɛ'stəʊnɪən, ɛ'sθəʊ-) ADJECTIVE [1] of, relating to, or characteristic of Estonia, its people, or their language. ◆ NOUN [2] the official language of Estonia: belongs to the Finno-Ugric family. [3] a native or inhabitant of Estonia.

estop (ɪ'stɒp) VERB **-tops, -topping, -topped.** (*tr*) [1] *Law* to preclude by estoppel. [2] *Archaic* to stop.
▷HISTORY C15: from Old French *estoper* to plug, ultimately from Latin *stuppa* tow; see STOP
▸**es'toppage** NOUN

estoppel (ɪ'stɒpᵊl) NOUN *Law* a rule of evidence whereby a person is precluded from denying the truth of a statement of facts he has previously asserted. See also **conclusion.**
▷HISTORY C16: from Old French *estoupail* plug, from *estoper* to stop up; see ESTOP

Estoril ('ɛʃtɔ:ˌri:l) NOUN a resort in W Portugal, near Lisbon, on the Atlantic Ocean: noted esp for a famous avenue of palm trees leading to the seafront. Pop.: 24 850 (1991).

estovers (ɛ'stəʊvəz) PLURAL NOUN *Law* a right allowed by law to tenants of land to cut timber, esp for fuel and repairs.
▷HISTORY C15: from Anglo-French, plural of *estover,* n use of Old French *estovoir* to be necessary, from Latin *est opus* there is need

estrade (ɪs'trɑ:d) NOUN a dais or raised platform.
▷HISTORY C17: from French, from Spanish *estrado* carpeted floor, from Latin: STRATUM

estradiol (ˌɛstrə'daɪɒl, ˌi:strə-) NOUN the US spelling of **oestradiol.**

estragon ('ɛstrəˌgɒn) NOUN another name for **tarragon.**

estrange (ɪ'streɪndʒ) VERB (*tr*) [1] (*usually passive; often foll by from*) to separate and live apart from (one's spouse): *he is estranged from his wife.* [2] (*usually passive; often foll by from*) to antagonize or lose the affection of (someone previously friendly); alienate.
▷HISTORY C15: from Old French *estranger,* from Late Latin *extrāneāre* to treat as a stranger, from Latin *extrāneus* foreign; see STRANGE
▸**es'trangement** NOUN

estranged (ɪ'streɪndʒd) ADJECTIVE [1] separated and living apart from one's spouse. [2] no longer friendly; alienated.

estray (ɪ'streɪ) NOUN *Law* a stray domestic animal of unknown ownership.
▷HISTORY C16: from Anglo-French, from Old French *estraier* to STRAY

estreat (ɪ'stri:t) *Law* ◆ NOUN [1] a true copy of or extract from a court record. ◆ VERB (*tr*) [2] to enforce (a recognizance that has been forfeited) by sending an extract of the court record to the proper authority.
▷HISTORY C14: from Old French *estraite,* feminine of *estrait* extracted, from *estraire* to EXTRACT

Estrela mountain dog (ɪs'treɪlə) NOUN a sturdy well-built dog of a Portuguese breed with a long

thick coat and a thick tuft of hair round the neck, often used as a guard dog.
▷HISTORY C20: after the Estrela mountain range in Portugal

estrin ('ɛstrɪn, 'i:strɪn) NOUN the US spelling of **oestrin**.

estriol ('ɛstrɪˌɒl, 'i:strɪ-) NOUN the usual US spelling of **oestriol**.

estrogen ('ɛstrədʒən, 'i:strə-) NOUN the usual US spelling of **oestrogen**.
▸**estrogenic** (ˌɛstrə'dʒɛnɪk, ˌi:strə-) ADJECTIVE
▸**ˌestro'genically** ADVERB

estrone ('ɛstrəʊn, 'i:strəʊn) NOUN the usual US spelling of **oestrone**.

estrus ('ɛstrəs, 'i:strəs) NOUN the usual US spelling of **oestrus**.
▸**'estrous** ADJECTIVE

estuarine ('ɛstjʊəˌraɪn, -rɪn) ADJECTIVE [1] formed or deposited in an estuary: *estuarine muds*. [2] growing in, inhabiting, or found in an estuary: *an estuarine fauna*.

estuary ('ɛstjʊərɪ) NOUN, *plural* **-aries**. [1] the widening channel of a river where it nears the sea, with a mixing of fresh water and salt (tidal) water. [2] an inlet of the sea.
▷HISTORY C16: from Latin *aestuārium* marsh, channel, from *aestus* tide, billowing movement, related to *aestās* summer
▸**estuarial** (ˌɛstjʊ'ɛərɪəl) ADJECTIVE

estuary English ADJECTIVE, NOUN a variety of standard British English in which the pronunciation reflects various features characteristic of London and the Southeast of England.
▷HISTORY C20: from the area around the Thames ESTUARY where it originated

e.s.u. *or* **ESU** ABBREVIATION FOR electrostatic unit.

esurient (ɪ'sjʊərɪənt) ADJECTIVE greedy; voracious.
▷HISTORY C17: from Latin *ēsurīre* to be hungry, from *edere* to eat
▸**e'surience** *or* **e'suriency** NOUN ▸**e'suriently** ADVERB

E. Sussex ABBREVIATION FOR East Sussex.

et THE INTERNET DOMAIN NAME FOR Ethiopia.

Et THE CHEMICAL SYMBOL FOR ethyl.

ET [1] ABBREVIATION FOR Employment Training: a government scheme offering training in technological and business skills to unemployed people. ◆ [2] INTERNATIONAL CAR REGISTRATION FOR Egypt.

-et SUFFIX OF NOUNS small or lesser: *islet*; *baronet*.
▷HISTORY from Old French *-et, -ete*

eta[1] ('i:tə) NOUN the seventh letter in the Greek alphabet (Η, η), a long vowel sound, transliterated as *e* or *ē*.
▷HISTORY Greek, of Phoenician origin; compare Hebrew HETH

eta[2] ('eɪtə) NOUN, *plural* **eta** *or* **etas**. (in Japan, formerly) a member of a class of outcasts who did menial and dirty tasks.
▷HISTORY C19: Japanese

ETA[1] ABBREVIATION FOR estimated time of arrival.

ETA[2] ('ɛtə) NOUN ACRONYM FOR Euzkadi ta Askatsuna: an organization of militant Basque nationalists attempting to gain independence for the Basques, esp those ruled by Spain, until a cease-fire in 1998, by means of guerrilla warfare.
▷HISTORY Basque, literally: Basque Nation and Liberty

etaerio (ɛ'tɪərɪəʊ) NOUN an aggregate fruit, as one consisting of drupes (raspberry) or achenes (traveller's joy).
▷HISTORY C19: from French *etairion*, from Greek *hetaireia* association

étagère *French* (etaʒɛr) NOUN a stand with open shelves for displaying ornaments, etc.
▷HISTORY C19: from French, from *étage* shelf; see STAGE

e-tail ('i:teɪl) *or* **e-tailing** ('i:teɪlɪŋ) NOUN retail conducted via the Internet.
▷HISTORY C20: E-[2] + (RE)TAIL
▸**'e-tailer** NOUN

et al. ABBREVIATION FOR: [1] et alibi. [Latin: and elsewhere] [2] et alii.
▷HISTORY Latin: and others

etalon ('ɛtəˌlɒn) NOUN *Physics* a device used in spectroscopy to measure wavelengths by interference effects produced by multiple reflections between parallel half-silvered glass or quartz plates.
▷HISTORY C20: French *étalon* a fixed standard of weights and measures, from Old French *estalon*; see also STALLION

etamine ('ɛtəˌmi:n) *or* **etamin** ('ɛtəmɪn) NOUN a cotton or worsted fabric of loose weave, used for clothing, curtains, etc.
▷HISTORY C18: from French, from Latin *stāminea*, from *stāmineus* made of threads, from *stamen* thread, warp

etc. ABBREVIATION FOR et cetera.

et cetera *or* **etcetera** (ɪt 'sɛtrə) [1] and the rest; and others; and so forth: used at the end of a list to indicate that other items of the same class or type should be considered or included. [2] or the like; or something else similar. Abbreviations: **etc., &c.** See also **etceteras**.
▷HISTORY from Latin, from *et* and + *cetera* the other (things)

> **Language note** It is unnecessary to use *and* before *etc.* as *etc.* (*et cetera*) already means *and other things*. The repetition of *etc.*, as in *he brought paper, ink, notebooks, etc., etc.*, is avoided except in informal contexts.

etceteras (ɪt'sɛtrəz) PLURAL NOUN miscellaneous extra things or persons.

etch (ɛtʃ) VERB [1] (*tr*) to wear away the surface of (a metal, glass, etc.) by chemical action, esp the action of an acid. [2] to cut or corrode (a design, decoration, etc.) on (a metal or other plate to be used for printing) by using the action of acid on parts not covered by wax or other acid-resistant coating. [3] (*tr*) to cut with or as if with a sharp implement: *he etched his name on the table*. [4] (*tr; usually passive*) to imprint vividly: *the event was etched on her memory*.
▷HISTORY C17: from Dutch *etsen*, from Old High German *azzen* to feed, bite
▸**'etcher** NOUN

etchant ('ɛtʃənt) NOUN any acid or corrosive used for etching.

etching ('ɛtʃɪŋ) NOUN [1] the art, act, or process of preparing etched surfaces or of printing designs from them. [2] an etched plate. [3] an impression made from an etched plate.

ETD ABBREVIATION FOR estimated time of departure.

Eteocles (ɪ'ti:əˌkli:z, 'ɛtɪə-) NOUN *Greek myth* a son of Oedipus and Jocasta. He expelled his brother Polynices from Thebes; they killed each other in single combat when Polynices returned as leader of the Seven against Thebes.

eternal (ɪ'tɜ:nᵊl) ADJECTIVE [1] **a** without beginning or end; lasting for ever: *eternal life*. **b** (*as noun*): *the eternal*. [2] (*often capital*) denoting or relating to that which is without beginning and end, regarded as an attribute of God. [3] unchanged by time, esp being true or valid for all time; immutable: *eternal truths*. [4] seemingly unceasing; occurring again and again: *eternal bickering*.
▷HISTORY C14: from Late Latin *aeternālis*, from Latin *aeternus*; related to Latin *aevum* age
▸**ˌeter'nality** *or* **e'ternalness** NOUN ▸**e'ternally** ADVERB

Eternal City NOUN **the.** Rome.

eternalize, eternalize (ɪ'tɜ:nəˌlaɪz), **eternize** (ɪ'tɜ:naɪz), **eternalise,** *or* **eternise** VERB (*tr*) [1] to make eternal. [2] to make famous for ever; immortalize.
▸**eˌternali'zation** *or* **eˌterni'zation** *or* **eˌternali'sation** *or* **eˌterni'sation** NOUN

eternal triangle NOUN an emotional relationship in which there are conflicts involving a man and two women or a woman and two men.

eterne (ɪ'tɜ:n) ADJECTIVE an archaic or poetic word for **eternal**.
▷HISTORY C14: from Old French, from Latin *aeternus*

eternity (ɪ'tɜ:nɪtɪ) NOUN, *plural* **-ties**. [1] endless or infinite time. [2] the quality, state, or condition of being eternal. [3] (*usually plural*) any of the aspects of life and thought that are considered to be timeless, esp timeless and true. [4] *Theol* the condition of timeless existence, believed by some to characterize the afterlife. [5] a seemingly endless period of time: *an eternity of waiting*.

eternity ring NOUN a ring given as a token of lasting affection, esp one set all around with stones to symbolize continuity.

etesian (ɪ'ti:ʒɪən) ADJECTIVE (of NW winds) recurring annually in the summer in the E Mediterranean.
▷HISTORY C17: from Latin *etēsius* yearly, from Greek *etēsios*, from *etos* year

ETF ABBREVIATION FOR **electronic transfer of funds**.

eth (ɛð, ɛθ) NOUN a variant of **edh**.

ETH INTERNATIONAL CAR REGISTRATION FOR Ethiopia.

Eth. ABBREVIATION FOR Ethiopia(n).

-eth[1] SUFFIX forming the archaic third person singular present indicative tense of verbs: *goeth*; *taketh*.
▷HISTORY Old English *-eth, -th*

-eth[2] *or* **-th** SUFFIX FORMING ORDINAL NUMBERS a variant of **-th**[2]. *twentieth*.

ethambutol (ɛ'θæmbjʊˌtɒl) NOUN a compound used in the treatment of tuberculosis.
▷HISTORY from ETH(YLENE) + AM(INE) + BUT(AN)OL

ethanal ('ɛθəˌnæl, 'i:θə-) NOUN the modern name for **acetaldehyde**.

ethane ('i:θeɪn, 'ɛθ-) NOUN a colourless odourless flammable gaseous alkane obtained from natural gas and petroleum: used as a fuel and in the manufacture of organic chemicals. Formula: C_2H_6.
▷HISTORY C19: from ETH(YL) + -ANE

ethanedioic acid (ˌi:θeɪndaɪ'əʊɪk, ˌɛθ-) NOUN the technical name for **oxalic acid**.
▷HISTORY C20: from ETHANE + DI-[1] + -O- + -IC

ethanediol ('i:θeɪnˌdaɪɒl, 'ɛθ-) NOUN a clear colourless syrupy soluble liquid substance, used as an antifreeze and solvent. Formula: CH_2OHCH_2OH. Also called: **glycol, ethylene glycol**.
▷HISTORY C20: from ETHANE + DI-[1] + -OL[1]

ethanoic acid (ˌɛθə'nəʊɪk, ˌi:θə-) NOUN the modern name for **acetic acid**.

ethanol ('ɛθəˌnɒl, 'i:θə-) NOUN the technical name for **alcohol** (sense 1).

ethanoyl ('ɛθəˌnɔɪl) NOUN (*modifier*) of, consisting of, or containing the monovalent group CH_3CO-: *ethanoyl group or radical*.
▷HISTORY C20: from ETH(YL) + -OYL

ethanoyl chloride NOUN another name for **acetyl chloride**.

ethene ('ɛθi:n) NOUN the technical name for **ethylene**.

ether ('i:θə) NOUN [1] Also called: **diethyl ether, ethyl ether, ethoxyethane**. a colourless volatile highly flammable liquid with a characteristic sweetish odour, made by the reaction of sulphuric acid with ethanol: used as a solvent and anaesthetic. Formula: $C_2H_5OC_2H_5$. [2] any of a class of organic compounds with the general formula ROR′ where R and R′ are alkyl groups, as in diethyl ether $C_2H_5OC_2H_5$. [3] **the ether.** the hypothetical medium formerly believed to fill all space and to support the propagation of electromagnetic waves. [4] *Greek myth* the upper regions of the atmosphere; clear sky or heaven. [5] a rare word for **air**. ◆ Also (for senses 3–5): **aether**.
▷HISTORY C17: from Latin *aether*, from Greek *aithēr*, from *aithein* to burn
▸**etheric** (i:'θɛrɪk) ADJECTIVE

ethereal (ɪ'θɪərɪəl) ADJECTIVE [1] extremely delicate or refined; exquisite. [2] almost as light as air; impalpable; airy. [3] celestial or spiritual. [4] of, containing, or dissolved in an ether, esp diethyl ether: *an ethereal solution*. [5] of or relating to the ether.
▷HISTORY C16: from Latin *aethereus*, from Greek *aitherios*, from *aithēr* ETHER
▸**eˌthere'ality** *or* **e'therealness** NOUN ▸**e'thereally** ADVERB

etherealize *or* **etherealise** (ɪ'θɪərɪəˌlaɪz) VERB (*tr*) [1] to make or regard as being ethereal. [2] to add ether to or make into ether or something resembling ether.
▸**eˌthereali'zation** *or* **eˌthereali'sation** NOUN

etherify ('i:θərɪˌfaɪ, i:'θɛrɪ-) VERB **-fies, -fying, -fied**. (*tr*) to change (a compound, such as an alcohol) into an ether.
▸**eˌtherifi'cation** NOUN

etherize *or* **etherise** ('i:θəˌraɪz) VERB (*tr*) *Obsolete*

to subject (a person) to the anaesthetic influence of ether fumes; anaesthetize.
▸ˌetheriˈzation *or* ˌetheriˈsation NOUN ▸ˈetherˌizer *or* ˈetherˌiser NOUN

Ethernet (ˈiːθəˌnɛt) NOUN *Trademark Computing* a widely used type of local area network.

ethic (ˈɛθɪk) NOUN [1] a moral principle or set of moral values held by an individual or group: *the Puritan ethic.* ◆ ADJECTIVE [2] another word for **ethical.** ◆ See also **ethics.**
▹HISTORY C15: from Latin *ēthicus,* from Greek *éthikos,* from *ēthos* custom; see ETHOS

ethical (ˈɛθɪkəl) ADJECTIVE [1] in accordance with principles of conduct that are considered correct, esp those of a given profession or group. [2] of or relating to ethics. [3] (of a medicinal agent) available legally only with a doctor's prescription or consent.
▸ˈethically ADVERB ▸ˈethicalness *or* ˌethiˈcality NOUN

ethical investment NOUN an investment in a company whose activities or products are not considered by the investor to be unethical.

ethicize *or* **ethicise** (ˈɛθɪˌsaɪz) VERB *(tr)* to make or consider as ethical.

ethics (ˈɛθɪks) NOUN [1] *(functioning as singular)* the philosophical study of the moral value of human conduct and of the rules and principles that ought to govern it; moral philosophy. See also **meta-ethics.** [2] *(functioning as plural)* a social, religious, or civil code of behaviour considered correct, esp that of a particular group, profession, or individual. [3] *(functioning as plural)* the moral fitness of a decision, course of action, etc.: *he doubted the ethics of their verdict.*
▸ˈethicist NOUN

Ethiop (ˈiːθɪˌɒp) *or* **Ethiope** (ˈiːθɪˌəʊp) ADJECTIVE archaic words for **Black[1].**

Ethiopia (ˌiːθɪˈəʊpɪə) NOUN a state in NE Africa, on the Red Sea: consolidated as an empire under Menelik II (1889–1913); federated with Eritrea from 1952 until 1993; Emperor Haile Selassie was deposed by the military in 1974 and the monarchy was abolished in 1975; an independence movement in Eritrea was engaged in war with the government from 1961 until 1993. It lies along the Great Rift Valley and consists of deserts in the southeast and northeast and a high central plateau with many rivers (including the Blue Nile) and mountains rising over 4500 m (15 000 ft.); the main export is coffee. Language: Amharic. Religion: Christian majority. Currency: birr. Capital: Addis Ababa. Pop.: 65 892 000 (2001 est). Area: 1 128 215 sq. km (435 614 sq. miles). Former name: **Abyssinia.**

Ethiopian (ˌiːθɪˈəʊpɪən) ADJECTIVE [1] of, relating to, or characteristic of Ethiopia, its people, or any of their languages. [2] of or denoting a zoogeographical region consisting of Africa south of the Sahara. [3] *Anthropol, obsolete* of or belonging to a postulated racial group characterized by dark skin, an oval elongated face, and thin lips, living chiefly in Africa south of the Sahara. ◆ NOUN [4] a native or inhabitant of Ethiopia. [5] any of the languages of Ethiopia, esp Amharic. ◆ NOUN, ADJECTIVE [6] an archaic word for **Black[1].**

Ethiopic (ˌiːθɪˈɒpɪk, -ˈəʊpɪk) NOUN [1] the ancient language of Ethiopia, belonging to the Semitic subfamily of the Afro-Asiatic family: a Christian liturgical language. See also **Ge'ez.** [2] the group of languages developed from this language, including Amharic, Tigre, and Tigrinya. ◆ ADJECTIVE [3] denoting or relating to this language or group of languages. [4] a less common word for **Ethiopian.**

ethmoid (ˈɛθmɔɪd) *Anatomy* ◆ ADJECTIVE *also* **ethmoidal.** [1] denoting or relating to a bone of the skull that forms part of the eye socket and the nasal cavity. ◆ NOUN [2] the ethmoid bone.
▹HISTORY C18: from Greek *ēthmoeidēs* like a sieve, from *ēthmos* sieve, from *ēthein* to sift

ethnarch (ˈɛθnɑːk) NOUN the ruler of a people or province, as in parts of the Roman and Byzantine Empires.
▹HISTORY C17: from Greek *ethnarkhēs,* from *ethnos* nation + *arkhein* to rule
▸ˈethnarchy NOUN

ethnic (ˈɛθnɪk) *or* **ethnical** ADJECTIVE [1] relating to or characteristic of a human group having racial, religious, linguistic, and certain other traits in common. [2] relating to the classification of mankind into groups, esp on the basis of racial characteristics. [3] denoting or deriving from the cultural traditions of a group of people: *the ethnic dances of Slovakia.* [4] characteristic of another culture, esp a peasant culture: *the ethnic look; ethnic food.* ◆ NOUN [5] *Chiefly US and Austral* a member of an ethnic group, esp a minority group.
▹HISTORY C14 (in the senses: heathen, Gentile): from Late Latin *ethnicus,* from Greek *ethnikos,* from *ethnos* race
▸ˈethnically ADVERB ▸ethnicity (ɛθˈnɪsɪtɪ) NOUN

ethnic cleansing NOUN *Euphemistic* the violent removal by one ethnic group of other ethnic groups from the population of a particular area: used esp of the activities of Serbs against Croats and Muslims in the former Yugoslavia.

ethnic minority NOUN an immigrant or racial group regarded by those claiming to speak for the cultural majority as distinct and unassimilated.

ethno- COMBINING FORM indicating race, people, or culture: *ethnology.*
▹HISTORY via French from Greek *ethnos* race

ethnobiology (ˌɛθnəʊbaɪˈɒlədʒɪ) NOUN the branch of biology involving the study of the uses of plants and animals in various human societies.

ethnobotany (ˌɛθnəʊˈbɒtənɪ) NOUN the branch of botany concerned with the use of plants in folklore, religion, etc.
▸ˌethnoˈbotanist NOUN

ethnocentrism (ˌɛθnəʊˈsɛnˌtrɪzəm) NOUN belief in the intrinsic superiority of the nation, culture, or group to which one belongs, often accompanied by feelings of dislike for other groups.
▸ˌethnoˈcentric ADJECTIVE ▸ˌethnoˈcentrically ADVERB ▸ˌethnocenˈtricity NOUN

ethnogeny (ɛθˈnɒdʒɪnɪ) NOUN the branch of ethnology that deals with the origin of races or peoples.
▸ethnogenic (ˌɛθnəʊˈdʒɛnɪk) ADJECTIVE ▸ethˈnogenist NOUN

ethnography (ɛθˈnɒgrəfɪ) NOUN the branch of anthropology that deals with the scientific description of individual human societies.
▸ˌethˈnographer NOUN ▸ethnographic (ˌɛθnəʊˈgræfɪk) *or* ˌethnoˈgraphical ADJECTIVE ▸ˌethnoˈgraphically ADVERB

ethnology (ɛθˈnɒlədʒɪ) NOUN the branch of anthropology that deals with races and peoples, their relations to one another, their origins, and their distinctive characteristics.
▸ethnologic (ˌɛθnəˈlɒdʒɪk) *or* ˌethnoˈlogical ADJECTIVE ▸ˌethnoˈlogically ADVERB ▸ethˈnologist NOUN

ethnomethodology (ˌɛθnəʊmɛθəˈdɒlədʒɪ) NOUN a method of studying linguistic communication that emphasizes common-sense views of conversation and the world. Compare **phenomenology.**

ethnomusicology (ˌɛθnəʊmjuːzɪˈkɒlədʒɪ) NOUN the study of the music of different cultures.
▸ˌethnomusiˈcologist NOUN

ethology (ɪˈθɒlədʒɪ) NOUN the study of the behaviour of animals in their normal environment.
▹HISTORY C17 (in the obsolete sense: mimicry): via Latin from Greek *ēthologia,* from *ēthos* character; current sense, C19
▸ethological (ˌɛθəˈlɒdʒɪkəl) ADJECTIVE ▸ˌethoˈlogically ADVERB ▸eˈthologist NOUN

ethonone (ˈɛθəˌnəʊn) NOUN another name for **ketene.**

ethos (ˈiːθɒs) NOUN the distinctive character, spirit, and attitudes of a people, culture, era, etc.: *the revolutionary ethos.*
▹HISTORY C19: from Late Latin: habit, from Greek

ethoxide (iːˈθɒksaɪd) NOUN any of a class of saltlike compounds with the formula MOC_2H_5, where M is a metal atom. Also called: **ethylate.**
▹HISTORY C20: from *ethox(yl)* (from ETH(YL) + OX(YGEN) + -YL) + -IDE

ethoxyethane (ɛˌθɒksɪˈiːθeɪn) NOUN the technical name for **ether** (sense 1).
▹HISTORY C20: from ETH(YL) + OXY-[2] + ETHANE

ethyl (ˈiːθaɪl, ˈɛθɪl) NOUN *(modifier)* of, consisting of, or containing the monovalent group C_2H_5-: *ethyl group or radical.*
▹HISTORY C19: from ETH(ER) + -YL
▸ethylic (ɪˈθɪlɪk) ADJECTIVE

ethyl acetate NOUN a colourless volatile flammable fragrant liquid ester, made from acetic acid and ethanol: used in perfumes and flavourings and as a solvent for plastics, etc. Formula: $CH_3COOC_2H_5$.

ethyl alcohol NOUN another name for **alcohol** (sense 1).

ethylate (ˈɛθɪˌleɪt) VERB [1] to undergo or cause to undergo a chemical reaction in which an ethyl group is introduced into a molecule. ◆ NOUN [2] another name for an **ethoxide.**
▸ˌethylˈation NOUN

ethyl carbamate NOUN a colourless odourless crystalline ester that is used in the manufacture of pesticides, fungicides, and pharmaceuticals. Formula: $CO(NH_2)OC_2H_5$. Also called: **urethane.**

ethylene (ˈɛθɪˌliːn) NOUN a colourless flammable gaseous alkene with a sweet odour, obtained from petroleum and natural gas and used in the manufacture of polythene and many other chemicals. Formula: CH_2:CH_2. Also called: **ethene.**
▸ethylenic (ˌɛθɪˈliːnɪk) ADJECTIVE

ethylene glycol NOUN another name for **ethanediol.**

ethylene group *or* **radical** NOUN *Chem* the divalent group, -CH_2CH_2-, derived from ethylene.

ethylene series NOUN *Chem* the homologous series of unsaturated hydrocarbons that contain one double bond and have the general formula, C_nH_{2n}; alkene series.

ethyl ether NOUN a more formal name for **ether** (sense 1).

ethyne (ˈiːθaɪn, ˈɛθaɪn) NOUN another name for **acetylene.**
▹HISTORY C20: from ETHYL + -INE[2]

etiolate (ˈiːtɪəʊˌleɪt) VERB [1] *Botany* to whiten (a green plant) through lack of sunlight. [2] to become or cause to become pale and weak, as from malnutrition.
▹HISTORY C18: from French *étioler* to make pale, probably from Old French *estuble* straw, from Latin *stipula*
▸ˌetioˈlation NOUN

etiology (ˌiːtɪˈɒlədʒɪ) NOUN, *plural* **-gies.** a variant spelling of **aetiology.**
▸etiological (ˌiːtɪəˈlɒdʒɪkəl) ADJECTIVE ▸ˌetioˈlogically ADVERB ▸etiˈologist NOUN

etiquette (ˈɛtɪˌkɛt, ˌɛtɪˈkɛt) NOUN [1] the customs or rules governing behaviour regarded as correct or acceptable in social or official life. [2] a conventional but unwritten code of practice followed by members of any of certain professions or groups: *medical etiquette.*
▹HISTORY C18: from French, from Old French *estiquette* label, from *estiquier* to attach; see STICK[2]

Etna (ˈɛtnə) NOUN **Mount.** an active volcano in E Sicily: the highest volcano in Europe and the highest peak in Italy south of the Alps. Height: 3323 m (10 902 ft.).

Eton (ˈiːtən) NOUN [1] a town in S England, in Windsor and Maidenhead unitary authority, Berkshire, near the River Thames: site of **Eton College,** a public school for boys founded in 1440. Pop.: 1974 (1991). [2] this college.

Eton collar NOUN a broad stiff white collar worn outside an Eton jacket.

Eton crop NOUN a short mannish hairstyle worn by women in the 1920s.

Etonian (iːˈtəʊnɪən) NOUN [1] a pupil of Eton College. ◆ ADJECTIVE [2] of or relating to Eton College.

Eton jacket NOUN a waist-length jacket with a V-shaped back, open in front, formerly worn by pupils of Eton College.

etonogestrel (ɪˌtɒnəʊˈdʒɛstrəl) NOUN a progestogen used as a male contraceptive, released from two tiny rods placed under the skin.

étrier *(French* etrije) NOUN *Mountaineering* a short portable ladder or set of webbing loops that can be attached to a karabiner or fifi hook. US name: **stirrup.**
▹HISTORY C20: from French: stirrup

Etruria (ɪˈtrʊərɪə) NOUN [1] an ancient country of central Italy, between the Rivers Arno and Tiber, roughly corresponding to present-day Tuscany and part of Umbria. [2] a factory established in Staffordshire by Josiah Wedgwood in 1769.

Etruscan (ɪˈtrʌskən) *or* **Etrurian** (ɪˈtrʊərɪən)

NOUN [1] a member of an ancient people of central Italy whose civilization influenced the Romans, who had suppressed them by about 200 B.C. [2] the non-Indo-European language of the ancient Etruscans, whose few surviving records have not been fully interpreted. ♦ ADJECTIVE [3] of, relating to, or characteristic of Etruria, the Etruscans, their culture, or their language.

et seq. ABBREVIATION FOR: [1] et sequens. [Latin: and the following] [2] Also: **et seqq.** et sequentia.
▷HISTORY Latin: and those that follow

-ette SUFFIX OF NOUNS [1] small: *cigarette*; *kitchenette*. [2] female: *majorette*; *suffragette*. [3] (esp in trade names) imitation: *Leatherette*.
▷HISTORY from French, feminine of -ET

étude (ˈeɪtjuːd; *French* etyd) NOUN a short musical composition for a solo instrument, esp one designed as an exercise or exploiting technical virtuosity.
▷HISTORY C19: from French: STUDY

étui (ɛˈtwiː) NOUN, *plural* **étuis**. a small usually ornamented case for holding needles, cosmetics, or other small articles.
▷HISTORY C17: from French, from Old French *estuier* to enclose; see TWEEZERS

ety., etym., *or* **etymol.** ABBREVIATION FOR: [1] etymological. [2] etymology.

etymologize *or* **etymologise** (ˌɛtɪˈmɒləˌdʒaɪz) VERB to trace, state, or suggest the etymology of (a word).

etymology (ˌɛtɪˈmɒlədʒɪ) NOUN, *plural* **-gies**. [1] the study of the sources and development of words and morphemes. [2] an account of the source and development of a word or morpheme.
▷HISTORY C14: via Latin from Greek *etumologia*; see ETYMON, -LOGY
▸**etymological** (ˌɛtɪməˈlɒdʒɪkᵊl) ADJECTIVE
▸**ˌetymoˈlogically** ADVERB ▸**ˌetyˈmologist** NOUN

etymon (ˈɛtɪˌmɒn) NOUN, *plural* **-mons** *or* **-ma** (-mə). a form of a word or morpheme, usually the earliest recorded form or a reconstructed form, from which another word or morpheme is derived: *the etymon of English "ewe" is Indo-European "*owi"*.
▷HISTORY C16: via Latin, from Greek *etumon* basic meaning, from *etumos* true, actual

e-type NOUN *Informal* a person who works in or is interested in electronics.
▷HISTORY C20: *e*lectronics

Etzel (ˈɛtsᵊl) NOUN *German legend* a great king who, according to the *Nibelungenlied,* was the second husband of Kriemhild after the death of Siegfried: identified with Attila the Hun. Compare **Atli**.

eu THE INTERNET DOMAIN NAME FOR the European Union.

Eu THE CHEMICAL SYMBOL FOR europium.

EU ABBREVIATION FOR **European Union**.

eu- COMBINING FORM well, pleasant, or good: *eupeptic*; *euphony*.
▷HISTORY via Latin from Greek, from *eus* good

eubacteria (ˌjuːbækˈtɪərɪə) PLURAL NOUN, *singular* **-rium** (-rɪəm). a large group of bacteria characterized by a rigid cell wall and, in motile types, flagella; the true bacteria.
▷HISTORY C20: via New Latin from Greek, from EU- (in the sense: true) + BACTERIUM

Euboea (juːˈbɪə) NOUN an island in the W Aegean Sea: the largest island after Crete of the Greek archipelago; linked with the mainland by a bridge across the Euripus channel. Capital: Chalcis. Pop.: 188 400 (latest est.). Area: 3908 sq. km (1509 sq. miles). Modern Greek name: **Évvoia**. Former English name: **Negropont**.

Euboean (juːˈbɪən) ADJECTIVE [1] of or relating to the Greek island of Euboea. ♦ NOUN [2] a native or inhabitant of Euboea.

eucaine (juːˈkeɪn) NOUN a crystalline optically active substance formerly used as a local anaesthetic. Formula: $C_{15}H_{21}NO_2$.

eucalyptol (ˌjuːkəˈlɪptɒl) *or* **eucalyptole** (ˌjuːkəˈlɪptəʊl) NOUN a colourless oily liquid with a camphor-like odour and a spicy taste, obtained from eucalyptus oil and used in perfumery and as a flavouring. Formula: $C_{10}H_{18}O$. Also called: **cineol**.

eucalyptus (ˌjuːkəˈlɪptəs) *or* **eucalypt** (ˈjuːkəˌlɪpt) NOUN, *plural* **-lyptuses** *or* **-lypti** (-ˈlɪptaɪ), *or* **-lypts**. any myrtaceous tree of the mostly Australian genus *Eucalyptus,* such as the blue gum and ironbark, widely cultivated for the medicinal oil in their leaves (**eucalyptus oil**), timber, and ornament.
▷HISTORY C19: New Latin, from EU- + Greek *kaluptos* covered, from *kaluptein* to cover, hide

eucaryote (juːˈkærɪɒt) NOUN a variant spelling of **eukaryote**.

eucharis (ˈjuːkərɪs) NOUN any amaryllidaceous plant of the South American genus *Eucharis,* cultivated for their large white fragrant flowers.
▷HISTORY C19: New Latin, from Late Latin: charming, from Greek *eukharis,* from EU- + *kharis* grace

Eucharist (ˈjuːkərɪst) NOUN [1] the Christian sacrament in which Christ's Last Supper is commemorated by the consecration of bread and wine. [2] the consecrated elements of bread and wine offered in the sacrament. [3] Mass, esp when regarded as the service where the sacrament of the Eucharist is administered.
▷HISTORY C14: via Church Latin from Greek *eukharistia,* from *eukharistos* thankful, from EU- + *kharizesthai* to show favour, from *kharis* favour
▸**ˌEuchaˈristic** *or* **ˌEuchaˈristical** ADJECTIVE
▸**ˌEuchaˈristically** ADVERB

euchlorine (juːˈklɔːriːn) *or* **euchlorin** (juːˈklɔːrɪn) NOUN an explosive gaseous mixture of chlorine and chlorine dioxide.

euchre (ˈjuːkə) NOUN [1] a US and Canadian card game similar to écarté for two to four players, using a poker pack with joker. [2] an instance of euchring another player, preventing him from making his contracted tricks. ♦ VERB *(tr)* [3] to prevent (a player) from making his contracted tricks. [4] (usually foll by *out*) *US, Canadian, Austral, and NZ informal* to outwit or cheat. [5] *Austral and NZ informal* to ruin or exhaust.
▷HISTORY C19: of unknown origin

euchromatin (juːˈkrəʊmətɪn) NOUN the part of a chromosome that constitutes the major genes and does not stain strongly with basic dyes when the cell is not dividing. Compare **heterochromatin**.
▸**euchromatic** (ˌjuːkrəʊˈmætɪk) ADJECTIVE

Euclid (ˈjuːklɪd) NOUN the works of Euclid (Greek mathematician of Alexandria, 3rd century B.C.), esp his system of geometry.

Euclidean *or* **Euclidian** (juːˈklɪdɪən) ADJECTIVE of or relating to Euclid, the 3rd century B.C. Greek mathematician, or his system of geometry.

eucryphia (juːˈkrɪfɪə) NOUN any tree or shrub of the mostly evergreen genus *Eucryphia,* native to Australia and S America, having leaves of a dark lustrous green and white flowers: family *Eucryphiaceae*.
▷HISTORY from Greek *eu* well + *kryphios* hidden, from *kryptein* to hide, referring to the sepals being joined at the top

eudemon *or* **eudaemon** (juːˈdiːmən) NOUN a benevolent spirit or demon.
▷HISTORY C17: from Greek *eudaimōn,* from EU- + *daimōn* in-dwelling spirit; see DEMON

eudemonia *or* **eudaemonia** (ˌjuːdɪˈməʊnɪə) NOUN happiness, esp (in the philosophy of Aristotle) that resulting from a rational active life.

eudemonics *or* **eudaemonics** (ˌjuːdɪˈmɒnɪks) NOUN *(functioning as singular)* [1] the art or theory of happiness. [2] another word for **eudemonism**.
▸**ˌeudeˈmonic** *or* **ˌeudaeˈmonic** ADJECTIVE

eudemonism *or* **eudaemonism** (juːˈdiːməˌnɪzəm) NOUN *Philosophy* an ethical doctrine holding that the value of moral action lies in its capacity to produce happiness.
▸**euˈdemonist** *or* **euˈdaemonist** NOUN ▸**euˌdemonˈistic** *or* **euˌdaemonˈistic** *or* **euˌdemonˈistical** *or* **euˌdaemonˈistical** ADJECTIVE ▸**euˌdemonˈistically** *or* **euˌdaemonˈistically** ADVERB

eudicotyledon (ˌjuːdaɪˌkɒtɪˈliːdᵊn) NOUN any plant belonging to one of the two major groups of flowering plants, comprising over 60 per cent of all plants, normally having net-veined leaves and two cotyledons in the seed.

eudiometer (ˌjuːdɪˈɒmɪtə) NOUN a graduated glass tube used in the study and volumetric analysis of gas reactions.
▷HISTORY C18: from Greek *eudios,* literally: clear skied (from EU- + *Dios,* genitive of *Zeus* god of the heavens) + -METER
▸**eudiometric** (ˌjuːdɪəˈmetrɪk) *or* **ˌeudioˈmetrical** ADJECTIVE ▸**ˌeudioˈmetrically** ADVERB ▸**ˌeudiˈometry** NOUN

eugarie (ˈjuːgərɪ) NOUN *Queensland dialect* another name for **pipi**.

eugenics (juːˈdʒɛnɪks) NOUN *(functioning as singular)* the study of methods of improving the quality of the human race, esp by selective breeding.
▷HISTORY C19: from Greek *eugenēs* well-born, from EU- + *-genēs* born; see -GEN
▸**euˈgenic** ADJECTIVE ▸**euˈgenically** ADVERB ▸**euˈgenicist** NOUN ▸**eugenist** (ˈjuːdʒənɪst) NOUN, ADJECTIVE

eugenol (ˈjuːdʒɪˌnɒl) NOUN a colourless or pale yellow oily liquid substance with a spicy taste and an odour of cloves, used in perfumery; 4-allyl-2-methoxyphenol. Formula: $C_{10}H_{12}O_2$.
▷HISTORY C19: *eugen-,* from *Eugenia caryophyllata* kind of clove from which oil may be obtained + -OL[1]

euglena (juːˈgliːnə) NOUN any freshwater unicellular organism of the genus *Euglena,* moving by means of flagella and typically having holophytic nutrition. It has been variously regarded as an alga or a protozoan but is now usually classified as a protoctist (phylum *Euglenophyta*).
▷HISTORY C19: from New Latin, from EU- + Greek *glēnē* eyeball, socket of a joint
▸**euˈglenoid** ADJECTIVE, NOUN

euhemerism (juːˈhiːməˌrɪzəm) NOUN [1] the theory that gods arose out of the deification of historical heroes. [2] any interpretation of myths that derives the gods from outstanding men and seeks the source of mythology in history.
▷HISTORY C19: named after *Euhemerus* (?300 B.C.), Greek philosopher who propounded this theory
▸**euˈhemerist** NOUN ▸**euˌhemerˈistic** ADJECTIVE
▸**euˌhemerˈistically** ADVERB

euhemerize *or* **euhemerise** (juːˈhiːməˌraɪz) VERB to deal with or explain (myths) by euhemerism.

eukaryote *or* **eucaryote** (juːˈkærɪɒt) NOUN any member of the *Eukarya,* a domain of organisms having cells each with a distinct nucleus within which the genetic material is contained. Eukaryotes include protoctists, fungi, plants, and animals. Compare **prokaryote**.
▷HISTORY from EU- + KARYO- + *-ote* as in *zygote*
▸**eukaryotic** *or* **eucaryotic** (ˌjuːkærɪˈɒtɪk) ADJECTIVE

eulachon (ˈjuːləˌkɒn) *or* **eulachan** NOUN, *plural* **-chons, -chon** *or* **-chans, -chan**. another name for **candlefish**.
▷HISTORY from Chinook Jargon *ulâkân*

Eulenspiegel (ˈɔɪlənˌʃpiːgᵊl) NOUN See **Till Eulenspiegel**.

Euler's circles (*German* ˈɔɪlər) PLURAL NOUN *Logic* a diagram in which the terms of categorial statements are represented by circles whose inclusion in one another represents the inclusion of the extensions of the terms in one another. Compare **Venn diagram**.
▷HISTORY named after Leonhard *Euler* (1707–83), Swiss mathematician

eulogia (juːˈləʊdʒɪə) NOUN [1] *Eastern Christian Church* blessed bread distributed to members of the congregation after the liturgy, esp to those who have not communed. [2] *Archaic* a blessing or something blessed.
▷HISTORY C18: from Greek: blessing; see EULOGY

eulogize *or* **eulogise** (ˈjuːləˌdʒaɪz) VERB to praise (a person or thing) highly in speech or writing.
▸**ˈeulogist** *or* **ˈeuloˌgizer** *or* **ˈeuloˌgiser** NOUN ▸**ˌeuloˈgistic** *or* **ˌeuloˈgistical** ADJECTIVE ▸**ˌeuloˈgistically** ADVERB

eulogy (ˈjuːlədʒɪ) NOUN, *plural* **-gies**. [1] a formal speech or piece of writing praising a person or thing, esp a person who has recently died. [2] high praise or commendation. Also called (archaic): **eulogium** (juːˈləʊdʒɪəm).
▷HISTORY C16: from Late Latin *eulogia,* from Greek: praise, from EU- + -LOGY; influenced by Latin *ēlogium* short saying, inscription

Language note Avoid confusion with **elegy**.

Eumenides (juːˈmɛnɪˌdiːz) PLURAL NOUN another name for the **Furies**, used by the Greeks as a euphemism
▷HISTORY from Greek, literally: the benevolent ones, from *eumenēs* benevolent, from EU- + *menos* spirit

eumung ('ju:mʌŋ) *or* **eumong** ('ju:mɒŋ) NOUN any of various Australian acacias.
▷HISTORY from a native Australian language

eunuch ('ju:nək) NOUN [1] a man who has been castrated, esp (formerly) for some office such as a guard in a harem. [2] *Informal* an ineffective man: *a political eunuch.*
▷HISTORY C15: via Latin from Greek *eunoukhos* attendant of the bedchamber, from *eunē* bed + *ekhein* to have, keep

euonymus (ju:'ɒnɪməs) *or* **evonymus** NOUN any tree or shrub of the N temperate genus *Euonymus,* such as the spindle tree, whose seeds are each enclosed in a fleshy, typically red, aril: family *Celastraceae.*
▷HISTORY C18: from Latin: spindle tree, from Greek *euōnumos* fortunately named, from EU- + *onoma* NAME

eupatorium (ˌju:pə'tɔ:rɪəm) NOUN any plant of the genus *Eupatorium,* of N temperate regions and tropical America: cultivated for their ornamental clusters of purple, pink, or white flowers: family *Asteraceae* (composites).
▷HISTORY C16: from New Latin, from Greek *eupatorion* hemp agrimony, from *Eupator* surname of Mithridates VI, king of Pontus and traditionally the first to have used it medicinally

eupatrid (ju:'pætrɪd) NOUN, *plural* **-patridae** (-'pætrɪˌdi:) *or* **-patrids.** (in ancient Greece) a hereditary noble or landowner.
▷HISTORY C19: via Latin from Greek *eupatridēs,* literally: having a good father, from EU- + *patēr* father

eupepsia (ju:'pɛpsɪə) *or* **eupepsy** (ju:'pɛpsɪ) NOUN *Physiol* good digestion.
▷HISTORY C18: from New Latin, from Greek, from EU- + *pepsis* digestion, from *peptein* to digest
▸**eupeptic** (ju:'pɛptɪk) ADJECTIVE

euphausiid (ju:'fɔ:zɪɪd) NOUN any small pelagic shrimplike crustacean of the order *Euphausiacea:* an important constituent of krill.
▷HISTORY C19: from New Latin *Euphausiacea,* perhaps from Greek EU- + *pha-* from *phainein* to reveal, show + *ousia* substance, stuff

euphemism ('ju:fɪˌmɪzəm) NOUN [1] an inoffensive word or phrase substituted for one considered offensive or hurtful, esp one concerned with religion, sex, death, or excreta. Examples of euphemisms are *sleep with* for *have sexual intercourse with; departed* for *dead; relieve oneself* for *urinate.* [2] the use of such inoffensive words or phrases.
▷HISTORY C17: from Greek *euphēmismos,* from EU- + *phēmē* speech
▸ˌ**euphe'mistic** ADJECTIVE ▸ˌ**euphe'mistically** ADVERB

euphemize *or* **euphemise** ('ju:fɪˌmaɪz) VERB to speak in euphemisms or refer to by means of a euphemism.
▸'**euphe**ˌ**mizer** *or* '**euphe**ˌ**miser** NOUN

euphonic (ju:'fɒnɪk) *or* **euphonious** (ju:'fəʊnɪəs) ADJECTIVE [1] denoting or relating to euphony; pleasing to the ear. [2] (of speech sounds) altered for ease of pronunciation.
▸**eu'phonically** *or* **eu'phoniously** ADVERB
▸**eu'phoniousness** NOUN

euphonium (ju:'fəʊnɪəm) NOUN a brass musical instrument with four valves; the tenor of the tuba family. It is used mainly in brass bands.
▷HISTORY C19: New Latin, from EUPH(ONY + HARM)ONIUM

euphonize *or* **euphonise** ('ju:fəˌnaɪz) VERB [1] to make pleasant to hear; render euphonious. [2] to change (speech sounds) so as to facilitate pronunciation.

euphony ('ju:fənɪ) NOUN, *plural* **-nies.** [1] the alteration of speech sounds, esp by assimilation, so as to make them easier to pronounce. [2] a pleasing sound, esp in speech.
▷HISTORY C17: from Late Latin *euphōnia,* from Greek, from EU- + *phōnē* voice

euphorbia (ju:'fɔ:bɪə) NOUN any plant of the genus *Euphorbia,* such as the spurges and poinsettia: family *Euphorbiaceae.*
▷HISTORY C14 *euforbia:* from Latin *euphorbea* African plant named after *Euphorbus,* first-century A.D. Greek physician

euphorbiaceous (ju:ˌfɔ:bɪ'eɪʃəs) ADJECTIVE of, relating to, or belonging to the *Euphorbiaceae,* a family of plants typically having capsular fruits: includes the spurges, the castor oil and cassava plants, cascarilla, and poinsettia.

euphoria (ju:'fɔ:rɪə) NOUN a feeling of great elation, esp when exaggerated.
▷HISTORY C19: from Greek: good ability to endure, from EU- + *pherein* to bear
▸**euphoric** (ju:'fɒrɪk) ADJECTIVE

euphoriant (ju:'fɔ:rɪənt) ADJECTIVE [1] relating to or able to produce euphoria. ◆ NOUN [2] a euphoriant drug or agent.

euphotic (ju:'fəʊtɪk, -'fɒt-) ADJECTIVE *Ecology* denoting or relating to the uppermost part of a sea or lake down to about 100 metres depth, which receives enough light to enable photosynthesis to take place.
▷HISTORY C20: from EU- + PHOTIC

euphrasy ('ju:frəsɪ) NOUN, *plural* **-sies.** another name for **eyebright.**
▷HISTORY C15 *eufrasie:* from Medieval Latin *eufrasia,* from Greek *euphrasia* gladness, from *euphrainein* to make glad, from EU- + *phrēn* mind

Euphrates (ju:'freɪti:z) NOUN a river in SW Asia, rising in E Turkey and flowing south across Syria and Iraq to join the Tigris, forming the Shatt-al-Arab, which flows to the head of the Persian Gulf: important in ancient times for the extensive irrigation of its valley (in Mesopotamia). Length: 3598 km (2235 miles).

euphroe *or* **uphroe** ('ju:frəʊ, -vrəʊ) NOUN *Nautical* a wooden block with holes through which the lines of a crowfoot are rove.
▷HISTORY C19: from Dutch *juffrouw* maiden, earlier *joncfrouwe* (from *jonc* YOUNG + *frouwe* woman)

Euphrosyne (ju:'frɒzɪˌni:) NOUN *Greek myth* one of the three Graces.
▷HISTORY from Greek: mirth, merriment

euphuism ('ju:fju:ˌɪzəm) NOUN [1] an artificial prose style of the Elizabethan period, marked by extreme use of antithesis, alliteration, and extended similes and allusions. [2] any stylish affectation in speech or writing, esp a rhetorical device or expression.
▷HISTORY C16: after *Euphues,* prose romance by John Lyly
▸'**euphuist** NOUN ▸ˌ**euphu'istic** *or* ˌ**euphu'istical** ADJECTIVE
▸ˌ**euphu'istically** ADVERB

euplastic (ju:'plæstɪk) ADJECTIVE healing quickly and well.
▷HISTORY C19: from Greek *euplastos* readily moulded; see EU-, PLASTIC

euploid ('ju:plɔɪd) ADJECTIVE [1] having chromosomes present in an exact multiple of the haploid number. ◆ NOUN [2] a euploid cell or individual. ◆ Compare **aneuploid.**
▷HISTORY C20: from EU- + *-ploid,* as in HAPLOID
▸'**euploidy** NOUN

eupnoea *or US* **eupnea** (ju:p'nɪə) NOUN *Physiol* normal relaxed breathing. Compare **dyspnoea.**
▷HISTORY C18: from New Latin, from Greek *eupnoia,* from *eupnous* breathing easily, from EU- + *pnoē,* from *pnein* to breathe
▸**eup'noeic** *or US* **eup'neic** ADJECTIVE

eur- COMBINING FORM a variant of **Euro-** before a vowel.

Eurasia (jʊə'reɪʃə, -ʒə) NOUN the continents of Europe and Asia considered as a whole.

Eurasian (jʊə'reɪʃən, -ʒən) ADJECTIVE [1] of or relating to Eurasia. [2] of mixed European and Asian descent. ◆ NOUN [3] a person of mixed European and Asian descent.

Euratom (jʊə'rætəm) NOUN short for **European Atomic Energy Community**; an authority established by the European Economic Community (now the European Union) to develop peaceful uses of nuclear energy.

Eure (*French* œr) NOUN a department of N France, in Haute-Normandie region. Capital: Évreux. Pop.: 541 054 (1999). Area: 6037 sq. km (2354 sq. miles).

Eure-et-Loir (*French* œrelwar) NOUN a department of N central France, in Centre region. Capital: Chartres. Pop.: 407 665 (1999). Area: 5940 sq. km (2317 sq. miles).

eureka (jʊ'ri:kə) INTERJECTION an exclamation of triumph on discovering or solving something.
▷HISTORY C17: from Greek *heurēka* I have found (it), from *heuriskein* to find; traditionally the exclamation of Archimedes when he realized, during bathing, that the volume of an irregular solid could be calculated by measuring the water displaced when it was immersed

Eureka Stockade NOUN a violent incident in Ballarat, Australia, in 1854 between gold miners and the military, as a result of which the miners won their democratic rights in the state parliament.

eurhythmic (ju:'rɪðmɪk), **eurhythmical,** *or esp US* **eurythmic, eurythmical** ADJECTIVE [1] having a pleasing and harmonious rhythm, order, or structure. [2] of or relating to eurhythmics.

eurhythmics *or esp US* **eurythmics** (ju:'rɪðmɪks) NOUN (*functioning as singular*) [1] a system of training through physical movement to music, originally taught by Émile Jaques-Dalcroze, to develop grace and musical understanding. [2] dancing of this style, expressing the rhythm and spirit of the music through body movements.

eurhythmy *or esp US* **eurythmy** (ju:'rɪðmɪ) NOUN [1] rhythmic movement. [2] harmonious structure.
▷HISTORY C17: from Latin *eurythmia,* from Greek *eurhuthmia,* from EU- + *rhuthmos* proportion, RHYTHM

euripus (jʊ'raɪpəs) NOUN, *plural* **-pi** (-paɪ). a strait or channel with a strong current or tide.
▷HISTORY C17: from Latin, from Greek *Euripos* the strait between Boeotia and Euboea, from *ripē* force, rush

euro ('jʊərəʊ) NOUN, *plural* **-os.** the official currency unit, divided into 100 cents, of the member countries of the European Union who have adopted European Monetary Union; these are Austria, Belgium, Finland, France, Germany, Greece, Ireland, Italy, Luxembourg, the Netherlands, Portgual, and Spain; also used by Andorra, Bosnia and Herzegovina, French Guiana, Guadeloupe, Kosovo, Martinique, Mayotte, Monaco, Montenegro, Réunion, San Marino, and the Vatican City.

euro- ('jʊərəʊ-) *or before a vowel* **eur-** COMBINING FORM (*sometimes capital*) Europe or European: *eurodollar.*

euro-ad ('jʊərəʊˌæd) NOUN an advertisement designed to be suitable for all countries in the European Union.

Eurobeach ('jʊərəʊˌbi:tʃ) NOUN a beach that has been designated as suitable for bathing from because it meets the limits set by European Union regulations for bacteria in bathing areas.

eurobond ('jʊərəʊˌbɒnd) NOUN (*sometimes capital*) a bond issued in a eurocurrency.

Eurocentric (ˌjʊərəʊ'sɛntrɪk) ADJECTIVE chiefly concerned with or concentrating on Europe and European culture: *the Eurocentric curriculum.*

eurocheque ('jʊərəʊˌtʃɛk) NOUN (*sometimes capital*) a cheque drawn on a European bank that can be cashed at any bank or bureau de change displaying the EC sign or that can be used to pay for goods or services at any outlet displaying this sign.

Euroclydon (jʊ'rɒklɪˌdɒn) NOUN [1] a stormy wind from the north or northeast that occurs in the Levant, which caused the ship in which St Paul was travelling to be wrecked (Acts 27:14). [2] any stormy wind.
▷HISTORY C17: from Greek *eurokludōn,* from *Euros* EURUS + Greek *akulōn* (unattested) north wind, from Latin *aquilō*

euro-commercial paper (ˌju:rəʊkə'mɜ:ʃəl) NOUN commercial paper issued in a eurocurrency.

Eurocommunism (ˌjʊərəʊ'kɒmjʊˌnɪzəm) NOUN the policies, doctrines, and practices of Communist Parties in Western Europe in the 1970s and 1980s, esp those rejecting democratic centralism and favouring nonalignment with the Soviet Union and China.
▸ˌ**Euro'communist** NOUN, ADJECTIVE

eurocrat ('jʊərəˌkræt) NOUN (*sometimes capital*) a member, esp a senior member, of the administration of the European Union.

eurocreep ('jʊərəˌkri:p) NOUN the gradual introduction of the euro into use in Britain.

eurocurrency ('jʊərəʊˌkʌrənsɪ) NOUN (*sometimes capital*) **a** the currency of any country held on deposit in Europe outside its home market: used as a source of short- or medium-term finance, esp in international trade, because of easy convertibility. **b** (*as modifier*): *the eurocurrency market.*

eurodeposit (ˌjʊərəʊdɪˈpɒzɪt) NOUN (*sometimes capital*) a deposit of the currency of any country in the eurocurrency market.

eurodollar (ˈjʊərəʊˌdɒlə) NOUN (*sometimes capital*) a US dollar as part of a European holding. See **eurocurrency.**

Euroland (ˈjʊərəʊˌlænd) NOUN the geographical area containing the countries that have joined the European single currency.

euromarket (ˈjʊərəʊˌmɑːkɪt) NOUN [1] a market for financing international trade backed by the central banks and commercial banks of the European Union. [2] the European Union treated as one large market for the sale of goods and services.

Euro MP NOUN *Informal* a member of the European Parliament.

Euronext (ˈjʊərəʊˌnɛkst) NOUN a European stock exchange formed by the amalgamation of the Paris, Brussels, and Amsterdam bourses.

euronote (ˈjuːrəʊˌnəʊt) NOUN a form of euro-commercial paper consisting of short-term negotiable bearer notes.

Europa[1] (jʊˈrəʊpə) NOUN *Greek myth* a Phoenician princess who had three children by Zeus in Crete, where he had taken her after assuming the guise of a white bull. Their offspring were Rhadamanthus, Minos, and Sarpedon.

Europa[2] (jʊˈrəʊpə) NOUN the smallest of the four Galilean satellites of Jupiter. Diameter: 3138 km; orbital radius: 671 000 km.

Europe (ˈjʊərəp) NOUN [1] the second smallest continent, forming the W extension of Eurasia: the border with Asia runs from the Urals to the Caspian and the Black Sea. The coastline is generally extremely indented and there are several peninsulas (notably Scandinavia, Italy, and Iberia) and offshore islands (including the British Isles and Iceland). It contains a series of great mountain systems in the south (Pyrenees, Alps, Apennines, Carpathians, Caucasus), a large central plain, and a N region of lakes and mountains in Scandinavia. Pop.: 729 370 000 (1996 est.). Area: about 10 400 000 sq. km (4 000 000 sq. miles). [2] *Brit* the continent of Europe except for the British Isles: *we're going to Europe for our holiday.* [3] *Brit* the European Union: *when did Britain go into Europe?*

European (ˌjʊərəˈpɪən) ADJECTIVE [1] of or relating to Europe or its inhabitants. [2] native to or derived from Europe. ◆ NOUN [3] a native or inhabitant of Europe. [4] a person of European descent. [5] a supporter of the European Union or of political union of the countries of Europe or a part of it.
▸ **ˌEuroˈpeanˌism** NOUN

European Central Bank NOUN the central bank of the European Union, established in 1998 to oversee the process of European Monetary Union and to direct monetary policy within the countries using the euro. Abbreviation: **ECB.**

European Commission NOUN the executive body of the European Union formed in 1967, which initiates action in the EU and mediates between member governments. Former name (until 1993): **Commission of the European Communities.**

European Community *or* **Communities** NOUN an economic and political association of European states that came into being in 1967, when the legislative and executive bodies of the European Economic Community merged with those of the European Coal and Steel Community and the European Atomic Energy Community: subsumed into the **European Union** in 1993. Abbreviation: **EC.**

European Council NOUN an executive body of the European Union, made up of the President of the European Commission and representatives of the Member states, including the foreign and other ministers. The Council acts at the request of the Commission.

European Currency Unit NOUN See **ECU.**

European Economic Area NOUN a free-trade area created in 1994 by an agreement between the European Free Trade Association (EFTA), excluding Switzerland, and the European Union (EU). Abbreviation: **EEA.**

European Economic Community NOUN the former W European economic association created by the Treaty of Rome in 1957; in 1967 its executive and legislative bodies merged with the European Coal and Steel Community and the European Atomic Energy Community to form the European Community (now part of the European Union). Informal name: **Common Market.** Abbreviation: **EEC.**

European Free Trade Association NOUN See **EFTA.**

Europeanize *or* **Europeanise** (ˌjʊərəˈpɪəˌnaɪz) VERB (*tr*) [1] to make European in culture, dress, etc. [2] to integrate (a country, economy, etc.) into the European Union.
▸ **ˌEuroˌpeaniˈzation** *or* **ˌEuroˌpeaniˈsation** NOUN

European Monetary Institute NOUN an organization set up in 1991 to coordinate economic and monetary policy within the European Union: superseded by the European Central Bank in 1998.

European Monetary System NOUN the system used in the European Union for stabilizing exchange rates between the currencies of member states and financing the balance-of-payments support mechanism. The original Exchange Rate Mechanism was formed in 1979 but superseded in 1999 when the euro was adopted as official currency of 11 EU member states. A new exchange rate mechanism (ERM II) based on the euro is used to regulate the currencies of participating states that have not adopted the euro. Abbreviation: **EMS.**

European Monetary Union NOUN the agreement between members of the European Union to establish a common currency. The current participating members are Austria, Belgium, Finland, France, Germany, Greece, Ireland, Italy, Luxembourg, the Netherlands, Portugal, and Spain. Abbreviation: **EMU.**

European Parliament NOUN the assembly of the European Union in Strasbourg. It consists of 626 directly elected members and its role is largely advisory.

European plan NOUN *US* a hotel rate of charging covering room and service but not meals. Compare **American plan.**

European Recovery Programme NOUN the official name for the **Marshall Plan.**

European Union NOUN an organization created in 1993 with the aim of achieving closer economic and political union between member states of the European Community. There are currently 15 members: Austria, Belgium, Denmark, Finland, France, Germany, Greece, Ireland, Italy, Luxembourg, the Netherlands, Portugal, Spain, Sweden, and the United Kingdom; Cyprus, the Czech Republic, Estonia, Hungary, Latvia, Lithuania, Malta, Poland, Slovenia, and Slovakia have been invited to join in 2004. Abbreviation: **EU.**

European wasp NOUN *Austral* a large black-and-yellow banded wasp, *Vespula germanica*, native to Europe, North Africa, and Asia, now established in Australasia and the US.

Europhile (ˈjʊərəʊˌfaɪl) (*sometimes not capital*) NOUN [1] a person who admires Europe, Europeans, or the European Union. ◆ ADJECTIVE [2] marked by or possessing admiration for Europe, Europeans, or the European Union.

Europhilia (ˌjʊərəʊˈfɪlɪə) (*sometimes not capital*) NOUN admiration for Europe, Europeans, or the European Union.

Europhobia (ˌjʊərəʊˈfəʊbɪə) (*sometimes not capital*) NOUN dislike for or hostility to Europe, Europeans, or the European Union.

Europhobic (ˌjʊərəʊˈfəʊbɪk) (*sometimes not capital*) ADJECTIVE hostile to Europe, Europeans, or the European Union.

europium (jʊˈrəʊpɪəm) NOUN a soft ductile reactive silvery-white element of the lanthanide series of metals: used as the red phosphor in colour television and in lasers. Symbol: Eu; atomic no.: 63; atomic wt.: 151.965; valency: 2 or 3; relative density: 5.244; melting pt.: 822°C; boiling pt.: 1527°C.
▷ HISTORY C20: named after EUROPE + -IUM

Europol (ˈjʊərəʊˌpɒl) NOUN ◆ ACRONYM FOR European Police Office, an international association devoted to fighting cross-border organized crime within the European Union.

Europoort (*Dutch* ˈøːroːpoːrt) NOUN a port in the Netherlands near Rotterdam: developed in the 1960s; handles chiefly oil.

Euro-sceptic (ˈjʊərəʊˌskɛptɪk) (in Britain) NOUN [1] a person who is opposed to closer links with the European Union. ◆ ADJECTIVE [2] opposing closer links with the European Union: *Euro-sceptic MPs.*

Eurostat (ˈjʊərəʊˌstæt) NOUN an organization within the European Union that collects and collates statistical information relating to member states. Full name: **Statistical Office of the European Communities.**

Eurosterling (ˈjʊərəʊˌstɜːlɪŋ) NOUN sterling as part of a European holding. See **eurocurrency.**

Eurotax (ˈjʊərəʊˌtæks) NOUN a tax imposed by the European Union.

Eurotrack (ˈjʊərəʊˌtræk) NOUN short for **Financial Times Stock Exchange Eurotrack 100 Index.**

Eurotunnel (ˈjʊərəʊˌtʌnᵊl) NOUN another name for **Channel Tunnel.**

Eurovision (ˈjʊərəʊˌvɪʒən) NOUN **a** the network of the European Broadcasting Union for the exchange of news and television programmes amongst its member organizations and for the relay of news and programmes from outside the network. **b** (*as modifier*): *the Eurovision song contest.*

Eurozone (ˈjʊərəʊˌzəʊn) NOUN another name for **Euroland.**

Eurus (ˈjʊərəs) NOUN *Greek myth* the east or southeast wind personified.
▷ HISTORY Latin, from Greek *euros*

eury- COMBINING FORM broad or wide: *eurythermal.*
▷ HISTORY New Latin, from Greek, from *eurus* wide

Euryale (jʊˈraɪəlɪ) NOUN *Greek myth* one of the three Gorgons.

Eurydice (jʊˈrɪdɪsɪ) NOUN *Greek myth* a dryad married to Orpheus, who sought her in Hades after she died. She could have left Hades with him had he not broken his pact and looked back at her.

euryhaline (ˌjʊərɪˈheɪliːn, -laɪn) ADJECTIVE (of certain aquatic animals) able to tolerate a wide range of salinity. Compare **stenohaline.**

eurypterid (jʊˈrɪptərɪd) NOUN any large extinct scorpion-like aquatic arthropod of the group *Eurypterida*, of Palaeozoic times, thought to be related to the horseshoe crabs.
▷ HISTORY C19: from New Latin *Eurypterida*, from EURY- + Greek *pteron* wing, feather

Eurystheus (jʊˈrɪsθjuːs, -θɪəs) NOUN *Greek myth* a grandson of Perseus, who, through the favour of Hera, inherited the kingship of Mycenae, which Zeus had intended for Hercules.

eurythermal (ˌjʊərɪˈθɜːməl), **eurythermic,** *or* **eurythermous** ADJECTIVE (of organisms) able to tolerate a wide range of temperatures in the environment. Compare **stenothermal.**

eurythmics (juːˈrɪðmɪks) NOUN a variant spelling (esp US) of **eurhythmics.**
▸ **euˈrythmic** *or* **euˈrythmical** ADJECTIVE ▸ **euˈrythmy** NOUN

eurytopic (ˌjʊərɪˈtɒpɪk) ADJECTIVE [1] *Ecology* (of a species) able to tolerate a wide range of environments. [2] *Ecology* having a wide geographical distribution. Compare **stenotopic.**
▷ HISTORY C20: from EURY- + *top* from Greek *topos* place + -IC

eusporangiate (ˌjuːspɔːˈrændʒɪɪt) ADJECTIVE (of ferns) having each sporangium developing from a group of cells, rather than a single cell, and with no specialized disperal of spores. ◆ Compare **leptosporangiate.**
▷ HISTORY from New Latin *eusporangiātus* (unattested), from EU- + SPORANGIUM

Eustachian tube (juːˈsteɪʃən) NOUN a tube that connects the middle ear with the nasopharynx and equalizes the pressure between the two sides of the eardrum.
▷ HISTORY C18: named after Bartolomeo *Eustachio*, 16th-century Italian anatomist

eustatic (juːˈstætɪk) ADJECTIVE denoting or relating to worldwide changes in sea level, caused by the melting of ice sheets, movements of the ocean floor, sedimentation, etc.
▷ HISTORY C20: from Greek, from EU- + STATIC
▸ **eustasy** (ˈjuːstəsɪ) NOUN ▸ **euˈstatically** ADVERB

eutaxia (juːˈtæksɪə) NOUN *Engineering* the condition of being easily melted.

eutectic (juːˈtɛktɪk) ADJECTIVE [1] (of a mixture of

substances, esp an alloy) having the lowest freezing point of all possible mixtures of the substances. [2] concerned with or suitable for the formation of eutectic mixtures. ◆ NOUN [3] a eutectic mixture. [4] the temperature on a phase diagram at which a eutectic mixture forms.
▷HISTORY C19: from Greek *eutēktos* melting readily, from EU- + *tēkein* to melt

eutectoid (juːˈtɛktɔɪd) NOUN [1] a mixture of substances similar to a eutectic, but forming two or three constituents from a solid instead of from a melt. ◆ ADJECTIVE [2] concerned with or suitable for eutectoid mixtures.
▷HISTORY C20: from EUTECT(IC) + -OID

Euterpe (juːˈtɜːpɪ) NOUN *Greek myth* the Muse of lyric poetry and music.
▸**Euˈterpean** ADJECTIVE

euthanasia (ˌjuːθəˈneɪzɪə) NOUN the act of killing someone painlessly, esp to relieve suffering from an incurable illness. Also called: **mercy killing.**
▷HISTORY C17: via New Latin from Greek: easy death, from EU- + *thanatos* death

euthenics (juːˈθɛnɪks) NOUN (*functioning as singular*) the study of the control of the environment, esp with a view to improving the health and living standards of the human race.
▷HISTORY C20: from Greek *euthēnein* to thrive
▸**euˈthenist** NOUN

eutherian (juːˈθɪərɪən) ADJECTIVE [1] of, relating to, or belonging to the *Eutheria*, a subclass of mammals all of which have a placenta and reach an advanced state of development before birth. The group includes all mammals except monotremes and marsupials. ◆ NOUN [2] any eutherian mammal. ◆ Compare **metatherian, prototherian.**
▷HISTORY C19: from New Latin *Euthēria*, from Greek EU- + *thēria*, plural of *thērion* beast

euthymia (juːˈθɪmɪə) NOUN *Psychol* a pleasant state of mind.
▷HISTORY EU- + -THYMIA

eutrophic (juːˈtrɒfɪk, -ˈtrəʊ-) ADJECTIVE (of lakes and similar habitats) rich in organic and mineral nutrients and supporting an abundant plant life, which in the process of decaying depletes the oxygen supply for animal life. Compare **oligotrophic.**
▷HISTORY C18: probably from *eutrophy*, from Greek *eutrophia* sound nutrition, from *eutrophos* well-fed, from EU- + *trephein* to nourish
▸**ˈeutrophy** NOUN

eutrophication (juːˌtrɒfɪˈkeɪʃən) NOUN a process by which pollution from such sources as sewage effluent or leachate from fertilized fields causes a lake, pond, or fen to become overrich in organic and mineral nutrients, so that algae and cyanobacteria grow rapidly and deplete the oxygen supply.

euxenite (ˈjuːksɪˌnaɪt) NOUN a rare brownish-black mineral containing erbium, cerium, uranium, columbium, and yttrium.
▷HISTORY C19: from Greek *euxenos* hospitable (literally: well-disposed to strangers), from EU- + *xenos* stranger; from its containing a number of rare elements

eV ABBREVIATION FOR electronvolt.

EV ABBREVIATION FOR English Version (of the Bible).

EVA *Astronautics* ABBREVIATION FOR extravehicular activity.

evacuant (ɪˈvækjʊənt) ADJECTIVE [1] serving to promote excretion, esp of the bowels. ◆ NOUN [2] an evacuant agent.

evacuate (ɪˈvækjʊˌeɪt) VERB (*mainly tr*) [1] (*also intr*) to withdraw or cause to withdraw from (a place of danger) to a place of greater safety. [2] to make empty by removing the contents of. [3] (*also intr*) *Physiol* **a** to eliminate or excrete (faeces); defecate. **b** to discharge (any waste product) from (a part of the body). [4] (*tr*) to create a vacuum in (a bulb, flask, reaction vessel, etc.).
▷HISTORY C16: from Latin *ēvacuāre* to void, from *vacuus* empty
▸**eˌvacuˈation** NOUN ▸**eˈvacuative** ADJECTIVE ▸**eˈvacuˌator** NOUN

evacuee (ɪˌvækjuˈiː) NOUN a person evacuated from a place of danger, esp in wartime.

evade (ɪˈveɪd) VERB (*mainly tr*) [1] to get away from or avoid (imprisonment, captors, etc.); escape. [2] to get around, shirk, or dodge (the law, a duty, etc.). [3] (*also intr*) to avoid answering (a question).
▷HISTORY C16: from French *évader*, from Latin *ēvādere* to go forth, from *vādere* to go
▸**eˈvadable** ADJECTIVE ▸**eˈvader** NOUN ▸**eˈvadingly** ADVERB

evaginate (ɪˈvædʒɪˌneɪt) VERB (*tr*) *Med* to turn (an organ or part) inside out; turn the outer surface (of an organ or part) back on itself.
▷HISTORY C17: from Late Latin *ēvāgīnāre* to unsheathe, from *vāgīna* sheath
▸**eˌvagiˈnation** NOUN

evaluate (ɪˈvæljʊˌeɪt) VERB (*tr*) [1] to ascertain or set the amount or value of. [2] to judge or assess the worth of; appraise. [3] *Maths, logic* to determine the unique member of the range of a function corresponding to a given member of its domain.
▷HISTORY C19: back formation from *evaluation*, from French, from *evaluer* to evaluate; see VALUE
▸**eˌvaluˈation** NOUN ▸**eˈvaluˌator** NOUN

evaluative (ɪˈvæljʊətɪv) ADJECTIVE [1] of, denoting, or based on an act of evaluating. [2] *Philosophy* expressing an attitude or value judgment; emotive.

evanesce (ˌɛvəˈnɛs) VERB (*intr*) (of smoke, mist, etc.) to fade gradually from sight; vanish.
▷HISTORY C19: from Latin *ēvānēscere* to disappear; see VANISH

evanescent (ˌɛvəˈnɛsᵊnt) ADJECTIVE [1] passing out of sight; fading away; vanishing. [2] ephemeral or transitory.
▸**ˌevaˈnescence** NOUN ▸**ˌevaˈnescently** ADVERB

evangel (ɪˈvændʒəl) NOUN [1] *Archaic* the gospel of Christianity. [2] (*often capital*) any of the four Gospels of the New Testament. [3] any body of teachings regarded as central or basic. [4] *US* an evangelist.
▷HISTORY C14: from Church Latin *ēvangelium*, from Greek *evangelion* good news, from EU- + *angelos* messenger; see ANGEL

evangelical (ˌiːvænˈdʒɛlɪkᵊl) *Christianity* ◆ ADJECTIVE [1] of, based upon, or following from the Gospels. [2] denoting or relating to any of certain Protestant sects or parties, which emphasize the importance of personal conversion and faith in atonement through the death of Christ as a means of salvation. [3] another word for **evangelistic.** ◆ NOUN [4] an upholder of evangelical doctrines or a member of an evangelical sect or party, esp the Low-Church party of the Church of England.
▸**ˌevanˈgelicalism** NOUN ▸**ˌevanˈgelically** ADVERB

evangelism (ɪˈvændʒɪˌlɪzəm) NOUN [1] (in Protestant churches) the practice of spreading the Christian gospel. RC Church term: **evangelization** *or* **evangelisation.** [2] ardent or missionary zeal for a cause. [3] the work, methods, or characteristic outlook of a revivalist or evangelist preacher. [4] a less common word for **evangelicalism.**

evangelist (ɪˈvændʒɪlɪst) NOUN [1] an occasional preacher, sometimes itinerant and often preaching at meetings in the open air. [2] a preacher of the Christian gospel. [3] any zealous advocate of a cause. [4] another word for **revivalist** (sense 1).

Evangelist (ɪˈvændʒɪlɪst) NOUN [1] any of the writers of the New Testament Gospels: Matthew, Mark, Luke, or John. [2] a senior official or dignitary of the Mormon Church.

evangelistic (ɪˌvændʒɪˈlɪstɪk) ADJECTIVE [1] denoting, resembling, or relating to evangelists or their methods and attitudes: *evangelistic zeal.* [2] zealously advocating a cause. [3] (*often capital*) of or relating to all or any of the four Evangelists.
▸**eˌvangeˈlistically** ADVERB

evangelize *or* **evangelise** (ɪˈvændʒɪˌlaɪz) VERB [1] to preach the Christian gospel or a particular interpretation of it (to). [2] (*intr*) to advocate a cause with the object of making converts.
▸**eˌvangeliˈzation** *or* **eˌvangeliˈsation** NOUN ▸**eˈvangeˌlizer** *or* **eˈvangeˌliser** NOUN

evanish (ɪˈvænɪʃ) VERB a poetic word for **vanish.**
▷HISTORY C15: from Old French *esvanir*, from Latin *ēvānēscere* to VANISH
▸**eˈvanishment** NOUN

evaporate (ɪˈvæpəˌreɪt) VERB [1] to change or cause to change from a liquid or solid state to a vapour. Compare **boil**[1] (sense 1). [2] to lose or cause to lose liquid by vaporization leaving a more concentrated residue. [3] to disappear or cause to disappear; fade away or cause to fade away: *all her doubts evaporated.* [4] (*tr*) to deposit (a film, metal, etc.) by vaporization of a liquid or solid and the subsequent condensation of its vapour.
▷HISTORY C16: from Late Latin *ēvapōrāre*, from Latin *vapor* steam; see VAPOUR
▸**eˈvaporable** ADJECTIVE ▸**eˌvaporaˈbility** NOUN ▸**eˌvapoˈration** NOUN ▸**eˈvaporative** ADJECTIVE ▸**eˈvapoˌrator** NOUN

evaporated milk NOUN thick unsweetened tinned milk from which some of the water has been evaporated.

evaporimeter (ɪˌvæpəˈrɪmɪtə) *or* **evaporometer** (ɪˌvæpəˈrɒmɪtə) NOUN another name for **atmometer.**

evaporite (ɪˈvæpəˌraɪt) NOUN any sedimentary rock, such as rock salt, gypsum, or anhydrite, formed by evaporation of former seas or salt-water lakes.
▷HISTORY C20: EVAPORATION + -ITE[1]

evapotranspiration (ɪˌvæpəʊˌtrænspəˈreɪʃən) NOUN the return of water vapour to the atmosphere by evaporation from land and water surfaces and by the transpiration of vegetation.

evasion (ɪˈveɪʒən) NOUN [1] the act of evading or escaping, esp from a distasteful duty, responsibility, etc., by trickery, cunning, or illegal means: *tax evasion.* [2] trickery, cunning, or deception used to dodge a question, duty, etc.; means of evading.
▷HISTORY C15: from Late Latin *ēvāsiō*, from Latin *ēvādere* to go forth; see EVADE

evasive (ɪˈveɪsɪv) ADJECTIVE [1] tending or seeking to evade; avoiding the issue; not straightforward. [2] avoiding or seeking to avoid trouble or difficulties: *to take evasive action.* [3] hard to catch or obtain; elusive.
▸**eˈvasively** ADVERB ▸**eˈvasiveness** NOUN

eve (iːv) NOUN [1] **a** the evening or day before some special event or festival. **b** (*capital when part of a name*): *New Year's Eve.* [2] the period immediately before an event: *on the eve of civil war.* [3] an archaic word for **evening.**
▷HISTORY C13: variant of EVEN[2]

Eve (iːv) NOUN *Old Testament* the first woman; mother of the human race, fashioned by God from the rib of Adam (Genesis 2:18-25).

evection (ɪˈvɛkʃən) NOUN irregularity in the moon's motion caused by perturbations of the sun and planets.
▷HISTORY C17: from Latin *ēvectiō* a going up, from *ēvehere* to lead forth, from *vehere* to carry
▸**eˈvectional** ADJECTIVE

even[1] (ˈiːvᵊn) ADJECTIVE [1] level and regular; flat: *an even surface.* [2] (*postpositive; foll by with*) on the same level or in the same plane (as): *one surface even with another.* [3] without variation or fluctuation; regular; constant: *an even rate of progress.* [4] not readily moved or excited; placid; calm: *an even temper.* [5] equally balanced between two sides: *an even game.* [6] equal or identical in number, quantity, etc.: *two even spoonfuls of sugar.* [7] **a** (of a number) divisible by two. **b** characterized or indicated by such a number: *maps are on the even pages.* Compare **odd** (sense 4). [8] relating to or denoting two or either of two alternatives, events, etc., that have an equal probability: *an even chance of missing or catching a train.* [9] having no balance of debt; neither owing nor being owed. [10] just and impartial; fair: *an even division.* [11] exact in number, amount, or extent: *an even pound.* [12] equal, as in score; level: *now the teams are even.* [13] *Maths* (of a function) unchanged in value when the sign of the independent variable is changed, as in $y = z^2$. Compare **odd** (sense 8). [14] **even money. a** a bet in which the winnings are the same as the amount staked. **b** (*as modifier*): *the even-money favourite.* [15] **get even (with).** *Informal* to exact revenge (on); settle accounts (with). [16] **of even date.** *Legal, formal, or obsolete* of the same or today's date. ◆ ADVERB [17] (intensifier; used to suggest that the content of a statement is unexpected or paradoxical): *even an idiot can do that.* [18] (intensifier; used with comparative forms): *this is even better.* [19] notwithstanding; in spite of: *even having started late she soon caught him up.* [20] used to introduce a more precise version of a word, phrase, or statement: *he is base, even depraved.* [21] used preceding a clause of supposition or hypothesis to emphasize the implication that whether or not the condition in it is fulfilled, the statement in the main clause remains valid: *even if she died he wouldn't care.* [22]

Archaic that is to say; namely (used for emphasis): *he, even he, hath spoken these things.* [23] *Archaic* all the way; fully: *I love thee even unto death.* [24] **even as.** (*conjunction*) at the very same moment or in the very same way that: *even as I spoke, it thundered.* [25] **even so.** in spite of any assertion to the contrary: nevertheless. ◆ VERB [26] to make or become even. ◆ See also **break even, even out, evens, even up.**
▷HISTORY Old English *efen;* related to Old Norse *jafn* even, equal, Gothic *ibns,* Old High German *eban*
▸'**evener** NOUN ▸'**evenly** ADVERB ▸'**evenness** NOUN

even² ('i:vᵊn) NOUN an archaic word for **eve** or **evening.**
▷HISTORY Old English *ǣfen;* related to Old Frisian *ēvend,* Old High German *āband*

evenfall ('i:vᵊn,fɔ:l) NOUN *Archaic* early evening; dusk.

even-handed ADJECTIVE dealing fairly with all; impartial.
▸,**even-'handedly** ADVERB ▸,**even-'handedness** NOUN

evening ('i:vnɪŋ) NOUN [1] the latter part of the day, esp from late afternoon until nightfall. [2] the latter or concluding period: *the evening of one's life.* [3] the early part of the night spent in a specified way: *an evening at the theatre.* [4] an entertainment, meeting, or reception held in the early part of the night. [5] *Southern US and Brit dialect* the period between noon and sunset. [6] (*modifier*) of, used, or occurring in the evening: *the evening papers.* ◆ See also **evenings.**
▷HISTORY Old English *ǣfnung;* related to Old Frisian *ēvend,* Old High German *āband*

evening class NOUN a class held in the evenings at certain colleges, normally for adults.

evening dress NOUN attire for wearing at a formal occasion during the evening, esp (for men) a dinner jacket and black tie, or (less commonly, for women) a floor-length gown.

evening primrose NOUN any onagraceous plant of the genus *Oenothera,* native to North America but widely cultivated and naturalized, typically having yellow flowers that open in the evening.

evening primrose oil NOUN an oil, obtained from the seeds of the evening primrose, that is claimed to stimulate the production of prostaglandins.

evenings ('i:vnɪŋz) ADVERB *Informal* in the evening, esp regularly.

evening star NOUN a planet, usually Venus, seen just after sunset during the time that the planet is east of the sun. Compare **morning star.**

Evenki (ə'vɛŋkɪ) NOUN [1] (*plural* **Evenki**) a Tungus people of E Siberia. [2] the language of this people.

even out VERB (*adverb*) to make or become even, as by the removal of bumps, inequalities, etc.: *the land evens out beyond that rise.*

evens ('i:vənz) ADJECTIVE, ADVERB [1] (of a bet) winning the same as the amount staked if successful. [2] (of a runner) offered at such odds.

evensong ('i:vᵊn,sɒŋ) NOUN [1] Also called: **Evening Prayer, vespers.** *Church of England* the daily evening service of Bible readings and prayers prescribed in the Book of Common Prayer. [2] *Archaic* another name for **vespers.** [3] an archaic or poetic word for **evening.**

event (ɪ'vɛnt) NOUN [1] anything that takes place or happens, esp something important; happening; incident. [2] the actual or final outcome; result (esp in the phrases **in the event, after the event**). [3] any one contest in a programme of sporting or other contests: *the high jump is his event.* [4] *Philosophy* **a** an occurrence regarded as a bare instant of space-time as contrasted with an object which fills space and has endurance. **b** an occurrence regarded in isolation from, or contrasted with, human agency. Compare **act** (sense 8). [5] **in any event** *or* **at all events.** regardless of circumstances; in any case. [6] **in the event of.** in case of; if (such a thing) happens: *in the event of rain the race will be cancelled.* [7] **in the event that.** if it should happen that. ◆ VERB [8] to take part or ride (a horse) in eventing.
▷HISTORY C16: from Latin *ēventus* a happening, from *ēvenīre* to come forth, happen, from *venīre* to come

even-tempered ADJECTIVE not easily angered or excited; calm.

eventful (ɪ'vɛntfʊl) ADJECTIVE full of events or incidents: *an eventful day.*
▸**e'ventfully** ADVERB ▸**e'ventfulness** NOUN

event horizon NOUN *Astronomy* the surface around a black hole enclosing the space from which electromagnetic radiation cannot escape due to gravitational attraction. For a non-rotating black hole, the radius is proportional to the mass of the black hole.

eventide ('i:vᵊn,taɪd) NOUN *Archaic or poetic* another word for **evening.**

eventide home ('i:vᵊn,taɪd) NOUN *Euphemistic* an old people's home.

eventing (ɪ'vɛntɪŋ) NOUN the sport of taking part in equestrian competitions (esp **three-day events**), usually consisting of three sections: dressage, cross-country riding, and showjumping.
▸**e'venter** NOUN

eventize *or* **eventise** (ɪ'vɛntaɪz) VERB (*tr*) to arrange (an occasion) so that it is seen as being a special event.

eventration (,i:vɛn'treɪʃən) NOUN *Pathol* protrusion of the bowel through the abdomen.

event television NOUN television programmes focusing on events which attract media attention and high ratings.

event theatre NOUN spectacular and extravagantly-mounted theatrical productions collectively.

eventual (ɪ'vɛntʃʊəl) ADJECTIVE (*prenominal*) happening in due course of time; ultimate: *the eventual outcome was his defeat.*

eventuality (ɪ,vɛntʃʊ'ælɪtɪ) NOUN, *plural* **-ties.** a possible event, occurrence, or result; contingency.

eventually (ɪ'vɛntʃʊəlɪ) ADVERB [1] at the very end; finally. [2] (*as sentence modifier*) after a long time or long delay: *eventually, he arrived.*

eventuate (ɪ'vɛntʃʊ,eɪt) VERB (*intr*) [1] (often foll by *in*) to result ultimately (in). [2] to come about as a result: *famine eventuated from the crop failure.*
▸**e,ventu'ation** NOUN

even up VERB (*adverb*) to make or become equal, esp in respect of claims or debts; settle or balance.

ever ('ɛvə) ADVERB [1] at any time: *have you ever seen it?* [2] by any chance; in any case: *how did you ever find out?* [3] at all times; always: *ever busy.* [4] in any possible way or manner: *come as fast as ever you can.* [5] *Informal, chiefly Brit* (intensifier, in the phrases **ever so, ever such,** and **ever such a**): *ever so good; ever such bad luck; ever such a waste.* [6] **ever and again** (*or* **anon**). *Archaic* now and then; from time to time. [7] **is he** *or* **she ever!** *US and Canadian slang* he or she displays the quality concerned in abundance. ◆ See also **forever.**
▷HISTORY Old English *ǣfre,* of uncertain origin

Everest ('ɛvərɪst) NOUN [1] **Mount.** a mountain in S Asia on the border between Nepal and Tibet, in the Himalayas: the highest mountain in the world; first climbed by a British expedition (1953). Height: 8850 m (29 035 ft.). [2] any high point of ambition or achievement.
▷HISTORY C19: named after Sir G. *Everest* (1790–1866), Surveyor-General of India

Everglades ('ɛvə,gleɪdz) PLURAL NOUN **the.** a subtropical marshy region of Florida, south of Lake Okeechobee: contains the **Everglades National Park** established to preserve the flora and fauna of the swamps. Area: over 13 000 sq. km (5000 sq. miles).

evergreen ('ɛvə,gri:n) ADJECTIVE [1] (of certain trees and shrubs) bearing foliage throughout the year; continually shedding and replacing leaves. Compare **deciduous.** [2] remaining fresh and vital. ◆ NOUN [3] an evergreen tree or shrub.

evergreen fund NOUN a fund that provides capital for new companies and makes regular injections of capital to support their development.

everlasting (,ɛvə'lɑ:stɪŋ) ADJECTIVE [1] never coming to an end; eternal. [2] lasting for an indefinitely long period. [3] lasting so long or occurring so often as to become tedious; incessant: *I cannot bear her everlasting complaints.* ◆ NOUN [4] endless duration; eternity. [5] Also called: **everlasting flower.** another name for **immortelle.** See also **cat's-foot.**
▸,**ever'lastingly** ADVERB ▸,**ever'lastingness** NOUN

evermore (,ɛvə'mɔ:) ADVERB (often preceded by *for*) all time to come.

evernet ('ɛvə,nɛt) NOUN a hypothetical form of Internet that is continuously accessible using a wide variety of devices.
▷HISTORY C20: from EVER + (INTER)NET

evert (ɪ'vɜ:t) VERB (*tr*) to turn (an eyelid, the intestines, or some other bodily part) outwards or inside out.
▷HISTORY C16: from Latin *ēvertere* to overthrow, from *vertere* to turn
▸**e'versible** ADJECTIVE ▸**e'version** NOUN

evertor (ɪ'vɜ:tə) NOUN any muscle that turns a part outwards.

every ('ɛvrɪ) DETERMINER [1] each one (of the class specified), without exception: *every child knows it.* [2] (*not used with a negative*) the greatest or best possible: *every hope of success.* [3] each: used before a noun phrase to indicate the recurrent, intermittent, or serial nature of a thing: *every third day; every now and then; every so often.* [4] **every bit.** (used in comparisons with *as*) quite; just; equally: *every bit as funny as the other show.* [5] **every other.** each alternate; every second: *every other day.* [6] **every which way. a** in all directions; everywhere: *I looked every which way for you.* **b** *US and Canadian* from all sides: *stones coming at me every which way.*
▷HISTORY C15 *everich,* from Old English *ǣfre ǣlc,* from *ǣfre* EVER + *ǣlc* EACH

everybody ('ɛvrɪ,bɒdɪ) PRONOUN every person; everyone.

> **Language note** See at **everyone.**

everyday ('ɛvrɪ,deɪ) ADJECTIVE [1] happening each day; daily. [2] commonplace or usual; ordinary. [3] suitable for or used on ordinary days as distinct from Sundays or special days.

Everyman ('ɛvrɪ,mæn) NOUN [1] a medieval English morality play in which the central figure represents mankind, whose earthly destiny is dramatized from the Christian viewpoint. [2] (*often not capital*) the ordinary person; common man.

everyone ('ɛvrɪ,wʌn, -wən) PRONOUN every person; everybody.

> **Language note** *Everyone* and *everybody* are interchangeable, as are *no one* and *nobody,* and *someone* and *somebody.* Care should be taken to distinguish between *everyone* and *someone* as single words and *every one* and *some one* as two words, the latter form correctly being used to refer to each individual person or thing in a particular group: *every one of them is wrong.*

every one PRONOUN each person or thing in a group, without exception: *every one of the large cats is a fast runner.*

everyplace ('ɛvrɪ,pleɪs) ADVERB *US* an informal word for **everywhere.**

everything ('ɛvrɪ,θɪŋ) PRONOUN [1] the entirety of a specified or implied class: *she lost everything in the War.* [2] a great deal, esp of something very important: *she means everything to me.*

everywhere ('ɛvrɪ,wɛə) ADVERB to or in all parts or places.

Evesham ('i:vʃəm) NOUN a town in W central England, in W Worcestershire, on the River Avon: scene of the Battle of Evesham in 1265 (Lord Edward's defeat of Simon de Montfort and the barons); centre of the **Vale of Evesham,** famous for market gardens and orchards. Pop.: 17 823 (1991).

Eve's pudding NOUN *Brit* a baked sponge pudding with a layer of apple at the bottom.

Évian-les-Bains *or* **Évian** (eviã lɛ bɛ̃) NOUN a resort and spa town in E France, on Lake Geneva opposite Lausanne; noted for its bottled mineral waters. Pop.: 6000 (latest est.).

evict (ɪ'vɪkt) VERB (*tr*) [1] to expel (a tenant) from property by process of law; turn out. [2] to recover (property or the title to property) by judicial process or by virtue of a superior title.
▷HISTORY C15: from Late Latin *ēvincere,* from Latin: to vanquish utterly, from *vincere* to conquer
▸**e'viction** NOUN ▸**e'victor** NOUN ▸,**evic'tee** NOUN

evidence ('ɛvɪdəns) NOUN 1 ground for belief or disbelief; data on which to base proof or to establish truth or falsehood. 2 a mark or sign that makes evident; indication: *his pallor was evidence of ill health.* 3 *Law* matter produced before a court of law in an attempt to prove or disprove a point in issue, such as the statements of witnesses, documents, material objects, etc. See also **circumstantial evidence, direct evidence.** 4 **turn queen's (king's, state's) evidence.** (of an accomplice) to act as witness for the prosecution and testify against those associated with him in crime. 5 **in evidence.** on display; apparent; conspicuous: *her engagement ring was in evidence.* ◆ VERB (*tr*) 6 to make evident; show clearly. 7 to give proof of or evidence for.

evident ('ɛvɪdənt) ADJECTIVE easy to see or understand; readily apparent.
▷**HISTORY** C14: from Latin *ēvidēns,* from *vidēre* to see

evidential (ˌɛvɪ'dɛnʃəl) ADJECTIVE relating to, serving as, or based on evidence.
▸ˌ**evi'dentially** ADVERB

evidently ('ɛvɪdəntlɪ) ADVERB 1 without question; clearly; undoubtedly. 2 to all appearances; apparently: *they are evidently related.*

evil ('i:vəl) ADJECTIVE 1 morally wrong or bad; wicked: *an evil ruler.* 2 causing harm or injury; harmful: *an evil plan.* 3 marked or accompanied by misfortune; unlucky: *an evil fate.* 4 (of temper, disposition, etc.) characterized by anger or spite. 5 not in high esteem; infamous: *an evil reputation.* 6 offensive or unpleasant: *an evil smell.* 7 *Slang* good; excellent. ◆ NOUN 8 the quality or an instance of being morally wrong; wickedness: *the evils of war.* 9 (*sometimes capital*) a force or power that brings about wickedness or harm: *evil is strong in the world.* 10 *Archaic* an illness or disease, esp scrofula (the **king's evil**). ◆ ADVERB 11 (*now usually in combination*) in an evil manner; badly: *evil-smelling.*
▷**HISTORY** Old English *yfel,* of Germanic origin; compare Old Frisian *evel,* Old High German *ubil* evil, Old Irish *adbal* excessive
▸'**evilly** ADVERB ▸'**evilness** NOUN

evildoer ('i:vəlˌdu:ə) NOUN a person who does evil.
▸'**evilˌdoing** NOUN

evil eye NOUN **the.** 1 a look or glance superstitiously supposed to have the power of inflicting harm or injury. 2 the power to inflict harm, etc., by such a look.
▸ˌ**evil-'eyed** ADJECTIVE

evil-minded ADJECTIVE inclined to evil thoughts; wicked; malicious or spiteful.
▸ˌ**evil-'mindedly** ADVERB ▸ˌ**evil-'mindedness** NOUN

Evil One NOUN **the.** the devil; Satan.

evince (ɪ'vɪns) VERB (*tr*) to make evident; show (something, such as an emotion) clearly.
▷**HISTORY** C17: from Latin *ēvincere* to overcome; see EVICT
▸**e'vincible** ADJECTIVE ▸**e'vincive** ADJECTIVE

> **Language note** *Evince* is sometimes wrongly used where *evoke* is meant: *the proposal evoked (not evinced) a storm of protest.*

eviscerate (ɪ'vɪsəˌreɪt) VERB 1 (*tr*) to remove the internal organs of; disembowel. 2 (*tr*) to deprive of meaning or significance. 3 (*tr*) *Surgery* to remove the contents of (the eyeball or other organ). 4 (*intr*) *Surgery* (of the viscera) to protrude through a weakened abdominal incision after an operation. ◆ ADJECTIVE 5 having been disembowelled.
▷**HISTORY** C17: from Latin *ēviscerāre* to disembowel, from *viscera* entrails
▸**eˌviscer'ation** NOUN ▸**e'viscerˌator** NOUN

evitable ('ɛvɪtəbəl) ADJECTIVE *Rare* able to be avoided.
▷**HISTORY** C16: from Latin *ēvītābilis,* from *ēvītāre,* from *vītāre* to avoid

evite (ɪ'vaɪt) VERB an archaic word for **avoid.**

evo ('i:vəʊ) NOUN *Austral* an informal word for **evening.**

evocation (ˌɛvə'keɪʃən) NOUN 1 the act or an instance of evoking. 2 *French law* the transference of a case from an inferior court for adjudication by a higher tribunal. 3 another word for **induction** (sense 6).
▷**HISTORY** C17: from Latin *ēvocātiō* a calling forth, from *ēvocāre* to EVOKE

evocative (ɪ'vɒkətɪv) ADJECTIVE tending or serving to evoke.
▸**e'vocatively** ADVERB ▸**e'vocativeness** NOUN

evocator ('ɛvəˌkeɪtə) NOUN 1 a person or thing that evokes. 2 *Embryol* a substance or tissue that induces morphogenesis.

evoke (ɪ'vəʊk) VERB (*tr*) 1 to call or summon up (a memory, feeling, etc.), esp from the past. 2 to call forth or provoke; produce; elicit: *his words evoked an angry reply.* 3 to cause (spirits) to appear; conjure up.
▷**HISTORY** C17: from Latin *ēvocāre* to call forth, from *vocāre* to call
▸**evocable** ('ɛvəkəbəl) ADJECTIVE ▸**e'voker** NOUN

> **Language note** See at **evince** and **invoke.**

evolute ('ɛvəˌlu:t) NOUN 1 a geometric curve that describes the locus of the centres of curvature of another curve (the **involute**). The tangents to the evolute are at right angles to the involute. ◆ ADJECTIVE 2 *Biology* having the margins rolled outwards.
▷**HISTORY** C19: from Latin *ēvolūtus* unrolled, from *ēvolvere* to roll out, EVOLVE

evolution (ˌi:və'lu:ʃən) NOUN 1 *Biology* a gradual change in the characteristics of a population of animals or plants over successive generations: accounts for the origin of existing species from ancestors unlike them. See also **natural selection.** 2 a gradual development, esp to a more complex form: *the evolution of modern art.* 3 the act of throwing off, as heat, gas, vapour, etc. 4 a pattern formed by a series of movements or something similar. 5 an algebraic operation in which the root of a number, expression, etc., is extracted. Compare **involution** (sense 6). 6 *Military* an exercise carried out in accordance with a set procedure or plan.
▷**HISTORY** C17: from Latin *ēvolūtiō* an unrolling, from *ēvolvere* to EVOLVE
▸ˌ**evo'lutionary** *or* ˌ**evo'lutional** ADJECTIVE

evolutionist (ˌi:və'lu:ʃənɪst) NOUN 1 a person who believes in a theory of evolution, esp Darwin's theory of the evolution of plant and animal species. ◆ ADJECTIVE 2 of or relating to a theory of evolution.
▸ˌ**evo'lutionism** NOUN ▸ˌ**evolution'istic** ADJECTIVE

evolutive (i:'vɒljʊtɪv) ADJECTIVE relating to, tending to, or promoting evolution.

evolve (ɪ'vɒlv) VERB 1 to develop or cause to develop gradually. 2 (*intr*) (of animal or plant species) to undergo evolution. 3 (*tr*) to yield, emit, or give off (heat, gas, vapour, etc.).
▷**HISTORY** C17: from Latin *ēvolvere* to unfold, from *volvere* to roll
▸**e'volvable** ADJECTIVE ▸**e'volvement** NOUN ▸**e'volver** NOUN

evonymus (ɛ'vɒnɪməs) NOUN a variant of **euonymus.**

Évora (*Portuguese* 'ɛvura) NOUN a city in S central Portugal: ancient Roman settlement; occupied by the Moors from 712 to 1166; residence of the Portuguese court in 15th and 16th centuries. Pop.: 34 100 (latest est.). Ancient name: **Ebora** ('i:bərə).

evulsion (ɪ'vʌlʃən) NOUN *Rare* the act of extracting by force.
▷**HISTORY** C17: from Latin *ēvulsiō,* from *ēvellere,* from *vellere* to pluck

evzone ('ɛvzəʊn) NOUN a soldier in an elite Greek infantry regiment.
▷**HISTORY** C19: from Modern Greek, from Greek *euzōnos* literally: well-girt, from EU- + *zōne* girdle

EW INTERNATIONAL CAR REGISTRATION FOR Estonia.

e-wallet NOUN computer software in which digital cash may be stored for use in paying for transactions on the Internet.

ewe (ju:) NOUN **a** a female sheep. **b** (*as modifier*): *a ewe lamb.*
▷**HISTORY** Old English *ēowu;* related to Old Norse *ær* ewe, Old High German *ou,* Latin *ovis* sheep, Sanskrit *avi*

Ewe ('ɛwɛ) NOUN 1 (*plural* **Ewe** *or* **Ewes**) a member of a Negroid people of W Africa living chiefly in the forests of E Ghana, Togo, and Benin. 2 the language of this people, belonging to the Kwa branch of the Niger-Congo family.

ewe equivalent NOUN *NZ* the basic measure for calculating stock unit: *one Jersey cow is equal to 6.5 ewe equivalents.*

ewe-neck NOUN 1 a condition in horses in which the neck is straight and sagging rather than arched. 2 a horse or other animal with this condition.
▸'**ewe-ˌnecked** ADJECTIVE

ewer ('ju:ə) NOUN a large jug or pitcher with a wide mouth.
▷**HISTORY** C14: from Old French *evier,* from Latin *aquārius* water carrier, from *aqua* water

EWO ABBREVIATION FOR **Educational Welfare Officer.**

ex[1] (ɛks) PREPOSITION 1 *Finance* not participating in; excluding; without: *ex bonus; ex dividend; ex rights.* 2 *Commerce* without charge to the buyer until removed from: *ex quay; ex ship; ex works.*
▷**HISTORY** C19: from Latin: out of, from

ex[2] (ɛks) NOUN *Informal* (a person's) former wife, husband, etc.

Ex. *Bible* ABBREVIATION FOR Exodus.

ex-[1] PREFIX 1 out of; outside of; from: *exclosure; exurbia.* 2 former: *ex-wife.*
▷**HISTORY** from Latin, from *ex* (prep), identical in meaning and origin with Greek *ex, ek;* see EC-

ex-[2] COMBINING FORM a variant of **exo-** before a vowel: *exergonic.*

exa- PREFIX denoting 10^{18}: *exametres.* Symbol: E.

exacerbate (ɪg'zæsəˌbeɪt, ɪk'sæs-) VERB (*tr*) 1 to make (pain, disease, emotion, etc.) more intense; aggravate. 2 to exasperate or irritate (a person).
▷**HISTORY** C17: from Latin *exacerbāre* to irritate, from *acerbus* bitter
▸**exˌacer'bation** NOUN

exact (ɪg'zækt) ADJECTIVE 1 correct in every detail; strictly accurate: *an exact copy.* 2 precise, as opposed to approximate; neither more nor less: *the exact sum.* 3 (*prenominal*) specific; particular: *this exact spot.* 4 operating with very great precision: *exact instruments.* 5 allowing no deviation from a standard; rigorous; strict: *an exact mind.* 6 based mainly on measurement and the formulation of laws, as opposed to description and classification: *physics is an exact science.* ◆ VERB (*tr*) 7 to force or compel (payment or performance); extort: *to exact tribute.* 8 to demand as a right; insist upon: *to exact respect from one's employees.* 9 to call for or require: *this work exacts careful effort.*
▷**HISTORY** C16: from Latin *exactus* driven out, from *exigere* to drive forth, from *agere* to drive
▸**ex'actable** ADJECTIVE ▸**ex'actness** NOUN ▸**ex'actor** *or* **ex'acter** NOUN

exacting (ɪg'zæktɪŋ) ADJECTIVE making rigorous or excessive demands: *an exacting job.*
▸**ex'actingly** ADVERB ▸**ex'actingness** NOUN

exaction (ɪg'zækʃən) NOUN 1 the act or an instance of exacting, esp money. 2 an excessive or harsh demand, esp for money; extortion. 3 a sum or payment exacted.

exactitude (ɪg'zæktɪˌtju:d) NOUN the quality of being exact; precision; accuracy.

exactly (ɪg'zæktlɪ) ADVERB 1 in an exact manner; accurately or precisely. 2 in every respect; just: *it is exactly what he wants.* ◆ SENTENCE SUBSTITUTE 3 just so! precisely! 4 **not exactly.** *Ironic* not at all; by no means.

exacum ('ɛksəkəm) NOUN any plant of the annual or perennial tropical genus *Exacum;* some are grown as greenhouse biennials for their bluish-purple platter-shaped flowers: family *Gentianaceae.*
▷**HISTORY** Latin, a name for centaury, from *ex* out + *agere* to drive

exaggerate (ɪg'zædʒəˌreɪt) VERB 1 to regard or represent as larger or greater, more important or more successful, etc., than is true. 2 (*tr*) to make greater, more noticeable, etc., than usual: *his new clothes exaggerated his awkwardness.*
▷**HISTORY** C16: from Latin *exaggerāre* to magnify, from *aggerāre* to heap, from *agger* heap
▸**ex'aggerˌatingly** ADVERB ▸**exˌagger'ation** NOUN ▸**ex'aggerative** *or* **ex'aggeratory** ADJECTIVE ▸**ex'aggerˌator** NOUN

exaggerated (ɪg'zædʒəˌreɪtɪd) ADJECTIVE 1 unduly or excessively magnified; enlarged beyond truth or reasonableness. 2 *Pathol* abnormally enlarged: *an exaggerated spleen.*
▸**ex'aggerˌatedly** ADVERB

ex all ADVERB *Finance* without the right to any benefits: *shares quoted ex all.*

exalt (ɪgˈzɔːlt) VERB *(tr)* 1 to raise or elevate in rank, position, dignity, etc. 2 to praise highly; glorify; extol. 3 to stimulate the mind or imagination of; excite. 4 to increase the intensity of (a colour, etc.). 5 to fill with joy or delight; elate. 6 *Obsolete* to lift up physically.
▷HISTORY C15: from Latin *exaltāre* to raise, from *altus* high
▸**exˈalter** NOUN

> **Language note** *Exalt* is sometimes wrongly used where *exult* is meant: *he was exulting* (not *exalting*) *in his win earlier that day.*

exaltation (ˌɛgzɔːlˈteɪʃən) NOUN 1 the act of exalting or state of being exalted. 2 a feeling of intense well-being or exhilaration; elation; rapture. 3 a flock of larks.

exalted (ɪgˈzɔːltɪd) ADJECTIVE 1 high or elevated in rank, position, dignity, etc. 2 elevated in character; noble; lofty: *an exalted ideal.* 3 *Informal* excessively high; inflated: *he has an exalted opinion of himself.* 4 intensely excited; elated.
▸**exˈaltedly** ADVERB ▸**exˈaltedness** NOUN

exam (ɪgˈzæm) NOUN short for **examination.**

examen (ɪgˈzeɪmɛn) NOUN *RC Church* an examination of conscience, usually made daily by Jesuits and others.
▷HISTORY C17: from Latin: tongue of a balance, from *exigere* to thrust out, from *agere* to thrust

examination (ɪgˌzæmɪˈneɪʃən) NOUN 1 the act of examining or state of being examined. 2 *Education* **a** written exercises, oral questions, or practical tasks, set to test a candidate's knowledge and skill. **b** (*as modifier*): *an examination paper.* 3 *Med* **a** a physical inspection of a patient or parts of his body, in order to verify health or diagnose disease. **b** laboratory study of secretory or excretory products, tissue samples, etc., esp in order to diagnose disease. 4 *Law* the formal interrogation of a person on oath, esp of an accused or a witness.
▸**exˌamiˈnational** ADJECTIVE

examine (ɪgˈzæmɪn) VERB *(tr)* 1 to look at, inspect, or scrutinize carefully or in detail; investigate. 2 *Education* to test the knowledge or skill of (a candidate) in (a subject or activity) by written or oral questions or by practical tests. 3 *Law* to interrogate (a witness or accused person) formally on oath. 4 *Med* to investigate the state of health of (a patient).
▷HISTORY C14: from Old French *examiner,* from Latin *exāmināre* to weigh, from *exāmen* means of weighing; see EXAMEN
▸**exˈaminable** ADJECTIVE ▸**exˈaminer** NOUN ▸**exˈamining** ADJECTIVE

examinee (ɪgˌzæmɪˈniː) NOUN a person who takes an examination.

examine-in-chief VERB *(tr) Law* to examine (one's own witness) in attempting to adduce a case. Compare **cross-examine.**
▸**exˌamiˈnation-in-chief** NOUN

example (ɪgˈzɑːmpᵊl) NOUN 1 a specimen or instance that is typical of the group or set of which it forms part; sample. 2 a person, action, thing, etc., that is worthy of imitation; pattern: *you must set an example to the younger children.* 3 a precedent, illustration of a principle, or model: *an example in a maths book.* 4 a punishment or the recipient of a punishment serving or intended to serve as a warning: *the headmaster made an example of him.* 5 **for example.** as an illustration; for instance. ◆ VERB 6 *(tr; now usually passive)* to present an example of; exemplify.
▷HISTORY C14: from Old French, from Latin *exemplum* pattern, from *eximere* to take out, from EX-[1] + *emere* to purchase

exanimate (ɪgˈzænɪmɪt, -ˌmeɪt) ADJECTIVE *Rare* lacking life; inanimate.
▷HISTORY C16: from Latin *exanimāre* to deprive of air, kill, from *anima* breath, spirit
▸**exˌaniˈmation** NOUN

exanthema (ˌɛksænˈθiːmə) *or* **exanthem** (ɛkˈsænθəm) NOUN, *plural* **-themata** (-ˈθiːmətə) *or* **-themas,** *or* **-thems.** a skin eruption or rash occurring as a symptom in a disease such as measles or scarlet fever.
▷HISTORY C17: via Late Latin from Greek, from *exanthein* to burst forth, from *anthein* to blossom, from *anthos* flower
▸**exanthematous** (ˌɛksænˈθɛmətəs) *or* **exanthematic** (ɛkˌsænθɪˈmætɪk) ADJECTIVE

exarate (ˈɛksəˌreɪt) ADJECTIVE (of the pupa of such insects as ants and bees) having the legs, wings, antennae, etc., free and movable.
▷HISTORY C19: from Latin *exarātus,* literally: ploughed up (apparently referring to the way this type of pupa throws off the larval skin), from *exarāre,* from *arā* plough

exarch[1] (ˈɛksɑːk) NOUN 1 the head of certain autonomous Orthodox Christian Churches, such as that of Bulgaria and Cyprus. 2 any of certain Eastern Orthodox bishops, lower in rank than a patriarch but higher than a metropolitan. 3 the governor of a province in the Byzantine Empire.
▷HISTORY C16: from Late Latin *exarchus* overseer, from Greek *exarkhos,* from *exarkhein* to take the lead, from *arkhein* to rule
▸**exˈarchal** ADJECTIVE

exarch[2] (ˈɛksɑːk) ADJECTIVE *Botany* (of a xylem strand) having the first-formed xylem external to that formed later. Compare **endarch, mesarch.**
▷HISTORY C19: from EX-[1] (outside) + Greek *arkhē* beginning, origin

exarchate (ˈɛksɑːˌkeɪt, ɛkˈsɑːkeɪt) *or* **exarchy** (ˈɛksɑːkɪ) NOUN, *plural* **-chates** *or* **-chies.** the office, rank, or jurisdiction of an exarch.

exasperate (ɪgˈzɑːspəˌreɪt) VERB *(tr)* 1 to cause great irritation or anger to; infuriate. 2 to cause (an unpleasant feeling, condition, etc.) to worsen; aggravate. ◆ ADJECTIVE 3 *Botany* having a rough prickly surface because of the presence of hard projecting points.
▷HISTORY C16: from Latin *exasperāre* to make rough, from *asper* rough
▸**exˈasperˌatedly** ADVERB ▸**exˈasperˌater** NOUN
▸**exˈasperˌating** ADJECTIVE ▸**exˈasperˌatingly** ADVERB
▸**exˌasperˈation** NOUN

exbi- (ˈɛksˌbaɪ) COMBINING FORM *Computing* denoting 2 to the power 60.
▷HISTORY C20: from EX(A-) + BI(NARY)

Exc. ABBREVIATION FOR Excellency.

Excalibur (ɛkˈskælɪbə) NOUN (in Arthurian legend) the magic sword of King Arthur.
▷HISTORY C14: from Old French *Escalibor,* from Medieval Latin *Caliburnus,* from Welsh *Caledvwlch,* perhaps related to Irish *Caladbolg* a legendary sword (literally: hard belly, hence, voracious)

ex cathedra (ɛks kəˈθiːdrə) ADJECTIVE, ADVERB 1 with authority. 2 *RC Church* (of doctrines of faith or morals) defined by the pope as infallibly true, to be accepted by all Catholics.
▷HISTORY Latin, literally: from the chair

excaudate (ɛksˈkɔːdeɪt) ADJECTIVE *Zoology* having no tail or tail-like process; tailless.

excavate (ˈɛkskəˌveɪt) VERB 1 to remove (soil, earth, etc.) by digging; dig out. 2 to make (a hole, cavity, or tunnel) in (solid matter) by hollowing or removing the centre or inner part: *to excavate a tooth.* 3 to unearth (buried objects) methodically in an attempt to discover information about the past.
▷HISTORY C16: from Latin *excavāre,* from *cavāre* to make hollow, from *cavus* hollow
▸**ˌexcaˈvation** NOUN

excavator (ˈɛkskəˌveɪtə) NOUN 1 a powered machine for digging earth, gravel, sand, etc., esp a caterpillar tractor so equipped. 2 any person, animal, or thing that excavates.

exceed (ɪkˈsiːd) VERB 1 to be superior to (a person or thing), esp in size or quality; excel. 2 *(tr)* to go beyond the limit or bounds of: *to exceed one's income; exceed a speed limit.* 3 to be greater in degree or quantity than (a person or thing).
▷HISTORY C14: from Latin *excēdere* to go beyond, from *cēdere* to go
▸**exˈceedable** ADJECTIVE ▸**exˈceeder** NOUN

exceeding (ɪkˈsiːdɪŋ) ADJECTIVE 1 very great; exceptional or excessive. ◆ ADVERB 2 an archaic word for **exceedingly.**

exceedingly (ɪkˈsiːdɪŋlɪ) ADVERB to a very great or unusual degree; extremely; exceptionally.

excel (ɪkˈsɛl) VERB **-cels, -celling, -celled.** 1 to be superior to (another or others); surpass. 2 *(intr;* foll by *in* or *at)* to be outstandingly good or proficient: *he excels at tennis.*
▷HISTORY C15: from Latin *excellere* to rise up

excellence (ˈɛksələns) NOUN 1 the state or quality of excelling or being exceptionally good; extreme merit; superiority. 2 an action, characteristic, feature, etc., in which a person excels.

Excellency (ˈɛksələnsɪ) *or* **Excellence** NOUN, *plural* **-lencies** *or* **-lences.** 1 (usually preceded by *Your, His,* or *Her)* a title used to address or refer to a high-ranking official, such as an ambassador or governor. 2 *RC Church* a title of bishops and archbishops in many non-English-speaking countries.

excellent (ˈɛksələnt) ADJECTIVE exceptionally good; extremely meritorious; superior.
▸**ˈexcellently** ADVERB

excelsior (ɪkˈsɛlsɪˌɔː) INTERJECTION, ADVERB, NOUN 1 excellent: used as a motto and as a trademark for various products, esp in the US for fine wood shavings used for packing breakable objects. 2 upwards.
▷HISTORY C19: from Latin: higher

except (ɪkˈsɛpt) PREPOSITION 1 Also: **except for.** other than; apart from; with the exception of: *he likes everyone except you; except for this mistake, you did very well.* 2 **except that.** (*conjunction*) but for the fact that; were it not true that. ◆ CONJUNCTION 3 an archaic word for **unless.** 4 *Informal; not standard in the US* except that; but for the fact that: *I would have arrived earlier, except I lost my way.* ◆ VERB 5 *(tr)* to leave out; omit; exclude. 6 *(intr;* often foll by *to) Rare* to take exception; object.
▷HISTORY C14: from Old French *excepter* to leave out, from Latin *exceptāre,* from *excipere* to take out, from *capere* to take

excepting (ɪkˈsɛptɪŋ) PREPOSITION 1 excluding; except; except for (esp in the phrase **not excepting**). ◆ CONJUNCTION 2 an archaic word for **unless.**

> **Language note** The use of *excepting* is considered by many people to be acceptable only after *not, only,* or *without.* Elsewhere *except* is preferred: *every country agreed to the proposal except* (not *excepting*) *Spain; he was well again except for* (not *excepting*) *a slight pain in his chest.*

exception (ɪkˈsɛpʃən) NOUN 1 the act of excepting or fact of being excepted; omission. 2 anything excluded from or not in conformance with a general rule, principle, class, etc. 3 criticism, esp when it is adverse; objection. 4 *Law* (formerly) a formal objection in the course of legal proceedings. 5 *Law* a clause or term in a document that restricts the usual legal effect of the document. 6 **a** (usually foll by *to*) to make objections (to); demur (at). **b** (often foll by *at*) to be offended (by); be resentful (at).

exceptionable (ɪkˈsɛpʃənəbᵊl) ADJECTIVE open to or subject to objection; objectionable.
▸**exˈceptionableness** NOUN ▸**exˈceptionably** ADVERB

exceptional (ɪkˈsɛpʃənᵊl) ADJECTIVE 1 forming an exception; not ordinary. 2 having much more than average intelligence, ability, or skill.
▸**exˈceptionally** ADVERB

exceptionalism (ɪkˈsɛpʃənᵊlɪzm) NOUN an attitude to other countries, cultures, etc. based on the idea of being quite distinct from, and often superior to, them in vital ways.

exceptive (ɪkˈsɛptɪv) ADJECTIVE relating to or forming an exception.

excerpt NOUN (ˈɛksɜːpt) 1 a part or passage taken from a book, speech, play, etc., and considered on its own; extract. ◆ VERB (ɛkˈsɜːpt) 2 *(tr)* to take (a part or passage) from a book, speech, play, etc.
▷HISTORY C17: from Latin *excerptum,* literally: (something) picked out, from *excerpere* to select, from *carpere* to pluck
▸**exˈcerptor** NOUN ▸**exˈcerptible** ADJECTIVE ▸**exˈcerption** NOUN

excess NOUN (ɪkˈsɛs, ˈɛksɛs) 1 the state or act of going beyond normal, sufficient, or permitted limits. 2 an immoderate or abnormal amount, number, extent, or degree too much or too many:

an excess of tolerance. [3] the amount, number, extent, or degree by which one thing exceeds another. [4] *Chem* a quantity of a reagent that is greater than the quantity required to complete a reaction: *add an excess of acid.* [5] overindulgence or intemperance. [6] *Insurance, chiefly Brit* a specified contribution towards the cost of a claim, stipulated on certain insurance policies as being payable by the policyholder. [7] **in excess of.** of more than; over. [8] **to excess.** to an inordinate extent; immoderately: *he drinks to excess.* ◆ ADJECTIVE (*usually prenominal*) (ˈɛksɛs, ɪkˈsɛs) [9] more than normal, necessary, or permitted; surplus: *excess weight.* [10] payable as a result of previous underpayment: *excess postage; an excess fare for a railway journey.*
▷**HISTORY** C14: from Latin *excessus,* from *excēdere* to go beyond; see EXCEED

excess demand NOUN *Economics* a situation in which the market demand for a commodity is greater than its market supply, thus causing its market price to rise.

excessive (ɪkˈsɛsɪv) ADJECTIVE exceeding the normal or permitted extents or limits; immoderate; inordinate.
▸**exˈcessively** ADVERB ▸**exˈcessiveness** NOUN

excess luggage *or* **baggage** NOUN luggage that is greater in weight or in number of pieces than an airline, etc., will carry free.

excess supply NOUN *Economics* a situation in which the market supply of a commodity is greater than the market demand for it, thus causing its market price to fall.

exchange (ɪksˈtʃeɪndʒ) VERB [1] (*tr*) to give up, part with, or transfer (one thing) for an equivalent: *to exchange gifts; to exchange francs for dollars.* [2] (*tr*) to give and receive (information, ideas, etc.); interchange. [3] (*tr*) to replace (one thing) with another, esp to replace unsatisfactory goods. [4] to transfer or hand over (goods) in return for the equivalent value in kind rather than in money; barter; trade. [5] (*tr*) *Chess* to capture and surrender (pieces, usually of the same value) in a single sequence of moves. ◆ NOUN [6] the act or process of exchanging. [7] **a** anything given or received as an equivalent, replacement, or substitute for something else. **b** (*as modifier*): *an exchange student.* [8] an argument or quarrel; altercation: *the two men had a bitter exchange.* [9] Also called: **telephone exchange.** a switching centre in which telephone lines are interconnected. [10] **a** a place where securities or commodities are sold, bought, or traded, esp by brokers or merchants: *a stock exchange; a corn exchange.* **b** (*as modifier*): *an exchange broker.* [11] **a** the system by which commercial debts between parties in different places are settled by commercial documents, esp bills of exchange, instead of by direct payment of money. **b** the percentage or fee charged for accepting payment in this manner. [12] a transfer or interchange of sums of money of equivalent value, as between different national currencies or different issues of the same currency. [13] (*often plural*) the cheques, drafts, bills, etc., exchanged or settled between banks in a clearing house. [14] *Chess* the capture by both players of pieces of equal value, usually on consecutive moves. [15] **win** (*or* **lose**) **the exchange.** *Chess* to win (or lose) a rook in return for a bishop or knight. [16] *Med* another word for **transfusion** (sense 2). [17] *Physics* a process in which a particle is transferred between two nucleons, such as the transfer of a meson between two nucleons. ◆ See also **bill of exchange, exchange rate, foreign exchange, labour exchange.**
▷**HISTORY** C14: from Anglo-French *eschaungier,* from Vulgar Latin *excambiāre* (unattested), from Latin *cambīre* to barter
▸**exˈchangeable** ADJECTIVE ▸**ex,changeaˈbility** NOUN
▸**exˈchangeably** ADVERB

exchange force NOUN *Physics* [1] a force between two elementary particles resulting from the exchange of a virtual particle. [2] the force causing the alignment of the magnetic dipole moments of atoms in ferromagnetic materials.

exchanger (ɪksˈtʃeɪndʒə) NOUN a person or thing that exchanges.

exchange rate NOUN the rate at which the currency unit of one country may be exchanged for that of another.

Exchange Rate Mechanism NOUN [1] the mechanism formerly used in the European Monetary System in which participating governments committed themselves to maintain the values of their currencies in relation to the ECU. Abbreviation: **ERM.** [2] Also: **Exchange Rate Mechanism II.** the mechanism used to stabilize the currencies of European Union States that have not adopted the euro but wish to maintain the value of their currency in relation to it. Abbreviation: **ERM II.**

exchequer (ɪksˈtʃɛkə) NOUN [1] (*often capital*) *Government* (in Britain and certain other countries) the accounting department of the Treasury, responsible for receiving and issuing funds. [2] *Informal* personal funds; finances.
▷**HISTORY** C13 (in the sense: chessboard, counting table): from Old French *eschequier,* from *eschec* CHECK

Exchequer (ɪksˈtʃɛkə) NOUN See **Court of Exchequer.**

excide (ɪkˈsaɪd) VERB (*tr*) *Rare* to cut out; excise.
▷**HISTORY** C18: from Latin *excīdere* to cut off, from *caedere* to cut

excimer (ˈɛk,saɪmə) NOUN *Physics* an excited dimer formed by the association of excited and unexcited molecules, which would remain dissociated in the ground state.

excipient (ɪkˈsɪpɪənt) NOUN a substance, such as sugar or gum, used to prepare a drug or drugs in a form suitable for administration.
▷**HISTORY** C18: from Latin *excipiēns* excepting, from *excipere* to EXCEPT

excisable (ɪkˈsaɪzəbᵊl) ADJECTIVE liable to an excise tax.

excise[1] NOUN (ˈɛksaɪz, ɛkˈsaɪz) [1] Also called: **excise tax.** a tax on goods, such as spirits, produced for the home market. [2] a tax paid for a licence to carry out various trades, sports, etc. [3] *Brit* that section of the government service responsible for the collection of excise, now the Board of Customs and Excise.
▷**HISTORY** C15: probably from Middle Dutch *excijs,* probably from Old French *assise* a sitting, assessment, from Latin *assidēre* to sit beside, assist in judging, from *sedēre* to sit
▸**exˈcisable** ADJECTIVE

excise[2] (ɪkˈsaɪz) VERB (*tr*) [1] to delete (a passage, sentence, etc.); expunge. [2] to remove (an organ, structure, or part) surgically.
▷**HISTORY** C16: from Latin *excīdere* to cut down; see EXCIDE
▸**excision** (ɪkˈsɪʒən) NOUN

exciseman (ˈɛksaɪz,mæn) NOUN, *plural* **-men.** *Brit* (formerly) a government agent whose function was to collect excise and prevent smuggling.

excitable (ɪkˈsaɪtəbᵊl) ADJECTIVE [1] easily excited; volatile. [2] (esp of a nerve) ready to respond to a stimulus.
▸**ex,citaˈbility** *or* **exˈcitableness** NOUN ▸**exˈcitably** ADVERB

excitant (ɪkˈsaɪtᵊnt, ˈɛksɪtənt) ADJECTIVE *also* **excitative** (ɪkˈsaɪtətɪv), **excitatory** (ɪkˈsaɪtətərɪ). [1] able to excite or stimulate. ◆ NOUN [2] something, such as a drug or other agent, able to excite; stimulant.

excitation (,ɛksɪˈteɪʃən) NOUN [1] the act or process of exciting or state of being excited. [2] a means of exciting or cause of excitement. [3] **a** the current in a field coil of a generator, motor, etc., or the magnetizing current in a transformer. **b** (*as modifier*): *an excitation current.* [4] the action of a stimulus on an animal or plant organ, inducing it to respond.

excite (ɪkˈsaɪt) VERB (*tr*) [1] to arouse (a person) to strong feeling, esp to pleasurable anticipation or nervous agitation. [2] to arouse or elicit (an emotion, response, etc.); evoke: *her answers excited curiosity.* [3] to cause or bring about; stir up: *to excite a rebellion.* [4] to arouse sexually. [5] *Physiol* to cause a response in or increase the activity of (an organ, tissue, or part); stimulate. [6] to raise (an atom, molecule, electron, nucleus, etc.) from the ground state to a higher energy level. [7] to supply electricity to (the coils of a generator or motor) in order to create a magnetic field. [8] to supply a signal to a stage of an active electronic circuit.
▷**HISTORY** C14: from Latin *excitāre,* from *exciēre* to stimulate, from *ciēre* to set in motion, rouse

excited (ɪkˈsaɪtɪd) ADJECTIVE [1] emotionally aroused, esp to pleasure or agitation. [2] characterized by excitement: *an excited dance.* [3] sexually aroused. [4] (of an atom, molecule, etc.) occupying an energy level above the ground state.
▸**exˈcitedly** ADVERB ▸**exˈcitedness** NOUN

excitement (ɪkˈsaɪtmənt) NOUN [1] the state of being excited. [2] a person or thing that excites; stimulation or thrill.

exciter (ɪkˈsaɪtə) NOUN [1] a person or thing that excites. [2] a small generator that excites a larger machine. [3] an oscillator producing a transmitter's carrier wave.

exciting (ɪkˈsaɪtɪŋ) ADJECTIVE causing excitement; stirring; stimulating.
▸**exˈcitingly** ADVERB

exciton (ˈɛksaɪ,tɒn) NOUN a mobile neutral entity in a crystalline solid consisting of an excited electron bound to the hole produced by its excitation.
▷**HISTORY** C20: from EXCIT(ATION) + -ON

excitor (ɪkˈsaɪtə) NOUN [1] a nerve that, when stimulated, causes increased activity in the organ or part it supplies. [2] a variant spelling of **exciter.**

exclaim (ɪkˈskleɪm) VERB to cry out or speak suddenly or excitedly, as from surprise, delight, horror, etc.
▷**HISTORY** C16: from Latin *exclāmāre,* from *clāmāre* to shout
▸**exˈclaimer** NOUN

exclamation (,ɛkskləˈmeɪʃən) NOUN [1] an abrupt, emphatic, or excited cry or utterance; interjection; ejaculation. [2] the act of exclaiming.
▸**,exclaˈmational** ADJECTIVE

exclamation mark *or US* **point** NOUN [1] the punctuation mark ! used after exclamations and vehement commands. [2] this mark used for any other purpose, as to draw attention to an obvious mistake, in road warning signs, (in chess commentaries) beside the notation of a move considered a good one, (in mathematics) as a symbol of the factorial function, or (in logic) occurring with an existential quantifier.

exclamatory (ɪkˈsklæmətərɪ, -trɪ) ADJECTIVE using, containing, or relating to exclamations.
▸**exˈclamatorily** ADVERB

exclaustration (,ɛksklɔːˈstreɪʃən) NOUN the return of a monk or nun to the outside world after being released from his or her religious vows.
▷**HISTORY** from EX-[1] + Latin *claustrum* cloister

exclave (ˈɛkskleɪv) NOUN a part of a country entirely surrounded by foreign territory: viewed from the position of the home country. Compare **enclave.**
▷**HISTORY** C20: from EX-[1] + *-clave,* on the model of ENCLAVE

exclosure (ɪkˈskləʊʒə) NOUN an area of land, esp in a forest, fenced round to keep out unwanted animals.

exclude (ɪkˈskluːd) VERB (*tr*) [1] to keep out; prevent from entering. [2] to reject or not consider; leave out. [3] to expel forcibly; eject. [4] to debar from school, either temporarily or permanently, as a form of punishment.
▷**HISTORY** C14: from Latin *exclūdere,* from *claudere* to shut
▸**exˈcludable** *or* **exˈcludible** ADJECTIVE ▸**exˈcluder** NOUN

excluded middle NOUN *Logic* the principle that every proposition is either true or false, so that there is no third truth-value and no statements lack truth-value.

excluding (ɪkˈskluːdɪŋ) PREPOSITION excepting.

exclusion (ɪkˈskluːʒən) NOUN the act or an instance of excluding or the state of being excluded.
▸**exˈclusionary** ADJECTIVE

exclusionist (ɪkˈskluːʒənɪst) ADJECTIVE [1] *Chiefly US* denoting or relating to a policy of excluding various types of immigrants, imports, etc. ◆ NOUN [2] a supporter of a policy of exclusion.
▸**exˈclusion,ism** NOUN

exclusion principle NOUN See **Pauli exclusion principle.**

exclusive (ɪkˈskluːsɪv) ADJECTIVE [1] excluding all else; rejecting other considerations, possibilities, events, etc.: *an exclusive preoccupation with money.* [2] belonging to a particular individual or group and to no other; not shared: *exclusive rights; an exclusive story.* [3] belonging to or catering for a privileged minority, esp a fashionable clique: *an exclusive restaurant.* [4] (*postpositive;* foll by *to*) limited (to); found only (in): *this model is exclusive to Harrods.* [5]

single; unique; only: *the exclusive means of transport on the island was the bicycle.* [6] separate and incompatible: *mutually exclusive principles.* [7] (*immediately postpositive*) not including the numbers, dates, letters, etc., mentioned: *1980–84 exclusive.* [8] (*postpositive;* foll by *of*) except (for); not taking account (of): *exclusive of bonus payments, you will earn this amount.* [9] *Commerce* (of a contract, agreement, etc.) binding the parties to do business only with each other with respect to a class of goods or services. [10] *Logic* (of a disjunction) true if only one rather than both of its component propositions is true. Compare **inclusive** (sense 5). ◆ NOUN [11] an exclusive story; a story reported in only one newspaper.
▸**ex'clusively** ADVERB ▸**exclusivity** (ˌɛksklu:ˈsɪvɪtɪ) *or* **ex'clusiveness** NOUN

Exclusive Brethren PLURAL NOUN one of the two main divisions of the Plymouth Brethren, which, in contrast to the Open Brethren, restricts its members' contacts with those outside the sect.

exclusive economic zone NOUN the coastal water and sea bed around a country's shores, to which it claims exclusive rights for fishing, oil exploration, etc. Sometimes shortened to: **economic zone.**

exclusive or NOUN *Logic* the connective that gives the value *true* to a disjunction if one or other, but not both, of the disjuncts are true. Also called: **exclusive disjunction.** Compare **inclusive or.**

exclusive OR circuit *or* **gate** NOUN *Electronics* a computer logic circuit having two or more input wires and one output wire and giving a high-voltage output signal if a low-voltage signal is fed to one or more, but not all, of the input wires. Compare **OR circuit.**

excogitate (ɛksˈkɒdʒɪˌteɪt) VERB (*tr*) [1] to devise, invent, or contrive. [2] to think out in detail.
▷HISTORY C16: from Latin *excōgitāre,* from *cōgitāre* to ponder, COGITATE
▸**ex'cogitable** ADJECTIVE ▸**exˌcogi'tation** NOUN ▸**ex'cogitative** ADJECTIVE ▸**ex'cogiˌtator** NOUN

excommunicate *RC Church* ◆ VERB (ˌɛkskəˈmju:nɪˌkeɪt) [1] (*tr*) to sentence (a member of the Church) to exclusion from the communion of believers and from the privileges and public prayers of the Church. ◆ ADJECTIVE (ˌɛkskəˈmju:nɪkɪt, -ˌkeɪt) [2] having incurred such a sentence. ◆ NOUN (ˌɛkskəˈmju:nɪkɪt, -ˌkeɪt) [3] an excommunicated person.
▷HISTORY C15: from Late Latin *excommūnicāre,* literally: to exclude from the community, from Latin *commūnis* COMMON
▸**ˌexcom'municable** ADJECTIVE ▸**ˌexcomˌmuni'cation** NOUN ▸**ˌexcom'municative** *or* **ˌexcom'municatory** ADJECTIVE ▸**ˌexcom'municator** NOUN

excoriate (ɪkˈskɔ:rɪˌeɪt) VERB (*tr*) [1] to strip (the skin) from (a person or animal); flay. [2] *Med* to lose (a superficial area of skin), as by scratching, the application of chemicals, etc. [3] to denounce vehemently; censure severely.
▷HISTORY C15: from Late Latin *excoriāre* to strip, flay, from Latin *corium* skin, hide
▸**exˌcori'ation** NOUN

excrement (ˈɛkskrɪmənt) NOUN waste matter discharged from the body, esp faeces; excreta.
▷HISTORY C16: from Latin *excrēmentum,* from *excernere* to sift, EXCRETE
▸**excremental** (ˌɛkskrɪˈmɛntᵊl) *or* **excrementitious** (ˌɛkskrɪmɛnˈtɪʃəs) ADJECTIVE

excrescence (ɪkˈskrɛsᵊns) NOUN a projection or protuberance, esp an outgrowth from an organ or part of the body.
▸**excrescential** (ˌɛkskrɪˈsɛnʃəl) ADJECTIVE

excrescency (ɪkˈskrɛsənsɪ) NOUN, *plural* **-cies.** [1] the state or condition of being excrescent. [2] another word for **excrescence.**

excrescent (ɪkˈskrɛsᵊnt) ADJECTIVE [1] denoting, relating to, or resembling an abnormal outgrowth. [2] uselessly added; not essential; superfluous. [3] denoting or relating to a speech sound or letter inserted into a word without etymological justification, such as the *b* in *nimble.*
▷HISTORY C17: from Latin *excrēscēns,* from *excrēscere,* from *crēscere* to grow
▸**ex'crescently** ADVERB

excreta (ɪkˈskri:tə) PLURAL NOUN waste matter, such as urine, faeces, or sweat, discharged from the body; excrement.
▷HISTORY C19: New Latin, from Latin *excernere* to EXCRETE
▸**ex'cretal** ADJECTIVE

excrete (ɪkˈskri:t) VERB [1] to discharge (waste matter, such as urine, sweat, carbon dioxide, or faeces) from the body through the kidneys, skin, lungs, bowels, etc. [2] (of plants) to eliminate (waste matter, such as carbon dioxide and salts) through the leaves, roots, etc.
▷HISTORY C17: from Latin *excernere* to separate, discharge, from *cernere* to sift
▸**ex'creter** NOUN ▸**ex'cretion** NOUN ▸**ex'cretive** *or* **ex'cretory** ADJECTIVE

excruciate (ɪkˈskru:ʃɪˌeɪt) VERB (*tr*) [1] to inflict mental suffering on; torment. [2] *Obsolete* to inflict physical pain on; torture.
▷HISTORY C16: from Latin *excruciāre,* from *cruciāre* to crucify, from *crux* cross
▸**exˌcruci'ation** NOUN

excruciating (ɪkˈskru:ʃɪˌeɪtɪŋ) ADJECTIVE [1] unbearably painful; agonizing. [2] intense; extreme: *he took excruciating pains to do it well.* [3] *Informal* irritating; trying. [4] *Humorous* very bad: *an excruciating pun.*
▸**ex'cruciˌatingly** ADVERB

exculpate (ˈɛkskʌlˌpeɪt, ɪkˈskʌlpeɪt) VERB (*tr*) to free from blame or guilt; vindicate or exonerate.
▷HISTORY C17: from Medieval Latin *exculpāre,* from Latin EX-[1] + *culpāre* to blame, from *culpa* fault, blame
▸**exculpable** (ɪkˈskʌlpəbᵊl) ADJECTIVE ▸**ˌexcul'pation** NOUN ▸**ex'culpatory** ADJECTIVE

excurrent (ɛkˈskʌrənt) ADJECTIVE [1] *Zoology* having an outward flow, as certain pores in sponges, ducts, etc. [2] *Botany* **a** (of veins) extending beyond the margin of the leaf. **b** having an undivided main stem or trunk, as the spruce and other conifers. [3] flowing or running in an outward direction.
▷HISTORY C19: from Latin *excurrere* to run forth; see EXCURSION

excursion (ɪkˈskɜ:ʃən, -ʒən) NOUN [1] a short outward and return journey, esp for relaxation, sightseeing, etc.; outing. [2] a group of people going on such a journey. [3] (*modifier*) of or relating to special reduced rates offered on certain journeys by rail: *an excursion ticket.* [4] a digression or deviation; diversion: *an excursion into politics.* [5] (formerly) a raid or attack. [6] *Physics* **a** a movement from an equilibrium position, as in an oscillation. **b** the magnitude of this displacement. [7] the normal movement of a movable bodily organ or part from its resting position, such as the lateral movement of the lower jaw. [8] *Machinery* the locus of a point on a moving part, esp the deflection of a whirling shaft.
▷HISTORY C16: from Latin *excursiō* an attack, from *excurrere* to run out, from *currere* to run

excursionist (ɪkˈskɜ:ʃənɪst, -ʒənɪst) NOUN a person who goes on an excursion.

excursive (ɪkˈskɜ:sɪv) ADJECTIVE [1] tending to digress. [2] involving detours; rambling.
▷HISTORY C17: from Latin *excursus,* from *excurrere* to run forth
▸**ex'cursively** ADVERB ▸**ex'cursiveness** NOUN

excursus (ɛkˈskɜ:səs) NOUN, *plural* **-suses** *or* **-sus.** an incidental digression from the main topic under discussion or from the main story in a narrative.
▷HISTORY C19: from Latin: a running forth, from *excurrere* to run out

excusatory (ɪkˈskju:zətərɪ, -trɪ) ADJECTIVE tending to or intended to excuse; apologetic.

excuse VERB (ɪkˈskju:z) (*tr*) [1] to pardon or forgive: *he always excuses her unpunctuality.* [2] to seek pardon or exemption for (a person, esp oneself): *to excuse oneself for one's mistakes.* [3] to make allowances for; judge leniently: *to excuse someone's ignorance.* [4] to serve as an apology or explanation for; vindicate or justify: *her age excuses her behaviour.* [5] to exempt from a task, obligation, etc.: *you are excused making breakfast.* [6] to dismiss or allow to leave: *he asked them to excuse him.* [7] to seek permission for (someone, esp oneself) to leave: *he excused himself and left.* [8] **be excused.** *Euphemistic* to go to the lavatory. [9] **excuse me!** an expression used to catch someone's attention or to apologize for an interruption, disagreement, or social indiscretion. ◆ NOUN (ɪkˈskju:s) [10] an explanation offered in defence of some fault or offensive behaviour or as a reason for not fulfilling an obligation, etc.: *he gave no excuse for his rudeness.* [11] *Informal* an inferior example of something specified; makeshift substitute: *she is a poor excuse for a hostess.* [12] the act of excusing.
▷HISTORY C13: from Latin *excūsāre,* from EX-[1] + *-cūsāre,* from *causa* cause, accusation
▸**ex'cusable** ADJECTIVE ▸**ex'cusableness** NOUN ▸**ex'cusably** ADVERB

excuse-me NOUN a dance in which a person may take another's partner.

ex-directory ADJECTIVE *Chiefly Brit* not listed in a telephone directory, by request, and not disclosed to inquirers. US and Canadian term: **unlisted.**

ex div. ABBREVIATION FOR ex dividend.

ex dividend ADVERB without the right to the current dividend: *to quote shares ex dividend.* Compare **cum dividend.**

exeat (ˈɛksɪət) NOUN *Brit* [1] leave of absence from school or some other institution. [2] a bishop's permission for a priest to leave his diocese in order to take up an appointment elsewhere.
▷HISTORY C18: Latin, literally: he may go out, from *exīre*

exec. ABBREVIATION FOR: [1] executive. [2] executor.

execrable (ˈɛksɪkrəbᵊl) ADJECTIVE [1] deserving to be execrated; abhorrent. [2] of very poor quality: *an execrable meal.*
▷HISTORY C14: from Latin *exsecrābilis,* from *exsecrārī* to EXECRATE
▸**'execrableness** NOUN ▸**'execrably** ADVERB

execrate (ˈɛksɪˌkreɪt) VERB [1] (*tr*) to loathe; detest; abhor. [2] (*tr*) to profess great abhorrence for; denounce; deplore. [3] to curse (a person or thing); damn.
▷HISTORY C16: from Latin *exsecrārī* to curse, from EX-[1] + *-secrārī* from *sacer* SACRED
▸**ˌexe'cration** NOUN ▸**'exeˌcrative** *or* **'exeˌcratory** ADJECTIVE ▸**'exeˌcratively** ADVERB

executant (ɪgˈzɛkjʊtənt) NOUN a performer, esp of musical works.

executary (ɪgˈzɛkjʊtrɪ) NOUN, *plural* **-aries.** a person whose job comprises tasks appropriate to a middle-management executive as well as those traditionally carried out by a secretary.
▷HISTORY C20: from EXECU(TIVE) + (SECRE)TARY

execute (ˈɛksɪˌkju:t) VERB (*tr*) [1] to put (a condemned person) to death; inflict capital punishment upon. [2] to carry out; complete; perform; do: *to execute an order.* [3] to perform; accomplish; effect: *to execute a pirouette.* [4] to make or produce: *to execute a drawing.* [5] to carry into effect (a judicial sentence, the law, etc.); enforce. [6] *Law* to comply with legal formalities in order to render (a deed, etc.) effective, as by signing, sealing, and delivering. [7] to sign (a will) in the presence of witnesses and in accordance with other legal formalities. [8] to carry out the terms of (a contract, will, etc.).
▷HISTORY C14: from Old French *executer,* back formation from *executeur* EXECUTOR
▸**'exeˌcutable** ADJECTIVE ▸**'exeˌcuter** NOUN

execution (ˌɛksɪˈkju:ʃən) NOUN [1] the act or process of executing. [2] the carrying out or undergoing of a sentence of death. [3] the style or manner in which something is accomplished or performed; technique: *as a pianist his execution is poor.* [4] **a** the enforcement of the judgment of a court of law. **b** the writ ordering such enforcement.

executioner (ˌɛksɪˈkju:ʃənə) NOUN [1] an official charged with carrying out the death sentence passed upon a condemned person. [2] an assassin, esp one appointed by a political or criminal organization.

executive (ɪgˈzɛkjʊtɪv) NOUN [1] **a** a person or group responsible for the administration of a project, activity, or business. **b** (*as modifier*): *executive duties; an executive position.* [2] **a** the branch of government responsible for carrying out laws, decrees, etc.; administration. **b** any administration. Compare **judiciary, legislature.** ◆ ADJECTIVE [3] having the function or purpose of carrying plans, orders, laws, etc., into practical effect. [4] of, relating to, or designed for an executive: *the executive suite.* [5] *Informal* of the most expensive or exclusive type: *executive housing; executive class.*
▸**ex'ecutively** ADVERB

Executive Council NOUN (in Australia and New Zealand) a body consisting of ministers of the Crown presided over by the Governor or Governor-General that formally approves Cabinet decisions, etc.

executive director NOUN a member of the board of directors of a company who is also an employee (usually full-time) of that company and who often has a specified area of responsibility, such as finance or production. Compare **nonexecutive director.**

executive officer NOUN [1] the second-in-command of any of certain military units. Abbreviation: *US* **XO.** [2] a specialist seaman officer, responsible under the captain for the routine efficient running of the ship in the US, British (formerly), and certain other navies.

executive session NOUN *US government* a session of the Senate for the discussion of executive business, such as the ratification of treaties: formerly held in secret.

executor (ɪɡˈzɛkjʊtə) NOUN [1] *Law* a person appointed by a testator to carry out the wishes expressed in his will. [2] a person who executes.
▷HISTORY C13: from Anglo-French *executour,* from Latin *execūtor,* from EX-[1] + *sequi* follow
▸**ex,ecu'torial** ADJECTIVE ▸**ex'ecutor,ship** NOUN

executory (ɪɡˈzɛkjʊtərɪ, -trɪ) ADJECTIVE [1] (of a law, agreement, etc.) coming into operation at a future date; not yet effective: *an executory contract.* [2] executive; administrative.

executrix (ɪɡˈzɛkjʊtrɪks) NOUN, *plural* **executrices** (ɪɡˌzɛkjʊˈtraɪsiːz) *or* **executrixes.** *Law* a female executor.

exedra (ˈɛksɪdrə, ɛkˈsiː-) NOUN [1] a building, room, portico, or apse containing a continuous bench, used in ancient Greece and Rome for holding discussions. [2] an outdoor bench in a recess.
▷HISTORY C18: via Latin from Greek, from *hedra* seat

exegesis (ˌɛksɪˈdʒiːsɪs) NOUN, *plural* **-ses** (-siːz). explanation or critical interpretation of a text, esp of the Bible. Compare **eisegesis.**
▷HISTORY C17: from Greek, from *exēgeisthai* to interpret, from EX-[1] + *hēgeisthai* to guide

exegete (ˈɛksɪˌdʒiːt) *or* **exegetist** (ˌɛksɪˈdʒiːtɪst, -ˈdʒɛt-) NOUN a person who practises exegesis.
▷HISTORY C18: from Greek *exēgētēs,* from *exēgeisthai* to interpret; see EXEGESIS

exegetic (ˌɛksɪˈdʒɛtɪk) *or* **exegetical** ADJECTIVE of or relating to exegesis; expository.
▸**ˌexe'getically** ADVERB

exegetics (ˌɛksɪˈdʒɛtɪks) NOUN (*functioning as singular*) the scientific study of exegesis and exegetical methods.

exemplar (ɪɡˈzɛmplə, -plɑː) NOUN [1] a person or thing to be copied or imitated; model. [2] a typical specimen or instance; example. [3] a copy of a book or text on which further printings have been based.
▷HISTORY C14: from Latin *exemplarium* model, from *exemplum* EXAMPLE

exemplary (ɪɡˈzɛmplərɪ) ADJECTIVE [1] fit for imitation; model: *an exemplary performance.* [2] serving as a warning; admonitory: *an exemplary jail sentence.* [3] representative; typical: *an action exemplary of his conduct.*
▸**ex'emplarily** ADVERB ▸**ex'emplariness** NOUN

exemplary damages PLURAL NOUN *Law* damages awarded to a plaintiff above the value of actual loss sustained so that they serve also as a punishment to the defendant and a deterrent to others.

exemplify (ɪɡˈzɛmplɪˌfaɪ) VERB **-fies, -fying, -fied.** (*tr*) [1] to show by example. [2] to serve as an example of. [3] *Law* **a** to make an official copy of (a document from public records) under seal. **b** to transcribe (a legal document).
▷HISTORY C15: via Old French from Medieval Latin *exemplificāre,* from Latin *exemplum* EXAMPLE + *facere* to make
▸**ex'empli,fiable** ADJECTIVE ▸**ex,emplifi'cation** NOUN ▸**ex'emplifi,cative** ADJECTIVE ▸**ex'empli,fier** NOUN

exempli gratia *Latin* (ɪɡˈzɛmplaɪ ˈɡrɑːtɪˌɑː) for the sake of example. Abbreviations: **e.g., eg.**

exemplum (ɪɡˈzɛmpləm) NOUN, *plural* **-pla** (-plə). [1] an anecdote that supports a moral point or sustains an argument, used esp in medieval sermons. [2] an example or illustration.
▷HISTORY from Latin: EXAMPLE

exempt (ɪɡˈzɛmpt) VERB [1] (*tr*) to release from an obligation, liability, tax, etc.; excuse: *to exempt a soldier from drill.* ◆ ADJECTIVE (*sometimes postpositive*) [2] freed from or not subject to an obligation, liability, tax, etc.; excused: *exempt gilts; tax-exempt bonus.* [3] *Obsolete* set apart; remote. ◆ NOUN [4] a person who is exempt from an obligation, tax, etc.
▷HISTORY C14: from Latin *exemptus* removed, from *eximere* to take out, from *emere* to buy, obtain
▸**ex'emption** NOUN

exenterate VERB (ɪɡˈzɛntəˌreɪt) (*tr*) [1] *Surgery* to remove (internal organs, an eyeball, etc.); eviscerate. [2] a rare word for **disembowel.** ◆ ADJECTIVE (ɪɡˈzɛntəˌreɪt, -rɪt) [3] *Rare* having been disembowelled.
▷HISTORY C17: from Latin *exenterāre,* from EX-[1] + Greek *enteron* intestine
▸**ex,enter'ation** NOUN

exequatur (ˌɛksɪˈkweɪtə) NOUN [1] an official authorization issued by a host country to a consular agent, permitting him to perform his official duties. [2] an act by which the civil governments of certain nations permit the laws of the Roman Catholic Church to take effect in their territories.
▷HISTORY C18: from Latin, literally: let him perform, from *exequī* to perform, from EX-[1] + *sequī* to follow

exequies (ˈɛksɪkwɪz) PLURAL NOUN, *singular* **-quy.** the rites and ceremonies used at funerals.
▷HISTORY C14: from Latin *exequiae* (plural) funeral procession, rites, from *exequī* to follow to the end, from *sequī* to follow

exercise (ˈɛksəˌsaɪz) VERB (*mainly tr*) [1] to put into use; employ: *to exercise tact.* [2] (*intr*) to take exercise or perform exercises; exert one's muscles, etc., esp in order to keep fit. [3] to practise using in order to develop or train: *to exercise one's voice.* [4] to perform or make proper use of: *to exercise one's rights.* [5] to bring to bear; exert: *to exercise one's influence.* [6] (*often passive*) to occupy the attentions of, esp so as to worry or vex: *to be exercised about a decision.* [7] *Military* to carry out or cause to carry out, manoeuvres, simulated combat operations, etc. ◆ NOUN [8] physical exertion, esp for the purpose of development, training, or keeping fit. [9] mental or other activity or practice, esp in order to develop a skill. [10] a set of movements, questions, tasks, etc., designed to train, improve, or test one's ability in a particular field: *piano exercises.* [11] a performance or work of art done as practice or to demonstrate a technique. [12] the performance of a function; discharge: *the exercise of one's rights; the object of the exercise is to win.* [13] (*sometimes plural*) *Military* a manoeuvre or simulated combat operation carried out for training and evaluation. [14] (*usually plural*) *US and Canadian* a ceremony or formal routine, esp at a school or college: *opening exercises; graduation exercises.* [15] *Gymnastics* a particular type of event, such as performing on the horizontal bar.
▷HISTORY C14: from Old French *exercice,* from Latin *exercitium,* from *exercēre* to drill, from EX-[1] + *arcēre* to ward off
▸**'exer,cisable** ADJECTIVE

exercise bike *or* **cycle** NOUN a stationary exercise machine that is pedalled like a bicycle as a method of increasing cardiovascular fitness.

exercise book NOUN a notebook used by pupils and students.

exercise price NOUN *Stock Exchange* the price at which the holder of a traded option may exercise his right to buy (or sell) a security.

exerciser (ˈɛksəˌsaɪzə) NOUN [1] a device with springs or elasticated cords for muscular exercise. [2] a person or thing that exercises.

exercitation (ɪɡˌzɜːsɪˈteɪʃən) NOUN a rare word for **exercise.**
▷HISTORY C14: from Latin *exercitātiō,* from *exercitāre* frequentative of *exercēre* to EXERCISE

exergonic (ˌɛksəˈɡɒnɪk) ADJECTIVE (of a biochemical reaction) producing energy and therefore occurring spontaneously. Compare **endergonic.**
▷HISTORY C20: from EX(O)- + Greek *ergon* work + -IC

exergue (ɛkˈsɜːɡ) NOUN a space on the reverse of a coin or medal below the central design, often containing the date, place of minting, etc.
▷HISTORY C17: from French, from Medieval Latin *exergum,* from Greek *ex* outside + *ergon* work
▸**ex'ergual** ADJECTIVE

exert (ɪɡˈzɜːt) VERB (*tr*) [1] to use (influence, authority, etc.) forcefully or effectively. [2] to apply (oneself) diligently; make a strenuous effort.
▷HISTORY C17 (in the sense: push forth, emit): from Latin *exserere* to thrust out, from EX-[1] + *serere* to bind together, entwine
▸**ex'ertion** NOUN ▸**ex'ertive** ADJECTIVE

Exeter (ˈɛksɪtə) NOUN a city in SW England, administrative centre of Devon; university (1955). Pop.: 94 717 (1991).

exeunt *Latin* (ˈɛksɪˌʌnt) they go out: used as a stage direction.

exeunt omnes *Latin* (ˈɛksɪˌʌnt ˈɒmneɪz) they all go out: used as a stage direction.

exfoliate (ɛksˈfəʊlɪˌeɪt) VERB [1] (of bark, skin, etc.) to peel off in (layers, flakes, or scales). [2] (*intr*) (of rocks or minerals) to shed the thin outermost layer because of weathering or heating. [3] (of some minerals, esp mica) to split or cause to split into thin flakes: *a factory to exfoliate vermiculite.*
▷HISTORY C17: from Late Latin *exfoliāre* to strip off leaves, from Latin *folium* leaf
▸**ex,foli'ation** NOUN ▸**ex'foliative** ADJECTIVE

ex gratia (ˈɡreɪʃə) ADJECTIVE given as a favour or gratuitously where no legal obligation exists: *an ex gratia payment.*
▷HISTORY New Latin, literally: out of kindness

exhalant (ɛksˈheɪlənt, ɪɡˈzeɪ-) ADJECTIVE [1] emitting a vapour or liquid; exhaling: *an exhalant siphon; exhalant duct.* ◆ NOUN [2] an organ or vessel that emits a vapour or liquid.

exhale (ɛksˈheɪl, ɪɡˈzeɪl) VERB [1] to expel (breath, tobacco smoke, etc.) from the lungs; breathe out. [2] to give off (air, vapour, fumes, etc.) or (of air, vapour, etc.) to be given off; emanate.
▷HISTORY C14: from Latin *exhālāre* to breathe out, from *hālāre* to breathe
▸**ex'halable** ADJECTIVE ▸**ˌexha'lation** NOUN

exhaust (ɪɡˈzɔːst) VERB (*mainly tr*) [1] to drain the energy of; tire out: *to exhaust someone by constant questioning.* [2] to deprive of resources, etc.: *a nation exhausted by war.* [3] to deplete totally; expend; consume: *to exhaust food supplies.* [4] to empty (a container) by drawing off or pumping out (the contents). [5] to develop or discuss thoroughly so that no further interest remains: *to exhaust a topic of conversation.* [6] to remove gas from (a vessel, etc.) in order to reduce the pressure or create a vacuum; evacuate. [7] to remove or use up the active ingredients from (a drug, solution, etc.). [8] to destroy the fertility of (soil) by excessive cultivation. [9] (*intr*) (of steam or other gases) to be emitted or to escape from an engine after being expanded. ◆ NOUN [10] gases ejected from an engine as waste products. [11] **a** the expulsion of expanded gas or steam from an engine. **b** (*as modifier*): *exhaust stroke.* [12] **a** the parts of an engine through which the exhausted gases or steam pass. **b** (*as modifier*): *exhaust valve; exhaust pipe.*
▷HISTORY C16: from Latin *exhaustus* made empty, from *exhaurīre* to draw out, from *haurīre* to draw, drain
▸**ex'hausted** ADJECTIVE ▸**ex'hauster** NOUN ▸**ex'haustible** ADJECTIVE ▸**ex,hausti'bility** NOUN ▸**ex'hausting** ADJECTIVE

exhaustion (ɪɡˈzɔːstʃən) NOUN [1] extreme tiredness; fatigue. [2] the condition of being used up; consumption: *exhaustion of the earth's resources.* [3] the act of exhausting or the state of being exhausted.

exhaustive (ɪɡˈzɔːstɪv) ADJECTIVE [1] comprehensive in scope; thorough: *an exhaustive survey.* [2] tending to exhaust.
▸**ex'haustively** ADVERB ▸**ex'haustiveness** NOUN

exhaust stroke NOUN another name for **scavenge stroke.**

exhibit (ɪɡˈzɪbɪt) VERB (*mainly tr*) [1] (*also intr*) to display (something) to the public for interest or instruction: *this artist exhibits all over the world.* [2] to manifest; display; show: *the child exhibited signs of distress.* [3] *Law* to produce (a document or object) in court to serve as evidence. ◆ NOUN [4] an object or collection exhibited to the public. [5] *Law* a document or object produced in court and referred to or identified by a witness in giving evidence.

▷HISTORY C15: from Latin *exhibēre* to hold forth, from *habēre* to have
▸**ex'hibitory** ADJECTIVE

exhibition (ˌɛksɪˈbɪʃən) NOUN [1] a public display of art, products, skills, activities, etc.: *a judo exhibition.* [2] the act of exhibiting or the state of being exhibited. [3] **make an exhibition of oneself.** to behave so foolishly in public that one excites notice or ridicule. [4] *Brit* an allowance or scholarship awarded to a student at a university or school.

exhibitioner (ˌɛksɪˈbɪʃənə) NOUN *Brit* a student who has been awarded an exhibition.

exhibitionism (ˌɛksɪˈbɪʃəˌnɪzəm) NOUN [1] a compulsive desire to attract attention to oneself, esp by absurd or exaggerated behaviour or boasting. [2] *Psychiatry* a compulsive desire to expose one's genital organs publicly.
▸**ˌexhi'bitionist** NOUN, ADJECTIVE ▸**ˌexhiˌbition'istic** ADJECTIVE

exhibitive (ɪgˈzɪbɪtɪv) ADJECTIVE (*usually postpositive and foll by of*) illustrative or demonstrative: *a masterpiece exhibitive of his talent.*
▸**ex'hibitively** ADVERB

exhibitor (ɪgˈzɪbɪtə) NOUN [1] a person or thing that exhibits. [2] an individual or company that shows films, esp the manager or owner of a cinema.

exhilarant (ɪgˈzɪlərənt) ADJECTIVE [1] exhilarating; invigorating. ◆ NOUN [2] something that exhilarates.

exhilarate (ɪgˈzɪləˌreɪt) VERB (*tr*) to make lively and cheerful; gladden; elate.
▷HISTORY C16: from Latin *exhilarāre*, from *hilarāre* to cheer; see HILARIOUS
▸**exˌhila'ration** NOUN ▸**ex'hilarative** *or* **ex'hilaratory** ADJECTIVE

exhilarating (ɪgˈzɪləˌreɪtɪŋ) ADJECTIVE causing strong feelings of excitement and happiness: *an exhilarating helicopter trip.*
▸**ex'hilaˌratingly** ADVERB

exhort (ɪgˈzɔːt) VERB to urge or persuade (someone) earnestly; advise strongly.
▷HISTORY C14: from Latin *exhortārī*, from *hortārī* to urge
▸**exhortative** (ɪgˈzɔːtətɪv) *or* **ex'hortatory** ADJECTIVE
▸**ex'horter** NOUN

exhortation (ˌɛgzɔːˈteɪʃən) NOUN [1] the act or process of exhorting. [2] a speech or written passage intended to persuade, inspire, or encourage.

exhume (ɛksˈhjuːm) VERB (*tr*) [1] to dig up (something buried, esp a corpse); disinter. [2] to reveal; disclose; unearth: *don't exhume that old argument.*
▷HISTORY C18: from Medieval Latin *exhumāre*, from Latin EX-[1] + *humāre* to bury, from *humus* the ground
▸**exhumation** (ˌɛkshjʊˈmeɪʃən) NOUN ▸**ex'humer** NOUN

ex hypothesi (ɛks haɪˈpɒθəsɪ) ADVERB in accordance with or following from the hypothesis stated.
▷HISTORY C17: New Latin

exigency (ˈɛksɪdʒənsɪ, ɪgˈzɪdʒənsɪ) *or* **exigence** (ˈɛksɪdʒəns) NOUN, *plural* **-gencies** *or* **-gences.** [1] the state of being exigent; urgency. [2] (*often plural*) an urgent demand; pressing requirement. [3] an emergency.

exigent (ˈɛksɪdʒənt) ADJECTIVE [1] urgent; pressing. [2] exacting; demanding.
▷HISTORY C15: from Latin *exigere* to drive out, weigh out, from *agere* to drive, compel
▸**'exigently** ADVERB

exigible (ˈɛksɪdʒəbᵊl) ADJECTIVE liable to be exacted or required: *part of the debt is exigible this month.*
▷HISTORY C17: from French, from *exiger* to demand, from Latin *exigere*; see EXIGENT

exiguous (ɪgˈzɪgjʊəs, ɪkˈsɪg-) ADJECTIVE scanty or slender; meagre: *an exiguous income.*
▷HISTORY C17: from Latin *exiguus*, from *exigere* to weigh out; see EXIGENT
▸**exiguity** (ˌɛksɪˈgjuːɪtɪ) *or* **ex'iguousness** NOUN
▸**ex'iguously** ADVERB

exile (ˈɛgzaɪl, ˈɛksaɪl) NOUN [1] a prolonged, usually enforced absence from one's home or country; banishment. [2] the expulsion of a person from his native land by official decree. [3] a person banished or living away from his home or country; expatriate. ◆ VERB [4] to expel from home or country, esp by official decree as a punishment; banish.
▷HISTORY C13: from Latin *exsilium* banishment, from *exsul* banished person; perhaps related to Greek *alasthai* to wander
▸**exilic** (ɛgˈzɪlɪk, ɛkˈsɪlɪk) *or* **ex'ilian** ADJECTIVE

Exile (ˈɛgzaɪl, ˈɛksaɪl) NOUN **the.** another name for the **Babylonian captivity** (of the Jews).

eximious (ɛgˈzɪmɪəs) ADJECTIVE *Rare* select and distinguished; eminent.
▷HISTORY C16: from Latin *eximius*, from *eximere* to take out, from *emere* to purchase
▸**ex'imiously** ADVERB

exine (ˈɛksɪn, -aɪn) *or* **extine** (ˈɛkstɪn, -tiːn, -taɪn) NOUN *Botany* the outermost coat of a pollen grain or a spore. Compare **intine.**

exist (ɪgˈzɪst) VERB (*intr*) [1] to have being or reality; to be. [2] to eke out a living; stay alive; survive: *he could barely exist on such a low wage.* [3] to be living; live. [4] to be present under specified conditions or in a specified place: *sharks exist in the Pacific.* [5] *Philosophy* **a** to be actual rather than merely possible. **b** to be a member of the domain of some theory, an element of some possible world, etc. **c** to have contingent being while free, responsible, and aware of one's situation.
▷HISTORY C17: from Latin *exsistere* to step forth, from EX-[1] + *sistere* to stand
▸**ex'isting** ADJECTIVE

existence (ɪgˈzɪstəns) NOUN [1] the fact or state of existing; being. [2] the continuance or maintenance of life; living, esp in adverse circumstances: *a struggle for existence; she has a wretched existence.* [3] something that exists; a being or entity. [4] everything that exists, esp that is living.

existent (ɪgˈzɪstənt) ADJECTIVE [1] in existence; extant; current. [2] having existence; living. ◆ NOUN [3] a person or a thing that exists.

existential (ˌɛgzɪˈstɛnʃəl) ADJECTIVE [1] of or relating to existence, esp human existence. [2] *Philosophy* pertaining to what exists, and is thus known by experience rather than reason; empirical as opposed to theoretical. [3] *Logic* denoting or relating to a formula or proposition asserting the existence of at least one object fulfilling a given condition; containing an existential quantifier. [4] of or relating to existentialism. ◆ NOUN *Logic* [5] **a** an existential statement or formula. **b** short for **existential quantifier.**
▸**ˌexis'tentially** ADVERB

existentialism (ˌɛgzɪˈstɛnʃəˌlɪzəm) NOUN a modern philosophical movement stressing the importance of personal experience and responsibility and the demands that they make on the individual, who is seen as a free agent in a deterministic and seemingly meaningless universe.
▸**ˌexis'tentialist** ADJECTIVE, NOUN

existential quantifier NOUN *Logic* a formal device, for which the conventional symbol is ∃, which indicates that the open sentence that follows is true of at least one member of the relevant universe of interpretation, as $(\exists x)\ Fx$ meaning "something is (an) F," "something Fs," or "there are (some) Fs.".

exit (ˈɛgzɪt, ˈɛksɪt) NOUN [1] a way out; door or gate by which people may leave. [2] the act or an instance of going out; departure. [3] **a** the act of leaving or right to leave a particular place. **b** (*as modifier*): *an exit visa.* [4] departure from life; death. [5] *Theatre* the act of going offstage. [6] (in Britain) a point at which vehicles may leave or join a motorway. [7] *Bridge* **a** the act of losing the lead deliberately. **b** a card enabling one to do this. ◆ VERB (*intr*) [8] to go away or out; depart; leave. [9] *Theatre* to go offstage: used as a stage direction: *exit Hamlet.* [10] *Bridge* to lose the lead deliberately. [11] (*sometimes tr*) *Computing* to leave (a computer program or system).
▷HISTORY C17: from Latin *exitus* a departure, from *exīre* to go out, from EX-[1] + *īre* to go

Exit (ˈɛgzɪt, ˈɛksɪt) NOUN (in Britain) a society that seeks to promote the legitimization of voluntary euthanasia.

exitance (ˈɛksɪtəns) NOUN a measure of the ability of a surface to emit radiation. See **luminous exitance, radiant exitance.**

exit poll NOUN a poll taken by an organization by asking people how they voted in an election as they leave a polling station.

exit pupil NOUN the smallest cross section of the beam of light from the eyepiece of a telescope through which all the light from the eyepiece passes. Its diameter is equal to the ratio of the focal length of the eyepiece to the focal ratio of the telescope.

exit strategy NOUN a method or plan for extricating oneself from an undesirable situation.

ex lib. ABBREVIATION FOR ex libris.

ex libris (ɛks ˈliːbrɪs) ADJECTIVE [1] from the collection or library of: frequently printed on bookplates. ◆ NOUN **ex-libris.** [2] a bookplate bearing the owner's name, coat of arms, etc.
▷HISTORY C19: from Latin, literally: from the books (of)

Exmoor (ˈɛksˌmʊə, -ˌmɔː) NOUN [1] a high moorland in SW England, in W Somerset and N Devon: chiefly grazing ground for Exmoor ponies, sheep, and red deer. [2] a small stocky breed of pony with a fawn-coloured nose, originally from Exmoor.

Exmouth (ˈɛksməθ) NOUN a town in SW England, in Devon, at the mouth of the River Exe: tourism, fishing. Pop.: 28 414 (1991).

ex new ADVERB, ADJECTIVE (of shares, etc.) without the right to take up any scrip issue or rights issue. Compare **cum new.**

exo (ˈɛksəʊ) ADJECTIVE *Austral* an informal word for **excellent.**

exo- COMBINING FORM external, outside, or beyond: *exobiology; exothermal.*
▷HISTORY from Greek *exō* outside

exobiology (ˌɛksəʊbaɪˈɒlədʒɪ) NOUN another name for **astrobiology.**
▸**ˌexobi'ologist** NOUN

exocarp (ˈɛksəʊˌkɑːp) NOUN another name for **epicarp.**

exocentric (ˌɛksəʊˈsɛntrɪk) ADJECTIVE *Grammar* (of a construction) not fulfilling the grammatical role of any of its constituents; as in *until last Easter*, where the constituents are prepositional, adjectival, and nominal, while the whole construction is adverbial. Compare **endocentric.**

Exocet (ˈɛksəʊsɛt) NOUN *Trademark* a tactical missile with a high-explosive warhead, which is guided by computer and radar, travels at a very low altitude at high subsonic speed, and has a range of up to 70 km. It may be launched from a ship, aircraft, or submarine.
▷HISTORY C20: from French, from New Latin *Exocoetus volitans* flying fish

exocrine (ˈɛksəʊˌkraɪn, -krɪn) ADJECTIVE [1] of or relating to exocrine glands or their secretions. ◆ NOUN [2] an exocrine gland. ◆ Compare **endocrine.**
▷HISTORY C20: EXO- + *-crine* from Greek *krinein* to separate

exocrine gland NOUN any gland, such as a salivary or sweat gland, that secretes its products through a duct onto an epithelial surface.

exocuticle (ˈɛksəʊˌkjuːtɪkᵊl) NOUN the layer of an insect's cuticle between the epicuticle and the endocuticle, which is often hard and dark in colour.

exocytosis (ˌɛksəʊsaɪˈtəʊsɪs) NOUN a process by which material is exported from a biological cell.

Exod. *Bible* ABBREVIATION FOR Exodus.

exoderm (ˈɛksəʊˌdɜːm) NOUN *Embryol* another name for **ectoderm.**

exodontics (ˌɛksəʊˈdɒntɪks) NOUN (*functioning as singular*) the branch of dental surgery concerned with the extraction of teeth. Also called: **exodontia** (ˌɛksəʊˈdɒnʃə).
▷HISTORY C20: New Latin, from EX-[1] + *-odontia*, from Greek *odōn* tooth
▸**ˌexo'dontist** NOUN

exodus (ˈɛksədəs) NOUN the act or an instance of going out.
▷HISTORY C17: via Latin from Greek *exodos* from EX-[1] + *hodos* way

Exodus (ˈɛksədəs) NOUN [1] **the.** the departure of the Israelites from Egypt led by Moses. [2] the second book of the Old Testament, recounting the events connected with this and the divine visitation of Moses at Mount Sinai.

exoenzyme (ˌɛksəʊˈɛnzaɪm) NOUN [1] any enzyme, esp an exopeptidase, that acts upon terminal chemical bonds in a chain of molecules.

Compare **endoenzyme.** [2] another name for **ectoenzyme.**

exoergic (ˌɛksəʊˈɜːdʒɪk) ADJECTIVE (of a nuclear reaction) occurring with evolution of energy. Compare **endoergic, exothermic.**
▷HISTORY EXO- + *-ergic,* from Greek *ergon* work

ex off. ABBREVIATION FOR ex officio.

ex officio (ˈɛks əˈfɪʃɪəʊ, əˈfɪsɪəʊ) ADVERB, ADJECTIVE by right of position or office. Abbreviation: **ex off.**
▷HISTORY Latin

exogamy (ɛkˈsɒgəmɪ) NOUN [1] *Sociol, anthropol* the custom or an act of marrying a person belonging to another tribe, clan, or similar social unit. Compare **endogamy.** [2] *Biology* fusion of gametes from parents that are not closely related.
▸**exogamous** (ɛkˈsɒgəməs) *or* **exogamic** (ˌɛksəʊˈgæmɪk) ADJECTIVE

exogenous (ɛkˈsɒdʒɪnəs) ADJECTIVE [1] having an external origin. [2] *Biology* **a** developing or originating outside an organism or part of an organism. **b** of or relating to external factors, such as light, that influence an organism. [3] *Psychiatry* (of a mental illness) caused by external factors.
▸**exˈogenously** ADVERB

exon[1] (ˈɛksɒn) NOUN *Brit* one of the four officers who command the Yeomen of the Guard.
▷HISTORY C17: a pronunciation spelling of French *exempt* EXEMPT

exon[2] (ˈɛksɒn) NOUN any segment of a discontinuous gene the segments of which are separated by introns. Compare **intron.**
▷HISTORY C20: from EX-[1] + -ON
▸**exˈonic** ADJECTIVE

exonerate (ɪgˈzɒnəˌreɪt) VERB (*tr*) [1] to clear or absolve from blame or a criminal charge. [2] to relieve from an obligation or task; exempt.
▷HISTORY C16: from Latin *exonerāre* to free from a burden, from *onus* a burden
▸**exˌonerˈation** NOUN ▸**exˈonerative** ADJECTIVE
▸**exˈonerˌator** NOUN

exonuclease (ˌɛksəʊˈnjuːklɪˌeɪz) NOUN an enzyme that is capable of detaching the terminal nucleotide from a nucleic acid chain. Compare **endonuclease.**

exonym (ˈɛksəˌnɪm) NOUN a name given to a place by foreigners: *Londres is an exonym of London.*
▷HISTORY C20: from Greek EX-[1] + -ONYM

exoparasite (ˌɛksəʊˈpærəˌsaɪt) NOUN another word for **ectoparasite.**
▸**exoparasitic** (ˌɛksəʊˌpærəˈsɪtɪk) ADJECTIVE

exopeptidase (ˌɛksəʊˈpɛptɪˌdeɪz) NOUN any proteolytic enzyme, such as erepsin, that acts on the terminal bonds in a peptide chain. Compare **endopeptidase.**

exophoric (ˌɛksəʊˈfɒrɪk) ADJECTIVE *Grammar* denoting or relating to a pronoun such as "I" or "you", the meaning of which is determined by reference outside the discourse rather than by a preceding or following expression. Compare **anaphora.**
▷HISTORY from EXO- + Greek *pherein* to carry

exophthalmic goitre NOUN a form of hyperthyroidism characterized by enlargement of the thyroid gland, protrusion of the eyeballs, increased basal metabolic rate, and weight loss. Also called: **Graves' disease.**

exophthalmos (ˌɛksɒfˈθælmɒs), **exophthalmus** (ˌɛksɒfˈθælməs), *or* **exophthalmia** (ˌɛksɒfˈθælmɪə) NOUN abnormal protrusion of the eyeball, as caused by hyperthyroidism. Also called: **proptosis, ocular proptosis.**
▷HISTORY C19: via New Latin from Greek, from EX-[1] + *ophthalmos* eye
▸**ˌexophˈthalmic** ADJECTIVE

exoplanet (ˈɛksəʊˌplænɪt) NOUN a planet that orbits a star in a solar system other than that of Earth.

exoplasm (ˈɛksəʊˌplæzəm) NOUN another name for **ectoplasm.**

exor. (ˈɛksɔː) *Brit* ABBREVIATION FOR executor.

exorable (ˈɛksərəbᵊl) ADJECTIVE able to be persuaded or moved by pleading.
▷HISTORY C16: from Latin *exōrābilis,* from *exōrāre* to persuade, from *ōrāre* to beseech
▸**ˌexoraˈbility** NOUN

exorbitant (ɪgˈzɔːbɪtᵊnt) ADJECTIVE (of prices, demands, etc.) in excess of what is reasonable; excessive; extravagant; immoderate.
▷HISTORY C15: from Late Latin *exorbitāre* to deviate, from Latin *orbita* track
▸**exˈorbitance** NOUN ▸**exˈorbitantly** ADVERB

exorcize *or* **exorcise** (ˈɛksɔːˌsaɪz) VERB (*tr*) to expel or attempt to expel (one or more evil spirits) from (a person or place believed to be possessed or haunted), by prayers, adjurations, and religious rites.
▷HISTORY C15: from Late Latin *exorcizāre,* from Greek *exorkizein,* from EX-[1] + *horkizein* to adjure
▸**ˈexorˌcizer** *or* **ˈexorˌciser** NOUN ▸**ˈexorcism** NOUN
▸**ˈexorcist** NOUN

exordium (ɛkˈsɔːdɪəm) NOUN, *plural* **-diums, -dia** (-dɪə). an introductory part or beginning, esp of an oration or discourse.
▷HISTORY C16: from Latin, from *exōrdīrī* to begin, from *ōrdīrī* to begin
▸**exˈordial** ADJECTIVE

exoskeleton (ˌɛksəʊˈskɛlɪtᵊn) NOUN the protective or supporting structure covering the outside of the body of many animals, such as the thick cuticle of arthropods. Compare **endoskeleton.**
▸**ˌexoˈskeletal** ADJECTIVE

exosmosis (ˌɛksɒzˈməʊsɪs, -sɒs-) NOUN *Biology* osmosis in which water flows from a cell or organism into the surrounding solution. Compare **endosmosis.**
▸**exosmotic** (ˌɛksɒzˈmɒtɪk, -sɒs-) *or* **exosmic** (ɛkˈsɒzmɪk, -ˈsɒs-) ADJECTIVE

exosphere (ˈɛksəʊˌsfɪə) NOUN the outermost layer of the earth's atmosphere. It extends from about 400 kilometres above the earth's surface.

exospore (ˈɛksəʊˌspɔː) NOUN the outer layer of the spores of some algae and fungi.
▸**ˌexoˈsporous** ADJECTIVE

exostosis (ˌɛksɒˈstəʊsɪs) NOUN, *plural* **-ses** (-siːz). an abnormal bony outgrowth from the surface of a bone.
▷HISTORY C18: via New Latin from Greek, from EX-[1] + *osteon* bone

exoteric (ˌɛksəʊˈtɛrɪk) ADJECTIVE [1] intelligible to or intended for more than a select or initiated minority: *an exoteric account of a philosophical doctrine.* [2] external; exterior.
▷HISTORY C17: from Latin *exōtericus* external, from Greek *exōterikos,* from *exōterō* further outside; see EXO-
▸**ˌexoˈterically** ADVERB ▸**ˌexoˈteriˌcism** NOUN

exothermic (ˌɛksəʊˈθɜːmɪk) *or* **exothermal** ADJECTIVE (of a chemical reaction or compound) occurring or formed with the evolution of heat. Compare **endothermic, exoergic.**
▸**ˌexoˈthermically** *or* **ˌexoˈthermally** ADVERB

exotic (ɪgˈzɒtɪk) ADJECTIVE [1] originating in a foreign country, esp one in the tropics; not native: *an exotic plant.* [2] having a strange or bizarre allure, beauty, or quality. [3] *NZ* (of trees, esp pine trees) native to the northern hemisphere but cultivated in New Zealand: *an exotic forest.* [4] of or relating to striptease. ◆ NOUN [5] an exotic person or thing.
▷HISTORY C16: from Latin *exōticus,* from Greek *exōtikos* foreign, from *exō* outside
▸**exˈotically** ADVERB ▸**exˈotiˌcism** NOUN ▸**exˈoticness** NOUN

exotica (ɪgˈzɒtɪkə) PLURAL NOUN exotic objects, esp when forming a collection.
▷HISTORY C19: Latin, neuter plural of *exōticus;* see EXOTIC

exotic dancer NOUN a striptease dancer or belly dancer.

exotoxin (ˌɛksəʊˈtɒksɪn) NOUN a toxin produced by a microorganism and secreted into the surrounding medium.
▸**ˌexoˈtoxic** ADJECTIVE

exp *Maths* SYMBOL FOR exponential (sense 2).

expand (ɪkˈspænd) VERB [1] to make or become greater in extent, volume, size, or scope; increase. [2] to spread out or be spread out; unfold; stretch out. [3] (*intr;* often foll by *on*) to enlarge or expatiate on (a story, topic, etc.) in detail. [4] (*intr*) to become increasingly relaxed, friendly, or talkative. [5] *Maths* to express (a function or expression) as the sum or product of terms.
▷HISTORY C15: from Latin *expandere* to spread out, from *pandere* to spread, extend
▸**exˈpandable** ADJECTIVE

expanded (ɪkˈspændɪd) ADJECTIVE [1] Also: **extended.** (of printer's type) wider than usual for a particular height. Compare **condensed.** [2] (of a plastic) having been foamed during manufacture by the introduction of a gas in order to make a light packaging material or heat insulator: *expanded polystyrene.* See also **expanded metal.**

expanded metal NOUN an open mesh of metal produced by stamping out alternating slots in a metal sheet and stretching it into an open pattern. It is used for reinforcing brittle or friable materials and in fencing.

expander (ɪkˈspændə) NOUN [1] a device for exercising and developing the muscles of the body: *a chest expander.* [2] an electronic device for increasing the variations in signal amplitude in a transmission system according to a specified law. Compare **compressor** (sense 5), **compander.**

expanding universe theory NOUN the theory, developed from the observed red shifts of celestial bodies, that the space between galaxies is expanding, so that they appear to recede from us at velocities that increase with their distance. See also **oscillating universe theory.**

expanse (ɪkˈspæns) NOUN [1] an uninterrupted surface of something that spreads or extends, esp over a wide area; stretch: *an expanse of water.* [2] expansion or extension.
▷HISTORY C17: from New Latin *expansum* the heavens, from Latin *expansus* spread out, from *expandere* to EXPAND

expansible (ɪkˈspænsəbᵊl) ADJECTIVE able to expand or be expanded.
▸**exˌpansiˈbility** NOUN

expansile (ɪkˈspænsaɪl) ADJECTIVE [1] able to expand or cause expansion. [2] of or relating to expansion.

expansion (ɪkˈspænʃən) NOUN [1] the act of expanding or the state of being expanded. [2] something expanded; an expanded surface or part. [3] the degree, extent, or amount by which something expands. [4] an increase, enlargement, or development, esp in the activities of a company. [5] *Maths* **a** the form of an expression or function when it is written as the sum or product of its terms. **b** the act or process of determining this expanded form. [6] the part of an engine cycle in which the working fluid does useful work by increasing in volume. [7] the increase in the dimensions of a body or substance when subjected to an increase in temperature, internal pressure, etc.
▸**exˈpansionary** ADJECTIVE

expansion bend NOUN *Engineering* a loop in a pipe conveying hot fluid that provides flexibility which takes up thermal expansion and thus reduces temperature-induced stress in the pipe to an acceptable level.

expansion bolt NOUN a bolt that expands on tightening, enabling it to be secured into an unthreaded hole.

expansionism (ɪkˈspænʃəˌnɪzəm) NOUN the doctrine or practice of expanding the economy or territory of a country.
▸**exˈpansionist** NOUN, ADJECTIVE ▸**exˌpansionˈistic** ADJECTIVE

expansion joint NOUN *Engineering* a gap in steel or concrete to allow for thermal expansion.

expansion slot NOUN a physical electronic interface provided in a computer system to enable extra facilities to be added easily at a later date.

expansive (ɪkˈspænsɪv) ADJECTIVE [1] able or tending to expand or characterized by expansion. [2] wide; extensive. [3] friendly, open, or talkative: *an expansive person.* [4] grand or extravagant: *an expansive way of life.* [5] *Psychiatry* lacking restraint in the expression of feelings, esp in having delusions of grandeur or being inclined to overvalue oneself or one's work.
▸**exˈpansively** ADVERB ▸**exˈpansiveness** NOUN

expansivity (ˌɛkspænˈsɪvɪtɪ) NOUN [1] the quality of being expansive. [2] another name for **coefficient of expansion.**

ex parte (ɛks ˈpɑːtɪ) ADJECTIVE *Law* (of an application in a judicial proceeding) on behalf of one side or party only: *an ex parte injunction.*
▷HISTORY Latin

expat (ˌɛksˈpæt) NOUN, ADJECTIVE *Informal* short for **expatriate.**

expatiate (ɪkˈspeɪʃɪˌeɪt) VERB (*intr*) 1 (foll by *on* or *upon*) to enlarge (on a theme, topic, etc.) at length or in detail; elaborate (on). 2 *Rare* to wander about.
▷HISTORY C16: from Latin *exspatiārī* to digress, from *spatiārī* to walk about
▸**exˌpatiˈation** NOUN ▸**exˈpatiˌator** NOUN

expatriate ADJECTIVE (ɛksˈpætrɪɪt, -ˌeɪt) 1 resident in a foreign country. 2 exiled or banished from one's native country: *an expatriate American.* ◆ NOUN (ɛksˈpætrɪɪt, -ˌeɪt) 3 a person who lives in a foreign country. 4 an exile; expatriate person. ◆ VERB (ɛksˈpætrɪˌeɪt) (*tr*) 5 to exile (oneself) from one's native country or cause (another) to go into exile. 6 to deprive (oneself or another) of citizenship.
▷HISTORY C18: from Medieval Latin *expatriāre,* from Latin EX-[1] + *patria* native land
▸**exˌpatriˈation** NOUN

expect (ɪkˈspɛkt) VERB (*tr; may take a clause as object or an infinitive*) 1 to regard as probable or likely; anticipate: *he expects to win.* 2 to look forward to or be waiting for: *we expect good news today.* 3 to decide that (something) is requisite or necessary; require: *the teacher expects us to work late today.* ◆ See also **expecting.**
▷HISTORY C16: from Latin *exspectāre* to watch for, from *spectāre* to look at
▸**exˈpectable** ADJECTIVE ▸**exˈpectably** ADVERB

expectancy (ɪkˈspɛktənsɪ) *or* **expectance** NOUN 1 something expected, esp on the basis of a norm or average: *his life expectancy was 30 years.* 2 anticipation; expectation. 3 the prospect of a future interest or possession, esp in property: *an estate in expectancy.*

expectant (ɪkˈspɛktənt) ADJECTIVE 1 expecting, anticipating, or hopeful: *an expectant glance.* 2 having expectations, esp of possession of something or prosperity. 3 pregnant: *an expectant mother.* ◆ NOUN 4 a person who expects something. 5 *Obsolete* a candidate for office, esp for ecclesiastical preferment.
▸**exˈpectantly** ADVERB

expectation (ˌɛkspɛkˈteɪʃən) NOUN 1 the act or state of expecting or the state of being expected. 2 (*usually plural*) something looked forward to, whether feared or hoped for: *we have great expectations for his future; their worst expectations.* 3 an attitude of expectancy or hope; anticipation: *to regard something with expectation.* 4 *Statistics* another term for **expected value.**
▸**expectative** (ɪkˈspɛktətɪv) ADJECTIVE

expected frequency NOUN *Statistics* the number of occasions on which an event may be presumed to occur on average in a given number of trials.

expected utility NOUN *Statistics* the weighted average utility of the possible outcomes of a probabilistic situation; the sum or integral of the product of the probability distribution and the utility function.

expected value NOUN *Statistics* the sum or integral of all possible values of a random variable, or any given function of it, multiplied by the respective probabilities of the values of the variable. Symbol: $E(X)$. $E(X)$ is the mean of the distribution; $E(X-c) = E(X)-c$ where c is a constant. Also called: **mathematical expectation.**

expecting (ɪkˈspɛktɪŋ) ADJECTIVE *Informal* pregnant.

expectorant (ɪkˈspɛktərənt) *Med* ◆ ADJECTIVE 1 promoting the secretion, liquefaction, or expulsion of sputum from the respiratory passages. ◆ NOUN 2 an expectorant drug or agent.

expectorate (ɪkˈspɛktəˌreɪt) VERB to cough up and spit out (sputum from the respiratory passages).
▷HISTORY C17: from Latin *expectorāre,* literally: to drive from the breast, expel, from *pectus* breast
▸**exˌpectoˈration** NOUN ▸**exˈpectoˌrator** NOUN

expediency (ɪkˈspiːdɪənsɪ) *or* **expedience** NOUN, *plural* **-encies** *or* **-ences.** 1 appropriateness; suitability. 2 the use of or inclination towards methods that are advantageous rather than fair or just. 3 another word for **expedient** (sense 3).

expedient (ɪkˈspiːdɪənt) ADJECTIVE 1 suitable to the circumstances; appropriate. 2 inclined towards methods or means that are advantageous rather than fair or just. ◆ NOUN *also* **expediency.** 3 something suitable or appropriate, esp something used during an urgent situation.
▷HISTORY C14: from Latin *expediēns* setting free; see EXPEDITE
▸**exˈpediently** ADVERB

expediential (ɪkˌspiːdɪˈɛnʃəl) ADJECTIVE denoting, based on, or involving expediency.
▸**exˌpediˈentially** ADVERB

expedite (ˈɛkspɪˌdaɪt) VERB (*tr*) 1 to hasten the progress of; hasten or assist. 2 to do or process (something, such as business matters) with speed and efficiency. 3 *Rare* to dispatch (documents, messages, etc.). ◆ ADJECTIVE *Obsolete* 4 unimpeded or prompt; expeditious. 5 alert or prepared.
▷HISTORY C17: from Latin *expedīre,* literally: to free the feet (as from a snare), hence, liberate, from EX-[1] + *pēs* foot

expediter *or* **expeditor** (ˈɛkspɪˌdaɪtə) NOUN a person who expedites something, esp a person employed in an industry to ensure that work on each job progresses efficiently.

expedition (ˌɛkspɪˈdɪʃən) NOUN 1 an organized journey or voyage for a specific purpose, esp for exploration or for a scientific or military purpose. 2 the people and equipment comprising an expedition. 3 a pleasure trip; excursion. 4 promptness in acting; dispatch.
▷HISTORY C15: from Latin *expedītiō,* from *expedīre* to prepare, EXPEDITE

expeditionary (ˌɛkspɪˈdɪʃənərɪ) ADJECTIVE relating to or constituting an expedition, esp a military one: *an expeditionary force.*

expeditious (ˌɛkspɪˈdɪʃəs) ADJECTIVE characterized by or done with speed and efficiency; prompt; quick.
▸**ˌexpeˈditiously** ADVERB ▸**ˌexpeˈditiousness** NOUN

expel (ɪkˈspɛl) VERB **-pels, -pelling, -pelled.** (*tr*) 1 to eject or drive out with force. 2 to deprive of participation in or membership of a school, club, etc.
▷HISTORY C14: from Latin *expellere* to drive out, from *pellere* to thrust, drive
▸**exˈpellable** ADJECTIVE ▸**expellee** (ˌɛkspɛˈliː) NOUN
▸**exˈpeller** NOUN

expellant *or* **expellent** (ɪkˈspɛlənt) ADJECTIVE 1 forcing out or having the capacity to force out. ◆ NOUN 2 a medicine used to expel undesirable substances or organisms from the body, esp worms from the digestive tract.

expellers (ɪkˈspɛləz) PLURAL NOUN the residue remaining after an oilseed has been crushed to expel the oil, used for animal fodder: *groundnut expellers.* Compare **extractions.**

expend (ɪkˈspɛnd) VERB (*tr*) 1 to spend; disburse. 2 to consume or use up.
▷HISTORY C15: from Latin *expendere,* from *pendere* to weigh
▸**exˈpender** NOUN

expendable (ɪkˈspɛndəbᵊl) ADJECTIVE 1 that may be expended or used up. 2 not essential; not worth preserving. 3 able to be sacrificed to achieve an objective, esp a military one. ◆ NOUN 4 something that is expendable.
▸**exˌpendaˈbility** NOUN

expenditure (ɪkˈspɛndɪtʃə) NOUN 1 something expended, such as time or money. 2 the act of expending.

expense (ɪkˈspɛns) NOUN 1 a particular payment of money; expenditure. 2 money needed for individual purchases; cost; charge. 3 (*plural*) incidental money spent in the performance of a job, commission, etc., usually reimbursed by an employer or allowable against tax. 4 something requiring money for its purchase or upkeep: *the car was more of an expense than he had expected.* 5 **at the expense of.** to the detriment of: *he succeeded at the expense of his health.* ◆ VERB 6 (*tr*) *US and Canadian* to treat as an expense for book-keeping or tax purposes.
▷HISTORY C14: from Late Latin *expēnsa,* from Latin *expēnsus* weighed out; see EXPEND

expense account NOUN 1 an arrangement by which expenses incurred in the course of a person's work are refunded by his employer or deducted from his income for tax purposes. 2 a record of such expenses. 3 (*modifier*) *Informal* paid for by an employer or by money allowable against tax: *an expense-account lunch.*

expensive (ɪkˈspɛnsɪv) ADJECTIVE high-priced; costly; dear.
▸**exˈpensively** ADVERB ▸**exˈpensiveness** NOUN

experience (ɪkˈspɪərɪəns) NOUN 1 direct personal participation or observation; actual knowledge or contact: *experience of prison life.* 2 a particular incident, feeling, etc., that a person has undergone: *an experience to remember.* 3 accumulated knowledge, esp of practical matters: *a man of experience.* 4 **a** the totality of characteristics, both past and present, that make up the particular quality of a person, place, or people. **b** the impact made on an individual by the culture of a people, nation, etc.: *the American experience.* 5 *Philosophy* **a** the content of a perception regarded as independent of whether the apparent object actually exists. Compare **sense datum. b** the faculty by which a person acquires knowledge of contingent facts about the world, as contrasted with reason. **c** the totality of a person's perceptions, feelings, and memories. ◆ VERB (*tr*) 6 to participate in or undergo. 7 to be emotionally or aesthetically moved by; feel: *to experience beauty.*
▷HISTORY C14: from Latin *experientia,* from *experīrī* to prove; related to Latin *perīculum* PERIL
▸**exˈperienceable** ADJECTIVE

experienced (ɪkˈspɪərɪənst) ADJECTIVE having become skilful or knowledgeable from extensive contact or participation or observation.

experience table NOUN *Insurance* an actuarial table, esp a mortality table based on past statistics.

experiential (ɪkˌspɪərɪˈɛnʃəl) ADJECTIVE *Philosophy* relating to or derived from experience; empirical.
▸**exˌperiˈentially** ADVERB

experiment NOUN (ɪkˈspɛrɪmənt) 1 a test or investigation, esp one planned to provide evidence for or against a hypothesis: a *scientific experiment.* 2 the act of conducting such an investigation or test; experimentation; research. 3 an attempt at something new or different; an effort to be original: *a poetic experiment.* 4 an obsolete word for **experience.** ◆ VERB (ɪkˈspɛrɪˌmɛnt) 5 (*intr*) to make an experiment or experiments.
▷HISTORY C14: from Latin *experīmentum* proof, trial, from *experīrī* to test; see EXPERIENCE
▸**exˈperiˌmenter** NOUN

experimental (ɪkˌspɛrɪˈmɛntᵊl) ADJECTIVE 1 relating to, based on, or having the nature of experiment: *an experimental study.* 2 based on or derived from experience; empirical: *experimental evidence.* 3 tending to experiment: *an experimental artist.* 4 tentative or provisional: *an experimental rule in football.*
▸**exˌperiˈmentally** ADVERB

experimental condition NOUN *Statistics* one of the distinct states of affairs or values of the independent variable for which the dependent variable is measured in order to carry out statistical tests or calculations. Also called: **condition.**

experimentalism (ɪkˌspɛrɪˈmɛntəˌlɪzəm) NOUN employment of or reliance upon experiments; empiricism.
▸**exˌperiˈmentalist** NOUN

experimentalize (ɪkˌspɛrɪˈmɛntəˌlaɪz) VERB (*intr*) to engage in experiments.

experimental psychology NOUN the scientific study of the individual behaviour of man and other animals, esp of perception, learning, memory, motor skills, and thinking.

experimentation (ɪkˌspɛrɪmɛnˈteɪʃən) NOUN the act, process, or practice of experimenting.

experimenter effect NOUN *Psychol* the influence of an experimenter's expectations on his results.

expert (ˈɛkspɜːt) NOUN 1 a person who has extensive skill or knowledge in a particular field. ◆ ADJECTIVE 2 skilful or knowledgeable. 3 of, involving, or done by an expert: *an expert job.*
▷HISTORY C14: from Latin *expertus* known by experience, from *experīrī* to test; see EXPERIENCE
▸**ˈexpertly** ADVERB ▸**ˈexpertness** NOUN

expertise (ˌɛkspɜːˈtiːz) NOUN special skill, knowledge, or judgment; expertness.
▷HISTORY C19: from French: expert skill, from EXPERT

expertize *or* **expertise** (ˈɛkspɜːˌtaɪz) VERB *US* to act as an expert or give an expert opinion (on).

expert system NOUN a computer program that can offer intelligent advice or make intelligent decisions using rule-based programs.

expiable ('ɛkspɪəbᵊl) ADJECTIVE capable of being expiated or atoned for.

expiate ('ɛkspɪˌeɪt) VERB *(tr)* to atone for or redress (sin or wrongdoing); make amends for.
▷HISTORY C16: from Latin *expiāre,* from *pius* dutiful; see PIOUS
▸ **'expiˌator** NOUN

expiation (ˌɛkspɪ'eɪʃən) NOUN the act, process, or a means of expiating; atonement.

expiatory ('ɛkspɪətərɪ, -trɪ) ADJECTIVE [1] capable of making expiation. [2] given or offered in expiation.

expiration (ˌɛkspɪ'reɪʃən) NOUN [1] the finish of something; ending; expiry. [2] the act, process, or sound of breathing out. [3] *Rare* a last breath; death.

expiratory (ɪk'spaɪərətərɪ, -trɪ) ADJECTIVE relating to the expulsion of air from the lungs during respiration.

expire (ɪk'spaɪə) VERB [1] *(intr)* to finish or run out; cease; come to an end. [2] to breathe out (air); exhale. [3] *(intr)* to die.
▷HISTORY C15: from Old French *expirer,* from Latin *exspīrāre* to breathe out, from *spīrāre* to breathe
▸ **ex'pirer** NOUN

expiry (ɪk'spaɪərɪ) NOUN, *plural* **-ries.** [1] **a** a coming to an end, esp of a contract period; termination: *expiry of a lease.* **b** *(as modifier)*: *the expiry date.* [2] death.

explain (ɪk'spleɪn) VERB [1] (when *tr, may take a clause as object*) to make (something) comprehensible, esp by giving a clear and detailed account of the relevant structure, operation, surrounding circumstances, etc. [2] *(tr)* to justify or attempt to justify (oneself) by giving reasons for one's actions or words.
▷HISTORY C15: from Latin *explānāre* to flatten, from *plānus* level
▸ **ex'plainable** ADJECTIVE ▸ **ex'plainer** NOUN

explain away VERB *(tr, adverb)* to offer excuses or reasons for (bad conduct, mistakes, etc.).

explanation (ˌɛksplə'neɪʃən) NOUN [1] the act or process of explaining. [2] a statement or occurrence that explains. [3] a clarification of disputed terms or points; reconciliation.

explanatory (ɪk'splænətərɪ, -trɪ) *or* **explanative** ADJECTIVE serving or intended to serve as an explanation.
▸ **ex'planatorily** ADVERB

explant (ɛks'plɑːnt) VERB [1] to transfer (living tissue) from its natural site to a new site or to a culture medium. ◆ NOUN [2] a piece of tissue treated in this way.
▸ **ˌexplan'tation** NOUN

expletive (ɪk'spliːtɪv) NOUN [1] an exclamation or swearword; an oath or a sound expressing an emotional reaction rather than any particular meaning. [2] any syllable, word, or phrase conveying no independent meaning, esp one inserted in a line of verse for the sake of the metre. ◆ ADJECTIVE *also* **expletory** (ɪk'spliːtərɪ). [3] expressing no particular meaning, esp when filling out a line of verse.
▷HISTORY C17: from Late Latin *explētīvus* for filling out, from *explēre,* from *plēre* to fill
▸ **ex'pletively** ADVERB

explicable ('ɛksplɪkəbᵊl, ɪk'splɪk-) ADJECTIVE capable of being explained.

explicate ('ɛksplɪˌkeɪt) VERB *(tr)* *Formal* [1] to make clear or explicit; explain. [2] to formulate or develop (a theory, hypothesis, etc.).
▷HISTORY C16: from Latin *explicāre* to unfold, from *plicāre* to fold
▸ **explicative** (ɪk'splɪkətɪv) *or* **explicatory** (ɪk'splɪkətərɪ, -trɪ) ADJECTIVE ▸ **'expliˌcator** NOUN

explication (ˌɛksplɪ'keɪʃən) NOUN [1] the act or process of explicating. [2] analysis or interpretation, esp of a literary passage or work or philosophical doctrine. [3] a comprehensive exposition or description.

explication de texte *French* (ɛksplikasjɔ̃ də tɛkst) NOUN, *plural* ***explications de texte*** (ɛksplikasjɔ̃ də tɛkst). a close textual analysis of a literary work.
▷HISTORY literally: explanation of (the) text

explicit[1] (ɪk'splɪsɪt) ADJECTIVE [1] precisely and clearly expressed, leaving nothing to implication; fully stated: *explicit instructions.* [2] graphically detailed, leaving little to the imagination: *sexually explicit scenes.* [3] openly expressed without reservations; unreserved. [4] *Maths* (of a function) having an equation of the form $y=f(x)$, in which y is expressed directly in terms of x, as in $y=x^4 + x + z$. Compare **implicit** (sense 4).
▷HISTORY C17: from Latin *explicitus* unfolded, from *explicāre;* see EXPLICATE
▸ **ex'plicitly** ADVERB ▸ **ex'plicitness** NOUN

explicit[2] (ɪk'splɪsɪt) the end; an indication, used esp by medieval scribes, of the end of a book, part of a manuscript, etc.
▷HISTORY Late Latin, probably short for *explicitus est liber* the book is unfolded (or complete); shortened by analogy with INCIPIT

explode (ɪk'spləʊd) VERB [1] to burst or cause to burst with great violence as a result of internal pressure, esp through the detonation of an explosive; blow up. [2] to destroy or be destroyed in this manner: *to explode a bridge.* [3] (of a gas) to undergo or cause (a gas) to undergo a sudden violent expansion, accompanied by heat, light, a shock wave, and a loud noise, as a result of a fast uncontrolled exothermic chemical or nuclear reaction. [4] *(intr)* to react suddenly or violently with emotion, etc.: *to explode with anger.* [5] *(intr)* (esp of a population) to increase rapidly. [6] *(tr)* to show (a theory, etc.) to be baseless; refute and make obsolete. [7] *(tr) Phonetics* to pronounce (a stop) with audible plosion. ◆ Compare **implode.**
▷HISTORY C16: from Latin *explōdere* to drive off by clapping, hiss (an actor) off, from EX-[1] + *plaudere* to clap
▸ **ex'ploder** NOUN

exploded view NOUN a drawing or photograph of a complicated mechanism that shows the individual parts separately, usually indicating their relative positions.

exploding star NOUN an irregular variable star, such as a nova, supernova, or flare star, in which rapid increases in luminosity occur, caused by some form of explosion.

exploit NOUN ('ɛksplɔɪt) [1] a notable deed or feat, esp one that is noble or heroic. ◆ VERB (ɪk'splɔɪt) *(tr)* [2] to take advantage of (a person, situation, etc.), esp unethically or unjustly for one's own ends. [3] to make the best use of: *to exploit natural resources.*
▷HISTORY C14: from Old French: accomplishment, from Latin *explicitum* (something) unfolded, from *explicāre* to EXPLICATE
▸ **ex'ploitable** ADJECTIVE ▸ **ˌexploi'tation** NOUN ▸ **ex'ploitive** *or* **ex'ploitative** ADJECTIVE

exploration (ˌɛksplə'reɪʃən) NOUN [1] the act or process of exploring. [2] *Med* examination of an organ or part for diagnostic purposes. [3] an organized trip into unfamiliar regions, esp for scientific purposes; expedition.
▸ **exploratory** (ɪk'splɒrətərɪ, -trɪ) *or* **ex'plorative** ADJECTIVE

explore (ɪk'splɔː) VERB [1] *(tr)* to examine or investigate, esp systematically. [2] to travel to or into (unfamiliar or unknown regions), esp for organized scientific purposes. [3] *(tr) Med* to examine (an organ or part) for diagnostic purposes. [4] *(tr) Obsolete* to search for or out.
▷HISTORY C16: from Latin *explōrāre,* from EX-[1] + *plōrāre* to cry aloud; probably from the shouts of hunters sighting prey
▸ **ex'plorer** NOUN

Explorer[1] (ɪk'splɔːrə) NOUN *US* a member of the senior branch of the Scouts. Brit equivalent: **Venture Scout.**

Explorer[2] (ɪk'splɔːrə) NOUN any of the first series of US satellites. **Explorer 1,** launched in 1958, confirmed the existence of intense radiation belts around the earth.

explosion (ɪk'spləʊʒən) NOUN [1] the act or an instance of exploding. [2] a violent release of energy resulting from a rapid chemical or nuclear reaction, esp one that produces a shock wave, loud noise, heat, and light. Compare **implosion** (sense 1). [3] a sudden or violent outburst of activity, noise, emotion, etc. [4] a rapid increase, esp in a population. [5] *Phonetics* another word for **plosion.**
▷HISTORY C17: from Latin *explōsiō,* from *explōdere* to EXPLODE

explosion welding NOUN *Engineering* the welding of two parts forced together by a controlled explosion.

explosive (ɪk'spləʊsɪv) ADJECTIVE [1] of, involving, or characterized by an explosion or explosions. [2] capable of exploding or tending to explode. [3] potentially violent or hazardous; dangerous: *an explosive situation.* [4] *Phonetics* another word for **plosive.** ◆ NOUN [5] a substance that decomposes rapidly under certain conditions with the production of gases, which expand by the heat of the reaction. The energy released is used in firearms, blasting, and rocket propulsion. [6] a plosive consonant; stop.
▸ **ex'plosively** ADVERB ▸ **ex'plosiveness** NOUN

explosive forming NOUN *Engineering* a rapid method of forming a metal object in which components are made by subjecting the metal to very high pressures generated by a controlled explosion.

expo ('ɛkspəʊ) NOUN, *plural* **-pos.** short for **exposition** (sense 3).

exponent (ɪk'spəʊnənt) NOUN [1] (usually foll by *of*) a person or thing that acts as an advocate (of an idea, cause, etc.). [2] a person or thing that explains or interprets. [3] a performer or interpretive artist, esp a musician. [4] Also called: **power, index.** *Maths* a number or variable placed as a superscript to the right of another number or quantity indicating the number of times the number or quantity is to be multiplied by itself. ◆ ADJECTIVE [5] offering a declaration, explanation, or interpretation.
▷HISTORY C16: from Latin *expōnere* to set out, expound, from *pōnere* to set, place

exponential (ˌɛkspəʊ'nɛnʃəl) ADJECTIVE [1] *Maths* (of a function, curve, series, or equation) of, containing, or involving one or more numbers or quantities raised to an exponent, esp e^x. [2] *Maths* raised to the power of e, the base of natural logarithms. Symbol: exp. [3] of or involving an exponent or exponents. [4] *Informal* very rapid. ◆ NOUN [5] *Maths* an exponential function, etc.
▸ **ˌexpo'nentially** ADVERB

exponential distribution NOUN *Statistics* a continuous single-parameter distribution used esp when making statements about the length of life of certain materials or waiting times between randomly occurring events. Its density function is $p(x) = \lambda e^{-\lambda x}$ for positive λ and nonnegative x, and it is a special case of the gamma distribution.

exponential horn NOUN a horn for the radiation of acoustic or high-frequency electromagnetic waves, of which the cross-sectional area increases exponentially with the length.

export NOUN ('ɛkspɔːt) [1] *(often plural)* **a** goods (**visible exports**) or services (**invisible exports**) sold to a foreign country or countries. **b** *(as modifier)*: *an export licence; export finance.* ◆ VERB (ɪk'spɔːt, 'ɛkspɔːt) [2] to sell (goods or services) or ship (goods) to a foreign country or countries. [3] *(tr)* to transmit or spread (an idea, social institution, etc.) abroad. ◆ Compare **import.**
▷HISTORY C15: from Latin *exportāre* to carry away, from *portāre* to carry
▸ **ex'portable** ADJECTIVE ▸ **exˌporta'bility** NOUN ▸ **ex'porter** NOUN

exportation (ˌɛkspɔː'teɪʃən) NOUN [1] the act, business, or process of exporting goods or services. [2] *Chiefly US* an exported product or service.

export reject NOUN an article that fails to meet a standard of quality required for export and that is sold on the home market.

expose (ɪk'spəʊz) VERB *(tr)* [1] to display for viewing; exhibit. [2] to bring to public notice; disclose; reveal: *to expose the facts.* [3] to divulge the identity of; unmask. [4] (foll by *to*) to make subject or susceptible (to attack, criticism, etc.). [5] to abandon (a child, animal, etc.) in the open to die. [6] (foll by *to*) to introduce (to) or acquaint (with): *he was exposed to the classics at an early age.* [7] *Photog* to subject (a photographic film or plate) to light, X-rays, or some other type of actinic radiation. [8] *RC Church* to exhibit (the consecrated Eucharistic Host or a relic) for public veneration. [9] **expose oneself.** to display one's sexual organs in public.
▷HISTORY C15: from Old French *exposer,* from Latin *expōnere* to set out; see EXPONENT
▸ **ex'posable** ADJECTIVE ▸ **ex'posal** NOUN ▸ **ex'poser** NOUN

exposé (ɛks'pəʊzeɪ) NOUN [1] the act or an instance

of bringing a scandal, crime, etc., to public notice. [2] an article, book, or statement that discloses a scandal, crime, etc.

exposed (ɪk'spəʊzd) ADJECTIVE [1] not concealed; displayed for viewing. [2] without shelter from the elements. [3] susceptible to attack or criticism; vulnerable. [4] *Mountaineering* (of a climb, pitch, or move) performed on a high, sheer, and unsheltered rock face.
▸**exposedness** (ɪk'spəʊzɪdnɪs) NOUN

exposition (ˌɛkspə'zɪʃən) NOUN [1] a systematic, usually written statement about, commentary on, or explanation of a specific subject. [2] the act of expounding or setting forth information or a viewpoint. [3] a large public exhibition, esp of industrial products or arts and crafts. [4] the act of exposing or the state of being exposed. [5] the part of a play, novel, etc., in which the theme and main characters are introduced. [6] *Music* the first statement of the subjects or themes of a movement in sonata form or a fugue. [7] *RC Church* the exhibiting of the consecrated Eucharistic Host or a relic for public veneration.
▷HISTORY C14: from Latin *expositiō* a setting forth, from *expōnere* to display; see EXPONENT
▸ˌ**expo'sitional** ADJECTIVE

expositor (ɪk'spɒzɪtə) NOUN a person who expounds.

expository (ɪk'spɒzɪtərɪ, -trɪ) *or* **expositive** ADJECTIVE of, involving, or assisting in exposition; explanatory.
▸**ex'positorily** *or* **ex'positively** ADVERB

ex post facto (ɛks pəʊst 'fæktəʊ) ADJECTIVE having retrospective effect: *an ex post facto law.*
▷HISTORY C17: from Latin *ex* from + *post* afterwards + *factus* done, from *facere* to do

expostulate (ɪk'spɒstjʊˌleɪt) VERB (*intr;* usually foll by *with*) to argue or reason (with), esp in order to dissuade from an action or intention.
▷HISTORY C16: from Latin *expostulāre* to require, from *postulāre* to demand; see POSTULATE
▸**ex'postuˌlatingly** ADVERB ▸**exˌpostu'lation** NOUN ▸**ex'postuˌlator** NOUN ▸**ex'postulatory** *or* **ex'postulative** ADJECTIVE

exposure (ɪk'spəʊʒə) NOUN [1] the act of exposing or the condition of being exposed. [2] the position or outlook of a house, building, etc.; aspect: *the bedroom has a southern exposure.* [3] lack of shelter from the weather, esp the cold: *to die of exposure.* [4] a surface that is exposed: *an exposure of granite.* [5] *Mountaineering* the degree to which a climb, etc. is exposed (see **exposed** (sense 4)). [6] *Photog* **a** the act of exposing a photographic film or plate to light, X-rays, etc. **b** an area on a film or plate that has been exposed to light, etc. **c** (*as modifier*): *exposure control.* [7] *Photog* **a** the intensity of light falling on a photographic film or plate multiplied by the time for which it is exposed. **b** a combination of lens aperture and shutter speed used in taking a photograph: *he used the wrong exposure.* [8] appearance or presentation before the public, as in a theatre, on television, or in films. [9] See **indecent exposure.**

exposure meter NOUN *Photog* an instrument for measuring the intensity of light, usually by means of a photocell, so that the suitable camera settings of shutter speed and f-number (or lens aperture) can be determined. Also called: **light meter.**

expound (ɪk'spaʊnd) VERB (when *intr,* foll by *on* or *about*) to explain or set forth (an argument, theory, etc.) in detail: *to expound on one's theories; he expounded his reasoning.*
▷HISTORY C13: from Old French *espondre,* from Latin *expōnere* to set forth, from *pōnere* to put
▸**ex'pounder** NOUN

express (ɪk'sprɛs) VERB (*tr*) [1] to transform (ideas) into words; utter; verbalize. [2] to show or reveal; indicate: *tears express grief.* [3] to communicate (emotion, etc.) without words, as through music, painting, etc. [4] to indicate through a symbol, formula, etc. [5] to force or squeeze out: *to express the juice from an orange.* [6] to send by rapid transport or special messenger. [7] **express oneself.** to communicate one's thoughts or ideas. ◆ ADJECTIVE (*prenominal*) [8] clearly indicated or shown; explicitly stated: *an express wish.* [9] done or planned for a definite reason or goal; particular: *an express purpose.* [10] of, concerned with, or designed for rapid transportation of people, merchandise, mail, money, etc.: *express delivery; an express depot.* ◆ NOUN [11] **a** a system for sending merchandise, mail, money, etc., rapidly. **b** merchandise, mail, etc., conveyed by such a system. **c** *Chiefly US and Canadian* an enterprise operating such a system. [12] Also called: **express train.** a fast train stopping at none or only a few of the intermediate stations between its two termini. [13] See **express rifle.** ◆ ADVERB [14] by means of a special delivery or express delivery: *it went express.*
▷HISTORY C14: from Latin *expressus,* literally: squeezed out, hence, prominent, from *exprimere* to force out, from EX-[1] + *premere* to press
▸**ex'presser** NOUN ▸**ex'pressible** ADJECTIVE

expressage (ɪk'sprɛsɪdʒ) NOUN [1] the conveyance of merchandise by express. [2] the fee charged for such conveyance.

expression (ɪk'sprɛʃən) NOUN [1] the act or an instance of transforming ideas into words. [2] a manifestation of an emotion, feeling, etc., without words: *tears are an expression of grief.* [3] communication of emotion through music, painting, etc. [4] a look on the face that indicates mood or emotion: *a joyful expression.* [5] the choice of words, phrases, syntax, intonation, etc., in communicating. [6] a particular phrase used conventionally to express something: *a dialect expression.* [7] the act or process of forcing or squeezing out a liquid. [8] *Maths* a variable, function, or some combination of constants, variables, or functions. [9] *Genetics* the effect of a particular gene on the phenotype.
▸**ex'pressional** ADJECTIVE ▸**ex'pressionless** ADJECTIVE ▸**ex'pressionlessly** ADVERB

expressionism (ɪk'sprɛʃəˌnɪzəm) NOUN (*sometimes capital*) an artistic and literary movement originating in Germany at the beginning of the 20th century, which sought to express emotions rather than to represent external reality: characterized by the use of symbolism and of exaggeration and distortion.
▸**ex'pressionist** NOUN, ADJECTIVE ▸**exˌpression'istic** ADJECTIVE

expression mark NOUN one of a set of musical directions, usually in Italian, indicating how a piece or passage is to be performed.

expressive (ɪk'sprɛsɪv) ADJECTIVE [1] of, involving, or full of expression. [2] (*postpositive;* foll by *of*) indicative or suggestive (of): *a look expressive of love.* [3] having a particular meaning, feeling, or force; significant.
▸**ex'pressively** ADVERB ▸**ex'pressiveness** NOUN

expressivity (ˌɛksprɛ'sɪvɪtɪ) NOUN [1] (esp of a work of art) the quality of being expressive. [2] *Genetics* the strength of the effect of a gene on the phenotype.

expressly (ɪk'sprɛslɪ) ADVERB [1] for an express purpose; with specific intentions. [2] plainly, exactly, or unmistakably.

expresso (ɪk'sprɛsəʊ) NOUN a variant of **espresso.**

express rifle NOUN a high-velocity hunting rifle for big game shooting.

expressway (ɪk'sprɛsˌweɪ) NOUN a motorway.

expropriate (ɛks'prəʊprɪˌeɪt) VERB (*tr*) to deprive (an owner) of (property), esp by taking it for public use. See also **eminent domain.**
▷HISTORY C17: from Medieval Latin *expropriāre* to deprive of possessions, from *proprius* own
▸**ex'propriable** ADJECTIVE ▸**exˌpropri'ation** NOUN ▸**ex'propriˌator** NOUN

expulsion (ɪk'spʌlʃən) NOUN the act of expelling or the fact or condition of being expelled.
▷HISTORY C14: from Latin *expulsiō* a driving out, from *expellere* to EXPEL

expulsive (ɪk'spʌlsɪv) ADJECTIVE tending or serving to expel.

expunge (ɪk'spʌndʒ) VERB (*tr*) [1] to delete or erase; blot out; obliterate. [2] to wipe out or destroy.
▷HISTORY C17: from Latin *expungere* to blot out, from *pungere* to prick
▸**expunction** (ɪk'spʌŋkʃən) NOUN ▸**ex'punger** NOUN

expurgate ('ɛkspəˌgeɪt) VERB (*tr*) to amend (a book, text, etc.) by removing (obscene or offensive sections).
▷HISTORY C17: from Latin *expurgāre* to clean out, from *purgāre* to purify; see PURGE
▸ˌ**expur'gation** NOUN ▸'**expurˌgator** NOUN ▸**expurgatory** (ɛks'pɜːgətərɪ, -trɪ) *or* **expurgatorial** (ɛkˌspɜːgə'tɔːrɪəl) ADJECTIVE

exquisite (ɪk'skwɪzɪt, 'ɛkskwɪzɪt) ADJECTIVE [1] possessing qualities of unusual delicacy and fine craftsmanship: *jewels in an exquisite setting.* [2] extremely beautiful and pleasing: *an exquisite face.* [3] outstanding or excellent: *an exquisite victory.* [4] sensitive; discriminating: *exquisite taste.* [5] fastidious and refined. [6] intense or sharp in feeling: *exquisite pleasure; exquisite pain.* ◆ NOUN [7] *Obsolete* a dandy.
▷HISTORY C15: from Latin *exquīsītus* excellent, from *exquīrere* to search out, from *quaerere* to seek
▸**ex'quisitely** ADVERB ▸**ex'quisiteness** NOUN

exr ABBREVIATION FOR executor.

exsanguinate (ɪk'sæŋgwɪneɪt) VERB (*tr*) *Rare* to drain the blood from.
▷HISTORY C19: from Latin *exsanguināre*
▸**exˌsanguin'ation** NOUN

exsanguine (ɪk'sæŋgwɪn) *or* **exsanguinous** ADJECTIVE without blood; bloodless or anaemic.
▷HISTORY C17: from Latin *exsanguis,* from *sanguis* blood
▸ˌ**exsan'guinity** NOUN

exscind (ɛk'sɪnd) VERB (*tr*) to cut off or out; excise.
▷HISTORY C17: *exscind,* from Latin *exscindere* to extirpate, destroy, from *scindere* to cut, tear, split

exsect (ɛk'sɛkt) VERB (*tr*) to cut out.
▷HISTORY C17: *exsect,* from Latin *exsecāre* to cut away, from *secāre* to cut
▸**exsection** (ɛk'sɛkʃən) NOUN

exsert (ɛk'sɜːt) VERB [1] (*tr*) to thrust out; protrude. ◆ ADJECTIVE *also* **exserted.** [2] protruded, stretched out, or (esp of stamens) projecting beyond the corolla of a flower.
▷HISTORY C19: from Latin *exserere* to thrust out; see EXERT
▸**ex'sertion** NOUN ▸**exsertile** (ɛk'sɜːtaɪl) ADJECTIVE

ex-service ADJECTIVE having formerly served in the armed forces.

ex-serviceman NOUN, *plural* **-men.** a man who has served in the army, navy, or air force.

ex-servicewoman NOUN, *plural* **-women.** a woman who has served in the army, navy, or air force.

exsiccate ('ɛksɪˌkeɪt) VERB to dry up; desiccate.
▷HISTORY C15: from Latin *exsiccāre,* from *siccus* dry
▸ˌ**exsic'cation** NOUN ▸'**exsiccative** ADJECTIVE ▸'**exsicˌcator** NOUN

ex silentio *Latin* (ɛks sɪ'lɛnʃɪˌəʊ) ADVERB, ADJECTIVE (of a theory, assumption, etc.) based on a lack of evidence to the contrary.
▷HISTORY literally: from silence

exstipulate (ɛk'stɪpjʊlɪt, -ˌleɪt) *or* **estipulate** ADJECTIVE (of a flowering plant) having no stipules.

exstrophy ('ɛkstrəfɪ) NOUN *Med* congenital eversion of a hollow organ, esp the urinary bladder.
▷HISTORY C19: from Greek EX-[1] + *strophein* to turn

ext ABBREVIATION FOR: [1] extinct. [2] extract.

extant (ɛk'stænt, 'ɛkstənt) ADJECTIVE [1] still in existence; surviving. [2] *Archaic* standing out; protruding.
▷HISTORY C16: from Latin *exstāns* standing out, from *exstāre,* from *stāre* to stand

> **Language note** *Extant* is sometimes wrongly used simply to say that something exists, without any connotation of survival: *plutonium is perhaps the deadliest element in existence* (not *the deadliest element extant*).

extemporaneous (ɪkˌstɛmpə'reɪnɪəs) *or* **extemporary** (ɪk'stɛmpərərɪ, -prərɪ) ADJECTIVE [1] spoken, performed, etc., without planning or preparation; impromptu; extempore. [2] done in a temporary manner; improvised.
▸**exˌtempo'raneously** *or* **ex'temporarily** ADVERB ▸**exˌtempo'raneousness** *or* **ex'temporariness** NOUN

extempore (ɪk'stɛmpərɪ) ADVERB, ADJECTIVE without planning or preparation; impromptu.
▷HISTORY C16: from Latin *ex tempore* instantaneously, from EX-[1] out of + *tempus* time

extemporize *or* **extemporise** (ɪkˈstɛmpəˌraɪz) VERB 1 to perform, speak, or compose (an act, speech, piece of music, etc.) without planning or preparation. 2 to use (a temporary solution) for an immediate need; improvise.
▸**exˌtemporiˈzation** *or* **exˌtemporiˈsation** NOUN
▸**exˈtempoˌrizer** *or* **exˈtempoˌriser** NOUN

extend (ɪkˈstɛnd) VERB 1 to draw out or be drawn out; stretch. 2 to last for a certain time: *his schooling extended for three years.* 3 (*intr*) to reach a certain point in time or distance: *the land extends five miles.* 4 (*intr*) to exist or occur: *the trees extended throughout the area.* 5 (*tr*) to increase (a building, etc.) in size or area; add to or enlarge. 6 (*tr*) to broaden the meaning or scope of: *the law was extended.* 7 (*tr*) to put forth, present, or offer: *to extend greetings.* 8 to stretch forth (an arm, etc.). 9 (*tr*) to lay out (a body) at full length. 10 (*tr*) to strain or exert (a person or animal) to the maximum. 11 (*tr*) to prolong (the time originally set) for payment of (a debt or loan), completion of (a task), etc. 12 (*tr*) *Book-keeping* **a** to carry forward. **b** to calculate the amount of (a total, balance, etc.). 13 (*tr*) *Law* (formerly in England) to value or assess (land).
▷HISTORY C14: from Latin *extendere* to stretch out, from *tendere* to stretch
▸**exˈtendible** *or* **exˈtendable** ADJECTIVE ▸**exˌtendiˈbility** *or* **exˌtendaˈbility** NOUN

extended (ɪkˈstɛndɪd) ADJECTIVE 1 stretched out in time, space, influence, application, etc. 2 (of a horse's pace) free-moving and with long steps: *an extended trot.* 3 *Printing* another word for **expanded** (sense 1).
▸**exˈtendedly** ADVERB ▸**exˈtendedness** NOUN

extended family NOUN *Sociol, anthropol* a social unit that contains the nuclear family together with blood relatives, often spanning three or more generations.

extended-play ADJECTIVE denoting an EP record.

extender (ɪkˈstɛndə) NOUN 1 a person or thing that extends. 2 a substance, such as French chalk or china clay, added to paints to give them body and decrease their rate of settlement. 3 a substance added to glues and resins to dilute them or to modify their viscosity. 4 a substance added to elastomers to assist the plasticizer. 5 *Printing* the part of certain lower-case letters that extends either above (the ascender) or below (the descender) the body of the letter.

extensible (ɪkˈstɛnsəbᵊl) *or* **extensile** (ɪkˈstɛnsaɪl) ADJECTIVE capable of being extended.
▸**exˌtensiˈbility** *or* **exˈtensibleness** NOUN

extension (ɪkˈstɛnʃən) NOUN 1 the act of extending or the condition of being extended. 2 something that can be extended or that extends another object. 3 the length, range, etc., over which something is extended; extent. 4 an additional telephone set connected to the same telephone line as another set or other sets. 5 a room or rooms added to an existing building. 6 a delay, esp one agreed by all parties, in the date originally set for payment of a debt or completion of a contract. 7 the property of matter by which it occupies space; size. 8 **a** the act of straightening or extending an arm or leg. **b** its position after being straightened or extended. 9 *Med* a steady pull applied to a fractured or dislocated arm or leg to restore it to its normal position. See also **traction** (sense 3). 10 **a** a service by which some of the facilities of an educational establishment, library, etc., are offered to outsiders. **b** (*as modifier*): *a university extension course.* 11 *Logic* **a** the class of entities to which a given word correctly applies: thus, the extension of *satellite of Mars* is the set containing only Deimos and Phobos. Compare **intension** (sense 1a). **b conservative extension.** a formal theory that includes among its theorems all the theorems of a given theory.
▷HISTORY C14: from Late Latin *extensiō* a stretching out; see EXTEND

extensional (ɪkˈstɛnʃənᵊl) ADJECTIVE 1 relating to or characterized by extension. 2 *Logic* explicable solely in terms of extensions; ignoring differences of meaning that do not affect the extension. See also **extensionality, substitutivity, transparent context.**
▸**exˈtensionally** ADVERB ▸**exˈtensionalism** NOUN

extensionality (ɪkˌstɛnʃəˈnælɪtɪ) NOUN *Logic* the principle that sets are definable in terms of their elements alone, whatever way they may have been selected. Thus {a, b}={b, a}={first two letters of the alphabet}.

extension ring *or* **tube** NOUN *Photog* a spacer element that can be fixed between the camera body and the lens to increase the distance between film and lens and allow closer focus than would be possible without it.

extensity (ɪkˈstɛnsɪtɪ) NOUN 1 *Psychol* that part of sensory perception relating to the spatial aspect of objects. 2 *Rare* the condition of being extensive or extended.

extensive (ɪkˈstɛnsɪv) ADJECTIVE 1 having a large extent, area, scope, degree, etc.; vast: *extensive deserts; an extensive inheritance.* 2 widespread: *extensive coverage in the press.* 3 *Agriculture* involving or farmed with minimum expenditure of capital or labour, esp depending on a large area of land. Compare **intensive** (sense 3). 4 *Physics* of or relating to a property, measurement, etc., of a macroscopic system that is proportional to the size of the system: *heat is an extensive property.* Compare **intensive** (sense 7). 5 *Logic* **a** of or relating to logical extension. **b** (of a definition) in terms of the objects to which the term applies rather than its meaning.
▸**exˈtensively** ADVERB ▸**exˈtensiveness** NOUN

extensometer (ˌɛkstɛnˈsɒmɪtə) *or* **extensimeter** (ˌɛkstɛnˈsɪmɪtə) NOUN an apparatus for studying small changes of length, as in the thermal expansion or mechanical compression of a solid.

extensor (ɪkˈstɛnsə, -sɔː) NOUN any muscle that stretches or extends an arm, leg, or other bodily part. Compare **flexor.**
▷HISTORY C18: from New Latin, from Latin *extensus* stretched out

extent (ɪkˈstɛnt) NOUN 1 the range over which something extends; scope: *the extent of the damage.* 2 an area or volume: *a vast extent of concrete.* 3 *US law* a writ authorizing a person to whom a debt is due to assume temporary possession of his debtor's lands. 4 *Logic* another word for **extension** (sense 11).
▷HISTORY C14: from Old French *extente,* from Latin *extentus* extensive, from *extendere* to EXTEND

extenuate (ɪkˈstɛnjʊˌeɪt) VERB (*tr*) 1 to represent (an offence, a fault, etc.) as being less serious than it appears, as by showing mitigating circumstances. 2 to cause to be or appear less serious; mitigate. 3 to underestimate or make light of. 4 *Archaic* **a** to emaciate or weaken. **b** to dilute or thin out.
▷HISTORY C16: from Latin *extenuāre* to make thin, from *tenuis* thin, frail
▸**exˈtenuˌating** ADJECTIVE ▸**exˌtenuˈation** NOUN
▸**exˈtenuˌator** NOUN ▸**exˈtenuatory** ADJECTIVE

exterior (ɪkˈstɪərɪə) NOUN 1 a part, surface, or region that is on the outside. 2 the observable outward behaviour or appearance of a person. 3 a film or scene shot outside a studio. ◆ ADJECTIVE 4 of, situated on, or suitable for the outside: *exterior cleaning.* 5 coming or acting from without; external: *exterior complications.* 6 of or involving foreign nations.
▷HISTORY C16: from Latin, comparative of *exterus* on the outside, from *ex* out of
▸**exˈteriorly** ADVERB

exterior angle NOUN 1 an angle of a polygon contained between one side extended and the adjacent side. 2 any of the four angles made by a transversal that are outside the region between the two intersected lines.

exteriorize *or* **exteriorise** (ɪkˈstɪərɪəˌraɪz) VERB (*tr*) 1 *Surgery* to expose (an attached organ or part) outside a body cavity, esp in order to remove it from an operating area. 2 another word for **externalize.**
▸**exˌterioriˈzation** *or* **exˌterioriˈsation** NOUN

exterminate (ɪkˈstɜːmɪˌneɪt) VERB (*tr*) to destroy (living things, esp pests or vermin) completely; annihilate; eliminate.
▷HISTORY C16: from Latin *extermināre* to drive away, from *terminus* boundary
▸**exˈterminable** ADJECTIVE ▸**exˌtermiˈnation** NOUN
▸**exˈterminative** *or* **exˈterminatory** ADJECTIVE
▸**exˈtermiˌnator** NOUN

extern *or* **externe** (ˈɛkstɜːn, ɪkˈstɜːn) NOUN *US* a person, such as a physician at a hospital, who has an official connection with an institution but does not reside in it.
▷HISTORY C16: from Latin *externus* EXTERNAL

external (ɪkˈstɜːnᵊl) ADJECTIVE 1 of, situated on, or suitable for the outside; outer. 2 coming or acting from without: *external evidence from an independent source.* 3 of or involving foreign nations; foreign. 4 of, relating to, or designating a medicine that is applied to the outside of the body. 5 *Anatomy* situated on or near the outside of the body: *the external ear.* 6 *Education* denoting assessment by examiners who are not employed at the candidate's place of study. 7 *Austral and NZ* (of a student) studying a university subject extramurally. 8 *Philosophy* (of objects, etc.) taken to exist independently of a perceiving mind. ◆ NOUN 9 (*often plural*) an external circumstance or aspect, esp one that is superficial or inessential. 10 *Austral and NZ* a student taking an extramural subject.
▷HISTORY C15: from Latin *externus* outward, from *exterus* on the outside, from *ex* out of
▸**exˈternally** ADVERB

External Affairs PLURAL NOUN *Canadian* (formerly) the Canadian federal Foreign Affairs department.

external-combustion engine NOUN a heat engine in which the working fluid is heated in an external boiler or heat exchanger and is thus isolated from the process of fuel combustion.

external ear NOUN the part of the ear consisting of the auricle and the auditory canal.

externalism (ɪkˈstɜːnəˌlɪzəm) NOUN 1 exaggerated emphasis on outward form, esp in religious worship. 2 a philosophical doctrine holding that only objects that can be perceived by the senses are real; phenomenalism.
▸**exˈternalist** NOUN

externality (ˌɛkstɜːˈnælɪtɪ) NOUN, *plural* **-ties.** 1 the state or condition of being external. 2 something external. 3 *Philosophy* the quality of existing independently of a perceiving mind. 4 an economic effect that results from an economic choice but is not reflected in market prices.

externalize (ɪkˈstɜːnəˌlaɪz), **exteriorize** (ɪkˈstɪərɪəˌraɪz), **externalise,** *or* **exteriorise** VERB (*tr*) 1 to make external; give outward shape to. 2 *Psychol* to attribute (one's own feelings) to one's surroundings.
▸**exˌternaliˈzation** *or* **exˌterioriˈzation** *or* **exˌternaliˈsation** *or* **exˌterioriˈsation** NOUN

exteroceptor (ˈɛkstərəʊˌsɛptə) NOUN any sensory organ or part of the body, such as the eye, able to receive stimuli from outside the body. Compare **interoceptor, proprioceptor.**
▷HISTORY C20 *extero-,* from Latin *exterus* EXTERIOR + (RE)CEPTOR
▸**ˌexteroˈceptive** ADJECTIVE

exterritorial (ˌɛkstɛrɪˈtɔːrɪəl) ADJECTIVE a variant of **extraterritorial.**
▸**exˌterriˌtoriˈality** NOUN ▸**ˌexterriˈtorially** ADVERB

extinct (ɪkˈstɪŋkt) ADJECTIVE 1 (of an animal or plant species) having no living representative; having died out. 2 quenched or extinguished. 3 (of a volcano) no longer liable to erupt; inactive. 4 void or obsolete: *an extinct political office.*
▷HISTORY C15: from Latin *exstinctus* quenched, from *exstinguere* to EXTINGUISH

extinction (ɪkˈstɪŋkʃən) NOUN 1 the act of making extinct or the state of being extinct. 2 the act of extinguishing or the state of being extinguished. 3 complete destruction; annihilation. 4 *Physics* reduction of the intensity of radiation as a result of absorption or scattering by matter. 5 *Astronomy* the dimming of light from a celestial body as it passes through an absorbing or scattering medium, such as the earth's atmosphere or interstellar dust. 6 *Psychol* a process in which the frequency or intensity of a learned response is decreased as a result of reinforcement being withdrawn. Compare **habituation.**

extinctive (ɪkˈstɪŋktɪv) ADJECTIVE tending or serving to extinguish or make extinct.

extine (ˈɛkstɪn, -tiːn, -taɪn) NOUN another name for **exine.**
▷HISTORY C19: from Latin *extimus* outermost + -INE[1]

extinguish (ɪkˈstɪŋgwɪʃ) VERB (*tr*) 1 to put out or quench (a light, flames, etc.). 2 to remove or destroy entirely; annihilate. 3 *Archaic* to eclipse or obscure by or as if by superior brilliance. 4 *Law* to discharge (a debt).

▷HISTORY C16: from Latin *exstinguere,* from *stinguere* to quench
▸**ex'tinguishable** ADJECTIVE ▸**ex'tinguisher** NOUN
▸**ex'tinguishment** NOUN

extinguishant (ɪk'stɪŋgwɪʃənt) NOUN a substance, such as a liquid, foam, powder, etc., used in extinguishing fires.

extirpate ('ɛkstəˌpeɪt) VERB (*tr*) 1 to remove or destroy completely. 2 to pull up or out; uproot. 3 to remove (an organ or part) surgically.
▷HISTORY C16: from Latin *exstirpāre* to root out, from *stirps* root, stock
▸ˌ**extir'pation** NOUN ▸'**extirˌpative** ADJECTIVE ▸'**extirˌpator** NOUN

extol *or US* **extoll** (ɪk'stəʊl) VERB **-tols, -tolling, -tolled** *or US* **-tolls, -tolling, -tolled.** (*tr*) to praise lavishly; exalt.
▷HISTORY C15: from Latin *extollere* to elevate, from *tollere* to raise
▸**ex'toller** NOUN ▸**ex'tollingly** ADVERB ▸**ex'tolment** NOUN

extort (ɪk'stɔːt) VERB (*tr*) 1 to secure (money, favours, etc.) by intimidation, violence, or the misuse of influence or authority. 2 to obtain by importunate demands: *the children extorted a promise of a trip to the zoo.* 3 to overcharge for (something, esp interest on a loan).
▷HISTORY C16: from Latin *extortus* wrenched out, from *extorquēre* to wrest away, from *torquēre* to twist, wrench
▸**ex'torter** NOUN ▸**ex'tortive** ADJECTIVE

extortion (ɪk'stɔːʃən) NOUN the act of securing money, favours, etc. by intimidation or violence; blackmail.
▸**ex'tortioner** *or* **ex'tortionist** NOUN

extortionate (ɪk'stɔːʃənɪt) ADJECTIVE 1 (of prices, etc.) excessive; exorbitant. 2 (of persons) using extortion.
▸**ex'tortionately** ADVERB

extra ('ɛkstrə) ADJECTIVE 1 being more than what is usual or expected; additional. ◆ NOUN 2 a person or thing that is additional. 3 something for which an additional charge is made: *the new car had many extras.* 4 an additional edition of a newspaper, esp to report a new development or crisis. 5 *Films* an actor or person temporarily engaged, usually for crowd scenes. 6 *Cricket* a run not scored from the bat, such as a wide, no-ball, bye, or leg bye. 7 *US* something that is better than usual in quality. ◆ ADVERB 8 unusually; exceptionally: *an extra fast car.*
▷HISTORY C18: perhaps shortened from EXTRAORDINARY

extra- PREFIX outside or beyond an area or scope: *extrasensory; extraterritorial.*
▷HISTORY from Latin *extrā* outside, beyond, changed from *extera,* from *exterus* outward

extracanonical (ˌɛkstrəkə'nɒnɪk^{ə}l) ADJECTIVE *Christianity* not included in the canon of Scripture.

extracellular (ˌɛkstrə'sɛljʊlə) ADJECTIVE *Biology* situated or occurring outside a cell or cells.
▸ˌ**extra'cellularly** ADVERB

extracorporeal (ˌɛkstrəkɔː'pɔːrɪəl) ADJECTIVE outside the body.

extra cover NOUN *Cricket* a fielding position between cover and mid-off.

extract VERB (ɪk'strækt) (*tr*) 1 to withdraw, pull out, or uproot by force. 2 to remove or separate. 3 to derive (pleasure, information, etc.) from some source or situation. 4 to deduce or develop (a doctrine, policy, etc.). 5 *Informal* to extort (money, etc.). 6 to obtain (a substance) from a mixture or material by a chemical or physical process, such as digestion, distillation, the action of a solvent, or mechanical separation. 7 to cut out or copy out (an article, passage, quotation, etc.) from a publication. 8 to determine the value of (the root of a number). ◆ NOUN ('ɛkstrækt) 9 something extracted, such as a part or passage from a book, speech, etc. 10 a preparation containing the active principle or concentrated essence of a material: *beef extract; yeast extract.* 11 *Pharmacol* a solution of plant or animal tissue containing the active principle.
▷HISTORY C15: from Latin *extractus* drawn forth, from *extrahere,* from *trahere* to drag
▸**ex'tractable** ADJECTIVE ▸**exˌtracta'bility** NOUN

> **Language note** *Extract* is sometimes wrongly used where *extricate* would be better: *he will find it difficult extricating* (not *extracting*) *himself from this situation.*

extraction (ɪk'strækʃən) NOUN 1 the act of extracting or the condition of being extracted. 2 something extracted; an extract. 3 **a** the act or an instance of extracting a tooth or teeth. **b** a tooth or teeth extracted. 4 origin, descent, lineage, or ancestry: *of German extraction.*

extractions (ɪk'strækʃənz) PLURAL NOUN the residue remaining after an oilseed has had the oil extracted by a solvent. Used as a feed for animals: *groundnut extractions.* Compare **expellers.**

extractive (ɪk'stræktɪv) ADJECTIVE 1 tending or serving to extract. 2 of, involving, or capable of extraction. ◆ NOUN 3 something extracted or capable of being extracted. 4 the part of an extract that is insoluble.

extractor (ɪk'stræktə) NOUN 1 a person or thing that extracts. 2 an instrument for pulling something out or removing tight-fitting components. 3 a device for extracting liquid from a solid, esp a centrifugal dryer. 4 short for **extractor fan.** 5 a fitting in many firearms for removing spent cartridges from the chamber.

extractor fan *or* **extraction fan** NOUN a fan used in kitchens, bathrooms, workshops, etc., to remove stale air or fumes.

extracurricular (ˌɛkstrəkə'rɪkjʊlə) ADJECTIVE 1 taking place outside the normal school timetable: *extracurricular activities.* 2 beyond the regular duties, schedule, etc.

extraditable ('ɛkstrəˌdaɪtəb^{ə}l) ADJECTIVE 1 (of a crime) rendering the offender liable to extradition: *an extraditable offence.* 2 (of a person) subject to extradition.

extradite ('ɛkstrəˌdaɪt) VERB (*tr*) 1 to surrender (an alleged offender) for trial to a foreign state. 2 to procure the extradition of.
▷HISTORY C19: back formation from EXTRADITION

extradition (ˌɛkstrə'dɪʃən) NOUN the surrender of an alleged offender or fugitive to the state in whose territory the alleged offence was committed.
▷HISTORY C19: from French, from Latin *trāditiō* a handing over; see TRADITION

extrados (ɛk'streɪdɒs) NOUN, *plural* **-dos** (-dəʊz) *or* **-doses.** *Architect* the outer curve or surface of an arch or vault. Compare **intrados.**
▷HISTORY C18: from French, from EXTRA- + *dos* back, from Latin *dorsum*

extradural (ˌɛkstrə'djʊərəl) ADJECTIVE another word for **epidural** (sense 1).

extrafloral (ˌɛkstrə'flɒrəl) ADJECTIVE produced or occurring outside a flower: *extrafloral nectar; extrafloral nectary.*

extragalactic (ˌɛkstrəgə'læktɪk) ADJECTIVE occurring or existing beyond the Galaxy.

extragalactic nebula NOUN the former name for **galaxy.**

extrajudicial (ˌɛkstrədʒuː'dɪʃəl) ADJECTIVE 1 outside the ordinary course of legal proceedings: *extrajudicial evidence.* 2 beyond the jurisdiction or authority of the court: *an extrajudicial opinion.*
▸ˌ**extraju'dicially** ADVERB

extramarital (ˌɛkstrə'mærɪt^{ə}l) ADJECTIVE (esp of sexual relations) occurring outside marriage.

extramundane (ˌɛkstrə'mʌndeɪn) ADJECTIVE not of the physical world or universe.

extramural (ˌɛkstrə'mjʊərəl) ADJECTIVE 1 connected with but outside the normal courses or programme of a university, college, etc.: *extramural studies.* 2 located beyond the boundaries or walls of a city, castle, etc.
▸ˌ**extra'murally** ADVERB

extraneous (ɪk'streɪnɪəs) ADJECTIVE 1 not essential. 2 not pertinent or applicable; irrelevant. 3 coming from without; of external origin. 4 not belonging; unrelated to that to which it is added or in which it is contained.
▷HISTORY C17: from Latin *extrāneus* external, from *extrā* outside
▸**ex'traneously** ADVERB ▸**ex'traneousness** NOUN

extranet ('ɛkstrəˌnɛt) NOUN *Computing* an intranet that is modified to allow outsiders access to it, esp one belonging to a business that allows access to customers.
▷HISTORY C20: from EXTRA- + NET[1] (sense 8), modelled on INTRANET

extranuclear (ˌɛkstrə'njuːklɪə) ADJECTIVE *Biology* situated or occurring in part of a cell outside the nucleus.

extraordinary (ɪk'strɔːd^{ə}nrɪ, -d^{ə}nərɪ) ADJECTIVE 1 very unusual, remarkable, or surprising. 2 not in an established manner, course, or order. 3 employed for particular events or purposes. 4 (*usually postpositive*) (of an official, etc.) additional or subordinate to the usual one: *a minister extraordinary.*
▷HISTORY C15: from Latin *extraordinārius* beyond what is usual; see ORDINARY
▸**ex'traordinarily** ADVERB ▸**ex'traordinariness** NOUN

extraordinary general meeting NOUN a meeting specially called to discuss a particular item of a company's business, usually one of some importance. The meeting may be called by a group of shareholders or by the directors. Abbreviation: **EGM.**

extraordinary ray NOUN *Optics* the plane-polarized ray of light that does not obey the laws of refraction in a doubly refracting crystal. See **double refraction.** Compare **ordinary ray.**

extrapolate (ɪk'stræpəˌleɪt) VERB 1 *Maths* to estimate (a value of a function or measurement) beyond the values already known, by the extension of a curve. Compare **interpolate** (sense 4). 2 to infer (something not known) by using but not strictly deducing from the known facts.
▷HISTORY C19: EXTRA- + *-polate,* as in INTERPOLATE
▸**exˌtrapo'lation** NOUN ▸**ex'trapolative** *or* **ex'trapolatory** ADJECTIVE ▸**ex'trapoˌlator** NOUN

extraposition (ˌɛkstrəpə'zɪʃən) NOUN 1 placement of something outside something else. 2 *Transformational grammar* a rule that moves embedded clauses out to the end of the main clause, converting, for example, *A man who will help has just arrived* into *A man has just arrived who will help.*

extrasensory (ˌɛkstrə'sɛnsərɪ) ADJECTIVE of or relating to extrasensory perception.

extrasensory perception NOUN the supposed ability of certain individuals to obtain information about the environment without the use of normal sensory channels. Also called: **cryptaesthesia.** See also **clairvoyance** (sense 1), **telepathy.** Abbreviation: **esp**

extrasolar (ˌɛkstrə'səʊlə) ADJECTIVE occurring or existing beyond the earth's solar system.

extraterrestrial (ˌɛkstrətɪ'rɛstrɪəl) ADJECTIVE 1 occurring or existing beyond the earth's atmosphere. ◆ NOUN 2 (in science fiction) a being from beyond the earth's atmosphere.

extraterritorial (ˌɛkstrəˌtɛrɪ'tɔːrɪəl) *or* **exterritorial** ADJECTIVE 1 beyond the limits of a country's territory. 2 of, relating to, or possessing extraterritoriality.
▸ˌ**extraˌterri'torially** *or* ˌ**exterri'torially** ADVERB

extraterritoriality (ˌɛkstrəˌtɛrɪˌtɔːrɪ'ælɪtɪ) NOUN *International law* 1 the privilege granted to some aliens, esp diplomats, of being exempt from the jurisdiction of the state in which they reside. 2 the right or privilege of a state to exercise authority in certain circumstances beyond the limits of its territory.

extra time NOUN *Sport* an additional period played at the end of a match, to compensate for time lost through injury or (in certain circumstances) to allow the teams to achieve a conclusive result.

extrauterine (ˌɛkstrə'juːtəˌraɪn) ADJECTIVE situated or developing outside the cavity of the uterus.

extravagance (ɪk'strævɪgəns) NOUN 1 excessive outlay of money; wasteful spending. 2 immoderate or absurd speech or behaviour.

extravagant (ɪk'strævɪgənt) ADJECTIVE 1 spending money excessively or immoderately. 2 going beyond usual bounds; unrestrained: *extravagant praise.* 3 ostentatious; showy. 4 exorbitant in price; overpriced.
▷HISTORY C14: from Medieval Latin *extravagāns,* from Latin EXTRA- + *vagārī* to wander
▸**ex'travagantly** ADVERB

Extravagantes (ɪkˌstrævəˈgæntiːz) PLURAL NOUN *RC Church* decretals circulating outside some recognized collection of canon law. Those of John XXII and the so-called Extravagantes communes form part of the Corpus Juris Canonici.
▷HISTORY Latin: wandering, circulating

extravaganza (ɪkˌstrævəˈgænzə) NOUN [1] an elaborately staged and costumed light entertainment. [2] any lavish or fanciful display, literary or other composition, etc.
▷HISTORY C18: from Italian: EXTRAVAGANCE

extravagate (ɪkˈstrævəˌgeɪt) VERB (*intr*) *Archaic* [1] to exceed normal limits or propriety. [2] to roam at will.
▷HISTORY C17: from Latin *extravagārī*; see EXTRAVAGANT
▸**exˌtravaˈgation** NOUN

extravasate (ɪkˈstrævəˌseɪt) VERB [1] *Pathol* to cause (blood or lymph) to escape or (of blood or lymph) to escape into the surrounding tissues from their proper vessels. [2] to exude (molten material, such as lava) or (of molten material) to be exuded. ◆ NOUN [3] *Pathol* the material extravasated.
▷HISTORY C17: from Latin EXTRA- + *vās* vessel
▸**exˌtravaˈsation** NOUN

extravascular (ˌɛkstrəˈvæskjʊlə) ADJECTIVE *Anatomy* situated or occurring outside a lymph or blood vessel.

extravehicular (ˌɛkstrəvɪˈhɪkjʊlə) ADJECTIVE occurring or used outside a spacecraft, either in space or on the surface of the moon or another planet: *extravehicular activity*.

extraversion (ˌɛkstrəˈvɜːʃən) NOUN a variant spelling of **extroversion.**
▸**ˌextraˈversive** ADJECTIVE

extravert (ˈɛkstrəˌvɜːt) NOUN, ADJECTIVE a variant spelling of **extrovert.**

extra virgin ADJECTIVE (of olive oil) of the highest quality, extracted by cold pressing rather than chemical treatment.

extremal (ɪkˈstriːməl) NOUN *Maths, logic* the clause in a recursive definition that specifies that no items other than those generated by the stated rules fall within the definition, as in *1 is an integer, if n is an integer so is n+1, and nothing else is*.

extreme (ɪkˈstriːm) ADJECTIVE [1] being of a high or of the highest degree or intensity: *extreme cold; extreme difficulty*. [2] exceeding what is usual or reasonable; immoderate: *extreme behaviour*. [3] very strict, rigid, or severe; drastic: *an extreme measure*. [4] (*prenominal*) farthest or outermost in direction: *the extreme boundary*. [5] *Meteorol* of, relating to, or characteristic of a continental climate. ◆ NOUN [6] the highest or furthest degree (often in the phrases **in the extreme, go to extremes**). [7] (*often plural*) either of the two limits or ends of a scale or range of possibilities: *extremes of temperature*. [8] *Maths* **a** the first or last term of a series or a proportion. **b** a maximum or minimum value of a function. [9] *Logic* the subject or predicate of the conclusion of a syllogism.
▷HISTORY C15: from Latin *extrēmus* outermost, from *exterus* on the outside; see EXTERIOR
▸**exˈtremeness** NOUN

extreme fighting NOUN a combat sport incorporating techniques from a range of martial arts, with little if any regulation of the types of blows permissible.

extremely (ɪkˈstriːmlɪ) ADVERB [1] to the extreme; exceedingly. [2] (intensifier): *she behaved extremely badly*.

Language note See at **very.**

extremely high frequency NOUN a radio frequency between 30 000 and 300 000 megahertz. Abbreviation: **EHF.**

extremely low frequency NOUN a radio frequency or radio-frequency band below 3 kilohertz. Abbreviation: **ELF.**

extreme sport NOUN a sport that is physically hazardous, such as bungee jumping or snowboarding.

extreme unction NOUN *RC Church* a former name for **anointing of the sick.**

extremist (ɪkˈstriːmɪst) NOUN [1] a person who favours or resorts to immoderate, uncompromising, or fanatical methods or behaviour, esp in being politically radical. ◆ ADJECTIVE [2] of, relating to, or characterized by immoderate or excessive actions, opinions, etc.
▸**exˈtremism** NOUN

extremity (ɪkˈstrɛmɪtɪ) NOUN, *plural* **-ties.** [1] the farthest or outermost point or section; termination. [2] the greatest or most intense degree. [3] an extreme condition or state, as of adversity or disease. [4] a limb, such as a leg, arm, or wing, or the part of such a limb farthest from the trunk. [5] (*usually plural*) *Archaic* a drastic or severe measure.

extricate (ˈɛkstrɪˌkeɪt) VERB (*tr*) to remove or free from complication, hindrance, or difficulty; disentangle.
▷HISTORY C17: from Latin *extrīcāre* to disentangle, from EX-[1] + *trīcae* trifles, vexations
▸**ˈextricable** ADJECTIVE ▸**ˌextriˈcation** NOUN

Language note See at **extract.**

extrinsic (ɛkˈstrɪnsɪk) ADJECTIVE [1] not contained or included within; extraneous. [2] originating or acting from outside; external.
▷HISTORY C16: from Late Latin *extrinsecus* (adj) outward, from Latin (adv) from without, on the outward side, from *exter* outward + *secus* alongside, related to *sequī* to follow
▸**exˈtrinsically** ADVERB

extrorse (ɛkˈstrɔːs) *or* **extrorsal** ADJECTIVE *Botany* turned or opening outwards or away from the axis: *extrorse anthers*.
▷HISTORY C19: from Late Latin *extrorsus* in an outward direction, from Latin EXTRA- + *versus* turned towards

extroversion *or* **extraversion** (ˌɛkstrəˈvɜːʃən) NOUN [1] *Psychol* the directing of one's interest outwards, esp towards social contacts. [2] *Pathol* a turning inside out of an organ or part. ◆ Compare **introversion.**
▷HISTORY C17: from *extro-* (variant of EXTRA-, contrasting with INTRO-) + *-version*, from Latin *vertere* to turn
▸**ˌextroˈversive** *or* **ˌextraˈversive** ADJECTIVE
▸**ˌextroˈversively** *or* **ˌextraˈversively** ADVERB

extrovert *or* **extravert** (ˈɛkstrəˌvɜːt) *Psychol* ◆ NOUN [1] a person concerned more with external reality than inner feelings. ◆ ADJECTIVE [2] of or characterized by extroversion: *extrovert tendencies*. Compare **introvert.**
▷HISTORY C20: from *extro-* (variant of EXTRA-, contrasting with INTRO-) + *-vert*, from Latin *vertere* to turn
▸**ˈextroˌverted** *or* **ˈextraˌverted** ADJECTIVE

extrude (ɪkˈstruːd) VERB [1] (*tr*) to squeeze or force out. [2] (*tr*) to produce (moulded sections of plastic, metal, etc.) by ejection under pressure through a suitably shaped nozzle or die. [3] (*tr*) to chop up or pulverize (an item of food) and re-form it to look like a whole: *a factory-made rod of extruded egg*. [4] a less common word for **protrude.**
▷HISTORY C16: from Latin *extrūdere* to thrust out, from *trūdere* to push, thrust
▸**exˈtruded** ADJECTIVE

extrusion (ɪkˈstruːʒən) NOUN [1] the act or process of extruding. [2] **a** the movement of magma onto the surface of the earth through volcano craters and cracks in the earth's crust, forming igneous rock. **b** any igneous rock formed in this way. [3] a component or length of material formed by the process of extruding.
▷HISTORY C16: from Medieval Latin *extrūsiō*, from *extrūdere* to EXTRUDE
▸**exˈtrusible** ADJECTIVE

extrusive (ɪkˈstruːsɪv) ADJECTIVE [1] tending to extrude. [2] (of igneous rocks) formed from magma issuing from volcanoes or cracks in the earth's crust; volcanic. Compare **intrusive** (sense 2).

exuberant (ɪgˈzjuːbərənt) ADJECTIVE [1] abounding in vigour and high spirits; full of vitality. [2] lavish or effusive; excessively elaborate: *exuberant compliments*. [3] growing luxuriantly or in profusion.
▷HISTORY C15: from Latin *exūberāns*, from *ūberāre* to be fruitful, from *ūber* fertile
▸**exuberance** NOUN ▸**exˈuberantly** ADVERB

exuberate (ɪgˈzjuːbəˌreɪt) VERB (*intr*) *Rare* [1] to be exuberant. [2] to abound or grow in profusion.
▷HISTORY C15: from Latin *exūberāre* to be abundant; see EXUBERANT

exudation (ˌɛksjʊˈdeɪʃən) NOUN [1] the act of exuding or oozing out. [2] Also called: **exudate** (ˈɛksjʊˌdeɪt). a fluid with a high content of protein in a body cavity. Compare **transudate.**
▸**exudative** (ɪgˈzjuːdətɪv) ADJECTIVE

exude (ɪgˈzjuːd) VERB [1] to release or be released through pores, incisions, etc., as sweat from the body or sap from trees. [2] (*tr*) to make apparent by mood or behaviour: *he exuded confidence*.
▷HISTORY C16: from Latin *exsūdāre*, from *sūdāre* to sweat

exult (ɪgˈzʌlt) VERB (*intr*) [1] to be joyful or jubilant, esp because of triumph or success; rejoice. [2] (often foll by *over*) to triumph (over); show or take delight in the defeat or discomfiture (of).
▷HISTORY C16: from Latin *exsultāre* to jump or leap for joy, from *saltāre* to leap
▸**exultation** (ˌɛgzʌlˈteɪʃən) NOUN ▸**exˈultingly** ADVERB

Language note See at **exalt.**

exultant (ɪgˈzʌltənt) ADJECTIVE elated or jubilant, esp because of triumph or success.
▸**exˈultance** *or* **exˈultancy** NOUN ▸**exˈultantly** ADVERB

exurbia (ɛksˈɜːbɪə) NOUN *Chiefly US* the region outside the suburbs of a city, consisting of residential areas (**exurbs**) that are occupied predominantly by rich commuters (**exurbanites**). Compare **stockbroker belt.**
▷HISTORY C20: from EX-[1] + Latin *urbs* city, on pattern of *suburbia*
▸**exˈurban** ADJECTIVE

exuviae (ɪgˈzjuːvɪˌiː) PLURAL NOUN layers of skin or cuticle shed by animals during ecdysis.
▷HISTORY C17: from Latin: something stripped off (the body), from *exuere* to strip off
▸**exˈuvial** ADJECTIVE

exuviate (ɪgˈzjuːvɪˌeɪt) VERB to shed (a skin or similar outer covering).
▸**exˌuviˈation** NOUN

ex voto *Latin* (ɛks ˈvəʊtəʊ) ADVERB, ADJECTIVE [1] in accordance with a vow. ◆ NOUN [2] an offering made in fulfilment of a vow.

ex works ADVERB, ADJECTIVE (**ex-works** when prenominal) *Brit* (of a price, value, etc.) excluding the cost of delivery from the factory and sometimes excluding the commission or profit of the distributor or retailer: *the price is £500 ex works*.

-ey SUFFIX a variant of **-y**[1], **-y**[2].

Eyam (ˈiːjəm) NOUN a village in N central England, in Derbyshire. When plague reached the village in 1665 the inhabitants isolated themselves to prevent it spreading further: as a result, most of them died.

eyas (ˈaɪəs) NOUN a nestling hawk or falcon, esp one reared for training in falconry.
▷HISTORY C15: mistaken division of earlier *a nyas*, from Old French *niais* nestling, from Latin *nīdus* nest

eye[1] (aɪ) NOUN [1] the organ of sight of animals, containing light-sensitive cells associated with nerve fibres, so that light entering the eye is converted to nervous impulses that reach the brain. In man and other vertebrates the iris controls the amount of light entering the eye and the lens focuses the light onto the retina. Related adjectives: **ocular, oculate, ophthalmic, optic.** [2] (*often plural*) the ability to see; sense of vision: *weak eyes*. [3] the visible external part of an eye, often including the area around it: *heavy-lidded eyes; piercing eyes*. [4] a look, glance, expression, or gaze: *a stern eye*. [5] a sexually inviting or provocative look (esp in the phrases **give (someone) the (glad) eye, make eyes at**). [6] attention or observation (often in the phrases **catch someone's eye, keep an eye on, cast an eye over**). [7] ability to recognize, judge, or appreciate: *an eye for antiques*. [8] (*often plural*) opinion, judgment, point of view, or authority: *in the eyes of the law*. [9] a structure or marking having the appearance of an eye, such as the bud on a twig or potato tuber or a spot on a butterfly wing. [10] a small loop or hole, as at one end of a needle. [11] a small area of low pressure and calm in the centre of a tornado or cyclone. [12] See **photocell.** [13] *Informal* See **private eye.** [14] **all eyes.** *Informal* acutely vigilant or observant: *the children were all eyes*. [15] **(all) my eye.**

Informal rubbish; nonsense. [16] **an eye for an eye.** retributive or vengeful justice; retaliation. [17] **cut one's eye after, at,** *or* **on (someone).** *Caribbean* to look rudely at (a person) and then turn one's face away sharply while closing one's eyes: a gesture of contempt. [18] *NZ* **eyes out.** with every possible effort: *he went at the job eyes out.* [19] **get one's eye in.** *Chiefly sport* to become accustomed to the conditions, light, etc., with a consequent improvement in one's performance. [20] **half an eye. a** a modicum of perceptiveness: *anyone with half an eye can see she's in love.* **b** continuing unobtrusive observation or awareness: *the dog had half an eye on the sheep.* [21] **have eyes for.** to be interested in: *she has eyes only for him.* [22] **in one's mind's eye.** pictured within the mind; imagined or remembered vividly. [23] **in the public eye.** exposed to public curiosity or publicity. [24] **keep an eye open** *or* **out (for).** to watch with special attention (for). [25] **keep one's eyes peeled** (*or* **skinned**). to watch vigilantly (for). [26] **look (someone) in the eye.** to look openly and without shame or embarrassment at. [27] **make (sheep's) eyes (at).** *Old-fashioned* to ogle amorously. [28] **more than meets the eye.** hidden motives, meaning, or facts. [29] **pick the eyes out (of).** *Austral and NZ* to select the best parts or pieces (of). [30] **see eye to eye (with).** to agree (with). [31] **set, lay,** *or* **clap eyes on.** (*usually used with a negative*) to see: *she had never laid eyes on him before.* [32] **the eye of the wind.** *Nautical* the direction from which the wind is blowing. [33] **turn a blind eye to** *or* **close one's eyes to.** to pretend not to notice or ignore deliberately. [34] **up to one's eyes (in).** extremely busy (with). [35] **with a ... eye.** in a ... manner: *he regards our success with a jealous eye.* [36] **with** *or* **having an eye to.** (*preposition*) **a** regarding; with reference to: *with an eye to one's own interests.* **b** with the intention or purpose of: *with an eye to reaching agreement.* [37] **with one's eyes open.** in the full knowledge of all relevant facts. [38] **with one's eyes shut. a** with great ease, esp as a result of thorough familiarity: *I could drive home with my eyes shut.* **b** without being aware of all the facts. ◆ VERB **eyes, eyeing** *or* **eying, eyed.** (*tr*) [39] to look at carefully or warily. [40] Also: **eye up.** to look at in a manner indicating sexual interest; ogle. ◆ See also **eyes.**

▷HISTORY Old English *ēage;* related to Old Norse *auga,* Old High German *ouga,* Sanskrit *aksi*

▸'**eyeless** ADJECTIVE ▸'**eye,like** ADJECTIVE

eye^2 (aɪ) NOUN another word for **nye.**

eyeball ('aɪˌbɔːl) NOUN [1] the entire ball-shaped part of the eye. [2] **eyeball to eyeball.** in close confrontation. ◆ VERB [3] (*tr*) *Slang* to stare at.

eyebank ('aɪˌbæŋk) NOUN a place in which corneas are stored for use in corneal grafts.

eyebath ('aɪˌbɑːθ) NOUN a small vessel with a rim shaped to fit round the eye, used for applying medicated or cleansing solutions to the eyeball. Also called (US and Canadian): **eyecup.**

eyeblack ('aɪˌblæk) NOUN another name for **mascara.**

eyebolt ('aɪˌbəʊlt) NOUN a threaded bolt, the head of which is formed into a ring or eye for lifting, pulling, or securing.

eyebright ('aɪˌbraɪt) NOUN any scrophulariaceous annual plant of the genus *Euphrasia,* esp *E. nemorosa,* having small white-and-purple two-lipped flowers: formerly used in the treatment of eye disorders. Also called: **euphrasy.**

eyebrow ('aɪˌbraʊ) NOUN [1] the transverse bony ridge over each eye. [2] the arch of hair that covers this ridge. Related adjective: **superciliary.** [3] **raise an eyebrow.** See **raise** (sense 31).

eyebrow pencil NOUN a cosmetic in pencil form for applying colour and shape to the eyebrows.

eye candy NOUN *Informal* [1] a person or people considered highly attractive to look at, often implying that they are lacking in intelligence or depth. [2] something intended to be attractive to the eye without being demanding or contributing anything essential.

eye-catching ADJECTIVE tending to attract attention; striking.

▸'**eye-ˌcatcher** NOUN

eye contact NOUN a direct look between two people; meeting of eyes: *he maintained eye contact with his interrogator.*

eyecup ('aɪˌkʌp) NOUN a US and Canadian name for an **eyebath.**

eyed (aɪd) ADJECTIVE **a** having an eye or eyes (as specified). **b** (*in combination*): *one-eyed; brown-eyed.*

eye dog NOUN *NZ* a dog trained to control sheep by staring fixedly at them. Also called: **strong-eye dog.** ◆ See also **seeing-eye dog.**

eyeful ('aɪfʊl) NOUN *Informal* [1] a view, glance, or gaze: *he got an eyeful of the secret before they blindfolded him.* [2] a very beautiful or attractive sight, esp a woman.

eyeglass ('aɪˌglɑːs) NOUN [1] a lens for aiding or correcting defective vision, esp a monocle. [2] another word for **eyepiece.**

eyeglasses ('aɪˌglɑːsɪz) PLURAL NOUN *Now chiefly US* another word for **spectacles.**

eyehole ('aɪˌhəʊl) NOUN [1] a hole through which something, such as a rope, hook, or bar, is passed. [2] the cavity that contains the eyeball; eye socket. [3] another word for **peephole.**

eyehook ('aɪˌhʊk) NOUN a hook attached to a ring at the extremity of a rope or chain.

eyelash ('aɪˌlæʃ) NOUN [1] any one of the short curved hairs that grow from the edge of the eyelids. [2] a row or fringe of these hairs. Related adjective: **ciliary.**

eyelet ('aɪlɪt) NOUN [1] a small hole for a lace or cord to be passed through or for a hook to be inserted into. [2] a small metal ring or tube with flared ends bent back, reinforcing an eyehole in fabric. [3] a chink or small opening, such as a peephole in a wall. [4] *Embroidery* **a** a small hole with finely stitched edges, forming part of an ornamental pattern. **b** Also called: **eyelet embroidery.** a piece of embroidery decorated with such work. [5] fabric decorated with such work produced by machine. [6] a small eye or eyelike marking. ◆ VERB [7] (*tr*) to supply with an eyelet or eyelets.

▷HISTORY C14: from Old French *oillet,* literally: a little eye, from *oill* eye, from Latin *oculus* eye; see EYE[1]

eyeleteer (ˌaɪlɪ'tɪə) NOUN a small bodkin or other pointed tool for making eyelet holes.

eyelevel ('aɪˌlevᵊl) ADJECTIVE level with a person's eyes when looking straight ahead: *an eyelevel grill.*

eyelid ('aɪˌlɪd) NOUN [1] either of the two muscular folds of skin that can be moved to cover the exposed portion of the eyeball. Related adjective: **palpebral.** [2] Also called: **clamshell.** *Aeronautics* a set of movable parts at the rear of a jet engine that redirect the exhaust flow to assist braking during landing.

eyeliner ('aɪˌlaɪnə) NOUN a cosmetic used to outline the eyes.

eye of day NOUN *Poetic* the sun.

eye-opener NOUN *Informal* [1] something startling or revealing. [2] *US and Canadian* an alcoholic drink taken early in the morning.

eyepiece ('aɪˌpiːs) NOUN the lens or combination of lenses in an optical instrument nearest the eye of the observer.

eye-popping ADJECTIVE *Informal* so amazing or astonishing as to make one's eyes protrude: *an eye-popping spending spree.*

eye rhyme NOUN a rhyme involving words that are similar in spelling but not in sound, such as *stone* and *none.*

eyes (aɪz) PLURAL NOUN *Nautical* the part of the bows of a ship that are furthest forward at the level of the main deck.

eyes front INTERJECTION [1] *Military* a command to troops to look ahead. [2] a demand for attention.

eyeshade ('aɪˌʃeɪd) NOUN an opaque or tinted translucent visor, worn on the head like a cap to protect the eyes from glare.

eye shadow NOUN a coloured cosmetic put around the eyes so as to enhance their colour or shape.

eyeshot ('aɪˌʃɒt) NOUN range of vision; view.

eyesight ('aɪˌsaɪt) NOUN the ability to see; faculty of sight.

eyes left INTERJECTION *Military* a command to troops to look left, esp as a salute when marching.

eye socket NOUN the nontechnical name for **orbit** (sense 3).

eyesore ('aɪˌsɔː) NOUN something very ugly.

eye splice NOUN an eye formed in a rope by splicing the end into its standing part.

eyespot ('aɪˌspɒt) NOUN [1] a small area of light-sensitive pigment in some protozoans, algae, and other simple organisms. [2] an eyelike marking, as on the wings of certain butterflies.

eyes right INTERJECTION *Military* a command to troops to look right, esp as a salute when marching.

eyestalk ('aɪˌstɔːk) NOUN a movable stalk bearing a compound eye at its tip: occurs in crustaceans and some molluscs.

eyestrain ('aɪˌstreɪn) NOUN fatigue or irritation of the eyes, resulting from excessive use, as from prolonged reading of small print, or uncorrected defects of vision.

Eyetie ('aɪtaɪ) NOUN, ADJECTIVE *Brit slang, offensive* Italian.

▷HISTORY C20: based on a jocular mispronunciation of *Italian*

eyetooth (ˌaɪ'tuːθ) NOUN, *plural* **-teeth.** [1] either of the two canine teeth in the upper jaw. [2] **give one's eyeteeth for.** to go to any lengths to achieve or obtain (something): *I'd give my eyeteeth for a radio as good as that.*

eyewash ('aɪˌwɒʃ) NOUN [1] a mild solution for applying to the eyes for relief of irritation, etc. [2] *Informal* nonsense; rubbish.

eyewitness ('aɪˌwɪtnɪs) NOUN **a** a person present at an event who can describe what happened. **b** (*as modifier*): *an eyewitness account.*

eyot (aɪt) NOUN *Brit rare* island.

▷HISTORY variant of AIT

eyra ('ɛərə, 'aɪərə) NOUN a reddish-brown variety of the jaguarondi.

▷HISTORY C19: from American Spanish, from Tupi *eirara*

eyre (ɛə) NOUN *English legal history* [1] any of the circuit courts held in each shire from 1176 until the late 13th century. [2] **justices in eyre.** the justices travelling on circuit and presiding over such courts.

▷HISTORY C13: from Old French *erre* journey, from *errer* to travel, from Latin *errāre* to wander

Eyre (ɛə) NOUN **Lake.** a shallow salt lake in NE central South Australia, about 11 m (35 ft.) below sea level. Area: 9600 sq. km (3700 sq. miles).

▷HISTORY C19: named after Edward John *Eyre* (1815–1901), British explorer and colonial administrator

Eyre Peninsula NOUN a peninsula of South Australia, between the Great Australian Bight and Spencer Gulf.

eyrie ('ɪərɪ, 'ɛərɪ, 'aɪərɪ) *or* **aerie** NOUN [1] the nest of an eagle or other bird of prey, built in a high inaccessible place. [2] the brood of a bird of prey, esp an eagle. [3] any high isolated position or place.

▷HISTORY C16: from Medieval Latin *airea,* from Latin *ārea* open field, hence nest

eyrir ('eɪrɪə) NOUN, *plural* **aurar** ('ɔːrɑː). an Icelandic monetary unit worth one hundredth of a krona.

▷HISTORY Old Norse: ounce (of silver), money; related to Latin *aureus* golden

Ez. *or* **Ezr.** *Bible* ABBREVIATION FOR Ezra.

Ezek. *Bible* ABBREVIATION FOR Ezekiel.

Ezekiel (ɪ'ziːkɪəl) NOUN *Old Testament* [1] a Hebrew prophet of the 6th century B.C., exiled to Babylon in 597 B.C. [2] the book containing his oracles, which describe the downfall of Judah and Jerusalem and their subsequent restoration. Douay spelling: **Ezechiel.**

e-zine ('iːziːn) NOUN a magazine available only in electronic form, for example on the World Wide Web.

Ezra ('ɛzrə) NOUN *Old Testament* [1] a Jewish priest of the 5th century B.C., who was sent from Babylon by the Persian king Artaxerxes I to reconstitute observance of the Jewish law and worship in Jerusalem after the captivity. [2] the book recounting his efforts to perform this task.

Ff

f *or* **F** (ɛf) NOUN, *plural* **f's, F's,** *or* **Fs.** [1] the sixth letter and fourth consonant of the modern English alphabet. [2] a speech sound represented by this letter, usually a voiceless labio-dental fricative, as in *fat.*

f SYMBOL FOR: [1] *Music* forte: an instruction to play loudly. [2] *Physics* frequency. [3] (formerly, in the Netherlands) guilder. [from Dutch: florin] [4] *Maths* function (of). [5] *Physics* femto-. [6] *Chess* See **algebraic notation.**

f, f/, *or* **f:** SYMBOL FOR f-number.

F SYMBOL FOR: [1] *Music* **a** a note having a frequency of 349.23 hertz (**F above middle C**) or this value multiplied or divided by any power of 2; the fourth note of the scale of C major. **b** a key, string, or pipe producing this note. **c** the major or minor key having this note as its tonic. [2] Fahrenheit. [3] Fellow. [4] *Chem* fluorine. [5] Helmholtz function. [6] *Physics* force. [7] franc(s). [8] farad(s). [9] *Genetics* a generation of filial offspring, F_1 being the first generation of offspring, F_2 being the second generation, etc. ◆ [10] INTERNATIONAL CAR REGISTRATION FOR France.

f. *or* **F.** ABBREVIATION FOR: [1] fathom(s). [2] female. [3] *Grammar* feminine. [4] (*plural* **ff.** *or* **FF.**) folio. [5] (*plural* **ff.**) following (page).

F- (of US military aircraft) ABBREVIATION FOR fighter: *F-106.*

fa (fɑː) NOUN *Music* a variant spelling of **fah.**

FA ABBREVIATION FOR: [1] *Military* field artillery. [2] (in Britain) Football Association. See also **FA Cup.**

f.a. *or* **FA** fanny adams.

faa *or* **fa'** (fɔː) VERB a Scot word for **fall.**

FAA ABBREVIATION FOR: [1] Fleet Air Arm. [2] (in the US) Federal Aviation Administration. [3] Fellow of the Australian Academy (of Science).

fab (fæb) ADJECTIVE, INTERJECTION *Informal, chiefly Brit* short for **fabulous**: an expression of approval or enthusiasm.

FAB ABBREVIATION FOR flavoured alcoholic beverage.

F.A.B. INTERJECTION *Brit* an expression of agreement to, or acknowledgment of, a command.
▷**HISTORY** C20: from British television series *Thunderbirds*

fabaceous (fəˈbeɪʃəs) ADJECTIVE a less common term for **leguminous.**
▷**HISTORY** C18: from Late Latin *fabāceus* of beans, from Latin *faba* bean

Fabian (ˈfeɪbɪən) ADJECTIVE [1] of, relating to, or resembling the delaying tactics of the Roman general Q. Fabius Maximus (died 203 B.C.) who withstood Hannibal while avoiding a pitched battle; cautious; circumspect. ◆ NOUN [2] a member of or sympathizer with the Fabian Society.
▷**HISTORY** C19: from Latin *Fabiānus* of Fabius

Fabianism (ˈfeɪbɪəˌnɪzəm) NOUN the beliefs, principles, or practices of the Fabian Society.
▸ˈ**Fabianist** NOUN, ADJECTIVE

Fabian Society NOUN an association of British socialists advocating the establishment of democratic socialism by gradual reforms within the law: founded in 1884.

fable (ˈfeɪbᵊl) NOUN [1] a short moral story, esp one with animals as characters. [2] a false, fictitious, or improbable account; fiction or lie. [3] a story or legend about supernatural or mythical characters or events. [4] legends or myths collectively. Related adjective: **fabulous.** [5] *Archaic* the plot of a play or of an epic or dramatic poem. ◆ VERB [6] to relate or tell (fables). [7] (*intr*) to speak untruthfully; tell lies. [8] (*tr*) to talk about or describe in the manner of a fable: *ghosts are fabled to appear at midnight.*
▷**HISTORY** C13: from Latin *fābula* story, narrative, from *fārī* to speak, say
▸ˈ**fabler** NOUN

fabled (ˈfeɪbᵊld) ADJECTIVE [1] made famous in fable. [2] fictitious.

fabliau (ˈfæblɪˌəʊ; *French* fɑblijo) NOUN, *plural* **fabliaux** (ˈfæblɪˌəʊz; *French* fɑblijo). a comic usually ribald verse tale, of a kind popular in France in the 12th and 13th centuries.
▷**HISTORY** C19: from French: a little tale, from *fable* tale

Fablon (ˈfæblən, -lɒn) NOUN *Trademark* a brand of adhesive-backed plastic material used to cover and decorate shelves, worktops, etc., and for handicraft purposes.

fabric (ˈfæbrɪk) NOUN [1] any cloth made from yarn or fibres by weaving, knitting, felting, etc. [2] the texture of a cloth. [3] a structure or framework: *the fabric of society.* [4] a style or method of construction. [5] *Rare* a building. [6] the texture, arrangement, and orientation of the constituents of a rock.
▷**HISTORY** C15: from Latin *fabrica* workshop, from *faber* craftsman

fabricant (ˈfæbrɪkənt) NOUN *Archaic* a manufacturer.

fabricate (ˈfæbrɪˌkeɪt) VERB (*tr*) [1] to make, build, or construct. [2] to devise, invent, or concoct (a story, lie, etc.). [3] to fake or forge.
▷**HISTORY** C15: from Latin *fabricāre* to build, make, from *fabrica* workshop; see FABRIC
▸ˌ**fabriˈcation** NOUN ▸ˈ**fabricative** ADJECTIVE ▸ˈ**fabriˌcator** NOUN

Fabrikoid (ˈfæbrɪˌkɔɪd) NOUN *Trademark* a waterproof fabric made of cloth coated with pyroxylin.

fabulist (ˈfæbjʊlɪst) NOUN [1] a person who invents or recounts fables. [2] a person who lies or falsifies.

fabulous (ˈfæbjʊləs) ADJECTIVE [1] almost unbelievable; astounding; legendary: *fabulous wealth.* [2] *Informal* extremely good: *a fabulous time at the party.* [3] of, relating to, or based upon fable: *a fabulous beast.*
▷**HISTORY** C15: from Latin *fābulōsus* celebrated in fable, from *fābula* FABLE
▸ˈ**fabulously** ADVERB ▸ˈ**fabulousness** NOUN

façade *or* **facade** (fəˈsɑːd, fæ-) NOUN [1] the face of a building, esp the main front. [2] a front or outer appearance, esp a deceptive one.
▷**HISTORY** C17: from French, from Italian *facciata,* from *faccia* FACE

face (feɪs) NOUN [1] **a** the front of the head from the forehead to the lower jaw; visage. **b** (*as modifier*): *face flannel; face cream.* [2] **a** the expression of the countenance; look: *a sad face.* **b** a distorted expression, esp to indicate disgust; grimace: *she made a face.* [3] *Informal* make-up (esp in the phrase **put one's face on**). [4] outward appearance: *the face of the countryside is changing.* [5] appearance or pretence (esp in the phrases **put a bold, good, bad,** etc., **face on**). [6] worth in the eyes of others; dignity (esp in the phrases **lose** or **save face**). [7] *Informal* impudence or effrontery. [8] the main side of an object, building, etc., or the front: *the face of a palace; a cliff face.* [9] the marked surface of an instrument, esp the dial of a timepiece. [10] the functional or working side of an object, as of a tool or playing card. [11] **a** the exposed area of a mine from which coal, ore, etc., may be mined. **b** (*as modifier*): *face worker.* [12] the uppermost part or surface: *the face of the earth.* [13] Also called: **side.** any one of the plane surfaces of a crystal or other solid figure. [14] *Mountaineering* a steep side of a mountain, bounded by ridges. [15] either of the surfaces of a coin, esp the one that bears the head of a ruler. [16] *Brit slang* a well-known or important person. [17] Also called: **typeface.** *Printing* **a** the printing surface of any type character. **b** the style, the design, or sometimes the size of any type fount. **c** the print made from type. [18] *Nautical, aeronautics* the aft or near side of a propeller blade. [19] **fly in the face of.** to act in defiance of. [20] **in one's face.** directly opposite or against one. [21] **in (the) face of.** despite. [22] **look (someone) in the face.** to look directly at a person without fear or shame. [23] **on the face of it.** to all appearances. [24] **set one's face against.** to oppose with determination. [25] **show one's face.** to make an appearance. [26] **shut one's face.** *Slang (often imperative)* to be silent. [27] **to someone's face.** in someone's presence; directly and openly: *I told him the truth to his face.* [28] **until one is blue in the face.** *Informal* to the utmost degree; indefinitely. ◆ VERB [29] (when *intr,* often foll by *to, towards,* or *on*) to look or be situated or placed (in a specified direction): *the house faces on the square.* [30] to be opposite: *facing page 9.* [31] (*tr*) to meet or be confronted by: *in his work he faces many problems.* [32] (*tr*) to provide with a surface of a different material: *the cuffs were faced with velvet.* [33] to dress the surface of (stone or other material). [34] (*tr*) to expose (a card) with the face uppermost. [35] *Military, chiefly US* to order (a formation) to turn in a certain direction or (of a formation) to turn as required: *right face!* [36] *Ice hockey* **a** (of the referee) to drop (the puck) between two opposing players, as when starting or restarting play. See also **face-off. b** to start or restart play in this manner. [37] **face the music.** *Informal* to confront the consequences of one's actions. ◆ See also **face down, face out, face up to.**
▷**HISTORY** C13: from Old French, from Vulgar Latin *facia* (unattested), from Latin *faciēs* form, related to *facere* to make
▸ˈ**faceable** ADJECTIVE

FACE ABBREVIATION FOR Fellow of the Australian College of Education.

face-ache NOUN [1] neuralgia. [2] *Slang* an ugly or miserable-looking person.

facebar (ˈfeɪsˌbɑː) NOUN a wrestling hold in which a wrestler stretches the skin on his opponent's face backwards.

face card NOUN the usual US and Canadian term for **court card.**

face-centred ADJECTIVE (of a crystal) having a lattice point at the centre of each face of each unit cell as well as at the corners. Compare **body-centred.**

face cloth *or* **face flannel** NOUN *Brit* a small piece of cloth used to wash the face and hands. US equivalent: **washcloth.**

face down VERB (*tr, adverb*) to confront and force (someone or something) to back down.

face flies NOUN flies (*musca autumnalis*) that attack cattle, feeding off their eye secretions.

face-harden VERB (*tr*) to harden the surface of (steel or iron) by the addition of carbon at high temperature.

faceless (ˈfeɪslɪs) ADJECTIVE [1] without a face. [2] without identity; anonymous.
▸ˈ**facelessness** NOUN

face-lift NOUN [1] a cosmetic surgical operation for tightening sagging skin and smoothing unwanted wrinkles on the face. [2] any improvement or renovation, as of a building, etc.

facemail (ˈfeɪsˌmeɪl) NOUN a computer program which uses an electronically generated face to deliver messages on screen.

face-off NOUN [1] *Ice hockey* the method of starting a game, in which the referee drops the puck, etc. between two opposing players. [2] a confrontation. ◆ VERB **face off.** (*adverb*) [3] to start play by (a face-off).

face out VERB (*tr, adverb*) [1] to endure (trouble). [2] to defy or act boldly in spite of (criticism, blame, etc.). [3] Also (esp US and Canadian): **face down.** to cause to concede by a bold stare.

face pack NOUN a cream treatment that cleanses and tones the skin.

faceplate (ˈfeɪsˌpleɪt) NOUN [1] a perforated circular metal plate that can be attached to the headstock of a lathe in order to hold flat or irregularly shaped workpieces. [2] Also called: **surface plate.** a flat rigid plate used to check the flatness and squareness of the faces of a component. [3] the part of a cathode-ray tube carrying the phosphor screen.

face powder NOUN a flesh-tinted cosmetic

powder worn to make the face look less shiny, softer, etc.

faceprint (ˈfeɪsˌprɪnt) NOUN a digitally recorded representation of a person's face that can be used for security purposes because it is as individual as a fingerprint.

facer (ˈfeɪsə) NOUN [1] a person or thing that faces. [2] a lathe tool used to turn a face perpendicular to the axis of rotation. [3] *Brit informal* a difficulty or problem.

face recognition NOUN the ability of a computer to scan, store, and recognize human faces for use in identifying people.

face-saver NOUN something that serves to maintain the dignity or prestige of someone or something.

face-saving ADJECTIVE maintaining dignity or prestige.

facet (ˈfæsɪt) NOUN [1] any of the surfaces of a cut gemstone. [2] an aspect or phase, as of a subject or personality. [3] *Architect* the raised surface between the flutes of a column. [4] any of the lenses that make up the compound eye of an insect or other arthropod. [5] *Anatomy* any small smooth area on a hard surface, as on a bone. ◆ VERB **-ets, -eting, -eted** *or* **-ets, -etting, -etted**. [6] *(tr)* to cut facets in (a gemstone).
▷HISTORY C17: from French *facette* a little FACE

facetiae (fəˈsiːʃɪˌiː) PLURAL NOUN [1] humorous or witty sayings. [2] obscene or coarsely witty books.
▷HISTORY C17: from Latin: jests, plural of *facētia* witticism, from *facētus* elegant

face time NOUN the time spent dealing with someone else face to face, esp in a place of work.

facetious (fəˈsiːʃəs) ADJECTIVE [1] characterized by levity of attitude and love of joking: *a facetious person*. [2] jocular or amusing, esp at inappropriate times: *facetious remarks*.
▷HISTORY C16: from Old French *facetieux*, from *facetie* witty saying; see FACETIAE
▸**faˈcetiously** ADVERB ▸**faˈcetiousness** NOUN

face to face ADVERB, ADJECTIVE (**face-to-face** *as adjective*) [1] opposite one another. [2] in confrontation.

face up to VERB *(intr, adverb + preposition)* to accept (an unpleasant fact, reality, etc.).

face validity NOUN *Psychol* the extent to which a psychological test appears to measure what it is intended to measure.

face value NOUN [1] the value written or stamped on the face of a commercial paper or coin. [2] apparent worth or value, as opposed to real worth.

facia (ˈfeɪʃɪə) NOUN a variant spelling of **fascia**.
▸**ˈfacial** ADJECTIVE

facial (ˈfeɪʃəl) ADJECTIVE [1] of or relating to the face. ◆ NOUN [2] a beauty treatment for the face, involving cleansing, massage, and cosmetic packs.
▸**ˈfacially** ADVERB

facial angle NOUN the angle formed between a line from the base of the nose to the opening of the ear and a line from the base of the nose to the most prominent part of the forehead: often used in comparative anthropology.

facial eczema NOUN a disease of sheep and cattle, occurring in warm areas of North Island, New Zealand. It is caused by a fungus, *Pithomyces chartarum*, and causes impairment of liver function and reddening, itching, scab formation, and swelling of the skin, esp on the face.

facial index NOUN the ratio of the length of the face to the width of the face multiplied by 100: often used in comparative anthropology. Compare **cranial index**.

facial nerve NOUN the seventh cranial nerve, supplying the muscles controlling facial expression, glands of the palate and nose, and the taste buds in the anterior two-thirds of the tongue.

-facient SUFFIX FORMING ADJECTIVES AND NOUNS indicating a state or quality: *absorbefacient; rubefacient*.
▷HISTORY from Latin *facient-, faciēns*, present participle of *facere* to do

facies (ˈfeɪʃɪˌiːz) NOUN, *plural* **-cies**. [1] the general form and appearance of an individual or a group of plants or animals. [2] the characteristics of a rock or series of rocks reflecting their appearance, composition, and conditions of formation. [3] *Med* the general facial expression of a patient, esp when typical of a specific disease or disorder. See **Hippocratic facies**.
▷HISTORY C17: from Latin: appearance, FACE

facile (ˈfæsaɪl) ADJECTIVE [1] easy to perform or achieve. [2] working or moving easily or smoothly. [3] without depth; superficial: *a facile solution*. [4] *Archaic* relaxed in manner; easygoing.
▷HISTORY C15: from Latin *facilis* easy, from *facere* to do
▸**ˈfacilely** ADVERB ▸**ˈfacileness** NOUN

facile princeps *Latin* (ˈfæsɪlɪ ˈprɪnsɛps) NOUN an obvious leader.
▷HISTORY literally: easily first

facilitate (fəˈsɪlɪˌteɪt) VERB *(tr)* to make easier; assist the progress of.
▸**faˈcilitative** ADJECTIVE ▸**faˈciliˌtator** NOUN

facilitation (fəˌsɪlɪˈteɪʃən) NOUN [1] the act or process of facilitating. [2] *Physiol* the increased ease of transmission of impulses in a nerve fibre, caused by prior excitation.

facility (fəˈsɪlɪtɪ) NOUN, *plural* **-ties**. [1] ease of action or performance; freedom from difficulty. [2] ready skill or ease deriving from practice or familiarity. [3] *(often plural)* the means or equipment facilitating the performance of an action. [4] *Rare* easy-going disposition. [5] *Military* an organization or building offering supporting capability. [6] *(usually plural)* a euphemistic word for **lavatory**.
▷HISTORY C15: from Latin *facilitās*, from *facilis* easy; see FACILE

facing (ˈfeɪsɪŋ) NOUN [1] a piece of material used esp to conceal the seam of a garment and prevent fraying. [2] *(usually plural)* a piece of additional cloth, esp in a different colour, on the collar, cuffs, etc., of the jacket of a military uniform, formerly used to denote the regiment. [3] an outer layer or coat of material applied to the surface of a wall. [4] *Marketing* an area of retail shelf space.

façonné *or* **faconne** (ˈfæsəˌneɪ) ADJECTIVE [1] denoting a fabric with the design woven in. ◆ NOUN [2] such a fabric.
▷HISTORY C19: French, from *façonner* to fashion

facsimile (fækˈsɪmɪlɪ) NOUN [1] **a** an exact copy or reproduction. **b** *(as modifier)*: *a facsimile publication*. [2] an image produced by facsimile transmission. ◆ VERB **-les, -leing, -led**. [3] *(tr)* to make an exact copy of.
▷HISTORY C17: from Latin *fac simile!* make something like it!, from *facere* to make + *similis* similar, like

facsimile machine NOUN a machine which transmits and receives documents in facsimile transmission. Often shortened to **fax, fax machine**.

facsimile transmission NOUN an international system of transmitting a written, printed, or pictorial document over the telephone system by scanning it photoelectrically and reproducing the image after transmission. Often shortened to **fax**.

fact (fækt) NOUN [1] an event or thing known to have happened or existed. [2] a truth verifiable from experience or observation. [3] a piece of information: *get me all the facts of this case*. [4] *Law* *(often plural)* an actual event, happening, etc., as distinguished from its legal consequences. Questions of fact are decided by the jury, questions of law by the court or judge. [5] *Philosophy* a proposition that may be either true or false, as contrasted with an evaluative statement. [6] **after** (*or* **before**) **the fact**. *Criminal law* after (or before) the commission of the offence: *an accessory after the fact*. [7] **as a matter of fact, in fact, in point of fact**. in reality or actuality. [8] **fact of life**. an inescapable truth, esp an unpleasant one. [9] **the fact of the matter**. the truth.
▷HISTORY C16: from Latin *factum* something done, from *factus* made, from *facere* to make
▸**ˈfactful** ADJECTIVE

fact-finding ADJECTIVE having the purpose of ascertaining facts: *a fact-finding tour of the Northeast*.

factice (ˈfæktɪs) NOUN a soft rubbery material made by reacting sulphur or sulphur chloride with vegetable oil.
▷HISTORY C19: from Greek *faktis* from Latin *factīcius* FACTITIOUS

faction[1] (ˈfækʃən) NOUN [1] a group of people forming a minority within a larger body, esp a dissentious group. [2] strife or dissension within a group.
▷HISTORY C16: from Latin *factiō* a making, from *facere* to make, do
▸**ˈfactional** ADJECTIVE ▸**ˈfactionalˌism** NOUN ▸**ˈfactionalist** NOUN

faction[2] (ˈfækʃən) NOUN a television programme, film, or literary work comprising a dramatized presentation of actual events.
▷HISTORY C20: a blend of FACT and FICTION

faction fight NOUN *South African* a fight between rival Black groups, usually originating in tribal or clan feuds.

factious (ˈfækʃəs) ADJECTIVE given to, producing, or characterized by faction.
▸**ˈfactiously** ADVERB ▸**ˈfactiousness** NOUN

> **Language note** See at **fractious**.

factitious (fækˈtɪʃəs) ADJECTIVE [1] artificial rather than natural: *factitious demands created by the mass media*. [2] not genuine; sham: *factitious enthusiasm*.
▷HISTORY C17: from Latin *factīcius*, from *facere* to make, do
▸**facˈtitiously** ADVERB ▸**facˈtitiousness** NOUN

factitive (ˈfæktɪtɪv) ADJECTIVE *Grammar* denoting a verb taking a direct object as well as a noun in apposition, as for example *elect* in *They elected John president*, where *John* is the direct object and *president* is the complement.
▷HISTORY C19: from New Latin *factitīvus*, from Latin *factitāre* to do frequently, from *facere* to do
▸**ˈfactitively** ADVERB

factive (ˈfæktɪv) ADJECTIVE *Logic, linguistics, philosophy* (of a linguistic context) giving rise to the presupposition that a sentence occurring in that context is true, as *John regrets that Mary did not attend*.

factoid (ˈfæktɔɪd) NOUN a piece of unreliable information believed to be true because of the way it is presented or repeated in print.
▷HISTORY C20: coined by Norman Mailer (born 1923), US author, from FACT + -OID

factor (ˈfæktə) NOUN [1] an element or cause that contributes to a result. [2] *Maths* **a** one of two or more integers or polynomials whose product is a given integer or polynomial: *2 and 3 are factors of 6*. **b** an integer or polynomial that can be exactly divided into another integer or polynomial: *1, 2, 3, and 6 are all factors of 6*. [3] (foll by identifying numeral) *Med* any of several substances that participate in the clotting of blood: *factor VIII*. [4] a person who acts on another's behalf, esp one who transacts business for another. [5] *Commerce* a business that makes loans in return for or on security of trade debts. [6] former name for a **gene**. [7] *Commercial law* a person to whom goods are consigned for sale and who is paid a factorage. [8] (in Scotland) the manager of an estate. ◆ VERB [9] *(intr)* to engage in the business of a factor. ◆ See also **factor in**.
▷HISTORY C15: from Latin: one who acts, from *facere* to do
▸**ˈfactorable** ADJECTIVE ▸**ˌfactoraˈbility** NOUN ▸**ˈfactorˌship** NOUN

> **Language note** *Factor* (sense 1) should only be used to refer to something which contributes to a result. It should not be used to refer to a part of something such as a plan or arrangement; instead a word such as *component* or *element* should be used.

factor VIII NOUN a protein that participates in the clotting of blood. It is extracted from donated serum and used in the treatment of the commonest type of haemophilia, in which it is absent.

factorage (ˈfæktərɪdʒ) NOUN the commission payable to a factor.

factor analysis NOUN *Statistics* any of several techniques for deriving from a number of given variables a smaller number of different, more useful, variables.

factor cost NOUN (in social accounting) valuation of goods and services at their overall commercial cost, including markups but excluding indirect taxes and subsidies.

factorial (fækˈtɔːrɪəl) *Maths* ◆ NOUN [1] the

product of all the positive integers from one up to and including a given integer. Factorial zero is assigned the value of one: *factorial four is 1 × 2 × 3 × 4*. Symbol: *n*!, where *n* is the given integer. ◆ ADJECTIVE [2] of or involving factorials or factors.
▸ **fac'torially** ADVERB

factor in VERB (*tr, adverb*) *Chiefly US* to take account of (something) when making a calculation.

factoring ('fæktərɪŋ) NOUN [1] the business of a factor. [2] the business of purchasing debts from clients at a discount and making a profit from their collection.

factorize *or* **factorise** ('fæktəˌraɪz) VERB (*tr*) *Maths* to resolve (an integer or polynomial) into factors.
▸ **ˌfactori'zation** *or* **ˌfactori'sation** NOUN

factor of production NOUN a resource or input entering the production of wealth, such as land, labour, capital, etc. Also called: **agent of production.**

factor of safety NOUN the ratio of the breaking stress of a material or structure to the calculated maximum stress when in use. Also called: **safety factor.**

factory ('fæktərɪ) NOUN, *plural* **-ries.** [1] **a** a building or group of buildings containing a plant assembly for the manufacture of goods. **b** (*as modifier*): *a factory worker.* [2] *Rare* a trading station maintained by factors in a foreign country. [3] *Canadian* (formerly) a main trading station for the exchange and transshipment of furs.
▷ **HISTORY** C16: from Late Latin *factorium*; see FACTOR
▸ **'factory-ˌlike** ADJECTIVE

factory farm NOUN a farm in which animals are bred and fattened using modern industrial methods.
▸ **factory farming** NOUN

factory outlet *or* **factory shop** NOUN a usually low-rent site leased by a factory to sell its end-of-line or damaged stock direct to the customer at reduced prices.

factory ship NOUN a fishing boat that processes the fish that are caught.

factotum (fæk'təʊtəm) NOUN a person employed to do all kinds of work.
▷ **HISTORY** C16: from Medieval Latin, from Latin *fac!* do! + *tōtum*, from *tōtus* (adjective) all

facts and figures PLURAL NOUN details; precise information.

factsheet ('fæktˌʃiːt) NOUN a printed sheet containing information relating to items covered in a television or radio programme.

facts of life PLURAL NOUN **the.** the details of sexual behaviour and reproduction, esp as told to children.

factual ('fæktʃʊəl) ADJECTIVE [1] of, relating to, or characterized by facts. [2] of the nature of fact; real; actual.
▸ **'factualism** NOUN ▸ **'factualist** NOUN ▸ **ˌfactual'istic** ADJECTIVE ▸ **'factually** ADVERB ▸ **'factualness** *or* **ˌfactu'ality** NOUN

facture ('fæktʃə) NOUN *Rare* [1] construction. [2] workmanship; quality.
▷ **HISTORY** C15: from Old French, from Latin *factūra*

facula ('fækjʊlə) NOUN, *plural* **-lae** (-ˌliː). any of the bright areas on the sun's surface, usually appearing just before a sunspot and subject to the same 11-year cycle.
▷ **HISTORY** C18: from Latin: little torch, from *fax* torch
▸ **'facular** ADJECTIVE

facultative ('fækəltətɪv) ADJECTIVE [1] empowering but not compelling the doing of an act. [2] *Philosophy* that may or may not occur. [3] *Insurance* denoting a form of reinsurance in which the reinsurer has no obligation to accept a particular risk nor the insurer to reinsure, terms and conditions being negotiated for each reinsurance. [4] *Biology* able to exist under more than one set of environmental conditions: *a facultative parasite can exist as a parasite or a saprotroph.* Compare **obligate** (sense 4). [5] of or relating to a faculty.
▸ **'facultatively** ADVERB

faculty ('fækəltɪ) NOUN, *plural* **-ties.** [1] one of the inherent powers of the mind or body, such as reason, memory, sight, or hearing. [2] any ability or power, whether acquired or inherent. [3] a conferred power or right. [4] **a** a department within a university or college devoted to a particular branch of knowledge. **b** the staff of such a department. **c** *Chiefly US and Canadian* all the teaching staff at a university, college, school, etc. [5] all members of a learned profession. [6] *Archaic* occupation.
▷ **HISTORY** C14 (in the sense: department of learning): from Latin *facultās* capability; related to Latin *facilis* easy

Faculty of Advocates NOUN *Law* the college or society of advocates in Scotland.

FA Cup NOUN *Soccer* (in England) [1] an annual knockout competition for a silver trophy, open to all member teams of the Football Association. [2] the trophy itself.

fad (fæd) NOUN *Informal* [1] an intense but short-lived fashion; craze. [2] a personal idiosyncrasy or whim.
▷ **HISTORY** C19: of uncertain origin
▸ **'faddish** ADJECTIVE ▸ **'faddishness** NOUN ▸ **'faddism** NOUN ▸ **'faddist** NOUN

FAD NOUN *Biochem* flavin adenine dinucleotide: an ester of riboflavin with ADP that acts as the prosthetic group for many flavoproteins. See also **FMN.**

faddy ('fædɪ) ADJECTIVE **-dier, -diest.** of, having, or involving personal and often transitory whims, esp about food.

fade (feɪd) VERB [1] to lose or cause to lose brightness, colour, or clarity. [2] (*intr*) to lose freshness, vigour, or youth; wither. [3] (*intr;* usually foll by *away* or *out*) to vanish slowly; die out. [4] **a** to decrease the brightness or volume of (a television or radio programme or film sequence) or (of a television programme, etc.) to decrease in this way. **b** to decrease the volume of (a sound) in a recording system or (of a sound) to be so reduced in volume. [5] (*intr*) (of the brakes of a vehicle) to lose power. [6] to cause (a golf ball) to move with a controlled left-to-right trajectory or (of a golf ball) to veer gradually from left to right. ◆ NOUN [7] the act or an instance of fading.
▷ **HISTORY** C14: from *fade* (adj) dull, from Old French, from Vulgar Latin *fatidus* (unattested), probably blend of Latin *vapidus* VAPID + Latin *fatuus* FATUOUS
▸ **'fadable** ADJECTIVE ▸ **'fadedness** NOUN ▸ **'fader** NOUN

fade-in NOUN [1] *Films* an optical effect in which a shot appears gradually out of darkness. [2] a gradual increase in the volume in a radio or television broadcast. ◆ VERB **fade in.** (*adverb*) [3] Also: **fade up.** to increase or cause to increase gradually, as vision or sound in a film or broadcast.

fadeless ('feɪdlɪs) ADJECTIVE not subject to fading.

fade-out NOUN [1] *Films* an optical effect in which a shot slowly disappears into darkness. [2] a gradual reduction in signal strength in a radio or television broadcast. [3] a gradual and temporary loss of a received radio or television signal due to atmospheric disturbances, magnetic storms, etc. [4] a slow or gradual disappearance. ◆ VERB **fade out.** (*adverb*) [5] to decrease or cause to decrease gradually, as vision or sound in a film or broadcast.

fadge (fædʒ) VERB (*intr*) *Archaic or dialect* [1] to agree. [2] to succeed. ◆ NOUN [3] *NZ* a package of wool in a wool-bale that weighs less than 100 kilograms.
▷ **HISTORY** C16: of uncertain origin

fading ('feɪdɪŋ) NOUN a variation in the strength of received radio signals due to variations in the conditions of the transmission medium.

fado *Portuguese* ('fɑːdu) NOUN a type of melancholy Portuguese folk song.
▷ **HISTORY** literally: FATE

fadometer (fə'dɒmɪtə) NOUN *Chem* an instrument used to determine the resistance to fading of a pigment or dye.

fae (feɪ) PREPOSITION a Scot word for **from.**

faecal *or esp US* **fecal** ('fiːkəl) ADJECTIVE of, relating to, or consisting of faeces.

faeces *or esp US* **feces** ('fiːsiːz) PLURAL NOUN bodily waste matter derived from ingested food and the secretions of the intestines and discharged through the anus.
▷ **HISTORY** C15: from Latin *faecēs*, plural of *faex* sediment, dregs

faena *Spanish* (fa'ena) NOUN *Bullfighting* the matador's final series of passes with sword and cape before the kill.
▷ **HISTORY** literally: task, from obsolete Catalan (modern *feina*), from Latin *facienda* things to be done, from *facere* to do

Faenza (*Italian* fa'ɛntsa) NOUN a city in N Italy, in Emilia-Romagna: famous in the 15th and 16th centuries for its majolica earthenware, esp faïence. Pop.: 54 050 (1990).

faerie *or* **faery** ('feɪərɪ, 'fɛərɪ) NOUN, *plural* **-ries.** *Archaic or poetic* [1] the land of fairies. [2] enchantment. ◆ ADJECTIVE, NOUN [3] a variant of **fairy.**

Faeroes *or* **Faroes** ('fɛərəʊz) PLURAL NOUN a group of 21 basalt islands in the North Atlantic between Iceland and the Shetland Islands: a self-governing community within the kingdom of Denmark; fishing. Capital: Thorshavn. Pop.: 46 600 (2001 est.). Area: 1400 sq. km (540 sq. miles). Also called: **Faeroe Islands** *or* **Faroe Islands.**

Faeroese *or* **Faroese** (ˌfɛərəʊ'iːz) ADJECTIVE [1] of, relating to, or characteristic of the Faeroes, their inhabitants, or their language. ◆ NOUN [2] the chief language of the Faeroes, closely related to Icelandic, although they are not mutually intelligible. [3] (*plural* **-ese**) a native or inhabitant of the Faeroes.

faff (fæf) VERB (*intr;* often foll by *about*) *Brit informal* to dither or fuss.
▷ **HISTORY** C19: of obscure origin

Fafnir ('fæfnɪə, 'fæv-) NOUN *Norse myth* the son of Hreidmar, whom he killed to gain the cursed treasure of Andvari. He became a dragon and was slain by Sigurd while guarding the treasure.

fag[1] (fæg) NOUN [1] *Informal* a boring or wearisome task: *it's a fag having to walk all that way.* [2] *Brit* (esp formerly) a young public school boy who performs menial chores for an older boy or prefect. ◆ VERB **fags, fagging, fagged.** [3] (when *tr,* often foll by *out*) *Informal* to become or cause to become exhausted by hard toil or work. [4] (*usually intr*) *Brit* to do or cause to do menial chores in a public school: *Brown fags for Lee.*
▷ **HISTORY** C18: of obscure origin

fag[2] (fæg) NOUN [1] *Brit* a slang word for **cigarette.** [2] a fag end, as of cloth.
▷ **HISTORY** C16 (in the sense: something hanging loose, flap): of obscure origin

fag[3] (fæg) NOUN *Slang, chiefly US and Canadian* short for **faggot**[2].

fagaceous (fə'geɪʃəs) ADJECTIVE of, relating to, or belonging to the *Fagaceae*, a family of trees, including beech, oak, and chestnut, whose fruit is partly or wholly enclosed in a husk (cupule).
▷ **HISTORY** C19: from New Latin *Fāgāceae*, from Latin *fāgus* beech

fag end NOUN [1] the last and worst part, esp when it is of little use. [2] *Brit informal* the stub of a cigarette.
▷ **HISTORY** C17: see FAG[2]

faggot[1] *or esp US* **fagot** ('fægət) NOUN [1] a bundle of sticks or twigs, esp when bound together and used as fuel. [2] a bundle of iron bars, esp a box formed by four pieces of wrought iron and filled with scrap to be forged into wrought iron. [3] a ball of chopped meat, usually pork liver, bound with herbs and bread and eaten fried. [4] a bundle of anything. ◆ VERB (*tr*) [5] to collect into a bundle or bundles. [6] *Needlework* to do faggoting on (a garment, piece of cloth, etc.).
▷ **HISTORY** C14: from Old French, perhaps from Greek *phakelos* bundle

faggot[2] ('fægət) NOUN *Slang, chiefly US and Canadian* a male homosexual. Often shortened to **fag.**
▷ **HISTORY** C20: special use of FAGGOT[1]
▸ **'faggoty** ADJECTIVE

faggoting *or esp US* **fagoting** ('fægətɪŋ) NOUN [1] decorative needlework done by tying vertical threads together in bundles. [2] a decorative way of joining two hems by crisscross stitches.

faggot vote NOUN (formerly) a vote created by the allotting of property to a person to give him the status of an elector.
▷ **HISTORY** C19: perhaps from the former use of FAGGOT[1] meaning a person spuriously entered on a military roll

fag hag NOUN *Slang, usually derogatory* a

heterosexual woman who prefers the company of homosexual men.

fah *or* **fa** (fɑː) NOUN *Music* 1 (in the fixed system of solmization) the note F. 2 (in tonic sol-fa) the fourth degree of any major scale; subdominant.
▷HISTORY C14: see GAMUT

FAHA ABBREVIATION FOR Fellow of the Australian Academy of the Humanities.

fahlband (ˈfɑːlˌbænd) NOUN a thin bed of schistose rock impregnated with metallic sulphides.
▷HISTORY C19: from German: pale band

Fahrenheit (ˈfærənˌhaɪt) ADJECTIVE of or measured according to the Fahrenheit scale of temperature. Symbol: F.
▷HISTORY named after G. D. *Fahrenheit* (1686–1736), German physicist and inventor of the scale

Fahrenheit scale NOUN a scale of temperatures in which 32° represents the melting point of ice and 212° represents the boiling point of pure water under standard atmospheric pressure. Compare **Celsius scale.**

FAI ABBREVIATION FOR: 1 Fédération aéronautique internationale. [French: International Aeronautical Federation] 2 Football Association of Ireland.

Faial *or* **Fayal** (*Portuguese* fəˈial) NOUN an island in the central Azores archipelago. Chief town: Horta. Area: 171 sq. km (66 sq. miles).

faïence (faɪˈɑːns, feɪ-) NOUN **a** tin-glazed earthenware, usually that of French, German, Italian, or Scandinavian origin. **b** (*as modifier*): *a faïence cup.*
▷HISTORY C18: from French, strictly: pottery from FAENZA

fail[1] (feɪl) VERB 1 to be unsuccessful in an attempt (at something or to do something). 2 (*intr*) to stop operating or working properly: *the steering failed suddenly.* 3 to judge or be judged as being below the officially accepted standard required for success in (a course, examination, etc.). 4 (*tr*) to prove disappointing, undependable, or useless to (someone). 5 (*tr*) to neglect or be unable (to do something). 6 (*intr*) to prove partly or completely insufficient in quantity, duration, or extent. 7 (*intr*) to weaken; fade away. 8 (*intr*) to go bankrupt or become insolvent. ◆ NOUN 9 a failure to attain the required standard, as in an examination. 10 **without fail.** definitely; with certainty.
▷HISTORY C13: from Old French *faillir*, ultimately from Latin *fallere* to disappoint; probably related to Greek *phēlos* deceitful

fail[2] (fel) NOUN *Scot* a turf; sod.
▷HISTORY perhaps from Scottish Gaelic *fàl*

failing (ˈfeɪlɪŋ) NOUN 1 a weak point; flaw. ◆ PREPOSITION 2 (*used to express a condition*) in default of: *failing a solution this afternoon, the problem will have to wait until Monday.*
▸ ˈ**failingly** ADVERB

faille (feɪl; *French* faj) NOUN a soft light ribbed fabric of silk, rayon, or taffeta.
▷HISTORY C16: from French: head covering, hence, fabric used for this, of obscure origin

fail-safe ADJECTIVE 1 designed to return to a safe condition in the event of a failure or malfunction. 2 (of a nuclear weapon) capable of being deactivated in the event of a failure or accident. 3 unlikely to fail; foolproof. ◆ VERB 4 (*intr*) to return to a safe condition in the event of a failure or malfunction.

failure (ˈfeɪljə) NOUN 1 the act or an instance of failing. 2 a person or thing that is unsuccessful or disappointing: *the evening was a failure.* 3 nonperformance of something required or expected: *failure to attend will be punished.* 4 cessation of normal operation; breakdown: *a power failure.* 5 an insufficiency or shortage: *a crop failure.* 6 a decline or loss, as in health or strength. 7 the fact of not reaching the required standard in an examination, test, course, etc. 8 the act or process of becoming bankrupt or the state of being bankrupt.

fain (feɪn) ADVERB 1 (usually with *would*) *Archaic* willingly; gladly: *she would fain be dead.* ◆ ADJECTIVE 2 *Obsolete* **a** willing or eager. **b** compelled.
▷HISTORY Old English *fægen*; related to Old Norse *fegiun* happy, Old High German *gifehan* to be glad, Gothic *fahehs* joy; see FAWN[2]

fainéant (ˈfeɪnɪənt; *French* fɛneɑ̃) NOUN 1 a lazy person; idler. ◆ ADJECTIVE 2 indolent.
▷HISTORY C17: from French, modification of earlier *fait-nient* (he) does nothing, by folk etymology from Old French *faignant* shirker, from *faindre* to be lazy
▸ ˈ**faineance** *or* ˈ**faineancy** NOUN

fainites (ˈfeɪnaɪts) *or* **fains** (feɪnz) INTERJECTION *Dialect* a cry for truce or respite from the rules of a game.
▷HISTORY C19: from *fains I* I decline, from *feine* feign, from Old French *se feindre* in the sense: back out, esp of battle

fáinne (ˈfaːɲə) NOUN *Irish* a small ring-shaped metal badge worn by advocates of the Irish language.
▷HISTORY Irish Gaelic, literally: ring

faint (feɪnt) ADJECTIVE 1 lacking clarity, brightness, volume, etc.: *a faint noise.* 2 lacking conviction or force; weak: *faint praise.* 3 feeling dizzy or weak as if about to lose consciousness. 4 without boldness or courage; timid (esp in the combination **faint-hearted**). 5 **not the faintest** (**idea** *or* **notion**). no idea whatsoever: *I haven't the faintest.* ◆ VERB (*intr*) 6 to lose consciousness, esp momentarily, as through weakness. 7 *Archaic or poetic* to fail or become weak, esp in hope or courage. ◆ NOUN 8 a sudden spontaneous loss of consciousness, usually momentary, caused by an insufficient supply of blood to the brain. Technical name: **syncope.**
▷HISTORY C13: from Old French, from *faindre* to be idle
▸ ˈ**fainter** NOUN ▸ ˈ**faintingly** ADVERB ▸ ˈ**faintish** ADJECTIVE ▸ ˈ**faintishness** NOUN ▸ ˈ**faintly** ADVERB ▸ ˈ**faintness** NOUN

faints (feɪnts) PLURAL NOUN a variant spelling of **feints.**

fair[1] (fɛə) ADJECTIVE 1 free from discrimination, dishonesty, etc.; just; impartial. 2 in conformity with rules or standards; legitimate: *a fair fight.* 3 (of the hair or complexion) light in colour. 4 beautiful or lovely to look at. 5 moderately or quite good: *a fair piece of work.* 6 unblemished; untainted. 7 (of the tide or wind) favourable to the passage of a vessel. 8 sunny, fine, or cloudless. 9 (*prenominal*) *Informal* thorough; real: *a fair battle to get to the counter.* 10 pleasant or courteous. 11 apparently good or valuable, but really false: *fair words.* 12 open or unobstructed: *a fair passage.* 13 (of handwriting) clear and legible. 14 **a fair crack of the whip** *or* (*Austral*) **a fair shake of the dice, a fair go.** *Informal* a fair opportunity; fair chance. 15 **fair and square.** in a correct or just way. 16 **fair do's. a** equal shares or treatment. **b** an expression of appeal for equal shares or treatment. 17 **fair enough!** an expression of agreement. 18 **fair go!** *Austral and NZ informal* come off it!; I don't believe it! 19 **fair to middling.** about average. ◆ ADVERB 20 in a fair way; correctly: *act fair, now!* 21 absolutely or squarely; quite: *the question caught him fair off his guard.* 22 *Dialect* really or very: *fair tired.* ◆ VERB 23 (*intr*) *Dialect* (of the weather) to become fine and mild. ◆ NOUN 24 *Archaic* a person or thing that is beautiful or valuable, esp a woman.
▷HISTORY Old English *fæger*; related to Old Norse *fagr*, Old Saxon, Old High German *fagar*, Gothic *fagrs* suitable
▸ ˈ**fairness** NOUN

fair[2] (fɛə) NOUN 1 a travelling entertainment with sideshows, rides, etc., esp one that visits places at the same time each year. 2 a gathering of producers of and dealers in a given class of products to facilitate business: *a book fair.* 3 an event including amusements and the sale of goods, esp for a charity; bazaar. 4 a regular assembly at a specific place for the sale of goods, esp livestock.
▷HISTORY C13: from Old French *feire*, from Late Latin *fēria* holiday, from Latin *fēriae* days of rest: related to *festus* FESTAL

Fairbanks (ˈfɛəˌbæŋks) NOUN a city in central Alaska, at the terminus of the Alaska Highway. Pop.: 30 800 (1990).

fair copy NOUN a clean copy of a document on which all corrections have been made.

fairfaced (ˈfɛəˌfeɪst) ADJECTIVE (of brickwork) having a neat smooth unplastered surface.

fair game NOUN 1 a legitimate object for ridicule or attack. 2 *Hunting, archaic* quarry that may legitimately be pursued according to the rules of a particular sport.

fairground (ˈfɛəˌgraʊnd) NOUN an open space used for a fair or exhibition.

fair-haired boy NOUN the usual US name for **blue-eyed boy.**

fairing[1] (ˈfɛərɪŋ) NOUN an external metal structure fitted around parts of an aircraft, car, vessel, etc., to reduce drag. Also called: **fillet.** Compare **cowling.**
▷HISTORY C20: FAIR[1] + -ING[1]

fairing[2] (ˈfɛərɪŋ) NOUN 1 *Archaic* a present, esp from a fair. 2 a sweet circular biscuit made with butter.

fairish (ˈfɛərɪʃ) ADJECTIVE 1 moderately good, well, etc. 2 (of the hair, complexion, etc.) moderately light in colour.

Fair Isle NOUN an intricate multicoloured pattern knitted with Shetland wool into various garments, such as sweaters.
▷HISTORY C19: named after one of the Shetland Islands where the pattern originated

fairlead (ˈfɛəˌliːd) *or* **fairleader** NOUN *Nautical* a block or ring through which a line is rove to keep it clear of obstructions, prevent chafing, or maintain it at an angle.

fairly (ˈfɛəlɪ) ADVERB 1 (*not used with a negative*) moderately. 2 as deserved; justly. 3 (*not used with a negative*) positively; absolutely: *the hall fairly rang with applause.* 4 *Archaic* clearly. 5 *Obsolete* courteously.

fair-minded ADJECTIVE just or impartial.
▸ ˌ**fair-**ˈ**mindedness** NOUN

fair play NOUN 1 an established standard of decency, honesty, etc. 2 abidance by this standard.

fair rent NOUN (in Britain) the rent for a private tenancy, fixed and registered by a rent officer, and based on the size, condition, and usefulness of the property, but not its scarcity value.

fair sex NOUN **the.** women collectively.

fair-spoken ADJECTIVE civil, courteous, or elegant in speech.
▸ ˌ**fair-**ˈ**spokenness** NOUN

fair trade NOUN **a** the practice of directly benefiting producers in the developing world by buying straight from them at a guaranteed price. **b** (*as modifier*): *fair-trade coffee.*

fairway (ˈfɛəˌweɪ) NOUN 1 (on a golf course) the areas of shorter grass between the tees and greens, esp the avenue approaching a green bordered by rough. 2 *Nautical* **a** the navigable part of a river, harbour, etc. **b** the customary course followed by vessels.

fair-weather ADJECTIVE 1 suitable for use in fair weather only. 2 not reliable or present in situations of hardship or difficulty (esp in the phrase **fair-weather friend**).

Fairweather (ˈfɛəˌwɛðə) NOUN **Mount.** a mountain in W North America, on the border between Alaska and British Columbia. Height: 4663 m (15 300 ft.).

fairy (ˈfɛərɪ) NOUN, *plural* **fairies.** 1 an imaginary supernatural being, usually represented in diminutive human form and characterized as clever, playful, and having magical powers. 2 *Slang* a male homosexual. 3 **away with the fairies.** *Informal* out of touch with reality. ◆ ADJECTIVE (*prenominal*) 4 of or relating to a fairy or fairies. 5 resembling a fairy or fairies, esp in being enchanted or delicate.
▷HISTORY C14: from Old French *faerie* fairyland, from *feie* fairy, from Latin *Fāta* the Fates; see FATE, FAY[1]
▸ ˈ**fairy-**ˌ**like** ADJECTIVE

fairy cycle NOUN a child's bicycle.

fairyfloss (ˈfɛərɪˌflɒs) NOUN the Austral word for **candyfloss.**

fairy godmother NOUN 1 a character in certain fairy stories who brings unexpected benefits to the hero or heroine. 2 any benefactress, esp an unknown one.

fairyland (ˈfɛərɪˌlænd) NOUN 1 the imaginary domain of the fairies; an enchanted or wonderful place. 2 a fantasy world, esp one resulting from a person's wild imaginings.

fairy lights PLURAL NOUN small coloured electric bulbs strung together and used for decoration, esp on a Christmas tree.

fairy penguin NOUN a small penguin, *Eudyptula minor*, with a bluish head and back, found on the Australian coast. Also called: **little** *or* **blue penguin.**

fairy ring NOUN 1 a ring of dark luxuriant vegetation in grassy ground corresponding to the edge of an underground fungal mycelium: popularly associated with the dancing of fairies: seasonally marked by a ring of mushrooms. 2 short for **fairy ring mushroom**, *Marasmius oreades*, a dainty buff-coloured edible basidiomycetous fungus, characteristically forming rings in grassland.

fairy shrimp NOUN any small freshwater branchiopod crustacean of the genera *Chirocephalus*, *Artemia*, etc., having a transparent body with many appendages and habitually swimming on its back: order *Anostraca*.

fairy swallow NOUN (*sometimes capitals*) a variety of domestic fancy pigeon having blue-and-white plumage and heavily muffed feet.

fairy tale *or* **story** NOUN 1 a story about fairies or other mythical or magical beings, esp one of traditional origin told to children. 2 a highly improbable account.

fairy-tale ADJECTIVE 1 of or relating to a fairy tale. 2 resembling a fairy tale, esp in being extremely happy or fortunate: *a true story with a fairy-tale ending*. 3 highly improbable: *he came out with a fairy-tale account of his achievements*.

Faisalabad (faɪ'ʒɑːləˌbɑːd) NOUN a city in NE Pakistan: commercial and manufacturing centre of a cotton- and wheat-growing region; university (1961). Pop.: 1 977 246 (1998). Former name (until 1979): **Lyallpur**.

fait accompli *French* (fɛt akɔ̃pli) NOUN, *plural* ***faits accomplis*** (fɛz akɔ̃pli). something already done and beyond alteration.
▷HISTORY literally: accomplished fact

faites vos jeux *French* (fɛt vo ʒø) place your bets! (a phrase used by croupiers in roulette and other casino gambling games).

faith (feɪθ) NOUN 1 strong or unshakeable belief in something, esp without proof or evidence. 2 a specific system of religious beliefs: *the Jewish faith*. 3 *Christianity* trust in God and in his actions and promises. 4 a conviction of the truth of certain doctrines of religion, esp when this is not based on reason. 5 complete confidence or trust in a person, remedy, etc. 6 any set of firmly held principles or beliefs. 7 allegiance or loyalty, as to a person or cause (esp in the phrases **keep faith**, **break faith**). 8 **bad faith.** insincerity or dishonesty. 9 **good faith.** honesty or sincerity, as of intention in business (esp in the phrase **in good faith**). ◆ INTERJECTION 10 *Archaic* indeed; really (also in the phrases **by my faith**, **in faith**).
▷HISTORY C12: from Anglo-French *feid*, from Latin *fidēs* trust, confidence

faith community NOUN a community of people sharing the same religious faith.

faither ('feðər) NOUN a Scot word for **father**.

faithful ('feɪθfʊl) ADJECTIVE 1 having faith; remaining true, constant, or loyal. 2 maintaining sexual loyalty to one's lover or spouse. 3 consistently reliable: *a faithful worker*. 4 reliable or truthful: *a faithful source*. 5 accurate in detail: *a faithful translation*. ◆ NOUN 6 **the faithful. a** the believers in and loyal adherents of a religious faith, esp Christianity. **b** any group of loyal and steadfast followers.
▸ **'faithfully** ADVERB ▸ **'faithfulness** NOUN

faith healing NOUN treatment of a sick person through the supposed power of religious faith.
▸ **faith healer** NOUN

faithless ('feɪθlɪs) ADJECTIVE 1 unreliable or treacherous. 2 dishonest or disloyal. 3 having no faith or trust. 4 lacking faith, esp religious faith.
▸ **'faithlessly** ADVERB ▸ **'faithlessness** NOUN

faith school NOUN *Brit* a school that provides a general education within a framework of a specific religious belief.

faitour ('feɪtə) NOUN *Obsolete* an impostor.
▷HISTORY C14: from Anglo-French: cheat, from Old French *faitor*, from Latin: FACTOR

Faiyûm *or* **Fayum** (faɪ'juːm) NOUN See **El Faiyûm**.

fajitas (fə'hiːtəz) PLURAL NOUN a Mexican dish of soft tortillas wrapped around fried strips of meat, vegetables, etc.
▷HISTORY Mexican Spanish

fake[1] (feɪk) VERB 1 (*tr*) to cause (something inferior or not genuine) to appear more valuable, desirable, or real by fraud or pretence. 2 to pretend to have (an illness, emotion, etc.): *to fake a headache*. 3 to improvise (music, stage dialogue, etc.). ◆ NOUN 4 an object, person, or act that is not genuine; sham, counterfeit, or forgery. ◆ ADJECTIVE 5 not genuine; spurious.
▷HISTORY originally (C18) thieves' slang to mug or do someone; probably via Polari from Italian *facciare* to make or do
▸ **'faker** NOUN ▸ **'fakery** NOUN

fake[2] (feɪk) *Nautical* ◆ VERB 1 (*tr*; *usually foll by down*) to coil (a rope) on deck. ◆ NOUN 2 one round of a coil of rope.
▷HISTORY Middle English *faken*, perhaps via Lingua Franca from Italian *facciare* to make or do; see FAKE[1]

fakir, faqir (fə'kɪə, 'feɪkə), *or* **fakeer** (fə'kɪə) NOUN 1 a Muslim ascetic who rejects wordly possessions. 2 a Hindu ascetic mendicant or holy man.
▷HISTORY C17: from Arabic *faqīr* poor

fa-la *or* **fal la** (fɑː'lɑː) NOUN (esp in 16th-century songs) a refrain sung to the syllables *fa-la-la*.

falafel *or* **felafel** (fəl'ɑːfəl) NOUN a ball or cake of ground spiced chickpeas, deep-fried and often served with pitta bread.
▷HISTORY C20: from Arabic *felāfil*

Falange ('fælændʒ; *Spanish* fa'lanxe) NOUN the Fascist movement founded in Spain in 1933; the one legal party in Spain under the regime (1939–75) of Francisco Franco (1892–1975), the Spanish general and statesman.
▷HISTORY Spanish: PHALANX
▸ **Fa'langist** NOUN, ADJECTIVE

Falasha (fə'læʃə) NOUN, *plural* **-sha** *or* **-shas**. a member of a tribe of Black Ethiopian Jews.
▷HISTORY from Amharic, from *fälasi* stranger

falbala ('fælbələ) NOUN a gathered flounce, frill, or ruffle.
▷HISTORY C18: from French, from (dialect) *ferbelà*; see FURBELOW

falcate ('fælkeɪt) *or* **falciform** ('fælsɪˌfɔːm) ADJECTIVE *Biology* shaped like a sickle.
▷HISTORY C19: from Latin *falcātus*, from *falx* sickle

falchion ('fɔːltʃən, 'fɔːlʃən) NOUN 1 a short and slightly curved medieval sword broader towards the point. 2 an archaic word for **sword**.
▷HISTORY C14: from Italian *falcione*, from *falce*, from Latin *falx* sickle

falcon ('fɔːlkən, 'fɔːkən) NOUN 1 any diurnal bird of prey of the family *Falconidae*, esp any of the genus *Falco* (gyrfalcon, peregrine falcon, etc.), typically having pointed wings and a long tail. 2 **a** any of these or related birds, trained to hunt small game. **b** the female of such a bird (compare **tercel**). Related adjective: **falconine.** 3 a light-medium cannon used from the 15th to 17th centuries.
▷HISTORY C13: from Old French *faucon*, from Late Latin *falcō* hawk, probably of Germanic origin; perhaps related to Latin *falx* sickle

falconer ('fɔːlkənə, 'fɔːkə-) NOUN a person who breeds or trains hawks or who follows the sport of falconry.

falconet ('fɔːlkəˌnɛt, 'fɔːkə-) NOUN 1 any of various small falcons, esp any of the Asiatic genus *Microhierax*. 2 a small light cannon used from the 15th to 17th centuries.

falcon-gentle *or* **falcon-gentil** NOUN *Falconry* a female falcon, esp a female peregrine falcon.
▷HISTORY C14: from Old French *faucon-gentil* literally: noble falcon

falconiform (fæl'kəʊnɪˌfɔːm) ADJECTIVE of, relating to, or belonging to the order *Falconiformes*, which includes the vultures, hawks, eagles, buzzards, and falcons.

falconine ('fɔːlkəˌnaɪn, 'fɔːkə-) ADJECTIVE 1 of, relating to, or resembling a falcon. 2 of, relating to, or belonging to the family *Falconidae*, which includes the falcons.

falconry ('fɔːlkənrɪ, 'fɔːkən-) NOUN 1 the art of keeping falcons and training them to return from flight to a lure or to hunt quarry. 2 the sport of causing falcons to return from flight to their trainer and to hunt quarry under his direction.

falcula ('fælkjʊlə) NOUN, *plural* **-lae** (-liː). *Zoology* a sharp curved claw, esp of a bird.
▸ **'falculate** ADJECTIVE

falderal ('fældɪˌræl), **falderol** ('fældɪˌrɒl), *or* **folderol** ('fɒldɪˌrɒl) NOUN 1 a showy but worthless trifle. 2 foolish nonsense. 3 a nonsensical refrain in old songs.

faldstool ('fɔːldˌstuːl) NOUN a backless seat, sometimes capable of being folded, used by bishops and certain other prelates.
▷HISTORY C11 *fyldestol*, probably a translation of Medieval Latin *faldistolium* folding stool, of Germanic origin; compare Old High German *faldstuol*

Falerii (fə'lɪərɪˌaɪ) NOUN an ancient city of S Italy, in Latium: important in pre-Roman times.

Faliscan (fə'lɪskən) NOUN an ancient language of Italy, spoken in the area north of the Tiber. It was closely related to Latin, which displaced it before 200 B.C.

Falkirk ('fɔːlkɜːk) NOUN 1 a town in Scotland, the administrative centre of Falkirk council area: scene of Edward I's defeat of Wallace (1298) and Prince Charles Edward's defeat of General Hawley (1746); iron works. Pop.: 35 610 (1991). 2 a council area in central Scotland, on the Firth of Forth: created in 1996 from part of Central Region: largely agricultural, with heavy industry in Falkirk and Grangemouth. Administrative centre: Falkirk. Pop.: 145 191 (2001). Area: 299 sq. km (115 sq. miles).

Falkland Islands ('fɔːklənd) PLURAL NOUN a group of over 100 islands in the S Atlantic: a UK Overseas Territory; invaded by Argentina, who had long laid claim to the islands, on 2 April 1982; recaptured by a British expeditionary force on 14 June 1982. Chief town: Stanley. Pop.: 2221 (1996). Area: about 12 200 sq. km (4700 sq. miles). Spanish name: **Islas Malvinas**.

Falkland Islands Dependencies PLURAL NOUN the former name (until 1985) for South Georgia and the South Sandwich Islands.

fall (fɔːl) VERB **falls, falling, fell** (fɛl), **fallen** ('fɔːlən). (*mainly intr*) 1 to descend by the force of gravity from a higher to a lower place. 2 to drop suddenly from an erect position. 3 to collapse to the ground, esp in pieces. 4 to become less or lower in number, quality, etc.: *prices fell in the summer*. 5 to become lower in pitch. 6 to extend downwards: *her hair fell to her waist*. 7 to be badly wounded or killed. 8 to slope in a downward direction. 9 *Christianity* to yield to temptation or sin. 10 to diminish in status, estimation, etc. 11 to yield to attack: *the city fell under the assault*. 12 to lose power: *the government fell after the riots*. 13 to pass into or take on a specified condition: *to fall asleep*; *fall in love*. 14 to adopt a despondent expression: *her face fell*. 15 to be averted: *her gaze fell*. 16 to come by chance or presumption: *suspicion fell on the butler*. 17 to occur; take place: *night fell*; *Easter falls early this year*. 18 (of payments) to be due. 19 to be directed to a specific point. 20 (foll by *back*, *behind*, etc.) to move in a specified direction. 21 to occur at a specified place: *the accent falls on the last syllable*. 22 (foll by *to*) to return (to); be inherited (by): *the estate falls to the eldest son*. 23 (often foll by *into*, *under*, etc.) to be classified or included: *the subject falls into two main areas*. 24 to issue forth: *a curse fell from her lips*. 25 (of animals, esp lambs) to be born. 26 *Brit dialect* to become pregnant. 27 (*tr*) *Austral and NZ dialect* to fell (trees). 28 *Cricket* (of a batsman's wicket) to be taken by the bowling side: *the sixth wicket fell for 96*. 29 *Archaic* to begin to do: *fall a-doing*; *fall to doing*. 30 **fall flat.** to fail to achieve a desired effect. 31 **fall foul of. a** to come into conflict with. **b** *Nautical* to come into collision with. 32 **fall short. a** to prove inadequate. **b** (often foll by *of*) to fail to reach or measure up to (a standard). ◆ NOUN 33 an act or instance of falling. 34 something that falls: *a fall of snow*. 35 *Chiefly US* autumn. 36 the distance that something falls: *a hundred-foot fall*. 37 a sudden drop from an upright position. 38 (*often plural*) **a** a waterfall or cataract. **b** (*capital when part of a name*): *Niagara Falls*. 39 a downward slope or decline. 40 a decrease in value, number, etc. 41 a decline in status or importance. 42 a moral lapse or failing. 43 a capture or overthrow: *the fall of the city*. 44 a long false hairpiece; switch. 45 a piece of loosely hanging material, such as a veil on a hat. 46 *Machinery, nautical* the end of a tackle to which power is applied to hoist it. 47 *Nautical* one of the lines of a davit for holding, lowering, or raising a boat. 48

Also called: **pinfall.** *Wrestling* a scoring move, pinning both shoulders of one's opponent to the floor for a specified period. **49** *Hunting* **a** another word for **deadfall. b** (*as modifier*): *a fall trap.* **50** **a** the birth of an animal. **b** the animals produced at a single birth. **51** **take the fall.** *Slang, chiefly US* to be blamed, punished, or imprisoned. ◆ See also **fall about, fall among, fall apart, fall away, fall back, fall behind, fall down, fall for, fall in, fall off, fall on, fallout, fall over, fall through, fall to.**

▷HISTORY Old English *feallan*; related to Old Norse *falla*, Old Saxon, Old High German *fallan* to fall; see FELL[2]

Fall (fɔːl) NOUN **the.** *Theol* Adam's sin of disobedience and the state of innate sinfulness ensuing from this for himself and all mankind. See also **original sin.**

fall about VERB (*intr, adverb*) to laugh in an uncontrolled manner: *we fell about when we saw him.*

fallacious (fəˈleɪʃəs) ADJECTIVE **1** containing or involving a fallacy; illogical; erroneous. **2** tending to mislead. **3** delusive or disappointing: *a fallacious hope.*

▸**falˈlaciously** ADVERB ▸**falˈlaciousness** NOUN

fallacy (ˈfæləsɪ) NOUN, *plural* **-cies. 1** an incorrect or misleading notion or opinion based on inaccurate facts or invalid reasoning. **2** unsound or invalid reasoning. **3** the tendency to mislead. **4** *Logic* an error in reasoning that renders an argument logically invalid.

▷HISTORY C15: from Latin *fallācia*, from *fallax* deceitful, from *fallere* to deceive

fallacy of many questions NOUN *Logic* the rhetorical trick of asking a question that cannot be answered without admitting a presupposition that may be false, as *have you stopped beating your wife?*

fallal (fælˈlæl) NOUN a showy ornament, trinket, or article of dress.

▷HISTORY C18: perhaps based on FALBALA

▸**falˈlalery** NOUN

fall among VERB (*intr, preposition*) to enter the company of (a group of people), esp by chance: *he fell among thieves.*

fall apart VERB (*intr, adverb*) **1** to break owing to long use or poor construction: *the chassis is falling apart.* **2** to become disorganized and ineffective: *since you resigned, the office has fallen apart.*

fall away VERB (*intr, adverb*) **1** (of friendship) to be withdrawn. **2** to slope down.

fall back VERB (*intr, adverb*) **1** to recede or retreat. **2** (foll by *on* or *upon*) to have recourse (to). ◆ NOUN **fall-back. 3** a retreat. **4** a reserve, esp money, that can be called upon in need. **5** **a** anything to which one can have recourse as a second choice. **b** (*as modifier*): *a fall-back position.*

fall behind VERB (*intr, adverb*) **1** to drop back; fail to keep up. **2** to be in arrears, as with a payment.

fall down VERB (*intr, adverb*) **1** to drop suddenly or collapse. **2** (often foll by *on*) *Informal* to prove unsuccessful; fail.

fallen (ˈfɔːlən) VERB **1** the past participle of **fall.** ◆ ADJECTIVE **2** having sunk in reputation or honour: *a fallen woman.* **3** killed in battle with glory: *our fallen heroes.* **4** defeated.

fallen arch NOUN collapse of the arch formed by the instep of the foot, resulting in flat feet.

faller (ˈfɔːlə) NOUN **1** any device that falls or operates machinery by falling, as in a spinning machine. **2** one that falls, esp a horse that falls at a fence in a steeplechase. **3** *US and Canadian* a person who fells trees.

fallfish (ˈfɔːlˌfɪʃ) NOUN, *plural* **-fish** *or* **-fishes.** a large North American freshwater cyprinid fish, *Semotilus corporalis*, resembling the chub.

fall for VERB (*intr, preposition*) **1** to become infatuated with (a person). **2** to allow oneself to be deceived by (a lie, trick, etc.).

fall guy NOUN *Informal* **1** a person who is the victim of a confidence trick. **2** a scapegoat.

fallible (ˈfælɪbᵊl) ADJECTIVE **1** capable of being mistaken; erring. **2** liable to mislead.

▷HISTORY C15: from Medieval Latin *fallibilis*, from Latin *fallere* to deceive

▸ˌ**falliˈbility** *or* ˈ**fallibleness** NOUN ▸ˈ**fallibly** ADVERB

fall in VERB (*intr, adverb*) **1** to collapse; no longer act as a support. **2** to adopt a military formation, esp as a soldier taking his place in a line. **3** (of a lease) to expire. **4** (of land) to come into the owner's possession on the expiry of the lease. **5** (often foll by *with*) **a** to meet and join. **b** to agree with or support a person, suggestion, etc. **6** *Austral and NZ* to make a mistake or come to grief. **7** *NZ* to become pregnant. ◆ SENTENCE SUBSTITUTE **8** the order to adopt a military formation.

falling band NOUN a man's large flat collar, often lace-trimmed, worn during the 17th century.

falling sickness *or* **evil** NOUN a former name (nontechnical) for **epilepsy.**

falling star NOUN an informal name for **meteor.**

fall line NOUN **1** *Skiing* the natural downward course between two points on a slope. **2** the edge of a plateau.

Fall Line NOUN a natural junction, running parallel to the E coast of the US, between the hard rocks of the Appalachians and the softer coastal plain, along which rivers form falls and rapids.

fall off VERB (*intr*) **1** to drop unintentionally to the ground from (a high object, bicycle, etc.), esp after losing one's balance. **2** (*adverb*) to diminish in size, intensity, etc.; decline or weaken: *business fell off after Christmas.* **3** (*adverb*) *Nautical* to allow or cause a vessel to sail downwind of her former heading. ◆ NOUN **fall-off. 4** a decline or drop.

fall on VERB (*intr, preposition*) **1** Also: **fall upon.** to attack or snatch (an army, booty, etc.). **2** **fall flat on one's face.** to fail, esp in a ridiculous or humiliating manner. **3** **fall on one's feet.** to emerge unexpectedly well from a difficult situation.

Fallopian tube (fəˈləupɪən) NOUN either of a pair of slender tubes through which ova pass from the ovaries to the uterus in female mammals. See **oviduct.** Related adjectives: **oviducal, oviductal.**

▷HISTORY C18: named after Gabriello *Fallopio* (1523–62), Italian anatomist who first described the tubes

Fallot's tetralogy (ˈfæləuz) NOUN a congenital heart disease in which there are four defects: pulmonary stenosis, enlarged right ventricle, a ventricular septal defect, and an aorta whose origin lies over the septal defect. In babies suffering this disease the defects can be corrected by surgery.

▷HISTORY C20: named after E. L. A. *Fallot* (1850–1911), French physician

fallout (ˈfɔːlˌaut) NOUN **1** the descent of solid material in the atmosphere onto the earth, esp of radioactive material following a nuclear explosion. **2** any solid particles that so descend. **3** *Informal* side-effects; secondary consequences. ◆ VERB **fall out.** (*intr, adverb*) **4** *Informal* to quarrel or disagree. **5** (*intr*) to happen or occur. **6** *Military* to leave a parade or disciplinary formation. ◆ SENTENCE SUBSTITUTE **7** *Military* the order to leave a parade or disciplinary formation.

fall over VERB (*intr, adverb*) **1** to lose one's balance and collapse to the ground. **2** to fall from an upright position: *the vase fell over.* **3** **fall over oneself.** to do everything within one's power: *he fell over himself to be as helpful as possible.*

fallow[1] (ˈfæləu) ADJECTIVE **1** (of land) left unseeded after being ploughed and harrowed to regain fertility for a crop. **2** (of an idea, state of mind, etc.) undeveloped or inactive, but potentially useful. ◆ NOUN **3** land treated in this way. ◆ VERB **4** (*tr*) to leave (land) unseeded after ploughing and harrowing it.

▷HISTORY Old English *fealga*; related to Greek *polos* ploughed field

▸ˈ**fallowness** NOUN

fallow[2] (ˈfæləu) ADJECTIVE of a light yellowish-brown colour.

▷HISTORY Old English *fealu*; related to Old Norse *fölr*, Old Saxon, Old High German *falo*, Latin *pallidus* Greek *polios* grey

fallow deer NOUN either of two deer, *Dama dama* or *D. mesopotamica*, native to the Mediterranean region and Persia respectively. The antlers are flattened and the summer coat is reddish with white spots.

fall through VERB (*intr, adverb*) to miscarry or fail.

fall to VERB (*intr*) **1** (*adverb*) to begin some activity, as eating, working, or fighting. **2** (*preposition*) to devolve on (a person): *the task fell to me.* **3** **fall to the ground.** (of a plan, theory, etc.) to be rendered invalid, esp because of lack of necessary information.

Falmouth (ˈfælməθ) NOUN a port and resort in SW England, in S Cornwall. Pop.: 20 297 (1991).

false (fɔːls) ADJECTIVE **1** not in accordance with the truth or facts. **2** irregular or invalid: *a false start.* **3** untruthful or lying: *a false account.* **4** not genuine, real, or natural; artificial; fake: *false eyelashes.* **5** being or intended to be misleading or deceptive: *a false rumour.* **6** disloyal or treacherous: *a false friend.* **7** based on mistaken or irrelevant ideas or facts: *false pride; a false argument.* **8** (*prenominal*) (esp of plants) superficially resembling the species specified: *false hellebore.* **9** serving to supplement or replace, often temporarily: *a false keel.* **10** *Music* **a** (of a note, interval, etc.) out of tune. **b** (of the interval of a perfect fourth or fifth) decreased by a semitone. **c** (of a cadence) interrupted or imperfect. ◆ ADVERB **11** in a false or dishonest manner (esp in the phrase **play (someone) false**).

▷HISTORY Old English *fals*, from Latin *falsus*, from *fallere* to deceive

▸ˈ**falsely** ADVERB ▸ˈ**falseness** NOUN

false acacia NOUN another name for the **locust tree** (see **locust** (sense 2)).

false alarm NOUN **1** a needless alarm given in error or with intent to deceive. **2** an occasion on which danger is perceived but fails to materialize.

false ankylosis NOUN a nontechnical name for **pseudoarthrosis.**

False Bay NOUN a bay in SW South Africa, near the Cape of Good Hope.

false bedding NOUN another name for **cross bedding.**

false-card VERB (*intr*) *Bridge* to play a misleading card, esp a high loser, in order to deceive an opponent.

false cirrus NOUN a type of thick cirrus cloud spreading from the top of a cumulonimbus cloud.

false colour NOUN colour used in a computer or photographic display to help in interpreting the image, as in the use of red to show high temperatures and blue to show low temperatures in an infrared image converter.

false colours PLURAL NOUN **1** a flag to which one is not entitled, flown esp in order to deceive: *the ship was sailing under false colours.* **2** an assumed or misleading name or guise: *to trade under false colours.*

false dawn NOUN zodiacal light appearing just before sunrise.

false diamond NOUN any of a number of semiprecious stones that resemble diamond, such as zircon and white topaz.

false friend NOUN a word or expression in one language that, because it resembles one in another language, is often wrongly taken to have the same meaning, for example, the French *agenda* which means *diary*, not *agenda*.

false fruit NOUN another name for **pseudocarp.**

falsehood (ˈfɔːlsˌhud) NOUN **1** the quality of being untrue. **2** an untrue statement; lie. **3** the act of deceiving or lying.

false imprisonment NOUN *Law* the restraint of a person's liberty without lawful authority.

false joint NOUN a nontechnical name for **pseudoarthrosis.**

false keel NOUN an extension to the keel of a vessel either for protecting the keel from damage or for reducing leeway.

false memory syndrome NOUN an alleged condition in which a person undergoing psychotherapy erroneously believes in traumatic events in his or her childhood. See also **recovered memory.**

false negative NOUN **1** a result in a medical test that wrongly indicates the absence of the condition being tested for. **2** a person from whom such a result is obtained.

false position NOUN a situation in which a person is forced to act or seems to be acting against his principles or interests.

false positive NOUN **1** a result in a medical test that wrongly indicates the presence of the condition being tested for. **2** a person from whom such a result is obtained.

false pregnancy NOUN another name for **phantom pregnancy.**

false pretences PLURAL NOUN 1 *Criminal law* a former name for **deception** (see **obtaining by deception**). 2 a similar misrepresentation used to obtain anything, such as trust or affection (esp in the phrase **under false pretences**).

false relation NOUN *Music* a harmonic clash that occurs when a note in one part sounds simultaneously with or immediately before or after its chromatically altered (sharpened or flattened) equivalent appearing in another part. Also called (esp US): **cross relation.**

false ribs PLURAL NOUN any of the lower five pairs of ribs in man, attached behind to the thoracic vertebrae but in front not attached directly to the breastbone. See **floating rib.**

false scorpion NOUN any small predatory arachnid of the order *Pseudoscorpionida*, which includes the **book scorpion** and is named from the claw-shaped palps, which are poison organs.

false step NOUN 1 an unwise action. 2 a stumble; slip.

false teeth PLURAL NOUN a denture, esp a removable complete set of artificial teeth for one or both jaws.

falsetto (fɔːlˈsɛtəʊ) NOUN, *plural* **-tos.** a form of vocal production used by male singers to extend their range upwards beyond its natural compass by limiting the vibration of the vocal cords.
▷HISTORY C18: from Italian, from *falso* FALSE

false vampire NOUN any large insectivorous bat of the family *Megadermatidae*, of Africa, S and SE Asia, and Australia. They eat insects and small vertebrates but do not feed on blood.

falsework (ˈfɔːlsˌwɜːk) NOUN a framework supporting something under construction.

falsies (ˈfɔːlsɪz) PLURAL NOUN *Informal* pads of soft material, such as foam rubber, worn to exaggerate the size of or simulate the appearance of a woman's breasts.

falsify (ˈfɔːlsɪˌfaɪ) VERB (*tr*) **-fies, -fying, -fied.** 1 to make (a report, evidence, accounts, etc.) false or inaccurate by alteration, esp in order to deceive. 2 to prove false; disprove.
▷HISTORY C15: from Old French *falsifier*, from Late Latin *falsificāre*, from Latin *falsus* FALSE + *facere* to make
▸ˈ**falsiˌfiable** ADJECTIVE ▸**falsification** (ˌfɔːlsɪfɪˈkeɪʃən) NOUN ▸ˈ**falsiˌfier** NOUN

falsity (ˈfɔːlsɪtɪ) NOUN, *plural* **-ties.** 1 the state of being false or untrue. 2 something false; a lie or deception.

Falstaffian (fɔːlˈstɑːfɪən) ADJECTIVE jovial, plump, and dissolute.
▷HISTORY C19: after Sir John *Falstaff*, a character in Shakespeare's *Henry IV, Parts I–II* (1597)

Falster (ˈfɑːlstə) NOUN an island in the Baltic Sea, part of SE Denmark. Chief town: Nykøbing. Pop.: 42 846 (1990 est.). Area: 513 sq. km (198 sq. miles).

faltboat (ˈfæltˌbəʊt) NOUN a collapsible boat made of waterproof material stretched over a light framework.
▷HISTORY German *Faltboot*, from *falten* to FOLD[1] + *Boot* BOAT

falter (ˈfɔːltə) VERB 1 (*intr*) to be hesitant, weak, or unsure; waver. 2 (*intr*) to move unsteadily or hesitantly; stumble. 3 to utter haltingly or hesitantly; stammer. ◆ NOUN 4 uncertainty or hesitancy in speech or action. 5 a quavering or irregular sound.
▷HISTORY C14: probably of Scandinavian origin; compare Icelandic *faltrast*
▸ˈ**falterer** NOUN ▸ˈ**falteringly** ADVERB

Falun (ˌfɑːˈlʌn) NOUN a city in central Sweden: iron and pyrites mines. Pop.: 55 014 (1994).

Falun Gong (ˌfæluːn ˈguːŋ) NOUN a modern religious movement combining aspects of Buddhism and Taoism, especially the practice of qi gong, founded by Li Hongzhi in 1992.
▷HISTORY C20: from Chinese, *falun* dharma wheel (from *fa* law, *lun* wheel) + *gong* practice

Famagusta (ˌfæməˈgʊstə) NOUN a port in E Cyprus, on **Famagusta Bay**: became one of the richest cities in Christendom in the 14th century. Pop.: 67 167 (1994).

fame (feɪm) NOUN 1 the state of being widely known or recognized; renown; celebrity. 2 *Archaic* rumour or public report. ◆ VERB 3 (*tr; now usually passive*) to make known or famous; celebrate: *he was famed for his ruthlessness.*
▷HISTORY C13: from Latin *fāma* report; related to *fārī* to say
▸**famed** ADJECTIVE

familial (fəˈmɪlɪəl) ADJECTIVE 1 of or relating to the family. 2 occurring in the members of a family: *a familial disease.*

familiar (fəˈmɪlɪə) ADJECTIVE 1 well-known; easily recognized: *a familiar figure.* 2 frequent or customary: *a familiar excuse.* 3 (*postpositive;* foll by *with*) acquainted. 4 friendly; informal. 5 close; intimate. 6 more intimate than is acceptable; presumptuous. 7 an archaic word for **familial.** ◆ NOUN 8 Also called: **familiar spirit.** a supernatural spirit often assuming animal form, supposed to attend and aid a witch, wizard, etc. 9 a person, attached to the household of the pope or a bishop, who renders service in return for support. 10 an officer of the Inquisition who arrested accused persons. 11 a friend or frequent companion.
▷HISTORY C14: from Latin *familiāris* domestic, from *familia* FAMILY
▸**faˈmiliarly** ADVERB ▸**faˈmiliarness** NOUN

familiarity (fəˌmɪlɪˈærɪtɪ) NOUN, *plural* **-ties.** 1 reasonable knowledge or acquaintance, as with a subject or place. 2 close acquaintanceship or intimacy. 3 undue intimacy. 4 (*sometimes plural*) an instance of unwarranted intimacy.

familiarize *or* **familiarise** (fəˈmɪljəˌraɪz) VERB (*tr*) 1 to make (oneself or someone else) familiar, as with a particular subject. 2 to make (something) generally known or accepted.
▸**faˌmiliariˈzation** *or* **faˌmiliariˈsation** NOUN ▸**faˈmiliarˌizer** *or* **faˈmiliarˌiser** NOUN

Familist (ˈfæmɪlɪst) NOUN a member of the Family of Love, a mystical Christian religious sect of the 16th and 17th centuries based upon love.
▸ˈ**Familism** NOUN

famille *French* (famij) NOUN a type of Chinese porcelain characterized either by a design on a background of yellow (***famille jaune***) or black (***famille noire***) or by a design in which the predominant colour is pink (***famille rose***) or green (***famille verte***).
▷HISTORY C19: literally: family

family (ˈfæmɪlɪ, ˈfæmlɪ) NOUN, *plural* **-lies.** 1 **a** a primary social group consisting of parents and their offspring, the principal function of which is provision for its members. **b** (*as modifier*): *family quarrels; a family unit.* 2 one's wife or husband and one's children. 3 one's children, as distinguished from one's husband or wife. 4 a group of persons related by blood; a group descended from a common ancestor. Compare **extended family.** 5 all the persons living together in one household. 6 any group of related things or beings, esp when scientifically categorized. 7 *Biology* any of the taxonomic groups into which an order is divided and which contains one or more genera. *Felidae* (cat family) and *Canidae* (dog family) are two families of the order *Carnivora.* 8 *Ecology* a group of organisms of the same species living together in a community. 9 a group of historically related languages assumed to derive from one original language. 10 *Chiefly US* an independent local group of the Mafia. 11 *Maths* a group of curves or surfaces whose equations differ from a given equation only in the values assigned to one or more constants in each curve: *a family of concentric circles.* 12 *Physics* the isotopes, collectively, that comprise a radioactive series. 13 **in the family way.** *Informal* pregnant.
▷HISTORY C15: from Latin *familia* a household, servants of the house, from *famulus* servant

family allowance NOUN 1 (in Britain) a former name for **child benefit.** 2 (*capitals*) the Canadian equivalent of **child benefit.**

family balancing NOUN *US* the choosing of the sex of a future child on the basis of how many children of each sex a family already has.

family Bible NOUN a large Bible used for family worship in which births, marriages, and deaths are recorded.

family circle NOUN 1 members of a family regarded as a closed group. 2 *Chiefly US* the cheap seating area in a theatre behind or above the dress circle.

Family Compact NOUN *Canadian* 1 **the.** the ruling oligarchy in Upper Canada in the early 19th century. 2 (*often not capital*) any influential clique.

family credit NOUN (formerly, in Britain) a means-tested allowance paid to low-earning families with one or more dependent children and one or both parents in work: replaced by Working Families Tax Credit in 1999.

Family Division NOUN *Brit, law* a division of the High Court of Justice dealing with divorce, the rights of access to children, etc.

family doctor NOUN See **general practitioner.**

family grouping NOUN a system, used usually in the infant school, of grouping children of various ages together, esp for project work. Also called: **vertical grouping.**

family man NOUN a man who is married and has children, esp one who is devoted to his family.

family name NOUN 1 a surname, esp when regarded as representing the family honour. 2 a first or middle name frequently used in a family, often originally a surname.

family planning NOUN the control of the number of children in a family and of the intervals between them, esp by the use of contraceptives. See also **birth control.**

family skeleton NOUN a closely guarded family secret.

family support NOUN *NZ* a means-tested allowance for families in need.

family therapy NOUN a form of psychotherapy in which the members of a family participate, with the aim of improving communications between them and the ways in which they relate to each other.

family tree NOUN a chart showing the genealogical relationships and lines of descent of a family. Also called: **genealogical tree.**

famine (ˈfæmɪn) NOUN 1 a severe shortage of food, as through crop failure or overpopulation. 2 acute shortage of anything. 3 violent hunger.
▷HISTORY C14: from Old French, via Vulgar Latin, from Latin *famēs* hunger

famish (ˈfæmɪʃ) VERB 1 (*now usually passive*) to be or make very hungry or weak. 2 *Archaic* to die or cause to die from starvation. 3 *Irish* to make very cold: *I was famished with the cold.*
▷HISTORY C14: from Old French *afamer*, via Vulgar Latin, from Latin *famēs* FAMINE
▸ˈ**famishment** NOUN

famous (ˈfeɪməs) ADJECTIVE 1 known to or recognized by many people; renowned. 2 *Informal* excellent; splendid. 3 *Archaic* of ill repute.
▷HISTORY C14: from Latin *fāmōsus;* see FAME
▸ˈ**famousness** NOUN

famously (ˈfeɪməslɪ) ADVERB 1 well-known: *her famously relaxed manner.* 2 very well: *the two got on famously.*

famulus (ˈfæmjʊləs) NOUN, *plural* **li** (-ˌlaɪ). (formerly) the attendant of a sorcerer or scholar.
▷HISTORY C19: from Latin: servant

fan[1] (fæn) NOUN 1 **a** any device for creating a current of air by movement of a surface or number of surfaces, esp a rotating device consisting of a number of blades attached to a central hub. **b** a machine that rotates such a device. 2 any of various hand-agitated devices for cooling onself, esp a collapsible semicircular series of flat segments of paper, ivory, etc. 3 something shaped like such a fan, such as the tail of certain birds. 4 *Agriculture* **a** a kind of basket formerly used for winnowing grain. **b** a machine equipped with a fan for winnowing or cleaning grain. ◆ VERB **fans, fanning, fanned.** (*mainly tr*) 5 to cause a current of air, esp cool air, to blow upon, as by means of a fan: *to fan one's face.* 6 to agitate or move (air, smoke, etc.) with or as if with a fan. 7 to make fiercer, more ardent, etc.: *fan one's passion.* 8 (*also intr;* often foll by *out*) to spread out or cause to spread out in the shape of a fan. 9 **a** to fire (an automatic gun) continuously by keeping the trigger depressed. **b** to fire (a nonautomatic gun) several times by repeatedly chopping back the hammer with the palm. 10 to winnow (grain) by blowing the chaff away from it.
▷HISTORY Old English *fann*, from Latin *vannus*
▸ˈ**fanlike** ADJECTIVE ▸ˈ**fanner** NOUN

fan² (fæn) NOUN [1] an ardent admirer of a pop star, film actor, football team, etc. [2] a devotee of a sport, hobby, etc.
▷HISTORY C17, re-formed C19: from FAN(ATIC)

Fanagalo ('fænəgələʊ) *or* **Fanakalo** NOUN (in South Africa) a Zulu-based pidgin with English and Afrikaans components, esp associated with the mines.
▷HISTORY C20: from Fanagalo *fana go lo*, literally: to be like this; compare Zulu *fand* to be like, *ka-lo* of this

fanatic (fə'nætɪk) NOUN [1] a person whose enthusiasm or zeal for something is extreme or beyond normal limits. [2] *Informal* a person devoted to a particular hobby or pastime; fan: *a jazz fanatic.* ◆ ADJECTIVE [3] a variant of **fanatical.**
▷HISTORY C16: from Latin *fānāticus* belonging to a temple, hence, inspired by a god, frenzied, from *fānum* temple

fanatical (fə'nætɪkᵊl) ADJECTIVE surpassing what is normal or accepted in enthusiasm for or belief in something; excessively or unusually dedicated or devoted.
▸**fa'natically** ADVERB

fanaticism (fə'nætɪˌsɪzəm) NOUN wildly excessive or irrational devotion, dedication, or enthusiasm.

fanaticize *or* **fanaticise** (fə'nætɪˌsaɪz) VERB to make or become fanatical.

fanbase ('fænˌbeɪs) NOUN the body of admirers of a particular pop singer, football team, etc.

fan belt NOUN any belt that drives a fan, esp the belt that drives a cooling fan together with a dynamo or alternator in a car engine.

fancied ('fænsɪd) ADJECTIVE [1] imaginary; unreal. [2] thought likely to win or succeed: *a fancied runner.*

fancier ('fænsɪə) NOUN [1] a person with a special interest in something. [2] a person who breeds plants or animals, often as a pastime: *a bird fancier.*

fanciful ('fænsɪfʊl) ADJECTIVE [1] not based on fact; dubious or imaginary: *fanciful notions.* [2] made or designed in a curious, intricate, or imaginative way. [3] indulging in or influenced by fancy; whimsical.
▸**'fancifully** ADVERB ▸**'fancifulness** NOUN

fan club NOUN [1] an organized group of admirers of a particular pop singer, film star, etc. [2] **be a member of someone's fan club.** *Informal* to approve of someone strongly.

fancy ('fænsɪ) ADJECTIVE **-cier, -ciest.** [1] not plain; ornamented or decorative: *a fancy cake; fancy clothes.* [2] requiring skill to perform; intricate: *a fancy dance routine.* [3] arising in the imagination; capricious or illusory. [4] (*often used ironically*) superior in quality or impressive: *a fancy course in business administration.* [5] higher than expected: *fancy prices.* [6] (of a domestic animal) bred for particular qualities. ◆ NOUN, *plural* **-cies.** [7] a sudden capricious idea; whim. [8] a sudden or irrational liking for a person or thing. [9] the power to conceive and represent decorative and novel imagery, esp in poetry. Fancy was held by Coleridge to be more casual and superficial than imagination. See **imagination** (sense 4). [10] an idea or thing produced by this. [11] a mental image. [12] taste or judgment, as in art of dress. [13] Also called: **fantasy, fantasia.** *Music* a composition for solo lute, keyboard, etc., current during the 16th and 17th centuries. [14] **the fancy.** *Archaic* those who follow a particular sport, esp prize fighting. ◆ VERB **-cies, -cying, -cied.** (*tr*) [15] to picture in the imagination. [16] to suppose; imagine: *I fancy it will rain.* [17] (*often used with a negative*) to like: *I don't fancy your chances!* [18] (*reflexive*) to have a high or ill-founded opinion of oneself: *he fancied himself as a doctor.* [19] *Informal* to have a wish for; desire: *she fancied some chocolate.* [20] *Brit informal* to be physically attracted to (another person). [21] to breed (animals) for particular characteristics. ◆ INTERJECTION [22] Also: **fancy that!** an exclamation of surprise or disbelief.
▷HISTORY C15 *fantsy*, shortened from *fantasie*; see FANTASY
▸**'fancily** ADVERB ▸**'fanciness** NOUN

fancy dress NOUN **a** costume worn at masquerades, etc., usually representing a particular role, historical figure, etc. **b** (*as modifier*): *a fancy-dress ball.*

fancy-free ADJECTIVE having no commitments; carefree.

fancy goods PLURAL NOUN small decorative gifts; knick-knacks.

fancy man NOUN *Slang* [1] a woman's lover. [2] a pimp.

fancy woman NOUN *Slang* a mistress or prostitute.

fancywork ('fænsɪˌwɜːk) NOUN any ornamental needlework, such as embroidery or crochet.

fan dance NOUN a dance in which large fans are manipulated in front of the body, partially revealing or suggesting nakedness.

fandangle (fæn'dæŋgᵊl) NOUN *Informal* [1] elaborate ornament. [2] nonsense.
▷HISTORY C19: perhaps from FANDANGO

fandango (fæn'dæŋgəʊ) NOUN, *plural* **-gos.** [1] an old Spanish courtship dance in triple time between a couple who dance closely and provocatively. [2] a piece of music composed for or in the rhythm of this dance.
▷HISTORY C18: from Spanish, of uncertain origin

fane (feɪn) NOUN *Archaic or poetic* a temple or shrine.
▷HISTORY C14: from Latin *fānum*

fanfare ('fænfeə) NOUN [1] a flourish or short tune played on brass instruments, used as a military signal, at a ceremonial event, etc. [2] an ostentatious flourish or display.
▷HISTORY C17: from French, back formation from *fanfarer* to play a flourish on trumpets; see FANFARONADE

fanfaronade (ˌfænfærə'nɑːd) NOUN *Rare* boasting or flaunting behaviour; bluster.
▷HISTORY C17: via French from Spanish *fanfaronada*, from *fanfarron* boaster, from Arabic *farfār* garrulous

fang¹ (fæŋ) NOUN [1] the long pointed hollow or grooved tooth of a venomous snake through which venom is injected. [2] any large pointed tooth, esp the canine or carnassial tooth of a carnivorous mammal. [3] the root of a tooth. [4] (*usually plural*) *Brit informal* tooth: *clean your fangs.*
▷HISTORY Old English *fang* what is caught, prey; related to Old Norse *fang* a grip, German *Fang* booty
▸**fanged** ADJECTIVE ▸**'fangless** ADJECTIVE ▸**'fangˌlike** ADJECTIVE

fang² (fæŋ) *Austral informal* ◆ VERB (*intr*) [1] to drive at great speed. ◆ NOUN [2] an act or instance of driving in such a way: *we took the car for a fang.*
▷HISTORY C20: from Juan Manuel *Fangio* (1911–95), Argentinian racing driver who was world champion five times

Fang (fæŋ, fɑːŋ) NOUN [1] (*plural* **Fangs** *or* **Fang**) a member of a Negroid people of W Africa, living chiefly in the rain forests of Gabon and Rio Muni: noted for their use of iron and copper money and for their sculpture. [2] the language of this people, belonging to the Bantu group of the Niger-Congo family.

fango ('fæŋgəʊ) NOUN mud from thermal springs in Italy, used in the treatment of rheumatic disease.
▷HISTORY from Italian

fan heater NOUN a space heater consisting of an electrically heated element with an electrically driven fan to disperse the heat by forced convection.

fanion ('fænjən) NOUN a small flag used by surveyors to mark stations.
▷HISTORY C18: from French, from *fanon* maniple, of Germanic origin

fanjet ('fænˌdʒɛt) NOUN another name for **turbofan** (senses 1, 2).

fankle ('fæŋkᵊl) *Scot dialect* ◆ VERB (*tr*) [1] to entangle. ◆ NOUN [2] a tangle; confusion.
▷HISTORY from *fank* a coil of rope, from *fang*, obsolete variant of VANG

fanlight ('fænˌlaɪt) NOUN [1] a semicircular window over a door or window, often having sash bars like the ribs of a fan. [2] a small rectangular window over a door. US name: **transom.** [3] another name for **skylight.**

fan mail NOUN mail sent to a famous person, such as a pop musician or film star, by admirers.

fanny ('fænɪ) NOUN, *plural* **-nies.** *Slang* [1] *Taboo, Brit* the female genitals. [2] *Chiefly US and Canadian* the buttocks.
▷HISTORY C20: perhaps from *Fanny*, pet name from *Frances*

> **Language note** Despite the theory that this word derives from the name 'Fanny', its use in British English is still considered taboo by many people, and is likely to cause offence. In the US the word refers to the buttocks. Serious misunderstanding may therefore arise when what people in Britain know as a 'bumbag' is referred to in the States as a 'fanny pack'.

fanny adams NOUN *Brit slang* [1] (usually preceded by *sweet*) absolutely nothing at all. Often shortened to: **f.a., FA,** *or* **SFA.** [2] *Chiefly nautical* (formerly) tinned meat, esp mutton.
▷HISTORY C19: from the name of a young murder victim whose body was cut up into small pieces. For sense 1: a euphemism for *fuck all*

fanon ('fænən) NOUN *RC Church* [1] a collar-shaped vestment worn by the pope when celebrating mass. [2] (formerly) various pieces of embroidered fabric used in the liturgy.
▷HISTORY Middle English, of Germanic origin; related to Old High German *fano* cloth

fan palm NOUN any of various palm trees, such as the talipot and palmetto, that have fan-shaped leaves. Compare **feather palm.**

fantail ('fænˌteɪl) NOUN [1] a breed of domestic pigeon having a large tail that can be opened like a fan. [2] any Old World flycatcher of the genus *Rhipidura*, of Australia, New Zealand, and SE Asia, having a broad fan-shaped tail. [3] a tail shaped like an outspread fan. [4] *Architect* a part or structure having a number of components radiating from a common centre. [5] a burner that ejects fuel to produce a wide flat flame in a lamp or furnace. [6] a flat jet of air and coal dust projected into the air stream of a pulverized-coal furnace. [7] an auxiliary sail on the upper portion of a windmill that turns the mill to face the wind. [8] *US* a curved part of the deck projecting aft of the sternpost of a ship.
▸**'fan-ˌtailed** ADJECTIVE

fan-tan NOUN [1] a Chinese gambling game in which a random number of counters are placed under a bowl and wagers laid on how many will remain after they have been divided by four. [2] a card game played in sequence, the winner being the first to use up all his cards.
▷HISTORY C19: from Chinese (Cantonese) *fan t'an* repeated divisions, from *fan* times + *t'an* division

fantasia (fæn'teɪzɪə, ˌfæntə'zɪə) NOUN [1] any musical composition of a free or improvisatory nature. [2] a potpourri of popular tunes woven freely into a loosely bound composition. [3] another word for **fancy** (sense 13).
▷HISTORY C18: from Italian: fancy; see FANTASY

fantasist ('fæntəsɪst) NOUN [1] a person who indulges in fantasies. [2] a person who writes musical or literary fantasies.

fantasize *or* **fantasise** ('fæntəˌsaɪz) VERB [1] (when *tr*, takes a clause as object) to conceive extravagant or whimsical ideas, images, etc. [2] (*intr*) to conceive pleasant or satisfying mental images.

fantasm ('fæntæzəm) NOUN an archaic spelling of **phantasm.**
▸**fan'tasmal** *or* **fan'tasmic** ADJECTIVE ▸**fan'tasmally** *or* **fan'tasmically** ADVERB

fantast ('fæntæst) NOUN a dreamer or visionary.
▷HISTORY C16: from German *Phantast*, from Greek *phantastēs* boaster; English word influenced in meaning by FANTASTIC

fantastic (fæn'tæstɪk) ADJECTIVE *also* **fantastical.** [1] strange, weird, or fanciful in appearance, conception, etc. [2] created in the mind; illusory. [3] extravagantly fanciful; unrealistic: *fantastic plans.* [4] incredible or preposterous; absurd: *a fantastic verdict.* [5] *Informal* very large or extreme; great: *a fantastic fortune; he suffered fantastic pain.* [6] *Informal* very good; excellent. [7] of, given to, or characterized by fantasy. [8] not constant; capricious; fitful: *given to fantastic moods.* ◆ NOUN [9] *Archaic* a person who dresses or behaves eccentrically.
▷HISTORY C14 *fantastik* imaginary, via Late Latin from Greek *phantastikos* capable of imagining, from *phantazein* to make visible
▸**ˌfantasti'cality** *or* **fan'tasticalness** NOUN

fantastically (fæn'tæstɪkəlɪ) ADVERB [1] in a

fantastic manner. [2] *Informal* (intensifier): *it's fantastically cheap*.

fantasy *or* **phantasy** ('fæntəsɪ) NOUN, *plural* **-sies.** [1] **a** imagination unrestricted by reality. **b** (*as modifier*): *a fantasy world*. [2] a creation of the imagination, esp a weird or bizarre one. [3] *Psychol* **a** a series of pleasing mental images, usually serving to fulfil a need not gratified in reality. **b** the activity of forming such images. [4] a whimsical or far-fetched notion. [5] an illusion, hallucination, or phantom. [6] a highly elaborate imaginative design or creation. [7] *Music* another word for **fantasia**[1] (sense 2), **fancy** (sense 13), (rarely) **development** (sense 5). [8] **a** literature having a large fantasy content. **b** a prose or dramatic composition of this type. [9] (*modifier*) of or relating to a competition, often in a newspaper, in which a participant selects players for an imaginary, ideal team, and points are awarded according to the actual performances of the chosen players: *fantasy football*. ◆ VERB **-sies, -sying, -sied.** [10] a less common word for **fantasize.**
▷HISTORY C14 *fantasie*, from Latin *phantasia*, from Greek *phantazein* to make visible

Fanti ('fæntɪ) NOUN [1] a language of Ghana: one of the two chief dialects of Akan. Compare **Twi.** [2] (*plural* **-tis** *or* **-ti**) a member of a Negroid people who speak this language, inhabiting the rain forests of Ghana and the Ivory Coast.

fantoccini (ˌfæntə'tʃiːnɪ) PLURAL NOUN [1] marionettes. [2] puppet shows in which they are used.
▷HISTORY C18: from Italian: little puppets, plural of *fantoccino*, from *fantoccio* puppet, from *fante* boy, from Latin *infāns* INFANT

fantod ('fæntəd) NOUN [1] crotchety or faddish behaviour. [2] (*plural*) a state of restlessness or unease.
▷HISTORY C19: of uncertain origin

fantom ('fæntəm) NOUN an archaic spelling of **phantom.**

fantoosh (fæn'tuːʃ) ADJECTIVE *Scot* pretentious; ostentatious.
▷HISTORY of uncertain origin

fan tracery NOUN *Architect* the carved ornamentation on fan vaulting.

fan vaulting NOUN *Architect* vaulting having ribs that radiate like those of a fan and spring from the top of a capital or corbel. Also called: **palm vaulting.**

fan worm NOUN any tube-dwelling polychaete worm of the family *Sabellidae*, having long tentacles that spread into a fan when the worm emerges from its tube.

FANY ('fænɪ) NOUN [1] ACRONYM FOR First Aid Nursing Yeomanry. [2] Also called: **Fany, Fanny,** *plural* **FANYs, Fanys, Fannies.** a member of this organization.

fanzine ('fænˌziːn) NOUN a small-circulation magazine produced by amateurs for fans of a specific interest, pop group, etc.
▷HISTORY C20: from FAN[2] + (MAGA)ZINE

FAO ABBREVIATION FOR: [1] Food and Agriculture Organization (of the United Nations). [2] for the attention of.

FAQ *Computing* ABBREVIATION FOR frequently asked question *or* questions: a text file containing basic information on a particular subject.

f.a.q. *Commerce* ABBREVIATION FOR fair average quality.

faqir (fə'kɪə, 'feɪkə) NOUN a variant spelling of **fakir.**

far (fɑː) ADVERB **farther** *or* **further, farthest** *or* **furthest.** [1] at, to, or from a great distance. [2] at or to a remote time: *far in the future*. [3] to a considerable degree; very much: *a far better plan*. [4] **as far as. a** to the degree or extent that. **b** to the distance or place of. [5] **by far.** by a considerable margin. [6] **far and away.** by a very great margin. [7] **far and wide.** over great distances; everywhere. [8] **far be it from me.** I would not presume; on no account: *far be it from me to tell you what to do*. [9] **far gone. a** in an advanced state of deterioration. **b** *Informal* extremely drunk. [10] **go far. a** to be successful; achieve much: *your son will go far*. **b** to be sufficient or last long: *the wine didn't go far*. [11] **go too far.** to exceed reasonable limits. [12] **how far?** to what extent, distance, or degree? [13] **in so far as.** to the degree or extent that. [14] **so far. a** up to the present moment. **b** up to a certain point, extent, degree, etc. [15] **so far, so good.** an expression of satisfaction with progress made. ◆ ADJECTIVE (*prenominal*) [16] remote in space or time: *a far country; in the far past*. [17] extending a great distance; long. [18] more distant: *the far end of the room*. [19] **a far cry. a** a long way. **b** something very different. [20] **far from.** in a degree, state, etc., remote from: *he is far from happy*.
▷HISTORY Old English *feorr*; related to Old Frisian *fīr*, Old High German *ferro*, Latin *porro* forwards, Greek *pera* further
▸'**farness** NOUN

farad ('færəd, -æd) NOUN *Physics* the derived SI unit of electric capacitance; the capacitance of a capacitor between the plates of which a potential of 1 volt is created by a charge of 1 coulomb. Symbol: F.
▷HISTORY C19: named after Michael *Faraday* (1791–1867), English physicist and chemist

faraday ('færəˌdeɪ) NOUN a quantity of electricity, used in electrochemical calculations, equivalent to unit amount of substance of electrons. It is equal to the product of the Avogadro number and the charge on the electron and has the value 96 487 coulombs per mole. Symbol: *F*.
▷HISTORY C20: named after Michael *Faraday* (1791–1867), English physicist and chemist

Faraday cage NOUN an earthed conducting cage or container used to protect electrical equipment against electric fields.
▷HISTORY C20: named after Michael *Faraday* (1791–1867), English physicist and chemist

faradic (fə'rædɪk) *or* **faradaic** (ˌfærə'deɪɪk) ADJECTIVE of or concerned with an intermittent asymmetric alternating current such as that induced in the secondary winding of an induction coil.
▷HISTORY C19: from French *faradique*, from Michael *Faraday* (1791–1867), English physicist and chemist

faradism ('færəˌdɪzəm) NOUN the therapeutic use of faradic currents.

faradize *or* **faradise** ('færəˌdaɪz) VERB (*tr*) *Obsolete* to treat (an organ or part) with faradic currents.
▸ˌ**faradi'zation** *or* ˌ**faradi'sation** NOUN ▸'**faraˌdizer** *or* '**faraˌdiser** NOUN

farandole ('færənˌdəʊl; *French* farɑ̃dɔl) NOUN [1] a lively dance in six-eight or four-four time from Provence. [2] a piece of music composed for or in the rhythm of this dance.
▷HISTORY C19: from French, from Provençal *farandoulo*, of uncertain origin; compare Spanish *farándula* itinerant group of actors

faraway ('fɑːrəˌweɪ) ADJECTIVE (**far away** *when postpositive*) [1] very distant; remote. [2] dreamy or absent-minded.

FARC (fɑːk) NOUN ACRONYM FOR *Fuerzas Armadas Revolucionarias de Colombia*, Revolutionary Armed Forces of Colombia, a Marxist revolutionary guerrilla force engaging in armed struggle against the government of Colombia.

farce (fɑːs) NOUN [1] a broadly humorous play based on the exploitation of improbable situations. [2] the genre of comedy represented by works of this kind. [3] a ludicrous situation or action. [4] Also: **farcemeat.** another name for **forcemeat.** ◆ VERB (*tr*) *Obsolete* [5] to enliven (a speech, etc.) with jokes. [6] to stuff (meat, fowl, etc.) with forcemeat.
▷HISTORY C14 (in the sense: stuffing): from Old French, from Latin *farcīre* to stuff, interpolate passages (in the mass, in religious plays, etc.)

farceur *French* (farsœr) NOUN [1] a writer of or performer in farces. [2] a joker.
▸**far'ceuse** FEMININE NOUN

farci (fɑː'siː) ADJECTIVE (of food) stuffed.
▷HISTORY French: stuffed; see FARCE

farcical ('fɑːsɪkəl) ADJECTIVE [1] ludicrous; absurd. [2] of or relating to farce.
▸ˌ**farci'cality** *or* '**farcicalness** NOUN ▸'**farcically** ADVERB

farcy ('fɑːsɪ) NOUN, *plural* **-cies.** *Vet science* a form of glanders in which lymph vessels near the skin become thickened, with skin lesions and abscess-forming nodules, caused by a bacterium, *Burkholderia mallei*.
▷HISTORY C15: from Old French *farcin*, from Late Latin *farcīminum* glanders, from Latin *farcīmen* a sausage, from *farcīre* to stuff

fard (fɑːd) NOUN *Archaic* paint for the face, esp white paint.
▷HISTORY C15: from Old French *farder* to use facial cosmetics, of Germanic origin

fardel ('fɑːdəl) NOUN *Archaic* a bundle or burden.
▷HISTORY C13: from Old French *farde*, ultimately from Arabic *fardah*

fare (fɛə) NOUN [1] the sum charged or paid for conveyance in a bus, train, aeroplane, etc. [2] a paying passenger, esp when carried by taxi. [3] a range of food and drink; diet. ◆ VERB (*intr*) [4] to get on (as specified); manage: *he fared well*. [5] (with *it* as a subject) to turn out or happen as specified: *it fared badly with him*. [6] *Archaic* to eat: *we fared sumptuously*. [7] (often foll by *forth*) *Archaic* to go or travel.
▷HISTORY Old English *faran*; related to Old Norse *fara* to travel, Old High German *faran* to go, Greek *poros* ford
▸'**farer** NOUN

Far East NOUN **the.** the countries of E Asia, usually including China, Japan, North and South Korea, Indonesia, Malaysia, and the Philippines: sometimes extended to include all territories east of Afghanistan.

Far Eastern ADJECTIVE of or relating to the Far East (E Asia) or its inhabitants.

Fareham ('fɛərəm) NOUN a market town in S England, in S Hampshire. Pop.: 54 866 (1991).

fare stage NOUN [1] a section of a bus journey for which a set charge is made. [2] a bus stop marking the end of such a section.

fare-thee-well *or* **fare-you-well** NOUN *Informal, chiefly US* a state of perfection: *the steak was cooked to a fare-thee-well*.

farewell (ˌfɛə'wɛl) SENTENCE SUBSTITUTE [1] goodbye; adieu. ◆ NOUN [2] a parting salutation. [3] an act of departure; leave-taking. [4] (*modifier*) expressing leave-taking: *a farewell speech*. ◆ VERB (*tr*) [5] *Austral and NZ* to honour (a person) at his departure, retirement, etc.

far-fetched ADJECTIVE improbable in nature; unlikely.

far-flung ADJECTIVE [1] widely distributed. [2] far distant; remote.

Faridabad (fæ'rɪdəbæd) NOUN a city in NE India, in Haryana: industrial centre. Pop.: 617 717 (1991).

farina (fə'riːnə) NOUN [1] flour or meal made from any kind of cereal grain. [2] *Chiefly Brit* starch, esp prepared from potato flour.
▷HISTORY C18: from Latin *fār* spelt, coarse meal

farinaceous (ˌfærɪ'neɪʃəs) ADJECTIVE [1] consisting or made of starch, such as bread, macaroni, and potatoes. [2] having a mealy texture or appearance. [3] containing starch: *farinaceous seeds*.

farinose ('færɪˌnəʊs, -ˌnəʊz) ADJECTIVE [1] similar to or yielding farina. [2] *Botany* covered with very short hairs resembling a whitish mealy dust.
▸'**fariˌnosely** ADVERB

farl *or* **farle** (fɑːl) NOUN a thin cake of oatmeal, often triangular in shape.
▷HISTORY C18: from earlier *fardel* fourth part, from Old English *fēortha* fourth + Middle English *del* part

farm (fɑːm) NOUN [1] **a** a tract of land, usually with house and buildings, cultivated as a unit or used to rear livestock. **b** (*as modifier*): *farm produce*. **c** (*in combination*): *farmland*. [2] a unit of land or water devoted to the growing or rearing of some particular type of vegetable, fruit, animal, or fish: *a fish farm*. [3] an installation for storage. [4] a district of which one or more taxes are leased. [5] *History* **a** a fixed sum paid by an individual or group for the right of collecting and retaining taxes, rents, etc. **b** a fixed sum paid regularly by a town, county, etc., in lieu of taxes. **c** the leasing of a source of revenue to an individual or group. **d** a fixed tax, rent, etc., paid regularly. ◆ VERB [6] (*tr*) **a** to cultivate (land). **b** to rear (stock, etc.) on a farm. [7] (*intr*) to engage in agricultural work, esp as a way of life. [8] (*tr*) to look after a child for a fixed sum. [9] **a** to collect the moneys due and retain the profits from (a tax district, business, etc.) for a specified period on payment of a sum or sums. **b** to operate (a franchise) under similar conditions. ◆ See also **farm out.**
▷HISTORY C13: from Old French *ferme* rented land, ultimately from Latin *firmāre* to settle
▸'**farmable** ADJECTIVE

farm-bike NOUN *NZ* a motorcycle built for off-road travel.

farmed (fɑːmd) ADJECTIVE (of fish and game) reared on a farm rather than caught in the wild.

farmer (ˈfɑːmə) NOUN [1] a person who operates or manages a farm. [2] a person who obtains the right to collect and retain a tax, rent, etc., or operate a franchise for a specified period on payment of a fee. [3] a person who looks after a child for a fixed sum.

farmer-general NOUN, *plural* **farmers-general**. (in France before 1789) a member of a group allowed to farm certain taxes.
▸ **ˈfarmer-ˈgeneralˌship** NOUN

farmer's lung NOUN inflammation of the alveoli of the lungs caused by an allergic response to fungal spores in hay.

farm-gate sale NOUN *NZ* the sale of produce direct from the producer.

farm hand NOUN a person who is hired to work on a farm.

farmhouse (ˈfɑːmˌhaʊs) NOUN [1] a house attached to a farm, esp the dwelling from which the farm is managed. [2] Also called: **farmhouse loaf.** *Brit* a large white loaf, baked in a tin, with slightly curved sides and top.

farming (ˈfɑːmɪŋ) NOUN **a** the business, art, or skill of agriculture. **b** (*as modifier*): *farming methods.*

farmland (ˈfɑːmˌlænd) NOUN land used or suitable for farming.

farm out VERB (*tr, adverb*) [1] to send (work) to be done by another person, firm, etc.; subcontract. [2] to put (a child, etc.) into the care of a private individual; foster. [3] to lease to another for a rent or fee the right to operate (a business for profit, land, etc.) or the right to collect (taxes).

farmstead (ˈfɑːmˌstɛd) NOUN a farm or the part of a farm comprising its main buildings together with adjacent grounds.

farm team NOUN *US and Canadian* a sports team in a smaller or lower league that is affiliated to one in a larger or higher league.

farm-toun (ˈfærmˌtʊn, ˈfɑːmˌtʊn) NOUN *Scot* a farmhouse together with its outbuildings.

farmyard (ˈfɑːmˌjɑːd) NOUN **a** an area surrounded by or adjacent to farm buildings. **b** (*as modifier*): *farmyard animals.*

farnarkel (ˈfɑːnɑːkəl) VERB (*intr; often foll by around*) *Austral slang* to spend time or act in a careless or inconsequential manner; waste time.
▹HISTORY C20: coined by the New Zealand-born comedian John Clarke as the name of a fictitious sport of doing nothing for which he commentated in an Australian TV series
▸ **ˈfarnarkeling** NOUN

Farnborough (ˈfɑːnbərə, -brə) NOUN a town in S England, in NE Hampshire: military base, with an aeronautical research centre. Pop.: 52 535 (1991).

farnesol (ˈfɑːnɪˌsɒl) NOUN a colourless aromatic sesquiterpene alcohol found in many essential oils and used in the form of its derivatives in perfumery; 3,7,11-trimethyl-2,6,10-dodecatrienol. Formula: $C_{15}H_{26}O$.
▹HISTORY C20: from New Latin (*Acacia*) *farnesiāna*; named after Odoardo *Farnese*, C17 Italian cardinal

Farnham (ˈfɑːnəm) NOUN a town in S England, in NW Surrey. Pop.: 36 178 (1991).

Far North NOUN **the.** the Arctic and sub-Arctic regions of the world.

faro (ˈfɛərəʊ) NOUN a gambling game in which players bet against the dealer on what cards he will turn up.
▹HISTORY C18: probably spelling variant of *Pharaoh*

Faro (ˈfɑːrəʊ) NOUN a port and resort in S Portugal: destroyed by earthquakes in 1722 and 1755. Pop.: 31 970 (1990).

Faroes (ˈfɛərəʊz) NOUN a variant spelling of **Faeroes.**

Faroese (ˌfɛərəʊˈiːz) ADJECTIVE, NOUN a variant spelling of **Faeroese.**

far-off ADJECTIVE (**far off** *when postpositive*) remote in space or time; distant.

farouche *French* (faruʃ) ADJECTIVE [1] sullen or shy. [2] socially inept.
▹HISTORY C18: from French, from Old French *faroche*, from Late Latin *forasticus* from without, from Latin *foras* out of doors

far-out *Slang* ◆ ADJECTIVE (**far out** *when postpositive*) [1] bizarre or avant-garde. [2] excellent; wonderful. ◆ INTERJECTION **far out.** [3] an expression of amazement or delight.

Farquhar Islands (ˈfɑːkwə, -kə) PLURAL NOUN an island group in the Indian Ocean: administratively part of the Seychelles.

farrago (fəˈrɑːgəʊ) NOUN, *plural* **-gos** *or* **-goes.** a hotchpotch.
▹HISTORY C17: from Latin: mash for cattle (hence, a mixture), from *fār* spelt
▸ **farraginous** (fəˈrædʒɪnəs) ADJECTIVE

far-reaching ADJECTIVE extensive in influence, effect, or range.

farrier (ˈfærɪə) NOUN *Chiefly Brit* [1] a person who shoes horses. [2] *Archaic* another name for **veterinary surgeon.** [3] *Military* a noncommissioned officer who looks after horses.
▹HISTORY C16: from Old French *ferrier*, from Latin *ferrārius* smith, from *ferrum* iron

farriery (ˈfærɪərɪ) NOUN, *plural* **-eries.** *Chiefly Brit* the art, work, or establishment of a farrier.

farrow¹ (ˈfærəʊ) NOUN [1] a litter of piglets. ◆ VERB [2] (of a sow) to give birth to (a litter).
▹HISTORY Old English *fearh*; related to Old High German *farah* young pig, Latin *porcus* pig, Greek *porkos*

farrow² (ˈfærəʊ) ADJECTIVE (of a cow) not calving in a given year.
▹HISTORY C15: from Middle Dutch *verwe-* (unattested) cow that has ceased to bear; compare Old English *fearr* ox

far-seeing ADJECTIVE having shrewd judgment; far-sighted.

Farsi (ˈfɑːsiː) NOUN the Indo-European language of modern Iran. See also **Persian** (sense 4).

far-sighted ADJECTIVE [1] possessing prudence and foresight. [2] *Med* of, relating to, or suffering from hyperopia. [3] another word for **long-sighted.**
▸ **ˌfar-ˈsightedly** ADVERB ▸ **ˌfar-ˈsightedness** NOUN

fart (fɑːt) *Slang* ◆ NOUN [1] an emission of intestinal gas from the anus, esp an audible one. [2] a contemptible person. ◆ VERB (*intr*) [3] to expel intestinal gas from the anus; to break wind. [4] **fart about** *or* **around. a** to behave foolishly or aimlessly. **b** to waste time.
▹HISTORY Middle English *farten*; related to Old Norse *freta*, Old High German *ferzan* to break wind, Sanskrit *pardatē* he breaks wind

farther (ˈfɑːðə) ADVERB [1] to or at a greater distance in space or time. [2] in addition. ◆ ADJECTIVE [3] more distant or remote in space or time. [4] additional.
▹HISTORY C13: see FAR, FURTHER

> **Language note** *Farther, farthest, further,* and *furthest* can all be used to refer to literal distance, but *further* and *furthest* are regarded as more correct for figurative senses denoting greater or additional amount, time, etc.: *further to my letter. Further* and *furthest* are also preferred for figurative distance.

farthermost (ˈfɑːðəˌməʊst) ADJECTIVE most distant or remote.

farthest (ˈfɑːðɪst) ADVERB [1] to or at the greatest distance in space or time. ◆ ADJECTIVE [2] most distant in space or time. [3] most extended.
▹HISTORY C14 *ferthest*, from *ferther* FURTHER

farthing (ˈfɑːðɪŋ) NOUN [1] a former British bronze coin, worth a quarter of an old penny, that ceased to be legal tender in 1961. [2] something of negligible value; jot.
▹HISTORY Old English *fēorthing* from *fēortha* FOURTH + -ING[1]

farthingale (ˈfɑːðɪŋˌgeɪl) NOUN a hoop or framework worn under skirts, esp in the Elizabethan period, to shape and spread them.
▹HISTORY C16: from French *verdugale*, from Old Spanish *verdugado*, from *verdugo* rod

fartlek (ˈfɑːtlɛk) NOUN *Sport* another name for **interval training.**
▹HISTORY Swedish, literally: speed play

FAS *or* **f.a.s.** ABBREVIATION FOR free alongside ship.

fasces (ˈfæsiːz) PLURAL NOUN, *singular* **-cis** (-sɪs). [1] (in ancient Rome) one or more bundles of rods containing an axe with its blade protruding; a symbol of a magistrate's power. [2] (in modern Italy) such an object used as the symbol of Fascism.
▹HISTORY C16: from Latin, plural of *fascis* bundle

fascia *or* **facia** (ˈfeɪʃɪə) NOUN, *plural* **-ciae** (-ʃɪˌiː). [1] the flat surface above a shop window. [2] *Architect* a flat band or surface, esp a part of an architrave or cornice. [3] (ˈfæʃɪə) fibrous connective tissue occurring in sheets beneath the surface of the skin and between muscles and groups of muscles. [4] *Biology* a distinctive band of colour, as on an insect or plant. [5] *Brit* a less common name for **dashboard** (sense 1).
▹HISTORY C16: from Latin: band: related to *fascis* bundle; see FASCES
▸ **ˈfascial** *or* **ˈfacial** ADJECTIVE

fasciate (ˈfæʃɪˌeɪt) *or* **fasciated** ADJECTIVE [1] *Botany* **a** (of stems and branches) abnormally flattened due to coalescence. **b** growing in a bundle. [2] (of birds, insects, etc.) marked by distinct bands of colour.
▹HISTORY C17: probably from New Latin *fasciātus* (unattested) having bands; see FASCIA
▸ **ˈfasciˌately** ADVERB

fasciation (ˌfæʃɪˈeɪʃən) NOUN *Botany* an abnormal flattening of stems due to failure of the lateral branches to separate from the main stem.

fascicle (ˈfæsɪkəl) NOUN [1] a bundle or cluster of branches, leaves, etc. [2] Also called: **fasciculus.** *Anatomy* a small bundle of fibres, esp nerve fibres. [3] *Printing* another name for **fascicule.** [4] any small bundle or cluster.
▹HISTORY C15: from Latin *fasciculus* a small bundle, from *fascis* a bundle
▸ **ˈfascicled** ADJECTIVE ▸ **fascicular** (fəˈsɪkjʊlə) *or* **fasciculate** (fəˈsɪkjʊˌleɪt, -lɪt) ADJECTIVE ▸ **fasˈciculately** ADVERB ▸ **fasˌcicuˈlation** NOUN

fascicule (ˈfæsɪˌkjuːl) NOUN one part of a printed work that is published in instalments. Also called: **fascicle, fasciculus.**

fasciculus (fəˈsɪkjʊləs) NOUN, *plural* **-li** (-ˌlaɪ). another name for **fascicle** (sense 2) or **fascicule.**

fasciitis (ˌfæʃɪˈaɪtɪs) NOUN inflammation of the fascia of a muscle.

fascinate (ˈfæsɪˌneɪt) VERB (*mainly tr*) [1] to attract and delight by arousing interest or curiosity: *his stories fascinated me for hours.* [2] to render motionless, as with a fixed stare or by arousing terror or awe. [3] *Archaic* to put under a spell.
▹HISTORY C16: from Latin *fascināre*, from *fascinum* a bewitching
▸ **ˈfasciˌnatedly** ADVERB ▸ **ˌfasciˈnation** NOUN ▸ **ˈfascinative** ADJECTIVE

> **Language note** A person can be fascinated *by* or *with* another person or thing. It is correct to speak of someone's fascination *with* a person or thing; one can also say a person or thing has a fascination *for* someone.

fascinating (ˈfæsɪˌneɪtɪŋ) ADJECTIVE [1] arousing great interest. [2] enchanting or alluring: *a fascinating woman.*
▸ **ˈfasciˌnatingly** ADVERB

fascinator (ˈfæsɪˌneɪtə) NOUN *Rare* a lace or crocheted head covering for women.

fascine (fæˈsiːn, fə-) NOUN a bundle of long sticks used for filling in ditches and in the construction of embankments, roads, fortifications, etc.
▹HISTORY C17: from French, from Latin *fascīna*; see FASCES

fascism (ˈfæʃɪzəm) NOUN (*sometimes capital*) [1] any ideology or movement inspired by Italian Fascism, such as German National Socialism; any right-wing nationalist ideology or movement with an authoritarian and hierarchical structure that is fundamentally opposed to democracy and liberalism. [2] any ideology, movement, programme, tendency, etc., that may be characterized as right-wing, chauvinist, authoritarian, etc. [3] prejudice in relation to the subject specified: *body fascism.*
▹HISTORY C20: from Italian *fascismo*, from *fascio* political group, from Latin *fascis* bundle; see FASCES

Fascism (ˈfæʃɪzəm) NOUN the political movement, doctrine, system, or regime (1922–43) in Italy of the dictator Benito Mussolini (1883–1945). Fascism encouraged militarism and nationalism, organizing the country along hierarchical authoritarian lines.

fascist ('fæʃɪst) (*sometimes capital*) ◆ NOUN [1] an adherent or practitioner of fascism. [2] any person regarded as having right-wing authoritarian views. ◆ ADJECTIVE *also* **fascistic** (fə'ʃɪstɪk). [3] characteristic of or relating to fascism.
▸**fa'scistically** ADVERB

Fascist ('fæʃɪst) NOUN [1] a supporter or member of the Italian Fascist movement. ◆ ADJECTIVE [2] of or relating to Italian Fascism.

fash (fæʃ) *Scot* ◆ NOUN [1] worry; trouble; bother. ◆ VERB [2] to trouble; bother; annoy.
▷**HISTORY** C16: from obsolete French *fascher* to annoy, ultimately from Latin *fastīdium* disgust, aversion

fashion ('fæʃən) NOUN [1] **a** style in clothes, cosmetics, behaviour, etc., esp the latest or most admired style. **b** (*as modifier*): *a fashion magazine.* [2] (*modifier*) (esp of accessories) designed to be in the current fashion, but not necessarily to last. [3] **a** manner of performance; mode; way: *in a striking fashion.* **b** (*in combination*): *crab-fashion.* [4] a way of life that revolves around the activities, dress, interests, etc., that are most fashionable. [5] shape, appearance, or form. [6] sort; kind; type. [7] **after** *or* **in a fashion. a** in some manner, but not very well: *I mended it, after a fashion.* **b** of a low order; of a sort: *he is a poet, after a fashion.* [8] **after the fashion of.** like; similar to. [9] **of fashion.** of high social standing. ◆ VERB (*tr*) [10] to give a particular form to. [11] to make suitable or fitting. [12] *Obsolete* to contrive; manage.
▷**HISTORY** C13 *facioun* form, manner, from Old French *faceon*, from Latin *factiō* a making, from *facere* to make
▸**'fashioner** NOUN

fashionable ('fæʃənəbᵊl) ADJECTIVE [1] conforming to fashion; in vogue. [2] of, characteristic of, or patronized by people of fashion: *a fashionable café.* [3] (usually foll by *with*) patronized (by); popular (with).
▸**ˌfashiona'bility** *or* **'fashionableness** NOUN ▸**'fashionably** ADVERB

fashion house NOUN an establishment in which fashionable clothes are designed, made, and sold.

fashion icon NOUN a person or thing that is very well known as being highly fashionable.

fashionista (ˌfæʃə'niːstə) NOUN *Informal* a person who follows trends in the fashion industry obsessively and strives continually to adopt the latest fashions.
▷**HISTORY** C20: from FASHION + *-ista* as in SANDINISTA

fashion plate NOUN [1] an illustration of the latest fashion in dress. [2] a fashionably dressed person.

fashion victim NOUN *Informal* a person who slavishly follows fashion.

fashiony ('fæʃənɪ) ADJECTIVE *Informal* of or relating to fashion; fashionable; trendy: *a more upbeat fashiony look.*

Fashoda (fə'ʃəudə) NOUN a small town in SE Sudan: scene of a diplomatic incident (1898) in which French occupation of the fort at Fashoda caused a crisis between France and Great Britain. Modern name: **Kodok.**

FASSA ABBREVIATION FOR Fellow of the Academy of Social Sciences in Australia.

fast¹ (fɑːst) ADJECTIVE [1] acting or moving or capable of acting or moving quickly; swift. [2] accomplished in or lasting a short time: *fast work; a fast visit.* [3] (*prenominal*) adapted to or facilitating rapid movement: *the fast lane of a motorway.* [4] requiring rapidity of action or movement: *a fast sport.* [5] (of a clock, etc.) indicating a time in advance of the correct time. [6] given to an active dissipated life. [7] of or characteristic of such activity: *a fast life.* [8] not easily moved; firmly fixed; secure. [9] firmly fastened, secured, or shut. [10] steadfast; constant (esp in the phrase **fast friends**). [11] *Sport* (of a playing surface, running track, etc.) conducive to rapid speed, as of a ball used on it or of competitors playing or racing on it. [12] that will not fade or change colour readily: *a fast dye.* [13] **a** proof against fading: *the colour is fast to sunlight.* **b** (*in combination*): *washfast.* [14] *Photog* **a** requiring a relatively short time of exposure to produce a given density: *a fast film.* **b** permitting a short exposure time: *a fast shutter.* [15] *Cricket* (of a bowler) characteristically delivering the ball rapidly. [16] *Informal* glib or unreliable; deceptive: *a fast talker.* [17] *Archaic* sound; deep: *a fast sleep.* [18] *Informal* a deceptive or unscrupulous trick (esp in the phrase **pull a fast one**). [19] **fast worker.** a person who achieves results quickly, esp in seductions. ◆ ADVERB [20] quickly; rapidly. [21] soundly; deeply: *fast asleep.* [22] firmly; tightly. [23] in quick succession. [24] in advance of the correct time: *my watch is running fast.* [25] in a reckless or dissipated way. [26] **fast by** *or* **beside.** *Archaic* close or hard by; very near. [27] **play fast and loose.** *Informal* to behave in an insincere or unreliable manner. ◆ INTERJECTION [28] *Archery* (said by the field captain to archers) stop shooting!
▷**HISTORY** Old English *fæst* strong, tight; related to Old High German *festi* firm, Old Norse *fastr*

fast² (fɑːst) VERB [1] (*intr*) to abstain from eating all or certain foods or meals, esp as a religious observance. ◆ NOUN [2] an act or period of fasting.
▷**HISTORY** Old English *fæstan*; related to Old High German *fastēn* to fast, Gothic *fastan*
▸**'faster** NOUN

fastback ('fɑːstˌbæk) NOUN [1] a car having a back that forms one continuous slope from roof to rear. [2] *Brit* a type of pig developed from the landrace or large white and bred for lean meat.

fastball ('fɑːstˌbɔːl) NOUN *Baseball* a ball pitched at the pitcher's top speed.

fast-breeder reactor NOUN a nuclear reactor that uses little or no moderator and produces more fissionable material than it consumes. See also **breeder reactor, fast reactor.**

fast casual NOUN a style of fast food involving healthier, fresher, and more varied dishes than traditional fast food, served in more attractive surroundings.

fasten ('fɑːsᵊn) VERB [1] to make or become fast or secure. [2] to make or become attached or joined. [3] to close or become closed by fixing firmly in place, locking, etc. [4] (*tr*; foll by *in* or *up*) to enclose or imprison. [5] (*tr*; usually foll by *on*) to cause (blame, a nickname, etc.) to be attached (to); place (on) or impute (to). [6] (usually foll by *on* or *upon*) to direct or be directed in a concentrated way; fix: *he fastened his gaze on the girl.* [7] (*intr*; usually foll by *on*) take firm hold (of).
▷**HISTORY** Old English *fæstnian*; related to Old Norse *fastna* to pledge, Old High German *fastinōn* to make fast; see FAST¹
▸**'fastener** NOUN

fastening ('fɑːsᵊnɪŋ) NOUN something that fastens, such as a clasp or lock.

fast follower NOUN a company that is quick to pick up good new ideas from other companies.

fast food NOUN [1] food that requires little preparation before being served. ◆ ADJECTIVE **fast-food.** [2] (of a restaurant, café, etc.) serving such food.

fast-forward NOUN [1] (*sometimes not hyphenated*) the control on a tape deck or video recorder used to wind the tape or video forward at speed. [2] *Informal* a state of urgency or rapid progress: *my mind went into fast forward.* ◆ VERB [3] (*tr*) to wind (a video or tape) forward using the fast-forward control. [4] to deal with speedily: *fast-forward the trials of the new drug.* [5] (*intr*) to move forward through a tape or video using the fast-forward control. [6] (usually foll by *to*) to direct one's attention towards a particular time or event, ignoring intervening material: *fast-forward to the summer of 2001.*
▷**HISTORY** C20: from the fast-forward wind control in a tape deck

fastidious (fæ'stɪdɪəs) ADJECTIVE [1] very critical; hard to please. [2] excessively particular about details. [3] exceedingly delicate; easily disgusted.
▷**HISTORY** C15: from Latin *fastīdiōsus* scornful, from *fastīdium* loathing, from *fastus* pride + *taedium* weariness
▸**fas'tidiously** ADVERB ▸**fas'tidiousness** NOUN

fastie ('fɑːstɪ) NOUN *Austral slang* [1] a deceitful act. [2] **pull a fastie.** to play a sly trick.

fastigiate (fæ'stɪdʒɪɪt, -ˌeɪt) *or* **fastigiated** ADJECTIVE *Biology* [1] (of plants) having erect branches, often appearing to form a single column with the stem. [2] (of parts or organs) united in a tapering group.
▷**HISTORY** C17: from Medieval Latin *fastīgiātus* lofty, from Latin *fastīgium* height

fast lane NOUN [1] the outside lane on a motorway or dual carriageway for vehicles overtaking or travelling at high speed. [2] *Informal* the quickest but most competitive route to success.

fast motion NOUN *Films* action that appears to have occurred at a faster speed than that at which it was filmed. Compare **slow motion** (sense 1).

fastness ('fɑːstnɪs) NOUN [1] a stronghold; fortress. [2] the state or quality of being firm or secure. [3] the ability of a dye to remain permanent and not run or fade. [4] *Archaic* swiftness.
▷**HISTORY** Old English *fæstnes*; see FAST¹

fast neutron NOUN *Physics* **a** a neutron produced by nuclear fission that has lost little energy by collision; a neutron with a kinetic energy in excess of 0.1 MeV. **b** a neutron with a kinetic energy in excess of 1.5 MeV, the fission threshold of uranium-238.

fast reactor NOUN a nuclear reactor using little or no moderator, fission being caused by fast neutrons.

fast talk *Slang* ◆ NOUN [1] fervent, deceptive patter. ◆ VERB **fast-talk.** [2] to influence (a person) by means of such patter.

fast-track ADJECTIVE [1] denoting the quickest or most direct route or system: *fast-track executives; a fast-track procedure for libel claims.* ◆ VERB [2] (*tr*) to speed up the progress of (a project or person).

fat (fæt) NOUN [1] any of a class of naturally occurring soft greasy solids that are esters of glycerol and certain fatty acids. They are present in some plants and in the adipose tissue of animals, forming a reserve energy source, and are used in making soap and paint and in the food industry. See also **oil** (sense 1). [2] vegetable or animal tissue containing fat. Related adjectives: **adipose, lipoid, stearic.** [3] corpulence, obesity, or plumpness. [4] the best or richest part of something. [5] a part in a play that gives an actor a good opportunity to show his talents. [6] **chew the fat.** *Slang* **a** to argue over a point. **b** to talk idly; gossip. [7] **the fat is in the fire.** an irrevocable action has been taken, esp one from which dire consequences are expected. [8] **the fat of the land.** the best that is obtainable. ◆ ADJECTIVE **fatter, fattest.** [9] having much or too much flesh or fat. [10] consisting of or containing fat; greasy: *fat pork.* [11] profitable; lucrative: *a fat year.* [12] affording great opportunities: *a fat part in the play.* [13] fertile or productive: *a fat land.* [14] thick, broad, or extended: *a fat log of wood.* [15] having a high content of a particular material or ingredient, such as resin in wood or oil in paint. [16] plentifully supplied: *a fat larder.* [17] *Slang* empty; stupid: *get this into your fat head.* [18] *Slang* very little or none; minimal (in phrases such as **a fat chance, a fat lot of good,** etc.). ◆ VERB **fats, fatting, fatted.** [19] to make or become fat; fatten.
▷**HISTORY** Old English *fǣtt*, past participle of *fǣtan* to cram; related to Old Norse *feita*, Old High German *feizen* to fatten; compare Gothic *fētjan* to adorn
▸**'fatless** ADJECTIVE ▸**'fatˌlike** ADJECTIVE ▸**'fatly** ADVERB ▸**'fatness** NOUN ▸**'fattish** ADJECTIVE

Fatah ('fætə) NOUN **Al.** a Palestinian terrorist organization, founded in 1956, with the aim of destroying the state of Israel: it has splintered into rival factions since 1988.

fatal ('feɪtᵊl) ADJECTIVE [1] resulting in or capable of causing death: *a fatal accident.* [2] bringing ruin; disastrous. [3] decisively important; fateful. [4] decreed by fate; destined; inevitable.
▷**HISTORY** C14: from Old French *fatal* or Latin *fātālis*, from *fātum*, see FATE

fatalism ('feɪtəˌlɪzəm) NOUN [1] the philosophical doctrine that all events are predetermined so that man is powerless to alter his destiny. [2] the acceptance of and submission to this doctrine. [3] a lack of effort or action in the face of difficulty.
▸**'fatalist** NOUN ▸**ˌfatal'istic** ADJECTIVE ▸**ˌfatal'istically** ADVERB

fatality (fə'tælɪtɪ) NOUN, *plural* **-ties.** [1] an accident or disaster resulting in death. [2] a person killed in an accident or disaster. [3] the power of causing death or disaster; deadliness. [4] the quality or condition of being fated. [5] something caused or dictated by fate.

fatally ('feɪtəlɪ) ADVERB [1] resulting in death or disaster. [2] as decreed by fate; inevitably.

Fata Morgana ('fɑːtə mɔː'ɡɑːnə; *Italian* 'faːta mɔr'gaːna) NOUN a mirage, esp one in the Strait of Messina attributed to the sorcery of Morgan le Fay.
▷HISTORY C19: from Italian: MORGAN LE FAY

fatback ('fætˌbæk) NOUN the fat, usually salted, from the upper part of a side of pork.

fat body NOUN *Zoology* [1] a mass of fatty tissue in insects, used as an energy source during hibernation and metamorphosis. [2] a similar tissue mass in amphibians and reptiles.

fat camp NOUN a residential camp at which children undergo a programme of exercise, diet change, etc., intended to help them lose weight.

fat cat NOUN *Slang* **a** a very wealthy or influential person. **b** (*as modifier*): *a fat-cat industrialist.*

fate (feɪt) NOUN [1] the ultimate agency that predetermines the course of events. [2] the inevitable fortune that befalls a person or thing; destiny. [3] the end or final result. [4] a calamitous or unfavourable outcome or result; death, destruction, or downfall. ◆ VERB [5] (*tr; usually passive*) to predetermine; doom: *he was fated to lose the game.*
▷HISTORY C14: from Latin *fātum* oracular utterance, from *fārī* to speak

fated ('feɪtɪd) ADJECTIVE [1] destined. [2] doomed to death or destruction.

fateful ('feɪtfʊl) ADJECTIVE [1] having important consequences; decisively important. [2] bringing death or disaster. [3] controlled by or as if by fate. [4] prophetic.
▸**'fatefully** ADVERB ▸**'fatefulness** NOUN

Fates (feɪts) PLURAL NOUN [1] *Greek myth* the three goddesses who control the destinies of the lives of man, which are likened to skeins of thread that they spin, measure out, and at last cut. See **Atropos, Clotho, Lachesis.** [2] *Norse myth* another name for the **Norns** (see **Norn**[1]).

fath. ABBREVIATION FOR fathom.

fathead ('fætˌhɛd) NOUN *Informal* a stupid person; fool.
▸**'fatˌheaded** ADJECTIVE

fat hen NOUN a common plant, *Chenopodium album*, with small green flowers and whitish scales on the stem and leaves: family *Chenopodiaceae* (chenopods). Also called (US): **pigweed, lamb's-quarters.**

father ('fɑːðə) NOUN [1] a male parent. [2] a person who founds a line or family; forefather. [3] any male acting in a paternal capacity. Related adjective: **paternal.** [4] (*often capital*) a respectful term of address for an old man. [5] a male who originates something: *the father of modern psychology.* [6] a leader of an association, council, etc.; elder: *a city father.* [7] *Brit* the eldest or most senior member in a society, profession, etc.: *father of the bar.* [8] (*often plural*) a senator or patrician in ancient Rome. [9] **the father of.** *Informal* a very large, severe, etc., example of a specified kind: *the father of a whipping.* ◆ VERB (*tr*) [10] to procreate or generate (offspring); beget. [11] to create, found, originate, etc. [12] to act as a father to. [13] to acknowledge oneself as father or originator of. [14] (foll by *on* or *upon*) to impose or place without a just reason.
▷HISTORY Old English *fæder*; related to Old Norse *fathir*, Old Frisian *feder*, Old High German *fater*, Latin *pater*, Greek *patēr*, Sanskrit *pitr*
▸**'fathering** NOUN

Father ('fɑːðə) NOUN [1] God, esp when considered as the first person of the Christian Trinity. [2] Also called: **Church Father.** any of the writers on Christian doctrine of the pre-Scholastic period. [3] a title used for Christian priests.

Father Christmas NOUN another name for **Santa Claus.**

father confessor NOUN [1] *Christianity* a priest who hears confessions and advises on religious or moral matters. [2] any person to whom one tells private matters.

fatherhood ('fɑːðəˌhʊd) NOUN the state or responsibility of being a father.

father-in-law NOUN, *plural* **fathers-in-law.** the father of one's wife or husband.

fatherland ('fɑːðəˌlænd) NOUN [1] a person's native country. [2] the country of a person's ancestors.

father lasher NOUN a large sea scorpion, *Myoxocephalus scorpius*, occurring in British and European coastal waters. Also called: **short-spined sea scorpion.**

fatherless ('fɑːðəlɪs) ADJECTIVE having no father.

fatherly ('fɑːðəlɪ) ADJECTIVE of, resembling, or suitable to a father.
▸**'fatherliness** NOUN

father of the chapel NOUN (in British trade unions in the publishing and printing industries) a shop steward. Abbreviation: **FoC.**

Father of the House NOUN (in Britain) the longest-serving member of the House of Commons.

Father's Day NOUN a day observed as a day in honour of fathers; in Britain the third Sunday in June.

Father Time NOUN time personified as an old bearded man, usually carrying a scythe and an hourglass.

fathom ('fæðəm) NOUN [1] a unit of length equal to six feet (1.829 metres), used to measure depths of water. [2] *Mining* a unit of volume usually equal to six cubic feet, used in measuring ore bodies. [3] *Forestry* a unit of volume equal to six cubic feet, used for measuring timber. ◆ VERB (*tr*) [4] to measure the depth of, esp with a sounding line; sound. [5] to penetrate (a mystery, problem, etc.); discover the meaning of.
▷HISTORY Old English *fæthm*; related to Old Frisian *fethem* outstretched arms, Old Norse *fathmr* embrace, Old High German *fadum* cubit, Latin *patēre* to gape
▸**'fathomable** ADJECTIVE ▸**'fathomer** NOUN

Fathometer (fə'ðɒmɪtə) NOUN *Trademark* a type of echo sounder used for measuring the depth of water.

fathomless ('fæðəmlɪs) ADJECTIVE another word for **unfathomable.**
▸**'fathomlessly** ADVERB ▸**'fathomlessness** NOUN

fatidic (feɪ'tɪdɪk) *or* **fatidical** ADJECTIVE *Rare* prophetic.
▷HISTORY C17: from Latin *fātidicus*, from *fātum* FATE + *dīcere* to say
▸**fa'tidically** ADVERB

fatigue (fə'tiːɡ) NOUN [1] physical or mental exhaustion due to exertion. [2] a tiring activity or effort. [3] *Physiol* the temporary inability of an organ or part to respond to a stimulus because of overactivity. [4] the progressive cracking of a material subjected to alternating stresses, esp vibrations. [5] the temporary inability to respond to a situation or perform a function, because of overexposure or overactivity: *compassion fatigue.* [6] **a** any of the mainly domestic duties performed by military personnel, esp as a punishment. **b** (*as modifier*): *fatigue duties.* [7] (*plural*) special clothing worn by military personnel to carry out such duties. ◆ VERB **-tigues, -tiguing, -tigued.** [8] to make or become weary or exhausted. [9] to crack or break (a material or part) by inducing fluctuating stresses in it, or (of a metal or part) to become weakened or fail as a result of fluctuating stresses.
▷HISTORY C17: from French, from *fatiguer* to tire, from Latin *fatīgāre*
▸**fatigable** ('fætɪɡəb^{ə}l) ADJECTIVE ▸**fa'tigueless** ADJECTIVE

Fátima (*Portuguese* 'fatimə) NOUN a village in central Portugal: Roman Catholic shrine and pilgrimage centre.

Fatimid ('fætɪmɪd) NOUN [1] a member of the Moslem dynasty, descended from Fatima, daughter of Mohammed, and Ali, her husband, that ruled over North Africa and parts of Egypt and Syria (909–1171). [2] Also called: **Fatimite** ('fætɪˌmaɪt). a descendant of Fatima and Ali.

fat lamb NOUN *Austral and NZ* a lamb bred for its tender meat, esp for export trade.

fatling ('fætlɪŋ) NOUN a young farm animal fattened for killing.

fat mouse NOUN any nocturnal African mouse of the genus *Steatomys*, of dry regions: eaten as a delicacy by Africans because of their high fat content: family *Muridae.*

Fatshan ('fɑːt'ʃɑːn) NOUN a variant transliteration of the Chinese name for **Foshan.**

fatshedera (fæts'hɛdərə) NOUN an evergreen garden shrub with shiny green leaves and umbels of pale green flowers; a bigeneric hybrid between *Fatsia japonica moseri* and *Hedera hibernica*: family *Araliaceae.*

fatsia ('fætsɪə) NOUN any shrub of the araliaceous genus *Fatsia*, esp *F. japonica*, with large deeply palmate leaves and umbels of white flowers.
▷HISTORY New Latin, from the Japanese name

fatso ('fætsəʊ) NOUN, *plural* **-sos** *or* **-soes.** *Slang* a fat person: used as an insulting or disparaging term of address.

fat-soluble ADJECTIVE soluble in nonpolar substances, such as ether, chloroform, and oils. Fat-soluble compounds are often insoluble in water.

fat stock NOUN livestock fattened and ready for market.

fatten ('fæt^{ə}n) VERB [1] to grow or cause to grow fat or fatter. [2] (*tr*) to cause (an animal or fowl) to become fat by feeding it. [3] (*tr*) to make fuller or richer. [4] (*tr*) to enrich (soil) by adding fertilizing agents.
▸**'fattenable** ADJECTIVE ▸**'fattener** NOUN ▸**'fattening** ADJECTIVE

fattism ('fætɪzəm) NOUN discrimination on the basis of weight, esp prejudice against those considered to be overweight.
▷HISTORY C20: from FAT + -ISM, on the model of RACISM
▸**'fattist** NOUN, ADJECTIVE

fatty ('fætɪ) ADJECTIVE **-tier, -tiest.** [1] containing, consisting of, or derived from fat. [2] having the properties of fat; greasy; oily. [3] (esp of tissues, organs, etc.) characterized by the excessive accumulation of fat. ◆ NOUN, *plural* **-ties.** [4] *Informal* a fat person.
▸**'fattily** ADVERB ▸**'fattiness** NOUN

fatty acid NOUN [1] any of a class of aliphatic carboxylic acids, such as palmitic acid, stearic acid, and oleic acid, that form part of a lipid molecule. [2] another name for **carboxylic acid**, esp a naturally occurring one

fatty degeneration NOUN *Pathol* the abnormal formation of tiny globules of fat within the cytoplasm of a cell.

fatty oil NOUN another name for **fixed oil.**

fatuity (fə'tjuːɪtɪ) NOUN, *plural* **-ties.** [1] complacent foolishness; inanity. [2] a fatuous remark, act, sentiment, etc. [3] *Archaic* idiocy.
▸**fa'tuitous** ADJECTIVE

fatuous ('fætjʊəs) ADJECTIVE complacently or inanely foolish.
▷HISTORY C17: from Latin *fatuus*; related to *fatiscere* to gape
▸**'fatuously** ADVERB ▸**'fatuousness** NOUN

fatwa *or* **fatwah** ('fætwɑː) NOUN a religious decree issued by a Muslim leader.
▷HISTORY Arabic

faubourg ('fəʊbʊəɡ; *French* fobur) NOUN a suburb or quarter, esp of a French city.
▷HISTORY C15: from French *fauxbourg*, perhaps a modification through folk etymology of Old French *forsborc*, from Latin *foris* outside + Old French *borc* BURG

faucal ('fɔːk^{ə}l) *or* **faucial** ('fɔːʃəl) ADJECTIVE [1] *Anatomy* of or relating to the fauces. [2] *Phonetics* articulated in that part of the vocal tract between the back of the mouth and the larynx; pharyngeal.

fauces ('fɔːsiːz) NOUN, *plural* **-ces.** *Anatomy* the area between the cavity of the mouth and the pharynx, including the surrounding tissues.
▷HISTORY C16: from Latin: throat

faucet ('fɔːsɪt) NOUN [1] a tap fitted to a barrel. [2] the US and Canadian name for a **tap**[2].
▷HISTORY C14: from Old French *fausset*, from Provençal *falset*, from *falsar* to bore

faugh (fɔː) INTERJECTION an exclamation of disgust, scorn, etc.

fault (fɔːlt) NOUN [1] an imperfection; failing or defect; flaw. [2] a mistake or error. [3] an offence; misdeed. [4] responsibility for a mistake or misdeed; culpability. [5] *Electronics* a defect in a circuit, component, or line, such as a short circuit. [6] *Geology* a fracture in the earth's crust resulting in the relative displacement and loss of continuity of the rocks on either side of it. [7] *Tennis, squash, badminton* an invalid serve, such as one that lands outside a prescribed area. [8] (in showjumping) a

penalty mark given for failing to clear or refusing a fence, exceeding a time limit, etc. 9 *Hunting* an instance of the hounds losing the scent. 10 deficiency; lack; want. 11 **at fault. a** guilty of error; culpable. **b** perplexed. **c** (of hounds) having temporarily lost the scent. 12 **find fault (with).** to seek out minor imperfections or errors (in); carp (at). 13 **to a fault.** excessively. ◆ VERB 14 *Geology* to undergo or cause to undergo a fault. 15 *(tr)* to find a fault in, criticize, or blame. 16 *(intr)* to commit a fault.
▷HISTORY C13: from Old French *faute*, from Vulgar Latin *fallita* (unattested), ultimately from Latin *fallere* to fail

fault-finding NOUN 1 continual and usually trivial criticism. 2 the systematic investigation of malfunctions in electronic apparatus. ◆ ADJECTIVE 3 given to finding fault.
▸ **'fault-ˌfinder** NOUN

faultless ('fɔːltlɪs) ADJECTIVE without fault; perfect or blameless.
▸ **'faultlessly** ADVERB ▸ **'faultlessness** NOUN

fault line NOUN 1 Also called: **fault plane.** *Geology* the surface of a fault fracture along which the rocks have been displaced. 2 a potentially disruptive division or area of contention: *Europe remains the main fault line in the Tory Party.*

fault tree NOUN a diagram providing a model of the interactions between the components of a system when a failure occurs.

faulty ('fɔːltɪ) ADJECTIVE **faultier, faultiest.** 1 defective or imperfect. 2 *Archaic* culpable.
▸ **'faultily** ADVERB ▸ **'faultiness** NOUN

faun (fɔːn) NOUN (in Roman legend) a rural deity represented as a man with a goat's ears, horns, tail, and hind legs.
▷HISTORY C14: back formation from *Faunes* (plural), from Latin FAUNUS
▸ **'faunˌlike** ADJECTIVE

fauna ('fɔːnə) NOUN, *plural* **-nas** *or* **-nae** (-niː). 1 all the animal life of a given place or time, esp when distinguished from the plant life (flora). 2 a descriptive list of such animals.
▷HISTORY C18: from New Latin, from Late Latin *Fauna* a goddess, sister of FAUNUS
▸ **'faunal** ADJECTIVE ▸ **'faunally** ADVERB

faunula ('fɔːnjʊlə) *or* **faunule** ('fɔːnjuːl) NOUN, *plural* **-ulae** (-juliː) *or* **-ules.** 1 the fauna of a small single environment. 2 fossil fauna, dominated by representatives of a single community, found in a single stratum or in several thin adjacent strata.
▷HISTORY C20: from FAUNA + -ULE

Faunus ('fɔːnəs) NOUN an ancient Italian deity of pastures and forests, later identified with the Greek Pan.

faur (fɔːr) ADJECTIVE a Scot word for **far.**

Faust (faust) *or* **Faustus** ('faustəs) NOUN *German legend* a magician and alchemist who sells his soul to the devil in exchange for knowledge and power.

Faustian ('faustɪən) ADJECTIVE of or relating to Faust, esp reminiscent of his bargain with the devil.

faut (fɔːt) NOUN, VERB a Scot word for **fault.**

faute de mieux *French* (fot də mjø; *English* ˌfəut də 'mjɜː) for lack of anything better.

fauteuil ('fəutɜːɪ; *French* fotœj) NOUN an armchair, the sides of which are not upholstered.
▷HISTORY C18: from French, from Old French *faudestuel*, folding chair, of Germanic origin; see FALDSTOOL

Fauve (*French* fov) NOUN 1 one of a group of French painters prominent from 1905, including Henri Matisse (1869–1954), Maurice de Vlaminck (1876–1958), and André Derain (1880–1954), characterized by the use of bright colours and simplified forms. ◆ ADJECTIVE 2 *(often not capital)* of this group or its style.
▷HISTORY C20: from French, literally: wild beast, alluding to the violence of colours, etc.
▸ **'Fauvism** NOUN ▸ **'Fauvist** NOUN, ADJECTIVE

faux-naïf *French* (fonaif) ADJECTIVE 1 appearing or seeking to appear simple and unsophisticated: *a faux-naïf narration.* ◆ NOUN 2 a person who pretends to be naïve.
▷HISTORY French: false naïve

faux pas (ˌfəu'pɑː; *French* fo pɑ) NOUN, *plural* **faux pas** (ˌfəu 'pɑːz; *French* fo pɑ). a social blunder or indiscretion.
▷HISTORY C17: from French: false step

fava bean ('fɑːvə) NOUN the US and Canadian name for **broad bean.**
▷HISTORY C20: Italian *fava* from Latin *faba* bean

fave (feɪv) ADJECTIVE, NOUN *Informal* short for **favourite** (senses 1, 2).

favela (fɑː'veɪlə) NOUN (in Brazil) a shanty or shantytown.
▷HISTORY C20: from Portuguese

faveolate (fə'viːəˌleɪt) *or* **favose** ('fævəus) ADJECTIVE pitted with cell-like cavities.
▷HISTORY C19: from New Latin *faveolus* a little honeycomb, blend of Latin *favus* honeycomb + *alveolus* a small hollow

favonian (fə'vəunɪən) ADJECTIVE 1 of or relating to the west wind. 2 *Poetic* favourable.
▷HISTORY C17: from Latin *Favōniānus*

favorite son NOUN (in the US) a politician popular in his home state but little admired beyond it.

favour *or US* **favor** ('feɪvə) NOUN 1 an approving attitude; good will. 2 an act performed out of good will, generosity, or mercy. 3 prejudice and partiality; favouritism. 4 a condition of being regarded with approval or good will (esp in the phrases **in favour, out of favour**). 5 *Archaic* leave; permission. 6 a token of love, goodwill, etc. 7 a small gift or toy given to a guest at a party. 8 *History* a badge or ribbon worn or given to indicate loyalty, often bestowed on a knight by a lady. 9 *Obsolete, chiefly Brit* a communication, esp a business letter. 10 *Archaic* appearance. 11 **find favour with.** to be approved of by someone. 12 **in favour of. a** approving. **b** to the benefit of. **c** (of a cheque, etc.) made out to. **d** in order to show preference for: *I rejected him in favour of George.* ◆ VERB *(tr)* 13 to regard with especial kindness or approval. 14 to treat with partiality or favouritism. 15 to support; advocate. 16 to perform a favour for; oblige. 17 to help; facilitate. 18 *Informal* to resemble: *he favours his father.* 19 to wear habitually: *she favours red.* 20 to treat gingerly or with tenderness; spare: *a footballer favouring an injured leg.* ◆ See also **favours.**
▷HISTORY C14: from Latin, from *favēre* to protect
▸ **'favourer** *or US* **'favorer** NOUN ▸ **'favouringly** *or US* **favoringly** ADVERB

favourable *or US* **favorable** ('feɪvərəbᵊl, 'feɪvrə-) ADJECTIVE 1 advantageous, encouraging, or promising. 2 giving consent.
▸ **'favourableness** *or US* **'favorableness** NOUN ▸ **'favourably** *or US* **favorably** ADVERB

favourable pressure gradient NOUN *Engineering* a decrease of pressure in the direction of flow.

-favoured ADJECTIVE *(in combination)* having an appearance (as specified): *ill-favoured.*

favourite *or US* **favorite** ('feɪvərɪt, 'feɪvrɪt) ADJECTIVE 1 *(prenominal)* most liked; preferred above all others. ◆ NOUN 2 **a** a person or thing regarded with especial preference or liking. **b** *(as modifier)*: *a favourite book.* 3 *Sport* a competitor thought likely to win. 4 **play favourites.** to display favouritism.
▷HISTORY C16: from Italian *favorito*, from *favorire* to favour, from Latin *favēre*

favouritism *or US* **favoritism** ('feɪvərɪˌtɪzəm, 'feɪvrɪ-) NOUN 1 the practice of giving special treatment to a person or group. 2 the state of being treated as a favourite.

favours *or US* **favors** ('feɪvəz) PLURAL NOUN sexual intimacy, as when consented to by a woman.

Favrile glass (fə'vriːl) NOUN a type of iridescent glass developed by L.C. Tiffany.

favus ('feɪvəs) NOUN an infectious fungal skin disease of man and some domestic animals, characterized by formation of a honeycomb-like mass of roundish dry cup-shaped crusts.
▷HISTORY C19: from New Latin, from Latin: honeycomb

fawn^{1} (fɔːn) NOUN 1 a young deer of either sex aged under one year. 2 **a** a light greyish-brown colour. **b** *(as adjective)*: *a fawn raincoat.* 3 **in fawn.** (of deer) pregnant. ◆ VERB 4 (of deer) to bear (young).
▷HISTORY C14: from Old French *faon*, from Latin *fētus* offspring; see FETUS
▸ **'fawnˌlike** ADJECTIVE

fawn^{2} (fɔːn) VERB *(intr; often foll by* on *or* upon*)* 1 to seek attention and admiration (from) by cringing and flattering. 2 (of animals, esp dogs) to try to please by a show of extreme friendliness and fondness (towards).
▷HISTORY Old English *fægnian* to be glad, from *fægen* glad; see FAIN
▸ **'fawner** NOUN ▸ **'fawningly** ADVERB ▸ **'fawningness** NOUN

fawn lily NOUN another name for **dogtooth violet.**

fax (fæks) NOUN 1 Also: **fax machine.** short for **facsimile machine.** 2 short for **facsimile transmission.** 3 a message or document sent by fax. ◆ VERB 4 *(tr)* to send (a message, document, etc.) by fax.

fay^{1} (feɪ) NOUN 1 a fairy or sprite. ◆ ADJECTIVE 2 of or resembling a fay. 3 *Informal* pretentious or precious.
▷HISTORY C14: from Old French *feie*, ultimately from Latin *fātum* FATE

fay^{2} (feɪ) VERB to fit or be fitted closely or tightly.
▷HISTORY Old English *fēgan* to join; related to Old High German *fuogen*, Latin *pangere* to fasten

fay^{3} (feɪ) NOUN an obsolete word for **faith.**
▷HISTORY C13: from Anglo-French *feid*; see FAITH

Fayal (*Portuguese* fə'ial) NOUN a variant spelling of **Faial.**

fayalite ('feɪəˌlaɪt, faɪ'ɑːlaɪt) NOUN a rare brown or black mineral of the olivine group, consisting of iron silicate. Formula: Fe_2SiO_4.
▷HISTORY C19: named after FAYAL

fayre (feə) NOUN a pseudo-archaic spelling of **fair**^{2} or **fare.**

Fayum (faɪ'juːm) NOUN See **El Faiyûm.**

faze (feɪz) VERB *(tr)* to disconcert; worry; disturb.
▷HISTORY C19: variant of FEEZE

fazed (feɪzd) ADJECTIVE disconcerted; worried; disturbed.

FBA ABBREVIATION FOR Fellow of the British Academy.

FBI (in the US) ABBREVIATION FOR Federal Bureau of Investigation; an agency of the Justice Department responsible for investigating violations of Federal laws.

FBL ABBREVIATION FOR fly-by-light.

FBW *Aeronautics* ABBREVIATION FOR fly-by-wire.

fc *Printing* ABBREVIATION FOR follow copy.

FC ABBREVIATION FOR: 1 (in Britain) Football Club. 2 (in Canada) Federal Court. 3 *Text messaging* fingers crossed.

FCA (in Britain) ABBREVIATION FOR Fellow of the Institute of Chartered Accountants.

fcap ABBREVIATION FOR foolscap.

FCC (in the US) ABBREVIATION FOR Federal Communications Commission.

FCCA (in Britain) ABBREVIATION FOR Fellow of the Chartered Association of Certified Accountants.

FCII (in Britain) ABBREVIATION FOR Fellow of the Chartered Insurance Institute.

F clef NOUN another name for **bass clef.**

FCO ABBREVIATION FOR Foreign and Commonwealth Office.

FD ABBREVIATION FOR Fidei Defensor.
▷HISTORY Latin: Defender of the Faith

FDA (in the US) ABBREVIATION FOR Food and Drug Administration: a federal agency responsible for monitoring trading and safety standards in the food and drug industries.

F distribution NOUN *Statistics* a continuous distribution obtained from the ratio of two chi-square distributions and used esp to test the equality of the variances of two normally distributed variances.

fdm ABBREVIATION FOR frequency-division multiplex. See **multiplex.**

FDP ABBREVIATION FOR Freie Demokratische Partei.
▷HISTORY German: Free Democratic Party

Fe THE CHEMICAL SYMBOL FOR iron.
▷HISTORY from New Latin *ferrum*

feal (fiːl) ADJECTIVE an archaic word for **faithful.**
▷HISTORY C16: from Old French *feeil*, from Latin *fidēlis*

fealty ('fiːəltɪ) NOUN, *plural* **-ties.** (in feudal society) the loyalty sworn to one's lord on becoming his vassal. See **homage** (sense 2).
▷HISTORY C14: from Old French *fealte*, from Latin *fidēlitās* FIDELITY

fear (fɪə) NOUN 1 a feeling of distress, apprehension, or alarm caused by impending danger, pain, etc. 2 a cause of this feeling. 3 awe; reverence: *fear of God.* 4 concern; anxiety. 5 possibility; chance: *there is no fear of that happening.* 6 **for fear of, that,** *or* **lest.** to forestall or avoid. 7 **no fear.** certainly not. 8 **put the fear of God into.** to frighten. ◆ VERB 9 to be afraid (to do something) or of (a person or thing); dread. 10 *(tr)* to revere; respect. 11 *(tr; takes a clause as object)* to be sorry: used to lessen the effect of an unpleasant statement: *I fear that you have not won.* 12 *(intr;* foll by *for)* to feel anxiety about something. 13 an archaic word for **frighten.**
▷HISTORY Old English *fǣr;* related to Old High German *fāra,* Old Norse *fār* hostility, Latin *perīculum* danger
▸ˈ**fearer** NOUN ▸ˈ**fearless** ADJECTIVE ▸ˈ**fearlessly** ADVERB ▸ˈ**fearlessness** NOUN

fearful (ˈfɪəfʊl) ADJECTIVE 1 having fear; afraid. 2 causing fear; frightening. 3 *Informal* very unpleasant or annoying: *a fearful cold.*
▸ˈ**fearfulness** NOUN

fearfully (ˈfɪəfʊlɪ) ADVERB 1 in a fearful manner. 2 (intensifier): *you're fearfully kind.*

fearnought *or* **fearnaught** (ˈfɪəˌnɔːt) NOUN 1 a heavy woollen fabric. 2 a coat made of such fabric.

fearsome (ˈfɪəsəm) ADJECTIVE 1 frightening. 2 timorous; afraid.
▸ˈ**fearsomely** ADVERB ▸ˈ**fearsomeness** NOUN

feasibility study NOUN a study designed to determine the practicability of a system or plan.

feasible (ˈfiːzəbᵊl) ADJECTIVE 1 able to be done or put into effect; possible. 2 likely; probable: *a feasible excuse.*
▷HISTORY C15: from Anglo-French *faisable,* from *faire* to do, from Latin *facere*
▸ˌ**feasiˈbility** *or* ˈ**feasibleness** NOUN ▸ˈ**feasibly** ADVERB

feast (fiːst) NOUN 1 a large and sumptuous meal, usually given as an entertainment for several people. 2 a periodic religious celebration. 3 something extremely pleasing or sumptuous: *a feast for the eyes.* 4 **movable feast.** a festival or other event of variable date. ◆ VERB 5 *(intr)* **a** to eat a feast. **b** (usually foll by *on)* to enjoy the eating (of), as if feasting: *to feast on cakes.* 6 *(tr)* to give a feast to. 7 *(intr;* foll by *on)* to take great delight (in): *to feast on beautiful paintings.* 8 *(tr)* to regale or delight: *to feast one's mind or one's eyes.*
▷HISTORY C13: from Old French *feste,* from Latin *festa,* neuter plural (later assumed to be feminine singular) of *festus* joyful; related to Latin *fānum* temple, *fēriae* festivals
▸ˈ**feaster** NOUN

Feast of Dedication NOUN *Judaism* a literal translation of **Chanukah.**

Feast of Lanterns NOUN 1 *Hinduism* another name for **Diwali.** 2 Also called: **Festival of Lanterns.** *Japanese Buddhism* another name for **Bon¹.**

Feast of Lights NOUN *Judaism* an English name for **Chanukah.**

Feast of Tabernacles NOUN *Judaism* a literal translation of **Sukkoth.**

Feast of Weeks NOUN *Judaism* a literal translation of **Shavuot.**

feat¹ (fiːt) NOUN a remarkable, skilful, or daring action; exploit; achievement: *feats of strength.*
▷HISTORY C14: from Anglo-French *fait,* from Latin *factum* deed; see FACT

feat² (fiːt) ADJECTIVE *Archaic* 1 another word for **skilful.** 2 another word for **neat¹** or **suitable.**
▷HISTORY C14: from Old French *fet,* from Latin *factus* made, from *facere* to make
▸ˈ**featly** ADVERB

feather (ˈfɛðə) NOUN 1 any of the flat light waterproof epidermal structures forming the plumage of birds, each consisting of a hollow shaft having a vane of barbs on either side. They are essential for flight and help maintain body temperature. 2 something resembling a feather, such as a tuft of hair or grass. 3 *Archery* **a** a bird's feather or artificial substitute fitted to an arrow to direct its flight. **b** the feathered end of an arrow, opposite the head. 4 a strip, spline, or tongue of wood fitted into a groove. 5 the wake created on the surface of the water by the raised periscope of a submarine. 6 *Rowing* the position of an oar turned parallel to the water between strokes. Compare **square** (sense 8). 7 a step in ballroom dancing in which a couple maintain the conventional hold but dance side by side. 8 condition of spirits; fettle: *in fine feather.* 9 something of negligible value; jot: *I don't care a feather.* 10 **birds of a feather.** people of the same type, character, or interests. 11 **feather in one's cap.** a cause for pleasure at one's achievements: *your promotion is a feather in your cap.* 12 **not take** *or* **knock a feather out of (someone).** *Irish* to fail to upset or injure (someone): *it didn't take a feather out of him.* ◆ VERB 13 *(tr)* to fit, cover, or supply with feathers. 14 *Rowing* to turn (an oar) parallel to the water during recovery between strokes, principally in order to lessen wind resistance. Compare **square** (sense 41). 15 (in canoeing) to turn (a paddle) parallel to the direction of the canoe between strokes, while keeping it in the water, principally in order to move silently. 16 to change the pitch of (an aircraft propeller) so that the chord lines of the blades are in line with the airflow. 17 *(tr)* to join (two boards) by means of a tongue-and-groove joint. 18 *(intr)* (of a bird) to grow feathers. 19 *(intr)* to move or grow like feathers. 20 **feather one's nest.** to provide oneself with comforts, esp financial. ◆ See also **feathers.**
▷HISTORY Old English *fether;* related to Old Frisian *fethere,* Old Norse *fjöthr* feather, Old High German *fedara* wing, Greek *petesthai* to fly, Sanskrit *patati* he flies
▸ˈ**featherless** ADJECTIVE ▸ˈ**feather-ˌlike** ADJECTIVE ▸ˈ**feathery** ADJECTIVE

feather bed NOUN 1 a mattress filled with feathers or down. ◆ VERB **featherbed, -beds, -bedding, -bedded.** 2 *(tr)* to pamper; spoil. 3 *(intr) US* to be subject to or engage in featherbedding.

featherbedding (ˈfɛðəˌbɛdɪŋ) NOUN the practice of limiting production, duplicating work, or overmanning, esp in accordance with a union contract, in order to prevent redundancies or create jobs.

featherbrain (ˈfɛðəˌbreɪn) *or* **featherhead** NOUN a frivolous or forgetful person.
▸ˈ**featherˌbrained** *or* ˈ**featherˌheaded** ADJECTIVE

featheredge (ˈfɛðərˌɛdʒ) NOUN a board or plank that tapers to a thin edge at one side.
▸ˈ**featherˌedged** ADJECTIVE

feather grass NOUN a perennial grass, *Stipa pennata,* native to the steppes of Europe and N Asia, cultivated as an ornament for its feathery inflorescence.

feathering (ˈfɛðərɪŋ) NOUN 1 the plumage of a bird; feathers. 2 another word for **feathers** (sense 2). 3 *Printing* **a** an imperfection in print caused by the spreading of ink. **b** the use of additional space between lines in typesetting in order to fill the page.

feather palm NOUN any of various palm trees, such as the wax palm and date palm, that have pinnate or feather-like leaves. Compare **fan palm.**

feathers (ˈfɛðəz) PLURAL NOUN 1 the plumage of a bird. 2 Also called: **feathering.** the long hair on the legs or tail of certain breeds of horses and dogs. 3 *Informal* dress; attire: *her best feathers.* 4 **ruffle feathers.** to cause upset or offence.

feather star NOUN any free-swimming crinoid echinoderm of the genus *Antedon* and related genera, living on muddy sea bottoms and having ten feathery arms radiating from a small central disc.

featherstitch (ˈfɛðəˌstɪtʃ) NOUN 1 a zigzag embroidery stitch. ◆ VERB 2 to decorate (cloth) with featherstitch.

feather-veined ADJECTIVE (of a leaf) having a network of veins branching from the midrib to the margin.

featherweight (ˈfɛðəˌweɪt) NOUN 1 **a** something very light or of little importance. **b** *(as modifier): featherweight considerations.* 2 **a** a professional boxer weighing 118–126 pounds (53.5–57 kg). **b** an amateur boxer weighing 54–57 kg (119–126 pounds). **c** *(as modifier): the featherweight challenger.* 3 a wrestler in a similar weight category (usually 126–139 pounds (57–63 kg)).

featly (ˈfiːtlɪ) ADVERB *Archaic* 1 neatly. 2 fitly.
▸ˈ**featliness** NOUN

feature (ˈfiːtʃə) NOUN 1 any one of the parts of the face, such as the nose, chin, or mouth. 2 a prominent or distinctive part or aspect, as of a landscape, building, book, etc. 3 the principal film in a programme at a cinema. 4 an item or article appearing regularly in a newspaper, magazine, etc.: *a gardening feature.* 5 Also called: **feature story.** a prominent story in a newspaper, etc.: *a feature on prison reform.* 6 a programme given special prominence on radio or television as indicated by attendant publicity. 7 an article offered for sale as a special attraction, as in a large retail establishment. 8 *Archaic* general form or make-up. 9 *Linguistics* a quality of a linguistic unit at some level of description: *grammatical feature; semantic feature.* ◆ VERB 10 *(tr)* to have as a feature or make a feature of. 11 to give prominence to (an actor, famous event, etc.) in a film or (of an actor, etc.) to have prominence in a film. 12 *(tr) US informal* to imagine; consider: *I can't feature that happening.*
▷HISTORY C14: from Anglo-French *feture,* from Latin *factūra* a making, from *facere* to make

featured ADJECTIVE *(in combination)* having features as specified: *heavy-featured.*

feature-length ADJECTIVE (of a film or programme) similar in extent to a feature although not classed as such.

featureless (ˈfiːtʃəlɪs) ADJECTIVE without distinctive points or qualities; undistinguished.
▸ˈ**featurelessness** NOUN

feaze¹ (fiːz) VERB *Nautical* to make or become unravelled or frayed.
▷HISTORY C16: perhaps from obsolete Dutch *vese* fringe, from Middle Dutch *vese, veze* fringe; related to Old English *fæs*

feaze² (fiːz) VERB, NOUN a variant of **feeze** or **faze.**

Feb. ABBREVIATION FOR February.

febri COMBINING FORM indicating fever: *febrifuge.*
▷HISTORY from Latin *febris* fever

febricity (fɪˈbrɪsɪtɪ) NOUN *Rare* the condition of having a fever.
▷HISTORY C19: from Medieval Latin *febricitās,* from Latin *febris* fever

febrifacient (ˌfɛbrɪˈfeɪʃənt) ADJECTIVE 1 producing fever. ◆ NOUN 2 something that produces fever.

febrific (fɪˈbrɪfɪk) *or* **febriferous** ADJECTIVE causing or having a fever.

febrifuge (ˈfɛbrɪˌfjuːdʒ) NOUN 1 any drug or agent for reducing fever. ◆ ADJECTIVE 2 serving to reduce fever.
▷HISTORY C17: from Medieval Latin *febrifugia* feverfew; see FEBRI-, -FUGE
▸**febrifugal** (fɪˈbrɪfjʊgᵊl, ˌfɛbrɪˈfjuːgᵊl) ADJECTIVE

febrile (ˈfiːbraɪl) ADJECTIVE of or relating to fever; feverish.
▷HISTORY C17: from medical Latin *febrīlis,* from Latin *febris* fever
▸**febrility** (fɪˈbrɪlɪtɪ) NOUN

February (ˈfɛbrʊərɪ) NOUN, *plural* **-aries.** the second month of the year, consisting of 28 or (in a leap year) 29 days.
▷HISTORY C13: from Latin *Februārius mēnsis* month of expiation, from *februa* Roman festival of purification held on February 15, from plural of *februum* a purgation

February Revolution NOUN another name for the **Russian Revolution** (sense 1).

fec. ABBREVIATION FOR fecit.

fecal (ˈfiːkᵊl) ADJECTIVE the usual US spelling of **faecal.**

feces (ˈfiːsiːz) PLURAL NOUN the usual US spelling of **faeces.**

fecht (fɛxt) VERB, NOUN a Scot word for **fight.**
▸ˈ**fechter** NOUN

fecit *Latin* (ˈfeɪkɪt) (he or she) made it: used formerly on works of art next to the artist's name. Abbreviation: **fec.**

feck¹ (fɛk) NOUN *Scot obsolete* **a** worth; value. **b** amount; quantity. **c** the greater part; the majority.
▷HISTORY C15 (Scottish dialect) *fek,* short for EFFECT

feck² (fɛk) VERB, NOUN, INTERJECTION *Slang* a variant of **fuck.**

feckless (ˈfɛklɪs) ADJECTIVE feeble; weak; ineffectual; irresponsible.
▷HISTORY C16: from obsolete *feck* value, effect + -LESS
▸ˈ**fecklessly** ADVERB ▸ˈ**fecklessness** NOUN

fecula (ˈfɛkjʊlə) NOUN, *plural* **-lae** (-ˌliː). 1 starch

obtained by washing the crushed parts of plants, such as the potato. [2] faecal material, esp of insects.
▷HISTORY C17: from Latin: burnt tartar, appearing as a crust in wine, from *faex* sediment

feculent ('fɛkjʊlənt) ADJECTIVE [1] filthy, scummy, muddy, or foul. [2] of the nature of or containing waste matter.
▷HISTORY C15: from Latin *faeculentus*; see FAECES
▸ **'feculence** NOUN

fecund ('fi:kənd, 'fɛk-) ADJECTIVE [1] greatly productive; fertile. [2] intellectually productive; prolific.
▷HISTORY C14: from Latin *fēcundus*; related to Latin *fētus* offspring

fecundate ('fi:kən,deɪt, 'fɛk-) VERB (*tr*) [1] to make fruitful. [2] to fertilize; impregnate.
▷HISTORY C17: from Latin *fēcundāre* to fertilize
▸ **,fecun'dation** NOUN ▸ **'fecun,dator** NOUN ▸ **fecundatory** (fɪ'kʌndətərɪ, -trɪ) ADJECTIVE

fecundity (fɪ'kʌndɪtɪ) NOUN [1] fertility; fruitfulness. [2] intellectual fruitfulness; creativity.

fed[1] (fɛd) VERB [1] the past tense and past participle of **feed.** [2] **fed to death** *or* **fed (up) to the (back) teeth.** *Informal* bored or annoyed.

fed[2] (fɛd) NOUN *US slang* an agent of the FBI.

Fed (fɛd) NOUN **the.** *US informal* the Federal Reserve Bank or Federal Reserve Board.

Fed. *or* **fed.** ABBREVIATION FOR: [1] Federal. [2] Federation. [3] Federated.

fedayee (fə'dɑ:ji:) NOUN, *plural* **-yeen** (-ji:n). (*sometimes capital*) (in Arab states) a commando, esp one fighting against Israel.
▷HISTORY from Arabic *fidā'i* one who risks his life in a cause, from *fidā'* redemption

federal ('fɛdərəl) ADJECTIVE [1] of or relating to a form of government or a country in which power is divided between one central and several regional governments. [2] of or relating to a treaty between provinces, states, etc., that establishes a political unit in which power is so divided. [3] of or relating to the central government of a federation. [4] of or relating to any union or association of parties or groups that retain some autonomy. [5] (of a university) comprised of relatively independent colleges. ♦ NOUN [6] a supporter of federal union or federation.
▷HISTORY C17: from Latin *foedus* league
▸ **'federally** ADVERB

Federal ('fɛdərəl) ADJECTIVE [1] **a** of or relating to the Federalist party or Federalism. **b** characteristic of or supporting the Union government during the American Civil War. ♦ NOUN [2] **a** a supporter of the Union government during the American Civil War. **b** a Federalist.

Federal Bureau of Investigation NOUN See **FBI.**

federal district *or* **territory** NOUN an area used as the seat of central government in a federal system.

Federal Government NOUN the national government of a federated state, such as that of Australia located in Canberra.

federalism ('fɛdərə,lɪzəm) NOUN [1] the principle or a system of federal union. [2] advocacy of federal union.
▸ **'federalist** NOUN, ADJECTIVE ▸ **,federal'istic** ADJECTIVE

Federalism ('fɛdərə,lɪzəm) NOUN *US history* the principles and policies of the Federalist party.

Federalist ('fɛdərəlɪst) *US history* ♦ NOUN [1] a supporter or member of the Federalist party. ♦ ADJECTIVE *also* **,Federal'istic.** [2] characteristic of the Federalists.

Federalist Party *or* **Federal Party** NOUN the American political party founded in 1787 and led initially by Alexander Hamilton. It took an active part in the shaping of the US Constitution and thereafter favoured strong centralized government and business interests.

federalize *or* **federalise** ('fɛdərə,laɪz) VERB (*tr*) [1] to unite in a federation or federal union; federate. [2] to subject to federal control.
▸ **,federali'zation** *or* **,federali'sation** NOUN

Federal Republic of Germany NOUN the official name of **Germany**, formerly of West Germany

Federal Reserve note NOUN a bank note issued by the Federal Reserve Banks and now serving as the prevailing paper currency in circulation in the US.

Federal Reserve System NOUN (in the US) a banking system consisting of twelve **Federal Reserve Districts**, each containing member banks regulated and served by a **Federal Reserve Bank**. It operates under the supervision of the **Federal Reserve Board** and performs functions similar to those of the Bank of England.

federate VERB ('fɛdə,reɪt) [1] to unite or cause to unite in a federal union. ♦ ADJECTIVE ('fɛdərɪt) [2] federal; federated.
▸ **'federative** ADJECTIVE

Federated Malay States PLURAL NOUN See **Malay States.**

federation (,fɛdə'reɪʃən) NOUN [1] the act of federating. [2] the union of several provinces, states, etc., to form a federal union. [3] a political unit formed in such a way. [4] any league, alliance, or confederacy. [5] a union of several parties, groups, etc. [6] any association or union for common action.

Federation (,fɛdə'reɪʃən) NOUN *Austral* [1] **the** the federation of the Australian colonies in 1901. [2] a style of domestic architecture of that period, characterized by red brick, terracotta roof tiles, sinuous curves, and heavy window frames.

Federation of Rhodesia and Nyasaland NOUN a federation (1953–63) of Northern Rhodesia, Southern Rhodesia, and Nyasaland.

Federation wheat NOUN *Austral* an early-maturing drought-resistant variety of wheat developed by William Farrar in 1902.

fedora (fɪ'dɔ:rə) NOUN a soft felt or velvet medium-brimmed hat, usually with a band.
▷HISTORY C19: allegedly named after *Fédora* (1882), play by Victorien Sardou (1831–1908)

fed up ADJECTIVE (*usually postpositive*) *Informal* annoyed, discontented, or bored: *I'm fed up with your conduct.*

fee (fi:) NOUN [1] a payment asked by professional people or public servants for their services: *a doctor's fee; school fees.* [2] a charge made for a privilege: *an entrance fee.* [3] *Property law* **a** an interest in land capable of being inherited. See **fee simple, fee tail. b** the land held in fee. [4] (in feudal Europe) the land granted by a lord to his vassal. [5] an obsolete word for a **gratuity.** [6] **in fee. a** *Law* (of land) in absolute ownership. **b** *Archaic* in complete subjection. ♦ VERB **fees, feeing, feed.** [7] *Rare* to give a fee to. [8] *Chiefly Scot* to hire for a fee.
▷HISTORY C14: from Old French *fie*, of Germanic origin; see FIEF
▸ **'feeless** ADJECTIVE

feeble ('fi:bᵊl) ADJECTIVE [1] lacking in physical or mental strength; frail; weak. [2] inadequate; unconvincing: *feeble excuses.* [3] easily influenced or indecisive.
▷HISTORY C12: from Old French *feble, fleible*, from Latin *flēbilis* to be lamented, from *flēre* to weep
▸ **'feebleness** NOUN ▸ **'feebly** ADVERB

feeble-minded ADJECTIVE [1] lacking in intelligence; stupid. [2] mentally defective. [3] lacking decision; irresolute.
▸ **,feeble-'mindedly** ADVERB ▸ **,feeble-'mindedness** NOUN

feed (fi:d) VERB **feeds, feeding, fed** (fɛd). (*mainly tr*) [1] to give food to: *to feed the cat.* [2] to give as food: *to feed meat to the cat.* [3] (*intr*) to eat food: *the horses feed at noon.* [4] to provide food for: *these supplies can feed 10 million people.* [5] to provide what is necessary for the existence or development of: *to feed one's imagination.* [6] to gratify; satisfy: *to feed one's eyes on a beautiful sight.* [7] (*also intr*) to supply (a machine, furnace, etc.) with (the necessary materials or fuel) for its operation, or (of such materials) to flow or move forwards into a machine, etc. [8] to use (land) as grazing. [9] *Theatre, informal* to cue (an actor, esp a comedian) with lines or actions. [10] *Sport* to pass a ball to (a team-mate). [11] *Electronics* to introduce (electrical energy) into a circuit, esp by means of a feeder. [12] (*also intr; foll by on or upon*) to eat or cause to eat. ♦ NOUN [13] the act or an instance of feeding. [14] food, esp that of animals or babies. [15] the process of supplying a machine or furnace with a material or fuel. [16] the quantity of material or fuel so supplied. [17] the rate of advance of a cutting tool in a lathe, drill, etc. [18] a mechanism that supplies material or fuel or controls the rate of advance of a cutting tool. [19] *Theatre, informal* a performer, esp a straight man, who provides cues. [20] an informal word for **meal.**
▷HISTORY Old English *fēdan*; related to Old Norse *fœtha* to feed, Old High German *fuotan*, Gothic *fōthjan*; see FOOD, FODDER
▸ **'feedable** ADJECTIVE

feedback ('fi:d,bæk) NOUN [1] **a** the return of part of the output of an electronic circuit, device, or mechanical system to its input, so modifying its characteristics. In **negative feedback** a rise in output energy reduces the input energy; in **positive feedback** an increase in output energy reinforces the input energy. **b** that part of the output signal fed back into the input. [2] the return of part of the sound output by a loudspeaker to the microphone or pick-up so that a high-pitched whistle is produced. [3] the whistling noise so produced. [4] **a** the effect of the product of a biological pathway on the rate of an earlier step in that pathway. **b** the substance or reaction causing such an effect, such as the release of a hormone in a biochemical pathway. [5] information in response to an inquiry, experiment, etc.: *there was little feedback from our questionnaire.* ♦ VERB **feed back.** (*adverb*) [6] (*tr*) to return (part of the output of a system) to its input. [7] to offer or suggest (information, ideas, etc.) in reaction to an inquiry, experiment, etc.

feedbag ('fi:d,bæg) NOUN [1] any bag in which feed for livestock is sacked. [2] the usual US and Canadian name for **nosebag.**

feeder ('fi:də) NOUN [1] a person or thing that feeds or is fed. [2] a child's feeding bottle or bib. [3] *Agriculture, chiefly US and Canadian* a head of livestock being fattened for slaughter. [4] a person or device that feeds the working material into a system or machine. [5] a tributary channel, esp one that supplies a reservoir or canal with water. [6] **a** a road, service, etc., that links secondary areas to the main traffic network. **b** (*as modifier*): *a feeder bus.* [7] **a** a transmission line connecting an aerial to a transmitter or receiver. **b** a power line for transmitting electrical power from a generating station to a distribution network.

feeding bottle NOUN a bottle fitted with a rubber teat from which infants or young animals suck liquids. Also called: **nursing bottle.**

feeding frenzy NOUN [1] a phenomenon in which aquatic predators, esp sharks, become so excited when eating that they attack each other. [2] a period of intense excitement over or interest in a person or thing: *the media erupt into a feeding frenzy.*

feedstuff ('fi:d,stʌf) *or* **feedingstuff** ('fi:dɪŋ,stʌf) NOUN any material used as a food, esp for animals.

feedlot ('fi:d,lɒt) NOUN an area or building where livestock are fattened rapidly for market.

feedstock ('fi:d,stɒk) NOUN the main raw material used in the manufacture of a product.

feedthrough ('fi:d,θru:) NOUN *Electronics* a conductor used to connect two sides of a part, such as a printed circuit board.

feedwater ('fi:d,wɔ:tə) NOUN water, previously purified to prevent scale deposit or corrosion, that is fed to boilers for steam generation.

feel (fi:l) VERB **feels, feeling, felt** (fɛlt). [1] to perceive (something) by touching. [2] to have a physical or emotional sensation of (something): *to feel heat; to feel anger.* [3] (*tr*) to examine (something) by touch. [4] (*tr*) to find (one's way) by testing or cautious exploration. [5] (*copula*) to seem or appear in respect of the sensation given: *I feel tired; it feels warm.* [6] to have an indistinct, esp emotional conviction; sense (esp in the phrase **feel in one's bones**). [7] (*intr; foll by for*) to show sympathy or compassion (towards): *I feel for you in your sorrow.* [8] to believe, think, or be of the opinion (that): *he feels he must resign.* [9] (*tr; often followed by up*) *Slang* to pass one's hands over the sexual organs of. [10] **feel like.** to have an inclination (for something or doing something): *I don't feel like going to the pictures.* [11] **feel (quite) oneself.** to be fit and sure of oneself. [12] **feel up to.** (*usually used with a negative or in a question*) to be fit enough for (something or doing something): *I don't feel up to going out tonight.* ♦ NOUN [13] the act or an instance of feeling, esp. by touching. [14] the

quality of or an impression from something perceived through feeling: *the house has a homely feel about it.* 15 the sense of touch: *the fabric is rough to the feel.* 16 an instinctive aptitude; knack: *she's got a feel for this sort of work.*
▷HISTORY Old English *fēlan*; related to Old High German *fuolen*, Old Norse *fālma* to grope, Latin *palma* PALM[1]

feeler ('fiːlə) NOUN 1 a person or thing that feels. 2 an organ in certain animals, such as an antenna or tentacle, that is sensitive to touch. 3 a remark designed to probe the reactions or intentions of other people.

feeler gauge NOUN a thin metal strip of known thickness used to measure a narrow gap or to set a gap between two parts.

feel-good ADJECTIVE causing or characterized by a feeling of self-satisfaction: *feel-good factor.*

feeling ('fiːlɪŋ) NOUN 1 the sense of touch. 2 **a** the ability to experience physical sensations, such as heat, pain, etc. **b** the sensation so experienced. 3 a state of mind. 4 a physical or mental impression: *a feeling of warmth.* 5 fondness; sympathy: *to have a great deal of feeling for someone.* 6 an ability to feel deeply: *a person of feeling.* 7 a sentiment: *a feeling that the project is feasible.* 8 an impression or mood; atmosphere: *the feeling of a foreign city.* 9 an emotional disturbance, esp anger or dislike: *a lot of bad feeling about the increase in taxes.* 10 intuitive appreciation and understanding: *a feeling for words.* 11 sensibility in the performance of something. 12 (*plural*) emotional or moral sensitivity, as in relation to principles or personal dignity (esp in the phrase **hurt** or **injure the feelings of**). 13 **have feelings for.** to be emotionally or sexually attracted to. ◆ ADJECTIVE 14 sentient; sensitive. 15 expressing or containing emotion. 16 warm-hearted; sympathetic.
▸ '**feelingly** ADVERB

fee simple NOUN *Property law* an absolute interest in land over which the holder has complete freedom of disposition during his life. Compare **fee tail.**
▷HISTORY C15: from Anglo-French: fee (or fief) simple

feet (fiːt) NOUN 1 the plural of **foot.** 2 **at (someone's) feet.** as someone's disciple. 3 **be run** *or* **rushed off one's feet.** to be very busy. 4 **carry** *or* **sweep off one's feet.** to fill with enthusiasm. 5 **feet of clay.** a weakness that is not widely known. 6 **get one's feet wet.** to begin to participate in something. 7 **have** (*or* **keep**) **one's feet on the ground.** to be practical and reliable. 8 **on one's** *or* **its feet. a** standing up. **b** in good health. **c** (of a business, company, etc.) thriving. 9 **put one's feet up.** to rest. 10 **stand on one's own feet.** to be independent.
▸ '**feetless** ADJECTIVE

fee tail NOUN *Property law* **a** a freehold interest in land restricted to a particular line of heirs. **b** an estate in land subject to such restriction. Compare **fee simple.**
▷HISTORY C15: from Anglo-French *fee tailé* fee (or fief) determined, from *taillier* to cut

feeze *or* **feaze** (fiːz) *Dialect* ◆ VERB 1 (*tr*) to beat. 2 to drive off. 3 *Chiefly US* to disconcert; worry. ◆ NOUN 4 a rush. 5 *Chiefly US* a state of agitation.
▷HISTORY Old English *fēsian*

feign (feɪn) VERB 1 to put on a show of (a quality or emotion); pretend: *to feign innocence.* 2 (*tr*) to make up; invent: *to feign an excuse.* 3 (*tr*) to copy; imitate: *to feign someone's laugh.*
▷HISTORY C13: from Old French *feindre* to pretend, from Latin *fingere* to form, shape, invent
▸ '**feigner** NOUN ▸ '**feigningly** ADVERB

feijoa (fiː'dʒəʊə) NOUN 1 an evergreen myrtaceous shrub, *Feijoa sellowiana*, of South America. 2 the fruit of this shrub.
▷HISTORY C19: from New Latin, named after J. da Silva *Feijo*, 19th-century Spanish botanist

feint[1] (feɪnt) NOUN 1 a mock attack or movement designed to distract an adversary, as in a military manoeuvre or in boxing, fencing, etc. 2 a misleading action or appearance. ◆ VERB 3 (*intr*) to make a feint.
▷HISTORY C17: from French *feinte*, from *feint* pretended, from Old French *feindre* to FEIGN

feint[2] (feɪnt) NOUN *Printing* the narrowest rule used in the production of ruled paper.

▷HISTORY C19: variant of FAINT

feints *or* **faints** (feɪnts) PLURAL NOUN the leavings of the second distillation of Scotch malt whisky.

feisty ('faɪstɪ) ADJECTIVE **feistier, feistiest.** *Informal* 1 lively, resilient, and self-reliant. 2 *US and Canadian* frisky. 3 *US and Canadian* irritable.
▷HISTORY C19: from dialect *feist, fist* small dog; related to Old English *fīsting* breaking wind

felafel (fəl'ɑːfəl) NOUN a variant spelling of **falafel.**

feldsher, feldscher, *or* **feldschar** ('fɛldʃə) NOUN (in Russia) a medical doctor's assistant.
▷HISTORY C19: Russian, from German *Feldscher* a field surgeon, from *Feld* field + *Scherer* surgeon, from *scheren* to shear

feldspar ('fɛldˌspɑː, 'fɛlˌspɑː) *or* **felspar** NOUN any of a group of hard rock-forming minerals consisting of aluminium silicates of potassium, sodium, calcium, or barium: the principal constituents of igneous rocks. The group includes orthoclase, microcline, and the plagioclase minerals.
▷HISTORY C18: from German *feldspat(h)*, from *feld* field + *spat(h)* SPAR[3]
▸**feldspathic** (fɛld'spæθɪk, fɛl'spæθ-), **fel'spathic,** '**feldspathˌose,** *or* '**felspathˌose** ADJECTIVE

feldspathoid ('fɛldspəˌθɔɪd) NOUN any of a group of rock-forming minerals, such as leucite and sodalite, that are similar to feldspars but contain less silica.

felicific (ˌfiːlɪ'sɪfɪk) ADJECTIVE making or tending to make happy.
▷HISTORY C19: from Latin *fēlix* happy + *facere* to make

felicitate (fɪ'lɪsɪˌteɪt) VERB to wish joy to; congratulate.
▸**fe'liciˌtator** NOUN

felicitation (fɪˌlɪsɪ'teɪʃən) NOUN a less common word for **congratulation.**

felicitous (fɪ'lɪsɪtəs) ADJECTIVE 1 well-chosen; apt. 2 possessing an agreeable style. 3 producing or marked by happiness.
▸**fe'licitously** ADVERB ▸**fe'licitousness** NOUN

felicity (fɪ'lɪsɪtɪ) NOUN, *plural* **-ties.** 1 happiness; joy. 2 a cause of happiness. 3 an appropriate expression or style. 4 the quality or display of such expressions or style. 5 *Philosophy* appropriateness (of a speech act). The performative *I appoint you ambassador* can only possess felicity if uttered by one in whom the authority for such appointments is vested.
▷HISTORY C14: from Latin *fēlīcitās* happiness, from *fēlix* happy

feline ('fiːlaɪn) ADJECTIVE 1 of, relating to, or belonging to the *Felidae*, a family of predatory mammals, including cats, lions, leopards, and cheetahs, typically having a round head and retractile claws: order *Carnivora* (carnivores). 2 resembling or suggestive of a cat, esp in stealth or grace. ◆ NOUN *also* **felid** ('fiːlɪd). 3 any animal belonging to the family *Felidae*; a cat.
▷HISTORY C17: from Latin *fēlīnus*, from *fēlēs* cat
▸ '**felinely** ADVERB ▸ '**felineness** *or* **felinity** (fɪ'lɪnɪtɪ) NOUN

Felixstowe ('fiːlɪkˌstəʊ) NOUN a port and resort in E England, in Suffolk: ferry connections to Rotterdam and Zeebrugge. Pop.: 28 606 (1991).

fell[1] (fɛl) VERB the past tense of **fall.**

fell[2] (fɛl) VERB (*tr*) 1 to cut or knock down: *to fell a tree; to fell an opponent.* 2 *Needlework* to fold under and sew flat (the edges of a seam). ◆ NOUN 3 *US and Canadian* the timber felled in one season. 4 a seam finished by felling.
▷HISTORY Old English *fellan*; related to Old Norse *fella*, Old High German *fellen*; see FALL
▸ '**fellable** ADJECTIVE

fell[3] (fɛl) ADJECTIVE 1 *Archaic* cruel or fierce; terrible. 2 *Archaic* destructive or deadly: *a fell disease.* 3 **one fell swoop.** a single hasty action or occurrence.
▷HISTORY C13 *fel*, from Old French: cruel, from Medieval Latin *fellō* villain; see FELON[1]
▸ '**fellness** NOUN

fell[4] (fɛl) NOUN an animal skin or hide.
▷HISTORY Old English; related to Old High German *fel* skin, Old Norse *berfjall* bearskin, Latin *pellis* skin; see PEEL[1]

fell[5] (fɛl) NOUN (*often plural*) *Northern English and Scot* **a** a mountain, hill, or tract of upland moor. **b** (*in combination*): *fell-walking.*
▷HISTORY C13: from Old Norse *fjall*; related to Old High German *felis* rock

fella ('fɛlə) NOUN a nonstandard variant of **fellow.**

fellah ('fɛlə) NOUN, *plural* **fellahs, fellahin,** *or* **fellaheen** (ˌfɛlə'hiːn). a peasant in Arab countries.
▷HISTORY C18: from Arabic, dialect variant of *fallāh*, from *falaha* to cultivate

fellate (fɛ'leɪt, fɪ-) VERB (*tr*) to perform fellatio on (a person).
▷HISTORY C20: back formation from FELLATIO

fellatio (fɪ'leɪʃɪəʊ, fɛ-) *or* **fellation** NOUN a sexual activity in which the penis is stimulated by the partner's mouth. Compare **cunnilingus.**
▷HISTORY C19: New Latin, from Latin *fellāre* to suck
▸**fel'lator** NOUN ▸**fel'latrix** FEMININE NOUN

feller[1] ('fɛlə) NOUN 1 a person or thing that fells. 2 an attachment on a sewing machine for felling seams.

feller[2] ('fɛlə) NOUN a nonstandard variant of **fellow.**

Felling ('fɛlɪŋ) NOUN a town in NE England, in Gateshead unitary authority, Tyne and Wear; formerly noted for coal mining. Pop.: 35 053 (1991).

fellmonger ('fɛlˌmʌŋgə) NOUN a person who deals in animal skins or hides.
▸ '**fellˌmongering** *or* '**fellˌmongery** NOUN

felloe ('fɛləʊ) *or* **felly** ('fɛlɪ) NOUN, *plural* **-loes** *or* **-lies.** a segment or the whole rim of a wooden wheel to which the spokes are attached and onto which a metal tyre is usually shrunk.
▷HISTORY Old English *felge*; related to Old High German *felga*, Middle Dutch *velge*, of unknown origin

fellow ('fɛləʊ) NOUN 1 a man or boy. 2 an informal word for **boyfriend.** 3 *Informal* one or oneself: *a fellow has to eat.* 4 a person considered to be of little importance or worth. 5 **a** (*often plural*) a companion; comrade; associate. **b** (*as modifier*): *fellow travellers.* 6 (at Oxford and Cambridge universities) a member of the governing body of a college, who is usually a member of the teaching staff. 7 a member of the governing body or established teaching staff at any of various universities or colleges. 8 a postgraduate student employed, esp for a fixed period, to undertake research and, often, to do some teaching. 9 **a** a person in the same group, class, or condition: *the surgeon asked his fellows.* **b** (*as modifier*): *fellow students; a fellow sufferer.* 10 one of a pair; counterpart; mate: *looking for the glove's fellow.*
▷HISTORY Old English *fēolaga*, from Old Norse *félagi*, one who lays down money, from *fé* money + *lag* a laying down

Fellow ('fɛləʊ) NOUN a member of any of various learned societies: *Fellow of the British Academy.*

fellow feeling NOUN 1 mutual sympathy or friendship. 2 an opinion held in common.

fellowship ('fɛləʊˌʃɪp) NOUN 1 the state of sharing mutual interests, experiences, activities, etc. 2 a society of people sharing mutual interests, experiences, activities, etc.; club. 3 companionship; friendship. 4 the state or relationship of being a fellow. 5 **a** mutual trust and charitableness between Christians. **b** a Church or religious association. 6 *Education* **a** a financed research post providing study facilities, privileges, etc., often in return for teaching services. **b** a foundation endowed to support a postgraduate research student. **c** an honorary title carrying certain privileges awarded to a postgraduate student. 7 (*often capital*) the body of fellows in a college, university, etc.

fellow traveller NOUN 1 a companion on a journey. 2 a non-Communist who sympathizes with Communism.

fell pony NOUN a British breed of large and heavy ponies, found in the hills of N England.

felo de se ('fiːləʊ dɪ 'siː, 'fɛləʊ) NOUN, *plural* **felones de se** ('fiːləʊˌniːz dɪ 'siː, 'fɛl-) *or* **felos de se.** *Law* **a** suicide. **b** a person who commits suicide.
▷HISTORY C17: from Anglo-Latin, from *felō* felon + Latin *dē* of + *sē* oneself

felon[1] ('fɛlən) NOUN 1 *Criminal law* (formerly) a person who has committed a felony. 2 *Obsolete* a

wicked person. ◆ ADJECTIVE [3] *Archaic or poetic* evil; cruel.
▷HISTORY C13: from Old French: villain, from Medieval Latin *fellō*, of uncertain origin

felon² (ˈfɛlən) NOUN a purulent inflammation of the end joint of a finger, sometimes affecting the bone.
▷HISTORY C12: from Medieval Latin *fellō* sore, perhaps from Latin *fel* poison

felonious (fɪˈləʊnɪəs) ADJECTIVE [1] *Criminal law* of, involving, or constituting a felony. [2] *Obsolete* wicked; base.
▸**feˈloniously** ADVERB ▸**feˈloniousness** NOUN

felonry (ˈfɛlənrɪ) NOUN, *plural* **-ries.** [1] felons collectively. [2] (formerly) the convict population of a penal colony, esp in Australia.

felony (ˈfɛlənɪ) NOUN, *plural* **-nies.** (formerly) a serious crime, such as murder or arson. All distinctions between felony and misdemeanour were abolished in England and Wales in 1967.

felsite (ˈfɛlsaɪt) *or* **felstone** (ˈfɛlˌstəʊn) NOUN any fine-grained igneous rock consisting essentially of quartz and feldspar.
▷HISTORY C18: FELS(*par*) + -ITE¹
▸**felsitic** (fɛlˈsɪtɪk) ADJECTIVE

felspar (ˈfɛlˌspɑː) NOUN a variant (esp Brit) of **feldspar.**
▸**felspathic** (fɛlˈspæθɪk) *or* **ˈfelspathˌose** ADJECTIVE

felt¹ (fɛlt) VERB the past tense and past participle of **feel.**

felt² (fɛlt) NOUN [1] **a** a matted fabric of wool, hair, etc., made by working the fibres together under pressure or by heat or chemical action. **b** (*as modifier*): *a felt hat.* [2] any material, such as asbestos, made by a similar process of matting. ◆ VERB [3] (*tr*) to make into or cover with felt. [4] (*intr*) to become matted.
▷HISTORY Old English; related to Old Saxon *filt*, Old High German *filz* felt, Latin *pellere* to beat, Greek *pelas* close; see ANVIL, FILTER

felting (ˈfɛltɪŋ) NOUN [1] felted material; felt. [2] the process of making felt. [3] materials for making felt.

felt-tip pen NOUN a pen having a writing point made from pressed fibres. Also called: **fibre-tip pen.**

felucca (fɛˈlʌkə) NOUN a narrow lateen-rigged vessel of the Mediterranean.
▷HISTORY C17: from Italian *felucca*, probably from obsolete Spanish *faluca*, probably from Arabic *fulūk* ships, from Greek *epholkion* small boat, from *ephelkein* to tow

felwort (ˈfɛlˌwɜːt) NOUN a biennial gentianaceous plant, *Gentianella amarella*, of Europe and SW China, having purple flowers and rosettes of leaves.
▷HISTORY Old English *feldwyrt*; see FIELD, WORT

fem. ABBREVIATION FOR: [1] female. [2] feminine.

female (ˈfiːmeɪl) ADJECTIVE [1] of, relating to, or designating the sex producing gametes (ova) that can be fertilized by male gametes (spermatozoa). [2] of, relating to, or characteristic of a woman: *female charm.* [3] for or composed of women or girls: *female suffrage; a female choir.* [4] (of reproductive organs such as the ovary and carpel) capable of producing female gametes. [5] (of gametes such as the ovum) capable of being fertilized by a male gamete in sexual reproduction. [6] (of flowers) lacking, or having nonfunctional, stamens. [7] having an internal cavity into which a projecting male counterpart can be fitted: *a female thread.* ◆ NOUN [8] **a** a female animal or plant. **b** *Mildly offensive* a woman or girl.
▷HISTORY C14: from earlier *femelle* (influenced by *male*), from Latin *fēmella* a young woman, from *fēmina* a woman
▸**ˈfemaleness** NOUN

female impersonator NOUN a male theatrical performer who acts as a woman.

female suffrage NOUN *Chiefly US* another name for **women's suffrage.**

feme (fɛm) NOUN *Law* a woman or wife.
▷HISTORY C16: from Anglo-French, ultimately from Latin *fēmina* woman

feme covert NOUN *Law* a married woman.
▷HISTORY C16: from Anglo-French: a covered woman, one protected by marriage

feme sole NOUN *Law* [1] a single woman, whether spinster, widow, or divorcee. [2] a woman whose marriage has been annulled or is otherwise independent of her husband, as by owning her own property.
▷HISTORY C16: from Anglo-French: a woman alone

femineity (ˌfɛmɪˈniːɪtɪ) NOUN the quality of being feminine; womanliness.

feminine (ˈfɛmɪnɪn) ADJECTIVE [1] suitable to or characteristic of a woman: *a feminine fashion.* [2] possessing qualities or characteristics considered typical of or appropriate to a woman. [3] effeminate; womanish. [4] *Grammar* **a** denoting or belonging to a gender of nouns, occurring in many inflected languages, that includes all kinds of referents as well as some female animate referents. **b** (*as noun*): *German* Zeit *"time" and* Ehe *"marriage" are feminines.*
▷HISTORY C14: from Latin *fēminīnus*, from *fēmina* woman
▸**ˈfemininely** ADVERB ▸**ˈfeminineness** NOUN

feminine ending NOUN *Prosody* an unstressed syllable at the end of a line of verse.

feminine rhyme NOUN *Prosody* a rhyme between words in which one, two, or more unstressed syllables follow a stressed one, as in *elation, nation* or *merrily, verily.* Compare **masculine rhyme.**

femininity (ˌfɛmɪˈnɪnɪtɪ) NOUN [1] the quality of being feminine. [2] womanhood.

feminism (ˈfɛmɪˌnɪzəm) NOUN a doctrine or movement that advocates equal rights for women.

feminist (ˈfɛmɪnɪst) NOUN [1] a person who advocates equal rights for women. ◆ ADJECTIVE [2] of, relating to, or advocating feminism.

feminize *or* **feminise** (ˈfɛmɪˌnaɪz) VERB [1] to make or become feminine. [2] to cause (a male animal) to develop female characteristics.
▸**ˌfeminiˈzation** *or* **ˌfeminiˈsation** NOUN

femme *French* (fam; *English* fɛm) NOUN a woman or wife.

femme de chambre *French* (fam də ʃɑ̃brə) NOUN, *plural* ***femmes de chambre*** (fam də ʃɑ̃brə). [1] a chambermaid. [2] *Rare* a personal maid.
▷HISTORY C18: woman of the bedroom

femme fatale *French* (fam fatal; *English* ˈfɛm fəˈtæl, -ˈtɑːl) NOUN, *plural* ***femmes fatales*** (fam fatal; *English* ˈfɛm fəˈtælz, -ˈtɑːlz). an alluring or seductive woman, esp one who causes men to love her to their own distress.
▷HISTORY fatal woman

femmy (ˈfɛmɪ) ADJECTIVE **-mier, -miest.** *Informal* markedly or exaggeratedly feminine in appearance, manner, etc.

femoral (ˈfɛmərəl) ADJECTIVE of or relating to the thigh or femur.

femto- PREFIX denoting 10^{-15}: *femtometer.* Symbol: f.
▷HISTORY from Danish or Norwegian *femten* fifteen

femur (ˈfiːmə) NOUN, *plural* **femurs** *or* **femora** (ˈfɛmərə). [1] the longest thickest bone of the human skeleton, articulating with the pelvis above and the knee below. Nontechnical name: **thighbone.** [2] the corresponding bone in other vertebrates. [3] the segment of an insect's leg nearest to the body.
▷HISTORY C18: from Latin: thigh

fen¹ (fɛn) NOUN low-lying flat land that is marshy or artificially drained.
▷HISTORY Old English *fenn*; related to Old High German *fenna*, Old Norse *fen*, Gothic *fani* clay, Sanskrit *panka* mud

fen² (fɛn) NOUN, *plural* **fen.** a monetary unit of the People's Republic of China, worth one hundredth of a yuan.
▷HISTORY from Mandarin Chinese

fence (fɛns) NOUN [1] a structure that serves to enclose an area such as a garden or field, usually made of posts of timber, concrete, or metal connected by wire, netting, rails, or boards. [2] *Slang* a dealer in stolen property. [3] an obstacle for a horse to jump in steeplechasing or showjumping. [4] *Machinery* a guard or guide, esp in a circular saw or plane. [5] a projection usually fitted to the top surface of a sweptback aircraft wing to prevent movement of the airflow towards the wing tips. [6] **mend one's fences. a** *Chiefly US and Canadian* to restore a position or reputation that has been damaged, esp in politics. **b** to re-establish friendly relations (with someone). [7] **(sit) on the fence.** (to be) unable or unwilling to commit oneself. [8] **over the fence.** *Austral and NZ informal* unreasonable, unfair, or unjust. ◆ VERB [9] (*tr*) to construct a fence on or around (a piece of land, etc.). [10] (*tr; foll by in or off*) to close (in) or separate (off) with or as if with a fence: *he fenced in the livestock.* [11] (*intr*) to fight using swords or foils. [12] (*intr*) to evade a question or argument, esp by quibbling over minor points. [13] (*intr*) to engage in skilful or witty debate, repartee, etc. [14] (*intr*) *Slang* to receive stolen property. [15] (*tr*) *Archaic* to ward off or keep out.
▷HISTORY C14 *fens*, shortened from *defens* DEFENCE
▸**ˈfenceless** ADJECTIVE ▸**ˈfenceˌlike** ADJECTIVE

fencer (ˈfɛnsə) NOUN [1] a person who fights with a sword, esp one who practises the art of fencing. [2] *Chiefly Austral and NZ* a person who erects and repairs fences.

fencible (ˈfɛnsəbᵊl) ADJECTIVE [1] a Scot word for **defensible.** ◆ NOUN [2] (formerly) a person who undertook military service in immediate defence of his homeland only.

fencing (ˈfɛnsɪŋ) NOUN [1] the practice, art, or sport of fighting with swords, esp the sport of using foils, épées, or sabres under a set of rules to score points. [2] **a** wire, stakes, etc., used as fences. **b** fences collectively. [3] skilful or witty debate. [4] the avoidance of direct answers; evasiveness. [5] *Slang* the business of buying and selling stolen property.

fencing wire NOUN a heavy-gauge galvanized wire used for farm fences.

fend (fɛnd) VERB [1] (*intr; foll by for*) to give support (to someone, esp oneself); provide (for). [2] (*tr; usually foll by off*) to ward off or turn aside (blows, questions, attackers, etc.). [3] (*tr*) *Archaic* to defend or resist. [4] (*intr*) *Scot and Northern English dialect* to struggle; strive. ◆ NOUN [5] *Scot and Northern English dialect* a shift or effort.
▷HISTORY C13 *fenden*, shortened from *defenden* to DEFEND

Fendalton tractor (ˌfɛnˈdɔːltən) NOUN *NZ informal* a four-wheel drive recreational vehicle. Also called: **Fendalton shopping cart.**
▷HISTORY from the name of a wealthy suburb of Christchurch

fender (ˈfɛndə) NOUN [1] a low metal frame which confines falling coals to the hearth. [2] *Chiefly US* a metal frame fitted to the front of locomotives to absorb shock, clear the track, etc. [3] a cushion-like device, such as a car tyre hung over the side of a vessel to reduce damage resulting from accidental contact or collision. [4] the US and Canadian name for **wing** (sense 10) or **mudguard.**
▸**ˈfendered** ADJECTIVE

Fender (ˈfɛndə) NOUN *Trademark* a type of solid-body electric guitar.
▷HISTORY C20: named after Leo *Fender*, its US inventor (1951)

fender pile NOUN an upright, usually freestanding, pile driven into the sea bed or a riverbed beside a berth to protect the dock wall or wharf from the impact of vessels.

fenestella (ˌfɛnɪˈstɛlə) NOUN, *plural* **-lae** (-liː). [1] *RC Church* a small aperture in the front of an altar, containing relics. [2] *Ecclesiast* a niche in the side wall of a chancel, in which the credence or piscina are set. [3] *Architect* a small window or an opening in a wall.
▷HISTORY C18: from Latin: a little window, from *fenestra* window

fenestra (fɪˈnɛstrə) NOUN, *plural* **-trae** (-triː). [1] *Biology* a small opening in or between bones, esp one of the openings between the middle and inner ears. [2] *Zoology* a transparent marking or spot, as on the wings of moths. [3] *Architect* a window or window-like opening in the outside wall of a building.
▷HISTORY C19: via New Latin from Latin: wall opening, window
▸**feˈnestral** ADJECTIVE

fenestrated (fɪˈnɛsˌtreɪtɪd, ˈfɛnɪˌstreɪtɪd) *or* **fenestrate** ADJECTIVE [1] *Architect* having windows or window-like openings. [2] *Biology* perforated or having fenestrae.

fenestration (ˌfɛnɪˈstreɪʃən) NOUN [1] the arrangement and design of windows in a building. [2] a surgical operation to restore hearing by making an artificial opening into the labyrinth of the ear.

F Eng ABBREVIATION FOR Fellow of the Fellowship of Engineering.

feng shui ('fʌŋ 'ʃweɪ) NOUN the Chinese art of determining the most propitious design and placement of a grave, building, room, etc., so that the maximum harmony is achieved between the flow of chi of the environment and that of the user, believed to bring good fortune.
▷HISTORY C20: from Chinese *feng* wind + *shui* water

Fenian ('fiːnɪən) NOUN [1] (formerly) a member of an Irish revolutionary organization founded in the US in the 19th century to fight for an independent Ireland. [2] *Irish myth* one of the Fianna. [3] *Derogatory, offensive* an Irish Catholic or a person of Irish Catholic descent. ◆ ADJECTIVE [4] of or relating to the Fenians.
▷HISTORY C19: from Irish Gaelic *fēinne*, plural of *fian* band of warriors
▸'**Fenianism** NOUN

fennec ('fɛnɛk) NOUN a very small nocturnal fox, *Fennecus zerda*, inhabiting deserts of N Africa and Arabia, having pale fur and enormous ears.
▷HISTORY C18: from Arabic *fenek* fox

fennel ('fɛnᵊl) NOUN [1] a strong-smelling yellow-flowered umbelliferous plant, *Foeniculum vulgare*, whose seeds and feathery leaves are used to season and flavour food. See also **finocchio.** [2] another name for **mayweed.**
▷HISTORY Old English *fenol*, from Latin *faeniculum* fennel, diminutive of *faenum* hay

fennelflower ('fɛnᵊlˌflaʊə) NOUN any of various Mediterranean ranunculaceous plants of the genus *Nigella*, having finely divided leaves and white, blue, or yellow flowers. See also **love-in-a-mist.**

fenny ('fɛnɪ) ADJECTIVE [1] boggy or marshy: *fenny country.* [2] found in, characteristic of, or growing in fens.

Fenrir ('fɛnrɪə), **Fenris** ('fɛnrɪs), *or* **Fenriswolf** ('fɛnrɪsˌwʊlf) NOUN *Norse myth* an enormous wolf, fathered by Loki, which killed Odin.

Fens (fɛnz) PLURAL NOUN **the.** a flat low-lying area of E England, west and south of the Wash: consisted of marshes until reclaimed in the 17th to 19th centuries.

fentanyl ('fɛntəˌnaɪl) NOUN a narcotic drug used in medicine to relieve pain.

fenugreek ('fɛnjʊˌgriːk) NOUN an annual heavily scented Mediterranean leguminous plant, *Trigonella foenum-graecum*, with hairy stems and white flowers: cultivated for forage and for its medicinal seeds.
▷HISTORY Old English *fēnogrēcum*, from Latin *fenum Graecum* literally: Greek hay

feoff (fiːf) *Medieval history* ◆ NOUN [1] a variant spelling of **fief.** ◆ VERB [2] (*tr*) to invest with a benefice or fief.
▷HISTORY C13: from Anglo-French *feoffer*, from *feoff* a FIEF
▸'**feoffor** *or* '**feoffer** NOUN

feoffee (fɛ'fiː, fiː'fiː) NOUN (in feudal society) a vassal granted a fief by his lord.

feoffment ('fiːfmənt) NOUN (in medieval Europe) a lord's act of granting a fief to his man.

-fer NOUN COMBINING FORM indicating a person or thing that bears something specified: *crucifer; conifer.*
▷HISTORY from Latin, from *ferre* to bear

feral[1] ('fɪərəl, 'fɛr-) ADJECTIVE [1] Also: **ferine.** (of animals and plants) existing in a wild or uncultivated state, esp after being domestic or cultivated. [2] Also: **ferine.** savage; brutal. [3] *Austral derogatory slang* (of a person) tending to be interested in environmental issues and having a rugged, unkempt appearance. ◆ NOUN [4] *Austral derogatory slang* a person who displays such tendencies and appearance. [5] *Austral slang* disgusting. [6] *Austral slang* excellent.
▷HISTORY C17: from Medieval Latin *ferālis*, from Latin *fera* a wild beast, from *ferus* savage
▸**ferity** ('fɛrɪtɪ) NOUN

feral[2] ('fɪərəl, 'fɛr-) ADJECTIVE *Archaic* [1] *Astrology* associated with death. [2] gloomy; funereal.
▷HISTORY C17: from Latin *fērālis* relating to corpses; perhaps related to *ferre* to carry

ferbam ('fɜːbæm) NOUN a black slightly water-soluble fluffy powder used as a fungicide. Formula: $[(CH_3)_2NCSS]_3Fe$.
▷HISTORY C20: from *fer(ric dimethyldithiocar)bam(ate)*

fer-de-lance (ˌfɛədə'lɑːns) NOUN a large highly venomous tropical American snake, *Trimeresurus* (or *Bothops*) *atrox*, with a greyish-brown mottled coloration: family *Crotalidae* (pit vipers).
▷HISTORY C19: from French, literally: iron (head) of a lance

fere (fɪə; *Scot* fiːr) NOUN *Scot* [1] a companion. [2] Also: **fier.** a husband or wife.
▷HISTORY Old English *gefēra*, from *fēran* to travel; see FARE

feretory ('fɛrɪtərɪ, -trɪ) NOUN, *plural* **-ries.** *Chiefly RC Church* [1] a shrine, usually portable, for a saint's relics. [2] the chapel in which a shrine is kept.
▷HISTORY C14: from Middle French *fiertre*, from Latin *feretrum* a bier, from Greek *pheretron*, from *pherein* to bear

Fergana *or* **Ferghana** (fə'gɑːnə) NOUN [1] a region of W central Asia, surrounded by high mountains and accessible only from the west; mainly in Uzbekistan and partly in Tajikistan and Kyrgyzstan. [2] the chief city of this region, in E Uzbekistan. Pop.: 203 000 (1998 est.).

Fergus ('fɜːgəs) NOUN (in Irish legend) a warrior king of Ulster, who was supplanted by Conchobar.

feria ('fɪərɪə) NOUN, *plural* **-rias** *or* **-riae** (-rɪˌiː). *RC Church* a weekday, other than Saturday, on which no feast occurs.
▷HISTORY C19: from Late Latin: day of the week (as in *prīma fēria* Sunday), singular of Latin *fēriae* festivals

ferial ('fɪərɪəl) ADJECTIVE [1] of or relating to a feria. [2] *Rare* of or relating to a holiday.

ferine ('fɪəraɪn) ADJECTIVE another word for **feral.**
▷HISTORY C17: from Latin *ferīnus*, of wild animals, from *fera* wild beast

ferity ('fɛrɪtɪ) NOUN, *plural* **-ties.** *Rare* [1] the state of being wild or uncultivated. [2] savagery; ferocity.
▷HISTORY C16: from Latin *feritās*, from *ferus* savage, untamed

ferly ('fɛrlɪ) *Scot* ◆ ADJECTIVE [1] wonderful; strange. ◆ NOUN, *plural* **-lies.** [2] a wonder; something strange or marvellous. ◆ VERB **-lies, -lying, -lied** (*intr*) [3] to wonder; be surprised.
▷HISTORY Old English *færlic* sudden

Fermanagh (fə'mænə) NOUN a district and historical county of SW Northern Ireland: contains the Upper and Lower Lough Erne. Pop.: 57 527 (2001). Area (excluding water): 1700 sq. km (656 sq. miles).

fermata (fə'mɑːtə) NOUN, *plural* **-tas** *or* **-te** (-tɪ). *Music* another word for **pause** (sense 5).
▷HISTORY from Italian, from *fermare* to stop, from Latin *firmāre* to establish; see FIRM[1]

Fermat's last theorem (fɜː'mæts) NOUN (in number theory) the assertion that the equation $x^n + y^n = z^n$ has no integral solutions for n greater than two. It was proved in 1993 by the British mathematician Andrew Wiles.
▷HISTORY named after Pierre de *Fermat* (1601–65), French mathematician

Fermat's principle NOUN *Physics* the principle that a ray of light passes from one point to another in such a way that the time taken is a minimum.

ferment NOUN ('fɜːmɛnt) [1] any agent or substance, such as a bacterium, mould, yeast, or enzyme, that causes fermentation. [2] another word for **fermentation.** [3] commotion; unrest. ◆ VERB (fə'mɛnt) [4] to undergo or cause to undergo fermentation. [5] to stir up or seethe with excitement.
▷HISTORY C15: from Latin *fermentum* yeast, from *fervēre* to seethe
▸**fer'mentable** ADJECTIVE ▸**ferˌmenta'bility** NOUN
▸**fer'menter** NOUN

Language note See at **foment.**

fermentation (ˌfɜːmɛn'teɪʃən) NOUN a chemical reaction in which a ferment causes an organic molecule to split into simpler substances, esp the anaerobic conversion of sugar to ethyl alcohol by yeast. Also called: **ferment.** Related adjective: **zymotic.**
▸**fer'mentative** ADJECTIVE ▸**fer'mentatively** ADVERB
▸**fer'mentativeness** NOUN

fermentation lock NOUN a valve placed on the top of bottles of fermenting wine to allow bubbles to escape.

fermi ('fɜːmɪ) NOUN a unit of length used in nuclear physics equal to 10^{-15} metre.

Fermi-Dirac statistics NOUN *Physics* the branch of quantum statistics used to calculate the permitted energy arrangements of the particles in a system in terms of the exclusion principle. Compare **Bose-Einstein statistics.**
▷HISTORY C20: named after Enrico *Fermi* (1901–54), Italian nuclear physicist and Paul *Dirac* (1902–84), English physicist

Fermi energy *or* **level** NOUN the level in the distribution of electron energies in a solid at which a quantum state is equally likely to be occupied or empty.
▷HISTORY C20: named after Enrico *Fermi* (1901–54), Italian nuclear physicist

fermion ('fɜːmɪˌɒn) NOUN any of a group of elementary particles, such as a nucleon, that has half-integral spin and obeys Fermi-Dirac statistics. Compare **boson.**
▷HISTORY C20: named after Enrico *Fermi* (1901–54), Italian nuclear physicist; see -ON

fermium ('fɜːmɪəm) NOUN a transuranic element artificially produced by neutron bombardment of plutonium. Symbol: Fm; atomic no.: 100; half-life of most stable isotope, ^{257}Fm: 80 days (approx.).
▷HISTORY C20: named after Enrico Fermi (1901–54), Italian nuclear physicist

fern (fɜːn) NOUN [1] any tracheophyte plant of the phylum *Filicinophyta*, having roots, stems, and fronds and reproducing by spores formed in structures (sori) on the fronds. See also **tree fern.** [2] any of certain similar but unrelated plants, such as the sweet fern.
▷HISTORY Old English *fearn*; related to Old High German *farn*, Sanskrit *parná* leaf
▸'**fernˌlike** ADJECTIVE ▸'**ferny** ADJECTIVE

Fernando de Noronha (*Portuguese* fer'nəndu di no'roɲa) NOUN a volcanic island in the S Atlantic northeast of Cape São Roque: constitutes a federal territory of Brazil; a penal colony since the 18th century; inhabited by military personnel. Area: 26 sq. km (10 sq. miles).

Fernando Po (fə'nændəʊ pəʊ) NOUN a former name (until 1973) of **Bioko.**

fernbird ('fɜːnˌbɜːd) NOUN a small brown and white New Zealand swamp bird, *Bowdleria punctata*, with a fernlike tail.

fernery ('fɜːnərɪ) NOUN, *plural* **-eries.** [1] a place where ferns are grown. [2] a collection of ferns grown in such a place.

fern seed NOUN the minute particles by which ferns reproduce themselves, formerly thought to be invisible. Possession of them was thought to make a person invisible.

ferocious (fə'rəʊʃəs) ADJECTIVE savagely fierce or cruel: *a ferocious tiger; a ferocious argument.*
▷HISTORY C17: from Latin *ferox* fierce, untamable, warlike
▸**fe'rociously** ADVERB ▸**ferocity** (fə'rɒsɪtɪ) *or* **fe'rociousness** NOUN

-ferous ADJECTIVE COMBINING FORM bearing or producing: *coniferous; crystalliferous.* Compare **-gerous.**
▷HISTORY from -FER + -OUS

Ferrara (fə'rɑːrə; *Italian* fer'rara) NOUN a city in N Italy, in Emilia-Romagna: a centre of the Renaissance under the House of Este; university (1391). Pop.: 132 127 (2000 est.).

ferrate ('fɛreɪt) NOUN a salt containing the divalent ion, FeO_4^{2-}. Ferrates are derivatives of the hypothetical acid H_2FeO_4.
▷HISTORY C19: from Latin *ferrum* iron

ferredoxin (ˌfɛrɪ'dɒksɪn) NOUN an iron- and sulphur-containing protein found in plants and microorganisms and involved in photosynthesis and nitrogen fixation.

ferreous ('fɛrɪəs) ADJECTIVE containing or resembling iron: *a ferreous alloy; a ferreous substance.*
▷HISTORY C17: from Latin *ferreus* made of iron, from *ferrum* iron

ferret[1] ('fɛrɪt) NOUN [1] a domesticated albino variety of the polecat *Mustela putorius*, bred for hunting rats, rabbits, etc. [2] **black-footed ferret.** a musteline mammal, *Mustela nigripes*, of W North America, closely related to the weasels. ◆ VERB **-rets, -reting, -reted.** [3] to hunt (rabbits, rats, etc.) with ferrets. [4] (*tr*; usually foll by *out*) to drive from hiding: *to ferret out snipers.* [5] (*tr*; usually foll by *out*)

to find by persistent investigation. 6 (*intr*) to search around.
▷HISTORY C14: from Old French *furet*, from Latin *fur* thief
▸ˈferreter NOUN ▸ˈferrety ADJECTIVE

ferret[2] (ˈfɛrɪt) *or* **ferreting** NOUN silk binding tape.
▷HISTORY C16: from Italian *fioretti* floss silk, plural of *fioretto*: a little flower, from *fiore* flower, from Latin *flōs*

ferret badger NOUN any small badger of the genus *Melogale*, of SE Asia, resembling a ferret in appearance and smell.

ferri- COMBINING FORM indicating the presence of iron, esp in the trivalent state: *ferricyanide*; *ferriferous*. Compare **ferro-**.
▷HISTORY from Latin *ferrum* iron

ferriage (ˈfɛrɪɪdʒ) NOUN 1 transportation by ferry. 2 the fee charged for passage on a ferry.

ferric (ˈfɛrɪk) ADJECTIVE of or containing iron in the trivalent state: *ferric oxide*; designating an iron(III) compound.
▷HISTORY C18: from Latin *ferrum* iron

ferric oxide NOUN a red crystalline insoluble oxide of iron that occurs as haematite and rust and is made by heating ferrous sulphate: used as a pigment and metal polish (**jeweller's rouge**), and as a sensitive coating on magnetic tape. Formula: Fe_2O_3. Systematic name: **iron(III) oxide.**

ferricyanic acid (ˌfɛrɪsaɪˈænɪk) NOUN a brown soluble unstable solid tribasic acid, usually known in the form of ferricyanide salts. Formula: $H_3Fe(CN)_6$.

ferricyanide (ˌfɛrɪˈsaɪəˌnaɪd) NOUN any salt of ferricyanic acid.

ferriferous (fɛˈrɪfərəs) ADJECTIVE producing or yielding iron; iron-bearing: *a ferriferous rock*.

ferrimagnetism (ˌfɛrɪˈmæɡnɪˌtɪzəm) NOUN a phenomenon exhibited by certain substances, such as ferrites, in which the magnetic moments of neighbouring ions are antiparallel and unequal in magnitude. The substances behave like ferromagnetic materials. See also **antiferromagnetism.**
▸**ferrimagnetic** (ˌfɛrɪmæɡˈnɛtɪk) ADJECTIVE

Ferris wheel (ˈfɛrɪs) NOUN a fairground wheel having seats freely suspended from its rim; the seats remain horizontal throughout its rotation.
▷HISTORY C19: named after G.W.G. *Ferris* (1859–96), American engineer

ferrite (ˈfɛraɪt) NOUN 1 any of a group of ferromagnetic highly resistive ceramic compounds with the formula MFe_2O_4, where M is usually a metal such as cobalt or zinc. 2 any of the body-centred cubic allotropes of iron, such as alpha iron, occurring in steel, cast iron, etc. 3 any of various microscopic grains, probably composed of iron compounds, in certain igneous rocks.
▷HISTORY C19: from FERRI- + -ITE[1]

ferrite-rod aerial NOUN a type of aerial, normally used in radio reception, consisting of a small coil of wire mounted on a ferrite core, the coil serving as a tuning inductance.

ferritin (ˈfɛrɪtɪn) NOUN *Biochem* a protein that contains iron and plays a part in the storage of iron in the body. It occurs in the liver and spleen.
▷HISTORY C20: from FERRITE + -IN

ferro- COMBINING FORM 1 indicating a property of iron or the presence of iron: *ferromagnetism*; *ferromanganese*. 2 indicating the presence of iron in the divalent state: *ferrocyanide*. Compare **ferri-**.
▷HISTORY from Latin *ferrum* iron

ferrocene (ˈfɛrəʊˌsiːn) NOUN a reddish-orange insoluble crystalline compound. Its molecules have an iron atom sandwiched between two cyclopentadiene rings. Formula: $Fe(C_5H_5)_2$.
▷HISTORY C20: from FERRO- + C(YCLOPENTADI)ENE

ferrochromium (ˌfɛrəʊˈkrəʊmɪəm) *or* **ferrochrome** NOUN an alloy of iron and chromium (60–72 per cent), used in the production of very hard steel.

ferroconcrete (ˌfɛrəʊˈkɒŋkriːt) NOUN another name for **reinforced concrete.**

ferrocyanic acid (ˌfɛrəʊsaɪˈænɪk) NOUN a white volatile unstable solid tetrabasic acid, usually known in the form of ferrocyanide salts. Formula: $H_4Fe(CN)_6$.

ferrocyanide (ˌfɛrəʊˈsaɪəˌnaɪd) NOUN any salt of ferrocyanic acid, such as potassium ferrocyanide, $K_4Fe(CN)_6$.

ferroelectric (ˌfɛrəʊɪˈlɛktrɪk) ADJECTIVE 1 (of a substance) exhibiting spontaneous polarization that can be reversed by the application of a suitable electric field. 2 of or relating to ferroelectric substances. ◆ NOUN 3 a ferroelectric substance.
▸ˌferroeˈlectrically ADVERB ▸**ferroelectricity** (ˌfɛrəʊɪlɛkˈtrɪsɪtɪ, -ˌiːlɛk-) NOUN

Ferrol (*Spanish* fɛˈrrɔl) NOUN See **El Ferrol.**

ferromagnesian (ˌfɛrəʊmæɡˈniːʒən) ADJECTIVE (of minerals such as biotite) containing a high proportion of iron and magnesium.

ferromagnetism (ˌfɛrəʊˈmæɡnɪˌtɪzəm) NOUN the phenomenon exhibited by substances, such as iron, that have relative permeabilities much greater than unity and increasing magnetization with applied magnetizing field. Certain of these substances retain their magnetization in the absence of the applied field. The effect is caused by the alignment of electron spin in regions called domains. Compare **diamagnetism, paramagnetism.** See also **magnet, Curie-Weiss law.**
▸**ferromagnetic** (ˌfɛrəʊmæɡˈnɛtɪk) ADJECTIVE

ferromanganese (ˌfɛrəʊˈmæŋɡəˌniːz) NOUN an alloy of iron and manganese, used in making additions of manganese to cast iron and steel.

ferromolybdenum (ˌfɛrəʊmɒˈlɪbdɪnəm) NOUN an alloy of iron and molybdenum used in making alloy steels.

ferronickel (ˌfɛrəʊˈnɪkəl) NOUN an alloy of iron and nickel used in making nickel steels.

ferrosilicon (ˌfɛrəʊˈsɪlɪkən) NOUN an alloy of iron and silicon, used in making cast iron and steel.

ferrotype (ˈfɛrəʊˌtaɪp) NOUN 1 a photographic print produced directly in a camera by exposing a sheet of iron or tin coated with a sensitized enamel. 2 the process by which such a print is produced. ◆ Also called: **tintype.**

ferrous (ˈfɛrəs) ADJECTIVE of or containing iron in the divalent state; designating an iron(II) compound.
▷HISTORY C19: from FERRI- + -OUS

ferrous sulphate NOUN an iron salt with a saline taste, usually obtained as greenish crystals of the heptahydrate, which are converted to the white monohydrate above 100°C: used in inks, tanning, water purification, and in the treatment of anaemia. Formula: $FeSO_4$. Systematic name: **iron(II) sulphate.** Also called: **copperas, green vitriol.**

ferruginous (fɛˈruːdʒɪnəs) ADJECTIVE 1 (of minerals, rocks, etc.) containing iron: *a ferruginous clay*. 2 rust-coloured.
▷HISTORY C17: from Latin *ferrūgineus* of a rusty colour, from *ferrūgō* iron rust, from *ferrum* iron

ferruginous duck NOUN a common European duck, *Aythyra nyroca*, having reddish-brown plumage with white wing bars.

ferrule *or* **ferule** (ˈfɛruːl, -rəl) NOUN 1 a metal ring, tube, or cap placed over the end of a stick, handle, or post for added strength or stability or to increase wear. 2 a side opening in a pipe that gives access for inspection or cleaning. 3 a bush, gland, small length of tube, etc., esp one used for making a joint. ◆ VERB 4 (*tr*) to equip (a stick, etc.) with a ferrule.
▷HISTORY C17: from Middle English *virole*, from Old French *virol*, from Latin *viriola* a little bracelet, from *viria* bracelet; influenced by Latin *ferrum* iron

ferry (ˈfɛrɪ) NOUN, *plural* **-ries.** 1 Also called: **ferryboat.** a vessel for transporting passengers and usually vehicles across a body of water, esp as a regular service. 2 **a** such a service. **b** (*in combination*): *a ferryman*. 3 a legal right to charge for transporting passengers by boat. 4 the act or method of delivering aircraft by flying them to their destination. ◆ VERB **-ries, -rying, -ried.** 5 to transport or go by ferry. 6 to deliver (an aircraft) by flying it to its destination. 7 (*tr*) to convey (passengers, goods, etc.): *the guests were ferried to the church in taxis*.
▷HISTORY Old English *ferian* to carry, bring; related to Old Norse *ferja* to transport, Gothic *farjan*; see FARE

fertile (ˈfɜːtaɪl) ADJECTIVE 1 capable of producing offspring. 2 **a** (of land) having nutrients capable of sustaining an abundant growth of plants. **b** (of farm animals) capable of breeding stock. 3 *Biology* **a** capable of undergoing growth and development: *fertile seeds*; *fertile eggs*. **b** (of plants) capable of producing gametes, spores, seeds, or fruits. 4 producing many offspring; prolific. 5 highly productive; rich; abundant: *a fertile brain*. 6 *Physics* (of a substance) able to be transformed into fissile or fissionable material, esp in a nuclear reactor. 7 conducive to productiveness: *fertile rain*.
▷HISTORY C15: from Latin *fertilis*, from *ferre* to bear
▸ˈfertilely ADVERB ▸ˈfertileness NOUN

Fertile Crescent NOUN an area of fertile land in the Middle East, extending around the Rivers Tigris and Euphrates in a semicircle from Israel to the Persian Gulf, where the Sumerian, Babylonian, Assyrian, Phoenician, and Hebrew civilizations flourished.

fertility (fɜːˈtɪlɪtɪ) NOUN 1 the ability to produce offspring, esp abundantly. 2 the state or quality of being fertile.

fertility cult NOUN the practice in some settled agricultural communities of performing religious or magical rites to ensure good weather and crops and the perpetuity of the tribe.

fertility symbol NOUN an object, esp a phallic symbol, used in fertility-cult ceremonies to symbolize regeneration.

fertilization *or* **fertilisation** (ˌfɜːtɪlaɪˈzeɪʃən) NOUN 1 the union of male and female gametes, during sexual reproduction, to form a zygote. 2 the act or process of fertilizing. 3 the state of being fertilized.

fertilize *or* **fertilise** (ˈfɜːtɪˌlaɪz) VERB (*tr*) 1 to provide (an animal, plant, or egg cell) with sperm or pollen to bring about fertilization. 2 to supply (soil or water) with mineral and organic nutrients to aid the growth of plants. 3 to make fertile or productive.
▸ˈfertiˌlizable *or* ˈfertiˌlisable ADJECTIVE

fertilizer *or* **fertiliser** (ˈfɜːtɪˌlaɪzə) NOUN 1 any substance, such as manure or a mixture of nitrates, added to soil or water to increase its productivity. 2 an object or organism such as an insect that fertilizes an animal or plant.

ferula (ˈfɛrʊlə, ˈfɛrjʊ-) NOUN, *plural* **-las** *or* **-lae** (-ˌliː). 1 any large umbelliferous plant of the Mediterranean genus *Ferula*, having thick stems and dissected leaves: cultivated as the source of several strongly scented gum resins, such as galbanum. 2 a rare word for **ferule**[1].
▷HISTORY C14: from Latin: giant fennel
▸**ferulaceous** (ˌfɛrʊˈleɪʃəs, ˌfɛrjʊ-) ADJECTIVE

ferule[1] (ˈfɛruːl, -rəl) NOUN 1 a flat piece of wood, such as a ruler, used in some schools to cane children on the hand. ◆ VERB 2 (*tr*) *Rare* to punish with a ferule.
▷HISTORY C16: from Latin *ferula* giant fennel, whip, rod; the stalk of the plant was used for punishment

ferule[2] (ˈfɛruːl, -rəl) NOUN a variant spelling of **ferrule.**

fervency (ˈfɜːvənsɪ) NOUN, *plural* **-cies.** another word for **fervour.**

fervent (ˈfɜːvənt) *or* **fervid** (ˈfɜːvɪd) ADJECTIVE 1 intensely passionate; ardent: *a fervent desire to change society*. 2 *Archaic or poetic* boiling, burning, or glowing: *fervent heat*.
▷HISTORY C14: from Latin *fervēre* to boil, glow
▸ˈfervently *or* ˈfervidly ADVERB ▸ˈferventness *or* ˈfervidness NOUN

Fervidor *French* (fɛrvidɔr) NOUN another name for **Thermidor.**
▷HISTORY probably from *ferveur* heat + THERMIDOR

fervour *or US* **fervor** (ˈfɜːvə) NOUN 1 great intensity of feeling or belief; ardour; zeal. 2 *Rare* intense heat.
▷HISTORY C14: from Latin *fervor* heat, from *fervēre* to glow, boil

Fès (fɛs) *or* **Fez** NOUN a city in N central Morocco, traditional capital of the north: became an independent kingdom in the 11th century, at its height in the 14th century; religious centre; university (850). Pop.: 263 828 (1994).

Fescennine (ˈfɛsɪˌnaɪn) ADJECTIVE *Rare* scurrilous or obscene.
▷HISTORY C17: from Latin *Fescennīnus* of *Fescennia*, a city in Etruria noted for the production of mocking or obscene verse

fescue ('fɛskjuː) *or* **fescue grass** NOUN any grass of the genus *Festuca*: widely cultivated as pasture and lawn grasses, having stiff narrow leaves. See also **meadow fescue, sheep's fescue.**
▷HISTORY C14: from Old French *festu*, ultimately from Latin *festūca* stem, straw

fess (fɛs) VERB (*intr;* foll by *up*) *Informal, chiefly US* to make a confession.
▷HISTORY C19: shortened from CONFESS

fesse *or* **fess** (fɛs) NOUN *Heraldry* an ordinary consisting of a horizontal band across a shield, conventionally occupying a third of its length and being wider than a bar.
▷HISTORY C15: from Anglo-French *fesse*, from Latin *fascia* band, fillet

fesse point NOUN *Heraldry* the midpoint of a shield.

fest (fɛst) NOUN **a** a meeting or event at which the emphasis is on a particular activity: *a fashion fest.* **b** (*in combination*): *schmaltz-fest; lovefest.*
▷HISTORY C19: from German *Fest* festival

festal ('fɛstᵊl) ADJECTIVE another word for **festive.**
▷HISTORY C15: from Latin *festum* holiday, banquet; see FEAST
▶ **'festally** ADVERB

fester ('fɛstə) VERB [1] to form or cause to form pus. [2] (*intr*) to become rotten; decay. [3] to become or cause to become bitter, irritated, etc., esp over a long period of time; rankle: *resentment festered his imagination.* [4] (*intr*) *Informal* to be idle or inactive. ◆ NOUN [5] a small ulcer or sore containing pus.
▷HISTORY C13: from Old French *festre* suppurating sore, from Latin: FISTULA

festina lente *Latin* (fɛs'tiːnə 'lɛntɪ) hasten slowly.

festination (ˌfɛstɪ'neɪʃən) NOUN an involuntary quickening of gait, as in some persons with Parkinson's disease.
▷HISTORY C16: from Latin *festīnātiō*, from *festīnāre* to hasten

festival ('fɛstɪvᵊl) NOUN [1] a day or period set aside for celebration or feasting, esp one of religious significance. [2] any occasion for celebration, esp one which commemorates an anniversary or other significant event. [3] an organized series of special events and performances, usually in one place: *a festival of drama.* [4] *Archaic* a time of revelry; merrymaking. [5] (*modifier*) relating to or characteristic of a festival.
▷HISTORY C14: from Church Latin *fēstīvālis* of a feast, from Latin *festīvus* FESTIVE

Festival Hall NOUN a concert hall in London, on the South Bank of the Thames: constructed for the 1951 Festival of Britain; completed 1964–65. Official name: **Royal Festival Hall.**

festive ('fɛstɪv) ADJECTIVE appropriate to or characteristic of a holiday, etc.; merry.
▷HISTORY C17: from Latin *festīvus* joyful, from *festus* of a FEAST
▶ **'festively** ADVERB ▶ **'festiveness** NOUN

festivity (fɛs'tɪvɪtɪ) NOUN, *plural* **-ties.** [1] merriment characteristic of a festival, party, etc. [2] any festival or other celebration. [3] (*plural*) festive proceedings; celebrations.

festoon (fɛ'stuːn) NOUN [1] a decorative chain of flowers, ribbons, etc., suspended in loops; garland. [2] a carved or painted representation of this, as in architecture, furniture, or pottery. [3] **a** the scalloped appearance of the gums where they meet the teeth. **b** a design carved on the base material of a denture to simulate this. [4] **a** either of two *Zerynthia* species of white pierid butterfly of southern Europe, typically mottled red, yellow, and brown. **b** an ochreous brown moth, *Apoda avellana* the unusual sluglike larvae of which feed on oak leaves. ◆ VERB (*tr*) [5] to decorate or join together with festoons. [6] to form into festoons.
▷HISTORY C17: from French *feston*, from Italian *festone* ornament for a feast, from *festa* FEAST

festoon blind NOUN a window blind consisting of vertical rows of horizontally gathered fabric that may be drawn up to form a series of ruches.

festoonery (fɛ'stuːnərɪ) NOUN an arrangement of festoons.

festschrift ('fɛstˌʃrɪft) NOUN, *plural* **-schriften** (-ˌʃrɪftən) *or* **-schrifts.** a collection of essays or learned papers contributed by a number of people to honour an eminent scholar, esp a colleague.
▷HISTORY German, from *Fest* celebration, FEAST + *Schrift* writing

festy ('fɛstɪ) ADJECTIVE *Austral slang* [1] dirty; malodorous. [2] very bad.
▷HISTORY C20: shortened form of *festering*

FET ABBREVIATION FOR **field-effect transistor.**

feta ('fɛtə) NOUN a white sheep or goat cheese popular in Greece.
▷HISTORY Modern Greek, from the phrase *turi pheta*, from *turi* cheese + *pheta*, from Italian *fetta* a slice

fetal *or* **foetal** ('fiːtᵊl) ADJECTIVE of, relating to, or resembling a fetus.

fetal alcohol syndrome NOUN a condition in newborn babies caused by excessive intake of alcohol by the mother during pregnancy: characterized by various defects including mental retardation.

fetal diagnosis NOUN prenatal determination of genetic or chemical abnormalities in a fetus, esp by amniocentesis.

fetal position NOUN a bodily position similar to that of a fetus in the womb, with the knees up towards the chest and the head bent forward.

fetation *or* **foetation** (fiː'teɪʃən) NOUN [1] the state of pregnancy. [2] the process of development of a fetus.

fetch¹ (fɛtʃ) VERB (*mainly tr*) [1] to go after and bring back; get: *to fetch help.* [2] to cause to come; bring or draw forth: *the noise fetched him from the cellar.* [3] (*also intr*) to cost or sell for (a certain price): *the table fetched six hundred pounds.* [4] to utter (a sigh, groan, etc.). [5] *Informal* to deal (a blow, slap, etc.). [6] (*also intr*) *Nautical* to arrive at or proceed by sailing. [7] *Informal* to attract: *to be fetched by an idea.* [8] (used esp as a command to dogs) to retrieve (shot game, an object thrown, etc.). [9] *Rare* to draw in (a breath, gasp, etc.), esp with difficulty. [10] **fetch and carry.** to perform menial tasks or run errands. ◆ NOUN [11] the reach, stretch, etc., of a mechanism. [12] a trick or stratagem. [13] the distance in the direction of the prevailing wind that air or water can travel continuously without obstruction.
▷HISTORY Old English *feccan;* related to Old Norse *feta* to step, Old High German *sih fazzōn* to climb
▶ **'fetcher** NOUN

fetch² (fɛtʃ) NOUN the ghost or apparition of a living person.
▷HISTORY C18: of unknown origin

fetching ('fɛtʃɪŋ) ADJECTIVE *Informal* [1] attractively befitting: *a fetching hat.* [2] charming: *a fetching personality.*
▶ **'fetchingly** ADVERB

fetch up VERB (*adverb*) [1] (*intr;* usually foll by *at* or *in*) *Informal* to arrive (at) or end up (in): *to fetch up in New York.* [2] (*intr*) *Nautical* to stop suddenly, as from running aground: *to fetch up on a rock.* [3] *Slang* to vomit (food, etc.). [4] (*tr*) *Brit dialect* to rear (children, animals, etc.).

fête *or* **fete** (feɪt) NOUN [1] a gala, bazaar, or similar entertainment, esp one held outdoors in aid of charity. [2] a feast day or holiday, esp one of religious significance. [3] *Caribbean informal* an organized group entertainment, esp a party or a dance. ◆ VERB [4] (*tr*) to honour or entertain with or as if with a fête: *the author was fêted by his publishers.* [5] (*intr*) *Caribbean informal* to join in a fête.
▷HISTORY C18: from French: FEAST

fête champêtre *French* (fɛt ʃɑ̃pɛtrə) NOUN, *plural* ***fêtes champêtres*** (fɛt ʃɑ̃pɛtrə). [1] a garden party, picnic, or similar outdoor entertainment. [2] Also called: **fête galante** (fɛt galɑ̃t). *Arts* **a** a genre of painting popular in France from the early 18th century, characterized by the depiction of figures in pastoral settings. Watteau was its most famous exponent. **b** a painting in this genre.
▷HISTORY C18: from French, literally: country festival

fetial ('fiːʃəl) NOUN, *plural* **fetiales** (ˌfiːʃɪ'eɪliːz). [1] (in ancient Rome) any of the 20 priestly heralds involved in declarations of war and in peace negotiations. ◆ ADJECTIVE [2] of or relating to the fetiales. [3] a less common word for **heraldic.**
▷HISTORY C16: from Latin *fētiālis*, probably from Old Latin *fētis* treaty

feticide *or* **foeticide** ('fiːtɪˌsaɪd) NOUN the destruction of a fetus in the uterus; aborticide.
▶ **ˌfeti'cidal** *or* **ˌfoeti'cidal** ADJECTIVE

fetid *or* **foetid** ('fɛtɪd, 'fiː-) ADJECTIVE having a stale nauseating smell, as of decay.
▷HISTORY C16: from Latin *fētidus*, from *fētēre* to stink; related to *fūmus* smoke
▶ **'fetidly** *or* **'foetidly** ADVERB ▶ **'fetidness** *or* **'foetidness** NOUN

fetiparous *or* **foetiparous** (fɪ'tɪpərəs) ADJECTIVE (of marsupials, such as the kangaroo) giving birth to incompletely developed offspring.
▷HISTORY C19: from FETUS + -PAROUS

fetish *or* **fetich** ('fɛtɪʃ, 'fiːtɪʃ) NOUN [1] something, esp an inanimate object, that is believed in certain cultures to be the embodiment or habitation of a spirit or magical powers. [2] **a** a form of behaviour involving fetishism. **b** any object that is involved in fetishism. [3] any object, activity, etc., to which one is excessively or irrationally devoted: *to make a fetish of cleanliness.*
▷HISTORY C17: from French *fétiche*, from Portuguese *feitiço* (n) sorcery, from adjective: artificial, from Latin *factīcius* made by art, FACTITIOUS
▶ **'fetish-ˌlike** *or* **'fetich-ˌlike** ADJECTIVE

fetishism *or* **fetichism** ('fɛtɪˌʃɪzəm, 'fiː-) NOUN [1] a condition in which the handling of an inanimate object or a specific part of the body other than the sexual organs is a source of sexual satisfaction. [2] belief in or recourse to a fetish for magical purposes. [3] excessive attention or attachment to something.
▶ **'fetishist** *or* **'fetichist** NOUN ▶ **ˌfetish'istic** *or* **ˌfetich'istic** ADJECTIVE

fetishize *or* **fetishise** ('fɛtɪʃˌaɪz) VERB (*tr*) to be excessively or irrationally devoted to (an object, activity, etc.).
▶ **ˌfetishi'zation** *or* **ˌfetishi'sation** NOUN

fetlock ('fɛtˌlɒk) *or* **fetterlock** NOUN [1] a projection behind and above a horse's hoof: the part of the leg between the cannon bone and the pastern. [2] Also called: **fetlock joint.** the joint at this part of the leg. [3] the tuft of hair growing from this part.
▷HISTORY C14 *fetlak;* related to Middle High German *vizzeloch* fetlock, from *vizzel* pastern + *-och;* see FOOT

fetor *or* **foetor** ('fiːtə, -tɔː) NOUN an offensive stale or putrid odour; stench.
▷HISTORY C15: from Latin, from *fētēre* to stink

fetoscope ('fiːtəʊˌskəʊp) NOUN a fibreoptic instrument that can be passed through the abdomen of a pregnant woman to enable examination of the fetus and withdrawal of blood for sampling in prenatal diagnosis.
▶ **fetoscopy** (fiː'tɒskəpɪ) NOUN

fetter ('fɛtə) NOUN [1] (*often plural*) a chain or bond fastened round the ankle; shackle. [2] (*usually plural*) a check or restraint: *in fetters.* ◆ VERB (*tr*) [3] to restrict or confine. [4] to bind in fetters.
▷HISTORY Old English *fetor;* related to Old Norse *fjöturr* fetter, Old High German *fezzera*, Latin *pedica* fetter, *impedīre* to hinder
▶ **'fetterer** NOUN ▶ **'fetterless** ADJECTIVE

fetter bone NOUN another name for **pastern** (sense 2).

fetterlock ('fɛtəˌlɒk) NOUN another name for **fetlock.**

fettle ('fɛtᵊl) VERB (*tr*) [1] to remove (excess moulding material and casting irregularities) from a cast component. [2] to line or repair (the walls of a furnace). [3] *Brit dialect* **a** to prepare or arrange (a thing, oneself, etc.), esp to put a finishing touch to. **b** to repair or mend (something). ◆ NOUN [4] state of health, spirits, etc. (esp in the phrase **in fine fettle**). [5] another name for **fettling.**
▷HISTORY C14 (in the sense: to put in order): back formation from *fetled* girded up, from Old English *fetel* belt

fettler ('fɛtlə) NOUN *Brit, Austral* a person employed to maintain railway tracks.

fettling ('fɛtlɪŋ) NOUN a refractory material used to line the hearth of puddling furnaces. Also called: **fettle.**

fettucine, fettuccine, *or* **fettucini** (ˌfɛtuː'tʃiːnɪ) NOUN a type of pasta in the form of narrow ribbons.
▷HISTORY Italian *fettuccine*, plural of *fettuccina*, diminutive of *fetta* slice

fetus *or* **foetus** ('fi:təs) NOUN, *plural* **-tuses.** the embryo of a mammal in the later stages of development, when it shows all the main recognizable features of the mature animal, esp a human embryo from the end of the second month of pregnancy until birth. Compare **embryo** (sense 2).
▷HISTORY C14: from Latin: offspring, brood

feu (fju:) NOUN [1] *Scot legal history* **a** a feudal tenure of land for which rent was paid in money or grain instead of by the performance of military service. **b** the land so held. [2] *Scots Law* a right to the use of land in return for a fixed annual payment (**feu duty**).
▷HISTORY C15: from Old French; see FEE

feuar ('fjʊə) NOUN *Scot* the tenant of a feu.

feud[1] (fju:d) NOUN [1] long and bitter hostility between two families, clans, or individuals; vendetta. [2] a quarrel or dispute. ◆ VERB [3] (*intr*) to take part in or carry on a feud.
▷HISTORY C13 *fede*, from Old French *feide*, from Old High German *fēhida*; related to Old English *fæhth* hostility; see FOE

feud[2] *or* **feod** (fju:d) NOUN *Feudal law* land held in return for service.
▷HISTORY C17: from Medieval Latin *feodum*, of Germanic origin; see FEE

feudal[1] ('fju:dᵊl) ADJECTIVE [1] of, resembling, relating to, or characteristic of feudalism or its institutions. [2] of, characteristic of, or relating to a fief. Compare **allodial.** [3] *Disparaging* old-fashioned, reactionary, etc.
▷HISTORY C17: from Medieval Latin *feudālis*, from *feudum* FEUD[2]

feudal[2] ('fju:dᵊl) ADJECTIVE of or relating to a feud or quarrel.

feudalism ('fju:dəˌlɪzəm) NOUN [1] Also called: **feudal system.** the legal and social system that evolved in W Europe in the 8th and 9th centuries, in which vassals were protected and maintained by their lords, usually through the granting of fiefs, and were required to serve under them in war. See also **vassalage, fief.** [2] any social system or society, such as medieval Japan or Ptolemaic Egypt, that resembles medieval European feudalism.
▸ **'feudalist** NOUN ▸ **ˌfeudal'istic** ADJECTIVE

feudality (fju:'dælɪtɪ) NOUN, *plural* **-ties.** [1] the state or quality of being feudal. [2] a fief or fee.

feudalize *or* **feudalise** ('fju:dəˌlaɪz) VERB (*tr*) to make feudal; create feudal institutions in (a society).
▸ **ˌfeudali'zation** *or* **ˌfeudali'sation** NOUN

feudatory ('fju:dətərɪ, -trɪ) (in feudal Europe) NOUN [1] a person holding a fief; vassal. ◆ ADJECTIVE [2] relating to or characteristic of the relationship between lord and vassal. [3] (esp of a kingdom) under the overlordship of another sovereign.
▷HISTORY C16: from Medieval Latin *feudātor*

feu de joie *French* (fø də ʒwa) NOUN, *plural* ***feux de joie*** (fø). a salute of musketry fired successively by each man in turn along a line and back.
▷HISTORY C18: literally: fire of joy

feudist ('fju:dɪst) NOUN *US* a person who takes part in a feud or quarrel.

Feuillant *French* (fœjɑ̃) NOUN *French history* a member of a club formed in 1791 by Lafayette advocating a limited constitutional monarchy: forced to disband in 1792 as the revolution became more violent and antimonarchical.
▷HISTORY from the convent of Notre Dame des *Feuillants*, where meetings were held

feuilleton ('fɜɪˌtɒn; *French* fœjtɔ̃) NOUN [1] the part of a European newspaper carrying reviews, serialized fiction, etc. [2] such a review or article.
▷HISTORY C19: from French, from *feuillet* sheet of paper, diminutive of *feuille* leaf, from Latin *folium*
▸ **'feuilletonism** NOUN ▸ **'feuilletonist** NOUN
▸ **ˌfeuilleton'istic** ADJECTIVE

fever ('fi:və) NOUN [1] an abnormally high body temperature, accompanied by a fast pulse rate, dry skin, etc. Related adjectives: **febrile, pyretic.** [2] any of various diseases, such as yellow fever or scarlet fever, characterized by a high temperature. [3] intense nervous excitement or agitation: *she was in a fever about her party.* ◆ VERB [4] (*tr*) to affect with or as if with fever.
▷HISTORY Old English *fēfor*, from Latin *febris*
▸ **'fevered** ADJECTIVE ▸ **'feverless** ADJECTIVE

fever blister *or* **sore** NOUN another name for **cold sore.**

feverfew ('fi:vəˌfju:) NOUN a bushy European strong-scented perennial plant, *Tanacetum parthenium*, with white flower heads, formerly used medicinally: family *Asteraceae* (composites).
▷HISTORY Old English *feferfuge*, from Late Latin *febrifugia*, from Latin *febris* fever + *fugāre* to put to flight

feverish ('fi:vərɪʃ) *or* **feverous** ADJECTIVE [1] suffering from fever, esp a slight fever. [2] in a state of restless excitement. [3] of, relating to, caused by, or causing fever.
▸ **'feverishly** *or* **'feverously** ADVERB ▸ **'feverishness** NOUN

fever pitch NOUN a state of intense excitement: *things were at fever pitch with the election coming up.*

fever therapy NOUN a former method of treating disease by raising the body temperature. Compare **cryotherapy.**

fever tree NOUN *US* [1] any of several trees that produce a febrifuge or tonic, esp *Pinckneya pubens*, a rubiaceous tree of SE North America. [2] a tall leguminous swamp tree, *Acacia xanthophloea*, of southern Africa, with fragrant yellow flowers.

feverwort ('fi:vəˌwɜ:t) NOUN *US* any of several plants considered to have medicinal properties, such as horse gentian and boneset.

few (fju:) DETERMINER [1] **a** a small number of; hardly any: *few men are so cruel.* **b** (*as pronoun; functioning as plural*): *many are called but few are chosen.* [2] (preceded by *a*) **a** a small number of: *a few drinks.* **b** (*as pronoun; functioning as plural*): *a few of you.* [3] **a good few.** *Informal* several. [4] **a** at great intervals; widely spaced. **b** not abundant; scarce. [5] **have a few** (**too many**). to consume several (*or* too many) alcoholic drinks. [6] **not** *or* **quite a few.** *Informal* several. ◆ NOUN [7] **the few.** a small number of people considered as a class: *the few who fell at Thermopylae.* Compare **many** (sense 4).
▷HISTORY Old English *fēawa*; related to Old High German *fao* little, Old Norse *fār* little, silent
▸ **'fewness** NOUN

Language note See at **less.**

fey (feɪ) ADJECTIVE [1] interested in or believing in the supernatural. [2] attuned to the supernatural; clairvoyant; visionary. [3] *Chiefly Scot* fated to die; doomed. [4] *Chiefly Scot* in a state of high spirits or unusual excitement, formerly believed to presage death.
▷HISTORY Old English *fæge* marked out for death; related to Old Norse *feigr* doomed, Old High German *feigi*
▸ **'feyness** NOUN

Feynman diagram ('faɪnmən) NOUN *Physics* a graphical representation of the interactions between elementary particles.
▷HISTORY C20: named after Richard *Feynman* (1918–88), US physicist

fez (fɛz) NOUN, *plural* **fezzes.** an originally Turkish brimless felt or wool cap, shaped like a truncated cone, usually red and with a tassel.
▷HISTORY C19: via French from Turkish, from FEZ
▸ **fezzed** ADJECTIVE

Fez (fɛz) NOUN a variant of **Fès.**

Fezzan (fɛ'zɑ:n) NOUN a region of SW Libya, in the Sahara: a former province (until 1963).

ff SYMBOL FOR: [1] Also: **ff.** folios. [2] Also: **ff.** following (pages, lines, etc.). [3] *Music* fortissimo: an instruction to play very loudly.

ffa *Commerce* ABBREVIATION FOR free from alongside (ship).

F-factor NOUN *Informal* the quality of being attractive to members of the opposite sex.
▷HISTORY C20: from *fanciability factor*

Ffestiniog (fɛs'tɪnjɒg) NOUN a town in N Wales, in Gwynedd: tourist attractions include former slate quarries and a narrow-gauge railway at nearby Blaenau Ffestiniog. Pop.: 800 (latest est.).

fi THE INTERNET DOMAIN NAME FOR Finland.

FI ABBREVIATION FOR Falkland Islands.

FIA ABBREVIATION FOR: [1] (in Britain) Fellow of the Institute of Actuaries. [2] *Motor Racing* Fédération Internationale l'Automobile, Formula One's governing body.

▷HISTORY (for sense 2) from French

fiacre (fɪ'ɑ:krə) NOUN a small four-wheeled horse-drawn carriage, usually with a folding roof.
▷HISTORY C17: named after the Hotel de St *Fiacre*, Paris, where these vehicles were first hired out

fiancé (fɪ'ɒnseɪ) NOUN a man who is engaged to be married.
▷HISTORY C19: from French, from Old French *fiancier* to promise, betroth, from *fiance* a vow, from *fier* to trust, from Latin *fīdere*

fiancée (fɪ'ɒnseɪ) NOUN a woman who is engaged to be married.

fianchetto (ˌfɪən'tʃetəʊ, -'kɛtəʊ) *Chess* ◆ NOUN, *plural* **-tos, -ti** (-ti:). [1] the development of a bishop on the second rank of the neighbouring knight's file or the third rank of the nearer rook's file. ◆ VERB **-toes, -toing, -toed.** [2] to develop (a bishop) thus.
▷HISTORY C19: from Italian diminutive of *fianco* FLANK

Fianna ('fɪənə) PLURAL NOUN a legendary band of Irish warriors noted for their heroic exploits, attributed to the 2nd and 3rd centuries A.D. Also called: **Fenians.**

Fianna Fáil ('fɪənə 'fɑ:l) NOUN one of the major Irish political parties, founded by de Valera in 1926 as a republican party.
▷HISTORY from Irish Gaelic *Fianna* warriors + *Fáil* of Ireland, from *Fál* an ancient and poetic name for Ireland

fiasco (fɪ'æskəʊ) NOUN, *plural* **-cos** *or* **-coes.** a complete failure, esp one that is ignominious or humiliating.
▷HISTORY C19: from Italian, literally: FLASK; sense development obscure

fiat ('faɪət, -æt) NOUN [1] official sanction; authoritative permission. [2] an arbitrary order or decree. [3] *Chiefly literary* any command, decision, or act of will that brings something about.
▷HISTORY C17: from Latin, literally: let it be done, from *fierī* to become

fiat money NOUN *Chiefly US* money declared by a government to be legal tender though it is not convertible into standard specie.

fib (fɪb) NOUN [1] a trivial and harmless lie. ◆ VERB **fibs, fibbing, fibbed.** [2] (*intr*) to tell such a lie.
▷HISTORY C17: perhaps from *fibble-fable* an unlikely story; see FABLE
▸ **'fibber** NOUN

fiber ('faɪbə) NOUN the usual US spelling of **fibre.**

Fibonacci sequence *or* **series** (ˌfɪbə'nɑ:tʃɪ) NOUN the infinite sequence of numbers, 0, 1, 1, 2, 3, 5, 8, etc., in which each member (**Fibonacci number**) is the sum of the previous two.
▷HISTORY named after Leonardo *Fibonacci* (?1170–?1250), Italian mathematician

fibre *or US* **fiber** ('faɪbə) NOUN [1] a natural or synthetic filament that may be spun into yarn, such as cotton or nylon. [2] cloth or other material made from such yarn. [3] a long fine continuous thread or filament. [4] the structure of any material or substance made of or as if of fibres; texture. [5] essential substance or nature: *all the fibres of his being were stirred.* [6] strength of character (esp in the phrase **moral fibre**). [7] See **dietary fibre.** [8] *Botany* **a** a narrow elongated thick-walled cell: a constituent of sclerenchyma tissue. **b** such tissue extracted from flax, hemp, etc., used to make linen, rope, etc. **c** a very small root or twig. [9] *Anatomy* any thread-shaped structure, such as a nerve fibre.
▷HISTORY C14: from Latin *fibra* filament, entrails
▸ **'fibred** *or US* **'fibered** ADJECTIVE ▸ **'fibreless** *or US* **'fiberless** ADJECTIVE

fibreboard *or US* **fiberboard** ('faɪbəˌbɔ:d) NOUN a building material made of compressed wood or other plant fibres, esp one in the form of a thin semirigid sheet.

fibrefill *or US* **fiberfill** ('faɪbəˌfɪl) NOUN a synthetic fibre used as a filling for pillows, quilted materials, etc.

fibreglass *or US* **fiberglass** ('faɪbəˌglɑ:s) NOUN [1] material consisting of matted fine glass fibres, used as insulation in buildings, in fireproof fabrics, etc. [2] a fabric woven from this material or a light strong material made by bonding fibreglass with a synthetic resin; used for car bodies, boat hulls, etc. Also called: **glass fibre.**

fibre optics NOUN (*functioning as singular*) the

transmission of information modulated on light carried down very thin flexible fibres of glass. See also **optical fibre.**
▸ ,**fibre'optic** ADJECTIVE

fibrescope *or US* **fiberscope** ('faɪbə,skəʊp) NOUN an endoscope that transmits images of the interior of a hollow organ by fibre optics.

fibriform ('faɪbrɪ,fɔ:m, 'fɪb-) ADJECTIVE having the form of a fibre or fibres.

fibril ('faɪbrɪl) *or* **fibrilla** (faɪ'brɪlə, fɪ-) NOUN, *plural* **-brils** *or* **-brillae** (-'brɪli:). 1 a small fibre or part of a fibre. 2 *Biology* a threadlike structure, such as a root hair or a thread of muscle tissue.
▹HISTORY C17: from New Latin *fibrilla* a little FIBRE
▸ '**fibrilar, fi'brillar,** *or* **fi'brillose** ADJECTIVE ▸**fi'brilli,form** ADJECTIVE

fibrillation (,faɪbrɪ'leɪʃən, ,fɪb-) NOUN 1 a local and uncontrollable twitching of muscle fibres, esp of the heart, not affecting the entire muscle. **Atrial fibrillation** results in rapid and irregular heart and pulse rate. In **ventricular fibrillation**, the heart stops beating. 2 irregular twitchings of the muscular wall of the heart, often interfering with the normal rhythmic contractions.

fibrin ('fɪbrɪn) NOUN a white insoluble elastic protein formed from fibrinogen when blood clots: forms a network that traps red cells and platelets.

fibrinogen (fɪ'brɪnədʒən) NOUN a soluble protein, a globulin, in blood plasma, converted to fibrin by the action of the enzyme thrombin when blood clots.
▸**fibrinogenic** (,faɪbrɪnəʊ'dʒɛnɪk) *or* **fibrinogenous** (,faɪbrɪ'nɒdʒənəs) ADJECTIVE

fibrinolysis (,fɪbrɪ'nɒlɪsɪs) NOUN the breakdown of fibrin in blood clots, esp by enzymes.
▸**fibrinolytic** (,faɪbrɪnəʊ'lɪtɪk) ADJECTIVE

fibrinous ('fɪbrɪnəs) ADJECTIVE of, containing, or resembling fibrin.

fibro ('faɪbrəʊ) NOUN *Austral informal* 1 **a** short for **fibrocement. b** (*as modifier*): *a fibro shack.* 2 a house built of fibrocement.

fibro- COMBINING FORM 1 indicating fibrous tissue: *fibroin; fibrosis.* 2 indicating fibre: *fibrocement.*
▹HISTORY from Latin *fibra* FIBRE

fibroblast ('faɪbrəʊ,blæst) NOUN a cell in connective tissue that synthesizes collagen.
▸ ,**fibro'blastic** ADJECTIVE

fibrocement (,faɪbrəʊsɪ'mɛnt) NOUN (formerly) cement combined with asbestos fibre, used esp in sheets for building.

fibroid ('faɪbrɔɪd) ADJECTIVE 1 *Anatomy* (of structures or tissues) containing or resembling fibres. ◆ NOUN 2 a benign tumour, composed of fibrous and muscular tissue, occurring in the wall of the uterus and often causing heavy menstruation.

fibroin ('faɪbrəʊɪn) NOUN a tough elastic protein that is the principal component of spiders' webs and raw silk.

Fibrolite ('faɪbrəlaɪt) NOUN *NZ Trademark* a type of building board containing asbestos and cement.

fibroma (faɪ'brəʊmə) NOUN, *plural* **-mata** (-mətə) *or* **-mas**. a benign tumour derived from fibrous connective tissue.
▸**fibromatous** (faɪ'brɒmətəs) ADJECTIVE

fibromyalgia (,faɪbrəʊmaɪ'ældʒɪə) NOUN a rheumatoid disorder characterized by muscle pain and headaches.

fibrosis (faɪ'brəʊsɪs) NOUN the formation of an abnormal amount of fibrous tissue in an organ or part as the result of inflammation, irritation, or healing.
▸**fibrotic** (faɪ'brɒtɪk) ADJECTIVE

fibrositis (,faɪbrə'saɪtɪs) NOUN inflammation of white fibrous tissue, esp that of muscle sheaths.

fibrous ('faɪbrəs) ADJECTIVE consisting of, containing, or resembling fibres: *fibrous tissue.*
▸ '**fibrously** ADVERB ▸ '**fibrousness** NOUN

fibrovascular (,faɪbrəʊ'væskjʊlə) ADJECTIVE *Botany* (of a vascular bundle) surrounded by sclerenchyma or within sclerenchymatous tissue.

fibula ('fɪbjʊlə) NOUN, *plural* **-lae** (-,li:) *or* **-las.** 1 the outer and thinner of the two bones between the knee and ankle of the human leg. Compare **tibia.** 2 the corresponding bone in other vertebrates. 3 a metal brooch resembling a safety pin, often highly decorated, common in Europe after 1300 B.C.
▹HISTORY C17: from Latin: clasp, probably from *fīgere* to fasten
▸ '**fibular** ADJECTIVE

-fic SUFFIX FORMING ADJECTIVES causing, making, or producing: *honorific.*
▹HISTORY from Latin *-ficus,* from *facere* to do, make

fiche (fi:ʃ) NOUN See **microfiche, ultrafiche.**

fichu ('fi:ʃu:) NOUN a woman's shawl or scarf of some light material, worn esp in the 18th century.
▹HISTORY C19: from French: small shawl, from *ficher* to fix with a pin, from Latin *fīgere* to fasten, FIX

fickle ('fɪk^{ə}l) ADJECTIVE changeable in purpose, affections, etc.; capricious.
▹HISTORY Old English *ficol* deceitful; related to *fician* to wheedle, *befician* to deceive
▸ '**fickleness** NOUN

fico ('fi:kəʊ) NOUN, *plural* **-coes.** *Archaic* 1 a worthless trifle. 2 another word for **fig**[1] (sense 7).
▹HISTORY C16: from Italian: FIG[1]

fictile ('fɪktaɪl) ADJECTIVE 1 moulded or capable of being moulded from clay; plastic. 2 made of clay by a potter. 3 relating to the craft of pottery.
▹HISTORY C17: from Latin *fictilis* that can be moulded, hence, made of clay, from *fingere* to shape

fiction ('fɪkʃən) NOUN 1 literary works invented by the imagination, such as novels or short stories. 2 an invented story or explanation; lie. 3 the act of inventing a story or explanation. 4 *Law* something assumed to be true for the sake of convenience, though probably false.
▹HISTORY C14: from Latin *fictiō* a fashioning, hence something imaginary, from *fingere* to shape
▸ '**fictional** ADJECTIVE ▸ '**fictionally** ADVERB ▸ ,**fiction'eer** *or* '**fictionist** NOUN

fictionalize *or* **fictionalise** ('fɪkʃənə,laɪz) VERB (*tr*) to make into fiction or give a fictional aspect to.
▸ ,**fictionali'zation** *or* ,**fictionali'sation** NOUN

fictitious (fɪk'tɪʃəs) ADJECTIVE 1 not genuine or authentic; assumed; false: *to give a fictitious address.* 2 of, related to, or characteristic of fiction; created by the imagination.
▸**fic'titiously** ADVERB ▸**fic'titiousness** NOUN

fictive ('fɪktɪv) ADJECTIVE 1 of, relating to, or able to create fiction. 2 a rare word for **fictitious.**
▸ '**fictively** ADVERB

ficus ('fi:kəs) NOUN any plant of the genus *Ficus,* which includes the edible fig and several greenhouse and house plants. See **rubber plant, weeping ivy.**

fid (fɪd) NOUN *Nautical* 1 a spike for separating strands of rope in splicing. 2 a wooden or metal bar for supporting the heel of a topmast.
▹HISTORY C17: of unknown origin

-fid ADJECTIVE COMBINING FORM divided into parts or lobes: *bifid; pinnatifid.*
▹HISTORY from Latin *-fidus,* from *findere* to split

Fid. Def. *or* **FID DEF** ABBREVIATION FOR Fidei Defensor.

fiddle ('fɪd^{ə}l) NOUN 1 *Informal or sometimes when used of a classical violin disparaging* any instrument of the viol or violin family, esp the violin. 2 a violin played as a folk instrument. 3 time-wasting or trifling behaviour; nonsense; triviality. 4 *Nautical* a small railing around the top of a table to prevent objects from falling off it in bad weather. 5 *Brit informal* an illegal or fraudulent transaction or arrangement. 6 *Brit informal* a manually delicate or tricky operation. 7 **at** *or* **on the fiddle.** *Informal* engaged in an illegal or fraudulent undertaking. 8 **face as long as a fiddle.** *Informal* a dismal or gloomy facial expression. 9 **fit as a fiddle.** *Informal* in very good health. 10 **play second fiddle.** *Informal* to be subordinate; play a minor part. ◆ VERB 11 to play (a tune) on the fiddle. 12 (*intr; often foll by with*) to make restless or aimless movements with the hands. 13 (when *intr,* often foll by *about* or *around*) *Informal* to spend (time) or act in a careless or inconsequential manner; waste (time). 14 (often foll by *with*) *Informal* to tamper or interfere (with). 15 *Informal* to contrive to do (something) by illicit means or deception: *he fiddled his way into a position of trust.* 16 (*tr*) *Informal* to falsify (accounts, etc.); swindle.
▹HISTORY Old English *fithele,* probably from Medieval Latin *vītula,* from Latin *vītulārī* to celebrate; compare Old High German *fidula* fiddle; see VIOLA[1]

fiddle-back NOUN 1 a chair with a fiddle-shaped back. 2 a chasuble with a fiddle-shaped front.

fiddle-de-dee, fiddlededee, *or* **fiddledeedee** (,fɪd^{ə}ldɪ'di:) INTERJECTION *Rare* an exclamation of impatience, disbelief, or disagreement.

fiddle-faddle ('fɪd^{ə}l,fæd^{ə}l) NOUN, INTERJECTION 1 trivial matter; nonsense. ◆ VERB 2 (*intr*) to fuss or waste time, esp over trivial matters.
▹HISTORY C16: reduplication of FIDDLE
▸ '**fiddle-,faddler** NOUN

fiddlehead ('fɪd^{ə}l,hɛd) *or* **fiddleneck** NOUN 1 *Nautical* an ornamental carving, in the shape of the scroll at the head end of a fiddle, fitted to the top of the stem or cutwater. 2 *US and Canadian* the edible coiled tip of a young fern frond.

fiddle pattern NOUN the style of a spoon or fork with a violin-shaped handle.

fiddler ('fɪdlə) NOUN 1 a person who plays the fiddle, esp in folk music. 2 See **fiddler crab.** 3 a person who wastes time or acts aimlessly. 4 *Informal* a cheat or petty rogue.

fiddler crab NOUN any of various burrowing crabs of the genus *Uca* of American coastal regions, the males of which have one of their anterior pincer-like claws very much enlarged.
▹HISTORY C19: referring to the rapid fiddling movement of the enlarged anterior claw of the males, used to attract females

fiddlestick ('fɪd^{ə}l,stɪk) NOUN 1 *Informal* a violin bow. 2 any meaningless or inconsequential thing; trifle. 3 **fiddlesticks!** an expression of annoyance or disagreement.

fiddlewood ('fɪd^{ə}l,wʊd) NOUN 1 any of various tropical American verbenaceous trees of the genus *Citharexylum* and related genera. 2 the hard durable wood of any of these trees.

fiddling ('fɪdlɪŋ) ADJECTIVE trifling or insignificant; petty.

fiddly ('fɪdlɪ) ADJECTIVE **-dlier, -dliest.** small and awkward to do or handle.

FIDE ABBREVIATION FOR Fédération Internationale des Echecs: International Chess Federation.

fideicommissary (,fɪdaɪ'kɒmɪsərɪ) *Civil law* ◆ NOUN, *plural* **-saries.** 1 a person who receives a fideicommissum. ◆ ADJECTIVE 2 of, relating to, or resembling a fideicommissum.

fideicommissum (,fɪdaɪkə'mɪsəm) NOUN, *plural* **-sa** (-sə). *Civil law* a gift of property, usually by will, to be held on behalf of another who cannot receive the gift directly.
▹HISTORY C18: from Late Latin: (something) bequeathed in trust, from Latin *fidēs* trust, faith + *committere* to entrust

Fidei Defensor *Latin* ('faɪdɪ,aɪ dɪ'fensɔ:) NOUN defender of the faith; a title given to Henry VIII by Pope Leo X, and appearing on Brit. coins as FID DEF or FD.

fideism ('fi:deɪ,ɪzəm) NOUN the theological doctrine that religious truth is a matter of faith and cannot be established by reason. Compare **natural theology.**
▹HISTORY C19: from Latin *fidēs* faith
▸ '**fideist** NOUN ▸ ,**fide'istic** ADJECTIVE

Fidelism (fi:'dɛlɪzəm) NOUN belief in, adherence to, or advocacy of the principles of Fidel Castro, the Cuban Communist statesman (born 1927). Also called: **Castroism.**
▸**Fi'delist** NOUN

fidelity (fɪ'dɛlɪtɪ) NOUN, *plural* **-ties.** 1 devotion to duties, obligations, etc.; faithfulness. 2 loyalty or devotion, as to a person or cause. 3 faithfulness to one's spouse, lover, etc. 4 adherence to truth; accuracy in reporting detail. 5 *Electronics* the degree to which the output of a system, such as an amplifier or radio, accurately reproduces the characteristics of the input signal. See also **high fidelity.**
▹HISTORY C15: from Latin *fidēlitās,* from *fidēlis* faithful, from *fidēs* faith, loyalty

fidge (fɪdʒ) VERB (*intr*) an obsolete word for **fidget.**
▹HISTORY C18: probably variant of dialect *fitch* to FIDGET

fidget ('fɪdʒɪt) VERB 1 (*intr*) to move about

restlessly. [2] (*intr; often foll by with*) to make restless or uneasy movements (with something); fiddle: *he fidgeted with his pen.* [3] (*tr*) to cause to fidget. [4] (*tr*) to cause to worry; make uneasy. ◆ NOUN [5] (*often plural*) a state of restlessness or unease, esp as expressed in continual motion: *he's got the fidgets.* [6] a person who fidgets.
▷HISTORY C17: from earlier *fidge*, probably from Old Norse *fikjast* to desire eagerly
▸ **'fidgetingly** ADVERB ▸ **'fidgety** ADJECTIVE

fiducial (fɪ'dju:ʃɪəl) ADJECTIVE [1] *Physics* used as a standard of reference or measurement: *a fiducial point.* [2] of or based on trust or faith. [3] *Law* a less common word for **fiduciary**.
▷HISTORY C17: from Late Latin *fīdūciālis* , from Latin *fīdūcia* confidence, reliance, from *fīdere* to trust
▸ **fi'ducially** ADVERB

fiduciary (fɪ'du:ʃɪərɪ) *Law* ◆ NOUN, *plural* **-aries** [1] a person bound to act for another's benefit, as a trustee in relation to his beneficiary. ◆ ADJECTIVE [2] **a** having the nature of a trust. **b** of or relating to a trust or trustee.
▷HISTORY C17: from Latin *fīdūciārius* relating to something held in trust, from *fīdūcia* trust; see FIDUCIAL
▸ **fi'duciarily** ADVERB

fiduciary issue NOUN an issue of banknotes not backed by gold.

fidus Achates ('faɪdəs ə'keɪti:z) NOUN a faithful friend or companion.
▷HISTORY Latin, literally: faithful Achates, the name of the faithful companion of Aeneas in Virgil's *Aeneid*

fie (faɪ) INTERJECTION *Obsolete or facetious* an exclamation of distaste or mock dismay.
▷HISTORY C13: from Old French *fi*, from Latin *fī*, exclamation of disgust

fief *or* **feoff** (fi:f) NOUN (in feudal Europe) the property or fee granted to a vassal for his maintenance by his lord in return for service.
▷HISTORY C17: from Old French *fie*, of Germanic origin; compare Old English *fēo* cattle, money, Latin *pecus* cattle, *pecūnia* money, Greek *pokos* fleece

fiefdom ('fi:fdəm) NOUN [1] (in feudal Europe) the property owned by a lord. [2] an area over which a person or organization exerts authority or influence.

field (fi:ld) NOUN [1] an open tract of uncultivated grassland; meadow. Related adjective: **campestral**. [2] a piece of land cleared of trees and undergrowth, usually enclosed with a fence or hedge and used for pasture or growing crops: *a field of barley.* [3] a limited or marked off area, usually of mown grass, on which any of various sports, athletic competitions, etc., are held: *a soccer field.* [4] an area that is rich in minerals or other natural resources: *a coalfield.* [5] short for **battlefield, airfield.** [6] the mounted followers that hunt with a pack of hounds. [7] **a** all the runners in a particular race or competitors in a competition. **b** the runners in a race or competitors in a competition excluding the favourite. [8] *Cricket* the fielders collectively, esp with regard to their positions. [9] a wide or open expanse: *a field of snow.* [10] **a** an area of human activity: *the field of human knowledge.* **b** a sphere or division of knowledge, interest, etc: *his field is physics.* [11] **a** a place away from the laboratory, office, library, etc., usually out of doors, where practical work is done or original material or data collected. **b** (*as modifier*): *a field course.* [12] the surface or background, as of a flag, coin, or heraldic shield, on which a design is displayed. [13] Also called: **field of view.** the area within which an object may be observed with a telescope, microscope, etc. [14] *Physics* **a** See **field of force. b** a region of space that is a vector field. **c** a region of space under the influence of some scalar quantity, such as temperature. [15] *Maths* a set of entities subject to two binary operations, addition and multiplication, such that the set is a commutative group under addition and the set, minus the zero, is a commutative group under multiplication and multiplication is distributive over addition. [16] *Maths, logic* the set of elements that are either arguments or values of a function; the union of its domain and range. [17] *Computing* **a** a set of one or more characters comprising a unit of information. **b** a predetermined section of a record. [18] *Television* one of two or more sets of scanning lines which when interlaced form the complete picture. [19] *Obsolete* the open country: *beasts of the field.* [20] **hold** *or* **keep the field.** to maintain one's position in the face of opposition. [21] **in the field. a** *Military* in an area in which operations are in progress. **b** actively or closely involved with or working on something (rather than being in a more remote or administrative position). [22] **lead the field.** to be in the leading or most pre-eminent position. [23] **leave the field.** *Informal* to back out of a competition, contest, etc. [24] **take the field.** to begin or carry on activity, esp in sport or military operations. [25] **play the field.** *Informal* to disperse one's interests or attentions among a number of activities, people, or objects. [26] (*modifier*) *Military* of or relating to equipment, personnel, etc., specifically designed or trained for operations in the field: *a field gun; a field army.* ◆ VERB [27] (*tr*) *Sport* to stop, catch, or return (the ball) as a fielder. [28] (*tr*) *Sport* to send (a player or team) onto the field to play. [29] (*intr*) *Sport* (of a player or team) to act or take turn as a fielder or fielders. [30] (*tr*) *Military* to put (an army, a unit, etc.) in the field. [31] (*tr*) to enter (a person) in a competition: *each party fielded a candidate.* [32] (*tr*) *Informal* to deal with or handle, esp adequately and by making a reciprocal gesture: *to field a question.*
▷HISTORY Old English *feld*; related to Old Saxon, Old High German *feld*, Old English *fold* earth, Greek *platus* broad

field ambulance NOUN *Military* a mobile medical unit that accepts casualties from forward units, treating the lightly wounded and stabilizing the condition of the seriously wounded before evacuating them to a hospital.

field army NOUN *Military* the largest formation of a land force, usually consisting of two or more corps with supporting arms and services.

field artillery NOUN artillery capable of deployment in support of front-line troops, due mainly to its mobility.

field battery NOUN a small unit of usually four field guns.

field boot NOUN a close-fitting knee-length boot.

field captain NOUN the senior official at an archery meeting, responsible for safety.

field centre NOUN a research centre equipped for field studies, usually located in or near an area of scientific interest.

field corn NOUN *US* any variety of corn that is grown as a feed for livestock.

field cornet NOUN *South African* a commander of burgher troops called up in time of war or in an emergency, esp during the 19th century. Often shortened to **cornet**.

fieldcraft ('fi:ld,krɑ:ft) NOUN ability and experience in matters concerned with living out-of-doors, esp in a wild area.

field day NOUN [1] a day spent in some special outdoor activity, such as nature study or sport. [2] a day-long competition between amateur radio operators using battery or generator power, the aim being to make the most contacts with other operators around the world. [3] *Military* a day devoted to manoeuvres or exercises, esp before an audience. [4] *Informal* a day or time of exciting or successful activity: *the children had a field day with their new toys.* [5] *Austral* **a** a day or series of days devoted to the demonstration of farm machinery in country centres. **b** a combined open day and sale on a stud property.

field drain *or* **tile** NOUN an underground earthenware pipe used for draining fields.

field-effect transistor NOUN a unipolar transistor consisting of three or more electrode regions, the source, one or more gates, and the drain. A current flowing in a channel between the highly doped source and drain is controlled by the electric field arising from a voltage applied between source and gate. Abbreviation: **FET.** See also **JFET, IGFET.**

field emission NOUN the emission of electrons from a solid or liquid subjected to a high electric field.

fielder ('fi:ldə) NOUN *Cricket, baseball* **a** a player in the field. **b** a member of the fielding rather than the batting side.

field event NOUN a competition, such as the discus, high jump, etc., that takes place on a field or similar area as opposed to those on the running track.

fieldfare ('fi:ld,fɛə) NOUN a large Old World thrush, *Turdus pilaris*, having a pale grey head and rump, brown wings and back, and a blackish tail.
▷HISTORY Old English *feldefare*; see FIELD, FARE

field glass NOUN [1] a small telescope often incorporating a prism and held in one hand. [2] a former name for **field glasses.**

field glasses PLURAL NOUN another name for **binoculars.** Former name: **field glass.**

field goal NOUN [1] *Basketball* a goal scored while the ball is in normal play rather than from a free throw. [2] *American football* a score of three points made by kicking the ball through the opponent's goalposts above the crossbar.

field guidance NOUN a method of guiding a missile to a point within a gravitational or radio field by means of the properties of the field.

field gun NOUN a gun specially designed for service in direct support of front-line troops.

field hockey NOUN *US and Canadian* hockey played on a field, as distinguished from ice hockey.

field-holler NOUN a cry employing falsetto, portamento, and sudden changes of pitch, used in African-American work songs, later integrated into the techniques of the blues.

field hospital NOUN a temporary hospital set up near a battlefield equipped to provide remedial surgery and post-operative care.

field layer NOUN See **layer** (sense 2).

field magnet NOUN a permanent magnet or an electromagnet that produces the magnetic field in a generator, electric motor, or similar device.

field marshal NOUN an officer holding the highest rank in the British and certain other armies.

fieldmouse ('fi:ld,maʊs) NOUN, *plural* **-mice.** [1] any nocturnal mouse of the genus *Apodemus*, inhabiting woods, fields, and gardens of the Old World: family *Muridae*. They have yellowish-brown fur and feed on fruit, vegetables, seeds, etc. [2] a former name for **vole**[1].

field officer NOUN an officer holding **field rank**, namely that of major, lieutenant colonel, or colonel.

field of fire NOUN the area that a weapon or group of weapons can cover with fire from a given position.

field of force NOUN the region of space surrounding a body, such as a charged particle or a magnet, within which it can exert a force on another similar body not in contact with it. See also **electric field, magnetic field, gravitational field.**

field of honour NOUN the place or scene of a battle or duel, esp of jousting tournaments in medieval times.

fieldpiece ('fi:ld,pi:s) NOUN a former name for **field gun.**

field poppy NOUN another name for **corn poppy.**

field post office NOUN a place to which mail intended for military units in the field is sent to be sorted and forwarded. Abbreviation: **FPO.**

fieldsman ('fi:ldzmən) NOUN, *plural* **-men.** *Cricket* another name for **fielder.**

field spaniel NOUN a robust, low-slung breed of spaniel developed by crossing the cocker spaniel with the Sussex spaniel.

field sports PLURAL NOUN sports carried on in the open countryside, such as hunting, shooting, or fishing.

fieldstone ('fi:ld,stəʊn) NOUN building stone found in fields.

field strength NOUN [1] *Radio, television* the intensity of an electromagnetic wave at any point in the area covered by a radio or television transmitter. [2] *Physics* the intensity of an electric or magnetic field. See **intensity.**

field study NOUN (*often plural*) a research project carried out in the field. See **field** (sense 11).

field tile NOUN *Brit and NZ* an earthenware drain used in farm drainage.

field trial NOUN [1] *Hunting* a test of or contest between gun dogs to determine their proficiency and standard of training in retrieving or pointing. 2 (*often plural*) a test to display performance, efficiency, or durability, as of a vehicle or invention.

field trip NOUN an expedition, as by a group of students or research workers, to study something at first hand.

field winding (ˈwaɪndɪŋ) NOUN the insulated current-carrying coils on a field magnet that produce the magnetic field intensity required to set up the electrical excitation in a generator or motor.

fieldwork (ˈfiːldˌwɜːk) NOUN *Military* a temporary structure used in defending or fortifying a place or position.

field work NOUN an investigation or search for material, data, etc., made in the field as opposed to the classroom, laboratory, or official headquarters. ▸**field worker** NOUN

fiend (fiːnd) NOUN 1 an evil spirit; demon; devil. 2 a person who is extremely wicked, esp in being very cruel or brutal. 3 *Informal* **a** a person who is intensely interested in or fond of something: *a fresh-air fiend; he is a fiend for cards.* **b** an addict: *a drug fiend.* 4 *Informal* a mischievous or spiteful person, esp a child.
▷HISTORY Old English *fēond*; related to Old Norse *fjāndi* enemy, Gothic *fijands*, Old High German *fiant*
▸ˈ**fiend,like** ADJECTIVE

Fiend (fiːnd) NOUN **the.** the devil; Satan.

fiendish (ˈfiːndɪʃ) ADJECTIVE 1 of or like a fiend. 2 diabolically wicked or cruel. 3 *Informal* extremely difficult or unpleasant: *a fiendish problem.* ▸ˈ**fiendishly** ADVERB ▸ˈ**fiendishness** NOUN

fier *or* **fiere** (fiːr) NOUN *Scot* variant spellings of **fere.**

fierce (fɪəs) ADJECTIVE 1 having a violent and unrestrained nature; savage: *a fierce dog.* 2 wild or turbulent in force, action, or intensity: *a fierce storm.* 3 vehement, intense, or strong: *fierce competition.* 4 *Informal* very disagreeable or unpleasant.
▷HISTORY C13: from Old French *fiers*, from Latin *ferus*
▸ˈ**fiercely** ADVERB ▸ˈ**fierceness** NOUN

fieri facias (ˈfaɪəˌraɪ ˈfeɪʃɪəs) NOUN *Law* a writ ordering a levy on the belongings of an adjudged debtor to satisfy the debt.
▷HISTORY C15: from Latin, literally: cause (it) to be done

fiery (ˈfaɪərɪ) ADJECTIVE **fierier, fieriest.** 1 of, containing, or composed of fire. 2 resembling fire in heat, colour, ardour, etc.: *a fiery desert wind; a fiery speaker.* 3 easily angered or aroused: *a fiery temper.* 4 (of food) producing a burning sensation: *a fiery curry.* 5 (of the skin or a sore) inflamed. 6 flammable or containing flammable gas. 7 (of a cricket pitch) making the ball bounce dangerously high.
▸ˈ**fierily** ADVERB ▸ˈ**fieriness** NOUN

fiery cross NOUN 1 a burning cross, used as a symbol by the Ku Klux Klan. 2 a wooden cross with ends charred or dipped in blood formerly used by Scottish Highlanders to summon the clans to battle.

Fiesole (*Italian* ˈfieːzole) NOUN a town in central Italy, in Tuscany near Florence: Etruscan and Roman remains. Pop.: 4 000 (latest est.). Ancient name: **Faesulae** (ˈfiːsʊliː).

fiesta (fɪˈɛstə; *Spanish* ˈfjesta) NOUN (esp in Spain and Latin America) 1 a religious festival or celebration, esp on a saint's day. 2 a holiday or carnival.
▷HISTORY Spanish, from Latin *festa*, plural of *festum* festival; see FEAST

FIFA (ˈfiːfə) NOUN ACRONYM FOR Fédération Internationale de Football Association.
▷HISTORY from French

fife (faɪf) NOUN 1 a small high-pitched flute similar to the piccolo and usually having no keys, used esp in military bands. ◆ VERB 2 to play (music) on a fife.
▷HISTORY C16: from Old High German *pfīfa*; see PIPE[1]
▸ˈ**fifer** NOUN

Fife (faɪf) NOUN a council area and historical county of E central Scotland, bordering on the North Sea between the Firths of Tay and Forth: coastal lowlands in the north and east, with several ranges of hills; mainly agricultural. Administrative centre: Glenrothes. Pop.: 349 429 (2001 est.). Area: 1323 sq. km (511 sq. miles).

fife rail NOUN *Nautical* a rail at the base of a mast of a sailing vessel, fitted with pins for belaying running rigging. Compare **pin rail.**
▷HISTORY C18: of unknown origin

fifi hook (ˈfiːfiː) NOUN *Mountaineering* a metal hook at the top of an étrier for attaching it to a peg and also connected by a cord to the climber's harness to pull the étrier up and prevent it being dropped.
▷HISTORY C20: of unknown origin

FIFO (ˈfaɪfəʊ) NOUN ACRONYM FOR first in, first out (as an accounting principle in costing stock). Compare **LIFO.**

fifteen (ˈfɪfˈtiːn) NOUN 1 the cardinal number that is the sum of ten and five. 2 a numeral, 15, XV, etc., representing this number. 3 something represented by, representing, or consisting of 15 units. 4 a rugby football team. ◆ DETERMINER 5 **a** amounting to fifteen: *fifteen jokes.* **b** (*as pronoun*): *fifteen of us danced.*
▷HISTORY Old English *fīftēne*

Fifteen (ˈfɪfˈtiːn) NOUN **the.** *Brit history* the Jacobite rising of 1715.

fifteenth (ˈfɪfˈtiːnθ) ADJECTIVE 1 **a** coming after the fourteenth in order, position, time, etc. Often written: 15th. **b** (*as noun*): *the fifteenth of the month.* ◆ NOUN 2 **a** one of 15 equal or nearly equal parts of something. **b** (*as modifier*): *a fifteenth part.* 3 the fraction equal to one divided by 15 (1/15). 4 **a** an interval of two octaves. **b** one of two notes constituting such an interval in relation to the other, esp the one higher in pitch. **c** an organ stop of diapason quality sounding a note two octaves higher than that normally produced by the key depressed; a two-foot stop.

fifth (fɪfθ) ADJECTIVE (*usually prenominal*) 1 **a** coming after the fourth in order, position, time, etc. Often written: 5th. **b** (*as noun*): *he came on the fifth.* ◆ NOUN 2 **a** one of five equal or nearly equal parts of an object, quantity, measurement, etc. **b** (*as modifier*): *a fifth part.* 3 the fraction equal to one divided by five (1/5). 4 *Music* **a** the interval between one note and another five notes away from it counting inclusively along the diatonic scale. **b** one of two notes constituting such an interval in relation to the other. See also **perfect** (sense 9), **diminished** (sense 2), **interval** (sense 5). 5 an additional high gear fitted to some motor vehicles. ◆ ADVERB 6 Also: **fifthly.** after the fourth person, position, event, etc. ◆ SENTENCE CONNECTOR 7 Also: **fifthly.** as the fifth point: linking what follows with the previous statements, as in a speech or argument.
▷HISTORY Old English *fifta*

Fifth Amendment NOUN 1 an amendment to the US Constitution stating that no person may be compelled to testify against himself and that no person may be tried for a second time on a charge for which he has already been acquitted. 2 **take the fifth (amendment).** *US* to refuse to answer a question on the grounds that it might incriminate oneself.

fifth column NOUN 1 (originally) a group of Falangist sympathizers in Madrid during the Spanish Civil War who were prepared to join the four columns of insurgents marching on the city. 2 any group of hostile or subversive infiltrators; an enemy in one's midst.
▸**fifth columnist** NOUN

fifth disease NOUN a mild infectious disease of childhood, caused by a virus, characterized by fever and a red rash spreading from the cheeks to the limbs and trunk. Also called: **slapped-cheek disease.** Technical name: **erythema infectiosum.**
▷HISTORY C20: from its being among the five most common childhood infections

fifth force NOUN a hypothetical non-Newtonian repulsive component of the force of gravity, postulated as an addition to the four known fundamental forces (gravitational, electromagnetic, strong, and weak).

fifth-generation ADJECTIVE denoting developments in computer design to produce machines with artifical intelligence.

Fifth Republic NOUN the French republic established in 1958 as the successor to the Fourth Republic. Its constitution is characterized by the strong position of the president.

fifth wheel NOUN 1 a spare wheel for a four-wheeled vehicle. 2 **a** the coupling table of an articulated vehicle. **b** a steering bearing that enables the front axle of a horse-drawn vehicle to rotate relative to the body. 3 a superfluous or unnecessary person or thing.

fiftieth (ˈfɪftɪɪθ) ADJECTIVE 1 **a** being the ordinal number of *fifty* in order, position, time, etc. Often written: 50th. **b** (*as noun*): *the fiftieth in the series.* ◆ NOUN 2 **a** one of 50 equal or approximately equal parts of something. **b** (*as modifier*): *a fiftieth part.* 3 the fraction equal to one divided by 50 (1/50).

fifty (ˈfɪftɪ) NOUN, *plural* **-ties.** 1 the cardinal number that is the product of ten and five. 2 a numeral, 50, L, etc., representing this number. 3 something represented by, representing, or consisting of 50 units. ◆ DETERMINER 4 **a** amounting to fifty: *fifty people.* **b** (*as pronoun*): *fifty should be sufficient.*
▷HISTORY Old English *fīftig*

fifty-fifty ADJECTIVE, ADVERB *Informal* shared or sharing equally; in equal parts.

fig[1] (fɪg) NOUN 1 any moraceous tree or shrub of the tropical and subtropical genus *Ficus*, in which the flowers are borne inside a pear-shaped receptacle. 2 the fruit of any of these trees, esp of *F. carica*, which develops from the receptacle and has sweet flesh containing numerous seedlike structures. 3 any of various plants or trees having a fruit similar to this. 4 **Hottentot** *or* **sour fig.** a succulent plant, *Mesembryanthemum edule*, of southern Africa, having a capsular fruit containing edible pulp: family *Aizoaceae*. 5 (*used with a negative*) something of negligible value; jot: *I don't care a fig for your opinion.* 6 Also: **feg.** *Dialect* a piece or segment from an orange. 7 Also called: **fico.** an insulting gesture made with the thumb between the first two fingers or under the upper teeth.
▷HISTORY C13: from Old French *figue*, from Old Provençal *figa*, from Latin *fīcus* fig tree

fig[2] (fɪg) *Slang* ◆ VERB **figs, figging, figged.** (*tr*) 1 (foll by *out* or *up*) to dress (up) or rig (out). 2 to administer stimulating drugs to (a horse). ◆ NOUN 3 dress, appearance, or array (esp in the phrase **in full fig**). 4 physical condition or form: *in bad fig.*
▷HISTORY C17 *feague*, of uncertain origin

fig. ABBREVIATION FOR: 1 figurative(ly). 2 figure.

fig-bird NOUN any Australian oriole of the genus *Sphecotheres*, feeding on figs and other fruit.

fight (faɪt) VERB **fights, fighting, fought.** 1 to oppose or struggle against (an enemy) in battle. 2 to oppose or struggle against (a person, thing, cause, etc.) in any manner. 3 (*tr*) to engage in or carry on (a battle, contest, etc.). 4 (when *intr* often foll by *for*) to uphold or maintain (a cause, ideal, etc.) by fighting or struggling: *to fight for freedom.* 5 (*tr*) to make or achieve (a way) by fighting. 6 (*intr*) *Boxing* **a** to box, as for a living. **b** to use aggressive rough tactics. 7 to engage (another or others) in combat. 8 **fight it out.** to contend or struggle until a decisive result is obtained. 9 **fight shy of.** to keep aloof from. ◆ NOUN 10 a battle, struggle, or physical combat. 11 a quarrel, dispute, or contest. 12 resistance (esp in the phrase **to put up a fight**). 13 the desire to take part in physical combat (esp in the phrase **to show fight**). 14 a boxing match. ◆ See also **fight back, fight off.**
▷HISTORY Old English *feohtan*; related to Old Frisian *fiuchta*, Old Saxon, Old High German *fehtan* to fight
▸ˈ**fighting** NOUN, ADJECTIVE

fight back VERB (*adverb*) 1 (*intr*) to resist an attack. 2 (*intr*) to counterattack. 3 (*tr*) to struggle to repress: *she tried to fight back her tears.* ◆ NOUN **fightback.** 4 an act or campaign of resistance. 5 a counterattack.

fighter (ˈfaɪtə) NOUN 1 a person who fights, esp a professional boxer. 2 a person who has determination. 3 *Military* an armed aircraft designed for destroying other aircraft.

fighter-bomber NOUN a high-performance aircraft that combines the roles of fighter and bomber.

fighting chance NOUN a slight chance of success dependent on a struggle.

fighting cock NOUN [1] another name for **gamecock.** [2] a pugnacious person.

fighting fish NOUN any of various labyrinth fishes of the genus *Betta*, esp the Siamese fighting fish.

fighting top NOUN one of the gun platforms on the lower masts of sailing men-of-war, used in attacking the crew of an enemy ship with swivel guns and muskets.

fight off VERB (*tr, adverb*) [1] to repulse; repel. [2] to struggle to avoid or repress: *to fight off a cold.*

fight-or-flight NOUN (*modifier*) involving or relating to an involuntary response to stress in which the hormone adrenaline is secreted into the blood in readiness for physical action, such as fighting or running away.

figjam ('fɪɡˌdʒæm) NOUN *Austral slang* a very conceited person.
▷HISTORY C20: from *f(uck) I('m) g(ood) j(ust) a(sk) m(e)*

fig leaf NOUN [1] a leaf from a fig tree. [2] a representation of a leaf, usually a vine leaf rather than an actual fig leaf, used in painting or sculpture to cover the genitals of nude figures. [3] a device intended to conceal something regarded as shameful or indecent.

fig marigold NOUN an erect species of mesembryanthemum, *M. tricolor*, grown as a garden annual for its red-orange flowers with yellow centres.

figment ('fɪɡmənt) NOUN a fantastic notion, invention, or fabrication: *a figment of the imagination.*
▷HISTORY C15: from Late Latin *figmentum* a fiction, from Latin *fingere* to shape

figuline ('fɪɡjʊˌlaɪn) *Rare* ◆ ADJECTIVE [1] of or resembling clay. ◆ NOUN [2] an article made of clay.
▷HISTORY C17: from Latin *figulīnus* of a potter, from *figulus* a potter, from *fingere* to mould

figural ('fɪɡərəl) ADJECTIVE composed of or relating to human or animal figures.

figurant ('fɪɡjʊrənt) NOUN [1] a ballet dancer who does group work but no solo roles. [2] *Theatre* a minor character, esp one who does not speak.
▷HISTORY C18: from French, from *figurer* to represent, appear, FIGURE
▸**figurante** (ˌfɪɡjʊ'rɒnt) FEMININE NOUN

figurate ('fɪɡjʊrɪt) ADJECTIVE [1] *Music* exhibiting or produced by figuration; florid or decorative. [2] having a definite or particular shape or figure.
▷HISTORY C15: from Latin *figūrāre* to shape
▸'**figurately** ADVERB

figuration (ˌfɪɡə'reɪʃən) NOUN [1] *Music* **a** the employment of characteristic patterns of notes, esp in variations on a theme. **b** decoration or florid ornamentation in general. [2] the act or an instance of representing figuratively, as by means of allegory or emblem. [3] a figurative or emblematic representation. [4] the act of decorating with a design.

figurative ('fɪɡərətɪv) ADJECTIVE [1] of the nature of, resembling, or involving a figure of speech; not literal; metaphorical. [2] using or filled with figures of speech. [3] representing by means of an emblem, likeness, figure, etc. [4] (in painting, sculpture, etc.) of, relating to, or characterized by the naturalistic representation of the external world.
▸'**figuratively** ADVERB ▸'**figurativeness** NOUN

figure ('fɪɡə; *US* 'fɪɡjər) NOUN [1] any written symbol other than a letter, esp a whole number. [2] another name for **digit** (sense 2). [3] an amount expressed numerically: *a figure of 1800 was suggested.* [4] (*plural*) calculations with numbers: *he's good at figures.* [5] visible shape or form; outline. [6] the human form, esp as regards size or shape: *a girl with a slender figure.* [7] a slim bodily shape (esp in the phrases **keep** *or* **lose one's figure**). [8] a character or personage, esp a prominent or notable one; personality: *a figure in politics.* [9] the impression created by a person through behaviour (esp in the phrase **to cut a fine, bold,** etc., **figure**). [10] **a** a person as impressed on the mind: *the figure of Napoleon.* **b** (*in combination*): *father-figure.* [11] a representation in painting or sculpture, esp of the human form. [12] an illustration or explanatory diagram in a text. [13] a representative object or symbol; emblem. [14] a pattern or design, as on fabric or in wood. [15] a predetermined set of movements in dancing or skating. [16] *Geometry* any combination of points, lines, curves, or planes. A **plane figure**, such as a circle, encloses an area; a **solid figure** such as a sphere, encloses a volume. [17] *Rhetoric* See **figure of speech.** [18] *Logic* one of the four possible arrangements of the three terms in the premises of a syllogism. Compare **mood**[2] (sense 2). [19] *Music* **a** a numeral written above or below a note in a part. See **figured bass, thorough bass. b** a characteristic short pattern of notes. ◆ VERB [20] (when *tr*, often foll by *up*) to calculate or compute (sums, amounts, etc.). [21] (*tr; usually takes a clause as object*) *Informal, chiefly US, Canadian, and NZ* to think or conclude; consider. [22] (*tr*) to represent by a diagram or illustration. [23] (*tr*) to pattern or mark with a design. [24] (*tr*) to depict or portray in a painting, etc. [25] (*tr*) *Rhetoric* to express by means of a figure of speech. [26] (*tr*) to imagine. [27] (*tr*) *Music* **a** to decorate (a melody line or part) with ornamentation. **b** to provide figures above or below (a bass part) as an indication of the accompanying harmonies required. See **figured bass, thorough bass.** [28] (*intr;* usually foll by *in*) to be included: *his name figures in the article.* [29] (*intr*) *Informal* to accord with expectation; be logical: *it figures that he wouldn't come.* [30] **go figure.** *Informal* an expression of surprise, astonishment, wonder, etc. ◆ See also **figure on, figure out.**
▷HISTORY C13: from Latin *figūra* a shape, from *fingere* to mould
▸'**figureless** ADJECTIVE ▸'**figurer** NOUN

figured ('fɪɡəd) ADJECTIVE [1] depicted as a figure in graphic art, painting, or sculpture. [2] decorated or patterned with a design. [3] having a form. [4] *Music* **a** ornamental. **b** (of a bass part) provided with numerals indicating accompanying harmonies.

figured bass (beɪs) NOUN a shorthand method of indicating a thorough-bass part in which each bass note is accompanied by figures indicating the intervals to be played in the chord above it in the realization.

figure-ground phenomenon NOUN the division of the perceptual field into background and objects that appear to stand out against it. The concept was evolved by the Gestalt psychologists, who invented *ambiguous* figures in which the same part could be seen either as figure or ground.

figurehead ('fɪɡəˌhɛd) NOUN [1] a person nominally having a prominent position, but no real authority. [2] a carved bust or full-length figure at the upper end of the stems of some sailing vessels.

figure of eight *or* **figure eight** NOUN [1] an outline of the number 8 traced on ice by a skater. [2] a flight manoeuvre by an aircraft outlining a figure 8. [3] **a** a knot in the shape of a figure 8 made to prevent the unreeving of a rope. **b** a climber's knot in the shape of a figure 8 made with a doubled rope to provide a secure loop. **c** an angler's knot sometimes used to attach a fly to a leader or dropper.

figure of merit NOUN [1] *Aeronautics* a measure of the efficiency of a helicopter in hover. [2] *Electrical engineering* a measure of the efficiency of a component, such as a circuit.

figure of speech NOUN an expression of language, such as simile, metaphor, or personification, by which the usual or literal meaning of a word is not employed.

figure on *or* **upon** VERB (*intr, preposition*) *Informal, chiefly US and Canadian* [1] to depend on (support or help). [2] to take into consideration.

figure out VERB (*tr, adverb; may take a clause as object*) *Informal* [1] to calculate or reckon. [2] to understand.

figure skating NOUN ice skating in which the skater traces outlines of selected patterns.
▸**figure skater** NOUN

figurine (ˌfɪɡə'riːn) NOUN a small carved or moulded figure; statuette.
▷HISTORY C19: from French, from Italian *figurina* a little FIGURE

figwort ('fɪɡˌwɜːt) NOUN any scrophulariaceous plant of the N temperate genus *Scrophularia*, having square stems and small brown or greenish flowers.

Fiji ('fiːdʒiː, fiː'dʒiː) NOUN [1] an independent republic, consisting of 844 islands (chiefly Viti Levu and Vanua Levu) in the SW Pacific: a British colony (1874–1970); a member of the Commonwealth (1970–87 and from 1997); the large islands are of volcanic origin, surrounded by coral reefs; smaller ones are of coral. Official language: English. Religion: Christian and Hindu. Currency: dollar. Capital: Suva. Pop.: 827 000 (2001 est.). Area: 18 272 sq. km (7055 sq. miles). ◆ NOUN, ADJECTIVE [2] another word for **Fijian.**

Fijian (fiː'dʒiːən) NOUN [1] a member of the indigenous people of mixed Melanesian and Polynesian descent inhabiting Fiji. [2] the language of this people, belonging to the Malayo-Polynesian family. ◆ ADJECTIVE [3] of, relating to, or characteristic of Fiji or its inhabitants. ◆ Also: **Fiji.**

filagree ('fɪləˌɡriː) NOUN, ADJECTIVE, VERB a less common variant of **filigree.**

filament ('fɪləmənt) NOUN [1] the thin wire, usually tungsten, inside a light bulb that emits light when heated to incandescence by an electric current. [2] *Electronics* a high-resistance wire or ribbon, forming the cathode in some valves. [3] a single strand of a natural or synthetic fibre; fibril. [4] *Botany* **a** the stalk of a stamen. **b** any of the long slender chains of cells into which some algae and fungi are divided. [5] *Ornithol* the barb of a down feather. [6] *Anatomy* any slender structure or part, such as the tail of a spermatozoon; filum. [7] *Astronomy* **a** a long structure of relatively cool material in the solar corona. **b** a long large-scale cluster of galaxies.
▷HISTORY C16: from New Latin *fīlāmentum*, from Medieval Latin *fīlāre* to spin, from Latin *fīlum* thread
▸**filamentary** (ˌfɪlə'mɛntərɪ, -trɪ) *or* ˌ**fila'mentous** ADJECTIVE

filar ('faɪlə) ADJECTIVE [1] of thread. [2] (of an optical instrument) having fine threads across the eyepiece forming a reticle or set of cross wires.
▷HISTORY C19: from Latin *fīlum* thread

filaria (fɪ'lɛərɪə) NOUN, *plural* **-iae** (-ɪˌiː). any parasitic nematode worm of the family *Filariidae*, living in the blood and tissues of vertebrates and transmitted by insects: the cause of filariasis.
▷HISTORY C19: New Latin (former name of genus), from Latin *fīlum* thread
▸**fi'larial** *or* **fi'larian** ADJECTIVE

filariasis (ˌfɪlə'raɪəsɪs, fɪˌlɛərɪ'eɪsɪs) NOUN a disease common in tropical and subtropical countries resulting from infestation of the lymphatic system with the nematode worms *Wuchereria bancrofti* or *Brugia malayi*, transmitted by mosquitoes: characterized by inflammation and obstruction of the lymphatic vessels. See also **elephantiasis.**
▷HISTORY C19: from New Latin; see FILARIA

filature ('fɪlətʃə) NOUN [1] the act or process of spinning silk, etc., into threads. [2] the reel used for this. [3] a place where such spinning or reeling is done.
▷HISTORY C18: from Medieval Latin *fīlātūra* the art of spinning, from *fīlāre* to spin thread; see FILAMENT

filbert ('fɪlbət) NOUN [1] any of several N temperate shrubs of the genus *Corylus*, esp *C. maxima*, that have edible rounded brown nuts: family *Corylaceae*. [2] Also called: **hazelnut, cobnut.** the nut of any of these shrubs. ◆ See also **hazel** (senses 1, 3).
▷HISTORY C14: named after St *Philbert*, 7th-century Frankish abbot, because the nuts are ripe around his feast day, Aug. 22

filch (fɪltʃ) VERB (*tr*) to steal or take surreptitiously in small amounts; pilfer.
▷HISTORY C16 *filchen* to steal, attack, perhaps from Old English *gefylce* band of men
▸'**filcher** NOUN

file[1] (faɪl) NOUN [1] a folder, box, etc., used to keep documents or other items in order. [2] the documents, etc., kept in this way. [3] documents or information about a specific subject, person, etc.: *we have a file on every known thief.* [4] an orderly line or row. [5] a line of people in marching formation, one behind another. Compare **rank**[1] (sense 6). [6] any of the eight vertical rows of squares on a chessboard. [7] *Computing* a named collection of information, in the form of text, programs, graphics, etc., held on a permanent storage device such as a magnetic disk. [8] *Obsolete* a list or catalogue. [9] **on file.** recorded or catalogued for reference, as in a file. ◆ VERB [10] to place (a document, letter, etc.) in a file. [11] (*tr*) to put on record, esp to place (a legal document) on public or

official record; register. **12** (*tr*) to bring (a suit, esp a divorce suit) in a court of law. **13** (*tr*) to submit (copy) to a newspaper or news agency. **14** (*intr*) to march or walk in a file or files: *the ants filed down the hill.*
▷HISTORY C16 (in the sense: string on which documents are hung): from Old French *filer*, from Medieval Latin *fīlāre*; see FILAMENT
▸'**filer** NOUN

file² (faɪl) NOUN **1** a hand tool consisting essentially of a steel blade with small cutting teeth on some or all of its faces. It is used for shaping or smoothing metal, wood, etc. **2** *Rare, Brit slang* a cunning or deceitful person. ◆ VERB **3** (*tr*) to shape or smooth (a surface) with a file.
▷HISTORY Old English *fīl*; related to Old Saxon *fīla*, Old High German *fīhala* file, Greek *pikros* bitter, sharp
▸'**filer** NOUN

file³ (faɪl) VERB (*tr*) *Obsolete* to pollute or defile.
▷HISTORY Old English *fӯlan*; related to Middle Low German *vülen*; see DEFILE¹, FILTH, FOUL

filecard ('faɪlˌkɑːd) NOUN a type of brush with sharp steel bristles, used for cleaning the teeth of a file.

filefish ('faɪlˌfɪʃ) NOUN, *plural* **-fish** *or* **-fishes**. any tropical triggerfish, such as *Alutera scripta*, having a narrow compressed body and a very long dorsal spine.
▷HISTORY C18: referring to its file-like scales

filename ('faɪlˌneɪm) NOUN an arrangement of characters that enables a computer system to permit the user to have access to a particular file.

file server NOUN *Computing* the central unit of a local area network that controls its operation and provides access to separately stored data files.

filet ('fɪlɪt, 'fɪleɪ; *French* filɛ) NOUN a variant spelling of **fillet** (senses 1–3).
▷HISTORY C20: from French: net, from Old Provençal *filat*, from *fil* thread, from Latin *fīlum*

filet mignon ('fɪleɪ 'miːnjɒn) NOUN a small tender boneless cut of beef from the inside of the loin.
▷HISTORY from French, literally: dainty fillet

file transfer protocol NOUN See **FTP**.

filial ('fɪljəl) ADJECTIVE **1** of, resembling, or suitable to a son or daughter: *filial affection.* **2** *Genetics* designating any of the generations following the parental generation. Abbreviation: **F**; F_1 indicates the first filial generation, F_2 the second, etc.
▷HISTORY C15: from Late Latin *fīliālis*, from Latin *fīlius* son
▸'**filially** ADVERB ▸'**filialness** NOUN

filiate ('fɪlɪˌeɪt) VERB (*tr*) **1** *Law* to fix judicially the paternity of (a child, esp one born out of wedlock). **2** *Law* a less common word for **affiliate**. **3** *Archaic* to affiliate or associate.
▷HISTORY C18: from Medieval Latin *fīliātus* acknowledged as a son, from Latin *fīlius* son

filiation (ˌfɪlɪ'eɪʃən) NOUN **1** line of descent; lineage; derivation. **2** the fact of being the child of certain parents. **3** *Law* the act or process of filiating. **4** *Law* a less common word for **affiliation order**. **5** the set of rules governing the attachment of children to their parents and its social consequences.

filibeg, fillibeg, *or* **philibeg** ('fɪlɪˌbɛg) NOUN the kilt worn by Scottish Highlanders.
▷HISTORY C18: from Scottish Gaelic *fēileadhbeag*, from *fēileadh* kilt + *beag* small

filibuster ('fɪlɪˌbʌstə) NOUN **1** the process or an instance of obstructing legislation by means of long speeches and other delaying tactics. **2** Also called: **filibusterer**. a legislator who engages in such obstruction. **3** a buccaneer, freebooter, or irregular military adventurer, esp a revolutionary in a foreign country. ◆ VERB **4** to obstruct (legislation) with delaying tactics. **5** (*intr*) to engage in unlawful and private military action.
▷HISTORY C16: from Spanish *filibustero*, from French *flibustier* probably from Dutch *vrijbuiter* pirate, literally: one plundering freely; see FREEBOOTER
▸'**filiˌbusterer** NOUN ▸'**filiˌbusterism** NOUN

filicide ('fɪlɪˌsaɪd) NOUN **1** the act of killing one's own son or daughter. **2** a person who does this.
▷HISTORY C17: from Latin *fīlius* son or *fīlia* daughter + -CIDE
▸ˌ**fili'cidal** ADJECTIVE

filiform ('fɪlɪˌfɔːm, 'faɪ-) ADJECTIVE *Biology* having the form of a thread.
▷HISTORY C18: from Latin *fīlum* thread

filigree ('fɪlɪˌgriː), **filagree,** *or* **fillagree** NOUN **1** delicate ornamental work of twisted gold, silver, or other wire. **2** any fanciful delicate ornamentation. ◆ ADJECTIVE **3** made of or as if with filigree. ◆ VERB **-grees, -greeing, -greed**. **4** (*tr*) to decorate with or as if with filigree.
▷HISTORY C17: from earlier *filigreen*, from French *filigrane*, from Latin *fīlum* thread + *grānum* GRAIN

filing clerk NOUN an employee who maintains office files.

filings ('faɪlɪŋz) PLURAL NOUN shavings or particles removed by a file: *iron filings.*

Filipino (ˌfɪlɪ'piːnəʊ) NOUN **1** (*plural* **-nos**) Also (feminine): **Filipina**. a native or inhabitant of the Philippines. **2** another name for **Tagalog**. ◆ ADJECTIVE **3** of or relating to the Philippines or their inhabitants.

fill (fɪl) VERB (*mainly tr*; often foll by *up*) **1** (*also intr*) to make or become full: *to fill up a bottle; the bath fills in two minutes.* **2** to occupy the whole of: *the party filled two floors of the house.* **3** to plug (a gap, crevice, cavity, etc.). **4** to meet (a requirement or need) satisfactorily. **5** to cover (a page or blank space) with writing, drawing, etc. **6** to hold and perform the duties of (an office or position). **7** to appoint or elect an occupant to (an office or position). **8** *Building trades* to build up (ground) with fill. **9** (*also intr*) to swell or cause to swell with wind, as in manoeuvring the sails of a sailing vessel. **10** to increase the bulk of by adding an inferior substance. **11** *Poker* to complete (a full house, etc.) by drawing the cards needed. **12** *Chiefly US and Canadian* to put together the necessary materials for (a prescription or order). **13** **fill the bill**. *Informal* to serve or perform adequately. ◆ NOUN **14** material such as gravel, stones, etc., used to bring an area of ground up to a required level. **15** **one's fill**. the quantity needed to satisfy one: *to eat your fill.* ◆ See also **fill away, fill in, fill out, fill up**.
▷HISTORY Old English *fyllan*; related to Old Frisian *fella*, Old Norse *fylla*, Gothic *fulljan*, Old High German *fullen*; see FULL¹, FULFIL

fillagree ('fɪləˌgriː) NOUN, ADJECTIVE, VERB a less common variant of **filigree**.

fill away VERB (*intr, adverb*) *Nautical* to cause a vessel's sails to fill, either by steering it off the wind or by bracing the yards.

fille de joie *French* (fij də ʒwa) NOUN, *plural* ***filles de joie*** (fij də ʒwa). a prostitute.
▷HISTORY girl of pleasure

filled gold NOUN another name (esp US) for **rolled gold**.

filler ('fɪlə) NOUN **1** a person or thing that fills. **2** an object or substance used to add weight or size to something or to fill in a gap. **3** a paste, used for filling in cracks, holes, etc., in a surface before painting. **4** *Architect* a small joist inserted between and supported by two beams. **5** **a** the inner portion of a cigar. **b** the cut tobacco for making cigarettes. **6** *Journalism* articles, photographs, etc., to fill space between more important articles in the layout of a newspaper or magazine. **7** *Informal* something, such as a musical selection, to fill time in a broadcast or stage presentation. **8** a small radio or television transmitter used to fill a gap in coverage.

filler cap NOUN a device sealing the filling pipe to the petrol tank in a motor vehicle.

filler metal NOUN metal supplied in the form of a welding rod, sometimes flux coated, melted by an arc or a flame into a joint between components to be joined.

fillet ('fɪlɪt) NOUN **1** **a** Also called: **fillet steak**. a strip of boneless meat, esp the undercut of a sirloin of beef. **b** the boned side of a fish. **c** the white meat of breast and wing of a chicken. **2** a narrow strip of any material. **3** a thin strip of ribbon, lace, etc., worn in the hair or around the neck. **4** a narrow flat moulding, esp one between other mouldings. **5** a narrow band between two adjacent flutings on the shaft of a column. **6** Also called: **fillet weld**. a narrow strip of welded metal of approximately triangular cross-section used to join steel members at right angles. **7** *Heraldry* a horizontal division of a shield, one quarter of the depth of the chief. **8** Also called: **listel, list**. the top member of a cornice. **9** *Anatomy* a band of sensory nerve fibres in the brain connected to the thalamus. Technical name: **lemniscus**. **10** **a** a narrow decorative line, impressed on the cover of a book. **b** a wheel tool used to impress such lines. **11** another name for **fairing¹**. ◆ VERB **-lets, -leting, -leted** (*tr*) **12** to cut or prepare (meat or fish) as a fillet. **13** to cut fillets from (meat or fish). **14** *Anatomy* to surgically remove a bone from (part of the body) so that only soft tissue remains. **15** to bind or decorate with or as if with a fillet. ◆ Also (for senses 1–3): **filet**.
▷HISTORY C14: from Old French *filet*, from *fil* thread, from Latin *fīlum*

fill in VERB (*adverb*) **1** (*tr*) to complete (a form, drawing, etc.). **2** (*intr*) to act as a substitute: *a girl is filling in while the typist is away.* **3** (*tr*) to put material into (a hole or cavity), esp so as to make it level with a surface. **4** (*tr*) *Informal* to inform with facts or news. **5** (*tr*) *Brit slang* to attack and injure severely. ◆ NOUN **fill-in**. **6** a substitute. **7** *US informal* a briefing to complete one's understanding.

filling ('fɪlɪŋ) NOUN **1** the substance or thing used to fill a space or container: *pie filling.* **2** *Dentistry* **a** any of various substances (metal, plastic, etc.) for inserting into the prepared cavity of a tooth. **b** the cavity of a tooth so filled. **3** *Textiles* another term for **weft**. ◆ ADJECTIVE **4** (of food or a meal) substantial and satisfying.

filling station NOUN a place where petrol and other supplies for motorists are sold.

fillip ('fɪlɪp) NOUN **1** something that adds stimulation or enjoyment. **2** the action of holding a finger towards the palm with the thumb and suddenly releasing it outwards to produce a snapping sound. **3** a quick blow or tap made by a finger snapped in this way. ◆ VERB **4** (*tr*) to stimulate or excite. **5** (*tr*) to strike or project sharply with a fillip. **6** (*intr*) to make a fillip.
▷HISTORY C15 *philippe*, of imitative origin

fillister, filister, *or* **fillester** ('fɪlɪstə) NOUN **1** Also called: **fillister plane**. an adjustable plane for cutting rabbets, grooves, etc. **2** Also called: **sash fillister**. a rabbet or groove, esp one in a window sash bar for a pane of glass.
▷HISTORY C19: of unknown origin

fill light NOUN *Photog* a light that supplements the key light without changing its character, used esp to lighten shadows.

fill out VERB (*adverb*) **1** to make or become fuller, thicker, or rounder: *her figure has filled out since her marriage.* **2** to make more substantial: *the writers were asked to fill their stories out.* **3** (*tr*) to complete (a form, application, etc.).

fill up VERB (*adverb*) **1** (*tr*) to complete (a form, application, etc.). **2** to make or become completely full. ◆ NOUN **fill-up**. **3** the act of filling something completely, esp the petrol tank of a car.

filly ('fɪlɪ) NOUN, *plural* **-lies**. **1** a female horse or pony under the age of four. **2** *Informal rare* a spirited girl or young woman.
▷HISTORY C15: from Old Norse *fylja*; related to Old High German *fulihha*; see FOAL

film (fɪlm) NOUN **1** **a** a sequence of images of moving objects photographed by a camera and providing the optical illusion of continuous movement when projected onto a screen. **b** a form of entertainment, information, etc., composed of such a sequence of images and shown in a cinema, etc. **c** (*as modifier*): *film techniques.* **2** a thin flexible strip of cellulose coated with a photographic emulsion, used to make negatives and transparencies. **3** a thin coating or layer. **4** a thin sheet of any material, as of plastic for packaging. **5** a fine haze, mist, or blur. **6** a gauzy web of filaments or fine threads. **7** *Pathol* an abnormally opaque tissue, such as the cornea in some eye diseases. ◆ VERB **8** **a** to photograph with a cine camera. **b** to make a film of (a screenplay, event, etc.). **9** (often foll by *over*) to cover or become covered or coated with a film.
▷HISTORY Old English *filmen* membrane; related to Old Frisian *filmene*, Greek *pelma* sole of the foot; see FELL⁴

film colour NOUN *Physiol* a misty appearance produced when no lines or edges are present in the visual field.

filmic ('fɪlmɪk) ADJECTIVE [1] of or relating to films or the cinema. [2] having characteristics that are suggestive of films or the cinema.
► **'filmically** ADVERB

film library NOUN a collection of films as archives or for loan or hire.

film noir (nwɑː) NOUN a gangster thriller, made esp in the 1940s in Hollywood characterized by contrasty lighting and often somewhat impenetrable plots.
▷ HISTORY C20: French, literally: black film

filmography (fɪl'mɒgrəfɪ) NOUN [1] a list of the films made by a particular director, actor, etc. [2] any writing that deals with films or the cinema.

film pack NOUN a box containing several sheets of film for use in a plate camera.

film set NOUN the scenery and props as arranged for shooting a film.

filmset ('fɪlm,sɛt) VERB **-sets, -setting, -set.** (*tr*) to set (type matter) by filmsetting.
► **'film,setter** NOUN

filmsetting ('fɪlm,sɛtɪŋ) NOUN *Printing* typesetting by exposing type characters onto photographic film from which printing plates are made.

film speed NOUN [1] the sensitivity to light of a photographic film, specified in terms of the film's ISO rating. [2] the rate at which the film passes through a motion picture camera or projector.

film star NOUN a popular film actor or actress.

film strip NOUN a strip of film composed of different images projected separately as slides.

filmy ('fɪlmɪ) ADJECTIVE **filmier, filmiest.** [1] composed of or resembling film; transparent or gauzy. [2] covered with or as if with a film; hazy; blurred.
► **'filmily** ADVERB ► **'filminess** NOUN

filmy fern NOUN any fern of the family *Hymenophyllaceae*, growing in humid regions and having thin translucent leaves.

filo ('fiːləʊ) NOUN a type of Greek flaky pastry in very thin sheets.
▷ HISTORY C20: Modern Greek *phullon* leaf

Filofax ('faɪləʊ,fæks) NOUN *Trademark* a type of loose-leaf ring binder with sets of different-coloured paper, used as a portable personal filing system, including appointments, addresses, etc.

filoplume ('fɪlə,pluːm, 'faɪ-) NOUN *Ornithol* any of the hairlike feathers that lack vanes and occur between the contour feathers.
▷ HISTORY C19: from New Latin *filoplūma*, from Latin *fīlum* thread + *plūma* feather

filose ('faɪləʊs, -ləʊz) ADJECTIVE *Biology* resembling or possessing a thread or threadlike process: *filose pseudopodia*.
▷ HISTORY C19: from Latin *fīlum* thread

filoselle (,fɪləʊ'sɛl) NOUN soft silk thread, used esp for embroidery.
▷ HISTORY C17: from French: silk, silkworm, from Italian *filosello*, perhaps from Latin *folliculus* little bag

filovirus ('faɪləʊ,vaɪrəs) NOUN any member of a family of viruses that includes the agents responsible for Ebola virus disease and Marburg disease.
▷ HISTORY C20: from Latin *fīlum* thread + VIRUS

fils[1] *French* (fis) an addition to a French surname to specify the son rather than the father of the same name: *a book by Dumas fils*. Compare ***père***.
▷ HISTORY French: son

fils[2] (fɪls) *or* **fil** (fɪl) NOUN, *plural* **fils. a** a fractional monetary unit of Bahrain, Iraq, Jordan, and Kuwait, worth one thousandth of a dinar. **b** a fractional monetary unit of the United Arab Emirates, worth one hundredth of a dirham. **c** a fractional monetary unit of Yemen, worth one hundredth of a riyal.
▷ HISTORY from Arabic

filter ('fɪltə) NOUN [1] a porous substance, such as paper or sand, that allows fluid to pass but retains suspended solid particles: used to clean fluids or collect solid particles. [2] any device containing such a porous substance for separating suspensions from fluids. [3] any of various porous substances built into the mouth end of a cigarette or cigar for absorbing impurities such as tar. [4] any electronic, optical, or acoustic device that blocks signals or radiations of certain frequencies while allowing others to pass. See also **band-pass filter.** [5] any transparent disc of gelatine or glass used to eliminate or reduce the intensity of given frequencies from the light leaving a lamp, entering a camera, etc. [6] *Brit* a traffic signal at a road junction consisting of a green arrow which when illuminated permits vehicles to turn either left or right when the main signals are red. ◆ VERB [7] (often foll by *out*) to remove or separate (suspended particles, wavelengths of radiation, etc.) from (a liquid, gas, radiation, etc.) by the action of a filter. [8] (*tr*) to obtain by filtering. [9] (*intr* foll by *through*) to pass (through a filter or something like a filter): *dust filtered through the screen*. [10] (*intr*) to flow slowly; trickle.
▷ HISTORY C16 *filtre* from Medieval Latin *filtrum* piece of felt used as a filter, of Germanic origin; see FELT[2]

filterable ('fɪltərəbᵊl) *or* **filtrable** ('fɪltrəbᵊl) ADJECTIVE [1] capable of being filtered. [2] (of most viruses and certain bacteria) capable of passing through the pores of a fine filter.
► **,filtera'bility** *or* **'filterableness** NOUN

filter bed NOUN [1] a layer of sand or gravel in a tank or reservoir through which a liquid is passed so as to purify it. Compare **bacteria bed.** [2] any layer of material through which a liquid is passed so as to filter it.

filter cake NOUN *Chem* the solid material accumulated by a filter press.

filter feeding NOUN *Zoology* a method of feeding occurring in some aquatic animals, such as planktonic invertebrates and whalebone whales, in which minute food particles are filtered from the surrounding water.
► **filter feeder** NOUN

filter out *or* **through** VERB (*intr, adverb*) to become known gradually; leak: *rumours filtered out about the divorce*.

filter paper NOUN a porous paper used for filtering liquids.

filter press NOUN an apparatus used for filtration consisting of a set of frames covered with filter cloth on both sides, between which the liquid to be filtered is pumped.

filter pump NOUN a vacuum pump used to assist laboratory filtrations in which a jet of water inside a glass tube entrains air molecules from the system to be evacuated.

filter tip NOUN [1] an attachment to the mouth end of a cigarette for trapping impurities such as tar during smoking. It consists of any of various dense porous substances, such as cotton. [2] a cigarette having such an attachment.
► **'filter-,tipped** ADJECTIVE

filth (fɪlθ) NOUN [1] foul or disgusting dirt; refuse. [2] extreme physical or moral uncleanliness; pollution. [3] vulgarity or obscenity, as in language. [4] **the.** *Derogatory slang* the police.
▷ HISTORY Old English *fȳlth*; related to Old Saxon, Old High German *fūlitha*; see FOUL, DEFILE

filthy ('fɪlθɪ) ADJECTIVE **filthier, filthiest.** [1] characterized by or full of filth; very dirty or obscene. [2] offensive or vicious: *that was a filthy trick to play*. [3] *Informal, chiefly Brit* extremely unpleasant: *filthy weather*. ◆ ADVERB [4] extremely; disgustingly: *filthy rich*.
► **'filthily** ADVERB ► **'filthiness** NOUN

filtrate ('fɪltreɪt) NOUN [1] a liquid or gas that has been filtered. ◆ VERB [2] another name for **filter** (sense 7).
▷ HISTORY C17: from Medieval Latin *filtrāre* to FILTER
► **'filtratable** ADJECTIVE

filtration (fɪl'treɪʃən) NOUN the act or process of filtering.

filum ('faɪləm) NOUN, *plural* **-la** (-lə). *Anatomy* any threadlike structure or part.
▷ HISTORY Latin: thread, cord, fibre

fimble ('fɪmbᵊl) NOUN the male plant of the hemp, which matures before the female plant.
▷ HISTORY C15: from Middle Dutch *femeel*, from Old French *chanvre femelle* female hemp, from *chanvre* hemp + *femelle* FEMALE

fimbria ('fɪmbrɪə) NOUN, *plural* **-briae** (-brɪ,iː). *Anatomy* a fringe or fringelike margin or border, esp at the opening of the Fallopian tubes.
▷ HISTORY C18: from Late Latin, from Latin *fimbriae* threads, shreds
► **'fimbrial** ADJECTIVE

fimbriate ('fɪmbrɪɪt, -,eɪt), **fimbriated,** *or* **fimbrillate** ('fɪmbrɪlɪt, -,leɪt) ADJECTIVE having a fringed margin, as some petals, antennae, etc.
► **,fimbri'ation** NOUN

fimicolous (fɪ'mɪkələs) ADJECTIVE *Biology* (esp of fungi) growing in or on dung.
▷ HISTORY C19: from Latin *fimus* dung + *colere* to inhabit

fin[1] (fɪn) NOUN [1] any of the firm appendages that are the organs of locomotion and balance in fishes and some other aquatic animals. Most fishes have paired and unpaired fins, the former corresponding to the limbs of higher vertebrates. [2] a part or appendage that resembles a fin. [3] **a** *Brit* a vertical surface to which the rudder is attached, usually placed at the rear of an aeroplane to give stability about the vertical axis. US name: **vertical stabilizer. b** a tail surface fixed to a rocket or missile to give stability. [4] *Nautical* a fixed or adjustable blade projecting under water from the hull of a vessel to give it stability or control. [5] a projecting rib to dissipate heat from the surface of an engine cylinder, motor casing, or radiator. [6] (*often plural*) another name for **flipper** (sense 2). ◆ VERB **fins, finning, finned.** [7] (*tr*) to provide with fins. [8] (*tr*) to remove the fins from (a dead fish). [9] (*intr*) (esp of a whale) to agitate the fins violently in the water.
▷ HISTORY Old English *finn*; related to Middle Dutch *vinne*, Old Swedish *fina*, Latin *pinna* wing
► **'finless** ADJECTIVE

fin[2] (fɪn) NOUN *US slang* a five-dollar bill.
▷ HISTORY from Yiddish *finf* five, ultimately from Old High German *funf, finf*

FIN INTERNATIONAL CAR REGISTRATION FOR Finland.

fin. ABBREVIATION FOR: [1] finance. [2] financial.

Fin. ABBREVIATION FOR: [1] Finland. [2] Finnish.

finable *or* **fineable** ('faɪnəbᵊl) ADJECTIVE liable to a fine.
► **'finableness** *or* **'fineableness** NOUN

finagle (fɪ'neɪgᵊl) VERB *Informal* [1] (*tr*) to get or achieve by trickery, craftiness, or persuasion; wangle. [2] to use trickery or craftiness on (a person).
▷ HISTORY C20: probably changed from dialect *fainaigue*
► **fi'nagler** NOUN

final ('faɪnᵊl) ADJECTIVE [1] of or occurring at the end; concluding; ultimate; last. [2] having no possibility for further discussion, action, or change; conclusive; decisive: *a final decree of judgment*. [3] relating to or constituting an end or purpose: *a final clause may be introduced by "in order to"*. [4] *Phonetics* at the end of a word: *"cat" has a final "t"*. Compare **medial** (sense 1), **initial** (sense 1). [5] *Music* another word for **perfect** (sense 9b). ◆ NOUN [6] a terminal or last thing; end. [7] a deciding contest between the winners of previous rounds in a competition. [8] *Music* the tonic note of a church mode. ◆ See also **finals.**
▷ HISTORY C14: from Latin *fīnālis*, from *fīnis* limit, boundary

final cause NOUN *Philosophy* the end or purpose of a thing or process, as opposed to its efficient cause. See **cause** (sense 7).

finale (fɪ'nɑːlɪ) NOUN [1] the concluding part of any performance or presentation. [2] the closing section or movement of a musical composition.
▷ HISTORY C18: from Italian, n use of adj *finale*, from Latin *fīnālis* FINAL

finalism ('faɪnə,lɪzəm) NOUN *Philosophy* the doctrine that final causes determine the course of all events.
► **,fina'listic** ADJECTIVE

finalist ('faɪnəlɪst) NOUN a contestant who has reached the last and decisive stage of a sports or other competition.

finality (faɪ'nælɪtɪ) NOUN, *plural* **-ties.** [1] the condition or quality of being final or settled; conclusiveness: *the finality of death*. [2] a final or conclusive act. [3] *Metaphysics* the doctrine of the efficacy of final causes. Compare **teleology.**

finalize *or* **finalise** ('faɪnə,laɪz) VERB [1] (*tr*) to put into final form; settle: *to finalize plans for the merger*.

2 (*intr*) to complete arrangements or negotiations; reach agreement on a transaction.
▸ ˌ**finaliˈzation** *or* ˌ**finaliˈsation** NOUN

> **Language note** Although *finalize* has been in widespread use for some time, many speakers and writers still prefer to use *complete, conclude*, or *make final*, esp in formal contexts.

finally (ˈfaɪnəlɪ) ADVERB 1 after a long delay; at last; eventually. 2 at the end or final point; lastly. 3 completely; conclusively; irrevocably. ◆ SENTENCE CONNECTOR 4 in the end; lastly: *finally, he put his tie on.* 5 as the last or final point: linking what follows with the previous statements, as in a speech or argument.

finals (ˈfaɪnᵊlz) PLURAL NOUN 1 the deciding part or parts of a sports or other competition. 2 *Education* the last examination series in an academic or professional course.

final-salary ADJECTIVE another name for **defined-benefit**.

finance (fɪˈnæns, ˈfaɪnæns) NOUN 1 the system of money, credit, etc., esp with respect to government revenues and expenditures. 2 funds or the provision of funds. 3 (*plural*) funds; financial condition. ◆ VERB 4 (*tr*) to provide or obtain funds, capital, or credit for. 5 (*intr*) to manage or secure financial resources.
▷HISTORY C14: from Old French, from *finer* to end, settle by payment

finance bill NOUN a legislative bill providing money for the public treasury.

finance company *or* **house** NOUN an enterprise engaged in the loan of money against collateral or speculatively to manufacturers and retailers, esp one specializing in the financing of hire-purchase contracts.

financial (fɪˈnænʃəl, faɪ-) ADJECTIVE 1 of or relating to finance or finances. 2 of or relating to persons who manage money, capital, or credit. 3 *Austral and NZ informal* having money; in funds. 4 *Austral and NZ* (of a club member) fully paid-up.
▸**fiˈnancially** ADVERB

financial futures PLURAL NOUN futures in a stock-exchange index, currency exchange rate, or interest rate enabling banks, building societies, brokers, and speculators to hedge their involvement in these markets.

Financial Ombudsman NOUN any of five British ombudsmen: the **Banking Ombudsman**, set up in 1986 to investigate complaints from bank customers; the **Building Society Ombudsman**, set up in 1987 to investigate complaints from building society customers; the **Insurance Ombudsman**, set up in 1981 to investigate complaints by policyholders (since 1988 this ombudsman has also operated a **Unit Trust Ombudsman** scheme); the **Investment Ombudsman** set up in 1989 to investigate complaints by investors (the **Personal Investment Authority Ombudsman** is responsible for investigating complaints by personal investors); and the **Pensions Ombudsman**, set up in 1993 to investigate complaints regarding pension schemes.

Financial Services Authority NOUN (in the United Kingdom) a regulatory body that oversees London's financial markets, each of which has its own self-regulatory organization: it succeeded the Securities and Investments Board. Abbreviation: **FSA**.

Financial Times Industrial Ordinary Share Index NOUN an index of share prices produced by the *Financial Times*, designed to reflect general price trends: based on the average price of thirty British shares.

Financial Times Stock Exchange 100 Index NOUN an index of share prices produced by the *Financial Times* based on an average of 100 securities and giving the best indication of daily movements. Abbreviation: **FTSE 100 Index.** Informal name: **Footsie.**

Financial Times Stock Exchange Eurotrack 100 Index NOUN an index of share prices produced by the *Financial Times* of 100 companies from Continental Europe, designed to reflect the wider European market. Usually shortened to **Eurotrack.**

financial year NOUN *Brit* 1 any annual period at the end of which a firm's accounts are made up. 2 the annual period ending April 5, over which Budget estimates are made by the British Government and which functions as the income-tax year. US and Canadian equivalent: **fiscal year.**

financier (fɪˈnænsɪə, faɪ-) NOUN a person who is engaged or skilled in large-scale financial operations.

financing gap NOUN the difference between a country's requirements for foreign exchange to finance its debts and imports and its income from overseas.

finback (ˈfɪnˌbæk) NOUN another name for **rorqual.**

finch (fɪntʃ) NOUN 1 any songbird of the family *Fringillidae*, having a short stout bill for feeding on seeds and, in most species, a bright plumage in the male. Common examples are the goldfinch, bullfinch, chaffinch, siskin, and canary. 2 any of various similar or related birds. Related adjective: **fringilline.**
▷HISTORY Old English *finc*; related to Old High German *finko*, Middle Dutch *vinker*, Greek *spingos*

Finchley (ˈfɪntʃlɪ) NOUN a residential district of N London, part of the Greater London borough of Barnet from 1965.

find (faɪnd) VERB **finds, finding, found** (faʊnd). (*mainly tr*) 1 to meet with or discover by chance. 2 to discover or obtain, esp by search or effort: *to find happiness.* 3 (*may take a clause as object*) to become aware of; realize: *he found that nobody knew.* 4 (*may take a clause as object*) to regard as being; consider: *I find this wine a little sour.* 5 to look for and point out (something to be criticized): *to find fault.* 6 (*also intr*) *Law* to determine an issue after judicial inquiry and pronounce a verdict (upon): *the court found the accused guilty.* 7 to regain (something lost or not functioning): *to find one's tongue.* 8 to reach (a target): *the bullet found its mark.* 9 to provide, esp with difficulty: *we'll find room for you too.* 10 to be able to pay: *I can't find that amount of money.* 11 **find oneself.** to realize and accept one's real character; discover one's true vocation. 12 **find one's feet.** to become capable or confident, as in a new job. ◆ NOUN 13 a person, thing, etc., that is found, esp a valuable or fortunate discovery.
▷HISTORY Old English *findan*; related to Old Norse *finna*, Gothic *finthan*, Old High German *fintan* to find
▸ˈ**findable** ADJECTIVE

finder (ˈfaɪndə) NOUN 1 a person or thing that finds. 2 *Physics* a small low-power wide-angle telescope fitted to a more powerful larger telescope, used to locate celestial objects to be studied by the larger instrument. 3 *Photog* short for **viewfinder.** 4 **finders keepers.** *Informal* whoever finds something has the right to keep it.

fin de siècle *French* (fɛ̃ də sjɛklə) NOUN 1 the end of the 19th century, when traditional social, moral, and artistic values were in transition. ◆ ADJECTIVE **fin-de-siècle.** 2 of or relating to the close of the 19th century. 3 decadent, esp in artistic tastes.

finding (ˈfaɪndɪŋ) NOUN 1 a thing that is found or discovered. 2 *Law* the conclusion reached after a judicial inquiry; verdict. 3 (*plural*) *US* the tools and equipment of an artisan.

find out VERB (*adverb*) 1 to gain knowledge of (something); learn: *he found out what he wanted.* 2 to detect the crime, deception, etc., of (someone).

find the lady NOUN another name for **three-card trick.**

fine[1] (faɪn) ADJECTIVE 1 excellent or choice in quality; very good of its kind: *a fine speech.* 2 superior in skill, ability, or accomplishment: *a fine violinist.* 3 (of weather) clear and dry. 4 enjoyable or satisfying: *a fine time.* 5 (*postpositive*) *Informal* quite well; in satisfactory health: *I feel fine.* 6 satisfactory; acceptable: *that's fine by me.* 7 of delicate composition or careful workmanship: *fine crystal.* 8 (of precious metals) pure or having a high or specified degree of purity: *fine silver; gold 98 per cent fine.* 9 subtle in perception; discriminating: *a fine eye for antique brasses.* 10 abstruse or subtle: *a fine point in argument.* 11 very thin or slender: *fine hair.* 12 very small: *fine dust; fine print.* 13 (of edges, blades, etc.) sharp; keen. 14 ornate, showy, or smart. 15 good-looking; handsome: *a fine young woman.* 16 polished, elegant, or refined: *a fine gentleman.* 17 morally upright and commendable: *a fine man.* 18 *Cricket* (of a fielding position) oblique to and behind the wicket: *fine leg.* 19 (*prenominal*) *Informal* disappointing or terrible: *a fine mess.* ◆ ADVERB 20 *Informal* quite well; all right: *that suits me fine.* 21 a nonstandard word for **finely.** 22 *Billiards, snooker* (of a stroke on the cue ball) so as to merely brush the object ball. 23 **cut it fine.** to allow little margin of time, space, etc. ◆ VERB 24 to make or become finer; refine. 25 (often foll by *down* or *away*) to make or become smaller. 26 (*tr*) to clarify (wine, etc.) by adding finings. 27 (*tr*) *Billiards, snooker* to hit (a cue ball) fine. 28 (*intr; foll by up*) *Austral and NZ informal* (of the weather) to become fine.
▷HISTORY C13: from Old French *fin*, from Latin *fīnis* end, boundary, as in *fīnis honōrum* the highest degree of honour

fine[2] (faɪn) NOUN 1 a certain amount of money exacted as a penalty: *a parking fine.* 2 a payment made by a tenant at the start of his tenancy to reduce his subsequent rent; premium. 3 *Feudal law* a sum of money paid by a man to his lord, esp for the privilege of transferring his land to another. 4 a method of transferring land in England by bringing a fictitious law suit: abolished 1833. 5 **in fine. a** in short; briefly. **b** in conclusion; finally. ◆ VERB 6 (*tr*) to impose a fine on.
▷HISTORY C12 (in the sense: conclusion, settlement): from Old French *fin*; see FINE[1]

fine[3] (ˈfiːneɪ) NOUN *Music* 1 the point at which a piece is to end, usually after a *da capo* or *dal segno*. 2 an ending or finale.
▷HISTORY Italian, from Latin *fīnis* end

***fine*[4]** *French* (fin) NOUN brandy of ordinary quality.
▷HISTORY literally: fine

fineable (ˈfaɪnəbᵊl) ADJECTIVE a variant spelling of **finable.**
▸ˈ**fineableness** NOUN

fine art NOUN 1 art produced chiefly for its aesthetic value, as opposed to applied art. 2 (*often plural*) Also called: **beaux arts.** any of the fields in which such art is produced, such as painting, sculpture, and engraving.

fine-cut ADJECTIVE (of tobacco) finely cut or shredded.

fine-draw VERB **-draws, -drawing, -drew, -drawn.** (*tr*) 1 to sew together so finely that the join is scarcely noticeable. 2 to carry out the last drawing-out operation on (wire, tube, etc.) to reduce its diameter.

fine-drawn ADJECTIVE 1 (of arguments, distinctions, etc.) precise or subtle. 2 (of wire) drawn out until very fine; attenuated. 3 (of features) delicate or refined.

Fine Gael (ˈfɪnə ˈgeːl) NOUN one of the major political parties in the Republic of Ireland, formed in 1933.
▷HISTORY from Irish Gaelic *fine* tribe, race + *Gael* of the Gaels

fine-grain ADJECTIVE *Photog* having or producing an image with grain of inconspicuous size: *a fine-grain image; a fine-grain developer.*

fine-grained ADJECTIVE (of wood, leather, etc.) having a fine smooth even grain.

fine leg NOUN *Cricket* **a** a fielding position between long leg and square leg. **b** a fielder in this position.

finely (ˈfaɪnlɪ) ADVERB 1 into small pieces; minutely. 2 precisely or subtly. 3 splendidly or delicately.

fineness (ˈfaɪnnɪs) NOUN 1 the state or quality of being fine. 2 a measurement of the purity of precious metal, expressed as the number of parts per thousand that is precious metal.

fine print NOUN matter set in small type, as in a contract, esp considered as containing unfavourable conditions that the signer might overlook. Also called: **small print.**

finery[1] (ˈfaɪnərɪ) NOUN elaborate or showy decoration, esp clothing and jewellery.

finery[2] (ˈfaɪnərɪ) NOUN, *plural* **-eries.** a hearth for converting cast iron into wrought iron.
▷HISTORY C17: from Old French *finerie*, from *finer* to refine; see FINE[1]

fines herbes (*French* finz ɛrb) PLURAL NOUN a

mixture of finely chopped herbs, used to flavour omelettes, salads, etc.

finespun ('faɪn'spʌn) ADJECTIVE 1 spun or drawn out to a fine thread. 2 excessively subtle or refined; not practical.

finesse (fɪ'nɛs) NOUN 1 elegant skill in style or performance. 2 subtlety and tact in handling difficult situations. 3 *Bridge, whist* an attempt to win a trick when opponents hold a high card in the suit led by playing a lower card, hoping the opponent who has already played holds the missing card. 4 a trick, artifice, or strategy. ◆ VERB 5 to manage or bring about with finesse. 6 to play (a card) as a finesse.
▷HISTORY C15: from Old French, from *fin* fine, delicate; see FINE[1]

fine structure NOUN the splitting of a spectral line into two or more closely spaced components as a result of interaction between the spin and orbital angular momenta of the atomic electrons. Compare **hyperfine structure.**

fine-tooth comb *or* **fine-toothed comb** NOUN 1 a comb with fine teeth set closely together. 2 **go over** (*or* **through**) **with a fine-tooth(ed) comb.** to examine very thoroughly.

fine-tune VERB (*tr*) to make fine adjustments to (something) in order to obtain optimum performance.

finfoot ('fɪnˌfʊt) NOUN, *plural* **-foots.** any aquatic bird of the tropical and subtropical family *Heliornithidae*, having broadly lobed toes, a long slender head and neck, and pale brown plumage: order *Gruiformes* (cranes, rails etc.). Also called: **sungrebe.**

Fingal's Cave ('fɪŋgᵊlz) NOUN a cave in W Scotland, on Staffa Island in the Inner Hebrides: basaltic pillars. Length: 69 m (227 ft.). Height: 36 m (117 ft.).

finger ('fɪŋgə) NOUN 1 **a** any of the digits of the hand, often excluding the thumb. Technical name: **digitus manus. b** (*as modifier*): *a finger bowl.* **c** (*in combination*): *a fingernail.* Related adjective: **digital.** 2 the part of a glove made to cover a finger. 3 something that resembles a finger in shape or function: *a finger of land.* 4 Also called: **digit.** the length or width of a finger used as a unit of measurement. 5 a quantity of liquid in a glass, etc., as deep as a finger is wide; tot. 6 a projecting machine part, esp one serving as an indicator, guide, or guard. 7 **burn one's fingers.** to suffer from having meddled or been rash. 8 **get** *or* **pull one's finger out.** *Brit informal* to begin or speed up activity, esp after initial delay or slackness. 9 **have a** (*or* **one's**) **finger in the pie. a** to have an interest in or take part in some activity. **b** to meddle or interfere. 10 **lay a finger on.** (*usually negative*) to harm. 11 **lay** *or* **put one's finger on.** to indicate, identify, or locate accurately. 12 **not lift** (*or* **raise**) **a finger.** (*foll by an infinitive*) not to make any effort (to do something). 13 **let slip through one's fingers.** to allow to escape; miss narrowly. 14 **point the finger at.** to accuse or blame. 15 **put the finger on.** *Informal* **a** to inform on or identify, esp for the police. **b** to choose (the victim or location of an intended crime). 16 **twist** *or* **wrap around one's little finger.** to have easy and complete control or influence over. ◆ VERB 17 (*tr*) to touch or manipulate with the fingers; handle. 18 (*tr*) *Informal, chiefly US* to identify as a criminal or suspect. 19 (*intr*) to extend like a finger. 20 to use one's fingers in playing (an instrument, such as a piano or clarinet). 21 to indicate on (a composition or part) the fingering required by a pianist, harpsichordist, etc. 22 (*tr; usually passive*) to arrange the keys of (a clarinet, flute, etc.) for playing in a certain way.
▷HISTORY Old English; related to Old Norse *fingr*, Gothic *figgrs*, Old High German *fingar*; see FIVE, FIST
▸'**fingerer** NOUN ▸'**fingerless** ADJECTIVE

fingerboard ('fɪŋgəˌbɔːd) NOUN the long strip of hard wood on a violin, guitar, or related stringed instrument upon which the strings are stopped by the fingers.

finger bowl NOUN a small bowl filled with water for rinsing the fingers at the table after a meal.

fingerbreadth ('fɪŋgəˌbrɛdθ, -ˌbrɛtθ) *or* **finger's breadth** NOUN the width of a finger, used as an indication of length.

finger buffet ('bʊfeɪ) NOUN a buffet meal at which food that may be picked up with the fingers (**finger food**), such as canapés or vol-au-vents, is served.

fingered ('fɪŋgəd) ADJECTIVE 1 marked or dirtied by handling. 2 **a** having a finger or fingers. **b** (*in combination*): *nine-fingered; red-fingered.* 3 (of a musical part) having numerals indicating the necessary fingering.

fingering[1] ('fɪŋgərɪŋ) NOUN 1 the technique or art of using one's fingers in playing a musical instrument, esp the piano. 2 the numerals in a musical part indicating this.

fingering[2] ('fɪŋgərɪŋ) NOUN fine wool for knitting.
▷HISTORY C17: from earlier *fingram*, perhaps from Old French *fin grain* fine grain

fingerling ('fɪŋgəlɪŋ) NOUN 1 a very young fish, esp the parr of salmon or trout. 2 a diminutive creature or object.

fingermark ('fɪŋgəˌmɑːk) NOUN a mark left by dirty or greasy fingers on paintwork, walls, etc.

fingernail ('fɪŋgəˌneɪl) NOUN a thin horny translucent plate covering part of the dorsal surface of the end joint of each finger. Related adjectives: **ungual, ungular.**

finger painting NOUN 1 the process or art of painting with **finger paints** of starch, glycerine, and pigments, using the fingers, hand, or arm. 2 a painting made in this way.

finger post NOUN a signpost showing a pointing finger or hand.

fingerprint ('fɪŋgəˌprɪnt) NOUN 1 an impression of the pattern of ridges on the palmar surface of the end joint of each finger and thumb. 2 any identifying characteristic. 3 *Biochem* the pattern of fragments obtained when a protein is digested by a proteolytic enzyme, usually observed following two-dimensional separation by chromatography and electrophoresis. ◆ VERB 4 (*tr*) to take an inked impression of the fingerprints of (a person). 5 to take a sample of (a person's) DNA.

fingerstall ('fɪŋgəˌstɔːl) NOUN a protective covering for a finger. Also called: **cot, fingertip.**

finger tight ADJECTIVE made as tight as possible by hand.

fingertip ('fɪŋgəˌtɪp) NOUN 1 the end joint or tip of a finger. 2 another term for **fingerstall.** 3 **at one's fingertips.** readily available and within one's mental grasp.

fingertip search NOUN a detailed search made by passing the fingers over the scene of a crime or incident.

finger trouble NOUN *Computing* trouble caused by operator error, such as striking the wrong key.

finger wave NOUN *Hairdressing* a wave set in wet hair by using fingers and comb only.

Fingo ('fɪŋgəʊ) NOUN, *plural* **-go** *or* **-gos.** a member of a Xhosa-speaking people settled in southern Africa in the Ciskei and Transkei: originally refugees from the Zulu wars of conquest.

finial ('faɪnɪəl) NOUN 1 an ornament on top of a spire, gable, etc., esp in the form of a foliated fleur-de-lys. 2 an ornament at the top of a piece of furniture, etc.
▷HISTORY C14: from *finial* (adj), variant of FINAL
▸'**finialed** ADJECTIVE

finical ('fɪnɪkᵊl) ADJECTIVE another word for **finicky.**
▸ˌ**fini'cality** NOUN ▸'**finically** ADVERB ▸'**finicalness** NOUN

finicky ('fɪnɪkɪ) *or* **finicking** ADJECTIVE 1 excessively particular, as in tastes or standards; fussy. 2 full of trivial detail; overelaborate.
▷HISTORY C19: from FINICAL

fining ('faɪnɪŋ) NOUN 1 the process of removing undissolved gas bubbles from molten glass. 2 the process of clarifying liquors by the addition of a coagulant. 3 (*plural*) a substance, such as isinglass, added to wine, beer, etc., to clarify it.
▷HISTORY C17: from FINE[1] (in the sense: to clarify, refine)

finis ('fɪnɪs) NOUN the end; finish: used at the end of books, films, etc.
▷HISTORY C15: from Latin

finish ('fɪnɪʃ) VERB (*mainly tr*) 1 to bring to an end; complete, conclude, or stop. 2 (*intr;* sometimes foll by *up*) to be at or come to the end; use up. 3 to bring to a desired or complete condition. 4 to put a particular surface texture on (wood, cloth, etc.). 5 (often foll by *off*) to destroy or defeat completely. 6 to train (a person) in social graces and talents. 7 (*intr;* foll by *with*) **a** to end a relationship or association. **b** to stop punishing a person: *I haven't finished with you yet!* ◆ NOUN 8 the final or last stage or part; end. 9 **a** the death, destruction, or absolute defeat of a person or one side in a conflict: *a fight to the finish.* **b** the person, event, or thing that brings this about. 10 **a** the surface texture or appearance of wood, cloth, etc.: *a rough finish.* **b** a preparation, such as varnish, used to produce such a texture. 11 a thing, event, etc., that completes. 12 completeness and high quality of workmanship. 13 refinement in social graces. 14 *Sport* ability to sprint at the end of a race: *he has a good finish.*
▷HISTORY C14: from Old French *finir*, from Latin *fīnīre* see FINE[1]

finished ('fɪnɪʃt) ADJECTIVE 1 perfected. 2 (*predicative*) at the end of a task, activity, etc.: *they were finished by four.* 3 (*predicative*) without further hope of success or continuation: *she was finished as a prima ballerina.*

finisher ('fɪnɪʃə) NOUN 1 a craftsman who carries out the final tasks in a manufacturing process. 2 *Boxing* a knockout blow.

finishing ('fɪnɪʃɪŋ) NOUN *Football* the act or skill of goal scoring: *Brattbakk's finishing is deadly.*

finishing school NOUN a private school for girls that prepares them for society by teaching social graces and accomplishments.

Finistère (ˌfɪnɪ'stɛə; *French* finistɛr) NOUN a department of NW France, at the tip of the Breton peninsula. Capital: Quimper. Pop.: 852 418 (1999). Area: 7029 sq. km (2741 sq. miles).

Finisterre (ˌfɪnɪ'stɛə) NOUN 1 **Cape.** a headland in NW Spain: the westernmost point of the Spanish mainland. 2 an English name for **Finistère.**

finite ('faɪnaɪt) ADJECTIVE 1 bounded in magnitude or spatial or temporal extent: *a finite difference.* 2 *Maths, logic* having a number of elements that is a natural number; able to be counted using the natural numbers less than some natural number. Compare **denumerable, infinite** (sense 4). 3 **a** limited or restricted in nature: *human existence is finite.* **b** (*as noun*): *the finite.* 4 denoting any form or occurrence of a verb inflected for grammatical features such as person, number, and tense.
▷HISTORY C15: from Latin *fīnītus* limited, from *fīnīre* to limit, end
▸'**finitely** ADVERB ▸'**finiteness** NOUN

finitism ('faɪnaɪtˌɪzəm) NOUN *Philosophy, logic* the view that only those entities may be admitted to mathematics that can be constructed in a finite number of steps, and only those propositions entertained whose truth can be proved in a finite number of steps. Compare **intuitionism.**

fink (fɪŋk) *Slang, chiefly US and Canadian* ◆ NOUN 1 a strikebreaker; blackleg. 2 an informer, such as one working for the police; spy. 3 an unpleasant, disappointing, or contemptible person. ◆ VERB 4 (*intr;* often foll by *on*) to inform (on someone), as to the police.
▷HISTORY C20: of uncertain origin

fin keel NOUN a projection from the keel of a vessel to give it additional stability.

fink out VERB (*intr, adverb*) *Slang, chiefly US* to fail to carry something out or through; give up.

Finland ('fɪnlənd) NOUN 1 a republic in N Europe, on the Baltic Sea: ceded to Russia by Sweden in 1809; gained independence in 1917; Soviet invasion successfully withstood in 1939–40, with the loss of Karelia; a member of the European Union. It is generally low-lying, with about 50 000 lakes, extensive forests, and peat bogs. Official languages: Finnish and Swedish. Religion: Christian, Lutheran majority. Currency: euro. Capital: Helsinki. Pop.: 5 185 000 (2001 est.). Area: 337 000 sq. km (130 120 sq. miles). Finnish name: **Suomi.** 2 **Gulf of.** an arm of the Baltic Sea between Finland, Estonia, and Russia.

Finlandization *or* **Finlandisation** (ˌfɪnləndaɪ'zeɪʃən) NOUN neutralization of a small country by a superpower, using conciliation, as the former Soviet Union did in relation to Finland.

Finn[1] (fɪn) NOUN 1 a native, inhabitant, or citizen of Finland. 2 a speaker of a Finnic language, esp

one of the original inhabitants of Russia, who were pushed northwards during the Slav migrations.
▷**HISTORY** Old English *Finnas* (plural); related to Old Norse *Finnr* Finn, Latin *Fennī* the Finns, Greek *Phinnoi*

Finn[2] (fɪn) NOUN known as *Finn MacCool*. (in Irish legend) chief of the Fianna, father of the heroic poet Ossian.

finnan haddock ('fɪnən) *or* **haddie** ('hædɪ) NOUN smoked haddock.
▷**HISTORY** C18: *finnan* after *Findon*, a village in Scotland south of Aberdeen + HADDOCK

finned (fɪnd) ADJECTIVE having one or more fins or finlike parts.

finner ('fɪnə) NOUN another name for **rorqual.**
▷**HISTORY** C18: from FIN[1] + -ER[1]

Finnic ('fɪnɪk) NOUN 1 one of the two branches of the Finno-Ugric family of languages, including Finnish and several languages of NE Europe. Compare **Ugric.** ◆ ADJECTIVE 2 of or relating to this group of languages or to the Finns.

Finnish ('fɪnɪʃ) ADJECTIVE 1 of, relating to, or characteristic of Finland, the Finns, or their language. ◆ NOUN 2 the official language of Finland, also spoken in Estonia and NW Russia, belonging to the Finno-Ugric family.

Finnmark ('fɪn,mɑːk) NOUN a county of N Norway: the largest, northernmost, and least populated county; mostly a barren plateau. Capital: Vadsø. Pop.: 74 059 (2000 est.). Area: 48 649 sq. km (18 779 sq. miles).

finnock ('fɪnək) NOUN a young sea trout on its first return to fresh water.
▷**HISTORY** originally Scot: from Gaelic *fionnag*, from *fionn* white

Finno-Ugric ('fɪnəʊ'uːgrɪk, -'juː-) *or* **Finno-Ugrian** NOUN 1 a family of languages spoken in Scandinavia, Hungary, and NE Europe, including Finnish, Estonian, Hungarian, Ostyak, and Vogul: generally regarded as a subfamily of Uralic. See also **Ural-Altaic.** ◆ ADJECTIVE 2 of, relating to, speaking, or belonging to this family of languages.

finny ('fɪnɪ) ADJECTIVE **-nier, -niest.** 1 *Poetic* relating to or containing many fishes. 2 having or resembling a fin or fins.

fino ('fiːnəʊ) NOUN a very dry sherry.
▷**HISTORY** from Spanish: FINE[1]

finocchio *or* **finochio** (fɪ'nɒkɪ,əʊ) NOUN a variety of fennel, *Foeniculum vulgare dulce*, with thickened stalks that resemble celery and are eaten as a vegetable, esp in S Europe. Also called: **Florence fennel.**
▷**HISTORY** C18: from Italian: FENNEL

Finsteraarhorn (*German* ˌfɪnstər'aːrhɔrn) NOUN a mountain in S central Switzerland: highest peak in the Bernese Alps. Height: 4274 m (14 022 ft.).

fiord (fjɔːd) NOUN a variant spelling of **fjord.**

fiorin ('faɪərɪn) NOUN a temperate perennial grass, *Agrostis stolonifera*. Also called: **creeping bent grass.** See **bent grass.**
▷**HISTORY** C19: from Irish Gaelic *fiorthann* wheat grass

fioritura (ˌfjɔːrɪ'tʊərə, ˌfiːərɪ-) NOUN, *plural* **-ture** (-'tʊəreɪ). *Music* embellishment, esp ornamentation added by the performer.
▷**HISTORY** Italian: a blossoming

fipple ('fɪpᵊl) NOUN 1 a wooden plug forming a flue in the end of a pipe, as the mouthpiece of a recorder. 2 a similar device in an organ pipe with a flutelike tone.
▷**HISTORY** C17: of unknown origin

fipple flute NOUN an end-blown flute provided with a fipple, such as the recorder or flageolet.

fir (fɜː) NOUN 1 any pyramidal coniferous tree of the N temperate genus *Abies*, having single needle-like leaves and erect cones: family *Pinaceae*. See also **red fir, silver fir, balsam fir.** 2 any of various other trees of the family *Pinaceae*, such as the Douglas fir. 3 the wood of any of these trees.
▷**HISTORY** Old English *furh*; related to Old Norse *fura*, Old High German *foraha* fir, Latin *quercus* oak

fire (faɪə) NOUN 1 the state of combustion in which inflammable material burns, producing heat, flames, and often smoke. 2 **a** a mass of burning coal, wood, etc., used esp in a hearth to heat a room. **b** (*in combination*): *firewood; firelighter*. 3 a destructive conflagration, as of a forest, building, etc. 4 a device for heating a room, etc. 5 something resembling a fire in light or brilliance: *a diamond's fire*. 6 a flash or spark of or as if of fire. 7 **a** the act of discharging weapons, artillery, etc. **b** the shells, etc., fired. 8 a burst or rapid volley: *a fire of questions*. 9 intense passion; ardour. 10 liveliness, as of imagination, thought, etc. 11 a burning sensation sometimes produced by drinking strong alcoholic liquor. 12 fever and inflammation. 13 a severe trial or torment (esp in the phrase **go through fire and water**). 14 **catch fire.** to ignite. 15 **draw someone's fire.** to attract the criticism or censure of someone. 16 **hang fire. a** to delay firing. **b** to delay or be delayed. 17 **no smoke without fire.** the evidence strongly suggests something has indeed happened. 18 **on fire. a** in a state of ignition. **b** ardent or eager. **c** *Informal* playing or performing at the height of one's abilities. 19 **open fire.** to start firing a gun, artillery, etc. 20 **play with fire.** to be involved in something risky. 21 **set fire to** *or* **set on fire. a** to ignite. **b** to arouse or excite. 22 **set the world** *or* (*Brit*) **the Thames** *or* (*Scot*) **the heather on fire.** *Informal* to cause a great sensation. 23 **under fire.** being attacked, as by weapons or by harsh criticism. 24 (*modifier*) *Astrology* of or relating to a group of three signs of the zodiac, Aries, Leo, and Sagittarius. Compare **earth** (sense 10), **air** (sense 20), **water** (sense 12). ◆ VERB 25 to discharge (a firearm or projectile) or (of a firearm, etc.) to be discharged. 26 to detonate (an explosive charge or device) or (of such a charge or device) to be detonated. 27 (*tr*) *Informal* to dismiss from employment. 28 (*tr*) *Ceramics* to bake in a kiln to harden the clay, fix the glaze, etc. 29 to kindle or be kindled; ignite. 30 (*tr*) to provide with fuel: *oil fires the heating system*. 31 (*intr*) to tend a fire. 32 (*tr*) to subject to heat. 33 (*tr*) to heat slowly so as to dry. 34 (*tr*) to arouse to strong emotion. 35 to glow or cause to glow. 36 (*intr*) (of an internal-combustion engine) to ignite. 37 (*intr*) (of grain) to become blotchy or yellow before maturity. 38 *Vet science* another word for **cauterize.** 39 (*intr*) *Austral informal* (of a sportsman, etc.) to play well or with enthusiasm. ◆ SENTENCE SUBSTITUTE 40 a cry to warn others of a fire. 41 the order to begin firing a gun, artillery, etc.
▷**HISTORY** Old English *fȳr*; related to Old Saxon *fiur*, Old Norse *fūrr*, Old High German *fūir*, Greek *pur*
▸ **'fireable** ADJECTIVE ▸ **'fireless** ADJECTIVE ▸ **'firer** NOUN

fire alarm NOUN 1 a device to give warning of fire, esp a bell, siren, or hooter. 2 a shout to warn that a fire has broken out.

fire-and-brimstone ADJECTIVE (of a sermon, preacher, etc.) zealous, esp in threatening eternal damnation.

fire ant NOUN any mound-building predatory ant of the genus *Solenopsis*, of tropical and subtropical America, that can inflict a painful sting.

firearm ('faɪər,ɑːm) NOUN a weapon, esp a portable gun or pistol, from which a projectile can be discharged by an explosion caused by igniting gunpowder, etc.

fire away VERB (*intr, adverb; often imperative*) *Informal* to begin to speak or to ask questions.

fireback ('faɪə,bæk) NOUN 1 Also called: **reredos.** an ornamental iron slab against the back wall of a hearth. 2 any pheasant of the genus *Lophura*, of SE Asia.

fireball ('faɪə,bɔːl) NOUN 1 a ball-shaped discharge of lightning. 2 the bright spherical region of hot ionized gas at the centre of a nuclear explosion. 3 *Astronomy* another name for **bolide.** 4 *Slang* an energetic person.

firebird ('faɪə,bɜːd) NOUN *Chiefly US* any of various songbirds having a bright red plumage, esp the Baltimore oriole.

fire blanket NOUN a large blanket-like piece of fire-resistant material such as fibreglass used in smothering a fire.

fire blight NOUN a disease of apples, pears, and similar fruit trees, caused by the bacterium *Erwinia amylovora* and characterized by blackening of the blossoms and leaves, and cankers on the branches.

fireboat ('faɪə,bəʊt) NOUN a motor vessel with fire-fighting apparatus.

firebomb ('faɪə,bɒm) NOUN another name for **incendiary** (sense 6).

firebox ('faɪə,bɒks) NOUN 1 the furnace chamber of a boiler in a steam locomotive. 2 an obsolete word for **tinderbox.**

firebrand ('faɪə,brænd) NOUN 1 a piece of burning or glowing wood or other material. 2 a person who causes unrest or is very energetic.

firebrat ('faɪə,bræt) NOUN a small primitive wingless insect, *Thermobia domestica*, that occurs in warm buildings, feeding on starchy food scraps, fabric, etc.: order *Thysanura* (bristletails).

firebreak ('faɪə,breɪk) NOUN 1 Also: **fireguard, fire line.** a strip of open land in forest or prairie, to arrest the advance of a fire. 2 a measure taken to arrest the advance of anything dangerous or harmful.

firebrick ('faɪə,brɪk) NOUN a refractory brick made of fire clay, used for lining furnaces, flues, etc.

fire brigade NOUN *Chiefly Brit* an organized body of firefighters.

firebug ('faɪə,bʌg) NOUN *Informal* a person who deliberately sets fire to property.

fire clay NOUN a heat-resistant clay used in the making of firebricks, furnace linings, etc.

fire company NOUN 1 an insurance company selling policies relating to fire risk. 2 *US* an organized body of firemen.

fire control NOUN *Military* the procedures by which weapons are brought to engage a target.

firecracker ('faɪə,krækə) NOUN 1 a small cardboard container filled with explosive powder and lit by a fuse. ◆ ADJECTIVE 2 impressively energetic: *a firecracker start to the race*.

firecrest ('faɪə,krest) NOUN a small European warbler, *Regulus ignicapillus*, having a crown striped with yellow, black, and white.

fire-cure VERB (*tr*) to cure (tobacco) by exposure to the smoke and heat of an open fire.

firedamp ('faɪə,dæmp) NOUN a mixture of hydrocarbons, chiefly methane, formed in coal mines. It forms explosive mixtures with air. See also **afterdamp.**

fire department NOUN *US and Canadian* the department of a local authority responsible for the prevention and extinguishing of fires.

firedog ('faɪə,dɒg) NOUN either of a pair of decorative metal stands used to support logs in an open fire.

fire door NOUN 1 a door made of noncombustible material, the purpose of which is to prevent a fire from spreading within a building. 2 a similar door, leading to the outside of a building, that can be easily opened from inside; emergency exit.

firedrake ('faɪə,dreɪk) *or* **firedragon** ('faɪə,drægən) NOUN *Myth* a fire-breathing dragon.

fire drill NOUN a rehearsal of duties or escape procedures to be followed in case of fire.

fire-eater NOUN 1 a performer who simulates the swallowing of fire. 2 a belligerent person.
▸ **'fire-ˌeating** NOUN, ADJECTIVE

fire engine NOUN a heavy road vehicle that carries firemen and fire-fighting equipment to a fire.

fire escape NOUN a means of evacuating persons from a building in the event of fire, esp a metal staircase outside the building.

fire-extinguisher NOUN a portable device for extinguishing fires, usually consisting of a canister with a directional nozzle used to direct a spray of water, chemically generated foam, inert gas, or fine powder onto the fire.

firefight ('faɪə,faɪt) NOUN a brief small-scale engagement between opposing military ground forces using short-range light weapons.

firefighter ('faɪə,faɪtə) NOUN a person who fights fires, usually a public employee or trained volunteer.

firefighting ('faɪə,faɪtɪŋ) NOUN 1 **a** the occupation of attempting to control and extinguish fires. **b** (*as modifier*): *firefighting equipment*. 2 the practice of reacting to urgent problems as they arise, as opposed to planning for the future.

firefly ('faɪə,flaɪ) NOUN, *plural* **-flies.** 1 any nocturnal beetle of the family *Lampyridae*, common in warm and tropical regions, having luminescent abdominal organs. See also **glow-worm.** 2 any tropical American click beetle of the genus

Pyrophorus, esp *P. noctiluca*, that have luminescent thoracic organs.

fireguard ('faɪəˌgɑːd) NOUN **1** Also called: **fire screen.** a metal panel or meshed frame put before an open fire to protect against falling logs, sparks, etc. **2** a less common word for **firebreak.**

fire hall NOUN *US and Canadian* a fire station.

fire hydrant NOUN a hydrant for use as an emergency supply for fighting fires, esp one in a street. Also called (esp US and NZ): **fireplug.**

fire insurance NOUN insurance covering damage or loss caused by fire or lightning.

fire irons PLURAL NOUN metal fireside implements, such as poker, shovel, and tongs.

fireless cooker NOUN an insulated container that retains enough heat to cook food or keep it warm.

firelock ('faɪəˌlɒk) NOUN **1** an obsolete type of gunlock with a priming mechanism ignited by sparks. **2** a gun or musket having such a lock.

fireman ('faɪəmən) NOUN, *plural* **-men. 1** a man who fights fires, usually a public employee or trained volunteer. **2 a** (on steam locomotives) the man who stokes the fire and controls the injectors feeding water to the boiler. **b** (on diesel and electric locomotives) the driver's assistant. **3** a man who tends furnaces; stoker. **4** Also called: **deputy.** a mine official responsible for safety precautions. US equivalent: **fire boss. 5** *US navy* a junior rating who works on marine engineering equipment.

fire marshal NOUN *US* **1** a public official responsible for investigating the causes of fires, enforcing fire prevention laws, etc. **2** the head of a fire prevention organization.

Firenze (fi'rɛntse) NOUN the Italian name for **Florence.**

fire opal NOUN an orange-red translucent variety of opal, valued as a gemstone.

firepan ('faɪəˌpæn) NOUN a metal container for a fire in a room.

fireplace ('faɪəˌpleɪs) NOUN **1** an open recess in a wall of a room, at the base of a chimney, etc., for a fire; hearth. **2** *Austral* an authorized place or installation for outside cooking, esp by a roadside.

fireplug ('faɪəˌplʌg) NOUN another name (esp US and NZ) for **fire hydrant.**

fire power NOUN *Military* **1** the amount of fire that may be delivered by a unit or weapon. **2** the capability of delivering fire.

fireproof ('faɪəˌpruːf) ADJECTIVE **1** capable of resisting damage by fire. ◆ VERB **2** (*tr*) to make resistant to fire.

fire raiser NOUN a person who deliberately sets fire to property.
▸**fire raising** NOUN

fire sale NOUN **1** a sale of goods at reduced prices after a fire at a shop or factory. **2** any instance of offering goods or assets at greatly reduced prices to ensure a quick sale.

fire screen NOUN **1** a decorative screen placed in the hearth when there is no fire. **2** a screen placed before a fire to protect the face from intense heat.

fire ship NOUN a vessel loaded with explosives and used, esp formerly, as a bomb by igniting it and directing it to drift among an enemy's warships.

fireside ('faɪəˌsaɪd) NOUN **1** the hearth. **2** family life; the home.

fire station NOUN a building where fire-fighting vehicles and equipment are stationed and where firefighters on duty wait. Also called (US): **firehouse, station house.**

firestone ('faɪəˌstəʊn) NOUN a sandstone that withstands intense heat, esp one used for lining kilns, furnaces, etc.

firestorm ('faɪəˌstɔːm) NOUN an uncontrollable blaze sustained by violent winds that are drawn into the column of rising hot air over the burning area: often the result of heavy bombing.

firethorn ('faɪəˌθɔːn) NOUN any rosaceous evergreen spiny shrub of the genus *Pyracantha*, of SE Europe and Asia, having bright red or orange fruits: cultivated for ornament.

fire trail NOUN *Austral* a permanent track cleared through the bush to provide access for fire-fighting.

firetrap ('faɪəˌtræp) NOUN a building that would burn easily or one without fire escapes.

fire walking NOUN a religious rite in which people walk barefoot over white-hot ashes, stones, etc.

firewall NOUN **1** a fireproof wall or partition used to impede the progress of a fire, as from one room or compartment to another. **2** *Computing* a computer system that isolates another computer from the Internet in order to prevent unauthorized access.

firewarden ('faɪəˌwɔːdᵊn) NOUN *US and Canadian* an officer responsible for fire prevention and control in an area, esp in a forest.

fire watcher NOUN a person who watches for fires, esp those caused by aerial bombardment.

firewater ('faɪəˌwɔːtə) NOUN any strong spirit, esp whisky.

fireweed ('faɪəˌwiːd) NOUN **1** any of various plants that appear as first vegetation in burnt-over areas, esp rosebay willowherb. **2** Also called: **pilewort.** a weedy North American plant, *Erechtites hieracifolia*, having small white or greenish flowers: family *Asteraceae* (composites).

firewheel tree ('faɪəˌwiːl) NOUN an Australian rainforest tree, *Stenocarpus sinuatus*, having whorls of bright red flowers.

firework ('faɪəˌwɜːk) NOUN a device, such as a Catherine wheel, Roman candle, or rocket, in which combustible materials are ignited and produce coloured flames, sparks, and smoke, sometimes accompanied by bangs.

fireworks ('faɪəˌwɜːks) PLURAL NOUN **1** a show in which large numbers of fireworks are let off simultaneously. **2** *Informal* an exciting or spectacular exhibition, as of musical virtuosity or wit. **3** *Informal* a burst of temper.

firing ('faɪərɪŋ) NOUN **1** the process of baking ceramics, etc., in a kiln or furnace: *a second firing.* **2** the act of stoking a fire or furnace. **3** a discharge of a firearm. **4** something used as fuel, such as coal or wood. **5** *US* a scorching of plants, as a result of disease, drought, or heat.

firing line NOUN **1** *Military* **a** the positions from which fire is delivered. **b** the soldiers occupying these positions. **2** the leading or most advanced position in an activity.

firing order NOUN the sequence of ignition in the cylinders of an internal-combustion engine.

firing party NOUN **1** a military detachment detailed to fire a salute at a funeral. **2** another name for **firing squad.**

firing pin NOUN the part of the firing mechanism of a firearm that ignites the charge by striking the primer.

firing squad NOUN a small military detachment formed to implement a death sentence by shooting.

firkin ('fɜːkɪn) NOUN **1** a small wooden barrel or similar container. **2** *Brit* a unit of capacity equal to nine gallons.
▷HISTORY C14 *fir*, from Middle Dutch *vierde* FOURTH + -KIN

firm[1] (fɜːm) ADJECTIVE **1** not soft or yielding to a touch or pressure; rigid; solid. **2** securely in position; stable or stationary. **3** definitely established; decided; settled. **4** enduring or steady; constant. **5** having determination or strength; resolute. **6** (of prices, markets, etc.) tending to rise. ◆ ADVERB **7** in a secure, stable, or unyielding manner: *he stood firm over his obligation to pay.* ◆ VERB **8** (sometimes foll by *up*) to make or become firm. **9** (*intr*) *Austral horse racing* (of a horse) to shorten in odds.
▷HISTORY C14: from Latin *firmus*
▸'**firmly** ADVERB ▸'**firmness** NOUN

firm[2] (fɜːm) NOUN **1** a business partnership. **2** any commercial enterprise. **3** a team of doctors and their assistants. **4** *Brit slang* **a** a gang of criminals. **b** a gang of football hooligans.
▷HISTORY C16 (in the sense: signature): from Spanish *firma* signature, title of a partnership or business concern, from *firmar* to sign, from Latin *firmāre* to confirm, from *firmus* firm

firmament ('fɜːməmənt) NOUN the expanse of the sky; heavens.
▷HISTORY C13: from Late Latin *firmāmentum* sky (considered as fixed above the earth), from Latin: prop, support, from *firmāre* to make FIRM[1]
▸**firmamental** (ˌfɜːmə'mɛntᵊl) ADJECTIVE

firman (fɜː'mɑːn, 'fɜː-) NOUN **1** an edict of an Oriental sovereign. **2** any authoritative grant of permission.
▷HISTORY C17: from Persian *fermān*

firmer chisel ('fɜːmə) NOUN a chisel or gouge with a thin blade, used on wood. Sometimes shortened to **firmer.**

firmware ('fɜːmˌwɛə) NOUN *Computing* a fixed form of software programmed into a read-only memory.

firn (fɪən) NOUN another name for **névé** (sense 1).
▷HISTORY C19: from German (Swiss dialect) *firn* of the previous year, from Old High German *firni* old

firn line NOUN **1** Also called: **firn limit.** the zone of a glacier between the lower region of solid ice and the upper region of névé, above which ablation occurs. **2** the snow line on a glacier.

firry ('fɜːrɪ) ADJECTIVE **1** of, relating to, or made from fir trees. **2** abounding in or dominated by firs.

first (fɜːst) ADJECTIVE (*usually prenominal*) **1 a** coming before all others; earliest, best, or foremost. **b** (*as noun*): *I was the first to arrive.* **2** preceding all others in numbering or counting order; the ordinal number of *one*. Often written: 1st. **3** rated, graded, or ranked above all other levels. **4** denoting the lowest forward ratio of a gearbox in a motor vehicle. **5** *Music* **a** denoting the highest part assigned to one of the voice parts in a chorus or one of the sections of an orchestra: *first soprano; the first violins.* **b** denoting the principal player in a specific orchestral section: *he plays first horn.* **6 first thing.** as the first action of the day: *I'll see you first thing tomorrow.* **7 first things first.** things must be done in order of priority. **8 the first thing, idea,** etc. (*in negative constructions*) even one thing, etc.: *he doesn't know the first thing about me.* ◆ NOUN **9** the beginning; outset: *I knew you were a rogue from the first; I couldn't see at first because of the mist.* **10** *Education, chiefly Brit* an honours degree of the highest class. Full term: **first-class honours degree. 11** the lowest forward ratio of a gearbox in a motor vehicle; low gear. **12** *Music* **a** the highest part in a particular section of a chorus or orchestra. **b** the instrument or voice taking such a part. **c** the chief or leading player in a section of an orchestra; principal. **13** *Music* a rare word for **prime** (sense 11). ◆ ADVERB **14** before anything else in order, time, preference, importance, etc.: *do this first; first, remove the head and tail of the fish.* **15 first and last.** on the whole; overall. **16 from first to last.** throughout. **17** for the first time: *I've loved you since I first saw you.* **18** (*sentence modifier*) in the first place or beginning of a series of actions: *first I want to talk about criminality.* ◆ See also **firsts.**
▷HISTORY Old English *fyrest*; related to Old Saxon *furist*, Old Norse *fyrstr*, German *Fürst* prince, one who is first in rank

first aid NOUN **1 a** immediate medical assistance given in an emergency. **b** (*as modifier*): *first-aid box.* **2** (in Barbados) a small shop that sells domestic items after hours.

first base NOUN **1** *Baseball* **a** the base that a runner must reach safely to score a hit, and the first of the three bases he must reach safely on the way to home plate in order to score a run. **b** the fielding position nearest this base. **2 get to first base.** *Informal, chiefly US and Canadian* to accomplish the first step of an undertaking.

first blood NOUN **1** the first killing or wounding in a fight or war. **2** the first damage or reverse inflicted on an opponent in a conflict.

first-born ADJECTIVE **1** eldest of the children in a family. ◆ NOUN **2** the eldest child in a family.

first cause NOUN **1** a source or cause of something. **2** (*often capitals*) (esp in philosophy) God considered as the uncaused creator of all beings apart from himself.

first class NOUN **1** the class or grade of the best or highest value, quality, etc. ◆ ADJECTIVE (**first-class** *when prenominal*) **2** of the best or highest class or grade: *a first-class citizen.* **3** excellent; first-rate. **4** of or denoting the most comfortable and expensive class of accommodation in a hotel, aircraft, train, etc. **5 a** (in Britain) of or relating to mail that is processed most quickly. **b** (in the US and Canada) of or relating to mail that consists mainly of written letters, cards, etc. 6 *Education* See **first** (sense 10). ◆ ADVERB **first-class.** 7 by first-class mail, means of transportation, etc.

first-day cover NOUN *Philately* a cover, usually an envelope, postmarked on the first day of the issue of its stamps.

first-degree burn NOUN *Pathol* See **burn**[1] (sense 22).

First Empire NOUN the period of imperial rule in France (1804–14) under Napoleon Bonaparte.

first estate NOUN the first of the three estates of the realm, such as the Lords Spiritual in England or the clergy in France until the revolution.

First Fleet NOUN *Austral* the fleet of convict ships that arrived at Port Jackson in 1788.
▸ **First Fleeter** NOUN

first floor NOUN 1 *Brit* the floor or storey of a building immediately above the ground floor. US and Canadian term: **second floor.** 2 *US and Canadian* another term for **ground floor.**

first-foot *Chiefly Scot* ◆ NOUN *also* **first-footer.** 1 the first person to enter a household in the New Year. By Hogmanay tradition a dark-haired man who crosses the threshold at midnight brings good luck. ◆ VERB 2 to enter (a house) as first-foot.
▸ **ˈfirst-ˈfooting** NOUN

first four ships PLURAL NOUN *NZ* 1 the earliest settlers' ships to arrive in the Canterbury Province. 2 **come with the first four ships.** to be a founder member of Canterbury.

first fruits PLURAL NOUN 1 the first results, products, or profits of an undertaking. 2 fruit that ripens first.

first-hand ADJECTIVE, ADVERB 1 from the original source; direct or directly: *first-hand news; he got the news first-hand.* 2 **at first hand.** from the original source; directly.

First International NOUN an association of socialists and labour leaders founded in London in 1864 and dissolved in Philadelphia in 1876. Official name: **International Workingmen's Association.**

first lady NOUN (*often capitals*) 1 (in the US) the wife or official hostess of a chief executive, esp of a state governor or a president. 2 a woman considered to be at the top of her profession or art: *the first lady of jazz.*

first language NOUN a person's native language.

first lieutenant NOUN 1 the officer responsible for the upkeep and maintenance of a warship, esp the executive officer of a smaller ship in the Royal Navy. 2 an officer holding commissioned rank in the US Army, Air Force, Marine Corps, or in certain other forces, senior to a second lieutenant and junior to a captain.

first light NOUN the time when light first appears in the morning; dawn.

first-line ADJECTIVE acting or used as a first resort: *first-line treatment; first-line batsmen.*

firstling (ˈfɜːstlɪŋ) NOUN the first, esp the first offspring.

first-loss policy NOUN an insurance policy for goods in which a total loss is extremely unlikely and the insurer agrees to provide cover for a sum less than the total value of the property.

firstly (ˈfɜːstlɪ) ADVERB coming before other points, questions, etc.

first mate NOUN an officer second in command to the captain of a merchant ship. Also called: **first officer.**

First Minister NOUN 1 the chief minister of the Northern Ireland Assembly. 2 the chief minister of the Scottish Parliament.

first mortgage NOUN a mortgage that has priority over other mortgages on the same property, except for taxation and other statutory liabilities.

First Mover NOUN the Aristotelian conception of God as the unmoved mover of everything else.

first name NOUN a name given to a person at birth, as opposed to a surname. Also called: **Christian name, forename, given name.**

First Nation NOUN (*also without capitals*) *Canadian* another name for **band**[1] (sense 5).

first night NOUN **a** the first public performance of a play or other production. **b** (*as modifier*): *first-night nerves.*

first-nighter NOUN a member of an opening night audience, esp one who habitually attends first nights.

first offender NOUN a person convicted of any criminal offence for the first time.

first officer NOUN 1 another name for **first mate.** 2 the member of an aircraft crew who is second in command to the captain.

first-order ADJECTIVE *Logic* quantifying only over individuals and not over predicates or clauses: **first-order predicate calculus** studies the logical properties of such quantification.

first-past-the-post NOUN (*modifier*) of or relating to a voting system in which a candidate may be elected by a simple majority rather than an absolute majority. Compare **proportional representation.**

First Peoples PLURAL NOUN *Canadian* a collective term for the Native Canadian peoples, the Inuit, and the Métis.

first person NOUN a grammatical category of pronouns and verbs used by the speaker to refer to or talk about himself, either alone (**first person singular**) or together with others (**first person plural**).

first post NOUN *Brit* the first of two military bugle calls ordering or giving notice of the time to retire for the night. The second is called **last post.**

first principle NOUN (*usually plural*) 1 one of the fundamental assumptions on which a particular theory or procedure is thought to be based. 2 an axiom of a mathematical or scientific theory.

first quarter NOUN one of the four principal phases of the moon, occurring between new moon and full moon, when half of the lighted surface is visible from earth. Compare **last quarter.**

first-rate ADJECTIVE 1 of the best or highest rated class or quality. 2 *Informal* very good; excellent. ◆ ADVERB 3 *Not standard* very well; excellently.

first reading NOUN the introduction of a bill in a legislative assembly.

first refusal NOUN the chance of buying a house, merchandise, etc., before the offer is made to other potential buyers.

First Republic NOUN the republic in France, which lasted from the abolition of the monarchy in 1792 until Napoleon Bonaparte proclaimed himself emperor in 1804.

firsts (fɜːsts) PLURAL NOUN saleable goods of the highest quality.

first school NOUN *Brit* a school for children aged between 5 and 8 or 9. Compare **middle school.**

First Secretary NOUN the chief minister of the National Assembly for Wales.

first-strike ADJECTIVE (of a nuclear missile) intended for use in an opening attack calculated to destroy the enemy's nuclear weapons.

first string NOUN 1 the top player of a team in an individual sport, such as squash. ◆ ADJECTIVE **first-string.** 2 being a regular member of a team rather than a substitute or reserve. 3 being the top player of a team in an individual sport. 4 of high rating; first-class.

first water NOUN 1 the finest quality of diamond or other precious stone. 2 the highest grade or best quality. 3 the most extreme kind: *a fool of the first water.*

First World War NOUN another name for **World War I.**

firth (fɜːθ) *or* **frith** NOUN a relatively narrow inlet of the sea, esp in Scotland.
▷ **HISTORY** C15: from Old Norse *fjörthr* FIORD

fisc (fɪsk) NOUN *Rare* a state or royal treasury.
▷ **HISTORY** C16: from Latin *fiscus* treasury, originally money-bag

fiscal (ˈfɪskᵊl) ADJECTIVE 1 of or relating to government finances, esp tax revenues. 2 of or involving financial matters. ◆ NOUN 3 **a** (in some countries) a public prosecutor. **b** *Scot* short for **procurator fiscal.** 4 a postage or other stamp signifying payment of a tax.
▷ **HISTORY** C16: from Latin *fiscālis* concerning the state treasury, from *fiscus* public money; see FISC
▸ **ˈfiscally** ADVERB

fiscal drag NOUN *Economics* the process by which, during inflation, rising incomes draw people into higher tax brackets, so that their real incomes may fall; this acts as a restraint on the expansion of the economy.

fiscal year NOUN the US and Canadian term for **financial year.**

fish (fɪʃ) NOUN, *plural* **fish** *or* **fishes.** 1 **a** any of a large group of cold-blooded aquatic vertebrates having jaws, gills, and usually fins and a skin covered in scales: includes the sharks and rays (class *Chondrichthyes*: **cartilaginous fishes**) and the teleosts, lungfish, etc. (class *Osteichthyes*: **bony fishes**). **b** (*in combination*): *fishpond.* Related adjectives: **ichthyic, ichthyoid, piscine.** 2 any of various similar but jawless vertebrates, such as the hagfish and lamprey. 3 (*not in technical use*) any of various aquatic invertebrates, such as the cuttlefish, jellyfish, and crayfish. 4 the flesh of fish used as food. 5 *Informal* a person of little emotion or intelligence: *a poor fish.* 6 short for **fishplate.** 7 Also called: **tin fish.** an informal word for **torpedo** (sense 1). 8 **a fine kettle of fish.** an awkward situation; mess. 9 **drink like a fish.** to drink (esp alcohol) to excess. 10 **have other fish to fry.** to have other activities to do, esp more important ones. 11 **like a fish out of water.** out of one's usual place. 12 **neither fish, flesh, nor fowl.** neither this nor that. 13 **make fish of one and flesh of another.** *Irish* to discriminate unfairly between people. ◆ VERB 14 (*intr*) to attempt to catch fish, as with a line and hook or with nets, traps, etc. 15 (*tr*) to fish in (a particular area of water). 16 to search (a body of water) for something or to search for something, esp in a body of water. 17 (*intr; foll by for*) to seek something indirectly: *to fish for compliments.* ◆ See also **fish out.**
▷ **HISTORY** Old English *fisc*; related to Old Norse *fiskr*, Gothic *fiscs*, Russian *piskar*, Latin *piscis*
▸ **ˈfishable** ADJECTIVE ▸ **ˈfishˌlike** ADJECTIVE

FISH (fɪʃ) NOUN ACRONYM FOR fluorescence in situ hybridization, a technique for detecting and locating gene mutations and chromosome abnormalities.

fish and brewis NOUN *Canadian* a Newfoundland dish of cooked salt cod and soaked hard bread.

fish and chips NOUN fish fillets coated with batter and deep-fried, eaten with potato chips.

fish-and-chip shop NOUN (esp in Britain) a place where fish and chips are cooked and sold.

fishbolt (ˈfɪʃˌbəʊlt) NOUN a bolt used for fastening a fishplate to a rail.

fishbone fern (ˈfɪʃˌbəʊn) NOUN a common Australian fern, *Nephrolepsis cordifolia*, having fronds with many pinnae.

fishbowl (ˈfɪʃˌbəʊl) NOUN another name for **goldfish bowl.**

fish cake NOUN a fried ball of flaked fish mixed with mashed potatoes.

fish eagle NOUN another name for the **osprey.**

fisher (ˈfɪʃə) NOUN 1 a person who fishes; fisherman. 2 Also called: **pekan. a** a large North American marten, *Martes pennanti*, having thick dark brown fur. **b** the fur of this animal. 3 **fisher of men.** an evangelist.

fisherman (ˈfɪʃəmən) NOUN, *plural* **-men.** 1 a person who fishes as a profession or for sport. 2 a vessel used for fishing.

fisherman's bend NOUN a knot used to fasten a rope to an anchor, ring, or spar.

fisherman's knot NOUN a knot for joining two ropes of equal thickness consisting of an overhand knot or double overhand knot by each rope round the other, so that the two knots jam when pulled tight.

fishery (ˈfɪʃərɪ) NOUN, *plural* **-eries.** 1 **a** the industry of catching, processing, and selling fish. **b** a place where this is carried on. 2 a place where fish are reared. 3 a fishing ground. 4 another word for **piscary** (sense 2).

Fishes (ˈfɪʃɪz) NOUN **the.** the constellation Pisces, the twelfth sign of the zodiac.

fisheye lens (ˈfɪʃˌaɪ) NOUN *Photog* a lens of small focal length, having a highly curved protruding front element, that covers an angle of view of almost 180°. It yields a circular image having considerable linear distortion.

fishfinger ('fɪʃˈfɪŋɡə) *or US and Canadian* **fish stick** NOUN an oblong piece of filleted or minced fish coated in breadcrumbs.

fish flake NOUN *Canadian* a platform on which fish are dried.

fishgig ('fɪʃˌɡɪɡ) NOUN a pole with barbed prongs for impaling fish. Also: **fizgig.**
▷HISTORY C17: of uncertain origin; perhaps altered from Spanish *fisga* harpoon

Fishguard ('fɪʃˌɡɑːd) NOUN a port and resort in SW Wales, in Pembrokeshire: ferry connections to Cork and Rosslare. Pop.: 2679 (1991).

fish hawk NOUN another name for the **osprey.**

fish-hook NOUN [1] a sharp hook used in angling, esp one with a barb. [2] *Logic* a symbol (—ɜ) for entailment.

fishing ('fɪʃɪŋ) NOUN [1] **a** the occupation of catching fish. **b** (*as modifier*): *a fishing match.* [2] another word for **piscary** (sense 2). Related adjective: **piscatorial.**

fishing ground NOUN an area of water that is good for fishing.

fishing rod NOUN a long tapered flexible pole, often in jointed sections, for use with a fishing line and, usually, a reel.

fishing tackle NOUN all the equipment, such as rods, lines, bait, etc., used in angling.

fish joint NOUN a connection formed by fishplates at the meeting point of two rails, beams, etc., as on a railway.

fish ladder NOUN a row of ascending pools or weirs connected by short falls to allow fish to pass barrages or dams.

fish louse NOUN any small flat rounded crustacean of the subclass *Branchiura*, having sucking mouth parts: parasites of fish.

fishmeal ('fɪʃˌmiːl) NOUN ground dried fish used as feed for farm animals, as a fertilizer, etc.

fishmonger ('fɪʃˌmʌŋɡə) NOUN *Chiefly Brit* a retailer of fish.

fishnet ('fɪʃˌnɛt) NOUN [1] *Chiefly US and Canadian* a net for catching fish. [2] **a** an open mesh fabric resembling netting. **b** (*as modifier*): *fishnet tights.*

fish out VERB (*tr, adverb*) to find or extract (something): *to fish keys out of a pocket.*

fishplate ('fɪʃˌpleɪt) NOUN a flat piece of metal joining one rail, stanchion, or beam to another.

fishskin disease ('fɪʃˌskɪn) NOUN *Pathol* a nontechnical name for **ichthyosis.**

fishtail ('fɪʃˌteɪl) NOUN [1] an aeroplane manoeuvre in which the tail is moved from side to side to reduce speed. [2] a nozzle having a long narrow slot at the top, placed over a Bunsen burner to produce a thin fanlike flame. ◆ VERB (*intr*) [3] to slow an aeroplane by moving the tail from side to side. [4] to drive with the rear of the vehicle moving from side to side in an uncontrolled fashion.

fish tail NOUN a step in ballroom dancing in which the feet are quickly crossed.

fishway ('fɪʃˌweɪ) NOUN *US and Canadian* another name for **fish ladder.**

fishwife ('fɪʃˌwaɪf) NOUN, *plural* **-wives.** [1] a woman who sells fish. [2] a coarse scolding woman.
▸'**fish,wifely** ADJECTIVE

fishy ('fɪʃɪ) ADJECTIVE **fishier, fishiest.** [1] of, involving, or suggestive of fish. [2] abounding in fish. [3] *Informal* suspicious, doubtful, or questionable: *their leaving at the same time looked fishy.* [4] dull and lifeless: *a fishy look.*
▸'**fishily** ADVERB ▸'**fishiness** NOUN

fissi- COMBINING FORM indicating a splitting or cleft: *fissirostral.*
▷HISTORY from Latin *fissus*, past participle of *findere* to split

fissile ('fɪsaɪl) ADJECTIVE [1] *Brit* capable of undergoing nuclear fission as a result of the impact of slow neutrons. [2] another word (esp US and Canadian) for **fissionable.** [3] tending to split or capable of being split.
▷HISTORY C17: from Latin *fissilis*, from *fissus* split; see FISSI-
▸**fissility** (fɪˈsɪlɪtɪ) NOUN

fission ('fɪʃən) NOUN [1] the act or process of splitting or breaking into parts. [2] *Biology* a form of asexual reproduction in single-celled animals and plants involving a division into two or more equal parts that develop into new cells. [3] short for **nuclear fission.**
▷HISTORY C19: from Latin *fissiō* a cleaving

fissionable ('fɪʃənəbᵊl) ADJECTIVE capable of undergoing nuclear fission as a result of any process. Compare **fissile** (sense 1).
▸ˌ**fissiona'bility** NOUN

fission bomb NOUN a bomb in which the energy is supplied by nuclear fission. See **atomic bomb.**

fission-fusion bomb NOUN another name for **fusion bomb.**

fission product NOUN a nuclide produced either directly by nuclear fission or by the radioactive decay of such a nuclide.

fission reactor NOUN a nuclear reactor in which a fission reaction takes place.

fission-track dating NOUN the dating of samples of minerals by comparing the tracks in them by fission fragments of the uranium nuclei they contain, before and after irradiation by neutrons.

fissipalmate (ˌfɪsɪˈpælmeɪt) ADJECTIVE (of some birds' feet) partially webbed, having lobes and fringes on separate toes.

fissiparous (fɪˈsɪpərəs) ADJECTIVE [1] *Biology* reproducing by fission. [2] having a tendency to divide into groups or factions.
▸**fis'siparously** ADVERB ▸**fis'siparousness** NOUN

fissiped ('fɪsɪˌpɛd) *or* **fissipedal** (fɪˈsɪpɪdᵊl, ˌfɪsɪˈpiːdᵊl) ADJECTIVE [1] having toes that are separated from one another, as dogs, cats, bears, and similar carnivores. ◆ NOUN [2] a fissiped animal. ◆ Compare **pinniped.**

fissirostral (ˌfɪsɪˈrɒstrəl) ADJECTIVE [1] (of the beaks of some birds) broad and deeply cleft. [2] having such a beak, as swifts and swallows.

fissure ('fɪʃə) NOUN [1] any long narrow cleft or crack, esp in a rock. [2] a weakness or flaw indicating impending disruption or discord: *fissures in a decaying empire.* [3] *Anatomy* a narrow split or groove that divides an organ such as the brain, lung, or liver into lobes. See also **sulcus.** [4] a small unnatural crack in the skin or mucous membrane, as between the toes or at the anus. [5] a minute crack in the surface of a tooth, caused by imperfect joining of enamel during development. ◆ VERB [6] to crack or split apart.
▷HISTORY C14: from medical Latin *fissūra*, from Latin *fissus* split

fissure eruption NOUN the emergence of lava from a fissure in the ground rather than from a volcanic cone or vent.

fissure of Rolando (rəʊˈlændəʊ) NOUN another name for **central sulcus.**
▷HISTORY C19: named after L. *Rolando* (died 1831), Italian anatomist

fissure of Sylvius ('sɪlvɪəs) NOUN a deep horizontal cleft in each cerebral hemisphere: marks the separation of the temporal lobe from the frontal and parietal lobes.
▷HISTORY named after Franciscus *Sylvius* (died 1652), German anatomist

fist (fɪst) NOUN [1] a hand with the fingers clenched into the palm, as for hitting. [2] Also called: **fistful.** the quantity that can be held in a fist or hand. [3] an informal word for **hand** or **index** (sense 9). ◆ VERB [4] (*tr*) to hit with the fist.
▷HISTORY Old English *fȳst*; related to Old Frisian *fest*, Old Saxon, Old High German *fūst*; see FIVE

fistic ('fɪstɪk) ADJECTIVE of or relating to fisticuffs or boxing.

fisticuffs ('fɪstɪˌkʌfs) PLURAL NOUN combat with the fists.
▷HISTORY C17: probably from *fisty* with the fist + CUFF²

fistmele ('fɪstˌmiːl) NOUN *Archery* a measure of the width of a hand and the extended thumb, used to calculate the approximate height of the string of a braced bow.
▷HISTORY C17: from FIST + *mele*, variant of obsolete *meal* measure

fistula ('fɪstjʊlə) NOUN, *plural* **-las** *or* **-lae** (-ˌliː). [1] *Pathol* an abnormal opening between one hollow organ and another or between a hollow organ and the surface of the skin, caused by ulceration, congenital malformation, etc. [2] *Obsolete* any musical wind instrument; a pipe.
▷HISTORY C14: from Latin: pipe, tube, hollow reed, ulcer

fistulous ('fɪstjʊləs), **fistular** ('fɪstjʊlə), *or* **fistulate** ('fɪstjʊlɪt) ADJECTIVE [1] *Pathol* containing, relating to, or resembling a fistula. [2] hollow, esp slender and hollow; reedlike or tubular. [3] containing tubes or tubelike parts.

fit¹ (fɪt) VERB **fits, fitting, fitted** *or US* **fit.** [1] to be appropriate or suitable for (a situation, etc.). [2] to be of the correct size or shape for (a connection, container, etc.). [3] (*tr*) to adjust in order to render appropriate: *they had to fit the idea to their philosophy.* [4] (*tr*) to supply with that which is needed. [5] (*tr*) to try clothes on (someone) in order to make adjustments if necessary. [6] (*tr*) to make competent or ready: *the experience helped to fit him for the task.* [7] (*tr*) to locate with care. [8] (*intr*) to correspond with the facts or circumstances. ◆ ADJECTIVE **fitter, fittest.** [9] suitable to a purpose or design; appropriate. [10] having the right qualifications; qualifying. [11] in good health. [12] worthy or deserving: *a book fit to be read.* [13] (*foll by an infinitive*) in such an extreme condition that a specified consequence is likely: *she was fit to scream; you look fit to drop.* ◆ NOUN [14] *Informal* (of a person) sexually attractive. [15] the manner in which something fits. [16] the act or process of fitting. [17] *Statistics* the correspondence between observed and predicted characteristics of a distribution or model. See **goodness of fit.** ◆ See also **fit in, fit out, fit up.**
▷HISTORY C14: probably from Middle Dutch *vitten*; related to Old Norse *fitja* to knit
▸'**fittable** ADJECTIVE

fit² (fɪt) NOUN [1] *Pathol* a sudden attack or convulsion, such as an epileptic seizure. [2] a sudden spell of emotion: *a fit of anger.* [3] an impulsive period of activity or lack of activity; mood: *a fit of laziness.* [4] **give (a person) a fit.** to surprise (a person) in an outrageous manner. [5] **have** *or* **throw a fit.** *Informal* to become very angry or excited. [6] **in** *or* **by fits and starts.** in spasmodic spells; irregularly. ◆ VERB **fits, fitting, fitted.** [7] (*intr*) *Informal* to have a sudden attack or convulsion, such as an epileptic seizure.
▷HISTORY Old English *fitt* conflict; see FIT³

fit³ (fɪt) NOUN *Archaic* a story or song or a section of a story or song.
▷HISTORY Old English *fitt*; related to Old Norse *fit* hem, Old High German *fizza* yarn

fitch (fɪtʃ) *or* **fitchet** ('fɪtʃɪt) NOUN [1] another name for **polecat** (sense 1). [2] the fur of the polecat or ferret.
▷HISTORY C16: probably from *ficheux* FITCHEW

fitchew ('fɪtʃuː) NOUN an archaic name for **polecat.**
▷HISTORY C14 *ficheux*, from Old French *ficheau*, from Middle Dutch *vitsau*, of obscure origin

fitful ('fɪtfʊl) ADJECTIVE characterized by or occurring in irregular spells: *fitful sleep.*
▸'**fitfully** ADVERB ▸'**fitfulness** NOUN

fit in VERB [1] (*tr*) to give a place or time to: *if my schedule allows it, I'll fit you in.* [2] (*intr, adverb*) to belong or conform, esp after adjustment: *he didn't fit in with their plans.*

fitly ('fɪtlɪ) ADVERB in a proper manner or place or at a proper time.

fitment ('fɪtmənt) NOUN [1] *Machinery* an accessory attached to an assembly of parts. [2] *Chiefly Brit* a detachable part of the furnishings of a room.

fitness ('fɪtnɪs) NOUN [1] the state of being fit. [2] *Biology* **a** the degree of adaptation of an organism to its environment, determined by its genetic constitution. **b** the ability of an organism to produce viable offspring capable of surviving to the next generation.

fit out VERB [1] (*tr, adverb*) to equip; supply with necessary or new equipment, clothes, etc. ◆ NOUN **fit-out.** [2] the act of equipping or supplying with necessary or new equipment; refurbishment.

fitted ('fɪtɪd) ADJECTIVE [1] designed for excellent fit: *a fitted suit.* [2] (of a carpet) cut, sewn, or otherwise adapted to cover a floor completely. [3] **a** (of furniture) built to fit a particular space: *a fitted cupboard.* **b** (of a room) equipped with fitted furniture: *a fitted kitchen.* [4] (of sheets) having ends that are elasticated and shaped to fit tightly over a mattress. [5] having accessory parts.

fitter ('fɪtə) NOUN [1] a person who fits a garment, esp when it is made for a particular person. [2] a person who is skilled in the assembly and adjustment of machinery, esp of a specified sort: *an electrical fitter.* [3] a person who supplies something for an expedition, activity, etc.

fitting ('fɪtɪŋ) ADJECTIVE [1] appropriate or proper; suitable. ♦ NOUN [2] an accessory or part: *an electrical fitting.* [3] (*plural*) furnishings or accessories in a building. [4] work carried out by a fitter. [5] the act of trying on clothes so that they can be adjusted to fit. [6] *Brit* size in clothes or shoes: *a narrow fitting.*
▸ **'fittingly** ADVERB ▸ **'fittingness** NOUN

fit up VERB (*tr, adverb*) [1] (often foll by *with*) to equip or provide: *the optician will soon fit you up with a new pair of glasses.* [2] *Brit slang* to incriminate (someone) on a false charge; frame: *he was fitted up for the bank job.* ♦ NOUN **fit-up.** [3] *Theatre, slang* a stage and accessories that can be erected quickly for plays. [4] *Brit slang* a frame-up.

Fitzgerald-Lorentz contraction (fɪts'dʒɛrəldlɔː'rɛnts) NOUN *Physics* the contraction that a moving body exhibits when its velocity approaches that of light.
▷**HISTORY** C19: named after G. F. *Fitzgerald* (1851–1901), Irish physicist and H. A. *Lorentz* (1853–1928), Dutch physicist

Fitzrovia (fɪts'rəʊvɪə) NOUN *Informal* the district north of Oxford Street, London, around Fitzroy Square and its pubs, noted in the 1930s and 40s as a haunt of poets.

Fitzwilliam Museum (ˌfɪtz'wɪljəm) NOUN a museum, attached to Cambridge University and founded in 1816, noted esp for its paintings and collections devoted to the applied arts.
▷**HISTORY** C19: named after the 7th Viscount *Fitzwilliam* of Merrion, who donated the first collection

Fiume ('fiu:me) NOUN the Italian name for **Rijeka.**

five (faɪv) NOUN [1] the cardinal number that is the sum of four and one. [2] a numeral, 5, V, etc., representing this number. [3] the amount or quantity that is one greater than four. [4] something representing, represented by, or consisting of five units, such as a playing card with five symbols on it. ♦ DETERMINER [5] **a** amounting to five: *five minutes; five nights.* **b** (*as pronoun*): *choose any five you like.* Related prefixes: **penta-, quinque-.** ♦ See also **fives.**
▷**HISTORY** Old English *fīf*; related to Old Norse *fimm*, Gothic *fimf*, Old High German *finf*, Latin *quinque*, Greek *pente*, Sanskrit *pañca*

five-a-side NOUN **a** a version of soccer with five players on each side. **b** (*as modifier*): *a five-a-side tournament.*

5BX NOUN a fitness exercise programme originally devised in the Canadian Air Force.
▷**HISTORY** from *5 b(asic) (e)x(ercises)*

five by five INTERJECTION an expression used in telecommunications to state that a signal is being received clearly.

five-eighth NOUN *Austral and NZ* a rugby player positioned between the halfbacks and three-quarters.

five-faced bishop NOUN *Brit* another name for **moschatel.**

five-finger NOUN any of various plants having five-petalled flowers or five lobed leaves, such as cinquefoil and Virginia creeper.

fivefold ('faɪvˌfəʊld) ADJECTIVE [1] equal to or having five times as many or as much. [2] composed of five parts. ♦ ADVERB [3] by or up to five times as many or as much.

five hundred NOUN a card game for three players, with 500 points for game.

five Ks PLURAL NOUN **the.** items traditionally worn or carried by Sikhs, each possessing a symbolic importance. See **Kachera, Kangha, Kara, Kesh, Kirpan.**
▷**HISTORY** translation of Punjabi *panch kakke*

Five Nations PLURAL NOUN (formerly) a confederacy of North American Indian peoples living mainly in and around present-day New York state, consisting of the Cayugas, Mohawks, Oneidas, Onondagas, and Senecas. Also called: **Iroquois.** See also **Six Nations.**

five-o'clock shadow NOUN beard growth visible late in the day on a man's shaven face.

fivepenny ('faɪvpənɪ) ADJECTIVE (*prenominal*) *US* (of a nail) one and three-quarters of an inch in length.

fivepins ('faɪvˌpɪnz) NOUN (*functioning as singular*) a bowling game using five pins, played esp in Canada. Also called: **five-pin bowling.**
▸ **'fiveˌpin** ADJECTIVE

fiver ('faɪvə) NOUN *Informal* [1] (in Britain) a five-pound note. [2] (in the US) a five-dollar bill.

fives (faɪvz) NOUN (*functioning as singular*) a ball game similar to squash but played with bats or the hands.

five-spot NOUN (in the US) a five-dollar bill.

five-star ADJECTIVE (of a hotel) first-class, top-quality, or offering exceptional luxury.

five stones NOUN the game of jacks played with five stones.

Five Towns NOUN **the.** the name given in his fiction by Arnold Bennett to the Potteries towns (actually six in number) of Burslem, Fenton, Hanley, Longton, Stoke-upon-Trent, and Tunstall, now part of the city of Stoke-on-Trent.

Five-Year Plan NOUN (formerly in socialist economies) a government plan for economic development over a period of five years.

fix (fɪks) VERB (*mainly tr*) [1] (*also intr*) to make or become firm, stable, or secure. [2] to attach or place permanently: *fix the mirror to the wall.* [3] (often foll by *up*) to settle definitely; decide: *let us fix a date.* [4] to hold or direct (eyes, attention, etc.) steadily: *he fixed his gaze on the woman.* [5] to call to attention or rivet. [6] to make rigid: *to fix one's jaw.* [7] to place or ascribe: *to fix the blame on someone.* [8] to mend or repair. [9] *Informal* to provide with: *how are you fixed for supplies?* [10] *Informal* to influence (a person, outcome of a contest, etc.) unfairly, as by bribery. [11] *Slang* to take revenge on; get even with, esp by killing. [12] *Informal* to give (someone) his just deserts: *that'll fix him.* [13] *Informal* to arrange or put in order: *to fix one's hair.* [14] *Informal* to prepare: *to fix a meal.* [15] *Dialect or informal* to spay or castrate (an animal). [16] *US dialect or informal* to prepare oneself: *I'm fixing to go out.* [17] *Photog* to treat (a film, plate, or paper) with fixer to make permanent the image rendered visible by developer. [18] *Cytology* to kill, preserve, and harden (tissue, cells, etc.) for subsequent microscopic study. [19] **a** to convert (atmospheric nitrogen) into nitrogen compounds, as in the manufacture of fertilizers or the action of bacteria in the soil. **b** to convert (carbon dioxide) into organic compounds, esp carbohydrates, as occurs in photosynthesis in plants and some microorganisms. [20] to reduce (a substance) to a solid or condensed state or a less volatile state. [21] (*intr*) *Slang* to inject a drug. ♦ NOUN [22] *Informal* a predicament; dilemma. [23] the ascertaining of the navigational position, as of a ship, by radar, observation, etc. [24] *Slang* an intravenous injection of a drug, esp heroin. [25] *Informal* an act or instance of bribery. ♦ See also **fix up.**
▷**HISTORY** C15: from Medieval Latin *fixāre*, from Latin *fixus* fixed, from Latin *fīgere*
▸ **'fixable** ADJECTIVE

fixate ('fɪkseɪt) VERB [1] to become or cause to become fixed. [2] to direct the eye or eyes at a point in space so that the image of the point falls on the centre (fovea) of the eye or eyes. [3] *Psychol* to engage in fixation. [4] (*tr; usually passive*) *Informal* to obsess or preoccupy.
▷**HISTORY** C19: from Latin *fixus* fixed + -ATE[1]

fixation (fɪk'seɪʃən) NOUN [1] the act of fixing or the state of being fixed. [2] a preoccupation or obsession. [3] *Psychol* **a** the act of fixating. **b** (in psychoanalytical schools) a strong attachment of a person to another person or an object in early life. [4] *Chem* **a** the conversion of nitrogen in the air into a compound, esp a fertilizer. **b** the conversion of a free element into one of its compounds. [5] the reduction of a substance from a volatile or fluid form to a nonvolatile or solid form.

fixative ('fɪksətɪv) ADJECTIVE [1] serving or tending to fix. ♦ NOUN [2] a fluid usually consisting of a transparent resin, such as shellac, dissolved in alcohol and sprayed over drawings to prevent smudging. [3] *Cytology* a fluid, such as formaldehyde or ethanol, that fixes tissues and cells for microscopic study. [4] a substance added to a liquid, such as a perfume, to make it less volatile.

fixed (fɪkst) ADJECTIVE [1] attached or placed so as to be immovable. [2] not subject to change; stable: *fixed prices.* [3] steadily directed: *a fixed expression.* [4] established as to relative position: *a fixed point.* [5] not fluctuating; always at the same time: *a fixed holiday.* [6] (of ideas, notions, etc.) firmly maintained. [7] (of an element) held in chemical combination: *fixed nitrogen.* [8] (of a substance) nonvolatile. [9] arranged. [10] *Astrology* of, relating to, or belonging to the group consisting of the four signs of the zodiac Taurus, Leo, Scorpio, and Aquarius, which are associated with stability. Compare **cardinal** (sense 9), **mutable** (sense 2). [11] *Informal* equipped or provided for, as with money, possessions, etc. [12] *Informal* illegally arranged: *a fixed trial.*
▸**fixedly** ('fɪksɪdlɪ) ADVERB ▸ **'fixedness** NOUN

fixed assets PLURAL NOUN nontrading business assets of a relatively permanent nature, such as plant, fixtures, or goodwill. Also called: **capital assets.** Compare **current assets.**

fixed charge NOUN [1] an invariable expense usually at regular intervals, such as rent. [2] a legal charge on specific assets or property, as of a company.

fixed costs PLURAL NOUN [1] another name for **overheads.** [2] costs that do not vary with output.

fixed-head coupé NOUN another name (esp Brit) for **coupé** (sense 1).

fixed idea NOUN an idea, esp one of an obsessional nature, that is persistently maintained and not subject to change. Also called: ***idée fixe.***

fixed oil NOUN a natural animal or vegetable oil that is not volatile: a mixture of esters of fatty acids, usually triglycerides. Also called: **fatty oil.** Compare **essential oil.**

fixed point NOUN [1] *Physics* a reproducible invariant temperature; the boiling point, freezing point, or triple point of a substance, such as water, that is used to calibrate a thermometer or define a temperature scale. [2] *Maths* a point that is not moved by a given transformation.

fixed-point representation NOUN *Computing* the representation of numbers by a single set of digits such that the radix point has a predetermined location, the value of the number depending on the position of each digit relative to the radix point. Compare **floating-point representation.**

fixed satellite NOUN a satellite in a geostationary orbit.

fixed star NOUN [1] any of the stars in the Ptolemaic system, all of which were thought to be attached to an outer crystal sphere thus explaining their apparent lack of movement. [2] an extremely distant star whose position appears to be almost stationary over a long period of time.

fixer ('fɪksə) NOUN [1] a person or thing that fixes. [2] *Photog* a solution containing one or more chemical compounds that is used, in fixing, to dissolve unexposed silver halides. It sometimes has an additive to stop the action of developer. [3] *Slang* a person who makes arrangements, esp by underhand or illegal means.

fixing ('fɪksɪŋ) NOUN a means of attaching one thing to another, as a pipe to a wall, slate to a roof, etc.

fixings ('fɪksɪŋz) PLURAL NOUN *Chiefly US and Canadian* [1] apparatus or equipment. [2] accompaniments for a dish; trimmings.

fixity ('fɪksɪtɪ) NOUN, *plural* **-ties.** [1] the state or quality of being fixed; stability. [2] something that is fixed; a fixture.

fixture ('fɪkstʃə) NOUN [1] an object firmly fixed in place, esp a household appliance. [2] a person or thing regarded as fixed in a particular place or position. [3] *Property law* an article attached to land and regarded as part of it. [4] a device to secure a workpiece in a machine tool. [5] *Chiefly Brit* **a** a sports match or social occasion. **b** the date of such an event. [6] *Rare* the act of fixing.
▷**HISTORY** C17: from Late Latin *fixūra* a fastening (with *-t-* by analogy with *mixture*)
▸ **'fixtureless** ADJECTIVE

fix up VERB (*tr, adverb*) [1] to arrange: *let's fix up a date.* [2] (often foll by *with*) to provide: *I'm sure we can fix you up with a room.* [3] *Informal* to repair or rearrange: *to fix up one's house.*

fizgig ('fɪz,gɪg) NOUN [1] a frivolous or flirtatious girl. [2] a firework or whirling top that fizzes as it moves. [3] a variant of **fishgig**. [4] *Austral slang* a police informer. ◆ VERB [5] *(intr) Austral slang* to inform on criminals to the police.
▷HISTORY C16: probably from obsolete *fise* a breaking of wind + *gig* girl

fizz (fɪz) VERB *(intr)* [1] to make a hissing or bubbling sound. [2] (of a drink) to produce bubbles of carbon dioxide, either through fermentation or aeration. ◆ NOUN [3] a hissing or bubbling sound. [4] the bubbly quality of a drink; effervescence. [5] any effervescent drink.
▷HISTORY C17: of imitative origin
▸'**fizzy** ADJECTIVE ▸'**fizziness** NOUN

fizzer ('fɪzə) NOUN [1] anything that fizzes. [2] *Austral slang* a person or thing that disappoints, fails to succeed, etc.: *the horse proved to be a fizzer*.

fizzle ('fɪz^{ə}l) VERB *(intr)* [1] to make a hissing or bubbling sound. [2] (often followed by *out*) *Informal* to fail or die out, esp after a promising start. ◆ NOUN [3] a hissing or bubbling sound; fizz. [4] *Informal* an outright failure; fiasco.
▷HISTORY C16: probably from obsolete *fist* to break wind

fj THE INTERNET DOMAIN NAME FOR Fiji.

fjeld *or* **field** (fjɛld) NOUN a high rocky plateau with little vegetation in Scandinavian countries.
▷HISTORY C19: Norwegian; related to Old Norse *fjall* mountain; see FELL[5]

FJI INTERNATIONAL CAR REGISTRATION FOR Fiji.

fjord *or* **fiord** (fjɔːd) NOUN (esp on the coast of Norway) a long narrow inlet of the sea between high steep cliffs formed by glacial action.
▷HISTORY C17: from Norwegian, from Old Norse *fjörthr*; see FIRTH, FORD

fk THE INTERNET DOMAIN NAME FOR Falkland Islands.

FL ABBREVIATION FOR: [1] Flight Lieutenant. [2] Florida. ◆ [3] INTERNATIONAL CAR REGISTRATION FOR Liechtenstein.
▷HISTORY (for sense 3) from German *Fürstentum Liechtenstein* Principality of Liechtenstein

fl. ABBREVIATION FOR: [1] *floruit*. ◆ [2] (formerly in the Netherlands) SYMBOL FOR guilder.

Fla. ABBREVIATION FOR Florida.

flab (flæb) NOUN unsightly or unwanted fat on the body; flabbiness.
▷HISTORY C20: back formation from FLABBY

flabbergast ('flæbə,gɑːst) VERB *(tr) Informal* to overcome with astonishment; amaze utterly; astound.
▷HISTORY C18: of uncertain origin

flabbergasted ('flæbə,gɑːstɪd) ADJECTIVE *Informal* overcome with astonishment; amazed; astounded.

flabby ('flæbɪ) ADJECTIVE **-bier, -biest.** [1] lacking firmness; loose or yielding: *flabby muscles*. [2] having flabby flesh, esp through being overweight. [3] lacking vitality; weak; ineffectual.
▷HISTORY C17: alteration of *flappy*, from FLAP + -Y[1]; compare Dutch *flabbe* drooping lip
▸'**flabbily** ADVERB ▸'**flabbiness** NOUN

flabellate (flə'bɛlɪt, -eɪt) *or* **flabelliform** (flə'bɛlɪ,fɔːm) ADJECTIVE *Biology* shaped like a fan.

flabellum (flə'bɛləm) NOUN, *plural* **-la** (-lə). [1] a fan-shaped organ or part, such as the tip of the proboscis of a honeybee. [2] *RC Church* a large ceremonial fan.
▷HISTORY C19: from Latin: small fan, from *flābra* breezes, from *flāre* to blow

flaccid ('flæksɪd, 'flæs-) ADJECTIVE lacking firmness; soft and limp; flabby.
▷HISTORY C17: from Latin *flaccidus*, from *flaccus*
▸**flac'cidity** *or* '**flaccidness** NOUN ▸'**flaccidly** ADVERB

flack[1] (flæk) NOUN *Chiefly US and Canadian* a press or publicity agent.
▷HISTORY C20: of unknown origin

flack[2] (flæk) NOUN a variant spelling of **flak**.

flacon (*French* flakɔ̃) NOUN a small stoppered bottle or flask, such as one used for perfume.
▷HISTORY C19: from French; see FLAGON

flag[1] (flæg) NOUN [1] a piece of cloth, esp bunting, often attached to a pole or staff, decorated with a design and used as an emblem, symbol, or standard or as a means of signalling. [2] a small paper flag, emblem, or sticker sold on flag days. [3] an indicator, that may be set or unset, used to indicate a condition or to stimulate a particular reaction in the execution of a computer program. [4] *Informal* short for **flag officer** and **flagship**. [5] *Journalism* another name for **masthead** (sense 2). [6] the fringe of long hair, tapering towards the tip, on the underside of the tail of certain breeds of dog, such as setters. [7] the conspicuously marked tail of a deer. [8] a less common name for **bookmark.** [9] *Austral and NZ* the part of a taximeter that is raised when a taxi is for hire. [10] **the.** (in Victoria, Australia) the Australian Rules premiership. [11] **fly the flag.** to represent or show support for one's country, an organization, etc. [12] **show the flag. a** to assert a claim, as to a territory or stretch of water, by military presence. **b** *Informal* to be present; make an appearance. [13] **strike** (*or* **lower**) **the flag. a** to relinquish command, esp of a ship. **b** to submit or surrender. ◆ VERB **flags, flagging, flagged.** *(tr)* [14] to decorate or mark with a flag or flags. [15] (often foll by *down*) to warn or signal (a vehicle) to stop. [16] to send or communicate (messages, information, etc.) by flag. [17] to decoy (game or wild animals) by waving a flag or similar object so as to attract their attention. [18] to mark (a page in a book, card, etc.) for attention by attaching a small tab or flag. [19] (foll by *away* or *by*) *NZ* to consider unimportant; brush aside. ◆ See also **flag out, flags.**
▷HISTORY C16: of uncertain origin
▸'**flagger** NOUN ▸'**flagless** ADJECTIVE

flag[2] (flæg) NOUN [1] any of various plants that have long swordlike leaves, esp the iris *Iris pseudacorus* (**yellow flag**). [2] the leaf of any such plant. ◆ See also **sweet flag.**
▷HISTORY C14: probably of Scandinavian origin; compare Dutch *flag*, Danish *flæg* yellow iris

flag[3] (flæg) VERB **flags, flagging, flagged.** *(intr)* [1] to hang down; become limp; droop. [2] to decline in strength or vigour; become weak or tired.
▷HISTORY C16: of unknown origin

flag[4] (flæg) NOUN [1] short for **flagstone.** ◆ VERB **flags, flagging, flagged.** [2] *(tr)* to furnish (a floor) with flagstones.

flag captain NOUN the captain of a flagship.

flag day NOUN *Brit* a day on which money is collected by a charity and small flags, emblems, or stickers are given to contributors.

Flag Day NOUN June 14, the annual holiday in the US to celebrate the adoption in 1777 of the Stars and Stripes.

flagellant ('flædʒɪlənt, flə'dʒɛlənt) *or* **flagellator** ('flædʒɪ,leɪtə) NOUN [1] a person who whips himself or others either as part of a religious penance or for sexual gratification. [2] (*often capital*) (in medieval Europe) a member of a religious sect who whipped themselves in public.
▷HISTORY C16: from Latin *flagellāre* to whip, from FLAGELLUM
▸'**flagellant,ism** NOUN

flagellate VERB ('flædʒɪ,leɪt) [1] *(tr)* to whip; scourge; flog. ◆ ADJECTIVE ('flædʒɪlɪt, -,leɪt) *also* **flagellated.** [2] possessing one or more flagella. [3] resembling a flagellum; whiplike. ◆ NOUN ('flædʒɪlɪt, -,leɪt) [4] a flagellate organism, esp any protozoan of the phylum *Zoomastigina*.
▸,**flagel'lation** NOUN

flagelliform (flə'dʒɛlɪ,fɔːm) ADJECTIVE slender, tapering, and whiplike, as the antennae of certain insects.

flagellin (flə'dʒɛlɪn) NOUN the structural protein of bacterial flagella.

flagellum (flə'dʒɛləm) NOUN, *plural* **-la** (-lə) *or* **-lums.** [1] *Biology* a long whiplike outgrowth from a cell that acts as an organ of locomotion: occurs in some protozoans, gametes, spores, etc. [2] *Botany* a long thin supple shoot or runner. [3] *Zoology* the terminal whiplike part of an arthropod's appendage, esp of the antenna of many insects.
▷HISTORY C19: from Latin: a little whip, from *flagrum* a whip, lash
▸**fla'gellar** ADJECTIVE

flageolet[1] (,flædʒə'lɛt) NOUN a high-pitched musical instrument of the recorder family having six or eight finger holes.
▷HISTORY C17: from French, modification of Old French *flajolet* a little flute, from *flajol* flute, from Vulgar Latin *flabeolum* (unattested), from Latin *flāre* to blow

flageolet[2] *or* **flageolet bean** ('flædʒə,leɪ) NOUN the pale green immature seed of a haricot bean, cooked and eaten as a vegetable.
▷HISTORY C19: from French *fageolet*, from Latin *phaseolus* bean; perhaps influenced by FLAGEOLET[1]

flag fall NOUN *Austral* the minimum charge for hiring a taxi, to which the rate per kilometre is added.

flagging ('flægɪŋ) NOUN flagstones or a flagged area.

flaggy[1] ('flægɪ) ADJECTIVE **-gier, -giest.** drooping; limp.

flaggy[2] ('flægɪ) ADJECTIVE made of or similar to flagstone.

flagitious (flə'dʒɪʃəs) ADJECTIVE atrociously wicked; vicious; outrageous.
▷HISTORY C14: from Latin *flāgitiōsus* infamous, from *flāgitium* a shameful act; related to Latin *flagrum* whip
▸**fla'gitiously** ADVERB ▸**fla'gitiousness** NOUN

flag lieutenant NOUN an admiral's ADC.

flagman ('flægmən) NOUN, *plural* **-men.** a person who has charge of, carries, or signals with a flag, esp a railway employee.

flag of convenience NOUN a national flag flown by a ship registered in that country to gain financial or legal advantage.

flag officer NOUN [1] an officer in certain navies of the rank of rear admiral or above and entitled to fly its flag. [2] the head of a boat or yacht club.

flag of truce NOUN a white flag indicating the peaceful intent of its bearer or an invitation to an enemy to negotiate.

flagon ('flægən) NOUN [1] a large bottle of wine, cider, etc. [2] a vessel having a handle, spout, and narrow neck.
▷HISTORY C15: from Old French *flascon*, from Late Latin *flascō*, probably of Germanic origin; see FLASK

flag out VERB *(adverb)* to register (a commercial vehicle) in a country other than the one in which it operates, usually in order to take advantage of favourable rates of taxation.

flagpole ('flæg,pəʊl) *or* **flagstaff** ('flæg,stɑːf) NOUN, *plural* **-poles, -staffs** *or* **-staves** (-,steɪvz). a pole or staff on which a flag is hoisted and displayed.

flag rank NOUN the rank of a flag officer.

flagrant ('fleɪgrənt) ADJECTIVE [1] openly outrageous. [2] *Obsolete* burning or blazing.
▷HISTORY C15: from Latin *flagrāre* to blaze, burn
▸'**flagrancy,** '**flagrance,** *or* '**flagrantness** NOUN
▸'**flagrantly** ADVERB

flagrante delicto (flə'grænti dɪ'lɪktəʊ) ADVERB See **in flagrante delicto.**

flags (flægz) PLURAL NOUN *Rare* the long feathers on the leg of a hawk or falcon.

flagship ('flæg,ʃɪp) NOUN [1] a ship, esp in a fleet, aboard which the commander of the fleet is quartered. [2] the most important ship belonging to a shipping company. [3] a single item from a related group considered as the most important, often in establishing a public image: *the nine o'clock news is the flagship of the BBC*.

flagstone ('flæg,stəʊn) *or* **flag** NOUN [1] a hard fine-textured rock, such as a sandstone or shale, that can be split up into slabs for paving. [2] a slab of such a rock.
▷HISTORY C15 *flag* (in the sense: sod, turf), from Old Norse *flaga* slab; compare Old English *flæcg* plaster, poultice

flag-waving NOUN *Informal* **a** an emotional appeal or display intended to arouse patriotic or nationalistic feeling. **b** (*as modifier*): *a flag-waving speech*.
▸'**flag-,waver** NOUN

flail (fleɪl) NOUN [1] an implement used for threshing grain, consisting of a wooden handle with a free-swinging metal or wooden bar attached to it. [2] a weapon so shaped used in the Middle Ages. ◆ VERB [3] *(tr)* to beat or thrash with or as if with a flail. [4] to move or be moved like a flail; thresh about: *with arms flailing*.
▷HISTORY C12 *fleil*, ultimately from Late Latin *flagellum* flail, from Latin: whip

flair[1] (flɛə) NOUN [1] natural ability; talent; aptitude. [2] instinctive discernment; perceptiveness. [3] stylishness or elegance; dash: *to*

dress with flair. [4] *Hunting, rare* **a** the scent left by quarry. **b** the sense of smell of a hound.
▷HISTORY C19: from French, literally: sense of smell, from Old French: scent, from *flairier* to give off a smell, ultimately from Latin *frāgrāre* to smell sweet; see FRAGRANT

flair² (fler) NOUN a Scot word for **floor**.

flak *or* **flack** (flæk) NOUN [1] anti-aircraft fire or artillery. [2] *Informal* a great deal of adverse criticism.
▷HISTORY C20: from German *Fl(ieger)a(bwehr)k(anone)*, literally: aircraft defence gun

flake¹ (fleɪk) NOUN [1] a small thin piece or layer chipped off or detached from an object or substance; scale. [2] a small piece or particle: *a flake of snow.* [3] a thin layer or stratum. [4] *Archaeol* **a** a fragment removed by chipping or hammering from a larger stone used as a tool or weapon. See also **blade. b** (*as modifier*): *flake tool.* [5] *Slang, chiefly US* an eccentric, crazy, or unreliable person. ◆ VERB [6] to peel or cause to peel off in flakes; chip. [7] to cover or become covered with or as with flakes. [8] (*tr*) to form into flakes.
▷HISTORY C14: of Scandinavian origin; compare Norwegian *flak* disc, Middle Dutch *vlacken* to flutter
▸'**flaker** NOUN

flake² (fleɪk) NOUN a rack or platform for drying fish or other produce.
▷HISTORY C14: from Old Norse *flaki*; related to Dutch *vlaak* hurdle

flake³ (fleɪk) VERB *Nautical* another word for **fake**.

flake⁴ (fleɪk) NOUN (in Australia) the commercial name for the meat of the gummy shark.

flake out VERB (*intr, adverb*) *Informal* to collapse or fall asleep as through extreme exhaustion.

flake white NOUN a pigment made from flakes of white lead.

flak jacket NOUN a reinforced sleeveless jacket for protection against gunfire or shrapnel worn by soldiers, policemen, etc.

flaky ('fleɪkɪ) ADJECTIVE **flakier, flakiest.** [1] like or made of flakes. [2] tending to peel off or break easily into flakes. [3] Also: **flakey.** *US slang* eccentric; crazy.
▸'**flakily** ADVERB ▸'**flakiness** NOUN

flaky pastry NOUN a rich pastry in the form of very thin layers, used for making pies, small cakes, etc.

flam¹ (flæm) *Now chiefly dialect* ◆ NOUN [1] a falsehood, deception, or sham. [2] nonsense; drivel. ◆ VERB **flams, flamming, flammed.** [3] (*tr*) to cheat or deceive.
▷HISTORY C16: probably short for FLIMFLAM

flam² (flæm) NOUN a drumbeat in which both sticks strike the head almost simultaneously but are heard to do so separately.
▷HISTORY C18: probably imitative of the sound

flambé *or* **flambée** ('flɑːmbeɪ, 'flæm-; *French* flɑ̃be) ADJECTIVE [1] (of food, such as steak or pancakes) served in flaming brandy. ◆ VERB **-béing** *or* **-béeing, -béd** *or* **-béed.** [2] (*tr*) to pour brandy over (food) and ignite it.
▷HISTORY French, past participle of *flamber* to FLAME

flambeau ('flæmbəʊ) NOUN, *plural* **-beaux** (-bəʊ, -bəʊz) *or* **-beaus.** [1] a burning torch, as used in night processions. [2] a large ornamental candlestick.
▷HISTORY C17: from Old French: torch, literally: a little flame, from *flambe* FLAME

Flamborough Head ('flæmbərə, -brə) NOUN a chalk promontory in NE England, on the coast of the East Riding of Yorkshire.

flamboyant (flæm'bɔɪənt) ADJECTIVE [1] elaborate or extravagant; florid; showy. [2] rich or brilliant in colour; resplendent. [3] of, denoting, or relating to the French Gothic style of architecture characterized by flamelike tracery and elaborate carving. ◆ NOUN [4] another name for **royal poinciana.**
▷HISTORY C19: from French: flaming, from *flamboyer* to FLAME
▸**flam'boyance** *or* **flam'boyancy** NOUN ▸**flam'boyantly** ADVERB

flame (fleɪm) NOUN [1] a hot usually luminous body of burning gas often containing small incandescent particles, typically emanating in flickering streams from burning material or produced by a jet of ignited gas. [2] (*often plural*) the state or condition of burning with flames: *to burst into flames.* [3] a brilliant light; fiery glow. [4] **a** a strong reddish-orange colour. **b** (*as adjective*): *a flame carpet.* [5] intense passion or ardour; burning emotion. [6] *Informal* a lover or sweetheart (esp in the phrase **an old flame**). [7] *Informal* an abusive message sent by electronic mail, esp to express anger or criticism of an Internet user by sending him or her large numbers of messages. ◆ VERB [8] to burn or cause to burn brightly; give off or cause to give off flame. [9] (*intr*) to burn or glow as if with fire; become red or fiery: *his face flamed with anger.* [10] (*intr*) to show great emotion; become angry or excited. [11] (*tr*) to apply a flame to (something). [12] (*tr*) *Archaic* to set on fire, either physically or with emotion. [13] *Informal* to send an abusive message by electronic mail. ◆ See also **flameout.**
▷HISTORY C14: from Anglo-French *flaume*, from Old French *flambe*, modification of *flamble*, from Latin *flammula* a little flame, from *flamma* flame
▸'**flamer** NOUN ▸'**flameless** ADJECTIVE ▸'**flamelet** NOUN ▸'**flame,like** ADJECTIVE ▸'**flamy** ADJECTIVE

flame-arc light NOUN *Electrical engineering* an arc light that uses flame carbons to colour the arc.

flame carbon NOUN *Electrical engineering* a carbon electrode containing metallic salts that colour the arc in a flame-arc light.

flame cell NOUN an organ of excretion in flatworms: a hollow cup-shaped cell containing a bunch of cilia, whose movement draws in waste products and wafts them to the outside through a connecting tubule.

flame cutting NOUN *Engineering* a method of cutting ferrous metals in which the metal is heated by a torch to about 800°C and is oxidized by a stream of oxygen from the torch.

flame gun NOUN a type of flame-thrower for destroying garden weeds.

flame hardening NOUN *Engineering* the surface hardening of ferrous metals by heating the metal with an oxyacetylene flame followed by rapid cooling.

flame lamp NOUN *Electrical engineering* a filament lamp in which the bulb resembles the shape of a flame.

flamen ('fleɪmɛn) NOUN, *plural* **flamens** *or* **flamines** ('flæmɪˌniːz). (in ancient Rome) any of 15 priests who each served a particular deity.
▷HISTORY C14: from Latin; probably related to Old English *blōtan* to sacrifice, Gothic *blotan* to worship

flamenco (flə'mɛŋkəʊ) NOUN, *plural* **-cos.** [1] a type of dance music for vocal soloist and guitar, characterized by elaborate melody and sad mood. [2] the dance performed to such music.
▷HISTORY from Spanish: like a gipsy, literally: Fleming, from Middle Dutch *Vlaminc* Fleming

flame-of-the-forest NOUN [1] (esp in Malaysia) another name for **royal poinciana.** [2] a leguminous tree, *Butea frondosa*, native to E India and Myanmar, having hanging clusters of scarlet flowers.

flameout ('fleɪmˌaʊt) NOUN [1] the failure of an aircraft jet engine in flight due to extinction of the flame. ◆ VERB **flame out.** (*adverb*) [2] (of a jet engine) to fail in flight or to cause (a jet engine) to fail in flight.

flameproof ('fleɪmˌpruːf) ADJECTIVE [1] not liable to catch fire or be damaged by fire. [2] (of electrical apparatus) designed so that an internal explosion will not ignite external flammable gas.

flame retarder NOUN a material that, while not incombustible, does not itself maintain combustion without an external heat source and therefore retards the spread of fire.

flame test NOUN a test for detecting the presence of certain metals in compounds by the coloration they give to a flame. Sodium, for example, turns a flame yellow.

flame-thrower NOUN a weapon that ejects a stream or spray of burning fluid.

flame tree NOUN any of various tropical trees with red or orange flowers, such as flame-of-the-forest.

flaming ('fleɪmɪŋ) ADJECTIVE [1] burning with or emitting flames. [2] glowing brightly; brilliant. [3] intense or ardent; vehement; passionate: *a flaming temper.* [4] *Informal* (intensifier): *you flaming idiot.* [5] an obsolete word for **flagrant.**
▸'**flamingly** ADVERB

flamingo (flə'mɪŋgəʊ) NOUN, *plural* **-gos** *or* **-goes.** [1] any large wading bird of the family *Phoenicopteridae*, having a pink-and-red plumage and downward-bent bill and inhabiting brackish lakes: order *Ciconiiformes.* [2] **a** a reddish-orange colour. **b** (*as adjective*): *flamingo gloves.*
▷HISTORY C16: from Portuguese *flamengo*, from Provençal *flamenc*, from Latin *flamma* flame + Germanic suffix *-ing* denoting descent from or membership of; compare -ING³

Flaminian Way (flə'mɪnɪən) NOUN an ancient road in Italy, extending north from Rome to Rimini: constructed in 220 B.C. by Gaius Flaminius. Length: over 322 km (200 miles). Latin name: **Via Flaminia.**

flammable ('flæməbᵊl) ADJECTIVE liable to catch fire; readily combustible; inflammable.
▸ˌ**flamma'bility** NOUN

> **Language note** *Flammable* and *inflammable* are interchangeable when used of the properties of materials. *Flammable* is, however, often preferred for warning labels as there is less likelihood of misunderstanding (*inflammable* being sometimes taken to mean *not flammable*). *Inflammable* is preferred in figurative contexts: *this could prove to be an inflammable situation.*

flan (flæn) NOUN [1] an open pastry or sponge tart filled with fruit or a savoury mixture. [2] a piece of metal ready to receive the die or stamp in the production of coins; shaped blank; planchet.
▷HISTORY C19: from French, from Old French *flaon*, from Late Latin *fladō* flat cake, of Germanic origin

flanch (flæntʃ) NOUN a variant of **flaunch.**

Flanders ('flɑːndəz) NOUN a powerful medieval principality in the SW part of the Low Countries, now in the Belgian provinces of East and West Flanders, the Netherlands province of Zeeland, and the French department of the Nord; scene of battles in many wars.

Flanders poppy NOUN another name for **corn poppy.**

flânerie *French* (flɑnri) NOUN aimless strolling or lounging; idleness.
▷HISTORY C19: from *flâner* to stroll, dawdle, ultimately from Old Norse *flana* to wander about

flâneur *French* (flɑnœr) NOUN an idler or loafer.
▷HISTORY C19: see FLÂNERIE

flange (flændʒ) NOUN [1] a projecting disc-shaped collar or rim on an object for locating or strengthening it or for attaching it to another object. [2] a flat outer face of a rolled-steel joist, esp of an I- or H-beam. [3] a tool for forming a flange. ◆ VERB [4] (*tr*) to attach or provide (a component) with a flange. [5] (*intr*) to take the form of a flange.
▷HISTORY C17: probably changed from earlier *flaunche* curved segment at side of a heraldic field, from French *flanc* FLANK
▸**flanged** ADJECTIVE ▸'**flangeless** ADJECTIVE ▸'**flanger** NOUN

flange coupling NOUN *Engineering* a driving coupling between rotating shafts that consists of flanges (or **half couplings**) one of which is fixed at the end of each shaft, the two flanges being bolted together with a ring of bolts to complete the drive.

flanged rail NOUN another name for **flat-bottomed rail.**

flank (flæŋk) NOUN [1] the side of a man or animal between the ribs and the hip. [2] (loosely) the outer part of the human thigh. [3] a cut of beef from the flank. [4] the side of anything, such as a mountain or building. [5] the side of a naval or military formation. ◆ VERB [6] (when *intr*, often foll by *on* or *upon*) to be located at the side of (an object, building, etc.). [7] *Military* to position or guard on or beside the flank of (a formation, etc.). [8] *Military* to move past or go round (a flank).
▷HISTORY C12: from Old French *flanc*, of Germanic origin

flanker ('flæŋkə) NOUN [1] one of a detachment of soldiers detailed to guard the flanks, esp of a formation. [2] a projecting fortification, used esp to protect or threaten a flank. [3] *Rugby* a wing forward.

flannel ('flænᵊl) NOUN [1] a soft light woollen

fabric with a slight nap, used for clothing. [2] (*plural*) trousers or other garments made of flannel. [3] See **cotton flannel.** [4] *Brit* a small piece of cloth used to wash the face and hands; face cloth. US and Canadian equivalent: **washcloth.** [5] *Brit informal* indirect or evasive talk; deceiving flattery. ◆ VERB **-nels, -nelling, -nelled** *or US* **-nels, -neling, -neled.** (*tr*) [6] to cover or wrap with flannel. [7] to rub, clean, or polish with flannel. [8] *Brit informal* to talk evasively to; flatter in order to mislead.
▷**HISTORY** C14: probably variant of *flanen* sackcloth, from Welsh *gwlanen* woollen fabric, from *gwlân* wool
▸'**flannelly** ADJECTIVE

flannelboard ('flæn^{ə}l,bɔːd) *or* **flannelgraph** ('flæn^{ə}l,grɑːf, -,græf) NOUN a visual aid used in teaching consisting of a board covered with flannel to which pictures, diagrams, etc. will stick when pressed on.

flannelette (,flæn^{ə}'lɛt) NOUN a cotton imitation of flannel.

flannel flower NOUN any Australian plant of the umbelliferous genus *Actinotus* having white flannel-like bracts beneath the flowers.

flap (flæp) VERB **flaps, flapping, flapped.** [1] to move (wings or arms) up and down, esp in or as if in flying, or (of wings or arms) to move in this way. [2] to move or cause to move noisily back and forth or up and down: *the curtains flapped in the breeze.* [3] (*intr*) *Informal* to become agitated or flustered; panic. [4] to deal (a person or thing) a blow with a broad flexible object. [5] (*tr; sometimes foll by down*) to toss, fling, slam, etc., abruptly or noisily. [6] (*tr*) *Phonetics* to pronounce (an (r) sound) by allowing the tongue to give a single light tap against the alveolar ridge or uvula. ◆ NOUN [7] the action, motion, or noise made by flapping: *with one flap of its wings the bird was off.* [8] a piece of material, etc., attached at one edge and usually used to cover an opening, as on a tent, envelope, or pocket. [9] a blow dealt with a flat object; slap. [10] a movable surface fixed to the trailing edge of an aircraft wing that increases lift during takeoff and drag during landing. [11] *Surgery* a piece of tissue partially connected to the body, either following an amputation or to be used as a graft. [12] *Informal* a state of panic, distress, or agitation. [13] *Phonetics* an (r) produced by allowing the tongue to give a single light tap against the alveolar ridge or uvula.
▷**HISTORY** C14: probably of imitative origin

flapdoodle ('flæp,duːd^{ə}l) NOUN *Slang* foolish talk; nonsense.
▷**HISTORY** C19: of unknown origin

flapjack ('flæp,dʒæk) NOUN [1] a chewy biscuit made with rolled oats. [2] *US, Canadian & NZ* another word for **pancake.**
▷**HISTORY** C17: from FLAP (in the sense: toss) + JACK[1]

flapper ('flæpə) NOUN [1] a person or thing that flaps. [2] (in the 1920s) a young woman, esp one flaunting her unconventional dress and behaviour.

flare (flɛə) VERB [1] to burn or cause to burn with an unsteady or sudden bright flame. [2] to spread or cause to spread outwards from a narrow to a wider shape. [3] (*tr*) to make a conspicuous display of. [4] to increase the temperature of (a molten metal or alloy) until a gaseous constituent of the melt burns with a characteristic flame or (of a molten metal or alloy) to show such a flame. [5] (*tr; sometimes foll by off*) (in the oil industry) to burn off (unwanted gas) at an oil well. ◆ NOUN [6] an unsteady flame. [7] a sudden burst of flame. [8] **a** a blaze of light or fire used to illuminate, identify, alert, signal distress, etc. **b** the device producing such a blaze. [9] a spreading shape or anything with a spreading shape: *a skirt with a flare.* [10] a sudden outburst, as of emotion. [11] *Optics* **a** the unwanted light reaching the image region of an optical device by reflections inside the instrument, etc. **b** the fogged area formed on a negative by such reflections. See also **solar flare.** [12] *Astronomy* short for **solar flare.** [13] *Aeronautics* the final transition phase of an aircraft landing, from the steady descent path to touchdown. [14] an open flame used to burn off unwanted gas at an oil well.
▷**HISTORY** C16 (to spread out): of unknown origin
▸**flared** ADJECTIVE

flare path NOUN an airstrip illuminated for use at night or in bad weather.

flares (flɛəz) PLURAL NOUN *Informal* trousers with legs that widen below the knee.

flare star NOUN a red dwarf star in which outbursts, thought to be analogous to solar flares, occur, increasing the luminosity by several magnitudes in a few minutes.

flare-up NOUN [1] a sudden burst of fire or light. [2] *Informal* a sudden burst of emotion or violence. ◆ VERB **flare up.** (*intr, adverb*) [3] to burst suddenly into fire or light. [4] *Informal* to burst into anger.

flash (flæʃ) NOUN [1] a sudden short blaze of intense light or flame: *a flash of sunlight.* [2] a sudden occurrence or display, esp one suggestive of brilliance: *a flash of understanding.* [3] a very brief space of time: *over in a flash.* [4] an ostentatious display: *a flash of her diamonds.* [5] Also called: **newsflash.** a short news announcement concerning a new event. [6] Also called: **patch.** *Chiefly Brit* an insignia or emblem worn on a uniform, vehicle, etc., to identify its military formation. [7] a patch of bright colour on a dark background, such as light marking on an animal. [8] a volatile mixture of inorganic salts used to produce a glaze on bricks or tiles. [9] **a** a sudden rush of water down a river or watercourse. **b** a device, such as a sluice, for producing such a rush. [10] *Photog, informal* short for **flashlight** (sense 2) or **flash photography.** [11] a ridge of thin metal or plastic formed on a moulded object by the extrusion of excess material between dies. [12] *Yorkshire and Lancashire dialect* a pond, esp one produced as a consequence of subsidence. [13] (*modifier*) involving, using, or produced by a flash of heat, light, etc.: *flash blindness; flash distillation.* [14] **flash in the pan.** a project, person, etc., that enjoys only short-lived success, notoriety, etc. ◆ ADJECTIVE [15] *Informal* ostentatious or vulgar. [16] *Informal* of or relating to gamblers and followers of boxing and racing. [17] sham or counterfeit. [18] *Informal* relating to or characteristic of the criminal underworld. [19] brief and rapid: *flash freezing.* ◆ VERB [20] to burst or cause to burst suddenly or intermittently into flame. [21] to emit or reflect or cause to emit or reflect light suddenly or intermittently. [22] (*intr*) to move very fast: *he flashed by on his bicycle.* [23] (*intr*) to come rapidly (into the mind or vision). [24] (*intr; foll by out or up*) to appear like a sudden light: *his anger really flashes out at times.* [25] **a** to signal or communicate very fast: *to flash a message.* **b** to signal by use of a light, such as car headlights. [26] (*tr*) *Informal* to display ostentatiously: *to flash money around.* [27] (*tr*) *Informal* to show suddenly and briefly. [28] (*intr*) *Brit slang* to expose oneself indecently. [29] (*tr*) to cover (a roof) with flashing. [30] to send a sudden rush of water down (a river, etc.), or to carry (a vessel) down by this method. [31] (in the making of glass) to coat (glass) with a thin layer of glass of a different colour. [32] (*tr*) to subject to a brief pulse of heat or radiation. [33] (*tr*) to change (a liquid) to a gas by causing it to hit a hot surface. [34] *Obsolete* to splash or dash (water).
▷**HISTORY** C14 (in the sense: to rush, as of water): of unknown origin

flashback ('flæʃ,bæk) NOUN [1] a transition in a novel, film, etc., to an earlier scene or event. ◆ VERB **flash back.** [2] (*intr, adverb*) to return in a novel, film, etc., to a past event.

flashboard ('flæʃ,bɔːd) NOUN a board or boarding that is placed along the top of a dam to increase its height and capacity. Also called: **stop log, stop plank.**

flashbulb ('flæʃ,bʌlb) NOUN *Photog* a small expendable glass light bulb formerly used to produce a bright flash of light. Also called: **photoflash.** Compare **electronic flash.**

flashbulb memory NOUN *Psychol* the clear recollections that a person may have of the circumstances associated with a dramatic event.

flash burn NOUN *Pathol* a burn caused by momentary exposure to intense radiant heat.

flash card NOUN a card on which are written or printed words for children to look at briefly, used as an aid to learning.

flash eliminator *or* **suppressor** NOUN a device fitted to the muzzle of a firearm to reduce the flash made by the ignited propellant gases.

flasher ('flæʃə) NOUN [1] something that flashes, such as a direction indicator on a vehicle. [2] *Brit slang* a person who indecently exposes himself.

flash flood NOUN a sudden short-lived torrent, usually caused by a heavy storm, esp in desert regions.

flash gun NOUN a type of electronic flash, attachable to or sometimes incorporated in a camera, that emits a very brief flash of light when the shutter is open.

flashing ('flæʃɪŋ) NOUN a weatherproof material, esp thin sheet metal, used to cover the valleys between the slopes of a roof, the junction between a chimney and a roof, etc.

flashlight ('flæʃ,laɪt) NOUN [1] another word (esp US and Canadian) for **torch.** [2] *Photog* the brief bright light emitted by an electronic flash unit. Sometimes shortened to **flash.** [3] *Chiefly US and Canadian* a light that flashes, used for signalling, in a lighthouse, etc.

flashover ('flæʃ,əʊvə) NOUN [1] an electric discharge over or around the surface of an insulator. [2] the sudden and rapid spread of fire through the air, caused by the ignition of smoke or fumes from surrounding objects.

flash photography NOUN photography in which a flashbulb or electronic flash is used to provide momentary illumination of a dark or insufficiently lit subject.

flash photolysis NOUN *Physics* a technique for producing and investigating free radicals. A low-pressure gas is subjected to a flash of radiation to produce the radicals, subsequent flashes being used to identify them and assess their lifetimes by absorption spectroscopy.

flash point *or* **flashing point** NOUN [1] the lowest temperature at which the vapour above a liquid can be ignited in air. [2] a critical moment beyond which a situation will inevitably erupt into violence: *the political mood has reached flash point.*

flash set NOUN *Civil engineering* undesirably rapid setting of cement in concrete.

flash smelting NOUN a smelting process for sulphur-containing ores in which the dried and powdered ore, mixed with oxygen, is ignited on discharge from a nozzle, melts, and drops to the bottom of a settling chamber. Sulphur is released mainly in its solid form, thus reducing atmospheric pollution.

flashy ('flæʃɪ) ADJECTIVE **flashier, flashiest.** [1] brilliant and dazzling, esp for a short time or in a superficial way. [2] cheap and ostentatious.
▸'**flashily** ADVERB ▸'**flashiness** NOUN

flask (flɑːsk) NOUN [1] a bottle with a narrow neck, esp used in a laboratory or for wine, oil, etc. [2] Also called: **hip flask.** a small flattened container of glass or metal designed to be carried in a pocket, esp for liquor. [3] See **powder flask.** [4] a container packed with sand to form a mould in a foundry. [5] See **vacuum flask.** [6] Also called: **cask, coffin.** *Engineering* a container used for transporting irradiated nuclear fuel.
▷**HISTORY** C14: from Old French *flasque, flaske,* from Medieval Latin *flasca, flasco,* perhaps of Germanic origin; compare Old English *flasce, flaxe*

flasket ('flɑːskɪt) NOUN [1] a long shallow basket. [2] a small flask.
▷**HISTORY** C15: from Old French *flasquet* a little FLASK

flat[1] (flæt) ADJECTIVE **flatter, flattest.** [1] horizontal; level: *flat ground; a flat roof.* [2] even or smooth, without projections or depressions: *a flat surface.* [3] lying stretched out at full length; prostrate: *he lay flat on the ground.* [4] having little depth or thickness; shallow: *a flat dish.* [5] (*postpositive; often foll by against*) having a surface or side in complete contact with another surface: *flat against the wall.* [6] spread out, unrolled, or levelled. [7] (of a tyre) deflated, either partially or completely. [8] (of shoes) having an unraised or only slightly raised heel. [9] *Chiefly Brit* **a** (of races, racetracks, or racecourses) not having obstacles to be jumped. **b** of, relating to, or connected with flat racing as opposed to steeplechasing and hurdling: *flat jockeys earn more.* [10] without qualification; total: *a flat denial.* [11] without possibility of change; fixed: *a flat rate.* [12] (*prenominal or immediately postpositive*) neither more nor less; exact: *he did the journey in thirty minutes flat; a flat thirty minutes.* [13] unexciting or lacking point or interest: *a flat joke.* [14] without variation or resonance; monotonous: *a flat voice.* [15]

(of food) stale or tasteless. 16 (of beer, sparkling wines, etc.) having lost effervescence, as by exposure to air. 17 (of trade, business, a market, etc.) commercially inactive; sluggish. 18 (of a battery) fully discharged; dead. 19 (of a print, photograph, or painting) lacking contrast or shading between tones. 20 (of paint) without gloss or lustre; matt. 21 (of a painting) lacking perspective. 22 (of lighting) diffuse. 23 *Music* **a** (*immediately postpositive*) denoting a note of a given letter name (or the sound it represents) that has been lowered in pitch by one chromatic semitone: *B flat.* **b** (of an instrument, voice, etc.) out of tune by being too low in pitch. Compare **sharp** (sense 12). 24 *Phonetics* another word for **lenis.** 25 **flat a.** *Phonetics* the vowel sound of *a* as in the usual US or S Brit pronunciation of *hand, cat,* usually represented by the symbol (æ). ◆ ADVERB 26 in or into a prostrate, level, or flat state or position: *he held his hand out flat.* 27 completely or utterly; absolutely: *he went flat against the rules.* 28 exactly; precisely: *in three minutes flat.* 29 *Music* **a** lower than a standard pitch. **b** too low in pitch: *she sings flat.* Compare **sharp** (sense 18). 30 **fall flat.** to fail to achieve a desired effect, etc. 31 **flat out.** *Informal* **a** with the maximum speed or effort. **b** totally exhausted. ◆ NOUN 32 a flat object, surface, or part. 33 (*often plural*) a low-lying tract of land, esp a marsh or swamp. 34 (*often plural*) a mud bank exposed at low tide. 35 *Music* **a** an accidental that lowers the pitch of the following note by one chromatic semitone. Usual symbol: ♭. **b** a note affected by this accidental. Compare **sharp** (sense 19). 36 *Theatre* a rectangular wooden frame covered with painted canvas, etc., used to form part of a stage setting. 37 a punctured car tyre. 38 (*often cap*; preceded by *the*) *Chiefly Brit* **a** flat racing, esp as opposed to steeplechasing and hurdling. **b** the season of flat racing. 39 *Nautical* a flatboat or lighter. 40 *US and Canadian* a shallow box or container, used for holding plants, growing seedlings, etc. ◆ VERB **flats, flatting, flatted.** 41 to make or become flat. 42 *Music* the usual US word for **flatten** (sense 3). ◆ See also **flats.**
▷HISTORY C14: from Old Norse *flatr*; related to Old High German *flaz* flat, Greek *platus* flat, broad
▸ **'flatly** ADVERB ▸ **'flatness** NOUN

flat[2] (flæt) NOUN 1 a set of rooms comprising a residence entirely on one floor of a building. Usual US and Canadian name: **apartment.** 2 *Brit and NZ* a portion of a house used as separate living quarters. 3 *NZ* a house shared with people who are not members of one's own family. ◆ VERB (*intr*) **flats, flatting, flatted.** 4 *Austral and NZ* to live in a flat (with someone).
▷HISTORY Old English *flett* floor, hall, house; related to FLAT[1]

flat-bed lorry ('flæt,bɛd) NOUN a lorry with a flat platform for its body.

flat-bed press NOUN a printing machine on which the type forme is carried on a flat bed under a revolving paper-bearing cylinder. Also called: **cylinder press.**

flat-bed scanner NOUN a computer-controlled device which electronically scans images placed on its flat plate, allowing them to be stored in digital form.

flatboat ('flæt,bəʊt) NOUN any boat with a flat bottom, usually for transporting goods on a canal or river.

flat-bottomed rail NOUN *Railways* a rail having a cross section like an inverted T, with the top extremity enlarged slightly to form the head. Also called: **flanged rail.**

flatbread ('flæt,brɛd) NOUN a type of thin unleavened bread.

flat cap NOUN 1 another name for **cloth cap** (sense 1). 2 an Elizabethan man's hat with a narrow down-turned brim.

flat-coated retriever NOUN a medium-sized variety of retriever having a dense flat black or liver-coloured coat with feathered legs and tail.

flat dog NOUN *Austral* another name for **crocodile.**

flat-earther NOUN *Informal* a person who does not accept or is out of touch with the realities of modern life.

flatette (,flæt'ɛt) NOUN *Austral* a very small flat.

flatfish ('flæt,fɪʃ) NOUN, *plural* **-fish** *or* **-fishes.** any marine spiny-finned fish of the order *Heterosomata*, including the halibut, plaice, turbot, and sole, all of which (when adult) swim along the sea floor on one side of the body, which is highly compressed and has both eyes on the uppermost side.

flatfoot ('flæt,fʊt) NOUN 1 Also called: **splayfoot.** a condition in which the entire sole of the foot is able to touch the ground because of flattening of the instep arch. 2 (*plural* **-foots** *or* **-feet**) a slang word (usually derogatory) for a **policeman.**

flat-footed (,flæt'fʊtɪd) ADJECTIVE 1 having flatfoot. 2 *Brit informal* **a** clumsy or awkward. **b** downright and uncompromising. 3 *Informal* off guard or unawares (often in the phrase **catch flat-footed**).
▸ **,flat-'footedly** ADVERB ▸ **,flat-'footedness** NOUN

flathead ('flæt,hɛd) NOUN, *plural* **-head** *or* **-heads.** any Pacific scorpaenoid food fish of the family *Platycephalidae*, which resemble gurnards.

flatiron ('flæt,aɪən) NOUN (formerly) an iron for pressing clothes that was heated by being placed on a stove, etc.

flat knot NOUN another name for **reef knot.**

flatlet ('flætlɪt) NOUN a flat having only a few rooms.

flatline ('flæt,laɪn) VERB (*intr*) *Informal* 1 to die or be so near death that the display of one's vital signs on medical monitoring equipment shows a flat line rather than peaks and troughs. 2 to remain at a continuous low level.

flatling ('flætlɪŋ) *Archaic or dialect* ◆ ADVERB 1 in a flat or prostrate position. ◆ ADJECTIVE, ADVERB 2 with the flat side, as of a sword. Also (for adverb): **flatlings.**

flatmate ('flæt,meɪt) NOUN *Brit* a person with whom one shares a flat.

flat-pack ADJECTIVE (of a piece of furniture, equipment, or other construction) supplied in pieces packed into a flat box for assembly by the buyer.

flat racing NOUN **a** the racing of horses on racecourses without jumps. **b** (*as modifier*): *the flat-racing season.*

flats (flæts) *or* **flatties** ('flætɪz) PLURAL NOUN shoes with flat heels or no heels.

flat-share NOUN 1 the state of living in a flat where each occupant shares the facilities and expenses. ◆ VERB (*intr*) 2 to live in a flat with other people who are not relatives.

flat spin NOUN 1 an aircraft spin in which the longitudinal axis is more nearly horizontal than vertical. 2 *Informal* a state of confusion; dither.

flat spot NOUN 1 *Engineering* a region of poor acceleration over a narrow range of throttle openings, caused by a weak mixture in the carburettor. 2 any narrow region of poor performance in a mechanical device.

flatten ('flætᵊn) VERB 1 (sometimes foll by *out*) to make or become flat or flatter. 2 (*tr*) *Informal* **a** to knock down or injure; prostrate. **b** to crush or subdue: *failure will flatten his self-esteem.* 3 (*tr*) *Music* to lower the pitch of (a note) by one chromatic semitone. Usual US word: **flat.** 4 (*intr;* foll by *out*) to manoeuvre an aircraft into horizontal flight, esp after a dive.
▸ **'flattener** NOUN

flatter[1] ('flætə) VERB 1 to praise insincerely, esp in order to win favour or reward. 2 to show to advantage: *that dress flatters her.* 3 (*tr*) to make to appear more attractive, etc., than in reality. 4 to play upon or gratify the vanity of (a person): *it flatters her to be remembered.* 5 (*tr*) to beguile with hope; encourage, esp falsely: *this success flattered him into believing himself a champion.* 6 (*tr*) to congratulate or deceive (oneself): *I flatter myself that I am the best.*
▷HISTORY C13: probably from Old French *flater* to lick, fawn upon, of Frankish origin
▸ **'flatterable** ADJECTIVE ▸ **'flatterer** NOUN ▸ **'flatteringly** ADVERB

flatter[2] ('flætə) NOUN 1 a blacksmith's tool, resembling a flat-faced hammer, that is placed on forged work and struck to smooth the surface of the forging. 2 a die with a narrow rectangular orifice for drawing flat sections.

flattery ('flætərɪ) NOUN, *plural* **-teries.** 1 the act of flattering. 2 excessive or insincere praise.

flattie ('flætɪ) NOUN *NZ informal* a flounder or other flatfish.

flatties ('flætɪz) PLURAL NOUN another word for **flats.**

flatting ('flætɪŋ) NOUN 1 *Metallurgy* the process of flattening metal into a sheet by rolling. 2 *NZ* the practice of sharing a house with people who are not members of one's own family. 3 *NZ* to leave the parental home and live independently in a flat, usually with people of the same age group.

flattish ('flætɪʃ) ADJECTIVE somewhat flat.

flattop ('flæt,tɒp) NOUN *US* an informal name for **aircraft carrier.**

flat top NOUN a style of haircut in which the hair is cut shortest on the top of the head so that it stands up from the scalp and appears flat from the crown to the forehead.

flat tuning NOUN the condition of a radio receiver that does not discriminate sharply between signals on different frequencies.

flatulent ('flætjʊlənt) ADJECTIVE 1 suffering from or caused by an excessive amount of gas in the alimentary canal, producing uncomfortable distension. 2 generating excessive gas in the alimentary canal. 3 pretentious or windy in style.
▷HISTORY C16: from New Latin *flātulentus*, from Latin: FLATUS
▸ **'flatulence** *or* **'flatulency** NOUN ▸ **'flatulently** ADVERB

flatus ('fleɪtəs) NOUN, *plural* **-tuses.** gas generated in the alimentary canal.
▷HISTORY C17: from Latin: a blowing, snorting, from *flāre* to breathe, blow

flatware ('flæt,wɛə) NOUN *US and Canadian* 1 cutlery. 2 any relatively flat tableware such as plates, saucers, etc. Compare **hollowware.**

flatways ('flæt,weɪz) *or US* **flatwise** ADVERB with the flat or broad side down or in contact with another surface.

flatworm ('flæt,wɜːm) NOUN any parasitic or free-living invertebrate of the phylum *Platyhelminthes*, including planarians, flukes, and tapeworms, having a flattened body with no circulatory system and only one opening to the intestine.

flat-woven ADJECTIVE (of a carpet) woven without pile.

flaunch (flɔːntʃ) NOUN a cement or mortar slope around a chimney top, manhole, etc., to throw off water. Also called: **flaunching.**
▷HISTORY C18: variant of FLANGE

flaunt (flɔːnt) VERB 1 to display (possessions, oneself, etc.) ostentatiously; show off. 2 to wave or cause to wave freely; flutter. ◆ NOUN 3 the act of flaunting.
▷HISTORY C16: perhaps of Scandinavian origin; compare Norwegian dialect *flanta* to wander about
▸ **'flaunter** NOUN ▸ **'flauntingly** ADVERB

> **Language note** *Flaunt* is sometimes wrongly used where *flout* is meant: *they must be prevented from flouting* (not *flaunting*) *the law.*

flaunty ('flɔːntɪ) ADJECTIVE **flauntier, flauntiest.** *Chiefly US* characterized by or inclined to ostentatious display or flaunting.
▸ **'flauntily** ADVERB ▸ **'flauntiness** NOUN

flautist ('flɔːtɪst) *or US and Canadian* **flutist** ('fluːtɪst) NOUN a player of the flute.
▷HISTORY C19: from Italian *flautista*, from *flauto* FLUTE

flavescent (flə'vɛsᵊnt) ADJECTIVE turning yellow; yellowish.
▷HISTORY C19: from Latin *flāvēscere* to become yellow, from *flāvēre* to be yellow, from *flāvus* yellow

flavin *or* **flavine** ('fleɪvɪn) NOUN 1 a heterocyclic ketone that forms the nucleus of certain natural yellow pigments, such as riboflavin. Formula: $C_{10}H_6N_4O_2$. See **flavoprotein.** 2 any yellow pigment based on flavin. 3 another name for **quercetin.**
▷HISTORY C19: from Latin *flāvus* yellow

flavine ('fleɪvɪn) NOUN 1 another name for **acriflavine hydrochloride.** 2 a variant spelling of **flavin.**

flavivirus ('fleɪvɪ,vaɪrəs) NOUN a type of arbovirus that causes a wide range of diseases in humans, including yellow fever, dengue, and West Nile fever. It is spread by ticks or mosquitoes.

flavone ('fleɪvəʊn) NOUN 1 a crystalline compound occurring in plants. Formula: $C_{15}H_{10}O_2$. 2 any of a class of yellow plant pigments derived from flavone.
▷HISTORY C19: from German *Flavon*, from Latin *flāvus* yellow + -ONE

flavonoid ('fleɪvəˌnɔɪd) NOUN any of a group of organic compounds that occur as pigments in fruit and flowers.
▷HISTORY C20: from FLAVONE + -OID

flavonol ('fleɪvəˌnɒl) NOUN a flavonoid that occurs in red wine and is said to offer protection against heart disease.

flavoprotein (ˌfleɪvəʊ'prəʊtiːn) NOUN any of a group of enzymes that contain a derivative of riboflavin linked to a protein and catalyse oxidation in cells. Also called: **cytochrome reductase**. See also **FMN, FAD.**
▷HISTORY C20: from FLAVIN + PROTEIN

flavopurpurin (ˌfleɪvəʊ'pɜːpjʊrɪn) NOUN a yellow crystalline dye derived from anthraquinone. Formula: $C_{14}H_5O_2(OH)_3$.
▷HISTORY C20: from Latin *flāvus* yellow + PURPURIN

flavorous ('fleɪvərəs) ADJECTIVE having flavour; tasty.

flavour *or US* **flavor** ('fleɪvə) NOUN 1 taste perceived in food or liquid in the mouth. 2 a substance added to food, etc., to impart a specific taste. 3 a distinctive quality or atmosphere; suggestion: *a poem with a Shakespearean flavour*. 4 a type or variety: *various flavours of graphical interface*. 5 *Physics* a property of quarks that enables them to be differentiated into six types: up, down, strange, charm, bottom (or beauty), and top (or truth). 6 **flavour of the month.** a person or thing that is the most popular at a certain time. ◆ VERB 7 (*tr*) to impart a flavour, taste, or quality to.
▷HISTORY C14: from Old French *flaour*, from Late Latin *flātor* (unattested) bad smell, breath, from Latin *flāre* to blow
▸ **'flavourer** *or US* **'flavorer** NOUN ▸ **'flavourless** *or US* **'flavorless** ADJECTIVE ▸ **'flavoursome** *or US* **'flavorsome** ADJECTIVE

flavour enhancer NOUN another term for **monosodium glutamate.**

flavourful *or US* **flavorful** ('fleɪvəfʊl) ADJECTIVE having a full pleasant taste or flavour.
▸ **'flavourfully** *or US* **'flavorfully** ADVERB

flavouring *or* **flavoring** ('fleɪvərɪŋ) NOUN a substance used to impart a particular flavour to food: *rum flavouring*.

flaw[1] (flɔː) NOUN 1 an imperfection, defect, or blemish. 2 a crack, breach, or rift. 3 *Law* an invalidating fault or defect in a document or proceeding. ◆ VERB 4 to make or become blemished, defective, or imperfect.
▷HISTORY C14: probably from Old Norse *flaga* stone slab; related to Swedish *flaga* chip, flake, flaw
▸ **'flawless** ADJECTIVE ▸ **'flawlessly** ADVERB ▸ **'flawlessness** NOUN

flaw[2] (flɔː) NOUN 1 **a** a sudden short gust of wind; squall. **b** a spell of bad, esp windy, weather. 2 *Obsolete* an outburst of strong feeling.
▷HISTORY C16: of Scandinavian origin; related to Norwegian *flaga* squall, gust, Middle Dutch *vlāghe*
▸ **'flawy** ADJECTIVE

flax (flæks) NOUN 1 any herbaceous plant or shrub of the genus *Linum*, esp *L. usitatissimum*, which has blue flowers and is cultivated for its seeds (flaxseed) and for the fibres of its stems: family *Linaceae*. 2 the fibre of this plant, made into thread and woven into linen fabrics. 3 any of various similar plants. 4 *NZ* a swamp plant producing a fibre that is used by Maoris for decorative work, baskets, etc.
▷HISTORY Old English *fleax*; related to Old Frisian *flax*, Old High German *flahs* flax, Greek *plekein* to plait

flaxen ('flæksən) *or* **flaxy** ADJECTIVE 1 of, relating to, or resembling flax. 2 of a soft yellow colour: *flaxen hair*.

flax kit NOUN *NZ* a basket woven from flax fibres.

flaxseed ('flæksˌsiːd) NOUN the seed of the flax plant, which yields linseed oil. Also called: **linseed.**

flay (fleɪ) VERB (*tr*) 1 to strip off the skin or outer covering of, esp by whipping; skin. 2 to attack with savage criticism. 3 to strip of money or goods, esp by cheating or extortion.
▷HISTORY Old English *flēan*; related to Old Norse *flā* to peel, Lithuanian *plėšti* to tear
▸ **'flayer** NOUN

flaysome ('fleɪsəm) ADJECTIVE *Northern English dialect* frightening.

fld ABBREVIATION FOR field.

fl. dr. ABBREVIATION FOR fluid dram.

flea (fliː) NOUN 1 any small wingless parasitic blood-sucking insect of the order *Siphonaptera*, living on the skin of mammals and birds and noted for its power of leaping. 2 any of various invertebrates that resemble fleas, such as the water flea and flea beetle. 3 **flea in one's ear.** *Informal* a sharp rebuke.
▷HISTORY Old English *flēah*; related to Old Norse *flō*, Old High German *flōh*

fleabag ('fliːˌbæg) NOUN *Slang* 1 *Brit* a dirty or unkempt person, esp a woman. 2 *US* a cheap or dirty hotel.

fleabane ('fliːˌbeɪn) NOUN 1 any of several plants of the genus *Erigeron*, such as *E. acer*, having purplish tubular flower heads with orange centres: family *Asteraceae* (composites). 2 any of several plants of the related genus *Pulicaria*, esp the Eurasian *P. dysenterica*, which has yellow daisy-like flower heads. 3 **Canadian fleabane.** a related plant, *Conyza* (or *Erigeron*) *canadensis*, with small white tubular flower heads. US name: **horseweed.** 4 any of various other plants reputed to ward off fleas.

flea beetle NOUN any small common beetle of the genera *Phyllotreta*, *Chalcoides*, etc., having enlarged hind legs and capable of jumping: family *Chrysomelidae*. The larvae of many species are very destructive to turnips and other cruciferous vegetables.

fleabite ('fliːˌbaɪt) NOUN 1 the bite of a flea. 2 a slight or trifling annoyance or discomfort.

flea-bitten ADJECTIVE 1 bitten by or infested with fleas. 2 *Informal* shabby or decrepit; mean. 3 (of the coat of a horse) having reddish-brown spots on a lighter background.

fleam (fliːm) NOUN *Archaic* a lancet used for letting blood.
▷HISTORY C16: from Old French *flieme*, alteration of Late Latin *phlebotomus* lancet (literally: vein cutter); see PHLEBOTOMY

flea market NOUN an open-air market selling cheap and often second-hand goods.

fleapit ('fliːˌpɪt) NOUN *Informal* a shabby cinema or theatre.

fleawort ('fliːˌwɜːt) NOUN 1 any of various plants of the genus *Senecio*, esp *S. integrifolius*, a European species with yellow daisy-like flowers and rosettes of downy leaves: family *Asteraceae* (composites). 2 a Eurasian plantain, *Plantago psyllium* (or *P. indica*), whose seeds resemble fleas and were formerly used as a flea repellent. 3 another name for **ploughman's spikenard.**

flèche (fleɪʃ, flɛʃ) NOUN 1 Also called: **spirelet.** a slender spire, esp over the intersection of the nave and transept ridges of a church roof. 2 a pointed part of a fortification directed towards the attackers. 3 *Fencing* a short running attack.
▷HISTORY C18: from French: spire (literally: arrow), probably of Germanic origin; related to Middle Low German *flieke* long arrow

fléchette (fleɪ'ʃɛt) NOUN a steel dart or missile dropped from an aircraft, as in World War I.
▷HISTORY from French; see FLÈCHE

fleck (flɛk) NOUN 1 a small marking or streak; speckle. 2 a small particle; speck: *a fleck of dust*. ◆ VERB 3 (*tr*) Also: **flecker.** to mark or cover with flecks; speckle.
▷HISTORY C16: probably from Old Norse *flekkr* stain, spot; related to Old High German *flec* spot, plot of land

flection ('flɛkʃən) NOUN 1 the act of bending or the state of being bent. 2 something bent; bend. 3 *Grammar* a less common word for **inflection.** ◆ See also **flexion.**
▷HISTORY C17: from Latin *flexiō* a bending, from *flectere* to curve, bow
▸ **'flectional** ADJECTIVE ▸ **'flectionless** ADJECTIVE

fled (flɛd) VERB the past tense and past participle of **flee.**

fledge (flɛdʒ) VERB 1 (*tr*) to feed and care for (a young bird) until it is able to fly. 2 (*tr*) Also called: **fletch.** to fit (something, esp an arrow) with a feather or feathers. 3 (*intr*) (of a young bird) to grow feathers. 4 (*tr*) to cover or adorn with or as if with feathers.
▷HISTORY Old English *-flycge*, as in *unflycge* unfledged; related to Old High German *flucki* able to fly; see FLY[1]

fledgling *or* **fledgeling** ('flɛdʒlɪŋ) NOUN 1 a young bird that has just fledged. 2 a young and inexperienced person.

fledgy ('flɛdʒɪ) ADJECTIVE **fledgier, fledgiest.** *Rare* feathery or feathered.

flee[1] (fliː) VERB **flees, fleeing, fled.** 1 to run away from (a place, danger, etc.); fly: *to flee the country*. 2 (*intr*) to run or move quickly; rush; speed: *she fled to the door*.
▷HISTORY Old English *flēon*; related to Old Frisian *fliā*, Old High German *fliohan*, Gothic *thliuhan*
▸ **'fleer** NOUN

flee[2] (fliː) VERB 1 a Scot word for **fly**[1]. ◆ NOUN 2 a Scot word for **fly**[2].

fleece (fliːs) NOUN 1 the coat of wool that covers the body of a sheep or similar animal and consists of a mass of crinkly hairs. 2 the wool removed from a single sheep. 3 something resembling a fleece in texture or warmth. 4 sheepskin or a fabric with soft pile, used as a lining for coats, etc. 5 a warm polyester fabric with a brushed nap, used for outdoor garments. 6 a jacket or top made from such a fabric. ◆ VERB (*tr*) 7 to defraud or charge exorbitantly; swindle. 8 another term for **shear** (sense 1).
▷HISTORY Old English *flēos*; related to Middle High German *vlius*, Dutch *vlies* fleece, Latin *plūma* feather, down

fleecie ('fliːsɪ) NOUN *NZ* a person who collects fleeces after shearing and prepares them for baling. Also called: **fleece-oh.**

fleecy ('fliːsɪ) ADJECTIVE **fleecier, fleeciest.** of or resembling fleece; woolly.
▸ **'fleecily** ADVERB ▸ **'fleeciness** NOUN

fleein' ('fliːɪn) ADJECTIVE *Scot dialect* drunk.
▷HISTORY literally: flying, from FLEE[2]

fleer (flɪə) *Archaic* ◆ VERB 1 to grin or laugh at; scoff; sneer. ◆ NOUN 2 a derisory glance or grin.
▷HISTORY C14: of Scandinavian origin; compare Norwegian *flire* to snigger
▸ **'fleeringly** ADVERB

fleet[1] (fliːt) NOUN 1 a number of warships organized as a tactical unit. 2 all the warships of a nation. 3 a number of aircraft, ships, buses, etc., operating together or under the same ownership.
▷HISTORY Old English *flēot* ship, flowing water, from *flēotan* to FLOAT

fleet[2] (fliːt) ADJECTIVE 1 rapid in movement; swift. 2 *Poetic* fleeting; transient. ◆ VERB 3 (*intr*) to move rapidly. 4 (*intr*) *Archaic* to fade away smoothly; glide. 5 (*tr*) *Nautical* **a** to change the position of (a hawser). **b** to pass (a messenger or lead) to a hawser from a winch for hauling in. **c** to spread apart (the blocks of a tackle). 6 (*intr*) *Obsolete* to float or swim. 7 (*tr*) *Obsolete* to cause (time) to pass rapidly.
▷HISTORY probably Old English *flēotan* to float, glide rapidly; related to Old High German *fliozzan* to flow, Latin *pluere* to rain
▸ **'fleetly** ADVERB ▸ **'fleetness** NOUN

fleet[3] (fliːt) NOUN *Chiefly Southeastern Brit* a small coastal inlet; creek.
▷HISTORY Old English *flēot* flowing water; see FLEET[1]

Fleet (fliːt) NOUN **the.** 1 a stream that formerly ran into the Thames between Ludgate Hill and Fleet Street and is now a covered sewer. 2 Also called: **Fleet Prison.** (formerly) a London prison, esp used for holding debtors.

fleet admiral NOUN an officer holding the most senior commissioned rank in the US and certain other navies.

Fleet Air Arm NOUN the aviation branch of the Royal Navy. Abbreviation: **FAA.**

fleet chief petty officer NOUN a noncommissioned officer in the Royal Navy comparable in rank to a warrant officer in the British Army or Royal Air Force.

fleeting (ˈfliːtɪŋ) ADJECTIVE rapid and transient: *a fleeting glimpse of the sea.*
▸ ˈ**fleetingly** ADVERB ▸ ˈ**fleetingness** NOUN

fleet rate *or* **fleet rating** NOUN a reduced rate quoted by an insurance company to underwrite the risks to a fleet of vehicles, aircraft, etc.

Fleet Street NOUN [1] a street in central London in which many newspaper offices were formerly situated. [2] British journalism or journalists collectively.

Fleetwood (ˈfliːtˌwʊd) NOUN a fishing port in NW England, in Lancashire. Pop.: 27 227 (1991).

fleishik *or* **fleishig** (ˈfleɪʃɪk, ˈflaɪ-) ADJECTIVE *Judaism* (of food) containing or derived from meat or meat products and therefore to be prepared and eaten separately from dairy foods. Also: **meaty.** Compare **milchik.** See also **kashruth.**

Flem. ABBREVIATION FOR Flemish.

Fleming (ˈflɛmɪŋ) NOUN a native or inhabitant of Flanders or a Flemish-speaking Belgian. Compare **Walloon.**
▹HISTORY C14: from Middle Dutch *Vlaminc*

Fleming's rules PLURAL NOUN *Physics* two rules used as mnemonics for the relationship between the directions of current flow, motion, and magnetic field in electromagnetic induction. The hand is held with the thumb, first, and second fingers at right angles, respectively indicating the directions of motion, field, and electric current. The left hand is used for electric motors and the right hand for dynamos.
▹HISTORY C19: named after Sir John Ambrose *Fleming* (1849–1945), English electrical engineer, who devised them

Flemish (ˈflɛmɪʃ) NOUN [1] one of the two official languages of Belgium, almost identical in form with Dutch. [2] **the.** (*functioning as plural*) the Flemings collectively. ♦ ADJECTIVE [3] of, relating to, or characteristic of Flanders, the Flemings, or their language.

Flemish bond NOUN a bond used in brickwork that has alternating stretchers and headers in each course, each header being placed centrally over a stretcher.

Flemish Brabant NOUN a province of central Belgium, formed in 1995 from the N part of Brabant province: densely populated and intensively farmed, with large industrial centres. Pop.: 1 041 704 (2000 est.). Area: 2106 sq. km (813 sq. miles).

Flensburg (*German* ˈflɛnsbʊrk) NOUN a port in N Germany, in Schleswig-Holstein: taken from Denmark by Prussia in 1864; voted to remain German in 1920. Pop.: 87 240 (1991).

flense (flɛns), **flench** (flɛntʃ), *or* **flinch** (flɪntʃ) VERB (*tr*) to strip (a whale, seal, etc.) of (its blubber or skin).
▹HISTORY C19: from Danish *flense*; related to Dutch *flensen*
▸ ˈ**flenser,** ˈ**flencher,** *or* ˈ**flincher** NOUN

flesh (flɛʃ) NOUN [1] the soft part of the body of an animal or human, esp muscular tissue, as distinct from bone and viscera. Related adjective: **sarcoid.** [2] *Informal* excess weight; fat. [3] *Archaic* the edible tissue of animals as opposed to that of fish or, sometimes, fowl; meat. [4] the thick usually soft part of a fruit or vegetable, as distinct from the skin, core, stone, etc. [5] the human body and its physical or sensual nature as opposed to the soul or spirit. Related adjective: **carnal.** [6] mankind in general. [7] animate creatures in general. [8] one's own family; kin (esp in the phrase **one's own flesh and blood**). [9] a yellowish-pink to greyish-yellow colour. [10] *Christian Science* belief on the physical plane which is considered erroneous, esp the belief that matter has sensation. [11] (*modifier*) *Tanning* of or relating to the inner or under layer of a skin or hide: *a flesh split.* [12] **in the flesh.** in person; actually present. [13] **make one's flesh creep.** (esp of something ghostly) to frighten and horrify one. [14] **press the flesh.** *Informal* to shake hands, usually with large numbers of people, esp in political campaigning. ♦ VERB [15] (*tr*) *Hunting* to stimulate the hunting instinct of (hounds or falcons) by giving them small quantities of raw flesh. [16] to wound the flesh of with a weapon. [17] *Archaic or poetic* to accustom or incite to bloodshed or battle by initial experience. [18] *Tanning* to remove the flesh layer of (a hide or skin). [19] to fatten; fill out.
▹HISTORY Old English *flǣsc*; related to Old Norse *flesk* ham, Old High German *fleisk* meat, flesh

flesher (ˈflɛʃə) NOUN [1] a person or machine that fleshes hides or skins. [2] *Scot* a person who sells meat; butcher.

flesh fly NOUN any dipterous fly of the genus *Sarcophaga*, esp *S. carnaria*, whose larvae feed on carrion or the tissues of living animals: family *Calliphoridae*.

fleshings (ˈflɛʃɪŋz) PLURAL NOUN [1] flesh-coloured tights. [2] bits of flesh scraped from the hides or skins of animals.

fleshly (ˈflɛʃlɪ) ADJECTIVE **-lier, -liest.** [1] relating to the body, esp its sensual nature; carnal: *fleshly desire.* [2] worldly as opposed to spiritual. [3] fleshy; fat.
▸ ˈ**fleshliness** NOUN

flesh out VERB (*adverb*) [1] (*tr*) to give substance to (an argument, description, etc.). [2] (*intr*) to expand or become more substantial.

fleshpots (ˈflɛʃˌpɒts) PLURAL NOUN *Often facetious* [1] luxurious or self-indulgent living. [2] places, such as striptease clubs, where bodily desires are gratified or titillated.
▹HISTORY C16: from the Biblical use as applied to Egypt (Exodus 16:3)

flesh wound (wuːnd) NOUN a wound affecting superficial tissues.

fleshy (ˈflɛʃɪ) ADJECTIVE **fleshier, fleshiest.** [1] fat; plump. [2] related to or resembling flesh. [3] *Botany* (of some fruits, leaves, etc.) thick and pulpy.
▸ ˈ**fleshiness** NOUN

fletch (flɛtʃ) VERB another word for **fledge** (sense 2).
▹HISTORY C17: probably back formation from FLETCHER

fletcher (ˈflɛtʃə) NOUN a person who makes arrows.
▹HISTORY C14: from Old French *flechier*, from *fleche* arrow; see FLÈCHE

Fletcherism (ˈflɛtʃəˌrɪzəm) NOUN the practice of chewing food thoroughly and drinking liquids in small sips to aid digestion.
▹HISTORY C20: named after Horace *Fletcher* (1849–1919), American nutritionist

fletchings (ˈflɛtʃɪŋz) PLURAL NOUN arrow feathers.
▹HISTORY plural of *fletching*, from FLETCH

fleur-de-lys *or* **fleur-de-lis** (ˌflɜːdəˈliː) NOUN, *plural* **fleurs-de-lys** *or* **fleurs-de-lis** (ˌflɜːdəˈliːz). [1] *Heraldry* a charge representing a lily with three distinct petals. [2] another name for **iris** (sense 2).
▹HISTORY C19: from Old French *flor de lis*, literally: lily flower

fleurette *or* **fleuret** (flʊəˈrɛt, flɜː-) NOUN an ornament resembling a flower.
▹HISTORY C19: French, literally: a small flower, from *fleur* flower

fleuron (ˈflʊərɒn, -rən, ˈflɜː-) NOUN [1] another name for **flower** (sense 8). [2] *Cookery* a decorative piece of pastry.
▹HISTORY C14: from French, from Old French *floron*, from *flor* FLOWER

flew[1] (fluː) VERB the past tense of **fly** (sense 1).

flew[2] (fluː) NOUN a variant spelling of **flue** (sense 3).

flews (fluːz) PLURAL NOUN the fleshy hanging upper lip of a bloodhound or similar dog.
▹HISTORY C16: of unknown origin

flex (flɛks) NOUN [1] *Brit* a flexible insulated electric cable, used esp to connect appliances to mains. US and Canadian name: **cord.** [2] *Informal* flexibility or pliability. ♦ VERB [3] to bend or be bent: *he flexed his arm; his arm flexed.* [4] to contract (a muscle) or (of a muscle) to contract. [5] (*intr*) to work according to flexitime. [6] to test or display (one's authority or strength).
▹HISTORY C16: from Latin *flexus* bent, winding, from *flectere* to bend, bow

flexecutive (flɛgˈzɛkjʊtɪv) NOUN an executive to whom the employer allows flexibility about times and locations of working.
▹HISTORY C20: from FLEX(IBLE)+ (EX)ECUTIVE

flexible (ˈflɛksɪbᵊl) ADJECTIVE [1] Also: **flexile** (ˈflɛksaɪl). able to be bent easily without breaking; pliable. [2] adaptable or variable: *flexible working hours.* [3] able to be persuaded easily; tractable.
▸ ˌ**flexiˈbility** *or* ˈ**flexibleness** NOUN ▸ ˈ**flexibly** ADVERB

flexion (ˈflɛkʃən) NOUN [1] the act of bending a joint or limb. [2] the condition of the joint or limb so bent. [3] a variant spelling of **flection.**
▸ ˈ**flexional** ADJECTIVE ▸ ˈ**flexionless** ADJECTIVE

flexitime (ˈflɛksɪˌtaɪm) *or* **flextime** (ˈflɛksˌtaɪm) NOUN a system permitting flexibility of working hours at the beginning or end of the day, provided an agreed period of each day (**core time**) is spent at work.

flexo (ˈflɛksəʊ) NOUN, ADJECTIVE, ADVERB short for **flexography, flexographic,** *or* **flexographically.**

flexography (flɛkˈsɒgrəfɪ) NOUN [1] a method of rotary letterpress printing using a resilient printing plate and solvent-based ink: used characteristically for printing on metal foil or plastic. [2] matter printed by this method. ♦ Abbreviation: **flexo.**
▸ **flexographic** (ˌflɛksəˈgræfɪk) ADJECTIVE
▸ ˌ**flexoˈgraphically** ADVERB

flexor (ˈflɛksə) NOUN any muscle whose contraction serves to bend a joint or limb. Compare **extensor.**
▹HISTORY C17: New Latin; see FLEX

flexuous (ˈflɛksjʊəs) *or* **flexuose** (ˈflɛksjʊˌəʊs) ADJECTIVE [1] full of bends or curves; winding. [2] variable; unsteady.
▹HISTORY C17: from Latin *flexuōsus* full of bends, tortuous, from *flexus* a bending; see FLEX
▸ ˈ**flexuously** ADVERB

flexure (ˈflɛkʃə) NOUN [1] the act of flexing or the state of being flexed. [2] a bend, turn, or fold.
▸ ˈ**flexural** ADJECTIVE

flex-wing NOUN *Aeronautics* a collapsible fabric delta wing, as used with hang-gliders.

fley *or* **flay** (fleɪ) VERB *Scot and Northern English dialect* [1] to be afraid or cause to be afraid. [2] (*tr*) to frighten away; scare.
▹HISTORY Old English *āflēgan* to put to flight; related to Old Norse *fleygja*

flibbert (ˈflɪbət) NOUN *Southwest English dialect* a small piece or bit.

flibbertigibbet (ˈflɪbətɪˌdʒɪbɪt) NOUN an irresponsible, silly, or gossipy person.
▹HISTORY C15: of uncertain origin

flick[1] (flɪk) VERB [1] (*tr*) to touch with or as if with the finger or hand in a quick jerky movement. [2] (*tr*) to propel or remove by a quick jerky movement, usually of the fingers or hand: *to flick a piece of paper at someone.* [3] to move or cause to move quickly or jerkily. [4] (*intr; foll by through*) to read or look at (a book, newspaper, etc.) quickly or idly. [5] to snap or click (the fingers) to produce a sharp sound. ♦ NOUN [6] a tap or quick stroke with the fingers, a whip, etc. [7] the sound made by such a stroke. [8] a fleck, streak, or particle.
▹HISTORY C15: of imitative origin; compare French *flicflac*

flick[2] (flɪk) NOUN *Slang* [1] a cinema film. [2] (*plural*) **the.** the cinema: *what's on at the flicks tonight?*

flicker[1] (ˈflɪkə) VERB [1] (*intr*) to shine with an unsteady or intermittent light: *a candle flickers.* [2] (*intr*) to move quickly to and fro; quiver, flutter, or vibrate. [3] (*tr*) to cause to flicker. ♦ NOUN [4] an unsteady or brief light or flame. [5] a swift quivering or fluttering movement. [6] a visual sensation, often seen in a television image, produced by periodic fluctuations in the brightness of light at a frequency below that covered by the persistence of vision. [7] (*plural*) **the.** a US word for **flick**[2] (sense 2).
▹HISTORY Old English *flicorian*; related to Dutch *flikkeren*, Old Norse *flökra* to flutter
▸ ˈ**flickeringly** ADVERB ▸ ˈ**flickery** ADJECTIVE

flicker[2] (ˈflɪkə) NOUN any North American woodpecker of the genus *Colaptes*, esp *C. auratus* (**yellow-shafted flicker**), which has a yellow undersurface to the wings and tail.
▹HISTORY C19: perhaps imitative of the bird's call

flick knife NOUN a knife with a retractable blade that springs out when a button is pressed. US and Canadian word: **switchblade.**

flier (ˈflaɪə) NOUN a variant spelling of **flyer.**

flight[1] (flaɪt) NOUN [1] the act, skill, or manner of flying. [2] a journey made by a flying animal or object. [3] **a** a scheduled airline journey. **b** an aircraft

flying on such a journey. 4 a group of flying birds or aircraft: *a flight of swallows*. 5 the basic tactical unit of a military air force. 6 a journey through space, esp of a spacecraft. 7 rapid movement or progress. 8 a soaring mental journey above or beyond the normal everyday world: *a flight of fancy*. 9 **a** a single line of hurdles across a track in a race. **b** a series of such hurdles. 10 a bird's wing or tail feather; flight feather. 11 a feather or plastic attachment fitted to an arrow or dart to give it stability in flight. 12 See **flight arrow.** 13 the distance covered by a flight arrow. 14 *Sport, esp cricket* **a** a flighted movement imparted to a ball, dart, etc. **b** the ability to flight a ball. 15 *Angling* a device on a spinning lure that revolves rapidly. 16 a set of steps or stairs between one landing or floor and the next. 17 a large enclosed area attached to an aviary or pigeon loft where the birds may fly but not escape. ◆ VERB 18 (*tr*) *Sport* to cause (a ball, dart, etc.) to float slowly or deceptively towards its target. 19 (*intr*) (of wild fowl) to fly in groups. 20 (*tr*) to shoot (a bird) in flight. 21 (*tr*) to fledge (an arrow or a dart).
▷HISTORY Old English *flyht*; related to Middle Dutch *vlucht*, Old Saxon *fluht*

flight² (flaɪt) NOUN 1 the act of fleeing or running away, as from danger. 2 **put to flight.** to cause to run away; rout. 3 **take (to) flight.** to run away or withdraw hastily; flee.
▷HISTORY Old English *flyht* (unattested); related to Old Frisian *flecht*, Old High German *fluht*, Old Norse *flōtti*

flight arrow NOUN a long thin arrow used for shooting long distances. Often shortened to: **flight.**

flight attendant NOUN a person who attends to the needs of passengers on a commercial flight.

flight capital NOUN funds transferred abroad in order to avoid high taxes or to provide for a person's needs if flight from the country becomes necessary.

flight deck NOUN 1 the crew compartment in an airliner. Compare **cockpit** (sense 1). 2 the upper deck of an aircraft carrier from which aircraft take off and on which they land.

flight engineer NOUN the member of an aircraft crew who is responsible for the operation of the aircraft's systems, including the engines, during flight.

flight feather NOUN any of the large stiff feathers that cover the wings and tail of a bird and are adapted for flying.

flight formation NOUN two or more aircraft flying together in a set pattern.

flightless ('flaɪtlɪs) ADJECTIVE (of certain birds and insects) unable to fly. See also **ratite.**

flight level NOUN *Aeronautics* a specified height at which an aircraft is allowed to fly.

flight lieutenant NOUN an officer holding a commissioned rank senior to a flying officer and junior to a squadron leader in the RAF and certain other air forces.

flight line NOUN an area of an airfield or airport on which aircraft, esp military aircraft, are parked and serviced.

flight management systems PLURAL NOUN a suite of computer programs in a computer on board an aircraft used to calculate the most economical flying speeds and altitudes during a flight and to identify possible choices in emergencies.

flight path NOUN the course through the air of an aircraft, rocket, or projectile. Compare **approach** (sense 10), **glide path.**

flight plan NOUN a written statement of the details of a proposed aircraft flight.

flight recorder NOUN an electronic device fitted to an aircraft for storing information concerning its performance in flight. It is often used to determine the cause of a crash. Also called: **black box.**

flight sergeant NOUN a noncommissioned officer in the Royal Air Force junior in rank to a master aircrew.

flight simulator NOUN a ground-training device that reproduces exactly the conditions experienced on the flight deck of an aircraft. Compare **Link trainer.**

flight strip NOUN 1 a strip of cleared land used as an emergency runway for aircraft. 2 another name for **runway** (sense 1). 3 a strip of continuous aerial photographs.

flight surgeon NOUN a medical officer specializing in aviation medicine in the US and certain other air forces.

flighty ('flaɪtɪ) ADJECTIVE **flightier, flightiest.** 1 frivolous and irresponsible; capricious; volatile. 2 mentally erratic, unstable, or wandering. 3 flirtatious; coquettish.
▸ **'flightily** ADVERB ▸ **'flightiness** NOUN

flim (flɪm) NOUN *Northern English dialect* a five-pound note.

flimflam ('flɪm,flæm) *Informal* ◆ NOUN 1 **a** nonsense; foolishness. **b** (*as modifier*): *flimflam arguments*. 2 a deception; swindle. ◆ VERB **-flams, -flamming, -flammed.** 3 (*tr*) to deceive; trick; swindle; cheat.
▷HISTORY C16: probably of Scandinavian origin; compare Old Norse *flīm* mockery, Norwegian *flire* to giggle
▸ **'flim,flammer** NOUN

flimsy ('flɪmzɪ) ADJECTIVE **-sier, -siest.** 1 not strong or substantial; fragile: *a flimsy building*. 2 light and thin: *a flimsy dress*. 3 unconvincing or inadequate; weak: *a flimsy excuse*. ◆ NOUN 4 thin paper used for making carbon copies of a letter, etc. 5 a copy made on such paper. 6 a slang word for **banknote.**
▷HISTORY C17: of uncertain origin
▸ **'flimsily** ADVERB ▸ **'flimsiness** NOUN

flinch¹ (flɪntʃ) VERB (*intr*) 1 to draw back suddenly, as from pain, shock, etc.; wince: *he flinched as the cold water struck him*. 2 (often foll by *from*) to avoid contact (with); shy away: *he never flinched from his duty*. ◆ NOUN 3 the act or an instance of drawing back. 4 a card game in which players build sequences.
▷HISTORY C16: from Old French *flenchir*; related to Middle High German *lenken* to bend, direct
▸ **'flincher** NOUN ▸ **'flinchingly** ADVERB

flinch² (flɪntʃ) VERB a variant of **flense.**

flinders ('flɪndəz) PLURAL NOUN *Rare* small fragments or splinters (esp in the phrase **fly into flinders**).
▷HISTORY C15: probably of Scandinavian origin; compare Norwegian *flindra* thin piece of stone

Flinders bar ('flɪndəz) NOUN *Navigation* a bar of soft iron mounted on a binnacle to compensate for local magnetism causing error to the compass.
▷HISTORY C19: named after Matthew *Flinders* (died 1814), English navigator

Flinders Island NOUN an island off the coast of NE Tasmania: the largest of the Furneaux Islands. Pop.: 1100 (latest est.). Area: 2077 sq. km (802 sq. miles).

Flinders Range NOUN a mountain range in E South Australia, between Lake Torrens and Lake Frome. Highest peak: 1188 m (3898 ft.).

fling (flɪŋ) VERB **flings, flinging, flung** (flʌŋ). (*mainly tr*) 1 to throw, esp with force or abandon; hurl or toss. 2 to put or send without warning or preparation: *to fling someone into jail*. 3 (*also intr*) to move (oneself or a part of the body) with abandon or speed: *he flung himself into a chair*. 4 (usually foll by *into*) to apply (oneself) diligently and with vigour (to). 5 to cast aside; disregard: *she flung away her scruples*. 6 to utter violently or offensively. 7 *Poetic* to give out; emit. ◆ NOUN 8 the act or an instance of flinging; toss; throw. 9 a period or occasion of unrestrained, impulsive, or extravagant behaviour: *to have a fling*. 10 any of various vigorous Scottish reels full of leaps and turns, such as the Highland fling. 11 a trial; try: *to have a fling at something different*.
▷HISTORY C13: of Scandinavian origin; related to Old Norse *flengja* to flog, Swedish *flänga*, Danish *flænge*
▸ **'flinger** NOUN

flint (flɪnt) NOUN 1 an impure opaque microcrystalline greyish-black form of quartz that occurs in chalk. It produces sparks when struck with steel and is used in the manufacture of pottery, flint glass, and road-construction materials. Formula: SiO_2. 2 any piece of flint, esp one used as a primitive tool or for striking fire. 3 a small cylindrical piece of an iron alloy, used in cigarette lighters. 4 Also called: **flint glass, white flint.** colourless glass other than plate glass. 5 See **optical flint.** ◆ VERB 6 (*tr*) to fit or provide with a flint.
▷HISTORY Old English; related to Old High German *flins*, Old Swedish *flinta* splinter of stone, Latin *splendēre* to shine

Flint (flɪnt) NOUN 1 a town in NE Wales, in Flintshire, on the Dee estuary. Pop.: 11 737 (1991). 2 a city in SE Michigan: closure of the car production plants led to a high level of unemployment. Pop.: 124 943 (2000).

flint glass NOUN another name for **optical flint, flint** (sense 4).

flintlock ('flɪnt,lɒk) NOUN 1 an obsolete gunlock in which the charge is ignited by a spark produced by a flint in the hammer. 2 a firearm having such a lock.

Flintshire ('flɪnt,ʃɪə, -ʃə) NOUN a county of NE Wales, on the Irish Sea and the Dee estuary: became part of Clwyd in 1974, reinstated with reduced borders in 1996: includes the industrialized Deeside region in the E and the Clwydian Hills in the SW. Administrative centre: Mold. Pop.: 148 565 (2001). Area: 437 sq. km (169 sq. miles).

flinty ('flɪntɪ) ADJECTIVE **flintier, flintiest.** 1 of, relating to, or resembling flint. 2 hard or cruel; obdurate; unyielding.
▸ **'flintily** ADVERB ▸ **'flintiness** NOUN

flip (flɪp) VERB **flips, flipping, flipped.** 1 to throw (something light or small) carelessly or briskly; toss: *he flipped me an envelope*. 2 to throw or flick (an object such as a coin) so that it turns or spins in the air. 3 to propel by a sudden movement of the finger; flick: *to flip a crumb across the room*. 4 (foll by *through*) to read or look at (a book, newspaper, etc.) quickly, idly, or incompletely. 5 (*intr*) (of small objects) to move or bounce jerkily. 6 (*intr*) to make a snapping movement or noise with the finger and thumb. 7 (*intr*) *Slang* to fly into a rage or an emotional outburst (also in the phrases **flip one's lid, flip one's top**). 8 (*intr*) *Slang* to become ecstatic or very excited: *he flipped over the jazz group*. ◆ NOUN 9 a snap or tap, usually with the fingers. 10 a rapid jerk. 11 a somersault, esp one performed in the air, as in a dive, rather than from a standing position. 12 same as **nog¹** (sense 1). ◆ ADJECTIVE 13 *Informal* impertinent, flippant, or pert.
▷HISTORY C16: probably of imitative origin; see FILLIP

flip chart NOUN a pad, containing large sheets of paper that can be easily turned over, mounted on a stand and used to present reports, data, etc.

flip-flop NOUN 1 a backward handspring. 2 Also called: **bistable.** an electronic device or circuit that can assume either of two stable states by the application of a suitable pulse. 3 *Informal, chiefly US* a complete change of opinion, policy, etc. 4 a repeated flapping or banging noise. 5 Also called (US, Canadian, Austral, and NZ): **thong.** a rubber-soled sandal attached to the foot by a thong between the big toe and the next toe. ◆ VERB **-flops, -flopping, -flopped.** (*intr*) 6 *Informal, chiefly US* to make a complete change of opinion, policy, etc. 7 to move with repeated flaps. ◆ ADVERB 8 with repeated flappings: *to go flip-flop*.
▷HISTORY C16: reduplication of FLIP

flippant ('flɪpənt) ADJECTIVE 1 marked by inappropriate levity; frivolous or offhand. 2 impertinent; saucy. 3 *Obsolete* talkative or nimble.
▷HISTORY C17: perhaps from FLIP
▸ **'flippancy** NOUN ▸ **'flippantly** ADVERB

flipper ('flɪpə) NOUN 1 the flat broad limb of seals, whales, penguins, and other aquatic animals, specialized for swimming. 2 (*often plural*) Also called: **fin.** either of a pair of rubber paddle-like devices worn on the feet as an aid in swimming, esp underwater. 3 *Cricket* a ball bowled with topspin imparted by the action of the bowler's wrist.

flipping ('flɪpɪŋ) ADJECTIVE, ADVERB *Brit slang* (intensifier): *a flipping idiot; it's flipping cold*.
▷HISTORY C19: perhaps a euphemism for FUCKING

flippy ('flɪpɪ) ADJECTIVE **-pier, -piest** *Informal* (of clothes) tending to move to and fro as the wearer walks: *little flippy skirts*.

flip side NOUN 1 another term for **B-side.** 2 another, less familiar aspect of a person or thing: *the flip side of John Lennon*.

flip-up ADJECTIVE (*prenominal*) able to be opened by being flipped upwards.

flirt (flɜːt) VERB 1 (*intr*) to behave or act amorously

without emotional commitment; toy or play with another's affections; dally. 2 (*intr;* usually foll by *with*) to deal playfully or carelessly (with something dangerous or serious); trifle: *the motorcyclist flirted with death.* 3 (*intr;* usually foll by *with*) to think casually (about); toy (with): *to flirt with the idea of leaving.* 4 (*intr*) to move jerkily; dart; flit. 5 (*tr*) to subject to a sudden swift motion; flick or toss. ◆ NOUN 6 a person who acts flirtatiously.
▷HISTORY C16: of uncertain origin
▸ 'flirter NOUN ▸ 'flirty ADJECTIVE ▸ 'flirtingly ADVERB

flirtation (flɜːˈteɪʃən) NOUN 1 behaviour intended to arouse sexual feelings or advances without emotional commitment; coquetry. 2 any casual involvement without commitment: *a flirtation with journalism.*

flirtatious (flɜːˈteɪʃəs) ADJECTIVE 1 given to flirtation. 2 expressive of playful sexual invitation: *a flirtatious glance.*
▸ flir'tatiously ADVERB ▸ flir'tatiousness NOUN

flit (flɪt) VERB **flits, flitting, flitted.** (*intr*) 1 to move along rapidly and lightly; skim or dart. 2 to fly rapidly and lightly; flutter. 3 to pass quickly; fleet: *a memory flitted into his mind.* 4 *Scot and Northern English dialect* to move house. 5 *Brit informal* to depart hurriedly and stealthily in order to avoid obligations. 6 an informal word for **elope.** ◆ NOUN 7 the act or an instance of flitting. 8 *Slang, chiefly US* a male homosexual. 9 *Brit informal* a hurried and stealthy departure in order to avoid obligations (esp in the phrase **do a flit**). 10 See **moonlight flit.**
▷HISTORY C12: from Old Norse *flytja* to carry
▸ 'flitter NOUN

flitch (flɪtʃ) NOUN 1 a side of pork salted and cured. 2 a steak cut from the side of certain fishes, esp halibut. 3 a piece of timber cut lengthways from a tree trunk, esp one that is larger than 4 by 12 inches. ◆ VERB 4 (*tr*) to cut (a tree trunk) into flitches.
▷HISTORY Old English *flicce;* related to Old Norse *flikki,* Middle Low German *vlicke,* Norwegian *flika;* see FLESH

flite *or* **flyte** (flaɪt; *Scot* flət) *Scot and Northern English dialect* ◆ VERB 1 (*tr*) to scold or rail at. ◆ NOUN 2 a dispute or scolding.
▷HISTORY Old English *flītan* to wrangle, of Germanic origin; related to Old Frisian *flīt* strife, Old High German *flīz* strife

flitter (ˈflɪtə) VERB a less common word for **flutter.**

flittermouse (ˈflɪtəˌmaʊs) NOUN, *plural* **-mice.** a dialect name for **bat²** (the animal).
▷HISTORY C16: translation of German *Fledermaus;* see FLITTER, MOUSE

flivver (ˈflɪvə) NOUN an old, cheap, or battered car.
▷HISTORY C20: of unknown origin

float (fləʊt) VERB 1 to rest or cause to rest on the surface of a fluid or in a fluid or space without sinking; be buoyant or cause to exhibit buoyancy: *oil floats on water; to float a ship.* 2 to move or cause to move buoyantly, lightly, or freely across a surface or through air, water, etc.; drift: *fog floated across the road.* 3 to move about aimlessly, esp in the mind: *thoughts floated before him.* 4 to suspend or be suspended without falling; hang: *lights floated above them.* 5 (*tr*) **a** to launch or establish (a commercial enterprise, etc.). **b** to offer for sale (stock or bond issues, etc.) on the stock market. 6 (*tr*) *Finance* to allow (a currency) to fluctuate against other currencies in accordance with market forces. 7 (*tr*) to flood, inundate, or irrigate (land), either artificially or naturally. 8 (*tr*) to spread, smooth, or level (a surface of plaster, rendering, etc.). ◆ NOUN 9 something that floats. 10 *Angling* an indicator attached to a baited line that sits on the water and moves when a fish bites. 11 a small hand tool with a rectangular blade used for floating plaster, etc. 12 *Chiefly US* any buoyant object, such as a platform or inflated tube, used offshore by swimmers or, when moored alongside a pier, as a dock by vessels. 13 Also called: **paddle.** a blade of a paddle wheel. 14 *Brit* a buoyant garment or device to aid a person in staying afloat. 15 a hollow watertight structure fitted to the underside of an aircraft to allow it to land on water. 16 another name for **air bladder** (sense 2). 17 an exhibit carried in a parade, esp a religious parade. 18 a motor vehicle used to carry a tableau or exhibit in a parade, esp a civic parade. 19 a small delivery vehicle, esp one powered by batteries: *a milk float.* 20 *Austral and NZ* a vehicle for transporting horses. 21 *Banking, chiefly US* the total value of uncollected cheques and other commercial papers. 22 *Chiefly US and Canadian* a sum to be applied to minor expenses; petty cash. 23 a sum of money used by shopkeepers to provide change at the start of the day's business, this sum being subtracted from the total at the end of the day when calculating the day's takings. 24 the hollow floating ball of a ballcock. 25 *Engineering* a hollow cylindrical structure in a carburettor that actuates the fuel valve. 26 *Chiefly US and Canadian* a carbonated soft drink with a scoop of ice cream in it. 27 (in textiles) a single thread brought to or above the surface of a woven fabric, esp to form a pattern. 28 *Forestry* a measure of timber equal to eighteen loads. ◆ See also **float off, floats.**
▷HISTORY Old English *flotian;* related to Old Norse *flota* , Old Saxon *flotōn;* see FLEET²
▸ 'floatable ADJECTIVE ▸ ˌfloata'bility NOUN

floatage (ˈfləʊtɪdʒ) NOUN a variant spelling of **flotage.**

floatation (fləʊˈteɪʃən) NOUN a variant spelling of **flotation.**

float chamber NOUN a chamber in a carburettor in which a floating valve controls the entry and level of petrol.

floatcut file (ˈfləʊtˌkʌt) NOUN *Engineering* a file having rows of parallel teeth.

floatel (fləʊˈtɛl) NOUN a variant spelling of **flotel.**

floater (ˈfləʊtə) NOUN 1 a person or thing that floats. 2 any of a number of dark spots that appear in one's vision as a result of dead cells or fragments in the lens or vitreous humour of the eye. 3 *US and Canadian* **a** a person of no fixed political opinion. **b** a person who votes illegally in more than one district at one election. **c** a voter who can be bribed. 4 Also called: **floating policy.** *US and Canadian insurance* a policy covering loss or theft of or damage to movable property, such as jewels or furs, regardless of its location. 5 *US informal* a person who often changes employment, residence, etc.; drifter. 6 *Austral* a loose gold- or opal-bearing rock. 7 *Austral* (esp in Adelaide) a meat pie in a plate of pea soup.

float-feed ADJECTIVE (of a fuel system) controlled by a float operating a needle valve.

float glass NOUN a type of flat polished transparent glass made by allowing the molten glass to harden as it floats on liquid of higher density.

floating (ˈfləʊtɪŋ) ADJECTIVE 1 having little or no attachment. 2 (of an organ or part) displaced from the normal position or abnormally movable: *a floating kidney.* 3 not definitely attached to one place or policy; uncommitted or unfixed: *the floating vote.* 4 *Finance* **a** (of capital) not allocated or invested; available for current use. **b** (of debt) short-term and unfunded, usually raised by a government or company to meet current expenses. **c** (of a currency) free to fluctuate against other currencies in accordance with market forces. 5 *Machinery* operating smoothly through being free from external constraints. 6 (of an electronic circuit or device) not connected to a source of voltage.
▸ 'floatingly ADVERB

floating assets PLURAL NOUN another term for **current assets.**

floating charge NOUN *Chiefly Brit* an unsecured charge on the assets of an enterprise that allows such assets to be used commercially until the enterprise ceases to operate or the creditor intervenes to demand collateral.

floating debt NOUN short-term government borrowing, esp by the issue of three-month Treasury bills.

floating dock NOUN a large boxlike structure that can be submerged to allow a vessel to enter it and then floated to raise the vessel out of the water for maintenance or repair. Also called: **floating dry dock.**

floating heart NOUN any perennial aquatic freshwater plant of the genus *Nymphoides,* esp *N. lacunosum,* having floating heart-shaped leaves: family *Menyanthaceae.*

floating island NOUN a floating mass of soil held together by vegetation.

floating-point representation NOUN *Computing* the representation of numbers by two sets of digits (*a, b*), the set *a* indicating the significant digits, the set *b* giving the position of the radix point. The number is the product ar^b, where *r* is the base of the number system used. Compare **fixed-point representation.**

floating policy NOUN 1 (in marine insurance) a policy covering loss of or damage to specified goods irrespective of the ship in which they are consigned. 2 another term for **floater** (sense 4).

floating-rate note NOUN a eurobond, often issued as a negotiable bearer bond, that has a floating rate of interest.

floating rib NOUN any rib of the lower two pairs of ribs in man, which are not attached to the breastbone.

floating voter NOUN a person who does not vote consistently for any single political party.

float off VERB (*tr, adverb*) to offer (shares in a subsidiary company) for sale on the stock market separately from the main company.

floats (fləʊts) PLURAL NOUN *Theatre* another word for **footlights.**

floaty (ˈfləʊtɪ) ADJECTIVE **floatier, floatiest.** 1 filmy and light: *floaty material.* 2 capable of floating; buoyant. 3 (of a vessel) riding high in the water; of shallow draught.

floc (flɒk) NOUN another word for **floccule.**
▷HISTORY C20: from Latin *floccus* a tuft of wool, FLOCK²

floccose (ˈflɒkəʊs) ADJECTIVE consisting of or covered with woolly tufts or hairs: *floccose growths of bacteria.*
▷HISTORY C18: from Latin *floccōsus* full of flocks of wool

flocculant (ˈflɒkjʊlənt) NOUN a substance added to a suspension to enhance aggregation of the suspended particles.

flocculate (ˈflɒkjʊˌleɪt) VERB to form or be formed into an aggregated flocculent mass.
▸ ˌfloccu'lation NOUN

floccule (ˈflɒkjuːl), **flocculus, flock,** *or* **floc** NOUN 1 a small aggregate of flocculent material. 2 something resembling a tuft of wool.
▷HISTORY C19: from Late Latin *flocculus* a little tuft; see FLOCK²

flocculent (ˈflɒkjʊlənt) ADJECTIVE 1 like wool; fleecy. 2 *Chem* aggregated in woolly cloudlike masses: *a flocculent precipitate.* 3 *Biology* covered with tufts or flakes of a waxy or wool-like substance.
▸ 'flocculence *or* 'flocculency NOUN ▸ 'flocculently ADVERB

flocculus (ˈflɒkjʊləs) NOUN, *plural* **-li** (-ˌlaɪ). 1 a marking on the sun's surface or in its atmosphere, as seen on a spectroheliogram. It consists of calcium when lighter than the surroundings and of hydrogen when darker. 2 *Anatomy* a tiny ovoid prominence on each side of the cerebellum. 3 another word for **floccule.**

floccus (ˈflɒkəs) NOUN, *plural* **flocci** (ˈflɒksaɪ). 1 a downy or woolly covering, as on the young of certain birds. 2 a small woolly tuft of hair. ◆ ADJECTIVE 3 (of a cloud) having the appearance of woolly tufts at odd intervals in its structure.
▷HISTORY C19: from Latin: tuft of hair or wool, FLOCK²

flock¹ (flɒk) NOUN (*sometimes functioning as plural*) 1 a group of animals of one kind, esp sheep or birds. 2 a large number of people; crowd. 3 a body of Christians regarded as the pastoral charge of a priest, a bishop, the pope, etc. 4 *Rare* a band of people; group. ◆ VERB (*intr*) 5 to gather together or move in a flock. 6 to go in large numbers: *people flocked to the church.*
▷HISTORY Old English *flocc;* related to Old Norse *flokkr* crowd, Middle Low German *vlocke*

flock² (flɒk) NOUN 1 a tuft, as of wool, hair, cotton, etc. 2 **a** waste from fabrics such as cotton, wool, or other cloth used for stuffing mattresses, upholstered chairs, etc. **b** (*as modifier*): *flock mattress.* 3 very small tufts of wool applied to fabrics, wallpaper, etc., to give a raised pattern. 4 another word for **floccule.** ◆ VERB 5 (*tr*) to fill, cover, or ornament with flock.
▷HISTORY C13: from Old French *floc,* from Latin

floccus; probably related to Old High German *floccho* down, Norwegian *flugsa* snowflake
▸ **'flocky** ADJECTIVE

flock paper NOUN a type of wallpaper with a raised pattern. See also **flock**[1] (sense 3).

Flodden ('flɒdᵊn) NOUN a hill in Northumberland where invading Scots were defeated by the English in 1513 and James IV of Scotland was killed. Also called: **Flodden Field.**

floe (fləʊ) NOUN See **ice floe.**
▷HISTORY C19: probably from Norwegian *flo* slab, layer, from Old Norse; see FLAW[1]

flog (flɒg) VERB **flogs, flogging, flogged.** 1 (*tr*) to beat harshly, esp with a whip, strap, etc. 2 (*tr*) *Brit slang* to sell. 3 (*intr*) (of a sail) to flap noisily in the wind. 4 (*intr*) to make progress by painful work. 5 *NZ* to steal. 6 **flog a dead horse.** *Chiefly Brit* **a** to harp on some long discarded subject. **b** to pursue the solution of a problem long realized to be insoluble. 7 **flog to death.** to persuade a person so persistently of the value of (an idea or venture) that he loses interest in it.
▷HISTORY C17: probably from Latin *flagellāre*; see FLAGELLANT
▸ **'flogger** NOUN ▸ **'flogging** NOUN

flokati (flə'kɑːtɪ) NOUN a Greek hand-woven shaggy woollen rug.
▷HISTORY C20: from Modern Greek *phlokatē* a peasant's blanket

flong (flɒŋ) NOUN 1 *Printing* a material, usually pulped paper or cardboard, used for making moulds in stereotyping. 2 *Journalism, slang* material that is not urgently topical.
▷HISTORY C20: variant of FLAN

flood (flʌd) NOUN 1 **a** the inundation of land that is normally dry through the overflowing of a body of water, esp a river. **b** the state of a river that is at an abnormally high level (esp in the phrase **in flood**). Related adjective: **diluvial.** 2 a great outpouring or flow: *a flood of words.* 3 **a** the rising of the tide from low to high water. **b** (*as modifier*): *the flood tide.* Compare **ebb** (sense 3). 4 *Theatre* short for **floodlight.** 5 *Archaic* a large body of water, as the sea or a river. ◆ VERB 6 (of water) to inundate or submerge (land) or (of land) to be inundated or submerged. 7 to fill or be filled to overflowing, as with a flood: *the children's home was flooded with gifts.* 8 (*intr*) to flow; surge: *relief flooded through him.* 9 to supply an excessive quantity of petrol to (a carburettor or petrol engine) or (of a carburettor, etc.) to be supplied with such an excess. 10 (*intr*) to rise to a flood; overflow. 11 (*intr*) **a** to bleed profusely from the uterus, as following childbirth. **b** to have an abnormally heavy flow of blood during a menstrual period.
▷HISTORY Old English *flōd*; related to Old Norse *flōth*, Gothic *flōdus*, Old High German *fluot* flood, Greek *plōtos* navigable; see FLOW, FLOAT
▸ **'floodable** ADJECTIVE ▸ **'flooder** NOUN ▸ **'floodless** ADJECTIVE

Flood (flʌd) NOUN *Old Testament* **the.** the flood extending over all the earth from which Noah and his family and livestock were saved in the ark. (Genesis 7–8); the Deluge.

flood basalt NOUN a very extensive lava flow of basaltic composition that has issued from a fissure, often to be found as part of a series of such flows one on top of another, forming a plateau. See **fissure eruption.**

flood control NOUN the technique or practice of preventing or controlling floods with dams, artificial channels, etc.

flooded gum NOUN any of various eucalyptus trees of Australia, esp *Eucalyptus saligna* (the Sydney blue gum), that grow in damp soil.

floodgate ('flʌd,geɪt) NOUN 1 Also called: **head gate, water gate.** a gate in a sluice that is used to control the flow of water. See also **sluicegate.** 2 (*often plural*) a control or barrier against an outpouring or flow: *to open the floodgates to immigration.*

flooding ('flʌdɪŋ) NOUN 1 the submerging of land under water, esp due to heavy rain, a lake or river overflowing, etc. 2 *Psychol* a method of eliminating anxiety in a given situation, by exposing a person to the situation until the anxiety subsides.

floodlight ('flʌd,laɪt) NOUN 1 a broad intense beam of artificial light, esp as used in the theatre or to illuminate the exterior of buildings. 2 the lamp or source producing such light. ◆ VERB **-lights, -lighting, -lit.** 3 (*tr*) to illuminate by or as if by a floodlight.

flood plain NOUN the flat area bordering a river, composed of sediment deposited during flooding.

floor (flɔː) NOUN 1 Also called: **flooring.** the inner lower surface of a room. 2 a storey of a building: *the second floor.* 3 a flat bottom surface in or on any structure: *the floor of a lift; a dance floor.* 4 the bottom surface of a tunnel, cave, river, sea, etc. 5 *Mining* an underlying stratum. 6 *Nautical* the bottom, or the lowermost framing members at the bottom, of a vessel. 7 that part of a legislative hall in which debate and other business is conducted. 8 the right to speak in a legislative or deliberative body (esp in the phrases **get, have,** or **be given the floor**). 9 the room in a stock exchange where trading takes place. 10 the earth; ground. 11 a minimum price charged or paid: *a wage floor.* 12 **take the floor.** to begin dancing on a dance floor. ◆ VERB 13 to cover with or construct a floor. 14 (*tr*) to knock to the floor or ground. 15 (*tr*) *Informal* to disconcert, confound, or defeat: *to be floored by a problem.*
▷HISTORY Old English *flōr*; related to Old Norse *flōrr*, Middle Low German *vlōr* floor, Latin *plānus* level, Greek *planan* to cause to wander

floorage ('flɔːrɪdʒ) NOUN an area of floor; floor space.

floorboard ('flɔː,bɔːd) NOUN one of the boards forming a floor.

floor-filler NOUN *Informal* a dance recording that is so catchy and popular that everyone in the place where it is played wants to dance.

flooring ('flɔːrɪŋ) NOUN 1 the material used in making a floor, esp the surface material. 2 another word for **floor** (sense 1).

flooring saw NOUN a type of saw curved at the end for cutting through floorboards.

floor leader NOUN *US government* a member of a legislative body who organizes his party's activities.

floor manager NOUN 1 the stage manager employed in the production of a television programme. 2 a person in overall charge of one floor of a large shop or department store.

floor plan NOUN a drawing to scale of the arrangement of rooms on one floor of a building. Compare **elevation** (sense 5).

floor show NOUN a series of entertainments, such as singing, dancing, and comedy acts, performed in a nightclub.

floor trading NOUN trading by personal contact on the floor of a market or exchange. Compare **screen trading.**

floorwalker ('flɔː,wɔːkə) NOUN the US name for **shopwalker.**

floozy, floozie, *or* **floosie** ('fluːzɪ) NOUN, *plural* **-zies** *or* **-sies.** *Slang* a disreputable woman.
▷HISTORY C20: of unknown origin

flop (flɒp) VERB **flops, flopping, flopped.** 1 (*intr*) to bend, fall, or collapse loosely or carelessly: *his head flopped backwards.* 2 (when *intr,* often foll by *into, onto,* etc) to fall, cause to fall, or move with a sudden noise: *the books flopped onto the floor.* 3 (*intr*) *Informal* to fail; be unsuccessful: *the scheme flopped.* 4 (*intr*) to fall flat onto the surface of water, hitting it with the front of the body. 5 (*intr; often followed by out*) *Slang* to go to sleep. ◆ NOUN 6 the act of flopping. 7 *Informal* a complete failure. 8 *US and Canadian slang* a place to sleep. 9 *Athletics* See **Fosbury flop.**
▷HISTORY C17: variant of FLAP

flophouse ('flɒp,haʊs) NOUN *Slang* the US and Canadian word for **dosshouse.**

floppy ('flɒpɪ) ADJECTIVE **-pier, -piest.** 1 limp or hanging loosely: *a dog with floppy ears.* ◆ NOUN, *plural* **-pies.** 2 short for **floppy disk.**
▸ **'floppily** ADVERB ▸ **'floppiness** NOUN

floppy disk NOUN a flexible removable magnetic disk that stores information and can be used to store data for use in a microprocessor. Also called: **diskette, flexible disk.**

flops *or* **FLOPS** NOUN ACRONYM FOR floating-point operations per second: used as a measure of computer processing power (in combination with a prefix): *megaflops; gigaflops.*

flop sweat NOUN *Informal* a sudden heavy perspiration caused by embarrassment.

flor. ABBREVIATION FOR *floruit.*

flora ('flɔːrə) NOUN, *plural* **-ras** *or* **-rae** (-riː). 1 all the plant life of a given place or time. 2 a descriptive list of such plants, often including a key for identification. 3 short for **intestinal flora.**
▷HISTORY C18: from New Latin, from Latin *Flōra* goddess of flowers, from *flōs* FLOWER

Flora ('flɔːrə) NOUN the Roman goddess of flowers.
▷HISTORY C16: from Latin, from *flōs* flower

floral ('flɔːrəl) ADJECTIVE 1 decorated with or consisting of flowers or patterns of flowers. 2 of, relating to, or associated with flowers: *floral leaves.*
▸ **'florally** ADVERB

floral envelope NOUN the part of a flower that surrounds the stamens and pistil: the calyx and corolla (considered together) or the perianth.

Floréal *French* (flɔreal) NOUN the month of flowers: the eighth month of the French revolutionary calendar, extending from April 21 to May 20.
▷HISTORY C19: ultimately from Latin *flōreus* of flowers, from *flōs* a flower

floreat *Latin* ('flɒrɪæt) VERB (*intr*), *plural* **floreant** may (a person, institution, etc.) flourish: *floreat Oxonia!*

floreated ('flɔːrɪ,eɪtɪd) ADJECTIVE a variant spelling of **floriated.**

Florence ('flɒrəns) NOUN a city in central Italy, on the River Arno in Tuscany: became an independent republic in the 14th century; under Austrian and other rule intermittently from 1737 to 1859; capital of Italy 1865–70. It was the major cultural and artistic centre of the Renaissance and is still one of the world's chief art centres. Pop.: 376 682 (2000 est.). Ancient name: **Florentia** (flɒ'rɛntsɪə, -'rɛntɪə). Italian name: **Firenze.**

Florence fennel NOUN another name for **finocchio.**

Florence flask NOUN a round flat-bottomed glass flask with a long neck, used in chemical experiments.

Florentine ('flɒrən,taɪn) ADJECTIVE 1 of or relating to Florence. 2 (*usually postpositive*) (of food) served or prepared with spinach. ◆ NOUN 3 a native or inhabitant of Florence. 4 a biscuit containing nuts and dried fruit and coated with chocolate. 5 a type of domestic fancy pigeon somewhat resembling the Modena.

Flores ('flɔːrɛs) NOUN 1 an island in Indonesia, one of the Lesser Sunda Islands, between the Flores Sea and the Savu Sea: mountainous, with active volcanoes and unexplored forests. Chief town: Ende. Area: 17 150 sq. km (6622 sq. miles). 2 (*also Portuguese* 'florɪʃ) an island in the Atlantic, the westernmost of the Azores. Chief town: Santa Cruz. Area: 142 sq. km (55 sq. miles).

florescence (flɔː'rɛsəns) NOUN the process, state, or period of flowering.
▷HISTORY C18: from New Latin *flōrēscentia*, from Latin *flōrēscere* to come into flower

Flores Sea NOUN a part of the Pacific Ocean in Indonesia between Celebes and the Lesser Sunda Islands.

floret ('flɔːrɪt) NOUN a small flower, esp one of many making up the head of a composite flower.
▷HISTORY C17: from Old French *florete* a little flower, from *flor* FLOWER

Florianópolis (*Portuguese* floriə'nɔpulis) NOUN a port in S Brazil, capital of Santa Caterina state, on the W coast of Santa Caterina Island. Pop.: 321 778 (2000).

floriated *or* **floreated** ('flɔːrɪ,eɪtɪd) ADJECTIVE *Architect* having ornamentation based on flowers and leaves.
▷HISTORY C19: from Latin *flōs* FLOWER

floribunda (,flɔːrɪ'bʌndə) NOUN any of several varieties of cultivated hybrid roses whose flowers grow in large sprays.
▷HISTORY C19: from New Latin, feminine of *flōribundus* flowering freely

floriculture ('flɔːrɪ,kʌltʃə) NOUN the cultivation of flowering plants.
▸ **,flori'cultural** ADJECTIVE ▸ **,flori'culturist** NOUN

florid ('flɒrɪd) ADJECTIVE [1] having a red or flushed complexion. [2] excessively ornate; flowery: *florid architecture*. [3] an archaic word for **flowery.**
▷HISTORY C17: from Latin *flōridus* blooming
▸**flo'ridity** *or* **'floridness** NOUN ▸**'floridly** ADVERB

Florida ('flɒrɪdə) NOUN [1] a state of the southeastern US, between the Atlantic and the Gulf of Mexico: consists mostly of a low-lying peninsula ending in the **Florida Keys** a chain of small islands off the coast of S Florida, extending southwest for over 160 km (100 miles). Capital: Tallahassee. Pop.: 15 982 378 (2000). Area: 143 900 sq. km (55 560 sq. miles). Abbreviations: **Fla.** (with zip code) **FL.** [2] **Straits of.** a sea passage between the Florida Keys and Cuba, linking the Atlantic with the Gulf of Mexico.

Floridian (flɒ'rɪdɪən) NOUN [1] a native or inhabitant of Florida. ◆ ADJECTIVE [2] of or relating to Florida or its inhabitants.

floriferous (flɔː'rɪfərəs) ADJECTIVE bearing or capable of bearing many flowers.

florigen ('flɒrɪdʒən) NOUN the hypothetical plant hormone that induces flowering, thought to be synthesized in the leaves as a photoperiodic response and transmitted to the flower buds.
▷HISTORY C20: from Latin *flōr-*, *flōs* FLOWER + -GEN

florilegium (ˌflɔːrɪ'liːdʒɪəm) NOUN, *plural* **-gia** (-dʒɪə). [1] (formerly) a lavishly illustrated book on flowers. [2] *Rare* an anthology.
▷HISTORY C17: Modern Latin, from Latin *florilegus* flower-collecting, from *flōs* flower + *legere* to collect

florin ('flɒrɪn) NOUN [1] a former British coin, originally silver and later cupronickel, equivalent to ten (new) pence. [2] the standard monetary unit of Aruba, divided into 100 cents. [3] (formerly) another name for **guilder** (sense 1). [4] any of various gold coins of Florence, Britain, or Austria.
▷HISTORY C14: from French, from Old Italian *fiorino* Florentine coin, from *fiore* flower, from Latin *flōs*

florist ('flɒrɪst) NOUN a person who grows or deals in flowers.

floristic (flɒ'rɪstɪk) ADJECTIVE of or relating to flowers or a flora.
▸**flo'ristically** ADVERB

floristics (flɒ'rɪstɪks) NOUN (*functioning as singular*) the branch of botany concerned with the types, numbers, and distribution of plant species in a particular area.

-florous ADJECTIVE COMBINING FORM indicating number or type of flowers: *tubuliflorous*.

floruit *Latin* ('flɒruːɪt) VERB (he or she) flourished: used to indicate the period when a historical figure, whose birth and death dates are unknown, was most active. Abbreviations: ***fl.***, ***flor.***

florula ('flɒrjʊlə) *or* **florule** ('flɒrjuːl) NOUN, *plural* **-ulae** (-jʊliː) *or* **-ules.** [1] the flora of a small single environment. [2] a fossil flower found in a single stratum or in several thin adjacent strata.
▷HISTORY C19: FLORA + -ULE

flory ('flɔːrɪ) *or* **fleury** ('flʊərɪ, 'flɜːrɪ) ADJECTIVE (*usually postpositive*) *Heraldry* containing a fleur-de-lys.
▷HISTORY C15: from Old French *floré*, from *flor* FLOWER

flos ferri ('flɒs 'fɛrɪ) NOUN a variety of aragonite that is deposited from hot springs in the form of a white branching mass.
▷HISTORY C18: from New Latin, literally: flower of iron

floss (flɒs) NOUN [1] the mass of fine silky fibres obtained from cotton and similar plants. [2] any similar fine silky material, such as the hairlike styles and stigmas of maize or the fibres prepared from silkworm cocoons. [3] untwisted silk thread used in embroidery, etc. [4] See **dental floss.** ◆ VERB [5] (*tr*) to clean (between one's teeth) with dental floss.
▷HISTORY C18: perhaps from Old French *flosche* down

flossy ('flɒsɪ) ADJECTIVE **flossier, flossiest.** [1] consisting of or resembling floss. [2] *US and Canadian slang* (esp of dress) showy.

flotage *or* **floatage** ('fləʊtɪdʒ) NOUN [1] the act or state of floating; flotation. [2] buoyancy; power or ability to float. [3] objects or material that float on the surface of the water; flotsam.

flotation *or* **floatation** (fləʊ'teɪʃən) NOUN [1] **a** the launching or financing of a commercial enterprise by bond or share issues. **b** the raising of a loan or new capital by bond or share issues. [2] power or ability to float; buoyancy. [3] Also called: **froth flotation.** a process to concentrate the valuable ore in low-grade ores. The ore is ground to a powder, mixed with water containing surface-active chemicals, and vigorously aerated. The bubbles formed trap the required ore fragments and carry them to the surface froth, which is then skimmed off.

flotation bags PLURAL NOUN bags inflated to keep a spacecraft or helicopter afloat and upright when it lands in the sea.

flotation tank *or* **chamber** NOUN an enclosed ventilated tank filled with a saline solution at body temperature, in which a person floats in darkness in order to relax or meditate.

flote grass (fləʊt) NOUN an aquatic perennial grass, *Glyceria fluitans*, whose metre-long stems and pale green leaves are often seen floating in still or sluggish water. The related **sweet grass** (*G. plicata*) has broader, darker leaves and owes its name to the fact that cattle like to eat it.
▷HISTORY C16: *flote* obsolete spelling of FLOAT

flotel *or* **floatel** (fləʊ'tɛl) NOUN (in the oil industry) an oil rig or boat used as accommodation for workers in off-shore oil fields.
▷HISTORY C20: from *float* + *hotel*

flotilla (flə'tɪlə) NOUN a small fleet or a fleet of small vessels.
▷HISTORY C18: from Spanish *flota* fleet, from French *flotte*, ultimately from Old Norse *floti*

flotsam ('flɒtsəm) NOUN [1] wreckage from a ship found floating. Compare **jetsam** (sense 1), **lagan.** [2] useless or discarded objects; odds and ends (esp in the phrase **flotsam and jetsam**). [3] vagrants.
▷HISTORY C16: from Anglo-French *floteson*, from *floter* to FLOAT

flounce[1] (flaʊns) VERB [1] (*intr; often foll by about, away, out,* etc) to move or go with emphatic or impatient movements. ◆ NOUN [2] the act of flouncing.
▷HISTORY C16: of Scandinavian origin; compare Norwegian *flunsa* to hurry, Swedish *flunsa* to splash

flounce[2] (flaʊns) NOUN an ornamental gathered ruffle sewn to a garment by its top edge.
▷HISTORY C18: from Old French *fronce* wrinkle, from *froncir* to wrinkle, of Germanic origin

flouncing ('flaʊnsɪŋ) NOUN material, such as lace or embroidered fabric, used for making flounces.

flounder[1] ('flaʊndə) VERB (*intr*) [1] to struggle; to move with difficulty, as in mud. [2] to behave awkwardly; make mistakes. ◆ NOUN [3] the act of floundering.
▷HISTORY C16: probably a blend of FOUNDER[2] + BLUNDER; perhaps influenced by FLOUNDER[2]

> **Language note** *Flounder* is sometimes wrongly used where *founder* is meant: *the project foundered* (not *floundered*) *because of a lack of funds.*

flounder[2] ('flaʊndə) NOUN, *plural* **-der** *or* **-ders.** [1] Also called: **fluke.** a European flatfish, *Platichthys flesus* having a greyish-brown body covered with prickly scales: family *Pleuronectidae*: an important food fish. [2] *US and Canadian* any flatfish of the families *Bothidae* (turbot, etc.) and *Pleuronectidae* (plaice, halibut, sand dab, etc.).
▷HISTORY C14: probably of Scandinavian origin; compare Old Norse *flythra*, Norwegian *flundra*

flour ('flaʊə) NOUN [1] a powder, which may be either fine or coarse, prepared by sifting and grinding the meal of a grass, esp wheat. [2] any finely powdered substance. ◆ VERB [3] (*tr*) to make (grain) into flour. [4] (*tr*) to dredge or sprinkle (food or cooking utensils) with flour. [5] (of mercury) to break into fine particles on the surface of a metal rather than amalgamating, or to produce such an effect on (a metal). The effect is caused by impurities, esp sulphur.
▷HISTORY C13 *flur* finer portion of meal, FLOWER
▸**'floury** ADJECTIVE

flourish ('flʌrɪʃ) VERB [1] (*intr*) to thrive; prosper. [2] (*intr*) to be at the peak of condition. [3] (*intr*) to be healthy: *plants flourish in the light.* [4] to wave or cause to wave in the air with sweeping strokes. [5] to display or make a display. [6] to play (a fanfare, etc.) on a musical instrument. [7] (*intr*) to embellish writing, characters, etc., with ornamental strokes. [8] to add decorations or embellishments to (speech or writing). [9] (*intr*) an obsolete word for **blossom.** ◆ NOUN [10] the act of waving or brandishing. [11] a showy gesture: *he entered with a flourish.* [12] an ornamental embellishment in writing. [13] a display of ornamental language or speech. [14] a grandiose passage of music. [15] an ostentatious display or parade. [16] *Obsolete* **a** the state of flourishing. **b** the state of flowering.
▷HISTORY C13: from Old French *florir*, ultimately from Latin *flōrēre* to flower, from *flōs* a flower
▸**'flourisher** NOUN

flour mite NOUN any of several mites that infest flour and other stored organic materials and may be a serious pest; some may cause itching in persons handling infected material.

flour moth NOUN a pyralid moth, *Ephestia Kuehniella*, the larvae of which are an important pest of flour mills and granaries.

flout (flaʊt) VERB (when *intr*, usually foll by *at*) to show contempt (for); scoff or jeer (at).
▷HISTORY C16: perhaps from Middle English *flouten* to play the flute, from Old French *flauter* compare Dutch *fluiten*; see FLUTE
▸**'flouter** NOUN ▸**'floutingly** ADVERB

> **Language note** See at **flaunt.**

flow (fləʊ) VERB (*mainly intr*) [1] (of liquids) to move or be conveyed as in a stream. [2] (of blood) to circulate around the body. [3] to move or progress freely as if in a stream: *the crowd flowed into the building.* [4] to proceed or be produced continuously and effortlessly: *ideas flowed from her pen.* [5] to show or be marked by smooth or easy movement. [6] to hang freely or loosely: *her hair flowed down her back.* [7] to be present in abundance: *wine flows at their parties.* [8] an informal word for **menstruate.** [9] (of tide water) to advance or rise. Compare **ebb** (sense 1). [10] (*tr*) to cover or swamp with liquid; flood. [11] (of rocks such as slate) to yield to pressure without breaking so that the structure and arrangement of the constituent minerals are altered. ◆ NOUN [12] the act, rate, or manner of flowing: *a fast flow.* [13] a continuous stream or discharge. [14] continuous progression. [15] the advancing of the tide. [16] a stream of molten or solidified lava. [17] the amount of liquid that flows in a given time. [18] an informal word for **menstruation.** [19] *Scot* **a** a marsh or swamp. **b** an inlet or basin of the sea. **c** (*capital when part of a name*): *Scapa Flow.* [20] **flow of spirits.** natural happiness.
▷HISTORY Old English *flōwan*; related to Old Norse *flōa*, Middle Low German *vlōien*, Greek *plein* to float, Sanskrit *plavate* he swims

flowage ('fləʊɪdʒ) NOUN [1] the act of flowing or overflowing or the state of having overflowed. [2] the liquid that flows or overflows. [3] a gradual deformation or motion of certain solids, such as asphalt, which flow without fracture.

flow chart *or* **sheet** NOUN a diagrammatic representation of the sequence of operations or equipment in an industrial process, computer program, etc.

Flow Country NOUN an area of moorland and peat bogs in northern Scotland known for its wildlife, now partly afforested.

flower ('flaʊə) NOUN [1] **a** a bloom or blossom on a plant. **b** a plant that bears blooms or blossoms. [2] the reproductive structure of angiosperm plants, consisting normally of stamens and carpels surrounded by petals and sepals all borne on the receptacle (one or more of these structures may be absent). In some plants it is conspicuous and brightly coloured and attracts insects or other animals for pollination. Related adjective: **floral.** Related prefix: **antho-.** [3] any similar reproductive structure in other plants. [4] the prime; peak: *in the flower of his youth.* [5] the choice or finest product, part, or representative: *the flower of the young men.* [6] a decoration or embellishment. [7] *Printing* a type ornament, used with others in borders, chapter headings, etc. [8] Also called: **fleuron.** an embellishment or ornamental symbol depicting a flower. [9] (*plural*) fine powder, usually produced by sublimation: *flowers of sulphur.* ◆ VERB [10] (*intr*) to

produce flowers; bloom. [11] (*intr*) to reach full growth or maturity. [12] (*tr*) to deck or decorate with flowers or floral designs.
▷HISTORY C13: from Old French *flor*, from Latin *flōs*; see BLOW[3]
▸**'flower-,like** ADJECTIVE

flowerage ('flauərɪdʒ) NOUN *Now rare* [1] a mass of flowers. [2] the process or act of flowering.

flowerbed ('flauə,bɛd) NOUN a plot of ground in which flowers are grown in a garden, park, etc.

flower bug NOUN any of a number of bugs of the family *Cimicidae*, related to the debris bugs but frequenting flowers and feeding on the small insects found there.

flower-de-luce ('flauədə'lu:s) NOUN, *plural* **flowers-de-luce**. an archaic name for the **iris** (sense 2) and **lily** (sense 1).
▷HISTORY C16: anglicized variant of French *fleur de lis*

flowered ('flauəd) ADJECTIVE [1] having or abounding in flowers. [2] decorated with flowers or a floral design.

flowerer ('flauərə) NOUN a plant that flowers at a specified time or in a specified way: *a late flowerer*.

floweret ('flauərɪt) NOUN another name for **floret**.

flower girl NOUN [1] a girl or woman who sells flowers in the street. [2] *US and Scot* a young girl who carries flowers in a procession, esp at weddings.

flower head NOUN an inflorescence in which stalkless florets are crowded together at the tip of the stem.

flowering ('flauərɪŋ) ADJECTIVE (of certain species of plants) capable of producing conspicuous flowers: *a flowering ash*.

flowering currant NOUN an ornamental shrub, *Ribes sanguineum*, growing to 2 to 3 metres (6 to 9ft.) in height, with red, crimson, yellow, or white flowers: family *Saxifragaceae*.

flowering maple NOUN any tropical shrub of the malvaceous genus *Abutilon*, esp *A. hybridum*, having lobed leaves like those of the maple and brightly coloured flowers.

flowerless ('flauəlɪs) ADJECTIVE designating any plant that does not produce seeds. See **cryptogam**.

flower-of-an-hour NOUN a malvaceous Old World herbaceous plant, *Hibiscus trionum*, having pale yellow flowers with a bladder-like calyx. Also called: **bladder ketmia**.

flower-pecker NOUN any small songbird of the family *Dicaeidae*, of SE Asia and Australasia, typically feeding on nectar, berries, and insects.

flowerpot ('flauə,pɒt) NOUN a pot in which plants are grown.

flower power NOUN *Informal* a youth cult of the late 1960s advocating peace and love, using the flower as a symbol; associated with drug-taking. Its adherents were known as **flower children** or **flower people**.

flowers of sulphur PLURAL NOUN minute crystals of sulphur obtained by condensing sulphur vapour on a cold surface.

flowery ('flauərɪ) ADJECTIVE [1] abounding in flowers. [2] decorated with flowers or floral patterns. [3] like or suggestive of flowers: *a flowery scent*. [4] (of language or style) elaborate; ornate.
▸**'floweriness** NOUN

flowmeter ('fləu,mi:tə) NOUN an instrument that measures the rate of flow of a liquid or gas within a pipe or tube.

flown[1] (fləun) VERB the past participle of **fly**.

flown[2] (fləun) ADJECTIVE relating to coloured (usually blue) decoration on porcelain that, during firing, has melted into the surrounding glaze giving a halo-like effect.
▷HISTORY probably from the obsolete past participle of FLOW

flow-on NOUN *Austral and NZ* a wage or salary increase granted to one group of workers as a consequence of a similar increase granted to another group.

flow sheet NOUN another name for **flow chart**.

fl. oz. ABBREVIATION FOR fluid ounce.

flu (flu:) NOUN *Informal* [1] (often preceded by *the*) short for **influenza**. [2] any of various viral infections, esp a respiratory or intestinal infection.

fluctuant ('flʌktjuənt) ADJECTIVE inclined to vary or fluctuate; unstable.

fluctuate ('flʌktju,eɪt) VERB [1] to change or cause to change position constantly; be or make unstable; waver or vary. [2] (*intr*) to rise and fall like a wave; undulate.
▷HISTORY C17: from Latin *fluctuāre*, from *fluctus* a wave, from *fluere* to flow

fluctuation (,flʌktju'eɪʃən) NOUN [1] constant change; vacillation; instability. [2] undulation. [3] a variation in an animal or plant that is determined by environment rather than heredity.

flue[1] (flu:) NOUN [1] a shaft, tube, or pipe, esp as used in a chimney, to carry off smoke, gas, etc. [2] *Music* the passage in an organ pipe or flute within which a vibrating air column is set up. See also **flue pipe**.
▷HISTORY C16: of unknown origin

flue[2] (flu:) NOUN loose fluffy matter; down.
▷HISTORY C16: from Flemish *vluwe*, from Old French *velu* shaggy

flue[3] *or* **flew** (flu:) NOUN a type of fishing net.
▷HISTORY Middle English, from Middle Dutch *vlūwe*

flue[4] (flu:) NOUN another word for **fluke**[1] (senses 1, 3).
▸**flued** ADJECTIVE

flue-cure VERB (*tr*) to cure (tobacco) by means of radiant heat from pipes or flues connected to a furnace.

flue gas NOUN the smoke in the uptake of a boiler fire: it consists mainly of carbon dioxide, carbon monoxide, and nitrogen.

fluellen *or* **fluellin** (flʊ'ɛlən) NOUN [1] either of two weedy scrophulariaceous annuals related to the toadflaxes, **round-leaved fluellen** (*Kickxia spuria*) and **sharp-leaved fluellen** (*K. elatine*). [2] *Obsolete* any of several speedwells, especially *Veronica officinalis*.
▷HISTORY C16: shortened from Welsh *llysiau Llewelyn* Llewelyn's flower

fluency ('flu:ənsɪ) NOUN the quality of being fluent, esp facility in speech or writing.

fluent ('flu:ənt) ADJECTIVE [1] able to speak or write a specified foreign language with facility. [2] spoken or written with facility: *his French is fluent*. [3] easy and graceful in motion or shape. [4] flowing or able to flow freely.
▷HISTORY C16: from Latin: flowing, from *fluere* to flow
▸**'fluently** ADVERB

flue pipe *or* **flue** NOUN an organ pipe or tubular instrument of the flute family whose sound is produced by the passage of air across a sharp-edged fissure in the side. This sets in motion a vibrating air column within the pipe or instrument.

flue stop NOUN an organ stop controlling a set of flue pipes.

fluey ('flu:ɪ) ADJECTIVE *Informal* involved in, caused by, or like influenza.

fluff (flʌf) NOUN [1] soft light particles, such as the down or nap of cotton or wool. [2] any light downy substance. [3] an object, matter, etc., of little importance; trifle. [4] *Informal* a mistake, esp in speaking or reading lines or performing music. [5] *Informal* a young woman (esp in the phrase **a bit of fluff**). ◆ VERB [6] to make or become soft and puffy by shaking or patting; puff up. [7] *Informal* to make a mistake in performing (an action, dramatic speech, music, etc.).
▷HISTORY C18: perhaps from FLUE[2]

fluffer ('flʌfə) NOUN a person employed on a pornographic film set to ensure that male actors are kept aroused.

fluffy ('flʌfɪ) ADJECTIVE **fluffier, fluffiest**. [1] of, resembling, or covered with fluff. [2] soft and light: *fluffy hair*. [3] **a** sentimental or overromantic; not very intelligent. **b** characterized by nonviolent methods: *fluffy environmentalist protestors*.
▸**'fluffily** ADVERB ▸**'fluffiness** NOUN

flugelhorn ('flu:gəl,hɔ:n) NOUN a type of valved brass instrument consisting of a tube of conical bore with a cup-shaped mouthpiece, used esp in brass bands. It is a transposing instrument in B flat or C, and has the same range as the cornet in B flat.
▷HISTORY German *Flügelhorn*, from *Flügel* wing + *Horn* HORN

fluid ('flu:ɪd) NOUN [1] a substance, such as a liquid or gas, that can flow, has no fixed shape, and offers little resistance to an external stress. ◆ ADJECTIVE [2] capable of flowing and easily changing shape. [3] of, concerned with, or using a fluid or fluids. [4] constantly changing or apt to change. [5] smooth in shape or movement; flowing.
▷HISTORY C15: from Latin *fluidus*, from *fluere* to flow
▸**'fluidal** ADJECTIVE ▸**'fluidness** NOUN ▸**'fluidly** *or* **'fluidally** ADVERB

fluid dram NOUN another name for **drachm**.

fluid drive NOUN a type of coupling for transmitting power from the engine of a motor vehicle to the transmission, using a torque converter. Also called: **fluid coupling, fluid clutch, fluid flywheel**.

fluidextract ('flu:ɪd'ɛkstrækt) NOUN an alcoholic solution of a vegetable drug, one millilitre of which has an activity equivalent to one gram of the powdered drug.

fluidics (flu:'ɪdɪks) NOUN (*functioning as singular*) the study and use of systems in which the flow of fluids in tubes simulates the flow of electricity in conductors. Such systems are used in place of electronics in certain applications, such as the control of apparatus.
▸**flu'idic** ADJECTIVE

fluidity (flu:'ɪdɪtɪ) NOUN [1] the state of being fluid. [2] *Physics* the reciprocal of viscosity.

fluidize *or* **fluidise** ('flu:ɪ,daɪz) VERB (*tr*) to make fluid, esp to make (solids) fluid by pulverizing them so that they can be transported in a stream of gas as if they were liquids: *fluidized coal*.
▸**,fluidi'zation** *or* **,fluidi'sation** NOUN ▸**'fluid,izer** *or* **'fluid,iser** NOUN

fluidized bed NOUN *Chemical engineering* a bed of fluidized solids used as a heat exchanger or mass transfer medium.

fluid lubrication NOUN *Engineering* lubrication in which bearing surfaces are separated by an oil film sustained by the motion of the parts.

fluid mechanics NOUN (*functioning as singular*) the study of the mechanical and flow properties of fluids, esp as they apply to practical engineering. Also called: **hydraulics**. See also **hydrodynamics, hydrostatics, hydrokinetics**.

fluid ounce NOUN a unit of capacity equal to the volume of one avoirdupois ounce of distilled water at 62°F: there are twenty fluid ounces in an Imperial pint and sixteen in a US pint.

fluid pressure NOUN the pressure exerted by a fluid at any point inside it. The difference of pressure between two levels is determined by the product of the difference of height, the density, and the acceleration of free fall.

fluke[1] (flu:k) NOUN [1] Also called: **flue**. a flat bladelike projection at the end of the arm of an anchor. [2] either of the two lobes of the tail of a whale or related animal. [3] Also called: **flue**. the barb or barbed head of a harpoon, arrow, etc.
▷HISTORY C16: perhaps a special use of FLUKE[3] (in the sense: a flounder)

fluke[2] (flu:k) NOUN [1] an accidental stroke of luck. [2] any chance happening. ◆ VERB [3] (*tr*) to gain, make, or hit by a fluke.
▷HISTORY C19: of unknown origin

fluke[3] (flu:k) NOUN [1] any parasitic flatworm, such as the blood fluke and liver fluke, of the classes *Monogenea* and *Digenea* (formerly united in a single class *Trematoda*). [2] another name for **flounder**[2] (sense 1).
▷HISTORY Old English *flōc*; related to Old Norse *flōki* flounder, Old Saxon *flaka* sole, Old High German *flah* smooth

fluky *or* **flukey** ('flu:kɪ) ADJECTIVE **flukier, flukiest**. *Informal* [1] done or gained by an accident, esp a lucky one. [2] variable; uncertain: *fluky weather*.
▸**'flukiness** NOUN

flume (flu:m) NOUN [1] a ravine through which a stream flows. [2] a narrow artificial channel made for providing water for power, floating logs, etc. [3] a slide in the form of a long and winding tube with a stream of water running through it that descends into a purpose-built pool. ◆ VERB [4] (*tr*) to transport (logs) in a flume.

▷HISTORY C12: from Old French *flum*, ultimately from Latin *flūmen* stream, from *fluere* to flow

flummery (ˈflʌmərɪ) NOUN, *plural* **-meries.** 1 *Informal* meaningless flattery; nonsense. 2 *Chiefly Brit* a cold pudding of oatmeal, etc.
▷HISTORY C17: from Welsh *llymru*

flummox (ˈflʌməks) VERB (*tr*) to perplex or bewilder.
▷HISTORY C19: of unknown origin

flung (flʌŋ) VERB the past tense and past participle of **fling.**

flunitrazepam (ˌfluːnaɪˈtræzəˌpæm) NOUN a drug similar to diazepam, used in treating long-term insomnia.

flunk (flʌŋk) *Informal, chiefly US, Canadian, and NZ* ◆ VERB 1 to fail or cause to fail to reach the required standard in (an examination, course, etc.). 2 (*intr; foll by out*) to be dismissed from a school or college through failure in examinations. ◆ NOUN 3 a low grade below the pass standard.
▷HISTORY C19: perhaps from FLINCH[1] + FUNK[1]

flunky *or* **flunkey** (ˈflʌŋkɪ) NOUN, *plural* **flunkies** *or* **flunkeys.** 1 a servile or fawning person. 2 a person who performs menial tasks. 3 *Usually derogatory* a manservant in livery.
▷HISTORY C18: of unknown origin

Fluon (ˈfluːɒn) NOUN a trademark for **polytetrafluoroethylene.**

fluor (ˈfluːɔː) NOUN another name for **fluorspar.**
▷HISTORY C17: from Latin: a flowing; so called from its use as a metallurgical flux

fluor- (*combining form*) a variant of **fluoro-** before a vowel: *fluorene; fluorine.*

fluorapatite (ˌflʊəˈræpətaɪt) NOUN a mineral consisting of calcium fluorophosphate; the most common form of apatite.

fluorene (ˈflʊəriːn) NOUN a white insoluble crystalline solid used in making dyes. Formula: $(C_6H_4)_2CH_2$.

fluoresce (ˌflʊəˈrɛs) VERB (*intr*) to exhibit fluorescence.
▷HISTORY C19: back formation from FLUORESCENCE

fluorescein *or* **fluoresceine** (ˌflʊəˈrɛsɪɪn) NOUN an orange-red crystalline compound that in aqueous solution exhibits a greenish-yellow fluorescence in reflected light and is reddish-orange in transmitted light: used as a marker in sea water and as an indicator. Formula: $C_{20}H_{12}O_5$.

fluorescence (ˌflʊəˈrɛsəns) NOUN 1 *Physics* **a** the emission of light or other radiation from atoms or molecules that are bombarded by particles, such as electrons, or by radiation from a separate source. The bombarding radiation produces excited atoms, molecules, or ions and these emit photons as they fall back to the ground state. **b** such an emission of photons that ceases as soon as the bombarding radiation is discontinued. **c** such an emission of photons for which the average lifetime of the excited atoms and molecules is less than about 10^{-8} seconds. 2 the radiation emitted as a result of fluorescence. Compare **phosphorescence.**
▷HISTORY C19: FLUOR + *-escence* (as in *opalescence*)

fluorescent (ˌflʊəˈrɛsᵊnt) ADJECTIVE exhibiting or having the property of fluorescence.

fluorescent lamp NOUN 1 a type of lamp in which an electrical gas discharge is maintained in a tube with a thin layer of phosphor on its inside surface. The gas, which is often mercury vapour, emits ultraviolet radiation causing the phosphor to fluoresce. 2 a type of lamp in which an electrical discharge is maintained in a tube containing a gas such as neon, mercury vapour, or sodium vapour at low pressure. Gas atoms in the discharge are struck by electrons and fluoresce.

fluorescent screen NOUN a transparent screen coated on one side with a phosphor that fluoresces when exposed to X-rays or cathode rays.

fluoric (fluːˈɔːrɪk) ADJECTIVE of, concerned with, or produced from fluorine or fluorspar.

fluoridate (ˈflʊərɪˌdeɪt) VERB to subject (water) to fluoridation.

fluoridation (ˌflʊərɪˈdeɪʃən) NOUN the addition of about one part per million of fluorides to the public water supply as a protection against tooth decay.

fluoride (ˈflʊəˌraɪd) NOUN 1 any salt of hydrofluoric acid, containing the fluoride ion, F^-. 2 any compound containing fluorine, such as methyl fluoride.

fluorinate (ˈflʊərɪˌneɪt) VERB to treat or combine with fluorine.
▸ˌ**fluoriˈnation** NOUN

fluorine (ˈflʊəriːn) *or* **fluorin** (ˈflʊərɪn) NOUN a toxic pungent pale yellow gas of the halogen group that is the most electronegative and reactive of all the elements, occurring principally in fluorspar and cryolite: used in the production of uranium, fluorocarbons, and other chemicals. Symbol: F; atomic no.: 9; atomic wt.: 18.9984032; valency: 1; density: 1.696 kg/m^3; relative density: 1.108; freezing pt.: –219.62°C; boiling pt.: –188.13°C.

fluorite (ˈflʊəraɪt) NOUN the US and Canadian name for **fluorspar.**

fluoro- *or before a vowel* **fluor-** COMBINING FORM 1 indicating the presence of fluorine: *fluorocarbon.* 2 indicating fluorescence: *fluoroscope.*

fluorocarbon (ˌflʊərəʊˈkɑːbᵊn) NOUN any compound derived by replacing all or some of the hydrogen atoms in hydrocarbons by fluorine atoms. Many of them are used as lubricants, solvents, and coatings. See also **Freon, polytetrafluoroethylene, CFC.**

fluorochrome (ˈflʊərəʊˌkrəʊm) NOUN a chemical entity, such as a molecule or group, that exhibits fluorescence.

fluorography (flʊəˈrɒgrəfɪ) NOUN the photographic recording of fluoroscopic images.

fluorometer (ˌflʊəˈrɒmɪtə) *or* **fluorimeter** (ˌflʊəˈrɪmɪtə) NOUN 1 an instrument for inducing fluorescence by irradiation and for examination of the emission spectrum of the resulting fluorescent light. 2 a device for detecting and measuring ultraviolet radiation by determining the amount of fluorescence that it produces from a phosphor.
▸**fluorometric** (ˌflʊərəʊˈmɛtrɪk) *or* **fluorimetric** (ˌflʊərɪˈmɛtrɪk) ADJECTIVE ▸ˌ**fluoˈrometry** *or* ˌ**fluoˈrimetry** NOUN

fluorophore (ˈflʊərəʊˌfɔː) NOUN a chemical group responsible for fluorescence.

fluoroscope (ˈflʊərəˌskəʊp) NOUN a device consisting of a fluorescent screen and an X-ray source that enables an X-ray image of an object, person, or part to be observed directly.
▸**fluoroscopic** (ˌflʊərəˈskɒpɪk) ADJECTIVE ▸ˌ**fluoroˈscopically** ADVERB

fluoroscopy (flʊəˈrɒskəpɪ) NOUN examination of a person or object by means of a fluoroscope.

fluorosis (flʊəˈrəʊsɪs) NOUN fluoride poisoning, due to ingestion of too much fluoride in drinking water over a long period or to ingestion of pesticides containing fluoride salts. Chronic fluorosis results in mottling of the teeth of children.

fluorspar (ˈflʊəˌspɑː), **fluor,** *or US and Canadian* **fluorite** NOUN a white or colourless mineral sometimes fluorescent and often tinted by impurities, found in veins and as deposits from hot gases. It is used in the manufacture of glass, enamel, and jewellery, and is the chief ore of fluorine. Composition: calcium fluoride. Formula: CaF_2. Crystal structure: cubic.

fluoxetine (fluːˈɒksɪˌtiːn) NOUN a drug that prolongs the action of serotonin in the brain. It is used as an antidepressant.

flurry (ˈflʌrɪ) NOUN, *plural* **-ries.** 1 a sudden commotion or burst of activity. 2 a light gust of wind or rain or fall of snow. 3 *Stock Exchange* a sudden brief increase in trading or fluctuation in stock prices. 4 the death spasms of a harpooned whale. ◆ VERB **-ries, -rying, -ried.** 5 to confuse or bewilder or be confused or bewildered.
▷HISTORY C17: from obsolete *flurr* to scatter, perhaps formed on analogy with HURRY

flush[1] (flʌʃ) VERB 1 to blush or cause to blush. 2 to flow or flood or cause to flow or flood with or as if with water. 3 to glow or shine or cause to glow or shine with a rosy colour. 4 to send a volume of water quickly through (a pipe, channel, etc.) or into (a toilet) for the purpose of cleansing, emptying, etc. 5 to cause (soluble substances in the soil) to be washed towards the surface, as by the action of underground springs, or (of such substances) to be washed towards the soil surface. 6 (*tr; usually passive*) to excite or elate. ◆ NOUN 7 a rosy colour, esp in the cheeks; blush. 8 a sudden flow or gush, as of water. 9 a feeling of excitement or elation: *the flush of success.* 10 early bloom; freshness: *the flush of youth.* 11 redness of the skin, esp of the face, as from the effects of a fever, alcohol, etc. 12 *Ecology* an area of boggy land fed by ground water. ◆ ADJECTIVE 13 having a ruddy or heightened colour.
▷HISTORY C16 (in the sense: to gush forth): perhaps from FLUSH[3]
▸ˈ**flusher** NOUN

flush[2] (flʌʃ) ADJECTIVE (*usually postpositive*) 1 level or even with another surface. 2 directly adjacent; continuous. 3 *Informal* having plenty of money. 4 *Informal* abundant or plentiful, as money. 5 full of vigour. 6 full to the brim or to the point of overflowing. 7 *Printing* having an even margin, right or left, with no indentations. 8 (of a blow) accurately delivered. 9 (of a vessel) having no superstructure built above the flat level of the deck. ◆ ADVERB 10 so as to be level or even. 11 directly or squarely. ◆ VERB (*tr*) 12 to cause (surfaces) to be on the same level or in the same plane. 13 to enrich the diet of (a ewe) during the breeding season. ◆ NOUN 14 a period of fresh growth of leaves, shoots, etc.
▷HISTORY C18: probably from FLUSH[1] (in the sense: spring out)
▸ˈ**flushness** NOUN

flush[3] (flʌʃ) VERB (*tr*) to rouse (game, wild creatures, etc.) and put to flight.
▷HISTORY C13 *flusshen*, perhaps of imitative origin

flush[4] (flʌʃ) NOUN (in poker and similar games) a hand containing only one suit.
▷HISTORY C16: from Old French *flus*, from Latin *fluxus* FLUX

flushing (ˈflʌʃɪŋ) NOUN an extra feeding given to ewes before mating to increase the lambing percentage.

Flushing (ˈflʌʃɪŋ) NOUN a port in the SW Netherlands, in Zeeland province, on Walcheren Island, at the mouth of the West Scheldt river: the first Dutch city to throw off Spanish rule (1572). Pop.: 43 945 (latest est.). Dutch name: **Vlissingen.**

flushwork (ˈflʌʃˌwɜːk) NOUN *Architect* decorative treatment of the surface of an outside wall with flints split to show their smooth black surface, combined with dressed stone to form patterns such as tracery or initials.

fluster (ˈflʌstə) VERB 1 to make or become confused, nervous, or upset. ◆ NOUN 2 a state of confusion or agitation.
▷HISTORY C15: probably of Scandinavian origin; compare Icelandic *flaustr* to hurry, *flaustra* to bustle

flute (fluːt) NOUN 1 a wind instrument consisting of an open cylindrical tube of wood or metal having holes in the side stopped either by the fingers or by pads controlled by keys. The breath is directed across a mouth hole cut in the side, causing the air in the tube to vibrate. Range: about three octaves upwards from middle C. 2 any pipe blown directly on the principle of a flue pipe, either by means of a mouth hole or through a fipple. 3 *Architect* a rounded shallow concave groove on the shaft of a column, pilaster, etc. 4 a groove or furrow in cloth, etc. 5 a tall narrow wineglass. 6 anything shaped like a flute. ◆ VERB 7 to produce or utter (sounds) in the manner or tone of a flute. 8 (*tr*) to make grooves or furrows in.
▷HISTORY C14: from Old French *flahute*, via Old Provençal, from Vulgar Latin *flabeolum* (unattested); perhaps also influenced by Old Provençal *laut* lute; see FLAGEOLET
▸ˈ**fluteˌlike** ADJECTIVE ▸ˈ**fluty** ADJECTIVE

fluted (ˈfluːtɪd) ADJECTIVE 1 (esp of the shaft of a column) having flutes. 2 sounding like a flute.

fluter (ˈfluːtə) NOUN 1 a craftsman who makes flutes or fluting. 2 a tool used to make flutes or fluting. 3 a less common word, used esp in folk music, for **flautist.**

fluting (ˈfluːtɪŋ) NOUN 1 a design or decoration of flutes on a column, pilaster, etc. 2 grooves or furrows, as in cloth.

flutist (ˈfluːtɪst) NOUN *Now chiefly US and Canadian* a variant of **flautist.**

flutter (ˈflʌtə) VERB 1 to wave or cause to wave rapidly; flap. 2 (*intr*) (of birds, butterflies, etc.) to flap the wings. 3 (*intr*) to move, esp downwards,

with an irregular motion. 4 (*intr*) *Pathol* (of the auricles of the heart) to beat abnormally rapidly, esp in a regular rhythm. 5 to be or make nervous or restless. 6 (*intr*) to move about restlessly. 7 *Swimming* to cause (the legs) to move up and down in a flutter kick or (of the legs) to move in this way. 8 (*tr*) *Brit informal* to wager or gamble (a small amount of money). ◆ NOUN 9 a quick flapping or vibrating motion. 10 a state of nervous excitement or confusion. 11 excited interest; sensation; stir. 12 *Brit informal* a modest bet or wager. 13 *Pathol* an abnormally rapid beating of the auricles of the heart (200 to 400 beats per minute), esp in a regular rhythm, sometimes resulting in heart block. 14 *Electronics* a slow variation in pitch in a sound-reproducing system, similar to wow but occurring at higher frequencies. 15 a potentially dangerous oscillation of an aircraft, or part of an aircraft, caused by the interaction of aerodynamic forces, structural elastic reactions, and inertia. 16 *Swimming* See **flutter kick.** 17 Also called: **flutter tonguing.** *Music* a method of sounding a wind instrument, esp the flute, with a rolling movement of the tongue.
▷HISTORY Old English *floterian* to float to and fro; related to German *flattern*; see FLOAT
▸ˈ**flutterer** NOUN ▸ˈ**flutteringly** ADVERB

flutterboard (ˈflʌtəˌbɔːd) NOUN *US and Canadian* an oblong board or piece of polystyrene plastic used by swimmers in training or practice. Brit word: **float.**

flutter kick NOUN a type of kick used in certain swimming strokes, such as the crawl, in which the legs are held straight and alternately moved up and down rapidly in the water.

fluttery (ˈflʌtərɪ) ADJECTIVE 1 flapping rapidly; fluttering. 2 showing nervousness or excitement. 3 light or insubstantial.

fluvial (ˈfluːvɪəl) *or* **fluviatile** (ˈfluːvɪəˌtaɪl, -tɪl) ADJECTIVE of, relating to, or occurring in a river: *fluvial deposits.*
▷HISTORY C14: from Latin *fluviālis*, from *fluvius* river, from *fluere* to flow

fluviomarine (ˌfluːvɪəʊməˈriːn) ADJECTIVE 1 (of deposits) formed by joint action of the sea and a river or stream. 2 (esp of fish) able to live in both rivers and the sea.
▷HISTORY C19: *fluvio-*, from Latin *fluvius* river + MARINE

fluvioterrestrial (ˌfluːvɪəʊtəˈrestrɪəl) ADJECTIVE (of animals) able to live in rivers and on land.

fluvoxamine (fluːˈvɒksəmiːn) NOUN an antidepressant drug that acts by preventing the re-uptake after release of serotonin in the brain, thereby prolonging its action. See **SSRI.**

flux (flʌks) NOUN 1 a flow or discharge. 2 continuous change; instability. 3 a substance, such as borax or salt, that gives a low melting-point mixture with a metal oxide. It is used for cleaning metal surfaces during soldering, etc., and for protecting the surfaces of liquid metals. 4 *Metallurgy* a chemical used to increase the fluidity of refining slags in order to promote the rate of chemical reaction. 5 a similar substance used in the making of glass. 6 *Physics* **a** the rate of flow of particles, energy, or a fluid, through a specified area, such as that of neutrons (**neutron flux**) or of light energy (**luminous flux**). **b** the strength of a field in a given area expressed as the product of the area and the component of the field strength at right angles to the area: *magnetic flux; electric flux.* 7 *Pathol* an excessive discharge of fluid from the body, such as watery faeces in diarrhoea. 8 the act or process of melting; fusion. 9 (in the philosophy of Heraclitus) the state of constant change in which all things exist. ◆ VERB 10 to make or become fluid. 11 (*tr*) to apply flux to (a metal, soldered joint, etc.). 12 (*tr*) an obsolete word for **purge.**
▷HISTORY C14: from Latin *fluxus* a flow, from *fluere* to flow

flux density NOUN *Physics* the amount of flux per unit of cross-sectional area.

fluxion (ˈflʌkʃən) NOUN 1 *Maths, obsolete* the rate of change of a function, especially the instantaneous velocity of a moving body; derivative. 2 a less common word for **flux** (senses 1, 2).
▷HISTORY C16: from Late Latin *fluxiō* a flowing
▸ˈ**fluxional** *or* ˈ**fluxionary** ADJECTIVE ▸ˈ**fluxionally** ADVERB

fluxmeter (ˈflʌksˌmiːtə) NOUN any instrument for measuring magnetic flux, usually by measuring the charge that flows through a coil when the flux changes.

fly¹ (flaɪ) VERB **flies, flying, flew, flown.** 1 (*intr*) (of birds, aircraft, etc.) to move through the air in a controlled manner using aerodynamic forces. 2 to travel over (an area of land or sea) in an aircraft. 3 to operate (an aircraft or spacecraft). 4 to float, flutter, or be displayed in the air or cause to float, etc., in this way: *to fly a kite; they flew the flag.* 5 to transport or be transported by or through the air by aircraft, wind, etc. 6 (*intr*) to move or be moved very quickly, forcibly, or suddenly: *she came flying towards me; the door flew open.* 7 (*intr*) to pass swiftly: *time flies.* 8 to escape from (an enemy, place, etc.); flee: *he flew the country.* 9 (*intr;* may be foll by *at* or *upon*) to attack a person. 10 (*intr*) to have a sudden outburst: *he flew into a rage again.* 11 (*intr*) (of money, etc.) to vanish rapidly. 12 (*tr*) *Falconry* (of hawks) to fly at (quarry) in attack: *peregrines fly rooks.* 13 (*tr*) *Theatre* to suspend (scenery) above the stage so that it may be lowered into view. 14 **fly a kite. a** to procure money by an accommodation bill. **b** to release information or take a step in order to test public opinion. 15 **fly high.** *Informal* **a** to have a high aim. **b** to prosper or flourish. 16 **fly in the face of.** See **face** (sense 19). 17 **fly off the handle.** *Informal* to lose one's temper. 18 **fly the coop.** *US and Canadian informal* to leave suddenly. 19 **go fly a kite.** *US and Canadian informal* go away. 20 **let fly.** *Informal* **a** to lose one's temper (with a person): *she really let fly at him.* **b** to shoot or throw (an object). ◆ NOUN, *plural* **flies.** 21 (*often plural*) Also called: **fly front.** a closure that conceals a zip, buttons, or other fastening, by having one side overlapping, as on trousers. 22 Also called: **fly sheet. a** a flap forming the entrance to a tent. **b** a piece of canvas drawn over the ridgepole of a tent to form an outer roof. 23 a small air brake used to control the chiming of large clocks. 24 the horizontal weighted arm of a fly press. 25 **a** the outer edge of a flag. **b** the distance from the outer edge of a flag to the staff. Compare **hoist** (sense 9). 26 *Brit* a light one-horse covered carriage formerly let out on hire. 27 *Austral and NZ* an attempt: *I'll give it a fly.* 28 *Printing* **a** a device for transferring printed sheets from the press to a flat pile. **b** Also called: **flyhand.** a person who collects and stacks printed matter from a printing press. **c** a piece of paper folded once to make four pages, with printing only on the first page. 29 (*plural*) *Theatre* the space above the stage out of view of the audience, used for storing scenery, etc. 30 *Rare* the act of flying.
▷HISTORY Old English *flēogan*; related to Old Frisian *fliāga*, Old High German *fliogan*, Old Norse *fljūga*
▸ˈ**flyable** ADJECTIVE

fly² (flaɪ) NOUN, *plural* **flies.** 1 any dipterous insect, esp the housefly, characterized by active flight. See also **horsefly, blowfly, tsetse fly, crane fly.** 2 any of various similar but unrelated insects, such as the caddis fly, firefly, dragonfly, and chalcid fly. 3 *Angling* a lure made from a fish-hook dressed with feathers, tinsel, etc., to resemble any of various flies or nymphs: used in fly-fishing. See also **dry fly, wet fly.** 4 (in southern Africa) an area that is infested with the tsetse fly. 5 **drink with the flies.** *Austral slang* to drink alone. 6 **fly in amber.** See **amber** (sense 2). 7 **fly in the ointment.** *Informal* a slight flaw that detracts from value, completeness, or enjoyment. 8 **fly on the wall.** a person who watches others, while not being noticed himself. 9 **there are no flies on him, her,** etc. *Informal* he, she, etc., is no fool.
▷HISTORY Old English *flēoge*; related to Old Norse *fluga* Old High German *flioga*; see FLY¹
▸ˈ**flyless** ADJECTIVE

fly³ (flaɪ) ADJECTIVE *Slang* 1 *Chiefly Brit* knowing and sharp; smart. 2 *Chiefly Scot* furtive or sneaky. 3 *Chiefly Scot* in secret; sneakily.
▷HISTORY C19: of uncertain origin

fly agaric NOUN a saprotrophic agaricaceous woodland fungus, *Amanita muscaria*, having a scarlet cap with white warts and white gills: poisonous but rarely fatal. See also **amanita.**
▷HISTORY so named from its use as a poison on flypaper

fly ash NOUN fine solid particles of ash carried into the air during combustion, esp the combustion of pulverized fuel in power stations.

flyaway (ˈflaɪəˌweɪ) ADJECTIVE 1 (of hair or clothing) loose and fluttering. 2 frivolous or flighty; giddy. ◆ NOUN 3 a person who is frivolous or flighty.

flyback (ˈflaɪˌbæk) NOUN the fast return of the spot on a cathode-ray tube after completion of each trace.

flyblow (ˈflaɪˌbləʊ) VERB **-blows, -blowing, -blew, -blown.** 1 (*tr*) to contaminate, esp with the eggs or larvae of the blowfly; taint. ◆ NOUN 2 (*usually plural*) the egg or young larva of a blowfly, deposited on meat, paper, etc.

flyblown (ˈflaɪˌbləʊn) ADJECTIVE 1 covered with flyblows. 2 contaminated; tainted.

flyboat (ˈflaɪˌbəʊt) NOUN any small swift boat.

flybook (ˈflaɪˌbʊk) NOUN a small case or wallet used by anglers for storing artificial flies.

flyby (ˈflaɪˌbaɪ) NOUN, *plural* **-bys.** a flight past a particular position or target, esp the close approach of a spacecraft to a planet or satellite for investigation of conditions.

fly-by-light NOUN aircraft control through systems operated by optical fibres rather than mechanical rods. Abbreviation: **FBL.**

fly-by-night *Informal* ◆ ADJECTIVE 1 unreliable or untrustworthy, esp in finance. 2 brief; impermanent. ◆ NOUN, *also* **fly-by-nighter.** 3 an untrustworthy person, esp one who departs secretly or by night to avoid paying debts. 4 a person who goes out at night to places of entertainment.

fly-by-wire NOUN aircraft control through systems operated by electronic circuits rather than mechanical rods. Abbreviation: **FBW.**

flycatcher (ˈflaɪˌkætʃə) NOUN 1 any small insectivorous songbird of the Old World subfamily *Muscicapinae*, having small slender bills fringed with bristles: family *Muscicapidae*. See also **spotted flycatcher.** 2 any American passerine bird of the family *Tyrannidae.*

fly-drive ADJECTIVE, ADVERB describing a type of package-deal holiday in which the price includes outward and return flights and car hire while away.

flyer *or* **flier** (ˈflaɪə) NOUN 1 a person or thing that flies or moves very fast. 2 an aviator or pilot. 3 *Informal* a long flying leap; bound. 4 a fast-moving machine part, esp one having periodic motion. 5 a rectangular step in a straight flight of stairs. Compare **winder** (sense 5). 6 *Athletics* an informal word for **flying start.** 7 *Chiefly US* a speculative business transaction. 8 a small handbill.

fly-fish VERB (*intr*) *Angling* to fish using artificial flies as lures. See **dry fly, wet fly.**
▸ˈ**fly-ˌfisher** NOUN ▸ˈ**fly-ˌfishing** NOUN

fly half NOUN *Rugby* another name for **stand-off half.**

flying (ˈflaɪɪŋ) ADJECTIVE 1 (*prenominal*) hurried; fleeting: *a flying visit.* 2 (*prenominal*) designed for fast action. 3 (*prenominal*) moving or passing quickly on or as if on wings: *a flying leap; the flying hours.* 4 hanging, waving, or floating freely: *flying hair.* 5 *Nautical* (of a sail) not hauled in tight against the wind. ◆ NOUN 6 the act of piloting, navigating, or travelling in an aircraft. 7 (*modifier*) relating to, capable of, accustomed to, or adapted for flight: *a flying machine.* Related adjective: **volar.**

flying boat NOUN a seaplane in which the fuselage consists of a hull that provides buoyancy in the water.

flying bomb NOUN another name for the **V-1.**

flying bridge NOUN an auxiliary bridge of a vessel, usually built above or far outboard of the main bridge.

flying buttress NOUN a buttress supporting a wall or other structure by an arch or part of an arch that transmits the thrust outwards and downwards. Also called: **arc-boutant.**

flying circus NOUN 1 an exhibition of aircraft aerobatics. 2 the aircraft and men who take part in such exhibitions.

flying colours PLURAL NOUN conspicuous success; triumph: *he passed his test with flying colours.*

flying doctor NOUN (in areas of sparse or scattered population) a doctor who visits patients by aircraft.

Flying Dutchman NOUN *Legend* 1 a phantom

ship sighted in bad weather, esp off the Cape of Good Hope. [2] the captain of this ship.

flying field NOUN a small airport; an airfield.

flying fish NOUN any marine teleost fish of the family *Exocoetidae*, common in warm and tropical seas, having enlarged winglike pectoral fins used for gliding above the surface of the water.

flying fox NOUN [1] any large fruit bat, esp any of the genus *Pteropus* of tropical Africa and Asia: family *Pteropodidae*. [2] *Austral and NZ* a cable mechanism used for transportation across a river, gorge, etc. [3] a cable mechanism ridden for fun at an adventure playground, etc.

flying frog NOUN any of several tropical frogs of the family *Rhacophoridae*, esp *Rhacophorus reinwardtii* of Malaya, that glide between trees by means of long webbed digits.

flying gurnard NOUN any marine spiny-finned gurnard-like fish of the mostly tropical family *Dactylopteridae*, having enlarged fan-shaped pectoral fins used to glide above the surface of the sea.

flying jib NOUN the jib set furthest forward or outboard on a vessel with two or more jibs.

flying lemur NOUN either of the two arboreal mammals of the genus *Cynocephalus*, family *Cynocephalidae*, and order *Dermoptera*, of S and SE Asia. They resemble lemurs but have a fold of skin between the limbs enabling movement by gliding leaps. Also called: **colugo**.

flying lizard *or* **dragon** NOUN any lizard of the genus *Draco*, of S and SE Asia, having an extensible fold of skin on each side of the body, used to make gliding leaps: family *Agamidae* (agamas).

flying mare NOUN a wrestling throw in which a wrestler seizes his opponent's arm or head (**flying head mare**) and turns to throw him over his shoulder.

flying officer NOUN an officer holding commissioned rank senior to a pilot officer but junior to a flight lieutenant in the British and certain other air forces.

flying phalanger NOUN any nocturnal arboreal phalanger of the genus *Petaurus*, of E Australia and New Guinea, having black-striped greyish fur and moving with gliding leaps using folds of skin between the hind limbs and forelimbs. Also called: **glider**.

flying picket NOUN (in industrial disputes) a member of a group of pickets organized to be able to move quickly from place to place.

flying saucer NOUN any disc-shaped flying object alleged to come from outer space.

flying-spot ADJECTIVE denoting an electronic system in which a rapidly moving spot of light is used to encode or decode data, for example to obtain a television signal by scanning a photographic film or slide.

flying squad NOUN a small group of police, soldiers, etc., ready to move into action quickly.

flying squirrel NOUN any nocturnal sciurine rodent of the subfamily *Petauristinae*, of Asia and North America. Furry folds of skin between the forelegs and hind legs enable these animals to move by gliding leaps.

flying start NOUN [1] Also called (informal): **flyer**. (in sprinting) a start by a competitor anticipating the starting signal. [2] a start to a race or time trial in which the competitor is already travelling at speed as he passes the starting line. [3] any promising beginning. [4] an initial advantage over others.

flying wing NOUN [1] an aircraft consisting mainly of one large wing and no fuselage or tailplane. [2] (in Canadian football) the twelfth player, who has a variable position behind the scrimmage line.

flyleaf ('flaɪˌliːf) NOUN, *plural* **-leaves**. the inner leaf of the endpaper of a book, pasted to the first leaf.

flyman ('flaɪmən) NOUN, *plural* **-men**. *Theatre* a stagehand who operates the scenery, curtains, etc., in the flies.

fly orchid NOUN a European orchid, *Ophrys insectifera*, whose flowers resemble and attract certain wasps: found in wood margins and scrub on lime-rich soils.

flyover ('flaɪˌəuvə) NOUN [1] Also called: **overpass**. *Brit* **a** an intersection of two roads at which one is carried over the other by a bridge. **b** such a bridge. [2] the US name for a **fly-past**.

flypaper ('flaɪˌpeɪpə) NOUN paper with a sticky and poisonous coating, usually hung from the ceiling to trap flies.

fly-past NOUN a ceremonial flight of aircraft over a given area. Also called (esp US): **flyover**.

flyposting ('flaɪˌpəustɪŋ) NOUN the posting of advertising or political bills, posters, etc. in unauthorized places.

fly press NOUN a hand-operated press in which a horizontal beam with heavy steel balls attached to the ends gives additional momentum to the descending member used to punch or compress material.

Fly River NOUN a river in W Papua New Guinea, flowing southeast to the Gulf of Papua. Length: about 1300 km (800 miles).

fly rod NOUN a light flexible rod, now usually made of fibreglass or split cane, used in fly-fishing.

Flysch (flɪʃ) NOUN (*sometimes not capital*) a marine sedimentary facies consisting of a sequence of sandstones, conglomerates, marls, shales, and clays that were formed by erosion during a period of mountain building and subsequently deformed as the mountain building continued. The phenomenon was first observed in the Alps.
▷HISTORY Swiss German

flyscreen ('flaɪˌskriːn) NOUN a wire-mesh screen over a window to prevent flies from entering a room.

fly sheet NOUN [1] another name for **fly** (sense 22). [2] a short handbill or circular.

flyspeck ('flaɪˌspɛk) NOUN [1] the small speck of the excrement of a fly. [2] a small spot or speck. ◆ VERB [3] (*tr*) to mark with flyspecks.

fly spray NOUN a liquid used to destroy flies and other insects, sprayed from an aerosol.

flystrike ('flaɪˌstraɪk) NOUN the infestation of wounded sheep by blowflies or maggots.

flyte (flaɪt; *Scot* fləɪt) VERB a variant spelling of **flite**.

fly-tipping NOUN the deliberate dumping of rubbish in an unauthorized place.

flytrap ('flaɪˌtræp) NOUN [1] any of various insectivorous plants, esp Venus's flytrap. [2] a device for catching flies.

fly way NOUN the usual route used by birds when migrating.

flyweight ('flaɪˌweɪt) NOUN [1] **a** a professional boxer weighing not more than 112 pounds (51 kg). **b** an amateur boxer weighing 48–51 kg (106–112 pounds). **c** (*as modifier*): *a flyweight contest*. [2] (in Olympic wrestling) a wrestler weighing not more than 115 pounds (52 kg).

flywheel ('flaɪˌwiːl) NOUN a heavy wheel that stores kinetic energy and smooths the operation of a reciprocating engine by maintaining a constant speed of rotation over the whole cycle.

fm ABBREVIATION FOR: [1] Also: **fm.** fathom. [2] from. ◆ [3] THE INTERNET DOMAIN NAME FOR Micronesia.

Fm THE CHEMICAL SYMBOL FOR fermium.

FM ABBREVIATION FOR: [1] frequency modulation. [2] Field Marshal. [3] *Aeronautics* figure of merit.

FMCG ABBREVIATION FOR fast-moving consumer goods.

FMD ABBREVIATION FOR **foot-and-mouth disease**.

FMN NOUN *Biochem* flavin mononucleotide; a phosphoric ester of riboflavin that acts as the prosthetic group for many flavoproteins. See also **FAD**.

FMRI ABBREVIATION FOR functional magnetic resonance imaging: a technique that directly measures the blood flow in the brain, thereby providing information on brain activity.

FMS *Aeronautics* ABBREVIATION FOR flight management systems.

f-number *or* **f number** NOUN *Photog* the numerical value of the relative aperture. If the relative aperture is f8, 8 is the f-number and indicates that the focal length of the lens is 8 times the size of the lens aperture. See also **T-number**.

fo THE INTERNET DOMAIN NAME FOR Faeroe Islands.

FO ABBREVIATION FOR: [1] *Army* Field Officer. [2] *Air Force* Flying Officer. [3] Foreign Office. ◆ [4] INTERNATIONAL CAR REGISTRATION FOR Faeroe Islands.
▷HISTORY (for sense 4) from Faeroese *Fōroyar*

fo. ABBREVIATION FOR folio.

foal (fəul) NOUN [1] the young of a horse or related animal. ◆ VERB [2] to give birth to (a foal).
▷HISTORY Old English *fola*; related to Old Frisian *fola*, Old High German *folo* foal, Latin *pullus* young creature, Greek *pōlos* foal

foam (fəum) NOUN [1] a mass of small bubbles of gas formed on the surface of a liquid, such as the froth produced by agitating a solution of soap or detergent in water. [2] frothy saliva sometimes formed in and expelled from the mouth, as in rabies. [3] the frothy sweat of a horse or similar animal. [4] **a** any of a number of light cellular solids made by creating bubbles of gas in the liquid material and solidifying it: used as insulators and in packaging. **b** (*as modifier*): *foam rubber; foam plastic*. [5] a colloid consisting of a gas suspended in a liquid. [6] a mixture of chemicals sprayed from a fire extinguisher onto a burning substance to create a stable layer of bubbles which smothers the flames. [7] a poetic word for the **sea**. ◆ VERB [8] to produce or cause to produce foam; froth. [9] (*intr*) to be very angry (esp in the phrase **foam at the mouth**).
▷HISTORY Old English *fām*; related to Old High German *feim*, Latin *spūma*, Sanskrit *phena*
▸ **'foamless** ADJECTIVE ▸ **'foam,like** ADJECTIVE

foamflower ('fəumˌflauə) NOUN a perennial saxifragaceous plant, *Tiarella cordifolia*, of North America and Asia, having spring-blooming white flowers.

foamy ('fəumɪ) ADJECTIVE **foamier, foamiest**. of, resembling, consisting of, or covered with foam.
▸ **'foamily** ADVERB ▸ **'foaminess** NOUN

fob[1] (fɒb) NOUN [1] a chain or ribbon by which a pocket watch is attached to a waistcoat. [2] any ornament hung on such a chain. [3] a small pocket in a man's waistcoat, for holding a watch. [4] a metal or plastic tab on a key ring.
▷HISTORY C17: probably of Germanic origin; compare German dialect *Fuppe* pocket

fob[2] (fɒb) VERB **fobs, fobbing, fobbed**. an archaic word for **cheat**.
▷HISTORY C15: probably from German *foppen* to trick

f.o.b. *or* **FOB** *Commerce* ABBREVIATION FOR free on board.

fob off VERB (*tr, adverb*) [1] to appease or trick (a person) with lies or excuses. [2] to dispose of (goods) by trickery.

FoC ABBREVIATION FOR father of the chapel.

focaccia (fəˈkætʃə) NOUN a flat Italian bread made with olive oil and yeast.
▷HISTORY from Italian

focal ('fəukəl) ADJECTIVE [1] of or relating to a focus. [2] situated at, passing through, or measured from the focus.
▸ **'focally** ADVERB

focal infection NOUN a bacterial infection limited to a specific part of the body, such as the tonsils or a gland.

focalize *or* **focalise** ('fəukəˌlaɪz) VERB a less common word for **focus**.
▸ **ˌfocali'zation** *or* **ˌfocali'sation** NOUN

focal length *or* **distance** NOUN the distance from the focal point of a lens or mirror to the reflecting surface of the mirror or the centre point of the lens.

focal plane NOUN [1] the plane that is perpendicular to the axis of a lens or mirror and passes through the focal point. [2] the plane in a telescope, camera, or other optical instrument in which a real image is in focus.

focal point NOUN [1] Also called: **principal focus, focus**. the point on the axis of a lens or mirror to which parallel rays of light converge or from which they appear to diverge after refraction or reflection. [2] a central point of attention or interest.

focal ratio NOUN *Photog* another name for **f-number**.

focometer (fəuˈkɒmɪtə) NOUN an instrument for measuring the focal length of a lens.

fo'c's'le *or* **fo'c'sle** ('fəuksəl) NOUN a variant spelling of **forecastle**.

focus ('fəʊkəs) NOUN, *plural* **-cuses** *or* **-ci** (-saɪ, -kaɪ, -kiː). 1 a point of convergence of light or other electromagnetic radiation, particles, sound waves, etc., or a point from which they appear to diverge. 2 another name for **focal point** (sense 1), **focal length.** 3 *Optics* the state of an optical image when it is distinct and clearly defined or the state of an instrument producing this image: *the picture is in focus; the telescope is out of focus.* 4 a point upon which attention, activity, etc., is directed or concentrated. 5 *Geometry* a fixed reference point on the concave side of a conic section, used when defining its eccentricity. 6 the point beneath the earth's surface at which an earthquake or underground nuclear explosion originates. Compare **epicentre.** 7 *Pathol* the main site of an infection or a localized region of diseased tissue. ◆ VERB **-cuses, -cusing, -cused** *or* **-cusses, -cussing, -cussed.** 8 to bring or come to a focus or into focus. 9 (*tr;* often foll by *on*) to fix attention (on); concentrate.
▷HISTORY C17: via New Latin from Latin: hearth, fireplace
▸ **'focusable** ADJECTIVE ▸ **'focuser** NOUN

focused strategy NOUN a business strategy in which an organization divests itself of all but its core activities, using the funds raised to enhance the distinctive abilities that give it an advantage over its rivals.

focus group NOUN a group of people brought together to give their opinions on a particular issue or product, often for the purpose of market research.

focus puller NOUN *Films* the member of a camera crew who adjusts the focus of the lens as the camera is tracked in or out.

fodder ('fɒdə) NOUN 1 bulk feed for livestock, esp hay, straw, etc. 2 raw experience or material: *fodder for the imagination.* ◆ VERB 3 (*tr*) to supply (livestock) with fodder.
▷HISTORY Old English *fōdor;* related to Old Norse *fōthr,* Old High German *fuotar;* see FOOD, FORAGE

foe (fəʊ) NOUN *Formal or literary* another word for **enemy.**
▷HISTORY Old English *fāh* hostile; related to Old High German *fēhan* to hate, Old Norse *feikn* dreadful; see FEUD[1]

FoE *or* **FOE** ABBREVIATION FOR Friends of the Earth.

foehn (fɜːn; *German* føːn) NOUN *Meteorol* a variant spelling of **föhn.**

foeman ('fəʊmən) NOUN, *plural* **-men.** *Archaic or poetic* an enemy in war; foe.

foetal ('fiːtᵊl) ADJECTIVE a variant spelling of **fetal.**

foetation (fiː'teɪʃən) NOUN a variant spelling of **fetation.**

foeticide ('fiːtɪˌsaɪd) NOUN a variant spelling of **feticide.**
▸ **ˌfoeti'cidal** ADJECTIVE

foetid ('fetɪd, 'fiː-) ADJECTIVE a variant spelling of **fetid.**
▸ **'foetidly** ADVERB ▸ **'foetidness** NOUN

foetor ('fiːtə) NOUN a variant spelling of **fetor.**

foetus ('fiːtəs) NOUN, *plural* **-tuses.** a variant spelling of **fetus.**

fog[1] (fɒg) NOUN 1 a mass of droplets of condensed water vapour suspended in the air, often greatly reducing visibility, corresponding to a cloud but at a lower level. 2 a cloud of any substance in the atmosphere reducing visibility. 3 a state of mental uncertainty or obscurity. 4 *Photog* a blurred or discoloured area on a developed negative, print, or transparency caused by the action of extraneous light, incorrect development, etc. 5 a colloid or suspension consisting of liquid particles dispersed in a gas. ◆ VERB **fogs, fogging, fogged.** 6 to envelop or become enveloped with or as if with fog. 7 to confuse or become confused: *to fog an issue.* 8 *Photog* to produce fog on (a negative, print, or transparency) or (of a negative, print, or transparency) to be affected by fog.
▷HISTORY C16: perhaps back formation from *foggy* damp, boggy, from FOG[2]

fog[2] (fɒg) NOUN **a** a second growth of grass after the first mowing. **b** grass left to grow long in winter.
▷HISTORY C14: probably of Scandinavian origin; compare Norwegian *fogg* rank grass

fog bank NOUN a distinct mass of fog, esp at sea.

fogbound ('fɒgˌbaʊnd) ADJECTIVE 1 prevented from operation by fog: *the airport was fogbound.* 2 obscured by or enveloped in fog: *the skyscraper was fogbound.*

fogbow ('fɒgˌbəʊ) NOUN a faint arc of light sometimes seen in a fog bank. Also called: **seadog, white rainbow.**

fogdog ('fɒgˌdɒg) NOUN a whitish spot sometimes seen in fog near the horizon. Also called: **seadog.**

fogey *or* **fogy** ('fəʊgɪ) NOUN, *plural* **-geys** *or* **-gies.** an extremely fussy, old-fashioned, or conservative person (esp in the phrase **old fogey**).
▷HISTORY C18: of unknown origin
▸ **'fogeyish** *or* **'fogyish** ADJECTIVE ▸ **'fogeyism** *or* **'fogyism** NOUN

fog fever NOUN *Vet science* an acute respiratory disease of cattle, with a high mortality, that can occur after grazing fog.

foggage ('fɒgɪdʒ) NOUN grass grown for winter grazing.

fogged (fɒgd) *or* **foggy** ADJECTIVE *Photog* affected or obscured by fog.

Foggia (*Italian* 'fɔddʒa) NOUN a city in SE Italy, in Apulia: seat of Emperor Frederick II; centre for Carbonari revolutionary societies in the revolts of 1820, 1848, and 1860. Pop.: 154 891 (2000 est.).

foggy ('fɒgɪ) ADJECTIVE **-gier, -giest.** 1 thick with fog. 2 obscure or confused. 3 another word for **fogged.** 4 **not the foggiest (idea** *or* **notion).** no idea whatsoever: *I haven't the foggiest.*
▸ **'foggily** ADVERB ▸ **'fogginess** NOUN

foghorn ('fɒgˌhɔːn) NOUN 1 a mechanical instrument sounded at intervals to serve as a warning to vessels in fog. 2 *Informal* a loud deep resounding voice.

fog lamp NOUN a powerful light for use in foggy conditions, usually positioned low down on the front or rear of a road vehicle.

fog level NOUN the density produced by the development of photographic materials that have not been exposed to light or other actinic radiation. It forms part of the characteristic curve of a particular material.

fog light NOUN another word for **fog lamp.**

fog signal NOUN a signal used to warn railway engine drivers in fog, consisting of a detonator placed on the line.

föhn *or* **foehn** (fɜːn; *German* føːn) NOUN a warm dry wind blowing down the northern slopes of the Alps. It originates as moist air blowing from the Mediterranean, rising on reaching the Alps and cooling at the saturated adiabatic lapse rate, and descending on the leeward side, warming at the dry adiabatic lapse rate, thus gaining heat. See also **lapse rate.**
▷HISTORY German, from Old High German *phōnno,* from Latin *favōnius;* related to *fovēre* to warm

foible ('fɔɪbᵊl) NOUN 1 a slight peculiarity or minor weakness; idiosyncrasy. 2 the most vulnerable part of a sword's blade, from the middle to the tip. Compare **forte**[1] (sense 2).
▷HISTORY C17: from obsolete French, from obsolete adjective: FEEBLE

foie gras (*French* fwa grɑ) NOUN See **pâté de foie gras.**

foil[1] (fɔɪl) VERB (*tr*) 1 to baffle or frustrate (a person, attempt, etc.). 2 *Hunting* (of hounds, hunters, etc.) to obliterate the scent left by a hunted animal or (of a hunted animal) to run back over its own trail. 3 *Archaic* to repulse or defeat (an attack or assailant). ◆ NOUN 4 *Hunting* any scent that obscures the trail left by a hunted animal. 5 *Archaic* a setback or defeat.
▷HISTORY C13 *foilen* to trample, from Old French *fouler,* from Old French *fuler* tread down, FULL[2]
▸ **'foilable** ADJECTIVE

foil[2] (fɔɪl) NOUN 1 metal in the form of very thin sheets: *gold foil; tin foil.* 2 the thin metallic sheet forming the backing of a mirror. 3 a thin leaf of shiny metal set under a gemstone to add brightness or colour. 4 a person or thing that gives contrast to another. 5 *Architect* a small arc between cusps, esp as used in Gothic window tracery. 6 short for **aerofoil** or **hydrofoil.** ◆ VERB (*tr*) 7 to back or cover with foil. 8 Also: **foliate.** *Architect* to ornament (windows) with foils.
▷HISTORY C14: from Old French *foille,* from Latin *folia* leaves, plural of *folium*

foil[3] (fɔɪl) NOUN a light slender flexible sword tipped by a button and usually having a bell-shaped guard.
▷HISTORY C16: of unknown origin

foilsman ('fɔɪlzmən) NOUN, *plural* **-men.** *Fencing* a person who uses or specializes in using a foil.

foin (fɔɪn) *Archaic* ◆ NOUN 1 a thrust or lunge with a weapon. ◆ VERB 2 to thrust with a weapon.
▷HISTORY C14: probably from Old French *foine,* from Latin *fuscina* trident

Foism ('fəʊˌɪzəm) NOUN Chinese Buddhism, the version introduced from India from the 4th century A.D. onwards and essentially belonging to the Mahayana school.
▷HISTORY from Mandarin Chinese *fo* BUDDHA
▸ **'Foist** NOUN, ADJECTIVE

foison ('fɔɪzᵊn) NOUN *Archaic or poetic* a plentiful supply or yield.
▷HISTORY C13: from Old French, from Latin *fūsiō* a pouring out, from *fundere* to pour; see FUSION

foist (fɔɪst) VERB (*tr*) 1 (often foll by *off* or *on*) to sell or pass off (something, esp an inferior article) as genuine, valuable, etc. 2 (usually foll by *in* or *into*) to insert surreptitiously or wrongfully.
▷HISTORY C16: probably from obsolete Dutch *vuisten* to enclose in one's hand, from Middle Dutch *vuist* fist

fol. ABBREVIATION FOR: 1 folio. 2 following.

folacin ('fɒləsɪn) NOUN another name for **folic acid.**
▷HISTORY C20: from FOL(IC) AC(ID) + -IN

fold[1] (fəʊld) VERB 1 to bend or be bent double so that one part covers another: *to fold a sheet of paper.* 2 (*tr*) to bring together and intertwine (the arms, legs, etc.): *she folded her hands.* 3 (*tr*) (of birds, insects, etc.) to close (the wings) together from an extended position. 4 (*tr;* often foll by *up* or *in*) to enclose in or as if in a surrounding material. 5 (*tr;* foll by *in*) to clasp (a person) in the arms. 6 (*tr;* usually foll by *round, about, etc*) to wind (around); entwine. 7 (*tr*) *Poetic* to cover completely: *night folded the earth.* 8 Also: **fold in.** (*tr*) to mix (a whisked mixture) with other ingredients by gently turning one part over the other with a spoon. 9 to produce a bend (in stratified rock) or (of stratified rock) to display a bend. 10 (*intr;* often foll by *up*) *Informal* to collapse; fail: *the business folded.* ◆ NOUN 11 a piece or section that has been folded: *a fold of cloth.* 12 a mark, crease, or hollow made by folding. 13 a hollow in undulating terrain. 14 a bend in stratified rocks that results from movements within the earth's crust and produces such structures as anticlines and synclines. 15 *Anatomy* another word for **plica** (sense 1). 16 a coil, as in a rope, etc. 17 an act of folding. ◆ See also **fold up.**
▷HISTORY Old English *fealdan;* related to Old Norse *falda* , Old High German *faldan,* Latin *duplus* double, Greek *haploos* simple
▸ **'foldable** ADJECTIVE

fold[2] (fəʊld) NOUN 1 **a** a small enclosure or pen for sheep or other livestock, where they can be gathered. **b** the sheep or other livestock gathered in such an enclosure. **c** a flock of sheep. 2 a church or the members of it. 3 any group or community sharing a way of life or holding the same values. ◆ VERB 4 (*tr*) to gather or confine (sheep or other livestock) in a fold.
▷HISTORY Old English *falod;* related to Old Saxon *faled,* Middle Dutch *vaelt*

-fold SUFFIX FORMING ADJECTIVES AND ADVERBS having so many parts, being so many times as much or as many, or multiplied by so much or so many: *threefold; three-hundredfold.*
▷HISTORY Old English *-fald, -feald*

fold-and-thrust belt NOUN *Geology* a linear or arcuate region of the earth's surface that has been subjected to severe folding and thrust faulting.

foldaway ('fəʊldəˌweɪ) ADJECTIVE (*prenominal*) (of a bed) able to be folded and put away when not in use.

foldback ('fəʊldˌbæk) NOUN (in multitrack recording) a process for returning a signal to a performer instantly. Also called: **cueing.**

foldboat ('fəʊldˌbəʊt) NOUN another name for **faltboat.**

folded dipole NOUN a type of aerial, widely used with television and VHF radio receivers, consisting of two parallel dipoles connected together at their outer ends and fed at the centre of one of them.

The length is usually half the operating wavelength.

folder (ˈfəʊldə) NOUN 1 a binder or file for holding loose papers, etc. 2 a folded circular. 3 a machine for folding printed sheets. 4 a person or thing that folds. 5 *Computing* another name for **directory** (sense 5).

folderol (ˈfɒldəˌrɒl) NOUN a variant of **falderal.**

folding door NOUN a door in the form of two or more vertical hinged leaves that can be folded one against another.

folding money NOUN *Informal* paper money.

folding press NOUN a fall in wrestling won by folding one's opponent's legs up to his head and pressing his shoulders to the floor.

foldout (ˈfəʊldˌaʊt) NOUN *Printing* another name for **gatefold.**

fold up VERB *(adverb)* 1 *(tr)* to make smaller or more compact. 2 *(intr)* to collapse, as with laughter or pain.

foley *or* **foley artist** (ˈfəʊlɪ) NOUN *Films* the US name for **footsteps editor.**
▷HISTORY C20: named after the inventor of the technique

folia (ˈfəʊlɪə) NOUN the plural of **folium.**

foliaceous (ˌfəʊlɪˈeɪʃəs) ADJECTIVE 1 having the appearance of the leaf of a plant. 2 bearing leaves or leaflike structures. 3 *Geology* (of certain rocks, esp schists) consisting of thin layers; foliated.
▷HISTORY C17: from Latin *foliāceus*

foliage (ˈfəʊlɪɪdʒ) NOUN 1 the green leaves of a plant. 2 sprays of leaves used for decoration. 3 an ornamental leaflike design.
▷HISTORY C15: from Old French *fuellage*, from *fuelle* leaf; influenced in form by Latin *folium*
▸ˈ**foliaged** ADJECTIVE

foliar (ˈfəʊlɪə) ADJECTIVE of or relating to a leaf or leaves.
▷HISTORY C19: from French *foliaire*, from Latin *folium* leaf

foliate ADJECTIVE (ˈfəʊlɪɪt, -ˌeɪt) 1 **a** relating to, possessing, or resembling leaves. **b** in combination: *trifoliate.* 2 (of certain metamorphic rocks, esp schists) having the constituent minerals arranged in thin leaflike layers. ◆ VERB (ˈfəʊlɪˌeɪt) 3 *(tr)* to ornament with foliage or with leaf forms such as foils. 4 to hammer or cut (metal) into thin plates or foil. 5 *(tr)* to coat or back (glass, etc.) with metal foil. 6 *(tr)* to number the leaves of (a book, manuscript, etc.). Compare **paginate.** 7 *(intr)* (of plants) to grow leaves.
▷HISTORY C17: from Latin *foliātus* leaved, leafy

foliated (ˈfəʊlɪˌeɪtɪd) ADJECTIVE 1 *Architect* ornamented with or made up of foliage or foils. 2 (of rocks and minerals, esp schists) composed of thin easily separable layers. 3 (esp of parts of animals or plants) resembling a leaf.

foliation (ˌfəʊlɪˈeɪʃən) NOUN 1 *Botany* **a** the process of producing leaves. **b** the state of being in leaf. **c** the arrangement of leaves in a leaf bud; vernation. 2 *Architect* **a** ornamentation consisting of foliage. **b** ornamentation consisting of cusps and foils. 3 any decoration with foliage. 4 the consecutive numbering of the leaves of a book. 5 *Geology* the arrangement of the constituents of a rock in leaflike layers, as in schists.

folic acid (ˈfəʊlɪk, ˈfɒl-) NOUN any of a group of vitamins of the B complex, including pteroylglutamic acid and its derivatives: used in the treatment of megaloblastic anaemia. Also called: **folacin.**
▷HISTORY C20: from Latin *folium* leaf; so called because it may be obtained from green leaves

folie à deux (ˈfɒlɪ æ ˈdɜː) NOUN *Psychiatry* mental illness occurring simultaneously in two intimately related persons who share some of the elements of the illness, such as delusions.
▷HISTORY French: madness involving two (people)

folie de grandeur *French* (fɔli də ɡrɑ̃dœr) NOUN delusions of grandeur.
▷HISTORY literally: madness of grandeur

folio (ˈfəʊlɪəʊ) NOUN, *plural* **-lios.** 1 a sheet of paper folded in half to make two leaves for a book or manuscript. 2 a book or manuscript of the largest common size made up of such sheets. 3 a leaf of paper or parchment numbered on the front side only. 4 a page number in a book. 5 *Law* a unit of measurement of the length of legal documents, determined by the number of words, generally 72 or 90 in Britain and 100 in the US. 6 *NZ* a collection of related material. ◆ ADJECTIVE 7 relating to or having the format of a folio: *a folio edition.* ◆ VERB **-lios, -lioing, -lioed.** 8 *(tr)* to number the leaves of (a book) consecutively.
▷HISTORY C16: from Latin phrase *in foliō* in a leaf, from *folium* leaf

foliolate (ˈfəʊlɪəˌleɪt, fəʊˈlɪəlɪt, -ˌleɪt) ADJECTIVE *Botany* possessing or relating to leaflets.
▷HISTORY C19: from Late Latin *foliolum* little leaf, from Latin *folium* leaf

foliose (ˈfəʊlɪˌəʊs, -ˌəʊz) ADJECTIVE another word for **foliaceous** (senses 1, 2).
▷HISTORY C18: from Latin *foliōsus* full of leaves

folium (ˈfəʊlɪəm) NOUN, *plural* **-lia** (-lɪə). 1 a plane geometrical curve consisting of a loop whose two ends, intersecting at a node, are asymptotic to the same line. Standard equation: $x^3 + y^3 - 3axy$ where $x = y + a$ is the equation of the line. 2 any thin leaflike layer, esp of some metamorphic rocks.
▷HISTORY C19: from Latin, literally: leaf

folk (fəʊk) NOUN, *plural* **folk** *or* **folks.** 1 *(functioning as plural; often plural in form)* people in general, esp those of a particular group or class: *country folk.* 2 *(functioning as plural; usually plural in form) Informal* members of a family. 3 *(functioning as singular) Informal* short for **folk music.** 4 a people or tribe. 5 *(modifier)* relating to, originating from, or traditional to the common people of a country: *a folk song.*
▷HISTORY Old English *folc*; related to Old Saxon, Old Norse, Old High German *folk*
▸ˈ**folkish** ADJECTIVE ▸ˈ**folkishness** NOUN

folk art NOUN the visual arts, music, drama, dance, or literature originating from, or traditional to, the common people of a country.

folk dance NOUN 1 any of various traditional rustic dances often originating from festivals or rituals. 2 a piece of music composed for such a dance. ◆ VERB **folk-dance.** *(intr)* 3 to perform a folk dance.
▸**folk dancing** NOUN

Folkestone (ˈfəʊkstən) NOUN a port and resort in SE England, in E Kent. Pop.: 45 587 (1991).

Folketing (ˈfəʊlkətɪŋ; *Danish* ˈfɔlgəteŋ) NOUN the unicameral Danish parliament.
▷HISTORY Danish, from *folk* the people, FOLK + Old Norse *thing* assembly

folk etymology NOUN 1 the gradual change in the form of a word through the influence of a more familiar word or phrase with which it becomes associated, as for example *sparrow-grass* for *asparagus.* 2 a popular but erroneous conception of the origin of a word.

folkie *or* **folky** (ˈfəʊkɪ) NOUN, *plural* **-ies.** a devotee of folk music.

folklore (ˈfəʊkˌlɔː) NOUN 1 the unwritten literature of a people as expressed in folk tales, proverbs, riddles, songs, etc. 2 the body of stories and legends attached to a particular place, group, activity, etc.: *Hollywood folklore; rugby folklore.* 3 the anthropological discipline concerned with the study of folkloric materials.
▸ˈ**folkˌloric** ADJECTIVE ▸ˈ**folkˌlorist** NOUN, ADJECTIVE
▸ˌ**folklorˈistic** ADJECTIVE

folk medicine NOUN the traditional art of medicine as practised among rustic communities and primitive peoples, consisting typically of the use of herbal remedies, fruits and vegetables thought to have healing power, etc.

folk memory NOUN the memory of past events as preserved in a community.

folkmoot (ˈfəʊkˌmuːt), **folkmote,** *or* **folkmot** (ˈfəʊkˌməʊt) NOUN (in early medieval England) an assembly of the people of a district, town, or shire.
▷HISTORY Old English *folcmōt*, from *folc* FOLK + *mōt* from *mǣtan* to MEET[1]

folk music NOUN 1 music that is passed on from generation to generation by oral tradition. Compare **art music.** 2 any music composed in the idiom of this oral tradition.

folk-rock NOUN a style of rock music influenced by folk, including traditional material arranged for electric instruments.

folk singer NOUN a person who sings folk songs or other songs in the folk idiom.
▸**folk singing** NOUN

folk song NOUN 1 a song of which the music and text have been handed down by oral tradition among the common people. 2 a modern song which employs or reflects the folk idiom.

folksy (ˈfəʊksɪ) ADJECTIVE **-sier, -siest.** 1 of or like ordinary people; sometimes used derogatorily to describe affected simplicity. 2 *Informal, chiefly US and Canadian* friendly; affable. 3 of or relating to folk art.
▸ˈ**folksiness** NOUN

folk tale *or* **story** NOUN a tale or legend originating among a people and typically becoming part of an oral tradition.

folkways (ˈfəʊkˌweɪz) PLURAL NOUN *Sociol* traditional and customary ways of living.

folk weave NOUN a type of fabric with a loose weave.

foll. ABBREVIATION FOR followed.

follicle (ˈfɒlɪkᵊl) NOUN 1 any small sac or cavity in the body having an excretory, secretory, or protective function: *a hair follicle.* 2 *Botany* a dry fruit, formed from a single carpel, that splits along one side only to release its seeds: occurs in larkspur and columbine.
▷HISTORY C17: from Latin *folliculus* small bag, from *follis* pair of bellows, leather money-bag
▸**follicular** (fɒˈlɪkjʊlə), **folliculate** (fɒˈlɪkjʊˌleɪt), *or* **folˈlicuˌlated** ADJECTIVE

follicle-stimulating hormone NOUN a gonadotrophic hormone secreted by the pituitary gland that stimulates maturation of ovarian follicles in female mammals and growth of seminiferous tubules in males. Abbreviation: **FSH.** See also **luteinizing hormone, prolactin.**

folliculin (fɒˈlɪkjʊlɪn) NOUN another name for **oestrone.**

follow (ˈfɒləʊ) VERB 1 to go or come after in the same direction: *he followed his friend home.* 2 *(tr)* to accompany; attend: *she followed her sister everywhere.* 3 to come after as a logical or natural consequence. 4 *(tr)* to keep to the course or track of: *she followed the towpath.* 5 *(tr)* to act in accordance with; obey: *to follow instructions.* 6 *(tr)* to accept the ideas or beliefs of (a previous authority, etc.): *he followed Donne in most of his teachings.* 7 to understand (an explanation, argument, etc.): *the lesson was difficult to follow.* 8 to watch closely or continuously: *she followed his progress carefully.* 9 *(tr)* to have a keen interest in: *to follow athletics.* 10 *(tr)* to help in the cause of or accept the leadership of: *the men who followed Napoleon.* 11 *(tr) Rare* to earn a living at or in: *to follow the Navy.* 12 **follow suit.** *Cards* **a** to play a card of the same suit as the card played immediately before it. **b** to do the same as someone else. ◆ NOUN 13 *Billiards, snooker* **a** a forward spin imparted to a cue ball causing it to roll after the object ball. **b** a shot made in this way. ◆ See also **follow-on, follow out, follow through, follow up.**
▷HISTORY Old English *folgian*; related to Old Frisian *folgia*, Old Saxon *folgōn*, Old High German *folgēn*
▸ˈ**followable** ADJECTIVE

follower (ˈfɒləʊə) NOUN 1 a person who accepts the teachings of another; disciple; adherent: *a follower of Marx.* 2 an attendant or henchman. 3 an enthusiast or supporter, as of a sport or team. 4 (esp formerly) a male admirer. 5 *Rare* a pursuer. 6 a machine part that derives its motion by following the motion of another part.

following (ˈfɒləʊɪŋ) ADJECTIVE 1 **a** *(prenominal)* about to be mentioned, specified, etc.: *the following items.* **b** *(as noun)*: *will the following please raise their hands?* 2 (of winds, currents, etc.) moving in the same direction as the course of a vessel. ◆ NOUN 3 a group of supporters or enthusiasts: *he attracted a large following wherever he played.* ◆ PREPOSITION 4 as a result of: *he was arrested following a tip-off.*

Language note The use of *following* to mean *as a result of* is very common in journalism, but should be avoided in other kinds of writing.

follow-my-leader NOUN a game in which the players must repeat the actions of the leader. US, Canadian, and Irish name: **follow-the-leader.**

follow-on *Cricket* ◆ NOUN 1 an immediate second innings forced on a team scoring a prescribed number of runs fewer than its opponents in the first innings. ◆ VERB **follow on.** 2 (*intr, adverb*) (of a team) to play a follow-on.

follow out VERB (*tr, adverb*) to implement (an idea or action) to a conclusion.

followship ('fɒləʊʃɪp) NOUN the practice of doing what other people suggest, rather than taking the lead.

follow through VERB (*adverb*) 1 *Sport* to complete (a stroke or shot) by continuing the movement to the end of its arc. 2 (*tr*) to pursue (an aim) to a conclusion. ◆ NOUN **follow-through.** 3 *Sport* **a** the act of following through. **b** the part of the stroke after the ball has been hit. 4 the completion of a procedure, esp after a first action.

follow up VERB (*tr, adverb*) 1 to pursue or investigate (a person, evidence, etc.) closely. 2 to continue (action) after a beginning, esp to increase its effect. ◆ NOUN **follow-up.** 3 **a** something done to reinforce an initial action. **b** (*as modifier*): *a follow-up letter.* 4 *Med* a routine examination of a patient at various intervals after medical or surgical treatment.

folly ('fɒlɪ) NOUN, *plural* **-lies.** 1 the state or quality of being foolish; stupidity; rashness. 2 a foolish action, mistake, idea, etc. 3 a building in the form of a castle, temple, etc., built to satisfy a fancy or conceit, often of an eccentric kind. 4 (*plural*) *Theatre* an elaborately costumed revue. 5 *Archaic* **a** evil; wickedness. **b** lewdness; wantonness.
▷HISTORY C13: from Old French *folie* madness, from *fou* mad; see FOOL[1]

Folsom man ('fɒlsəm) NOUN a type of early man from a North American culture of the Pleistocene period, thought to have used flint tools and to have subsisted mainly by hunting bison.
▷HISTORY C20: named after *Folsom*, a settlement in New Mexico, where archaeological evidence was found

Fomalhaut ('fəʊməˌləʊt) NOUN the brightest star in the constellation Piscis Austrinus, possessing a protoplanetary disc. Distance: 25 light years. Spectral type A3V.
▷HISTORY C16: from Arabic *fum'l-hūt* mouth of the fish, referring to its position in the constellation

foment (fə'mɛnt) VERB (*tr*) 1 to encourage or instigate (trouble, discord, etc.); stir up. 2 *Med* to apply heat and moisture to (a part of the body) to relieve pain and inflammation.
▷HISTORY C15: from Late Latin *fōmentāre*, from Latin *fōmentum* a poultice, ultimately from *fovēre* to foster
▸**fomentation** (ˌfəʊmɛn'teɪʃən) NOUN ▸**fo'menter** NOUN

> **Language note** Both *foment* and *ferment* can be used to talk about stirring up trouble: *he was accused of fomenting/fermenting unrest.* Only *ferment* can be used intransitively or as a noun: *his anger continued to ferment* (not *foment*); *rural areas were unaffected by the ferment in the cities.*

fomes ('fəʊmiːz) NOUN, *plural* **-mites** (-mɪtiːz). *Med* any material, such as bedding or clothing, that may harbour pathogens and therefore convey disease.
▷HISTORY C18: from Latin *fōmes* tinder

fond[1] (fɒnd) ADJECTIVE 1 (*postpositive; foll by* of) predisposed (to); having a liking (for). 2 loving; tender: *a fond embrace.* 3 indulgent; doting: *a fond mother.* 4 (of hopes, wishes, etc.) cherished but unlikely to be realized: *he had fond hopes of starting his own business.* 5 *Archaic or dialect* **a** foolish. **b** credulous.
▷HISTORY C14 *fonned*, from *fonnen* to be foolish, from *fonne* a fool
▸'**fondly** ADVERB ▸'**fondness** NOUN

fond[2] (fɒnd; *French* fɔ̃) NOUN 1 the background of a design, as in lace. 2 *Obsolete* fund; stock.
▷HISTORY C17: from French, from Latin *fundus* bottom; see FUND

fondant ('fɒndənt) NOUN 1 a thick flavoured paste of sugar and water, used in sweets and icings. 2 a sweet made of this mixture. ◆ ADJECTIVE 3 (of a colour) soft; pastel.
▷HISTORY C19: from French, literally: melting, from *fondre* to melt, from Latin *fundere*; see FOUND[3]

fondle ('fɒndᵊl) VERB 1 (*tr*) to touch or stroke tenderly; caress. 2 (*intr*) *Archaic* to act in a loving manner.
▷HISTORY C17: from (obsolete) vb *fond* to fondle; see FOND[1]
▸'**fondler** NOUN ▸'**fondlingly** ADVERB

fondue ('fɒndjuː; *French* fɔ̃dy) NOUN a Swiss dish, consisting of cheese melted in white wine or cider, into which small pieces of bread are dipped and then eaten.
▷HISTORY C19: from French, feminine of *fondu* melted, from *fondre* to melt; see FONDANT

fondue Bourguignonne ('bʊəgɪˌnjɒn; *French* burgiɲɔn) NOUN a dish consisting of pieces of steak impaled on forks, cooked in oil at the table and dipped in sauces.
▷HISTORY French: Burgundy fondue

FONE *Text messaging* ABBREVIATION FOR phone.

Fonseca (*Spanish* fɔn'seka) NOUN **Gulf of.** an inlet of the Pacific Ocean in W Central America.

fons et origo *Latin* (fɒnz ɛt 'ɒrɪgəʊ) NOUN the source and origin.

font[1] (fɒnt) NOUN 1 **a** a large bowl for baptismal water, usually mounted on a pedestal. **b** a receptacle for holy water. 2 the reservoir for oil in an oil lamp. 3 *Archaic or poetic* a fountain or well.
▷HISTORY Old English, from Church Latin *fons*, from Latin: fountain
▸'**fontal** ADJECTIVE

font[2] (fɒnt) NOUN *Printing* another name (esp US and Canadian) for **fount**[2].

Fontainebleau ('fɒntɪnˌbləʊ; *French* fɔ̃tɛnblo) NOUN a town in N France, in the **Forest of Fontainebleau:** famous for its palace (now a museum), one of the largest royal residences in France, built largely by Francis I (16th century). Pop.: 18 753 (latest est.).

fontanelle *or chiefly US* **fontanel** (ˌfɒntə'nɛl) NOUN *Anatomy* any of several soft membranous gaps between the bones of the skull in a fetus or infant.
▷HISTORY C16 (in the sense: hollow between muscles): from Old French *fontanele*, literally: a little spring, from *fontaine* FOUNTAIN

Fonthill Abbey ('fɒnthɪl) NOUN a ruined Gothic Revival mansion in Wiltshire: rebuilt (1790–1810) for William Beckford by James Wyatt; the main tower collapsed in 1800 and, after rebuilding, again in 1827.

fontina (fɒn'tiːnə) NOUN a semihard, pale yellow, mild Italian cheese made from cow's milk.
▷HISTORY C20: from Italian dialect, of unknown origin

Foochow ('fuː'tʃaʊ) NOUN a variant transliteration of the Chinese name for **Fuzhou.**

food (fuːd) NOUN 1 any substance containing nutrients, such as carbohydrates, proteins, and fats, that can be ingested by a living organism and metabolized into energy and body tissue. Related adjective: **alimentary.** 2 nourishment in more or less solid form as opposed to liquid form: *food and drink.* 3 anything that provides mental nourishment or stimulus: *food for thought.*
▷HISTORY Old English *fōda*; related to Old Frisian *fōdia* to nourish, feed, Old Norse *fœthi*, Gothic *fōdeins* food; see FEED, FODDER
▸'**foodless** ADJECTIVE

food additive NOUN any of various natural or synthetic substances, such as salt, monosodium glutamate, or citric acid, used in the commercial processing of food as preservatives, antioxidants, emulsifiers, etc., in order to preserve or add flavour, colour, or texture to processed food.

food body NOUN *Botany* a mass of nutrients attached to a seed coat, which attracts ants and thus aids dispersal of the seed.

food chain NOUN *Ecology* a sequence of organisms in an ecosystem in which each species is the food of the next member of the chain. 2 *Informal* the hierarchy in an organization or society.

food combining NOUN the practice of keeping carbohydrates separate from proteins in one's daily diet, as a way of losing weight and also for some medical conditions.

food conversion ratio NOUN a ratio expressing the weight of food required to produce a unit gain in the live weight of an animal.

foodie *or* **foody** ('fuːdɪ) NOUN, *plural* **-ies.** a person having an enthusiastic interest in the preparation and consumption of good food.

food mile NOUN a unit used to measure the distance that a food product travels from where it is produced to where it is sold or consumed.

food poisoning NOUN an acute illness typically characterized by gastrointestinal inflammation, vomiting, and diarrhoea, caused by food that is either naturally poisonous or contaminated by pathogenic bacteria (esp *Salmonella*).

food pollen NOUN infertile pollen produced by some plants that attracts insects and thus aids pollination.

food processor NOUN *Cookery* an electric domestic appliance designed to speed the preparation and mixing of ingredients by automatic chopping, grating, blending, etc.

foodstuff ('fuːdˌstʌf) NOUN any material, substance, etc., that can be used as food.

food stylist NOUN a person who prepares food for photographs used in magazines, cookery books, etc.

food vacuole NOUN *Biology* a cavity surrounding ingested food particles in some protozoans.

food web NOUN a combination of food chains that integrate to form a network.

fool[1] (fuːl) NOUN 1 a person who lacks sense or judgement. 2 a person who is made to appear ridiculous. 3 (formerly) a professional jester living in a royal or noble household. 4 *Obsolete* an idiot or imbecile: *the village fool.* 5 **form the fool.** *Caribbean* to play the fool or behave irritatingly. 6 **no fool.** a wise or sensible person. 7 **play** *or* **act the fool.** to deliberately act foolishly; indulge in buffoonery. ◆ VERB 8 (*tr*) to deceive (someone), esp in order to make him look ridiculous. 9 (*intr; foll by* with, around with, *or* about with) *Informal* to act or play (with) irresponsibly or aimlessly: *to fool around with a woman.* 10 (*intr*) to speak or act in a playful, teasing, or jesting manner. 11 (*tr; foll by* away) to squander; fritter: *he fooled away a fortune.* 12 **fool along.** *US* to move or proceed in a leisurely way. ◆ ADJECTIVE 13 *Informal* short for **foolish.**
▷HISTORY C13: from Old French *fol* mad person, from Late Latin *follis* empty-headed fellow, from Latin: bellows; related to Latin *flāre* to blow

fool[2] (fuːl) NOUN *Chiefly Brit* a dessert made from a purée of fruit with cream or custard: *gooseberry fool.*
▷HISTORY C16: perhaps from FOOL[1]

foolery ('fuːlərɪ) NOUN, *plural* **-eries.** 1 foolish behaviour. 2 an instance of this, esp a prank or trick.

foolhardy ('fuːlˌhɑːdɪ) ADJECTIVE **-hardier, -hardiest.** heedlessly rash or adventurous.
▷HISTORY C13: from Old French *fol hardi*, from *fol* foolish + *hardi* bold
▸'**foolˌhardily** ADVERB ▸'**foolˌhardiness** NOUN

foolish ('fuːlɪʃ) ADJECTIVE 1 unwise; silly. 2 resulting from folly or stupidity. 3 ridiculous or absurd; not worthy of consideration. 4 weak-minded; simple. 5 an archaic word for **insignificant.**
▸'**foolishly** ADVERB ▸'**foolishness** NOUN

foolproof ('fuːlˌpruːf) ADJECTIVE 1 proof against failure; infallible: *a foolproof idea.* 2 (esp of machines) proof against human misuse, error, etc.

foolscap ('fuːlzˌkæp) NOUN 1 *Chiefly Brit* a size of writing or printing paper, 13½ by 17 inches or 13¼ by 16½ inches. 2 a book size, 4¼ by 6¾ inches (**foolscap octavo**) or (chiefly Brit.) 6¾ by 8½ inches (**foolscap quarto**). 3 a variant spelling of **fool's cap.**
▷HISTORY C17: see FOOL[1], CAP; so called from the watermark formerly used on this kind of paper

fool's cap NOUN 1 a hood or cap with bells or tassels, worn by court jesters. 2 a dunce's cap.

fool's errand NOUN a fruitless undertaking.

fool's gold NOUN any of various yellow minerals, esp pyrite or chalcopyrite, that can be mistaken for gold.

fool's mate NOUN *Chess* a checkmate achieved by Black's second move: the quickest possible mate.

fool's paradise NOUN illusory happiness.

fool's-parsley NOUN an evil-smelling Eurasian umbelliferous plant, *Aethusa cynapium*, with small white flowers: contains the poison coniine.

foot (fʊt) NOUN, *plural* **feet** (fiːt). 1 the part of the vertebrate leg below the ankle joint that is in

contact with the ground during standing and walking. Related adjective: **pedal.** 2 any of various organs of locomotion or attachment in invertebrates, including molluscs. 3 *Botany* the lower part of some plant structures, as of a developing moss sporophyte embedded in the parental tissue. 4 **a** a unit of length equal to one third of a yard or 12 inches. 1 Imperial foot is equivalent to 0.3048 metre. Abbreviation: **ft. b** any of various units of length used at different times and places, typically about 10 per cent greater than the Imperial foot. 5 any part resembling a foot in form or function: *the foot of a chair.* 6 the lower part of something; base; bottom: *the foot of the page; the foot of a hill.* 7 the end of a series or group: *the foot of the list.* 8 manner of walking or moving; tread; step: *a heavy foot.* 9 **a** infantry, esp in the British army. **b** (*as modifier*): *a foot soldier.* 10 any of various attachments on a sewing machine that hold the fabric in position, such as a presser foot for ordinary sewing and a zipper foot. 11 *Music* **a** a unit used in classifying organ pipes according to their pitch, in terms of the length of an equivalent column of air. **b** this unit applied to stops and registers on other instruments. 12 *Printing* **a** the margin at the bottom of a page. **b** the undersurface of a piece of type. 13 *Prosody* a group of two or more syllables in which one syllable has the major stress, forming the basic unit of poetic rhythm. 14 **a foot in the door.** an action, appointment, etc., that provides an initial step towards a desired goal, esp one that is not easily attainable. 15 **kick with the wrong foot.** *Scot and Irish* to be of the opposite religion to that which is regarded as acceptable or to that of the person who is speaking. 16 **my foot!** an expression of disbelief, often of the speaker's own preceding statement: *he didn't know, my foot! Of course he did!* 17 **of foot.** *Archaic* in manner of movement: *fleet of foot.* 18 **on foot. a** walking or running. **b** in progress; astir; afoot. 19 **one foot in the grave.** *Informal* near to death. 20 **on the wrong** (*or* **right**) **foot.** *Informal* in an inauspicious (or auspicious) manner. 21 **put a foot wrong.** to make a mistake. 22 **put one's best foot forward. a** to try to do one's best. **b** to hurry. 23 **put one's foot down.** *Informal* **a** to act firmly. **b** to increase speed (in a motor vehicle) by pressing down on the accelerator. 24 **put one's foot in it.** *Informal* to blunder. 25 **set on foot.** to initiate or start (something). 26 **tread under foot.** to oppress. 27 **under foot.** on the ground; beneath one's feet. ◆ VERB 28 to dance to music (esp in the phrase **foot it**). 29 (*tr*) to walk over or set foot on; traverse (esp in the phrase **foot it**). 30 (*tr*) to pay the entire cost of (esp in the phrase **foot the bill**). 31 (usually foll by *up*) *Archaic or dialect* to add up. ◆ See also **feet, foots.**
▷**HISTORY** Old English *fōt*; related to Old Norse *fōtr*, Gothic *fōtus*, Old High German *fuoz*, Latin *pēs*, Greek *pous*, Sanskrit *pad*
▸ **'footless** ADJECTIVE

> **Language note** In front of another noun, the plural for the unit of length is *foot: a 20-foot putt; his 70-foot ketch. Foot* can also be used instead of *feet* when mentioning a quantity and in front of words like *tall: four foot of snow; he is at least six foot tall.*

footage ('fʊtɪdʒ) NOUN 1 a length or distance measured in feet. 2 **a** the extent of film material shot and exposed. **b** the sequences of filmed material. 3 **a** payment, by the linear foot of work done. **b** the amount paid.

foot-and-mouth disease NOUN an acute highly infectious viral disease of cattle, pigs, sheep, and goats, characterized by the formation of vesicular eruptions in the mouth and on the feet, esp around the hoofs. Also called: **hoof-and-mouth disease, aphtha, aphthous fever.** Technical name: **contagious stomatitis.**

football ('fʊtˌbɔːl) NOUN 1 **a** any of various games played with a round or oval ball and usually based on two teams competing to kick, head, carry, or otherwise propel the ball into each other's goal, territory, etc. See **association football, rugby, Australian Rules, American football, Gaelic football. b** (*as modifier*): *a football ground; a football supporter.* 2 the ball used in any of these games or their variants. 3 a problem, issue, etc., that is continually passed from one group or person to another and treated as a pretext for argument instead of being resolved: *he accused the government of using the strike as a political football.*
▸ **'footˌballer** NOUN

footboard ('fʊtˌbɔːd) NOUN 1 a treadle or foot-operated lever on a machine. 2 a vertical board at the foot of a bed.

footboy ('fʊtˌbɔɪ) NOUN a boy servant; page.

foot brake NOUN a brake operated by applying pressure to a foot pedal. Also called: **pedal brake.**

footbridge ('fʊtˌbrɪdʒ) NOUN a narrow bridge for the use of pedestrians.

foot-candle NOUN a former unit of illumination, equal to one lumen per square foot or 10.764 lux.

footcloth ('fʊtˌklɒθ) NOUN an obsolete word for **caparison** (sense 1).

-footed ADJECTIVE 1 having a foot or feet as specified: *four-footed.* 2 having a tread as specified: *heavy-footed.*

footer[1] ('fʊtə) NOUN 1 *Archaic* a person who goes on foot; walker. 2 (*in combination*) a person or thing of a specified length or height in feet: *a six-footer.*

footer[2] ('fʊtə) NOUN *Brit informal* short for **football** (the game).

footer[3] *or* **fouter** ('fuːtər, 'fuːtə) *Scot* ◆ VERB (*intr*) 1 to potter; occupy oneself trivially or to little effect. ◆ NOUN 2 a person who footers.
▷**HISTORY** perhaps from French *foutre*; see FOOTLE

footfall ('fʊtˌfɔːl) NOUN the sound of a footstep.

foot fault NOUN *Tennis* a fault that occurs when the server fails to keep both feet behind the baseline until he has served.

footgear ('fʊtˌɡɪə) NOUN another name for **footwear.**

foothill ('fʊtˌhɪl) NOUN (*often plural*) a lower slope of a mountain or a relatively low hill at the foot of a mountain.

foothold ('fʊtˌhəʊld) NOUN 1 a ledge, hollow, or other place affording a secure grip for the foot, as during climbing. 2 a secure position from which further progress may be made: *a foothold for a successful career.*

footie ('fʊtɪ) NOUN a variant spelling of **footy.**

footing ('fʊtɪŋ) NOUN 1 the basis or foundation on which something is established: *the business was on a secure footing.* 2 the relationship or status existing between two persons, groups, etc.: *the two countries were on a friendly footing.* 3 a secure grip by or for the feet. 4 the lower part of a foundation of a column, wall, building, etc. 5 *Chiefly US* **a** the act of adding a column of figures. **b** the total obtained. 6 *Rare* a fee paid upon entrance into a craft, society, etc., or such an entrance itself.

foot-lambert NOUN a former unit of luminance equal to the luminance of a surface emitting or reflecting 1 lumen per square foot. A completely reflecting surface illuminated by 1 foot-candle has a luminance of 1 foot-lambert. Abbreviation: **ft-L.**

footle ('fuːtᵊl) *Informal* ◆ VERB (*intr*) 1 (often foll by *around* or *about*) to loiter aimlessly; potter. 2 to talk nonsense. ◆ NOUN 3 *Rare* foolishness.
▷**HISTORY** C19: probably from French *foutre* to copulate with, from Latin *futuere*

footlights ('fʊtˌlaɪts) PLURAL NOUN *Theatre* 1 lights set in a row along the front of the stage floor and shielded on the audience side. 2 *Informal* the acting profession; the stage.

footling ('fuːtlɪŋ) ADJECTIVE *Informal* silly, trivial, or petty.

footloose ('fʊtˌluːs) ADJECTIVE 1 free to go or do as one wishes. 2 eager to travel; restless: *to feel footloose.*

footman ('fʊtmən) NOUN, *plural* **-men.** 1 a male servant, esp one in livery. 2 a low four-legged metal stand used in a fireplace for utensils, etc. 3 (formerly) a foot soldier. 4 any of several arctiid moths related to the tiger moths, esp the **common footman** (*Eilema lurideola*), with yellowish hind wings and brown forewings with a yellow front stripe; they produce woolly bear larvae.

footmark ('fʊtˌmɑːk) NOUN a mark or trace of mud, wetness, etc., left by a person's foot on a surface.

footnote ('fʊtˌnəʊt) NOUN 1 a note printed at the bottom of a page, to which attention is drawn by means of a reference mark in the body of the text. 2 an additional comment, as to a main statement. ◆ VERB 3 (*tr*) to supply (a page, book, etc.) with footnotes.

footpace ('fʊtˌpeɪs) NOUN 1 a normal or walking pace. 2 Also called (in the Roman Catholic Church): **predella.** the platform immediately before an altar at the top of the altar steps.

footpad ('fʊtˌpæd) NOUN *Archaic* a robber or highwayman, on foot rather than horseback.

footpath ('fʊtˌpɑːθ) NOUN 1 a narrow path for walkers only. 2 *Chiefly Austral and NZ* another word for **pavement.**

footplate ('fʊtˌpleɪt) NOUN *Chiefly Brit* **a** a platform in the cab of a locomotive on which the crew stand to operate the controls. **b** (*as modifier*): *a footplate man.*

foot-pound NOUN an fps unit of work or energy equal to the work done when a force of 1 pound moves through a distance of 1 foot. Abbreviation: **ft-lb.**

foot-poundal NOUN a unit of work or energy equal to the work done when a force of one poundal moves through a distance of one foot: it is equal to 0.042 14 joule.

foot-pound-second NOUN See **fps units.**

footprint ('fʊtˌprɪnt) NOUN 1 an indentation or outline of the foot of a person or animal on a surface. 2 an identifying characteristic on land or water, such as the area in which an aircraft's sonic boom can be heard or the area covered by the down-blast of a hovercraft. 3 the area in which the signal from a direct broadcasting satellite is receivable.

footrest ('fʊtˌrɛst) NOUN something that provides a support for the feet, such as a low stool, rail, etc.

footrope ('fʊtˌrəʊp) NOUN *Nautical* 1 the part of a boltrope to which the foot of a sail is stitched. 2 a rope fixed so as to hang below a yard to serve as a foothold.

foot rot NOUN *Vet science* See **rot**[1] (sense 11).

foot rule NOUN a rigid measure, one foot in length.

foots (fʊts) PLURAL NOUN (*sometimes singular*) the sediment that accumulates at the bottom of a vessel containing any of certain liquids, such as vegetable oil or varnish; dregs.

footsie ('fʊtsɪ) NOUN *Informal* flirtation involving the touching together of feet, knees, etc. (esp in the phrase **play footsie**).

Footsie ('fʊtsɪ) NOUN an informal name for **Financial Times Stock Exchange 100 Index.**

footslog ('fʊtˌslɒɡ) VERB **-slogs, -slogging, -slogged.** (*intr*) to march; tramp.
▸ **'footˌslogger** NOUN

foot soldier NOUN an infantryman.

footsore ('fʊtˌsɔː) ADJECTIVE having sore or tired feet, esp from much walking.
▸ **'footˌsoreness** NOUN

footstalk ('fʊtˌstɔːk) NOUN a small supporting stalk in animals and plants; a pedicel, peduncle, or pedicle.

footstall ('fʊtˌstɔːl) NOUN 1 the pedestal, plinth, or base of a column, pier, or statue. 2 the stirrup on a sidesaddle.

footstep ('fʊtˌstɛp) NOUN 1 the action of taking a step in walking. 2 the sound made by stepping or walking. 3 the distance covered with a step; pace. 4 a footmark. 5 a single stair; step. 6 to continue the tradition or example of another.

footsteps editor NOUN *Brit films* the technician who adds sound effects, such as doors closing, rain falling, etc., during the postproduction sound-dubbing process. US name: **foley** *or* **foley artist.**

footstock ('fʊtˌstɒk) NOUN another name for **tailstock.**

footstool ('fʊtˌstuːl) NOUN a low stool used for supporting or resting the feet of a seated person.

foot-ton NOUN a unit of work or energy equal to 2240 foot-pounds.

foot valve NOUN 1 another name for **suction valve.** 2 a nonreturn valve at the inlet end of a pipe.

footwall ('fʊtˌwɔːl) NOUN the rocks on the lower

side of an inclined fault plane or mineral vein. Compare **hanging wall.**

footway (ˈfʊtˌweɪ) NOUN a way or path for pedestrians, such as a raised walk along the edge of a bridge.

footwear (ˈfʊtˌwɛə) NOUN anything worn to cover the feet.

footwork (ˈfʊtˌwɜːk) NOUN 1 skilful use of the feet, as in sports, dancing, etc. 2 *Informal* clever manoeuvring: *deft political footwork.* 3 *Informal* preliminary groundwork: *many estate agents now do the footwork – you only need to visit.*

footworn (ˈfʊtˌwɔːn) ADJECTIVE 1 Also: **footweary.** footsore. 2 worn away by the feet: *a footworn staircase.*

footy *or* **footie** (ˈfʊtɪ) NOUN *Informal* **a** football. **b** (*as modifier*): *footy boots.*

foo yong (ˈfuː ˈjɒŋ), **foo yoong** (ˈfuː ˈjʊŋ), **foo yung,** *or* **fu yung** (ˈfuː ˈjʌŋ) NOUN a Chinese dish made of eggs mixed with chicken, crab meat, etc., and cooked like an omelette.
▷HISTORY from Chinese *fu yung* hibiscus

foozle (ˈfuːzᵊl) *Chiefly golf* ◆ VERB 1 to bungle (a shot). ◆ NOUN 2 a bungled shot.
▷HISTORY C19: perhaps from German dialect *fuseln* to do slipshod work
▸ˈ**foozler** NOUN

fop (fɒp) NOUN a man who is excessively concerned with fashion and elegance.
▷HISTORY C15: related to German *foppen* to trick; see FOB[2]
▸ˈ**foppish** ADJECTIVE ▸ˈ**foppishly** ADVERB ▸ˈ**foppishness** NOUN

foppery (ˈfɒpərɪ) NOUN, *plural* **-peries.** the clothes, affectations, obsessions, etc., of or befitting a fop.

for (fɔː; *unstressed* fə) PREPOSITION 1 intended to reach; directed or belonging to: *there's a phone call for you.* 2 to the advantage of: *I only did it for you.* 3 in the direction of: *heading for the border.* 4 over a span of (time or distance): *working for six days; the river ran for six miles.* 5 in favour of; in support of: *those for the proposal; vote for me.* 6 in order to get or achieve: *I do it for money; he does it for pleasure; what did you do that for?* 7 appropriate to; designed to meet the needs of; meant to be used in: *these kennels are for puppies.* 8 in exchange for; at a cost of; to the amount of: *I got it for hardly any money.* 9 such as explains or results in: *his reason for changing his job was not given.* 10 in place of: *a substitute for the injured player.* 11 because of; through: *she wept for pure relief.* 12 with regard or consideration to the usual characteristics of: *he's short for a man; it's cool for this time of year.* 13 concerning; as regards: *desire for money.* 14 as being: *we took him for the owner; I know that for a fact.* 15 at a specified time: *a date for the next evening.* 16 to do or partake of: *an appointment for supper.* 17 in the duty or task of: *that's for him to say.* 18 to allow of: *too big a job for us to handle.* 19 despite; notwithstanding: *she's a good wife, for all her nagging.* 20 in order to preserve, retain, etc.: *to fight for survival.* 21 as a direct equivalent to: *word for word; weight for weight.* 22 in order to become or enter: *to go for a soldier; to train for the priesthood.* 23 in recompense for: *I paid for it last week; he took the punishment for his crime.* 24 **for it.** *Brit informal* liable for punishment or blame: *you'll be for it if she catches you.* 25 **nothing for it.** no choice; no other course. ◆ CONJUNCTION 26 (*coordinating*) for the following reason; because; seeing that: *I couldn't stay, for the area was violent.*
▷HISTORY Old English; related to Old Norse *fyr* for, Old High German *fora* before, Latin *per* through, *prō* before, Greek *pro* before, in front

f.o.r. *or* **FOR** *Commerce* ABBREVIATION FOR free on rail.

for- PREFIX 1 indicating rejection or prohibition: *forbear; forbid.* 2 indicating falsity or wrongness: *forswear.* 3 used to give intensive force: *forgive; forlorn.*
▷HISTORY Old English *for-*; related to German *ver-*, Latin *per-*, Greek *peri-*

forage (ˈfɒrɪdʒ) NOUN 1 food for horses or cattle, esp hay or straw. 2 the act of searching for food or provisions. 3 *Military* a raid or incursion. ◆ VERB 4 to search (the countryside or a town) for food, provisions, etc. 5 (*intr*) *Military* to carry out a raid. 6 (*tr*) to obtain by searching about. 7 (*tr*) to give food or other provisions to. 8 (*tr*) to feed (cattle or horses) with such food.
▷HISTORY C14: from Old French *fourrage*, probably of Germanic origin; see FOOD, FODDER
▸ˈ**forager** NOUN

forage cap NOUN a soldier's undress cap.

forage mite NOUN a mite normally occurring in forage but sometimes infesting the skin of mammals, esp horses, and birds.

foramen (fɒˈreɪmɛn) NOUN, *plural* **-ramina** (-ˈræmɪnə) *or* **-ramens.** a natural hole, esp one in a bone through which nerves and blood vessels pass.
▷HISTORY C17: from Latin, from *forāre* to bore, pierce
▸**foraminal** (fɒˈræmɪnᵊl) ADJECTIVE

foramen magnum NOUN the large opening at the base of the skull through which the spinal cord passes.
▷HISTORY New Latin: large hole

foraminifer (ˌfɒrəˈmɪnɪfə) NOUN any marine protozoan of the phylum *Foraminifera*, having a shell with numerous openings through which cytoplasmic processes protrude. Often shortened to: **foram.** See also **globigerina, nummulite.**
▷HISTORY C19: from New Latin, from FORAMEN + -FER
▸**foraminiferal** (fɒˌræmɪˈnɪfərəl) *or* **foˌramiˈniferous** ADJECTIVE

forasmuch as (fərəzˈmʌtʃ) CONJUNCTION (*subordinating*) *Archaic or legal* seeing that; since.

foray (ˈfɒreɪ) NOUN 1 a short raid or incursion. 2 a first attempt or new undertaking. ◆ VERB 3 to raid or ravage (a town, district, etc.).
▷HISTORY C14: from *forrayen* to pillage, from Old French *forreier*, from *forrier* forager, from *fuerre* fodder; see FORAGE
▸ˈ**forayer** NOUN

forb (fɔːb) NOUN any herbaceous plant that is not a grass.
▷HISTORY C20: from Greek *phorbē* food, from *pherbein* to graze

forbade (fəˈbæd, -ˈbeɪd) *or* **forbad** (fəˈbæd) VERB the past tense of **forbid.**

forbear[1] (fɔːˈbɛə) VERB **-bears, -bearing, -bore, -borne.** 1 (when *intr*, often foll by *from* or an infinitive) to cease or refrain (from doing something). 2 *Archaic* to tolerate or endure (misbehaviour, mistakes, etc.).
▷HISTORY Old English *forberan*; related to Gothic *frabairan* to endure
▸**forˈbearer** NOUN ▸**forˈbearingly** ADVERB

forbear[2] (ˈfɔːˌbɛə) NOUN a variant spelling of **forebear.**

forbearance (fɔːˈbɛərəns) NOUN 1 the act of forbearing. 2 self-control; patience. 3 *Law* abstention from or postponement of the enforcement of a legal right, esp by a creditor allowing his debtor time to pay.

forbid (fəˈbɪd) VERB **-bids, -bidding, -bade** *or* **-bad, -bidden** *or* **-bid.** (*tr*) 1 to prohibit (a person) in a forceful or authoritative manner (from doing something or having something). 2 to make impossible; hinder. 3 to shut out or exclude. 4 **God forbid!** may it not happen.
▷HISTORY Old English *forbēodan*; related to Old High German *farbiotan*, Gothic *faurbiudan*; see FOR-, BID
▸**forˈbiddance** NOUN ▸**forˈbidder** NOUN

> **Language note** It was formerly considered incorrect to talk of *forbidding* someone *from* doing something, but in modern usage either *from* or *to* can be used: *he was forbidden from entering/to enter the building.*

forbidden (fəˈbɪdᵊn) ADJECTIVE 1 not permitted by order or law. 2 *Physics* involving a change in quantum numbers that is not permitted by certain rules derived from quantum mechanics, esp rules for changes in the electrical dipole moment of the system.

forbidden band NOUN See **energy band.**

Forbidden City NOUN **the.** 1 Lhasa, Tibet: once famed for its inaccessibility and hostility to strangers. 2 a walled section of Beijing, China, enclosing the Imperial Palace and associated buildings of the former Chinese Empire.

forbidden fruit NOUN any pleasure or enjoyment regarded as illicit, esp sexual indulgence.

forbidden transition NOUN *Physics* an electronic transition in an atom, molecule, etc., that is not permitted by electric dipole selection rules.

forbidding (fəˈbɪdɪŋ) ADJECTIVE 1 hostile or unfriendly. 2 dangerous or ominous.
▸**forˈbiddingly** ADVERB ▸**forˈbiddingness** NOUN

forbore (fɔːˈbɔː) VERB the past tense of **forbear.**

forborne (fɔːˈbɔːn) VERB the past participle of **forbear.**

forby *or* **forbye** (fɔːˈbaɪ; *Scot* fərˈbaɪ) PREPOSITION, ADVERB *Scot* 1 besides; in addition (to). 2 *Obsolete* near; nearby.

force[1] (fɔːs) NOUN 1 strength or energy; might; power: *the force of the blow; a gale of great force.* 2 exertion or the use of exertion against a person or thing that resists; coercion. 3 *Physics* **a** a dynamic influence that changes a body from a state of rest to one of motion or changes its rate of motion. The magnitude of the force is equal to the product of the mass of the body and its acceleration. **b** a static influence that produces an elastic strain in a body or system or bears weight. Symbol: F. 4 *Physics* any operating influence that produces or tends to produce a change in a physical quantity: *electromotive force; coercive force.* 5 **a** intellectual, social, political, or moral influence or strength: *the force of his argument; the forces of evil.* **b** a person or thing with such influence: *he was a force in the land.* 6 vehemence or intensity: *he spoke with great force.* 7 a group of persons organized for military or police functions: *armed forces.* 8 (*sometimes capital; preceded by the*) *Informal* the police force. 9 a group of persons organized for particular duties or tasks: *a workforce.* 10 *Criminal law* violence unlawfully committed or threatened. 11 *Philosophy, logic* that which an expression is normally used to achieve. See **speech act, illocution, perlocution.** 12 **in force. a** (of a law) having legal validity or binding effect. **b** in great strength or numbers. 13 **join forces.** to combine strengths, efforts, etc. ◆ VERB (*tr*) 14 to compel or cause (a person, group, etc.) to do something through effort, superior strength, etc.; coerce. 15 to acquire, secure, or produce through effort, superior strength, etc.: *to force a confession.* 16 to propel or drive despite resistance: *to force a nail into wood.* 17 to break down or open (a lock, safe, door, etc.). 18 to impose or inflict: *he forced his views on them.* 19 to cause (plants or farm animals) to grow or fatten artificially at an increased rate. 20 to strain or exert to the utmost: *to force the voice.* 21 to rape; ravish. 22 *Cards* **a** to compel (a player) to trump in order to take a trick. **b** to compel a player by the lead of a particular suit to play (a certain card). **c** (in bridge) to induce (a bid) from one's partner by bidding in a certain way. 23 **force down.** to compel an aircraft to land. 24 **force a smile.** to make oneself smile. 25 **force the pace.** to adopt a high speed or rate of procedure.
▷HISTORY C13: from Old French, from Vulgar Latin *fortia* (unattested), from Latin *fortis* strong
▸ˈ**forceable** ADJECTIVE ▸ˈ**forceless** ADJECTIVE ▸ˈ**forcer** NOUN ▸ˈ**forcingly** ADVERB

force[2] (fɔːs) NOUN (in northern England) a waterfall.
▷HISTORY C17: from Old Norse *fors*

forced (fɔːst) ADJECTIVE 1 done because of force; compulsory: *forced labour.* 2 false or unnatural: *a forced smile.* 3 due to an emergency or necessity: *a forced landing.* 4 *Physics* caused by an external agency: *a forced vibration; a forced draught.*
▸**forcedly** (ˈfɔːsɪdlɪ) ADVERB ▸ˈ**forcedness** NOUN

forced development NOUN the processing of underexposed photographic film to increase the image density.

force de frappe (*French* fɔrs də frap) NOUN a military strike force, esp the independent nuclear strike force of France.
▷HISTORY C20: literally: striking force

forced march NOUN *Military* a march in which normal needs are subordinated to the need for speed.

force-feed VERB **-feeds, -feeding, -fed.** (*tr*) 1 to force (a person or animal) to eat or swallow food. 2 to force (someone) to receive opinions, propaganda, etc. ◆ NOUN **force feed.** 3 a method of lubrication in which a pump forces oil into the bearings of an engine, etc.

force-field analysis NOUN a decision-making technique, often presented graphically, that identifies all the positive and negative forces impinging on a problem.

forceful (ˈfɔːsfʊl) ADJECTIVE [1] powerful. [2] persuasive or effective.
► **ˈforcefully** ADVERB ► **ˈforcefulness** NOUN

force majeure (ˈfɔːs mæˈʒɜː, -ˈdʒʊə) NOUN *Law* irresistible force or compulsion such as will excuse a party from performing his part of a contract.
▷HISTORY from French: superior force

forcemeat (ˈfɔːsˌmiːt) NOUN a mixture of chopped or minced ingredients used for stuffing. Also called: **farce, farcemeat.**
▷HISTORY C17: from *force* (see FARCE) + MEAT

forceps (ˈfɔːsɪps) NOUN, *plural* **-ceps** *or* **-cipes** (-sɪˌpiːz). [1] **a** a surgical instrument in the form of a pair of pincers, used esp in the delivery of babies. **b** (*as modifier*): *a forceps baby.* [2] any pincer-like instrument. [3] any part or structure of an organism shaped like a forceps.
▷HISTORY C17: from Latin, from *formus* hot + *capere* to seize
► **ˈforceps-ˌlike** ADJECTIVE

force pump NOUN a pump that ejects fluid under pressure. Compare **lift pump.**

force-ripe *Caribbean* ◆ ADJECTIVE [1] (of fruit) prematurely picked and ripened by squeezing or warm storage. [2] precocious, esp sexually. ◆ VERB [3] (*tr*) to ripen (prematurely picked fruit) by squeezing or warm storage.

Forces (ˈfɔːsɪz) PLURAL NOUN (usually preceded by *the*) the armed services of a nation.

forcible (ˈfɔːsəbᵊl) ADJECTIVE [1] done by, involving, or having force. [2] convincing or effective: *a forcible argument.*
► **ˈforcibleness** *or* **ˌforciˈbility** NOUN ► **ˈforcibly** ADVERB

forcing bid NOUN *Contract bridge* a bid, often at a higher level than is required, that is understood to oblige the bidder's partner to reply.

forcing frequency NOUN *Physics* the frequency of an oscillating force applied to a system. Compare **natural frequency.**

forcing house NOUN a place where growth or maturity (as of fruit, animals, etc.) is artificially hastened.

ford (fɔːd) NOUN [1] a shallow area in a river that can be crossed by car, horseback, etc. ◆ VERB [2] (*tr*) to cross (a river, brook, etc.) over a shallow area.
▷HISTORY Old English; related to Old Frisian *forda*, Old High German *furt* ford, Latin *porta* door, *portus* PORT[1]
► **ˈfordable** ADJECTIVE

fordo *or* **foredo** (fɔːˈduː) VERB **-does, -doing, -did, -done.** (*tr*) *Archaic* [1] to destroy. [2] to exhaust.
▷HISTORY Old English *fordōn*; related to Old Saxon *fardōn*, Old High German *fartuon*, Dutch *verdoen*; see FOR-, DO[1]

fore[1] (fɔː) ADJECTIVE [1] (*usually in combination*) located at, in, or towards the front: *the forelegs of a horse.* ◆ NOUN [2] the front part. [3] something located at, in, or towards the front. [4] short for **foremast.** [5] **fore and aft.** located at or directed towards both ends of a vessel: *a fore-and-aft rig.* [6] **to the fore. a** to or into the front or conspicuous position. **b** *Scot and Irish* alive or active: *is your grandfather still to the fore?* ◆ ADVERB [7] at or towards a ship's bow. [8] *Obsolete* before. ◆ PREPOSITION, CONJUNCTION [9] a less common word for **before.**
▷HISTORY Old English; related to Old Saxon, Old High German *fora*, Gothic *faura*, Greek *para*, Sanskrit *pura*

fore[2] (fɔː) INTERJECTION (in golf) a warning shout made by a player about to make a shot.
▷HISTORY C19: probably short for BEFORE

fore- PREFIX [1] before in time or rank: *foresight; forefather; foreman.* [2] at or near the front; before in place: *forehead; forecourt.*
▷HISTORY Old English, from *fore* (adverb)

fore-and-after NOUN *Nautical* [1] any vessel with a fore-and-aft rig. [2] a double-ended vessel.

forearm[1] (ˈfɔːrˌɑːm) NOUN the part of the arm from the elbow to the wrist. Related adjectives: **cubital, radial.**
▷HISTORY C18: from FORE- + ARM[1]

forearm[2] (fɔːrˈɑːm) VERB (*tr*) to prepare or arm (someone, esp oneself) in advance.
▷HISTORY C16: from FORE- + ARM[2]

forearm smash (ˈfɔːrˌɑːm) NOUN a blow like a punch delivered with the forearm in certain types of wrestling.

forebear *or* **forbear** (ˈfɔːˌbɛə) NOUN an ancestor; forefather.

forebode (fɔːˈbəʊd) VERB [1] to warn of or indicate (an event, result, etc.) in advance. [2] to have an intuition or premonition of (an event).
► **foreˈboder** NOUN

foreboding (fɔːˈbəʊdɪŋ) NOUN [1] a feeling of impending evil, disaster, etc. [2] an omen or portent. ◆ ADJECTIVE [3] presaging something.
► **foreˈbodingly** ADVERB ► **foreˈbodingness** NOUN

forebrain (ˈfɔːˌbreɪn) NOUN the nontechnical name for **prosencephalon.**

forecast (ˈfɔːˌkɑːst) VERB **-casts, -casting, -cast** *or* **-casted.** [1] to predict or calculate (weather, events, etc.), in advance. [2] (*tr*) to serve as an early indication of. [3] (*tr*) to plan in advance. ◆ NOUN [4] a statement of probable future weather conditions calculated from meteorological data. [5] a prophecy or prediction. [6] the practice or power of forecasting.
► **ˈforeˌcaster** NOUN

forecastle, fo'c's'le, *or* **fo'c'sle** (ˈfəʊksᵊl) NOUN the part of a vessel at the bow where the crew is quartered and stores, machines, etc., may be stowed.

foreclose (fɔːˈkləʊz) VERB [1] *Law* to deprive (a mortgagor, etc.) of the right to redeem (a mortgage or pledge). [2] (*tr*) to shut out; bar. [3] (*tr*) to prevent or hinder. [4] (*tr*) to answer or settle (an obligation, promise, etc.) in advance. [5] (*tr*) to make an exclusive claim to.
▷HISTORY C15: from Old French *forclore*, from *for-* out + *clore* to close, from Latin *claudere*
► **foreˈclosable** ADJECTIVE ► **foreclosure** (fɔːˈkləʊʒə) NOUN

forecourse (ˈfɔːˌkɔːs) NOUN *Nautical* the lowest foresail on a square-rigged vessel.

forecourt (ˈfɔːˌkɔːt) NOUN [1] a courtyard in front of a building, as one in a filling station. [2] Also called: **front court.** the front section of the court in tennis, badminton, etc., esp the area between the service line and the net.

foredeck (ˈfɔːˌdɛk) NOUN *Nautical* the deck between the bridge and the forecastle.

foredo (fɔːˈduː) VERB **-does, -doing, -did, -done.** (*tr*) a variant spelling of **fordo.**

foredoom (fɔːˈduːm) VERB (*tr*) to doom or condemn beforehand.

fore-edge NOUN the outer edge of the pages of a book.

forefather (ˈfɔːˌfɑːðə) NOUN an ancestor, esp a male.
► **ˈforeˌfatherly** ADJECTIVE

forefend (fɔːˈfɛnd) VERB (*tr*) a variant spelling of **forfend.**

forefinger (ˈfɔːˌfɪŋgə) NOUN the finger next to the thumb. Also called: **index finger.**

forefoot (ˈfɔːˌfʊt) NOUN, *plural* **-feet.** [1] either of the front feet of a quadruped. [2] *Nautical* the forward end of the keel.

forefront (ˈfɔːˌfrʌnt) NOUN [1] the extreme front. [2] the position of most prominence, responsibility, or action.

foregather *or* **forgather** (fɔːˈgæðə) VERB (*intr*) [1] to gather together; assemble. [2] *Rare* to meet, esp unexpectedly. [3] (foll by *with*) to socialize.

forego[1] (fɔːˈgəʊ) VERB **-goes, -going, -went, -gone.** to precede in time, place, etc.
▷HISTORY Old English *foregān*
► **foreˈgoer** NOUN

forego[2] (fɔːˈgəʊ) VERB **-goes, -going, -went, -gone.** (*tr*) a variant spelling of **forgo.**
► **foreˈgoer** NOUN

foregoing (fɔːˈgəʊɪŋ) ADJECTIVE (*prenominal*) (esp of writing or speech) going before; preceding.

foregone (fɔːˈgɒn, ˈfɔːˌgɒn) ADJECTIVE gone or completed; past.
► **foreˈgoneness** NOUN

foregone conclusion NOUN an inevitable result or conclusion.

foreground (ˈfɔːˌgraʊnd) NOUN [1] the part of a scene situated towards the front or nearest to the viewer. [2] the area of space in a perspective picture, depicted as nearest the viewer. [3] a conspicuous or active position. ◆ VERB [4] (*tr*) to emphasize (an issue, idea, or word).

foregut (ˈfɔːˌgʌt) NOUN [1] the anterior part of the digestive tract of vertebrates, between the buccal cavity and the bile duct. [2] the anterior part of the digestive tract of arthropods. ◆ See also **midgut, hindgut.**

forehand (ˈfɔːˌhænd) ADJECTIVE (*prenominal*) [1] *Sport* **a** (of a stroke) made with the racket held so that the wrist is facing the direction of the stroke. **b** of or relating to the right side of a right-handed player or the left side of a left-handed player. [2] foremost or paramount. [3] done or given beforehand. ◆ NOUN [4] *Sport* **a** a forehand stroke. **b** the side on which such strokes are made. [5] the part of a horse in front of the saddle. [6] a frontal position. ◆ ADVERB [7] *Sport* with a forehand stroke. ◆ VERB [8] *Sport* to play (a shot) forehand.

forehanded (ˌfɔːˈhændɪd) ADJECTIVE [1] *US* **a** thrifty. **b** well-off. ◆ ADVERB, ADJECTIVE [2] *Sport* a less common word for **forehand.**
► **ˌforeˈhandedly** ADVERB ► **ˌforeˈhandedness** NOUN

forehead (ˈfɒrɪd, ˈfɔːˌhɛd) NOUN the part of the face between the natural hairline and the eyes, formed skeletally by the frontal bone of the skull; brow. Related adjective: **frontal.**
▷HISTORY Old English *forhēafod*; related to Old Frisian *forhāfd*, Middle Low German *vorhōved*

forehock (ˈfɔːˌhɒk) NOUN a foreleg cut of bacon or pork.

foreign (ˈfɒrɪn) ADJECTIVE [1] of, involving, located in, or coming from another country, area, people, etc.: *a foreign resident.* [2] dealing or concerned with another country, area, people, etc.: *a foreign office.* [3] not pertinent or related: *a matter foreign to the discussion.* [4] not familiar; strange. [5] in an abnormal place or position: *foreign matter; foreign bodies.* [6] *Law* outside the jurisdiction of a particular state; alien.
▷HISTORY C13: from Old French *forain*, from Vulgar Latin *forānus* (unattested) situated on the outside, from Latin *foris* outside
► **ˈforeignly** ADVERB ► **ˈforeignness** NOUN

foreign affairs PLURAL NOUN [1] matters abroad that involve the homeland, such as relations with another country. [2] matters that do not involve the homeland.

foreign aid NOUN economic and other assistance given by one country to another.

foreign bill *or* **draft** NOUN a bill of exchange that is drawn in one country and made payable in another: used extensively in foreign trade. Compare **inland bill.**

foreign correspondent NOUN *Journalism* a reporter who visits or resides in a foreign country in order to report on its affairs.

foreigner (ˈfɒrɪnə) NOUN [1] a person from a foreign country; alien. [2] an outsider or interloper. [3] something from a foreign country, such as a ship or product.

foreign exchange NOUN [1] the system by which one currency is converted into another, enabling international transactions to take place without the physical transportation of gold. [2] foreign bills and currencies.

foreignism (ˈfɒrɪˌnɪzəm) NOUN [1] a custom, mannerism, idiom, etc., that is foreign. [2] imitation of something foreign.

foreign legion NOUN a body of foreign volunteers serving in an army, esp that of France.

foreign minister *or* **secretary** NOUN (*often capitals*) a cabinet minister who is responsible for a country's dealings with other countries. US equivalent: **secretary of state.**
► **foreign ministry** NOUN

foreign mission NOUN [1] a body of persons sent to a non-Christian country in order to propagate Christianity. [2] a diplomatic or other mission sent by one country to another.

foreign office NOUN the ministry of a country or state that is concerned with dealings with other states. US equivalent: **State Department.** Canadian equivalent: (**department of**) **external affairs.**

foreign service NOUN *Chiefly US* the diplomatic and usually consular personnel of a foreign affairs ministry or foreign office collectively who represent their country abroad, deal with foreign diplomats at home, etc.

forejudge[1] (fɔːˈdʒʌdʒ) VERB to judge (someone or an event, circumstance, etc.) before the facts are known; prejudge.

forejudge[2] (fɔːˈdʒʌdʒ) VERB *Law* a variant spelling of **forjudge**.
▸**foreˈjudgment** NOUN

foreknow (fɔːˈnəʊ) VERB **-knows, -knowing, -knew, -known.** (*tr*) to know in advance.
▸**foreˈknowable** ADJECTIVE ▸**foreˈknowledge** NOUN ▸**foreˈknowingly** ADVERB

foreland (ˈfɔːlənd) NOUN [1] a headland, cape, or coastal promontory. [2] land lying in front of something, such as water.

Foreland (ˈfɔːlənd) NOUN either of two headlands (**North Foreland** and **South Foreland**) in SE England, on the coast of Kent.

foreleg (ˈfɔːˌlɛg) NOUN either of the front legs of a horse, sheep, or other quadruped.

forelimb (ˈfɔːˌlɪm) NOUN either of the front or anterior limbs of a four-limbed vertebrate: a foreleg, flipper, or wing.

forelock[1] (ˈfɔːˌlɒk) NOUN [1] a lock of hair growing or falling over the forehead. [2] a lock of a horse's mane that grows forwards between the ears.

forelock[2] (ˈfɔːˌlɒk) NOUN [1] a wedge or peg passed through the tip of a bolt to prevent withdrawal. ◆ VERB [2] (*tr*) to secure (a bolt) by means of a forelock.

foreman (ˈfɔːmən) NOUN, *plural* **-men.** [1] a person, often experienced, who supervises other workmen. Female equivalent: **forewoman.** [2] *Law* the principal juror, who presides at the deliberations of a jury.
▸ **ˈforemanˌship** NOUN

foremast (ˈfɔːˌmɑːst; *Nautical* ˈfɔːməst) NOUN the mast nearest the bow on vessels with two or more masts.

foremilk (ˈfɔːˌmɪlk) NOUN [1] another word for **colostrum.** [2] the first milk drawn from a cow's udder prior to milking.

foremost (ˈfɔːˌməʊst) ADJECTIVE, ADVERB first in time, place, rank, etc.
▷**HISTORY** Old English *formest*, from *forma* first; related to Old Saxon *formo* first, Old High German *fruma* advantage

foremother (ˈfɔːˌmʌðə) NOUN a female ancestor.

forename (ˈfɔːˌneɪm) NOUN a first or Christian name.

forenamed (ˈfɔːˌneɪmd) ADJECTIVE (*prenominal*) named or mentioned previously; aforesaid.

forenoon (ˈfɔːˌnuːn) NOUN **a** the daylight hours before or just before noon. **b** (*as modifier*): *a forenoon conference.*

forensic (fəˈrɛnsɪk) ADJECTIVE relating to, used in, or connected with a court of law: *forensic science.*
▷**HISTORY** C17: from Latin *forēnsis* public, from FORUM
▸**forensicality** (fəˌrɛnsɪˈkælɪtɪ) NOUN ▸**foˈrensically** ADVERB

forensic accountant NOUN an accountant who specializes in applying accountancy skills to the purposes of the law.

forensic medicine NOUN the applied use of medical knowledge or practice, esp pathology, to the purposes of the law, as in determining the cause of death. Also called: **medical jurisprudence, legal medicine.**

forensics (fəˈrɛnsɪks) NOUN (*functioning as singular or plural*) the art or study of formal debating.

foreordain (ˌfɔːrɔːˈdeɪn) VERB (*tr; may take a clause as object*) to determine (events, results, etc.) in the future.
▸ **ˌforeorˈdainment** *or* **foreordination** (ˌfɔːrɔːdɪˈneɪʃən) NOUN

forepart (ˈfɔːˌpɑːt) NOUN the first or front part in place, order, or time.

forepaw (ˈfɔːˌpɔː) NOUN either of the front feet of most land mammals that do not have hoofs.

forepeak (ˈfɔːˌpiːk) NOUN *Nautical* the interior part of a vessel that is furthest forward.

foreplay (ˈfɔːˌpleɪ) NOUN mutual sexual stimulation preceding sexual intercourse.

forequarter (ˈfɔːˌkwɔːtə) NOUN the front portion, including the leg, of half of a carcass, as of beef or lamb.

forequarters (ˈfɔːˌkwɔːtəz) PLURAL NOUN the part of the body of a horse or similar quadruped that consists of the forelegs, shoulders, and adjoining parts.

forereach (fɔːˈriːtʃ) VERB [1] (*intr*) *Nautical* to keep moving under momentum without engine or sails. [2] (*tr*) to surpass or outdo.

forerun (fɔːˈrʌn) VERB **-runs, -running, -ran, -run.** (*tr*) [1] to serve as a herald for. [2] to go before; precede. [3] to prevent or forestall.

forerunner (ˈfɔːˌrʌnə) NOUN [1] a person or thing that precedes another; precursor. [2] a person or thing coming in advance to herald the arrival of someone or something; harbinger. [3] an indication beforehand of something to follow; omen; portent.

foresaid (ˈfɔːˌsɛd) ADJECTIVE a less common word for **aforesaid.**

foresail (ˈfɔːˌseɪl; *Nautical* ˈfɔːsᵊl) NOUN *Nautical* [1] the aftermost headsail of a fore-and-aft rigged vessel. [2] the lowest sail set on the foremast of a square-rigged vessel.

foresee (fɔːˈsiː) VERB **-sees, -seeing, -saw, -seen.** (*tr; may take a clause as object*) to see or know beforehand: *he did not foresee that.*
▸**foreˈseeable** ADJECTIVE ▸**foreˈseer** NOUN

foreshadow (fɔːˈʃædəʊ) VERB (*tr*) to show, indicate, or suggest in advance; presage.
▸**foreˈshadower** NOUN

foreshank (ˈfɔːˌʃæŋk) NOUN [1] the top of the front leg of an animal. [2] a cut of meat from this part.

foresheet (ˈfɔːˌʃiːt) NOUN [1] the sheet of a foresail. [2] (*plural*) the part forward of the foremost thwart of a boat.

foreshock (ˈfɔːˌʃɒk) NOUN a relatively small earthquake heralding the arrival of a much larger one. Some large earthquakes are preceded by a series of foreshocks. Compare **aftershock.**

foreshore (ˈfɔːˌʃɔː) NOUN [1] the part of the shore that lies between the limits for high and low tides. [2] the part of the shore that lies just above the high-water mark.

foreshorten (fɔːˈʃɔːtᵊn) VERB (*tr*) [1] to represent (a line, form, object, etc.) as shorter than actual length in order to give an illusion of recession or projection, in accordance with the laws of linear perspective. [2] to make shorter or more condensed; reduce or abridge.

foreshow (fɔːˈʃəʊ) VERB **-shows, -showing, -showed, -shown.** (*tr*) *Archaic* to indicate in advance; foreshadow.

foreside (ˈfɔːˌsaɪd) NOUN [1] the front or upper side or part. [2] *US* land extending along the sea.

foresight (ˈfɔːˌsaɪt) NOUN [1] provision for or insight into future problems, needs, etc. [2] the act or ability of foreseeing. [3] the act of looking forward. [4] *Surveying* a reading taken looking forwards to a new station, esp in levelling from a point of known elevation to a point the elevation of which is to be determined. Compare **backsight.** [5] the front sight on a firearm.
▸ **ˌforeˈsighted** ADJECTIVE ▸ **ˌforeˈsightedly** ADVERB ▸ **ˌforeˈsightedness** NOUN

foreskin (ˈfɔːˌskɪn) NOUN *Anatomy* the nontechnical name for **prepuce** (sense 1). Related adjective: **preputial.**

forespeak (fɔːˈspiːk) VERB **-speaks, -speaking, -spoke, -spoken.** (*tr*) *Rare* [1] to predict; foresee. [2] to arrange or speak of in advance.

forespent (fɔːˈspɛnt) ADJECTIVE a variant spelling of **forspent.**

forest (ˈfɒrɪst) NOUN [1] a large wooded area having a thick growth of trees and plants. [2] the trees of such an area. [3] *NZ* an area planted with exotic pines or similar trees. Compare **bush**[1] (sense 4). [4] something resembling a large wooded area, esp in density: *a forest of telegraph poles.* [5] *Law* (formerly) an area of woodland, esp one owned by the sovereign and set apart as a hunting ground with its own laws and officers. Compare **park** (sense 5). [6] (*modifier*) of, involving, or living in a forest or forests: *a forest glade.* ◆ VERB [7] (*tr*) to create a forest (in); plant with trees.
▷**HISTORY** C13: from Old French, from Medieval Latin *forestis* unfenced woodland, from Latin *foris* outside
▸**ˈforestal** *or* **foresteal** (fəˈrɛstɪəl) ADJECTIVE ▸**ˈforested** ADJECTIVE ▸**ˈforestless** ADJECTIVE ▸**ˈforest-ˌlike** ADJECTIVE

forestall (fɔːˈstɔːl) VERB (*tr*) [1] to delay, stop, or guard against beforehand. [2] to anticipate. [3] **a** to prevent or hinder sales at (a market, etc.) by buying up merchandise in advance, etc. **b** to buy up (merchandise) for profitable resale. Compare **corner** (sense 21).
▷**HISTORY** C14 *forestallen* to waylay, from Old English *foresteall* an ambush, from *fore-* in front of + *steall* place
▸**foreˈstaller** NOUN ▸**foreˈstalment** *or esp US* **foreˈstallment** NOUN

forestation (ˌfɒrɪˈsteɪʃən) NOUN the planting of trees over a wide area.

forestay (ˈfɔːˌsteɪ) NOUN *Nautical* an adjustable stay leading from the truck of the foremast to the deck, stem, or bowsprit, for controlling the motion or bending of the mast.

forestaysail (fɔːˈsteɪˌseɪl; *Nautical* fɔːˈsteɪsᵊl) NOUN *Nautical* the triangular headsail set aftermost on a vessel.

forester (ˈfɒrɪstə) NOUN [1] a person skilled in forestry or in charge of a forest. [2] any of various Old World moths of the genus *Ino*, characterized by brilliant metallic green wings: family *Zygaenidae*. [3] a person or animal that lives in a forest. [4] (*capital*) a member of the Ancient Order of Foresters, a friendly society.

forest park NOUN *NZ* a recreational reserve which may include bush and exotic trees.

forest ranger NOUN *Chiefly US and Canadian* a government official who patrols and protects forests, wildlife, etc.

forestry (ˈfɒrɪstrɪ) NOUN [1] the science of planting and caring for trees. [2] the planting and management of forests. [3] *Rare* forest land.

foretaste NOUN (ˈfɔːˌteɪst) [1] an early but limited experience or awareness of something to come. ◆ VERB (fɔːˈteɪst) [2] (*tr*) to have a foretaste of.

foretell (fɔːˈtɛl) VERB **-tells, -telling, -told.** (*tr; may take a clause as object*) to tell or indicate (an event, a result, etc.) beforehand; predict.
▸**foreˈteller** NOUN

forethought (ˈfɔːˌθɔːt) NOUN [1] advance consideration or deliberation. [2] thoughtful anticipation of future events.
▸**foreˈthoughtful** ADJECTIVE ▸**foreˈthoughtfully** ADVERB ▸**foreˈthoughtfulness** NOUN

foretime (ˈfɔːˌtaɪm) NOUN time already gone; the past.

foretoken NOUN (ˈfɔːˌtəʊkən) [1] a sign of a future event. ◆ VERB (fɔːˈtəʊkən) [2] (*tr*) to foreshadow.

foretooth (ˈfɔːˌtuːθ) NOUN, *plural* **-teeth** (-ˌtiːθ). *Dentistry* another word for an **incisor.**

foretop (ˈfɔːˌtɒp; *Nautical* ˈfɔːtəp) NOUN *Nautical* a platform at the top of the foremast.

fore-topgallant (ˌfɔːtɒpˈgælənt; *Nautical* ˌfɔːtəˈgælənt) ADJECTIVE *Nautical* of, relating to, or being the topmost portion of a foremast, above the topmast: *the fore-topgallant mast.*

fore-topmast (fɔːˈtɒpˌmɑːst; *Nautical* fɔːˈtɒpməst) NOUN *Nautical* a mast stepped above a foremast.

fore-topsail (fɔːˈtɒpˌseɪl; *Nautical* fɔːˈtɒpsᵊl) NOUN *Nautical* a sail set on a fore-topmast.

foretriangle (ˈfɔːtraɪˌæŋgᵊl) NOUN the triangular area formed by the deck, foremast, and headstay of a sailing vessel.

4EVA *Text messaging* ABBREVIATION FOR for ever.

forever (fɔːˈrɛvə, fə-) ADVERB [1] Also: **for ever.** without end; everlastingly; eternally. [2] at all times; incessantly. [3] *Informal* for a very long time: *he went on speaking forever.* ◆ NOUN [4] (*as object*) *Informal* a very long time: *it took him forever to reply.* [5] **...forever!** an exclamation expressing support or loyalty: *Scotland forever!*

> **Language note** *Forever* and *for ever* can both be used to say that something is without end. For all other meanings, *forever* is the preferred form.

for evermore *or* **forevermore** (fɔːˌrɛvəˈmɔː, fə-) ADVERB a more emphatic or emotive term for **forever.**

forewarn (fɔːˈwɔːn) VERB (*tr*) to warn beforehand. ▸foreˈwarner NOUN ▸foreˈwarningly ADVERB

forewent (fɔːˈwɛnt) VERB the past tense of **forego**.

forewind (ˈfɔːˌwɪnd) NOUN *Nautical* a favourable wind.

forewing (ˈfɔːˌwɪŋ) NOUN either wing of the anterior pair of an insect's two pairs of wings.

foreword (ˈfɔːˌwɜːd) NOUN an introductory statement to a book.
▷HISTORY C19: literal translation of German *Vorwort*

foreworn (fɔːˈwɔːn) ADJECTIVE a variant spelling of **forworn**.

forex (ˈfɒrɛks) NOUN short for **foreign exchange**.

foreyard (ˈfɔːˌjɑːd) NOUN *Nautical* a yard for supporting the foresail of a square-rigger.

forfaiting (ˈfɔːˌfeɪtɪŋ) NOUN the financial service of discounting, without recourse, a promissory note, bill of exchange, letter of credit, etc., received from an overseas buyer by an exporter; a form of debt discounting.
▷HISTORY C20: from French *forfaire* to forfeit or surrender

Forfar (ˈfɔːfər, -fɑː) NOUN a market town in E Scotland, the administrative centre of Angus: site of a castle, residence of Scottish kings between the 11th and 14th centuries. Pop.: 12 961 (1991).

forfeit (ˈfɔːfɪt) NOUN 1 something lost or given up as a penalty for a fault, mistake, etc. 2 the act of losing or surrendering something in this manner. 3 *Law* something confiscated as a penalty for an offence, breach of contract, etc. 4 (*sometimes plural*) **a** a game in which a player has to give up an object, perform a specified action, etc., if he commits a fault. **b** an object so given up. ◆ VERB 5 (*tr*) to lose or be liable to lose in consequence of a mistake, fault, etc. 6 (*tr*) *Law* **a** to confiscate as punishment. **b** to surrender (something exacted as a penalty). ◆ ADJECTIVE 7 surrendered or liable to be surrendered as a penalty.
▷HISTORY C13: from Old French *forfet* offence, from *forfaire* to commit a crime, from Medieval Latin *foris facere* to act outside (what is lawful), from Latin *foris* outside + *facere* to do
▸ˈforfeitable ADJECTIVE ▸ˈforfeiter NOUN

forfeiture (ˈfɔːfɪtʃə) NOUN 1 something forfeited. 2 the act of forfeiting or paying a penalty.

forfend *or* **forefend** (fɔːˈfɛnd) VERB (*tr*) 1 *US* to protect or secure. 2 *Obsolete* to prohibit or prevent.

forfex (ˈfɔːfɛks) NOUN *Entomol* a pair of pincers, esp the paired terminal appendages of an earwig.
▷HISTORY C18: Latin: a pair of scissors

forficate (ˈfɔːfɪkɪt, -ˌkeɪt) ADJECTIVE (esp of the tails of certain birds) deeply forked.
▷HISTORY C19: from Latin *forfex* scissors

forfochen (fərˈfoxᵊn) ADJECTIVE *Scot* exhausted.
▷HISTORY a variant of earlier *forfoughten* worn out by fighting

forgat (fəˈgæt) VERB *Archaic* a past tense of **forget**.

forgather (fɔːˈgæðə) VERB a variant spelling of **foregather**.

forgave (fəˈgeɪv) VERB the past tense of **forgive**.

forge¹ (fɔːdʒ) NOUN 1 a place in which metal is worked by heating and hammering; smithy. 2 a hearth or furnace used for heating metal. 3 a machine used to shape metals by hammering. ◆ VERB 4 (*tr*) to shape (metal) by heating and hammering. 5 (*tr*) to form, shape, make, or fashion (objects, articles, etc.). 6 (*tr*) to invent or devise (an agreement, understanding, etc.). 7 to make or produce a fraudulent imitation of (a signature, banknote, etc.) or to commit forgery.
▷HISTORY C14: from Old French *forgier* to construct, from Latin *fabricāre*, from *faber* craftsman
▸ˈforgeable ADJECTIVE ▸ˈforger NOUN

forge² (fɔːdʒ) VERB (*intr*) 1 to move at a steady and persevering pace. 2 to increase speed; spurt.
▷HISTORY C17: of unknown origin

forgery (ˈfɔːdʒərɪ) NOUN, *plural* **-geries**. 1 the act of reproducing something for a deceitful or fraudulent purpose. 2 something forged, such as a work of art or an antique. 3 *Criminal law* **a** the false making or altering of any document, such as a cheque or character reference (and including a postage stamp), or any tape or disc on which information is stored, intending that anyone shall accept it as genuine and so act to his or another's prejudice. **b** something forged. 4 *Criminal law* the counterfeiting of a seal or die with intention to defraud.

forget (fəˈgɛt) VERB **-gets, -getting, -got, -gotten** *or archaic or dialect* **-got**. 1 (when *tr, may take a clause as object or an infinitive*) to fail to recall (someone or something once known); be unable to remember. 2 (*tr; may take a clause as object or an infinitive*) to neglect, usually as the result of an unintentional error. 3 (*tr*) to leave behind by mistake. 4 (*tr*) to disregard intentionally. 5 (when *tr, may take a clause as object*) to fail to mention. 6 **a** forget oneself. a. to act in an improper manner. **b** to be unselfish. **c** to be deep in thought. 7 **forget it!** an exclamation of annoyed or forgiving dismissal of a matter or topic.
▷HISTORY Old English *forgietan*; related to Old Frisian *forgeta*, Old Saxon *fargetan*, Old High German *firgezzan*
▸forˈgettable ADJECTIVE ▸forˈgetter NOUN

forgetful (fəˈgɛtfʊl) ADJECTIVE 1 tending to forget. 2 (*often postpositive; foll by of*) inattentive (to) or neglectful (of). 3 *Poetic* causing loss of memory.
▸forˈgetfully ADVERB ▸forˈgetfulness NOUN

forget-me-not NOUN any temperate low-growing plant of the mainly European boraginaceous genus *Myosotis*, having clusters of small typically blue flowers. Also called: **scorpion grass**.

forging (ˈfɔːdʒɪŋ) NOUN 1 the process of producing a metal component by hammering. 2 the act of a forger. 3 a metal component produced by this process. 4 the collision of a horse's hind shoe and fore shoe.

forgive (fəˈgɪv) VERB **-gives, -giving, -gave, -given**. 1 to cease to blame or hold resentment against (someone or something). 2 to grant pardon for (a mistake, wrongdoing, etc.). 3 (*tr*) to free or pardon (someone) from penalty. 4 (*tr*) to free from the obligation of (a debt, payment, etc.).
▷HISTORY Old English *forgiefan*; see FOR-, GIVE
▸forˈgivable ADJECTIVE ▸forˈgivably ADVERB ▸forˈgiver NOUN

forgiveness (fəˈgɪvnɪs) NOUN 1 the act of forgiving or the state of being forgiven. 2 willingness to forgive.

forgiving (fəˈgɪvɪŋ) ADJECTIVE willing to forgive; merciful.
▸forˈgivingly ADVERB ▸forˈgivingness NOUN

forgo *or* **forego** (fɔːˈgəʊ) VERB **-goes, -going, -went, -gone**. (*tr*) 1 to give up or do without. 2 *Archaic* to leave.
▷HISTORY Old English *forgān*; see FOR-, GO[1]
▸forˈgoer *or* foreˈgoer NOUN

forgot (fəˈgɒt) VERB 1 the past tense of **forget**. 2 *Archaic or dialect* a past participle of **forget**.

forgotten (fəˈgɒtᵊn) VERB a past participle of **forget**.

forint (*Hungarian* ˈforint) NOUN the standard monetary unit of Hungary, divided into 100 fillér.
▷HISTORY from Hungarian, from Italian *fiorino* FLORIN

forjudge *or* **forejudge** (fɔːˈdʒʌdʒ) VERB (*tr*) *Law* 1 to deprive of a right by the judgment of a court. 2 *Chiefly US* to expel (an officer or attorney) from court for misconduct.
▸forˈjudgment *or* foreˈjudgment NOUN

fork (fɔːk) NOUN 1 a small usually metal implement consisting of two, three, or four long thin prongs on the end of a handle, used for lifting food to the mouth or turning it in cooking, etc. 2 an agricultural tool consisting of a handle and three or four metal prongs, used for lifting, digging, etc. 3 a pronged part of any machine, device, etc. 4 (of a road, river, etc.) **a** a division into two or more branches. **b** the point where the division begins. **c** such a branch. 5 *Chiefly US* the main tributary of a river. 6 *Chess* a position in which two pieces are forked. ◆ VERB 7 (*tr*) to pick up, dig, etc., with a fork. 8 (*tr*) *Chess* to place (two enemy pieces) under attack with one of one's own pieces, esp a knight. 9 (*tr*) to make into the shape of a fork. 10 (*intr*) to be divided into two or more branches. 11 to take one or other branch at a fork in a road, river, etc.
▷HISTORY Old English *forca*, from Latin *furca*
▸ˈforkful NOUN

forked (fɔːkt, ˈfɔːkɪd) ADJECTIVE 1 **a** having a fork or forklike parts. **b** (*in combination*): *two-forked*. 2 having sharp angles; zigzag. 3 insincere or equivocal (esp in the phrase **forked tongue**).
▸forkedly (ˈfɔːkɪdlɪ) ADVERB ▸ˈforkedness NOUN

forked lightning NOUN a zigzag form of lightning. Also called: **chain lightning**.

fork-lift truck NOUN a vehicle having two power-operated horizontal prongs that can be raised and lowered for loading, transporting, and unloading goods, esp goods that are stacked on wooden pallets. Sometimes shortened to **forklift**.

fork out, over, *or* **up** VERB (*adverb*) *Slang* to pay (money, goods, etc.), esp with reluctance.

Forlì (*Italian* forˈli) NOUN a city in N Italy, in Emilia-Romagna. Pop.: 107 475 (2000 est.). Ancient name: **Forum Livii** (ˈlɪvɪaɪ).

forlorn (fəˈlɔːn) ADJECTIVE 1 miserable, wretched, or cheerless; desolate. 2 deserted; forsaken. 3 (*postpositive; foll by of*) destitute; bereft: *forlorn of hope*. 4 desperate: *the last forlorn attempt*.
▷HISTORY Old English *forloren* lost, from *forlēosan* to lose; related to Old Saxon *farliosan*, Gothic *fraliusan*, Greek *luein* to release
▸forˈlornly ADVERB ▸forˈlornness NOUN

forlorn hope NOUN 1 a hopeless or desperate enterprise. 2 a faint hope. 3 *Obsolete* a group of soldiers assigned to an extremely dangerous duty.
▷HISTORY C16 (in the obsolete sense): changed (by folk etymology) from Dutch *verloren hoop* lost troop, from *verloren*, past participle of *verliezen* to lose + *hoop* troop (literally: heap)

form (fɔːm) NOUN 1 the shape or configuration of something as distinct from its colour, texture, etc. 2 the particular mode, appearance, etc., in which a thing or person manifests itself: *water in the form of ice; in the form of a bat*. 3 a type or kind: *imprisonment is a form of punishment*. 4 **a** a printed document, esp one with spaces in which to insert facts or answers: *an application form*. **b** (*as modifier*): *a form letter*. 5 physical or mental condition, esp good condition, with reference to ability to perform: *off form*. 6 the previous record of a horse, athlete, etc., esp with regard to fitness. 7 *Brit slang* a criminal record. 8 style, arrangement, or design in the arts, as opposed to content. 9 a fixed mode of artistic expression or representation in literary, musical, or other artistic works: *sonata form; sonnet form*. 10 a mould, frame, etc., that gives shape to something. 11 organized structure or order, as in an artistic work. 12 *Education, chiefly Brit* a group of children who are taught together; class. 13 manner, method, or style of doing something, esp with regard to recognized standards. 14 behaviour or procedure, esp as governed by custom or etiquette: *good form*. 15 formality or ceremony. 16 a prescribed set or order of words, terms, etc., as in a religious ceremony or legal document. 17 *Philosophy* **a** the structure of anything as opposed to its constitution or content. **b** essence as opposed to matter. **c** (*often capital*) (in the philosophy of Plato) the ideal universal that exists independently of the particulars which fall under it. See also **Form**. **d** (in the philosophy of Aristotle) the constitution of matter to form a substance; by virtue of this its nature can be understood. 18 See **logical form**. 19 *Brit* a bench, esp one that is long, low, and backless. 20 the nest or hollow in which a hare lives. 21 a group of organisms within a species that differ from similar groups by trivial differences, as of colour. 22 *Linguistics* **a** the phonological or orthographic shape or appearance of a linguistic element, such as a word. **b** a linguistic element considered from the point of view of its shape or sound rather than, for example, its meaning. 23 *Crystallog* See **crystal form**. 24 *Taxonomy* a group distinguished from other groups by a single characteristic: ranked below a variety. ◆ VERB 25 to give shape or form to or to take shape or form, esp a specified or particular shape. 26 to come or bring into existence: *a scum formed on the surface*. 27 to make, produce, or construct or be made, produced, or constructed. 28 to construct or develop in the mind: *to form an opinion*. 29 (*tr*) to train, develop, or mould by instruction, discipline, or example. 30 (*tr*) to acquire, contract, or develop: *to form a habit*. 31 (*tr*) to be an element of, serve as, or constitute: *this plank will form a bridge*. 32 (*tr*) to draw up; organize: *to form a club*.
▷HISTORY C13: from Old French *forme*, from Latin *forma* shape, model
▸ˈformable ADJECTIVE

Form (fɔːm) NOUN (in the philosophy of Plato) an ideal archetype existing independently of those individuals which fall under it, supposedly explaining their common properties and serving as the only objects of true knowledge as opposed to the mere opinion obtainable of matters of fact. Also called: **Idea.**

-form ADJECTIVE COMBINING FORM having the shape or form of or resembling: *cruciform; vermiform.*
▷HISTORY from New Latin *-formis*, from Latin, from *fōrma* FORM

formal¹ (ˈfɔːməl) ADJECTIVE 1 of, according to, or following established or prescribed forms, conventions, etc.: *a formal document.* 2 characterized by observation of conventional forms of ceremony, behaviour, dress, etc.: *a formal dinner.* 3 methodical, precise, or stiff. 4 suitable for occasions organized according to conventional ceremony: *formal dress.* 5 denoting or characterized by idiom, vocabulary, etc., used by educated speakers and writers of a language. 6 acquired by study in academic institutions: *a formal education.* 7 regular or symmetrical in form: *a formal garden.* 8 of or relating to the appearance, form, etc., of something as distinguished from its substance. 9 logically deductive: *formal proof.* 10 *Philosophy* **a** of or relating to form as opposed to matter or content. **b** pertaining to the essence or nature of something: *formal cause.* **c** (in the writings of Descartes) pertaining to the correspondence between an image or idea and its object. **d** being in the formal mode. 11 denoting a second-person pronoun in some languages used when the addressee is a stranger, social superior, etc.: *in French the pronoun "vous" is formal, while "tu" is informal.*
▷HISTORY C14: from Latin *formālis*
▸ˈ**formally** ADVERB ▸ˈ**formalness** NOUN

formal² (ˈfɔːmæl) NOUN another name for **methylal.**
▷HISTORY C19: from FORM(IC) + -AL³

formaldehyde (fɔːˈmældɪˌhaɪd) NOUN a colourless poisonous irritating gas with a pungent characteristic odour, made by the oxidation of methanol and used as formalin and in the manufacture of synthetic resins. Formula: HCHO. Systematic name: **methanal.**
▷HISTORY C19: FORM(IC) + ALDEHYDE; on the model of German *Formaldehyd*

formal equivalence NOUN *Logic* the relation that holds between two open sentences when their universal closures are materially equivalent.

formalin (ˈfɔːməlɪn) *or* **formol** (ˈfɔːmɒl) NOUN a 40 per cent solution of formaldehyde in water, used as a disinfectant, preservative for biological specimens, etc.

formalism (ˈfɔːməˌlɪzəm) NOUN 1 scrupulous or excessive adherence to outward form at the expense of inner reality or content. 2 **a** the mathematical or logical structure of a scientific argument as distinguished from its subject matter. **b** the notation, and its structure, in which information is expressed. 3 *Theatre* a stylized mode of production. 4 (in Marxist criticism) excessive concern with artistic technique at the expense of social values, etc. 5 the philosophical theory that a mathematical statement has no meaning but that its symbols, regarded as physical objects, exhibit a structure that has useful applications. Compare **logicism, intuitionism.**
▸ˈ**formalist** NOUN ▸ˌ**formalˈistic** ADJECTIVE
▸ˌ**formalˈistically** ADVERB

formality (fɔːˈmælɪtɪ) NOUN, *plural* **-ties.** 1 a requirement of rule, custom, etiquette, etc. 2 the condition or quality of being formal or conventional. 3 strict or excessive observance of form, ceremony, etc. 4 an established, proper, or conventional method, act, or procedure.

formalize *or* **formalise** (ˈfɔːməˌlaɪz) VERB 1 to be or make formal. 2 (*tr*) to make official or valid. 3 (*tr*) to give a definite shape or form to. 4 *Logic* to extract the logical form of (an expression), to express in the symbols of some formal system.
▸ˌ**formaliˈzation** *or* ˌ**formaliˈsation** NOUN ▸ˈ**formalˌizer** *or* ˈ**formalˌiser** NOUN

formal language NOUN 1 a language designed for use in situations in which natural language is unsuitable, as for example in mathematics, logic, or computer programming. The symbols and formulas of such languages stand in precisely specified syntactic and semantic relations to one another. 2 *Logic* a logistic system for which an interpretation is provided: distinguished from formal calculus in that the semantics enable it to be regarded as *about* some subject matter.

formal logic NOUN 1 the study of systems of deductive argument in which symbols are used to represent precisely defined categories of expressions. Also called: **symbolic logic.** Compare **philosophical logic.** 2 a specific formal system that can be interpreted as representing a fragment of natural argument.

formal mode NOUN *Philosophy* the style in which words are explicitly mentioned rather than used of their subject matter. *"Fido" is a dog's name* is in the formal mode, while *"Fido is a dog"* is in the material mode. See also **mention** (sense 7).

formal system NOUN *Logic* an uninterpreted symbolic system whose syntax is precisely defined, and on which a relation of deducibility is defined in purely syntactic terms; a logistic system. Also called: **formal theory, formal calculus.** Compare **formal language.**

formant (ˈfɔːmənt) NOUN *Acoustics, phonetics* any of several frequency ranges within which the partials of a sound, esp a vowel sound, are at their strongest, thus imparting to the sound its own special quality, tone colour, or timbre.

format (ˈfɔːmæt) NOUN 1 the general appearance of a publication, including type style, paper, binding, etc. 2 an approximate indication of the size of a publication as determined by the number of times the original sheet of paper is folded to make a leaf. See also **duodecimo, quarto.** 3 style, plan, or arrangement, as of a television programme. 4 *Computing* **a** the defined arrangement of data encoded in a file or for example on magnetic disk or CD-ROM, essential for the correct recording and recovery of data on different devices. **b** the arrangement of text on printed output or a display screen, or a coded description of such an arrangement. ◆ VERB **-mats, -matting, -matted.** (*tr*) 5 to arrange (a book, page, etc.) into a specified format.
▷HISTORY C19: via French from German, from Latin *liber formātus* volume formed

formate (ˈfɔːmeɪt) NOUN any salt or ester of formic acid containing the ion $HCOO^-$ or the group HCOO–.
▷HISTORY C19: from FORM(IC) + -ATE¹

formation (fɔːˈmeɪʃən) NOUN 1 the act of giving or taking form, shape, or existence. 2 something that is formed. 3 the manner in which something is formed or arranged. 4 a formal arrangement of a number of persons or things acting as a unit, such as a troop of soldiers, aircraft in flight, or a football team. 5 *Geology* **a** the fundamental lithostratigraphic unit. **b** a series of rocks with certain characteristics in common. 6 *Ecology* a community of plants, such as a tropical rainforest, extending over a very large area.
▸**forˈmational** ADJECTIVE

formation dance NOUN any dance in which a number of couples form a certain arrangement, such as two facing lines or a circle, and perform a series of figures within or based on that arrangement.
▸**formation dancing** NOUN

formation rules PLURAL NOUN *Logic* the set of rules that specify the syntax of a formal system; the algorithm that generates the well-formed formulae.

formative (ˈfɔːmətɪv) ADJECTIVE 1 of or relating to formation, development, or growth: *formative years.* 2 shaping; moulding: *a formative experience.* 3 (of tissues and cells in certain parts of an organism) capable of growth and differentiation. 4 functioning in the formation of derived, inflected, or compound words. ◆ NOUN 5 an inflectional or derivational affix. 6 (in generative grammar) any of the minimum units of a sentence that have syntactic function.
▸ˈ**formatively** ADVERB ▸ˈ**formativeness** NOUN

formative assessment NOUN ongoing assessment of a pupil's educational development within a particular subject area. Compare **summative assessment.**

form class NOUN 1 another term for **part of speech.** 2 a group of words distinguished by common inflections, such as the weak verbs of English.

form criticism NOUN literary criticism concerned esp with analysing the Bible in terms of the literary forms used, such as proverbs, songs, or stories, and relating them to their historical forms and background.
▸**form critic** NOUN ▸**form critical** ADJECTIVE

form drag NOUN the drag on a body moving through a fluid as a result of the shape of the body. It can be reduced by streamlining.

forme *or US* **form** (fɔːm) NOUN *Printing* type matter, blocks, etc., assembled in a chase and ready for printing.
▷HISTORY C15: from French: FORM

former¹ (ˈfɔːmə) ADJECTIVE (*prenominal*) 1 belonging to or occurring in an earlier time: *former glory.* 2 having been at a previous time: *a former colleague.* 3 denoting the first or first mentioned of two: *in the former case.* 4 near the beginning. ◆ NOUN 5 **the former.** the first or first mentioned of two: distinguished from *latter.*

former² (ˈfɔːmə) NOUN 1 a person or thing that forms or shapes. 2 *Electrical engineering* a tool for giving a coil or winding the required shape, sometimes consisting of a frame on which the wire can be wound, the frame then being removed.

formerly (ˈfɔːməlɪ) ADVERB 1 at or in a former time; in the past. 2 *Obsolete* in the immediate past; just now.

form genus NOUN a group of species (**form species**) that have similar structural characteristics but are not closely related.

formic (ˈfɔːmɪk) ADJECTIVE 1 of, relating to, or derived from ants. 2 of, containing, or derived from formic acid.
▷HISTORY C18: from Latin *formīca* ant; the acid occurs naturally in ants

Formica (fɔːˈmaɪkə) NOUN *Trademark* any of various laminated plastic sheets, containing melamine, used esp for heat-resistant surfaces that can be easily cleaned.

formic acid NOUN a colourless corrosive liquid carboxylic acid found in some insects, esp ants, and many plants: used in dyeing textiles and the manufacture of insecticides and refrigerants. Formula: HCOOH. Systematic name: **methanoic acid.**

formicary (ˈfɔːmɪkərɪ) *or* **formicarium** (ˌfɔːmɪˈkɛərɪəm) NOUN, *plural* **-caries, -caria** (-ˈkɛərɪə). less common names for **ant hill.**
▷HISTORY C19: from Medieval Latin *formīcārium* see FORMIC

formicate (ˈfɔːmɪˌkeɪt) VERB (*intr*) *Now rare* 1 to crawl around like ants. 2 to swarm with ants or other crawling things.
▷HISTORY C17: from Latin *formīcāre*, from *formīca* ant

formication (ˌfɔːmɪˈkeɪʃən) NOUN a sensation of insects crawling on the skin; symptom of a nerve disorder.

formidable (ˈfɔːmɪdəbᵊl) ADJECTIVE 1 arousing or likely to inspire fear or dread. 2 extremely difficult to defeat, overcome, manage, etc.: *a formidable problem.* 3 tending to inspire awe or admiration because of great size, strength, excellence, etc.
▷HISTORY C15: from Latin *formīdābilis*, from *formīdāre* to dread, from *formīdō* fear
▸ˌ**formidaˈbility** *or* ˈ**formidableness** NOUN ▸ˈ**formidably** ADVERB

formless (ˈfɔːmlɪs) ADJECTIVE without a definite shape or form; amorphous.
▸ˈ**formlessly** ADVERB ▸ˈ**formlessness** NOUN

form letter NOUN a single copy of a letter that has been mechanically reproduced in large numbers for circulation.

Formosa (fɔːˈməʊsə) NOUN the former name of **Taiwan.**

Formosa Strait NOUN an arm of the Pacific between Taiwan and mainland China, linking the East and South China Seas. Also called: **Taiwan Strait.**

formula (ˈfɔːmjʊlə) NOUN, *plural* **-las, -lae** (-ˌliː). 1 an established form or set of words, as used in religious ceremonies, legal proceedings, etc. 2 *Maths, physics* a general relationship, principle, or rule stated, often as an equation, in the form of symbols. 3 *Chem* a representation of molecules, radicals, ions, etc., expressed in the symbols of the

atoms of their constituent elements. See **molecular formula, empirical formula, structural formula.** 4 **a** a method, pattern, or rule for doing or producing something, often one proved to be successful. **b** (*as modifier*): *formula fiction.* 5 **a** a prescription for making up a medicine, baby's food, etc. **b** a substance prepared according to such a prescription. 6 *Motor racing* the specific category in which a particular type of car competes, judged according to engine size, weight, and fuel capacity.
▷HISTORY C17: from Latin: diminutive of *forma* FORM
▸**formulaic** (ˌfɔːmjʊˈleɪɪk) ADJECTIVE

Formula One NOUN 1 the top class of professional motor racing. 2 the most important world championship in motor racing.

formularize *or* **formularise** (ˈfɔːmjʊləˌraɪz) VERB a less common word for **formulate** (sense 1).
▸ˌ**formulariˈzation** *or* ˌ**formulariˈsation** NOUN
▸ˈ**formularˌizer** *or* ˈ**formularˌiser** NOUN

formulary (ˈfɔːmjʊlərɪ) NOUN, *plural* **-laries.** 1 a book or system of prescribed formulas, esp relating to religious procedure or doctrine. 2 a formula. 3 *Pharmacol* a book containing a list of pharmaceutical products, with their formulas and means of preparation. ◆ ADJECTIVE 4 of, relating to, or of the nature of a formula.

formulate (ˈfɔːmjʊˌleɪt) VERB (*tr*) 1 to put into or express in systematic terms; express in or as if in a formula. 2 to devise.
▸ˈ**formuˌlator** NOUN

formulation (ˌfɔːmjʊˈleɪʃən) NOUN (*tr*) 1 the act or process of formulating. 2 any mixture or substance prepared according to a particular formula. 3 a medicinal preparation administered in a specific form, such as a tablet, linctus, ointment, or injection.

formulism (ˈfɔːmjʊˌlɪzəm) NOUN adherence to or belief in formulas.
▸ˈ**formulist** NOUN, ADJECTIVE ▸ˌ**formuˈlistic** ADJECTIVE

formwork (ˈfɔːmˌwɜːk) NOUN an arrangement of wooden boards, bolts, etc., used to shape reinforced concrete while it is setting. Also called (esp Brit): **shuttering.**

formyl (ˈfɔːmaɪl) NOUN (*modifier*) of, consisting of, or containing the monovalent group HCO-: *a formyl group or radical.*
▷HISTORY C19: from FORM(IC) + -YL

Fornax (ˈfɔːnæks) NOUN, *Latin genitive* **Fornacis** (fɔːˈneɪsɪs, -ˈnæs-). a faint constellation in the S hemisphere lying between Cetus and Phoenix.
▷HISTORY Latin: oven, kiln

fornenst (fɔːˈnɛnst) PREPOSITION *Scot and Northeast English dialect* situated against or facing towards.
▷HISTORY from Scottish, from FORE[1] + *anenst* a variant of archaic ANENT

fornicate[1] (ˈfɔːnɪˌkeɪt) VERB (*intr*) to indulge in or commit fornication.
▷HISTORY C16: from Late Latin *fornicārī*, from Latin *fornix* vault, brothel situated therein
▸ˈ**forniˌcator** NOUN

fornicate[2] (ˈfɔːnɪkɪt, -ˌkeɪt) *or* **fornicated** ADJECTIVE *Biology* arched or hoodlike in form.
▷HISTORY C19: from Latin *fornicātus* arched, from *fornix* vault

fornication (ˌfɔːnɪˈkeɪʃən) NOUN 1 voluntary sexual intercourse outside marriage. 2 *Law* voluntary sexual intercourse between two persons of the opposite sex, where one is or both are unmarried. 3 *Bible* sexual immorality in general, esp adultery.

fornix (ˈfɔːnɪks) NOUN, *plural* **-nices** (-nɪˌsiːz). *Anatomy* any archlike structure, esp the arched band of white fibres at the base of the brain.
▷HISTORY C17: from Latin; see FORNICATE[2]
▸ˈ**fornical** ADJECTIVE

forsake (fəˈseɪk) VERB **-sakes, -saking, -sook** (-ˈsʊk), **-saken** (-ˈseɪkən). (*tr*) 1 to abandon. 2 to give up (something valued or enjoyed).
▷HISTORY Old English *forsacan*
▸**forˈsaker** NOUN

forsaken (fəˈseɪkən) VERB 1 the past participle of **forsake.** ◆ ADJECTIVE 2 completely deserted or helpless; abandoned.
▸**forˈsakenly** ADVERB ▸**forˈsakenness** NOUN

forsook (fəˈsʊk) VERB the past tense of **forsake.**

forsooth (fəˈsuːθ) ADVERB *Archaic* in truth; indeed.
▷HISTORY Old English *forsōth*

forspeak (fɔːˈspiːk) VERB **-speaks, -speaking, -spoke, -spoken.** (*tr*) *Scot archaic* to bewitch.

forspent *or* **forespent** (fɔːˈspɛnt) ADJECTIVE *Archaic* tired out; exhausted.

forsterite (ˈfɔːstəˌraɪt) NOUN a white, yellow, or green mineral of the olivine group consisting of magnesium silicate. Formula: Mg_2SiO_4.
▷HISTORY C19: named after J. R. *Forster* (1729–98), German naturalist

forswear (fɔːˈswɛə) VERB **-swears, -swearing, -swore, -sworn.** 1 (*tr*) to reject or renounce with determination or as upon oath. 2 (*tr*) to deny or disavow absolutely or upon oath: *he forswore any knowledge of the crime.* 3 to perjure (oneself).
▷HISTORY Old English *forswerian*
▸**forˈswearer** NOUN

forsworn (fɔːˈswɔːn) VERB the past participle of **forswear.**
▸**forˈswornness** NOUN

forsythia (fɔːˈsaɪθɪə) NOUN any oleaceous shrub of the genus *Forsythia*, native to China, Japan, and SE Europe but widely cultivated for its showy yellow bell-shaped flowers, which appear in spring before the foliage.
▷HISTORY C19: New Latin, named after William *Forsyth* (1737–1804), English botanist

fort (fɔːt) NOUN 1 a fortified enclosure, building, or position able to be defended against an enemy. 2 **hold the fort.** *Informal* to maintain or guard something temporarily.
▷HISTORY C15: from Old French, from *fort* (adj) strong, from Latin *fortis*

Fortaleza (*Portuguese* fortaˈleza) NOUN a port in NE Brazil, capital of Ceará state. Pop.: 2 138 234 (2000). Also called: **Ceará.**

fortalice (ˈfɔːtəlɪs) NOUN a small fort or outwork of a fortification.
▷HISTORY C15: from Medieval Latin *fortalitia*, from Latin *fortis* strong; see FORTRESS

Fort-de-France (*French* fɔrdəfrɑ̃s) NOUN the capital of Martinique, a port on the W coast: commercial centre of the French Antilles. Pop.: 94 049 (1999 est.).

forte[1] (fɔːt, ˈfɔːteɪ) NOUN 1 something at which a person excels; strong point: *cooking is my forte.* 2 *Fencing* the stronger section of a sword blade, between the hilt and the middle. Compare **foible.**
▷HISTORY C17: from French *fort*, from *fort* (adj) strong, from Latin *fortis*

forte[2] (ˈfɔːtɪ) *Music* ◆ ADJECTIVE, ADVERB 1 loud or loudly. Symbol: f. ◆ NOUN 2 a loud passage in music.
▷HISTORY C18: from Italian, from Latin *fortis* strong

fortepiano (ˌfɔːtɪpɪˈænəʊ) NOUN an early type of piano popular in the late 18th century.
▷HISTORY from Italian, loud-soft

forte-piano (ˌfɔːtɪˈpjɑːnəʊ) *Music* ◆ ADJECTIVE, ADVERB 1 loud and then immediately soft. Symbol: fp. ◆ NOUN 2 a note played in this way.

forth (fɔːθ) ADVERB 1 forward in place, time, order, or degree. 2 out, as from concealment, seclusion, or inaction. 3 away, as from a place or country. 4 and so on; et cetera. ◆ PREPOSITION 5 *Archaic* out of; away from.
▷HISTORY Old English; related to Middle High German *vort*; see FOR, FURTHER

Forth (fɔːθ) NOUN 1 **Firth of.** an inlet of the North Sea in SE Scotland: spanned by a cantilever railway bridge 1600 m (almost exactly 1 mile) long (1889), and by a road bridge (1964). 2 a river in S Scotland, flowing generally east to the Firth of Forth. Length: about 104 km (65 miles).

forthcoming (ˌfɔːθˈkʌmɪŋ) ADJECTIVE 1 approaching in time: *the forthcoming debate.* 2 about to appear: *his forthcoming book.* 3 available or ready: *the money wasn't forthcoming.* 4 open or sociable.
▸ˌ**forthˈcomingness** NOUN

forthright ADJECTIVE (ˈfɔːθˌraɪt) 1 direct and outspoken. ◆ ADVERB (ˌfɔːθˈraɪt, ˈfɔːθˌraɪt) *also* **forthrightly.** 2 in a direct manner; frankly. 3 at once.
▸ˈ**forthˌrightness** NOUN

forthwith (ˌfɔːθˈwɪθ, -ˈwɪð) ADVERB at once; immediately.

fortieth (ˈfɔːtɪɪθ) ADJECTIVE 1 **a** being the ordinal number of *forty* in numbering or counting order, position, time, etc. Often written: 40th. **b** (*as noun*): *he was the fortieth.* ◆ NOUN 2 **a** one of 40 approximately equal parts of something. **b** (*as modifier*): *a fortieth part.* 3 the fraction equal to one divided by 40 (1/40).
▷HISTORY Old English *fēowertigotha*

fortification (ˌfɔːtɪfɪˈkeɪʃən) NOUN 1 the act, art, or science of fortifying or strengthening. 2 **a** a wall, mound, etc., used to fortify a place. **b** such works collectively. 3 any place that can be militarily defended.

fortified pa NOUN *NZ history* a Maori hilltop dwelling with trenches and palisades for defensive occupation.

fortified wine NOUN wine treated by the addition of brandy or alcohol, such as port, marsala, and sherry.

fortify (ˈfɔːtɪˌfaɪ) VERB **-fies, -fying, -fied.** (*mainly tr*) 1 (*also intr*) to make (a place) defensible, as by building walls, digging trenches, etc. 2 to strengthen physically, mentally, or morally. 3 to strengthen, support, or reinforce (a garment, structure, etc.). 4 to add spirits or alcohol to (wine), in order to produce sherry, port, etc. 5 to increase the nutritious value of (a food), as by adding vitamins and minerals. 6 to support or confirm: *to fortify an argument with facts.*
▷HISTORY C15: from Old French *fortifier*, from Late Latin *fortificāre*, from Latin *fortis* strong + *facere* to make
▸ˈ**fortiˌfiable** ADJECTIVE ▸ˈ**fortiˌfier** NOUN ▸ˈ**fortiˌfyingly** ADVERB

fortis (ˈfɔːtɪs) *Phonetics* ◆ ADJECTIVE 1 (of a consonant) articulated with considerable muscular tension of the speech organs or with a great deal of breath pressure or plosion. ◆ NOUN, *plural* **-tes** (-tiːz). 2 a consonant, such as English *p* or *f*, pronounced with considerable muscular force or breath pressure. ◆ Compare **lenis.**
▷HISTORY Latin: strong

fortissimo (fɔːˈtɪsɪˌməʊ) *Music* ◆ ADJECTIVE, ADVERB 1 very loud. Symbol: ff. ◆ NOUN 2 a very loud passage in music.
▷HISTORY C18: from Italian, from Latin *fortissimus*, from *fortis* strong

fortitude (ˈfɔːtɪˌtjuːd) NOUN strength and firmness of mind; resolute endurance.
▷HISTORY C15: from Latin *fortitūdō* courage
▸ˌ**fortiˈtudinous** ADJECTIVE

Fort Knox (nɒks) NOUN a military reservation in N Kentucky: site of the US Gold Bullion Depository. Pop.: 38 280 (latest est.).

Fort Lamy (ˈfɔːt ˈlɑːmɪ; *French* fɔr lami) NOUN the former name (until 1973) of **Ndjamena.**

Fort Lauderdale (ˈlɔːdəˌdeɪl) NOUN a city in SE Florida, on the Atlantic. Pop.: 152 397 (2000).

fortnight (ˈfɔːtˌnaɪt) NOUN a period of 14 consecutive days; two weeks.
▷HISTORY Old English *fēowertīene niht* fourteen nights

fortnightly (ˈfɔːtˌnaɪtlɪ) *Chiefly Brit* ◆ ADJECTIVE 1 occurring or appearing once each fortnight. ◆ ADVERB 2 once a fortnight. ◆ NOUN, *plural* **-lies.** 3 a publication issued at intervals of two weeks.

FORTRAN *or* **Fortran** (ˈfɔːtræn) NOUN a high-level computer programming language for mathematical and scientific purposes, designed to facilitate and speed up the solving of complex problems.
▷HISTORY C20: from *for(mula) tran(slation)*

fortress (ˈfɔːtrɪs) NOUN 1 a large fort or fortified town. 2 a place or source of refuge or support. ◆ VERB 3 (*tr*) to protect with or as if with a fortress.
▷HISTORY C13: from Old French *forteresse*, from Medieval Latin *fortalitia*, from Latin *fortis* strong

Fort Sumter (ˈsʌmtə) NOUN a fort in SE South Carolina, guarding Charleston Harbour. Its capture by Confederate forces (1861) was the first action of the Civil War.

fortuitism (fɔːˈtjuːɪˌtɪzəm) NOUN *Philosophy* the doctrine that evolutionary adaptations are the result of chance. Compare **tychism.**
▸**forˈtuitist** NOUN, ADJECTIVE

fortuitous (fɔːˈtjuːɪtəs) ADJECTIVE happening by chance, esp by a lucky chance; unplanned; accidental.

▷HISTORY C17: from Latin *fortuitus* happening by chance, from *forte* by chance, from *fors* chance, luck ▸**for'tuitously** ADVERB ▸**for'tuitousness** NOUN

fortuity (fɔːˈtjuːɪtɪ) NOUN, *plural* **-ties.** [1] a chance or accidental occurrence. [2] fortuitousness. [3] chance or accident.

Fortuna (fɔːˈtjuːnə) NOUN the Roman goddess of fortune and good luck. Greek counterpart: **Tyche.**

fortunate (ˈfɔːtʃənɪt) ADJECTIVE [1] having good luck; lucky. [2] occurring by or bringing good fortune or luck; auspicious.
▸ˈ**fortunateness** NOUN

fortunately (ˈfɔːtʃənɪtlɪ) ADVERB [1] (*sentence modifier*) it is fortunate that; luckily. [2] in a fortunate manner.

fortune (ˈfɔːtʃən) NOUN [1] an amount of wealth or material prosperity, esp, when unqualified, a great amount. [2] **small fortune.** a large sum of money. [3] a power or force, often personalized, regarded as being responsible for human affairs; chance. [4] luck, esp when favourable. [5] (*often plural*) a person's lot or destiny. ◆ VERB [6] *Archaic* **a** (*tr*) to endow with great wealth. **b** (*intr*) to happen by chance.
▷HISTORY C13: from Old French, from Latin *fortūna*, from *fors* chance
▸ˈ**fortuneless** ADJECTIVE

fortune-hunter NOUN a person who seeks to secure a fortune, esp through marriage.
▸ˈ**fortune-ˌhunting** ADJECTIVE, NOUN

fortune-teller NOUN a person who makes predictions about the future as by looking into a crystal ball, reading palms, etc.
▸ˈ**fortune-ˌtelling** ADJECTIVE, NOUN

Fort Wayne (weɪn) NOUN a city in NE Indiana. Pop.: 205 727 (2000).

Fort William (ˈwɪljəm) NOUN a town in W Scotland, in Highland at the head of Loch Linnhe: tourist centre; the fort itself, built in 1655 and renamed after William III in 1690, was demolished in 1866. Pop.: 10 391 (1991).

Fort Worth (wɜːθ) NOUN a city in N Texas, at the junction of the Clear and West forks of the Trinity River: aircraft works, electronics. Pop.: 534 694 (2000).

forty (ˈfɔːtɪ) NOUN, *plural* **-ties.** [1] the cardinal number that is the product of ten and four. See also **number** (sense 1). [2] a numeral, 40, XL, etc., representing this number. [3] something representing, represented by, or consisting of 40 units. ◆ DETERMINER [4] **a** amounting to forty: *forty thieves.* **b** (*as pronoun*): *there were forty in the herd.*
▷HISTORY Old English *fēowertig*

forty-five NOUN [1] a gramophone record played at 45 revolutions per minute. [2] *US and Canadian* a pistol having .45 calibre.

Forty-Five NOUN **the.** *Brit history* another name for the **Jacobite Rebellion** (sense 2).

forty-niner NOUN (*sometimes capital*) *US history* a prospector who took part in the California gold rush of 1849.

forty-ninth parallel NOUN *Canadian* an informal name for the border with the USA., which is in part delineated by the parallel line of latitude at 49°N.

forty winks NOUN (*functioning as singular or plural*) *Informal* a short light sleep; nap.

forum (ˈfɔːrəm) NOUN, *plural* **-rums, -ra** (-rə). [1] a meeting or assembly for the open discussion of subjects of public interest. [2] a medium for open discussion, such as a magazine. [3] a public meeting place for open discussion. [4] a court; tribunal. [5] (in South Africa) a pressure group of leaders or representatives, esp Black leaders or representatives. [6] (in ancient Italy) an open space, usually rectangular in shape, serving as a city's marketplace and centre of public business.
▷HISTORY C15: from Latin: public place; related to Latin *foris* outside

Forum *or* **Forum Romanum** (rəʊˈmɑːnəm) NOUN **the.** the main forum of ancient Rome, situated between the Capitoline and the Palatine Hills.

forward (ˈfɔːwəd) ADJECTIVE [1] directed or moving ahead. [2] lying or situated in or near the front part of something. [3] presumptuous, pert, or impudent: *a forward remark.* [4] well developed or advanced, esp in physical, material, or intellectual growth or development: *forward ideas.* [5] *Archaic* (*often postpositive*) ready, eager, or willing. [6] **a** of or relating to the future or favouring change; progressive. **b** (*in combination*): *forward-looking.* [7] *NZ* (of an animal) in good condition. ◆ NOUN [8] **a** an attacking player in any of various sports, such as soccer, hockey, or basketball. **b** (in American football) a lineman. ◆ ADVERB [9] a variant of **forwards.** [10] (ˈfɔːwəd; *Nautical* ˈfɒrəd) towards the front or bow of an aircraft or ship. [11] into prominence or a position of being subject to public scrutiny; out; forth: *the witness came forward.* ◆ VERB (*tr*) [12] to send forward or pass on to an ultimate destination: *the letter was forwarded from a previous address.* [13] to advance, help, or promote: *to forward one's career.* [14] *Bookbinding* to prepare (a book) for the finisher.
▷HISTORY Old English *foreweard*
▸ˈ**forwardly** ADVERB

forward bias *or* **voltage** NOUN a voltage applied to a circuit or device, esp a semiconductor device, in the direction that produces the larger current.

forward delivery NOUN (in commerce) delivery at a future date.

forwarder (ˈfɔːwədə) NOUN [1] a person or thing that forwards. [2] a person engaged in the bookbinding process of forwarding. [3] See **forwarding agent.**

forwarding (ˈfɔːwədɪŋ) NOUN all the processes involved in the binding of a book subsequent to cutting and up to the fitting of its cover.

forwarding agent NOUN a person, agency, or enterprise engaged in the collection, shipment, and delivery of goods.

forward market NOUN a market in which contracts are made to buy or sell currencies, commodities, etc., at some future date at a price fixed at the date of the contract. Compare **spot market.**

forwardness (ˈfɔːwədnɪs) NOUN [1] lack of modesty; presumption; boldness. [2] willing readiness; eagerness. [3] a state or condition of advanced progress or development.

forward pass NOUN *Rugby* an illegal pass towards the opponent's dead-ball line. Also called: **throw-forward.**

forward quotation NOUN (in commerce) the price quoted for goods sent on forward delivery.

forward roll NOUN a gymnastic movement in which the body is turned heels over head with the back of the neck resting on the ground.

forwards (ˈfɔːwədz) *or* **forward** ADVERB [1] towards or at a place ahead or in advance, esp in space but also in time. [2] towards the front.

forwent (fɔːˈwent) VERB the past tense of **forgo.**

forwhy (fɔːˈwaɪ) *Archaic* ◆ ADVERB [1] for what reason; why. ◆ CONJUNCTION [2] (*subordinating*) because.
▷HISTORY Old English *for hwī*

forworn *or* **foreworn** (fɔːˈwɔːn) ADJECTIVE *Archaic* weary.
▷HISTORY C16: past participle of obsolete *forwear* to wear out, from Middle English *forweren* to hollow out

forza (ˈfɔːtsə) NOUN *Music* force.
▷HISTORY C19: Italian, literally: force

forzando (fɔːˈtsændəʊ) ADJECTIVE, ADVERB, NOUN another word for **sforzando.**

Fosbury flop (ˈfɒzbərɪ, -brɪ) NOUN *Athletics* a modern high-jumping technique whereby the jumper clears the bar headfirst and backwards.
▷HISTORY C20: named after Dick *Fosbury*, US winner of men's high jump at Mexico Olympics in 1968, who perfected the technique

Foshan (ˈfɔːˈʃɑːn) *or* **Fatshan** NOUN a city in SE China, in W Guangdong province. Pop.: 411 107 (1999 est.). Also called: **Namhoi.**

fossa[1] (ˈfɒsə) NOUN, *plural* **-sae** (-siː). an anatomical depression, trench, or hollow area.
▷HISTORY C19: from Latin: ditch, from *fossus* dug up, from *fodere* to dig up

fossa[2] (ˈfɒsə) NOUN a large primitive catlike viverrine mammal, *Cryptoprocta ferox*, inhabiting the forests of Madagascar: order *Carnivora* (carnivores). It has thick reddish-brown fur and preys on lemurs, poultry, etc.
▷HISTORY from Malagasy

fosse *or* **foss** (fɒs) NOUN a ditch or moat, esp one dug as a fortification.
▷HISTORY C14: from Old French, from Latin *fossa*; see FOSSA[1]

fossette (fɒˈset) NOUN [1] *Anatomy* a small depression or fossa, as in a bone. [2] *Pathol* a small deep ulcer of the cornea.
▷HISTORY C19: from French: dimple, from *fosse* ditch

Fosse Way (fɒs) NOUN a Roman road in Britain between Lincoln and Exeter, with a fosse on each side.

fossick (ˈfɒsɪk) VERB *Austral and NZ* [1] (*intr*) to search for gold or precious stones in abandoned workings, rivers, etc. [2] to rummage or search for (something).
▷HISTORY C19: Australian, probably from English dialect *fussock* to bustle about, from FUSS
▸ˈ**fossicker** NOUN

fossil (ˈfɒsəl) NOUN [1] **a** a relic, remnant, or representation of an organism that existed in a past geological age, or of the activity of such an organism, occurring in the form of mineralized bones, shells, etc., as casts, impressions, and moulds, and as frozen perfectly preserved organisms. **b** (*as modifier*): *fossil insects.* [2] *Informal derogatory* **a** a person, idea, thing, etc., that is outdated or incapable of change. **b** (*as modifier*): *fossil politicians.* [3] *Linguistics* a form once current but now appearing only in one or two special contexts, as for example *stead*, which is found now only in *instead* (*of*) and in phrases like *in his stead.* [4] *Obsolete* any rock or mineral dug out of the earth.
▷HISTORY C17: from Latin *fossilis* dug up, from *fodere* to dig

fossil energy NOUN heat energy released by burning fossil fuel.

fossil fuel NOUN any naturally occurring carbon or hydrocarbon fuel, such as coal, petroleum, peat, and natural gas, formed by the decomposition of prehistoric organisms.

fossiliferous (ˌfɒsɪˈlɪfərəs) ADJECTIVE (of sedimentary rocks) containing fossils.

fossilize *or* **fossilise** (ˈfɒsɪˌlaɪz) VERB [1] to convert or be converted into a fossil. [2] to become or cause to become antiquated or inflexible.
▸ˈ**fossilˌizable** *or* ˈ**fossilˌisable** ADJECTIVE ▸ˌ**fossiliˈzation** *or* ˌ**fossiliˈsation** NOUN

fossorial (fɒˈsɔːrɪəl) ADJECTIVE [1] (of the forelimbs and skeleton of burrowing animals) adapted for digging. [2] (of burrowing animals, such as the mole and armadillo) having limbs of this type.
▷HISTORY C19: from Medieval Latin *fossōrius* from Latin *fossor* digger, from *fodere* to dig

foster (ˈfɒstə) VERB (*tr*) [1] to promote the growth or development of. [2] to bring up (a child, etc.); rear. [3] to cherish (a plan, hope, etc.) in one's mind. [4] *Chiefly Brit* **a** to place (a child) in the care of foster parents. **b** to bring up under fosterage. ◆ ADJECTIVE [5] (*in combination*) of or involved in the rearing of a child by persons other than his natural or adopted parents: *foster parents; foster home.*
▷HISTORY Old English *fōstrian* to feed, from *fōstor* FOOD
▸ˈ**fosterer** NOUN ▸ˈ**fosteringly** ADVERB

fosterage (ˈfɒstərɪdʒ) NOUN [1] the act of caring for or bringing up a foster child. [2] the condition or state of being a foster child. [3] the act of encouraging or promoting.

foster child NOUN a child looked after temporarily or brought up by people other than its natural or adoptive parents.

foster father NOUN a man who looks after or brings up a child or children as a father, in place of the natural or adoptive father.

fosterling (ˈfɒstəlɪŋ) NOUN a less common word for **foster child.**

foster mother NOUN a woman who looks after or brings up a child or children as a mother, in place of the natural or adoptive mother.

Fotheringhay (ˈfɒðərɪŋˌgeɪ) NOUN a village in E England, in NE Northamptonshire: ruined castle, scene of the imprisonment and execution of Mary Queen of Scots (1587).

fou (fuː) ADJECTIVE *Scot* [1] full. [2] drunk.
▷HISTORY perhaps a Scot variant of *full*

Foucault current (*French* fuko) NOUN another name for **eddy current.**
▷HISTORY named after J. B. L. *Foucault* (1819–68), French physicist

foudroyant (fuːˈdrɔɪənt) ADJECTIVE 1 (of a disease) occurring suddenly and with great severity. 2 *Rare* stunning, dazzling, or overwhelming.
▷HISTORY C19: from French, from *foudroyer* to strike with lightning, from Old French *foudre* lightning, from Latin *fulgur*

fouetté *French* (fwete) NOUN a step in ballet in which the dancer stands on one foot and makes a whiplike movement with the other.
▷HISTORY C19: French, past participle of *fouetter* to whip, from *fouet* a whip

fought (fɔːt) VERB the past tense and past participle of **fight.**

foul (faʊl) ADJECTIVE 1 offensive to the senses; revolting. 2 offensive in odour; stinking. 3 charged with or full of dirt or offensive matter; filthy. 4 (of food) putrid; rotten. 5 morally or spiritually offensive; wicked; vile. 6 obscene; vulgar: *foul language.* 7 not in accordance with accepted standards or established rules; unfair: *to resort to foul means.* 8 (esp of weather) unpleasant or adverse. 9 blocked or obstructed with dirt or foreign matter: *a foul drain.* 10 entangled or impeded: *a foul anchor.* 11 (of the bottom of a vessel) covered with barnacles and other growth that slow forward motion. 12 *Informal* unsatisfactory or uninteresting; bad: *a foul book.* 13 *Archaic* ugly. ◆ NOUN 14 *Sport* **a** a violation of the rules. **b** (*as modifier*): *a foul shot; a foul blow.* 15 something foul. 16 an entanglement or collision, esp in sailing or fishing. ◆ VERB 17 to make or become dirty or polluted. 18 to become or cause to become entangled or snarled. 19 (*tr*) to disgrace or dishonour. 20 to become or cause to become clogged or choked. 21 (*tr*) *Nautical* (of underwater growth) to cling to (the bottom of a vessel) so as to slow its motion. 22 (*tr*) *Sport* to commit a foul against (an opponent). 23 (*tr*) *Baseball* to hit (a ball) in an illegal manner. 24 (*intr*) *Sport* to infringe the rules. 25 to collide with (a boat, etc.). ◆ ADVERB 26 in a foul or unfair manner. 27 **fall foul of. a** to come into conflict with. **b** *Nautical* to come into collision with. ◆ See also **foul up.**
▷HISTORY Old English *fūl*; related to Old Norse *fúll*, Gothic *fūls* smelling offensively, Latin *pūs* PUS, Greek *puol* pus
▸ˈ**foully** ADVERB

foulard (fuːˈlɑːd, ˈfuːlɑː) NOUN 1 a soft light fabric of plain-weave or twill-weave silk or rayon, usually with a printed design. 2 something made of this fabric, esp a scarf or handkerchief.
▷HISTORY C19: from French, of unknown origin

foulie (ˈfaʊlɪ) NOUN *Austral informal* a bad mood.
▷HISTORY C20: from FOUL

foul marten NOUN another name for the **polecat** (sense 1). See also **sweet marten.**

foul-mouthed ADJECTIVE given to using obscene, abusive, or blasphemous language.

foulness (ˈfaʊlnɪs) NOUN 1 the state or quality of being foul. 2 obscenity; vulgarity. 3 viciousness or inhumanity. 4 foul matter; filth.

Foulness (faʊlˈnɛs) NOUN a flat marshy island in SE England, in Essex north of the Thames estuary.

foul play NOUN 1 unfair or treacherous conduct esp with violence. 2 a violation of the rules in a game or sport.

foul shot NOUN *Basketball* another term (esp US and Canadian) for **free throw.**

foul up VERB (*adverb*) 1 (*tr*) to bungle; mismanage. 2 (*tr*) to make dirty; contaminate. 3 to be or cause to be blocked, choked, or entangled. ◆ NOUN **foul-up.** 4 a state of confusion or muddle caused by bungling.

foumart (ˈfuːmɑːt, -mət) NOUN a former name for the **polecat** (sense 1).
▷HISTORY C15 *folmarde*: from Old English *fūl* foul + *mearth* a marten

found[1] (faʊnd) VERB 1 the past tense and past participle of **find.** ◆ ADJECTIVE 2 furnished, or fitted out: *the boat is well found.* 3 *Brit* with meals, heating, bed linen, etc., provided without extra charge (esp in the phrase **all found**).

found[2] (faʊnd) VERB 1 (*tr*) to bring into being, set up, or establish (something, such as an institution, society, etc.). 2 (*tr*) to build or establish the foundation or basis of. 3 (*also intr;* foll by *on* or *upon*) to have a basis (in); depend (on).
▷HISTORY C13: from Old French *fonder*, from Latin *fundāre*, from *fundus* bottom

found[3] (faʊnd) VERB (*tr*) 1 to cast (a material, such as metal or glass) by melting and pouring into a mould. 2 to shape or make (articles) in this way; cast.
▷HISTORY C14: from Old French *fondre*, from Latin *fundere* to melt

foundation (faʊnˈdeɪʃən) NOUN 1 that on which something is founded; basis. 2 (*often plural*) a construction below the ground that distributes the load of a building, wall, etc. 3 the base on which something stands. 4 the act of founding or establishing or the state of being founded or established. 5 **a** an endowment or legacy for the perpetual support of an institution such as a school or hospital. **b on the foundation.** entitled to benefit from the funds of a foundation. 6 an institution supported by an endowment, often one that provides funds for charities, research, etc. 7 the charter incorporating or establishing a society or institution and the statutes or rules governing its affairs. 8 a cosmetic in cream or cake form used as a base for make-up. 9 See **foundation garment.** 10 *Cards* a card on which a sequence may be built.
▸**founˈdational** ADJECTIVE ▸**founˈdationally** ADVERB
▸**founˈdationary** ADJECTIVE

foundation garment NOUN a woman's undergarment worn to shape and support the figure; brassiere or corset.

foundation stone NOUN a stone laid at a ceremony to mark the foundation of a new building.

foundation subjects PLURAL NOUN *Brit education* the subjects studied as part of the National Curriculum, including the compulsory core subjects.

founder[1] (ˈfaʊndə) NOUN a person who establishes an institution, company, society, etc.
▷HISTORY C14: see FOUND[2]

founder[2] (ˈfaʊndə) VERB (*intr*) 1 (of a ship) to sink. 2 to break down or fail: *the project foundered.* 3 to sink into or become stuck in soft ground. 4 to fall in or give way; collapse. 5 (of a horse) to stumble or go lame. 6 *Archaic* (of animals, esp livestock) to become ill from overeating. ◆ NOUN 7 *Vet science* another name for **laminitis.**
▷HISTORY C13: from Old French *fondrer* to submerge, from Latin *fundus* bottom; see FOUND[2]

> **Language note** *Founder* is sometimes wrongly used where *flounder* is meant: *this unexpected turn of events left him floundering* (not *foundering*).

founder[3] (ˈfaʊndə) NOUN **a** a person who makes metal castings. **b** (*in combination*): *an iron founder.*
▷HISTORY C15: see FOUND[3]

founders' shares PLURAL NOUN shares awarded to the founders of a company and often granting special privileges.

founder's type NOUN *Printing* special type cast by a type founder for hand composition, as opposed to type cast in a mechanical composing machine.

founding father NOUN (*often capitals*) a person who founds or establishes an important institution, esp a member of the US Constitutional Convention (1787).

foundling (ˈfaʊndlɪŋ) NOUN an abandoned infant whose parents are not known.
▷HISTORY C13: *foundeling*; see FIND

found object NOUN another name for ***objet trouvé.***

foundry (ˈfaʊndrɪ) NOUN, *plural* **-ries.** 1 a place in which metal castings are produced. 2 the science or practice of casting metal. 3 cast-metal articles collectively.
▷HISTORY C17: from Old French *fonderie*, from *fondre*; see FOUND[3]

foundry proof NOUN *Printing* a proof taken from a forme before duplicate plates are made from it.

foundry sand NOUN silica-based sand mixed with clay, oil, etc., to improve its cohesive strength, used in moulding.

fount[1] (faʊnt) NOUN 1 *Poetic* a spring or fountain. 2 source or origin.
▷HISTORY C16: back formation from FOUNTAIN

fount[2] (faʊnt, fɒnt) NOUN *Printing* a complete set of type of one style and size. Also called (esp US and Canadian): **font.**
▷HISTORY C16: from Old French *fonte* a founding, casting, from Vulgar Latin *funditus* (unattested) a casting, from Latin *fundere* to melt; see FOUND[3]

fountain (ˈfaʊntɪn) NOUN 1 a jet or spray of water or some other liquid. 2 a structure from which such a jet or a number of such jets spurt, often incorporating figures, basins, etc. 3 a natural spring of water, esp the source of a stream. 4 a stream, jet, or cascade of sparks, lava, etc. 5 a principal source or origin. 6 a reservoir or supply chamber, as for oil in a lamp. 7 short for **drinking fountain** or **soda fountain.**
▷HISTORY C15: from Old French *fontaine*, from Late Latin *fontāna*, from Latin *fons* spring, source
▸ˈ**fountained** ADJECTIVE ▸ˈ**fountainless** ADJECTIVE
▸ˈ**fountain-ˌlike** ADJECTIVE

fountainhead (ˈfaʊntɪnˌhɛd) NOUN 1 a spring that is the source of a stream. 2 a principal or original source.

fountain pen NOUN a pen the nib of which is supplied with ink from a cartridge or a reservoir in its barrel.

Fountains Abbey (ˈfaʊntɪns) NOUN a ruined Cistercian abbey near Ripon in Yorkshire: founded 1132, dissolved 1539; landscaped 1720.

four (fɔː) NOUN 1 the cardinal number that is the sum of three and one. 2 a numeral, 4, IV, etc., representing this number. 3 something representing, represented by, or consisting of four units, such as a playing card with four symbols on it. 4 Also called: **four o'clock.** four hours after noon or midnight. 5 *Cricket* **a** a shot that crosses the boundary after hitting the ground. **b** the four runs scored for such a shot. 6 *Rowing* **a** a racing shell propelled by four oarsmen pulling one oar each, with or without a cox. **b** the crew of such a shell. ◆ DETERMINER 7 **a** amounting to four: *four thousand eggs; four times.* **b** (*as pronoun*): *four are ready.* ◆ Related prefixes: **quadri-, tetra-.**
▷HISTORY Old English *fēower*; related to Old Frisian *fiūwer*, Old Norse *fjōrir*, Old High German *fior*, Latin *quattuor*, Greek *tessares*, Sanskrit *catur*

four-ball NOUN *Golf* a match for two pairs in which each player uses his own ball, the better score of each pair being counted at every hole. Compare **foursome** (sense 2), **greensome.**

four-by-four NOUN a vehicle equipped with four-wheel drive.

four-by-two NOUN *Austral and NZ* a piece of timber with a cross section that measures 4 inches by 2 inches.

fourchette (fʊəˈʃɛt) NOUN 1 *Anatomy* the bandlike fold of skin, about one inch from the anus, forming the posterior margin of the vulva. 2 a less common name for **furcula** or **frog**[3].
▷HISTORY C18: from French: a little fork, from Old French *forche* , from Latin *furca* FORK

four-colour NOUN (*modifier*) (of a print or photographic process) using the principle in which four colours (magenta, cyan, yellow, and black) are used in combination to produce almost any other colour.

four-cycle ADJECTIVE the US and Canadian word for **four-stroke.**

four-deal bridge NOUN a version of bridge in which four hands only are played, the players then cutting for new partners.

four-dimensional ADJECTIVE having or specified by four dimensions, esp the three spatial dimensions and the dimension of time: *a four-dimensional continuum.*

Fourdrinier (fʊəˈdrɪnɪə) NOUN a particular type of paper-making machine that forms the paper in a continuous web.
▷HISTORY C19: named after Henry (died 1854) and Sealy (died 1847) *Fourdrinier*, English paper makers

four-eyed fish NOUN either of two viviparous tropical American freshwater cyprinodont fishes, *Anableps anableps* or *A. microlepis*, that swim at the surface of the water and have half of each eye specialized for seeing in air, the other half for seeing in water.

four-eyes NOUN a disparaging term of address for a person wearing spectacles.
▸ **'four-,eyed** ADJECTIVE

four flush NOUN [1] a useless poker hand, containing four of a suit and one odd card. ◆ VERB **four-flush.** (*intr*) [2] to bid confidently on a poor hand such as a four flush. [3] *US and Canadian* a slang word for **bluff**[1].

four-flusher ('fɔːˌflʌʃə) NOUN *US and Canadian slang* a person who bluffs or attempts to deceive.

fourfold ('fɔːˌfəʊld) ADJECTIVE [1] equal to or having four times as many or as much. [2] composed of four parts. ◆ ADVERB [3] by or up to four times as many or as much.

four-four time NOUN *Music* a form of simple quadruple time in which there are four crotchets to the bar, indicated by the time signature $\frac{4}{4}$. Often shortened to: **four-four.** Also called: **common time.**

fourgon *French* (furgɔ̃) NOUN a long covered wagon, used mainly for carrying baggage, supplies, etc.
▷ **HISTORY** C19: from French: from Old French *forgon* poker, from *furgier* to search, ultimately from Latin *fūr* thief

four-handed ADJECTIVE [1] (of a card game) arranged for four players. [2] (of a musical composition) written for two performers at the same piano.
▸ **ˌfour-'handedly** ADVERB

Four Hundred NOUN **the.** *US* the most exclusive or affluent social clique in a particular place.

Fourier analysis ('fʊərɪˌeɪ) NOUN the analysis of a periodic function into its simple sinusoidal or harmonic components, whose sum forms a Fourier series.
▷ **HISTORY** C19: named after Baron Jean Baptiste Joseph *Fourier* (1768–1830), French mathematician, Egyptologist, and administrator

Fourierism ('fʊərɪəˌrɪzəm) NOUN the system of Charles Fourier (1772–1837), the French social reformer, under which society was to be organized into self-sufficient cooperatives.
▸ **'Fourierist** *or* **Fourierite** ('fʊərɪəˌraɪt) NOUN, ADJECTIVE
▸ **ˌFourier'istic** ADJECTIVE

Fourier series NOUN an infinite trigonometric series of the form $\frac{1}{2}a_0 + a_1\cos x + b_1\sin x + a_2\cos 2x + b_2\sin 2x + \ldots$, where $a_0, a_1, b_1, a_2, b_2 \ldots$ are the **Fourier coefficients.** It is used, esp in mathematics and physics, to represent or approximate any periodic function by assigning suitable values to the coefficients.

Fourier transform NOUN an integral transform, used in many branches of science, of the form $F(x) = [1/\sqrt{(2\pi)}]\int e^{ixy}f(y)dy$, where the limits of integration are from $-\infty$ to $+\infty$ and the function F is the transform of the function f.

four-in-hand NOUN [1] Also called: **tally-ho.** a road vehicle drawn by four horses and driven by one driver. [2] a four-horse team in a coach or carriage. [3] a long narrow tie formerly worn tied in a flat slipknot with the ends dangling.

four-leaf clover *or* **four-leaved clover** NOUN [1] a clover with four leaves rather than three, supposed to bring good luck. [2] another name for **cloverleaf** (sense 1).

four-letter word NOUN any of several short English words referring to sex or excrement: often used as swearwords and regarded generally as offensive or obscene.

four-o'clock NOUN [1] Also called: **marvel-of-Peru.** a tropical American nyctaginaceous plant, *Mirabilis jalapa*, cultivated for its tubular yellow, red, or white flowers that open in late afternoon. [2] an Australian name for **friarbird**, esp the noisy friarbird (*Philemon corniculatus*): so called because of its cry

four-part ADJECTIVE *Music* arranged for four voices or instruments.

fourpence ('fɔːpəns) NOUN a former English silver coin then worth four pennies.

fourpenny ('fɔːpənɪ) ADJECTIVE **fourpenny one.** *Brit slang* a blow, esp with the fist.

four-poster NOUN a bed with posts at each corner supporting a canopy and curtains. Also called: **four-poster bed.**

fourragère ('fʊərəˌʒɛə; *French* furaʒɛr) NOUN an ornamental cord worn on the shoulder of a uniform for identification or as an award, esp in the US and French Armies.
▷ **HISTORY** French, feminine adj of *fourrager* relating to forage, from *fourrage* FORAGE

fourscore (ˌfɔː'skɔː) DETERMINER an archaic word for **eighty.**

foursome ('fɔːsəm) NOUN [1] a set or company of four. [2] *Sport* a game between two pairs of players, esp a form of golf in which each partner in a pair takes alternate strokes at the same ball. Compare **four-ball, greensome.** [3] (*modifier*) of or performed by a company of four: *a foursome competition.*

foursquare (ˌfɔː'skwɛə) ADVERB [1] squarely; firmly. ◆ ADJECTIVE [2] solid and strong. [3] forthright; honest. [4] a rare word for **square.**
▸ **ˌfour'squarely** ADVERB ▸ **ˌfour'squareness** NOUN

four-stroke ADJECTIVE relating to or designating an internal-combustion engine in which the piston makes four strokes for every explosion. US and Canadian name: **four-cycle.** Compare **two-stroke.**

fourteen ('fɔː'tiːn) NOUN [1] the cardinal number that is the sum of ten and four. [2] a numeral, 14, XIV, etc., representing this number. [3] something represented by, representing, or consisting of 14 units. ◆ DETERMINER [4] **a** amounting to fourteen: *fourteen cats.* **b** (*as pronoun*): *the fourteen who remained.*
▷ **HISTORY** Old English *fēowertīene*

Fourteen Points PLURAL NOUN the principles expounded by President Wilson in 1918 as war aims of the US.

fourteenth ('fɔː'tiːnθ) ADJECTIVE [1] **a** coming after the thirteenth in order, position, time etc. Often written: 14th. **b** (*as noun*): *the fourteenth in succession.* ◆ NOUN [2] **a** one of 14 equal or nearly equal parts of something. **b** (*as modifier*): *a fourteenth part.* [3] the fraction equal to one divided by 14 (1/14).

fourth (fɔːθ) ADJECTIVE (*usually prenominal*) [1] **a** coming after the third in order, position, time, etc. Often written: 4th. **b** (*as noun*): *the fourth in succession.* [2] denoting the fourth forward ratio of a gearbox in motor vehicles. ◆ NOUN [3] *Music* **a** the interval between one note and another four notes away from it counting inclusively along the diatonic scale. **b** one of two notes constituting such an interval in relation to the other. See also **perfect** (sense 9), **interval** (sense 5), **diminished** (sense 2). [4] the fourth forward ratio of a gearbox in a motor vehicle: *he changed into fourth as soon as he had passed me.* [5] a less common word for **quarter** (sense 2). ◆ ADVERB *also* **fourthly.** [6] after the third person, position, event, etc. ◆ SENTENCE CONNECTOR *also* **fourthly.** [7] as the fourth point: linking what follows with the previous statements, as in a speech or argument.

fourth-class *US* ◆ ADJECTIVE [1] of or relating to mail that is carried at the lowest rate. ◆ ADVERB [2] by fourth-class mail.

fourth dimension NOUN [1] the dimension of time, which is necessary in addition to three spatial dimensions to specify fully the position and behaviour of a point or particle. [2] the concept in science fiction of a dimension in addition to three spatial dimensions, used to explain supranatural phenomena, events, etc.
▸ **ˌfourth-di'mensional** ADJECTIVE

fourth estate NOUN (*sometimes capitals*) journalists or their profession; the press. See **estate** (sense 4).

Fourth International NOUN another name for any of the **Trotskyist Internationals.**

Fourth of July NOUN (preceded by *the*) a holiday in the United States, traditionally celebrated with fireworks: the day of the adoption of the Declaration of Independence in 1776. Official name: **Independence Day.**

Fourth Republic NOUN the fourth period of republican government in France or the republic itself (1945–58).

Fourth World NOUN [1] the poorest countries in the most undeveloped parts of the world in Africa, Asia, and Latin America. [2] the poorest people in developed countries.

four-way ADJECTIVE (*usually prenominal*) [1] giving passage in four directions. [2] made up of four elements.

four-wheel drive NOUN a system used in motor vehicles in which all four wheels are connected to the source of power.

fovea ('fəʊvɪə) NOUN, *plural* **-veae** (-vɪˌiː). [1] *Anatomy* any small pit or depression in the surface of a bodily organ or part. [2] See **fovea centralis.**
▷ **HISTORY** C19: from Latin: a small pit
▸ **'foveal** ADJECTIVE ▸ **'foveate** *or* **'foveˌated** ADJECTIVE

fovea centralis (sɛn'trɑːlɪs) NOUN a small depression in the centre of the retina that contains only cone cells and is therefore the area of sharpest vision.
▷ **HISTORY** C19: from New Latin: central fovea

foveola (fəʊ'viːələ) NOUN, *plural* **-lae** (-ˌliː). *Biology* a small fovea.
▷ **HISTORY** C19: from New Latin, diminutive of FOVEA
▸ **fo'veolar** ADJECTIVE ▸ **foveolate** ('fəʊvɪəˌleɪt) *or* **'foveoˌlated** ADJECTIVE

Fowey (fɔɪ) NOUN a resort and fishing village in SW England, in Cornwall, linked administratively with St Austell in 1968. Pop.: 1939 (1991).

fowl (faʊl) NOUN [1] See **domestic fowl.** [2] any other bird, esp any gallinaceous bird, that is used as food or hunted as game. See also **waterfowl, wildfowl.** [3] the flesh or meat of fowl, esp of chicken. [4] an archaic word for any **bird.** ◆ VERB [5] (*intr*) to hunt or snare wildfowl.
▷ **HISTORY** Old English *fugol*; related to Old Frisian *fugel*, Old Norse *fogl*, Gothic *fugls*, Old High German *fogal*

fowl cholera NOUN *Vet science* a contagious disease of poultry and other fowl, usually resulting in sudden death; caused by the organism *Pasteurella multocida.*

Fowliang *or* **Fou-liang** ('fuː'ljæŋ) NOUN a variant transliteration of the Chinese name for **Jingdezhen.**

fowling ('faʊlɪŋ) NOUN the shooting or trapping of birds for sport or as a livelihood.
▸ **'fowler** NOUN

fowl mite NOUN any of various mites parasitic in birds, usually bloodsucking and including the **red fowl mite** (*Dermanyssus gallinae*) and the **northern fowl mite** (*Ornithonyssus sylviarum*), both pests of poultry.

fowl pest NOUN [1] an acute and usually fatal viral disease of domestic fowl, characterized by refusal to eat, high temperature, and discoloration of the comb and wattles. [2] another name for **Newcastle disease.**

fox (fɒks) NOUN, *plural* **foxes** *or* **fox.** [1] any canine mammal of the genus *Vulpes* and related genera. They are mostly predators that do not hunt in packs and typically have large pointed ears, a pointed muzzle, and a bushy tail. Related adjective: **vulpine.** [2] the fur of any of these animals, usually reddish-brown or grey in colour. [3] a person who is cunning and sly. [4] *Slang, chiefly US* a sexually attractive woman. [5] *Bible* **a** a jackal. **b** an image of a false prophet. [6] *Nautical* small stuff made from yarns twisted together and then tarred. ◆ VERB [7] (*tr*) to perplex or confound: *to fox a person with a problem.* [8] to cause (paper, wood, etc.) to become discoloured with spots, or (of paper, etc.) to become discoloured, as through mildew. [9] (*tr*) to trick; deceive. [10] (*intr*) to act deceitfully or craftily. [11] (*tr*) *Austral informal* to pursue stealthily; tail. [12] (*tr*) *Austral informal* to chase and retrieve (a ball). [13] (*tr*) *Obsolete* to befuddle with alcoholic drink.
▷ **HISTORY** Old English; related to Old High German *fuhs*, Old Norse *fōa* fox, Sanskrit *puccha* tail; see VIXEN
▸ **'foxˌlike** ADJECTIVE

Fox (fɒks) NOUN [1] (*plural* **Fox** *or* **Foxes**) a member of a North American Indian people formerly living west of Lake Michigan along the Fox River. [2] the language of this people, belonging to the Algonquian family.

Foxe Basin (fɒks) NOUN an arm of the Atlantic in NE Canada, between Melville Peninsula and Baffin Island.

foxfire ('fɒksˌfaɪə) NOUN a luminescent glow emitted by certain fungi on rotting wood. See also **bioluminescence.**

foxglove ('fɒksˌglʌv) NOUN any Eurasian scrophulariaceous plant of the genus *Digitalis*, esp *D. purpurea*, having spikes of purple or white thimble-like flowers. The soft wrinkled leaves are a source of digitalis.

fox grape NOUN a common wild grape, *Vitis labrusca* of the northern US, having purplish-black fruit and woolly leaves: the source of many cultivated grapes, including the catawba.

foxhole (ˈfɒksˌhəʊl) NOUN *Military* a small pit dug during an action to provide individual shelter against hostile fire.

foxhound (ˈfɒksˌhaʊnd) NOUN either of two breeds (the English and the American) of dog having a short smooth coat and pendent ears. Though not large (height about 60 cm or 23 in.) they have great stamina and are usually kept for hunting foxes.

fox hunt NOUN [1] **a** the hunting of foxes with hounds. **b** an instance of this. [2] an organization for fox-hunting within a particular area.

fox-hunting NOUN a sport in which hunters follow a pack of hounds in pursuit of a fox.
▸ **ˈfox-ˌhunter** NOUN

foxie (ˈfɒksɪ) NOUN *Austral* an informal name for **fox terrier**.

foxing (ˈfɒksɪŋ) NOUN a piece of leather used to reinforce or trim part of the upper of a shoe.

fox moth NOUN a coppery-brown European eggar moth, *Macrothylacia rubi*, whose black-and-yellow woolly larvae are commonly found on heather and bramble.

fox squirrel NOUN a large squirrel, *Sciurus niger*, occurring in E North America.

foxtail (ˈfɒksˌteɪl) NOUN [1] any grass of the genus *Alopecurus*, esp *A. pratensis*, of Europe, Asia, and South America, having soft cylindrical spikes of flowers: cultivated as a pasture grass. [2] any of various similar and related grasses, esp any of the genus *Setaria*.

fox terrier NOUN either of two breeds of small terrier, the wire-haired and the smooth, having a white coat with markings of black or tan or both.

foxtrot (ˈfɒksˌtrɒt) NOUN [1] a ballroom dance in quadruple time, combining short and long steps in various sequences. ◆ VERB **-trots, -trotting, -trotted.** [2] (*intr*) to perform this dance.

Foxtrot (ˈfɒksˌtrɒt) NOUN *Communications* a code word for the letter *f*.

foxy (ˈfɒksɪ) ADJECTIVE **foxier, foxiest.** [1] of or resembling a fox, esp in craftiness. [2] smelling strongly like a fox. [3] of a reddish-brown colour. [4] (of paper, wood, etc.) spotted, esp by mildew. [5] (of wine) having the flavour of fox grapes. [6] (of oats) having a musty smell as a result of getting wet, fermenting, and drying out. [7] *Slang* sexy; sexually attractive.
▸ **ˈfoxily** ADVERB ▸ **ˈfoxiness** NOUN

foyboat (ˈfɔɪˌbəʊt) NOUN *Tyneside dialect* **a** a small rowing boat. **b** (*in combination*): *a foyboatman*.
▷ **HISTORY** C19: from *foy* to provide aid for ships, esp those in distress

foyer (ˈfɔɪeɪ, ˈfɔɪə) NOUN [1] a hall, lobby, or anteroom, used for reception and as a meeting place, as in a hotel, theatre, cinema, etc. [2] (in Britain) a centre providing accommodation and employment training, etc. for homeless young people.
▷ **HISTORY** C19: from French: fireplace, from Medieval Latin *focārius*, from Latin *focus* fire

fp [1] ABBREVIATION FOR fine point. ◆ [2] *Music* SYMBOL FOR fortepiano.

FP *or* **fp** ABBREVIATION FOR: [1] freezing point. [2] fully paid.

FPA ABBREVIATION FOR Family Planning Association.

FPO ABBREVIATION FOR field post office.

fps ABBREVIATION FOR: [1] feet per second. [2] foot-pound-second. [3] *Photog* frames per second.

fps units PLURAL NOUN an Imperial system of units based on the foot, pound, and second as the units of length, mass, and time. For scientific and most technical purposes these units have been replaced by SI units.

fr THE INTERNET DOMAIN NAME FOR France.

Fr [1] *Christianity* ABBREVIATION FOR **a** Frater. **b** Father. ◆ [2] THE CHEMICAL SYMBOL FOR francium.
▷ **HISTORY** (for sense 1) Latin: brother

FR INTERNATIONAL CAR REGISTRATION FOR Faeroes.

fr. franc.

Fr. ABBREVIATION FOR: [1] *Christianity* Father. [2] France. [3] French. [4] the German equivalent of **Mrs.**
▷ **HISTORY** from German *Frau*

Fra (frɑː) NOUN brother: a title given to an Italian monk or friar.
▷ **HISTORY** Italian, short for *frate* brother (in either natural or religious sense), from Latin *frāter* BROTHER

fracas (ˈfrækɑː) NOUN a noisy quarrel; brawl.
▷ **HISTORY** C18: from French, from *fracasser* to shatter, from Latin *frangere* to break, influenced by *quassāre* to shatter

FRACP ABBREVIATION FOR Fellow of the Royal Australasian College of Physicians.

FRACS ABBREVIATION FOR Fellow of the Royal Australasian College of Surgeons.

fractal (ˈfræktəl) *Maths* ◆ NOUN [1] a figure or surface generated by successive subdivisions of a simpler polygon or polyhedron, according to some iterative process. ◆ ADJECTIVE [2] of, relating to, or involving such a process: *fractal geometry*; *fractal curve*.
▷ **HISTORY** C20: from Latin *frāctus* past participle of *frangere* to break

fraction (ˈfrækʃən) NOUN [1] *Maths* **a** a ratio of two expressions or numbers other than zero. **b** any rational number that is not an integer. [2] any part or subdivision: *a substantial fraction of the nation*. [3] a small piece; fragment. [4] *Chem* a component of a mixture separated by a fractional process, such as fractional distillation. [5] *Christianity* the formal breaking of the bread in Communion. [6] the act of breaking. ◆ VERB [7] (*tr*) to divide.
▷ **HISTORY** C14: from Late Latin *fractiō* a breaking into pieces, from Latin *fractus* broken, from *frangere* to break

fractional (ˈfrækʃənᵊl) ADJECTIVE [1] relating to, containing, or constituting one or more fractions. [2] of or denoting a process in which components of a mixture are separated by exploiting differences in their physical properties, such as boiling points, solubility, etc.: *fractional distillation*; *fractional crystallization*. [3] very small or insignificant. [4] broken up; fragmented. ◆ Also: **fractionary** (ˈfrækʃənərɪ).
▸ **ˈfractionally** ADVERB

fractional crystallization NOUN *Chem* the process of separating the components of a solution on the basis of their different solubilities, by means of evaporating the solution until the least soluble component crystallizes out.

fractional currency NOUN paper or metal money of smaller denomination than the standard monetary unit.

fractional distillation NOUN [1] the process of separating the constituents of a liquid mixture by heating it and condensing separately the components according to their different boiling points. [2] a distillation in which the vapour is brought into contact with a countercurrent of condensed liquid to increase the purity of the final products. ◆ Sometimes shortened to **distillation**.

fractionate (ˈfrækʃəˌneɪt) VERB [1] to separate or cause to separate into constituents or into fractions containing concentrated constituents. [2] (*tr*) *Chem* to obtain (a constituent of a mixture) by a fractional process.
▸ **ˌfractionˈation** NOUN ▸ **ˈfractionˌator** NOUN

fractionating column NOUN *Chem* a long vertical cylinder used in fractional distillation, in which internal reflux enables separation of high and low boiling fractions to take place.

fractionize *or* **fractionise** (ˈfrækʃəˌnaɪz) VERB to divide (a number or quantity) into fractions.
▸ **ˌfractioniˈzation** *or* **ˌfractioniˈsation** NOUN

fractious (ˈfrækʃəs) ADJECTIVE [1] irritable. [2] unruly.
▷ **HISTORY** C18: from (obsolete) *fraction* discord + -OUS
▸ **ˈfractiously** ADVERB ▸ **ˈfractiousness** NOUN

> **Language note** *Fractious* is sometimes wrongly used where *factious* is meant: *this factious (not fractious) dispute has split the party still further.*

fractocumulus (ˌfræktəʊˈkjuːmjʊləs) NOUN, *plural* **-li** (-ˌlaɪ). low ragged slightly bulbous cloud, often appearing below nimbostratus clouds during rain. Also called: **fractocumulus cloud.**
▷ **HISTORY** C19: from Latin *fractus* broken + CUMULUS

fractostratus (ˌfræktəʊˈstrɑːtəs, -ˈstræt-) NOUN, *plural* **-ti** (-taɪ). low ragged layered cloud often appearing below nimbostratus clouds during rain.
▷ **HISTORY** C19: from Latin *fractus* broken + STRATUS

fracture (ˈfræktʃə) NOUN [1] the act of breaking or the state of being broken. [2] **a** the breaking or cracking of a bone or the tearing of a cartilage. **b** the resulting condition. See also **Colles' fracture, comminuted fracture, compound fracture, greenstick fracture, impacted** (sense 2). [3] a division, split, or breach. [4] *Mineralogy* **a** the characteristic appearance of the surface of a freshly broken mineral or rock. **b** the way in which a mineral or rock naturally breaks. ◆ VERB [5] to break or cause to break; split. [6] to break or crack (a bone) or (of a bone) to become broken or cracked. [7] to tear (a cartilage) or (of a cartilage) to become torn.
▷ **HISTORY** C15: from Old French, from Latin *fractūra*, from *frangere* to break
▸ **ˈfracturable** ADJECTIVE ▸ **ˈfractural** ADJECTIVE

frae (freɪ) PREPOSITION a Scot word for **from.**

fraenum *or* **frenum** (ˈfriːnəm) NOUN, *plural* **-na** (-nə). a fold of membrane or skin, such as the fold beneath the tongue, that supports an organ.
▷ **HISTORY** C18: from Latin: bridle

frag (fræg) VERB **frags, fragging, fragged.** (*tr*) *US military slang* to kill or wound (a fellow soldier or superior officer) deliberately with an explosive device.
▷ **HISTORY** C20: short for *fragmentation grenade*, as used in Vietnam
▸ **ˈfragging** NOUN

fragile (ˈfrædʒaɪl) ADJECTIVE [1] able to be broken easily. [2] in a weakened physical state. [3] delicate; light: *a fragile touch*. [4] slight; tenuous: *a fragile link with the past*.
▷ **HISTORY** C17: from Latin *fragilis*, from *frangere* to break
▸ **ˈfragilely** ADVERB ▸ **fragility** (frəˈdʒɪlɪtɪ) *or* **fragileness** NOUN

fragile-X syndrome NOUN an inherited condition characterized by mental subnormality: affected individuals have an X-chromosome that is easily damaged under certain conditions.

fragment NOUN (ˈfrægmənt) [1] a piece broken off or detached: *fragments of rock*. [2] an incomplete piece; portion: *fragments of a novel*. [3] a scrap; morsel; bit. ◆ VERB (frægˈmɛnt), *also US* **fragmentize** (ˈfrægmənˌtaɪz). [4] to break or cause to break into fragments.
▷ **HISTORY** C15: from Latin *fragmentum*, from *frangere* to break

fragmental (frægˈmɛntᵊl) ADJECTIVE [1] (of rocks or deposits) composed of fragments of pre-existing rocks and minerals. [2] another word for **fragmentary.**
▸ **fragˈmentally** ADVERB

fragmentary (ˈfrægməntərɪ, -trɪ) ADJECTIVE made up of fragments; disconnected; incomplete. Also: **fragmental.**
▸ **ˈfragmentarily** ADVERB ▸ **ˈfragmentariness** NOUN

fragmentation (ˌfrægmɛnˈteɪʃən) NOUN [1] the act of fragmenting or the state of being fragmented. [2] the disintegration of norms regulating behaviour, thought, and social relationships. [3] the steel particles of an exploded projectile. [4] (*modifier*) of or relating to a weapon designed to explode into many small pieces, esp as an antipersonnel weapon: *a fragmentation bomb*.

fragrance (ˈfreɪgrəns) *or* **fragrancy** NOUN, *plural* **-grances** *or* **-grancies.** [1] a pleasant or sweet odour; scent; perfume. [2] the state of being fragrant.

fragrant (ˈfreɪgrənt) ADJECTIVE having a pleasant or sweet smell.
▷ **HISTORY** C15: from Latin *frāgrāns*, from *frāgrāre* to emit a smell
▸ **ˈfragrantly** ADVERB

fragrant orchid NOUN another name for **scented orchid.**

frail[1] (freɪl) ADJECTIVE [1] physically weak and delicate. [2] fragile: *a frail craft*. [3] easily corrupted or tempted.
▷ **HISTORY** C13: from Old French *frele*, from Latin *fragilis*, FRAGILE
▸ **ˈfrailly** ADVERB ▸ **ˈfrailness** NOUN

frail² (freɪl) NOUN [1] a rush basket for figs or raisins. [2] a quantity of raisins or figs equal to between 50 and 75 pounds.
▷HISTORY C13: from Old French *fraiel*, of uncertain origin

frailty (ˈfreɪltɪ) NOUN, *plural* **-ties.** [1] physical or moral weakness. [2] (*often plural*) a fault symptomatic of moral weakness.

fraise (freɪz) NOUN [1] a neck ruff worn during the 16th century. [2] a sloping or horizontal rampart of pointed stakes. [3] **a** a tool for enlarging a drill hole. **b** a tool for cutting teeth on watch wheels.
▷HISTORY C18: from French: mesentery of a calf, from Old French *fraiser* to remove a shell, from Latin *frendere* to crush

Fraktur (*German* frakˈtuːr) NOUN a style of typeface, formerly used in German typesetting for many printed works.
▷HISTORY German, from Latin *fractūra* a breaking, FRACTURE; from the curlicues that seem to interrupt the continuous line of a word

framboesia *or US* **frambesia** (fræmˈbiːzɪə) NOUN *Pathol* another name for **yaws.**
▷HISTORY C19: from New Latin, from French *framboise* raspberry; see FRAMBOISE; so called because of its raspberry-like excrescences

framboise *French* (frɑ̃bwaz) NOUN a brandy distilled from raspberries in the Alsace-Lorraine region.
▷HISTORY C16: from Old French: raspberry, probably of Germanic origin

frame (freɪm) NOUN [1] an open structure that gives shape and support to something, such as the transverse stiffening ribs of a ship's hull or an aircraft's fuselage or the skeletal beams and uprights of a building. [2] an enclosing case or border into which something is fitted: *the frame of a picture.* [3] the system around which something is built up: *the frame of government.* [4] the structure of the human body. [5] a condition; state (esp in the phrase **frame of mind**). [6] **a** one of a series of individual exposures on a strip of film used in making motion pictures. **b** an individual exposure on a film used in still photography. **c** an individual picture in a comic strip. [7] **a** a television picture scanned by one or more electron beams at a particular frequency. **b** the area of the picture so formed. [8] *Billiards, snooker* **a** the wooden triangle used to set up the balls. **b** the balls when set up. **c** a single game finished when all the balls have been potted. ◆ US and Canadian equivalent (for senses 8a, 8b): **rack.** [9] short for **cold frame.** [10] one of the sections of which a beehive is composed, esp one designed to hold a honeycomb. [11] a machine or part of a machine over which yarn is stretched in the production of textiles. [12] (in language teaching, etc.) a syntactic construction with a gap in it, used for assigning words to syntactic classes by seeing which words may fill the gap. [13] *Statistics* an enumeration of a population for the purposes of sampling, esp as the basis of a stratified sample. [14] (in telecommunications, computers, etc.) one cycle of a regularly recurring number of pulses in a pulse train. [15] *Slang* another word for **frame-up.** [16] *Obsolete* shape; form. [17] **in the frame.** likely to be awarded or to achieve: *I'm in the frame for the top job.* ◆ VERB (*mainly tr*) [18] to construct by fitting parts together. [19] to draw up the plans or basic details for; outline: *to frame a policy.* [20] to compose, contrive, or conceive: *to frame a reply.* [21] to provide, support, or enclose with a frame: *to frame a picture.* [22] to form (words) with the lips, esp silently. [23] *Slang* to conspire to incriminate (someone) on a false charge. [24] *Slang* to contrive the dishonest outcome of (a contest, match, etc.); rig. [25] (*intr*) *Yorkshire and Northeastern English dialect* **a** (*usually imperative or dependent imperative*) to make an effort. **b** to have ability.
▷HISTORY Old English *framiae* to avail; related to Old Frisian *framia* to carry out, Old Norse *frama*
▸ **ˈframable** *or* **ˈframeable** ADJECTIVE ▸ **ˈframeless** ADJECTIVE
▸ **ˈframer** NOUN

frame aerial NOUN another name for **loop aerial.**

frame house NOUN a house that has a timber framework and cladding.

frame line NOUN *Films* a black horizontal bar appearing between successive picture images.

frame of reference NOUN [1] a set of basic assumptions or standards that determines and sanctions behaviour. [2] any set of planes or curves, such as the three coordinate axes, used to locate or measure movement of a point in space.

frame saw NOUN a saw with a thin blade held in a specially shaped frame. Also called: **span saw.**

frame-up NOUN *Slang* [1] a conspiracy to incriminate someone on a false charge. [2] a plot to bring about a dishonest result, as in a contest.

framework (ˈfreɪmˌwɜːk) NOUN [1] a structural plan or basis of a project. [2] a structure or frame supporting or containing something. [3] frames collectively. [4] work such as embroidery or weaving done in or on a frame.

framing (ˈfreɪmɪŋ) NOUN [1] a frame, framework, or system of frames. [2] the way in which something is framed. [3] adjustment of the longitudinal position of the film in a projector gate to secure proper vertical positioning of the picture on the screen.

franc (fræŋk; *French* frɑ̃) NOUN [1] the former standard monetary unit of France, most French dependencies, Andorra, and Monaco, divided into 100 centimes; replaced by the euro in 2002. Also called: **French franc.** [2] the former standard monetary unit of Belgium (**Belgian franc**) and Luxembourg (**Luxembourg franc**), divided into 100 centimes; replaced by the euro in 2002. [3] the standard monetary unit of Switzerland and Liechtenstein, divided into 100 centimes. Also called: **Swiss franc.** [4] the standard monetary unit, comprising 100 centimes, of the following countries: Benin, Burkina-Faso, Cameroon, the Central African Republic, Chad, Congo-Brazzaville, Côte d'Ivoire, Equatorial Guinea, Gabon, Guinea-Bissau, Mali, Niger, Senegal, and Togo. Also called: **franc CFA, CFA franc, franc of the African financial community.** [5] the standard monetary unit of Burundi (**Burundi franc**), Comoros (**Comorian franc**), Democratic Republic of Congo (formerly Zaïre; **Congolese franc**), Djibouti (**Djibouti franc**), Guinea (**Guinea franc**), Madagascar (**franc malgache**), Rwanda (**Rwanda franc**), and French Polynesia and New Caledonia (**French Pacific franc**).

France (frɑːns) NOUN a republic in W Europe, between the English Channel, the Mediterranean, and the Atlantic: the largest country wholly in Europe; became a republic in 1793 after the French Revolution and an empire in 1804 under Napoleon; reverted to a monarchy (1815–48), followed by the Second Republic (1848–52), the Second Empire (1852–70), the Third Republic (1870–1940), and the Fourth and Fifth Republics (1946 and 1958); a member of the European Union. It is generally flat or undulating in the north and west and mountainous in the south and east. Official language: French. Religion: Roman Catholic majority. Currency: euro. Capital: Paris. Pop.: 59 090 000 (2001 est.). Area: (including Corsica) 551 600 sq. km (212 973 sq. miles). Related adjectives: **French, Gallic.**

Franche-Comté (*French* frɑ̃ʃkɔ̃te) NOUN a region of E France, covering the Jura and the low country east of the Saône: part of the Kingdom of Burgundy (6th cent. A.D.–1137); autonomous as the Free County of Burgundy (1137–1384); under Burgundian rule again (1384–1477) and Hapsburg rule (1493–1674); annexed by France (1678).

franchise (ˈfræntʃaɪz) NOUN [1] (usually preceded by *the*) the right to vote, esp for representatives in a legislative body; suffrage. [2] any exemption, privilege, or right granted to an individual or group by a public authority, such as the right to use public property for a business. [3] *Commerce* authorization granted by a manufacturing enterprise to a distributor to market the manufacturer's products. [4] the full rights of citizenship. [5] *Films* a film that is or has the potential to be part of a series and lends itself to merchandising. [6] (in marine insurance) a sum or percentage stated in a policy, below which the insurer disclaims all liability. ◆ VERB [7] (*tr*) *Commerce, chiefly US and Canadian* to grant (a person, firm, etc.) a franchise. [8] an obsolete word for **enfranchise.**
▷HISTORY C13: from Old French, from *franchir* to set free, from *franc* free; see FRANK
▸ **franchisement** (ˈfræntʃɪzmənt) NOUN

Franciscan (frænˈsɪskən) NOUN **a** a member of any of several Christian religious orders of mendicant friars or nuns tracing their origins back to Saint Francis of Assisi; a Grey Friar. **b** (*as modifier*): *a Franciscan friar.*

Francis turbine (frɑːnˈsɪs) NOUN a water turbine designed to produce high flow from a low head of pressure: used esp in hydroelectric power generation.
▷HISTORY named after J. B. *Francis* (1815–92), English-born hydraulic engineer, who invented it

francium (ˈfrænsɪəm) NOUN an unstable radioactive element of the alkali-metal group, occurring in minute amounts in uranium ores. Symbol: Fr; atomic no.: 87; half-life of most stable isotope, ^{223}Fr: 22 minutes; valency: 1; melting pt.: 27°C; boiling pt.: 677°C.
▷HISTORY C20: from New Latin, from FRANCE + -IUM; so-called because first found in France

Franco- (ˈfræŋkəʊ-) COMBINING FORM indicating France or French: *Franco-Prussian.*
▷HISTORY from Medieval Latin *Francus*, from Late Latin: FRANK

francolin (ˈfræŋkəʊlɪn) NOUN any African or Asian partridge of the genus *Francolinus.*
▷HISTORY C17: from French, from Old Italian *francolino*, of unknown origin

Franconia (fræŋˈkəʊnɪə) NOUN a medieval duchy of Germany, inhabited by the Franks from the 7th century, now chiefly in Bavaria, Hesse, and Baden-Württemberg.

Franconian (fræŋˈkəʊnɪən) NOUN [1] a group of medieval Germanic dialects spoken by the Franks in an area from N Bavaria and Alsace to the mouth of the Rhine. **Low Franconian** developed into Dutch, while **Upper Franconian** contributed to High German, of which it remains a recognizable dialect. See also **Old Low German, Old High German, Frankish.** ◆ ADJECTIVE [2] of or relating to Franconia, the Franks, or their languages.

Francophile (ˈfræŋkəʊˌfaɪl) *or* **Francophil** (ˈfræŋkəʊfɪl) (*sometimes not capital*) NOUN [1] a person who admires France and the French. ◆ ADJECTIVE [2] marked by or possessing admiration of France and the French.

Francophobe (ˈfræŋkəʊˌfəʊb) NOUN (*sometimes not capital*) [1] a person who hates or despises France or its people. [2] *Canadian* a person who hates or fears Canadian Francophones.

Francophone (ˈfræŋkəʊˌfəʊn) (*often not capital*) NOUN [1] a person who speaks French, esp a native speaker. ◆ ADJECTIVE [2] speaking French as a native language. [3] using French as a lingua franca. ◆ Compare **Anglophone.**

Franco-Prussian War NOUN the war of 1870–71 between France and Prussia culminating in the fall of the French Second Empire and the founding of the German empire.

franc-tireur *French* (frɑ̃tirœr) NOUN [1] a sniper. [2] a guerrilla or irregular soldier.
▷HISTORY C19: from *franc* free + *tireur* shooter, from *tirer* to shoot, of unknown origin

franger (ˈfræŋə) NOUN *Austral slang* a condom.
▷HISTORY C20: perhaps related to FRENCH LETTER

frangible (ˈfrændʒɪbᵊl) ADJECTIVE breakable or fragile.
▷HISTORY C15: from Old French, ultimately from Latin *frangere* to break
▸ **ˌfrangiˈbility** *or* **ˈfrangibleness** NOUN

frangipane (ˈfrændʒɪˌpeɪn) NOUN [1] **a** a pastry filled with cream and flavoured with almonds. **b** a rich cake mixture containing ground almonds. [2] a variant of **frangipani** (the perfume).

frangipani (ˌfrændʒɪˈpɑːnɪ) NOUN, *plural* **-panis, -pani.** [1] any tropical American apocynaceous shrub of the genus *Plumeria*, esp *P. rubra*, cultivated for its waxy typically white or pink flowers, which have a sweet overpowering scent. [2] a perfume prepared from this plant or resembling the odour of its flowers. [3] **native frangipani.** *Austral* an Australian evergreen tree, *Hymenosporum flavum*, with large fragrant yellow flowers: family *Pittosporaceae.*
▷HISTORY C17: via French from Italian: perfume for scenting gloves, named after the Marquis Muzio *Frangipani*, 16th-century Roman nobleman who invented it

Franglais (*French* frɑ̃glɛ) NOUN informal French containing a high proportion of words of English origin.

▷HISTORY C20: from French *français* French + *anglais* English

frank (fræŋk) ADJECTIVE 1 honest and straightforward in speech or attitude: *a frank person.* 2 outspoken or blunt. 3 open and avowed; undisguised: *frank interest.* 4 an obsolete word for **free** or **generous.** ◆ VERB (*tr*) 5 *Chiefly Brit* to put a mark on (a letter, parcel, etc.), either cancelling the postage stamp or in place of a stamp, ensuring free carriage. See also **postmark.** 6 to mark (a letter, parcel, etc.) with an official mark or signature, indicating the right of free delivery. 7 to facilitate or assist (a person) to come and go, pass, or enter easily. 8 to obtain immunity for or exempt (a person). ◆ NOUN 9 an official mark or signature affixed to a letter, parcel, etc., ensuring free delivery or delivery without stamps. 10 the privilege, issued to certain people and establishments, entitling them to delivery without postage stamps.
▷HISTORY C13: from Old French *franc*, from Medieval Latin *francus* free; identical with FRANK (in Frankish Gaul only members of this people enjoyed full freedom)
▸**'frankable** ADJECTIVE ▸**'franker** NOUN ▸**'frankness** NOUN

Frank (fræŋk) NOUN a member of a group of West Germanic peoples who spread from the east bank of the middle Rhine into the Roman Empire in the late 4th century A.D., gradually conquering most of Gaul and Germany. The Franks achieved their greatest power under Charlemagne.
▷HISTORY Old English *Franca*; related to Old High German *Franko*; perhaps from the name of a typical Frankish weapon (compare Old English *franca* javelin)

frankalmoign ('fræŋkəl,mɔɪn) NOUN *English legal history* a form of tenure by which religious bodies held lands, esp on condition of praying for the soul of the donor.
▷HISTORY C16: from Anglo-French *fraunke almoigne*, from *fraunke* FRANK + *almoign* church treasury, alms chest

franked investment income NOUN (formerly) dividends from one UK company received by another on which the paying company had paid corporation tax so that the receiving company had no corporation tax to pay: discontinued from 1999.

Frankenstein ('fræŋkɪn,staɪn) NOUN 1 a person who creates something that brings about his ruin. 2 Also called: **Frankenstein's monster.** a thing that destroys its creator.
▷HISTORY C19: after Baron *Frankenstein*, who created a destructive monster from parts of corpses in the novel by Mary Shelley (1818)
▸**,Franken'steinian** ADJECTIVE

Frankenstein food *or* **Frankenfood** ('fræŋkən,fuːd) NOUN *Facetious* any foodstuff that has been genetically modified.
▷HISTORY C20: from FRANKENSTEIN, alluding to its unnatural origin

Frankfurt (am Main) (*German* 'fraŋkfʊrt (am 'main)) NOUN a city in central Germany, in Hesse on the Main River: a Roman settlement in the 1st century; a free imperial city (1372–1806); seat of the federal assembly (1815–66); university (1914); trade fairs since the 13th century. Pop.: 644 700 (1999 est.).

Frankfurt (an der Oder) (*German* 'fraŋkfʊrt (an der 'oːdər)) NOUN a city in E Germany on the Polish border: member of the Hanseatic League (1368–1450). Pop.: 85 360 (1991).

frankfurter ('fræŋk,fɜːtə) NOUN a light brown smoked sausage, made of finely minced pork or beef, often served in a bread roll.
▷HISTORY C20: short for German *Frankfurter Wurst* sausage from FRANKFURT (AM MAIN)

Frankfurter ('fræŋk,fɜːtə) NOUN an inhabitant or native of Frankfurt.

Frankfurt School NOUN *Philosophy* a school of thought, founded at the University of Frankfurt in 1923 by Theodor Adorno, Herbert Marcuse and others, derived from Marxist, Freudian, and Hegelian theory.

frankincense ('fræŋkɪn,sɛns) NOUN an aromatic gum resin obtained from trees of the burseraceous genus *Boswellia*, which occur in Asia and Africa. Also called: **olibanum.**
▷HISTORY C14: from Old French *franc* free, pure + *encens* INCENSE[1]; see FRANK

Frankish ('fræŋkɪʃ) NOUN 1 the ancient West Germanic language of the Franks, esp the dialect that contributed to the vocabulary of modern French. See also **Franconian, Old High German.** ◆ ADJECTIVE 2 of or relating to the Franks or their language.

franklin ('fræŋklɪn) NOUN (in 14th- and 15th-century England) a substantial landholder of free but not noble birth.
▷HISTORY C13: from Anglo-French *fraunclein*, from Old French *franc* free, on the model of CHAMBERLAIN

franklinite ('fræŋklɪ,naɪt) NOUN a black mineral consisting of an oxide of iron, manganese, and zinc: a source of iron and zinc. Formula: $(Fe,Mn,Zn)(Fe,Mn)_2O_4$.
▷HISTORY C19: from *Franklin*, New Jersey, where it is found, + -ITE[1]

frankly ('fræŋklɪ) ADVERB 1 (*sentence modifier*) in truth; to be honest: *frankly, I can't bear him.* 2 in a frank manner.

frankpledge ('fræŋk,plɛdʒ) NOUN (in medieval England) 1 the corporate responsibility of members of a tithing for the good behaviour of each other. 2 a member of a tithing. 3 a tithing itself.
▷HISTORY C15: via Anglo-French from Old French *franc* free (see FRANK) + *plege* PLEDGE

frantic ('fræntɪk) ADJECTIVE 1 distracted with fear, pain, joy, etc. 2 marked by or showing frenzy: *frantic efforts.* 3 *Archaic* insane.
▷HISTORY C14: from Old French *frenetique*, from Latin *phrenēticus* mad, FRENETIC
▸**'frantically** *or* **'franticly** ADVERB ▸**'franticness** NOUN

Franz Josef Land (*German* frants 'joːzɛf) NOUN an archipelago of over 100 islands in the Arctic Ocean, administratively part of Russia. Area: about 21 000 sq. km (8000 sq. miles). Russian name: **Zemlya Frantsa Iosifa** (zji'mlja 'frantsə 'jɔsifə).

frap (fræp) VERB **fraps, frapping, frapped.** (*tr*) *Nautical* to lash down or together.
▷HISTORY C14: from Old French *fraper* to hit, probably of imitative origin

frape (freɪp) ADJECTIVE *Southwest English dialect* tightly bound.
▷HISTORY see FRAP

frappé ('fræpeɪ; *French* frape) NOUN 1 a drink consisting of a liqueur, etc., poured over crushed ice. ◆ ADJECTIVE 2 (*postpositive*) (esp of drinks) chilled; iced.
▷HISTORY C19: from French, from *frapper* to strike, hence, chill; see FRAP

Frascati (fræ'skɑːtɪ) NOUN a dry or semisweet white wine from the Lazio region of Italy.

Fraser ('freɪzə) NOUN a river in SW Canada, in S central British Columbia, flowing northwest, south, and west through spectacular canyons in the Coast Mountains to the Strait of Georgia. Length: 1370 km (850 miles).

frass (fræs) NOUN excrement or other refuse left by insects and insect larvae.
▷HISTORY C19: from German, from *fressen* to devour

frat (fræt) NOUN *US slang* **a** a member of a fraternity. **b** (*as modifier*): *the frat kid.*

fratch (frætʃ) NOUN *English dialect* a quarrel.
▷HISTORY C19: from obsolete *fratch* to make a harsh noise; perhaps of imitative origin
▸**'fratchy** ADJECTIVE

frater[1] ('freɪtə) NOUN a mendicant friar or a lay brother in a monastery or priory.
▷HISTORY C16: from Latin: BROTHER

frater[2] ('freɪtə) NOUN *Archaic* a refectory.
▷HISTORY C13: from Old French *fraiteur*, aphetic variant of *refreitor*, from Late Latin *rēfectōrium* REFECTORY

fraternal (frə'tɜːnᵊl) ADJECTIVE 1 of or suitable to a brother; brotherly. 2 of or relating to a fraternity. 3 designating either or both of a pair of twins of the same or opposite sex that developed from two separate fertilized ova. Compare **identical** (sense 3).
▷HISTORY C15: from Latin *frāternus*, from *frāter* brother
▸**fra'ternalism** NOUN ▸**fra'ternally** ADVERB

fraternity (frə'tɜːnɪtɪ) NOUN, *plural* **-ties.** 1 a body of people united in interests, aims, etc.: *the teaching fraternity.* 2 brotherhood. 3 *US and Canadian* a secret society joined by male students, usually functioning as a social club.

fraternize *or* **fraternise** ('frætə,naɪz) VERB (*intr*; often foll by *with*) to associate on friendly terms.
▸**,fraterni'zation** *or* **,fraterni'sation** NOUN ▸**'frater,nizer** *or* **'frater,niser** NOUN

fratricide ('frætrɪ,saɪd, 'freɪ-) NOUN 1 the act of killing one's brother. 2 a person who kills his brother. 3 *Military* the destruction of or interference with a nuclear missile before it can strike its target caused by the earlier explosion of a warhead at a nearby target.
▷HISTORY C15: from Latin *frātricīda*; see FRATER[1], -CIDE
▸**,fratri'cidal** ADJECTIVE

Frau (frau) NOUN, *plural* **Frauen** ('frauən) *or* **Fraus.** a married German woman: usually used as a title equivalent to *Mrs* and sometimes extended to older unmarried women.
▷HISTORY from Old High German *frouwa*; related to Dutch *vrouw*

fraud (frɔːd) NOUN 1 deliberate deception, trickery, or cheating intended to gain an advantage. 2 an act or instance of such deception. 3 something false or spurious: *his explanation was a fraud.* 4 *Informal* a person who acts in a false or deceitful way.
▷HISTORY C14: from Old French *fraude*, from Latin *fraus* deception

Fraud Squad NOUN (in Britain) the department of a police force that is concerned with criminal fraud.

fraudster ('frɔːdstə) NOUN a swindler.

fraudulent ('frɔːdjʊlənt) ADJECTIVE 1 acting with or having the intent to deceive. 2 relating to or proceeding from fraud or dishonest action.
▷HISTORY C15: from Latin *fraudulentus* deceitful
▸**'fraudulence** *or* **'fraudulency** NOUN ▸**'fraudulently** ADVERB

fraughan ('frɒhən) NOUN an Irish word for **whortleberry** (senses 1, 2).
▷HISTORY from Irish Gaelic *fraochán*, diminutive of *fraoch* heather

fraught (frɔːt) ADJECTIVE 1 (*usually postpositive* and foll by *with*) filled or charged; attended: *a venture fraught with peril.* 2 *Informal* showing or producing tension or anxiety: *she looks rather fraught; a fraught situation.* 3 *Archaic* (*usually postpositive* and foll by *with*) freighted. ◆ NOUN 4 an obsolete word for **freight.**
▷HISTORY C14: from Middle Dutch *vrachten*, from *vracht* FREIGHT

Fräulein (*German* 'frɔylain; *English* 'frɔːlaɪn, 'frau-) NOUN, *plural* **-lein** *or English* **-leins.** an unmarried German woman: formerly used as a title equivalent to *Miss.* Abbreviation: **Frl.**
▷HISTORY from Middle High German *vrouwelīn*, diminutive of *vrouwe* lady

Fraunhofer lines (*German* 'fraunhoːfər) PLURAL NOUN a set of dark lines appearing in the continuous emission spectrum of the sun. It is caused by the absorption of light of certain wavelengths coming from the hotter region of the sun by elements in the cooler outer atmosphere.
▷HISTORY named after J. von *Fraunhofer* (1787–1826), German physicist

frawzey ('frɔːzɪ) NOUN *Southwest English dialect* a celebration; treat.

fraxinella (,fræksɪ'nɛlə) NOUN another name for **gas plant.**
▷HISTORY C17: from New Latin: a little ash tree, from Latin *frāxinus* ash

fray[1] (freɪ) NOUN 1 a noisy quarrel. 2 a fight or brawl. 3 an archaic word for **fright.** ◆ VERB *Archaic* 4 (*tr*) to frighten.
▷HISTORY C14: short for AFFRAY

fray[2] (freɪ) VERB 1 to wear or cause to wear away into tatters or loose threads, esp at an edge or end. 2 to make or become strained or irritated. 3 to rub or chafe (another object) or (of two objects) to rub against one another. ◆ NOUN 4 a frayed place, as in cloth.
▷HISTORY C14: from French *frayer* to rub, from Latin *fricāre*; see FRICTION, FRIABLE

Fray Bentos (,freɪ 'bɛntɒs) NOUN a port in W Uruguay, on the River Uruguay: noted for meat-packing. Pop.: 21 400 (1995 est.).

frazil ('freɪzɪl) NOUN small pieces of ice that form in water moving turbulently enough to prevent the formation of a sheet of ice.
▷HISTORY C19: from Canadian French *frasil*, from French *fraisil* cinders, ultimately from Latin *fax* torch

frazzle ('fræzᵊl) VERB 1 *Informal* to make or become exhausted or weary; tire out. 2 a less common word for **fray**[2] (sense 1). ◆ NOUN 3 *Informal* the state of being frazzled or exhausted. 4 a frayed end or remnant. 5 **to a frazzle.** *Informal* absolutely; completely (esp in the phrase **burnt to a frazzle**).
▷HISTORY C19: probably from Middle English *faselen* to fray, from *fasel* fringe; influenced by FRAY[2]

FRCM (in Britain) ABBREVIATION FOR Fellow of the Royal College of Music.

FRCO (in Britain) ABBREVIATION FOR Fellow of the Royal College of Organists.

FRCP (in Britain) ABBREVIATION FOR Fellow of the Royal College of Physicians.

FRCS (in Britain) ABBREVIATION FOR Fellow of the Royal College of Surgeons.

FRCVS (in Britain) ABBREVIATION FOR Fellow of the Royal College of Veterinary Surgeons.

freak[1] (fri:k) NOUN 1 a person, animal, or plant that is abnormal or deformed; monstrosity. 2 **a** an object, event, etc., that is abnormal or extremely unusual. **b** (*as modifier*): *a freak storm*. 3 a personal whim or caprice. 4 *Informal* a person who acts or dresses in a markedly unconventional or strange way. 5 *Informal* a person who is obsessed with something specified: *a jazz freak*. ◆ VERB 6 See **freak out**.
▷HISTORY C16: of obscure origin

freak[2] (fri:k) *Rare* ◆ NOUN 1 a fleck or streak of colour. ◆ VERB 2 (*tr*) to streak with colour; variegate.
▷HISTORY C17: from earlier *freaked*, probably coined by Milton, based on STREAK[1] + obsolete *freckt* freckled; see FRECKLE

freaking ('fri:kɪŋ) ADJECTIVE (*prenominal*), ADVERB *Slang, chiefly US* (intensifier): *his freaking mother; this is freaking weird*.
▷HISTORY C20: euphemism for FUCKING

freakish ('fri:kɪʃ) ADJECTIVE 1 of, related to, or characteristic of a freak; abnormal or unusual. 2 unpredictable or changeable: *freakish weather*.
▸ **'freakishly** ADVERB ▸ **'freakishness** NOUN

freak out VERB (*adverb*) *Informal* to be or cause to be in a heightened emotional state, such as that of fear, anger, or excitement.

freaky ('fri:kɪ) ADJECTIVE **freakier, freakiest.** 1 *Slang* strange; unconventional; bizarre. 2 another word for **freakish.**
▸ **'freakily** ADVERB ▸ **'freakiness** NOUN

freckle ('frɛkᵊl) NOUN 1 a small brownish spot on the skin: a localized deposit of the pigment melanin, developed by exposure to sunlight. Technical name: **lentigo.** 2 any small area of discoloration; a spot. 3 *Austral slang* the anus. ◆ VERB 4 to mark or become marked with freckles or spots.
▷HISTORY C14: from Old Norse *freknur* freckles; related to Swedish *fräkne*, Danish *fregne*
▸ **'freckled** *or* **'freckly** ADJECTIVE

Fredericton ('frɛdrɪktən) NOUN a city in SE Canada, capital of New Brunswick, on the St John River. Pop.: 45 364 (1991).

Frederiksberg (*Danish* freðregs'bɛr) NOUN a city in E Denmark, within the area of greater Copenhagen: founded in 1651 by King Frederick III. Pop.: 88 002 (1995 est.).

free (fri:) ADJECTIVE **freer, freest.** 1 able to act at will; not under compulsion or restraint. 2 **a** having personal rights or liberty; not enslaved or confined. **b** (*as noun*): *land of the free*. 3 (*often postpositive* and foll by *from*) not subject (to) or restricted (by some regulation, constraint, etc.); exempt: *a free market; free from pain*. 4 (of a country, etc.) autonomous or independent. 5 exempt from external direction or restriction; not forced or induced: *free will*. 6 not subject to conventional constraints: *free verse*. 7 (of jazz) totally improvised, with no preset melodic, harmonic, or rhythmic basis. 8 not exact or literal: *a free translation*. 9 costing nothing; provided without charge: *free entertainment*. 10 *Law* (of property) **a** not subject to payment of rent or performance of services; freehold. **b** not subject to any burden or charge, such as a mortgage or lien; unencumbered. 11 (*postpositive;* often foll by *of* or *with*) ready or generous in using or giving; liberal; lavish: *free with advice*. 12 unrestrained by propriety or good manners; licentious. 13 not occupied or in use; available: *a free cubicle*. 14 not occupied or busy; without previous engagements: *I'm not free until Wednesday*. 15 open or available to all; public. 16 without charge to the subscriber or user: *freepost; freephone*. 17 not fixed or joined; loose: *the free end of a chain*. 18 without obstruction or impediment: *free passage*. 19 *Chem* chemically uncombined: *free nitrogen*. 20 *Phonetics* denoting a vowel that can occur in an open syllable, such as the vowel in *see* as opposed to the vowel in *cat*. 21 *Grammar* denoting a morpheme that can occur as a separate word. Compare **bound**[1] (sense 8a). 22 *Logic* denoting an occurrence of a variable not bound by a quantifier. Compare **bound**[1] (sense 9). 23 (of some materials, such as certain kinds of stone) easily worked. 24 *Nautical* (of the wind) blowing from the quarter. 25 **for free.** *Not standard* without charge or cost. 26 **free and easy.** casual or tolerant; easy-going. 27 **feel free.** (*usually imperative*) to regard oneself as having permission to perform a specified action. 28 **make free with.** to take liberties with; behave too familiarly towards. ◆ ADVERB 29 in a free manner; freely. 30 without charge or cost. 31 *Nautical* with the wind blowing from the quarter: *a yacht sailing free*. ◆ VERB **frees, freeing, freed.** (*tr*) 32 (sometimes foll by *up*) to set at liberty; release. 33 to remove obstructions, attachments, or impediments from; disengage. 34 (often foll by *of* or *from*) to relieve or rid (of obstacles, pain, etc.). ◆ NOUN 35 *Informal* a freesheet.
▷HISTORY Old English *frēo*; related to Old Saxon, Old High German *frī*, Gothic *freis* free, Sanskrit *priya* dear
▸ **'freer** NOUN ▸ **'freely** ADVERB ▸ **'freeness** NOUN

-free ADJECTIVE COMBINING FORM free from: *trouble-free; lead-free petrol*.

free agent NOUN a person whose actions are not constrained by others.

free alongside ship ADJECTIVE (of a shipment of goods) delivered to the dock without charge to the buyer, but excluding the cost of loading onto the vessel. Compare **free on board.** Abbreviations: **FAS, f.a.s.** Also: **free alongside vessel.**

free association NOUN 1 *Psychoanal* a method of exploring a person's unconscious by eliciting words and thoughts that are associated with key words provided by a psychoanalyst. 2 a spontaneous mental process whereby ideas, words, or images suggest other ideas, etc., in a nonlogical chain reaction.

freebase ('fri:ˌbeɪs) NOUN 1 *Slang* cocaine that has been refined by heating it in ether or some other solvent. ◆ VERB **freebases, freebasing, freebased.** 2 to refine (cocaine) in this way. 3 to smoke or inhale the fumes from (refined cocaine).

freebie ('fri:bɪ) *Slang* ◆ NOUN 1 something provided without charge. ◆ ADJECTIVE 2 without charge; free.

freeboard ('fri:ˌbɔ:d) NOUN the space or distance between the deck of a vessel and the waterline.

freeboot ('fri:ˌbu:t) VERB (*intr*) to act as a freebooter; pillage.

freebooter ('fri:ˌbu:tə) NOUN 1 a person, such as a pirate, living from plunder. 2 *Informal* a person, esp an itinerant, who seeks pleasure, wealth, etc., without responsibility.
▷HISTORY C16: from Dutch *vrijbuiter*, from *vrijbuit* booty; see FILIBUSTER

freeborn ('fri:ˌbɔ:n) ADJECTIVE 1 not born in slavery. 2 of, relating to, or suitable for people not born in slavery.

Free Church NOUN *Chiefly Brit* **a** any Protestant Church, esp the Presbyterian, other than the Established Church. **b** (*as modifier*): *Free-Church attitudes*.

free city NOUN a sovereign or autonomous city; city-state.

free climbing NOUN *Mountaineering* climbing without using pitons, étriers, etc., as direct aids to ascent, but using ropes, belays, etc., at discretion for security. Compare **aid climbing.**

free coinage NOUN *US* coinage of bullion brought to the mint by any individual.

free companion NOUN (in medieval Europe) a member of a company of mercenary soldiers.

free company NOUN *European history* a band of mercenary soldiers during the Middle Ages.

freedman ('fri:dˌmæn) NOUN, *plural* **-men.** a man who has been freed from slavery.
▸ **'freedˌwoman** FEMININE NOUN

freedom ('fri:dəm) NOUN 1 personal liberty, as from slavery, bondage, serfdom, etc. 2 liberation or deliverance, as from confinement or bondage. 3 the quality or state of being free, esp to enjoy political and civil liberties. 4 (usually foll by *from*) the state of being without something unpleasant or bad; exemption or immunity: *freedom from taxation*. 5 the right or privilege of unrestricted use or access: *the freedom of a city*. 6 autonomy, self-government, or independence. 7 the power or liberty to order one's own actions. 8 *Philosophy* the quality, esp of the will or the individual, of not being totally constrained; able to choose between alternative actions in identical circumstances. 9 ease or frankness of manner; candour: *she talked with complete freedom*. 10 excessive familiarity of manner; boldness. 11 ease and grace, as of movement; lack of effort.
▷HISTORY Old English *frēodōm*

freedom fighter NOUN a militant revolutionary.

Freedom Food NOUN (in Britain) food that is produced by farmers conforming to the guidelines for humane farming set by the Freedom Food programme set up by the RSPCA in conjunction with some major supermarkets.

Freedomites ('fri:dəˌmaɪts) PLURAL NOUN another name for **Sons of Freedom.**

freedom of the seas NOUN *International law* 1 the right of ships of all nations to sail the high seas in peacetime. 2 (in wartime) the immunity accorded to neutral ships from attack. 3 the exclusive jurisdiction possessed by a state over its own ships sailing the high seas in peacetime.

freedom rider NOUN *US* a person who participated, esp in the 1960s, in an organized tour, usually by public transport in the South, in order to protest against racism and put federal laws on integration to the test.

free electron NOUN any electron that is not attached to an ion, atom, or molecule and is free to move under the influence of an applied electric or magnetic field.

free energy NOUN a thermodynamic property that expresses the capacity of a system to perform work under certain conditions. See **Gibbs function, Helmholtz function.**

free enterprise NOUN an economic system in which commercial organizations compete for profit with little state control.

free fall NOUN 1 free descent of a body in which the gravitational force is the only force acting on it. 2 the part of a parachute descent before the parachute opens.

free flight NOUN the flight of a rocket, missile, etc., when its engine has ceased to produce thrust.

free-floating ADJECTIVE unattached or uncommitted, as to a cause, a party, etc.
▸ **ˌfree-'floater** NOUN

free-floating anxiety NOUN *Psychiatry* chronic anxiety occurring for no identifiable cause.

Freefone ('fri:ˌfəʊn) NOUN *Brit, trademark* a system of telephone use in which the cost of calls in response to an advertisement is borne by the advertiser.

free-for-all NOUN *Informal* a disorganized brawl or argument, usually involving all those present.

free form *Arts* ◆ NOUN 1 an irregular flowing shape, often used in industrial or fabric design. ◆ ADJECTIVE **free-form.** 2 freely flowing, spontaneous.

free gift NOUN something given away, esp as an incentive to a purchaser.

free gold NOUN 1 gold, uncombined with other minerals, found in a pure state. 2 *US* the excess of gold held by the Federal Reserve Banks over the legal reserve.

free hand NOUN 1 unrestricted freedom to act (esp in the phrase **give (someone) a free hand**). ◆

ADJECTIVE, ADVERB **freehand.** 2 (done) by hand without the use of guiding instruments: *a freehand drawing.*

free-handed ADJECTIVE generous or liberal; unstinting.
▸ ˌ**free-ˈhandedly** ADVERB ▸ ˌ**free-ˈhandedness** NOUN

free-hearted ADJECTIVE frank and spontaneous; open; generous.
▸ ˌ**free-ˈheartedly** ADVERB ▸ ˌ**free-ˈheartedness** NOUN

freehold (ˈfriːˌhəʊld) *Property law* ◆ NOUN 1 **a** a tenure by which land is held in fee simple, fee tail, or for life. **b** an estate held by such tenure. ◆ ADJECTIVE 2 relating to or having the nature of freehold.

freeholder (ˈfriːˌhəʊldə) NOUN *Property law* a person in possession of a freehold building or estate in land.

free house NOUN *Brit* a public house not bound to sell only one brewer's products.

free kick NOUN *Soccer* a place kick awarded for a foul or infringement, either direct, from which a goal may be scored, or indirect, from which the ball must be touched by at least one other player for a goal to be allowed.

free labour NOUN 1 the labour of workers who are not members of trade unions. 2 such workers collectively.

freelance (ˈfriːˌlɑːns) NOUN 1 **a** Also called: **freelancer.** a self-employed person, esp a writer or artist, who is not employed continuously but hired to do specific assignments. **b** (*as modifier*): *a freelance journalist.* 2 a person, esp a politician, who supports several causes or parties without total commitment to any one. 3 (in medieval Europe) a mercenary soldier or adventurer. ◆ VERB 4 to work as a freelance on (an assignment, etc.). ◆ ADVERB 5 as a freelance.
▷**HISTORY** C19 (in sense 3): later applied to politicians, writers, etc.

free list NOUN 1 *Commerce, chiefly US* a list of commodities not subject to tariffs. 2 a list of people admitted free.

free-living ADJECTIVE 1 given to ready indulgence of the appetites. 2 (of animals and plants) not parasitic; existing independently.
▸ ˌ**free-ˈliver** NOUN

freeload (ˈfriːˌləʊd) VERB (*intr*) *Slang* to act as a freeloader; sponge.

freeloader (ˈfriːˌləʊdə) NOUN *Slang* a person who habitually depends on the charity of others for food, shelter, etc.
▸ ˈ**freeˌloading** NOUN

free love NOUN the practice of sexual relationships without fidelity to a single partner or without formal or legal ties.

freeman (ˈfriːmən) NOUN, *plural* **-men.** 1 a person who is not a slave or in bondage. 2 a person who enjoys political and civil liberties; citizen. 3 a person who enjoys a privilege or franchise, such as the freedom of a city.

free market NOUN **a** an economic system that allows supply and demand to regulate prices, wages, etc., rather than government policy. **b** (*as modifier*): *a free-market economy.*

freemartin (ˈfriːˌmɑːtɪn) NOUN the female of a pair of twin calves of unlike sex that is imperfectly developed and sterile, probably due to the influence of the male hormones of its twin during development in the uterus.
▷**HISTORY** C17: of uncertain origin

freemason (ˈfriːˌmeɪsᵊn) NOUN *Medieval history* a member of a guild of itinerant skilled stonemasons, who had a system of secret signs and passwords with which they recognized each other.
▸**freemasonic** (ˌfriːməˈsɒnɪk) ADJECTIVE

Freemason (ˈfriːˌmeɪsᵊn) NOUN a member of the widespread secret order, constituted in London in 1717, of **Free and Accepted Masons,** pledged to brotherly love, faith, and charity. Sometimes shortened to: **Mason.**
▸**Freemasonic** (ˌfriːməˈsɒnɪk) ADJECTIVE

freemasonry (ˈfriːˌmeɪsᵊnrɪ) NOUN natural or tacit sympathy and understanding.

Freemasonry (ˈfriːˌmeɪsᵊnrɪ) NOUN 1 the institutions, rites, practices, etc., of Freemasons. 2 Freemasons collectively.

free on board ADJECTIVE (of a shipment of goods) delivered on board ship or other carrier without charge to the buyer. Compare **free alongside ship.** Abbreviations: **FOB, f.o.b.**

free on rail ADJECTIVE (of a consignment of goods) delivered to a railway station and loaded onto a train without charge to the buyer. Abbreviations: **FOR, f.o.r.**

freephone (ˈfriːˌfəʊn) NOUN a common spelling of **Freefone.**

free port NOUN 1 a port open to all commercial vessels on equal terms. 2 Also called: **free zone.** a zone adjoining a port that permits the duty-free entry of foreign goods intended for re-export.

Freepost (ˈfriːˌpəʊst) NOUN *Brit, trademark* a method of postage by which the cost of replies to an advertisement is borne by the advertiser.

free radical NOUN an atom or group of atoms containing at least one unpaired electron and existing for a brief period of time before reacting to produce a stable molecule. Sometimes shortened to: **radical.** Compare **group** (sense 10).

free-range ADJECTIVE *Chiefly Brit* kept or produced in natural nonintensive conditions: *free-range hens; free-range eggs.*

free recall NOUN *Psychol* the recollection of the members of a list of items without regard to their serial order.

free-running ADJECTIVE 1 (of a mechanism, material, etc.) moving smoothly and uninterruptedly. 2 *Electronics* of or relating to a periodic signal that is not synchronized to a timing source: *free-running interference produces moving patterns on a television screen.*

free-select VERB (*tr*) *Austral history* to select (areas of crown land) and acquire the freehold by a series of annual payments.
▸ ˌ**free-seˈlection** NOUN ▸ ˌ**free-seˈlector** NOUN

freesheet (ˈfriːˌʃiːt) NOUN a newspaper that is distributed free, paid for by its advertisers. Also called: **giveaway.**

freesia (ˈfriːzɪə, ˈfriːʒə) NOUN any iridaceous plant of the genus *Freesia,* of southern Africa, cultivated for their white, yellow, or pink tubular fragrant flowers.
▷**HISTORY** C19: New Latin, named after F. H. T. *Freese* (died 1876), German physician

free silver NOUN the unlimited minting of silver coins, esp when at a fixed ratio to gold.

free skating NOUN either the short programme of specified movements or the long programme chosen by a skater in a figure-skating competition.

Free Soil Party NOUN a former US political party opposing slavery from 1848 until 1854 when it merged with the Republican party.

free space NOUN a region that has no gravitational and electromagnetic fields: used as an absolute standard. Also called (no longer in technical usage): **vacuum.**

free speech NOUN the right to express one's opinions publicly.

free-spoken ADJECTIVE speaking frankly or without restraint.
▸ ˌ**free-ˈspokenly** ADVERB ▸ ˌ**free-ˈspokenness** NOUN

freestanding (ˌfriːˈstændɪŋ) ADJECTIVE 1 standing apart; not attached to or supported by another object. 2 (in systemic grammar) denoting a clause that can stand alone as a sentence; denoting or being a main clause. Compare **bound**¹ (sense 8b).

Free State NOUN 1 a province of central South Africa; replaced the former province of Orange Free State in 1994: gold and uranium mining. Capital: Bloemfontein. Pop.: 2 714 654 (1999 est.). Area: 129 480 sq. km (49 992 sq. miles). 2 *US history* (before the Civil War) any state prohibiting slavery. 3 short for the **Irish Free State.**

freestone (ˈfriːˌstəʊn) NOUN 1 **a** any fine-grained stone, esp sandstone or limestone, that can be cut and worked in any direction without breaking. **b** (*as modifier*): *a freestone house.* 2 *Botany* **a** a fruit, such as a peach, in which the flesh separates readily from the stone. **b** (*as modifier*): *a freestone peach.* Compare **clingstone.**

freestyle (ˈfriːˌstaɪl) NOUN 1 a competition or race, as in swimming, in which each participant may use a style of his or her choice instead of a specified style. 2 **a** an amateur style of wrestling with an agreed set of rules. **b** Also called: **all-in wrestling.** a style of professional wrestling with no internationally agreed set of rules. 3 a series of acrobatics performed in skiing, etc. 4 (*as modifier*): *a freestyle event.*

freestyling (ˈfriːˌstaɪlɪŋ) NOUN the practice of improvising scenes when making a film or performing a play.

free-swimming ADJECTIVE (of aquatic animals or larvae) not sessile or attached to any object and therefore able to swim freely in the water.
▸ ˌ**free-ˈswimmer** NOUN

freethinker (ˌfriːˈθɪŋkə) NOUN a person who forms his ideas and opinions independently of authority or accepted views, esp in matters of religion.
▸ ˌ**freeˈthinking** NOUN, ADJECTIVE

free thought NOUN thought unrestrained and uninfluenced by dogma or authority, esp in religious matters.

free throw NOUN *Basketball* an unimpeded shot at the basket from the **free-throw line** given for a technical fault (one free shot) or a foul (two free shots).

free-to-air NOUN **a** a system of television for which viewers do not have to subscribe or pay. **b** (*as modifier*): *free-to-air networks.* ◆ Compare **pay-per-view, pay television.**

Freetown (ˈfriːˌtaʊn) NOUN the capital and chief port of Sierra Leone: founded in 1787 for slaves freed and destitute in England. Pop.: 822 000 (1999 est.).

free trade NOUN 1 international trade that is free of such government interference as import quotas, export subsidies, protective tariffs, etc. Compare **protection** (sense 3). 2 *Archaic* illicit trade; smuggling.

free-trader NOUN 1 a person who supports or advocates free trade. 2 *Archaic* a smuggler or smuggling vessel.

free verse NOUN unrhymed verse without a metrical pattern.

free vibration NOUN the vibration of a structure that occurs at its natural frequency, as opposed to a forced vibration.

free vote NOUN *Chiefly Brit* a parliamentary division in which members are not constrained by a party whip.

freeware (ˈfriːˌwɛə) NOUN computer software that may be distributed and used without payment.

freeway (ˈfriːˌweɪ) NOUN *US* 1 another name for **expressway.** 2 a major road that can be used without paying a toll.

freewheel (ˌfriːˈwiːl) NOUN 1 a ratchet device in the rear hub of a bicycle wheel that permits the wheel to rotate freely while the pedals are stationary. 2 a device in the transmission of some vehicles that automatically disengages the drive shaft when it rotates more rapidly than the engine shaft, so that the drive shaft can turn freely. ◆ VERB 3 (*intr*) to coast in a vehicle or on a bicycle using the freewheel.

freewheeling (ˌfriːˈwiːlɪŋ) ADJECTIVE 1 relating to, operating as, or having a freewheel; coasting. 2 *Informal* free of restraints; carefree or uninhibited.

free will NOUN 1 **a** the apparent human ability to make choices that are not externally determined. **b** the doctrine that such human freedom of choice is not illusory. Compare **determinism. c** (*as modifier*): *a free-will decision.* 2 the ability to make a choice without coercion: *he left of his own free will: I did not influence him.*

Free World NOUN **the.** the non-Communist countries collectively, esp those that are actively anti-Communist.

freeze (friːz) VERB **freezes, freezing, froze** (frəʊz), **frozen** (ˈfrəʊzᵊn). 1 to change (a liquid) into a solid as a result of a reduction in temperature, or (of a liquid) to solidify in this way, esp to convert or be converted into ice. 2 (when *intr,* sometimes foll by *over* or *up*) to cover, clog, or harden with ice, or become so covered, clogged, or hardened: *the lake froze over last week.* 3 to fix fast or become fixed (to something) because of the action of frost. 4 (*tr*) to preserve (food) by subjection to extreme cold, as in a freezer. 5 to feel or cause to feel the sensation or effects of extreme cold. 6 to die or cause to die of

frost or extreme cold. [7] to become or cause to become paralysed, fixed, or motionless, esp through fear, shock, etc.: *he froze in his tracks.* [8] *(tr)* to cause (moving film) to stop at a particular frame. [9] to decrease or cause to decrease in animation or vigour. [10] to make or become formal, haughty, etc., in manner. [11] *(tr)* to fix (prices, incomes, etc.) at a particular level, usually by government direction. [12] *(tr)* to forbid by law the exchange, liquidation, or collection of (loans, assets, etc.). [13] *(tr)* to prohibit the manufacture, sale, or use of (something specified). [14] *(tr)* to stop (a process) at a particular stage of development. [15] *(tr) Informal* to render (tissue or a part of the body) insensitive, as by the application or injection of a local anaesthetic. [16] *(intr; foll by onto) Informal, chiefly US* to cling. ◆ NOUN [17] the act of freezing or state of being frozen. [18] *Meteorol* a spell of temperatures below freezing point, usually over a wide area. [19] the fixing of incomes, prices, etc., by legislation. [20] another word for **frost.** ◆ SENTENCE SUBSTITUTE. [21] *Chiefly US* a command to stop still instantly or risk being shot.
▷HISTORY Old English *frēosan*; related to Old Norse *frjōsa*, Old High German *friosan*, Latin *prūrīre* to itch; see FROST
▸ **ˈfreezable** ADJECTIVE

freeze-dry VERB **-dries, -drying, -dried.** *(tr)* to preserve (a substance) by rapid freezing and subsequently drying in a vacuum.

freeze-frame NOUN [1] *Films, television* a single frame of a film repeated to give an effect like a still photograph. [2] a single frame of a video recording viewed as a still by stopping the tape. ◆ VERB *(tr)* [3] to make a freeze-frame of (an image).

freeze out VERB *(tr, adverb) Informal* to force out or exclude, as by unfriendly behaviour, boycotting, etc.

freezer (ˈfriːzə) NOUN [1] Also called: **deepfreeze.** a device that freezes or chills, esp an insulated cold-storage cabinet for long-term storage of perishable foodstuffs. [2] a former name for a **refrigerator.**

freeze-up NOUN *Informal* [1] a period of freezing or extremely cold weather. [2] *US, Canadian* **a** the freezing of lakes, rivers, and topsoil in autumn or early winter. **b** the time of year when this occurs.

freezing (ˈfriːzɪŋ) ADJECTIVE *Informal* extremely cold.

freezing injunction NOUN *Law* an order enabling the court to freeze the assets of a defendant, esp to prevent him or her taking them abroad. Formerly called: **Mareva injunction.**

freezing mixture NOUN a mixture of two substances, usually salt and ice, to give a temperature below 0°C.

freezing point NOUN the temperature below which a liquid turns into a solid. It is equal to the melting point.

freezing works NOUN *Austral and NZ* a slaughterhouse at which animal carcasses are frozen for export. See also **chamber** (sense 10).

free zone NOUN an area at a port where certain customs restrictions are not implemented. See also **free port.**

F region NOUN the highest region of the ionosphere, extending from a height of about 150 kilometres to about 1000 kilometres. It contains the highest proportion of free electrons and is the most useful region for long-range radio transmission. Also called: **Appleton layer.** See also **ionosphere.**

Freiburg (*German* ˈfraibʊrk) NOUN [1] a city in SW Germany, in SW Baden-Württemberg: under Austrian rule (1368–1805); university (1457). Pop.: 201 000 (1999 est.). Official name: **Freiburg im Breisgau** (ɪm ˈbraisgau). [2] the German name for **Fribourg.**

freight (freɪt) NOUN [1] **a** commercial transport that is slower and cheaper than express. **b** the price charged for such transport. **c** goods transported by this means. **d** *(as modifier)*: *freight transport.* [2] *Chiefly Brit* a ship's cargo or part of it. ◆ VERB *(tr)* [3] to load with goods for transport. [4] *Chiefly US and Canadian* to convey commercially as or by freight. [5] to load or burden; charge.
▷HISTORY C16: from Middle Dutch *vrecht*; related to French *fret*, Spanish *flete*, Portuguese *frete*
▸ **ˈfreightless** ADJECTIVE

freightage (ˈfreɪtɪdʒ) NOUN [1] the commercial conveyance of goods. [2] the goods so transported. [3] the price charged for such conveyance.

freighter (ˈfreɪtə) NOUN [1] a ship or aircraft designed for transporting cargo. [2] a person concerned with the loading or chartering of a ship.

Freightliner (ˈfreɪtˌlaɪnə) NOUN *Trademark* [1] a goods train carrying containers that can be transferred onto lorries or ships. [2] (in Britain) a containerized transportation service involving both rail and road.

freight ton NOUN the full name for **ton**[1] (sense 4).

Fremantle (ˈfriːˌmæntᵊl) NOUN a port in SW Western Australia, on the Indian Ocean. Pop.: 24 000 (latest est.).

fremd (frɛmd, freɪmd) ADJECTIVE *Archaic* alien or strange.
▷HISTORY Old English *fremde*; related to Old High German *fremidi*

fremitus (ˈfrɛmɪtəs) NOUN, *plural* **-tus.** a vibration felt by the hand when placed on a part of the body, esp the chest, when the patient is speaking or coughing.
▷HISTORY C19: from Latin: a roaring sound, a humming, from *fremere* to make a low roaring, murmur

French (frɛntʃ) NOUN [1] the official language of France: also an official language of Switzerland, Belgium, Canada, and certain other countries. It is the native language of approximately 70 million people; also used for diplomacy. Historically, French is an Indo-European language belonging to the Romance group. See also **Old French, Anglo-French.** [2] **the French.** *(functioning as plural)* the natives, citizens, or inhabitants of France collectively. [3] See **French vermouth.** ◆ ADJECTIVE [4] relating to, denoting, or characteristic of France, the French, or their language. ◆ Related prefixes: **Franco-, Gallo-.** [5] (in Canada) of or relating to French Canadians.
▷HISTORY Old English *Frencisc* French, Frankish; see FRANK
▸ **ˈFrenchness** NOUN

French Academy NOUN an association of 40 French scholars and writers, founded by Cardinal Richelieu in 1635, devoted chiefly to preserving the purity of the French language.

French and Indian War NOUN the war (1755–60) between the French and British, each aided by different Indian tribes, that formed part of the North American Seven Years' War.

French bean NOUN [1] a small twining bushy or annual bean plant, *Phaseolus vulgaris*, with white or lilac flowers and slender green edible pods. [2] the pod of this plant. See also **haricot.** Also called: **dwarf bean, kidney bean.**

French bread NOUN white bread in a long slender loaf that is made from a water dough and has a crisp brown crust.

French bulldog NOUN a small stocky breed of dog with a sleek coat, usually brindled or pied, a large square head, and large erect rounded ears.

French Canada NOUN the areas of Canada, esp in the province of Quebec, where French Canadians predominate.

French Canadian NOUN [1] a Canadian citizen whose native language is French. ◆ ADJECTIVE **French-Canadian.** [2] of or relating to French Canadians or their language.

French chalk NOUN a compact variety of talc used to mark cloth or remove grease stains from materials.

French Community NOUN an international association consisting of France and a number of former French colonies: founded in 1958 as a successor to the French Union.

French cricket NOUN a child's game resembling cricket, in which the batsman's legs are used as the wicket.

French cuff NOUN a double cuff formed by a backward fold of the material.

French curve NOUN a thin plastic sheet with profiles of several curves, used by draughtsmen for drawing curves.

French doors PLURAL NOUN the US and Canadian name for **French windows.**

French dressing NOUN a salad dressing made from oil and vinegar with seasonings; vinaigrette.

French Equatorial Africa NOUN the former French overseas territories of Chad, Gabon, Middle Congo, and Ubangi-Shari (1910–58).

French fact NOUN (in Canada) the presence of French Canada as a distinct cultural force within Confederation.

French Foreign Legion NOUN a unit of the French Army formerly serving esp in French North African colonies. It is largely recruited from foreigners, with French senior officers.

French fried potatoes PLURAL NOUN a more formal name for **chips.** Also called (US and Canadian): **French fries.**

French Guiana NOUN a French overseas region in NE South America, on the Atlantic: colonized by the French in about 1637; tropical forests. Capital: Cayenne. Pop.: 168 000 (2001 est.). Area: about 91 000 sq. km (23 000 sq. miles).

French Guianese *or* **Guianan** ADJECTIVE [1] of or relating to French Guiana or its inhabitants. ◆ NOUN [2] a native or inhabitant of French Guiana.

French heel NOUN a fairly high and narrow-waisted heel on women's shoes.
▸ **ˌFrench-ˈheeled** ADJECTIVE

French horn NOUN *Music* a valved brass instrument with a funnel-shaped mouthpiece and a tube of conical bore coiled into a spiral. It is a transposing instrument in F. Range: about three and a half octaves upwards from B on the second leger line below the bass staff. See **horn.**

Frenchify (ˈfrɛntʃɪˌfaɪ) VERB **-fies, -fying, -fied.** *Informal* to make or become French in appearance, behaviour, etc.
▸ **ˌFrenchifiˈcation** NOUN

French Indochina NOUN the territories of SE Asia that were colonized by France and held mostly until 1954: included Cochin China, Annam, and Tonkin (now largely Vietnam), Cambodia, Laos, and Kuang-Chou Wan (returned to China in 1945, now Zhanjiang).

French kiss NOUN a kiss involving insertion of the tongue into the partner's mouth.

French knickers PLURAL NOUN women's wide-legged underpants.

French knot NOUN an ornamental stitch made by looping the thread three or four times around the needle before putting it into the fabric.

French leave NOUN an unauthorized or unannounced absence or departure.
▷HISTORY C18: alluding to a custom in France of leaving without saying goodbye to one's host or hostess

French letter NOUN *Brit* a slang term for **condom.**

French lilac NOUN another name for **goat's-rue** (sense 1).

Frenchman (ˈfrɛntʃmən) NOUN, *plural* **-men.** a native, citizen, or inhabitant of France.
▸ **ˈFrenchˌwoman** FEMININE NOUN

French Morocco NOUN a former French protectorate in NW Africa, united in 1956 with Spanish Morocco and Tangier to form the kingdom of Morocco.

French mustard NOUN a mild mustard paste made with vinegar rather than water.

French navy NOUN **a** a dark dull navy blue. **b** *(as adjective)*: *a French-navy dress.*

French North Africa NOUN the former French possessions of Algeria, French Morocco, and Tunisia.

French paradox NOUN the theory that the lower incidence of heart disease in Mediterranean countries compared to that in the US is a consequence of the larger intake of flavonoids from red wine in these countries.

French pastry NOUN a rich pastry made esp from puff pastry and filled with cream, fruit, etc.

French pleat *or* **roll** NOUN a woman's hair style with the hair gathered at the back into a cylindrical roll.

French polish NOUN [1] a varnish for wood consisting of shellac dissolved in alcohol. [2] the gloss finish produced by repeated applications of this polish.

French-polish VERB to treat with French polish or give a French polish (to).

French Polynesia NOUN a French Overseas Territory in the S Pacific Ocean, including the Society Islands, the Tuamotu group, the Gambier group, the Tubuai Islands, and the Marquesas Islands. Capital: Papeete, on Tahiti. Pop.: 238 000 (2001 est.). Area: about 4000 sq. km (1500 sq. miles). Former name (until 1958): **French Oceania.**

French Revolution NOUN the anticlerical and republican revolution in France from 1789 until 1799, when Napoleon seized power.

French Revolutionary calendar NOUN the full name for the **Revolutionary calendar.**

French seam NOUN a seam in which the edges are not visible.

French sixth NOUN (in musical harmony) an augmented sixth chord having a major third and an augmented fourth between the root and the augmented sixth.

French Southern and Antarctic Territories PLURAL NOUN a French overseas territory, comprising Adélie Land in Antarctica and the islands of Amsterdam and St Paul and the Kerguelen and Crozet archipelagos in the S Indian Ocean.

French stick NOUN *Brit* a long straight notched stick loaf. Also called: **French stick loaf.**

French toast NOUN [1] *Brit* toast cooked on one side only. [2] bread dipped in beaten egg and lightly fried.

French Union NOUN a union of France with its dependencies (1946–58): replaced by the French Community.

French vermouth NOUN a dry aromatic white wine. Also called: **French.**

French West Africa NOUN a former group (1895–1958) of French Overseas Territories: consisted of Senegal, Mauritania, French Sudan, Burkina-Faso, Niger, French Guinea, the Ivory Coast, and Dahomey.

French West Indies PLURAL NOUN **the.** a group of islands in the Lesser Antilles, administered by France. Pop.: 632 754 (latest est.). Area: 2792 sq. km (1077 sq. miles).

French windows PLURAL NOUN (*sometimes singular*) *Brit* a pair of casement windows extending to floor level and opening onto a balcony, garden, etc. US and Canadian name: **French doors.**

Frenchy (ˈfrɛntʃɪ) ADJECTIVE [1] *Informal* characteristic of or resembling the French. ◆ NOUN, *plural* **-ies.** [2] an informal name for a French person.

frenetic (frɪˈnɛtɪk) ADJECTIVE distracted or frantic; frenzied.
▷HISTORY C14: via Old French *frenetique* from Latin *phrenēticus*, from Greek *phrenētikos*, from *phrenitis* insanity, from *phrēn* mind
▸**freˈnetically** ADVERB ▸**freˈneticness** NOUN

Frenkel defect (ˈfrɛnkᵊl) NOUN *Physics* a crystal defect in which a lattice ion has moved to an interstitial position leaving a vacant lattice site.
▷HISTORY C20: named after I. I. *Frenkel* (1894–1952), Russian physicist

frenulum (ˈfrɛnjʊləm) NOUN, *plural* **-la** (-lə). [1] a strong bristle or group of bristles on the hind wing of some moths and other insects, by which the forewing and hind wing are united during flight. [2] a small fraenum.
▷HISTORY C18: New Latin, diminutive of Latin *frēnum* bridle

frenum (ˈfriːnəm) NOUN, *plural* **-na** (-nə). a variant spelling (esp US) of **fraenum.**

frenzied (ˈfrɛnzɪd) ADJECTIVE filled with or as if with frenzy; wild; frantic.
▸**ˈfrenziedly** ADVERB

frenzy (ˈfrɛnzɪ) NOUN, *plural* **-zies.** [1] violent mental derangement. [2] wild excitement or agitation; distraction. [3] a bout of wild or agitated activity: *a frenzy of preparations.* ◆ VERB **-zies, -zying, -zied.** [4] (*tr*) to make frantic; drive into a frenzy.
▷HISTORY C14: from Old French *frenesie*, from Late Latin *phrēnēsis* madness, delirium, from Late Greek, ultimately from Greek *phrēn* mind; compare FRENETIC

Freon (ˈfriːɒn) NOUN *Trademark* any of a group of chemically unreactive chlorofluorocarbons used as aerosol propellants, refrigerants, and solvents.

frequency (ˈfriːkwənsɪ) NOUN, *plural* **-cies.** [1] the state of being frequent; frequent occurrence. [2] the number of times that an event occurs within a given period; rate of recurrence. [3] *Physics* the number of times that a periodic function or vibration repeats itself in a specified time, often 1 second. It is usually measured in hertz. Symbol: ν or *f.* [4] *Statistics* **a** the number of individuals in a class (**absolute frequency**). **b** the ratio of this number to the total number of individuals under survey (**relative frequency**). [5] *Ecology* **a** the number of individuals of a species within a given area. **b** the percentage of quadrats that contains individuals of a species. Also called (for senses 1, 2): **frequence.**
▷HISTORY C16: from Latin *frequentia* a large gathering, from *frequēns* numerous, crowded

frequency band NOUN a continuous range of frequencies, esp in the radio spectrum, between two limiting frequencies.

frequency distribution NOUN *Statistics* the function of the distribution of a sample corresponding to the probability density function of the underlying population and tending to it as the sample size increases, the set of relative frequencies of sample points falling within given intervals of the range of the random variable.

frequency-division multiplex NOUN See **multiplex** (sense 1).

frequency modulation NOUN a method of transmitting information using a radio-frequency carrier wave. The frequency of the carrier wave is varied in accordance with the amplitude and polarity of the input signal, the amplitude of the carrier remaining unchanged. Abbreviation: **FM.** Compare **amplitude modulation.**

frequent ADJECTIVE (ˈfriːkwənt) [1] recurring at short intervals. [2] constant or habitual. ◆ VERB (frɪˈkwɛnt) [3] (*tr*) to visit repeatedly or habitually.
▷HISTORY C16: from Latin *frequēns* numerous; perhaps related to Latin *farcīre* to stuff
▸**freˈquentable** ADJECTIVE ▸**freˈquenter** NOUN ▸**ˈfrequently** ADVERB ▸**ˈfrequentness** NOUN

frequentation (ˌfriːkwɛnˈteɪʃən) NOUN the act or practice of frequenting or visiting often.

frequentative (frɪˈkwɛntətɪv) *Grammar* ◆ ADJECTIVE [1] denoting an aspect of verbs in some languages used to express repeated or habitual action. [2] (in English) denoting a verb or an affix having meaning that involves repeated or habitual action, such as the verb *wrestle*, from *wrest.* ◆ NOUN [3] **a** a frequentative verb or affix. **b** the frequentative aspect of verbs.

fresco (ˈfrɛskəʊ) NOUN, *plural* **-coes** *or* **-cos.** [1] a very durable method of wall-painting using watercolours on wet plaster or, less properly, dry plaster (**fresco secco**), with a less durable result. [2] a painting done in this way.
▷HISTORY C16: from Italian: fresh plaster, coolness, from *fresco* (adjective) fresh, cool, of Germanic origin

fresh (frɛʃ) ADJECTIVE [1] not stale or deteriorated; newly made, harvested, etc.: *fresh bread; fresh strawberries.* [2] newly acquired, created, found, etc.: *fresh publications.* [3] novel; original: *a fresh outlook.* [4] latest; most recent: *fresh developments.* [5] further; additional; more: *fresh supplies.* [6] not canned, frozen, or otherwise preserved: *fresh fruit.* [7] (of water) not salt. [8] bright or clear: *a fresh morning.* [9] chilly or invigorating: *a fresh breeze.* [10] not tired; alert; refreshed. [11] not worn or faded: *fresh colours.* [12] having a healthy or ruddy appearance. [13] newly or just arrived; straight: *fresh from the presses.* [14] youthful or inexperienced. [15] *Chiefly US* designating a female farm animal, esp a cow, that has recently given birth. [16] *Informal* presumptuous or disrespectful; forward. [17] *Northern English dialect* partially intoxicated; tipsy. ◆ NOUN [18] the fresh part or time of something. [19] another name for **freshet.** ◆ VERB [20] *Obsolete* to make or become fresh; freshen. ◆ ADVERB [21] in a fresh manner; freshly. [22] **fresh out of.** *Informal* having just run out of supplies of.
▷HISTORY Old English *fersc* fresh, unsalted; related to Old High German *frisc*, Old French *freis*, Old Norse *ferskr*
▸**ˈfreshly** ADVERB ▸**ˈfreshness** NOUN

fresh breeze NOUN a fairly strong breeze of force five on the Beaufort scale.

freshen (ˈfrɛʃən) VERB [1] to make or become fresh or fresher. [2] (often foll by *up*) to refresh (oneself), esp by washing. [3] (*intr*) (of the wind) to increase. [4] to lose or cause to lose saltiness. [5] (*intr*) *Chiefly US* **a** (of farm animals) to give birth. **b** (of cows) to commence giving milk after calving.
▸**ˈfreshener** NOUN

fresher (ˈfrɛʃə) *or* **freshman** (ˈfrɛʃmən) NOUN, *plural* **-ers** *or* **-men.** a first-year student at college or university.

freshet (ˈfrɛʃɪt) NOUN [1] the sudden overflowing of a river caused by heavy rain or melting snow. [2] a stream of fresh water emptying into the sea.

fresh gale NOUN a gale of force eight on the Beaufort scale.

fresh-run ADJECTIVE (of fish) newly migrated upstream from the sea, esp to spawn.

freshwater (ˈfrɛʃˌwɔːtə) NOUN (*modifier*) [1] of, relating to, or living in fresh water. [2] (esp of a sailor who has not sailed on the sea) unskilled or inexperienced. [3] *US* small and little known: *a freshwater school.*

fresnel (ˈfreɪnɛl; *French* frɛnɛl) NOUN a unit of frequency equivalent to 10^{12} hertz.
▷HISTORY C20: named after Augustin Jean *Fresnel* (1788–1827), French physicist

Fresnel lens NOUN a lens consisting of a number of smaller lenses arranged to give a flat surface of short focal length.
▷HISTORY C20: named after Augustin Jean *Fresnel* (1788–1827), French physicist

fret¹ (frɛt) VERB **frets, fretting, fretted.** [1] to distress or be distressed; worry. [2] to rub or wear away. [3] to irritate or be irritated; feel or give annoyance or vexation. [4] to eat away or be eaten away by chemical action; corrode. [5] (*intr*) (of a road surface) to become loose so that potholes develop; scab. [6] to agitate (water) or (of water) to be agitated. [7] (*tr*) to make by wearing away; erode. ◆ NOUN [8] a state of irritation or anxiety. [9] the result of fretting; corrosion. [10] a hole or channel caused by fretting.
▷HISTORY Old English *fretan* to EAT; related to Old High German *frezzan*, Gothic *fraitan*, Latin *peredere*

fret² (frɛt) NOUN [1] a repetitive geometrical figure, esp one used as an ornamental border. [2] such a pattern made in relief and with numerous small openings; fretwork. [3] *Heraldry* a charge on a shield consisting of a mascle crossed by a saltire. ◆ VERB **frets, fretting, fretted.** [4] (*tr*) to ornament with fret or fretwork.
▷HISTORY C14: from Old French *frete* interlaced design used on a shield, probably of Germanic origin
▸**ˈfretless** ADJECTIVE

fret³ (frɛt) NOUN any of several small metal bars set across the fingerboard of a musical instrument of the lute, guitar, or viol family at various points along its length so as to produce the desired notes when the strings are stopped by the fingers.
▷HISTORY C16: of unknown origin
▸**ˈfretless** ADJECTIVE

fret⁴ (frɛt) NOUN short for **sea fret.**

fretboard (ˈfrɛtbɔːd) NOUN a fingerboard with frets on a stringed musical instrument.

fretful (ˈfrɛtfʊl) ADJECTIVE peevish, irritable, or upset.
▸**ˈfretfully** ADVERB ▸**ˈfretfulness** NOUN

fret saw NOUN a fine-toothed saw with a long thin narrow blade, used for cutting designs in thin wood or metal.

fretted (ˈfrɛtɪd) ADJECTIVE [1] ornamented with angular designs or frets. [2] decorated with fretwork.

fretwork (ˈfrɛtˌwɜːk) NOUN [1] decorative geometrical carving or openwork. [2] any similar pattern of light and dark. [3] ornamental work of three-dimensional frets.

Freudian (ˈfrɔɪdɪən) ADJECTIVE [1] of or relating to Sigmund Freud (1856–1939), the Austrian psychiatrist, or his ideas. ◆ NOUN [2] a person who follows or believes in the basic ideas of Sigmund Freud.
▸**ˈFreudianˌism** NOUN

Freudian slip NOUN any action, such as a slip of

the tongue, that may reveal an unconscious thought.

Frey (freɪ) *or* **Freyr** (freɪə) NOUN *Norse myth* the god of earth's fertility and dispenser of prosperity.

Freya *or* **Freyja** ('freɪə) NOUN *Norse myth* the goddess of love and fecundity, sister of Frey.

FRG ABBREVIATION FOR Federal Republic of Germany.

FRGS (in Britain) ABBREVIATION FOR Fellow of the Royal Geographical Society.

Fri. ABBREVIATION FOR Friday.

friable ('fraɪəbᵊl) ADJECTIVE easily broken up; crumbly.
▷HISTORY C16: from Latin *friābilis*, from *friāre* to crumble; related to Latin *fricāre* to rub down
▸ **ˌfria'bility** *or* **'friableness** NOUN

friar ('fraɪə) NOUN a member of any of various chiefly mendicant religious orders of the Roman Catholic Church, the main orders being the **Black Friars** (Dominicans), **Grey Friars** (Franciscans), **White Friars** (Carmelites), and **Austin Friars** (Augustinians).
▷HISTORY C13 *frere*, from Old French: brother, from Latin *frāter* BROTHER
▸ **'friarly** ADJECTIVE

friarbird ('fraɪəˌbɜːd) NOUN any of various Australian honeyeaters of the genus *Philemon*, having a naked head.

Friar Minor NOUN, *plural* **Friars Minor**. *Christianity* a member of either of two of the three orders into which the order founded by St Francis of Assisi came to be divided, namely the **Order of Friars Minor** and the **Order of Friars Minor Conventual**. Compare **Capuchin**.

friar's balsam NOUN a compound containing benzoin, mixed with hot water, and used as an inhalant to relieve colds and sore throats.

friar's lantern NOUN another name for **will-o'-the-wisp**.

Friar Tuck NOUN *English legend* a jolly friar who joined Robin Hood's band and aided their exploits.

friary ('fraɪərɪ) NOUN, *plural* **-aries**. *Christianity* a convent or house of friars.

frib (frɪb) NOUN *Austral and NZ* a short heavy-conditioned piece of wool removed from a fleece during classing.
▷HISTORY of unknown origin

fribble ('frɪbᵊl) VERB [1] (*tr*) to fritter away; waste. [2] (*intr*) to act frivolously; trifle. ◆ NOUN [3] a wasteful or frivolous person or action. ◆ ADJECTIVE [4] frivolous; trifling.
▷HISTORY C17: of unknown origin
▸ **'fribbler** NOUN

Fribourg (*French* fribur) NOUN [1] a canton in W Switzerland. Capital: Fribourg. Pop.: 234 300 (2000 est.). Area: 1676 sq. km (645 sq. miles). [2] a town in W Switzerland, capital of Fribourg canton: university (1889). Pop.: 35 000 (latest est.). German name: **Freiburg**.

fricandeau *or* **fricando** ('frɪkənˌdəʊ) NOUN, *plural* **-deaus, -deaux,** *or* **-does** (-ˌdəʊz). a larded and braised veal fillet.
▷HISTORY C18: from Old French, probably based on FRICASSEE

fricassee (ˌfrɪkə'siː, 'frɪkəsɪ, 'frɪkəˌseɪ) NOUN [1] stewed meat, esp chicken or veal, and vegetables, served in a thick white sauce. ◆ VERB **-sees, -seeing, -seed**. [2] (*tr*) to prepare (meat) as a fricassee.
▷HISTORY C16: from Old French, from *fricasser* to fricassee; probably related to *frire* to FRY[1]

fricative ('frɪkətɪv) NOUN [1] a continuant consonant produced by partial occlusion of the airstream, such as (f) or (z). ◆ ADJECTIVE [2] relating to or denoting a fricative.
▷HISTORY C19: from New Latin *fricātīvus*, from Latin *fricāre* to rub

fricking ('frɪkɪŋ) ADJECTIVE *Slang* (intensifier): *surrounded by fricking idiots*.
▷HISTORY C20: euphemism for FUCKING

FRICS (in Britain) ABBREVIATION FOR Fellow of the Royal Institution of Chartered Surveyors.

friction ('frɪkʃən) NOUN [1] a resistance encountered when one body moves relative to another body with which it is in contact. [2] the act, effect, or an instance of rubbing one object against another. [3] disagreement or conflict; discord. [4] *Phonetics* the hissing element of a speech sound, such as a fricative. [5] perfumed alcohol used on the hair to stimulate the scalp.
▷HISTORY C16: from French, from Latin *frictiō* a rubbing, from *fricāre* to rub, rub down; related to Latin *friāre* to crumble
▸ **'frictional** ADJECTIVE ▸ **'frictionless** ADJECTIVE

frictional soil NOUN another term for **cohesionless soil**.

frictional unemployment NOUN those people who are in the process of moving from one job to another and who therefore appear in the unemployment statistics collected at any given time.

friction clutch NOUN a mechanical clutch in which the drive is transmitted by the friction between surfaces, lined with cork, asbestos, or other fibrous materials, attached to the driving and driven shafts.

friction layer NOUN the atmospheric layer extending up to about 600 m, in which the aerodynamic effects of surface friction are appreciable.

friction match NOUN a match that ignites as a result of the heat produced by friction when it is struck on a rough surface. See also **safety match**.

friction rub *or* **murmur** NOUN *Med* the sound, heard through a stethoscope, made by the rubbing together of the two inflamed layers of pericardium in patients with pericarditis or of pleura in patients with pleurisy.

friction tape NOUN the US and Canadian name for **insulating tape**.

friction welding NOUN a form of welding in which the welding heat is generated by pressure and relative movement at the interface in the area of the weld.

Friday ('fraɪdɪ) NOUN [1] the sixth day of the week; fifth day of the working week. [2] See **girl Friday, man Friday**.
▷HISTORY Old English *Frīgedæg*, literally: Freya's day; related to Old Frisian *frīadei*, Old High German *frīatag*

fridge (frɪdʒ) NOUN *Informal* short for **refrigerator**.

fried (fraɪd) VERB the past tense and past participle of **fry**[1].

friend (frɛnd) NOUN [1] a person known well to another and regarded with liking, affection, and loyalty; an intimate. [2] an acquaintance or associate. [3] an ally in a fight or cause; supporter. [4] a fellow member of a party, society, etc. [5] a patron or supporter: *a friend of the opera*. [6] **be friends (with)**. to be friendly (with). [7] **make friends (with)**. to become friendly (with). ◆ VERB [8] (*tr*) an archaic word for **befriend**.
▷HISTORY Old English *frēond*; related to Old Saxon *friund*, Old Norse *frǣndi*, Gothic *frijōnds*, Old High German *friunt*
▸ **'friendless** ADJECTIVE ▸ **'friendlessness** NOUN
▸ **'friendship** NOUN

Friend[1] (frɛnd) NOUN a member of the Religious Society of Friends; Quaker.

Friend[2] (frɛnd) NOUN *Trademark, mountaineering* a device consisting of a shaft with double-headed spring-loaded cams that can be wedged in a crack to provide an anchor point.

friend at court NOUN an influential acquaintance who can promote one's interests.

friendly ('frɛndlɪ) ADJECTIVE **-lier, -liest**. [1] showing or expressing liking, goodwill, or trust: *a friendly smile*. [2] on the same side; not hostile. [3] tending or disposed to help or support; favourable: *a friendly breeze helped them escape*. ◆ NOUN, *plural* **-lies**. [4] Also called: **friendly match**. *Sport* a match played for its own sake, and not as part of a competition, etc.
▸ **'friendlily** ADVERB ▸ **'friendliness** NOUN

-friendly ADJECTIVE COMBINING FORM helpful, easy, or good for the person or thing specified: *ozone-friendly*.

friendly fire NOUN *Military* firing by one's own side, esp when it harms one's own personnel.

Friendly Islands PLURAL NOUN another name for **Tonga**[2].

friendly society NOUN *Brit* an association of people who pay regular dues or other sums in return for old-age pensions, sickness benefits, etc. US term: **benefit society**.

friend of Dorothy ('dɒrəθɪ) NOUN *Informal* a male homosexual.
▷HISTORY C20: after a character in the 1939 film *The Wizard of Oz* played by the US actress Judy Garland (1922–69), who has a large gay following

Friends of the Earth NOUN (*functioning as singular or plural*) an organization of environmentalists and conservationists whose aim is to promote the sustainable use of the earth's resources. Abbrevs: **FoE, FOE**.

frier ('fraɪə) NOUN a variant spelling of **fryer**.

fries (fraɪz) PLURAL NOUN another name for **French fried potatoes**.

Friesian[1] ('friːʒən) NOUN *Brit* any of several breeds of black-and-white dairy cattle having a high milk yield. Usual US and Canadian name: **Holstein**.

Friesian[2] ('friːʒən) NOUN, ADJECTIVE a variant of **Frisian**.

Friesland ('friːzlənd; *Dutch* 'friːslɑnt) NOUN [1] a province of the N Netherlands, on the IJsselmeer and the North Sea: includes four of the West Frisian Islands; flat, with sand dunes and fens (under reclamation), canals, and lakes. Capital: Leeuwarden. Pop.: 624 500 (2000 est.). Area: 3319 sq. km (1294 sq. miles). Official and Frisian name: **Fryslân**. [2] an area comprising the province of Friesland in the Netherlands along with the regions of **East Friesland** and **North Friesland** in Germany.

frieze[1] (friːz) NOUN [1] *Architect* **a** the horizontal band between the architrave and cornice of a classical entablature, esp one that is decorated with sculpture. **b** the upper part of the wall of a room, below the cornice, esp one that is decorated. [2] any ornamental band or strip on a wall.
▷HISTORY C16: from French *frise*, perhaps from Medieval Latin *frisium*, changed from Latin *Phrygium* Phrygian (work), from *Phrygia* Phrygia, famous for embroidery in gold

frieze[2] (friːz) NOUN a heavy woollen fabric with a long nap, used for coats, etc.
▷HISTORY C15: from Old French *frise*, from Middle Dutch *friese, vriese*, perhaps from *Vriese* Frisian

frig (frɪg) VERB **frigs, frigging, frigged**. *Taboo slang* [1] to have sexual intercourse (with). [2] to masturbate. [3] (*intr; foll by around, about,* etc.) to behave foolishly or aimlessly.
▷HISTORY C15 (in the sense: to wriggle): of uncertain origin; perhaps related to obsolete *frike* strong, or to Old English *frīgan* to love

frigate ('frɪgɪt) NOUN [1] a medium-sized square-rigged warship of the 18th and 19th centuries. [2] **a** *Brit* a warship larger than a corvette and smaller than a destroyer. **b** *US* (formerly) a warship larger than a destroyer and smaller than a cruiser. **c** *US* a small escort vessel.
▷HISTORY C16: from French *frégate*, from Italian *fregata*, of unknown origin

frigate bird NOUN any bird of the genus *Fregata* and family *Fregatidae*, of tropical and subtropical seas, having a long bill with a downturned tip, a wide wingspan, and a forked tail: order *Pelecaniformes* (pelicans, cormorants, etc.). Also called: **man-of-war bird**.

Frigg (frɪg) *or* **Frigga** ('frɪgə) NOUN *Norse myth* the wife of Odin; goddess of the heavens and married love.

frigging ('frɪgɪŋ) ADJECTIVE (*prenominal*), ADVERB *Slang* (intensifier): *it's only a frigging game; frigging hopeless*.
▷HISTORY C20: euphemism for FUCKING

fright (fraɪt) NOUN [1] sudden intense fear or alarm. [2] a sudden alarming shock. [3] *Informal* a horrifying, grotesque, or ludicrous person or thing: *she looks a fright in that hat*. [4] **take fright**. to become frightened. ◆ VERB [5] a poetic word for **frighten**.
▷HISTORY Old English *fryhto*; related to Gothic *faurhtei*, Old Frisian *fruchte*, Old High German *forhta*

frighten ('fraɪtᵊn) VERB (*tr*) [1] to cause fear in; terrify; scare. [2] to drive or force to go (away, off, out, in, etc.) by making afraid.
▸ **'frightenable** ADJECTIVE ▸ **'frighteningly** ADVERB

frightener ('fraɪtᵊnə) NOUN [1] a person or thing that causes fear. [2] **put the frighteners on**. *Brit informal* to intimidate.

frightful ('fraɪtfʊl) ADJECTIVE [1] very alarming, distressing, or horrifying. [2] unpleasant, annoying, or extreme: *a frightful hurry*.
▸ **'frightfulness** NOUN

frightfully (ˈfraɪtfəlɪ) ADVERB (intensifier): *I'm frightfully glad.*

fright wig NOUN **a** a wig with frizzy hair standing straight up from the surface. **b** a hairstyle resembling this.

frigid (ˈfrɪdʒɪd) ADJECTIVE [1] formal or stiff in behaviour or temperament; lacking in affection or warmth. [2] (esp of a woman) **a** lacking sexual responsiveness. **b** averse to sexual intercourse or unable to achieve orgasm during intercourse. [3] characterized by physical coldness: *a frigid zone.*
▷HISTORY C15: from Latin *frigidus* cold, from *frīgēre* to be cold, freeze; related to Latin *frīgus* frost
▸**friˈgidity** *or* **ˈfrigidness** NOUN ▸**ˈfrigidly** ADVERB

Frigid Zone NOUN *Archaic* the cold region inside the Arctic or Antarctic Circle where the sun's rays are very oblique.

frigorific (ˌfrɪgəˈrɪfɪk) ADJECTIVE *Obsolete* causing cold or freezing.
▷HISTORY C17: from French *frigorifique*, from Latin *frīgorificus*, from *frīgus* cold, coldness + *facere* to make

frijol (ˈfriːhəʊl; *Spanish* friˈxol) NOUN, *plural* **-joles** (-həʊlz; *Spanish* -ˈxoles). a variety of bean, esp of the French bean, extensively cultivated for food in Mexico.
▷HISTORY C16: from Spanish, ultimately from Latin *phaseolus*, diminutive of *phasēlus*, from Greek *phasēlos* bean with edible pod

frill (frɪl) NOUN [1] a gathered, ruched, or pleated strip of cloth sewn on at one edge only, as on garments, as ornament, or to give extra body. [2] a ruff of hair or feathers around the neck of a dog or bird or a fold of skin around the neck of a reptile or amphibian. [3] Full name: **oriental frill.** (*often capital*) a variety of domestic fancy pigeon having a ruff of curled feathers on the chest and crop. [4] *Photog* a wrinkling or loosening of the emulsion at the edges of a negative or print. [5] (*often plural*) *Informal* a superfluous or pretentious thing or manner; affectation: *he made a plain speech with no frills.* ◆ VERB [6] (*tr*) to adorn or fit with a frill or frills. [7] to form into a frill or frills. [8] (*intr*) *Photog* (of an emulsion) to develop a frill.
▷HISTORY C14: perhaps of Flemish origin
▸**ˈfrilliness** NOUN ▸**ˈfrilly** ADJECTIVE

frill-necked lizard NOUN a large arboreal insectivorous Australian lizard, *Chlamydosaurus kingi*, having an erectile fold of skin around the neck: family *Agamidae* (agamas). Also called: **frilled lizard.**

Frimaire *French* (frimɛr) NOUN the frosty month: the third month of the French Revolutionary calendar, extending from Nov. 22 to Dec. 21.
▷HISTORY C19: from French, from *frimas* hoarfrost, from Old French *frim*, of Germanic origin; related to Old Norse *hrīm* RIME[1]

fringe (frɪndʒ) NOUN [1] an edging consisting of hanging threads, tassels, etc. [2] **a** an outer edge; periphery. **b** (*as modifier*): *fringe dwellers; a fringe area.* [3] (*modifier*) unofficial; not conventional in form: *fringe theatre.* [4] *Chiefly Brit* a section of the front hair cut short over the forehead. [5] an ornamental border or margin. [6] *Physics* any of the light and dark or coloured bands produced by diffraction or interference of light. ◆ VERB (*tr*) [7] to adorn or fit with a fringe or fringes. [8] to be a fringe for: *fur fringes the satin.*
▷HISTORY C14: from Old French *frenge*, ultimately from Latin *fimbria* fringe, border; see FIMBRIA
▸**ˈfringeless** ADJECTIVE

fringe benefit NOUN an incidental or additional advantage, esp a benefit provided by an employer to supplement an employee's regular pay, such as a pension, company car, luncheon vouchers, etc.

fringed orchis NOUN any orchid of the genus *Habenaria*, having yellow, white, purple, or greenish flowers with fringed petals. See also **purple-fringed orchid.**

fringe tree NOUN either of two ornamental oleaceous shrubs or small trees of the genus *Chionanthus*, of North America and China, having clusters of white narrow-petalled flowers.

fringilline (frɪnˈdʒɪlaɪn, -ɪn) *or* **fringillid** (frɪnˈdʒɪlɪd) ADJECTIVE of, relating to, or belonging to the *Fringillidae*, a family of songbirds that includes the finches.
▷HISTORY C19: from New Latin *Fringilla* type genus, from Latin *fringilla* a small bird, perhaps a chaffinch

fringing reef NOUN a coral reef close to the shore to which it is attached, having a steep seaward edge.

frippery (ˈfrɪpərɪ) NOUN, *plural* **-peries.** [1] ornate or showy clothing or adornment. [2] showiness; ostentation. [3] unimportant considerations; trifles; trivia.
▷HISTORY C16: from Old French *freperie*, from *frepe* frill, rag, old garment, from Medieval Latin *faluppa* a straw, splinter, of obscure origin

frippet (ˈfrɪpɪt) NOUN *Brit old-fashioned informal* a frivolous or flamboyant young woman.

Frisbee (ˈfrɪzbiː) NOUN *Trademark* a light plastic disc, usually 20–25 centimetres in diameter, thrown with a spinning motion for recreation or in competition.

frisé (ˈfriːzeɪ) NOUN a fabric with a long normally uncut nap used for upholstery and rugs.
▷HISTORY from French, literally: curled

frisette *or* **frizette** (frɪˈzɛt) NOUN a curly or frizzed fringe, often an artificial hairpiece, worn by women on the forehead.
▷HISTORY C19: from French, literally: little curl, from *friser* to curl, shrivel up, probably from *frire* to FRY[1]

friseur *French* (frizœr) NOUN a hairdresser.
▷HISTORY C18: literally: one who curls (hair); see FRISETTE

Frisian (ˈfrɪʒən) *or* **Friesian** NOUN [1] a language spoken in the NW Netherlands, parts of N Germany, and adjacent islands, belonging to the West Germanic branch of the Indo-European family: the nearest relative of the English language; it has three main dialects. [2] a native or inhabitant of Friesland or a speaker of the Frisian language. ◆ ADJECTIVE [3] **a** of or relating to the Frisian language or its speakers. **b** of or relating to Friesland or its peoples and culture.
▷HISTORY C16: from Latin *Frīsiī* people of northern Germany

Frisian Islands PLURAL NOUN a chain of islands in the North Sea along the coasts of the Netherlands, Germany, and Denmark: separated from the mainland by shallows.

frisk (frɪsk) VERB [1] (*intr*) to leap, move about, or act in a playful manner; frolic. [2] (*tr*) (esp of animals) to whisk or wave briskly: *the dog frisked its tail.* [3] (*tr*) *Informal* **a** to search (someone) by feeling for concealed weapons, etc. **b** to rob by searching in this way. ◆ NOUN [4] a playful antic or movement; frolic. [5] *Informal* the act or an instance of frisking a person.
▷HISTORY C16: from Old French *frisque*, of Germanic origin; related to Old High German *frisc* lively, FRESH
▸**ˈfrisker** NOUN ▸**ˈfriskingly** ADVERB

frisket (ˈfrɪskɪt) NOUN *Printing* a light rectangular frame, attached to the tympan of a hand printing press, that carries a parchment sheet to protect the nonprinting areas.
▷HISTORY C17: from French *frisquette*, of obscure origin

frisky (ˈfrɪskɪ) ADJECTIVE **friskier, friskiest.** lively, high-spirited, or playful.
▸**ˈfriskily** ADVERB ▸**ˈfriskiness** NOUN

frisson *French* (frisɔ̃) NOUN a shudder or shiver; thrill.
▷HISTORY C18 (but in common use only from C20): literally: shiver

frit *or* **fritt** (frɪt) NOUN [1] **a** the basic materials, partially or wholly fused, for making glass, glazes for pottery, enamel, etc. **b** a glassy substance used in some soft-paste porcelain. [2] the material used for making the glaze for artificial teeth. ◆ VERB **frits** *or* **fritts, fritting, fritted.** [3] (*tr*) to fuse (materials) in making frit.
▷HISTORY C17: from Italian *fritta*, literally: fried, from *friggere* to fry, from Latin *frīgere*

frit fly NOUN a small black dipterous fly, *Oscinella frit*, whose larvae are destructive to barley, wheat, rye, oats, etc.: family *Chloropidae.*

frith (frɪθ) NOUN a variant of **firth.**

fritillary (frɪˈtɪlərɪ) NOUN, *plural* **-laries.** [1] any N temperate liliaceous plant of the genus *Fritillaria*, having purple or white drooping bell-shaped flowers, typically marked in a chequered pattern. See also **snake's head.** [2] any of various nymphalid butterflies of the genera *Argynnis, Boloria*, etc., having brownish wings chequered with black and silver.
▷HISTORY C17: from New Latin *fritillāria*, from Latin *fritillus* dice box; probably with reference to the spotted markings

frittata (frɪˈtɑːtə) NOUN an Italian dish made with eggs and chopped vegetables or meat, resembling a flat thick omelette.
▷HISTORY C20: Italian, from *fritto*, past participle of *friggere* to fry

fritter[1] (ˈfrɪtə) VERB (*tr*) [1] (usually foll by *away*) to waste or squander: *to fritter away time.* [2] to break or tear into small pieces; shred. ◆ NOUN [3] a small piece; shred.
▷HISTORY C18: probably from obsolete *fitter* to break into small pieces, ultimately from Old English *fitt* a piece
▸**ˈfritterer** NOUN

fritter[2] (ˈfrɪtə) NOUN a piece of food, such as apple or clam, that is dipped in batter and fried in deep fat.
▷HISTORY C14: from Old French *friture*, from Latin *frictus* fried, roasted, from *frīgere* to fry, parch

Friulian (frɪˈuːlɪən) NOUN [1] the Rhaetian dialect spoken in parts of Friuli. See also **Ladin, Romansch.** [2] an inhabitant of Friuli or a speaker of Friulian. ◆ ADJECTIVE [3] of or relating to Friuli, its inhabitants, or their language.

Friuli-Venezia Giulia (*Italian* ˈdʒuːlja) NOUN a region of NE Italy, formed in 1947 from **Venetian Friuli** and part of **Eastern Friuli.** Capital: Trieste. Pop.: 1 185 172 (2000 est.). Area: 7851 sq. km (3031 sq. miles).

frivol (ˈfrɪvəl) VERB **-ols, -olling, -olled** *or US* **-ols, -oling, -oled.** *Informal* [1] (*intr*) to behave frivolously; trifle. [2] (*tr*; often foll by *away*) to waste on frivolous pursuits.
▷HISTORY C19: back formation from FRIVOLOUS
▸**ˈfrivoller** *or US* **ˈfrivoler** NOUN

frivolous (ˈfrɪvələs) ADJECTIVE [1] not serious or sensible in content, attitude, or behaviour; silly: *a frivolous remark.* [2] unworthy of serious or sensible treatment; unimportant: *frivolous details.*
▷HISTORY C15: from Latin *frīvolus* silly, worthless
▸**ˈfrivolously** ADVERB ▸**ˈfrivolousness** *or* **frivolity** (frɪˈvɒlɪtɪ) NOUN

frizette (frɪˈzɛt) NOUN a variant spelling of **frisette.**

frizz (frɪz) VERB [1] (of the hair, nap, etc.) to form or cause (the hair, etc.) to form tight wiry curls or crisp tufts. ◆ NOUN [2] hair that has been frizzed. [3] the state of being frizzed.
▷HISTORY C19: from French *friser* to curl, shrivel up (see FRISETTE): influenced by FRIZZLE[1]
▸**ˈfrizzer** NOUN

frizzante (frɪˈzæntɪ; *Italian* fridˈdzante) ADJECTIVE (of wine) slightly effervescent.
▷HISTORY Italian, from *frizzare* to sparkle

frizzle[1] (ˈfrɪzəl) VERB [1] to form (the hair) into tight crisp curls; frizz. ◆ NOUN [2] a tight crisp curl.
▷HISTORY C16: probably related to Old English *frīs* curly, Old Frisian *frēsle* curl, ringlet
▸**ˈfrizzler** NOUN ▸**ˈfrizzly** ADJECTIVE

frizzle[2] (ˈfrɪzəl) VERB [1] to scorch or be scorched, esp with a sizzling noise. [2] (*tr*) to fry (bacon, etc.) until crisp.
▷HISTORY C16: probably blend of FRY[1] + SIZZLE

frizzy (ˈfrɪzɪ) *or* **frizzly** (ˈfrɪzlɪ) ADJECTIVE **-zier, -ziest** *or* **-zlier, -zliest.** (of the hair) in tight crisp wiry curls.
▸**ˈfrizzily** ADVERB ▸**ˈfrizziness** *or* **ˈfrizzliness** NOUN

Frl. ABBREVIATION FOR Fräulein.
▷HISTORY German: Miss

fro (frəʊbɪ) ADVERB back or from. See **to and fro.**
▷HISTORY C12: from Old Norse *frā*; related to Old English *fram* FROM

Frobisher Bay (ˈfrəʊbɪʃə) NOUN [1] an inlet of the Atlantic in NE Canada, in the SE coast of Baffin Island. [2] the former name of **Iqaluit.**

frock (frɒk) NOUN [1] a girl's or woman's dress. [2] a loose garment of several types, such as a peasant's smock. [3] a coarse wide-sleeved outer garment worn by members of some religious orders. ◆ VERB [4] (*tr*) to invest (a person) with the office or status of a cleric.
▷HISTORY C14: from Old French *froc*; related to Old Saxon, Old High German *hroc* coat

frock coat NOUN a man's single- or

double-breasted skirted coat, as worn in the 19th century.

frocking ('frɒkɪŋ) NOUN coarse material suitable for making frocks or work clothes.

frock tart NOUN *NZ slang* a person who makes or designs costumes for films or television.

froe *or* **frow** (frəʊ) NOUN a cutting tool with handle and blade at right angles, used for stripping young trees, etc.
▷**HISTORY** C16: from *frower*, from *froward* (in the sense: turned away)

frog[1] (frɒg) NOUN [1] any insectivorous anuran amphibian of the family *Ranidae*, such as *Rana temporaria* of Europe, having a short squat tailless body with a moist smooth skin and very long hind legs specialized for hopping. [2] any of various similar amphibians of related families, such as the tree frog. Related adjective: **batrachian.** [3] any spiked or perforated object used to support plant stems in a flower arrangement. [4] a recess in a brick to reduce its weight. [5] **a frog in one's throat.** phlegm on the vocal cords that affects one's speech. ◆ VERB **frogs, frogging, frogged.** [6] *(intr)* to hunt or catch frogs.
▷**HISTORY** Old English *frogga*; related to Old Norse *froskr*, Old High German *forsk*
▸ **'froggy** ADJECTIVE

frog[2] (frɒg) NOUN [1] *(often plural)* a decorative fastening of looped braid or cord, as on the front of a 19th-century military uniform. [2] a loop or other attachment on a belt to hold the scabbard of a sword, etc. [3] *Music* another name (esp US and Canadian) for **nut** (sense 11).
▷**HISTORY** C18: perhaps ultimately from Latin *floccus* tuft of hair, FLOCK[2]

frog[3] (frɒg) NOUN a tough elastic horny material in the centre of the sole of a horse's foot.
▷**HISTORY** C17: of uncertain origin

frog[4] (frɒg) NOUN a grooved plate of iron or steel placed to guide train wheels over an intersection of railway lines.
▷**HISTORY** C19: of uncertain origin; perhaps a special use of FROG[1]

Frog (frɒg) *or* **Froggy** ('frɒgɪ) NOUN, *plural* **Frogs** *or* **Froggies.** a derogatory word for a French person.

frog-bit NOUN a floating aquatic Eurasian plant, *Hydrocharis morsus-ranae*, with heart-shaped leaves and white flowers: family *Hydrocharitaceae*.

frogfish ('frɒg,fɪʃ) NOUN, *plural* **-fish** *or* **-fishes.** any angler (fish) of the family *Antennariidae*, in which the body is covered with fleshy processes, including a fleshy lure on top of the head.

frogged (frɒgd) ADJECTIVE (of a coat) fitted with ornamental frogs.

frogging ('frɒgɪŋ) NOUN the ornamental frogs on a coat collectively.

froggy ('frɒgɪ) ADJECTIVE **-gier, -giest.** of, like, or relating to frogs; full of frogs.

froghopper ('frɒg,hɒpə) NOUN any small leaping herbivorous homopterous insect of the family *Cercopidae*, whose larvae secrete a protective spittle-like substance around themselves. Also called: **spittle insect, spittlebug.**

frog kick NOUN a type of kick used in swimming, as in the breast stroke, in which the legs are simultaneously drawn towards the body and bent at the knees with the feet together, straightened out with the legs apart, and then brought together again quickly.

frogman ('frɒgmən) NOUN, *plural* **-men.** a swimmer equipped with a rubber suit, flippers, and breathing equipment for working underwater.

frogmarch ('frɒg,mɑːtʃ) NOUN [1] a method of carrying a resisting person in which each limb is held by one person and the victim is carried horizontally and face downwards. [2] any method of making a resisting person move forward against his will. ◆ VERB [3] *(tr)* to carry in a frogmarch or cause to move forward unwillingly.

frogmouth ('frɒg,maʊθ) NOUN any nocturnal insectivorous bird of the genera *Podargus* and *Batrachostomus*, of SE Asia and Australia, similar to the nightjars: family *Podargidae*, order *Caprimulgiformes*.

frog orchid NOUN any of several orchids having greenish flowers thought to resemble small frogs, esp *Coeloglossum viride* of calcareous turf.

frog pad NOUN a rubber or leather cushion fixed to a leather sole and fitted under a horseshoe to reduce shock to a horse's foot.

frogspawn ('frɒg,spɔːn) NOUN a mass of fertilized frogs' eggs or developing tadpoles, each egg being surrounded by a protective nutrient jelly.

frog spit *or* **spittle** NOUN [1] another name for **cuckoo spit.** [2] a foamy mass of threadlike green algae floating on ponds.

frolic ('frɒlɪk) NOUN [1] a light-hearted entertainment or occasion. [2] light-hearted activity; gaiety; merriment. ◆ VERB **-ics, -icking, -icked.** [3] *(intr)* to caper about; act or behave playfully. ◆ ADJECTIVE [4] *Archaic or literary* full of merriment or fun.
▷**HISTORY** C16: from Dutch *vrolijk*, from Middle Dutch *vro* happy, glad; related to Old High German *frō* happy
▸ **'frolicker** NOUN

frolicsome ('frɒlɪksəm) *or* **frolicky** ADJECTIVE given to frolicking; merry and playful.
▸ **'frolicsomely** ADVERB ▸ **'frolicsomeness** NOUN

from (frɒm; *unstressed* frəm) PREPOSITION [1] used to indicate the original location, situation, etc.: *from Paris to Rome; from behind the bushes; from childhood to adulthood.* [2] in a period of time starting at: *he lived from 1910 to 1970.* [3] used to indicate the distance between two things or places: *a hundred miles from here.* [4] used to indicate a lower amount: *from five to fifty pounds.* [5] showing the model of: *painted from life.* [6] used with the gerund to mark prohibition, restraint, etc.: *nothing prevents him from leaving.* [7] because of: *exhausted from his walk.*
▷**HISTORY** Old English *fram*; related to Old Norse *frā*, Old Saxon, Old High German, Gothic *fram* from, Greek *promos* foremost

fromage frais ('frɒmɑːʒ 'freɪ) NOUN a low-fat soft cheese with a smooth light texture.
▷**HISTORY** French, literally: fresh cheese

Frome (frəʊm) NOUN **Lake** a shallow salt lake in NE South Australia: intermittently filled with water. Length: 100 km (60 miles). Width: 48 km (30 miles).

fromenty ('frəʊməntɪ) NOUN a variant of **frumenty.**

frond (frɒnd) NOUN [1] a large compound leaf, esp of a fern. [2] the thallus of a seaweed or a lichen.
▷**HISTORY** C18: from Latin *frōns*
▸ **'fronded** ADJECTIVE ▸ **'frondless** ADJECTIVE

Fronde (frɒnd; *French* frɔ̃d) NOUN *French history* either of two rebellious movements against the ministry of Cardinal Mazarin in the reign of Louis XIV, the first led by the parlement of Paris (1648–49) and the second by the princes (1650–53).
▷**HISTORY** C18: from French, literally: sling, the insurgent parliamentarians being likened to naughty schoolboys using slings

frondescence (frɒn'dɛsəns) NOUN [1] *Now rare* the process or state of producing leaves. [2] a less common name for **foliage.**
▷**HISTORY** C19: from New Latin *frondēscentia*, from Latin *frondēscere* to put forth leaves, from *frōns* foliage; see FROND
▸ **fron'descent, 'frondose,** *or* **'frondous** ADJECTIVE

Frondeur (frɒn'dɜː; *French* frɔ̃dœr) NOUN [1] *French history* a member of the Fronde. [2] any malcontent or troublemaker.

frons (frɒnz) NOUN, *plural* **frontes** ('frɒntiːz). an anterior cuticular plate on the head of some insects, in front of the clypeus.
▷**HISTORY** C19: from Latin: forehead, brow, FRONT

front (frʌnt) NOUN [1] that part or side that is forward, prominent, or most often seen or used. [2] a position or place directly before or ahead: *a fountain stood at the front of the building.* [3] the beginning, opening, or first part: *the front of the book.* [4] the position of leadership; forefront; vanguard: *in the front of scientific knowledge.* [5] land bordering a lake, street, etc. [6] land along a seashore or large lake, esp a promenade. [7] *Military* **a** the total area in which opposing armies face each other. **b** the lateral space in which a military unit or formation is operating: *to advance on a broad front.* **c** the direction in which troops are facing when in a formed line. [8] *Meteorol* the dividing line or plane between two air masses or water masses of different origins and having different characteristics. See also **warm front, cold front.** [9] outward aspect or bearing, as when dealing with a situation: *a bold front.* [10] assurance, overconfidence, or effrontery. [11] *Informal* a business or other activity serving as a respectable cover for another, usually criminal, organization. [12] *Chiefly US* a nominal leader of an organization, etc., who lacks real power or authority; figurehead. [13] *Informal* outward appearance of rank or wealth. [14] a particular field of activity involving some kind of struggle: *on the wages front.* [15] a group of people with a common goal: *a national liberation front.* [16] a false shirt front; a dicky. [17] *Archaic* the forehead or the face. ◆ ADJECTIVE *(prenominal)* [18] of, at, or in the front: *a front seat.* [19] *Phonetics* of, relating to, or denoting a vowel articulated with the blade of the tongue brought forward and raised towards the hard palate, as for the sound of *ee* in English *see* or *a* in English *hat.* [20] **on the front foot.** at an advantage, outclassing and outmaneouvring one's opponents.◆ VERB [21] (when *intr*, foll by *on* or *onto*) to be opposite (to); face (onto): *this house fronts the river.* [22] *(tr)* to be a front of or for. [23] *(tr) Informal* to appear as a presenter in (a television show). [24] *(tr)* to be the lead singer or player in (a band). [25] *(tr)* to confront, esp in hostility or opposition. [26] *(tr)* to supply a front for. [27] *(intr;* often foll by *up) Austral and NZ informal* to appear (at): *to front up at the police station.*
▷**HISTORY** C13 (in the sense: forehead, face): from Latin *frōns* forehead, foremost part
▸ **'frontless** ADJECTIVE

front. ABBREVIATION FOR frontispiece.

frontage ('frʌntɪdʒ) NOUN [1] the façade of a building or the front of a plot of ground. [2] the extent of the front of a shop, plot of land, etc., esp along a street, river, etc. [3] the direction in which a building faces: *a frontage on the river.*

frontal ('frʌnt^{ə}l) ADJECTIVE [1] of, at, or in the front. [2] of or relating to the forehead: *frontal artery.* [3] of or relating to the anterior part of a body or organ. [4] *Meteorol* of, relating to, or resulting from a front or its passage: *frontal rainfall.* ◆ NOUN [5] a decorative hanging for the front of an altar. [6] See **frontal lobe, frontal bone.** [7] another name for **frontlet** (sense 1).
▷**HISTORY** C14 (in the sense: adornment for forehead, altar cloth): via Old French *frontel*, from Latin *frontālia* (pl) ornament worn on forehead, *frontellum* altar cloth, both from *frōns* forehead, FRONT
▸ **'frontally** ADVERB

frontal bone NOUN the bone forming the forehead and the upper parts of the orbits. It contains several air spaces.

frontality (frən'tælɪtɪ) NOUN *Fine arts* a frontal view, as in a painting or other work of art.

frontal lobe NOUN *Anatomy* the anterior portion of each cerebral hemisphere, situated in front of the central sulcus.

front bench NOUN *Brit* **a** the foremost bench of either the Government or Opposition in the House of Commons. **b** the leadership (**frontbenchers**) of either group, who occupy this bench. **c** (*as modifier*): *a front-bench decision.*

front door NOUN [1] the main entrance to a house. [2] an open legitimate means of obtaining a job, position, etc.: *to get in by the front door.*

front-end ADJECTIVE (of money, costs, etc.) required or incurred in advance of a project in order to get it under way.

front-end load NOUN commission and other expenses paid for as a large proportion of the early payments made by an investor in an insurance policy or a long-term investment plan.
▸ **front-end loading** NOUN

front-end processor NOUN a small computer that receives data from input devices and performs some initial processing tasks on it before passing it to a more powerful computer for final processing.

frontier ('frʌntɪə, frʌn'tɪə) NOUN [1] **a** the region of a country bordering on another or a line, barrier, etc., marking such a boundary. **b** (*as modifier*): *a frontier post.* [2] *US and Canadian* **a** the edge of the settled area of a country. **b** (*as modifier*): *the frontier spirit.* [3] *(often plural)* the limit of knowledge in a particular field: *the frontiers of physics have been pushed back.*
▷**HISTORY** C14: from Old French *frontiere*, from *front* (in the sense: part which is opposite); see FRONT

frontier orbital NOUN the highest-energy occupied orbital or lowest-energy unoccupied orbital in a molecule. Such orbitals have a large influence on chemical properties.

frontiersman ('frʌntɪəzmən, frʌn'tɪəz-) NOUN, *plural* **-men.** (formerly) a man living on a frontier, esp in a newly pioneered territory of the US.

frontierswoman ('frʌntɪəzwʊmən, frʌn'tɪəz-) NOUN, *plural* **-women.** (formerly) a woman living on a frontier, esp in a newly pioneered territory of the US.

frontispiece ('frʌntɪsˌpiːs) NOUN [1] an illustration facing the title page of a book. [2] the principal façade of a building; front. [3] a pediment, esp an ornamented one, over a door, window, etc.
▷HISTORY C16 *frontispice*, from French, from Late Latin *frontispicium* façade, inspection of the forehead, from Latin *frōns* forehead + *specere* to look at; influenced by PIECE

frontlet ('frʌntlɪt) NOUN [1] Also called: **frontal.** a small decorative loop worn on a woman's forehead, projecting from under her headdress, in the 15th century. [2] the forehead of an animal, esp of a bird when it is a different colour from the rest of the head. [3] the decorated border of an altar frontal. [4] *Judaism* a phylactery worn on the forehead. See also **tefillah.**
▷HISTORY C15: from Old French *frontelet* a little FRONTAL

front line NOUN [1] *Military* the most advanced military units or elements in a battle. [2] the most advanced, exposed, or conspicuous element in any activity or situation. [3] (*modifier*) **a** of, relating to, or suitable for the front line of a military formation: *frontline troops*. **b** to the fore; advanced, conspicuous, etc.: *frontline news*. **c** of or relating to a country bordering on or close to a hostile country or scene of armed conflict: *leaders of the frontline states attended the summit*.

front list NOUN **a** a publisher's list of forthcoming books. **b** (*as modifier*): *a front-list writer*. See also **backlist, mid-list.**

front loader NOUN a washing machine with a door at the front which opens one side of the drum into which washing is placed.

front man NOUN *Informal* [1] a nominal leader of an organization, etc., who lacks real power or authority, esp one who lends respectability to some nefarious activity. [2] the leader or visual focus of a group of musicians, usually the singer.
◆ Also called: **front person.**

front matter NOUN another name for **prelims** (sense 1).

front of house NOUN the areas of a theatre, opera house, etc., used by the audience.

frontogenesis (ˌfrʌntəʊ'dʒɛnɪsɪs) NOUN *Meteorol* the formation or development of a front through the meeting of air or water masses from different origins.
▸**frontogenetic** (ˌfrʌntəʊdʒə'nɛtɪk) ADJECTIVE
▸**ˌfrontoge'netically** ADVERB

frontolysis (frʌn'tɒlɪsɪs) NOUN *Meteorol* the weakening or dissipation of a front.

fronton ('frɒntɒn, frɒn'tɒn) NOUN a wall against which pelota or jai alai is played.
▷HISTORY C17: from Spanish *frontón*, from *frente* forehead, from Latin *frōns*

front-page NOUN (*modifier*) important or newsworthy enough to be put on the front page of a newspaper.

frontrunner ('frʌntˌrʌnə) NOUN *Informal* the leader or a favoured contestant in a race, election, etc.

frontrunning ('frʌntˌrʌnɪŋ) NOUN *Stock Exchange* the practice by market makers of using advance information provided by their own investment analysts before it has been given to clients.

frontwards ('frʌntwədz) *or* **frontward** ADVERB towards the front.

frore (frɔː) ADJECTIVE *Archaic* very cold or frosty.
▷HISTORY C13 *froren*, past participle of Old English *frēosan* to FREEZE

frost (frɒst) NOUN [1] a white deposit of ice particles, esp one formed on objects out of doors at night. See also **hoarfrost.** [2] an atmospheric temperature of below freezing point, characterized by the production of this deposit. [3] degrees below freezing point: eight degrees of frost indicates a temperature of either –8°C or 24°F. [4] *Informal* something given a cold reception; failure. [5] *Informal* coolness of manner. [6] the act of freezing. ◆ VERB [7] to cover or be covered with frost. [8] (*tr*) to give a frostlike appearance to (glass, etc.), as by means of a fine-grained surface. [9] (*tr*) *Chiefly US and Canadian* to decorate (cakes, etc.) with icing or frosting. [10] (*tr*) to kill or damage (crops, etc.) with frost.
▷HISTORY Old English *frost*; related to Old Norse, Old Saxon, Old High German *frost*; see FREEZE
▸**'frostˌlike** ADJECTIVE

frostbite ('frɒstˌbaɪt) NOUN [1] destruction of tissues, esp those of the fingers, ears, toes, and nose, by freezing, characterized by tingling, blister formation, and gangrene. [2] *NZ* a type of small sailing dinghy.

frostbitten ('frɒstˌbɪtᵊn) ADJECTIVE of or affected with frostbite.

frost cog NOUN another name for **frost stud.**

frosted ('frɒstɪd) ADJECTIVE [1] covered or injured by frost. [2] covered with icing, as a cake. [3] (of glass, etc.) having a surface roughened, as if covered with frost, to prevent clear vision through it.

frost heave NOUN the upthrust and cracking of a ground surface through the freezing and expansion of water underneath. Also called: **frost heaving.**

frost hollow NOUN a depression in a hilly area in which cold air collects, becoming very cold at night.

frosting ('frɒstɪŋ) NOUN [1] a soft icing based on sugar and egg whites. [2] another word (esp US and Canadian) for **icing.** [3] a rough or matt finish on glass, silver, etc. [4] *Slang* the practice of stealing a car while the owner has left it idling in order to defrost the windows and heat the engine.

frost line NOUN [1] the deepest point in the ground to which frost will penetrate. [2] the limit towards the equator beyond which frosts do not occur.

frost stud NOUN an antislip device fitted to a horse's shoe. Also called: **frost cog.**

frostwork ('frɒstˌwɜːk) NOUN [1] the patterns made by frost on glass, metal, etc. [2] similar artificial ornamentation.

frosty ('frɒstɪ) ADJECTIVE **frostier, frostiest.** [1] characterized by frost: *a frosty night*. [2] covered by or decorated with frost. [3] lacking warmth or enthusiasm: *the new plan had a frosty reception*. [4] like frost in appearance or colour; hoary.
▸**'frostily** ADVERB ▸**'frostiness** NOUN

froth (frɒθ) NOUN [1] a mass of small bubbles of air or a gas in a liquid, produced by fermentation, detergent, etc. [2] a mixture of saliva and air bubbles formed at the lips in certain diseases, such as rabies. [3] trivial ideas, talk, or entertainment. ◆ VERB [4] to produce or cause to produce froth. [5] (*tr*) to give out in the form of froth. [6] (*tr*) to cover with froth.
▷HISTORY C14: from Old Norse *frotha* or *frauth*; related to Old English *āfrēothan* to foam, Sanskrit *prothati* he snorts
▸**'frothy** ADJECTIVE ▸**'frothily** ADVERB ▸**'frothiness** NOUN

froth flotation NOUN another name for **flotation** (in metallurgy).

frottage ('frɒtɑːʒ; *French* frɔtaʒ) NOUN [1] the act or process of taking a rubbing from a rough surface, such as wood, for a work of art. [2] sexual excitement obtained by rubbing against another person's clothed body.
▷HISTORY French, from *frotter* to rub

Froude number (fraʊd) NOUN a dimensionless number used in hydrodynamics for model simulation of actual conditions.
▷HISTORY named after William *Froude* (1810–79), English civil engineer

froufrou ('fruːˌfruː) NOUN [1] a swishing sound, as made by a long silk dress. [2] elaborate dress or ornamentation, esp worn by women.
▷HISTORY C19: from French, of imitative origin

frow (frəʊ) NOUN a variant spelling of **froe.**

froward ('frəʊəd) ADJECTIVE *Archaic* obstinate; contrary.
▷HISTORY C14: see FRO, -WARD
▸**'frowardly** ADVERB ▸**'frowardness** NOUN

frown (fraʊn) VERB [1] (*intr*) to draw the brows together and wrinkle the forehead, esp in worry, anger, or concentration. [2] (*intr*; foll by *on* or *upon*) to have a dislike (of); look disapprovingly (upon): *the club frowned upon political activity by its members*. [3] (*tr*) to express (worry, etc.) by frowning. [4] (*tr*; often foll by *down*) to force, silence, etc., by a frowning look. ◆ NOUN [5] the act of frowning. [6] a show of dislike or displeasure.
▷HISTORY C14: from Old French *froignier*, of Celtic origin; compare Welsh *ffroen* nostril, Middle Breton *froan*
▸**'frowner** NOUN ▸**'frowningly** ADVERB

frowst (fraʊst) NOUN *Brit informal* a hot and stale atmosphere; fug.
▷HISTORY C19: back formation from *frowsty* musty, stuffy, variant of FROWZY

frowsty ('fraʊstɪ) ADJECTIVE **-stier, -stiest.** ill-smelling; stale; musty.
▸**'frowstiness** NOUN

frowzy, frouzy, *or* **frowsy** ('fraʊzɪ) ADJECTIVE **frowzier, frowziest; frouzier, frouziest; frowsier, frowsiest.** [1] untidy or unkempt in appearance; shabby. [2] ill-smelling; frowsty.
▷HISTORY C17: of unknown origin
▸**'frowziness, 'frouziness,** *or* **'frowsiness** NOUN

froze (frəʊz) VERB the past tense of **freeze.**

frozen ('frəʊzᵊn) VERB [1] the past participle of **freeze.** ◆ ADJECTIVE [2] turned into or covered with ice. [3] obstructed or blocked by ice. [4] killed, injured, or stiffened by extreme cold. [5] (of a region or climate) icy or snowy. [6] (of food) preserved by a freezing process. [7] **a** (of prices, wages, etc.) arbitrarily pegged at a certain level. **b** (of business assets) not convertible into cash, as by government direction or business conditions. [8] frigid, unfeeling, or disdainful in manner. [9] motionless or unyielding: *he was frozen with horror*.
▸**'frozenly** ADVERB ▸**'frozenness** NOUN

frozen shoulder NOUN *Pathol* a painful stiffness in a shoulder joint.

FRPS (in Britain) ABBREVIATION FOR Fellow of the Royal Photographic Society.

FRS (in Britain) ABBREVIATION FOR Fellow of the Royal Society.

FRSC (in Britain) ABBREVIATION FOR Fellow of the Royal Society of Chemistry.

FRSNZ ABBREVIATION FOR Fellow of the Royal Society of New Zealand.

frt ABBREVIATION FOR freight.

fructan ('frʌktən) NOUN a type of polymer of fructose, present in certain fruits.

Fructidor *French* (fryktidɔr) NOUN the month of fruit: the twelfth month of the French Revolutionary calendar, extending from Aug. 19 to Sept. 22.
▷HISTORY C18: from Latin *frūctus* fruit + Greek *dōron* gift

fructiferous (frʌk'tɪfərəs, frʊk-) ADJECTIVE (of plants or trees) bearing or yielding fruit.
▸**fruc'tiferously** ADVERB

fructification (ˌfrʌktɪfɪ'keɪʃən, ˌfrʊk-) NOUN [1] the act or state of fructifying. [2] the fruit of a seed-bearing plant. [3] any spore-bearing structure in ferns, mosses, fungi, etc.

fructify ('frʌktɪˌfaɪ, 'frʊk-) VERB **-fies, -fying, -fied.** [1] to bear or cause to bear fruit. [2] to make or become productive or fruitful.
▷HISTORY C14: from Old French *fructifier*, from Late Latin *frūctificāre* to bear fruit, from Latin *frūctus* fruit + *facere* to make, produce
▸**'fructiˌfier** NOUN

fructose ('frʌktəʊs, -təʊz, 'frʊk-) NOUN a white crystalline water-soluble sugar occurring in honey and many fruits. Formula: $C_6H_{12}O_6$. Also called: **laevulose, fruit sugar.**
▷HISTORY C19: from Latin *frūctus* fruit + -OSE[2]

fructuous ('frʌktjʊəs, 'frʊk-) ADJECTIVE productive or fruitful; fertile.
▷HISTORY C14: from Latin *frūctuōsus*, from *frūctus* fruit + -OUS
▸**'fructuously** ADVERB ▸**'fructuousness** NOUN

frugal ('fruːgᵊl) ADJECTIVE [1] practising economy; living without waste; thrifty. [2] not costly; meagre.
▷HISTORY C16: from Latin *frūgālis*, from *frūgī* useful, temperate, from *frux* fruit
▸**fru'gality** *or* **'frugalness** NOUN ▸**'frugally** ADVERB

frugivorous (fruːˈdʒɪvərəs) ADJECTIVE feeding on fruit; fruit-eating.
▷HISTORY C18: from *frugi-* (as in FRUGAL) + -VOROUS

fruit (fruːt) NOUN [1] *Botany* the ripened ovary of a flowering plant, containing one or more seeds. It may be dry, as in the poppy, or fleshy, as in the peach. [2] any fleshy part of a plant, other than the above structure, that supports the seeds and is edible, such as the strawberry. [3] the specialized spore-producing structure of plants that do not bear seeds. [4] any plant product useful to man, including grain, vegetables, etc. [5] (*often plural*) the result or consequence of an action or effort. [6] *Brit old-fashioned slang* chap; fellow: used as a term of address. [7] *Slang, chiefly Brit* a person considered to be eccentric or insane. [8] *Slang, chiefly US and Canadian* a male homosexual. [9] *Archaic* offspring of man or animals; progeny. ◆ VERB [10] to bear or cause to bear fruit.
▷HISTORY C12: from Old French, from Latin *frūctus* enjoyment, profit, fruit, from *fruī* to enjoy
▸ˈ**fruit,like** ADJECTIVE

fruitage (ˈfruːtɪdʒ) NOUN [1] the process, state, or season of producing fruit. [2] fruit collectively.

fruitarian (fruːˈtɛərɪən) NOUN [1] a person who eats only fruit. ◆ ADJECTIVE [2] of or relating to a fruitarian: *a fruitarian diet.*
▸**fruiˈtarian,ism** NOUN

fruit bat NOUN any large Old World bat of the suborder *Megachiroptera*, occurring in tropical and subtropical regions and feeding on fruit. Compare **insectivorous bat.**

fruit body NOUN a variant of **fruiting body.**

fruitcake (ˈfruːtˌkeɪk) NOUN [1] a rich cake containing mixed dried fruit, lemon peel, nuts, etc. [2] *Slang, chiefly Brit* a person considered to be eccentric or insane.

fruitcaked (ˈfruːtˌkeɪkt) ADJECTIVE *Slang* disturbed; driven mad.

fruit cocktail NOUN fruit salad consisting of small or diced fruits.

fruit cup NOUN a variety of fruits served in a cup or glass as an appetizer or dessert.

fruit drop NOUN [1] the premature shedding of fruit from a tree before fully ripe. [2] a boiled sweet with a fruity flavour.

fruiter (ˈfruːtə) NOUN [1] a fruit grower. [2] any tree that bears fruit, esp edible fruit.

fruiterer (ˈfruːtərə) NOUN *Chiefly Brit* a fruit dealer or seller.

fruit fly NOUN [1] any small dipterous fly of the family *Trypetidae*, which feed on and lay their eggs in plant tissues. See also **gallfly.** [2] any dipterous fly of the genus *Drosophila*. See **drosophila.**

fruitful (ˈfruːtfʊl) ADJECTIVE [1] bearing fruit in abundance. [2] productive or prolific, esp in bearing offspring. [3] causing or assisting prolific growth. [4] producing results or profits: *a fruitful discussion.*
▸ˈ**fruitfully** ADVERB ▸ˈ**fruitfulness** NOUN

fruiting body NOUN the part of a fungus in which the spores are produced. Also: **fruit body.**

fruition (fruːˈɪʃən) NOUN [1] the attainment or realization of something worked for or desired; fulfilment. [2] enjoyment of this. [3] the act or condition of bearing fruit.
▷HISTORY C15: from Late Latin *fruitiō* enjoyment, from Latin *fruī* to enjoy

fruit knife NOUN a small stainless knife for cutting fruit.

fruitless (ˈfruːtlɪs) ADJECTIVE [1] yielding nothing or nothing of value; unproductive; ineffectual. [2] without fruit.
▸ˈ**fruitlessly** ADVERB ▸ˈ**fruitlessness** NOUN

fruit machine NOUN *Brit* a gambling machine that pays out when certain combinations of diagrams, usually of fruit, are displayed.

fruit salad NOUN a dish consisting of sweet fruits cut up and served in a syrup: often sold canned.

fruit sugar NOUN another name for **fructose.**

fruit tree NOUN any tree that bears edible fruit.

fruity (ˈfruːtɪ) ADJECTIVE **fruitier, fruitiest.** [1] of or resembling fruit. [2] (of a voice) mellow or rich. [3] ingratiating or unctuous. [4] *Informal, chiefly Brit* erotically stimulating; salacious. [5] *Slang* eccentric or insane. [6] *Chiefly US and Canadian* a slang word for **homosexual.**
▸ˈ**fruitiness** NOUN ▸ˈ**fruitily** ADVERB

frumentaceous (ˌfruːmɛnˈteɪʃəs) ADJECTIVE resembling or made of wheat or similar grain.
▷HISTORY C17: from Late Latin *frūmentāceus*, from Latin *frūmentum* corn, grain

frumenty (ˈfruːməntɪ), **fromenty, furmenty,** *or* **furmity** NOUN *Brit* a kind of porridge made from hulled wheat boiled with milk, sweetened, and spiced.
▷HISTORY C14: from Old French *frumentee*, from *frument* grain, from Latin *frūmentum*

frump (frʌmp) NOUN a woman who is dowdy, drab, or unattractive.
▷HISTORY C16 (in the sense: to be sullen; C19: dowdy woman): from Middle Dutch *verrompelen* to wrinkle, RUMPLE

frumpy (ˈfrʌmpɪ) *or* **frumpish** (ˈfrʌmpɪʃ) ADJECTIVE (of a woman, clothes, etc) dowdy, drab, or unattractive.
▸ˈ**frumpily** *or* ˈ**frumpishly** ADVERB ▸ˈ**frumpiness** *or* ˈ**frumpishness** NOUN

frusemide (ˈfrʌsəˌmaɪd) *or* **furosemide** (ˈfjʊərˌəʊsəˌmaɪd) NOUN a diuretic used to relieve oedema, for example caused by heart or kidney disease.

frustrate (frʌˈstreɪt) VERB (*tr*) [1] to hinder or prevent (the efforts, plans, or desires) of; thwart. [2] to upset, agitate, or tire: *her constant complaints began to frustrate him.* ◆ ADJECTIVE [3] *Archaic* frustrated or thwarted; baffled.
▷HISTORY C15: from Latin *frustrāre* to cheat, from *frustrā* in error
▸**frusˈtrater** NOUN

frustrated (frʌˈstreɪtɪd) ADJECTIVE having feelings of dissatisfaction or lack of fulfilment.

frustration (frʌˈstreɪʃən) NOUN [1] the condition of being frustrated. [2] something that frustrates. [3] *Psychol* **a** the prevention or hindering of a potentially satisfying activity. **b** the emotional reaction to such prevention that may involve aggression.

frustule (ˈfrʌstjuːl) NOUN *Botany* the hard siliceous cell wall of a diatom.
▷HISTORY C19: from French, from Late Latin *frustulum* a small piece, from *frustum* a bit

frustum (ˈfrʌstəm) NOUN, *plural* **-tums** *or* **-ta** (-tə). [1] *Geometry* **a** the part of a solid, such as a cone or pyramid, contained between the base and a plane parallel to the base that intersects the solid. **b** the part of such a solid contained between two parallel planes intersecting the solid. [2] *Architect* a single drum of a column or a single stone used to construct a pier.
▷HISTORY C17: from Latin: piece; probably related to Old English *brȳsan* to crush, BRUISE

frutescent (fruːˈtɛsᵊnt) *or* **fruticose** (ˈfruːtɪˌkəʊs, -ˌkəʊz) ADJECTIVE having the appearance or habit of a shrub; shrubby.
▷HISTORY C18: from Latin *frutex* shrub, bush
▸**fruˈtescence** NOUN

fry¹ (fraɪ) VERB **fries, frying, fried.** [1] (when *tr*, sometimes foll by *up*) to cook or be cooked in fat, oil, etc., usually over direct heat. [2] (*intr*) *Informal* to be excessively hot. [3] *Slang, chiefly US* to kill or be killed by electrocution, esp in the electric chair. ◆ NOUN, *plural* **fries.** [4] a dish of something fried, esp the offal of a specified animal: *pig's fry.* [5] *US and Canadian* a social occasion, often outdoors, at which the chief food is fried. [6] *Brit informal* the act of preparing a mixed fried dish or the dish itself.
▷HISTORY C13: from Old French *frire*, from Latin *frīgere* to roast, fry

fry² (fraɪ) PLURAL NOUN [1] the young of various species of fish. [2] the young of certain other animals, such as frogs. [3] young children. See also **small fry.**
▷HISTORY C14 (in the sense: young, offspring): perhaps via Norman French from Old French *freier* to spawn, rub, from Latin *fricāre* to rub

fryer *or* **frier** (ˈfraɪə) NOUN [1] a person or thing that fries. [2] a young chicken suitable for frying.

frying pan *or esp US* **fry-pan** NOUN [1] a long-handled shallow pan used for frying. [2] **out of the frying pan into the fire.** from a bad situation to a worse one.

f.s. ABBREVIATION FOR foot-second.

FSA ABBREVIATION FOR: [1] Fellow of the Society of Antiquaries. [2] Financial Services Authority. [3] (in Britain) Food Standards Association.

FSB ABBREVIATION FOR the Russian Federal Security Service, founded in 1995.
▷HISTORY C20: Russian *Federalnaya sluzhba bezopasnosti*

FSH ABBREVIATION FOR follicle-stimulating hormone.

f-stop NOUN any of the settings for the f-number of a camera.

ft ABBREVIATION FOR fort.

FT (in Britain) ABBREVIATION FOR Financial Times.

ft. ABBREVIATION FOR: [1] foot *or* feet. [2] fortification.

fth. *or* **fthm.** ABBREVIATION FOR fathom.

ft-l ABBREVIATION FOR foot-lambert.

ft-lb ABBREVIATION FOR foot-pound.

FTP *or* **ftp** NOUN [1] file transfer protocol; the standard protocol used to transfer files across the Internet, or a similar network, between computer systems. [2] the program implementing this. ◆ VERB (*tr*) [3] to transfer (a file) in this way.

FT-SE 100 Index ABBREVIATION FOR Financial Times Stock Exchange 100 Index.

FT Share Indexes PLURAL NOUN any of a number of share indexes published by the *Financial Times* to reflect various aspects of stock exchange prices. See **Financial Times Industrial Ordinary Share Index, Financial Times Stock Exchange 100 Index.**

fubar *or* **foobar** (ˈfuːbɑː) ADJECTIVE *Slang* irreparably damaged or bungled.
▷HISTORY C20: acronym for *f(ucked) u(p) b(eyond) a(ll) r(epair)*

fubsy (ˈfʌbzɪ) ADJECTIVE **-sier, -siest.** *Archaic or dialect* short and stout; squat.
▷HISTORY C18: from obsolete *fubs* plump person

Fu-chou (ˈfuːˈtʃaʊ) NOUN a variant transliteration of the Chinese name for **Fuzhou.**

fuchsia (ˈfjuːʃə) NOUN [1] any onagraceous shrub of the mostly tropical genus *Fuchsia*, widely cultivated for their showy drooping purple, red, or white flowers. [2] Also called: **California fuchsia.** a North American onagraceous plant, *Zauschneria californica*, with tubular scarlet flowers. [3] **a** a reddish-purple to purplish-pink colour. **b** (*as adjective*): *a fuchsia dress.*
▷HISTORY C18: from New Latin, named after Leonhard *Fuchs* (1501–66), German botanist

fuchsin (ˈfuːksɪn) *or* **fuchsine** (ˈfuːksiːn, -sɪn) NOUN a greenish crystalline substance, the quaternary chloride of rosaniline, forming a red solution in water: used as a textile dye and a biological stain. Formula: $C_{20}H_{19}N_3HCl$. Also called: **magenta.**
▷HISTORY C19: from FUCHS(IA) + -IN; from its similarity in colour to the flower

fucivorous (fjuːˈsɪvərəs) ADJECTIVE *Zoology* feeding on seaweed.
▷HISTORY C19: from Greek *phukos* seaweed + -VOROUS

fuck (fʌk) *Taboo* ◆ VERB [1] to have sexual intercourse with (someone). ◆ NOUN [2] an act of sexual intercourse. [3] *Slang* a partner in sexual intercourse, esp one of specified competence or experience: *she was a good fuck.* [4] **not care** *or* **give a fuck.** not to care at all. ◆ INTERJECTION [5] *Offensive* an expression of strong disgust or anger (often in exclamatory phrases such as **fuck you! fuck it!** etc.).
▷HISTORY C16: of Germanic origin; related to Middle Dutch *fokken* to strike

> **Language note** The use and overuse of *fuck* in the everyday speech of many people has led, to some extent, to a lessening of its impact as an expletive. However, the word still retains its shock value, although it is less now than it was when the critic Kenneth Tynan caused controversy by saying it on British television in 1965.

fuck about *or* **around** VERB (*adverb*) *Offensive taboo slang* [1] (*intr*) to act in a stupid or aimless manner. [2] (*tr*) to treat (someone) in an inconsiderate or selfish way.

fucker (ˈfʌkə) NOUN *Taboo* [1] *Slang* a despicable or obnoxious person. [2] *Slang* a person; fellow. [3] a person who fucks.

fucking ('fʌkɪŋ) ADJECTIVE (*prenominal*), ADVERB *Taboo slang* (intensifier): *turn off that fucking phone; a fucking good time.*

fucking A INTERJECTION *Taboo slang, US* an emphatic exclamation of approval.

fuck off *Offensive taboo slang* ◆ INTERJECTION [1] a forceful expression of dismissal or contempt. ◆ VERB (*adverb*) [2] (*intr*) to go away. [3] (*tr*) to irritate or annoy (a person). ◆ ADJECTIVE [4] (*prenominal*) very large or impressive: *a huge fuck-off cigar.*

fuck up *Offensive taboo slang* ◆ VERB (*tr, adverb*) [1] to damage or bungle: *to fuck up a machine.* [2] to make confused. ◆ NOUN **fuck-up.** [3] an act or an instance of bungling.

fuckwit ('fʌkwɪt) NOUN *Taboo slang* a fool or idiot.

fucoid ('fjuːkɔɪd) ADJECTIVE, *also* **fucoidal, fucous** ('fjuːkəs). [1] of, relating to, or resembling seaweeds of the genus *Fucus*. ◆ NOUN [2] any seaweed of the genus *Fucus*.

fucoxanthin (ˌfjuːkəʊ'zænθɪn) NOUN a carotenoid pigment that gives brown algae and diatoms their colour: functions in photosynthesis. Formula: $C_{40}H_{56}O_6$ or $C_{40}H_{60}O_6$.

fucus ('fjuːkəs) NOUN, *plural* **-ci** (-saɪ) *or* **-cuses.** any seaweed of the genus *Fucus*, common in the intertidal regions of many shores and typically having greenish-brown slimy fronds. See also **wrack**[2] (sense 2).
▷HISTORY C16: from Latin: rock lichen, from Greek *phukos* seaweed, dye, of Semitic origin

fuddle ('fʌdᵊl) VERB [1] (*tr; often passive*) to cause to be confused or intoxicated. [2] (*intr*) to drink excessively; tipple. ◆ NOUN [3] a muddled or confused state.
▷HISTORY C16: of unknown origin

fuddy-duddy ('fʌdɪˌdʌdɪ) NOUN, *plural* **-dies.** *Informal* a person, esp an elderly one, who is extremely conservative or dull.
▷HISTORY C20: of uncertain origin

fudge[1] (fʌdʒ) NOUN a soft variously flavoured sweet made from sugar, butter, cream, etc.
▷HISTORY C19: of unknown origin

fudge[2] (fʌdʒ) NOUN [1] foolishness; nonsense. ◆ INTERJECTION [2] a mild exclamation of annoyance. ◆ VERB [3] (*intr*) to talk foolishly or emptily.
▷HISTORY C18: of uncertain origin

fudge[3] (fʌdʒ) NOUN [1] a small section of type matter in a box in a newspaper allowing late news to be included without the whole page having to be remade. [2] the box in which such type matter is placed. [3] the late news so inserted. [4] a machine attached to a newspaper press for printing this. [5] an unsatisfactory compromise reached to evade a difficult problem or controversial issue. ◆ VERB [6] (*tr*) to make or adjust in a false or clumsy way. [7] (*tr*) to misrepresent; falsify. [8] to evade (a problem, issue, etc.); dodge; avoid.
▷HISTORY C19: see FADGE

Fuegian (fjuː'iːdʒɪən, 'fweɪdʒ-) ADJECTIVE [1] of or relating to Tierra del Fuego or its indigenous Indians. ◆ NOUN [2] an Indian of Tierra del Fuego.

fuel (fjʊəl) NOUN [1] any substance burned as a source of heat or power, such as coal or petrol. [2] **a** the material, containing a fissile substance, such as uranium-235, that produces energy in a nuclear reactor. **b** a substance that releases energy in a fusion reactor. [3] something that nourishes or builds up emotion, action, etc. ◆ VERB **fuels, fuelling, fuelled** *or US* **fuels, fueling, fueled.** [4] to supply with or receive fuel.
▷HISTORY C14: from Old French *feuaile*, from *feu* fire, ultimately from Latin *focus* fireplace, hearth
▸'**fueller** *or US* '**fueler** NOUN

fuel air bomb NOUN a type of bomb that spreads a cloud of gas, which is then detonated, over the target area, causing extensive destruction.

fuel cell NOUN a cell in which the energy produced by oxidation of a fuel is converted directly into electrical energy.

fuel element NOUN a can containing nuclear fuel for use in a fission reactor.

fuel injection NOUN a system for introducing atomized liquid fuel under pressure directly into the combustion chambers of an internal-combustion engine without the use of a carburettor.

fuel oil NOUN a liquid petroleum product having a flash point above 37.8°C: used as a substitute for coal in industrial furnaces, domestic heaters, ships, and locomotives.

fuel rod NOUN a long tube, often made of a zirconium alloy and containing uranium-oxide pellets, that is stacked in bundles of about 200 to provide the fuel in certain types of nuclear reactor.

fug (fʌg) NOUN *Chiefly Brit* a hot, stale, or suffocating atmosphere.
▷HISTORY C19: perhaps variant of FOG[1]
▸'**fuggy** ADJECTIVE

fugacious (fjuː'geɪʃəs) ADJECTIVE [1] passing quickly away; transitory; fleeting. [2] *Botany* lasting for only a short time: *fugacious petals.*
▷HISTORY C17: from Latin *fugax* inclined to flee, swift, from *fugere* to flee; see FUGITIVE
▸**fu'gaciously** ADVERB ▸**fu'gaciousness** NOUN

fugacity (fjuː'gæsɪtɪ) NOUN [1] Also called: **escaping tendency.** *Thermodynamics* a property of a gas, related to its partial pressure, that expresses its tendency to escape or expand, given by $d(\log_e f) = d\mu/RT$, where μ is the chemical potential, R the gas constant, and T the thermodynamic temperature. Symbol: f. [2] the state or quality of being fugacious.

fugal ('fjuːgᵊl) ADJECTIVE of, relating to, or in the style of a fugue.
▸'**fugally** ADVERB

fugato (fjʊ'gɑːtəʊ) *Music* ◆ ADVERB, ADJECTIVE [1] in the manner or style of a fugue. ◆ NOUN [2] a movement, section, or piece in this style.
▷HISTORY C19: from Italian, from *fugare* to compose in the style of a FUGUE

-fuge NOUN COMBINING FORM indicating an agent or substance that expels or drives away: *vermifuge.*
▷HISTORY from Latin *fugāre* to expel, put to flight
▸**-fugal** ADJECTIVE COMBINING FORM

fugio ('fjuːdʒɪəʊ) NOUN, *plural* **-gios.** a former US copper coin worth one dollar, the first authorized by Congress (1787).
▷HISTORY C18: Latin: I flee; one of the words inscribed on the coin

fugitive ('fjuːdʒɪtɪv) NOUN [1] a person who flees. [2] a thing that is elusive or fleeting. ◆ ADJECTIVE [3] fleeing, esp from arrest or pursuit. [4] not permanent; fleeting; transient. [5] moving or roving about.
▷HISTORY C14: from Latin *fugitīvus* fleeing away, from *fugere* to take flight, run away
▸'**fugitively** ADVERB ▸'**fugitiveness** NOUN

fugitometer (ˌfjuːdʒɪ'tɒmɪtə) NOUN an instrument used for measuring the fastness to light of dyed materials.

fugleman ('fjuːgᵊlmən) NOUN, *plural* **-men.** [1] (formerly) a soldier used as an example for those learning drill. [2] any person who acts as a leader or example.
▷HISTORY C19: from German *Flügelmann*, from *Flügel* wing, flank + *Mann* MAN

fugue (fjuːg) NOUN [1] a musical form consisting essentially of a theme repeated a fifth above or a fourth below the continuing first statement. [2] *Psychiatry* a dreamlike altered state of consciousness, lasting from a few hours to several days, during which a person loses his memory for his previous life and often wanders away from home.
▷HISTORY C16: from French, from Italian *fuga*, from Latin: a running away, flight
▸'**fugue,like** ADJECTIVE

fuguist ('fjuːgɪst) NOUN a composer of fugues.

Führer *or* ***Fuehrer*** *German* ('fyːrər; *English* 'fjʊərə) NOUN a leader: applied esp to Adolf Hitler (***der Führer***) while he was Chancellor.
▷HISTORY German, from *führen* to lead

Fuji ('fuːdʒɪ) NOUN **Mount.** an extinct volcano in central Japan, in S central Honshu: the highest mountain in Japan, famous for its symmetrical snow-capped cone. Height: 3776 m (12 388 ft.). Also called: **Fujiyama, Fuji-san.**

Fukuyama (ˌfuːkuː'jɑːmə) NOUN a city in Japan, in SW Honshu: industrial and commercial centre. Pop.: 374 510 (1995).

-ful SUFFIX [1] (*forming adjectives*) full of or characterized by: *painful; spiteful; restful.* [2] (*forming adjectives*) able or tending to: *helpful; useful.* [3] (*forming nouns*) indicating as much as will fill the thing specified: *mouthful; spoonful.*
▷HISTORY Old English *-ful, -full*, from FULL[1]

> **Language note** Where the amount held by a spoon, etc., is used as a rough unit of measurement, the correct form is *spoonful*, etc.: *take a spoonful of this medicine every day. Spoon full* is used in a sentence such as *he held out a spoon full of dark liquid*, where *full of* describes the spoon. A plural form such as *spoonfuls* is preferred by many speakers and writers to *spoonsful*.

Fula ('fuːlə) *or* **Fulah** ('fuːlɑː) NOUN [1] (*plural* **-la, -las** *or* **-lah, -lahs**) a member of a pastoral nomadic people of W and central Africa, living chiefly in the sub-Sahara region from Senegal to N Cameroon: a racial mixture of light-skinned Berber peoples of the North and darker-skinned W Africans. [2] the language of this people; Fulani.

Fulani (fuː'lɑːnɪ, 'fuːlənɪ) NOUN [1] the language of the Fula, belonging to the West Atlantic branch of the Niger-Congo family, widely used as a trade pidgin in W Africa. [2] (*plural* **-nis, -ni**) another name for **Fula** (the people). [3] (*plural* **-nis, -ni**) a humped breed of cattle from W Africa. ◆ ADJECTIVE [4] of or relating to the Fula or their language.

fulcrum ('fulkrəm, 'fʌl-) NOUN, *plural* **-crums** *or* **-cra** (-krə). [1] the pivot about which a lever turns. [2] something that supports or sustains; prop. [3] a spinelike scale occurring in rows along the anterior edge of the fins in primitive bony fishes such as the sturgeon.
▷HISTORY C17: from Latin: foot of a couch, bedpost, from *fulcīre* to prop up

fulfil *or US* **fulfill** (fʊl'fɪl) VERB **-fils** *or US* **-fills, -filling, -filled.** (*tr*) [1] to bring about the completion or achievement of (a desire, promise, etc.). [2] to carry out or execute (a request, etc.). [3] to conform with or satisfy (regulations, demands, etc.). [4] to finish or reach the end of: *he fulfilled his prison sentence.* [5] **fulfil oneself.** to achieve one's potential or desires.
▷HISTORY Old English *fulfyllan*
▸**ful'filler** NOUN ▸**ful'filment** *or US* **ful'fillment** NOUN

fulgent ('fʌldʒənt) *or* **fulgid** ('fʌldʒɪd) ADJECTIVE *Poetic* shining brilliantly; resplendent; gleaming.
▷HISTORY C15: from Latin *fulgēre* to shine, flash
▸'**fulgently** ADVERB

fulgurate ('fʌlgjʊˌreɪt) VERB (*intr*) *Rare* to flash like lightning.
▷HISTORY C17: from Latin *fulgurāre*, from *fulgur* lightning
▸**fulgurant** ('fʌlgjʊrənt) ADJECTIVE

fulgurating ('fʌlgjʊˌreɪtɪŋ) ADJECTIVE [1] *Pathol* (of pain) sudden and sharp; piercing. [2] *Surgery* of or relating to fulguration.

fulguration (ˌfʌlgjʊ'reɪʃən) NOUN *Surgery* destruction of tissue by means of high-frequency (more than 10 000 per second) electric sparks.

fulgurite ('fʌlgjʊˌraɪt) NOUN a tube of glassy mineral matter found in sand and rock, formed by the action of lightning.
▷HISTORY C19: from Latin *fulgur* lightning

fulgurous ('fʌlgjʊrəs) ADJECTIVE *Rare* flashing like or resembling lightning; fulgurant.
▷HISTORY C17: from Latin *fulgur* lightning

Fulham ('fʊləm) NOUN a district of the Greater London borough of Hammersmith and Fulham (since 1965): contains **Fulham Palace** (16th century), residence of the Bishop of London.

fuliginous (fjuː'lɪdʒɪnəs) ADJECTIVE [1] sooty or smoky. [2] of the colour of soot; dull greyish-black or brown.
▷HISTORY C16: from Late Latin *fūlīginōsus* full of soot, from Latin *fūlīgō* soot
▸**fu'liginously** ADVERB ▸**fu'liginousness** NOUN

full[1] (fʊl) ADJECTIVE [1] holding or containing as much as possible; filled to capacity or near capacity. [2] abundant in supply, quantity, number, etc.: *full of energy.* [3] having consumed enough food or drink. [4] (esp of the face or figure) rounded or plump; not thin. [5] (*prenominal*) with no part lacking; complete: *a full dozen.* [6] (*prenominal*) with all privileges, rights, etc.; not restricted: *a full member.* [7] (*prenominal*) of, relating to, or designating a relationship established by descent from the same parents: *full brother.* [8] filled with emotion or sentiment: *a full heart.* [9] (*postpositive;*

foll by *of*) occupied or engrossed (with): *full of his own projects.* 10 *Music* **a** powerful or rich in volume and sound. **b** completing a piece or section; concluding: *a full close.* 11 (of a garment, esp a skirt) containing a large amount of fabric; of ample cut. 12 (of sails, etc.) distended by wind. 13 (of wine, such as a burgundy) having a heavy body. 14 (of a colour) containing a large quantity of pure hue as opposed to white or grey; rich; saturated. 15 *Informal* drunk. 16 **full and by.** *Nautical* another term for **close-hauled.** 17 **full of oneself.** full of pride or conceit; egoistic. 18 **full up.** filled to capacity: *the cinema was full up.* 19 **in full cry.** (esp of a pack of hounds) in hot pursuit of quarry. 20 **in full swing.** at the height of activity: *the party was in full swing.* ◆ ADVERB 21 **a** completely; entirely. **b** (*in combination*): *full-grown; full-fledged.* 22 exactly; directly; right: *he hit him full in the stomach.* 23 very; extremely (esp in the phrase **full well**). 24 **full out.** with maximum effort or speed. ◆ NOUN 25 the greatest degree, extent, etc. 26 *Brit* a ridge of sand or shingle along a seashore. 27 **in full.** without omitting, decreasing, or shortening: *we paid in full for our mistake.* 28 **to the full.** to the greatest extent; thoroughly; fully. ◆ VERB 29 (*tr*) *Needlework* to gather or tuck. 30 (*intr*) (of the moon) to be fully illuminated.
▷HISTORY Old English; related to Old Norse *fullr,* Old High German *foll,* Latin *plēnus,* Greek *plērēs;* see FILL
▸ **'fullness** *or esp US* **'fulness** NOUN

full² (fʊl) VERB (of cloth, yarn, etc.) to become or to make (cloth, yarn, etc.) heavier and more compact during manufacture through shrinking and beating or pressing.
▷HISTORY C14: from Old French *fouler,* ultimately from Latin *fullō* a FULLER¹

fullback ('fʊl,bæk) NOUN 1 *Soccer, hockey* one of two defensive players positioned in front of the goalkeeper. 2 *Rugby* a defensive player positioned close to his own line. 3 the position held by any of these players.

full blood NOUN 1 an individual, esp a horse or similar domestic animal, of unmixed race or breed. 2 the relationship between individuals having the same parents.

full-blooded ADJECTIVE 1 (esp of horses) of unmixed ancestry; thoroughbred. 2 having great vigour or health; hearty; virile.
▸ **,full-'bloodedness** NOUN

full-blown ADJECTIVE 1 characterized by the fullest, strongest, or best development. 2 in full bloom.

full board NOUN **a** the provision by a hotel of a bed and all meals. **b** (*as modifier*): *full board accommodation.*

full-bodied ADJECTIVE having a full rich flavour or quality.

full-bottomed ADJECTIVE (of a wig) long at the back.

full-court press NOUN *Basketball* the tactic of harrying the opposing team in all areas of the court, as opposed to the more usual practice of trying to defend one's own basket.

full-cream ADJECTIVE denoting or made with whole unskimmed milk.

full dress NOUN **a** a formal or ceremonial style of dress, such as white tie and tails for a man and a full-length evening dress for a woman. **b** (*as modifier*): *full-dress uniform.*

full employment NOUN a state in which the labour force and other economic resources of a country are utilized to their maximum.

fuller¹ ('fʊlə) NOUN a person who fulls cloth for his living.
▷HISTORY Old English *fullere,* from Latin *fullō*

fuller² ('fʊlə) NOUN 1 Also called: **fullering tool.** a tool for forging a groove. 2 a tool for caulking a riveted joint. ◆ VERB 3 (*tr*) to forge (a groove) or caulk (a riveted joint) with a fuller.
▷HISTORY C19: perhaps from the name *Fuller*

fullerene ('fʊlə,riːn) NOUN 1 short for **buckminsterfullerene.** 2 any of various carbon molecules with a polyhedral structure similar to that of buckminsterfullerene, such as C_{70}, C_{76}, and C_{84}.

fulleride ('fʊlə,raɪd) NOUN a compound of a fullerene in which atoms are trapped inside the cage of carbon atoms.

fullerite ('fʊlə,raɪt) NOUN a crystalline form of a fullerene.

fuller's earth NOUN a natural absorbent clay used, after heating, for decolorizing oils and fats, fulling cloth, etc.

fuller's teasel NOUN 1 a Eurasian teasel plant, *Dipsacus fullonum,* whose prickly flower heads are used for raising the nap on woollen cloth. 2 a similar and related plant, *Dipsacus sativum.*

full-faced ADJECTIVE 1 having a round full face. 2 Also: **full face.** facing towards the viewer, with the entire face visible. 3 another name for **bold face.**
▸ **'full'face** NOUN, ADVERB

full-fledged ADJECTIVE See **fully fledged.**

full-frontal ADJECTIVE 1 *Informal* (of a nude person or a photograph of a nude person) exposing the genitals to full view. 2 all-out; unrestrained. ◆ NOUN **full frontal.** 3 a full-frontal photograph.

full house NOUN 1 *Poker* a hand with three cards of the same value and another pair. 2 a theatre, etc., filled to capacity. 3 (in bingo, etc.) the set of numbers needed to win.

full-length NOUN (*modifier*) 1 extending to or showing the complete length: *a full-length mirror.* 2 of the original length; not abridged.

full monty ('mɒntɪ) NOUN **the.** *Informal* something in its entirety.
▷HISTORY of unknown origin

full moon NOUN 1 one of the four phases of the moon, occurring when the earth lies between the sun and the moon so that the moon is visible as a fully illuminated disc. 2 the moon in this phase. 3 the time at which this occurs.

full-mouthed ADJECTIVE 1 (of livestock) having a full adult set of teeth. 2 uttered loudly: *a full-mouthed oath.*

full nelson NOUN a wrestling hold, illegal in amateur wrestling, in which a wrestler places both arms under his opponent's arms from behind and exerts pressure with both palms on the back of the neck. Compare **half-nelson.**

full-on ADJECTIVE *Informal* complete; unrestrained: *full-on military intervention; full-on hard rock.*

full pitch NOUN *Cricket* another term for **full toss.**

full professor NOUN *US and Canadian* a university teacher of the highest academic rank.

full radiator NOUN *Physics* another name for **black body.**

full-rigged ADJECTIVE (of a sailing vessel) having three or more masts rigged square.

full sail ADVERB 1 at top speed. ◆ ADJECTIVE (*postpositive*), ADVERB 2 with all sails set.
▸ **,full-'sailed** ADJECTIVE

full-scale NOUN (*modifier*) 1 (of a plan, etc.) of actual size; having the same dimensions as the original. 2 done with thoroughness or urgency; using all resources; all-out.

full score NOUN the entire score of a musical composition, showing each part separately.

full stop *or* **full point** NOUN the punctuation mark (.) used at the end of a sentence that is not a question or exclamation, after abbreviations, etc. Also called (esp US and Canadian): **period.**

full time NOUN the end of a football or other match. Compare **half-time.**

full-time ADJECTIVE 1 for the entire time appropriate to an activity: *a full-time job; a full-time student.* ◆ ADVERB **full time.** 2 on a full-time basis: *he works full time.* ◆ Compare **part-time.**
▸ **,full-'timer** NOUN

full toss *or* **full pitch** NOUN *Cricket* a bowled ball that reaches the batsman without bouncing.

full-wave rectifier NOUN an electronic circuit in which both half-cycles of incoming alternating current furnish the direct current output.

fully ('fʊlɪ) ADVERB 1 to the greatest degree or extent; totally; entirely. 2 amply; sufficiently; adequately: *they were fully fed.* 3 at least: *it was fully an hour before she came.*

fully fashioned ADJECTIVE (of stockings, knitwear, etc.) shaped and seamed so as to fit closely.

fully fledged *or* **full-fledged** ADJECTIVE 1 (of a young bird) having acquired its adult feathers and thus able to fly. 2 developed or matured to the fullest degree. 3 of full rank or status.

fulmar ('fʊlmə) NOUN any heavily built short-tailed oceanic bird of the genus *Fulmarus* and related genera, of polar regions: family *Procellariidae,* order *Procellariiformes* (petrels).
▷HISTORY C17: of Scandinavian origin; related to Old Norse *fūlmār,* from *fūll* foul + *mār* gull

fulminant ('fʌlmɪnənt, 'fʊl-) ADJECTIVE 1 sudden and violent; fulminating. 2 *Pathol* (of pain) sudden and sharp; piercing.
▷HISTORY C17: from Latin *fulmināre* to cause lightning, from *fulmen* lightning that strikes

fulminate ('fʌlmɪ,neɪt, 'fʊl-) VERB 1 (*intr;* often foll by *against*) to make criticisms or denunciations; rail. 2 to explode with noise and violence. 3 (*intr*) *Archaic* to thunder and lighten. ◆ NOUN 4 any salt or ester of fulminic acid, esp the mercury salt, which is used as a detonator.
▷HISTORY C15: from Medieval Latin *fulmināre;* see FULMINANT
▸ **,fulmi'nation** NOUN ▸ **'fulmi,nator** NOUN ▸ **'fulmi,natory** ADJECTIVE

fulminating powder NOUN powder that detonates by percussion.

fulminic acid (fʌl'mɪnɪk, fʊl-) NOUN an unstable volatile acid known only in solution and in the form of its salts and esters. Formula: HONC. Compare **cyanic acid.**
▷HISTORY C19: from Latin *fulmen* lightning

fulminous ('fʌlmɪnəs, 'fʊl-) ADJECTIVE *Rare* 1 harshly critical. 2 of, involving, or resembling thunder and lightning.

fulsome ('fʊlsəm) ADJECTIVE 1 excessive or insincere, esp in an offensive or distasteful way: *fulsome compliments.* 2 *Not standard* extremely complimentary. 3 *Informal* full, rich or abundant: *a fulsome figure; a fulsome flavour; fulsome detail.* 4 *Archaic* disgusting; loathsome.
▸ **'fulsomely** ADVERB ▸ **'fulsomeness** NOUN

> **Language note** The use of *fulsome* to mean *extremely complimentary* or *full, rich or abundant* is common in journalism, but should be avoided in other kinds of writing.

fulvous ('fʌlvəs, 'fʊl-) ADJECTIVE of a dull brownish-yellow colour; tawny.
▷HISTORY C17: from Latin *fulvus* reddish yellow, gold-coloured, tawny; probably related to *fulgēre* to shine

fumaric acid (fjuː'mærɪk) NOUN a colourless crystalline acid with a fruity taste, found in some plants and manufactured from benzene; *trans*-butenedioic acid: used esp in synthetic resins. Formula: HCOOCH:CHCOOH.
▷HISTORY C19: from New Latin *Fumāria* name of genus, from Late Latin: fumitory, from Latin *fūmus* smoke

fumarole ('fjuːmə,rəʊl) NOUN a vent in or near a volcano from which hot gases, esp steam, are emitted.
▷HISTORY C19: from French *fumerolle,* from Late Latin *fūmāriolum* smoke hole, from Latin *fūmus* smoke
▸ **fumarolic** (,fjuːmə'rɒlɪk) ADJECTIVE

fumatorium (,fjuːmə'tɔːrɪəm) NOUN, *plural* **-riums** *or* **-ria** (-rɪə). an airtight chamber in which insects and fungi on organic matter or plants are destroyed by fumigation. Also called: **fumatory.**
▷HISTORY New Latin, from Latin *fūmāre* to smoke

fumatory ('fjuːmətərɪ, -trɪ) ADJECTIVE 1 of or relating to smoking or fumigation. ◆ NOUN, *plural* **-ries.** 2 another name for a **fumatorium.**

fumble ('fʌmbᵊl) VERB 1 (*intr;* often foll by *for* or *with*) to grope about clumsily or blindly, esp in searching: *he was fumbling in the dark for the money he had dropped.* 2 (*intr;* foll by *at* or *with*) to finger or play with, esp in an absent-minded way. 3 to say or do hesitantly or awkwardly: *he fumbled the introduction badly.* 4 to fail to catch or grasp (a ball, etc.) cleanly. ◆ NOUN 5 the act of fumbling.
▷HISTORY C16: probably of Scandinavian origin; related to Swedish *fumla*
▸ **'fumbler** NOUN ▸ **'fumblingly** ADVERB ▸ **'fumblingness** NOUN

fume (fju:m) VERB [1] (*intr*) to be overcome with anger or fury; rage. [2] to give off (fumes) or (of fumes) to be given off, esp during a chemical reaction. [3] (*tr*) to subject to or treat with fumes; fumigate. ◆ NOUN [4] (*often plural*) a pungent or toxic vapour. [5] a sharp or pungent odour. [6] a condition of anger.
▷HISTORY C14: from Old French *fum*, from Latin *fūmus* smoke, vapour
▸ **'fumeless** ADJECTIVE ▸ **'fume,like** ADJECTIVE ▸ **'fumer** NOUN ▸ **'fumingly** ADVERB ▸ **'fumy** ADJECTIVE

fume cupboard NOUN a ventilated enclosure for storing or experimenting with chemicals with harmful vapours.

fumed (fju:md) ADJECTIVE (of wood, esp oak) having a dark colour and distinctive grain from exposure to ammonia fumes.

fumet¹ (fju:'mɛt) NOUN a strong-flavoured liquor from cooking fish, meat, or game: used to flavour sauces.
▷HISTORY French, literally: aroma

fumet² ('fju:mət) NOUN (*often plural*) *Archaic* the dropping of a deer.
▷HISTORY C16 *fewmet:* probably via Old French from Latin *fimāre* to spread dung on, from *fimus* dung

fumigant ('fju:mɪgənt) NOUN a substance used for fumigating.

fumigate ('fju:mɪ,geɪt) VERB to treat (something contaminated or infected) with fumes or smoke.
▷HISTORY C16: from Latin *fūmigāre* to smoke, steam, from *fūmus* smoke + *agere* to drive, produce
▸ **,fumi'gation** NOUN ▸ **'fumi,gator** NOUN

fuming sulphuric acid NOUN a mixture of pyrosulphuric acid, $H_2S_2O_7$, and other condensed acids, made by dissolving sulphur trioxide in concentrated sulphuric acid. Also called: **oleum, Nordhausen acid** ('nɔ:dhaʊzᵊn).

fumitory ('fju:mɪtərɪ, -trɪ) NOUN, *plural* **-ries**. any plant of the chiefly European genus *Fumaria*, esp *F. officinalis*, having spurred flowers and formerly used medicinally: family *Fumariaceae*.
▷HISTORY C14: from Old French *fumetere*, from Medieval Latin *fūmus terrae*, literally: smoke of the earth; see FUME

fun (fʌn) NOUN [1] a source of enjoyment, amusement, diversion, etc. [2] pleasure, gaiety, or merriment. [3] jest or sport (esp in the phrases **in** or **for fun**). [4] **fun and games.** *Ironic or facetious* amusement; frivolous activity. [5] **like fun.** *Informal* **a** (*adverb*) quickly; vigorously. **b** (*interjection*) not at all! certainly not! [6] **make fun of** *or* **poke fun at.** to ridicule or deride. [7] (*modifier*) full of amusement, diversion, gaiety, etc.: *a fun sport*. ◆ VERB **funs, funning, funned.** [8] (*intr*) *Informal* to act in a joking or sporting manner.
▷HISTORY C17: perhaps from obsolete *fon* to make a fool of; see FOND¹

funambulist (fju:'næmbjʊlɪst) NOUN a tightrope walker.
▷HISTORY C18: from Latin *fūnambulus* rope dancer, from *fūnis* rope + *ambulāre* to walk
▸ **fu'nambulism** NOUN

Funchal (*Portuguese* fũ'ʃal) NOUN the capital and chief port of the Madeira Islands, on the S coast of Madeira. Pop.: 44 110 (latest est.).

function ('fʌŋkʃən) NOUN [1] the natural action or intended purpose of a person or thing in a specific role: *the function of a hammer is to hit nails into wood*. [2] an official or formal social gathering or ceremony. [3] a factor dependent upon another or other factors: *the length of the flight is a function of the weather*. [4] Also called: **map, mapping.** *Maths, logic* a relation between two sets that associates a unique element (the value) of the second (the range) with each element (the argument) of the first (the domain): a many-one relation. Symbol: f(x) The value of f(x) for x = 2 is f(2). ◆ VERB (*intr*) [5] to operate or perform as specified; work properly. [6] (foll by *as*) to perform the action or role (of something or someone else): *a coin may function as a screwdriver*.
▷HISTORY C16: from Latin *functiō*, from *fungī* to perform, discharge
▸ **'functionless** ADJECTIVE

functional ('fʌŋkʃənᵊl) ADJECTIVE [1] of, involving, or containing a function or functions. [2] practical rather than decorative; utilitarian: *functional architecture*. [3] capable of functioning; working. [4] *Psychol* **a** relating to the purpose or context of a behaviour. **b** denoting a psychosis such as schizophrenia assumed not to have a direct organic cause, like deterioration or poisoning of the brain. ◆ NOUN [5] *Maths* a function whose domain is a set of functions and whose range is a set of functions or a set of numbers.
▸ **'functionally** ADVERB

functional calculus NOUN another name for **predicate calculus.**

functional disease NOUN a disease in which there is no observable change in the structure of an organ or part. Compare **organic disease.**

functional food NOUN a food containing additives which provide extra nutritional value. Also called: **nutraceutical.**

functional group NOUN *Chem* the group of atoms in a compound, such as the hydroxyl group in an alcohol, that determines the chemical behaviour of the compound.

functional illiterate NOUN a person whose literacy is insufficient for most work and normal daily situations.
▸ **functional illiteracy** NOUN

functionalism ('fʌŋkʃənə,lɪzəm) NOUN [1] the theory of design that the form of a thing should be determined by its use. [2] any doctrine that stresses utility or purpose. [3] *Psychol* a system of thought based on the premise that all mental processes derive from their usefulness to the organism in adapting to the environment.
▸ **'functionalist** NOUN, ADJECTIVE

functionality (,fʌŋkʃən'alɪtɪ) NOUN [1] the quality of being functional. [2] *Computing* a function or range of functions in a computer, program, package, etc.

functionary ('fʌŋkʃənərɪ) NOUN, *plural* **-aries**. [1] a person acting in an official capacity, as for a government; an official. ◆ ADJECTIVE [2] a less common word for **functional** or **official.**

function key NOUN *Computing* a key on the keyboard of a microcomputer, etc. that gives special commands to the computer.

function shift *or* **change** NOUN [1] *Grammar* a change in the syntactic function of a word, as when the noun *mushroom* is used as an intransitive verb. [2] *Linguistics* sound change involving a realignment of the phonemic system of a language.

function word NOUN *Grammar* a word, such as *the*, with a particular grammatical role but little identifiable meaning. Compare **content word, grammatical meaning.**

fund (fʌnd) NOUN [1] a reserve of money, etc., set aside for a certain purpose. [2] a supply or store of something; stock: *it exhausted his fund of wisdom*. ◆ VERB (*tr*) [3] to furnish money to in the form of a fund. [4] to place or store up in a fund. [5] to convert (short-term floating debt) into long-term debt bearing fixed interest and represented by bonds. [6] to provide a fund for the redemption of principal or payment of interest of. [7] to accumulate a fund for the discharge of (a recurrent liability): *to fund a pension plan*. [8] to invest (money) in government securities. See also **funds.**
▷HISTORY C17: from Latin *fundus* the bottom, piece of land, estate; compare FOND²
▸ **'funder** NOUN

fundament ('fʌndəmənt) NOUN [1] *Euphemistic or facetious* the buttocks. [2] the natural features of the earth's surface, unaltered by man. [3] a base or foundation, esp of a building. [4] a theory, principle, or underlying basis.
▷HISTORY C13: from Latin *fundāmentum* foundation, from *fundāre* to FOUND²

fundamental (,fʌndə'mɛntᵊl) ADJECTIVE [1] of, involving, or comprising a foundation; basic. [2] of, involving, or comprising a source; primary. [3] *Music* denoting or relating to the principal or lowest note of a harmonic series. [4] of or concerned with the component of lowest frequency in a complex vibration. ◆ NOUN [5] a principle, law, etc., that serves as the basis of an idea or system. [6] **a** the principal or lowest note of a harmonic series. **b** the bass note of a chord in root position. [7] Also called: **fundamental frequency, first harmonic.** *Physics* **a** the component of lowest frequency in a complex vibration. **b** the frequency of this component.
▸ **,fundamen'tality** *or* **,funda'mentalness** NOUN

fundamental constant NOUN a physical constant, such as the gravitational constant or speed of light, that plays a fundamental role in physics and chemistry and usually has an accurately known value.

fundamental interaction NOUN any of the four basic interactions that occur in nature: the gravitational, electromagnetic, strong, and weak interactions.

fundamentalism (,fʌndə'mɛntə,lɪzəm) NOUN [1] *Christianity* (esp among certain Protestant sects) the belief that every word of the Bible is divinely inspired and therefore true. [2] *Islam* a movement favouring strict observance of the teachings of the Koran and Islamic law. [3] strict adherence to the fundamental principles of any set of beliefs.
▸ **,funda'mentalist** NOUN, ADJECTIVE ▸ **,funda,mental'istic** ADJECTIVE

fundamental law NOUN the law determining the constitution of the government of a state; organic law.

fundamentally (,fʌndə'mɛntᵊlɪ) ADVERB [1] in a way that affects the basis or essentials; utterly: *the terms of engagement have been fundamentally altered*. [2] (*sentence modifier*) in essence; at heart: *fundamentally, we want our lives to be safe*.

fundamental particle NOUN another name for **elementary particle.**

fundamental unit NOUN one of a set of unrelated units that form the basis of a system of units. For example, the metre, kilogram, and second are fundamental units of the SI system.

funded debt NOUN the part of the national debt, consisting mostly of consols, that the government has no obligation to repay by a specified date.

fundholding ('fʌnd,həʊldɪŋ) NOUN (formerly, in the National Health Service in Britain) the system enabling general practitioners to receive a fixed budget from which to pay for primary care, drugs, and nonurgent hospital treatment for patients.
▸ **'fund,holder** NOUN

fundi¹ ('fʊndi:) NOUN *E African* a person skilled in repairing or maintaining machinery; mechanic.
▷HISTORY C20: from Swahili

fundi² ('fʊndi:) NOUN *South African* an expert.
▷HISTORY C20: from Nguni *umfindisi* a teacher

fundie ('fʌndɪ) NOUN *Austral derogatory slang* a fundamentalist Christian.

funding operations PLURAL NOUN *Finance* the conversion of government floating stock or short-term debt into holdings of long-term bonds.

fund manager NOUN an employee of an insurance company, pension fund, investment trust, etc., who manages its fund of investments.

fundraise ('fʌnd,reɪz) VERB (*intr*) to raise money for a cause.

fundraiser ('fʌnd,reɪzə) NOUN [1] a person who raises money for a cause. [2] an event held to raise money for a cause.

funds (fʌndz) PLURAL NOUN [1] money that is readily available. [2] British government securities representing national debt.

fund supermarket NOUN an online facility offering discounted investment opportunities and advice.

fundus ('fʌndəs) NOUN, *plural* **-di** (-daɪ). *Anatomy* the base of an organ or the part farthest away from its opening.
▷HISTORY C18: from Latin, literally: the bottom, a farm, estate
▸ **'fundic** ADJECTIVE

Fundy ('fʌndɪ) NOUN **Bay of.** an inlet of the Atlantic in SE Canada, between S New Brunswick and W Nova Scotia: remarkable for its swift tides of up to 21 m (70 ft.).

funeral ('fju:nərəl) NOUN [1] **a** a ceremony at which a dead person is buried or cremated. **b** (*as modifier*): *a funeral service*. [2] a procession of people escorting a corpse to burial. [3] *Informal* worry; concern; affair: *that's your funeral*.
▷HISTORY C14: from Medieval Latin *fūnerālia*, from Late Latin *fūnerālis* (adjective), from Latin *fūnus* funeral

funeral director NOUN an undertaker.

funeral parlour NOUN a place where the dead are

prepared for burial or cremation. Usual US name: **funeral home.**

funerary ('fju:nərərɪ) ADJECTIVE of, relating to, or for a funeral.

funereal (fju:'nɪərɪəl) ADJECTIVE suggestive of a funeral; gloomy or mournful. Also: **funebrial** (fju:'ni:brɪəl).
▷HISTORY C18: from Latin *fūnereus*
▸**fu'nereally** ADVERB

funfair ('fʌn,fɛə) NOUN *Brit* an amusement park or fairground.

fun fur NOUN a relatively inexpensive synthetic fur garment.

fungal ('fʌŋgəl) ADJECTIVE of, derived from, or caused by a fungus or fungi: *fungal spores; a fungal disease.*

fungi ('fʌŋgaɪ, 'fʌndʒaɪ, 'fʌndʒɪ) NOUN a plural of **fungus.**

fungi- *or before a vowel* **fung-** COMBINING FORM fungus: *fungicide; fungoid.*

fungible ('fʌndʒɪbəl) *Law* ◆ NOUN 1 (*often plural*) moveable perishable goods of a sort that may be estimated by number or weight, such as grain, wine, etc. ◆ ADJECTIVE 2 having the nature or quality of fungibles.
▷HISTORY C18: from Medieval Latin *fungibilis*, from Latin *fungī* to perform; see FUNCTION
▸,**fungi'bility** NOUN

fungible issue NOUN *Finance* a bond issued by a company on the same terms as a bond previously issued by that company, although the redemption yield will probably be different.

fungicide ('fʌndʒɪ,saɪd) NOUN a substance or agent that destroys or is capable of destroying fungi.
▸,**fungi'cidal** ADJECTIVE

fungiform ('fʌndʒɪ,fɔ:m) ADJECTIVE shaped like a mushroom or similar fungus: *the fungiform papillae of the tongue.*

fungistat ('fʌndʒɪ,stæt) NOUN a substance that inhibits the growth of fungi.
▸,**fungi'static** ADJECTIVE

fungoid ('fʌŋgɔɪd) ADJECTIVE resembling a fungus or fungi: *a fungoid growth.*

fungous ('fʌŋgəs) ADJECTIVE 1 appearing suddenly and spreading quickly like a fungus, but not lasting. 2 a less common word for **fungal.**

fungus ('fʌŋgəs) NOUN, *plural* **fungi** ('fʌŋgaɪ, 'fʌndʒaɪ, 'fʌndʒɪ) *or* **funguses.** 1 any member of a kingdom of organisms (Fungi) that lack chlorophyll, leaves, true stems, and roots, reproduce by spores, and live as saprotrophs or parasites. The group includes moulds, mildews, rusts, yeasts, and mushrooms. 2 something resembling a fungus, esp in suddenly growing and spreading rapidly. 3 *Pathol* any soft tumorous growth.
▷HISTORY C16: from Latin: mushroom, fungus; probably related to Greek *spongos* SPONGE
▸**fungic** ('fʌndʒɪk) ADJECTIVE ▸**'fungus-,like** ADJECTIVE

funicle ('fju:nɪkəl) NOUN *Botany* the stalk that attaches an ovule or seed to the wall of the ovary. Also called: **funiculus.**
▷HISTORY C17: from Latin *fūniculus* a thin rope, from *fūnis* rope
▸**funiculate** (fjʊ'nɪkjʊlɪt, -,leɪt) ADJECTIVE

funicular (fju:'nɪkjʊlə) NOUN 1 Also called: **funicular railway.** a railway up the side of a mountain, consisting of two counterbalanced cars at either end of a cable passing round a driving wheel at the summit. ◆ ADJECTIVE 2 relating to or operated by a rope, cable, etc. 3 of or relating to a funicle.

funiculus (fju:'nɪkjʊləs) NOUN, *plural* **-li** (-,laɪ). 1 *Anatomy* a cordlike part or structure, esp a small bundle of nerve fibres in the spinal cord. 2 a variant of **funicle.**
▷HISTORY C17: from Latin; see FUNICLE

funk¹ (fʌŋk) *Informal, chiefly Brit* ◆ NOUN 1 Also called: **blue funk.** a state of nervousness, fear, or depression (esp in the phrase **in a funk**). 2 a coward. ◆ VERB 3 to flinch from (responsibility) through fear. 4 (*tr; usually passive*) to make afraid.
▷HISTORY C18: university slang, perhaps related to FUNK²
▸**'funker** NOUN

funk² (fʌŋk) NOUN *US slang* a strong foul odour.
▷HISTORY C17 (in the sense: tobacco smoke): from *funk* (verb) to smoke (tobacco), probably of French dialect origin; compare Old French *funkier* to smoke, from Latin *fūmigāre*

funk³ (fʌŋk) NOUN *Informal* a type of polyrhythmic Black dance music with heavy syncopation.
▷HISTORY C20: back formation from FUNKY¹

funk hole NOUN *Informal* 1 *Military* a dugout. 2 a job that affords exemption from military service.

funkster ('fʌŋkstə) NOUN 1 a performer or fan of funk music. 2 someone who follows the latest trends in music, ideas, or fashion.

funky¹ ('fʌŋkɪ) ADJECTIVE **funkier, funkiest.** *Informal* 1 (of music) passionate, soulful; of or pertaining to funk. 2 authentic; earthy. 3 stylish and exciting; cool: *funky jeans.*
▷HISTORY C20: from FUNK², perhaps alluding to music that was smelly, that is, earthy (like the early blues)

funky² ('fʌŋkɪ) ADJECTIVE **funkier, funkiest.** *Slang, chiefly US* evil-smelling; foul.
▷HISTORY C18: from FUNK²

funnel ('fʌnəl) NOUN 1 a hollow utensil with a wide mouth tapering to a small hole, used for pouring liquids, powders, etc., into a narrow-necked vessel. 2 something resembling this in shape or function. 3 a smokestack for smoke and exhaust gases, as on a steamship or steam locomotive. 4 a shaft or tube, as in a building, for ventilation. ◆ VERB **-nels, -nelling, -nelled** *or US* **-nels, -neling, -neled.** 5 to move or cause to move or pour through or as if through a funnel. 6 to concentrate or focus or be concentrated or focused in a particular direction: *they funnelled their attention on the problem.* 7 (*intr*) to take on a funnel-like shape.
▷HISTORY C15: from Old Provençal *fonilh*, ultimately from Latin *infundibulum* funnel, hopper (in a mill), from *infundere* to pour in
▸**'funnel-,like** ADJECTIVE

funnel cap NOUN any of various basidiomycetous fungi of the genus *Clitocybe*, characterized by the funnel-shaped caps and, usually, markedly decurrent gills.

funnel cloud NOUN a whirling column of cloud extending downwards from the base of a cumulonimbus cloud: part of a waterspout or tornado.

funnel-web NOUN *Austral* any large poisonous black spider of the family *Dipluridae*, constructing funnel-shaped webs.

funnies ('fʌnɪz) PLURAL NOUN *US and Canadian informal* comic strips in a newspaper.

funny ('fʌnɪ) ADJECTIVE **-nier, -niest.** 1 causing amusement or laughter; humorous; comical. 2 peculiar; odd. 3 suspicious or dubious (esp in the phrase **funny business**). 4 *Informal* faint or ill: *to feel funny.* ◆ NOUN, *plural* **-nies.** 5 *Informal* a joke or witticism.
▸**'funnily** ADVERB ▸**'funniness** NOUN

funny bone NOUN the area near the elbow where the ulnar nerve is close to the surface of the skin: when it is struck, a sharp tingling sensation is experienced along the forearm and hand. Also called (US): **crazy bone.**

funny farm NOUN *Facetious* a mental institution.

funny money NOUN 1 a sum of money so large as to be considered unreal. 2 counterfeit money. 3 *Derogatory* foreign currency.

funny paper NOUN *US and Canadian* a section or separate supplement of a newspaper, etc., containing comic strips.

fun run NOUN a long run or part-marathon run for exercise and pleasure, often by large numbers of people.

fur (fɜ:) NOUN 1 the dense coat of fine silky hairs on such mammals as the cat, seal, and mink. 2 **a** the dressed skin of certain fur-bearing animals, with the hair left on. **b** (*as modifier*): *a fur coat.* 3 a garment made of fur, such as a coat or stole. 4 **a** a pile fabric made in imitation of animal fur. **b** a garment made from such a fabric. 5 *Heraldry* any of various stylized representations of animal pelts or their tinctures, esp ermine or vair, used in coats of arms. 6 **make the fur fly.** to cause a scene or disturbance. 7 *Informal* a whitish coating of cellular debris on the tongue, caused by excessive smoking, an upset stomach, etc. 8 *Brit* a whitish-grey deposit consisting chiefly of calcium carbonate precipitated from hard water onto the insides of pipes, boilers, and kettles. ◆ VERB **furs, furring, furred.** 9 (*tr*) to line or trim a garment, etc., with fur. 10 (often foll by *up*) to cover or become covered with a furlike lining or deposit. 11 (*tr*) to clothe (a person) in a fur garment or garments.
▷HISTORY C14: from Old French *forrer* to line a garment, from *fuerre* sheath, of Germanic origin; related to Old English *fōdder* case, Old Frisian *fōder* coat lining
▸**'furless** ADJECTIVE

fur. ABBREVIATION FOR furlong.

furaldehyde (fjʊə'rældə,haɪd) NOUN either of two aldehydes derived from furan, esp **2-furaldehyde** (see **furfuraldehyde**).
▷HISTORY C20: shortened from *furfuraldehyde*, from *furfurol* (see FURFUR, -OL¹) + ALDEHYDE

furan ('fjʊəræn, fjʊə'ræn) NOUN a colourless flammable toxic liquid heterocyclic compound, used in the manufacture of cotton textiles and in the synthesis of nylon. Formula: C_4H_4O. Also called: **furfuran.**
▷HISTORY C19: shortened form of *furfuran*, from FURFUR

furbelow ('fɜ:bɪ,ləʊ) NOUN 1 a flounce, ruffle, or other ornamental trim. 2 (*often plural*) showy ornamentation. ◆ VERB 3 (*tr*) to put a furbelow on (a garment).
▷HISTORY C18: by folk etymology from French dialect *farbella*; see FALBALA

furbish ('fɜ:bɪʃ) VERB (*tr*) 1 to make bright by polishing; burnish. 2 (often foll by *up*) to improve the appearance or condition of; renovate; restore.
▷HISTORY C14: from Old French *fourbir* to polish, of Germanic origin
▸**'furbisher** NOUN

fur brigade NOUN *Canadian* (formerly) a convoy of canoes, horses, or dog sleighs that transported furs and other goods between trading posts and towns or factories.

furca ('fɜ:kə) NOUN, *plural* **-cae** (-ki:). *Zoology* any forklike structure, esp in insects.
▷HISTORY Latin: fork
▸**'furcal** ADJECTIVE

furcate VERB ('fɜ:keɪt) 1 to divide into two parts; fork. ◆ ADJECTIVE ('fɜ:keɪt, -kɪt) *or* **furcated.** 2 forked; divided: *furcate branches.*
▷HISTORY C19: from Late Latin *furcātus* forked, from Latin *furca* a fork
▸**fur'cation** NOUN

furcula ('fɜ:kjʊlə) *or* **furculum** ('fɜ:kjʊləm) NOUN, *plural* **-lae** (-,li:) *or* **-la** (-lə). any forklike part or organ, esp the fused clavicles (wishbone) of birds.
▷HISTORY C19: from Latin: a forked support for a wall, diminutive of *furca* fork

furfur ('fɜ:fə) NOUN, *plural* **furfures** ('fɜ:fjʊ,ri:z, -fə,ri:z). 1 a scaling of the skin; dandruff. 2 any scale of the epidermis.
▷HISTORY C17: from Latin: bran, scurf

furfuraceous (,fɜ:fjʊ'reɪʃəs, -fə'reɪ-) ADJECTIVE 1 relating to or resembling bran. 2 *Med* resembling dandruff; scaly.
▸,**furfu'raceously** ADVERB

furfuraldehyde (,fɜ:fjə'rældə,haɪd) NOUN a colourless flammable soluble mobile liquid with a penetrating odour, present in oat and rice hulls; 2-furaldehyde: used as a solvent and in the manufacture of resins. Formula: $C_5H_4O_2$. Also called: **furfural.**

furfuran ('fɜ:fə,ræn, 'fɜ:fjʊ-) NOUN another name for **furan.**

Furies ('fjʊərɪz) PLURAL NOUN, *singular* **Fury.** *Classical myth* the snake-haired goddesses of vengeance, usually three in number, who pursued unpunished criminals. Also called: **Erinyes, Eumenides.**

furioso (,fjʊərɪ'əʊsəʊ) *Music* ◆ ADJECTIVE, ADVERB 1 in a frantically rushing manner. ◆ NOUN 2 a passage or piece to be performed in this way.
▷HISTORY C19: Italian, literally: furious; see FURY

furious ('fjʊərɪəs) ADJECTIVE 1 extremely angry or annoyed; raging. 2 violent, wild, or unrestrained, as in speed, vigour, energy, etc.
▸**'furiously** ADVERB ▸**'furiousness** NOUN

furl (fɜ:l) VERB 1 to roll up (an umbrella, a flag, etc.) neatly and securely or (of an umbrella, flag,

etc.) to be rolled up in this way. 2 (tr) *Nautical* to gather in (a square sail). ◆ NOUN 3 the act or an instance of furling. 4 a single rolled-up section.
▷HISTORY C16: from Old French *ferlier* to bind tightly, from *ferm* tight (from Latin *firmus* FIRM[1]) + *lier* to tie, bind, from Latin *ligāre*
▸ 'furlable ADJECTIVE ▸ 'furler NOUN

furlong ('fɜːˌlɒŋ) NOUN a unit of length equal to 220 yards (201.168 metres).
▷HISTORY Old English *furlang*, from *furh* FURROW + *lang* LONG[1]

furlough ('fɜːləʊ) NOUN 1 leave of absence from military duty. 2 *US* a temporary laying-off of employees, usually because there is insufficient work to occupy them. ◆ VERB (tr) 3 to grant a furlough to. 4 *US* to lay off (staff) temporarily.
▷HISTORY C17: from Dutch *verlof*, from *ver-* FOR- + *lof* leave, permission; related to Swedish *förlof*

furmenty ('fɜːməntɪ) *or* **furmity** ('fɜːmɪtɪ) NOUN variants of **frumenty**.

furnace ('fɜːnɪs) NOUN 1 an enclosed chamber in which heat is produced to generate steam, destroy refuse, smelt or refine ores, etc. 2 a very hot or stifling place.
▷HISTORY C13: from Old French *fornais*, from Latin *fornax* oven, furnace; related to Latin *formus* warm
▸ 'furnace-ˌlike ADJECTIVE

Furness ('fɜːnɪs) NOUN a region in NW England in Cumbria, forming a peninsula between the Irish Sea and Morecambe Bay.

furnish ('fɜːnɪʃ) VERB (tr) 1 to provide (a house, room, etc.) with furniture, carpets, etc. 2 to equip with what is necessary; fit out. 3 to give; supply: *the records furnished the information required.*
▷HISTORY C15: from Old French *fournir*, of Germanic origin; related to Old High German *frummen* to carry out
▸ 'furnisher NOUN

furnishings ('fɜːnɪʃɪŋz) PLURAL NOUN 1 furniture and accessories, including carpets and curtains, with which a room, house, etc., is furnished. 2 *US and Canadian* articles of dress and accessories.

furniture ('fɜːnɪtʃə) NOUN 1 the movable, generally functional, articles that equip a room, house, etc. 2 the equipment necessary for a ship, factory, etc. 3 *Printing* lengths of wood, plastic, or metal, used in assembling formes to create the blank areas and to surround the type. 4 the wooden parts of a rifle. 5 *Obsolete* the full armour, trappings, etc., for a man and horse. 6 the attitudes or characteristics that are typical of a person or thing: *the furniture of the murderer's mind.* 7 **part of the furniture.** *Informal* someone or something that is so long established in an environment as to be accepted as an integral part of it: *he has been here so long that he is part of the furniture.* 8 See **door furniture** and **street furniture**.
▷HISTORY C16: from French *fourniture*, from *fournir* to equip, FURNISH

furniture beetle NOUN See **anobiid.**

furore (fjʊ'rɔːrɪ) *or esp US* **furor** ('fjʊərɔː) NOUN 1 a public outburst, esp of protest; uproar. 2 a sudden widespread enthusiasm for something; craze. 3 frenzy; rage; madness.
▷HISTORY C15: from Latin: frenzy, rage, from *furere* to rave

furphy ('fɜːfɪ) NOUN, *plural* **-phies.** *Austral slang* a rumour or fictitious story.
▷HISTORY C20: from *Furphy* carts (used for water or sewage in World War I), made at a foundry established by the Furphy family

furred (fɜːd) ADJECTIVE 1 made of, lined with, or covered in fur. 2 wearing fur. 3 (of animals) having fur. 4 another word for **furry** (sense 4). 5 Also: **furry.** provided with furring strips. 6 (of a pipe, kettle, etc.) lined with hard lime or other salts deposited from water.

furrier ('fʌrɪə) NOUN a person whose occupation is selling, making, dressing, or repairing fur garments.
▷HISTORY C14: *furour*, from Old French *fourrer* to trim or line with FUR

furriery ('fʌrɪərɪ) NOUN, *plural* **-eries.** 1 the occupation of a furrier. 2 furs worn as a garment or trim collectively.

furring ('fɜːrɪŋ) NOUN 1 **a** short for **furring strip. b** the fixing of furring strips. **c** furring strips collectively. 2 the formation of fur on the tongue. 3 trimming of animal fur, as on a coat or other garment, or furs collectively.

furring strip NOUN a strip of wood or metal fixed to a wall, floor, or ceiling to provide a surface for the fixing of plasterboard, floorboards, etc. Sometimes shortened to **furring.**

furrow ('fʌrəʊ) NOUN 1 a long narrow trench made in the ground by a plough or a trench resembling this. 2 any long deep groove, esp a deep wrinkle on the forehead. ◆ VERB 3 to develop or cause to develop furrows or wrinkles. 4 to make a furrow or furrows in (land).
▷HISTORY Old English *furh*; related to Old Frisian *furch*, Old Norse *for*, Old High German *furuh* furrow, Latin *porca* ridge between furrows
▸ 'furrower NOUN ▸ 'furrowless ADJECTIVE ▸ 'furrow-ˌlike *or* 'furrowy ADJECTIVE

furry ('fɜːrɪ) ADJECTIVE **-rier, -riest.** 1 covered with fur or something furlike. 2 of, relating to, or resembling fur. 3 another word for **furred** (sense 5). 4 Also: **furred.** (of the tongue) coated with whitish cellular debris.
▸ 'furrily ADVERB ▸ 'furriness NOUN

fur seal NOUN any of various eared seals, esp of the genus *Arctocephalus*, that have a fine dense underfur and are hunted as a source of sealskin.

furth (fʌrθ) ADVERB *Scot* out; outside; to the outside.
▷HISTORY a Scot variant of FORTH

further ('fɜːðə) ADVERB 1 in addition; furthermore. 2 to a greater degree or extent. 3 to or at a more advanced point. 4 to or at a greater distance in time or space; farther. ◆ ADJECTIVE 5 additional; more. 6 more distant or remote in time or space; farther. ◆ VERB 7 (tr) to assist the progress of; promote. ◆ See also **far, furthest.**
▷HISTORY Old English *furthor*; related to Old Frisian *further*, Old Saxon *furthor*, Old High German *furdar*; see FORTH
▸ 'furtherer NOUN

Language note See at **farther.**

furtherance ('fɜːðərəns) NOUN 1 the act of furthering; advancement. 2 something that furthers or advances.

further education NOUN (in Britain) formal education beyond school other than at a university or polytechnic.

furthermore ('fɜːðəˌmɔː) ADVERB in addition; moreover.

furthermost ('fɜːðəˌməʊst) ADJECTIVE most distant; furthest.

furthest ('fɜːðɪst) ADVERB 1 to the greatest degree or extent. 2 to or at the greatest distance in time or space; farthest. ◆ ADJECTIVE 3 most distant or remote in time or space; farthest.

furtive ('fɜːtɪv) ADJECTIVE characterized by stealth; sly and secretive.
▷HISTORY C15: from Latin *furtīvus* stolen, clandestine, from *furtum* a theft, from *fūr* a thief; related to Greek *phōr* thief
▸ 'furtively ADVERB ▸ 'furtiveness NOUN

furuncle ('fjʊərʌŋkᵊl) NOUN *Pathol* the technical name for **boil.**
▷HISTORY C17: from Latin *fūrunculus* pilferer, petty thief, sore on the body, from *fūr* thief
▸ **furuncular** (fjʊ'rʌŋkjʊlə) *or* **fu'runculous** ADJECTIVE

furunculosis (fjʊˌrʌŋkjʊ'ləʊsɪs) NOUN 1 a skin condition characterized by the presence of multiple boils. 2 an infectious ulcerative disease of salmon and trout caused by the bacterium *Aeromonas salmonicida.*

fury ('fjʊərɪ) NOUN, *plural* **-ries.** 1 violent or uncontrolled anger; wild rage. 2 an outburst of such anger. 3 uncontrolled violence: *the fury of the storm.* 4 a person, esp. a woman, with a violent temper. 5 See **Furies.** 6 **like fury.** *Informal* violently; furiously: *they rode like fury.*
▷HISTORY C14: from Latin *furia* rage, from *furere* to be furious

furze (fɜːz) NOUN another name for **gorse.**
▷HISTORY Old English *fyrs*
▸ 'furzy ADJECTIVE

fusain (fjuː'zeɪn; *French* fyzɛ̃) NOUN 1 a fine charcoal pencil or stick made from the spindle tree. 2 a drawing done with such a pencil. 3 a dull black brittle form of carbon resembling charcoal, found in certain coals.
▷HISTORY C19: from French: spindle tree or charcoal made from it, from Vulgar Latin *fūsāgō* (unattested) a spindle (generally made from the spindle tree), from Latin *fūsus*

fuscous ('fʌskəs) ADJECTIVE of a brownish-grey colour.
▷HISTORY C17: from Latin *fuscus* dark, swarthy, tawny

fuse[1] *or US* **fuze** (fjuːz) NOUN 1 a lead of combustible black powder in a waterproof covering (**safety fuse**), or a lead containing an explosive (**detonating fuse**), used to fire an explosive charge. 2 any device by which an explosive charge is ignited. 3 **blow a fuse.** See **blow[1]** (sense 12). ◆ VERB 4 (tr) to provide or equip with such a fuse.
▷HISTORY C17: from Italian *fuso* spindle, from Latin *fūsus*
▸ 'fuseless ADJECTIVE

fuse[2] (fjuːz) VERB 1 to unite or become united by melting, esp by the action of heat: *to fuse borax and copper sulphate at a high temperature.* 2 to become or cause to become liquid, esp by the action of heat; melt. 3 to join or become combined; integrate. 4 (tr) to equip (an electric circuit, plug, etc.) with a fuse. 5 *Brit* to fail or cause to fail as a result of the blowing of a fuse: *the lights fused.* ◆ NOUN 6 a protective device for safeguarding electric circuits, etc., containing a wire that melts and breaks the circuit when the current exceeds a certain value.
▷HISTORY C17: from Latin *fūsus* melted, cast, poured out, from *fundere* to pour out, shed; sense 5 influenced by FUSE[1]

fuse box NOUN a housing for electric fuses.

fusee *or* **fuzee** (fjuː'ziː) NOUN 1 (in early clocks and watches) a spirally grooved spindle, functioning as an equalizing force on the unwinding of the mainspring. 2 a friction match with a large head, capable of remaining alight in a wind. 3 an explosive fuse.
▷HISTORY C16: from French *fusée* spindleful of thread, from Old French *fus* spindle, from Latin *fūsus*

fuselage ('fjuːzɪˌlɑːʒ) NOUN the main body of an aircraft, excluding the wings, tailplane, and fin.
▷HISTORY C20: from French, from *fuseler* to shape like a spindle, from Old French *fusel* spindle; see FUSEE

fusel oil *or* **fusel** ('fjuːzᵊl) NOUN a mixture of amyl alcohols, propanol, and butanol: a by-product in the distillation of fermented liquors used as a source of amyl alcohols.
▷HISTORY C19: from German *Fusel* bad spirits

Fushun ('fuː'ʃʌn) NOUN a city in NE China, in central Liaoning province near Shenyang: situated on one of the richest coalfields in the world; site of the largest thermal power plant in NE Asia. Pop.: 1 271 113 (1999 est.).

fusible ('fjuːzəbᵊl) ADJECTIVE capable of being fused or melted.
▸ ˌfusi'bility *or* 'fusibleness NOUN ▸ 'fusibly ADVERB

fusible metal *or* **alloy** NOUN any of various alloys with low melting points that contain bismuth, lead, and tin. They are used as solders and in safety devices.

fusiform ('fjuːzɪˌfɔːm) ADJECTIVE elongated and tapering at both ends; spindle-shaped.
▷HISTORY C18: from Latin *fūsus* spindle

fusil[1] ('fjuːzɪl) NOUN a light flintlock musket.
▷HISTORY C16 (in the sense: steel for a tinderbox): from Old French *fuisil*, from Vulgar Latin *focīlis* (unattested), from Latin *focus* fire

fusil[2] ('fjuːzɪl) NOUN *Heraldry* a charge shaped like a lengthened lozenge.
▷HISTORY C15: from Old French *fusel*, ultimately from Latin *fūsus* spindle, FUSE[1] (the heraldic lozenge originally represented a spindle covered with tow for spinning)

fusile ('fjuːzaɪl) *or* **fusil** ADJECTIVE 1 easily melted; fusible. 2 formed by casting or melting; founded.
▷HISTORY C14: from Latin *fūsilis* molten, from *fundere* to pour out, melt

fusilier (ˌfjuːzɪ'lɪə) NOUN 1 (formerly) an infantryman armed with a light musket. 2 Also: **fusileer. a** a soldier, esp a private, serving in any of

certain British or other infantry regiments. **b** (*pl; cap. when part of a name*): *the Royal Welch Fusiliers*.
▷HISTORY C17: from French; see FUSIL[1]

fusillade (ˌfjuːzɪˈleɪd, -ˈlɑːd) NOUN [1] a simultaneous or rapid continual discharge of firearms. [2] a sudden outburst, as of criticism. ◆ VERB [3] (*tr*) to attack with a fusillade.
▷HISTORY C19: from French, from *fusiller* to shoot; see FUSIL[1]

fusion (ˈfjuːʒən) NOUN [1] the act or process of fusing or melting together; union. [2] the state of being fused. [3] something produced by fusing. [4] See **nuclear fusion.** [5] the merging of juxtaposed speech sounds, morphemes, or words. [6] a coalition of political parties or other groups, esp to support common candidates at an election. [7] a kind of popular music that is a blend of two or more styles, such as jazz and funk. [8] *Psychol* the processing by the mind of elements falling on the two eyes so that they yield a single percept. [9] (*modifier*) relating to a style of cooking which combines traditional Western techniques and ingredients with those used in Eastern cuisine: *fusion cuisine*; *fusion food*.
▷HISTORY C16: from Latin *fūsiō* a pouring out, melting, casting, from *fundere* to pour out, FOUND[3]

fusion bomb NOUN a type of bomb in which most of the energy is provided by nuclear fusion, esp the fusion of hydrogen isotopes. Also called: **thermonuclear bomb, fission-fusion bomb.** See also **hydrogen bomb.**

fusionism (ˈfjuːʒəˌnɪzəm) NOUN the favouring of coalitions among political groups.
▸ **ˈfusionist** NOUN, ADJECTIVE

fusion reactor NOUN a nuclear reactor in which a thermonuclear fusion reaction takes place.

fuss (fʌs) NOUN [1] nervous activity or agitation, esp when disproportionate or unnecessary. [2] complaint or objection: *he made a fuss over the bill*. [3] an exhibition of affection or admiration, esp if excessive: *they made a great fuss over the new baby*. [4] a quarrel; dispute. ◆ VERB [5] (*intr*) to worry unnecessarily. [6] (*intr*) to be excessively concerned over trifles. [7] (when *intr*, usually foll by *over*) to show great or excessive concern, affection, etc. (for). [8] (*intr;* foll by *with*) *Jamaican* to quarrel violently. [9] (*tr*) to bother (a person).
▷HISTORY C18: of uncertain origin
▸ **ˈfusser** NOUN

fusspot (ˈfʌsˌpɒt) NOUN *Brit informal* a person who fusses unnecessarily. Also called (US): **fuss-budget.**

fussy (ˈfʌsɪ) ADJECTIVE **fussier, fussiest.** [1] inclined to fuss over minor points. [2] very particular about detail. [3] characterized by overelaborate detail: *the furniture was too fussy to be elegant*.
▸ **ˈfussily** ADVERB ▸ **ˈfussiness** NOUN

fustanella (ˌfʌstəˈnɛlə) *or* **fustanelle** NOUN a white knee-length pleated skirt worn by men in Greece and Albania.
▷HISTORY C19: from Italian, from Modern Greek *phoustani*, probably from Italian *fustagno* FUSTIAN

fustian (ˈfʌstɪən) NOUN [1] **a** a hard-wearing fabric of cotton mixed with flax or wool with a slight nap. **b** (*as modifier*): *a fustian jacket*. [2] pompous or pretentious talk or writing. ◆ ADJECTIVE [3] cheap; worthless. [4] pompous; bombastic.
▷HISTORY C12: from Old French *fustaigne*, from Medieval Latin *fustāneum*, from Latin *fustis* cudgel

fustic (ˈfʌstɪk) NOUN [1] Also called: **old fustic. a** large tropical American moraceous tree, *Chlorophora tinctoria*. [2] the yellow dye obtained from the wood of this tree. [3] any of various trees or shrubs that yield a similar dye, esp *Rhus cotinus* (**young fustic**), a European sumach.
▷HISTORY C15: from French *fustoc*, from Spanish, from Arabic *fustuq*, from Greek *pistakē* pistachio tree

fustigate (ˈfʌstɪˌgeɪt) VERB (*tr*) *Archaic* to beat; cudgel.
▷HISTORY C17: from Late Latin *fūstīgāre* to cudgel to death, from Latin *fūstis* cudgel
▸ **ˌfustiˈgation** NOUN ▸ **ˈfustiˌgator** NOUN ▸ **ˈfustiˌgatory** ADJECTIVE

fusty (ˈfʌstɪ) ADJECTIVE **-tier, -tiest.** [1] smelling of damp or mould; musty. [2] old-fashioned in attitude.
▷HISTORY C14: from *fust* wine cask, from Old French: cask, tree trunk, from Latin *fūstis* cudgel, club

▸ **ˈfustily** ADVERB ▸ **ˈfustiness** NOUN

futhark, futharc (ˈfuːθɑːk), **futhorc,** *or* **futhork** (ˈfuːθɔːk) NOUN a phonetic alphabet consisting of runes.
▷HISTORY C19: from the first six letters: *f, u, th, a, r, k*; compare ALPHABET

futile (ˈfjuːtaɪl) ADJECTIVE [1] having no effective result; unsuccessful. [2] pointless; unimportant; trifling. [3] inane or foolish: *don't be so futile!*
▷HISTORY C16: from Latin *futtilis* pouring out easily, worthless, from *fundere* to pour out
▸ **ˈfutilely** ADVERB ▸ **ˈfutileness** NOUN

futilitarian (fjuːˌtɪlɪˈtɛərɪən) ADJECTIVE [1] of or relating to the belief that human endeavour can serve no useful purpose. ◆ NOUN [2] one who holds this belief.
▷HISTORY C19: facetious coinage from FUTILE + UTILITARIAN
▸ **fuˌtiliˈtarianˌism** NOUN

futility (fjuːˈtɪlɪtɪ) NOUN, *plural* **-ties.** [1] lack of effectiveness or success. [2] lack of purpose or meaning. [3] something futile.

futon (ˈfuːˌtɒn) NOUN a Japanese padded quilt, laid on the floor for use as a bed.
▷HISTORY C19: from Japanese

futtock (ˈfʌtək) NOUN *Nautical* one of the ribs in the frame of a wooden vessel.
▷HISTORY C13: perhaps variant of *foothook*

futtock plate NOUN *Nautical* a horizontal metal disc fixed at the top of a lower mast for holding the futtock shrouds.

futtock shroud NOUN *Nautical* any of several metal rods serving as a brace between the futtock plate on a lower mast and the topmast.

future (ˈfjuːtʃə) NOUN [1] the time yet to come. [2] undetermined events that will occur in that time. [3] the condition of a person or thing at a later date: *the future of the school is undecided*. [4] likelihood of later improvement or advancement: *he has a future as a singer*. [5] *Grammar* **a** a tense of verbs used when the action or event described is to occur after the time of utterance. **b** a verb in this tense. [6] **in future.** from now on; henceforth. ◆ ADJECTIVE [7] that is yet to come or be. [8] of or expressing time yet to come. [9] (*prenominal*) destined to become: *a future president*. [10] *Grammar* in or denoting the future as a tense of verbs. ◆ See also **futures.**
▷HISTORY C14: from Latin *fūtūrus* about to be, from *esse* to be
▸ **ˈfutureless** ADJECTIVE

future life NOUN a life after death; afterlife.

future perfect *Grammar* ◆ ADJECTIVE [1] denoting a tense of verbs describing an action that will have been performed by a certain time. In English this is formed with *will have* or *shall have* plus the past participle. ◆ NOUN [2] **a** the future perfect tense. **b** a verb in this tense.

future-proof ADJECTIVE (of a system, computer, program, etc.) guaranteed not to be superseded by future versions, developments, etc.

futures (ˈfjuːtʃəz) PLURAL NOUN **a** commodities or other financial products bought or sold at an agreed price for delivery at a specified future date. See also **financial futures. b** (*as modifier*): *futures contract*; *futures market*.

future value NOUN the value that a sum of money invested at compound interest will have after a specified period.

futurism (ˈfjuːtʃəˌrɪzəm) NOUN an artistic movement that arose in Italy in 1909 to replace traditional aesthetic values with the characteristics of the machine age.
▸ **ˈfuturist** NOUN, ADJECTIVE

futuristic (ˌfjuːtʃəˈrɪstɪk) ADJECTIVE [1] denoting or relating to design, technology, etc., that is thought likely to be current or fashionable at some future time; ultramodern. [2] of or relating to futurism.
▸ **ˌfuturˈistically** ADVERB

futurity (fjuːˈtjʊərɪtɪ) NOUN, *plural* **-ties.** [1] a less common word for **future.** [2] the quality of being in the future. [3] a future event.

futurology (ˌfjuːtʃəˈrɒlədʒɪ) NOUN the study or prediction of the future of mankind.
▸ **ˌfuturˈologist** NOUN

fuze (fjuːz) NOUN *Chiefly US* a variant spelling of **fuse.**

fuzee (fjuːˈziː) NOUN a variant spelling of **fusee.**

fuzz[1] (fʌz) NOUN [1] a mass or covering of fine or curly hairs, fibres, etc. [2] a blur. ◆ VERB [3] to make or become fuzzy. [4] to make or become indistinct; blur.
▷HISTORY C17: perhaps from Low German *fussig* loose

fuzz[2] (fʌz) NOUN a slang word for **police** or **policeman.**
▷HISTORY C20: of uncertain origin

fuzz box NOUN *Music* an electronic device that breaks up the sound passing through it, used esp by guitarists.

fuzzy (ˈfʌzɪ) ADJECTIVE **fuzzier, fuzziest.** [1] of, resembling, or covered with fuzz. [2] indistinct; unclear or distorted. [3] not clearly thought out or expressed. [4] (of the hair) tightly curled or very wavy. [5] *Maths* of or relating to a form of set theory in which set membership depends on a likelihood function: *fuzzy set*; *fuzzy logic*. [6] (of a computer program or system) designed to operate according to the principles of fuzzy logic, so as to be able to deal with data which is imprecise or has uncertain boundaries.
▸ **ˈfuzzily** ADVERB ▸ **ˈfuzziness** NOUN

fuzzy logic NOUN a branch of logic designed to allow degrees of imprecision in reasoning and knowledge, typified by terms such as 'very', 'quite possibly', and 'unlikely', to be represented in such a way that the information can be processed by computer.

fuzzy-wuzzy (ˈfʌzɪˌwʌzɪ) NOUN, *plural* **-wuzzies** *or* **-wuzzy.** *Archaic, offensive slang* a Black fuzzy-haired native of any of various countries.

fuzzy-wuzzy angel NOUN *Austral informal* any native of Papua New Guinea who assisted as a stretcher-bearer in World War II.

fv ABBREVIATION FOR folio verso.
▷HISTORY Latin: on the reverse (that is left-hand) page

FWA NOUN flexible working arrangement: an agreement between an employer and employee that the employee's working hours may be adapted to suit his or her particular needs.

fwd ABBREVIATION FOR forward.

FWD *Text messaging* ABBREVIATION FOR forward.

f.w.d. ABBREVIATION FOR: [1] four-wheel drive. [2] front-wheel drive.

FWIW *Text messaging* ABBREVIATION FOR for what it's worth.

f-word NOUN (*sometimes capital;* preceded by *the*) a euphemistic way of referring to the word **fuck.**

FX NOUN [1] *Films, informal* short for **special effects.** [2] (in the US and Canada) ABBREVIATION FOR foreign exchange.
▷HISTORY C20: (for sense 1) a phonetic respelling of EFFECTS

-fy SUFFIX FORMING VERBS to make or become: *beautify*; *simplify*; *liquefy*.
▷HISTORY from Old French *-fier*, from Latin *-ficāre*, verbal ending formed from *-ficus* -FIC

FYI *Text messaging* ABBREVIATION FOR for your information.

fyke (faɪk) NOUN *US* a fish trap consisting of a net suspended over a series of hoops, laid horizontally in the water.
▷HISTORY C19: from Middle Dutch *fuycke*

Fylde (faɪld) NOUN a region in NW England in Lancashire between the Wyre and Ribble estuaries.

fylfot (ˈfaɪlfɒt) NOUN a rare word for **swastika.**
▷HISTORY C16 (apparently meaning: a sign or device for the lower part or foot of a painted window): from *fillen* to FILL + *fot* FOOT

fyrd (fɪəd, faɪəd) NOUN *History* the local militia of an Anglo-Saxon shire, in which all freemen had to serve.

FYROM ABBREVIATION FOR Former Yugoslav Republic of Macedonia.

FZS ABBREVIATION FOR Fellow of the Zoological Society.

Gg

g *or* **G** (dʒiː) NOUN, *plural* **g's, G's** *or* **Gs.** [1] the seventh letter and fifth consonant of the modern English alphabet. [2] a speech sound represented by this letter, in English usually either a voiced velar stop, as in *grass*, or a voiced palato-alveolar affricate, as in *page*.

g SYMBOL FOR: [1] gallon(s). [2] gram(s). [3] acceleration of free fall (due to gravity) near the surface of the earth. [4] grav. [5] *Chess* See **algebraic notation.**

G SYMBOL FOR: [1] *Music* **a** a note having a frequency of 392 hertz (**G above middle C**) or this value multiplied or divided by any power of 2; the fifth note of the scale of C major. **b** a key, string, or pipe producing this note. **c** the major or minor key having this note as its tonic. [2] gauss. [3] gravitational constant. [4] *Physics* conductance. [5] *Biochem* guanine. [6] German. [7] Gibbs function. [8] giga. [9] good. [10] *Slang, chiefly US* grand (a thousand dollars or pounds). [11] (in Australia) **a** general exhibition (used to describe a category of film certified as suitable for viewing by anyone). **b** (*as modifier*): *a G film.*

G. *or* **g.** ABBREVIATION FOR: [1] Gulf. [2] guilder(s). [3] guinea(s).

2G ABBREVIATION FOR second generation; a system for mobile phones characterized by digital technology, Internet access, and a short-message service.

3G ABBREVIATION FOR third generation; a system for mobile phones allowing fast connection, Internet access, digital photography, graphics transmission and display, and other advanced features.

G3 ABBREVIATION FOR Group of Three.

G5 ABBREVIATION FOR Group of Five.

G7 ABBREVIATION FOR Group of Seven.

G8 ABBREVIATION FOR Group of Eight.

G9 *Text messaging* ABBREVIATION FOR genius.

G10 ABBREVIATION FOR Group of Ten.

G24 ABBREVIATION FOR Group of Twenty-Four.

G77 ABBREVIATION FOR Group of Seventy-Seven.

ga THE INTERNET DOMAIN NAME FOR Gabon.

Ga[1] THE CHEMICAL SYMBOL FOR gallium.

Ga[2] *or* **Gã** (gɑː) NOUN [1] (*plural* **Ga, Gas** *or* **Gã, Gãs**) a member of a Negroid people of W Africa living chiefly in S Ghana. [2] the language of this people, belonging to the Kwa branch of the Niger-Congo family.

GA ABBREVIATION FOR: [1] General Assembly (of the United Nations). [2] **general average.** [3] Georgia.

Ga. ABBREVIATION FOR Georgia.

GAA (in Ireland) ABBREVIATION FOR Gaelic Athletic Association.

gab[1] (gæb) *Informal* ◆ VERB **gabs, gabbing, gabbed.** [1] (*intr*) to talk excessively or idly, esp about trivial matters; gossip; chatter. ◆ NOUN [2] idle or trivial talk. [3] **gift of the gab.** ability to speak effortlessly, glibly, or persuasively.
▷HISTORY C18: variant of Northern dialect *gob* mouth, probably from Irish Gaelic *gob* beak, mouth
▸'**gabber** NOUN

gab[2] (gæb) NOUN [1] a hook or open notch in a rod or lever that drops over the spindle of a valve to form a temporary connection for operating the valve. [2] a pointed tool used in masonry.
▷HISTORY C18: probably from Flemish *gabbe* notch, gash

GAB INTERNATIONAL CAR REGISTRATION FOR Gabon.

GABA ('gæbə) NOUN ACRONYM FOR gamma-aminobutyric acid: a biologically active substance found in plants and in brain and other animal tissues; it is a neurotransmitter that inhibits activation of neurones.

gabapentin (ˌgæbə'pentɪn) NOUN an antiepileptic drug that is also used to control neurological pain.

Gabar ('gɑːbə), **Gheber,** *or* **Ghebre** NOUN [1] a member of an Iranian religious sect practising a modern version of Zoroastrianism. ◆ ADJECTIVE [2] of, relating to, or characterizing the Gabar sect or its beliefs.

gabardine *or* **gaberdine** ('gæbəˌdiːn, ˌgæbə'diːn) NOUN [1] a twill-weave worsted, cotton, or spun-rayon fabric. [2] an ankle-length loose coat or frock worn by men, esp by Jews, in the Middle Ages. [3] any of various other garments made of gabardine, esp a child's raincoat.
▷HISTORY C16: from Old French *gauvardine* pilgrim's garment, from Middle High German *wallewart* pilgrimage; related to Spanish *gabardina*

gabble ('gæbᵊl) VERB [1] to utter (words, etc.) rapidly and indistinctly; jabber. [2] (*intr*) (of geese and some other birds or animals) to utter rapid cackling noises. ◆ NOUN [3] rapid and indistinct speech or noises.
▷HISTORY C17: from Middle Dutch *gabbelen*, of imitative origin
▸'**gabbler** NOUN

gabbro ('gæbrəʊ) NOUN, *plural* **-bros.** a dark coarse-grained basic plutonic igneous rock consisting of plagioclase feldspar, pyroxene, and often olivine.
▷HISTORY C19: from Italian, probably from Latin *glaber* smooth, bald
▸**gab'broic** *or* ˌ**gabbro'itic** ADJECTIVE

gabby ('gæbɪ) ADJECTIVE **-bier, -biest.** *Informal* inclined to chatter; talkative.

gabelle (gæ'bɛl) NOUN *French history* a salt tax levied until 1790.
▷HISTORY C15: from Old Italian *gabella*, from Arabic *qabālah* tribute, from *qabala* he received
▸**ga'belled** ADJECTIVE

gaberdine ('gæbəˌdiːn, ˌgæbə'diːn) NOUN a variant spelling of **gabardine.**

gaberlunzie (ˌgæbə'lʌnzɪ, -'luːnjɪ) NOUN *Scot archaic or literary* a wandering beggar. Also called: **gaberlunzie-man.**
▷HISTORY C16: variant of earlier *gaberlungy*

Gaberones (ˌgæbə'rəʊnɛs) NOUN the former name for **Gaborone.**

Gabès ('gɑːbɛs; *French* gabɛs) NOUN [1] a port in E Tunisia. Pop.: 98 800 (1994). [2] **Gulf of.** an inlet of the Mediterranean on the E coast of Tunisia. Ancient name: **Syrtis Minor.** Arabic name: **Qabis.**

gabfest ('gæbfest) NOUN *Informal, chiefly US and Canadian* [1] prolonged gossiping or conversation. [2] an informal gathering for conversation.
▷HISTORY C19: from GAB[1] + FEST

gabion ('geɪbɪən) NOUN [1] a cylindrical metal container filled with stones, used in the construction of underwater foundations. [2] a wickerwork basket filled with stones or earth, used (esp formerly) as part of a fortification.
▷HISTORY C16: from French: basket, from Italian *gabbione*, from *gabbia* cage, from Latin *cavea*; see CAGE

gabionade *or* **gabionnade** (ˌgeɪbɪə'neɪd) NOUN [1] a row of gabions submerged in a waterway, stream, river, etc., to control the flow of water. [2] a fortification constructed of gabions.
▷HISTORY C18: from French; see GABION

gable ('geɪbᵊl) NOUN [1] the triangular upper part of a wall between the sloping ends of a pitched roof (**gable roof**). [2] a triangular ornamental feature in the form of a gable, esp as used over a door or window. [3] the triangular wall on both ends of a gambrel roof.
▷HISTORY C14: Old French *gable*, probably from Old Norse *gafl*; related to Old English *geafol* fork, Old High German *gibil* gable
▸'**gabled** ADJECTIVE ▸'**gable-**ˌ**like** ADJECTIVE

gable end NOUN the end wall of a building on the side which is topped by a gable.

gablet ('geɪblɪt) NOUN a small gable.

gable window NOUN a window positioned in a gable or having a small gable over it.

Gabon (gə'bɒn; *French* gabɔ̃) NOUN a republic in W central Africa, on the Atlantic: settled by the French in 1839; made part of the French Congo in 1888; became independent in 1960; almost wholly forested. Official language: French. Religion: Christian majority; significant animist minority. Currency: franc. Capital: Libreville. Pop.: 1 221 000 (2001 est). Area: 267 675 sq. km (103 350 sq. miles).

Gabonese (ˌgæbə'niːz) ADJECTIVE [1] of or relating to Gabon or its inhabitants. ◆ NOUN [2] a native or inhabitant of Gabon.

gaboon (gə'buːn) NOUN the dark mahogany-like wood from a western and central African burseraceous tree, *Aucoumea klaineana*, used in plywood, for furniture, and as a veneer.
▷HISTORY C20: altered from GABON

gaboon viper NOUN a large venomous viper, *Bitis gabonica*, that occurs in African rainforests. It has brown and purple markings and hornlike projections on its snout.

Gaborone (ˌgæbə'rəʊnɪ) NOUN the capital of Botswana (since 1964), in the extreme southeast. Pop.: 183 487 (1997 est.). Former name: **Gaberones.**

Gabriel ('geɪbrɪəl) NOUN *Bible* one of the archangels, the messenger of good news (Daniel 8:16–26; Luke 1:11–20, 26–38).

gaby ('geɪbɪ) NOUN, *plural* **-bies.** *Archaic or dialect* a simpleton.
▷HISTORY C18: of unknown origin

gad[1] (gæd) VERB **gads, gadding, gadded.** [1] (*intr; often foll by about* or *around*) to go out in search of pleasure, esp in an aimless manner; gallivant. ◆ NOUN [2] carefree adventure (esp in the phrase **on** *or* **upon the gad**).
▷HISTORY C15: back formation from obsolete *gadling* companion, from Old English, from *gæd* fellowship; related to Old High German *gatuling*
▸'**gadder** NOUN

gad[2] (gæd) NOUN [1] *Mining* a short chisel-like instrument for breaking rock or coal from the face. [2] a goad for driving cattle. [3] a western US word for **spur** (sense 1). ◆ VERB **gads, gadding, gadded.** [4] (*tr*) *Mining* to break up or loosen with a gad.
▷HISTORY C13: from Old Norse *gaddr* spike; related to Old High German *gart*, Gothic *gazds* spike

Gad[1] (gæd) NOUN, INTERJECTION an archaic euphemism for **God**: used as or in an oath.

Gad[2] (gæd) NOUN *Old Testament* [1] **a** Jacob's sixth son, whose mother was Zilpah, Leah's maid. **b** the Israelite tribe descended from him. **c** the territory of this tribe, lying to the east of the Jordan and extending southwards from the Sea of Galilee. [2] a prophet and admonisher of David (I Samuel 22; II Samuel 24).

gadabout ('gædəˌbaʊt) NOUN *Informal* a person who restlessly seeks amusement.

Gadarene ('gædəˌriːn) ADJECTIVE relating to or engaged in a headlong rush.
▷HISTORY C19: via Late Latin from Greek *Gadarēnos*, of Gadara (Palestine), alluding to the Biblical Gadarene swine (Matthew 8:28ff.)

gadfly ('gædˌflaɪ) NOUN, *plural* **-flies.** [1] any of various large dipterous flies, esp the horsefly, that annoy livestock by sucking their blood. [2] a constantly irritating or harassing person.
▷HISTORY C16: from GAD[2] (sting) + FLY[2]

gadget ('gædʒɪt) NOUN [1] a small mechanical device or appliance. [2] any object that is interesting for its ingenuity or novelty rather than for its practical use.
▷HISTORY C19: perhaps from French *gâchette* lock catch, trigger, diminutive of *gâche* staple
▸'**gadgety** ADJECTIVE

gadgeteer (ˌgædʒɪ'tɪə) NOUN a person who delights in gadgetry.

gadgetry ('gædʒɪtrɪ) NOUN [1] gadgets collectively. [2] use of or preoccupation with gadgets and their design.

gadgie (ˈgædʒɪ) NOUN *Scot dialect* a fellow.
▷HISTORY from Romany

Gadhelic (gædˈhɛlɪk) NOUN, ADJECTIVE another term for **Goidelic.**
▷HISTORY C19: from Old Irish *Gaídelc, Goídelc* the Gaelic language

gadid (ˈgeɪdɪd) NOUN [1] any marine teleost fish of the family *Gadidae,* which includes the cod, haddock, whiting, and pollack. ◆ ADJECTIVE [2] of, relating to, or belonging to the *Gadidae.*
▷HISTORY C19: see GADOID

gadoid (ˈgeɪdɔɪd) ADJECTIVE [1] of, relating to, or belonging to the *Anacanthini,* an order of marine soft-finned fishes typically having the pectoral and pelvic fins close together and small cycloid scales. The group includes gadid fishes and hake. ◆ NOUN [2] any gadoid fish.
▷HISTORY C19: from New Latin *Gadidae,* from *gadus* cod; see -OID

gadolinite (ˈgædəlɪˌnaɪt) NOUN a rare brown or black mineral consisting of a silicate of iron, beryllium, and yttrium in monoclinic crystalline form. Formula: $2BeO.FeO.Y_2O_3.2SiO_2$. Also called: **ytterbite.**
▷HISTORY C19: named after Johan *Gadolin* (1760–1852), Finnish mineralogist

gadolinium (ˌgædəˈlɪnɪəm) NOUN a ductile malleable silvery-white ferromagnetic element of the lanthanide series of metals: occurs principally in monazite and bastnaesite. Symbol: Gd; atomic no.: 64; atomic wt.: 157.25; valency: 3; relative density: 7.901; melting pt.: 1313±°C; boiling pt.: 3273°C (approx.).
▷HISTORY C19: New Latin, from GADOLINITE
▸ **ˌgadoˈlinic** ADJECTIVE

gadroon *or* **godroon** (gəˈdruːn) NOUN [1] a moulding composed of a series of convex flutes and curves joined to form a decorative pattern, used esp as an edge to silver articles. [2] *Architect* a carved ornamental moulding having a convex cross section.
▷HISTORY C18: from French *godron,* perhaps from Old French *godet* cup, goblet, drinking vessel
▸ **gaˈdrooned** *or* **goˈdrooned** ADJECTIVE

Gadsden Purchase (ˈgædzdən) NOUN an area of about 77 000 sq. km (30 000 sq. miles) in present-day Arizona and New Mexico, bought by the US from Mexico for 10 million dollars in 1853. The purchase was negotiated by James Gadsden (1788–1858), US diplomat.

gadwall (ˈgædˌwɔːl) NOUN, *plural* **-walls** *or* **-wall.** a duck, *Anas strepera,* related to the mallard. The male has a grey body and black tail.
▷HISTORY C17: of unknown origin

gadzooks (gædˈzuːks) INTERJECTION *Archaic* a mild oath.
▷HISTORY C17: perhaps from *God's hooks* (the nails of the cross); see GAD^1

gae (ge) VERB **gaes, gaun, gaed, gane.** a Scot word for **go^1.**

Gaea (ˈdʒiːə) NOUN *Greek myth* a variant of **Gaia.**

Gaekwar *or* **Gaikwar** (ˈgaɪkwɑː) NOUN *History* the title of the ruler of the former native state of Baroda in India.
▷HISTORY C19: from Marathi *Gaekvād,* literally: Guardian of the Cows, from Sanskrit *gauh* cow + *-vad* guardian

Gael (geɪl) NOUN a person who speaks a Gaelic language, esp a Highland Scot or an Irishman.
▷HISTORY C19: from Gaelic *Gaidheal;* related to Old Irish *goidel,* Old Welsh *gwyddel* Irishman
▸ **ˈGaeldom** NOUN

Gaelic (ˈgeɪlɪk, ˈgæl-) NOUN [1] any of the closely related languages of the Celts in Ireland, Scotland, or (formerly) the Isle of Man. Compare **Goidelic.** ◆ ADJECTIVE [2] of, denoting, or relating to the Celtic people of Ireland, Scotland, or the Isle of Man or their language or customs.

Gaelic coffee NOUN another name for **Irish coffee.**

Gaelic football NOUN an Irish game played with 15 men on each side and goals resembling rugby posts with a net on the bottom part. Players are allowed to kick, punch, and bounce the ball and attempt to get it over the bar or in the net.

Gaeltacht (ˈgɛːltəxt) *or* **Gaedhealtacht** (ˈgeɪlˌtæxt, ˈgaɛl-) NOUN any of the regions in Ireland in which Irish Gaelic is the vernacular speech. The form *Gaeltacht* is sometimes also used to mean the region of Scotland in which Scottish Gaelic is spoken. See also **Gaidhealtachd.**
▷HISTORY C20: from Irish Gaelic

gaff^1 (gæf) NOUN [1] *Angling* a stiff pole with a stout prong or hook attached for landing large fish. [2] *Nautical* a boom hoisted aft of a mast to support a gaffsail. [3] a metal spur fixed to the leg of a gamecock. ◆ VERB *(tr)* [4] *Angling* to hook or land (a fish) with a gaff. [5] *Slang* to cheat; hoax.
▷HISTORY C13: from French *gaffe,* from Provençal *gaf* boathook

gaff^2 (gæf) NOUN [1] *Slang* foolish talk; nonsense. [2] **blow the gaff.** *Brit slang* to divulge a secret. [3] **stand the gaff.** *Slang, chiefly US and Canadian* to endure ridicule, difficulties, etc.
▷HISTORY C19: of unknown origin

gaff^3 (gæf) NOUN *Brit slang archaic* [1] a person's home, esp a flat. [2] Also called: **penny-gaff.** a cheap or low-class place of entertainment, esp a cheap theatre or music hall in Victorian England.
▷HISTORY C18: of unknown origin

gaffe (gæf) NOUN a social blunder, esp a tactless remark.
▷HISTORY C19: from French

gaffer (ˈgæfə) NOUN [1] an old man, esp one living in the country: often used affectionately or patronizingly. Compare **gammer.** [2] *Informal, chiefly Brit* a boss, foreman, or owner of a factory, mine, etc. [3] the senior electrician on a television or film set.
▷HISTORY C16: alteration of GODFATHER

gaffer tape NOUN *Brit* strong adhesive tape used in electrical repairs.

gaff-rigged ADJECTIVE (of a sailing vessel) rigged with one or more gaffsails.

gaffsail (ˈgæfˌseɪl, -səl) NOUN a quadrilateral fore-and-aft sail on a sailing vessel.

gaff-topsail NOUN a sail set above a gaffsail.

gag^1 (gæg) VERB **gags, gagging, gagged.** [1] *(tr)* to stop up (a person's mouth), esp with a piece of cloth, etc., to prevent him or her from speaking or crying out. [2] *(tr)* to suppress or censor (free expression, information, etc.). [3] to retch or cause to retch. [4] *(intr)* to struggle for breath; choke. [5] *(tr)* to hold (the jaws) of (a person or animal) apart with a surgical gag. [6] *(tr)* to apply a gag-bit to (a horse). [7] **be gagging for** *or* **to.** *Slang* to be very eager to have or do something. ◆ NOUN [8] a piece of cloth, rope, etc., stuffed into or tied across the mouth. [9] any restraint on or suppression of information, free speech, etc. [10] a surgical device for keeping the jaws apart, as during a tonsillectomy. [11] *Parliamentary procedure* another word for **closure** (sense 4).
▷HISTORY C15 *gaggen;* perhaps imitative of a gasping sound

gag^2 (gæg) *Informal* ◆ NOUN [1] a joke or humorous story, esp one told by a professional comedian. [2] a hoax, practical joke, etc.: *he did it for a gag.* ◆ VERB **gags, gagging, gagged.** [3] *(intr)* to tell jokes or funny stories, as comedians in nightclubs, etc. [4] (often foll by *up) Theatre* **a** to interpolate lines or business not in the actor's stage part, usually comic and improvised. **b** to perform a stage jest, either spoken or based on movement.
▷HISTORY C19: perhaps special use of GAG^1

gaga (ˈgɑːgɑː) ADJECTIVE *Informal* [1] senile; doting. [2] slightly crazy.
▷HISTORY C20: from French, of imitative origin

Gagauzi (gəˈgɔːzɪ) NOUN a language spoken chiefly in the Ukraine, on the NW coast of the Black Sea, belonging to the Turkic branch of the Altaic family.

gag-bit NOUN a powerful type of bit used in breaking horses.

gage^1 (geɪdʒ) NOUN [1] something deposited as security against the fulfilment of an obligation; pledge. [2] (formerly) a glove or other object thrown down to indicate a challenge to combat. ◆ VERB [3] *(tr) Archaic* to stake, pledge, or wager.
▷HISTORY C14: from Old French *gage,* of Germanic origin; compare Gothic *wadi* pledge

gage^2 (geɪdʒ) NOUN short for **greengage.**

gage^3 (geɪdʒ) NOUN *US dated slang* marijuana.
▷HISTORY C20: of uncertain origin; compare GANJA

gage^4 (geɪdʒ) NOUN, VERB *US* a variant spelling (esp in technical senses) of **gauge.**

gager (ˈgeɪdʒə) NOUN a variant spelling of **gauger.**

gagger (ˈgægə) NOUN [1] a person or thing that gags. [2] a wedge for a core in a casting mould.

gaggery (ˈgægərɪ) NOUN the practice of telling jokes.

gaggle (ˈgægᵊl) VERB [1] *(intr)* (of geese) to cackle. ◆ NOUN [2] a flock of geese. [3] *Informal* a disorderly group of people. [4] a gabbling or cackling sound.
▷HISTORY C14: of Germanic origin; compare Old Norse *gagl* gosling, Dutch *gaggelen* to cackle, all of imitative origin

gag rule *or* **resolution** NOUN *US* any closure regulation adopted by a deliberative body.

gahnite (ˈgɑːnaɪt) NOUN a dark green mineral of the spinel group consisting of zinc aluminium oxide. Formula: $ZnAl_2O_4$.
▷HISTORY C19: named after J. G. *Gahn* (1745–1818), Swedish chemist; see -ITE^1

GAI (geɪn) NOUN (in Canada) ◆ ABBREVIATION FOR Guaranteed Annual Income.

Gaia (ˈgeɪə), **Gaea,** *or* **Ge** NOUN the goddess of the earth, who bore Uranus and by him Oceanus, Cronus, and the Titans.
▷HISTORY from Greek *gaia* earth

Gaia hypothesis *or* **theory** (ˈgaɪə) NOUN the theory that the earth and everything on it constitutes a single self-regulating living entity.

Gaidhealtachd (ˈgeɪlˌtæxt, ˈgaɛlˌtaxg) NOUN [1] the area of Scotland in which Scottish Gaelic is the vernacular speech. See also **Gaeltacht.** [2] the culture and traditions of the Scottish Gaels.
▷HISTORY Scottish Gaelic

gaiety (ˈgeɪətɪ) NOUN, *plural* **-ties.** [1] the state or condition of being merry, bright, or lively. [2] festivity; merrymaking. ◆ Also (esp US): **gayety.**

> **Language note** See at **gay.**

gaijin (gaɪˈdʒɪn) NOUN (in Japan) a foreigner.
▷HISTORY C20: Japanese, a contraction of *gaikoku-jin,* from *gaikoku* foreign country + *jin* person

Gaikwar (ˈgaɪkwɑː) NOUN a variant spelling of **Gaekwar.**

Gaillard Cut (gɪlˈjɑːd, ˈgeɪlɑːd) NOUN the SE section of the Panama Canal, cut through Culebra Mountain. Length: about 13 km (8 miles). Former name: **Culebra Cut.**
▷HISTORY C19: named after David Du Bose *Gaillard* (1859–1913), US engineer in charge of the work

gaillardia (geɪˈlɑːdɪə) NOUN any plant of the North American genus *Gaillardia,* having ornamental flower heads with yellow or red rays and purple discs: family *Asteraceae* (composites).
▷HISTORY C19: from New Latin, named after *Gaillard* de Marentonneau, 18th-century French amateur botanist

gaily (ˈgeɪlɪ) ADVERB [1] in a lively manner; cheerfully. [2] with bright colours; showily.

gain^1 (geɪn) VERB [1] *(tr)* to acquire (something desirable); obtain. [2] *(tr)* to win in competition: *to gain the victory.* [3] to increase, improve, or advance: *the car gained speed; the shares gained in value.* [4] *(tr)* to earn (a wage, living, etc.). [5] *(intr;* usually foll by *on* or *upon)* **a** to get nearer (to) or catch up (on). **b** to get farther away (from). [6] *(tr)* (esp of ships) to get to; reach: *the steamer gained port.* [7] (of a timepiece) to operate too fast, so as to indicate a time ahead of the true time or to run fast by a specified amount: *this watch gains; it gains ten minutes a day.* [8] **gain ground.** to make progress or obtain an advantage. [9] **gain time. a** to obtain extra time by a delay or postponement. **b** (of a timepiece) to operate too fast. ◆ NOUN [10] something won, acquired, earned, etc.; profit; advantage. [11] an increase in size, amount, etc. [12] the act of gaining; attainment; acquisition. [13] Also called: **amplification.** *Electronics* the ratio of the output signal of an amplifier to the input signal, usually measured in decibels. ◆ See also **gains.**
▷HISTORY C15: from Old French *gaaignier,* of Germanic origin; related to Old High German *weidenen* to forage, hunt
▸ **ˈgainable** ADJECTIVE

gain² (geɪn) NOUN [1] a notch, mortise, or groove, esp one cut to take the flap of a butt hinge. ◆ VERB [2] (*tr*) to cut a gain or gains in.
▷HISTORY C17: of obscure origin

GAIN (geɪn) NOUN (in Canada) ABBREVIATION OR ACRONYM FOR Guaranteed Annual Income.

gainer ('geɪnə) NOUN [1] a person or thing that gains. [2] Also called: **full gainer.** a type of dive in which the diver leaves the board facing forward and completes a full backward somersault to enter the water feet first with his back to the diving board. Compare **half gainer.**

gainful ('geɪnfʊl) ADJECTIVE profitable; lucrative: *gainful employment.*
▸'**gainfully** ADVERB ▸'**gainfulness** NOUN

gainings ('geɪnɪŋz) PLURAL NOUN profits or earnings.

gainly ('geɪnlɪ) *Obsolete or dialect* ◆ ADJECTIVE [1] graceful or well-formed; shapely. ◆ ADVERB [2] conveniently or suitably.
▸'**gainliness** NOUN

gains (geɪnz) PLURAL NOUN profits or winnings: *ill-gotten gains.*

gainsay (geɪn'seɪ) VERB **-says, -saying, -said.** (*tr*) *Archaic or literary* to deny (an allegation, a statement, etc.); contradict.
▷HISTORY C13 *gainsaien,* from *gain-* AGAINST + *saien* to SAY[1]
▸**gain'sayer** NOUN

'gainst *or* **gainst** (genst, geɪnst) PREPOSITION *Poetic* short for **against.**

gait (geɪt) NOUN [1] manner of walking or running; bearing. [2] (used esp of horses and dogs) the pattern of footsteps at various speeds, as the walk, trot, canter, etc., each pattern being distinguished by a particular rhythm and footfall. ◆ VERB [3] (*tr*) to teach (a horse) a particular gait.
▷HISTORY C16: variant of GATE[1]

-gaited ('geɪtɪd) ADJECTIVE (*in combination*) having a gait as specified: *slow-gaited.*

gaiter ('geɪtə) NOUN (*often plural*) [1] a cloth or leather covering for the leg or ankle buttoned on one side and usually strapped under the foot. [2] Also called: **spat.** a similar covering extending from the ankle to the instep. [3] a waterproof covering for the ankle worn by climbers and walkers to prevent snow, mud, or gravel entering over the top of the boot.
▷HISTORY C18: from French *guêtre,* probably of Germanic origin and related to WRIST
▸'**gaiterless** ADJECTIVE

gal¹ (gæl) NOUN *Slang* a girl.

gal² (gæl) NOUN a unit of acceleration equal to 1 centimetre per second per second.
▷HISTORY C20: named after Galileo Galilei (1564–1642), Italian mathematician, astronomer, and physicist

GAL *Text messaging* ABBREVIATION FOR get a life.

gal. *or* **gall.** ABBREVIATION FOR gallon.

Gal. *Bible* ABBREVIATION FOR Galatians.

gala ('gɑːlə, 'geɪlə) NOUN [1] **a** a celebration; festive occasion. **b** (*as modifier*): *a gala occasion.* [2] *Chiefly Brit* a sporting occasion involving competitions in several events: *a swimming gala.*
▷HISTORY C17: from French or Italian, from Old French *gale* pleasure, from Old French *galer* to make merry, probably of Germanic origin; compare GALLANT

galactagogue (gə'læktəˌgɒg) ADJECTIVE [1] inducing milk secretion. ◆ NOUN [2] a galactagogue agent.
▷HISTORY C19: from Greek *gala, galaktos,* milk + -AGOGUE

galactic (gə'læktɪk) ADJECTIVE [1] *Astronomy* of or relating to a galaxy, esp the Galaxy: *the galactic plane.* [2] *Med* of or relating to milk.
▷HISTORY C19: from Greek *galaktikos;* see GALAXY

galactic equator *or* **circle** NOUN the great circle on the celestial sphere containing the galactic plane.

galactic halo NOUN *Astronomy* a spheroidal aggregation of globular clusters, individual stars, dust, and gas that surrounds the Galaxy.

galactic plane NOUN the plane passing through the spiral arms of the Galaxy.

galactic poles PLURAL NOUN the two points on the celestial sphere, diametrically opposite each other, that can be joined by an imaginary line perpendicular to the galactic plane.

galacto- *or before a vowel* **galact-** COMBINING FORM milk or milky: *galactometer.*
▷HISTORY from Greek *galakt-, gala*

galactometer (ˌgæləkˈtɒmɪtə) NOUN an instrument, similar to a hydrometer, for measuring the relative density of milk. It is used to determine the fat content.
▸ˌ**galac'tometry** NOUN

galactopoietic (gəˌlæktəʊpɔɪ'ɛtɪk) ADJECTIVE [1] inducing or increasing the secretion of milk. ◆ NOUN [2] a galactopoietic agent.
▸**galactopoiesis** (gəˌlæktəʊpɔɪ'iːsɪs) NOUN

galactose (gə'læktəʊz, -əʊs) NOUN a white water-soluble monosaccharide found in lactose. Formula: $C_6H_{12}O_6$.

galago (gə'lɑːgəʊ) NOUN, *plural* **-gos.** another name for **bushbaby.**
▷HISTORY C19: from New Latin, perhaps from Wolof *golokh* monkey

galah (gə'lɑː) NOUN [1] an Australian cockatoo, *Kakatoe roseicapilla,* having grey wings, back, and crest and a pink body. [2] *Austral slang* a fool or simpleton.
▷HISTORY C19: from a native Australian language

Galahad ('gæləˌhæd) NOUN [1] **Sir.** (in Arthurian legend) the most virtuous knight of the Round Table, destined to regain the Holy Grail; son of Lancelot and Elaine. [2] a pure or noble man.

galah session NOUN *Austral informal* an occasion on which people from remote areas converse with each other by radio.

galangal (gə'læŋgᵊl) NOUN [1] another name for **galingale.** [2] a zingiberaceous plant, *Alpinia officinarum,* of China and the East Indies. [3] the pungent aromatic root of this plant, dried and used as a seasoning and in medicine.

galant (gə'lɑːnt) NOUN an 18th-century style of music characterized by homophony and elaborate ornamentation.
▷HISTORY C17: from Old French *galant,* from *galer* to make merry, from *gale* enjoyment, pleasure

galantamine (gə'læntəˌmiːn) NOUN a drug that, by blocking the action of the enzyme acetylcholinesterase in the cortex of the brain, has been used to slow down the cognitive decline that characterizes Alzheimer's disease.

galantine ('gælənˌtiːn) NOUN a cold dish of meat or poultry, which is boned, cooked, stuffed, then pressed into a neat shape and glazed.
▷HISTORY C14: from Old French, from Medieval Latin *galatina,* probably from Latin *gelātus* frozen, set; see GELATINE

galanty show (gə'læntɪ) NOUN (formerly) a pantomime shadow play, esp one in miniature using figures cut from paper.
▷HISTORY C19: perhaps from Italian *galante* GALLANT

Galápagos Islands (gə'læpəgəs; *Spanish* ga'lapaɣos) PLURAL NOUN a group of 15 islands in the Pacific west of Ecuador, of which they form a province: discovered (1535) by the Spanish; main settlement on San Cristóbal. Pop.: 17 000 (2000 est.). Area: 7844 sq. km (3028 sq. miles). Official Spanish name: **Archipiélago de Colón.**

Galashiels (ˌgælə'ʃiːlz) NOUN a town in SE Scotland, in central Scottish Borders. Pop.: 13 753 (1997).

Galata ('gælətə) NOUN a port in NW Turkey, a suburb and the chief business section of Istanbul.

galatea (ˌgælə'tɪə) NOUN a strong twill-weave cotton fabric, striped or plain, for clothing.
▷HISTORY C19: named after the man-of-war HMS *Galatea* (the fabric was at one time in demand for children's sailor suits)

Galatea (ˌgælə'tɪə) NOUN *Greek myth* a statue of a maiden brought to life by Aphrodite in response to the prayers of the sculptor Pygmalion, who had fallen in love with his creation.

Galaţi (*Romanian* ga'latsj) NOUN an inland port in SE Romania, on the River Danube. Pop.: 331 360 (1997 est.).

Galatia (gə'leɪʃə, -ʃɪə) NOUN an ancient region in central Asia Minor, conquered by Gauls 278–277 B.C.: later a Roman province.

Galatian (gə'leɪʃən, -ʃɪən) ADJECTIVE [1] of or relating to Galatia or its inhabitants. ◆ NOUN [2] a native or inhabitant of Galatia.

Galatians (gə'leɪʃənz, -ʃɪənz) NOUN (*functioning as singular*) a book of the New Testament (in full **The Epistle of Paul the Apostle to the Galatians**).

galaxy ('gæləksɪ) NOUN, *plural* **-axies.** [1] any of a vast number of star systems held together by gravitational attraction in an asymmetric shape (an **irregular galaxy**) or, more usually, in a symmetrical shape (a **regular galaxy**), which is either a spiral or an ellipse. Former names: **island universe, extragalactic nebula.** ◆ Related adjective **galactic.** [2] a splendid gathering, esp one of famous or distinguished people.
▷HISTORY C14 (in the sense: the Milky Way), from Medieval Latin *galaxia,* from Latin *galaxias,* from Greek, from *gala* milk; related to Latin *lac* milk

Galaxy ('gæləksɪ) NOUN **the.** the spiral galaxy, approximately 100 000 light years in diameter, that contains the solar system about three fifths of the distance from its centre. Also called: **the Milky Way System.** See also **Magellanic Cloud.**

galbanum ('gælbənəm) NOUN a bitter aromatic gum resin extracted from any of several Asian umbelliferous plants of the genus *Ferula,* esp *F. galbaniflua,* and used in incense and medicinally as a counterirritant.
▷HISTORY C14: from Latin, from Greek *khalbanē,* from Hebrew *helbenāh*

gale¹ (geɪl) NOUN [1] a strong wind, specifically one of force seven to ten on the Beaufort scale or from 45 to 90 kilometres per hour. [2] (*often plural*) a loud outburst, esp of laughter. [3] *Archaic and poetic* a gentle breeze.
▷HISTORY C16: of unknown origin

gale² (geɪl) NOUN short for **sweet gale.**
▷HISTORY Old English *gagel;* related to Middle Low German *gagel*

galea ('geɪlɪə) NOUN, *plural* **-leae** (-lɪˌiː). a part or organ shaped like a helmet or hood, such as the petals of certain flowers.
▷HISTORY C18: from Latin: helmet
▸'**galeˌate** *or* '**galeˌated** ADJECTIVE ▸'**galeiˌform** ADJECTIVE

galena (gə'liːnə) *or* **galenite** (gə'liːnaɪt) NOUN a grey mineral, found in hydrothermal veins. It is the chief source of lead. Composition: lead sulphide. Formula: PbS. Crystal structure: cubic.
▷HISTORY C17: from Latin: lead ore, dross left after melting lead

Galenic (geɪ'lɛnɪk, gə-) ADJECTIVE of or relating to Galen (Latin name *Claudius Galenus* ?130–?200 A.D.), the Greek physician, anatomist, and physiologist, or his teachings or methods.

galenical (geɪ'lɛnɪkᵊl, gə-) *Pharmacol* ◆ NOUN [1] any drug prepared from plant or animal tissue, esp vegetables, rather than being chemically synthesized. ◆ ADJECTIVE [2] denoting or belonging to this group of drugs.
▷HISTORY C17: after *Galen* (?130–?200 A.D.), Greek physician, anatomist, and physiologist

Galenism ('geɪlɪˌnɪzəm) NOUN a system of medicine based on the 84 surviving technical treatises of Galen (Latin name *Claudius Galenus* ?130–?200 A.D.), Greek physician, anatomist, and physiologist, including the theory of the four bodily humours.
▸'**Galenist** ADJECTIVE, NOUN

galère *French* (galɛr) NOUN [1] a group of people having a common interest, esp a coterie of undesirable people. [2] an unpleasant situation.
▷HISTORY C18: literally: a galley

Galibi (gɑː'liːbɪ) NOUN [1] (*plural* **-bi** *or* **-bis**) a member of an American Indian people of French Guiana. [2] the language of this people, belonging to the Carib family.

Galicia NOUN [1] (gə'lɪʃɪə, -'lɪʃə) a region of E central Europe on the N side of the Carpathians, now in SE Poland and the Ukraine. [2] (*Spanish* ga'liθja) an autonomous region and former kingdom of NW Spain, on the Bay of Biscay and the Atlantic. Pop.: 2 731 900 (2000 est.).

Galician (gə'lɪʃɪən, -ʃən) ADJECTIVE [1] of or relating to Galicia in E central Europe. [2] of or relating to Galicia in NW Spain. ◆ NOUN [3] a native or inhabitant of either Galicia. [4] the Romance language or dialect of Spanish Galicia, sometimes regarded as a dialect of Spanish, although historically it is more closely related to Portuguese.

Galilean[1] (ˌgælɪˈliːən) NOUN 1 a native or inhabitant of Galilee. 2 **a the.** an epithet of Jesus Christ (?4 B.C.–?29 A.D.), the founder of Christianity. **b** (*often plural*) a Christian. ◆ ADJECTIVE 3 of Galilee.

Galilean[2] (ˌgælɪˈleɪən) ADJECTIVE of or relating to Galileo Galilei (1564–1642), the Italian mathematician, astronomer, and physicist.

Galilean satellite (ˌgælɪˈleɪən) NOUN any of the four large satellites of the planet Jupiter – Io, Europa, Ganymede, or Callisto – discovered in 1610 by Galileo.

Galilean telescope (ˌgælɪˈleɪən) NOUN a type of telescope with a convex objective lens and a concave eyepiece; it produces an erect image and is suitable for terrestrial use.

galilee (ˈgælɪˌliː) NOUN a porch or chapel at the entrance to some medieval churches and cathedrals in England.

Galilee (ˈgælɪˌliː) NOUN 1 **Sea of.** Also called: Lake **Tiberias**, Lake **Kinneret.** a lake in NE Israel, 209 m (686 ft.) below sea level, through which the River Jordan flows. Area: 165 sq. km (64 sq. miles). 2 a northern region of Israel: scene of Christ's early ministry.

Galileo (ˌgælɪˈleɪəʊ) NOUN a US spacecraft, launched 1989, that entered orbit around Jupiter in late 1995 to study the planet and its major satellites.

galimatias (ˌgælɪˈmeɪʃɪəs, -ˈmætɪəs) NOUN *Rare* confused talk; gibberish.
▷**HISTORY** C17: from French, of unknown origin

galingale (ˈgælɪŋˌgeɪl) *or* **galangal** NOUN a European cyperaceous plant, *Cyperus longus,* with rough-edged leaves, reddish spikelets of flowers, and aromatic roots.
▷**HISTORY** C13: from Old French *galingal,* from Arabic *khalanjān,* from Chinese *kaoliang-chiang,* from *Kaoliang* district in Guangdong province + *chiang* ginger

galiot *or* **galliot** (ˈgælɪət) NOUN 1 a small swift galley formerly sailed on the Mediterranean. 2 a shallow-draught ketch formerly used along the coasts of Germany and the Netherlands.
▷**HISTORY** C14: from Old French *galiote,* from Italian *galeotta,* from Medieval Latin *galea* GALLEY

galipot *or* **gallipot** (ˈgælɪˌpɒt) NOUN a resin obtained from several species of pine, esp from the S European *Pinus pinaster.*
▷**HISTORY** C18: from French, of unknown origin

gall[1] (gɔːl) NOUN 1 *Informal* impudence. 2 bitterness; rancour. 3 something bitter or disagreeable. 4 *Physiol* an obsolete term for **bile.** 5 an obsolete term for **gall bladder.**
▷**HISTORY** from Old Norse, replacing Old English *gealla;* related to Old High German *galla,* Greek *kholē*

gall[2] (gɔːl) NOUN 1 a sore on the skin caused by chafing. 2 something that causes vexation or annoyance: *a gall to the spirits.* 3 irritation; exasperation. ◆ VERB 4 *Pathol* to abrade (the skin, etc.) as by rubbing. 5 (*tr*) to irritate or annoy; vex.
▷**HISTORY** C14: of Germanic origin; related to Old English *gealla* sore on a horse, and perhaps to GALL[1]

gall[3] (gɔːl) NOUN an abnormal outgrowth in plant tissue caused by certain parasitic insects, fungi, bacteria, or mechanical injury.
▷**HISTORY** C14: from Old French *galle,* from Latin *galla*

gall. *or* **gal.** ABBREVIATION FOR gallon.

Galla (ˈgælə) NOUN 1 (*plural* **-las** *or* **-la**) a member of a tall dark-skinned people inhabiting Somalia and SE Ethiopia. 2 the language of this people, belonging to the Cushitic subfamily of the Afro-Asiatic family of languages.

gallant ADJECTIVE (ˈgælənt) 1 brave and high-spirited; courageous and honourable; dashing: *a gallant warrior.* 2 (gəˈlænt, ˈgælənt) (of a man) attentive to women; chivalrous. 3 imposing; dignified; stately: *a gallant ship.* 4 *Archaic* showy in dress. ◆ NOUN (ˈgælənt, gəˈlænt) *Archaic* 5 a woman's lover or suitor. 6 a dashing or fashionable young man, esp one who pursues women. 7 a brave, high-spirited, or adventurous man. ◆ VERB (gəˈlænt, ˈgælənt) *Rare* 8 (when *intr,* usually foll by *with*) to court or flirt (with). 9 (*tr*) to attend or escort (a woman).
▷**HISTORY** C15: from Old French *galant,* from *galer* to make merry, from *gale* enjoyment, pleasure, of Germanic origin; related to Old English *wela* WEAL[2]
▸ˈ**gallantly** ADVERB ▸ˈ**gallantness** NOUN

gallantry (ˈgæləntrɪ) NOUN, *plural* **-ries.** 1 conspicuous courage, esp in war: *the gallantry of the troops.* 2 polite attentiveness to women. 3 a gallant action, speech, etc.

gallant soldier NOUN a South American plant, *Galinsoga parviflora,* widely distributed as a weed, having small daisy-like flowers surrounded by silvery scales: family *Asteraceae* (composites). Also called: **Joey Hooker.**
▷**HISTORY** C20: by folk etymology from New Latin *Galinsoga*

gall bladder NOUN a muscular pear-shaped sac, lying underneath the right lobe of the liver, that stores bile and ejects it into the duodenum through the common bile duct.

Galle (gɔːl) NOUN a port in SW Sri Lanka. Pop.: 123 616 (1997 est.). Former name: **Point de Galle.**

galleass *or* **galliass** (ˈgælɪˌæs) NOUN *Nautical* a three-masted lateen-rigged galley used as a warship in the Mediterranean from the 15th to the 18th centuries.
▷**HISTORY** C16: from French *galleasse,* from Italian *galeazza,* from *galea* GALLEY

galleon (ˈgælɪən) NOUN *Nautical* a large sailing ship having three or more masts, lateen-rigged on the after masts and square-rigged on the foremast and mainmast, used as a warship or trader from the 15th to the 18th centuries.
▷**HISTORY** C16: from Spanish *galeón,* from French *galion,* from Old French *galie* GALLEY

galleria (ˌgæləˈriːə) NOUN a central court through several storeys of a shopping centre or department store onto which shops or departments open at each level.
▷**HISTORY** C20: from Italian; see GALLERY

galleried (ˈgælərɪd) ADJECTIVE having a gallery or galleries.

gallerist (ˈgæləˌrɪst) NOUN a person who owns or runs an art gallery.

gallery (ˈgælərɪ) NOUN, *plural* **-leries.** 1 a room or building for exhibiting works of art. 2 a covered passageway open on one side or on both sides. See also **colonnade** (sense 1). 3 **a** a balcony running along or around the inside wall of a church, hall, etc. **b** a covered balcony, sometimes with columns on the outside. 4 *Theatre* **a** an upper floor that projects from the rear over the main floor and contains the cheapest seats. **b** the seats there. **c** the audience seated there. 5 a long narrow room, esp one used for a specific purpose: *a shooting gallery.* 6 *Chiefly US* a building or room where articles are sold at auction. 7 an underground passage, as in a mine, the burrow of an animal, etc. 8 *Theatre* a narrow raised platform at the side or along the back of the stage for the use of technicians and stagehands. 9 (in a TV studio) a glass-fronted soundproof room high up to one side of the studio looking into it. One gallery is used by the director and an assistant and one is for lighting, etc. 10 *Nautical* a balcony or platform at the quarter or stern of a ship, sometimes used as a gun emplacement. 11 a small ornamental metal or wooden balustrade or railing on a piece of furniture, esp one surrounding the top of a desk, table, etc. 12 any group of spectators, as at a golf match. 13 **play to the gallery.** to try to gain popular favour, esp by crude appeals.
▷**HISTORY** C15: from Old French *galerie,* from Medieval Latin *galeria,* probably from *galilea* GALILEE

gallery forest NOUN a stretch of forest along a river in an area of otherwise open country.

gallery tray NOUN a tray usually of silver with a raised rim, used for serving drinks.

galley (ˈgælɪ) NOUN 1 any of various kinds of ship propelled by oars or sails used in ancient or medieval times as a warship or as a trader. 2 the kitchen of a ship, boat, or aircraft. 3 any of various long rowing boats. 4 *Printing* **a** (in hot-metal composition) a tray open at one end for holding composed type. **b** short for **galley proof.**
▷**HISTORY** C13: from Old French *galie,* from Medieval Latin *galea,* from Greek *galaia,* of unknown origin; the sense development apparently is due to the association of a galley or slave ship with a ship's kitchen and hence with a hot furnace, trough, printer's tray, etc.

galley proof NOUN a printer's proof, esp one taken on a long strip of paper from type in a galley, used to make corrections before the matter has been split into pages. Often shortened to: **galley.**

galley slave NOUN 1 a criminal or slave condemned to row in a galley. 2 *Informal* a drudge.

galley-west ADVERB *Slang, chiefly US* into confusion, inaction, or unconsciousness (esp in the phrase **knock (someone** *or* **something) galley-west).**
▷**HISTORY** C19: from English dialect *colly-west* awry, perhaps from *Collyweston,* a village in Northamptonshire

gallfly (ˈgɔːlˌflaɪ) NOUN, *plural* **-flies.** any of several small insects that produce galls in plant tissues, such as the gall wasp and gall midge.

Gallia (ˈgælɪə) NOUN the Latin name of **Gaul.**

galliambic (ˌgælɪˈæmbɪk) *Prosody* ◆ ADJECTIVE 1 of or relating to a metre consisting of four lesser Ionics, used by Callimachus and Catullus and imitated by Tennyson in *Boadicea.* ◆ NOUN 2 a verse in this metre.
▷**HISTORY** C19: from Latin *galliambus* song of the *Galli* (priests of Cybele)

galliard (ˈgæljəd) NOUN 1 a spirited dance in triple time for two persons, popular in the 16th and 17th centuries. 2 a piece of music composed for this dance. ◆ ADJECTIVE 3 *Archaic* lively; spirited.
▷**HISTORY** C14: from Old French *gaillard* valiant, perhaps of Celtic origin

gallic[1] (ˈgælɪk) ADJECTIVE of or containing gallium in the trivalent state.
▷**HISTORY** C18: from GALL(IUM) + -IC

gallic[2] (ˈgælɪk) ADJECTIVE of, relating to, or derived from plant galls.
▷**HISTORY** C18: from French *gallique;* see GALL[3]

Gallic (ˈgælɪk) ADJECTIVE 1 of or relating to France. 2 of or relating to ancient Gaul or the Gauls.

gallic acid NOUN a colourless crystalline compound obtained from tannin: used as a tanning agent and in making inks, paper, and pyrogallol; 3,4,5-trihydroxybenzoic acid. Formula: $C_6H_2(OH)_3COOH$.

Gallican (ˈgælɪkən) ADJECTIVE 1 of or relating to Gallicanism. ◆ NOUN 2 an upholder of Gallicanism.

Gallicanism (ˈgælɪkəˌnɪzəm) NOUN a movement among French Roman Catholic clergy that favoured the restriction of papal control and greater autonomy for the French church. Compare **ultramontanism.**

Gallice (ˈgælɪsɪ) ADVERB in French.
▷**HISTORY** C19: from Latin

Gallicism (ˈgælɪˌsɪzəm) NOUN a word or idiom borrowed from French.

Gallicize *or* **Gallicise** (ˈgælɪˌsaɪz) VERB to make or become French in attitude, language, etc.
▸ˌ**Galliciˈzation** *or* ˌ**Galliciˈsation** NOUN ▸ˈ**Galliˌcizer** *or* ˈ**Galliˌciser** NOUN

galligaskins *or* **gallygaskins** (ˌgælɪˈgæskɪnz) PLURAL NOUN 1 loose wide breeches or hose, esp as worn by men in the 17th century. 2 leather leggings, as worn in the 19th century.
▷**HISTORY** C16: from obsolete French *garguesques,* from Italian *grechesco* Greek, from Latin *Graecus*

gallimaufry (ˌgælɪˈmɔːfrɪ) NOUN, *plural* **-fries.** a jumble; hotchpotch.
▷**HISTORY** C16: from French *galimafrée* ragout, hash, of unknown origin

gallinacean (ˌgælɪˈneɪʃən) NOUN any gallinaceous bird.

gallinaceous (ˌgælɪˈneɪʃəs) ADJECTIVE 1 of, relating to, or belonging to the *Galliformes,* an order of birds, including domestic fowl, pheasants, grouse, etc., having a heavy rounded body, short bill, and strong legs. 2 of, relating to, or resembling the domestic fowl.
▷**HISTORY** C18: from Latin *gallīnāceus,* from *gallīna* hen

Gallinas Point (gɑːˈjiːnəs) NOUN a cape in NE Colombia: the northernmost point of South America. Spanish name: **Punta Gallinas** (ˈpunta gaˈʎinas).

galling (ˈgɔːlɪŋ) ADJECTIVE 1 irritating,

exasperating, or bitterly humiliating. [2] *Obsolete* rubbing painfully; chafing.
▸ **'gallingly** ADVERB

gallinule ('gælɪˌnjuːl) NOUN [1] any of various aquatic birds of the genera *Porphyrio* and *Porphyrula*, typically having a dark plumage, red bill, and a red shield above the bill: family *Rallidae* (rails). [2] **common gallinule**. the US name for **moorhen** (sense 1).
▹HISTORY C18: from New Latin *Gallīnula* genus name, from Late Latin: pullet, chicken, from Latin *gallīna* hen

galliot ('gælɪət) NOUN a variant spelling of **galiot**.

Gallipoli (gə'lɪpəlɪ) NOUN [1] a peninsula in NW Turkey, between the Dardanelles and the Gulf of Saros: scene of a costly but unsuccessful Allied campaign in 1915. [2] a port in NW Turkey, at the entrance to the Sea of Marmara: historically important for its strategic position. Pop.: 16 751 (latest est.). Turkish name: **Gelibolu**.

gallipot[1] ('gælɪˌpɒt) NOUN a small earthenware pot used by pharmacists as a container for ointments, etc.
▹HISTORY C16: probably from GALLEY + POT[1]; so called because imported in galleys

gallipot[2] ('gælɪˌpɒt) NOUN a variant spelling of **galipot**.

gallium ('gælɪəm) NOUN a silvery metallic element that is liquid for a wide temperature range. It occurs in trace amounts in some ores and is used in high-temperature thermometers and low-melting alloys. **Gallium arsenide** is a semiconductor. Symbol: Ga; atomic no.: 31; atomic wt.: 69.723; valency: 2 or 3; relative density: 5.904; melting pt.: 29.77°C; boiling pt.: 2205°C.
▹HISTORY C19: from New Latin, from Latin *gallus* cock, translation of French *coq* in the name of its discoverer, *Lecoq* de Boisbaudran, 19th-century French chemist

gallivant, galivant, *or* **galavant** ('gælɪˌvænt) VERB (*intr*) to go about in search of pleasure; gad about.
▹HISTORY C19: perhaps whimsical modification of GALLANT

Gällivare (*Swedish* 'jelivɑːrə) NOUN a town in N Sweden, within the Arctic Circle: iron mines. Pop.: 22 400 (1990).

galliwasp ('gælɪˌwɒsp) NOUN any lizard of the Central American genus *Diploglossus*, esp *D. monotropis* of the Caribbean: family *Anguidae*.
▹HISTORY C18: of unknown origin

gall midge NOUN any of various small fragile mosquito-like dipterous flies constituting the widely distributed family *Cecidomyidae*, many of which have larvae that produce galls on plants. Also called: **gallfly, gall gnat**. See also **Hessian fly**.

gall mite NOUN any of various plant-feeding mites of the family *Phytoptidae* that cause galls or blisters on buds, leaves, or fruit.

gallnut ('gɔːlˌnʌt) *or* **gall-apple** NOUN a type of plant gall that resembles a nut.

Gallo- ('gæləʊ) COMBINING FORM denoting Gaul or France: *Gallo-Roman*.
▹HISTORY from Latin *Gallus* a Gaul

gallock ('gælək) ADJECTIVE *Northern English dialect* [1] left-handed. [2] left-handed.

galloglass *or* **gallowglass** ('gæləʊˌglɑːs) NOUN a heavily armed mercenary soldier, originally Hebridean (Gaelic-Norse), maintained by Irish and some other Celtic chiefs from about 1235 to the 16th century.
▹HISTORY C16: from Irish Gaelic *gallóglach*, from *gall* foreigner + *óglach*, young warrior-servant, from *og* young + *-lach* a noun suffix

gallon ('gælən) NOUN [1] Also called: **imperial gallon**. *Brit* a unit of capacity equal to 277.42 cubic inches. 1 Brit. gallon is equivalent to 1.20 US gallons or 4.55 litres. [2] *US* a unit of capacity equal to 231 cubic inches. 1 US gallon is equivalent to 0.83 imperial gallon or 3.79 litres.
▹HISTORY C13: from Old Northern French *galon* (Old French *jalon*), perhaps of Celtic origin

gallonage ('gælənɪdʒ) NOUN [1] a capacity measured in gallons. [2] the rate of pumping, transmission, or consumption of a fluid in gallons per unit of time.

galloon (gə'luːn) NOUN a narrow band of cord, embroidery, silver or gold braid, etc., used on clothes and furniture.
▹HISTORY C17: from French *galon*, from Old French *galonner* to trim with braid, of unknown origin
▸ **gal'looned** ADJECTIVE

galloot (gə'luːt) NOUN a variant spelling of **galoot**.

gallop ('gæləp) VERB **-lops, -loping, -loped**. [1] (*intr*) (of a horse or other quadruped) to run fast with a two-beat stride in which all four legs are off the ground at once. [2] to ride (a horse, etc.) at a gallop. [3] (*intr*) to move, read, talk, etc., rapidly; hurry. ◆ NOUN [4] the fast two-beat gait of horses and other quadrupeds. [5] an instance of galloping.
▹HISTORY C16: from Old French *galoper*, of uncertain origin
▸ **'galloper** NOUN

gallopade *or* **galopade** (ˌgælə'peɪd) NOUN another word for **galop**.

galloping ('gæləpɪŋ) ADJECTIVE (*prenominal*) progressing at or as if at a gallop: *galloping consumption*.

Gallo-Romance *or* **Gallo-Roman** NOUN [1] the vernacular language or group of dialects, of which few records survive, spoken in France between about 600 A.D. and 900 A.D.; the intermediate stage between Vulgar Latin and Old French. ◆ ADJECTIVE [2] denoting or relating to this language or the period during which it was spoken.

gallous ('gæləs) ADJECTIVE of or containing gallium in the divalent state.

Gallovidian (ˌgæləʊ'vɪdɪən) NOUN [1] a native or inhabitant of Galloway. ◆ ADJECTIVE [2] of or relating to Galloway. ◆ Also: **Galwegian**.

Galloway ('gæləˌweɪ) NOUN [1] an area of SW Scotland, on the Solway Firth: consists of the former counties of Kirkcudbright and Wigtown, now part of Dumfries and Galloway; in the west is a large peninsula, the **Rhinns of Galloway**, with the **Mull of Galloway**, a promontory, at the south end of it (the southernmost point of Scotland). Related adjectives: **Gallovidian, Galwegian**. [2] a breed of hardy beef cattle, usually black, originally bred in Galloway.

gallows ('gæləʊz) NOUN, *plural* **-lowses** *or* **-lows**. [1] a wooden structure usually consisting of two upright posts with a crossbeam from which a rope is suspended, used for hanging criminals. [2] any timber structure resembling this, such as (in Australia and New Zealand) a frame for hoisting up the bodies of slaughtered cattle. [3] **the gallows**. execution by hanging.
▹HISTORY C13: from Old Norse *galgi*, replacing Old English *gealga*; related to Old High German *galgo*

gallows bird NOUN *Informal* a person considered deserving of hanging.

gallows humour NOUN sinister and ironic humour.

gallows tree *or* **gallow tree** NOUN another name for **gallows** (sense 1).

gallsickness ('gɔːlˌsɪknɪs) NOUN a disease of cattle and sheep, caused by infection with rickettsiae of the genus *Anaplasma*, resulting in anaemia and jaundice. Also called: **anaplasmosis**.

gallstone ('gɔːlˌstəʊn) NOUN *Pathol* a small hard concretion of cholesterol, bile pigments, and lime salts, formed in the gall bladder or its ducts. Also called: **bilestone**.

Gallup Poll ('gæləp) NOUN a sampling by the American Institute of Public Opinion or its British counterpart of the views of a representative cross section of the population, used esp as a means of forecasting voting.

gallus ('gæləs) ADJECTIVE *Scot* bold; daring; reckless.
▹HISTORY a variant of *gallows* used as an adjective, meaning fit for the gallows

galluses ('gæləsɪz) PLURAL NOUN *Dialect* braces for trousers.
▹HISTORY C18: variant spelling of *gallowses*, from GALLOWS (in the obsolete sense: braces)

gall wasp NOUN any small solitary wasp of the family *Cynipidae* and related families that produces galls in plant tissue, which provide shelter and food for the larvae.

Galois theory ('gælwɑː) NOUN *Maths* the theory applying group theory to solving algebraic equations.
▹HISTORY C19: named after Évariste *Galois* (1811–32), French mathematician

galoot *or* **galloot** (gə'luːt) NOUN *Slang, chiefly US* a clumsy or uncouth person.
▹HISTORY C19: of unknown origin

galop ('gæləp) NOUN [1] a 19th-century couple dance in quick duple time. [2] a piece of music composed for this dance. ◆ Also called: **gallopade**.
▹HISTORY C19: from French; see GALLOP

galore (gə'lɔː) DETERMINER (*immediately postpositive*) in great numbers or quantity: *there were daffodils galore in the park*.
▹HISTORY C17: from Irish Gaelic *go leór* to sufficiency

galoshes *or* **goloshes** (gə'lɒʃɪz) PLURAL NOUN (*sometimes singular*) a pair of waterproof overshoes.
▹HISTORY C14 (in the sense: wooden shoe): from Old French *galoche*, from Late Latin *gallicula* Gallic shoe

gal pal NOUN *Informal* [1] a female friend. [2] a lesbian lover.

galtonia (gɔːl'təʊnɪə) NOUN any plant of the bulbous genus *Galtonia*, esp *G. candicans*, with lanceolate leaves, drooping racemes of waxy white flowers, and a fragrant scent: family *Liliaceae*.
▹HISTORY named after Sir Francis *Galton* (1822–1911), English explorer and scientist

galumph (gə'lʌmpf, -'lʌmf) VERB (*intr*) *Informal* to leap or move about clumsily or joyfully.
▹HISTORY C19 (coined by Lewis Carroll): probably a blend of GALLOP + TRIUMPH

galvanic (gæl'vænɪk) *or* **galvanical** ADJECTIVE [1] Also: **voltaic**. of, producing, or concerned with an electric current, esp a direct current produced chemically: *a galvanic cell*. [2] *Informal* resembling the effect of an electric shock; convulsive, startling, or energetic: *galvanic reflexes*.
▸ **gal'vanically** ADVERB

galvanic pile NOUN another name for **voltaic pile**.

galvanic skin response NOUN a change in the electrical resistance of the skin occurring in moments of strong emotion; measurements of this change are used in lie detector tests. Abbreviation: **GSR**.

galvanism ('gælvəˌnɪzəm) NOUN [1] *Obsolete* electricity, esp when produced by chemical means as in a cell or battery. [2] *Med* treatment involving the application of electric currents to tissues.
▹HISTORY C18: via French from Italian *galvanismo*, after Luigi Galvani (1737–98), Italian physiologist

galvanize *or* **galvanise** ('gælvəˌnaɪz) VERB (*tr*) [1] to stimulate to action; excite; startle. [2] to cover (iron, steel, etc.) with a protective zinc coating by dipping into molten zinc or by electrodeposition. [3] to stimulate by application of an electric current. ◆ NOUN [4] *Caribbean* galvanized iron, usually in the form of corrugated sheets as used in roofing.
▸ **ˌgalvani'zation** *or* **ˌgalvani'sation** NOUN ▸ **'galvaˌnizer** *or* **'galvaˌniser** NOUN

galvanized iron *or* **galvanised iron** NOUN *Building trades* iron, esp a sheet of corrugated iron, covered with a protective coating of zinc.

galvano- COMBINING FORM indicating a galvanic current: *galvanometer*.

galvanometer (ˌgælvə'nɒmɪtə) NOUN any sensitive instrument for detecting or measuring small electric currents.
▸ **galvanometric** (ˌgælvənəʊ'mɛtrɪk, gælˌvænə-) *or* **ˌgalvano'metrical** ADJECTIVE ▸ **ˌgalvano'metrically** ADVERB ▸ **ˌgalva'nometry** NOUN

galvanoscope ('gælvənəˌskəʊp, gæl'vænə-) NOUN a galvanometer that depends for its action on the deflection of a magnetic needle in a magnetic field produced by the electric current that is to be detected.
▸ **galvanoscopic** (ˌgælvənə'skɒpɪk, gælˌvænə-) ADJECTIVE ▸ **ˌgalva'noscopy** NOUN

galvanotropism (ˌgælvə'nɒtrəˌpɪzəm) NOUN the directional growth of an organism, esp a plant, in response to an electrical stimulus.
▸ **galvanotropic** (ˌgælvənəʊ'trɒpɪk, gælˌvænəʊ-) ADJECTIVE

Galveston plan ('gælvɪstən) NOUN another term for **commission plan**.

galvo ('gælvəʊ) NOUN, *plural* **-vos**. an informal name for a **galvanometer**.

Galway ('gɔːlweɪ) NOUN [1] a county of W Republic

of Ireland, in S Connacht, on **Galway Bay** and the Atlantic: it has a deeply indented coastline and many offshore islands, including the Aran Islands. County town: Galway. Pop.: 188 854 (1996). Area: 5939 sq. km (2293 sq. miles). [2] a port in W Republic of Ireland, county town of Co. Galway, on Galway Bay: important fisheries (esp for salmon). Pop.: 57 241 (1996). [3] Former name: **Roscommon.** a breed of sheep with long wool, originally from W Ireland.

Galwegian (gæl'wi:dʒən) NOUN [1] another word for **Gallovidian** (sense 1). [2] a native or inhabitant of the town or county of Galway in W Republic of Ireland. ♦ ADJECTIVE [3] another word for **Gallovidian** (sense 2).
▷HISTORY C18: influenced by *Norway, Norwegian*

galyak *or* **galyac** ('gæljæk, gæl'jæk) NOUN a smooth glossy fur obtained from the skins of newborn or premature lambs and kids.
▷HISTORY from Russian (Uzbek dialect)

gam[1] (gæm) NOUN [1] a school of whales. [2] *Nautical* an informal visit between crew members of whalers. [3] *NZ* a flock of large sea birds. ♦ VERB **gams, gamming, gammed.** [4] (*intr*) (of whales) to form a school. [5] *Nautical* (of members of the crews of whalers) to visit (each other) informally. [6] (*tr*) *US* to visit or exchange visits with.
▷HISTORY C19: perhaps dialect variant of GAME[1]

gam[2] (gæm) NOUN *Slang* a leg, esp a woman's shapely leg.
▷HISTORY C18: probably from Old Northern French *gambe* or Lingua Franca *gambe;* see JAMB

gama grass ('gɑ:mə) NOUN a tall perennial grass, *Tripsacum dactyloides,* of SE North America: cultivated for fodder.
▷HISTORY C19: *gama,* probably changed from GRAMA

gamahuche ('gæmə,hu:ʃ) *or* **gamaruche** ('gæmə,ru:ʃ) *Taboo* ♦ VERB (*tr*) [1] to practise cunnilingus or fellatio on. ♦ NOUN [2] cunnilingus or fellatio.
▷HISTORY C19: from French *gamahucher*

gamba ('gæmbə) NOUN short for **viola da gamba.**

gambado[1] (gæm'beɪdəʊ) NOUN, *plural* **-dos** *or* **-does.** [1] either of two leather holders for the feet attached to a horse's saddle like stirrups. [2] either of a pair of leggings.
▷HISTORY C17: from Italian *gamba* leg, from Late Latin: leg, hoof; see JAMB

gambado[2] (gæm'beɪdəʊ) *or* **gambade** (gæm'beɪd, -'bɑ:d) NOUN, *plural* **-bados, -badoes** *or* **-bades.** [1] *Dressage* another word for **curvet.** [2] a leap or gambol; caper.
▷HISTORY C19: from French *gambade* spring (of a horse), ultimately from Spanish or Italian *gamba* leg

gamba stop NOUN an organ stop with a tone resembling that of stringed instruments.

gambeson ('gæmbɪsᵊn) NOUN a quilted and padded or stuffed leather or cloth garment worn under chain mail in the Middle Ages and later as a doublet by men and women.
▷HISTORY C13: from Old French, of Germanic origin; related to Old High German *wamba* belly; see WOMB

Gambia ('gæmbɪə) NOUN **The.** a republic in W Africa, entirely surrounded by Senegal except for an outlet to the Atlantic: sold to English merchants by the Portuguese in 1588; became a British colony in 1843; gained independence and became a member of the Commonwealth in 1965; joined with Senegal to form the Confederation of Senegambia (1982–89); consists of a strip of land about 16 km (10 miles) wide, on both banks of the **Gambia River,** extending inland for about 480 km (300 miles). Official language: English. Religion: Muslim majority. Currency: dalasi. Capital: Banjul. Pop.: 1 411 000 (2001 est.). Area: 11 295 sq. km (4361 sq. miles).

Gambian ('gæmbɪən) ADJECTIVE [1] of or relating to Gambia or its inhabitants. ♦ NOUN [2] a native or inhabitant of Gambia.

gambier *or* **gambir** ('gæmbɪə) NOUN an astringent resinous substance obtained from a rubiaceous tropical Asian woody climbing plant, *Uncaria gambir* (or *U. gambier*): used as an astringent and tonic and in tanning.
▷HISTORY C19: from Malay

Gambier Islands ('gæmbɪə) PLURAL NOUN a group of islands in the S Pacific Ocean, in French Polynesia. Chief settlement: Rikitéa. Pop.: 580 (latest est.) Area: 30 sq. km (11 sq. miles).

gambit ('gæmbɪt) NOUN [1] *Chess* an opening move in which a chessman, usually a pawn, is sacrificed to secure an advantageous position. [2] an opening comment, manoeuvre, etc., intended to secure an advantage or promote a point of view.
▷HISTORY C17: from French, from Italian *gambetto* a tripping up, from *gamba* leg

gamble ('gæmbᵊl) VERB [1] (*intr*) to play games of chance to win money. [2] to risk or bet (money) on the outcome of an event, sport, etc. [3] (*intr; often foll by on*) to act with the expectation of: *to gamble on its being a sunny day.* [4] (often foll by *away*) to lose by or as if by betting; squander. ♦ NOUN [5] a risky act or venture. [6] a bet, wager, or other risk or chance taken for possible monetary gain.
▷HISTORY C18: probably variant of GAME[1]
▸'**gambler** NOUN ▸'**gambling** NOUN

gamblers' fallacy NOUN *Psychol* the fallacy that in a series of chance events the probability of one event occurring increases with the number of times another event has occurred in succession.

gamboge (gæm'bəʊdʒ, -'bu:ʒ) NOUN [1] **a** a gum resin used as the source of a yellow pigment and as a purgative. **b** the pigment made from this resin. [2] **gamboge tree.** any of several tropical Asian trees of the genus *Garcinia,* esp *G. hanburyi,* that yield this resin: family *Clusiaceae.* [3] a strong yellow colour. ♦ Also called (for senses 1, 2): **cambogia.**
▷HISTORY C18: from New Latin *gambaugium,* from CAMBODIA
▸**gam'bogian** ADJECTIVE

gambol ('gæmbᵊl) VERB **-bols, -bolling, -bolled** *or US* **-bols, -boling, -boled.** [1] (*intr*) to skip or jump about in a playful manner; frolic. ♦ NOUN [2] a playful antic; frolic.
▷HISTORY C16: from French *gambade;* see GAMBADO[2], JAMB

gambrel ('gæmbrəl) NOUN [1] the hock of a horse or similar animal. [2] a frame of wood or metal shaped like a horse's hind leg, used by butchers for suspending carcasses of meat. [3] short for **gambrel roof.**
▷HISTORY C16: from Old Northern French *gamberel,* from *gambe* leg

gambrel roof NOUN [1] *Chiefly Brit* a hipped roof having a small gable at both ends. [2] *Chiefly US and Canadian* a roof having two slopes on both sides, the lower slopes being steeper than the upper. Compare **mansard** (sense 1). ♦ Sometimes shortened to: **gambrel.**
▸'**gambrel-,roofed** ADJECTIVE

Gambrinus (gæm'braɪnəs) NOUN a legendary Flemish king who was said to have invented beer.

game[1] (geɪm) NOUN [1] an amusement or pastime; diversion. [2] a contest with rules, the result being determined by skill, strength, or chance. [3] a single period of play in such a contest, sport, etc. [4] the score needed to win a contest. [5] a single contest in a series; match. [6] (*plural; often capital*) an event consisting of various sporting contests, esp in athletics: *Olympic Games; Highland Games.* [7] equipment needed for playing certain games. [8] short for **computer game.** [9] style or ability in playing a game: *he is a keen player but his game is not good.* [10] a scheme, proceeding, etc., practised like a game: *the game of politics.* [11] an activity undertaken in a spirit of levity; joke: *marriage is just a game to him.* [12] **a** wild animals, including birds and fish, hunted for sport, food, or profit. **b** (*as modifier*): *game laws.* [13] the flesh of such animals, used as food: generally taken not to include fish. [14] an object of pursuit; quarry; prey (esp in the phrase **fair game**). [15] *Informal* work or occupation. [16] *Informal* a trick, strategy, or device: *I can see through your little game.* [17] *Obsolete* pluck or courage; bravery. [18] *Slang, chiefly Brit* prostitution (esp in the phrase **on the game**). [19] **give the game away.** to reveal one's intentions or a secret. [20] **make (a) game of.** to make fun of; ridicule; mock. [21] **on** (*or* **off**) **one's game.** playing well (or badly). [22] **play the game.** to behave fairly or in accordance with rules. [23] **the game is up.** there is no longer a chance of success. ♦ ADJECTIVE [24] *Informal* full of fighting spirit; plucky; brave. [25] **(as) game as Ned Kelly.** *Austral informal* extremely brave; indomitable. [26] (usually foll by *for*) *Informal* prepared or ready; willing: *I'm game for a try.* ♦ VERB [27] (*intr*) to play games of chance for money, stakes, etc.; gamble.
▷HISTORY Old English *gamen;* related to Old Norse *gaman,* Old High German *gaman* amusement
▸'**game,like** ADJECTIVE

game[2] (geɪm) ADJECTIVE a less common word for **lame**[1] (esp in the phrase **game leg**).
▷HISTORY C18: probably from Irish *cam* crooked

game-ball ADJECTIVE *Irish* [1] (of a person) in perfect health. [2] (of an arrangement, plan, etc.) excellent.

game bird NOUN a bird of any species hunted as game.

gamebreaker ('geɪm,breɪkə) NOUN a person who makes a significant contribution to a team's sporting success.

game chips PLURAL NOUN round thin potato chips served with game.

gamecock ('geɪm,kɒk) NOUN a cock bred and trained for fighting. Also called: **fighting cock.**

game fish NOUN any fish providing sport for the angler.

game fowl NOUN any of several breeds of domestic fowl reared for cockfighting.

gamekeeper ('geɪm,ki:pə) NOUN a person employed to take care of game and wildlife, as on an estate.
▸'**game,keeping** NOUN

gamelan ('gæmɪ,læn) NOUN a type of percussion orchestra common in the East Indies.
▷HISTORY from Javanese

game laws PLURAL NOUN laws governing the hunting and preservation of game.

gamely ('geɪmlɪ) ADVERB in a brave or sporting manner.

gameness ('geɪmnɪs) NOUN courage or bravery; pluck.

game park NOUN (esp in Africa) a large area of country set aside as a reserve for wild animals.

game plan NOUN [1] a strategy. [2] a plan of campaign, esp in politics.

gameplay ('geɪm,pleɪ) NOUN the plot of a computer or video game or the way that it is played.

game point NOUN *Tennis, squash, badminton* a stage at which winning one further point would enable one player or side to win a game.

gamer ('geɪmə) NOUN a person who plays computer games or participates in a role-playing game.

gamesmanship ('geɪmzmən,ʃɪp) NOUN *Informal* the art of winning games or defeating opponents by clever or cunning practices without actually cheating.
▸'**gamesman** NOUN

gamesome ('geɪmsəm) ADJECTIVE full of merriment; sportive.
▸'**gamesomely** ADVERB ▸'**gamesomeness** NOUN

gamester ('geɪmstə) NOUN a person who habitually plays games for money; gambler.

gametangium (,gæmɪ'tændʒɪəm) NOUN, *plural* **-gia** (-dʒɪə). *Biology* an organ or cell in which gametes are produced, esp in algae and fungi.
▷HISTORY C19: New Latin, from GAMETO- + Greek *angeion* vessel
▸,**game'tangial** ADJECTIVE

gamete ('gæmi:t, gə'mi:t) NOUN a haploid germ cell, such as a spermatozoon or ovum, that fuses with another germ cell during fertilization.
▷HISTORY C19: from New Latin, from Greek *gametē* wife, from *gamos* marriage
▸**ga'metal** *or* **gametic** (gə'mɛtɪk) ADJECTIVE

gamete intrafallopian transfer (,ɪntrəfə'ləʊpɪən) NOUN the full name for **GIFT.**

game theory NOUN mathematical theory concerned with the optimum choice of strategy in situations involving a conflict of interest. Also called: **theory of games.**
▸,**game-,theo'retic** ADJECTIVE

gameto- *or sometimes before a vowel* **gamet-** COMBINING FORM gamete: *gametocyte.*

gametocyte (gə'mi:təʊ,saɪt) NOUN an animal or plant cell that develops into gametes by meiosis. See also **oocyte, spermatocyte.**

gametogenesis (,gæmɪtəʊ'dʒɛnɪsɪs) *or* **gametogeny** (,gæmɪ'tɒdʒɪnɪ) NOUN the

formation and maturation of gametes. See also **spermatogenesis, oogenesis.**
▸ **ˌgametoˈgenic** *or* **ˌgameˈtogenous** ADJECTIVE

gametophore (gəˈmiːtəʊˌfɔː) NOUN the part of a plant that bears the reproductive organs.
▸ **gaˌmetoˈphoric** ADJECTIVE

gametophyte (gəˈmiːtəʊˌfaɪt) NOUN the plant body, in species showing alternation of generations, that produces the gametes. Compare **sporophyte.**
▸ **gametophytic** (ˌgæmɪtəʊˈfɪtɪk) ADJECTIVE

game warden NOUN a person who looks after game, as in a game reserve.

gamey *or* **gamy** (ˈgeɪmɪ) ADJECTIVE **gamier, gamiest.** 1 having the smell or flavour of game, esp high game. 2 *Informal* spirited; plucky; brave.
▸ **ˈgamily** ADVERB ▸ **ˈgaminess** NOUN

gamic (ˈgæmɪk) ADJECTIVE (esp of reproduction) requiring the fusion of gametes; sexual.
▷ HISTORY C19: from Greek *gamikos* of marriage; see GAMETE

gamin (ˈgæmɪn; *French* gamɛ̃) NOUN a street urchin; waif.
▷ HISTORY from French

gamine (ˈgæmiːn; *French* gamin) NOUN **a** a slim and boyish girl or young woman; an elfish tomboy. **b** (*as modifier*): *a gamine style of haircut.*
▷ HISTORY from French

gaming (ˈgeɪmɪŋ) NOUN **a** gambling on games of chance. **b** (*as modifier*): *gaming house; gaming losses.*

gamma (ˈgæmə) NOUN 1 the third letter in the Greek alphabet (Γ, γ), a consonant, transliterated as *g*. When double, it is transcribed and pronounced as *ng*. 2 the third highest grade or mark, as in an examination. 3 a unit of magnetic field strength equal to 10^{-5} oersted. 1 gamma is equivalent to $0.795\ 775 \times 10^{-3}$ ampere per metre. 4 *Photog, television* the numerical value of the slope of the characteristic curve of a photographic emulsion or television camera; a measure of the contrast reproduced in a photographic or television image. 5 (*modifier*) **a** involving or relating to photons of very high energy: *a gamma detector.* **b** relating to one of two or more allotropes or crystal structures of a solid: *gamma iron.* **c** relating to one of two or more isomeric forms of a chemical compound, esp one in which a group is attached to the carbon atom next but one to the atom to which the principal group is attached.
▷ HISTORY C14: from Greek; related to Hebrew *gīmel* third letter of the Hebrew alphabet (probably: camel)

Gamma (ˈgæmə) NOUN (*foll by the genitive case of a specified constellation*) the third brightest star in a constellation: *Gamma Leonis.*

gamma-aminobutyric acid (ˌgæməəˌmiːnəʊbjuːˈtɪrɪk) NOUN the full name for **GABA.**

gamma camera NOUN a medical apparatus that detects gamma rays emitted from a person's body after the administration of a radioactive drug and so produces images of the organ being investigated.

gammadion (gæˈmeɪdɪən) NOUN, *plural* **-dia** (-dɪə). a decorative figure composed of a number of Greek capital gammas, esp radiating from a centre, as in a swastika.
▷ HISTORY C19: from Late Greek, literally: little GAMMA

gamma distribution NOUN *Statistics* a continuous two-parameter distribution from which the chi-square and exponential distributions are derived, written Gamma(α,β), where α and β are greater than zero, and defined in terms of the gamma function.

gamma function NOUN *Maths* a function defined by $\Gamma(x) = \int_0^\infty t^{x-1}e^{-t}dt$, where *x* is real and greater than zero.

gamma globulin NOUN any of a group of proteins in blood plasma that includes most known antibodies.

gamma-hydroxybutyrate (ˌgæməhaɪˌdrɒksɪˈbjuːtɪreɪt) NOUN a substance that occurs naturally in the brain, used medically as a sedative but also as a recreational drug and alleged aphrodisiac: known as 'liquid ecstasy' when mixed with alcohol. Abbreviation: **GHB.**

gamma iron NOUN an allotrope of iron that is nonmagnetic and exists between 910°C and 1400°C.

gamma radiation NOUN 1 electromagnetic radiation emitted by atomic nuclei; the wavelength is generally in the range 1×10^{-10} to 2×10^{-13} metres. 2 electromagnetic radiation of very short wavelength emitted by any source, esp the portion of the electromagnetic spectrum with a wavelength less than about 1×10^{-11} metres.

gamma-ray astronomy NOUN the investigation of cosmic gamma rays, such as those from quasars.

gamma-ray burst NOUN *Astronomy* an intense but short-lived burst of gamma rays from an unknown celestial source. First detected in 1970, they have since been found to be widely distributed in the sky.

gamma rays PLURAL NOUN streams of gamma radiation.

gamma stock NOUN any of the third rank of active securities on the London Stock Exchange. Prices displayed by market makers are given as an indication rather than an offer to buy or sell.

gammat (xamat) NOUN *South African derogatory* a reference to the accent of Cape Coloured people.
▷ HISTORY C20: corruption of *Achmet,* a common Arabic name

gammer (ˈgæmə) NOUN *Rare, chiefly Brit* a dialect word for an old woman: now chiefly humorous or contemptuous. Compare **gaffer** (sense 1).
▷ HISTORY C16: probably alteration of GODMOTHER or GRANDMOTHER

gammon[1] (ˈgæmən) NOUN 1 a cured or smoked ham. 2 the hindquarter of a side of bacon, cooked either whole or cut into large rashers.
▷ HISTORY C15: from Old Northern French *gambon,* from *gambe* leg; see GAMBREL

gammon[2] (ˈgæmən) NOUN 1 a double victory in backgammon in which one player throws off all his pieces before his opponent throws any. 2 *Archaic* the game of backgammon. ◆ VERB 3 (*tr*) to score a gammon over.
▷ HISTORY C18: probably special use of Middle English *gamen* GAME[1]

gammon[3] (ˈgæmən) *Brit informal* ◆ NOUN 1 deceitful nonsense; humbug. ◆ VERB 2 to deceive (a person).
▷ HISTORY C18: perhaps special use of GAMMON[2]
▸ **ˈgammoner** NOUN

gammon[4] (ˈgæmən) VERB (*tr*) *Nautical* to fix (a bowsprit) to the stemhead of a vessel.
▷ HISTORY C18: perhaps related to GAMMON[1], with reference to the tying up of a ham

gammy (ˈgæmɪ) ADJECTIVE **-mier, -miest.** *Brit slang* (esp of the leg) malfunctioning, injured, or lame; game. US equivalent: **gimpy.**
▷ HISTORY C19: from Shelta *gyamyath* bad, altered form of Irish *cam* crooked; see GAME[2]

gamo- *or before a vowel* **gam-** COMBINING FORM 1 indicating sexual union or reproduction: *gamogenesis.* 2 united or fused: *gamopetalous.*
▷ HISTORY from Greek *gamos* marriage

gamogenesis (ˌgæməʊˈdʒɛnɪsɪs) NOUN another name for **sexual reproduction.**
▸ **gamogenetic** (ˌgæməʊdʒɪˈnɛtɪk) *or* **ˌgamogeˈnetical** ADJECTIVE ▸ **ˌgamogeˈnetically** ADVERB

gamone (ˈgæməʊn) NOUN *Botany* any chemical substance secreted by a gamete that attracts another gamete during sexual reproduction.

gamopetalous (ˌgæməʊˈpɛtələs) ADJECTIVE (of flowers) having petals that are united or partly united, as the primrose. Also: **sympetalous.** Compare **polypetalous.**

gamophyllous (ˌgæməʊˈfɪləs) ADJECTIVE (of flowers) having united leaves or perianth segments.

gamosepalous (ˌgæməʊˈsɛpələs) ADJECTIVE (of flowers) having united or partly united sepals, as the primrose. Compare **polysepalous.**

-gamous ADJECTIVE COMBINING FORM denoting marrying or uniting sexually: *monogamous.*
▷ HISTORY from Greek *gamos;* see -GAMY

gamp (gæmp) NOUN *Brit informal* an umbrella.
▷ HISTORY C19: after Mrs Sarah *Gamp,* a nurse in Dickens' *Martin Chuzzlewit,* who carried a faded cotton umbrella

gamut (ˈgæmət) NOUN 1 entire range or scale, as of emotions. 2 *Music* **a** a scale, esp (in medieval theory) one starting on the G on the bottom line of the bass staff. **b** the whole range of notes. 3 *Physics* the range of chromaticities that can be obtained by mixing three colours.
▷ HISTORY C15: from Medieval Latin, changed from *gamma ut,* from *gamma,* the lowest note of the hexachord as established by Guido d'Arezzo + *ut* (now, *doh*), the first of the notes of the scale *ut, re, mi, fa, sol, la, si,* derived from a Latin hymn to St John: *Ut* queant laxis *re*sonare fibris, *Mi*ra gestorum *fa*muli tuorum, *Sol*ve polluti *la*bi reatum, *S*ancte *I*ohannes

-gamy NOUN COMBINING FORM denoting marriage or sexual union: *bigamy.*
▷ HISTORY from Greek *-gamia,* from *gamos* marriage

gan[1] (gæn) VERB *Archaic or poetic* the past tense of **gin**[3].

gan[2] (gæn) VERB **gans, ganning, ganned.** (*intr*) *Northeast English dialect* to go.
▷ HISTORY from Old English *gangan;* related to Old Norse *ganga.* See GANG[1]

Gäncä (ˈganʒə) NOUN a variant transliteration of the Azerbaijani name for **Gandzha.**

Gand (gɑ̃) NOUN the French name for **Ghent.**

Ganda (ˈgændə) NOUN 1 (*plural* **-das** *or* **-da**) a member of the Buganda people of Uganda, whose kingdom was formerly the largest in E Africa. See also **Luganda.** 2 the Luganda language of this people.

gander (ˈgændə) NOUN 1 a male goose. 2 *Informal* a quick look (esp in the phrase **take** (*or* **have**) **a gander**). 3 *Informal* a simpleton.
▷ HISTORY Old English *gandra, ganra;* related to Low German and Dutch *gander* and to GANNET

Gandhian (ˈgændɪən) ADJECTIVE 1 of or relating to Mohandas Karamchand Gandhi (1869–1948), the Indian political and spiritual leader and social reformer, or his ideas. ◆ NOUN 2 a follower of Gandhi or his ideas.

Gandhi cap NOUN a cap made of white hand-woven cloth worn by some men in India.

Gandhiism (ˈgændɪˌɪzəm) *or* **Gandhism** (ˈgænˌdɪzəm) NOUN the political principles of M. K. Gandhi, the Indian political and spiritual leader and social reformer (1869–1948), esp civil disobedience and passive resistance as means of achieving reform.

gandy dancer (ˈgændɪ) NOUN *Slang* a railway track maintenance worker.
▷ HISTORY C20: of uncertain origin

Gandzha (*Russian* ganˈdʒa) *or* **Gäncä** NOUN a city in NW Azerbaijan: annexed by the Russians in 1804; centre of a cotton-growing region. Pop.: 291 900 (1997 est.). Former names: **Yelisavetpol** (1813–1920), **Kirovabad** (1936–91).

gane (gen) VERB the past participle of **gae.**

ganef, ganev, ganof (ˈgɑːnəf), **gonif,** *or* **gonof** NOUN *US slang* an unscrupulous opportunist who stoops to sharp practice.
▷ HISTORY from Yiddish, from Hebrew *gannābh* thief, from *gānnabh* he stole

Ganesh (gæˈniːʃ) NOUN the Hindu god of prophecy, represented as having an elephant's head.

gang[1] (gæŋ) NOUN 1 a group of people who associate together or act as an organized body, esp for criminal or illegal purposes. 2 an organized group of workmen. 3 a herd of buffaloes or elks or a pack of wild dogs. 4 *NZ* a group of shearers who travel to different shearing sheds, shearing, classing, and baling wool. 5 **a** a series of similar tools arranged to work simultaneously in parallel. **b** (*as modifier*): *a gang saw.* ◆ VERB 6 to form into, become part of, or act as a gang. 7 (*tr*) *Electronics* to mount (two or more components, such as variable capacitors) on the same shaft, permitting adjustment by a single control. ◆ See also **gang up.**
▷ HISTORY Old English *gang* journey; related to Old Norse *gangr,* Old High German *gang,* Sanskrit *jangha* foot
▸ **ganged** ADJECTIVE

gang[2] (gæŋ) VERB *Scot* to go.
▷ HISTORY Old English *gangan* to GO[1]

gang[3] (gæŋ) NOUN a variant spelling of **gangue.**

Ganga jal (ˈgʌŋgɑː dʒʌl) NOUN sacred water from the River Ganges in India.
▷ HISTORY Hindi, from *Ganga* GANGES + *jal* water

gangbang ('gæŋˌbæŋ) *Slang* ◆ NOUN 1 an instance of sexual intercourse between one woman and several men one after the other, esp against her will. ◆ VERB 2 (*tr*) to force (a woman) to take part in a gangbang. 3 (*intr*) to take part in a gangbang. ◆ Also called: **gangshag** ('gæŋˌʃæg).

gang-banger NOUN *US slang* a member of a street gang.
▸ **'gang-ˌbanging** NOUN

ganger ('gæŋə) NOUN *Chiefly Brit* the foreman of a gang of labourers.

Ganges ('gændʒiːz) NOUN the great river of N India and central Bangladesh: rises in two headstreams in the Himalayas and flows southeast to Allahabad, where it is joined by the Jumna; continues southeast into Bangladesh, where it enters the Bay of Bengal in a great delta; the most sacred river to Hindus, with many places of pilgrimage, esp Varanasi. Length: 2507 km (1557 miles). Hindi name: **Ganga** ('gʌŋgə, 'gɑːŋ-).

Gangetic (gæn'dʒetɪk) ADJECTIVE of or relating to the river Ganges.

gang-gang ('gæŋˌgæŋ) NOUN a small black cockatoo, *Callocephalon fimbriatum*, of SE Australia, the male of which has a scarlet head.
▷ HISTORY C19: from a native Australian language

gangland ('gæŋˌlænd, -lənd) NOUN the criminal underworld.

gangling ('gæŋglɪŋ) *or* **gangly** ('gæŋglɪ) ADJECTIVE tall, lanky, and awkward in movement.
▷ HISTORY perhaps related to GANGREL; see GANG[2]

ganglion ('gæŋglɪən) NOUN, *plural* **-glia** (-glɪə) *or* **-glions.** 1 an encapsulated collection of nerve-cell bodies, usually located outside the brain and spinal cord. 2 any concentration of energy, activity, or strength. 3 a cystic tumour on a tendon sheath or joint capsule.
▷ HISTORY C17: from Late Latin: swelling, from Greek: cystic tumour
▸ **'ganglial** *or* **'gangliar** ADJECTIVE ▸ **ˌgangli'onic** *or* **'gangliˌated** ADJECTIVE

Gangnail ('gæŋˌneɪl) NOUN *Trademark* a particular arrangement of nails on a metal plate, used as a connecting piece in strong timber joints.

Gang of Four NOUN **the.** a radical faction within the Chinese Communist Party that emerged as a political force in the spring of 1976 and was suppressed later that year. Its members, Zhang Chunqiao, Wang Hongwen, Yao Wenyuan, and Jiang Qing, were tried and imprisoned (1981).

gangplank ('gæŋˌplæŋk) *or* **gangway** NOUN *Nautical* a portable bridge for boarding and leaving a vessel at dockside.

gang plough NOUN a plough having two or more shares, coulters, and mouldboards designed to work simultaneously.

gangrel ('gæŋgrəl, 'gæŋrəl) NOUN *Scot archaic or literary* 1 a wandering beggar. 2 a child just able to walk; toddler.
▷ HISTORY C16: from Old English *gangan* to GO[1]

gangrene ('gæŋgriːn) NOUN 1 death and decay of tissue as the result of interrupted blood supply, disease, or injury. 2 moral decay or corruption. ◆ VERB 3 to become or cause to become affected with gangrene.
▷ HISTORY C16: from Latin *gangraena,* from Greek *gangraina* an eating sore; related to Greek *gran* to gnaw
▸ **gangrenous** ('gæŋgrɪnəs) ADJECTIVE

gang saw NOUN a saw having several parallel blades making simultaneous cuts.
▸ **gang sawyer** NOUN

gangsta rap ('gæŋstə) NOUN a style of rap music, usually characterized by lyrics about Black street gangs in the US, often with violent, nihilistic, and misogynistic themes.
▷ HISTORY C20: phonetic rendering of GANGSTER
▸ **gangsta rapper** NOUN

gangster ('gæŋstə) NOUN a member of an organized gang of criminals, esp one who resorts to violence.

gangster chic NOUN a cinematic or literary genre which seeks to glamorize the criminal underworld.

gangsterism ('gæŋstəˌrɪzəm) NOUN the culture of belonging to organized gangs of criminals, esp involving violence.

Gangtok ('gʌŋtɒk) NOUN a city in NE India: capital of Sikkim state. Pop.: 24 970 (1991).

gangue *or* **gang** (gæŋ) NOUN valueless and undesirable material, such as quartz in small quantities, in an ore.
▷ HISTORY C19: from French *gangue,* from German *Gang* vein of metal, course; see GANG[1]

gang up VERB (often foll by *on* or *against*) *Informal* to combine in a group (against).

gangway ('gæŋˌweɪ) NOUN 1 an opening in a ship's side to take a gangplank. 2 another word for **gangplank.** 3 *Brit* an aisle between rows of seats. 4 Also called: **logway.** *Chiefly US* a ramp for logs leading into a sawmill. 5 a main passage in a mine. 6 temporary planks over mud or earth, as on a building site. ◆ SENTENCE SUBSTITUTE 7 clear a path!

ganister *or* **gannister** ('gænɪstə) NOUN 1 a highly refractory siliceous sedimentary rock occurring beneath coal seams: used for lining furnaces. 2 a similar material synthesized from ground quartz and fireclay.
▷ HISTORY C19: of unknown origin

ganja ('gɑːndʒə) NOUN a highly potent form of cannabis, usually used for smoking.
▷ HISTORY from Hindi *gājā,* from Sanskrit *grñja*

gannet ('gænɪt) NOUN 1 any of several heavily built marine birds of the genus *Morus* (or *Sula*), having a long stout bill and typically white plumage with dark markings: family *Sulidae,* order *Pelecaniformes* (pelicans, cormorants, etc.). See also **booby** (sense 3). 2 *Slang* a gluttonous or greedy person.
▷ HISTORY Old English *ganot;* related to Old High German *gannazzo* gander

ganof ('gɑːnəf) NOUN a variant spelling of **ganef.**

ganoid ('gænɔɪd) ADJECTIVE 1 (of the scales of certain fishes) consisting of an inner bony layer and an outer layer of an enamel-like substance (ganoin). 2 denoting fishes, including the sturgeon and bowfin, having such scales. ◆ NOUN 3 a ganoid fish.
▷ HISTORY C19: from French *ganoïde,* from Greek *ganos* brightness + -OID

gansey ('gænzɪ) NOUN *Dialect* a jersey or pullover.
▷ HISTORY from the island of GUERNSEY

Gansu ('gæn'suː) *or* **Kansu** NOUN a province of NW China, between Tibet and Inner Mongolia: mountainous, with desert regions; forms a corridor, the Old Silk Road, much used in early and medieval times for trade with Turkestan, India, and Persia. Capital: Lanzhou. Pop.: 25 620 000 (2000 est.). Area: 366 500 sq. km (141 500 sq. miles).

gantlet[1] ('gæntlɪt, 'gɔːnt-) NOUN 1 a section of a railway where two tracks overlap. 2 *US* a variant spelling of **gauntlet[2]**.
▷ HISTORY C17 *gantlope* (modern spelling influenced by GAUNTLET[1]), from Swedish *gatlopp,* literally: passageway, from *gata* way (related to GATE[3]) + *lop* course

gantlet[2] ('gæntlɪt, 'gɔːnt-) NOUN a variant of **gauntlet[1]**.

gantline ('gæntˌlaɪn, -lɪn) NOUN *Nautical* a line rove through a sheave for hoisting men or gear.
▷ HISTORY C19: variant of *girtline;* see GIRT[1], LINE

gantry ('gæntrɪ) *or* **gauntry** NOUN, *plural* **-tries.** 1 a bridgelike framework used to support a travelling crane, signals over a railway track, etc. 2 Also called: **gantry scaffold.** the framework tower used to attend to a large rocket on its launching pad. 3 a supporting framework for a barrel or cask. 4 **a** the area behind a bar where bottles, esp spirit bottles mounted in optics, are kept for use or display. **b** the range or quality of the spirits on view: *this pub's got a good gantry.*
▷ HISTORY C16 (in the sense: wooden platform for barrels): from Old French *chantier,* from Medieval Latin *cantārius,* changed from Latin *canthērius* supporting frame, pack ass; related to Greek *kanthēlios* pack ass

Gantt chart (gænt) NOUN a chart showing, in horizontal lines, activity planned to take place during specified periods, which are indicated in vertical bands.
▷ HISTORY C20: named after Henry L. *Gantt* (1861–1919), US management consultant

Ganymede[1] ('gænɪˌmiːd) NOUN *Classical myth* a beautiful Trojan youth who was abducted by Zeus to Olympus and made the cupbearer of the gods.

Ganymede[2] ('gænɪˌmiːd) NOUN the brightest and largest of the four Galilean satellites of Jupiter, and the largest in the solar system. Diameter: 5262 km; orbital radius: 1 070 000 km.

Gao ('gɑːəʊ, gaʊ) NOUN a town in E Mali, on the River Niger: a small river port. Pop.: 54 875 (latest est.).

gaol (dʒeɪl) NOUN, VERB *Brit* a variant spelling of **jail.**
▸ **'gaoler** NOUN

Gaoxiong (ˌjaʊə'ʃɒŋ) NOUN a variant transliteration of the Chinese name for **Kaohsiung.**

gap (gæp) NOUN 1 a break or opening in a wall, fence, etc. 2 a break in continuity; interruption; hiatus: *there is a serious gap in the accounts.* 3 a break in a line of hills or mountains affording a route through. 4 *Chiefly US* a gorge or ravine. 5 a divergence or difference; disparity: *there is a gap between his version of the event and hers; the generation gap.* 6 *Electronics* **a** a break in a magnetic circuit that increases the inductance and saturation point of the circuit. **b** See **spark gap.** 7 **bridge, close, fill,** *or* **stop a gap.** to remedy a deficiency. ◆ VERB **gaps, gapping, gapped.** 8 (*tr*) to make a breach or opening in.
▷ HISTORY C14: from Old Norse *gap* chasm; related to *gapa* to GAPE, Swedish *gap,* Danish *gab* open mouth, opening
▸ **'gapless** ADJECTIVE ▸ **'gappy** ADJECTIVE

gape (geɪp) VERB (*intr*) 1 to stare in wonder or amazement, esp with the mouth open. 2 to open the mouth wide, esp involuntarily, as in yawning or hunger. 3 to be or become wide open: *the crater gaped under his feet.* ◆ NOUN 4 the act of gaping. 5 a wide opening; breach. 6 the width of the widely opened mouth of a vertebrate. 7 a stare or expression of astonishment. ◆ See also **gapes.**
▷ HISTORY C13: from Old Norse *gapa;* related to Middle Dutch *gapen,* Danish *gabe*

gaper ('geɪpə) NOUN 1 a person or thing that gapes. 2 any of various large marine bivalve molluscs of the genera *Mya* and *Lutraria* that burrow in muddy sand. *M. arenaria* is the American soft-shelled clam and the two species of *Lutraria* are the otter shells. The valves have a permanent gap at the hind end.

gapes (geɪps) NOUN (*functioning as singular*) 1 a disease of young domestic fowl, characterized by gaping or gasping for breath and caused by gapeworms. 2 *Informal* a fit of yawning.
▸ **'gapy** ADJECTIVE

gapeworm ('geɪpˌwɜːm) NOUN a parasitic nematode worm, *Syngamus trachea,* that lives in the trachea of birds and causes gapes in domestic fowl: family *Syngamidae.*

gaping ('geɪpɪŋ) ADJECTIVE wide open; extremely wide: *a gaping hole.*
▸ **'gapingly** ADVERB

gapped scale NOUN *Music* a scale, such as a pentatonic scale, containing fewer than seven notes.

gapping ('gæpɪŋ) NOUN 1 (in transformational grammar) a rule that deletes repetitions of a verb, as in the sentence *Bill voted for Smith, Sam for McKay, and Dave for Harris.* 2 the act or practice of taking a gap year.

gap-toothed ADJECTIVE having wide spaces between the teeth.

gap year NOUN a year's break taken by a student between leaving school and starting further education.

gar[1] (gɑː) NOUN, *plural* **gar** *or* **gars.** short for **garpike** or **garfish.**

gar[2] (gɑːr) VERB (*tr*) *Scot* to cause or compel.
▷ HISTORY from Old Norse

garage ('gærɑːʒ, -rɪdʒ) NOUN 1 a building or part of a building used to house a motor vehicle. 2 a commercial establishment in which motor vehicles are repaired, serviced, bought, and sold, and which usually also sells motor fuels. 3 **a** a rough-and-ready style of rock music. **b** a type of disco music based on soul. ◆ VERB 4 (*tr*) to put into, keep in, or take to a garage.
▷ HISTORY C20: from French, from *garer* to dock (a ship), from Old French: to protect, from Old High German *warōn;* see BEWARE

garage band NOUN a rough-and-ready amateurish rock group.
▷HISTORY perhaps from the practice of such bands rehearsing in a garage

garage sale NOUN a sale of personal belongings or household effects held at a person's home, usually in the garage.

garaging (ˈgærədʒɪŋ) NOUN accommodation for housing a motor vehicle: *there is garaging for two cars.*

garam masala (ˈgɑːrəm mɑːˈsɑːlə) NOUN an aromatic mixture of spices, extensively used in curries.
▷HISTORY from Hindi

Garamond (ˈgærəmɒnd) NOUN a typeface, designed by Claude Garamond (?1480–1561), French type founder.

Garand rifle (ˈgærənd, gəˈrænd) NOUN another name for **M-1 rifle.**
▷HISTORY C20: named after John C. *Garand* (1888–1974), US gun designer

garb (gɑːb) NOUN [1] clothes, esp the distinctive attire of an occupation or profession: *clerical garb.* [2] style of dress; fashion. [3] external appearance, covering, or attire. ◆ VERB [4] (*tr*) to clothe or cover; attire.
▷HISTORY C16: from Old French *garbe* graceful contour, from Old Italian *garbo* grace, probably of Germanic origin
▸ˈ**garbless** ADJECTIVE

garbage (ˈgɑːbɪdʒ) NOUN [1] worthless, useless, or unwanted matter. [2] another word (esp US and Canadian) for **rubbish.** [3] *Computing* invalid data. [4] *Informal* nonsense.
▷HISTORY C15: probably from Anglo-French *garbelage* removal of discarded matter, of uncertain origin; compare Old Italian *garbuglio* confusion

garbage can NOUN a US and Canadian name for **dustbin.** Also called: **ash bin, ash can, trash can.**

garbage collection NOUN *Computing* a systems routine for eliminating invalid or out-of-date data and releasing storage locations.

garbage truck NOUN a US and Canadian name for **dustcart.**

garbanzo (gɑːˈbænzəʊ) NOUN, *plural* **-zos.** another name for **chickpea.**
▷HISTORY C18: from Spanish, from *arvanço,* probably of Germanic origin; compare Old High German *araweiz* pea

garble (ˈgɑːbᵊl) VERB (*tr*) [1] to jumble (a story, quotation, etc.), esp unintentionally. [2] to distort the meaning of (an account, text, etc.), as by making misleading omissions; corrupt. [3] *Rare* to select the best part of. ◆ NOUN [4] **a** the act of garbling. **b** garbled matter.
▷HISTORY C15: from Old Italian *garbellare* to strain, sift, from Arabic *gharbala,* from *ghirbāl* sieve, from Late Latin *crībellum* small sieve, from *crībrum* sieve
▸ˈ**garbler** NOUN

garbled (ˈgɑːbᵊld) ADJECTIVE jumbled or unclear because of distortion or omissions.

garbo (ˈgɑːbəʊ) NOUN, *plural* **garbos.** *Austral informal* a dustman.
▷HISTORY C20: from GARBAGE

garboard (ˈgɑːˌbɔːd) NOUN *Nautical* the bottommost plank of a vessel's hull. Also called: **garboard plank, garboard strake.**
▷HISTORY C17: from Dutch *gaarboord,* probably from Middle Dutch *gaderen* to GATHER + *boord* BOARD

garboil (ˈgɑːbɔɪl) NOUN *Archaic* confusion or disturbance; uproar.
▷HISTORY C16: from Old French *garbouil,* from Old Italian *garbuglio,* ultimately from Latin *bullīre* to boil, hence, seethe with indignation

garbology (gɑːˈbɒlədʒɪ) NOUN the study of the contents of domestic dustbins to analyse the consumption patterns of households.
▷HISTORY C20: from GARB(AGE) + OLOGY
▸**garˈbologist** NOUN

garçon (garsɔn; *French* garsɔ̃) NOUN a waiter or male servant, esp if French.
▷HISTORY C19: from Old French *gars* lad, probably of Germanic origin

Gard (*French* gar) NOUN a department of S France, in Languedoc-Roussillon region. Capital: Nîmes. Pop.: 623 125 (1999). Area: 5881 sq. km (2294 sq. miles).

garda (ˈgɑːrdə) NOUN, *plural* **gardaí** (ˈgɑːrdiː). a member of the **Garda Síochána.**

Garda (ˈgɑːdə) NOUN **Lake.** a lake in N Italy: the largest lake in the country. Area: 370 sq. km (143 sq. miles).

gardant (ˈgɑːdᵊnt) ADJECTIVE a less common spelling of **guardant.**

Garda Síochána (ˈgɑːrdə ˌʃɪəˈxɑːnə) NOUN the police force of the Republic of Ireland.
▷HISTORY C20: from Irish Gaelic *garda* guard + *síochána* of the peace, from *síocháin* peace

garden (ˈgɑːdᵊn) NOUN [1] *Brit* **a** an area of land, usually planted with grass, trees, flowerbeds, etc., adjoining a house. US and Canadian word: **yard. b** (*as modifier*): *a garden chair.* [2] **a** an area of land used for the cultivation of ornamental plants, herbs, fruit, vegetables, trees, etc. **b** (*as modifier*): *garden tools.* Related adjective: **horticultural.** [3] (*often plural*) such an area of land that is open to the public, sometimes part of a park: *botanical gardens.* [4] **a** a fertile and beautiful region. **b** (*as modifier*): *a garden paradise.* [5] (*modifier*) provided with or surrounded by a garden or gardens: *a garden flat.* [6] **lead (a person) up the garden path.** *Informal* to mislead or deceive (a person). ◆ ADJECTIVE [7] **common or garden.** *Informal* ordinary; unexceptional. ◆ VERB [8] to work in, cultivate, or take care of (a garden, plot of land, etc.).
▷HISTORY C14: from Old French *gardin,* of Germanic origin; compare Old High German *gart* enclosure; see YARD² (sense 1)
▸ˈ**gardenless** ADJECTIVE ▸ˈ**garden-ˌlike** ADJECTIVE

garden centre NOUN a place where gardening tools and equipment, plants, seeds, etc., are sold.

garden city NOUN *Brit* a planned town of limited size with broad streets and spacious layout, containing trees and open spaces and surrounded by a rural belt. See also **garden suburb.**

garden cress NOUN a pungent-tasting plant, *Lepidium sativum,* with white or reddish flowers: cultivated for salads, as a garnish, etc.: family Brassicaceae (crucifers).

gardener (ˈgɑːdnə) NOUN [1] a person who works in or takes care of a garden as an occupation or pastime. [2] any bowerbird of the genus *Amblyornis.*

garden flat NOUN a flat with direct access to a garden: typically, a garden flat consists of basement accommodation in prewar property, but some are in purpose-built blocks in urban areas.

garden frame NOUN another name for a **cold frame.**

gardenia (gɑːˈdiːnɪə) NOUN [1] any evergreen shrub or tree of the Old World tropical rubiaceous genus *Gardenia,* cultivated for their large fragrant waxlike typically white flowers. [2] the flower of any of these shrubs.
▷HISTORY C18: New Latin, named after Dr Alexander *Garden* (1730–91), American botanist

gardening (ˈgɑːdᵊnɪŋ) NOUN **a** the planning and cultivation of a garden. **b** (*as modifier*): *gardening gloves.*

gardening leave NOUN *Brit informal* a period during which an employee who is about to leave a company continues to receive a salary but does not work.

Garden of Eden NOUN the full name for **Eden.**

garden party NOUN a social gathering held in the grounds of a house, school, etc., usually with light refreshments.

garden snail NOUN any of several land snails common in gardens, where they may become pests, esp *Helix aspersa,* and sometimes including *Cepaea nemoralis,* common in woods and hedgerows.

garden suburb NOUN *Brit* a suburb of a large established town or city, planned along the lines of a garden city.

garden warbler NOUN any of several small brownish-grey European songbirds of the genus *Sylvia* (warblers), esp *S. borin,* common in woods and hedges: in some parts of Europe they are esteemed as a delicacy.

garderobe (ˈgɑːdˌrəʊb) NOUN *Archaic* [1] a wardrobe or the contents of a wardrobe. [2] a bedroom or private room. [3] a privy.
▷HISTORY C14: from French, from *garder* to keep + *robe* dress, clothing; see WARDROBE

garfish (ˈgɑːˌfɪʃ) NOUN, *plural* **-fish** *or* **-fishes.** [1] another name for **garpike** (sense 1). [2] an elongated European marine teleost fish, *Belone belone,* with long toothed jaws: related to the flying fishes. [3] any of various marine or estuarine fish with a long needle-like lower jaw.
▷HISTORY Old English *gār* spear + FISH

garganey (ˈgɑːgənɪ) NOUN a small Eurasian duck, *Anas querquedula,* closely related to the mallard. The male has a white stripe over each eye.
▷HISTORY C17: from Italian dialect *garganei,* of imitative origin

Gargantua (gɑːˈgæntjʊə) NOUN a gigantic king noted for his great capacity for food and drink, in Rabelais' satire *Gargantua and Pantagruel* (1534).

gargantuan (gɑːˈgæntjʊən) ADJECTIVE (*sometimes capital*) huge; enormous.

> **Language note** Some people think that *gargantuan* should only be used to describe things connected with food: *a gargantuan meal; his gargantuan appetite.*

garget (ˈgɑːgɪt) NOUN *Archaic* inflammation of the mammary gland of domestic animals, esp cattle.
▷HISTORY C16 (in the sense: throat): from Old French *gargate,* perhaps from Latin *gurges* gulf
▸ˈ**gargety** ADJECTIVE

gargle (ˈgɑːgᵊl) VERB [1] to rinse (the mouth and throat) with a liquid, esp a medicinal fluid by slowly breathing out through the liquid. [2] to utter (words, sounds, etc.) with the throaty bubbling noise of gargling. ◆ NOUN [3] the liquid used for gargling. [4] the sound produced by gargling. [C16: from Old French *gargouiller* to gargle, make a gurgling sound, from *gargouille* throat, perhaps of imitative origin] [5] *Brit informal* an alcoholic drink: *what was her favourite gargle?*
▸ˈ**gargler** NOUN

gargoyle (ˈgɑːgɔɪl) NOUN [1] a waterspout carved in the form of a grotesque face or creature and projecting from a roof gutter, esp of a Gothic church. [2] any grotesque ornament or projection, esp on a building. [3] a person with a grotesque appearance.
▷HISTORY C15: from Old French *gargouille* gargoyle, throat; see GARGLE
▸ˈ**gargoyled** ADJECTIVE

gari (ˈgɑːrɪ) NOUN thinly sliced pickled ginger, often served with sushi.
▷HISTORY C20: Japanese

garibaldi (ˌgærɪˈbɔːldɪ) NOUN [1] a woman's loose blouse with long sleeves popular in the 1860s, copied from the red flannel shirt worn by Garibaldi's soldiers. [2] *Brit* a type of biscuit having a layer of currants in the centre.

garigue *or* ***garrigue*** *French* (garig) NOUN open shrubby vegetation of dry Mediterranean regions, consisting of spiny or aromatic dwarf shrubs interspersed with colourful ephemeral species.

garish (ˈgɛərɪʃ) ADJECTIVE gay or colourful in a crude or vulgar manner; gaudy.
▷HISTORY C16: from earlier *gaure* to stare + -ISH
▸ˈ**garishly** ADVERB ▸ˈ**garishness** NOUN

garland (ˈgɑːlənd) NOUN [1] a wreath or festoon of flowers, leaves, etc., worn round the head or neck or hung up. [2] a representation of such a wreath, as in painting, sculpture, etc. [3] a collection of short literary pieces, such as ballads or poems; miscellany or anthology. [4] *Nautical* a ring or grommet of rope. ◆ VERB [5] (*tr*) to deck or adorn with a garland or garlands.
▷HISTORY C14: from Old French *garlande,* perhaps of Germanic origin

garlic (ˈgɑːlɪk) NOUN [1] a hardy widely cultivated Asian alliaceous plant, *Allium sativum,* having a stem bearing whitish flowers and bulbils. [2] **a** the bulb of this plant, made up of small segments (cloves) that have a strong odour and pungent taste and are used in cooking. **b** (*as modifier*): *a garlic taste.* [3] any of various other plants of the genus *Allium.*
▷HISTORY Old English *gārlēac,* from *gār* spear + *lēac* LEEK

garlicky (ˈgɑːlɪkɪ) ADJECTIVE containing or resembling the taste or odour of garlic.

garlic mustard NOUN a plant, *Alliaria petiolata,* of N temperate regions, with small white flowers and an odour of garlic: family Brassicaceae (crucifers).

Also called: **jack-by-the-hedge, hedge garlic.** Compare **garlic.**

garment ('gɑːmənt) NOUN 1 (*often plural*) an article of clothing. 2 outer covering. ◆ VERB 3 (*tr; usually passive*) to cover or clothe.
▷HISTORY C14: from Old French *garniment,* from *garnir* to equip; see GARNISH
▸'**garmentless** ADJECTIVE

garner ('gɑːnə) VERB (*tr*) 1 to gather or store in or as if in a granary. ◆ NOUN 2 an archaic word for **granary.** 3 *Archaic* a place for storage or safekeeping.
▷HISTORY C12: from Old French *gernier* granary, from Latin *grānārium,* from *grānum* grain

garnet[1] ('gɑːnɪt) NOUN any of a group of hard glassy red, yellow, or green minerals consisting of the silicates of calcium, iron, manganese, chromium, magnesium, and aluminium in cubic crystalline form: used as a gemstone and abrasive. Formula: $A_3B_2(SiO_4)_3$ where A is a divalent metal and B is a trivalent metal.
▷HISTORY C13: from Old French *grenat,* from *grenat* (adj) red, from *pome grenate* POMEGRANATE
▸'**garnet-ˌlike** ADJECTIVE

garnet[2] ('gɑːnɪt) NOUN *Nautical* a tackle used for lifting cargo.
▷HISTORY C15: probably from Middle Dutch *garnaat*

garnet paper NOUN sandpaper having powdered garnet as the abrasive.

garnierite ('gɑːnɪəˌraɪt) NOUN a green amorphous mineral consisting of hydrated nickel magnesium silicate: a source of nickel.
▷HISTORY C19: named after Jules *Garnier* (died 1904), French geologist

garnish ('gɑːnɪʃ) VERB (*tr*) 1 to decorate; trim. 2 to add something to (food) in order to improve its appearance or flavour. 3 *Law* **a** to serve with notice of proceedings; warn. **b** *Obsolete* to summon to proceedings already in progress. **c** to attach (a debt). 4 *Slang* to extort money from. ◆ NOUN 5 a decoration; trimming. 6 something, such as parsley, added to a dish for its flavour or decorative effect. 7 *Obsolete slang* a payment illegally extorted, as from a prisoner by his jailer.
▷HISTORY C14: from Old French *garnir* to adorn, equip, of Germanic origin; compare Old High German *warnōn* to pay heed
▸'**garnisher** NOUN

garnishee (ˌgɑːnɪ'ʃiː) *Law* ◆ NOUN 1 a person upon whom a garnishment has been served. ◆ VERB **-nishees, -nisheeing, -nisheed.** (*tr*) 2 to attach (a debt or other property) by garnishment. 3 to serve (a person) with a garnishment.

garnishment ('gɑːnɪʃmənt) NOUN 1 the act of garnishing. 2 decoration or embellishment; garnish. 3 *Law* **a** a notice or warning. **b** *Obsolete* a summons to court proceedings already in progress. **c** a notice warning a person holding money or property belonging to a debtor whose debt has been attached to hold such property until directed by the court to apply it.

garniture ('gɑːnɪtʃə) NOUN decoration or embellishment.
▷HISTORY C16: from French, from *garnir* to GARNISH

Garonne (*French* garɔn) NOUN a river in SW France, rising in the central Pyrenees in Spain and flowing northeast then northwest into the Gironde estuary. Length: 580 km (360 miles).

garotte (gə'rɒt) NOUN, VERB a variant spelling of **garrotte.**
▸**ga'rotter** NOUN

garpike ('gɑːˌpaɪk) NOUN 1 Also called: **garfish, gar.** any primitive freshwater elongated bony fish of the genus *Lepisosteus,* of North and Central America, having very long toothed jaws and a body covering of thick scales. 2 another name for **garfish** (sense 2).

garret ('gærɪt) NOUN another word for **attic** (sense 1).
▷HISTORY C14: from Old French *garite* watchtower, from *garir* to protect, of Germanic origin; see WARY

garret window NOUN a skylight that lies along the slope of the roof.

garrigue *French* (garig) NOUN a variant spelling of **garigue.**

garrison ('gærɪsᵊn) NOUN 1 the troops who maintain and guard a base or fortified place. 2 **a** the place itself. **b** (*as modifier*): *a garrison town.* ◆ VERB 3 (*tr*) to station (troops) in (a fort).
▷HISTORY C13: from Old French *garison,* from *garir* to defend, of Germanic origin; compare Old Norse *verja* to defend, Old English, Old High German *werian*

garron ('gærən) NOUN a small sturdy pony bred and used chiefly in Scotland and Ireland.
▷HISTORY C16: from Gaelic *gearran*

garrotte, garrote, *or* **garotte** (gə'rɒt) NOUN 1 a Spanish method of execution by strangulation or by breaking the neck. 2 the device, usually an iron collar, used in such executions. 3 *Obsolete* strangulation of one's victim while committing robbery. ◆ VERB (*tr*) 4 to execute by means of the garrotte. 5 to strangle, esp in order to commit robbery.
▷HISTORY C17: from Spanish *garrote,* perhaps from Old French *garrot* cudgel; of obscure origin
▸**gar'rotter** *or* **gar'roter** *or* **ga'rotter** NOUN

garrulous ('gærʊləs) ADJECTIVE 1 given to constant and frivolous chatter; loquacious; talkative. 2 wordy or diffuse; prolix.
▷HISTORY C17: from Latin *garrulus,* from *garrīre* to chatter
▸'**garrulously** ADVERB ▸'**garrulousness** *or* **garrulity** (gæ'ruːlɪtɪ) NOUN

garrya ('gærɪə) NOUN any ornamental catkin-bearing evergreen shrub of the North American genus *Garrya:* family *Garryaceae.*
▷HISTORY C19: named after Nicholas *Garry* (1781–1856), an officer of the Hudson's Bay Company

garryowen (ˌgærɪ'əʊɪn) NOUN (in rugby union) another term for **up-and-under.**
▷HISTORY C20: named after *Garryowen* RFC, Ireland

garter ('gɑːtə) NOUN 1 a band, usually of elastic, worn round the arm or leg to hold up a shirtsleeve, sock, or stocking. 2 the US and Canadian word for **suspender.** 3 **have someone's guts for garters.** See **gut** (sense 10). ◆ VERB 4 (*tr*) to fasten, support, or secure with or as if with a garter.
▷HISTORY C14: from Old Northern French *gartier,* from *garet* bend of the knee, probably of Celtic origin

Garter ('gɑːtə) NOUN **the.** 1 See **Order of the Garter.** 2 (*sometimes not capital*) **a** the badge of this Order. **b** membership of this Order.

garter snake NOUN any nonvenomous North American colubrid snake of the genus *Thamnophis,* typically marked with longitudinal stripes.

garter stitch NOUN knitting in which all the rows are knitted in plain stitch instead of alternating with purl rows.

garth[1] (gɑːθ) NOUN 1 a courtyard surrounded by a cloister. 2 *Archaic* a yard or garden.
▷HISTORY C14: from Old Norse *garthr;* related to Old English *geard* YARD[2]

garth[2] (gɑːθ) NOUN *Northern English dialect* a child's hoop, often the rim of a bicycle wheel.
▷HISTORY dialect variant of GIRTH

Gary ('gærɪ) NOUN a port in NW Indiana, on Lake Michigan: a major world steel producer. Pop.: 102 746 (1996 est.).

gas (gæs) NOUN, *plural* **gases** *or* **gasses.** 1 a substance in a physical state in which it does not resist change of shape and will expand indefinitely to fill any container. If very high pressure is applied a gas may become liquid or solid, otherwise its density tends towards that of the condensed phase. Compare **liquid** (sense 1), **solid** (sense 1). 2 any substance that is gaseous at room temperature and atmospheric pressure. 3 any gaseous substance that is above its critical temperature and therefore not liquefiable by pressure alone. Compare **vapour** (sense 2). 4 **a** a fossil fuel in the form of a gas, used as a source of domestic and industrial heat. See also **coal gas, natural gas. b** (*as modifier*): *a gas cooker; gas fire.* 5 a gaseous anaesthetic, such as nitrous oxide. 6 *Mining* firedamp or the explosive mixture of firedamp and air. 7 the usual US, Canadian, and New Zealand word for **petrol,** a shortened form of **gasoline.** 8 **step on the gas.** *Informal* **a** to increase the speed of a motor vehicle; accelerate. **b** to hurry. 9 a toxic or suffocating substance in suspension in air used against an enemy. 10 *Informal* idle talk or boasting. 11 *Slang* a delightful or successful person or thing: *his latest record is a gas.* 12 *US* an informal name for **flatus.** ◆ VERB **gases** *or* **gasses, gassing, gassed.** 13 (*tr*) to provide or fill with gas. 14 (*tr*) to subject to gas fumes, esp so as to asphyxiate or render unconscious. 15 (*intr*) to give off gas, as in the charging of a battery. 16 (*tr*) (in textiles) to singe (fabric) with a flame from a gas burner to remove unwanted fibres. 17 (*intr; foll by to*) *Informal* to talk in an idle or boastful way (to a person). 18 (*tr*) *Slang, chiefly US and Canadian* to thrill or delight.
▷HISTORY C17 (coined by J. B. van Helmont (1577–1644), Flemish chemist): modification of Greek *khaos* atmosphere
▸'**gasless** ADJECTIVE

gasbag ('gæsˌbæg) *Informal* ◆ NOUN 1 a person who talks in a voluble way, esp about unimportant matters. ◆ VERB **-bags, -bagging, -bagged.** 2 (*intr*) *Irish* to talk in a voluble way, esp about unimportant matters.

gas black NOUN finely powdered carbon produced by burning natural gas. It is used as a pigment in paints, etc.

gas burner NOUN 1 Also called: **gas jet.** a jet or nozzle from which a combustible gas issues in order to form a stable flame. 2 an assembly of such jets or nozzles, used esp in cooking.

gas chamber *or* **oven** NOUN an airtight room into which poison gas is introduced to kill people or animals.

gas chromatography NOUN a technique for analysing a mixture of volatile substances in which the mixture is carried by an inert gas through a column packed with a selective adsorbent and a detector records on a moving strip the conductivity of the gas leaving the tube. Peaks on the resulting graph indicate the presence of a particular component. Also called: **gas-liquid chromatography.**

gas coal NOUN coal that is rich in volatile hydrocarbons, making it a suitable source of domestic gas.

gascon ('gæskən) NOUN *Rare* a boaster; braggart.
▷HISTORY C14: from Old French *gascoun;* compare Latin *Vasconēs* Basque

Gascon ('gæskən) NOUN 1 a native or inhabitant of Gascony. 2 the dialect of French spoken in Gascony. ◆ ADJECTIVE 3 of or relating to Gascony, its inhabitants, or their dialect of French.

gasconade (ˌgæskə'neɪd) *Rare* ◆ NOUN 1 boastful talk, bragging, or bluster. ◆ VERB 2 (*intr*) to boast, brag, or bluster.
▷HISTORY C18: from French *gasconnade,* from *gasconner* to chatter, boast like a GASCON
▸ˌ**gascon'ader** NOUN

gas constant NOUN the constant in the gas equation. It is equal to 8.31472 joules per kelvin per mole. Symbol: *R.* Also called: **universal gas constant.**

Gascony ('gæskənɪ) NOUN a former province of SW France. French name: **Gascogne** (gaskɔɲ).

gas-cooled reactor NOUN a nuclear reactor using a gas as the coolant. In the Mark I type the coolant is carbon dioxide, the moderator is graphite, and the fuel is uranium cased in magnox. See also **advanced gas-cooled reactor.**

gas-discharge tube NOUN *Electronics* any tube in which an electric discharge takes place through a gas.

gaselier (ˌgæsə'lɪə) NOUN a variant spelling of **gasolier.**

gas engine NOUN a type of internal-combustion engine using a flammable gas, such as coal gas or natural gas, as fuel.

gaseous ('gæsɪəs, -ʃəs, -ʃɪəs, 'geɪ-) ADJECTIVE of, concerned with, or having the characteristics of a gas.
▸'**gaseousness** NOUN

gas equation NOUN an equation that equates the product of the pressure and the volume of one mole of a gas to the product of its thermodynamic temperature and the **gas constant.** The equation is exact for an ideal gas and is a good approximation for real gases at low pressures. Also called: **ideal gas equation** *or* **law.**

gas gangrene NOUN gangrene resulting from infection of a wound by anaerobic bacteria (esp *Clostridium welchii*) that cause gas bubbles and swelling in the surrounding tissues.

gas guzzler NOUN *Informal* a large car with very high petrol consumption.

gash¹ (gæʃ) VERB [1] (*tr*) to make a long deep cut or wound in; slash. ♦ NOUN [2] a long deep cut or wound.
▷HISTORY C16: from Old French *garser* to scratch, wound, from Vulgar Latin *charissāre* (unattested), from Greek *kharassein* to scratch

gash² (gæʃ) ADJECTIVE *Slang* surplus to requirements; unnecessary, extra, or spare.
▷HISTORY C20: of unknown origin

gasholder (ˈgæsˌhəʊldə) NOUN [1] Also called: **gasometer.** a large tank for storing coal gas or natural gas prior to distribution to users. [2] any vessel for storing or measuring a gas.

gasiform (ˈgæsɪˌfɔːm) ADJECTIVE in a gaseous form.

gasify (ˈgæsɪˌfaɪ) VERB **-fies, -fying, -fied.** [1] to make into or become a gas. [2] to subject (coal, etc.) to destructive distillation to produce gas, esp for use as a fuel.
▸**ˈgasiˌfiable** ADJECTIVE ▸**ˌgasifiˈcation** NOUN ▸**ˈgasiˌfier** NOUN

gasket (ˈgæskɪt) NOUN [1] a compressible packing piece of paper, rubber, asbestos, etc., sandwiched between the faces or flanges of a joint to provide a seal. [2] *Nautical* a piece of line used as a sail stop. [3] **blow a gasket.** *Slang* to burst out in anger.
▷HISTORY C17 (in the sense: rope lashing a furled sail): probably from French *garcette* rope's end, literally: little girl, from Old French *garce* girl, feminine of *gars* boy, servant

gaskin (ˈgæskɪn) NOUN the lower part of a horse's thigh, between the hock and the stifle.
▷HISTORY C16: perhaps shortened from GALLIGASKINS

gas laws PLURAL NOUN the physical laws obeyed by gases, esp Boyle's law and Charles' law. See also **gas equation.**

gaslight (ˈgæsˌlaɪt) NOUN [1] a type of lamp in which the illumination is produced by an incandescent mantle heated by a jet of gas. [2] the light produced by such a lamp.

gas lighter NOUN [1] a device for igniting a jet of gas. [2] a cigarette lighter using a gas as fuel.

gas-liquid chromatography NOUN another name for **gas chromatography.**

gas main NOUN a large pipeline in which gas is carried for distribution through smaller pipes to consumers.

gasman (ˈgæsˌmæn) NOUN, *plural* **-men.** a man employed to read household gas meters, supervise gas fittings, etc.

gas mantle NOUN a mantle for use in a gaslight. See **mantle** (sense 4).

gas mask NOUN a mask fitted with a chemical filter to enable the wearer to breathe air free of poisonous or corrosive gases: used for military or industrial purposes. Also called (in Britain): **respirator.**

gas meter NOUN an apparatus for measuring and recording the amount of gas passed through it.

gasohol (ˈgæsəˌhɒl) NOUN a mixture of 80% or 90% petrol with 20% or 10% ethyl alcohol, for use as a fuel in internal-combustion engines.

gas oil NOUN a fuel oil obtained in the distillation of petroleum, intermediate in viscosity and boiling point between paraffin and lubricating oils. It boils above about 250°C.

gasolier *or* **gaselier** (ˌgæsəˈlɪə) NOUN a branched hanging fitting for gaslights.
▷HISTORY C19: from GAS + (CHAND)ELIER

gasoline *or* **gasolene** (ˈgæsəˌliːn) NOUN a US and Canadian name for **petrol.**
▸**gasolinic** (ˌgæsəˈlɪnɪk) ADJECTIVE

gasometer (gæsˈɒmɪtə) NOUN a nontechnical name for **gasholder.**

gasometry (gæsˈɒmɪtrɪ) NOUN the measurement of quantities of gases.
▸**gasometric** (ˌgæsəˈmɛtrɪk) *or* **ˌgasoˈmetrical** ADJECTIVE

gas oven NOUN [1] a domestic oven heated by gas. [2] a gas-fuelled cremation chamber. [3] another name for **gas chamber.**

gasp (gɑːsp) VERB [1] (*intr*) to draw in the breath sharply, convulsively, or with effort, esp in expressing awe, horror, etc. [2] (*intr; foll by after or for*) to crave. [3] (*tr; often foll by out*) to utter or emit breathlessly. ♦ NOUN [4] a short convulsive intake of breath. [5] a short convulsive burst of speech. [6] **at the last gasp. a** at the point of death. **b** at the last moment.
▷HISTORY C14: from Old Norse *geispa* to yawn; related to Swedish dialect *gispa,* Danish *gispe*
▸**ˈgaspingly** ADVERB

Gaspar (ˈgæspə, ˈgæspɑː) NOUN a variant of **Caspar.**

Gaspé Peninsula (gæˈspeɪ; *French* gaspe) NOUN a peninsula in E Canada, in SE Quebec between the St Lawrence River and New Brunswick: mountainous and wooded with many lakes and rivers. Area: about 29 500 sq. km (11 400 sq. miles). Also called: **the Gaspé.**

gasper (ˈgɑːspə) NOUN [1] a person who gasps. [2] *Brit dated slang* a cheap cigarette. [3] *Informal* something that shocks one or causes one to gasp in astonishment.

gaspereau (ˈgæspərəʊ) NOUN *Canadian* another name for **alewife.**
▷HISTORY from Canadian French

gas-permeable lens NOUN a contact lens made of rigid plastic that is more permeable to air than a standard hard lens. Abbreviation: **GP.** Compare **hard lens, soft lens.**

gas plant NOUN an aromatic white-flowered Eurasian rutaceous plant, *Dictamnus albus,* that emits a vapour capable of being ignited. Also called: **burning bush, dittany, fraxinella.**

gas poker NOUN a long tubular gas burner used to kindle a fire.

gas ring NOUN a circular assembly of gas jets, used esp for cooking.

gassed (gæst) ADJECTIVE *Slang* drunk.

gasser (ˈgæsə) NOUN a drilling or well that yields natural gas.

gassing (ˈgæsɪŋ) NOUN [1] the act or process of supplying or treating with gas. [2] the affecting or poisoning of persons with gas or fumes. [3] the evolution of a gas, esp in electrolysis.

gas station NOUN *Chiefly US and Canadian* another term for **filling station.**

gassy (ˈgæsɪ) ADJECTIVE **-sier, -siest.** [1] filled with, containing, or resembling gas. [2] *Informal* full of idle or vapid talk.
▸**ˈgassiness** NOUN

gasteropod (ˈgæstərəˌpɒd) NOUN, ADJECTIVE a variant of **gastropod.**

gas thermometer NOUN a device for measuring temperature by observing the pressure of gas at a constant volume or the volume of a gas kept at a constant pressure.

gastight (ˈgæsˌtaɪt) ADJECTIVE not allowing gas to enter or escape.

gastralgia (gæsˈtrældʒɪə) NOUN pain in the stomach.
▸**gasˈtralgic** ADJECTIVE

gastrectomy (gæsˈtrɛktəmɪ) NOUN, *plural* **-mies.** surgical removal of all or part of the stomach.

gastric (ˈgæstrɪk) ADJECTIVE of, relating to, near, or involving the stomach: *gastric pains.*

gastric juice NOUN a digestive fluid secreted by the stomach, containing hydrochloric acid, pepsin, rennin, etc.

gastric ulcer NOUN an ulcer of the mucous membrane lining the stomach. Compare **peptic ulcer.**

gastrin (ˈgæstrɪn) NOUN a polypeptide hormone secreted by the stomach: stimulates secretion of gastric juice.

gastritis (gæsˈtraɪtɪs) NOUN inflammation of the lining of the stomach.
▸**gastritic** (gæsˈtrɪtɪk) ADJECTIVE

gastro- *or often before a vowel* **gastr-** COMBINING FORM stomach: *gastroenteritis; gastritis.*
▷HISTORY from Greek *gastēr*

gastrocolic (ˌgæstrəʊˈkɒlɪk) ADJECTIVE of or relating to the stomach and colon: *gastrocolic reflex.*

gastroduodenostomy (ˌgæstrəʊˌdjuːəʊdiːˈnɒstəmɪ) NOUN a surgical operation in which the duodenum is joined to a new opening in the stomach, esp to bypass an obstruction.

gastroenteric (ˌgæstrəʊenˈtɛrɪk) ADJECTIVE another word for **gastrointestinal.**

gastroenteritis (ˌgæstrəʊˌɛntəˈraɪtɪs) NOUN inflammation of the stomach and intestines.
▸**gastroenteritic** (ˌgæstrəʊˌɛntəˈrɪtɪk) ADJECTIVE

gastroenterology (ˌgæstrəʊˌɛntəˈrɒlədʒɪ) NOUN the branch of medical science concerned with diseases of the stomach and intestines.
▸**ˌgastroˌenterˈologist** NOUN

gastroenterostomy (ˌgæstrəʊˌɛntəˈrɒstəmɪ) NOUN, *plural* **-mies.** surgical formation of an artificial opening between the stomach and the small intestine.

gastrointestinal (ˌgæstrəʊɪnˈtɛstɪnᵊl) ADJECTIVE of or relating to the stomach and intestinal tract.

gastrolith (ˈgæstrəlɪθ) NOUN *Pathol* a stone in the stomach; gastric calculus.

gastrology (gæsˈtrɒlədʒɪ) NOUN a former name for **gastroenterology.**
▸**gastrological** (ˌgæstrəˈlɒdʒɪkᵊl) ADJECTIVE
▸**gasˈtrologist** NOUN

gastronome (ˈgæstrəˌnəʊm), **gastronomer** (gæsˈtrɒnəmə), *or* **gastronomist** NOUN less common words for **gourmet.**

gastronomic (ˌgæstrəˈnɒmɪk) *or* **gastronomical** ADJECTIVE of or relating to food and cookery, esp the art of good eating.
▸**ˌgastroˈnomically** ADVERB

gastronomy (gæsˈtrɒnəmɪ) NOUN [1] the art of good eating. [2] the type of cookery of a particular region: *the gastronomy of Provence.*
▷HISTORY C19: from French *gastronomie,* from Greek *gastronomia,* from *gastēr* stomach; see -NOMY

gastropod (ˈgæstrəˌpɒd) *or* **gasteropod** NOUN [1] any mollusc of the class *Gastropoda,* typically having a flattened muscular foot for locomotion and a head that bears stalked eyes. The class includes the snails, whelks, limpets, and slugs. ♦ ADJECTIVE [2] of, relating to, or belonging to the *Gastropoda.*
▸**gastropodan** (gæsˈtrɒpədᵊn) ADJECTIVE, NOUN
▸**gasˈtropodous** ADJECTIVE

gastro-pub NOUN a pub serving restaurant-quality food.

gastroscope (ˈgæstrəˌskəʊp) NOUN a medical instrument for examining the interior of the stomach.
▸**gastroscopic** (ˌgæstrəˈskɒpɪk) ADJECTIVE ▸**gastroscopist** (gæsˈtrɒskəpɪst) NOUN ▸**gasˈtroscopy** NOUN

gastrostomy (gæsˈtrɒstəmɪ) NOUN, *plural* **-mies.** surgical formation of an artificial opening into the stomach from the skin surface: used for feeding.

gastrotomy (gæsˈtrɒtəmɪ) NOUN, *plural* **-mies.** surgical incision into the stomach.

gastrotrich (ˈgæstrətrɪk) NOUN any minute aquatic multicellular animal of the phylum *Gastrotricha,* having a wormlike body covered with cilia and bristles.
▷HISTORY from New Latin *gastrotricha,* from GASTRO- + Greek *-trichos* -haired: see TRICHO-

gastrovascular (ˌgæstrəʊˈvæskjʊlə) ADJECTIVE (esp of the body cavities of coelenterates) functioning in digestion and circulation.

gastrula (ˈgæstrʊlə) NOUN, *plural* **-las** *or* **-lae** (-ˌliː). a saclike animal embryo consisting of three layers of cells (see **ectoderm, mesoderm,** and **endoderm**) surrounding a central cavity (archenteron) with a small opening (blastopore) to the exterior.
▷HISTORY C19: New Latin: little stomach, from Greek *gastēr* belly
▸**ˈgastrular** ADJECTIVE

gastrulation (ˌgæstrʊˈleɪʃən) NOUN *Embryol* the process in which a gastrula is formed from a blastula by the inward migration of cells.

gas turbine NOUN an internal-combustion engine in which the expanding gases emerging from one or more combustion chambers drive a turbine. A rotary compressor driven by the turbine compresses the air used for combustion, power being taken either as torque from the turbine or thrust from the expanding gases.

gas vacuole NOUN *Biology* a gas-filled structure that provides buoyancy in some aquatic bacteria.

gas welding NOUN a method of welding in which a combination of gases, usually oxyacetylene, is used to provide a hot flame.

gas well NOUN a well for obtaining natural gas.

gasworks (ˈgæsˌwɜːks) NOUN (*functioning as singular*) a plant in which gas, esp coal gas, is made.

gat¹ (gæt) VERB *Archaic* a past tense of **get.**

gat² (gæt) NOUN *Slang, chiefly US* a pistol or revolver.
▷HISTORY C20: shortened from GATLING GUN

gat³ (gæt) NOUN a narrow channel of water.
▷HISTORY C18: probably from Old Norse *gat* passage; related to GATE¹

gate¹ (geɪt) NOUN 1 a movable barrier, usually hinged, for closing an opening in a wall, fence, etc. 2 an opening to allow passage into or out of an enclosed place. 3 any means of entrance or access. 4 a mountain pass or gap, esp one providing entry into another country or region. 5 **a** the number of people admitted to a sporting event or entertainment. **b** the total entrance money received from them. 6 (in a large airport) any of the numbered exits leading to the airfield or aircraft: *passengers for Paris should proceed to gate 14.* 7 *Horse racing* short for **starting gate.** 8 *Electronics* **a** a logic circuit having one or more input terminals and one output terminal, the output being switched between two voltage levels determined by the combination of input signals. **b** a circuit used in radar that allows only a fraction of the input signal to pass. 9 the electrode region or regions in a field-effect transistor that is biased to control the conductivity of the channel between the source and drain. 10 a component in a motion-picture camera or projector that holds each frame flat and momentarily stationary behind the lens. 11 a slotted metal frame that controls the positions of the gear lever in a motor vehicle. 12 *Rowing* a hinged clasp to prevent the oar from jumping out of a rowlock. 13 a frame surrounding the blade or blades of a saw. ◆ VERB (*tr*) 14 to provide with a gate or gates. 15 *Brit* to restrict (a student) to the school or college grounds as a punishment. 16 to select (part of a waveform) in terms of amplitude or time.
▷HISTORY Old English *geat;* related to Old Frisian *jet* opening, Old Norse *gat* opening, passage
▸ **'gateless** ADJECTIVE ▸ **'gate,like** ADJECTIVE

gate² (geɪt) NOUN *Dialect* 1 the channels by which molten metal is poured into a mould. 2 the metal that solidifies in such channels.
▷HISTORY C17: probably related to Old English *gyte* a pouring out, *geotan* to pour

gate³ (geɪt) NOUN *Scot and northern English dialect* 1 a way, road, street, or path. 2 a way or method of doing something.
▷HISTORY C13: from Old Norse *gata* path; related to Old High German *gazza* road, street

-gate NOUN COMBINING FORM indicating a person or thing that has been the cause of, or is associated with, a public scandal.
▷HISTORY C20: on the analogy of WATERGATE

gateau *or* **gâteau** ('gætəʊ) NOUN, *plural* **-teaux** (-təʊz). any of various elaborate cakes, usually layered with cream and richly decorated.
▷HISTORY French: cake

gate-crash VERB to gain entry to (a party, concert, etc.) without invitation or payment.
▸ **'gate-,crasher** NOUN

gatefold ('geɪt,fəʊld) NOUN an oversize page in a book or magazine that is folded in. Also called: **foldout.**

gatefold sleeve NOUN a record sleeve that opens out like a book.

gatehouse ('geɪt,haʊs) NOUN 1 a building above or beside an entrance gate to a city, university, etc., often housing a porter or guard, or (formerly) used as a fortification. 2 a small house at the entrance to the grounds of a country mansion. 3 a structure that houses the controls operating lock gates or dam sluices.

gatekeeper ('geɪt,kiːpə) NOUN 1 a person who has charge of a gate and controls who may pass through it. 2 any of several Eurasian butterflies of the genus *Pyronia*, esp *P. tithonus,* having brown-bordered orange wings with a black-and-white eyespot on each forewing: family *Satyridae.* 3 a manager in a large organization who controls the flow of information, esp to parent and subsidiary companies.

gate-leg table *or* **gate-legged table** NOUN a table with one or two drop leaves that are supported when in use by a hinged leg swung out from the frame.

gate money NOUN the total receipts taken for admission to a sporting event or other entertainment.

gatepost ('geɪt,pəʊst) NOUN 1 **a** the post on which a gate is hung. **b** the post to which a gate is fastened when closed. 2 **between you, me, and the gatepost.** confidentially. 3 *Logic* another name for **turnstile** (sense 3).

Gateshead ('geɪts,hɛd) NOUN 1 a port in NE England, in Gateshead unitary authority, Tyne and Wear: engineering works, cultural centre. Pop.: 83 159 (1991). 2 a unitary authority in NE England, in Tyne and Wear. Pop.: 191 151 (2001). Area: 142 sq. km (55 sq. miles).

gate valve NOUN a valve in a pipe or channel having a sliding plate that controls the flow.

gateway ('geɪt,weɪ) NOUN 1 an entrance that may be closed by or as by a gate. 2 a means of entry or access: *Bombay, gateway to India.* 3 *Computing* hardware and software that connect incompatible computer networks, allowing information to be passed from one to another.

gateway drug NOUN a recreational drug such as cannabis, the use of which is believed by some to encourage the user to try stronger drugs.

Gath (gæθ) NOUN *Old Testament* one of the five cities of the Philistines, from which Goliath came (I Samuel 17:4) and near which Saul fell in battle (II Samuel 1:20). Douay spelling: **Geth** (geθ).

Gatha ('gɑːtə) NOUN *Zoroastrianism* any of a number of versified sermons in the Avesta that are in a more ancient dialect than the rest.
▷HISTORY from Avestan *gāthā-;* related to Sanskrit *gāthā* song

gather ('gæðə) VERB 1 to assemble or cause to assemble. 2 to collect or be collected gradually; muster. 3 (*tr*) to learn from information given; conclude or assume. 4 (*tr*) to pick or harvest (flowers, fruit, etc.). 5 (*tr; foll by to or into*) to clasp or embrace: *the mother gathered the child into her arms.* 6 (*tr*) to bring close (to) or wrap (around): *she gathered her shawl about her shoulders.* 7 to increase or cause to increase gradually, as in force, speed, intensity, etc. 8 to contract (the brow) or (of the brow) to become contracted into wrinkles; knit. 9 (*tr*) to assemble (sections of a book) in the correct sequence for binding. 10 (*tr*) to collect by making a selection. 11 (*tr*) to prepare or make ready: *to gather one's wits.* 12 to draw (material) into a series of small tucks or folds by passing a thread through it and then pulling it tight. 13 (*intr*) (of a boil or other sore) to come to a head; form pus. ◆ NOUN 14 **a** the act of gathering. **b** the amount gathered. 15 a small fold in material, as made by a tightly pulled stitch; tuck. 16 *Printing* an informal name for **section** (sense 17).
▷HISTORY Old English *gadrian;* related to Old Frisian *gaderia,* Middle Low German *gaderen*
▸ **'gatherable** ADJECTIVE ▸ **'gatherer** NOUN

gathering ('gæðərɪŋ) NOUN 1 a group of people, things, etc., that are gathered together; assembly. 2 *Sewing* a gather or series of gathers in material. 3 **a** the formation of pus in a boil. **b** the pus so formed. 4 *Printing* an informal name for **section** (sense 17).

Gatling gun ('gætlɪŋ) NOUN a hand-cranked automatic machine gun equipped with a rotating cluster of barrels that are fired in succession using brass cartridges.
▷HISTORY C19: named after R. J. *Gatling* (1818–1903), its US inventor

GATT (gæt) NOUN ACRONYM FOR General Agreement on Tariffs and Trade: a multilateral international treaty signed in 1947 to promote trade, esp by means of the reduction and elimination of tariffs and import quotas; replaced in 1995 by the World Trade Organization.

Gatún Lake (*Spanish* ga'tun) NOUN a lake in Panama, part of the Panama Canal: formed in 1912 on the completion of the **Gatún Dam** across the Chagres River. Area: 424 sq. km (164 sq. miles).

gauche (gəʊʃ) ADJECTIVE lacking ease of manner; tactless.
▷HISTORY C18: French: awkward, left, from Old French *gauchir* to swerve, ultimately of Germanic origin; related to Old High German *wankōn* to stagger
▸ **'gauchely** ADVERB ▸ **'gaucheness** NOUN

gaucherie (,gəʊʃə'riː, 'gəʊʃərɪ; *French* goʃri) NOUN 1 the quality of being gauche. 2 a gauche act.

gaucho ('gaʊtʃəʊ) NOUN, *plural* **-chos.** a cowboy of the South American pampas, usually one of mixed Spanish and Indian descent.
▷HISTORY C19: from American Spanish, probably from Quechuan *wáhcha* orphan, vagabond

gaud (gɔːd) NOUN an article of cheap finery; trinket; bauble.
▷HISTORY C14: probably from Old French *gaudir* to be joyful, from Latin *gaudēre*

gaudeamus igitur *Latin* (,gaʊdɪ'ɑːmʊs 'ɪgɪ,tʊə, ,gɔːdɪ'eɪməs 'ɪdʒɪtə) INTERJECTION let us therefore rejoice.
▷HISTORY from a medieval student song

gaudery ('gɔːdərɪ) NOUN, *plural* **-eries.** cheap finery or display.

gaudy¹ ('gɔːdɪ) ADJECTIVE **gaudier, gaudiest.** gay, bright, or colourful in a crude or vulgar manner; garish.
▷HISTORY C16: from GAUD
▸ **'gaudily** ADVERB ▸ **'gaudiness** NOUN

gaudy² ('gɔːdɪ) NOUN, *plural* **gaudies.** *Brit* a celebratory festival or feast held at some schools and colleges.
▷HISTORY C16: from Latin *gaudium* joy, from *gaudēre* to rejoice

gauffer ('gəʊfə) NOUN, VERB a less common spelling of **goffer.**

gauge *or* **gage** (geɪdʒ) VERB (*tr*) 1 to measure or determine the amount, quantity, size, condition, etc., of. 2 to estimate or appraise; judge. 3 to check for conformity or bring into conformity with a standard measurement, dimension, etc. ◆ NOUN 4 a standard measurement, dimension, capacity, or quantity. 5 any of various instruments for measuring a quantity: *a pressure gauge.* 6 any of various devices used to check for conformity with a standard measurement. 7 a standard or means for assessing; test; criterion. 8 scope, capacity, or extent. 9 the diameter of the barrel of a gun, esp a shotgun. 10 the thickness of sheet metal or the diameter of wire. 11 the distance between the rails of a railway track: in Britain 4 ft. 8½ in. (1.435 m). 12 the distance between two wheels on the same axle of a vehicle, truck, etc. 13 *Nautical* the position of a vessel in relation to the wind and another vessel. One vessel may be windward (**weather gauge**) or leeward (**lee gauge**) of the other. 14 the proportion of plaster of Paris added to mortar to accelerate its setting. 15 the distance between the nails securing the slates, tiles, etc., of a roof. 16 a measure of the fineness of woven or knitted fabric, usually expressed as the number of needles used per inch. 17 the width of motion-picture film or magnetic tape. ◆ ADJECTIVE 18 (of a pressure measurement) measured on a pressure gauge that registers zero at atmospheric pressure; above or below atmospheric pressure: *5 bar gauge.* See also **absolute** (sense 10).
▷HISTORY C15: from Old Northern French, probably of Germanic origin
▸ **'gaugeable** *or* **'gageable** ADJECTIVE ▸ **'gaugeably** *or* **'gageably** ADVERB

gauge boson NOUN *Physics* a boson that mediates the interaction between elementary particles. There are several types: photons for electromagnetic interactions, W and Z intermediate vector bosons for weak interactions, and gravitons for gravitational interactions.

gauger *or* **gager** ('geɪdʒə) NOUN 1 a person or thing that gauges. 2 *Chiefly Brit* a customs officer who inspects bulk merchandise, esp liquor casks, for excise duty purposes. 3 a collector of excise taxes.

gauge theory NOUN *Physics* a type of theory of elementary particles designed to explain the strong, weak, and electromagnetic interactions in terms of exchange of virtual particles.

Gauhati (gaʊ'hɑːtɪ) NOUN a city in NE India, in Assam on the River Brahmaputra: centre of British administration in Assam (1826–74). Pop.: 584 342 (1991).

Gaul (gɔːl) NOUN 1 an ancient region of W Europe corresponding to N Italy, France, Belgium, part of Germany, and the S Netherlands: divided into Cisalpine Gaul, which became a Roman province before 100 B.C., and Transalpine Gaul, which was conquered by Julius Caesar (58–51 B.C.). Latin name: **Gallia.** 2 a native of ancient Gaul. 3 a Frenchman.

Gauleiter ('gaʊˌlaɪtə) NOUN 1 a provincial governor in Germany under Hitler. 2 *(sometimes not capital) Informal* a person in a position of petty or local authority who behaves in an overbearing authoritarian manner.
▷HISTORY from German, from *Gau* district + *Leiter* LEADER

Gaulish ('gɔːlɪʃ) NOUN 1 the extinct language of the pre-Roman Gauls, belonging to the Celtic branch of the Indo-European family. ◆ ADJECTIVE 2 of or relating to ancient Gaul, the Gauls, or their language.

Gaullism ('gəʊlɪzəm, 'gɔː-) NOUN 1 the conservative French nationalist policies and principles associated with General Charles de Gaulle (1890–1970), the French general and statesman. 2 a political movement founded on and supporting General de Gaulle's principles and policies.

Gaullist ('gəʊlɪst, 'gɔː-) NOUN 1 a supporter of Gaullism. ◆ ADJECTIVE 2 of, characteristic of, supporting, or relating to Gaullism.

gault (gɔːlt) NOUN a stiff compact clay or thick heavy clayey soil.
▷HISTORY C16: of obscure origin

Gault (gɔːlt) NOUN **the.** the Lower Cretaceous clay formation in eastern England.

gaultheria (gɔːl'θɪərɪə) NOUN any aromatic evergreen shrub of the ericaceous genus *Gaultheria,* of America, Asia, Australia, and New Zealand, esp the wintergreen.
▷HISTORY C19: New Latin, after Jean-François *Gaultier,* 18th-century Canadian physician and botanist

gaumless ('gɔːmlɪs) ADJECTIVE a variant spelling of **gormless.**

gaun (gɔːn) VERB the present participle of **gae.**

gaunt (gɔːnt) ADJECTIVE 1 bony and emaciated in appearance. 2 (of places) bleak or desolate.
▷HISTORY C15: perhaps of Scandinavian origin; compare Norwegian dialect *gand* tall lean person
▸ **'gauntly** ADVERB ▸ **'gauntness** NOUN

gauntlet[1] ('gɔːntlɪt) *or* **gantlet** NOUN 1 a medieval armoured leather glove. 2 a heavy glove with a long cuff. 3 **take up** (*or* **throw down**) **the gauntlet.** to accept (or offer) a challenge.
▷HISTORY C15: from Old French *gantelet,* diminutive of *gant* glove, of Germanic origin

gauntlet[2] ('gɔːntlɪt) NOUN 1 a punishment in which the victim is forced to run between two rows of men who strike at him as he passes: formerly a military punishment. 2 **run the gauntlet. a** to suffer this punishment. **b** to endure an onslaught or ordeal, as of criticism. 3 a testing ordeal; trial. 4 a variant spelling of **gantlet**[1] (sense 1).
▷HISTORY C15: changed (through influence of GAUNTLET[1]) from earlier *gantlope;* see GANTLET[1]

gauntry ('gɔːntrɪ) NOUN, *plural* **-tries.** a variant of **gantry.**

gaup (gɔːp) VERB a variant spelling of **gawp.**

gaur (gaʊə) NOUN a large wild member of the cattle tribe, *Bos gaurus,* inhabiting mountainous regions of S Asia.
▷HISTORY C19: from Hindi, from Sanskrit *gāura*

Gause's principle ('gaʊzəz) NOUN *Ecology* the principle that similar species cannot coexist for long in the same ecological niche.
▷HISTORY named after G. F. *Gause,* 20th-century Soviet biologist

gauss (gaʊs) NOUN, *plural* **gauss.** the cgs unit of magnetic flux density; the flux density that will induce an emf of 1 abvolt (10^{-8} volt) per centimetre in a wire moving across the field at a velocity of 1 centimetre per second. 1 gauss is equivalent to 10^{-4} tesla.
▷HISTORY after Karl Friedrich *Gauss* (1777–1855), German mathematician

Gaussian distribution NOUN another name for **normal distribution.**

gaussmeter ('gaʊsˌmiːtə) NOUN an instrument for measuring the intensity of a magnetic field.

Gautama ('gaʊtəmə) NOUN the Sanskrit form of the family name of Siddhartha, the historical Buddha.

Gauteng (xaʊ'tɛŋ) NOUN a province of N South Africa; formed in 1994 from part of the former province of Transvaal: service industries, mining, and manufacturing. Capital: Johannesburg. Pop.: 7 807 273 (1999 est.). Area: 18 810 sq. km (7262 sq. miles).

gauze (gɔːz) NOUN 1 **a** a transparent cloth of loose plain or leno weave. **b** *(as modifier): a gauze veil.* 2 a surgical dressing of muslin or similar material. 3 any thin openwork material, such as wire. 4 a fine mist or haze.
▷HISTORY C16: from French *gaze,* perhaps from GAZA, where it was believed to originate

gauzy ('gɔːzɪ) ADJECTIVE **gauzier, gauziest.** resembling gauze; thin and transparent.
▸ **'gauzily** ADVERB ▸ **'gauziness** NOUN

gavage ('gævɑːʒ) NOUN forced feeding by means of a tube inserted into the stomach through the mouth.
▷HISTORY C19: from French, from *gaver,* from Old French (dialect) *gave* throat

gave (geɪv) VERB the past tense of **give.**

gavel ('gævᵊl) NOUN 1 a small hammer used by a chairman, auctioneer, etc., to call for order or attention. 2 a hammer used by masons to trim rough edges off stones.
▷HISTORY C19: of unknown origin

gavelkind ('gævᵊlˌkaɪnd) NOUN 1 a former system of land tenure peculiar to Kent based on the payment of rent to the lord instead of the performance of services by the tenant. 2 the land subject to such tenure. 3 *English law* (formerly) land held under this system.
▷HISTORY C13: from Old English *gafol* tribute + *gecynd* KIND[2]

gavial ('geɪvɪəl), **gharial,** *or* **garial** ('gærɪəl) NOUN 1 a large fish-eating Indian crocodilian, *Gavialis gangeticus,* with a very long slender snout: family *Gavialidae.* 2 **false gavial.** a SE Asian crocodile, *Tomistoma schlegeli,* similar to but smaller than the gavial.
▷HISTORY C19: from French, from Hindi *ghariyāl*

Gävle (*Swedish* 'jɛːvlə) NOUN a port in E Sweden, on an inlet of the Gulf of Bothnia. Pop.: 90 270 (1994).

gavotte *or* **gavot** (gə'vɒt) NOUN 1 an old formal dance in quadruple time. 2 a piece of music composed for or in the rhythm of this dance.
▷HISTORY C17: from French, from Provençal *gavoto,* from *gavot* mountaineer, dweller in the Alps (where the dance originated), from *gava* goitre (widespread in the Alps), from Old Latin *gaba* (unattested) throat

gawk (gɔːk) NOUN 1 a clumsy stupid person; lout. ◆ VERB 2 *(intr)* to stare in a stupid way; gape.
▷HISTORY C18: from Old Danish *gaukr;* probably related to GAPE

gawky ('gɔːkɪ) *or* **gawkish** ADJECTIVE **gawkier, gawkiest.** 1 clumsy or ungainly; awkward. 2 *West Yorkshire dialect* left-handed.
▸ **'gawkily** *or* **'gawkishly** ADVERB ▸ **'gawkiness** *or* **'gawkishness** NOUN

gawp *or* **gaup** (gɔːp) VERB *(intr; often foll by at) Brit slang* to stare stupidly; gape.
▷HISTORY C14 *galpen;* probably related to Old English *gielpan* to boast, YELP. Compare Dutch *galpen* to yelp
▸ **'gawper** NOUN

gay (geɪ) ADJECTIVE 1 **a** homosexual. **b** *(as noun): a group of gays.* 2 **a** carefree and merry: *a gay temperament.* **b** brightly coloured; brilliant: *a gay hat.* **c** given to pleasure, esp in social entertainment: *a gay life.*
▷HISTORY C13: from Old French *gai,* from Old Provençal, of Germanic origin
▸ **'gayness** NOUN

> **Language note** *Gayness* is the state of being homosexual. The noun which refers to the state of being carefree and merry is *gaiety.*

Gaya ('gɑːjə, 'gaɪə) NOUN a city in NE India, in Bihar: Hindu place of pilgrimage and one of the holiest sites of Buddhism. Pop.: 291 675 (1991).

gayal (gə'jæl) NOUN, *plural* **gayal** *or* **gayals.** an ox of India and Myanmar, *Bibos frontalis,* possibly a semidomesticated variety of gaur, black or brown with white stockings.
▷HISTORY C19: from Bengali *gayāl,* from Sanskrit *gāura;* compare GAUR

gaydar ('geɪdɑː) NOUN *Informal* the ability of a homosexual person to recognize whether another person is homosexual.
▷HISTORY C20 from GAY + (RA)DAR

Gay Gordons ('gɔːdᵊnz) NOUN *(functioning as singular) Brit* an energetic old-time dance.

Gay-Lussac's law NOUN 1 the principle that gases react together in volumes (measured at the same temperature and pressure) that bear a simple ratio to each other and to the gaseous products. 2 another name for **Charles' law.**

Gayomart (gɑː'jəʊmɑːt) NOUN *Zoroastrianism* the first man, whose seed was buried in the earth for 40 years and then produced the first human couple.

Gaza ('gɑːzə) NOUN a city in the Gaza Strip: a Philistine city in biblical times. It was under Egyptian administration from 1949 until occupied by Israel (1967). Pop.: 388 031 (1999 est.). Arabic name: **Ghazzah.**

gazania (gə'zeɪnɪə) NOUN any plant of the S. African genus *Gazania,* grown for their rayed flowers in variegated colours; the flowers close in the afternoon: family *Asteraceae.* Also called: **treasure flower.**
▷HISTORY named after Theodore of *Gaza,* 1398–1478, translator of the botanical treatises of Theophrastus

Gazankulu (ˌgazaŋ'kuːluː) NOUN (formerly) a Bantu homeland in South Africa; abolished in 1993. Capital: Giyani.

Gaza Strip NOUN a coastal region on the SE corner of the Mediterranean: administered by Egypt from 1949; occupied by Israel from 1967; granted autonomy in 1993 and administered by the Palestinian National Authority from 1994. Pop.: 1 147 000 (2000 est.).

gaze (geɪz) VERB 1 *(intr)* to look long and fixedly, esp in wonder or admiration. ◆ NOUN 2 a fixed look; stare.
▷HISTORY C14: from Swedish dialect *gasa* to gape at
▸ **'gazer** NOUN

gazebo (gə'ziːbəʊ) NOUN, *plural* **-bos** *or* **-boes.** a summerhouse, garden pavilion, or belvedere, sited to command a view.
▷HISTORY C18: perhaps a pseudo-Latin coinage based on GAZE

gazehound ('geɪzˌhaʊnd) NOUN 1 a hound such as a greyhound that hunts by sight rather than by scent. 2 another name for a **Saluki.**

gazelle (gə'zɛl) NOUN, *plural* **-zelles** *or* **-zelle.** any small graceful usually fawn-coloured antelope of the genera *Gazella* and *Procapra,* of Africa and Asia, such as *G. thomsoni* (**Thomson's gazelle**).
▷HISTORY C17: from Old French, from Arabic *ghazāl*
▸ **ga'zelle-ˌlike** ADJECTIVE

gazelle hound NOUN another name for **Saluki.**

gazette (gə'zɛt) NOUN 1 **a** a newspaper or official journal. **b** *(capital when part of the name of a newspaper): the Thame Gazette.* 2 *Brit* an official document containing public notices, appointments, etc. Abbreviation: **gaz.** ◆ VERB 3 *(tr) Brit* to announce or report (facts or an event) in a gazette.
▷HISTORY C17: from French, from Italian *gazzetta,* from Venetian dialect *gazeta* news-sheet costing one *gazet,* small copper coin, perhaps from *gaza* magpie, from Latin *gaia, gaius* jay

gazetted officer NOUN (in India) a senior official whose appointment is published in the government gazette.

gazetteer (ˌgæzɪ'tɪə) NOUN 1 a book or section of a book that lists and describes places. Abbreviation: **gaz.** 2 *Archaic* a writer for a gazette or newspaper; journalist.

Gaziantep (ˌgɑːziːɑːn'tɛp) NOUN a city in S Turkey: base for Ibrahim Pasha's campaign against the Turks (1839) and centre of Turkish resistance to French forces (1921). Pop.: 712 800 (1997). Former name (until 1921): **Aintab.**

gazpacho (gəz'pɑːtʃəʊ, gæs-) NOUN a Spanish soup made from tomatoes, peppers, etc., and served cold.
▷HISTORY from Spanish

gazump (gə'zʌmp) *Brit* ◆ VERB 1 to raise the price of something, esp a house, after agreeing a price verbally with (an intending buyer). 2 *(tr)* to

swindle or overcharge. ◆ NOUN [3] the act or an instance of gazumping.
▷HISTORY C20: of uncertain origin
▸ga'zumper NOUN

gazunder (gə'zʌndə) *Brit* ◆ VERB [1] to reduce an offer on a property immediately before exchanging contracts, having previously agreed a higher price with (the seller). ◆ NOUN [2] an act or instance of gazundering.
▷HISTORY C20: modelled on GAZUMP
▸ga'zunderer NOUN

Gb [1] SYMBOL FOR gilbert. [2] Also: **GB.** ◆ ABBREVIATION FOR gigabyte.

GB ABBREVIATION FOR: [1] Great Britain. [2] Also: **Gb.** gigabyte. ◆ [3] INTERNATIONAL CAR REGISTRATION FOR Great Britain.

GBA INTERNATIONAL CAR REGISTRATION FOR Alderney.

GBE ABBREVIATION FOR (Knight or Dame) Grand Cross of the British Empire (a Brit. title).

GBG INTERNATIONAL CAR REGISTRATION FOR Guernsey.

GBH ABBREVIATION FOR **grievous bodily harm.**

GBJ INTERNATIONAL CAR REGISTRATION FOR Jersey.

GBM INTERNATIONAL CAR REGISTRATION FOR Isle of Man.

GBS ABBREVIATION FOR George Bernard Shaw.

GBZ INTERNATIONAL CAR REGISTRATION FOR Gibraltar.

GC ABBREVIATION FOR George Cross (a Brit. award for bravery).

GCA [1] *Aeronautics* ◆ ABBREVIATION FOR ground control approach. ◆ [2] INTERNATIONAL CAR REGISTRATION FOR Guatemala.

GCB ABBREVIATION FOR (Knight) Grand Cross of the Bath (a Brit. title).

GCE ABBREVIATION FOR General Certificate of Education: a public examination in specified subjects taken in English and Welsh schools at the ages of 17 and 18. The GCSE has replaced the former GCE O-level for 16-year-olds. See also **AS level, S level.**

GCF *or* **gcf** ABBREVIATION FOR greatest common factor.

GCHQ (in Britain) ABBREVIATION FOR Government Communications Headquarters.

G clef NOUN another name for **treble clef.**

GCMG ABBREVIATION FOR (Knight or Dame) Grand Cross of the Order of St Michael and St George (a Brit. title).

G-cramp NOUN another name for **cramp**[2] (sense 2).

GCSE (in Britain) ABBREVIATION FOR General Certificate of Secondary Education: a public examination in specified subjects for 16-year-old schoolchildren. It replaced the GCE O-level and CSE.

GCVO ABBREVIATION FOR (Knight or Dame) Grand Cross of the Royal Victorian Order (a Brit title).

gd THE INTERNET DOMAIN NAME FOR Grenada.

Gd THE CHEMICAL SYMBOL FOR gadolinium.

Gdańsk (*Polish* gdajinsk) NOUN [1] the chief port of Poland, on the Baltic: a member of the Hanseatic league; under Prussian rule (1793–1807 and 1814–1919); a free city under the League of Nations from 1919 until annexed by Germany in 1939; returned to Poland in 1945. Pop.: 445 988 (1999 est.). German name: **Danzig.** [2] **Bay of.** a wide inlet of the Baltic Sea on the N coast of Poland.

g'day *or* **gidday** (gə'daɪ) SENTENCE SUBSTITUTE an Austral and NZ informal variant of **good day.**

Gdns ABBREVIATION FOR Gardens.

GDP *or* **gdp** ABBREVIATION FOR gross domestic product.

GDR ABBREVIATION FOR German Democratic Republic (East Germany; DDR).

gds ABBREVIATION FOR goods.

Gdynia (*Polish* 'gdɪnja) NOUN a port in N Poland, near Gdańsk: developed 1924–39 as the outlet for trade through the Polish Corridor; naval base. Pop.: 253 521 (1999 est.).

ge THE INTERNET DOMAIN NAME FOR Georgia.

Ge[1] (dʒi:) NOUN another name for **Gaia.**

Ge[2] THE CHEMICAL SYMBOL FOR germanium.

GE INTERNATIONAL CAR REGISTRATION FOR Georgia.

gean (gi:n) NOUN [1] Also called: **wild cherry.** a white-flowered rosaceous tree, *Prunus avium,* of Europe, W Asia, and N Africa, the ancestor of the cultivated sweet cherries. [2] See **sweet cherry** (sense 1).

geanticline (dʒi:'æntɪˌklaɪn) NOUN a gently sloping anticline covering a large area.
▷HISTORY C19: from Greek *gē* earth, land + ANTICLINE
▸geˌanti'clinal ADJECTIVE

gear (gɪə) NOUN [1] a toothed wheel that engages with another toothed wheel or with a rack in order to change the speed or direction of transmitted motion. [2] a mechanism for transmitting motion by gears, esp for a specific purpose: *the steering gear of a boat.* [3] the engagement or specific ratio of a system of gears: *in gear; high gear.* [4] personal equipment and accoutrements; belongings. [5] equipment and supplies for a particular operation, sport, etc.: *fishing gear.* [6] *Nautical* all equipment or appurtenances belonging to a certain vessel, sailor, etc. [7] short for **landing gear.** [8] *Informal* up-to-date clothes and accessories, esp those bought by young people. [9] *Slang* **a** stolen goods. **b** illegal drugs. [10] a less common word for **harness** (sense 1). [11] **in gear.** working or performing effectively or properly. [12] **out of gear.** out of order; not functioning properly. ◆ VERB [13] (*tr*) to adjust or adapt (one thing) so as to fit in or work with another: *to gear our output to current demand.* [14] (*tr*) to equip with or connect by gears. [15] (*intr*) to be in or come into gear. [16] (*tr*) to equip with harness.
▷HISTORY C13: from Old Norse *gervi;* related to Old High German *garawī* equipment, Old English *gearwe*
▸'gearless ADJECTIVE

gearbox ('gɪəˌbɒks) NOUN [1] the metal casing within which a train of gears is sealed. [2] this metal casing and its contents, esp in a motor vehicle.

gear cluster NOUN *Engineering* an assembly of gears permanently attached to a shaft.

gear down VERB (*tr, adverb*) to adapt to a new situation by decreasing output, intensity of operations, etc.

gearing ('gɪərɪŋ) NOUN [1] an assembly of gears designed to transmit motion. [2] the act or technique of providing gears to transmit motion. [3] Also called: **capital gearing.** *Accounting, Brit* the ratio of a company's debt capital to its equity capital. US word: **leverage.**

gear knob NOUN *Brit* a gear lever.

gear lever *or US and Canadian* **gearshift** ('gɪəˌʃɪft) NOUN a lever used to move gearwheels relative to each other, esp in a motor vehicle.

gear train NOUN *Engineering* a system of gears that transmits power from one shaft to another.

gear up VERB (*adverb*) [1] (*tr*) to equip with gears. [2] to prepare, esp for greater efficiency: *is our industry geared up for these new challenges?*

gearwheel ('gɪəˌwi:l) NOUN another name for **gear** (sense 1).

gecko ('gɛkəʊ) NOUN, *plural* **-os** *or* **-oes.** any small insectivorous terrestrial lizard of the family *Gekkonidae,* of warm regions. The digits have adhesive pads, which enable these animals to climb on smooth surfaces.
▷HISTORY C18: from Malay *ge'kok,* of imitative origin

gedact (gə'dɑ:kt, -'dækt) *or* **gedeckt** (gə'dɛkt) NOUN *Music* a flutelike stopped metal diapason organ pipe.
▷HISTORY (*gedeckt*) from German: covered, from *decken* to cover

geddit ('gɛdɪt) INTERJECTION *Slang* an exclamation meaning *do you understand it?: they nicknamed him 'Treasure', because of his sunken chest, geddit?*
▷HISTORY C20: from *Do you get it?* from GET understand

gee[1] (dʒi:) INTERJECTION [1] Also: **gee up!** an exclamation, as to a horse or draught animal, to encourage it to turn to the right, go on, or go faster. ◆ VERB **gees, geeing, geed.** [2] (usually foll by *up*) to move (an animal, esp a horse) ahead; urge on. [3] (followed by *up*) to encourage (someone) to greater effort or activity. ◆ NOUN [4] *Slang* See **gee-gee.**
▷HISTORY C17: origin uncertain

gee[2] (dʒi:) INTERJECTION *US and Canadian informal* a mild exclamation of surprise, admiration, etc. Also: **gee whizz.**
▷HISTORY C20: euphemism for JESUS

geebung ('dʒi:bʌŋ) NOUN [1] any of various trees and shrubs of the genus *Persoonia* of Australia having an edible but tasteless fruit. [2] the fruit of these trees. [3] (in the 19th century) an uncultivated Australian from the country districts.
▷HISTORY from a native Australian language

gee-gee ('dʒi:ˌdʒi:) NOUN *Slang* a horse.
▷HISTORY C19: reduplication of GEE[1]

geek (gi:k) NOUN *Slang* [1] a boring and unattractive social misfit. [2] a person who is preoccupied with or very knowledgeable about computing. [3] a degenerate.
▷HISTORY C19: probably variant of Scottish *geck* fool, from Middle Low German *geck*
▸'geeky ADJECTIVE

geelbek ('xɪəlˌbɛk) NOUN *South African* a yellow-jawed edible marine fish.
▷HISTORY from Afrikaans *geel* yellow + *bek* mouth

Geelong (dʒə'lɒŋ) NOUN a port in SE Australia, in S Victoria on Port Phillip Bay. Pop.: 186 307 (1998 est.).

geepound ('dʒi:ˌpaʊnd) NOUN another name for **slug**[2] (sense 1).
▷HISTORY C20: from *gee,* representing G(RAVITY) + POUND[2]

geese (gi:s) NOUN the plural of **goose.**

geest (gi:st) NOUN an area of sandy heathland in N Germany and adjacent areas.
▷HISTORY C19: Low German *Geest* dry soil

gee-whiz ADJECTIVE *Informal* impressive or amazing: *gee-whiz special effects.*
▷HISTORY C20: from GEE[2]

Ge'ez ('gi:ɛz) NOUN the classical form of the ancient Ethiopic language, having an extensive Christian literature and still used in Ethiopia as a liturgical language.

geezah ('gi:zə) NOUN a variant spelling of **geezer.**

geezer ('gi:zə) NOUN *Informal* a man.
▷HISTORY C19: probably from dialect pronunciation of *guiser,* from GUISE + -ER[1]

gefilte fish *or* **gefüllte fish** (gə'fɪltə) NOUN *Jewish cookery* a dish consisting of fish and matzo meal rolled into balls and poached, formerly served stuffed into the skin of a fish.
▷HISTORY Yiddish, literally: filled fish

gegenschein ('geɪgənˌʃaɪn) NOUN a faint glow in the sky, just visible at a position opposite to that of the sun and having a similar origin to zodiacal light. Also called: **counterglow.**
▷HISTORY German, from *gegen* against, opposite + *Schein* light; see SHINE

geggie ('gɛgɪ) NOUN a Scottish, esp Glaswegian, slang word for the **mouth.**

Gehenna (gɪ'hɛnə) NOUN [1] *Old Testament* the valley below Jerusalem, where children were sacrificed and where idolatry was practised (II Kings 23:10; Jeremiah 19:6) and where later offal and refuse were slowly burned. [2] *New Testament, Judaism* a place where the wicked are punished after death. [3] a place or state of pain and torment.
▷HISTORY C16: from Late Latin, from Greek *Geena,* from Hebrew *Gê' Hinnōm,* literally: valley of Hinnom, symbolic of hell

gehlenite ('geɪləˌnaɪt) NOUN a green mineral consisting of calcium aluminium silicate in tetragonal crystalline form. Formula: $Ca_2Al_2SiO_7$.
▷HISTORY named after A. F. *Gehlen* (1775–1815), German chemist; see -ITE[1]

Geiger counter *or* **Geiger-Müller counter** ('gaɪgə'mʊlə) NOUN an instrument for detecting and measuring the intensity of ionizing radiation. It consists of a gas-filled tube containing a fine wire anode along the axis of a cylindrical cathode with a potential difference of several hundred volts. Any particle or photon which ionizes any number of gas molecules in the tube causes a discharge which is registered by electronic equipment. The magnitude of the discharge does not depend upon the nature or the energy of the ionizing particle. Compare **proportional counter.**
▷HISTORY C20: named after Hans *Geiger* (1882–1945), German physicist and W. *Müller,* 20th-century German physicist

geisha ('geɪʃə) NOUN, *plural* **-sha** *or* **-shas.** a professional female companion for men in Japan, trained in music, dancing, and the art of conversation.

▷HISTORY C19: from Japanese, from *gei* art + *sha* person, from Ancient Chinese *ngi* and *che*

Geissler tube ('gaɪslə) NOUN a glass or quartz vessel, usually having two bulbs containing electrodes separated by a capillary tube, for maintaining an electric discharge in a low-pressure gas as a source of visible or ultraviolet light for spectroscopy.
▷HISTORY C19: named after Heinrich *Geissler* (1814–79), German mechanic

geitonogamy (ˌgaɪtəˈnɒgəmɪ) NOUN *Botany* the transfer of pollen to a stigma of a different flower on the same plant.
▷HISTORY C19: from Greek *geitōn* neighbour + -GAMY

gel (dʒɛl) NOUN [1] a semirigid jelly-like colloid in which a liquid is dispersed in a solid: *nondrip paint is a gel.* [2] See **hair gel.** [3] *Theatre, informal* See **gelatine** (sense 4). ◆ VERB **gels, gelling, gelled.** [4] to become or cause to become a gel. [5] a variant spelling of **jell.**
▷HISTORY C19: by shortening from GELATINE

gelada ('dʒɛlədə, 'gɛl-, dʒɪ'lɑːdə, gɪ-) NOUN a NE African baboon, *Theropithecus gelada,* with dark brown hair forming a mane over the shoulders, a bare red chest, and a ridge muzzle: family *Cercopithecidae.* Also called: **gelada baboon.**
▷HISTORY probably from Arabic *qilādah* mane

Geländesprung (gəˈlɛndəˌʃprʊŋ) *or* **gelände jump** (gəˈlɛndə) NOUN *Skiing* a jump made in downhill skiing, usually over an obstacle.
▷HISTORY German, from *Gelände* terrain + *Sprung* jump

gelatine ('dʒɛləˌtiːn) *or* **gelatin** ('dʒɛlətɪn) NOUN [1] a colourless or yellowish water-soluble protein prepared by boiling animal hides and bones: used in foods, glue, photographic emulsions, etc. [2] an edible jelly made of this substance, sweetened and flavoured. [3] any of various substances that resemble gelatine. [4] Also called (informal): **gel.** a translucent substance used for colour effects in theatrical lighting.
▷HISTORY C19: from French *gélatine,* from Medieval Latin *gelātina,* from Latin *gelāre* to freeze

gelatinize *or* **gelatinise** (dʒɪˈlætɪˌnaɪz) VERB [1] to make or become gelatinous. [2] (*tr*) *Photog* to coat (glass, paper, etc.) with gelatine.
▸**geˌlatiniˈzation** *or* **geˌlatiniˈsation** NOUN ▸**geˈlatiˌnizer** *or* **geˈlatiˌniser** NOUN

gelatinoid (dʒɪˈlætɪˌnɔɪd) ADJECTIVE [1] resembling gelatine. ◆ NOUN [2] a gelatinoid substance, such as collagen.

gelatinous (dʒɪˈlætɪnəs) ADJECTIVE [1] consisting of or resembling jelly; viscous. [2] of, containing, or resembling gelatine.
▸**geˈlatinously** ADVERB ▸**geˈlatinousness** NOUN

gelation[1] (dʒɪˈleɪʃən) NOUN the act or process of freezing a liquid.
▷HISTORY C19: from Latin *gelātiō* a freezing; see GELATINE

gelation[2] (dʒɪˈleɪʃən) NOUN the act or process of forming into a gel.
▷HISTORY C20: from GEL

geld[1] (gɛld) VERB **gelds, gelding, gelded** *or* **gelt.** (*tr*) [1] to castrate (a horse or other animal). [2] to deprive of virility or vitality; emasculate; weaken.
▷HISTORY C13: from Old Norse *gelda,* from *geldr* barren
▸ˈ**gelder** NOUN

geld[2] (gɛld) NOUN a tax on land levied in late Anglo-Saxon and Norman England.
▷HISTORY Old English *gield* service, tax; related to Old Norse *gjald* tribute, Old Frisian *jeld,* Old High German *gelt* retribution, income

Gelderland *or* **Guelderland** ('gɛldəˌlænd; *Dutch* 'xɛldərlɑnt) NOUN a province of the E Netherlands: formerly a duchy, belonging successively to several different European powers. Capital: Arnhem. Pop.: 1 919 200 (2000 est.). Area: 5014 sq. km (1955 sq. miles). Also called: **Guelders.**

gelding ('gɛldɪŋ) NOUN a castrated male horse.
▷HISTORY C14: from Old Norse *geldingr;* see GELD[1], -ING[1]

Gelibolu (geˈlibɔlu) NOUN the Turkish name for **Gallipoli.**

gelid ('dʒɛlɪd) ADJECTIVE very cold, icy, or frosty.
▷HISTORY C17: from Latin *gelidus* icy cold, from *gelu* frost
▸**geˈlidity** *or* ˈ**gelidness** NOUN ▸ˈ**gelidly** ADVERB

gelignite ('dʒɛlɪgˌnaɪt) NOUN a type of dynamite in which the nitrogelatine is absorbed in a base of wood pulp and potassium or sodium nitrate. Also called (informal): **gelly** ('dʒɛlɪ).
▷HISTORY C19: from GEL(ATINE) + Latin *ignis* fire + -ITE[1]

Gelligaer (*Welsh* ˌgɛhliːˈgaɪr) NOUN a town in S Wales, in Caerphilly county borough. Pop.: 15 906 (1991).

gelsemium (dʒɛlˈsiːmɪəm) NOUN, *plural* **-miums** *or* **-mia** (-mɪə). [1] any climbing shrub of the loganiaceous genus *Gelsemium,* of SE Asia and North America, esp the yellow jasmine, having fragrant yellow flowers. [2] the powdered root of the yellow jasmine, formerly used as a sedative.
▷HISTORY C19: New Latin, from Italian *gelsomino* JASMINE

Gelsenkirchen (*German* gelzənˈkɪrçən) NOUN an industrial city in W Germany, in North Rhine-Westphalia. Pop.: 283 300 (1999 est.).

gelt[1] (gelt) VERB *Archaic or dialect* a past tense and past participle of **geld**[1].

gelt[2] (gelt) NOUN *Slang, chiefly US* cash or funds; money.
▷HISTORY C19: from Yiddish, from Old High German *gelt* reward

gem (dʒɛm) NOUN [1] a precious or semiprecious stone used in jewellery as a decoration; jewel. [2] a person or thing held to be a perfect example; treasure. [3] a size of printer's type, approximately equal to 4 point. [4] *NZ* a type of small sweet cake. ◆ VERB **gems, gemming, gemmed.** [5] (*tr*) to set or ornament with gems.
▷HISTORY C14: from Old French *gemme,* from Latin *gemma* bud, precious stone
▸ˈ**gemˌlike** ADJECTIVE ▸ˈ**gemmy** ADJECTIVE

Gemara (gɛˈmɔrə; *Hebrew* gemaˈra) NOUN *Judaism* the main body of the Talmud, consisting of a record of ancient rabbinical debates about the interpretation of the Mishna and constituting the primary source of Jewish religious law. See also **Talmud.**
▷HISTORY C17: from Aramaic *gemārā* completion, from *gemār* to complete
▸**Geˈmaric** ADJECTIVE ▸**Geˈmarist** NOUN

gemclip ('dʒɛmˌklɪp) NOUN *South African* a paperclip.

gemeinschaft (*German* gəˈmainʃaft) NOUN, *plural* **-schaften** (*German* -ʃaftən). (*often capital*) a social group united by common beliefs, family ties, etc. Compare **gesellschaft.**
▷HISTORY German, literally: community

gemfibrozil (dʒɛmˈfaɪbrəʊzɪl) NOUN a drug that lowers the concentration of low-density lipoproteins in the blood and is therefore used to treat patients with hyperlipoproteinaemia.

gemfish ('dʒɛmˌfɪʃ) NOUN, *plural* **-fish** *or* **-fishes.** a food fish, *Rexea solandri,* of Australia, having a delicate flavour.

geminate ADJECTIVE ('dʒɛmɪnɪt, -ˌneɪt) *also* **geminated.** [1] combined in pairs; doubled: *a geminate leaf; a geminate consonant.* ◆ VERB ('dʒɛmɪˌneɪt) [2] to arrange or be arranged in pairs: *the "t"s in "fitted" are geminated.*
▷HISTORY C17: from Latin *gemināre* to double, from *geminus* born at the same time, twin
▸ˈ**geminately** ADVERB

gemination (ˌdʒɛmɪˈneɪʃən) NOUN [1] the act or state of being doubled or paired. [2] the doubling of a consonant. [3] the immediate repetition of a word, phrase, or clause for rhetorical effect.

Geminga NOUN *Astronomy* one of the brightest and nearest gamma-ray sources, situated in the constellation Gemini. A pulsar, it is believed to be a spinning neutron star.
▷HISTORY C20: from GEMINI + *gamma ray*

Gemini ('dʒɛmɪˌnaɪ, -ˌniː) NOUN, *Latin genitive* **Geminorum** (ˌdʒɛmɪˈnɔːrəm). [1] *Astronomy* a zodiacal constellation in the N hemisphere lying between Taurus and Cancer on the ecliptic and containing the stars Castor and Pollux. [2] *Classical myth* another name for **Castor and Pollux.** [3] *Astronautics* any of a series of manned US spacecraft launched between the Mercury and Apollo projects to improve orbital rendezvous and docking techniques. [4] *Astrology* **a** Also called: **the Twins.** the third sign of the zodiac, symbol ♊, having a mutable air classification and ruled by the planet Mercury. The sun is in this sign between about May 21 and June 20. **b** a person born when the sun is in this sign. ◆ ADJECTIVE [5] *Astrology* born under or characteristic of Gemini. ◆ Also (for senses 4b, 5): **Geminian** (ˌdʒɛmɪˈnaɪən).

Geminid ('dʒɛmɪˌnɪd) NOUN a member of a shower of meteors (the *Geminids*) occurring annually around December 13.

Gemini telescope NOUN either of two identical 8-metre telescopes for optical and near-infrared observations built by an international consortium. **Gemini North** is in Hawaii at an altitude of 4200 m on Mauna Kea and **Gemini South** is in Chile at 2715 m on Cerro Pachón.

gem iron NOUN *NZ* a heavy, usually cast-iron oven dish used for baking small cakes (gems).

gemma ('dʒɛmə) NOUN, *plural* **-mae** (-miː). [1] a small asexual reproductive structure in liverworts, mosses, etc., that becomes detached from the parent and develops into a new individual. [2] *Zoology* another name for **gemmule** (sense 1).
▷HISTORY C18: from Latin: bud, GEM
▸**gemmaceous** (dʒɛˈmeɪʃəs) ADJECTIVE

gemmate ('dʒɛmeɪt) ADJECTIVE [1] (of some plants and animals) having or reproducing by gemmae. ◆ VERB [2] (*intr*) to produce or reproduce by gemmae.
▸**gemˈmation** NOUN

gemmiparous (dʒɛˈmɪpərəs) ADJECTIVE (of plants and animals) reproducing by gemmae or buds. Also: **gemmiferous** (dʒɛˈmɪfərəs).
▸**gemˈmiparously** ADVERB

gemmulation (ˌdʒɛmjʊˈleɪʃən) NOUN the process of reproducing by or bearing gemmules.

gemmule ('dʒɛmjuːl) NOUN [1] *Zoology* a cell or mass of cells produced asexually by sponges and developing into a new individual; bud. [2] *Botany* a small gemma. [3] a small hereditary particle postulated by Darwin in his theory of pangenesis.
▷HISTORY C19: from French, from Latin *gemmula* a little bud; see GEM

gemology *or* **gemmology** (dʒɛˈmɒlədʒɪ) NOUN the branch of mineralogy that is concerned with gems and gemstones.
▸**gemological** *or* **gemmological** (ˌdʒɛməˈlɒdʒɪkᵊl) ADJECTIVE ▸**gemˈologist** *or* **gemˈmologist** NOUN

gemot *or* **gemote** (gɪˈməʊt) NOUN (in Anglo-Saxon England) a legal or administrative assembly of a community, such as a shire or hundred.
▷HISTORY Old English *gemōt* MOOT

gemsbok *or* **gemsbuck** ('gɛmzˌbʌk) NOUN, *plural* **-bok, -boks** *or* **-buck, -bucks.** *South African* another word for **oryx.**
▷HISTORY C18: from Afrikaans, from German *Gemsbock,* from *Gemse* chamois + *Bock* BUCK[1]

gemstone ('dʒɛmˌstəʊn) NOUN a precious or semiprecious stone, esp one cut and polished for setting in jewellery. Related adjective: **lapidary.**

gemütlich *German* (gəˈmyːtlɪç) ADJECTIVE having a feeling or atmosphere of warmth and friendliness; cosy.

gen (dʒɛn) NOUN *Informal* information: *give me the gen on your latest project.* See also **gen up.**
▷HISTORY C20: from *gen(eral information)*

Gen. ABBREVIATION FOR: [1] General. [2] *Bible* Genesis.

-gen SUFFIX FORMING NOUNS [1] producing or that which produces: *hydrogen.* [2] something produced: *carcinogen.*
▷HISTORY via French *-gène,* from Greek *-genēs* born

genappe (dʒəˈnæp) NOUN a smooth worsted yarn used for braid, etc.
▷HISTORY C19: from *Genappe,* Belgium, where originally manufactured

Genck (*Flemish* xɛŋk) NOUN a variant spelling of **Genk.**

gendarme ('ʒɒndɑːm; *French* ʒɑ̃darm) NOUN [1] a member of the police force in France or in countries formerly influenced or controlled by France. [2] a slang word for a **policeman.** [3] a sharp pinnacle of rock on a mountain ridge, esp in the Alps.
▷HISTORY C16: from French, from *gens d'armes* people of arms

gendarmerie *or* **gendarmery** (ʒɒnˈdɑːmərɪ; *French* ʒɑ̃darməri) NOUN [1] the whole corps of gendarmes. [2] the headquarters or barracks of a body of gendarmes.

gender (ˈdʒɛndə) NOUN 1 a set of two or more grammatical categories into which the nouns of certain languages are divided, sometimes but not necessarily corresponding to the sex of the referent when animate. See also **natural gender.** 2 any of the categories, such as masculine, feminine, neuter, or common, within such a set. 3 *Informal* the state of being male, female, or neuter. 4 *Informal* all the members of one sex: *the female gender.*
▷HISTORY C14: from Old French *gendre,* from Latin *genus* kind
▶ **ˈgenderless** ADJECTIVE

gender-bender NOUN *Informal* a person who adopts an androgynous style of dress, hair, make-up, etc.

gender-blind ADJECTIVE not discriminating on the basis of gender, or not making a distinction between the sexes.

gender reassignment NOUN male-to-female or female-to-male transformation involving surgery and hormone treatment.

gene (dʒiːn) NOUN a unit of heredity composed of DNA occupying a fixed position on a chromosome (some viral genes are composed of RNA). A gene may determine a characteristic of an individual by specifying a polypeptide chain that forms a protein or part of a protein (**structural gene**); or encode an RNA molecule; or regulate the operation of other genes or repress such operation. See also **operon.**
▷HISTORY C20: from German *Gen,* shortened from *Pangen;* see PAN-, -GEN

-gene SUFFIX FORMING NOUNS a variant of **-gen.**

geneal. ABBREVIATION FOR genealogy.

genealogical tree NOUN another name for a **family tree.**

genealogy (ˌdʒiːnɪˈælədʒɪ) NOUN, *plural* **-gies.** 1 the direct descent of an individual or group from an ancestor. 2 the study of the evolutionary development of animals and plants from earlier forms. 3 a chart showing the relationships and descent of an individual, group, genes, etc.
▷HISTORY C13: from Old French *genealogie,* from Late Latin *geneālogia,* from Greek, from *genea* race
▶ **genealogical** (ˌdʒiːnɪəˈlɒdʒɪkᵊl) *or* **ˌgeneaˈlogic** ADJECTIVE ▶ **ˌgeneaˈlogically** ADVERB ▶ **ˌgeneˈalogist** NOUN

gene bank NOUN *Botany* 1 a collection of seeds, plants, tissue cultures, etc., of potentially useful species, esp species containing genes of significance to the breeding of crops. 2 another name for **gene library.**

gene clone NOUN See **clone** (sense 2).

genecology (ˌdʒɛnɪˈkɒlədʒɪ) NOUN the study of the gene frequency of a species in relation to its population distribution within a particular environment.

gene flow NOUN the movement and exchange of genes between interbreeding populations.

gene frequency NOUN the frequency of occurrence of a particular allele in a population.

gene library NOUN a collection of gene clones that represents the genetic material of an organism: used in genetic engineering. Also called: **gene bank.**

gene pool NOUN the sum of all the genes in an interbreeding population.

genera (ˈdʒɛnərə) NOUN a plural of **genus.**

generable (ˈdʒɛnərəbᵊl) ADJECTIVE able to be generated.
▷HISTORY C15: from Late Latin *generābilis,* from Latin *generāre* to beget

general (ˈdʒɛnərəl, ˈdʒɛnrəl) ADJECTIVE 1 common; widespread: *a general feeling of horror at the crime.* 2 of, including, applying to, or participated in by all or most of the members of a group, category, or community. 3 relating to various branches of an activity, profession, etc.; not specialized: *general office work.* 4 including various or miscellaneous items: *general knowledge; a general store.* 5 not specific as to detail; overall: *a general description of the merchandise.* 6 not definite; vague: *give me a general idea of when you will finish.* 7 applicable or true in most cases; usual. 8 (*prenominal or immediately postpositive*) having superior or extended authority or rank: *general manager; consul general.* 9 Also: **pass.** designating a degree awarded at some universities, studied at a lower academic standard than an honours degree. See **honours** (sense 2). 10 *Med* relating to or involving the entire body or many of its parts; systemic. 11 *Logic* (of a statement) not specifying an individual subject but quantifying over a domain. ◆ NOUN 12 an officer of a rank senior to lieutenant general, esp one who commands a large military formation. 13 any person acting as a leader and applying strategy or tactics. 14 a general condition or principle: opposed to *particular.* 15 a title for the head of a religious order, congregation, etc. 16 *Med* short for **general anaesthetic.** 17 *Archaic* the people; public. 18 **in general.** generally; mostly or usually.
▷HISTORY C13: from Latin *generālis* of a particular kind, from *genus* kind
▶ **ˈgeneralness** NOUN

general anaesthetic NOUN a drug producing anaesthesia of the entire body, with loss of consciousness.

General Assembly NOUN 1 the deliberative assembly of the United Nations. Abbreviation: **GA.** 2 the former name for the parliament of New Zealand. 3 the supreme governing body of certain religious denominations, esp of the Presbyterian Church.

general average NOUN *Insurance* loss or damage to a ship or its cargo that is shared among the shipowners and all the cargo owners. Abbreviation: **GA.** Compare **particular average.**

General Certificate of Education NOUN See **GCE.**

General Certificate of Secondary Education NOUN See **GCSE.**

general delivery NOUN the US and Canadian equivalent of **poste restante.**

general election NOUN 1 an election in which representatives are chosen in all constituencies of a state. 2 *US* a final election from which successful candidates are sent to a legislative body. Compare **primary.** 3 *US and Canadian* (in the US) a national or state election or (in Canada) a federal or provincial election in contrast to a local election.

general hospital NOUN a hospital not specializing in the treatment of particular illnesses or of patients of a particular sex or age group.

generalissimo (ˌdʒɛnərəˈlɪsɪˌməʊ, ˌdʒɛnrə-) NOUN, *plural* **-mos.** a supreme commander of combined military, naval, and air forces, esp one who wields political as well as military power.
▷HISTORY C17: from Italian, superlative of *generale* GENERAL

generalist (ˈdʒɛnərəlɪst, ˈdʒɛnrə-) NOUN 1 **a** a person who is knowledgeable in many fields of study. **b** (*as modifier*): *a generalist profession.* 2 *Ecology* an organism able to utilize many food sources and therefore able to flourish in many habitats. Compare **specialist** (sense 3).

generality (ˌdʒɛnəˈrælɪtɪ) NOUN, *plural* **-ties.** 1 a principle or observation having general application, esp when imprecise or unable to be proved. 2 the state or quality of being general. 3 *Archaic* the majority.

generalization *or* **generalisation** (ˌdʒɛnrəlaɪˈzeɪʃən) NOUN 1 a principle, theory, etc., with general application. 2 the act or an instance of generalizing. 3 *Psychol* the evoking of a response learned to one stimulus by a different but similar stimulus. See also **conditioning.** 4 *Logic* the derivation of a general statement from a particular one, formally by prefixing a quantifier and replacing a subject term by a bound variable. If the quantifier is universal (**universal generalization**) the argument is not in general valid; if it is existential (**existential generalization**) it is valid. 5 *Logic* any statement ascribing a property to every member of a class (**universal generalization**) or to one or more members (**existential generalization**).

generalize *or* **generalise** (ˈdʒɛnrəˌlaɪz) VERB 1 to form (general principles or conclusions) from (detailed facts, experience, etc.); infer. 2 (*intr*) to think or speak in generalities, esp in a prejudiced way. 3 (*tr; usually passive*) to cause to become widely used or known. 4 (*intr*) (of a disease) **a** to spread throughout the body. **b** to change from a localized infection or condition to a systemic one: *generalized infection.*
▶ **ˈgeneralˌizer** *or* **ˈgeneralˌiser** NOUN

generalized other NOUN *Psychol* an individual's concept of other people.

generally (ˈdʒɛnrəlɪ) ADVERB 1 usually; as a rule. 2 commonly or widely. 3 without reference to specific details or facts; broadly.

general officer NOUN an officer holding a commission of brigadier's rank or above in the army, air force, or marine corps.

general paralysis of the insane NOUN a disease of the central nervous system: a late manifestation of syphilis, often occurring up to 15 years after the original infection, characterized by mental deterioration, speech defects, and progressive paralysis. Abbreviation: **GPI.** Also called: **general paresis, dementia paralytica.**

General Post Office NOUN 1 (in Britain until 1969) the department of the central Government that provided postal and telephone services. 2 the main post office in a locality.

general practitioner NOUN a physician who does not specialize but has a medical practice (**general practice**) in which he deals with all illnesses. Informal name: **family doctor.** Abbreviation: **GP.**

general-purpose ADJECTIVE having a range of uses or applications; not restricted to one function.

general semantics NOUN (*functioning as singular*) a school of thought, founded by Alfred Korzybski, that stresses the arbitrary nature of language and other symbols and the problems that result from misunderstanding their nature.

generalship (ˈdʒɛnrəlˌʃɪp) NOUN 1 the art or duties of exercising command of a major military formation or formations. 2 tactical or administrative skill.

general staff NOUN officers assigned to advise commanders in the planning and execution of military operations.

general strike NOUN a strike by all or most of the workers of a country, province, city, etc., esp (*caps.*) such a strike that took place in Britain in 1926.

General Synod NOUN the governing body, under Parliament, of the Church of England, made up of the bishops and elected clerical and lay representatives.

general theory of relativity NOUN the theory of gravitation, developed by Einstein in 1916, extending the special theory of relativity to include acceleration and leading to the conclusion that gravitational forces are equivalent to forces caused by acceleration.

general will NOUN (in the philosophy of Rousseau) the source of legitimate authority residing in the collective will as contrasted with individual interests.

generate (ˈdʒɛnəˌreɪt) VERB (*mainly tr*) 1 to produce or bring into being; create. 2 (*also intr*) to produce (electricity), esp in a power station. 3 to produce (a substance) by a chemical process. 4 *Maths, linguistics* to provide a precise criterion or specification for membership in (a set): *these rules will generate all the noun phrases in English.* 5 *Geometry* to trace or form by moving a point, line, or plane in a specific way: *circular motion of a line generates a cylinder.*
▷HISTORY C16: from Latin *generāre* to beget, from *genus* kind

generation (ˌdʒɛnəˈreɪʃən) NOUN 1 the act or process of bringing into being; production or reproduction, esp of offspring. 2 **a** a successive stage in natural descent of organisms: the time between when an organism comes into being and when it reproduces. **b** the individuals produced at each stage. 3 the normal or average time between two such generations of a species: about 35 years for humans. 4 a phase or form in the life cycle of a plant or animal characterized by a particular type of reproduction: *the gametophyte generation.* 5 all the people of approximately the same age, esp when considered as sharing certain attitudes, etc. 6 production of electricity, heat, etc. 7 *Physics* a set of nuclei formed directly from a preceding set in a chain reaction. 8 (*modifier, in combination*) **a** belonging to a generation specified as having been born in or as having parents, grandparents, etc., born in a given country: *a third-generation American.* **b** belonging to a specified stage of development in manufacture, usually implying improvement: *a second-generation computer.*
▶ **ˌgenerˈational** ADJECTIVE

generation gap NOUN the years separating one generation from the generation that precedes or follows it, esp when regarded as representing the difference in outlook and the lack of understanding between them.

Generation X NOUN members of the generation of people born between the mid-1960s and the mid-1970s who are highly educated and underemployed, reject consumer culture, and have little hope for the future.
▷HISTORY C20: from the novel *Generation X: Tales for an Accelerated Culture* by Douglas Coupland
▸**ˌGeneration ˈXer** NOUN

Generation Y NOUN members of the generation of people born since the early 1980s who are seen as being discerning consumers with a high disposable income.

generative (ˈdʒɛnərətɪv) ADJECTIVE 1 of or relating to the production of offspring, parts, etc.: *a generative cell.* 2 capable of producing or originating.

generative grammar NOUN a description of a language in terms of explicit rules that ideally generate all and only the grammatical sentences of the language. Compare **transformational grammar.**

generative semantics NOUN (*functioning as singular*) a school of semantic theory based on the doctrine that syntactic and semantic structure are of the same formal nature and that there is a single system of rules that relates surface structure to meaning. Compare **interpretive semantics.**

generator (ˈdʒɛnəˌreɪtə) NOUN 1 *Physics* **a** any device for converting mechanical energy into electrical energy by electromagnetic induction, esp a large one as in a power station. **b** a device for producing a voltage electrostatically. **c** any device that converts one form of energy into another form: *an acoustic generator.* 2 an apparatus for producing a gas. 3 a person or thing that generates.

generatrix (ˈdʒɛnəˌreɪtrɪks) NOUN, *plural* **generatrices** (ˈdʒɛnəˌreɪtrɪˌsiːz). a point, line, or plane that is moved in a specific way to produce a geometric figure.

generic (dʒɪˈnɛrɪk) *or* **generical** ADJECTIVE 1 applicable or referring to a whole class or group; general. 2 *Biology* of, relating to, or belonging to a genus: *the generic name.* 3 denoting the nonproprietary name of a drug, food product, etc. ◆ NOUN 4 a drug, food product, etc. that does not have a trademark.
▷HISTORY C17: from French; see GENUS
▸**geˈnerically** ADVERB

generosity (ˌdʒɛnəˈrɒsɪtɪ) NOUN, *plural* **-ties.** 1 willingness and liberality in giving away one's money, time, etc.; magnanimity. 2 freedom from pettiness in character and mind. 3 a generous act. 4 abundance; plenty.

generous (ˈdʒɛnərəs, ˈdʒɛnrəs) ADJECTIVE 1 willing and liberal in giving away one's money, time, etc.; munificent. 2 free from pettiness in character and mind. 3 full or plentiful: *a generous portion.* 4 (of wine) rich in alcohol. 5 (of a soil type) fertile.
▷HISTORY C16: via Old French from Latin *generōsus* nobly born, from *genus* race; see GENUS
▸**ˈgenerously** ADVERB ▸**ˈgenerousness** NOUN

genesis (ˈdʒɛnɪsɪs) NOUN, *plural* **-ses** (-ˌsiːz). a beginning or origin of anything.
▷HISTORY Old English: via Latin from Greek; related to Greek *gignesthai* to be born

Genesis (ˈdʒɛnɪsɪs) NOUN the first book of the Old Testament recounting the events from the Creation of the world to the sojourning of the Israelites in Egypt.

-genesis NOUN COMBINING FORM indicating genesis, development, or generation: *biogenesis; parthenogenesis.*
▷HISTORY New Latin, from Latin: GENESIS
▸**-genetic** *or* **-genic** ADJECTIVE COMBINING FORM

genet[1] (ˈdʒɛnɪt) *or* **genette** (dʒɪˈnɛt) NOUN 1 any agile catlike viverrine mammal of the genus *Genetta,* inhabiting wooded regions of Africa and S Europe, having an elongated head, thick spotted or blotched fur, and a very long tail. 2 the fur of such an animal.
▷HISTORY C15: from Old French *genette,* from Arabic *jarnayt*

genet[2] (ˈdʒɛnɪt) NOUN an obsolete spelling of **jennet.**

gene therapy NOUN the replacement or alteration of defective genes in order to prevent the occurrence of such inherited diseases as haemophilia. Effected by genetic engineering techniques, it is still at the experimental stage.

genetic (dʒɪˈnɛtɪk) *or* **genetical** ADJECTIVE of or relating to genetics, genes, or the origin of something.
▷HISTORY C19: from GENESIS
▸**geˈnetically** ADVERB

genetic code NOUN *Biochem* the order in which the nitrogenous bases of DNA are arranged in the molecule, which determines the type and amount of protein synthesized in the cell. The four bases are arranged in groups of three in a specific order, each group acting as a unit (codon), which specifies a particular amino acid. See also **messenger RNA, transfer RNA.**

genetically modified ADJECTIVE denoting or derived from an organism whose DNA has been altered for the purpose of improvement or correction of defects: *genetically modified food.* Abbreviation: **GM.**
▸**genetic modification** NOUN

genetic counselling NOUN the provision of advice for couples with a history of inherited disorders who wish to have children, including the likelihood of having affected children and the course and management of the disorder, etc.

genetic engineering NOUN alteration of the DNA of a cell for purposes of research, as a means of manufacturing animal proteins, correcting genetic defects, or making improvements to plants and animals bred by man.

genetic fingerprint NOUN the pattern of DNA unique to each individual that can be analysed in a sample of blood, saliva, or tissue: used as a means of identification.

geneticist (dʒɪˈnɛtɪsɪst) NOUN a person who studies or specializes in genetics.

genetic map NOUN a graphic representation of the order of genes within chromosomes by means of detailed analysis of the DNA. See also **chromosome map.**
▸**genetic mapping** NOUN

genetic marker NOUN a gene with two or more alternative forms, producing readily identifiable variations in a particular character, used in studies of linkage, genetic mapping, and identification of the presence of other genes that are closely linked to, and therefore usually inherited with, it.

genetics (dʒɪˈnɛtɪks) NOUN 1 (*functioning as singular*) the branch of biology concerned with the study of heredity and variation in organisms. 2 the genetic features and constitution of a single organism, species, or group.

Geneva (dʒɪˈniːvə) NOUN 1 a city in SW Switzerland, in the Rhône valley on Lake Geneva: centre of Calvinism; headquarters of the International Red Cross (1864), the International Labour Office (1925), the League of Nations (1929–46), the World Health Organization, and the European office of the United Nations; banking centre. Pop.: 172 809 (1999 est.). 2 a canton in SW Switzerland. Capital: Geneva. Pop.: 403 100 (2000 est.). Area: 282 sq. km (109 sq. miles). ◆ French name: **Genève.** German name: **Genf.** 3 **Lake.** a lake between SW Switzerland and E France: fed and drained by the River Rhône, it is the largest of the Alpine lakes; the surface is subject to considerable changes of level. Area: 580 sq. km (224 sq. miles). French name: **Lac Léman.** German name: **Genfersee.**

Geneva bands PLURAL NOUN a pair of white lawn or linen strips hanging from the front of the neck or collar of some ecclesiastical and academic robes.
▷HISTORY C19: named after GENEVA, where originally worn by Swiss Calvinist clergy

Geneva Convention NOUN the international agreement, first formulated in 1864 at Geneva, establishing a code for wartime treatment of the sick or wounded: revised and extended on several occasions to cover maritime warfare and prisoners of war.

Geneva gown NOUN a long loose black gown with very wide sleeves worn by academics or Protestant clerics.
▷HISTORY C19: named after GENEVA; see GENEVA BANDS

Genevan (dʒɪˈniːvᵊn) *or* **Genevese** (ˌdʒɛnɪˈviːz) ADJECTIVE 1 of, relating to, or characteristic of Geneva. 2 of, adhering to, or relating to the teachings of Calvin or the Calvinists. ◆ NOUN, *plural* **-vans** *or* **-vese.** 3 a native or inhabitant of Geneva. 4 a less common name for a **Calvinist.**

Geneva protocol NOUN the agreement in 1925 to ban the use of asphyxiating, poisonous, or other gases in war. It does not ban the development or manufacture of such gases.

Genève (ʒənɛv) NOUN the French name for **Geneva.**

Genf (gɛnf) NOUN the German name for **Geneva** (senses 1, 2).

Genfersee (ˈgɛnfərzeː) NOUN the German name for (Lake) **Geneva.**

genial[1] (ˈdʒiːnjəl, -nɪəl) ADJECTIVE 1 cheerful, easy-going, and warm in manner or behaviour. 2 pleasantly warm, so as to give life, growth, or health: *the genial sunshine.*
▷HISTORY C16: from Latin *geniālis* relating to birth or marriage, from *genius* tutelary deity; see GENIUS
▸**geniality** (ˌdʒiːnɪˈælɪtɪ) *or* **ˈgenialness** NOUN ▸**ˈgenially** ADVERB

genial[2] (dʒɪˈniːəl) ADJECTIVE *Anatomy* of or relating to the chin.
▷HISTORY C19: from Greek *geneion,* from *genus* jaw

genic (ˈdʒɛnɪk) ADJECTIVE of or relating to a gene or genes.

-genic ADJECTIVE COMBINING FORM 1 relating to production or generation: *carcinogenic.* 2 well suited to or suitable for: *photogenic.*
▷HISTORY from -GEN + -IC

genicular (dʒɪˈnɪkjʊlə) ADJECTIVE *Anatomy* of or relating to the knee: *genicular artery.*
▷HISTORY C19: from Latin *genu* knee

geniculate (dʒɪˈnɪkjʊlɪt, -ˌleɪt) ADJECTIVE 1 *Biology* bent at a sharp angle: *geniculate antennae.* 2 having a joint or joints capable of bending sharply.
▷HISTORY C17: from Latin *geniculātus* jointed, from *geniculum* a little knee, small joint, from *genu* knee
▸**geˈniculately** ADVERB ▸**geˌnicuˈlation** NOUN

genie (ˈdʒiːnɪ) NOUN 1 (in fairy tales and stories) a servant who appears by magic and fulfils a person's wishes. 2 another word for **jinni.**
▷HISTORY C18: from French *génie,* from Arabic *jinni* demon, influenced by Latin *genius* attendant spirit; see GENIUS

genii (ˈdʒiːnɪˌaɪ) NOUN the plural of **genius** (senses 5, 6).

genip (ˈdʒɛnɪp) NOUN another word for **genipap.**
▷HISTORY C18: from Spanish *genipa,* from French, from Guarani

genipap (ˈdʒɛnɪˌpæp) *or* **genip** NOUN 1 an evergreen Caribbean rubiaceous tree, *Genipa americana,* with reddish-brown edible orange-like fruits. 2 the fruit of this tree.
▷HISTORY C17: from Portuguese *genipapo,* from Tupi

genit. ABBREVIATION FOR genitive.

genital (ˈdʒɛnɪtᵊl) ADJECTIVE 1 of or relating to the sexual organs or to reproduction. 2 *Psychoanal* relating to the mature stage of psychosexual development in which an affectionate relationship with one's sex partner is established. Compare **anal** (sense 2), **oral** (sense 7), **phallic** (sense 2).
▷HISTORY C14: from Latin *genitālis* concerning birth, from *gignere* to beget

genital herpes NOUN a sexually transmitted disease caused by a variety of the herpes simplex virus in which painful blisters occur in the genital region.

genitals (ˈdʒɛnɪtᵊlz) *or* **genitalia** (ˌdʒɛnɪˈteɪlɪə, -ˈteɪljə) PLURAL NOUN the sexual organs; the testicles and penis of a male or the labia, clitoris, and vagina of a female. Related adjective: **venereal.**
▸**genitalic** (ˌdʒɛnɪˈtælɪk) ADJECTIVE

genitive (ˈdʒɛnɪtɪv) *Grammar* ◆ ADJECTIVE 1 denoting a case of nouns, pronouns, and adjectives in inflected languages used to indicate a relation of ownership or association, usually translated by English *of.* ◆ NOUN 2 **a** the genitive case. **b** a word or speech element in this case.
▷HISTORY C14: from Latin *genetīvus* relating to birth, from *gignere* to produce
▸**genitival** (ˌdʒɛnɪˈtaɪvᵊl) ADJECTIVE ▸**ˌgeniˈtivally** ADVERB

genitor (ˈdʒɛnɪtə, -tɔː) NOUN the biological father as distinguished from the pater or legal father.
▷HISTORY C15: from Latin, from *gignere* to beget

genitourinary (ˌdʒɛnɪtəʊˈjʊərɪnərɪ) ADJECTIVE of or relating to both the reproductive and excretory organs; urogenital.

genitourinary medicine NOUN the branch of medical science concerned with the study and treatment of diseases of the genital and urinary organs, esp sexually transmitted diseases. Abbreviation: **GUM.**

genius (ˈdʒiːnɪəs, -njəs) NOUN, *plural* **-uses** *or for senses 5, 6* **genii** (ˈdʒiːnɪˌaɪ). [1] a person with exceptional ability, esp of a highly original kind. [2] such ability or capacity: *Mozart's musical genius.* [3] the distinctive spirit or creative nature of a nation, era, language, etc. [4] a person considered as exerting great influence of a certain sort: *an evil genius.* [5] *Roman myth* **a** the guiding spirit who attends a person from birth to death. **b** the guardian spirit of a place, group of people, or institution. [6] *Arabic myth* (*usually plural*) a demon; jinn.
▷HISTORY C16: from Latin, from *gignere* to beget

genius loci *Latin* (ˈdʒiːnɪəs ˈləʊsaɪ) NOUN [1] the guardian spirit of a place. [2] the special atmosphere of a particular place.
▷HISTORY genius of the place

genizah (geˈniːzə) NOUN *Judaism* a repository (usually in a synagogue) for books and other sacred objects which can no longer be used but which may not be destroyed.
▷HISTORY C19: from Hebrew, literally: a hiding place, from *gānaz* to hide, set aside

Genk *or* **Genck** (*Flemish* xɛŋk) NOUN a town in NE Belgium, in Limburg province: coal-mining. Pop.: 61 996 (1995 est.).

Genl *or* **genl** ABBREVIATION FOR General *or* general.

genoa (ˈdʒɛnəʊə) NOUN *Yachting* a large triangular jib sail, often with a foot that extends as far aft as the clew of the mainsail. Also called: **genoa jib.** Sometimes shortened to: **genny, jenny.**

Genoa (ˈdʒɛnəʊə) NOUN a port in NW Italy, capital of Liguria, on the **Gulf of Genoa:** Italy's main port; an independent commercial city with many colonies in the Middle Ages; university (1243); heavy industries. Pop.: 636 104 (2000 est.). Italian name: **Genova.**

Genoa cake NOUN a rich fruit cake, usually decorated with almonds.

genocide (ˈdʒɛnəʊˌsaɪd) NOUN the policy of deliberately killing a nationality or ethnic group.
▷HISTORY C20: from *geno-*, from Greek *genos* race + -CIDE
▸ˌ**genoˈcidal** ADJECTIVE

Genoese (ˌdʒɛnəʊˈiːz) *or* **Genovese** (ˌdʒɛnəˈviːz) NOUN, *plural* **-ese** *or* **-vese.** [1] a native or inhabitant of Genoa. ◆ ADJECTIVE [2] of or relating to Genoa or its inhabitants.

genome *or* **genom** (ˈdʒiːnəʊm) NOUN [1] the full complement of genetic material within an organism. [2] all the genes comprising a haploid set of chromosomes.
▷HISTORY C20: from German *Genom,* from *Gen* GENE + (CHROMOS)OME
▸**genomic** (dʒɪˈnɒmɪk) ADJECTIVE

genomics (dʒɪˈnɒmɪks) NOUN (*functioning as singular*) the branch of molecular genetics concerned with the study of genomes, specifically the identification and sequencing of their constituent genes and the application of this knowledge in medicine, pharmacy, agriculture, etc.

genotype (ˈdʒɛnəʊˌtaɪp) NOUN [1] the genetic constitution of an organism. [2] a group of organisms with the same genetic constitution. ◆ Compare **phenotype.**
▸**genotypic** (ˌdʒɛnəʊˈtɪpɪk) *or* ˌ**genoˈtypical** ADJECTIVE ▸ˌ**genoˈtypically** ADVERB ▸**genotypicity** (ˌdʒɛnəʊtɪˈpɪsɪtɪ) NOUN

-genous ADJECTIVE COMBINING FORM [1] yielding or generating: *androgenous; erogenous.* [2] generated by or issuing from: *endogenous.*
▷HISTORY from -GEN + -OUS

Genova (ˈdʒɛːnova) NOUN the Italian name for **Genoa.**

genre (ˈʒɑːnrə) NOUN [1] **a** kind, category, or sort, esp of literary or artistic work. **b** (*as modifier*): *genre fiction.* [2] a category of painting in which domestic scenes or incidents from everyday life are depicted.
▷HISTORY C19: from French, from Old French *gendre;* see GENDER

genre-busting ADJECTIVE not conforming to established patterns, styles, etc.

genro (ˈgenˈrəʊ) NOUN [1] (*functioning as singular or plural*) a group of highly respected elder statesmen in late 19th- and early 20th-century Japan. [2] a member of this group.
▷HISTORY C20: from Japanese, from Ancient Chinese *nguan lao,* from *nguan* first + *lao* elder

gens (dʒɛnz) NOUN, *plural* **gentes** (ˈdʒɛntiːz). [1] (in ancient Rome) any of a group of aristocratic families, having a common name and claiming descent from a common ancestor in the male line. [2] *Anthropol* a group based on descent in the male line.
▷HISTORY C19: from Latin: race; compare GENUS, GENDER

gent (dʒɛnt) NOUN *Informal* short for **gentleman.**

Gent (xɛnt) NOUN the Flemish name for **Ghent.**

genteel (dʒɛnˈtiːl) ADJECTIVE [1] affectedly proper or refined; excessively polite. [2] respectable, polite, and well-bred: *a genteel old lady.* [3] appropriate to polite or fashionable society: *genteel behaviour.*
▷HISTORY C16: from French *gentil* well-born; see GENTLE
▸**genˈteelly** ADVERB ▸**genˈteelness** NOUN

genteelism (dʒɛnˈtiːlɪzəm) NOUN a word or phrase used in place of a less genteel one.

gentian (ˈdʒɛnʃən) NOUN [1] any gentianaceous plant of the genera *Gentiana* or *Gentianella,* having blue, yellow, white, or red showy flowers. [2] the bitter-tasting dried rhizome and roots of *Gentiana lutea* (**European** or **yellow gentian**), which can be used as a tonic. [3] any of several similar plants, such as the horse gentian.
▷HISTORY C14: from Latin *gentiāna;* perhaps named after *Gentius,* a second-century B.C. Illyrian king, reputedly the first to use it medicinally

gentianaceous (ˌdʒɛnʃɪəˈneɪʃəs) ADJECTIVE of, relating to, or belonging to the *Gentianaceae,* a family of flowering plants that includes centaury, felwort, and gentian.

gentian blue NOUN **a** a purplish-blue colour. **b** (*as adjective*): *gentian-blue shoes.*

gentianella (ˌdʒɛnʃəˈnɛlə, -ʃɪə-) NOUN [1] any of various gentianaceous plants, esp the alpine species *Gentiana acaulis,* which has showy blue flowers. [2] any of several related plants of the genus *Gentianella.*
▷HISTORY C17: from New Latin, literally: a little GENTIAN

gentian violet NOUN a greenish crystalline substance, obtained from rosaniline, that forms a violet solution in water, used as an indicator, antiseptic, and in the treatment of burns. Also called: **crystal violet.**

gentile (ˈdʒɛntaɪl) ADJECTIVE [1] denoting an adjective or proper noun used to designate a place or the inhabitants of a place, as *Spanish* and *Spaniard.* [2] of or relating to a tribe or people.
▷HISTORY C14: from Late Latin *gentīlis,* from Latin: one belonging to the same tribe or family; see GENS

Gentile (ˈdʒɛntaɪl) NOUN [1] a person who is not a Jew. [2] a Christian, as contrasted with a Jew. [3] a person who is not a member of one's own church: used esp by Mormons. [4] a heathen or pagan. ◆ ADJECTIVE [5] of or relating to a race or religion that is not Jewish. [6] Christian, as contrasted with Jewish. [7] not being a member of one's own church: used esp by Mormons. [8] pagan or heathen.

gentilesse (ˈdʒɛntəˌlɛs) NOUN *Archaic* politeness or good breeding.
▷HISTORY C14: from Old French *gentillesse;* see GENTEEL

gentility (dʒɛnˈtɪlɪtɪ) NOUN, *plural* **-ties.** [1] respectability and polite good breeding. [2] affected politeness. [3] noble birth or ancestry. [4] people of noble birth.
▷HISTORY C14: from Old French *gentilite,* from Latin *gentīlitās* relationship of those belonging to the same tribe or family; see GENS

gentle (ˈdʒɛntəl) ADJECTIVE [1] having a mild or kindly nature or character. [2] soft or temperate; mild; moderate: *a gentle scolding.* [3] gradual: *a gentle slope.* [4] easily controlled; tame: *a gentle horse.* [5] *Archaic* of good breeding; noble: *gentle blood.* [6] *Archaic* gallant; chivalrous. ◆ VERB (*tr*) [7] to tame or subdue (a horse). [8] to appease or mollify. [9] *Obsolete* to ennoble or dignify. ◆ NOUN [10] a maggot, esp when used as bait in fishing. [11] *Archaic* a person who is of good breeding.
▷HISTORY C13: from Old French *gentil* noble, from Latin *gentīlis* belonging to the same family; see GENS
▸ˈ**gently** ADVERB

gentle breeze NOUN *Meteorol* a light breeze of force three on the Beaufort scale, blowing at 8–12 mph.

gentlefolk (ˈdʒɛntəlˌfəʊk) *or* **gentlefolks** PLURAL NOUN persons regarded as being of good breeding.

gentleman (ˈdʒɛntəlmən) NOUN, *plural* **-men.** [1] a man regarded as having qualities of refinement associated with a good family. [2] a man who is cultured, courteous, and well-educated. [3] a polite name for a man. [4] the personal servant of a gentleman (esp in the phrase **gentleman's gentleman**). [5] *Brit history* a man of gentle birth, who was entitled to bear arms, ranking above a yeoman in social position. [6] (formerly) a euphemistic word for a **smuggler.**
▸ˈ**gentlemanly** ADJECTIVE ▸ˈ**gentlemanliness** NOUN

gentleman-at-arms NOUN, *plural* **gentlemen-at-arms.** a member of the guard who attend the British sovereign on ceremonial and state occasions.

gentleman-farmer NOUN, *plural* **gentlemen-farmers.** [1] a person who engages in farming but does not depend on it for his living. [2] a person who owns farmland but does not farm it personally.

gentlemen's agreement *or* **gentleman's agreement** NOUN a personal understanding or arrangement based on honour and not legally binding.

gentleness (ˈdʒɛntəlnɪs) NOUN [1] the quality of being gentle. [2] *Physics* a property of elementary particles, conserved in certain strong interactions. See also **charm** (sense 7).

gentlewoman (ˈdʒɛntəlˌwʊmən) NOUN, *plural* **-women.** [1] *Archaic* a woman regarded as being of good family or breeding; lady. [2] *Rare* a woman who is cultured, courteous, and well-educated. [3] *History* a woman in personal attendance on a high-ranking lady.
▸ˈ**gentleˌwomanly** ADJECTIVE ▸ˈ**gentleˌwomanliness** NOUN

Gentoo (ˈdʒɛntuː) NOUN, *plural* **-toos.** (*sometimes not capital*) *Archaic* a Hindu, esp as distinguished from a Muslim.
▷HISTORY C17: from Portuguese *gentio* pagan (literally: GENTILE)

gentrification (ˌdʒɛntrɪfɪˈkeɪʃən) NOUN *Brit* a process by which middle-class people take up residence in a traditionally working-class area of a city, changing the character of the area.
▷HISTORY C20: from *gentrify* (to become GENTRY)
▸ˈ**gentriˌfier** NOUN

gentry (ˈdʒɛntrɪ) NOUN [1] persons of high birth or social standing; aristocracy. [2] *Brit* persons just below the nobility in social rank. [3] *Informal, often derogatory* people, esp of a particular group or kind.
▷HISTORY C14: from Old French *genterie,* from *gentil* GENTLE

gents (dʒɛnts) NOUN (*functioning as singular*) *Brit informal* a men's public lavatory.

genu (ˈdʒɛnjuː) NOUN, *plural* **genua** (ˈdʒɛnjʊə). *Anatomy* [1] the technical name for the **knee.** [2] any kneelike bend in a structure or part.
▷HISTORY Latin: knee

genuflect (ˈdʒɛnjʊˌflɛkt) VERB (*intr*) [1] to act in a servile or deferential manner. [2] *RC Church* to bend one or both knees as a sign of reverence, esp when passing before the Blessed Sacrament.
▷HISTORY C17: from Medieval Latin *genūflectere,* from Latin *genu* knee + *flectere* to bend
▸ˌ**genuˈflection** *or* (*esp Brit*) ˌ**genuˈflexion** NOUN ▸ˈ**genuˌflector** NOUN

genuine (ˈdʒɛnjʊɪn) ADJECTIVE [1] not fake or counterfeit; original; real; authentic. [2] not pretending; frank; sincere. [3] being of authentic or original stock.
▷HISTORY C16: from Latin *genuīnus* inborn, hence (in Late Latin) authentic, from *gignere* to produce
▸ˈ**genuinely** ADVERB ▸ˈ**genuineness** NOUN

gen up VERB **gens up, genning up, genned up.** (*adverb; often passive;* when *intr,* usually foll by *on*) *Brit* *informal* to brief (someone) or study (something) in detail; make or become fully conversant with: *I can only take over this job if I am properly genned up.*

genus ('dʒiːnəs) NOUN, *plural* **genera** ('dʒɛnərə) *or* **genuses.** 1 *Biology* any of the taxonomic groups into which a family is divided and which contains one or more species. For example, *Vulpes* (foxes) is a genus of the dog family (*Canidae*). 2 *Logic* a class of objects or individuals that can be divided into two or more groups or species. 3 a class, group, etc., with common characteristics. 4 *Maths* a number characterizing a closed surface in topology equal to the number of handles added to a sphere to form the surface. A sphere has genus 0, a torus genus 1, etc.
▷HISTORY C16: from Latin: race

-geny NOUN COMBINING FORM indicating origin or manner of development: *phylogeny.*
▷HISTORY from Greek *-geneia,* from *-genēs* born
▸**-genic** ADJECTIVE COMBINING FORM

geo *or* **gio** ('dʒiːəʊ) NOUN, *plural* **geos** *or* **gios.** (esp in Shetland) a small fjord or gully.
▷HISTORY C18: from Old Norse *gjā* ravine; related to Old English *gionian* to YAWN

geo- COMBINING FORM indicating earth: *geomorphology.*
▷HISTORY from Greek, from *gē* earth

geocarpy ('dʒiːəʊˌkɑːpɪ) NOUN *Botany* the ripening of fruits below ground, as occurs in the peanut.

geocentric (ˌdʒiːəʊ'sɛntrɪk) ADJECTIVE 1 having the earth at its centre: *the Ptolemaic system postulated a geocentric universe.* 2 measured from or relating to the centre of the earth.
▸**ˌgeo'centrically** ADVERB

geocentric parallax NOUN See **parallax** (sense 2).

geochemistry (ˌdʒiːəʊ'kɛmɪstrɪ) NOUN the geology and chemistry concerned with the chemical composition of, and chemical reactions taking place within, the earth's crust.
▸**geochemical** (ˌdʒiːəʊ'kɛmɪkᵊl) ADJECTIVE ▸**ˌgeo'chemist** NOUN

geochronology (ˌdʒiːəʊkrə'nɒlədʒɪ) NOUN the branch of geology concerned with ordering and dating of events in the earth's history, including the origin of the earth itself.
▸**geochronological** (ˌdʒiːəʊˌkrɒnᵊ'lɒdʒɪkᵊl) ADJECTIVE

geod. ABBREVIATION FOR: 1 geodesy. 2 geodetic.

geode ('dʒiːəʊd) NOUN a cavity, usually lined with crystals, within a rock mass or nodule.
▷HISTORY C17: from Latin *geōdēs* a precious stone, from Greek: earthlike; see GEO-, -ODE[1]
▸**geodic** (dʒɪ'ɒdɪk) ADJECTIVE

geodemographics (ˌdʒiːəʊdɛmə'græfɪks) PLURAL NOUN (*functioning as singular*) the study and grouping of the people in a geographical area according to socioeconomic criteria, esp for market research.

geodesic (ˌdʒiːəʊ'dɛsɪk, -'diː-) ADJECTIVE 1 Also: **geodetic, geodesical.** relating to or involving the geometry of curved surfaces. ◆ NOUN 2 Also called: **geodesic line.** the shortest line between two points on a curved or plane surface.

geodesic dome NOUN a light structural framework arranged as a set of polygons in the form of a shell and covered with sheeting made of plastic, plywood, metal, etc.; developed by Buckminster Fuller.

geodesy (dʒɪ'ɒdɪsɪ) *or* **geodetics** (ˌdʒiːəʊ'dɛtɪks) NOUN the branch of science concerned with determining the exact position of geographical points and the shape and size of the earth.
▷HISTORY C16: from French *géodésie,* from Greek *geōdaisia,* from GEO- + *daiein* to divide
▸**ge'odesist** NOUN

geodetic (ˌdʒiːəʊ'dɛtɪk) ADJECTIVE 1 of or relating to geodesy. 2 another word for **geodesic.**
▸**ˌgeo'detically** ADVERB

geodetic surveying NOUN the surveying of the earth's surface, making allowance for its curvature and giving an accurate framework for smaller-scale surveys.

geodynamics (ˌdʒiːəʊdaɪ'næmɪks) NOUN (*functioning as singular*) the branch of geology concerned with the forces and processes, esp large-scale, of the earth's interior, particularly as regards their effects on the crust or lithosphere.
▸**ˌgeody'namic** ADJECTIVE ▸**ˌgeody'namicist** NOUN

geog. 1 geographic(al). 2 geography.

geognosy (dʒɪ'ɒgnəsɪ) NOUN the study of the origin and distribution of minerals and rocks in the earth's crust: superseded generally by the term **geology.**
▷HISTORY C18: from French *géognosie,* from GEO- + Greek *gnōsis* a seeking to know, knowledge
▸**geognostic** (ˌdʒiːɒg'nɒstɪk) ADJECTIVE

geographical determinism NOUN *Sociol* the theory that human activity is determined by geographical conditions.

geographical mile NOUN a former name for **nautical mile.**

geographic north NOUN another name for **true north.**

geography (dʒɪ'ɒgrəfɪ) NOUN, *plural* **-phies.** 1 the study of the natural features of the earth's surface, including topography, climate, soil, vegetation, etc., and man's response to them. 2 the natural features of a region. 3 an arrangement of constituent parts; plan; layout.
▸**ge'ographer** NOUN ▸**geographical** (ˌdʒɪə'græfɪkᵊl) *or* **ˌgeo'graphic** ADJECTIVE ▸**ˌgeo'graphically** ADVERB

geoid ('dʒiːɔɪd) NOUN 1 a hypothetical surface that corresponds to mean sea level and extends at the same level under the continents. 2 the shape of the earth.

geol. ABBREVIATION FOR: 1 geologic(al). 2 geology.

geological cycle NOUN the series of events in which a rock of one type is converted to one or more other types and then back to the original type. Also called: **rock cycle.**

Geological Survey NOUN a government-sponsored organization working in the field of geology, such as the US Geological Survey, the Geological Survey of India, or the Institute of Geological Sciences (UK).

geological timescale NOUN any division of geological time into chronological units, whether relative (with units in the correct temporal sequence) or absolute (with numerical ages attached).

geologize *or* **geologise** (dʒɪ'ɒləˌdʒaɪz) VERB to study the geological features of (an area).

geology (dʒɪ'ɒlədʒɪ) NOUN 1 the scientific study of the origin, history, structure, and composition of the earth. 2 the geological features of a district or country.
▸**geological** (ˌdʒɪə'lɒdʒɪkᵊl) *or* **ˌgeo'logic** ADJECTIVE ▸**ˌgeo'logically** ADVERB ▸**ge'ologist** *or* **ge'ologer** NOUN

geom. ABBREVIATION FOR: 1 geometric(al). 2 geometry.

geomagnetism (ˌdʒiːəʊ'mægnɪˌtɪzəm) NOUN 1 the magnetic field of the earth. 2 the branch of physics concerned with this.
▸**geomagnetic** (ˌdʒiːəʊmæg'nɛtɪk) ADJECTIVE

geomancy ('dʒiːəʊˌmænsɪ) NOUN prophecy from the pattern made when a handful of earth is cast down or dots are drawn at random and connected with lines.
▸**'geoˌmancer** NOUN ▸**ˌgeo'mantic** ADJECTIVE

geomechanics (ˌdʒiːəʊmɪ'kænɪks) NOUN (*functioning as singular*) the study and application of rock and soil mechanics.

geometer (dʒɪ'ɒmɪtə) *or* **geometrician** (dʒɪˌɒmɪ'trɪʃən, ˌdʒiːəʊmɪ-) NOUN a person who is practised in or who studies geometry.

geometric (ˌdʒɪə'mɛtrɪk) *or* **geometrical** ADJECTIVE 1 of, relating to, or following the methods and principles of geometry. 2 consisting of, formed by, or characterized by points, lines, curves, or surfaces: *a geometric figure.* 3 (of design or ornamentation) composed predominantly of simple geometric forms, such as circles, rectangles, triangles, etc.
▸**ˌgeo'metrically** ADVERB

geometric distribution NOUN *Statistics* the distribution of the number, x, of independent trials required to obtain a first success: where the probability in each is p, the probability that $x = r$ is $p(1-p)^{r-1}$, where $r = 1, 2, 3, \ldots$, with mean $1/p$. See also **Bernoulli trial.**

geometric mean NOUN the average value of a set of n integers, terms, or quantities, expressed as the nth root of their product. Compare **arithmetic mean.**

geometric pace NOUN a modern form of a Roman pace, a measure of length taken as 5 feet.

geometric progression NOUN a sequence of numbers, each of which differs from the succeeding one by a constant ratio, as 1, 2, 4, 8, ... Compare **arithmetic progression.**

geometric series NOUN a geometric progression written as a sum, as in 1 + 2 + 4 + 8.

geometrid (dʒɪ'ɒmɪtrɪd) NOUN 1 any moth of the family *Geometridae,* the larvae of which are called measuring worms, inchworms, or loopers. ◆ ADJECTIVE 2 of, relating to, or belonging to the *Geometridae.*
▷HISTORY C19: from New Latin *Geōmetridae,* from Latin, from Greek *geometrēs:* land measurer, from the looping gait of the larvae

geometrize *or* **geometrise** (dʒɪ'ɒmɪˌtraɪz) VERB 1 to use or apply geometric methods or principles (to). 2 (*tr*) to represent in geometric form.

geometry (dʒɪ'ɒmɪtrɪ) NOUN 1 the branch of mathematics concerned with the properties, relationships, and measurement of points, lines, curves, and surfaces. See also **analytical geometry, non-Euclidean geometry.** 2 **a** any branch of geometry using a particular notation or set of assumptions: *analytical geometry.* **b** any branch of geometry referring to a particular set of objects: *solid geometry.* 3 a shape, configuration, or arrangement. 4 *Arts* the shape of a solid or a surface.
▷HISTORY C14: from Latin *geōmetria,* from Greek, from *geōmetrein* to measure the land

geomorphic (ˌdʒiːəʊ'mɔːfɪk) ADJECTIVE of, relating to, or resembling the earth's surface.

geomorphology (ˌdʒiːəʊmɔː'fɒlədʒɪ) *or* **geomorphogeny** (ˌdʒiːəʊmɔː'fɒdʒənɪ) NOUN the branch of geology that is concerned with the structure, origin, and development of the topographical features of the earth's surface.
▸**geomorphological** (ˌdʒiːəʊˌmɔːfə'lɒdʒɪkᵊl) *or* **ˌgeoˌmorpho'logic** ADJECTIVE ▸**ˌgeoˌmorpho'logically** ADVERB

geophagy (dʒɪ'ɒfədʒɪ), **geophagia** (ˌdʒɪə'feɪdʒə, -dʒɪə), *or* **geophagism** (dʒɪ'ɒfədʒɪzəm) NOUN 1 the practice of eating earth, clay, chalk, etc., found in some primitive tribes. 2 *Zoology* the habit of some animals, esp earthworms, of eating soil.
▸**ge'ophagist** NOUN ▸**geophagous** (dʒɪ'ɒfəgəs) ADJECTIVE

geophysical (ˌdʒiːəʊ'fɪzɪkᵊl) ADJECTIVE of or relating to geophysics.

geophysics (ˌdʒiːəʊ'fɪzɪks) NOUN (*functioning as singular*) the study of the earth's physical properties and of the physical processes acting upon, above, and within the earth. It includes seismology, geomagnetism, meteorology, and oceanography.
▸**ˌgeo'physicist** NOUN

geophyte ('dʒiːəʊˌfaɪt) NOUN a perennial plant that propagates by means of buds below the soil surface.
▸**geophytic** (ˌdʒiːəʊ'fɪtɪk) ADJECTIVE

geopolitical (ˌdʒiːəʊpə'lɪtɪkᵊl) ADJECTIVE of or relating to geopolitics; involving geographical and political elements.

geopolitics (ˌdʒiːəʊ'pɒlɪtɪks) NOUN 1 (*functioning as singular*) the study of the effect of geographical factors on politics, esp international politics; political geography. 2 (*functioning as plural*) the combination of geographical and political factors affecting a country or area.
▸**ˌgeoˌpoli'tician** NOUN

geoponic (ˌdʒiːəʊ'pɒnɪk) ADJECTIVE 1 of or relating to agriculture, esp as a science. 2 rural; rustic.
▷HISTORY C17: from Greek *geōponikos* concerning land cultivation, from *geōponein* to till the soil, from GEO- + *ponein* to labour

geoponics (ˌdʒiːəʊ'pɒnɪks) NOUN (*functioning as singular*) the science of agriculture.

Geordie ('dʒɔːdɪ) *Brit* ◆ NOUN 1 a person who comes from or lives in Tyneside. 2 the dialect spoken by these people. ◆ ADJECTIVE 3 of or relating to these people or their dialect.
▷HISTORY C19: a diminutive of *George*

George (dʒɔːdʒ) NOUN *Brit informal* the automatic pilot in an aircraft.
▷HISTORY C20: originally a slang name for an airman

George Cross NOUN a British award for bravery, esp of civilians: instituted 1940. Abbreviation: **GC.**

Georgetown ('dʒɔːdʒˌtaʊn) NOUN 1 the capital

and chief port of Guyana, at the mouth of the Demerara River: became capital of the Dutch colonies of Essequibo and Demerara in 1784; seat of the University of Guyana. Pop.: 275 000 (1999 est.). Former name (until 1812): **Stabroek.** 2 the capital of the Cayman Islands: a port on Grand Cayman Island. Pop.: 16 600 (1995 est.).

George Town NOUN a port in NW Malaysia, capital of Penang state, in NE Penang Island: the first chartered city of the Malayan federation. Pop.: 219 376 (1991). Also called: **Penang.**

georgette *or* **georgette crepe** (dʒɔːˈdʒɛt) NOUN **a** a thin silk or cotton crepe fabric with a mat finish. **b** (*as modifier*): *a georgette blouse.*
▷HISTORY C20: from the name Mme *Georgette,* a French modiste

Georgia (ˈdʒɔːdʒjə) NOUN 1 a republic in NW Asia, on the Black Sea: an independent kingdom during the middle ages, it was divided by Turkey and Persia in 1555; became part of Russia in 1918 and a separate Soviet republic in 1936; its independence was recognized internationally in 1992. It is rich in minerals and has hydroelectric resources. Official language: Georgian. Religion: believers are mainly Christian or Muslim. Currency: lari. Capital: Tbilisi. Pop.: 4 989 000 (2001 est.). Area: 69 493 sq. km (26 831 sq. miles). 2 a state of the southeastern US, on the Atlantic: consists of coastal plains with forests and swamps, rising to the Cumberland Plateau and the Appalachians in the northwest. Capital: Atlanta. Pop.: 8 186 453 (2000). Area: 152 489 sq. km (58 876 sq. miles). Abbreviations: **Ga,** (with zip code) **GA.**

Georgian (ˈdʒɔːdʒjən) ADJECTIVE 1 of, characteristic of, or relating to any or all of the four kings who ruled Great Britain and Ireland from 1714 to 1830, or to their reigns. 2 of or relating to George V of Great Britain and Northern Ireland or his reign (1910–36): *the Georgian poets.* 3 of or relating to the republic of Georgia, its people, or their language. 4 of or relating to the American State of Georgia or its inhabitants. 5 in or imitative of the style prevalent in England during the 18th century (reigns of George I, II, and III); in architecture, dominated by the ideas of Palladio, and in furniture represented typically by the designs of Sheraton. ◆ NOUN 6 the official language of Georgia, belonging to the South Caucasian family. 7 a native or inhabitant of Georgia. 8 an aboriginal inhabitant of the Caucasus. 9 a native or inhabitant of the American State of Georgia. 10 a person belonging to or imitating the styles of either of the Georgian periods in England.

Georgian Bay NOUN a bay in S central Canada, in Ontario, containing many small islands: the NE part of Lake Huron. Area: 15 000 sq. km (5800 sq. miles).

georgic (ˈdʒɔːdʒɪk) ADJECTIVE 1 *Literary* agricultural. ◆ NOUN 2 a poem about rural or agricultural life.
▷HISTORY C16: from Latin *geōrgicus,* from Greek *geōrgikos,* from *geōrgos* farmer, from *gē* land, earth + *-ourgos,* from *ergon* work

geoscience (ˌdʒiːəʊˈsaɪəns) NOUN 1 any science, such as geology, geophysics, geochemistry, or geodesy, concerned with the earth; an earth science. 2 these sciences collectively.

geosphere (ˈdʒiːəʊˌsfɪə) NOUN another name for **lithosphere.**

geostatic (ˌdʒiːəʊˈstætɪk) ADJECTIVE 1 denoting or relating to the pressure exerted by a mass of rock or a similar substance. also: **lithostatic.** 2 (of a construction) able to resist the pressure of a mass of earth or similar material.

geostatics (ˌdʒiːəʊˈstætɪks) NOUN (*functioning as singular*) the branch of physics concerned with the statics of rigid bodies, esp the balance of forces within the earth.

geostationary (ˌdʒiːəʊˈsteɪʃənərɪ) ADJECTIVE (of a satellite) in a circular equatorial orbit in which it circles the earth once per sidereal day so that it appears stationary in relation to the earth's surface. Also: **geosynchronous.**

geostrategy (ˌdʒiːəʊˈstrætədʒɪ) NOUN the study of geopolitics and strategics, esp as they affect the analysis of a region.

geostrophic (ˌdʒiːəʊˈstrɒfɪk) ADJECTIVE of, relating to, or caused by the force produced by the rotation of the earth: *geostrophic wind.*

geosynchronous (ˌdʒiːəʊˈsɪŋkrənəs) ADJECTIVE another word for: **geostationary.**

geosyncline (ˌdʒiːəʊˈsɪŋklaɪn) NOUN a broad elongated depression in the earth's crust containing great thicknesses of sediment.
▸ **ˌgeosynˈclinal** ADJECTIVE

geotaxis (ˌdʒiːəʊˈtæksɪs) NOUN movement of an organism in response to the stimulus of gravity.
▸ **ˌgeoˈtactic** ADJECTIVE ▸ **ˌgeoˈtactically** ADVERB

geotectonic (ˌdʒiːəʊtɛkˈtɒnɪk) ADJECTIVE of or relating to the formation, arrangement, and structure of the rocks of the earth's crust.

geotextile (ˌdʒiːəʊˈtɛkstaɪl) NOUN any strong synthetic fabric used in civil engineering, as to retain an embankment.

geotherm (ˈdʒiːəʊˌθɜːm) NOUN 1 a line or surface within or on the earth connecting points of equal temperature. 2 the representation of such a line or surface on a map or diagram.

geothermal (ˌdʒiːəʊˈθɜːməl) *or* **geothermic** ADJECTIVE of or relating to the heat in the interior of the earth.

geothermal power NOUN power generated using steam produced by heat emanating from the molten core of the earth.

geotropism (dʒɪˈɒtrəˌpɪzəm) NOUN the response of a plant part to the stimulus of gravity. Plant stems, which grow upwards irrespective of the position in which they are placed, show **negative geotropism.**
▸ **geotropic** (ˌdʒiːəʊˈtrɒpɪk) ADJECTIVE ▸ **ˌgeoˈtropically** ADVERB

ger. ABBREVIATION FOR: 1 gerund. 2 gerundive.

Ger. ABBREVIATION FOR: 1 German. 2 Germany.

Gera (*German* ˈgeːra) NOUN an industrial city in E central Germany, in Thuringia. Pop.: 115 800 (1999 est.).

gerah (ˈgɪərə) NOUN 1 an ancient Hebrew unit of weight. 2 an ancient Hebrew coin equal to one twentieth of a shekel.
▷HISTORY C16: from Hebrew *gērāh* bean

Geraldton waxflower (ˈdʒɛrəldtən ˈwæksˌflaʊə) NOUN an evergreen shrub, *Chamelaucium uncinatum,* native to W Australia, cultivated for its pale pink flowers. Also called: **Geraldton wax.**
▷HISTORY named after *Geraldton,* a port in W Australia

geraniaceous (dʒɪˌreɪnɪˈeɪʃəs) ADJECTIVE of, relating to, or belonging to the *Geraniaceae,* a family of plants with typically hairy stems and beaklike fruits: includes the geranium, pelargonium, storksbill, and cranesbill.
▷HISTORY C19: from New Latin *Geraniāceae;* see GERANIUM

geranial (dʒɪˈreɪnɪəl) NOUN the *cis-* isomer of citral.
▷HISTORY C19: from GERANI(UM) + AL(DEHYDE)

geraniol (dʒɪˈreɪnɪˌɒl, dʒɪˈrɑː-) NOUN a colourless or pale yellow terpine alcohol with an odour of roses, found in many essential oils: used in perfumery. Formula: $C_{10}H_{18}O$.
▷HISTORY C19: from GERANI(UM + ALCOH)OL

geranium (dʒɪˈreɪnɪəm) NOUN 1 any cultivated geraniaceous plant of the genus *Pelargonium,* having scarlet, pink, or white showy flowers. See also **pelargonium, rose geranium, lemon geranium.** 2 any geraniaceous plant of the genus *Geranium,* such as cranesbill and herb Robert, having divided leaves and pink or purplish flowers. 3 a strong red to a moderate or strong pink colour.
▷HISTORY C16: from Latin: cranesbill, from Greek *geranion,* from *geranos* CRANE

geratology (ˌdʒɛrəˈtɒlədʒɪ) NOUN the branch of medicine concerned with the elderly and the phenomena associated with ageing; geriatrics and gerontology.
▷HISTORY C19: from *gerato-,* from Greek *gēras* old age + -LOGY
▸ **geratological** (ˌdʒɛrətəˈlɒdʒɪkᵊl) ADJECTIVE
▸ **ˌgeraˈtologist** NOUN

gerbera (ˈdʒɜːbərə) NOUN any plant of the perennial genus *Gerbera,* esp the Barberton daisy from S. Africa, *G. jamesonii,* grown, usually as a greenhouse plant, for its large brightly coloured daisy-like flowers: family *Asteraceae.*
▷HISTORY named after Traugott *Gerber* (died 1743), German naturalist

gerbil *or* **gerbille** (ˈdʒɜːbɪl) NOUN any burrowing rodent of the subfamily *Gerbillinae,* inhabiting hot dry regions of Asia and Africa and having soft pale fur: family *Cricetidae.*
▷HISTORY C19: from French *gerbille,* from New Latin *gerbillus* a little JERBOA

gerent (ˈdʒɛrənt) NOUN *Rare* a person who rules or manages.
▷HISTORY C16: from Latin *gerēns* managing, from *gerere* to bear

gerenuk (ˈgɛrɪˌnʊk) NOUN a slender E African antelope, *Litocranius walleri,* with a long thin neck and backward-curving horns.
▷HISTORY from Somali *garanug*

gerfalcon (ˈdʒɜːˌfɔːlkən, -ˌfɔːkən) NOUN a variant spelling of **gyrfalcon.**

geriatric (ˌdʒɛrɪˈætrɪk) ADJECTIVE 1 of or relating to geriatrics or to elderly people. 2 *Facetious, derogatory, or offensive* (of people or machines) old, obsolescent, worn out, or useless. ◆ NOUN 3 an elderly person. 4 *Derogatory* an older person considered as one who may be disregarded as senile or irresponsible. ◆ See also **psychogeriatric.**
▷HISTORY C20: from Greek *gēras* old age + IATRIC

geriatrician (ˌdʒɛrɪəˈtrɪʃən) *or* **geriatrist** (ˌdʒɛrɪˈætrɪst) NOUN a physician who specializes in geriatrics.

geriatrics (ˌdʒɛrɪˈætrɪks) NOUN (*functioning as singular*) the branch of medical science concerned with the diagnosis and treatment of diseases affecting elderly people. Compare **gerontology.**

Gerlachovka (*Czech* ˈgɛrlaɔxfka) NOUN a mountain in N Slovakia, in the Tatra Mountains: the highest peak of the Carpathian Mountains. Height: 2663 m (8737 ft.).

germ (dʒɜːm) NOUN 1 a microorganism, esp one that produces disease in animals or plants. 2 (*often plural*) the rudimentary or initial form of something: *the germs of revolution.* 3 a simple structure, such as a fertilized egg, that is capable of developing into a complete organism.
▷HISTORY C17: from French *germe,* from Latin *germen* sprig, bud, sprout, seed

german¹ (ˈdʒɜːmən) NOUN *US* a dance consisting of complicated figures and changes of partners.
▷HISTORY C19: shortened from *German cotillion*

german² (ˈdʒɜːmən) ADJECTIVE 1 (used in combination) **a** having the same parents as oneself: *a brother-german.* **b** having a parent that is a brother or sister of either of one's own parents: *cousin-german.* 2 a less common word for **germane.**
▷HISTORY C14: via Old French *germain,* from Latin *germānus* of the same race, from *germen* sprout, offshoot

German (ˈdʒɜːmən) NOUN 1 the official language of Germany and Austria and one of the official languages of Switzerland; the native language of approximately 100 million people. It is an Indo-European language belonging to the West Germanic branch, closely related to English and Dutch. There is considerable diversity of dialects; modern standard German is a development of Old High German, influenced by Martin Luther's translation of the Bible. See also **High German, Low German.** 2 a native, inhabitant, or citizen of Germany. 3 a person whose native language is German: *Swiss Germans; Volga Germans.* ◆ ADJECTIVE 4 denoting, relating to, or using the German language. 5 relating to, denoting, or characteristic of any German state or its people. ◆ Related prefixes **Germano-, Teuto-.**

German Baptist Brethren PLURAL NOUN a Protestant sect founded in 1708 in Germany but who migrated to the US in 1719–29, the members of which (Dunkers) insist on adult baptism by total immersion. Also called: **Church of the Brethren.**

German cockroach NOUN a small cockroach, *Blattella germanica:* a common household pest. Also called (US): **Croton bug.**

German Democratic Republic NOUN (formerly) the official name of **East Germany.** Abbreviations: **GDR, DDR.**

germander (dʒɜːˈmændə) NOUN any of several plants of the genus *Teucrium,* esp *T. chamaedrys* (**wall germander**) of Europe, having two-lipped flowers

with a very small upper lip: family *Lamiaceae* (labiates).
▷HISTORY C15: from Medieval Latin *germandrea*, from Late Greek *khamandrua*, from Greek *khamaidrus*, from *khamai* on the ground + *drus* oak tree

germander speedwell NOUN a creeping scrophulariaceous Eurasian plant, *Veronica chamaedrys*, naturalized in North America, having small bright blue flowers with white centres. Usual US name: **bird's-eye speedwell.**

germane (dʒɜːˈmeɪn) ADJECTIVE (*postpositive; usually foll by to*) related (to the topic being considered); akin; relevant: *an idea germane to the conversation.*
▷HISTORY variant of GERMAN[2]
▸**gerˈmanely** ADVERB ▸**gerˈmaneness** NOUN

German East Africa NOUN a former German territory in E Africa, consisting of Tanganyika and Ruanda-Urundi: divided in 1919 between Great Britain and Belgium; now in Tanzania, Rwanda, and Burundi.

germanic (dʒɜːˈmænɪk) ADJECTIVE of or containing germanium in the tetravalent state.

Germanic (dʒɜːˈmænɪk) NOUN 1 a branch of the Indo-European family of languages that includes English, Dutch, German, the Scandinavian languages, and Gothic. See **East Germanic, West Germanic, North Germanic.** Abbreviation: **Gmc.** 2 the unrecorded language from which all of these languages developed; Proto-Germanic. ♦ ADJECTIVE 3 of, denoting, or relating to this group of languages. 4 of, relating to, or characteristic of Germany, the German language, or any people that speaks a Germanic language.

Germanism (ˈdʒɜːməˌnɪzəm) NOUN 1 a word or idiom borrowed from or modelled on German. 2 a German custom, trait, practice, etc. 3 attachment to or high regard for German customs, institutions, etc.

germanite (ˈdʒɜːməˌnaɪt) NOUN a mineral consisting of a complex copper arsenic sulphide containing germanium, gallium, iron, zinc, and lead: an ore of germanium and gallium.
▷HISTORY from GERMANIUM + -ITE[1]

germanium (dʒɜːˈmeɪnɪəm) NOUN a brittle crystalline grey element that is a semiconducting metalloid, occurring principally in zinc ores and argyrodite: used in transistors, as a catalyst, and to strengthen and harden alloys. Symbol: Ge; atomic no.: 32; atomic wt.: 72.61; valency: 2 or 4; relative density: 5.323; melting pt.: 938.35°C; boiling pt.: 2834°C.
▷HISTORY C19: New Latin, named after GERMANY

Germanize *or* **Germanise** (ˈdʒɜːməˌnaɪz) VERB to adopt or cause to adopt German customs, speech, institutions, etc.
▸**ˌGermaniˈzation** *or* **ˌGermaniˈsation** NOUN ▸**ˈGermanˌizer** *or* **ˈGermanˌiser** NOUN

German measles NOUN (*functioning as singular*) a nontechnical name for **rubella.**

German Ocean NOUN a former name for the **North Sea.**

Germanophile (dʒɜːˈmænəˌfaɪl) *or* **Germanophil** NOUN a person having admiration for or devotion to Germany and the Germans.
▸**Germanophilia** (dʒɜːˌmænəˈfɪlɪə) NOUN

Germanophobe (dʒɜːˈmænəˌfəʊb) NOUN a person who hates Germany or its people.
▸**Gerˌmanoˈphobia** NOUN

germanous (dʒɜːˈmænəs) ADJECTIVE of or containing germanium in the divalent state.

German shepherd *or* **German shepherd dog** NOUN another name for **Alsatian** (sense 1).

German short-haired pointer NOUN a medium-sized short-haired variety of pointer having a liver-coloured or black coat, sometimes with white markings.

German silver NOUN another name for **nickel silver.**

German sixth NOUN (in musical harmony) an augmented sixth chord having a major third and a perfect fifth between the root and the augmented sixth. Compare **Italian sixth, French sixth.**

German wire-haired pointer NOUN a medium-sized powerfully-built variety of pointer with a wiry coat in liver, liver and white, or black and white, and a short beard.

Germany (ˈdʒɜːmənɪ) NOUN a country in central Europe: in the Middle Ages the centre of the Holy Roman Empire; dissolved into numerous principalities; united under the leadership of Prussia in 1871 after the Franco-Prussian War; became a republic with reduced size in 1919 after being defeated in World War I; under the dictatorship of Hitler from 1933 to 1945; defeated in World War II and divided by the Allied Powers into four zones, which became established as East and West Germany in the late 1940s; reunified in 1990: a member of the European Union. It is flat and low-lying in the north with plateaus and uplands (including the Black Forest and the Bavarian Alps) in the centre and south. Official language: German. Religion: Christianity, Protestant majority. Currency: euro. Capital: Berlin. Pop.: 82 386 000 (2001 est.). Area: 357 041 sq. km (137 825 sq. miles). German name: **Deutschland.** Official name: **Federal Republic of Germany.** See also **East Germany, West Germany.** Related adjective: **Teutonic.**

germ cell NOUN a sexual reproductive cell; gamete. Compare **somatic cell.**

germen (ˈdʒɜːmən) NOUN, *plural* **-mens** *or* **-mina** (-mɪnə). *Biology, now rare* the mass of undifferentiated cells that gives rise to the germ cells.
▷HISTORY C17: from Latin; see GERM

germicide (ˈdʒɜːmɪˌsaɪd) NOUN any substance that kills germs or other microorganisms.
▸**ˌgermiˈcidal** ADJECTIVE

germinal (ˈdʒɜːmɪnəl) ADJECTIVE 1 of, relating to, or like germs or a germ cell. 2 of, or in the earliest stage of development; embryonic.
▷HISTORY C19: from New Latin *germinālis*, from Latin *germen* bud; see GERM
▸**ˈgerminally** ADVERB

Germinal *French* (ʒɛrminal) NOUN the month of buds: the seventh month of the French revolutionary calendar, from March 22 to April 20.

germinal vesicle NOUN *Biology* the large nucleus of an oocyte before it develops into an ovum.

germinant (ˈdʒɜːmɪnənt) ADJECTIVE in the process of germinating; sprouting.

germinate (ˈdʒɜːmɪˌneɪt) VERB 1 to cause (seeds or spores) to sprout or (of seeds or spores) to sprout or form new tissue following increased metabolism. 2 to grow or cause to grow; develop. 3 to come or bring into existence; originate: *the idea germinated with me.*
▷HISTORY C17: from Latin *germināre* to sprout; see GERM
▸**ˈgerminable** *or* **ˈgerminative** ADJECTIVE ▸**ˌgermiˈnation** NOUN ▸**ˈgermiˌnator** NOUN

Germiston (ˈdʒɜːmɪstən) NOUN a city in South Africa, southeast of Johannesburg: industrial centre, with the world's largest gold refinery, serving the Witwatersrand mines. Pop.: 134 005 (1991).

germ layer NOUN *Embryol* any of the three layers of cells formed during gastrulation. See **ectoderm, mesoderm, endoderm.**

germ line NOUN the lineage of cells culminating in the germ cells.

germ plasm NOUN **a** the part of a germ cell that contains hereditary material; the chromosomes and genes. **b** the germ cells collectively. Compare **somatoplasm.**

germ theory NOUN 1 the theory that all infectious diseases are caused by microorganisms. 2 the theory that living organisms develop from other living organisms by the growth and differentiation of germ cells.

germ tube NOUN *Botany* a tube produced by a germinating spore, such as the pollen tube produced by a pollen grain.

germ warfare NOUN the military use of disease-spreading bacteria against an enemy. Also called: **bacteriological warfare.**

Gerona (*Spanish* xeˈrona) NOUN a city in NE Spain: city walls and 14th-century cathedral; often besieged, in particular by the French (1809). Pop.: 67 580 (latest est.). Ancient name: **Gerunda** (dʒəˈruːndə).

Geronimo (dʒəˈrɒnɪˌməʊ) INTERJECTION 1 *US* a shout given by paratroopers as they jump into battle. 2 an exclamation expressing exhilaration, esp when jumping from a great height.
▷HISTORY from *Geronimo* (1829–1909), Apache Indian chieftain

gerontic (dʒɛˈrɒntɪk) ADJECTIVE *Biology* of or relating to the senescence of an organism.

geronto- *or before a vowel* **geront-** COMBINING FORM indicating old age: *gerontology; gerontophilia.*
▷HISTORY from Greek *gerōn, geront-* old man

gerontocracy (ˌdʒɛrɒnˈtɒkrəsɪ) NOUN, *plural* **-cies.** 1 government by old people. 2 a governing body of old people.
▸**gerontocratic** (dʒəˌrɒntəˈkrætɪk) ADJECTIVE
▸**geˈrontoˌcrat** NOUN

gerontology (ˌdʒɛrɒnˈtɒlədʒɪ) NOUN the scientific study of ageing and the problems associated with elderly people. Compare **geriatrics.**
▸**gerontological** (ˌdʒɛrɒntəˈlɒdʒɪkəl) ADJECTIVE
▸**ˌgeronˈtologist** NOUN

-gerous ADJECTIVE COMBINING FORM bearing or producing: *armigerous.* Compare **-ferous.**
▷HISTORY from Latin *-ger* bearing + -OUS

gerrymander (ˈdʒɛrɪˌmændə) VERB 1 to divide the constituencies of (a voting area) so as to give one party an unfair advantage. 2 to manipulate or adapt to one's advantage. ♦ NOUN 3 an act or result of gerrymandering.
▷HISTORY C19: from Elbridge *Gerry*, US politician + (SALA)MANDER; from the salamander-like outline of an electoral district reshaped (1812) for political purposes while Gerry was governor of Massachusetts
▸**ˌgerryˈmandering** NOUN

Gers (*French* ʒɛr) NOUN a department of SW France, in Midi-Pyrénées region. Capital: Auch. Pop.: 172 335 (1999). Area: 6291 sq. km (2453 sq. miles).

gerund (ˈdʒɛrənd) NOUN a noun formed from a verb, denoting an action or state. In English, the gerund, like the present participle, is formed in *-ing*: *the living is easy.*
▷HISTORY C16: from Late Latin *gerundium*, from Latin *gerundum* something to be carried on, from *gerere* to wage
▸**gerundial** (dʒɪˈrʌndɪəl) ADJECTIVE

gerundive (dʒɪˈrʌndɪv) NOUN 1 (in Latin grammar) an adjective formed from a verb, expressing the desirability of the activity denoted by the verb. ♦ ADJECTIVE 2 of or relating to the gerund or gerundive.
▷HISTORY C17: from Late Latin *gerundīvus*, from *gerundium* GERUND
▸**gerundival** (ˌdʒɛrənˈdaɪvəl) ADJECTIVE ▸**geˈrundively** ADVERB

Geryon (ˈgɛrɪən) NOUN *Greek myth* a winged monster with three bodies joined at the waist, killed by Hercules, who stole the monster's cattle as his tenth labour.

gesellschaft (*German* gəˈzɛlʃaft) NOUN, *plural* **-schaften** (*German* -ʃaftən). (*often capital*) a social group held together by practical concerns, formal and impersonal relationships, etc. Compare **gemeinschaft.**
▷HISTORY German, literally: society

gesneria (gesˈnɪərɪə) NOUN any plant of the mostly tuberous-rooted S. American genus *Gesneria*, grown as a greenhouse plant for its large leaves and showy tubular flowers in a range of bright colours: family *Gesneriaceae.*
▷HISTORY named after Conrad *Gesner*, 1516–65, Swiss naturalist

gesso (ˈdʒɛsəʊ) NOUN 1 a white ground of plaster and size, used esp in the Middle Ages and Renaissance to prepare panels or canvas for painting or gilding. 2 any white substance, esp plaster of Paris, that forms a ground when mixed with water.
▷HISTORY C16: from Italian: chalk, GYPSUM

gest *or* **geste** (dʒɛst) NOUN *Archaic* 1 a notable deed or exploit. 2 a tale of adventure or romance, esp in verse. See also **chanson de geste.**
▷HISTORY C14: from Old French, from Latin *gesta* deeds, from *gerere* to carry out

Gestalt (gəˈʃtælt) NOUN, *plural* **-stalts** *or* **-stalten** (-ˈʃtæltən). (*sometimes not capital*) a perceptual pattern or structure possessing qualities as a whole that cannot be described merely as a sum of its parts. See also **Gestalt psychology.**

▷HISTORY C20: German: form, from Old High German *stellen* to shape

Gestalt psychology NOUN a system of thought, derived from experiments carried out by German psychologists, that regards all mental phenomena as being arranged in gestalts.

Gestalt psychotherapy NOUN a therapy devised in the US in the 1960s in which patients are encouraged to concentrate on the immediate present and to express their true feelings.

Gestapo (ge'stɑːpəʊ; *German* ge'ʃtaːpo) NOUN the secret state police in Nazi Germany, noted for its brutal methods of interrogation.
▷HISTORY from German *Ge(heime) Sta(ats)po(lizei)*, literally: secret state police

Gesta Romanorum ('dʒɛstə ˌrəʊmə'nɔːrəm) NOUN a popular collection of tales in Latin with moral applications, compiled in the late 13th century as a manual for preachers.
▷HISTORY Latin: deeds of the Romans

gestate ('dʒesteɪt) VERB [1] (*tr*) to carry (developing young) in the uterus during pregnancy. [2] (*tr*) to develop (a plan or idea) in the mind. [3] (*intr*) to be in the process of gestating.
▷HISTORY C19: back formation from GESTATION

gestation (dʒɛ'steɪʃən) NOUN [1] **a** the development of the embryo of a viviparous mammal, between conception and birth: about 266 days in humans, 624 days in elephants, and 63 days in cats. **b** (*as modifier*): *gestation period.* [2] the development of an idea or plan in the mind. [3] the period of such a development.
▷HISTORY C16: from Latin *gestātiō* a bearing, from *gestāre* to bear, frequentative of *gerere* to carry
▸**ges'tational** *or* **gestative** ('dʒɛstətɪv, dʒɛ'steɪ-) ADJECTIVE ▸**'gestatory** ADJECTIVE

gestatorial chair (ˌdʒɛstə'tɔːrɪəl) NOUN a ceremonial chair on which the pope is carried.

gesticulate (dʒɛ'stɪkjʊˌleɪt) VERB to express by or make gestures.
▷HISTORY C17: from Latin *gesticulārī*, from Latin *gesticulus* (unattested except in Late Latin) gesture, diminutive of *gestus* gesture, from *gerere* to bear, conduct
▸**ges'ticulative** ADJECTIVE ▸**ges'ticuˌlator** NOUN

gesticulation (dʒɛˌstɪkjʊ'leɪʃən) NOUN [1] the act of gesticulating. [2] an animated or expressive gesture.
▸**ges'ticulatory** ADJECTIVE

gesture ('dʒɛstʃə) NOUN [1] a motion of the hands, head, or body to emphasize an idea or emotion, esp while speaking. [2] something said or done as a formality or as an indication of intention: *a political gesture.* [3] *Obsolete* the manner in which a person bears himself; posture. ◆ VERB [4] to express by or make gestures; gesticulate.
▷HISTORY C15: from Medieval Latin *gestūra* bearing, from Latin *gestus*, past participle of *gerere* to bear
▸**'gestural** ADJECTIVE ▸**'gesturer** NOUN

gesundheit *German* (gə'zʊnthait) SENTENCE SUBSTITUTE an expression used to wish good health to someone who has just sneezed.
▷HISTORY from *gesund* healthy + *-heit* -HOOD; see SOUND[2]

get (get) VERB **gets, getting, got** (gɒt). (*mainly tr*) [1] to come into possession of; receive or earn. [2] to bring or fetch. [3] to contract or be affected by: *he got a chill at the picnic.* [4] to capture or seize: *the police finally got him.* [5] (*also intr*) to become or cause to become or act as specified: *to get a window open; get one's hair cut; get wet.* [6] (*intr*; foll by a preposition or adverbial particle) to succeed in going, coming, leaving, etc.: *get off the bus.* [7] (*takes an infinitive*) to manage or contrive: *how did you get to be captain?* [8] to make ready or prepare: *to get a meal.* [9] to hear, notice, or understand: *I didn't get your meaning.* [10] *US and Canadian informal* to learn or master by study. [11] (*intr*; often foll by *to*) to come (to) or arrive (at): *we got home safely; to get to London.* [12] to catch or enter: *to get a train.* [13] to induce or persuade: *get him to leave at once.* [14] to reach by calculation: *add 2 and 2 and you will get 4.* [15] to receive (a broadcast signal). [16] to communicate with (a person or place), as by telephone. [17] (*also intr*; foll by *to*) *Informal* to have an emotional effect (on): *that music really gets me.* [18] *Informal* to annoy or irritate: *her high voice gets me.* [19] *Informal* to bring a person into a difficult position from which he or she cannot escape. [20] *Informal* to puzzle; baffle. [21] *Informal* to hit: *the blow got him in the back.* [22] *Informal* to be revenged on, esp by killing. [23] *US slang* **a** (foll by *to*) to gain access (to a person) with the purpose of bribing him. **b** (often foll by *to*) to obtain access (to someone) and kill or silence him. [24] *Informal* to have the better of: *your extravagant habits will get you in the end.* [25] (*intr*; foll by present participle) *Informal* to begin: *get moving.* [26] (used as a command) *Informal* go! leave now! [27] *Archaic* to beget or conceive. [28] **get even with.** See **even**[1] (sense 15). [29] **get it (in the neck).** *Informal* to be reprimanded or punished severely. [30] **get with it.** *Slang* to allow oneself to respond to new ideas, styles, etc. [31] **get with child.** *Archaic* to make pregnant. ◆ NOUN [32] *Rare* the act of begetting. [33] *Rare* something begotten; offspring. [34] *Brit slang* a variant of **git.** [35] *Informal* (in tennis) a successful return of a shot that was difficult to reach. ◆ See also **get about, get across, get ahead, get along, get at, get away, get back, get by. get down, get in, get into, get off, get on, get onto, get out, get over. get round, get through, get-together, get up, got, gotten.**
▷HISTORY Old English *gietan*; related to Old Norse *geta* to get, learn, Old High German *bigezzan* to obtain
▸**'getable** *or* **'gettable** ADJECTIVE

> **Language note** The use of *off* after *get* as in *I got this chair off an antique dealer* is acceptable in conversation, but should not be used in formal writing.

GeT ABBREVIATION FOR Greenwich Electronic Time.

get about *or* **around** VERB (*intr, adverb*) [1] to move around, as when recovering from an illness. [2] to be socially active. [3] (of news, rumour, etc.) to become known; spread.

get across VERB [1] to cross or cause or help to cross. [2] (*adverb*) to be or cause to be readily understood. [3] (*intr, preposition*) *Informal* to annoy: *her constant interference really got across him.*

get ahead VERB (*intr, adverb*) [1] to be successful; prosper. [2] (foll by *of*) to surpass or excel.

get along VERB (*intr, adverb*) [1] (often foll by *with*) to be friendly or compatible: *my brother gets along well with everybody.* [2] to manage, cope, or fare: *how are you getting along in your job?* [3] (*also preposition; often imperative*) to go or move away; leave. ◆ INTERJECTION [4] *Brit informal* an exclamation indicating mild disbelief.

get around VERB See **get about, get round.**

get at VERB (*intr, preposition*) [1] to gain access to: *the dog could not get at the meat on the high shelf.* [2] to mean or intend: *what are you getting at when you look at me like that?* [3] to irritate or annoy persistently; criticize: *she is always getting at him.* [4] to influence or seek to influence, esp illegally by bribery, intimidation, etc.: *someone had got at the witness before the trial.*

get-at-able ADJECTIVE *Informal* accessible.

get away VERB (*adverb, mainly intr*) [1] to make an escape; leave. [2] to make a start. [3] **get away with. a** to steal and escape (with money, goods, etc.). **b** to do (something wrong, illegal, etc.) without being discovered or punished or with only a minor punishment. ◆ INTERJECTION [4] an exclamation indicating mild disbelief. ◆ NOUN **getaway.** [5] the act of escaping, esp by criminals. [6] a start or acceleration. [7] (*modifier*) used for escaping: *a getaway car.*

get back VERB (*adverb*) [1] (*tr*) to recover or retrieve. [2] (*intr*; often foll by *to*) to return, esp to a former position or activity: *let's get back to the original question.* [3] (*intr*; foll by *at*) to retaliate (against); wreak vengeance (on). [4] **get one's own back.** *Informal* to obtain one's revenge.

get by VERB [1] to pass; go past or overtake. [2] (*intr, adverb*) *Informal* to manage, esp in spite of difficulties: *I can get by with little money.* [3] (*intr*) to be accepted or permitted: *that book will never get by the authorities.*

get down VERB (*mainly adverb*) [1] (*intr; also preposition*) to dismount or descend. [2] (*tr; also preposition*) to bring down: *we could not get the wardrobe down the stairs.* [3] (*tr*) to write down. [4] (*tr*) to make depressed: *your nagging gets me down.* [5] (*tr*) to swallow: *he couldn't get the meal down.* [6] (*intr*; foll by *to*) to attend seriously (to); concentrate (on) (esp in the phrases **get down to business** *or* **brass tacks**). [7] (*intr*) *Informal, chiefly US* to enjoy oneself uninhibitedly, esp by dancing.

get-go NOUN **from the get-go.** *Informal* from the beginning: *I've been your friend from the get-go.*

Gethsemane (geθ'sɛmənɪ) NOUN *New Testament* the garden in Jerusalem where Christ was betrayed on the night before his Crucifixion (Matthew 26:36–56).

get in VERB (*mainly adverb*) [1] (*intr*) to enter a car, train, etc. [2] (*intr*) to arrive, esp at one's home or place of work: *I got in at midnight.* [3] (*tr*) to bring in or inside: *get the milk in.* [4] (*tr*) to insert or slip in: *he got his suggestion in before anyone else.* [5] (*tr*) to gather or collect (crops, debts, etc.). [6] (*tr*) to ask (a person, esp a specialist) to give a service: *shall I get the doctor in?* [7] to be elected or cause to be elected: *he got in by 400 votes.* [8] (*tr*) to succeed in doing (something), esp during a specified period: *I doubt if I can get this task in today.* [9] (*intr*) to obtain a place at university, college, etc. [10] (foll by *on*) to join or cause to join (an activity or organization). [11] **get in with.** to be or cause to be on friendly terms with (a person). [12] (*preposition*) See **get into.** ◆ NOUN **get-in.** [13] *Theatre* the process of moving into a theatre the scenery, props, and costumes for a production.

get into VERB (*preposition*) [1] (*intr*) to enter. [2] (*intr*) to reach (a destination): *the train got into London at noon.* [3] to get dressed in (clothes). [4] (*intr*) to preoccupy or obsess (a person's emotions or thoughts): *what's got into him tonight?* [5] to assume or cause to assume (a specified condition, habit, etc.): *to get into debt; get a person into a mess.* [6] to be elected to or cause to be elected to: *to get into Parliament.* [7] (*usually intr*) *Informal* to become or cause to become familiar with (a skill): *once you get into driving you'll enjoy it.* [8] (*usually intr*) *Informal* to develop or cause to develop an absorbing interest in (a hobby, subject, or book).

get off VERB [1] (*intr, adverb*) to escape the consequences of an action: *he got off very lightly in the accident.* [2] (*adverb*) to be or cause to be acquitted: *a good lawyer got him off.* [3] (*adverb*) to depart or cause to depart: *to get the children off to school.* [4] (*intr*) to descend (from a bus, train, etc.); dismount: *she got off at the terminus.* [5] to move or cause to move to a distance (from): *get off the field.* [6] (*tr, adverb*) to remove; take off: *get your coat off.* [7] (*adverb*) to go or send to sleep. [8] (*adverb*) to send (letters) or (of letters) to be sent. [9] (*intr, adverb*) *Slang* to become high on or as on heroin or some other drug. [10] **get off with.** *Brit informal* to establish an amorous or sexual relationship with. [11] **tell (someone) where to get off.** *Informal* to rebuke or criticize harshly.

get on VERB (*mainly adverb*) [1] Also (when *preposition*): **get onto.** to board or cause or help to board (a bus, train, etc.). [2] (*tr*) to dress in (clothes as specified). [3] (*intr*) to grow late or (of time) to elapse: *it's getting on and I must go.* [4] (*intr*) (of a person) to grow old. [5] (*intr*; foll by *for*) to approach (a time, age, amount, etc.): *she is getting on for seventy.* [6] (*intr*) to make progress, manage, or fare: *how did you get on in your exam?* [7] (*intr*; often foll by *with*) to establish a friendly relationship: *he gets on well with other people.* [8] (*intr*; foll by *with*) to continue to do: *get on with your homework!* ◆ INTERJECTION [9] I don't believe you!

get onto VERB (*preposition*) [1] Also: **get on.** to board or cause or help to board (a bus, train, etc.). [2] (*intr*) to make contact with; communicate with. [3] (*intr*) to become aware of (something illicit or secret): *the boss will get onto their pilfering unless they're careful.* [4] (*intr*) to deliver a demand, request, or rebuke to: *I'll get onto the manufacturers to replace these damaged goods.* ◆ See usage note at **onto.**

get out VERB (*adverb*) [1] to leave or escape or cause to leave or escape: used in the imperative when dismissing a person. [2] to make or become known; publish or be published. [3] (*tr*) to express with difficulty. [4] (*tr*; often foll by *of*) to extract (information or money) (from a person): *to get a confession out of a criminal.* [5] (*tr*) to gain or receive something, esp something of significance or value: *you get out of life what you put into it.* [6] (foll by *of*) to avoid or cause to avoid: *she always gets out of swimming.* [7] (*tr*) to solve (a puzzle or problem) successfully. 8 *Cricket* to dismiss or be dismissed. ◆ NOUN **get-out.** 9 an escape, as from a difficult situation. 10 *Theatre* the process of moving out of a theatre the scenery, props, and costumes after a production.

get over VERB 1 to cross or surmount (something): *the children got over the fence.* 2 (*intr, preposition*) to recover from (an illness, shock, etc.). 3 (*intr, preposition*) to overcome or master (a problem): *you'll soon get over your shyness.* 4 (*intr, preposition*) to appreciate fully: *I just can't get over seeing you again.* 5 (*tr, adverb*) to communicate effectively: *he had difficulty getting the message over.* 6 (*tr, adverb;* sometimes foll by *with*) to bring (something necessary but unpleasant) to an end: *let's get this job over with quickly.*

get round *or* **around** VERB (*intr*) 1 (*preposition*) to circumvent or overcome: *he got round the problem by an ingenious trick.* 2 (*preposition*) *Informal* to have one's way with; cajole: *that girl can get round anyone.* 3 (*preposition*) to evade (a law or rules). 4 (*adverb;* foll by *to*) to reach or come to at length: *I'll get round to that job in an hour.*

getter ('gɛtə) NOUN 1 a person or thing that gets. 2 a substance, usually a metal such as titanium, evaporated onto the walls of a vacuum tube, vessel, etc., to adsorb the residual gas and lower the pressure. ◆ VERB 3 (*tr*) to remove (a gas) by the action of a getter.

get through VERB 1 to succeed or cause or help to succeed in an examination, test, etc. 2 to bring or come to a destination, esp after overcoming problems: *we got through the blizzards to the survivors.* 3 (*intr, adverb*) to contact, as by telephone. 4 (*intr, preposition*) to use, spend, or consume (money, supplies, etc.). 5 to complete or cause to complete (a task, process, etc.): *to get a bill through Parliament.* 6 (*adverb;* foll by *to*) to reach the awareness and understanding (of a person): *I just can't get the message through to him.* 7 (*intr, adverb*) *US slang* to obtain drugs.

get-together NOUN 1 *Informal* a small informal meeting or social gathering. ◆ VERB **get together.** (*adverb*) 2 (*tr*) to gather or collect. 3 (*intr*) (of people) to meet socially. 4 (*intr*) to discuss, esp in order to reach an agreement. 5 **get it together.** *Informal* **a** to achieve one's full potential, either generally as a person or in a particular field of activity. **b** to achieve a harmonious frame of mind.

Gettysburg ('gɛtɪz,bɜːg) NOUN a small town in S Pennsylvania, southwest of Harrisburg: scene of a crucial battle (1863) during the American Civil War, in which Meade's Union forces defeated Lee's Confederate army; site of the national cemetery dedicated by President Lincoln. Pop.: 7195 (latest est.).

Gettysburg Address NOUN *US history* the speech made by President Lincoln at the dedication of the national cemetery on the Civil War battlefield at Gettysburg in Nov. 1863.

get up VERB (*mainly adverb*) 1 to wake and rise from one's bed or cause to wake and rise from bed. 2 (*intr*) to rise to one's feet; stand up. 3 (*also preposition*) to ascend or cause to ascend: *the old van couldn't get up the hill.* 4 to mount or help to mount (a bicycle, horse, etc.). 5 to increase or cause to increase in strength: *the wind got up at noon.* 6 (*tr*) *Informal* to dress (oneself) in a particular way, esp showily or elaborately. 7 (*tr*) *Informal* to devise or create: *to get up an entertainment for Christmas.* 8 (*tr*) *Informal* to study or improve one's knowledge of: *I must get up my history.* 9 (*intr;* foll by *to*) *Informal* to be involved in: *he's always getting up to mischief.* 10 (*intr*) *Austral informal* to win, esp in a sporting event. ◆ NOUN **get-up.** 11 *Informal* a costume or outfit, esp one that is striking or bizarre. 12 *Informal* the arrangement or production of a book, etc.

get-up-and-go NOUN *Informal* energy, drive, or ambition.

geum ('dʒiːəm) NOUN any herbaceous plant of the rosaceous genus *Geum,* having compound leaves and red, orange, or white flowers. See also **avens.**
▷HISTORY C19: New Latin, from Latin: herb bennet, avens

GeV ABBREVIATION FOR giga-electronvolts (10^9 electronvolts). Sometimes written (esp US and Canadian) **BeV** (billion electronvolts).

gewgaw ('gjuːgɔː, 'guː-) NOUN 1 a showy but valueless trinket. ◆ ADJECTIVE 2 showy and valueless; gaudy.
▷HISTORY C15: of unknown origin

Gewürztraminer (gə,vɜːts'træmɪnə; *German* gə,vyrts'tramiːnər) NOUN 1 a white grape grown in Alsace, Germany, and elsewhere, used for making wine. 2 any of various fragrant white wines made from this grape.
▷HISTORY German, from *Gewürz* spice, seasoning + *Traminer* a variety of grape first grown in the *Tramin* area of the South Tyrol

gey (gaɪ; *Scot* gəɪ) ADVERB *Scot and Northumberland dialect* (intensifier): *it's gey cold.*
▷HISTORY variant of GAY

geyser ('giːzə; *US* 'gaɪzər) NOUN 1 a spring that discharges steam and hot water. 2 *Brit* a domestic gas water heater.
▷HISTORY C18: from Icelandic *Geysir,* from Old Norse *geysa* to gush

geyserite ('giːzə,raɪt) NOUN a mineral form of hydrated silica resembling opal, deposited from the waters of geysers and hot springs. Formula: $SiO_2.nH_2O$.

Gezira (dʒə'zɪərə) NOUN a region of the E central Sudan between the Blue and White Niles: site of a large-scale irrigation system.

gf THE INTERNET DOMAIN NAME FOR French Guiana.

G-force NOUN the force of gravity.

gg THE INTERNET DOMAIN NAME FOR Guernsey.

GG *Text messaging* ◆ ABBREVIATION FOR: 1 Girl Guides. 2 Governor General. 3 good game.

gh THE INTERNET DOMAIN NAME FOR Ghana.

GH INTERNATIONAL CAR REGISTRATION FOR Ghana.

Ghan (gæn) NOUN *Austral* 1 short for **Afghan** (sense 3). 2 **the.** the train connecting Adelaide and Alice Springs.
▷HISTORY from the number of Afghan camelmen at the Oodnadatta railhead

Ghana ('gɑːnə) NOUN a republic in W Africa, on the Gulf of Guinea: a powerful empire from the 4th to the 13th centuries; a major source of gold and slaves for Europeans after 1471; British colony of the Gold Coast established in 1874; united with British Togoland in 1957 and became a republic and a member of the Commonwealth in 1960. Official language: English. Religions: Christian, Muslim, and animist. Currency: cedi. Capital: Accra. Pop.: 19 894 000 (2001 est.). Area: 238 539 sq. km (92 100 sq. miles).

Ghanaian (gɑː'neɪən) *or* **Ghanian** ('gɑːnɪən) ADJECTIVE 1 of or relating to Ghana or its inhabitants. ◆ NOUN 2 a native or inhabitant of Ghana.

gharial ('gærɪəl) NOUN another name for for **gavial.**

gharry *or* **gharri** ('gærɪ) NOUN, *plural* **-ries.** (in India) a horse-drawn vehicle available for hire.
▷HISTORY C19: from Hindi *gārī*

ghastly ('gɑːstlɪ) ADJECTIVE **-lier, -liest.** 1 *Informal* very bad or unpleasant. 2 deathly pale; wan. 3 *Informal* extremely unwell; ill: *they felt ghastly after the party.* 4 terrifying; horrible. ◆ ADVERB 5 unhealthily; sickly: *ghastly pale.* 6 *Archaic* in a horrible or hideous manner.
▷HISTORY Old English *gāstlīc* spiritual; see GHOSTLY
▸ **'ghastliness** NOUN

ghat (gɔːt) NOUN (in India) 1 stairs or a passage leading down to a river. 2 a mountain pass or mountain range. 3 a place of cremation.
▷HISTORY C17: from Hindi *ghāt,* from Sanskrit *ghatta*

Ghats (gɔːts) PLURAL NOUN See **Eastern Ghats** and **Western Ghats.**

ghaut (gʌt) NOUN *Caribbean* a small cleft in a hill through which a rivulet runs down to the sea.
▷HISTORY C17 *gaot,* a mountain pass, from Hindi: GHAT

ghazi ('gɑːzɪ) NOUN, *plural* **-zis.** 1 a Muslim fighter against infidels. 2 (*often capital*) a Turkish warrior of high rank.
▷HISTORY C18: from Arabic, from *ghazā* he made war

Ghazzah ('gɑːzə, 'gʌzə) NOUN transliteration of the Arabic name for **Gaza.**

GHB ABBREVIATION FOR **gamma hydroxybutyrate.**

Gheber *or* **Ghebre** ('geɪbə, 'giː-) NOUN other words for **Gabar.**

ghee (giː) NOUN butter, clarified by boiling, used in Indian cookery.
▷HISTORY C17: from Hindi *ghī,* from Sanskrit *ghri* sprinkle

Ghent (gɛnt) NOUN an industrial city and port in NW Belgium, capital of East Flanders province, at the confluence of the Rivers Lys and Scheldt: formerly famous for its cloth industry; university (1816). Pop.: 224 180 (2000 est.). Flemish name: **Gent.** French name: **Gand.**

gherao (ge'raʊ) NOUN a form of industrial action in India in which workers imprison their employers on the premises until their demands are met.
▷HISTORY from Hindi *gherna* to besiege

gherkin ('gɜːkɪn) NOUN 1 the immature fruit of any of various cucumbers, used for pickling. 2 **a** a tropical American cucurbitaceous climbing plant, *Cucumis anguria.* **b** the small edible fruit of this plant.
▷HISTORY C17: from early modern Dutch *agurkkijn,* diminutive of *gurk,* from Slavonic, ultimately from Greek *angourion*

ghetto ('gɛtəʊ) NOUN, *plural* **-tos** *or* **-toes.** 1 *Sociol* a densely populated slum area of a city inhabited by a socially and economically deprived minority. 2 an area in a European city in which Jews were formerly required to live. 3 a group or class of people that is segregated in some way.
▷HISTORY C17: from Italian, perhaps shortened from *borghetto,* diminutive of *borgo* settlement outside a walled city; or from the Venetian *ghetto* the medieval iron-founding district, largely inhabited by Jews

ghetto blaster NOUN *Informal* a large portable cassette recorder or CD player with built-in speakers.

ghetto fabulous ADJECTIVE (of fashion) characterized by gaudy, extravagant, and often sexually alluring clothes.

ghettoize *or* **ghettoise** ('gɛtəʊ,aɪz) VERB (*tr*) to confine or restrict to a particular area, activity, or category: *to ghettoize women as housewives.*
▸ **,ghettoi'zation** *or* **,ghettoi'sation** NOUN

Ghibelline ('gɪbɪ,laɪn, -,liːn) NOUN 1 a member of the political faction in medieval Italy originally based on support for the German emperor. 2 (*modifier*) of or relating to the Ghibellines. Compare **Guelph**[1].
▷HISTORY C16: from Italian *Ghibellino,* probably from Middle High German *Waiblingen,* a Hohenstaufen estate
▸ **'Ghibel,linism** NOUN

ghibli *or* **gibli** ('gɪblɪ) NOUN a fiercely hot wind of North Africa.
▷HISTORY C20: from Arabic *gibliy* south wind

ghillie ('gɪlɪ) NOUN 1 a type of tongueless shoe with lacing up the instep, originally worn by the Scots. 2 a variant spelling of **gillie.**
▷HISTORY from Scottish Gaelic *gille* boy

ghost (gəʊst) NOUN 1 the disembodied spirit of a dead person, supposed to haunt the living as a pale or shadowy vision; phantom. Related adjective: **spectral.** 2 a haunting memory: *the ghost of his former life rose up before him.* 3 a faint trace or possibility of something; glimmer: *a ghost of a smile.* 4 the spirit; soul (archaic, except in the phrase **the Holy Ghost**). 5 *Physics* **a** a faint secondary image produced by an optical system. **b** a similar image on a television screen, formed by reflection of the transmitting waves or by a defect in the receiver. 6 See **ghost word.** 7 Also called: **ghost edition.** an entry recorded in a bibliography of which no actual proof exists. 8 See **ghostwriter.** 9 (*modifier*) falsely recorded as doing a particular job or fulfilling a particular function in order that some benefit, esp money, may be obtained: *a ghost worker.* 10 **give up the ghost. a** to die. **b** (of a machine) to stop working. ◆ VERB 11 See **ghostwrite.** 12 (*tr*) to haunt. 13 (*intr*) to move effortlessly and smoothly, esp unnoticed: *he ghosted into the penalty area.*
▷HISTORY Old English *gāst;* related to Old Frisian *jēst,* Old High German *geist* spirit, Sanskrit *hēda* fury, anger
▸ **'ghost,like** ADJECTIVE

ghost car NOUN *Canadian* an unmarked police car.

ghost dance NOUN a religious dance of certain North American Indians, connected with a political movement (from about 1888) that looked to reunion with the dead and a return to an idealized state of affairs before Europeans came.

ghost gum NOUN *Austral* a eucalyptus tree with white trunk and branches.

ghostly ('gəʊstlɪ) ADJECTIVE **-lier, -liest.** 1 of or resembling a ghost; spectral: *a ghostly face appeared at the window.* 2 suggesting the presence of ghosts; eerie. 3 *Archaic* of or relating to the soul or spirit. ▸ **'ghostliness** NOUN

ghost moth NOUN any of various large pale moths of the family *Hepialidae* that are active at dusk.

ghost town NOUN a deserted town, esp one in the western US that was formerly a boom town.

ghost word NOUN a word that has entered the language through the perpetuation, in dictionaries, etc., of an error.

ghostwrite ('gəʊstˌraɪt) VERB **-writes, -writing, -wrote, -written.** to write (an autobiographical or other article) on behalf of a person who is then credited as author. Often shortened to: **ghost.** ▸ **'ghostˌwriter** NOUN

ghoul (guːl) NOUN 1 a malevolent spirit or ghost. 2 a person interested in morbid or disgusting things. 3 a person who robs graves. 4 (in Muslim legend) an evil demon thought to eat human bodies, either stolen corpses or children. ▷ HISTORY C18: from Arabic *ghūl*, from *ghāla* he seized

ghoulish ('guːlɪʃ) ADJECTIVE of or relating to ghouls; morbid or disgusting; unhealthily interested in death. ▸ **'ghoulishly** ADVERB ▸ **'ghoulishness** NOUN

GHQ *Military* ABBREVIATION FOR General Headquarters.

ghyll (gɪl) NOUN a variant spelling of **gill**[3].

gi (giː) NOUN a loose-fitting white suit worn in judo, karate, and other martial arts: *a karate gi.* ▷ HISTORY from Japanese *-gi* costume, from *ki* to wear

gi THE INTERNET DOMAIN NAME FOR Gibraltar.

Gi *Electronics* ABBREVIATION FOR gilbert.

GI[1] NOUN *US informal* 1 (*plural* **GIs** *or* **GI's**) a soldier in the US Army, esp an enlisted man. ◆ ADJECTIVE 2 conforming to US Army regulations; of standard government issue. ▷ HISTORY C20: abbrev. of *government issue*

GI[2] *or* **g.i.** ABBREVIATION FOR: 1 gastrointestinal. 2 glycaemic index.

giant ('dʒaɪənt) NOUN 1 Also (feminine): **giantess** ('dʒaɪəntɪs). a mythical figure of superhuman size and strength, esp in folklore or fairy tales. 2 a person or thing of exceptional size, reputation, etc.: *a giant in nuclear physics.* 3 *Greek myth* any of the large and powerful offspring of Uranus (sky) and Gaea (earth) who rebelled against the Olympian gods but were defeated in battle. 4 *Pathol* a person suffering from gigantism. 5 *Astronomy* See **giant star.** 6 *Mining* another word for **monitor** (sense 8). ◆ ADJECTIVE 7 remarkably or supernaturally large. 8 *Architect* another word for **colossal.** ▷ HISTORY C13: from Old French *geant*, from Vulgar Latin *gagās* (unattested), from Latin *gigās, gigant-*, from Greek ▸ **'giant-ˌlike** ADJECTIVE

giant cell NOUN *Histology* an exceptionally large cell, often possessing several nuclei, such as an osteoclast.

giant hogweed NOUN an umbelliferous garden escape, *Heracleum mantegazzianum*, a tall species of cow parsley that grows up to 3½ metres (10 ft.) and whose irritant hairs and sap can cause a severe reaction if handled. Also called: **cartwheel flower.**

giantism ('dʒaɪənˌtɪzəm) NOUN another term for **gigantism.**

giant killer NOUN a person, sports team, etc., that defeats an apparently superior opponent.

giant panda NOUN See **panda** (sense 1).

giant peacock moth NOUN the largest European moth, an emperor, *Saturnia pyri*, reaching 15 cm (6 in.) in wingspan. It is mottled brown with a prominent ocellus on each wing and being night-flying can be mistaken for a bat.

giant planet NOUN any of the planets Jupiter, Saturn, Uranus, and Neptune, characterized by large mass, low density, and an extensive atmosphere.

giant powder NOUN dynamite composed of trinitroglycerine absorbed in kieselguhr.

Giant's Causeway NOUN a promontory of columnar basalt on the N coast of Northern Ireland, in Antrim: consists of several thousand pillars, mostly hexagonal, that were formed by the rapid cooling of lava and the inward contraction of the lava flow.

giant slalom NOUN *Skiing* a type of slalom in which the course is longer and the obstacles are further apart than in a standard slalom.

giant star NOUN any of a class of stars, such as Capella and Arcturus, that have swelled and brightened considerably as they approach the end of their life, their energy supply having changed. Sometimes shortened to: **giant.** Compare **supergiant.**

giant tortoise NOUN any of various very large tortoises of the genus *Testudo*, of the Galápagos, Seychelles, and certain other islands, weighing up to 225 kilograms (495 lbs.).

giaour ('dʒaʊə) NOUN a derogatory term for a non-Muslim, esp a Christian, used esp by the Turks. ▷ HISTORY C16: from Turkish *giaur* unbeliever, from Persian *gaur*, variant of *gäbr*

giardiasis (ˌdʒaɪɑː'daɪəsɪs) NOUN infection with the parasitic protozoan *Giardia lamblia*, which can cause severe diarrhoea.

gib[1] (gɪb) NOUN 1 a metal wedge, pad, or thrust bearing, esp a brass plate let into a steam engine crosshead. ◆ VERB **gibs, gibbing, gibbed.** 2 (*tr*) to fasten or supply with a gib. ▷ HISTORY C18: of unknown origin

gib[2] (gɪb) NOUN a male cat, esp a castrated one. ▷ HISTORY C14: probably a shortening and alteration of the proper name *Gilbert*

Gib (dʒɪb) NOUN an informal name for **Gibraltar.**

gibber[1] ('dʒɪbə) VERB 1 to utter rapidly and unintelligibly; prattle. 2 (*intr*) (of monkeys and related animals) to make characteristic chattering sounds. ◆ NOUN 3 a less common word for **gibberish.** ▷ HISTORY C17: of imitative origin

gibber[2] ('gɪbə) NOUN *Austral* 1 a stone or boulder. 2 (*modifier*) of or relating to a dry flat area of land covered with wind-polished stones: *gibber plains.* ▷ HISTORY C19: from a native Australian language

gibberellic acid (ˌdʒɪbə'relɪk) NOUN a slightly soluble crystalline plant hormone first isolated from the fungus *Gibberella fujikuroi*: a gibberellin. Formula: $C_{19}H_{22}O_6$. ▷ HISTORY C20: from New Latin *Gibberella*, literally: a little hump, from Latin *gibber* hump + -IC

gibberellin (ˌdʒɪbə'relɪn) NOUN any of several plant hormones, including gibberellic acid, whose main action is to cause elongation of the stem: used in promoting the growth of plants, in the malting of barley, etc.

gibberish ('dʒɪbərɪʃ) NOUN 1 rapid chatter like that of monkeys. 2 incomprehensible talk; nonsense.

gibbet ('dʒɪbɪt) NOUN 1 **a** a wooden structure resembling a gallows, from which the bodies of executed criminals were formerly hung to public view. **b** a gallows. ◆ VERB (*tr*) 2 to put to death by hanging on a gibbet. 3 to hang (a corpse) on a gibbet. 4 to expose to public ridicule. ▷ HISTORY C13: from Old French *gibet* gallows, literally: little cudgel, from *gibe* cudgel; of uncertain origin

Gib board NOUN *NZ informal* short for **Gibraltar board.**

gibbon ('gɪbᵊn) NOUN any small agile arboreal anthropoid ape of the genus *Hylobates*, inhabiting forests in S Asia. ▷ HISTORY C18: from French, probably from an Indian dialect word

gibbosity (gɪ'bɒsɪtɪ) NOUN, *plural* **-ties.** *Rare* 1 the state of being gibbous. 2 *Biology* a bulge or protuberance.

gibbous ('gɪbəs) *or* **gibbose** ('gɪbəʊs) ADJECTIVE 1 (of the moon or a planet) more than half but less than fully illuminated. 2 having a hunchback; hunchbacked. 3 bulging. ▷ HISTORY C17: from Late Latin *gibbōsus* humpbacked, from Latin *gibba* hump ▸ **'gibbously** ADVERB ▸ **'gibbousness** NOUN

Gibbs function (gɪbz) NOUN a thermodynamic property of a system equal to the difference between its enthalpy and the product of its temperature and its entropy. It is usually measured in joules. Symbol: *G*, (esp US) *F*. Also called: **Gibbs free energy, free enthalpy.** Compare **Helmholtz function.** ▷ HISTORY C19: named after Josiah Willard *Gibbs* (1839–1903), US physicist and mathematician

gibbsite ('gɪbzaɪt) NOUN a mineral consisting of hydrated aluminium oxide: a constituent of bauxite and a source of alumina. Formula: $Al(OH)_3$. ▷ HISTORY C19: named after George *Gibbs* (died 1833), American mineralogist

gibe[1] *or* **jibe** (dʒaɪb) VERB 1 to make jeering or scoffing remarks (at); taunt. ◆ NOUN 2 a derisive or provoking remark. ▷ HISTORY C16: perhaps from Old French *giber* to treat roughly, of uncertain origin ▸ **'giber** *or* **'jiber** NOUN ▸ **'gibingly** *or* **'jibingly** ADVERB

gibe[2] (dʒaɪb) VERB, NOUN *Nautical* a variant spelling of **gybe.**

Gibeon ('gɪbɪən) NOUN an ancient town of Palestine: the excavated site thought to be its remains lies about 9 kilometres (6 miles) northwest of Jerusalem.

Gibeonite ('gɪbɪəˌnaɪt) NOUN *Old Testament* one of the inhabitants of the town of Gibeon, who were compelled by Joshua to serve the Hebrews (Joshua 9).

giblets ('dʒɪblɪts) PLURAL NOUN (*sometimes singular*) the gizzard, liver, heart, and neck of a fowl. ▷ HISTORY C14: from Old French *gibelet* stew of game birds, probably from *gibier* game, of Germanic origin

gibli ('gɪblɪ) NOUN a variant spelling of **ghibli.**

Gibraltar (dʒɪ'brɔːltə) NOUN 1 **City of.** a city on the **Rock of Gibraltar,** a limestone promontory at the tip of S Spain: settled by Moors in 711 and taken by Spain in 1462; ceded to Britain in 1713; a British crown colony (1830–1969), still politically associated with Britain; a naval and air base of strategic importance. Pop.: 27 100 (1998 est.). Area: 6.5 sq. km (2.5 sq. miles). Ancient name: **Calpe.** 2 **Strait of.** a narrow strait between the S tip of Spain and the NW tip of Africa, linking the Mediterranean with the Atlantic.

Gibraltar board NOUN *Trademark, NZ* a type of lining board with a cardboard surface and a gypsum core.

Gibraltarian (ˌdʒɪbrɔːl'teərɪən) ADJECTIVE 1 of or relating to Gibraltar or its inhabitants. ◆ NOUN 2 a native or inhabitant of Gibraltar.

Gibson ('gɪbsᵊn) NOUN *Chiefly US* a cocktail consisting of four or more parts dry gin and one part dry vermouth, iced and served with a pickled pearl onion.

Gibson Desert NOUN a desert in W central Australia, between the Great Sandy Desert and the Victoria Desert: salt marshes, salt lakes, and scrub. Area: about 220 000 sq. km (85 000 sq. miles).

Gibson girl NOUN the ideal fashionable American girl of the late 1890s and early 1900s, as portrayed in the drawings of Charles Dana Gibson, 1867–1944, US illustrator.

gibus ('dʒaɪbəs) NOUN another name for **opera hat.** ▷ HISTORY C19: named after *Gibus*, 19th-century Frenchman who invented it

gid (gɪd) NOUN a disease of sheep characterized by an unsteady gait and staggering, caused by infestation of the brain with tapeworms (*Taenia caenuris*). ▷ HISTORY C17: back formation from GIDDY

giddap (gɪ'dæp) *or* **giddy-up** (ˌgɪdɪ'ʌp) INTERJECTION an exclamation used to make a horse go faster. ▷ HISTORY C20: colloquial form of *get up*

giddy ('gɪdɪ) ADJECTIVE **-dier, -diest.** 1 affected with a reeling sensation and feeling as if about to fall; dizzy. 2 causing or tending to cause vertigo. 3 impulsive; scatterbrained. 4 **my giddy aunt.** an exclamation of surprise. ◆ VERB **-dies, -dying, -died.** 5 to make or become giddy. ▷ HISTORY Old English *gydig* mad, frenzied, possessed by God; related to GOD ▸ **'giddily** ADVERB ▸ **'giddiness** NOUN

Gideon ('gɪdɪən) NOUN *Old Testament* a Hebrew

judge who led the Israelites to victory over their Midianite oppressors (Judges 6:11–8:35).

Gideon Bible NOUN a Bible purchased by members of a Christian organization (**Gideons**) and placed in a hotel room, hospital ward, etc.

gidgee *or* **gidjee** ('gɪdʒiː) NOUN *Austral* any of various small acacia trees, esp *Acacia cambagei,* which at times emits an unpleasant smell.
▷HISTORY C19: from a native Australian language

gie (giː) VERB a Scot word for **give.**

Giessen (*German* 'giːsən) NOUN a city in central Germany, in Hesse: university (1607). Pop.: 71 750 (latest est.).

GIF (gɪf) NOUN ACRONYM FOR graphics interchange format; a compressed format for images, widely used on the Internet.

gift (gɪft) NOUN [1] something given; a present. [2] a special aptitude, ability, or power; talent. [3] the power or right to give or bestow (esp in the phrases **in the gift of, in (someone's) gift**). [4] the act or process of giving. [5] **look a gift-horse in the mouth.** (*usually negative*) to find fault with a free gift or chance benefit. ◆ VERB (*tr*) [6] to present (something) as a gift to (a person). [7] (often foll by *with*) to present (someone) with a gift. [8] *Rare* to endow with; bestow.
▷HISTORY Old English *gift* payment for a wife, dowry; related to Old Norse *gipt,* Old High German *gift,* Gothic *fragifts* endowment, engagement; see GIVE
▸ '**giftless** ADJECTIVE

GIFT (gɪft) NOUN ACRONYM FOR gamete intrafallopian transfer: a technique, similar to in vitro fertilization, that enables some women who are unable to conceive to bear children. Egg cells are removed from the woman's ovary, mixed with sperm, and introduced into one of her Fallopian tubes.

gifted ('gɪftɪd) ADJECTIVE having or showing natural talent or aptitude: *a gifted musician; a gifted performance.*
▸ '**giftedly** ADVERB ▸ '**giftedness** NOUN

gift of tongues NOUN an utterance, partly or wholly unintelligible, produced under the influence of ecstatic religious emotion and conceived to be a manifestation of the Holy Ghost: practised in certain Christian churches, usually called Pentecostal. Also called: **glossolalia.**

gift tax NOUN another name for (the former) **capital transfer tax.**

giftwrap ('gɪftˌræp) VERB **-wraps, -wrapping, -wrapped.** to wrap (an article intended as a gift) attractively.

Gifu ('giːfuː) NOUN a city in Japan, on central Honshu: hot springs, textile and paper lantern manufacturing. Pop.: 407 145 (1995).

gig[1] (gɪg) NOUN [1] a light two-wheeled one-horse carriage without a hood. [2] *Nautical* a light tender for a vessel, often for the personal use of the captain. [3] a long light rowing boat, used esp for racing. [4] a machine for raising the nap of a fabric. ◆ VERB **gigs, gigging, gigged.** [5] (*intr*) to travel in a gig. [6] (*tr*) to raise the nap of (fabric).
▷HISTORY C13 (in the sense: flighty girl, spinning top): perhaps of Scandinavian origin; compare Danish *gig* top, Norwegian *giga* to shake about

gig[2] (gɪg) NOUN [1] a cluster of barbless hooks drawn through a shoal of fish to try to impale them. [2] short for **fishgig.** ◆ VERB **gigs, gigging, gigged.** [3] to catch (fish) with a gig.
▷HISTORY C18: shortened from FISHGIG

gig[3] (gɪg) *Informal* ◆ NOUN [1] a job, esp a single booking for jazz or pop musicians to play at a concert or club. [2] the performance itself. ◆ VERB **gigs, gigging, gigged.** [3] (*intr*) to perform at a gig or gigs.
▷HISTORY C20: of unknown origin

gig[4] (gɪg) NOUN *Informal* short for **gigabyte.**

giga- COMBINING FORM [1] denoting 10^9: *gigavolt.* Symbol: G. [2] (in computer technology) denoting 2^{30}: *gigabyte.*
▷HISTORY from Greek *gigas* GIANT

gigabyte ('gaɪgəˌbaɪt) NOUN *Computing* one thousand and twenty-four megabytes. See also **giga-** (sense 2).

gigaflop ('gaɪgəˌflɒp) NOUN *Computing* a measure of processing speed, consisting of a thousand million floating-point operations a second.
▷HISTORY C20: from GIGA- + *flo(ating) p(oint)*

gigahertz ('gaɪgəˌhɜːts, 'dʒɪg-) NOUN, *plural* **-hertz.** a unit of frequency equal to 10^9 hertz. Symbol: GHz.

gigantic (dʒaɪ'gæntɪk) ADJECTIVE [1] very large; enormous: *a gigantic error.* [2] Also: **gigantesque** (ˌdʒaɪgæn'tɛsk). of or suitable for giants.
▷HISTORY C17: from Greek *gigantikos,* from *gigas* GIANT
▸ **gi'gantically** ADVERB ▸ **gi'ganticness** NOUN

gigantism ('dʒaɪgænˌtɪzəm, dʒaɪ'gæntɪzəm) NOUN [1] Also called: **giantism.** excessive growth of the entire body, caused by over-production of growth hormone by the pituitary gland during childhood or adolescence. Compare **acromegaly.** [2] the state or quality of being gigantic.

gigantomachy (ˌdʒaɪgæn'tɒməkɪ) *or* **gigantomachia** (dʒaɪˌgæntəʊ'meɪkɪə) NOUN, *plural* **-chies** *or* **-chias.** [1] *Greek myth* the war fought between the gods of Olympus and the rebelling giants. See **giant** (sense 3). [2] any battle fought between or as if between giants.
▷HISTORY C17: from Greek *gigantomakhia,* from *gigas* giant + *makhē* battle

giggle ('gɪgᵊl) VERB [1] (*intr*) to laugh nervously or foolishly. ◆ NOUN [2] such a laugh. [3] *Informal* something or someone that provokes amusement. [4] **the giggles.** a fit of prolonged and uncontrollable giggling. [5] **for a giggle.** *Informal* as a joke or prank; not seriously.
▷HISTORY C16: of imitative origin
▸ '**giggler** NOUN ▸ '**giggling** NOUN, ADJECTIVE ▸ '**gigglingly** ADVERB ▸ '**giggly** ADJECTIVE

gig-lamps PLURAL NOUN an old-fashioned slang term for **spectacles.**

GIGO ('gaɪgəʊ) NOUN *Computing, slang* ◆ ACRONYM FOR garbage in, garbage out.

gigolo ('ʒɪgəˌləʊ) NOUN, *plural* **-los.** [1] a man who is kept by a woman, esp an older woman. [2] a man who is paid to dance with or escort women.
▷HISTORY C20: from French, back formation from *gigolette* girl for hire as a dancing partner, prostitute, from *giguer* to dance, from *gigue* a fiddle; compare GIGOT, GIGUE, JIG

gigot ('ʒiːgəʊ, 'dʒɪgət) NOUN [1] a leg of lamb or mutton. [2] a leg-of-mutton sleeve.
▷HISTORY C16: from Old French: leg, a small fiddle, from *gigue* a fiddle, of Germanic origin

gigue (ʒiːg) NOUN [1] a piece of music, usually in six-eight time and often fugal, incorporated into the classical suite. [2] a formal couple dance of the 16th and 17th centuries, derived from the jig.
▷HISTORY C17: from French, from Italian *giga,* literally: a fiddle; see GIGOT

GI Joe NOUN *US informal* a US enlisted soldier; a GI.

Gijón (giː'hɔːn; *Spanish* xi'ɔxn) NOUN a port in NW Spain, on the Bay of Biscay: capital of the kingdom of Asturias until 791. Pop.: 265 491 (1998 est.). Ancient name: **Gigia.**

Gila monster ('hiːlə) NOUN a large venomous brightly coloured lizard, *Heloderma suspectum,* inhabiting deserts of the southwestern US and Mexico and feeding mostly on eggs and small mammals: family *Helodermatidae.*
▷HISTORY C19: after the *Gila,* a river in New Mexico and Arizona

gilbert ('gɪlbət) NOUN a unit of magnetomotive force; the magnetomotive force resulting from the passage of 4π abamperes through one turn of a coil. 1 gilbert is equivalent to $10/4\pi = 0.795\ 775$ ampere-turn. Symbols: **Gb** *or* **Gi.**
▷HISTORY C19: named after William *Gilbert* (1540–1603), English physician and physicist

Gilbertine ('gɪlbətaɪn, -tɪn) NOUN [1] a member of a Christian order founded in approximately 1135 by St Gilbert of Sempringham, composed of nuns who followed the Cistercian rule and Augustinian canons who ministered to them. It was the only religious order of English origin and never spread to Europe. ◆ ADJECTIVE [2] of, relating to, or belonging to this order.

Gilbert Islands PLURAL NOUN a group of islands in the W Pacific: with Banaba, the Phoenix Islands, and three of the Line Islands they constitute the independent state of Kiribati; until 1975 they formed part of the British colony of **Gilbert and Ellice Islands;** achieved full independence in 1979. Pop.: 71 757 (1995). Area: 295 sq. km (114 sq. miles).

gild[1] (gɪld) VERB **gilds, gilding, gilded** *or* **gilt** (gɪlt). (*tr*) [1] to cover with or as if with gold. [2] **gild the lily. a** to adorn unnecessarily something already beautiful. **b** to praise someone inordinately. [3] to give a falsely attractive or valuable appearance to. [4] *Archaic* to smear with blood.
▷HISTORY Old English *gyldan,* from *gold* GOLD; related to Old Norse *gylla,* Middle High German *vergülden*
▸ '**gilder** NOUN

gild[2] (gɪld) NOUN a variant spelling of **guild** (sense 2).
▸ '**gildsman** NOUN

gilder ('gɪldə) NOUN a variant spelling of **guilder.**

gilding ('gɪldɪŋ) NOUN [1] the act or art of applying gilt to a surface. [2] the surface so produced. [3] another word for **gilt**[1] (sense 2).

Gilead[1] ('gɪlɪˌæd) NOUN a historic mountainous region east of the River Jordan, rising over 1200 m (4000 ft.).

Gilead[2] ('gɪlɪˌæd) NOUN *Old Testament* a grandson of Manasseh; ancestor of the Coileadites (Numbers 26: 29–30).

Gileadite ('gɪlɪəˌdaɪt) NOUN [1] an inhabitant of the region of Gilead. [2] a descendant of Gilead (the man).

gilet (dʒɪ'leɪ) NOUN [1] a waist- or hip-length garment, usually sleeveless, fastening up the front; sometimes made from a quilted fabric, and designed to be worn over a blouse, shirt, etc. [2] a bodice resembling a waistcoat in a woman's dress. [3] such a bodice as part of a ballet dancer's costume.
▷HISTORY C19: French, literally: waistcoat

gilgai ('gɪlgaɪ) NOUN *Austral* a natural water hole.
▷HISTORY C19: from a native Australian language

Gilgamesh ('gɪlgəˌmɛʃ) NOUN a legendary Sumerian king.

gill[1] (gɪl) NOUN [1] the respiratory organ in many aquatic animals, consisting of a membrane or outgrowth well supplied with blood vessels. **External gills** occur in tadpoles, some molluscs, etc.; **internal gills,** within gill slits, occur in most fishes. Related adjective: **branchial.** [2] any of the radiating leaflike spore-producing structures on the undersurface of the cap of a mushroom. ◆ VERB [3] to catch (fish) or (of fish) to be caught in a gill net. [4] (*tr*) to gut (fish). ◆ See also **gills.**
▷HISTORY C14: of Scandinavian origin; compare Swedish *gäl,* Danish *gjælle,* Greek *khelunē* lip
▸ **gilled** ADJECTIVE ▸ '**gill-less** ADJECTIVE ▸ '**gill-ˌlike** ADJECTIVE

gill[2] (dʒɪl) NOUN [1] a unit of liquid measure equal to one quarter of a pint. [2] *Northern Brit dialect* half a pint, esp of beer.
▷HISTORY C14: from Old French *gille* vat, tub, from Late Latin *gillō* cooling vessel for liquids, of obscure origin

gill[3] *or* **ghyll** (gɪl) NOUN *Dialect* [1] a narrow stream; rivulet. [2] a wooded ravine. [3] (*capital when part of place name*) a deep natural hole in rock; pothole: *Gaping Gill.*
▷HISTORY C11: from Old Norse *gil* steep-sided valley

gill[4] (dʒɪl) NOUN [1] *Archaic* a girl or sweetheart. [2] *Dialect* Also spelt: **jill.** a female ferret. [3] an archaic or dialect name for **ground ivy.**
▷HISTORY C15: special use of *Gill,* short for *Gillian,* girl's name

Gilles de la Tourette syndrome (dʒiːl də læ tʊə'rɛt) NOUN another name for **Tourette syndrome.**

gill fungus (gɪl) NOUN any fungus of the basidiomycetous family *Agaricaceae,* in which the spores are produced on gills underneath a cap. See also **agaric.**

gillie, ghillie, *or* **gilly** ('gɪlɪ) NOUN, *plural* **-lies.** *Scot* [1] an attendant or guide for hunting or fishing. [2] (formerly) a Highland chieftain's male attendant or personal servant.
▷HISTORY C17: from Scottish Gaelic *gille* boy, servant

Gillingham ('dʒɪlɪŋəm) NOUN a town in SE England, in Medway unitary authority, Kent, on the Medway estuary: former dockyards. Pop.: 94 923 (1991).

gillion ('dʒɪljən) NOUN *Brit* (no longer in technical use) one thousand million. US and Canadian equivalent: **billion.**
▷HISTORY C20: from G(IGA-) + (M)ILLION

gill net (gɪl) NOUN *Fishing* a net suspended vertically in the water to trap fish by their gills in its meshes.

gill pouch (gɪl) NOUN any of a series of paired linear pouches in chordate embryos, arising as outgrowths of the wall of the pharynx. In fish and some amphibians they become the gill slits.

gills (gɪlz) PLURAL NOUN 1 (*sometimes singular*) the wattle of birds such as domestic fowl. 2 **green around** *or* **about the gills.** *Informal* looking or feeling nauseated.

gill slit (gɪl) NOUN any of a series of paired linear openings to the exterior from the sides of the pharynx in fishes and some amphibians. They contain the gills.

gillyflower *or* **gilliflower** ('dʒɪlɪˌflaʊə) NOUN 1 any of several plants having fragrant flowers, such as the stock and wallflower. 2 an archaic name for **carnation.**
▷HISTORY C14: changed (through influence of *flower*) from *gilofre,* from Old French *girofle,* from Medieval Latin, from Greek *karuophullon* clove tree, from *karuon* nut + *phullon* leaf

Gilolo (dʒaɪ'ləʊləʊ, dʒɪ-) NOUN See **Halmahera.**

Gilsonite ('gɪlsəˌnaɪt) NOUN *Trademark* a very pure form of asphalt found in Utah and Colorado; used for making paints, varnishes, and linoleum.
▷HISTORY C19: named after S. H. *Gilson* of Salt Lake City, Utah, who discovered it

gilt¹ (gɪlt) VERB 1 a past tense and past participle of **gild¹**. ◆ NOUN 2 gold or a substance simulating it, applied in gilding. 3 another word for **gilding** (senses 1, 2). 4 superficial or false appearance of excellence; glamour. 5 a gilt-edged security. 6 **take the gilt off the gingerbread.** to destroy the part of something that gives it its appeal. ◆ ADJECTIVE 7 covered with or as if with gold or gilt; gilded.

gilt² (gɪlt) NOUN a young female pig, esp one that has not had a litter.
▷HISTORY C15: from Old Norse *gyltr;* related to Old English *gelte,* Old High German *gelza,* Middle Low German *gelte*

gilt-edged ADJECTIVE 1 *Stock Exchange* denoting government securities on which interest payments will certainly be met and that will certainly be repaid at par on the due date. 2 of the highest quality: *the last track on the album is a gilt-edged classic.* 3 (of books, papers, etc.) having gilded edges.

gilthead ('gɪltˌhɛd) NOUN 1 a sparid fish, *Sparus aurata,* of Mediterranean and European Atlantic waters, having a gold-coloured band between the eyes. 2 any similar or related fish.

gimbals ('dʒɪmbᵊlz, 'gɪm-) PLURAL NOUN a device, consisting of two or three pivoted rings at right angles to each other, that provides free suspension in all planes for an object such as a gyroscope, compass, chronometer, etc. Also called: **gimbal ring.**
▷HISTORY C16: variant of earlier *gimmal* finger ring, from Old French *gemel,* from Latin *gemellus,* diminutive of *geminus* twin

gimcrack ('dʒɪmˌkræk) ADJECTIVE 1 cheap; shoddy. ◆ NOUN 2 a cheap showy trifle or gadget.
▷HISTORY C18: changed from C14 *gibecrake* little ornament, of unknown origin
▸ **'gimˌcrackery** NOUN

gimel ('gɪməl; *Hebrew* 'giːmɛl) NOUN the third letter of the Hebrew alphabet (ג) transliterated as *g* or, when final, *gh.*
▷HISTORY literally: camel

gimlet ('gɪmlɪt) NOUN 1 a small hand tool consisting of a pointed spiral tip attached at right angles to a handle, used for boring small holes in wood. 2 *US* a cocktail consisting of half gin or vodka and half lime juice. 3 a eucalyptus of W Australia having a twisted bole. ◆ VERB 4 (*tr*) to make holes in (wood) using a gimlet. ◆ ADJECTIVE 5 penetrating; piercing (esp in the phrase **gimlet-eyed**).
▷HISTORY C15: from Old French *guimbelet,* of Germanic origin, see WIMBLE

gimme ('gɪmiː) INTERJECTION 1 *Slang* give me! ◆ NOUN 2 *Golf* a short putt that one is excused by one's opponent from playing because it is considered too easy to miss.

gimmick ('gɪmɪk) NOUN 1 something designed to attract extra attention, interest, or publicity. 2 any clever device, gadget, or stratagem, esp one used to deceive. 3 *Chiefly US* a device or trick of legerdemain that enables a magician to deceive the audience.
▷HISTORY C20: originally US slang, of unknown origin
▸ **'gimmickry** NOUN ▸ **'gimmicky** ADJECTIVE

gimp¹ *or* **guimpe** (gɪmp) NOUN a tapelike trimming of silk, wool, or cotton, often stiffened with wire.
▷HISTORY C17: probably from Dutch *gimp,* of unknown origin

gimp² (gɪmp) NOUN 1 *US & Canadian offensive slang* a physically disabled person, esp one who is lame. 2 *Slang* a sexual fetishist who likes to be dominated and who dresses in a leather or rubber body suit with mask, zips, and chains.
▷HISTORY C20: of unknown origin

gimpy ('gɪmpɪ) ADJECTIVE the US equivalent of **gammy.**

gin¹ (dʒɪn) NOUN 1 an alcoholic drink obtained by distillation and rectification of the grain of malted barley, rye, or maize, flavoured with juniper berries. 2 any of various grain spirits flavoured with other fruit or aromatic essences: *sloe gin.* 3 an alcoholic drink made from any rectified spirit.
▷HISTORY C18: shortened from Dutch *genever* juniper, via Old French from Latin *jūniperus* JUNIPER

gin² (dʒɪn) NOUN 1 a primitive engine in which a vertical shaft is turned by horses driving a horizontal beam or yoke in a circle. 2 Also called: **cotton gin.** a machine of this type used for separating seeds from raw cotton. 3 a trap for catching small mammals, consisting of a noose of thin strong wire. 4 a hand-operated hoist that consists of a drum winder turned by a crank. ◆ VERB **gins, ginning, ginned.** (*tr*) 5 to free (cotton) of seeds with a gin. 6 to trap or snare (game) with a gin.
▷HISTORY C13 *gyn,* shortened from ENGINE
▸ **'ginner** NOUN

gin³ (gɪn) VERB **gins, ginning, gan, gun.** an archaic word for **begin.**

gin⁴ (gɪn) CONJUNCTION *Scot* if.
▷HISTORY perhaps related to *gif,* an earlier form of *if*

gin⁵ (dʒɪn) NOUN *Austral offensive slang* an Aboriginal woman.
▷HISTORY C19: from a native Australian language

ging (gɪŋ) NOUN *Austral slang* a child's catapult.
▷HISTORY of unknown origin

ginge (dʒɪndʒ) NOUN *Informal* a person with ginger hair.

ginger ('dʒɪndʒə) NOUN 1 any of several zingiberaceous plants of the genus *Zingiber,* esp *Z. officinale* of the East Indies, cultivated throughout the tropics for its spicy hot-tasting underground stem. See also **galangal.** Compare **wild ginger.** 2 the underground stem of this plant, which is used fresh or powdered as a flavouring or crystallized as a sweetmeat. 3 any of certain related plants. 4 **a** a reddish-brown or yellowish-brown colour. **b** (*as adjective*): *ginger hair.* 5 *Informal* liveliness; vigour. ◆ VERB 6 (*tr*) to add the spice ginger to (a dish). ◆ See also **ginger up.**
▷HISTORY C13: from Old French *gingivre,* from Medieval Latin *gingiber,* from Latin *zinziberi,* from Greek *zingiberis,* probably from Sanskrit *śṛṅgaveram,* from *śṛṅga-* horn + *vera-* body, referring to its shape

ginger ale NOUN a sweetened effervescent nonalcoholic drink flavoured with ginger extract.

ginger beer NOUN a slightly alcoholic drink made by fermenting a mixture of syrup and root ginger.

gingerbread ('dʒɪndʒəˌbrɛd) NOUN 1 a moist brown cake, flavoured with ginger and treacle or syrup. 2 **a** a rolled biscuit, similarly flavoured, cut into various shapes and sometimes covered with icing. **b** (*as modifier*): *gingerbread man.* 3 **a** an elaborate but unsubstantial ornamentation. **b** (*as modifier*): *gingerbread style of architecture.*

gingerbread tree NOUN a W African tree, *Parinari macrophyllum,* with large mealy edible fruits (**gingerbread plums**): family *Chrysobalanaceae.*

ginger group NOUN *Chiefly Brit* a group within a party, association, etc., that enlivens or radicalizes its parent body.

gingerly ('dʒɪndʒəlɪ) ADVERB 1 in a cautious, reluctant, or timid manner. ◆ ADJECTIVE 2 cautious, reluctant, or timid.
▷HISTORY C16: perhaps from Old French *gensor* dainty, from *gent* of noble birth; see GENTLE
▸ **'gingerliness** NOUN

ginger nut *or* **snap** NOUN a crisp biscuit flavoured with ginger.

ginger up VERB (*tr, adverb*) to enliven (an activity, group, etc.).

ginger wine NOUN an alcoholic drink made from fermented bruised ginger, sugar, and water.

gingery ('dʒɪndʒərɪ) ADJECTIVE 1 like or tasting of ginger. 2 of or like the colour ginger. 3 full of vigour; high-spirited. 4 pointed; biting: *a gingery remark.*

gingham ('gɪŋəm) NOUN *Textiles* **a** a cotton fabric, usually woven of two coloured yarns in a checked or striped design. **b** (*as modifier*): *a gingham dress.*
▷HISTORY C17: from French *guingan,* from Malay *ginggang* striped cloth

gingili, gingelli, *or* **gingelly** ('dʒɪndʒɪlɪ) NOUN 1 the oil obtained from sesame seeds. 2 another name for **sesame.**
▷HISTORY C18: from Hindi *jingalī*

gingiva ('dʒɪndʒɪvə, dʒɪn'dʒaɪvə) NOUN, *plural* **-givae** (-dʒɪˌviː, -'dʒaɪviː). *Anatomy* the technical name for the **gum²**.
▷HISTORY from Latin
▸ **'gingival** ADJECTIVE

gingivitis (ˌdʒɪndʒɪ'vaɪtɪs) NOUN inflammation of the gums.

ginglymus ('dʒɪŋglɪməs, 'gɪŋ-) NOUN, *plural* **-mi** (-ˌmaɪ). *Anatomy* a hinge joint. See **hinge** (sense 2).
▷HISTORY C17: New Latin, from Greek *ginglumos* hinge

gink (gɪŋk) NOUN *Slang* a man or boy, esp one considered to be odd.
▷HISTORY C20: of unknown origin

ginkgo ('gɪŋkgəʊ) *or* **gingko** ('gɪŋkəʊ) NOUN, *plural* **-goes** *or* **-koes.** a widely planted ornamental Chinese gymnosperm tree, *Ginkgo biloba,* with fan-shaped deciduous leaves and fleshy yellow fruit: phylum *Ginkgophyta.* It is used in herbal remedies and as a food supplement. Also called: **maidenhair tree.**
▷HISTORY C18: from Japanese *ginkyō,* from Ancient Chinese *yin* silver + *hang* apricot

ginnel ('gɪnᵊl, 'dʒɪn-) NOUN *Northern English dialect* a narrow passageway between buildings.
▷HISTORY C17: perhaps a corruption of CHANNEL¹

ginormous (dʒaɪ'nɔːməs) ADJECTIVE *Informal* very large.
▷HISTORY C20: blend of *giant* or *gigantic* and *enormous*

gin palace (dʒɪn) NOUN (formerly) a gaudy drinking house.

gin rummy (dʒɪn) NOUN a version of rummy in which a player may go out if the odd cards outside his sequences total less than ten points. Often shortened to: **gin.**
▷HISTORY C20: from GIN¹ + RUMMY¹, apparently from a humorous allusion to gin and rum

ginseng ('dʒɪnsɛŋ) NOUN 1 either of two araliaceous plants, *Panax schinseng* of China or *P. quinquefolius* of North America, whose forked aromatic roots are used medicinally. 2 the root of either of these plants or a substance obtained from the roots, believed to possess stimulant, tonic, and energy-giving properties.
▷HISTORY C17: from Mandarin Chinese *jen shen,* from *jen* man (from a resemblance of the roots to human legs) + *shen* ginseng

gin sling (dʒɪn) NOUN an iced drink made from gin and water, sweetened, and flavoured with lemon or lime juice.

gio ('dʒiːəʊ) NOUN an older variant of **geo.**

Gioconda (*Italian* dʒo'konda) NOUN **La.** See **Mona Lisa.**
▷HISTORY Italian: the smiling (lady)

Giorgi system ('dʒɔːdʒɪ) NOUN a system of units based on the metre, kilogram, second, and ampere, in which the magnetic constant has the value $4\pi \times 10^{-7}$ henries per metre. It was used as a basis for SI units. Also called: **MKSA system.**

▷HISTORY C20: named after Giovanni *Giorgi* (1871–1950), Italian physicist

Giotto (ˈdʒɒtəʊ) NOUN a European spacecraft that intercepted the path of Halley's comet in March 1986, gathering data and recording images, esp of the comet's nucleus.

gip (dʒɪp) VERB **gips, gipping, gipped.** [1] a variant spelling of **gyp**[1]. ◆ NOUN [2] a variant spelling of **gyp**[2].

gipon (dʒɪˈpɒn, ˈdʒɪpɒn) NOUN another word for **jupon.**

Gippsland (ˈgɪpsˌlænd) NOUN a fertile region of SE Australia, in SE Victoria, extending east along the coast from Melbourne to the New South Wales border. Area: 35 200 sq. km (13 600 sq. miles).

gippy (ˈdʒɪpɪ) *Slang* ◆ NOUN, *plural* **-pies.** [1] an Egyptian person or thing. [2] Also called: **gippo** *plural* **-poes.** a Gypsy. ◆ ADJECTIVE [3] Egyptian. [4] **gippy tummy.** diarrhoea, esp as experienced by visitors to hot climates.
▷HISTORY C19: from GYPSY and EGYPTIAN

gippy (ˈgɪpɪ) NOUN, *plural* **-ies.** *Northern English dialect* a starling.

Gipsy (ˈdʒɪpsɪ) NOUN, *plural* **-sies.** (*sometimes not capital*) a variant spelling of **Gypsy.**
▸ˈ**Gipsyish** ADJECTIVE ▸ˈ**Gipsydom** NOUN ▸ˈ**Gipsyˌhood** NOUN ▸ˈ**Gipsy-ˌlike** ADJECTIVE

gipsy moth NOUN a European moth, *Lymantria dispar,* introduced into North America, where it is a serious pest of shade trees: family *Lymantriidae* (or *Liparidae*). See also **tussock moth.**

gipsywort (ˈdʒɪpsɪˌwɜːt) NOUN a hairy Eurasian plant, *Lycopus europaeus,* having two-lipped white flowers with purple dots on the lower lip: family *Lamiaceae* (labiates). See also **bugleweed** (sense 1).

giraffe (dʒɪˈrɑːf, -ˈræf) NOUN, *plural* **-raffes** *or* **-raffe.** a large ruminant mammal, *Giraffa camelopardalis,* inhabiting savannas of tropical Africa: the tallest mammal, with very long legs and neck and a colouring of regular reddish-brown patches on a beige ground: family *Giraffidae.*
▷HISTORY C17: from Italian *giraffa,* from Arabic *zarāfah,* probably of African origin

girandole (ˈdʒɪrənˌdəʊl) *or* **girandola** (dʒɪˈrændələ) NOUN [1] an ornamental branched wall candleholder, usually incorporating a mirror. [2] an earring or pendant having a central gem surrounded by smaller ones. [3] a kind of revolving firework. [4] *Artillery* a group of connected mines.
▷HISTORY C17: from French, from Italian *girandola,* from *girare* to revolve, from Latin *gȳrāre* to GYRATE

girasol, girosol, *or* **girasole** (ˈdʒɪrəˌsɒl, -ˌsəʊl) NOUN a type of opal that has a red or pink glow in bright light; fire opal.
▷HISTORY C16: from Italian, from *girare* to revolve (see GYRATE) + *sole* the sun, from Latin *sōl*

gird[1] (gɜːd) VERB **girds, girding, girded** *or* **girt.** (*tr*) [1] to put a belt, girdle, etc., around (the waist or hips). [2] to bind or secure with or as if with a belt: *to gird on one's armour.* [3] to surround; encircle. [4] to prepare (oneself) for action (esp in the phrase **gird (up) one's loins**). [5] to endow with a rank, attribute, etc., esp knighthood.
▷HISTORY Old English *gyrdan,* of Germanic origin; related to Old Norse *gyrtha,* Old High German *gurten*

gird[2] (gɜːd) *Northern English dialect* ◆ VERB [1] (when *intr,* foll by *at*) to jeer (at someone); mock. [2] (*tr*) to strike (a blow at someone). [3] (*intr*) to move at high speed. ◆ NOUN [4] **a** a blow or stroke. **b** a taunt; gibe. [5] a display of bad temper or anger (esp in the phrases **in a gird; throw a gird**).
▷HISTORY C13 *girden* to strike, cut, of unknown origin

gird[3] (gɪrd) NOUN *Scot* a hoop, esp a child's hoop. Also: **girr.**
▷HISTORY a Scot variant of GIRTH

girder (ˈgɜːdə) NOUN [1] a large beam, esp one made of steel, used in the construction of bridges, buildings, etc. [2] *Botany* the structure composed of tissue providing mechanical support for a stem or leaf.

girdle[1] (ˈgɜːdᵊl) NOUN [1] a woman's elastic corset covering the waist to the thigh. [2] anything that surrounds or encircles. [3] a belt or sash. [4] *Jewellery* the outer edge of a gem. [5] *Anatomy* any encircling structure or part. See **pectoral girdle, pelvic girdle.** [6] the mark left on a tree trunk after the removal of a ring of bark. ◆ VERB (*tr*) [7] to put a girdle on or around. [8] to surround or encircle. [9] to remove a ring of bark from (a tree or branch), thus causing it to die.
▷HISTORY Old English *gyrdel,* of Germanic origin; related to Old Norse *gyrthill,* Old Frisian *gerdel,* Old High German *gurtila;* see GIRD[1]
▸ˈ**girdle-ˌlike** ADJECTIVE

girdle[2] (ˈgɜːdᵊl) NOUN *Scot and northern English dialect* another word for **griddle.**

girdler (ˈgɜːdlə) NOUN [1] a person or thing that girdles. [2] a maker of girdles. [3] any insect, such as the twig girdler, that bores circular grooves around the stems or twigs in which it lays its eggs.

girdlescone (ˈgɜːdᵊlˌskəʊn, -ˌskɒn), **girdle scone,** *or* **girdlecake** (ˈgɜːdᵊlˌkeɪk) NOUN less common names for **drop scone.**

girdle traverse NOUN *Mountaineering* a climb that consists of a complete traverse of a face or crag.

Girgenti (*Italian* dʒirˈdʒɛnti) NOUN a former name (until 1927) of **Agrigento.**

girl (gɜːl) NOUN [1] a female child from birth to young womanhood. [2] a young unmarried woman; lass; maid. [3] *Informal* a sweetheart or girlfriend. [4] *Informal* a woman of any age. [5] an informal word for **daughter.** [6] a female employee, esp a female servant. [7] *South African derogatory* a Black female servant of any age. [8] (*usually plural* and preceded by *the*) *Informal* a group of women, esp acquaintances.
▷HISTORY C13: of uncertain origin; perhaps related to Low German *Göre* boy, girl

girl band NOUN an all-female vocal pop group created to appeal to a young audience.

girl Friday NOUN a female employee who has a wide range of duties, usually including secretarial and clerical work.
▷HISTORY C20: coined on the pattern of MAN FRIDAY

girlfriend (ˈgɜːlˌfrɛnd) NOUN [1] a female friend with whom a man or boy is romantically or sexually involved; sweetheart. [2] any female friend.

Girl Guide NOUN See **Guide.**

girlhood (ˈgɜːlˌhʊd) NOUN the state or time of being a girl.

girlie (ˈgɜːlɪ) *or* **girly** NOUN [1] a little girl. ◆ ADJECTIVE [2] displaying or featuring nude or scantily dressed women: *a girlie magazine.* [3] suited to or designed to appeal to young women: *a girlie night out.*

girlish (ˈgɜːlɪʃ) ADJECTIVE of or like a girl in looks, behaviour, innocence, etc.
▸ˈ**girlishly** ADVERB ▸ˈ**girlishness** NOUN

Girls' Brigade NOUN (in Britain) an organization for girls, founded in 1893, with the aim of promoting self-discipline and self-respect.

Girl Scout NOUN *US* a member of the equivalent organization for girls to the Scouts. Brit equivalent: **Guide.**

girn (gərn, gɜːn) VERB (*intr*) *Scot and northern English dialect* [1] to snarl. [2] to grimace; pull grotesque faces. [3] to complain fretfully or peevishly.
▷HISTORY C14: a variant of GRIN

giro (ˈdʒaɪrəʊ) NOUN, *plural* **-ros.** [1] a system of transferring money within the financial institutions of a country, such as banks and post offices, by which bills, etc. may be paid by filling in a giro form authorizing the debit of a specified sum from one's own account to the credit of the payee's account. [2] *Brit informal* an unemployment or income support payment by giro cheque, posted fortnightly.
▷HISTORY C20: ultimately from Greek *guros* circuit

girolle (ʒiːˈrɒl) NOUN another word for **chanterelle.**
▷HISTORY C20: French

giron *or* **gyron** (ˈdʒaɪrɒn) NOUN *Heraldry* a charge consisting of the lower half of a diagonally divided quarter, usually in the top left corner of the shield.
▷HISTORY C16: from Old French *giron* a triangular piece of material, of Germanic origin; related to Old High German *gēro* triangular object; compare GORE[3]

Gironde (*French* ʒirɔ̃d) NOUN [1] a department of SW France, in Aquitaine region. Capital: Bordeaux. Pop.: 1 287 334 (1999). Area: 10 726 sq. km (4183 sq. miles). [2] an estuary in SW France, formed by the confluence of the Rivers Garonne and Dordogne. Length: 72 km (45 miles).

Girondist (dʒɪˈrɒndɪst) NOUN [1] a member of a party of moderate republicans during the French Revolution, many of whom came from Gironde: overthrown (1793) by their rivals the Jacobins. See also **Jacobin** (sense 1). ◆ ADJECTIVE [2] of or relating to the Girondists or their principles.
▸**Giˈrondism** NOUN

gironny *or* **gyronny** (dʒaɪˈrɒnɪ) ADJECTIVE (*usually postpositive*) *Heraldry* divided into segments from the fesse point.

girosol (ˈdʒɪrəˌsɒl, -ˌsəʊl) NOUN a variant spelling of **girasol.**

girr (gɪr) NOUN *Scot* a variant of **gird**[3].

girt[1] (gɜːt) VERB [1] a past tense and past participle of **gird**[1]. ◆ ADJECTIVE [2] *Nautical* moored securely to prevent swinging.

girt[2] (gɜːt) VERB [1] (*tr*) to bind or encircle; gird. [2] to measure the girth of (something).

girth (gɜːθ) NOUN [1] the distance around something; circumference. [2] size or bulk: *a man of great girth.* [3] a band around a horse's belly to keep the saddle in position. ◆ VERB [4] (usually foll by *up*) to fasten a girth on (a horse). [5] (*tr*) to encircle or surround.
▷HISTORY C14: from Old Norse *gjörth* belt; related to Gothic *gairda* GIRDLE[1]; see GIRD[1]

GIS (in Canada) ABBREVIATION FOR guaranteed income supplement.

gisarme (gɪˈzɑːm) NOUN a long-shafted battle-axe with a sharp point on the back of the axe head.
▷HISTORY C13: from Old French *guisarme,* probably from Old High German *getīsarn* weeding tool, from *getan* to weed + *īsarn* IRON

Gisborne (ˈgɪzbən) NOUN a port in N New Zealand, on E North Island on Poverty Bay. Pop.: 31 700 (1994).

gist (dʒɪst) NOUN [1] the point or substance of an argument, speech, etc. [2] *Law* the essential point of an action.
▷HISTORY C18: from Anglo-French, as in *cest action gist en* this action consists in, literally: lies in, from Old French *gésir* to lie, from Latin *jacēre,* from *jacere* to throw

git (gɪt) NOUN *Brit slang* [1] a contemptible person, often a fool. [2] a bastard.
▷HISTORY C20: from GET (in the sense: *to beget,* hence a bastard, fool)

gîte (ʒiːt) NOUN a self-catering holiday cottage for let in France.
▷HISTORY C20: French

gittarone (ˌgɪtəˈrəʊnɪ) NOUN *Music* an acoustic bass guitar.

gittern (ˈgɪtɜːn) NOUN *Music* an obsolete medieval stringed instrument resembling the guitar. Compare **cittern.**
▷HISTORY C14: from Old French *guiterne,* ultimately from Old Spanish *guitarra* GUITAR; see CITTERN

giusto (ˈdʒuːstəʊ) ADVERB *Music* (of a tempo marking) **a** to be observed strictly. **b** to be observed appropriately: *allegro giusto.*
▷HISTORY Italian: just, proper

give (gɪv) VERB **gives, giving, gave** (geɪv), **given** (ˈgɪvᵊn). (*mainly tr*) [1] (*also intr*) to present or deliver voluntarily (something that is one's own) to the permanent possession of another or others. [2] (often foll by *for*) to transfer (something that is one's own, esp money) to the possession of another as part of an exchange: *to give fifty pounds for a painting.* [3] to place in the temporary possession of another: *I gave him my watch while I went swimming.* [4] (when *intr,* foll by *of*) to grant, provide, or bestow: *give me some advice.* [5] to administer: *to give a reprimand.* [6] to award or attribute: *to give blame, praise,* etc. [7] to be a source of: *he gives no trouble.* [8] to impart or communicate: *to give news; give a person a cold.* [9] to utter or emit: *to give a shout.* [10] to perform, make, or do: *the car gave a jolt and stopped.* [11] to sacrifice or devote: *he gave his life for his country.* [12] to surrender: *to give place to others.* [13] to concede or yield: *I will give you this game.* [14] (*intr*) *Informal* to happen: *what gives?* [15] (often foll by *to*) to cause; lead: *she gave me to believe that she would come.* [16] (foll by *for*) to value (something) at: *I don't give anything for his promises.* [17] to perform or present as an entertainment: *to give a play.* [18] to propose as a toast: *I give you the Queen.* [19] (*intr*) to yield or break under force or pressure: *this surface will give if you sit on it; his courage will never give.* [20]

give as good as one gets. to respond to verbal or bodily blows to at least an equal extent as those received. [21] **give battle.** to commence fighting. [22] **give birth.** (often foll by *to*) **a** to bear (offspring). **b** to produce, originate, or create (an idea, plan, etc.). [23] **give (a person) five** *or* **some skin.** *Slang* to greet or congratulate (someone) by slapping raised hands. [24] **give ground.** to draw back or retreat. [25] **give it up for (someone).** *Slang* to applaud (someone). [26] **give (someone) one.** *Brit slang* to have sex with someone. [27] **give rise to.** to be the cause of. [28] **give me.** *Informal* I prefer: *give me hot weather any day!* [29] **give or take.** plus or minus: *three thousand people came, give or take a few hundred.* [30] **give way.** See **way** (sense 24). [31] **give (a person) what for.** *Informal* to punish or reprimand (a person) severely. ◆ NOUN [32] a tendency to yield under pressure; resilience: *there's bound to be some give in a long plank; there is no give in his moral views.* ◆ See also **give away, give in, give off, give onto, give out, give over, give up.**
▷HISTORY Old English *giefan;* related to Old Norse *gefa,* Gothic *giban,* Old High German *geban,* Swedish *giva*
▸ **'givable** *or* **'giveable** ADJECTIVE ▸ **'giver** NOUN

give-and-take NOUN [1] mutual concessions, shared benefits, and cooperation. [2] a smoothly flowing exchange of ideas and talk. ◆ VERB **give and take.** (*intr*) [3] to make mutual concessions.

give away VERB (*tr, adverb*) [1] to donate or bestow as a gift, prize, etc. [2] to sell very cheaply. [3] to reveal or betray (esp in the phrases **give the game** *or* **show away**). [4] to fail to use (an opportunity) through folly or neglect. [5] to present (a bride) formally to her husband in a marriage ceremony. [6] *Austral and NZ informal* to give up or abandon (something). ◆ NOUN **giveaway.** [7] a betrayal or disclosure of information, esp when unintentional. [8] *Chiefly US and Canadian* something given, esp with articles on sale, at little or no charge to increase sales, attract publicity, etc. [9] *Journalism* another name for **freesheet.** [10] *Chiefly US and Canadian* a radio or television programme characterized by the award of money and prizes. [11] (*modifier*) **a** very cheap (esp in the phrase **giveaway prices**). **b** free of charge: *a giveaway property magazine.*

give in VERB (*adverb*) [1] (*intr*) to yield; admit defeat. [2] (*tr*) to submit or deliver (a document).

given ('gɪvᵊn) VERB [1] the past participle of **give.** ◆ ADJECTIVE [2] (*postpositive;* foll by *to*) tending (to); inclined or addicted (to). [3] specific or previously stated. [4] assumed as a premise. [5] *Maths* known or determined independently: *a given volume.* [6] (on official documents) issued or executed, as on a stated date. ◆ NOUN [7] an assumed fact. [8] *Philosophy* the supposed raw data of experience. See also **sense datum.**

given name NOUN another term for **first name.**

give off VERB (*tr, adverb*) to emit or discharge: *the mothballs gave off an acrid odour.*

give onto VERB (*intr; preposition*) to afford a view or prospect of: *their new house gives onto the sea.*

give out VERB (*adverb*) [1] (*tr*) to emit or discharge. [2] (*tr*) to publish or make known: *the chairman gave out that he would resign.* [3] (*tr*) to hand out or distribute: *they gave out free chewing gum on the street.* [4] (*intr*) to become exhausted; fail: *the supply of candles gave out.* [5] (*intr;* foll by *to*) *Irish informal* to reprimand (someone) at length. [6] (*tr*) *Cricket* (of an umpire) to declare (a batsman) dismissed.

give over VERB (*adverb*) [1] (*tr*) to transfer, esp to the care or custody of another. [2] (*tr*) to assign or resign to a specific purpose or function: *the day was given over to pleasure.* [3] *Informal* to cease (an activity): *give over fighting, will you!*

give up VERB (*adverb*) [1] to abandon hope (for). [2] (*tr*) to renounce (an activity, belief, etc.): *I have given up smoking.* [3] (*tr*) to relinquish or resign from: *he gave up the presidency.* [4] (*tr; usually reflexive*) to surrender: *the escaped convict gave himself up.* [5] (*tr*) to reveal or disclose (information). [6] (*intr*) to admit one's defeat or inability to do something. [7] (*tr; often passive or reflexive*) to devote completely (to): *she gave herself up to caring for the sick.*

Gîza ('gi:zə) NOUN See **El Gîza.**

gizmo *or* **gismo** ('gɪzməʊ) NOUN, *plural* **-mos.** *Slang* a device; gadget.
▷HISTORY C20: of unknown origin

gizzard ('gɪzəd) NOUN [1] the thick-walled part of a bird's stomach, in which hard food is broken up by muscular action and contact with grit and small stones. [2] a similar structure in many invertebrates. [3] *Informal* the stomach and entrails generally.
▷HISTORY C14: from Old North French *guisier* fowl's liver, alteration of Latin *gigēria* entrails of poultry when cooked, of uncertain origin

Gk ABBREVIATION FOR Greek.

gl THE INTERNET DOMAIN NAME FOR Greenland.

GLA ABBREVIATION FOR Greater London Assembly, established in 2000.

glabella (glə'bɛlə) NOUN, *plural* **-lae** (-li:). *Anatomy* a smooth elevation of the frontal bone just above the bridge of the nose: a reference point in physical anthropology or craniometry.
▷HISTORY C19: New Latin, from Latin *glabellus* smooth, from *glaber bald, smooth*
▸ **gla'bellar** ADJECTIVE

glabrescent (gleɪ'brɛsənt) ADJECTIVE *Botany* [1] becoming hairless at maturity: *glabrescent stems.* [2] nearly hairless.
▷HISTORY C19: from Latin *glabrescere* to become smooth

glabrous ('gleɪbrəs) *or* **glabrate** ('gleɪbreɪt, -brɪt) ADJECTIVE *Biology* without hair or a similar growth; smooth: *a glabrous stem.*
▷HISTORY C17 *glabrous,* from Latin *glaber*
▸ **'glabrousness** NOUN

glacé ('glæseɪ) ADJECTIVE [1] crystallized or candied: *glacé cherries.* [2] covered in icing. [3] (of leather, silk, etc.) having a glossy finish. [4] *Chiefly US* frozen or iced. ◆ VERB **-cés, -céing, -céed.** [5] (*tr*) to ice or candy (cakes, fruits, etc.).
▷HISTORY C19: from French *glacé,* literally: iced, from *glacer* to freeze, from *glace* ice, from Latin *glaciēs*

glacial ('gleɪsɪəl, -ʃəl) ADJECTIVE [1] characterized by the presence of masses of ice. [2] relating to, caused by, or deposited by a glacier. [3] extremely cold; icy. [4] cold or hostile in manner: *a glacial look.* [5] (of a chemical compound) of or tending to form crystals that resemble ice: *glacial acetic acid.* [6] very slow in progress: *a glacial pace.*
▸ **'glacially** ADVERB

glacial acetic acid NOUN pure acetic acid (more than 99.8 per cent).

glacial period NOUN [1] any period of time during which a large part of the earth's surface was covered with ice, due to the advance of glaciers, as in the late Carboniferous period, and during most of the Pleistocene; glaciation. [2] (*often capitals*) the Pleistocene epoch. ◆ Also called: **glacial epoch, ice age.**

glaciate ('gleɪsɪˌeɪt) VERB [1] to cover or become covered with glaciers or masses of ice. [2] (*tr*) to subject to the effects of glaciers, such as denudation and erosion.
▸ **ˌglaci'ation** NOUN

glacier ('glæsɪə, 'gleɪs-) NOUN a slowly moving mass of ice originating from an accumulation of snow. It can either spread out from a central mass (**continental glacier**) or descend from a high valley (**alpine glacier**).
▷HISTORY C18: from French (Savoy dialect), from Old French *glace* ice, from Late Latin *glacia,* from Latin *glaciēs* ice

glacier cream NOUN *Mountaineering* a barrier cream, esp against ultraviolet radiation, used when climbing above the snow line.

glacier milk NOUN water flowing in a stream from the snout of a glacier and containing particles of rock.

glacier table NOUN a rock sitting on a pillar of ice on top of a glacier, as a result of the ice immediately beneath the rock being protected from the heat of the sun and not melting.

glaciology (ˌglæsɪ'ɒlədʒɪ, ˌgleɪ-) NOUN the study of the distribution, character, and effects of glaciers.
▸ **glaciological** (ˌglæsɪə'lɒdʒɪkᵊl, ˌgleɪ-) *or* **ˌglacio'logic** ADJECTIVE ▸ **ˌglaci'ologist** *or* **'glacialist** NOUN

glacis ('glæsɪs, 'glæsɪ, 'gleɪ-) NOUN, *plural* **-ises** *or* **-is** (-i:z, -ɪz). [1] a slight incline; slope. [2] an open slope in front of a fortified place. [3] short for **glacis plate.**
▷HISTORY C17: from French, from Old French *glacier* to freeze, slip, from Latin *glaciāre,* from *glaciēs* ice

glacis plate NOUN [1] the frontal plate armour on a tank. [2] a section of armour plate shielding an opening on a naval vessel.

glad¹ (glæd) ADJECTIVE **gladder, gladdest.** [1] happy and pleased; contented. [2] causing happiness or contentment. [3] (*postpositive;* foll by *to*) very willing: *he was glad to help.* [4] (*postpositive;* foll by *of*) happy or pleased to have: *glad of her help.* ◆ VERB **glads, gladding, gladded.** [5] an archaic word for **gladden.**
▷HISTORY Old English *glæd;* related to Old Norse *glathr,* Old High German *glat* smooth, shining, Latin *glaber* smooth, Lithuanian *glodùs* fitting closely
▸ **'gladly** ADVERB ▸ **'gladness** NOUN

glad² (glæd) NOUN *Informal* short for **gladiolus.** Also called (Austral): **gladdie** ('glædɪ).

Gladbeck (*German* 'glatbɛk) NOUN a city in NW Germany, in North Rhine-Westphalia. Pop.: 79 190 (latest est.).

gladden ('glædᵊn) VERB to make or become glad and joyful.
▸ **'gladdener** NOUN

gladdon ('glædᵊn) NOUN another name for the **stinking iris.**
▷HISTORY Old English, of uncertain origin

glade (gleɪd) NOUN an open place in a forest; clearing.
▷HISTORY C16: of uncertain origin; perhaps related to GLAD¹ (in obsolete sense: bright); see GLEAM
▸ **'gladeˌlike** ADJECTIVE

glad eye NOUN *Informal* an inviting or seductive glance (esp in the phrase **give (someone) the glad eye**).

glad hand NOUN [1] **a** a welcoming hand. **b** a welcome. ◆ VERB **glad-hand.** [2] (*tr*) to welcome by or as if by offering a hand.

gladiate ('glædɪɪt, -ˌeɪt, 'gleɪ-) ADJECTIVE *Botany* shaped like a sword: *gladiate leaves.*
▷HISTORY C18: from Latin *gladius* sword

gladiator ('glædɪˌeɪtə) NOUN [1] (in ancient Rome and Etruria) a man trained to fight in arenas to provide entertainment. [2] a person who supports and fights publicly for a cause.
▷HISTORY C16: from Latin: swordsman, from *gladius* sword

gladiatorial (ˌglædɪə'tɔ:rɪəl) ADJECTIVE of, characteristic of, or relating to gladiators, combat, etc.

gladiolus (ˌglædɪ'əʊləs) NOUN, *plural* **-lus, -li** (-laɪ) *or* **-luses.** [1] Also called: **sword lily, gladiola.** any iridaceous plant of the widely cultivated genus *Gladiolus,* having sword-shaped leaves and spikes of funnel-shaped brightly coloured flowers. [2] *Anatomy* the large central part of the breastbone.
▷HISTORY C16: from Latin: a small sword, sword lily, from *gladius* a sword

glad rags PLURAL NOUN *Informal* best clothes or clothes used on special occasions.

gladsome ('glædsəm) ADJECTIVE an archaic word for **glad¹.**
▸ **'gladsomely** ADVERB ▸ **'gladsomeness** NOUN

Gladstone ('glædstən) NOUN a light four-wheeled horse-drawn vehicle.
▷HISTORY C19: named after William Ewart *Gladstone* (1809–98), British Liberal statesman

Gladstone bag NOUN a piece of hand luggage consisting of two equal-sized hinged compartments.
▷HISTORY C19: named after William Ewart *Gladstone* (1809–98), British Liberal statesman

Glagolitic (ˌglægə'lɪtɪk) ADJECTIVE of, relating to, or denoting a Slavic alphabet whose invention is attributed to Saint Cyril, preserved only in certain Roman Catholic liturgical books found in Dalmatia.
▷HISTORY C19: from New Latin *glagoliticus,* from Serbo-Croat *glagolica* the Glagolitic alphabet; related to Old Church Slavonic *glagolŭ* word

glaikit *or* **glaiket** ('gleɪkɪt) ADJECTIVE *Scot* foolish; silly; thoughtless.
▷HISTORY C15: of obscure origin
▸ **'glaikitness** *or* **'glaiketness** NOUN

glair (glɛə) NOUN [1] white of egg, esp when used as a size, glaze, or adhesive, usually in bookbinding. [2] any substance resembling this. ◆ VERB [3] (*tr*) to apply glair to (something).
▷HISTORY C14: from Old French *glaire,* from Vulgar Latin *clāria* (unattested) CLEAR, from Latin *clārus*
▸ **'glairy** *or* **'glaireous** ADJECTIVE ▸ **'glairiness** NOUN

glaive (gleɪv) NOUN an archaic word for **sword.**

▷HISTORY C13: from Old French: javelin, from Latin *gladius* sword
▸**glaived** ADJECTIVE

glam (glæm) ADJECTIVE *Slang* short for **glamorous.**

Glamis Castle (glɑːmz) NOUN a castle near Glamis in Angus, Scotland: ancestral seat of the Lyons family, forebears of Elizabeth, the Queen Mother; famous for its legend of a secret chamber.

Glamorgan (ɡləˈmɔːɡən) *or* **Glamorganshire** (ɡləˈmɔːɡənˌʃɪə, -ʃə) NOUN a former county of SE Wales: divided into West Glamorgan, Mid Glamorgan, and South Glamorgan in 1974; since 1996 administered by the county of Swansea and the county boroughs of Neath Port Talbot, Bridgend, Rhondda Cynon Taff, Vale of Glamorgan, Merthyr Tydfil, and part of Caerphilly.

glamorize, glamorise, *or sometimes US* **glamourize** (ˈɡlæməˌraɪz) VERB (*tr*) to cause to be or seem glamorous; romanticize or beautify.
▸**ˌglamoriˈzation** *or* **ˌglamoriˈsation** NOUN ▸**ˈglamorˌizer** *or* **ˈglamorˌiser** NOUN

glamorous *or* **glamourous** (ˈɡlæmərəs) ADJECTIVE 1 possessing glamour; alluring and fascinating: *a glamorous career.* 2 beautiful and smart, esp in a showy way: *a glamorous woman.*
▸**ˈglamorously** *or* **ˈglamourously** ADVERB ▸**ˈglamorousness** *or* **ˈglamourousness** NOUN

glamour *or sometimes US* **glamor** (ˈɡlæmə) NOUN 1 charm and allure; fascination. 2 **a** fascinating or voluptuous beauty, often dependent on artifice. **b** (*as modifier*): *a glamour girl.* 3 *Archaic* a magic spell; charm.
▷HISTORY C18: Scottish variant of GRAMMAR (hence a magic spell, because occult practices were popularly associated with learning)

glam rock NOUN a style of rock music of the early 1970s, characterized by the glittery flamboyance and androgynous image of its performers.

glance[1] (ɡlɑːns) VERB 1 (*intr*) to look hastily or briefly. 2 (*intr; foll by over, through,* etc.) to look over briefly: *to glance through a report.* 3 (*intr*) to reflect, glint, or gleam: *the sun glanced on the water.* 4 (*intr; usually foll by off*) to depart (from an object struck) at an oblique angle: *the arrow glanced off the tree.* 5 (*tr*) to strike at an oblique angle: *the arrow glanced the tree.* ◆ NOUN 6 a hasty or brief look; peep. 7 **at a glance.** from one's first look; immediately. 8 a flash or glint of light; gleam. 9 the act or an instance of an object glancing or glancing off another. 10 a brief allusion or reference. 11 *Cricket* a stroke in which the ball is deflected off the bat to the leg side; glide.
▷HISTORY C15: modification of *glacen* to strike obliquely, from Old French *glacier* to slide (see GLACIS); compare Middle English *glenten* to make a rapid sideways movement, GLINT
▸**ˈglancingly** ADVERB

> **Language note** *Glance* is sometimes wrongly used where *glimpse* is meant: *he caught a glimpse* (not *glance*) *of her making her way through the crowd.*

glance[2] (ɡlɑːns) NOUN any mineral having a metallic lustre, esp a simple sulphide: *copper glance.*
▷HISTORY C19: from German *Glanz* brightness, lustre

gland[1] (ɡlænd) NOUN 1 a cell or organ in man and other animals that synthesizes chemical substances and secretes them for the body to use or eliminate, either through a duct (see **exocrine gland**) or directly into the bloodstream (see **endocrine gland**). 2 a structure, such as a lymph node, that resembles a gland in form. 3 a cell or organ in plants that synthesizes and secretes a particular substance. ◆ Related adjective **adenoid.**
▷HISTORY C17: from Latin *glāns* acorn
▸**ˈglandˌlike** ADJECTIVE

gland[2] (ɡlænd) NOUN a device that prevents leakage of fluid along a rotating shaft or reciprocating rod passing through a boundary between areas of high and low pressure. It often consists of a flanged metal sleeve bedding into a stuffing box.
▷HISTORY C19: of unknown origin

glanders (ˈɡlændəz) NOUN (*functioning as singular*) a highly infectious bacterial disease of horses, sometimes transmitted to man, caused by *Actinobacillus mallei* and characterized by inflammation and ulceration of the mucous membranes of the air passages, skin, and lymph glands.
▷HISTORY C16: from Old French *glandres* enlarged glands, from Latin *glandulae,* literally: little acorns, from *glāns* acorn; see GLAND[1]
▸**ˈglandered** ADJECTIVE ▸**ˈglanderous** ADJECTIVE

glandular (ˈɡlændjʊlə) *or* **glandulous** (ˈɡlændjʊləs) ADJECTIVE of, relating to, containing, functioning as, or affecting a gland: *glandular tissue.*
▷HISTORY C18: from Latin *glandula,* literally: a little acorn; see GLANDERS
▸**ˈglandularly** *or* **ˈglandulously** ADVERB

glandular fever NOUN another name for **infectious mononucleosis.**

glandule (ˈɡlændjuːl) NOUN a small gland.

glans (ɡlænz) NOUN, *plural* **glandes** (ˈɡlændiːz). *Anatomy* any small rounded body or glandlike mass, such as the head of the penis (**glans penis**).
▷HISTORY C17: from Latin: acorn; see GLAND[1]

glare[1] (ɡlɛə) VERB 1 (*intr*) to stare angrily; glower. 2 (*tr*) to express by glowering. 3 (*intr*) (of light, colour, etc.) to be very bright and intense. 4 (*intr*) to be dazzlingly ornamented or garish. ◆ NOUN 5 an angry stare. 6 a dazzling light or brilliance. 7 garish ornamentation or appearance; gaudiness.
▷HISTORY C13: probably from Middle Low German, Middle Dutch *glaren* to gleam; probably related to Old English *glæren* glassy; see GLASS
▸**ˈglareless** ADJECTIVE ▸**ˈglary** ADJECTIVE

glare[2] (ɡlɛə) ADJECTIVE *Chiefly US and Canadian* smooth and glassy: *glare ice.*
▷HISTORY C16: special use of GLARE[1]

glaring (ˈɡlɛərɪŋ) ADJECTIVE 1 conspicuous: *a glaring omission.* 2 dazzling or garish.
▸**ˈglaringly** ADVERB ▸**ˈglaringness** NOUN

Glarus (*German* ˈɡlaːrʊs) NOUN 1 an Alpine canton of E central Switzerland. Capital: Glarus. Pop.: 38 700 (2000 est.). Area 684 sq. km (264 sq. miles). 2 a town in E central Switzerland, the capital of Glarus canton. Pop.: 5541 (1990). ◆ French name: **Glaris** (ɡlari).

Glasgow (ˈɡlɑːzɡəʊ, ˈɡlæz-) NOUN 1 a city in W central Scotland, in City of Glasgow council area on the River Clyde: the largest city in Scotland; centre of a major industrial region, formerly an important port; universities (1451, 1964, 1992). Pop.: 662 954 (1991). Related adjective: **Glaswegian.** 2 **City of.** a council area in W central Scotland. Pop.: 577 869 (2001). Area: 175 sq. km (68 sq. miles).

glasnost (ˈɡlæsˌnɒst) NOUN the policy of public frankness and accountability developed in the former Soviet Union under the leadership of Mikhail Gorbachov.
▷HISTORY C20: Russian, literally: openness

glass (ɡlɑːs) NOUN 1 **a** a hard brittle transparent or translucent noncrystalline solid, consisting of metal silicates or similar compounds. It is made from a fused mixture of oxides, such as lime, silicon dioxide, etc., and is used for making windows, mirrors, bottles, etc. **b** (*as modifier*): *a glass bottle.* Related adjectives: **vitreous, vitric.** 2 any compound that has solidified from a molten state into a noncrystalline form. 3 something made of glass, esp a drinking vessel, a barometer, or a mirror. 4 Also called: **glassful.** the amount contained in a drinking glass. 5 glassware collectively. 6 See **volcanic glass.** 7 See **fibreglass.** ◆ VERB (*tr*) 8 to cover with, enclose in, or fit with glass. 9 *Informal* to hit (someone) in the face with a glass or a bottle.
▷HISTORY Old English *glæs;* related to Old Norse *gler,* Old High German *glas,* Middle High German *glast* brightness; see GLARE[1]
▸**ˈglassless** ADJECTIVE ▸**ˈglassˌlike** ADJECTIVE

glass-blowing NOUN the process of shaping a mass of molten or softened glass into a vessel, shape, etc., by blowing air into it through a tube.
▸**ˈglass-ˌblower** NOUN

glass can NOUN *Austral slang* a short squat beer bottle.

glass ceiling NOUN a situation in which progress, esp promotion, appears to be possible but restrictions or discrimination create a barrier that prevents it.

glasses (ˈɡlɑːsɪz) PLURAL NOUN a pair of lenses for correcting faulty vision, in a frame that rests on the bridge of the nose and hooks behind the ears. Also called: **spectacles, eyeglasses.**

glass eye NOUN an artificial eye made of glass.

glass fibre NOUN another name for **fibreglass.**

glass harmonica NOUN a musical instrument of the 18th century consisting of a set of glass bowls of graduated pitches, played by rubbing the fingers over the moistened rims or by a keyboard mechanism. Sometimes shortened to: **harmonica.** Also called: **musical glasses.**

glasshouse (ˈɡlɑːsˌhaʊs) NOUN 1 *Brit* a glass building, esp a greenhouse, used for growing plants in protected or controlled conditions. 2 *Obsolete informal, chiefly Brit* a military detention centre. 3 *US* another word for **glassworks.**

glassine (ɡlæˈsiːn) NOUN a glazed translucent paper used for book jackets.

glass jaw NOUN *Boxing, informal* a jaw that is excessively fragile or susceptible to punches.

glass-maker NOUN a person who makes glass or glass objects.
▸**ˈglass-ˌmaking** NOUN

glassman (ˈɡlɑːsmən) NOUN, *plural* **-men.** 1 a man whose work is making or selling glassware. 2 a less common word for **glazier.**

glasspaper (ˈɡlɑːsˌpeɪpə) NOUN 1 strong paper coated with powdered glass or other abrasive material for smoothing and polishing. ◆ VERB 2 to smooth or polish with glasspaper.

glass snake NOUN any snakelike lizard of the genus *Ophisaurus,* of Europe, Asia, and North America, with vestigial hind limbs and a tail that breaks off easily: family *Anguidae.*

glass string NOUN (in Malaysia) the string of a kite used in kite fighting that has an abrasive coating of glue and crushed glass.

glassware (ˈɡlɑːsˌwɛə) NOUN articles made of glass.

glass wool NOUN fine spun glass massed into a wool-like bulk, used in insulation, filtering, etc.

glasswork (ˈɡlɑːsˌwɜːk) NOUN 1 the production of glassware. 2 the fitting of glass. 3 articles of glass.
▸**ˈglass-ˌworker** NOUN

glassworks (ˈɡlɑːsˌwɜːks) NOUN (*functioning as singular*) a factory for the moulding of glass.

glasswort (ˈɡlɑːsˌwɜːt) NOUN 1 Also called: **marsh samphire.** any plant of the chenopodiaceous genus *Salicornia,* of salt marshes, having fleshy stems and scalelike leaves: formerly used as a source of soda for glass-making. 2 another name for **saltwort** (sense 1).

glassy (ˈɡlɑːsɪ) ADJECTIVE **glassier, glassiest.** 1 resembling glass, esp in smoothness, slipperiness, or transparency. 2 void of expression, life, or warmth: *a glassy stare.*
▸**ˈglassily** ADVERB ▸**ˈglassiness** NOUN

Glastonbury (ˈɡlæstənbərɪ, -brɪ) NOUN a town in SW England, in Somerset: remains of prehistoric lake villages; the reputed burial place of King Arthur; site of a ruined Benedictine abbey, probably the oldest in England. Pop.: 7747 (1991).

Glaswegian (ɡlæzˈwiːdʒən) ADJECTIVE 1 of or relating to Glasgow or its inhabitants. ◆ NOUN 2 a native or inhabitant of Glasgow.
▷HISTORY C19: influenced by *Norway, Norwegian*

Glauber's salt (ˈɡlaʊbəz) *or* **Glauber salt** (ˈɡlaʊbə) NOUN the crystalline decahydrate of sodium sulphate.
▷HISTORY C18: named after J. R. *Glauber* (1604–68), German chemist

Glauce (ˈɡlɔːsɪ) NOUN *Greek myth* 1 the second bride of Jason, murdered on her wedding day by Medea, whom Jason had deserted. 2 a sea nymph, one of the Nereids.

glaucoma (ɡlɔːˈkəʊmə) NOUN a disease of the eye in which pressure within the eyeball damages the optic disc, impairing vision, sometimes progressing to blindness.
▷HISTORY C17: from Latin, from Greek *glaukōma,* from *glaukos;* see GLAUCOUS
▸**glauˈcomatous** ADJECTIVE

glauconite (ˈɡlɔːkəˌnaɪt) NOUN a green mineral consisting of the hydrated silicate of iron, potassium, aluminium, and magnesium: found in

greensand and other similar rocks. Formula: $(K,Na,Ca)_{0.5-1}(Fe,Al,Mg)_2(Si,Al)_4O_{10}(OH)_2.nH_2O$.
▷**HISTORY** C19: from Greek *glaukon,* neuter of *glaukos* bluish-green + -ITE[1]; see GLAUCOUS
▸**glauconitic** (ˌglɔːkəˈnɪtɪk) ADJECTIVE

glaucous (ˈglɔːkəs) ADJECTIVE 1 *Botany* covered with a bluish waxy or powdery bloom. 2 bluish-green.
▷**HISTORY** C17: from Latin *glaucus* silvery, bluish-green, from Greek *glaukos*
▸ˈ**glaucously** ADVERB

glaucous gull NOUN a gull, *Larus hyperboreus,* of northern and arctic regions, with a white head and tail and pale grey back and wings.

glaur (glɔːr) NOUN *Scot* mud or mire.
▷**HISTORY** C16: of unknown origin
▸ˈ**glaury** ADJECTIVE

glaze (gleɪz) VERB 1 (*tr*) to fit or cover with glass. 2 (*tr*) *Ceramics* to cover with a vitreous solution, rendering impervious to liquid and smooth to the touch. 3 (*tr*) to cover (a painting) with a layer of semitransparent colour to modify the tones. 4 (*tr*) to cover (foods) with a shiny coating by applying beaten egg, sugar, etc. 5 (*tr*) to make glossy or shiny. 6 (when *intr,* often foll by *over*) to become or cause to become glassy: *his eyes were glazing over.* ◆ NOUN 7 *Ceramics* **a** a vitreous or glossy coating. **b** the substance used to produce such a coating. 8 a semitransparent coating applied to a painting to modify the tones. 9 a smooth lustrous finish on a fabric produced by applying various chemicals. 10 something used to give a glossy surface to foods: *a syrup glaze.*
▷**HISTORY** C14 *glasen,* from *glas* GLASS
▸**glazed** ADJECTIVE ▸ˈ**glazer** NOUN ▸ˈ**glazy** ADJECTIVE

glaze ice *or* **glazed frost** NOUN *Brit* a thin clear layer of ice caused by the freezing of rain or water droplets in the air on impact with a cool surface or by refreezing after a thaw. Also called: **silver frost.** US term: **glaze.**

glazier (ˈgleɪzɪə) NOUN a person who glazes windows, etc.
▸ˈ**glaziery** NOUN

glazing (ˈgleɪzɪŋ) NOUN 1 the surface of a glazed object. 2 glass fitted, or to be fitted, in a door, frame, etc.

glazing-bar NOUN a supporting or strengthening bar for a glass window, door, etc. Usual US word: **muntin.**

GLC ABBREVIATION FOR Greater London Council, abolished 1986.

gld ABBREVIATION FOR guilder.

gleam (gliːm) NOUN 1 a small beam or glow of light, esp reflected light. 2 a brief or dim indication: *a gleam of hope.* ◆ VERB (*intr*) 3 to send forth or reflect a beam of light. 4 to appear, esp briefly: *intelligence gleamed in his eyes.*
▷**HISTORY** Old English *glǣm;* related to Old Norse *glja* to flicker, Old High German *gleimo* glow-worm, *glīmo* brightness, Old Irish *glē* bright
▸ˈ**gleaming** ADJECTIVE ▸ˈ**gleamy** ADJECTIVE

glean (gliːn) VERB 1 to gather (something) slowly and carefully in small pieces: *to glean information from the newspapers.* 2 to gather (the useful remnants of a crop) from the field after harvesting.
▷**HISTORY** C14: from Old French *glener,* from Late Latin *glennāre,* probably of Celtic origin
▸ˈ**gleanable** ADJECTIVE ▸ˈ**gleaner** NOUN

gleanings (ˈgliːnɪŋz) PLURAL NOUN the useful remnants of a crop that can be gathered from the field after harvesting.

glebe (gliːb) NOUN 1 *Brit* land granted to a clergyman as part of his benefice. 2 *Poetic* land, esp when regarded as the source of growing things.
▷**HISTORY** C14: from Latin *glaeba*

glede (gliːd) *or* **gled** (glɛd) NOUN a former Brit name for the **red kite.** See **kite** (sense 4).
▷**HISTORY** Old English *glida;* related to Old Norse *gletha,* Middle Low German *glede*

glee (gliː) NOUN 1 great merriment or delight, often caused by someone else's misfortune. 2 a type of song originating in 18th-century England, sung by three or more unaccompanied voices. Compare **madrigal** (sense 1).
▷**HISTORY** Old English *glēo;* related to Old Norse *glȳ*

glee club NOUN *Now chiefly US and Canadian* a club or society organized for the singing of choral music.

gleed (gliːd) NOUN *Archaic or dialect* a burning ember or hot coal.
▷**HISTORY** Old English glēd; related to German *Glut,* Dutch *gloed,* Swedish glöd

gleeful (ˈgliːfʊl) ADJECTIVE full of glee; merry.
▸ˈ**gleefully** ADVERB ▸ˈ**gleefulness** NOUN

gleeman (ˈgliːmən) NOUN, *plural* **-men.** *Obsolete* a minstrel.

gleenie (ˈgliːnɪ) NOUN *Southwest English dialect* a guinea fowl.

gleet (gliːt) NOUN 1 inflammation of the urethra with a slight discharge of thin pus and mucus: a stage of chronic gonorrhoea. 2 the pus and mucus discharged.
▷**HISTORY** C14: from Old French *glette* slime, from Latin *glittus* sticky
▸ˈ**gleety** ADJECTIVE

Gleichschaltung (ˈglaɪkˌʃæltʊŋ) NOUN the enforcement of standardization and the elimination of all opposition within the political, economic, and cultural institutions of a state.
▷**HISTORY** C20: German

Gleiwitz (ˈglaɪvɪts) NOUN the German name for **Gliwice.**

glen (glɛn) NOUN a narrow and deep mountain valley, esp in Scotland or Ireland.
▷**HISTORY** C15: from Scottish Gaelic *gleann,* from Old Irish *glend*
▸ˈ**glen,like** ADJECTIVE

Glen Albyn (ˈælbɪn, ˈɔːl-) NOUN another name for the **Great Glen.**

Glencoe (glɛnˈkəʊ) NOUN a glen in W Scotland, in S Highland: site of a massacre of Macdonalds by Campbells and English troops (1692).

glengarry (glɛnˈgærɪ) NOUN, *plural* **-ries.** a brimless Scottish woollen cap with a crease down the crown, often with ribbons dangling at the back. Also called: **glengarry bonnet.**
▷**HISTORY** C19: after *Glengarry,* Scotland

Glen More (mɔː) NOUN another name for the **Great Glen.**

Glen of Imaal terrier (ɪˈmɑːl) NOUN a strongly-built medium-sized variety of terrier with a medium-length coat and short forelegs.

glenoid (ˈgliːnɔɪd) ADJECTIVE *Anatomy* 1 resembling or having a shallow cavity. 2 denoting the cavity in the shoulder blade into which the head of the upper arm bone fits.
▷**HISTORY** C18: from Greek *glēnoeidēs,* from *glēnē* socket of a joint

Glenrothes (glɛnˈrɒθɪs) NOUN a new town in E central Scotland, the administrative centre of Fife: founded in 1948. Pop.: 38 650 (1991).

gley *or* **glei** (gleɪ) NOUN a bluish-grey compact sticky soil occurring in certain humid regions.
▷**HISTORY** C20: from Russian *glei* clay

glia (ˈgliːə) NOUN the delicate web of connective tissue that surrounds and supports nerve cells. Also called: **neuroglia.**
▸ˈ**glial** ADJECTIVE

gliadin (ˈglaɪədɪn) *or* **gliadine** (ˈglaɪəˌdiːn, -dɪn) NOUN a protein of cereals, esp wheat, with a high proline content: forms a sticky mass with water that binds flour into dough. Compare **glutelin.**
▷**HISTORY** C19: from Italian *gliadina,* from Greek *glia* glue

glib (glɪb) ADJECTIVE **glibber, glibbest.** fluent and easy, often in an insincere or deceptive way.
▷**HISTORY** C16: probably from Middle Low German *glibberich* slippery
▸ˈ**glibly** ADVERB ▸ˈ**glibness** NOUN

glib ice NOUN *Canadian* ice that is particularly smooth and slippery.

glide (glaɪd) VERB 1 to move or cause to move easily without jerks or hesitations: *to glide in a boat down the river.* 2 (*intr*) to pass slowly or without perceptible change: *to glide into sleep.* 3 to cause (an aircraft) to come into land without engine power, or (of an aircraft) to land in this way. 4 (*intr*) to fly a glider. 5 (*intr*) *Music* to execute a portamento from one note to another. 6 (*intr*) *Phonetics* to produce a glide. ◆ NOUN 7 a smooth easy movement. 8 **a** any of various dances featuring gliding steps. **b** a step in such a dance. 9 a manoeuvre in which an aircraft makes a gentle descent without engine power. See also **glide path.** 10 the act or process of gliding. 11 *Music* **a** a long portion of tubing slipped in and out of a trombone to increase its length for the production of lower harmonic series. See also **valve** (sense 5). **b** a portamento or slur. 12 *Phonetics* **a** a transitional sound as the speech organs pass from the articulatory position of one speech sound to that of the next, as the (w) sound in some pronunciations of the word *doing.* **b** another word for **semivowel.** 13 *Crystallog* another name for **slip**[1] (sense 33). 14 *Cricket* another word for **glance**[1] (sense 11).
▷**HISTORY** Old English *glīdan;* related to Old High German *glītan*
▸ˈ**glidingly** ADVERB

glide path *or* **glide slope** NOUN the approach path of an aircraft when landing, usually defined by a radar beam.

glider (ˈglaɪdə) NOUN 1 an aircraft capable of gliding and soaring in air currents without the use of an engine. See also **sailplane.** 2 a person or thing that glides. 3 another name for **flying phalanger.**

glide time NOUN the New Zealand term for **flexitime.**

gliding (ˈglaɪdɪŋ) NOUN the sport of flying in a glider.

glim (glɪm) NOUN *Slang* 1 a light or lamp. 2 an eye.
▷**HISTORY** C17: probably short for GLIMMER; compare GLIMPSE

glimmer (ˈglɪmə) VERB (*intr*) 1 (of a light, candle, etc.) to glow faintly or flickeringly. 2 to be indicated faintly: *hope glimmered in his face.* ◆ NOUN 3 a glow or twinkle of light. 4 a faint indication.
▷**HISTORY** C14: compare Middle High German *glimmern,* Swedish *glimra,* Danish *glimre*
▸ˈ**glimmeringly** ADVERB

glimpse (glɪmps) NOUN 1 a brief or incomplete view: *to catch a glimpse of the sea.* 2 a vague indication: *he had a glimpse of what the lecturer meant.* 3 *Archaic* a glimmer of light. ◆ VERB 4 (*tr*) to catch sight of briefly or momentarily. 5 (*intr;* usually foll by *at*) *Chiefly US* to look (at) briefly or cursorily; glance (at). 6 (*intr*) *Archaic* to shine faintly; glimmer.
▷**HISTORY** C14: of Germanic origin; compare Middle High German *glimsen* to glimmer
▸ˈ**glimpser** NOUN

> **Language note** *Glimpse* is sometimes wrongly used where *glance* is meant: *he gave a quick glance* (not *glimpse*) *at his watch.*

glint (glɪnt) VERB 1 to gleam or cause to gleam brightly. ◆ NOUN 2 a bright gleam or flash. 3 brightness or gloss. 4 a brief indication.
▷**HISTORY** C15: probably of Scandinavian origin; compare Swedish dialect *glänta, glinta* to gleam

glioma (glaɪˈəʊmə) NOUN, *plural* **-mata** (-mətə) *or* **-mas.** a tumour of the brain and spinal cord, composed of neuroglia cells and fibres.
▷**HISTORY** C19: from New Latin, from Greek *glia* glue + -OMA
▸**gliˈomatous** ADJECTIVE

glissade (glɪˈsɑːd, -ˈseɪd) NOUN 1 a gliding step in ballet, in which one foot slides forwards, sideways, or backwards. 2 a controlled slide down a snow slope. ◆ VERB 3 (*intr*) to perform a glissade.
▷**HISTORY** C19: from French, from *glisser* to slip, from Old French *glicier,* of Frankish origin; compare Old High German *glītan* to GLIDE
▸**glisˈsader** NOUN

glissando (glɪˈsændəʊ) NOUN, *plural* **-di** (-diː) *or* **-dos.** 1 a rapidly executed series of notes on the harp or piano, each note of which is discretely audible. 2 a portamento, esp as executed on the violin, viola, etc.
▷**HISTORY** C19: probably Italianized variant of GLISSADE

glisten (ˈglɪsᵊn) VERB (*intr*) 1 (of a wet or glossy surface) to gleam by reflecting light: *wet leaves glisten in the sunlight.* 2 (of light) to reflect with brightness: *the sunlight glistens on wet leaves.* ◆ NOUN 3 *Rare* a gleam or gloss.
▷**HISTORY** Old English *glisnian;* related to *glisian* to glitter, Middle High German *glistern*
▸ˈ**glisteningly** ADVERB

glister (ˈglɪstə) VERB, NOUN an archaic word for **glitter.**

▷**HISTORY** C14: probably from Middle Dutch *glisteren*
▸**'glisteringly** ADVERB

glitch (glɪtʃ) NOUN 1 a sudden instance of malfunctioning or irregularity in an electronic system. 2 a change in the rotation rate of a pulsar.
▷**HISTORY** C20: of unknown origin

glitter ('glɪtə) VERB (*intr*) 1 (of a hard, wet, or polished surface) to reflect light in bright flashes. 2 (of light) to be reflected in bright flashes. 3 (usually foll by *with*) to be decorated or enhanced by the glamour (of): *the show glitters with famous actors.* ◆ NOUN 4 sparkle or brilliance. 5 show and glamour. 6 tiny pieces of shiny decorative material used for ornamentation, as on the skin. 7 *Canadian* Also called: **silver thaw.** ice formed from freezing rain.
▷**HISTORY** C14: from Old Norse *glitra;* related to Old High German *glīzan* to shine
▸**'glitteringly** ADVERB ▸**'glittery** ADJECTIVE

glitterati (ˌglɪtə'rɑːtiː) PLURAL NOUN *Informal* the leaders of society, esp the rich and beautiful; fashionable celebrities.
▷**HISTORY** C20: from GLITTER + *-ati* as in LITERATI

glitz (glɪts) NOUN *Slang* ostentatious showiness; gaudiness or glitter.
▷**HISTORY** C20: back formation from GLITZY

glitzy ('glɪtsɪ) ADJECTIVE **glitzier, glitziest.** *Slang* showily attractive; flashy or glittery.
▷**HISTORY** C20: originally US, probably via Yiddish from German *glitzern* to glitter

Gliwice (*Polish* gli'vitsɛ) NOUN an industrial city in S Poland. Pop.: 212 164 (1999 est.). German name: **Gleiwitz.**

gloaming ('gləʊmɪŋ) NOUN *Poetic* twilight or dusk.
▷**HISTORY** Old English *glōmung,* from *glōm;* related to Old Norse *glāmr* moon

gloat (gləʊt) VERB 1 (*intr;* often foll by *over*) to dwell (on) with malevolent smugness or exultation. ◆ NOUN 2 the act of gloating.
▷**HISTORY** C16: probably of Scandinavian origin; compare Old Norse *glotta* to grin, Middle High German *glotzen* to stare
▸**'gloater** NOUN ▸**'gloatingly** ADVERB

glob (glɒb) NOUN *Informal* a rounded mass of some thick fluid or pliable substance: *a glob of cream.*
▷**HISTORY** C20: probably from GLOBE, influenced by BLOB

global ('gləʊbᵊl) ADJECTIVE 1 covering, influencing, or relating to the whole world. 2 comprehensive.
▸**'globally** ADVERB

global community NOUN the people or nations of the world, considered as being closely connected by modern telecommunications, and as being economically, socially, and politically interdependent.

globalization *or* **globalisation** (ˌgləʊbᵊlaɪ'zeɪʃən) NOUN 1 the process enabling financial and investment markets to operate internationally, largely as a result of deregulation and improved communications. 2 the emergence since the 1980s of a single world market dominated by multinational companies, leading to a diminishing capacity for national governments to control their economies. 3 the process by which a company, etc., expands to operate internationally.

globalize *or* **globalise** ('gləʊbᵊˌlaɪz) VERB (*tr*) to put into effect or spread worldwide.

global positioning system NOUN a system of earth-orbiting satellites, transmitting signals continuously towards the earth, that enables the position of a receiving device on or near the earth's surface to be accurately estimated from the difference in arrival times of the signals. Abbreviation: **GPS.**

global product NOUN a commercial product, such as Coca Cola, that is marketed throughout the world under the same brand name.

global rule NOUN (in transformational grammar) a rule that makes reference to nonconsecutive stages of a derivation.

global search NOUN a word-processing operation in which a complete computer file or set of files is searched for every occurrence of a particular word or other sequence of characters.

global village NOUN the whole world considered as being closely connected by modern telecommunications and as being interdependent economically, socially, and politically.
▷**HISTORY** C20: coined by Marshall McLuhan (1911–80), Canadian author of works analysing the mass media

global warming NOUN an increase in the average temperature worldwide believed to be caused by the greenhouse effect.

globate ('gləʊbeɪt) *or* **globated** ADJECTIVE shaped like a globe.

globe (gləʊb) NOUN 1 a sphere on which a map of the world or the heavens is drawn or represented. 2 **the.** the world; the earth. 3 a planet or some other astronomical body. 4 an object shaped like a sphere, such as a glass lampshade or fish-bowl. 5 *Austral, NZ, and South African* an electric light bulb. 6 an orb, usually of gold, symbolic of authority or sovereignty. ◆ VERB 7 to form or cause to form into a globe.
▷**HISTORY** C16: from Old French, from Latin *globus*
▸**'globe,like** ADJECTIVE

globe artichoke NOUN See **artichoke** (senses 1, 2).

globefish ('gləʊbˌfɪʃ) NOUN, *plural* **-fish** *or* **-fishes.** another name for **puffer** (sense 2) or **porcupine fish.**

globeflower ('gləʊbˌflaʊə) NOUN any ranunculaceous plant of the genus *Trollius,* having pale yellow, white, or orange globe-shaped flowers.

globetrotter ('gləʊbˌtrɒtə) NOUN a habitual worldwide traveller, esp a tourist or businessman.
▸**'globe,trotting** NOUN, ADJECTIVE

globigerina (gləʊˌbɪdʒə'raɪnə) NOUN, *plural* **-nas** *or* **-nae** (-niː). 1 any marine protozoan of the genus *Globigerina,* having a rounded shell with spiny processes: phylum *Foraminifera* (foraminifers). 2 **globigerina ooze.** a deposit on the ocean floor consisting of the shells of these protozoans.
▷**HISTORY** C19: from New Latin, from Latin *globus* GLOBE + *gerere* to carry, bear

globin ('gləʊbɪn) NOUN *Biochem* the protein component of the pigments myoglobin and haemoglobin.
▷**HISTORY** C19: from Latin *globus* ball, sphere + -IN

globoid ('gləʊbɔɪd) ADJECTIVE 1 shaped approximately like a globe. ◆ NOUN 2 a globoid body, such as any of those occurring in certain plant granules.

globose ('gləʊbəʊs, gləʊ'bəʊs) *or* **globous** ('gləʊbəs) ADJECTIVE spherical or approximately spherical.
▷**HISTORY** C15: from Latin *globōsus;* see GLOBE
▸**'globosely** ADVERB ▸**globosity** (gləʊ'bɒsɪtɪ) NOUN

globular ('glɒbjʊlə) *or* **globulous** ADJECTIVE 1 shaped like a globe or globule. 2 having or consisting of globules.
▸**globularity** (ˌglɒbjʊ'lærɪtɪ) *or* **'globularness** NOUN
▸**'globularly** ADVERB

globular cluster NOUN *Astronomy* a densely populated spheroidal star cluster with the highest concentration of stars near its centre, found in the galactic halo and in other galaxies.

globule ('glɒbjuːl) NOUN 1 a small globe, esp a drop of liquid. 2 *Astronomy* a small dark nebula thought to be a site of star formation.
▷**HISTORY** C17: from Latin *globulus,* diminutive of *globus* GLOBE

globuliferous (ˌglɒbjʊ'lɪfərəs) ADJECTIVE producing, containing, or having globules.

globulin ('glɒbjʊlɪn) NOUN any of a group of simple proteins, including gamma globulin, that are generally insoluble in water but soluble in salt solutions and coagulated by heat.
▷**HISTORY** C19: from GLOBULE + -IN

globus ('gləʊbəs) NOUN *Anatomy* any spherelike structure.

globus hystericus (hɪ'stɛrɪkəs) NOUN the technical name for a **lump in the throat.** See **lump** (sense 8).

glochidium (gləʊ'kɪdɪəm) NOUN, *plural* **-chidia** (-'kɪdɪə). 1 a barbed hair, esp among the spore masses of water ferns and on certain other plants. 2 a parasitic larva of certain freshwater mussels that attaches itself to the fins or gills of fish by hooks or suckers.
▷**HISTORY** C19: from New Latin, from Greek *glōkhis* projecting point
▸**glo'chidiate** ADJECTIVE

glockenspiel ('glɒkənˌspiːl, -ˌʃpiːl) NOUN a percussion instrument consisting of a set of tuned metal plates played with a pair of small hammers.
▷**HISTORY** C19: German, from *Glocken* bells + *Spiel* play

glogg (glɒg) NOUN a hot alcoholic mixed drink, originally from Sweden, consisting of sweetened brandy, red wine, bitters or other flavourings, and blanched almonds.
▷**HISTORY** from Swedish *glögg,* from *glödga* to burn

glom (glɒm) VERB (*tr;* followed by *on to*) *Slang* to attach oneself to.

glomerate ('glɒmərɪt) ADJECTIVE 1 gathered into a compact rounded mass. 2 wound up like a ball of thread. 3 *Anatomy* (esp of glands) conglomerate in structure.
▷**HISTORY** C18: from Latin *glomerāre* to wind into a ball, from *glomus* ball

glomeration (ˌglɒmə'reɪʃən) NOUN a conglomeration or cluster.

glomerule ('glɒməˌruːl) NOUN *Botany* 1 a cymose inflorescence in the form of a ball-like cluster of flowers. 2 a ball-like cluster of spores.
▷**HISTORY** C18: from New Latin GLOMERULUS
▸**glomerulate** (glɒ'mɛrʊlɪt, -ˌleɪt) ADJECTIVE

glomerulonephritis (glɒˌmɛrʊləʊnɪ'fraɪtɪs) NOUN any of various kidney diseases in which the glomeruli are affected.

glomerulus (glɒ'mɛrʊləs) NOUN, *plural* **-li** (-ˌlaɪ). 1 a knot of blood vessels in the kidney projecting into the capsular end of a urine-secreting tubule. 2 any cluster or coil of blood vessels, nerve fibres, etc., in the body.
▷**HISTORY** C18: from New Latin, diminutive of *glomus* ball
▸**glo'merular** ADJECTIVE

Glomma (*Norwegian* 'glɔma) NOUN a river in SE Norway, rising near the border with Sweden and flowing generally south to the Skagerrak: the largest river in Scandinavia; important for hydroelectric power and floating timber. Length: 588 km (365 miles).

gloom (gluːm) NOUN 1 partial or total darkness. 2 a state of depression or melancholy. 3 an appearance or expression of despondency or melancholy. 4 *Poetic* a dim or dark place. ◆ VERB 5 (*intr*) to look sullen or depressed. 6 to make or become dark or gloomy.
▷**HISTORY** C14 *gloumben* to look sullen; related to Norwegian dialect *glome* to eye suspiciously
▸**'gloomful** ADJECTIVE ▸**'gloomfully** ADVERB ▸**'gloomless** ADJECTIVE

gloomy ('gluːmɪ) ADJECTIVE **gloomier, gloomiest.** 1 dark or dismal. 2 causing depression, dejection, or gloom: *gloomy news.* 3 despairing; sad.
▸**'gloomily** ADVERB ▸**'gloominess** NOUN

Glooscap, Gluscap, *or* **Gluskap** ('gluːskæp) NOUN (among the Micmac and other Native North American peoples) a traditional trickster hero.
▷**HISTORY** of Algonquian origin

gloria ('glɔːrɪə) NOUN 1 a silk, wool, cotton, or nylon fabric used esp for umbrellas. 2 a halo or nimbus, esp as represented in art.
▷**HISTORY** C16: from Latin: GLORY

Gloria ('glɔːrɪə, -ˌɑː) NOUN 1 any of several doxologies beginning with the word *Gloria,* esp the Greater and the Lesser Doxologies. 2 a musical setting of one of these.

Gloria in Excelsis Deo ('glɔːrɪə ɪn ɛk'sɛlsɪs'deɪəʊ, 'glɔːrɪˌɑː, ɛks'tʃɛlsɪs) NOUN 1 the Greater Doxology (see **doxology**), beginning in Latin with these words. 2 a musical setting of this, usually incorporated into the Ordinary of the Mass. Often shortened to: **Gloria.**
▷**HISTORY** literally: glory to God in the highest

Gloria Patri ('glɔːrɪə 'pɑːtrɪ, 'glɔːrɪˌɑː, 'pæt-) NOUN 1 the Lesser Doxology (see **doxology**), beginning in Latin with these words. 2 a musical setting of this.
▷**HISTORY** literally: glory to the father

glorification (ˌglɔːrɪfɪ'keɪʃən) NOUN 1 the act of glorifying or state of being glorified. 2 *Informal* an enhanced or favourably exaggerated version or account. 3 *Brit informal* a celebration.

glorify ('glɔːrɪˌfaɪ) VERB **-fies, -fying, -fied.** (*tr*) 1 to make glorious. 2 to make more splendid; adorn. 3

to worship, exalt, or adore. [4] to extol. [5] to cause to seem more splendid or imposing than reality.
▸**'glori,fiable** ADJECTIVE ▸**'glori,fier** NOUN

gloriole ('glɔːrɪ,əʊl) NOUN another name for a **halo** or **nimbus** (senses 2, 3).
▷HISTORY C19: from Latin *glōriola,* literally: a small GLORY

gloriosa (,glɔːrɪ'əʊsə) NOUN any plant of the bulbous tropical African genus *Gloriosa,* some species of which are grown as ornamental greenhouse climbers for their showy flowers of yellow, orange, and red: family *Liliaceae.* Also called: **glory lily.**
▷HISTORY New Latin, from Latin *gloriosus* glorious

glorious ('glɔːrɪəs) ADJECTIVE [1] having or full of glory; illustrious. [2] conferring glory or renown: *a glorious victory.* [3] brilliantly beautiful. [4] delightful or enjoyable. [5] *Informal* drunk.
▸**'gloriously** ADVERB ▸**'gloriousness** NOUN

Glorious Revolution NOUN the events of 1688–89 in England that resulted in the ousting of James II and the establishment of William III and Mary II as joint monarchs. Also called: **Bloodless Revolution.**

glory ('glɔːrɪ) NOUN, *plural* **-ries.** [1] exaltation, praise, or honour, as that accorded by general consent: *the glory for the exploit went to the captain.* [2] something that brings or is worthy of praise (esp in the phrase **crowning glory**). [3] thanksgiving, adoration, or worship: *glory be to God.* [4] pomp; splendour: *the glory of the king's reign.* [5] radiant beauty; resplendence: *the glory of the sunset.* [6] the beauty and bliss of heaven. [7] a state of extreme happiness or prosperity. [8] another word for **halo** or **nimbus.** ◆ VERB **-ries, -rying, -ried.** [9] (*intr;* often foll by *in*) to triumph or exult. [10] (*intr*) *Obsolete* to brag. ◆ INTERJECTION [11] *Informal* a mild interjection to express pleasure or surprise (often in the exclamatory phrase **glory be!**).
▷HISTORY C13: from Old French *glorie,* from Latin *glōria,* of obscure origin

glory box NOUN *Austral and NZ informal* a box in which a young woman stores clothes, etc., in preparation for marriage.

glory hole NOUN [1] *Informal* a room, cupboard, or other storage space that contains an untidy and miscellaneous collection of objects. [2] *Nautical* another term for **lazaretto** (sense 1).

glory-of-the-snow NOUN a small W Asian liliaceous plant, *Chionodoxa luciliae,* cultivated for its early-blooming blue flowers.

Glos ABBREVIATION FOR Gloucestershire.

gloss[1] (glɒs) NOUN [1] lustre or sheen, as of a smooth surface. [2] a superficially attractive appearance. [3] See **gloss paint.** [4] a cosmetic preparation applied to the skin to give it a faint sheen: *lip gloss.* ◆ VERB [5] to give a gloss to or obtain a gloss. ◆ See also **gloss over.**
▷HISTORY C16: probably of Scandinavian origin; compare Icelandic *glossi* flame, Middle High German *glosen* to glow
▸**'glosser** NOUN ▸**'glossless** ADJECTIVE

gloss[2] (glɒs) NOUN [1] a short or expanded explanation or interpretation of a word, expression, or foreign phrase in the margin or text of a manuscript, etc. [2] an intentionally misleading explanation or interpretation. [3] short for **glossary.** ◆ VERB (*tr*) [4] to add glosses to.
▷HISTORY C16: from Latin *glōssa* unusual word requiring explanatory note, from Ionic Greek
▸**'glosser** NOUN ▸**'glossingly** ADVERB

gloss. ABBREVIATION FOR glossary.

glossa ('glɒsə) NOUN, *plural* **-sae** (-siː) *or* **-sas.** [1] *Anatomy* a technical word for the **tongue.** [2] a paired tonguelike lobe in the labium of an insect.
▸**'glossal** ADJECTIVE

glossary ('glɒsərɪ) NOUN, *plural* **-ries.** an alphabetical list of terms peculiar to a field of knowledge with definitions or explanations. Sometimes called: **gloss.**
▷HISTORY C14: from Late Latin *glossārium;* see GLOSS[2]
▸**glossarial** (glɒ'sɛərɪəl) ADJECTIVE ▸**glos'sarially** ADVERB ▸**'glossarist** NOUN

glossator (glɒ'seɪtə) NOUN [1] Also called: **glossarist, glossist, glossographer.** a writer of glosses and commentaries, esp (in the Middle Ages) an interpreter of Roman and Canon Law. [2] a compiler of a glossary.

glossectomy (glɒ'sɛktəmɪ) NOUN, *plural* **-mies.** surgical removal of all or part of the tongue.

glosseme ('glɒsiːm) NOUN the smallest meaningful unit of a language, such as stress, form, etc.
▷HISTORY C20: from Greek *glōssēma;* see GLOSS[2], -EME

glossitis (glɒ'saɪtɪs) NOUN inflammation of the tongue.
▸**glossitic** (glɒ'sɪtɪk) ADJECTIVE

glosso- *or before a vowel* **gloss-** COMBINING FORM indicating a tongue or language: *glossolaryngeal.*
▷HISTORY from Greek *glossa* tongue

glossography (glɒ'sɒgrəfɪ) NOUN the art of writing textual glosses or commentaries.
▸**glos'sographer** NOUN

glossolalia (,glɒsə'leɪlɪə) NOUN [1] another term for **gift of tongues.** [2] *Psychol* babbling in a nonexistent language.
▷HISTORY C19: New Latin, from GLOSSO- + Greek *lalein* to speak, babble

glossology (glɒ'sɒlədʒɪ) NOUN an obsolete term for **linguistics.**
▸**glossological** (,glɒsə'lɒdʒɪk^{ə}l) ADJECTIVE ▸**glos'sologist** NOUN

glossopharyngeal nerve (,glɒsəʊ,færɪn'dʒiːəl) NOUN the ninth cranial nerve, which supplies the muscles of the pharynx, the tongue, the middle ear, and the parotid gland.

gloss over VERB (*tr, adverb*) [1] to hide under a deceptively attractive surface or appearance. [2] to deal with (unpleasant facts) rapidly and cursorily, or to omit them altogether from an account of something.

gloss paint NOUN a type of paint composed of pigments ground up in a varnish medium, which produces a hard, shiny, and usually durable finish. Also called: **gloss.**

glossy ('glɒsɪ) ADJECTIVE **glossier, glossiest.** [1] smooth and shiny; lustrous. [2] superficially attractive; plausible. [3] (of a magazine) lavishly produced on shiny paper and usually with many colour photographs. ◆ NOUN, *plural* **glossies.** [4] Also called (US): **slick.** an expensively produced magazine, typically a sophisticated fashion or glamour magazine, printed on shiny paper and containing high quality colour photography. Compare **pulp** (sense 3). [5] a photograph printed on paper that has a smooth shiny surface.
▸**'glossily** ADVERB ▸**'glossiness** NOUN

glottal ('glɒt^{ə}l) ADJECTIVE [1] of or relating to the glottis. [2] *Phonetics* articulated or pronounced at or with the glottis.

glottal stop NOUN a plosive speech sound produced as the sudden onset of a vowel in several languages, such as German, by first tightly closing the glottis and then allowing the air pressure to build up in the trachea before opening the glottis, causing the air to escape with force.

glottic ('glɒtɪk) ADJECTIVE of or relating to the tongue or the glottis.

glottis ('glɒtɪs) NOUN, *plural* **-tises** *or* **-tides** (-tɪ,diːz). the vocal apparatus of the larynx, consisting of the two true vocal cords and the opening between them.
▷HISTORY C16: from New Latin, from Greek *glōttis,* from *glōtta,* Attic form of Ionic *glōssa* tongue; see GLOSS[2]
▸**glottidean** (glɒ'tɪdɪən) ADJECTIVE

glottochronology (,glɒtəʊkrə'nɒlədʒɪ) NOUN the use of lexicostatistics to establish that languages are historically related.
▷HISTORY C20 *glotto-,* from Greek *glōtta* tongue

Gloucester ('glɒstə) NOUN a city in SW England, administrative centre of Gloucestershire, on the River Severn; cathedral (founded 1100). Pop.: 104 800 (1993 est.). Latin name: **Glevum** ('gliːvʊm).

Gloucester Old Spot NOUN a hardy rare breed of pig, white with a few black markings, that originally lived off windfalls in orchards in the Severn valley.

Gloucestershire ('glɒstə,ʃɪə, -ʃə) NOUN a county of SW England, situated around the lower Severn valley: contains the Forest of Dean and the main part of the Cotswold Hills: the geographical and ceremonial county includes the unitary authority of South Gloucestershire (part of Avon county from 1974 to 1996). Administrative centre: Gloucester. Pop. (excluding South Gloucestershire): 564 559 (1996 est.). Area (excluding South Gloucestershire): 2643 sq. km (1020 sq. miles). Abbreviation: **Glos.**

glove (glʌv) NOUN [1] (*often plural*) a shaped covering for the hand with individual sheaths for the fingers and thumb, made of leather, fabric, etc. See also **gauntlet[1]** (sense 2). [2] any of various large protective hand covers worn in sports, such as a boxing glove. [3] **hand in glove.** *Informal* in an intimate relationship or close association. [4] **handle with kid gloves.** *Informal* to treat with extreme care. [5] **with the gloves off.** *Informal* (of a dispute, argument, etc.) conducted mercilessly and in earnest, with no reservations. ◆ VERB [6] (*tr; usually passive*) to cover or provide with or as if with gloves.
▷HISTORY Old English *glōfe;* related to Old Norse *glōfi*
▸**'gloved** ADJECTIVE ▸**'gloveless** ADJECTIVE

glove box NOUN a closed box in which toxic or radioactive substances can be handled by an operator who places his hands through protective gloves sealed to the box.

glove compartment NOUN a small compartment in a car dashboard for the storage of miscellaneous articles.

glove puppet NOUN a small figure of a person or animal that fits over and is manipulated by the hand.

glover ('glʌvə) NOUN a person who makes or sells gloves.

glow (gləʊ) NOUN [1] light emitted by a substance or object at a high temperature. [2] a steady even light without flames. [3] brilliance or vividness of colour. [4] brightness or ruddiness of complexion. [5] a feeling of wellbeing or satisfaction. [6] intensity of emotion; ardour. ◆ VERB (*intr*) [7] to emit a steady even light without flames. [8] to shine intensely, as if from great heat. [9] to be exuberant or high-spirited, as from excellent health or intense emotion. [10] to experience a feeling of wellbeing or satisfaction: *to glow with pride.* [11] (esp of the complexion) to show a strong bright colour, esp a shade of red. [12] to be very hot.
▷HISTORY Old English *glōwan;* related to Old Norse *glōa,* Old High German *gluoen,* Icelandic *glōra* to sparkle

glow discharge NOUN a silent luminous discharge of electricity through a low-pressure gas.

glower ('glaʊə) VERB [1] (*intr*) to stare hard and angrily. ◆ NOUN [2] a sullen or angry stare.
▷HISTORY C16: probably of Scandinavian origin; related to Middle Low German *glūren* to watch
▸**'gloweringly** ADVERB

glowing ('gləʊɪŋ) ADJECTIVE [1] emitting a steady bright light without flames: *glowing embers.* [2] warm and rich in colour: *the room was decorated in glowing shades of gold and orange.* [3] flushed and rosy, as from exercise or excitement: *glowing cheeks.* [4] displaying or indicative of extreme satisfaction, pride, or emotion: *he gave a glowing account of his son's achievements.*
▸**'glowingly** ADVERB

glow lamp NOUN a small light consisting of two or more electrodes in an inert gas, such as neon, at low pressure, across which an electrical discharge occurs when the voltage applied to the electrodes exceeds the ionization potential.

glow plug NOUN one of usually four plugs fitted to the cylinder block of a diesel engine that warms the engine chamber to facilitate starting in cold weather. Also called: **heater plug.**

glowstick ('gləʊ,stɪk) NOUN a plastic tube containing a luminescent material, waved or held aloft esp at gigs, raves, etc.

glow-worm NOUN [1] a European beetle, *Lampyris noctiluca,* the females and larvae of which bear luminescent organs producing a greenish light: family *Lampyridae.* [2] any of various other beetles or larvae of the family *Lampyridae.* ◆ See also **firefly** (sense 1).

gloxinia (glɒk'sɪnɪə) NOUN any of several tropical plants of the genus *Sinningia,* esp the South American *S. speciosa,* cultivated for its large white, red, or purple bell-shaped flowers: family *Gesneriaceae.*
▷HISTORY C19: named after Benjamin P. *Gloxin,* 18th-century German physician and botanist who first described it

gloze (gləʊz) *Archaic* ◆ VERB [1] (*tr;* often foll by *over*) to explain away; minimize the effect or importance of. [2] to make explanatory notes or glosses on (a text). [3] to use flattery (on). ◆ NOUN [4] flattery or deceit. [5] an explanatory note or gloss. [6] specious or deceptive talk or action.
▷HISTORY C13: from Old French *glosser* to comment; see GLOSS[2]

glucagon (ˈgluːkəˌgɒn, -gən) NOUN a polypeptide hormone, produced in the pancreas by the islets of Langerhans, that stimulates the release of glucose into the blood. Compare **insulin.**
▷HISTORY C20: from GLUC(OSE) + *-agon,* perhaps from Greek *agein* to lead

glucan (ˈgluːˌkæn) NOUN any polysaccharide consisting of a polymer of glucose, such as cellulose or starch.

glucinum (gluːˈsaɪnəm) *or* **glucinium** (gluːˈsɪnɪəm) NOUN a former name for **beryllium.**
▷HISTORY C19: New Latin *glucina* beryllium oxide, from Greek *glukus* sweet + -IN; alluding to the sweet taste of some of the salts

glucocorticoid (ˌgluːkəʊˈkɔːtɪˌkɔɪd) NOUN any of a class of corticosteroids that control carbohydrate, protein, and fat metabolism and have anti-inflammatory activity.

gluconeogenesis (ˌgluːkəʊˌniːəʊˈdʒɛnɪsɪs) NOUN *Biochem* the sequence of metabolic reactions by which glucose is synthesized, esp in the liver, from noncarbohydrate sources, such as amino acids, pyruvic acid, or glycerol. Also called: **glyconeogenesis.**

glucophore (ˈgluːkəʊˌfɔː) NOUN a chemical group responsible for sweetness of taste.

glucoprotein (ˌgluːkəʊˈprəʊtiːn) NOUN another name for **glycoprotein.**

glucosamine (gluːˈkəʊzˈəmiːn) NOUN the amino derivative of glucose that occurs in chitin. It has been used in some herbal remedies.

glucose (ˈgluːkəʊz, -kəʊs) NOUN [1] a white crystalline monosaccharide sugar that has several optically active forms, the most abundant being dextrose: a major energy source in metabolism. Formula: $C_6H_{12}O_6$. [2] a yellowish syrup (or, after desiccation, a solid) containing dextrose, maltose, and dextrin, obtained by incomplete hydrolysis of starch: used in confectionery, fermentation, etc.
▷HISTORY C19: from French, from Greek *gleukos* sweet wine; related to Greek *glukus* sweet
▸**glucosic** (gluːˈkɒsɪk) ADJECTIVE

glucoside (ˈgluːkəʊˌsaɪd) NOUN *Biochem* any of a large group of glycosides that yield glucose on hydrolysis.
▸**ˌglucoˈsidal** *or* **glucosidic** (ˌgluːkəʊˈsɪdɪk) ADJECTIVE

glucosuria (ˌgluːkəʊˈsjʊərɪə) NOUN *Pathol* a less common word for **glycosuria.**
▸**ˌglucoˈsuric** ADJECTIVE

glue (gluː) NOUN [1] any natural or synthetic adhesive, esp a sticky gelatinous substance prepared by boiling animal products such as bones, skin, and horns. [2] any other sticky or adhesive substance. ◆ VERB **glues, gluing** *or* **glueing, glued.** [3] (*tr*) to join or stick together with or as if with glue.
▷HISTORY C14: from Old French *glu,* from Late Latin *glūs;* compare Greek *gloios*
▸**ˈglueˌlike** ADJECTIVE ▸**ˈgluer** NOUN ▸**ˈgluey** ADJECTIVE

glue ear NOUN accumulation of fluid in the middle ear in children, caused by infection and sometimes resulting in deafness.

glue-sniffing NOUN the practice of inhaling the fumes of certain types of glue to produce intoxicating or hallucinatory effects.
▸**ˈglue-ˌsniffer** NOUN

glug (glʌg) NOUN a word representing a gurgling sound, as of liquid being poured from a bottle or swallowed.
▷HISTORY C19: of imitative origin

gluggable (ˈglʌgəbᵊl) ADJECTIVE *Informal* (of wine) easy and pleasant to drink.

gluhwein (ˈgluːˌvaɪn) NOUN mulled wine.
▷HISTORY German

glum (glʌm) ADJECTIVE **glummer, glummest.** silent or sullen, as from gloom.
▷HISTORY C16: variant of GLOOM
▸**ˈglumly** ADVERB ▸**ˈglumness** NOUN

glum bum NOUN *Austral slang* a pessimistic person.

glume (gluːm) NOUN [1] *Botany* one of a pair of dry membranous bracts at the base of the spikelet of grasses. [2] the bract beneath each flower in a sedge or related plant.
▷HISTORY C18: from Latin *glūma* husk of corn; related to Latin *glūbere* to remove the bark from
▸**gluˈmaceous** ADJECTIVE ▸**ˈglumeˌlike** ADJECTIVE

gluon (ˈgluːɒn) NOUN a hypothetical particle believed to be exchanged between quarks in order to bind them together to form particles.
▷HISTORY C20: from GLUE + -ON

glut (glʌt) NOUN [1] an excessive amount, as in the production of a crop, often leading to a fall in price. [2] the act of glutting or state of being glutted. ◆ VERB **gluts, glutting, glutted.** (*tr*) [3] to feed or supply beyond capacity. [4] to supply (a market) with a commodity in excess of the demand for it. [5] to cram full or choke up: *to glut a passage.*
▷HISTORY C14: probably from Old French *gloutir,* from Latin *gluttīre;* see GLUTTON[1]
▸**ˈgluttingly** ADVERB

glutamate (ˈgluːtəˌmeɪt) NOUN any salt of glutamic acid, esp its sodium salt (see **monosodium glutamate**).
▷HISTORY C19: from GLUTAM(IC ACID) + -ATE[1]

glutamic acid (gluːˈtæmɪk) *or* **glutaminic acid** (ˌgluːtəˈmɪnɪk) NOUN a nonessential amino acid, occurring in proteins, that acts as a neurotransmitter and plays a part in nitrogen metabolism.

glutamine (ˈgluːtəˌmiːn, -mɪn) NOUN a nonessential amino acid occurring in proteins: plays an important role in protein metabolism.
▷HISTORY C19: from GLUT(EN) + -AMINE

glutaraldehyde (ˌgluːtəˈældɪˌhaɪd) NOUN a water-soluble oil used as a disinfectant, tanning agent, and in resins. Formula: $C_5H_8O_2$.

glutathione (ˌgluːtəˈθaɪəʊn, -θaɪˈəʊn) NOUN *Biochem* a tripeptide consisting of glutamic acid, cysteine, and glycine: important in biological oxidations and the activation of some enzymes. Formula: $C_{10}H_{17}N_3O_6S$.
▷HISTORY C20: from GLUTA(MIC ACID) + THI- + -ONE

glutelin (ˈgluːtɪlɪn) NOUN any of a group of water-insoluble plant proteins found in cereals. They are precipitated by alcohol and are not coagulated by heat. Compare **gliadin.**
▷HISTORY C20: See GLUTEN, -IN

gluten (ˈgluːtᵊn) NOUN a protein consisting of a mixture of glutelin and gliadin, present in cereal grains, esp wheat. A gluten-free diet is necessary in cases of coeliac disease.
▷HISTORY C16: from Latin: GLUE
▸**ˈglutenous** ADJECTIVE

gluten bread NOUN bread made from flour containing a high proportion of gluten.

gluteus *or* **glutaeus** (gluˈtiːəs) NOUN, *plural* **-tei** *or* **-taei** (-ˈtiːaɪ). any one of the three large muscles that form the human buttock and move the thigh, esp the **gluteus maximus.**
▷HISTORY C17: from New Latin, from Greek *gloutos* buttock, rump
▸**gluˈteal** *or* **gluˈtaeal** ADJECTIVE

glutinous (ˈgluːtɪnəs) ADJECTIVE resembling glue in texture; sticky.
▸**ˈglutinously** ADVERB ▸**ˈglutinousness** *or* **glutinosity** (ˌgluːtɪˈnɒsɪtɪ) NOUN

glutton[1] (ˈglʌtᵊn) NOUN [1] a person devoted to eating and drinking to excess; greedy person. [2] *Often ironic* a person who has or appears to have a voracious appetite for something: *a glutton for punishment.*
▷HISTORY C13: from Old French *glouton,* from Latin *glutto,* from *gluttīre* to swallow
▸**ˈgluttonous** ADJECTIVE ▸**ˈgluttonously** ADVERB

glutton[2] (ˈglʌtᵊn) NOUN another name for **wolverine.**
▷HISTORY C17: from GLUTTON[1], apparently translating German *Vielfrass* great eater

gluttony (ˈglʌtənɪ) NOUN the act or practice of eating to excess.

glycaemic index (ˌglaɪˈsiːmɪk) NOUN an index indicating the effects of various foods on blood sugar. Fast-releasing foods that raise blood sugar levels quickly are high on the index, while slow-releasing foods, at the bottom of the index, give a slow but sustained release of sugar. Abbreviation: **GI.**

glyceric (glɪˈsɛrɪk) ADJECTIVE of, containing, or derived from glycerol.

glyceric acid NOUN a viscous liquid carboxylic acid produced by the oxidation of glycerol; 2,3-dihydroxypropanoic acid. Formula: $C_3H_6O_4$.

glyceride (ˈglɪsəˌraɪd) NOUN any fatty-acid ester of glycerol.

glycerine (ˈglɪsərɪn, ˌglɪsəˈriːn) *or* **glycerin** (ˈglɪsərɪn) NOUN another name (not in technical usage) for **glycerol.**
▷HISTORY C19: from French *glycérine,* from Greek *glukeros* sweet + *-ine* -IN; related to Greek *glukus* sweet

glycerol (ˈglɪsəˌrɒl) NOUN a colourless or pale yellow odourless sweet-tasting syrupy liquid; 1,2,3-propanetriol: a by-product of soap manufacture, used as a solvent, antifreeze, plasticizer, and sweetener (**E422**). Formula: $C_3H_8O_3$. Also called (not in technical usage): **glycerine, glycerin.**
▷HISTORY C19: from GLYCER(INE) + -OL[1]

glyceryl (ˈglɪsərɪl) NOUN (*modifier*) derived from glycerol by replacing or removing one or more of its hydroxyl groups: *a glyceryl group or radical.*

glyceryl trinitrate NOUN another name for **nitroglycerine.**

glycine (ˈglaɪsiːn, glaɪˈsiːn) NOUN a nonessential amino acid occurring in most proteins that acts as a neurotransmitter; aminoacetic acid.
▷HISTORY C19: GLYCO- + -INE[2]

glyco- *or before a vowel* **glyc-** COMBINING FORM indicating sugar: *glycogen.*
▷HISTORY from Greek *glukus* sweet

glycogen (ˈglaɪkəʊdʒən, -dʒɛn) NOUN a polysaccharide consisting of glucose units: the form in which carbohydrate is stored in the liver and muscles in man and animals. It can easily be hydrolysed to glucose. Also called: **animal starch.**
▸**glycogenic** (ˌglaɪkəʊˈdʒɛnɪk) ADJECTIVE

glycogenesis (ˌglaɪkəʊˈdʒɛnɪsɪs) NOUN the formation of sugar, esp (in animals) from glycogen.
▸**glycogenetic** (ˌglaɪkəʊdʒɪˈnɛtɪk) ADJECTIVE

glycol (ˈglaɪkɒl) NOUN another name (not in technical usage) for **ethanediol** or a **diol.**
▸**glycolic** *or* **glycollic** (glaɪˈkɒlɪk) ADJECTIVE

glycolic acid NOUN a colourless crystalline soluble hygroscopic compound found in sugar cane and sugar beet: used in tanning and in the manufacture of pharmaceuticals, pesticides, adhesives, and plasticizers; hydroxyacetic acid. Formula: $CH_2(OH)COOH$.

glycolipid (ˌglaɪkəʊˈlɪpɪd) NOUN any of a group of lipids containing a carbohydrate group, commonly glucose or galactose.

glycolysis (glaɪˈkɒlɪsɪs) NOUN *Biochem* the breakdown of glucose by enzymes into pyruvic and lactic acids with the liberation of energy.

glyconeogenesis (ˌglaɪkəʊˌniːəʊˈdʒɛnɪsɪs) NOUN another name for **gluconeogenesis.**

glycophyte (ˈglaɪkəʊˌfaɪt) NOUN any plant that will only grow healthily in soils with a low content of sodium salts.
▸**glycophytic** (ˌglaɪkəʊˈfɪtɪk) ADJECTIVE

glycoprotein (ˌglaɪkəʊˈprəʊtiːn), **glucoprotein,** *or* **glycopeptide** (ˌglaɪkəʊˈpeptaɪd) NOUN any of a group of conjugated proteins containing small amounts of carbohydrates as prosthetic groups. See also **mucoprotein.**

glycose (ˈglaɪkəʊz, -kəʊs) NOUN [1] an older word for **glucose.** [2] any of various monosaccharides.

glycoside (ˈglaɪkəʊˌsaɪd) NOUN any of a group of substances, such as digitoxin, derived from monosaccharides by replacing the hydroxyl group by another group. Many are important medicinal drugs. See also **glucoside.**
▸**glycosidic** (ˌglaɪkəʊˈsɪdɪk) ADJECTIVE

glycosuria (ˌglaɪkəʊˈsjʊərɪə) *or* **glucosuria** NOUN the presence of excess sugar in the urine, as in diabetes.
▷HISTORY C19: from New Latin, from French *glycose* GLUCOSE + -URIA
▸**ˌglycoˈsuric** *or* **ˌglucoˈsuric** ADJECTIVE

glycosylation (ˌglaɪkəʊsəˈleɪʃən) NOUN the

process by which sugars are chemically attached to proteins to form glycoproteins.
▷HISTORY from *glycosyl* radical derived from *glycose* + -ATION

Glyndebourne (ˈglaɪndˌbɔːn) NOUN an estate in SE England, in East Sussex: site of a famous annual festival of opera founded in 1934 by John Christie.

glyoxaline (glaɪˈɒksəlɪn) NOUN another name (not in technical usage) for **imidazole.**

glyph (glɪf) NOUN [1] a carved channel or groove, esp a vertical one as used on a Doric frieze. [2] *Now rare* another word for **hieroglyphic.**
▷HISTORY C18: from French *glyphe,* from Greek *gluphē* carving, from *gluphein* to carve
▸ˈ**glyphic** ADJECTIVE

glyphography (glɪˈfɒgrəfɪ) NOUN a plate-making process in which an electrotype is made from an engraved copper plate.
▷HISTORY C19: from Greek *gluphē* carving + -GRAPHY
▸**glyphograph** (ˈglɪfəˌgrɑːf, -ˌgræf) NOUN
▸**glyˈphographer** NOUN ▸**glyphographic** (ˌglɪfəˈgræfɪk) *or* ˌ**glyphoˈgraphical** ADJECTIVE

glyptal (ˈglɪptəl) NOUN an alkyd resin obtained from polyhydric alcohols and polybasic organic acids or their anhydrides; used for surface coatings.
▷HISTORY C20: a trademark, perhaps from GLY(CEROL) + P(H)T(H)AL(IC)

glyptic (ˈglɪptɪk) ADJECTIVE of or relating to engraving or carving, esp on precious stones.
▷HISTORY C19: from French *glyptique,* from Greek *gluptikos,* from *gluptos,* from *gluphein* to carve

glyptics (ˈglɪptɪks) NOUN (*functioning as singular*) the art of engraving precious stones.

glyptodont (ˈglɪptəˌdɒnt) NOUN any extinct late Cenozoic edentate mammal of the genus *Glyptodon* and related genera, of South America, which resembled giant armadillos.
▷HISTORY C19: from Greek *gluptos* carved + -ODONT

glyptography (glɪpˈtɒgrəfɪ) NOUN the art of carving or engraving upon gemstones.
▸**glypˈtographer** NOUN ▸**glyptographic** (ˌglɪptəˈgræfɪk) *or* ˌ**glyptoˈgraphical** ADJECTIVE

gm THE INTERNET DOMAIN NAME FOR Gambia.

GM ABBREVIATION FOR: [1] general manager. [2] genetically modified. [3] (in Britain) George Medal. [4] Grand Master. [5] **grant-maintained.**

G-man NOUN, *plural* **G-men.** [1] *US slang* an FBI agent. [2] *Irish* a political detective.

GMB ABBREVIATION FOR: [1] Grand Master Bowman; the highest standard of archer. [2] General, Municipal, and Boilermakers (trades union).

GmbH (in Germany) ABBREVIATION FOR Gesellschaft mit beschränkter Haftung; a limited company.
▷HISTORY German: company with limited liabilities

Gmc ABBREVIATION FOR Germanic.

GMC ABBREVIATION FOR: [1] general management committee. [2] General Medical Council.

GMDSS ABBREVIATION FOR Global Marine Distress and Safety System: a worldwide satellite communication system used for transmitting messages (esp distress messages) at sea; officially superseded Morse code in 1999.

GMO ABBREVIATION FOR genetically modified organism.

GMT ABBREVIATION FOR **Greenwich Mean Time.**

GMTA *Text messaging* ABBREVIATION FOR great minds think alike.

gn THE INTERNET DOMAIN NAME FOR Guinea.

gnamma hole (ˈnæmə) NOUN a variant spelling of **namma hole.**

gnarl[1] (nɑːl) NOUN [1] any knotty protuberance or swelling on a tree. ◆ VERB [2] (*tr*) to knot or cause to knot.
▷HISTORY C19: back formation from *gnarled,* probably variant of *knurled;* see KNURL

gnarl[2] (nɑːl) *or* **gnar** (nɑː) VERB (*intr*) *Obsolete* to growl or snarl.
▷HISTORY C16: of imitative origin

gnarled (nɑːld) ADJECTIVE [1] having gnarls. [2] (esp of hands) rough, twisted, and weather-beaten in appearance. [3] perverse or ill-tempered.

gnarly (ˈnɑːlɪ) ADJECTIVE [1] another word for **gnarled.** [2] *NZ informal* good; great.

gnash (næʃ) VERB [1] to grind (the teeth) together, as in pain or anger. [2] (*tr*) to bite or chew as by grinding the teeth. ◆ NOUN [3] the act of gnashing the teeth.
▷HISTORY C15: probably of Scandinavian origin; compare Old Norse *gnastan* gnashing of teeth, *gnesta* to clatter
▸ˈ**gnashingly** ADVERB

gnashers (ˈnæʃəz) PLURAL NOUN *Slang* teeth, esp false ones.

gnat (næt) NOUN any of various small fragile biting dipterous insects of the suborder *Nematocera,* esp *Culex pipiens* (**common gnat**), which abounds near stagnant water.
▷HISTORY Old English *gnætt;* related to Middle High German *gnaz* scurf, German dialect *Gnitze* gnat
▸ˈ**gnatˌlike** ADJECTIVE

gnatcatcher (ˈnætˌkætʃə) NOUN any of various small American songbirds of the genus *Polioptila* and related genera, typically having a long tail and a pale bluish-grey plumage: family *Muscicapidae* (Old World flycatchers, etc.).

gnathic (ˈnæθɪk) *or* **gnathal** ADJECTIVE *Anatomy* of or relating to the jaw.
▷HISTORY C19: from Greek *gnathos* jaw

gnathion (ˈneɪθɪˌɒn, ˈnæθ-) NOUN the lowest point of the midline of the lower jaw: a reference point in craniometry.
▷HISTORY C19: from New Latin, from Greek *gnathos* jaw

gnathite (ˈneɪθaɪt, ˈnæθ-) NOUN *Zoology* an appendage of an arthropod that is specialized for grasping or chewing; mouthpart.
▷HISTORY C19: from Greek *gnathos* jaw

gnathonic (næˈθɒnɪk) ADJECTIVE *Literary* deceitfully flattering; sycophantic.
▷HISTORY C17: from Latin *gnathōnicus,* from *Gnathō,* such a character in the *Eunuchus,* Roman comedy by Terence
▸**gnaˈthonically** ADVERB

gnathostome (ˈneɪθəʊˌstəʊm) NOUN any vertebrate of the superclass *Gnathostomata,* having a mouth with jaws, including all vertebrates except the agnathans.
▷HISTORY from New Latin *Gnathostomata,* from Greek *gnathos* jaw + *stoma* mouth
▸ˌ**gnathoˈstomatous** ADJECTIVE

-gnathous ADJECTIVE COMBINING FORM indicating or having a jaw of a specified kind: *prognathous.*
▷HISTORY from New Latin *-gnathus,* from Greek *gnathos* jaw

gnaw (nɔː) VERB **gnaws, gnawing, gnawed; gnawed** *or* **gnawn** (nɔːn). [1] (when *intr,* often foll by *at* or *upon*) to bite (at) or chew (upon) constantly so as to wear away little by little. [2] (*tr*) to form by gnawing: *to gnaw a hole.* [3] to cause erosion of (something). [4] (when *intr,* often foll by *at*) to cause constant distress or anxiety (to). ◆ NOUN [5] the act or an instance of gnawing.
▷HISTORY Old English *gnagan;* related to Old Norse *gnaga,* Old High German *gnagan*
▸ˈ**gnawable** ADJECTIVE ▸ˈ**gnawer** NOUN ▸ˈ**gnawing** ADJECTIVE, NOUN ▸ˈ**gnawingly** ADVERB

GNC (in Britain) ABBREVIATION FOR General Nursing Council.

gneiss (naɪs) NOUN any coarse-grained metamorphic rock that is banded and foliated: represents the last stage in the metamorphism of rocks before melting.
▷HISTORY C18: from German *Gneis,* probably from Middle High German *ganeist* spark; related to Old Norse *gneista* to give off sparks
▸ˈ**gneissic** *or* ˈ**gneissoid** *or* ˈ**gneissose** ADJECTIVE

gnetophyte (ˈniːtəʊˌfaɪt) NOUN any gymnosperm plant of the phylum *Genetophyta,* which includes three genera: *Gnetum,* consisting of small tropical trees and vines, *Ephedra* (see **ephedra**), and *Welwitschia* (see **welwitschia**).

gnocchi (ˈnɒkɪ, gəˈnɒkɪ, ˈgnɒkɪ) PLURAL NOUN dumplings made of pieces of semolina pasta, or sometimes potato, used to garnish soup or served alone with sauce.
▷HISTORY Italian, plural of *gnocco* lump, probably of Germanic origin; compare Middle High German *knoche* bone

gnome[1] (nəʊm) NOUN [1] one of a species of legendary creatures, usually resembling small misshapen old men, said to live in the depths of the earth and guard buried treasure. [2] the statue of a gnome, esp in a garden. [3] a very small or ugly person. [4] *Facetious or derogatory* an international banker or financier (esp in the phrase **gnomes of Zürich**).
▷HISTORY C18: from French, from New Latin *gnomus,* coined by Paracelsus, of obscure origin
▸ˈ**gnomish** ADJECTIVE

gnome[2] (nəʊm) NOUN a short pithy saying or maxim expressing a general truth or principle.
▷HISTORY C16: from Greek *gnōmē,* from *gignōskein* to know

gnomic (ˈnəʊmɪk, ˈnɒm-) *or* **gnomical** ADJECTIVE [1] consisting of, containing, or relating to gnomes or aphorisms. [2] of or relating to a writer of such sayings.
▸ˈ**gnomically** ADVERB

gnomon (ˈnəʊmɒn) NOUN [1] the stationary arm that projects the shadow on a sundial. [2] a geometric figure remaining after a parallelogram has been removed from one corner of a larger parallelogram.
▷HISTORY C16: from Latin, from Greek: interpreter, from *gignōskein* to know
▸**gnoˈmonic** ADJECTIVE ▸**gnoˈmonically** ADVERB

gnosis (ˈnəʊsɪs) NOUN, *plural* **-ses** (-siːz). supposedly revealed knowledge of various spiritual truths, esp that said to have been possessed by ancient Gnostics.
▷HISTORY C18: ultimately from Greek: knowledge, from *gignōskein* to know

-gnosis NOUN COMBINING FORM (esp in medicine) recognition or knowledge: *prognosis; diagnosis.*
▷HISTORY via Latin from Greek: GNOSIS
▸**-gnostic** ADJECTIVE COMBINING FORM

gnostic (ˈnɒstɪk) *or* **gnostical** ADJECTIVE of, relating to, or possessing knowledge, esp esoteric spiritual knowledge.
▸ˈ**gnostically** ADVERB

Gnostic (ˈnɒstɪk) NOUN [1] an adherent of Gnosticism. ◆ ADJECTIVE [2] of or relating to Gnostics or to Gnosticism.
▷HISTORY C16: from Late Latin *Gnosticī* the Gnostics, from Greek *gnōstikos* relating to knowledge, from *gnōstos* known, from *gignōskein* to know

Gnosticism (ˈnɒstɪˌsɪzəm) NOUN a religious movement characterized by a belief in gnosis, through which the spiritual element in man could be released from its bondage in matter: regarded as a heresy by the Christian Church.

Gnosticize *or* **Gnosticise** (ˈnɒstɪˌsaɪz) VERB [1] (*intr*) to maintain or profess Gnostic views. [2] to put a Gnostic interpretation upon (something).
▸ˈ**Gnostiˌcizer** *or* ˈ**Gnostiˌciser** NOUN

gnotobiotics (ˌnəʊtəʊbaɪˈɒtɪks) NOUN (*functioning as singular*) the study of organisms living in germ-free conditions or when inoculated with known microorganisms.
▷HISTORY C20: from Greek, from *gnōtos,* from *gignōskein* to know + *bios* known life
▸ˌ**gnotobiˈotic** ADJECTIVE ▸ˌ**gnotobiˈotically** ADVERB

gnow (naʊ) NOUN *W Austral* another name for **mallee fowl.**

GNP ABBREVIATION FOR **gross national product.**

GnRH *Biochem* ABBREVIATION FOR gonadotrophin-releasing hormone: a peptide that is released from the brain and stimulates the pituitary gland to secrete gonadotrophic hormones that act in turn on the sex glands.

gns. ABBREVIATION FOR guineas.

gnu (nuː) NOUN, *plural* **gnus** *or* **gnu.** either of two sturdy antelopes, *Connochaetes taurinus* (**brindled gnu**) or the much rarer *C. gnou* (**white-tailed gnu**), inhabiting the savannas of Africa, having an oxlike head and a long tufted tail. Also called: **wildebeest.**
▷HISTORY C18: from Xhosa *nqu*

GNVQ (in Britain) ABBREVIATION FOR general national vocational qualification: a qualification which rewards the development of skills which are likely to be of use to employers.

go[1] (gəʊ) VERB **goes, going, went, gone.** (*mainly intr*) [1] to move or proceed, esp to or from a point or in a certain direction: *to go to London; to go home.* [2] (*tr; takes an infinitive,* often with *to* omitted or replaced by *and*) to proceed towards a particular person or place with some specified intention or purpose: *I must go and get that book.* [3] to depart: *we'll have to go at eleven.* [4] to start, as in a race: often used in commands. 5 to make regular journeys: *this train service goes to the east coast.* 6 to operate or function effectively: *the radio won't go.* 7 (*copula*) to become: *his face went red with embarrassment.* 8 to make a noise as specified: *the gun went bang.* 9 to enter into a specified state or condition: *to go into hysterics; to go into action.* 10 to be or continue to be in a specified state or condition: *to go in rags; to go in poverty.* 11 to lead, extend, or afford access: *this route goes to the north.* 12 to proceed towards an activity: *to go to supper; to go to sleep.* 13 (*tr; takes an infinitive*) to serve or contribute: *this letter goes to prove my point.* 14 to follow a course as specified; fare: *the lecture went badly.* 15 to be applied or allotted to a particular purpose or recipient: *her wealth went to her son; his money went on drink.* 16 to be sold or otherwise transferred to a recipient: *the necklace went for three thousand pounds.* 17 to be ranked; compare: *this meal is good as my meals go.* 18 to blend or harmonize: *these chairs won't go with the rest of your furniture.* 19 (foll by *by* or *under*) to be known (by a name or disguise). 20 to fit or extend: *that skirt won't go round your waist.* 21 to have a usual or proper place: *those books go on this shelf.* 22 (of music, poetry, etc.) to be sounded; expressed, etc.: *how does that song go?* 23 to fail or give way: *my eyesight is going.* 24 to break down or collapse abruptly: *the ladder went at the critical moment.* 25 to die: *the old man went at 2 a.m.* 26 (often foll by *by*) **a** (of time) to elapse: *the hours go by so slowly at the office.* **b** to travel past: *the train goes by her house at four.* **c** to be guided (by). 27 to occur: *happiness does not always go with riches.* 28 to be eliminated, abolished, or given up: *this entry must go to save space.* 29 to be spent or finished: *all his money has gone.* 30 to circulate or be transmitted: *the infection went around the whole community.* 31 to attend: *go to school; go to church.* 32 to join a stated profession: *go to the bar; go on the stage.* 33 (foll by *to*) to have recourse (to); turn: *to go to arbitration.* 34 (foll by *to*) to subject or put oneself (to): *she goes to great pains to please him.* 35 to proceed, esp. up to or beyond certain limits: *you will go too far one day and then you will be punished.* 36 to be acceptable or tolerated: *anything goes in this place.* 37 to carry the weight of final authority: *what the boss says goes.* 38 (foll by *into*) to be contained in: *four goes into twelve three times.* 39 (often foll by *for*) to endure or last out: *we can't go for much longer without water in this heat.* 40 (*tr*) *Cards* to bet or bid: *I go two hearts.* 41 (*tr*) *Informal, chiefly US* to have as one's weight: *I went 112 pounds a year ago.* 42 *US and Canadian* (*usually used in commands;* takes an infinitive without *to*) **a** to start to act so as to: *go shut the door.* **b** to leave so as to: *go blow your brains out.* 43 *Informal* to perform well; be successful: *that group can really go.* 44 (*tr*) *Not standard* to say: widely used, esp. in the historic present, in reporting dialogue: *Then she goes, "Give it to me!" and she just snatched it.* 45 **go and.** *Informal* to be so foolish or unlucky as to: *then she had to go and lose her hat.* 46 **be going.** to intend or be about to start (to do or be doing something): often used as an alternative future construction: *what's going to happen to us?* 47 **go ape.** *Slang* to become crazy, enraged, or out of control. 48 **go ape over.** *Slang* to become crazy or extremely enthusiastic about. 49 **go astray.** to be mislaid; go missing. 50 **go bail.** to act as surety. 51 **go bush.** See **bush** (sense 13). 52 **go halves.** See **half** (sense 15). 53 **go hard.** (often foll by *with*) to cause trouble or unhappiness (to). 54 **go it.** *Slang* to do something or move energetically. 55 **go it alone.** *Informal* to act or proceed without allies or help. 56 **go much on.** *Informal* to approve of or be in agreement with (something): usually used in the negative: *I don't go much on the idea.* 57 **go one better.** *Informal* to surpass or outdo (someone). 58 **go the whole hog.** *Informal* See **hog** (sense 9). 59 **let go.** **a** to relax one's hold (on); release. **b** *Euphemistic* to dismiss (from employment). **c** to discuss or consider no further. 60 **let oneself go.** **a** to act in an uninhibited manner. **b** to lose interest in one's appearance, manners, etc. 61 **to go.** **a** remaining. **b** *US and Canadian informal* (of food served by a restaurant) for taking away. ♦ NOUN, *plural* **goes.** 62 the act of going. 63 *Informal* **a** an attempt or try: *he had a go at the stamp business.* **b** an attempt at stopping a person suspected of a crime: *the police are not always in favour of the public having a go.* **c** an attack, esp. verbal: *she had a real go at them.* 64 a turn: *it's my go next.* 65 *Informal* the quality of being active and energetic: *she has much more go than I.* 66 *Informal* hard or energetic work: *it's all go.* 67 *Informal* a successful venture or achievement: *he made a go of it.* 68 *Informal* a bout or attack (of an illness): *he had a bad go of flu last winter.* 69 *Informal* an unforeseen, usually embarrassing or awkward, turn of events: *here's a rum go.* 70 *Informal* a bargain or agreement. 71 **all the go.** *Informal* very popular; in fashion. 72 **from the word go.** *Informal* from the very beginning. 73 See **get-up-and-go.** 74 **no go.** *Informal* impossible; abortive or futile: *it's no go, I'm afraid.* 75 **on the go.** *Informal* active and energetic. ♦ ADJECTIVE 76 (*postpositive*) *Informal* functioning properly and ready for action: esp. used in astronautics: *all systems are go.* ♦ See also **go about, go against, go ahead, go along, go around, go at, go away, go back, go by, go down, go for, go forth, go in, going, go into, gone, go off, go on, go out, go over, go through, go to, go together, go under, go up, go with, go without.**

▷HISTORY Old English *gān;* related to Old High German *gēn,* Greek *kikhanein* to reach, Sanskrit *jahāti* he forsakes

go² (gəʊ) *or* **I-go** NOUN a game for two players in which stones are placed on a board marked with a grid, the object being to capture territory on the board.

▷HISTORY from Japanese

GO *Military* ABBREVIATION FOR general order.

goa (ˈgəʊə) NOUN a gazelle, *Procapra picticaudata,* inhabiting the plains of the Tibetan plateau, having a brownish-grey coat and backward-curving horns.

▷HISTORY C19: from Tibetan *dgoba*

Goa (ˈgəʊə) NOUN a state on the W coast of India: a Portuguese overseas territory from 1510 until annexed by India in 1961. Pop.: 1 343 998 (2001). Area: 3702 sq. km (1430 sq. miles).

go about VERB (*intr*) 1 (*adverb*) to move from place to place. 2 (*preposition*) to busy oneself with: *to go about one's duties.* 3 (*preposition*) to tackle (a problem or task). 4 (*preposition*) to be actively and constantly engaged in (doing something): *he went about doing good.* 5 to circulate (in): *there's a lot of flu going about.* 6 (*adverb*) (of a sailing ship) to change from one tack to another.

goad (gəʊd) NOUN 1 a sharp pointed stick for urging on cattle, etc. 2 anything that acts as a spur or incitement. ♦ VERB 3 (*tr*) to drive with or as if with a goad; spur; incite.

▷HISTORY Old English *gād,* of Germanic origin, related to Old English *gār,* Old Norse *geirr* spear

▸ˈ**goad,like** ADJECTIVE

Goa, Daman, and Diu NOUN a former Union Territory of India consisting of the widely separated districts of Goa and Daman and the island of Diu. Capital: Panaji. Area: 3814 sq. km (1472 sq. miles).

go against VERB (*intr, preposition*) 1 to be contrary to (principles or beliefs). 2 to be unfavourable to (a person): *the case went against him.*

go ahead VERB 1 (*intr, adverb*) to start or continue, often after obtaining permission. ♦ NOUN **go-ahead.** 2 (usually preceded by *the*) *Informal* permission to proceed. ♦ ADJECTIVE **go-ahead.** 3 enterprising or ambitious.

goal (gəʊl) NOUN 1 the aim or object towards which an endeavour is directed. 2 the terminal point of a journey or race. 3 (in various sports) the net, basket, etc. into or over which players try to propel the ball, puck, etc., to score. 4 *Sport* **a** a successful attempt at scoring. **b** the score so made. 5 (in soccer, hockey, etc.) the position of goalkeeper.

▷HISTORY C16: perhaps related to Middle English *gol* boundary, Old English *gǣlan* to hinder, impede

▸ˈ**goalless** ADJECTIVE

goal area NOUN *Soccer* a rectangular area to the sides and front of the goal, measuring 20 × 6 yards on a full-sized pitch, from which goal kicks are taken. Also called: **six-yard area.**

goalball (ˈgəʊl,bɔːl) NOUN 1 a game played by two teams who compete to score goals by throwing a ball that emits audible sound when in motion. Players, who may be blind or sighted, are blindfolded during play. 2 the ball used in this game.

goalie (ˈgəʊlɪ) NOUN *Informal* short for **goalkeeper.**

goalkeeper (ˈgəʊl,kiːpə) NOUN *Sport* a player in the goal whose duty is to prevent the ball, puck, etc., from entering or crossing it.

▸ˈ**goal,keeping** NOUN

goal kick NOUN *Soccer* a kick taken from the six-yard line by the defending team after the ball has been put out of play by an opposing player.

goal line NOUN *Sport* the line marking each end of the pitch, on which the goals stand.

goalmouth (ˈgəʊl,maʊθ) NOUN *Sport* the area in front of the goal.

go along VERB (*intr, adverb;* often foll by *with*) to refrain from disagreement; assent.

goalpost (ˈgəʊl,pəʊst) NOUN 1 either of two upright posts supporting the crossbar of a goal. 2 **move the goalposts.** to change the aims of an activity to ensure the desired results.

goanna (gəʊˈænə) NOUN 1 any of various Australian monitor lizards. 2 *Austral slang* a piano.

▷HISTORY C19: sense 1 changed from IGUANA; sense 2 from rhyming slang *pianna*

Goa powder NOUN another name for **araroba** (sense 2).

go around *or* **round** VERB (*intr*) 1 (*adverb*) to move about. 2 (*adverb;* foll by *with*) to frequent the society (of a person or group of people): *she went around with older men.* 3 (*adverb*) to be sufficient: *are there enough sweets to go round?* 4 to circulate (in): *measles is going round the school.* 5 (*preposition*) to be actively and constantly engaged in (doing something): *she went around caring for the sick.* 6 to be long enough to encircle: *will that belt go round you?*

goat (gəʊt) NOUN 1 any sure-footed agile bovid mammal of the genus *Capra,* naturally inhabiting rough stony ground in Europe, Asia, and N Africa, typically having a brown-grey colouring and a beard. Domesticated varieties (*C. hircus*) are reared for milk, meat, and wool. Related adjectives: **caprine, hircine.** 2 short for **Rocky Mountain goat.** 3 *Informal* a lecherous man. 4 a bad or inferior member of any group (esp in the phrase **separate the sheep from the goats**). 5 short for **scapegoat.** 6 **act** (*or* **play**) **the** (**giddy**) **goat.** to fool around. 7 **get** (**someone's**) **goat.** *Slang* to cause annoyance to (someone).

▷HISTORY Old English *gāt;* related to Old Norse *geit,* Old High German *geiz,* Latin *haedus* kid

▸ˈ**goat,like** ADJECTIVE

Goat (gəʊt) NOUN **the.** the constellation Capricorn, the tenth sign of the zodiac.

go at VERB (*intr, preposition*) 1 to make an energetic attempt at (something). 2 to attack vehemently.

goat antelope NOUN any bovid mammal of the tribe *Rupicaprini,* including the chamois, goral, serow, and Rocky Mountain goat, having characteristics of both goats and antelopes.

goatee (gəʊˈtiː) NOUN a pointed tuftlike beard on the chin.

▷HISTORY C19: from GOAT + *-ee* (see -Y²)

▸**goatˈeed** ADJECTIVE

goatfish (ˈgəʊt,fɪʃ) NOUN, *plural* **-fish** *or* **-fishes.** the US name for the **red mullet.**

goatherd (ˈgəʊt,hɜːd) NOUN a person employed to tend or herd goats.

goatish (ˈgəʊtɪʃ) ADJECTIVE 1 of, like, or relating to a goat. 2 *Archaic or literary* lustful or lecherous.

▸ˈ**goatishly** ADVERB ▸ˈ**goatishness** NOUN

goat moth NOUN a large European moth, *Cossus cossus,* with pale brownish-grey variably marked wings: family *Cossidae.*

goatsbeard *or* **goat's-beard** (ˈgəʊts,bɪəd) NOUN 1 Also called: **Jack-go-to-bed-at-noon.** a Eurasian plant, *Tragopogon pratensis,* with woolly stems and large heads of yellow rayed flowers surrounded by large green bracts: family *Asteraceae* (composites). 2 an American rosaceous plant, *Aruncus sylvester,* with long spikes of small white flowers.

goatskin (ˈgəʊt,skɪn) NOUN 1 the hide of a goat. 2 **a** something made from the hide of a goat, such as leather or a container for wine. **b** (*as modifier*): *a goatskin rug.*

goat's-rue NOUN 1 Also called: **French lilac.** a Eurasian leguminous plant, *Galega officinalis,* cultivated for its white, mauve, or pinkish flowers: formerly used medicinally. 2 a North American leguminous plant, *Tephrosia virginiana,* with pink-and-yellow flowers.

goatsucker (ˈgəʊt,sʌkə) NOUN the US and Canadian name for **nightjar.**

go away VERB (*intr, adverb*) to leave, as when starting from home on holiday.

go-away bird NOUN *South African* a common name for a grey-plumaged **lourie** of the genus *Corythaixoides*.
▷HISTORY C19: imitative of its call

gob[1] (gɒb) NOUN **1** a lump or chunk, esp of a soft substance. **2** (*often plural*) *Informal* a great quantity or amount. **3** *Mining* **a** a waste material such as clay, shale, etc. **b** a worked-out area in a mine often packed with this. **4** a lump of molten glass used to make a piece of glassware. **5** *Informal* a globule of spittle or saliva. ◆ VERB **gobs, gobbing, gobbed**. **6** (*intr*) *Brit informal* to spit.
▷HISTORY C14: from Old French *gobe* lump, from *gober* to gulp down; see GOBBET

gob[2] (gɒb) NOUN *US slang* an enlisted ordinary seaman in the US Navy.
▷HISTORY C20: of unknown origin

gob[3] (gɒb) NOUN a slang word (esp Brit) for the **mouth.**
▷HISTORY C16: perhaps from Gaelic *gob*

go back VERB (*intr, adverb*) **1** to return. **2** (often foll by *to*) to originate (in): *the links with France go back to the Norman Conquest.* **3** (foll by *on*) to change one's mind about; repudiate (esp in the phrase **go back on one's word**). **4** (of clocks and watches) to be set to an earlier time, as during British Summer Time: *when do the clocks go back this year?*

gobbet (ˈgɒbɪt) NOUN a chunk, lump, or fragment, esp of raw meat.
▷HISTORY C14: from Old French *gobet,* from *gober* to gulp down

gobble[1] (ˈgɒbəl) VERB **1** (when *tr,* often foll by *up*) to eat or swallow (food) hastily and in large mouthfuls. **2** (*tr;* often foll by *up*) *Informal* to snatch.
▷HISTORY C17: probably from GOB[1]

gobble[2] (ˈgɒbəl) NOUN **1** the loud rapid gurgling sound made by male turkeys. ◆ INTERJECTION **2** an imitation of this sound. ◆ VERB **3** (*intr*) (of a turkey) to make this sound.
▷HISTORY C17: probably of imitative origin

gobbledegook *or* **gobbledygook** (ˈgɒbəldɪˌguːk) NOUN pretentious or unintelligible jargon, such as that used by officials.
▷HISTORY C20: whimsical formation from GOBBLE[2]

gobbler (ˈgɒblə) NOUN *Informal* a male turkey.

gobby (ˈgɒbɪ) ADJECTIVE **-bier, -biest**. *Informal* loudmouthed and offensive.

Gobelin (ˈgəʊbəlɪn; *French* gɔblɛ̃) ADJECTIVE **1** of or resembling tapestry made at the Gobelins' factory in Paris, having vivid pictorial scenes. ◆ NOUN **2** a tapestry of this kind.
▷HISTORY C19: from the *Gobelin* family, who founded the factory

go-between NOUN a person who acts as agent or intermediary for two people or groups in a transaction or dealing.

Gobi (ˈgəʊbɪ) NOUN a desert in E Asia, mostly in Mongolia and the Inner Mongolian Autonomous Region of China: sometimes considered to include all the arid regions east of the Pamirs and north of the plateau of Tibet and the Great Wall of China: one of the largest deserts in the world. Length: about 1600 km (1000 miles). Width: about 1000 km (625 miles). Average height: 900 m (3000 ft.). Chinese name: **Shamo.**
▸ˈ**Gobian** ADJECTIVE

Gobian (ˈgəʊbɪən) ADJECTIVE of or relating to the Gobi desert.

gobioid (ˈgəʊbɪˌɔɪd) ADJECTIVE **1** of or relating to the *Gobioidea,* a suborder of spiny-finned teleost fishes that includes gobies and mudskippers (family *Gobiidae*) and sleepers (family *Eleotridae*). ◆ NOUN **2** any gobioid fish.
▷HISTORY C19: from New Latin *Gobioidea,* from Latin *gōbius* gudgeon

goblet (ˈgɒblɪt) NOUN **1** a vessel for drinking, usually of glass or metal, with a base and stem but without handles. **2** *Archaic* a large drinking cup shaped like a bowl.
▷HISTORY C14: from Old French *gobelet* a little cup, from *gobel* ultimately of Celtic origin

goblin (ˈgɒblɪn) NOUN (in folklore) a small grotesque supernatural creature, regarded as malevolent towards human beings.
▷HISTORY C14: from Old French, from Middle High German *kobolt;* compare COBALT

gobo (ˈgəʊbəʊ) NOUN, *plural* **-bos** *or* **-boes**. **1** a shield placed around a microphone to exclude unwanted sounds. **2** a black screen placed around a camera lens, television lens, etc., to reduce the incident light.
▷HISTORY C20: of unknown origin

gobshite (ˈgɒbˌʃaɪt) NOUN *Slang* a stupid person.
▷HISTORY C20: from GOB[3] + *shite* excrement; see SHIT

> **Language note** This word was formerly considered to be taboo, and it was labelled as such in previous editions of *Collins English Dictionary*. However, it has now become acceptable in speech, although some older or more conservative people may object to its use.

gobsmacked (ˈgɒbˌsmækt) ADJECTIVE *Brit slang* astounded; astonished.
▷HISTORY C20: from GOB[3] + SMACK[2]

gobstopper (ˈgɒbˌstɒpə) NOUN *Brit* a large hard sweet consisting of different coloured concentric layers that are revealed as it is sucked.

goby (ˈgəʊbɪ) NOUN, *plural* **-by** *or* **-bies**. **1** any small spiny-finned fish of the family *Gobiidae,* of coastal or brackish waters, having a large head, an elongated tapering body, and the ventral fins modified as a sucker. **2** any other gobioid fish.
▷HISTORY C18: from Latin *gōbius* gudgeon, fish of little value, from Greek *kōbios*

go-by NOUN *Slang* a deliberate snub or slight (esp in the phrase **give (a person) the go-by**).

go by VERB (*intr*) **1** to pass: *the cars went by; as the years go by we all get older; don't let those opportunities go by!* **2** (*preposition*) to be guided by: *in the darkness we could only go by the stars.* **3** (*preposition*) to use as a basis for forming an opinion or judgment: *it's wise not to go only by appearances.*

go-cart NOUN **1** *Chiefly US and Canadian* a small wagon for young children to ride in or pull. **2** *Chiefly US and Canadian* a light frame on casters or wheels that supports a baby while learning to walk. Brit word: **baby-walker. 3** *Motor racing* See **kart. 4** another word for **handcart.**

GOC(-in-C) ABBREVIATION FOR General Officer Commanding(-in-Chief).

god (gɒd) NOUN **1** a supernatural being, who is worshipped as the controller of some part of the universe or some aspect of life in the world or is the personification of some force. Related adjective: **divine. 2** an image, idol, or symbolic representation of such a deity. **3** any person or thing to which excessive attention is given: *money was his god.* **4** a man who has qualities regarded as making him superior to other men. **5** (*in plural*) the gallery of a theatre.
▷HISTORY Old English *god;* related to Old Norse *goth,* Old High German *got,* Old Irish *guth* voice

God (gɒd) NOUN **1** *Theol* the sole Supreme Being, eternal, spiritual, and transcendent, who is the Creator and ruler of all and is infinite in all attributes; the object of worship in monotheistic religions. **2 play God.** to behave in an imperious or superior manner. ◆ INTERJECTION **3** an oath or exclamation used to indicate surprise, annoyance, etc. (and in such expressions as **My God!** or **God Almighty!**).

Godavari (gəʊˈdɑːvərɪ) NOUN a river in central India, rising in the Western Ghats and flowing southeast to the Bay of Bengal: extensive delta, linked by canal with the Krishna delta; a sacred river to Hindus. Length: about 1500 km (900 miles).

God-botherer (ˈgɒdˌbɒðərə) NOUN *Informal* an over-zealous Christian.

godchild (ˈgɒdˌtʃaɪld) NOUN, *plural* **-children** (-ˌtʃɪldrən). a person, usually an infant, who is sponsored by adults at baptism.

goddamn (ˈgɒdˈdæm) *Informal, chiefly US and Canadian* ◆ INTERJECTION *also* **God damn. 1** an oath expressing anger, surprise, etc. ◆ ADVERB *also* **goddam.** ◆ ADJECTIVE *also* **goddam, goddamned. 2** (intensifier): *a goddamn fool.*

goddaughter (ˈgɒdˌdɔːtə) NOUN a female godchild.

goddess (ˈgɒdɪs) NOUN **1** a female divinity. **2** a woman who is adored or idealized, esp by a man.
▸ˈ**goddessˌhood** *or* ˈ**goddess-ˌship** NOUN

Gödel's proof (ˈgɜːdəl) NOUN a proof that in a formal axiomatic system such as logic or mathematics it is possible to prove consistency without using methods from outside the system, demonstrated by Kurt Gödel (1906–78).

Godesberg (*German* ˈgoːdəsbɛrk) NOUN a town and spa in W Germany, in North Rhine-Westphalia on the Rhine: a SE suburb of Bonn. Official name: **Bad Godesberg.**

godet (ˈgəʊdeɪ, gəʊˈdɛt) NOUN a triangular piece of material inserted into a garment, such as into a skirt to create a flare.
▷HISTORY C19: from French

godetia (gəˈdiːʃə) NOUN any plant of the American onagraceous genus *Godetia,* esp one grown as a showy-flowered annual garden plant.
▷HISTORY C19: named after C. H. *Godet* (died 1879), Swiss botanist

godfather (ˈgɒdˌfɑːðə) NOUN **1** a male godparent. **2** the head of a Mafia family or other organized criminal ring. **3** an originator or leading exponent: *the godfather of South African pop.*

godfather offer NOUN *Informal* a takeover bid pitched so high that the management of the target company is unable to dissuade shareholders from accepting it.
▷HISTORY C20: from the 1972 film *The Godfather,* in which a character was made an offer he could not refuse by a threatening mafioso

God-fearing ADJECTIVE pious; devout: *a God-fearing people.*

godforsaken (ˈgɒdfəˌseɪkən, ˌgɒdfəˈseɪkən) ADJECTIVE (*sometimes capital*) **1** (*usually prenominal*) desolate; dreary; forlorn. **2** wicked.

Godhead (ˈgɒdˌhɛd) NOUN (*sometimes not capital*) **1** the essential nature and condition of being God. **2 the Godhead.** God.

godhood (ˈgɒdˌhʊd) NOUN the state of being divine.

godless (ˈgɒdlɪs) ADJECTIVE **1** wicked or unprincipled. **2** lacking a god. **3** refusing to acknowledge God.
▸ˈ**godlessly** ADVERB ▸ˈ**godlessness** NOUN

godlike (ˈgɒdˌlaɪk) ADJECTIVE resembling or befitting a god or God; divine.

godly (ˈgɒdlɪ) ADJECTIVE **-lier, -liest**. having a religious character; pious; devout: *a godly man.*
▸ˈ**godliness** NOUN

God man NOUN a person, such as Jesus Christ, who unites humanity with God.

godmother (ˈgɒdˌmʌðə) NOUN a female godparent.

godown (ˈgəʊˌdaʊn) NOUN (in East Asia and India) a warehouse.
▷HISTORY C16: from Malay *godong*

go down VERB (*intr, mainly adverb*) **1** (*also preposition*) to move or lead to or as if to a lower place or level; sink, decline, decrease, etc.: *the ship went down this morning; prices are going down; the path goes down to the sea.* **2** to be defeated; lose. **3** to be remembered or recorded (esp in the phrase **go down in history**). **4** to be received: *his speech went down well.* **5** (of food) to be swallowed. **6** *Bridge* to fail to make the number of tricks previously contracted for. **7** *Brit* to leave a college or university at the end of a term or the academic year. **8** (usually foll by *with*) to fall ill; be infected. **9** (of a celestial body) to sink or set: *the sun went down before we arrived.* **10** *Brit slang* to go to prison, esp for a specified period: *he went down for six months.* **11** *Slang, chiefly US* to happen.

godparent (ˈgɒdˌpɛərənt) NOUN a person who stands sponsor to another at baptism.

godroon (gəˈdruːn) NOUN a variant spelling of **gadroon.**
▸**goˈdrooned** ADJECTIVE

God's acre NOUN *Literary* a churchyard or burial ground.
▷HISTORY C17: translation of German *Gottesacker*

godsend (ˈgɒdˌsɛnd) NOUN a person or thing that comes unexpectedly but is particularly welcome.

▷HISTORY C19: changed from C17 *God's send,* alteration of *goddes sand* God's message, from Old English *sand;* see SEND[1]

godslot ('gɒd,slɒt) NOUN *Informal* a time in a television or radio schedule traditionally reserved for religious broadcasts.

godson ('gɒd,sʌn) NOUN a male godchild.

Godspeed ('gɒd'spi:d) INTERJECTION, NOUN an expression of one's good wishes for a person's success and safety.
▷HISTORY C15: from *God spede* may God prosper (you)

godsquad ('gɒd,skwɒd) NOUN *Informal, derogatory* any group of evangelical Christians, members of which are regarded as intrusive and exuberantly pious.

Godthaab (*Danish* 'gɔdhɔ:b) NOUN the former name for **Nuuk**.

Godwin Austen NOUN another name for **K2**.

godwit ('gɒdwɪt) NOUN any large shore bird of the genus *Limosa,* of northern and arctic regions, having long legs and a long upturned bill: family *Scolopacidae* (sandpipers, etc.), order *Charadriiformes.*
▷HISTORY C16: of unknown origin

Godzone NOUN *Austral informal* one's home country.
▷HISTORY from *God's own country*

goer ('gəʊə) NOUN [1] **a** a person who attends something regularly. **b** (*in combination*): *filmgoer.* [2] an energetic person. [3] *Informal* an acceptable or feasible idea, proposal, etc. [4] *Austral and NZ informal* a person trying to succeed.

goethite *or* **göthite** ('gəʊθaɪt; *German* 'gø:ti:t) NOUN a black, brown, or yellow mineral consisting of hydrated iron oxide in the form of orthorhombic crystals or fibrous masses. Formula: FeO(OH).
▷HISTORY C19: named after Johann Wolfgang von *Goethe* (1749–1832), German poet, novelist, and dramatist

go-faster stripe NOUN *Informal* a decorative line, often suggestive of high speed, on the bodywork of a car.

gofer ('gəʊfə) NOUN *Slang, chiefly US and Canadian* an employee or assistant whose duties include menial tasks such as running errands.
▷HISTORY C20: originally US: alteration of *go for*

goffer *or* **gauffer** ('gəʊfə) VERB (*tr*) [1] to press pleats into (a frill). [2] to decorate (the gilt edges of a book) with a repeating pattern. ◆ NOUN [3] an ornamental frill made by pressing pleats. [4] the decoration formed by goffering books. [5] the iron or tool used in making goffers.
▷HISTORY C18: from French *gaufrer* to impress a pattern, from *gaufre,* from Middle Low German *wāfel;* see WAFFLE[1], WAFER

go for VERB (*intr, preposition*) [1] to go somewhere in order to have or fetch: *he went for a drink; shall I go for a doctor?* [2] to seek to obtain: *I'd go for that job if I were you.* [3] to apply to: *what I told him goes for you too.* [4] to prefer or choose; like: *I really go for that new idea of yours.* [5] to be to the advantage of: *you'll have great things going for you in the New Year.* [6] to make a physical or verbal attack on. [7] to be considered to be of a stated importance or value: *his twenty years went for nothing when he was made redundant.* [8] **go for it.** *Informal* to make the maximum effort to achieve a particular goal.

go forth VERB (*intr, adverb*) *Archaic or formal* [1] to be issued: *the command went forth that taxes should be collected.* [2] to go out: *the army went forth to battle.*

Gog and Magog (gɒg, 'meɪgɒg) NOUN [1] *Old Testament* a hostile prince and the land from which he comes to attack Israel (Ezekiel 38). [2] *New Testament* two kings, who are to attack the Church in a climactic battle, but are then to be destroyed by God (Revelation 20:8–10). [3] *Brit folklore* two giants, the only survivors of a race of giants destroyed by Brutus, the legendary founder of Britain.

go-getter NOUN *Informal* an ambitious enterprising person.
▸'**go-,getting** ADJECTIVE

gogga ('xɒxə) NOUN *South African informal* any small animal that crawls or flies, esp an insect.
▷HISTORY C20: from Khoikhoi *xoxon* insects collectively

goggle ('gɒgᵊl) VERB [1] (*intr*) to stare stupidly or fixedly, as in astonishment. [2] to cause (the eyes) to roll or bulge or (of the eyes) to roll or bulge. ◆ NOUN [3] a fixed or bulging stare. [4] (*plural*) spectacles, often of coloured glass or covered with gauze: used to protect the eyes.
▷HISTORY C14: from *gogelen* to look aside, of uncertain origin; see AGOG
▸'**goggly** ADJECTIVE

gogglebox ('gɒgᵊl,bɒks) NOUN *Brit slang* a television set.

goggle-eyed ADJECTIVE (*often postpositive*) with a surprised, staring, or fixed expression.

goglet ('gɒglɪt) *or* **gurglet** NOUN a long-necked water-cooling vessel of porous earthenware, used esp in India. Also called: **guglet** ('gʌglɪt).
▷HISTORY C17: from Portuguese *gorgoleta* a little throat, from *gorja* throat; related to French *gargoule;* see GARGLE

go-go ADJECTIVE *Informal, chiefly US and Canadian* [1] of or relating to discos or the lively music and dancing performed in them. [2] dynamic or forceful.
▷HISTORY C20: altered from French *à-gogo* aplenty, ad lib: sense influenced by English verb *go*

go-go dancer NOUN a dancer, usually scantily dressed, who performs rhythmic and often erotic modern dance routines, esp in a nightclub or disco.

Gogolian (,gəʊ'gɒlɪən) ADJECTIVE of, relating to, or like the Russian writer Gogol (1809–52) or his works.

Gogra ('gɒgrə) NOUN a river in N India, rising in Tibet, in the Himalayas, and flowing southeast through Nepal as the Karnali, then through Uttar Pradesh to join the Ganges. Length: about 1000 km (600 miles).

gohonzon (gəʊ'hɒnzɒn) NOUN (in Nichiren Buddhism) the paper scroll to which devotional chanting is directed.
▷HISTORY from Japanese *go* an honorific prefix + *honzon* object of respect

Goiânia (gɔɪ'ɑ:nɪə; *Portuguese* go'jənja) NOUN a city in central Brazil, capital of Goiás state: planned in 1933 to replace the old capital, Goiás; two universities. Pop.: 1 083 396 (2000).

Goiás (*Portuguese* gɔ'jas) NOUN a state of central Brazil, in the Brazilian Highlands: contains Brasília, the capital of Brazil. Capital: Goiânia. Pop.: 4 994 897 (1995 est.). Area: 341 289 sq. km (131 772 sq. miles).

Goidel ('gɔɪdᵊl) NOUN a Celt who speaks a Goidelic language; Gael. Compare **Brython**.

Goidelic, Goidhelic (gɔɪ'delɪk), *or* **Gadhelic** NOUN [1] the N group of Celtic languages, consisting of Irish Gaelic, Scottish Gaelic, and Manx. Compare **Brythonic**. ◆ ADJECTIVE [2] of, relating to, or characteristic of this group of languages.
▷HISTORY C19: from Old Irish *Goidel* a Celt, from Old Welsh *gwyddel,* from *gwydd* savage

go in VERB (*intr, mainly adverb*) [1] to enter. [2] (*preposition*) See **go into**. [3] (of the sun) to become hidden behind a cloud. [4] to be assimilated or grasped: *nothing much goes in if I try to read in the evenings.* [5] *Cricket* to begin an innings. [6] **go in for. a** to enter as a competitor or contestant. **b** to adopt as an activity, interest, or guiding principle: *she went in for nursing; some men go in for football in a big way.*

going ('gəʊɪŋ) NOUN [1] a departure or farewell. [2] the condition of a surface such as a road or field with regard to walking, riding, etc.: *muddy going.* [3] *Informal* speed, progress, etc.: *we made good going on the trip.* ◆ ADJECTIVE [4] thriving (esp in the phrase **a going concern**). [5] current or accepted, as from past negotiations or commercial operation: *the going rate for electricians; the going value of the firm.* [6] (*postpositive*) available: *the best going.* [7] **going, going, gone!** a statement by an auctioneer that the bidding has almost finished.

going-over NOUN, *plural* **goings-over**. *Informal* [1] a check, examination, or investigation. [2] a castigation or thrashing.

goings-on PLURAL NOUN *Informal* [1] actions or conduct, esp when regarded with disapproval. [2] happenings or events, esp when mysterious or suspicious: *there were strange goings-on up at the Hall.*

go into VERB (*intr, preposition*) [1] to enter. [2] to start a career in: *to go into publishing.* [3] to investigate or examine: *to go into the problem of price increases.* [4] to discuss: *we won't go into that now.* [5] to dress oneself differently in: *to go into mourning.* [6] to hit: *the car had gone into a lamppost.* [7] to go to live in or be admitted to, esp temporarily: *she went into hospital on Tuesday.* [8] to enter a specified state: *she went into fits of laughter.*

goitre *or US* **goiter** ('gɔɪtə) NOUN *Pathol* a swelling of the thyroid gland, in some cases nearly doubling the size of the neck, usually caused by under- or overproduction of hormone by the gland.
▷HISTORY C17: from French *goitre,* from Old French *goitron,* ultimately from Latin *guttur* throat
▸'**goitred** *or US* '**goitered** ADJECTIVE ▸'**goitrous** ADJECTIVE

go-juice NOUN *Informal* fuel for an engine, esp petrol.

go-kart *or* **go-cart** NOUN See **kart**.

Golan Heights ('gəʊ,læn) PLURAL NOUN a range of hills in the Middle East, possession of which is disputed between Israel and Syria: under Syrian control until 1967 when they were stormed by Israeli forces; Jewish settlements have since been established. Highest peak: 2224 m (7297 ft.).

Golconda (gɒl'kɒndə) NOUN [1] a ruined town and fortress in S central India, in W Andhra Pradesh near Hyderabad city: capital of one of the five Muslim kingdoms of the Deccan from 1512 to 1687, then annexed to the Mogul empire; renowned for its diamonds. [2] (*sometimes not capital*) a source of wealth or riches, esp a mine.

gold (gəʊld) NOUN [1] **a** a dense inert bright yellow element that is the most malleable and ductile metal, occurring in rocks and alluvial deposits: used as a monetary standard and in jewellery, dentistry, and plating. The radioisotope gold-198 (**radiogold**), with a half-life of 2.69 days, is used in radiotherapy. Symbol: Au; atomic no.: 79; atomic wt.: 196.96654; valency: 1 or 3; relative density: 19.3; melting pt.: 1064.43°C; boiling pt.: 2857°C. Related adjectives: **aurous, auric. b** (*as modifier*): *a gold mine.* [2] a coin or coins made of this metal. [3] money; wealth. [4] something precious, beautiful, etc., such as a noble nature (esp in the phrase **heart of gold**). [5] **a** a deep yellow colour, sometimes with a brownish tinge. **b** (*as adjective*): *a gold carpet.* [6] *Archery* the bull's eye of a target, scoring nine points. [7] short for **gold medal**.
▷HISTORY Old English *gold;* related to Old Norse *gull,* Gothic *gulth,* Old High German *gold*

goldarn (gɒl'dɑ:n) INTERJECTION, ADVERB *US and Canadian slang* a euphemistic variant of **goddamn**.

Goldbach's conjecture ('gəʊld,bɑ:xs) NOUN the conjecture that every even number greater than two is the sum of two prime numbers.
▷HISTORY named after C. *Goldbach* (1690–1764), German mathematician

gold basis NOUN the gold standard as a criterion for the determination of prices.

goldbeater's skin ('gəʊld,bi:təz) NOUN animal membrane used to separate sheets of gold that are being hammered into gold leaf.

gold-beating NOUN the act, process, or skill of hammering sheets of gold into gold leaf.
▸'**gold-,beater** NOUN

gold beetle *or* **goldbug** ('gəʊld,bʌg) NOUN any American beetle of the family *Chrysomelidae* having a bright metallic lustre.

gold brick NOUN [1] something with only a superficial appearance of value. [2] *US slang* an idler or shirker.

gold card NOUN a credit card issued by credit-card companies to favoured clients, entitling them to high unsecured overdrafts, some insurance cover, etc.

gold certificate NOUN (in the US) [1] a currency note issued exclusively to the Federal Reserve Banks by the US Treasury. It forms a claim on gold reserves deposited by the Federal Reserve Banks at the Treasury and is used to transfer interbank balances within the Federal Reserve System. [2] Also called: **gold note**. (formerly) a banknote issued by the US Treasury to the public and redeemable in gold.

Gold Coast NOUN [1] the former name (until 1957) of **Ghana**. [2] a line of resort towns and beaches in E Australia, extending for over 30 km (20 miles) along the SE coast of Queensland and the NE coast of New South Wales.

goldcrest ('gəʊld,krest) NOUN a small Old World

warbler, *Regulus regulus,* having a greenish plumage and a bright yellow-and-black crown.

gold-digger NOUN [1] a person who prospects or digs for gold. [2] *Informal* a woman who uses her sexual attractions to accumulate gifts and wealth or advance her social position.
▸ **ˈgold-ˌdigging** NOUN

gold disc NOUN **a** (in Britain) an LP record certified to have sold 250 000 copies or a single certified to have sold 500 000 copies. **b** (in the US) an LP record or single certified to have sold 1 000 000 copies or a single certified to have sold 500 000 copies. Compare **silver disc, platinum disc.**

gold dust NOUN [1] gold in the form of small particles or powder, as found in placer-mining. [2] a valuable or rare thing: *tickets for this match are gold dust.*

golden (ˈɡəʊldən) ADJECTIVE [1] of the yellowish or brownish-yellow metallic colour of gold: *golden hair.* [2] made from or largely consisting of gold: *a golden statue.* [3] happy or prosperous: *golden days.* [4] (*sometimes capital*) (of anniversaries) the 50th in a series: *Golden Jubilee; golden wedding.* [5] *Informal* very successful or destined for success: *the golden girl of tennis.* [6] extremely valuable or advantageous: *a golden opportunity.*
▸ **ˈgoldenly** ADVERB ▸ **ˈgoldenness** NOUN

golden age NOUN [1] *Classical myth* the first and best age of mankind, when existence was happy, prosperous, and innocent. [2] the most flourishing and outstanding period, esp in the history of an art or nation: *the golden age of poetry.* [3] the great classical period of Latin literature, occupying approximately the 1st century B.C. and represented by such writers as Cicero and Virgil.

golden aster NOUN any North American plant of the genus *Chrysopsis,* esp *C. mariana* of the eastern US, having yellow rayed flowers: family *Asteraceae* (composites).

golden calf NOUN [1] *Old Testament* **a** an idol made by Aaron and set up for the Israelites to worship (Exodus 32). **b** either of two similar idols set up by Jeroboam I at Dan and Bethel in the northern kingdom (I Kings 12:28–30). [2] *Informal* the pursuit or idolization of material wealth.

golden chain NOUN another name for **laburnum.**

Golden Delicious NOUN a variety of eating apple having sweet flesh and greenish-yellow skin.

golden eagle NOUN a large eagle, *Aquila chrysaetos,* of mountainous regions of the N hemisphere, having a plumage that is golden brown on the back and brown elsewhere.

goldeneye (ˈɡəʊldənˌaɪ) NOUN, *plural* **-eyes** *or* **-eye.** [1] either of two black-and-white diving ducks, *Bucephala clangula* or *B. islandica,* of northern regions. [2] any lacewing of the family *Chrysopidae* that has a greenish body and eyes of a metallic lustre.

Golden Fleece NOUN *Greek myth* the fleece of a winged ram that rescued Phrixus and brought him to Colchis, where he sacrificed it to Zeus. Phrixus gave the fleece to King Aeëtes who kept it in a sacred grove, whence Jason and the Argonauts stole it with the help of Aeëtes' daughter. See also **Phrixus.**

Golden Gate NOUN a strait between the Pacific and San Francisco Bay: crossed by the **Golden Gate Bridge,** with a central span of 1280 m (4200 ft.).

golden goal NOUN *Soccer* (in certain matches) the first goal scored in extra time, which wins the match for the side scoring it.

golden goose NOUN a goose in folklore that laid a golden egg a day until its greedy owner killed it in an attempt to get all the gold at once.

golden handcuffs PLURAL NOUN *Informal* payments deferred over a number of years that induce a person to stay with a particular company or in a particular job.

golden handshake NOUN *Informal* a sum of money, usually large, given to an employee, either on retirement in recognition of long or excellent service or as compensation for loss of employment.

Goldenhar's syndrome (ˈɡəʊldən ˌhaːz) NOUN a congenital disorder in which one side of the face is malformed, often with an enlargement of one side of the mouth. There may also be hearing loss, curvature of the spine, and mild retardation. technical name **oculoauriculovertebral displasia.**
▷ **HISTORY** C20: named after Maurice *Goldenhar,* Swiss physician

golden hello NOUN *Informal* a payment made to a sought-after recruit on signing a contract of employment with a company.

Golden Horde NOUN the Mongol horde that devastated E Europe in the early 13th century. It established the westernmost Mongol khanate, which at its height ruled most of European Russia. Defeated by the power of Muscovy (1380), the realm split into four smaller khanates in 1405.

Golden Horn NOUN an inlet of the Bosporus in NW Turkey, forming the harbour of Istanbul. Turkish name: **Haliç.**

golden hour NOUN the first hour after a serious accident, when it is crucial that the victim receives medical treatment in order to have a chance of surviving.

golden mean NOUN [1] the middle course between extremes. [2] another term for **golden section.**

golden number NOUN a number between 1 and 19, used to indicate the position of any year in the Metonic cycle, calculated as the remainder when 1 is added to the given year and the sum is divided by 19. If the remainder is zero the number is 19: *the golden number of 1984 is 9.*

golden oldie NOUN something old or long-established, esp a hit record or song that has remained popular or is enjoying a revival. Also called: **oldie.**

golden oriole NOUN a European oriole, *Oriolus oriolus,* the male of which has a bright yellow head and body with black wings and tail.

golden parachute NOUN *Informal* a clause in the employment contract of a senior executive providing for special benefits if the executive's employment is terminated as a result of a takeover.

golden perch NOUN another name for **callop.**

golden pheasant NOUN a brightly coloured pheasant, *Chrysolophus pictus,* of the mountainous regions of W and central Asia, the males of which have a crest and ruff.

golden plover NOUN any of several plovers of the genus *Pluvialis,* such as *P. apricaria* of Europe and Asia, that have golden brown back, head, and wings.

golden ratio NOUN the ratio of two lengths, equal in value to $(1 + \sqrt{5})/2$ and given by $b/a = (b + a)/b$; it is the reciprocal of the **golden section** and also equal to (1 + golden section). Symbol: Φ.

golden retriever NOUN a compact large breed of dog having a silky coat of flat or wavy hair of a gold or dark-cream colour, well-feathered on the legs and tail.

goldenrod (ˌɡəʊldənˈrɒd) NOUN [1] any plant of the genus *Solidago,* of North America, Europe, and Asia, having spikes made up of inflorescences of minute yellow florets: family *Asteraceae* (composites). See also **yellowweed.** [2] any of various similar related plants, such as *Brachychaeta sphacelata* (**false goldenrod**) of the southern US.

golden rule NOUN [1] any of a number of rules of fair conduct, such as *Whatsoever ye would that men should do to you, do ye even so to them* (Matthew 7:12) or *thou shalt love thy neighbour as thyself* (Leviticus 19:28). [2] any important principle: *a golden rule of sailing is to wear a life jacket.* [3] another name for **rule of three.**

goldenseal (ˌɡəʊldənˈsiːl) NOUN a ranunculaceous woodland plant, *Hydrastis canadensis,* of E North America, whose thick yellow rootstock contains such alkaloids as berberine and hydrastine and was formerly used medicinally.

golden section *or* **mean** NOUN the proportion of the two divisions of a straight line or the two dimensions of a plane figure such that the smaller is to the larger as the larger is to the sum of the two. If the sides of a rectangle are in this proportion and a square is constructed internally on the shorter side, the rectangle that remains will also have sides in the same proportion. Compare **golden ratio.**

golden share NOUN a share in a company that controls at least 51% of the voting rights, esp one retained by the UK government in some privatization issues.

Golden Starfish NOUN an award given to a bathing beach that meets EU standards of cleanliness.

golden syrup NOUN *Brit* a light golden-coloured treacle produced by the evaporation of cane sugar juice, used to sweeten and flavour cakes, puddings, etc.

golden triangle NOUN **the.** an opium-producing area of SE Asia, comprising parts of Myanmar, Laos, and Thailand. [2] any more or less triangular area or region noted for its success, prosperity, influence, etc. [3] *Maths* a triangle which has two 72-degree angles and one 36-degree angle.

golden wattle NOUN [1] an Australian yellow-flowered leguminous plant, *Acacia pycnantha,* that yields a useful gum and bark. [2] any of several similar and related plants, esp *Acacia longifolia* of Australia.

gold-exchange standard NOUN a monetary system by which one country's currency, which is not itself based on the gold standard, is kept at a par with another currency that is based on the gold standard.

goldeye (ˈɡəʊldˌaɪ) NOUN, *plural* **-eyes** *or* **-eye.** a North American clupeoid fish, *Hiodon alosoides,* with yellowish eyes, silvery sides, and a dark blue back: family *Hiodontidae* (mooneyes).

goldfinch (ˈɡəʊldˌfɪntʃ) NOUN [1] a common European finch, *Carduelis carduelis,* the adult of which has a red-and-white face and yellow-and-black wings. [2] any of several North American finches of the genus *Spinus,* esp the yellow-and-black species *S. tristis.*

goldfinny (ˈɡəʊldˌfɪnɪ) NOUN, *plural* **-nies.** another name for **goldsinny.**

goldfish (ˈɡəʊldˌfɪʃ) NOUN, *plural* **-fish** *or* **-fishes.** [1] a freshwater cyprinid fish, *Carassius auratus,* of E Europe and Asia, esp China, widely introduced as a pond or aquarium fish. It resembles the carp and has a typically golden or orange-red coloration. [2] any of certain similar ornamental fishes, esp the golden orfe (see **orfe**).

goldfish bowl NOUN [1] Also called: **fishbowl.** a glass bowl, typically spherical, in which fish are kept as pets. [2] a place or situation open to observation by onlookers.

gold foil NOUN thin gold sheet that is thicker than gold leaf.

goldilocks (ˈɡəʊldɪˌlɒks) NOUN (*functioning as singular*) [1] a Eurasian plant, *Aster linosyris* (or *Linosyris vulgaris*), with clusters of small yellow flowers: family *Asteraceae* (composites). [2] a Eurasian ranunculaceous woodland plant, *Ranunculus auricomus,* with yellow flowers. See also **buttercup.** [3] (*sometimes capital*) a person, esp a girl, with light blond hair. [4] (*modifier; sometimes capital*) not prone to extremes of temperature, volatility, etc.: *a goldilocks planet; a goldilocks economy.*
▷ **HISTORY** (for sense 4): C20: from the fairy tale *Goldilocks and the Three Bears,* in which the heroine prefers the porridge that is neither too hot nor too cold

gold leaf NOUN very thin gold sheet with a thickness usually between 0.076 and 0.127 micrometre, produced by rolling or hammering gold and used for gilding woodwork, etc.

gold medal NOUN a medal of gold, awarded to the winner of a competition or race. Compare **silver medal, bronze medal.**

gold mine NOUN [1] a place where gold ore is mined. [2] a source of great wealth, profit, etc.
▸ **ˈgold-ˌminer** NOUN ▸ **ˈgold-ˌmining** NOUN

gold note NOUN (in the US) another name for **gold certificate.**

gold-of-pleasure NOUN a yellow-flowered Eurasian plant, *Camelina sativa,* widespread as a weed, esp in flax fields, and formerly cultivated for its oil-rich seeds: family *Brassicaceae* (crucifers).

gold-plate VERB (*tr*) to coat (other metal) with gold, usually by electroplating.

gold plate NOUN [1] a thin coating of gold, usually produced by electroplating. [2] vessels or utensils made of gold.

gold point NOUN *Finance* either of two exchange rates (the **gold export point** and the **gold import point**) at which it is as cheap to settle international accounts by exporting or importing gold bullion as by selling or buying bills of exchange. Also called: **specie point.**

gold record NOUN a former name for **gold disc.**

gold reserve NOUN the gold reserved by a central bank to support domestic credit expansion, to cover balance of payments deficits, and to protect currency.

gold rush NOUN a large-scale migration of people to a territory where gold has been found.

goldsinny ('gəʊldˌsɪnɪ) NOUN, *plural* **-nies.** any of various small European wrasses, esp the brightly coloured *Ctenolabrus rupestris.* Also called: **goldfinny.**
▷HISTORY origin obscure, but probably has reference to the colour of the fins and tail

goldsmith ('gəʊldˌsmɪθ) NOUN 1 **a** a dealer in articles made of gold. **b** an artisan who makes such articles. 2 (formerly) a dealer or manufacturer of gold articles who also engaged in banking or other financial business. 3 (in Malaysia) a Chinese jeweller.

goldsmith beetle NOUN any of various scarabaeid beetles that have a metallic golden lustre, esp the rose chafer.

gold standard NOUN 1 a monetary system in which the unit of currency is defined with reference to gold. 2 the supreme example of something against which others are judged or measured: *the current gold standard for breast cancer detection.*

Gold Stick NOUN (*sometimes not capitals*) 1 a gilt rod carried by the colonel of the Life Guards or the captain of the gentlemen-at-arms. 2 the bearer of this rod.

goldstone ('gəʊldˌstəʊn) NOUN another name for **aventurine** (senses 2, 3).

goldtail moth ('gəʊldˌteɪl) NOUN a European moth, *Euproctis chrysorrhoea* (or *similis*), having white wings and a soft white furry body with a yellow tail tuft: its hairy caterpillars are known as palmer worms: family *Lymantriidae.* Also called: **yellowtail, yellowtail moth.**

goldthread ('gəʊldˌθrɛd) NOUN 1 a North American woodland ranunculaceous plant, *Coptis trifolia* (or *C. groenlandica*), with slender yellow roots. 2 the root of this plant, which yields a medicinal tonic and a dye.

gold tranche NOUN former name for **reserve tranche.**

golem ('gəʊlɛm) NOUN (in Jewish legend) an artificially created human being brought to life by supernatural means.
▷HISTORY from Yiddish *goylem,* from Hebrew *gōlem* formless thing

golf (gɒlf) NOUN 1 **a** a game played on a large open course, the object of which is to hit a ball using clubs, with as few strokes as possible, into each of usually 18 holes. **b** (*as modifier*): *a golf bag.* ♦ VERB 2 (*intr*) to play golf.
▷HISTORY C15: perhaps from Middle Dutch *colf* CLUB

Golf (gɒlf) NOUN *Communications* a code word for the letter *g.*

golf ball NOUN 1 a small resilient, usually white, ball of either two-piece or three-piece construction, the former consisting of a solid inner core with a thick covering of toughened material, the latter consisting of a liquid centre, rubber-wound core, and a thin layer of balata. 2 (in some electric typewriters) a small detachable metal sphere, around the surface of which type characters are arranged.

golf cart NOUN 1 a small motorized vehicle for transporting golfers and their equipment round a golf course. 2 a two-wheeled trolley with a long handle used for carrying golf clubs.

golf club NOUN 1 any of various long-shafted clubs with wood or metal heads used to strike a golf ball. 2 **a** an association of golf players, usually having its own course and facilities. **b** the premises of such an association.

golf course NOUN a general term for an area of ground, either inland or beside the sea, laid out for the playing of golf.

golfer ('gɒlfə) NOUN 1 a person who plays golf. 2 a type of cardigan.

golfer's elbow NOUN a painful inflammation of the muscles on the inside of the forearm caused by exertion in playing golf.

golf links PLURAL NOUN a large open undulating stretch of land beside the sea laid out for the playing of golf. See also **links.**

Golgi body, apparatus, *or* **complex** NOUN a membranous complex of vesicles, vacuoles, and flattened sacs in the cytoplasm of most cells: involved in intracellular secretion and transport.
▷HISTORY C20: named after Camillo *Golgi* (1844–1926), Italian neurologist and histologist

Golgotha ('gɒlgəθə) NOUN 1 another name for **Calvary.** 2 (*sometimes not capital*) *Now rare* a place of burial.
▷HISTORY C17: from Late Latin, from Greek, from Aramaic, based on Hebrew *gulgōleth* skull

goliard ('gəʊljəd) NOUN one of a number of wandering scholars in 12th- and 13th-century Europe famed for their riotous behaviour, intemperance, and composition of satirical and ribald Latin verse.
▷HISTORY C15: from Old French *goliart* glutton, from Latin *gula* gluttony
▸**goliardic** (gəʊl'jɑːdɪk) ADJECTIVE

goliardery (gəʊl'jɑːdərɪ) NOUN the poems of the goliards.

Goliath (gə'laɪəθ) NOUN *Old Testament* a Philistine giant from Gath who terrorized the Hebrews until he was killed by David with a stone from his sling (I Samuel 17).

Goliathan (gə'laɪəθən) ADJECTIVE huge; gigantic.

goliath beetle NOUN any very large tropical scarabaeid beetle of the genus *Goliathus,* esp *G. giganteus* of Africa, which may grow to a length of 20 centimetres.

goliath frog NOUN the largest living frog, *Rana goliath,* which occurs in the Congo region of Africa and can grow to a length of 30 centimetres.

golliwog *or* **golliwogg** ('gɒlɪˌwɒg) NOUN a soft doll with a black face, usually made of cloth or rags.
▷HISTORY C19: from the name of a doll character in children's books by Bertha Upton (died 1912), US writer, and Florence Upton (died 1922), US illustrator

gollop ('gɒləp) VERB to eat or drink (something) quickly or greedily.
▷HISTORY dialect variant of GULP
▸'**golloper** NOUN

golly[1] ('gɒlɪ) INTERJECTION an exclamation of mild surprise or wonder.
▷HISTORY C19: originally a euphemism for GOD

golly[2] ('gɒlɪ) NOUN, *plural* **-lies.** *Brit informal* short for **golliwog**: used chiefly by children.

golly[3] ('gɒlɪ) *Austral slang* ♦ VERB **-lies, -lying, -lied.** 1 to spit. ♦ NOUN, *plural* **-lies.** 2 a gob of spit.
▷HISTORY C20: altered from *gollion* a gob of phlegm, probably of imitative origin

goloshes (gə'lɒʃɪz) PLURAL NOUN a less common spelling of **galoshes.**

GOM ABBREVIATION FOR Grand Old Man: used to describe an old and respected person or institution.

gombeenism ('gɒmbiːnɪzəm) NOUN *Irish* the practice of usury.
▷HISTORY C19: from Irish Gaelic *gaimbín* interest on a loan, from Middle English *cambie* exchange, barter, from Latin *cambium*

gombeen-man ('gɒmbiːnˌmæn) NOUN *Irish* a shopkeeper who practises usury.

gombroon (gɒm'bruːn) NOUN Persian and Chinese pottery and porcelain wares.
▷HISTORY C17: named after *Gombroon,* Iran, from which it was originally exported

Gomel (*Russian* 'gɔmɪlj) NOUN an industrial city in SE Belarus, on the River Sozh; an industrial centre. Pop.: 513 000 (1998 est.).

gomeril ('gɒmərɪl) NOUN *Scot* a slow-witted or stupid person.
▷HISTORY C19: of uncertain origin

Gomorrah *or* **Gomorrha** (gə'mɒrə) NOUN 1 *Old Testament* one of two ancient cities near the Dead Sea, the other being Sodom, that were destroyed by God as a punishment for the wickedness of their inhabitants (Genesis 19:24). 2 any place notorious for vice and depravity.
▸**Go'morrean** *or* **Go'morrhean** ADJECTIVE

gomphosis (gɒm'fəʊsɪs) NOUN, *plural* **-ses** (-siːz). *Anatomy* a form of immovable articulation in which a peglike part fits into a cavity, as in the setting of a tooth in its socket.
▷HISTORY C16: from New Latin, from Greek *gomphoein* to bolt together, from *gomphos* tooth, peg

gomuti *or* **gomuti palm** (gə'muːtɪ) NOUN, *plural* **gomutis** *or* **gomuti palms.** 1 an East Indian feather palm, *Arenga pinnata,* whose sweet sap is a source of sugar. 2 a black wiry fibre obtained from the leafstalks of this plant, used for making rope, etc. 3 a Malaysian sago palm, *Metroxylon sagu.*
▷HISTORY from Malay *gĕmuti*

gon- COMBINING FORM a variant of **gono-** before a vowel: *gonidium.*

-gon NOUN COMBINING FORM indicating a figure having a specified number of angles: *pentagon.*
▷HISTORY from Greek *-gōnon,* from *gōnia* angle

gonad ('gɒnæd) NOUN an animal organ in which gametes are produced, such as a testis or an ovary. 2 *Slang* a foolish or stupid person.
▷HISTORY C19: from New Latin *gonas,* from Greek *gonos* seed
▸'**gonadal** *or* **gonadial** (gɒ'neɪdɪəl) *or* **go'nadic** ADJECTIVE

gonadotrophin (ˌgɒnədəʊ'trəʊfɪn) *or* **gonadotropin** (ˌgɒnədəʊ'trəʊpɪn) NOUN any of several glycoprotein hormones secreted by the pituitary gland and placenta that stimulate the gonads and control reproductive activity. See **chorionic gonadotrophin, follicle-stimulating hormone, luteinizing hormone, prolactin.**
▸ˌ**gonado'trophic** *or* ˌ**gonado'tropic** ADJECTIVE

Gonaïves (*French* gɔnaiv) NOUN a port in W Haiti, on the **Gulf of Gonaïves;** scene of the proclamation of Haiti's independence (1804). Pop.: 63 291 (1992).

Gond (gɒnd) NOUN a member of a formerly tribal people now living in scattered enclaves throughout S central India.

Gondar ('gɒndɑː) NOUN a city in NW Ethiopia: capital of Ethiopia from the 17th century until 1868. Pop.: 112 249 (1999 est.).

Gondi ('gɒndɪ) NOUN the language or group of languages spoken by the Gonds, belonging to the Dravidian family of languages.

gondola ('gɒndələ) NOUN 1 a long narrow flat-bottomed boat with a high ornamented stem and a platform at the stern where an oarsman stands and propels the boat by sculling or punting: traditionally used on the canals of Venice. 2 **a** a car or cabin suspended from an airship or balloon. **b** a moving cabin suspended from a cable across a valley, etc. 3 a flat-bottomed barge used on canals and rivers of the US as far west as the Mississippi. 4 *US and Canadian* a low open flat-bottomed railway goods wagon. 5 a set of island shelves in a self-service shop: used for displaying goods. 6 *Canadian* a broadcasting booth built close to the roof over an ice-hockey arena, used by commentators.
▷HISTORY C16: from Italian (Venetian dialect), from Medieval Latin *gondula,* perhaps ultimately from Greek *kondu* drinking vessel

gondolier (ˌgɒndə'lɪə) NOUN a man who propels a gondola.

Gondwanaland (gɒnd'wɑːnəˌlænd) *or* **Gondwana** NOUN one of the two ancient supercontinents produced by the first split of the even larger supercontinent Pangaea about 200 million years ago, comprising chiefly what are now Africa, South America, Australia, Antarctica, and the Indian subcontinent.
▷HISTORY C19: from *Gondwana* region in central north India, where the rock series was originally found

gone (gɒn) VERB 1 the past participle of **go**[1]. ♦ ADJECTIVE (*usually postpositive*) 2 ended; past. 3 lost; ruined (esp in the phrases **gone goose** *or* **gosling**). 4 dead or near to death. 5 spent; consumed; used up. 6 *Informal* faint or weak. 7 *Informal* having been pregnant (for a specified time): *six months gone.* 8 (usually foll by *on*) *Slang* in love (with). 9 *Slang* in an exhilarated state, as through music or the use of drugs. 10 **gone out.** *Informal* blankly and without comprehension, as if stupefied in surprise. ♦ ADVERB 11 past: *it's gone midnight.*

goner ('gɒnə) NOUN *Slang* a person or thing beyond help or recovery, esp a person who is dead or about to die.

gonfalon ('gɒnfələn) *or* **gonfanon** ('gɒnfənən)

NOUN 1 a banner hanging from a crossbar, used esp by certain medieval Italian republics or in ecclesiastical processions. 2 a battle flag suspended crosswise on a staff, usually having a serrated edge to give the appearance of streamers.
▷HISTORY C16: from Old Italian *gonfalone,* from Old French *gonfalon,* of Germanic origin; compare Old English *gūthfana* war banner, Old Norse *gunnfani*

gonfalonier (ˌgɒnfələˈnɪə) NOUN the chief magistrate or other official of a medieval Italian republic, esp the bearer of the republic's gonfalon.

gong (gɒŋ) NOUN 1 Also called: **tam-tam.** a percussion instrument of indefinite pitch, consisting of a metal platelike disc struck with a soft-headed drumstick. 2 a rimmed metal disc, hollow metal hemisphere, or metal strip, tube, or wire that produces a note when struck. It may be used to give alarm signals when operated electromagnetically. 3 a fixed saucer-shaped bell, as on an alarm clock, struck by a mechanically operated hammer. 4 *Brit slang* a medal, esp a military one. ◆ VERB 5 (*intr*) to sound a gong. 6 (*tr*) (of traffic police) to summon (a driver) to stop by sounding a gong.
▷HISTORY C17: from Malay, of imitative origin
▸ˈ**gong,like** ADJECTIVE

Gongorism (ˈgɒŋgəˌrɪzəm) NOUN 1 an affected literary style characterized by intricate language and obscurity. 2 an example of this.
▷HISTORY C19: from Spanish *gongorismo;* named after Luis de Góngora y Argote (1561–1627), Spanish lyric poet, noted for his exaggerated pedantic style
▸ˈ**Gongorist** NOUN ▸ˌ**Gongoˈristic** ADJECTIVE

gongyo (ˈgɒngjəʊ) NOUN (in Nichiren Buddhism) a ceremony, performed twice a day, involving reciting parts of the Lotus Sutra and chanting the Daimoku to the Gohonzon.
▷HISTORY from Japanese, literally: assiduous practice

goniatite (ˈgəʊnɪəˌtaɪt) NOUN any extinct cephalopod mollusc of the genus *Goniatites* and related genera, similar to ammonites: a common fossil of Devonian and Carboniferous rocks.
▷HISTORY C19: from Greek *gōnia* angle, referring to the angular sutures in some species + -ITE[1]

gonidium (gəˈnɪdɪəm) NOUN, *plural* **-ia** (-ɪə). 1 a green algal cell in the thallus of a lichen. 2 an asexual reproductive cell in some colonial algae.
▷HISTORY C19: from New Latin, diminutive from GONO-
▸**goˈnidial** *or* **goˈnidic** ADJECTIVE

goniometer (ˌgəʊnɪˈɒmɪtə) NOUN 1 an instrument for measuring the angles between the faces of a crystal. 2 an instrument consisting of a transformer circuit connected to two directional aerials, used to determine the bearing of a distant radio station.
▷HISTORY C18: via French from Greek *gōnia* angle
▸**goniometric** (ˌgəʊnɪəˈmɛtrɪk) *or* ˌ**gonioˈmetrical** ADJECTIVE ▸ˌ**gonioˈmetrically** ADVERB ▸ˌ**goniˈometry** NOUN

gonion (ˈgəʊnɪən) NOUN, *plural* **-nia** (-nɪə). *Anatomy* the point or apex of the angle of the lower jaw.
▷HISTORY C19: from New Latin, from Greek *gōnia* angle

gonioscope (ˈgəʊnɪəʊˌskəʊp) NOUN an instrument used for examining the structures of the eye between the cornea and the lens that are not directly visible.

-gonium NOUN COMBINING FORM indicating a seed or reproductive cell: *archegonium.*
▷HISTORY from New Latin *gonium,* from Greek *gonos* seed

gonk (gɒŋk) NOUN a stuffed toy, often used as a mascot.

gonna (ˈgɒnə) VERB *Slang* ◆ CONTRACTION OF going to.

gono- *or before a vowel* **gon-** COMBINING FORM sexual or reproductive: *gonorrhoea.*
▷HISTORY New Latin, from Greek *gonos* seed

gonococcus (ˌgɒnəʊˈkɒkəs) NOUN, *plural* **-cocci** (-ˈkɒksaɪ). a spherical Gram-negative bacterium, *Neisseria gonorrhoeae,* that causes gonorrhoea: family *Neisseriaceae.*
▸ˌ**gonoˈcoccal** *or* ˌ**gonoˈcoccic** ADJECTIVE ▸ˌ**gonoˈcoccoid** ADJECTIVE

gonocyte (ˈgɒnəʊˌsaɪt) NOUN an oocyte or spermatocyte.

gonoduct (ˈgɒnəʊˌdʌkt) NOUN *Zoology* a duct leading from a gonad to the exterior, through which gametes pass.

gonof *or* **gonif** (ˈgɒnəf) NOUN a variant of **ganef.**

gonophore (ˈgɒnəʊˌfɔː) NOUN 1 *Zoology* a polyp in certain coelenterates that bears gonads. 2 *Botany* an elongated structure in certain flowers that bears the stamens and pistil above the level of the other flower parts.
▸**gonophoric** (ˌgɒnəʊˈfɒrɪk) *or* **gonophorous** (gəʊˈnɒfərəs) ADJECTIVE

gonopod (ˈgɒnəʊˌpɒd) NOUN *Zoology* either member of a pair of appendages that are the external reproductive organs of insects and some other arthropods.

gonopore (ˈgɒnəˌpɔː) NOUN an external pore in insects, earthworms, etc., through which the gametes are extruded.

gonorrhoea *or esp US* **gonorrhea** (ˌgɒnəˈrɪə) NOUN an infectious venereal disease caused by a gonococcus, characterized by a burning sensation when urinating and a mucopurulent discharge from the urethra or vagina.
▷HISTORY C16: from Late Latin, from Greek, from *gonos* seed + *rhoia* flux, flow
▸ˌ**gonorˈrhoeal** *or* ˌ**gonorˈrhoeic** *or* (*esp US*) ˌ**gonorˈrheal** *or* ˌ**gonorˈrheic** ADJECTIVE

gonosome (ˈgɒnəʊˌsəʊm) NOUN *Zoology* the individuals, collectively, in a colonial animal that are involved with reproduction.

-gony NOUN COMBINING FORM genesis, origin, or production: *cosmogony.*
▷HISTORY from Latin *-gonia,* from Greek, *-goneia,* from *gonos* seed, procreation

gonzo (ˈgɒnzəʊ) ADJECTIVE *Slang* 1 wild or crazy. 2 (of journalism) explicitly including the writer's feelings at the time of witnessing the events or undergoing the experiences written about.
▷HISTORY C20: perhaps from Italian, literally: fool, or Spanish *ganso* idiot, bumpkin (literally: goose)

goo (guː) NOUN *Informal* 1 a sticky or viscous substance. 2 coy or sentimental language or ideas.
▷HISTORY C20: of uncertain origin

goober *or* **goober pea** (ˈguːbə) NOUN another name for **peanut.**
▷HISTORY C19: of African (Angolan) origin; related to Kongo *nguba*

gooby (ˈguːbɪ) NOUN, *plural* **goobies.** *NZ informal* spittle.

good (gʊd) ADJECTIVE **better, best.** 1 having admirable, pleasing, superior, or positive qualities; not negative, bad or mediocre: *a good idea; a good teacher.* 2 **a** morally excellent or admirable; virtuous; righteous: *a good man.* **b** (*as collective noun; preceded by the*): *the good.* 3 suitable or efficient for a purpose: *a good secretary; a good winter coat.* 4 beneficial or advantageous: *vegetables are good for you.* 5 not ruined or decayed; sound or whole: *the meat is still good.* 6 kindly, generous, or approving: *you are good to him.* 7 right or acceptable: *your qualifications are good for the job.* 8 rich and fertile: *good land.* 9 valid or genuine: *I would not do this without good reason.* 10 honourable or held in high esteem: *a good family.* 11 commercially or financially secure, sound, or safe: *good securities; a good investment.* 12 (of a draft) drawn for a stated sum. 13 (of debts) expected to be fully paid. 14 clever, competent, or talented: *he's good at science.* 15 obedient or well-behaved: *a good dog.* 16 reliable, safe, or recommended: *a good make of clothes.* 17 affording material pleasure or indulgence: *the good things in life; the good life.* 18 having a well-proportioned, beautiful, or generally fine appearance: *a good figure; a good complexion.* 19 complete; full: *I took a good look round the house.* 20 propitious; opportune: *a good time to ask the manager for a rise.* 21 satisfying or gratifying: *a good rest.* 22 comfortable: *did you have a good night?* 23 newest or of the best quality: *to keep the good plates for important guests.* 24 fairly large, extensive, or long: *a good distance away.* 25 sufficient; ample: *we have a good supply of food.* 26 *US* (of meat) of the third government grade, above *standard* and below *choice.* 27 serious or intellectual: *good music.* 28 used in a traditional description: *the good ship "America".* 29 used in polite or patronizing phrases or to express anger (often intended ironically): *how is your good lady?; look here, my good man!* 30 **a good one. a** an unbelievable assertion. **b** a very funny joke. 31 **as good as.** virtually; practically: *it's as good as finished.* 32 **as good as gold.** excellent; very good indeed. 33 **be as** *or* **so good as to.** would you please. 34 **come good.** to recover and perform well after a bad start or setback. 35 **good and.** *Informal* (intensifier): *good and mad.* 36 (intensifier; used in mild oaths): *good grief!; good heavens!* ◆ INTERJECTION 37 an exclamation of approval, agreement, pleasure, etc. ◆ NOUN 38 moral or material advantage or use; benefit or profit: *for the good of our workers; what is the good of worrying?* 39 positive moral qualities; goodness; virtue; righteousness; piety. 40 (*sometimes capital*) moral qualities seen as a single abstract entity: *we must pursue the Good.* 41 a good thing. 42 *Economics* a commodity or service that satisfies a human need. 43 **for good (and all).** forever; permanently: *I have left them for good.* 44 **make good. a** to recompense or repair damage or injury. **b** to be successful. **c** to demonstrate or prove the truth of (a statement or accusation). **d** to secure and retain (a position). **e** to effect or fulfil (something intended or promised). 45 **good on** *or* **for you (him,** etc.**).** well done, well said, etc.: a term of congratulation. 46 **get any** (*or* **some**) **good of.** *Irish* **a** to handle to good effect: *I never got any good of this machine.* **b** to understand properly: *I could never get any good of him.* **c** to receive cooperation from. ◆ See also **goods.**
▷HISTORY Old English *gōd;* related to Old Norse *gōthr,* Old High German *guot* good
▸ˈ**goodish** ADJECTIVE

good afternoon SENTENCE SUBSTITUTE a conventional expression of greeting or farewell used in the afternoon.

Good Book NOUN a name for the **Bible.** Also called: **the Book.**

goodbye (ˌgʊdˈbaɪ) SENTENCE SUBSTITUTE 1 farewell: a conventional expression used at leave-taking or parting with people and at the loss or rejection of things or ideas. ◆ NOUN 2 a leave-taking; parting: *they prolonged their goodbyes for a few more minutes.* 3 a farewell: *they said goodbyes to each other.*
▷HISTORY C16: contraction of *God be with ye*

good day SENTENCE SUBSTITUTE a conventional expression of greeting or farewell used during the day.

good evening SENTENCE SUBSTITUTE a conventional expression of greeting or farewell used in the evening.

good-for-nothing NOUN 1 an irresponsible or worthless person. ◆ ADJECTIVE 2 irresponsible; worthless.

Good Friday NOUN the Friday before Easter, observed as a commemoration of the Crucifixion of Jesus.

good hair NOUN *Caribbean* hair showing evidence of some European strain in a person's blood.

Good Hope NOUN **Cape of.** See **Cape of Good Hope.**

good-humoured ADJECTIVE being in or expressing a pleasant, tolerant, and kindly state of mind.
▸ˌ**good-ˈhumouredly** ADVERB ▸ˌ**good-ˈhumouredness** NOUN

goodies (ˈgʊdɪz) PLURAL NOUN any objects, rewards, prizes, etc., considered particularly desirable, attractive, or pleasurable.

Good King Henry NOUN a weedy edible chenopodiaceous plant, *Chenopodium bonus-henricus,* of N Europe, W Asia, and North America, having arrow-shaped leaves and clusters of small green flowers.

good-looker NOUN a handsome or pretty person.

good-looking ADJECTIVE handsome or pretty.

good looks PLURAL NOUN personal attractiveness or beauty.

goodly (ˈgʊdlɪ) ADJECTIVE **-lier, -liest.** 1 considerable: *a goodly amount of money.* 2 *Obsolete* attractive, pleasing, or fine: *a goodly man.*
▸ˈ**goodliness** NOUN

goodman (ˈgʊdmən) NOUN, *plural* **-men.** *Archaic* 1 a husband. 2 a man not of gentle birth: used as a title. 3 a master of a household.

good morning SENTENCE SUBSTITUTE a conventional expression of greeting or farewell used in the morning.

good-natured ADJECTIVE of a tolerant and kindly disposition.
▸ˌ**good-ˈnaturedly** ADVERB ▸ˌ**good-ˈnaturedness** NOUN

goodness (ˈgʊdnɪs) NOUN 1 the state or quality

of being good. 2 generosity; kindness. 3 moral excellence; piety; virtue. ◆ INTERJECTION 4 a euphemism for **God**: used as an exclamation of surprise (often in phrases such as **goodness knows!**, **thank goodness!**).

goodness of fit NOUN *Statistics* the extent to which observed sample values of a variable approximate to values derived from a theoretical density, often measured by a chi-square test.

good night SENTENCE SUBSTITUTE a conventional expression of farewell, or, rarely, of greeting, used in the late afternoon, the evening, or at night, esp when departing to bed.

good-oh *or* **good-o** ('gʊd'əʊ) *Informal* ◆ INTERJECTION 1 *Brit and Austral* an exclamation of pleasure, agreement, approval, etc. ◆ ADJECTIVE, ADVERB 2 *Austral* all right: *it was good-oh; I was getting on good-oh.*

good oil NOUN (usually preceded by *the*) *Austral slang* true or reliable facts, information, etc.

good ol' boy NOUN *Informal* **a** a man considered as being trustworthy and dependable because of his ordinary and down-to-earth background and upbringing. **b** (*as modifier*): *he was expected to bring some good-ol'-boy informality to the White House.*

good people PLURAL NOUN **the.** *Folklore* fairies.

good question NOUN a question that is hard to answer immediately.

goods (gʊdz) PLURAL NOUN 1 possessions and personal property. 2 (*sometimes singular*) *Economics* commodities that are tangible, usually movable, and generally not consumed at the same time as they are produced. Compare **services.** 3 articles of commerce; merchandise. 4 *Chiefly Brit* **a** merchandise when transported, esp by rail; freight. **b** (*as modifier*): *a goods train.* 5 **the goods.** **a** *Informal* that which is expected or promised: *to deliver the goods.* **b** *Slang* the real thing. **c** *US and Canadian slang* incriminating evidence (esp in the phrase **have the goods on someone**). 6 **a piece of goods.** *Slang* a person, esp a woman.

Good Samaritan NOUN 1 *New Testament* a figure in one of Christ's parables (Luke 10:30–37) who is an example of compassion towards those in distress. 2 a kindly person who helps another in difficulty or distress.

goods and chattels PLURAL NOUN any property that is not freehold, usually limited to include only moveable property.

Good Shepherd NOUN *New Testament* a title given to Jesus Christ in John 10:11–12.

good-sized ADJECTIVE quite large.

good sort NOUN *Informal* 1 a person of a kindly and likable disposition. 2 *Austral* an agreeable or attractive woman.

good-tempered ADJECTIVE of a kindly and generous disposition.

good-time ADJECTIVE (of a person) wildly seeking pleasure.

good turn NOUN a helpful and friendly act; good deed; favour.

goodwife ('gʊd,waɪf) NOUN, *plural* **-wives.** *Archaic* 1 the mistress of a household. 2 a woman not of gentle birth: used as a title.

goodwill (,gʊd'wɪl) NOUN 1 a feeling of benevolence, approval, and kindly interest. 2 (*modifier*) resulting from, showing, or designed to show goodwill: *the government sent a goodwill mission to Moscow; a goodwill ambassador for UNICEF.* 3 willingness or acquiescence. 4 *Accounting* an intangible asset taken into account in assessing the value of an enterprise and reflecting its commercial reputation, customer connections, etc.

Goodwin Sands ('gʊdwɪn) PLURAL NOUN a dangerous stretch of shoals at the entrance to the Strait of Dover: separated from the E coast of Kent by the Downs roadstead.

Goodwood ('gʊd,wʊd) NOUN an area in SE England, in Sussex: site of a famous racecourse and of **Goodwood House,** built 1780–1800.

goody[1] ('gʊdɪ) INTERJECTION 1 a child's exclamation of pleasure and approval. ◆ NOUN, *plural* **goodies.** 2 short for **goody-goody.** 3 *Informal* the hero in a film, book, etc. 4 something particularly pleasant to have or (often) to eat. See also **goodies.**

goody[2] ('gʊdɪ) NOUN, *plural* **goodies.** *Archaic or literary* a married woman of low rank: used as a title: *Goody Two-Shoes.*
▷**HISTORY** C16: shortened from GOODWIFE

goody-goody NOUN, *plural* **-goodies.** 1 a smugly virtuous or sanctimonious person. ◆ ADJECTIVE 2 smug and sanctimonious.

gooey ('gu:ɪ) ADJECTIVE **gooier, gooiest.** *Informal* 1 sticky, soft, and often sweet. 2 oversweet and sentimental.
▸ **'gooily** ADVERB

goof (gu:f) *Informal* ◆ NOUN 1 a foolish error or mistake. 2 a stupid person. ◆ VERB 3 to bungle (something); botch. 4 (*intr;* often foll by *about* or *around*) to fool (around); mess (about). 5 (*tr*) to dope with drugs. 6 (*intr;* often foll by *off*) *US and Canadian* to waste time; idle.
▷**HISTORY** C20: probably from (dialect) *goff* simpleton, from Old French *goffe* clumsy, from Italian *goffo,* of obscure origin

goofball ('gu:f,bɔ:l) NOUN *US and Canadian slang* 1 a barbiturate sleeping pill. 2 a fool.

go off VERB (*intr*) 1 (*adverb*) (of power, a water supply, etc.) to cease to be available, running, or functioning: *the lights suddenly went off.* 2 (*adverb*) to be discharged or activated; explode. 3 (*adverb*) to occur as specified: *the meeting went off well.* 4 to leave (a place): *the actors went off stage.* 5 (*adverb*) (of a sensation) to gradually cease to be felt or perceived. 6 (*adverb*) to fall asleep. 7 (*adverb*) to enter a specified state or condition: *she went off into hysterics.* 8 (*adverb;* foll by *with*) to abscond (with). 9 (*adverb*) (of concrete, mortar, etc.) to harden. 10 (*adverb*) *Brit informal* (of food, milk, etc.) to become stale or rotten. 11 (*preposition*) *Brit informal* to cease to like: *she went off him after their marriage.* 12 (*adverb*) *Informal* to become bad-tempered. 13 (*adverb*) *Slang* to have an orgasm. 14 (*adverb*) *Austral slang* (of premises) to be raided by the police. 15 (*adverb*) *Austral slang* (of a racehorse) to win a fixed race. 16 (*adverb*) *Austral slang* to be stolen.

goofy ('gu:fɪ) ADJECTIVE **goofier, goofiest.** *Informal* 1 foolish; silly; stupid. 2 *Brit* (of teeth) sticking out; protruding.
▸ **'goofily** ADVERB ▸ **'goofiness** NOUN

goofy-footer NOUN *Austral informal* a surfboard rider who stands with his right foot forward instead of his left foot forward.

goog (gʊg) NOUN *Austral informal* 1 an egg. 2 **full as a goog.** drunk.

google ('gu:gəl) VERB (*tr*) 1 to search for (something on the Internet) using a search engine. 2 to check (the credentials of someone) by searching for websites containing his or name.
▷**HISTORY** C20: from *Google,* a popular search engine on the World Wide Web

googly ('gu:glɪ) NOUN, *plural* **-lies.** *Cricket* an off break bowled with a leg break action.
▷**HISTORY** C20: Australian, of unknown origin

googol ('gu:gɒl, -gəl) NOUN the number represented as one followed by 100 zeros (10^{100}).
▷**HISTORY** C20: coined by E. Kasner (1878–1955), American mathematician

googolplex ('gu:gɒl,plɛks, -gəl-) NOUN the number represented as one followed by a googol (10^{100}) of zeros.
▷**HISTORY** C20: from GOOGOL + (DU)PLEX

gook (gʊk, gu:k) NOUN *US* 1 *Slang* a derogatory word for a person from a Far Eastern country. 2 *Informal* a messy sticky substance; muck.
▷**HISTORY** C20: of uncertain origin

Goole (gu:l) NOUN an inland port in NE England, in the East Riding of Yorkshire at the confluence of the Ouse and Don Rivers, 75 km (47 miles) from the North Sea. Pop.: 19 410 (1991).

goolie *or* **gooly** ('gu:lɪ) NOUN, *plural* **-lies.** 1 (*usually plural*) *Slang* a testicle. 2 *Austral slang* a stone or pebble.
▷**HISTORY** from Hindustani *goli* a ball, bullet

> **Language note** This word was formerly considered to be taboo, and it was labelled as such in previous editions of *Collins English Dictionary*. However, it has now become acceptable in speech, although some older or more conservative people may object to its use.

goon (gu:n) NOUN 1 a stupid or deliberately foolish person. 2 *US informal* a thug hired to commit acts of violence or intimidation, esp in an industrial dispute.
▷**HISTORY** C20: partly from dialect *gooney* fool, partly after the character Alice the *Goon,* created by E. C. Segar (1894–1938), American cartoonist

go on VERB (*intr, mainly adverb*) 1 to continue or proceed. 2 to happen or take place: *there's something peculiar going on here.* 3 (of power, water supply, etc.) to start running or functioning. 4 (*preposition*) to mount or board and ride on, esp as a treat: *children love to go on donkeys at the seaside.* 5 *Theatre* to make an entrance on stage. 6 to act or behave: *he goes on as though he's rich.* 7 to talk excessively; chatter. 8 to continue talking, esp after a short pause: *"When I am Prime Minister," he went on, "we shall abolish taxes.".* 9 (foll by *at*) to criticize or nag: *stop going on at me all the time!* 10 (*preposition*) to use as a basis for further thought or action: *the police had no evidence at all to go on in the murder case.* 11 (foll by *for*) *Brit* to approach (a time, age, amount, etc.): *he's going on for his hundredth birthday.* 12 *Cricket* to start to bowl. 13 to take one's turn. 14 (of clothes) to be capable of being put on. 15 **go much on.** (*used with a negative*) *Brit* to care for; like. 16 **something to go on** *or* **to be going on with.** something that is adequate for the present time. ◆ INTERJECTION 17 I don't believe what you're saying.

gooney bird ('gu:nɪ) NOUN an informal name for **albatross**, esp the black-footed albatross (*Diomedea nigripes*)
▷**HISTORY** C19 *gony* (originally sailors' slang), probably from dialect *gooney* fool, of obscure origin; compare GOON

goop (gu:p) NOUN *US and Canadian slang* 1 a rude or ill-mannered person. 2 any sticky or semiliquid substance.
▷**HISTORY** C20: coined by G. Burgess (1866–1951), American humorist
▸ **'goopy** ADJECTIVE

goorie *or* **goory** ('gu:rɪ) NOUN, *plural* **-ries.** See **kuri.**

goosander (gu:'sændə) NOUN a common merganser (a duck), *Mergus merganser,* of Europe and North America, having a dark head and white body in the male.
▷**HISTORY** C17: probably from GOOSE[1] + Old Norse *önd* (genitive *andar*) duck

goose[1] (gu:s) NOUN, *plural* **geese** (gi:s). 1 any of various web-footed long-necked birds of the family *Anatidae:* order *Anseriformes.* They are typically larger and less aquatic than ducks and are gregarious and migratory. Related adjective: **anserine.** See also **brent goose, barnacle goose, greylag, snow goose.** 2 the female of such a bird, as opposed to the male (gander). 3 *Informal* a silly person. 4 (*plural* **gooses**) a pressing iron with a long curving handle, used esp by tailors. 5 the flesh of the goose, used as food. 6 **all his geese are swans.** he constantly exaggerates the importance of a person or thing. 7 **cook someone's goose.** *Informal* **a** to spoil someone's plans. **b** to bring about someone's ruin, downfall, etc. 8 **kill the goose that lays the golden eggs.** to sacrifice future benefits for the sake of momentary present needs. See also **golden goose.**
▷**HISTORY** Old English *gōs;* related to Old Norse *gās,* Old High German *gans,* Old Irish *gēiss* swan, Greek *khēn,* Sanskrit *haṁsas*

goose[2] (gu:s) *Slang* ◆ VERB 1 (*tr*) to prod (a person) playfully in the behind. ◆ NOUN, *plural* **gooses.** 2 a playful prod in the behind.
▷**HISTORY** C19: from GOOSE[1], probably from a comparison with the jabbing of a goose's bill

goose barnacle NOUN any barnacle of the genus *Lepas,* living attached by a stalk to pieces of wood, having long feathery appendages (cirri) and flattened shells.

gooseberry ('gʊzbərɪ, -brɪ) NOUN, *plural* **-ries.** 1 a Eurasian shrub, *Ribes uva-crispa* (or *R. grossularia*), having greenish, purple-tinged flowers and ovoid yellow-green or red-purple berries: family *Grossulariaceae.* See also **currant** (sense 2). 2 **a** the berry of this plant. **b** (*as modifier*): *gooseberry jam.* 3 *Brit informal* an unwanted single person in a group of couples, esp a third person with a couple (often in the phrase **play gooseberry**). 4 **Cape gooseberry.** a tropical American solanaceous plant, *Physalis peruviana,* naturalized in southern Africa, having yellow flowers and edible yellow berries. See also **ground cherry.**

gooseberry bush NOUN [1] See **gooseberry** (sense 1). [2] **under a gooseberry bush.** used humorously in answering children's questions regarding their birth.

gooseberry stone NOUN another name for **grossularite.**

goosefish ('gu:sˌfɪʃ) NOUN, *plural* **-fish** *or* **-fishes.** *US* another name for **monkfish** (sense 1).

goose flesh NOUN the bumpy condition of the skin induced by cold, fear, etc., caused by contraction of the muscles at the base of the hair follicles with consequent erection of papillae: so called because of the resemblance to the skin of a freshly-plucked fowl. Also called: **goose bumps, goose pimples, goose skin.**

goosefoot ('gu:sˌfʊt) NOUN, *plural* **-foots.** any typically weedy chenopodiaceous plant of the genus *Chenopodium,* having small greenish flowers and leaves shaped like a goose's foot. See also **Good King Henry, fat hen.**

goosegog ('gʊzgɒg) *or* **goosegob** NOUN *Brit* a dialect or informal word for **gooseberry.**
▷**HISTORY** from *goose* in GOOSEBERRY + *gog,* variant of GOB[1]

goosegrass ('gu:sˌgrɑ:s) NOUN another name for **cleavers.**

gooseneck ('gu:sˌnɛk) NOUN [1] *Nautical* a pivot between the forward end of a boom and a mast, to allow the boom to swing freely. [2] something in the form of a neck of a goose.
▸ **'gooseˌnecked** ADJECTIVE

goose step NOUN [1] a military march step in which the leg is swung rigidly to an exaggerated height, esp as in the German army in the Third Reich. [2] an abnormal gait in animals. ◆ VERB **goose-step, -steps, -stepping, -stepped.** [3] (*intr*) to march in goose step.

goosy *or* **goosey** ('gu:sɪ) ADJECTIVE **goosier, goosiest.** [1] of or like a goose. [2] having goose flesh. [3] silly and foolish.
▸ **'goosiness** NOUN

go out VERB (*intr, adverb*) [1] to depart from a room, house, country, etc. [2] to cease to illuminate, burn, or function: *the fire has gone out.* [3] to cease to be fashionable or popular: *that style went out ages ago!* [4] to become unconscious or fall asleep: *she went out like a light.* [5] (of a broadcast) to be transmitted. [6] to go to entertainments, social functions, etc. [7] (usually foll by *with* or *together*) to associate (with a person of the opposite sex) regularly; date. [8] (of workers) to begin to strike. [9] (foll by *to*) to be extended (to): *our sympathy went out to her on the death of her sister.* [10] *Cards* to get rid of the last card, token, etc., in one's hand. [11] **go all out.** to make a great effort to achieve or obtain something: *he went all out to pass the exam.*

go over VERB (*intr*) [1] to be received in a specified manner: *the concert went over very well.* [2] (*preposition*) Also: **go through.** to examine and revise as necessary: *he went over the accounts.* [3] (*preposition*) Also: **go through.** to clean: *she went over the room before her mother came.* [4] (*preposition*) to check and repair: *can you go over my car please?* [5] (*preposition*) Also: **go through.** to rehearse: *I'll go over my lines before the play.* [6] (*adverb;* foll by *to*) **a** to change (to a different practice or system): *will Britain ever go over to driving on the right?* **b** to change one's allegiances. [7] (*preposition*) *Slang* to do physical violence to: *they went over him with an iron bar.*

GOP (in the US) ABBREVIATION FOR **Grand Old Party.**

gopak ('gəʊˌpæk) NOUN a spectacular high-leaping Russian peasant dance for men.
▷**HISTORY** from Russian, from Ukrainian *hopak,* from *hop!* a cry in the dance, from German *hopp!*

Go-Ped ('gəʊˌpɛd) NOUN *Trademark* a motorized vehicle consisting of a low footboard on wheels, steered by handlebars.

gopher ('gəʊfə) NOUN [1] Also called: **pocket gopher.** any burrowing rodent of the family *Geomyidae,* of North and Central America, having a thickset body, short legs, and cheek pouches. [2] another name for **ground squirrel.** [3] any burrowing tortoise of the genus *Gopherus,* of SE North America. [4] **gopher snake.** another name for **bull snake.**
▷**HISTORY** C19: shortened from earlier *megopher* or *magopher,* of obscure origin

gopherwood ('gəʊfəˌwʊd) NOUN *US* another name for **yellowwood** (sense 1).

gopher wood NOUN the wood used in the construction of Noah's ark, thought to be a type of cypress (Genesis 6:14).
▷**HISTORY** from Hebrew *gōpher*

Gorakhpur ('gɔ:rəkˌpʊə) NOUN a city in N India, in SE Uttar Pradesh: formerly an important Muslim garrison. Pop.: 505 566 (1991).

goral ('gɔ:rəl) NOUN a small goat antelope, *Naemorhedus goral,* inhabiting mountainous regions of S Asia. It has a yellowish-grey and black coat and small conical horns.
▷**HISTORY** C19: from Hindi, probably of Sanskrit origin

Gorbals ('gɔ:bəlz) NOUN **the.** a district of Glasgow, formerly known for its slums.

gorblimey (gɔ:'blaɪmɪ) INTERJECTION a variant of **cor blimey.**

gorcock ('gɔ:ˌkɒk) NOUN the male of the red grouse.
▷**HISTORY** C17: *gor-* (of unknown origin) + COCK[1]

Gordian knot ('gɔ:dɪən) NOUN [1] (in Greek legend) a complicated knot, tied by King Gordius of Phrygia, that Alexander the Great cut with a sword. [2] a complicated and intricate problem (esp in the phrase **cut the Gordian knot**).

Gordon setter NOUN a breed of large setter originating in Scotland, with a black-and-tan coat.
▷**HISTORY** C19: named after Alexander *Gordon* (1743–1827), Scottish nobleman who promoted this breed

gore[1] (gɔ:) NOUN [1] blood shed from a wound, esp when coagulated. [2] *Informal* killing, fighting, etc.
▷**HISTORY** Old English *gor* dirt; related to Old Norse *gor* half-digested food, Middle Low German *göre,* Dutch *goor*

gore[2] (gɔ:) VERB (*tr*) (of an animal, such as a bull) to pierce or stab (a person or another animal) with a horn or tusk.
▷**HISTORY** C16: probably from Old English *gār* spear

gore[3] (gɔ:) NOUN [1] a tapering or triangular piece of material used in making a shaped skirt, umbrella, etc. [2] a similarly shaped piece, esp of land. ◆ VERB [3] (*tr*) to make into or with a gore or gores.
▷**HISTORY** Old English *gāra;* related to Old Norse *geiri* gore, Old High German *gēro*
▸ **gored** ADJECTIVE

gorehound ('gɔ:ˌhaʊnd) NOUN an enthusiast of gory horror films.

Gore-Tex ('gɔ:ˌtɛks) NOUN *Trademark* a type of synthetic fabric which is waterproof yet allows the wearer's skin to breathe, used for sportswear.

gorge (gɔ:dʒ) NOUN [1] a deep ravine, esp one through which a river runs. [2] the contents of the stomach. [3] feelings of disgust or resentment (esp in the phrase **one's gorge rises**). [4] an obstructing mass: *an ice gorge.* [5] *Fortifications* **a** a narrow rear entrance to a work. **b** the narrow part of a bastion or outwork. [6] *Archaic* the throat or gullet. ◆ VERB *also* **engorge.** [7] (*intr*) *Falconry* (of hawks) to eat until the crop is completely full. [8] to swallow (food) ravenously. [9] (*tr*) to stuff (oneself) with food.
▷**HISTORY** C14: from Old French *gorger* to stuff, from *gorge* throat, from Late Latin *gurga,* modification of Latin *gurges* whirlpool
▸ **'gorgeable** ADJECTIVE ▸ **'gorger** NOUN

gorgeous ('gɔ:dʒəs) ADJECTIVE [1] strikingly beautiful or magnificent: *gorgeous array; a gorgeous girl.* [2] *Informal* extremely pleasing, fine, or good: *gorgeous weather.*
▷**HISTORY** C15: from Old French *gorgias* elegant, from *gorgias* wimple, from *gorge;* see GORGE
▸ **'gorgeously** ADVERB ▸ **'gorgeousness** NOUN

gorgerin ('gɔ:dʒərɪn) NOUN *Architect* another name for **necking.**
▷**HISTORY** C17: from French, from *gorge* throat; see GORGE

gorget ('gɔ:dʒɪt) NOUN [1] a collar-like piece of armour worn to protect the throat. [2] a part of a wimple worn by women to cover the throat and chest, esp in the 14th century. [3] a band of distinctive colour on the throat of an animal, esp a bird.
▷**HISTORY** C15: from Old French, from *gorge;* see GORGE
▸ **'gorgeted** ADJECTIVE

Gorgio ('gɔ:dʒəʊ, -dʒɪəʊ) NOUN, *plural* **-gios.** (*sometimes not capital*) a word used by Gypsies for a non-Gypsy.
▷**HISTORY** from Romany

Gorgon ('gɔ:gən) NOUN [1] *Greek myth* any of three winged monstrous sisters, Stheno, Euryale, and Medusa, who had live snakes for hair, huge teeth, and brazen claws. [2] (*often not capital*) *Informal* a fierce or unpleasant woman.
▷**HISTORY** via Latin *Gorgō* from Greek, from *gorgos* terrible

gorgoneion (ˌgɔ:gə'ni:ɒn) NOUN, *plural* **-neia** (-'ni:ə). a representation of a Gorgon's head, esp Medusa's.
▷**HISTORY** C19: from Greek, from *gorgoneios* of a GORGON

gorgonian (gɔ:'gəʊnɪən) NOUN [1] any coral of the order *Gorgonacea,* having a horny or calcareous branching skeleton: includes the sea fans and red corals. ◆ ADJECTIVE [2] of, relating to, or belonging to the *Gorgonacea.*

Gorgonian (gɔ:'gəʊnɪən) ADJECTIVE of or resembling a Gorgon.

Gorgonzola *or* **Gorgonzola cheese** (ˌgɔ:gən'zəʊlə) NOUN a semihard blue-veined cheese of sharp flavour, made from pressed milk.
▷**HISTORY** C19: named after *Gorgonzola,* Italian town where it originated

Gorica ('gɔritsa) NOUN the Serbo-Croat name for **Gorizia.**

gorilla (gə'rɪlə) NOUN [1] the largest anthropoid ape, *Gorilla gorilla,* inhabiting the forests of central W Africa. It is stocky and massive, with a short muzzle and coarse dark hair. [2] *Informal* a large, strong, and brutal-looking man.
▷**HISTORY** C19: New Latin, from Greek *Gorillai,* an African tribe renowned for their hirsute appearance
▸ **go'rilla-ˌlike** ADJECTIVE ▸ **go'rillian** *or* **gorilline** (gə'rɪlaɪn) ADJECTIVE ▸ **go'rilloid** ADJECTIVE

gorillagram (gə'rɪləˌgræm) NOUN *Informal* a jocular greetings message delivered to someone celebrating a birthday, engagement, etc., by a person dressed as a gorilla.
▷**HISTORY** C20: from GORILLA + (TELE)GRAM

Gorizia (*Italian* go'rittsja) NOUN a city in NE Italy, in Friuli-Venezia Giulia, on the Isonzo River: cultural centre under the Hapsburgs. Pop.: 39 230 (1990). German name: **Görz.** Serbo-Croat name: **Gorica.**

Gorki *or* **Gorky** (*Russian* 'gɔrjkij) NOUN the former name (until 1991) of **Nizhni Novgorod.**

Gorlin syndrome ('gɔ:lɪn) NOUN a rare congenital disorder in which cancer destroys the facial skin and causes blindness; skeletal anomalies and some mental retardation can also occur.
▷**HISTORY** C20: named after R. J. *Gorlin* (born 1923), US oral pathologist

Görlitz (*German* 'gœrlɪts) NOUN a city in E Germany, in Saxony on the Neisse River: divided in 1945, the area on the E bank of the river becoming the Polish town of **Zgorzelec.** Pop.: 70 450 (1991).

Gorlovka (*Russian* 'gɔrləfkə) NOUN a city in SE Ukraine in the centre of the Donets Basin: a major coal-mining centre. Pop.: 309 300 (1998 est.).

gorm ('gɔ:m) NOUN *Northern English dialect* a foolish person.

gormand ('gɔ:mənd) NOUN a less common variant of **gourmand.**

gormandize *or* **gormandise** VERB ('gɔ:mənˌdaɪz) [1] to eat (food) greedily and voraciously. ◆ NOUN ('gɔ:mənˌdi:z) [2] a less common variant of **gourmandise.**
▸ **'gormandˌizer** *or* **'gormandˌiser** NOUN

gormless ('gɔ:mlɪs) ADJECTIVE *Brit informal* stupid; dull.
▷**HISTORY** C19: variant of C18 *gaumless,* from dialect *gome,* from Old English *gom, gome,* from Old Norse *gaumr* heed

Gorno-Altai Republic ('gɔ:nəʊæl'taɪ, -'æltaɪ) NOUN a constituent republic of S Russia: mountainous, rising over 4350 m (14 500 ft.) in the Altai Mountains of the south. Capital: Gorno-Altaisk. Pop.: 205 000 (2000 est.). Area:

92 600 sq. km (35 740 sq. miles). Also called: **Altai Republic.**

Gorno-Badakhshan Autonomous Republic (-bəˈdækʃɑːn) NOUN an administrative division of Tajikistan: generally mountainous and inaccessible. Capital: Khorog. Pop.: 206 000 (1999 est.). Area: 63 700 sq. km (24 590 sq. miles). Also called: **Badakhshan.**

gorse (gɔːs) NOUN any evergreen shrub of the leguminous genus *Ulex*, esp the European species *U. europeaus*, which has yellow flowers and thick green spines instead of leaves. Also called: **furze, whin.**
▷HISTORY Old English *gors;* related to Old Irish *garb* rough, Latin *horrēre* to bristle, Old High German *gersta* barley, Greek *khēr* hedgehog
▸ˈ**gorsy** ADJECTIVE

Gorsedd (ˈgɔːsɛð) NOUN (in Wales) the bardic institution associated with the eisteddfod, esp a meeting of bards and druids held daily before the eisteddfod.
▷HISTORY from Welsh, literally: throne

gory (ˈgɔːrɪ) ADJECTIVE **gorier, goriest.** [1] horrific or bloodthirsty: *a gory story.* [2] involving bloodshed and killing: *a gory battle.* [3] covered in gore.
▸ˈ**gorily** ADVERB ▸ˈ**goriness** NOUN

Görz (gœrts) NOUN the German name for **Gorizia.**

gosh (gɒʃ) INTERJECTION an exclamation of mild surprise or wonder.
▷HISTORY C18: euphemistic for *God,* as in *by gosh!*

goshawk (ˈgɒsˌhɔːk) NOUN a large hawk, *Accipiter gentilis,* of Europe, Asia, and North America, having a bluish-grey back and wings and paler underparts: used in falconry.
▷HISTORY Old English *gōshafoc;* see GOOSE[1], HAWK[1]

Goshen (ˈgəʊʃən) NOUN [1] a region of ancient Egypt, east of the Nile delta: granted to Jacob and his descendants by the king of Egypt and inhabited by them until the Exodus (Genesis 45:10). [2] a place of comfort and plenty.

Goslar (ˈgɒslɑː) NOUN a city in N central Germany, in Lower Saxony: imperial palace and other medieval buildings, silver mines. Pop.: 46 000 (latest est.).

gosling (ˈgɒzlɪŋ) NOUN [1] a young goose. [2] an inexperienced or youthful person.
▷HISTORY C15: from Old Norse *gæslingr;* related to Danish *gäsling;* see GOOSE[1], -LING[1]

go-slow NOUN [1] *Brit* **a** a deliberate slackening of the rate of production by organized labour as a tactic in industrial conflict. **b** (*as modifier*): *go-slow tactics.* US and Canadian equivalent: **slowdown.** ◆ VERB **go slow.** [2] (*intr*) to work deliberately slowly as a tactic in industrial conflict.

gospel (ˈgɒspᵊl) NOUN [1] Also called: **gospel truth.** an unquestionable truth: *to take someone's word as gospel.* [2] a doctrine maintained to be of great importance. [3] Black religious music originating in the churches of the Southern states of the United States. [4] the message or doctrine of a religious teacher. [5] **a** the story of Christ's life and teachings as narrated in the Gospels. **b** the good news of salvation in Jesus Christ. **c** (*as modifier*): *the gospel story.*
▷HISTORY Old English *gōdspell,* from *gōd* GOOD + *spell* message; see SPELL[2]; compare Old Norse *guthspjall,* Old High German *guotspell*

Gospel (ˈgɒspᵊl) NOUN [1] any of the first four books of the New Testament, namely Matthew, Mark, Luke, and John. [2] a reading from one of these in a religious service.

gospeller (ˈgɒspələ) NOUN [1] a person who reads or chants the Gospel in a religious service. [2] a person who professes to preach a gospel held exclusively by him and others of a like mind.

gospel oath NOUN an oath sworn on the Gospels.

Gosplan (ˈgɒsˌplæn) NOUN the state planning commission of the former Soviet Union or any of its constituent republics: it was responsible for coordination and development of the economy, social services, etc.
▷HISTORY C20: from Russian *Gos(udarstvennaya) Plan(ovaya Comissiya)* State Planning Committee

gospodin *Russian* (gɐspaˈdin) NOUN, *plural* **-poda** (-paˈda). a Russian title of address, often indicating respect, equivalent to *sir* when used alone or to *Mr* when before a name.
▷HISTORY literally: lord

Gosport (ˈgɒsˌpɔːt) NOUN a town in S England, in Hampshire on Portsmouth harbour: naval base since the 16th century. Pop.: 67 802 (1991).

goss (gɒs) VERB (*intr*) *English dialect* to spit.

gossamer (ˈgɒsəmə) NOUN [1] a gauze or silk fabric of the very finest texture. [2] a filmy cobweb often seen on foliage or floating in the air. [3] anything resembling gossamer in fineness or filminess. [4] (*modifier*) made of or resembling gossamer: *gossamer wings.*
▷HISTORY C14 (in the sense: a filmy cobweb): probably from *gos* GOOSE[1] + *somer* SUMMER[1]; the phrase refers to *St Martin's summer,* a period in November when goose was traditionally eaten; from the prevalence of the cobweb in the autumn; compare German *Gänsemonat,* literally: goosemonth, used for November
▸ˈ**gossamery** ADJECTIVE

gossip (ˈgɒsɪp) NOUN [1] casual and idle chat: *to have a gossip with a friend.* [2] a conversation involving malicious chatter or rumours about other people: *a gossip about the neighbours.* [3] Also called: **gossipmonger.** a person who habitually talks about others, esp maliciously. [4] light easy communication: *to write a letter full of gossip.* [5] *Archaic* a close woman friend. ◆ VERB **-sips, -siping, -siped.** [6] (*intr;* often foll by *about*) to talk casually or maliciously (about other people).
▷HISTORY Old English *godsibb* godparent, from GOD + SIB; the term came to be applied to familiar friends, esp a woman's female friends at the birth of a child, hence a person, esp a woman, fond of light talk
▸ˈ**gossiper** NOUN ▸ˈ**gossiping** NOUN, ADJECTIVE ▸ˈ**gossipingly** ADVERB ▸ˈ**gossipy** ADJECTIVE

gossipmonger (ˈgɒsɪpˌmʌŋgə) NOUN another word for **gossip** (sense 3).

gossoon (gɒˈsuːn) NOUN *Irish* a boy, esp a servant boy.
▷HISTORY C17: from Old French *garçon*

gossypol (ˈgɒsɪˌpɒl) NOUN a toxic crystalline pigment that is a constituent of cottonseed oil.
▷HISTORY C19: from Modern Latin *gossypium* cotton plant + -OL[1]

goster (ˈgɒstə) VERB (*intr*) *Northern English dialect* [1] to laugh uncontrollably. [2] to gossip.
▷HISTORY C18: from earlier *gauster,* from Middle English *galstre,* of obscure origin

got (gɒt) VERB [1] the past tense and past participle of **get.** [2] **have got. a** to possess: *he has got three apples.* **b** (*takes an infinitive*) used as an auxiliary to express compulsion felt to be imposed by or upon the speaker: *I've got to get a new coat.* [3] **have got it bad** *or* **badly.** *Informal* to be infatuated.

Göta (*Swedish* ˈjøːta) NOUN a river in S Sweden, draining Lake Vänern and flowing south-southwest to the Kattegat: forms part of the **Göta Canal,** which links Göteborg in the west with Stockholm in the east. Length: 93 km (58 miles).

Gotama (ˈgəʊtəmə) NOUN the Pali form of the name **Gautama.**

gotcha lizard (ˈgɒtʃə) NOUN *Austral* another name for **crocodile.**

Göteborg (*Swedish* jœtəˈbɔrj) *or* **Gothenburg** NOUN a port in SW Sweden, at the mouth of the Göta River: the largest port and second largest city in the country; developed through the Swedish East India Company and grew through Napoleon's continental blockade and with the opening of the Göta Canal (1832); university (1891). Pop.: 462 470 (2000 est.).

Goth (gɒθ) NOUN [1] a member of an East Germanic people from Scandinavia who settled south of the Baltic early in the first millennium A.D. They moved on to the Ukrainian steppes and raided and later invaded many parts of the Roman Empire from the 3rd to the 5th century. See also **Ostrogoth, Visigoth.** [2] a rude or barbaric person. [3] (*sometimes not capital*) Also called: **Gothic.** an aficionado of Goth music and fashion. ◆ ADJECTIVE [4] (*sometimes not capital*) Also: **Gothic. a** (of music) in a style of guitar-based rock with some similarities to heavy metal and punk and usually characterized by depressing or mournful lyrics. **b** (of fashion) characterized by black clothes and heavy make-up, often creating a ghostly appearance.

Gotha (ˈgəʊθə; *German* ˈgoːta) NOUN a town in central Germany, in Thuringia on the N edge of the Thuringian forest: capital of Saxe-Coburg-Gotha (1826–1918); noted for the *Almanach de Gotha* (a record of the royal and noble houses of Europe, first published in 1764). Pop.: 57 360 (latest est.).

Gothamite (ˈgɒθəˌmaɪt) NOUN *US* a native or inhabitant of New York City.
▷HISTORY C20: from *Gotham,* a nickname for New York City

Gothenburg (ˈgɒθənˌbɜːg) NOUN the English name for **Göteborg.**

Gothic (ˈgɒθɪk) ADJECTIVE [1] denoting, relating to, or resembling the style of architecture that was used in W Europe from the 12th to the 16th centuries, characterized by the lancet arch, the ribbed vault, and the flying buttress. See also **Gothic Revival.** [2] of or relating to the style of sculpture, painting, or other arts as practised in W Europe from the 12th to the 16th centuries. [3] (*sometimes not capital*) of or relating to a literary style characterized by gloom, the grotesque, and the supernatural, popular esp in the late 18th century: when used of modern literature, films, etc., sometimes spelt: **Gothick.** [4] of, relating to, or characteristic of the Goths or their language. [5] (*sometimes not capital*) primitive and barbarous in style, behaviour, etc. [6] of or relating to the Middle Ages. [7] another word for **Goth** (sense 4). ◆ NOUN [8] Gothic architecture or art. [9] the extinct language of the ancient Goths, known mainly from fragments of a translation of the Bible made in the 4th century by Bishop Wulfila. See also **East Germanic.** [10] Also called (esp Brit): **black letter.** the family of heavy script typefaces. [11] another word for **Goth** (sense 3).
▸ˈ**Gothically** ADVERB

Gothic arch NOUN another name for **lancet arch.**

Gothicism (ˈgɒθɪˌsɪzəm) NOUN [1] conformity to, use of, or imitation of the Gothic style, esp in architecture. [2] crudeness of manner or style.

Gothicize *or* **Gothicise** (ˈgɒθɪˌsaɪz) VERB (*tr*) to make Gothic in style.
▸ˈ**Gothiˌcizer** *or* ˈ**Gothiˌciser** NOUN

Gothic Revival NOUN a Gothic style of architecture popular between the late 18th and late 19th centuries, exemplified by the Houses of Parliament in London (1840). Also called: **neogothic.**

go through VERB (*intr*) [1] (*adverb*) to be approved or accepted: *the amendment went through.* [2] (*preposition*) to consume; exhaust: *we went through our supplies in a day; some men go through a pair of socks in no time.* [3] (*preposition*) Also: **go over.** to examine and revise as necessary: *he went through the figures.* [4] (*preposition*) to suffer: *she went through tremendous pain.* [5] (*preposition*) Also: **go over.** to rehearse: *let's just go through the details again.* [6] (*preposition*) Also: **go over.** to clean: *she went through the cupboards in the spring-cleaning.* [7] (*preposition*) to participate in: *she went through the degree ceremony without getting too nervous.* [8] (*adverb;* foll by *with*) to bring to a successful conclusion, often by persistence. [9] (*preposition*) (of a book) to be published in: *that book has gone through three printings this year alone.* [10] to proceed to the next round of a competition.

Gotland (ˈgɒtlənd; *Swedish* ˈgɔtlant), **Gothland** (ˈgɒθlənd), *or* **Gottland** (ˈgɒtlənd) NOUN an island in the Baltic Sea, off the SE coast of Sweden: important trading centre since the Bronze Age; long disputed between Sweden and Denmark, finally becoming Swedish in 1645; tourism and agriculture now important. Capital: Visby. Pop.: (including associated islands) 57 313 (2001 est.). Area: 3140 sq. km (1212 sq. miles).

go to VERB (*intr, preposition*) [1] to be awarded to: *the Nobel prize last year went to a Scot.* [2] **go to it.** to tackle a task vigorously. ◆ INTERJECTION [3] *Archaic* an exclamation expressing surprise, encouragement, etc.

go together VERB (*intr, adverb*) [1] to be mutually suited; harmonize: *the colours go well together.* [2] *Informal* (of two people) to have a romantic or sexual relationship: *they had been going together for two years.*

gotta (ˈgɒtə) VERB *Slang* ◆ CONTRACTION OF got to.

gotten (ˈgɒtᵊn) VERB *US* [1] a past participle of **get.** [2] **have gotten.** (*not usually in the infinitive*) **a** to have obtained: *he had gotten a car for his 21st birthday.* **b** to have become: *I've gotten sick of your constant bickering.*

Götterdämmerung (ˌgɒtəˈdɛməˌrʊŋ; *German* gœtərˈdɛmərʊŋ) NOUN *German myth* the twilight of the gods; their ultimate destruction in a battle with the forces of evil. Norse equivalent: **Ragnarök**.

Göttingen (ˈgœtɪŋən) NOUN a city in central Germany, in Lower Saxony: important member of the Hanseatic League (14th century); university, founded in 1734 by George II of England. Pop.: 127 366 (1999 est.).

gouache (guˈɑːʃ) NOUN 1 Also called: **body colour.** a painting technique using opaque watercolour paint in which the pigments are bound with glue and the lighter tones contain white. 2 the paint used in this technique. 3 a painting done by this method.
▷HISTORY C19: from French, from Italian *guazzo* puddle, from Latin *aquātiō* a watering place, from *aqua* water

Gouda (ˈgaʊdə; *Dutch* ˈɔxudaː) NOUN 1 a town in the W Netherlands, in South Holland province: important medieval cloth trade; famous for its cheese. Pop.: 69 917 (1994). 2 a large round Dutch cheese, mild and similar in taste to Edam.

gouge (gaʊdʒ) VERB (*mainly tr*) 1 (usually foll by *out*) to scoop or force (something) out of its position, esp with the fingers or a pointed instrument. 2 (sometimes foll by *out*) to cut (a hole or groove) in (something) with a sharp instrument or tool. 3 *US and Canadian informal* to extort from. 4 (*also intr*) *Austral* to dig for (opal). ◆ NOUN 5 a type of chisel with a blade that has a concavo-convex section. 6 a mark or groove made with, or as if with, a gouge. 7 *Geology* a fine deposit of rock fragments, esp clay, occurring between the walls of a fault or mineral vein. 8 *US and Canadian informal* extortion; swindling.
▷HISTORY C15: from French, from Late Latin *gulbia* a chisel, of Celtic origin

gouger (ˈgaʊdʒə) NOUN 1 a person or tool that gouges. 2 *Irish dialect* a low-class city lout.

goujon (ˈguːʒɒn) NOUN a small strip of fish or chicken, coated in breadcrumbs and deep-fried.
▷HISTORY French, literally: gudgeon

goulash (ˈguːlæʃ) NOUN 1 Also called: **Hungarian goulash.** a rich stew, originating in Hungary, made of beef, lamb, or veal highly seasoned with paprika. 2 *Bridge* a method of dealing in threes and fours without first shuffling the cards, to produce freak hands.
▷HISTORY C19: from Hungarian *gulyás hus* herdsman's meat, from *gulya* herd

Gouldian finch (ˈguːldɪən) NOUN a multicoloured finch, *Chloebia gouldiae*, of tropical N Australia.
▷HISTORY named after Elizabeth *Gould* (1804–41), British natural history artist

go under VERB (*intr, mainly adverb*) 1 (*also preposition*) to sink below (a surface). 2 to founder or drown. 3 to be conquered or overwhelmed: *the firm went under in the economic crisis.*

go up VERB (*intr, mainly adverb*) 1 (*also preposition*) to move or lead to or as if to a higher place or level; rise; increase: *prices are always going up; the curtain goes up at eight o'clock; new buildings are going up all around us.* 2 to be destroyed: *the house went up in flames.* 3 *Brit* to go or return (to college or university) at the beginning of a term or academic year.

gourami (ˈgʊərəmɪ) NOUN, *plural* **-mi** *or* **-mis.** 1 a large SE Asian labyrinth fish, *Osphronemus goramy*, used for food and (when young) as an aquarium fish. 2 any of various other labyrinth fishes, such as *Helostoma temmincki* (**kissing gourami**), many of which are brightly coloured and popular aquarium fishes.
▷HISTORY from Malay *gurami*

gourd (gʊəd) NOUN 1 the fruit of any of various cucurbitaceous or similar plants, esp the bottle gourd and some squashes, whose dried shells are used for ornament, drinking cups, etc. 2 any plant that bears this fruit. See also **sour gourd, dishcloth gourd, calabash.** 3 a bottle or flask made from the dried shell of the bottle gourd. 4 a small bottle shaped like a gourd.
▷HISTORY C14: from Old French *gourde*, ultimately from Latin *cucurbita*
▸ˈ**gourd**ˌ**like** ADJECTIVE ▸ˈ**gourd**-ˌ**shaped** ADJECTIVE

gourde (gʊəd) NOUN the standard monetary unit of Haiti, divided into 100 centimes.
▷HISTORY C19: from French, feminine of *gourd* heavy, from Latin *gurdus* a stupid person

gourmand (ˈgʊəmənd; *French* gurmɑ̃) *or* **gormand** NOUN a person devoted to eating and drinking, esp to excess.
▷HISTORY C15: from Old French *gourmant*, of uncertain origin
▸ˈ**gourmand**ˌ**ism** NOUN

gourmandise (ˌgʊəmənˈdiːz) *or* **gormandize** NOUN a love of and taste for good food.

gourmet (ˈgʊəmeɪ; *French* gurmɛ) NOUN a person who cultivates a discriminating palate for the enjoyment of good food and drink.
▷HISTORY C19: from French, from Old French *gromet* serving boy

gout (gaʊt) NOUN 1 a metabolic disease characterized by painful inflammation of certain joints, esp of the big toe and foot, caused by deposits of sodium urate in them. 2 *Archaic* a drop or splash, esp of blood.
▷HISTORY C13: from Old French *goute* gout (thought to result from drops of humours), from Latin *gutta* a drop
▸ˈ**gouty** ADJECTIVE ▸ˈ**goutily** ADVERB ▸ˈ**goutiness** NOUN

goût *French* (gu) NOUN taste or good taste.

goutweed (ˈgaʊtˌwiːd) NOUN a widely naturalized Eurasian umbelliferous plant, *Aegopodium podagraria*, with white flowers and creeping underground stems. Also called: **bishop's weed, ground elder, herb Gerard.**

gov AN INTERNET DOMAIN NAME FOR a US government organization.

Gov. *or* **gov.** governor.

govern (ˈgʌvᵊn) VERB (*mainly tr*) 1 (*also intr*) to direct and control the actions, affairs, policies, functions, etc., of (a political unit, organization, nation, etc.); rule. 2 to exercise restraint over; regulate or direct: *to govern one's temper.* 3 to be a predominant influence on (something); decide or determine (something): *his injury governed his decision to avoid sports.* 4 to control the speed of (an engine, machine, etc.) using a governor. 5 to control the rate of flow of (a fluid) by using an automatic valve. 6 (of a word) to determine the inflection of (another word): *Latin nouns govern adjectives that modify them.*
▷HISTORY C13: from Old French *gouverner*, from Latin *gubernāre* to steer, from Greek *kubernan*
▸ˈ**governable** ADJECTIVE ▸ˌ**governa**ˈ**bility** *or* ˈ**governableness** NOUN

governance (ˈgʌvənəns) NOUN 1 government, control, or authority. 2 the action, manner, or system of governing.

governess (ˈgʌvənɪs) NOUN a woman teacher employed in a private household to teach and train the children.

government (ˈgʌvənmənt, ˈgʌvəmənt) NOUN 1 the exercise of political authority over the actions, affairs, etc., of a political unit, people, etc., as well as the performance of certain functions for this unit or body; the action of governing; political rule and administration. 2 the system or form by which a community, etc., is ruled: *tyrannical government.* 3 **a** the executive policy-making body of a political unit, community, etc.; ministry or administration: *yesterday we got a new government.* **b** (*capital when of a specific country*): *the British Government.* 4 **a** the state and its administration: *blame it on the government.* **b** (*as modifier*): *a government agency.* 5 regulation; direction. 6 *Grammar* the determination of the form of one word by another word.
▸**governmental** (ˌgʌvənˈmɛntᵊl, ˌgʌvəˈmɛntᵊl) ADJECTIVE ▸ˌ**govern**ˈ**mentally** ADVERB

Government House NOUN the official residence of a representative of the British Crown (such as a Canadian Lieutenant-Governor or an Australian Governor General) in a state or province that recognizes the British sovereign as Head of the Commonwealth.

government issue ADJECTIVE supplied by a government or government agency.

government man NOUN *Austral* (in the 19th century) a convict.

governor (ˈgʌvənə) NOUN 1 a person who governs. 2 the ruler or chief magistrate of a colony, province, etc. 3 the representative of the Crown in a British colony. 4 *Brit* the senior administrator or head of a society, prison, etc. 5 the chief executive of any state in the US. 6 a device that controls the speed of an engine, esp by regulating the supply of fuel, etc., either to limit the maximum speed or to maintain a constant speed. 7 *Grammar* Also called: **head. a** a word in a phrase or clause that is the principal item and gives the function of the whole, as *hat* in *the big red hat.* **b** (*as modifier*): *a governor noun.* 8 *Brit informal* a name or title of respect for a father, employer, etc. ◆ Related adjective **gubernatorial.**

governor general NOUN, *plural* **governors general** *or* **governor generals.** 1 the representative of the Crown in a dominion of the Commonwealth or a British colony; vicegerent. 2 *Brit* a governor with jurisdiction or precedence over other governors.
▸ˌ**governor**-ˈ**general**ˌ**ship** NOUN

governorship (ˈgʌvənəˌʃɪp) NOUN the office, jurisdiction, or term of a governor.

Govt *or* **govt** ABBREVIATION FOR government.

gowan (ˈgaʊən) NOUN *Scot* any of various yellow or white flowers growing in fields, esp the common daisy.
▷HISTORY C16: variant of *gollan*, probably of Scandinavian origin; compare Old Norse *gullin* golden
▸ˈ**gowaned** ADJECTIVE ▸ˈ**gowany** ADJECTIVE

Gower (ˈgaʊə) NOUN **the.** a peninsula in S Wales, in Swansea county on the Bristol Channel: mainly agricultural with several resorts.

go with VERB (*intr, preposition*) 1 to accompany. 2 to blend or harmonize: *that new wallpaper goes well with the furniture.* 3 to be a normal part of: *three acres of land go with the house.* 4 to be of the same opinion as: *I'm sorry I can't go with you on your new plan.* 5 (of two people) to associate frequently with (each other).

go without VERB (*intr*) 1 *Chiefly Brit* to be denied or deprived of (something, esp food): *if you don't like your tea you can go without.* 2 **that goes without saying.** that is obvious or self-evident.

gowk (gaʊk) NOUN *Scot and northern English dialect* 1 a stupid person; fool. 2 a cuckoo.
▷HISTORY from Old Norse *gaukr* cuckoo; related to Old High German *gouh*

gowl (gaʊl) NOUN *Midland English dialect* the substance often found in the corner of the eyes after sleep.

gown (gaʊn) NOUN 1 any of various outer garments, such as a woman's elegant or formal dress, a dressing robe, or a protective garment, esp one worn by surgeons during operations. 2 a loose wide garment indicating status, such as worn by academics. 3 the members of a university as opposed to the other residents of the university town. Compare **town** (sense 7). ◆ VERB 4 (*tr*) to supply with or dress in a gown.
▷HISTORY C14: from Old French *goune*, from Late Latin *gunna* garment made of leather or fur, of Celtic origin

goy (gɔɪ) NOUN, *plural* **goyim** (ˈgɔɪɪm) *or* **goys.** a Jewish word for a gentile.
▷HISTORY from Yiddish, from Hebrew *goi* people
▸ˈ**goyish** ADJECTIVE

gp THE INTERNET DOMAIN NAME FOR Guadeloupe.

GP ABBREVIATION FOR: 1 general practitioner. 2 **Gallup Poll.** 3 (in Britain) graduated pension. 4 Grand Prix. 5 gas-permeable (contact lens). 6 *Music* general pause.

GPI ABBREVIATION FOR general paralysis of the insane (general paresis).

GPMU (in Britain) ABBREVIATION FOR Graphical, Paper and Media Union.

GPO ABBREVIATION FOR general post office.

GPRS ABBREVIATION FOR general packet radio service: a telecommunications system providing very fast internet connections for mobile phones.

GPS ABBREVIATION FOR: 1 **global positioning system.** 2 (in Australia) Great Public Schools; used of a group of mainly nonstate schools, and of sporting competitions between them.

GPU ABBREVIATION FOR State Political Administration; the Soviet police and secret police from 1922 to 1923.
▷HISTORY from Russian *Gosudarstvennoye politicheskoye upravlenie*

gq THE INTERNET DOMAIN NAME FOR Equatorial Guinea.

GQ *Military* ABBREVIATION FOR general quarters.

gr THE INTERNET DOMAIN NAME FOR Greece.

GR INTERNATIONAL CAR REGISTRATION FOR Greece.

GR8 *Text messaging* ABBREVIATION FOR great.

Gr. ABBREVIATION FOR: 1 Grecian. 2 Greece. 3 Greek.

Graafian follicle ('grɑːfɪən) NOUN a fluid-filled vesicle in the mammalian ovary containing a developing egg cell.
▷HISTORY C17: named after R. de *Graaf* (1641–73), Dutch anatomist

grab (græb) VERB **grabs, grabbing, grabbed.** 1 to seize hold of (something). 2 (*tr*) to seize illegally or unscrupulously. 3 (*tr*) to arrest; catch. 4 (*intr*) (of a brake or clutch in a vehicle) to grip and release intermittently causing juddering. 5 (*tr*) *Informal* to catch the attention or interest of; impress. ◆ NOUN 6 the act or an instance of grabbing. 7 a mechanical device for gripping objects, esp the hinged jaws of a mechanical excavator. 8 something that is grabbed. 9 **up for grabs.** *Informal* available to be bought, claimed, or won.
▷HISTORY C16: probably from Middle Low German or Middle Dutch *grabben;* related to Swedish *grabba,* Sanskrit *grbhnāti* he seizes
▸ '**grabber** NOUN

grab bag NOUN 1 a collection of miscellaneous things. 2 *US, Canadian, and Austral* a bag or other container from which gifts are drawn at random.

grabble ('græbᵊl) VERB 1 (*intr*) to scratch or feel about with the hands. 2 (*intr*) to fall to the ground; sprawl. 3 (*tr*) *Caribbean* to seize rashly.
▷HISTORY C16: probably from Dutch *grabbelen,* from *grabben* to GRAB
▸ '**grabbler** NOUN

grabby ('grabɪ) ADJECTIVE **-bier, -biest.** 1 greedy or selfish. 2 direct, stimulating, or attention-grabbing: *grabbier opening paragraphs.*

graben ('grɑːbᵊn) NOUN an elongated trough of land produced by subsidence of the earth's crust between two faults.
▷HISTORY C19: from German, from Old High German *graban* to dig

grace (greɪs) NOUN 1 elegance and beauty of movement, form, expression, or proportion. 2 a pleasing or charming quality. 3 goodwill or favour. 4 the granting of a favour or the manifestation of goodwill, esp by a superior. 5 a sense of propriety and consideration for others. 6 (*plural*) **a** affectation of manner (esp in the phrase **airs and graces**). **b in (someone's) good graces.** regarded favourably and with kindness by (someone). 7 mercy; clemency. 8 *Christianity* **a** the free and unmerited favour of God shown towards man. **b** the divine assistance and power given to man in spiritual rebirth and sanctification. **c** the condition of being favoured or sanctified by God. **d** an unmerited gift, favour, etc., granted by God. 9 a short prayer recited before or after a meal to invoke a blessing upon the food or give thanks for it. 10 *Music* a melodic ornament or decoration. 11 See **days of grace.** 12 **with (a) bad grace.** unwillingly or grudgingly. 13 **with (a) good grace.** willingly or cheerfully. ◆ VERB 14 (*tr*) to add elegance and beauty to: *flowers graced the room.* 15 (*tr*) to honour or favour: *to grace a party with one's presence.* 16 to ornament or decorate (a melody, part, etc.) with nonessential notes.
▷HISTORY C12: from Old French, from Latin *grātia,* from *grātus* pleasing

Grace (greɪs) NOUN (preceded by *your, his,* or *her*) a title used to address or refer to a duke, duchess, or archbishop.

grace-and-favour NOUN (*modifier*) *Brit* (of a house, flat, etc.) owned by the sovereign and granted free of rent to a person to whom the sovereign wishes to express gratitude.

grace cup NOUN a cup, as of wine, passed around at the end of the meal for the final toast.

graceful ('greɪsfʊl) ADJECTIVE characterized by beauty of movement, style, form, etc.
▸ '**gracefully** ADVERB ▸ '**gracefulness** NOUN

graceless ('greɪslɪs) ADJECTIVE 1 lacking any sense of right and wrong; depraved. 2 lacking grace or excellence.
▸ '**gracelessly** ADVERB ▸ '**gracelessness** NOUN

grace note NOUN *Music* a note printed in small type to indicate that it is melodically and harmonically nonessential.

Graces ('greɪsɪz) PLURAL NOUN *Greek myth* three sisters, the goddesses Aglaia, Euphrosyne, and Thalia, givers of charm and beauty.

gracile ('græsaɪl) ADJECTIVE 1 gracefully thin or slender. 2 a less common word for **graceful.**
▷HISTORY C17: from Latin *gracilis* slender
▸**gracility** (græ'sɪlɪtɪ) *or* '**gracileness** NOUN

gracioso (ˌgræsɪ'əʊsəʊ; *Spanish* gra'θjoso) NOUN, *plural* **-sos.** a clown in Spanish comedy.
▷HISTORY C17: from Spanish: GRACIOUS

gracious ('greɪʃəs) ADJECTIVE 1 characterized by or showing kindness and courtesy. 2 condescendingly courteous, benevolent, or indulgent. 3 characterized by or suitable for a life of elegance, ease, and indulgence: *gracious living; gracious furnishings.* 4 merciful or compassionate. 5 *Obsolete* fortunate, prosperous, or happy. ◆ INTERJECTION 6 an expression of mild surprise or wonder (often in exclamatory phrases such as **good gracious!, gracious me!**).
▸ '**graciously** ADVERB ▸ '**graciousness** NOUN

grackle ('grækᵊl) NOUN 1 Also called: **crow blackbird.** any American songbird of the genera *Quiscalus* and *Cassidix,* having a dark iridescent plumage: family *Icteridae* (American orioles). 2 any of various starlings of the genus *Gracula,* such as *G. religiosa* (**Indian grackle** or **hill mynah**).
▷HISTORY C18: from New Latin *Grācula,* from Latin *grāculus* jackdaw

grad (græd) NOUN *Informal* a graduate.

grad. ABBREVIATION FOR: 1 *Maths* gradient. 2 *Education* graduate(d).

gradable ('greɪdəbᵊl) ADJECTIVE 1 capable of being graded. 2 *Linguistics* denoting or relating to a word in whose meaning there is some implicit relationship to a standard: *"big" and "small" are gradable adjectives.* ◆ NOUN 3 *Linguistics* a word of this kind.
▸ ˌ**grada'bility** *or* '**gradableness** NOUN

gradate (grə'deɪt) VERB 1 to change or cause to change imperceptibly, as from one colour, tone, or degree to another. 2 (*tr*) to arrange in grades or ranks.

gradation (grə'deɪʃən) NOUN 1 a series of systematic stages; gradual progression. 2 (*often plural*) a stage or degree in such a series or progression. 3 the act or process of arranging or forming in stages, grades, etc., or of progressing evenly. 4 (in painting, drawing, or sculpture) transition from one colour, tone, or surface to another through a series of very slight changes. 5 *Linguistics* any change in the quality or length of a vowel within a word indicating certain distinctions, such as inflectional or tense differentiations. See **ablaut.** 6 *Geology* the natural levelling of land as a result of the building up or wearing down of pre-existing formations.
▸**gra'dational** ADJECTIVE ▸**gra'dationally** ADVERB

grade (greɪd) NOUN 1 a position or degree in a scale, as of quality, rank, size, or progression: *small-grade eggs; high-grade timber.* 2 a group of people or things of the same category. 3 *Chiefly US* a military or other rank. 4 a stage in a course of progression. 5 a mark or rating indicating achievement or the worth of work done, as at school. 6 *US and Canadian* a unit of pupils of similar age or ability taught together at school. 7 another word (esp US and Canadian) for **gradient** (senses 1, 2). 8 a unit of angle equal to one hundredth of a right angle or 0.9 degree. 9 *Stockbreeding* **a** an animal with one purebred parent and one of unknown or unimproved breeding. **b** (*as modifier*): *a grade sheep.* Compare **crossbred** (sense 2), **purebred** (sense 2). 10 *Linguistics* one of the forms of the vowel in a morpheme when this vowel varies because of gradation. 11 **at grade. a** on the same level. **b** (of a river profile or land surface) at an equilibrium level and slope, because there is a balance between erosion and deposition. 12 **make the grade.** *Informal* **a** to reach the required standard. **b** to succeed. ◆ VERB 13 (*tr*) to arrange according to quality, rank, etc. 14 (*tr*) to determine the grade of or assign a grade to. 15 (*intr*) to achieve or deserve a grade or rank. 16 to change or blend (something) gradually; merge. 17 (*tr*) to level (ground, a road, etc.) to a suitable gradient. 18 (*tr*) *Stockbreeding* to cross (one animal) with another to produce a grade animal.
▷HISTORY C16: from French, from Latin *gradus* step, from *gradī* to step

-grade ADJECTIVE COMBINING FORM indicating a kind or manner of movement or progression: *plantigrade; retrograde.*
▷HISTORY via French from Latin *-gradus,* from *gradus* a step, from *gradī* to walk

grade cricket NOUN *Austral* competitive cricket, in which cricket club teams are arranged in grades.

grade crossing NOUN the US and Canadian name for **level crossing.**

graded post NOUN *Brit* a position in a school having special responsibility for which additional payment is given.

grade inflation NOUN an apparently continual increase in numbers of students attaining high examination grades, or the practice of awarding grades in this way.

gradely ('greɪdlɪ) ADJECTIVE **-lier, -liest.** *Midland English dialect* fine; excellent.
▷HISTORY C13 *greithlic, greithli,* from Old Norse *greidhligr,* from *greidhr* ready

grader ('greɪdə) NOUN 1 a person or thing that grades. 2 a machine, either self-powered or towed by a tractor, that levels earth, rubble, etc., as in road construction.

grade school NOUN *US* another name for **elementary school.**

gradient ('greɪdɪənt) NOUN 1 Also called (esp US): **grade.** a part of a railway, road, etc., that slopes upwards or downwards; inclination. 2 Also called (esp US and Canadian): **grade.** a measure of such a slope, esp the ratio of the vertical distance between two points on the slope to the horizontal distance between them. 3 *Physics* a measure of the change of some physical quantity, such as temperature or electric potential, over a specified distance. 4 *Maths* **a** (of a curve) the slope of the tangent at any point on a curve with respect to the horizontal axis. **b** (of a function, $f(x, y, z)$) the vector whose components along the axes are the partial derivatives of the function with respect to each variable, and whose direction is that in which the derivative of the function has its maximum value. Usually written: grad **f**, ∇f or ∇**f**. Compare **curl** (sense 11), **divergence** (sense 4). ◆ ADJECTIVE 5 sloping uniformly.
▷HISTORY C19: from Latin *gradiēns* stepping, from *gradī* to go

gradient post NOUN a small white post beside a railway line at a point where the gradient changes having arms set at angles representing the gradients.

gradin ('greɪdɪn) *or* **gradine** (grə'diːn) NOUN 1 a ledge above or behind an altar on which candles, a cross, or other ornaments stand. 2 one of a set of steps or seats arranged on a slope, as in an amphitheatre.
▷HISTORY C19: from French, from Italian *gradino,* a little step, from *grado* step; see GRADE

gradiometer (ˌgrædɪ'ɒmɪtə) NOUN 1 *Physics* an instrument for measuring the gradient of a magnetic field. 2 *Surveying* an instrument used to ensure that a long gradient remains constant.

gradual ('grædjʊəl) ADJECTIVE 1 occurring, developing, moving, etc., in small stages: *a gradual improvement in health.* 2 not steep or abrupt: *a gradual slope.* ◆ NOUN 3 (*often capital*) *Christianity* **a** an antiphon or group of several antiphons, usually from the Psalms, sung or recited immediately after the epistle at Mass. **b** a book of plainsong containing the words and music of the parts of the Mass that are sung by the cantors and choir.
▷HISTORY C16: from Medieval Latin *graduālis* relating to steps, from Latin *gradus* a step
▸ '**gradually** ADVERB ▸ '**gradualness** NOUN

gradualism ('grædjʊəˌlɪzəm) NOUN 1 the policy of seeking to change something or achieve a goal gradually rather than quickly or violently, esp in politics. 2 the theory that explains major changes in rock strata, fossils, etc. in terms of gradual evolutionary processes rather than sudden violent catastrophes. Compare **catastrophism.**
▸ '**gradualist** NOUN, ADJECTIVE ▸ˌ**gradual'istic** ADJECTIVE

graduand ('grædjʊˌænd) NOUN *Chiefly Brit* a person who is about to graduate.

▷HISTORY C19: from Medieval Latin *graduandus,* gerundive of *graduārī* to GRADUATE

graduate NOUN (ˈgrædjʊɪt) 1 **a** a person who has been awarded a first degree from a university or college. **b** (*as modifier*): *a graduate profession.* 2 *US and Canadian* a student who has completed a course of studies at a high school and received a diploma. 3 *US* a container, such as a flask, marked to indicate its capacity. ◆ VERB (ˈgrædjʊˌeɪt) 4 to receive or cause to receive a degree or diploma. 5 (*tr*) *Chiefly US and Canadian* to confer a degree, diploma, etc. upon. 6 (*tr*) to mark (a thermometer, flask, etc.) with units of measurement; calibrate. 7 (*tr*) to arrange or sort into groups according to type, quality, etc. 8 (*intr; often foll by to*) to change by degrees (from something to something else).
▷HISTORY C15: from Medieval Latin *graduārī* to take a degree, from Latin *gradus* a step
▸ **ˈgraduˌator** NOUN

graduation (ˌgrædjʊˈeɪʃən) NOUN 1 the act of graduating or the state of being graduated. 2 the ceremony at which school or college degrees and diplomas are conferred. 3 a mark or division or all the marks or divisions that indicate measure on an instrument or vessel.

gradus (ˈgreɪdəs) NOUN, *plural* **-duses.** 1 a book of études or other musical exercises arranged in order of increasing difficulty. 2 *Prosody* a dictionary or textbook of prosody for use in writing Latin or Greek verse.
▷HISTORY C18: shortened from Latin *Gradus ad Parnassum* a step towards Parnassus, a dictionary of prosody used in the 18th and 19th centuries

Graeae (ˈgriːiː) *or* **Graiae** PLURAL NOUN *Greek myth* three aged sea deities, having only one eye and one tooth among them, guardians of their sisters, the Gorgons.

Graecism *or esp US* **Grecism** (ˈgriːsɪzəm) NOUN 1 Greek characteristics or style. 2 admiration for or imitation of these, as in sculpture or architecture. 3 a form of words characteristic or imitative of the idiom of the Greek language.

Graecize, Graecise, *or esp US* **Grecize** (ˈgriːsaɪz) VERB another word for **Hellenize.**
▷HISTORY C17: from Latin *graecizāre* to imitate the Greeks, from Greek *graikizein*

Graeco- *or esp US* **Greco-** (ˈgriːkəʊ, ˈgrɛkəʊ) COMBINING FORM Greek: *Graeco-Roman.*

Graeco-Roman *or esp US* **Greco-Roman** ADJECTIVE 1 of, characteristic of, or relating to Greek and Roman influences, as found in Roman sculpture. 2 denoting a style of wrestling in which the legs may not be used to obtain a fall and no hold may be applied below the waist.

Graf *German* (graːf) NOUN, *plural* ***Grafen*** (ˈgraːfən). a German count: often used as a title.
▷HISTORY German, from Old High German *grāvo*

graffiti (græˈfiːtiː) PLURAL NOUN, *singular* **-to** (-təʊ). 1 (*sometimes with singular verb*) drawings, messages, etc., often obscene, scribbled on the walls of public lavatories, advertising posters, etc. 2 *Archaeol* inscriptions or drawings scratched or carved onto a surface, esp rock or pottery.
▷HISTORY C19: *graffito* from Italian: a little scratch, from *graffio,* from Latin *graphium* stylus, from Greek *grapheion;* see GRAFT[1]
▸ **grafˈfitist** NOUN

graft[1] (grɑːft) NOUN 1 *Horticulture* **a** a piece of plant tissue (the scion), normally a stem, that is made to unite with an established plant (the stock), which supports and nourishes it. **b** the plant resulting from the union of scion and stock. **c** the point of union between the scion and the stock. 2 *Surgery* a piece of tissue or an organ transplanted from a donor or from the patient's own body to an area of the body in need of the tissue. 3 the act of joining one thing to another by or as if by grafting. ◆ VERB 4 *Horticulture* **a** to induce (a plant or part of a plant) to unite with another part or (of a plant or part of a plant) to unite in this way. **b** to produce (fruit, flowers, etc.) by this means or (of fruit, flowers, etc.) to grow by this means. 5 to transplant (tissue) or (of tissue) to be transplanted. 6 to attach or incorporate or become attached or incorporated: *to graft a happy ending onto a sad tale.*
▷HISTORY C15: from Old French *graffe,* from Medieval Latin *graphium,* from Latin: stylus, from Greek *grapheion,* from *graphein* to write
▸ **ˈgrafter** NOUN ▸ **ˈgrafting** NOUN

graft[2] (grɑːft) *Informal* ◆ NOUN 1 work (esp in the phrase **hard graft**). 2 **a** the acquisition of money, power, etc., by dishonest or unfair means, esp by taking advantage of a position of trust. **b** something gained in this way, such as profit from government business. **c** a payment made to a person profiting by such a practice. ◆ VERB 3 (*intr*) to work. 4 to acquire by or practise graft.
▷HISTORY C19: of uncertain origin
▸ **ˈgrafter** NOUN

graft hybrid NOUN a plant produced by grafting a scion and stock from dissimilar plants such that cells of both stock and scion are mixed in the visible parts, giving an intermediate appearance in at least some parts; chimera.

graham (ˈgreɪəm) NOUN (*modifier*) *Chiefly US and Canadian* made of graham flour: *graham crackers.*
▷HISTORY C19: named after S. *Graham* (1794–1851), American dietetic reformer

graham flour NOUN *Chiefly US and Canadian* unbolted wheat flour ground from whole-wheat grain, similar to whole-wheat flour.

Graham Land NOUN the N part of the Antarctic Peninsula: became part of the British Antarctic Territory in 1962 (formerly part of the Falkland Islands Dependencies).

Graham's Law NOUN the principle that the rates of diffusion and effusion of a gas are inversely proportional to the square root of its density, proposed by Thomas Graham (1805-69) in 1831.

Graiae (ˈgreɪiː, ˈgraɪiː) PLURAL NOUN a variant of **Graeae.**

Graian Alps (ˈgreɪən, ˈgraɪ-) PLURAL NOUN the N part of the Western Alps, in France and NW Piedmont, Italy. Highest peak: Gran Paradiso, 4061 m (13 323 ft.).

Grail (greɪl) NOUN See **Holy Grail.**

grain (greɪn) NOUN 1 the small hard seedlike fruit of a grass, esp a cereal plant. 2 a mass of such fruits, esp when gathered for food. 3 the plants, collectively, from which such fruits are harvested. 4 a small hard particle: *a grain of sand.* 5 **a** the general direction or arrangement of the fibrous elements in paper or wood: *to saw across the grain.* **b** the pattern or texture of wood resulting from such an arrangement: *the attractive grain of the table.* 6 the relative size of the particles of a substance: *sugar of fine grain.* 7 **a** the granular texture of a rock, mineral, etc. **b** the appearance of a rock, mineral, etc., determined by the size and arrangement of its constituents. 8 **a** the outer (hair-side) layer of a hide or skin from which the hair or wool has been removed. **b** the pattern on the outer surface of such a hide or skin. 9 a surface artificially imitating the grain of wood, leather, stone, etc.; graining. 10 the smallest unit of weight in the avoirdupois, Troy, and apothecaries' systems, based on the average weight of a grain of wheat: in the avoirdupois system it equals 1/7000 of a pound, and in the Troy and apothecaries' systems it equals 1/5760 of a pound. 1 grain is equal to 0.0648 gram. Abbreviation: **gr.** 11 Also called: **metric grain.** a metric unit of weight used for pearls or diamonds, equal to 50 milligrams or one quarter of a carat. 12 the threads or direction of threads in a woven fabric. 13 *Photog* any of a large number of particles in a photographic emulsion, the size of which limit the extent to which an image can be enlarged without serious loss of definition. 14 *Television* a granular effect in a television picture caused by electrical noise. 15 cleavage lines in crystalline material, parallel to growth planes. 16 *Chem* any of a large number of small crystals forming a polycrystalline solid, each having a regular array of atoms that differs in orientation from that of the surrounding crystallites. 17 a state of crystallization: *to boil syrup to the grain.* 18 a very small amount: *a grain of truth.* 19 natural disposition, inclination, or character (esp in the phrase **go against the grain**). 20 *Astronautics* a homogenous mass of solid propellant in a form designed to give the required combustion characteristics for a particular rocket. 21 (*not in technical usage*) kermes or a red dye made from this insect. 22 *Dyeing* an obsolete word for **colour.** 23 **with a grain** *or* **pinch of salt.** without wholly believing: sceptically. ◆ VERB (*mainly tr*) 24 (*also intr*) to form grains or cause to form into grains; granulate; crystallize. 25 to give a granular or roughened appearance or texture to. 26 to paint, stain, etc., in imitation of the grain of wood or leather. 27 **a** to remove the hair or wool from (a hide or skin) before tanning. **b** to raise the grain pattern on (leather).
▷HISTORY C13: from Old French, from Latin *grānum*
▸ **ˈgrainer** NOUN ▸ **ˈgrainless** ADJECTIVE

grain alcohol NOUN ethanol containing about 10 per cent of water, made by the fermentation of grain.

grain elevator NOUN a machine for raising grain to a higher level, esp one having an endless belt fitted with scoops.

graining (ˈgreɪnɪŋ) NOUN 1 the pattern or texture of the grain of wood, leather, etc. 2 the process of painting, printing, staining, etc., a surface in imitation of a grain. 3 a surface produced by such a process.

grains of paradise PLURAL NOUN the peppery seeds of either of two African zingiberaceous plants, *Aframomum melegueta* or *A. granum-paradisi,* used as stimulants, diuretics, etc. Also called: **guinea grains.**

grainy (ˈgreɪnɪ) ADJECTIVE **grainier, grainiest.** 1 resembling, full of, or composed of grain; granular. 2 resembling the grain of wood, leather, etc. 3 *Photog* having poor definition because of large grain size.
▸ **ˈgraininess** NOUN

grallatorial (ˌgræləˈtɔːrɪəl) ADJECTIVE of or relating to long-legged wading birds, such as cranes, herons, and storks.
▷HISTORY C19: from New Latin *grallātōrius,* from Latin *grallātor* one who walks on stilts, from *grallae* stilts

gralloch (ˈgrælək; *Scot* ˈgrælɒx) *Brit* ◆ NOUN 1 the entrails of a deer. 2 the act or an instance of disembowelling a deer killed in a hunt. ◆ VERB (*tr*) 3 to disembowel (a deer killed in a hunt).
▷HISTORY C19: from Scottish Gaelic *grealach* intestines

gram[1] (græm) NOUN a metric unit of mass equal to one thousandth of a kilogram. It is equivalent to 15.432 grains or 0.002 205 pounds. Symbol: g.
▷HISTORY C18: from French *gramme,* from Late Latin *gramma,* from Greek: small weight, from *graphein* to write

gram[2] (græm) NOUN 1 any of several leguminous plants, such as the beans *Phaseolus mungo* (**black gram** or **urd**) and *P. aureus* (**green gram**), whose seeds are used as food in India. 2 the seed of any of these plants.
▷HISTORY C18: from Portuguese *gram* (modern spelling *grão*), from Latin *grānum* GRAIN

gram[3] (grɑːm) NOUN (in India) a village.
▷HISTORY Hindi

gram. ABBREVIATION FOR: 1 grammar. 2 grammatical.

-gram NOUN COMBINING FORM indicating a drawing or something written or recorded: *hexagram; telegram.*
▷HISTORY from Latin *-gramma,* from Greek, from *gramma* letter and *grammē* line

grama *or* **grama grass** (ˈgrɑːmə) NOUN any of various grasses of the genus *Bouteloua,* of W North America and South America: often used as pasture grasses.
▷HISTORY C19: from Spanish, ultimately from Latin *grāmen* grass

gramarye *or* **gramary** (ˈgræmərɪ) NOUN *Archaic* magic, necromancy, or occult learning.
▷HISTORY C14: from Old French *gramaire* GRAMMAR

gram atom *or* **gram-atomic weight** NOUN an amount of an element equal to its atomic weight expressed in grams: now replaced by the mole. See **mole**[3].

gram calorie NOUN another name for **calorie.**

gram equivalent *or* **gram-equivalent weight** NOUN an amount of a substance equal to its equivalent weight expressed in grams.

gramercy (grəˈmɜːsɪ) INTERJECTION *Archaic* 1 many thanks. 2 an expression of surprise, wonder, etc.
▷HISTORY C13: from Old French *grand merci* great thanks

gramicidin *or* **gramicidin D** (ˌgræmɪˈsaɪdɪn) NOUN an antibiotic used in treating local

Gram-positive bacterial infections: obtained from the soil bacterium *Bacillus brevis*.
▷**HISTORY** C20: from GRAM(-POSITIVE) + -CID(E) + -IN

gramineous (grəˈmɪnɪəs) resembling a grass; grasslike. Also: **graminaceous** (ˌgræmɪˈneɪʃəs).
▷**HISTORY** C17: from Latin *grāmineus* of grass, grassy, from *grāmen* grass

graminicolous (ˌgræmɪˈnɪkələs) ADJECTIVE (esp of parasitic fungi) living on grass.

graminivorous (ˌgræmɪˈnɪvərəs) ADJECTIVE (of animals) feeding on grass.
▷**HISTORY** C18: from Latin *grāmen* grass + -VOROUS

graminology (ˌgræmɪˈnɒlədʒɪ) NOUN the branch of botany concerned with the study of grasses.

grammage (ˈgræmɪdʒ) NOUN the weight of paper expressed as grams per square metre.

grammalogue (ˈgræməˌlɒg) NOUN (in shorthand) a sign or symbol representing a word.
▷**HISTORY** C19: from Greek, *gramma* letter + *logos* word

grammar (ˈgræmə) NOUN 1 the branch of linguistics that deals with syntax and morphology, sometimes also phonology and semantics. 2 the abstract system of rules in terms of which a person's mastery of his native language can be explained. 3 a systematic description of the grammatical facts of a language. 4 a book containing an account of the grammatical facts of a language or recommendations as to rules for the proper use of a language. 5 **a** the use of language with regard to its correctness or social propriety, esp in syntax: *the teacher told him to watch his grammar*. **b** (*as modifier*): *a grammar book*. 6 the elementary principles of a science or art: *the grammar of drawing*.
▷**HISTORY** C14: from Old French *gramaire*, from Latin *grammatica*, from Greek *grammatikē* (*tekhnē*) the grammatical (art), from *grammatikos* concerning letters, from *gramma* letter
▸ˈ**grammarless** ADJECTIVE

grammarian (grəˈmɛərɪən) NOUN 1 a person whose occupation is the study of grammar. 2 the author of a grammar.

grammar school NOUN 1 *Brit* (esp formerly) a state-maintained secondary school providing an education with an academic bias for children who are selected by the eleven-plus examination, teachers' reports, or other means. Compare **secondary modern school, comprehensive school.** 2 *US* another term for **elementary school.** 3 *NZ* a secondary school forming part of the public education system.

grammatical (grəˈmætɪkəl) ADJECTIVE 1 of or relating to grammar. 2 (of a sentence) well formed; regarded as correct and acceptable by native speakers of the language.
▸**gramˈmatically** ADVERB ▸**gramˈmaticalness** NOUN

grammatical meaning NOUN the meaning of a word by reference to its function within a sentence rather than to a world outside the sentence. Compare **lexical meaning, function word.**

grammatology (ˌgræməˈtɒlədʒɪ) NOUN the scientific study of writing systems.
▸ˌ**grammaˈtologist** NOUN

gram molecule *or* **gram-molecular weight** NOUN an amount of a compound equal to its molecular weight expressed in grams: now replaced by the mole. See **mole**[3].
▸ˌ**gram-moˈlecular** *or* **gram-molar** (ˌgræmˈməʊlə) ADJECTIVE

Grammy (ˈgræmɪ) NOUN, *plural* **-mys** *or* **-mies.** (in the US) one of the gold-plated discs awarded annually for outstanding achievement in the record industry.
▷**HISTORY** C20: from GRAM(OPHONE) + *my* as in EMMY

Gram-negative ADJECTIVE designating bacteria that fail to retain the violet stain in Gram's method.

gramophone (ˈgræməˌfəʊn) NOUN 1 **a** Also called: **acoustic gramophone.** a device for reproducing the sounds stored on a record: now usually applied to the nearly obsolete type that uses a clockwork motor and acoustic horn. US and Canadian name: **phonograph. b** (*as modifier*): *a gramophone record*. 2 the technique and practice of recording sound on disc: *the gramophone has made music widely available*.
▷**HISTORY** C19: originally a trademark, perhaps based on an inversion of *phonogram;* see PHONO-, -GRAM
▸**gramophonic** (ˌgræməˈfɒnɪk) ADJECTIVE

Grampian Mountains (ˈgræmpɪən) PLURAL NOUN 1 a mountain system of central Scotland, extending from the southwest to the northeast and separating the Highlands from the Lowlands. Highest peak: Ben Nevis, 1343 m (4406 ft.). 2 a mountain range in SE Australia, in W Victoria. ◆ Also called: **the Grampians.**

Grampian Region NOUN a former local government region in NE Scotland, formed in 1975 from Aberdeenshire, Kincardineshire, and most of Banffshire and Morayshire; replaced in 1996 by the council areas of Aberdeenshire, City of Aberdeen, and Moray.

Gram-positive ADJECTIVE designating bacteria that retain the violet stain in Gram's method.

grampus (ˈgræmpəs) NOUN, *plural* **-puses.** 1 a widely distributed slaty-grey dolphin, *Grampus griseus*, with a blunt snout. 2 another name for **killer whale.**
▷**HISTORY** C16: from Old French *graspois*, from *gras* fat (from Latin *crassus*) + *pois* fish (from Latin *piscis*)

Gram's method NOUN *Bacteriol* a staining technique used to classify bacteria, based on their ability to retain or lose a violet colour, produced by crystal violet and iodine, after treatment with a decolorizing agent. See also **Gram-negative, Gram-positive.**
▷**HISTORY** C19: named after Hans Christian Joachim *Gram* (1853–1938), Danish physician

gran (græn) NOUN an informal word for **grandmother.**

Granada (grəˈnɑːdə) NOUN 1 a former kingdom of S Spain, in Andalusia: founded in the 13th century and divided in 1833 into the present-day provinces of Granada, Almería, and Málaga, in Andalusia. 2 a city in S Spain, in Andalusia: capital of the Moorish kingdom of Granada from 1238 to 1492 and a great commercial and cultural centre, containing the Alhambra palace (13th and 14th centuries); university (1531). Pop.: 241 471 (1998 est.). 3 a city in SW Nicaragua, on the NW shore of Lake Nicaragua: the oldest city in the country, founded in 1523 by Córdoba; attacked frequently by pirates in the 17th century. Pop.: 74 396 (1995 est.).

granadilla (ˌgrænəˈdɪlə) NOUN 1 any of various passionflowers, such as *Passiflora quadrangularis* (**giant granadilla**), that have edible egg-shaped fleshy fruit. 2 Also called: **passion fruit.** the fruit of such a plant.
▷**HISTORY** C18: from Spanish, diminutive of *granada* pomegranate, from Late Latin *grānātum*

granary (ˈgrænərɪ; *US* ˈgreɪnərɪ) NOUN, *plural* **-ries.** 1 a building or store room for storing threshed grain, farm feed, etc. 2 a region that produces a large amount of grain.
▷**HISTORY** C16: from Latin *grānārium*, from *grānum* GRAIN

Granary (ˈgrænərɪ) ADJECTIVE *Trademark* (of bread, flour, etc.) containing malted wheat grain.

Gran Canaria (graŋ kaˈnarja) NOUN the Spanish name for **Grand Canary.**

gran cassa (*Italian* gran ˈkassa) NOUN *Music* another name for **bass drum.**
▷**HISTORY** Italian: great drum

Gran Chaco (*Spanish* gran ˈtʃako) NOUN a plain of S central South America, between the Andes and the Paraguay River in SE Bolivia, E Paraguay, and N Argentina: huge swamps and scrub forest. Area: about 780 000 sq. km (300 000 sq. miles). Often shortened to: **Chaco.**

grand (grænd) ADJECTIVE 1 large or impressive in size, extent, or consequence: *grand mountain scenery*. 2 characterized by or attended with magnificence or display; sumptuous: *a grand feast*. 3 of great distinction or pretension; dignified or haughty. 4 designed to impress: *he punctuated his story with grand gestures*. 5 very good; wonderful. 6 comprehensive; complete: *a grand total*. 7 worthy of respect; fine: *a grand old man*. 8 large or impressive in conception or execution: *grand ideas*. 9 most important; chief: *the grand arena*. ◆ NOUN 10 short for **grand piano.** 11 (*plural* **grand**) *Slang* a thousand pounds or dollars.
▷**HISTORY** C16: from Old French, from Latin *grandis*
▸ˈ**grandly** ADVERB ▸ˈ**grandness** NOUN

grand- PREFIX (in designations of kinship) one generation removed in ascent or descent: *grandson; grandfather*.
▷**HISTORY** from French *grand-*, on the model of Latin *magnus* in such phrases as *avunculus magnus* great-uncle

grandad, granddad (ˈgrænˌdæd), **grandaddy,** *or* **granddaddy** (ˈgrænˌdædɪ) NOUN, *plural* **-dads** *or* **-daddies.** informal words for **grandfather.**

grandad shirt NOUN a long-sleeved collarless shirt.

grandam (ˈgrændəm, -dæm) *or* **grandame** (ˈgrændeɪm, -dəm) NOUN an archaic word for **grandmother.**
▷**HISTORY** C13: from Anglo-French *grandame*, from Old French GRAND- + *dame* lady, mother

grandaunt (ˈgrændˌɑːnt) NOUN another name for **great-aunt.**

Grand Bahama NOUN an island in the Atlantic, in the W Bahamas. Pop.: 40 898 (1990). Area: 1114 sq. km (430 sq. miles).

Grand Banks PLURAL NOUN a part of the continental shelf in the Atlantic, extending for about 560 km (350 miles) off the SE coast of Newfoundland: meeting place of the cold Labrador Current and the warm Gulf Stream, producing frequent fogs and rich fishing grounds.

Grand Canal NOUN 1 a canal in E China, extending north from Hangzhou to Tianjin: the longest canal in China, now partly silted up; central section, linking the Yangtze and Yellow Rivers, finished in 486 B.C.; north section finished by Kublai Khan between 1282 and 1292. Length: about 1600 km (1000 miles). Chinese name: **Da Yunhe.** 2 a canal in Venice, forming the main water thoroughfare: noted for its bridges, the Rialto, and the fine palaces along its banks.

Grand Canary NOUN an island in the Atlantic, in the Canary Islands: part of the Spanish province of Las Palmas. Capital: Las Palmas. Pop.: 631 000 (latest est.). Area: 1533 sq. km (592 sq. miles). Spanish name: **Gran Canaria.**

Grand Canyon NOUN a gorge of the Colorado River in N Arizona, extending from its junction with the Little Colorado River to Lake Mead; cut by vertical river erosion through the multicoloured strata of a high plateau; partly contained in the **Grand Canyon National Park,** covering 2610 sq. km (1008 sq. miles). Length: 451 km (280 miles). Width: 6 km (4 miles) to 29 km (18 miles). Greatest depth: over 1.5 km (1 mile).

grand chain NOUN a figure in formation dances, such as the lancers and Scottish reels, in which couples split up and move around in a circle in opposite directions, passing all other dancers until reaching their original partners.

grandchild (ˈgrænˌtʃaɪld) NOUN, *plural* **-children** (-ˌtʃɪldrən). the son or daughter of one's child.

Grand Coulee (ˈkuːlɪ) NOUN a canyon in central Washington State, over 120 m (400 ft.) deep, at the N end of which is situated the **Grand Coulee Dam,** on the Columbia River. Height of dam: 168 m (550 ft.). Length of dam: 1310 m (4300 ft.).

granddaughter (ˈgrænˌdɔːtə) NOUN a daughter of one's son or daughter.

grand duchess NOUN 1 the wife or a widow of a grand duke. 2 a woman who holds the rank of grand duke in her own right.

grand duchy NOUN the territory, state, or principality of a grand duke or grand duchess.

grand duke NOUN 1 a prince or nobleman who rules a territory, state, or principality. 2 a son or a male descendant in the male line of a Russian tsar. 3 a medieval Russian prince who ruled over other princes.

grande dame *French* (grɑ̃d dam) NOUN a woman regarded as the most experienced, prominent, or venerable member of her profession, etc.: *the* grande dame *of fashion*.

grandee (grænˈdiː) NOUN 1 a Spanish or Portuguese prince or nobleman of the highest rank. 2 a man of great rank or eminence.
▷**HISTORY** C16: from Spanish *grande*
▸**granˈdeeship** NOUN

Grande-Terre (*French* grɑ̃dtɛr) NOUN a French

island in the Caribbean, in the Lesser Antilles: one of the two main islands which constitute Guadeloupe. Chief town: Pointe-à-Pitre.

grandeur ('grændʒə) NOUN 1 personal greatness, esp when based on dignity, character, or accomplishments. 2 magnificence; splendour. 3 pretentious or bombastic behaviour.

Grand Falls PLURAL NOUN the former name (until 1965) of **Churchill Falls.**

grandfather ('græn,fɑːðə, 'grænd-) NOUN 1 the father of one's father or mother. 2 *(often plural)* a male ancestor. 3 *(often capital)* a familiar term of address for an old man. 4 *Dialect* a caterpillar or woodlouse.

grandfather clause NOUN 1 *US history* a clause in the constitutions of several Southern states that waived electoral literacy requirements for lineal descendants of people voting before 1867, thus ensuring the franchise for illiterate Whites: declared unconstitutional in 1915. 2 a clause in legislation that forbids or regulates an activity so that those engaged in it are exempted from the ban.

grandfather clock NOUN any of various types of long-pendulum clocks in tall standing wooden cases, usually between six and eight feet tall. Also called: **longcase clock.**

grandfatherly ('græn,fɑːðəlɪ, 'grænd-) ADJECTIVE of, resembling, or suitable to a grandfather, esp in being kindly.

grand final NOUN *Austral* the final game of the season in any of various sports, esp football.

Grand Guignol *French* (grɑ̃ giɲɔl) NOUN **a** a brief sensational play intended to horrify. **b** *(modifier)* of, relating to, or like plays of this kind.
▷HISTORY C20: after *Le Grand Guignol,* a small theatre in Montmartre, Paris

grandiloquent (græn'dɪləkwənt) ADJECTIVE inflated, pompous, or bombastic in style or expression.
▷HISTORY C16: from Latin *grandiloquus,* from *grandis* great + *loquī* to speak
▸**gran'diloquence** NOUN ▸**gran'diloquently** ADVERB

grandiose ('grændɪ,əʊs) ADJECTIVE 1 pretentiously grand or stately. 2 imposing in conception or execution.
▷HISTORY C19: from French, from Italian *grandioso,* from *grande* great; see GRAND
▸**'grandi,osely** ADVERB ▸**grandiosity** (,grændɪ'ɒsɪtɪ) NOUN

grandioso (,grændɪ'əʊsəʊ) ADJECTIVE, ADVERB *Music* (to be played) in a grand manner.

grand jury NOUN *Law* (esp in the US and, now rarely, in Canada) a jury of between 12 and 23 persons summoned to inquire into accusations of crime and ascertain whether the evidence is adequate to found an indictment. Abolished in Britain in 1948. Compare **petit jury.**

Grand Lama NOUN either of two high priests of Lamaism, the Dalai Lama or the Panchen Lama.

grand larceny NOUN 1 (formerly in England) the theft of property valued at over 12 pence. Abolished in 1827. 2 (in some states of the US) the theft of property of which the value is above a specified figure, varying from state to state but usually being between $25 and $60. ◆ Compare **petit larceny.**

grandma ('græn,mɑː, 'grænd-, 'græm-), **grandmama,** *or* **grandmamma** ('grænmə,mɑː, 'grænd-) NOUN informal words for **grandmother.**

grand mal (grɒn mæl; *French* grɑ̃ mal) NOUN a form of epilepsy characterized by loss of consciousness for up to five minutes and violent convulsions. Compare **petit mal.**
▷HISTORY French: great illness

Grand Manan (mə'næn) NOUN a Canadian island, off the SW coast of New Brunswick: separated from the coast of Maine by the **Grand Manan Channel.** Area: 147 sq. km (57 sq. miles).

Grand Marnier ('grɒn 'mɑːnɪ,eɪ; *French* grɑ̃ marnje) NOUN *Trademark* a French cognac-based liqueur with an orange flavour.

grandmaster ('grænd,mɑːstə) NOUN 1 *Chess* **a** one of the top chess players of a particular country. **b** *(capital as part of title)*: *Grandmaster of the USSR.* 2 *Chess* Also called: **International Grandmaster.** a player who has been awarded the highest title by the Fédération Internationale des Échecs. 3 a leading exponent of any of various arts.

Grand Master NOUN the title borne by the head of any of various societies, orders, and other organizations, such as the Templars or Freemasons, or the various martial arts.

grandmother ('græn,mʌðə, 'grænd-) NOUN 1 the mother of one's father or mother. 2 *(often plural)* a female ancestor. 3 *(often capital)* a familiar term of address for an old woman. 4 **teach one's grandmother to suck eggs.** See **egg**[1] (sense 8).

grandmother clock NOUN a longcase clock with a pendulum, about two thirds the size of a grandfather clock.

grandmotherly ('græn,mʌðəlɪ, 'grænd-) ADJECTIVE of, resembling, or suitable to a grandmother, esp in being protective, indulgent, or solicitous.

Grand Mufti NOUN 1 the titular head of the Muslim community in Jerusalem and formerly the chief constitutional administrator there. 2 (in Turkey) the former official head of the state religion.

Grand National NOUN **the.** an annual steeplechase run at Aintree, Liverpool, since 1839.

grandnephew ('græn,nɛvjuː, -,nɛfjuː, 'grænd-) NOUN another name for **great-nephew.**

grandniece ('græn,niːs, 'grænd-) NOUN another name for **great-niece.**

Grand Old Party NOUN (in the US) a nickname for the Republican Party since 1880. Abbreviation: **GOP.**

grand opera NOUN an opera that has a serious plot and is entirely in musical form, with no spoken dialogue.

grandpa ('græn,pɑː, 'grænd-, 'græm-) *or* **grandpapa** ('grænpə,pɑː, 'grænd-) NOUN informal words for **grandfather.**

grandparent ('græn,pɛərənt, 'grænd-) NOUN the father or mother of either of one's parents.

grand piano NOUN a form of piano in which the strings are arranged horizontally. Grand pianos exist in three sizes (see **baby grand, boudoir grand, concert grand**). Compare **upright piano.**

Grand Pré (grɒn preɪ; *French* grɑ̃ pre) NOUN a village in SE Canada, in W Nova Scotia: setting of Longfellow's *Evangeline.*

Grand Prix (*French* grɑ̃ pri) NOUN 1 **a** any of a series of formula motor races held to determine the annual Drivers' World Championship. **b** *(as modifier)*: *a Grand Prix car.* 2 *Horse racing* a race for three-year-old horses run at Maisons Lafitte near Paris. 3 a very important competitive event in various other sports, such as athletics, snooker, or powerboating.
▷HISTORY French: great prize

Grand Rapids NOUN *(functioning as singular)* a city in SW Michigan: electronics, car parts. Pop.: 197 800 (2000).

Grand Remonstrance NOUN **the.** *English history* the document prepared by the Long Parliament in 1640 listing the evils of the king's government, the abuses already rectified, and the reforms Parliament advocated.

grand seigneur *French* (grɑ̃ sɛɲœr) NOUN, *plural* ***grands seigneurs*** (grɑ̃ sɛɲœr). *Often ironic* a dignified or aristocratic man.
▷HISTORY literally: great lord

grand siècle *French* (grɑ̃ sjɛklə) NOUN, *plural* ***grands siècles*** (grɑ̃ sjɛklə). the 17th century in French art and literature, esp the classical period of Louis XIV.
▷HISTORY literally: great century

grandsire[1] ('græn,saɪə, 'grænd-) NOUN an archaic word for **grandfather.**

grandsire[2] ('grændsə, -,saɪə) NOUN *Bell-ringing* a well-established method used in change-ringing. See **method** (sense 4).

grand slam NOUN 1 *Bridge* the winning of 13 tricks by one player or side or the contract to do so. 2 the winning of all major competitions in a season, esp in tennis and golf. 3 *(often capital)* *Rugby Union* the winning of all five games in the annual Six Nations Championship involving England, Scotland, Wales, Ireland, France, and Italy. Compare **triple crown** (sense 3).

grandson ('grænsʌn, 'grænd-) NOUN a son of one's son or daughter.

grandstand ('græn,stænd, 'grænd-) NOUN 1 **a** a terraced block of seats, usually under a roof, commanding the best view at racecourses, football pitches, etc. **b** *(as modifier)*: *grandstand tickets.* 2 the spectators in a grandstand. 3 *(modifier)* as if from a grandstand; unimpeded (esp in the phrase **grandstand view**). ◆ VERB 4 *(intr)* *Informal, chiefly US and Canadian* to behave ostentatiously in an attempt to impress onlookers.
▸**'grand,stander** NOUN

grandstand finish NOUN a close or exciting ending to a sports match or competition.

grand tour NOUN 1 (formerly) an extended tour through the major cities of Europe, esp one undertaken by a rich or aristocratic Englishman to complete his education. 2 *Informal* an extended sightseeing trip, tour of inspection, etc.

granduncle ('grænd,ʌŋkᵊl) NOUN another name for **great-uncle.**

grand unified theory NOUN *Physics* any of a number of theories of elementary particles and fundamental interactions designed to explain the gravitational, electromagnetic, strong, and weak interactions in terms of a single mathematical formalism. Abbreviation: **GUT.**

Grand Union Canal NOUN a canal in S England linking London and the Midlands: opened in 1801.

grand vizier NOUN (formerly) the chief officer or minister of state in the Ottoman Empire and other Muslim countries.

grange (greɪndʒ) NOUN 1 *Chiefly Brit* a farm, esp a farmhouse or country house with its various outbuildings. 2 *History* an outlying farmhouse in which a religious establishment or feudal lord stored crops and tithes in kind. 3 *Archaic* a granary or barn.
▷HISTORY C13: from Anglo-French *graunge,* from Medieval Latin *grānica,* from Latin *grānum* GRAIN

Grange (greɪndʒ) NOUN (in the US) 1 **the.** an association of farmers that strongly influenced state legislatures in the late 19th century. 2 a lodge of this association.

Grangemouth ('greɪndʒmaʊθ, -məθ) NOUN a port in Scotland, in Falkirk council area: now Scotland's second port, with oil refineries, shipyards, and chemical industries. Pop.: 18 739 (1991).

grangerize *or* **grangerise** ('greɪndʒə,raɪz) VERB *(tr)* 1 to illustrate (a book) by inserting prints, drawings, etc., taken from other works. 2 to raid (books) to acquire material for illustrating another book.
▷HISTORY C19: named after Joseph *Granger,* 18th-century English writer, whose *Biographical History of England* (1769) included blank pages for illustrations to be supplied by the reader
▸**'grangerism** NOUN ▸**,grangeri'zation** *or* **,grangeri'sation** NOUN ▸**'granger,izer** *or* **'granger,iser** NOUN

grani- COMBINING FORM indicating grain: *graniform.*
▷HISTORY from Latin, from *grānum* GRAIN

Granicus (grə'naɪkəs) NOUN an ancient river in NW Asia Minor where Alexander the Great won his first major battle against the Persians (334 B.C.).

granite ('grænɪt) NOUN 1 a light-coloured coarse-grained acid plutonic igneous rock consisting of quartz, feldspars, and such ferromagnesian minerals as biotite or hornblende: widely used for building. 2 great hardness, endurance, or resolution. 3 another name for a **stone** (sense 9).
▷HISTORY C17: from Italian *granito* grained, from *granire* to grain, from *grano* grain, from Latin *grānum*
▸**'granite-,like** ADJECTIVE ▸**granitic** (grə'nɪtɪk) *or* **'granit,oid** ADJECTIVE

graniteware ('grænɪt,wɛə) NOUN 1 iron vessels coated with enamel of a granite-like appearance. 2 a type of very durable white semivitreous pottery. 3 a type of pottery with a speckled glaze.

granitite ('grænɪ,taɪt) NOUN any granite with a high content of biotite.

granitization *or* **granitisation** (,grænɪtaɪ'zeɪʃən) NOUN the metamorphic conversion of a rock into granite.

granivorous (græ'nɪvərəs) ADJECTIVE (of animals) feeding on seeds and grain.
▸**granivore** ('grænɪ,vɔː) NOUN

grannies ('grænɪz) PLURAL NOUN *NZ informal* Granny Smith apples.

grannom ('grænəm) NOUN a widespread caddis fly, *Brachycentrus subnubilus,* the larvae of which attach their cases to vegetation under running water and are esteemed as a bait by anglers.
▷HISTORY C18: altered from *green tail*

granny *or* **grannie** ('grænɪ) NOUN, *plural* **-nies.** 1 informal words for **grandmother.** 2 *Informal* an irritatingly fussy person. 3 a revolving cap on a chimneypot that keeps out rain, etc. 4 *Southern US* a midwife or nurse. 5 See **granny knot.**

granny bond NOUN (in Britain) an informal name for **retirement issue certificate,** an index-linked savings certificate, originally available only to people over retirement age.

granny flat NOUN self-contained accommodation within or built onto a house, suitable for an elderly parent. Also called: **granny annexe.**

grannyish ('granɪjɪʃ) ADJECTIVE typical of or suitable for an elderly woman; old-fashioned.

granny knot *or* **granny's knot** NOUN a reef knot with the ends crossed the wrong way, making it liable to slip or jam.

Granny Smith NOUN a variety of hard green-skinned apple eaten raw or cooked.
▷HISTORY C19: named after Maria Ann Smith, known as *Granny Smith* (died 1870), who first produced them at Eastwood, Sydney

grano- COMBINING FORM of or resembling granite: *granolith.*
▷HISTORY from German, from *Granit* GRANITE

granodiorite (ˌgrænəʊ'daɪəˌraɪt) NOUN a coarse-grained acid igneous rock containing almost twice as much plagioclase as orthoclase: intermediate in composition between granite and diorite.
▷HISTORY C19: from *grano* + DIORITE

granolith ('grænəʊˌlɪθ) NOUN a paving material consisting of a mixture of cement and crushed granite or granite chippings.
▸ˌ**grano'lithic** ADJECTIVE, NOUN

granophyre ('grænəʊˌfaɪə) NOUN a fine-grained granitic rock in which irregular crystals of intergrown quartz and feldspar are embedded in a groundmass of these minerals.
▷HISTORY C19: from GRAN(ITE) + *-phyre* after *porphyry*
▸**granophyric** (ˌgrænəʊ'fɪrɪk) ADJECTIVE

Gran Paradiso (*Italian* gram para'di:zo) NOUN a mountain in NW Italy, in NW Piedmont: the highest peak of the Graian Alps. Height: 4061 m (13 323 ft.).

grant (grɑ:nt) VERB (*tr*) 1 to consent to perform or fulfil: *to grant a wish.* 2 (*may take a clause as object*) to permit as a favour, indulgence, etc.: *to grant an interview.* 3 (*may take a clause as object*) to acknowledge the validity of; concede: *I grant what you say is true.* 4 to bestow, esp in a formal manner. 5 to transfer (property) to another, esp by deed; convey. 6 **take for granted. a** to accept or assume without question: *one takes certain amenities for granted.* **b** to fail to appreciate the value, merit, etc., of (a person). ◆ NOUN 7 a sum of money provided by a government, local authority, or public fund to finance educational study, overseas aid, building repairs, etc. 8 a privilege, right, etc., that has been granted. 9 the act of granting. 10 a transfer of property by deed or other written instrument; conveyance. 11 *US* a territorial unit in Maine, New Hampshire, and Vermont, originally granted to an individual or organization.
▷HISTORY C13: from Old French *graunter,* from Vulgar Latin *credentāre* (unattested), from Latin *crēdere* to believe
▸'**grantable** ADJECTIVE ▸'**granter** NOUN

Granta ('græntə, 'grɑ:ntə) NOUN the original name, still in use locally, for the River Cam.

grantee (grɑ:n'ti:) NOUN *Law* a person to whom a grant is made.

Grantham ('grænθəm) NOUN a town in E England, in Lincolnshire: birthplace of Sir Isaac Newton and Margaret Thatcher. Pop.: 33 243 (1991).

Granthi ('grʌnˌti:) NOUN the caretaker of a gurdwara and the reader of the Guru Granth, who officiates at Sikh ceremonies.
▷HISTORY from Punjabi: keeper of the (GURU) GRANTH

grant-in-aid NOUN, *plural* **grants-in-aid.** 1 a sum of money granted by one government to a lower level of government or to a dependency for a programme, etc. 2 *Education* a grant provided by the central government or local education authority to ensure consistent standards in buildings and other facilities.

grant-maintained ADJECTIVE (**grant maintained** when postpostive) (of schools or educational institutions) funded directly by central government.

grant of probate NOUN *Law* a certificate stating that a will is valid.

grantor (grɑ:n'tɔ:, 'grɑ:ntə) NOUN *Law* a person who makes a grant.

gran turismo ('græn tʊə'rɪzməʊ) NOUN, *plural* **gran turismos.** the full form of **GT.**
▷HISTORY C20: Italian, literally: great touring (i.e., touring on a grand scale)

granular ('grænjʊlə) ADJECTIVE 1 of, like, containing, or resembling a granule or granules. 2 having a grainy or granulated surface.
▸'**granularly** ADVERB

granularity (ˌgrænjʊ'lærɪtɪ) NOUN 1 the state or quality of being grainy or granular. 2 the state or quality of being composed of many individual pieces or elements.

granulate ('grænjʊˌleɪt) VERB 1 (*tr*) to make into grains. 2 to make or become roughened in surface texture. 3 (*intr*) (of a wound, ulcer, etc.) to form granulation tissue.
▸'**granulative** ADJECTIVE ▸'**granuˌlator** *or* '**granuˌlater** NOUN

granulated sugar NOUN a coarsely ground white sugar.

granulation (ˌgrænjʊ'leɪʃən) NOUN 1 the act or process of granulating. 2 a granulated texture or surface. 3 a single bump or grain in such a surface. 4 See **granulation tissue.** 5 Also called: **granule.** *Astronomy* any of numerous bright regions (approximate diameter 900 km) having a fine granular structure that can appear briefly on any part of the sun's surface.

granulation tissue NOUN a mass of new connective tissue and capillaries formed on the surface of a healing ulcer or wound, usually leaving a scar. Nontechnical name: **proud flesh.**

granule ('grænju:l) NOUN 1 a small grain. 2 *Geology* a single rock fragment in gravel, smaller than a pebble but larger than a sand grain. 3 *Astronomy* another name for **granulation** (sense 5).
▷HISTORY C17: from Late Latin *grānulum* a small GRAIN

granulite ('grænjʊˌlaɪt) NOUN a granular foliated metamorphic rock in which the minerals form a mosaic of equal-sized granules.
▸**granulitic** (ˌgrænjʊ'lɪtɪk) ADJECTIVE

granulocyte ('grænjʊləˌsaɪt) NOUN any of a group of phagocytic leucocytes having cytoplasmic granules that take up various dyes. See also **eosinophil, neutrophil** (sense 1), **basophil** (sense 2).
▸**granulocytic** (ˌgrænjʊlə'sɪtɪk) ADJECTIVE

granulocytopenia (ˌgrænjʊləʊˌsaɪtəʊ'pi:nɪə) NOUN a diminished number of granulocytes in the blood, which occurs in certain forms of anaemia.

granuloma (ˌgrænjʊ'ləʊmə) NOUN, *plural* **-mas** *or* **-mata** (-mətə). a tumour composed of granulation tissue produced in response to chronic infection, inflammation, a foreign body, or to unknown causes.
▸**granulomatous** (ˌgrænjʊ'lɒmətəs) ADJECTIVE

granulose ('grænjʊˌləʊs, -ˌləʊz) ADJECTIVE a less common word for **granular.**

grape (greɪp) NOUN 1 the fruit of the grapevine, which has a purple or green skin and sweet flesh: eaten raw, dried to make raisins, currants, or sultanas, or used for making wine. 2 any of various plants that bear grapelike fruit, such as the Oregon grape. 3 See **grapevine** (sense 1). 4 **the.** an informal term for **wine.** 5 See **grapeshot.**
▷HISTORY C13: from Old French *grape* bunch of grapes, of Germanic origin; compare Old High German *krāpfo;* related to CRAMP², GRAPPLE
▸'**grapeless** ADJECTIVE ▸'**grapeˌlike** ADJECTIVE ▸'**grapey** *or* '**grapy** ADJECTIVE

grapefruit ('greɪpˌfru:t) NOUN, *plural* **-fruit** *or* **-fruits.** 1 a tropical or subtropical cultivated evergreen rutaceous tree, *Citrus paradisi.* 2 the large round edible fruit of this tree, which has yellow rind and juicy slightly bitter pulp.

grape hyacinth NOUN any of various Eurasian liliaceous plants of the genus *Muscari,* esp *M. botryoides,* with clusters of rounded blue flowers resembling tiny grapes.

grape ivy NOUN See **rhoicissus.**

grapes (greɪps) NOUN (*functioning as singular*) *Vet science, archaic* an abnormal growth, resembling a bunch of grapes, on the fetlock of a horse.

grapeshot ('greɪpˌʃɒt) NOUN ammunition for cannons consisting of a canvas tube containing a cluster of small iron or lead balls that scatter after firing.

grape sugar NOUN another name for **dextrose.**

grapevine ('greɪpˌvaɪn) NOUN 1 any of several vitaceous vines of the genus *Vitis,* esp *V. vinifera* of E Asia, widely cultivated for its fruit (grapes): family *Vitaceae.* 2 *Informal* an unofficial means of relaying information, esp from person to person. 3 a wrestling hold in which a wrestler entwines his own leg around his opponent's and exerts pressure against various joints.

grapey *or* **grapy** ('greɪpɪ) ADJECTIVE **-pier, -piest.** tasting or smelling of grapes.

graph (grɑ:f, græf) NOUN 1 Also called: **chart.** a drawing depicting the relation between certain sets of numbers or quantities by means of a series of dots, lines, etc., plotted with reference to a set of axes. See also **bar graph.** 2 *Maths* a drawing depicting a functional relation between two or three variables by means of a curve or surface containing only those points whose coordinates satisfy the relation. 3 *Maths* a structure represented by a diagram consisting of points (vertices) joined by lines (edges). 4 *Linguistics* a symbol in a writing system not further subdivisible into other such symbols. ◆ VERB 5 (*tr*) to draw or represent in a graph.
▷HISTORY C19: short for *graphic formula*

-graph NOUN COMBINING FORM 1 an instrument that writes or records: *telegraph.* 2 a writing, record, or drawing: *autograph; lithograph.*
▷HISTORY via Latin from Greek *-graphos,* from *graphein* to write
▸**-graphic** *or* **-graphical** ADJECTIVE COMBINING FORM
▸**-graphically** ADVERB COMBINING FORM

grapheme ('græfi:m) NOUN *Linguistics* one of a set of orthographic symbols (letters or combinations of letters) in a given language that serve to distinguish one word from another and usually correspond to or represent phonemes, e.g. the *f* in *fun,* the *ph* in *phantom,* and the *gh* in *laugh.*
▷HISTORY C20: from Greek *graphēma* a letter
▸**gra'phemically** ADVERB

-grapher NOUN COMBINING FORM 1 indicating a person who writes about or is skilled in a subject: *geographer; photographer.* 2 indicating a person who writes, records, or draws in a specified way: *stenographer; lithographer.*

graphic ('græfɪk) *or* **graphical** ADJECTIVE 1 vividly or clearly described: *a graphic account of the disaster.* 2 sexually explicit. 3 of or relating to writing or other inscribed representations: *graphic symbols.* 4 *Maths* using, relating to, or determined by a graph: *a graphic representation of the figures.* 5 of or relating to the graphic arts. 6 *Geology* having or denoting a texture formed by intergrowth of the crystals to resemble writing: *graphic granite.*
▷HISTORY C17: from Latin *graphicus,* from Greek *graphikos,* from *graphein* to write; see CARVE
▸'**graphically** *or* '**graphicly** ADVERB ▸'**graphicalness** *or* '**graphicness** NOUN

graphicacy ('græfɪkəsɪ) NOUN the ability to understand and use maps, plans, symbols, etc.
▷HISTORY C20: formed on the model of *literacy*

graphical user interface NOUN an interface between a user and a computer system that involves the use of a mouse-controlled screen cursor to select options from menus, make choices with buttons, start programs by clicking icons, etc. Abbreviation: **GUI.**

graphic arts PLURAL NOUN any of the fine or applied visual arts based on drawing or the use of line, as opposed to colour or relief, on a plane surface, esp illustration and printmaking of all kinds.

graphic equalizer NOUN an electronic device for cutting or boosting selected frequencies, using small linear faders. Compare **parametric equalizer.**

graphic novel NOUN a novel in the form of a comic strip.

graphics ('græfɪks) NOUN [1] (*functioning as singular*) the process or art of drawing in accordance with mathematical principles. [2] (*functioning as singular*) the study of writing systems. [3] (*functioning as plural*) the drawings, photographs, etc., in the layout of a magazine or book, or in a television or film production. [4] (*functioning as plural*) the information displayed on a visual display unit or on a computer printout in the form of diagrams, graphs, pictures, and symbols.

graphite ('græfaɪt) NOUN a blackish soft allotropic form of carbon in hexagonal crystalline form: used in pencils, crucibles, and electrodes, as a lubricant, as a moderator in nuclear reactors, and, in a carbon fibre form, as a tough lightweight material for sporting equipment. Also called: **plumbago.**
▷HISTORY C18: from German *Graphit;* from Greek *graphein* to write + -ITE[1]
▸**graphitic** (grə'fɪtɪk) ADJECTIVE

graphitize *or* **graphitise** ('græfɪˌtaɪz) VERB (*tr*) [1] to convert (a substance) into graphite, usually by heating. [2] to coat or impregnate with graphite.
▸ˌ**graphiti'zation** *or* ˌ**graphiti'sation** NOUN

graphology (græ'fɒlədʒɪ) NOUN [1] the study of handwriting, esp to analyse the writer's character. [2] *Linguistics* the study of writing systems.
▸**graphologic** (ˌgræfə'lɒdʒɪk) *or* ˌ**grapho'logical** ADJECTIVE ▸**gra'phologist** NOUN

graphomotor ('græfəˌməʊtə) ADJECTIVE of or relating to the muscular movements used or required in writing.

graph paper NOUN paper printed with intersecting lines, usually horizontal and vertical and equally spaced, for drawing graphs, diagrams, etc.

-graphy NOUN COMBINING FORM [1] indicating a form or process of writing, representing, etc.: *calligraphy; photography.* [2] indicating an art or descriptive science: *choreography; oceanography.*
▷HISTORY via Latin from Greek *-graphia,* from *graphein* to write

grapnel ('græpnᵊl) NOUN [1] a device with a multiple hook at one end and attached to a rope, which is thrown or hooked over a firm mooring to secure an object attached to the other end of the rope. [2] a light anchor for small boats.
▷HISTORY C14: from Old French *grapin* a little hook, from *grape* a hook; see GRAPE

grappa ('græpə) NOUN a spirit distilled from the fermented remains of grapes after pressing.
▷HISTORY Italian: grape stalk, of Germanic origin; see GRAPE

grapple ('græpᵊl) VERB [1] to come to grips with (one or more persons), esp to struggle in hand-to-hand combat. [2] (*intr;* foll by *with*) to cope or contend: *to grapple with a financial problem.* [3] (*tr*) to secure with a grapple. ◆ NOUN [4] any form of hook or metal instrument by which something is secured, such as a grapnel. [5] **a** the act of gripping or seizing, as in wrestling. **b** a grip or hold. [6] a contest of grappling, esp a wrestling match.
▷HISTORY C16: from Old French *grappelle* a little hook, from *grape* hook; see GRAPNEL
▸'**grappler** NOUN

grapple plant NOUN a herbaceous plant, *Harpagophytum procumbens,* of southern Africa, whose fruits are covered with large woody barbed hooks: family *Pedaliaceae.* Also called: **wait-a-bit.**

grappling ('græplɪŋ) NOUN [1] the act of gripping or seizing, as in wrestling. [2] a hook used for securing something.

grappling iron *or* **hook** NOUN a grapnel, esp one used for securing ships.

graptolite ('græptəˌlaɪt) NOUN any extinct Palaeozoic colonial animal of the class *Graptolithina,* usually regarded as related to either the hemichordates or the coelenterates: a common fossil, used to determine the age of sedimentary rocks.
▷HISTORY C19: from Greek *graptos* written, from *graphein* to write + -LITE

Grasmere ('grɑːsˌmɪə) NOUN a village in NW England, in Cumbria at the head of **Lake Grasmere:** home of William Wordsworth and of Thomas de Quincey.

grasp (grɑːsp) VERB [1] to grip (something) firmly with or as if with the hands. [2] (when *intr,* often foll by *at*) to struggle, snatch, or grope (for). [3] (*tr*) to understand, esp with effort. ◆ NOUN [4] the act of grasping. [5] a grip or clasp, as of a hand. [6] the capacity to accomplish (esp in the phrase **within one's grasp**). [7] total rule or possession. [8] understanding; comprehension.
▷HISTORY C14: from Low German *grapsen;* related to Old English *græppian* to seize, Old Norse *grāpa* to steal
▸'**graspable** ADJECTIVE ▸'**grasper** NOUN

grasping ('grɑːspɪŋ) ADJECTIVE greedy; avaricious; rapacious.
▸'**graspingly** ADVERB

grass (grɑːs) NOUN [1] any monocotyledonous plant of the family *Poaceae* (formerly *Gramineae*), having jointed stems sheathed by long narrow leaves, flowers in spikes, and seedlike fruits. The family includes cereals, bamboo, etc. [2] such plants collectively, in a lawn, meadow, etc. Related adjectives: **gramineous, verdant.** [3] any similar plant, such as knotgrass, deergrass, or scurvy grass. [4] ground on which such plants grow; a lawn, field, etc. [5] ground on which animals are grazed; pasture. [6] a slang word for **marijuana.** [7] *Brit slang* a person who informs, esp on criminals. [8] short for **sparrowgrass.** [9] **get off the grass.** *NZ informal* an exclamation of disbelief. [10] **let the grass grow under one's feet.** to squander time or opportunity. [11] **put out to grass. a** to retire (a racehorse). **b** *Informal* to retire (a person). ◆ VERB [12] to cover or become covered with grass. [13] to feed or be fed with grass. [14] (*tr*) to spread (cloth) out on grass for drying or bleaching in the sun. [15] (*tr*) *Sport* to knock or bring down (an opponent). [16] (*tr*) to shoot down (a bird). [17] (*tr*) to land (a fish) on a river bank. [18] (*intr;* usually foll by *on*) *Brit slang* to inform, esp to the police. ◆ See also **grass up.**
▷HISTORY Old English *græs;* related to Old Norse, Gothic, Old High German *gras,* Middle High German *gruose* sap
▸'**grassless** ADJECTIVE ▸'**grassˌlike** ADJECTIVE

grass box NOUN a container attached to a lawn mower that receives grass after it has been cut.

grass cloth NOUN a cloth made from plant fibres, such as jute or hemp.

grass court NOUN a tennis court covered with grass. See also **hard court.**

grassfinch ('grɑːsˌfɪntʃ) NOUN any Australian weaverbird of the genus *Poephila* and related genera, many of which are brightly coloured and kept as cagebirds.

grass hockey NOUN *Canadian* field hockey, as contrasted with ice hockey.

grasshook ('grɑːsˌhʊk) NOUN another name for **sickle.**

grasshopper ('grɑːsˌhɒpə) NOUN [1] any orthopterous insect of the families *Acrididae* (**short-horned grasshoppers**) and *Tettigoniidae* (**long-horned grasshoppers**), typically terrestrial, feeding on plants, and producing a ticking sound by rubbing the hind legs against the leathery forewings. See also **locust** (sense 1), **katydid.** [2] **knee-high to a grasshopper.** *Informal* very young or very small. [3] an iced cocktail of equal parts of crème de menthe, crème de cacao, and cream. [4] (*modifier*) unable to concentrate on any one subject for long: *a grasshopper mind.*

grassland ('grɑːsˌlænd) NOUN [1] land, such as a prairie, on which grass predominates. [2] land reserved for natural grass pasture.

grass moth NOUN any of a large subfamily of small night-flying pyralid moths, esp *Crambus pratellus,* that during the day cling to grass stems.

grass-of-Parnassus NOUN a herbaceous perennial N temperate marsh plant, *Parnassia palustris,* with solitary whitish flowers: family *Parnassiaceae.*

grassquit ('grɑːsˌkwɪt) NOUN any tropical American finch of the genus *Tiaris* and related genera, such as *T. olivacea* (**yellow-faced grassquit**).
▷HISTORY from GRASS + *quit,* a bird name in Jamaica

grass roots PLURAL NOUN [1] **a** the ordinary people as distinct from the active leadership of a party or organization: used esp of the rank-and-file members of a political party, or of the voters themselves. **b** (*as modifier*): *the newly elected MP expressed a wish for greater contact with people at grass-roots level.* [2] the origin or essentials.
▷HISTORY C20: sense 1 originally US, with reference to rural areas in contrast to the towns

grass snake NOUN [1] a harmless nonvenomous European colubrid snake, *Natrix natrix,* having a brownish-green body with variable markings. [2] any of several similar related European snakes, such as *Natrix maura* (**viperine grass snake**).

grass tree NOUN [1] Also called: **black boy.** any plant of the Australian genus *Xanthorrhoea,* having a woody stem, stiff grasslike leaves, and a spike of small white flowers: family *Xanthorrhoeaceae.* Some species produce fragrant resins. Also called: **yacca, yacka.** See also **acaroid gum.** [2] any of several similar Australasian plants.

grass up VERB (*tr, adverb*) *Slang* to inform on (someone), esp to the police.

grass widow NOUN [1] a woman divorced, separated, or living away from her spouse. [2] a woman whose spouse is regularly away for short periods.
▷HISTORY C16, meaning a discarded mistress: perhaps an allusion to a grass bed as representing an illicit relationship; compare BASTARD; C19 in the modern sense

grass widower NOUN [1] a man divorced, separated, or living away from his spouse. [2] a man whose spouse is regularly away for short periods.

grassy ('grɑːsɪ) ADJECTIVE **grassier, grassiest.** covered with, containing, or resembling grass.
▸'**grassiness** NOUN

grate[1] (greɪt) VERB [1] (*tr*) to reduce to small shreds by rubbing against a rough or sharp perforated surface: *to grate carrots.* [2] to scrape (an object) against something or (objects) together, producing a harsh rasping sound, or (of objects) to scrape with such a sound. [3] (*intr;* foll by *on* or *upon*) to annoy. ◆ NOUN [4] a harsh rasping sound.
▷HISTORY C15: from Old French *grater* to scrape, of Germanic origin; compare Old High German *krazzōn*

grate[2] (greɪt) NOUN [1] a framework of metal bars for holding fuel in a fireplace, stove, or furnace. [2] a less common word for **fireplace.** [3] another name for **grating**[1] (sense 1). [4] *Mining* a perforated metal screen for grading crushed ore. ◆ VERB [5] (*tr*) to provide with a grate or grates.
▷HISTORY C14: from Old French *grate,* from Latin *crātis* hurdle

grateful ('greɪtfʊl) ADJECTIVE [1] thankful for gifts, favours, etc.; appreciative. [2] showing gratitude: *a grateful letter.* [3] favourable or pleasant: *a grateful rest.*
▷HISTORY C16: from obsolete *grate,* from Latin *grātus* + -FUL
▸'**gratefully** ADVERB ▸'**gratefulness** NOUN

grater ('greɪtə) NOUN [1] a kitchen utensil with sharp-edged perforations for grating carrots, cheese, etc. [2] a person or thing that grates.

graticule ('grætɪˌkjuːl) NOUN [1] the grid of intersecting lines, esp of latitude and longitude on which a map is drawn. [2] another name for **reticle.** [3] a transparent scale in front of a cathode-ray oscilloscope or other measuring instrument.
▷HISTORY C19: from French, from Latin *crāticula,* from *crātis* wickerwork

gratification (ˌgrætɪfɪ'keɪʃən) NOUN [1] the act of gratifying or the state of being gratified. [2] something that gratifies. [3] an obsolete word for **gratuity.**

gratify ('grætɪˌfaɪ) VERB **-fies, -fying, -fied.** (*tr*) [1] to satisfy or please. [2] to yield to or indulge (a desire, whim, etc.). [3] *Obsolete* to reward.
▷HISTORY C16: from Latin *grātificārī* to do a favour to, from *grātus* grateful + *facere* to make
▸'**gratiˌfier** NOUN

gratify ('grætɪˌfaɪɪŋ) ADJECTIVE giving one satisfaction or pleasure.
▸'**gratiˌfyingly** ADVERB

gratin (*French* gratɛ̃) See **au gratin.**

grating[1] ('greɪtɪŋ) NOUN [1] Also called: **grate.** a framework of metal bars in the form of a grille set into a wall, pavement, etc., serving as a cover or guard but admitting air and sometimes light. [2] short for **diffraction grating.**

grating[2] ('greɪtɪŋ) ADJECTIVE [1] (of sounds) harsh

and rasping. 2 annoying; irritating. ◆ NOUN 3 (*often plural*) something produced by grating.
▸ **'gratingly** ADVERB

gratis ('greɪtɪs, 'grætɪs, 'grɑːtɪs) ADVERB, ADJECTIVE (*postpositive*) without payment; free of charge.
▷ HISTORY C15: from Latin: out of kindness, from *grātīs*, ablative pl of *grātia* favour

gratitude ('grætɪˌtjuːd) NOUN a feeling of thankfulness or appreciation, as for gifts or favours.
▷ HISTORY C16: from Medieval Latin *grātitūdō*, from Latin *grātus* GRATEFUL

gratuitous (grə'tjuːɪtəs) ADJECTIVE 1 given or received without payment or obligation. 2 without cause; unjustified. 3 *Law* given or made without receiving any value in return: *a gratuitous agreement*.
▷ HISTORY C17: from Latin *grātuītus*, from *grātia* favour
▸ **gra'tuitously** ADVERB ▸ **gra'tuitousness** NOUN

gratuity (grə'tjuːɪtɪ) NOUN, *plural* **-ties**. 1 a gift or reward, usually of money, for services rendered; tip. 2 something given without claim or obligation. 3 *Military* a financial award granted for long or meritorious service.

gratulate ('grætjʊˌleɪt) VERB (*tr*) *Archaic* 1 to greet joyously. 2 to congratulate.
▷ HISTORY C16: from Latin *grātulārī*, from *grātus* pleasing
▸ **'gratulant** ADJECTIVE ▸ **ˌgratu'lation** NOUN ▸ **'gratulatory** ADJECTIVE

Graubünden (*German* grau'byndən) NOUN an Alpine canton of E Switzerland: the largest of the cantons, but sparsely populated. Capital: Chur. Pop.: 186 000 (2000 est.). Area: 7109 sq. km (2773 sq. miles). Italian name: **Grigioni**. Romansch name: **Grishun**. French name: **Grisons**.

graunch (grɔːntʃ) VERB (*tr*) *NZ* to crush or destroy.
▷ HISTORY C19: from English dialect word, of imitative origin

graupel ('graʊpᵊl) NOUN soft hail or snow pellets.
▷ HISTORY German, from *Graupe*, probably from Serbo-Croat *krupa*; related to Russian *krupá* peeled grain

grav (græv) NOUN a unit of acceleration equal to the standard acceleration of free fall. 1 grav is equivalent to 9.806 65 metres per second per second. Symbol: g.

gravadlax ('grævədˌlæks) NOUN another name for **gravlax**.

gravamen (grə'veɪmɛn) NOUN, *plural* **-vamina** (-'væmɪnə). 1 *Law* that part of an accusation weighing most heavily against an accused. 2 *Law* the substance or material grounds of a complaint. 3 a rare word for **grievance**.
▷ HISTORY C17: from Late Latin: trouble, from Latin *gravāre* to load, from *gravis* heavy; see GRAVE²

grave¹ (greɪv) NOUN 1 a place for the burial of a corpse, esp beneath the ground and usually marked by a tombstone. Related adjective: **sepulchral**. 2 something resembling a grave or resting place: *the ship went to its grave*. 3 (often preceded by *the*) a poetic term for **death**. 4 **have one foot in the grave**. *Informal* to be near death. 5 **to make (someone) turn (over) in his grave**. to do something that would have shocked or distressed (someone now dead): *many modern dictionaries would make Dr Johnson turn in his grave*.
▷ HISTORY Old English *græf*; related to Old Frisian *gref*, Old High German *grab*, Old Slavonic *grobŭ*; see GRAVE³

grave² (greɪv) ADJECTIVE 1 serious and solemn: *a grave look*. 2 full of or suggesting danger: *a grave situation*. 3 important; crucial: *grave matters of state*. 4 (of colours) sober or dull. 5 (*also* grɑːv) *Phonetics* **a** (of a vowel or syllable in some languages with a pitch accent, such as ancient Greek) spoken on a lower or falling musical pitch relative to neighbouring syllables or vowels. **b** of or relating to an accent (`) over vowels, denoting a pronunciation with lower or falling musical pitch (as in ancient Greek), with certain special quality (as in French), or in a manner that gives the vowel status as a syllable nucleus not usually possessed by it in that position (as in English *agèd*). Compare **acute** (sense 8), **circumflex**. ◆ NOUN 6 (*also* grɑːv) a grave accent.
▷ HISTORY C16: from Old French, from Latin *gravis*; related to Greek *barus* heavy; see GRAVAMEN
▸ **'gravely** ADVERB ▸ **'graveness** NOUN

grave³ (greɪv) VERB **graves, graving, graved; graved** *or* **graven**. (*tr*) *Archaic* 1 to cut, carve, sculpt, or engrave. 2 to fix firmly in the mind.
▷ HISTORY Old English *grafan*; related to Old Norse *grafa*, Old High German *graban* to dig

grave⁴ (greɪv) VERB (*tr*) *Nautical* to clean and apply a coating of pitch to (the bottom of a vessel).
▷ HISTORY C15: perhaps from Old French *grave* GRAVEL

grave⁵ ('grɑːvɪ) ADJECTIVE, ADVERB *Music* to be performed in a solemn manner.
▷ HISTORY C17: from Italian: heavy, from Latin *gravis*

grave clothes PLURAL NOUN the wrappings in which a dead body is interred.

gravel ('grævᵊl) NOUN 1 an unconsolidated mixture of rock fragments that is coarser than sand. 2 *Geology* a mixture of rock fragments with diameters in the range 4–76 mm. 3 *Pathol* small rough calculi in the kidneys or bladder. ◆ VERB **-els, -elling, -elled** *or US* **-els, -eling, -eled**. (*tr*) 4 to cover with gravel. 5 to confound or confuse. 6 *US informal* to annoy or disturb.
▷ HISTORY C13: from Old French *gravele*, diminutive of *grave* gravel, perhaps of Celtic origin
▸ **'gravelish** ADJECTIVE

gravel-blind ADJECTIVE *Literary* almost entirely blind.
▷ HISTORY C16: from GRAVEL + BLIND, formed on the model of SAND-BLIND

gravelly ('grævəlɪ) ADJECTIVE 1 consisting of or abounding in gravel. 2 of or like gravel. 3 (esp of a voice) harsh and grating.

gravel-voiced ADJECTIVE speaking in a rough and rasping tone.

graven ('greɪvᵊn) VERB 1 a past participle of **grave³**. ◆ ADJECTIVE 2 strongly fixed.

Gravenhage (xraːvən'haːxə) NOUN **'s.** a Dutch name for (The) **Hague**.

graven image NOUN *Chiefly Bible* a carved image used as an idol.

graveolent ('grævɪələnt) ADJECTIVE (of plants) having a strong fetid smell.
▷ HISTORY C17: from Latin *gravis* heavy + *olēre* to smell

graver ('greɪvə) NOUN any of various engraving, chasing, or sculpting tools, such as a burin.

Graves (grɑːv) NOUN (*sometimes not capital*) a white or red wine from the district around Bordeaux, France.

Graves' disease (greɪvz) NOUN another name for **exophthalmic goitre**.
▷ HISTORY C19: named after R. J. *Graves* (1796–1853), Irish physician

Gravesend (ˌgreɪvz'ɛnd) NOUN a river port in SE England, in NW Kent on the Thames. Pop.: 51 435 (1991).

gravestone ('greɪvˌstəʊn) NOUN a stone marking a grave and usually inscribed with the name and dates of the person buried.

Gravettian (grə'vɛtɪən) ADJECTIVE of, referring to, or characteristic of an Upper Palaeolithic culture, characterized esp by small pointed blades with blunt backs.
▷ HISTORY C20: from *La Gravette* on the Dordogne, France

grave-wax NOUN the nontechnical name for **adipocere**.

graveyard ('greɪvˌjɑːd) NOUN a place for graves; a burial ground, esp a small one or one in a churchyard.

graveyard orbit NOUN another name for **dump orbit**.

graveyard shift NOUN *US* the working shift between midnight and morning.

graveyard slot NOUN *Television* the hours from late night until early morning when the number of people watching television is at its lowest.

gravid ('grævɪd) ADJECTIVE the technical word for **pregnant**.
▷ HISTORY C16: from Latin *gravidus*, from *gravis* heavy
▸ **gra'vidity** *or* **'gravidness** NOUN ▸ **'gravidly** ADVERB

gravimeter (grə'vɪmɪtə) NOUN 1 an instrument for measuring the earth's gravitational field at points on its surface. 2 an instrument for measuring relative density.
▷ HISTORY C18: from French *gravimètre*, from Latin *gravis* heavy
▸ **gra'vimetry** NOUN

gravimetric (ˌgrævɪ'mɛtrɪk) *or* **gravimetrical** ADJECTIVE of, concerned with, or using measurement by weight. Compare **volumetric**.
▸ **ˌgravi'metrically** ADVERB

gravimetric analysis NOUN *Chem* quantitative analysis by weight, usually involving the precipitation, filtration, drying, and weighing of the precipitate. Compare **volumetric analysis**.

graving dock NOUN another term for **dry dock**.

graviperception (ˌgrævɪpə'sɛpʃən) NOUN the perception of gravity by plants.

gravitas ('grævɪˌtæs) NOUN seriousness, solemnity, or importance.
▷ HISTORY C20: from Latin *gravitās* weight, from *gravis* heavy

gravitate ('grævɪˌteɪt) VERB (*intr*) 1 *Physics* to move under the influence of gravity. 2 (usually foll by *to* or *towards*) to be influenced or drawn, as by strong impulses. 3 to sink or settle.
▸ **'graviˌtater** NOUN

gravitation (ˌgrævɪ'teɪʃən) NOUN 1 the force of attraction that bodies exert on one another as a result of their mass. 2 any process or result caused by this interaction, such as the fall of a body to the surface of the earth. ◆ Also called: **gravity**. See also **Newton's law of gravitation**.

gravitational (ˌgrævɪ'teɪʃənəl) ADJECTIVE of, relating to, or involving gravitation.
▸ **ˌgravi'tationally** ADVERB

gravitational constant NOUN the factor relating force to mass and distance in Newton's law of gravitation. It is a universal constant with the value 6.673×10^{-11} N m^2 kg^{-2}. Symbol: *G*.

gravitational field NOUN the field of force surrounding a body of finite mass in which another body would experience an attractive force that is proportional to the product of the masses and inversely proportional to the square of the distance between them.

gravitational interaction *or* **force** NOUN an interaction between particles or bodies resulting from their mass. It is very weak and occurs at all distances. See **interaction** (sense 2).

gravitational lens NOUN *Astronomy* a lenslike effect in which light rays are bent when passing through the gravitational field of such massive objects as galaxies or black holes.

gravitational mass NOUN the mass of a body determined by its response to the force of gravity. Compare **inertial mass**.

gravitational wave NOUN *Physics* another name for **gravity wave**.

gravitative ('grævɪˌteɪtɪv) ADJECTIVE 1 of, involving, or produced by gravitation. 2 tending or causing to gravitate.

graviton ('grævɪˌtɒn) NOUN a postulated quantum of gravitational energy, usually considered to be a particle with zero charge and rest mass and a spin of 2. Compare **photon**.

gravity ('grævɪtɪ) NOUN, *plural* **-ties**. 1 the force of attraction that moves or tends to move bodies towards the centre of a celestial body, such as the earth or moon. 2 the property of being heavy or having weight. See also **specific gravity, centre of gravity**. 3 another name for **gravitation**. 4 seriousness or importance, esp as a consequence of an action or opinion. 5 manner or conduct that is solemn or dignified. 6 lowness in pitch. 7 (*modifier*) of or relating to gravity or gravitation or their effects: *gravity wave*; *gravity feed*.
▷ HISTORY C16: from Latin *gravitās* weight, from *gravis* heavy

gravity cell NOUN an electrolytic cell in which the electrodes lie in two different electrolytes, which are separated into two layers by the difference in their relative densities.

gravity dam NOUN a dam whose weight alone is great enough to prevent it from tipping over.

gravity fault NOUN a fault in which the rocks on the upper side of an inclined fault plane have been displaced downwards; normal fault.

gravity platform NOUN (in the oil industry) a drilling platform that rests directly on the sea bed and is kept in position by its own weight; it is usually made of reinforced concrete.

gravity scale NOUN a scale giving the relative density of fluids. See **API gravity scale.**

gravity wave NOUN *Physics* 1 a wave propagated in a gravitational field, predicted to occur as a result of an accelerating mass. 2 a surface wave on water or other liquid propagated because of the weight of liquid in the crests. ◆ Also called: **gravitational wave.**

gravlax ('græv,læks) *or* **gravadlax** NOUN dry-cured salmon, marinated in salt, sugar, and spices, as served in Scandinavia.
▷HISTORY C20: from Norwegian, from *grav* grave (because the salmon is left to ferment) + *laks* or Swedish *lax* salmon

gravure (grə'vjʊə) NOUN 1 a method of intaglio printing using a plate with many small etched recesses. See also **rotogravure.** 2 See **photogravure.** 3 matter printed by this process.
▷HISTORY C19: from French, from *graver* to engrave, of Germanic origin; see GRAVE[3]

gravy ('greɪvɪ) NOUN, *plural* **-vies.** 1 **a** the juices that exude from meat during cooking. **b** the sauce made by thickening and flavouring such juices. 2 *Slang* money or gain acquired with little effort, esp above that needed for ordinary living. 3 *Slang* wonderful; excellent: *it's all gravy.*
▷HISTORY C14: from Old French *gravé,* of uncertain origin

gravy boat NOUN a small often boat-shaped vessel for serving gravy or other sauces.

gravy train NOUN *Slang* a job requiring comparatively little work for good pay, benefits, etc.

gray[1] (greɪ) ADJECTIVE, NOUN, VERB a variant spelling (now esp US) of **grey.**
► **'grayish** ADJECTIVE ► **'grayly** ADVERB ► **'grayness** NOUN

gray[2] (greɪ) NOUN the derived SI unit of absorbed ionizing radiation dose or kerma equivalent to an absorption per unit mass of one joule per kilogram of irradiated material. 1 gray is equivalent to 100 rads. Symbol: Gy.
▷HISTORY C20: named after Louis Harold *Gray* (1905–65), English physicist

Gray code NOUN a modification of a number system, esp a binary code, in which any adjacent pair of numbers, in counting order, differ in their digits at one position only, the absolute difference being the value 1.
▷HISTORY named after Frank *Gray,* 20th-century American physicist

grayling ('greɪlɪŋ) NOUN, *plural* **-ling** *or* **-lings.** 1 any freshwater salmonoid food fish of the genus *Thymallus* and family *Thymallidae,* of the N hemisphere, having a long spiny dorsal fin, a silvery back, and greyish-green sides. 2 any butterfly of the satyrid genus *Hipparchia* and related genera, esp *H. semele* of Europe, having grey or greyish-brown wings.

Gray's Inn NOUN (in England) one of the four legal societies in London that together form the Inns of Court.

Graz (*German* gra:ts) NOUN an industrial city in SE Austria, capital of Styria province: the second largest city in the country. Pop.: 226 424 (2001).

graze[1] (greɪz) VERB 1 to allow (animals) to consume the vegetation on (an area of land), or (of animals, esp cows and sheep) to feed thus. 2 (*tr*) to tend (livestock) while at pasture. 3 *Informal* to eat snacks throughout the day rather than formal meals. 4 (*intr*) *Informal* to switch between television channels while viewing without watching any channel for long. 5 *US* to pilfer and eat sweets, vegetables, etc., from supermarket shelves while shopping.
▷HISTORY Old English *grasian,* from *græs* GRASS; related to Old High German *grasōn,* Dutch *grazen,* Norwegian *grasa*

graze[2] (greɪz) VERB 1 (when *intr,* often foll by *against* or *along*) to brush or scrape (against) gently, esp in passing. 2 (*tr*) to break the skin of (a part of the body) by scraping. ◆ NOUN 3 the act of grazing. 4 a scrape or abrasion made by grazing.
▷HISTORY C17: probably special use of GRAZE[1]; related to Swedish *gräsa*
► **'grazer** NOUN ► **'grazingly** ADVERB

grazier ('greɪzɪə) NOUN a rancher or farmer who rears or fattens cattle or sheep on grazing land.

grazing ('greɪzɪŋ) NOUN 1 the vegetation on pastures that is available for livestock to feed upon. 2 the land on which this is growing.

grease NOUN (gri:s, gri:z) 1 animal fat in a soft or melted condition. 2 any thick fatty oil, esp one used as a lubricant for machinery, etc. 3 Also called: **grease wool.** shorn fleece before it has been cleaned. 4 Also called: **seborrhoea.** *Vet science* inflammation of the skin of horses around the fetlocks, usually covered with an oily secretion. ◆ VERB (gri:z, gri:s) (*tr*) 5 to soil, coat, or lubricate with grease. 6 to ease the course of: *his education greased his path to success.* 7 **grease the palm** (*or* **hand**) **of.** *Slang* to bribe; influence by giving money to.
▷HISTORY C13: from Old French *craisse,* from Latin *crassus* thick
► **'greaseless** ADJECTIVE

grease cup NOUN a container that stores grease and feeds it through a small hole into a bearing.

grease gun NOUN a device for forcing grease through nipples into bearings, usually consisting of a cylinder with a plunger and nozzle fitted to it.

grease monkey NOUN *Informal* a mechanic, esp one who works on cars or aircraft.

grease nipple NOUN a metal nipple designed to engage with a grease gun for injecting grease into a bearing, etc.

greasepaint ('gri:s,peɪnt) NOUN 1 a waxy or greasy substance used as make-up by actors. 2 theatrical make-up.

greaseproof paper ('gri:s,pru:f) NOUN any paper that is resistant to penetration by greases and oils.

greaser ('gri:zə, 'gri:sə) NOUN *Brit slang* 1 a mechanic, esp of motor vehicles. 2 a semiskilled engine attendant aboard a merchant ship. 3 a young long-haired motorcyclist, usually one of a gang. 4 an unpleasant person, esp one who ingratiates himself with superiors.

greasewood ('gri:s,wʊd) *or* **greasebush** ('gri:s,bʊʃ) NOUN 1 Also called: **chico.** a spiny chenopodiaceous shrub, *Sarcobatus vermiculatus* of W North America, that yields an oil used as a fuel. 2 any of various similar or related plants, such as the creosote bush.

greasies ('gri:sɪz) PLURAL NOUN *NZ informal* fish and chips.

greasy ('gri:zɪ, -sɪ) ADJECTIVE **greasier, greasiest.** 1 coated or soiled with or as if with grease. 2 composed of or full of grease. 3 resembling grease. 4 unctuous or oily in manner. ◆ NOUN, *plural* **greasies.** *Austral slang* 5 a shearer. 6 an outback cook, esp cooking for a number of men.
► **'greasily** ADVERB ► **'greasiness** NOUN

greasy spoon NOUN *Slang* a small, cheap, and often unsanitary restaurant, usually specializing in fried foods.

greasy wool NOUN untreated wool, still retaining the lanolin, which is used for waterproof clothing.

great (greɪt) ADJECTIVE 1 relatively large in size or extent; big. 2 relatively large in number; having many parts or members: *a great assembly.* 3 of relatively long duration: *a great wait.* 4 of larger size or more importance than others of its kind: *the great auk.* 5 extreme or more than usual: *great worry.* 6 of significant importance or consequence: *a great decision.* 7 **a** of exceptional talents or achievements; remarkable: *a great writer.* **b** (*as noun*): *the great; one of the greats.* 8 arising from or possessing idealism in thought, action, etc.; heroic: *great deeds.* 9 illustrious or eminent: *a great history.* 10 impressive or striking: *a great show of wealth.* 11 much in use; favoured: *poetry was a great convention of the Romantic era.* 12 active or enthusiastic: *a great walker.* 13 doing or exemplifying (a characteristic or pursuit) on a large scale: *what a great buffoon; he's not a great one for reading.* 14 (often foll by *at*) skilful or adroit: *a great carpenter; you are great at singing.* 15 *Informal* excellent; fantastic. 16 *Brit informal* (intensifier): *a dirty great smack in the face.* 17 (*postpositive;* foll by *with*) *Archaic* **a** pregnant: *great with child.* **b** full (of): *great with hope.* 18 (intensifier, used in mild oaths): *Great Scott!* 19 **be great on.** *Informal* **a** to be informed about. **b** to be enthusiastic about or for. ◆ ADVERB 20 *Informal* very well; excellently: *it was working great.* ◆ NOUN 21 Also called: **great organ.** the principal manual on an organ. Compare **choir** (sense 4), **swell** (sense 16).
▷HISTORY Old English *grēat;* related to Old Frisian *grāt,* Old High German *grōz;* see GRIT, GROAT
► **'greatly** ADVERB ► **'greatness** NOUN

great- PREFIX 1 being the parent of a person's grandparent (in the combinations **great-grandfather, great-grandmother, great-grandparent**). 2 being the child of a person's grandchild (in the combinations **great-grandson, great-granddaughter, great-grandchild**).

great ape NOUN any of the larger anthropoid apes, such as the chimpanzee, orang-utan, or gorilla.

Great Attractor NOUN *Astronomy* a large mass, possibly a gigantic cluster of galaxies, postulated to explain the fact that many galaxies appear to be moving towards a particular point in the sky.

great auk NOUN a large flightless auk, *Pinguinus impennis,* extinct since the middle of the 19th century.

great-aunt *or* **grandaunt** NOUN an aunt of one's father or mother; sister of one's grandfather or grandmother.

Great Australian Bight NOUN a wide bay of the Indian Ocean, in S Australia, extending from Cape Pasley to the Eyre Peninsula: notorious for storms.

Great Barrier Reef NOUN a coral reef in the Coral Sea, off the NE coast of Australia, extending for about 2000 km (1250 miles) from the Torres Strait along the coast of Queensland; the largest coral reef in the world.

Great Basin NOUN a semiarid region of the western US, between the Wasatch and the Sierra Nevada Mountains, having no drainage to the ocean: includes Nevada, W Utah, and parts of E California, S Oregon, and Idaho. Area: about 490 000 sq. km (189 000 sq. miles).

Great Bear NOUN **the.** the English name for **Ursa Major.**

Great Bear Lake NOUN a lake in NW Canada, in the Northwest Territories: the largest freshwater lake entirely in Canada; drained by the **Great Bear River,** which flows to the Mackenzie River. Area: 31 792 sq. km (12 275 sq. miles).

Great Belt NOUN a strait in Denmark, between Zealand and Funen islands, linking the Kattegat with the Baltic. Danish name: **Store Bælt.**

Great Britain NOUN England, Wales, and Scotland including those adjacent islands governed from the mainland (i.e. excluding the Isle of Man and the Channel Islands). The United Kingdom of Great Britain was formed by the Act of Union (1707), although the term Great Britain had been in use since 1603, when James VI of Scotland became James I of England (including Wales). Later unions created the United Kingdom of Great Britain and Ireland (1801) and the United Kingdom of Great Britain and Northern Ireland (1922). Pop.: 57 103 927 (2001 est.). Area: 229 523 sq. km (88 619 sq. miles). See also **United Kingdom.**

great circle NOUN a circular section of a sphere that has a radius equal to that of the sphere. Compare **small circle.**

greatcoat ('greɪt,kəʊt) NOUN a heavy overcoat, now worn esp by men in the armed forces.
► **'great,coated** ADJECTIVE

great council NOUN (in medieval England) an assembly of the great nobles and prelates to advise the king.

great crested grebe NOUN a European grebe, *Podiceps cristatus,* having blackish ear tufts and, in the breeding season, a dark brown frill around the head.

Great Dane NOUN one of a very large powerful yet graceful breed of dog with a short smooth coat.

Great Divide NOUN another name for the **continental divide.**

Great Dividing Range PLURAL NOUN a series of mountain ranges and plateaus roughly parallel to the E coast of Australia, in Queensland, New South Wales, and Victoria; the highest range is the Australian Alps, in the south.

Great Dog NOUN **the.** the English name for **Canis Major.**

greaten ('greɪtᵊn) VERB *Archaic* to make or become great.

Greater ('greɪtə) ADJECTIVE (of a city) considered with the inclusion of the outer suburbs: *Greater London.*

Greater Antilles PLURAL NOUN **the.** a group of islands in the Caribbean, including Cuba, Jamaica, Hispaniola, and Puerto Rico.

greater celandine NOUN a Eurasian papaveraceous plant, *Chelidonium majus,* with yellow flowers and deeply divided leaves. Also called: **swallowwort.** Compare **lesser celandine.**

Greater London NOUN See **London** (sense 2).

Greater Manchester NOUN a metropolitan county of NW England, administered since 1986 by the unitary authorities of Wigan, Bolton, Bury, Rochdale, Salford, Manchester, Oldham, Trafford, Stockport, and Tameside. Area: 1286 sq. km (496 sq. miles).

Greater Sunda Islands PLURAL NOUN a group of islands in the W Malay Archipelago, forming the larger part of the Sunda Islands: consists of Borneo, Sumatra, Java, and Sulawesi.

greatest ('greɪtɪst) ADJECTIVE 1 the superlative of **great.** ◆ NOUN 2 **the greatest.** *Slang* an exceptional person.

greatest common divisor NOUN another name for **highest common factor.**

greatest happiness principle NOUN the ethical principle that an action is right in so far as it promotes the greatest happiness of the greatest number of those affected. See **utilitarianism.**

Great Glen NOUN **the.** a fault valley across the whole of Scotland, extending southwest from the Moray Firth in the east to Loch Linnhe and containing Loch Ness and Loch Lochy. Also called: **Glen More, Glen Albyn.**

great gross NOUN a unit of quantity equal to one dozen gross (or 1728).

great-hearted ADJECTIVE benevolent or noble; magnanimous.
▸ **ˌgreat-ˈheartedness** NOUN

Great Indian Desert NOUN another name for the **Thar Desert.**

Great Lakes PLURAL NOUN a group of five lakes in central North America with connecting waterways: the largest group of lakes in the world: consists of Lakes Superior, Huron, Erie, and Ontario, which are divided by the border between the US and Canada and Lake Michigan, which is wholly in the US; constitutes the most important system of inland waterways in the world, discharging through the St Lawrence into the Atlantic. Total length: 3767 km (2340 miles). Area: 246 490 sq. km (95 170 sq. miles).

Great Leap Forward NOUN **the.** the attempt by the People's Republic of China in 1959–60 to solve the country's economic problems by labour-intensive industrialization.

Great Mogul NOUN any of the Muslim emperors of India (1526–1857).

great mountain buttercup NOUN *NZ* See **Mount Cook lily.**

great-nephew *or* **grandnephew** NOUN a son of one's nephew or niece; grandson of one's brother or sister.

great-niece *or* **grandniece** NOUN a daughter of one's nephew or niece; granddaughter of one's brother or sister.

great northern diver NOUN a large northern bird, *Gavia immer,* with a black-and-white chequered back and a black head and neck in summer: family *Gaviidae* (divers).

great organ NOUN the full name for **great** (sense 21).

Great Ouse NOUN See **Ouse** (sense 1).

Great Plains PLURAL NOUN a vast region of North America east of the Rocky Mountains, extending from the lowlands of the Mackenzie River (Canada), south to the Big Bend of the Rio Grande.

Great Power NOUN a nation that has exceptional political influence, resources, and military strength.

great primer NOUN (formerly) a size of printer's type approximately equal to 18 point.

Great Rebellion NOUN **the.** another name for the English **Civil War.**

Great Red Spot NOUN a large long-lived oval feature, south of Jupiter's equator, that is an anticyclonic disturbance in the atmosphere.

Great Rift Valley NOUN the most extensive rift in the earth's surface, extending from the Jordan valley in Syria to Mozambique; marked by a chain of steep-sided lakes, volcanoes, and escarpments.

Great Russian NOUN 1 *Linguistics* the technical name for **Russian.** Compare **Belarussian, Ukrainian.** 2 a member of the chief East Slavonic people of Russia. ◆ ADJECTIVE 3 of or relating to this people or their language.

Greats (greɪts) PLURAL NOUN (at Oxford University) 1 the Honour School of Literae Humaniores, involving the study of Greek and Roman history and literature and philosophy. 2 the final examinations at the end of this course.

Great Salt Lake NOUN a shallow salt lake in NW Utah, in the Great Basin at an altitude of 1260 m (4200 ft.): the area has fluctuated from less than 2500 sq. km (1000 sq. miles) to over 5000 sq. km (2000 sq. miles).

Great Sandy Desert NOUN 1 a desert in NW Australia. Area: about 415 000 sq. km (160 000 sq. miles). 2 the English name for the **Rub' al Khali.**

Great Schism NOUN 1 the breach between the Eastern and Western churches, usually dated from 1054. 2 the division within the Roman Catholic Church from 1378 to 1429, during which rival popes reigned at Rome and Avignon.

great seal NOUN (*often capitals*) the principal seal of a nation, sovereign, etc., used to authenticate signatures and documents of the highest importance.

Great Slave Lake NOUN a lake in NW Canada, in the Northwest Territories: drained by the Mackenzie River into the Arctic Ocean. Area: 28 440 sq. km (10 980 sq. miles).

Great Slave River NOUN another name for the **Slave River.**

Great Smoky Mountains *or* **Great Smokies** PLURAL NOUN the W part of the Appalachians, in W North Carolina and E Tennessee. Highest peak: Clingman's Dome, 2024 m (6642 ft.).

Great St Bernard Pass NOUN a pass over the W Alps, between SW central Switzerland and N Italy: noted for the hospice at the summit, founded in the 11th century. Height: 2469 m (8100 ft.).

Great Stour NOUN another name for **Stour** (sense 1).

great tit NOUN a large common Eurasian tit, *Parus major,* with yellow-and-black underparts and a black-and-white head.

Great Trek NOUN **the.** *South African history* the migration of Boer farmers from the Cape Colony to the north and east from about 1836 to 1845 to escape British authority.

great-uncle *or* **granduncle** NOUN an uncle of one's father or mother; brother of one's grandfather or grandmother.

Great Victoria Desert NOUN a desert in S Australia, in SE Western Australia and W South Australia. Area: 323 750 sq. km (125 000 sq. miles).

Great Vowel Shift NOUN *Linguistics* a phonetic change that took place during the transition from Middle to Modern English, whereby the long vowels were raised (e: became i:, o: became u:, etc.). The vowels (i:) and (u:) underwent breaking and became the diphthongs (aɪ) and (aʊ).

Great Wall NOUN *Astronomy* a vast sheet of many thousands of gravitationally associated galaxies detected in the universe.

Great Wall of China NOUN a defensive wall in N China, extending from W Gansu to the Gulf of Liaodong: constructed in the 3rd century B.C. as a defence against the Mongols; substantially rebuilt in the 15th century. Length: over 2400 km (1500 miles). Average height: 6 m (20 ft.). Average width: 6 m (20 ft.).

Great War NOUN another name for **World War I.**

Great Week NOUN *Eastern Church* the week preceding Easter, the equivalent of Holy Week in the Western Church.

great white heron NOUN 1 a large white heron, *Ardea occidentalis,* of S North America. 2 a widely distributed white egret, *Egretta* (or *Casmerodius*) *albus.*

Great White Way NOUN the theatre district on Broadway in New York City.

Great Yarmouth ('jɑːməθ) NOUN a port and resort in E England, in E Norfolk. Pop.: 56 190 (1991).

great year NOUN one complete cycle of the precession of the equinoxes; about 25 800 years.

greave (griːv) NOUN (*often plural*) a piece of armour worn to protect the shin from the ankle to the knee.
▷ **HISTORY** C14: from Old French *greve,* perhaps from *graver* to part the hair, of Germanic origin
▸ **greaved** ADJECTIVE

greaves (griːvz) PLURAL NOUN the residue left after the rendering of tallow.
▷ **HISTORY** C17: from Low German *greven;* related to Old High German *griubo*

grebe (griːb) NOUN any aquatic bird, such as *Podiceps cristatus* (**great crested grebe**), of the order *Podicipediformes,* similar to the divers but with lobate rather than webbed toes and a vestigial tail.
▷ **HISTORY** C18: from French *grèbe,* of unknown origin

Grecian ('griːʃən) ADJECTIVE 1 (esp of beauty or architecture) conforming to Greek ideals, esp in being classically simple. ◆ NOUN 2 a scholar of or expert in the Greek language or literature. ◆ ADJECTIVE, NOUN 3 another word for **Greek.**

Grecism ('griːˌsɪzəm) NOUN a variant spelling (esp US) of **Graecism.**

Grecize ('griːsaɪz) VERB a variant spelling (esp US) of **Graecize.**

Greco- ('griːkəʊ, 'grɛkəʊ) COMBINING FORM a variant (esp US) of **Graeco-.**

gree[1] (griː) NOUN *Scot archaic* 1 superiority or victory. 2 the prize for a victory.
▷ **HISTORY** C14: from Old French *gré,* from Latin *gradus* step

gree[2] (griː) NOUN *Obsolete* 1 goodwill; favour. 2 satisfaction for an insult or injury.
▷ **HISTORY** C14: from Old French *gré,* from Latin *grātum* what is pleasing; see GRATEFUL

gree[3] (griː) VERB **grees, greeing, greed.** *Archaic or dialect* to come or cause to come to agreement or harmony.
▷ **HISTORY** C14: variant of AGREE

greebo ('griːbəʊ) NOUN, *plural* **greeboes.** an unkempt or dirty-looking young man.

Greece (griːs) NOUN a republic in SE Europe, occupying the S part of the Balkan Peninsula and many islands in the Ionian and Aegean Seas; site of two of Europe's earliest civilizations (the Minoan and Mycenaean); in the classical era divided into many small independent city-states, the most important being Athens and Sparta; part of the Roman and Byzantine Empires; passed under Turkish rule in the late Middle Ages; became an independent kingdom in 1827; taken over by a military junta (1967–74); the monarchy was abolished in 1973; became a republic in 1975; a member of the European Union. Official language: Greek. Official religion: Eastern (Greek) Orthodox. Currency: euro. Capital: Athens. Pop.: 10 975 000 (2001 est.). Area: 131 944 sq. km (50 944 sq. miles). Modern Greek name: **Ellás.** Related adjective: **Hellenic.**

greed (griːd) NOUN 1 excessive consumption of or desire for food; gluttony. 2 excessive desire, as for wealth or power.
▷ **HISTORY** C17: back formation from GREEDY
▸ **ˈgreedless** ADJECTIVE

greedy ('griːdɪ) ADJECTIVE **greedier, greediest.** 1 excessively desirous of food or wealth, esp in large amounts; voracious. 2 (*postpositive;* foll by *for*) eager (for): *a man greedy for success.*
▷ **HISTORY** Old English *grǣdig;* related to Old Norse *grāthugr,* Gothic *grēdags* hungry, Old High German *grātac*
▸ **ˈgreedily** ADVERB ▸ **ˈgreediness** NOUN

greedy guts NOUN (*functioning as singular*) *Slang* a glutton.

greegree ('griːgriː) NOUN a variant spelling of **grigri.**

Greek (griːk) NOUN [1] the official language of Greece, constituting the Hellenic branch of the Indo-European family of languages. See **Ancient Greek, Late Greek, Medieval Greek, Modern Greek.** [2] a native or inhabitant of Greece or a descendant of such a native. [3] a member of the Greek Orthodox Church. [4] *Informal* anything incomprehensible (esp in the phrase **it's (all) Greek to me**). [5] **Greek meets Greek.** equals meet. ◆ ADJECTIVE [6] denoting, relating to, or characteristic of Greece, the Greeks, or the Greek language; Hellenic. [7] of, relating to, or designating the Greek Orthodox Church.
▷HISTORY from Old English *Grēcas* (plural), or Latin *Graecus,* from Greek *Graikos*
▸ **'Greekness** NOUN

Greek Catholic NOUN [1] a member of an Eastern Church in communion with the Greek patriarchal see of Constantinople. [2] a member of one of the Uniat Greek Churches, which acknowledge the Pope's authority while retaining their own institutions, discipline, and liturgy.

Greek Church NOUN another name for the **Greek Orthodox Church.**

Greek cross NOUN a cross with each of the four arms of the same length.

greeked text (griːkt) NOUN *Computing* words which appear on screen as grey lines when the type size is too small for actual letters to be shown.

Greek fire NOUN [1] a Byzantine weapon employed in naval warfare from 670 A.D. It consisted of an unknown mixture that, when wetted, exploded and was projected, burning, from tubes. [2] any of several other inflammable mixtures used in warfare up to the 19th century.

Greek gift NOUN a gift given with the intention of tricking and causing harm to the recipient.
▷HISTORY C19: in allusion to Virgil's *Aeneid* ii 49; see also TROJAN HORSE

Greek mallow NOUN See **sidalcea.**

Greek Orthodox Church NOUN [1] Also called: **Greek Church.** the established Church of Greece, governed by the holy synod of Greece, in which the Metropolitan of Athens has primacy of honour. [2] another name for **Orthodox Church.**

Greek Revival NOUN (*modifier*) denoting, relating to, or having the style of architecture used in Western Europe in the late 18th and early 19th centuries, based upon ancient Greek classical examples.
▸ **Greek Revivalism** NOUN ▸ **Greek Revivalist** ADJECTIVE, NOUN

green (griːn) NOUN [1] any of a group of colours, such as that of fresh grass, that lie between yellow and blue in the visible spectrum in the wavelength range 575–500 nanometres. Green is the complementary colour of magenta and with red and blue forms a set of primary colours. Related adjective: **verdant.** [2] a dye or pigment of or producing these colours. [3] something of the colour green. [4] a small area of grassland, esp in the centre of a village. [5] an area of ground used for a purpose: *a putting green.* [6] (*plural*) **a** the edible leaves and stems of certain plants, eaten as a vegetable. **b** freshly cut branches of ornamental trees, shrubs, etc., used as a decoration. [7] (*sometimes capital*) a person, esp a politician, who supports environmentalist issues (see sense 13). [8] *Slang* money. [9] *Slang* marijuana of low quality. [10] (*plural*) *Slang* sexual intercourse. ◆ ADJECTIVE [11] of the colour green. [12] greenish in colour or having parts or marks that are greenish: *a green monkey.* [13] (*sometimes capital*) concerned with or relating to conservation of the world's natural resources and improvement of the environment: *green policies; the green consumer.* [14] vigorous; not faded: *a green old age.* [15] envious or jealous. [16] immature, unsophisticated, or gullible. [17] characterized by foliage or green plants: *a green wood; a green salad.* [18] fresh, raw, or unripe: *green bananas.* [19] unhealthily pale in appearance: *he was green after his boat trip.* [20] denoting a unit of account that is adjusted in accordance with fluctuations between the currencies of the EU nations and is used to make payments to agricultural producers within the EU: *green pound; green franc.* [21] (of pottery) not fired. [22] (of meat) not smoked or cured; unprocessed: *green bacon.* [23] *Metallurgy* (of a product, such as a sand mould or cermet) compacted but not yet fired; ready for firing. [24] (of timber) freshly felled; not dried or seasoned. [25] (of concrete) not having matured to design strength. ◆ VERB [26] to make or become green.
▷HISTORY Old English *grēne;* related to Old High German *gruoni;* see GROW
▸ **'greenish** ADJECTIVE ▸ **'greenly** ADVERB ▸ **'greenness** NOUN ▸ **'greeny** ADJECTIVE

green algae PLURAL NOUN the algae of the phylum *Chlorophyta,* which possess the green pigment chlorophyll. The group includes sea lettuce and spirogyra.

greenback ('griːnˌbæk) NOUN [1] *US informal* an inconvertible legal-tender US currency note originally issued during the Civil War in 1862. [2] *US slang* a dollar bill.

Greenback Party NOUN *US history* a political party formed after the Civil War advocating the use of fiat money and opposing the reduction of paper currency.
▸ **'Greenˌbacker** NOUN ▸ **'Greenˌbackism** NOUN

green ban NOUN *Austral* a trade union ban on any development that might be considered harmful to the environment.

green bean NOUN any bean plant, such as the French bean, having narrow green edible pods when unripe.

green belt NOUN a zone of farmland, parks, and open country surrounding a town or city: usually officially designated as such and preserved from urban development.

Green Beret NOUN an informal name for a member of the US Army Special Forces.

greenbone ('griːnˌbəʊn) NOUN *NZ* another name for **butterfish** (sense 2).

greenbottle ('griːnˌbɒtᵊl) NOUN a common dipterous fly, *Lucilia caesar,* that has a dark greenish body with a metallic lustre and lays its eggs in carrion: family *Calliphoridae.*

greenbrier ('griːnˌbraɪə) NOUN any of several prickly climbing plants of the liliaceous genus *Smilax,* esp *S. rotundifolia* of the eastern US, which has small green flowers and blackish berries. Also called: **cat brier.**

green card NOUN [1] an official permit allowing the holder permanent residence and employment, issued to foreign nationals in the US. [2] an insurance document covering motorists against accidents abroad. [3] *Social welfare* (in Britain) an identification card issued by the Manpower Services Commission to a disabled person, to show registration for employment purposes and eligibility for special services. See also **handicap register, registered disabled.**

green corn NOUN another name for **sweet corn** (sense 1).

Green Cross Code NOUN (in Britain) a code for children giving rules for road safety: first issued in 1971.

green dragon NOUN a North American aroid plant, *Arisaema dracontium,* with a long slender spadix projecting from a green or white long narrow spathe. Also called: **dragonroot.**

greenery ('griːnərɪ) NOUN green foliage or vegetation, esp when used for decoration.

green-eyed ADJECTIVE [1] jealous or envious. [2] **the green-eyed monster.** jealousy or envy.

greenfield ('griːnˌfiːld) NOUN (*modifier*) denoting or located in a rural area which has not previously been built on: *new factories were erected on greenfield sites.*

greenfinch ('griːnˌfɪntʃ) NOUN a common European finch, *Carduelis chloris,* the male of which has a dull green plumage with yellow patches on the wings and tail.

green fingers PLURAL NOUN considerable talent or ability to grow plants. US and Canadian equivalent: **green thumb.**

Green Flag NOUN an award given to a bathing beach that meets EU standards of cleanliness.

green flash NOUN *Astronomy* a flash of bright green light sometimes seen as the sun passes below the horizon, caused by a combination of the dispersion, scattering, and refraction of light.

greenfly ('griːnˌflaɪ) NOUN, *plural* **-flies.** a greenish aphid commonly occurring as a pest on garden and crop plants.

greengage ('griːnˌgeɪdʒ) NOUN [1] a cultivated variety of plum tree, *Prunus domestica italica,* with edible green plumlike fruits. [2] the fruit of this tree.
▷HISTORY C18: GREEN + *-gage,* after Sir W. *Gage* (1777–1864), English botanist who brought it from France

green gland NOUN one of a pair of excretory organs in some crustaceans that open at the base of each antenna.

green glass NOUN glass in its natural colour, usually greenish as a result of metallic substances in the raw materials.

Green Goddess NOUN *Brit* an army fire engine.
▷HISTORY C20: so-called because of its green livery

greengrocer ('griːnˌgrəʊsə) NOUN *Chiefly Brit* a retail trader in fruit and vegetables.
▸ **'greenˌgrocery** NOUN

Greenham Common ('griːnəm) NOUN a village in West Berkshire unitary authority, Berkshire; site of a US cruise missile base, and, from 1981, a camp of women protesters against nuclear weapons; although the base had closed by 1991 a small number of women remained until 2000.

greenhead ('griːnˌhɛd) NOUN a male mallard.

greenheart ('griːnˌhɑːt) NOUN [1] Also called: **bebeeru.** a tropical American lauraceous tree, *Ocotea* (or *Nectandra*) *rodiaei,* that has dark green durable wood and bark that yields the alkaloid bebeerine. [2] any of various similar trees. [3] the wood of any of these trees.

green heron NOUN a small heron, *Butorides virescens,* of subtropical North America, with dark greenish wings and back.

greenhorn ('griːnˌhɔːn) NOUN [1] an inexperienced person, esp one who is extremely gullible. [2] *Chiefly US* a newcomer or immigrant.
▷HISTORY C17: originally an animal with *green* (that is, young) horns

greenhouse ('griːnˌhaʊs) NOUN [1] a building with transparent walls and roof, usually of glass, for the cultivation and exhibition of plants under controlled conditions. ◆ ADJECTIVE [2] relating to or contributing to the greenhouse effect: *greenhouse gases such as carbon dioxide.*

greenhouse effect NOUN [1] an effect occurring in greenhouses, etc., in which radiant heat from the sun passes through the glass warming the contents, the radiant heat from inside being trapped by the glass. [2] the application of this effect to a planet's atmosphere; carbon dioxide and some other gases in the planet's atmosphere can absorb the infrared radiation emitted by the planet's surface as a result of exposure to solar radiation, thus increasing the mean temperature of the planet.

greenie ('griːnɪ) NOUN *Austral informal* a conservationist.

greening ('griːnɪŋ) NOUN the process of making or becoming more aware of environmental considerations.
▷HISTORY C20: from GREEN (sense 13)

green-ink brigade NOUN *Informal* a collective term for people who write abusive or threatening letters to people in the public eye.
▷HISTORY C20: from the idea that only the eccentric would write in green ink

green keeper NOUN a person in charge of a golf course or bowling green.

Greenland ('griːnlənd) NOUN a large island, lying mostly within the Arctic Circle off the NE coast of North America: first settled by Icelanders in 986; resettled by Danes from 1721 onwards; integral part of Denmark (1953–79); granted internal autonomy 1979; mostly covered by an icecap up to 3300 m (11 000 ft.) thick, with ice-free coastal strips and coastal mountains; the population is largely Eskimo, with a European minority; fishing, hunting, and mining. Capital: Nuuk. Pop.: 56 300 (2001 est.). Area: 175 600 sq. km (840 000 sq. miles). Danish name: **Grønland.** Greenlandic name: **Kalaallit Nunaat.**

Greenlander ('griːnləndə) NOUN a native or inhabitant of Greenland.

Greenlandic (griːn'lændɪk) ADJECTIVE [1] of, relating to, or characteristic of Greenland, the Greenlanders, or the Inuit dialect spoken in

Greenland. ◆ NOUN 2 the dialect of Inuit Eskimo spoken in Greenland.

Greenland Sea NOUN the S part of the Arctic Ocean, off the NE coast of Greenland.

Greenland whale NOUN an arctic right whale, *Balaena mysticetus,* that is black with a cream-coloured throat.

green leek NOUN any of several Australian parrots with a green or mostly green plumage.

greenlet (ˈgriːnlɪt) NOUN a vireo, esp one of the genus *Hylophilus.*

green light NOUN 1 a signal to go, esp a green traffic light. 2 permission to proceed with a project. ◆ VERB **greenlight, -lights, -lighting, -lighted.** (*tr*) 3 to permit (a project, etc.) to proceed.

green line NOUN (*sometimes capitals*) a line of demarcation between two hostile communities.

greenling (ˈgriːnlɪŋ) NOUN any scorpaenoid food fish of the family *Hexagrammidae* of the North Pacific Ocean.

green lung NOUN an area of parkland within a town or city, considered in terms of the healthier environment it provides.

greenmail (ˈgriːnˌmeɪl) NOUN (esp in the US) the practice of a company buying sufficient shares in another company to threaten takeover and making a quick profit as a result of the threatened company buying back its shares at a higher price.

green manure NOUN 1 a growing crop that is ploughed under to enrich the soil. 2 manure that has not yet decomposed.

green monkey NOUN a W African variety of a common guenon monkey, *Cercopithecus aethiops,* having greenish-brown fur and a dark face. Compare **grivet, vervet.**

green monkey disease NOUN another name for **Marburg disease.**

green mould NOUN another name for **blue mould** (sense 1).

Green Mountain Boys PLURAL NOUN the members of the armed bands of Vermont organized in 1770 to oppose New York's territorial claims. Under Ethan Allen they won fame in the War of American Independence.

Green Mountains PLURAL NOUN a mountain range in E North America, extending from Canada through Vermont into W Massachusetts: part of the Appalachian system. Highest peak: Mount Mansfield, 1338 m (4393 ft.).

Greenock (ˈgriːnək) NOUN a port in SW Scotland, in Inverclyde on the Firth of Clyde: shipbuilding and other marine industries. Pop.: 50 013 (1991).

greenockite (ˈgriːnəˌkaɪt) NOUN a rare yellowish mineral consisting of cadmium sulphide in hexagonal crystalline form: the only ore of cadmium. Formula: CdS.
▷HISTORY C19: named after Lord C. C. *Greenock,* 19th-century English soldier

green paper NOUN (*often capitals*) (in Britain) a command paper containing policy proposals to be discussed, esp by Parliament.

Green Party NOUN a political party whose policies are based on concern for the environment.

Greenpeace (ˈgriːnˌpiːs) NOUN an organization founded in 1971 that stresses the need to maintain a balance between human progress and environmental conservation. Members take active but nonviolent measures against what are regarded as threats to environmental safety, such as the dumping of nuclear waste in the sea.

green pepper NOUN 1 the green unripe fruit of the sweet pepper, eaten raw or cooked. 2 the unripe fruit of various other pepper plants, eaten as a green vegetable.

green plover NOUN another name for **lapwing.**

green pound NOUN a unit of account used in calculating Britain's contributions to and payments from the Community Agricultural Fund of the EU.

green revolution NOUN the introduction of high-yielding seeds and modern agricultural techniques in developing countries.

Green River NOUN a river in the western US, rising in W central Wyoming and flowing south into Utah, east through NW Colorado, re-entering Utah before joining the Colorado River. Length: 1175 km (730 miles).

greenroom (ˈgriːnˌruːm, -ˌrʊm) NOUN (esp formerly) a backstage room in a theatre where performers may rest or receive visitors.
▷HISTORY C18: probably from its original colour

green run NOUN *Skiing* a very easy run, suitable for complete beginners.

greensand (ˈgriːnˌsænd) NOUN an olive-green sandstone consisting mainly of quartz and glauconite.

Greensboro (ˈgriːnzbərə, -brə) NOUN a city in N central North Carolina. Pop.: 223 891 (2000).

greenshank (ˈgriːnˌʃæŋk) NOUN a large European sandpiper, *Tringa nebularia,* with greenish legs and a slightly upturned bill.

greensickness (ˈgriːnˌsɪknɪs) NOUN another name for **chlorosis.**
▸ˈ**green,sick** ADJECTIVE

green soap NOUN *Med* a soft or liquid alkaline soap made from vegetable oils, used in treating certain chronic skin diseases. Also called: **soft soap.**

greensome (ˈgriːnsəm) NOUN *Golf* a match for two pairs in which each of the four players tees off and after selecting the better drive the partners of each pair play that ball alternately. Compare **four-ball, foursome** (sense 2).

greenstick fracture (ˈgriːnˌstɪk) NOUN a fracture in children in which the bone is partly bent and splinters only on the convex side of the bend.
▷HISTORY C20: alluding to the similar way in which a green stick splinters

greenstone (ˈgriːnˌstəʊn) NOUN 1 any basic igneous rock that is dark green because of the presence of chlorite, actinolite, or epidote. 2 a variety of jade used in New Zealand for ornaments and tools.

greenstuff (ˈgriːnˌstʌf) NOUN green vegetables, such as cabbage or lettuce.

greensward (ˈgriːnˌswɔːd) NOUN *Archaic or literary* fresh green turf or an area of such turf.

green tea NOUN a sharp tea made from tea leaves that have been steamed and dried quickly without fermenting.

green thumb NOUN the US and Canadian term for **green fingers.**

green turtle NOUN a mainly tropical edible turtle, *Chelonia mydas,* with greenish flesh used to prepare turtle soup: family *Chelonidae.*

green vitriol NOUN another name for **ferrous sulphate.**

greenwash (ˈgriːnˌwɒʃ) NOUN a superficial or insincere display of concern for the environment that is shown by an organization.

green-wellie NOUN (*modifier*) characterizing or belonging to the upper-class set devoted to hunting, shooting, and fishing: *the green-wellie brigade.*

Greenwich (ˈgrɪnɪdʒ, -ɪtʃ, ˈgren-) NOUN a Greater London borough on the Thames: site of a Royal Naval College and of the original Royal Observatory designed by Christopher Wren (1675), accepted internationally as the prime meridian of longitude since 1884, and the basis of Greenwich Mean Time; also site of the Millennium Dome. Pop.: 214 540 (2001). Area: 46 sq. km (18 sq. miles).

Greenwich Mean Time *or* **Greenwich Time** NOUN mean solar time on the 0° meridian passing through Greenwich, England, measured from midnight: formerly a standard time in Britain and a basis for calculating times throughout most of the world, it has been replaced by an atomic timescale. See **universal time.** Abbreviation: **GMT.**

> **Language note** The name **Greenwich mean time** is ambiguous, having been measured from mean midday in astronomy up to 1925, and is not used for scientific purposes. It is generally and incorrectly used in the sense of **universal coordinated time**, an atomic timescale available since 1972 from broadcast signals, in addition to the earliest sense of **universal time**, adopted internationally in 1928 as the name for GMT measured from midnight.

Greenwich Village (ˈgrenɪtʃ, ˈgrɪn-) NOUN a part of New York City in the lower west side of Manhattan; traditionally the home of many artists and writers.

greenwood (ˈgriːnˌwʊd) NOUN a forest or wood when the leaves are green: the traditional setting of stories about English outlaws, esp Robin Hood.

green woodpecker NOUN a European woodpecker, *Picus viridis,* with a dull green back and wings and a red crown.

greet[1] (griːt) VERB (*tr*) 1 to meet or receive with expressions of gladness or welcome. 2 to send a message of friendship to. 3 to receive in a specified manner: *her remarks were greeted by silence.* 4 to become apparent to: *the smell of bread greeted him.*
▷HISTORY Old English *grētan;* related to Old High German *gruozzen* to address

greet[2] (griːt) *Scot* ◆ VERB 1 (*intr*) to weep; lament. ◆ NOUN 2 weeping; lamentation.
▷HISTORY from Old English *grētan,* northern dialect variant of *grǣtan;* compare Old Norse *grāta,* Middle High German *grazen*

greeter (ˈgriːtə) NOUN a person who greets people at the entrance of a shop, restaurant, casino, etc.

greeting (ˈgriːtɪŋ) NOUN 1 the act or an instance of welcoming or saluting on meeting. 2 (*often plural*) **a** an expression of friendly salutation. **b** (*as modifier*): *a greetings card.*

gregarine (ˈgregəˌriːn, -rɪn) NOUN 1 any parasitic protozoan of the order *Gregarinida,* typically occurring in the digestive tract and body cavity of other invertebrates: phylum *Apicomplexa* (sporozoans). ◆ ADJECTIVE *also* **gregarinian** (ˌgregəˈrɪnɪən). 2 of, relating to, or belonging to the *Gregarinida.*
▷HISTORY C19: from New Latin *Gregarīna* genus name, from Latin *gregārius;* see GREGARIOUS

gregarious (grɪˈgeərɪəs) ADJECTIVE 1 enjoying the company of others. 2 (of animals) living together in herds or flocks. Compare **solitary** (sense 6). 3 (of plants) growing close together but not in dense clusters. 4 of, relating to, or characteristic of crowds or communities.
▷HISTORY C17: from Latin *gregārius* belonging to a flock, from *grex* flock
▸**greˈgariously** ADVERB ▸**greˈgariousness** NOUN

Gregorian (grɪˈgɔːrɪən) ADJECTIVE relating to, associated with, or introduced by any of the popes named Gregory, esp Gregory I (?540–604 A.D., pope (590–604)), or Gregory XIII (1502–85, pope (1572–85)).

Gregorian calendar NOUN the revision of the Julian calendar introduced in 1582 by Pope Gregory XIII and still in force, whereby the ordinary year is made to consist of 365 days and a leap year occurs in every year whose number is divisible by four, except those centenary years, such as 1900, whose numbers are not divisible by 400.

Gregorian chant NOUN another name for **plainsong.**

Gregorian telescope NOUN a form of reflecting astronomical telescope with a concave ellipsoidal secondary mirror and the eyepiece set behind the centre of the parabolic primary mirror.
▷HISTORY C18: named after J. *Gregory* (died 1675), Scottish mathematician who invented it

Gregorian tone NOUN a plainsong melody. See **tone** (sense 6).

Gregory's powder NOUN a formulation of rhubarb powder used as a laxative or purgative.
▷HISTORY C19: named after Dr James *Gregory* (1753–1821), who first made it

greige (greɪʒ) *Chiefly US* ◆ ADJECTIVE 1 (of a fabric or material) not yet dyed. ◆ NOUN 2 an unbleached or undyed cloth or yarn.
▷HISTORY C20: from French *grège* raw

greisen (ˈgraɪzᵊn) NOUN a light-coloured metamorphic rock consisting mainly of quartz, white mica, and topaz formed by the pneumatolysis of granite.
▷HISTORY C19: from German, from *greissen* to split

gremial (ˈgriːmɪəl) NOUN *RC Church* a cloth spread upon the lap of a bishop when seated during Mass.
▷HISTORY C17: from Latin *gremium* lap

gremlin (ˈgremlɪn) NOUN 1 an imaginary imp jokingly said to be responsible for malfunctions in machinery. 2 any mischievous troublemaker.
▷HISTORY C20: of unknown origin

Grenada (grɛˈneɪdə) NOUN an island state in the Caribbean, in the Windward Islands: formerly a British colony (1783–1967); since 1974 an independent state within the Commonwealth; occupied by US troops (1983–85); mainly agricultural. Official language: English. Religion: Christian majority. Currency: East Caribbean dollar. Capital: St George's. Pop.: 102 000 (2001 est.). Area: 344 sq. km (133 sq. miles).

grenade (ɡrɪˈneɪd) NOUN 1 a small container filled with explosive thrown by hand or fired from a rifle. 2 a sealed glass vessel that is thrown and shatters to release chemicals, such as tear gas or a fire extinguishing agent.
▷HISTORY C16: from French, from Spanish *granada* pomegranate, from Late Latin *grānāta,* from Latin *grānātus* seedy; see GRAIN

Grenadian (grɛˈneɪdɪən) ADJECTIVE 1 of or relating to Grenada or its inhabitants. ◆ NOUN 2 a native or inhabitant of Grenada.

grenadier (ˌɡrɛnəˈdɪə) NOUN 1 *Military* **a** (in the British Army) a member of the senior regiment of infantry in the Household Brigade. **b** (formerly) a member of a special formation, usually selected for strength and height. **c** (formerly) a soldier trained to throw grenades. 2 Also called: **rat-tail.** any deep-sea gadoid fish of the family *Macrouridae,* typically having a large head and trunk and a long tapering tail. 3 any of various African weaverbirds of the genus *Estrilda.* See **waxbill.**
▷HISTORY C17: from French; see GRENADE

grenadine[1] (ˌɡrɛnəˈdiːn) NOUN a light thin leno-weave fabric of silk, wool, rayon, or nylon, used esp for dresses.
▷HISTORY C19: from French, from earlier *grenade* silk with a grained texture, from *grenu* grained; see GRAIN

grenadine[2] (ˌɡrɛnəˈdiːn, ˈɡrɛnəˌdiːn) NOUN 1 a syrup made from pomegranate juice, used as a sweetening and colouring agent in various drinks. 2 **a** a moderate reddish-orange colour. **b** (*as adjective*): *a grenadine coat.*
▷HISTORY C19: from French: a little pomegranate, from *grenade* pomegranate; see GRENADE

Grenadines (ˌɡrɛnəˈdiːnz, ˈɡrɛnəˌdiːnz) PLURAL NOUN **the.** a chain of about 600 islets in the Caribbean, part of the Windward Islands, extending for about 100 km (60 miles) between St Vincent and Grenada and divided administratively between the two states. Largest island: Carriacou.

Grendel (ˈɡrɛndᵊl) NOUN (in Old English legend) a man-eating monster defeated by the hero Beowulf.

Grenoble (ɡrəˈnəʊbᵊl; *French* ɡrənɔblə) NOUN a city in SE France, on the Isère River: university (1339). Pop.: 153 317 (1999).

grenz rays (ɡrɛnz) NOUN *Physics* X-rays of long wavelength produced in a device when electrons are accelerated through 25 kilovolts or less.
▷HISTORY C20: from *grenz* from German *Grenze* boundary

Gresham's law *or* **theorem** NOUN the economic hypothesis that bad money drives good money out of circulation; the superior currency will tend to be hoarded and the inferior will thus dominate the circulation.
▷HISTORY C16: named after Sir Thomas *Gresham* (?1519–79), English financier

gressorial (ɡrɛˈsɔːrɪəl) *or* **gressorious** ADJECTIVE 1 (of the feet of certain birds) specialized for walking. 2 (of birds, such as the ostrich) having such feet.
▷HISTORY C19: from New Latin *gressōrius,* from *gressus* having walked, from *gradī* to step

Gretna Green (ˈɡrɛtnə) NOUN a village in S Scotland, in Dumfries and Galloway on the border with England: famous smithy where eloping couples were married by the blacksmith from 1754 until 1940, when such marriages became illegal. Pop.: 3149 (1991).

grevillea (ɡrəˈvɪljə) NOUN any of a large variety of evergreen trees and shrubs that comprise the genus *Grevillea,* native to Australia, Tasmania, and New Caledonia: family *Proteaceae.*
▷HISTORY named after C. F. *Greville* (1749–1809), a founder of the Royal Horticultural Society

grew (ɡruː) VERB the past tense of **grow.**

grewsome (ˈɡruːsəm) ADJECTIVE an archaic or US spelling of **gruesome.**

grex (ɡrɛks) NOUN a group of plants that has arisen from the same hybrid parent group.
▷HISTORY C20: from Latin *grex* flock

grey *or now esp US* **gray** (ɡreɪ) ADJECTIVE 1 of a neutral tone, intermediate between black and white, that has no hue and reflects and transmits only a little light. 2 greyish in colour or having parts or marks that are greyish. 3 dismal or dark, esp from lack of light; gloomy. 4 neutral or dull, esp in character or opinion. 5 having grey hair. 6 of or relating to people of middle age or above: *grey power.* 7 ancient; venerable. 8 (of textiles) natural, unbleached, undyed, and untreated. ◆ NOUN 9 any of a group of grey tones. 10 grey cloth or clothing: *dressed in grey.* 11 an animal, esp a horse, that is grey or whitish. ◆ VERB 12 to become or make grey.
▷HISTORY Old English *grǣg;* related to Old High German *grāo,* Old Norse *grar*
▸ˈ**greyish** *or* (*now esp US*) ˈ**grayish** ADJECTIVE ▸ˈ**greyly** *or* (*now esp US*) ˈ**grayly** ADVERB ▸ˈ**greyness** *or* (*now esp US*) ˈ**grayness** NOUN

grey area NOUN 1 (in Britain) a region in which unemployment is relatively high. 2 an area or part of something existing between two extremes and having mixed characteristics of both. 3 an area, situation, etc., lacking clearly defined characteristics.

greyback *or US* **grayback** (ˈɡreɪˌbæk) NOUN any of various animals having a grey back, such as the grey whale and the hooded crow.

greybeard *or US* **graybeard** (ˈɡreɪˌbɪəd) NOUN 1 an old man, esp a sage. 2 a large stoneware or earthenware jar or jug for spirits.
▸ˈ**grey,bearded** *or US* ˈ**gray,bearded** ADJECTIVE

grey body NOUN *Physics* a body that emits radiation in constant proportion to the corresponding black-body radiation.

grey-crowned babbler NOUN an insect-eating Australian bird, *Pomatostomus temporalis* of the family *Timaliidae.*

grey eminence NOUN the English equivalent of ***éminence grise.***

grey fox NOUN 1 a greyish American fox, *Urocyon cinereoargenteus,* inhabiting arid and woody regions from S North America to N South America. 2 **island grey fox.** a similar and related animal, *U. littoralis,* inhabiting islands off North America.

Grey Friar NOUN a Franciscan friar.

grey gum NOUN any of various eucalyptus trees of New South Wales having dull grey bark, esp *Eucalyptus punctata.*

greyhen (ˈɡreɪˌhɛn) NOUN the female of the black grouse. Compare **blackcock.**

grey heron NOUN a large European heron, *Ardea cinerea,* with grey wings and back and a long black drooping crest.

greyhound (ˈɡreɪˌhaʊnd) NOUN a tall slender fast-moving dog of an ancient breed originally used for coursing.

greyhound racing NOUN a sport in which a mechanically propelled dummy hare is pursued by greyhounds around a race track.

grey knight NOUN *Informal* an ambiguous intervener in a takeover battle, who makes a counterbid for the shares of the target company without having made his intentions clear. Compare **black knight, white knight.**

greylag *or* **greylag goose** (ˈɡreɪˌlæɡ) NOUN a large grey Eurasian goose, *Anser anser:* the ancestor of many domestic breeds of goose. US spelling: **graylag.**
▷HISTORY C18: from GREY + LAG[1], from its migrating later than other species

greylist (ˈɡreɪˌlɪst) VERB (*tr*) to hold (someone) in suspicion, without actually excluding him or her from a particular activity.

grey market NOUN 1 a system involving the secret but not illegal sale of goods at excessive prices. Compare **black market.** 2 *Stock Exchange* a market in the shares of a new issue, in which market makers deal with investors who have applied for shares but not yet received an allotment. 3 the market for goods and services created by older people with a comfortable disposable income and increased opportunities for spending it.

grey matter NOUN 1 the greyish tissue of the brain and spinal cord, containing nerve cell bodies, dendrites, and bare (unmyelinated) axons. Technical name: **substantia grisea.** Compare **white matter.** 2 *Informal* brains or intellect.

grey mullet NOUN any teleost food fish of the family *Mugilidae,* mostly occurring in coastal regions, having a spindle-shaped body and a broad fleshy mouth. US name: **mullet.** Compare **red mullet.**

grey nurse shark NOUN a common greyish Australian shark, *Odontaspis arenarius.*

grey panther NOUN a member of the generation of affluent older consumers, who regard themselves as young, active, and sociable.

grey power NOUN the political, financial, or social influence of elderly people.

grey propaganda NOUN propaganda that does not identify its source. Compare **black propaganda, white propaganda.**

Greys PLURAL NOUN **the.** another name for (the) **Royal Scots Greys.**

grey sedge NOUN *Brit* an angler's name for a greyish caddis fly, *Odontocerum albicorne,* that frequents running water, in which its larvae make cases from grains of sand.

grey squirrel NOUN a grey-furred squirrel, *Sciurus carolinensis,* native to E North America but now widely established.

grey-state NOUN (*modifier*) (of a fabric or material) not yet dyed.

grey vote NOUN the body of elderly people's votes, or elderly people regarded collectively as voters.

greywacke *or US* **graywacke** (ˈɡreɪˌwækə) NOUN any dark sandstone or grit having a matrix of clay minerals.
▷HISTORY C19: partial translation of German *Grauwacke;* see WACKE

grey warbler NOUN *NZ* a small bush bird that hatches the eggs of the shining cuckoo. Also called: **riroriro.**

grey water NOUN water that has been used for one purpose but can be used again without repurification, e.g. bath water, which can be used to water plants.

grey-wave ADJECTIVE *Informal* denoting a company or an investment that is potentially profitable but is unlikely to fulfil expectations before the investor has grey hair.

greywether (ˈɡreɪˌwɛðə) NOUN *Geology* another name for **sarsen.**
▷HISTORY from its resemblance to a grey sheep; see WETHER

grey whale NOUN a large N Pacific whalebone whale, *Eschrichtius glaucus,* that is grey or black with white spots and patches: family *Eschrichtidae.*

grey wolf NOUN another name for **timber wolf.**

GRF *Biochem* ABBREVIATION FOR growth hormone-releasing factor: a peptide that is released from the brain and stimulates the pituitary gland to secrete growth hormone.

gribble (ˈɡrɪbᵊl) NOUN any small marine isopod crustacean of the genus *Limnoria,* which bores into and damages wharves and other submerged wooden structures.
▷HISTORY C19: perhaps related to GRUB

grice (ˈɡraɪs) VERB 1 (*intr*) (of a railway enthusiast) to collect objects or visit places connected with trains and railways. ◆ NOUN 2 an object collected or place visited by a railway enthusiast.
▷HISTORY C20: origin obscure
▸ˈ**gricer** NOUN ▸ˈ**gricing** NOUN

grid (ɡrɪd) NOUN 1 See **gridiron.** 2 a network of horizontal and vertical lines superimposed over a map, building plan, etc., for locating points. 3 a grating consisting of parallel bars. 4 **the grid.** the national network of transmission lines, pipes, etc., by which electricity, gas, or water is distributed. 5 *NZ* short for **national grid.** 6 Also called: **control grid.** *Electronics* **a** an electrode situated between the cathode and anode of a valve usually consisting of a cylindrical mesh of wires, that controls the flow of electrons between cathode and anode. See also **screen grid, suppressor grid. b** (*as modifier*): *the grid bias.* 7 See **starting grid.** 8 a plate in an accumulator that carries the active substance. 9 any interconnecting

system of links: *the bus service formed a grid across the country.* [10] Northern English dialect word for **face.**
▷HISTORY C19: back formation from GRIDIRON
▸'**gridded** ADJECTIVE

grid bias NOUN the fixed voltage applied between the control grid and cathode of a valve.

grid declination NOUN the angular difference between true north and grid north on a map.

griddle ('grɪdᵊl) NOUN [1] Also called: **girdle.** *Brit* a thick round iron plate with a half hoop handle over the top, for making scones, etc. [2] any flat heated surface, esp on the top of a stove, for cooking food. ◆ VERB [3] (*tr*) to cook (food) on a griddle.
▷HISTORY C13: from Old French *gridil,* from Late Latin *crāticulum* (unattested) fine wickerwork; see GRILL[1]

griddlebread ('grɪdᵊlˌbrɛd) *or* **griddlecake** ('grɪdᵊlˌkeɪk) NOUN bread or cake made on a griddle.

gride (graɪd) VERB [1] (*intr*) *Literary* to grate or scrape harshly. [2] *Obsolete* to pierce or wound. ◆ NOUN [3] *Literary* a harsh or piercing sound.
▷HISTORY C14: variant of *girde* GIRD[2]

gridiron ('grɪdˌaɪən) NOUN [1] a utensil of parallel metal bars, used to grill meat, fish, etc. [2] any framework resembling this utensil. [3] a framework above the stage in a theatre from which suspended scenery, lights, etc., are manipulated. [4] **a** the field of play in American football. **b** an informal name for American football. **c** (*as modifier*): *a gridiron hero.* ◆ Often shortened to: **grid.**
▷HISTORY C13 *gredire,* perhaps variant (through influence of *ire* IRON) of *gredile* GRIDDLE

gridlock ('grɪdˌlɒk) *Chiefly US* ◆ NOUN [1] obstruction of urban traffic caused by queues of vehicles forming across junctions and causing further queues to form in the intersecting streets. [2] a point in a dispute at which no agreement can be reached; deadlock: *political gridlock.* ◆ VERB [3] (*tr*) (of traffic) to block or obstruct (an area).

grid reference NOUN a method of locating a point on a map or plan by a number referring to the lines of a grid drawn upon the map or plan and to subdivisions of the space between the lines.

grid road NOUN (in Canada) a road that follows a surveyed division between areas of a township, municipality, etc.

grid variation NOUN *Navigation* the angle between grid north and magnetic north at a point on a map or chart. Also called: **grivation.**

grief (gri:f) NOUN [1] deep or intense sorrow or distress, esp at the death of someone. [2] something that causes keen distress or suffering. [3] *Informal* trouble or annoyance: *people were giving me grief for leaving ten minutes early.* [4] **come to grief.** *Informal* to end unsuccessfully or disastrously.
▷HISTORY C13: from Anglo-French *gref,* from *grever* to GRIEVE[1]
▸'**griefless** ADJECTIVE

grief-stricken ADJECTIVE deeply affected by sorrow or distress.

grief tourism NOUN the practice of travelling to a place specifically in order to take part in public mourning.

grievance ('gri:vᵊns) NOUN [1] a real or imaginary wrong causing resentment and regarded as grounds for complaint. [2] a feeling of resentment or injustice at having been unfairly treated. [3] *Obsolete* affliction or hardship.
▷HISTORY C15 *grevance,* from Old French, from *grever* to GRIEVE[1]

grieve[1] (gri:v) VERB [1] to feel or cause to feel great sorrow or distress, esp at the death of someone. [2] (*tr*) *Obsolete* to inflict injury, hardship, or sorrow on.
▷HISTORY C13: from Old French *grever,* from Latin *gravāre* to burden, from *gravis* heavy
▸'**griever** NOUN ▸'**grieving** NOUN, ADJECTIVE ▸'**grievingly** ADVERB

grieve[2] (gri:v) NOUN *Scot* a farm manager or overseer.
▷HISTORY C15: from Old English (Northumbrian) *grǣfa* reeve

grievous ('gri:vəs) ADJECTIVE [1] very severe or painful: *a grievous injury.* [2] very serious; heinous: *a grievous sin.* [3] showing or marked by grief: *a grievous cry.* [4] causing great pain or suffering: *a grievous attack.*
▸'**grievously** ADVERB ▸'**grievousness** NOUN

grievous bodily harm NOUN *Criminal law* really serious injury caused by one person to another. Abbreviation: **GBH.**

griff (grɪf) NOUN *Slang* information; news.
▷HISTORY C20: from GRIFFIN[2]

griffe (grɪf) NOUN *Architect* a carved ornament at the base of a column, often in the form of a claw.
▷HISTORY C19: from French: claw, of Germanic origin

griffin[1] ('grɪfɪn), **griffon,** *or* **gryphon** NOUN a winged monster with an eagle-like head and the body of a lion.
▷HISTORY C14: from Old French *grifon,* from Latin *grӯphus,* from Greek *grups,* from *grupos* hooked

griffin[2] ('grɪfɪn) NOUN a newcomer to the Orient, esp one from W Europe.
▷HISTORY C18: of unknown origin

griffon[1] ('grɪfᵊn) NOUN [1] any of various small wire-haired breeds of dog, originally from Belgium. [2] any large vulture of the genus *Gyps,* of Africa, S Europe, and SW Asia, having a pale plumage with black wings: family *Accipitridae* (hawks).
▷HISTORY C19: from French: GRIFFIN[1]

griffon[2] ('grɪfᵊn) NOUN a variant of **griffin[1].**

grig (grɪg) NOUN *Dialect* [1] a lively person. [2] a short-legged hen. [3] a young eel.
▷HISTORY C14: dwarf, perhaps of Scandinavian origin; compare Swedish *krik* a little creature

Grigioni (gri'dʒo:ni) NOUN the Italian name for **Graubünden.**

Grignard reagent ('gri:njɑ:; *French* griɲar) NOUN *Chem* any of a class of organometallic reagents, having the general formula RMgX, where R is an organic group and X is a halogen atom: used in the synthesis of organic compounds.
▷HISTORY C20: named after Victor *Grignard* (1871–1934), French chemist

grigri, gris-gris, *or* **greegree** ('gri:gri:) NOUN, *plural* **-gris** (-gri:z) *or* **-grees.** an African talisman, amulet, or charm.
▷HISTORY of African origin

grike *or* **gryke** (graɪk) NOUN a solution fissure, a vertical crack about 0.5 m wide formed by the dissolving of limestone by water, that divides an exposed limestone surface into sections or clints.
▷HISTORY C20 in geological sense: from northern dialect

Grikwa ('gri:kwə, 'grɪk-) NOUN, *plural* **-kwa** *or* **-kwas.** a variant spelling of **Griqua.**

grill[1] (grɪl) VERB [1] to cook (meat, fish, etc.) by direct heat, as under a grill or over a hot fire, or (of meat, fish, etc.) to be cooked in this way. Usual US and Canadian word: **broil.** [2] (*tr; usually passive*) to torment with or as if with extreme heat: *the travellers were grilled by the scorching sun.* [3] (*tr*) *Informal* to subject to insistent or prolonged questioning. ◆ NOUN [4] a device with parallel bars of thin metal on which meat, fish, etc., may be cooked by a fire; gridiron. [5] a device on a cooker that radiates heat downwards for grilling meat, fish, etc. [6] food cooked by grilling. [7] See **grillroom.**
▷HISTORY C17: from French *gril* gridiron, from Latin *crāticula* fine wickerwork; see GRILLE
▸'**griller** NOUN

grill[2] (grɪl) NOUN a variant spelling of **grille.**
▷HISTORY C17: see GRILLE

grillage ('grɪlɪdʒ) NOUN an arrangement of beams and crossbeams used as a foundation on soft ground.
▷HISTORY C18: from French, from *griller* to furnish with a grille

grille *or* **grill** (grɪl) NOUN [1] Also called: **grillwork.** a framework, esp of metal bars arranged to form an ornamental pattern, used as a screen or partition. [2] Also called: **radiator grille.** a grating, often chromium-plated, that admits cooling air to the radiator of a motor vehicle. [3] a metal or wooden openwork grating used as a screen or divider. [4] a protective screen, usually plastic or metal, in front of the loudspeaker in a radio, record player, etc. [5] *Real Tennis* the opening in one corner of the receiver's end of the court. [6] a group of small pyramidal marks impressed in parallel rows into a stamp to prevent reuse.
▷HISTORY C17: from Old French, from Latin *crāticula* fine hurdlework, from *crātis* a hurdle

grilled (grɪld) ADJECTIVE [1] cooked on a grill or gridiron. [2] having a grille.

grillion (grɪljən) NOUN, *plural* **-lions** *or* **-lion.** *Informal* [1] (*often plural*) an extremely large but unspecified number, quantity, or amount: *he had grillions more goes than me.* ◆ DETERMINER [2] amounting to a grillion: *a grillion years old.*
▷HISTORY C20: on the model of *million*

grillroom ('grɪlˌru:m, -ˌrʊm) NOUN a restaurant or room in a restaurant, etc., where grilled steaks and other meat are served.

grilse (grɪls) NOUN, *plural* **grilses** *or* **grilse.** a young salmon that returns to fresh water after one winter in the sea.
▷HISTORY C15 *grilles* (plural), of uncertain origin

grim (grɪm) ADJECTIVE **grimmer, grimmest.** [1] stern; resolute: *grim determination.* [2] harsh or formidable in manner or appearance. [3] harshly ironic or sinister: *grim laughter.* [4] cruel, severe, or ghastly: *a grim accident.* [5] *Archaic or poetic* fierce: *a grim warrior.* [6] *Informal* unpleasant; disagreeable. [7] **hold on like grim death.** to hold very firmly or resolutely.
▷HISTORY Old English *grimm;* related to Old Norse *grimmr,* Old High German *grimm* savage, Greek *khremizein* to neigh
▸'**grimly** ADVERB ▸'**grimness** NOUN

grimace (grɪ'meɪs) NOUN [1] an ugly or distorted facial expression, as of wry humour, disgust, etc. ◆ VERB [2] (*intr*) to contort the face.
▷HISTORY C17: from French *grimace,* of Germanic origin; related to Spanish *grimazo* caricature; see GRIM
▸**gri'macer** NOUN ▸**gri'macingly** ADVERB

Grimaldi man NOUN *Anthropol* a type of Aurignacian man having a negroid appearance, thought to be a race of Cro-Magnon man.
▷HISTORY C20: named after the *Grimaldi* caves, Italy, where skeletons of this type were found

grimalkin (grɪ'mælkɪn, -'mɔ:l-) NOUN [1] an old cat, esp an old female cat. [2] a crotchety or shrewish old woman.
▷HISTORY C17: from GREY + MALKIN

grim dig NOUN *NZ informal, obsolete* an obdurate soldier.

grime (graɪm) NOUN [1] dirt, soot, or filth, esp when thickly accumulated or ingrained. ◆ VERB [2] (*tr*) to make dirty or coat with filth.
▷HISTORY C15: from Middle Dutch *grime;* compare Flemish *grijm,* Old English *grīma* mask
▸'**grimy** ADJECTIVE ▸'**griminess** NOUN

Grimm's law NOUN the rules accounting for systematic correspondences between consonants in the Germanic languages and consonants in other Indo-European languages; it states that Proto-Indo-European voiced aspirated stops, voiced unaspirated stops, and voiceless stops became voiced unaspirated stops, voiceless stops, and voiceless fricatives respectively.
▷HISTORY formulated by Jakob Ludwig Karl *Grimm* (1785–1863), German philologist and folklorist

grimoire (gri:m'wɑ:) NOUN a textbook of sorcery and magic.
▷HISTORY C19: from French, altered from *grammaire* GRAMMAR; compare GLAMOUR

Grimsby ('grɪmzbɪ) NOUN a port in E England, in North East Lincolnshire unitary authority, Lincolnshire, formerly important for fishing. Pop.: 90 703 (1991).

grin (grɪn) VERB **grins, grinning, grinned.** [1] to smile with the lips drawn back revealing the teeth or express (something) by such a smile: *to grin a welcome.* [2] (*intr*) to draw back the lips revealing the teeth, as in a snarl or grimace. [3] **grin and bear it.** *Informal* to suffer trouble or hardship without complaint. ◆ NOUN [4] a broad smile. [5] a snarl or grimace.
▷HISTORY Old English *grennian;* related to Old High German *grennen* to snarl, Old Norse *grenja* to howl; see GRUNT
▸'**grinner** NOUN ▸'**grinning** ADJECTIVE, NOUN

grinch (grɪntʃ) NOUN *US informal* a person whose lack of enthusiasm or bad temper has a depressing effect on others.
▷HISTORY C20: from a character in the 1957 children's book *How the Grinch stole Christmas* by Dr Seuss (1904–91), US writer and illustrator, whose full name was Theodor Seuss Geisel

grind (graɪnd) VERB **grinds, grinding, ground.** [1] to

reduce or be reduced to small particles by pounding or abrading: *to grind corn; to grind flour.* **2** (*tr*) to smooth, sharpen, or polish by friction or abrasion: *to grind a knife.* **3** to scrape or grate together (two things, esp the teeth) with a harsh rasping sound or (of such objects) to be scraped together. **4** (*tr; foll by out*) to speak or say (something) in a rough voice. **5** (*tr; often foll by down*) to hold down; oppress; tyrannize. **6** (*tr*) to operate (a machine) by turning a handle. **7** (*tr; foll by out*) to produce in a routine or uninspired manner: *he ground out his weekly article for the paper.* **8** (*tr; foll by out*) to continue to play in a dull or insipid manner: *the band only ground out old tunes all evening.* **9** (*tr; often foll by into*) to instil (facts, information, etc.) by persistent effort: *they ground into the recruits the need for vigilance.* **10** (*intr*) *Informal* to study or work laboriously. **11** (*intr*) *Chiefly US* to dance erotically by rotating the pelvis (esp in the phrase **bump and grind**). ◆ NOUN **12** *Informal* laborious or routine work or study. **13** *Slang, chiefly US* a person, esp a student, who works excessively hard. **14** a specific grade of pulverization, as of coffee beans: *coarse grind.* **15** *Brit slang* the act of sexual intercourse. **16** *Chiefly US* a dance movement involving an erotic rotation of the pelvis. **17** the act or sound of grinding. ◆ See also **grind on.**
▷HISTORY Old English *grindan;* related to Latin *frendere,* Lithuanian *gréndu* I rub, Low German *grand* sand
▸'**grindingly** ADVERB

grindelia (grɪn'diːlɪə) NOUN **1** any coarse plant of the American genus *Grindelia,* having yellow daisy-like flower heads: family *Asteraceae* (composites). See also **gum plant. 2** the dried leaves and tops of certain species of these plants, used in tonics and sedatives.
▷HISTORY C19: named after David Hieronymus *Grindel* (1777–1836), Russian botanist

Grindelwald (*German* 'grɪndəlvalt) NOUN a valley and resort in central Switzerland, in the Bernese Oberland: mountaineering centre, with the Wetterhorn and the Eiger nearby.

grinder ('graɪndə) NOUN **1** a person who grinds, esp one who grinds cutting tools. **2** a machine for grinding. **3** a molar tooth.

grindery ('graɪndərɪ) NOUN, *plural* **-eries. 1** a place in which tools and cutlery are sharpened. **2** the equipment of a shoemaker.

grind in VERB (*tr, adverb*) *Engineering* to make (a conical valve) fit its seating by grinding them together in the presence of an abrasive paste.

grinding wheel NOUN an abrasive wheel, usually a composite of hard particles in a resin filler, used for grinding.

grind on VERB (*intr, adverb*) to move further relentlessly: *the enemy's invasion ground slowly on.*

grindstone ('graɪnd,stəʊn) NOUN **1 a** a machine having a circular block of stone or composite abrasive rotated for sharpening tools or grinding metal. **b** the stone used in this machine. **c** any stone used for sharpening; whetstone. **2** another name for **millstone. 3 keep** *or* **have one's nose to the grindstone.** to work hard and perseveringly.

gringo ('grɪŋgəʊ) NOUN, *plural* **-gos.** a person from an English-speaking country: used as a derogatory term by Latin Americans.
▷HISTORY C19: from Spanish: foreigner, probably from *griego* Greek, hence an alien

griot ('griːəʊ, griː'ɒt) NOUN (in Western Africa) a member of a caste responsible for maintaining an oral record of tribal history in the form of music, poetry, and storytelling.
▷HISTORY C20: from French *guirot,* perhaps from Portuguese *criado* domestic servant

grip^{1} (grɪp) NOUN **1** the act or an instance of grasping and holding firmly: *he lost his grip on the slope.* **2** Also called: **handgrip.** the strength or pressure of such a grasp, as in a handshake: *a feeble grip.* **3** the style or manner of grasping an object, such as a tennis racket. **4** understanding, control, or mastery of a subject, problem, etc. (esp in such phrases as **get** *or* **have a grip on**). **5** Also called: **handgrip.** a part by which an object is grasped; handle. **6** Also called: **handgrip.** a travelling bag or holdall. **7** See **hairgrip. 8** any device that holds by friction, such as certain types of brake. **9** a method of clasping or shaking hands used by members of secret societies to greet or identify one another. **10** a spasm of pain: *a grip in one's stomach.* **11** a worker in a camera crew or a stagehand who shifts sets and props, etc. **12** a small drainage channel cut above an excavation to conduct surface water away from the excavation. **13 get** *or* **come to grips.** (often foll by *with*) **a** to deal with (a problem or subject). **b** to tackle (an assailant). ◆ VERB **grips, gripping, gripped. 14** to take hold of firmly or tightly, as by a clutch. **15** to hold the interest or attention of: *to grip an audience.*
▷HISTORY Old English *gripe* grasp; related to Old Norse *gripr* property, Old High German *grif*
▸'**gripper** NOUN ▸'**grippingly** ADVERB

grip^{2} (grɪp) NOUN *Med* a variant spelling of **grippe.**

gripe (graɪp) VERB **1** (*intr*) *Informal* to complain, esp in a persistent nagging manner. **2** to cause sudden intense pain in the intestines of (a person) or (of a person) to experience this pain. **3** (*intr*) *Nautical* (of a ship) to tend to come up into the wind in spite of the helm. **4** *Archaic* to clutch; grasp. **5** (*tr*) *Archaic* to afflict. ◆ NOUN **6** (*usually plural*) a sudden intense pain in the intestines; colic. **7** *Informal* a complaint or grievance. **8** *Now rare* **a** the act of gripping. **b** a firm grip. **c** a device that grips. **9** (*in plural*) *Nautical* the lashings that secure a boat.
▷HISTORY Old English *grīpan;* related to Gothic *greipan,* Old High German *grīfan* to seize, Lithuanian *greibiu*
▸'**griper** NOUN ▸'**gripingly** ADVERB

gripe water NOUN *Brit* a solution given to infants to relieve colic.

grippe *or* **grip** (grɪp) NOUN a former name for **influenza.**
▷HISTORY C18: from French *grippe,* from *gripper* to seize, of Germanic origin; see GRIP^{1}

grip tape NOUN a rough tape for sticking to a surface to provide a greater grip.

Griqua *or* **Grikwa** ('griːkwə, 'grɪk-) NOUN **1** (*plural* **-qua, -quas** *or* **-kwa, -kwas**) a member of a people of mixed European and Khoikhoi ancestry, living chiefly in Griqualand. **2** the language or dialect of Khoikhoi spoken by this people, belonging to the Khoisan family.

Griqualand East ('griːkwə,lænd, 'grɪk-) NOUN an area of central South Africa: settled in 1861 by Griquas led by Adam Kok III; annexed to the Cape Colony in 1879; part of the Transkei in 1903–94. Chief town: Kokstad. Area: 17 100 sq. km (6602 sq. miles).

Griqualand West NOUN an area of N South Africa, north of the Orange river: settled after 1803 by the Griquas; annexed by the British in 1871 following a dispute with the Orange Free State; became part of the Cape Colony in 1880. Chief town: Kimberley. Area: 39 360 sq. km (15 197 sq. miles).

grisaille (grɪ'zeɪl; *French* grizɑj) NOUN **1** a technique of monochrome painting in shades of grey, as in an oil painting or a wall decoration, imitating the effect of relief. **2** a painting, stained glass window, etc., in this manner.
▷HISTORY C19: from French, from *gris* grey

griseofulvin (,grɪzɪəʊ'fʊlvɪn) NOUN an antibiotic used to treat fungal infections.
▷HISTORY C20: from New Latin, from *Penicillium griseofulvum dierckx* (fungus from which it was isolated), from Medieval Latin *griseus* grey + Latin *fulvus* reddish yellow

griseous ('grɪsɪəs, 'grɪz-) ADJECTIVE streaked or mixed with grey; somewhat grey.
▷HISTORY C19: from Medieval Latin *griseus,* of Germanic origin

grisette (grɪ'zɛt) NOUN **1** (esp formerly) a French working-class girl, esp a pretty or flirtatious one. **2** an edible toadstool of the genus *Amanita* of broad-leaved and birch woods.
▷HISTORY C18: from French, from *grisette* grey fabric used for dresses, from *gris* grey

gris-gris ('griːgriː) NOUN, *plural* **-gris** (-griːz). a variant spelling of **grigri.**

Grishun (griː'ʃuːn) NOUN the Romansch name for **Graubünden.**

griskin ('grɪskɪn) NOUN *Brit* the lean part of a loin of pork.
▷HISTORY C17: probably from dialect *gris* pig, from Old Norse *griss*

grisly^{1} ('grɪzlɪ) ADJECTIVE **-lier, -liest.** causing horror or dread; gruesome.
▷HISTORY Old English *grislic;* related to Old Frisian *grislik,* Old High German *grīsenlīh*
▸'**grisliness** NOUN

Language note See at **grizzly.**

grisly^{2} ('grɪzlɪ) NOUN, *plural* **-lies.** *Obsolete* a variant spelling of **grizzly.**

grison ('graɪs^{ə}n, 'grɪz^{ə}n) NOUN either of two musteline mammals, *Grison* (or *Galictis*) *cuja* or *G. vittata,* of Central and South America, having a greyish back and black face and underparts.
▷HISTORY C18: from French, from *grison* grey animal, from Old French *gris* grey

Grisons (grizɔ̃) NOUN the French name for **Graubünden.**

grist (grɪst) NOUN **1 a** grain intended to be or that has been ground. **b** the quantity of such grain processed in one grinding. **2** *Brewing* malt grains that have been cleaned and cracked. **3 grist to** (*or* **for**) **the** (*or* **one's**) **mill.** anything that can be turned to profit or advantage.
▷HISTORY Old English *grīst;* related to Old Saxon *grist-grimmo* gnashing of teeth, Old High German *grist-grimmōn*

gristle ('grɪs^{ə}l) NOUN cartilage, esp when in meat.
▷HISTORY Old English *gristle;* related to Old Frisian, Middle Low German *gristel*
▸'**gristly** ADJECTIVE ▸'**gristliness** NOUN

gristmill ('grɪst,mɪl) NOUN a mill, esp one equipped with large grinding stones for grinding grain.

grit (grɪt) NOUN **1** small hard particles of sand, earth, stone, etc. **2** Also called: **gritstone.** any coarse sandstone that can be used as a grindstone or millstone. **3** the texture or grain of stone. **4** indomitable courage, toughness, or resolution. **5** *Engineering* an arbitrary measure of the size of abrasive particles used in a grinding wheel or other abrasive process. ◆ VERB **grits, gritting, gritted. 6** to clench or grind together (two objects, esp the teeth). **7** to cover (a surface, such as icy roads) with grit.
▷HISTORY Old English *grēot;* related to Old Norse *grjōt* pebble, Old High German *grioz;* see GREAT, GROATS, GRUEL
▸'**gritless** ADJECTIVE

Grit (grɪt) NOUN, ADJECTIVE *Canadian* an informal word for **Liberal.**

grith (grɪθ) NOUN **1** *English legal history* security, peace, or protection, guaranteed either in a certain place, such as a church, or for a period of time. **2** a place of safety or protection.
▷HISTORY Old English *grith;* related to Old Norse *grith* home

grits (grɪts) PLURAL NOUN **1** hulled and coarsely ground grain. **2** *US* See **hominy grits.**
▷HISTORY Old English *grytt;* related to Old High German *gruzzi;* see GREAT, GRIT

gritter ('grɪtə) NOUN *Brit* a vehicle which spreads grit on roads during icy weather, or when icy conditions are expected.

gritting ('grɪtɪŋ) NOUN *Brit* **a** the spreading of grit on road surfaces to render them less slippery for vehicles during icy weather. **b** (*as modifier*): *gritting lorries.*

gritty ('grɪtɪ) ADJECTIVE **-tier, -tiest. 1** courageous; hardy; resolute. **2** of, like, or containing grit.
▸'**grittily** ADVERB ▸'**grittiness** NOUN

grivation (grɪ'veɪʃən) NOUN *Navigation* short for **grid variation.**

grivet ('grɪvɪt) NOUN an E African variety of a common guenon monkey, *Cercopithecus aethiops,* having long white tufts of hair on either side of the face. Compare **green monkey, vervet.**
▷HISTORY C19: from French, of unknown origin

grizzle^{1} ('grɪz^{ə}l) VERB **1** to make or become grey. ◆ NOUN **2** a grey colour. **3** grey or partly grey hair. **4** a grey wig.
▷HISTORY C15: from Old French *grisel,* from *gris,* of Germanic origin; compare Middle High German *grīs* grey

grizzle^{2} ('grɪz^{ə}l) VERB (*intr*) *Informal, chiefly Brit* **1**

(esp of a child) to fret; whine. 2 to sulk or grumble.
▷HISTORY C18: of Germanic origin; compare Old High German *grist-grimmōn* gnashing of teeth, German *Griesgram* unpleasant person
▸'**grizzler** NOUN

grizzled ('grɪzəld) ADJECTIVE 1 streaked or mixed with grey; grizzly; griseous. 2 having grey or partly grey hair.

grizzly ('grɪzlɪ) ADJECTIVE **-zlier, -zliest.** 1 somewhat grey; grizzled. ◆ NOUN, *plural* **-zlies.** 2 See **grizzly bear.**

> **Language note** *Grizzly* is sometimes wrongly used where *grisly* is meant: *a grisly* (not *grizzly*) *murder.*

grizzly bear NOUN a variety of the brown bear, *Ursus arctos horribilis,* formerly widespread in W North America; its brown fur has cream or white hair tips on the back, giving a grizzled appearance. Often shortened to: **grizzly.**

gro. ABBREVIATION FOR gross (unit of quantity).

groan (grəʊn) NOUN 1 a prolonged stressed dull cry expressive of agony, pain, or disapproval. 2 a loud harsh creaking sound, as of a tree bending in the wind. 3 *Informal* a grumble or complaint, esp a persistent one. ◆ VERB 4 to utter (low inarticulate sounds) expressive of pain, grief, disapproval, etc.: *they all groaned at Larry's puns.* 5 (*intr*) to make a sound like a groan. 6 (*intr,* usually foll by *beneath* or *under*) to be weighed down (by) or suffer greatly (under): *the country groaned under the dictator's rule.* 7 (*intr*) *Informal* to complain or grumble.
▷HISTORY Old English *grānian*; related to Old Norse *grīna,* Old High German *grīnan;* see GRIN
▸'**groaning** NOUN, ADJECTIVE ▸'**groaningly** ADVERB

groaner ('grəʊnə) NOUN 1 a person or thing that groans. 2 *Informal* a bad or corny joke or pun.

groat (grəʊt) NOUN an English silver coin worth four pennies, taken out of circulation in the 17th century.
▷HISTORY C14: from Middle Dutch *groot,* from Middle Low German *gros,* from Medieval Latin (*denarius*) *grossus* thick (coin); see GROSCHEN

groats (grəʊts) PLURAL NOUN 1 the hulled and crushed grain of oats, wheat, or certain other cereals. 2 the parts of oat kernels used as food.
▷HISTORY Old English *grot* particle; related to *grota* fragment, as in *meregrota* pearl; see GRIT, GROUT

grocer ('grəʊsə) NOUN a dealer in foodstuffs and other household supplies.
▷HISTORY C15: from Old French *grossier,* from *gros* large; see GROSS

groceries ('grəʊsərɪz) PLURAL NOUN merchandise, esp foodstuffs, sold by a grocer.

grocery ('grəʊsərɪ) NOUN, *plural* **-ceries.** the business or premises of a grocer.

grockle ('grɒkəl) NOUN *Southwest English dialect* a tourist, esp one from the Midlands or the North of England.
▷HISTORY C20: of unknown origin

Grodno (*Russian* 'grɔdnə) NOUN a city in W Belarus on the Neman River: part of Poland (1921–39); an industrial centre. Pop.: 306 000 (1998 est.).

grog (grɒg) NOUN 1 diluted spirit, usually rum, as an alcoholic drink. 2 *Informal, chiefly Austral and NZ* alcoholic drink in general, esp spirits.
▷HISTORY C18: from Old *Grog,* nickname of Edward Vernon (1684–1757), British admiral, who in 1740 issued naval rum diluted with water; his nickname arose from his grogram cloak

groggy ('grɒgɪ) ADJECTIVE **-gier, -giest.** *Informal* 1 dazed or staggering, as from exhaustion, blows, or drunkenness. 2 faint or weak.
▸'**groggily** ADVERB ▸'**grogginess** NOUN

grogram ('grɒgrəm) NOUN a coarse fabric of silk, wool, or silk mixed with wool or mohair, often stiffened with gum, formerly used for clothing.
▷HISTORY C16: from French *gros grain* coarse grain; see GROSGRAIN

grogshop ('grɒg,ʃɒp) NOUN 1 *Rare* a drinking place, esp one of disreputable character. 2 *Austral and NZ informal* a shop where liquor can be bought for drinking off the premises.

groin (grɔɪn) NOUN 1 the depression or fold where the legs join the abdomen. Related adjective: **inguinal.** 2 *Euphemistic* the genitals, esp the testicles. 3 a variant spelling (esp US) of **groyne.** 4 *Architect* a curved arris formed where two intersecting vaults meet. ◆ VERB 5 (*tr*) *Architect* to provide or construct with groins.
▷HISTORY C15: perhaps from English *grynde* abyss; related to GROUND[1]

Grolier ('grəʊlɪə; *French* grɔlje) ADJECTIVE relating to or denoting a decorative style of bookbinding using interlaced leather straps, gilded ornamental scrolls, etc.
▷HISTORY C19: named after Jean *Grolier de Servières* (1479–1565), French bibliophile

grommet ('grɒmɪt) *or* **grummet** NOUN 1 a ring of rubber or plastic or a metal eyelet designed to line a hole to prevent a cable or pipe passed through it from chafing. 2 a ring of rope hemp used to stuff the gland of a pipe joint. 3 *Med* a small tube inserted into the eardrum in cases of glue ear in order to allow air to enter the middle ear. 4 *Austral informal* a young or inexperienced surfer.
▷HISTORY C15: from obsolete French *gourmette* chain linking the ends of a bit, from *gourmer* bridle, of unknown origin

gromwell ('grɒmwəl) NOUN any of various hairy plants of the boraginaceous genus *Lithospermum,* esp *L. officinale,* having small greenish-white, yellow, or blue flowers, and smooth nutlike fruits. See also **puccoon** (sense 1).
▷HISTORY C13: from Old French *gromil,* from *gres* sandstone + *mil* millet, from Latin *milium*

Groningen ('grəʊnɪŋən; *Dutch* 'xroːnɪŋə) NOUN 1 a province in the NE Netherlands: mainly agricultural. Capital: Groningen. Pop.: 562 600 (2000 est.). Area: 2336 sq. km (902 sq. miles). 2 a city in the NE Netherlands, capital of Groningen province. Pop.: 171 193 (1999 est.).

Grønland ('grœnlan) NOUN the Danish name for **Greenland.**

groom (gruːm, grʊm) NOUN 1 a person employed to clean and look after horses. 2 See **bridegroom.** 3 any of various officers of a royal or noble household. 4 *Archaic* a male servant or attendant. 5 *Archaic and poetic* a young man. ◆ VERB (*tr*) 6 to make or keep (clothes, appearance, etc.) clean and tidy. 7 to rub down, clean, and smarten (a horse, dog, etc.). 8 to train or prepare for a particular task, occupation, etc.: *to groom someone for the Presidency.* 9 to win the confidence of (a victim) in order to a commit sexual assault on him or her.
▷HISTORY C13 *grom* manservant; perhaps related to Old English *grōwan* to GROW
▸'**groomer** NOUN ▸'**grooming** NOUN

groomsman ('gruːmzmən, 'grʊmz-) NOUN, *plural* **-men.** a man who attends the bridegroom at a wedding, usually the best man.

groove (gruːv) NOUN 1 a long narrow channel or furrow, esp one cut into wood by a tool. 2 the spiral channel, usually V-shaped, in a gramophone record. See also **microgroove.** 3 one of the spiral cuts in the bore of a gun. 4 *Anatomy* any furrow or channel on a bodily structure or part; sulcus. 5 *Mountaineering* a shallow fissure in a rock face or between two rock faces, forming an angle of more than 120°. 6 a settled existence, routine, etc., to which one is suited or accustomed, esp one from which it is difficult to escape. 7 *Slang* an experience, event, etc., that is groovy. 8 **in the groove. a** *Jazz* playing well and apparently effortlessly, with a good beat, etc. **b** *US* fashionable. ◆ VERB 9 (*tr*) to form or cut a groove in. 10 (*intr*) *Dated slang* to enjoy oneself or feel in rapport with one's surroundings. 11 (*intr*) *Jazz* to play well, with a good beat, etc.
▷HISTORY C15: from obsolete Dutch *groeve,* of Germanic origin; compare Old High German *gruoba* pit, Old Norse *grof*
▸'**grooveless** ADJECTIVE ▸'**groove,like** ADJECTIVE

grooving saw NOUN a circular saw used for making grooves.

groovy ('gruːvɪ) ADJECTIVE **groovier, grooviest.** *Slang, often jocular* attractive, fashionable, or exciting.

grope (grəʊp) VERB 1 (*intr;* usually foll by *for*) to feel or search about uncertainly (for something) with the hands. 2 (*intr;* usually foll by *for* or *after*) to search uncertainly or with difficulty (for a solution, answer, etc.). 3 (*tr*) to find or make (one's way) by groping. 4 (*tr*) *Slang* to feel or fondle the body of (someone) for sexual gratification. ◆ NOUN 5 the act of groping.
▷HISTORY Old English *grāpian;* related to Old High German *greifōn,* Norwegian *greipa;* compare GRIPE
▸'**gropingly** ADVERB

groper ('grəʊpə) *or* **grouper** NOUN, *plural* **-er** *or* **-ers.** any large marine serranid fish of the genus *Epinephelus* and related genera, of warm and tropical seas.
▷HISTORY C17: from Portuguese *garupa,* probably from a South American Indian word

grosbeak ('grəʊs,biːk, 'grɒs-) NOUN 1 any of various finches, such as *Pinicola enucleator* (**pine grosbeak**), that have a massive powerful bill. 2 **cardinal grosbeak.** any of various mostly tropical American buntings, such as the cardinal and pyrrhuloxia, the males of which have brightly coloured plumage.
▷HISTORY C17: from French *grosbec,* from Old French *gros* large, thick + *bec* BEAK[1]

groschen ('grəʊʃən; *German* 'grɔʃən) NOUN, *plural* **-schen.** 1 a former Austrian monetary unit worth one hundredth of a schilling. 2 a former German coin worth ten pfennigs. 3 a former German silver coin.
▷HISTORY C17: from German: Bohemian dialect alteration of Middle High German *grosse,* from Medieval Latin (*denarius*) *grossus* thick (penny); see GROSS, GROAT

gros de Londres *French* (gro də lɔ̃drə) NOUN a lightweight shiny ribbed silk fabric, the ribs alternating between wide and narrow between different colours or between different textures of yarn.
▷HISTORY literally: heavy (fabric) from London

grosgrain ('grəʊ,greɪn) NOUN a heavy ribbed silk or rayon fabric or tape for trimming clothes, etc.
▷HISTORY C19: from French *gros grain* coarse grain; see GROSS, GRAIN

gros point ('grəʊ 'pɔɪnt; *French* gro pwɛ̃) NOUN 1 a needlepoint stitch covering two horizontal and two vertical threads. 2 work done in this stitch. ◆ Compare **petit point.**

gross (grəʊs) ADJECTIVE 1 repellently or excessively fat or bulky. 2 with no deductions for expenses, tax, etc.; total: *gross sales; gross income.* Compare **net**[2] (sense 1). 3 (of personal qualities, tastes, etc.) conspicuously coarse or vulgar. 4 obviously or exceptionally culpable or wrong; flagrant: *gross inefficiency.* 5 lacking in perception, sensitivity, or discrimination: *gross judgments.* 6 (esp of vegetation) dense; thick; luxuriant. 7 *Obsolete* coarse in texture or quality. 8 *Rare* rude; uneducated; ignorant. ◆ INTERJECTION *Slang* 9 an exclamation indicating disgust. ◆ NOUN 10 (*plural* **gross**) a unit of quantity equal to 12 dozen. 11 (*plural* **grosses**) **a** the entire amount. **b** the great majority. ◆ VERB (*tr*) 12 to earn as total revenue, before deductions for expenses, tax, etc. ◆ See also **gross out, gross up.**
▷HISTORY C14: from Old French *gros* large, from Late Latin *grossus* thick
▸'**grossly** ADVERB ▸'**grossness** NOUN

gross domestic product NOUN the total value of all goods and services produced domestically by a nation during a year. It is equivalent to gross national product minus net investment incomes from foreign nations. Abbreviation: **GDP.**

gross national product NOUN the total value of all final goods and services produced annually by a nation. Abbreviation: **GNP.**

gross out *US slang* ◆ VERB (*tr, adverb*) 1 to cause (a person) to feel distaste or strong dislike for (something). ◆ NOUN **gross-out.** 2 a person or thing regarded as disgusting or objectionable. ◆ ADJECTIVE **gross-out.** 3 disgusting, boring, or objectionable.

gross profit NOUN *Accounting* the difference between total revenue from sales and the total cost of purchases or materials, with an adjustment for stock.

gross ton NOUN another name for **long ton:** see **ton**[1] (sense 1).

grossularite ('grɒsjʊlə,raɪt) NOUN a green or greenish-grey garnet, used as a gemstone. Formula: $Ca_3Al_2(SiO_4)_3$. Also called: **gooseberry stone.**
▷HISTORY C19: from New Latin *grossulāria* gooseberry, from Old French *groselle* + -ITE[1]

gross up VERB (*tr, adverb*) to increase (net income) to its pretax value.

Grosswardein (groːsvar'dain) NOUN the German name for **Oradea**.

gross weight NOUN total weight of an article inclusive of the weight of the container and packaging.

grosz (grɔːʃ) NOUN, *plural* **groszy** ('grɔːʃɪ). a Polish monetary unit worth one hundredth of a zloty.
▷HISTORY from Polish, from Czech *grosh;* see GROSCHEN

grot[1] (grɒt) NOUN *Slang* rubbish; dirt.
▷HISTORY C20: from GROTTY

grot[2] (grɒt) NOUN a poetic word for **grotto**.
▷HISTORY C16: from French *grotte,* from Old Italian *grotta;* see GROTTO

grotesque (grəʊ'tɛsk) ADJECTIVE [1] strangely or fantastically distorted; bizarre: *a grotesque reflection in the mirror.* [2] of or characteristic of the grotesque in art. [3] absurdly incongruous; in a ludicrous context: *a grotesque turn of phrase.* ◆ NOUN [4] a 16th-century decorative style in which parts of human, animal, and plant forms are distorted and mixed. [5] a decorative device, as in painting or sculpture, in this style. [6] *Printing* the family of 19th-century sans serif display types. [7] any grotesque person or thing.
▷HISTORY C16: from French, from Old Italian (*pittura*) *grottesca* cave painting, from *grottesco* of a cave, from *grotta* cave; see GROTTO
▸**gro'tesquely** ADVERB ▸**gro'tesqueness** NOUN

grotesquery *or* **grotesquerie** (grəʊ'tɛskərɪ) NOUN, *plural* **-queries.** [1] the state of being grotesque. [2] something that is grotesque, esp an object such as a sculpture.

grotto ('grɒtəʊ) NOUN, *plural* **-toes** *or* **-tos.** [1] a small cave, esp one with attractive features. [2] a construction in the form of a cave, esp as in landscaped gardens during the 18th century.
▷HISTORY C17: from Old Italian *grotta,* from Late Latin *crypta* vault; see CRYPT

grotty ('grɒtɪ) ADJECTIVE **-tier, -tiest.** *Brit slang* [1] unpleasant, nasty, or unattractive. [2] of poor quality or in bad condition; unsatisfactory or useless.
▷HISTORY C20: from GROTESQUE

grouch (graʊtʃ) *Informal* ◆ VERB (*intr*) [1] to complain; grumble. ◆ NOUN [2] a complaint, esp a persistent one. [3] a person who is always grumbling.
▷HISTORY C20: from obsolete *grutch,* from Old French *grouchier* to complain; see GRUDGE

grouchy ('graʊtʃɪ) *Informal* **grouchier, grouchiest** bad-tempered; tending to complain; peevish.
▸**'grouchily** ADVERB ▸**'grouchiness** NOUN

grough (grʌf) NOUN *Mountaineering* a natural channel or fissure in a peat moor; a peat hag.
▷HISTORY C20: possibly the same as *grough,* an obsolete variant of GRUFF in the obsolete sense: "rough" (of terrain)

ground[1] (graʊnd) NOUN [1] the land surface. [2] earth or soil: *he dug into the ground outside his house.* [3] (*plural*) the land around a dwelling house or other building. [4] (*sometimes plural*) an area of land given over to a purpose: *football ground; burial grounds.* [5] land having a particular characteristic: *level ground; high ground.* [6] matter for consideration or debate; field of research or inquiry: *the lecture was familiar ground to him; the report covered a lot of ground.* [7] a position or viewpoint, as in an argument or controversy (esp in the phrases **give ground, hold, stand,** *or* **shift one's ground**). [8] position or advantage, as in a subject or competition (esp in the phrases **gain ground, lose ground,** etc.). [9] (*often plural*) reason; justification: *grounds for complaint.* [10] *Arts* **a** the prepared surface applied to the support of a painting, such as a wall, canvas, etc., to prevent it reacting with or absorbing the paint. **b** the support of a painting. **c** the background of a painting or main surface against which the other parts of a work of art appear superimposed. [11] **a** the first coat of paint applied to a surface. **b** (*as modifier*): *ground colour.* [12] the bottom of a river or the sea. [13] (*plural*) sediment or dregs, esp from coffee. [14] *Chiefly Brit* the floor of a room. [15] *Cricket* **a** the area from the popping crease back past the stumps, in which a batsman may legally stand. **b** ground staff. [16] See **ground bass.** [17] a mesh or network supporting the main pattern of a piece of lace. [18] *Electrical* the usual US and Canadian word for **earth** (sense 8). [19] **above ground.** alive. [20] **below ground.** dead and buried. [21] **break new ground.** to do something that has not been done before. [22] **cut the ground from under someone's feet.** to anticipate someone's action or argument and thus make it irrelevant or meaningless. [23] **(down) to the ground.** *Brit informal* completely; absolutely: *it suited him down to the ground.* [24] **get off the ground.** *Informal* to make a beginning, esp one that is successful. [25] **go to ground.** to go into hiding. [26] **into the ground.** beyond what is requisite or can be endured; to exhaustion. [27] **meet someone on his own ground.** to meet someone according to terms he has laid down himself. [28] **the (moral) high ground.** a position of moral or ethical superiority in a dispute. [29] **touch ground. a** (of a ship) to strike the sea bed. **b** to arrive at something solid or stable after discussing or dealing with topics that are abstract or inconclusive. [30] (*modifier*) situated on, living on, or used on the ground: *ground frost; ground forces.* [31] (*modifier*) concerned with or operating on the ground, esp as distinct from in the air: *ground crew; ground hostess.* [32] (*modifier*) (used in names of plants) low-growing and often trailing or spreading. ◆ VERB [33] (*tr*) to put or place on the ground. [34] (*tr*) to instruct in fundamentals. [35] (*tr*) to provide a basis or foundation for; establish. [36] (*tr*) to confine (an aircraft, pilot, etc.) to the ground. [37] (*tr*) *Informal* to confine (a child) to the house as a punishment. [38] the usual US word for **earth** (sense 16). [39] (*tr*) *Nautical* to run (a vessel) aground. [40] (*tr*) to cover (a surface) with a preparatory coat of paint. [41] (*intr*) to hit or reach the ground.
▷HISTORY Old English *grund;* related to Old Norse *grunn* shallow, *grunnr, grund* plain, Old High German *grunt*

ground[2] (graʊnd) VERB [1] the past tense and past participle of **grind.** ◆ ADJECTIVE [2] having the surface finished, thickness reduced, or an edge sharpened by grinding. [3] reduced to fine particles by grinding.

groundage ('graʊndɪdʒ) NOUN *Brit* a fee levied on a vessel entering a port or anchored off a shore.

groundbait ('graʊnd,beɪt) *Angling* ◆ NOUN [1] bait, such as scraps of bread, maggots, etc., thrown into an area of water to attract fish. See **chum**[2]. ◆ VERB [2] (*tr*) to prepare (an area of water) with groundbait.

ground bass *or* **ground** (beɪs) NOUN *Music* a short melodic bass line that is repeated over and over again.

ground beetle NOUN [1] any beetle of the family *Carabidae,* often found under logs, stones, etc., having long legs and a dark coloration. [2] any beetle of the family *Tenebrionidae,* feeding on plants and plant products. [3] any of various other beetles that live close to or beneath the ground.

ground-breaking ADJECTIVE innovative: *a ground-breaking novel.*

ground bug NOUN any member of a family (*Lygaeidae*) of hemipterous plant-eating insects, having generally dark bodies, sometimes marked with red, and lighter, yellowish wings.

ground cherry NOUN any of various American solanaceous plants of the genus *Physalis,* esp *P. pubescens,* having round fleshy fruit enclosed in a bladder-like husk. See also **winter cherry, gooseberry** (sense 4).

ground control NOUN [1] the personnel, radar, computers, etc., on the ground that monitor the progress of aircraft or spacecraft. [2] a system for feeding continuous radio messages to an aircraft pilot to enable him to make a blind landing.

ground cover NOUN **a** dense low herbaceous plants and shrubs that grow over the surface of the ground, esp, in a forest, preventing soil erosion or, in a garden, stifling weeds. **b** (*as modifier*): *ground-cover plants.*

grounded ('graʊndɪd) ADJECTIVE sensible and down-to-earth; having one's feet on the ground.

ground effect NOUN the improvement to the aerodynamic qualities of a low-slung motor vehicle resulting from a cushion of air beneath it.

ground elder NOUN another name for **goutweed.**

ground engineer NOUN an engineer qualified and licensed to certify the airworthiness of an aircraft. Official name: **licensed aircraft engineer.**

ground floor NOUN [1] the floor of a building level or almost level with the ground. [2] **get in on** (*or* **start from**) **the ground floor.** *Informal* **a** to enter a business, organization, etc., at the lowest level. **b** to be in a project, undertaking, etc., from its inception.

ground frost NOUN the condition resulting from a temperature reading of 0°C or below on a thermometer in contact with a grass surface.

ground game NOUN *Brit* game animals, such as hares or deer, found on the earth's surface: distinguished from game birds.

ground glass NOUN [1] glass that has a rough surface produced by grinding, used for diffusing light. [2] glass in the form of fine particles produced by grinding, used as an abrasive.

groundhog ('graʊnd,hɒg) NOUN another name for **woodchuck.**

Groundhog Day NOUN [1] (in the US and Canada) February 2nd, when, according to tradition, the groundhog emerges from hibernation; if it sees its shadow, it returns to its burrow for six weeks as a sunny day indicates a late spring, while a cloudy day would mean an early spring. [2] a situation in which events are or appear to be continually repeated.
▷HISTORY C20: sense 2 from the 1993 film *Groundhog Day,* in which the lead character experiences the same day repeatedly

ground ice NOUN sea ice that is in contact with the coast or sea bed and thus not floating freely.

grounding ('graʊndɪŋ) NOUN a basic knowledge of or training in a subject.

ground ivy NOUN a creeping or trailing Eurasian aromatic herbaceous plant, *Glechoma* (or *Nepeta*) *hederacea,* with scalloped leaves and purplish-blue flowers: family *Lamiaceae* (labiates).

ground layer NOUN See **layer** (sense 2).

groundless ('graʊndlɪs) ADJECTIVE without reason or justification: *his suspicions were groundless.*
▸**'groundlessly** ADVERB ▸**'groundlessness** NOUN

groundling ('graʊndlɪŋ) NOUN [1] any animal or plant that lives close to the ground or at the bottom of a lake, river, etc. [2] **a** (in Elizabethan theatre) a spectator standing in the yard in front of the stage and paying least. **b** a spectator in the cheapest section of any theatre. [3] a person on the ground as distinguished from one in an aircraft.

ground loop NOUN a sudden uncontrolled turn by an aircraft on the ground, while moving under its own power.

groundmass ('graʊnd,mæs) NOUN the matrix of igneous rocks, such as porphyry, in which larger crystals (phenocrysts) are embedded.

groundnut ('graʊnd,nʌt) NOUN [1] a North American climbing leguminous plant, *Apios tuberosa,* with fragrant brown flowers and small edible underground tubers. [2] the tuber of this plant. [3] any of several other plants having underground nutlike parts. [4] *Brit* another name for **peanut.**

groundnut oil NOUN a mild-tasting oil extracted from peanuts and used in cooking.

ground pine NOUN [1] a hairy plant, *Ajuga chamaepitys,* of Europe and N Africa, having two-lipped yellow flowers marked with red spots: family *Lamiaceae* (labiates). It smells of pine when crushed. See also **bugle**[2]. [2] any of certain North American club mosses, esp *Lycopodium obscurum.*

ground plan NOUN [1] a drawing of the ground floor of a building, esp one to scale. See also **plan** (sense 3). Compare **elevation** (sense 5). [2] a preliminary or basic outline.

ground-plane aerial NOUN *Electronics* a quarter-wave vertical dipole aerial in which the electrical image forming the other quarter-wave section is formed by reflection in a system of radially disposed metal rods or in a conductive sheet.

ground plate NOUN a joist forming the lowest member of a timber frame. Also called: **groundsill, soleplate.**

ground plum NOUN [1] a North American leguminous plant, *Astragalus caryocarpus,* with purple or white flowers and green thick-walled plumlike edible pods. [2] the pod of this plant.

ground provisions PLURAL NOUN *Caribbean* starchy vegetables, esp root crops and plantains.

ground rent NOUN *Law* the rent reserved by a lessor on granting a lease, esp one for a long period of years.

ground rule NOUN a procedural rule or principle.

ground run NOUN the distance taken by an aircraft to brake from its landing speed to its taxiing speed or a stop.

groundsel ('graʊnsəl) NOUN [1] any of certain plants of the genus *Senecio*, esp *S. vulgaris*, a Eurasian weed with heads of small yellow flowers: family *Asteraceae* (composites). See also **ragwort.** [2] **groundsel tree.** a shrub, *Baccharis halimifolia*, of E North America, with white plumelike fruits: family *Asteraceae*.
▷HISTORY Old English *grundeswelge*, changed from *gundeswilge*, from *gund* pus + *swelgan* to swallow; after its use in poultices on abscesses

groundsheet ('graʊnd,ʃiːt) *or* **ground cloth** NOUN [1] a waterproof rubber, plastic, or polythene sheet placed on the ground in a tent, etc., to keep out damp. [2] a similar sheet put over a sports field to protect it against rain.

groundsill ('graʊnd,sɪl) NOUN another name for **ground plate.**

groundsman ('graʊndzmən) NOUN, *plural* **-men.** a person employed to maintain a sports ground, park, etc.

groundspeed ('graʊnd,spiːd) NOUN the speed of an aircraft relative to the ground. Compare **airspeed.**

ground squirrel NOUN any burrowing sciurine rodent of the genus *Citellus* and related genera, resembling chipmunks and occurring in North America, E Europe, and Asia. Also called: **gopher.**

ground state *or* **level** NOUN the lowest energy state of an atom, molecule, particle, etc. Compare **excited** (sense 4).

ground stroke NOUN *Tennis* any return made to a ball that has touched the ground, as opposed to a volley.

groundswell ('graʊnd,swɛl) NOUN [1] a considerable swell of the sea, often caused by a distant storm or earthquake or by the passage of waves into shallow water. [2] a strong public feeling or opinion that is detectable even though not openly expressed: *a groundswell of discontent.*

ground water NOUN underground water that has come mainly from the seepage of surface water and is held in pervious rocks.

ground wave *or* **ray** NOUN a radio wave that travels directly between a transmitting and a receiving aerial. Compare **sky wave.**

groundwork ('graʊnd,wɜːk) NOUN [1] preliminary work as a foundation or basis. [2] the ground or background of a painting, etc.

ground zero NOUN [1] a point on the surface of land or water at or directly above or below the centre of a nuclear explosion. [2] a scene of great devastation. [3] (*sometimes capitals*) the name given to the devastated site of the collapsed World Trade Center towers in New York after September 11 2001.

group (gruːp) NOUN [1] a number of persons or things considered as a collective unit. [2] **a** a number of persons bound together by common social standards, interests, etc. **b** (*as modifier*): *group behaviour.* [3] a small band of players or singers, esp of pop music. [4] a number of animals or plants considered as a unit because of common characteristics, habits, etc. [5] *Grammar* another word, esp in systemic grammar, for **phrase** (sense 1). [6] an association of companies under a single ownership and control, consisting of a holding company, subsidiary companies, and sometimes associated companies. [7] two or more figures or objects forming a design or unit in a design, in a painting or sculpture. [8] a military formation comprising complementary arms and services, usually for a purpose: *a brigade group.* [9] an air force organization of higher level than a squadron. [10] Also called: **radical.** *Chem* two or more atoms that are bound together in a molecule and behave as a single unit: *a methyl group* $-CH_3$. Compare **free radical.** [11] a vertical column of elements in the periodic table that all have similar electronic structures, properties, and valencies. Compare **period** (sense 8). [12] *Geology* any stratigraphical unit, esp the unit for two or more formations. [13] *Maths* a set that has an associated operation that combines any two members of the set to give another member and that also contains an identity element and an inverse for each element. [14] See **blood group.** ◆ VERB [15] to arrange or place (things, people, etc.) in or into a group or (of things, etc.) to form into a group.
▷HISTORY C17: from French *groupe*, of Germanic origin; compare Italian *gruppo;* see CROP

group captain NOUN an officer holding commissioned rank senior to a wing commander but junior to an air commodore in the British RAF and certain other air forces.

group dynamics NOUN (*functioning as singular*) *Psychol* a field of social psychology concerned with the nature of human groups, their development, and their interactions with individuals, other groups, and larger organizations.

grouper ('gruːpə) NOUN a variant of **groper.**

groupie ('gruːpɪ) NOUN *Slang* an ardent fan of a celebrity, esp a pop star: originally, often a girl who followed the members of a pop group on tour in order to have sexual relations with them.

grouping ('gruːpɪŋ) NOUN a planned arrangement of things, people, etc., within a group.

group insurance NOUN *Chiefly US and Canadian* insurance relating to life, health, or accident and covering several persons, esp the employees of a firm, under a single contract at reduced premiums.

group marriage NOUN an arrangement in which several males live together with several females, forming a conjugal unit.

Group of Eight NOUN the Group of Seven nations and Russia, whose heads of government meet to discuss economic matters and international relations. Abbreviation: **G8.**

Group of Five NOUN France, Japan, UK, US, and Germany acting as a group to stabilize their currency exchange rates. Abbreviation: **G5.**

Group of Seven NOUN the seven leading industrial nations, Canada, France, Germany, Italy, Japan, UK, and the US, whose heads of government and finance ministers meet regularly to coordinate economic policy. Abbreviation: **G7.**

Group of Seventy Seven NOUN the developing countries of the world. Abbreviation: **G77.**

Group of Ten NOUN the ten nations who met in Paris in 1961 to arrange the special drawing rights of the IMF; Belgium, Canada, France, Italy, Japan, Netherlands, Sweden, UK, US, and West Germany. Abbreviation: **G10.**

Group of Three NOUN Japan, US, and Germany (formerly West Germany), regarded as the largest western industrialized nations.

Group of Twenty-Four NOUN the twenty-four richest and most industrialized countries of the world. Abbreviation: **G24.**

group practice NOUN a medical practice undertaken by a group of associated doctors who work together as partners or as specialists in different areas.

group speed *or* **velocity** NOUN *Physics* the speed at which energy is propagated in a wave. This is the quantity determined when one measures the distance which the radiation travels in a given time. In a medium in which the speed increases with wavelength the group speed is less than the phase speed, and vice versa.

group therapy NOUN *Psychol* the simultaneous treatment of a number of individuals who are members of a natural group or who are brought together to share their problems in group discussion.

groupthink ('gruːp,θɪŋk) NOUN a tendency within organizations or society to promote or establish the view of the predominant group.

groupuscule ('gruːpə,skjuːl) NOUN *Usually derogatory* a small group within a political party or movement.
▷HISTORY C20: from French: small group

groupware ('gruːp,wɛə) NOUN software that enables computers within a group or organization to work together, allowing users to exchange electronic-mail messages, access shared files and databases, use video conferencing, etc.

grouse[1] (graʊs) NOUN, *plural* **grouse** *or* **grouses.** [1] any gallinaceous bird of the family *Tetraonidae*, occurring mainly in the N hemisphere, having a stocky body and feathered legs and feet. They are popular game birds. See also **black grouse, red grouse.** ◆ ADJECTIVE [2] *Austral and NZ slang* excellent.
▷HISTORY C16: of unknown origin
▸ **'grouse,like** ADJECTIVE

grouse[2] (graʊs) VERB [1] (*intr*) to grumble; complain. ◆ NOUN [2] a persistent complaint.
▷HISTORY C19: of unknown origin
▸ **'grouser** NOUN

grout (graʊt) NOUN [1] a thin mortar for filling joints between tiles, masonry, etc. [2] a fine plaster used as a finishing coat. [3] coarse meal or porridge. ◆ VERB [4] (*tr*) to fill (joints) or finish (walls, etc.) with grout.
▷HISTORY Old English *grūt;* related to Old Frisian *grēt* sand, Middle High German *grūz*, Middle Dutch *grūte* coarse meal; see GRIT, GROATS
▸ **'grouter** NOUN

grouts (graʊts) PLURAL NOUN [1] *Chiefly Brit* sediment or grounds, as from making coffee. [2] a variant of **groats.**

grove (grəʊv) NOUN [1] a small wooded area or plantation. [2] **a** a road lined with houses and often trees, esp in a suburban area. **b** (*capital as part of a street name*): *Ladbroke Grove.*
▷HISTORY Old English *grāf;* related to *grǣfa* thicket, GREAVE, Norwegian *greivla* to intertwine

grovel ('grɒvᵊl) VERB **-els, -elling, -elled** *or US* **-els, -eling, -eled.** (*intr*) [1] to humble or abase oneself, as in making apologies or showing respect. [2] to lie or crawl face downwards, as in fear or humility. [3] (often foll by *in*) to indulge or take pleasure (in sensuality or vice).
▷HISTORY C16: back formation from obsolete *groveling* (adv), from Middle English *on grufe* on the face, of Scandinavian origin; compare Old Norse *ā grūfu*, from *grūfa* prone position; see -LING[2]
▸ **'groveller** NOUN ▸ **'grovelling** NOUN, ADJECTIVE
▸ **'grovellingly** ADVERB

grovet ('grɒvət) NOUN a wrestling hold in which a wrestler in a kneeling position grips the head of his kneeling opponent with one arm and forces his shoulders down with the other.

grow (grəʊ) VERB **grows, growing, grew** (gruː), **grown** (grəʊn). [1] (of an organism or part of an organism) to increase in size or develop (hair, leaves, or other structures). [2] (*intr;* usually foll by *out of* or *from*) to originate, as from an initial cause or source: *the federation grew out of the Empire.* [3] (*intr*) to increase in size, number, degree, etc.: *the population is growing rapidly.* [4] (*intr*) to change in length or amount in a specified direction: *some plants grow downwards; profits over the years grew downwards.* [5] (*copula; may take an infinitive*) (esp of emotions, physical states, etc.) to develop or come into existence or being gradually: *to grow cold; to grow morose; he grew to like her.* [6] (*intr;* usually foll by *up*) to come into existence: *a close friendship grew up between them.* [7] (*intr;* foll by *together*) to be joined gradually by or as by growth: *the branches on the tree grew together.* [8] (*intr;* foll by *away, together,* etc.) to develop a specified state of friendship: *the lovers grew together gradually; many friends grow apart over the years.* [9] (when *intr*, foll by *with*) to become covered with a growth: *the path grew with weeds.* [10] to produce (plants) by controlling or encouraging their growth, esp for home consumption or on a commercial basis. ◆ See also **grow into, grow on, grow out of, grow up.**
▷HISTORY Old English *grōwan;* related to Old Norse *grōa*, Old Frisian *grōia*, Old High German *gruoen;* see GREEN, GRASS

grow bag NOUN a plastic bag containing a sufficient amount of a sterile growing medium and nutrients to enable a plant, such as a tomato or pepper, to be grown to full size in it, usually for one season only.
▷HISTORY C20: from *Gro-bag*, trademark for the first ones marketed

grower ('grəʊə) NOUN [1] a person who grows plants: *a vegetable grower.* [2] a plant that grows in a specified way: *a fast grower.* [3] a piece of music that is initially unimpressive but becomes more enjoyable after further hearings.

growing pains PLURAL NOUN 1 pains in muscles or joints sometimes experienced by children during a period of unusually rapid growth. 2 difficulties besetting a new enterprise in its early stages.

grow into VERB (*intr, preposition*) to become big or mature enough for: *his clothes were always big enough for him to grow into.*

growl (graʊl) VERB 1 (of animals, esp when hostile) to utter (sounds) in a low inarticulate manner: *the dog growled at us.* 2 to utter (words) in a gruff or angry manner: *he growled an apology.* 3 (*intr*) to make sounds suggestive of an animal growling: *the thunder growled around the lake.* ◆ NOUN 4 the act or sound of growling. 5 *Jazz* an effect resembling a growl, produced at the back of the throat when playing a wind instrument.
▷HISTORY C18: from earlier *grolle,* from Old French *grouller* to grumble
▸ ˈ**growlingly** ADVERB

growler (ˈgraʊlə) NOUN 1 a person, animal, or thing that growls. 2 *Brit slang, obsolete* a four-wheeled hansom cab. 3 *Canadian* a small iceberg that has broken off from a larger iceberg or from a glacier, often hazardous to shipping. 4 *US slang* any container, such as a can, for draught beer.

grown (grəʊn) ADJECTIVE **a** developed or advanced: *fully grown.* **b** (*in combination*): *half-grown.*

grown-up ADJECTIVE 1 having reached maturity; adult. 2 suitable for or characteristic of an adult. ◆ NOUN 3 an adult.

grow on VERB (*intr, preposition*) to become progressively more acceptable or pleasant to: *I don't think much of your new record, but I suppose it will grow on me.*

grow out of VERB (*intr, adverb + preposition*) to become too big or mature for: *she soon grew out of her girlish ways.*

growth (grəʊθ) NOUN 1 the process or act of growing, esp in organisms following assimilation of food. 2 an increase in size, number, significance, etc. 3 something grown or growing: *a new growth of hair.* 4 a stage of development. 5 any abnormal tissue, such as a tumour. 6 (*modifier*) of, relating to, causing or characterized by growth: *a growth industry; growth hormone.*

growth curve NOUN a curve on a graph in which a variable is plotted against time to illustrate the growth of the variable.

growth factor NOUN any of several substances present in serum that induce growth of cells. Excessive amounts of growth factor may be associated with the production of cancer cells.

growth hormone NOUN a hormone synthesized in and secreted by the anterior lobe of the pituitary gland that promotes growth of the long bones in the limbs and increases the synthesis of protein essential for growth. Also called: **somatotrophin.**

growth ring NOUN another name for **annual ring.**

growth shares PLURAL NOUN *Finance* ordinary shares with good prospects of appreciation in yield and value.

growth substance NOUN *Botany* any substance, produced naturally by a plant or manufactured commercially, that, in very low concentrations, affects plant growth; a plant hormone.

grow up VERB (*intr, adverb*) 1 to reach maturity; become adult. 2 to come into existence; develop.

groyne *or esp US* **groin** (grɔɪn) NOUN a wall or jetty built out from a riverbank or seashore to control erosion. Also called: **spur, breakwater.**
▷HISTORY C16: origin uncertain: perhaps altered from GROIN

grozing iron (ˈgrəʊzɪŋ) NOUN an iron for smoothing joints between lead pipes.
▷HISTORY C17: part translation of Dutch *gruisijzer,* from *gruizen* to crush, from *gruis* gravel + *yzer* iron

Grozny (*Russian* ˈgroznij) NOUN a city in S Russia, capital of the Chechen Republic: a major oil centre: it was badly damaged during fighting between separatists and Russian troops (1994–95, 1999–2000). Pop.: 186 000 (1999 est.).

GRU ABBREV (formerly) the Soviet military intelligence service; the military counterpart of the **KGB.**
▷HISTORY from Russian *Glavnoye Razvedyvatelnoye Upravleniye* Main Intelligence Directorate

grub (grʌb) VERB **grubs, grubbing, grubbed.** 1 (when *tr,* often foll by *up* or *out*) to search for and pull up (roots, stumps, etc.) by digging in the ground. 2 to dig up the surface of (ground, soil, etc.), esp to clear away roots, stumps, etc. 3 (*intr;* often foll by *in* or *among*) to search carefully. 4 (*intr*) to work unceasingly, esp at a dull task or research. 5 *Slang* to provide (a person) with food or (of a person) to take food. 6 (*tr*) *Slang, chiefly US* to scrounge: *to grub a cigarette.* ◆ NOUN 7 the short legless larva of certain insects, esp beetles. 8 *Slang* food; victuals. 9 a person who works hard, esp in a dull plodding way. 10 *Brit informal* a dirty child.
▷HISTORY C13: of Germanic origin; compare Old High German *grubilōn* to dig, German *grübeln* to rack one's brain, Middle Dutch *grobben* to scrape together; see GRAVE[3], GROOVE

grubber (ˈgrʌbə) NOUN 1 a person who grubs. 2 another name for **grub hoe.**

grubby (ˈgrʌbɪ) ADJECTIVE **-bier, -biest.** 1 dirty; slovenly. 2 mean; beggarly. 3 infested with grubs.
▸ ˈ**grubbily** ADVERB ▸ ˈ**grubbiness** NOUN

grub hoe *or* **grubbing hoe** NOUN a heavy hoe for grubbing up roots. Also called: **grubber.**

grub screw NOUN a small headless screw having a slot cut for a screwdriver or a socket for a hexagon key and used to secure a sliding component in a determined position.

grubstake (ˈgrʌbˌsteɪk) NOUN 1 *US and Canadian informal* supplies provided for a prospector on the condition that the donor has a stake in any finds. ◆ VERB (*tr*) 2 *US informal* to furnish with such supplies. 3 *Chiefly US and Canadian* to supply (a person) with a stake in a gambling game.
▸ ˈ**grubˌstaker** NOUN

Grub Street NOUN 1 a former street in London frequented by literary hacks and needy authors. 2 the world or class of literary hacks, etc. ◆ ADJECTIVE *also* ˈ**Grubˌstreet.** 3 (*sometimes not capital*) relating to or characteristic of hack literature.

grudge (grʌdʒ) NOUN 1 a persistent feeling of resentment, esp one due to some cause, such as an insult or injury. 2 (*modifier*) planned or carried out in order to settle a grudge: *a grudge fight.* ◆ VERB 3 (*tr*) to give or allow unwillingly. 4 to feel resentful or envious about (someone else's success, possessions, etc.).
▷HISTORY C15: from Old French *grouchier* to grumble, probably of Germanic origin; compare Old High German *grunnizōn* to grunt
▸ ˈ**grudgeless** ADJECTIVE ▸ ˈ**grudger** NOUN ▸ ˈ**grudging** ADJECTIVE ▸ ˈ**grudgingly** ADVERB

grue (gru:) *Scot* ◆ NOUN 1 a shiver or shudder; a creeping of the flesh. ◆ VERB (*intr*) 2 to shiver or shudder. 3 to feel strong aversion.
▷HISTORY C14: of Scandinavian origin; compare Old Swedish *grua,* Old Danish *grue;* related to German *graven,* Dutch *gruwen* to abhor

gruel (ˈgru:əl) NOUN a drink or thin porridge, made by boiling meal, esp oatmeal, in water or milk.
▷HISTORY C14: from Old French, of Germanic origin; see GROUT

gruelling *or US* **grueling** (ˈgru:əlɪŋ) ADJECTIVE 1 severe or tiring: *a gruelling interview.* ◆ NOUN 2 *Informal* a severe experience, esp punishment.
▷HISTORY C19: from now obsolete vb *gruel* to exhaust, punish

gruesome (ˈgru:səm) ADJECTIVE inspiring repugnance and horror; ghastly.
▷HISTORY C16: originally Northern English and Scottish; see GRUE, -SOME[1]
▸ ˈ**gruesomely** ADVERB ▸ ˈ**gruesomeness** NOUN

gruff (grʌf) ADJECTIVE 1 rough or surly in manner, speech, etc.: *a gruff reply.* 2 (of a voice, bark, etc.) low and throaty.
▷HISTORY C16: originally Scottish, from Dutch *grof,* of Germanic origin; compare Old High German *girob;* related to Old English *hrēof,* Lithuanian *kraupùs*
▸ ˈ**gruffish** ADJECTIVE ▸ ˈ**gruffly** ADVERB ▸ ˈ**gruffness** NOUN

grugru (ˈgru:gru:) NOUN 1 any of several tropical American palms, esp *Acrocomia sclerocarpa,* which has a spiny trunk and leaves and edible nuts. 2 the large edible wormlike larva of a weevil, *Rhynchophorus palmarum,* that infests this palm.
▷HISTORY C18: from American Spanish (Puerto Rican dialect) *grugrú,* of Cariban origin

grumble (ˈgrʌmbᵊl) VERB 1 to utter (complaints) in a nagging or discontented way. 2 (*intr*) to make low dull rumbling sounds. ◆ NOUN 3 a complaint; grouse. 4 a low rumbling sound.
▷HISTORY C16: from Middle Low German *grommelen,* of Germanic origin; see GRIM
▸ ˈ**grumbler** NOUN ▸ ˈ**grumblingly** ADVERB ▸ ˈ**grumbly** ADJECTIVE

grumbling appendix NOUN *Informal* a condition in which the appendix causes intermittent pain but appendicitis has not developed.

grummet (ˈgrʌmɪt) NOUN another word for **grommet.**

grumous (ˈgru:məs) *or* **grumose** (ˈgru:məʊs) ADJECTIVE (esp of plant parts) consisting of granular tissue.
▷HISTORY C17: from *grume* a clot of blood, from Latin *grumus* a little heap; related to CRUMB

grump (grʌmp) *Informal* ◆ NOUN 1 a surly or bad-tempered person. 2 (*plural*) a sulky or morose mood (esp in the phrase **have the grumps**). ◆ VERB 3 (*intr*) to complain or grumble.
▷HISTORY C18: dialect *grump* surly remark, probably of imitative origin

grumpy (ˈgrʌmpɪ) *or* **grumpish** (ˈgrʌmpɪʃ) ADJECTIVE **grumpier, grumpiest.** peevish; sulky.
▷HISTORY C18: from GRUMP + -Y[1]
▸ ˈ**grumpily** *or* ˈ**grumpishly** ADVERB ▸ ˈ**grumpiness** *or* ˈ**grumpishness** NOUN

grundies (ˈgrʌndɪz) PLURAL NOUN *NZ informal* men's underpants.

Grundy (ˈgrʌndɪ) NOUN a narrow-minded person who keeps critical watch on the propriety of others.
▷HISTORY C18: named after Mrs *Grundy,* the character in T. Morton's play *Speed the Plough* (1798)
▸ ˈ**Grundyˌism** NOUN ▸ ˈ**Grundyist** *or* ˈ**Grundyite** NOUN

grunge (grʌndʒ) NOUN 1 *US slang* dirt or rubbish. 2 a style of rock music originating in the US in the late 1980s, featuring a distorted guitar sound. 3 a deliberately untidy and uncoordinated fashion style.
▷HISTORY C20: possibly a coinage imitating GRIME + SLUDGE

grungy (ˈgrʌndʒɪ) ADJECTIVE **-gier, -giest.** *Slang* 1 *Chiefly US and Canadian* squalid or seedy. 2 (of pop music) characterized by a loud fuzzy guitar sound.

grunion (ˈgrʌnjən) NOUN a Californian marine teleost fish, *Leuresthes tenuis,* that spawns on beaches: family *Atherinidae* (silversides).
▷HISTORY C20: probably from Spanish *gruñón* a grunter

grunt (grʌnt) VERB 1 (*intr*) (esp of pigs and some other animals) to emit a low short gruff noise. 2 (when *tr, may take a clause as object*) to express something gruffly: *he grunted his answer.* ◆ NOUN 3 the characteristic low short gruff noise of pigs, etc., or a similar sound, as of disgust. 4 any of various mainly tropical marine sciaenid fishes, such as *Haemulon macrostomum* (**Spanish grunt**), that utter a grunting sound when caught. 5 *US slang* an infantry soldier or US marine, esp in the Vietnam War.
▷HISTORY Old English *grunnettan,* probably of imitative origin; compare Old High German *grunnizōn, grunni* moaning, Latin *grunnīre*
▸ ˈ**gruntingly** ADVERB

grunter (ˈgrʌntə) NOUN 1 a person or animal that grunts, esp a pig. 2 another name for **grunt** (sense 4).

gruntled (ˈgrʌntᵊld) ADJECTIVE *Informal* happy or contented; satisfied.
▷HISTORY C20: back formation from DISGRUNTLED

gruppetto (grʊˈpetəʊ) NOUN, *plural* **-ti** (-ti:). *Music* a turn.
▷HISTORY C19: from Italian, diminutive of *gruppo* a group, a turn

Grus (grʊs) NOUN, *Latin genitive* **Gruis** (ˈgru:ɪs). a constellation in the S hemisphere lying near Phoenix and Piscis Austrinus and containing a first and a second magnitude star.
▷HISTORY via New Latin from Latin: crane

Gruyère *or* **Gruyère cheese** (ˈgru:jɛə; *French* gryjɛr) NOUN a hard flat whole-milk cheese, pale yellow in colour and with holes.
▷HISTORY C19: after *Gruyère,* Switzerland where it originated

gr. wt. ABBREVIATION FOR gross weight.

gryke (graɪk) NOUN a variant spelling of **grike.**

gryphon (ˈgrɪfᵊn) NOUN a variant of **griffin[1].**

grysbok ('graɪsˌbɒk) NOUN either of two small antelopes, *Raphicerus melanotis* or *R. sharpei*, of central and southern Africa, having small straight horns.
▷HISTORY C18: Afrikaans, from Dutch *grijs* grey + *bok* BUCK[1]

gs THE INTERNET DOMAIN NAME FOR South Georgia and the South Sandwich Islands.

GS ABBREVIATION FOR: 1 General Secretary. 2 General Staff.

gsm ABBREVIATION FOR grams per square metre: the term used to specify the weight of paper.

GSM ABBREVIATION FOR Global System for Mobile Communications.

GSOH ABBREVIATION FOR good sense of humour: used in lonely hearts columns and personal advertisements.

G-spot NOUN an area in the front wall of the vagina which is alleged to produce an extremely intense orgasm when stimulated.
▷HISTORY C20: short for *Gräfenberg spot,* named after Ernst *Gräfenberg* (1881–1957), German gynaecologist

GSR ABBREVIATION FOR **galvanic skin response**.

GST (in Australia, New Zealand, and Canada) ABBREVIATION FOR goods and services tax.

G-string NOUN 1 a piece of cloth attached to a narrow waistband covering the pubic area, worn esp by strippers. 2 a strip of cloth attached to the front and back of a waistband and covering the loins. 3 *Music* a string tuned to G, such as the lowest string of a violin.

G-suit NOUN a close-fitting garment covering the legs and abdomen that is worn by the crew of high-speed aircraft and can be pressurized to prevent blackout during certain manoeuvres. Also called: **anti-G suit**.
▷HISTORY C20: from *g(ravity) suit*

GSVQ (in Britain) ABBREVIATION FOR General Scottish Vocational Qualification. Compare **GNVQ**.

gt THE INTERNET DOMAIN NAME FOR Guatemala.

GT ABBREVIATION FOR gran turismo: a high-performance luxury sports car with a hard fixed roof, designed for covering long distances.

GTC ABBREVIATION FOR: 1 Also: **gtc.** (on a commercial order for goods) good till cancelled (*or* countermanded). 2 (in Scotland) General Teaching Council.

gtd ABBREVIATION FOR guaranteed.

gu THE INTERNET DOMAIN NAME FOR Guam.

g.u. *or* **GU** ABBREVIATION FOR genitourinary.

guacamole *or* **guachamole** (ˌgwɑːkəˈməʊlɪ) NOUN 1 a spread of mashed avocado, tomato pulp, mayonnaise, and seasoning. 2 any of various Mexican or South American salads containing avocado.
▷HISTORY from American Spanish, from Nahuatl *ahuacamolli,* from *ahuacatl* avocado + *molli* sauce

guacharo (ˈgwɑːtʃəˌrəʊ) NOUN, *plural* **-ros**. another name for **oilbird**.
▷HISTORY C19: from Spanish *guácharo*

guaco (ˈgwɑːkəʊ) NOUN, *plural* **-cos**. 1 any of several tropical American plants whose leaves are used as an antidote to snakebite, esp the climbers *Mikania guaco,* family *Asteraceae* (composites), or *Aristolochia maxima* (*A. serpentina*), family *Aristolochiaceae*. 2 the leaves of any of these plants.
▷HISTORY C19: from American Spanish

Guadalajara (ˌgwɑːdəˈləˈhɑːrə; *Spanish* gwaðalaˈxara) NOUN 1 a city in W Mexico, capital of Jalisco state: the second largest city of Mexico: centre of the Indian slave trade until its abolition, declared here in 1810; two universities (1792 and 1935). Pop.: 1 647 000 (2000 est.). 2 a city in central Spain, in New Castile. Pop.: 67 200 (1991).

Guadalcanal (ˌgwɑːdəlkəˈnæl; *Spanish* gwaðalkaˈnal) NOUN a mountainous island in the SW Pacific, the largest of the Solomon Islands: under British protection until 1978; occupied by the Japanese (1942–43). Pop.: 61 243 (1997 est.). Area: 6475 sq. km (2500 sq. miles).

Guadalquivir (ˌgwɑːdəlˈkwɪvɪə; *Spanish* gwaðalkiˈβir) NOUN the chief river of S Spain, rising in the Sierra de Segura and flowing west and southwest to the Gulf of Cádiz: navigable by ocean-going vessels to Seville. Length: 560 km (348 miles).

Guadalupe Hidalgo (ˌgwɑːdəˈluːp hɪˈdælgəʊ; *Spanish* gwaðaˈlupe iˈðalɣo) NOUN a city in central Mexico, northwest of Mexico City: became a pilgrimage centre after an Indian convert had a vision of the Virgin Mary here in 1531. Pop.: 668 500 (2000 est.). Former name (1931–71): **Gustavo A. Madero**.

Guadeloupe (ˌgwɑːdəˈluːp) NOUN an overseas region of France in the E Caribbean, in the Leeward Islands, formed by the islands of Basse Terre and Grande Terre and their five dependencies. Capital: Basse-Terre. Pop.: 432 000 (2001 est.). Area: 1780 sq. km (687 sq. miles).

Guadiana (*Spanish* gwaˈðjana; *Portuguese* gwəˈðjənə) NOUN a river in SW Europe, rising in S central Spain and flowing west, then south as part of the border between Spain and Portugal, to the Gulf of Cádiz. Length: 578 km (359 miles).

guaiacol (ˈgwaɪəˌkɒl) NOUN a yellowish oily creosote-like liquid extracted from guaiacum resin and hardwood tar, used medicinally as an expectorant. Formula: $C_7H_8O_2$.
▷HISTORY from GUAIAC(UM) + -OL[2]

guaiacum *or* **guaiocum** (ˈgwaɪəkəm) NOUN 1 any tropical American evergreen tree of the zygophyllaceous genus *Guaiacum,* such as the lignum vitae. 2 the hard heavy wood of any of these trees. 3 Also called: **guaiac** (ˈgwaɪæk). a brownish resin obtained from the lignum vitae, used medicinally and in making varnishes.
▷HISTORY C16: New Latin, from Spanish *guayaco,* of Taino origin

Guam (gwɑːm) NOUN an island in the N Pacific, the largest and southernmost of the Marianas: belonged to Spain from the 17th century until 1898, when it was ceded to the US; site of naval and air force bases. Capital: Agaña. Pop.: 158 000 (2001 est.). Area: 541 sq. km (209 sq. miles).

Guamanian (gwɑːˈmeɪnɪən) ADJECTIVE 1 of or relating to Guam or its inhabitants. ◆ NOUN 2 a native or inhabitant of Guam.

guan (gwɑːn) NOUN any gallinaceous bird of the genera *Penelope, Pipile,* etc., of Central and South America: family *Cracidae* (curassows).
▷HISTORY C18: from American Spanish

Guanabara (*Portuguese* gwənaˈbara) NOUN (until 1975) a state of SE Brazil, on the Atlantic and **Guanabara Bay,** now amalgamated with the state of Rio de Janeiro.

guanaco (gwɑːˈnɑːkəʊ) NOUN, *plural* **-cos**. a cud-chewing South American artiodactyl mammal, *Lama guanicoe,* closely related to the domesticated llama: family *Camelidae*.
▷HISTORY C17: from Spanish, from Quechuan *huanacu*

Guanajuato (*Spanish* gwanaˈxwato) NOUN 1 a state of central Mexico, on the great central plateau: mountainous in the north, with fertile plains in the south; important mineral resources. Capital: Guanajuato. Pop.: 4 656 761 (2000). Area: 30 588 sq. km (11 810 sq. miles). 2 a city in central Mexico, capital of Guanajuato state: founded in 1554, it became one of the world's richest silver-mining centres. Pop.: 113 580 (1990).

guanase (ˈgwɑːneɪz) NOUN an enzyme that converts guanine to xanthine by removal of an amino group.
▷HISTORY C20: from GUAN(INE) + -ASE

Guangdong (ˈgwæŋˈdʊŋ) *or* **Kwangtung** NOUN a province of SE China, on the South China Sea: includes the Leizhou Peninsula, with densely populated river valleys, Macao and Hong Kong; the only true tropical climate in China. Capital: Canton. Pop.: 86 420 000 (2000 est.). Area: 197 100 sq. km (76 100 sq. miles).

Guangxi Zhuang Autonomous Region (ˈgwæŋˈsiː ˈdʒwæŋ) *or* **Kwangsi-Chuang Autonomous Region** NOUN an administrative division of S China. Capital: Nanning. Pop.: 44 890 000 (2000 est.). Area: 220 400 sq. km (85 100 sq. miles).

Guangzhou (ˈgwæŋˈdzəʊ) NOUN the Pinyin transliteration of the Chinese name for **Canton**.

guanidine (ˈgwɑːnɪˌdiːn, -dɪn, ˈgwænɪ-) *or* **guanidin** (ˈgwɑːnɪdɪn, ˈgwænɪ-) NOUN a strongly alkaline crystalline substance, soluble in water and found in plant and animal tissues. It is used in organic synthesis. Formula: $HNC(NH_2)_2$. Also called: **carbamidine, iminourea**.
▷HISTORY C19: from GUANO + -ID[3] + -INE[2]

guanine (ˈgwɑːniːn, ˈguːəˌniːn) NOUN a white almost insoluble compound: one of the purine bases in nucleic acids. Formula: $C_5H_5N_5O$.
▷HISTORY C19: from GUANO + -INE[2]

guano (ˈgwɑːnəʊ) NOUN, *plural* **-nos**. 1 **a** the dried excrement of fish-eating sea birds, deposited in rocky coastal regions of South America: contains the urates, oxalates, and phosphates of ammonium and calcium; used as a fertilizer. **b** the accumulated droppings of bats and seals. 2 any similar but artificial substance used as a fertilizer.
▷HISTORY C17: from Spanish, from Quechuan *huano* dung

guanosine (ˈgwɑːnəˌsiːn, -ˌziːn) NOUN *Biochem* a nucleoside consisting of guanine and ribose.

Guantánamo (*Spanish* gwanˈtanamo) NOUN a city in SE Cuba, on **Guantánamo Bay:** site of a US naval base. Pop.: 207 796 (1994 est.).

guanylic acid (gwəˈnɪlɪk) NOUN a nucleotide consisting of guanine, ribose or deoxyribose, and a phosphate group. It is a constituent of DNA or RNA. Also called: **guanosine monophosphate**.

Guaporé (*Portuguese* gwapoˈrɛ) NOUN 1 a river in W central South America, rising in SW Brazil and flowing northwest as part of the border between Brazil and Bolivia, to join the Mamoré River. Length: 1750 km (1087 miles). Spanish name: **Iténez**. 2 the former name (until 1956) of **Rondônia**.

guar (gwɑː) NOUN 1 a leguminous Indian plant, *Cyamopsis tetragonolobus*, grown as a fodder crop and for the gum obtained from its seeds. 2 Also called: **guar gum**. a gum obtained from the seeds of this plant, used as a stabilizer and thickening agent in food (E412) and as sizing for paper.
▷HISTORY C19: from Hindi

guaraní (ˈgwɑːrənɪ) NOUN, *plural* **-ní** *or* **-nís**. the standard monetary unit of Paraguay, divided into 100 céntimos.

Guarani (ˌgwɑːrəˈniː) NOUN 1 (*plural* **-ni** *or* **-nis**) a member of a South American Indian people of Paraguay, S Brazil, and Bolivia. 2 the language of this people, belonging to the Tupi-Guarani family; one of the official languages of Paraguay, along with Spanish.

guarantee (ˌgærənˈtiː) NOUN 1 a formal assurance, esp in writing, that a product, service, etc., will meet certain standards or specifications. 2 *Law* a promise, esp a collateral agreement, to answer for the debt, default, or miscarriage of another. 3 **a** a person, company, etc., to whom a guarantee is made. **b** a person, company, etc., who gives a guarantee. 4 a person who acts as a guarantor. 5 something that makes a specified condition or outcome certain. 6 a variant spelling of **guaranty**. ◆ VERB **-tees, -teeing, -teed**. (*mainly tr*) 7 (*also tr*) to take responsibility for (someone else's debts, obligations, etc.). 8 to serve as a guarantee for. 9 to secure or furnish security for: *a small deposit will guarantee any dress.* 10 (usually foll by *from* or *against*) to undertake to protect or keep secure, as against injury, loss, etc. 11 to ensure: *good planning will guarantee success.* 12 (*may take a clause as object or an infinitive*) to promise or make certain.
▷HISTORY C17: perhaps from Spanish *garante* or French *garant,* of Germanic origin; compare WARRANT

guarantor (ˌgærənˈtɔː) NOUN a person who gives or is bound by a guarantee or guaranty; surety.

guaranty (ˈgærəntɪ) NOUN, *plural* **-ties**. 1 a pledge of responsibility for fulfilling another person's obligations in case of that person's default. 2 a thing given or taken as security for a guaranty. 3 the act of providing security. 4 a person who acts as a guarantor. ◆ VERB **-ties, -tying, -tied**. 5 a variant of **guarantee**.
▷HISTORY C16: from Old French *garantie,* variant of *warantie,* of Germanic origin; see WARRANTY

guard (gɑːd) VERB 1 to watch over or shield (a person or thing) from danger or harm; protect. 2 to keep watch over (a prisoner or other potentially dangerous person or thing), as to prevent escape. 3 (*tr*) to control: *to guard one's tongue.* 4 (*intr;* usually foll by *against*) to take precautions. 5 to control entrance and exit through (a gate, door, etc.). 6 (*tr*) to provide (machinery, etc.) with a device to protect the operator. 7 (*tr*) **a** *Chess, cards* to protect or cover (a chess man or card) with another. **b** *Curling, bowling* to protect or cover (a stone or bowl) by placing one's own stone or bowl between it and another player. 8 (*tr*) *Archaic* to accompany as a guard. ◆ NOUN 9 a person or group who keeps a protecting, supervising, or restraining watch or control over people, such as prisoners, things, etc. Related adjective: **custodial.** 10 a person or group of people, such as soldiers, who form a ceremonial escort: *guard of honour.* 11 *Brit* the official in charge of a train. 12 **a** the act or duty of protecting, restraining, or supervising. **b** (*as modifier*): *guard duty.* 13 *Irish* another word for **garda.** 14 a device, part, or attachment on an object, such as a weapon or machine tool, designed to protect the user against injury, as on the hilt of a sword or the trigger of a firearm. 15 anything that provides or is intended to provide protection: *a guard against infection.* 16 **a** another name for **safety chain. b** a long neck chain often holding a chatelaine. 17 See **guard ring.** 18 *Sport* an article of light tough material worn to protect any of various parts of the body. 19 *Basketball* **a** the position of the two players in a team who play furthest from the basket. **b** a player in this position. 20 the posture of defence or readiness in fencing, boxing, cricket, etc. 21 **take guard.** *Cricket* (of a batsman) to choose a position in front of the wicket to receive the bowling, esp by requesting the umpire to indicate his position relative to the stumps. 22 **give guard.** *Cricket* (of an umpire) to indicate such a position to a batsman. 23 **off (one's) guard.** having one's defences down; unprepared. 24 **on (one's) guard.** prepared to face danger, difficulties, etc. 25 **stand guard.** (of a military sentry, etc.) to keep watch. 26 **mount guard. a** (of a sentry) to begin to keep watch. **b** (with *over*) to take up a protective or defensive stance (over something).

▷HISTORY C15: from Old French *garde,* from *garder* to protect, of Germanic origin; compare Spanish *guardar;* see WARD

▸'**guardable** ADJECTIVE ▸'**guarder** NOUN ▸'**guardless** ADJECTIVE ▸'**guard,like** ADJECTIVE

Guardafui (ˌgwɑːdəˈfuːɪ) NOUN **Cape.** a cape at the NE tip of Somalia, extending into the Indian Ocean.

guardant *or* **gardant** (ˈgɑːdənt) ADJECTIVE (*usually postpositive*) *Heraldry* (of a beast) shown full face.

▷HISTORY C16: from French *gardant* guarding, from *garder* to GUARD

guard band NOUN a space left vacant between two radio frequency bands, or between two tracks on a magnetic tape recording, to avoid mutual interference.

guard cell NOUN *Botany* one of a pair of crescent-shaped cells that surround a pore (stoma) in the epidermis. Changes in the turgidity of the cells cause the opening and closing of the stoma.

guarded (ˈgɑːdɪd) ADJECTIVE 1 protected or kept under surveillance. 2 prudent, restrained, or noncommittal: *a guarded reply.*

▸'**guardedly** ADVERB ▸'**guardedness** NOUN

guardee (ˌgɑːˈdiː) NOUN *Brit informal* a guardsman, esp considered as representing smartness and dash.

guard hair NOUN any of the coarse hairs that form the outer fur in certain mammals, rising above the underfur.

guardhouse (ˈgɑːdˌhaus) NOUN *Military* a building serving as the headquarters or a post for military police and in which military prisoners are detained.

guardian (ˈgɑːdɪən) NOUN 1 one who looks after, protects, or defends: *the guardian of public morals.* 2 **a** *Law* someone legally appointed to manage the affairs of a person incapable of acting for himself, as a minor or person of unsound mind. **b** *Social welfare* (in England) a local authority, or person accepted by it, named under the Mental Health Act 1983 as having the powers to require a mentally disordered person to live at a specified place, attend for treatment, and be accessible to a doctor or social worker. 3 (*often capital*) (in England) another word for **custos.** ◆ ADJECTIVE 4 protecting or safeguarding.

▸'**guardian,ship** NOUN

Guardian Angels PLURAL NOUN vigilante volunteers who patrol the underground railway in New York, London, and elsewhere, wearing red berets, to deter violent crime.

Guardianista (ˈgɑːdɪənˈiːstə) NOUN *Brit informal* a reader of the *Guardian* newspaper, seen as being typically left-wing, liberal, and politically correct.

▷HISTORY C20: from the *Guardian* newspaper + (SANDIN)ISTA

guardrail (ˈgɑːdˌreɪl) NOUN 1 a railing at the side of a staircase, road, etc., as a safety barrier. 2 Also called (Brit): **checkrail.** *Railways* a short metal rail fitted to the inside of the main rail to provide additional support in keeping a train's wheels on the track.

guard ring NOUN 1 Also called: **guard, keeper ring.** *Jewellery* an extra ring worn to prevent another from slipping off the finger. 2 an electrode used to counteract distortion of the electric fields at the edges of other electrodes in a capacitor or electron lens.

guardroom (ˈgɑːdˌruːm, -ˌrʊm) NOUN 1 a room used by guards. 2 a room in which prisoners are confined under guard.

Guards (gɑːdz) PLURAL NOUN **a** (esp in European armies) any of various regiments responsible for ceremonial duties and, formerly, the protection of the head of state: *the Life Guards; the Grenadier Guards.* **b** (*as modifier*): *a Guards regiment.*

guardsman (ˈgɑːdzmən) NOUN, *plural* **-men.** 1 (in Britain) a member of a Guards battalion or regiment. 2 (in the US) a member of the National Guard. 3 a guard.

guard's van NOUN *Railways, Brit and NZ* the van in which the guard travels, usually attached to the rear of a train. US and Canadian equivalent: **caboose.**

Guarneri (gwɑːˈnɪərɪ; *Italian* gwarˈnɛːri), **Guarnieri** (*Italian* gwarˈnjɛːri), *or* **Guarnerius** (gwɑːˈnɛərɪəs) NOUN, *plural* **Guarneris, Guarnieris** *or* **Guarneriuses.** any violin made by a member of the Guarneri family (active in Italy in the 17th and 18th centuries).

Guat. ABBREVIATION FOR Guatemala.

Guatemala (ˌgwɑːtəˈmɑːlə) NOUN a republic in Central America: original Maya Indians conquered by the Spanish in 1523; became the centre of Spanish administration in Central America; gained independence and was annexed to Mexico in 1821, becoming an independent republic in 1839. Official language: Spanish. Religion: Roman Catholic majority. Currency: quetzal and US dollar. Capital: Guatemala City. Pop.: 11 687 000 (2001 est.). Area: 108 889 sq. km (42 042 sq. miles).

Guatemala City NOUN the capital of Guatemala, in the southeast: founded in 1776 to replace the former capital, Antigua Guatemala, after an earthquake; university (1676). Pop.: 2 578 526 (2000 est.).

Guatemalan (ˌgwɑːtəˈmɑːlən) ADJECTIVE 1 of or relating to Guatemala or its inhabitants. ◆ NOUN 2 a native or inhabitant of Guatemala.

guava (ˈgwɑːvə) NOUN 1 any of various tropical American trees of the myrtaceous genus *Psidium,* esp *P. guajava,* grown in tropical regions for their edible fruit. 2 the fruit of such a tree, having yellow skin and pink pulp: used to make jellies, jams, etc.

▷HISTORY C16: from Spanish *guayaba,* from a South American Indian word

Guayaquil (*Spanish* gwajaˈkil) NOUN a port in W Ecuador: the largest city in the country and its chief port; university (1867). Pop.: 1 973 880 (1997 est.).

guayule (gwəˈjuːlɪ) NOUN 1 a bushy shrub, *Parthenium argentatum,* of the southwestern US: family *Asteraceae* (composites). 2 rubber derived from the sap of this plant.

▷HISTORY from American Spanish, from Nahuatl *cuauhuli,* from *cuahuitl* tree + *uli* gum

gubbins (ˈgʌbɪnz) NOUN *Informal* 1 an object of little or no value. 2 a small device or gadget. 3 odds and ends; litter or rubbish. 4 a silly person.

▷HISTORY C16 (meaning: fragments): from obsolete *gobbon,* probably related to GOBBET

gubernatorial (ˌgjuːbənəˈtɔːrɪəl, ˌguː-) ADJECTIVE *Chiefly US* of or relating to a governor.

▷HISTORY C18: from Latin *gubernātor* governor

guberniya *Russian* (guˈbjɛrnɪjə) NOUN 1 a territorial division of imperial Russia. 2 a territorial and administrative subdivision in the former Soviet Union.

▷HISTORY from Russian: government, ultimately from Latin *gubernāre* to GOVERN

guck (gʌk, gʊk) NOUN slimy matter; gunk.

▷HISTORY C20: perhaps a blend of GOO and MUCK

guddle (ˈgʌdəl) *Scot* ◆ VERB 1 to catch (fish) by groping with the hands under the banks or stones of a stream. ◆ NOUN 2 a muddle; confusion.

▷HISTORY C19: of unknown origin

gudgeon[1] (ˈgʌdʒən) NOUN 1 a small slender European freshwater cyprinid fish, *Gobio gobio,* with a barbel on each side of the mouth: used as bait by anglers. 2 any of various other fishes, such as the goby. 3 bait or enticement. 4 *Slang* a person who is easy to trick or cheat. ◆ VERB 5 (*tr*) *Slang* to trick or cheat.

▷HISTORY C15: from Old French *gougon,* probably from Latin *gōbius;* see GOBY

gudgeon[2] (ˈgʌdʒən) NOUN 1 **a** a pivot at the end of a beam or axle. **b** the female or socket portion of a pinned hinge. 2 *Nautical* one of two or more looplike sockets, fixed to the transom of a boat, into which the pintles of a rudder are fitted.

▷HISTORY C14: from Old French *goujon,* perhaps from Late Latin *gulbia* chisel

gudgeon pin NOUN *Brit* the pin through the skirt of a piston in an internal-combustion engine, to which the little end of the connecting rod is attached. US and Canadian name: **wrist pin.**

Gudrun (ˈgʊdruːn), **Guthrun** (ˈgʊðruːn), *or* **Kudrun** (ˈkʊdruːn) NOUN *Norse myth* the wife of Sigurd and, after his death, of Atli, whom she slew for his murder of her brother Gunnar. She corresponds to Kriemhild in the *Nibelungenlied.*

guelder-rose (ˈgɛldəˌrəʊz) NOUN a Eurasian caprifoliaceous shrub, *Viburnum opulus,* with clusters of white flowers and small red fruits.

▷HISTORY C16: from Dutch *geldersche roos,* from *Gelderland* or *Gelders,* province of Holland

Guelders (ˈgɛldəz) NOUN another name for **Gelderland.**

Guelph[1] *or* **Guelf** (gwɛlf) NOUN 1 a member of the political faction in medieval Italy that supported the power of the pope against the German emperors. Compare **Ghibelline.** 2 a member of a secret society in 19th-century Italy opposed to foreign rule.

▸'**Guelphic** *or* '**Guelfic** ADJECTIVE ▸'**Guelphism** *or* '**Guelfism** NOUN

Guelph[2] (gwɛlf) NOUN a city in Canada, in SE Ontario. Pop.: 95 821 (1996).

guenon (gəˈnɒn) NOUN any slender agile Old World monkey of the genus *Cercopithecus,* inhabiting wooded regions of Africa and having long hind limbs and tail and long hair surrounding the face.

▷HISTORY C19: from French, of unknown origin

guerdon (ˈgɜːdən) *Poetic* ◆ NOUN 1 a reward or payment. ◆ VERB 2 (*tr*) to give a guerdon to.

▷HISTORY C14: from Old French *gueredon,* of Germanic origin; compare Old High German *widarlōn,* Old English *witherlēan;* final element influenced by Latin *dōnum* gift

▸'**guerdoner** NOUN

guereza (gəˈrɛzə) NOUN a handsome colobus monkey of the mountain forests of Ethiopia.

▷HISTORY C19: its native name

Guernica (gɜːˈniːkə, ˈgɜːnɪkə; *Spanish* gɛrˈnika) NOUN a town in N Spain: formerly the seat of a Basque parliament; destroyed in 1937 by German bombers during the Spanish Civil War, an event depicted in one of Picasso's most famous paintings. Pop.: 16 380 (latest est.).

Guernsey (ˈgɜːnzɪ) NOUN 1 an island in the English Channel: the second largest of the Channel Islands, which, with Alderney and Sark, Herm, Jethou, and some islets, forms the bailiwick of Guernsey; finance, market gardening, dairy farming, and tourism. Capital: St Peter Port. Pop.: 64 300 (2001 est.). Area: 63 sq. km (24.5 sq. miles). 2 a breed of dairy cattle producing rich creamy milk, originating from the island of Guernsey. 3 (*sometimes not capital*) a seaman's knitted woollen sweater. 4 (*not capital*) *Austral* a sleeveless woollen shirt or jumper worn by a football player. 5 **get a guernsey.** *Austral* to be selected or gain recognition for something.

Guernsey lily NOUN See **nerine.**

Guerrero (*Spanish* ge'rrero) NOUN a mountainous state of S Mexico, on the Pacific: rich mineral resources. Capital: Chilpancingo. Pop.: 3 075 083 (2000 est.). Area: 63 794 sq. km (24 631 sq. miles).

guerrilla *or* **guerilla** (gə'rɪlə) NOUN 1 **a** a member of an irregular usually politically motivated armed force that combats stronger regular forces, such as the army or police. **b** (*as modifier*): *guerrilla warfare.* 2 a form of vegetative spread in which the advance is from several individual rhizomes or stolons growing rapidly away from the centre, as in some clovers. ◆ Compare **phalanx.**
▷**HISTORY** C19: from Spanish, diminutive of *guerra* WAR
▸**guer'rillaism** *or* **gue'rillaism** NOUN

guess (gɛs) VERB (when *tr, may take a clause as object*) 1 (when *intr,* often foll by *at* or *about*) to form or express an uncertain estimate or conclusion (about something), based on insufficient information: *guess what we're having for dinner.* 2 to arrive at a correct estimate of (something) by guessing: *he guessed my age.* 3 *Informal, chiefly US and Canadian* to believe, think, or suppose (something): *I guess I'll go now.* 4 **keep a person guessing.** to let a person remain in a state of uncertainty. ◆ NOUN 5 an estimate or conclusion arrived at by guessing: *a bad guess.* 6 the act of guessing. 7 **anyone's guess.** something difficult to predict.
▷**HISTORY** C13: probably of Scandinavian origin; compare Old Swedish *gissa,* Old Danish *gitse,* Middle Dutch *gissen;* see GET
▸**'guessable** ADJECTIVE ▸**'guesser** NOUN ▸**'guessingly** ADVERB

guesstimate *or* **guestimate** *Informal* ◆ NOUN ('gɛstɪmɪt) 1 an estimate calculated mainly or only by guesswork. ◆ VERB ('gɛstɪˌmeɪt) 2 to form a guesstimate of.

guesswork ('gɛsˌwɜːk) NOUN 1 a set of conclusions, estimates, etc., arrived at by guessing. 2 the process of making guesses.

guest (gɛst) NOUN 1 a person who is entertained, taken out to eat, etc., and paid for by another. 2 **a** a person who receives hospitality at the home of another: *a weekend guest.* **b** (*as modifier*): *the guest room.* 3 **a** a person who receives the hospitality of a government, establishment, or organization. **b** (*as modifier*): *a guest speaker.* 4 **a** an actor, contestant, entertainer, etc., taking part as a visitor in a programme in which there are also regular participants. **b** (*as modifier*): *a guest appearance.* 5 a patron of a hotel, boarding house, restaurant, etc. 6 *Zoology* a nontechnical name for **inquiline.** 7 **be my guest.** *Informal* do as you like. ◆ VERB 8 (*intr*) (in theatre and broadcasting) to be a guest: *to guest on a show.*
▷**HISTORY** Old English *giest* guest, stranger, enemy; related to Old Norse *gestr,* Gothic *gasts,* Old High German *gast,* Old Slavonic *gostĭ,* Latin *hostis* enemy

guest beer NOUN a draught beer stocked by a bar, often for a limited period, in addition to its usual range.

guesthouse ('gɛstˌhaʊs) NOUN a private home or boarding house offering accommodation, esp to travellers.

guest rope NOUN *Nautical* any line sent or trailed over the side of a vessel as a convenience for boats drawing alongside, as an aid in warping or towing, etc.

guff (gʌf) NOUN *Slang* ridiculous or insolent talk.
▷**HISTORY** C19: imitative of empty talk; compare dialect Norwegian *gufs* puff of wind

guffaw (gʌ'fɔː) NOUN 1 a crude and boisterous laugh. ◆ VERB 2 to laugh crudely and boisterously or express (something) in this way.
▷**HISTORY** C18: of imitative origin

Guggenheim Museum ('gʊgənˌhaɪm) NOUN a museum of modern art in New York: designed by Frank Lloyd Wright (1956–59).

GUI ('guːiː) NOUN ACRONYM FOR graphical user interface.

Guiana (gaɪ'ænə, gɪ'ɑːnə) *or* **The Guianas** NOUN a region of NE South America, including Guyana, Surinam, French Guiana, and the **Guiana Highlands** (largely in SE Venezuela and partly in N Brazil). Area: about 1 787 000 sq. km (690 000 sq. miles).
▸**Guianese** (ˌgaɪə'niːz, ˌgɪə-) *or* **Guianan** (gaɪ'ænən, gɪ'ɑːnən) ADJECTIVE, NOUN

Guianese (ˌgaɪə'niːz, ˌgɪə-) *or* **Guianan** (gaɪ'ænən, gɪ'ɑːnən) ADJECTIVE 1 of or relating to the South American region of Guiana or its inhabitants. ◆ NOUN 2 a native or inhabitant of Guiana.

guichet ('giːʃeɪ) NOUN a grating, hatch, or small opening in a wall, esp a ticket-office window.
▷**HISTORY** C19: from French

guid (gyd, gɪd) ADJECTIVE a Scot word for **good.**

guidance ('gaɪdᵊns) NOUN 1 leadership, instruction, or direction. 2 **a** counselling or advice on educational, vocational, or psychological matters. **b** (*as modifier*): *the marriage-guidance counsellor.* 3 something that guides. 4 any process by which the flight path of a missile is controlled in flight. See also **guided missile.**

guide (gaɪd) VERB 1 to lead the way for (a person). 2 to control the movement or course of (an animal, vehicle, etc.) by physical action; steer. 3 to supervise or instruct (a person). 4 (*tr*) to direct the affairs of (a person, company, nation, etc.): *he guided the country through the war.* 5 (*tr*) to advise or influence (a person) in his standards or opinions: *let truth guide you always.* ◆ NOUN 6 **a** a person, animal, or thing that guides. **b** (*as modifier*): *a guide dog.* 7 a person, usually paid, who conducts tour expeditions, etc. 8 a model or criterion, as in moral standards or accuracy. 9 See **guidebook.** 10 a book that instructs or explains the fundamentals of a subject or skill: *a guide to better living.* 11 any device that directs the motion of a tool or machine part. 12 **a** a mark, sign, etc., that points the way. **b** (*in combination*): *guidepost.* 13 *Spiritualism* a spirit believed to influence a medium so as to direct what he utters and convey messages through him. 14 **a** *Naval* a ship in a formation used as a reference for manoeuvres, esp with relation to maintaining the correct formation and disposition. **b** *Military* a soldier stationed to one side of a column or line to regulate alignment, show the way, etc.
▷**HISTORY** C14: from (Old) French *guider,* of Germanic origin; compare Old English *wītan* to observe
▸**'guidable** ADJECTIVE ▸**'guideless** ADJECTIVE ▸**'guider** NOUN ▸**'guiding** ADJECTIVE, NOUN

Guide (gaɪd) NOUN (*sometimes not capital*) a member of an organization for girls equivalent to the Scouts. US equivalent: **Girl Scout.**

guidebook ('gaɪdˌbʊk) NOUN a handbook with information for visitors to a place, as a historic building, museum, or foreign country. Also called: **guide.**

guided missile NOUN a missile, esp one that is rocket-propelled, having a flight path controlled during flight either by radio signals or by internal preset or self-actuating homing devices. See also **command guidance, field guidance, homing guidance, inertial guidance, terrestrial guidance.**

guide dog NOUN a dog that has been specially trained to live with and accompany someone who is blind, enabling the blind person to move about safely.

guideline ('gaɪdˌlaɪn) NOUN a principle put forward to set standards or determine a course of action.

guidepost ('gaɪdˌpəʊst) NOUN 1 a sign on a post by a road indicating directions. 2 a principle or guideline.

Guider ('gaɪdə) NOUN (*sometimes not capital*) 1 In full: **Guide Guider.** a woman leader of a company of Guides. 2 **Brownie Guider.** a woman leader of a pack of Brownie Guides.

guide rope NOUN 1 a stay or rope attached to another rope that is lifting a load, either to steady the load or guide the rope. 2 another name for **dragrope** (sense 2).

guide vanes PLURAL NOUN fixed aerofoils that direct air, gas, or water into the moving blades of a turbine or into or around bends in ducts with minimum loss of energy.

guidon ('gaɪdᵊn) NOUN 1 a small pennant, used as a marker or standard, esp by cavalry regiments. 2 the man or vehicle that carries this.
▷**HISTORY** C16: from French, from Old Provençal *guidoo,* from *guida* GUIDE

Guienne *or* **Guyenne** (*French* gɥijɛn) NOUN a former province of SW France: formed, with Gascony, the duchy of Aquitaine during the 12th century.

guild *or* **gild** (gɪld) NOUN 1 an organization, club, or fellowship. 2 (esp in medieval Europe) an association of men sharing the same interests, such as merchants or artisans: formed for mutual aid and protection and to maintain craft standards or pursue some other purpose such as communal worship. 3 *Ecology* a group of plants, such as a group of epiphytes, that share certain habits or characteristics.
▷**HISTORY** C14: of Scandinavian origin; compare Old Norse *gjald* payment, *gildi* guild; related to Old English *gield* offering, Old High German *gelt* money

guilder, gilder ('gɪldə), *or* **gulden** NOUN, *plural* **-ders, -der** *or* **-dens, -den.** 1 the former standard monetary unit of the Netherlands, divided into 100 cents; replaced by the euro in 2002. Also called: **florin.** 2 the standard monetary unit of the Netherlands Antilles and Surinam, divided into 100 cents. 3 any of various former gold or silver coins of Germany, Austria, or the Netherlands.
▷**HISTORY** C15: changed from Middle Dutch *gulden,* literally: GOLDEN

Guildford ('gɪlfəd) NOUN a city in S England, in Surrey: cathedral (1936–68); seat of the University of Surrey (1966). Pop.: 65 998 (1991).

guildhall ('gɪldˌhɔːl) NOUN 1 *Brit* **a** the hall of a guild or corporation. **b** a town hall. 2 Also: **gildhall.** the meeting place of a medieval guild.

guildsman *or* **gildsman** ('gɪldzmən) NOUN, *plural* **-men.** a man who is a member of a guild.

guild socialism NOUN a form of socialism advocated in Britain in the early 20th century. Industry was to be owned by the state but managed and controlled by worker-controlled guilds.
▸**guild socialist** NOUN

guildswoman *or* **gildswoman** ('gɪldzwʊmən) NOUN, *plural* **-women.** a woman who is a member of a guild.

guile (gaɪl) NOUN clever or crafty character or behaviour.
▷**HISTORY** C18: from Old French *guile,* of Germanic origin; see WILE
▸**'guileful** ADJECTIVE ▸**'guilefully** ADVERB ▸**'guilefulness** NOUN

guileless ('gaɪllɪs) ADJECTIVE free from guile; ingenuous.
▸**'guilelessly** ADVERB ▸**'guilelessness** NOUN

Guilin ('gweɪ'lɪn), **Kweilin,** *or* **Kuei-lin** NOUN a city in S China, in Guangxi Zhuang AR on the Li River: noted for the unusual caves and formations of the surrounding karst scenery; trade and manufacturing centre. Pop.: 458 333 (1999 est.).

Guillain-Barré syndrome (*French* ˌgije 'bareɪ) NOUN an acute neurological disorder, usually following a virus or bacterial infection, that causes progressive muscle weakness and partial paralysis.
▷**HISTORY** C20: named after Georges *Guillain* (1876–1961) and Jean Alexandre *Barré* (1880–1967), French neurologists

guillemet ('gɪlɪˌmɛt) NOUN *Printing* another name for **duckfoot quote.**

guillemot ('gɪlɪˌmɒt) NOUN any northern oceanic diving bird of the genera *Uria* and *Cepphus,* having a black-and-white plumage and long narrow bill: family *Alcidae* (auks, etc.), order *Charadriiformes.*
▷**HISTORY** C17: from French, diminutive of *Guillaume* William

guilloche (gɪ'lɒʃ) NOUN an ornamental band or border with a repeating pattern of two or more interwoven wavy lines, as in architecture.
▷**HISTORY** C19: from French: tool used in ornamental work, perhaps from *Guillaume* William

guillotine NOUN ('gɪləˌtiːn) 1 **a** a device for beheading persons, consisting of a weighted blade set between two upright posts. **b the guillotine.** execution by this instrument. 2 a device for cutting or trimming sheet material, such as paper or sheet metal, consisting of a blade inclined at a small angle that descends onto the sheet. 3 a surgical instrument for removing tonsils, growths in the throat, etc. 4 Also called: **closure by compartment.** (in Parliament, etc.) a form of closure under which a bill is divided into compartments, groups of which must be completely dealt with

each day. ◆ VERB (ˌgɪlə'tiːn) (tr) 5 to behead (a person) by guillotine. 6 (in Parliament, etc.) to limit debate on (a bill, motion, etc.) by the guillotine.
▷HISTORY C18: from French, named after Joseph Ignace *Guillotin* (1738–1814), French physician, who advocated its use in 1789
▸ˌ**guillo'tiner** NOUN

guilt (gɪlt) NOUN 1 the fact or state of having done wrong or committed an offence. 2 responsibility for a criminal or moral offence deserving punishment or a penalty. 3 remorse or self-reproach caused by feeling that one is responsible for a wrong or offence. 4 *Archaic* sin or crime.
▷HISTORY Old English *gylt,* of obscure origin

guiltless ('gɪltlɪs) ADJECTIVE free of all responsibility for wrongdoing or crime; innocent.
▸'**guiltlessly** ADVERB ▸'**guiltlessness** NOUN

guilty ('gɪltɪ) ADJECTIVE **guiltier, guiltiest.** 1 responsible for an offence or misdeed. 2 *Law* having committed an offence or adjudged to have done so: *the accused was found guilty.* 3 **plead guilty.** *Law* (of a person charged with an offence) to admit responsibility; confess. 4 of, showing, or characterized by guilt.
▸'**guiltily** ADVERB ▸'**guiltiness** NOUN

guimpe (gɪmp, gæmp) NOUN 1 a short blouse with sleeves worn under a pinafore dress. 2 a fill-in for a low-cut dress. 3 a piece of starched cloth covering the chest and shoulders of a nun's habit. 4 a variant spelling of **gimp.**
▷HISTORY C19: variant of GIMP

Guin. ABBREVIATION FOR Guinea.

guinea ('gɪnɪ) NOUN 1 **a** a British gold coin taken out of circulation in 1813, worth 21 shillings. **b** the sum of 21 shillings (£1.05), still used in some contexts, as in quoting professional fees. 2 See **guinea fowl.** 3 *US slang, derogatory* an Italian or a person of Italian descent.
▷HISTORY C16: the coin was originally made of gold from Guinea

Guinea ('gɪnɪ) NOUN 1 a republic in West Africa, on the Atlantic: established as the colony of French Guinea in 1890 and became an independent republic in 1958. Official language: French. Religion: Muslim majority and animist. Currency: franc. Capital: Conakry. Pop.: 7 614 000 (2001 est.). Area: 245 855 sq. km (94 925 sq. miles). 2 (formerly) the coastal region of West Africa, between Cape Verde and Namibe (formerly Moçâmedes; Angola): divided by a line of volcanic peaks into **Upper Guinea** (between The Gambia and Cameroon) and **Lower Guinea** (between Cameroon and S Angola). 3 **Gulf of.** a large inlet of the S Atlantic on the W coast of Africa, extending from Cape Palmas, Liberia, to Cape Lopez, Gabon: contains two large bays, the Bight of Biafra and the Bight of Benin, separated by the Niger delta.

Guinea-Bissau NOUN a republic in West Africa, on the Atlantic: first discovered by the Portuguese in 1446 and of subsequent importance in the slave trade; made a colony in 1879; became an independent republic in 1974. Official language: Portuguese; Cape Verde creole is widely spoken. Religion: animist majority and Muslim. Currency: franc. Capital: Bissau. Pop.: 1 316 000 (2001 est.). Area: 36 125 sq. km (13 948 sq. miles). Former name (until 1974): **Portuguese Guinea.**

Guinea corn NOUN another name for **durra.**

guinea fowl *or* **guinea** NOUN any gallinaceous bird, esp *Numida meleagris,* of the family *Numididae* of Africa and SW Asia, having a dark plumage mottled with white, a naked head and neck, and a heavy rounded body.

guinea grains PLURAL NOUN another name for **grains of paradise.**

guinea hen NOUN a guinea fowl, esp a female.

Guinean ('gɪnɪən) ADJECTIVE 1 of or relating to Guinea or its inhabitants. ◆ NOUN 2 a native or inhabitant of Guinea.

Guinea pepper NOUN a variety of the pepper plant *Capsicum frutescens,* from which cayenne pepper is obtained.

guinea pig NOUN 1 a domesticated cavy, probably descended from *Cavia porcellus,* commonly kept as a pet and used in scientific experiments. 2 a person or thing used for experimentation.
▷HISTORY C17: origin uncertain: perhaps from old use of the name *Guinea* to mean any remote unknown land

Guinea worm NOUN a parasitic nematode worm, *Dracunculus medinensis,* that lives beneath the skin in man and other vertebrates and is common in India and Africa.

Guinevere ('gwɪnɪˌvɪə), **Guenevere** ('gwɛnɪˌvɪə), *or* **Guinever** ('gwɪnɪvə) NOUN (in Arthurian legend) the wife of King Arthur and paramour of Lancelot.

guipure (gɪ'pjʊə) NOUN 1 Also called: **guipure lace.** any of many types of heavy lace that have their pattern connected by brides, rather than supported on a net mesh. 2 a heavy corded trimming; gimp.
▷HISTORY C19: from Old French *guipure,* from *guiper* to cover with cloth, of Germanic origin; see WIPE, WHIP

guise (gaɪz) NOUN 1 semblance or pretence: *under the guise of friendship.* 2 external appearance in general. 3 *Archaic* manner or style of dress. 4 *Obsolete* customary behaviour or manner. ◆ VERB 5 *Dialect* to disguise or be disguised in fancy dress. 6 (tr) *Archaic* to dress or dress up.
▷HISTORY C13: from Old French *guise,* of Germanic origin; see WISE[2]

guiser ('gaɪzə) NOUN a mummer, esp at Christmas or Halloween revels.

guitar (gɪ'tɑː) NOUN *Music* a plucked stringed instrument originating in Spain, usually having six strings, a flat sounding board with a circular sound hole in the centre, a flat back, and a fretted fingerboard. Range: more than three octaves upwards from E on the first leger line below the bass staff. See also **electric guitar, bass guitar, Hawaiian guitar.**
▷HISTORY C17: from Spanish *guitarra,* from Arabic *qītār,* from Greek *kithara* CITHARA
▸**gui'tarist** NOUN ▸**gui'tar-ˌlike** ADJECTIVE

guitarfish (gɪ'tɑːˌfɪʃ) NOUN, *plural* **-fish** *or* **-fishes.** any marine sharklike ray of the family *Rhinobatidae,* having a guitar-shaped body with a stout tail and occurring at the bottom of the sea.

Guiyang ('gweɪ'jæŋ), **Kweiyang,** *or* **Kuei-yang** NOUN a city in S China, capital of Guizhou province: reached by rail in 1959, with subsequent industrial growth. Pop.: 1 320 566 (1999 est.).

Guizhou ('gweɪ'dʒəʊ), **Kweichow,** *or* **Kueichou** NOUN a province of SW China, between the Yangtze and Xi Rivers: a high plateau. Capital: Guiyang. Pop.: 35 250 000 (2000 est.). Area: 174 000 sq. km (69 278 sq. miles).

Gujarat *or* **Gujerat** (ˌgʊdʒə'rɑːt) NOUN 1 a state of W India: formed in 1960 from the N and W parts of Bombay State; one of India's most industrialized states. Capital: Gandhinagar. Pop.: 50 596 992 (2001). Area: 196 024 sq. km (75 268 sq. miles). 2 a region of W India, north of the Narmada River: generally includes the areas north of Bombay city where Gujarati is spoken.

Gujarati *or* **Gujerati** (ˌgʊdʒə'rɑːtɪ) NOUN 1 (*plural* **-ti**) a member of a people of India living chiefly in Gujarat. 2 the state language of Gujarat, belonging to the Indic branch of the Indo-European family. ◆ ADJECTIVE 3 of or relating to Gujarat, its people, or their language.

Gujranwala (guːdʒ'rɑːnˌwʌlə) NOUN a city in NE Pakistan: textile manufacturing. Pop.: 1 124 799 (1998).

Gulag ('guːlæg) NOUN (formerly) the central administrative department of the Soviet security service, established in 1930, responsible for maintaining prisons and forced labour camps.
▷HISTORY C20: from Russian *G(lavnoye) U(pravleniye Ispravitelno-Trudovykh) Lag(erei)* Main Administration for Corrective Labour Camps

gular ('guːlə, 'gjuː-) ADJECTIVE *Anatomy* of, relating to, or situated in the throat or oesophagus.
▷HISTORY C19: from Latin *gula* throat

gulch (gʌltʃ) NOUN *US and Canadian* a narrow ravine cut by a fast stream.
▷HISTORY C19: of obscure origin

gulden ('gʊldᵊn) NOUN, *plural* **-dens** *or* **-den.** a variant of **guilder.**

Gülek Bogaz (guː'lɛk bəʊ'gɑːz) NOUN the Turkish name for the **Cilician Gates.**

gules (gjuːlz) ADJECTIVE (*usually postpositive*), NOUN *Heraldry* red.
▷HISTORY C14: from Old French *gueules* red fur worn around the neck, from *gole* throat, from Latin *gula* GULLET

gulf (gʌlf) NOUN 1 a large deep bay. 2 a deep chasm. 3 something that divides or separates, such as a lack of understanding. 4 something that engulfs, such as a whirlpool. ◆ VERB 5 (tr) to swallow up; engulf.
▷HISTORY C14: from Old French *golfe,* from Italian *golfo,* from Greek *kolpos*
▸'**gulfˌlike** ADJECTIVE ▸'**gulfy** ADJECTIVE

Gulf (gʌlf) NOUN **the.** 1 the Persian Gulf. 2 *Austral* **a** the Gulf of Carpentaria. **b** (*modifier*) of, relating to, or adjoining the Gulf: *Gulf country.* 3 *NZ* the Hauraki Gulf.

Gulf States PLURAL NOUN **the.** 1 the oil-producing states around the Persian Gulf: Iran, Iraq, Kuwait, Saudi Arabia, Bahrain, Qatar, the United Arab Emirates, and Oman. 2 the states of the US that border on the Gulf of Mexico: Alabama, Florida, Louisiana, Mississippi, and Texas.

Gulf Stream NOUN 1 a relatively warm ocean current flowing northeastwards off the Atlantic coast of the US from the Gulf of Mexico. 2 another name for **North Atlantic Drift.**

Gulf War NOUN 1 the war (1991) between US-led UN forces and Iraq, following Iraq's invasion of Kuwait. 2 See **Iran-Iraq War.**

Gulf War syndrome NOUN a group of various debilitating symptoms experienced by many soldiers who served in the Gulf War of 1991. It is claimed to be associated with damage to the central nervous system, caused by exposure to pesticides containing organophosphates.

gulfweed ('gʌlfˌwiːd) NOUN any brown seaweed of the genus *Sargassum,* esp *S. bacciferum,* having air bladders and forming dense floating masses in tropical Atlantic waters, esp the Gulf Stream. Also called: **sargasso, sargasso weed.**

gull[1] (gʌl) NOUN any aquatic bird of the genus *Larus* and related genera, such as *L. canus* (**common gull** or **mew**) having long pointed wings, short legs, and a mostly white plumage: family *Laridae,* order *Charadriiformes.* Related adjective: **larine.**
▷HISTORY C15: of Celtic origin; compare Welsh *gwylan*
▸'**gull-ˌlike** ADJECTIVE

gull[2] (gʌl) *Archaic* ◆ NOUN 1 a person who is easily fooled or cheated. ◆ VERB 2 (tr) to fool, cheat, or hoax.
▷HISTORY C16: perhaps from dialect *gull* unfledged bird, probably from *gul,* from Old Norse *gulr* yellow

Gullah ('gʌlə) NOUN 1 (*plural* **-lahs** *or* **-lah**) a member of a Negroid people living on the Sea Islands or in the coastal regions of South Carolina, Georgia, and NE Florida. 2 the creolized English spoken by these people.

gullet ('gʌlɪt) NOUN 1 a less formal name for the **oesophagus.** Related adjective: **oesophageal.** 2 the throat or pharynx. 3 *Mining, quarrying* a preliminary cut in excavating, wide enough to take the vehicle that removes the earth.
▷HISTORY C14: from Old French *goulet,* diminutive of *goule* throat, from Latin *gula* throat

gullible ('gʌləbᵊl) ADJECTIVE easily taken in or tricked.
▸ˌ**gulli'bility** NOUN ▸'**gullibly** ADVERB

gull-wing ('gʌlˌwɪŋ) ADJECTIVE 1 (of a car door) opening upwards. 2 (of an aircraft wing) having a short upward-sloping inner section and a longer horizontal outer section.

gully[1] *or* **gulley** ('gʌlɪ) NOUN, *plural* **-lies** *or* **-leys.** 1 a channel or small valley, esp one cut by heavy rainwater. 2 *NZ* a small bush-clad valley. 3 a deep, wide fissure between two buttresses in a mountain face, sometimes containing a stream or scree. 4 *Cricket* **a** a fielding position between the slips and point. **b** a fielder in this position. 5 either of the two channels at the side of a tenpin bowling lane. ◆ VERB **-lies, -lying, -lied.** 6 (tr) to make (channels) in (the ground, sand, etc.).
▷HISTORY C16: from French *goulet* neck of a bottle; see GULLET

gully[2] ('gʌlɪ) NOUN, *plural* **-lies.** *Scot* a large knife, such as a butcher's knife.
▷HISTORY C16: of obscure origin

gulosity (gjʊˈlɒsɪtɪ) NOUN *Archaic* greed or gluttony.
▷HISTORY C16: from Late Latin *gulōsitās,* from Latin *gulōsus* gluttonous, from *gula* gullet

gulp (gʌlp) VERB 1 (*tr; often foll by down*) to swallow rapidly, esp in large mouthfuls: *to gulp down food.* 2 (*tr; often foll by back*) to stifle or choke: *to gulp back sobs.* 3 (*intr*) to swallow air convulsively, as while drinking, because of nervousness, surprise, etc. 4 (*intr*) to make a noise, as when swallowing too quickly. ◆ NOUN 5 the act of gulping. 6 the quantity taken in a gulp.
▷HISTORY C15: from Middle Dutch *gulpen,* of imitative origin
▸ **ˈgulper** NOUN ▸ **ˈgulpingly** ADVERB ▸ **ˈgulpy** ADJECTIVE

gulper eel *or* **fish** NOUN any deep-sea eel-like fish of the genera *Eurypharynx* and *Saccopharynx* and order *Lyomeri,* having the ability to swallow large prey.

gum[1] (gʌm) NOUN 1 any of various sticky substances that exude from certain plants, hardening on exposure to air and dissolving or forming viscous masses in water. 2 any of various products, such as adhesives, that are made from such exudates. 3 any sticky substance used as an adhesive; mucilage; glue. 4 *NZ* short for **kauri gum.** 5 See **chewing gum, bubble gum,** and **gumtree.** 6 *Chiefly Brit* a gumdrop. ◆ VERB **gums, gumming, gummed.** 7 to cover or become covered, clogged, or stiffened with or as if with gum. 8 (*tr*) to stick together or in place with gum. 9 (*intr*) to emit or form gum. ◆ See also **gum up.**
▷HISTORY C14: from Old French *gomme,* from Latin *gummi,* from Greek *kommi,* from Egyptian *kemai*
▸ **ˈgumless** ADJECTIVE ▸ **ˈgumˌlike** ADJECTIVE

gum[2] (gʌm) NOUN the fleshy tissue that covers the jawbones around the bases of the teeth. Technical name: **gingiva.** Related adjective: **gingival.**
▷HISTORY Old English *gōma* jaw; related to Old Norse *gōmr,* Middle High German *gūme,* Lithuanian *gomurīs*

gum[3] (gʌm) NOUN used in the mild oath *by gum!*
▷HISTORY C19: euphemism for GOD

GUM ABBREVIATION FOR genitourinary medicine.

gum accroides (əˈkrɔɪdiːz) NOUN another name for **acaroid gum.**

gum ammoniac NOUN another name for **ammoniac**[2].

gum arabic NOUN a gum exuded by certain acacia trees, esp *Acacia senegal:* used in the manufacture of ink, food thickeners, pills, emulsifiers, etc. Also called: **acacia, gum acacia.**

gum benzoin NOUN another name for **benzoin.**

gumbo *or* **gombo** (ˈgʌmbəʊ) NOUN, *plural* **-bos.** *US and Canadian* 1 the mucilaginous pods of okra. 2 another name for **okra.** 3 a soup or stew thickened with okra pods. 4 a fine soil in the W prairies that becomes muddy when wet.
▷HISTORY C19: from Louisiana French *gombo,* of Bantu origin

Gumbo (ˈgʌmbəʊ) NOUN (*sometimes not capital*) a French patois spoken by Creoles in Louisiana and the Caribbean.
▷HISTORY see GUMBO

gumboil (ˈgʌmˌbɔɪl) NOUN an abscess on the gums, often at the root of a decayed tooth. Also called: **parulis.**

gumboots (ˈgʌmˌbuːts) PLURAL NOUN another name for **Wellington boots** (sense 1).

gumbotil (ˈgʌmbətɪl) NOUN a sticky clay formed by the weathering of glacial drift.
▷HISTORY C20: from GUMBO + TIL(L)[4]

gum digger NOUN *NZ* a person who digs for fossilized kauri gum in a gum field.

gum digger's spear NOUN *NZ* a long steel probe used by gum diggers digging for kauri gum.

gumdrop (ˈgʌmˌdrɒp) NOUN a small jelly-like sweet containing gum arabic and various colourings and flavourings. Also called (esp Brit): **gum.**

gum elastic NOUN another name for **rubber**[1] (sense 1).

gum elemi NOUN another name for **elemi.**

gum field NOUN *NZ* an area of land containing buried fossilized kauri gum.

gumlands (ˈgʌmˌlændz) PLURAL NOUN *NZ* infertile land from which the original kauri bush has been removed or burnt producing only kauri gum.

gumma (ˈgʌmə) NOUN, *plural* **-mas** *or* **-mata** (-mətə). *Pathol* a rubbery tumour characteristic of advanced syphilis, occurring esp on the skin, liver, brain or heart.
▷HISTORY C18: from New Latin, from Latin *gummi* GUM[1]
▸ **ˈgummatous** ADJECTIVE

gummite (ˈgʌmaɪt) NOUN an orange or yellowish amorphous secondary mineral consisting of hydrated uranium oxides.

gummosis (gʌˈməʊsɪs) NOUN the abnormal production of excessive gum in certain trees, esp fruit trees, as a result of wounding, infection, adverse weather conditions, severe pruning, etc.
▷HISTORY C19: from New Latin; see GUMMA

gummous (ˈgʌməs) *or* **gummose** (ˈgʌməʊs) ADJECTIVE *Rare* resembling or consisting of gum.

gummy[1] (ˈgʌmɪ) ADJECTIVE **-mier, -miest.** 1 sticky or tacky. 2 consisting of, coated with, or clogged by gum or a similar substance. 3 producing gum.
▷HISTORY C14: from GUM[1] + -Y[1]
▸ **ˈgumminess** NOUN

gummy[2] (ˈgʌmɪ) ADJECTIVE **-mier, -miest.** 1 toothless; not showing one's teeth. ◆ NOUN, *plural* **-mies.** 2 *Austral* a small crustacean-eating shark, *Mustelus antarcticus,* with bony ridges resembling gums in its mouth. 3 *NZ* an old ewe that has lost its incisor teeth.
▷HISTORY C20: from GUM[2] + -Y[1]
▸ **ˈgummily** ADVERB

gummy shark NOUN *Austral* another term for **gummy**[2] (sense 2).

Gum Nebula NOUN *Astronomy* a large, almost circular, emission nebula in the constellation Vela and Puppis. Thought to be the remains of a supernova explosion 1 million years ago, it is estimated to lie 1300 light years away.
▷HISTORY C20: discovered by C. S. *Gum* (1924–60), Australian astronomer

gum nut NOUN *Austral* the hardened seed container of the gum tree *Eucalyptus gummifera.*

gum plant *or* **gumweed** (ˈgʌmˌwiːd) NOUN any of several American yellow-flowered plants of the genus *Grindelia,* esp *G. robusta,* that have sticky flower heads: family *Asteraceae* (composites).

gumption (ˈgʌmpʃən) NOUN *Informal* 1 *Brit* common sense or resourcefulness. 2 initiative or courage: *you haven't the gumption to try.*
▷HISTORY C18: originally Scottish, of unknown origin

gum resin NOUN a mixture of resin and gum obtained from various plants and trees. See also **bdellium, gamboge.**

gumshield (ˈgʌmˌʃiːld) NOUN a plate or strip of soft waxy substance used by boxers to protect the teeth and gums. Also called: **mouthpiece.**

gumshoe (ˈgʌmˌʃuː) NOUN 1 a waterproof overshoe. 2 *US and Canadian* a rubber-soled shoe. 3 *US and Canadian slang* a detective or one who moves about stealthily. 4 *US and Canadian slang* a stealthy action or movement. ◆ VERB **-shoes, -shoeing, -shoed.** 5 (*intr*) *US and Canadian slang* to act stealthily.

gumsucker (ˈgʌmˌsʌkə) NOUN *Austral informal* (in the 19th century) **a** a native-born Australian. **b** a native of Victoria.

gumtree (ˈgʌmˌtriː) NOUN 1 any of various trees that yield gum, such as the eucalyptus, sweet gum, and sour gum. Sometimes shortened to: **gum.** 2 Also called: **gumwood.** the wood of the eucalyptus tree. 3 **up a gumtree.** *Informal* in a very awkward position; in difficulties.

gum up VERB (*tr, adverb*) 1 to cover, dab, or stiffen with gum. 2 *Informal* to make a mess of; bungle (often in the phrase **gum up the works**).

gun (gʌn) NOUN 1 **a** a weapon with a metallic tube or barrel from which a missile is discharged, usually by force of an explosion. It may be portable or mounted. In a military context the term applies specifically to a flat-trajectory artillery piece. **b** (*as modifier*): *a gun barrel.* 2 the firing of a gun as a salute or signal, as in military ceremonial. 3 a member of or a place in a shooting party or syndicate. 4 any device used to project something under pressure: *a grease gun; a spray gun.* 5 *US slang* an armed criminal; gunman. 6 *Austral and NZ slang* **a** an expert. **b** (*as modifier*): *a gun shearer; a gun batsman.* 7 **go great guns.** *Slang* to act or function with great speed, intensity, etc. 8 **jump** *or* **beat the gun. a** (of a runner, etc.) to set off before the starting signal is given. **b** *Informal* to act prematurely. 9 **spike someone's guns.** See **spike**[1] (sense 15). 10 **stick to one's guns.** *Informal* to maintain one's opinions or intentions in spite of opposition. ◆ VERB **guns, gunning, gunned.** 11 (when *tr,* often foll by *down*) to shoot (someone) with a gun. 12 (*tr*) to press hard on the accelerator of (an engine): *to gun the engine of a car.* 13 (*intr*) to hunt with a gun. ◆ See also **gun for.**
▷HISTORY C14: probably from a female pet name shortened from the Scandinavian name *Gunnhildr* (from Old Norse *gunnr* war + *hildr* war)

gunboat (ˈgʌnˌbəʊt) NOUN a small shallow-draft vessel carrying mounted guns and used by coastal patrols, etc.

gunboat diplomacy NOUN diplomacy conducted by threats of military intervention, esp by a major power against a militarily weak state.

gun carriage NOUN a mechanical frame on which a gun is mounted for adjustment and firing or for transportation.

guncotton (ˈgʌnˌkɒtᵊn) NOUN cellulose nitrate containing a relatively large amount of nitrogen: used as an explosive.

gun dog NOUN 1 a dog trained to work with a hunter or gamekeeper, esp in retrieving, pointing at, or flushing game. 2 a dog belonging to any breed adapted to these activities.

gunfight (ˈgʌnˌfaɪt) NOUN *Chiefly US* a fight between persons using firearms.
▸ **ˈgunˌfighter** NOUN ▸ **ˈgunˌfighting** NOUN

gunfire (ˈgʌnˌfaɪə) NOUN 1 the firing of one or more guns, esp when done repeatedly. 2 the use of firearms, as contrasted with other military tactics.

gunflint (ˈgʌnˌflɪnt) NOUN a piece of flint in a flintlock's hammer used to strike the spark that ignites the charge.

gun for VERB (*intr, preposition*) 1 to search for in order to reprimand, punish, or kill. 2 to try earnestly for: *he was gunning for promotion.*

gunge (gʌndʒ) *Informal* ◆ NOUN 1 sticky, rubbery, or congealed matter. ◆ VERB 2 (*tr; usually passive; foll by up*) to block or encrust with gunge; clog.
▷HISTORY C20: of imitative origin, perhaps influenced by GOO and SPONGE
▸ **ˈgungy** ADJECTIVE

gung ho (gʌŋ həʊ) ADJECTIVE 1 extremely enthusiastic and enterprising, sometimes to excess. 2 extremely keen to participate in military combat.
▷HISTORY C20: pidgin English, from Mandarin Chinese *kung* work + *ho* together

gunite (ˈgʌnˌaɪt) NOUN *Civil engineering* a cement-sand mortar that is sprayed onto formwork, walls, or rock by a compressed air ejector giving a very dense strong concrete layer: used to repair reinforced concrete, to line tunnel walls or mine airways, etc.
▷HISTORY C20: from GUN + -ITE[1]

gunk (gʌŋk) NOUN *Informal* slimy, oily, or filthy matter.
▷HISTORY C20: perhaps of imitative origin

gunlock (ˈgʌnˌlɒk) NOUN the mechanism in some firearms that causes the charge to be exploded.

gunman (ˈgʌnmən) NOUN, *plural* **-men.** 1 a man who is armed with a gun, esp unlawfully. 2 a man who is skilled with a gun. 3 *US* a person who makes, repairs, or has expert knowledge of guns.
▸ **ˈgunmanˌship** NOUN

gunmetal (ˈgʌnˌmetᵊl) NOUN 1 a type of bronze containing copper (88 per cent), tin (8–10 per cent), and zinc (2–4 per cent): used for parts that are subject to wear or to corrosion, esp by sea water. 2 any of various dark grey metals used for toys, belt buckles, etc. 3 a dark grey colour with a purplish or bluish tinge.

gun moll NOUN *Slang* a female criminal or a woman who associates with criminals.

Gunnar (ˈgʊnɑː) NOUN *Norse myth* brother of Gudrun and husband of Brynhild, won for him by Sigurd. He corresponds to Gunther in the *Nibelungenlied.*

gunned (gʌnd) ADJECTIVE **a** having a gun or guns as specified: *heavily gunned.* **b** (*in combination*): *three-gunned.*

Gunn effect (gʌn) NOUN a phenomenon observed in some semiconductors in which a steady electric field of magnitude greater than a threshold value generates electrical oscillations with microwave frequencies.
▷HISTORY C20: named after John Battiscombe *Gunn* (born 1928), British physicist

gunnel[1] (ˈgʌnᵊl) NOUN any eel-like blennioid fish of the family *Pholidae,* occurring in coastal regions of northern seas. See also **butterfish.**
▷HISTORY C17: of unknown origin

gunnel[2] (ˈgʌnᵊl) NOUN a variant spelling of **gunwale.**

gunner (ˈgʌnə) NOUN 1 a serviceman who works with, uses, or specializes in guns. 2 *Naval* (formerly) a warrant officer responsible for the training of gun crews, their performance in action, and accounting for ammunition. 3 (in the British Army) an artilleryman, esp a private. Abbreviation: **gnr.** 4 a person who hunts with a rifle or shotgun.
▸ **ˈgunner,ship** NOUN

gunnera (ˈgʌnərə) NOUN any herbaceous perennial plant of the genus *Gunnera,* found throughout the S hemisphere and cultivated for its large leaves.
▷HISTORY C18: named after J. E. *Gunnerus* (1718–73), Norwegian bishop and botanist

gunnery (ˈgʌnərɪ) NOUN 1 the art and science of the efficient design and use of ordnance, esp artillery. 2 guns collectively. 3 the use and firing of guns. 4 (*modifier*) of, relating to, or concerned with heavy guns, as in warfare: *a gunnery officer.*

gunning (ˈgʌnɪŋ) NOUN 1 the act or an instance of shooting with guns. 2 the art, practice, or act of hunting game with guns.

gunny (ˈgʌnɪ) NOUN, *plural* **-nies.** *Chiefly US* 1 a coarse hard-wearing fabric usually made from jute and used for sacks, etc. 2 Also called: **gunny sack.** a sack made from this fabric.
▷HISTORY C18: from Hindi *gōnī,* from Sanskrit *goṇī* sack, probably of Dravidian origin

gunpaper (ˈgʌn,peɪpə) NOUN a cellulose nitrate explosive made by treating paper with nitric acid.

gunplay (ˈgʌn,pleɪ) NOUN *Chiefly US* the use of firearms, as by criminals.

gunpoint (ˈgʌn,pɔɪnt) NOUN 1 the muzzle of a gun. 2 **at gunpoint.** being under or using the threat of being shot.

gunpowder (ˈgʌn,paʊdə) NOUN an explosive mixture of potassium nitrate, charcoal, and sulphur (typical proportions are 75:15:10): used in time fuses, blasting, and fireworks. Also called: **black powder.**
▸ **ˈgun,powdery** ADJECTIVE

Gunpowder Plot NOUN the unsuccessful conspiracy to blow up James I and Parliament at Westminster on Nov. 5, 1605. See also **Guy Fawkes Day.**

gunpowder tea NOUN a fine variety of green tea, each leaf of which is rolled into a pellet.

gun room NOUN 1 (esp in the Royal Navy) the mess allocated to subordinate or junior officers. 2 a room where guns are stored.

gunrunning (ˈgʌn,rʌnɪŋ) NOUN the smuggling of guns and ammunition or other weapons of war into a country.
▸ **ˈgun,runner** NOUN

gunsel (ˈgʌnsᵊl) NOUN *US slang* 1 a catamite. 2 a stupid or inexperienced person, esp a youth. 3 a criminal who carries a gun.
▷HISTORY C20: probably from Yiddish *genzel;* compare German *ganslein* gosling, from *gans* GOOSE[1]

gunshot (ˈgʌn,ʃɒt) NOUN 1 **a** shot fired from a gun. **b** (*as modifier*): *gunshot wounds.* 2 the range of a gun. 3 the shooting of a gun.

gun-shy ADJECTIVE afraid of a gun or the sound it makes: *a gun-shy dog is useless for shooting.*

gunslinger (ˈgʌn,slɪŋə) NOUN *Slang* a gunfighter or gunman, esp in the Old West.
▸ **ˈgun,slinging** NOUN

gunsmith (ˈgʌn,smɪθ) NOUN a person who manufactures or repairs firearms, esp portable guns.
▸ **ˈgun,smithing** NOUN

gunstock (ˈgʌn,stɒk) NOUN the wooden or metallic handle or support to which is attached the barrel of a rifle.

gunter rig (ˈgʌntə) NOUN *Nautical* a type of gaffing in which the gaff is hoisted parallel to the mast.
▷HISTORY C18: named after Edmund *Gunter* (1581–1626), English mathematician and astronomer
▸ **ˈgunter-,rigged** ADJECTIVE

Gunter's chain NOUN *Surveying* a measuring chain 22 yards in length, or this length as a unit. See **chain** (sense 7).
▷HISTORY C17: named after Edmund *Gunter* (1581–1626), English mathematician and astronomer

Gunther (ˈgʊntə) NOUN (in the *Nibelungenlied*) a king of Burgundy, allied with Siegfried, who won for him his wife Brunhild. He corresponds to Gunnar in Norse mythology.

Guntur (gʊnˈtʊə) NOUN a city in E India, in central Andhra Pradesh: founded by the French in the 18th century; ceded to Britain in 1788. Pop.: 471 051 (1991).

gunwale *or* **gunnel** (ˈgʌnᵊl) NOUN 1 *Nautical* the top of the side of a boat or the topmost plank of a wooden vessel. 2 **full to the gunwales.** completely full; full to overflowing.

gunyah (ˈgʌnjə) NOUN *Austral* a bush hut or shelter.
▷HISTORY C19: from a native Australian language

Günz (gʊnts) NOUN the first major Pleistocene glaciation of the Alps. See also **Mindel, Riss, Würm.**
▷HISTORY named after the river *Günz* in Germany

guppy (ˈgʌpɪ) NOUN, *plural* **-pies.** a small brightly coloured freshwater viviparous cyprinodont fish, *Lebistes reticulatus,* of N South America and the Caribbean: a popular aquarium fish.
▷HISTORY C20: named after R. J. L. *Guppy,* 19th-century clergyman of Trinidad who first presented specimens to the British Museum

Gupta (ˈgʌptə) NOUN the dynasty ruling northern India from the early 4th century to the late 6th century A.D.: the period is famous for achievements in art, science, and mathematics.

Gur (gʊə) NOUN a small group of languages of W Africa, spoken chiefly in Burkina-Faso and Ghana, forming a branch of the Niger-Congo family. Also called: **Voltaic.**

gurdwara (ˈgɜːdwɑːrə) NOUN a Sikh place of worship.
▷HISTORY C20: from Punjabi *gurduārā,* from Sanskrit *guru* teacher + *dvārā* DOOR

gurgitation (,gɜːdʒɪˈteɪʃən) NOUN surging or swirling motion, esp of water.
▷HISTORY C16: from Late Latin *gurgitātus* engulfed, from *gurgitāre* to engulf, from Latin *gurges* whirlpool

gurgle (ˈgɜːgᵊl) VERB (*intr*) 1 (of liquids, esp of rivers, streams, etc.) to make low bubbling noises when flowing. 2 to utter low throaty bubbling noises, esp as a sign of contentment: *the baby gurgled with delight.* ◆ NOUN 3 the act or sound of gurgling.
▷HISTORY C16: perhaps from Vulgar Latin *gurgulāre,* from Latin *gurguliō* gullet
▸ **ˈgurgling** ADJECTIVE

gurglet (ˈgɜːglɪt) NOUN another word for **goglet.**

Gurindji (gʊˈrɪndʒɪ) NOUN 1 an Aboriginal people of N central Australia. 2 the language of this people.

gurjun (ˈgɜːdʒən) NOUN 1 any of several S or SE Asian dipterocarpaceous trees of the genus *Dipterocarpus* that yield a resin. 2 Also called: **gurjun balsam.** the resin from any of these trees, used as a varnish.
▷HISTORY C19: from Bengali *garjon*

Gurkha (ˈgʊəkɑː, ˈgɜːkə) NOUN, *plural* **-khas** *or* **-kha.** 1 a member of a Hindu people, descended from Brahmins and Rajputs, living chiefly in Nepal, where they achieved dominance after being driven from India by the Muslims. 2 a member of this people serving as a soldier in the Indian or British army.

Gurkhali (,gʊəˈkɑːlɪ, ,gɜː-) NOUN the language of the Gurkhas, belonging to the Indic branch of the Indo-European family.

Gurmukhi (ˈgʊəmʊkɪ) NOUN the script used for writing the Punjabi language.
▷HISTORY Sanskrit, from *guru* teacher + *mukh* mouth

gurn (gərn, gɜːn) VERB (*intr*) a variant spelling of **girn.**

gurnard (ˈgɜːnəd) *or* **gurnet** (ˈgɜːnɪt) NOUN, *plural* **-nard, -nards** *or* **-net, -nets.** any European marine scorpaenoid fish of the family *Triglidae,* such as *Trigla lucerna* (**tub** or **yellow gurnard**), having a heavily armoured head and finger-like pectoral fins.
▷HISTORY C14: from Old French *gornard* grunter, from *grognier* to grunt, from Latin *grunnīre*

gurney (ˈgɜːnɪ) NOUN *US* a wheeled stretcher for transporting hospital patients.
▷HISTORY C20: of unknown origin

gurrier (ˈgʌrɪər) NOUN *Dublin dialect* a low-class tough ill-mannered person.
▷HISTORY perhaps from CURRIER

guru (ˈgʊruː, ˈguːruː) NOUN 1 a Hindu or Sikh religious teacher or leader, giving personal spiritual guidance to his disciples. 2 *Often derogatory* a leader or chief theoretician of a movement, esp a spiritual or religious cult. 3 *Often facetious* a leading authority in a particular field: *a cricketing guru.*
▷HISTORY C17: from Hindi *gurū,* from Sanskrit *guruḥ* weighty
▸ **ˈguru,ship** NOUN

Guru Granth *or* **Guru Granth Sahib** (grʌnt) NOUN the sacred scripture of the Sikhs, believed by them to be the embodiment of the gurus. Also called: **Adi Granth.**
▷HISTORY from Punjabi, from Sanskrit *grantha* a book

gush (gʌʃ) VERB 1 to pour out or cause to pour out suddenly and profusely, usually with a rushing sound. 2 to act or utter in an overeffusive, affected, or sentimental manner. ◆ NOUN 3 a sudden copious flow or emission, esp of liquid. 4 something that flows out or is emitted. 5 an extravagant and insincere expression of admiration, sentiment, etc.
▷HISTORY C14: probably of imitative origin; compare Old Norse *gjósa,* Icelandic *gusa*
▸ **ˈgushing** ADJECTIVE ▸ **ˈgushingly** ADVERB

gusher (ˈgʌʃə) NOUN 1 a person who gushes, as in being unusually effusive or sentimental. 2 something, such as a spurting oil well, that gushes.

gushy (ˈgʌʃɪ) ADJECTIVE **gushier, gushiest.** *Informal* displaying excessive admiration or sentimentality.
▸ **ˈgushily** ADVERB ▸ **ˈgushiness** NOUN

gusset (ˈgʌsɪt) NOUN 1 an inset piece of material used esp to strengthen or enlarge a garment. 2 a triangular metal plate for strengthening a corner joist between two structural members. 3 a piece of mail fitted between armour plates or into the leather or cloth underclothes worn with armour, to give added protection. ◆ VERB 4 (*tr*) to put a gusset in (a garment).
▷HISTORY C15: from Old French *gousset* a piece of mail, a diminutive of *gousse* pod, of unknown origin
▸ **ˈgusseted** ADJECTIVE

gussy up (ˈgʌsɪ) VERB (*tr, adverb*) **-sies, -sying, -sied** *Slang, chiefly US* to give (a person or thing) a smarter or more interesting appearance.
▷HISTORY C20: probably from the name *Gussie,* diminutive of *Augusta*

gust (gʌst) NOUN 1 a sudden blast of wind. 2 a sudden rush of smoke, sound, etc. 3 an outburst of emotion. ◆ VERB (*intr*) 4 to blow in gusts: *the wind was gusting to more than 50 mph.*
▷HISTORY C16: from Old Norse *gustr;* related to *gjōsa* to GUSH; see GEYSER

gustation (gʌˈsteɪʃən) NOUN the act of tasting or the faculty of taste.
▷HISTORY C16: from Latin *gustātiō,* from *gustāre* to taste
▸ **gustatory** (ˈgʌstətərɪ, -trɪ) *or* **ˈgustative** ADJECTIVE

Gustavo A. Madero (*Spanish* gusˈtaβo a maˈðero) NOUN the former name (1931–71) of **Guadalupe Hidalgo.**

gusto (ˈgʌstəʊ) NOUN vigorous enjoyment, zest, or relish, esp in the performance of an action: *the aria was sung with great gusto.*
▷HISTORY C17: from Spanish: taste, from Latin *gustus* a tasting; see GUSTATION

gusty (ˈgʌstɪ) ADJECTIVE **gustier, gustiest.** 1 blowing or occurring in gusts or characterized by blustery weather: *a gusty wind.* 2 given to sudden outbursts, as of emotion or temperament.
▸ **ˈgustily** ADVERB ▸ **ˈgustiness** NOUN

gut (gʌt) NOUN 1 **a** the lower part of the alimentary canal; intestine. **b** the entire alimentary

canal. Related adjective: **visceral.** [2] (*often plural*) the bowels or entrails, esp of an animal. [3] *Slang* the belly; paunch. [4] See **catgut.** [5] a silky fibrous substance extracted from silkworms, used in the manufacture of fishing tackle. [6] a narrow channel or passage. [7] (*plural*) *Informal* courage, willpower, or daring; forcefulness. [8] (*plural*) *Informal* the essential part: *the guts of a problem.* [9] **bust a gut.** *Informal* to make an intense effort. [10] **have someone's guts for garters.** *Informal* to be extremely angry with someone. [11] **hate a person's guts.** *Informal* to dislike a person very strongly. [12] **sweat** *or* **work one's guts out.** *Informal* to work very hard. ◆ VERB **guts, gutting, gutted.** (*tr*) [13] to remove the entrails from (fish, etc.). [14] (esp of fire) to destroy the inside of (a building). [15] to plunder; despoil: *the raiders gutted the city.* [16] to take out the central points of (an article), esp in summary form. ◆ ADJECTIVE [17] *Informal* arising from or characterized by what is basic, essential, or natural: *a gut problem; a gut reaction.*
▷HISTORY Old English *gutt;* related to *gēotan* to flow; see FUSION
▸**'gut,like** ADJECTIVE

GUT (gʌt) NOUN ACRONYM FOR grand unified theory.

gutbucket ('gʌt,bʌkɪt) NOUN a highly emotional style of jazz playing.
▷HISTORY C20: from US *gutbucket* a cheap gambling saloon where musicians could play for hand-outs

Gütersloh (*German* 'gy:tərslo:) NOUN a town in NW Germany, in North Rhine-Westphalia. Pop.: 83 400 (latest est.).

Guthrun ('gʊðru:n) NOUN a variant of **Gudrun.**

gutless ('gʌtlɪs) ADJECTIVE *Informal* lacking courage or determination.

gut reaction NOUN a reaction to a situation derived from a person's instinct and experience.

gutser ('gʌtsə) NOUN **come a gutser.** *Austral and NZ slang* [1] to fall heavily to the ground. [2] to fail through error or misfortune.
▷HISTORY C20: from *guts* + -ER[1]

gutsy ('gʌtsɪ) ADJECTIVE **gutsier, gutsiest.** *Slang* [1] gluttonous; greedy. [2] full of courage, determination, or boldness.

gutta ('gʌtə) NOUN, *plural* **-tae** (-ti:). [1] *Architect* one of a set of small droplike ornaments, esp as used on the architrave of a Doric entablature. [2] *Med* (formerly used in writing prescriptions) a technical name for a **drop.** Abbreviation: **gt.**
▷HISTORY C16: from Latin: a drop

gutta-percha ('gʌtə'pɜ:tʃə) NOUN [1] any of several tropical trees of the sapotaceous genera *Palaquium* and *Payena,* esp *Palaquium gutta.* [2] a whitish rubber substance derived from the coagulated milky latex of any of these trees: used in electrical insulation and dentistry.
▷HISTORY C19: from Malay *getah* gum + *percha* name of a tree that produces it

guttate ('gʌteɪt) *or* **guttated** ADJECTIVE *Biology* [1] (esp of plants) covered with small drops or droplike markings, esp oil glands. [2] resembling a drop or drops.
▷HISTORY C19: from Latin *guttātus* dappled, from *gutta* a drop
▸**gut'tation** NOUN

gutted ('gʌtɪd) ADJECTIVE *Informal* disappointed and upset.

gutter ('gʌtə) NOUN [1] a channel along the eaves or on the roof of a building, used to collect and carry away rainwater. [2] a channel running along the kerb or the centre of a road to collect and carry away rainwater. [3] a trench running beside a canal lined with clay puddle. [4] either of the two channels running parallel to a tenpin bowling lane. [5] *Printing* **a** the space between two pages in a forme. **b** the white space between the facing pages of an open book. **c** the space between two columns of type. [6] the space left between stamps on a sheet in order to separate them. [7] *Surfing* a dangerous deep channel formed by currents and waves. [8] *Austral* (in gold-mining) the channel of a former watercourse that is now a vein of gold. [9] **the gutter.** a poverty-stricken, degraded, or criminal environment. ◆ VERB [10] (*tr*) to make gutters in. [11] (*intr*) to flow in a stream or rivulet. [12] (*intr*) (of a candle) to melt away by the wax forming channels and running down in drops. [13] (*intr*) (of a flame) to flicker and be about to go out.
▷HISTORY C13: from Anglo-French *goutiere,* from Old French *goute* a drop, from Latin *gutta*
▸**'gutter-,like** ADJECTIVE

guttering ('gʌtərɪŋ) NOUN [1] the gutters, downpipes, etc., that make up the rainwater disposal system on the outside of a building. [2] the materials used in this system.

gutter press NOUN the section of the popular press that seeks sensationalism in its coverage.

guttersnipe ('gʌtə,snaɪp) NOUN [1] a child who spends most of his time in the streets, esp in a slum area. [2] a person regarded as having the behaviour, morals, etc., of one brought up in squalor.
▷HISTORY C19: originally a name applied to the common snipe (the bird), then to a person who gathered refuse from gutters in city streets
▸**'gutter,snipish** ADJECTIVE

guttural ('gʌtərəl) ADJECTIVE [1] *Anatomy* of or relating to the throat. [2] *Phonetics* pronounced in the throat or the back of the mouth; velar or uvular. [3] raucous. ◆ NOUN [4] *Phonetics* a guttural consonant.
▷HISTORY C16: from New Latin *gutturālis* concerning the throat, from Latin *guttur* gullet
▸**'gutturally** ADVERB ▸**'gutturalness** *or* **,guttur'ality** *or* **'gutturalism** NOUN

gutturalize *or* **gutturalise** ('gʌtərə,laɪz) VERB [1] (*tr*) *Phonetics* to change into a guttural speech sound or pronounce with guttural articulation or pharyngeal constriction. [2] to speak or utter in harsh raucous tones.
▸**,gutturali'zation** *or* **,gutturali'sation** NOUN

gutty ('gʌtɪ) NOUN, *plural* **-ties.** *Irish dialect* [1] an urchin or delinquent. [2] a low-class person.
▷HISTORY probably from GUTTER, perhaps from the compound GUTTERSNIPE

gut-wrenching ADJECTIVE *Informal* causing great distress or suffering: *gut-wrenching scenes.*

guv (gʌv) *or* **guv'nor** ('gʌvnə) NOUN *Brit* an informal name for **governor.**

guy¹ (gaɪ) NOUN [1] *Informal* a man or youth. [2] *Brit* a crude effigy of Guy Fawkes, usually made of old clothes stuffed with straw or rags, that is burnt on top of a bonfire on Guy Fawkes Day. [3] *Brit* a person in shabby or ludicrously odd clothes. [4] (*plural*) *Informal* persons of either sex. ◆ VERB [5] (*tr*) to make fun of; ridicule.
▷HISTORY C19: short for *Guy* Fawkes (1570–1606), English conspirator in the Gunpowder Plot

guy² (gaɪ) NOUN [1] a rope, chain, wire, etc., for anchoring an object, such as a radio mast, in position or for steadying or guiding it while being hoisted or lowered. ◆ VERB [2] (*tr*) to anchor, steady, or guide with a guy or guys.
▷HISTORY C14: probably from Low German; compare Dutch *gei* brail, *geiblok* pulley, Old French *guie* guide, from *guier* to GUIDE

GUY INTERNATIONAL CAR REGISTRATION FOR Guyana.

Guyana (gaɪ'ænə) NOUN a republic in NE South America, on the Atlantic: colonized chiefly by the Dutch in the 17th and 18th centuries; became a British colony in 1831 and an independent republic within the Commonwealth in 1966. Official language: English. Religions: Christian and Hindu. Currency: dollar. Capital: Georgetown. Pop.: 776 000 (2001 est.). Area: about 215 000 sq. km (83 000 sq. miles). Former name (until 1966): **British Guiana.**

Guyanese (,gaɪə'ni:z) *or* **Guyanan** (gaɪ'ænən) ADJECTIVE [1] of or relating to Guyana or its inhabitants. ◆ ADJECTIVE [2] a native or inhabitant of Guyana.

Guyenne (*French* gɥijɛn) NOUN a variant spelling of **Guienne.**

Guy Fawkes Day NOUN the anniversary of the discovery of the Gunpowder Plot, celebrated on Nov. 5 in Britain with fireworks and bonfires.

guyot ('gi:,əʊ) NOUN a flat-topped submarine mountain, common in the Pacific Ocean, usually an extinct volcano whose summit did not reach above the sea surface. Compare **seamount.**
▷HISTORY C20: named after A. H. *Guyot* (1807–84), Swiss geographer and geologist

guzzle ('gʌzᵊl) VERB to consume (food or drink) excessively or greedily.
▷HISTORY C16: of unknown origin

guzzler ('gʌzlə) NOUN **a** a person or thing that guzzles. **b** (*in combination*) *a gas-guzzler.*

gv ABBREVIATION FOR gravimetric volume.

gw THE INTERNET DOMAIN NAME FOR Guinea-Bissau.

Gwalior ('gwɑ:lɪ,ɔ:) NOUN [1] a city in N central India, in Madhya Pradesh: built around the fort, which dates from before 525; industrial and commercial centre. Pop.: 690 765 (1991). [2] a former princely state of central India, established in the 18th century: merged with Madhya Bharat in 1948, which in turn merged with Madhya Pradesh in 1956.

Gwent (gwɛnt) NOUN a former county of SE Wales: formed in 1974 from most of Monmouthshire and part of Breconshire; replaced in 1996 by Monmouthshire and the county boroughs of Newport, Torfaen, Blaenau Gwent, and part of Caerphilly.

Gweru ('gweɪru:) NOUN a city in central Zimbabwe. Pop.: 170 000 (1998 est.). Former name (until 1982): **Gwelo** ('gwi:ləʊ).

Gwynedd ('gwɪnəð) NOUN a county of NW Wales, formed in 1974 from Anglesey, Caernarvonshire, part of Denbighshire, and most of Merionethshire; lost Anglesey and part of the NE in 1996: generally mountainous with many lakes, much of it lying in the Snowdonia National Park. Administrative centre: Caernarfon. Pop.: 116 838 (2001). Area: 2550 sq. km (869 sq. miles).

gwyniad ('gwɪnɪ,æd) NOUN a freshwater white fish, *Coregonus pennantii,* occurring in Lake Bala in Wales: related to the powan.
▷HISTORY C17: Welsh, from *gwyn* white, related to Scottish Gaelic *fionn;* see FINNOCK

gy THE INTERNET DOMAIN NAME FOR Guyana.

Gyani ('gjɑ:nɪ) NOUN (in India) a title placed before the name of a Punjabi scholar.
▷HISTORY Hindi, from Sanskrit *gyan* knowledge

gybe *or* **jibe** (dʒaɪb) *Nautical* ◆ VERB [1] (*intr*) (of a fore-and-aft sail) to shift suddenly from one side of the vessel to the other when running before the wind, as the result of allowing the wind to catch the leech. [2] to cause (a sailing vessel) to gybe or (of a sailing vessel) to undergo gybing. ◆ NOUN [3] an instance of gybing.
▷HISTORY C17: from obsolete Dutch *gijben* (now *gijpen*), of obscure origin

gym (dʒɪm) NOUN, ADJECTIVE short for **gymnasium, gymnastics, gymnastic.**

gym bunny NOUN *Informal* a person who spends a lot of time exercising at a gymnasium.

gymkhana (dʒɪm'kɑ:nə) NOUN [1] *Chiefly Brit* an event in which horses and riders display skill and aptitude in various races and contests. [2] (esp in Anglo-India) a place providing sporting and athletic facilities.
▷HISTORY C19: from Hindi *gend-khānā,* literally: ball house, from *khāna* house; influenced by GYMNASIUM

gymnasiarch (dʒɪm'neɪzɪ,ɑ:k) NOUN [1] (in ancient Greece) an official who supervised athletic schools and contests. [2] *Obsolete* the governor or chief tutor of an academy or college.
▷HISTORY C17: from Latin, from Greek *gymnasiarchos,* from *gymnasion* gymnasium + *-archos* ruling

gymnasiast (dʒɪm'neɪzɪ,æst) NOUN a student in a gymnasium.

gymnasium (dʒɪm'neɪzɪəm) NOUN, *plural* **-siums** *or* **-sia** (-zɪə). [1] a large room or hall equipped with bars, weights, ropes, etc., for games or physical training. [2] (in various European countries) a secondary school that prepares pupils for university.
▷HISTORY C16: from Latin: school for gymnastics, from Greek *gumnasion,* from *gumnazein* to exercise naked, from *gumnos* naked

gymnast ('dʒɪmnæst) NOUN a person who is skilled or trained in gymnastics.

gymnastic (dʒɪm'næstɪk) ADJECTIVE of, relating to, like, or involving gymnastics.
▸**gym'nastically** ADVERB

gymnastics (dʒɪm'næstɪks) NOUN [1] (*functioning as singular*) practice or training in exercises that develop physical strength and agility or mental capacity. [2] (*functioning as plural*) gymnastic exercises.

gymno- COMBINING FORM naked, bare, or exposed: *gymnosperm*.
▷HISTORY from Greek *gumnos* naked

gymnosophist (dʒɪm'nɒsəfɪst) NOUN one of a sect of naked Indian ascetics who regarded food or clothing as detrimental to purity of thought.
▷HISTORY C16: from Latin *gymnosophistae,* from Greek *gumnosophistai* naked philosophers
▸**gym'nosophy** NOUN

gymnosperm ('dʒɪmnəʊˌspɜːm, 'gɪm-) NOUN any seed-bearing plant in which the ovules are borne naked on the surface of the megasporophylls, which are often arranged in cones. Gymnosperms, which include conifers and cycads, are traditionally classified in the division *Gymnospermae* but in modern classifications are split into separate phyla. Compare **angiosperm.**
▸**ˌgymno'spermous** ADJECTIVE

gympie ('gɪmpɪ) NOUN *Austral* [1] a tall tree with stinging hairs on its leaves. [2] a hammer.
▷HISTORY C19: from a native Australian language

gym shoe NOUN another name for **plimsoll.**

gymslip ('dʒɪmˌslɪp) NOUN a tunic or pinafore dress worn by schoolgirls, often part of a school uniform.

gyn. ABBREVIATION FOR: [1] gynaecological. [2] gynaecology.

gyn- COMBINING FORM variant of **gyno-** before a vowel.

gynae ('gaɪnɪ) ADJECTIVE *Informal* gynaecological.

gynaeceum (ˌdʒaɪnɪ'siːəm) NOUN, *plural* **-cea** (-'siːə). [1] (in ancient Greece and Rome) the inner section of a house, used as women's quarters. [2] (dʒaɪ'niːsɪəm, gaɪ-) a variant spelling of **gynoecium.**
▷HISTORY C17: from Latin: women's apartments, from Greek *gunaikeion,* from *gunē* a woman

gynaeco- *or US* **gyneco-** COMBINING FORM relating to women; female: *gynaecology*.
▷HISTORY from Greek, from *gunē, gunaik-* woman, female

gynaecocracy *or US* **gynecocracy** (ˌdʒaɪnɪ'kɒkrəsɪ, ˌgaɪ-) NOUN, *plural* **-cies.** government by women or by a single woman. Also called: **gynarchy.**
▸**gynaecocratic** *or US* **gynecocratic** (dʒaɪˌniːkə'krætɪk, gaɪ-) ADJECTIVE

gynaecoid *or US* **gynecoid** ('dʒaɪnɪˌkɔɪd, 'gaɪ-) ADJECTIVE resembling, relating to, or like a woman.

gynaecology *or US* **gynecology** (ˌgaɪnɪ'kɒlədʒɪ) NOUN the branch of medicine concerned with diseases in women, esp those of the genitourinary tract.
▸**gynaecological** (ˌgaɪnɪkə'lɒdʒɪkᵊl) *or* **ˌgynaeco'logic** *or US* **ˌgyneco'logical** *or* **ˌgyneco'logic** ADJECTIVE
▸**ˌgynae'cologist** *or US* **ˌgyne'cologist** NOUN

gynaecomastia *or US* **gynecomastia** (ˌgaɪnɪkəʊ'mæstrɪə) NOUN abnormal overdevelopment of the breasts in a man.
▷HISTORY C19: from GYNAECO- + Greek *mastos* breast

gynandromorph (dʒɪ'nændrəʊˌmɔːf, gaɪ-, dʒaɪ-) NOUN an organism, esp an insect, that has both male and female physical characteristics. Compare **hermaphrodite** (sense 1).
▸**gyˌnandro'morphic** *or* **gyˌnandro'morphous** ADJECTIVE
▸**gyˌnandro'morphism** *or* **gy'nandroˌmorphy** NOUN

gynandrous (dʒaɪ'nændrəs, dʒɪ-, gaɪ-) ADJECTIVE [1] (of flowers such as the orchid) having the stamens and styles united in a column. [2] hermaphroditic.
▷HISTORY C19: from Greek *gunandros* of uncertain sex, from *gunē* woman + *anēr* man
▸**gy'nandry** *or* **gy'nandrism** NOUN

gynarchy ('dʒaɪˌnɑːkɪ, 'gaɪ-) NOUN, *plural* **-chies.** another word for **gynaecocracy.**

gynecium (dʒaɪ'niːsɪəm, gaɪ-) NOUN, *plural* **-cia** (-sɪə). a variant spelling (esp US) of **gynoecium.**

gyneco- COMBINING FORM a variant (esp US) of **gynaeco-.**

gyniatrics (ˌdʒaɪnɪ'ætrɪks, ˌgaɪ-) *or* **gyniatry** (dʒaɪ'naɪətrɪ, gaɪ-) NOUN *Med* less common words for **gynaecology.**

gyno- *or before a vowel* **gyn-** COMBINING FORM [1] relating to women; female: *gynarchy*. [2] denoting a female reproductive organ: *gynophore*.
▷HISTORY from Greek, from *gunē* woman

gynodioecious (ˌgaɪnəʊdaɪ'iːʃəs) ADJECTIVE (of a plant species) having some individuals bearing female flowers only and others bearing hermaphrodite flowers only.

gynoecium, gynaeceum, gynaecium, *or esp US* **gynecium** (dʒaɪ'niːsɪəm, gaɪ-) NOUN, *plural* **-cia** *or* **-cea** (-sɪə). the carpels of a flowering plant collectively.
▷HISTORY C18: New Latin, from Greek *gunaikeion* women's quarters, from *gunaik-, gunē* woman + *-eion,* suffix indicating place

gynomonoecious (ˌgaɪnəʊmɔː'niːʃəs) ADJECTIVE (of a plant species) having each individual bearing both female and hermaphrodite flowers.

gynophore ('dʒaɪnəʊˌfɔː, 'gaɪ-) NOUN a stalk in some plants that bears the gynoecium above the level of the other flower parts.
▸**gynophoric** (ˌdʒaɪnəʊ'fɒrɪk, ˌgaɪ-) ADJECTIVE

-gynous ADJECTIVE COMBINING FORM [1] of or relating to women or females: *androgynous; misogynous*. [2] relating to female organs: *epigynous*.
▷HISTORY from New Latin *-gynus,* from Greek *-gunos,* from *gunē* woman
▸**-gyny** NOUN COMBINING FORM

Györ (*Hungarian* djøːr) NOUN an industrial town in NW Hungary: medieval Benedictine abbey. Pop.: 127 119 (2000 est.).

gyoza (giː'əʊzə) NOUN a Japanese fried dumpling.
▷HISTORY Japanese

gyp[1] *or* **gip** (dʒɪp) *Slang* ◆ VERB **gyps, gypping, gypped** *or* **gips, gipping, gipped.** [1] (*tr*) to swindle, cheat, or defraud. ◆ NOUN [2] an act of cheating. [3] a person who gyps.
▷HISTORY C18: back formation from GYPSY

gyp[2] (dʒɪp) NOUN *Brit and NZ slang* severe pain; torture: *his arthritis gave him gyp*.
▷HISTORY C19: probably a contraction of *gee up!;* see GEE[1]

gyp[3] (dʒɪp) NOUN a college servant at the universities of Cambridge and Durham. Compare **scout[1]** (sense 5).
▷HISTORY C18: perhaps from GYPSY, or from obsolete *gippo* a scullion

gyppo ('dʒɪpəʊ) NOUN, *plural* **-pos.** *Slang* a derogatory term for **Gypsy.**

gypsophila (dʒɪp'sɒfɪlə) NOUN any caryophyllaceous plant of the mainly Eurasian genus *Gypsophila,* such as baby's-breath, having small white or pink flowers.
▷HISTORY C18: New Latin, from Greek *gupsos* chalk + *philos* loving

gypsum ('dʒɪpsəm) NOUN a colourless or white mineral sometimes tinted by impurities, found in beds as an evaporite. It is used in the manufacture of plaster of Paris, cement, paint, school chalk, glass, and fertilizer. Composition: hydrated calcium sulphate. Formula: $CaSO_4.2H_2O$. Crystal structure: monoclinic.
▷HISTORY C17: from Latin, from Greek *gupsos* chalk, plaster, cement, of Semitic origin
▸**gypseous** ('dʒɪpsɪəs) ADJECTIVE ▸**gypsiferous** (dʒɪp'sɪfərəs) ADJECTIVE

Gypsy *or* **Gipsy** ('dʒɪpsɪ) NOUN, *plural* **-sies.** (*sometimes not capital*) [1] **a** a member of a people scattered throughout Europe and North America, who maintain a nomadic way of life in industrialized societies. They migrated from NW India from about the 9th century onwards. **b** (*as modifier*): *a Gypsy fortune-teller*. [2] the language of the Gypsies; Romany. [3] a person who looks or behaves like a Gypsy.
▷HISTORY C16: from EGYPTIAN, since they were thought to have come originally from Egypt
▸**'Gypsydom** *or* **'Gipsydom** NOUN ▸**'Gypsyˌhood** *or* **'Gipsyˌhood** NOUN ▸**'Gypsyish** *or* **'Gipsyish** ADJECTIVE
▸**'Gypsy-ˌlike** *or* **'Gipsy-ˌlike** ADJECTIVE

gypsy moth NOUN a variant spelling of **gipsy moth.**

gyral ('dʒaɪrəl) ADJECTIVE [1] having a circular, spiral, or rotating motion; gyratory. [2] *Anatomy* of or relating to a convolution (gyrus) of the brain.
▸**'gyrally** ADVERB

gyrate VERB (dʒɪ'reɪt, dʒaɪ-) [1] (*intr*) to rotate or spiral, esp about a fixed point or axis. ◆ ADJECTIVE ('dʒaɪrɪt, -reɪt) [2] *Biology* curved or coiled into a circle; circinate.
▷HISTORY C19: from Late Latin *gȳrāre,* from Latin *gȳrus* circle, from Greek *guros*
▸**gyratory** ('dʒaɪrətərɪ, -trɪ, dʒaɪ'reɪtərɪ) ADJECTIVE

gyration (dʒaɪ'reɪʃən) NOUN [1] the act or process of gyrating; rotation. [2] any one of the whorls of a spiral-shaped shell.

gyrator (dʒaɪ'reɪtə) NOUN an electronic circuit that inverts the impedance.

gyre (dʒaɪə) *Chiefly literary* ◆ NOUN [1] a circular or spiral movement or path. [2] a ring, circle, or spiral. ◆ VERB [3] (*intr*) to whirl.
▷HISTORY C16: from Latin *gȳrus* circle, from Greek *guros*

gyrfalcon *or* **gerfalcon** ('dʒɜːˌfɔːlkən, -ˌfɔːkən) NOUN a very large rare falcon, *Falco rusticolus,* of northern and arctic regions: often used for hunting.
▷HISTORY C14: from Old French *gerfaucon,* perhaps from Old Norse *geirfalki,* from *geirr* spear + *falki* falcon

gyro ('dʒaɪrəʊ) NOUN, *plural* **-ros.** [1] See **gyrocompass.** [2] See **gyroscope.**

gyro- *or before a vowel* **gyr-** COMBINING FORM [1] indicating rotating or gyrating motion: *gyroscope*. [2] indicating a spiral. [3] indicating a gyroscope: *gyrocompass*.
▷HISTORY via Latin from Greek *guro-,* from *guros* circle

gyrocompass ('dʒaɪrəʊˌkʌmpəs) NOUN *Navigation* a nonmagnetic compass that uses a motor-driven gyroscope to indicate true north. Sometimes shortened to: **gyro.**

gyrodyne ('dʒaɪrəʊˌdaɪn) NOUN an aircraft that uses a powered rotor to take off and manoeuvre, but uses autorotation when cruising.

gyro horizon NOUN another name for **artificial horizon** (sense 1).

gyromagnetic (ˌdʒaɪrəʊmæg'nɛtɪk) ADJECTIVE of or caused by magnetic properties resulting from the spin of a charged particle, such as an electron.

gyromagnetic ratio NOUN *Physics* the ratio of the magnetic moment of a rotating charged particle, such as an electron, to its angular momentum.

gyron ('dʒaɪrɒn) NOUN a variant spelling of **giron.**

gyronny (dʒaɪ'rɒnɪ) ADJECTIVE a variant spelling of **gironny.**

gyroplane ('dʒaɪrəˌpleɪn) NOUN another name for **autogiro.**

gyroscope ('dʒaɪrəˌskəʊp) *or* **gyrostat** NOUN a device containing a disc rotating on an axis that can turn freely in any direction so that the disc resists the action of an applied couple and tends to maintain the same orientation in space irrespective of the movement of the surrounding structure. Sometimes shortened to: **gyro.**
▸**gyroscopic** (ˌdʒaɪrə'skɒpɪk) ADJECTIVE
▸**ˌgyro'scopically** ADVERB ▸**ˌgyro'scopics** NOUN

gyrose ('dʒaɪrəʊz) ADJECTIVE *Botany* marked with sinuous lines.

gyrostabilizer *or* **gyrostabiliser** (ˌdʒaɪrəʊ'steɪbɪˌlaɪzə) NOUN a gyroscopic device used to stabilize the rolling motion of a ship.

gyrostatic (ˌdʒaɪrəʊ'stætɪk) ADJECTIVE of or concerned with the gyroscope or with gyrostatics.
▸**ˌgyro'statically** ADVERB

gyrostatics (ˌdʒaɪrəʊ'stætɪks) NOUN (*functioning as singular*) the science of rotating bodies.

gyrus ('dʒaɪrəs) NOUN, *plural* **gyri** ('dʒaɪraɪ). another name for **convolution** (sense 3).
▷HISTORY C19: from Latin; see GYRE

gyve (dʒaɪv) *Archaic* ◆ VERB [1] (*tr*) to shackle or fetter. ◆ NOUN [2] (*usually plural*) fetters.
▷HISTORY C13: of unknown origin

Hh

h *or* **H** (eɪtʃ) NOUN, *plural* **h's, H's,** *or* **Hs.** [1] the eighth letter and sixth consonant of the modern English alphabet. [2] a speech sound represented by this letter, in English usually a voiceless glottal fricative, as in *hat.* [3] **a** something shaped like an H. **b** (*in combination*): *an H-beam.*

h SYMBOL FOR: [1] *Physics* Planck constant. [2] hecto-. [3] *Chess* See **algebraic notation.**

H SYMBOL FOR: [1] *Chem* hydrogen. [2] *Physics* **a** magnetic field strength. **b** Hamiltonian. [3] *Electronics* henry or henries. [4] *Thermodynamics* enthalpy. [5] (on Brit. pencils, signifying degree of hardness of lead) hard: *H; 2H; 3H.* Compare **B** (sense 9). [6] *Slang* heroin. ◆ [7] INTERNATIONAL CAR REGISTRATION FOR Hungary.

H8 *Text messaging* ABBREVIATION FOR hate.

h. *or* **H.** ABBREVIATION FOR: [1] harbour. [2] height. [3] hour. [4] husband.

ha[1] *or* **hah** (hɑː) INTERJECTION [1] an exclamation expressing derision, triumph, surprise, etc., according to the intonation of the speaker. [2] (*reiterated*) a representation of the sound of laughter.

ha[2] SYMBOL FOR hectare.

Ha ABBREVIATION FOR Hawaii.

h.a. ABBREVIATION FOR hoc anno.
▷HISTORY Latin: in this year

HAA ABBREVIATION FOR hepatitis-associated antigen; an antigen that occurs in the blood serum of some people, esp those with serum hepatitis.

haaf (hɑːf) NOUN a deep-sea fishing ground off the Shetland and Orkney Islands.
▷HISTORY Old English *hæf* sea; related to Old Norse *haf;* see HEAVE

haar (hɑː) NOUN *Eastern Brit* a cold sea mist or fog off the North Sea.
▷HISTORY C17: related to Dutch dialect *harig* damp

Haarlem (*Dutch* 'haːrlɛm) NOUN a city in the W Netherlands, capital of North Holland province. Pop.: 148 262 (1999 est.).

Hab. *Bible* ABBREVIATION FOR Habakkuk.

Habakkuk ('hæbəkək) NOUN *Old Testament* [1] a Hebrew prophet. [2] the book containing his oracles and canticle. Douay spelling: **Habacuc.**

Habana (a'βana) NOUN the Spanish name for **Havana.**

habanera (ˌhæbə'nɛərə) NOUN [1] a slow Cuban dance in duple time. [2] a piece of music composed for or in the rhythm of this dance.
▷HISTORY from Spanish *danza habanera* dance from Havana

Habanero (*Spanish* aβa'nero) NOUN, *plural* **-ros** (-ros). a native or inhabitant of Havana.

habeas corpus ('heɪbɪəs 'kɔːpəs) NOUN *Law* a writ ordering a person to be brought before a court or judge, esp so that the court may ascertain whether his detention is lawful.
▷HISTORY C15: from the opening of the Latin writ, literally: you may have the body

haberdasher ('hæbəˌdæʃə) NOUN [1] *Brit* a dealer in small articles for sewing, such as buttons, zips, and ribbons. [2] *US* a men's outfitter.
▷HISTORY C14: from Anglo-French *hapertas* small items of merchandise, of obscure origin

haberdashery ('hæbəˌdæʃərɪ) NOUN, *plural* **-eries.** the goods or business kept by a haberdasher.

habergeon ('hæbədʒən) *or* **haubergeon** NOUN a light sleeveless coat of mail worn in the 14th century under the plated hauberk.
▷HISTORY C14: from Old French *haubergeon* a little HAUBERK

Haber process ('hɑːbə) NOUN an industrial process for producing ammonia by reacting atmospheric nitrogen with hydrogen at about 200 atmospheres (2×10^7 pascals) and 500°C in the presence of a catalyst, usually iron.
▷HISTORY named after Fritz *Haber* (1868–1934), German chemist

habile ('hæbiːl) ADJECTIVE [1] *Rare* skilful. [2] *Obsolete* fit.
▷HISTORY C14: from Latin *habilis,* from *habēre* to have; see ABLE

habiliment (hə'bɪlɪmənt) NOUN (*often plural*) dress or attire.
▷HISTORY C15: from Old French *habillement,* from *habiller* to dress, from *bille* log; see BILLET[2]

habilitate (hə'bɪlɪˌteɪt) VERB [1] (*tr*) *US, chiefly Western* to equip and finance (a mine). [2] (*intr*) to qualify for office. [3] (*tr*) *Archaic* to clothe.
▷HISTORY C17: from Medieval Latin *habilitāre* to make fit, from Latin *habilitās* aptness, readiness; see ABILITY
▸**haˌbili'tation** NOUN ▸**ha'biliˌtator** NOUN

habit ('hæbɪt) NOUN [1] a tendency or disposition to act in a particular way. [2] established custom, usual practice, etc. [3] *Psychol* a learned behavioural response that has become associated with a particular situation, esp one frequently repeated. [4] mental disposition or attitude: *a good working habit of mind.* [5] **a** a practice or substance to which a person is addicted: *drink has become a habit with him.* **b** the state of being dependent on something, esp a drug. [6] *Botany, zoology* the method of growth, type of existence, behaviour, or general appearance of a plant or animal: *a climbing habit; a burrowing habit.* [7] the customary apparel of a particular occupation, rank, etc., now esp the costume of a nun or monk. [8] Also called: **riding habit.** a woman's riding dress. [9] *Crystallog* short for **crystal habit.** ◆ VERB (*tr*) [10] to clothe. [11] an archaic word for **inhabit** or **habituate.**
▷HISTORY C13: from Latin *habitus* custom, from *habēre* to have

habitable ('hæbɪtəbᵊl) ADJECTIVE able to be lived in.
▸**ˌhabita'bility** *or* **'habitableness** NOUN ▸**'habitably** ADVERB

habitant ('hæbɪtᵊnt) NOUN [1] a less common word for **inhabitant.** [2] ('hæbɪtᵊnt; *French* abitɑ̃) **a** an early French settler in Canada or Louisiana, esp a small farmer. **b** a descendant of these settlers, esp a farmer.

habitat ('hæbɪˌtæt) NOUN [1] the environment in which an animal or plant normally lives or grows. [2] the place in which a person, group, class, etc., is normally found.
▷HISTORY C18: from Latin: it inhabits, from *habitāre* to dwell, from *habēre* to have

habitation (ˌhæbɪ'teɪʃən) NOUN [1] a dwelling place. [2] occupation of a dwelling place.
▸**ˌhabi'tational** ADJECTIVE

habited ('hæbɪtɪd) ADJECTIVE [1] dressed in a habit. [2] clothed.

habit-forming ADJECTIVE (of an activity, indulgence, etc.) tending to become a habit or addiction.

habitual (hə'bɪtjʊəl) ADJECTIVE [1] (*usually prenominal*) done or experienced regularly and repeatedly: *the habitual Sunday walk.* [2] (*usually prenominal*) by habit: *a habitual drinker.* [3] customary; usual: *his habitual comment.*
▸**ha'bitually** ADVERB ▸**ha'bitualness** NOUN

habituate (hə'bɪtjʊˌeɪt) VERB [1] to accustom; make used (to). [2] *US and Canadian archaic* to frequent.

habituation (həˌbɪtjʊ'eɪʃən) NOUN [1] the act or process of habituating. [2] *Psychol* the temporary waning of an innate response that occurs when it is elicited many times in succession. Compare **extinction** (sense 6).

habitude ('hæbɪˌtjuːd) NOUN *Rare* habit or tendency.
▸**ˌhabi'tudinal** ADJECTIVE

habitué (hə'bɪtjʊˌeɪ) NOUN a frequent visitor to a place.
▷HISTORY C19: from French, from *habituer* to frequent

habitus ('hæbɪtəs) NOUN, *plural* **-tus.** [1] *Med* general physical state, esp with regard to susceptibility to disease. [2] tendency or inclination, esp of plant or animal growth; habit.
▷HISTORY C19: from Latin: state, HABIT

habu ('hɑːbuː) NOUN a large venomous snake, *Trimeresurus flavoviridis,* of Okinawa and other Ryukyu Islands: family *Crotalidae* (pit vipers).
▷HISTORY from the native name originally used in the Ryukyu Islands

HAC ABBREVIATION FOR Honourable Artillery Company.

háček ('hɑːtʃɛk) NOUN a diacritic mark (ˇ) placed over certain letters in order to modify their sounds, esp used in Slavonic languages to indicate various forms of palatal articulation, as in the affricate *č* and the fricative trill *ř* used in Czech.
▷HISTORY from Czech

hachure (hæ'ʃjʊə) NOUN [1] another word for **hatching (see hatch**[3]**).** [2] shading of short lines drawn on a relief map to indicate gradients. ◆ VERB [3] (*tr*) to mark or show by hachures.
▷HISTORY C19: from French, from *hacher* to chop up, HATCH[3]

hacienda (ˌhæsɪ'ɛndə) NOUN (in Spain or Spanish-speaking countries) [1] **a** a ranch or large estate. **b** any substantial stock-raising, mining, or manufacturing establishment in the country. [2] the main house on such a ranch or plantation.
▷HISTORY C18: from Spanish, from Latin *facienda* things to be done, from *facere* to do

hack[1] (hæk) VERB [1] (when *intr,* usually foll by *at* or *away*) to cut or chop (at) irregularly, roughly, or violently. [2] to cut and clear (a way, path, etc.), as through undergrowth. [3] (in sport, esp rugby) to foul (an opposing player) by kicking or striking his shins. [4] *Basketball* to commit the foul of striking (an opposing player) on the arm. [5] (*intr*) to cough in short dry spasmodic bursts. [6] (*tr*) to reduce or cut (a story, article, etc.) in a damaging way. [7] to manipulate a computer program skilfully, esp, to gain unauthorized access to another computer system. [8] (*tr*) *Slang* to tolerate; cope with: *I joined the army but I couldn't hack it.* [9] **hack to bits.** to damage severely: *his reputation was hacked to bits.* ◆ NOUN [10] a cut, chop, notch, or gash, esp as made by a knife or axe. [11] any tool used for shallow digging, such as a mattock or pick. [12] a chopping blow. [13] a dry spasmodic cough. [14] a kick on the shins, as in rugby. [15] a wound from a sharp kick.
▷HISTORY Old English *haccian;* related to Old Frisian *hackia,* Middle High German *hacken*

hack[2] (hæk) NOUN [1] a horse kept for riding or (more rarely) for driving. [2] an old, ill-bred, or overworked horse. [3] a horse kept for hire. [4] *Brit* a country ride on horseback. [5] a drudge. [6] a person who produces mediocre literary or journalistic work. [7] Also called: **hackney.** *US* a coach or carriage that is for hire. [8] Also called: **hackie.** *US informal* **a** a cab driver. **b** a taxi. ◆ VERB [9] *Brit* to ride (a horse) cross-country for pleasure. [10] (*tr*) to let (a horse) out for hire. [11] (*tr*) *Informal* to write (an article) as or in the manner of a hack. [12] (*intr*) *US informal* to drive a taxi. ◆ ADJECTIVE [13] (*prenominal*) banal, mediocre, or unoriginal: *hack writing.*
▷HISTORY C17: short for HACKNEY

hack[3] (hæk) NOUN [1] a rack used for fodder for livestock. [2] a board on which meat is placed for a hawk. [3] a pile or row of unfired bricks stacked to dry. ◆ VERB (*tr*) [4] to place (fodder) in a hack. [5] to place (bricks) in a hack.
▷HISTORY C16: variant of HATCH[2]

hackamore ('hækəˌmɔː) NOUN *US and NZ* a rope or rawhide halter used for unbroken foals.
▷HISTORY C19: by folk etymology from Spanish *jáquima* headstall, from Old Spanish *xaquima,* from Arabic *shaqīmah*

hackberry (ˈhækˌbɛrɪ) NOUN, *plural* **-ries.** 1 any American tree or shrub of the ulmaceous genus *Celtis,* having edible cherry-like fruits. 2 the fruit or soft yellowish wood of such a tree.
▷ HISTORY C18: variant of **C16** *hagberry,* of Scandinavian origin; compare Old Norse *heggr* hackberry

hackbut (ˈhækbʌt) *or* **hagbut** NOUN another word for **arquebus.**
▸ ˌ**hackbut**ˈ**eer** *or* ˈ**hackbutter** *or* ˌ**hagbut**ˈ**eer** *or* ˈ**hagbutter** NOUN

hacker (ˈhækə) NOUN 1 a person that hacks. 2 *Slang* a computer fanatic, esp one who through a personal computer breaks into the computer system of a company, government, etc.

hackery (ˈhækərɪ) NOUN 1 *Ironic* journalism; hackwork. 2 *Informal* the practice of gaining illegal access to a computer system.

hackette (ˌhæˈkɛt) *Informal, derogatory* a female journalist.
▷ HISTORY C20: from HACK² (sense 3) + -ETTE

hack hammer NOUN an adzelike tool, used for dressing stone.

hacking (ˈhækɪŋ) ADJECTIVE (of a cough) harsh, dry, and spasmodic.

hacking jacket *or* **coat** NOUN *Chiefly Brit* a riding jacket with side or back vents and slanting pockets.

hackle (ˈhækᵊl) NOUN 1 any of the long slender feathers on the necks of poultry and other birds. 2 *Angling* **a** parts of an artificial fly made from hackle feathers, representing the legs and sometimes the wings of a real fly. **b** short for **hackle fly.** 3 a feathered ornament worn in the headdress of some British regiments. 4 a steel flax comb. ◆ VERB (*tr*) 5 to comb (flax) using a hackle. ◆ See also **hackles.**
▷ HISTORY C15 *hakell,* probably from Old English; variant of HECKLE; see HATCHEL
▸ ˈ**hackler** NOUN

hackle fly NOUN *Angling* an artificial fly in which the legs and wings are represented by hackle feathers.

hackles (ˈhækᵊlz) PLURAL NOUN 1 the hairs on the back of the neck and the back of a dog, cat, etc., which rise when the animal is angry or afraid. 2 anger or resentment (esp in the phrases **get one's hackles up, make one's hackles rise**).

hackney (ˈhæknɪ) NOUN 1 a compact breed of harness horse with a high-stepping trot. 2 **a** a coach or carriage that is for hire. **b** (*as modifier*): *a hackney carriage.* 3 a popular term for **hack²** (sense 1). ◆ VERB 4 (*tr; usually passive*) to make commonplace and banal by too frequent use.
▷ HISTORY C14: probably after HACKNEY, where horses were formerly raised; sense 4 meaning derives from the allusion to a weakened hired horse
▸ ˈ**hackneyism** NOUN

Hackney (ˈhæknɪ) NOUN a borough of NE Greater London: formed in 1965 from the former boroughs of Shoreditch, Stoke Newington, and Hackney; nearby are **Hackney Marshes,** the largest recreation ground in London. Pop.: 202 819 (2001). Area: 19 sq. km (8 sq. miles).

hackneyed (ˈhæknɪd) ADJECTIVE (of phrases, fashions, etc.) used so often as to be trite, dull, and stereotyped.

hacksaw (ˈhækˌsɔː) NOUN 1 a handsaw for cutting metal, with a hard-steel blade in a frame under tension. ◆ VERB **-saws, -sawing, -sawed, -sawed** *or* **-sawn** (-ˌsɔːn). 2 (*tr*) to cut with a hacksaw.

hackwork (ˈhækˌwɜːk) NOUN undistinguished literary work produced to order.

had (hæd) VERB the past tense and past participle of **have.**

hadal (ˈheɪdᵊl) ADJECTIVE of, relating to, or constituting the zones of the oceans deeper than **abyssal**: below about 6000 metres (18 000 ft.).
▷ HISTORY C20: from French, from *Hadès* HADES

hadaway (ˌhædəˈweɪ) SENTENCE SUBSTITUTE *Northeastern English dialect* an exclamation urging the hearer to refrain from delay in the execution of a task.
▷ HISTORY perhaps from HOLD¹ + AWAY

haddock (ˈhædək) NOUN, *plural* **-docks** *or* **-dock.** a North Atlantic gadoid food fish, *Melanogrammus aeglefinus:* similar to but smaller than the cod.
▷ HISTORY C14: of uncertain origin

hade (heɪd) *Geology* ◆ NOUN 1 the angle made to the vertical by the plane of a fault or vein. ◆ *obsolete* VERB 2 (*intr*) (of faults or veins) to incline from the vertical.
▷ HISTORY C18: of unknown origin

hadedah (ˈhɑːdɪˌdɑː) NOUN *South African* a large greyish-green ibis, *Hagedeshia hagedash,* having a greenish metallic sheen on the wing coverts and shoulders.
▷ HISTORY probably imitative of the bird's call

Hades (ˈheɪdiːz) NOUN 1 *Greek myth* **a** the underworld abode of the souls of the dead. **b** Pluto, the god of the underworld, brother of Zeus and husband of Persephone. 2 *New Testament* the abode or state of the dead. 3 (*often not capital*) *Informal* hell.
▸ **Hadean** (heɪˈdiːən, ˈheɪdɪən) ADJECTIVE

Hadhramaut *or* **Hadramaut** (ˌhɑːdrəˈmɔːt) NOUN a plateau region of the S Arabian Peninsula, in SE Yemen on the Indian Ocean; formerly in South Yemen: corresponds roughly to the former East Aden Protectorate. Area: about 151 500 sq. km (58 500 sq. miles).

Hadith (ˈhædɪθ, hɑːˈdiːθ) NOUN the body of tradition and legend about Mohammed and his followers, used as a basis of Islamic law.
▷ HISTORY Arabic

hadj (hædʒ) NOUN, *plural* **hadjes.** a variant spelling of **hajj.**

hadji (ˈhædʒɪ) NOUN, *plural* **hadjis.** a variant spelling of **hajji.**

hadn't (ˈhædᵊnt) VERB CONTRACTION OF had not.

Hadrian's Wall NOUN a fortified Roman wall, of which substantial parts remain, extending across N England from the Solway Firth in the west to the mouth of the River Tyne in the east. It was built in 120–123 A.D. on the orders of the emperor Hadrian as a defence against the N British tribes.

hadron (ˈhædrɒn) NOUN any elementary particle capable of taking part in a strong nuclear interaction and therefore excluding leptons and photons.
▷ HISTORY C20: from Greek *hadros* heavy, from *hadēn* enough + -ON
▸ **had**ˈ**ronic** ADJECTIVE

hadrosaur (ˈhædrəˌsɔː) *or* **hadrosaurus** (ˌhædrəˈsɔːrəs) NOUN any one of a large group of bipedal Upper Cretaceous dinosaurs of the genus *Anatosaurus, Maiasaura, Edmontosaurus,* and related genera: partly aquatic, with a duck-billed skull and webbed feet. Also called: **duck-billed dinosaur.**
▷ HISTORY C19: from Greek *hadros* thick, fat + -SAUR

hadst (hædst) VERB *Archaic or dialect* (used with the pronoun *thou*) a singular form of the past tense (indicative mood) of **have.**

hae (heɪ, hæ) VERB a Scot variant of **have.**

haecceity (hɛkˈsiːɪtɪ, hiːk-) NOUN, *plural* **-ties.** *Philosophy* the property that uniquely identifies an object. Compare **quiddity.**
▷ HISTORY C17: from Medieval Latin *haecceitas,* literally: thisness, from *haec,* feminine of *hic* this

haem *or US* **heme** (hiːm) NOUN *Biochem* a complex red organic pigment containing ferrous iron, present in haemoglobin.
▷ HISTORY C20: shortened from HAEMATIN

haem- COMBINING FORM a variant of **haemo-** before a vowel. Also (US): **hem-.**

haema- COMBINING FORM a variant of **haemo-.** Also (US): **hema-.**

haemachrome *or US* **hemachrome** (ˈhiːməˌkrəʊm, ˈhɛm-) NOUN variants of **haemochrome.**

haemacytometer *or US* **hemacytometer** (ˌhiːməsaɪˈtɒmɪtə) NOUN *Med* variants of **haemocytometer.**

haemagglutinate *or US* **hemagglutinate** (ˌhiːməˈgluːtɪˌneɪt, ˌhɛm-) VERB (*tr*) to cause the clumping of red blood cells in (a blood sample).

haemagglutinin *or US* **hemagglutinin** (ˌhiːməˈgluːtɪnɪn, ˌhɛm-) NOUN an antibody that causes the clumping of red blood cells.

haemagogue, *or US* **hemagogue, hemagog** (ˈhiːməˌgɒg) ADJECTIVE 1 promoting the flow of blood. ◆ NOUN 2 a drug or agent that promotes the flow of blood, esp the menstrual flow.
▷ HISTORY C18: from HAEMO- + Greek *agōgos* leading

haemal *or US* **hemal** (ˈhiːməl) ADJECTIVE 1 of or relating to the blood or the blood vessels. 2 denoting or relating to the region of the body containing the heart.

haemangioma *or esp US* **hemangioma** (hɪˌmændʒɪˈəʊmə) NOUN, *plural* **-mas** *or* **-mata** (-mətə). a nonmalignant tumour of blood vessels, esp affecting those of the skin. See **strawberry mark.**
▷ HISTORY from HAEM(O)- + ANGI(O)- + -OMA

haematein *or US* **hematein** (ˌhiːməˈtiːɪn, ˌhɛm-) NOUN a dark purple water-insoluble crystalline substance obtained from logwood and used as an indicator and biological stain. Formula: $C_{16}H_{12}O_6$.

haematemesis *or US* **hematemesis** (ˌhiːməˈtɛmɪsɪs, ˌhɛm-) NOUN vomiting of blood, esp as the result of a bleeding ulcer. Compare **haemoptysis.**
▷ HISTORY C19: from HAEMATO- + Greek *emesis* vomiting

haematic *or US* **hematic** (hiːˈmætɪk) ADJECTIVE 1 Also: **haemic.** relating to, acting on, having the colour of, or containing blood. ◆ NOUN 2 *Med* another name for a **haematinic.**

haematin *or US* **hematin** (ˈhɛmətɪn, ˈhiː-) NOUN *Biochem* a dark bluish or brownish pigment containing iron in the ferric state, obtained by the oxidation of haem.

haematinic *or US* **hematinic** (ˌhɛməˈtɪnɪk, ˌhiː-) NOUN 1 Also called: **haematic.** an agent that stimulates the production of red blood cells or increases the amount of haemoglobin in the blood. ◆ ADJECTIVE 2 having the effect of enriching the blood.

haematite (ˈhiːməˌtaɪt, ˈhɛm-) NOUN a variant spelling of **hematite.**
▸ **haematitic** (ˌhiːməˈtɪtɪk, ˌhɛm-) ADJECTIVE

haemato- *or before a vowel* **haemat-** COMBINING FORM indicating blood: *haematolysis.* Also: **haemo-,** (US) **hemato-,** (US) **hemat-.**
▷ HISTORY from Greek *haima, haimat-* blood

haematoblast *or US* **hematoblast** (hiːˈmætəʊˌblæst) NOUN any of the undifferentiated cells in the bone marrow that develop into blood cells.
▸ **hae**ˌ**mato**ˈ**blastic** *or US* **he**ˌ**mato**ˈ**blastic** ADJECTIVE

haematocele *or US* **hematocele** (ˈhɛmətəʊˌsiːl, ˈhiː-) NOUN *Pathol* a collection of blood in a body cavity, as in the space surrounding the testis; blood cyst.

haematocrit *or US* **hematocrit** (ˈhɛmətəʊkrɪt, ˈhiː-) NOUN 1 a centrifuge for separating blood cells from plasma. 2 Also called: **packed cell volume.** the ratio of the volume occupied by these cells, esp the red cells, to the total volume of blood, expressed as a percentage.
▷ HISTORY C20: from HAEMATO- + Greek *kritēs* judge, from *krinein* to separate

haematocryal *or US* **hematocryal** (ˌhɛmətəʊˈkraɪəl, ˌhiː-) ADJECTIVE *Zoology* another word for **poikilothermic.**

haematogenesis *or US* **hematogenesis** (ˌhɛmətəʊˈdʒɛnɪsɪs, ˌhiː-) NOUN another name for **haematopoiesis.**
▸ ˌ**haemato**ˈ**genic** *or* **haematogenetic** (ˌhɛmətəʊdʒɪˈnɛtɪk, ˌhiː-) *or US* ˌ**hemato**ˈ**genic** *or* ˌ**hematoge**ˈ**netic** ADJECTIVE

haematogenous *or US* **hematogenous** (ˌhɛməˈtɒdʒɪnəs, ˌhiː-) ADJECTIVE 1 producing blood. 2 produced by, derived from, or originating in the blood. 3 (of bacteria, cancer cells, etc.) borne by or distributed by the blood.

haematoid (ˈhiːməˌtɔɪd, ˈhɛm-), **haemoid,** *or US* **hematoid, hemoid** ADJECTIVE resembling blood.

haematology *or US* **hematology** (ˌhiːməˈtɒlədʒɪ) NOUN the branch of medical science concerned with diseases of the blood and blood-forming tissues.
▸ **haematologic** (ˌhiːmətəˈlɒdʒɪk) *or* ˌ**haemato**ˈ**logical** *or US* ˌ**hemato**ˈ**logic** *or* ˌ**hemato**ˈ**logical** ADJECTIVE
▸ ˌ**haema**ˈ**tologist** *or US* ˌ**hema**ˈ**tologist** NOUN

haematolysis *or US* **hematolysis** (ˌhiːməˈtɒlɪsɪs) NOUN, *plural* **-ses** (-ˌsiːz). another name for **haemolysis.**

haematoma *or US* **hematoma** (ˌhiːməˈtəʊmə, ˌhɛm-) NOUN, *plural* **-mas** *or* **-mata** (-mətə). *Pathol* a tumour of clotted or partially clotted blood.

haematophagous *or US* **hematophagous** (ˌhiːməˈtɒfəgəs) ADJECTIVE (of certain animals) feeding on blood.

haematopoiesis (ˌhɛmətəʊpɔɪˈiːsɪs, ˌhiː-), **haemopoiesis,** *or US* **hematopoiesis, hemopoiesis** NOUN *Physiol* the formation of blood. Also called: **haematosis, haematogenesis.**
▸**haematopoietic** (ˌhɛmətəʊpɔɪˈɛtɪk, ˌhiː-) *or* **haemopoietic** (ˌhiːməpɔɪˈɛtɪk, ˌhɛm-) *or US* **ˌhematopoiˈetic** *or* **ˌhemopoiˈetic** ADJECTIVE

haematosis *or US* **hematosis** (ˌhiːməˈtəʊsɪs, ˌhɛm-) NOUN *Physiol* [1] another word for **haematopoiesis.** [2] the oxygenation of venous blood in the lungs.

haematothermal *or US* **hematothermal** (ˌhɛmətəʊˈθɜːməl, ˌhiː-) ADJECTIVE *Zoology* another word for **homoiothermic.**

haematoxylin *or US* **hematoxylin** (ˌhiːməˈtɒksɪlɪn, ˌhɛm-) NOUN [1] a colourless or yellowish crystalline compound that turns red on exposure to light: obtained from logwood and used in dyes and as a biological stain. Formula: $C_{16}H_{14}O_6.3H_2O$. [2] a variant spelling of **haematoxylon.**
▷HISTORY C19: from New Latin *Haematoxylon* genus name of logwood, from HAEMATO- + Greek *xulon* wood + -IN

haematoxylon (ˌhiːməˈtɒksɪlɒn) *or* **haematoxylin** NOUN any thorny leguminous tree of the genus *Haematoxylon,* esp the logwood, of tropical America and SW Africa. The heartwood yields the dye haematoxylin.
▷HISTORY C19: see HAEMATOXYLIN
▸**haematoxylic** (ˌhiːmətɒkˈsɪlɪk) ADJECTIVE

haematozoon *or US* **hematozoon** (ˌhiːmətəʊˈzəʊɒn, ˌhɛm-) NOUN, *plural* **-zoa** (-ˈzəʊə). any microorganism, esp a protozoan, that is parasitic in the blood.

haematuria *or esp US* **hematuria** (ˌhiːməˈtjʊərɪə, ˌhɛm-) NOUN *Pathol* the presence of blood or red blood cells in the urine.
▸**ˌhaemaˈturic** *or US* **ˌhemaˈturic** ADJECTIVE

haemia *or esp US* **-hemia** NOUN COMBINING FORM variants of **-aemia.**

haemic *or US* **hemic** (ˈhiːmɪk, ˈhɛm-) ADJECTIVE another word for **haematic.**

haemin *or US* **hemin** (ˈhiːmɪn) NOUN *Biochem* haematin chloride; insoluble reddish-brown crystals formed by the action of hydrochloric acid on haematin in a test for the presence of blood.
▷HISTORY C20: from HAEMO- + -IN

haemo-, haema-, *or before a vowel* **haem-** COMBINING FORM denoting blood: *haemophobia*. Also: **haemato-,** (US) **hemo-,** (US) **hema-,** (US) **hem-.**
▷HISTORY from Greek *haima* blood

haemochrome *or US* **hemochrome** (ˈhiːməˌkrəʊm, ˈhɛm-) NOUN a blood pigment, such as haemoglobin, that carries oxygen.

haemocoel *or US* **hemocoel** (ˈhiːməˌsiːl) NOUN the body cavity of many invertebrates, including arthropods and molluscs, developed from part of the blood system.
▷HISTORY C19: from HAEMO- + New Latin *coel,* from Greek *koilos* hollow

haemocyanin *or US* **hemocyanin** (ˌhiːməʊˈsaɪənɪn) NOUN a blue copper-containing respiratory pigment in crustaceans and molluscs that functions as haemoglobin.

haemocyte *or US* **hemocyte** (ˈhiːməʊˌsaɪt, ˈhɛm-) NOUN any blood cell, esp a red blood cell.

haemocytometer (ˌhiːməʊsaɪˈtɒmɪtə), **haemacytometer,** *or US* **hemocytometer, hemacytometer** NOUN *Med* an apparatus for counting the number of cells in a quantity of blood, typically consisting of a graduated pipette for drawing and diluting the blood and a ruled glass slide on which the cells are counted under a microscope.

haemodialysis *or US* **hemodialysis** (ˌhiːməʊdaɪˈælɪsɪs) NOUN, *plural* **-ses** (-ˌsiːz). *Med* the filtering of circulating blood through a semipermeable membrane in an apparatus (**haemodialyser** or **artificial kidney**) to remove waste products: performed in cases of kidney failure. Also called: **extracorporeal dialysis.** See also **dialysis.**
▷HISTORY C20: from HAEMO- + DIALYSIS

haemoflagellate *or US* **hemoflagellate** (ˌhiːməˈflædʒəˌleɪt, ˌhɛm-) NOUN a flagellate protozoan, such as a trypanosome, that is parasitic in the blood.

haemoglobin *or US* **hemoglobin** (ˌhiːməʊˈgləʊbɪn, ˌhɛm-) NOUN a conjugated protein, consisting of haem and the protein globin, that gives red blood cells their characteristic colour. It combines reversibly with oxygen and is thus very important in the transportation of oxygen to tissues. See also **oxyhaemoglobin.**
▷HISTORY C19: shortened from *haematoglobulin,* from HAEMATIN + GLOBULIN the two components

haemoglobinometer *or US* **hemoglobinometer** (ˌhiːməʊgləʊbɪˈnɒmɪtə) NOUN an instrument used to determine the haemoglobin content of blood.

haemoglobinopathy *or US* **hemoglobinopathy** (ˌhiːməʊgləʊbɪˈnɒpəθɪ) NOUN any of various inherited diseases, including sickle-cell anaemia and thalassaemia, characterized by abnormal haemoglobin.

haemoglobinuria *or US* **hemoglobinuria** (ˌhiːməʊgləʊbɪˈnjʊərɪə, ˌhɛm-) NOUN *Pathol* the presence of haemoglobin in the urine.

haemoid *or US* **hemoid** (ˈhiːmɔɪd) ADJECTIVE a former word for **haematoid.**

haemolysin *or US* **hemolysin** (ˌhiːməʊˈlaɪsɪn, ˌhɛməʊ-, hɪˈmɒlɪsɪn) NOUN *Biochem* any substance, esp an antibody, that causes the breakdown of red blood cells.

haemolysis (hɪˈmɒlɪsɪs), **haematolysis,** *or US* **hemolysis, hematolysis** NOUN, *plural* **-ses** (-ˌsiːz). the disintegration of red blood cells, with the release of haemoglobin, occurring in the living organism or in a blood sample.

haemolytic *or US* **hemolytic** (ˌhiːməʊˈlɪtɪk, ˌhɛm-) ADJECTIVE of or relating to the disintegration of red blood cells.

haemophile *or US* **hemophile** (ˈhiːməʊˌfaɪl, ˈhɛm-) NOUN [1] another name for **haemophiliac.** [2] a haemophilic bacterium.

haemophilia *or US* **hemophilia** (ˌhiːməʊˈfɪlɪə, ˌhɛm-) NOUN an inheritable disease, usually affecting only males but transmitted by women to their male children, characterized by loss or impairment of the normal clotting ability of blood so that a minor wound may result in fatal bleeding.
▸**ˌhaemoˈphiliˌoid** *or US* **ˌhemoˈphiliˌoid** ADJECTIVE

haemophiliac *or US* **hemophiliac** (ˌhiːməʊˈfɪlɪˌæk, ˌhɛm-) NOUN a person having haemophilia. Nontechnical name: **bleeder.** Also called: **haemophile.**

haemophilic *or US* **hemophilic** (ˌhiːməʊˈfɪlɪk, ˌhɛm-) ADJECTIVE [1] of, relating to, or affected by haemophilia. [2] (of bacteria) growing well in a culture medium containing blood.

haemopoiesis *or US* **hemopoiesis** (ˌhiːməʊpɔɪˈiːsɪs, ˌhɛm-) NOUN *Physiol* another name for **haematopoiesis.**
▸**haemopoietic** *or US* **hemopoietic** (ˌhiːməʊpɔɪˈɛtɪk, ˌhɛm-) ADJECTIVE

haemoptysis *or US* **hemoptysis** (hɪˈmɒptɪsɪs) NOUN, *plural* **-ses** (-ˌsiːz). spitting or coughing up of blood or blood-streaked mucus, as in tuberculosis. Compare **haematemesis.**
▷HISTORY C17: from HAEMO- + *-ptysis,* from Greek *ptyein* to spit

haemorrhage *or US* **hemorrhage** (ˈhɛmərɪdʒ) NOUN [1] profuse bleeding from ruptured blood vessels. [2] a steady or severe loss or depletion of resources, staff, etc. ◆ VERB [3] (*intr*) to bleed profusely. [4] (*tr*) to undergo a steady or severe loss or depletion of (resources, staff, etc.).
▷HISTORY C17: from Latin *haemorrhagia;* see HAEMO-, -RRHAGIA
▸**haemorrhagic** *or US* **hemorrhagic** (ˌhɛməˈrædʒɪk) ADJECTIVE

haemorrhagic fever NOUN any of a group of fevers, such as Ebola virus disease and yellow fever, characterized by internal bleeding or bleeding into the skin.

haemorrhoidectomy *or US* **hemorrhoidectomy** (ˌhɛmərɔɪˈdɛktəmɪ) NOUN, *plural* **-mies.** surgical removal of haemorrhoids.

haemorrhoids *or US* **hemorrhoids** (ˈhɛməˌrɔɪdz) PLURAL NOUN *Pathol* swollen and twisted veins in the region of the anus and lower rectum, often painful and bleeding. Nontechnical name: **piles.**
▷HISTORY C14: from Latin *haemorrhoidae* (plural), from Greek, from *haimorrhoos* discharging blood, from *haimo-* HAEMO- + *rhein* to flow
▸**ˌhaemorˈrhoidal** *or US* **ˌhemorˈrhoidal** ADJECTIVE

haemostasis (ˌhiːməʊˈsteɪsɪs, ˌhɛm-), **haemostasia** (ˌhiːməʊˈsteɪʒɪə, -ʒə, ˌhɛm-), *or US* **hemostasis, hemostasia** NOUN [1] the stopping of bleeding or arrest of blood circulation in an organ or part, as during a surgical operation. [2] stagnation of the blood.
▷HISTORY C18: from New Latin, from HAEMO- + Greek *stasis* a standing still

haemostat *or US* **hemostat** (ˈhiːməʊˌstæt, ˈhɛm-) NOUN [1] a surgical instrument that stops bleeding by compression of a blood vessel. [2] a chemical agent that retards or stops bleeding.

haemostatic *or US* **hemostatic** (ˌhiːməʊˈstætɪk, ˌhɛm-) ADJECTIVE [1] retarding or stopping the flow of blood within the blood vessels. [2] retarding or stopping bleeding. ◆ NOUN [3] a drug or agent that retards or stops bleeding.

haeremai (ˈhaɪrəˌmaɪ) INTERJECTION *NZ* a Maori expression of welcome.
▷HISTORY C18: Maori, literally: come hither

haeres (ˈhɪəriːz) NOUN, *plural* **haeredes** (hɪˈriːdiːz). a variant spelling of **heres.**

Ha-erh-pin (ˈhɑːˈɛəˈpɪn) NOUN transliteration of the Chinese name for **Harbin.**

haet (het) NOUN *Scot* a whit; iota; the least amount.
▷HISTORY C16: originally in the phrase *deil hae' it* devil have it

hafiz (ˈhɑːfɪz) NOUN *Islam* a title for a person who knows the Koran by heart.
▷HISTORY from Persian, from Arabic *hāfiz,* from *hafiza* to guard

hafnium (ˈhæfnɪəm) NOUN a bright metallic element found in zirconium ores: used in tungsten filaments and as a neutron absorber in nuclear reactors. Symbol: Hf; atomic no.: 72; atomic wt.: 178.49; valency: 4; relative density: 13.31; melting pt.: 2231±20°C; boiling pt.: 4603°C.
▷HISTORY C20: New Latin, named after *Hafnia,* Latin name of Copenhagen + -IUM

haft (hɑːft) NOUN [1] the handle of an axe, knife, etc. ◆ VERB [2] (*tr*) to provide with a haft.
▷HISTORY Old English *hæft;* related to Old Norse *hapt,* Old High German *haft* fetter, *hefti* handle
▸**ˈhafter** NOUN

Haftarah *or* **Haphtarah** (hɑːfˈtəʊrə; *Hebrew* haftaˈraː) NOUN, *plural* **-taroth** (-ˈtəʊrəʊt; *Hebrew* -taˈroːt). *Judaism* a short reading from the Prophets which follows the reading from the Torah on Sabbaths and festivals, and relates either to the theme of the Torah reading or to the observances of the day. See also **maftir.**

hag[1] (hæg) NOUN [1] an unpleasant or ugly old woman. [2] a witch. [3] short for **hagfish.** [4] *Obsolete* a female demon.
▷HISTORY Old English *hægtesse* witch; related to Old High German *hagazussa,* Middle Dutch *haghetisse*
▸**ˈhaggish** ADJECTIVE ▸**ˈhaggishly** ADVERB ▸**ˈhaggishness** NOUN ▸**ˈhagˌlike** ADJECTIVE

hag[2] (hæg, hɑːg) NOUN *Scot and northern English dialect* [1] a firm spot in a bog. [2] a soft place in a moor.
▷HISTORY C13: of Scandinavian origin; compare Old Norse *högg* gap; see HEW

Hag. *Bible* ABBREVIATION FOR Haggai.

Hagar (ˈheɪgɑː, -gə) NOUN *Old Testament* an Egyptian maid of Sarah, who bore Ishmael to Abraham, Sarah's husband.

hagbut (ˈhægbʌt) NOUN another word for **arquebus.**
▸**ˌhagbutˈeer** *or* **ˈhagbutter** NOUN

Hagen[1] (ˈhɑːgən) NOUN (in the *Nibelungenlied*) Siegfried's killer, who in turn is killed by Siegfried's wife, Kriemhild.

Hagen[2] (*German* ˈhaːgən) NOUN an industrial city in NW Germany, in North Rhine-Westphalia. Pop.: 206 400 (1999 est.).

hagfish (ˈhægˌfɪʃ) NOUN, *plural* **-fish** *or* **-fishes.** any eel-like marine cyclostome vertebrate of the family *Myxinidae,* having a round sucking mouth and feeding on the tissues of other animals and on dead organic material. Often shortened to **hag.**

Haggadah *or* **Haggodoh** (həˈgɑːdə; *Hebrew* hagaˈdaː, -gɔˈdɔ) NOUN, *plural* **-dahs, -das** *or* **-doth** (*Hebrew* -ˈdoːt). *Judaism* [1] **a** a book containing the order of service of the traditional Passover meal. **b**

the narrative of the Exodus from Egypt that constitutes the main part of that service. ◆ See also **Seder.** 2 another word for **Aggadah.**
▷HISTORY C19: from Hebrew *haggādāh* a story, from *hagged* to tell
▸**haggadic** (həˈgædɪk, -ˈgɑː-) *or* **hagˈgadical** ADJECTIVE

haggadist (həˈgɑːdɪst) NOUN *Judaism* 1 a writer of Aggadoth. 2 an expert in or a student of haggadic literature.
▸**haggadistic** (ˌhægəˈdɪstɪk) ADJECTIVE

Haggai (ˈhægeɪˌaɪ) NOUN *Old Testament* 1 a Hebrew prophet, whose oracles are usually dated between August and December of 520 B.C. 2 the book in which these oracles are contained, chiefly concerned with the rebuilding of the Temple after the Exile. Douay spelling: **Aggeus** (əˈdʒiːəs).

haggard¹ (ˈhægəd) ADJECTIVE 1 careworn or gaunt, as from lack of sleep, anxiety, or starvation. 2 wild or unruly. 3 (of a hawk) having reached maturity in the wild before being caught. ◆ NOUN 4 *Falconry* a hawk that has reached maturity before being caught. Compare **eyas, passage hawk.**
▷HISTORY C16: from Old French *hagard* wild; perhaps related to HEDGE
▸**ˈhaggardly** ADVERB ▸**ˈhaggardness** NOUN

haggard² (ˈhægərd) NOUN (in Ireland and the Isle of Man) an enclosure beside a farmhouse in which crops are stored.
▷HISTORY C16: related to Old Norse *heygarthr,* from *hey* hay + *garthr* yard

haggis (ˈhægɪs) NOUN a Scottish dish made from sheep's or calf's offal, oatmeal, suet, and seasonings boiled in a skin made from the animal's stomach.
▷HISTORY C15: perhaps from *haggen* to HACK¹

haggle (ˈhægᵊl) VERB 1 (*intr;* often foll by *over*) to bargain or wrangle (over a price, terms of an agreement, etc.); barter. 2 (*tr*) *Rare* to hack.
▷HISTORY C16: of Scandinavian origin; compare Old Norse *haggva* to HEW
▸**ˈhaggler** NOUN

hagiarchy (ˈhægɪˌɑːkɪ) NOUN, *plural* **-archies.** 1 government by saints, holy men, or men in holy orders. 2 an order of saints.

hagio- *or before a vowel* **hagi-** COMBINING FORM indicating a saint, saints, or holiness: *hagiography.*
▷HISTORY via Late Latin from Greek, from *hagios* holy

hagiocracy (ˌhægɪˈɒkrəsɪ) NOUN, *plural* **-cies.** 1 government by holy men. 2 a state, community, etc., governed by holy men.

Hagiographa (ˌhægɪˈɒgrəfə) NOUN the third of the three main parts into which the books of the Old Testament are divided in Jewish tradition (the other two parts being the Law and the Prophets), comprising Psalms, Proverbs, Job, the Song of Solomon, Ruth, Lamentations, Ecclesiastes, Esther, Daniel, Ezra, Nehemiah, and Chronicles. Also called: **Writings.**

hagiographer (ˌhægɪˈɒgrəfə) *or* **hagiographist** NOUN 1 a person who writes about the lives of the saints. 2 one of the writers of the Hagiographa.

hagiography (ˌhægɪˈɒgrəfɪ) NOUN, *plural* **-phies.** 1 the writing of the lives of the saints. 2 biography of the saints. 3 any biography that idealizes or idolizes its subject.
▸**hagiographic** (ˌhægɪəˈgræfɪk) *or* **ˌhagioˈgraphical** ADJECTIVE

hagiolatry (ˌhægɪˈɒlətrɪ) NOUN worship or veneration of saints.
▸**ˌhagiˈolater** NOUN ▸**ˌhagiˈolatrous** ADJECTIVE

hagiology (ˌhægɪˈɒlədʒɪ) NOUN, *plural* **-gies.** 1 literature concerned with the lives and legends of saints. 2 **a** a biography of a saint. **b** a collection of such biographies. 3 an authoritative canon of saints. 4 a history of sacred writings.
▸**hagiologic** (ˌhægɪəˈlɒdʒɪk) *or* **ˌhagioˈlogical** ADJECTIVE
▸**ˌhagiˈologist** NOUN

hagioscope (ˈhægɪəˌskəʊp) NOUN *Architect* another name for **squint** (sense 6).
▸**hagioscopic** (ˌhægɪəˈskɒpɪk) ADJECTIVE

hag-ridden ADJECTIVE 1 tormented or worried, as if by a witch. 2 *Facetious* (of a man) harassed by women.

Hague (heɪg) NOUN **The.** the seat of government of the Netherlands and capital of South Holland province, situated about 3 km (2 miles) from the North Sea. Pop.: 440 743 (1999 est.). Dutch names: **'s Gravenhage, Den Haag.**

Hague Tribunal NOUN a tribunal of judges at The Hague, founded in 1899 to provide a panel of arbitrators for international disputes. It also chooses nominees for election by the United Nations to the International Court of Justice. Official name: **Permanent Court of Arbitration.**

hah (hɑː) INTERJECTION a variant spelling of **ha.**

ha-ha¹ (ˈhɑː ˈhɑː) *or* **haw-haw** INTERJECTION 1 a representation of the sound of laughter. 2 an exclamation expressing derision, mockery, surprise, etc.

ha-ha² (ˈhɑː hɑː) *or* **haw-haw** NOUN a wall or other boundary marker that is set in a ditch so as not to interrupt the landscape.
▷HISTORY C18: from French *haha,* probably based on *ha!* ejaculation denoting surprise

hahnium (ˈhɑːnɪəm) NOUN a transuranic element artificially produced from californium. Symbol: Ha; atomic no.: 105; half-life of most stable isotope, ^{262}Ha: 40 seconds.
▷HISTORY C20: named after Otto *Hahn* (1879–1968), German physicist

Haida (ˈhaɪdə) NOUN 1 (*plural* **-das** *or* **-da**) a member of a seafaring group of North American Indian peoples inhabiting the coast of British Columbia and SW Alaska. 2 the language of these peoples, belonging to the Na-Dene phylum.
▸**ˈHaidan** ADJECTIVE

Haiduk, Heyduck, *or* **Heiduc** (ˈhaɪdʊk) NOUN a rural brigand in the European part of the Ottoman Empire.
▷HISTORY C17: from Hungarian *hajdúk* brigands

Haifa (ˈhaɪfə) NOUN a port in NW Israel, near Mount Carmel, on the Bay of Acre: Israel's chief port, with an oil refinery and other heavy industry. Pop.: 265 700 (1999 est.).

haik *or* **haick** (haɪk, heɪk) NOUN an Arab's outer garment of cotton, wool, or silk, for the head and body.
▷HISTORY C18: from Arabic *hā'ik*

haiku (ˈhaɪkuː) *or* **hokku** NOUN, *plural* **-ku.** an epigrammatic Japanese verse form in 17 syllables.
▷HISTORY from Japanese, from *hai* amusement + *ku* verse

hail¹ (heɪl) NOUN 1 small pellets of ice falling from cumulonimbus clouds when there are very strong rising air currents. 2 a shower or storm of such pellets. 3 words, ideas, etc., directed with force and in great quantity: *a hail of abuse.* 4 a collection of objects, esp bullets, spears, etc., directed at someone with violent force. ◆ VERB 5 (*intr;* with *it* as subject) to be the case that hail is falling. 6 (often with *it* as subject) to fall or cause to fall as or like hail: *to hail criticism; bad language hailed about him.*
▷HISTORY Old English *hægl;* related to Old Frisian *heil,* Old High German *hagal* hail, Greek *kakhlēx* pebble

hail² (heɪl) VERB (*mainly tr*) 1 to greet, esp enthusiastically: *the crowd hailed the actress with joy.* 2 to acclaim or acknowledge: *they hailed him as their hero.* 3 to attract the attention of by shouting or gesturing: *to hail a taxi; to hail a passing ship.* 4 (*intr;* foll by *from*) to be a native (of); originate (in): *she hails from India.* ◆ NOUN 5 the act or an instance of hailing. 6 a shout or greeting. 7 distance across which one can attract attention (esp in the phrase **within hail**). ◆ SENTENCE SUBSTITUTE 8 *Poetic* an exclamation of greeting.
▷HISTORY C12: from Old Norse *heill* WHOLE; see HALE¹, WASSAIL
▸**ˈhailer** NOUN

hail-fellow-well-met ADJECTIVE genial and familiar, esp in an offensive or ingratiating way: *a hail-fellow-well-met slap on the back.*

Hail Mary NOUN 1 *RC Church* a prayer to the Virgin Mary, based on the salutations of the angel Gabriel (Luke 1:28) and Elizabeth (Luke 1:42) to her. Also called: **Ave Maria.** 2 *American football, slang* a very long high pass into the end zone, made in the final seconds of a half or of a game.

hailstone (ˈheɪlˌstəʊn) NOUN a pellet of hail.

hailstorm (ˈheɪlˌstɔːm) NOUN a storm during which hail falls.

Hainan (ˈhaɪˈnæn) *or* **Hainan Tao** (taʊ) NOUN an island and province in the South China Sea, separated from the mainland of S China by **Hainan Strait**: part of Guangdong province until 1988; China's second largest offshore island. Pop.: 7 240 000 (1996 est.). Area: 33 572 sq. km (12 962 sq. miles).

Hainaut *or* **Hainault** (*French* ɛno) NOUN a province of SW Belgium: stretches from the Flanders Plain in the north to the Ardennes in the south. Capital: Mons. Pop.: 1 279 467 (2000 est.). Area: 3797 sq. km (1466 sq. miles).

hain't (heɪnt) *Archaic or dialect* CONTRACTION OF has not, have not, *or* is not.

Haiphong (ˈhaɪˈfɒŋ) NOUN a port in N Vietnam, on the Red River delta: a major industrial centre. Pop.: 783 133 (1992 est.).

hair (hɛə) NOUN 1 any of the threadlike pigmented structures that grow from follicles beneath the skin of mammals and consist of layers of dead keratinized cells. 2 a growth of such structures, as on the human head or animal body, which helps prevent heat loss from the body. 3 *Botany* any threadlike outgrowth from the epidermis, such as a root hair. 4 **a** a fabric or material made from the hair of some animals. **b** (*as modifier*): *a hair carpet; a hair shirt.* 5 another word for **hair's-breadth**: *to lose by a hair.* 6 **get in someone's hair.** *Informal* to annoy someone persistently. 7 **hair of the dog (that bit one).** an alcoholic drink taken as an antidote to a hangover. 8 **keep your hair on!** *Brit informal* keep calm. 9 **let one's hair down.** to behave without reserve. 10 **not turn a hair.** to show no surprise, anger, fear, etc. 11 **split hairs.** to make petty and unnecessary distinctions.
▷HISTORY Old English *hær;* related to Old Norse *hār,* Old High German *hār* hair, Norwegian *herren* stiff, hard, Lettish *sari* bristles, Latin *crescere* to grow
▸**ˈhairˌlike** ADJECTIVE

hairball (ˈhɛəˌbɔːl) NOUN a compact mass of hair that forms in the stomach of cats, calves, etc., as a result of licking and swallowing the fur, and causes vomiting, coughing, bloat, weight loss, and depression.

hairbrush (ˈhɛəˌbrʌʃ) NOUN a brush for grooming the hair.

haircloth (ˈhɛəˌklɒθ) NOUN a cloth woven from horsehair, used in upholstery.

haircut (ˈhɛəˌkʌt) NOUN 1 the act or an instance of cutting the hair. 2 the style in which hair has been cut.

hairdo (ˈhɛəˌduː) NOUN, *plural* **-dos.** the arrangement of a person's hair, esp after styling and setting.

hairdresser (ˈhɛəˌdrɛsə) NOUN 1 a person whose business is cutting, curling, colouring and arranging hair, esp that of women. 2 a hairdresser's establishment. ◆ Related adjective: **tonsorial.**
▸**ˈhairˌdressing** NOUN

hairdryer *or* **hairdrier** (ˈhɛəˌdraɪə) NOUN 1 a hand-held electric device that blows out hot air and is used to dry and, sometimes, assist in styling the hair, as in blow-drying. 2 a device for drying the hair in which hot air is blown into a hood that surrounds the head of a seated person.

-haired ADJECTIVE having hair as specified: *long-haired.*

hair follicle NOUN a narrow tubular cavity that contains the root of a hair, formed by an infolding of the epidermis and corium of the skin.

hair gel NOUN a jelly-like substance applied to the hair before styling in order to retain the shape of the style.

hair grass NOUN any grass of the genera *Aira, Deschampsia,* etc., having very narrow stems and leaves.

hairgrip (ˈhɛəˌgrɪp) NOUN *Chiefly Brit* a small tightly bent metal hair clip. Also called (esp US, Canadian, and NZ): **bobby pin.**

hairif (ˈhɛərɪf) NOUN another name for **cleavers.**

hair lacquer NOUN another name for **hairspray.**

hairless (ˈhɛəlɪs) ADJECTIVE 1 having little or no hair. 2 *Brit slang* very angry; raging.

hairline (ˈhɛəˌlaɪn) NOUN 1 the natural margin formed by hair on the head. 2 **a** a very narrow line. **b** (*as modifier*): *a hairline crack.* 3 *Printing* **a** a thin stroke in a typeface. **b** any typeface consisting of such strokes. **c** thin lines beside a character, produced by worn or poorly cast type. 4 a rope or line of hair.

hairline fracture NOUN a very fine crack in a bone.

hairnet (ˈhɛəˌnɛt) NOUN any of several kinds of light netting worn over the hair to keep it in place.

hairpiece (ˈhɛəˌpiːs) NOUN 1 a wig or toupee. 2 Also called: **postiche.** a section of extra hair attached to a woman's real hair to give it greater bulk or length.

hairpin (ˈhɛəˌpɪn) NOUN 1 a thin double-pronged pin used by women to fasten the hair. 2 *(modifier)* (esp of a bend in a road) curving very sharply.

hair-raising ADJECTIVE inspiring horror; terrifying: *a hair-raising drop of 600 feet.*
▸ ˈ**hair-ˌraiser** NOUN

hair restorer NOUN a lotion claimed to promote hair growth.

hair's-breadth NOUN **a** a very short or imperceptible margin or distance. **b** *(as modifier)*: *a hair's-breadth escape.*

hair seal NOUN any earless seal, esp the harbour seal, having a coat of stiff hair with no underfur.

hair sheep NOUN any variety of sheep growing hair instead of wool, yielding hides with a finer and tougher grain than those of wool sheep.

hair shirt NOUN 1 a shirt made of haircloth worn next to the skin as a penance. 2 a secret trouble or affliction.

hair slide NOUN a hinged clip with a tortoiseshell, bone, or similar back, used to fasten the hair.

hair space NOUN *Printing* the thinnest of the metal spaces used in setting type to separate letters or words.

hairsplitting (ˈhɛəˌsplɪtɪŋ) NOUN 1 the making of petty distinctions. ◆ ADJECTIVE 2 occupied with or based on petty distinctions.
▸ ˈ**hairˌsplitter** NOUN

hairspray (ˈhɛəˌspreɪ) NOUN a fixative solution sprayed onto the hair to keep a hairstyle in shape. Also called: **hair lacquer.**

hairspring (ˈhɛəˌsprɪŋ) NOUN *Horology* a very fine spiral spring in some timepieces, which, in combination with the balance wheel, controls the timekeeping.

hairstreak (ˈhɛəˌstriːk) NOUN any small butterfly of the genus *Callophrys* and related genera, having fringed wings marked with narrow white streaks: family *Lycaenidae.*

hair stroke NOUN a very fine line in a written character.

hairstyle (ˈhɛəˌstaɪl) NOUN a particular mode of arranging, cutting, or setting the hair.
▸ ˈ**hairˌstylist** NOUN

hairtail (ˈhɛəˌteɪl) NOUN any marine spiny-finned fish of the family *Trichiuridae,* most common in warm seas, having a long whiplike scaleless body and long sharp teeth. Usual US name: **cutlass fish.**

hair trigger NOUN 1 a trigger of a firearm that responds to very slight pressure. 2 *Informal* **a** any mechanism, reaction, etc., set in operation by slight provocation. **b** *(as modifier)*: *a hair-trigger temper.*

hairweaving (ˈhɛəˌwiːvɪŋ) NOUN the interweaving of false hair with the hair on a balding person's head.

hairworm (ˈhɛəˌwɜːm) NOUN 1 any hairlike nematode worm of the family *Trichostrongylidae,* such as the stomach worm, parasitic in the intestines of vertebrates. 2 Also called: **horsehair worm.** any very thin long worm of the phylum (or class) *Nematomorpha,* the larvae of which are parasitic in arthropods.

hairy (ˈhɛərɪ) ADJECTIVE **hairier, hairiest.** 1 having or covered with hair. 2 *Slang* **a** difficult or problematic. **b** scaring, dangerous, or exciting.
▸ ˈ**hairiness** NOUN

hairyback NOUN (ˈhɛərɪbæk), NOUN *South African slang* an offensive word for an Afrikaner.

hairy frog NOUN a W African frog, *Astylosternus robustus,* the males of which have glandular hairlike processes on the flanks.

hairy willowherb NOUN another name for **codlins-and-cream.**

Haiti (ˈheɪtɪ, hɑːˈiːtɪ) NOUN 1 a republic occupying the W part of the island of Hispaniola in the Caribbean, the E part consisting of the Dominican Republic: ceded by Spain to France in 1697 and became one of the richest colonial possessions in the world, with numerous plantations; slaves rebelled under Toussaint L'Ouverture in 1793 and defeated the French; taken over by the US (1915–41) after long political and economic chaos; under the authoritarian regimes of François Duvalier (1957–71) and his son Jean-Claude Duvalier (1971–86); returned to civilian rule in 1990, but another coup in 1991 brought military rule, which was ended in 1994 with US intervention. Official languages: French and Haitian creole. Religions: Roman Catholic and voodoo. Currency: gourde. Capital: Port-au-Prince. Pop.: 6 965 000 (2001 est.). Area: 27 749 sq. km (10 714 sq. miles). 2 a former name for **Hispaniola.**

Haitian *or* **Haytian** (ˈheɪʃɪən, hɑːˈiːʃən) ADJECTIVE 1 relating to or characteristic of Haiti, its inhabitants, or their language. ◆ NOUN 2 a native, citizen, or inhabitant of Haiti. 3 the creolized French spoken in Haiti.

hajj *or* **hadj** (hædʒ) NOUN, *plural* **hajjes** *or* **hadjes.** the pilgrimage to Mecca that every Muslim is required to make at least once in his life, provided he has enough money and the health to do so.
▷HISTORY from Arabic *hajj* pilgrimage

hajji, hadji, *or* **haji** (ˈhædʒɪ) NOUN, *plural* **hajis, hadjis,** *or* **hajis.** 1 a Muslim who has made a pilgrimage to Mecca: also used as a title. 2 a Christian of the Greek Orthodox or Armenian Churches who has visited Jerusalem.
▸ ˈ**hajjah** (ˈhædʒə) FEMININE NOUN

haka (ˈhɒkə) NOUN *NZ* 1 a Maori war chant accompanied by gestures. 2 a similar performance by a rugby team.
▷HISTORY Maori

hake^{1} (heɪk) NOUN, *plural* **hake** *or* **hakes.** 1 any gadoid food fish of the genus *Merluccius,* such as *M. merluccius* (European hake), of the N hemisphere, having an elongated body with a large head and two dorsal fins. 2 any North American fish of the genus *Urophycis,* similar and related to *Merluccius* species. 3 *Austral* another name for **barracouta.**
▷HISTORY C15: perhaps from Old Norse *haki* hook; compare Old English *hacod* pike; see HOOK

hake^{2} (heɪk) NOUN a wooden frame for drying cheese or fish.
▷HISTORY C18: variant of HECK^{2}

hakea (ˈhɑːkɪə, ˈheɪkɪə) NOUN any shrub or tree of the Australian genus *Hakea,* having a hard woody fruit and often yielding a useful wood: family *Proteaceae.*
▷HISTORY C19: New Latin, named after C. L. von Hake (died 1818), German botanist

Hakenkreuz *German* (ˈhɑːkənˌkrɔɪts) NOUN the swastika.
▷HISTORY literally: hooked cross

hakim *or* **hakeem** (hɑːˈkiːm, ˈhɑːkiːm) NOUN 1 a Muslim judge, ruler, or administrator. 2 a Muslim physician.
▷HISTORY C17: from Arabic, from *hakama* to rule

Hakodate (ˌhɑːkəʊˈdɑːteɪ) NOUN a port in N Japan, on S Hokkaido: fishing industry and shipbuilding. Pop.: 298 868 (1995).

hakuna mathata (ˌhɑːˈkuːnə ˌmɑːˈtɑːtə) SENTENCE SUBSTITUTE no problem.
▷HISTORY from Swahili, there is no difficulty

hal- COMBINING FORM a variant of **halo-** before a vowel.

Halacha, Halaka, *or* **Halakha** (*Hebrew* hɑlɑˈxɑː; *Yiddish* hɑˈloxə) NOUN 1 **a** Jewish religious law. **b** a ruling on some specific matter. 2 **a** that part of the Talmud which is concerned with legal matters as distinct from homiletics. **b** Jewish legal literature in general. ◆ Compare **Aggadah** (sense 1).
▷HISTORY from Hebrew *hălākhāh* way

Halafian (həˈlɑːfɪən) ADJECTIVE of or relating to the Neolithic culture extending from Iran to the Mediterranean.

halal *or* **hallal** (hɑːˈlɑːl) NOUN 1 meat from animals that have been killed according to Muslim law. ◆ ADJECTIVE 2 of or relating to such meat: *a halal butcher.* ◆ VERB **-als, -alling, -alled.** *(tr)* 3 to kill (animals) in this way.
▷HISTORY from Arabic: lawful

halation (həˈleɪʃən) NOUN *Photog* fogging usually seen as a bright ring surrounding a source of light: caused by reflection from the back of the film.
▷HISTORY C19: from HALO + -ATION

halberd (ˈhælbəd) *or* **halbert** (ˈhælbət) NOUN a weapon consisting of a long shaft with an axe blade and a pick, topped by a spearhead: used in 15th- and 16th-century warfare.
▷HISTORY C15: from Old French *hallebarde,* from Middle High German *helm* handle, HELM^{1} + *barde* axe, from Old High German *bart* BEARD
▸ ˌ**halberˈdier** NOUN

Halberstadt (ˈhælbəˌstæt) NOUN a town in central Germany, in Saxony-Anhalt: industrial centre noted for its historic buildings. Pop.: 47 500 (latest est.).

halcyon (ˈhælsɪən) ADJECTIVE *also* **halcyonian** (ˌhælsɪˈəʊnɪən), **halcyonic** (ˌhælsɪˈɒnɪk). 1 peaceful, gentle, and calm. 2 happy and carefree. ◆ NOUN 3 *Greek myth* a fabulous bird associated with the winter solstice. 4 a poetic name for the **kingfisher.** 5 **halcyon days. a** a fortnight of calm weather during the winter solstice. **b** a period of peace and happiness.
▷HISTORY C14: from Latin *alcyon,* from Greek *alkuōn* kingfisher, of uncertain origin

Halcyone (hælˈsaɪənɪ) NOUN a variant of **Alcyone.**

hale^{1} (heɪl) ADJECTIVE 1 healthy and robust (esp in the phrase **hale and hearty**). 2 *Scot and northern English dialect* whole.
▷HISTORY Old English *hæl* WHOLE
▸ ˈ**haleness** NOUN

hale^{2} (heɪl) VERB *(tr)* to pull or drag; haul.
▷HISTORY C13: from Old French *haler,* of Germanic origin; compare Old High German *halōn* to fetch, Old English *geholian* to acquire
▸ ˈ**haler** NOUN

Haleakala (ˌhɑːliːˌɑːkɑːˈlɑː) NOUN a volcano in Hawaii, on E Mani Island. Height: 3057 m (10 032 ft.). Area of crater: 49 sq. km (19 sq. miles). Depth of crater: 829 m (2720 ft.).

haler (ˈhɑːlə) NOUN, *plural* **-lers** *or* **-leru** (-ləˌruː). a variant of **heller** (sense 1).

Halesowen (heɪlzˈəʊɪn) NOUN a town in W central England, in Dudley unitary authority, West Midlands. Pop.: 57 918 (1991).

half (hɑːf) NOUN, *plural* **halves** (hɑːvz). 1 **a** either of two equal or corresponding parts that together comprise a whole. **b** a quantity equalling such a part: *half a dozen.* 2 half a pint, esp of beer. 3 *Scot* a small drink of spirits, esp whisky. 4 *Sport* the half of the pitch regarded as belonging to one team. 5 *Golf* an equal score on a hole or round with an opponent. 6 (in various games) either of two periods of play separated by an interval (the **first half** and **second half**). 7 a half-price ticket on a bus, train, etc. 8 short for **half-hour.** 9 short for **halfpenny** (sense 1). 10 *Sport* short for **halfback.** 11 *Obsolete* a half-year period. 12 **better half.** *Humorous* a person's wife or husband. 13 **by half.** by an excessive amount or to an excessive degree: *he's too arrogant by half.* 14 **by halves.** *(used with a negative)* without being thorough or exhaustive: *we don't do things by halves.* 15 **go halves.** (often foll by *on, in,* etc.) **a** to share the expenses (of something with one other person). **b** to share the whole amount (of something with another person): *to go halves on an orange.* ◆ DETERMINER 16 **a** being a half or approximately a half: *half the kingdom.* **b** *(as pronoun; functioning as singular or plural)*: *half of them came.* ◆ ADJECTIVE 17 not perfect or complete; partial: *he only did a half job on it.* ◆ ADVERB 18 to the amount or extent of a half. 19 to a great amount or extent. 20 partially; to an extent. 21 **half two,** etc. *Informal* 30 minutes after two o'clock. 22 **have half a mind to.** to have the intention of. 23 **not half.** *Informal* **a** not in any way: *he's not half clever enough.* **b** *Brit* really; very; indeed: *he isn't half stupid.* **c** certainly; yes, indeed. ◆ Related prefixes **bi-, demi-, hemi-, semi-.**
▷HISTORY Old English *healf;* related to Old Norse *halfr,* Old High German *halb,* Dutch *half*

half-a-crown NOUN another name for a **half-crown.**

half-a-dollar NOUN *Brit slang* another name for a **half-crown.**

half-and-half NOUN 1 a mixture of half one thing and half another thing. 2 a drink consisting of equal parts of beer and stout, or equal parts of bitter and mild. ◆ ADJECTIVE 3 of half one thing and half another thing. ◆ ADVERB 4 in two equal parts.

half-arsed ADJECTIVE *Slang* incompetent; inept; badly organized.

half-asleep ADJECTIVE neither fully asleep nor awake.

half-assed ADJECTIVE *US and Canadian slang* 1 incompetent; inept. 2 lacking efficiency or organization.

half-awake ADJECTIVE not fully awake.

halfback ('hɑːf,bæk) NOUN 1 *Rugby* either the scrum half or the stand-off half. 2 *Soccer, old-fashioned* any of three players positioned behind the line of forwards and in front of the fullbacks. 3 any of certain similar players in other team sports. 4 the position of a player who is halfback.

half-baked ADJECTIVE 1 insufficiently baked. 2 *Informal* foolish; stupid. 3 *Informal* poorly planned or conceived.

half-ball NOUN **a** a contact in billiards, etc., in which the player aims through the centre of the cue ball to the edge of the object ball, so that half the object ball is covered. **b** (*as modifier*): *a half-ball stroke.*

halfbeak ('hɑːf,biːk) NOUN any marine and freshwater teleost fish of the tropical and subtropical family *Hemiramphidae,* having an elongated body with a short upper jaw and a long protruding lower jaw.

half-binding NOUN a type of hardback bookbinding in which the spine and corners are bound in one material, such as leather, and the sides in another, such as cloth.

half-blind ADJECTIVE having a limited capacity to see.

half-blood NOUN 1 **a** the relationship between individuals having only one parent in common. **b** an individual having such a relationship. 2 a less common name for a **half-breed.** 3 a half-blooded domestic animal.

half-blooded ADJECTIVE 1 being related to another individual through only one parent. 2 having parents of different races. 3 (of a domestic animal) having only one parent of known pedigree.

half-blue NOUN (at Oxford and Cambridge universities) a sportsman who substitutes for a full blue or who represents the university in a minor sport. Compare **blue** (sense 4).

half board NOUN **a** the daily provision by a hotel of bed, breakfast, and one main meal. **b** (*as modifier*): *half-board accommodation.* Also called: **demi-pension.**

half-board NOUN a manoeuvre by a sailing ship enabling it to gain distance to windward by luffing up into the wind.

half-boot NOUN a boot reaching to the midcalf.

half-bottle NOUN a bottle half the size of a standard bottle of wine, spirits, etc.

half-bound ADJECTIVE (of a book) having a half-binding.

half-breed NOUN 1 *Offensive* a person whose parents are of different races, esp the offspring of a White person and an American Indian. ◆ ADJECTIVE *also* **half-bred.** 2 of, relating to, or designating offspring of people or animals of different races or breeds.

half-brother NOUN the son of either of one's parents by another partner.

half-buried ADJECTIVE partially buried: *a ring half-buried in the mud.*

half-butt NOUN a snooker cue longer than an ordinary cue, usually used with a long rest.

half-caste NOUN 1 *Offensive* a person having parents of different races, esp the offspring of a European and an Indian. ◆ ADJECTIVE 2 of, relating to, or designating such a person.

half-century NOUN, *plural* **-ies.** 1 a period of 50 years: *during the past half-century.* 2 **a** a score or grouping of 50: *a half-century of points.* **b** (*as modifier*): *as I near the half-century mark.*

half-circle NOUN 1 **a** one half of a circle. **b** half the circumference of a circle. 2 anything having the shape or form of half a circle.

half-closed ADJECTIVE partially closed: *with half-closed eyes.*

half-cock NOUN 1 on a single-action firearm, a halfway position in which the hammer can be set for safety; in this position the trigger is cocked by the hammer which cannot reach the primer to fire the weapon. 2 **go off at half-cock** *or* **half-cocked. a** to fail as a result of inadequate preparation or premature starting. **b** to act or function prematurely.

half-cocked ADJECTIVE (of a firearm) at half-cock.

half-completed ADJECTIVE (of a job, task, project, etc.) only partially completed.

half-concealed ADJECTIVE partially hidden: *little half-concealed paths.*

half-conscious ADJECTIVE only partially alert and awake.

half-convinced ADJECTIVE not entirely convinced.

half-cooked ADJECTIVE not cooked thoroughly.

half-covered ADJECTIVE partially covered or concealed.

half-crown NOUN a British silver or cupronickel coin worth two shillings and sixpence (now equivalent to 12½p), taken out of circulation in 1970. Also called: **half-a-crown.**

half-cut ADJECTIVE 1 partially severed or divided: *half-cut citrus fruits lying around.* 2 *Informal* intoxicated with alcohol: *he looks half-cut already.*

half-day NOUN a day when one works only in the morning or only in the afternoon.

half-dead ADJECTIVE *Brit informal* very tired.

half-deserted ADJECTIVE (of a place) not having many inhabitants, visitors, etc.

half-digested ADJECTIVE 1 (of food, drink, etc.) partially digested. 2 (of ideas, beliefs, etc.) not entirely assimilated mentally: *half-digested tenets of the latest intellectual fads.*

half-dollar NOUN (in the US) a 50-cent piece.

half-done ADJECTIVE (of a job, task, project, etc.) only partially completed.

half-dozen DETERMINER 1 (preceded by *a*) **a** six or a group of six: *a half-dozen roses.* **b** (*as pronoun; functioning as singular or plural*) *at least a half-dozen.*

half-dressed ADJECTIVE partially clothed.

half-drowned ADJECTIVE 1 nearly dead or killed by immersion in liquid: *half-drowned crewmen lay on the planks.*

half-drunk ADJECTIVE partially intoxicated with alcohol.

half eagle NOUN a former US gold coin worth five dollars.

half-eaten ADJECTIVE (of food, a meal, etc.) partially consumed: *he pushed his half-eaten meal away.*

half-educated ADJECTIVE not having benefited from a comprehensive education.

half-empty ADJECTIVE (of a vessel, place, etc.) holding or containing half its capacity.

half-English ADJECTIVE having partial English citizenship through the nationality of one parent.

half-filled ADJECTIVE (of a vessel, place, etc.) holding or containing half its capacity.

half-finished ADJECTIVE only partially completed: *a half-finished jigsaw puzzle.*

half-forgotten ADJECTIVE having been nearly forgotten: *a half-forgotten dream.*

half-formed ADJECTIVE not or not having been fully formed.

half-forward NOUN *Australian Rules football* any of three forwards positioned between the centre line and the forward line.

half frame NOUN **a** a photograph taking up half the normal area of a frame on a particular film, taken esp on 35-millimetre film. **b** (*as modifier*): *a half-frame camera.*

half-frozen ADJECTIVE 1 extremely cold: *the half-frozen, but still conscious boy.* 2 (of food, ice, etc.) partially defrosted.

half-full ADJECTIVE (of a vessel, place, etc.) holding or containing half its capacity.

half gainer NOUN a type of dive in which the diver completes a half backward somersault to enter the water headfirst facing the diving board. Compare **gainer.**

half-grown ADJECTIVE not yet fully grown.

half-hardy ADJECTIVE (of a cultivated plant) able to survive out of doors except during severe frost.

half-hearted ADJECTIVE without enthusiasm or determination.
▸ ,**half-'heartedly** ADVERB ▸ ,**half-'heartedness** NOUN

half-hitch NOUN a knot made by passing the end of a piece of rope around itself and through the loop thus made.

half holiday NOUN a day of which either the morning or the afternoon is a holiday.

half-hoping ADJECTIVE having or expressing some hope.

half-hour NOUN 1 **a** a period of 30 minutes. **b** (*as modifier*): *a half-hour stint.* 2 **a** the point of time 30 minutes after the beginning of an hour. **b** (*as modifier*): *a half-hour chime.*
▸ ,**half-'hourly** ADVERB, ADJECTIVE

half-human ADJECTIVE having half the properties of, characterizing, or relating to man and mankind.

half-hunter NOUN a watch with a hinged lid in which a small circular opening or crystal allows the approximate time to be read. See **hunter** (sense 5).

half-inch NOUN 1 a measure of length approximately equivalent to 13 millimetres. ◆ VERB 2 *Slang, old-fashioned* to steal.
▷**HISTORY** sense 2: from rhyming slang for PINCH to steal

half-jack NOUN *South African informal* a flat pocket-sized bottle of alcohol.
▷**HISTORY** C20 *jack,* probably from C16 *jack* a leather-covered vessel, from Old French *jaque,* of uncertain origin

half-joking ADJECTIVE said, done, or acting in a seemingly jokey manner, but with some serious intent.
▸ ,**half-'jokingly** ADVERB

half landing NOUN a landing halfway up a flight of stairs.

half-leather NOUN a type of half-binding in which the backs and corners of a book are bound in leather.

half-length ADJECTIVE 1 (of a portrait) showing only the body from the waist up and including the hands. 2 of half the entire or original length. ◆ NOUN 3 a half-length portrait.

half-life NOUN 1 the time taken for half of the atoms in a radioactive material to undergo decay. Symbol: τ. 2 the time required for half of a quantity of radioactive material absorbed by a living tissue or organism to be naturally eliminated (**biological half-life**) or removed by both elimination and decay (**effective half-life**).

half-light NOUN a dim light, as at dawn or dusk.

half-mad ADJECTIVE 1 not entirely sane. 2 extremely upset or distracted: *half-mad with fear.*

half-marathon NOUN a race on foot of 13 miles 352 yards (21.243 kilometres).

half-mast NOUN 1 the lower than normal position to which a flag is lowered on a mast as a sign of mourning or distress. ◆ VERB 2 (*tr*) to put (a flag) in this position.

half measure NOUN (*often plural*) an inadequate measure.

half-mile NOUN 1 **a** half a mile. **b** (*as modifier*): *a half-mile stretch of the river.*

half-miler NOUN a runner who specializes in running races over half a mile or a similar metric distance.

half-minute NOUN 1 **a** 30 seconds. **b** (*as modifier*): *a half-minute lead.* 2 a short period of time; moment: *I'll be a half-minute.*

half-moon NOUN 1 the moon at first or last quarter when half its face is illuminated. 2 the time at which a half-moon occurs. 3 **a** something shaped like a half-moon. **b** (*as modifier*): *half-moon spectacles.* 4 *Anatomy* a nontechnical name for **lunula.**

half-mourning NOUN dark grey clothes worn by some during a period after full formal mourning.

half-naked ADJECTIVE partially clothed: *a half-naked body.*

half-nelson NOUN a wrestling hold in which a wrestler places an arm under one of his opponent's arms from behind and exerts pressure with his palm on the back of his opponent's neck. Compare **full nelson**.

half-note NOUN the usual US and Canadian name for **minim** (sense 2).

half-open ADJECTIVE *Chess* (of a file) having a pawn or pawns of only one colour on it.

half-p NOUN, *plural* **-ps**. an informal name for a **halfpenny** (sense 1).

half-pedalling NOUN a technique of piano playing in which the sustaining pedal is raised and immediately depressed thus allowing the lower strings to continue sounding.

halfpenny *or* **ha'penny** ('heɪpnɪ; *for sense 1* 'hɑːfˌpenɪ) NOUN [1] (*plural* **-pennies**) Also called: **half**. a small British coin worth half a new penny, withdrawn from circulation in 1985. [2] (*plural* **-pennies**) an old British coin worth half an old penny. [3] (*plural* **-pence**) the sum represented by half a penny. [4] (*plural* **-pence**) something of negligible value. [5] (*modifier*) having the value or price of a halfpenny. [6] (*modifier*) of negligible value.

halfpennyworth *or* **ha'p'orth** ('heɪpəθ) NOUN [1] an amount that may be bought for a halfpenny. [2] a trifling or very small amount.

half-pie ADJECTIVE the NZ term for **half-baked** (sense 3).
▷HISTORY from Maori *pai* good

half-pipe NOUN a structure with a U-shaped cross-section, used in performing stunts in skateboarding, snowboarding, rollerblading, etc.

half-plate NOUN *Photog* a size of plate measuring 6½ × 4¼ inches.

half-price ADJECTIVE, ADVERB for half the normal price: *children go half-price*.

half-quartern NOUN *Brit* a loaf having a weight, when baked, of 800 g.

half-remembered ADJECTIVE (of a memory, idea, etc.) partially remembered or recalled.

half-rhyme NOUN a rhyme in which the vowel sounds are not identical, such as *years* and *yours*. See **consonance** (sense 2).

half-right ADJECTIVE not entirely correct: *they were only half-right*.

half-round chisel NOUN a cold chisel with a semicircular cutting edge used for making narrow channels.

half-round file NOUN *Engineering* a file having a semicircular cross-section.

half-ruined ADJECTIVE badly damaged, decayed, or ruined.

half seas over ADJECTIVE *Brit informal* drunk.

half-second NOUN [1] **a** 1/120 of a minute of time. **b** (*as modifier*): *a half-second lead over the Finn*. [2] a very short period of time; moment.

half-section NOUN *Engineering* a scale drawing of a section through a symmetrical object that shows only half the object.

half-serious ADJECTIVE not entirely serious.
▸ˌ**half'seriously** ADVERB

half-silvered ADJECTIVE (of a mirror) having an incomplete reflective coating, so that half the incident light is reflected and half transmitted: used in optical instruments and two-way mirrors.

half-sister NOUN the daughter of either of one's parents by another partner.

half-size NOUN any size, esp in clothing, that is halfway between two sizes.

half-slip NOUN a woman's topless slip that hangs from the waist. Also called: **waist-slip**.

half-smile NOUN a smile that is uncertain or short-lived.

half-sole NOUN [1] a sole from the shank of a shoe to the toe. ◆ VERB [2] (*tr*) to replace the half-sole of (a shoe).

half-starved ADJECTIVE having been deprived of food; malnourished.

half-step NOUN *Music, US and Canadian* another word for **semitone**.

half term NOUN *Brit education* **a** a short holiday midway through an academic term. **b** (*as modifier*): *a half-term holiday*.

half-tide NOUN the state of the tide between flood and ebb.

half-timbered *or* **half-timber** ADJECTIVE (of a building, wall, etc.) having an exposed timber framework filled with brick, stone, or plastered laths, as in Tudor architecture.
▸ˌ**half-'timbering** NOUN

half-time NOUN *Sport* **a** a rest period between the two halves of a game. **b** (*as modifier*): *the half-time score*.

half-title NOUN [1] the short title of a book as printed on the right-hand page preceding the title page. [2] a title on a separate page preceding a section of a book.

halftone ('hɑːfˌtəʊn) NOUN [1] **a** a process used to reproduce an illustration by photographing it through a fine screen to break it up into dots. **b** the etched plate thus obtained. **c** the print obtained from such a plate. [2] *Art* a tonal value midway between highlight and dark shading. ◆ ADJECTIVE [3] relating to, used in, or made by halftone.

half-track NOUN a vehicle with caterpillar tracks on the wheels that supply motive power only.
▸'**half-ˌtracked** ADJECTIVE

half-truth NOUN a partially true statement intended to mislead.
▸'**half-'true** ADJECTIVE

half-used ADJECTIVE having been partially used: *half-used tubes of toothpaste*.

half volley *Sport* ◆ NOUN [1] a stroke or shot in which the ball is hit immediately after it bounces. ◆ VERB **half-volley**. [2] to hit or kick (a ball) immediately after it bounces.

halfway (ˌhɑːf'weɪ) ADVERB, ADJECTIVE [1] at or to half the distance; at or to the middle. [2] in or of an incomplete manner or nature. [3] **meet halfway**. to compromise with.

halfway house NOUN [1] a place to rest midway on a journey. [2] the halfway point in any progression. [3] a centre or hostel designed to facilitate the readjustment to private life of released prisoners, mental patients, etc. [4] *Brit* a compromise: *a halfway house between fixed and floating exchange rates*.

halfwit ('hɑːfˌwɪt) NOUN [1] a feeble-minded person. [2] a foolish or inane person.
▸ˌ**half'witted** ADJECTIVE ▸ˌ**half'wittedly** ADVERB
▸ˌ**half'wittedness** NOUN

half-year NOUN **a** a period of 6 months: *the campaign lasted nearly a half-year*. **b** (*as modifier*): *a half-year break*.

hali- COMBINING FORM a variant of **halo-**.

halibut ('hælɪbət) *or* **holibut** ('hɒlɪbət) NOUN, *plural* **-buts** *or* **-but**. [1] the largest flatfish: a dark green North Atlantic species, *Hippoglossus hippoglossus*, that is a very important food fish: family *Pleuronectidae*. [2] any of several similar and related flatfishes, such as *Reinhardtius hippoglossoides* (**Greenland halibut**).
▷HISTORY C15: from *hali* HOLY (because it was eaten on holy days) + *butte* flat fish, from Middle Dutch *butte*

Haliç (ha'liːtʃ) NOUN the Turkish name for the **Golden Horn**.

Halicarnassian (ˌhælɪkɑː'næsɪən) ADJECTIVE of or relating to the ancient Greek city of Halicarnassus.

Halicarnassus (ˌhælɪkɑː'næsəs) NOUN a Greek colony on the SW coast of Asia Minor: one of the major Hellenistic cities.

halide ('hælaɪd) *or* **halid** ('hælɪd) NOUN [1] a binary compound containing a halogen atom or ion in combination with a more electropositive element. [2] any organic compound containing halogen atoms in its molecules.

halidom ('hælɪdəm) NOUN *Archaic* a holy place or thing.
▷HISTORY Old English *hāligdōm*; see HOLY, -DOM

Halifax ('hælɪˌfæks) NOUN [1] a port in SE Canada, capital of Nova Scotia, on the Atlantic: founded in 1749 as a British stronghold. Pop.: 113 910 (1996). [2] a town in N England, in Calderdale unitary authority, West Yorkshire: textiles. Pop.: 91 069 (1991).

haliplankton ('hælɪˌplæŋktən) NOUN plankton living in sea water.

halite ('hælaɪt) NOUN a colourless or white mineral sometimes tinted by impurities, found in beds as an evaporite. It is used to produce common salt and chlorine. Composition: sodium chloride. Formula: NaCl. Crystal structure: cubic. Also called: **rock salt**.
▷HISTORY C19: from New Latin *halītes*; see HALO-, -ITE[2]

halitosis (ˌhælɪ'təʊsɪs) NOUN the state or condition of having bad breath.
▷HISTORY C19: New Latin, from Latin *hālitus* breath, from *hālāre* to breathe

hall (hɔːl) NOUN [1] a room serving as an entry area within a house or building. [2] (*sometimes capital*) a building for public meetings. [3] (*often capital*) the great house of an estate; manor. [4] a large building or room used for assemblies, worship, concerts, dances, etc. [5] a residential building, esp in a university; hall of residence. [6] **a** a large room, esp for dining, in a college or university. **b** a meal eaten in this room. [7] the large room of a house, castle, etc. [8] *US and Canadian* a passage or corridor into which rooms open. [9] (*often plural*) *Informal* short for **music hall**.
▷HISTORY Old English *heall*; related to Old Norse *höll*, Old High German *halla* hall, Latin *cela* CELL[1], Old Irish *cuile* cellar, Sanskrit *śālā* hut; see HELL

hallah ('hɑːlə; *Hebrew* xa'la) NOUN, *plural* **-lahs** *or* **-lot** (*Hebrew* -'lɔt). a variant spelling of **challah**.

Halle (*German* 'halə) NOUN a city in E central Germany, in Saxony-Anhalt, on the River Saale: early saltworks; a Hanseatic city in the late Middle Ages; university (1694). Pop.: 258 500 (1999 est.). Official name: **Halle an der Saale** (an der 'zaːlə).

Hall effect NOUN the production of a potential difference across a conductor carrying an electric current when a magnetic field is applied in a direction perpendicular to that of the current flow.
▷HISTORY named after Edwin Herbert *Hall* (1855–1938), American physicist who discovered it

Hallel (*Hebrew* hɑ'lel; *Yiddish* hɑː'leɪl) NOUN *Judaism* a section of the liturgy consisting of Psalms 113–18, read during the morning service on festivals, Chanukah, and Rosh Chodesh.
▷HISTORY C18: from Hebrew *hallēl*, from *hellēl* to praise

hallelujah, halleluiah (ˌhælɪ'luːjə), *or* **alleluia** (ˌælɪ'luːjə) INTERJECTION [1] an exclamation of praise to God. [2] an expression of relief or a similar emotion. ◆ NOUN [3] an exclamation of "Hallelujah". [4] a musical composition that uses the word *Hallelujah* as its text.
▷HISTORY C16: from Hebrew *hallelūyāh* praise the Lord, from *hellēl* to praise + *yāh* the Lord, YAHWEH

Halley's Comet NOUN a comet revolving around the sun in a period of about 76 years, last seen in 1985–86, whose return was predicted by Edmund Halley (1656–1742).

halliard ('hæljəd) NOUN a variant spelling of **halyard**.

hallmark ('hɔːlˌmɑːk) NOUN [1] *Brit* an official series of marks, instituted by statute in 1300, and subsequently modified, stamped by the Guild of Goldsmiths at one of its assay offices on gold, silver, or platinum (since 1975) articles to guarantee purity, date of manufacture, etc. [2] a mark or sign of authenticity or excellence. [3] an outstanding or distinguishing feature. ◆ VERB [4] (*tr*) to stamp with or as if with a hallmark. ◆ Also (for senses 1, 4): **platemark**.
▷HISTORY C18: named after Goldsmiths' *Hall* in London, where items were graded and stamped

hallo (hə'ləʊ) SENTENCE SUBSTITUTE, NOUN [1] a variant spelling of **hello**. ◆ SENTENCE SUBSTITUTE, NOUN, VERB [2] a variant spelling of **halloo**.

Hall of Fame NOUN *Chiefly US and Canadian* (*sometimes not capitals*) [1] a building containing plaques or busts honouring famous people. [2] a group of famous people.

hall of residence NOUN a residential block in or attached to a university, college, etc.

halloo (hə'luː), **hallo,** *or* **halloa** (hə'ləʊ) SENTENCE SUBSTITUTE [1] a shout to attract attention, esp to call hounds at a hunt. ◆ NOUN, *plural* **-loos, -los,** *or* **-loas**. [2] a shout of "halloo". ◆ VERB **-loos, -looing, -looed; -los, -loing, -loed,** *or* **-loas, -loaing, -loaed**. [3] to shout (something) to (someone). [4] (*tr*) to urge on or incite (dogs) with shouts.
▷HISTORY C16: perhaps variant of *hallow* to encourage hounds by shouting

halloumi *or* **haloumi** (hə'luːmɪ) NOUN a salty

white sheep's-milk cheese from Greece or Turkey, usually eaten grilled.
▷**HISTORY** probably from Arabic *haluma* be mild

hallow ('hæləʊ) VERB (*tr*) 1 to consecrate or set apart as being holy. 2 to venerate as being holy.
▷**HISTORY** Old English *hālgian,* from *hālig* HOLY
▸ **'hallower** NOUN

hallowed ('hæləʊd; *liturgical* 'hæləʊɪd) ADJECTIVE 1 set apart as sacred. 2 consecrated or holy.
▸ **'hallowedness** NOUN

Halloween *or* **Hallowe'en** (ˌhæləʊ'iːn) NOUN the eve of All Saints' Day celebrated on Oct. 31 by masquerading; Allhallows Eve.
▷**HISTORY** C18: see ALLHALLOWS, EVEN[2]

Hallowmas *or* **Hallowmass** ('hæləʊˌmæs) NOUN *Archaic* the feast celebrating All Saints' Day.
▷**HISTORY** C14: see ALLHALLOWS, MASS

hall stand *or esp US* **hall tree** NOUN a piece of furniture on which are hung coats, hats, etc.

Hallstatt ('hælstæt) *or* **Hallstattian** (hæl'stætɪən) ADJECTIVE of or relating to a late Bronze Age culture extending from central Europe to Britain and lasting from the 9th to the 5th century B.C., characterized by distinctive burial customs, bronze and iron tools, etc.
▷**HISTORY** C19: named after *Hallstatt,* Austrian village where remains were found

hallucinate (hə'luːsɪˌneɪt) VERB (*intr*) to experience hallucinations.
▷**HISTORY** C17: from Latin *ālūcinārī* to wander in mind; compare Greek *aluein* to be distraught
▸ **hal'luciˌnator** NOUN

hallucination (həˌluːsɪ'neɪʃən) NOUN the alleged perception of an object when no object is present, occurring under hypnosis, in some mental disorders, etc.
▸ **halˌluci'national** *or* **hal'lucinative** *or* **hal'lucinatory** ADJECTIVE

hallucinogen (hə'luːsɪnəˌdʒɛn) NOUN any drug, such as LSD or mescaline, that induces hallucinations.

hallucinogenic (həˌluːsɪnəʊ'dʒɛnɪk) ADJECTIVE 1 (of drugs, plants, substances, etc.) inducing hallucinations. 2 having qualities suggestive of hallucination or hallucinogens: *strange, hallucinogenic scenes.*

hallucinosis (həˌluːsɪ'nəʊsɪs) NOUN *Psychiatry* a mental disorder the symptom of which is hallucinations, commonly associated with the ingestion of alcohol or other drugs.

hallux ('hæləks) NOUN the first digit on the hind foot of a mammal, bird, reptile, or amphibian; the big toe of man.
▷**HISTORY** C19: New Latin, from Late Latin *allex* big toe

hallux valgus NOUN an abnormal bending or deviation of the big toe towards the other toes of the same foot.

hallway ('hɔːlˌweɪ) NOUN a hall or corridor.

halm (hɔːm) NOUN a variant spelling of **haulm.**

halma ('hælmə) NOUN a board game in which players attempt to transfer their pieces from their own to their opponents' bases.
▷**HISTORY** C19: from Greek *halma* leap, from *hallesthai* to leap

Halmahera (ˌhælmə'hɪərə) NOUN an island in NE Indonesia, the largest of the Moluccas: consists of four peninsulas enclosing three bays; mountainous and forested. Area: 17 780 sq. km (6865 sq. miles). Dutch name: **Djailolo, Gilolo** *or* **Jilolo.**

Halmstad (*Swedish* 'halmstaːd) NOUN a port in SW Sweden, on the Kattegat. Pop.: 83 080 (1994).

halo ('heɪləʊ) NOUN, *plural* **-loes** *or* **-los.** 1 a disc or ring of light around the head of an angel, saint, etc., as in painting or sculpture. 2 the aura surrounding an idealized, famous, or admired person, thing, or event. 3 a circle of light around the sun or moon, caused by the refraction of light by particles of ice. 4 *Astronomy* a spherical cloud of stars surrounding the Galaxy and other spiral galaxies. ◆ VERB **-loes** *or* **-los, -loing, -loed.** 5 to surround with or form a halo.
▷**HISTORY** C16: from Medieval Latin, from Latin *halōs* circular threshing floor, from Greek
▸ **'halo-ˌlike** ADJECTIVE

halo-, hali-, *or before a vowel* **hal-** COMBINING FORM 1 indicating salt or the sea: *halophyte.* 2 relating to or containing a halogen: *halothane.*
▷**HISTORY** from Greek *hals, hal-* sea, salt

halobiont (ˌhæləʊ'baɪɒnt) NOUN a plant or animal that lives in a salty environment such as the sea.
▷**HISTORY** C20: from HALO- + *-biont* from Greek *bios* life
▸ **ˌhalobi'ontic** ADJECTIVE

halo effect NOUN See **horns and halo effect.**

halogen ('hæləˌdʒɛn) NOUN any of the chemical elements fluorine, chlorine, bromine, iodine, and astatine. They are all monovalent and readily form negative ions.
▷**HISTORY** C19: from Swedish; see HALO-, -GEN
▸ **'halogenˌoid** ADJECTIVE ▸ **halogenous** (hə'lɒdʒɪnəs) ADJECTIVE

halogenate ('hælədʒəˌneɪt) VERB *Chem* to treat or combine with a halogen.
▸ **ˌhalogen'ation** NOUN

haloid ('hælɔɪd) *Chem* ◆ ADJECTIVE 1 resembling or derived from a halogen: *a haloid salt.* ◆ NOUN 2 a compound containing halogen atoms in its molecules; halide.

halon ('hælɒn) NOUN any of a class of chemical compounds derived from hydrocarbons by replacing one or more hydrogen atoms by bromine atoms and other hydrogen atoms by other halogen atoms (chlorine, fluorine, or iodine). Halons are stable compounds that are used in fire extinguishers, although they may contribute to depletion of the ozone layer.

halophile ('hæləʊˌfaɪl) NOUN an organism that thrives in an extremely salty environment, such as the Dead Sea.
▸ **ˌhalo'philic** ADJECTIVE

halophyte ('hæləʊˌfaɪt) NOUN a plant that grows in very salty soil, as in a salt marsh.
▸ **halophytic** (ˌhælə'fɪtɪk) ADJECTIVE ▸ **'haloˌphytism** NOUN

halosere ('hæləʊˌsɪə) NOUN *Ecology* a plant community that originates and develops in conditions of high salinity.

halothane ('hæləʊˌθeɪn) NOUN a colourless volatile slightly soluble liquid with an odour resembling that of chloroform; 2-bromo-2-chloro-1,1,1-trifluoroethane: a general anaesthetic. Formula: $CF_3CHBrCl$.
▷**HISTORY** C20: from HALO- + *-thane,* as in METHANE

haloumi (hə'luːmɪ) NOUN a variant spelling of **halloumi.**

Hälsingborg (*Swedish* hɛlsiŋ'bɔrj) NOUN the former name (until 1971) of **Helsingborg.**

halt[1] (hɔːlt) NOUN 1 an interruption or end to activity, movement, or progress. 2 *Chiefly Brit* a minor railway station, without permanent buildings. 3 **call a halt** (**to**). to put an end (to something); stop. ◆ NOUN, SENTENCE SUBSTITUTE 4 a command to halt, esp as an order when marching. ◆ VERB 5 to come or bring to a halt.
▷**HISTORY** C17: from the phrase *to make halt,* translation of German *halt machen,* from *halten* to HOLD[1], STOP

halt[2] (hɔːlt) VERB (*intr*) 1 (esp of logic or verse) to falter or be defective. 2 to waver or be unsure. 3 *Archaic* to be lame. ◆ ADJECTIVE 4 *Archaic* **a** lame. **b** (*as collective noun;* preceded by *the*): *the halt.* ◆ NOUN 5 *Archaic* lameness.
▷**HISTORY** Old English *healt* lame; related to Old Norse *haltr,* Old High German *halz* lame, Greek *kólos* maimed, Old Slavonic *kladivo* hammer

halter ('hɔːltə) NOUN 1 a rope or canvas headgear for a horse, usually with a rope for leading. 2 Also called: **halterneck.** a style of woman's top fastened behind the neck and waist, leaving the back and arms bare. 3 a rope having a noose for hanging a person. 4 death by hanging. ◆ VERB (*tr*) 5 to secure with a halter or put a halter on. 6 to hang (someone).
▷**HISTORY** Old English *hælfter;* related to Old High German *halftra,* Middle Dutch *heliftra*

haltere ('hæltɪə) *or* **halter** ('hæltə) NOUN, *plural* **halteres** (hæl'tɪəriːz). one of a pair of short projections in dipterous insects that are modified hind wings, used for maintaining equilibrium during flight. Also called: **balancer.**
▷**HISTORY** C18: from Greek *haltēres* (plural) hand-held weights used as balancers or to give impetus in leaping, from *hallesthai* to leap

halting ('hɔːltɪŋ) ADJECTIVE 1 hesitant: *halting speech.* 2 lame.
▸ **'haltingly** ADVERB ▸ **'haltingness** NOUN

Halton ('hɔːltən) NOUN a unitary authority in NW England, in N Cheshire. Pop.: 118 215 (2001). Area: 75 sq. km (29 sq. miles).

halutz *Hebrew* (xa'luts; *English* hɑː'luːts) NOUN a variant spelling of **chalutz.**

halvah, halva ('hælvɑː), *or* **halavah** ('hæləvɑː) NOUN an Eastern Mediterranean, Middle Eastern, or Indian sweetmeat made of honey and containing sesame seeds, nuts, rose water, saffron, etc.
▷**HISTORY** from Yiddish *halva,* from Romanian, from Turkish *helve,* from Arabic *halwā* sweetmeat

halve (hɑːv) VERB (*tr*) 1 to divide into two approximately equal parts. 2 to share equally. 3 to reduce by half, as by cutting. 4 *Golf* to take the same number of strokes on (a hole or round) as one's opponent.
▷**HISTORY** Old English *hielfan;* related to Middle High German *helben;* see HALF

halyard *or* **halliard** ('hæljəd) NOUN *Nautical* a line for hoisting or lowering a sail, flag, or spar.
▷**HISTORY** C14 *halier,* influenced by YARD[1]; see HALE[2]

ham[1] (hæm) NOUN 1 the part of the hindquarters of a pig or similar animal between the hock and the hip. 2 the meat of this part, esp when salted or smoked. 3 *Informal* **a** the back of the leg above the knee. **b** the space or area behind the knee. 4 *Needlework* a cushion used for moulding curves.
▷**HISTORY** Old English *hamm;* related to Old High German *hamma* haunch, Old Irish *cnāim* bone, *camm* bent, Latin *camur* bent

ham[2] (hæm) NOUN 1 *Theatre, informal* **a** an actor who overacts or relies on stock gestures or mannerisms. **b** overacting or clumsy acting. **c** (*as modifier*): *a ham actor.* 2 *Informal* **a** a licensed amateur radio operator. **b** (*as modifier*): *a ham licence.* ◆ VERB **hams, hamming, hammed.** 3 *Informal* to overact.
▷**HISTORY** C19: special use of HAM[1]; in some senses probably influenced by AMATEUR

Hama ('hɑːmɑː) NOUN a city in W Syria, on the Orontes River: an early Hittite settlement; famous for its huge water wheels, used for irrigation since the Middle Ages. Pop.: 264 348 (1994). Biblical name: **Hamath.**

Hamadān *or* **Hamedān** ('hæməˌdæn) NOUN city in W central Iran, at an altitude of over 1830 m (6000 ft.): changed hands several times from the 17th century between Iraq, Persia, and Turkey; trading centre. Pop.: 401 281 (1998).

hamadryad (ˌhæmə'draɪəd, -æd) NOUN 1 *Classical myth* one of a class of nymphs, each of which inhabits a tree and dies with it. 2 another name for **king cobra.**
▷**HISTORY** C14: from Latin *Hamādryas,* from Greek *Hamadruas,* from *hama* together with + *drus* tree; see DRYAD

hamadryas (ˌhæmə'draɪəs) NOUN a baboon, *Papio* (or *Comopithecus*) *hamadryas,* of Arabia and NE Africa, having long silvery hair on the head, neck, and chest: regarded as sacred by the ancient Egyptians: family *Cercopithecidae.* Also called: **hamadryas baboon, sacred baboon.**
▷**HISTORY** C19: via New Latin from Latin; see HAMADRYAD

hamal, hammal, *or* **hamaul** (hə'mɑːl) NOUN (in Middle Eastern countries) a porter, bearer, or servant.
▷**HISTORY** from Arabic *hamala* to carry

Hamamatsu (ˌhæmə'mætsuː) NOUN a city in central Japan, in S central Honshu: cotton textiles and musical instruments. Pop.: 561 568 (1995).

hamamelidaceous (ˌhæməˌmiːlɪ'deɪʃəs, -ˌmɛlɪ-) ADJECTIVE of, relating to, or belonging to the *Hamamelidaceae,* a chiefly subtropical family of trees and shrubs that includes the witch hazel.
▷**HISTORY** C19: from New Latin *Hamamelis* type genus, from Greek: medlar, from *hama* together with + *mēlon* fruit

hamamelis (ˌhæmə'miːlɪs) NOUN any of several trees or shrubs constituting the hamameliaceous genus *Hamamelis,* native to E Asia and North America and cultivated as ornamentals. ◆ See **witch hazel.**

hamartia (hə'mɑːtɪə) NOUN *Literature* the flaw in

character which leads to the downfall of the protagonist in a tragedy.
▷HISTORY C19: from Greek

hamartiology (hə,mɑːtɪˈɒlədʒɪ) NOUN the doctrine of sin in Christian theology.
▷HISTORY C19: from Greek *hamartia* sin + -LOGY

Hamas (ˈhæmæs) NOUN an organization founded in 1987 with the aim of establishing an Islamic state in Palestine.
▷HISTORY C20: Arabic: zeal; also an acronym for *haraka musallaha islamya* Islamic Armed Movement

hamate (ˈheɪmeɪt) ADJECTIVE *Rare* hook-shaped.
▷HISTORY C18: from Latin *hāmātus,* from *hāmus* hook

hamba (ˈhæmbə) INTERJECTION *South African usually offensive* go away; be off.
▷HISTORY from Nguni *ukuttamba* to go

hamba kahle (ˈhæmbə ˈgɑːʃlɪ) SENTENCE SUBSTITUTE goodbye, farewell.
▷HISTORY from Nguni, literally: go well

Hambletonian (,hæmbᵊlˈtəʊnɪən) NOUN one of a breed of trotting horses descended from a stallion of that name.

Hamburg (ˈhæmbɜːg) NOUN a city-state and port in NW Germany, on the River Elbe: the largest port in Germany; a founder member of the Hanseatic League; became a free imperial city in 1510 and a state of the German empire in 1871; university (1919); extensive shipyards. Pop.: 1 701 800 (1999 est.).

hamburger (ˈhæm,bɜːgə) *or* **hamburg** NOUN a flat fried cake of minced beef, often served in a bread roll. Also called: **Hamburger steak, beefburger.**
▷HISTORY C20: shortened from *Hamburger steak* (that is, steak in the fashion of HAMBURG)

hame¹ (heɪm) NOUN either of the two curved bars holding the traces of the harness, attached to the collar of a draught animal.
▷HISTORY C14: from Middle Dutch *hame;* related to Middle High German *hame* fishing rod

hame² (hem) NOUN, ADVERB a Scot word for **home.**

Hameln (*German* ˈhaːməln) NOUN an industrial town in N Germany, in Lower Saxony on the Weser River: famous for the legend of the Pied Piper (supposedly took place in 1284). Pop.: 57 640 (latest est.). English name: **Hamelin** (ˈhæməlɪn, ˈhæmlɪn).

Hamersley Range (ˈhæməzlɪ) NOUN a mountain range in N Western Australia: iron-ore deposits. Highest peak: 1236 m (4056 ft.).

hames (heɪmz) NOUN **make a hames of.** *Irish informal* to spoil through clumsiness or ineptitude.
▷HISTORY of unknown origin

ham-fisted *or* **ham-handed** ADJECTIVE *Informal* lacking dexterity or elegance; clumsy.

Hamhung *or* **Hamheung** (ˈhɑːmˈhʊŋ) NOUN an industrial city in central North Korea: commercial and governmental centre of NE Korea during the Yi dynasty (1392–1910). Pop.: 701 000 (latest est.).

Hamilton (ˈhæməltən) NOUN [1] a port in central Canada, in S Ontario on Lake Ontario: iron and steel industry. Pop.: 322 352 (1996). [2] a city in New Zealand, on central North Island. Pop.: 117 100 (1999 est.). [3] a town in S Scotland, in South Lanarkshire near Glasgow. Pop.: 49 991 (1991). [4] the capital and chief port of Bermuda. Pop.: 1100 (1995 est.). [5] the former name of the **Churchill** River in Labrador.

Hamiltonian (,hæməlˈtəʊnɪən) *Physics, maths* ◆ NOUN [1] a mathematical function of the coordinates and momenta of a system of particles used to express their equations of motion. [2] a mathematical operator that generates such a function. Symbol: H. ◆ ADJECTIVE [3] denoting or relating to the Irish mathematician Sir William Rowan Hamilton (1805–65), or to the theory of mechanics or mathematical operator devised by him.

Hamiltonstovare (,hæmɪltən,stəˈvɑːrɪ) NOUN a large strong short-haired breed of hound with a black, brown, and white coat.
▷HISTORY C20: named after Count Adolf Patrik *Hamilton,* the founder of the Swedish Kennel Club, who created the breed in the 1880s

Hamite (ˈhæmaɪt) NOUN a member of a group of peoples of N Africa supposedly descended from Noah's son Ham (Genesis 5:32, 10:6), including the ancient Egyptians, the Berbers, etc.

Hamitic (hæˈmɪtɪk, hə-) NOUN [1] a group of N African languages related to Semitic. They are now classified in four separate subfamilies of the Afro-Asiatic family: Egyptian, Berber, Cushitic, and Chadic. ◆ ADJECTIVE [2] denoting, relating to, or belonging to this group of languages. [3] denoting, belonging to, or characteristic of the Hamites.

Hamito-Semitic NOUN [1] a former name for the **Afro-Asiatic** family of languages. ◆ ADJECTIVE [2] denoting or belonging to this family of languages.

hamlet (ˈhæmlɪt) NOUN [1] a small village or group of houses. [2] (in Britain) a village without its own church.
▷HISTORY C14: from Old French *hamelet,* diminutive of *hamel,* from *ham,* of Germanic origin; compare Old English *hamm* plot of pasture, Low German *hamm* enclosed land; see HOME

Hamm (*German* ham) NOUN an industrial city in NW Germany, in North Rhine-Westphalia: a Hanse town from 1417; severely damaged in World War II. Pop.: 181 500 (1999 est.).

hammam (hʌmˈɑːm) NOUN a bathing establishment, such as a Turkish bath.
▷HISTORY Arabic: literally, bath

hammer (ˈhæmə) NOUN [1] a hand tool consisting of a heavy usually steel head held transversely on the end of a handle, used for driving in nails, beating metal, etc. [2] any tool or device with a similar function, such as the moving part of a door knocker, the striking head on a bell, etc. [3] a power-driven striking tool, esp one used in forging. A **pneumatic hammer** delivers a repeated blow from a pneumatic ram, a **drop hammer** uses the energy of a falling weight. [4] a part of a gunlock that rotates about a fulcrum to strike the primer or percussion cap, either directly or via a firing pin. [5] *Athletics* **a** a heavy metal ball attached to a flexible wire: thrown in competitions. **b** the event or sport of throwing the hammer. [6] an auctioneer's gavel. [7] a device on a piano that is made to strike a string or group of strings causing them to vibrate. [8] *Anatomy* the nontechnical name for **malleus.** [9] *Curling* the last stone thrown in an end. [10] **go** (*or* **come**) **under the hammer.** to be offered for sale by an auctioneer. [11] **hammer and tongs.** with great effort or energy: *fighting hammer and tongs.* [12] **on someone's hammer.** *Austral and NZ slang* **a** persistently demanding and critical of someone. **b** in hot pursuit of someone. ◆ VERB [13] to strike or beat (a nail, wood, etc.) with or as if with a hammer. [14] (*tr*) to shape or fashion with or as if with a hammer. [15] (*tr; foll by in or into*) to impress or force (facts, ideas, etc.) into (someone) through constant repetition. [16] (*intr*) to feel or sound like hammering: *his pulse was hammering.* [17] (*intr; often foll by away*) to work at constantly. [18] (*tr*) *Brit* **a** to question in a relentless manner. **b** to criticize severely. [19] *Informal* to inflict a defeat on. [20] (*tr*) *Slang* to beat, punish, or chastise. [21] (*tr*) *Stock Exchange* **a** to announce the default of (a member). **b** to cause prices of (securities, the market, etc.) to fall by bearish selling. ◆ See also **hammer out.**
▷HISTORY Old English *hamor;* related to Old Norse *hamarr* crag, Old High German *hamar* hammer, Old Slavonic *kamy* stone
▸ˈ**hammerer** NOUN ▸ˈ**hammer-,like** ADJECTIVE

hammer and sickle NOUN [1] the emblem on the flag of the former Soviet Union, representing the industrial workers and the peasants respectively. [2] a symbolic representation of the former Soviet Union or of Communism in general.

hammer beam NOUN either of a pair of short horizontal beams that project from opposite walls to support arched braces and struts.

hammer blow NOUN [1] a blow from a hammer. [2] a severe shock or setback: *Liam's death was a hammer blow.*

hammer drill NOUN [1] a rock drill operated by compressed air in which the boring bit is not attached to the reciprocating piston. [2] an electric hand drill providing hammering in addition to rotating action.

Hammerfest (*Norwegian* ˈhamərfɛst) NOUN a port in N Norway, on the W coast of Kvalöy Island: the northernmost town in Europe, with uninterrupted daylight from May 17 to July 29 and no sun between Nov. 21 and Jan. 21; fishing and tourist centre. Pop.: 6900 (1991).

hammerhead (ˈhæmə,hɛd) NOUN [1] any shark of the genus *Sphyrna* and family *Sphyrnidae,* having a flattened hammer-shaped head. [2] a heavily built tropical African wading bird, *Scopus umbretta,* related to the herons, having a dark plumage and a long backward-pointing crest: family *Scopidae,* order *Ciconiiformes.* [3] a large African fruit bat, *Hypsignathus monstrosus,* with a large square head and hammer-shaped muzzle.
▸ˈ**hammer,headed** ADJECTIVE

hammerless (ˈhæməlɪs) ADJECTIVE (of a firearm) having the hammer enclosed so that it is not visible.

hammerlock (ˈhæmə,lɒk) NOUN a wrestling hold in which a wrestler twists his opponent's arm upwards behind his back.

hammer out VERB (*tr, adverb*) [1] to shape or remove with or as if with a hammer. [2] to form or produce (an agreement, plan, etc.) after much discussion or dispute.

hammer price NOUN the price offered as the winning bid in a public auction.

Hammersmith and Fulham (ˈhæmə,smɪθ) NOUN a borough of Greater London on the River Thames: established in 1965 by the amalgamation of Fulham and Hammersmith. Pop.: 165 243 (2001). Area: 16 sq. km (6 sq. miles).

hammerstone (ˈhæmə,stəʊn) NOUN a stone used as a hammer in the production of tools during the Acheulian period.

hammertoe (ˈhæmə,təʊ) NOUN [1] a deformity of the bones of a toe causing the toe to be bent in a clawlike arch. [2] such a toe.

hammock¹ (ˈhæmək) NOUN a length of canvas, net, etc., suspended at the ends and used as a bed.
▷HISTORY C16: from Spanish *hamaca,* of Taino origin
▸ˈ**hammock-,like** ADJECTIVE

hammock² (ˈhæmək) NOUN a variant of **hummock** (sense 3).

Hammond (ˈhæmənd) NOUN a city in NW Indiana, adjacent to Chicago. Pop.: 83 048 (2000).

Hammond organ NOUN *Trademark* an electric organ with two keyboards, electronic tone generation, and a wide variety of tone colours: invented in 1934.
▷HISTORY C20: named after Laurens *Hammond* (1895–1973), US mechanical engineer

hammy (ˈhæmɪ) ADJECTIVE **-mier, -miest.** *Informal* [1] (of an actor) overacting or tending to overact. [2] (of a play, performance, etc.) overacted or exaggerated.

hamper¹ (ˈhæmpə) VERB [1] (*tr*) to prevent the progress or free movement of. ◆ NOUN [2] *Nautical* gear aboard a vessel that, though essential, is often in the way.
▷HISTORY C14: of obscure origin; perhaps related to Old English *hamm* enclosure, *hemm* HEM¹
▸ˈ**hamperedness** NOUN ▸ˈ**hamperer** NOUN

hamper² (ˈhæmpə) NOUN [1] a large basket, usually with a cover. [2] *Brit* such a basket and its contents, usually food. [3] *US* a laundry basket.
▷HISTORY C14: variant of HANAPER

Hampshire (ˈhæmp,ʃɪə, -ʃə) NOUN a county of S England, on the English Channel: crossed by the **Hampshire Downs** and the South Downs, with the New Forest in the southwest and many prehistoric and Roman remains: the geographical and ceremonial county includes Portsmouth and Southampton, which became independent unitary authorities in 1997. Administrative centre: Winchester. Pop. (excluding unitary authorities): 1 240 032 (2001). Area (excluding unitary authorities): 3679 sq. km (1420 sq. miles). Abbreviation: **Hants.**

Hampshire Down NOUN a breed of stocky sheep having a dark face and dense close wool, originating from Hampshire, S England.

Hampstead (ˈhæmpstɪd) NOUN a residential district in N London: part of the Greater London borough of Camden since 1965; nearby is **Hampstead Heath,** a popular recreation area.

Hampton (ˈhæmptən) NOUN [1] a city in SE Virginia, on the harbour of **Hampton Roads** on Chesapeake Bay. Pop.: 146 437 (2000). [2] a district of the Greater London borough of Richmond-upon-Thames, on the River Thames: famous for **Hampton Court Palace** (built in 1515 by Cardinal Wolsey).

hamshackle ('hæmʃæk^{ə}l) VERB (*tr*) to hobble (a cow, horse, etc.) by tying a rope around the head and one of the legs.

hamster ('hæmstə) NOUN any Eurasian burrowing rodent of the tribe *Cricetini,* such as *Mesocricetus auratus* (**golden hamster**), having a stocky body, short tail, and cheek pouches: family *Cricetidae.* They are popular pets.
▷HISTORY C17: from German, from Old High German *hamustro,* of Slavic origin

hamstring ('hæm,strɪŋ) NOUN [1] *Anatomy* any of the tendons at the back of the knee. Related adjective: **popliteal.** [2] the large tendon at the back of the hock in the hind leg of a horse, etc. ◆ VERB **-strings, -stringing, -strung.** (*tr*) [3] to cripple by cutting the hamstring of. [4] to ruin or thwart.
▷HISTORY C16: HAM[1] + STRING

hamulus ('hæmjʊləs) NOUN, *plural* **-li** (-,laɪ). *Biology* a hook or hooklike process at the end of some bones or between the fore and hind wings of a bee or similar insect.
▷HISTORY C18: from Latin: a little hook, from *hāmus* hook
▸ **'hamular** *or* **'hamu,late** *or* **'hamu,lose** *or* **'hamulous** ADJECTIVE

hamza *or* **hamzah** ('hɑːmzɑː, -zə) NOUN the sign used in Arabic to represent the glottal stop.
▷HISTORY from Arabic *hamzah,* literally: a compression

Han (hæn) NOUN a river in E central China, rising in S Shaanxi and flowing southeast through Hubei to the Yangtze River at Wuhan. Length: about 1450 km (900 miles).

hanaper ('hænəpə) NOUN a small wickerwork basket, often used to hold official papers.
▷HISTORY C15: from Old French *hanapier,* from *hanap* cup, of Germanic origin; compare Old High German *hnapf* bowl, Old English *hnæp*

Hanau (*German* 'haːnau) NOUN a city in central Germany, in Hesse east of Frankfurt am Main: a centre of the jewellery industry. Pop.: 84 420 (latest est.).

hance (hæns) NOUN a variant of **haunch** (sense 3).

Han Cities PLURAL NOUN a group of three cities in E central China, in SE Hubei at the confluence of the Han and Yangtze Rivers: Hanyang, Hankow, and Wuchang; united in 1950 to form the conurbation of Wuhan, the capital of Hubei province.

hand (hænd) NOUN [1] **a** the prehensile part of the body at the end of the arm, consisting of a thumb, four fingers, and a palm. **b** the bones of this part. Related adjective: **manual.** [2] the corresponding or similar part in animals. [3] something resembling this in shape or function. [4] **a** the cards dealt to one or all players in one round of a card game. **b** a player holding such cards. **c** one round of a card game. [5] agency or influence: *the hand of God.* [6] a part in something done: *he had a hand in the victory.* [7] assistance: *to give someone a hand with his work.* [8] a pointer on a dial, indicator, or gauge, esp on a clock: *the minute hand.* [9] acceptance or pledge of partnership, as in marriage: *he asked for her hand; he gave me his hand on the merger.* [10] a position or direction indicated by its location to the side of an object or the observer: *on the right hand; on every hand.* [11] a contrastive aspect, condition, etc. (in the phrases **on the one hand, on the other hand**). [12] (preceded by an ordinal number) source or origin: *a story heard at third hand.* [13] a person, esp one who creates something: *a good hand at painting.* [14] a labourer or manual worker: *we've just taken on a new hand at the farm.* [15] a member of a ship's crew: *all hands on deck.* [16] *Printing* another name for **index** (sense 9). [17] a person's handwriting: *the letter was in his own hand.* [18] a round of applause: *give him a hand.* [19] ability or skill: *a hand for woodwork.* [20] a manner or characteristic way of doing something: *the hand of a master.* [21] a unit of length measurement equalling four inches, used for measuring the height of horses, usually from the front hoof to the withers. [22] a cluster or bundle, esp of bananas. [23] a shoulder of pork. [24] one of the two possible mirror-image forms of an asymmetric object, such as the direction of the helix in a screw thread. [25] **a free hand.** freedom to do as desired. [26] **a hand's turn.** (*usually used with a negative*) a small amount of work: *he hasn't done a hand's turn.* [27] **a heavy hand.** tyranny, persecution, or oppression: *he ruled with a heavy hand.* [28] **a high hand.** an oppressive or dictatorial manner. [29] **(near) at hand.** very near or close, esp in time. [30] **at someone's hand(s).** from: *the acts of kindness received at their hands.* [31] **by hand. a** by manual rather than mechanical means. **b** by messenger or personally: *the letter was delivered by hand.* [32] **come to hand.** to become available; be received. [33] **force someone's hand.** to force someone to act. [34] **from hand to hand.** from one person to another. [35] **from hand to mouth. a** in poverty: *living from hand to mouth.* **b** without preparation or planning. [36] **hand and foot.** in all ways possible; completely: *they waited on him hand and foot.* [37] **hand in glove.** in an intimate relationship or close association. [38] **hand in hand. a** together; jointly. **b** clasping each other's hands. [39] **hand over fist.** steadily and quickly; with rapid progress: *he makes money hand over fist.* [40] **hold one's hand.** to stop or postpone a planned action or punishment. [41] **hold someone's hand.** to support, help, or guide someone, esp by giving sympathy or moral support. [42] **in hand. a** in possession. **b** under control. **c** receiving attention or being acted on. **d** available for use; in reserve. **e** with deferred payment: *he works a week in hand.* [43] **keep one's hand in.** to continue or practise. [44] **lend a hand.** to help. [45] **on hand.** close by; present: *I'll be on hand to help you.* [46] **out of hand. a** beyond control. **b** without reservation or deeper examination: *he condemned him out of hand.* [47] **set one's hand to. a** to sign (a document). **b** to start (a task or undertaking). [48] **show one's hand.** to reveal one's stand, opinion, or plans. [49] **take in hand.** to discipline; control. [50] **throw one's hand in.** See **throw in** (sense 3). [51] **to hand.** accessible. [52] **try one's hand.** to attempt to do something. [53] (*modifier*) **a** of or involving the hand: *a hand grenade.* **b** made to be carried in or worn on the hand: *hand luggage.* **c** operated by hand: *a hand drill.* [54] (*in combination*) made by hand rather than by a machine: *hand-sewn.* ◆ VERB (*tr*) [55] to transmit or offer by the hand or hands. [56] to help or lead with the hand. [57] *Nautical* to furl (a sail). [58] **hand it to someone.** to give credit to someone. ◆ See also **hand down, hand in, hand-off, hand on, hand-out, hand over, hands.**
▷HISTORY Old English *hand;* related to Old Norse *hönd,* Gothic *handus,* Old High German *hant*
▸ **'handless** ADJECTIVE ▸ **'hand,like** ADJECTIVE

HAND *Text messaging* ABBREVIATION FOR have a nice day.

handba' ('handbɔ:, -bɑː) NOUN *Scot* another name for **ba'** (sense 2).

handbag ('hænd,bæg) NOUN [1] Also called: **bag, purse** (US and Canadian), **pocketbook** (chiefly US). a woman's small bag carried to contain personal articles. [2] a small suitcase that can be carried by hand. [3] a commercial style of House music.
▷HISTORY (for sense 3) C20: humorous allusion to the trend for groups of women to dance round their handbags in discos, nightclubs, etc.

handbags ('hænd,bægz) PLURAL NOUN *Facetious* an incident in which people, esp sportsmen, fight or threaten to fight, but without real intent to inflict harm (esp in the phrases **handbags at dawn, handbags at twenty paces,** etc.).

handball ('hænd,bɔːl) NOUN [1] a game in which two teams of seven players try to throw a ball into their opponent's goal. [2] a game in which two or four people strike a ball against a wall or walls with the hand, usually gloved. [3] the small hard rubber ball used in this game. [4] *Soccer* the offence committed when a player other than a goalkeeper in his own penalty area touches the ball with a hand. ◆ VERB [5] *Australian Rules football* to pass (the ball) with a blow of the fist.
▸ **'hand,baller** NOUN

handbarrow ('hænd,bærəʊ) NOUN a flat tray for transporting loads, usually carried by two men.

handbell ('hænd,bɛl) NOUN a bell rung by hand, esp one of a tuned set used in musical performance.

handbill ('hænd,bɪl) NOUN a small printed notice for distribution by hand.

handbook ('hænd,bʊk) NOUN a reference book listing brief facts on a subject or place or directions for maintenance or repair, as of a car: *a tourists' handbook.*

handbrake ('hænd,breɪk) NOUN [1] a brake operated by a hand lever. [2] the lever that operates the handbrake.

handbrake turn NOUN a turn sharply reversing the direction of a vehicle by speedily applying the handbrake while turning the steering wheel.

handbreadth ('hænd,brɛtθ, -,brɛdθ) *or* **hand's-breadth** NOUN the width of a hand used as an indication of length.

h and c ABBREVIATION FOR hot and cold (water).

handcart ('hænd,kɑːt) NOUN a simple cart, usually with one or two wheels, pushed or drawn by hand.

handclasp ('hænd,klɑːsp) NOUN *US* another word for **handshake.**

handcraft ('hænd,krɑːft) NOUN [1] another word for **handicraft.** ◆ VERB [2] (*tr*) to make by handicraft.

handcrafted ('hænd,krɑːftɪd) ADJECTIVE made by handicraft.

handcuff ('hænd,kʌf) VERB [1] (*tr*) to put handcuffs on (a person); manacle. ◆ NOUN [2] (*plural*) a pair of locking metal rings joined by a short bar or chain for securing prisoners, etc.

hand down VERB (*tr, adverb*) [1] to leave to a later period or generation; bequeath. [2] to pass (an outgrown garment) on from one member of a family to a younger one. [3] *Law* to announce or deliver (a verdict).

-handed ADJECTIVE [1] having a hand or hands as specified: *broad-handed; a four-handed game of cards.* [2] made as specified for either left- or right-hand operation or positioning.

handedness ('hændɪdnɪs) NOUN [1] the tendency to use one hand more skilfully or in preference to the other. [2] the property of some chemical substances of rotating the plane of polarized light in one direction rather than another. See also **dextrorotation, laevorotation.** [3] the relation between the vectors of spin and momentum of neutrinos and certain other elementary particles. See also **helicity.**

handfast ('hænd,fɑːst) *Archaic* ◆ NOUN [1] an agreement, esp of marriage, confirmed by a handshake. [2] a firm grip. ◆ VERB (*tr*) [3] to betroth or marry (two persons or another person) by joining the hands. [4] to grip with the hand.

handfasting ('hænd,fɑːstɪŋ) NOUN [1] an archaic word for **betrothal.** [2] (formerly) a kind of trial marriage marked by the formal joining of hands.

handfeed ('hænd,fiːd) VERB **-feeds, -feeding, -fed** (-,fɛd). (*tr*) [1] to feed (a person or an animal) by hand. [2] *Agriculture* to give food to (poultry or livestock) in fixed amounts and at fixed times, rather than use a self-feeding system.

hand, foot, and mouth disease NOUN a usually mild disease, mainly affecting children under seven, in which the sufferers develop mouth ulcers accompanied by blisters or rashes on their hands and feet. Caused by the Coxsackie virus A16, it has no known cure. Abbreviation: **HFMD.**

handful ('hændfʊl) NOUN, *plural* **-fuls.** [1] the amount or number that can be held in the hand. [2] a small number or quantity. [3] *Informal* a person or thing difficult to manage or control.

hand glass NOUN [1] a magnifying glass with a handle. [2] a small mirror with a handle. [3] a small glazed frame for seedlings or plants.

hand grenade NOUN a small metal or plastic canister containing explosives, usually activated by a short fuse and used in close combat.

handgrip ('hænd,grɪp) NOUN [1] another word for **grip**[1] (senses 2, 5, and 6). [2] *Sport* a covering, usually of towelling or rubber, that makes the handle of a racket or club easier to hold.

handgun ('hænd,gʌn) NOUN a firearm that can be held, carried, and fired with one hand, such as a pistol.

hand-held ADJECTIVE [1] held in position by the hand. [2] (of a film camera) held rather than mounted, as in close-up action shots. [3] (of a computer) able to be held in the hand and not requiring connection to a fixed power source. ◆ NOUN [4] a computer that can be held in the hand.

handhold ('hænd,həʊld) NOUN [1] an object, crevice, etc., that can be used as a grip or support, as in climbing. 2 a grip or secure hold with the hand or hands.

handicap ('hændɪˌkæp) NOUN 1 something that hampers or hinders. 2 **a** a contest, esp a race, in which competitors are given advantages or disadvantages of weight, distance, time, etc., in an attempt to equalize their chances of winning. **b** the advantage or disadvantage prescribed. 3 *Golf* the number of strokes by which a player's averaged score exceeds the standard scratch score for the particular course: used as the basis for handicapping in competitive play. 4 any physical disability or disadvantage resulting from physical, mental, or social impairment or abnormality. ◆ VERB **-caps, -capping, -capped**. (*tr*) 5 to be a hindrance or disadvantage to. 6 to assign a handicap or handicaps to. 7 to organize (a contest) by handicapping. 8 *US and Canadian* **a** to attempt to forecast the winner of (a contest, esp a horse race). **b** to assign odds for or against (a contestant).
▷HISTORY C17: probably from *hand in cap*, a lottery game in which players drew forfeits from a cap or deposited money in it
▸ **'handiˌcapper** NOUN

handicapped ('hændɪˌkæpt) ADJECTIVE 1 physically disabled. 2 *Psychol* denoting a person whose social behaviour or emotional reactions are in some way impaired. 3 (of a competitor) assigned a handicap.

handicapper ('hændɪˌkæpə) NOUN 1 an official appointed to assign handicaps to competitors in such sports as golf and horse racing. 2 a newspaper columnist employed to estimate the chances that horses have of winning races.

handicap register NOUN *Social welfare* (in Britain) 1 a list of the handicapped people in its area that a local authority has a duty to compile under the Chronically Sick and Disabled Persons Act 1970. Eligibility for certain welfare benefits may depend on registration. 2 a different list of handicapped people, kept by the Manpower Services Commission for employment purposes. See also **green card, registered disabled.**

handicraft ('hændɪˌkrɑːft) NOUN 1 skill or dexterity in working with the hands. 2 a particular skill or art performed with the hands, such as weaving, pottery, etc. 3 the work produced by such a skill or art: *local handicraft is on sale*. Also called: **handcraft.**
▷HISTORY C15: changed from HANDCRAFT through the influence of HANDIWORK, which was analysed as if HANDY + WORK
▸ **'handiˌcraftsman** NOUN

handily ('hændɪlɪ) ADVERB 1 in a handy way or manner. 2 conveniently or suitably: *handily nearby*. 3 *US and Canadian* easily: *the horse won handily*.

hand in VERB (*tr, adverb*) to return or submit (something, such as an examination paper).

handiwork ('hændɪˌwɜːk) NOUN 1 work performed or produced by hand, such as embroidery or pottery. 2 the result of the action or endeavours of a person or thing.
▷HISTORY Old English *handgeweorc*, from HAND + *geweorc*, from *ge-* (collective prefix) + *weorc* WORK

handkerchief ('hæŋkətʃɪf, -tʃiːf) NOUN a small square of soft absorbent material, such as linen, silk, or soft paper, carried and used to wipe the nose, etc.

hand-knit ADJECTIVE *also* **hand-knitted.** 1 knitted by hand, not on a machine. ◆ VERB **-knits, -knitting, -knitted** *or* **-knit.** 2 to knit (garments) by hand.

handlanger ('hændˌlæŋə) NOUN *South African* an unskilled assistant to a tradesman.
▷HISTORY from Dutch

handle ('hændᵊl) NOUN 1 the part of a utensil, drawer, etc., designed to be held in order to move, use, or pick up the object. 2 *NZ* a glass beer mug with a handle. 3 *Slang* a person's name or title. 4 a CB radio slang name for **call sign.** 5 an opportunity, reason, or excuse for doing something: *his background served as a handle for their mockery*. 6 the quality, as of textiles, perceived by touching or feeling. 7 the total amount of a bet on a horse race or similar event. 8 **fly off the handle.** *Informal* to become suddenly extremely angry. ◆ VERB (*mainly tr*) 9 to pick up and hold, move, or touch with the hands. 10 to operate or employ using the hands: *the boy handled the reins well*. 11 to have power or control over: *my wife handles my investments*. 12 to manage successfully: *a secretary must be able to handle clients*. 13 to discuss (a theme, subject, etc.). 14 to deal with or treat in a specified way: *I was handled with great tact*. 15 to trade or deal in (specified merchandise). 16 (*intr*) to react or respond in a specified way to operation or control: *the car handles well on bends*.
▷HISTORY Old English; related to Old Saxon *handlon* (vb), Old High German *hantilla* towel
▸ **'handleable** ADJECTIVE ▸ **'handled** ADJECTIVE ▸ **'handleless** ADJECTIVE

handlebar moustache ('hændᵊlˌbɑː) NOUN a bushy extended moustache with curled ends that resembles handlebars.

handlebars ('hændᵊlˌbɑːz) PLURAL NOUN (*sometimes singular*) a metal tube having its ends curved to form handles, used for steering a bicycle, motorcycle, etc.

handler ('hændlə) NOUN 1 a person, esp a police officer, in charge of a specially trained dog. 2 a person who handles some specified thing: *a baggage handler*. 3 a person who holds or incites a dog, gamecock, etc., esp in a race or contest. 4 the trainer or second of a boxer.

handling ('hændlɪŋ) NOUN 1 the act or an instance of picking up, turning over, or touching something. 2 treatment, as of a theme in literature. 3 **a** the process by which a commodity is packaged, transported, etc. **b** (*as modifier*): *handling charges*. 4 *Law* the act of receiving property that one knows or believes to be stolen.

hand-loomed ADJECTIVE (of a garment) made on a hand loom.

handmade (ˌhænd'meɪd) ADJECTIVE made by hand, not by machine, esp with care or craftsmanship.

handmaiden ('hændˌmeɪdᵊn) *or* **handmaid** NOUN 1 a person or thing that serves a useful but subordinate purpose: *logic is the handmaid of philosophy*. 2 *Archaic* a female servant or attendant.

hand-me-down NOUN *Informal* 1 **a** something, esp an outgrown garment, passed down from one person to another. **b** (*as modifier*): *a hand-me-down dress*. 2 **a** anything that has already been used by another. **b** (*as modifier*): *hand-me-down ideas*.

hand-off *Rugby* ◆ NOUN 1 the act of warding off an opposing player with the open hand. ◆ VERB **hand off.** 2 (*tr, adverb*) to ward off (an opponent) using a hand-off.

hand on VERB (*tr, adverb*) to pass to the next in a succession.

hand organ NOUN another name for **barrel organ.**

hand-out NOUN, *plural* **hand-outs.** 1 clothing, food, or money given to a needy person. 2 a leaflet, free sample, etc., given out to publicize something. 3 a statement or other document distributed to the press or an audience to confirm, supplement, or replace an oral presentation. ◆ VERB **hand out.** (*tr, adverb*) 4 to distribute.

hand over VERB (*tr, adverb*) 1 to surrender possession of; transfer. ◆ NOUN **handover.** 2 a transfer, surrender.

hand-pick VERB (*tr*) to choose or select with great care, as for a special job or purpose.

hand-picked ADJECTIVE selected with great care, as for a special job or purpose; chosen.

hand-piece NOUN *Austral and NZ* hand-held, power-operated shears used by a shearer. See also **comb** (sense 3).

handrail ('hændˌreɪl) NOUN a rail alongside a stairway, etc., at a convenient height to be grasped to provide support.

hands (hændz) PLURAL NOUN 1 power or keeping: *your welfare is in his hands*. 2 Also called: **handling.** *Soccer* the infringement of touching the ball with any part of the hand or arm. 3 **change hands.** to pass from the possession of one person or group to another. 4 **clean hands.** freedom from guilt. 5 **hands down.** without effort; easily. 6 **hands off.** do not touch or interfere. 7 **hands up!** raise the hands above the level of the shoulders, an order usually given by an armed robber to a victim, etc. 8 **have one's hands full. a** to be completely occupied. **b** to be beset with problems. 9 **have one's hands tied.** to be wholly unable to act. 10 **in good hands.** in protective care. 11 **join hands.** See **join** (sense 12). 12 **lay hands on** *or* **upon. a** to seize or get possession of. **b** to beat up; assault. **c** to find: *I just can't lay my hands on it anywhere*. **d** *Christianity* to confirm or ordain by the imposition of hands. 13 **off one's hands.** for which one is no longer responsible. 14 **on one's hands. a** for which one is responsible: *I've got too much on my hands to help*. **b** to spare: *time on my hands*. 15 **out of one's hands.** no longer one's responsibility. 16 **throw up one's hands.** to give up in despair. 17 **wash one's hands of.** to have nothing more to do with.

handsaw ('hændˌsɔː) NOUN any saw for use in one hand only.

hand's-breadth NOUN another name for **handbreadth.**

handsel *or* **hansel** ('hænsᵊl) *Archaic or dialect* ◆ NOUN 1 a gift for good luck at the beginning of a new year, new venture, etc. ◆ VERB **-sels, -selling, -selled** *or US* **-sels, -seling, -seled.** (*tr*) 2 to give a handsel to (a person). 3 to begin (a venture) with ceremony; inaugurate.
▷HISTORY Old English *handselen* delivery into the hand; related to Old Norse *handsal* promise sealed with a handshake, Swedish *handsöl* gratuity; see HAND, SELL

handset ('hændˌsɛt) NOUN a telephone mouthpiece and earpiece mounted so that they can be held simultaneously to mouth and ear.

hand setting NOUN *Printing* text matter composed in metal type by hand, rather than by machine.

handshake ('hændˌʃeɪk) NOUN the act of grasping and shaking a person's hand, as when being introduced or agreeing on a deal.

handshaking ('hændˌʃeɪkɪŋ) NOUN *Computing* communication between a computer system and an external device, by which each tells the other that data is ready to be transferred, and that the receiver is ready to accept it.

hands-off ADJECTIVE (of a machine, device, etc.) without need of manual operation.

handsome ('hændsəm) ADJECTIVE 1 (of a man) good-looking, esp in having regular, pleasing, and well-defined features. 2 (of a woman) fine-looking in a dignified way. 3 well-proportioned, stately, or comely: *a handsome room*. 4 liberal or ample: *a handsome allowance*. 5 gracious or generous: *a handsome action*. 6 *Southwest English* pleasant: *handsome weather*. ◆ NOUN 7 *Southwest English* a term of endearment for a beloved person, esp in **my handsome.**
▷HISTORY C15 *handsom* easily handled; compare Dutch *handzaam;* see HAND, -SOME[1]
▸ **'handsomely** ADVERB ▸ **'handsomeness** NOUN

hands-on ADJECTIVE involving practical experience of equipment, etc.: *hands-on training in the use of computers*.

handspike ('hændˌspaɪk) NOUN a bar or length of pipe used as a lever.

handspring ('hændˌsprɪŋ) NOUN a gymnastic feat in which a person starts from a standing position and leaps forwards or backwards into a handstand and then onto his feet.

handstand ('hændˌstænd) NOUN the act or instance of supporting the body on the hands alone in an upside down position.

handstroke ('hændˌstrəʊk) NOUN *Bell-ringing* the downward movement of the bell rope as the bell swings around allowing the ringer to grasp and pull it. Compare **backstroke** (sense 4).

hand-to-hand ADJECTIVE, ADVERB at close quarters: *they fought hand-to-hand*.

hand-to-mouth ADJECTIVE, ADVERB with barely enough money or food to satisfy immediate needs: *a hand-to-mouth existence*.

handwork ('hændˌwɜːk) NOUN work done by hand rather than by machine.
▸ **'handˌworked** ADJECTIVE

hand-wringing NOUN *Informal* an extended debate over the correct course of action in a situation.

handwriting ('hændˌraɪtɪŋ) NOUN 1 writing by hand rather than by typing or printing. 2 a person's characteristic writing style: *that signature is in my handwriting*.

handwritten ('hændˌrɪtᵊn) ADJECTIVE written by hand; not printed or typed.

handy ('hændɪ) ADJECTIVE **handier, handiest.** 1

conveniently or easily within reach. 2 easy to manoeuvre, handle, or use: *a handy tool.* 3 skilful with one's hands.
▸ 'handiness NOUN

handyman ('hændɪ,mæn) NOUN, *plural* **-men.** 1 a man employed to do various tasks. 2 a man skilled in odd jobs, etc.

hanepoot ('hɑːnə,puət) NOUN *South African* a variety of muscat grape used as a dessert fruit and in making wine.
▷HISTORY from Afrikaans *hane* cock + *poot* claw

hang (hæŋ) VERB **hangs, hanging, hung** (hʌŋ). 1 to fasten or be fastened from above, esp by a cord, chain, etc.; suspend: *the picture hung on the wall; to hang laundry.* 2 to place or be placed in position as by a hinge so as to allow free movement around or at the place of suspension: *to hang a door.* 3 (*intr;* sometimes foll by *over*) to be suspended or poised; hover: *a pall of smoke hung over the city.* 4 (*intr;* sometimes foll by *over*) to be imminent; threaten. 5 (*intr*) to be or remain doubtful or unresolved (esp in the phrase **hang in the balance**). 6 (*past tense and past participle* **hanged**) to suspend or be suspended by the neck until dead. 7 (*tr*) to fasten, fix, or attach in position or at an appropriate angle: *to hang a scythe to its handle.* 8 (*tr*) to decorate, furnish, or cover with something suspended or fastened: *to hang a wall with tapestry.* 9 (*tr*) to fasten to or suspend from a wall: *to hang wallpaper.* 10 to exhibit (a picture or pictures) by (a particular painter, printmaker, etc.) or (of a picture or a painter, etc.) to be exhibited in an art gallery, etc. 11 to fall or droop or allow to fall or droop: *to hang one's head in shame.* 12 (of cloth, clothing, etc.) to drape, fall, or flow, esp in a specified manner: *her skirt hangs well.* 13 (*tr*) to suspend (game such as pheasant) so that it becomes slightly decomposed and therefore more tender and tasty. 14 (of a jury) to prevent or be prevented from reaching a verdict. 15 (*past tense and past participle* **hanged**) *Slang* to damn or be damned: used in mild curses or interjections: *I'll be hanged before I'll go out in that storm.* 16 (*intr*) to pass slowly (esp in the phrase **time hangs heavily**). 17 **hang fire. a** to be delayed. **b** to procrastinate. See also **fire** (sense 16). 18 **hang tough.** See **tough** (sense 10). ◆ NOUN 19 the way in which something hangs. 20 (*usually used with a negative*) *Slang* a damn: *I don't care a hang for what you say.* 21 **get the hang of.** *Informal* **a** to understand the technique of doing something. **b** to perceive the meaning or significance of. ◆ See also **hang about, hang back, hang behind, hang in, hang on, hang out, hang together, hang up, hang with.**
▷HISTORY Old English *hangian;* related to Old Norse *hanga,* Old High German *hangēn*

hang about *or* **around** VERB (*intr*) 1 to waste time; loiter. 2 (*adverb;* foll by *with*) to frequent the company (of someone). ◆ INTERJECTION 3 wait a moment! stop!

hangar ('hæŋə) NOUN a large workshop or building for storing and maintaining aircraft.
▷HISTORY C19: from French: shed, perhaps from Medieval Latin *angārium* shed used as a smithy, of obscure origin

hang back VERB (*intr, adverb;* often foll by *from*) to be reluctant to go forward or carry on (with some activity).

hang behind VERB (*intr, adverb*) to remain in a place after others have left; linger.

hangbird ('hæŋ,bɜːd) NOUN *US and Canadian* any bird, esp the Baltimore oriole, that builds a hanging nest.

Hangchow NOUN a variant transliteration of the Chinese name for **Hangzhou.**

hangdog ('hæŋ,dɒg) ADJECTIVE 1 downcast, furtive, or guilty in appearance or manner. ◆ NOUN 2 a furtive or sneaky person.

hanger ('hæŋə) NOUN 1 **a** any support, such as a hook, strap, peg, or loop, on or by which something may be hung. **b** See **coat hanger.** 2 **a** a person who hangs something. **b** (*in combination*): *paperhanger.* 3 a bracket designed to attach one part of a mechanical structure to another, such as the one that attaches the spring shackle of a motor car to the chassis. 4 a wood on a steep hillside, characteristically beech growing on chalk in southern England. 5 **a** a loop or strap on a sword belt from which a short sword or dagger was hung. **b** the weapon itself.

hanger-on NOUN, *plural* **hangers-on.** a sycophantic follower or dependant, esp one hoping for personal gain.

hang-glider NOUN an unpowered aircraft consisting of a large cloth wing stretched over a light framework from which the pilot hangs in a harness, using a horizontal bar to control the flight.
▸ 'hang-gliding NOUN

hangi ('hʌŋiː) NOUN *NZ* 1 an open-air cooking pit. 2 the food cooked in it. 3 the social gathering at the resultant meal.
▷HISTORY Maori

hang in VERB (*intr, preposition*) *Informal* to persist: *just hang in there for a bit longer.*

hanging ('hæŋɪŋ) NOUN 1 **a** the putting of a person to death by suspending the body by the neck from a noose. **b** (*as modifier*): *a hanging offence.* 2 (*often plural*) a decorative textile such as a tapestry or drapery hung on a wall or over a window. 3 the act of a person or thing that hangs. ◆ ADJECTIVE 4 not supported from below; suspended. 5 undecided; still under discussion. 6 inclining or projecting downwards; overhanging. 7 situated on a steep slope or in a high place. 8 (*prenominal*) given to issuing harsh sentences, esp death sentences: *a hanging judge.* 9 *Northern English informal* unpleasant. 10 *Chess* See **hanging pawn.**

Hanging Gardens of Babylon NOUN (in ancient Babylon) gardens, probably planted on terraces of a ziggurat: one of the Seven Wonders of the World.

hanging glacier NOUN a glacier situated on a shelf above a valley or another glacier; it may be joined to the lower level by an icefall or separate from it.

hanging indentation NOUN *Printing* a style of text-setting in which the first line of a paragraph is set to the full measure and subsequent lines are indented at the left-hand side.

hanging pawn NOUN *Chess* one of two or more adjacent pawns on central half-open files with no pawns of the same colour on the files immediately to left and right of them.

hanging valley NOUN *Geography* a tributary valley entering a main valley at a much higher level because of overdeepening of the main valley, esp by glacial erosion.

hanging wall NOUN the rocks on the upper side of an inclined fault plane or mineral vein. Compare **footwall.**

hangman ('hæŋmən) NOUN, *plural* **-men.** an official who carries out a sentence of hanging on condemned criminals.

hangnail ('hæŋ,neɪl) NOUN a piece of skin torn away from, but still attached to, the base or side of a fingernail.
▷HISTORY C17: from Old English *angnægl,* from *enge* tight + *nægl* NAIL; influenced by HANG

hang on VERB (*intr*) 1 (*adverb*) to continue or persist in an activity, esp with effort or difficulty: *hang on at your present job until you can get another.* 2 (*adverb*) to cling, grasp, or hold: *she hangs on to her mother's arm.* 3 (*preposition*) to be conditioned or contingent on; depend on: *everything hangs on this business deal.* 4 (*preposition*) Also: **hang onto, hang upon.** to listen attentively to: *she hung on his every word.* 5 (*adverb*) *Informal* to wait or remain: *hang on for a few minutes.*

hang out VERB (*adverb*) 1 to suspend, be suspended, or lean, esp from an opening, as for display or airing: *to hang out the washing.* 2 (*intr*) *Informal* to live at or frequent a place: *the police know where the thieves hang out.* 3 (*intr;* foll by *with*) *Informal* to frequent the company (of someone). 4 *Slang* to relax completely in an unassuming way (esp in the phrase **let it all hang out**). 5 (*intr*) *US informal* to act or speak freely, in an open, cooperative, or indiscreet manner. ◆ NOUN **hang-out.** 6 *Informal* a place where one lives or that one frequently visits.

hangover ('hæŋ,əʊvə) NOUN 1 the delayed aftereffects of drinking too much alcohol in a relatively short period of time, characterized by headache and sometimes nausea and dizziness. 2 a person or thing left over from or influenced by a past age.

Hang Seng Index (hæŋ sɛŋ) NOUN an index of share prices based on an average of 33 stocks quoted on the Hong Kong Stock Exchange.
▷HISTORY name of a Hong Kong bank

hang together VERB (*intr, adverb*) 1 to be cohesive or united. 2 to be consistent: *your statements don't quite hang together.*

Hanguk ('hæn'gʊk) NOUN the Korean name for **South Korea.**

hang up VERB (*adverb*) 1 (*tr*) to put on a hook, hanger, etc.: *please hang up your coat.* 2 to replace (a telephone receiver) on its cradle at the end of a conversation, often breaking a conversation off abruptly. 3 (*tr; usually passive;* usually foll by *on*) *Informal* to cause to have an emotional or psychological preoccupation or problem: *he's really hung up on his mother.* ◆ NOUN **hang-up.** *Informal.* 4 an emotional or psychological preoccupation or problem. 5 a persistent cause of annoyance.

hang with VERB (*intr, preposition*) *US informal* to frequent the company of (someone).

Hangzhou ('hæŋ'dʒəʊ) *or* **Hangchow** NOUN a port in E China, capital of Zhejiang province, on **Hangzhou Bay** (an inlet of the East China Sea), at the foot of the Eye of Heaven Mountains: regarded by Marco Polo as the finest city in the world; seat of two universities (1927, 1959). Pop.: 1 346 148 (1999 est.).

Hania ('hɑːnɪə) NOUN a variant spelling of **Chania.**

hank (hæŋk) NOUN 1 a loop, coil, or skein, as of rope, wool, or yarn. 2 *Nautical* a ringlike fitting that can be opened to admit a stay for attaching the luff of a sail. 3 a unit of measurement of cloth, yarn, etc., such as a length of 840 yards (767 m) of cotton or 560 yards (512 m) of worsted yarn. ◆ VERB 4 (*tr*) *Nautical* to attach (a sail) to a stay by hanks.
▷HISTORY C13: of Scandinavian origin; compare Old Norse *hanka* to coil, Swedish *hank* string

hanker ('hæŋkə) VERB (foll by *for, after,* or an infinitive) to have a yearning (for something or to do something).
▷HISTORY C17: probably from Dutch dialect *hankeren*
▸ 'hankering NOUN

Hankow *or* **Han-k'ou** ('hæn'kaʊ) NOUN a former city in SE China, in SE Hubei at the confluence of the Han and Yangtze Rivers: one of the Han Cities; merged with Hanyang and Wuchang in 1950 to form the conurbation of Wuhan.

hanky *or* **hankie** ('hæŋkɪ) NOUN, *plural* **hankies.** *Informal* short for **handkerchief.**

hanky-panky ('hæŋkɪ'pæŋkɪ) NOUN *Informal* 1 dubious or suspicious behaviour. 2 foolish behaviour or talk. 3 illicit sexual relations.
▷HISTORY C19: variant of HOCUS-POCUS

Hannah ('hænə) NOUN *Old Testament* the woman who gave birth to Samuel (I Samuel 1–2).

Hannover (*German* ha'noːfər) NOUN a city in N Germany, capital of Lower Saxony: capital of the kingdom of Hannover (1815–66); situated on the Mittelland canal. Pop.: 515 200 (1999 est.). English spelling: **Hanover.**

Hanoi (hæ'nɔɪ) NOUN the capital of Vietnam, on the Red River: became capital of Tonkin in 1802, of French Indochina in 1887, of Vietnam in 1945, and of North Vietnam (1954–75); university (1917); industrial centre. Pop. (urban area): 2 154 900 (1993 est.).

Hanover ('hænəʊvə) NOUN the English spelling of **Hannover.**

Hanoverian (,hænə'vɪərɪən) ADJECTIVE 1 of, relating to, or situated in Hannover. 2 of or relating to the princely house of Hanover or to the monarchs of England or their reigns from 1714 to 1901. ◆ NOUN 3 a member or supporter of the house of Hanover.

Hansard ('hænsɑːd) NOUN 1 the official report of the proceedings of the British Parliament. 2 a similar report kept by other legislative bodies.
▷HISTORY C19: named after T.C. *Hansard* (1752–1828) and his son, who compiled the reports until 1889

Hanse (hæns) *or* **Hansa** ('hænsə, -zə) NOUN 1 a medieval guild of merchants. 2 a fee paid by the new members of a medieval trading guild. 3 **a** another name for the **Hanseatic League. b** (*as modifier*): *a Hanse town.*

▷HISTORY C12: of Germanic origin; compare Old High German *hansa,* Old English *hōs* troop

Hanseatic (ˌhænsɪˈætɪk) ADJECTIVE 1 of or relating to the Hanseatic League. ◆ NOUN 2 a member of the Hanseatic League.

Hanseatic League NOUN a commercial association of towns in N Germany formed in the mid-14th century to protect and control trade. It was at its most powerful in the 15th century. Also called: **Hansa, Hanse.**

hansel (ˈhænsəl) NOUN, VERB a variant spelling of **handsel.**

Hansen's disease (ˈhænsənz) NOUN *Pathol* another name for **leprosy.**
▷HISTORY C20: named after G. H. *Hansen* (1841–1912), Norwegian physician

hansom (ˈhænsəm) NOUN (*sometimes capital*) a two-wheeled one-horse carriage with a fixed hood. The driver sits on a high outside seat at the rear. Also called: **hansom cab.**
▷HISTORY C19: short for *hansom cab,* named after its designer J. A. *Hansom* (1803–82)

hantavirus (ˈhæntəˌvaɪrəs) NOUN any one of a group of viruses that are transmitted to humans by rodents and cause disease of varying severity, ranging from a mild form of influenza to respiratory or kidney failure.
▷HISTORY C20: from *Hanta(an),* river in North and South Korea where the disease was first reported + VIRUS

Hants (hænts) ABBREVIATION FOR Hampshire.

hanukiah *or* **chanukiah** (ˈhɑːnukɪə, ˌhɑːnəkiːə; *Hebrew* xanuˈkiːa) NOUN a candelabrum having nine branches that is lit during the festival of Hanukkah.
▷HISTORY from Hebrew

Hanukkah, Hanukah, *or* **Chanukah** (ˈhɑːnəkə, -nʊˌkɑː; *Hebrew* xanuˈka) NOUN the eight-day Jewish festival of lights beginning on the 25th of Kislev and commemorating the rededication of the temple by Judas Maccabaeus in 165 B.C. Also called: **Feast of Dedication, Feast of Lights.**
▷HISTORY from Hebrew, literally: a dedication

Hanuman (ˌhʌnʊˈmɑːn) NOUN 1 another word for **entellus** (the monkey). 2 the monkey chief of Hindu mythology and devoted helper of Rama.
▷HISTORY from Hindi *Hanumān,* from Sanskrit *hanumant* having (conspicuous) jaws, from *hanu* jaw

Hanyang *or* **Han-yang** (ˈhænˈjæŋ) NOUN a former city in SE China, in SE Hubei at the confluence of the Han and Yangtze Rivers: one of the Han Cities; merged with Hankow and Wuchang in 1950 to form the conurbation of Wuhan.

hào (haʊ) NOUN a monetary unit of Vietnam, worth one tenth of a dông.

hap[1] (hæp) NOUN *Archaic* 1 luck; chance. 2 an occurrence. ◆ VERB **haps, happing, happed.** 3 (*intr*) an archaic word for **happen.**
▷HISTORY C13: from Old Norse *happ* good luck; related to Old English *gehæplic* convenient, Old Slavonic *kobŭ* fate

hap[2] (hæp) *Scot and eastern English dialect* ◆ VERB (*tr*) 1 to cover up; wrap up warmly. ◆ NOUN 2 a covering of any kind.
▷HISTORY C14: perhaps of Norse origin

hapaxanthic (ˌhæpəˈzænθɪk) *or* **hapaxanthous** (ˌhæpəˈzænθəs) ADJECTIVE *Botany* another word for **semelparous.**
▷HISTORY from Greek: fruiting only once

hapax legomenon (ˈhæpæks ləˈgɒmɪˌnɒn) NOUN, *plural* **hapax legomena** (ləˈgɒmɪnə). another term for **nonce word.**
▷HISTORY Greek: thing said only once

ha'penny (ˈheɪpnɪ) NOUN, *plural* **-nies.** *Brit* a variant spelling of **halfpenny.**

haphazard (hæpˈhæzəd) ADVERB, ADJECTIVE 1 at random. ◆ ADJECTIVE 2 careless; slipshod. ◆ NOUN 3 *Rare* chance.
▸**hapˈhazardly** ADVERB ▸**hapˈhazardness** NOUN

Haphtarah (hɑːfˈtəʊrə; *Hebrew* haftaˈraː) NOUN, *plural* **-taroth** (-ˈtəʊrəʊt; *Hebrew* -taˈroːt) *or* **-tarahs.** a variant spelling of **Haftarah.**

hapless (ˈhæplɪs) ADJECTIVE unfortunate; wretched.
▸**ˈhaplessly** ADVERB ▸**ˈhaplessness** NOUN

haplite (ˈhæplaɪt) NOUN a variant of **aplite.**
▸**haplitic** (hæpˈlɪtɪk) ADJECTIVE

haplo- *or before a vowel* **hapl-** COMBINING FORM single or simple: *haplology; haplosis.*
▷HISTORY from Greek *haplous* simple

haplobiont (ˌhæpləʊˈbaɪɒnt) NOUN *Biology* an organism, esp a plant, that exists in either the diploid form or the haploid form (but never alternates between these forms) during its life cycle.
▸ˌ**haplobiˈontic** ADJECTIVE

haplography (hæpˈlɒgrəfɪ) NOUN, *plural* **-phies.** the accidental writing of only one letter or syllable where there should be two similar letters or syllables, as in spelling *endodontics* as *endontics.*
▷HISTORY C19: from Greek, from *haplous* single + -GRAPHY

haploid (ˈhæplɔɪd) *Biology* ◆ ADJECTIVE *also* **haploidic.** 1 (esp of gametes) having a single set of unpaired chromosomes. ◆ NOUN 2 a haploid cell or organism. Compare **diploid.**
▷HISTORY C20: from Greek *haploeidēs* single, from *haplous* single
▸**ˈhaploidy** NOUN

haplology (hæpˈlɒlədʒɪ) NOUN omission of a repeated occurrence of a sound or syllable in fluent speech, as for example in the pronunciation of *library* as (ˈlaɪbrɪ).
▸**haplologic** (ˌhæpləˈlɒdʒɪk) ADJECTIVE

haplont (ˈhæplɒnt) NOUN *Biology* an organism, esp a plant, that has the haploid number of chromosomes in its somatic cells.
▸**haˈplontic** ADJECTIVE

haplosis (hæpˈləʊsɪs) NOUN *Biology* the production of a haploid number of chromosomes during meiosis.

haplostemonous (ˈhæpləʊˈstiːmənəs, -ˈstɛm-) ADJECTIVE (of plants) having the stamens arranged in a single whorl.
▷HISTORY C19: from New Latin, from HAPLO- + *-stemonus* relating to a STAMEN

haply (ˈhæplɪ) ADVERB (*sentence modifier*) an archaic word for **perhaps.**

ha'p'orth (ˈheɪpəθ) NOUN *Brit* 1 a variant spelling of **halfpennyworth.** 2 *Informal* a person considered as specified: *daft ha'p'orth.*

happen (ˈhæpən) VERB 1 (*intr*) (of an event in time) to come about or take place; occur. 2 (*intr; foll by* to) (of some unforeseen circumstance or event, esp death), to fall to the lot (of); be a source of good or bad fortune (to): *if anything happens to me it'll be your fault.* 3 (*tr*) to chance (to be or do something): *I happen to know him.* 4 (*tr; takes a clause as object*) to be the case, esp if by chance, that: *it happens that I know him.* ◆ ADVERB, SENTENCE SUBSTITUTE 5 *Northern English dialect* **a** another word for **perhaps. b** (*as sentence modifier*): *happen I'll see thee tomorrow.*
▷HISTORY C14: see HAP[1], -EN[1]

Language note See at **occur.**

happen by, past, along, *or* **in** VERB (*intr, adverb*) *Informal, chiefly US* to appear, arrive, or come casually or by chance.

happening (ˈhæpənɪŋ, ˈhæpnɪŋ) NOUN 1 an occurrence; event. 2 an improvised or spontaneous display or performance consisting of bizarre and haphazard events. ◆ ADJECTIVE 3 *Informal* fashionable and up-to-the-minute.

happen on *or* **upon** VERB (*intr, preposition*) to find by chance: *I happened upon a five-pound note lying in the street.*

happenstance (ˈhæpənˌstæns) NOUN 1 chance. 2 a chance occurrence.

happy (ˈhæpɪ) ADJECTIVE **-pier, -piest.** 1 feeling, showing, or expressing joy; pleased. 2 willing: *I'd be happy to show you around.* 3 causing joy or gladness. 4 fortunate; lucky: *the happy position of not having to work.* 5 aptly expressed; appropriate: *a happy turn of phrase.* 6 (*postpositive*) *Informal* slightly intoxicated. ◆ INTERJECTION 7 (*in combination*): *happy birthday; happy Christmas.* ◆ See also **trigger-happy.**
▷HISTORY C14: see HAP[1], -Y[1]
▸**ˈhappily** ADVERB ▸**ˈhappiness** NOUN

-happy ADJECTIVE COMBINING FORM denoting excessive enthusiasm for or devotion to: *gun-happy.*

happy camper NOUN *Informal* a happy, satisifed person (esp in the phrase **not a happy camper**).

happy-clappy (ˈhæpɪˈklæpɪ) *Derogatory* ◆ ADJECTIVE 1 of or denoting a form of evangelical Christianity in which members of the congregation sing and clap enthusiastically during acts of worship. ◆ NOUN, *plural* **-pies.** 2 Also called: **happy clapper.** an enthusiastic evangelical Christian.

happy event NOUN *Informal* the birth of a child.

happy family *or* **happy family bird** NOUN *Austral* 1 another name for **grey-crowned babbler.** 2 another name for **apostle bird.**

happy-go-lucky ADJECTIVE carefree or easy-going.

happy hour NOUN a time, usually in the early evening, when some pubs or bars sell drinks at reduced prices.

happy hunting ground NOUN 1 (in American Indian legend) the paradise to which a person passes after death. 2 a productive or profitable area for a person with a particular interest or requirement: *jumble sales proved happy hunting grounds in her search for old stone jars.*

Happy Jack NOUN *Austral* another name for **grey-crowned babbler.**

happy medium NOUN a course or state that avoids extremes.

happy release NOUN liberation, esp by death, from an unpleasant condition.

hapten (ˈhæptən) *or* **haptene** (ˈhæptiːn) NOUN *Immunol* an incomplete antigen that can stimulate antibody production only when it is chemically combined with a particular protein.
▷HISTORY C20: from German, from Greek *haptein* to fasten

hapteron (ˈhæptərɒn) NOUN a cell or group of cells that occurs in certain plants, esp seaweeds, and attaches the plant to its substratum; holdfast.
▷HISTORY C20: from Greek *haptein* to make fast

haptic (ˈhæptɪk) ADJECTIVE relating to or based on the sense of touch.
▷HISTORY C19: from Greek, from *haptein* to touch

haptotropism (ˌhæptəʊˈtrəʊpɪzəm) NOUN another name for **thigmotropism.**

hapu (ˈhɑːpuː) NOUN *NZ* a subtribe.
▷HISTORY Maori

hapuka *or* **hapuku** (həˈpuːkə, ˈhɑːpʊkə) NOUN *NZ* another name for **groper.**
▷HISTORY Maori

hara-kiri (ˌhærəˈkɪrɪ) *or* **hari-kari** (ˌhærɪˈkɑːrɪ) NOUN (formerly, in Japan) ritual suicide by disembowelment with a sword when disgraced or under sentence of death. Also called: **seppuku.**
▷HISTORY C19: from Japanese taboo slang, from *hara* belly + *kiri* cutting

haram (ˈhɑːˌrɑːm) NOUN anything that is forbidden by Islamic law.
▷HISTORY from Arabic, literally: forbidden

harambee (ˌhɑːrɑːmˈbeɪ) NOUN 1 a work chant used on the E African coast. 2 a rallying cry used in Kenya. ◆ INTERJECTION 3 a cry of harambee.
▷HISTORY Swahili: pull together

harangue (həˈræŋ) VERB 1 to address (a person or crowd) in an angry, vehement, or forcefully persuasive way. ◆ NOUN 2 a loud, forceful, or angry speech.
▷HISTORY C15: from Old French, from Old Italian *aringa* public speech, probably of Germanic origin; related to Medieval Latin *harenga;* see HARRY, RING[1]
▸**haˈranguer** NOUN

Harappa (həˈræpə) NOUN an ancient city in the Punjab in NW Pakistan: one of the centres of the Indus civilization that flourished from 2500 to 1700 B.C.; probably destroyed by Indo-European invaders.

Harappan (həˈræpən) ADJECTIVE 1 of or relating to Harappa (an ancient city in the Punjab) or its inhabitants. ◆ NOUN 2 a native or inhabitant of Harappa.

Harar *or* **Harrer** (ˈhɑːrə) NOUN a city in E Ethiopia: former capital of the Muslim state of Adal. Pop.: 122 932 (1994 est.).

Harare (həˈrɑːrɪ) NOUN the capital of Zimbabwe, in the northeast: University of Zimbabwe (1957); industrial and commercial centre. Pop.: 1 686 169 (1998 est.). Former name (until 1982): **Salisbury.**

harass (ˈhærəs, həˈræs) VERB (*tr*) to trouble, torment, or confuse by continual persistent attacks, questions, etc.

▷HISTORY C17: from French *harasser,* variant of Old French *harer* to set a dog on, of Germanic origin; compare Old High German *harēn* to cry out
▸ˈ**harassed** ADJECTIVE ▸ˈ**harassing** ADJECTIVE, NOUN
▸ˈ**harassment** NOUN

Harbin (hɑːˈbiːn, -ˈbɪn) NOUN a city in NE China, capital of Heilongjiang province on the Songhua River: founded by the Russians in 1897; centre of tsarist activities after the October Revolution in Russia (1917). Pop.: 2 586 978 (1999 est.). Also called: **Ha-erh-pin.**

harbinger (ˈhɑːbɪndʒə) NOUN 1 a person or thing that announces or indicates the approach of something; forerunner. 2 *Obsolete* a person sent in advance of a royal party or army to obtain lodgings for them. ◆ VERB 3 (*tr*) to announce the approach or arrival of.
▷HISTORY C12: from Old French *herbergere,* from *herberge* lodging, from Old Saxon *heriberga;* compare Old High German *heriberga* army shelter; see HARRY, BOROUGH

harbour *or US* **harbor** (ˈhɑːbə) NOUN 1 a sheltered port. 2 a place of refuge or safety. ◆ VERB 3 (*tr*) to give shelter to: *to harbour a criminal.* 4 (*tr*) to maintain secretly: *to harbour a grudge.* 5 to shelter (a vessel) in a harbour or (of a vessel) to seek shelter.
▷HISTORY Old English *herebeorg,* from *here* troop, army + *beorg* shelter; related to Old High German *heriberga* hostelry, Old Norse *herbergi*
▸ˈ**harbourer** *or US* ˈ**harborer** NOUN ▸ˈ**harbourless** *or US* ˈ**harborless** ADJECTIVE

harbourage *or US* **harborage** (ˈhɑːbərɪdʒ) NOUN shelter or refuge, as for a ship, or a place providing shelter.

harbour master NOUN an official in charge of a harbour.

harbour seal NOUN a common earless seal, *Phoca vitulina,* that is greyish-black with paler markings: occurs off the coasts of North America, N Europe, and NE Asia.

hard (hɑːd) ADJECTIVE 1 firm or rigid; not easily dented, crushed, or pierced. 2 toughened by or as if by physical labour; not soft or smooth: *hard hands.* 3 difficult to do or accomplish; arduous: *a hard task.* 4 difficult to understand or perceive: *a hard question.* 5 showing or requiring considerable physical or mental energy, effort, or application: *hard work; a hard drinker.* 6 stern, cold, or intractable: *a hard judge.* 7 exacting; demanding: *a hard master.* 8 harsh; cruel: *a hard fate.* 9 inflicting pain, sorrow, distress, or hardship: *hard times.* 10 tough or adamant: *a hard man.* 11 forceful or violent: *a hard knock.* 12 cool or uncompromising: *we took a long hard look at our profit factor.* 13 indisputable; real: *hard facts.* 14 *Chem* (of water) impairing the formation of a lather by soap. See **hardness** (sense 3). 15 practical, shrewd, or calculating: *he is a hard man in business.* 16 too harsh to be pleasant: *hard light.* 17 **a** (of cash, money, etc.) in coin and paper rather than cheques. **b** (of currency) in strong demand, esp as a result of a good balance of payments situation. **c** (of credit) difficult to obtain; tight. 18 (of alcoholic drink) being a spirit rather than a wine, beer, etc.: *the hard stuff.* 19 (of a drug such as heroin, morphine, or cocaine) highly addictive. Compare **soft** (sense 20). 20 *Physics* (of radiation, such as gamma rays and X-rays) having high energy and the ability to penetrate solids. 21 *Physics* (of a vacuum) almost complete. 22 *Chiefly US* (of goods) durable. 23 short for **hard-core.** 24 (of news coverage) concentrating on serious stories. 25 *Phonetics* **a** an older word for **fortis. b** (not in modern technical usage) denoting the consonants *c* and *g* in English when they are pronounced as velar stops (k, g). **c** (of consonants in the Slavonic languages) not palatalized. 26 **a** being heavily fortified and protected. **b** (of nuclear missiles) located underground in massively reinforced silos. 27 politically extreme: *the hard left.* 28 *Brit and NZ informal* incorrigible or disreputable (esp in the phrase **a hard case**). 29 (of bread, etc.) stale and old. 30 **a hard nut to crack. a** a person not easily persuaded or won over. **b** a thing not easily understood. 31 **hard by.** near; close by. 32 **hard doer.** *NZ* a tough worker at anything. 33 **hard done by.** unfairly or badly treated. 34 **hard up.** *Informal* **a** in need of money; poor. **b** (foll by *for*) in great need (of): *hard up for suggestions.* 35 **put the hard word on.** *Austral and NZ informal* to ask or demand something from. ◆ ADVERB 36 with great energy, force, or vigour: *the team always played hard.* 37 as far as possible; all the way: *hard left.* 38 with application; earnestly or intently: *she thought hard about the formula.* 39 with great intensity, force, or violence: *his son's death hit him hard.* 40 (foll by *on, upon, by,* or *after*) close; near: *hard on his heels.* 41 (foll by *at*) assiduously; devotedly. 42 **a** with effort or difficulty: *their victory was hard won.* **b** (*in combination*): *hard-earned.* 43 slowly and reluctantly: *prejudice dies hard.* 44 **go hard with.** to cause pain or difficulty to (someone): *it will go hard with you if you don't tell the truth.* 45 **hard at it.** working hard. 46 **hard put (to it).** scarcely having the capacity (to do something): *he's hard put to get to work by 9:30.* ◆ NOUN 47 any colorant that produces a harsh coarse appearance. 48 *Brit* a roadway across a foreshore. 49 *Slang* hard labour. 50 *Slang* an erection of the penis (esp in the phrase **get** or **have a hard on**).
▷HISTORY Old English *heard;* related to Old Norse *harthr,* Old Frisian *herd,* Old High German *herti,* Gothic *hardus* hard, Greek *kratus* strong

hard and fast ADJECTIVE (**hard-and-fast** *when prenominal*) (esp of rules) invariable or strict.

hardback (ˈhɑːdˌbæk) NOUN 1 a book or edition with covers of cloth, cardboard, or leather. Compare **paperback.** ◆ ADJECTIVE 2 Also: **casebound, hardbound** (ˈhɑːdˌbaʊnd), **hardcover** (ˈhɑːdˌkʌvə). of or denoting a hardback or the publication of hardbacks.

hardbake (ˈhɑːdˌbeɪk) NOUN almond toffee.

hardball (ˈhɑːdbɔːl) NOUN 1 *US and Canadian* baseball as distinct from softball. 2 **play hardball.** *Informal, chiefly US and Canadian* to act in a ruthless or uncompromising way.

hard-bitten ADJECTIVE tough and realistic.

hardboard (ˈhɑːdˌbɔːd) NOUN a thin stiff sheet made of compressed sawdust and wood pulp bound together with plastic adhesive or resin under heat and pressure.

hard-boiled ADJECTIVE 1 (of an egg) boiled until the yolk and white are solid. 2 *Informal* **a** tough, realistic. **b** cynical.

hard bop NOUN a form of jazz originating in the late 1950s that is rhythmically less complex than bop.

hard cash NOUN money or payment in the form of coins or notes rather than cheques or credit.

hard cheese SENTENCE SUBSTITUTE, NOUN *Brit slang* bad luck.

hard cider NOUN *US and Canadian* fermented apple juice. Compare **sweet cider.**

hard coal NOUN another name for **anthracite.** Compare **soft coal.**

hard copy NOUN computer output printed on paper, as contrasted with machine-readable output such as magnetic tape.

hardcore (ˈhɑːdˌkɔː) NOUN 1 a style of rock music characterized by short fast numbers with minimal melody and aggressive delivery. 2 a type of dance music with a very fast beat.

hard core NOUN 1 the members of a group or movement who form an intransigent nucleus resisting change. 2 material, such as broken bricks, stones, etc., used to form a foundation for a road, paving, building, etc. ◆ ADJECTIVE **hard-core.** 3 (of pornography) describing or depicting sexual acts in explicit detail. 4 extremely committed or fanatical: *a hard-core Communist.*

hard court NOUN a tennis court made of asphalt, concrete, etc. See also **grass court.**

hard disk NOUN a disk of rigid magnetizable material that is used to store data for computers: it is permanently mounted in its disk drive and usually has a storage capacity of a few gigabytes.

hard-edge ADJECTIVE of, relating to, or denoting a style of painting in which vividly coloured subjects are clearly delineated.

harden[1] (ˈhɑːdᵊn) VERB 1 to make or become hard or harder; freeze, stiffen, or set. 2 to make or become more hardy, tough, or unfeeling. 3 to make or become stronger or firmer: *they hardened defences.* 4 to make or become more resolute or set: *hardened in his resolve.* 5 (*intr*) *Commerce* **a** (of prices, a market, etc.) to cease to fluctuate. **b** (of price) to rise higher. ◆ See also **harden off, harden up.**

harden[2] (ˈhɑːdᵊn) NOUN a rough fabric made from hards.

hardened (ˈhɑːdᵊnd) ADJECTIVE 1 rigidly set, as in a mode of behaviour. 2 toughened, as by custom; seasoned. 3 (of a nuclear missile site) constructed to withstand a nuclear attack.

hardener (ˈhɑːdᵊnə) NOUN 1 a person or thing that hardens. 2 a substance added to paint or varnish to increase durability. 3 an ingredient of certain adhesives and synthetic resins that accelerates or promotes setting.

hardening (ˈhɑːdᵊnɪŋ) NOUN 1 the act or process of becoming or making hard. 2 a substance added to another substance or material to make it harder.

hardening of the arteries NOUN a nontechnical name for **arteriosclerosis.**

harden off VERB (*adverb*) to accustom (a cultivated plant) or (of such a plant) to become accustomed to outdoor conditions by repeated exposure.

harden up VERB (*intr*) *Nautical* to tighten the sheets of a sailing vessel so as to prevent luffing.

hard-faced ADJECTIVE *Northern English dialect* cheeky.

hard feeling NOUN (*often plural; often used with a negative*) resentment; ill will: *no hard feelings?*

hard fern NOUN a common tufted erect fern of the polypody family, *Blechnum spicant,* having dark-green lanceolate leaves: it prefers acid soils, and in the US is sometimes grown as deer feed. US name: **deer fern.**

hardhack (ˈhɑːdˌhæk) NOUN a woody North American rosaceous plant, *Spiraea tomentosa,* with downy leaves and tapering clusters of small pink or white flowers. Also called: **steeplebush.**

hard hat NOUN 1 a hat made of a hard material for protection, worn esp by construction workers, equestrians, etc. 2 *Informal, chiefly US and Canadian* a construction worker. ◆ ADJECTIVE **hard-hat.** 3 *Informal, chiefly US* characteristic of the presumed conservative attitudes and prejudices typified by construction workers.

hard-headed ADJECTIVE 1 tough, realistic, or shrewd; not moved by sentiment. 2 *Chiefly US and Canadian* stubborn; obstinate.
▸ˌ**hard-ˈheadedly** ADVERB ▸ˌ**hard-ˈheadedness** NOUN

hardheads (ˈhɑːdˌhɛdz) NOUN (*functioning as singular*) a thistle-like plant, *Centaurea nigra,* native to Europe and introduced into North America and New Zealand, that has reddish-purple flower heads: family *Asteraceae* (composites). Also called: **knapweed.** See also **centaury** (sense 2).

hardhearted (ˌhɑːdˈhɑːtɪd) ADJECTIVE unkind or intolerant.
▸ˌ**hardˈheartedly** ADVERB ▸ˌ**hardˈheartedness** NOUN

hard-hit ADJECTIVE seriously affected or hurt: *hard-hit by taxation.*

hard hitter NOUN *NZ informal* a bowler hat.

hard-hitting ADJECTIVE uncompromising; tough: *a hard-hitting report on urban deprivation.*

hardihood (ˈhɑːdɪˌhʊd) NOUN courage, daring, or audacity.

hardily (ˈhɑːdɪlɪ) ADVERB in a hardy manner; toughly or boldly.

hardiness (ˈhɑːdɪnɪs) NOUN the condition or quality of being hardy, robust, or bold.

hard labour NOUN *Criminal law* (formerly) the penalty of compulsory physical labour imposed in addition to a sentence of imprisonment: abolished in England in 1948.

hard landing NOUN 1 a landing by a rocket or spacecraft in which the vehicle is destroyed on impact. 2 a sharp fall into recession following a sustained period of economic growth. Compare **soft landing.**

hard lens NOUN a rigid plastic lens which floats on the layer of tears in front of the cornea, worn to correct defects of vision. Compare **gas-permeable lens, soft lens.**

hard line NOUN **a** an uncompromising course or policy. **b hardline.** (*as modifier*): *a hardline policy.*
▸ˌ**hardˈliner** NOUN

hard lines SENTENCE SUBSTITUTE, NOUN *Brit informal* bad luck. Also: **hard cheese.**

hardly ('hɑːdlɪ) ADVERB 1 scarcely; barely: *we hardly knew the family.* 2 just; only just: *he could hardly hold the cup.* 3 *Often used ironically* almost or probably not or not at all: *he will hardly incriminate himself.* 4 with difficulty or effort. 5 *Rare* harshly or cruelly.

> **Language note** Since *hardly, scarcely,* and *barely* already have negative force, it is redundant to use another negative in the same clause: *he had hardly had* (not *he hadn't hardly had*) *time to think; there was scarcely any* (not *scarcely no*) *bread left.*

hardman ('hɑːdˌmæn) NOUN a tough, ruthless, or violent man.

hard money NOUN *Politics* (in the US) money given directly to a candidate in an election to assist his or her campaign. Compare **soft money.**

hard-mouthed ADJECTIVE 1 (of a horse) not responding satisfactorily to a pull on the bit. 2 stubborn; obstinate.

hard neck NOUN *Irish informal* audacity; nerve.

hardness ('hɑːdnɪs) NOUN 1 the quality or condition of being hard. 2 one of several measures of resistance to indentation, deformation, or abrasion. See **Mohs scale, Brinell number.** 3 the quality of water that causes it to impair the lathering of soap: caused by the presence of certain calcium salts. **Temporary hardness** can be removed by boiling whereas **permanent hardness** cannot.

hard-nosed ADJECTIVE *Informal* tough, shrewd, and practical.

hard of hearing ADJECTIVE **a** deaf or partly deaf. **b** (*as collective noun;* preceded by *the*): *the hard of hearing.*

hard pad NOUN (in dogs) an abnormal increase in the thickness of the foot pads: one of the clinical signs of canine distemper. See **distemper**[1] (sense 1).

hard palate NOUN the anterior bony portion of the roof of the mouth, extending backwards to the soft palate.

hardpan ('hɑːdˌpæn) NOUN a hard impervious layer of clay below the soil, resistant to drainage and root growth.

hard paste NOUN **a** porcelain made with kaolin and petuntse, of Chinese origin and made in Europe from the early 18th century. **b** (*as modifier*): *hard-paste porcelain.*

hard-pressed ADJECTIVE 1 in difficulties: *the swimmer was hard-pressed.* 2 subject to severe competition. 3 subject to severe attack. 4 closely pursued.

hardrock ('hɑːdˌrɒk) *Canadian* ◆ ADJECTIVE 1 (of mining) concerned with extracting minerals other than coal, usually from solid rock. ◆ NOUN 2 *Slang* a tough uncompromising man.

hard rock NOUN *Music* a rhythmically simple and usually highly amplified style of rock and roll.

hard rubber NOUN a hard fairly inelastic material made by vulcanizing natural rubber. See **vulcanite.**

hards (hɑːdz) *or* **hurds** PLURAL NOUN coarse fibres and other refuse from flax and hemp.
▷ HISTORY Old English *heordan* (plural); related to Middle Dutch *hēde,* Greek *keskeon* tow

hard sauce NOUN another name for **brandy butter.**

hard science NOUN **a** one of the natural or physical sciences, such as physics, chemistry, biology, geology, or astronomy. **b** (*as modifier*): *a hard-science lecture.*
▸ **hard scientist** NOUN

hardscrabble ('hɑːdˌskræbᵊl) NOUN *US informal* 1 (*modifier*) (of a place) difficult to make a living in; barren. 2 great effort made in the face of difficulties.

hard sell NOUN an aggressive insistent technique of selling or advertising. Compare **soft sell.**

hard-shell ADJECTIVE *also* **hard-shelled.** 1 *Zoology* having a shell or carapace that is thick, heavy, or hard. 2 *US* strictly orthodox. ◆ NOUN 3 another name for the **quahog.**

hard-shell clam NOUN another name for the **quahog.**

hard-shell crab NOUN a crab, esp of the edible species *Cancer pagurus,* that has not recently moulted and therefore has a hard shell. Compare **soft-shell crab.**

hardship ('hɑːdʃɪp) NOUN 1 conditions of life difficult to endure. 2 something that causes suffering or privation.

hard shoulder NOUN *Brit* a surfaced verge running along the edge of a motorway for emergency stops.

hard-spun ADJECTIVE (of yarn) spun with a firm close twist.

hard standing NOUN a hard surface on which vehicles, such as cars or aircraft, may be parked.

hardtack ('hɑːdˌtæk) NOUN a kind of hard saltless biscuit, formerly eaten esp by sailors as a staple aboard ship. Also called: **pilot biscuit, ship's biscuit, sea biscuit.**

hard tack NOUN *Irish informal* whisky.

hardtop ('hɑːdˌtɒp) NOUN 1 a car equipped with a metal or plastic roof that is sometimes detachable. 2 the detachable hard roof of some sports cars.

hardware ('hɑːdˌwɛə) NOUN 1 metal tools, implements, etc., esp cutlery or cooking utensils. 2 *Computing* the physical equipment used in a computer system, such as the central processing unit, peripheral devices, and memory. Compare **software.** 3 mechanical equipment, components, etc. 4 heavy military equipment, such as tanks and missiles or their parts. 5 *Informal* a gun or guns collectively.

hard-wearing ADJECTIVE resilient, durable, and tough.

hard wheat NOUN a type of wheat with hard kernels, yielding a strong flour and used for bread, macaroni, etc.

Hardwick Hall ('hɑːdwɪk) NOUN an Elizabethan mansion near Chesterfield in Derbyshire: built 1591–97 for Elizabeth, Countess of Shrewsbury (Bess of Hardwick).

hard-wired ADJECTIVE 1 (of a circuit or instruction) permanently wired into a computer, replacing separate software. 2 (of human behaviour) innate; not learned: *humans have a hard-wired ability for acquiring language.*

hardwood ('hɑːdˌwʊd) NOUN 1 the wood of any of numerous broad-leaved dicotyledonous trees, such as oak, beech, ash, etc., as distinguished from the wood of a conifer. 2 any tree from which this wood is obtained. ◆ Compare **softwood.**

hard-working ADJECTIVE (of a person) industrious; diligent.

hardy[1] ('hɑːdɪ) ADJECTIVE **-dier, -diest.** 1 having or demanding a tough constitution; robust. 2 bold; courageous. 3 foolhardy; rash. 4 (of plants) able to live out of doors throughout the winter.
▷ HISTORY C13: from Old French *hardi* bold, past participle of *hardir* to become bold, of Germanic origin; compare Old English *hierdan* to HARDEN[1], Old Norse *hertha,* Old High German *herten*

hardy[2] ('hɑːdɪ) NOUN, *plural* **-dies.** any blacksmith's tool made with a square shank so that it can be lodged in a square hole in an anvil.
▷ HISTORY C19: probably from HARD

hard yards PLURAL NOUN a great deal of effort or hard work, esp in playing a sport: *Dallaglio's ability to make the hard yards and cross the gain line.*

hare (hɛə) NOUN, *plural* **hares** *or* **hare.** 1 any solitary leporid mammal of the genus *Lepus,* such as *L. europaeus* (**European hare**). Hares are larger than rabbits, having longer ears and legs, and live in shallow nests (forms). Related adjective: **leporine.** 2 **make a hare of (someone).** *Irish informal* to defeat (someone) completely. 3 **run with the hare and hunt with the hounds.** to be on good terms with both sides. ◆ VERB 4 (*intr;* often foll by *off, after,* etc.) *Brit informal* to go or run fast or wildly.
▷ HISTORY Old English *hara;* related to Old Norse *heri,* Old High German *haso,* Swedish *hare,* Sanskrit *śaśá*
▸ **'hare,like** ADJECTIVE

Hare (hɛə) NOUN a member of a Dene Native Canadian people of northern Canada.
▷ HISTORY of Athaspascan origin

hare and hounds NOUN (*functioning as singular*) a game in which certain players (**hares**) run across country scattering pieces of paper that the other players (**hounds**) follow in an attempt to catch the hares.

harebell ('hɛəˌbɛl) NOUN a N temperate campanulaceous plant, *Campanula rotundifolia,* having slender stems and leaves, and bell-shaped pale blue flowers. Also called (in Scotland): **bluebell.**

harebrained *or* **hairbrained** ('hɛəˌbreɪnd) ADJECTIVE rash, foolish, or badly thought out: *harebrained schemes.*

Hare Krishna ('hɑːrɪ 'krɪʃnə) NOUN 1 a Hindu sect devoted to a form of Hinduism (**Krishna Consciousness**) based on the worship of the god Krishna. 2 (*plural* **Hare Krishnas**) a member or follower of this sect.
▷ HISTORY C20: from Hindi, literally: Lord Krishna (vocative): the opening words of a sacred verse often chanted in public by adherents of the movement

harelip ('hɛəˌlɪp) NOUN a congenital cleft or fissure in the midline of the upper lip, resembling the cleft upper lip of a hare, often occurring with cleft palate.
▸ **'hare,lipped** ADJECTIVE

harem ('hɛərəm, hɑː'riːm) *or* **hareem** (hɑː'riːm) NOUN 1 the part of an Oriental house reserved strictly for wives, concubines, etc. 2 a Muslim's wives and concubines collectively. 3 a group of female animals of the same species that are the mates of a single male.
▷ HISTORY C17: from Arabic *harīm* forbidden (place)

hare's-foot NOUN a leguminous annual plant, *Trifolium arvense,* that grows on sandy soils in Europe and NW Asia and has downy heads of white or pink flowers. Also called: **hare's-foot clover.**

harestail ('hɛəsˌteɪl) NOUN a species of cotton grass, *Eriophorum vaginatum,* more tussocky than common cotton grass and having only a single flower head.

Harewood House ('hɛəwʊd) NOUN a mansion near Harrogate in Yorkshire: built 1759–71 by John Carr for the Lascelles family; interior decoration by Robert Adam.

Harfleur ('hɑːflɜː; *French* arflœr) NOUN a port in N France, in the Seine-Maritime department: important centre in the Middle Ages. Pop.: 9700 (latest est.).

Hargeisa (hɑː'geɪsə) NOUN a city in NW Somalia: former capital of British Somaliland (1941–60); trading centre for nomadic herders. Pop.: 400 000 (latest est.).

haricot ('hærɪkəʊ) NOUN 1 a variety of French bean with light-coloured edible seeds, which can be dried and stored. 2 another name for **French bean.** 3 the seed or pod of any of these plants, eaten as a vegetable.
▷ HISTORY C17: from French, perhaps from Nahuatl *ayecotli*

Harijan ('hʌrɪdʒən) NOUN a member of certain classes in India, formerly considered inferior and untouchable. See **scheduled castes.**
▷ HISTORY Hindi, literally: man of God (so called by Mahatma Gandhi), from *Hari* god + *jan* man

hari-kari (ˌhærɪ'kɑːrɪ) NOUN a non-Japanese variant of **hara-kiri.**

Haringey ('hærɪŋˌgeɪ) NOUN a borough of N Greater London. Pop.: 216 510 (2001 est.). Area: 30 sq. km (12 sq. miles).

harira (hə'rɪərə) NOUN a Moroccan soup made from a variety of vegetables with lentils, chickpeas, and coriander.
▷ HISTORY Arabic

hark (hɑːk) VERB (*intr; usually imperative*) to listen; pay attention.
▷ HISTORY Old English *heorcnian* to HEARKEN; related to Old Frisian *herkia,* Old High German *hōrechen;* see HEAR

hark back VERB (*intr, adverb*) to return to an earlier subject, point, or position, as in speech or thought.

harken ('hɑːkən) VERB a variant spelling (esp US) of **hearken.**
▸ **'harkener** NOUN

harl[1] (hærl, hɑːl) *Scot* ◆ VERB 1 (*tr*) to drag (something) along the ground. 2 (*intr*) to drag oneself; trail along. 3 (*tr*) to cover (a building) with a mixture of lime and gravel; roughcast. 4 (*intr*) to troll for fish. ◆ NOUN 5 the act of harling or

dragging. [6] a small quantity; a scraping. [7] a mixture of lime and gravel; roughcast.
▷HISTORY C18: of unknown origin
▸ **'harling** NOUN

harl² (hɑːl) NOUN *Angling* a variant of **herl.**

Harlech ('hɑːˌlɪk) NOUN a town in N Wales, in Gwynedd: noted for its ruined 13th-century castle overlooking Cardigan Bay: tourism. Pop.: 1233 (1991).

Harlem ('hɑːləm) NOUN a district of New York City, in NE Manhattan: now largely a Black ghetto.

harlequin ('hɑːlɪkwɪn) NOUN [1] *(sometimes capital) Theatre* a stock comic character originating in the commedia dell'arte; the foppish lover of Columbine in the English harlequinade. He is usually represented in diamond-patterned multicoloured tights, wearing a black mask. [2] a clown or buffoon. ◆ ADJECTIVE [3] varied in colour or decoration. [4] (of certain animals) having a white coat with irregular patches of black or other dark colour: *harlequin Great Dane.* [5] comic; ludicrous.
▷HISTORY C16: from Old French *Herlequin, Hellequin* leader of band of demon horsemen, perhaps from Middle English *Herle king* (unattested) King Herle, mythical being identified with Woden

harlequinade (ˌhɑːlɪkwɪ'neɪd) NOUN [1] *(sometimes capital) Theatre* a play or part of a pantomime in which harlequin has a leading role. [2] buffoonery.

harlequin bug NOUN a brightly coloured heteropterous insect, *Murgantia histrionica,* of the US and Central America: a pest of cabbages and related plants: family *Pentatomidae.*

harlequin duck NOUN a northern sea duck, *Histrionicus histrionicus,* the male of which has a blue and red plumage with black and white markings.

Harley Street NOUN a street in central London famous for its large number of medical specialists' consulting rooms.

harlot ('hɑːlət) NOUN [1] a prostitute or promiscuous woman. ◆ ADJECTIVE [2] *Archaic* of or like a harlot.
▷HISTORY C13: from Old French *herlot* rascal, of obscure origin
▸ **'harlotry** NOUN

Harlow ('hɑːləʊ) NOUN a town in SE England, in W Essex: designated a new town in 1947, with a planned population of 80 000. Pop.: 74 629 (1991).

harm (hɑːm) NOUN [1] physical or mental injury or damage. [2] moral evil or wrongdoing. ◆ VERB [3] *(tr)* to injure physically, morally, or mentally.
▷HISTORY Old English *hearm;* related to Old Norse *harmr* grief, Old High German *harm* injury, Old Slavonic *sramŭ* disgrace
▸ **'harmer** NOUN

harmattan (hɑː'mætᵊn) NOUN a dry dusty wind from the Sahara blowing towards the W African coast, esp from November to March.
▷HISTORY C17: from Twi *haramata,* perhaps from Arabic *harām* forbidden thing; see HAREM

harmful ('hɑːmfʊl) ADJECTIVE causing or tending to cause harm; injurious.
▸ **'harmfully** ADVERB ▸ **'harmfulness** NOUN

harmless ('hɑːmlɪs) ADJECTIVE [1] not causing any physical or mental damage or injury. [2] unlikely to annoy or worry people: *a harmless sort of man.*
▸ **'harmlessly** ADVERB ▸ **'harmlessness** NOUN

harmolodics (ˌhɑːmə'lɒdɪks) NOUN *(functioning as singular) Jazz* the technique of each musician in a group simultaneously improvising around the melodic and rhythmic patterns in a tune, rather than one musician improvising on its underlying harmonic pattern while the others play an accompaniment.
▷HISTORY C20: of unknown origin
▸ **ˌharmo'lodic** ADJECTIVE

harmonic (hɑː'mɒnɪk) ADJECTIVE [1] of, involving, producing, or characterized by harmony; harmonious. [2] *Music* of, relating to, or belonging to harmony. [3] *Maths* **a** capable of expression in the form of sine and cosine functions. **b** of or relating to numbers whose reciprocals form an arithmetic progression. [4] *Physics* of or concerned with an oscillation that has a frequency that is an integral multiple of a fundamental frequency. [5] *Physics* of or concerned with harmonics. ◆ NOUN [6] *Physics, music* a component of a periodic quantity, such as a musical tone, with a frequency that is an integral multiple of the fundamental frequency. The **first harmonic** is the fundamental, the **second harmonic** (twice the fundamental frequency) is the **first overtone**, the **third harmonic** (three times the fundamental frequency) is the **second overtone**, etc. [7] *Music* (not in technical use) overtone: in this case, the first overtone is the first harmonic, etc. ◆ See also **harmonics.**
▷HISTORY C16: from Latin *harmonicus* relating to HARMONY
▸ **har'monically** ADVERB

harmonica (hɑː'mɒnɪkə) NOUN [1] a small wind instrument of the reed organ family in which reeds of graduated lengths set into a metal plate enclosed in a narrow oblong box are made to vibrate by blowing and sucking. Also called: **mouth organ.** [2] See **glass harmonica.**
▷HISTORY C18: from Latin *harmonicus* relating to HARMONY

harmonic analysis NOUN [1] the representation of a periodic function by means of the summation and integration of simple trigonometric functions. [2] the study of this means of representation.

harmonic distortion NOUN *Electronics* distortion caused by nonlinear characteristics of electronic apparatus, esp of audio amplifiers, that generate unwanted harmonics of the input frequencies.

harmonic mean NOUN the reciprocal of the arithmetic mean of the reciprocals of a set of specified numbers: the harmonic mean of 2, 3, and 4 is $3(\frac{1}{2} + \frac{1}{3} + \frac{1}{4})^{-1} = 36/13$.

harmonic minor scale NOUN *Music* a minor scale modified from the state of being natural by the sharpening of the seventh degree. See **minor.** Compare **melodic minor scale.**

harmonic motion NOUN a periodic motion in which the displacement is symmetrical about a point or a periodic motion that is composed of such motions. See also **simple harmonic motion.**

harmonic progression NOUN a sequence of numbers whose reciprocals form an arithmetic progression, as 1, ½, ⅓, ...

harmonics (hɑː'mɒnɪks) NOUN [1] *(functioning as singular)* the science of musical sounds and their acoustic properties. [2] *(functioning as plural)* the overtones of a fundamental note, as produced by lightly touching the string of a stringed instrument at one of its node points while playing. See **harmonic** (sense 6).

harmonic series NOUN [1] *Maths* a series whose terms are in harmonic progression, as in $1 + \frac{1}{2} + \frac{1}{3} + \ldots$. [2] *Acoustics* the series of tones with frequencies strictly related to one another and to the fundamental tone, as obtained by touching lightly the node points of a string while playing it. Its most important application is in the playing of brass instruments.

harmonious (hɑː'məʊnɪəs) ADJECTIVE [1] (esp of colours or sounds) fitting together well. [2] having agreement or consensus. [3] tuneful, consonant, or melodious.
▸ **har'moniously** ADVERB

harmonist ('hɑːmənɪst) NOUN [1] a person skilled in the art and techniques of harmony. [2] a person who combines and collates parallel narratives.
▸ **ˌharmo'nistic** ADJECTIVE ▸ **ˌharmo'nistically** ADVERB

harmonium (hɑː'məʊnɪəm) NOUN a musical keyboard instrument of the reed organ family, in which air from pedal-operated bellows causes the reeds to vibrate.
▷HISTORY C19: from French, from *harmonie* HARMONY

harmonization *or* **harmonisation** (ˌhɑːmənaɪ'zeɪʃən) NOUN [1] the act of harmonizing. [2] a system, particularly used in the EU, whereby the blue-collar workers and the white-collar workers in an organization have similar status and any former differences in terms and conditions of employment are levelled up.

harmonize *or* **harmonise** ('hɑːməˌnaɪz) VERB [1] to make or become harmonious. [2] *(tr) Music* to provide a harmony for (a melody, tune, etc.). [3] *(intr)* to sing in harmony, as with other singers. [4] to collate parallel narratives.
▸ **'harmoˌnizable** *or* **'harmoˌnisable** ADJECTIVE

harmonizer *or* **harmoniser** ('hɑːməˌnaɪzə) NOUN *Music* [1] a person skilled in the theory of composition of harmony. [2] a device that electronically duplicates a signal at a different pitch or different pitches.

harmony ('hɑːmənɪ) NOUN, *plural* **-nies.** [1] agreement in action, opinion, feeling, etc.; accord. [2] order or congruity of parts to their whole or to one another. [3] agreeable sounds. [4] *Music* **a** any combination of notes sounded simultaneously. **b** the vertically represented structure of a piece of music. Compare **melody** (sense 1b), **rhythm** (sense 1). **c** the art or science concerned with the structure and combinations of chords. [5] a collation of the material of parallel narratives, esp of the four Gospels.
▷HISTORY C14: from Latin *harmonia* concord of sounds, from Greek: harmony, from *harmos* a joint

harmotome ('hɑːməˌtəʊm) NOUN a mineral of the zeolite group consisting of hydrated aluminium barium silicate in the form of monoclinic twinned crystals. Formula: $Ba(Al_2Si_6O_{16}).6H_2O$.
▷HISTORY C19: from French, from Greek *harmos* a joint + *tomē* a slice, from *temnein* to cut

harness ('hɑːnɪs) NOUN [1] an arrangement of leather straps buckled or looped together, fitted to a draught animal in order that the animal can be attached to and pull a cart. [2] something resembling this, esp for attaching something to the body: *a parachute harness.* [3] *Mountaineering* an arrangement of webbing straps that enables a climber to attach himself to the rope so that the impact of a fall is minimized. [4] the total system of electrical leads for a vehicle or aircraft. [5] *Weaving* the part of a loom that raises and lowers the warp threads, creating the shed. [6] *Archaic* armour collectively. [7] **in harness.** at one's routine work. ◆ VERB *(tr)* [8] to put harness on (a horse). [9] (usually foll by *to*) to attach (a draught animal) by means of harness to (a cart, etc.). [10] to control so as to employ the energy or potential power of: *to harness the atom.* [11] to equip or clothe with armour.
▷HISTORY C13: from Old French *harneis* baggage, probably from Old Norse *hernest* (unattested) provisions, from *herr* army + *nest* provisions
▸ **'harnesser** NOUN ▸ **'harnessless** ADJECTIVE
▸ **'harness-ˌlike** ADJECTIVE

harnessed antelope NOUN any of various antelopes with vertical white stripes on the back, esp the bushbuck.

harness hitch NOUN a knot forming a loop with no free ends.

harness race NOUN *Horse racing* a trotting or pacing race for standardbred horses driven in sulkies and harnessed in a special way to cause them to use the correct gait.

Harney Peak ('hɑːnɪ) NOUN a mountain in SW South Dakota: the highest peak in the Black Hills. Height: 2207 m (7242 ft.).

harp (hɑːp) NOUN [1] a large triangular plucked stringed instrument consisting of a soundboard connected to an upright pillar by means of a curved crossbar from which the strings extend downwards. The strings are tuned diatonically and may be raised in pitch either one or two semitones by the use of pedals (**double-action harp**). Basic key: B major; range: nearly seven octaves. [2] something resembling this, esp in shape. [3] an informal name (esp in pop music) for **harmonica.** ◆ VERB [4] *(intr)* to play the harp. [5] *(tr) Archaic* to speak; utter; express. [6] *(intr;* foll by *on* or *upon)* to speak or write in a persistent and tedious manner.
▷HISTORY Old English *hearpe;* related to Old Norse *harpa,* Old High German *harfa,* Latin *corbis* basket, Russian *korobit* to warp
▸ **'harper** *or* **'harpist** NOUN

Harper's Ferry ('hɑːpəz) NOUN a village in NE West Virginia, at the confluence of the Potomac and Shenandoah Rivers: site of an arsenal seized by John Brown (1859). Pop.: 308 (1990).

harpings ('hɑːpɪŋz) *or* **harpins** ('hɑːpɪnz) PLURAL NOUN [1] *Nautical* wooden members used for strengthening the bow of a vessel. [2] *Shipbuilding* wooden supports used in construction.
▷HISTORY C17: perhaps related to French *harpe* cramp iron

harpoon (hɑː'puːn) NOUN [1] **a** a barbed missile attached to a long cord and hurled or fired from a gun when hunting whales, etc. **b** *(as modifier)*: *a harpoon gun.* ◆ VERB [2] *(tr)* to spear with or as if with a harpoon.

▷HISTORY C17: probably from Dutch *harpoen*, from Old French *harpon* clasp, from *harper* to seize, perhaps of Scandinavian origin
▸**har'pooner** *or* **,harpoon'eer** NOUN ▸**har'poon-,like** ADJECTIVE

harp seal NOUN a brownish-grey earless seal, *Pagophilus groenlandicus*, of the North Atlantic and Arctic Oceans.

harpsichord ('hɑːpsɪˌkɔːd) NOUN a horizontally strung stringed keyboard instrument, triangular in shape, consisting usually of two manuals controlling various sets of strings plucked by pivoted plectrums mounted on jacks. Some harpsichords have a pedal keyboard and stops by which the tone colour may be varied.
▷HISTORY C17: from New Latin *harpichordium*, from Late Latin *harpa* HARP + Latin *chorda* CHORD[1]
▸**'harpsi,chordist** NOUN

harpy ('hɑːpɪ) NOUN, *plural* **-pies**. a cruel grasping woman.
▷HISTORY C16: from Latin *Harpyia*, from Greek *Harpuiai* the Harpies, literally: snatchers, from *harpazein* to seize

Harpy ('hɑːpɪ) NOUN, *plural* **-pies**. *Greek myth* a ravenous creature with a woman's head and trunk and a bird's wings and claws.

harpy eagle NOUN a very large tropical American eagle, *Harpia harpyja*, with a black-and-white plumage and a head crest.

harquebus ('hɑːkwɪbəs) NOUN, *plural* **-buses**. a variant of **arquebus**.

harquebusier (ˌhɑːkwɪbə'sɪə) NOUN (formerly) a soldier armed with an arquebus. Also called: **arquebusier**.

Harrer ('hɑːrə) NOUN a variant spelling of **Harar**.

harridan ('hærɪdᵊn) NOUN a scolding old woman; nag.
▷HISTORY C17: of uncertain origin; perhaps related to French *haridelle*, literally: broken-down horse; of obscure origin

harrier[1] ('hærɪə) NOUN **1** a person or thing that harries. **2** any diurnal bird of prey of the genus *Circus*, having broad wings and long legs and tail and typically preying on small terrestrial animals: family *Accipitridae* (hawks, etc.). See also **marsh harrier, Montagu's harrier**.

harrier[2] ('hærɪə) NOUN **1** a smallish breed of hound used originally for hare-hunting. **2** a cross-country runner.
▷HISTORY C16: from HARE + -ER[1]; influenced by HARRIER[1]

Harrier ('hærɪə) NOUN a British subsonic multipurpose military jet plane capable of vertical takeoff and landing by means of vectoring the engine thrust.

Harris ('hærɪs) NOUN the S part of the island of Lewis with Harris, in the Outer Hebrides. Pop.: (including Lewis) 23 390 (latest est.). Area: 500 sq. km (193 sq. miles).

Harrisburg ('hærɪsˌbɜːg) NOUN a city in S Pennsylvania, on the Susquehanna River: the state capital. Pop.: 53 430 (1992 est.).

Harris Tweed NOUN *Trademark* a loose-woven tweed made in the Outer Hebrides, esp Lewis and Harris.

Harrogate ('hærəgɪt) NOUN a town in N England, in North Yorkshire: a former spa, now a centre for tourism and conferences. Pop.: 66 178 (1991).

Harrovian (hə'rəʊvɪən) NOUN **1** a person educated at Harrow School. ◆ ADJECTIVE **2** of or concerning Harrow.
▷HISTORY C19: from New Latin *Harrōvia* HARROW + -AN

harrow[1] ('hærəʊ) NOUN **1** any of various implements used to level the ground, stir the soil, break up clods, destroy weeds, etc., in soil. ◆ VERB **2** (*tr*) to draw a harrow over (land). **3** (*intr*) (of soil) to become broken up through harrowing. **4** (*tr*) to distress; vex.
▷HISTORY C13: of Scandinavian origin; compare Danish *harv*, Swedish *harf*; related to Middle Dutch *harke* rake
▸**'harrower** NOUN ▸**'harrowing** ADJECTIVE, NOUN

harrow[2] ('hærəʊ) VERB (*tr*) *Archaic* **1** to plunder or ravish. **2** (of Christ) to descend into (hell) to rescue righteous souls.
▷HISTORY C13: variant of Old English *hergian* to HARRY
▸**'harrowment** NOUN

Harrow ('hærəʊ) NOUN a borough of NW Greater London; site of an English boys' public school founded in 1571 at **Harrow-on-the-Hill**, a part of this borough. Pop.: 207 389 (2001). Area: 51 sq. km (20 sq. miles).

harrumph (hə'rʌmf) VERB (*intr*) to clear or make the noise of clearing the throat.

harry ('hærɪ) VERB **-ries, -rying, -ried**. **1** (*tr*) to harass; worry. **2** to ravage (a town, etc.), esp in war.
▷HISTORY Old English *hergian*; related to *here* army, Old Norse *herja* to lay waste, Old High German *heriōn*

harsh (hɑːʃ) ADJECTIVE **1** rough or grating to the senses. **2** stern, severe, or cruel.
▷HISTORY C16: probably of Scandinavian origin; compare Middle Low German *harsch*, Norwegian *harsk* rancid
▸**'harshly** ADVERB ▸**'harshness** NOUN

harslet ('hɑːzlɪt, 'hɑːs-) NOUN a variant of **haslet**.

hart (hɑːt) NOUN, *plural* **harts** *or* **hart**. the male of the deer, esp the red deer aged five years or more.
▷HISTORY Old English *heorot*; related to Old Norse *hjörtr*, Old High German *hiruz* hart, Latin *cervus* stag, Lithuanian *kárve* cow; see HORN

hartal (hɑː'tɑːl) NOUN (in India) the act of closing shops or suspending work, esp in political protest.
▷HISTORY C20: from Hindi *hartāl*, from *hāt* shop (from Sanskrit *hatta*) + *tālā* bolt for a door (from Sanskrit: latch)

hartebeest ('hɑːtɪˌbiːst) *or* **hartbeest** ('hɑːtˌbiːst) NOUN **1** either of two large African antelopes, *Alcelaphus buselaphus* or *A. lichtensteini*, having an elongated muzzle, lyre-shaped horns, and a fawn-coloured coat. **2** any similar and related animal, such as *Damaliscus hunteri* (**Hunter's hartebeest**).
▷HISTORY C18: via Afrikaans from Dutch; see HART, BEAST

Hartford ('hɑːtfəd) NOUN a port in central Connecticut, on the Connecticut River: the state capital. Pop.: 121 578 (2000).

Hartlepool ('hɑːtlɪˌpuːl) NOUN **1** a port in NE England, in Hartlepool unitary authority, Co. Durham, on the North Sea: greatly enlarged in 1967 by its amalgamation with West Hartlepool; engineering, clothing, food processing. Pop.: 87 310 (1991). **2** a unitary authority in NE England, in Co. Durham: formerly (1974–96) part of the county of Cleveland. Pop.: 88 629 (2001). Area: 93 sq. km (36 sq. miles).

hartshorn ('hɑːtsˌhɔːn) NOUN an obsolete name for **sal volatile** (sense 2).
▷HISTORY Old English *heortes horn* hart's horn (formerly a chief source of ammonia)

hart's-tongue NOUN an evergreen Eurasian fern, *Asplenium scolopendrium*, with narrow undivided fronds bearing rows of sori: family *Polypodiaceae*.

harum-scarum ('hɛərəm'skɛərəm) ADJECTIVE, ADVERB **1** in a reckless way or of a reckless nature. ◆ NOUN **2** a person who is impetuous or rash.
▷HISTORY C17: perhaps from *hare* (in obsolete sense: harass) + *scare*, variant of STARE[1]; compare HELTER-SKELTER

haruspex (hə'rʌspɛks) NOUN, *plural* **haruspices** (hə'rʌspɪˌsiːz). (in ancient Rome) a priest who practised divination, esp by examining the entrails of animals.
▷HISTORY C16: from Latin, probably from *hīra* gut + *specere* to look
▸**haruspical** (hə'rʌspɪkᵊl) ADJECTIVE ▸**haruspicy** (hə'rʌspɪsɪ) NOUN

Harvard classification ('hɑːvəd) NOUN a classification of stars based on the characteristic spectral absorption lines and bands of the chemical elements present. See **spectral type**.
▷HISTORY C20: named after the observatory at *Harvard*, Massachusetts, where it was prepared and published as part of *The Henry Draper Catalogue* (1924)

harvest ('hɑːvɪst) NOUN **1** the gathering of a ripened crop. **2** the crop itself or the yield from it in a single growing season. **3** the season for gathering crops. **4** the product of an effort, action, etc.: *a harvest of love*. ◆ VERB **5** to gather or reap (a ripened crop) from (the place where it has been growing). **6** (*tr*) to receive or reap (benefits, consequences, etc.). **7** (*tr*) *Chiefly US* to remove (an organ) from the body for transplantation.
▷HISTORY Old English *hærfest*; related to Old Norse *harfr* harrow, Old High German *herbist* autumn, Latin *carpere* to pluck, Greek *karpos* fruit, Sanskrit *krpāna* shears
▸**'harvesting** NOUN ▸**'harvestless** ADJECTIVE

harvester ('hɑːvɪstə) NOUN **1** a person who harvests. **2** a harvesting machine, esp a combine harvester.

harvest home NOUN **1** the bringing in of the harvest. **2** *Chiefly Brit* a harvest supper.

harvestman ('hɑːvɪstmən) NOUN, *plural* **-men**. **1** a person engaged in harvesting. **2** Also called (US and Canadian): **daddy-longlegs**. any arachnid of the order *Opiliones* (or *Phalangida*), having a small rounded body and very long thin legs.

harvest mite *or* **tick** NOUN the bright red parasitic larva of any of various free-living mites of the genus *Trombicula* and related genera, which causes intense itching of human skin.

harvest moon NOUN the full moon occurring nearest to the autumnal equinox.

harvest mouse NOUN **1** a very small reddish-brown Eurasian mouse, *Micromys minutus*, inhabiting cornfields, hedgerows, etc., and feeding on grain and seeds: family *Muridae*. **2** **American harvest mouse**. any small greyish mouse of the American genus *Reithrodontomys*: family *Cricetidae*.

Harwell ('hɑːˌwɛl) NOUN a village in S England, in Oxfordshire: atomic research station (1947).

Harwich ('hærɪtʃ) NOUN a port in SE England, in NE Essex on the North Sea. Pop.: 18 436 (1991).

Haryana (hər'jɑːnə) NOUN a state of NE India, formed in 1966 from the Hindi-speaking parts of the state of Punjab. Capital: Chandigarh (shared with Punjab). Pop.: 21 082 989 (2001 est.). Area: 44 506 sq. km (17 182 sq. miles).

Harz *or* **Harz Mountains** (hɑːts) PLURAL NOUN a range of wooded hills in central Germany, between the Rivers Weser and Elbe: source of many legends. Highest peak: Brocken, 1142 m (3746 ft.).

has (hæz) VERB (used with *he, she, it*, or a singular noun) a form of the present tense (indicative mood) of **have**.

has-been NOUN *Informal* a person or thing that is no longer popular, successful, effective, etc.

hash[1] (hæʃ) NOUN **1** a dish of diced cooked meat, vegetables, etc., reheated in a sauce. **2** something mixed up. **3** a reuse or rework of old material. **4** **make a hash of**. *Informal* **a** to mix or mess up. **b** to defeat or destroy. **5** **settle** (*or* **fix**) **someone's hash**. *Informal* to subdue or silence someone. ◆ VERB (*tr*) **6** to chop into small pieces. **7** to mix or mess up.
▷HISTORY C17: from Old French *hacher* to chop up, from *hache* HATCHET

hash[2] (hæʃ) NOUN *Slang* short for **hashish**.

hash[3] (hæʃ) *or* **hash mark** NOUN **1** the character (#) used to precede a number. **2** this sign used in printing or writing to indicate that a space should be inserted.

hash browns PLURAL NOUN diced boiled potatoes mixed with chopped onion, shaped and fried until brown.

HaShem (hɑ'ʃɛm) *Judaism* a periphrastic way of referring to God in contexts other than prayer, scriptural reading, etc. because the name itself is considered too holy for such use.
▷HISTORY from Hebrew, literally: The Name

Hashemite Kingdom of Jordan ('hæʃɪˌmaɪt) NOUN the official name of **Jordan**.

hash house NOUN *US slang* a cheap café or restaurant.

hashish ('hæʃiːʃ, -ɪʃ) *or* **hasheesh** ('hæʃiːʃ) NOUN **1** a purified resinous extract of the dried flower tops of the female hemp plant, used as a hallucinogenic. See also **cannabis**. **2** any hallucinogenic substance prepared from this resin.
▷HISTORY C16: from Arabic *hashīsh* hemp, dried herbage

haslet ('hæzlɪt) *or* **harslet** NOUN a loaf of cooked minced pig's offal, eaten cold.
▷HISTORY C14: from Old French *hastelet* piece of

spit roasted meat, from *haste* spit, of Germanic origin; compare Old High German *harsta* frying pan

hasn't ('hæzənt) VERB CONTRACTION OF has not.

hasp (hɑːsp) NOUN 1 a metal fastening consisting of a hinged strap with a slot that fits over a staple and is secured by a pin, bolt, or padlock. ◆ VERB 2 (*tr*) to secure (a door, window, etc.) with a hasp.
▷HISTORY Old English *hæpse; related to Old Norse hespa,* Old High German *haspa* hasp, Dutch *haspel* reel, Sanskrit *capa* bow

Hasselt (*Flemish* 'hɑsəlt; *French* asɛlt) NOUN a market town in E Belgium, capital of Limbourg province. Pop.: 67 486 (1995 est.).

Hassid *or* **Hasid** ('hæsɪd; *Hebrew* xa'sid) NOUN variant spellings of **Chassid.**

hassium ('hæsɪəm) NOUN a synthetic element produced in small quantities by high-energy ion bombardment. Symbol: Hs; atomic no. 108.
▷HISTORY C20: from Latin, from HESSE, German state where it was discovered

hassle ('hæsəl) *Informal* ◆ NOUN 1 a prolonged argument; wrangle. 2 a great deal of trouble; difficulty; nuisance. ◆ VERB 3 (*intr*) to quarrel or wrangle. 4 (*tr*) to cause annoyance or trouble to (someone); harass.
▷HISTORY C20: of unknown origin

hassock ('hæsək) NOUN 1 a firm upholstered cushion used for kneeling on, esp in church. 2 a thick clump of grass.
▷HISTORY Old English *hassuc* matted grass

hast (hæst) VERB *Archaic or dialect* (used with the pronoun *thou* or its relative equivalent) a singular form of the present tense (indicative mood) of **have.**

hastate ('hæsteɪt) ADJECTIVE (of a leaf) having a pointed tip and two outward-pointing lobes at the base.
▷HISTORY C18: from Latin *hastātus* with a spear, from *hasta* spear

haste (heɪst) NOUN 1 speed, esp in an action; swiftness; rapidity. 2 the act of hurrying in a careless or rash manner. 3 a necessity for hurrying; urgency. 4 **make haste.** to hurry; rush. ◆ VERB 5 a poetic word for **hasten.**
▷HISTORY C14: from Old French *haste,* of Germanic origin; compare Old Norse *heifst* hate, Old English *hǣst* strife, Old High German *heisti* powerful
▸'**hasteful** ADJECTIVE ▸'**hastefully** ADVERB

hasten ('heɪsən) VERB 1 (*may take an infinitive*) to hurry or cause to hurry; rush. 2 (*tr*) to be anxious (to say something): *I hasten to add that we are just good friends.*
▸'**hastener** NOUN

Hastings ('heɪstɪŋz) NOUN 1 a port in SE England, in East Sussex on the English Channel: near the site of the **Battle of Hastings** (1066), in which William the Conqueror defeated King Harold; chief of the Cinque Ports. Pop.: 81 139 (1991). 2 a town in New Zealand, on E North Island: centre of a rich agricultural and fruit-growing region. Pop. (urban area): 58 700 (1995 est.).

hasty ('heɪstɪ) ADJECTIVE **-tier, -tiest.** 1 rapid; swift; quick. 2 excessively or rashly quick. 3 short-tempered. 4 showing irritation or anger: *hasty words.*
▸'**hastily** ADVERB ▸'**hastiness** NOUN

hasty pudding NOUN 1 *Brit* a simple pudding made from milk thickened with tapioca, semolina, etc., and sweetened. 2 *US* a mush of cornmeal, served with treacle sugar.

hat (hæt) NOUN 1 **a** any of various head coverings, esp one with a brim and a shaped crown. **b** (*in combination*): *hatrack.* 2 *Informal* a role or capacity. 3 **at the drop of a hat.** without hesitation or delay. 4 **I'll eat my hat.** *Informal* I will be greatly surprised if (something that proves me wrong) happens: *I'll eat my hat if this book comes out late.* 5 **hat in hand.** humbly or servilely. 6 **keep (something) under one's hat.** to keep (something) secret. 7 **my hat.** (*interjection*) *Brit informal* **a** my word! my goodness! **b** nonsense! 8 **old hat.** something stale or old-fashioned. 9 **out of a hat. a** as if by magic. **b** at random. 10 **pass** (*or* **send**) **the hat round.** to collect money, as for a cause. 11 **take off one's hat to.** to admire or congratulate. 12 **talk through one's hat. a** to talk foolishly. **b** to deceive or bluff. 13 **throw one's hat at (it).** *Irish* to give up all hope of getting or achieving (something): *you can throw your hat at it now.* 14 **throw** (*or* **toss**) **one's hat in the ring.** to announce one's intentions to be a candidate or contestant. ◆ VERB **hats, hatting, hatted.** 15 (*tr*) to supply (a person, etc.) with a hat or put a hat on (someone).
▷HISTORY Old English *hætt;* related to Old Norse *höttr* cap, Latin *cassis* helmet; see HOOD[1]
▸'**hatless** ADJECTIVE ▸'**hat,like** ADJECTIVE

hatband ('hæt,bænd) NOUN a band or ribbon around the base of the crown of a hat.

hatbox ('hæt,bɒks) NOUN a box or case for a hat or hats.

hatch[1] (hætʃ) VERB 1 to cause (the young of various animals, esp birds) to emerge from the egg or (of young birds, etc.) to emerge from the egg. 2 to cause (eggs) to break and release the fully developed young or (of eggs) to break and release the young animal within. 3 (*tr*) to contrive or devise (a scheme, plot, etc.). ◆ NOUN 4 the act or process of hatching. 5 a group of newly hatched animals.
▷HISTORY C13: of Germanic origin; compare Middle High German *hecken* to mate (used of birds), Swedish *häcka* to hatch, Danish *hække*
▸'**hatchable** ADJECTIVE ▸'**hatcher** NOUN

hatch[2] (hætʃ) NOUN 1 a covering for a hatchway. 2 short for **hatchway.** 3 Also called: **serving hatch.** an opening in a wall between a kitchen and a dining area. 4 the lower half of a divided door. 5 a sluice or sliding gate in a dam, dyke, or weir. 6 **down the hatch.** *Slang* (used as a toast) drink up! 7 **under hatches. a** below decks. **b** out of sight. **c** brought low; dead.
▷HISTORY Old English *hæcc;* related to Middle High German *heck,* Dutch *hek* gate

hatch[3] (hætʃ) VERB *Art* to mark (a figure, shade, etc.) with fine parallel or crossed lines to indicate shading. Compare **hachure.**
▷HISTORY C15: from Old French *hacher* to chop, from *hache* HATCHET
▸'**hatching** NOUN

hatch[4] (hætʃ) NOUN *Informal* short for **hatchback.**

hatchback ('hætʃ,bæk) NOUN 1 **a** a sloping rear end of a car having a single door that is lifted to open. **b** (*as modifier*): *a hatchback model.* 2 a car having such a rear end.

hatchel ('hætʃəl) VERB **-els, -elling, -elled** *or US* **-els, -eling, -eled,** NOUN another word for **heckle** (senses 2, 3).
▷HISTORY C13 *hechele,* of Germanic origin; related to Old High German *hāko* hook, Middle Dutch *hekele* HACKLE
▸'**hatcheller** NOUN

hatchery ('hætʃərɪ) NOUN, *plural* **-eries.** a place where eggs are hatched under artificial conditions.

hatchet ('hætʃɪt) NOUN 1 a short axe used for chopping wood, etc. 2 a tomahawk. 3 (*modifier*) of narrow dimensions and sharp features: *a hatchet face.* 4 **bury the hatchet.** to cease hostilities and become reconciled.
▷HISTORY C14: from Old French *hachette,* from *hache* axe, of Germanic origin; compare Old High German *happa* knife
▸'**hatchet-,like** ADJECTIVE

hatchet job NOUN *Informal* a malicious or devastating verbal or written attack.

hatchet man NOUN *Informal* 1 a person carrying out unpleasant assignments for an employer or superior. 2 *US and Canadian* a hired murderer. 3 a severe or malicious critic.

hatchling ('hætʃlɪŋ) NOUN a young animal that has newly emerged from an egg.
▷HISTORY C19: from HATCH[1] + -LING[1]

hatchment ('hætʃmənt) NOUN *Heraldry* a diamond-shaped tablet displaying the coat of arms of a dead person. Also called: **achievement.**
▷HISTORY C16: changed from ACHIEVEMENT

hatchway ('hætʃ,weɪ) NOUN 1 an opening in the deck of a vessel to provide access below. 2 a similar opening in a wall, floor, ceiling, or roof, usually fitted with a lid or door. ◆ Often shortened to **hatch.**

hate (heɪt) VERB 1 to dislike (something) intensely; detest. 2 (*intr*) to be unwilling (to be or do something). ◆ NOUN 3 intense dislike. 4 *Informal* a person or thing that is hated (esp in the phrase **pet hate**). 5 (*modifier*) expressing or arousing feelings of hatred: *hate mail.*
▷HISTORY Old English *hatian;* related to Old Norse *hata,* Old Saxon *hatōn,* Old High German *hazzēn*
▸'**hateable** *or* '**hatable** ADJECTIVE

hate crime NOUN a crime, esp of violence, in which the victim is targeted because of his or her race, religion, sexuality, etc.

hateful ('heɪtfʊl) ADJECTIVE 1 causing or deserving hate; loathsome; detestable. 2 full of or showing hate.
▸'**hatefully** ADVERB ▸'**hatefulness** NOUN

Hatfield ('hæt,fiːld) NOUN a market town in S central England, in Hertfordshire, with a new town of the same name built on the outskirts: university (1992); site of **Hatfield House** (1607–11), the seat of the Cecil family. Pop.: 31 104 (1991).

hath (hæθ) VERB *Archaic or dialect* (used with the pronouns *he, she,* or *it* or a singular noun) a form of the present tense (indicative mood) of **have.**

hatha yoga ('hʌtə, 'hæθə) NOUN (*sometimes capitals*) a form of yoga concerned chiefly with the regulation of breathing by exercises consisting of various postures designed to maintain healthy functioning of the body and to induce mental calm. Compare **raja yoga.**
▷HISTORY C20: from Sanskrit *hatha* force + YOGA

Hathor ('hæθɔː) NOUN (in ancient Egyptian religion) the mother of Horus and goddess of creation.
▸**Hathoric** (hæ'θɔːrɪk, -'θɒr-) ADJECTIVE

hatpin ('hæt,pɪn) NOUN a sturdy pin used to secure a woman's hat to her hair, often having a decorative head.

hatred ('heɪtrɪd) NOUN a feeling of intense dislike; enmity.

hat stand *or esp US* **hat tree** NOUN a frame or pole equipped with hooks or arms for hanging up hats, coats, etc.

hatter ('hætə) NOUN 1 a person who makes and sells hats. 2 **mad as a hatter.** crazily eccentric.

Hatteras ('hætərəs) NOUN **Cape.** a promontory off the E coast of North Carolina, on **Hatteras Island,** which is situated between Pamlico Sound and the Atlantic: known as the "Graveyard of the Atlantic" for its danger to shipping.

hat trick NOUN 1 *Cricket* the achievement of a bowler in taking three wickets with three successive balls. 2 any achievement of three successive points, victories, etc.

haubergeon ('hɔːbədʒən) NOUN a variant of **habergeon.**

hauberk ('hɔːbɜːk) NOUN a long coat of mail, often sleeveless.
▷HISTORY C13: from Old French *hauberc,* of Germanic origin; compare Old High German *halsberc,* Old English *healsbeorg,* from *heals* neck + *beorg* protection, shelter

haud (hɔːd, hʌd) VERB, NOUN a Scot word for **hold.**

hauf (hɔːf) NOUN, DETERMINER, ADJECTIVE, ADVERB a Scot word for **half.**

haugh (hɑːk, hɑːf; *Scot* hɒx) NOUN *Scot and northern English dialect* a low-lying often alluvial riverside meadow.
▷HISTORY Old English *healh* corner of land; see HOLLOW

haughty ('hɔːtɪ) ADJECTIVE **-tier, -tiest.** 1 having or showing arrogance. 2 *Archaic* noble or exalted.
▷HISTORY C16: from Old French *haut,* literally: lofty, from Latin *altus* high
▸'**haughtily** ADVERB ▸'**haughtiness** NOUN

Hauhau ('haʊhaʊ) NOUN *NZ history* a 19th-century Maori religious sect.
▷HISTORY Maori

haul (hɔːl) VERB 1 to drag or draw (something) with effort. 2 (*tr*) to transport, as in a lorry. 3 *Nautical* to alter the course of (a vessel), esp so as to sail closer to the wind. 4 (*tr*) *Nautical* to draw or hoist (a vessel) out of the water onto land or a dock for repair, storage, etc. 5 (*intr*) *Nautical* (of the wind) to blow from a direction nearer the bow. Compare **veer**[1] (sense 3b). 6 (*intr*) to change one's opinion or action. ◆ NOUN 7 the act of dragging with effort. 8 (esp of fish) the amount caught at a single time. 9 something that is hauled. 10 the goods obtained from a robbery. 11 a distance of hauling: *a three-mile haul.* 12 the amount of a contraband seizure: *arms haul; drugs haul.* 13 **in** (*or*

over) the long haul. a in a future time. **b** over a lengthy period of time.
▷HISTORY C16: from Old French *haler,* of Germanic origin; see HALE[2]

haulage ('hɔːlɪdʒ) NOUN [1] the act or labour of hauling. [2] a rate or charge levied for the transportation of goods, esp by rail.

haulier ('hɔːljə) *or US* **hauler** ('hɔːlə) NOUN [1] a person or firm that transports goods by lorry; one engaged in road haulage. [2] a person that hauls, esp a mine worker who conveys coal from the workings to the foot of the shaft.

haulm *or* **halm** (hɔːm) NOUN [1] the stems or stalks of beans, peas, potatoes, grasses, etc., collectively, as used for thatching, bedding, etc. [2] a single stem of such a plant.
▷HISTORY Old English *healm;* related to Old Norse *halmr,* Old High German *halm* stem, straw, Latin *culmus* stalk, Greek *kalamos* reed, Old Slavonic *slama* straw

haul off VERB *(intr, adverb)* [1] (foll by *and) US and Canadian informal* to draw back in preparation (esp to strike or fight): *I hauled off and slugged him.* [2] *Nautical* to alter the course of a vessel so as to avoid an obstruction, shallow waters, etc.

haul up VERB *(adverb)* [1] *(tr) Informal* to call to account or criticize. [2] *Nautical* to sail (a vessel) closer to the wind.

haunch (hɔːntʃ) NOUN [1] the human hip or fleshy hindquarter of an animal, esp a horse or similar quadruped. [2] the leg and loin of an animal, used for food: *a haunch of venison.* [3] Also called: **hance.** *Architect* the part of an arch between the impost and the apex.
▷HISTORY C13: from Old French *hanche;* related to Spanish, Italian *anca,* of Germanic origin; compare Low German *hanke*
▸**haunched** ADJECTIVE

haunch bone NOUN a nontechnical name for the **ilium** or **hipbone.**

haunt (hɔːnt) VERB [1] to visit (a person or place) in the form of a ghost. [2] *(tr)* to intrude upon or recur to (the memory, thoughts, etc.): *he was haunted by the fear of insanity.* [3] to visit (a place) frequently. [4] to associate with (someone) frequently. ◆ NOUN [5] *(often plural)* a place visited frequently: *an old haunt of hers.* [6] a place to which animals habitually resort for food, drink, shelter, etc.
▷HISTORY C13: from Old French *hanter,* of Germanic origin; compare Old Norse *heimta* to bring home, Old English *hāmettan* to give a home to; see HOME
▸'**haunter** NOUN

haunted ('hɔːntɪd) ADJECTIVE [1] frequented or visited by ghosts. [2] *(postpositive)* obsessed or worried.

haunting ('hɔːntɪŋ) ADJECTIVE [1] (of memories) poignant or persistent. [2] poignantly sentimental; enchantingly or eerily evocative.
▸'**hauntingly** ADVERB

Hauraki Gulf (haʊ'rækɪ) NOUN an inlet of the Pacific in New Zealand, on the N coast of North Island.

Hausa ('haʊsə) NOUN [1] *(plural* **-sas** *or* **-sa)** a member of a Negroid people of W Africa, living chiefly in N Nigeria. [2] the language of this people: the chief member of the Chadic subfamily of the Afro-Asiatic family of languages. It is widely used as a trading language throughout W Africa and the S Sahara.

hausfrau ('haʊsˌfraʊ) NOUN a German housewife.
▷HISTORY German, from *Haus* HOUSE + *Frau* woman, wife

haustellum (hɔː'stɛləm) NOUN, *plural* **-la** (-lə). the tip of the proboscis of a housefly or similar insect, specialized for sucking food.
▷HISTORY C19: New Latin, diminutive of Latin *haustrum* device for drawing water, from *haurīre* to draw up; see EXHAUST
▸**haus'tellate** ADJECTIVE

haustorium (hɔː'stɔːrɪəm) NOUN, *plural* **-ria** (-rɪə). the organ of a parasitic plant that penetrates the host tissues and absorbs food and water from them.
▷HISTORY C19: from New Latin, from Late Latin *haustor* a water-drawer; see HAUSTELLUM
▸**haus'torial** ADJECTIVE

hautboy ('əʊbɔɪ) NOUN [1] Also called: **hautbois strawberry, haubois** ('əʊbɔɪ). a strawberry, *Fragaria moschata,* of central Europe and Asia, with large fruit. [2] an archaic word for **oboe.**
▷HISTORY C16: from French *hautbois,* from *haut* high + *bois* wood, of Germanic origin; see BUSH[1]

haute couture *French* (ot kutyr) NOUN high fashion.
▷HISTORY literally: high dressmaking

haute cuisine *French* (ot kwizin) NOUN high-class cooking.
▷HISTORY literally: high cookery

haute école *French* (ot ekɔl) NOUN the classical art of riding.
▷HISTORY literally: high school

Haute-Garonne *(French* otgarɔn) NOUN a department of SW France, in Midi-Pyrénées region. Capital: Toulouse. Pop.: 1 046 338 (1999). Area: 6367 sq. km (2483 sq. miles).

Haute-Loire *(French* otlwar) NOUN a department of S central France, in Auvergne region. Capital: Le Puy. Pop.: 209 113 (1999). Area: 5001 sq. km (1950 sq. miles).

Haute-Marne *(French* otmarn) NOUN a department of NE France, in Champagne-Ardenne region. Capital: Chaumont. Pop.: 194 873 (1999). Area: 6257 sq. km (2440 sq. miles).

Haute-Normandie *(French* otnɔrmɑ̃di) NOUN a region of NW France, on the English Channel: generally fertile and flat.

Hautes-Alpes *(French* otzalp) NOUN a department of SE France in Provence-Alpes-Côte d'Azur region. Capital: Gap. Pop.: 121 419 (1999). Area: 5643 sq. km (2201 sq. miles).

Haute-Saône *(French* otson) NOUN a department of E France, in Franche-Comté region. Capital: Vesoul. Pop.: 229 732 (1999). Area: 5375 sq. km (2096 sq. miles).

Haute-Savoie *(French* otsavwa) NOUN a department of E France, in Rhône-Alpes region. Capital: Annecy. Pop.: 631 679 (1999). Area: 4958 sq. km (1934 sq. miles).

Hautes-Pyrénées *(French* otpirene) NOUN a department of SW France, in Midi-Pyrénées region. Capital: Tarbes. Pop.: 222 368 (1999). Area: 4534 sq. km (1768 sq. miles).

hauteur (əʊ'tɜː) NOUN pride; haughtiness.
▷HISTORY C17: from French, from *haut* high; see HAUGHTY

Haute-Vienne *(French* otvjɛn) NOUN a department of W central France, in Limousin region. Capital: Limoges. Pop.: 353 893 (1999). Area: 5555 sq. km (2166 sq. miles).

haut monde *French* (o mɔ̃d) NOUN high society.
▷HISTORY literally: high world

Haut-Rhin *(French* orɛ̃) NOUN a department of E France in Alsace region. Capital: Colmar. Pop.: 708 025 (1999). Area: 3566 sq. km (1377 sq. miles).

Hauts-de-Seine *(French* odəsɛn) NOUN a department of N central France, in Île-de-France region just west of Paris: formed in 1964. Capital: Nanterre. Pop.: 1 428 238 (1999). Area: 175 sq. km (68 sq. miles).

Havana (hə'vænə) NOUN the capital of Cuba, a port in the northwest on the Gulf of Mexico: the largest city in the Caribbean; founded in 1514 as San Cristóbal de la Habana by Diego Velásquez. Pop.: 2 198 392 (1994 est.). Spanish name: **Habana.** Related adjective: **Habanero.**

Havana Brown NOUN a breed of medium-sized cat with large eyes, large ears, and a sleek brown coat.

Havana cigar NOUN any of various cigars hand-rolled in Cuba, known esp for their high quality. Also called: **Havana.**

Havant ('hævᵊnt) NOUN a market town in S England, in SE Hampshire. Pop.: 46 510 (1991).

havdalah *or* ***havdoloh*** *Hebrew* (hɑvdɑ'lɑ; *Yiddish* hɑv'dɔlə) NOUN *Judaism* the ceremony marking the end of the sabbath or of a festival, including the blessings over wine, candles, and spices.
▷HISTORY literally: separation

have (hæv) VERB **has, having, had.** *(mainly tr)* [1] to be in material possession of; own: *he has two cars.* [2] to possess as a characteristic quality or attribute: *he has dark hair.* [3] to receive, take, or obtain: *she had a present from him; have a look.* [4] to hold or entertain in the mind: *to have an idea.* [5] to possess a knowledge or understanding of: *I have no German.* [6] to experience or undergo: *to have a shock.* [7] to be infected with or suffer from: *to have a cold.* [8] to gain control of or advantage over: *you have me on that point.* [9] *(usually passive) Slang* to cheat or outwit: *he was had by that dishonest salesman.* [10] (foll by *on)* to exhibit (mercy, compassion, etc., towards): *have mercy on us, Lord.* [11] to engage or take part in: *to have a conversation.* [12] to arrange, carry out, or hold: *to have a party.* [13] to cause, compel, or require to (be, do, or be done): *have my shoes mended.* [14] (takes an infinitive with *to)* used as an auxiliary to express compulsion or necessity: *I had to run quickly to escape him.* [15] to eat, drink, or partake of: *to have a good meal.* [16] *Slang* to have sexual intercourse with: *he had her on the sofa.* [17] *(used with a negative)* to tolerate or allow: *I won't have all this noise.* [18] to declare, state, or assert: *rumour has it that they will marry.* [19] to put or place: *I'll have the sofa in this room.* [20] to receive as a guest: *to have three people to stay.* [21] to beget or bear (offspring): *she had three children.* [22] *(takes a past participle)* used as an auxiliary to form compound tenses expressing completed action: *I have gone; I shall have gone; I would have gone; I had gone.* [23] **had better** *or* **best.** ought to: used to express compulsion, obligation, etc.: *you had better go.* [24] **had rather** *or* **sooner.** to consider or find preferable that: *I had rather you left at once.* [25] **have done.** See **done** (sense 3). [26] **have had it.** *Informal* **a** to be exhausted, defeated, or killed. **b** to have lost one's last chance. **c** to become unfashionable. [27] **have it.** to win a victory. [28] **have it away** *(or* **off).** *Brit slang* to have sexual intercourse. [29] **have it coming.** *Informal* to be about to receive or to merit punishment or retribution. [30] **have it in for.** *Informal* to wish or intend harm towards. [31] **have it so good.** to have so many benefits, esp material benefits. [32] **have to do with. a** to have dealings or associate with: *I have nothing to do with her.* **b** to be of relevance to: *this has nothing to do with you.* [33] **I have it.** *Informal* I know the answer. [34] **let (someone) have it.** *Slang* to launch or deliver an attack on, esp to discharge a firearm at (someone). [35] **not having any.** (foll by *of) Informal* refusing to take part or be involved (in). ◆ NOUN [36] *(usually plural)* a person or group of people in possession of wealth, security, etc.: *the haves and the have-nots.* ◆ See also **have at, have in, have on, have out, have up.**
▷HISTORY Old English *habban;* related to Old Norse *hafa,* Old Saxon *hebbian,* Old High German *habēn,* Latin *habēre*

have-a-go ADJECTIVE *Informal* (of people attempting arduous or dangerous tasks) brave or spirited: *a have-a-go pensioner.*

have at VERB *(intr, preposition) Archaic* to make an opening attack on, esp in fencing.

have in VERB *(tr, adverb)* [1] to ask (a person) to give a service: *we must have the electrician in to mend the fire.* [2] to invite to one's home.

Havel *(German* 'haːfəl) NOUN a river in E Germany, flowing south to Berlin, then west and north to join the River Elbe. Length: about 362 km (225 miles).

havelock ('hævlɒk) NOUN a light-coloured cover for a service cap with a flap extending over the back of the neck to protect the head and neck from the sun.
▷HISTORY C19: named after Sir H. *Havelock* (1795–1857), English general in India

haven ('heɪvᵊn) NOUN [1] a port, harbour, or other sheltered place for shipping. [2] a place of safety or sanctuary; shelter. ◆ VERB [3] *(tr)* to secure or shelter in or as if in a haven.
▷HISTORY Old English *hæfen,* from Old Norse *höfn;* related to Middle Dutch *havene,* Old Irish *cuan* to bend
▸'**havenless** ADJECTIVE

have-not NOUN *(usually plural)* a person or group of people in possession of relatively little material wealth.

haven't ('hævᵊnt) VERB CONTRACTION OF have not.

have on VERB *(tr)* [1] *(usually adverb)* to wear. [2] *(usually adverb)* to have (a meeting or engagement) arranged as a commitment: *what does your boss have on this afternoon?* [3] *(adverb) Informal* to trick or tease (a person). [4] *(preposition)* to have available (information or evidence, esp when incriminating) about (a person): *the police had nothing on him, so they let him go.*

have out VERB *(tr, adverb)* 1 to settle (a matter) or come to (a final decision), esp by fighting or by frank discussion (often in the phrase **have it out**). 2 to have extracted or removed: *I had a tooth out.*

haver ('heɪvə) VERB *(intr) Brit* 1 to dither. 2 *Scot and northern English dialect* to talk nonsense; babble. ◆ NOUN 3 *(usually plural) Scot* nonsense.
▷**HISTORY** C18: of unknown origin

Havering ('heɪvərɪŋ) NOUN a borough of NE Greater London, formed in 1965 from Romford and Hornchurch (both previously in Essex). Pop.: 224 248 (2001). Area: 120 sq. km (46 sq. miles).

haversack ('hævəˌsæk) NOUN a canvas bag for provisions or equipment, carried on the back or shoulder.
▷**HISTORY** C18: from French *havresac,* from German *Habersack* oat bag, from Old High German *habaro* oats + *Sack* SACK[1]

Haversian canal (hæ'vɜːʃən) NOUN *Histology* any of the channels that form a network in bone and contain blood vessels and nerves.
▷**HISTORY** C19: named after C. *Havers* (died 1702), English anatomist who discovered them

haversine ('hævəˌsaɪn) NOUN *Obsolete* half the value of the versed sine.
▷**HISTORY** C19: combination of *half* + *versed* + SINE[1]

have up VERB *(tr, adverb; usually passive)* to cause to appear for trial: *he was had up for breaking and entering.*

havildar ('hævɪlˌdɑː) NOUN a noncommissioned officer in the Indian army, equivalent in rank to sergeant.
▷**HISTORY** C17: from Hindi, from Persian *hawāldār* one in charge

havoc ('hævək) NOUN 1 destruction; devastation; ruin. 2 *Informal* confusion; chaos. 3 **cry havoc.** *Archaic* to give the signal for pillage and destruction. 4 **play havoc.** (often foll by *with*) to cause a great deal of damage, distress, or confusion (to). ◆ VERB **-ocs, -ocking, -ocked.** 5 *(tr) Archaic* to lay waste.
▷**HISTORY** C15: from Old French *havot* pillage, probably of Germanic origin

Havre ('hɑːvrə; *French* ɑvrə) NOUN See **Le Havre.**

haw[1] (hɔː) NOUN 1 the round or oval fruit (a pome) of the hawthorn, usually red or yellow, containing one to five seeds. 2 another name for **hawthorn.**
▷**HISTORY** Old English *haga,* identical with *haga* HEDGE; related to Old Norse *hagi* pasture

haw[2] (hɔː) NOUN, INTERJECTION 1 an inarticulate utterance, as of hesitation, embarrassment, etc.; hem. ◆ VERB 2 *(intr)* to make this sound. 3 **hem** (*or* **hum**) **and haw.** See **hem[2]** (sense 3).
▷**HISTORY** C17: of imitative origin

haw[3] (hɔː) NOUN *Archaic* a yard or close.
▷**HISTORY** of unknown origin

haw[4] (hɔː) NOUN the nictitating membrane of a horse or other domestic animal.
▷**HISTORY** C15: of unknown origin

Hawaii (hə'waɪɪ) NOUN a state of the US in the central Pacific, consisting of over 20 volcanic islands and atolls, including Hawaii, Maui, Oahu, Kauai, and Molokai: discovered by Captain Cook in 1778; annexed by the US in 1898; naval base at Pearl Harbor attacked by the Japanese in 1941, a major cause of US entry into World War II; became a state in 1959. Capital: Honolulu. Pop.: 1 211 537 (2000). Area: 16 640 sq. km (6425 sq. miles). Former name: **Sandwich Islands.** Abbreviations: **Ha,** (with zip code) **HI.**

Hawaiian (hə'waɪən) ADJECTIVE 1 of or relating to Hawaii, its people, or their language. ◆ NOUN 2 a native or inhabitant of Hawaii, esp one descended from Melanesian or Tahitian immigrants. 3 a language of Hawaii belonging to the Malayo-Polynesian family.

Hawaiian guitar NOUN a lap-held steel-strung guitar with a wood or metal body, tuned to an open chord and played with a slide. Compare **Dobro, pedal steel guitar.**

Hawaiki ('hɑːwaɪkiː) NOUN *NZ* a legendary Pacific island from which the Maoris migrated to New Zealand by canoe.
▷**HISTORY** Maori

Hawes Water (hɔːz) NOUN a lake in NW England, in the Lake District: provides part of Manchester's water supply; extended by damming from 4 km (2.5 miles) to 6 km (4 miles).

hawfinch ('hɔːˌfɪntʃ) NOUN an uncommon European finch, *Coccothraustes coccothraustes,* having a very stout bill and brown plumage with black-and-white wings.

haw-haw[1] ('hɔː'hɔː) INTERJECTION a variant of **ha-ha[1].**

haw-haw[2] ('hɔːhɔː) NOUN a variant of **ha-ha[2].**

Hawick ('hɔːɪk) NOUN a town in SE Scotland, in S central Scottish Borders: knitwear industry. Pop.: 15 812 (1991).

hawk[1] (hɔːk) NOUN 1 any of various diurnal birds of prey of the family *Accipitridae,* such as the goshawk and Cooper's hawk, typically having short rounded wings and a long tail. Related adjective: **accipitrine.** 2 *US and Canadian* any of various other falconiform birds, including the falcons but not the eagles or vultures. 3 a person who advocates or supports war or warlike policies. Compare **dove[1]** (sense 2). 4 a ruthless or rapacious person. 5 **know a hawk from a handsaw.** to be able to judge things; be discerning. [from Shakespeare (*Hamlet* II:2:375); *handsaw* is probably a corruption of dialect *heronshaw* heron] ◆ VERB 6 *(intr)* to hunt with falcons, hawks, etc. 7 *(intr)* (of falcons or hawks) to fly in quest of prey. 8 to pursue or attack on the wing, as a hawk.
▷**HISTORY** Old English *hafoc;* related to Old Norse *haukr,* Old Frisian *havek,* Old High German *habuh,* Polish *kobuz*
▸ **'hawkˌlike** ADJECTIVE

hawk[2] (hɔːk) VERB 1 to offer (goods) for sale, as in the street. 2 *(tr; often foll by about)* to spread (news, gossip, etc.).
▷**HISTORY** C16: back formation from HAWKER[1]

hawk[3] (hɔːk) VERB 1 *(intr)* to clear the throat noisily. 2 *(tr)* to force (phlegm) up from the throat. 3 *Brit* a slang word for **spit.** ◆ NOUN 4 a noisy clearing of the throat.
▷**HISTORY** C16: of imitative origin; see HAW[2]

hawk[4] (hɔːk) NOUN a small square board with a handle underneath, used for carrying wet plaster or mortar. Also called: **mortar board.**
▷**HISTORY** of unknown origin

hawkbill ('hɔːkˌbɪl) NOUN another name for **hawksbill turtle.**

hawkbit ('hɔːkˌbɪt) NOUN any of three composite perennial plants of the genus *Leontodon,* with yellow dandelion-like flowers and lobed leaves in a rosette, erect or prostrate: found in grassland.
▷**HISTORY** C18: from HAWK(WEED) + (DEVIL'S) BIT

hawker[1] ('hɔːkə) NOUN a person who travels from place to place selling goods.
▷**HISTORY** C16: probably from Middle Low German *hōker,* from *hōken* to peddle; see HUCKSTER

hawker[2] ('hɔːkə) NOUN a person who hunts with hawks, falcons, etc.
▷**HISTORY** Old English *hafecere;* see HAWK[1], -ER[1]

Hawk-Eye NOUN *Trademark, cricket* a machine, employed by TV commentators, that uses a missile tracking system to spot legitimate leg before wickets by determining whether the ball would have hit the stumps.

hawk-eyed ADJECTIVE 1 having extremely keen sight. 2 vigilant, watchful, or observant: *hawk-eyed scrutiny.*

hawking ('hɔːkɪŋ) NOUN another name for **falconry.**

Hawking radiation NOUN *Astronomy* the emission of particles by a black hole. Pairs of virtual particles in the intense gravitational field around a black hole may live long enough for one to move outward when the other is pulled into the black hole, making it appear that the black hole is emitting radiation.
▷**HISTORY** C20: discovered by Stephen *Hawking* (born 1942), British physicist

hawkish ('hɔːkɪʃ) ADJECTIVE favouring the use or display of force rather than diplomacy to achieve foreign policy goals.

hawk moth NOUN any of various moths of the family *Sphingidae,* having long narrow wings and powerful flight, with the ability to hover over flowers when feeding from the nectar. Also called: **sphinx moth, hummingbird moth.** See also **death's-head moth.**

hawk owl NOUN a hawklike northern owl, *Surnia ulula,* with a long slender tail and brownish speckled plumage.

hawk's-beard NOUN any plant of the genus *Crepis,* having a ring of fine hairs surrounding the fruit and clusters of small dandelion-like flowers: family *Asteraceae* (composites).

hawksbill turtle *or* **hawksbill** ('hɔːksˌbɪl) NOUN a small tropical turtle, *Eretmochelys imbricata,* with a hooked beaklike mouth: a source of tortoiseshell: family *Chelonidae.* Also called: **hawkbill, tortoiseshell turtle.**

hawk's-eye NOUN a dark blue variety of the mineral crocidolite: a semiprecious gemstone.

hawkweed ('hɔːkˌwiːd) NOUN any typically hairy plant of the genus *Hieracium,* with clusters of dandelion-like flowers: family *Asteraceae* (composites).

Haworth ('hauəθ) NOUN a village in N England, in Bradford unitary authority, West Yorkshire: home of Charlotte, Emily, and Anne Brontë. Pop.: 4956 (1991).

hawse (hɔːz) *Nautical* ◆ NOUN 1 the part of the bows of a vessel where the hawseholes are. 2 short for **hawsehole** or **hawsepipe.** 3 the distance from the bow of an anchored vessel to the anchor. 4 the arrangement of port and starboard anchor ropes when a vessel is riding on both anchors. ◆ VERB 5 *(intr)* (of a vessel) to pitch violently when at anchor.
▷**HISTORY** C14: from earlier *halse,* probably from Old Norse *háls;* related to Old English *heals* neck

hawsehole ('hɔːzˌhəʊl) NOUN *Nautical* one of the holes in the upper part of the bows of a vessel through which the anchor ropes pass. Often shortened to **hawse.**

hawsepipe ('hɔːzˌpaɪp) NOUN *Nautical* a strong metal pipe through which an anchor rope passes. Often shortened to **hawse.**

hawser ('hɔːzə) NOUN *Nautical* a large heavy rope.
▷**HISTORY** C14: from Anglo-French *hauceour,* from Old French *haucier* to hoist, ultimately from Latin *altus* high

hawser bend NOUN a knot for tying two ropes together.

hawser-laid ADJECTIVE (of a rope) made up of three strands, the fibres (or yarns) of which have been twisted together in a left-handed direction. These three strands are then twisted together in a right-handed direction to make the rope.

hawthorn ('hɔːˌθɔːn) NOUN any of various thorny trees or shrubs of the N temperate rosaceous genus *Crataegus,* esp *C. oxyacantha,* having white or pink flowers and reddish fruits (haws). Also called (in Britain): **may, may tree, mayflower.**
▷**HISTORY** Old English *haguthorn* from *haga* hedge + *thorn* thorn; related to Old Norse *hagthorn,* Middle High German *hagendorn,* Dutch *haagdoorn*

Hawthorne effect NOUN improvement in the performance of employees, students, etc., brought about by making changes in working methods, resulting from research into means of improving performance. Compare **iatrogenic, placebo effect.**
▷**HISTORY** from the Western Electric Company's *Hawthorne* works in Chicago, USA, where it was discovered during experiments in the 1920s

hay[1] (heɪ) NOUN 1 **a** grass, clover, etc., cut and dried as fodder. **b** *(in combination)*: *a hayfield; a hayloft.* 2 **hit the hay.** *Slang* to go to bed. 3 **make hay of.** to throw into confusion. 4 **make hay while the sun shines.** to take full advantage of an opportunity. 5 **roll in the hay.** *Informal* sexual intercourse or heavy petting. ◆ VERB 6 to cut, dry, and store (grass, clover, etc.) as fodder. 7 *(tr)* to feed with hay.
▷**HISTORY** Old English *hieg;* related to Old Norse *hey,* Gothic *hawi,* Old Frisian *hē,* Old High German *houwi;* see HEW

hay[2] *or* **hey** (heɪ) NOUN 1 a circular figure in country dancing. 2 a former country dance in which the dancers wove in and out of a circle.
▷**HISTORY** C16: of uncertain origin

haybox ('heɪˌbɒks) NOUN an airtight box full of hay or other insulating material used to keep partially cooked food warm and allow cooking by retained heat.

haycock ('heɪˌkɒk) NOUN a small cone-shaped pile

of hay left in the field until dry enough to carry to the rick or barn.

hay fever NOUN an allergic reaction to pollen, dust, etc., characterized by sneezing, runny nose, and watery eyes due to inflammation of the mucous membranes of the eyes and nose. Technical names **allergic rhinitis, pollinosis.**

hayfork ('heɪˌfɔːk) NOUN a long-handled fork with two long curved prongs, used for moving or turning hay; pitchfork.

haymaker ('heɪˌmeɪkə) NOUN [1] a person who helps to cut, turn, toss, spread, or carry hay. [2] Also called: **hay conditioner.** either of two machines, one designed to crush stems of hay, the other to break and bend them, in order to cause more rapid and even drying. [3] *Boxing, slang* a wild swinging punch.
▸ **'hayˌmaking** ADJECTIVE, NOUN

haymow ('heɪˌmaʊ) NOUN [1] a part of a barn where hay is stored. [2] a quantity of hay stored in a barn or loft.

hayrack ('heɪˌræk) NOUN [1] a rack for holding hay for feeding to animals. [2] a rack fixed to a cart or wagon to increase the quantity of hay or straw that it can carry.

hayseed ('heɪˌsiːd) NOUN [1] seeds or fragments of grass or straw. [2] *US and Canadian informal, derogatory* a yokel.

haystack ('heɪˌstæk) *or* **hayrick** ('heɪˌrɪk) NOUN a large pile of hay, esp one built in the open air and covered with thatch.

hayward ('heɪˌwɔːd) NOUN *Brit obsolete* a parish officer in charge of enclosures and fences.

haywire ('heɪˌwaɪə) ADJECTIVE (*postpositive*) *Informal* [1] (of things) not functioning properly; disorganized (esp in the phrase **go haywire**). [2] (of people) erratic or crazy.
▷HISTORY C20: alluding to the disorderly tangle of wire removed from bales of hay

hazan *or* ***hazzan*** *Hebrew* (xa'zan; *English* 'hɑːzᵊn) NOUN variant spellings of **chazan.**

hazard ('hæzəd) NOUN [1] exposure or vulnerability to injury, loss, evil, etc. [2] **at hazard.** at risk; in danger. [3] a thing likely to cause injury, etc. [4] *Golf* an obstacle such as a bunker, a road, rough, water, etc. [5] chance; accident (esp in the phrase **by hazard**). [6] a gambling game played with two dice. [7] *Real Tennis* **a** the receiver's side of the court. **b** one of the winning openings. [8] *Billiards* a scoring stroke made either when a ball other than the striker's is pocketed (**winning hazard**) or the striker's cue ball itself (**losing hazard**). ◆ VERB (*tr*) [9] to chance or risk. [10] to venture (an opinion, guess, etc.). [11] to expose to danger.
▷HISTORY C13: from Old French *hasard,* from Arabic *az-zahr* the die
▸ **'hazardable** ADJECTIVE ▸ **'hazard-ˌfree** ADJECTIVE

hazard lights ADJECTIVE, PLURAL NOUN the indicator lights of a motor vehicle when flashing simultaneously to indicate that the vehicle is stationary and temporarily obstructing the traffic. Also called: **hazard warning lights, hazards.**

hazardous ('hæzədəs) ADJECTIVE [1] involving great risk. [2] depending on chance.
▸ **'hazardously** ADVERB ▸ **'hazardousness** NOUN

hazard warning device NOUN an appliance fitted to a motor vehicle that operates the hazard lights.

Hazchem ('hæzˌkɛm) NOUN a word used on warning signs to indicate the presence of hazardous chemicals.

haze¹ (heɪz) NOUN [1] *Meteorol* **a** reduced visibility in the air as a result of condensed water vapour, dust, etc., in the atmosphere. **b** the moisture or dust causing this. [2] obscurity of perception, feeling, etc. ◆ VERB [3] (when *intr,* often foll by *over*) to make or become hazy.
▷HISTORY C18: back formation from HAZY

haze² (heɪz) VERB (*tr*) [1] *Chiefly US and Canadian* to subject (fellow students) to ridicule or abuse. [2] *Nautical* to harass with humiliating tasks.
▷HISTORY C17: of uncertain origin
▸ **'hazer** NOUN

hazel ('heɪzᵊl) NOUN [1] Also called: **cob.** any of several shrubs of the N temperate genus *Corylus,* esp *C. avellana,* having oval serrated leaves and edible rounded brown nuts: family *Corylaceae.* [2] the wood of any of these trees. [3] short for **hazelnut.** [4] **a** a light yellowish-brown colour. **b** (*as adjective*): *hazel eyes.*
▷HISTORY Old English *hæsel;* related to Old Norse *hasl,* Old High German *hasala,* Latin *corylus,* Old Irish *coll*

hazelhen ('heɪzᵊlˌhɛn) NOUN a European woodland gallinaceous bird, *Tetrastes bonasia,* with a speckled brown plumage and slightly crested crown: family *Tetraonidae* (grouse).

hazelnut ('heɪzᵊlˌnʌt) NOUN the nut of a hazel shrub, having a smooth shiny hard shell. Also called: **filbert,** (Brit) **cobnut,** (Brit) **cob.**

hazelnut oil NOUN an oil extracted from hazelnuts and used mostly in cooking.

hazy ('heɪzɪ) ADJECTIVE **-zier, -ziest.** [1] characterized by reduced visibility; misty. [2] indistinct; vague.
▷HISTORY C17: of unknown origin
▸ **'hazily** ADVERB ▸ **'haziness** NOUN

hazzan *Hebrew* (xa'zan; *English* 'hɑːzᵊn) NOUN a variant spelling of **chazan.**

Hb SYMBOL FOR haemoglobin.

HB (on Brit pencils) SYMBOL FOR hard-black: denoting a medium-hard lead. Compare **H** (sense 5), **B** (sense 9).

H.B.C. (in Canada) ABBREVIATION FOR **Hudson's Bay Company.**

H-beam NOUN a rolled steel joist or girder with a cross section in the form of a capital letter *H.* Compare **I-beam.**

HBM (in Britain) ABBREVIATION FOR His (*or* Her) Britannic Majesty.

H-bomb NOUN short for **hydrogen bomb.**

HC ABBREVIATION FOR: [1] Holy Communion. [2] (in Britain) House of Commons.

HCF *or* **hcf** ABBREVIATION FOR **highest common factor.**

HCG ABBREVIATION FOR human chorionic gonadotrophin. See **gonadotrophin.**

hcp ABBREVIATION FOR handicap.

hd ABBREVIATION FOR: [1] hand. [2] head.

hdbk ABBREVIATION FOR handbook.

HDL ABBREVIATION FOR high-density lipoprotein.

hdqrs ABBREVIATION FOR headquarters: replaced in military use by **HQ.**

HDR energy NOUN hot dry rock energy; energy extracted from hot rocks below the earth's surface by pumping water around a circuit in the hot region and back to the surface.

HDTV ABBREVIATION FOR **high definition television.**

he¹ (hiː; *unstressed* iː) PRONOUN (*subjective*) [1] refers to a male person or animal: *he looks interesting; he's a fine stallion.* [2] refers to an indefinite antecedent such as *one, whoever,* or *anybody*: *everybody can do as he likes in this country.* [3] refers to a person or animal of unknown or unspecified sex: *a member of the party may vote as he sees fit.* ◆ NOUN [4] **a** a male person or animal. **b** (*in combination*): *he-goat.* [5] **a** a children's game in which one player chases the others in an attempt to touch one of them, who then becomes the chaser. Compare **tag².** **b** the person chasing. Compare **it** (sense 7).
▷HISTORY Old English *hē;* related to Old Saxon *hie,* Old High German *her* he, Old Slavonic *sĭ* this, Latin *cis* on this side

he² (heɪ; *Hebrew* he) NOUN the fifth letter of the Hebrew alphabet (ה), transliterated as *h.*

he³ (hiː, heɪ) INTERJECTION an expression of amusement or derision. Also: **he-he!** *or* **hee-hee!**

He THE CHEMICAL SYMBOL FOR helium.

HE ABBREVIATION FOR: [1] high explosive. [2] His Eminence. [3] His (*or* Her) Excellency.

head (hɛd) NOUN [1] the upper or front part of the body in vertebrates, including man, that contains and protects the brain, eyes, mouth, and nose and ears when present. Related adjective: **cephalic.** [2] the corresponding part of an invertebrate animal. [3] something resembling a head in form or function, such as the top of a tool. [4] **a** the person commanding most authority within a group, organization, etc. **b** (*as modifier*): *head buyer.* **c** (*in combination*): *headmaster.* [5] the position of leadership or command: *at the head of his class.* [6] **a** the most forward part of a thing; a part that juts out; front: *the head of a queue.* **b** (*as modifier*): *head point.* [7] the highest part of a thing; upper end: *the head of the pass.* [8] the froth on the top of a glass of beer. [9] aptitude, intelligence, and emotions (esp in the phrases **above** or **over one's head, have a head for, keep one's head, lose one's head,** etc.): *she has a good head for figures; a wise old head.* [10] (*plural* **head**) a person or animal considered as a unit: *the show was two pounds per head; six hundred head of cattle.* [11] the head considered as a measure of length or height: *he's a head taller than his mother.* [12] *Botany* **a** a dense inflorescence such as that of the daisy and other composite plants. **b** any other compact terminal part of a plant, such as the leaves of a cabbage or lettuce. [13] a culmination or crisis (esp in the phrase **bring** or **come to a head**). [14] the pus-filled tip or central part of a pimple, boil, etc. [15] the head considered as the part of the body on which hair grows densely: *a fine head of hair.* [16] the source or origin of a river or stream. [17] (*capital when part of name*) a headland or promontory, esp a high one. [18] the obverse of a coin, usually bearing a portrait of the head or a full figure of a monarch, deity, etc. Compare **tail¹.** [19] a main point or division of an argument, discourse, etc. [20] (*often plural*) the headline at the top of a newspaper article or the heading of a section within an article. [21] *Nautical* **a** the front part of a ship or boat. **b** (in sailing ships) the upper corner or edge of a sail. **c** the top of any spar or derrick. **d** any vertical timber cut to shape. **e** (*often plural*) a slang word for **lavatory.** [22] *Grammar* another word for **governor** (sense 7). [23] the taut membrane of a drum, tambourine, etc. [24] **a** the height of the surface of liquid above a specific point, esp when considered or used as a measure of the pressure at that point: *a head of four feet.* **b** pressure of water, caused by height or velocity, measured in terms of a vertical column of water. **c** any pressure: *a head of steam in the boiler.* [25] *Slang* **a** a person who regularly takes drugs, esp LSD or cannabis. **b** (*in combination*): *an acidhead; a pothead.* [26] *Mining* a road driven into the coal face. [27] **a** the terminal point of a route. **b** (*in combination*): *railhead.* [28] a device on a turning or boring machine, such as a lathe, that is equipped with one or more cutting tools held to the work by this device. [29] See **cylinder head.** [30] an electromagnet that can read, write, or erase information on a magnetic medium such as a magnetic tape, disk, or drum, used in computers, tape recorders, etc. [31] *Informal* short for **headmaster** or **headmistress.** [32] **a** the head of a horse considered as a narrow margin in the outcome of a race (in the phrase **win by a head**). **b** any narrow margin of victory (in the phrase (**win**) **by a head**). [33] *Informal* short for **headache.** [34] *Curling* the stones lying in the house after all 16 have been played. [35] **against the head.** *Rugby* from the opposing side's put-in to the scrum. [36] **bite** *or* **or snap someone's head off.** to speak sharply and angrily to someone. [37] **bring** *or* **come to a head.** **a** to bring or be brought to a crisis: *matters came to a head.* **b** (of a boil) to cause to be or be about to burst. [38] **get it into one's head.** to come to believe (an idea, esp a whimsical one): *he got it into his head that the earth was flat.* [39] **give head.** *Slang* to perform fellatio. [40] **give someone** (*or* **something**) **his** (*or* **its**) **head.** **a** to allow a person greater freedom or responsibility. **b** to allow a horse to gallop by lengthening the reins. [41] **go to one's head.** **a** to make one dizzy or confused, as might an alcoholic drink. **b** to make one conceited: *his success has gone to his head.* [42] **head and shoulders above.** greatly superior to. [43] **head over heels.** **a** turning a complete somersault. **b** completely; utterly (esp in the phrase **head over heels in love**). [44] **hold up one's head.** to be unashamed. [45] **keep one's head.** to remain calm. [46] **keep one's head above water.** to manage to survive a difficult experience. [47] **make head.** to make progress. [48] **make head or tail of.** (*used with a negative*) to attempt to understand (a problem, etc.): *he couldn't make head or tail of the case.* [49] **off** (*or* **out of**) **one's head.** *Slang* insane or delirious. [50] **off the top of one's head.** without previous thought; impromptu. [51] **on one's** (**own**) **head.** at one's (own) risk or responsibility. [52] **one's head off.** *Slang* loudly or excessively: *the baby cried its head off.* [53] **over someone's head.** **a** without a person in the obvious position being considered, esp for promotion: *the graduate was promoted over the heads of several of his seniors.* **b** without consulting a person in the obvious position but referring to a higher authority: *in making his complaint he went straight to the director, over the head of his immediate boss.* **c** beyond a person's comprehension. 54 **put (our, their, etc.) heads together.** *Informal* to consult together. 55 **take it into one's head.** to conceive a notion, desire, or wish (to do something). 56 **turn heads.** to be so beautiful, unusual, or impressive as to attract a lot of attention. 57 **turn** *or* **stand (something) on its head.** to treat or present (something) in a completely new and different way: *health care which has turned orthodox medicine on its head.* 58 **turn someone's head.** to make someone vain, conceited, etc. ◆ VERB 59 (*tr*) to be at the front or top of: *to head the field.* 60 (*tr; often foll by up*) to be in the commanding or most important position. 61 (often foll by *for*) to go or cause to go (towards): *where are you heading?* 62 to turn or steer (a vessel) as specified: *to head into the wind.* 63 *Soccer* to propel (the ball) by striking it with the head. 64 (*tr*) to provide with or be a head or heading: *to head a letter; the quotation which heads chapter 6.* 65 (*tr*) to cut the top branches or shoots off (a tree or plant). 66 (*intr*) to form a head, as a boil or plant. 67 (*intr; often foll by in*) (of streams, rivers, etc.) to originate or rise in. 68 **head them.** *Austral* to toss the coins in a game of two-up. ◆ See also **head for, head off, heads.**

▷**HISTORY** Old English *hēafod;* related to Old Norse *haufuth,* Old Frisian *hāved,* Old Saxon *hōbid,* Old High German *houbit*

▸ **'head,like** ADJECTIVE

-head COMBINING FORM indicating a person having a preoccupation as specified: *breadhead.*

headache ('hɛd,eɪk) NOUN 1 pain in the head, caused by dilation of cerebral arteries, muscle contraction, insufficient oxygen in the cerebral blood, reaction to drugs, etc. Technical name: **cephalalgia.** 2 *Informal* any cause of worry, difficulty, or annoyance.

headachy *or* **headachey** ('hɛd,eɪkɪ) ADJECTIVE suffering from, caused by, or likely to cause a headache.

head arrangement NOUN *Jazz* a spontaneous orchestration.

headband ('hɛd,bænd) NOUN 1 a ribbon or band worn around the head. 2 a narrow cloth band attached to the top of the spine of a book for protection or decoration.

headbang ('hɛd,bæŋ) VERB (*intr*) *Slang* to nod one's head violently to the beat of loud rock music.

head-banger NOUN *Slang* 1 a heavy-metal rock fan. 2 a crazy or stupid person.

headboard ('hɛd,bɔːd) NOUN a vertical board or terminal at the head of a bed.

head-butt VERB (*tr*) 1 to deliberately strike (someone) with the head. ◆ NOUN **head butt.** 2 an act or an instance of deliberately striking someone with the head.

headcase ('hɛd,keɪs) NOUN *Informal* an insane person.

headcheese ('hɛd,tʃiːz) NOUN the US and Canadian name for **brawn** (sense 3).

head collar NOUN the part of a bridle that fits round a horse's head. Also called (esp US): **headstall.**

headdress ('hɛd,drɛs) NOUN any head covering, esp an ornate one or one denoting a rank or occupation.

headed ('hɛdɪd) ADJECTIVE 1 **a** having a head or heads. **b** (*in combination*): *two-headed; bullet-headed.* 2 having a heading: *headed notepaper.* 3 (*in combination*) having a mind or intellect as specified: *thickheaded.*

header ('hɛdə) NOUN 1 Also called: **header tank.** a reservoir, tank, or hopper that maintains a gravity feed or a static fluid pressure in an apparatus. 2 a manifold for distributing a fluid supply amongst a number of passages. 3 a machine that trims the heads from castings, forgings, etc., or one that forms heads, as in wire, to make nails. 4 a person who operates such a machine. 5 a brick or stone laid across a wall so that its end is flush with the outer surface. Compare **stretcher** (sense 5). 6 the action of striking a ball with the head. 7 *Informal* a headlong fall or dive. 8 *Computing* a block of data on a tape or disk providing information about the size, location, etc., of a file. 9 *Dialect* a mentally unbalanced person.

headfast ('hɛdfɑːst) NOUN a mooring rope at the bows of a ship.

▷**HISTORY** C16: from HEAD (in the sense: front) + *fast* a mooring rope, from Middle English *fest,* from Old Norse *festr;* related to FAST[1]

headfirst ('hɛd'fɜːst) ADJECTIVE, ADVERB 1 with the head foremost; headlong: *he fell headfirst.* ◆ ADVERB 2 rashly or carelessly.

head for VERB (*preposition*) 1 to go or cause to go (towards). 2 to be destined for: *to head for trouble.*

headfuck ('hɛdfʌk) NOUN *Taboo slang* an experience that is wildly exciting or impressive.

head gate NOUN 1 a gate that is used to control the flow of water at the upper end of a lock or conduit. Compare **tail gate.** 2 another name for **floodgate** (sense 1).

headgear ('hɛd,gɪə) NOUN 1 any head covering, esp a hat. 2 any part of a horse's harness that is worn on the head. 3 the hoisting mechanism at the pithead of a mine.

head-hunting NOUN 1 the practice among certain peoples of removing the heads of slain enemies and preserving them as trophies. 2 the recruitment, esp through an agency, of executives from one company to another, often rival, company. 3 *US slang* the destruction or neutralization of political opponents.

▸ **'head-,hunter** NOUN

heading ('hɛdɪŋ) NOUN 1 a title for a page, paragraph, chapter, etc. 2 a main division, as of a lecture, speech, essay, etc. 3 *Mining* **a** a horizontal tunnel. **b** the end of such a tunnel. 4 the angle between the direction of an aircraft and a specified meridian, often due north. 5 the compass direction parallel to the keel of a vessel. 6 the act of heading. 7 anything that serves as a head.

heading dog NOUN *NZ* a dog that heads off a flock of sheep or a single sheep.

headland NOUN 1 ('hɛdlənd) a narrow area of land jutting out into a sea, lake, etc. 2 ('hɛd,lænd) a strip of land along the edge of an arable field left unploughed to allow space for machines.

headless ('hɛdlɪs) ADJECTIVE 1 without a head. 2 without a leader. 3 foolish or stupid. 4 *Prosody* another word for **catalectic.**

headlight ('hɛd,laɪt) *or* **headlamp** NOUN a powerful light, equipped with a reflector and attached to the front of a motor vehicle, locomotive, etc. See also **quartz-iodine lamp.**

headline ('hɛd,laɪn) NOUN 1 Also called: **head, heading. a** a phrase at the top of a newspaper or magazine article indicating the subject of the article, usually in larger and heavier type. **b** a line at the top of a page indicating the title, page number, etc. 2 (*usually plural*) the main points of a television or radio news broadcast, read out before the full broadcast and summarized at the end. 3 **hit the headlines.** to become prominent in the news. ◆ VERB 4 (*tr*) to furnish (a story or page) with a headline. 5 to have top billing (in).

headliner ('hɛd,laɪnə) NOUN a performer given prominent billing; star.

headline rate NOUN a basic rate of inflation, taxation, etc., before distorting factors have been removed: *the headline rate of inflation.*

head-load *African* ◆ NOUN 1 baggage or goods arranged so as to be carried on the heads of African porters. ◆ VERB 2 (*tr*) to convey or carry (goods) on the head.

headlock ('hɛd,lɒk) NOUN a wrestling hold in which a wrestler locks his opponent's head between the crook of his elbow and the side of his body.

headlong ('hɛd,lɒŋ) ADVERB, ADJECTIVE 1 with the head foremost; headfirst. 2 with great haste. ◆ ADJECTIVE 3 *Archaic* (of slopes, etc.) very steep; precipitous.

headman ('hɛdmən) NOUN, *plural* **-men.** 1 *Anthropol* a chief or leader. 2 a foreman or overseer.

headmaster (,hɛd'mɑːstə) NOUN a male principal of a school.

▸ **,head'master,ship** NOUN

headmasterly (,hɛd'mæstəlɪ) ADJECTIVE typical of the duties and behaviour of a headmaster.

headmistress (,hɛd'mɪstrəs) NOUN a female principal of a school.

▸ **,head'mistress,ship** NOUN

headmistressy (,hɛd'mɪstrɪsɪ) ADJECTIVE typical of the duties and behaviour of a headmistress.

head money NOUN 1 a reward paid for the capture or slaying of a fugitive, outlaw, etc. 2 an archaic term for **poll tax.**

headmost ('hɛd,məʊst) ADJECTIVE a less common word for **foremost.**

head off VERB (*tr, adverb*) 1 to intercept and force to change direction: *to head off the stampede.* 2 to prevent or forestall (something that is likely to happen). 3 to depart or set out: *to head off to school.*

head of the river NOUN **a** any of various annual rowing regattas held on particular rivers. **b** the boat or team winning such a regatta: *Eton are head of the river again this year.*

head-on ADVERB, ADJECTIVE 1 with the front or fronts foremost: *a head-on collision.* 2 with directness or without compromise: *in his usual head-on fashion.*

headphones ('hɛd,fəʊnz) PLURAL NOUN an electrical device consisting of two earphones held in position by a flexible metallic strap passing over the head. Informal name: **cans.**

headpiece ('hɛd,piːs) NOUN 1 *Printing* a decorative band at the top of a page, chapter, etc. 2 any covering for the head, esp a helmet. 3 *Archaic* the intellect. 4 a less common word for **crownpiece** (sense 2).

headpin ('hɛd,pɪn) NOUN *Tenpin bowling* another word for **kingpin.**

headquarter (,hɛd'kwɔːtə) VERB *Informal, chiefly US* to place in or establish as headquarters.

headquarters (,hɛd'kwɔːtəz) PLURAL NOUN (*sometimes functioning as singular*) 1 any centre or building from which operations are directed, as in the military, the police, etc. 2 a military formation comprising the commander, his staff, and supporting echelons. ◆ Abbreviations: **HQ, h.q.**

headrace ('hɛd,reɪs) NOUN a channel that carries water to a water wheel, turbine, etc. Compare **tailrace.**

headrail ('hɛd,reɪl) NOUN *Billiards, snooker* the end of the table from which play is started, nearest the baulkline.

headreach ('hɛd,riːtʃ) *Nautical* ◆ NOUN 1 the distance made to windward while tacking. ◆ VERB 2 (*tr*) to gain distance over (another boat) when tacking.

headrest ('hɛd,rɛst) NOUN a support for the head, as on a dentist's chair or car seat.

head restraint NOUN an adjustable support for the head, attached to a car seat, to prevent the neck from being jolted backwards sharply in the event of a crash or sudden stop.

headroom ('hɛd,rʊm, -,ruːm) *or* **headway** NOUN the height of a bridge, room, etc.; clearance.

heads (hɛdz) INTERJECTION, ADVERB 1 with the obverse side of a coin uppermost, esp if it has a head on it: used as a call before tossing a coin. Compare **tails.** 2 **the.** *Austral informal* people in authority.

headsail ('hɛd,seɪl; *Nautical* 'hɛdsəl) NOUN any sail set forward of the foremast.

headscarf ('hɛd,skɑːf) NOUN, *plural* **-scarves** (-,skɑːvz). a scarf for the head, often worn tied under the chin.

head sea NOUN a sea in which the waves run directly against the course of a ship.

headset ('hɛd,sɛt) NOUN a pair of headphones, esp with a microphone attached.

headship ('hɛdʃɪp) NOUN 1 the position or state of being a leader; command; leadership. 2 *Education Brit* the position of headmaster or headmistress of a school.

headshrinker ('hɛd,ʃrɪŋkə) NOUN 1 a slang name for **psychiatrist.** Often shortened to **shrink.** 2 a head-hunter who shrinks the heads of his victims.

headsman ('hɛdzmən) NOUN, *plural* **-men.** (formerly) an executioner who beheaded condemned persons.

headspring ('hɛd,sprɪŋ) NOUN 1 a spring that is the source of a stream. 2 a spring using the head as a lever from a position lying on the ground. 3 *Rare* a source.

headsquare ('hɛd,skwɛə) NOUN a scarf worn on the head.

headstall (ˈhɛdˌstɔːl) NOUN another word (esp US) for **head collar.**

headstand (ˈhɛdˌstænd) NOUN the act or an instance of balancing on the head, usually with the hands as support.

head start NOUN an initial advantage in a competitive situation.
▷HISTORY originally referring to a horse's having its head in front of others at the start of a race

head station NOUN *Austral* the main buildings on a large sheep or cattle farm.

headstock (ˈhɛdˌstɒk) NOUN 1 the part of a machine that supports and transmits the drive to the chuck. Compare **tailstock.** 2 the wooden or metal block on which a church bell is hung.

headstone (ˈhɛdˌstəʊn) NOUN 1 a memorial stone at the head of a grave. 2 *Architect* another name for **keystone.**

headstream (ˈhɛdˌstriːm) NOUN a stream that is the source or a source of a river.

headstrong (ˈhɛdˌstrɒŋ) ADJECTIVE 1 self-willed; obstinate. 2 (of an action) heedless; rash.
▸ **ˈheadˌstrongly** ADVERB ▸ **ˈheadˌstrongness** NOUN

heads up NOUN *US and Canadian* a tip-off or small amount of information given in advance.

head teacher NOUN a headmaster or headmistress.

head-to-head *Informal* ◆ ADJECTIVE 1 in direct competition. ◆ NOUN 2 a competition involving two people, teams, etc.

head-up display NOUN the projection of readings from instruments onto a windscreen, enabling an aircraft pilot or car driver to see them without looking down.

head voice *or* **register** NOUN the high register of the human voice, in which the vibrations of sung notes are felt in the head.

head waiter NOUN a waiter who supervises the activities of other waiters and arranges the seating of guests.

headward (ˈhɛdwəd) ADJECTIVE 1 (of river erosion) cutting backwards or upstream above the original source, which recedes. ◆ ADVERB 2 a variant of **headwards.**

headwards (ˈhɛdwədz) *or* **headward** ADVERB backwards beyond the original source: *a river erodes headwards.*

headwaters (ˈhɛdˌwɔːtəz) PLURAL NOUN the tributary streams of a river in the area in which it rises; headstreams.

headway (ˈhɛdˌweɪ) NOUN 1 motion in a forward direction: *the vessel made no headway.* 2 progress or rate of progress: *he made no headway with the problem.* 3 another name for **headroom.** 4 the distance or time between consecutive trains, buses, etc., on the same route.

headwind (ˈhɛdˌwɪnd) NOUN a wind blowing directly against the course of an aircraft or ship. Compare **tailwind.**

headword (ˈhɛdˌwɜːd) NOUN a key word placed at the beginning of a line, paragraph, etc., as in a dictionary entry.

headwork (ˈhɛdˌwɜːk) NOUN 1 mental work. 2 the ornamentation of the keystone of an arch.
▸ **ˈheadˌworker** NOUN

heady (ˈhɛdɪ) ADJECTIVE **headier, headiest.** 1 (of alcoholic drink) intoxicating. 2 strongly affecting the mind or senses; extremely exciting. 3 rash; impetuous.
▸ **ˈheadily** ADVERB ▸ **ˈheadiness** NOUN

heal (hiːl) VERB 1 to restore or be restored to health. 2 (*intr;* often foll by *over* or *up*) (of a wound, burn, etc.) to repair by natural processes, as by scar formation. 3 (*tr*) **a** to treat (a wound, etc.) by assisting in its natural repair. **b** to cure (a disease or disorder). 4 to restore or be restored to friendly relations, harmony, etc.
▷HISTORY Old English *hǣlan;* related to Old Norse *heila,* Gothic *hailjan,* Old High German *heilen;* see HALE[1], WHOLE
▸ **ˈhealable** ADJECTIVE ▸ **ˈhealer** NOUN ▸ **ˈhealing** NOUN, ADJECTIVE

heal-all NOUN another name for **selfheal.**

healee (hiːˈliː) NOUN a person who is being healed.

health (hɛlθ) NOUN 1 the state of being bodily and mentally vigorous and free from disease. 2 the general condition of body and mind: *in poor health.* 3 the condition of any unit, society, etc.: *the economic health of a nation.* 4 a toast to a person, wishing him or her good health, happiness, etc. 5 (*modifier*) of or relating to food or other goods reputed to be beneficial to the health: *health food; a health store.* 6 (*modifier*) of or relating to health, esp to the administration of health: *a health committee; health resort; health service.* ◆ INTERJECTION 7 an exclamation wishing someone good health as part of a toast (in the phrases **your health, good health,** etc.).
▷HISTORY Old English *hǣlth;* related to *hāl* HALE[1]

health camp NOUN *NZ* a camp, usually at the seaside, for children requiring health care.

health card NOUN *Canadian* an identity card required to obtain public health insurance services.

health centre NOUN (in Britain) premises, owned by a local authority, providing health care for the local community and usually housing a group practice, nursing staff, a child-health clinic, X-ray facilities, etc.

health farm NOUN a residential establishment, often in the country, visited by those who wish to improve their health by losing weight, eating healthy foods, taking exercise, etc.

health food NOUN **a** vegetarian food organically grown and with no additives, eaten for its dietary value and benefit to health. **b** (*as modifier*): *a health-food shop.*

healthful (ˈhɛlθfʊl) ADJECTIVE a less common word for **healthy** (senses 1–3).
▸ **ˈhealthfully** ADVERB ▸ **ˈhealthfulness** NOUN

healthism (ˈhɛlθɪzəm) NOUN a lifestyle that prioritizes health and fitness over anything else.

health physics NOUN (*functioning as singular*) the branch of physics concerned with the health and safety of people in medical, scientific, and industrial work, esp with protection from the biological effects of ionizing radiation.

health salts PLURAL NOUN magnesium sulphate or similar salts taken as a mild laxative.

Health Service Commissioner NOUN (in Britain) the official name for an ombudsman who investigates personal complaints of injustice or hardship resulting from the failure, absence, or maladministration of a service for which a Regional or District Health Authority or Family Practitioner Committee is responsible, after other attempts to obtain redress have failed. See also **Commissioner for Local Administration, Parliamentary Commissioner.**

health stamp NOUN *NZ* a postage stamp with a surcharge that is used to support a health camp.

health visitor NOUN (in Britain) a nurse employed by a district health authority to visit people in their homes and give help and advice on health and social welfare, esp to mothers of preschool children, to the handicapped, and to elderly people.

healthy (ˈhɛlθɪ) ADJECTIVE **healthier, healthiest.** 1 enjoying good health. 2 functioning well or being sound: *the company's finances are not very healthy.* 3 conducive to health; salutary. 4 indicating soundness of body or mind: *a healthy appetite.* 5 *Informal* considerable in size or amount: *a healthy sum.*
▸ **ˈhealthily** ADVERB ▸ **ˈhealthiness** NOUN

heap (hiːp) NOUN 1 a collection of articles or mass of material gathered together in one place. 2 (*often plural;* usually foll by *of*) *Informal* a large number or quantity. 3 **give them heaps.** *Austral slang* to contend strenuously with an opposing sporting team. 4 **give it heaps.** *NZ slang* to try very hard. 5 *Informal* a place or thing that is very old, untidy, unreliable, etc.: *the car was a heap.* ◆ ADVERB 6 **heaps.** (intensifier): *he said he was feeling heaps better.* ◆ VERB 7 (often foll by *up* or *together*) to collect or be collected into or as if into a heap or pile: *to heap up wealth.* 8 (*tr;* often foll by *with, on,* or *upon*) to load or supply (with) abundantly: *to heap with riches.*
▷HISTORY Old English *héap;* related to Old Frisian *hāp,* Old Saxon *hōp,* Old High German *houf*
▸ **ˈheaper** NOUN

heaping (ˈhiːpɪŋ) ADJECTIVE *US and Canadian* (of a spoonful) heaped.

hear (hɪə) VERB **hears, hearing, heard** (hɜːd). 1 (*tr*) to perceive (a sound) with the sense of hearing. 2 (*tr; may take a clause as object*) to listen to: *did you hear what I said?* 3 (when *intr,* sometimes foll by *of* or *about;* when *tr, may take a clause as object*) to be informed (of); receive information (about): *to hear of his success; have you heard?* 4 *Law* to give a hearing to (a case). 5 (when *intr,* usually foll by *of* and used with a negative) to listen (to) with favour, assent, etc.: *she wouldn't hear of it.* 6 (*intr;* foll by *from*) to receive a letter, news, etc. (from). 7 **hear! hear!** an exclamation used to show approval of something said. 8 **hear tell (of).** *Dialect* to be told (about); learn (of).
▷HISTORY Old English *hieran;* related to Old Norse *heyra,* Gothic *hausjan,* Old High German *hōren,* Greek *akouein*
▸ **ˈhearable** ADJECTIVE ▸ **ˈhearer** NOUN

Heard and McDonald Islands (hɜːd, məkˈdɒnəld) PLURAL NOUN a group of islands in the S Indian Ocean: an external territory of Australia from 1947. Area: 412 sq. km (159 sq. miles).

hearing (ˈhɪərɪŋ) NOUN 1 the faculty or sense by which sound is perceived. Related adjective: **audio.** 2 an opportunity to be listened to. 3 the range within which sound can be heard; earshot. 4 the investigation of a matter by a court of law, esp the preliminary inquiry into an indictable crime by magistrates. 5 a formal or official trial of an action or lawsuit.

hearing aid NOUN a device for assisting the hearing of partially deaf people, typically consisting of a small battery-powered electronic amplifier with microphone and earphone, worn by a deaf person in or behind the ear. Also called: **deaf aid.**

hearing dog NOUN a dog that has been specially trained to help deaf or partially deaf people by alerting them to sounds such as a ringing doorbell, an alarm, etc.

hearing loss NOUN an increase in the threshold of audibility caused by age, infirmity, or prolonged exposure to intense noise.

hearken *or sometimes US* **harken** (ˈhɑːkən) VERB *Archaic* to listen to (something).
▷HISTORY Old English *heorcnian;* see HARK
▸ **ˈhearkener** NOUN

hear out VERB (*tr, adverb*) to listen in regard to every detail and give a proper or full hearing to.

hearsay (ˈhɪəˌseɪ) NOUN gossip; rumour.

hearsay evidence NOUN *Law* evidence based on what has been reported to a witness by others rather than what he has himself observed or experienced (not generally admissible as evidence).

hearse (hɜːs) NOUN a vehicle, such as a specially designed car or carriage, used to carry a coffin to a place of worship and ultimately to a cemetery or crematorium.
▷HISTORY C14: from Old French *herce,* from Latin *hirpex* harrow

heart (hɑːt) NOUN 1 the hollow muscular organ in vertebrates whose contractions propel the blood through the circulatory system. In mammals it consists of a right and left atrium and a right and left ventricle. Related adjective: **cardiac.** 2 the corresponding organ or part in invertebrates. 3 this organ considered as the seat of life and emotions, esp love. 4 emotional mood or disposition: *a happy heart; a change of heart.* 5 tenderness or pity: *you have no heart.* 6 courage or spirit; bravery. 7 the inmost or most central part of a thing: *the heart of the city.* 8 the most important or vital part: *the heart of the matter.* 9 (of vegetables such as cabbage) the inner compact part. 10 the core of a tree. 11 the part nearest the heart of a person; breast: *she held him to her heart.* 12 a dearly loved person: usually used as a term of address: *dearest heart.* 13 a conventionalized representation of the heart, having two rounded lobes at the top meeting in a point at the bottom. 14 **a** a red heart-shaped symbol on a playing card. **b** a card with one or more of these symbols or (*when pl.*) the suit of cards so marked. 15 a fertile condition in land, conducive to vigorous growth in crops or herbage (esp in the phrase **in good heart**). 16 **after one's own heart.** appealing to one's own disposition, taste, or tendencies. 17 **at heart.** in reality or fundamentally. 18 **break one's** (*or* **someone's**) **heart.** to grieve (or cause to grieve) very deeply, esp through love. 19 **by heart.** by committing to memory. 20 **cross my heart (and hope to die)!** I promise! 21 **eat one's heart out.** to brood or pine with grief or longing. 22 **from (the bottom of) one's heart.** very sincerely or deeply. 23 **have a heart!** be kind or merciful. 24 **have one's heart in it.** (*usually used with a negative*) to have enthusiasm for something. 25 **have one's heart in one's boots.** to be depressed or down-hearted. 26 **have one's heart in one's mouth** (*or* **throat**). to be full of apprehension, excitement, or fear. 27 **have one's heart in the right place. a** to be kind, thoughtful, or generous. **b** to mean well. 28 **have the heart.** (*usually used with a negative*) to have the necessary will, callousness, etc., (to do something): *I didn't have the heart to tell him.* 29 **heart and soul.** absolutely; completely. 30 **heart of hearts.** the depths of one's conscience or emotions. 31 **heart of oak.** a brave person. 32 **in one's heart.** secretly; fundamentally. 33 **lose heart.** to become despondent or disillusioned (over something). 34 **lose one's heart to.** to fall in love with. 35 **near** *or* **close to one's heart.** cherished or important. 36 **set one's heart on.** to have as one's ambition to obtain; covet. 37 **take heart.** to become encouraged. 38 **take to heart.** to take seriously or be upset about. 39 **to one's heart's content.** as much as one wishes. 40 **wear one's heart on one's sleeve.** to show one's feelings openly. 41 **with all one's** (*or* **one's whole**) **heart.** very willingly. ◆ VERB 42 (*intr*) (of vegetables) to form a heart. 43 an archaic word for **hearten.** ◆ See also **hearts.**

▷HISTORY Old English *heorte;* related to Old Norse *hjarta,* Gothic *hairtō,* Old High German *herza,* Latin *cor,* Greek *kardia,* Old Irish *cride*

heartache ('hɑːtˌeɪk) NOUN intense anguish or mental suffering.

heart attack NOUN any sudden severe instance of abnormal heart functioning, esp coronary thrombosis.

heartbeat ('hɑːtˌbiːt) NOUN one complete pulsation of the heart. See **diastole, systole.**

heart block NOUN impaired conduction or blocking of the impulse that regulates the heartbeat, resulting in a lack of coordination between the beating of the atria and the ventricles. Also called: **Adams-Stokes syndrome, atrioventricular block.**

heartbreak ('hɑːtˌbreɪk) NOUN intense and overwhelming grief, esp through disappointment in love.

heartbreaker ('hɑːtˌbreɪkə) NOUN a person or thing that causes intense sadness or disappointment.

heartbreaking ('hɑːtˌbreɪkɪŋ) ADJECTIVE extremely sad, disappointing, or pitiful.
▸ **'heartˌbreakingly** ADVERB

heartbroken ('hɑːtˌbrəʊkən) ADJECTIVE suffering from intense grief.
▸ **'heartˌbrokenly** ADVERB ▸ **'heartˌbrokenness** NOUN

heartburn ('hɑːtˌbɜːn) NOUN a burning sensation beneath the breastbone caused by irritation of the oesophagus, as from regurgitation of the contents of the stomach. Technical names: **cardialgia, pyrosis.**

heart cherry NOUN a heart-shaped variety of sweet cherry.

-hearted ADJECTIVE having a heart or disposition as specified: *good-hearted; cold-hearted; great-hearted; heavy-hearted.*

hearten ('hɑːtᵊn) VERB to make or become cheerful.

heartening ('hɑːtᵊnɪŋ) ADJECTIVE causing cheerfulness; encouraging.

heart failure NOUN 1 a condition in which the heart is unable to pump an adequate amount of blood to the tissues, usually resulting in breathlessness, swollen ankles, etc. 2 sudden and permanent cessation of the heartbeat, resulting in death.

heartfelt ('hɑːtˌfelt) ADJECTIVE sincerely and strongly felt.

hearth (hɑːθ) NOUN 1 **a** the floor of a fireplace, esp one that extends outwards into the room. **b** (*as modifier*): *hearth rug.* 2 this part of a fireplace as a symbol of the home, etc. 3 the bottom part of a metallurgical furnace in which the molten metal is produced or contained.

▷HISTORY Old English *heorth;* related to Old High German *herd* hearth, Latin *carbō* charcoal

hearthstone ('hɑːθˌstəʊn) NOUN 1 a stone that forms a hearth. 2 a less common word for **hearth** (sense 1). 3 soft stone used to clean and whiten floors, steps, etc.

heartily ('hɑːtɪlɪ) ADVERB 1 thoroughly or vigorously: *to eat heartily.* 2 in a sincere manner: *he congratulated me heartily.*

heartland ('hɑːtˌlænd) NOUN 1 the central region of a country or continent. 2 the core or most vital area: *the industrial heartland of England.*

heartless ('hɑːtlɪs) ADJECTIVE unkind or cruel; hard-hearted.
▸ **'heartlessly** ADVERB ▸ **'heartlessness** NOUN

heart-lung machine NOUN a machine used to maintain the circulation and oxygenation of the blood during heart surgery.

heart murmur NOUN an abnormal sound heard through a stethoscope over the region of the heart.

heart-rending ADJECTIVE causing great mental pain and sorrow.
▸ **'heart-ˌrendingly** ADVERB

hearts (hɑːts) NOUN (*functioning as singular*) a card game in which players must avoid winning tricks containing hearts or the queen of spades. Also called: **Black Maria.**

heart-searching NOUN examination of one's feelings or conscience.

heartsease *or* **heart's-ease** ('hɑːtsˌiːz) NOUN 1 another name for the **wild pansy.** 2 peace of mind.

heartsick ('hɑːtˌsɪk) ADJECTIVE deeply dejected or despondent.
▸ **'heartˌsickness** NOUN

heartsome ('hɑːtsəm) ADJECTIVE *Chiefly Scot* 1 cheering or encouraging: *heartsome news.* 2 gay; cheerful.
▸ **'heartsomely** ADVERB ▸ **'heartsomeness** NOUN

heart starter NOUN *Austral slang* the first drink of the day.

heartstrings ('hɑːtˌstrɪŋz) PLURAL NOUN *Often facetious* deep emotions or feelings.

▷HISTORY C15: originally referring to the tendons supposed to support the heart

heart-throb NOUN 1 an object of infatuation. 2 a heart beat.

heart-to-heart ADJECTIVE 1 (esp of a conversation or discussion) concerned with personal problems or intimate feelings. ◆ NOUN 2 an intimate conversation or discussion.

heart urchin NOUN any echinoderm of the genus *Echinocardium,* having a heart-shaped body enclosed in a rigid spiny test: class *Echinoidea* (sea urchins).

heart-warming ADJECTIVE 1 pleasing; gratifying. 2 emotionally moving.

heart-water NOUN *Vet science* a tick-borne disease of cattle, sheep, and goats characterized by fluid accumulation in the pericardial sac. It is caused by the organism *Rickettsia ruminantium.*

heart-whole ADJECTIVE *Rare* 1 not in love. 2 sincere. 3 stout-hearted.
▸ **ˌheart-'wholeness** NOUN

heartwood ('hɑːtˌwʊd) NOUN the central core of dark hard wood in tree trunks, consisting of nonfunctioning xylem tissue that has become blocked with resins, tannins, and oils. Compare **sapwood.**

heartworm ('hɑːtˌwɜːm) NOUN a parasitic nematode worm, *Dirofilaria immitis,* that lives in the heart and bloodstream of vertebrates.

hearty ('hɑːtɪ) ADJECTIVE **heartier, heartiest.** 1 warm and unreserved in manner or behaviour. 2 vigorous and enthusiastic: *a hearty slap on the back.* 3 sincere and heartfelt: *hearty dislike.* 4 healthy and strong (esp in the phrase **hale and hearty**). 5 substantial and nourishing. ◆ NOUN *Informal* 6 a comrade, esp a sailor. 7 a vigorous sporting man: *a rugby hearty.*
▸ **'heartiness** NOUN

heat (hiːt) NOUN 1 **a** the energy transferred as a result of a difference in temperature. **b** the random kinetic energy of the atoms, molecules, or ions in a substance or body. Related adjectives: **thermal, calorific.** 2 the sensation caused in the body by heat energy; warmth. 3 the state or quality of being hot. 4 hot weather: *the heat of summer.* 5 intensity of feeling; passion: *the heat of rage.* 6 pressure: *the political heat on the government over the economy.* 7 the most intense or active part: *the heat of the battle.* 8 a period or condition of sexual excitement in female mammals that occurs at oestrus. 9 *Sport* **a** a preliminary eliminating contest in a competition. **b** a single section of a contest. 10 *Slang* police activity after a crime: *the heat is off.* 11 *Chiefly US slang* criticism or abuse: *he took a lot of heat for that mistake.* 12 **in the heat of the moment.** without pausing to think. 13 **on** *or* **in heat. a** Also: **in season.** (of some female mammals) sexually receptive. **b** in a state of sexual excitement. 14 **the heat.** *Slang* the police. 15 **turn up** *or* **on the heat.** *Informal* to increase the intensity of activity, coercion, etc. ◆ VERB 16 to make or become hot or warm. 17 to make or become excited or intense.

▷HISTORY Old English *hǣtu;* related to *hāt* HOT, Old Frisian *hēte* heat, Old High German *heizī*
▸ **'heatless** ADJECTIVE

heat barrier NOUN another name for **thermal barrier.**

heat capacity NOUN the heat required to raise the temperature of a substance by unit temperature interval under specified conditions, usually measured in joules per kelvin. Symbol: C_p (for constant pressure) or C_V (for constant volume).

heat content NOUN another name for **enthalpy.**

heat death NOUN *Thermodynamics* the condition of any closed system when its total entropy is a maximum and it has no available energy. If the universe is a closed system it should eventually reach this state.

heated ('hiːtɪd) ADJECTIVE 1 made hot; warmed. 2 impassioned or highly emotional.
▸ **'heatedly** ADVERB ▸ **'heatedness** NOUN

heat engine NOUN an engine that converts heat energy into mechanical energy.

heater ('hiːtə) NOUN 1 any device for supplying heat, such as a hot-air blower, radiator, convector, etc. 2 *US slang* a pistol. 3 *Electronics* a conductor carrying a current that indirectly heats the cathode in some types of valve.

heat exchanger NOUN a device for transferring heat from one fluid to another without allowing them to mix.

heat exhaustion NOUN a condition resulting from exposure to intense heat, characterized by dizziness, abdominal cramp, and prostration. Also called: **heat prostration.** Compare **heatstroke.**

heath (hiːθ) NOUN 1 *Brit* a large open area, usually with sandy soil and scrubby vegetation, esp heather. 2 Also called: **heather.** any low-growing evergreen ericaceous shrub of the Old World genus *Erica* and related genera, having small bell-shaped typically pink or purple flowers. 3 any of several nonericaceous heathlike plants, such as sea heath. 4 *Austral* any of various heathlike plants of the genus *Epacris*: family *Epacridaceae.* 5 any of various small brown satyrid butterflies of the genus *Coenonympha,* with coppery-brown wings, esp the **large heath** (*C. tullia*).

▷HISTORY Old English *hǣth;* related to Old Norse *heithr* field, Old High German *heida* heather
▸ **'heathˌlike** ADJECTIVE ▸ **'heathy** ADJECTIVE

heathberry ('hiːθˌbɛrɪ) NOUN, *plural* **-ries.** any of various plants that have berry-like fruits and grow on heaths, such as the bilberry and crowberry.

heath cock NOUN another name for **blackcock.**

heathen ('hiːðən) NOUN, *plural* **-thens** *or* **-then.** 1 a person who does not acknowledge the God of Christianity, Judaism, or Islam; pagan. 2 an uncivilized or barbaric person. 3 **the heathen.** (*functioning as plural*) heathens collectively. ◆ ADJECTIVE 4 irreligious; pagan. 5 unenlightened; uncivilized; barbaric. 6 of or relating to heathen peoples or their religious, moral, and other customs, practices, and beliefs.

▷HISTORY Old English *hǣthen;* related to Old Norse *heithinn,* Old Frisian *hēthin,* Old High German *heidan*
▸ **'heathenism** *or* **'heathenry** NOUN ▸ **'heathenness** NOUN

heathendom ('hiːðəndəm) NOUN heathen lands, peoples, or beliefs.

heathenish ('hiːðənɪʃ) ADJECTIVE of, relating to, or resembling a heathen or heathen culture.
▸ **'heathenishly** ADVERB ▸ **'heathenishness** NOUN

heathenize *or* **heathenise** ('hiːðəˌnaɪz) VERB 1 to render or become heathen, or bring or come under heathen influence. 2 (*intr*) to engage in heathen practices.

heather ('hɛðə) NOUN 1 Also called: **ling, heath.** a low-growing evergreen Eurasian ericaceous shrub, *Calluna vulgaris,* that grows in dense masses on open ground and has clusters of small bell-shaped typically pinkish-purple flowers. 2 any of certain similar plants. 3 a purplish-red to pinkish-purple colour. ◆ ADJECTIVE 4 of a heather colour. 5 of or relating to interwoven yarns of mixed colours: *heather mixture.*
▷HISTORY C14: originally Scottish and Northern English, probably from HEATH
▸ **'heathered** ADJECTIVE ▸ **'heathery** ADJECTIVE

heathfowl ('hiːθ,faʊl) NOUN (in British game laws) an archaic name for the **black grouse.** Compare **moorfowl.**

heath grass *or* **heather grass** NOUN a perennial European grass, *Danthonia decumbens,* with flat hairless leaves.

heath hen NOUN 1 another name for **greyhen.** 2 a recently extinct variety of the prairie chicken.

Heath Robinson (rɒbɪnsᵊn) ADJECTIVE (of a mechanical device) absurdly complicated in design and having a simple function.
▷HISTORY C20: named after William *Heath Robinson* (1872–1944), British cartoonist

heath wren NOUN either of two ground-nesting warblers of southern Australia, *Hylacola pyrrhopygia* or *H. cauta,* noted for their song and their powers of mimicry.

heating ('hiːtɪŋ) NOUN 1 a device or system for supplying heat, esp central heating, to a building. 2 the heat supplied.

heating element NOUN a coil or other arrangement of wire in which heat is produced by an electric current.

heat-island NOUN *Meteorol* the mass of air over a large city, characteristically having a slightly higher average temperature than that of the surrounding air.

heat lightning NOUN flashes of light seen near the horizon, esp on hot evenings: reflections of more distant lightning.

heat of combustion NOUN *Chem* the heat evolved when one mole of a substance is burnt in oxygen at constant volume.

heat of formation NOUN *Chem* the heat evolved or absorbed when one mole of a compound is formed from its constituent atoms.

heat of reaction NOUN *Chem* the heat evolved or absorbed when one mole of a product is formed at constant pressure.

heat of solution NOUN *Chem* the heat evolved or absorbed when one mole of a substance dissolves completely in a large volume of solvent.

heat prostration NOUN another name for **heat exhaustion.**

heat pump NOUN a device, as used in a refrigerator, for extracting heat from a source and delivering it elsewhere at a much higher temperature.

heat rash NOUN a nontechnical name for **miliaria.**

heat-seeking ADJECTIVE 1 (of a detecting device) able to detect sources of infrared radiation: *a heat-seeking camera.* 2 (of a missile) able to detect and follow a source of heat, as from an aircraft engine: *a heat-seeking missile.*
▸ **heat seeker** NOUN

heat shield NOUN a coating or barrier for shielding from excessive heat, such as that experienced by a spacecraft on re-entry into the earth's atmosphere.

heat sink NOUN 1 a metal plate specially designed to conduct and radiate heat from an electrical component. 2 a layer of material placed within the outer skin of high-speed aircraft to absorb heat.

heatstroke ('hiːt,strəʊk) NOUN a condition resulting from prolonged exposure to intense heat, characterized by high fever and in severe cases convulsions and coma. See **sunstroke.**

heat-treat VERB (*tr*) to apply heat to (a metal or alloy) in one or more temperature cycles to give it desirable properties.
▸ **heat treatment** NOUN

heat wave NOUN 1 a continuous spell of abnormally hot weather. 2 (*not in technical use*) an extensive slow-moving air mass at a relatively high temperature.

heaume (həʊm) NOUN (in the 12th and 13th centuries) a large helmet reaching and supported by the shoulders.
▷HISTORY C16: from Old French *helme;* see HELMET

heave (hiːv) VERB **heaves, heaving, heaved** *or chiefly nautical* **hove.** 1 (*tr*) to lift or move with a great effort. 2 (*tr*) to throw (something heavy) with effort. 3 to utter (sounds, sighs, etc.) or breathe noisily or unhappily: *to heave a sigh.* 4 to rise and fall or cause to rise and fall heavily. 5 (*past tense and past participle* **hove**) *Nautical* **a** to move or cause to move in a specified way, direction, or position: *to heave in sight.* **b** (*intr*) (of a vessel) to pitch or roll. 6 (*tr*) to displace (rock strata, mineral veins, etc.) in a horizontal direction. 7 (*intr*) to retch. ◆ NOUN 8 the act or an instance of heaving. 9 a fling. 10 the horizontal displacement of rock strata at a fault. ◆ See also **heave down, heaves, heave to.**
▷HISTORY Old English *hebban;* related to Old Norse *hefja,* Old Saxon *hebbian,* Old High German *heffen* to raise, Latin *capere* to take, Sanskrit *kapatī* two hands full
▸ **'heaver** NOUN

heave down VERB (*intr, adverb*) *Nautical* to turn a vessel on its side for cleaning.

heave-ho SENTENCE SUBSTITUTE 1 a sailors' cry, as when hoisting anchor. ◆ NOUN 2 *Informal* dismissal, as from employment.

heaven ('hɛvᵊn) NOUN 1 (*sometimes capital*) *Christianity* **a** the abode of God and the angels. **b** a place or state of communion with God after death. Compare **hell.** 2 (*usually plural*) the sky, firmament or space surrounding the earth. 3 (in any of various mythologies) a place, such as Elysium or Valhalla, to which those who have died in the gods' favour are brought to dwell in happiness. 4 a place or state of joy and happiness. 5 (*singular* or *plural; sometimes capital*) God or the gods, used in exclamatory phrases of surprise, exasperation, etc.: *for heaven's sake; heavens above.* 6 **in seventh heaven.** ecstatically happy. 7 **move heaven and earth.** to do everything possible (to achieve something).
▷HISTORY Old English *heofon;* related to Old Saxon *heban*

heavenly ('hɛvᵊnlɪ) ADJECTIVE 1 *Informal* alluring, wonderful, or sublime. 2 of or occurring in space: *a heavenly body.* 3 divine; holy.
▸ **'heavenliness** NOUN

heaven-sent ADJECTIVE providential; fortunate: *a heaven-sent opportunity.*

heavenward ('hɛvᵊnwəd) ADJECTIVE 1 directed towards heaven or the sky. ◆ ADVERB 2 a variant of **heavenwards.**

heavenwards ('hɛvᵊnwədz) *or* **heavenward** ADVERB towards heaven or the sky.

heaves (hiːvz) NOUN (*functioning as singular or plural*) 1 Also called: **broken wind.** a chronic respiratory disorder of animals of the horse family caused by allergies and dust. 2 **the heaves.** *Slang* an attack of vomiting or retching.

heave to VERB (*adverb*) to stop (a vessel) or (of a vessel) to stop, as by trimming the sails, etc. Also: **lay to.**

heavier-than-air ADJECTIVE 1 having a density greater than that of air. 2 of or relating to an aircraft that does not depend on buoyancy for support but gains lift from aerodynamic forces.

Heaviside layer NOUN another name for **E region** (of the ionosphere), predicted by English physicist Oliver Heaviside (1850–1925) in 1902.

heavy ('hɛvɪ) ADJECTIVE **heavier, heaviest.** 1 of comparatively great weight: *a heavy stone.* 2 having a relatively high density: *lead is a heavy metal.* 3 great in yield, quality, or quantity: *heavy rain; heavy traffic.* 4 great or considerable: *heavy emphasis.* 5 hard to bear, accomplish, or fulfil: *heavy demands.* 6 sad or dejected in spirit or mood: *heavy at heart.* 7 coarse or broad: *a heavy line; heavy features.* 8 (of soil) having a high clay content; cloggy. 9 solid or fat: *heavy legs.* 10 (of an industry) engaged in the large-scale complex manufacture of capital goods or extraction of raw materials. Compare **light²** (sense 19). 11 serious; grave. 12 *Military* **a** armed or equipped with large weapons, armour, etc. **b** (of guns, etc.) of a large and powerful type. 13 (of a syllable) having stress or accentuation. Compare **light²** (sense 24). 14 dull and uninteresting: *a heavy style.* 15 prodigious: *a heavy drinker.* 16 (of cakes, bread, etc.) insufficiently leavened. 17 deep and loud: *a heavy thud.* 18 (of music, literature, etc.) **a** dramatic and powerful; grandiose. **b** not immediately comprehensible or appealing. 19 *Slang* **a** unpleasant or tedious. **b** wonderful. **c** (of rock music) having a powerful beat; hard. 20 weighted; burdened: *heavy with child.* 21 clumsy and slow: *heavy going.* 22 permeating: *a heavy smell.* 23 cloudy or overcast, esp threatening rain: *heavy skies.* 24 not easily digestible: *a heavy meal.* 25 (of an element or compound) being or containing an isotope with greater atomic weight than that of the naturally occurring element: *heavy hydrogen; heavy water.* 26 *Horse racing* (of the going on a racecourse) soft and muddy. 27 *Slang* using, or prepared to use, violence or brutality: *the heavy mob.* 28 **heavy on.** *Informal* using large quantities of: *this car is heavy on petrol.* ◆ NOUN, *plural* **heavies.** 29 **a** a villainous role. **b** an actor who plays such a part. 30 *Military* **a** a large fleet unit, esp an aircraft carrier or battleship. **b** a large calibre or weighty piece of artillery. 31 *Informal* (*usually plural,* often preceded by *the*) a serious newspaper: *the Sunday heavies.* 32 *Informal* a heavyweight boxer, wrestler, etc. 33 *Slang* a man hired to threaten violence or deter others by his presence. 34 *Scot* strong bitter beer. ◆ ADVERB 35 **a** in a heavy manner; heavily: *time hangs heavy.* **b** (*in combination*): *heavy-laden.*
▷HISTORY Old English *hefig;* related to *hebban* to HEAVE, Old High German *hebīg*
▸ **'heavily** ADVERB ▸ **'heaviness** NOUN

heavy breather NOUN 1 a person who breathes stertorously or with difficulty. 2 an anonymous telephone caller who imitates such sounds, as being suggestive of sexual excitement.

heavy chain NOUN *Immunol* a type of polypeptide chain present in an immunoglobulin molecule.

heavy-duty NOUN (*modifier*) 1 made to withstand hard wear, bad weather, etc.: *heavy-duty uniforms.* 2 subject to high import or export taxes.

heavy earth NOUN another name for **barium oxide.**

heavy-footed ADJECTIVE having a heavy or clumsy tread.

heavy-handed ADJECTIVE 1 clumsy. 2 harsh and oppressive.
▸ **,heavy-'handedly** ADVERB ▸ **,heavy-'handedness** NOUN

heavy-hearted ADJECTIVE sad; melancholy.

heavy hitter NOUN *Informal* another term for **big hitter** (sense 2).

heavy hydrogen NOUN another name for **deuterium.**

heavy metal NOUN 1 **a** a type of rock music characterized by a strong beat and amplified instrumental effects, often with violent, nihilistic, and misogynistic lyrics. **b** (*as modifier*): *a heavy-metal band.* 2 a metal with a high specific gravity. 3 *Military* large guns or shot.

heavy oil NOUN a hydrocarbon mixture, heavier than water, distilled from coal tar.

heavy spar NOUN another name for **barytes.**

heavy water NOUN water that has been electrolytically decomposed to enrich it in the deuterium isotope in the form HDO or D_2O.

heavy-water reactor NOUN a nuclear reactor that uses heavy water as moderator.

heavyweight ('hɛvɪ,weɪt) NOUN 1 a person or thing that is heavier than average. 2 **a** a professional boxer weighing more than 175 pounds (79 kg). **b** an amateur boxer weighing more than 81 kg (179 pounds). **c** (*as modifier*): *the world heavyweight championship.* 3 a wrestler in a similar weight category (usually over 214 pounds (97 kg)). 4 *Informal* an important or highly influential person.

Heb. *or* **Hebr.** ABBREVIATION FOR: 1 Hebrew (language). 2 *Bible* Hebrews.

hebdomad ('hɛbdə,mæd) NOUN 1 *Obsolete* the number seven or a group of seven. 2 a rare word for **week.**
▷HISTORY C16: from Greek, from *hebdomos* seventh, from *heptas* seven

hebdomadal (hɛb'dɒmədᵊl) *or* **hebdomadary** (hɛb'dɒmədərɪ, -drɪ) ADJECTIVE a rare word for **weekly.**
▸ **heb'domadally** ADVERB

Hebdomadal Council NOUN the governing council or senate of Oxford University.

Hebe ('hi:bɪ) NOUN *Greek myth* the goddess of youth and spring, daughter of Zeus and Hera and wife of Hercules.

Hebei ('hʌ'beɪ), **Hopeh,** *or* **Hopei** NOUN a province of NE China, on the Gulf of Chihli: important for the production of winter wheat, cotton, and coal. Capital: Shijiazhuang. Pop.: 67 440 000 (2000 est.). Area: 202 700 sq. km (79 053 sq. miles).

hebephrenia (ˌhi:bɪ'fri:nɪə) NOUN a form of pubertal schizophrenia, characterized by hallucinations, delusions, foolish behaviour, and senseless laughter.
▷HISTORY C20: New Latin, from Greek *hēbē* youth + *-phrenia* mental disorder, from *phrēn* mind
▸**hebephrenic** (ˌhi:bɪ'frɛnɪk) ADJECTIVE

hebetate ('hɛbɪˌteɪt) ADJECTIVE [1] (of plant parts) having a blunt or soft point. ◆ VERB [2] *Rare* to make or become blunted.
▷HISTORY C16: from Latin *hebetāre* to make blunt, from *hebes* blunt
▸**ˌhebe'tation** NOUN ▸**'hebeˌtative** ADJECTIVE

hebetic (hɪ'bɛtɪk) ADJECTIVE of or relating to puberty.
▷HISTORY C19: from Greek *hēbētikos* youth, from *hēbē* youth

hebetude ('hɛbɪˌtju:d) NOUN *Rare* mental dullness or lethargy.
▷HISTORY C17: from Late Latin *hebetūdō,* from Latin *hebes* blunt
▸**ˌhebe'tudinous** ADJECTIVE

Hebraic (hɪ'breɪɪk), **Hebraical,** *or* **Hebrew** ADJECTIVE of, relating to, or characteristic of the Hebrews or their language or culture.
▸**He'braically** ADVERB

Hebraism ('hi:breɪˌɪzəm) NOUN a linguistic usage, custom, or other feature borrowed from or particular to the Hebrew language, or to the Jewish people or their culture.

Hebraist ('hi:breɪɪst) NOUN a person who studies the Hebrew language and culture.
▸**ˌHebra'istic** *or* **ˌHebra'istical** ADJECTIVE ▸**ˌHebra'istically** ADVERB

Hebraize *or* **Hebraise** ('hi:breɪˌaɪz) VERB to become or cause to become Hebrew or Hebraic.
▸**ˌHebrai'zation** *or* **ˌHebrai'sation** NOUN ▸**'Hebraˌizer** *or* **'HebraˌIser** NOUN

Hebrew ('hi:bru:) NOUN [1] the ancient language of the Hebrews, revived as the official language of Israel. It belongs to the Canaanitic branch of the Semitic subfamily of the Afro-Asiatic family of languages. [2] a member of an ancient Semitic people claiming descent from Abraham; an Israelite. [3] *Archaic or offensive* a Jew. ◆ ADJECTIVE [4] of or relating to the Hebrews or their language. [5] *Archaic or offensive* Jewish.
▷HISTORY C13: from Old French *Ebreu,* from Latin *Hebraeus,* from Greek *Hebraios,* from Aramaic *'ibhray,* from Hebrew *'ibhrī* one from beyond (the river)

Hebrew calendar NOUN another term for the **Jewish calendar.**

Hebrews ('hi:bru:z) NOUN (*functioning as singular*) a book of the New Testament.

Hebridean (ˌhɛbrɪ'di:ən) *or* **Hebridian** (he'brɪdɪən) ADJECTIVE [1] of or relating to the Hebrides or their inhabitants. ◆ NOUN [2] a native or inhabitant of the Hebrides.

Hebrides ('hɛbrɪˌdi:z) PLURAL NOUN **the.** a group of over 500 islands off the W coast of Scotland: separated by the North Minch, Little Minch, and the Sea of the Hebrides: the chief islands are Skye, Raasay, Rhum, Eigg, Coll, Tiree, Mull, Jura, Colonsay, and Islay (**Inner Hebrides**), and Lewis with Harris, North Uist, Benbecula, South Uist, and Barra (**Outer Hebrides**). Also called: **Western Isles.**

Hebron ('hɛbrɒn, 'hi:-) NOUN a city in the West Bank: famous for the Haram, which includes the cenotaphs of Abraham and Sarah, Isaac and Rebecca, and Jacob and Leah. Pop.: 119 401 (1997). Arabic name: **El Khalil.**

Hecate *or* **Hekate** ('hɛkətɪ) NOUN *Greek myth* a goddess of the underworld.

hecatomb ('hɛkəˌtəʊm, -ˌtu:m) NOUN [1] (in ancient Greece or Rome) any great public sacrifice and feast, originally one in which 100 oxen were sacrificed. [2] a great sacrifice.
▷HISTORY C16: from Latin *hecatombē,* from Greek *hekatombē,* from *hekaton* hundred + *bous* ox

heck[1] (hɛk) INTERJECTION a mild exclamation of surprise, irritation, etc.
▷HISTORY C19: euphemistic for *hell*

heck[2] (hɛk) NOUN *Northern English dialect* a frame for obstructing the passage of fish in a river.
▷HISTORY C14: variant of HATCH[2]

heckelphone ('hɛkəlˌfəʊn) NOUN *Music* a type of bass oboe.
▷HISTORY C20: named after W. *Heckel* (1856–1909), German inventor

heckle ('hɛk^{ə}l) VERB [1] to interrupt (a public speaker, performer, etc.) by comments, questions, or taunts. [2] (*tr*) Also: **hackle, hatchel.** to comb (hemp or flax). ◆ NOUN [3] an instrument for combing flax or hemp.
▷HISTORY C15: Northern and East Anglian form of HACKLE
▸**'heckler** NOUN

hectare ('hɛktɑ:) NOUN one hundred ares. 1 hectare is equivalent to 10 000 square metres or 2.471 acres. Symbol: ha.
▷HISTORY C19: from French; see HECTO-, ARE[2]

hectic ('hɛktɪk) ADJECTIVE [1] characterized by extreme activity or excitement. [2] associated with, peculiar to, or symptomatic of tuberculosis (esp in the phrases **hectic fever, hectic flush**). ◆ NOUN [3] a hectic fever or flush. [4] *Rare* a person who is consumptive or who experiences a hectic fever or flush.
▷HISTORY C14: from Late Latin *hecticus,* from Greek *hektikos* habitual, from *hexis* state, from *ekhein* to have
▸**'hectically** ADVERB

hecto- *or before a vowel* **hect-** PREFIX denoting 100: *hectogram.* Symbol: h.
▷HISTORY via French from Greek *hekaton* hundred

hectocotylus (ˌhɛktəʊ'kɒtɪləs) NOUN, *plural* **-li** (-ˌlaɪ). a tentacle in certain male cephalopod molluscs, such as the octopus, that is specialized for transferring spermatozoa to the female.
▷HISTORY C19: New Latin, from HECTO- + Greek *kotulē* cup

hectogram *or* **hectogramme** ('hɛktəʊˌgræm) NOUN one hundred grams. 1 hectogram is equivalent to 3.527 ounces. Symbol: hg.

hectograph ('hɛktəʊˌgrɑ:f, -ˌgræf) NOUN [1] Also called: **copygraph.** a process for copying type or manuscript from a glycerine-coated gelatine master to which the original has been transferred. [2] a machine using this process.
▸**hectographic** (ˌhɛktəʊ'græfɪk) ADJECTIVE ▸**ˌhecto'graphically** ADVERB ▸**hectography** (hɛk'tɒgrəfɪ) NOUN

hectolitre *or US* **hectoliter** ('hɛktəʊˌli:tə) NOUN one hundred litres. A measure of capacity equivalent to 3.531 cubic feet. Symbol: hl.

hectometre *or US* **hectometer** ('hɛktəʊˌmi:tə) NOUN one hundred metres: 1 hectometre is equivalent to 328.089 feet. Symbol: hm.

hector ('hɛktə) VERB [1] to bully or torment. ◆ NOUN [2] a blustering bully.
▷HISTORY C17: after HECTOR (the son of Priam), in the sense: a bully

Hector ('hɛktə) NOUN *Classical myth* a son of King Priam of Troy, who was killed by Achilles.

Hecuba ('hɛkjʊbə) NOUN *Classical myth* the wife of King Priam of Troy, and mother of Hector and Paris.

he'd (hi:d; *unstressed* i:d, hɪd, ɪd) CONTRACTION OF he had *or* he would.

heddle ('hɛd^{ə}l) NOUN one of a set of frames of vertical wires on a loom, each wire having an eye through which a warp thread can be passed.
▷HISTORY Old English *hefeld* chain; related to Old Norse *hafald,* Middle Low German *hevelte*

heder *Hebrew* ('xɛdɛr; *English* 'heɪdə) NOUN, *plural* ***hadarim*** (xada'ri:m). a variant spelling of **cheder.**

hedera ('hɛdərə) NOUN See **ivy** (sense 1).
▷HISTORY Latin: ivy

hedge (hɛdʒ) NOUN [1] a row of shrubs, bushes, or trees forming a boundary to a field, garden, etc. [2] a barrier or protection against something. [3] the act or a method of reducing the risk of financial loss on an investment, bet, etc. [4] a cautious or evasive statement. [5] (*modifier; often in combination*) low, inferior, or illiterate: *a hedge lawyer.* ◆ VERB [6] (*tr*) to enclose or separate with or as if with a hedge. [7] (*intr*) to make or maintain a hedge, as by cutting and laying. [8] (*tr; often foll by in, about,* or *around*) to hinder, obstruct, or restrict. [9] (*intr*) to evade decision or action, esp by making noncommittal statements. [10] (*tr*) to guard against the risk of loss in (a bet, the paying out of a win, etc.), esp by laying bets with other bookmakers. [11] (*intr*) to protect against financial loss through future price fluctuations, as by investing in futures.
▷HISTORY Old English *hecg;* related to Old High German *heckia,* Middle Dutch *hegge;* see HAW[1]
▸**'hedger** NOUN ▸**'hedging** NOUN ▸**'hedgy** ADJECTIVE

hedge fund NOUN a largely unregulated speculative fund which offers substantial returns for high-risk investments.

hedge garlic NOUN another name for **garlic mustard.**

hedgehog ('hɛdʒˌhɒg) NOUN [1] any small nocturnal Old World mammal of the genus *Erinaceus,* such as *E. europaeus,* and related genera, having a protective covering of spines on the back: family *Erinaceidae,* order *Insectivora* (insectivores). Related adjective: **erinaceous.** [2] any other insectivores of the family *Erinaceidae,* such as the moon rat. [3] *US* any of various other spiny animals, esp the porcupine.

hedgehop ('hɛdʒˌhɒp) VERB **-hops, -hopping, -hopped.** (*intr*) (of an aircraft) to fly close to the ground, as in crop spraying.
▸**'hedgeˌhopper** NOUN ▸**'hedgeˌhopping** NOUN, ADJECTIVE

hedge hyssop NOUN any of several North American scrophulariaceous plants of the genus *Gratiola,* esp *G. aurea,* having small yellow or white flowers.

hedge laying NOUN the art or practice of making or maintaining a hedge by cutting branches partway through, laying them horizontally, and pegging them in position in order to create a strong thick hedge.

hedgerow ('hɛdʒˌrəʊ) NOUN a hedge of shrubs or low trees growing along a bank, esp one bordering a field or lane.

hedge-school NOUN *Irish history* a school held out of doors in favourable weather, indoors in winter.
▸**'hedge-schoolˌmaster** NOUN

hedge sparrow NOUN a small brownish European songbird, *Prunella modularis:* family *Prunellidae* (accentors). Also called: **dunnock.**

Hedjaz (hi:'dʒæz) NOUN a variant spelling of **Hejaz.**

hedonics (hi:'dɒnɪks) NOUN (*functioning as singular*) [1] the branch of psychology concerned with the study of pleasant and unpleasant sensations. [2] (in philosophy) the study of pleasure, esp in its relation to duty.

hedonism ('hi:d^{ə}ˌnɪzəm, 'hɛd-) NOUN [1] *Ethics* **a** the doctrine that moral value can be defined in terms of pleasure. See **utilitarianism. b** the doctrine that the pursuit of pleasure is the highest good. [2] the pursuit of pleasure as a matter of principle. [3] indulgence in sensual pleasures.
▷HISTORY C19: from Greek *hēdonē* pleasure
▸**he'donic** *or* **ˌhedon'istic** ADJECTIVE ▸**'hedonist** NOUN

-hedron NOUN COMBINING FORM indicating a geometric solid having a specified number of faces or surfaces: *tetrahedron.*
▷HISTORY from Greek *-edron* -sided, from *hedra* seat, base
▸**-hedral** ADJECTIVE COMBINING FORM

heebie-jeebies ('hi:bɪ'dʒi:bɪz) PLURAL NOUN **the.** *Slang* apprehension and nervousness.
▷HISTORY C20: coined by W. De Beck (1890–1942), American cartoonist

heed (hi:d) NOUN [1] close and careful attention; notice (often in the phrases **give, pay,** *or* **take heed**). ◆ VERB [2] to pay close attention to (someone or something).
▷HISTORY Old English *hēdan;* related to Old Saxon *hōdian,* Old High German *huoten*
▸**'heeder** NOUN ▸**'heedful** ADJECTIVE ▸**'heedfully** ADVERB ▸**'heedfulness** NOUN

heedless ('hi:dlɪs) ADJECTIVE taking little or no notice; careless or thoughtless.
▸**'heedlessly** ADVERB ▸**'heedlessness** NOUN

heehaw (ˌhi:'hɔ:) INTERJECTION an imitation or representation of the braying sound of a donkey.

heel[1] (hi:l) NOUN 1 the back part of the human foot from the instep to the lower part of the ankle. Compare **calcaneus.** 2 the corresponding part in other vertebrates. 3 the part of a shoe, stocking, etc., designed to fit the heel. 4 the outer part of a shoe underneath the heel. 5 the part of the palm of a glove nearest the wrist. 6 the lower, end, or back section of something: *the heel of a loaf.* 7 *Horticulture* the small part of the parent plant that remains attached to a young shoot cut for propagation and that ensures more successful rooting. 8 *Nautical* **a** the bottom of a mast. **b** the after end of a ship's keel. 9 the back part of a golf club head where it bends to join the shaft. 10 *Rugby* possession of the ball as obtained from a scrum (esp in the phrase **get the heel**). 11 *Slang* a contemptible person. 12 **at** (*or* **on**) **one's heels.** just behind or following closely. 13 **dig one's heels in.** See **dig in** (sense 5). 14 **down at heel. a** shabby or worn. **b** slovenly or careless. 15 **kick** (*or* **cool**) **one's heels.** to wait or be kept waiting. 16 **rock back on one's heels.** to astonish or be astonished. 17 **show a clean pair of heels.** to run off. 18 **take to one's heels.** to run off. 19 **to heel.** disciplined or under control, as a dog walking by a person's heel. ◆ VERB 20 (*tr*) to repair or replace the heel of (shoes, boots, etc.). 21 to perform (a dance) with the heels. 22 (*tr*) *Golf* to strike (the ball) with the heel of the club. 23 *Rugby* to kick (the ball) backwards using the sole and heel of the boot. 24 to follow at the heels of (a person). 25 (*tr*) to arm (a gamecock) with spurs. 26 (*tr*) *NZ* (of a cattle dog) to drive (cattle) by biting their heels.
▷HISTORY Old English *hēla;* related to Old Norse *hǣll,* Old Frisian *hêl*
▸'**heelless** ADJECTIVE

heel[2] (hi:l) VERB 1 (of a vessel) to lean over; list. ◆ NOUN 2 inclined position from the vertical: *the boat is at ten degrees of heel.*
▷HISTORY Old English *hieldan;* related to Old Norse *hallr* inclined, Old High German *helden* to bow

heel-and-toe ADJECTIVE 1 of or denoting a style of walking in which the heel of the front foot touches the ground before the toes of the rear one leave it. ◆ VERB 2 (*intr*) (esp in motor racing) to use the heel and toe of the same foot to operate the brake and accelerator.

heelball ('hi:lˌbɔ:l) NOUN **a** a black waxy substance used by shoemakers to blacken the edges of heels and soles. **b** a similar substance used to take rubbings, esp brass rubbings.

heel bar NOUN a small shop or a counter in a department store where shoes are mended while the customer waits.

heel bone NOUN the nontechnical name for **calcaneus.**

heeled (hi:ld) ADJECTIVE 1 **a** having a heel or heels. **b** (*in combination*): *high-heeled.* 2 **well-heeled.** wealthy.

heeler ('hi:lə) NOUN 1 *US* See **ward heeler.** 2 a person or thing that heels. 3 *Austral and NZ* a dog that herds cattle by biting at their heels.

heel in *or dialect* **hele in** VERB (*tr, adverb*) to insert (cuttings, shoots, etc.) into the soil before planting to keep them moist.

heelpiece ('hi:lˌpi:s) NOUN the piece of a shoe, stocking, etc., designed to fit the heel.

heelpost ('hi:lˌpəust) NOUN a post for carrying the hinges of a door or gate.

heeltap ('hi:lˌtæp) NOUN 1 Also called: **lift.** a layer of leather, etc., in the heel of a shoe. 2 a small amount of alcoholic drink left at the bottom of a glass after drinking.

Heerlen ('hɪələn; *Dutch* 'he:rlə) NOUN a city in the SE Netherlands, in Limburg province: industrial centre of a coal-mining region. Pop.: 95 794 (1994).

Hefei ('hʌ'feɪ) *or* **Hofei** NOUN a city in SE China, capital of Anhui province: administrative and commercial centre in a rice- and cotton-growing region. Pop.:1 000 655 (1999 est.).

heft (hɛft) VERB (*tr*) 1 to assess the weight of (something) by lifting. 2 to lift. ◆ NOUN 3 *US* weight. 4 *US* the main part.
▷HISTORY C19: probably from HEAVE, by analogy with *thieve, theft, cleave, cleft*
▸'**hefter** NOUN

hefty ('hɛftɪ) ADJECTIVE **heftier, heftiest.** *Informal* 1 big and strong. 2 characterized by vigour or force: *a hefty blow.* 3 large, bulky, or heavy. 4 sizable; involving a large amount of money: *a hefty bill; a hefty wage.*
▸'**heftily** ADVERB ▸'**heftiness** NOUN

Hegelian dialectic NOUN *Philosophy* an interpretive method in which the contradiction between a proposition (thesis) and its antithesis is resolved at a higher level of truth (synthesis).

hegemony (hɪ'gɛmənɪ) NOUN, *plural* **-nies.** ascendancy or domination of one power or state within a league, confederation, etc., or of one social class over others.
▷HISTORY C16: from Greek *hēgemonia* authority, from *hēgemōn* leader, from *hēgeisthai* to lead
▸**hegemonic** (ˌhɛgə'mɒnɪk) ADJECTIVE

Hegira *or* **Hejira** ('hɛdʒɪrə) NOUN 1 the departure of Mohammed from Mecca to Medina in 622 A.D.; the starting point of the Muslim era. 2 the Muslim era itself. See also **AH.** 3 (*often not capital*) an emigration escape or flight. ◆ Also called: **Hijrah.**
▷HISTORY C16: from Medieval Latin, from Arabic *hijrah* emigration or flight

hegumen (hɪ'gju:mɛn) *or* **hegumenos** (hɪ'gju:mɪˌnəus) NOUN the head of a monastery of the Eastern Church.
▷HISTORY C16: from Medieval Latin *hēgūmenus,* from Late Greek *hēgoumenos* leader, from Greek *hēgeisthai* to lead

heh (heɪ) INTERJECTION an exclamation of surprise or inquiry.

heid (hi:d) NOUN a Scot word for **head.**

Heidelberg ('haɪdᵊlˌbɜ:g; *German* 'haidəlbɛrk) NOUN a city in SW Germany, in NW Baden-Württemberg on the River Neckar: capital of the Palatinate from the 13th century until 1719; famous castle (begun in the 12th century) and university (1386), the oldest in Germany. Pop.: 139 400 (1999 est.).

Heidelberg man NOUN a type of primitive man, *Homo heidelbergensis,* occurring in Europe in the middle Palaeolithic age, known only from a single fossil lower jaw.
▷HISTORY C20: referring to the site where remains were found, at Mauer, near *Heidelberg,* Germany (1907)

Heiduc ('haɪdʊk) NOUN a variant spelling of **Haiduk.**

heifer ('hɛfə) NOUN a young cow.
▷HISTORY Old English *heahfore;* related to Greek *poris* calf; see HIGH

heigh-ho ('heɪ'həu) INTERJECTION an exclamation of weariness, disappointment, surprise, or happiness.

height (haɪt) NOUN 1 the vertical distance from the bottom or lowest part of something to the top or apex. 2 the vertical distance of an object or place above the ground or above sea level; altitude. 3 relatively great altitude or distance from the bottom to the top. 4 the topmost point; summit. 5 *Astronomy* the angular distance of a celestial body above the horizon. 6 the period of greatest activity or intensity: *the height of the battle.* 7 an extreme example of its kind: *the height of rudeness.* 8 (*often plural*) an area of high ground. 9 (*often plural*) the state of being far above the ground: *I don't like heights.* 10 (*often plural*) a position of influence, fame, or power: *the giddy heights they occupied in the 1980s.*
▷HISTORY Old English *hīehthu;* related to Old Norse *hǣthe,* Gothic *hauhitha,* Old High German *hōhida;* see HIGH

heighten ('haɪtᵊn) VERB 1 to make or become high or higher. 2 to make or become more extreme or intense.
▸'**heightened** ADJECTIVE ▸'**heightener** NOUN

height of land NOUN *US and Canadian* a watershed.

height-to-paper NOUN the overall height of printing plates and type, standardized as 0.9175 inch (Brit.) and 0.9186 inch (US).

Heilbronn (*German* hail'brɔn) NOUN a city in SW Germany, in N Baden-Württemberg on the River Neckar. Pop.: 119 900 (1999 est.).

Heilongjiang ('heɪ'lʊŋdʒaɪ'æŋ) *or* **Heilungkiang** ('heɪ'lʊŋ'kjæŋ, -kaɪ'æŋ) NOUN a province of NE China, in Manchuria: coal-mining, with placer gold in some rivers. Capital: Harbin. Pop.: 36 890 000 (2000 est.). Area: 464 000 sq. km (179 000 sq. miles).

Heilong Jiang ('heɪ'lʊŋ 'dʒaɪ'æŋ) NOUN the Pinyin transliteration of the Chinese name for the **Amur.**

Heiltsuk ('haɪlˌtsʊk) NOUN a member of a coastal Native Canadian people living in British Columbia. Formerly called: **Bella Bella.**
▷HISTORY of Wakashan origin

Heimdall, Heimdal ('heɪmˌdɑ:l), *or* **Heimdallr** ('heɪmˌdɑ:lə) NOUN *Norse myth* the god of light and the dawn, and the guardian of the rainbow bridge Bifrost.

Heimlich manoeuvre ('haɪmlɪk) NOUN a technique in first aid to dislodge a foreign body in a person's windpipe by applying sudden upward pressure on the upper abdomen. Also called: **abdominal thrust.**
▷HISTORY C20: named after Henry J. *Heimlich* (born 1920), American surgeon

heinous ('heɪnəs, 'hi:-) ADJECTIVE evil; atrocious.
▷HISTORY C14: from Old French *haineus,* from *haine* hatred, from *hair* to hate, of Germanic origin; see HATE
▸'**heinously** ADVERB ▸'**heinousness** NOUN

heir (ɛə) NOUN 1 *Civil law* the person legally succeeding to all property of a deceased person, irrespective of whether such person died testate or intestate, and upon whom devolves as well as the rights the duties and liabilities attached to the estate. 2 any person or thing that carries on some tradition, circumstance, etc., from a forerunner. 3 an archaic word for **offspring.**
▷HISTORY C13: from Old French, from Latin *hērēs;* related to Greek *khēros* bereaved
▸'**heirless** ADJECTIVE

heir apparent NOUN, *plural* **heirs apparent.** *Property law* a person whose right to succeed to certain property cannot be defeated, provided such person survives his ancestor. Compare **heir presumptive.**

heir-at-law NOUN, *plural* **heirs-at-law.** *Property law* the person entitled to succeed to the real property of a person who dies intestate.

heirdom ('ɛədəm) NOUN *Property law* succession by right of blood; inheritance.

heiress ('ɛərɪs) NOUN 1 a woman who inherits or expects to inherit great wealth. 2 *Property law* a female heir.

heirloom ('ɛəˌlu:m) NOUN 1 an object that has been in a family for generations. 2 *Property law* a chattel inherited by special custom or in accordance with the terms of a will.
▷HISTORY C15: from HEIR + *lome* tool; see LOOM[1]

heir presumptive NOUN *Property law* a person who expects to succeed to an estate but whose right may be defeated by the birth of one nearer in blood to the ancestor. Compare **heir apparent.**

heirship ('ɛəʃɪp) NOUN *Law* 1 the state or condition of being an heir. 2 the right to inherit; inheritance.

Heisenberg uncertainty principle NOUN a more formal name for **uncertainty principle.**

heist (haɪst) *Slang, chiefly US and Canadian* ◆ NOUN 1 a robbery. ◆ VERB 2 (*tr*) to steal or burgle.
▷HISTORY variant of HOIST
▸'**heister** NOUN

heitiki (heɪ'ti:ki:) NOUN *NZ* a Maori neck ornament of greenstone.
▷HISTORY C19: from Maori, from *hei* to hang + TIKI

hejab (hɛ'dʒɑ:b) NOUN a variant of **hijab.**

Hejaz, Hedjaz, *or* **Hijaz** (hi:'dʒæz) NOUN a region of W Saudi Arabia, along the Red Sea and the Gulf of Aqaba: formerly an independent kingdom; united with Nejd in 1932 to form Saudi Arabia. Area: about 348 600 sq. km (134 600 sq. miles).

Hejira ('hɛdʒɪrə) NOUN a variant spelling of **Hegira.**

Hekate ('hɛkətɪ) NOUN a variant spelling of **Hecate.**

Hekla ('hɛklə) NOUN a volcano in SW Iceland: several craters, with the last eruption in 1970. Height: 1491 m (4892 ft.).

Hel (hɛl) *or* **Hela** ('hɛlɑ:) NOUN *Norse myth* 1 the goddess of the dead. 2 the underworld realm of the dead.

held (hɛld) VERB the past tense and past participle of **hold**[1].

Heldentenor *German* ('hɛldənteno:r) NOUN, *plural*

-tenöre (-te'nø:rə). a tenor with a powerful voice suited to singing heroic roles, esp in Wagner.
▷HISTORY literally: hero tenor

hele in VERB (*tr, adverb*) a dialect variant of **heel in.**
▷HISTORY Old English *helian* hide

Helen ('hɛlɪn) NOUN *Greek myth* the beautiful daughter of Zeus and Leda, whose abduction by Paris from her husband Menelaus caused the Trojan War.

Helena ('hɛlənə) NOUN a city in W Montana: the state capital. Pop.: 24 569 (1990).

helenium (hə'li:nɪəm) NOUN any plant of the American genus *Helenium*, up to 1.6 m (5 ft.) tall, some species of which are grown as border plants for their daisy-like yellow or variegated flowers: family *Asteraceae*.
▷HISTORY New Latin, from Greek *helenion*, a plant name

Helgoland ('hɛlgolant) NOUN the German name for **Heligoland.**

heli- COMBINING FORM helicopter: *helipad*.
▷HISTORY C20: shortened from HELICOPTER

heliacal rising (hɪ'laɪək^{ə}l) NOUN [1] the rising of a celestial object at approximately the same time as the rising of the sun. [2] the date at which such a celestial object first becomes visible in the dawn sky.
▷HISTORY C17: from Late Latin *hēliacus* relating to the sun, from Greek *hēliakos*, from *hēlios* the sun

helianthemum (hi:lɪ'ænθəməm) NOUN any plant of the dwarf evergreen genus *Helianthemum*, some species of which are grown as rock-garden plants for their numerous papery yellow or orange flowers; related to the rockrose, which they resemble: family *Cistaceae*. Also called: **Cape primrose.**
▷HISTORY New Latin, from Greek *hēlios* sun + *anthemon* flower

helianthus (ˌhi:lɪ'ænθəs) NOUN, *plural* **-thuses.** any plant of the genus *Helianthus*, such as the sunflower and Jerusalem artichoke, typically having large yellow daisy-like flowers with yellow, brown, or purple centres: family *Asteraceae* (composites).
▷HISTORY C18: New Latin, from Greek *hēlios* sun + *anthos* flower

heli-boarding NOUN *NZ* the sport of snowboarding on mountains or glaciers accessible only by helicopter or skiplane.

helical ('hɛlɪk^{ə}l) ADJECTIVE of or shaped like a helix; spiral.
▸**'helically** ADVERB

helical gear NOUN a cylindrical gearwheel having the tooth form generated on a helical path about the axis of the wheel.

helical scan NOUN (*modifier*) denoting a recording technique used with video tapes in which the recorded tracks on the tape are segments of a helix: *a helical-scan tape*.

helices ('hɛlɪˌsi:z) NOUN a plural of **helix.**

helichrysum (ˌhɛlɪ'kraɪzəm) NOUN any plant of the widely cultivated genus *Helichrysum*, whose flowers retain their shape and colour when dried: family *Asteraceae* (composites).
▷HISTORY C16: from Latin, from Greek *helikhrusos*, from *helix* spiral + *khrusos* gold

helicity (hɪ'lɪsɪtɪ) NOUN, *plural* **-ties.** *Physics* the projection of the spin of an elementary particle on the direction of propagation.
▷HISTORY C20: from HELIX + -ITY

helicline ('hɛlɪˌklaɪn) NOUN *Architect* a spiral-shaped ramp.
▷HISTORY from HELICO- + -CLINE

helico- *or before a vowel* **helic-** COMBINING FORM spiral or helical: *helicograph*.
▷HISTORY from Latin, from Greek *helix* spiral

helicograph ('hɛlɪkəʊˌgrɑ:f, -ˌgræf) NOUN an instrument for drawing spiral curves.

helicoid ('hɛlɪˌkɔɪd) ADJECTIVE *also* **helicoidal.** [1] *Biology* shaped like a spiral: *a helicoid shell*. ◆ NOUN [2] *Geometry* any surface resembling that of a screw thread.

helicon ('hɛlɪkən) NOUN a bass tuba made to coil over the shoulder of a band musician.
▷HISTORY C19: probably from HELICON, associated with Greek *helix* spiral

Helicon ('hɛlɪkən) NOUN a mountain in Greece, in Boeotia: location of the springs of Hippocrene and Aganippe, believed by the Ancient Greeks to be the source of poetic inspiration and the home of the Muses. Height: 1749 m (5738 ft.). Modern Greek name: **Elikón.**

helicopter ('hɛlɪˌkɒptə) NOUN [1] an aircraft capable of hover, vertical flight, and horizontal flight in any direction. Most get all of their lift and propulsion from the rotation of overhead blades. See also **autogiro.** ◆ VERB [2] to transport (people or things) or (of people or things) to be transported by helicopter.
▷HISTORY C19: from French *hélicoptère*, from HELICO- + Greek *pteron* wing

helicopter gunship NOUN a large heavily armed helicopter used for ground attack.

helicopter view NOUN an overview of a situation without any details.

helideck ('hɛlɪˌdɛk) NOUN a landing deck for helicopters on ships, oil platforms, etc.
▷HISTORY C20: from HELI- + DECK

Heligoland ('hɛlɪgəʊˌlænd) NOUN a small island in the North Sea, one of the North Frisian Islands, separated from the coast of NW Germany by **Heligoland Bight**: administratively part of the German state of Schleswig-Holstein: a large island in early medieval times, now eroded to an area of about 150 hectares (380 acres); ceded by Britain to Germany in 1890 in exchange for Zanzibar. German name: **Helgoland.**

helio- *or before a vowel* **heli-** COMBINING FORM indicating the sun: *heliocentric; heliolithic*.
▷HISTORY from Greek, from *hēlios* sun

heliocentric (ˌhi:lɪəʊ'sɛntrɪk) ADJECTIVE [1] having the sun at its centre. [2] measured from or in relation to the centre of the sun.
▸ˌ**helio'centrically** ADVERB ▸**heliocentricity** (ˌhi:lɪəʊsɛn'trɪsɪtɪ) *or* **heliocentricism** (ˌhi:lɪəʊ'sɛntrɪˌsɪzəm) NOUN

heliocentric parallax NOUN See **parallax** (sense 2).

Heliochrome ('hi:lɪəʊˌkrəʊm) NOUN *Trademark* a photograph that reproduces the natural colours of the subject.
▸ˌ**helio'chromic** ADJECTIVE

heliodor ('hi:lɪəʊˌdɔ:) NOUN a clear yellow form of beryl used as a gemstone.

heliograph ('hi:lɪəʊˌgrɑ:f, -ˌgræf) NOUN [1] an instrument with mirrors and a shutter used for sending messages in Morse code by reflecting the sun's rays. [2] a device used to photograph the sun.
▸**heliographer** (ˌhi:lɪ'ɒgrəfə) NOUN ▸**heliographic** (ˌhi:lɪəʊ'græfɪk) *or* ˌ**helio'graphical** ADJECTIVE
▸ˌ**heli'ography** NOUN

heliolatry (ˌhi:lɪ'ɒlətrɪ) NOUN worship of the sun.
▸ˌ**heli'olater** NOUN ▸ˌ**heli'olatrous** ADJECTIVE

heliolithic (ˌhi:lɪəʊ'lɪθɪk) ADJECTIVE of or relating to a civilization characterized by sun worship and megaliths.

heliometer (ˌhi:lɪ'ɒmɪtə) NOUN a refracting telescope having a split objective lens that is used to determine very small angular distances between celestial bodies.
▸**heliometric** (ˌhi:lɪəʊ'mɛtrɪk) *or* ˌ**helio'metrical** ADJECTIVE ▸ˌ**helio'metrically** ADVERB ▸ˌ**heli'ometry** NOUN

heliopause ('hi:lɪəʊˌpɔ:z) NOUN the boundary between the region of space dominated by the solar wind and the interstellar medium.

heliophyte ('hi:lɪəʊˌfaɪt) NOUN any plant that grows best in direct sunlight.

Heliopolis (ˌhi:lɪ'ɒpəlɪs) NOUN [1] (in ancient Egypt) a city near the apex of the Nile delta: a centre of sun worship. Ancient Egyptian name: **On.** [2] the Ancient Greek name for **Baalbek.**

Helios ('hi:lɪˌɒs) NOUN *Greek myth* the god of the sun, who drove his chariot daily across the sky. Roman counterpart: **Sol.**

heliosphere ('hi:lɪəʊˌsfɪə) NOUN the region around the sun outside of which the sun's influence is negligible and interstellar space begins.

heliostat ('hi:lɪəʊˌstæt) NOUN an astronomical instrument used to reflect the light of the sun in a constant direction.
▸ˌ**helio'static** ADJECTIVE

heliotaxis (ˌhi:lɪəʊ'tæksɪs) NOUN movement of an entire organism in response to the stimulus of sunlight.
▸**heliotactic** (ˌhi:lɪəʊ'tæktɪk) ADJECTIVE

heliotherapy (ˌhi:lɪəʊ'θɛrəpɪ) NOUN the therapeutic use of sunlight.

heliotrope ('hi:lɪəˌtrəʊp, 'hɛljə-) NOUN [1] any boraginaceous plant of the genus *Heliotropium*, esp the South American *H. arborescens*, cultivated for its small fragrant purple flowers. [2] **garden heliotrope.** a widely cultivated valerian, *Valeriana officinalis*, with clusters of small pink, purple, or white flowers. [3] any of various plants that turn towards the sun. [4] **a** a bluish-violet to purple colour. **b** (*as adjective*): *a heliotrope dress*. [5] an instrument used in geodetic surveying employing the sun's rays reflected by a mirror as a signal for the sighting of stations over long distances. [6] another name for **bloodstone.**
▷HISTORY C17: from Latin *hēliotropium*, from Greek *hēliotropion*, from *hēlios* sun + *trepein* to turn

heliotropin (ˌhi:lɪ'ɒtrəpɪn) NOUN another term for **piperonal.**

heliotropism (ˌhi:lɪ'ɒtrəˌpɪzəm) NOUN the growth of plants or plant parts (esp flowers) in response to the stimulus of sunlight, so that they turn to face the sun.
▸**heliotropic** (ˌhi:lɪəʊ'trɒpɪk) ADJECTIVE ▸ˌ**helio'tropically** ADVERB

heliotype ('hi:lɪəʊˌtaɪp) NOUN [1] a printing process in which an impression is taken in ink from a gelatine surface that has been exposed under a negative and prepared for printing. Also called: **heliotypy.** [2] the gelatine plate produced by such a process. [3] a print produced from such a plate.
▸**heliotypic** (ˌhi:lɪəʊ'tɪpɪk) ADJECTIVE

heliozoan (ˌhi:lɪəʊ'zəʊən) NOUN any protozoan of the mostly freshwater group *Heliozoa*, typically having a siliceous shell and stiff radiating cytoplasmic projections: phylum *Actinopoda* (actinopods).

helipad ('hɛlɪˌpæd) NOUN a place for helicopters to land and take off.
▷HISTORY C20: from HELI- + PAD[1]

heliport ('hɛlɪˌpɔ:t) NOUN an airport for helicopters.
▷HISTORY C20: from HELI- + PORT[1]

heli-skiing NOUN skiing in which skiers are transported by helicopter to remote slopes.
▸**'heli-ˌskier** NOUN

helium ('hi:lɪəm) NOUN a very light nonflammable colourless odourless element that is an inert gas, occurring in certain natural gases: used in balloons and in cryogenic research. Symbol: He; atomic no.: 2; atomic wt.: 4.002602; density: 0.1785 kg/m^3; at normal pressures it is liquid down to absolute zero; melting pt.: below –272.2°C; boiling pt.: –268.90°C. See also **alpha particle.**
▷HISTORY C19: New Latin, from HELIO- + -IUM; named from its having first been detected in the solar spectrum

helium flash NOUN *Astronomy* the explosive burning of helium in the case of a star of low mass that occurs when the core is so dense that the matter has become degenerate. The burning causes a rapid rise in temperature until it is so high that the gas ceases to be degenerate, after which there is a rapid expansion.

helix ('hi:lɪks) NOUN, *plural* **helices** ('hɛlɪˌsi:z) *or* **helixes.** [1] a curve that lies on a cylinder or cone, at a constant angle to the line segments making up the surface; spiral. [2] a spiral shape or form. [3] the incurving fold that forms the margin of the external ear. [4] another name for **volute** (sense 2). [5] any terrestrial gastropod mollusc of the genus *Helix*, which includes the garden snail (*H. aspersa*).
▷HISTORY C16: from Latin, from Greek: spiral; probably related to Greek *helissein* to twist

hell (hɛl) NOUN [1] *Christianity* (*sometimes capital*) **a** the place or state of eternal punishment of the wicked after death, with Satan as its ruler. **b** forces of evil regarded as residing there. [2] (*sometimes capital*) (in various religions and cultures) the abode of the spirits of the dead. See also **Hel, Hades, Sheol.** [3] pain, extreme difficulty, etc. [4] *Informal* a cause of such difficulty or suffering: *war is hell*. [5] *US and Canadian* high spirits or mischievousness: *there's hell in that boy*. [6] a box used by a tailor for discarded material. [7] *Now rare* a gambling house, booth, etc. [8] **as hell.** (intensifier): *tired as hell*. [9] **for the hell of it.** *Informal* for the fun of it. [10] **from hell.** *Informal* denoting a person or thing that is particularly bad or alarming: *neighbour from hell; hangover from hell*.

[11] **give someone hell.** *Informal* **a** to give someone a severe reprimand or punishment. **b** to be a source of annoyance or torment to someone. [12] **hell of a** *or* **helluva.** *Informal* (intensifier): *a hell of a good performance.* [13] **hell for leather.** at great speed. [14] **(come) hell or high water.** *Informal* whatever difficulties may arise. [15] **hell to pay.** *Informal* serious consequences, as of a foolish action. [16] **like hell.** *Informal* **a** (*adverb*) (intensifier): *he works like hell.* **b** an expression of strong disagreement with a previous statement, request, order, etc. [17] **play (merry) hell with.** *Informal* to throw into confusion and disorder; disrupt. [18] **raise hell. a** to create a noisy disturbance, as in fun. **b** to react strongly and unfavourably. [19] **the hell.** *Informal* **a** (intensifier) used in such phrases as **what the hell, who the hell,** etc. **b** an expression of strong disagreement or disfavour: *the hell I will.* See **like hell.** ◆ INTERJECTION [20] *Informal* an exclamation of anger, annoyance, surprise, etc. (Also in exclamations such as **hell's bells, hell's teeth,** etc.).
▷**HISTORY** Old English *hell;* related to *helan* to cover, Old Norse *hel,* Gothic *halja* hell, Old High German *hella*

he'll (hi:l; *unstressed* i:l, hɪl, ɪl) CONTRACTION OF he will *or* he shall.

hellacious (hɛ'leɪʃəs) ADJECTIVE *US slang* [1] remarkable; horrifying. [2] wonderful; excellent.
▷**HISTORY** C20: from HELL + *-acious* as in AUDACIOUS

Helladic (hɛ'lædɪk) ADJECTIVE of, characteristic of, or related to the Bronze Age civilization that flourished about 2900 to 1100 B.C. on the Greek mainland and islands.

Hellas ('hɛləs) NOUN transliteration of the Ancient Greek name for **Greece.**

hellbender ('hɛl,bɛndə) NOUN a very large dark grey aquatic salamander, *Cryptobranchus alleganiensis,* with internal gills: inhabits rivers in E and central US: family *Cryptobranchidae.*

hellbent (,hɛl'bɛnt) ADJECTIVE (*postpositive* and foll by *on*) *Informal* strongly or rashly intent.

hellcat ('hɛl,kæt) NOUN a spiteful fierce-tempered woman.

helldiver ('hɛl,daɪvə) NOUN *US informal* a small greyish-brown North American grebe, *Podilymbus podiceps,* with a small bill. Also called: **pied-billed grebe, dabchick.**

Helle ('hɛlɪ) NOUN *Greek myth* a daughter of King Athamas, who was borne away with her brother Phrixus on the golden winged ram. She fell from its back and was drowned in the Hellespont. See also **Phrixus, Golden Fleece.**

hellebore ('hɛlɪ,bɔ:) NOUN [1] any plant of the Eurasian ranunculaceous genus *Helleborus,* esp *H. niger* (black hellebore), typically having showy flowers and poisonous parts. See also **Christmas rose.** [2] any of various liliaceous plants of the N temperate genus *Veratrum,* esp *V. album,* that have greenish flowers and yield alkaloids used in the treatment of heart disease.
▷**HISTORY** C14: from Greek *helleboros,* of uncertain origin

helleborine (,hɛlɪ'bɔ:ri:n) NOUN any of various N temperate orchids of the genera *Cephalanthera* and *Epipactis.*
▷**HISTORY** C16: ultimately from Greek *helleborinē* a plant resembling hellebore

Hellen ('hɛlɪn) NOUN (in Greek legend) a Thessalian king and eponymous ancestor of the Hellenes.

Hellene ('hɛli:n) *or* **Hellenian** (hɛ'li:nɪən) NOUN another name for a **Greek.**

Hellenic (hɛ'lɛnɪk, -'li:-) ADJECTIVE [1] of or relating to the ancient or modern Greeks or their language. [2] of or relating to ancient Greece or the Greeks of the classical period (776–323 B.C.). Compare **Hellenistic.** [3] another word for **Greek.** ◆ NOUN [4] a branch of the Indo-European family of languages consisting of Greek in its various ancient and modern dialects.
▸**Hel'lenically** ADVERB

Hellenism ('hɛlɪ,nɪzəm) NOUN [1] the principles, ideals, and pursuits associated with classical Greek civilization. [2] the spirit or national character of the Greeks. [3] conformity to, imitation of, or devotion to the culture of ancient Greece. [4] the cosmopolitan civilization of the Hellenistic world.

Hellenist ('hɛlɪnɪst) NOUN [1] Also called: **Hellenizer.** (in the Hellenistic world) a non-Greek, esp a Jew, who adopted Greek culture. [2] a student of the Greek civilization or language.

Hellenistic (,hɛlɪ'nɪstɪk) *or* **Hellenistical** ADJECTIVE [1] characteristic of or relating to Greek civilization in the Mediterranean world, esp from the death of Alexander the Great (323 B.C.) to the defeat of Antony and Cleopatra (30 B.C.). [2] of or relating to the Greeks or to Hellenism.
▸**,Hellen'istically** ADVERB

Hellenize *or* **Hellenise** ('hɛlɪ,naɪz) VERB to make or become like the ancient Greeks.
▸**,Helleni'zation** *or* **,Helleni'sation** NOUN ▸**'Hellen,izer** *or* **'Hellen,iser** NOUN

heller[1] ('hɛlə) NOUN, *plural* **-ler.** [1] a monetary unit of the Czech Republic and Slovakia, worth one hundredth of a koruna. [2] any of various old German or Austrian coins of low denomination.
▷**HISTORY** from German *haller* a silver coin, after *Hall,* town in Swabia where the coins were minted

heller[2] ('hɛlə) NOUN another word for **hellion.**

Hellerwork ('hɛlə,wɜ:k) NOUN a form of deep tissue massage intended to release the build-up of physical and emotional traumas in the body.

hellery ('hɛlərɪ) NOUN *Canadian slang, rare* wild or mischievous behaviour.

Helles ('hɛlɪs) NOUN **Cape.** a cape in NW Turkey, at the S end of the Gallipoli Peninsula.

Hellespont ('hɛlɪ,spɒnt) NOUN the ancient name for the **Dardanelles.**

hellfire ('hɛl,faɪə) NOUN [1] the torment and punishment of hell, envisaged as eternal fire. [2] (*modifier*) characterizing sermons or preachers that emphasize this aspect of Christian belief.

hellgrammite ('hɛlgrə,maɪt) NOUN *US* the larva of the dobsonfly, about 10 cm long with biting mouthparts: used as bait for bass. Also called: **Dobson.**
▷**HISTORY** C19: of unknown origin

hellhole ('hɛl,həʊl) NOUN an unpleasant or evil place.

hellhound ('hɛl,haʊnd) NOUN [1] a hound of hell. [2] a fiend.

hellion ('hɛljən) NOUN *US informal* a rough or rowdy person, esp a child; troublemaker. Also called: **heller.**
▷**HISTORY** C19: probably from dialect *hallion* rogue, of unknown origin

hellish ('hɛlɪʃ) ADJECTIVE [1] of or resembling hell. [2] wicked; cruel. [3] *Informal* very difficult or unpleasant. ◆ ADVERB [4] *Brit informal* (intensifier): *a hellish good idea.*
▸**'hellishly** ADVERB ▸**'hellishness** NOUN

hello, hallo, *or* **hullo** (hɛ'ləʊ, hə-, 'hɛləʊ) SENTENCE SUBSTITUTE [1] an expression of greeting used on meeting a person or at the start of a telephone call. [2] a call used to attract attention. [3] an expression of surprise. [4] an expression used to indicate that the speaker thinks his or her listener is naive or slow to realise something: *Hello? Have you been on Mars for the past two weeks or something?* ◆ NOUN, *plural* **-los.** [4] the act of saying or calling "hello".
▷**HISTORY** C19: see HALLO

hello money NOUN a charge made by a retailer to a supplier for introducing the supplier's goods to its stores.

Hell's Angel NOUN a member of a motorcycle gang of a kind originating in the US in the 1950s, who typically dress in denim and Nazi-style paraphernalia and are noted for their initiation rites, lawless behaviour, etc.

helluva ('hɛləvə) ADVERB, ADJECTIVE *Informal* (intensifier): *a helluva difficult job; he's a helluva guy.*

helm[1] (hɛlm) NOUN [1] *Nautical* **a** the wheel, tiller, or entire apparatus by which a vessel is steered. **b** the position of the helm: that is, on the side of the keel opposite from that of the rudder. [2] a position of leadership or control (esp in the phrase **at the helm**). ◆ VERB [3] (*tr*) to direct or steer.
▷**HISTORY** Old English *helma;* related to Old Norse *hjalm* rudder, Old High German *halmo*
▸**'helmless** ADJECTIVE

helm[2] (hɛlm) NOUN [1] an archaic or poetic word for **helmet.** ◆ VERB [2] (*tr*) *Archaic or poetic* to supply with a helmet.
▷**HISTORY** Old English *helm;* related to *helan* to cover, Old Norse *hjalmr,* Gothic *hilms,* Old High German *helm* helmet, Sanskrit *śárman* protection

Helmand ('hɛlmənd) NOUN a river in S Asia, rising in E Afghanistan and flowing generally southwest to a marshy lake, Hamun Helmand, on the border with Iran. Length: 1400 km (870 miles).

helmer ('hɛlmə) NOUN *Informal* a film director.

helmet ('hɛlmɪt) NOUN [1] a piece of protective or defensive armour for the head worn by soldiers, policemen, firemen, divers, etc. [2] *Biology* a part or structure resembling a helmet, esp the upper part of the calyx of certain flowers.
▷**HISTORY** C15: from Old French, diminutive of *helme,* of Germanic origin
▸**'helmeted** ADJECTIVE

Helmholtz function NOUN a thermodynamic property of a system equal to the difference between its internal energy and the product of its temperature and its entropy. Symbol: *A or F.* Also called: **Helmholtz free energy.**
▷**HISTORY** C20: named after Baron Hermann Ludwig Ferdinand von *Helmholtz* (1821–94), German physiologist, physicist, and mathematician

helminth ('hɛlmɪnθ) NOUN any parasitic worm, esp a nematode or fluke.
▷**HISTORY** C19: from Greek *helmins* parasitic worm
▸**helminthoid** ('hɛlmɪn,θɔɪd, hɛl'mɪnθɔɪd) ADJECTIVE

helminthiasis (,hɛlmɪn'θaɪəsɪs) NOUN infestation of the body with parasitic worms.
▷**HISTORY** C19: from New Latin, from Greek *helminthian* to be infested with worms

helminthic (hɛl'mɪnθɪk) ADJECTIVE [1] of, relating to, or caused by parasitic worms. ◆ NOUN, ADJECTIVE [2] another word for **vermifuge.**

helminthology (,hɛlmɪn'θɒlədʒɪ) NOUN the study of parasitic worms.
▸**helminthological** (,hɛlmɪnθə'lɒdʒɪkəl) ADJECTIVE
▸**,helmin'thologist** NOUN

helmsman ('hɛlmzmən) NOUN, *plural* **-men.** the person at the helm who steers the ship; steersman.

helophyte ('hɛləfaɪt) NOUN any perennial marsh plant that bears its overwintering buds in the mud below the surface.
▷**HISTORY** C20: from Modern Greek *helos* marsh + -PHYTE

Helot ('hɛlət, 'hi:-) NOUN [1] (in ancient Greece, esp Sparta) a member of the class of unfree men above slaves owned by the state. [2] (*usually not capital*) a serf or slave.
▷**HISTORY** C16: from Latin *Hēlōtēs,* from Greek *Heilōtes,* alleged to have meant originally: inhabitants of Helos, who, after its conquest, were serfs of the Spartans

helotism ('hɛlə,tɪzəm, 'hi:-) NOUN [1] the condition or quality of being a Helot. [2] a sociopolitical system in which a class, minority, nation, etc., is held in a state of subjection. [3] *Zoology* another name for **dulosis.** ◆ Also called (for senses 1, 2): **helotage.**

helotry ('hɛlətrɪ, 'hi:-) NOUN [1] serfdom or slavery. [2] serfs or slaves as a class.

help (hɛlp) VERB [1] to assist or aid (someone to do something), esp by sharing the work, cost, or burden of something: *he helped his friend to escape; she helped him climb out of the boat.* [2] to alleviate the burden of (someone else) by giving assistance. [3] (*tr*) to assist (a person) to go in a specified direction: *help the old lady up from the chair.* [4] to promote or contribute to: *to help the relief operations.* [5] to cause improvement in (a situation, person, etc.): *crying won't help.* [6] (*tr;* preceded by *can, could,* etc.; *usually used with a negative*) **a** to avoid or refrain from: *we can't help wondering who he is.* **b** (usually foll by *it*) to prevent or be responsible for: *I can't help it if it rains.* [7] to alleviate (an illness, etc.). [8] (*tr*) to serve (a customer): *can I help you, madam?* [9] (*tr;* foll by *to*) **a** to serve (someone with food, etc.) (usually in the phrase **help oneself**): *may I help you to some more vegetables?; help yourself to peas.* **b** to provide (oneself with) without permission: *he's been helping himself to money out of the petty cash.* [10] **cannot help but.** to be unable to do anything else except: *I cannot help but laugh.* [11] **help a person on** *or* **off with.** to assist a person in the putting on or removal of (clothes). [12] **so help me. a** on my honour. **b** no matter what: *so help me, I'll get revenge.* ◆ NOUN [13] the act of helping, or being helped, or a person or thing that

helps: *she's a great help.* [14] a helping. [15] **a** a person hired for a job; employee, esp a farm worker or domestic servant. **b** (*functioning as singular*) several employees collectively. [16] a means of remedy: *there's no help for it.* ◆ INTERJECTION [17] used to ask for assistance. ◆ See also **help out.**
▷HISTORY Old English *helpan;* related to Old Norse *hjalpa,* Gothic *hilpan,* Old High German *helfan*
▸**'helpable** ADJECTIVE ▸**'helper** NOUN

helpful ('hɛlpfʊl) ADJECTIVE serving a useful function; giving help.
▸**'helpfully** ADVERB ▸**'helpfulness** NOUN

helping ('hɛlpɪŋ) NOUN a single portion of food taken at a meal.

helping hand NOUN assistance: *many people lent a helping hand in making arrangements for the party.*

helpless ('hɛlplɪs) ADJECTIVE [1] unable to manage independently. [2] made powerless or weak: *they were helpless from so much giggling.* [3] without help.
▸**'helplessly** ADVERB ▸**'helplessness** NOUN

helpline ('hɛlp,laɪn) NOUN [1] a telephone line operated by a charitable organization for people in distress. [2] a telephone line operated by a commercial organization to provide information.

helpmate ('hɛlp,meɪt) NOUN a companion and helper, esp a wife.

helpmeet ('hɛlp,mi:t) NOUN a less common word for **helpmate.**
▷HISTORY C17: from the phrase *an helpe meet* (suitable) *for him* Genesis 2:18

help out VERB (*adverb*) [1] to assist or aid (someone), esp by sharing the burden. [2] to share the burden or cost of something with (another person).

help screens PLURAL NOUN computer instructions displayed on a visual display unit.

Helsingborg (*Swedish* hɛlsiŋ'bɔrj) NOUN a port in SW Sweden, on the Sound opposite Helsingør, Denmark: changed hands several times between Denmark and Sweden, finally becoming Swedish in 1710; shipbuilding. Pop.: 116 870 (2000 est.). Former name (until 1971): **Hälsingborg.**

Helsingør (*Danish* helsəŋ'ø:r) NOUN a port in NE Denmark, in NE Zealand: site of Kronborg Castle (16th century), famous as the scene of Shakespeare's *Hamlet.* Pop.: 56 855 (1995). English name: **Elsinore.**

Helsinki ('hɛlsɪŋkɪ, hɛl'sɪŋ-) NOUN the capital of Finland, a port in the south on the Gulf of Finland: founded by Gustavus I of Sweden in 1550; replaced Turku as capital in 1812, while under Russian rule; university. Pop.: 551 123 (2000 est.). Swedish name: **Helsingfors** (hɛlsɪŋ'fɔrs).

helter-skelter ('hɛltə'skɛltə) ADJECTIVE [1] haphazard or carelessly hurried. ◆ ADVERB [2] in a helter-skelter manner. ◆ NOUN [3] *Brit* a high spiral slide, as at a fairground. [4] disorder or haste.
▷HISTORY C16: probably of imitative origin

helve (hɛlv) NOUN [1] the handle of a hand tool such as an axe or pick. ◆ VERB [2] (*tr*) to fit a helve to (a tool).
▷HISTORY Old English *hielfe;* related to Old Saxon *hèlvi,* Old High German *halb,* Lithuanian *kìlpa* stirrup; see HALTER

Helvellyn (hɛl'vɛlɪn) NOUN a mountain in NW England, in the Lake District. Height: 950 m (3118 ft.).

Helvetia (hɛl'vi:ʃə) NOUN [1] the Latin name for Switzerland. [2] a Roman province in central Europe (1st century B.C. to the 5th century A.D.), corresponding to part of S Germany and parts of W and N Switzerland.

Helvetian (hɛl'vi:ʃən) ADJECTIVE [1] of or relating to the Helvetii. [2] another word for **Swiss.** ◆ NOUN [3] a native or citizen of Switzerland. [4] a member of the Helvetii.

Helvetic (hɛl'vɛtɪk) ADJECTIVE [1] Helvetian or Swiss. [2] of or relating to the Helvetic Confessions or to Swiss Protestantism. ◆ NOUN [3] a Swiss Protestant or reformed Calvinist who subscribes to one of the two **Helvetic Confessions** (of faith) formulated in 1536 and 1566.

Helvetii (hɛl'vi:ʃɪ,aɪ) PLURAL NOUN a Celtic tribe from SW Germany who settled in Helvetia from about 200 B.C.

hem[1] (hɛm) NOUN [1] an edge to a piece of cloth, made by folding the raw edge under and stitching it down. [2] short for **hemline.** ◆ VERB **hems, hemming, hemmed.** (*tr*) [3] to provide with a hem. [4] (usually foll by *in, around,* or *about*) to enclose or confine.
▷HISTORY Old English *hemm;* related to Old Frisian *hemme* enclosed land

hem[2] (hɛm) NOUN, INTERJECTION [1] a representation of the sound of clearing the throat, used to gain attention, express hesitation, etc. ◆ VERB **hems, hemming, hemmed.** [2] (*intr*) to utter this sound. [3] **hem** (*or* **hum**) **and haw.** to hesitate in speaking or in making a decision.

hem- COMBINING FORM a US variant of **haemo-** before a vowel.

hema- COMBINING FORM a US variant of **haemo-.**

he-man NOUN, *plural* **-men.** *Informal* a strongly built muscular man.

hematite ('hɛmətaɪt) *or* **haematite** ('hɛmətaɪt, 'hi:m-) NOUN a red, grey, or black mineral, found as massive beds and in veins and igneous rocks. It is the chief source of iron. Composition: iron (ferric) oxide. Formula: Fe_2O_3. Crystal structure: hexagonal (rhombohedral).
▷HISTORY C16: via Latin from Greek *haimatitēs* resembling blood, from *haima* blood
▸**hematitic** *or* **haematitic** (,hɛmə'tɪtɪk, ,hi:-) ADJECTIVE

hemato- *or before a vowel* **hemat-** COMBINING FORM US variants of **haemato-.**

Hemel Hempstead ('hɛməl 'hɛmstɪd) NOUN a town in SE England, in W Hertfordshire: designated a new town in 1947. Pop.: 79 235 (1991).

hemelytron (hɛ'mɛlɪ,trɒn) *or* **hemielytron** (,hɛmɪ'ɛlɪ,trɒn) NOUN, *plural* **-tra** (-trə). the forewing of plant bugs and related insects, having a thickened base and a membranous apex.
▷HISTORY C19: from New Latin *hemielytron,* from HEMI- + Greek *elutron* a covering
▸**hem'elytral** *or* **,hemi'elytral** ADJECTIVE

hemeralopia (,hɛmərə'ləʊpɪə) NOUN inability to see clearly in bright light. Nontechnical name: **day blindness.** Compare **nyctalopia.**
▷HISTORY C18: New Latin, from Greek *hēmeralōps,* from *hēmera* day + *alaos* blind + *ōps* eye
▸**hemeralopic** (,hɛmərə'lɒpɪk) ADJECTIVE

hemerocallis (,hɛmərəʊ'kælɪs) NOUN See **day lily.**
▷HISTORY from Greek *hemera* day + *kallos* beautiful

hemi- PREFIX half: *hemicycle; hemisphere.* Compare **demi-** (sense 1), **semi-** (sense 1).
▷HISTORY from Latin, from Greek *hēmi-*

-hemia NOUN COMBINING FORM US variant of **-aemia.**

hemialgia (,hɛmɪ'ældʒɪə) NOUN pain limited to one side of the body.

hemianopia (,hɛmɪæn'əʊpɪə) NOUN loss of vision in either the whole left or the whole right half of the field of vision. Also called: **hemianopsia** (,hɛmɪæn'ɒpsɪə).
▷HISTORY C19: from HEMI- + AN- + Greek *opsis* sight

hemicellulose (,hɛmɪ'sɛljʊ,ləʊz) NOUN any of a group of plant polysaccharides that occur chiefly in the cell wall.

hemichordate (,hɛmɪ'kɔ:,deɪt) NOUN [1] any small wormlike marine animal of the subphylum *Hemichordata* (or *Hemichorda*), having numerous gill slits in the pharynx: phylum *Chordata* (chordates). ◆ ADJECTIVE [2] of, relating to, or belonging to the subphylum *Hemichordata.* ◆ See also **acorn worm.**

hemicryptophyte (,hɛmɪ'krɪptəfaɪt) NOUN any perennial plant that bears its overwintering buds at soil level, where they are often partly covered by surface debris.
▷HISTORY C20: HEMI- + CRYPTOPHYTE

hemicrystalline (,hɛmɪ'krɪstə,laɪn) ADJECTIVE a former name for **hypocrystalline.** Compare **holocrystalline.**

hemicycle ('hɛmɪ,saɪkᵊl) NOUN [1] a semicircular structure, room, arena, wall, etc. [2] a rare word for **semicircle.**
▸**hemicyclic** (,hɛmɪ'saɪklɪk, -'sɪk-) ADJECTIVE

hemidemisemiquaver (,hɛmɪ,dɛmɪ'sɛmɪ,kweɪvə) NOUN *Music* a note having the time value of one sixty-fourth of a semibreve. Usual US and Canadian name: **sixty-fourth note.**

hemielytron (,hɛmɪ'ɛlɪ,trɒn) NOUN, *plural* **-tra** (-trə). a variant of **hemelytron.**
▸**,hemi'elytral** ADJECTIVE

hemihedral (,hɛmɪ'hi:drəl) ADJECTIVE (of a crystal) exhibiting only half the number of planes necessary for complete symmetry.

hemihydrate (,hɛmɪ'haɪdreɪt) NOUN *Chem* a hydrate in which there are two molecules of substance to every molecule of water.
▸**,hemi'hydrated** ADJECTIVE

hemimorphic (,hɛmɪ'mɔ:fɪk) ADJECTIVE (of a crystal) having different forms at each end of an axis.
▸**,hemi'morphism** *or* **'hemi,morphy** NOUN

hemimorphite (,hɛmɪ'mɔ:faɪt) NOUN a white mineral consisting of hydrated zinc silicate in orthorhombic crystalline form: a common ore of zinc. Formula: $Zn_4Si_2O_7(OH)_2.H_2O$. Also called (US): **calamine.**

hemiola (,hɛmɪ'əʊlə) *or* **hemiolia** NOUN *Music* a rhythmic device involving the superimposition of, for example, two notes in the time of three. Also called: **sesquialtera.**
▷HISTORY New Latin, from Greek *hēmiolia* ratio of one to one and a half, from HEMI- + *(h)olos* whole
▸**hemiolic** (,hɛmɪ'ɒlɪk) ADJECTIVE

hemiparasite (,hɛmɪ'pærɪ,saɪt) *or* **semiparasite** NOUN [1] a parasitic plant, such as mistletoe, that carries out photosynthesis but also obtains food from its host. [2] an organism that can live independently or parasitically.
▸**hemiparasitic** (,hɛmɪ,pærə'sɪtɪk) ADJECTIVE

hemiplegia (,hɛmɪ'pli:dʒɪə) NOUN paralysis of one side of the body, usually as the result of injury to the brain. Compare **paraplegia, quadriplegia.**
▸**,hemi'plegic** ADJECTIVE

hemipode ('hɛmɪ,pəʊd) *or* **hemipod** ('hɛmɪ,pɒd) NOUN other names for **button quail.**

hemipteran (hɪ'mɪptərən) NOUN [1] Also called: **hemipteron** (hɪ'mɪptə,rɒn). any hemipterous insect. ◆ ADJECTIVE [2] another word for **hemipterous.**
▷HISTORY C19: from HEMI- + Greek *pteron* wing

hemipterous (hɪ'mɪptərəs) *or* **hemipteran** ADJECTIVE of, relating to, or belonging to the *Hemiptera,* a large order of insects having sucking or piercing mouthparts specialized as a beak (rostrum). The group is divided into the suborders *Homoptera* (aphids, cicadas, etc.) and *Heteroptera* (water bugs, bedbugs, etc.).

hemisphere ('hɛmɪ,sfɪə) NOUN [1] one half of a sphere. [2] **a** half of the terrestrial globe, divided into **northern** and **southern hemispheres** by the equator or into **eastern** and **western hemispheres** by some meridians, usually 0° and 180°. **b** a map or projection of one of the hemispheres. [3] either of the two halves of the celestial sphere that lie north or south of the celestial equator. [4] *Anatomy* short for **cerebral hemisphere.**
▸**hemispheric** (,hɛmɪ'sfɛrɪk) *or* **,hemi'spherical** ADJECTIVE

hemispheroid (,hɛmɪ'sfɪərɔɪd) NOUN half of a spheroid.
▸**,hemispher'oidal** ADJECTIVE

hemistich ('hɛmɪ,stɪk) NOUN *Prosody* a half line of verse.

hemiterpene (,hɛmɪ'tɜ:pi:n) NOUN any of a class of simple unsaturated hydrocarbons, such as isoprene, having the formula C_5H_8.

hemitrope ('hɛmɪ,trəʊp) NOUN *Chem* another name for **twin** (sense 3).
▸**hemitropic** (,hɛmɪ'trɒpɪk) ADJECTIVE ▸**,hemi'tropism** *or* **hemitropy** (hi:'mɪtrəpɪ) NOUN

hemizygous (,hɛmɪ'zaɪgəs) ADJECTIVE *Genetics* (of a chromosome or gene) not having a homologue; not paired in a diploid cell.

hemline ('hɛm,laɪn) NOUN the level to which the hem of a skirt or dress hangs; hem: *knee-length hemlines.*

hemlock ('hɛm,lɒk) NOUN [1] an umbelliferous poisonous Eurasian plant, *Conium maculatum,* having finely divided leaves, spotted stems, and small white flowers. US name: **poison hemlock.** See also **water hemlock.** [2] a poisonous drug derived from this plant. [3] Also called: **hemlock spruce.** any coniferous tree of the genus *Tsuga,* of North America and E Asia, having short flat needles: family *Pinaceae.* See also **western hemlock.** [4] the wood of any of these trees, used for lumber and as a source of wood pulp.
▷HISTORY Old English *hymlic;* perhaps related to *hymele* hop plant, Middle Low German *homele,* Old Norwegian *humli,* Old Slavonic *chŭmelĭ*

hemmer ('hɛmə) NOUN an attachment on a sewing machine for hemming.

hemo- COMBINING FORM a US variant of **haemo-**.

hemp (hɛmp) NOUN 1 Also called: **cannabis, marijuana.** an annual strong-smelling Asian plant, *Cannabis sativa*, having tough fibres, deeply lobed leaves, and small greenish flowers: family *Cannabidaceae*. See also **Indian hemp.** 2 the fibre of this plant, used to make canvas, rope, etc. 3 any of several narcotic drugs obtained from some varieties of this plant, esp from Indian hemp. See **bhang, cannabis, hashish. marijuana.** ◆ See also **bowstring hemp.**
▷HISTORY Old English *hænep;* related to Old Norse *hampr,* Old High German *hanaf,* Greek *kannabis,* Dutch *hennep*
▸ **'hempen** *or* **'hemp,like** ADJECTIVE

hemp agrimony NOUN a Eurasian plant, *Eupatorium cannabinum,* with clusters of small pink flower heads: family *Asteraceae* (composites).

hemp nettle NOUN 1 a hairy weedy plant, *Galeopsis tetrahit,* of northern regions, having helmet-shaped pink, purple, and white flowers and toothed leaves: family *Lamiaceae* (labiates). 2 any of various other plants of the genus *Galeopsis.*

hemstitch ('hɛm,stɪtʃ) NOUN 1 a decorative edging stitch, usually for a hem, in which the cross threads are stitched in groups. ◆ VERB 2 to decorate (a hem, etc.) with hemstitches.
▸ **'hem,stitcher** NOUN

hen (hɛn) NOUN 1 the female of any bird, esp the adult female of the domestic fowl. 2 the female of certain other animals, such as the lobster. 3 *Informal* a woman regarded as gossipy or foolish. 4 *Scot dialect* a term of address (often affectionate), used to women and girls. 5 **scarce as hen's teeth.** extremely rare.
▷HISTORY Old English *henn;* related to Old High German *henna,* Old Frisian *henne*

Henan ('hʌ'næn) *or* **Honan** NOUN a province of N central China: the chief centre of early Chinese culture; mainly agricultural (the largest wheat-producing province in China). Capital: Zhengzhou. Pop.: 95 560 000 (2000 est.).

hen-and-chickens NOUN, *plural* **hens-and-chickens.** *(functioning as singular or plural)* any of several plants, such as the houseleek and ground ivy, that produce many offsets or runners.

henbane ('hɛn,beɪn) NOUN a poisonous solanaceous European plant, *Hyoscyamus niger,* with sticky hairy leaves and funnel-shaped greenish flowers: yields the drug hyoscyamine.

henbit ('hɛn,bɪt) NOUN a plant, *Lamium amplexicaule,* that is native to Europe and has toothed opposite leaves and small dark red flowers: family *Lamiaceae* (labiates).

hence (hɛns) SENTENCE CONNECTOR 1 for this reason; following from this; therefore. ◆ ADVERB 2 from this time: *a year hence.* 3 *Archaic* **a** from here or from this world; away. **b** from this origin or source. ◆ INTERJECTION 4 *Archaic* begone! away!
▷HISTORY Old English *hionane;* related to Old High German *hinana* away from here, Old Irish *cen* on this side

henceforth ('hɛns'fɔːθ), **henceforwards,** *or* **henceforward** ADVERB from this time forward; from now on.

henchman ('hɛntʃmən) NOUN, *plural* **-men.** 1 a faithful attendant or supporter. 2 *Archaic* a squire; page.
▷HISTORY C14 *hengestman,* from Old English *hengest* stallion + MAN; related to Old Norse *hestr* horse, Old High German *hengist* gelding

hencoop ('hɛn,kuːp) NOUN a cage for poultry.

hendeca- COMBINING FORM eleven: *hendecagon; hendecahedron; hendecasyllable.*
▷HISTORY from Greek *hendeka,* from *hen,* neuter of *heis* one + *deka* ten

hendecagon (hɛn'dɛkəgən) NOUN a polygon having 11 sides.
▸ **hendecagonal** (,hɛndɪ'kægənᵊl) ADJECTIVE

hendecahedron (,hɛndɛkə'hɛdrən, -'hiːdrən) NOUN, *plural* **-drons** *or* **-dra** (-drə). a solid figure having 11 plane faces. See also **polyhedron.**

hendecasyllable ('hɛndɛkə,sɪləbᵊl) NOUN *Prosody* a verse line of 11 syllables.
▷HISTORY C18: via Latin from Greek *hendekasullabos*
▸ **hendecasyllabic** (hɛn,dɛkəsɪ'læbɪk) ADJECTIVE

hendiadys (hɛn'daɪədɪs) NOUN a rhetorical device by which two nouns joined by a conjunction, usually *and,* are used instead of a noun and a modifier, as in *to run with fear and haste* instead of *to run with fearful haste.*
▷HISTORY C16: from Medieval Latin, changed from Greek phrase *hen dia duoin,* literally: one through two

henequen, henequin, *or* **heniquen** ('hɛnɪkɪn) NOUN 1 an agave plant, *Agave fourcroydes,* that is native to Yucatán. 2 the fibre of this plant, used in making rope, twine, and coarse fabrics.
▷HISTORY C19: from American Spanish *henequén,* probably of Taino origin

henge (hɛndʒ) NOUN a circular area, often containing a circle of stones or sometimes wooden posts, dating from the Neolithic and Bronze Ages.
▷HISTORY back formation from STONEHENGE

Hengelo (*Dutch* 'hɛŋəloː) NOUN a city in the E Netherlands, in Overijssel province on the Twente Canal: industrial centre, esp for textiles. Pop.: 77 514 (1994).

Hengyang ('hɛŋ'jæŋ) NOUN a city in SE central China, in Hunan province on the Xiang River. Pop.: 584 346 (1999 est.).

hen harrier NOUN a common harrier, *Circus cyaneus,* that flies over fields and marshes and nests in marshes and open land. US and Canadian names: **marsh hawk, marsh harrier.**

henhouse ('hɛn,haʊs) NOUN a coop for hens.

Henle's loop ('hɛnlɪz) NOUN *Anatomy* See **loop**[1] (sense 10b).
▷HISTORY C19: named after F. G. J. *Henle* (1809–85), German anatomist

Henley-on-Thames ('hɛnlɪ-) NOUN a town in S England, in SE Oxfordshire on the River Thames: a riverside resort with an annual regatta. Pop.: 10 558 (1991). Often shortened to **Henley.**

henna ('hɛnə) NOUN 1 a lythraceous shrub or tree, *Lawsonia inermis,* of Asia and N Africa, with white or reddish fragrant flowers. 2 a reddish dye obtained from the powdered leaves of this plant, used as a cosmetic and industrial dye. 3 a reddish-brown or brown colour. ◆ VERB 4 *(tr)* to dye with henna. ◆ Archaic name (for senses 1, 2): **camphire.**
▷HISTORY C16: from Arabic *hinnā';* see ALKANET

hennery ('hɛnərɪ) NOUN, *plural* **-neries.** a place or farm for keeping poultry.

hen night NOUN *Informal* a party for women only, esp held for a woman shortly before she is married. Compare **hen party, stag night.**

henotheism ('hɛnəʊθiː,ɪzəm) NOUN the worship of one deity (of several) as the special god of one's family, clan, or tribe.
▷HISTORY C19: from Greek *heis* one + *theos* god
▸ **'henotheist** NOUN ▸ **,henothe'istic** ADJECTIVE

hen party NOUN *Informal* a party at which only women are present. Compare **hen night, stag night.**

henpeck ('hɛn,pɛk) VERB *(tr)* (of a woman) to harass or torment (a man, esp her husband) by persistent nagging.

henpecked ('hɛn,pɛkd) ADJECTIVE (of a man) continually harassed or tormented by the persistent nagging of a woman (esp his wife).

hen run NOUN an enclosure for hens, esp one made of chicken wire.

henry ('hɛnrɪ) NOUN, *plural* **-ry, -ries,** *or* **-rys.** the derived SI unit of electric inductance; the inductance of a closed circuit in which an emf of 1 volt is produced when the current varies uniformly at the rate of 1 ampere per second. Symbol: H.
▷HISTORY C19: named after Joseph *Henry* (1797–1878), US physicist

Henry's law NOUN *Chem* the principle that the amount of a gas dissolved at equilibrium in a given quantity of a liquid is proportional to the pressure of the gas in contact with the liquid.
▷HISTORY C19: named after William *Henry* (1774–1836), English chemist

hent[1] (hɛnt) *Archaic* ◆ VERB 1 *(tr)* to seize; grasp. ◆ NOUN 2 anything that has been grasped, esp by the mind.
▷HISTORY Old English *hentan* to pursue; related to *huntian* to HUNT

hent[2] (hɛnt) VERB *(tr) Southwestern English dialect* to empty: *I'll hent the water out in the garden.*

hep (hɛp) ADJECTIVE **hepper, heppest.** *Slang* an earlier word for **hip**[4].

heparin ('hɛpərɪn) NOUN a polysaccharide, containing sulphate groups, present in most body tissues: an anticoagulant used in the treatment of thrombosis.
▷HISTORY C20: from Greek *hēpar* the liver + -IN
▸ **'heparin,oid** ADJECTIVE

hepatic (hɪ'pætɪk) ADJECTIVE 1 of or relating to the liver. 2 *Botany* of or relating to the liverworts. 3 having the colour of liver. ◆ NOUN 4 *Obsolete* any of various drugs for use in treating diseases of the liver. 5 a less common name for a **liverwort.**
▷HISTORY C15: from Latin *hēpaticus,* from Greek *hēpar* liver

hepatica (hɪ'pætɪkə) NOUN any ranunculaceous woodland plant of the N temperate genus *Hepatica,* having three-lobed leaves and white, mauve, or pink flowers.
▷HISTORY C16: from Medieval Latin: liverwort, from Latin *hēpaticus* of the liver

hepatitis (,hɛpə'taɪtɪs) NOUN inflammation of the liver, characterized by fever, jaundice, and weakness. See **hepatitis A, hepatitis B, hepatitis C.**

hepatitis A NOUN a form of hepatitis caused by a virus transmitted in contaminated food or drink.

hepatitis B NOUN a form of hepatitis caused by a virus transmitted by infected blood (as in transfusions), contaminated hypodermic needles, sexual contact, or by contact with any other body fluid. Former name: **serum hepatitis.**

hepatitis C NOUN a form of hepatitis caused by a virus that is transmitted in the same ways as that responsible for hepatitis B. Former name: **non-A, non-B hepatitis.**

hepato- *or before a vowel* **hepat-** COMBINING FORM denoting the liver: *hepatitis.*
▷HISTORY from Greek *hēpat-, hēpar*

hepatogenous (,hɛpə'tɒdʒɪnəs) ADJECTIVE originating in the liver.

hepatomegaly (,hɛpətəʊ'mɛgəlɪ) NOUN an abnormal enlargement of the liver, caused by congestion, inflammation, or a tumour.
▷HISTORY C20: from HEPATO- + New Latin *megalia,* from Greek *megas* great

hepcat ('hɛp,kæt) NOUN *Obsolete slang* a person who is hep, esp a player or admirer of jazz and swing in the 1940s.

Hephaestus (hɪ'fiːstəs) *or* **Hephaistos** (hɪ'faɪstɒs) NOUN *Greek myth* the lame god of fire and metal-working. Roman counterpart: **Vulcan.**

Hepplewhite ('hɛpᵊl,waɪt) ADJECTIVE of, denoting, or made in a style of ornamental and carved 18th-century English furniture, of which oval or shield-shaped open chairbacks are characteristic.
▷HISTORY C18: named after George *Hepplewhite* (1727–86), English cabinetmaker

hepta- *or before a vowel* **hept-** COMBINING FORM seven: *heptameter.*
▷HISTORY from Greek

heptad ('hɛptæd) NOUN 1 a group or series of seven. 2 the number or sum of seven. 3 an atom or element with a valency of seven.
▷HISTORY C17: from Greek *heptas* seven

heptadecanoic acid (,hɛptə,dɛkə'nəʊɪk) NOUN a colourless crystalline water-insoluble carboxylic acid used in organic synthesis. Formula: $CH_3(CH_2)_{15}COOH$. Also called: **margaric acid.**

heptagon ('hɛptəgən) NOUN a polygon having seven sides.
▸ **heptagonal** (hɛp'tægənᵊl) ADJECTIVE

heptahedron (,hɛptə'hiːdrən) NOUN a solid figure having seven plane faces. See also **polyhedron.**
▸ **,hepta'hedral** ADJECTIVE

heptamerous (hɛp'tæmərəs) ADJECTIVE (esp of plant parts such as petals or sepals) arranged in groups of seven.

heptameter (hɛp'tæmɪtə) NOUN *Prosody* a verse line of seven metrical feet.
▸ **heptametrical** (,hɛptə'mɛtrɪkᵊl) ADJECTIVE

heptane ('hɛpteɪn) NOUN an alkane existing in nine isomeric forms, esp the isomer with a straight chain of carbon atoms (*n*-heptane), which is found in petroleum and used as an anaesthetic. Formula: C_7H_{16}.

▷**HISTORY** C19: from HEPTA- + -ANE, so called because it has seven carbon atoms

heptangular (hɛp'tæŋgjʊlə) ADJECTIVE having seven angles.

heptarchy ('hɛptɑːkɪ) NOUN, *plural* **-chies.** [1] government by seven rulers. [2] a state divided into seven regions each under its own ruler. [3] **a** the seven kingdoms into which Anglo-Saxon England is thought to have been divided from about the 7th to the 9th centuries A.D.: Kent, East Anglia, Essex, Sussex, Wessex, Mercia, and Northumbria. **b** the period when this grouping existed.
▸'**heptarch** NOUN ▸**hep'tarchic** *or* **hep'tarchal** ADJECTIVE

heptastich ('hɛptəˌstɪk) NOUN *Prosody* a poem, strophe, or stanza that consists of seven lines.

Heptateuch ('hɛptəˌtjuːk) NOUN the first seven books of the Old Testament.
▷**HISTORY** C17: from Late Latin *Heptateuchos,* from Greek HEPTA- + *teukhos* book

heptathlon (hɛp'tæθlɒn) NOUN an athletic contest for women in which each athlete competes in seven different events.
▷**HISTORY** C20: from HEPTA- + Greek *athlon* contest
▸**hep'tathlete** NOUN

heptavalent (hɛp'tævələnt, ˌhɛptə'veɪlənt) ADJECTIVE *Chem* having a valency of seven. Also: **septivalent.**

heptose ('hɛptəʊs, -təʊz) NOUN any monosaccharide that has seven carbon atoms per molecule.

her (hɜː; *unstressed* hə, ə) PRONOUN (*objective*) [1] refers to a female person or animal: *he loves her; they sold her a bag; something odd about her; lucky her!* [2] refers to things personified as feminine or traditionally to ships and nations. [3] *Chiefly US* a dialect word for **herself** when used as an indirect object: *she needs to get her a better job.* ◆ DETERMINER [4] of, belonging to, or associated with her: *her silly ideas; her hair; her smoking annoys me.*
▷**HISTORY** Old English *hire,* genitive and dative of *hēo* SHE, feminine of *hē* HE[1]; related to Old High German *ira,* Gothic *izōs,* Middle Dutch *hare*

Language note See at **me**[1].

her. ABBREVIATION FOR: [1] heraldic. [2] heraldry.

Hera *or* **Here** ('hɪərə) NOUN *Greek myth* the queen of the Olympian gods and sister and wife of Zeus. Roman counterpart: **Juno.**

Heraclea (ˌhɛrə'kliːə) NOUN any of several ancient Greek colonies. The most famous is the S Italian site where Pyrrhus of Epirus defeated the Romans (280 B.C.).

Heracles *or* **Herakles** ('hɛrəˌkliːz) NOUN the usual name (in Greek) for **Hercules.**
▸ˌ**Hera'clean** *or* ˌ**Hera'klean** ADJECTIVE

Heraclid *or* **Heraklid** ('hɛrəklɪd) NOUN, *plural* **Heraclidae** *or* **Heraklidae** (ˌhɛrə'klaɪdiː). any person claiming descent from Hercules, esp one of the Dorian aristocrats of Sparta.
▸**Heraclidan** *or* **Heraklidan** (ˌhɛrə'klaɪdən) ADJECTIVE

Herakleion *or* **Heraklion** (*Greek* he'raːkliɔn) NOUN variants of **Iráklion.**

herald ('hɛrəld) NOUN [1] **a** a person who announces important news. **b** (*as modifier*): *herald angels.* [2] *Often literary* a forerunner; harbinger. [3] the intermediate rank of heraldic officer, between king-of-arms and pursuivant. [4] (in the Middle Ages) an official at a tournament. ◆ VERB *tr.* [5] to announce publicly. [6] to precede or usher in.
▷**HISTORY** C14: from Old French *herault,* of Germanic origin; compare Old English *here* war; see WIELD

heraldic (hɛ'rældɪk) ADJECTIVE [1] of or relating to heraldry. [2] of or relating to heralds.
▸**he'raldically** ADVERB

herald moth NOUN a noctuid moth, *Scoliopteryx libatrix,* having brownish cryptically mottled forewings and plain dull hind wings. The adult hibernates and has a prolonged life.

heraldry ('hɛrəldrɪ) NOUN, *plural* **-ries.** [1] the occupation or study concerned with the classification of armorial bearings, the allocation of rights to bear arms, the tracing of genealogies, etc. [2] the duties and pursuit of a herald. [3] armorial bearings, insignia, devices, etc. [4] heraldic symbols or symbolism. [5] the show and ceremony of heraldry.
▸'**heraldist** NOUN

heralds' college NOUN another name for **college of arms.**

Herat (hɛ'ræt) NOUN a city in NW Afghanistan, on the Hari Rud River: on the site of several ancient cities; at its height as a cultural centre in the 15th century. Pop.: 186 800 (1990 est.).

Hérault (*French* ero) NOUN a department of S France, in Languedoc-Roussillon region. Capital: Montpellier. Pop.: 896 441 (1999). Area: 6224 sq. km (2427 sq. miles).

herb (hɜːb; *US* ɜːrb) NOUN [1] a seed-bearing plant whose aerial parts do not persist above ground at the end of the growing season; herbaceous plant. [2] **a** any of various usually aromatic plants, such as parsley, rue, and rosemary, that are used in cookery and medicine. **b** (*as modifier*): *a herb garden.* [3] *Caribbean* a slang term for **marijuana.**
▷**HISTORY** C13: from Old French *herbe,* from Latin *herba* grass, green plants
▸'**herbˌlike** ADJECTIVE

herbaceous (hɜː'beɪʃəs) ADJECTIVE [1] designating or relating to plants or plant parts that are fleshy as opposed to woody: *a herbaceous plant.* [2] (of petals and sepals) green and leaflike. [3] of or relating to herbs.
▸**her'baceously** ADVERB

herbaceous border NOUN a flower bed that primarily contains nonwoody perennials rather than annuals.

herbage ('hɜːbɪdʒ) NOUN [1] herbaceous plants collectively, esp the edible parts on which cattle, sheep, etc., graze. [2] the vegetation of pasture land; pasturage.

herbal ('hɜːbᵊl) ADJECTIVE [1] of or relating to herbs, usually culinary or medicinal herbs. [2] *Austral informal* interested or participating in activities relating to esoteric philosophies, traditional remedies, etc. ◆ NOUN [3] a book describing and listing the properties of plants.

herbalist ('hɜːbᵊlɪst) NOUN [1] a person who grows, collects, sells, or specializes in the use of herbs, esp medicinal herbs. [2] (formerly) a descriptive botanist.

herbarium (hɜː'bɛərɪəm) NOUN, *plural* **-iums** *or* **-ia** (-ɪə). [1] a collection of dried plants that are mounted and classified systematically. [2] a building, room, etc., in which such a collection is kept.
▸**her'barial** ADJECTIVE

herb bennet NOUN a Eurasian and N African rosaceous plant, *Geum urbanum,* with yellow flowers. Also called: **wood avens, bennet.**
▷**HISTORY** C13 *herbe beneit,* from Old French *herbe benoite,* literally: blessed herb, from Medieval Latin *herba benedicta*

herb Christopher NOUN, *plural* **herbs Christopher.** another name for **baneberry.**
▷**HISTORY** C16: named after St *Christopher*

herb Gerard ('dʒɛˌrɑːd) NOUN, *plural* **herbs Gerard.** another name for **goutweed.**
▷**HISTORY** C16: named after St *Gerard* (feast day April 23), who was invoked by those suffering from gout

herbicide ('hɜːbɪˌsaɪd) NOUN a chemical that destroys plants, esp one used to control weeds.
▸ˌ**herbi'cidal** ADJECTIVE

herbivore ('hɜːbɪˌvɔː) NOUN [1] an animal that feeds on grass and other plants. [2] *Informal* a liberal, idealistic, or nonmaterialistic person.
▷**HISTORY** C19: from New Latin *herbivora* grass-eaters

herbivorous (hɜː'bɪvərəs) ADJECTIVE [1] (of animals) feeding on grass and other plants. [2] *Informal* liberal, idealistic, or nonmaterialistic.
▸**her'bivorously** ADVERB ▸**her'bivorousness** NOUN

herb layer NOUN See **layer** (sense 2).

herb of grace NOUN an archaic name for **rue** (the plant).

herb Paris NOUN, *plural* **herbs Paris.** a Eurasian woodland plant, *Paris quadrifolia,* with a whorl of four leaves and a solitary yellow flower: formerly used medicinally: family *Trilliaceae.*
▷**HISTORY** C16: from Medieval Latin *herba paris,* literally: herb of a pair: so called because the four leaves on the stalk look like a true lovers' knot; associated in folk etymology with *Paris,* France

herb Robert NOUN, *plural* **herbs Robert.** a low-growing N temperate geraniaceous plant, *Geranium robertianum,* with strongly scented divided leaves and small pink flowers.
▷**HISTORY** C13: from Medieval Latin *herba Roberti* herb of Robert, probably named after St *Robert,* 11th-century French ecclesiastic

herby ('hɜːbɪ) ADJECTIVE **herbier, herbiest.** [1] abounding in herbs. [2] of or relating to medicinal or culinary herbs.

Hercegovina (*Serbo-Croat* 'hɛrtsɛgɔvina) NOUN a variant of **Herzegovina.**

Herculaneum (ˌhɜːkjʊ'leɪnɪəm) NOUN an ancient city in SW Italy, of marked Greek character, on the S slope of Vesuvius: buried along with Pompeii by an eruption of the volcano (79 A.D.). Excavation has uncovered well preserved streets, houses, etc.

herculean (ˌhɜːkjʊ'liːən) ADJECTIVE [1] requiring tremendous effort, strength, etc.: *a herculean task.* [2] (*sometimes capital*) resembling Hercules in strength, courage, etc.

Hercules[1] ('hɜːkjʊˌliːz), **Heracles,** *or* **Herakles** NOUN [1] Also called: **Alcides.** *Classical myth* a hero noted for his great strength, courage, and for the performance of twelve immense labours. [2] a man of outstanding strength or size.
▸ˌ**Hercu'lean** *or* ˌ**Hera'clean** *or* ˌ**Hera'klean** ADJECTIVE

Hercules[2] ('hɜːkjʊˌliːz) NOUN, *Latin genitive* **Herculeis** (ˌhɜːkjʊ'liːɪs). [1] a large constellation in the N hemisphere lying between Lyra and Corona Borealis. [2] a conspicuous crater in the NW quadrant of the moon, about 70 kilometres in diameter.

hercules beetle NOUN a very large tropical American scarabaeid beetle, *Dynastes hercules:* the male has two large anterior curved horns.

Hercules'-club NOUN [1] a prickly North American araliaceous shrub, *Aralia spinosa,* with medicinal bark and leaves. [2] a prickly North American rutaceous tree, *Zanthoxylum clava-herculis,* with medicinal bark and berries.

Hercynian (hɜː'sɪnɪən) ADJECTIVE denoting a period of mountain building in Europe in the late Palaeozoic.
▷**HISTORY** C16: from Latin *Hercynia silva* the Hercynian forest (i.e., the wooded mountains of central Germany, esp the Erzgebirge)

herd[1] (hɜːd) NOUN [1] a large group of mammals living and feeding together, esp a group of cattle, sheep, etc. [2] *Often disparaging* a large group of people. [3] *Derogatory* the large mass of ordinary people. ◆ VERB [4] to collect or be collected into or as if into a herd.
▷**HISTORY** Old English *heord;* related to Old Norse *hjörth,* Gothic *hairda,* Old High German *herta,* Greek *kórthus* troop

herd[2] (hɜːd) NOUN [1] **a** *Archaic or dialect* a man or boy who tends livestock; herdsman. **b** (*in combination*): *goatherd; swineherd.* ◆ VERB (*tr*) [2] to drive forwards in a large group. [3] to look after (livestock).
▷**HISTORY** Old English *hirde;* related to Old Norse *hirthir,* Gothic *hairdeis,* Old High German *hirti,* Old Saxon *hirdi, herdi;* see HERD[1]

herd-book NOUN a book containing the pedigrees of breeds of pigs, cattle, etc.

herder ('hɜːdə) NOUN *Chiefly US* a person who cares for or drives herds of cattle or flocks of sheep, esp on an open range. Brit equivalent: **herdsman.**

herdic ('hɜːdɪk) NOUN *US* a small horse-drawn carriage with a rear entrance and side seats.
▷**HISTORY** C19: named after P. *Herdic,* 19th-century American inventor

herd instinct NOUN *Psychol* the inborn tendency to associate with others and follow the group's behaviour.

herdsman ('hɜːdzmən) NOUN, *plural* **-men.** *Chiefly Brit* a person who breeds, rears, or cares for cattle or (rarely) other livestock in the herd. US equivalent: **herder.**

herd tester NOUN *NZ* a technician trained to test the health and production of milk and butterfat of dairy cows.
▸**herd testing** NOUN

Herdwick ('hɜːdwɪk) NOUN a hardy breed of coarse-woolled sheep from NW England.
▷HISTORY C19: from obsolete *herdwick* pasture, sheep farm (see HERD² (sense 1), WICK²); the breed is thought to have originated on the herdwicks of Furness Abbey

here (hɪə) ADVERB [1] in, at, or to this place, point, case, or respect: *we come here every summer; here, the policemen do not usually carry guns; here comes Roy.* [2] **here and there.** at several places in or throughout an area. [3] **here goes.** an exclamation indicating that the speaker is about to perform an action. [4] **here's to.** a formula used in proposing a toast to someone or something. [5] **here today, gone tomorrow.** short-lived; transitory. [6] **here we go again.** an event or process is about to repeat itself. [7] **neither here nor there.** of no relevance or importance. [8] **this here.** See **this** (senses 1–3). ◆ NOUN [9] this place: *they leave here tonight.* [10] (**the**) **here and now.** the present time.
▷HISTORY Old English *hēr;* related to Old Norse *hēr,* Old High German *hiar,* Old Saxon *hīr*

hereabouts ('hɪərəˌbaʊts) *or* **hereabout** ADVERB in this region or neighbourhood; near this place.

hereafter (ˌhɪər'ɑːftə) ADVERB [1] *Formal* in a subsequent part of this document, matter, case, etc. [2] a less common word for **henceforth.** [3] at some time in the future. [4] in a future life after death. ◆ NOUN (usually preceded by *the*) [5] life after death. [6] the future.

hereat (ˌhɪər'æt) ADVERB *Archaic* because of this.

hereby (ˌhɪə'baɪ) ADVERB [1] (used in official statements, proclamations, etc.) by means of or as a result of this. [2] *Archaic* nearby.

heredes (hɪ'riːdiːz) NOUN the plural of **heres.**

hereditable (hɪ'rɛdɪtəbᵊl) ADJECTIVE a less common word for **heritable.**
▸**heˌredita'bility** NOUN ▸**he'reditably** ADVERB

hereditament (ˌhɛrɪ'dɪtəmənt) NOUN *Property law* [1] any kind of property capable of being inherited. [2] property that before 1926 passed to an heir if not otherwise disposed of by will.

hereditarianism (həˌrɛdɪ'tɛərɪəˌnɪzəm) NOUN *Psychol* a school of thought that emphasizes the influence of heredity in the determination of human behaviour. Compare **environmentalism.**

hereditary (hɪ'rɛdɪtərɪ, -trɪ) ADJECTIVE [1] of, relating to, or denoting factors that can be transmitted genetically from one generation to another. [2] *Law* **a** descending or capable of descending to succeeding generations by inheritance. **b** transmitted or transmissible according to established rules of descent. [3] derived from one's ancestors; traditional: *hereditary feuds.* [4] *Maths, logic* **a** (of a set) containing all those elements which have a given relation to any element of the set. **b** (of a property) transferred by the given relation, so that if *x* has the property *P* and *xRy,* then *y* also has the property *P.*
▸**he'reditarily** ADVERB ▸**he'reditariness** NOUN

hereditist (hə'rɛdɪtɪst) NOUN any person who places the role of heredity above that of the environment as the determining factor in human or animal behaviour.

heredity (hɪ'rɛdɪtɪ) NOUN, *plural* **-ties.** [1] the transmission from one generation to another of genetic factors that determine individual characteristics: responsible for the resemblances between parents and offspring. [2] the sum total of the inherited factors or their characteristics in an organism.
▷HISTORY C16: from Old French *heredite,* from Latin *hērēditās* inheritance; see HEIR

heredo-familial (həˌrɛdəʊfə'mɪlɪəl) ADJECTIVE denoting a condition or disease that may be passed from generation to generation and to several members of one family.

Hereford ('hɛrɪfəd) NOUN [1] a city in W England, in Herefordshire on the River Wye: trading centre for agricultural produce; cathedral (begun 1079). Pop.: 54 326 (1991). [2] a hardy breed of beef cattle characterized by a red body, red and white head, and white markings.

Hereford and Worcester NOUN a former county of the W Midlands of England, created in 1974 from the historic counties of Herefordshire and (most of) Worcestershire: abolished in 1998 when Herefordshire became an independent unitary authority.

Herefordshire ('hɛrɪfədˌʃɪə, -ʃə) NOUN a county of W England: from 1974 to 1998 part of Hereford and Worcester: drained chiefly by the River Wye; agricultural (esp fruit and cattle). Administrative centre: Hereford. Pop.: 174 844 (2001). Area: 2180 sq. km (842 sq. miles).

herein (ˌhɪər'ɪn) ADVERB [1] *Formal* in or into this place, thing, document, etc. [2] *Rare* in this respect, circumstance, etc.

hereinafter (ˌhɪərɪn'ɑːftə) ADVERB *Formal* in a subsequent part or from this point on in this document, statement, etc.

hereinbefore (ˌhɪərɪnbɪ'fɔː) ADVERB *Formal* in a previous part of or previously in this document, statement, etc.

hereinto (ˌhɪər'ɪntuː) ADVERB *Formal* into this place, circumstance, etc.

hereof (ˌhɪər'ɒv) ADVERB *Formal* of or concerning this.

hereon (ˌhɪər'ɒn) ADVERB an archaic word for **hereupon.**

Herero (hə'rɛərəʊ, 'hɛərəˌrəʊ) NOUN [1] (*plural* **-ro** *or* **-ros**) a member of a formerly rich cattle-keeping Negroid people of southern Africa, living chiefly in central Namibia. [2] the language of this people, belonging to the Bantu group of the Niger-Congo family.

heres *or* **haeres** ('hɪəriːz) NOUN, *plural* **heredes** *or* **haeredes** (hɪ'riːdiːz). *Civil law* an heir.
▷HISTORY from Latin

heresiarch (hɪ'riːzɪˌɑːk) NOUN the leader or originator of a heretical movement or sect.

heresthetic (ˌhɛrəs'θɛtɪk) NOUN a political strategy by which a person or group sets or manipulates the context and structure of a decision-making process in order to win or be more likely to win.
▷HISTORY C20: coined, originally in the form *heresthetics,* by the US political scientist William Riker (1921–93), from Greek *hairein* to choose
▸**ˌheres'thetical** ADJECTIVE ▸**heresthetician** (ˌhɛrəsθə'tɪʃən) NOUN

heresy ('hɛrəsɪ) NOUN, *plural* **-sies.** [1] **a** an opinion or doctrine contrary to the orthodox tenets of a religious body or church. **b** the act of maintaining such an opinion or doctrine. [2] any opinion or belief that is or is thought to be contrary to official or established theory. [3] belief in or adherence to unorthodox opinion.
▷HISTORY C13: from Old French *eresie,* from Late Latin *haeresis,* from Latin: sect, from Greek *hairesis* a choosing, from *hairein* to choose

heretic ('hɛrətɪk) NOUN [1] *Now chiefly RC Church* a person who maintains beliefs contrary to the established teachings of the Church. [2] a person who holds unorthodox opinions in any field.
▸**heretical** (hɪ'rɛtɪkᵊl) ADJECTIVE ▸**he'retically** ADVERB

hereto (ˌhɪə'tuː) ADVERB [1] *Formal* to this place, thing, matter, document, etc. [2] an obsolete word for **hitherto.**

heretofore (ˌhɪətʊ'fɔː) ADVERB [1] *Formal* until now; before this time. ◆ ADJECTIVE [2] *Obsolete* previous; former. ◆ NOUN [3] (preceded by *the*) *Archaic* the past.

hereunder (ˌhɪər'ʌndə) ADVERB *Formal* [1] (in documents, etc.) below this; subsequently; hereafter. [2] under the terms or authority of this.

hereunto (ˌhɪərʌn'tuː) ADVERB an archaic word for **hereto** (sense 1).

hereupon (ˌhɪərə'pɒn) ADVERB [1] following immediately after this; at this stage. [2] *Formal* upon this thing, point, subject, etc.

herewith (ˌhɪə'wɪð, -'wɪθ) ADVERB [1] *Formal* together with this: *we send you herewith your statement of account.* [2] a less common word for **hereby** (sense 1).

heriot ('hɛrɪət) NOUN (in medieval England) a death duty paid by villeins and free tenants to their lord, often consisting of the dead man's best beast or chattel.
▷HISTORY Old English *heregeatwa,* from *here* army + *geatwa* equipment

Herisau (*German* 'heːrizau) NOUN a town in NE Switzerland, capital of Appenzell Outer Rhodes demicanton. Pop.: 14 955 (latest est.).

heritable ('hɛrɪtəbᵊl) ADJECTIVE [1] capable of being inherited; inheritable. [2] *Chiefly law* capable of inheriting.
▷HISTORY C14: from Old French, from *heriter* to INHERIT
▸**ˌherita'bility** NOUN ▸**'heritably** ADVERB

heritage ('hɛrɪtɪdʒ) NOUN [1] something inherited at birth, such as personal characteristics, status, and possessions. [2] anything that has been transmitted from the past or handed down by tradition. [3] **a** the evidence of the past, such as historical sites, buildings, and the unspoilt natural environment, considered collectively as the inheritance of present-day society. **b** (*as modifier; capital as part of name*): *Bannockburn Heritage Centre.* [4] something that is reserved for a particular person or group or the outcome of an action, way of life, etc.: *the sea was their heritage; the heritage of violence.* [5] *Law* any property, esp land, that by law has descended or may descend to an heir. [6] *Bible* **a** the Israelites regarded as belonging inalienably to God. **b** the land of Canaan regarded as God's gift to the Israelites.
▷HISTORY C13: from Old French; see HEIR

heritor ('hɛrɪtə) NOUN *Scots Law* a person who inherits; inheritor.
▸**heritress** ('hɛrɪtrɪs) *or* **'heritrix** FEMININE NOUN

herl (hɜːl) *or* **harl** NOUN *Angling* [1] the barb or barbs of a feather, used to dress fishing flies. [2] an artificial fly dressed with such barbs.
▷HISTORY C15: from Middle Low German *herle,* of obscure origin

herm (hɜːm) *or* **herma** ('hɜːmə) NOUN, *plural* **herms, hermae** ('hɜːmiː) *or* **hermai** ('hɜːmaɪ). (in ancient Greece) a stone head of Hermes surmounting a square stone pillar.
▷HISTORY C16: from Latin *herma,* from Greek *hermēs* HERMES¹

Hermannstadt ('hɛrmanʃtat) NOUN the German name for **Sibiu.**

hermaphrodite (hɜː'mæfrəˌdaɪt) NOUN [1] *Biology* an individual animal or flower that has both male and female reproductive organs. [2] a person having both male and female sexual characteristics and genital tissues. [3] a person or thing in which two opposite forces or qualities are combined. ◆ ADJECTIVE [4] having the characteristics of a hermaphrodite.
▷HISTORY C15: from Latin *hermaphrodītus,* from Greek, after HERMAPHRODITUS
▸**herˌmaphro'ditic** *or* **herˌmaphro'dital** ADJECTIVE
▸**herˌmaphro'ditically** ADVERB ▸**her'maphroditˌism** NOUN

hermaphrodite brig NOUN a sailing vessel with two masts, rigged square on the foremast and fore-and-aft on the aftermast. Also called: **brigantine.**

Hermaphroditus (hɜːˌmæfrə'daɪtəs) NOUN *Greek myth* a son of Hermes and Aphrodite who merged with the nymph Salmacis to form one body.

hermeneutic (ˌhɜːmɪ'njuːtɪk) *or* **hermeneutical** ADJECTIVE [1] of or relating to the interpretation of Scripture; using or relating to hermeneutics. [2] interpretive.
▸**ˌherme'neutically** ADVERB ▸**ˌherme'neutist** NOUN

hermeneutics (ˌhɜːmɪ'njuːtɪks) NOUN (*functioning as singular*) [1] the science of interpretation, esp of Scripture. [2] the branch of theology that deals with the principles and methodology of exegesis. [3] *Philosophy* **a** the study and interpretation of human behaviour and social institutions. **b** (in existentialist thought) discussion of the purpose of life.
▷HISTORY C18: from Greek *hermēneutikos* expert in interpretation, from *hermēneuein* to interpret, from *hermēneus* interpreter, of uncertain origin

Hermes¹ ('hɜːmiːz) NOUN *Greek myth* the messenger and herald of the gods; the divinity of commerce, cunning, theft, travellers, and rascals. He was represented as wearing winged sandals. Roman counterpart: **Mercury.**

Hermes² ('hɜːmiːz) NOUN a small asteroid some 800 m in diameter that passed within 670 000 kilometres of the earth in 1937, and is now lost.

Hermes Trismegistus (ˌtrɪsmə'dʒɪstəs) NOUN a Greek name for the Egyptian god Thoth, credited with various works on mysticism and magic.
▷HISTORY Greek: Hermes thrice-greatest

hermetic (hɜː'mɛtɪk) *or* **hermetical** ADJECTIVE sealed so as to be airtight.
▷HISTORY C17: from Medieval Latin *hermēticus*

belonging to HERMES TRISMEGISTUS, traditionally the inventor of a magic seal
▸**her'metically** ADVERB

hermit ('hɜːmɪt) NOUN [1] one of the early Christian recluses. [2] any person living in solitude.
▷HISTORY C13: from Old French *hermite,* from Late Latin *erēmīta,* from Greek *erēmitēs* living in the desert, from *erēmia* desert, from *erēmos* lonely
▸**her'mitic** *or* **her'mitical** ADJECTIVE ▸**her'mitically** ADVERB
▸**'hermit-ˌlike** ADJECTIVE

hermitage ('hɜːmɪtɪdʒ) NOUN [1] the abode of a hermit. [2] any place where a person may live in seclusion; retreat.

Hermitage[1] ('hɜːmɪtɪdʒ) NOUN **the.** an art museum in Leningrad, originally a palace built by Catherine the Great.

Hermitage[2] ('hɜːmɪtɪdʒ) NOUN a full-bodied red or white wine from the Rhône valley at Tain-l'Ermitage, in SE France.

hermit crab NOUN any small soft-bodied decapod crustacean of the genus *Pagurus* and related genera, living in and carrying about the empty shells of whelks or similar molluscs.

Hermitian conjugate (hɜː'mɪtɪən) NOUN *Maths* a matrix that is the transpose of the matrix of the complex conjugates of the entries of a given matrix. Also called: **adjoint.**
▷HISTORY C19: named after Charles *Hermite* (1822–1901), French mathematician

Hermitian matrix NOUN *Maths* a matrix whose transpose is equal to the matrix of the complex conjugates of its entries.
▷HISTORY C20: named after Charles *Hermite* (1822–1901), French mathematician

Hermon ('hɜːmən) NOUN **Mount.** a mountain on the border between Lebanon and SW Syria, in the Anti-Lebanon Range: represented the NE limits of Israeli conquests under Moses and Joshua. Height: 2814 m (9232 ft.).

Hermosillo (*Spanish* ɛrmo'siʎo) NOUN a city in NW Mexico, capital of Sonora state, on the Sonora River: university (1938); winter resort and commercial centre for an agricultural and mining region. Pop.: 544 889 (2000).

Hermoupolis (hɜː'muːpəlɪs) NOUN a port in Greece, capital of Cyclades department, on the E coast of Syros Island. Pop.: 14 115 (latest est.).

hern (hɜːn) NOUN an archaic or dialect word for **heron.**

Herne (*German* 'hɛrnə) NOUN an industrial city in W Germany, in North Rhine-Westphalia, in the Ruhr on the Rhine-Herne Canal. Pop.: 176 200 (1999 est.).

hernia ('hɜːnɪə) NOUN, *plural* **-nias** *or* **-niae** (-nɪˌiː). the projection of an organ or part through the lining of the cavity in which it is normally situated, esp the protrusion of intestine through the front wall of the abdominal cavity. It is caused by muscular strain, injury, etc. Also called: **rupture.**
▷HISTORY C14: from Latin
▸**'hernial** ADJECTIVE ▸**'herniˌated** ADJECTIVE

herniorrhaphy (ˌhɜːnɪ'ɒrəfɪ) NOUN, *plural* **-phies.** surgical repair of a hernia by means of a suturing operation.

hero ('hɪərəʊ) NOUN, *plural* **-roes.** [1] a man distinguished by exceptional courage, nobility, fortitude, etc. [2] a man who is idealized for possessing superior qualities in any field. [3] *Classical myth* a being of extraordinary strength and courage, often the offspring of a mortal and a god, who is celebrated for his exploits. [4] the principal male character in a novel, play, etc.
▷HISTORY C14: from Latin *hērōs,* from Greek

Hero ('hɪərəʊ) NOUN *Greek myth* a priestess of Aphrodite, who killed herself when her lover Leander drowned while swimming the Hellespont to visit her.

heroic (hɪ'rəʊɪk) *or* **heroical** ADJECTIVE [1] of, like, or befitting a hero. [2] courageous but desperate. [3] relating to or treating of heroes and their deeds. [4] of, relating to, or resembling the heroes of classical mythology. [5] (of language, manner, etc.) extravagant. [6] *Prosody* of, relating to, or resembling heroic verse. [7] (of the arts, esp sculpture) larger than life-size; smaller than colossal. [8] *RC Church* **a** held to such a degree as to enable a person to perform virtuous actions with exceptional promptness, ease and pleasure, and with self-abnegation and self-control: *heroic virtue.* **b** performed or undergone by such a person: *the heroic witness of martyrdom.* ◆ See also **heroics.**
▸**he'roically** ADVERB ▸**he'roicalness** *or* **he'roicness** NOUN

heroic age NOUN the period in an ancient culture, when legendary heroes are said to have lived.

heroic couplet NOUN *Prosody* a verse form consisting of two rhyming lines in iambic pentameter.

heroics (hɪ'rəʊɪks) PLURAL NOUN [1] *Prosody* short for **heroic verse.** [2] extravagant or melodramatic language, behaviour, etc.

heroic stanza NOUN *Poetry* a quatrain having the rhyme scheme a b a b.

heroic tenor NOUN a tenor with a dramatic voice.

heroic verse NOUN *Prosody* a type of verse suitable for epic or heroic subjects, such as the classical hexameter, the French Alexandrine, or the English iambic pentameter.

heroin ('hɛrəʊɪn) NOUN a white odourless bitter-tasting crystalline powder related to morphine: a highly addictive narcotic. Formula: $C_{21}H_{23}NO_5$. Technical names: **diamorphine, diacetylmorphine.**
▷HISTORY C19: coined in German as a trademark, probably from HERO, referring to its aggrandizing effect on the personality

heroin chic NOUN the perceived glamorization of heroin and the characteristics associated with heroin addicts, such as gauntness and hollow eyes.

heroine ('hɛrəʊɪn) NOUN [1] a woman possessing heroic qualities. [2] a woman idealized for possessing superior qualities. [3] the main female character in a novel, play, film, etc.

heroism ('hɛrəʊˌɪzəm) NOUN the state or quality of being a hero.

heron ('hɛrən) NOUN any of various wading birds of the genera *Butorides, Ardea,* etc., having a long neck, slim body, and a plumage that is commonly grey or white: family *Ardeidae,* order *Ciconiiformes.*
▷HISTORY C14: from Old French *hairon,* of Germanic origin; compare Old High German *heigaro,* Old Norse *hegri*

heronry ('hɛrənrɪ) NOUN, *plural* **-ries.** a colony of breeding herons.

hero worship NOUN [1] admiration for heroes or idealized persons. [2] worship by the ancient Greeks and Romans of heroes. ◆ VERB **hero-worship, -ships, -shipping, -shipped** *or US* **-ships, -shiping, -shiped.** [3] (*tr*) to feel admiration or adulation for.
▸**'hero-ˌworshipper** NOUN

herpes ('hɜːpiːz) NOUN any of several inflammatory diseases of the skin, esp herpes simplex, characterized by the formation of small watery blisters. See also **genital herpes.**
▷HISTORY C17: via Latin from Greek: a creeping, from *herpein* to creep

herpes labialis (ˌleɪbɪ'ælɪs) NOUN a technical name for **cold sore.**
▷HISTORY New Latin: herpes of the lip

herpes simplex ('sɪmplɛks) NOUN an acute viral disease characterized by formation of clusters of watery blisters, esp on the margins of the lips and nostrils or on the genitals. It can be sexually transmitted and may recur fitfully.
▷HISTORY New Latin: simple herpes

herpesvirus ('hɜːpiːzˌvaɪrəs) NOUN any one of a family of DNA-containing viruses that includes the agents causing herpes, the Epstein-Barr virus, and the cytomegalovirus.

herpes zoster ('zɒstə) NOUN a technical name for **shingles.**
▷HISTORY New Latin: girdle herpes, from HERPES + Greek *zōstēr* girdle

herpetic (hɜː'pɛtɪk) ADJECTIVE [1] of or relating to any of the herpes diseases. ◆ NOUN [2] a person suffering from any of the herpes diseases.

herpetology (ˌhɜːpɪ'tɒlədʒɪ) NOUN the study of reptiles and amphibians.
▷HISTORY C19: from Greek *herpeton* creeping animal, from *herpein* to creep
▸**herpetologic** (ˌhɜːpɪtə'lɒdʒɪk) *or* ˌ**herpeto'logical** ADJECTIVE ▸ˌ**herpeto'logically** ADVERB ▸ˌ**herpe'tologist** NOUN

herptile ('hɜːpˌtaɪl) ADJECTIVE *Chiefly US* denoting, relating to, or characterizing both reptiles and amphibians.
▷HISTORY from Greek *herp(eton)* (see HERPETOLOGY) + (REP)TILE

Herr (*German* hɛr) NOUN, *plural* **Herren** ('hɛrən). a German man: used before a name as a title equivalent to *Mr.*
▷HISTORY German, from Old High German *herro* lord

Herrenvolk *German* ('hɛrənfɔlk) NOUN See **master race.**

herring ('hɛrɪŋ) NOUN, *plural* **-rings** *or* **-ring.** any marine soft-finned teleost fish of the family *Clupeidae,* esp *Clupea harengus,* an important food fish of northern seas, having an elongated body covered, except in the head region, with large fragile silvery scales.
▷HISTORY Old English *hǣring;* related to Old High German *hāring,* Old Frisian *hēring,* Dutch *haring*

herringbone ('hɛrɪŋˌbəʊn) NOUN [1] **a** a pattern used in textiles, brickwork, etc., consisting of two or more rows of short parallel strokes slanting in alternate directions to form a series of parallel Vs or zigzags. **b** (*as modifier*): *a herringbone jacket; a herringbone pattern of very long, narrow bricks.* [2] *Skiing* a method of ascending a slope by walking with the skis pointing outwards and one's weight on the inside edges. ◆ VERB [3] to decorate (textiles, brickwork, etc.) with herringbone. [4] (*intr*) *Skiing* to ascend a slope in herringbone fashion.

herringbone bond NOUN a type of bricklaying in which the bricks are laid on the slant to form a herringbone pattern.

herringbone gear NOUN a gearwheel having two sets of helical teeth, one set inclined at an acute angle to the other so that V-shaped teeth are formed. Also called: **double-helical gear.**

herring gull NOUN a common gull, *Larus argentatus,* that has a white plumage with black-tipped wings and pink legs.

hers (hɜːz) PRONOUN [1] something or someone belonging to or associated with her: *hers is the nicest dress; that cat is hers.* [2] **of hers.** belonging to or associated with her.
▷HISTORY C14 *hires;* see HER

herself (hə'sɛlf) PRONOUN [1] **a** the reflexive form of *she* or *her.* **b** (intensifier): *the queen herself signed the letter.* [2] (*preceded by a copula*) her normal or usual self: *she looks herself again after the operation.* [3] *Irish and Scot* the wife or woman of the house: *is herself at home?*

Herstmonceux *or* **Hurstmonceux** ('hɜːstmənˌsuː, -ˌsəʊ) NOUN a village in S England, in E Sussex north of Eastbourne: 15th-century castle, site of the Royal Observatory, which was transferred from Greenwich between 1948 and 1958, until 1990.

herstory ('hɜːstərɪ) NOUN history from a female point of view or as it relates to women.
▷HISTORY C20: from changing the initial *his* in HISTORY to *her,* as if HISTORY were derived from *his* + *story* rather than from Latin *historia*

Hertford ('hɑːtfəd) NOUN a town in SE England, administrative centre of Hertfordshire. Pop.: 21 665 (1991).

Hertfordshire ('hɑːtfədˌʃɪə, -ʃə) NOUN a county of S England, bordering on Greater London in the south: mainly low-lying, with the Chiltern Hills in the northwest; largely agricultural; expanding light industries, esp in the new towns. Administrative centre: Hertford. Pop.: 1 033 977 (2001). Area: 1634 sq. km (631 sq. miles).

Hertogenbosch (*Dutch* hɛrtoːxən'bɔs) NOUN **'s.** See **'s Hertogenbosch.**

Herts (hɑːts) ABBREVIATION FOR Hertfordshire.

hertz (hɜːts) NOUN, *plural* **hertz.** the derived SI unit of frequency; the frequency of a periodic phenomenon that has a periodic time of 1 second; 1 cycle per second. Symbol: Hz.
▷HISTORY C20: named after Heinrich Rudolph Hertz (1857–94), German physicist

Hertzian wave NOUN an electromagnetic with a frequency in the range from about hertz to about 1.5×10^5 hertz.
▷HISTORY C19: named after Heinrich Hertz (1857–94), German physicist

Hertzsprung-Russell diagram (ˈhɜːtsspɹʌŋˈrʌsᵊl) NOUN a graph in which the spectral types of stars are plotted against their absolute magnitudes. Stars fall into different groupings in different parts of the graph. See also **main sequence.**
▷HISTORY C20: named after Ejnar Hertzsprung (1873–1967), Danish astronomer, and Henry Norris Russell (1877–1957), US astronomer and astrophysicist

Herzegovina (ˌhɜːtsəgəʊˈviːnə) *or* **Hercegovina** NOUN a region in Bosnia-Herzegovina: originally under Austro-Hungarian rule; became part of the province of Bosnia-Herzegovina (1878), which was a constituent republic of Yugoslavia (1946–92).

he's (hiːz) CONTRACTION OF he is *or* he has.

Heshvan (xɜʃˈvɑn) NOUN a variant spelling of **Cheshvan.**

Hesione (hɪˈsaɪənɪ) NOUN *Greek myth* daughter of King Laomedon, rescued by Hercules from a sea monster.

hesitant (ˈhɛzɪtᵊnt) ADJECTIVE wavering, hesitating, or irresolute.
▸ **ˈhesitance** *or* **ˈhesitancy** NOUN ▸ **ˈhesitantly** ADVERB

hesitate (ˈhɛzɪˌteɪt) VERB *(intr)* 1 to hold back or be slow in acting; be uncertain. 2 to be unwilling or reluctant (to do something). 3 to stammer or pause in speaking.
▷HISTORY C17: from Latin *haesitāre,* from *haerēre* to cling to
▸ **ˈhesiˌtater** *or* **ˈhesiˌtator** NOUN ▸ **ˈhesiˌtatingly** ADVERB ▸ **ˌhesiˈtation** NOUN ▸ **ˈhesiˌtative** ADJECTIVE

Hesperia (hɛˈspɪərɪə) NOUN a poetic name used by the ancient Greeks for Italy and by the Romans for Spain or beyond.
▷HISTORY Latin, from Greek: land of the west, from *hesperos* western

Hesperian (hɛˈspɪərɪən) ADJECTIVE 1 *Poetic* western. 2 of or relating to the Hesperides. ◆ NOUN 3 a native or inhabitant of a western land.

Hesperides (hɛˈspɛrɪˌdiːz) PLURAL NOUN *Greek myth* 1 the daughters of Hesperus, nymphs who kept watch with a dragon over the garden of the golden apples in the Islands of the Blessed. 2 *(functioning as singular)* the gardens themselves. 3 another name for the **Islands of the Blessed.**
▸ **Hesperidian** (ˌhɛspəˈrɪdɪən) *or* **ˌHesperˈidean** ADJECTIVE

hesperidin (hɛˈspɛrɪdɪn) NOUN a glycoside extracted from orange peel or other citrus fruits and used to treat capillary fragility.
▷HISTORY C19: from New Latin HESPERIDIUM + -IN

hesperidium (ˌhɛspəˈrɪdɪəm) NOUN *Botany* the fruit of citrus plants, in which the flesh consists of fluid-filled hairs and is protected by a tough rind.
▷HISTORY C19: New Latin; alluding to the fruit in the garden of the HESPERIDES

Hesperus (ˈhɛspərəs) NOUN an evening star, esp Venus.
▷HISTORY from Latin, from Greek *Hesperos,* from *hesperos* western

Hesse (hɛs) NOUN a state of central Germany, formed in 1945 from the former Prussian province of Hesse-Nassau and part of the former state of Hesse; part of West Germany until 1990. Capital: Wiesbaden. Pop.: 6 052 000 (2000 est.). Area: 21 111 sq. km (8151 sq. miles). German name: **Hessen** (ˈhɛsᵊn).

Hesse-Nassau NOUN a former province of Prussia, now part of the state of Hesse, Germany; part of West Germany until 1990.

hessian (ˈhɛsɪən) NOUN a coarse jute fabric similar to sacking, used for bags, upholstery, etc.
▷HISTORY C18: from HESSE + -IAN

Hessian (ˈhɛsɪən) NOUN 1 a native or inhabitant of Hesse. 2 **a** a Hessian soldier in any of the mercenary units of the British Army in the War of American Independence or the Napoleonic Wars. **b** *US* any German mercenary in the British Army during the War of American Independence. 3 *Chiefly US* a mercenary or ruffian. ◆ ADJECTIVE 4 of or relating to Hesse or its inhabitants.

Hessian boots PLURAL NOUN men's high boots with tassels around the top, fashionable in England in the early 19th century.

Hessian fly NOUN a small dipterous fly, *Mayetiola destructor,* whose larvae damage wheat, barley, and rye: family *Cecidomyidae* (gall midges).
▷HISTORY C18: so called because it was thought to have been introduced into America by Hessian soldiers

hessite (ˈhɛsaɪt) NOUN a black or grey metallic mineral consisting of silver telluride in cubic crystalline form. Formula: Ag_2Te.
▷HISTORY C19: from German *Hessit;* named after Henry *Hess,* 19th-century chemist of Swiss origin who worked in Russia; see -ITE[1]

hessonite (ˈhɛsəˌnaɪt) NOUN an orange-brown variety of grossularite garnet. Also called: **essonite, cinnamon stone.**
▷HISTORY C19: from French, from Greek *hēssōn* less, inferior + -ITE[1]; so called because it is less hard than genuine hyacinth

hest (hɛst) NOUN an archaic word for **behest.**
▷HISTORY Old English *hǣs;* related to *hātan* to promise, command

Hestia (ˈhɛstɪə) NOUN *Greek myth* the goddess of the hearth. Roman counterpart: **Vesta.**

Hesychast (ˈhɛsɪˌkæst) NOUN *Greek Orthodox Church* a member of a school of mysticism developed by the monks of Mount Athos in the 14th century.
▷HISTORY C18: from Medieval Latin *hesychasta* mystic, from Greek *hēsukhastēs,* from *hēsukhazein* to be tranquil, from *hēsukhos* quiet
▸ **ˌHesyˈchastic** ADJECTIVE

het[1] (hɛt) NOUN *Slang* short for **heterosexual.**

het[2] (hɛt) VERB 1 *Archaic or dialect* a past tense and past participle of **heat.** ◆ ADJECTIVE 2 a Scot word for **hot.** ◆ See also **het up.**

hetaera (hɪˈtɪərə) *or* **hetaira** (hɪˈtaɪrə) NOUN, *plural* **-taerae** (-ˈtɪəriː) *or* **-tairai** (-ˈtaɪraɪ). (esp in ancient Greece) a female prostitute, esp an educated courtesan.
▷HISTORY C19: from Greek *hetaira* concubine
▸ **heˈtaeric** *or* **heˈtairic** ADJECTIVE

hetaerism (hɪˈtɪərɪzəm) *or* **hetairism** (hɪˈtaɪrɪzəm) NOUN 1 the state of being a concubine. 2 *Sociol, anthropol* a social system attributed to some primitive societies, in which women are communally shared.
▸ **heˈtaerist** *or* **heˈtairist** NOUN ▸ **ˌhetaeˈristic** *or* **ˌhetaiˈristic** ADJECTIVE

heterarchy (ˈhɛtərɑːkɪ) NOUN *Linguistics* a formal structure, usually represented by a diagram of connected nodes, without any single permanent uppermost node. Compare **hierarchy** (sense 5), **tree** (sense 6).
▷HISTORY from Greek *heteros* other, different + *archē* sovereignty

hetero (ˈhɛtərəʊ) NOUN, *plural* **-os,** ADJECTIVE *Informal* short for **heterosexual.**

hetero- COMBINING FORM other, another, or different: *heterodyne; heterophony; heterosexual.* Compare **homo-.**
▷HISTORY from Greek *heteros* other

heteroblastic (ˌhɛtərəʊˈblæstɪk) ADJECTIVE *Botany* (of a plant or plant part) showing a marked difference in form between the juvenile and the adult structures. Compare **homoblastic.**

heterocercal (ˌhɛtərəʊˈsɜːkᵊl) ADJECTIVE *Ichthyol* of or possessing a tail in which the vertebral column turns upwards and extends into the upper, usually larger, lobe, as in sharks. Compare **homocercal.**
▷HISTORY C19: from HETERO- + Greek *kerkos* tail

heterochlamydeous (ˌhɛtərəʊkləˈmɪdɪəs) ADJECTIVE (of a plant) having a perianth consisting of distinct sepals and petals. Compare **homochlamydeous.**

heterochromatic (ˌhɛtərəʊkrəʊˈmætɪk) ADJECTIVE 1 of or involving many different colours. 2 *Physics* consisting of or concerned with different frequencies or wavelengths.
▸ **ˌheteroˈchromatism** NOUN

heterochromatin (ˌhɛtərəʊˈkrəʊmətɪn) NOUN the condensed part of a chromosome that stains strongly with basic dyes in nondividing cells and has little genetic activity. Compare **euchromatin.**

heterochromosome (ˌhɛtərəʊˈkrəʊməˌsəʊm) NOUN 1 an atypical chromosome, esp a sex chromosome. 2 a chromosome composed mainly of heterochromatin.

heterochromous (ˌhɛtərəʊˈkrəʊməs) ADJECTIVE (esp of plant parts) of different colours: *the heterochromous florets of a daisy flower.*

heteroclite (ˈhɛtərəˌklaɪt) ADJECTIVE *also* **heteroclitic** (ˌhɛtərəˈklɪtɪk). 1 (esp of the form of a word) irregular or unusual. ◆ NOUN 2 an irregularly formed word.
▷HISTORY C16: from Late Latin *heteroclitus* declining irregularly, from Greek *heteroklitos,* from HETERO- + *klinein* to bend, inflect

heterocyclic (ˌhɛtərəʊˈsaɪklɪk, -ˈsɪk-) ADJECTIVE (of an organic compound) containing a closed ring of atoms, at least one of which is not a carbon atom. Compare **homocyclic.**

heterodactyl (ˌhɛtərəʊˈdæktɪl) ADJECTIVE 1 (of the feet of certain birds) having the first and second toes directed backwards and the third and fourth forwards. ◆ NOUN 2 a bird with heterodactyl feet. ◆ Compare **zygodactyl.**

heterodont (ˈhɛtərəˌdɒnt) ADJECTIVE (of most mammals) having teeth of different types. Compare **homodont.**

heterodox (ˈhɛtərəʊˌdɒks) ADJECTIVE 1 at variance with established, orthodox, or accepted doctrines or beliefs. 2 holding unorthodox opinions.
▷HISTORY C17: from Greek *heterodoxos* holding another opinion, from HETERO- + *doxa* opinion
▸ **ˈheteroˌdoxy** NOUN

heterodyne (ˈhɛtərəʊˌdaɪn) VERB 1 *Electronics* to combine by intermodulation (two alternating signals, esp radio signals) to produce two signals having frequencies corresponding to the sum and the difference of the original frequencies. See also **superheterodyne receiver.** ◆ ADJECTIVE 2 produced by, operating by, or involved in heterodyning two signals.

heteroecious (ˌhɛtəˈriːʃəs) ADJECTIVE (of parasites, esp rust fungi) undergoing different stages of the life cycle on different host species. Compare **autoecious.**
▷HISTORY from HETERO- + *-oecious,* from Greek *oikia* house
▸ **ˌheterˈoecism** NOUN

heterogamete (ˌhɛtərəʊgæˈmiːt) NOUN a gamete that differs in size and form from the one with which it unites in fertilization. Compare **isogamete.**

heterogametic (ˌhɛtərəʊgəˈmɛtɪk) ADJECTIVE *Genetics* denoting the sex that possesses dissimilar sex chromosomes. In humans and many other mammals it is the male sex, possessing one X-chromosome and one Y-chromosome. Compare **homogametic.**

heterogamy (ˌhɛtəˈrɒgəmɪ) NOUN 1 a type of sexual reproduction in which the gametes differ in both size and form. Compare **isogamy.** 2 a condition in which different types of reproduction occur in successive generations of an organism. 3 the presence of both male and female flowers in one inflorescence. Compare **homogamy** (sense 1).
▸ **ˌheterˈogamous** ADJECTIVE

heterogeneous (ˌhɛtərəʊˈdʒiːnɪəs) ADJECTIVE 1 composed of unrelated or differing parts or elements. 2 not of the same kind or type. 3 *Chem* of, composed of, or concerned with two or more different phases. Compare **homogeneous.**
▷HISTORY C17: from Medieval Latin *heterogeneus,* from Greek *heterogenēs,* from HETERO- + *genos* sort
▸ **heterogeneity** (ˌhɛtərəʊdʒɪˈniːɪtɪ) *or* **ˌheteroˈgeneousness** NOUN ▸ **ˌheteroˈgeneously** ADVERB

heterogenesis (ˌhɛtərəʊˈdʒɛnɪsɪs) NOUN another name for **alternation of generations** or **abiogenesis.**
▸ **heterogenetic** (ˌhɛtərəʊdʒɪˈnɛtɪk) *or* **ˌheteroˈgenic** ADJECTIVE ▸ **ˌheterogeˈnetically** ADVERB

heterogenous (ˌhɛtəˈrɒdʒɪnəs) ADJECTIVE *Biology, med* not originating within the body; of foreign origin: *a heterogenous skin graft.* Compare **autogenous.**

heterogony (ˌhɛtəˈrɒgənɪ) NOUN 1 *Biology* the alternation of parthenogenetic and sexual generations in rotifers and similar animals. 2 the condition in plants, such as the primrose, of having flowers that differ from each other in the length of their stamens and styles. Compare **homogony.**
▸ **ˌheterˈogonous** ADJECTIVE ▸ **ˌheterˈogonously** ADVERB

heterograft (ˈhɛtərəʊˌgrɑːft) NOUN a tissue graft obtained from a donor of a different species from the recipient.

heterography (ˌhɛtəˈrɒgrəfɪ) NOUN 1 the phenomenon of different letters or sequences of letters representing the same sound in different words, as for example *-ight* and *-ite* in *blight* and *bite.*

2 any writing system in which this phenomenon occurs.
▸**heterographic** (ˌhɛtərəʊˈɡræfɪk) *or* **ˌheteroˌgraphical** ADJECTIVE

heterogynous (ˌhɛtəˈrɒdʒɪnəs) ADJECTIVE (of ants, bees, etc.) having two types of female, one fertile and the other infertile.

heterokaryon (ˌhɛtərəʊˈkærɪɒn) NOUN *Biology* a fungal cell or mycelium containing two or more nuclei of different genetic constitution.
▷**HISTORY** from HETERO- + *karyon,* from Greek *karuon* kernel

heterokont (ˈhɛtərəʊˌkɒnt) NOUN 1 any organism that possesses two flagella of unequal length. Heterokonts include diatoms and some other algae. ◆ ADJECTIVE 2 possessing two flagella of unequal length.

heterolecithal (ˌhɛtərəʊˈlɛsɪθəl) ADJECTIVE (of the eggs of birds) having an unequally distributed yolk. Compare **isolecithal.**
▷**HISTORY** C19: HETERO- + Greek *lekithos* egg yolk

heterologous (ˌhɛtəˈrɒləɡəs) ADJECTIVE 1 *Pathol* of, relating to, or designating cells or tissues not normally present in a particular part of the body. 2 (esp of parts of an organism or of different organisms) differing in structure or origin.
▸**ˌheterˈology** NOUN

heterolysis (ˌhɛtəˈrɒlɪsɪs) NOUN 1 the dissolution of the cells of one organism by the lysins of another. Compare **autolysis.** 2 Also called: **heterolytic fission.** *Chem* the dissociation of a molecule into two ions with opposite charges. Compare **homolysis.**
▸**heterolytic** (ˌhɛtərəʊˈlɪtɪk) ADJECTIVE

heteromerous (ˌhɛtəˈrɒmərəs) ADJECTIVE *Biology* having or consisting of parts that differ, esp in number.

heteromorphic (ˌhɛtərəʊˈmɔːfɪk) *or* **heteromorphous** ADJECTIVE *Biology* 1 differing from the normal form in size, shape, and function. 2 (of pairs of homologous chromosomes) differing from each other in size or form. 3 (esp of insects) having different forms at different stages of the life cycle.
▸**ˌheteroˈmorphism** *or* **ˌheteroˈmorphy** NOUN

heteronomous (ˌhɛtəˈrɒnɪməs) ADJECTIVE 1 subject to an external law, rule, or authority. Compare **autonomous.** 2 (of the parts of an organism) differing in the manner of growth, development, or specialization. 3 (in philosophy) directed to an end other than duty for its own sake. Compare **autonomous** (sense 4b).
▸**ˌheterˈonomously** ADVERB ▸**ˌheterˈonomy** NOUN

heteronym (ˈhɛtərəʊˌnɪm) NOUN one of two or more words pronounced differently but spelt alike: *the two English words spelt "bow" are heteronyms.* Compare **homograph.**
▷**HISTORY** C17: from Late Greek *heteronumos,* from Greek HETERO- + *onoma* name
▸**heteronymous** (ˌhɛtəˈrɒnɪməs) ADJECTIVE
▸**ˌheterˈonymously** ADVERB

Heteroousian (ˌhɛtərəʊˈuːsɪən, -ˈaʊsɪən) NOUN 1 a Christian who maintains that God the Father and God the Son are different in substance. ◆ ADJECTIVE 2 of or relating to this belief.
▷**HISTORY** C17: from Late Greek *heteroousios,* from Greek HETERO- + *ousia* nature

heterophony (ˌhɛtəˈrɒfənɪ) NOUN the simultaneous performance of different versions of the same melody by different voices or instruments.

heterophyllous (ˌhɛtərəʊˈfɪləs, ˌhɛtəˈrɒfɪləs) ADJECTIVE (of plants such as arrowhead) having more than one type of leaf on the same plant. Also: **anisophyllous.**
▸**ˈheteroˌphylly** NOUN

heteroplasty (ˈhɛtərəʊˌplæstɪ) NOUN, *plural* **-ties.** the surgical transplantation of tissue obtained from another person or animal.
▸**ˌheteroˈplastic** ADJECTIVE

heteroploid (ˈhɛtərəʊˌplɔɪd) ADJECTIVE 1 of a chromosome number that is neither the haploid nor diploid number characteristic of the species. ◆ NOUN 2 such a chromosome number.

heteropolar (ˌhɛtərəʊˈpəʊlə) ADJECTIVE a less common word for **polar** (sense 5a).
▸**heteropolarity** (ˌhɛtərəʊpəʊˈlærɪtɪ) NOUN

heteropterous (ˌhɛtəˈrɒptərəs) *or* **heteropteran** ADJECTIVE of, relating to, or belonging to the *Heteroptera,* a suborder of hemipterous insects, including bedbugs, water bugs, etc., in which the forewings are membranous but have leathery tips. Compare **homopterous.**
▷**HISTORY** C19: from New Latin *Heteroptera,* from HETERO- + Greek *pteron* wing

heteroscedastic (ˌhɛtərəʊskɪˈdæstɪk) ADJECTIVE *Statistics* 1 (of several distributions) having different variances. 2 (of a bivariate or multivariate distribution) not having any variable whose variance is the same for all values of the other or others. 3 (of a random variable) having different variances for different values of the others in a multivariate distribution. ◆ Compare **homoscedastic.**
▷**HISTORY** C20: from HETERO- + *scedastic,* from Greek *skedasis* a scattering, dispersal
▸**heteroscedasticity** (ˌhɛtərəʊskɪdæsˈtɪsɪtɪ) NOUN

heterosexism (ˌhɛtərəʊˈsɛkˌsɪzəm) NOUN discrimination on the basis of sexual orientation, practised by heterosexuals against homosexuals.
▸**ˌheteroˈsexist** ADJECTIVE, NOUN

heterosexual (ˌhɛtərəʊˈsɛksjʊəl) NOUN 1 a person who is sexually attracted to the opposite sex. ◆ ADJECTIVE 2 of or relating to heterosexuality. ◆ Compare **homosexual.**

heterosexuality (ˌhɛtərəʊˌsɛksjʊˈælɪtɪ) NOUN sexual attraction to or sexual relations with a person or persons of the opposite sex. Compare **homosexuality.**

heterosis (ˌhɛtəˈrəʊsɪs) NOUN *Biology* another name for **hybrid vigour.**
▷**HISTORY** C19: from Late Greek: alteration, from Greek *heteroioun* to alter, from *heteros* other, different

heterosocial (ˌhɛtərəʊˈsəʊʃəl) ADJECTIVE relating to or denoting mixed-sex social relationships.
▸**heterosociality** (ˌhɛtərəʊˌsəʊʃɪˈælɪtɪ) NOUN ◆ Compare **homosocial.**

heterosporous (ˌhɛtəˈrɒspərəs) ADJECTIVE (of seed plants and some ferns and club mosses) producing megaspores and microspores. Compare **homosporous.**
▸**ˌheterˈospory** NOUN

heterostyly (ˈhɛtərəˌstaɪlɪ) NOUN the condition in certain plants, such as primroses, of having styles of different lengths, each type of style in flowers on different plants, which promotes cross-pollination.
▷**HISTORY** C20: from Greek, from *heteros* different + *stylos* pillar
▸**ˌheteroˈstylous** ADJECTIVE

heterotaxis (ˌhɛtərəʊˈtæksɪs), **heterotaxy,** *or* **heterotaxia** NOUN an abnormal or asymmetrical arrangement of parts, as of the organs of the body or the constituents of a rock.
▸**ˌheteroˈtactic** *or* **ˌheteroˈtactous** *or* **ˌheteroˈtaxic** ADJECTIVE

heterothallic (ˌhɛtərəʊˈθælɪk) ADJECTIVE 1 (of some algae and fungi) having male and female reproductive organs on different thalli. 2 (of some fungi) having sexual reproduction that occurs only between two self-sterile mycelia. ◆ Compare **homothallic.**
▷**HISTORY** C20: from HETERO- + Greek *thallos* green shoot, young twig
▸**ˌheteroˈthallism** NOUN

heterotopia (ˌhɛtərəʊˈtəʊpɪə) *or* **heterotopy** (ˌhɛtəˈrɒtəpɪ) NOUN abnormal displacement of a bodily organ or part.
▷**HISTORY** C19: from New Latin, from HETERO- + Greek *topos* place
▸**ˌheteroˈtopic** *or* **ˌheterˈotopous** ADJECTIVE

heterotrophic (ˌhɛtərəʊˈtrɒfɪk) ADJECTIVE (of organisms, such as animals) obtaining carbon for growth and energy from complex organic compounds. Compare **autotrophic.**
▷**HISTORY** C20: from HETERO- + Greek *trophikos* concerning food, from *trophē* nourishment
▸**ˈheteroˌtroph** NOUN

heterotypic (ˌhɛtərəʊˈtɪpɪk) *or* **heterotypical** ADJECTIVE denoting or relating to the first nuclear division of meiosis, in which the chromosome number is halved. Compare **homeotypic.**

heterozygote (ˌhɛtərəʊˈzaɪɡəʊt, -ˈzɪɡəʊt) NOUN an animal or plant that is heterozygous; a hybrid. Compare **homozygote.**
▸**ˌheterozyˈgosis** NOUN

heterozygous (ˌhɛtərəʊˈzaɪɡəs) ADJECTIVE *Genetics* (of an organism) having different alleles for any one gene: *heterozygous for eye colour.* Compare **homozygous.**

heth *or* **cheth** (hɛt; *Hebrew* xɛt) NOUN the eighth letter of the Hebrew alphabet (ח), transliterated as *h* and pronounced as a pharyngeal fricative.
▷**HISTORY** from Hebrew

hetman (ˈhɛtmən) NOUN, *plural* **-mans.** another word for **ataman.**
▷**HISTORY** C18: from Polish, from German *Hauptmann* headman

het up ADJECTIVE angry; excited: *don't get het up.*

HEU ABBREVIATION FOR highly enriched uranium.

heuchera (ˈhjuːkərə) NOUN any plant of the N. American genus *Heuchera,* with low-growing heart-shaped leaves and mostly red flowers carried in sprays on slender graceful stems: family *Saxifragaceae.* See also **alumroot.**
▷**HISTORY** named after J. H. *Heucher* (1677–1747), German doctor and botanist

heulandite (ˈhjuːlənˌdaɪt) NOUN a white, grey, red, or brown zeolite mineral that consists essentially of hydrated calcium aluminium silicate in the form of elongated tabular crystals. Formula: $CaAl_2Si_7O_{18}.6H_2O$.
▷**HISTORY** C19: named after H. *Heuland,* 19th-century English mineral collector; see -ITE[1]

heuristic (hjʊəˈrɪstɪk) ADJECTIVE 1 helping to learn; guiding in discovery or investigation. 2 (of a method of teaching) allowing pupils to learn things for themselves. 3 **a** *Maths, science, philosophy* using or obtained by exploration of possibilities rather than by following set rules. **b** *Computing* denoting a rule of thumb for solving a problem without the exhaustive application of an algorithm: *a heuristic solution.* ◆ NOUN 4 (*plural*) the science of heuristic procedure.
▷**HISTORY** C19: from New Latin *heuristicus,* from Greek *heuriskein* to discover
▸**heuˈristically** ADVERB

heuristics (hjʊəˈrɪstɪks) NOUN (*functioning as singular*) *Maths, logic* a method or set of rules for solving problems other than by algorithm. See also **algorithm** (sense 1), **artificial intelligence.**

hevea (ˈhiːvjə) NOUN any tree of the South American euphorbiaceous genus *Hevea,* having a milky sap which provides rubber.
▷**HISTORY** C19: New Latin from native name *hevé*

Hever Castle (ˈhiːvə) NOUN a Tudor mansion near Edenbridge in Kent: home of Anne Boleyn before her marriage; Italian garden added in the 20th century by the Astor family.

hew (hjuː) VERB **hews, hewing, hewed, hewed** *or* **hewn** (hjuːn). 1 to strike (something, esp wood) with cutting blows, as with an axe. 2 (*tr;* often foll by *out*) to shape or carve from a substance. 3 (*tr;* often foll by *away, down, from, off,* etc.) to sever from a larger or another portion. 4 (*intr;* often foll by *to*) *US and Canadian* to conform (to a code, principle, etc.).
▷**HISTORY** Old English *hēawan;* related to Old Norse *heggva,* Old Saxon *hāwa,* Old High German *houwan,* Latin *cūdere* to beat
▸**ˈhewer** NOUN

HEW (in the US) ABBREVIATION FOR Department of Health, Education, and Welfare.

hex[1] (hɛks) NOUN **a** short for **hexadecimal notation** or **hexadecimal. b** (*as modifier*): *hex code.*

hex[2] (hɛks) *Informal* ◆ VERB 1 (*tr*) to bewitch. ◆ NOUN 2 an evil spell or symbol of bad luck. 3 a witch.
▷**HISTORY** C19: via Pennsylvania Dutch from German *Hexe* witch, from Middle High German *hecse,* perhaps from Old High German *hagzissa;* see HAG[1]
▸**ˈhexer** NOUN

hexa- *or before a vowel* **hex-** COMBINING FORM six: *hexachord; hexameter.*
▷**HISTORY** from Greek, from *hex* six

hexachlorocyclohexane (ˌhɛksəˌklɔːrəˌsaɪkləʊˈhɛkseɪn) NOUN a white or yellowish powder existing in many isomeric forms. A mixture of isomers, including lindane, is used as an insecticide. Formula: $C_6H_6Cl_6$.

hexachloroethane (ˌhɛksəˌklɔːrəʊˈɛθeɪn) *or* **hexachlorethane** NOUN a colourless cryst insoluble compound with a camphor-like odour: used in pyrotechnics and explosives. Formula: C_2Cl_6.

hexachlorophene (ˌhɛksəˈklɔːrəfiːn) NOUN an insoluble almost odourless white bactericidal substance used in antiseptic soaps, deodorants, etc. Formula: $(C_6HCl_3OH)_2CH_2$.

hexachord (ˈhɛksəˌkɔːd) NOUN (in medieval musical theory) any of three diatonic scales based upon C, F, and G, each consisting of six notes, from which solmization was developed.

hexacosanoic acid (ˌhɛksəkəʊsəˈnəʊɪk) NOUN a white insoluble odourless wax present in beeswax, carnauba, and Chinese wax. Formula: $CH_3(CH_2)_{24}COOH$. Also called: **cerotic acid.**

hexad (ˈhɛksæd) NOUN [1] a group or series of six. [2] the number or sum of six.
▷HISTORY C17: from Greek *hexas*, from *hex* six
▸**hexˈadic** ADJECTIVE

hexadecane (ˈhɛksədɛˌkeɪn, ˌhɛksəˈdɛkeɪn) NOUN the systematic name for **cetane.**
▷HISTORY C19: from HEXA- + DECA- + -ANE

hexadecanoic acid (ˈhɛksəˌdɛkənəʊɪk) NOUN the systematic name for **palmitic acid.**

hexadecimal notation *or* **hexadecimal** (ˌhɛksəˈdɛsɪməl) NOUN a number system having a base 16; the symbols for the numbers 0–9 are the same as those used in the decimal system, and the numbers 10–15 are usually represented by the letters A–F. The system is used as a convenient way of representing the internal binary code of a computer.

hexaemeron (ˌhɛksəˈɛmərɒn) *or* **hexahemeron** NOUN **a** the period of six days in which God created the world. **b** the account of the Creation in Genesis 1.
▷HISTORY C16: via Late Latin from Greek, from *hexaēmeros* (adj) of six days, from HEXA- + *hēmera* day
▸ˌ**hexaˈemeric** *or* ˌ**hexaˈhemeric** ADJECTIVE

hexagon (ˈhɛksəgən) NOUN a polygon having six sides.

hexagonal (hɛkˈsægənᵊl) ADJECTIVE [1] having six sides and six angles. [2] of or relating to a hexagon. [3] *Crystallog* relating or belonging to the crystal system characterized by three equal coplanar axes inclined at 60° to each other and a fourth longer or shorter axis at right angles to their plane. See also **trigonal.**
▸**hexˈagonally** ADVERB

hexagram (ˈhɛksəˌgræm) NOUN [1] a star-shaped figure formed by extending the sides of a regular hexagon to meet at six points. [2] a group of six broken or unbroken lines which may be combined into 64 different patterns, as used in the *I Ching*.
▸ˌ**hexaˈgrammoid** ADJECTIVE, NOUN

hexahedron (ˌhɛksəˈhiːdrən) NOUN a solid figure having six plane faces. A **regular hexahedron** (cube) has square faces. See also **polyhedron.**
▸ˌ**hexaˈhedral** ADJECTIVE

hexahydrate (ˌhɛksəˈhaɪdreɪt) NOUN a hydrate, such as magnesium chloride, $MgCl_2.6H_2O$, with six molecules of water per molecule of substance.
▸ˌ**hexaˈhydrated** ADJECTIVE

hexahydropiridine (ˌhɛksəhaɪdrəʊˈpɪrɪˌdiːn) NOUN the systematic name for **piperidine.**

hexahydropyrazine (ˌhɛksəhaɪdrəʊˈpaɪrəˌziːn) NOUN the systematic name for **piperazine.**

hexamerous (hɛkˈsæmərəs) *or* **hexameral** ADJECTIVE (esp of the parts of a plant) arranged in groups of six.
▸**hexˈamerism** NOUN

hexameter (hɛkˈsæmɪtə) NOUN *Prosody* [1] a verse line consisting of six metrical feet. [2] (in Greek and Latin epic poetry) a verse line of six metrical feet, of which the first four are usually dactyls or spondees, the fifth almost always a dactyl, and the sixth a spondee or trochee.
▸**hexametric** (ˌhɛksəˈmɛtrɪk) *or* **hexˈametral** *or* ˌ**hexaˈmetrical** ADJECTIVE

hexamethylenetetramine (ˌhɛksəˌmɛθɪliːnˈtɛtrəˌmiːn) NOUN a colourless crystalline organic compound used as a urinary antiseptic. Formula: $C_6H_{12}N_4$. Also called: **hexamine, methenamine.**

hexamine (ˈhɛksəmiːn) NOUN [1] another name for **hexamethylenetetramine.** [2] a type of fuel produced in small solid blocks or tablets for use in miniature camping stoves.

hexane (ˈhɛkseɪn) NOUN a liquid alkane existing in five isomeric forms that are found in petroleum and used as solvents, esp the isomer with a straight chain of carbon atoms (*n*-hexane). Formula: C_6H_{14}.
▷HISTORY C19: from HEXA- + -ANE

hexangular (hɛkˈsæŋgjʊlə) ADJECTIVE having six angles.

hexanoic acid (ˌhɛksəˈnəʊɪk) NOUN an insoluble oily carboxylic acid found in coconut and palm oils and in milk. Formula: $C_5H_{11}COOH$.
▷HISTORY C20: from HEXANE + *-oic*

hexapla (ˈhɛksəplə) NOUN an edition of the Old Testament compiled by Origen, containing six versions of the text.
▷HISTORY C17: from Greek *hexaploos* sixfold
▸ˈ**hexaplar** *or* **hexaplaric** (ˌhɛksəˈplærɪk) *or* **hexaplarian** (ˌhɛksəˈplɛərɪən) ADJECTIVE

hexapod (ˈhɛksəˌpɒd) NOUN any arthropod of the class *Hexapoda* (or *Insecta*); an insect.

hexapody (hɛkˈsæpədɪ) NOUN, *plural* **-dies.** *Prosody* a verse measure consisting of six metrical feet.
▸**hexapodic** (ˌhɛksəˈpɒdɪk) ADJECTIVE

hexastich (ˈhɛksəˌstɪk) *or* **hexastichon** (hɛkˈsæstɪˌkɒn) NOUN *Prosody* a poem, stanza, or strophe that consists of six lines.
▸ˌ**hexaˈstichic** ADJECTIVE

hexastyle (ˈhɛksəˌstaɪl) *Architect* ◆ NOUN [1] a portico or façade with six columns. ◆ ADJECTIVE [2] having six columns.

Hexateuch (ˈhɛksəˌtjuːk) NOUN the first six books of the Old Testament.
▷HISTORY C19: from HEXA- + Greek *teukhos* a book
▸ˈ**Hexaˌteuchal** ADJECTIVE

hexavalent (ˌhɛksəˈveɪlənt) ADJECTIVE *Chem* having a valency of six. Also: **sexivalent.**

hexone (ˈhɛksəʊn) NOUN another name for **methyl isobutyl ketone.**

hexosan (ˈhɛksəˌsæn) NOUN any of a group of polysaccharides that yield hexose on hydrolysis.

hexose (ˈhɛksəʊs, -əʊz) NOUN a monosaccharide, such as glucose, that contains six carbon atoms per molecule.

hexyl (ˈhɛksɪl) NOUN (*modifier*) of, consisting of, or containing the group of atoms C_6H_{13}, esp the isomeric form of this group, $CH_3(CH_2)_4CH_2$-: *a hexyl group or radical.*

hexylresorcinol (ˌhɛksɪlrɪˈzɔːsɪˌnɒl) NOUN a yellowish-white crystalline phenol that has a fatty odour and sharp taste; 2,4-dihydroxy-1-hexylbenzene: used for treating bacterial infections of the urinary tract. Formula: $C_{12}H_{18}O_2$.

hey (heɪ) INTERJECTION [1] an expression indicating surprise, dismay, discovery, etc., or calling for another's attention. [2] **hey presto.** an exclamation used by conjurors to herald the climax of a trick.
▷HISTORY C13: compare Old French *hay*, German *hei*, Swedish *hej*

heyday (ˈheɪˌdeɪ) NOUN the time of most power, popularity, vigour, etc.; prime.
▷HISTORY C16: probably based on HEY

Heyduck (ˈhaɪdʊk) NOUN a variant spelling of **Haiduk.**

Heysham (ˈheɪʃəm) NOUN a port in NW England, in NW Lancashire. Pop. (with Morecambe): 46 657 (1991).

Heywood (ˈheɪˌwʊd) NOUN a town in NW England, in Rochdale unitary authority, Greater Manchester, near Bury. Pop.: 29 286 (1991).

Hezbollah (ˌhɛzbəˈlɑː) *or* **Hizbollah** NOUN an organization of militant Shiite Muslims based in Lebanon.
▷HISTORY C20: Arabic, literally: party of God

Hezekiah (ˌhɛzəˈkaɪə) NOUN a king of Judah ?715–?687 B.C., noted for his religious reforms (II Kings 18–19). Douay spelling: **Ezechias.**
▷HISTORY from Hebrew *hizqīyyāh ū* God has strengthened

hf ABBREVIATION FOR half.

Hf THE CHEMICAL SYMBOL FOR hafnium.

HF *or* **h.f.** ABBREVIATIONS. FOR **high frequency.**

HFEA (in Britain) ABBREVIATION FOR Human Fertilization and Embryology Authority.

HFMD ABBREVIATION FOR hand, foot, and mouth disease.

hg ABBREVIATION FOR hectogram.

Hg THE CHEMICAL SYMBOL FOR mercury.
▷HISTORY from New Latin HYDRARGYRUM

HG ABBREVIATION FOR: [1] High German. [2] His (*or* Her) Grace. [3] (formerly, in Britain) **Home Guard.**

HGH ABBREVIATION FOR human growth hormone.

hgt ABBREVIATION FOR height.

HGV (formerly, in Britain) ABBREVIATION FOR heavy goods vehicle.

HH ABBREVIATION FOR: [1] His (*or* Her) Highness. [2] His Holiness (title of the Pope). [3] (on Brit pencils) ◆ SYMBOL FOR double hard.

hhd ABBREVIATION FOR hogshead.

H-hour NOUN *Military* the specific hour at which any operation commences. Also called: **zero hour.**

hi[1] (haɪ) SENTENCE SUBSTITUTE an informal word for **hello.**
▷HISTORY C20: originally US, from HIYA

hi[2] (haɪ) INTERJECTION an expression used to attract attention.
▷HISTORY C15 *hy;* compare HEY

HI ABBREVIATION FOR: [1] Hawaii (state). [2] Hawaiian Islands.

Hialeah (ˌhaɪəˈliːə) NOUN a city in SE Florida, near Miami: racetrack. Pop.: 226 419 (2000).

hiatus (haɪˈeɪtəs) NOUN, *plural* **-tuses** *or* **-tus.** [1] (esp in manuscripts) a break or gap where something is missing. [2] a break or interruption in continuity. [3] a break between adjacent vowels in the pronunciation of a word. [4] *Anatomy* a natural opening or aperture; foramen. [5] *Anatomy* a less common word for **vulva.**
▷HISTORY C16: from Latin: gap, cleft, aperture, from *hiāre* to gape, yawn
▸**hiˈatal** ADJECTIVE

hiatus hernia *or* **hiatal hernia** NOUN protrusion of part of the stomach through the diaphragm at the oesophageal opening.

Hib (hɪb) NOUN ACRONYM FOR *Haemophilus influenzae* type b: a vaccine against a type of bacterial meningitis, administered to children.

hibachi (hɪˈbɑːtʃɪ) NOUN a portable brazier for heating and cooking food.
▷HISTORY from Japanese, from *hi* fire + *bachi* bowl

hibakusha (hɪˈbɑːkʊʃə) NOUN, *plural* **-sha** *or* **-shas.** a survivor of either of the atomic-bomb attacks on Hiroshima and Nagasaki in 1945.
▷HISTORY C20: from Japanese, from *hibaku* exposed + *-sha* -person

hibernaculum (ˌhaɪbəˈnækjʊləm) *or* **hibernacle** (ˈhaɪbəˌnækᵊl) NOUN, *plural* **-ula** (-jʊlə) *or* **-les.** *Rare* [1] the winter quarters of a hibernating animal. [2] the protective case or covering of a plant bud or animal.
▷HISTORY C17: from Latin: winter residence; see HIBERNATE

hibernal (haɪˈbɜːnᵊl) ADJECTIVE of or occurring in winter.
▷HISTORY C17: from Latin *hībernālis*, from *hiems* winter

hibernate (ˈhaɪbəˌneɪt) VERB (*intr*) [1] (of some mammals, reptiles, and amphibians) to pass the winter in a dormant condition with metabolism greatly slowed down. Compare **aestivate.** [2] to cease from activity.
▷HISTORY C19: from Latin *hībernāre* to spend the winter, from *hībernus* of winter, from *hiems* winter
▸ˌ**hiberˈnation** NOUN ▸ˈ**hiberˌnator** NOUN

Hibernia (haɪˈbɜːnɪə) NOUN the Roman name for **Ireland**: used poetically in later times.

Hibernian (haɪˈbɜːnɪən) ADJECTIVE [1] of or relating to Ireland or its inhabitants. ◆ NOUN [2] a native or inhabitant of Ireland.
▷HISTORY from *Hibernia*, the Roman name for Ireland

Hibernicism (haɪˈbɜːnɪˌsɪzəm) *or* **Hibernianism** (haɪˈbɜːnɪəˌnɪzəm) NOUN an Irish expression, idiom, trait, custom, etc.

Hiberno- (haɪˈbɜːnəʊ) COMBINING FORM denoting Irish or Ireland: *Hiberno-English.*

hibiscus (haɪˈbɪskəs) NOUN, *plural* **-cuses.** any plant of the chiefly tropical and subtropical malvaceous

genus *Hibiscus,* esp *H. rosa-sinensis,* cultivated for its large brightly coloured flowers.
▷HISTORY C18: from Latin, from Greek *hibiskos* marsh mallow

hic (hɪk) INTERJECTION a representation of the sound of a hiccup.

hiccup ('hɪkʌp) NOUN [1] a spasm of the diaphragm producing a sudden breathing in followed by a closing of the glottis, resulting in a sharp sound. Technical name: **singultus.** [2] the state or condition of having such spasms. [3] *Informal* a minor difficulty or problem. ◆ VERB **-cups, -cuping, -cuped** *or* **-cups, -cupping, -cupped.** [4] *(intr)* to make a hiccup or hiccups. [5] *(tr)* to utter with a hiccup or hiccups. Also: **hiccough** ('hɪkʌp).
▷HISTORY C16: of imitative origin

hic jacet *Latin* (hɪk 'jækɛt) (on gravestones) here lies.

hick (hɪk) NOUN *Informal* **a** a country person; bumpkin. **b** *(as modifier)*: *hick ideas.*
▷HISTORY C16: after *Hick,* familiar form of *Richard*

hickey ('hɪkɪ) NOUN [1] *US and Canadian informal* an object or gadget: used as a name when the correct name is forgotten, etc.; doodah. [2] *US and Canadian informal* a mark on the skin, esp a lovebite. [3] *Printing* a spot on a printed sheet caused by an imperfection or a speck on the printing plate.
▷HISTORY C20: of unknown origin

hickory ('hɪkərɪ) NOUN, *plural* **-ries.** [1] any juglandaceous tree of the chiefly North American genus *Carya,* having nuts with edible kernels and hard smooth shells. See also **pecan, pignut** (sense 1), **bitternut** (sense 1), **shagbark.** [2] the hard tough wood of any of these trees. [3] the nut of any of these trees. [4] a switch or cane made of hickory wood.
▷HISTORY C17: from earlier *pohickery,* from Algonquian *pawcohiccora* food made from ground hickory nuts

hickymal ('hɪkɪməl) NOUN *Southwest English dialect* a titmouse.

hid (hɪd) VERB the past tense and a past participle of **hide**[1].

hidalgo (hɪ'dælgəʊ; *Spanish* i'ðalɣo) NOUN, *plural* **-gos** (-gəʊz; *Spanish* -ɣos). a member of the lower nobility in Spain.
▷HISTORY C16: from Spanish, from Old Spanish *fijo dalgo* nobleman, from Latin *filius* son + *dē* of + *aliquid* something

Hidalgo (hɪ'dælgəʊ; *Spanish* i'ðalɣo) NOUN a state of central Mexico: consists of a high plateau, with the Sierra Madre Oriental in the north and east; ancient remains of Teltec culture (at Tula); rich mineral resources. Capital: Pachuca. Pop.: 2 231 392 (2000). Area: 20 987 sq. km (8103 sq. miles).

hidden ('hɪdᵊn) VERB [1] a past participle of **hide**[1]. ◆ ADJECTIVE [2] concealed or obscured: *a hidden cave; a hidden meaning.*
▸'**hiddenly** ADVERB ▸'**hiddenness** NOUN

hidden agenda NOUN a hidden motive or intention behind an overt action, policy, etc.

hidden hand NOUN an unknown force or influence believed to be the cause of certain, often unfortunate, events.

hiddenite ('hɪdəˌnaɪt) NOUN a green transparent variety of the mineral spodumene, used as a gemstone.
▷HISTORY C19: named after W. E. *Hidden* (1853–1918), American mineralogist who discovered it

hide[1] (haɪd) VERB **hides, hiding, hid** (hɪd), **hidden** ('hɪdᵊn) *or* **hid.** [1] to put or keep (oneself or an object) in a secret place; conceal (oneself or an object) from view or discovery: *to hide a pencil; to hide from the police.* [2] *(tr)* to conceal or obscure: *the clouds hid the sun.* [3] *(tr)* to keep secret. [4] *(tr)* to turn (one's head, eyes, etc.) away. ◆ NOUN [5] *Brit* a place of concealment, usually disguised to appear as part of the natural environment, used by hunters, birdwatchers, etc. US and Canadian equivalent: **blind.** ◆ See also **hide-out.**
▷HISTORY Old English *hȳdan;* related to Old Frisian *hēda,* Middle Low German *hüden,* Greek *keuthein*
▸'**hidable** ADJECTIVE ▸'**hider** NOUN

hide[2] (haɪd) NOUN [1] the skin of an animal, esp the tough thick skin of a large mammal, either tanned or raw. [2] *Informal* the human skin. [3] *Austral and NZ informal* impudence. ◆ VERB **hides, hiding, hided.** [4] *(tr) Informal* to flog.
▷HISTORY Old English *hȳd;* related to Old Norse *hūth,* Old Frisian *hēd,* Old High German *hūt,* Latin *cutis* skin, Greek *kutos;* see CUTICLE
▸'**hideless** ADJECTIVE

hide[3] (haɪd) NOUN an obsolete Brit. unit of land measure, varying in magnitude from about 60 to 120 acres.
▷HISTORY Old English *hīgid;* related to *hīw* family, household, Latin *cīvis* citizen

hide-and-seek *or US and Canadian* **hide-and-go-seek** NOUN a game in which one player covers his eyes and waits while the others hide, and then he tries to find them.

hideaway ('haɪdəˌweɪ) NOUN a hiding place or secluded spot.

hidebound ('haɪdˌbaʊnd) ADJECTIVE [1] restricted by petty rules, a conservative attitude, etc. [2] (of cattle, etc.) having the skin closely attached to the flesh as a result of poor feeding. [3] (of trees) having a very tight bark that impairs growth.

hideous ('hɪdɪəs) ADJECTIVE [1] extremely ugly; repulsive: *a hideous person.* [2] terrifying and horrific.
▷HISTORY C13: from Old French *hisdos,* from *hisde* fear; of uncertain origin
▸'**hideously** ADVERB ▸'**hideousness** *or* **hideosity** (ˌhɪdɪ'ɒsɪtɪ) NOUN

hide-out NOUN [1] a hiding place, esp a remote place used by outlaws, etc.; hideaway. ◆ VERB **hide out.** *(intr)* [2] to remain deliberately concealed, esp for a prolonged period of time.

hiding[1] ('haɪdɪŋ) NOUN [1] the state of concealment (esp in the phrase **in hiding**). [2] **hiding place.** a place of concealment.

hiding[2] ('haɪdɪŋ) NOUN [1] *Informal* a flogging; beating. [2] **be on a hiding to nothing.** to be bound to fail; to face impossible odds.

hidrosis (hɪ'drəʊsɪs) NOUN [1] a technical word for **sweating** or **sweat.** [2] any skin disease affecting the sweat glands. [3] Also called: **hyperhidrosis** (ˌhaɪpəhɪ'drəʊsɪs, -haɪ'drəʊsɪs). *Pathol* excessive perspiration.
▷HISTORY C18: via New Latin from Greek: sweating, from *hidrōs* sweat
▸**hidrotic** (hɪ'drɒtɪk) ADJECTIVE

hidy-hole *or* **hidey-hole** ('haɪdɪˌhəʊl) NOUN *Informal* a hiding place.

hie (haɪ) VERB **hies, hieing** *or* **hying, hied.** *Archaic or poetic* to hurry; hasten; speed.
▷HISTORY Old English *hīgian* to strive

HIE (in Scotland) ABBREVIATION FOR Highlands and Islands Enterprise.

hieland ('hiːlənd) ADJECTIVE *Scot dialect* [1] a variant of **Highland.** [2] characteristic of Highlanders, esp alluding to their supposed gullibility or foolishness in towns or cities.

hiemal ('haɪəməl) ADJECTIVE a less common word for **hibernal.**
▷HISTORY C16: from Latin *hiems* winter; see HIBERNATE

hieracosphinx (ˌhaɪə'reɪkəʊˌsfɪŋks) NOUN, *plural* **-sphinxes** *or* **-sphinges** (-ˌsfɪndʒiːz). (in ancient Egyptian art) a hawk-headed sphinx.
▷HISTORY C18: from Greek *hierax* hawk + SPHINX

hierarch ('haɪəˌrɑːk) NOUN [1] **a** a person in a position of high priestly authority. **b** a person holding high rank in a religious hierarchy. [2] a person at a high level in a hierarchy.
▸ˌ**hier'archal** ADJECTIVE

hierarchy ('haɪəˌrɑːkɪ) NOUN, *plural* **-chies.** [1] a system of persons or things arranged in a graded order. [2] a body of persons in holy orders organized into graded ranks. [3] the collective body of those so organized. [4] a series of ordered groupings within a system, such as the arrangement of plants and animals into classes, orders, families, etc. [5] *Linguistics, maths* a formal structure, usually represented by a diagram of connected nodes, with a single uppermost element. Compare **ordering, heterarchy, tree** (sense 6). [6] government by an organized priesthood.
▷HISTORY C14: from Medieval Latin *hierarchia,* from Late Greek *hierarkhia,* from *hierarkhēs* high priest; see HIERO-, -ARCHY
▸ˌ**hier'archical** *or* ˌ**hier'archic** ADJECTIVE ▸ˌ**hier'archically** ADVERB ▸'**hierˌarchism** NOUN

hieratic (ˌhaɪə'rætɪk) ADJECTIVE *also* **hieratical.** [1] of or relating to priests. [2] of or relating to a cursive form of hieroglyphics used by priests in ancient Egypt. [3] of or relating to styles in art that adhere to certain fixed types or methods, as in ancient Egypt. ◆ NOUN [4] the hieratic script of ancient Egypt.
▷HISTORY C17: from Latin *hierāticus,* from Greek *hieratikos,* from *hiereus* a priest, from *hieros* holy
▸ˌ**hier'atically** ADVERB

hiero- *or before a vowel* **hier-** COMBINING FORM holy or divine: *hierocracy; hierarchy.*
▷HISTORY from Greek, from *hieros*

hierocracy (ˌhaɪə'rɒkrəsɪ) NOUN, *plural* **-cies.** government by priests or ecclesiastics.
▸**hierocratic** (ˌhaɪərə'krætɪk) *or* ˌ**hiero'cratical** ADJECTIVE

hierodule ('haɪərəˌdjuːl) NOUN (in ancient Greece) a temple slave, esp a sacral prostitute.
▷HISTORY C19: from Greek *hierodoulos,* from HIERO- + *doulos* slave
▸ˌ**hiero'dulic** ADJECTIVE

hieroglyphic (ˌhaɪərə'glɪfɪk) ADJECTIVE *also* **hieroglyphical.** [1] of or relating to a form of writing using picture symbols, esp as used in ancient Egypt. [2] written with hieroglyphic symbols. [3] difficult to read or decipher. ◆ NOUN *also* **hieroglyph.** [4] a picture or symbol representing an object, concept, or sound. [5] a symbol or picture that is difficult to read or decipher.
▷HISTORY C16: from Late Latin *hieroglyphicus,* from Greek *hierogluphikos,* from HIERO- + *gluphē* carving, from *gluphein* to carve
▸ˌ**hiero'glyphically** ADVERB ▸**hieroglyphist** (ˌhaɪərə'glɪfɪst, ˌhaɪə'rɒg-) NOUN

hieroglyphics (ˌhaɪərə'glɪfɪks) NOUN *(functioning as singular or plural)* [1] a form of writing, esp as used in ancient Egypt, in which pictures or symbols are used to represent objects, concepts, or sounds. [2] difficult or undecipherable writing.

hierogram ('haɪərəˌgræm) NOUN a sacred symbol.

hierology (ˌhaɪə'rɒlədʒɪ) NOUN, *plural* **-gies.** [1] sacred literature. [2] a biography of a saint.
▸**hierologic** (ˌhaɪərə'lɒdʒɪk) *or* ˌ**hiero'logical** ADJECTIVE
▸ˌ**hier'ologist** NOUN

hierophant ('haɪərəˌfænt) NOUN [1] (in ancient Greece) an official high priest of religious mysteries, esp those of Eleusis. [2] a person who interprets and explains esoteric mysteries.
▷HISTORY C17: from Late Latin *hierophanta,* from Greek *hierophantēs,* from HIERO- + *phainein* to reveal
▸ˌ**hiero'phantic** ADJECTIVE ▸ˌ**hiero'phantically** ADVERB

hifalutin (ˌhaɪfə'luːtɪn) ADJECTIVE a variant spelling of **highfalutin.**

hi-fi ('haɪ'faɪ) NOUN *Informal* [1] **a** short for **high fidelity. b** *(as modifier)*: *hi-fi equipment.* [2] a set of high-quality sound-reproducing equipment.

higgle ('hɪgᵊl) VERB a less common word for **haggle.**
▸'**higgler** NOUN

higgledy-piggledy ('hɪgᵊldɪ'pɪgᵊldɪ) *Informal* ◆ ADJECTIVE, ADVERB [1] in a jumble. ◆ NOUN [2] a muddle.

Higgs boson *or* **Higgs particle** (hɪgs) NOUN *Physics* an elementary particle with zero spin and mass greater than zero, predicted to exist by electroweak theory and other gauge theories.
▷HISTORY C20: named after Peter *Higgs* (born 1929), British theoretical physicist

high (haɪ) ADJECTIVE [1] being a relatively great distance from top to bottom; tall: *a high building.* [2] situated at or extending to a relatively great distance above the ground or above sea level: *a high plateau.* [3] **a** *(postpositive)* being a specified distance from top to bottom: *three feet high.* **b** *(in combination)*: *a seven-foot-high wall.* [4] extending from an elevation: *a high dive.* [5] *(in combination)* coming up to a specified level: *knee-high.* [6] being at its peak or point of culmination: *high noon.* [7] of greater than average height: *a high collar.* [8] greater than normal in degree, intensity, or amount: *high prices; a high temperature; a high wind.* [9] of large or relatively large numerical value: *high frequency; high voltage; high mileage.* [10] (of sound) acute in pitch; having a high frequency. [11] (of latitudes) situated relatively far north or south from the equator. [12] (of meat) slightly decomposed or tainted, regarded as enhancing the flavour of game. [13] of great eminence; very important: *the high priestess.* [14] exalted in style or character; elevated: *high drama.*

[15] expressing or feeling contempt or arrogance: *high words.* [16] elated; cheerful: *high spirits.* [17] (*predicative*) *Informal* overexcited: *by the end of term the children are really high.* [18] *Informal* being in a state of altered consciousness, characterized esp by euphoria and often induced by the use of alcohol, narcotics, etc. [19] luxurious or extravagant: *high life.* [20] advanced in complexity or development: *high finance.* [21] (of a gear) providing a relatively great forward speed for a given engine speed. Compare **low**[1] (sense 21). [22] *Phonetics* of, relating to, or denoting a vowel whose articulation is produced by raising the back of the tongue towards the soft palate or the blade towards the hard palate, such as for the *ee* in English *see* or *oo* in English *moon.* Compare **low**[1] (sense 20). [23] (*capital when part of name*) formal and elaborate in style: *High Mass.* [24] (*usually capital*) of or relating to the High Church. [25] remote, esp in time. [26] *Cards* **a** having a relatively great value in a suit. **b** able to win a trick. [27] **high and dry.** stranded; helpless; destitute. [28] **high and low.** in all places; everywhere. [29] **high and mighty.** *Informal* arrogant. [30] **high as a kite.** *Informal* **a** very drunk. **b** overexcited. **c** euphoric from drugs. [31] **high opinion.** a favourable opinion. ◆ ADVERB [32] at or to a height: *he jumped high.* [33] in a high manner. [34] *Nautical* close to the wind with sails full. ◆ NOUN [35] a high place or level. [36] *Informal* a state of altered consciousness, often induced by alcohol, narcotics, etc. [37] another word for **anticyclone.** [38] short for **high school.** [39] (*capital*) (esp in Oxford) the High Street. [40] *Electronics* the voltage level in a logic circuit corresponding to logical one. Compare **low**[1] (sense 30). [41] **on high. a** at a height. **b** in heaven.
▷HISTORY Old English *hēah;* related to Old Norse *hār,* Gothic *hauhs,* Old High German *hōh* high, Lithuanian *kaũkas* bump, Russian *kúchča* heap, Sanskrit *kuča* bosom

high altar NOUN the principal altar of a church.

High Arctic NOUN the regions of Canada, esp the northern islands, within the Arctic Circle.

highball (ˈhaɪˌbɔːl) *Chiefly US* ◆ NOUN [1] a long iced drink consisting of a spirit base with water, soda water, etc. [2] (originally in railway use) a signal that the way ahead is clear and one may proceed. ◆ VERB [3] (*intr*) to move at great speed. [4] (*tr*) to drive (a vehicle) at great speed.
▷HISTORY C19: (in sense 2) from the early railway signal consisting of a ball hoisted to the top of a pole

highbinder (ˈhaɪˌbaɪndə) NOUN *US informal* [1] a gangster. [2] a corrupt politician. [3] (formerly) a member of a Chinese-American secret society that engaged in blackmail, murder, etc.
▷HISTORY C19: named after the *High-binders,* a New York city gang

highborn (ˈhaɪˌbɔːn) ADJECTIVE of noble or aristocratic birth.

highboy (ˈhaɪˌbɔɪ) NOUN *US and Canadian* a tall chest of drawers in two sections, the lower section being a lowboy. Brit equivalent: **tallboy.**

high brass NOUN brass containing 65 per cent copper and 35 per cent zinc, used for most applications.

highbrow (ˈhaɪˌbraʊ) *Often disparaging* ◆ NOUN [1] a person of scholarly and erudite tastes. ◆ ADJECTIVE *also* **highbrowed.** [2] appealing to highbrows: *highbrow literature.*

high camp NOUN a sophisticated form of **camp**[2] (the style).

high-carb NOUN (*modifier*) having a high carbohydrate content: *high-carb foods.*

high-carbon steel NOUN steel containing between 0.5 and 1.5 per cent carbon.

highchair (ˈhaɪˌtʃɛə) NOUN a long-legged chair for a child, esp one with a table-like tray used at meal times.

High Church NOUN [1] the party or movement within the Church of England stressing continuity with Catholic Christendom, the authority of bishops, and the importance of sacraments, rituals, and ceremonies. Compare **Broad Church, Low Church.** ◆ ADJECTIVE **High-Church.** [2] of or relating to this party or movement.
▶ˈ**High-**ˈ**Churchman** NOUN

high-class ADJECTIVE [1] of very good quality; superior: *a high-class grocer.* [2] belonging to, associated with, or exhibiting the characteristics of an upper social class: *a high-class lady; a high-class prostitute.*

high-coloured ADJECTIVE (of the complexion) deep red or purplish; florid.

high comedy NOUN comedy set largely among cultured and articulate people and featuring witty dialogue. Compare **low comedy.**
▶**high comedian** NOUN

high command NOUN the commander-in-chief and senior officers of a nation's armed forces.

high commissioner NOUN [1] the senior diplomatic representative sent by one Commonwealth country to another instead of an ambassador. [2] the head of an international commission. [3] the chief officer in a colony or other dependency.

high concept NOUN **a** popular appeal. **b** **high-concept.** (*as modifier*): *Baz Luhrmann's high-concept Romeo and Juliet.*

high-context ADJECTIVE preferring to communicate in person, rather than by electronic methods such as email. Compare **low-context.**

high country NOUN (often preceded by *the*) sheep pastures in the foothills of the Southern Alps, New Zealand.

High Court NOUN [1] a shortened form of. **a** (in England and Wales) High Court of Justice. **b** (in Scotland) High Court of Justiciary. [2] (in New Zealand) a court of law inferior to the Court of Appeal. Formerly called: **Supreme Court.**

High Court of Justice NOUN (in England) one of the two divisions of the Supreme Court of Judicature. See also **Court of Appeal.**

High Court of Justiciary NOUN the senior criminal court in Scotland, to which all cases of murder and rape and all cases involving heavy penalties are referred.

high day NOUN a day of celebration; festival (esp in the phrase **high days and holidays**).

high definition television NOUN a television system offering a picture with superior definition, using 1000 or more scanning lines, and possibly a higher field repetition rate to reduce flicker effects. Abbreviation: **HDTV.**

high-density ADJECTIVE *Computing* (of a floppy disk) having a relatively high storage capacity, usually of 1.44 megabytes.

high-density lipoprotein NOUN a lipoprotein that is the form in which cholesterol is transported in the bloodstream from the tissues to the liver. Abbreviation: **HDL.**

high-dependency ADJECTIVE needing or providing a more than usually high level of healthcare: *a shortage of high-dependency beds.*

high-end ADJECTIVE (*prenominal*) (esp of computers, electronic equipment, etc.) of the greatest power or sophistication.

high-energy physics NOUN another name for **particle physics.**

higher (ˈhaɪə) ADJECTIVE [1] the comparative of **high.** ◆ NOUN (*usually capital*) (in Scotland) [2] **a** the advanced level of the Scottish Certificate of Education. **b** (*as modifier*): *Higher Latin.* [3] a pass in a particular subject at Higher level: *she has four Highers.*

higher criticism NOUN the use of scientific techniques of literary criticism to establish the sources of the books of the Bible. Compare **lower criticism.**

higher education NOUN education and training at colleges, universities, polytechnics, etc.

higher mathematics NOUN (*functioning as singular*) abstract mathematics, including number theory and topology, that is more advanced than basic arithmetic, algebra, geometry, and trigonometry.

higher rate NOUN (in Britain) a rate of income tax that is higher than the basic rate and becomes payable on taxable income in excess of a specified limit.

higher self NOUN a person's spiritual self, as the focus of many meditation techniques, as opposed to the physical body.

Higher Still NOUN (in Scotland) **a** a system of post-Standard Grade qualifications offered at five levels including Higher and Advanced Higher. **b** (*as modifier*): *Higher Still courses.*

higher-up NOUN *Informal* a person of higher rank or in a superior position.

highest common factor NOUN the largest number or quantity that is a factor of each member of a group of numbers or quantities. Abbreviation: **HCF, h.c.f.** Also called: **greatest common divisor.**

high explosive NOUN an extremely powerful chemical explosive, such as TNT or gelignite.

highfalutin, hifalutin (ˌhaɪfəˈluːtɪn), *or* **highfaluting** ADJECTIVE *Informal* pompous or pretentious.
▷HISTORY C19: from HIGH + *-falutin,* perhaps variant of *fluting,* from FLUTE

high fashion NOUN another name for **haute couture.**

high fidelity NOUN **a** the reproduction of sound using electronic equipment that gives faithful reproduction with little or no distortion. **b** (*as modifier*): *a high-fidelity amplifier.* ◆ Often shortened to **hi-fi.**

high-five *Slang* ◆ NOUN [1] a gesture of greeting or congratulation in which two people slap raised right palms together. ◆ VERB [2] to greet or congratulate (a person) in this way.

high-flown ADJECTIVE extravagant or pretentious in conceptioon or intention: *high-flown ideas.*

high-flyer *or* **high-flier** NOUN [1] a person who is extreme in aims, ambition, etc. [2] a person of great ability, esp in a career.

high-flying ADJECTIVE having great ambition or ability.

high frequency NOUN a radio-frequency band or radio frequency lying between 3 and 30 megahertz. Abbreviation: **HF.**

High German NOUN [1] the standard German language, historically developed from the form of West Germanic spoken in S Germany. Abbreviation: **HG.** See also **German, Low German.** [2] any of the German dialects of S Germany, Austria, or Switzerland.

high-handed ADJECTIVE tactlessly overbearing and inconsiderate.
▶ˌ**high-**ˈ**handedly** ADVERB ▶ˌ**high-**ˈ**handedness** NOUN

high hat NOUN another name for **top hat.**

high-hat ADJECTIVE [1] *Informal* snobbish and arrogant. ◆ VERB **-hats, -hatting, -hatted.** (*tr*) [2] *Informal, chiefly US and Canadian* to treat in a snobbish or offhand way. ◆ NOUN [3] *Informal* a snobbish person. [4] two facing brass cymbals triggered by means of a foot pedal.

High Holidays PLURAL NOUN *Judaism* the festivals of Rosh Hashanah and Yom Kippur, the period of repentance in the first ten days of the Jewish new year. Also called: **Days of Awe, Yamim Nora'im.**

high hurdles NOUN (*functioning as singular*) a race in which competitors leap over hurdles 42 inches (107 cm) high.

high-impact ADJECTIVE (*prenominal*) [1] (of a plastic or other material) able to withstand great force. [2] (of aerobic or other exercise) placing great stress on various areas of the body. [3] *Informal* having great effect: *high-impact sound.*

highjack (ˈhaɪˌdʒæk) VERB, NOUN a less common spelling of **hijack.**
▶ˈ**high**ˌ**jacker** NOUN

high jinks *or* **hijinks** (ˈhaɪˌdʒɪŋks) NOUN lively enjoyment.

high jump NOUN [1] **a** (usually preceded by *the*) an athletic event in which a competitor has to jump over a high bar set between two vertical supports. **b** (*as modifier*): *high-jump techniques.* [2] **be for the high jump.** *Brit informal* to be liable to receive a severe reprimand or punishment.
▶**high jumper** NOUN ▶**high jumping** NOUN

high-key ADJECTIVE (of a photograph, painting, etc.) having a predominance of light grey tones or light colours. Compare **low-key** (sense 3).

high-keyed ADJECTIVE [1] having a high pitch; shrill. [2] *US* highly strung. [3] bright in colour.

highland (ˈhaɪlənd) NOUN [1] relatively high ground. [2] (*modifier*) of or relating to a highland.
▶ˈ**highlander** NOUN

Highland (ˈhaɪlənd) NOUN [1] a council area in N Scotland, formed in 1975 (as Highland Region) from Caithness, Sutherland, Nairnshire, most of Inverness-shire, and Ross and Cromarty except for the Outer Hebrides. Administrative centre: Inverness. Pop.: 208 914 (2001). Area: 25 149 sq. km (9710 sq. miles). 2 (*modifier*) of, relating to, or denoting the Highlands of Scotland.

Highland cattle NOUN a breed of cattle with shaggy hair, usually reddish-brown in colour, and long horns.

Highland Clearances PLURAL NOUN in Scotland, the removal, often by force, of the people from some parts of the Highlands to make way for sheep, during the eighteenth and nineteenth centuries. Also called: **the Clearances.**

Highland dress NOUN 1 the historical costume, including the plaid, kilt or filibeg, and bonnet, as worn by Highland clansmen and soldiers. 2 a modern version of this worn for formal occasions.

Highlander ('haɪləndə) NOUN 1 a native of the Highlands of Scotland. 2 a member of a Scottish Highland regiment.

Highland fling NOUN a vigorous Scottish solo dance.

Highland Games NOUN (*functioning as singular or plural*) a meeting in which competitions in sport, piping, and dancing are held: originating in the Highlands of Scotland.

Highlands ('haɪləndz) NOUN **the.** 1 **a** the part of Scotland that lies to the northwest of the great fault that runs from Dumbarton to Stonehaven. **b** a smaller area consisting of the mountainous north of Scotland: distinguished by Gaelic culture. 2 (*often not capital*) the highland region of any country.

high-level ADJECTIVE (of conferences, talks, etc.) involving very important people.

high-level language NOUN a computer programming language that resembles natural language or mathematical notation and is designed to reflect the requirements of a problem; examples include Ada, BASIC, C, COBOL, FORTRAN, Pascal. See also **machine code.**

high-level waste NOUN radioactive waste material, such as spent nuclear fuel initially having a high activity and thus needing constant cooling for several decades by its producers before it can be reprocessed or treated. Compare **intermediate-level waste, low-level waste.**

highlife ('haɪˌlaɪf) NOUN **a** a style of music combining West African elements with US jazz forms, found esp in the cities of West Africa. **b** (*as modifier*): *a highlife band.*

highlight ('haɪˌlaɪt) NOUN 1 an area of the lightest tone in a painting, drawing, photograph, etc. 2 the most exciting or memorable part of an event or period of time. 3 (*often plural*) a bleached blond streak in the hair. ◆ VERB (*tr*) 4 *Painting, drawing, photog* to mark (any brightly illuminated or prominent part of a form or figure) with light tone. 5 to bring notice or emphasis to. 6 to be the highlight of. 7 to produce blond streaks in (the hair) by bleaching.

highlighter ('haɪˌlaɪtə) NOUN 1 a cosmetic cream or powder applied to the face to highlight the cheekbones, eyes, etc. 2 a fluorescent felt-tip pen used as a marker to emphasize a section of text without obscuring it.

highly ('haɪlɪ) ADVERB 1 (intensifier): *highly pleased; highly disappointed.* 2 with great approbation or favour: *we spoke highly of it.* 3 in a high position: *placed highly in class.* 4 at or for a high price or cost.

highly strung *or US and Canadian* **high-strung** ADJECTIVE tense and easily upset; excitable; nervous.

High Mass NOUN a solemn and elaborate sung Mass. Compare **Low Mass.**

high-minded ADJECTIVE 1 having or characterized by high moral principles. 2 *Archaic* arrogant; haughty.
▸ **ˌhigh-ˈmindedly** ADVERB ▸ **ˌhigh-ˈmindedness** NOUN

high-muck-a-muck NOUN a conceited or haughty person.
▷ HISTORY C19: from Chinook Jargon *hiu muckamuck,* literally: plenty (of) food

highness ('haɪnɪs) NOUN the condition of being high or lofty.

Highness ('haɪnɪs) NOUN (preceded by *Your, His,* or *Her*) a title used to address or refer to a royal person.

high-octane ADJECTIVE 1 (of petrol) having a high octane number. 2 *Informal* dynamic, forceful, or intense: *high-octane drive and efficiency.*

high-pass filter NOUN *Electronics* a filter that transmits all frequencies above a specified value, substantially attenuating frequencies below this value. Compare **low-pass filter, band-pass filter.**

high-pitched ADJECTIVE 1 pitched high in volume or tone. See **high** (sense 10). 2 (of a roof) having steeply sloping sides. 3 (of an argument, style, etc.) lofty or intense.

high place NOUN *Old Testament* a place of idolatrous worship, esp a hilltop.

high places PLURAL NOUN positions and offices of influence and importance: *a scandal in high places.*

high point NOUN a moment or occasion of great intensity, interest, happiness, etc.: *the award marked a high point in his life.*

high-powered ADJECTIVE 1 (of an optical instrument or lens) having a high magnification: *a high-powered telescope.* 2 dynamic and energetic; highly capable. 3 possessing great strength, power, etc.: *a high-powered engine.*

high-pressure ADJECTIVE 1 having, using, involving, or designed to withstand a pressure above normal pressure: *a high-pressure gas; a high-pressure cylinder.* 2 *Informal* (of selling) persuasive in an aggressive and persistent manner.

high priest NOUN 1 *Judaism* the priest of highest rank who alone was permitted to enter the holy of holies of the tabernacle and Temple. 2 *Mormon Church* a priest of the order of Melchizedek priesthood. 3 Also (feminine): **high priestess.** the head of a group or cult.
▸ **high priesthood** NOUN

high profile NOUN **a** a position or approach characterized by a deliberate seeking of prominence or publicity. **b** (*as modifier*): *a high-profile campaign.* Compare **low profile.**

high relief NOUN relief in which forms and figures stand out from the background to half or more than half of their natural depth. Also called: **alto-relievo.**

High Renaissance NOUN **a the.** the period from about the 1490s to the 1520s in painting, sculpture, and architecture in Europe, esp in Italy, when the Renaissance ideals were considered to have been attained through the mastery of Leonardo, Michelangelo, and Raphael. **b** (*as modifier*): *High Renaissance art.*

high-rise ADJECTIVE **a** (*prenominal*) of or relating to a building that has many storeys, esp one used for flats or offices: *a high-rise block.* Compare **low-rise. b** (*as noun*): *a high-rise in Atlanta.*

high-risk ADJECTIVE denoting a group, part, etc., that is particularly subject or exposed to a danger.

highroad ('haɪˌrəʊd) NOUN 1 a main road; highway. 2 (usually preceded by *the*) the sure way: *the highroad to fame.*

high roller NOUN *Slang, chiefly US and Canadian* a person who spends money extravagantly or gambles recklessly.
▸ **high rolling** NOUN, ADJECTIVE

high school NOUN 1 *Brit* another term for **grammar school.** 2 *US and NZ* a secondary school from grade 7 to grade 12. 3 *Canadian* a secondary school, the grades covered depending on the province.

high seas PLURAL NOUN (*sometimes singular*) the open seas of the world, outside the jurisdiction of any one nation.

high season NOUN the most popular time of year at a holiday resort, etc.

high society NOUN **a** the upper classes, esp when fashionable. **b** (*as modifier*): *her high-society image.*

high-sounding ADJECTIVE another term for **high-flown.**

high-speed ADJECTIVE *Photog* 1 employing or requiring a very short exposure time: *high-speed film.* 2 recording or making exposures at a rate usually exceeding 50 and up to several million frames per second. 3 working, moving, or operating at a high speed.

high-speed steel NOUN any of various steels that retain their hardness at high temperatures and are thus suitable for making tools used on lathes and other high-speed machines.

high-spirited ADJECTIVE vivacious, bold, or lively.
▸ **ˌhigh-ˈspiritedly** ADVERB ▸ **ˌhigh-ˈspiritedness** NOUN

high spot NOUN *Informal* another word for **highlight** (sense 2).

high-stepper NOUN a horse trained to lift its feet high off the ground when walking or trotting.

High Street (*often not capitals*) NOUN (usually preceded by *the*) 1 *Brit* the main street of a town, usually where the principal shops are situated. 2 the market constituted by the general public. 3 (*modifier*) geared to meet the requirements of, and readily available for purchase by, the general public: *High-Street fashion.*

hight (haɪt) VERB (*tr; used only as a past tense in the passive or as a past participle*) *Archaic and poetic* to name; call: *a maid hight Mary.*
▷ HISTORY Old English *heht,* from *hatan* to call; related to Old Norse *heita,* Old Frisian *hēta,* Old High German *heizzan*

high table NOUN (*sometimes capitals*) the table, sometimes elevated, in the dining hall of a school, college, etc., at which the principal teachers, fellows, etc., sit.

hightail ('haɪˌteɪl) VERB (*intr*) *Informal, chiefly US and Canadian* to go or move in a great hurry. Also: **hightail it.**

High Tatra NOUN another name for the **Tatra Mountains.**

high tea NOUN *Brit* See **tea** (sense 4c).

high tech (tɛk) NOUN a variant spelling of **hi tech.**

high technology NOUN highly sophisticated, often electronic, techniques used in manufacturing and other processes.

high-tension NOUN (*modifier*) subjected to, carrying, or capable of operating at a relatively high voltage: *a high-tension wire.* Abbreviation: **HT.**

high tide NOUN 1 **a** the tide at its highest level. **b** the time at which it reaches this. 2 a culminating point.

high time *Informal* ◆ ADVERB 1 the latest possible time; a time that is almost too late: *it's high time you mended this shelf.* ◆ NOUN 2 Also called: **high old time.** an enjoyable and exciting time.

high-toned ADJECTIVE 1 having a superior social, moral, or intellectual quality. 2 affectedly superior. 3 high in tone.

high tops PLURAL NOUN training shoes that reach above the ankles.

high treason NOUN an act of treason directly affecting a sovereign or state.

high-up NOUN *Informal* a person who holds an important or influential position.

highveld ('haɪˌfɛlt, -ˌvɛlt) NOUN **the.** the high-altitude grassland region of E South Africa.

high water NOUN 1 another name for **high tide** (sense 1). 2 the state of any stretch of water at its highest level, as during a flood. Abbreviation: **HW.**

high-water mark NOUN 1 **a** the level reached by sea water at high tide or by other stretches of water in flood. **b** the mark indicating this level. 2 the highest point.

highway ('haɪˌweɪ) NOUN 1 a public road that all may use. 2 *Now chiefly US and Canadian except in legal contexts* a main road, esp one that connects towns or cities. 3 a main route for any form of transport. 4 a direct path or course.

Highway Code NOUN (in Britain) an official government booklet giving guidance to users of public roads.

highwayman ('haɪˌweɪmən) NOUN, *plural* **-men.** (formerly) a robber, usually on horseback, who held up travellers.

highway robbery NOUN *Informal* blatant overcharging.

high wire NOUN a tightrope stretched high in the air for balancing acts.

High Wycombe ('wɪkəm) NOUN a town in S central England, in S Buckinghamshire: furniture industry. Pop.: 71 718 (1991).

HIH ABBREVIATION FOR His (*or* Her) Imperial Highness.

hi-hat NOUN a variant spelling of **high-hat** (sense 4).

hijab (hɪ'dʒæb, he'dʒɑ:b) *or* **hejab** NOUN a covering for the head and face, worn by Muslim women.
▷HISTORY from Arabic, literally: curtain

hijack *or* **highjack** ('haɪˌdʒæk) VERB [1] (*tr*) to seize, divert, or appropriate (a vehicle or the goods it carries) while in transit: *to hijack an aircraft.* [2] to rob (a person or vehicle) by force: *to hijack a traveller.* [3] (esp in the US during Prohibition) to rob (a bootlegger or smuggler) of his illicit goods or to steal (illicit goods) in transit. ◆ NOUN [4] the act or an instance of hijacking.
▷HISTORY C20: of unknown origin
▸'**hiˌjacker** *or* '**highˌjacker** NOUN

Hijaz (hi:'dʒæz) NOUN a variant spelling of **Hejaz.**

Hijrah ('hɪdʒrə) NOUN a variant of **Hegira.**

hike (haɪk) VERB [1] (*intr*) to walk a long way, usually for pleasure or exercise, esp in the country. [2] (usually foll by *up*) to pull or be pulled; hitch. [3] (*tr*) to increase (a price). ◆ NOUN [4] a long walk. [5] a rise in prices, wages, etc.
▷HISTORY C18: of uncertain origin
▸'**hiker** NOUN

hike out VERB (*intr, adverb*) *Nautical* the US and Canadian term for **sit out** (sense 3).

hikoi ('hi:kɔɪ) NOUN *NZ* a walk or march, esp a Maori protest march.
▷HISTORY Maori

hilarious (hɪ'lɛərɪəs) ADJECTIVE very funny or merry.
▷HISTORY C19: from Latin *hilaris* glad, from Greek *hilaros*
▸**hi'lariously** ADVERB ▸**hi'lariousness** NOUN

hilarity (hɪ'lærɪtɪ) NOUN mirth and merriment; cheerfulness.

Hilary term NOUN the spring term at Oxford University, the Inns of Court, and some other educational establishments.
▷HISTORY C16: named after Saint Hilary of Poitiers (?315–?367 A.D.), French bishop, whose feast day is Jan. 13 or 14

Hildesheim (*German* 'hɪldəshaim) NOUN a city in N central Germany, in Lower Saxony: a member of the Hanseatic League. Pop.: 105 405 (1999 est.).

hill (hɪl) NOUN [1] **a** a conspicuous and often rounded natural elevation of the earth's surface, less high or craggy than a mountain. **b** (*in combination*): *a hillside; a hilltop.* [2] **a** a heap or mound made by a person or animal. **b** (*in combination*): *a dunghill.* [3] an incline; slope. [4] **over the hill. a** *Informal* beyond one's prime. **b** *Military, slang* absent without leave or deserting. [5] **up hill and down dale.** strenuously and persistently. ◆ VERB (*tr*) [6] to form into a hill or mound. [7] to cover or surround with a mound or heap of earth. ◆ See also **hills.**
▷HISTORY Old English *hyll;* related to Old Frisian *holla* head, Latin *collis* hill, Low German *hull* hill
▸'**hiller** NOUN ▸'**hilly** ADJECTIVE

Hilla ('hɪlə) NOUN a market town in central Iraq, on a branch of the Euphrates: built partly of bricks from the nearby site of Babylon. Pop.: 268 834 (latest est.). Also called: **Al Hillah.**

hillbilly ('hɪlˌbɪlɪ) NOUN, *plural* **-lies.** [1] *Usually disparaging* an unsophisticated person, esp from the mountainous areas in the southeastern US. [2] another name for **country and western.**
▷HISTORY C20: from HILL + *Billy* (the nickname)

hill climb NOUN a competition in which motor vehicles attempt singly to ascend a steep slope as fast as possible.

hill country NOUN *NZ* (in North Island) elevated pasture land for sheep or cattle.

hillfort ('hɪlˌfɔ:t) NOUN *Archaeol* a hilltop fortified with ramparts and ditches, dating from the second millennium B.C.

Hillingdon ('hɪlɪŋdən) NOUN a residential borough of W Greater London. Pop.: 242 435 (2001). Area: 110 sq. km (43 sq. miles).

hill mynah NOUN a starling, *Gracula religiosa,* of S and SE Asia: a popular cage bird because of its ability to talk. Also called: **Indian grackle.**

hillock ('hɪlək) NOUN a small hill or mound.
▷HISTORY C14 *hilloc,* from HILL + -OCK
▸'**hillocked** *or* '**hillocky** ADJECTIVE

hills (hɪlz) PLURAL NOUN [1] **the.** a hilly and often remote region. [2] **as old as the hills.** very old.

hill station NOUN (in northern India) a settlement or resort at a high altitude.

hilt (hɪlt) NOUN [1] the handle or shaft of a sword, dagger, etc. [2] **to the hilt.** to the full. ◆ VERB [3] (*tr*) to supply with a hilt.
▷HISTORY Old English; related to Old Norse *hjalt,* Old Saxon *helta* oar handle, Old High German *helza*

hilum ('haɪləm) NOUN, *plural* **-la** (-lə). [1] *Botany* **a** a scar on the surface of a seed marking its point of attachment to the seed stalk (funicle). **b** the nucleus of a starch grain. [2] a deep fissure or depression on the surface of a bodily organ around the point of entrance or exit of vessels, nerves, or ducts.
▷HISTORY C17: from Latin: trifle; see NIHIL

hilus ('haɪləs) NOUN a rare word for **hilum** (sense 2).
▷HISTORY C19: via New Latin from Latin: a trifle
▸'**hilar** ADJECTIVE

Hilversum ('hɪlvəsəm; *Dutch* 'hɪlvərsym) NOUN a city in the central Netherlands, in North Holland province: Dutch radio and television centre. Pop.: 84 213 (1994).

him (hɪm; *unstressed* ɪm) PRONOUN (*objective*) [1] refers to a male person or animal: *they needed him; she baked him a cake; not him again!* [2] *Chiefly US* a dialect word for **himself** when used as an indirect object: *he ought to find him a wife.*
▷HISTORY Old English *him,* dative of *hē* HE[1]

Language note See at **me**[1].

HIM ABBREVIATION FOR His (*or* Her) Imperial Majesty.

Himachal Pradesh (hɪ'mɑ:tʃəl prɑ:'dɛʃ) NOUN a state of N India, in the W Himalayas: rises to about 6700 m (22 000 ft.) and is densely forested. Capital: Simla. Pop.: 6 077 248 (2001). Area: 55 658 sq. km (21 707 sq. miles).

Himalayan (ˌhɪmə'leɪən) ADJECTIVE of or relating to the Himalayas or their inhabitants.

Himalayan cat NOUN the US name for **colourpoint cat.**

Himalayan guinea pig NOUN a variety of short-haired guinea pig with markings on its nose, ears, and feet.

Himalayas (ˌhɪmə'leɪəz, hɪ'mɑ:ljəz) PLURAL NOUN **the.** a vast mountain system in S Asia, extending 2400 km (1500 miles) from Kashmir (west) to Assam (east), between the valleys of the Rivers Indus and Brahmaputra: covers most of Nepal, Sikkim, Bhutan, and the S edge of Tibet; the highest range in the world, with several peaks over 7500 m (25 000 ft.). Highest peak: Mount Everest, 8848 m (29 028 ft.).

Himalia (hɪ'mɑ:lɪə) NOUN *Astronomy* a satellite of Jupiter in an intermediate orbit.

himation (hɪ'mætɪˌɒn) NOUN, *plural* **-ia** (-ɪə). (in ancient Greece) a cloak draped around the body.
▷HISTORY C19: from Greek: a little garment, from *heima* dress, from *hennunai* to clothe

himbo ('hɪmbəʊ) NOUN, *plural* **-bos.** *Slang, usually derogatory* an attractive, but empty-headed man.
▷HISTORY C20: from HIM + (BIM)BO

Himeji ('hi:mɛˌdʒi:) NOUN a city in central Japan, on W Honshu: cotton textile centre. Pop.: 470 986 (1995).

Hims (hɪmz) NOUN a former name of **Homs.**

himself (hɪm'sɛlf; *medially often* ɪm'sɛlf) PRONOUN [1] **a** the reflexive form of *he* or *him.* **b** (intensifier): *the king himself waved to me.* [2] (*preceded by a copula*) his normal or usual self: *he seems himself once more.* [3] *Irish and Scot* the man of the house: *how is himself?*
▷HISTORY Old English *him selfum,* dative singular of *hē self;* see HE[1], SELF

Himyarite ('hɪmjəˌraɪt) NOUN [1] a member of an ancient people of SW Arabia, sometimes regarded as including the Sabeans. ◆ ADJECTIVE [2] of or relating to this people or their culture.
▷HISTORY C19: named after *Himyar* legendary king in ancient Yemen

Himyaritic (ˌhɪmjə'rɪtɪk) NOUN [1] the extinct language of the Himyarites, belonging to the SE Semitic subfamily of the Afro-Asiatic family. ◆ ADJECTIVE [2] of, relating to, or using this language.

hin (hɪn) NOUN a Hebrew unit of capacity equal to about 12 pints or 3.5 litres.
▷HISTORY from Late Latin, from Greek, from Hebrew *hīn,* from Egyptian *hnw*

Hinayana (ˌhi:nə'jɑ:nə) NOUN **a** any of various early forms of Buddhism. **b** (*as modifier*): *Hinayana Buddhism.*
▷HISTORY from Sanskrit *hīnayāna,* from *hīna* lesser + *yāna* vehicle
▸ˌ**Hina'yanist** NOUN ▸ˌ**Hinaya'nistic** ADJECTIVE

Hinckley ('hɪŋklɪ) NOUN a town in central England, in Leicestershire. Pop.: 40 608 (1991 est.).

hind[1] (haɪnd) ADJECTIVE **hinder, hindmost** *or* **hindermost.** (*prenominal*) (esp of parts of the body) situated at the back or rear: *a hind leg.*
▷HISTORY Old English *hindan* at the back, related to German *hinten;* see BEHIND, HINDER[2]

hind[2] (haɪnd) NOUN, *plural* **hinds** *or* **hind.** [1] the female of the deer, esp the red deer when aged three years or more. [2] any of several marine serranid fishes of the genus *Epinephelus,* closely related and similar to the gropers.
▷HISTORY Old English *hind;* related to Old High German *hinta,* Greek *kemas* young deer, Lithuanian *szmúlas* hornless

hind[3] (haɪnd) NOUN (formerly) [1] a simple peasant. [2] (in N Britain) a skilled farm worker. [3] a steward.
▷HISTORY Old English *hīne,* from *hīgna,* genitive plural of *hīgan* servants

Hind. ABBREVIATION FOR: [1] Hindi. [2] Hindu. [3] Hindustan. [4] Hindustani.

hindbrain ('haɪndˌbreɪn) NOUN the nontechnical name for **rhombencephalon.**

Hindenburg ('hɪndənbʊrk) NOUN the German name for **Zabrze.**

Hindenburg line NOUN a line of strong fortifications built by the German army near the Franco-Belgian border in 1916–17: breached by the Allies in August 1918.
▷HISTORY C20: named after Paul von Beneckendorff und von Hindenburg (1847–1934), German field marshal and statesman

hinder[1] ('hɪndə) VERB [1] to be or get in the way of (someone or something); hamper. [2] (*tr*) to prevent.
▷HISTORY Old English *hindrian;* related to Old Norse *hindra,* Old High German *hintarōn*
▸'**hinderer** NOUN ▸'**hindering** ADJECTIVE, NOUN

hinder[2] ('haɪndə) ADJECTIVE (*prenominal*) situated at or further towards the back or rear; posterior.
▷HISTORY Old English; related to Old Norse *hindri* latter, Gothic *hindar* beyond, Old High German *hintar* behind

hindgut ('haɪndˌgʌt) NOUN [1] the part of the vertebrate digestive tract comprising the colon and rectum. [2] the posterior part of the digestive tract of arthropods. ◆ See also **foregut, midgut.**

Hindi ('hɪndɪ) NOUN [1] a language or group of dialects of N central India. It belongs to the Indic branch of the Indo-European family and is closely related to Urdu. See also **Hindustani.** [2] a formal literary dialect of this language, the official language of India, usually written in Nagari script. [3] a person whose native language is Hindi.
▷HISTORY C18: from Hindi *hindī,* from *Hind* India, from Old Persian *Hindu* the river Indus

hindmost ('haɪndˌməʊst) *or* **hindermost** ('haɪndəˌməʊst) ADJECTIVE furthest back; last.

Hindoo ('hɪndu:, hɪn'du:) NOUN, *plural* **-doos,** ADJECTIVE an older spelling of **Hindu.**
▸**Hindooism** ('hɪnduˌɪzəm) NOUN

hindquarter ('haɪndˌkwɔ:tə) NOUN [1] one of the two back quarters of a carcass of beef, lamb, etc. [2] (*plural*) the rear, esp of a four-legged animal.

hindrance ('hɪndrəns) NOUN [1] an obstruction or snag; impediment. [2] the act of hindering; prevention.

hindsight ('haɪndˌsaɪt) NOUN [1] the ability to understand, after something has happened, what should have been done or what caused the event. [2] a firearm's rear sight.

Hindu *or* **Hindoo** ('hɪndu:, hɪn'du:) NOUN, *plural* **-dus, -doos.** [1] a person who adheres to Hinduism. [2] an inhabitant or native of Hindustan or India, esp one adhering to Hinduism. ◆ ADJECTIVE [3] relating to Hinduism, Hindus, or India.
▷HISTORY C17: from Persian *Hindū,* from *Hind* India; see HINDI

Hinduism *or* **Hindooism** (ˈhɪnduˌɪzəm) NOUN the complex of beliefs, values, and customs comprising the dominant religion of India, characterized by the worship of many gods, including Brahma as supreme being, a caste system, belief in reincarnation, etc.

Hindu Kush (kʊʃ, kuːʃ) PLURAL NOUN a mountain range in central Asia, extending about 800 km (500 miles) east from the Koh-i-Baba Mountains of central Afghanistan to the Pamirs. Highest peak: Tirich Mir, 7690 m (25 230 ft.).

Hindustan (ˌhɪnduˈstɑːn) NOUN 1 the land of the Hindus, esp India north of the Deccan and excluding Bengal. 2 the general area around the Ganges where Hindi is the predominant language. 3 the areas of India where Hinduism predominates, as contrasted with those areas where Islam predominates.

Hindustani, Hindoostani (ˌhɪnduˈstɑːnɪ), *or* **Hindostani** (ˌhɪndəʊˈstɑːnɪ) NOUN 1 the dialect of Hindi spoken in Delhi: used as a lingua franca throughout India. 2 a group of languages or dialects consisting of all spoken forms of Hindi and Urdu considered together. ◆ ADJECTIVE 3 of or relating to these languages or Hindustan.

hinge (hɪndʒ) NOUN 1 a device for holding together two parts such that one can swing relative to the other, typically having two interlocking metal leaves held by a pin about which they pivot. 2 *Anatomy* a type of joint, such as the knee joint, that moves only backwards and forwards; a joint that functions in only one plane. Technical name: **ginglymus.** 3 a similar structure in invertebrate animals, such as the joint between the two halves of a bivalve shell. 4 something on which events, opinions, etc., turn. 5 Also called: **mount.** *Philately* a small thin transparent strip of gummed paper for affixing a stamp to a page. ◆ VERB 6 (*tr*) to attach or fit a hinge to (something). 7 (*intr;* usually foll by *on* or *upon*) to depend (on). 8 (*intr*) to hang or turn on or as if on a hinge.
▷HISTORY C13: probably of Germanic origin; compare Middle Dutch *henge;* see HANG
▸**hinged** ADJECTIVE ▸**ˈhingeless** ADJECTIVE ▸**ˈhingeˌlike** ADJECTIVE

hinny[1] (ˈhɪnɪ) NOUN, *plural* **-nies.** the sterile hybrid offspring of a male horse and a female donkey or ass. Compare **mule[1]** (sense 1).
▷HISTORY C17: from Latin *hinnus,* from Greek *hinnos*

hinny[2] (ˈhɪnɪ) VERB **-nies, -nying, -nied.** a less common word for **whinny.**

hinny[3] (ˈhɪnɪ) NOUN *Scot and northern English dialect* a term of endearment, esp for a woman or child.
▷HISTORY variant of HONEY

hint (hɪnt) NOUN 1 a suggestion or implication given in an indirect or subtle manner: *he dropped a hint.* 2 a helpful piece of advice or practical suggestion. 3 a small amount; trace. ◆ VERB 4 (when *intr,* often foll by *at;* when *tr, takes a clause as object*) to suggest or imply indirectly.
▷HISTORY C17: of uncertain origin
▸**ˈhinter** NOUN ▸**ˈhinting** NOUN ▸**ˈhintingly** ADVERB

hinterland (ˈhɪntəˌlænd) NOUN 1 land lying behind something, esp a coast or the shore of a river. 2 remote or undeveloped areas of a country. 3 an area located near and dependent on a large city, esp a port.
▷HISTORY C19: from German, from *hinter* behind + *land* LAND; see HINDER[2]

hip[1] (hɪp) NOUN 1 (*often plural*) either side of the body below the waist and above the thigh, overlying the lateral part of the pelvis and its articulation with the thighbones. 2 another name for **pelvis** (sense 1). 3 short for **hip joint.** 4 the angle formed where two sloping sides of a roof meet or where a sloping side meets a sloping end.
▷HISTORY Old English *hype;* related to Old High German *huf,* Gothic *hups,* Dutch *heup*
▸**ˈhipless** ADJECTIVE ▸**ˈhipˌlike** ADJECTIVE

hip[2] (hɪp) NOUN the berry-like brightly coloured fruit of a rose plant: a swollen receptacle, rich in vitamin C, containing several small hairy achenes. Also called: **rosehip.**
▷HISTORY Old English *héopa;* related to Old Saxon *hiopo,* Old High German *hiufo,* Dutch *joop,* Norwegian dialect *hjūpa*

hip[3] (hɪp) INTERJECTION an exclamation used to introduce cheers (in the phrase **hip, hip, hurrah**).
▷HISTORY C18: of unknown origin

hip[4] (hɪp) *or* **hep** ADJECTIVE **hipper, hippest** *or* **hepper, heppest.** *Slang* 1 aware of or following the latest trends in music, ideas, fashion, etc. 2 (*often postpositive;* foll by *to*) informed (about).
▷HISTORY C20: variant of earlier *hep*

hip bath NOUN a portable bath in which the bather sits.

hipbone (ˈhɪpˌbəʊn) NOUN the nontechnical name for **innominate bone.**

hip dysplasia NOUN *Vet science* a common disorder of large and giant-breed dogs, as well as other species, in which the femoral head does not sit properly in the socket of the hip joint.

hip flask NOUN a small metal flask for spirits, etc., often carried in a hip pocket.

hip-hop (ˈhɪpˌhɒp) NOUN a US pop culture movement originating in the 1980s comprising rap music, graffiti, and break dancing.

hip-huggers PLURAL NOUN *Chiefly US* trousers that begin at the hips instead of the waist. Usual Brit word: **hipsters.**

hip joint NOUN the ball-and-socket joint that connects each leg to the trunk of the body, in which the head of the femur articulates with the socket (acetabulum) of the pelvis.

hipparch (ˈhɪpɑːk) NOUN (in ancient Greece) a cavalry commander.
▷HISTORY C17: from Greek *hippos* horse + -ARCH

Hipparchus (hɪˈpɑːkəs) NOUN a large crater in the SW quadrant of the moon, about 130 kilometres in diameter.
▷HISTORY after *Hipparchus,* Greek astronomer (2nd century B.C.)

Hipparchus satellite (hɪˈpɑːkəs) NOUN an astronometric satellite launched in 1989 by the European Space Agency that measured the position, proper motion, and brightness of 118 218 stars down to 12th magnitude and the magnitude and colour of a million stars down to 10th magnitude.
▷HISTORY after *Hipparchus,* Greek astronomer (2nd century B.C.)

hippeastrum (hɪpɪˈæstrəm) NOUN any plant of the South American amaryllidaceous genus *Hippeastrum:* cultivated for their large funnel-shaped typically red flowers.
▷HISTORY C19: New Latin, from Greek *hippeus* knight + *astron* star

hipped[1] (hɪpt) ADJECTIVE 1 **a** having a hip or hips. **b** (*in combination*): *broad-hipped; low-hipped.* 2 (esp of cows, sheep, reindeer, elk, etc.) having an injury to the hip, such as a dislocation of the bones. 3 *Architect* having a hip or hips. See also **hipped roof.**

hipped[2] (hɪpt) ADJECTIVE (*often postpositive;* foll by *on*) *US and Canadian dated slang* very enthusiastic (about).
▷HISTORY C20: from HIP[4]

hipped roof NOUN a roof having sloping ends and sides.

hippie (ˈhɪpɪ) NOUN a variant spelling of **hippy[1]**.

hippo (ˈhɪpəʊ) NOUN, *plural* **-pos.** *Informal* 1 short for **hippopotamus.** 2 *South African* an armoured police car.

hippocampus (ˌhɪpəʊˈkæmpəs) NOUN, *plural* **-pi** (-paɪ). 1 a mythological sea creature with the forelegs of a horse and the tail of a fish. 2 any marine teleost fish of the genus *Hippocampus,* having a horselike head. See **sea horse.** 3 an area of cerebral cortex that forms a ridge in the floor of the lateral ventricle of the brain, which in cross section has the shape of a sea horse. It functions as part of the limbic system.
▷HISTORY C16: from Latin, from Greek *hippos* horse + *kampos* a sea monster
▸**ˌhippoˈcampal** ADJECTIVE

hip pocket NOUN a pocket at the back of a pair of trousers.

hippocras (ˈhɪpəʊˌkræs) NOUN an old English drink of wine flavoured with spices.
▷HISTORY C14 *ypocras,* from Old French: Hippocrates (?460–?377 B.C.), Greek physician, probably referring to a filter called *Hippocrates' sleeve*

Hippocratic facies (ˌhɪpəʊˈkrætɪk) NOUN the sallow facial expression, with listless staring eyes, often regarded as denoting approaching death.

Hippocratic oath (ˌhɪpəʊˈkrætɪk) NOUN an oath taken by a doctor to observe a code of medical ethics supposedly derived from that of Hippocrates (?460–?337), Greek physician commonly regarded as the father of medicine.

Hippocrene (ˈhɪpəʊˌkriːn, ˌhɪpəʊˈkriːnɪ) NOUN a spring on Mount Helicon in Greece, said to engender poetic inspiration.
▷HISTORY C17: via Latin from Greek *hippos* horse + *krēnē* spring
▸**ˌHippoˈcrenian** ADJECTIVE

hippodrome (ˈhɪpəˌdrəʊm) NOUN 1 a music hall, variety theatre, or circus. 2 (in ancient Greece or Rome) an open-air course for horse and chariot races.
▷HISTORY C16: from Latin *hippodromos,* from Greek *hippos* horse + *dromos* a race

hippogriff *or* **hippogryph** (ˈhɪpəʊˌgrɪf) NOUN a monster of Greek mythology with a griffin's head, wings, and claws and a horse's body.
▷HISTORY C17: from Italian *ippogrifo,* from *ippo-* horse (from Greek *hippos*) + *grifo* GRIFFIN[1]

Hippolyta (hɪˈpɒlɪtə) *or* **Hippolyte** (hɪˈpɒlɪˌtiː) NOUN *Greek myth* a queen of the Amazons, slain by Hercules in battle for her belt, which he obtained as his ninth labour.

Hippolytus (hɪˈpɒlɪtəs) NOUN *Greek myth* a son of Theseus, killed after his stepmother Phaedra falsely accused him of raping her.
▸**Hipˈpolytan** ADJECTIVE

Hippomenes (hɪˈpɒmɪˌniːz) NOUN *Greek myth* the husband, in some traditions, of Atalanta.

hippopotamus (ˌhɪpəˈpɒtəməs) NOUN, *plural* **-muses** *or* **-mi** (-ˌmaɪ). 1 a very large massive gregarious artiodactyl mammal, *Hippopotamus amphibius,* living in or around the rivers of tropical Africa: family *Hippopotamidae.* It has short legs and a thick skin sparsely covered with hair. 2 **pigmy hippopotamus.** a related but smaller animal, *Choeropsis liberiensis.*
▷HISTORY C16: from Latin, from Greek *hippopotamos* river horse, from *hippos* horse + *potamos* river

Hippo Regius (ˈhɪpəʊ ˈriːdʒɪəs) NOUN an ancient Numidian city, adjoining present-day Annaba, Algeria. Often shortened to **Hippo.**

hippuric acid (hɪˈpjʊərɪk) NOUN a crystalline solid excreted in the urine of mammals. Formula: $C_9H_9NO_3$.

hippy[1] *or* **hippie** (ˈhɪpɪ) NOUN, *plural* **-pies. a** (esp during the 1960s) a person whose behaviour, dress, use of drugs, etc., implied a rejection of conventional values. **b** (*as modifier*): *hippy language.*
▷HISTORY C20: see HIP[4]

hippy[2] (ˈhɪpɪ) ADJECTIVE **-pier, -piest.** *Informal* (esp of a woman) having large hips.

hip roof NOUN a roof having sloping ends and sides.

hipster (ˈhɪpstə) NOUN 1 *Slang, now rare* **a** an enthusiast of modern jazz. **b** an outmoded word for **hippy[1]**. 2 (*modifier*) (of trousers) cut so that the top encircles the hips.

hipsters (ˈhɪpstəz) PLURAL NOUN *Brit* trousers cut so that the top encircles the hips. Usual US word: **hip-huggers.**

hiragana (ˌhɪərəˈgɑːnə) NOUN one of the Japanese systems of syllabic writing based on Chinese cursive ideograms. The more widely used of the two current systems, it is employed in newspapers and general literature. Compare **katakana.**
▷HISTORY from Japanese: flat kana

hircine (ˈhɜːsaɪn, -sɪn) ADJECTIVE 1 *Archaic* of or like a goat, esp in smell. 2 *Literary* lustful; lascivious.
▷HISTORY C17: from Latin *hircīnus,* from *hircus* goat

hire (ˈhaɪə) VERB (*tr*) 1 to acquire the temporary use of (a thing) or the services of (a person) in exchange for payment. 2 to employ (a person) for wages. 3 (often foll by *out*) to provide (something) or the services of (oneself or others) for an agreed payment, usually for an agreed period. 4 (*tr;* foll by *out*) *Chiefly Brit* to pay independent contractors for (work to be done). ◆ NOUN 5 **a** the act of hiring or the state of being hired. **b** (*as modifier*): *a hire car.* 6 **a** the price paid or payable for a person's services or

the temporary use of something. **b** (*as modifier*): *the hire charge.* [7] **for** *or* **on hire.** available for service or temporary use in exchange for payment.
▷HISTORY Old English *hȳrian;* related to Old Frisian *hēra* to lease, Middle Dutch *hūren*
▸'**hirable** *or* '**hireable** ADJECTIVE ▸'**hirer** NOUN

hireling ('haɪəlɪŋ) NOUN *Derogatory* a person who works only for money, esp one paid to do something unpleasant.
▷HISTORY Old English *hȳrling;* related to Dutch *huurling;* see HIRE, -LING[1]

hire-purchase NOUN *Brit* **a** a system for purchasing merchandise, such as cars or furniture, in which the buyer takes possession of the merchandise on payment of a deposit and completes the purchase by paying a series of regular instalments while the seller retains ownership until the final instalment is paid. **b** (*as modifier*): *hire-purchase legislation.* Abbreviation: **HP, h.p.** US and Canadian equivalents: **installment plan, instalment plan.**

Hiri Motu ('hɪərɪ 'məʊtuː) NOUN another name for **Motu** (the language).

hiring-fair NOUN (formerly, in rural areas) a fair or market at which agricultural labourers were hired.

Hiroshima (ˌhɪrɒ'ʃiːmə, hɪ'rɒʃɪmə) NOUN a port in SW Japan, on SW Honshu on the delta of the Ota River: largely destroyed on August 6, 1945, by the first atomic bomb to be used in warfare, dropped by the US, which killed over 75 000 of its inhabitants. Pop.: 1 108 868 (1995).

hirple ('hɪrpᵊl) *Scot* ◆ VERB (*intr*) [1] to limp. ◆ NOUN [2] a limping gait.
▷HISTORY C15: of unknown origin

hirsute ('hɜːsjuːt) ADJECTIVE [1] covered with hair. [2] (of plants or their parts) covered with long but not stiff hairs. [3] (of a person) having long, thick, or untrimmed hair.
▷HISTORY C17: from Latin *hirsūtus* shaggy; related to Latin *horrēre* to bristle, *hirtus* hairy; see HORRID
▸'**hirsuteness** NOUN

hirudin (hɪ'ruːdɪn) NOUN *Med* an anticoagulant extracted from the mouth glands of leeches.
▷HISTORY C20: from Latin *hirudin-*, *hirudo* leech + -IN

hirundine (hɪ'rʌndɪn, -daɪn) ADJECTIVE [1] of or resembling a swallow. [2] belonging to the bird family *Hirundinidae,* which includes swallows and martins.
▷HISTORY C19: from Late Latin *hirundineus,* from Latin *hirundō* a swallow

his (hɪz; *unstressed* ɪz) DETERMINER [1] **a** of, belonging to, or associated with him: *his own fault; his knee; I don't like his being out so late.* **b** *as pronoun*: *his is on the left; that book is his.* [2] **his and hers.** (of paired objects) for a man and woman respectively. ◆ PRONOUN [3] **of his.** belonging to or associated with him.
▷HISTORY Old English *his,* genitive of *hē* HE[1] and of *hit* IT

Hispania (hɪ'spænɪə) NOUN the Iberian peninsula in the Roman world.

Hispanic (hɪ'spænɪk) ADJECTIVE [1] relating to, characteristic of, or derived from Spain or the Spanish. ◆ NOUN [2] *US* a US citizen of Spanish or Latin-American descent.

Hispanicism (hɪ'spænɪˌsɪzəm) NOUN a word or expression borrowed from Spanish or modelled on the form of a Spanish word or expression.

Hispanicize *or* **Hispanicise** (hɪ'spænɪˌsaɪz) VERB (*tr*) to make Spanish, as in custom or culture; bring under Spanish control or influence.
▸**His'panicist** NOUN ▸**Hisˌpanici'zation** *or* **Hisˌpanici'sation** NOUN

Hispaniola (ˌhɪspən'jəʊlə; *Spanish* ispa'ɲola) NOUN the second largest island in the Caribbean, in the Greater Antilles: divided politically into Haiti and the Dominican Republic; discovered in 1492 by Christopher Columbus, who named it La Isla Española. Area: 18 703 sq. km (29 418 sq. miles). Former name: **Santo Domingo.**

hispid ('hɪspɪd) ADJECTIVE *Biology* covered with stiff hairs or bristles.
▷HISTORY C17: from Latin *hispidus* bristly
▸**his'pidity** NOUN

hiss (hɪs) NOUN [1] a voiceless fricative sound like that of a prolonged *s.* [2] such a sound uttered as an exclamation of derision, contempt, etc., esp by an audience or crowd. [3] *Electronics* receiver noise with a continuous spectrum, caused by thermal agitation, shot noise, etc. ◆ INTERJECTION [4] an exclamation of derision or disapproval. ◆ VERB [5] (*intr*) to produce or utter a hiss. [6] (*tr*) to express with a hiss, usually to indicate derision or anger. [7] (*tr*) to show derision or anger towards (a speaker, performer, etc.) by hissing.
▷HISTORY C14: of imitative origin
▸'**hisser** NOUN

hissy fit NOUN *Informal* a childish temper tantrum.

hist (hɪst) INTERJECTION an exclamation used to attract attention or as a warning to be silent.

histaminase (hɪ'stæmɪˌneɪs) NOUN an enzyme, occurring in the digestive system, that inactivates histamine by removal of its amino group. Also called: **diamine oxidase.**

histamine ('hɪstəˌmiːn, -mɪn) NOUN an amine formed from histidine and released by the body tissues in allergic reactions, causing irritation. It also stimulates gastric secretions, dilates blood vessels, and contracts smooth muscle. Formula: $C_5H_9N_3$. See also **antihistamine.**
▷HISTORY C20: from HIST(IDINE) + -AMINE
▸**histaminic** (ˌhɪstə'mɪnɪk) ADJECTIVE

histidine ('hɪstɪˌdiːn, -dɪn) NOUN a nonessential amino acid that occurs in most proteins: a precursor of histamine.

histiocyte ('hɪstɪəˌsaɪt) NOUN *Physiol* a macrophage that occurs in connective tissue.
▷HISTORY C20: alteration of German *histiozyt,* from Greek *histion* a little web, from *histos* web + -CYTE
▸**histiocytic** (ˌhɪstɪə'sɪtɪk) ADJECTIVE

histo- *or before a vowel* **hist-** COMBINING FORM indicating animal or plant tissue: *histology; histamine.*
▷HISTORY from Greek, from *histos* web

histochemistry (ˌhɪstəʊ'kɛmɪstrɪ) NOUN the chemistry of tissues, such as liver and bone, often studied with the aid of a microscope.
▸ˌ**histo'chemical** ADJECTIVE

histocompatibility (ˌhɪstəʊkəmˌpætɪ'bɪlɪtɪ) NOUN the degree of similarity between the histocompatibility antigens of two individuals. Histocompatibility determines whether an organ transplant will be tolerated.
▸ˌ**histocom'patible** ADJECTIVE

histocompatibility antigen NOUN a molecule occurring on the surface of tissue cells that can take several different forms. The differences between histocompatibility antigens are inherited and determine organ transplant rejection.

histogen ('hɪstəˌdʒɛn) NOUN (formerly) any of three layers in an apical meristem that were thought to give rise to the different parts of the plant: the apical meristem is now regarded as comprising two layers. ◆ See **corpus, tunica.**

histogenesis (ˌhɪstəʊ'dʒɛnɪsɪs) *or* **histogeny** (hɪ'stɒdʒənɪ) NOUN the formation of tissues and organs from undifferentiated cells.
▸**histogenetic** (ˌhɪstəʊdʒə'nɛtɪk) *or* ˌ**histo'genic** ADJECTIVE ▸ˌ**histoge'netically** *or* ˌ**histo'genically** ADVERB

histogram ('hɪstəˌɡræm) NOUN a statistical graph that represents the frequency of values of a quantity by vertical rectangles of varying heights and widths. The width of the rectangles is in proportion to the class interval under consideration, and their areas represent the relative frequency of the phenomenon in question. See also **stem-and-leaf diagram.**
▷HISTORY C20: perhaps from HISTO(RY) + -GRAM

histoid ('hɪstɔɪd) ADJECTIVE (esp of a tumour). [1] resembling normal tissue. [2] composed of one kind of tissue.

histology (hɪ'stɒlədʒɪ) NOUN [1] the study, esp the microscopic study, of the tissues of an animal or plant. [2] the structure of a tissue or organ.
▸**histological** (ˌhɪstə'lɒdʒɪkᵊl) *or* ˌ**histo'logic** ADJECTIVE ▸ˌ**histo'logically** ADVERB ▸**his'tologist** NOUN

histolysis (hɪ'stɒlɪsɪs) NOUN the disintegration of organic tissues.
▸**histolytic** (ˌhɪstə'lɪtɪk) ADJECTIVE ▸ˌ**histo'lytically** ADVERB

histone ('hɪstəʊn) NOUN any of a group of basic proteins present in cell nuclei and implicated in the spatial organization of DNA.

histopathology (ˌhɪstəʊpə'θɒlədʒɪ) NOUN the study of the microscopic structure of diseased tissues.
▸**histopathological** (ˌhɪstəʊˌpæθə'lɒdʒɪkᵊl) ADJECTIVE

histoplasmosis (ˌhɪstəʊplæz'məʊsɪs) NOUN a severe fungal disease of the lungs caused by *Histoplasma capsulatum.*

historian (hɪ'stɔːrɪən) NOUN a person who writes or studies history, esp one who is an authority on it.

historiated (hɪ'stɔːrɪˌeɪtɪd) ADJECTIVE decorated with flowers or animals. Also: **storiated.**
▷HISTORY C19: from Medieval Latin *historiāre* to tell a story in pictures, from Latin *historia* story

historic (hɪ'stɒrɪk) ADJECTIVE [1] famous or likely to become famous in history; significant. [2] a less common word for **historical** (senses 1–5). [3] Also: **secondary.** *Linguistics* (of Latin, Greek, or Sanskrit verb tenses) referring to past time.

historical (hɪ'stɒrɪkᵊl) ADJECTIVE [1] belonging to or typical of the study of history: *historical methods.* [2] concerned with or treating of events of the past: *historical accounts.* [3] based on or constituting factual material as distinct from legend or supposition. [4] based on or inspired by history: *a historical novel.* [5] occurring or prominent in history. [6] a less common word for **historic** (sense 1).
▸**his'torically** ADVERB ▸**his'toricalness** NOUN

> **Language note** A distinction is usually made between *historic* (important, significant) and *historical* (pertaining to history): *a historic decision; a historical perspective.*

historical-cost accounting NOUN a method of accounting that values assets at the original cost. In times of high inflation profits can be overstated. Compare **current-cost accounting.**

historical geology NOUN the branch of geology concerned with the evolution of the earth and its life forms from its origins to the present.

historical linguistics NOUN (*functioning as singular*) the study of language as it changes in the course of time, with a view either to discovering general principles of linguistic change or to establishing the correct genealogical classification of particular languages. Also called: **diachronic linguistics.** Compare **descriptive linguistics.**

historical materialism NOUN the part of Marxist theory maintaining that social structures derive from economic structures and that these are transformed as a result of class struggles, each ruling class producing another, which will overcome and destroy it, the final phase being the emergence of a communist society.

historical method NOUN a means of learning about something by considering its origins and development.

historical present NOUN the present tense used to narrate past events, usually employed in English for special effect or in informal use, as in *a week ago I'm walking down the street and I see this accident.*

historical school NOUN [1] a group of 19th-century German economists who maintained that modern economies evolved from historical institutions. [2] the school of jurists maintaining that laws are based on social and historical circumstances rather than made by a sovereign power.

historic episcopate NOUN *Christian Church* the derivation of the episcopate of a Church in historic succession from the apostles.

historicism (hɪ'stɒrɪˌsɪzəm) NOUN [1] the belief that natural laws govern historical events which in turn determine social and cultural phenomena. [2] the doctrine that each period of history has its own beliefs and values inapplicable to any other, so that nothing can be understood independently of its historical context. [3] the conduct of any enquiry in accordance with these views. [4] excessive emphasis on history, historicism, past styles, etc.
▸**his'toricist** NOUN, ADJECTIVE

historicity (ˌhɪstə'rɪsɪtɪ) NOUN historical authenticity.

Historic Places Trust NOUN (in New Zealand) the statutory body concerned with the conservation of historic buildings, esp with ancient Maori sites.

historiographer (hɪˌstɔːrɪ'ɒɡrəfə) NOUN [1] a historian, esp one concerned with historical method and the writings of other historians. [2] a historian employed to write the history of a group or public institution.

historiography (ˌhɪstɔːrɪ'ɒɡrəfɪ) NOUN [1] the writing of history. [2] the study of the development of historical method, historical research, and writing. [3] any body of historical literature.
▸**historiographic** (hɪˌstɔːrɪə'ɡræfɪk) *or* **hisˌtorio'graphical** ADJECTIVE

history ('hɪstərɪ, 'hɪstrɪ) NOUN, *plural* **-ries.** [1] **a** a record or account, often chronological in approach, of past events, developments, etc. **b** (*as modifier*): *a history book; a history play.* [2] all that is preserved or remembered of the past, esp in written form. [3] the discipline of recording and interpreting past events involving human beings. [4] past events, esp when considered as an aggregate. [5] an event in the past, esp one that has been forgotten or reduced in importance: *their quarrel was just history.* [6] the past, background, previous experiences, etc., of a thing or person: *the house had a strange history.* [7] *Computing* a stored list of the websites that a user has recently visited. [8] a play that depicts or is based on historical events. [9] a narrative relating the events of a character's life: *the history of Joseph Andrews.* Abbreviation (for senses 1–3): **hist.**
▷**HISTORY** C15: from Latin *historia,* from Greek: enquiry, from *historein* to narrate, from *histōr* judge

histrionic (ˌhɪstrɪ'ɒnɪk) *or* **histrionical** ADJECTIVE [1] excessively dramatic, insincere, or artificial: *histrionic gestures.* [2] *Now rare* dramatic. ◆ NOUN [3] (*plural*) melodramatic displays of temperament. [4] *Rare* (*plural, functioning as singular*) dramatics.
▷**HISTORY** C17: from Late Latin *histriōnicus* of a player, from *histriō* actor
▸**ˌhistri'onically** ADVERB

hit (hɪt) VERB **hits, hitting, hit.** (*mainly tr*) [1] (*also intr*) to deal (a blow or stroke) to (a person or thing); strike: *the man hit the child.* [2] to come into violent contact with: *the car hit the tree.* [3] to reach or strike with a missile, thrown object, etc.: *to hit a target.* [4] to make or cause to make forceful contact; knock or bump: *I hit my arm on the table.* [5] to propel or cause to move by striking: *to hit a ball.* [6] *Cricket* to score (runs). [7] to affect (a person, place, or thing) suddenly or adversely: *his illness hit his wife very hard.* [8] to become suddenly apparent to (a person): *the reason for his behaviour hit me and made the whole episode clear.* [9] to achieve or reach: *to hit the jackpot; unemployment hit a new high.* [10] to experience or encounter: *I've hit a slight snag here.* [11] *Slang* to murder (a rival criminal) in fulfilment of an underworld contract or vendetta. [12] to accord or suit (esp in the phrase **hit one's fancy**). [13] to guess correctly or find out by accident: *you have hit the answer.* [14] *Informal* to set out on (a road, path, etc.): *let's hit the road.* [15] *Informal* to arrive or appear in: *he will hit town tomorrow night.* [16] *Informal, chiefly US and Canadian* to demand or request from: *he hit me for a pound.* [17] *Slang* to drink an excessive amount of (alcohol): *to hit the bottle.* [18] **hit it.** *Music, slang* start playing. [19] **hit the sack** (*or* **hay**). *Slang* to go to bed. [20] **not know what has hit one.** to be completely taken by surprise. ◆ NOUN [21] an impact or collision. [22] a shot, blow, etc., that reaches its object. [23] an apt, witty, or telling remark. [24] *Informal* **a** a person or thing that gains wide appeal: *she's a hit with everyone.* **b** (*as modifier*): *a hit record.* [25] *Informal* a stroke of luck. [26] *Slang* **a** a murder carried out as the result of an underworld vendetta or rivalry. **b** (*as modifier*): *a hit squad.* [27] *Slang* a drag on a cigarette, a swig from a bottle, a line of a drug, or an injection of heroin. [28] *Computing* a single visit to a website. [29] **make** (*or* **score**) **a hit with.** *Informal* to make a favourable impression on. ◆ See also **hit off, hit on, hit out.**
▷**HISTORY** Old English *hittan,* from Old Norse *hitta*

Hitachi (hɪ'tætʃɪ) NOUN a city in Japan, in E Honshu: a centre of the electronics industry. Pop.: 199 241 (1995).

hit-and-miss ADJECTIVE *Informal* random; haphazard: *a hit-and-miss affair; the technique is very hit and miss.* Also: **hit or miss.**

hit-and-run ADJECTIVE (*prenominal*) [1] **a** involved in or denoting a motor-vehicle accident in which the driver leaves the scene without stopping to give assistance, inform the police, etc. **b** (*as noun*): *a hit-and-run.* [2] (of an attack, raid, etc.) relying on surprise allied to a rapid departure from the scene of operations for the desired effect: *hit-and-run tactics.* [3] *Baseball* denoting a play in which a base runner begins to run as the pitcher throws the ball to the batter.

hitch (hɪtʃ) VERB [1] to fasten or become fastened with a knot or tie, esp temporarily. [2] (often foll by *up*) to connect (a horse, team, etc.); harness. [3] (*tr;* often foll by *up*) to pull up (the trousers, a skirt, etc.) with a quick jerk. [4] (*intr*) *Chiefly US* to move in a halting manner: *to hitch along.* [5] to entangle or become entangled: *the thread was hitched on the reel.* [6] (*tr; passive*) *Slang* to marry (esp in the phrase **get hitched**). [7] *Informal* to obtain (a ride or rides) by hitchhiking. ◆ NOUN [8] an impediment or obstacle, esp one that is temporary or minor: *a hitch in the proceedings.* [9] a knot for fastening a rope to posts, other ropes, etc., that can be undone by pulling against the direction of the strain that holds it. [10] a sudden jerk; tug; pull: *he gave it a hitch and it came loose.* [11] *Chiefly US* a hobbling gait: *to walk with a hitch.* [12] a device used for fastening. [13] *Informal* a ride obtained by hitchhiking. [14] *US and Canadian slang* a period of time spent in prison, in the army, etc.
▷**HISTORY** C15: of uncertain origin
▸**'hitcher** NOUN

hitchhike ('hɪtʃˌhaɪk) VERB (*intr*) to travel by obtaining free lifts in motor vehicles.
▸**'hitchˌhiker** NOUN

hitching post NOUN a post or rail to which the reins of a horse, etc., are tied.

hi tech *or* **high tech** (tɛk) NOUN [1] short for **high technology.** [2] a style of interior design using features of industrial equipment. ◆ ADJECTIVE **hi-tech, high-tech.** [3] designed for or using high technology. [4] of or in the interior design style. Compare **low tech.**

hither ('hɪðə) ADVERB [1] Also (archaic): **hitherward, hitherwards.** to or towards this place (esp in the phrase **come hither**). [2] **hither and thither.** this way and that, as in a state of confusion. ◆ ADJECTIVE [3] *Archaic or dialect* (of a side or part, esp of a hill or valley) nearer; closer.
▷**HISTORY** Old English *hider;* related to Old Norse *hethra* here, Gothic *hidrē,* Latin *citrā* on this side, *citrō*

hithermost ('hɪðəˌməʊst) ADJECTIVE *Now rare* nearest to this place or in this direction.

hitherto ('hɪðə'tuː) ADVERB [1] until this time: *hitherto, there have been no problems.* [2] *Archaic* to this place or point.

Hitler ('hɪtlə) NOUN a person who displays dictatorial characteristics.
▷**HISTORY** from Adolf *Hitler* (1889–1945), president of the National Socialist German Workers' Party (Nazi party) and German dictator

Hitlerism ('hɪtləˌrɪzəm) NOUN the policies, principles, and methods of the Nazi party as developed by its leader Adolf Hitler (1889–1945).

hit list NOUN *Informal* [1] a list of people to be murdered: *a terrorist hit list.* [2] a list of targets to be eliminated in some way: *a hit list of pits to be closed.*

hit man NOUN *Slang* a hired assassin, esp one employed by gangsters.

hit off VERB [1] (*tr, adverb*) to represent or mimic accurately. [2] **hit it off.** *Informal* to have a good relationship with.

hit on VERB (*tr, preposition*) [1] to strike. [2] Also: **hit upon.** to discover unexpectedly or guess correctly. [3] *US and Canadian slang* to make sexual advances to.

hit out VERB (*intr, adverb;* often foll by *at*) [1] to direct blows forcefully and vigorously. [2] to make a verbal attack (upon someone).

hit parade NOUN *Old-fashioned* a listing or playing of the current most popular songs.

hitter ('hɪtə) NOUN [1] *Informal* a boxer who has a hard punch rather than skill or finesse. [2] a person who hits something.

Hittite ('hɪtaɪt) NOUN [1] a member of an ancient people of Anatolia, who built a great empire in N Syria and Asia Minor in the second millennium B.C. [2] the extinct language of this people, deciphered from cuneiform inscriptions found at Boğazköy and elsewhere. It is clearly related to the Indo-European family of languages, although the precise relationship is disputed. ◆ ADJECTIVE [3] of or relating to this people, their civilization, or their language.

hit wicket NOUN *Cricket* an instance of a batsman breaking the wicket with the bat or a part of the body while playing a stroke and so being out.

HIV ABBREVIATION FOR human immunodeficiency virus; the cause of AIDS. Two strains have been identified: HIV-1 and HIV-2.

hive (haɪv) NOUN [1] a structure in which social bees live and rear their young. [2] a colony of social bees. [3] a place showing signs of great industry (esp in the phrase **a hive of activity**). [4] a teeming crowd; multitude. [5] an object in the form of a hive. ◆ VERB [6] to cause (bees) to collect or (of bees) to collect inside a hive. [7] to live or cause to live in or as if in a hive. [8] (*tr*) (of bees) to store (honey, pollen, etc.) in the hive. [9] (*tr;* often foll by *up* or *away*) to store, esp for future use: *he used to hive away a small sum every week.*
▷**HISTORY** Old English *hȳf;* related to Westphalian *hüwe,* Old Norse *hūfr* ship's hull, Latin *cūpa* barrel, Greek *kupē,* Sanskrit *kūpa* cave
▸**'hiveˌlike** ADJECTIVE

hive bee NOUN another name for a **honeybee.**

hive dross NOUN another name for **propolis.**

hive off VERB (*adverb*) [1] to transfer or be transferred from a larger group or unit. [2] (*usually tr*) to transfer (profitable activities of a nationalized industry) back to private ownership.

hives (haɪvz) NOUN (*functioning as singular or plural*) *Pathol* a nontechnical name for **urticaria.**
▷**HISTORY** C16: of uncertain origin

hiya ('haɪjə, ˌhaɪ'jɑː) SENTENCE SUBSTITUTE an informal term of greeting.
▷**HISTORY** C20: shortened from *how are you?*

Hizbollah (ˌhɪzbə'lɑː) NOUN a variant spelling of **Hezbollah.**

HJ (on gravestones) ABBREVIATION FOR hic jacet.
▷**HISTORY** Latin: here lies

HJS (on gravestones) ABBREVIATION FOR hic jacet sepultus.
▷**HISTORY** Latin: here lies buried

hk THE INTERNET DOMAIN NAME FOR Hong Kong.

HK [1] ABBREVIATION FOR House of Keys (Manx Parliament). ◆ [2] INTERNATIONAL CAR REGISTRATION FOR Hong Kong.

HKJ INTERNATIONAL CAR REGISTRATION FOR (Hashemite Kingdom of) Jordan.

hl SYMBOL FOR hectolitre.

HL (in Britain) ABBREVIATION FOR House of Lords.

HLA system NOUN human leucocyte antigen system; a group of the most important antigens responsible for tissue compatibility, together with the genes that encode them. For tissue and organ transplantation to be successful there needs to be a minimum number of HLA differences between the donor's and recipient's tissue.

hm[1] SYMBOL FOR hectometre.

hm[2] THE INTERNET DOMAIN NAME FOR Heard and McDonald Islands.

HM ABBREVIATION FOR: [1] His (*or* Her) Majesty. [2] heavy metal (sense 1). [3] headmaster; headmistress.

h'm (*spelling pron* hmmm) INTERJECTION used to indicate hesitation, doubt, assent, pleasure, etc.

HMAS ABBREVIATION FOR His (*or* Her) Majesty's Australian Ship.

HMCS ABBREVIATION FOR His (*or* Her) Majesty's Canadian Ship.

HMG ABBREVIATION FOR His (*or* Her) Majesty's Government.

HMI (in Britain) ABBREVIATION FOR Her Majesty's Inspector; a government official who examines and supervises schools.

H.M.S. *or* **HMS** ABBREVIATION FOR: [1] His (*or* Her) Majesty's Service. [2] His (*or* Her) Majesty's Ship.

HMSO (formerly, in Britain) ABBREVIATION FOR His (*or* Her) Majesty's Stationery Office, now The Stationery Office (TSO).

hn THE INTERNET DOMAIN NAME FOR Honduras.

HNC (in Britain) ABBREVIATION FOR Higher National Certificate; a qualification recognized by many national technical and professional institutions.

HND (in Britain) ABBREVIATION FOR Higher National Diploma; a qualification in technical subjects equivalent to an ordinary degree.

ho[1] (həʊ) INTERJECTION [1] Also: **ho-ho.** an imitation or representation of the sound of a deep laugh. [2] an exclamation used to attract attention, announce a destination, etc.: *what ho!; land ho!; westward ho!*
▷HISTORY C13: of imitative origin; compare Old Norse *hó,* Old French *ho!* halt!

ho[2] (həʊ) NOUN *US black slang* a derogatory term for a woman.
▷HISTORY C20: from Black or Southern US pronunciation of WHORE

Ho THE CHEMICAL SYMBOL FOR holmium.

HO *or* **H.O.** ABBREVIATION FOR: [1] head office. [2] *Brit government* Home Office.

ho. ABBREVIATION FOR house.

hoactzin (həʊˈæktsɪn) NOUN a variant of **hoatzin.**

hoar (hɔː) NOUN [1] short for **hoarfrost.** ◆ ADJECTIVE [2] *Rare* covered with hoarfrost. [3] *Archaic* a poetic variant of **hoary.**
▷HISTORY Old English *hār;* related to Old Norse *hārr,* Old High German *hēr,* Old Slavonic *sěrŭ* grey

hoard (hɔːd) NOUN [1] an accumulated store hidden away for future use. [2] a cache of ancient coins, treasure, etc. ◆ VERB [3] to gather or accumulate (a hoard).
▷HISTORY Old English *hord;* related to Old Norse *hodd,* Gothic *huzd,* German *Hort,* Swedish *hydda* hut
▸ˈ**hoarder** NOUN

> **Language note** *Hoard* is sometimes wrongly written where *horde* is meant: *hordes* (not *hoards*) *of tourists.*

hoarding (ˈhɔːdɪŋ) NOUN [1] a large board used for displaying advertising posters, as by a road. Also called (esp US and Canadian): **billboard.** [2] a temporary wooden fence erected round a building or demolition site.
▷HISTORY C19: from C15 *hoard* fence, from Old French *hourd* palisade, of Germanic origin, related to Gothic *haurds,* Old Norse *hurth* door

hoarfrost (ˈhɔːˌfrɒst) NOUN a deposit of needle-like ice crystals formed on the ground by direct condensation at temperatures below freezing point. Also called: **white frost.**

hoarhound (ˈhɔːˌhaʊnd) NOUN a variant spelling of **horehound.**

hoarse (hɔːs) ADJECTIVE [1] gratingly harsh or raucous in tone. [2] low, harsh, and lacking in intensity: *a hoarse whisper.* [3] having a husky voice, as through illness, shouting, etc.
▷HISTORY C14: of Scandinavian origin; related to Old Norse *hās,* Old Saxon *hēs*
▸ˈ**hoarsely** ADVERB ▸ˈ**hoarseness** NOUN

hoarsen (ˈhɔːsən) VERB to make or become hoarse.

hoary (ˈhɔːrɪ) ADJECTIVE **hoarier, hoariest.** [1] having grey or white hair. [2] white or whitish-grey in colour. [3] ancient or venerable.
▸ˈ**hoarily** ADVERB ▸ˈ**hoariness** NOUN

hoary cress NOUN a perennial Mediterranean plant, *Cardaria* (or *Lepidium*) *draba,* with small white flowers: a widespread troublesome weed: family *Brassicaceae* (crucifers).

hoast (host) *Scot* ◆ NOUN [1] a cough. ◆ VERB (*intr*) [2] to cough.
▷HISTORY from Old Norse

hoatching (ˈhəʊtʃɪŋ) ADJECTIVE *Scot* infested; swarming: *this food's hoatching with flies.*
▷HISTORY of unknown origin

hoatzin (həʊˈætsɪn) *or* **hoactzin** NOUN a unique South American gallinaceous bird, *Opisthocomus hoazin,* with a brownish plumage, a very small crested head, and clawed wing digits in the young: family *Opisthocomidae.*
▷HISTORY C17: from American Spanish, from Nahuatl *uatzin* pheasant

hoax (həʊks) NOUN [1] a deception, esp a practical joke. ◆ VERB [2] (*tr*) to deceive or play a joke on (someone).
▷HISTORY C18: probably from HOCUS
▸ˈ**hoaxer** NOUN

hob[1] (hɒb) NOUN [1] the flat top part of a cooking stove, or a separate flat surface, containing hotplates or burners. [2] a shelf beside an open fire, for keeping kettles, etc., hot. [3] a steel pattern used in forming a mould or die in cold metal. [4] a hard steel rotating cutting tool used in machines for cutting gears. ◆ VERB **hobs, hobbing, hobbed.** [5] (*tr*) to cut or form with a hob.
▷HISTORY C16: variant of obsolete *hubbe,* of unknown origin; perhaps related to HUB

hob[2] (hɒb) NOUN [1] a hobgoblin or elf. [2] **raise** *or* **play hob.** *US informal* to cause mischief or disturbance. [3] a male ferret.
▷HISTORY C14: variant of *Rob,* short for *Robin* or *Robert*
▸ˈ**hobˌlike** ADJECTIVE

Hobart (ˈhəʊbɑːt) NOUN a port in Australia, capital of the island state of Tasmania on the estuary of the Derwent: excellent natural harbour; University of Tasmania (1890). Pop.: 194 700 (1995 est.).

Hobbesian (ˈhɒbzɪən) ADJECTIVE of or relating to Thomas Hobbes, the English political philosopher (1588–1679).

Hobbism (ˈhɒbɪzəm) NOUN the mechanistic political philosophy of Thomas Hobbes, the English political philosopher (1588–1679), which stresses the necessity for a powerful sovereign to control human beings.
▸ˈ**Hobbist** NOUN

hobbit (ˈhɒbɪt) NOUN one of an imaginary race of half-size people living in holes.
▷HISTORY C20: coined by British writer J. R. R. Tolkien (1892–1973), with the meaning "hole-builder"
▸ˈ**hobbitry** NOUN

hobble (ˈhɒbəl) VERB [1] (*intr*) to walk with a lame awkward movement. [2] (*tr*) to fetter the legs of (a horse) in order to restrict movement. [3] to progress unevenly or with difficulty. [4] (*tr*) to hamper or restrict (the actions or scope of a person, organization, etc.). ◆ NOUN [5] a strap, rope, etc., used to hobble a horse. [6] a limping gait. [7] *Brit dialect* a difficult or embarrassing situation. ◆ Also (for senses 2, 5): **hopple.**
▷HISTORY C14: probably from Low German; compare Flemish *hoppelen,* Middle Dutch *hobbelen* to stammer
▸ˈ**hobbler** NOUN

hobbledehoy (ˌhɒbəldɪˈhɔɪ) NOUN *Archaic or dialect* a clumsy or bad-mannered youth.
▷HISTORY C16: from earlier *hobbard de hoy,* of uncertain origin

hobble skirt NOUN a long skirt, popular between 1910 and 1914, cut so narrow at the ankles that it hindered walking.

hobby[1] (ˈhɒbɪ) NOUN, *plural* **-bies.** [1] an activity pursued in spare time for pleasure or relaxation. [2] *Archaic or dialect* a small horse or pony. [3] short for **hobbyhorse** (sense 1). [4] an early form of bicycle, without pedals.
▷HISTORY C14 *hobyn,* probably variant of proper name *Robin;* compare DOBBIN
▸ˈ**hobbyist** NOUN

hobby[2] (ˈhɒbɪ) NOUN, *plural* **-bies.** any of several small Old World falcons, esp the European *Falco subbuteo,* formerly used in falconry.
▷HISTORY C15: from Old French *hobet,* from *hobe* falcon; probably related to Middle Dutch *hobbelen* to roll, turn

hobby farmer NOUN a person who runs a farm as a hobby rather than a means of making a living.

hobbyhorse (ˈhɒbɪˌhɔːs) NOUN [1] a toy consisting of a stick with a figure of a horse's head at one end. [2] another word for **rocking horse.** [3] a figure of a horse attached to a performer's waist in a pantomime, morris dance, etc. [4] a favourite topic or obsessive fixed idea (esp in the phrase **on one's hobbyhorse**). ◆ VERB [5] (*intr*) *Nautical* (of a vessel) to pitch violently.
▷HISTORY C16: from HOBBY[1], originally a small horse, hence sense 3; then generalized to apply to any pastime

hobday (ˈhɒbˌdeɪ) VERB (*tr*) to alleviate (a breathing problem in certain horses) by the surgical operation of removing soft tissue ventricles to pull back the vocal fold.
▷HISTORY C20: named after F. T. *Hobday* (1869–1939), English veterinary surgeon, who devised the operation
▸ˈ**hobˌdayed** ADJECTIVE

hobgoblin (ˌhɒbˈgɒblɪn) NOUN [1] an evil or mischievous goblin. [2] a bogey; bugbear.
▷HISTORY C16: from HOB[2] + GOBLIN

hobnail (ˈhɒbˌneɪl) NOUN **a** a short nail with a large head for protecting the soles of heavy footwear. **b** (*as modifier*): *hobnail boots.*
▷HISTORY C16: from HOB[1] (in the archaic sense: peg) + NAIL
▸ˈ**hobˌnailed** ADJECTIVE

hobnob (ˈhɒbˌnɒb) VERB **-nobs, -nobbing, -nobbed.** (*intr; often foll by with*) [1] to socialize or talk informally. [2] *Obsolete* to drink (with).
▷HISTORY C18: from *hob or nob* to drink to one another in turns, hence, to be familiar, ultimately from Old English *habban* to HAVE + *nabban* not to have

hobo (ˈhəʊbəʊ) NOUN, *plural* **-bos** *or* **-boes.** *Chiefly US and Canadian* [1] a tramp; vagrant. [2] a migratory worker, esp an unskilled labourer.
▷HISTORY C19 (US): origin unknown
▸ˈ**hoboism** NOUN

Hoboken (ˈhəʊbəʊkən) NOUN a city in N Belgium, in Antwerp province, on the River Scheldt. Pop.: 35 000 (latest est.).

hobson-jobson (ˌhɒbsənˈdʒɒbsən) NOUN another word for **folk etymology.**
▷HISTORY C19: Anglo-Indian folk-etymological variant of Arabic *yā Hasan! yā Husayn!* O Hasan! O Husain! (ritual lament for the grandsons of Mohammed); influenced by the surnames *Hobson* and *Jobson*

Hobson's choice (ˈhɒbsənz) NOUN the choice of taking what is offered or nothing at all.
▷HISTORY C16: named after Thomas *Hobson* (1544–1631), English liveryman who gave his customers no choice but had them take the nearest horse

Hochheimer (ˈhɒkˌhaɪmə; *German* ˈhoːxhaimər) NOUN a German white wine from the area around Hochheim near Mainz. Also called: **Hochheim.**

Ho Chi Minh City NOUN a port in S Vietnam, 97 km (60 miles) from the South China Sea, on the Saigon River: captured by the French in 1859; merged with adjoining Cholon in 1932; capital of the former Republic of Vietnam (South Vietnam) from 1954 to 1976; university (1917); US headquarters during the Vietnam War. Pop.: 4 322 300 (1993 est.). Former name (until 1976): **Saigon.**

hochmagandy *or* **houghmagandie** (ˌhɒxməˈgændɪ) NOUN *Scot* a mainly jocular or literary word for **sexual intercourse.**
▷HISTORY of uncertain origin

hock[1] (hɒk) NOUN [1] the joint at the tarsus of a horse or similar animal, pointing backwards and corresponding to the human ankle. [2] the corresponding joint in domestic fowl. ◆ VERB [3] another word for **hamstring.**
▷HISTORY C16: short for *hockshin,* from Old English *hōhsinu* heel sinew

hock[2] (hɒk) NOUN [1] any of several white wines from the German Rhine. [2] (not in technical usage) any dry white wine.
▷HISTORY C17: short for obsolete *hockamore* HOCHHEIMER

hock[3] (hɒk) *Informal, chiefly US and Canadian* ◆ VERB [1] (*tr*) to pawn or pledge. ◆ NOUN [2] the state of being in pawn (esp in the phrase **in hock**). [3] **in hock. a** in prison. **b** in debt.
▷HISTORY C19: from Dutch *hok* prison, debt
▸ˈ**hocker** NOUN

hockey[1] (ˈhɒkɪ) NOUN [1] Also called (esp US and Canadian): **field hockey. a** a game played on a field by two opposing teams of 11 players each, who try to hit a ball into their opponents' goal using long sticks curved at the end. **b** (*as modifier*): *hockey stick; hockey ball.* [2] See **ice hockey.**
▷HISTORY C19: from earlier *hawkey,* of unknown origin

hockey[2] (ˈhɒkɪ) NOUN *East Anglian dialect* **a** the feast at harvest home; harvest supper. **b** (*as modifier*): *the hockey cart.* Also: **hawkey, horkey.**
▷HISTORY C16: of unknown origin

hockle (ˈhɒkəl) VERB **hockles, hockled, hockling.** (*intr*) *Northumbrian English dialect* to spit.

Hocktide (ˈhɒkˌtaɪd) NOUN *Brit history* a former festival celebrated on the second Monday and Tuesday after Easter.

▷HISTORY C15: from *hock-, hoke-* (of unknown origin) + TIDE[1]

hocus ('həʊkəs) VERB **-cuses, -cusing, -cused** *or* **-cuses, -cussing, -cussed.** (*tr*) *Now rare* 1 to take in; trick. 2 to stupefy, esp with a drug. 3 to add a drug to (a drink).

hocus-pocus ('həʊkəs'pəʊkəs) NOUN 1 trickery or chicanery. 2 mystifying jargon. 3 an incantation used by conjurors or magicians when performing tricks. 4 conjuring skill or practice. ◆ VERB **-cuses, -cusing, -cused** *or* **-cuses, -cussing, -cussed.** 5 to deceive or trick (someone).
▷HISTORY C17: perhaps a dog-Latin formation invented by jugglers

hod (hɒd) NOUN 1 an open metal or plastic box fitted with a handle, for carrying bricks, mortar, etc. 2 a tall narrow coal scuttle.
▷HISTORY C14: perhaps alteration of C13 dialect *hot,* from Old French *hotte* pannier, creel, probably from Germanic

hod carrier NOUN a labourer who carries the materials in a hod for a plasterer, bricklayer, etc. Also called: **hodman.**

hodden ('hɒdᵊn) *or* **hoddin** ('hɒdɪn) NOUN a coarse homespun cloth produced in Scotland: **hodden grey** is made by mixing black and white wools.
▷HISTORY C18: Scottish, of obscure origin

Hodeida (hɒ'deɪdə) NOUN a port in N Yemen, on the Red Sea; formerly in North Yemen. Pop.: 298 500 (1994).

Hodge (hɒdʒ) NOUN a typical name for a farm labourer; rustic.
▷HISTORY C14 *hogge,* from familiar form of *Roger*

hodgepodge ('hɒdʒˌpɒdʒ) NOUN a variant (esp US and Canadian) of **hotchpotch.**

Hodgkin's disease NOUN a malignant disease, a form of lymphoma, characterized by painless enlargement of the lymph nodes, spleen, and liver. Also called: **lymphoadenoma, lymphogranulomatosis.**
▷HISTORY C19: named after Thomas *Hodgkin* (1798–1866), London physician, who first described it

hodman ('hɒdmən) NOUN, *plural* **-men.** *Brit* another name for a **hod carrier.**

hodograph ('hɒdəˌgrɑːf, -ˌgræf) NOUN a curve of which the radius vector represents the velocity of a moving particle.
▷HISTORY C19: from Greek *hodos* way + -GRAPH
▸ ˌ**hodo'graphic** ADJECTIVE

hodometer (hɒ'dɒmɪtə) NOUN *US* another name for **odometer.**
▸ **ho'dometry** NOUN

hodoscope ('hɒdəˌskəʊp) NOUN *Physics* any device for tracing the path of a charged particle, esp a particle found in cosmic rays.
▷HISTORY C20: from Greek *hodos* way, path + -SCOPE

hoe (həʊ) NOUN 1 any of several kinds of long-handled hand implement equipped with a light blade and used to till the soil, eradicate weeds, etc. ◆ VERB **hoes, hoeing, hoed.** 2 to dig, scrape, weed, or till (surface soil) with or as if with a hoe.
▷HISTORY C14: via Old French *houe* from Germanic: compare Old High German *houwā, houwan* to HEW, German *Haue* hoe
▸ '**hoer** NOUN ▸ '**hoe**ˌ**like** ADJECTIVE

hoedown ('həʊˌdaʊn) NOUN *US and Canadian* 1 a boisterous square dance. 2 a party at which hoedowns are danced.

hoe in VERB (*intr, adverb*) *Austral and NZ informal* to eat food heartily.

hoe into VERB (*intr, preposition*) *Austral and NZ informal* to eat (food) heartily.

Hoek van Holland ('huːk fɑn 'hɔlɑnt) NOUN the Dutch name for the **Hook of Holland.**

Hofei ('həʊ'feɪ) NOUN a variant transliteration of the Chinese name for **Hefei.**

Hofuf (hʊ'fuːf) NOUN another name for **Al Hufuf.**

hog (hɒg) NOUN 1 a domesticated pig, esp a castrated male weighing more than 102 kg. 2 *US and Canadian* any artiodactyl mammal of the family *Suidae;* pig. 3 Also: **hogg.** *Brit dialect Austral, and NZ* another name for **hogget.** 4 *Informal* a selfish, greedy or slovenly person. 5 *Nautical* a stiff brush, for scraping a vessel's bottom. 6 *Nautical* the amount or extent to which a vessel is hogged. Compare **sag** (sense 6). 7 another word for **camber** (sense 4). 8 *Slang, chiefly US* a large powerful motorcycle. 9 **go the whole hog.** *Informal* to do something thoroughly or unreservedly: *if you are redecorating one room, why not go the whole hog and paint the entire house?* 10 **live high on the hog.** *Informal, chiefly US* to have an extravagant lifestyle. ◆ VERB **hogs, hogging, hogged.** (*tr*) 11 *Slang* to take more than one's share of. 12 to arch (the back) like a hog. 13 to cut (the mane) of (a horse) very short.
▷HISTORY Old English *hogg,* from Celtic; compare Cornish *hoch*
▸ '**hogger** NOUN ▸ '**hog**ˌ**like** ADJECTIVE

hogan ('həʊgən) NOUN a wooden dwelling covered with earth, typical of the Navaho Indians of N America.
▷HISTORY from Navaho

Hogarthian (ˌhəʊ'gɑːθɪən) ADJECTIVE reminiscent of the engravings of William Hogarth, the English engraver and painter (1697–1764), in which he satirized contemporary vices and affectations.

hogback ('hɒgˌbæk) NOUN 1 Also called: **hog's back.** a narrow ridge that consists of steeply inclined rock strata. 2 *Archaeol* a Saxon or Scandinavian tomb with sloping sides.

hog badger NOUN a SE Asian badger, *Arctonyx collaris,* with a piglike mobile snout. Also called: **sand badger.**

hog cholera NOUN the US term for **swine fever.**

hogfish ('hɒgˌfɪʃ) NOUN, *plural* **-fish** *or* **-fishes.** 1 a wrasse, *Lachnolaimus maximus,* that occurs in the Atlantic off the SE coast of North America. The head of the male resembles a pig's snout. 2 another name for **pigfish** (sense 1).

hogg (hɒg) NOUN 1 an uncastrated male pig. 2 a sheep of either sex aged between birth and second shearing.

hogged (hɒgd) ADJECTIVE *Nautical* (of a vessel) having a keel that droops at both ends. Compare **sag** (sense 6).

hogget ('hɒgɪt) NOUN *Brit dialect Austral, and NZ* 1 a sheep up to the age of one year that has yet to be sheared. 2 the meat of this sheep.

hoggin ('hɒgɪn) *or* **hogging** ('hɒgɪŋ) NOUN a finely sifted gravel containing enough clay binder for it to be used in its natural form for making paths or roads.
▷HISTORY C19: perhaps the same as *hogging* from HOG in the sense of arching the back, from the shape given to a road to facilitate drainage

hogging moment NOUN a bending moment that produces convex bending at the supports of a continuously supported beam. Also called: **negative bending moment.**

hoggish ('hɒgɪʃ) ADJECTIVE selfish, gluttonous, or dirty.
▸ '**hoggishly** ADVERB ▸ '**hoggishness** NOUN

Hogmanay (ˌhɒgmə'neɪ) NOUN (*sometimes not capital*) **a** New Year's Eve in Scotland. **b** (*as modifier*): *a Hogmanay party.* See also **first-foot.**
▷HISTORY C17: Scottish and Northern English, perhaps from Norman French *hoguinane,* from Old French *aguillanneuf* the last day of the year; also, a New Year's eve gift

hognosed skunk ('hɒgˌnəʊzd) NOUN any of several American skunks of the genus *Conepatus,* esp *C. leuconotus,* having a broad snoutlike nose.

hognose snake ('hɒgˌnəʊz) NOUN any North American nonvenomous colubrid snake of the genus *Heterodon,* having a trowel-shaped snout and inflating the body when alarmed. Also called: **puff adder.**

hognut ('hɒgˌnʌt) NOUN another name for **pignut.**

hog peanut NOUN a North American leguminous climbing plant, *Amphicarpa bracteata,* having fleshy curved one-seeded pods, which ripen in or on the ground.

hog's fennel NOUN any of several Eurasian umbelliferous marsh plants of the genus *Peucedanum,* esp *P. officinale,* having clusters of small whitish flowers.

hogshead ('hɒgzˌhed) NOUN 1 a unit of capacity, used esp for alcoholic beverages. It has several values, being 54 imperial gallons in the case of beer and 52.5 imperial gallons in the case of wine. 2 a large cask used for shipment of wines and spirits.
▷HISTORY C14: of obscure origin

hogtie ('hɒgˌtaɪ) VERB **-ties, -tying, -tied.** (*tr*) *Chiefly US* 1 to tie together the legs or the arms and legs of. 2 to impede, hamper, or thwart.

Hogtown ('hɒgˌtaʊn) NOUN *Canadian* a slang name for **Toronto.**

Hogue (*French* ɔg) NOUN See **La Hogue.**

hogwash ('hɒgˌwɒʃ) NOUN 1 nonsense. 2 pigswill.

hogweed ('hɒgˌwiːd) NOUN any of several coarse weedy umbelliferous plants, esp cow parsnip. See also **giant hogweed.**

Hohenlinden (*German* hoːən'lɪndən) NOUN a village in S Germany, in Bavaria east of Munich: scene of the defeat of the Austrians by the French during the Napoleonic Wars (1800).

Hohhot ('hɒ'hɒt), **Huhehot,** *or* **Hu-ho-hao-t'e** NOUN a city in N China, capital of Inner Mongolia Autonomous Region (since 1954); previously capital of the former Suiyüan province; Inner Mongolia University (1957). Pop.: 754 749 (1999 est.).

ho-hum ('həʊˌhʌm) ADJECTIVE *Informal* lacking interest or inspiration; dull; mediocre: *a ho-hum collection of new releases.*

hoick (hɔɪk) VERB 1 *Informal* to rise or raise abruptly and sharply: *She hoicked her dress above her knees.* 2 *NZ informal* to clear the throat and spit.
▷HISTORY C20: perhaps a variant of *hike*

hoicks (hɔɪks) INTERJECTION a cry used to encourage hounds to hunt. Also: **yoicks.**

hoiden ('hɔɪdᵊn) NOUN a variant spelling of **hoyden.**
▸ '**hoidenish** ADJECTIVE ▸ '**hoidenishness** NOUN

hoi polloi (ˌhɔɪ pə'lɔɪ) PLURAL NOUN *Often derogatory* the masses; common people.
▷HISTORY Greek, literally: the many

hoist (hɔɪst) VERB 1 (*tr*) to raise or lift up, esp by mechanical means. 2 **hoist with one's own petard.** See **petard** (sense 2). ◆ NOUN 3 any apparatus or device for hoisting. 4 the act of hoisting. 5 See **rotary clothesline.** 6 *Nautical* **a** the amidships height of a sail bent to the yard with which it is hoisted. Compare **drop** (sense 15). **b** the difference between the set and lowered positions of this yard. 7 *Nautical* the length of the luff of a fore-and-aft sail. 8 *Nautical* a group of signal flags. 9 the inner edge of a flag next to the staff. Compare **fly**[1] (sense 25).
▷HISTORY C16: variant of *hoise,* probably from Low German; compare Dutch *hijschen,* German *hissen*
▸ '**hoister** NOUN

hoity-toity (ˌhɔɪtɪ'tɔɪtɪ) ADJECTIVE *Informal* arrogant or haughty: *we have had enough of her hoity-toity manner.*
▷HISTORY C17: rhyming compound based on C16 *hoit* to romp, of obscure origin

hoke (həʊk) VERB (*tr; usually foll by up*) to overplay (a part, etc.).
▷HISTORY C20: perhaps from HOKUM

hokey ('həʊkɪ) ADJECTIVE *Slang, chiefly US and Canadian* 1 corny; sentimental. 2 contrived; phoney.
▷HISTORY C20: from HOKUM

hokey cokey ('həʊkɪ 'kəʊkɪ) NOUN a Cockney song with a traditional dance routine to match the words.

hokey-pokey (ˌhəʊkɪ'pəʊkɪ) NOUN 1 another word for **hocus-pocus** (senses 1, 2). 2 *NZ* a brittle toffee sold in lumps.

Hokkaido (hɒ'kaɪdəʊ) NOUN the second largest and northernmost of the four main islands of Japan, separated from Honshu by the Tsugaru Strait and from the island of Sakhalin, Russia, by La Pérouse Strait: constitutes an autonomous administrative division. Capital: Sapporo. Pop.: 5 683 000 (2000 est.). Area: 78 508 sq. km (30 312 sq. miles).

hokku ('hɒkuː) NOUN, *plural* **-ku.** *Prosody* another word for **haiku.**
▷HISTORY from Japanese, from *hok* beginning + *ku* hemistich

hokonui (həʊkə'nuːiː) NOUN *NZ obsolete* illicit whisky.
▷HISTORY from *Hokonui,* district of Southland region, NZ

hokum ('həʊkəm) NOUN *Slang* 1 claptrap; bunk. 2 obvious or hackneyed material of a sentimental nature in a play, film, etc.

▷HISTORY C20: probably a blend of HOCUS-POCUS and BUNKUM

hol- COMBINING FORM a variant of **holo-** before a vowel.

holarchy (ˈhəʊlˌɑːkɪ) NOUN a system composed of interacting holons.
▷HISTORY C20: from HOLO- + -ARCHY

Holarctic (həʊˈlɑːktɪk) ADJECTIVE of or denoting a zoogeographical region consisting of the Palaearctic and Nearctic regions.
▷HISTORY C19: from HOLO- + ARCTIC

hold¹ (həʊld) VERB **holds, holding, held** (hɛld). [1] to have or keep (an object) with or within the hands, arms, etc.; clasp. [2] (*tr*) to support or bear: *to hold a drowning man's head above water.* [3] to maintain or be maintained in a specified state or condition: *to hold one's emotions in check; hold firm.* [4] (*tr*) to set aside or reserve: *they will hold our tickets until tomorrow.* [5] (when *intr, usually used in commands*) to restrain or be restrained from motion, action, departure, etc.: *hold that man until the police come.* [6] (*intr*) to remain fast or unbroken: *that cable won't hold much longer.* [7] (*intr*) (of the weather) to remain dry and bright: *how long will the weather hold?* [8] (*tr*) to keep the attention of: *her singing held the audience.* [9] (*tr*) to engage in or carry on: *to hold a meeting.* [10] (*tr*) to have the ownership, possession, etc., of: *he holds a law degree from London; who's holding the ace of spades?* [11] (*tr*) to have the use of or responsibility for: *to hold the office of director.* [12] (*tr*) to have the space or capacity for: *the carton will hold only eight books.* [13] (*tr*) to be able to control the outward effects of drinking beer, spirits, etc.: *he can hold his drink well.* [14] (often foll by *to* or *by*) to remain or cause to remain committed to: *hold him to his promise; he held by his views in spite of opposition.* [15] (*tr; takes a clause as object*) to claim: *he holds that the theory is incorrect.* [16] (*intr*) to remain relevant, valid, or true: *the old philosophies don't hold nowadays.* [17] (*tr*) to keep in the mind: *to hold affection for someone.* [18] (*tr*) to regard or consider in a specified manner: *I hold him very dear.* [19] (*tr*) to guard or defend successfully: *hold the fort against the attack.* [20] (*intr*) to continue to go: *hold on one's way.* [21] (sometimes foll by *on*) *Music* to sustain the sound of (a note) throughout its specified duration: *to hold on a semibreve for its full value.* [22] (*tr*) *Computing* to retain (data) in a storage device after copying onto another storage device or onto another location in the same device. Compare **clear** (sense 49). [23] (*tr*) to be in possession of illegal drugs. [24] **hold (good) for.** to apply or be relevant to: *the same rules hold for everyone.* [25] **hold it!** **a** stop! wait! **b** stay in the same position! as when being photographed. [26] **hold one's head high.** to conduct oneself in a proud and confident manner. [27] **hold one's own.** to maintain one's situation or position esp in spite of opposition or difficulty. [28] **hold one's peace** *or* **tongue.** to keep silent. [29] **hold water.** to prove credible, logical, or consistent. [30] **there is no holding him.** he is so spirited or resolute that he cannot be restrained. ◆ NOUN [31] the act or method of holding fast or grasping, as with the hands. [32] something to hold onto, as for support or control. [33] an object or device that holds fast or grips something else so as to hold it fast. [34] controlling force or influence: *she has a hold on him.* [35] a short delay or pause. [36] **on hold.** in a state of temporary postponement or delay. [37] a prison or a cell in a prison. [38] *Wrestling* a way of seizing one's opponent: *a wrist hold.* [39] *Music* a pause or fermata. [40] **a** a tenure or holding, esp of land. **b** (*in combination*): *leasehold; freehold; copyhold.* [41] a container. [42] *Archaic* a fortified place. [43] **get hold of. a** to obtain. **b** to come into contact with. [44] **no holds barred.** all limitations removed. ◆ See also **hold back, hold down, hold forth, hold in, hold off, hold on, hold out, hold over. hold together, hold-up, hold with.**
▷HISTORY Old English *healdan;* related to Old Norse *halla,* Gothic *haldan,* German *halten*
▸ˈ**holdable** ADJECTIVE

hold² (həʊld) NOUN the space in a ship or aircraft for storing cargo.
▷HISTORY C16: variant of HOLE

holdall (ˈhəʊldˌɔːl) NOUN *Brit* a large strong bag with handles. Usual US and Canadian name: **carryall.**

hold back VERB (*adverb*) [1] to restrain or be restrained. [2] (*tr*) to withhold: *he held back part of the payment.* ◆ NOUN **holdback.** [3] a strap of the harness joining the breeching to the shaft, so that the horse can hold back the vehicle. [4] something that restrains or hinders.

hold down VERB (*tr, adverb*) [1] to restrain or control. [2] *Informal* to manage to retain or keep possession of: *to hold down two jobs at once.*

holden (ˈhəʊldən) VERB *Archaic or dialect* a past participle of **hold¹**.

holder (ˈhəʊldə) NOUN [1] a person or thing that holds. [2] **a** a person, such as an owner, who has possession or control of something. **b** (*in combination*): *householder.* [3] *Law* a person who has possession of a bill of exchange, cheque, or promissory note that he is legally entitled to enforce.
▸ˈ**holderˌship** NOUN

holdfast (ˈhəʊldˌfɑːst) NOUN [1] **a** the act of gripping strongly. **b** such a grip. [2] any device used to secure an object, such as a hook, clamp, etc. [3] the organ of attachment of a seaweed or related plant.

hold forth VERB (*adverb*) [1] (*intr*) to speak for a long time or in public. [2] (*tr*) to offer (an attraction or enticement).

hold in VERB (*tr, adverb*) [1] to curb, control, or keep in check. [2] to conceal or restrain (feelings).

holding (ˈhəʊldɪŋ) NOUN [1] land held under a lease and used for agriculture or similar purposes. [2] (*often plural*) property to which the holder has legal title, such as land, stocks, shares, and other investments. [3] *Sport* the obstruction of an opponent with the hands or arms, esp in boxing. ◆ ADJECTIVE [4] *Austral informal* in funds; having money.

holding company NOUN a company with controlling shareholdings in one or more other companies.

holding operation NOUN a plan or procedure devised to prolong the existing situation.

holding paddock NOUN *Austral and NZ* a paddock in which cattle or sheep are kept temporarily, as before shearing, etc.

holding pattern NOUN the oval or circular path of an aircraft flying around an airport awaiting permission to land.

hold off VERB (*adverb*) [1] (*tr*) to keep apart or at a distance. [2] (*intr;* often foll by *from*) to refrain (from doing something): *he held off buying the house until prices fell slightly.*

hold on VERB (*intr, adverb*) [1] to maintain a firm grasp: *she held on with all her strength.* [2] to continue or persist. [3] (foll by *to*) to keep or retain: *hold on to those stamps as they'll soon be valuable.* [4] to keep a telephone line open. ◆ INTERJECTION [5] *Informal* stop! wait!

hold out VERB (*adverb*) [1] (*tr*) to offer or present. [2] (*intr*) to last or endure. [3] (*intr*) to continue to resist or stand firm, as a city under siege or a person refusing to succumb to persuasion. [4] *Chiefly US* to withhold (something due or expected). [5] **hold out for.** to wait patiently or uncompromisingly for (the fulfilment of one's demands). [6] **hold out on.** *Informal* to delay in or keep from telling (a person) some new or important information. ◆ NOUN **holdout.** *US* [7] a person, country, organization, etc., that continues to resist or refuses to change: *Honecker was one of the staunchest holdouts against reform.* [8] a person, country, organization, etc., that declines to cooperate or participate: *they remain the only holdouts to signing the accord.*

hold over VERB (*tr, mainly adverb*) [1] to defer consideration of or action on. [2] to postpone for a further period. [3] to prolong (a note, chord, etc.) from one bar to the next. [4] (*preposition*) to intimidate (a person) with (a threat). ◆ NOUN **holdover.** *US and Canadian informal* [5] an elected official who continues in office after his term has expired. [6] a performer or performance continuing beyond the original engagement.

hold together VERB (*adverb*) [1] to cohere or remain or cause to cohere or remain in one piece: *your old coat holds together very well.* [2] to stay or cause to stay united: *the children held the family together.*

hold-up NOUN [1] a robbery, esp an armed one. [2] a delay; stoppage. [3] *US* an excessive charge; extortion. [4] (*usually plural*) a stocking that is held up by an elasticated top without suspenders. ◆ VERB **hold up.** (*adverb*) [5] (*tr*) to delay; hinder: *we were held up by traffic.* [6] (*tr*) to keep from falling; support. [7] (*tr*) to stop forcibly or waylay in order to rob, esp using a weapon. [8] (*tr*) to exhibit or present: *he held up his achievements for our admiration.* [9] (*intr*) to survive or last: *how are your shoes holding up?* [10] *Bridge* to refrain from playing a high card, so delaying the establishment of (a suit). [11] **hold up one's hands.** to confess a mistake or misdeed.

hold with VERB (*intr, preposition*) to support; approve of.

hole (həʊl) NOUN [1] an area hollowed out in a solid. [2] an opening made in or through something. [3] an animal's hiding place or burrow. [4] *Informal* an unattractive place, such as a town or a dwelling. [5] *Informal* a cell or dungeon. [6] *US informal* a small anchorage. [7] a fault (esp in the phrase **pick holes in**). [8] *Slang* a difficult and embarrassing situation. [9] the cavity in various games into which the ball must be thrust. [10] (on a golf course) **a** the cup on each of the greens. **b** each of the divisions of a course (usually 18) represented by the distance between the tee and a green. **c** the score made in striking the ball from the tee into the hole. [11] *Physics* **a** a vacancy in a nearly full band of quantum states of electrons in a semiconductor or an insulator. Under the action of an electric field holes behave as carriers of positive charge. **b** (*as modifier*): *hole current.* **c** a vacancy in the nearly full continuum of quantum states of negative energy of fermions. A hole appears as the antiparticle of the fermion. [12] **in holes.** so worn as to be full of holes: *his socks were in holes.* [13] **in the hole.** *Chiefly US* **a** in debt. **b** (of a card, the **hole card,** in stud poker) dealt face down in the first round. [14] **make a hole in.** to consume or use a great amount of (food, drink, money, etc.): *to make a hole in a bottle of brandy.* ◆ VERB [15] to make a hole or holes in (something). [16] (when *intr,* often foll by *out*) *Golf* to hit (the ball) into the hole.
▷HISTORY Old English *hol;* related to Gothic *hulundi,* German *Höhle,* Old Norse *hylr* pool, Latin *caulis* hollow stem; see HOLLOW

hole-and-corner ADJECTIVE (*usually prenominal*) *Informal* furtive or secretive.

hole in one *Golf* ◆ NOUN [1] a shot from the tee that finishes in the hole. ◆ VERB [2] (*intr*) to score a hole in one. ◆ Also (esp US): **ace.**

hole in the heart NOUN **a** a defect of the heart in which there is an abnormal opening in any of the walls dividing the four heart chambers. **b** (*as modifier*): *a hole-in-the-heart operation.*

hole in the wall NOUN *Informal* [1] *Chiefly Brit* another name for **cash dispenser.** [2] a small dingy place, esp one difficult to find.

hole up VERB (*intr, adverb*) [1] (of an animal) to hibernate, esp in a cave. [2] *Informal* to hide or remain secluded.

holey (ˈhəʊlɪ) ADJECTIVE **holeyer, holeyest.** full of holes.

Holguín (*Spanish* ɔlˈγin) NOUN a city in NE Cuba, in Holguín province: trading centre. Pop.: 242 085 (1994 est.).

Holi (ˈhɒˌliː) NOUN a Hindu spring festival, celebrated for two to five days, commemorating Krishna's dalliance with the cowgirls. Bonfires are lit and coloured powder and water thrown over celebrants.
▷HISTORY named after *Holika,* legendary female demon

-holic SUFFIX FORMING NOUNS indicating a person having an abnormal desire for or dependence on: *workaholic; chocoholic.*
▷HISTORY C20: on the pattern of *alcoholic*

holiday (ˈhɒlɪˌdeɪ, -dɪ) NOUN [1] (*often plural*) *Chiefly Brit* **a** a period in which a break is taken from work or studies for rest, travel, or recreation. US and Canadian word: **vacation. b** (*as modifier*): *a holiday mood.* [2] a day on which work is suspended by law or custom, such as a religious festival, bank holiday, etc. Related adjective: **ferial.** ◆ VERB [3] (*intr*) *Chiefly Brit* to spend a holiday.
▷HISTORY Old English *hāligdæg,* literally: holy day

holiday camp NOUN *Brit* a place, esp one at the seaside, providing accommodation, recreational facilities, etc., for holiday-makers.

holiday-maker NOUN *Brit* a person who goes on holiday. US and Canadian equivalents: **vacationer, vacationist.**

holily (ˈhəʊlɪlɪ) ADVERB in a holy, devout, or sacred manner.

holiness (ˈhəʊlɪnɪs) NOUN the state or quality of being holy.

Holiness (ˈhəʊlɪnɪs) NOUN (preceded by *his* or *your*) a title once given to all bishops, but now reserved for the pope.

holism (ˈhəʊlɪzəm) NOUN 1 any doctrine that a system may have properties over and above those of its parts and their organization. 2 the treatment of any subject as a whole integrated system, esp, in medicine, the consideration of the complete person, physically and psychologically, in the treatment of a disease. See also **alternative medicine.** 3 *Philosophy* one of a number of methodological theses holding that the significance of the parts can only be understood in terms of their contribution to the significance of the whole and that the latter must therefore be epistemologically prior. Compare **reductionism, atomism** (sense 2).
▷HISTORY C20: from HOLO- + -ISM

holistic (həʊˈlɪstɪk) ADJECTIVE 1 of or relating to a doctrine of holism. 2 of or relating to the the medical consideration of the complete person, physically and psychologically, in the treatment of a disease.
▸**hoˈlistically** ADVERB

Holkar State (hɒlˈkɑː) NOUN a former state of central India, ruled by the Holkar dynasty of Maratha rulers of Indore (18th century until 1947).

Holkham Hall (ˈhəʊlkəm, ˈhɒlkəm) NOUN a Palladian mansion near Wells in Norfolk: built 1734–59 by William Kent for Thomas Coke.

holland (ˈhɒlənd) NOUN a coarse linen cloth, used esp for furnishing.
▷HISTORY C15: after HOLLAND, where it was made

Holland (ˈhɒlənd) NOUN 1 another name for the **Netherlands.** 2 a county of the Holy Roman Empire, corresponding to the present-day North and South Holland provinces of the Netherlands. 3 **Parts of.** an area in E England constituting a former administrative division of Lincolnshire.

hollandaise sauce (ˌhɒlənˈdeɪz, ˈhɒlənˌdeɪz) NOUN a rich sauce of egg yolks, butter, vinegar, etc., served esp with fish.
▷HISTORY C19: from French *sauce hollandaise* Dutch sauce

Hollander (ˈhɒləndə) NOUN another name for a **Dutchman.**

Hollandia (hɒˈlændɪə) NOUN a former name of **Jayapura.**

Hollands (ˈhɒləndz) NOUN Dutch gin, often sold in stone bottles.
▷HISTORY C18: from Dutch *hollandsch genever*

holler (ˈhɒlə) *Informal* ◆ VERB 1 to shout or yell (something). ◆ NOUN 2 a shout; call.
▷HISTORY variant of C16 *hollow,* from *holla,* from French *holà* stop! (literally: ho there!)

hollo (ˈhɒləʊ), **holla** (ˈhɒlə), *or* **holloa** (həˈləʊ) NOUN, *plural* **-los, -las,** *or* **-loas** (-ˈləʊz), INTERJECTION 1 a cry for attention, or of encouragement. ◆ VERB 2 (*intr*) to shout.
▷HISTORY C16: from French *holà* ho there!

hollow (ˈhɒləʊ) ADJECTIVE 1 having a hole, cavity, or space within; not solid. 2 having a sunken area; concave. 3 recessed or deeply set: *hollow cheeks.* 4 (of sounds) as if resounding in a hollow place. 5 without substance or validity. 6 hungry or empty. 7 insincere; cynical. 8 **a hollow leg** *or* **hollow legs.** the capacity to eat or drink a lot without ill effects. ◆ ADVERB 9 **beat (someone) hollow.** *Brit informal* to defeat (someone) thoroughly and convincingly. ◆ NOUN 10 a cavity, opening, or space in or within something. 11 a depression or dip in the land. ◆ VERB (often foll by *out,* usually when *tr*) 12 to make or become hollow. 13 to form (a hole, cavity, etc.) or (of a hole, etc.) to be formed.
▷HISTORY C12: from *holu,* inflected form of Old English *holh* cave; related to Old Norse *holr,* German *hohl;* see HOLE
▸**ˈhollowly** ADVERB ▸**ˈhollowness** NOUN

hollow-back NOUN *Pathol* the nontechnical name for **lordosis.** Compare **hunchback.**

hollow-eyed ADJECTIVE with the eyes appearing to be sunk into the face, as from excessive fatigue.

hollowware (ˈhɒləʊˌwɛə) NOUN hollow articles made of metal, china, etc., such as pots, jugs, and kettles. Compare **flatware** (sense 2).

holly (ˈhɒlɪ) NOUN, *plural* **-lies.** 1 any tree or shrub of the genus *Ilex,* such as the Eurasian *I. aquifolium,* having bright red berries and shiny evergreen leaves with prickly edges. 2 branches of any of these trees, used for Christmas decorations. 3 **holly oak.** another name for **holm oak.** ◆ See also **sea holly.**
▷HISTORY Old English *holegn;* related to Old Norse *hulfr,* Old High German *hulis,* German *Hulst,* Old Slavonic *kolja* prick

hollyhock (ˈhɒlɪˌhɒk) NOUN a tall widely cultivated malvaceous plant, *Althaea rosea,* with stout hairy stems and spikes of white, yellow, red, or purple flowers. Also called (US): **rose mallow.**
▷HISTORY C16: from HOLY + *hock,* from Old English *hoc* mallow

Hollywood (ˈhɒlɪˌwʊd) NOUN 1 a NW suburb of Los Angeles, California: centre of the American film industry. Pop.: 250 000 (latest est.). 2 **a** the American film industry. **b** (*as modifier*): *a Hollywood star.*

holm¹ (həʊm) NOUN *Dialect, chiefly northwestern English* 1 an island in a river, lake, or estuary. 2 low flat land near a river.
▷HISTORY Old English *holm* sea, island; related to Old Saxon *holm* hill, Old Norse *holmr* island, Latin *culmen* tip

holm² (həʊm) NOUN 1 short for **holm oak.** 2 *Chiefly Brit* a dialect word for **holly.**
▷HISTORY C14: variant of obsolete *holin,* from Old English *holegn* HOLLY

holmic (ˈhɒlmɪk) ADJECTIVE of or containing holmium.

holmium (ˈhɒlmɪəm) NOUN a malleable silver-white metallic element of the lanthanide series. Symbol: Ho; atomic no.: 67; atomic wt.: 164.93032; valency: 3; relative density: 8.795; melting pt.: 1474°C; boiling pt.: 2700°C.
▷HISTORY C19: from New Latin *Holmia* Stockholm

holm oak NOUN an evergreen Mediterranean oak tree, *Quercus ilex,* widely planted for ornament: the leaves are holly-like when young but become smooth-edged with age. Also called: **holm, holly oak, ilex.**

holo- *or before a vowel* **hol-** COMBINING FORM whole or wholly: *holograph; holotype; Holarctic.*
▷HISTORY from Greek *holos*

holobenthic (ˌhɒləˈbɛnθɪk) ADJECTIVE (of an animal) completing its life cycle in the ocean depths.

holoblastic (ˌhɒləˈblæstɪk) ADJECTIVE *Embryol* of or showing cleavage of the entire zygote into blastomeres, as in eggs with little yolk. Compare **meroblastic.**
▸**ˌholoˈblastically** ADVERB

Holocaine (ˈhɒləˌkeɪn) NOUN a trademark for **phenacaine.**

holocaust (ˈhɒləˌkɔːst) NOUN 1 great destruction or loss of life or the source of such destruction, esp fire. 2 (*usually capital*) **the.** Also called: **Churban, Shoah.** the mass murder by the Nazis of the Jews of continental Europe between 1940 and 1945. 3 a rare word for **burnt offering.**
▷HISTORY C13: from Late Latin *holocaustum* whole burnt offering, from Greek *holokauston,* from HOLO- + *kaustos,* from *kaiein* to burn
▸**ˌholoˈcaustal** *or* **ˌholoˈcaustic** ADJECTIVE

Holocene (ˈhɒləˌsiːn) ADJECTIVE 1 of, denoting, or formed in the second and most recent epoch of the Quaternary period, which began 10 000 years ago at the end of the Pleistocene. ◆ NOUN 2 **the.** the Holocene epoch or rock series. ◆ Also: **Recent.**

holocrine (ˈhɒləkrɪn) ADJECTIVE (of the secretion of glands) characterized by disintegration of the entire glandular cell in releasing its product, as in sebaceous glands. Compare **merocrine, apocrine.**
▷HISTORY C20: from HOLO- + Greek *krinein* to separate, decide

holocrystalline (ˌhɒləˈkrɪstəˌlaɪn) ADJECTIVE (of igneous rocks) having only crystalline components and no glass. Compare **hemicrystalline.**

holoenzyme (ˌhɒləʊˈɛnzaɪm) NOUN an active enzyme consisting of a protein component (apoenzyme) and its coenzyme.

Holofernes (ˌhɒləˈfɜːniːz, həˈlɒfəˌniːz) NOUN the Assyrian general, who was killed by the biblical heroine Judith.

hologram (ˈhɒləˌɡræm) NOUN a photographic record produced by illuminating the object with coherent light (as from a laser) and, without using lenses, exposing a film to light reflected from this object and to a direct beam of coherent light. When interference patterns on the film are illuminated by the coherent light a three-dimensional image is produced.

holograph (ˈhɒləˌɡræf, -ˌɡrɑːf) NOUN **a** a book or document handwritten by its author; original manuscript; autograph. **b** (*as modifier*): *a holograph document.*

holographic (ˌhɒləˈɡræfɪk) ADJECTIVE of, relating to, or produced using holograms; three-dimensional.
▸**ˌholoˈgraphically** ADVERB

holography (hɒˈlɒɡrəfɪ) NOUN the science or practice of producing holograms.

holohedral (ˌhɒləˈhiːdrəl) ADJECTIVE (of a crystal) exhibiting all the planes required for the symmetry of the crystal system.
▸**ˌholoˈhedrism** NOUN

holomorphic (ˌhɒləˈmɔːfɪk) ADJECTIVE *Maths* another word for **analytic** (sense 5).

holon (ˈhəʊlən) NOUN an autonomous self-reliant unit, esp in manufacturing.
▷HISTORY C20: from HOLO- + -ON
▸**hoˈlonic** ADJECTIVE

holophrastic (ˌhɒləˈfræstɪk) ADJECTIVE 1 denoting the stage in a child's acquisition of syntax when most utterances are single words. 2 (of languages) tending to express in one word what would be expressed in several words in other languages; polysynthetic.
▷HISTORY C19: from HOLO- + Greek *phrastikos* expressive, from *phrazein* to express

holophytic (ˌhɒləˈfɪtɪk) ADJECTIVE (of plants) capable of synthesizing their food from inorganic molecules, esp by photosynthesis.
▸**holophyte** (ˈhɒləˌfaɪt) NOUN

holoplankton (ˌhɒləˈplæŋktən) NOUN organisms, such as diatoms and algae, that spend all stages of their life cycle as plankton. Compare **meroplankton.**

holothurian (ˌhɒləˈθjʊərɪən) NOUN 1 any echinoderm of the class *Holothuroidea,* including the sea cucumbers, having a leathery elongated body with a ring of tentacles around the mouth. ◆ ADJECTIVE 2 of, relating to, or belonging to the *Holothuroidea.*
▷HISTORY C19: from New Latin *Holothūria* name of type genus, from Latin: water polyp, from Greek *holothourion,* of obscure origin

holotype (ˈhɒləˌtaɪp) NOUN *Biology* another name for **type specimen.**
▸**holotypic** (ˌhɒləˈtɪpɪk) ADJECTIVE

holozoic (ˌhɒləˈzəʊɪk) ADJECTIVE (of animals) obtaining nourishment by feeding on plants or other animals.

holp (həʊlp) VERB *Archaic or dialect* a past tense of **help.**

holpen (ˈhəʊlpən) VERB *Archaic* a past participle of **help.**

hols (hɒlz) PLURAL NOUN *Brit school slang* holidays.

Holstein¹ (ˈhəʊlstaɪn) NOUN the usual US and Canadian name for **Friesian** (the cattle).

Holstein² (*German* ˈhɔlʃtain) NOUN a region of N Germany, in S Schleswig-Holstein: in early times a German duchy of Saxony; became a duchy of Denmark in 1474; finally incorporated into Prussia in 1866.

holster (ˈhəʊlstə) NOUN 1 a sheathlike leather case for a pistol, attached to a belt or saddle. 2 *Mountaineering* a similar case for an ice axe or piton hammer.
▷HISTORY C17: via Dutch *holster* from Germanic; compare Old Norse *hulstr* sheath, Old English *heolstor* darkness, Gothic *hulistr* cover
▸**ˈholstered** ADJECTIVE

holt¹ (həʊlt) NOUN *Archaic or poetic* a wood or wooded hill.
▷HISTORY Old English *holt;* related to Old Norse

holt, Old High German *holz,* Old Slavonic *kladŭ* log, Greek *klados* twig

holt[2] (həʊlt) NOUN the burrowed lair of an animal, esp an otter.
▷HISTORY C16: a phonetic variant of HOLD[2]

holus-bolus ('həʊləs'bəʊləs) ADVERB *Informal* all at once.
▷HISTORY C19: pseudo-Latin based on *whole bolus;* see BOLUS

holy ('həʊlɪ) ADJECTIVE **holier, holiest.** [1] of, relating to, or associated with God or a deity; sacred. [2] endowed or invested with extreme purity or sublimity. [3] devout, godly, or virtuous. [4] **holier-than-thou.** offensively sanctimonious or self-righteous: *a holier-than-thou attitude.* [5] **holy terror. a** a difficult or frightening person. **b** *Irish informal* a person who is an active gambler, womanizer, etc. ◆ NOUN, *plural* **-lies.** [6] **a** a sacred place. **b the holy.** (*functioning as plural*) persons or things invested with holiness.
▷HISTORY Old English *hālig, hǣlig;* related to Old Saxon *hēlag,* Gothic *hailags,* German *heilig;* see HALLOW

Holy Alliance NOUN [1] a document advocating government according to Christian principles that was signed in 1815 by the rulers of Russia, Prussia, and Austria. [2] the informal alliance that resulted from this agreement.

Holy Bible NOUN another name for the **Bible.**

Holy City NOUN **the.** [1] Jerusalem, esp when regarded as the focal point of the religions of Judaism, Christianity, or Islam. [2] *Christianity* heaven regarded as the perfect counterpart of Jerusalem. [3] any city regarded as especially sacred by a particular religion.

Holy Communion NOUN [1] the celebration of the Eucharist. [2] the consecrated elements of the Eucharist. ◆ Often shortened to **Communion.**

holy day NOUN a day on which a religious festival is observed.

holy day of obligation NOUN a major feastday of the Roman Catholic Church on which Catholics are bound to attend Mass and refrain from servile work.

Holy Family NOUN **the.** *Christianity* the infant Jesus, Mary, and St Joseph.

Holy Father NOUN *RC Church* a title of the pope.

Holy Ghost NOUN another name for the **Holy Spirit.**

Holy Grail NOUN [1] **a** Also called: **Grail, Sangraal.** (in medieval legend) the bowl used by Jesus at the Last Supper. It was allegedly brought to Britain by Joseph of Arimathea, where it became the quest of many knights. **b** (in modern spirituality) a symbol of the spiritual wholeness that leads a person to union with the divine. [2] *Informal* any desired ambition or goal: *the Holy Grail of infrared astronomy.*
▷HISTORY C14 *grail* from Old French *graal,* from Medieval Latin *gradālis* bowl, of unknown origin

Holyhead ('hɒlɪˌhɛd) NOUN a town in NW Wales, in Anglesey, the chief town of Holy Island: a port on the N coast. Pop.: 11 796 (1991).

Holy Hour NOUN [1] *RC Church* an hour set aside for prayer and reflection. [2] (*not capitals*) *Irish informal* a period during the afternoon when public houses are obliged to close by law.

Holy Innocents' Day NOUN Dec. 28, a day commemorating the massacre of male children at Bethlehem by Herod's order (Matthew 2:16); Childermas.

Holy Island NOUN [1] an island off the NE coast of Northumberland, linked to the mainland by road but accessible only at low water: site of a monastery founded by St Aidan in 635. Also called: **Lindisfarne.** [2] an island off the NW coast of Anglesey. Area: about 62 sq. km (24 sq. miles).

Holy Joe NOUN *Informal* [1] a minister or chaplain. [2] any sanctimonious or self-righteous person.

Holy Land NOUN **the.** another name for **Palestine** (sense 1).

holy Mary NOUN *Irish* a pietistic person: *he's a real holy Mary.*

Holy Office NOUN *RC Church* a congregation established in 1542 as the final court of appeal in heresy trials; it now deals with matters of doctrine.

holy of holies NOUN [1] any place of special sanctity. [2] (*capitals*) the innermost compartment of the Jewish tabernacle, and later of the Temple, where the Ark was enshrined.

holy orders PLURAL NOUN [1] the sacrament or rite whereby a person is admitted to the Christian ministry. [2] the grades of the Christian ministry. [3] the rank or status of an ordained Christian minister. ◆ See also **orders.**

holy place NOUN [1] the outer chamber of a Jewish sanctuary. [2] a place of pilgrimage.

Holy Roller NOUN *Derogatory* a member of a sect that expresses religious fervour in an ecstatic or frenzied way.

Holy Roman Empire NOUN the complex of European territories under the rule of the Frankish or German king who bore the title of Roman emperor, beginning with the coronation of Charlemagne in 800 A.D. The last emperor, Francis II, relinquished his crown in 1806.

holy rood NOUN [1] a cross or crucifix, esp one placed upon the rood screen in a church. [2] (*often capital*) the cross on which Christ was crucified.

Holyroodhouse (ˌhɒlɪru:d'haʊs) NOUN a royal palace in Edinburgh in Scotland: official residence of the Queen when in Scotland; begun in 1501 by James IV of Scotland; scene of the murder of David Rizzio in 1566.

Holy Saturday NOUN the Saturday before Easter Sunday.

Holy Scripture NOUN another term for **Scripture.**

Holy See NOUN *RC Church* [1] the see of the pope as bishop of Rome and head of the Church. [2] the Roman curia.

Holy Sepulchre NOUN *New Testament* the tomb in which the body of Christ was laid after the Crucifixion.

Holy Spirit *or* **Ghost** NOUN *Christianity* the third person of the Trinity.

holystone ('həʊlɪˌstəʊn) NOUN [1] a soft sandstone used for scrubbing the decks of a vessel. ◆ VERB [2] (*tr*) to scrub (a vessel's decks) with a holystone.
▷HISTORY C19: perhaps so named from its being used in a kneeling position

holy synod NOUN the governing body of any of the Orthodox Churches.

Holy Thursday NOUN *RC Church* [1] another name for **Maundy Thursday.** [2] a rare name for **Ascension Day.**

holy war NOUN a war waged in the cause of a religion.

holy water NOUN water that has been blessed by a priest for use in symbolic rituals of purification.

Holy Week NOUN the week preceding Easter Sunday.

Holy Willie ('wɪlɪ) NOUN a person who is hypocritically pious.
▷HISTORY C18: from Burns' *Holy Willie's Prayer*

Holy Writ NOUN another term for **Scripture.**

Holy Year NOUN *RC Church* a period of remission from sin, esp one granted every 25 years.

hom (hɒm) *or* **homa** ('hɒmə) NOUN [1] a sacred plant of the Parsees and ancient Persians. [2] a drink made from this plant.
▷HISTORY from Persian, from Avestan *haoma*

homage ('hɒmɪdʒ) NOUN [1] a public show of respect or honour towards someone or something (esp in the phrases **pay** *or* **do homage to**). [2] (in feudal society) **a** the act of respect and allegiance made by a vassal to his lord. See also **fealty. b** something done in acknowledgment of vassalage. ◆ VERB (*tr*) [3] *Archaic or poetic* to render homage to.
▷HISTORY C13: from Old French, from *home* man, from Latin *homo*

hombre[1] ('ɒmbreɪ, -brɪ) NOUN *Western US* a slang word for **man.**
▷HISTORY C19: from Spanish: man

hombre[2] ('hɒmbə) NOUN a variant of **ombre.**

homburg ('hɒmbɜ:g) NOUN a man's hat of soft felt with a dented crown and a stiff upturned brim.
▷HISTORY C20: named after *Homburg,* in Germany, town where it was originally made

home (həʊm) NOUN [1] the place or a place where one lives: *have you no home to go to?* [2] a house or other dwelling. [3] a family or other group living in a house or other place. [4] a person's country, city, etc., esp viewed as a birthplace, a residence during one's early years, or a place dear to one. [5] the environment or habitat of a person or animal. [6] the place where something is invented, founded, or developed: *the US is the home of baseball.* [7] **a** a building or organization set up to care for orphans, the aged, etc. **b** an informal name for a **mental home.** [8] *Sport* one's own ground: *the match is at home.* [9] **a** the objective towards which a player strives in certain sports. **b** an area where a player is safe from attack. [10] *Lacrosse* **a** one of two positions of play nearest the opponents' goal. **b** a player assigned to such a position: *inside home.* [11] *Baseball* another name for **home plate.** [12] *NZ informal, obsolete* Britain, esp England. [13] **a home from home.** a place other than one's own home where one can be at ease. [14] **at home. a** in one's own home or country. **b** at ease, as if at one's own home. **c** giving an informal party at one's own home. **d** *Brit* such a party. [15] **at home in, on,** *or* **with.** familiar or conversant with. [16] **home and dry.** *Brit informal* definitely safe or successful: *we will not be home and dry until the votes have been counted.* Austral and NZ equivalent: **home and hosed.** [17] **near home.** concerning one deeply. ◆ ADJECTIVE (*usually prenominal*) [18] of, relating to, or involving one's home, country, etc.; domestic. [19] (of an activity) done in one's house: *home taping.* [20] effective or deadly: *a home thrust.* [21] *Sport* relating to one's own ground: *a home game.* [22] *US* central; principal: *the company's home office.* ◆ ADVERB [23] to or at home: *I'll be home tomorrow.* [24] to or on the point. [25] to the fullest extent: *hammer the nail home.* [26] (of nautical gear) into or in the best or proper position: *the boom is home.* [27] **bring home to. a** to make clear to. **b** to place the blame on. [28] **come home.** *Nautical* (of an anchor) to fail to hold. [29] **come home to.** to become absolutely clear to. [30] **nothing to write home about.** *Informal* to be of no particular interest: *the film was nothing to write home about.* ◆ VERB [31] (*intr*) (of birds and other animals) to return home accurately from a distance. [32] (often foll by *on* or *onto*) to direct or be directed onto a point or target, esp by automatic navigational aids. [33] to send or go home. [34] to furnish with or have a home. [35] (*intr;* often foll by *in* or *in on*) to be directed towards a goal, target, etc.
▷HISTORY Old English *hām;* related to Old Norse *heimr,* Gothic *haims,* Old High German *heim,* Dutch *heem,* Greek *kōmi* village
▸**'home,like** ADJECTIVE

home aid NOUN *NZ* another name for **home help.**

home-alone ADJECTIVE *Informal* (esp of a young child) left in a house, flat, etc. unattended.

home banking NOUN a system whereby a person at home or in an office can use a computer with a modem to call up information from a bank or to transfer funds electronically.

homebody ('həʊmˌbɒdɪ) NOUN, *plural* **-bodies.** a person whose life and interests are centred on the home.

homeboy ('həʊmˌbɔɪ) NOUN *Slang, chiefly US* [1] a close friend. [2] a person from one's home town or neighbourhood.
▷HISTORY C20: US rap-music usage
▸**'home,girl** FEMININE NOUN

home brand NOUN an Australian term for **own brand.**

homebred ('həʊmˌbrɛd) ADJECTIVE [1] raised or bred at home. [2] lacking sophistication or cultivation; crude.

home-brew NOUN a beer or other alcoholic drink brewed at home rather than commercially.
▸**'home-'brewed** ADJECTIVE

homecoming ('həʊmˌkʌmɪŋ) NOUN [1] the act of coming home. [2] *US* an annual celebration held by a university, college, or school, for former students.

Home Counties PLURAL NOUN the counties surrounding London.

home economics NOUN (*functioning as singular or plural*) the study of diet, budgeting, child care, textiles, and other subjects concerned with running a home.
▸**home economist** NOUN

home farm NOUN *Brit* (esp formerly) a farm belonging to and providing food for a large country house.

home ground NOUN a familiar area or topic.

home-grown ADJECTIVE (esp of fruit and

vegetables) produced in one's own country, district, estate, or garden.

Home Guard NOUN 1 a volunteer part-time military force recruited for the defence of the United Kingdom in World War II. 2 (in various countries) a civil defence and reserve militia organization.

home help NOUN *Social welfare* (in Britain and New Zealand) 1 a person who is paid to do domestic chores for persons unable to look after themselves adequately. 2 Also called: **home care.** such a service provided by a local authority social services department to those whom it judges most need it. ♦ Also called (NZ): **home aid.**

home invasion NOUN *Austral and NZ* aggravated burglary.

homeland ('həʊm,lænd) NOUN 1 the country in which one lives or was born. 2 the official name for a **Bantustan.**

homelands movement NOUN *Austral* the programme to resettle native Australians on their tribal lands.

homeless ('həʊmlɪs) ADJECTIVE **a** having nowhere to live. **b** (*as collective noun;* preceded by *the*): *the homeless.*
▸ **'homelessness** NOUN

home loan NOUN an informal name for **mortgage** (sense 1).

homely ('həʊmlɪ) ADJECTIVE **-lier, -liest.** 1 characteristic of or suited to the ordinary home; unpretentious. 2 (of a person) **a** *Brit* warm and domesticated in manner or appearance. **b** *Chiefly US and Canadian* plain or ugly.
▸ **'homeliness** NOUN

home-made ADJECTIVE 1 (esp of cakes, jam, and other foods) made at home or on the premises, esp of high-quality ingredients. 2 crudely fashioned.

homemaker ('həʊm,meɪkə) NOUN 1 *Chiefly US and Canadian* a person, esp a housewife, who manages a home. 2 *US and Canadian* a social worker who manages a household during the incapacity of the housewife.
▸ **'home,making** NOUN, ADJECTIVE

homeo-, homoeo-, *or* **homoio-** COMBINING FORM like or similar: *homeomorphism.*
▷HISTORY from Latin *homoeo-,* from Greek *homoio-,* from *homos* same

Home Office NOUN *Brit government* the national department responsible for the maintenance of law and order, immigration control, and all other domestic affairs not specifically assigned to another department.

homeomorphism *or* **homoeomorphism** (,həʊmɪə'mɔːfɪzəm) NOUN 1 the property, shown by certain chemical compounds, of having the same crystal form but different chemical composition. 2 *Maths* a one-to-one correspondence, continuous in both directions, between the points of two geometric figures or between two topological spaces.
▸ **,homeo'morphic** *or* **,homeo'morphous** *or* **,homoeo'morphic** *or* **,homoeo'morphous** ADJECTIVE

homeopathy *or* **homoeopathy** (,həʊmɪ'ɒpəθɪ) NOUN a method of treating disease by the use of small amounts of a drug that, in healthy persons, produces symptoms similar to those of the disease being treated. Compare **allopathy.**
▸ **homeopathic** *or* **homoeopathic** (,həʊmɪə'pæθɪk) ADJECTIVE ▸ **,homeo'pathically** *or* **,homoeo'pathically** ADVERB ▸ **homeopathist** *or* **homoeopathist** (,həʊmɪ'ɒpəθɪst) *or* **homeopath** *or* **homoeopath** ('həʊmɪə,pæθ) NOUN

homeostasis *or* **homoeostasis** (,həʊmɪəʊ'steɪsɪs) NOUN 1 the maintenance of metabolic equilibrium within an animal by a tendency to compensate for disrupting changes. 2 the maintenance of equilibrium within a social group, person, etc.
▸ **homeostatic** *or* **homoeostatic** (,həʊmɪəʊ'stætɪk) ADJECTIVE

homeotypic (,həʊmɪəʊ'tɪpɪk), **homeotypical, homoeotypic,** *or* **homoeotypical** ADJECTIVE denoting or relating to the second nuclear division of meiosis, which resembles mitosis. Compare **heterotypic.**

homeowner ('həʊm,əʊnə) NOUN a person who owns the house in which he or she lives.
▸ **,home'ownership** NOUN

home page NOUN *Computing* (on a website) the main document relating to an individual or institution that provides introductory information about a website with links to the actual details of services or information provided.

home plate NOUN *Baseball* a flat often five-sided piece of hard rubber or other material that serves to define the area over which the pitcher must throw the ball for a strike and that a base runner must safely reach on his way from third base to score a run. Also called: **plate, home, home base.**

homer ('həʊmə) NOUN 1 another word for **homing pigeon.** 2 *US and Canadian* an informal word for **home run.**

home range NOUN *Ecology* the area in which an animal normally ranges.

Homeric (həʊ'merɪk) *or* **Homerian** (həʊ'mɪərɪən) ADJECTIVE 1 of, relating to, or resembling Homer (c. 800 B.C.), the Greek poet to whom are attributed the *Iliad* and the *Odyssey,* or his poems. 2 imposing or heroic. 3 of or relating to the archaic form of Greek used by Homer. See **epic.**
▸ **Ho'merically** ADVERB

Homeric laughter NOUN loud unrestrained laughter, as that of the gods.

home rule NOUN 1 self-government, esp in domestic affairs. 2 *US government* the partial autonomy of cities and (in some states) counties, under which they manage their own affairs, with their own charters, etc., within the limits set by the state constitution and laws. 3 the partial autonomy sometimes granted to a national minority or a colony.

Home Rule NOUN self-government for Ireland: the goal of the Irish Nationalists from about 1870 to 1920.

home run NOUN *Baseball* a hit that enables the batter to run round all four bases, usually by hitting the ball out of the playing area.

home-school VERB 1 **a** to teach one's child at home instead of sending him or her to school. ♦ ADJECTIVE 2 **a** being educated at home rather than in school: *home-school kids.* **b** relating to the education of children in their own homes instead of in school: *home-school parents.*

home-schooler NOUN 1 a child who is educated at home, esp by his or her parents. 2 a parent who educates a child at home.

homescreetch ('həʊm,skriːtʃ) NOUN *Southwest English dialect* a mistle thrush.

Home Secretary NOUN *Brit government* short for **Secretary of State for the Home Department**; the head of the Home Office.

homesick ('həʊm,sɪk) ADJECTIVE depressed or melancholy at being away from home and family.
▸ **'home,sickness** NOUN

homespun ('həʊm,spʌn) ADJECTIVE 1 having plain or unsophisticated character. 2 woven or spun at home. ♦ NOUN 3 cloth made at home or made of yarn spun at home. 4 a cloth resembling this but made on a power loom.

homestead ('həʊm,sted, -stɪd) NOUN 1 a house or estate and the adjoining land, buildings, etc., esp a farm. 2 (in the US) a house and adjoining land designated by the owner as his fixed residence and exempt under the homestead laws from seizure and forced sale for debts. 3 (in western Canada) a piece of land, usually 160 acres, granted to a settler by the federal government. 4 *Austral and NZ* the owner's or manager's residence on a sheep or cattle station; in New Zealand the term includes all outbuildings.

Homestead Act NOUN 1 an act passed by the US Congress in 1862 making available to settlers 160-acre tracts of public land for cultivation. 2 (in Canada) a similar act passed by the Canadian Parliament in 1872.

homesteader ('həʊm,stedə) NOUN 1 a person owning a homestead. 2 *US and Canadian* a person who acquires or possesses land under a homestead law. 3 a person taking part in a homesteading scheme.

homesteading ('həʊm,stedɪŋ) NOUN (in Britain) **a** a scheme whereby council tenants are enabled to buy derelict property from the council and renovate it with the aid of Government grants. **b** (*as modifier*): *a homesteading scheme.*

homestead law NOUN (in the US and Canada) any of various laws conferring certain privileges on owners of homesteads.

home straight NOUN 1 *Horse racing* the section of a racecourse forming the approach to the finish. 2 the final stage of an undertaking or journey. ♦ Also (chiefly US): **home stretch.**

home teacher NOUN *Brit* a teacher who educates ill or disabled children in their homes.

home truth NOUN (*often plural*) an unpleasant fact told to a person about himself.

home unit NOUN *Austral and NZ* a self-contained residence which is part of a series of similar residences. Often shortened to **unit.**

homeward ('həʊmwəd) ADJECTIVE 1 directed or going home. 2 (of a ship, part of a voyage, etc.) returning to the home port. ♦ ADVERB *also* **homewards.** 3 towards home.

homeware ('həʊmweə) NOUN crockery, furniture, and furnishings with which a house, room, etc., is furnished.
▷HISTORY C20: HOME + WARE[1]

homework ('həʊm,wɜːk) NOUN 1 school work done out of lessons, esp at home. 2 any preparatory study. 3 work done at home for pay.

homeworker ('həʊm,wɜːkə) NOUN a person who does paid work at home, rather than in an office.

homey ('həʊmɪ) ADJECTIVE **homier, homiest.** 1 a variant spelling (esp US) of **homy.** ♦ NOUN 2 *NZ informal* a British person.
▸ **'homeyness** NOUN

homicidal (,hɒmɪ'saɪdᵊl) ADJECTIVE 1 of, involving, or characterized by homicide. 2 likely to commit homicide: *a homicidal maniac.*
▸ **,homi'cidally** ADVERB

homicide ('hɒmɪ,saɪd) NOUN 1 the killing of a human being by another person. 2 a person who kills another.
▷HISTORY C14: from Old French, from Latin *homo* man + *caedere* to slay

homie ('həʊmɪ) NOUN *Slang, chiefly US* short for **homeboy** or **homegirl.**

homiletic (,hɒmɪ'letɪk) *or* **homiletical** ADJECTIVE 1 of or relating to a homily or sermon. 2 of, relating to, or characteristic of homiletics.
▸ **,homi'letically** ADVERB

homiletics (,hɒmɪ'letɪks) NOUN (*functioning as singular*) the art of preaching or writing sermons.
▷HISTORY C17: from Greek *homilētikos* cordial, from *homilein* to converse with; see HOMILY

homily ('hɒmɪlɪ) NOUN, *plural* **-lies.** 1 a sermon or discourse on a moral or religious topic. 2 moralizing talk or writing.
▷HISTORY C14: from Church Latin *homīlia,* from Greek: discourse, from *homilein* to converse with, from *homilos* crowd, from *homou* together + *ilē* crowd
▸ **'homilist** NOUN

homing ('həʊmɪŋ) NOUN (*modifier*) 1 *Zoology* relating to the ability to return home after travelling great distances: *homing instinct.* 2 (of an aircraft, a missile, etc.) capable of guiding itself onto a target or to a specified point.

homing guidance NOUN a method of missile guidance in which internal equipment enables it to steer itself onto the target, as by sensing the target's heat radiation.

homing pigeon NOUN any breed of pigeon developed for its homing instinct, used for carrying messages or for racing. Also called: **homer.**

hominid ('hɒmɪnɪd) NOUN 1 any primate of the family *Hominidae,* which includes modern man (*Homo sapiens*) and the extinct precursors of man. ♦ ADJECTIVE 2 of, relating to, or belonging to the *Hominidae.*
▷HISTORY C19: via New Latin from Latin *homo* man + -ID[2]

hominoid ('hɒmɪ,nɔɪd) ADJECTIVE 1 of or like man; manlike. 2 of, relating to, or belonging to the primate superfamily *Hominoidea,* which includes

the anthropoid apes and man. ◆ NOUN 3 a hominoid animal.
▷HISTORY C20: from Latin *homin-, homo* man + -OID

hominy (ˈhɒmɪnɪ) NOUN *Chiefly US* coarsely ground maize prepared as a food by boiling in milk or water.
▷HISTORY C17: probably of Algonquian origin

hominy grits PLURAL NOUN *US* finely ground hominy. Often shortened to **grits**.

homo[1] (ˈhəʊməʊ) NOUN, *plural* **-mos**. *Informal* short for **homosexual**.

homo[2] (ˈhəʊməʊ) NOUN *Canadian informal* short for **homogenized milk**.

Homo (ˈhəʊməʊ) NOUN a genus of hominids including modern man (see ***Homo sapiens***) and several extinct species of primitive man, including *H. habilis* and *H. erectus*.
▷HISTORY Latin: man

homo- COMBINING FORM being the same or like: *homologous; homosexual*. Compare **hetero-**.
▷HISTORY via Latin from Greek, from *homos* same

homoblastic (ˌhəʊməʊˈblæstɪk) ADJECTIVE (of a plant or plant part) showing no difference in form between the juvenile and the adult structures. Compare **heteroblastic**.

homocentric (ˌhəʊməʊˈsɛntrɪk, ˌhɒm-) ADJECTIVE having the same centre; concentric.
▸ **ˌhomoˈcentrically** ADVERB

homocercal (ˌhəʊməʊˈsɜːkᵊl, ˌhɒm-) ADJECTIVE *Ichthyol* of or possessing a symmetrical tail that extends beyond the end of the vertebral column, as in most bony fishes. Compare **heterocercal**.
▷HISTORY C19: from HOMO- + Greek *kerkos* tail

homochlamydeous (ˌhəʊməkləˈmɪdɪəs) ADJECTIVE (of a plant) having a perianth in which the sepals and petals are fused together and indistinguishable. Compare **heterochlamydeous**.

homochromatic (ˌhəʊməʊkrəʊˈmætɪk, ˌhɒm-) ADJECTIVE a less common word for **monochromatic** (sense 1).
▸ **homochromatism** (ˌhəʊməʊˈkrəʊməˌtɪzəm, ˌhɒm-) NOUN

homochromous (ˌhəʊməˈkrəʊməs, ˌhɒm-) ADJECTIVE (esp of plant parts) of only one colour.

homocyclic (ˌhəʊməʊˈsaɪklɪk, -ˈsɪk-, ˌhɒm-) ADJECTIVE (of an organic compound) containing a closed ring of atoms of the same kind, esp carbon atoms. Compare **heterocyclic**.

homocysteine (ˌhəʊməʊˈsɪstiːn) NOUN an amino acid occurring as an intermediate in the metabolism of methionine. Elevated levels in the blood may indicate increased risk of cardiovascular disease.

homodont (ˈhəʊməˌdɒnt) ADJECTIVE (of most nonmammalian vertebrates) having teeth that are all of the same type. Compare **heterodont**.
▷HISTORY C19: from HOMO- + -ODONT

homoeo- COMBINING FORM a variant of **homeo-**.

homoerotic (ˌhəʊməʊɪˈrɒtɪk) ADJECTIVE of, concerning, or arousing sexual desire for persons of one's own sex.

homoeroticism (ˌhəʊməʊɪˈrɒtɪˌsɪzəm) *or* **homoerotism** (ˌhəʊməʊˈɛrəˌtɪzəm) NOUN eroticism centred on or aroused by persons of one's own sex.

homogametic (ˌhəʊməgəˈmɛtɪk) ADJECTIVE *Genetics* denoting the sex that possesses two similar sex chromosomes. In humans and many other mammals it is the female sex, possessing two X-chromosomes. Compare **heterogametic**.

homogamy (hɒˈmɒgəmɪ) NOUN 1 a condition in which all the flowers of an inflorescence are either of the same sex or hermaphrodite. Compare **heterogamy** (sense 3). 2 the maturation of the anthers and stigmas of a flower at the same time, ensuring self-pollination. Compare **dichogamy**.
▸ **hoˈmogamous** ADJECTIVE

homogenate (hɒˈmɒdʒɪnɪt, -ˌneɪt) NOUN a substance produced by homogenizing.
▷HISTORY C20: from HOMOGENIZE + -ATE[1]

homogeneous (ˌhəʊməˈdʒiːnɪəs, ˌhɒm-) ADJECTIVE 1 composed of similar or identical parts or elements. 2 of uniform nature. 3 similar in kind or nature. 4 having a constant property, such as density, throughout. 5 *Maths* **a** (of a polynomial) containing terms of the same degree with respect to all the variables, as in $x^2 + 2xy + y^2$. **b** (of a function) containing a set of variables such that when each is multiplied by a constant, this constant can be eliminated without altering the value of the function, as in cos $x/y + x/y$. **c** (of an equation) containing a homogeneous function made equal to 0. 6 *Chem* of, composed of, or concerned with a single phase. Compare **heterogeneous**. ◆ Also (for senses 1–4): **homogenous**.
▸ **homogeneity** (ˌhəʊməʊdʒɪˈniːɪtɪ, ˌhɒm-) NOUN
▸ **ˌhomoˈgeneously** ADVERB ▸ **ˌhomoˈgeneousness** NOUN

homogenize *or* **homogenise** (hɒˈmɒdʒɪˌnaɪz) VERB 1 (*tr*) to break up the fat globules in (milk or cream) so that they are evenly distributed. 2 to make or become homogeneous.
▸ **hoˌmogeniˈzation** *or* **hoˌmogeniˈsation** NOUN
▸ **hoˈmogeˌnizer** *or* **hoˈmogeˌniser** NOUN

homogenous (həˈmɒdʒɪnəs) ADJECTIVE 1 another word for **homogeneous** (senses 1–4). 2 of, relating to, or exhibiting homogeny.

homogeny (hɒˈmɒdʒɪnɪ) NOUN *Biology* similarity in structure of individuals or parts because of common ancestry.
▷HISTORY C19: from Greek *homogeneia* community of origin, from *homogenēs* of the same kind

homogony (hɒˈmɒgənɪ) NOUN the condition in a plant of having stamens and styles of the same length in all the flowers. Compare **heterogony** (sense 2).
▸ **hoˈmogonous** ADJECTIVE ▸ **hoˈmogonously** ADVERB

homograft (ˈhɒməˌgrɑːft) NOUN a tissue graft obtained from an organism of the same species as the recipient.

homograph (ˈhɒməˌgræf, -ˌgrɑːf) NOUN one of a group of words spelt in the same way but having different meanings. Compare **heteronym**.
▸ **ˌhomoˈgraphic** ADJECTIVE

homoio- COMBINING FORM a variant of **homeo-**.

homoiothermic (həʊˌmɔɪəˈθɜːmɪk) *or* **homothermal** ADJECTIVE (of birds and mammals) having a constant body temperature, usually higher than the temperature of the surroundings; warm-blooded. Compare **poikilothermic**.
▸ **hoˈmoioˌthermy** *or* **ˈhomoˌthermy** NOUN

Homoiousian (ˌhəʊmɔɪˈuːsɪən, -ˈaʊ-, ˌhɒm-) NOUN 1 a Christian who believes that the Son is of like (and not identical) substance with the Father. Compare **Homoousian**. ◆ ADJECTIVE 2 of or relating to the Homoiousians.
▷HISTORY C18: from Late Greek *homoiousios* of like substance, from Greek *homoio-* like + *ousia* nature
▸ **ˌHomoiˈousianism** NOUN

homologate (hɒˈmɒləˌgeɪt) VERB (*tr*) 1 *Law, chiefly Scots* to approve or ratify (a deed or contract, esp one that is defective). 2 *Law* to confirm (a proceeding, etc.). 3 to recognize (a particular type of car or car component) as a production model or component rather than a prototype, as in making it eligible for a motor race.
▷HISTORY C17: from Medieval Latin *homologāre* to agree, from Greek *homologein* to approve, from *homologos* agreeing, from HOMO- + *legein* to speak
▸ **hoˌmoloˈgation** NOUN

homologize *or* **homologise** (hɒˈmɒləˌdʒaɪz) VERB to be, show to be, or make homologous.
▸ **hoˈmoloˌgizer** *or* **hoˈmoloˌgiser** NOUN

homologous (həʊˈmɒləgəs, hɒ-), **homological** (ˌhəʊməˈlɒdʒɪkᵊl, ˌhɒm-), *or* **homologic** ADJECTIVE 1 having a related or similar position, structure, etc. 2 *Chem* (of a series of organic compounds) having similar characteristics and structure but differing by a number of CH_2 groups. 3 *Med* **a** (of two or more tissues) identical in structure. **b** (of a vaccine) prepared from the infecting microorganism. 4 *Biology* (of organs and parts) having the same evolutionary origin but different functions: *the wing of a bat and the paddle of a whale are homologous*. Compare **analogous** (sense 2). 5 *Maths* (of elements) playing a similar role in distinct figures or functions.
▸ **ˌhomoˈlogically** ADVERB

homologous chromosomes PLURAL NOUN two chromosomes, one of paternal origin, the other of maternal origin, that are identical in appearance and pair during meiosis.

homolographic (həʊˌmɒləˈgræfɪk) *or* **homalographic** ADJECTIVE *Cartography* another term for **equal-area**.

homologue *or sometimes US* **homolog** (ˈhɒməˌlɒg) NOUN 1 *Biology* a homologous part or organ. 2 *Chem* any homologous compound.

homology (həʊˈmɒlədʒɪ) NOUN, *plural* **-gies**. 1 the condition of being homologous. 2 *Chem* the similarities in chemical behaviour shown by members of a homologous series. 3 *Zoology* the measurable likenesses between animals, as used in grouping them according to the theory of cladistics.
▷HISTORY C17: from Greek *homologia* agreement, from *homologos* agreeing; see HOMOLOGATE

homolosine projection (hɒˈmɒləˌsaɪn) NOUN a map projection of the world on which the oceans are distorted to allow for greater accuracy in representing the continents, combining the sinusoidal and equal-area projections.
▷HISTORY C20: from HOMOLOGRAPHIC + SINE[1]

homolysis (hɒˈmɒlɪsɪs) NOUN the dissociation of a molecule into two neutral fragments. Also called: **homolytic fission**. Compare **heterolysis** (sense 2).
▸ **homolytic** (ˌhəʊməʊˈlɪtɪk, ˌhɒm-) ADJECTIVE

homomorphism (ˌhəʊməʊˈmɔːfɪzəm, ˌhɒm-) *or* **homomorphy** NOUN *Biology* similarity in form.
▸ **ˌhomoˈmorphic** *or* **ˌhomoˈmorphous** ADJECTIVE

homonym (ˈhɒmənɪm) NOUN 1 one of a group of words pronounced or spelt in the same way but having different meanings. Compare **homograph**, **homophone**. 2 a person with the same name as another. 3 *Biology* a name for a species or genus that should be unique but has been used for two or more different organisms.
▷HISTORY C17: from Latin *homōnymum*, from Greek *homōnumon*, from *homōnumos* of the same name; see HOMO-, -ONYM
▸ **ˌhomoˈnymic** *or* **hoˈmonymous** ADJECTIVE ▸ **ˌhomoˈnymity** *or* **hoˈmonymy** NOUN

Homoousian (ˌhəʊməʊˈuːsɪən, -ˈaʊ-, ˌhɒm-) NOUN 1 a Christian who believes that the Son is of the same substance as the Father. Compare **Homoiousian**. ◆ ADJECTIVE 2 of or relating to the Homoousians.
▷HISTORY C16: from Late Greek *homoousios* of the same substance, from Greek HOMO- + *ousia* nature
▸ **ˌHomoˈousianism** NOUN

homophile (ˈhəʊməˌfaɪl, ˈhɒm-) NOUN a rare word for **homosexual**.

homophobia (ˌhəʊməʊˈfəʊbɪə) NOUN intense hatred or fear of homosexuals or homosexuality.
▷HISTORY C20: from HOMO(SEXUAL) + -PHOBIA
▸ **ˈhomoˌphobe** NOUN ▸ **ˌhomoˈphobic** ADJECTIVE

homophone (ˈhɒməˌfəʊn) NOUN 1 one of a group of words pronounced in the same way but differing in meaning or spelling or both, as for example *bear* and *bare*. 2 a written letter or combination of letters that represents the same speech sound as another: *"ph" is a homophone of "f" in English*.

homophonic (ˌhɒməˈfɒnɪk) ADJECTIVE 1 of or relating to homophony. 2 of or relating to music in which the parts move together rather than independently.
▸ **ˌhomoˈphonically** ADVERB

homophonous (hɒˈmɒfənəs) ADJECTIVE of, relating to, or denoting a homophone.

homophony (hɒˈmɒfənɪ) NOUN 1 the linguistic phenomenon whereby words of different origins become identical in pronunciation. 2 part music composed in a homophonic style.

homophyly (hɒˈmɒfəlɪ) NOUN resemblance due to common ancestry.
▷HISTORY C19: from Greek, from HOMO- + PHYLUM
▸ **homophyllic** (ˌhəʊməˈfɪlɪk, ˌhɒm-) ADJECTIVE

homoplastic (ˌhəʊməʊˈplæstɪk, ˌhɒm-) ADJECTIVE 1 (of a tissue graft) derived from an individual of the same species as the recipient. 2 another word for **analogous** (sense 2).
▸ **ˌhomoˈplastically** ADVERB ▸ **ˈhomoˌplasty** NOUN
▸ **homoplasy** (ˈhəʊməʊˌpleɪsɪ, ˈhɒm-) NOUN

homopolar (ˌhəʊməʊˈpəʊlə) ADJECTIVE *Chem* of uniform charge; not ionic; covalent: *a homopolar bond*.
▸ **homopolarity** (ˌhəʊməʊpəʊˈlærɪtɪ, ˌhɒm-) NOUN

homopterous (həʊˈmɒptərəs) *or* **homopteran** ADJECTIVE of, relating to, or belonging to the *Homoptera*, a suborder of hemipterous insects, including cicadas, aphids, and scale insects, having

wings of a uniform texture held over the back at rest. Compare **heteropterous.**
▷HISTORY C19: from Greek *homopteros,* from HOMO- + *pteron* wing

homorganic (ˌhəʊmɔːˈgænɪk, ˌhɒm-) ADJECTIVE *Phonetics* (of a consonant) articulated at the same point in the vocal tract as a consonant in a different class. Thus ŋ is the homorganic nasal of *k.*

Homo sapiens (ˈsæpɪˌɛnz) NOUN the specific name of modern man; the only extant species of the genus *Homo.* This species also includes extinct types of primitive man such as Cro-Magnon man. See also **man** (sense 5).
▷HISTORY New Latin, from Latin *homo* man + *sapiens* wise

homoscedastic (ˌhəʊməʊskɪˈdæstɪk) ADJECTIVE *Statistics* 1 (of several distributions) having equal variance. 2 (of a bivariate or multivariate distribution) having one variable whose variance is the same for all values of the other or others. 3 (of a random variable) having this property. ◆ Compare **heteroscedastic.**
▷HISTORY C20: from HOMO- + *scedastic,* from Greek *skedasis* a scattering, dispersal
▸**homoscedasticity** (ˌhəʊməʊskɪdæsˈtɪsɪtɪ) NOUN

homosexual (ˌhəʊməʊˈsɛksjʊəl, ˌhɒm-) NOUN 1 a person who is sexually attracted to members of the same sex. ◆ ADJECTIVE 2 of or relating to homosexuals or homosexuality. 3 of or relating to the same sex. ◆ Compare **heterosexual.**

homosexuality (ˌhəʊməʊˌsɛksjʊˈælɪtɪ, ˌhɒm-) NOUN sexual attraction to or sexual relations with members of the same sex. Compare **heterosexuality.**

homosocial (ˌhəʊməʊˈsəʊʃəl) ADJECTIVE relating to or denoting same-sex social relationships. ◆ Compare **heterosocial.**
▸**homosociality** (ˌhəʊməʊˌsəʊʃɪˈælɪtɪ) NOUN

homosporous (hɒˈmɒspərəs, ˌhəʊməʊˈspɔːrəs) ADJECTIVE (of most ferns and some other spore-bearing plants) producing spores of one kind only, which develop into hermaphrodite gametophytes. Compare **heterosporous.**
▸**homospory** (həʊˈmɒspərɪ) NOUN

homotaxis (ˌhəʊməʊˈtæksɪs, ˌhɒm-) NOUN similarity of composition and arrangement in rock strata of different ages or in different regions.
▸ˌ**homoˈtaxic** *or* ˌ**homoˈtaxial** ADJECTIVE ▸ˌ**homoˈtaxially** ADVERB

homothallic (ˌhəʊməʊˈθælɪk) ADJECTIVE (of some algae and fungi) having both male and female reproductive organs on the same thallus, which can be self-fertilizing. Compare **heterothallic.**
▷HISTORY C20: from HOMO- + Greek *thallos* green shoot
▸ˌ**homoˈthallism** NOUN

homothermal (ˌhəʊməʊˈθɜːməl, ˌhɒm-) ADJECTIVE another word for **homoiothermic.**

homozygote (ˌhəʊməʊˈzaɪgəʊt, -ˈzɪg-, ˌhɒm-) NOUN an animal or plant that is homozygous and breeds true to type. Compare **heterozygote.**
▸ˌ**homozyˈgosis** NOUN ▸**homozygotic** (ˌhəʊməʊzaɪˈgɒtɪk, -zɪ-, ˌhɒm-) ADJECTIVE

homozygous (ˌhəʊməʊˈzaɪgəs, -ˈzɪg-, ˌhɒm-) ADJECTIVE *Genetics* (of an organism) having identical alleles for any one gene: *these two fruit flies are homozygous for red eye colour.* Compare **heterozygous.**
▸ˌ**homoˈzygously** ADVERB

Homs (hɒms) *or* **Hums** (hʊms) NOUN a city in W Syria, near the Orontes River: important in Roman times as the capital of Phoenicia-Lebanesia. Pop.: 644 204 (1994 est.). Ancient name: **Emesa** (ˈɛmɛsə). Former name: **Hims.**

homunculus (hɒˈmʌŋkjʊləs) NOUN, *plural* **-li** (-ˌlaɪ). 1 a miniature man; midget. 2 (in early biological theory) a fully-formed miniature human being existing in a spermatozoon or egg. ◆ Also called: **homuncule** (həʊˈmʌŋkjuːl).
▷HISTORY C17: from Latin, diminutive of *homo* man
▸**hoˈmuncular** ADJECTIVE

homy *or esp US* **homey** (ˈhəʊmɪ) ADJECTIVE **homier, homiest.** like a home, esp in comfort or informality; cosy.
▸ˈ**hominess** *or esp US* ˈ**homeyness** NOUN

hon. ABBREVIATION FOR: 1 honorary. 2 honourable.

Hon. ABBREVIATION FOR Honourable (title).

honan (ˈhəʊˈnæn) NOUN (*sometimes capital*) a silk fabric of rough weave.
▷HISTORY C20: from *Honan,* former name of HENAN, where it is made

Honan (ˈhəʊˈnæn) NOUN a variant transliteration of the Chinese name for **Henan.**

honcho (ˈhɒntʃəʊ) *Informal, chiefly US* ◆ NOUN, *plural* **-chos.** 1 the person in charge; the boss. ◆ VERB 2 to supervise or be in charge of.
▷HISTORY C20: from Japanese *han'chō* group leader

Hond. ABBREVIATION FOR Honduras.

Hondo (ˈhɒndəʊ) NOUN another name for **Honshu.**

Honduran (hɒnˈdjʊərən) ADJECTIVE 1 of or relating to Honduras or its inhabitants. ◆ NOUN 2 a native or inhabitant of Honduras.

Honduras (hɒnˈdjʊərəs) NOUN 1 a republic in Central America: an early centre of Mayan civilization; colonized by the Spanish from 1524 onwards; gained independence in 1821. Official language: Spanish; English is also widely spoken. Religion: Roman Catholic majority. Currency: lempira. Capital: Tegucigalpa. Pop.: 6 626 000 (2001 est.). Area: 112 088 sq. km (43 277 sq. miles). 2 **Gulf of.** an inlet of the Caribbean, on the coasts of Honduras, Guatemala, and Belize.

hone[1] (həʊn) NOUN 1 a fine whetstone, esp for sharpening razors. 2 a tool consisting of a number of fine abrasive slips held in a machine head, rotated and reciprocated to impart a smooth finish to cylinder bores, etc. ◆ VERB 3 (*tr*) to sharpen or polish with or as if with a hone.
▷HISTORY Old English *hān* stone; related to Old Norse *hein*

> **Language note** *Hone* is sometimes wrongly used where *home* is meant: *this device makes it easier to home in on* (not *hone in on*) *the target.*

hone[2] (həʊn) VERB (*intr*) *Dialect* 1 (often foll by *for* or *after*) to yearn or pine. 2 to moan or grieve.
▷HISTORY C17: from Old French *hogner* to growl, probably of Germanic origin; compare Old High German *hōnen* to revile

honest (ˈɒnɪst) ADJECTIVE 1 not given to lying, cheating, stealing, etc.; trustworthy. 2 not false or misleading; genuine. 3 just or fair: *honest wages.* 4 characterized by sincerity and candour: *an honest appraisal.* 5 without pretensions or artificial traits: *honest farmers.* 6 *Archaic* (of a woman) respectable. 7 **honest broker.** a mediator in disputes, esp international ones. 8 **make an honest woman of.** to marry (a woman, esp one who is pregnant) to prevent scandal. 9 **honest Injun.** (*interjection*) *School slang* genuinely, really. 10 **honest to God** (*or* **goodness**). **a** (*adjective*) completely authentic. **b** (*interjection*) an expression of affirmation or surprise.
▷HISTORY C13: from Old French *honeste,* from Latin *honestus* distinguished, from *honōs* HONOUR
▸ˈ**honestness** NOUN

honestly (ˈɒnɪstlɪ) ADVERB 1 in an honest manner. 2 (intensifier): *I honestly don't believe it.* ◆ INTERJECTION 3 an expression of disgust, surprise, etc.

honesty (ˈɒnɪstɪ) NOUN, *plural* **-ties.** 1 the condition of being honest. 2 sincerity or fairness. 3 *Archaic* virtue or respect. 4 a purple-flowered SE European plant, *Lunaria annua,* cultivated for its flattened silvery pods, which are used for indoor decoration: family *Brassicaceae* (crucifers). Also called: **moonwort, satinpod.**

honesty box NOUN a container into which members of the public are trusted to place payments when there is no attendant to collect them.

honewort (ˈhəʊnˌwɜːt) NOUN 1 a European umbelliferous plant, *Trinia glauca,* with clusters of small white flowers. 2 any of several similar and related plants.
▷HISTORY C17: apparently from obsolete dialect *hone* a swelling, of obscure origin; the plant was believed to relieve swellings

honey (ˈhʌnɪ) NOUN 1 a sweet viscid substance made by bees from nectar and stored in their nests or hives as food. It is spread on bread or used as a sweetening agent. 2 any similar sweet substance, esp the nectar of flowers. 3 anything that is sweet or delightful. 4 (*often capital*) *Chiefly US and Canadian* a term of endearment. 5 *Informal, chiefly US and Canadian* something considered to be very good of its kind: *a honey of a car.* 6 (*modifier*) of, concerned with, or resembling honey. ◆ VERB **honeys, honeying, honeyed** *or* **honied.** 7 (*tr*) to sweeten with or as if with honey. 8 (often foll by *up*) to talk to (someone) in a fond or flattering way.
▷HISTORY Old English *huneg;* related to Old Norse *hunang,* Old Saxon *hanig,* German *Honig,* Greek *knēkos* yellowish, Sanskrit *kánaka-* gold
▸ˈ**honey-ˌlike** ADJECTIVE

honey badger NOUN another name for **ratel.**

honey bear NOUN another name for **kinkajou** (sense 1) or **sun bear.**

honeybee (ˈhʌnɪˌbiː) NOUN any of various social honey-producing bees of the genus *Apis,* esp *A. mellifera,* which has been widely domesticated as a source of honey and beeswax. Also called: **hive bee.**

honeybunch (ˈhʌnɪˌbʌntʃ) *or* **honeybun** (ˈhʌnɪˌbʌn) NOUN *Informal, chiefly US* honey; darling: a term of endearment.

honey buzzard NOUN a common European bird of prey, *Pernis apivorus,* having broad wings and a typically dull brown plumage with white-streaked underparts: family *Accipitridae* (hawks, buzzards, etc.). It feeds on grubs and honey from bees' nests.

honeycomb (ˈhʌnɪˌkəʊm) NOUN 1 a waxy structure, constructed by bees in a hive, that consists of adjacent hexagonal cells in which honey is stored, eggs are laid, and larvae develop. 2 something resembling this in structure or appearance. 3 *Zoology* another name for **reticulum** (sense 2). ◆ VERB (*tr*) 4 to pierce or fill with holes, cavities, etc. 5 to permeate: *honeycombed with spies.*

honeycomb moth NOUN another name for the **wax moth.**

honey creeper NOUN 1 any small tropical American songbird of the genus *Dacnis* and related genera, closely related to the tanagers and buntings, having a slender downward-curving bill and feeding on nectar. 2 any bird of the family *Drepanididae* of Hawaii.

honeydew (ˈhʌnɪˌdjuː) NOUN 1 a sugary substance excreted by aphids and similar insects. 2 a similar substance exuded by certain plants. 3 short for **honeydew melon.**
▸ˈ**honeyˌdewed** ADJECTIVE

honeydew melon NOUN a variety of muskmelon with a smooth greenish-white rind and sweet greenish flesh.

honey-eater (ˈhʌnɪˌiːtə) NOUN any small arboreal songbird of the Australasian family *Meliphagidae,* having a downward-curving bill and a brushlike tongue specialized for extracting nectar from flowers.

honeyed *or* **honied** (ˈhʌnɪd) ADJECTIVE *Poetic* 1 flattering or soothing. 2 made sweet or agreeable: *honeyed words.* 3 of, full of, or resembling honey.
▸ˈ**honeyedly** *or* ˈ**honiedly** ADVERB

honey fungus NOUN an edible basidiomycetous fungus, *Armillaria mellea,* having a yellow-spotted cap and wrinkled stems, parasitic on the roots of woody plants, which it may kill by root rot. It spreads by thin black underground strands. Also called: **bootlace fungus.**

honey guide NOUN any small bird of the family *Indicatoridae,* inhabiting tropical forests of Africa and Asia and feeding on beeswax, honey, and insects: order *Piciformes* (woodpeckers, etc.).

honey locust NOUN 1 a thorny leguminous tree, *Gleditsia triacanthos* of E North America, that has long pods containing a sweet-tasting pulp. 2 another name for **mesquite.**

honey mesquite NOUN another name for **mesquite.**

honeymoon (ˈhʌnɪˌmuːn) NOUN 1 **a** a holiday taken by a newly married couple. **b** (*as modifier*): *a honeymoon cottage.* 2 a holiday considered to resemble a honeymoon: *a second honeymoon.* 3 the early, usually calm period of a relationship, such as a political or business one. ◆ VERB 4 (*intr*) to take a honeymoon.
▷HISTORY C16: traditionally explained as an

allusion to the feelings of married couples as changing with the phases of the moon
▸ **'honey,mooner** NOUN

honey mouse *or* **phalanger** NOUN a small agile Australian marsupial, *Tarsipes spenserae,* having dark-striped pale brown fur, a long prehensile tail, and a very long snout and tongue with which it feeds on honey, pollen, and insects: family *Phalangeridae*. Also called: **honeysucker.**

honey plant NOUN any of various plants that are particularly useful in providing bees with nectar.

honeypot ('hʌnɪ,pɒt) NOUN 1 a container for honey. 2 something which attracts people in great numbers: *Cornwall is a honeypot for tourists.*

honeysucker ('hʌnɪ,sʌkə) NOUN 1 any bird, esp a honey-eater, that feeds on nectar. 2 another name for **honey mouse.**

honeysuckle ('hʌnɪ,sʌk^{ə}l) NOUN 1 any temperate caprifoliaceous shrub or vine of the genus *Lonicera:* cultivated for their fragrant white, yellow, or pink tubular flowers. 2 any of several similar plants. 3 any of various Australian trees or shrubs of the genus *Banksia,* having flowers in dense spikes: family *Proteaceae.*
▹HISTORY Old English *hunigsūce,* from HONEY + SUCK; see SUCKLE
▸ **'honey,suckled** ADJECTIVE

honeysuckle ornament NOUN *Arts* another term for **anthemion.**

honey-sweet ADJECTIVE sweet or endearing.

honeytrap ('hʌnɪ,træp) NOUN *Informal* a scheme in which a victim is lured into a compromising sexual situation to provide an opportunity for blackmail.

hong (hɒŋ) NOUN 1 (in China) a factory, warehouse, etc. 2 (formerly, in Canton) a foreign commercial establishment.
▹HISTORY C18: from Chinese (Cantonese dialect)

hongi ('hɒŋi:) NOUN *NZ* a form of salutation expressed by touching noses.
▹HISTORY Maori

Hong Kong (,hɒŋ 'kɒŋ) NOUN 1 a Special Administrative Region of S China, with some autonomy; formerly a British Crown Colony: consists of Hong Kong Island, leased by China to Britain from 1842 until 1997, Kowloon Peninsula, Stonecutters Island, the New Territories (mainland), leased by China in 1898 for a 99-year period, and over 230 small islands; important entrepôt trade and manufacturing centre, esp for textiles and other consumer goods; university (1912). Administrative centre: Victoria. Pop.: 6 732 000 (2001 est.). Area: 1046 sq. km (404 sq. miles). 2 an island in Hong Kong region, south of Kowloon Peninsula: contains the capital, Victoria. Pop.: 1 337 800 (2001). Area: 75 sq. km (29 sq. miles).

Honiara (,həʊnɪ'ɑ:rə) NOUN the capital of the Solomon Islands, on NW Guadalcanal Island. Pop.: 50 100 (2000 est.).

honied ('hʌnɪd) ADJECTIVE a variant spelling of **honeyed.**
▸ **'honiedly** ADVERB

honi soit qui mal y pense *French* (ɔni swa ki mal i pɑ̃s) shamed be he who thinks evil of it: the motto of the Order of the Garter.

Honiton ('hɒnɪt^{ə}n, 'hʌn-) *or* **Honiton lace** NOUN a type of lace with a floral sprig pattern.
▹HISTORY C19: named after *Honiton,* Devon, where it was first made

honk (hɒŋk) NOUN 1 a representation of the sound made by a goose. 2 any sound resembling this, esp a motor horn. ◆ VERB 3 to make or cause (something) to make such a sound. 4 (*intr*) *Brit* a slang word for **vomit.**

honker ('hɒŋkə) NOUN 1 a person or thing that honks. 2 *Canadian* an informal name for the **Canada goose.** 3 *Slang* a nose, esp a large nose.

honky ('hɒŋkɪ) NOUN, *plural* **honkies.** *Derogatory slang, chiefly US* a White man or White men collectively.
▹HISTORY C20: of unknown origin

honky-tonk ('hɒŋkɪ,tɒŋk) NOUN 1 *US and Canadian slang* **a** a cheap disreputable nightclub, bar, etc. **b** (*as modifier*): *a honky-tonk district.* 2 a style of ragtime piano-playing, esp on a tinny-sounding piano. 3 a type of country music, usually performed by a small band with electric and steel guitars. 4 (*as modifier*): *honky-tonk music.*
▹HISTORY C19: rhyming compound based on HONK

Honolulu (,hɒnə'lu:lu:) NOUN a port in Hawaii, on S Oahu Island: the state capital. Pop.: 371 657 (2000).

honor ('ɒnə) NOUN, VERB the US spelling of **honour.**

honorarium (,ɒnə'rɛərɪəm) NOUN, *plural* **-iums** *or* **-ia** (-ɪə). a fee paid for a nominally free service.
▹HISTORY C17: from Latin: something presented on being admitted to a post of HONOUR

honorary ('ɒnərərɪ, 'ɒnrərɪ) ADJECTIVE (*usually prenominal*) 1 **a** (esp of a position, title, etc.) held or given only as an honour, without the normal privileges or duties: *an honorary degree.* **b** (of a secretary, treasurer, etc.) unpaid. 2 having such a position or title. 3 depending on honour rather than legal agreement.

honorific (,ɒnə'rɪfɪk) ADJECTIVE 1 showing or conferring honour or respect. 2 **a** (of a pronoun, verb inflection, etc.) indicating the speaker's respect for the addressee or his acknowledgment of inferior status. **b** (*as noun*): *a Japanese honorific.*
▸ **,honor'ifically** ADVERB

honoris causa *Latin* (hɒ'nɔ:rɪs 'kaʊzɑ:) for the sake of honour.

honour *or US* **honor** ('ɒnə) NOUN 1 personal integrity; allegiance to moral principles. 2 **a** fame or glory. **b** a person or thing that wins this for another: *he is an honour to the school.* 3 (*often plural*) great respect, regard, esteem, etc., or an outward sign of this. 4 (*often plural*) high or noble rank. 5 a privilege or pleasure: *it is an honour to serve you.* 6 a woman's virtue or chastity. 7 **a** *Bridge, poker* any of the top five cards in a suit or any of the four aces at no trumps. **b** *Whist* any of the top four cards. 8 *Golf* the right to tee off first. 9 **do honour to. a** to pay homage to. **b** to be a credit to. 10 **do the honours. a** to serve as host or hostess. **b** to perform a social act, such as carving meat, proposing a toast, etc. 11 **honour bright.** *Brit school slang* an exclamation pledging honour. 12 **in honour bound.** under a moral obligation. 13 **in honour of.** out of respect for. 14 **on** (*or*) **upon one's honour.** on the pledge of one's word or good name. ◆ VERB (*tr*) 15 to hold in respect or esteem. 16 to show courteous behaviour towards. 17 to worship. 18 to confer a distinction upon. 19 to accept and then pay when due (a cheque, draft, etc.). 20 to keep (one's promise); fulfil (a previous agreement). 21 to bow or curtsy to (one's dancing partner). ◆ See also **honours.**
▹HISTORY C12: from Old French *onor,* from Latin *honor* esteem
▸ **'honourer** *or US* **'honorer** NOUN ▸ **'honourless** *or US* **'honorless** ADJECTIVE

Honour ('ɒnə) NOUN (preceded by *Your, His,* or *Her*) **a** a title used to or of certain judges. **b** (in Ireland) a form of address in general use.

honourable *or US* **honorable** ('ɒnərəb^{ə}l, 'ɒnrəb^{ə}l) ADJECTIVE 1 possessing or characterized by high principles: *honourable intentions.* 2 worthy of or entitled to honour or esteem. 3 consistent with or bestowing honour.
▸ **'honourableness** *or US* **'honorableness** NOUN
▸ **'honourably** *or US* **'honorably** ADVERB

Honourable *or US* **Honorable** ('ɒnərəb^{ə}l, 'ɒnrəb^{ə}l) ADJECTIVE (*prenominal*) **the.** a title of respect placed before a name: employed before the names of various officials in the English-speaking world, as a courtesy title in Britain for the children of viscounts and barons and the younger sons of earls, and in Parliament by one member speaking of another. Abbreviation: **Hon.**

honourable discharge NOUN See **discharge** (sense 15).

Honour Moderations PLURAL NOUN (at Oxford University) the first public examination, in which candidates are placed into one of three classes of honours. Sometimes shortened to **Moderations** *or* **Mods.**

honours *or US* **honors** ('ɒnəz) PLURAL NOUN 1 observances of respect. 2 (*often capital*) **a** (in a university degree or degree course) a rank of the highest academic standard. **b** (*as modifier*): *an honours degree.* Abbreviation: **Hons.** Compare **general** (sense 9), **pass** (sense 35). 3 a high mark awarded for an examination; distinction. 4 **last** (*or* **funeral**) **honours.** observances of respect at a funeral. 5 **military honours.** ceremonies performed by troops in honour of royalty, at the burial of an officer, etc.

honour school NOUN (at Oxford University) one of the courses of study leading to an honours degree.

honours list NOUN *Brit* a list of those who have had or are having an honour, esp a peerage or membership of an order of chivalry, conferred on them.

honours of war PLURAL NOUN *Military* the honours granted by the victorious to the defeated, esp as of marching out with all arms and flags flying.

Hons (ɑnz) NOUN short for **honours** (sense 2).

Hon. Sec. ABBREVIATION FOR Honorary Secretary.

Honshu ('hɒnʃu:) NOUN the largest of the four main islands of Japan, between the Pacific and the Sea of Japan; regarded as the Japanese mainland; includes a number of offshore islands and contains most of the main cities. Pop.: 100 995 000 (1995). Area: 230 448 sq. km (88 976 sq. miles). Also called: **Hondo.**

hoo (hu:) PRONOUN *West Yorkshire and south Lancashire dialect* she.
▹HISTORY from Old English *heo*

hooch *or* **hootch** (hu:tʃ) NOUN *Informal, chiefly US and Canadian* alcoholic drink, esp illicitly distilled spirits.
▹HISTORY C20: shortened from Tlingit *Hootchinoo,* name of a tribe that distilled a type of liquor

hood[1] (hʊd) NOUN 1 a loose head covering either attached to a cloak or coat or made as a separate garment. 2 something resembling this in shape or use. 3 the US and Canadian name for **bonnet** (of a car). 4 the folding roof of a convertible car. 5 a hoodlike garment worn over an academic gown, indicating its wearer's degree and university. 6 *Falconry* a close-fitting cover, placed over the head and eyes of a falcon to keep it quiet when not hunting. 7 *Biology* a structure or marking, such as the fold of skin on the head of a cobra, that covers or appears to cover the head or some similar part. ◆ VERB 8 (*tr*) to cover or provide with or as if with a hood.
▹HISTORY Old English *hōd;* related to Old High German *huot* hat, Middle Dutch *hoet,* Latin *cassis* helmet; see HAT
▸ **'hoodless** ADJECTIVE ▸ **'hood,like** ADJECTIVE

hood[2] (hʊd) NOUN *Slang* short for **hoodlum** (gangster).

-hood SUFFIX FORMING NOUNS 1 indicating state or condition of being: *manhood.* 2 indicating a body of persons: *knighthood; priesthood.*
▹HISTORY Old English *-hād*

'hood (hʊd) NOUN *Slang, chiefly US* short for **neighbourhood.**

hooded ('hʊdɪd) ADJECTIVE 1 covered with, having, or shaped like a hood. 2 (of eyes) having heavy eyelids that appear to be half closed.

hooded crow NOUN a subspecies of the carrion crow, *Corvus corone cornix,* that has a grey body and black head, wings, and tail. Also called (Scot): **hoodie** ('hʊdɪ), **hoodie crow.**

hooded seal NOUN a large greyish earless seal, *Cystophora cristata,* of the N Atlantic and Arctic Oceans, having an inflatable hoodlike sac over the nasal region. Also called: **bladdernose.**

hoodia ('hʊdɪə) NOUN any of several succulent asclepiadaceous plants of the genus *Hoodia,* of southern Africa, the sap of which suppresses appetite.

hoodie ('hʊdɪ) NOUN a hooded sweatshirt.

hoodlum ('hu:dləm) NOUN 1 a petty gangster or ruffian. 2 a lawless youth.
▹HISTORY C19: perhaps from Southern German dialect *Haderlump* ragged good-for-nothing
▸ **'hoodlumism** NOUN

hoodman-blind NOUN *Brit archaic* blind man's buff.

hood mould NOUN another name for **dripstone** (sense 2).

hoodoo ('hu:du:) NOUN, *plural* **-doos.** 1 a variant of **voodoo.** 2 *Informal* a person or thing that brings bad luck. 3 *Informal* bad luck. 4 (in the western US and Canada) a strangely shaped column of rock.

◆ VERB **-doos, -dooing, -dooed.** 5 (*tr*) *Informal* to bring bad luck to.
▷HISTORY C19: variant of VOODOO
▸'**hoodooism** NOUN

hoodwink ('hʊd,wɪŋk) VERB (*tr*) 1 to dupe; trick. 2 *Obsolete* to cover or hide.
▷HISTORY C16: originally, to cover the eyes with a hood, blindfold
▸'**hood,winker** NOUN

hooey ('huːɪ) NOUN, INTERJECTION *Slang* nonsense; rubbish.
▷HISTORY C20: of unknown origin

hoof (huːf) NOUN, *plural* **hooves** (huːvz) *or* **hoofs.** 1 **a** the horny covering of the end of the foot in the horse, deer, and all other ungulate mammals. **b** (*in combination*): *a hoofbeat.* Related adjective: **ungular.** 2 the foot of an ungulate mammal. 3 a hoofed animal. 4 *Facetious* a person's foot. 5 **on the hoof. a** (of livestock) alive. **b** in an impromptu manner: *he did his thinking on the hoof.* ◆ VERB 6 (*tr*) to kick or trample with the hoofs. 7 **hoof it.** *Slang* **a** to walk. **b** to dance.
▷HISTORY Old English *hōf;* related to Old Norse *hōfr,* Old High German *huof* (German *Huf*), Sanskrit *saphás*
▸'**hoofless** ADJECTIVE ▸'**hoof,like** ADJECTIVE

hoofbound ('huːf,baʊnd) ADJECTIVE *Vet science* (of a horse) having dry contracted hooves, with resultant pain and lameness.

hoofed (huːft) ADJECTIVE **a** having a hoof or hoofs. **b** (*in combination*): *four-hoofed; cloven-hoofed.*

hoofer ('huːfə) NOUN *Slang* a professional dancer, esp a tap-dancer.

Hooghly ('huːglɪ) NOUN a river in NE India, in West Bengal: the westernmost and commercially most important channel by which the River Ganges enters the Bay of Bengal. Length: 232 km (144 miles).

hoo-ha ('huː,hɑː) NOUN a noisy commotion or fuss.
▷HISTORY C20: of unknown origin

hook (hʊk) NOUN 1 a piece of material, usually metal, curved or bent and used to suspend, catch, hold, or pull something. 2 short for **fish-hook.** 3 a trap or snare. 4 *Chiefly US* something that attracts or is intended to be an attraction. 5 something resembling a hook in design or use. 6 **a** a sharp bend or angle in a geological formation, esp a river. **b** a sharply curved spit of land. 7 *Boxing* a short swinging blow delivered from the side with the elbow bent. 8 *Cricket* a shot in which the ball is hit square on the leg side with the bat held horizontally. 9 *Golf* a shot that causes the ball to swerve sharply from right to left. 10 *Surfing* the top of a breaking wave. 11 Also called: **hookcheck.** *Ice hockey* the act of hooking an opposing player. 12 *Music* a stroke added to the stem of a written or printed note to indicate time values shorter than a crotchet. 13 a catchy musical phrase in a pop song. 14 another name for a **sickle.** 15 a nautical word for **anchor.** 16 **by hook or** (**by**) **crook.** by any means. 17 **get the hook.** *US and Canadian slang* to be dismissed from employment. 18 **hook, line, and sinker.** *Informal* completely: *he fell for it hook, line, and sinker.* 19 **off the hook. a** *Slang* out of danger; free from obligation or guilt. **b** (of a telephone receiver) not on the support, so that incoming calls cannot be received. 20 **on one's own hook.** *Slang, chiefly US* on one's own initiative. 21 **on the hook.** *Slang* **a** waiting. **b** in a dangerous or difficult situation. 22 **sling one's hook.** *Brit slang* to leave. ◆ VERB 23 (often foll by *up*) to fasten or be fastened with or as if with a hook or hooks. 24 (*tr*) to catch (something, such as a fish) on a hook. 25 to curve like or into the shape of a hook. 26 (*tr*) (of bulls, elks, etc.) to catch or gore with the horns. 27 (*tr*) to make (a rug) by hooking yarn through a stiff fabric backing with a special instrument. 28 (*tr;* often foll by *down*) to cut (grass or herbage) with a sickle: *to hook down weeds.* 29 *Boxing* to hit (an opponent) with a hook. 30 *Ice hockey* to impede (an opposing player) by catching hold of him with the stick. 31 *Golf* to play (a ball) with a hook. 32 *Rugby* to obtain and pass (the ball) backwards from a scrum to a member of one's team, using the feet. 33 *Cricket* to play (a ball) with a hook. 34 (*tr*) *Informal* to trick. 35 (*tr*) a slang word for **steal.** 36 **hook it.** *Slang* to run or go quickly away. ◆ See also **hook-up.**
▷HISTORY Old English *hōc;* related to Middle Dutch *hōk,* Old Norse *haki*
▸'**hookless** ADJECTIVE ▸'**hook,like** ADJECTIVE

hookah *or* **hooka** ('hʊkə) NOUN an oriental pipe for smoking marijuana, tobacco, etc., consisting of one or more long flexible stems connected to a container of water or other liquid through which smoke is drawn and cooled. Also called: **hubble-bubble, kalian, narghile, water pipe.**
▷HISTORY C18: from Arabic *huqqah*

hook and eye NOUN a fastening for clothes consisting of a small hook hooked onto a small metal or thread loop.

hooked (hʊkt) ADJECTIVE 1 bent like a hook. 2 having a hook or hooks. 3 caught or trapped. 4 a slang word for **married.** 5 *Slang* addicted to a drug. 6 (often foll by *on*) obsessed (with).
▸**hookedness** ('hʊkɪdnɪs) NOUN

hooker[1] ('hʊkə) NOUN 1 a commercial fishing boat using hooks and lines instead of nets. 2 a sailing boat of the west of Ireland formerly used for cargo and now for pleasure sailing and racing.
▷HISTORY C17: from Dutch *hoeker*

hooker[2] ('hʊkə) NOUN 1 a person or thing that hooks. 2 *US and Canadian slang* **a** a draught of alcoholic drink, esp of spirits. **b** a prostitute. 3 *Rugby* the central forward in the front row of a scrum whose main job is to hook the ball.

Hooke's law NOUN the principle that the stress imposed on a solid is directly proportional to the strain produced, within the elastic limit.
▷HISTORY C18: named after Robert *Hooke* (1635–1703), English physicist, chemist, and inventor

hooknose ('hʊk,nəʊz) NOUN a nose with a pronounced outward and downward curve; aquiline nose.
▸'**hook,nosed** ADJECTIVE

Hook of Holland NOUN **the.** 1 a cape on the SW coast of the Netherlands, in South Holland province. 2 a port on this cape. ◆ Dutch name: **Hoek van Holland.**

hook-tip NOUN 1 any of several moths of the genus *Daepana,* characterized by the hooked point on each forewing. 2 **beautiful hook-tip.** a similar but unrelated species, *Laspeyria flexula.*

hook-up NOUN 1 the contact of an aircraft in flight with the refuelling hose of a tanker aircraft. 2 an alliance or relationship, esp an unlikely one, between people, countries, etc. 3 the linking of broadcasting equipment or stations to transmit a special programme. ◆ VERB **hook up.** (*adverb*) 4 to connect (two or more people or things). 5 (often foll by *with*) *Slang* to get married (to).

hookworm ('hʊk,wɜːm) NOUN any parasitic blood-sucking nematode worm of the family *Ancylostomatidae,* esp *Ancylostoma duodenale* or *Necator americanus,* both of which cause disease. They have hooked mouthparts and enter their hosts by boring through the skin.

hookworm disease NOUN the nontechnical name for **ancylostomiasis.**

hooky *or* **hookey** ('hʊkɪ) NOUN *Informal, chiefly US, Canadian, and NZ* truancy, usually from school (esp in the phrase **play hooky**).
▷HISTORY C20: perhaps from *hook it* to escape

hooley *or* **hoolie** ('huːlɪ) NOUN, *plural* **-leys** *or* **-lies.** *Chiefly Irish and NZ* a lively party.
▷HISTORY C19: of unknown origin

hoolie ('huːlɪ) NOUN *Slang* a hooligan.

hooligan ('huːlɪgən) NOUN *Slang* a rough lawless young person.
▷HISTORY C19: perhaps variant of *Houlihan,* Irish surname
▸'**hooliganism** NOUN

hoon (huːn) NOUN *Austral and NZ informal* a hooligan.
▷HISTORY of unknown origin

hoop[1] (huːp) NOUN 1 a rigid circular band of metal or wood. 2 something resembling this. 3 **a** a band of iron that holds the staves of a barrel or cask together. **b** (*as modifier*): *hoop iron.* 4 a child's toy shaped like a hoop and rolled on the ground or whirled around the body. 5 *Croquet* any of the iron arches through which the ball is driven. 6 **a** a light curved frame to spread out a skirt. **b** (*as modifier*): *a hoop skirt; a hoop petticoat.* 7 *Basketball* the round metal frame to which the net is attached to form the basket. 8 a large ring through which performers or animals jump. 9 *Jewellery* **a** an earring consisting of one or more circles of metal, plastic, etc. **b** the part of a finger ring through which the finger fits. 10 *Austral informal* a jockey. 11 **go** *or* **be put through the hoop.** to be subjected to an ordeal. ◆ VERB 12 (*tr*) to surround with or as if with a hoop.
▷HISTORY Old English *hōp;* related to Dutch *hoep,* Old Norse *hōp* bay, Lithuanian *kabẽ* hook
▸**hooped** ADJECTIVE ▸'**hoop,like** ADJECTIVE

hoop[2] (huːp) NOUN, VERB a variant spelling of **whoop.**

hooper ('huːpə) NOUN a rare word for **cooper.**

hoopla ('huːplɑː) NOUN 1 *Brit* a fairground game in which a player tries to throw a hoop over an object and so win it. 2 *US and Canadian slang* noise; bustle. 3 *US slang* nonsense; ballyhoo.
▷HISTORY C20: see WHOOP, LA[2]

hoopoe ('huːpuː) NOUN an Old World bird, *Upupa epops,* having a pinkish-brown plumage with black-and-white wings and an erectile crest: family *Upupidae,* order *Coraciiformes* (kingfishers, etc.).
▷HISTORY C17: from earlier *hoopoop,* of imitative origin; compare Latin *upupa*

hoop pine NOUN a fast-growing timber tree of Australia, *Araucaria cunninghamii,* having rough bark with hoop-like cracks around the trunk and branches: family *Araucariaceae.*

hoop snake NOUN any of various North American snakes, such as the mud snake (*Farancia abacura*), that were formerly thought to hold the tail in the mouth and roll along like a hoop.

hooray (huːˈreɪ) INTERJECTION, NOUN, VERB 1 a variant of **hurrah.** ◆ INTERJECTION 2 Also: **hooroo** (huːˈruː). *Austral and NZ* goodbye; cheerio.

Hooray Henry ('huː,reɪ) NOUN, *plural* **Hooray Henries** *or* **-rys.** a young upper-class man, often with affectedly hearty voice and manners. Sometimes shortened to **Hooray.**

hoosegow *or* **hoosgow** ('huːsgaʊ) NOUN *US* a slang word for **jail.**
▷HISTORY C20: from Mexican Spanish *jusgado* prison, from Spanish: court of justice, from *juzgar* to judge, from Latin *jūdicāre,* from *judex* a JUDGE; compare JUG

Hoosier ('huːʒɪə) NOUN *US* a native or inhabitant of Indiana.
▷HISTORY C19: origin unknown

hoot[1] (huːt) NOUN 1 the mournful wavering cry of some owls. 2 a similar sound, such as that of a train whistle. 3 a jeer of derision. 4 *Informal* an amusing person or thing. 5 **not give a hoot.** not to care at all. ◆ VERB 6 (often foll by *at*) to jeer or yell (something) contemptuously (at someone). 7 (*tr*) to drive (political speakers, actors on stage, etc.) off or away by hooting. 8 (*intr*) to make a hoot. 9 (*intr*) *Brit* to blow a horn.
▷HISTORY C13 *hoten,* of imitative origin

hoot[2] (huːt) *or* **hoots** (huːts) INTERJECTION an exclamation of impatience or dissatisfaction: a supposed Scotticism.
▷HISTORY C17: of unknown origin

hoot[3] (huːt) NOUN *Austral and NZ* a slang word for **money.**
▷HISTORY from Maori *utu* price

hootch (huːtʃ) NOUN a variant spelling of **hooch.**

hootenanny ('huːtᵊ,nænɪ) *or* **hootnanny** ('huːt,nænɪ) NOUN, *plural* **-nies.** 1 an informal performance by folk singers. 2 *Chiefly US* something the name of which is unspecified or forgotten.
▷HISTORY C20: of unknown origin

hooter ('huːtə) NOUN *Chiefly Brit* 1 a person or thing that hoots, esp a car horn. 2 *Slang* a nose.

hoot owl NOUN any owl that utters a hooting cry, as distinct from a screech owl.

Hoover ('huːvə) NOUN 1 *Trademark* a type of vacuum cleaner. ◆ VERB (*usually not capital*) 2 to vacuum-clean (a carpet, furniture, etc.). 3 (*tr;* often foll by *up*) to consume or dispose of (something) quickly and completely: *he hoovered up his grilled fish.*

Hoover Dam NOUN a dam in the western US, on the Colorado River on the border between Nevada and Arizona; forms Lake Mead. Height: 222 m (727 ft.). Length: 354 m (1180 ft.). Former name (1933–47): **Boulder Dam.**

hooves (huːvz) NOUN a plural of **hoof.**

hop[1] (hɒp) VERB **hops, hopping, hopped.** [1] (*intr*) to make a jump forwards or upwards, esp on one foot. [2] (*intr*) (esp of frogs, birds, rabbits, etc.) to move forwards in short jumps. [3] (*tr*) to jump over: *he hopped the hedge.* [4] (*intr*) *Informal* to move or proceed quickly (in, on, out of, etc.): *hop on a bus.* [5] (*tr*) *Informal* to cross (an ocean) in an aircraft: *they hopped the Atlantic in seven hours.* [6] (*tr*) *US and Canadian informal* to travel by means of (an aircraft, bus, etc.): *he hopped a train to Chicago.* [7] *US and Canadian* to bounce or cause to bounce: *he hopped the flat stone over the lake's surface.* [8] (*intr*) *US and Canadian informal* to begin intense activity, esp work. [9] (*intr*) another word for **limp**[1]. [10] **hop it** (*or* **off**). *Brit slang* to go away. ◆ NOUN [11] the act or an instance of hopping. [12] *Old-fashioned informal* a dance, esp one at which popular music is played: *we're all going to the school hop tonight.* [13] *Informal* a trip, esp in an aircraft. [14] *US* a bounce, as of a ball. [15] **on the hop.** *Informal* **a** active or busy. **b** *Brit* unawares or unprepared: *the new ruling caught me on the hop.* ◆ See also **hop into.**
▷HISTORY Old English *hoppian;* related to Old Norse *hoppa* to hop, Middle Low German *hupfen*

hop[2] (hɒp) NOUN [1] any climbing plant of the N temperate genus *Humulus,* esp *H. lupulus,* which has green conelike female flowers and clusters of small male flowers: family *Cannabiaceae* (or *Cannabidaceae*). See also **hops.** [2] **hop garden.** a field of hops. [3] *Obsolete slang* opium or any other narcotic drug.
▷HISTORY C15: from Middle Dutch *hoppe;* related to Old High German *hopfo,* Norwegian *hupp* tassel

hop clover NOUN the US name for **hop trefoil.**

hope (həʊp) NOUN [1] (*sometimes plural*) a feeling of desire for something and confidence in the possibility of its fulfilment: *his hope for peace was justified; their hopes were dashed.* [2] a reasonable ground for this feeling: *there is still hope.* [3] a person or thing that gives cause for hope. [4] a thing, situation, or event that is desired: *my hope is that prices will fall.* [5] **not a hope** *or* **some hope.** used ironically to express little confidence that expectations will be fulfilled. ◆ VERB [6] (*tr; takes a clause as object or an infinitive*) to desire (something) with some possibility of fulfilment: *we hope you can come; I hope to tell you.* [7] (*intr;* often foll by *for*) to have a wish (for a future event, situation, etc.). [8] (*tr; takes a clause as object*) to trust, expect, or believe: *we hope that this is satisfactory.*
▷HISTORY Old English *hopa;* related to Old Frisian *hope,* Dutch *hoop,* Middle High German *hoffe*
▸ **'hoper** NOUN

hope chest NOUN the US and Canadian name for **bottom drawer.**

hopeful ('həʊpfʊl) ADJECTIVE [1] having or expressing hope. [2] giving or inspiring hope; promising. ◆ NOUN [3] a person considered to be on the brink of success (esp in the phrase **a young hopeful**).
▸ **'hopefulness** NOUN

hopefully ('həʊpfʊlɪ) ADVERB [1] in a hopeful manner. [2] *Informal* it is hoped: *hopefully they will be married soon.*

> **Language note** The use of *hopefully* to mean *it is hoped* used to be considered incorrect by some people but has now become acceptable in informal contexts.

Hopeh *or* **Hopei** ('həʊ'peɪ) NOUN a variant transliteration of the Chinese name for **Hebei.**

hopeless ('həʊplɪs) ADJECTIVE [1] having or offering no hope. [2] impossible to analyse or solve. [3] unable to learn, function, etc. [4] *Informal* without skill or ability.
▸ **'hopelessly** ADVERB ▸ **'hopelessness** NOUN

hophead ('hɒp,hɛd) NOUN *Slang, chiefly US* a heroin or opium addict.
▷HISTORY C20: from obsolete slang *hop* opium; see HOP[2]

Hopi ('həʊpɪ) NOUN [1] (*plural* **-pis** *or* **-pi**) a member of a North American Indian people of NE Arizona. [2] the language of this people, belonging to the Shoshonean subfamily of the Uto-Aztecan family.
▷HISTORY from Hopi *Hópi* peaceful

hop into VERB (*intr, preposition*) *Austral and NZ slang* [1] to attack (a person). [2] to start or set about (a task).

hoplite ('hɒplaɪt) NOUN (in ancient Greece) a heavily armed infantryman.
▷HISTORY C18: from Greek *hoplitēs,* from *hoplon* weapon, from *hepein* to prepare
▸ **hoplitic** (hɒp'lɪtɪk) ADJECTIVE

hoplology (hɒp'lɒlədʒɪ) NOUN the study of weapons or armour.
▷HISTORY C19: from Greek, from *hoplon* weapon + -LOGY
▸ **hop'lologist** NOUN

hopper ('hɒpə) NOUN [1] a person or thing that hops. [2] a funnel-shaped chamber or reservoir from which solid materials can be discharged under gravity into a receptacle below, esp for feeding fuel to a furnace, loading a railway truck with grain, etc. [3] a machine used for picking hops. [4] any of various long-legged hopping insects, esp the grasshopper, leaf hopper, and immature locust. [5] Also called: **hoppercar.** an open-topped railway truck for bulk transport of loose minerals, etc., unloaded through doors on the underside. [6] *Computing* a device formerly used for holding punched cards and feeding them to a card punch or card reader.

hop-picker NOUN a person employed or a machine used to pick hops.

hopping ('hɒpɪŋ) NOUN [1] the action of a person or animal that hops. [2] *Tyneside dialect* a fair, esp (**the Hoppings**) an annual fair in Newcastle. ◆ ADJECTIVE [3] **hopping mad.** in a terrible rage.

hopple ('hɒp[ə]l) VERB, NOUN a less common word for **hobble** (senses 2, 5).
▸ **'hoppler** NOUN

Hoppus foot ('hɒpəs) NOUN a unit of volume equal to 1.27 cubic feet, applied to timber in the round, the cross-sectional area being taken as the square of one quarter of the circumference.
▷HISTORY C20: named after Edward *Hoppus,* 18th-century English surveyor

hops (hɒps) PLURAL NOUN the dried ripe flowers, esp the female flowers, of the hop plant, used to give a bitter taste to beer.

hopsack ('hɒp,sæk) NOUN [1] a roughly woven fabric of wool, cotton, etc., used for clothing. [2] Also called: **hopsacking.** a coarse fabric used for bags, etc., made generally of hemp or jute.

hopscotch ('hɒp,skɒtʃ) NOUN a children's game in which a player throws a small stone or other object to land in one of a pattern of squares marked on the ground and then hops over to it to pick it up.
▷HISTORY C19: HOP[1] + SCOTCH[1]

hop, step, and jump NOUN [1] an older term for **triple jump.** [2] Also called: **hop, skip, and jump.** a short distance: *the shops are only a hop, step, and jump from our house.*

hop trefoil NOUN a leguminous plant, *Trifolium campestre,* of N temperate grasslands, with globular yellow flower heads and trifoliate leaves. US and Canadian name: **hop clover.**

hora ('hɔːrə) NOUN a traditional Israeli or Romanian circle dance.
▷HISTORY from Modern Hebrew *hōrāh,* from Romanian *horă,* from Turkish

Horae ('hɔːriː) PLURAL NOUN *Classical myth* the goddesses of the seasons. Also called: **the Hours.**
▷HISTORY Latin: hours

horal ('hɔːrəl) ADJECTIVE a less common word for **hourly.**
▷HISTORY C18: from Late Latin *hōrālis* of an HOUR

horary ('hɔːrərɪ) ADJECTIVE *Archaic* [1] relating to the hours. [2] hourly.
▷HISTORY C17: from Medieval Latin *hōrārius;* see HOUR

Horatian ode NOUN an ode of several stanzas, each of the same metrical pattern. Also called: **Sapphic ode.**

horde (hɔːd) NOUN [1] a vast crowd; throng; mob. [2] a local group of people in a nomadic society. [3] a nomadic group of people, esp an Asiatic group. [4] a large moving mass of animals, esp insects. ◆ VERB [5] (*intr*) to form, move in, or live in a horde.
▷HISTORY C16: from Polish *horda,* from Turkish *ordū* camp; compare *Urdu*

> **Language note** *Horde* is sometimes wrongly written where *hoard* is meant: *a hoard* (not *horde*) *of gold coins.*

hordein ('hɔːdiːɪn) NOUN a simple protein, rich in proline, that occurs in barley.
▷HISTORY C19: from French *hordéine,* from Latin *hordeum* barley + French *-ine* -IN

hordeolum (,hɔːdɪ'əʊləm) NOUN medical name for a **stye** (of the eye).

Horeb ('hɔːrɛb) NOUN *Bible* a mountain, probably Mount Sinai.

horehound *or* **hoarhound** ('hɔː,haʊnd) NOUN [1] Also called: **white horehound.** a downy perennial herbaceous Old World plant, *Marrubium vulgare,* with small white flowers that contain a bitter juice formerly used as a cough medicine and flavouring: family *Lamiaceae* (labiates). See also **black horehound.** [2] **water horehound.** another name for **bugleweed** (sense 1).
▷HISTORY Old English *hārhūne,* from *hār* grey + *hūne* horehound, of obscure origin

hori ('hɔːriː) NOUN, *plural* **horis.** *NZ informal, derogatory* a Maori.
▷HISTORY Maori

horizon (hə'raɪz[ə]n) NOUN [1] Also called: **visible horizon, apparent horizon.** the apparent line that divides the earth and the sky. [2] *Astronomy* **a** Also called: **sensible horizon.** the circular intersection with the celestial sphere of the plane tangential to the earth at the position of the observer. **b** Also called: **celestial horizon.** the great circle on the celestial sphere, the plane of which passes through the centre of the earth and is parallel to the sensible horizon. [3] the range or limit of scope, interest, knowledge, etc. [4] a thin layer of rock within a stratum that has a distinct composition, esp of fossils, by which the stratum may be dated. [5] a layer in a soil profile having particular characteristics. See **A horizon, B horizon, C horizon.** [6] **on the horizon.** likely or about to happen or appear.
▷HISTORY C14: from Latin, from Greek *horizōn kuklos* limiting circle, from *horizein* to limit, from *horos* limit
▸ **ho'rizonless** ADJECTIVE

horizontal (,hɒrɪ'zɒnt[ə]l) ADJECTIVE [1] parallel to the plane of the horizon; level; flat. Compare **vertical** (sense 1). [2] of or relating to the horizon. [3] measured or contained in a plane parallel to that of the horizon. [4] applied uniformly or equally to all members of a group. [5] *Economics* relating to identical stages of commercial activity: *horizontal integration.* ◆ NOUN [6] a horizontal plane, position, line, etc.
▸ **,hori'zontalness** *or* **,horizon'tality** NOUN ▸ **,hori'zontally** ADVERB

horizontal bar NOUN *Gymnastics* a raised bar on which swinging and vaulting exercises are performed. Also called: **high bar.**

horizontal mobility NOUN *Sociol* the movement of groups or individuals to positions that differ from those previously held but do not involve any change in class, status, or power. Compare **vertical mobility.** See also **upward mobility, downward mobility.**

horizontal stabilizer NOUN the US name for **tailplane.**

horizontal union NOUN another name (esp US) for **craft union.**

horlicks ('hɔːlɪks) NOUN **make a horlicks.** *Brit informal* to make a mistake or a mess: *his boss is making a horlicks of his job.*
▷HISTORY C20: from *Horlicks* a drink meant to induce sleep

horme ('hɔːmɪ) NOUN (in the psychology of C. G. Jung) fundamental vital energy.
▷HISTORY C20: from Greek *hormē* impulse
▸ **'hormic** ADJECTIVE

hormone ('hɔːməʊn) NOUN [1] a chemical substance produced in an endocrine gland and transported in the blood to a certain tissue, on which it exerts a specific effect. [2] an organic compound produced by a plant that is essential for growth. [3] any synthetic substance having the same effects.

▷HISTORY C20: from Greek *hormōn,* from *horman* to stir up, urge on, from *hormē* impulse, assault
▸**hor'monal** ADJECTIVE

hormone replacement therapy NOUN a form of oestrogen treatment used to control menopausal symptoms and in the prevention of osteoporosis. Abbreviation: **HRT.**

Hormuz (hɔː'muːz, 'hɔːmʌz) *or* **Ormuz** NOUN an island off the SE coast of Iran, in the **Strait of Hormuz:** ruins of the ancient city of Hormuz, a major trading centre in the Middle Ages. Area: about 41 sq. km (16 sq. miles).

horn (hɔːn) NOUN 1 either of a pair of permanent outgrowths on the heads of cattle, antelopes, sheep, etc., consisting of a central bony core covered with layers of keratin. Related adjectives: **corneous, keratoid.** 2 the outgrowth from the nasal bone of a rhinoceros, consisting of a mass of fused hairs. 3 any hornlike projection or process, such as the eyestalk of a snail. 4 the antler of a deer. 5 **a** the constituent substance, mainly keratin, of horns, hooves, etc. **b** (*in combination*): *horn-rimmed spectacles.* 6 a container or device made from this substance or an artificial substitute: *a shoe horn; a drinking horn.* 7 an object or part resembling a horn in shape, such as the points at either end of a crescent, the point of an anvil, the pommel of a saddle, or a cornucopia. 8 a primitive musical wind instrument made from the horn of an animal. 9 any musical instrument consisting of a pipe or tube of brass fitted with a mouthpiece, with or without valves. See **hunting horn, French horn, cor anglais.** 10 *Jazz, slang* any wind instrument. 11 **a** a device for producing a warning or signalling noise. **b** (*in combination*): *a foghorn.* 12 (*usually plural*) the hornlike projection attributed to certain devils, deities, etc. 13 (*usually plural*) the imaginary hornlike parts formerly supposed to appear on the forehead of a cuckold. 14 Also called: **horn balance.** an extension of an aircraft control surface that projects in front of the hinge providing aerodynamic assistance in moving the control. 15 **a** Also called: **acoustic horn, exponential horn.** a hollow conical device coupled to the diaphragm of a gramophone to control the direction and quality of the sound. **b** any such device used to spread or focus sound, such as the device attached to an electrical loudspeaker in a public address system. **c** Also called: **horn antenna.** a microwave aerial, formed by flaring out the end of a waveguide. 16 *Geology* another name for **pyramidal peak.** 17 a stretch of land or water shaped like a horn. 18 *Brit slang* an erection of the penis. 19 *Bible* a symbol of power, victory, or success: *in my name shall his horn be exalted.* 20 **blow one's horn.** *US and Canadian* to boast about oneself; brag. Brit equivalent: **blow one's own trumpet.** 21 **draw** (*or* **pull**) **in one's horns. a** to suppress or control one's feelings, esp of anger, enthusiasm, or passion. **b** to withdraw a previous statement. **c** to economize. 22 **on the horns of a dilemma. a** in a situation involving a choice between two equally unpalatable alternatives. **b** in an awkward situation. ◆ VERB (*tr*) 23 to provide with a horn or horns. 24 to gore or butt with a horn. ◆ See also **horn in.**
▷HISTORY Old English; related to Old Norse *horn,* Gothic *haurn,* Latin *cornu* horn
▸**'hornless** ADJECTIVE ▸**'horn,like** ADJECTIVE

Horn (hɔːn) NOUN **Cape.** See **Cape Horn.**

hornbeam ('hɔːn,biːm) NOUN 1 any tree of the betulaceous genus *Carpinus,* such as *C. betulus* of Europe and Asia, having smooth grey bark and hard white wood. 2 the wood of any of these trees. ◆ Also called: **ironwood.**
▷HISTORY C14: from HORN + BEAM, referring to its tough wood

hornbill ('hɔːn,bɪl) NOUN any bird of the family *Bucerotidae* of tropical Africa and Asia, having a very large bill with a basal bony protuberance: order *Coraciiformes* (kingfishers, etc.).

hornblende ('hɔːn,blɛnd) NOUN a black or greenish-black mineral of the amphibole group, found in igneous and metamorphic rocks. Composition: calcium magnesium iron sodium aluminium aluminosilicate. General formula: $(Ca,Na)_{2.3}(Mg,Fe,Al)_5Si_6(Si,Al)_2O_{22}(OH)_2$.
▷HISTORY C18: from German *Horn* horn + BLENDE
▸**,horn'blendic** ADJECTIVE

hornbook ('hɔːn,bʊk) NOUN 1 a page bearing a religious text or the alphabet, held in a frame with a thin window of flattened cattle horn over it. 2 any elementary primer.

horned (hɔːnd) ADJECTIVE having a horn, horns, or hornlike parts.
▸**hornedness** ('hɔːnɪdnɪs) NOUN

horned owl NOUN any large owl of the genus *Bubo,* having prominent ear tufts: family *Strigidae.*

horned poppy NOUN any of several Eurasian papaveraceous plants of the genera *Glaucium* and *Roemeria,* having large brightly coloured flowers and long curved seed capsules.

horned pout NOUN a North American catfish, *Ameiurus* (or *Ictalurus*) *nebulosus,* with a sharp spine on the dorsal and pectoral fins and eight long barbels around the mouth: family *Ameiuridae.* Also called: **brown bullhead.**

horned toad *or* **lizard** NOUN any small insectivorous burrowing lizard of the genus *Phrynosoma,* inhabiting desert regions of America, having a flattened toadlike body covered with spines: family *Iguanidae* (iguanas).

horned viper NOUN a venomous snake, *Cerastes cornutus,* that occurs in desert regions of N Africa and SW Asia and has a small horny spine above each eye: family *Viperidae* (vipers). Also called: **sand viper.**

hornet ('hɔːnɪt) NOUN 1 any of various large social wasps of the family *Vespidae,* esp *Vespa crabro* of Europe, that can inflict a severe sting. 2 **hornet's nest.** a strongly unfavourable reaction (often in the phrase **stir up a hornet's nest**).
▷HISTORY Old English *hyrnetu;* related to Old Saxon *hornut,* Old High German *hornuz*

hornet clearwing NOUN See **clearwing.**

hornfels ('hɔːnfɛlz) NOUN a hard compact fine-grained metamorphic rock formed by the action of heat from a magmatic intrusion on neighbouring sedimentary rocks. Also called: **hornstone.**
▷HISTORY German: literally, horn rock

horn in VERB (*intr, adverb;* often foll by *on*) *Slang* to interrupt or intrude: *don't horn in on our conversation.*

Horn of Africa NOUN a region of NE Africa, comprising Somalia and adjacent territories.

horn of plenty NOUN 1 another term for **cornucopia.** 2 an edible basidiomycetous fungus, *Craterellus cornucopioides,* related to the chanterelle and like it funnel shaped but dark brown inside and dark grey outside: found in broad-leaved woodland.

hornpipe ('hɔːn,paɪp) NOUN 1 an obsolete reed instrument with a mouthpiece made of horn. 2 an old British solo dance to a hornpipe accompaniment, traditionally performed by sailors. 3 a piece of music for such a dance.

horns and halo effect NOUN a tendency to allow one's judgement of another person, esp in a job interview, to be unduly influenced by an unfavourable (horns) or favourable (halo) first impression based on appearances.

horn silver NOUN another name for **chlorargyrite.**

hornstone ('hɔːn,stəʊn) NOUN another name for **chert** or **hornfels.**
▷HISTORY C17: translation of German *Hornstein;* so called from its appearance

hornswoggle ('hɔːn,swɒgᵊl) VERB (*tr*) *Slang* to cheat or trick; bamboozle.
▷HISTORY C19: of unknown origin

horntail ('hɔːn,teɪl) NOUN any of various large wasplike insects of the hymenopterous family *Siricidae,* the females of which have a strong stout ovipositor and lay their eggs in the wood of felled trees. Also called: **wood wasp.**

hornwort ('hɔːn,wɜːt) NOUN 1 any aquatic plant of the genus *Ceratophyllum,* forming submerged branching masses in ponds and slow-flowing streams: family *Ceratophyllaceae.* 2 any of a group of bryophytes belonging to the phylum *Anthocerophyta,* resembling liverworts but with hornlike sporophytes.

hornwrack ('hɔːn,ræk) NOUN a yellowish bryozoan or sea mat sometimes found on beaches after a storm.

horny ('hɔːnɪ) ADJECTIVE **hornier, horniest.** 1 of, like, or hard as horn. 2 having a horn or horns. 3 *Slang* **a** sexually aroused. **b** provoking or intended to provoke sexual arousal. **c** sexually eager or lustful.
▸**'hornily** ADVERB ▸**'horniness** NOUN

hornywink ('hɔːnɪ,wɪŋk) NOUN *Southwest English dialect* a lapwing.

horol. ABBREVIATION FOR horology.

horologe ('hɒrə,lɒdʒ) NOUN a rare word for **timepiece.**
▷HISTORY C14: from Latin *hōrologium,* from Greek *hōrologion,* from *hōra* HOUR + *-logos* from *legein* to tell

horologist (hɒ'rɒlədʒɪst) *or* **horologer** (hɒ'rɒlədʒə) NOUN a person skilled in horology, esp an expert maker of timepieces.

horologium (,hɒrə'ləʊdʒɪəm) NOUN, *plural* **-gia** (-dʒɪə). 1 a clocktower. 2 Also called: **horologion.** (in the Eastern Church) a liturgical book of the offices for the canonical hours, corresponding to the Western breviary.
▷HISTORY C17: from Latin; see HOROLOGE

Horologium (,hɒrə'ləʊdʒɪəm) NOUN, *Latin genitive* **Horologii** (,hɒrə'ləʊdʒɪaɪ). a faint constellation in the S hemisphere lying near Eridanus and Hydrus.

horology (hɒ'rɒlədʒɪ) NOUN the art or science of making timepieces or of measuring time.
▸**horologic** (,hɒrə'lɒdʒɪk) *or* **,horo'logical** ADJECTIVE

horopter (hɒ'rɒptə) NOUN *Optics* the locus of all points in space that stimulate points on each eye that yield the same visual direction as each other.
▷HISTORY C18: from Greek *horos* boundary + *optēr,* from *ops* eye

horoscope ('hɒrə,skəʊp) NOUN 1 the prediction of a person's future based on a comparison of the zodiacal data for the time of birth with the data from the period under consideration. 2 the configuration of the planets, the sun, and the moon in the sky at a particular moment. 3 Also called: **chart.** a diagram showing the positions of the planets, sun, moon, etc., at a particular time and place.
▷HISTORY Old English *horoscopus,* from Latin, from Greek *hōroskopos* ascendant birth sign, from *hōra* HOUR + -SCOPE
▸**horoscopic** (,hɒrə'skɒpɪk) ADJECTIVE

horoscopy (hɒ'rɒskəpɪ) NOUN, *plural* **-pies.** the casting and interpretation of horoscopes.

horrendous (hɒ'rɛndəs) ADJECTIVE another word for **horrific.**
▷HISTORY C17: from Latin *horrendus* fearful, from *horrēre* to bristle, shudder, tremble; see HORROR
▸**hor'rendously** ADVERB

horrible ('hɒrəbᵊl) ADJECTIVE 1 causing horror; dreadful. 2 disagreeable; unpleasant. 3 *Informal* cruel or unkind.
▷HISTORY C14: via Old French from Latin *horribilis,* from *horrēre* to tremble
▸**'horribleness** NOUN

horribly ('hɒrɪblɪ) ADVERB 1 in a horrible manner. 2 (intensifier): *I'm horribly bored.*

horrid ('hɒrɪd) ADJECTIVE 1 disagreeable; unpleasant: *a horrid meal.* 2 repulsive or frightening. 3 *Informal* unkind.
▷HISTORY C16 (in the sense: bristling, shaggy): from Latin *horridus* prickly, rough, from *horrēre* to bristle
▸**'horridly** ADVERB ▸**'horridness** NOUN

horrific (hɒ'rɪfɪk, hə-) ADJECTIVE provoking horror; horrible.
▸**hor'rifically** ADVERB

horrify ('hɒrɪ,faɪ) VERB **-fies, -fying, -fied.** (*tr*) 1 to cause feelings of horror in; terrify; frighten. 2 to dismay or shock greatly.
▸**,horrifi'cation** NOUN ▸**'horrified** ADJECTIVE

horrifying ('hɒrɪ,faɪɪŋ) ADJECTIVE 1 causing feelings of horror in; awful; terrifying;. 2 dismaying or greatly shocking; dreadful.
▸**'horri,fyingly** ADVERB

horripilation (hɒ,rɪpɪ'leɪʃən) NOUN *Physiol* 1 a technical name for **goose flesh.** 2 the erection of any short bodily hairs.
▷HISTORY C17: from Late Latin *horripilātiō* a bristling, from Latin *horrēre* to stand on end + *pilus* hair

horror ('hɒrə) NOUN 1 extreme fear; terror; dread. 2 intense loathing; hatred. 3 (*often plural*) a thing or person causing fear, loathing, etc. 4 (*modifier*) having a frightening subject, esp a supernatural one: *a horror film.*
▷HISTORY C14: from Latin: a trembling with fear; compare HIRSUTE

horrors ('hɒrəz) PLURAL NOUN 1 *Slang* a fit of depression or anxiety. 2 *Informal* See **delirium tremens.** ◆ INTERJECTION 3 an expression of dismay, sometimes facetious.

horror-struck *or* **horror-stricken** ADJECTIVE shocked; horrified.

hors concours *French* (ɔr kɔ̃kur) ADJECTIVE (*postpositive,*), ADVERB 1 (of an artist, exhibitor, etc.) excluded from competing. 2 without equal; unrivalled.
▷HISTORY literally: out of the competition

hors de combat *French* (ɔr də kɔ̃ba) ADJECTIVE (*postpositive,*), ADVERB disabled or injured.
▷HISTORY literally: out of (the) fight

hors d'oeuvre (ɔː 'dɜːvr; *French* ɔr dœvrə) NOUN, *plural* ***hors d'oeuvre*** *or* ***hors d'oeuvres*** ('dɜːvr; *French* dœvrə). an additional dish served as an appetizer, usually before the main meal.
▷HISTORY C18: from French, literally: outside the work, not part of the main course

horse (hɔːs) NOUN 1 a domesticated perissodactyl mammal, *Equus caballus,* used for draught work and riding: family *Equidae.* Related adjective: **equine.** 2 the adult male of this species; stallion. 3 **wild horse. a** a horse (*Equus caballus*) that has become feral. **b** another name for **Przewalski's horse.** 4 **a** any other member of the family *Equidae,* such as the zebra or ass. **b** (*as modifier*): *the horse family.* 5 (*functioning as plural*) horsemen, esp cavalry: *a regiment of horse.* 6 Also called: **buck.** *Gymnastics* a padded apparatus on legs, used for vaulting, etc. 7 a narrow board supported by a pair of legs at each end, used as a frame for sawing or as a trestle, barrier, etc. 8 a contrivance on which a person may ride and exercise. 9 a slang word for **heroin.** 10 *Mining* a mass of rock within a vein of ore. 11 *Nautical* a rod, rope, or cable, fixed at the ends, along which something may slide by means of a thimble, shackle, or other fitting; traveller. 12 *Chess* an informal name for **knight.** 13 *Informal* short for **horsepower.** 14 (*modifier*) drawn by a horse or horses: *a horse cart.* 15 **be** (*or* **get**) **on one's high horse.** *Informal* to be disdainfully aloof. 16 **flog a dead horse.** See **flog** (sense 6). 17 **hold one's horses.** to hold back; restrain oneself. 18 **a horse of another** *or* **a different colour.** a completely different topic, argument, etc. 19 **horses for courses.** a policy, course of action, etc. modified slightly to take account of specific circumstances without departing in essentials from the original. 20 **the horse's mouth.** the most reliable source. 21 **to horse!** an order to mount horses. ◆ VERB 22 (*tr*) to provide with a horse or horses. 23 to put or be put on horseback. 24 (*tr*) to move (something heavy) into position by sheer physical strength.
▷HISTORY Old English *hors;* related to Old Frisian *hors,* Old High German *hros,* Old Norse *hross*
▸**'horseless** ADJECTIVE ▸**'horse,like** ADJECTIVE

horse around *or* **about** VERB (*intr, adverb*) *Informal* to indulge in horseplay.

horseback ('hɔːs,bæk) NOUN **a** a horse's back (esp in the phrase **on horseback**). **b** (*as modifier*): *horseback riding.*

horse bean NOUN another name for **broad bean.**

horsebox ('hɔːs,bɒks) NOUN *Brit* a van or trailer used for carrying horses.

horse brass NOUN a decorative brass ornament, usually circular, originally attached to a horse's harness.

horse chestnut NOUN 1 any of several trees of the genus *Aesculus,* esp the Eurasian *A. hippocastanum,* having palmate leaves, erect clusters of white, pink, or red flowers, and brown shiny inedible nuts enclosed in a spiky bur: family *Hippocastanaceae.* 2 Also called: **conker.** the nut of this tree.
▷HISTORY C16: so called from its having been used in the treatment of respiratory disease in horses

horseflesh ('hɔːs,flɛʃ) NOUN 1 horses collectively. 2 the flesh of a horse, esp edible horse meat.

horsefly ('hɔːs,flaɪ) NOUN, *plural* **-flies.** any large stout-bodied dipterous fly of the family *Tabanidae,* the females of which suck the blood of mammals, esp horses, cattle, and man. Also called: **gadfly, cleg.**

horse gentian NOUN any caprifoliaceous plant of the genus *Triosteum,* of Asia and North America, having small purplish-brown flowers. Also called: **feverwort.**

Horse Guards PLURAL NOUN 1 the cavalry regiment that, together with the Life Guards, comprises the cavalry part of the British sovereign's Household Brigade. 2 their headquarters in Whitehall, London: also the headquarters of the British Army.

horsehair ('hɔːs,hɛə) NOUN **a** hair taken chiefly from the tail or mane of a horse, used in upholstery and for fabric, etc. **b** (*as modifier*): *a horsehair mattress.*

horsehair toadstool *or* **fungus** NOUN a small basidiomycetous fungus, *Marasmius androsaceus,* having a rusty coloured cap and very slender black stems. It is related to the fairy ring mushroom, but is commonly found among conifers and heather.

horsehair worm NOUN another name for **hairworm** (sense 2).

Horsehead nebula ('hɔːs,hɛd) NOUN *Astronomy* a dark nebula lying in the constellation of Orion and resembling the head of a horse.

horsehide ('hɔːs,haɪd) NOUN 1 the hide of a horse. 2 leather made from this hide. 3 (*modifier*) made of horsehide.

horse latitudes PLURAL NOUN *Nautical* the latitudes near 30°N or 30°S at sea, characterized by baffling winds, calms, and high barometric pressure.
▷HISTORY C18: referring either to the high mortality of horses on board ship in these latitudes or to *dead horse* (nautical slang: advance pay), which sailors expected to work off by this stage of a voyage

horse laugh NOUN a coarse, mocking, or raucous laugh; guffaw.

horseleech ('hɔːs,liːtʃ) NOUN 1 any of several large carnivorous freshwater leeches of the genus *Haemopis,* esp *H. sanguisuga.* 2 an archaic name for a **veterinary surgeon.**

horse mackerel NOUN 1 Also called: **scad.** a mackerel-like carangid fish, *Trachurus* of European Atlantic waters, with a row of bony scales along the lateral line. Sometimes called (US): **saurel.** 2 any of various large tunnies or related fishes.

horseman ('hɔːsmən) NOUN, *plural* **-men.** 1 a person who is skilled in riding or horsemanship. 2 a person who rides a horse.
▸**'horse,woman** FEMININE NOUN

horsemanship ('hɔːsmən,ʃɪp) NOUN 1 the art of riding on horseback. 2 skill in riding horses.

horse marine NOUN *US* 1 (formerly) a mounted marine or cavalryman serving in a ship. 2 someone out of his natural element, as if a member of an imaginary body of marine cavalry.

horsemint ('hɔːs,mɪnt) NOUN 1 a hairy European mint plant, *Mentha longifolia,* with small mauve flowers: family *Lamiaceae* (labiates). 2 any of several similar and related plants, such as *Monarda punctata* of North America.

horse mushroom NOUN a large edible agaricaceous field mushroom, *Agaricus arvensis,* with a white cap and greyish gills.

horse nettle NOUN a weedy solanaceous North American plant, *Solanum carolinense,* with yellow prickles, white or blue flowers, and yellow berries.

Horsens (*Danish* 'hɔrsəns) NOUN a port in Denmark, in E Jutland at the head of **Horsens Fjord.** Pop.: 55 252 (1995).

horse opera NOUN *Informal* another term for **Western** (sense 4).

horse pistol NOUN a large holstered pistol formerly carried by horsemen.

horseplay ('hɔːs,pleɪ) NOUN rough, boisterous, or rowdy play.

horsepower ('hɔːs,paʊə) NOUN 1 an fps unit of power, equal to 550 foot-pounds per second (equivalent to 745.7 watts). 2 a US standard unit of power, equal to 746 watts. ◆ Abbreviations: **HP, h.p.**

horsepower-hour NOUN an fps unit of work or energy equal to the work done by 1 horsepower in 1 hour. 1 horsepower-hour is equivalent to 2.686×10^6 joules.

horseradish ('hɔːs,rædɪʃ) NOUN 1 a coarse Eurasian plant, *Armoracia rusticana,* cultivated for its thick white pungent root: family *Brassicaceae* (crucifers). 2 the root of this plant, which is ground and combined with vinegar, etc., to make a sauce.

horse sense NOUN another term for **common sense.**

horseshit ('hɔːs,ʃɪt) NOUN *Slang* rubbish; nonsense.

> **Language note** This word was formerly considered to be taboo, and it was labelled as such in previous editions of *Collins English Dictionary*. However, it has now become acceptable in speech, although some older or more conservative people may object to its use.

horseshoe ('hɔːs,ʃuː) NOUN 1 a piece of iron shaped like a U with the ends curving inwards that is nailed to the underside of the hoof of a horse to protect the soft part of the foot from hard surfaces: commonly thought to be a token of good luck. 2 an object of similar shape. ◆ VERB **-shoes, -shoeing, -shoed.** 3 (*tr*) to fit with a horseshoe; shoe.

horseshoe arch NOUN an arch formed in the shape of a horseshoe, esp as used in Moorish architecture.

horseshoe bat NOUN any of numerous large-eared Old World insectivorous bats, mostly of the genus *Rhinolophus,* with a fleshy growth around the nostrils, used in echolocation: family *Rhinolophidae.*

horseshoe crab NOUN any marine chelicerate arthropod of the genus *Limulus,* of North America and Asia, having a rounded heavily armoured body with a long pointed tail: class *Merostomata.* Also called: **king crab.**

horseshoes ('hɔːs,ʃuːz) NOUN (*functioning as singular*) a game in which the players try to throw horseshoes so that they encircle a stake in the ground some distance away.

horsetail ('hɔːs,teɪl) NOUN 1 any tracheophyte plant of the genus *Equisetum,* having jointed stems with whorls of small dark toothlike leaves and producing spores within conelike structures at the tips of the stems: phylum *Sphenophyta.* 2 a stylized horse's tail formerly used as the emblem of a pasha, the number of tails increasing with rank.

horse trading NOUN hard bargaining to obtain equal concessions by both sides in a dispute.

horseweed ('hɔːs,wiːd) NOUN the US name for **Canadian fleabane** (see **fleabane** (sense 3)).

horsewhip ('hɔːs,wɪp) NOUN 1 a whip, usually with a long thong, used for managing horses. ◆ VERB **-whips, -whipping, -whipped.** 2 (*tr*) to flog with such a whip.
▸**'horse,whipper** NOUN

horsey *or* **horsy** ('hɔːsɪ) ADJECTIVE **horsier, horsiest.** 1 of or relating to horses: *a horsey smell.* 2 dealing with or devoted to horses. 3 like a horse: *a horsey face.*
▸**'horsily** ADVERB ▸**'horsiness** NOUN

horst (hɔːst) NOUN a ridge of land that has been forced upwards between two parallel faults.
▷HISTORY C20: from German: thicket

Horta (*Portuguese* 'ɔrtə) NOUN a port in the Azores, on the SE coast of Fayal Island.

hortatory ('hɔːtətərɪ, -trɪ) *or* **hortative** ('hɔːtətɪv) ADJECTIVE tending to exhort; encouraging.
▷HISTORY C16: from Late Latin *hortātōrius,* from Latin *hortārī* to EXHORT
▸**hor'tation** NOUN ▸**'hortatorily** *or* **'hortatively** ADVERB

horticultural (,hɔːtɪ'kʌltʃərəl) ADJECTIVE of or relating to horticulture.
▸**,horti'culturally** ADVERB ▸**,horti'culturalist** NOUN

horticulture ('hɔːtɪ,kʌltʃə) NOUN the art or science of cultivating gardens.
▷HISTORY C17: from Latin *hortus* garden + CULTURE, on the model of AGRICULTURE
▸**,horti'culturist** NOUN

hortus siccus ('hɔːtəs 'sɪkəs) NOUN a less common name for **herbarium.**
▷HISTORY C17: Latin, literally: dry garden

Horus ('hɔːrəs) NOUN a solar god of Egyptian mythology, usually depicted with a falcon's head.
▷HISTORY via Late Latin from Greek *Hōros,* from Egyptian *Hur* hawk

Hos. *Bible* ABBREVIATION FOR Hosea.

hosanna (həʊ'zænə) INTERJECTION 1 an exclamation of praise, esp one to God. ◆ NOUN 2 the act of crying "hosanna".
▷HISTORY Old English *osanna,* via Late Latin from Greek, from Hebrew *hōshi 'āh nnā* save now, we pray

hose[1] (həʊz) NOUN 1 a flexible pipe, for conveying a liquid or gas. ◆ VERB 2 (sometimes foll by *down*) to wash, water, or sprinkle (a person or thing) with or as if with a hose.
▷HISTORY C15: later use of HOSE[2]

hose[2] (həʊz) NOUN, *plural* **hose** *or* **hosen.** 1 stockings, socks, and tights collectively. 2 *History* a man's garment covering the legs and reaching up to the waist; worn with a doublet. 3 **half-hose.** socks.
▷HISTORY Old English *hosa;* related to Old High German *hosa,* Dutch *hoos,* Old Norse *hosa*

Hosea (həʊ'zɪə) NOUN *Old Testament* 1 a Hebrew prophet of the 8th century B.C. 2 the book containing his oracles.

hoser (həʊzə) NOUN 1 *US slang* a person who swindles or deceives others. 2 *Canadian slang* an unsophisticated, esp rural, person.

hosier ('həʊzɪə) NOUN a person who sells stockings, etc.

hosiery ('həʊzɪərɪ) NOUN stockings, socks, and knitted underclothing collectively.

hospice ('hɒspɪs) NOUN, *plural* **hospices.** 1 a nursing home that specializes in caring for the terminally ill. 2 Also called: **hospitium** (hɒ'spɪtɪəm). ◆ PLURAL **hospitia** (hɒ'spɪtɪə). *Archaic* a place of shelter for travellers, esp one kept by a monastic order.
▷HISTORY C19: from French, from Latin *hospitium* hospitality, from *hospes* guest, HOST[1]

hospitable ('hɒspɪtəbᵊl, hɒ'spɪt-) ADJECTIVE 1 welcoming to guests or strangers. 2 fond of entertaining. 3 receptive: *hospitable to new ideas.*
▷HISTORY C16: from Medieval Latin *hospitāre* to receive as a guest, from Latin *hospes* guest, HOST[1]
▸ **'hospitableness** NOUN ▸ **'hospitably** ADVERB

hospital ('hɒspɪtᵊl) NOUN 1 an institution for the medical, surgical, obstetric, or psychiatric care and treatment of patients. 2 (*modifier*) having the function of a hospital: *a hospital ship.* 3 a repair shop for something specified: *a dolls' hospital.* 4 *Archaic* a charitable home, hospice, or school.
▷HISTORY C13: from Medieval Latin *hospitāle* hospice, from Latin *hospitālis* relating to a guest, from *hospes, hospit-* guest, HOST[1]

hospital corner NOUN a corner of a made-up bed in which the bedclothes have been neatly and securely folded, esp as in hospitals.

Hospitalet (*Spanish* ɔspita'lɛt) NOUN a city in NE Spain, a SW suburb of Barcelona. Pop.: 248 521 (1998 est.).

hospitality (ˌhɒspɪ'tælɪtɪ) NOUN, *plural* **-ties.** 1 kindness in welcoming strangers or guests. 2 receptiveness.

hospitality suite NOUN a room or suite, as at a conference, where free drinks are offered.

hospitalization *or* **hospitalisation** (ˌhɒspɪtəlaɪ'zeɪʃən) NOUN 1 the act or an instance of being hospitalized. 2 the duration of a stay in a hospital.

hospitalize *or* **hospitalise** ('hɒspɪtəˌlaɪz) VERB (*tr*) to admit or send (a person) into a hospital.

hospitaller *or US* **hospitaler** ('hɒspɪtələ) NOUN a person, esp a member of certain religious orders, dedicated to hospital work, ambulance services, etc.
▷HISTORY C14: from Old French *hospitalier,* from Medieval Latin *hospitālārius,* from *hospitāle* hospice; see HOSPITAL

Hospitaller *or US* **Hospitaler** ('hɒspɪtələ) NOUN a member of the order of the Knights Hospitallers.

hospital pass NOUN *Informal* 1 *Sport* a pass made to a team-mate who will be tackled heavily as soon as the ball is received. 2 a task or project that will inevitably bring heavy criticism on the person to whom it has been assigned.
▷HISTORY C20

hospodar ('hɒspəˌdɑː) NOUN (formerly) the governor or prince of Moldavia or Wallachia under Ottoman rule.
▷HISTORY C17: via Romanian from Ukrainian, from *hospod'* lord; related to Russian *gospodin* courtesy title, Old Slavonic *gospodĭ* lord

host[1] (həʊst) NOUN 1 a person who receives or entertains guests, esp in his own home. 2 **a** a country or organization which provides facilities for and receives visitors to an event. **b** (*as modifier*): *the host nation.* 3 the compere of a show or television programme. 4 *Biology* **a** an animal or plant that nourishes and supports a parasite. **b** an animal, esp an embryo, into which tissue is experimentally grafted. 5 *Computing* a computer connected to a network and providing facilities to other computers and their users. 6 the owner or manager of an inn. ◆ VERB 7 to be the host of (a party, programme, etc.): *to host one's own show.* 8 (*tr*) *US informal* to leave (a restaurant) without paying the bill.
▷HISTORY C13: from French *hoste,* from Latin *hospes* guest, foreigner, from *hostis* enemy

host[2] (həʊst) NOUN 1 a great number; multitude. 2 an archaic word for **army.**
▷HISTORY C13: from Old French *hoste,* from Latin *hostis* stranger, enemy

Host (həʊst) NOUN the bread consecrated in the Eucharist.
▷HISTORY C14: from Old French *oiste,* from Latin *hostia* victim

hosta ('hɒstə) NOUN any plant of the liliaceous genus *Hosta,* of China and Japan: cultivated esp for their ornamental foliage.
▷HISTORY C19: New Latin, named after N. T. *Host* (1761–1834), Austrian physician

hostage ('hɒstɪdʒ) NOUN 1 a person given to or held by a person, organization, etc., as a security or pledge or for ransom, release, exchange for prisoners, etc. 2 the state of being held as a hostage. 3 any security or pledge. 4 **give hostages to fortune.** to place oneself in a position in which misfortune may strike through the loss of what one values most.
▷HISTORY C13: from Old French, from *hoste* guest, HOST[1]

hostel ('hɒstᵊl) NOUN 1 a building providing overnight accommodation, as for the homeless, etc. 2 See **youth hostel.** 3 *Brit* a supervised lodging house for nurses, workers, etc. 4 *Archaic* another word for **hostelry.**
▷HISTORY C13: from Old French, from Medieval Latin *hospitāle* hospice; see HOSPITAL

hosteller *or US* **hosteler** ('hɒstələ) NOUN 1 a person who stays at youth hostels. 2 an archaic word for **innkeeper.**

hostelling *or US* **hosteling** ('hɒstəlɪŋ) NOUN the practice of staying at youth hostels when travelling.

hostelry ('hɒstəlrɪ) NOUN, *plural* **-ries.** *Archaic or facetious* an inn.

hostel school NOUN (in N Canada) a government boarding school for Native American and Inuit students.

hostess ('həʊstɪs) NOUN 1 a woman acting as host. 2 a woman who receives and entertains patrons of a club, restaurant, etc. 3 See **air hostess.**

hostie ('həʊstɪ) NOUN *Austral informal* short for **air hostess.**

hostile ('hɒstaɪl) ADJECTIVE 1 antagonistic; opposed. 2 of or relating to an enemy. 3 unfriendly. ◆ NOUN 4 a hostile person; enemy.
▷HISTORY C16: from Latin *hostīlis,* from *hostis* enemy
▸ **'hostilely** ADVERB

hostile witness NOUN a witness who gives evidence against the party calling him.

hostility (hɒ'stɪlɪtɪ) NOUN, *plural* **-ties.** 1 enmity or antagonism. 2 an act expressing enmity or opposition. 3 (*plural*) fighting; warfare.

hostler ('ɒslə) NOUN another name (esp Brit) for **ostler.**

hot (hɒt) ADJECTIVE **hotter, hottest.** 1 having a relatively high temperature. 2 having a temperature higher than desirable. 3 causing or having a sensation of bodily heat. 4 causing a burning sensation on the tongue: *hot mustard; a hot curry.* 5 expressing or feeling intense emotion, such as embarrassment, anger, or lust. 6 intense or vehement: *a hot argument.* 7 recent; fresh; new: *a hot trial; hot from the press.* 8 *Ball games* (of a ball) thrown or struck hard, and so difficult to respond to. 9 much favoured or approved: *a hot tip; a hot favourite.* 10 *Informal* having a dangerously high level of radioactivity: *a hot laboratory.* 11 *Slang* (of goods or money) stolen, smuggled, or otherwise illegally obtained. 12 *Slang* (of people) being sought by the police. 13 *Informal* sexually attractive. 14 (of a colour) intense; striking: *hot pink.* 15 close or following closely: *hot on the scent.* 16 *Informal* at a dangerously high electric potential: *a hot terminal.* 17 *Physics* having an energy level higher than that of the ground state: *a hot atom.* 18 *Slang* impressive or good of its kind (esp in the phrase **not so hot**). 19 *Jazz, slang* arousing great excitement or enthusiasm by inspired improvisation, strong rhythms, etc. 20 *Informal* dangerous or unpleasant (esp in the phrase **make it hot for someone**). 21 (in various searching or guessing games) very near the answer or object to be found. 22 *Metallurgy* (of a process) at a sufficiently high temperature for metal to be in a soft workable state. 23 *Austral and NZ informal* (of a price, charge, etc.) excessive. 24 **give it (to someone) hot.** to punish or thrash (someone). 25 **hot on.** *Informal* **a** very severe: *the police are hot on drunk drivers.* **b** particularly skilled at or knowledgeable about: *he's hot on vintage cars.* 26 **hot under the collar.** *Informal* aroused with anger, annoyance, etc. 27 **in hot water.** *Informal* in trouble, esp with those in authority. ◆ ADVERB 28 in a hot manner; hotly. ◆ See also **hots, hot up.**
▷HISTORY Old English *hāt;* related to Old High German *heiz,* Old Norse *heitr,* Gothic *heito* fever
▸ **'hotly** ADVERB ▸ **'hotness** NOUN

hot air NOUN *Informal* empty and usually boastful talk.

hot-air balloon NOUN a lighter-than-air craft in which air heated by a flame is trapped in a large fabric bag.

Hotan ('həʊ'tæn), **Hotien,** *or* **Ho-t'ien** ('həʊ'tjɛn) NOUN 1 an oasis in W China, in the Taklimakan Shamo desert of central Xinjiang Uygur Autonomous Region, around the seasonal Hotan River. 2 the chief town of this oasis, situated at the foot of the Kunlun Mountains. Pop.: 71 600 (latest est.). Also called: **Khotan, Hetian.**

hotbed ('hɒtˌbɛd) NOUN 1 a glass-covered bed of soil, usually heated by fermenting material, used for propagating plants, forcing early vegetables, etc. 2 a place offering ideal conditions for the growth of an idea, activity, etc., esp one considered bad: *a hotbed of insurrection.*

hot-blooded ADJECTIVE 1 passionate or excitable. 2 (of a horse) being of thoroughbred stock.
▸ **ˌhot-'bloodedness** NOUN

hot button NOUN *Informal* **a** a controversial subject or issue that is likely to arouse strong emotions. **b** (*as modifier*): *the hot-button issue of abortion.*

hotchpot ('hɒtʃˌpɒt) NOUN *Property law* the collecting of property so that it may be redistributed in equal shares, esp on the intestacy of a parent who has given property to his children in his lifetime.
▷HISTORY C14: from Old French *hochepot,* from *hocher* to shake, of Germanic origin + POT[1]

hotchpotch ('hɒtʃˌpɒtʃ) *or esp US and Canadian* **hodgepodge** NOUN 1 a jumbled mixture. 2 a thick soup or stew made from meat and vegetables.
▷HISTORY C15: variant of HOTCHPOT

hot cockles NOUN (*functioning as singular*) (formerly) a children's game in which one blindfolded player has to guess which other player has hit him.

hot cross bun NOUN a yeast bun with spices, currants, and sometimes candied peel, marked with a cross and traditionally eaten on Good Friday.

hot-desking ('dɛskɪŋ) NOUN the practice of not assigning permanent desks in a workplace, so that employees may work at any available desk.

hot dog[1] NOUN a sausage, esp a frankfurter, served hot in a long roll split lengthways.
▷HISTORY C20: from the supposed resemblance of the sausage to a dachshund

hot dog[2] NOUN 1 *Chiefly US* a person who performs showy acrobatic manoeuvres when skiing or surfing. ◆ VERB **hot-dog, -dogs, -dogging, -dogged.** 2 (*intr*) to perform a series of manoeuvres in skiing, surfing, etc., esp in a showy manner.
▷HISTORY C20: from US *hot dog!,* exclamation of pleasure, approval, etc.

hotel (həʊ'tɛl) NOUN a commercially run establishment providing lodging and usually meals for guests, and often containing a public bar.
▷HISTORY C17: from French *hôtel,* from Old French *hostel;* see HOSTEL

Hotel (həʊ'tɛl) NOUN *Communications* a code word for the letter *h.*

hotelier (həʊ'tɛljeɪ) NOUN an owner or manager of one or more hotels.

hot fence NOUN *NZ* an electric fence surrounding a farm.

hot flush *or US* **hot flash** NOUN a sudden unpleasant hot feeling in the skin, caused by endocrine imbalance, esp experienced by women at menopause.

hotfoot ('hɒt,fʊt) ADVERB [1] with all possible speed; quickly. ◆ VERB [2] to move quickly.

hothead ('hɒt,hɛd) NOUN an excitable or fiery person.

hot-headed ADJECTIVE impetuous, rash, or hot-tempered.
▶,**hot-'headedly** ADVERB ▶,**hot-'headedness** NOUN

hothouse ('hɒt,haʊs) NOUN [1] **a** a greenhouse in which the temperature is maintained at a fixed level above that of the surroundings. **b** (*as modifier*): *a hothouse plant.* [2] a place offering ideal conditions for the growth of an idea, activity, etc.: *the cultural hothouse of Europe and America.* [3] an environment where there is great pressure: *showjumping is a tough, hothouse world.*

Hotien *or* **Ho-t'ien** ('həʊ'tjɛn) NOUN a variant transliteration of the Chinese name for **Hotan.**

hot key NOUN *Computing* a single key or combination of keys on the keyboard of a computer that carries out a series of commands.

hotline ('hɒt,laɪn) NOUN [1] a direct telephone, teletype, or other communications link between heads of government, for emergency use. [2] any such direct line kept for urgent use.

hot link NOUN a word or phrase in a hypertext document that when selected by mouse or keyboard causes information that has been associated with that word or phrase to be displayed. See **hypertext.**

hot metal NOUN **a** metallic type cast into shape in the molten state. **b** (*as modifier*): *hot-metal printing.*

hot money NOUN capital transferred from one financial centre to another seeking the highest interest rates or the best opportunity for short-term gain, esp from changes in exchange rates.

hot pants PLURAL NOUN [1] very brief skin-tight shorts, worn by young women. [2] *Slang* a feeling of sexual arousal: *he has hot pants for her.*

hot pepper NOUN [1] any of several varieties of the pepper *Capsicum frutescens,* esp chilli pepper. [2] the pungent usually small fruit of any of these plants.

hotplate ('hɒt,pleɪt) NOUN [1] an electrically heated plate on a cooker. [2] a portable device, heated electrically or by spirit lamps, etc., on which food can be kept warm.

hotpot ('hɒt,pɒt) NOUN [1] *Brit* a baked stew or casserole made with meat or fish and covered with a layer of potatoes. [2] *Austral slang* a heavily backed horse.

hot potato NOUN *Slang* an awkward or delicate matter.

hot-press NOUN [1] a machine for applying a combination of heat and pressure to give a smooth surface to paper, to express oil from it, etc. ◆ VERB [2] (*tr*) to subject (paper, cloth, etc.) to heat and pressure to give it a smooth surface or extract oil.

hot rod NOUN a car with an engine that has been radically modified to produce increased power.

hots (hɒts) PLURAL NOUN **the.** *Slang* intense sexual desire; lust (esp in the phrase **have the hots for someone**).

hot seat NOUN [1] *Informal* a precarious, difficult, or dangerous position. [2] *US* a slang term for **electric chair.**

hot shoe NOUN *Photog* an accessory shoe on a camera through which electrical contact is made to an electronic flash device.

hotshot ('hɒt,ʃɒt) NOUN *Informal* an important person or expert, esp when showy.

hot spot NOUN [1] an area of potential violence or political unrest. [2] a lively nightclub or other place of entertainment. [3] an area of great activity of a specific type: *the world's economic hot spots.* [4] **a** any local area of high temperature in a part of an engine, etc. **b** part of the inlet manifold of a paraffin engine that is heated by exhaust gases to vaporize the fuel. [5] *Med* **a** a small area on the surface of or within a body with an exceptionally high concentration of radioactivity or of some chemical or mineral considered harmful. **b** a similar area that generates an abnormal amount of heat, as revealed by thermography. [6] *Genetics* a part of a chromosome that has a tendency for mutation or recombination.

hot spring NOUN a natural spring of mineral water at a temperature of 21°C (70°F) or above, found in areas of volcanic activity. Also called: **thermal spring.**

hotspur ('hɒt,spɜː) NOUN an impetuous or fiery person.
▷HISTORY C15: from *Hotspur,* nickname of Sir Henry Percy (1364–1403), English rebel

hot stuff NOUN *Informal* [1] a person, object, etc., considered important, attractive, sexually exciting, etc. [2] a pornographic or erotic book, play, film, etc.

Hottentot ('hɒtᵊn,tɒt) NOUN *Offensive* [1] (*plural* **-tot** *or* **-tots**) another name for the **Khoikhoi** people. [2] any of the languages of this people, belonging to the Khoisan family.
▷HISTORY C17: from Afrikaans, of uncertain origin

Hottentot fig NOUN a perennial plant, *Mesembryanthemum* (or *Carpobrotus*) *edule,* originally South African, having fleshy prostrate leaves, showy yellow or purple flowers, and edible fruits.

hottie *or* **hotty** ('hɒtɪ) NOUN, *plural* **-ties.** *Informal* [1] *US* a sexually attractive person. [2] a hot-water bottle.

hotting ('hɒtɪŋ) NOUN *Informal* the practice of stealing fast cars and putting on a show of skilful but dangerous driving.
▶**'hotter** NOUN

hottish ('hɒtɪʃ) ADJECTIVE fairly hot.

hot up VERB (*adverb*) *Informal* [1] to make or become more exciting, active, or intense: *the chase was hotting up.* [2] (*tr*) another term for **soup up.**

hot-water bottle NOUN a receptacle, now usually made of rubber, designed to be filled with hot water, used for warming a bed or parts of the body.

hot-wire VERB (*tr*) *Slang* to start the engine of (a motor vehicle) by bypassing the ignition switch.

hot-work VERB (*tr*) to shape (metal) when hot.

hot zone NOUN *Computing* a variable area towards the end of a line of text that informs the operator that a decision must be taken as to whether to hyphenate or begin a new line.

houdah ('haʊdə) NOUN a variant spelling of **howdah.**

Houdan ('huːdæn) NOUN a breed of light domestic fowl originally from France, with a distinctive full crest.
▷HISTORY C19: named after *Houdan,* village near Paris where the breed originated

hough (hɒk) *Brit* ◆ NOUN [1] another word for **hock**[1]. [2] (hɒx) in Scotland, a cut of meat corresponding to shin. ◆ VERB (*tr*) [3] to hamstring (cattle, horses, etc.).
▷HISTORY C14: from Old English *hōh* heel

houghmagandie (,hɒxmə'gændɪ) NOUN *Scot* a variant spelling of **hochmagandy.**

Houghton-le-Spring ('haʊtᵊnlə'sprɪŋ) NOUN a town in N England, in Sunderland unitary authority, Tyne and Wear: coal-mining. Pop.: 35 100 (1991).

hoummos, houmous, *or* **houmus** ('huːməs) NOUN variant spellings of **hummus.**

hound[1] (haʊnd) NOUN [1] **a** any of several breeds of dog used for hunting. **b** (*in combination*): *an otterhound; a deerhound.* [2] **the hounds.** a pack of foxhounds, etc. [3] a dog, esp one regarded as annoying. [4] a despicable person. [5] (in hare and hounds) a runner who pursues a hare. [6] *Slang, chiefly US and Canadian* an enthusiast: *an autograph hound.* [7] short for **houndfish.** See also **nursehound.** [8] **ride to hounds** *or* **follow the hounds.** to take part in a fox hunt with hounds. ◆ VERB (*tr*) [9] to pursue or chase relentlessly. [10] to urge on.
▷HISTORY Old English *hund;* related to Old High German *hunt,* Old Norse *hundr,* Gothic *hunds*
▶**'hounder** NOUN

hound[2] (haʊnd) NOUN [1] either of a pair of horizontal bars that reinforce the running gear of a horse-drawn vehicle. [2] *Nautical* either of a pair of fore-and-aft braces that serve as supports for a topmast.
▷HISTORY C15: of Scandinavian origin; related to Old Norse *hūnn* knob, cube

houndfish ('haʊnd,fɪʃ) NOUN, *plural* **-fish** *or* **-fishes.** a name given to various small sharks or dogfish. See also **nursehound.**

hound's-tongue NOUN any boraginaceous weedy plant of the genus *Cynoglossum,* esp the Eurasian *C. officinale,* which has small reddish-purple flowers and spiny fruits. Also called: **dog's-tongue.**
▷HISTORY Old English *hundestunge,* translation of Latin *cynoglōssos,* from Greek *kunoglōssos,* from *kuōn* dog + *glōssa* tongue; referring to the shape of its leaves

hound's-tooth check NOUN a pattern of broken or jagged checks, esp one printed on or woven into cloth. Also called: **dog's-tooth check, dogtooth check.**

houngan *or* **hungan** ('huːŋgᵊn, 'uːŋgᵊn) NOUN a voodoo priest.
▷HISTORY C20: from Haitian Creole, from Fon *hun* deity + *ga* chief

Hounslow ('haʊnzləʊ) NOUN a borough of Greater London, on the River Thames: site of London's first civil airport (1919). Pop.: 212 344 (2001). Area: 59 sq. km (23 sq. miles).

hour (aʊə) NOUN [1] a period of time equal to 3600 seconds; 1/24th of a calendar day. Related adjectives: **horal, horary.** [2] any of the points on the face of a timepiece that indicate intervals of 60 minutes. [3] **the hour.** an exact number of complete hours: *the bus leaves on the hour.* [4] the time of day as indicated by a watch, clock, etc. [5] the period of time allowed for or used for something: *the lunch hour; the hour of prayer.* [6] a special moment or period: *our finest hour.* [7] **the hour.** the present time: *the man of the hour.* [8] the distance covered in an hour: *we live an hour from the city.* [9] *Astronomy* an angular measurement of right ascension equal to 15° or a 24th part of the celestial equator. [10] **one's hour. a** a time of success, fame, etc. **b** Also: **one's last hour.** the time of one's death: *his hour had come.* [11] **take one's hour.** *Irish informal* to do something in a leisurely manner. ◆ See also **hours.**
▷HISTORY C13: from Old French *hore,* from Latin *hōra,* from Greek: season

hour angle NOUN the angular distance along the celestial equator from the meridian of the observer to the hour circle of a particular celestial body.

hour circle NOUN a great circle on the celestial sphere passing through the celestial poles and a specified point, such as a star.

hourglass ('aʊə,glɑːs) NOUN [1] a device consisting of two transparent chambers linked by a narrow channel, containing a quantity of sand that takes a specified time to trickle to one chamber from the other. [2] (*modifier*) well-proportioned with a small waist: *an hourglass figure.*

hour hand NOUN the pointer on a timepiece that indicates the hour. Compare **minute hand, second hand.**

houri ('hʊərɪ) NOUN, *plural* **-ris.** [1] (in Muslim belief) any of the nymphs of Paradise. [2] any alluring woman.
▷HISTORY C18: from French, from Persian *hūri,* from Arabic *hūr,* plural of *haurā'* woman with dark eyes

hourlong ('aʊə,lɒŋ) ADJECTIVE, ADVERB lasting an hour.

hourly ('aʊəlɪ) ADJECTIVE [1] of, occurring, or done every hour. [2] done in or measured by the hour: *we are paid an hourly rate.* [3] continual or frequent. ◆ ADVERB [4] every hour. [5] at any moment or time.

hours (aʊəz) PLURAL NOUN [1] a period regularly or customarily appointed for work, business, etc. [2] one's times of rising and going to bed (esp in the phrases **keep regular, irregular,** or **late hours**). [3] **the small hours.** the hours just after midnight. [4] **till all hours.** until very late. [5] an indefinite period of time. [6] Also called (in the Roman Catholic

Church): **canonical hours. a** the seven times of the day laid down for the recitation of the prayers of the divine office. **b** the prayers recited at these times.

Hours (auəz) PLURAL NOUN another word for the **Horae.**

house NOUN (haus), *plural* **houses** ('hauzɪz). 1 **a** a building used as a home; dwelling. **b** (*as modifier*): *house dog.* 2 the people present in a house, esp its usual occupants. 3 **a** a building used for some specific purpose. **b** (*in combination*): *a schoolhouse.* 4 (*often capital*) a family line including ancestors and relatives, esp a noble one: *the House of York.* 5 **a** a commercial company; firm: *a publishing house.* **b** (*as modifier*): *house style; a house journal.* 6 an official deliberative or legislative body, such as one chamber of a bicameral legislature. 7 a quorum in such a body (esp in the phrase **make a house**). 8 a dwelling for a religious community. 9 *Astrology* any of the 12 divisions of the zodiac. See also **planet** (sense 3). 10 **a** any of several divisions, esp residential, of a large school. **b** (*as modifier*): *house spirit.* 11 **a** a hotel, restaurant, bar, inn, club, etc., or the management of such an establishment. **b** (*as modifier*): *house rules.* **c** (*in combination*): *steakhouse.* 12 (*modifier*) (of wine) sold unnamed by a restaurant, at a lower price than wines specified on the wine list: *the house red.* 13 the audience in a theatre or cinema. 14 an informal word for **brothel.** 15 a hall in which an official deliberative or legislative body meets. 16 See **full house.** 17 *Curling* the 12-foot target circle around the tee. 18 *Nautical* any structure or shelter on the weather deck of a vessel. 19 **bring the house down.** *Theatre* to win great applause. 20 **house and home.** an emphatic form of **home.** 21 **keep open house.** to be always ready to provide hospitality. 22 **like a house on fire.** *Informal* very well, quickly, or intensely. 23 **on the house.** (usually of drinks) paid for by the management of the hotel, bar, etc. 24 **put one's house in order.** to settle or organize one's affairs. 25 **safe as houses.** *Brit* very secure. ◆ VERB (hauz) 26 (*tr*) to provide with or serve as accommodation. 27 to give or receive shelter or lodging. 28 (*tr*) to contain or cover, esp in order to protect. 29 (*tr*) to fit (a piece of wood) into a mortise, joint, etc. 30 (*tr*) *Nautical* **a** to secure or stow. **b** to secure (a topmast). **c** to secure and stow (an anchor).
▷HISTORY Old English *hūs;* related to Old High German *hūs,* Gothic *gudhūs* temple, Old Norse *hūs* house
▸'**houseless** ADJECTIVE

House (haus) **the.** NOUN 1 See **House of Commons.** 2 *Brit informal* the Stock Exchange.

house agent NOUN *Brit* another name for **estate agent.**

house arrest NOUN confinement to one's own home.

houseboat ('haus,bəut) NOUN a stationary boat or barge used as a home.

housebound ('haus,baund) ADJECTIVE unable to leave one's house because of illness, injury, etc.

houseboy ('haus,bɔɪ) NOUN a male domestic servant.

housebreaking ('haus,breɪkɪŋ) NOUN *Criminal law* the act of entering a building as a trespasser for an unlawful purpose. Assimilated with burglary, 1968.
▸'**house,breaker** NOUN

house-broken ADJECTIVE another word for **house-trained.**

housecarl ('haus,kɑːl) NOUN (in medieval Europe) a household warrior of Danish kings and noblemen.
▷HISTORY Old English *hūscarl,* from Old Norse *hūskarl* manservant, from *hūs* HOUSE + *karl* man; see CHURL

house church NOUN 1 a group of Christians meeting for worship in a private house. 2 a nondenominational charismatic Church movement.

housecoat ('haus,kəut) NOUN a woman's loose robelike informal garment.

house-craft NOUN skill in domestic management.

house factor NOUN a Scot term for **estate agent.**

housefather ('haus,fɑːðə) NOUN a man in charge of the welfare of a particular group of children in an institution such as a children's home or approved school.
▸'**house,mother** FEMININE NOUN

housefly ('haus,flaɪ) NOUN, *plural* **-flies.** a common dipterous fly, *Musca domestica,* that frequents human habitations, spreads disease, and lays its eggs in carrion, decaying vegetables, etc.: family *Muscidae.*

houseful ('hausful) NOUN the full amount or number that can be accommodated in a particular house.

house group *or* **church** NOUN a group of Christians who regularly meet to worship, study the Bible, etc., in someone's house.

house guest NOUN a guest at a house, esp one who stays for a comparatively long time.

household ('haus,həuld) NOUN 1 the people living together in one house collectively. 2 (*modifier*) of, relating to, or used in the running of a household; domestic: *household management.*

householder ('haus,həuldə) NOUN a person who owns or rents a house.
▸'**house,holder,ship** NOUN

household gods PLURAL NOUN 1 (in ancient Rome) deities of the home; lares and penates. 2 *Brit informal* the essentials of domestic life.

household name *or* **word** NOUN a person or thing that is very well known.

household troops PLURAL NOUN the infantry and cavalry regiments that carry out escort and guard duties for a head of state.

househusband ('haus,hʌzbənd) NOUN a married man who keeps house, usually without having paid employment.

housekeeper ('haus,kiːpə) NOUN 1 a person, esp a woman, employed to run a household. 2 **good** (*or* **bad**) **housekeeper.** a person who is (or is not) an efficient and thrifty domestic manager.

housekeeping ('haus,kiːpɪŋ) NOUN 1 the running of a household. 2 money allocated for the running of a household. 3 organization and tidiness in general, as of an office, shop, etc. 4 the general maintenance of a computer storage system, including removal of obsolete files, documentation, security copying, etc.

housel ('hauzᵊl) NOUN 1 a medieval name for **Eucharist.** ◆ VERB **-sels, -selling, -selled** *or US* **-sels, -seling, -seled.** 2 (*tr*) to give the Eucharist to (someone).
▷HISTORY Old English *hūsl;* related to Gothic *hunsl* sacrifice, Old Norse *hūsl*

houseleek ('haus,liːk) NOUN any Old World crassulaceous plant of the genus *Sempervivum,* esp *S. tectorum,* which has a rosette of succulent leaves and pinkish flowers: grows on walls. Also called: **hen-and-chickens.**

house lights PLURAL NOUN the lights in the auditorium of a theatre, cinema, etc.

houseline ('haus,laɪn) NOUN *Nautical* tarred marline. Also called: **housing.**

housemaid ('haus,meɪd) NOUN a girl or woman employed to do housework, esp one who is resident in the household.

housemaid's knee NOUN inflammation and swelling of the bursa in front of the kneecap, caused esp by constant kneeling on a hard surface. Technical name: **prepatellar bursitis.**

houseman ('hausmən) NOUN, *plural* **-men.** *Med* a junior doctor who is a member of the medical staff of a hospital. US and Canadian equivalent: **intern.**

house martin NOUN a Eurasian swallow, *Delichon urbica,* with a slightly forked tail and a white and bluish-black plumage.

housemaster ('haus,mɑːstə) NOUN a teacher, esp in a boarding school, responsible for the pupils in his house.
▸**housemistress** ('haus,mɪstrɪs) FEMININE NOUN

housemate ('haus,meɪt) NOUN a person who is not part of the same family, but with whom one shares a house.

house moth NOUN either of two species of micro moth, esp the **brown house moth** (*Hofmannophila pseudospretella*) which, although it usually inhabits birds' nests, sometimes enters houses where its larvae can be very destructive of stored fabrics and foodstuffs.

house mouse NOUN any of various greyish mice of the Old World genus *Mus,* esp *M. musculus,* a common household pest in most parts of the world: family *Muridae.*

House music *or* **House** NOUN a type of disco music originating in the late 1980s, based on funk, with fragments of other recordings edited in electronically.

House of Assembly NOUN a legislative assembly or the lower chamber of such an assembly, esp in various British colonies and countries of the Commonwealth.

house of cards NOUN 1 a tiered structure created by balancing playing cards on their edges. 2 an unstable situation, plan, etc.

House of Commons NOUN (in Britain, Canada, etc.) the lower chamber of Parliament.

house of correction NOUN (formerly) a place of confinement for persons convicted of minor offences.

house officer *or* **houseman** ('hausmən) NOUN, *plural* **-men.** *Med* a doctor who is the most junior member of the medical staff of a hospital, usually resident in the hospital. US and Canadian equivalent: **intern.**

house of God NOUN a church, temple, or chapel.

house of ill repute *or* **ill fame** NOUN a euphemistic name for **brothel.**

House of Keys NOUN the lower chamber of the legislature of the Isle of Man.

House of Lords NOUN (in Britain) the upper chamber of Parliament, composed of the peers of the realm.

House of Representatives NOUN 1 (in the US) the lower chamber of Congress. 2 (in Australia) the lower chamber of Parliament. 3 the sole chamber of New Zealand's Parliament: formerly the lower chamber. 4 (in the US) the lower chamber in many state legislatures.

House of the People NOUN another name for **Lok Sabha.**

house organ NOUN a periodical published by an organization for its employees or clients.

house party NOUN 1 a party, usually in a country house, at which guests are invited to stay for several days. 2 the guests who are invited.

house physician *or* **doctor** NOUN 1 a house officer working in a medical as opposed to a surgical discipline. Compare **house surgeon.** 2 a physician who lives in a hospital or other institution in which he is employed. Also called: **house doctor.** Compare **resident** (sense 7).

house plant NOUN a plant that can be grown indoors.

house-proud ADJECTIVE proud of the appearance, cleanliness, etc., of one's house, sometimes excessively so.

houseroom ('haus,rum, -,ruːm) NOUN 1 room for storage or lodging. 2 **give (something) houseroom.** (*used with a negative*) to have or keep (something) in one's house: *I wouldn't give that vase houseroom.*

house-sit VERB **-sits, -sitting, -sat.** (*intr*) to live in and look after a house during the absence of its owner or owners.
▸'**house-,sitter** NOUN

Houses of Parliament NOUN (in Britain) 1 the building in which the House of Commons and the House of Lords assemble. 2 these two chambers considered together.

house sparrow NOUN a small Eurasian weaverbird, *Passer domesticus,* now established in North America and Australia. It has a brown streaked plumage with grey underparts. Also called (US): **English sparrow.**

house spider NOUN any largish dark spider of the genus *Tegenaria* that is common in houses, such as the cardinal spider.

house style NOUN a set of rules concerning spellings, typography, etc., observed by editorial and printing staff in a particular publishing or printing company.

house surgeon a house officer working in a surgical as opposed to a medical discipline. Compare **house physician.**

house-train VERB (*tr*) *Brit* to train (pets) to urinate

and defecate outside the house or in a special place, such as a litter tray.
▸ 'house-ˌtrained ADJECTIVE

House Un-American Activities Committee NOUN the former name of the **Internal Security Committee** of the US House of Representatives: notorious for its anti-Communist investigations in the late 1940s and 1950s.

house-warming NOUN **a** a party given after moving into a new home. **b** (*as modifier*): *a house-warming party.*

housewife ('haʊsˌwaɪf) NOUN, *plural* **-wives.** [1] a woman, typically a married woman, who keeps house, usually without having paid employment. [2] ('hʌzɪf) Also called: **hussy, huswife.** *Chiefly Brit* a small sewing kit issued to soldiers.
▸ **housewifery** ('haʊsˌwɪfərɪ, -ˌwɪfrɪ) NOUN

housewifely ('haʊsˌwaɪflɪ) ADJECTIVE prudent and neat; domestic: *housewifely virtues.*
▸ '**houseˌwifeliness** NOUN

housewifey ('haʊsˌwaɪfɪ) ADJECTIVE suitable for or typical of a housewife.

housework ('haʊsˌwɜːk) NOUN the work of running a home, such as cleaning, cooking, etc.
▸ '**houseˌworker** NOUN

housey-housey ('haʊzɪ'haʊzɪ) NOUN another name for **bingo** or **lotto.**
▹ HISTORY C20: so called from the cry of "house!" shouted by the winner of a game, probably from FULL HOUSE

housing[1] ('haʊzɪŋ) NOUN [1] **a** houses or dwellings collectively. **b** (*as modifier*): *a housing problem.* [2] the act of providing with accommodation. [3] a hole, recess, groove, or slot made in one wooden member to receive another. [4] a part designed to shelter, cover, contain, or support a component, such as a bearing, or a mechanism, such as a pump or wheel: *a bearing housing; a motor housing; a wheel housing.* [5] another word for **houseline.**

housing[2] ('haʊzɪŋ) NOUN (*often plural*) *Archaic* another word for **trappings** (sense 2).
▹ HISTORY C14: from Old French *houce* covering, of Germanic origin

housing association NOUN *Social welfare* (in Britain) a non-profit-making body whose purpose is to build, convert, or improve houses for letting at fair rents.

housing benefit NOUN *Social welfare* (in Britain) a payment made by a local authority in the form of a rent rebate to a council tenant or a rent allowance to a private tenant.

housing estate NOUN a planned area of housing, often with its own shops and other amenities.

housing project NOUN *US* a housing development built and maintained by a local authority, usually intended for people with a low or moderate income.

housing scheme NOUN *Brit* [1] a local-authority housing plan. [2] the houses built according to such a plan; housing estate. ◆ Often shortened to **scheme.**

Houston ('hjuːstən) NOUN an inland port in SE Texas, linked by the **Houston Ship Canal** to the Gulf of Mexico and the Gulf Intracoastal Waterway: capital of the Republic of Texas (1837–39; 1842–45); site of the Manned Spacecraft Center (1964). Pop.: 1 953 631 (2000).

houstonia (huː'stəʊnɪə) NOUN any small North American rubiaceous plant of the genus *Houstonia,* having blue, white or purple flowers.
▹ HISTORY C19: named after Dr. William *Houston* (died 1733), Scottish botanist

houting ('haʊtɪŋ) NOUN a European whitefish, *Coregonus oxyrhynchus,* that lives in salt water but spawns in freshwater lakes: a valued food fish.
▹ HISTORY C19: from Dutch, from Middle Dutch *houtic,* of uncertain origin

Hovawart ('həʊfəˌvɑːt) NOUN a medium-sized strongly-built dog of a breed with a long thick coat, a thick tuft of hair round the neck, and a long bushy tail.
▹ HISTORY from Middle High German *hova* yard + *wart* watchman

hove (həʊv) VERB *Chiefly nautical* a past tense and past participle of **heave.**

Hove (həʊv) NOUN a town and coastal resort in S England, in Brighton and Hove unitary authority, East Sussex. Pop.: 67 602 (1991).

hovea ('həʊvɪə) NOUN any of various plants of the Australian genus *Hovea,* having clusters of small purple flowers.

hovel ('hʌvᵊl, 'hɒv-) NOUN [1] a ramshackle dwelling place. [2] an open shed for livestock, carts, etc. [3] the conical building enclosing a kiln. ◆ VERB **-els, -elling, -elled** *or US* **-els, -eling, -eled.** [4] to shelter or be sheltered in a hovel.
▹ HISTORY C15: of unknown origin

hover ('hɒvə) VERB (*intr*) [1] to remain suspended in one place. [2] (of certain birds, esp hawks) to remain in one place in the air by rapidly beating the wings. [3] to linger uncertainly in a nervous or solicitous way. [4] to be in a state of indecision: *she was hovering between the two suitors.* ◆ NOUN [5] the act of hovering.
▹ HISTORY C14: *hoveren,* variant of *hoven,* of obscure origin
▸ '**hoverer** NOUN ▸ '**hoveringly** ADVERB

hovercraft ('hɒvəˌkrɑːft) NOUN a vehicle that is able to travel across both land and water on a cushion of air. The cushion is produced by a fan continuously forcing air under the vehicle.

hover fly NOUN any dipterous fly of the family *Syrphidae,* with a typically hovering flight, esp *Syrphus ribesii,* which mimics a wasp.

hoverport ('hɒvəˌpɔːt) NOUN a port for hovercraft.

hovertrain ('hɒvəˌtreɪn) NOUN a train that moves over a concrete track and is supported while in motion by a cushion of air supplied by powerful fans.

how[1] (haʊ) ADVERB [1] in what way? in what manner? by what means?: *how did it happen?* Also used in indirect questions: *tell me how he did it.* [2] to what extent?: *how tall is he?* [3] how good? how well? what…like?: *how did she sing?; how was the holiday?* [4] **how about?** used to suggest something: *how about asking her?; how about a cup of tea?* [5] **how are you?** what is your state of health? [6] **how come?** *Informal* what is the reason (that)?: *how come you told him?* [7] **how's that for…?** **a** is this satisfactory as regards…?: *how's that for size?* **b** an exclamation used to draw attention to a quality, deed, etc.: *how is that for endurance?* [8] **how's that?** **a** what is your opinion? **b** *Cricket* Also written: **howzat** (haʊ'zæt). (an appeal to the umpire) is the batsman out? [9] **how now?** *or* **how so?** *Archaic* what is the meaning of this? [10] Also: **as how.** *Not standard* that: *he told me as how the shop was closed.* [11] in whatever way: *do it how you wish.* [12] used in exclamations to emphasize extent: *how happy I was!* [13] **and how!** (intensifier) very much so! [14] **here's how!** (as a toast) good health! ◆ NOUN [15] the way a thing is done: *the how of it.*
▹ HISTORY Old English *hu;* related to Old Frisian *hū,* Old High German *hweo*

how[2] (haʊ) SENTENCE SUBSTITUTE a greeting supposed to be or have been used by American Indians and often used humorously.
▹ HISTORY C19: of Siouan origin; related to Dakota *háo*

howbeit (haʊ'biːɪt) *Archaic* ◆ SENTENCE CONNECTOR [1] however. ◆ CONJUNCTION [2] (*subordinating*) though; although.

howdah *or* **houdah** ('haʊdə) NOUN a seat for riding on an elephant's back, esp one with a canopy.
▹ HISTORY C18: from Hindi *haudah,* from Arabic *haudaj* load carried by elephant or camel

how do you do SENTENCE SUBSTITUTE [1] Also: **how do?, how d'ye do?** a formal greeting said by people who are being introduced to each other or are meeting for the first time. ◆ NOUN **how-do-you-do.** [2] *Informal* a difficult situation.

howdy ('haʊdɪ) SENTENCE SUBSTITUTE *Chiefly US* an informal word for **hello.**
▹ HISTORY C16: from the phrase *how d'ye do*

howe (haʊ) NOUN *Scot and northern English dialect* a depression in the earth's surface, such as a basin or valley.
▹ HISTORY C16: from HOLE

howe'er (haʊ'ɛə) SENTENCE CONNECTOR, ADVERB a poetic contraction of **however.**

however (haʊ'ɛvə) SENTENCE CONNECTOR [1] still; nevertheless. [2] on the other hand; yet. ◆ ADVERB [3] by whatever means; in whatever manner. [4] (*used with adjectives expressing or admitting of quantity or degree*) no matter how: *however long it takes, finish it.* [5] an emphatic form of **how**[1] (sense 1).

howf *or* **howff** (haʊf, həʊf) NOUN *Scot* a haunt, esp a public house.
▹ HISTORY C16: of uncertain origin

howitzer ('haʊɪtsə) NOUN a cannon having a short or medium barrel with a low muzzle velocity and a steep angle of fire.
▹ HISTORY C16: from Dutch *houwitser,* from German *Haubitze,* from Czech *houfnice* stone-sling

howk (haʊk) VERB *Scot* to dig (out or up).
▹ HISTORY C17: from earlier *holk*

howl (haʊl) NOUN [1] a long plaintive cry or wail characteristic of a wolf or hound. [2] a similar cry of pain or sorrow. [3] *Slang* **a** a person or thing that is very funny. **b** a prolonged outburst of laughter. [4] *Electronics* an unwanted prolonged high-pitched sound produced by a sound-producing system as a result of feedback. ◆ VERB [5] to express in a howl or utter such cries. [6] (*intr*) (of the wind, etc.) to make a wailing noise. [7] (*intr*) *Informal* to shout or laugh.
▹ HISTORY C14: *houlen;* related to Middle High German *hiuweln,* Middle Dutch *hūlen,* Danish *hyle*

howl down VERB (*tr, adverb*) to prevent (a speaker) from being heard by shouting disapprovingly.

howler ('haʊlə) NOUN [1] Also called: **howler monkey.** any large New World monkey of the genus *Alouatta,* inhabiting tropical forests in South America and having a loud howling cry. [2] *Informal* a glaring mistake. [3] *Brit* (formerly) a device that produces a loud tone in a telephone receiver to attract attention when the receiver is incorrectly replaced. [4] a person or thing that howls.

howlet ('haʊlɪt) NOUN *Archaic, poetic* another word for **owl.**
▹ HISTORY C15: diminutive of *howle* OWL

howling ('haʊlɪŋ) ADJECTIVE (*prenominal*) *Informal* (intensifier): *a howling success; a howling error.*
▸ '**howlingly** ADVERB

howlround ('haʊlˌraʊnd) NOUN the condition, resulting in a howling noise, when sound from a loudspeaker is fed back into the microphone of a public-address or recording system. Also called: **howlback.**

Howrah ('haʊrə) NOUN an industrial city in E India, in West Bengal on the Hooghly River opposite Calcutta. Pop.: 950 435 (1991).

howsoever (ˌhaʊsəʊ'ɛvə) SENTENCE CONNECTOR, ADVERB a less common word for **however.**

how-to ADJECTIVE (of a book or guide) giving basic instructions to the lay person on how to do or make something, esp as a hobby or for practical purposes: *a how-to book on carpentry.*

howtowdie (haʊ'taʊdɪ) NOUN a Scottish dish of boiled chicken with poached eggs and spinach.
▹ HISTORY C18: from Old French *hétoudeau, estaudeau* a fat young chicken for cooking

howzit ('haʊzɪt) SENTENCE SUBSTITUTE *South African* an informal word for **hello.**
▹ HISTORY C20: from the phrase *how is it?*

hoy[1] (hɔɪ) NOUN *Nautical* [1] a freight barge. [2] a coastal fishing and trading vessel, usually sloop-rigged, used during the 17th and 18th centuries.
▹ HISTORY C15: from Middle Dutch *hoei*

hoy[2] (hɔɪ) INTERJECTION a cry used to attract attention or drive animals.
▹ HISTORY C14: variant of HEY

hoya ('hɔɪə) NOUN any plant of the asclepiadaceous genus *Hoya,* of E Asia and Australia, esp the waxplant popular as a house plant.
▹ HISTORY C19: named after Thomas *Hoy* (died 1821), English gardener

hoyden *or* **hoiden** ('hɔɪdᵊn) NOUN a wild boisterous girl; tomboy.
▹ HISTORY C16: perhaps from Middle Dutch *heidijn* heathen
▸ '**hoydenish** *or* '**hoidenish** ADJECTIVE ▸ '**hoydenishness** *or* '**hoidenishness** NOUN

Hoylake ('hɔɪˌleɪk) NOUN a town and resort in NW England, in Wirral unitary authority, Merseyside, on the Irish Sea. Pop.: 25 554 (1991).

Hoyle (hɔɪl) NOUN an authoritative book of rules for card games.
▹ HISTORY after Edmond *Hoyle* (1672–1769), English authority on games, its compiler

HP *or* **h.p.** ABBREVIATION FOR: 1 *Brit* hire-purchase. 2 horsepower. 3 high pressure. 4 (in Britain) Houses of Parliament.

HPV ABBREVIATION FOR **human papilloma virus.**

HQ *or* **h.q.** ABBREVIATION FOR headquarters.

hr¹ ABBREVIATION FOR: 1 hour. 2 *Baseball.* home run.

hr² THE INTERNET DOMAIN NAME FOR Croatia.

HR ABBREVIATION FOR: 1 *Brit* Home Rule. 2 *US* House of Representatives. 3 human resources. 4 human rights. ◆ 5 INTERNATIONAL CAR REGISTRATION FOR Croatia.
▷HISTORY (for sense 5) from Serbo-Croat *Hrvatska*

Hradec Králové (*Czech* 'hradɛts 'kraːlɔvɛː) NOUN a town in the N Czech Republic, on the Elbe River. Pop.: 100 528 (1996 est.). German name: **Königgrätz.**

HRE ABBREVIATION FOR Holy Roman Emperor *or* Empire.

HRH ABBREVIATION FOR His (*or* Her) Royal Highness.

HRT ABBREVIATION FOR **hormone replacement therapy.**

Hrvatska ('hrvaːtskaː) NOUN the Serbo-Croat name for **Croatia.**

hryvna ('hrʌvnə) *or* **hryvnya** ('hrʌvnjə) NOUN the standard monetary unit of the Ukraine, divided into 100 kopiykas.

HS ABBREVIATION FOR: 1 High School. 2 (in Britain) Home Secretary.

HSE (in Britain) ABBREVIATION FOR Health and Safety Executive.

HSH ABBREVIATION FOR His (*or* Her) Serene Highness.

Hsi (ʃiː) NOUN a variant spelling of **Xi.**

Hsia-men ('ʃjɑː'mɛn) NOUN a transliteration of the modern Chinese name for **Amoy.**

Hsian (ʃjɑːn) NOUN a variant transliteration of the Chinese name for **Xi An.**

Hsiang (ʃjɑːŋ) NOUN a variant transliteration of the Chinese name for **Xiang.**

Hsining ('ʃiː'nɪŋ) NOUN a variant transliteration of the Chinese name for **Xining.**

HSM ABBREVIATION FOR His (*or* Her) Serene Majesty.

HSRC ABBREVIATION FOR Human Sciences Research Council.

HST ABBREVIATION FOR: 1 (in Britain) high speed train. 2 Hubble Space Telescope. See **Hubble telescope.**

Hsü-chou ('ʃuː'tʃaʊ) NOUN a variant transliteration of the Chinese name for **Xuzhou.**

ht¹ ABBREVIATION FOR height.

ht² THE INTERNET DOMAIN NAME FOR Haiti.

HT *Physics* ABBREVIATION FOR high tension.

HTLV ABBREVIATION FOR human T-cell lymphotrophic virus: any one of a small family of viruses that cause certain rare diseases in the T-cells of human beings; for instance, HTLV I causes a form of leukaemia.

HTML ABBREVIATION FOR hypertext markup language: a text description language that is used for electronic publishing, esp on the World Wide Web.

Hts (in place names) ABBREVIATION FOR Heights.

HTTP ABBREVIATION FOR hypertext transfer protocol, used esp on the World Wide Web. See also **hypertext.**

hu THE INTERNET DOMAIN NAME FOR Hungary.

Huang Hai ('hwæŋ 'haɪ) NOUN the Pinyin transliteration of the Chinese name for the **Yellow Sea.**

Huang Ho ('hwæŋ 'həʊ) NOUN the Pinyin transliteration of the Chinese name for the **Yellow River.**

Huascarán (*Spanish* uaska'ran) *or* **Huascán** (*Spanish* uas'kan) NOUN an extinct volcano in W Peru, in the Peruvian Andes: the highest peak in Peru; avalanche in 1962 killed over 3000 people. Height: 6768 m (22 205 ft.).

hub (hʌb) NOUN 1 the central portion of a wheel, propeller, fan, etc., through which the axle passes. 2 the focal point.
▷HISTORY C17: probably variant of HOB¹

hub-and-spoke NOUN (*modifier*) denoting a method of organizing intercontinental air traffic in which one major airport is used as a feeder for local airports. Sometimes shortened to **hub.**

hubble-bubble ('hʌbᵊl'bʌbᵊl) NOUN 1 another name for **hookah.** 2 hubbub; turmoil. 3 a bubbling or gargling sound.
▷HISTORY C17: rhyming jingle based on BUBBLE

Hubble classification NOUN a method of classifying galaxies depending on whether they are elliptical, spiral, barred spiral, or irregular.
▷HISTORY C20: named after Edwin Powell Hubble (1889–1953), US astronomer

Hubble constant NOUN the rate at which the expansion velocity of the universe depends on distance away. It is currently estimated to lie in the range 60–80 km s^{-1} megaparsec^{-1}. Also called: **Hubble parameter.**

Hubble's law NOUN *Astronomy* a law stating that the velocity of recession of a galaxy is proportional to its distance from the observer.

Hubble telescope NOUN a telescope launched into orbit around the earth in 1990 to provide information about the universe in the visible, infrared, and ultraviolet ranges. Also called: **Hubble space telescope.**
▷HISTORY C20: named after Edwin Powell Hubble (1889–1953), US astronomer

hubbub ('hʌbʌb) NOUN 1 a confused noise of many voices. 2 uproar.
▷HISTORY C16: probably from Irish *hooboobbes;* compare Scottish Gaelic *ubub!* an exclamation of contempt

hubby ('hʌbɪ) NOUN, *plural* **-bies.** an informal word for **husband.**
▷HISTORY C17: by shortening and altering

hubcap ('hʌb,kæp) NOUN a metal cap fitting onto the hub of a wheel, esp a stainless steel or chromium-plated one.

Hubei ('huː'beɪ), **Hupeh,** *or* **Hupei** NOUN a province of central China: largely low-lying with many lakes. Capital: Wuhan. Pop.: 60 280 000 (2000 est.). Area: 187 500 sq. km (72 394 sq. miles).

hubris ('hjuːbrɪs) *or* **hybris** NOUN 1 pride or arrogance. 2 (in Greek tragedy) an excess of ambition, pride, etc., ultimately causing the transgressor's ruin.
▷HISTORY C19: from Greek
▸**hu'bristic** *or* **hy'bristic** ADJECTIVE

huckaback ('hʌkə,bæk) NOUN a coarse absorbent linen or cotton fabric used for towels and informal shirts, etc. Also called: **huck** (hʌk).
▷HISTORY C17: of unknown origin

huckery ('hʌkərɪ) ADJECTIVE *NZ informal* ugly.

huckle ('hʌkᵊl) NOUN *Rare* 1 the hip or haunch. 2 a projecting or humped part.
▷HISTORY C16: diminutive of Middle English *huck* hip, haunch; perhaps related to Old Norse *hūka* to squat

huckleberry ('hʌkᵊl,bɛrɪ) NOUN, *plural* **-ries.** 1 any American ericaceous shrub of the genus *Gaylussacia,* having edible dark blue berries with large seeds. 2 the fruit of any of these shrubs. 3 another name for **blueberry.** 4 a Brit name for **whortleberry** (sense 1).
▷HISTORY C17: probably a variant of *hurtleberry,* of unknown origin

hucklebone ('hʌkᵊl,bəʊn) NOUN *Archaic* 1 the anklebone; talus. 2 the hipbone; innominate bone.

huckster ('hʌkstə) NOUN 1 a person who uses aggressive or questionable methods of selling. 2 *Now rare* a person who sells small articles or fruit in the street. 3 *US* a person who writes for radio or television advertisements. ◆ VERB 4 (*tr*) to peddle. 5 (*tr*) to sell or advertise aggressively or questionably. 6 to haggle (over).
▷HISTORY C12: perhaps from Middle Dutch *hoekster,* from *hoeken* to carry on the back
▸**'hucksterism** NOUN

HUD ABBREVIATION FOR **head-up display.**

Huddersfield ('hʌdəz,fiːld) NOUN a town in N England, in Kirklees unitary authority, West Yorkshire, on the River Colne: former textile centre, now with varied manufacturing and services; university 1992. Pop.: 143 726 (1991).

huddle ('hʌdᵊl) NOUN 1 a heaped or crowded mass of people or things. 2 *Informal* a private or impromptu conference (esp in the phrase **go into a huddle**). ◆ VERB 3 to crowd or cause to crowd or nestle closely together. 4 (often foll by *up*) to draw or hunch (oneself), as through cold. 5 (*intr*) *Informal* to meet and confer privately. 6 (*tr*) *Chiefly Brit* to do (something) in a careless way. 7 (*tr*) *Rare* to put on (clothes) hurriedly.
▷HISTORY C16: of uncertain origin; compare Middle English *hoderen* to wrap up
▸**'huddler** NOUN

hudibrastic (,hjuːdɪ'bræstɪk) ADJECTIVE mock-heroic in style.
▷HISTORY C18: after *Hudibras,* poem (1663–68) by Samuel Butler

Hudson Bay NOUN an inland sea in NE Canada: linked with the Atlantic by **Hudson Strait;** the S extension forms James Bay; discovered in 1610 by Henry Hudson. Area (excluding James Bay): 647 500 sq. km (250 000 sq. miles).

Hudson River NOUN a river in E New York State, flowing generally south into Upper New York Bay: linked to the Great Lakes, the St Lawrence Seaway, and Lake Champlain by the New York State Barge Canal and the canalized Mohawk River. Length: 492 km (306 miles).

Hudson's Bay blanket NOUN *Canadian* a woollen blanket with wide stripes.
▷HISTORY C19: from a type of blanket originally sold by the Hudson's Bay Company

Hudson's Bay Company NOUN an English company chartered in 1670 to trade in all parts of North America drained by rivers flowing into Hudson Bay.

Hudson seal NOUN muskrat fur that has been dressed and dyed to resemble sealskin.

hue (hjuː) NOUN 1 the attribute of colour that enables an observer to classify it as red, green, blue, purple, etc., and excludes white, black, and shades of grey. See also **colour.** 2 a shade of a colour. 3 aspect; complexion: *a different hue on matters.*
▷HISTORY Old English *hīw* beauty; related to Old Norse *hȳ* fine hair, Gothic *hiwi* form

Hué (*French* ɥe) NOUN a port in central Vietnam, on the delta of the **Hué River** near the South China Sea: former capital of the kingdom of Annam, of French Indochina (1883–1946), and of Central Vietnam (1946–54). Pop.: 219 149 (1992 est.).

hue and cry NOUN 1 (formerly) the pursuit of a suspected criminal with loud cries in order to raise the alarm. 2 any loud public outcry.
▷HISTORY C16: from Anglo-French *hu et cri,* from Old French *hue* outcry, from *huer* to shout, from *hu!* shout of warning + *cri* CRY

hued (hjuːd) ADJECTIVE *Archaic or poetic* **a** having a hue or colour as specified. **b** (*in combination*): *rosy-hued dawn.*

huff (hʌf) NOUN 1 a passing mood of anger or pique (esp in the phrase **in a huff**). ◆ VERB 2 to make or become angry or resentful. 3 (*intr*) to blow or puff heavily. 4 Also: **blow.** *Draughts* to remove (an opponent's draught) from the board for failure to make a capture. 5 (*tr*) *Obsolete* to bully. 6 **huffing and puffing.** empty threats or objections; bluster.
▷HISTORY C16: of imitative origin; compare PUFF
▸**'huffish** *or* **'huffy** ADJECTIVE ▸**'huffily** *or* **'huffishly** ADVERB
▸**'huffiness** *or* **'huffishness** NOUN

Hufuf (hʊ'fuːf) NOUN See **Al Hufuf.**

hug (hʌg) VERB **hugs, hugging, hugged.** (*mainly tr*) 1 (*also intr*) to clasp (another person or thing) tightly or (of two people) to cling close together; embrace. 2 to keep close to a shore, kerb, etc. 3 to cling to (beliefs, etc.); cherish. 4 to congratulate (oneself); be delighted with (oneself). ◆ NOUN 5 a tight or fond embrace.
▷HISTORY C16: probably of Scandinavian origin; related to Old Norse *hugga* to comfort, Old English *hogian* to take care of
▸**'huggable** ADJECTIVE ▸**'hugger** NOUN

huge (hjuːdʒ) ADJECTIVE extremely large in size, amount, or scope. Archaic form: **hugeous.**
▷HISTORY C13: from Old French *ahuge,* of uncertain origin
▸**'hugeness** NOUN

hugely ('hjuːdʒlɪ) ADVERB very much; enormously.

hugger-mugger ('hʌgə,mʌgə) NOUN 1 confusion. 2 *Rare* secrecy. ◆ ADJECTIVE, ADVERB *Archaic* 3 with secrecy. 4 in confusion. ◆ VERB *Obsolete* 5 (*tr*) to keep secret. 6 (*intr*) to act secretly.
▷HISTORY C16: of uncertain origin

huggy ('hʌgɪ) ADJECTIVE *Informal* sensitive and caring: *a soft, lovely, huggy person.*

hug-me-tight NOUN a woman's knitted jacket.

Huguenot ('hjuːgəˌnəʊ, -ˌnɒt) NOUN 1 a French Calvinist, esp of the 16th or 17th centuries. ◆ ADJECTIVE 2 designating the French Protestant Church.
▷HISTORY C16: from French, from Genevan dialect *eyguenot* one who opposed annexation by Savoy, ultimately from Swiss German *Eidgenoss* confederate; influenced by *Hugues,* surname of 16th-century Genevan burgomaster
▸ˌHugue'notic ADJECTIVE ▸'Hugueˌnotism NOUN

huh (*spelling pron* hʌ) INTERJECTION an exclamation of derision, bewilderment, inquiry, etc.

Huhehot (ˌhuːhɪ'hɒt ˌhuːɪ-) *or* **Hu-ho-hao-t'e** (ˌhuːhəʊ-haʊ'teɪ) NOUN a variant transliteration of the Chinese name for **Hohhot**.

huhu ('huːhuː) NOUN a New Zealand beetle, *Prionoplus reticularis,* with a hairy body.
▷HISTORY Maori

hui ('huːɪ) NOUN, *plural* **huies**. *NZ* a conference, meeting, or other gathering.
▷HISTORY Maori

huia ('hʊɪjə) NOUN an extinct bird of New Zealand, *Heteralocha acutirostris,* prized by early Maoris for its distinctive tail feathers.
▷HISTORY Maori

hula ('huːlə) *or* **hula-hula** NOUN a Hawaiian dance performed by a woman.
▷HISTORY from Hawaiian

Hula Hoop NOUN *Trademark* a light hoop that is whirled around the body by movements of the waist and hips.

hula skirt NOUN a skirt made of long grass attached to a waistband and worn by hula dancers.

hulk (hʌlk) NOUN 1 the body of an abandoned vessel. 2 *Disparaging* a large or unwieldy vessel. 3 *Disparaging* a large ungainly person or thing. 4 (*often plural*) the frame or hull of a ship, used as a storehouse, etc., or (esp in 19th-century Britain) as a prison. ◆ VERB 5 (*intr*) *Brit informal* to move clumsily. 6 (*intr;* often foll by *up*) to rise massively.
▷HISTORY Old English *hulc,* from Medieval Latin *hulca,* from Greek *holkas* barge, from *helkein* to tow

hulking ('hʌlkɪŋ) ADJECTIVE big and ungainly. Also: **hulky**.

hull (hʌl) NOUN 1 the main body of a vessel, tank, flying boat, etc. 2 the shell or pod of peas or beans; the outer covering of any fruit or seed; husk. 3 the persistent calyx at the base of a strawberry, raspberry, or similar fruit. 4 the outer casing of a missile, rocket, etc. ◆ VERB 5 to remove the hulls from (fruit or seeds). 6 (*tr*) to pierce the hull of (a vessel, tank, etc.).
▷HISTORY Old English *hulu;* related to Old High German *helawa,* Old English *helan* to hide
▸'huller NOUN ▸'hull-less ADJECTIVE

Hull (hʌl) NOUN 1 a city and port in NE England, in Kingston upon Hull unitary authority, East Riding of Yorkshire: fishing, food processing; two universities. Pop.: 310 636 (1991). Official name: **Kingston upon Hull**. 2 a city in SE Canada, in SW Quebec on the River Ottawa: a centre of the timber trade and associated industries. Pop.: 60 707 (1991).

hullabaloo *or* **hullaballoo** (ˌhʌləbə'luː) NOUN, *plural* **-loos**. loud confused noise, esp of protest; commotion.
▷HISTORY C18: perhaps from interjection HALLO + Scottish *baloo* lullaby

hull down ADJECTIVE 1 (of a ship) having its hull concealed by the horizon. 2 (of a tank) having only its turret visible.

hullo (hʌ'ləʊ) SENTENCE SUBSTITUTE, NOUN a variant of **hello**.

hum (hʌm) VERB **hums, humming, hummed**. 1 (*intr*) to make a low continuous vibrating sound like that of a prolonged *m*. 2 (*intr*) (of a person) to sing with the lips closed. 3 (*intr*) to utter an indistinct sound, as in hesitation; hem. 4 (*intr*) *Informal* to be in a state of feverish activity. 5 (*intr*) *Brit and Irish slang* to smell unpleasant. 6 (*intr*) *Austral slang* to scrounge. 7 **hum and haw**. See **hem**² (sense 3). ◆ NOUN 8 a low continuous murmuring sound. 9 *Electronics* an undesired low-frequency noise in the output of an amplifier or receiver, esp one caused by the power supply. 10 *Austral slang* a scrounger; cadger. 11 *Brit and Irish slang* an unpleasant odour. ◆ INTERJECTION, NOUN 12 an indistinct sound of hesitation, embarrassment, etc.; hem.
▷HISTORY C14: of imitative origin; compare Dutch *hommelen,* Old High German *humbal* bumblebee
▸'hummer NOUN

human ('hjuːmən) ADJECTIVE 1 of, characterizing, or relating to man and mankind: *human nature.* 2 consisting of people: *the human race; a human chain.* 3 having the attributes of man as opposed to animals, divine beings, or machines: *human failings.* 4 **a** kind or considerate. **b** natural. ◆ NOUN 5 a human being; person. Related prefix: **anthropo-**.
▷HISTORY C14: from Latin *hūmānus;* related to Latin *homō* man
▸'human-ˌlike ADJECTIVE ▸'humanness NOUN

human being NOUN a member of any of the races of *Homo sapiens;* person; man, woman, or child.

human capital NOUN *Economics* the abilities and skills of any individual, esp those acquired through investment in education and training, that enhance potential income earning.

humane (hjuː'meɪn) ADJECTIVE 1 characterized by kindness, mercy, sympathy, etc. 2 inflicting as little pain as possible: *a humane killing.* 3 civilizing or liberal (esp in the phrases **humane studies, humane education**).
▷HISTORY C16: variant of HUMAN
▸hu'manely ADVERB ▸hu'maneness NOUN

humane society NOUN an organization for promotion of humane ideals, esp in dealing with animals.

Human Fertilization and Embryology Authority NOUN an organization set up by act of Parliament (1990) to control and review research involving embryos. It maintains a register of persons whose gametes are used for assisted conception. Abbreviation: **HFEA**.

human immunodeficiency virus NOUN the full name for **HIV**.

human interest NOUN (in a newspaper story, news broadcasting, etc.) reference to individuals and their emotions.

humanism ('hjuːməˌnɪzəm) NOUN 1 the denial of any power or moral value superior to that of humanity; the rejection of religion in favour of a belief in the advancement of humanity by its own efforts. 2 a philosophical position that stresses the autonomy of human reason in contradistinction to the authority of the Church. 3 (*often capital*) a cultural movement of the Renaissance, based on classical studies. 4 interest in the welfare of people.
▸'humanist NOUN ▸ˌhuman'istic ADJECTIVE

humanistic psychology NOUN approach to psychology advocated by some that emphasizes feelings and emotions and the better understanding of the self in terms of observation of oneself and one's relations with others.

humanitarian (hjuːˌmænɪ'tɛərɪən) ADJECTIVE 1 having the interests of mankind at heart. 2 of or relating to ethical or theological humanitarianism. ◆ NOUN 3 a philanthropist. 4 an adherent of humanitarianism.

humanitarianism (hjuːˌmænɪ'tɛərɪəˌnɪzəm) NOUN 1 humanitarian principles. 2 *Ethics* **a** the doctrine that man's duty is to strive to promote the welfare of mankind. **b** the doctrine that man can achieve perfection through his own resources. 3 *Theol* the belief that Jesus Christ was only a mortal man.
▸huˌmani'tarianist NOUN

humanity (hjuː'mænɪtɪ) NOUN, *plural* **-ties**. 1 the human race. 2 the quality of being human. 3 kindness or mercy. 4 (*plural;* usually preceded by *the*) the study of literature, philosophy, and the arts. 5 the study of Ancient Greek and Roman language, literature, etc.

humanize *or* **humanise** ('hjuːməˌnaɪz) VERB 1 to make or become human. 2 to make or become humane.
▸ˌhumani'zation *or* ˌhumani'sation NOUN ▸'humanˌizer *or* 'humanˌiser NOUN

humankind (ˌhjuːmən'kaɪnd) NOUN the human race; humanity.

Language note See at **mankind**.

humanly ('hjuːmənlɪ) ADVERB 1 by human powers or means. 2 in a human or humane manner.

human nature NOUN 1 the qualities common to humanity. 2 ordinary human behaviour, esp considered as less than perfect. 3 *Sociol* the unique elements that form a basic part of human life and distinguish it from other animal life.

humanoid ('hjuːməˌnɔɪd) ADJECTIVE 1 like a human being in appearance. ◆ NOUN 2 a being with human rather than anthropoid characteristics. 3 (in science fiction) a robot or creature resembling a human being.

human papilloma virus NOUN any one of a class of viruses that cause tumours, including warts, in humans. Certain strains infect the cervix and have been implicated as a cause of cervical cancer. Abbreviation: **HPV**.

human resources PLURAL NOUN 1 **a** the workforce of an organization. **b** (*as modifier*): *human-resources management; human-resources officer.* 2 **a** the office or department in an organization that interviews, appoints, or keeps records of employees. **b** (*as modifier*): *a human-resources consultancy.* 3 the contribution to an employing organization which its workforce could provide in effort, skills, knowledge, etc.

human rights PLURAL NOUN the rights of individuals to liberty, justice, etc.

Humber ('hʌmbə) NOUN an estuary in NE England, into which flow the Rivers Ouse and Trent: flows east into the North Sea; navigable for large ocean-going ships as far as Hull; crossed by the **Humber Bridge** (1981), a single-span suspension bridge with a main span of 1410 m (4626 ft.). Length: 64 km (40 miles).

Humberside ('hʌmbəˌsaɪd) NOUN a former county of N England around the Humber estuary, formed in 1974 from parts of the East and West Ridings of Yorkshire and N Lincolnshire: replaced in 1996 by the unitary authorities of East Riding of Yorkshire, Kingston upon Hull, North Lincolnshire, and North East Lincolnshire.

humble ('hʌmbᵊl) ADJECTIVE 1 conscious of one's failings. 2 unpretentious; lowly: *a humble cottage; my humble opinion.* 3 deferential or servile. ◆ VERB (*tr*) 4 to cause to become humble; humiliate. 5 to lower in status.
▷HISTORY C13: from Old French, from Latin *humilis* low, from *humus* the ground
▸'humbled ADJECTIVE ▸'humbleness NOUN ▸'humbler NOUN ▸'humbling ADJECTIVE ▸'humblingly ADVERB ▸'humbly ADVERB

humblebee ('hʌmbᵊlˌbiː) NOUN another name for the **bumblebee**.
▷HISTORY C15: related to Middle Dutch *hommel* bumblebee, Old High German *humbal;* see HUM

humble pie NOUN 1 (formerly) a pie made from the heart, entrails, etc., of a deer. 2 **eat humble pie**. to behave or be forced to behave humbly; be humiliated.
▷HISTORY C17: earlier *an umble pie,* by mistaken word division from *a numble pie,* from *numbles* offal of a deer, from Old French *nombles,* ultimately from Latin *lumbulus* a little loin, from *lumbus* loin

Humboldt Current NOUN a cold ocean current of the S Pacific, flowing north along the coasts of Chile and Peru. Also called: **Peru Current**.

humbucker ('hʌmˌbʌkə) NOUN a twin-coil guitar pick-up.

humbug ('hʌmˌbʌg) NOUN 1 a person or thing that tricks or deceives. 2 nonsense; rubbish. 3 *Brit* a hard boiled sweet, usually flavoured with peppermint and often having a striped pattern. ◆ VERB **-bugs, -bugging, -bugged**. 4 to cheat or deceive (someone).
▷HISTORY C18: of unknown origin
▸'humˌbugger NOUN ▸'humˌbuggery NOUN

humdinger ('hʌmˌdɪŋə) NOUN *Slang* 1 something unusually large: *a humdinger of a recession.* 2 an excellent person or thing: *a humdinger of a party.*
▷HISTORY C20: of unknown origin

humdrum ('hʌmˌdrʌm) ADJECTIVE 1 ordinary; dull. ◆ NOUN 2 a monotonous routine, task, or person.
▷HISTORY C16: rhyming compound, probably based on HUM
▸'humˌdrumness NOUN

humectant (hjuːˈmɛktənt) ADJECTIVE [1] producing moisture. ◆ NOUN [2] a substance added to another substance to keep it moist.
▷HISTORY C17: from Latin *ūmectāre* to wet, from *ūmēre* to be moist, from *ūmor* moisture; see HUMOUR

humeral (ˈhjuːmərəl) ADJECTIVE [1] *Anatomy* of or relating to the humerus. [2] of or near the shoulder.

humeral veil NOUN *RC Church* a silk shawl worn by a priest at High Mass, etc. Often shortened to **veil**.

humerus (ˈhjuːmərəs) NOUN, *plural* **-meri** (-məˌraɪ). [1] the bone that extends from the shoulder to the elbow. [2] the corresponding bone in other vertebrates.
▷HISTORY C17: from Latin *umerus;* related to Gothic *ams* shoulder, Greek *ōmos*

Hume's law NOUN the philosophical doctrine that an evaluative statement cannot be derived from purely factual premises, often formulated as: *one can't derive an "ought" from an "is".* See also **naturalistic fallacy**.
▷HISTORY named after David *Hume* (1711–76), Scottish empiricist philosopher, economist, and historian

humic (ˈhjuːmɪk) ADJECTIVE of, relating to, derived from, or resembling humus: *humic acids.*
▷HISTORY C19: from Latin *humus* ground + -IC

humicole (ˈhjuːmɪˌkəʊl) NOUN *Now rare* any plant that thrives on humus.
▸**humicolous** (hjuːˈmɪkələs) ADJECTIVE

humid (ˈhjuːmɪd) ADJECTIVE moist; damp: *a humid day.*
▷HISTORY C16: from Latin *ūmidus,* from *ūmēre* to be wet; see HUMECTANT, HUMOUR
▸ˈ**humidly** ADVERB ▸ˈ**humidness** NOUN

humidex (ˈhjuːmɪˌdeks) NOUN *Canadian* a scale indicating the levels of heat and humidity in current weather conditions.
▷HISTORY C20: from HUMID + (IN)DEX

humidifier (hjuːˈmɪdɪˌfaɪə) NOUN a device for increasing or controlling the water vapour in a room, building, etc.

humidify (hjuːˈmɪdɪˌfaɪ) VERB **-fies, -fying, -fied.** (*tr*) to make (air) humid or damp.
▸**huˌmidifiˈcation** NOUN

humidistat (hjuːˈmɪdɪˌstæt) NOUN a device for maintaining constant humidity. Also called: **hygrostat.**

humidity (hjuːˈmɪdɪtɪ) NOUN [1] the state of being humid; dampness. [2] a measure of the amount of moisture in the air. See **relative humidity, absolute humidity.**

humidor (ˈhjuːmɪˌdɔː) NOUN a humid place or container for storing cigars, tobacco, etc.

humify (ˈhjuːmɪˌfaɪ) VERB **-fies, -fying, -fied.** to convert or be converted into humus.
▸ˌ**humifiˈcation** NOUN

humiliate (hjuːˈmɪlɪˌeɪt) VERB (*tr*) to lower or hurt the dignity or pride of.
▷HISTORY C16: from Late Latin *humiliāre,* from Latin *humilis* HUMBLE
▸**huˈmiliˌated** ADJECTIVE ▸**huˈmiliˌating** ADJECTIVE ▸**huˈmiliˌatingly** ADVERB ▸**huˌmiliˈation** NOUN ▸**humiliative** (hjuːˈmɪljətɪv) ADJECTIVE ▸**huˈmiliˌator** NOUN ▸**huˈmiliatory** ADJECTIVE

humility (hjuːˈmɪlɪtɪ) NOUN, *plural* **-ties.** the state or quality of being humble.

hummel (ˈhʌməl) ADJECTIVE *Scot* [1] (of cattle) hornless. [2] (of grain) awnless.
▷HISTORY C15: of Germanic origin; compare Low German *hummel* hornless animal

hummingbird (ˈhʌmɪŋˌbɜːd) NOUN any very small American bird of the family *Trochilidae,* having a brilliant iridescent plumage, long slender bill, and wings specialized for very powerful vibrating flight: order *Apodiformes.*

hummingbird moth NOUN *US* another name for the **hawk moth.**

humming top NOUN a top that hums as it spins.

hummock (ˈhʌmək) NOUN [1] a hillock; knoll. [2] a ridge or mound of ice in an ice field. [3] Also called: **hammock.** *Chiefly southern US* a wooded area lying above the level of an adjacent marsh.
▷HISTORY C16: of uncertain origin; compare HUMP, HAMMOCK
▸ˈ**hummocky** ADJECTIVE

hummus, hoummos, *or* **houmous** (ˈhʊməs) NOUN a creamy dip originating in the Middle East, made from puréed chickpeas, tahina, etc.
▷HISTORY from Turkish *humus*

> **Language note** Avoid confusion with **humus.**

humoral (ˈhjuːmərəl) ADJECTIVE [1] *Immunol* denoting or relating to a type of immunity caused by free antibodies circulating in the blood. [2] *Obsolete* of or relating to the four bodily fluids (humours).

humoresque (ˌhjuːməˈrɛsk) NOUN a short lively piece of music.
▷HISTORY C19: from German *Humoreske,* ultimately from English HUMOUR

humorist (ˈhjuːmərɪst) NOUN a person who acts, speaks, or writes in a humorous way.
▸ˌ**humorˈistic** ADJECTIVE

humorous (ˈhjuːmərəs) ADJECTIVE [1] funny; comical; amusing. [2] displaying or creating humour. [3] *Archaic* another word for **capricious.**
▸ˈ**humorously** ADVERB ▸ˈ**humorousness** NOUN

humour *or US* **humor** (ˈhjuːmə) NOUN [1] the quality of being funny. [2] Also called: **sense of humour.** the ability to appreciate or express that which is humorous. [3] situations, speech, or writings that are thought to be humorous. [4] **a** a state of mind; temper; mood. **b** (*in combination*): *ill humour; good humour.* [5] temperament or disposition. [6] a caprice or whim. [7] any of various fluids in the body, esp the aqueous humour and vitreous humour. [8] Also called: **cardinal humour.** *Archaic* any of the four bodily fluids (blood, phlegm, choler or yellow bile, melancholy or black bile) formerly thought to determine emotional and physical disposition. [9] **out of humour.** in a bad mood. ◆ VERB (*tr*) [10] to attempt to gratify; indulge: *he humoured the boy's whims.* [11] to adapt oneself to: *to humour someone's fantasies.*
▷HISTORY C14: from Latin *humor* liquid; related to Latin *ūmēre* to be wet, Old Norse *vökr* moist, Greek *hugros* wet
▸ˈ**humourful** *or US* ˈ**humorful** ADJECTIVE ▸ˈ**humourless** *or US* ˈ**humorless** ADJECTIVE ▸ˈ**humourlessness** *or US* ˈ**humorlessness** NOUN

humoursome *or US* **humorsome** (ˈhjuːməsəm) ADJECTIVE [1] capricious; fanciful. [2] inclined to humour (someone).

hump (hʌmp) NOUN [1] a rounded protuberance or projection, as of earth, sand, etc. [2] *Pathol* a rounded deformity of the back in persons with kyphosis, consisting of a convex spinal curvature. [3] a rounded protuberance on the back of a camel or related animal. [4] **the hump.** *Brit informal* a fit of depression or sulking (esp in the phrase **it gives me the hump**). [5] **over the hump.** past the largest or most difficult portion of work, time, etc. ◆ VERB [6] to form or become a hump; hunch; arch. [7] (*tr*) *Brit slang* to carry or heave. [8] *Slang* to have sexual intercourse with (someone). [9] **hump one's swag.** *Austral and NZ informal* (of a tramp) to carry one's belongings from place to place on one's back.
▷HISTORY C18: probably from earlier HUMPBACKED
▸ˈ**humpˌlike** ADJECTIVE

humpback (ˈhʌmpˌbæk) NOUN [1] another word for **hunchback.** [2] Also called: **humpback whale.** a large whalebone whale, *Megaptera novaeangliae,* closely related and similar to the rorquals but with a humped back and long flippers: family *Balaenopteridae.* [3] a Pacific salmon, *Oncorhynchus gorbuscha,* the male of which has a humped back and hooked jaws. [4] Also called: **humpback bridge.** *Brit* a road bridge having a sharp incline and decline and usually a narrow roadway.
▷HISTORY C17: alteration of earlier *crumpbacked,* perhaps influenced by HUNCHBACK; perhaps related to Dutch *homp* lump
▸ˈ**humpˌbacked** ADJECTIVE

humph (*spelling pron* hʌmf) INTERJECTION an exclamation of annoyance, dissatisfaction, scepticism, etc.

humpty (ˈhʌmptɪ) NOUN *Brit* a low padded seat; pouffe.
▷HISTORY C20: from *humpty* hunchbacked, perhaps influenced by *Humpty Dumpty* (nursery rhyme)

humpty dumpty (ˈhʌmptɪ ˈdʌmptɪ) NOUN *Chiefly Brit* [1] a short fat person. [2] a person or thing that once overthrown or broken cannot be restored or mended.
▷HISTORY C18: after the nursery rhyme *Humpty Dumpty*

humpy[1] (ˈhʌmpɪ) ADJECTIVE **humpier, humpiest.** [1] full of humps. [2] *Brit informal* angry or gloomy.
▸ˈ**humpiness** NOUN

humpy[2] (ˈhʌmpɪ) NOUN, *plural* **humpies.** *Austral* a primitive hut.
▷HISTORY C19: from a native Australian language

Hums (hʊms) NOUN a variant of **Homs.**

hum tone NOUN a note produced by a bell when struck, lying an octave or (in many English bells) a sixth or seventh below the strike tone. Also called (esp Brit): **hum note.**

humus (ˈhjuːməs) NOUN a dark brown or black colloidal mass of partially decomposed organic matter in the soil. It improves the fertility and water retention of the soil and is therefore important for plant growth.
▷HISTORY C18: from Latin: soil, earth

> **Language note** Avoid confusion with **hummus.**

Hun (hʌn) NOUN [1] a member of any of several Asiatic nomadic peoples speaking Mongoloid or Turkic languages who dominated much of Asia and E Europe from before 300 B.C., invading the Roman Empire in the 4th and 5th centuries A.D. [2] *Informal* (esp in World War I) a derogatory name for a **German.** [3] *Informal* a vandal.
▷HISTORY Old English *Hūnas,* from Late Latin *Hūnī,* from Turkish *Hun-yū*
▸ˈ**HunˌlIke** ADJECTIVE

Hunan (ˈhuːˈnæn) NOUN a province of S China, between the Yangtze River and the Nan Ling Mountains: drained chiefly by the Xiang and Yüan Rivers; valuable mineral resources. Capital: Changsha. Pop.: 64 400 000 (2000 est.). Area: 210 500 sq. km (82 095 sq. miles).

hunch (hʌntʃ) NOUN [1] an intuitive guess or feeling. [2] another word for **hump.** [3] a lump or large piece. ◆ VERB [4] to bend or draw (oneself or a part of the body) up or together. [5] (*intr;* usually foll by *up*) to sit in a hunched position.
▷HISTORY C16: of unknown origin

hunchback (ˈhʌntʃˌbæk) NOUN [1] a person having an abnormal convex curvature of the thoracic spine. [2] such a curvature. Also called: **humpback.** See **kyphosis.** Compare **hollow-back.**
▷HISTORY C18: from earlier *hunchbacked, huckbacked* humpbacked, influenced by *bunchbacked,* from *bunch* (in obsolete sense of *hump*) + BACKED
▸ˈ**hunchˌbacked** ADJECTIVE

hundred (ˈhʌndrəd) NOUN, *plural* **-dreds** *or* **-dred.** [1] the cardinal number that is the product of ten and ten; five score. See also **number** (sense 1). [2] a numeral, 100, C, etc., representing this number. [3] (*often plural*) a large but unspecified number, amount, or quantity: *there will be hundreds of people there.* [4] **the hundreds. a** the numbers 100 to 109: *the temperature was in the hundreds.* **b** the numbers 100 to 199: *his score went into the hundreds.* **c** the numbers 100 to 999: *the price was in the hundreds.* [5] (*plural*) the 100 years of a specified century: *in the sixteen hundreds.* [6] something representing, represented by, or consisting of 100 units. [7] *Maths* the position containing a digit representing that number followed by two zeros: *in 4376, 3 is in the hundred's place.* [8] an ancient division of a county in England, Ireland, and parts of the US. ◆ DETERMINER [9] **a** amounting to or approximately a hundred: *a hundred reasons for that.* **b** (*as pronoun*): *the hundred I chose.* [10] amounting to 100 times a particular scientific quantity: *a hundred volts.* Related prefix: **hecto-.**
▷HISTORY Old English; related to Old Frisian *hunderd,* Old Norse *hundrath,* German *hundert,* Gothic *hund,* Latin *centum,* Greek *hekaton*

hundred days PLURAL NOUN *French history* the period between Napoleon Bonaparte's arrival in Paris from Elba on March 20, 1815, and his abdication on June 29, 1815.

hundred-percenter NOUN *US* an extreme or unjustified nationalist.
▸ˈ**hundred-perˈcentism** NOUN

hundreds and thousands PLURAL NOUN tiny

beads of brightly coloured sugar, used in decorating cakes, sweets, etc.

hundredth (ˈhʌndrədθ) ADJECTIVE [1] (*usually prenominal*) **a** being the ordinal number of 100 in numbering or counting order, position, time, etc. **b** (*as noun*): *the hundredth in line.* ◆ NOUN [2] **a** one of 100 approximately equal parts of something. **b** (*as modifier*): *a hundredth part.* [3] one of 100 equal divisions of a particular scientific quantity. Related prefix: **centi-**: *centimetre.* [4] the fraction equal to one divided by 100 (1/100).

hundredweight (ˈhʌndrədˌweɪt) NOUN, *plural* **-weights** *or* **-weight.** [1] Also called: **long hundredweight.** *Brit* a unit of weight equal to 112 pounds or 50.802 35 kilograms. [2] Also called: **short hundredweight.** *US and Canadian* a unit of weight equal to 100 pounds or 45.359 24 kilograms. [3] Also called: **metric hundredweight.** a metric unit of weight equal to 50 kilograms. ◆ Abbreviation (for senses 1, 2): **cwt.**

Hundred Years' War NOUN the series of wars fought intermittently between England and France from 1337–1453: after early victories the English were expelled from all of France except Calais.

hung (hʌŋ) VERB [1] the past tense and past participle of **hang** (except in the sense of *to execute* or in the idiom *I'll be hanged.*). ◆ ADJECTIVE [2] **a** (of a legislative assembly) not having a party with a working majority: *a hung parliament.* **b** unable to reach a decision: *a hung jury.* **c** (of a situation) unable to be resolved. [3] **hung over.** *Informal* suffering from the effects of a hangover. [4] **hung up.** *Slang* **a** impeded by some difficulty or delay. **b** in a state of confusion; emotionally disturbed. [5] **hung up on.** *Slang* obsessively or exclusively interested in: *he's hung up on modern art these days.*

Hung. ABBREVIATION FOR: [1] Hungarian. [2] Hungary.

Hungarian (hʌŋˈgɛərɪən) NOUN [1] the official language of Hungary, also spoken in Romania and elsewhere, belonging to the Finno-Ugric family and most closely related to the Ostyak and Vogul languages of NW Siberia. [2] a native, inhabitant, or citizen of Hungary. [3] a Hungarian-speaking person who is not a citizen of Hungary. ◆ ADJECTIVE [4] of or relating to Hungary, its people, or their language. ◆ Compare **Magyar.**

Hungarian goulash NOUN the full name of **goulash.**

Hungary (ˈhʌŋgərɪ) NOUN a republic in central Europe: Magyars first unified under Saint Stephen, the first Hungarian king (1001–38); taken by the Hapsburgs from the Turks at the end of the 17th century; gained autonomy with the establishment of the dual monarchy of Austria-Hungary (1867) and became a republic in 1918; passed under Communist control in 1949; a popular rising in 1956 was suppressed by Soviet troops; a multi-party democracy replaced Communism in 1989 after mass protests. It consists chiefly of the Middle Danube basin and plains. Official language: Hungarian. Religion: Christian majority. Currency: forint. Capital: Budapest. Pop.: 10 190 000 (2001 est.). Area: 93 030 sq. km (35 919 sq. miles). Hungarian name: **Magyarország.**

hunger (ˈhʌŋgə) NOUN [1] a feeling of pain, emptiness, or weakness induced by lack of food. [2] an appetite, desire, need, or craving: *hunger for a woman.* ◆ VERB [3] to have or cause to have a need or craving for food. [4] (*intr;* usually foll by *for* or *after*) to have a great appetite or desire (for).
▷HISTORY Old English *hungor;* related to Old High German *hungar,* Old Norse *hungr,* Gothic *hūhrus*

hunger march NOUN a procession of protest or demonstration by the unemployed.

hunger strike NOUN a voluntary fast undertaken, usually by a prisoner, as a means of protest.
▸**hunger striker** NOUN

hungry (ˈhʌŋgrɪ) ADJECTIVE **-grier, -griest.** [1] desiring food. [2] experiencing pain, weakness, or nausea through lack of food. [3] (*postpositive;* foll by *for*) having a craving, desire, or need (for). [4] expressing or appearing to express greed, craving, or desire. [5] lacking fertility; poor. [6] *NZ* (of timber) dry and bare.
▸ˈ**hungrily** *or* ˈ**hungeringly** ADVERB ▸ˈ**hungriness** NOUN

hunk (hʌŋk) NOUN [1] a large piece. [2] Also called: **hunk of a man.** *Slang* a well-built, sexually attractive man.
▷HISTORY C19: probably related to Flemish *hunke;* compare Dutch *homp* lump

hunker (ˈhʌŋkə) VERB (*intr:* often foll by *down*) to squat; crouch.

hunkers (ˈhʌŋkəz) PLURAL NOUN haunches.
▷HISTORY C18: of uncertain origin

hunks (hʌŋks) NOUN (*functioning as singular*) *Rare* [1] a crotchety old person. [2] a miserly person.
▷HISTORY C17: of unknown origin

hunky-dory (ˌhʌŋkɪˈdɔːrɪ) ADJECTIVE *Informal* very satisfactory; fine.
▷HISTORY C20: of uncertain origin

Hunnish (ˈhʌnɪʃ) ADJECTIVE [1] of, relating to, or characteristic of the Huns. [2] barbarously destructive; vandalistic.
▸ˈ**Hunnishly** ADVERB ▸ˈ**Hunnishness** NOUN

hunt (hʌnt) VERB [1] to seek out and kill or capture (game or wild animals) for food or sport. [2] (*intr;* often foll by *for*) to look (for); search (for): *to hunt for a book; to hunt up a friend.* [3] (*tr*) to use (hounds, horses, etc.) in the pursuit of wild animals, game, etc.: *to hunt a pack of hounds.* [4] (*tr*) to search or draw (country) to hunt wild animals, game, etc.: *to hunt the parkland.* [5] (*tr;* often foll by *down*) to track or chase diligently, esp so as to capture: *to hunt down a criminal.* [6] (*tr; usually passive*) to persecute; hound. [7] (*intr*) (of a gauge indicator, engine speed, etc.) to oscillate about a mean value or position. [8] (*intr*) (of an aircraft, rocket, etc.) to oscillate about a flight path. ◆ NOUN [9] the act or an instance of hunting. [10] chase or search, esp of animals or game. [11] the area of a hunt. [12] a party or institution organized for the pursuit of wild animals or game, esp for sport. [13] the participants in or members of such a party or institution. [14] **in the hunt.** *Informal* having a chance of success: *that result keeps us in the hunt.* See also **hunt down, hunt up.**
▷HISTORY Old English *huntian;* related to Old English *hentan,* Old Norse *henda* to grasp
▸ˈ**huntedly** ADVERB

huntaway (ˈhʌntəˌweɪ) NOUN *NZ* a dog trained to drive sheep at a long distance from the shepherd.

hunt down VERB (*adverb*) [1] (*tr*) to pursue successfully by diligent searching and chasing: *they finally hunted down the killer in Mexico.* [2] (*intr*) (of a bell) to be rung progressively later during a set of changes.

hunted (ˈhʌntɪd) ADJECTIVE harassed and worn: *he has a hunted look.*

hunter (ˈhʌntə) NOUN [1] a person or animal that seeks out and kills or captures game. Female equivalent: **huntress** (ˈhʌntrɪs). [2] **a** a person who looks diligently for something. **b** (*in combination*): *a fortune-hunter.* [3] a specially bred horse used in hunting, usually characterized by strength and stamina. [4] a specially bred dog used to hunt game. [5] a watch with a hinged metal lid or case (**hunting case**) to protect the crystal. Also called: **hunting watch.** See also **half-hunter.**

hunter-gatherer *Anthropol* ◆ ADJECTIVE [1] (of a society, lifestyle, etc.) surviving by hunting animals and gathering plants for subsistence. ◆ NOUN [2] a member of such a society.

hunter-killer ADJECTIVE denoting a type of naval vessel, esp a submarine, designed and equipped to pursue and destroy enemy craft.

hunter's moon NOUN the full moon following the harvest moon.

hunting (ˈhʌntɪŋ) NOUN **a** the pursuit and killing or capture of game and wild animals, regarded as a sport. **b** (*as modifier*): *hunting boots; hunting lodge.* Related adjective: **venatic.**

hunting cat *or* **leopard** NOUN another name for **cheetah.**

Huntingdon (ˈhʌntɪŋdən) NOUN a town in E central England, in Cambridgeshire: birthplace of Oliver Cromwell. Pop. (with Godmanchester): 15 575 (1991).

Huntingdonshire (ˈhʌntɪŋdənˌʃɪə, -ʃə) NOUN (until 1974) a former county of E England, now part of Cambridgeshire.

hunting ground NOUN [1] the area of a hunt. [2] Also called: **happy hunting ground.** any place containing a supply of what is wanted or in which a search is conducted: *some resorts are a happy hunting ground for souvenirs.*

hunting horn NOUN [1] a long straight metal tube with a flared end and a cylindrical bore, used in giving signals in hunting. See **horn** (sense 9). [2] an obsolete brass instrument from which the modern French horn was developed.

hunting knife NOUN a knife used for flaying and cutting up game and sometimes for killing it.

hunting spider NOUN another name for **wolf spider.**

Huntington's disease (ˈhʌntɪŋtən) NOUN a rare hereditary type of chorea, marked by involuntary jerky movements, impaired speech, and increasing dementia. Former name: **Huntington's chorea.**
▷HISTORY C19: named after George *Huntington* (1850–1916), US neurologist

huntsman (ˈhʌntsmən) NOUN, *plural* **-men.** [1] a person who hunts. [2] a person who looks after and trains hounds, beagles, etc., and manages them during a hunt.

huntsman's-cup NOUN *US* any of various pitcher plants of the genus *Sarracenia,* whose leaves are modified to form tubular pitchers.

Huntsville (ˈhʌntsvɪl) NOUN a city in NE Alabama: space-flight and guided-missile research centre. Pop.: 152 216 (2000).

hunt the slipper NOUN a children's game in which the players look for a hidden slipper or other object, such as a thimble (**hunt the thimble**).

hunt up VERB (*adverb*) [1] (*tr*) to search for, esp successfully: *I couldn't hunt up a copy of it anywhere.* [2] (*intr*) (of a bell) to be rung progressively earlier during a set of changes.

Huon pine (ˈhjuːɒn) NOUN a Tasmanian coniferous tree, *Dacrydium franklinii,* with scalelike leaves and cup-shaped berry-like fruits: family *Podocarpaceae.* It is among the oldest living individual plants, thought to be up to 10 000 years old.
▷HISTORY named after the *Huon* River, Tasmania

Hupeh *or* **Hupei** (ˈxuːˈpeɪ) NOUN a variant transliteration of the Chinese name for **Hubei.**

huppah (ˈhʊpə) NOUN a variant spelling of **chuppah.**

Hurban *Hebrew* (xuːrˈbɑn; *Yiddish* ˈxuːrbᵊn) NOUN a variant spelling of **Churban.**

hurdies (ˈhʌrdɪz) PLURAL NOUN *Scot* the buttocks or haunches.
▷HISTORY C16: of unknown origin

hurdle (ˈhɜːdᵊl) NOUN [1] **a** *Athletics* one of a number of light barriers over which runners leap in certain events. **b** a low barrier used in certain horse races. [2] an obstacle to be overcome: *the next hurdle in his career.* [3] a light framework of interlaced osiers, wattle, etc., used as a temporary fence. [4] *Brit* a sledge on which criminals were dragged to their executions. ◆ VERB [5] to jump (a hurdle, etc.), as in racing. [6] (*tr*) to surround with hurdles. [7] (*tr*) to overcome.
▷HISTORY Old English *hyrdel;* related to Gothic *haurds* door, Old Norse *hurth* door, Old High German *hurd,* Latin *crātis,* Greek *kurtos* basket
▸ˈ**hurdler** NOUN

hurdle rate NOUN *Finance* the rate of return that a proposed project must provide if it is to be worth considering: usually calculated as the cost of the capital involved adjusted by a risk factor.

hurds (hɜːdz) PLURAL NOUN another word for **hards.**

hurdy-gurdy (ˈhɜːdɪˈgɜːdɪ) NOUN, *plural* **-dies.** [1] any mechanical musical instrument, such as a barrel organ. [2] a medieval instrument shaped like a viol in which a rosined wheel rotated by a handle sounds the strings.
▷HISTORY C18: rhyming compound, probably of imitative origin

hurl (hɜːl) VERB [1] (*tr*) to throw or propel with great force. [2] (*tr*) to utter with force; yell: *to hurl insults.* [3] (hʌrl) *Scot* to transport or be transported in a driven vehicle. ◆ NOUN [4] the act or an instance of hurling. [5] (hʌrl) *Scot* a ride in a driven vehicle.
▷HISTORY C13: probably of imitative origin
▸ˈ**hurler** NOUN

hurley (ˈhɜːlɪ) NOUN [1] *Chiefly Brit* another word for **hurling** (the game). [2] Also called: **hurley stick.** the stick used in playing hurling.

hurling (ˈhɜːlɪŋ) NOUN a traditional Irish game resembling hockey and lacrosse, played with sticks and a ball between two teams of 15 players each.

hurly-burly (ˈhɜːlɪˈbɜːlɪ) NOUN, *plural* **hurly-burlies.**

[1] confusion or commotion. ◆ ADJECTIVE [2] turbulent.
▷**HISTORY** C16: from earlier *hurling and burling,* rhyming phrase based on *hurling* in obsolete sense of uproar

Huron ('hjʊərən) NOUN [1] **Lake.** a lake in North America, between the US and Canada: the second largest of the Great Lakes. Area: 59 570 sq. km (23 000 sq. miles). [2] (*plural* **-rons** *or* **-ron**) a member of a North American Indian people formerly living in the region east of Lake Huron. [3] the Iroquoian language of this people.

hurrah (hʊ'rɑː), **hooray** (huː'reɪ), *or* **hurray** (hʊ'reɪ) INTERJECTION, NOUN [1] a cheer of joy, victory, etc. ◆ VERB [2] to shout "hurrah".
▷**HISTORY** C17: probably from German *hurra;* compare HUZZAH

hurricane ('hʌrɪkən, -keɪn) NOUN [1] a severe, often destructive storm, esp a tropical cyclone. [2] **a** a wind of force 12 or above on the Beaufort scale. **b** (*as modifier*): *a wind of hurricane force.* [3] anything acting like such a wind.
▷**HISTORY** C16: from Spanish *huracán,* from Taino *hurakán,* from *hura* wind

hurricane deck NOUN a ship's deck that is covered by a light deck as a sunshade.

hurricane lamp NOUN a paraffin lamp, with a glass covering to prevent the flame from being blown out. Also called: **storm lantern.**

hurried ('hʌrɪd) ADJECTIVE performed with great or excessive haste: *a hurried visit.*
▸ **'hurriedly** ADVERB ▸ **'hurriedness** NOUN

hurry ('hʌrɪ) VERB **-ries, -rying, -ried.** [1] (*intr;* often foll by *up*) to hasten (to do something); rush. [2] (*tr;* often foll by *along*) to speed up the completion, progress, etc., of. ◆ NOUN [3] haste. [4] urgency or eagerness. [5] **in a hurry.** *Informal* **a** easily: *you won't beat him in a hurry.* **b** willingly: *we won't go there again in a hurry.*
▷**HISTORY** C16 *horyen,* probably of imitative origin; compare Middle High German *hurren;* see SCURRY
▸ **'hurrying** NOUN, ADJECTIVE ▸ **'hurryingly** ADVERB

hurry-scurry ADVERB [1] in frantic haste. ◆ ADJECTIVE [2] hasty and disorderly. ◆ NOUN [3] disordered haste. ◆ VERB (*intr*) [4] to rush about in confusion.
▷**HISTORY** C18: reduplication of HURRY; compare HELTER-SKELTER

hurst (hɜːst) NOUN *Archaic* [1] a wood. [2] a sandbank.
▷**HISTORY** Old English *hyrst;* related to Old High German *hurst*

Hurstmonceux ('hɜːstmən,suː, -,səʊ) NOUN a variant spelling of **Herstmonceux.**

hurt[1] (hɜːt) VERB **hurts, hurting, hurt.** [1] to cause physical pain to (someone or something). [2] to cause emotional pain or distress to (someone). [3] to produce a painful sensation in (someone): *the bruise hurts.* [4] (*intr*) *Informal* to feel pain. ◆ NOUN [5] physical, moral, or mental pain or suffering. [6] a wound, cut, or sore. [7] damage or injury; harm. ◆ ADJECTIVE [8] injured or pained physically or emotionally: *a hurt knee; a hurt look.*
▷**HISTORY** C12 *hurten* to hit, from Old French *hurter* to knock against, probably of Germanic origin; compare Old Norse *hrūtr* ram, Middle High German *hurt* a collision
▸ **'hurter** NOUN

hurt[2] (hɜːt) *or* **whort** (hwɜːt) NOUN *Southern English dialect* another name for **whortleberry.**

hurter ('hɜːtə) NOUN an object or part that gives protection, such as a concrete block that protects a building from traffic or the shoulder of an axle against which the hub strikes.
▷**HISTORY** C14 *hurtour,* from Old French *hurtoir* something that knocks or strikes, from *hurter* to HURT[1]

hurtful ('hɜːtfʊl) ADJECTIVE causing distress or injury: *to say hurtful things.*
▸ **'hurtfully** ADVERB ▸ **'hurtfulness** NOUN

hurtle ('hɜːtəl) VERB [1] to project or be projected very quickly, noisily, or violently. [2] (*intr*) *Rare* to collide or crash.
▷**HISTORY** C13 *hurtlen,* from *hurten* to strike; see HURT[1]

husband ('hʌzbənd) NOUN [1] a woman's partner in marriage. [2] *Archaic* **a** a manager of an estate. **b** a frugal person. ◆ VERB [3] to manage or use (resources, finances, etc.) thriftily. [4] *Archaic* **a** (*tr*) to find a husband for. **b** (of a woman) to marry (a man). [5] (*tr*) *Obsolete* to till (the soil).
▷**HISTORY** Old English *hūsbonda,* from Old Norse *hūsbōndi,* from *hūs* house + *bōndi* one who has a household, from *bōa* to dwell
▸ **'husbander** NOUN ▸ **'husbandless** ADJECTIVE

husbandman ('hʌzbəndmən) NOUN, *plural* **-men.** a farmer.

husbandry ('hʌzbəndrɪ) NOUN [1] farming, esp when regarded as a science, skill, or art. [2] management of affairs and resources.

hush[1] (hʌʃ) VERB [1] to make or become silent; quieten. [2] to soothe or be soothed. ◆ NOUN [3] stillness; silence. [4] an act of hushing. ◆ INTERJECTION [5] a plea or demand for silence.
▷**HISTORY** C16: probably from earlier *husht* quiet!, the *-t* being thought to indicate a past participle
▸ **hushed** ADJECTIVE

hush[2] (hʌʃ) *Mining northern English* ◆ VERB (*tr*) [1] to run water over the ground to erode (surface soil), revealing the underlying strata and any valuable minerals present. [2] to wash (an ore) by removing particles of earth with rushing water. ◆ NOUN [3] a gush of water, esp when artificially produced.
▷**HISTORY** C18: of imitative origin

hushaby ('hʌʃə,baɪ) INTERJECTION [1] used in quietening a baby or child to sleep. ◆ NOUN [2] a lullaby.
▷**HISTORY** C18: from HUSH[1] + *by,* as in BYE-BYE

hush-hush ADJECTIVE *Informal* (esp of official work, documents, etc.) secret; confidential.

hush money NOUN *Slang* money given to a person, such as an accomplice, to ensure that something is kept secret.

hush up VERB (*tr, adverb*) to suppress information or rumours about.

husk[1] (hʌsk) NOUN [1] the external green or membranous covering of certain fruits and seeds. [2] any worthless outer covering. ◆ VERB [3] (*tr*) to remove the husk from.
▷**HISTORY** C14: probably based on Middle Dutch *huusken* little house, from *hūs* house; related to Old English *hosu* husk, *hūs* HOUSE
▸ **'husker** NOUN ▸ **'husk,like** ADJECTIVE

husk[2] NOUN bronchitis in cattle, sheep, and goats, usually caused by lungworm infestation.

husky[1] ('hʌskɪ) ADJECTIVE **huskier, huskiest.** [1] (of a voice, an utterance, etc.) slightly hoarse or rasping. [2] of, like, or containing husks. [3] *Informal* big, strong, and well-built.
▷**HISTORY** C19: probably from HUSK, from the toughness of a corn husk
▸ **'huskily** ADVERB ▸ **'huskiness** NOUN

husky[2] ('hʌskɪ) NOUN, *plural* **huskies.** a breed of Arctic sled dog with a thick dense coat, pricked ears, and a curled tail.
▷**HISTORY** C19: probably based on ESKIMO

huss (hʌs) NOUN the flesh of the European dogfish, when used as food.
▷**HISTORY** C15 *husk, huske,* C16 *huss:* of obscure origin

hussar (hʊ'zɑː) NOUN [1] **a** a member of any of various light cavalry regiments in European armies, renowned for their elegant dress. **b** (*pl; cap when part of a name*): *the Queen's own Hussars.* [2] a Hungarian horseman of the 15th century.
▷**HISTORY** C15: from Hungarian *huszár* hussar, formerly freebooter, from Old Serbian *husar,* from Old Italian *corsaro* CORSAIR

Hussite ('hʌsaɪt) NOUN [1] an adherent of the religious ideas of John Huss (?1372–1415), the Bohemian religious reformer, or a member of the movement initiated by him. ◆ ADJECTIVE [2] of or relating to John Huss, his teachings, followers, etc.
▸ **'Hussism** *or* **'Hussitism** NOUN

hussy ('hʌsɪ, -zɪ) NOUN, *plural* **-sies.** [1] a shameless or promiscuous woman. [2] *Dialect* a folder for needles, thread, etc.
▷**HISTORY** C16 (in the sense: housewife): from *hussif* HOUSEWIFE

hustings ('hʌstɪŋz) NOUN (*functioning as plural or singular*) [1] *Brit* (before 1872) the platform on which candidates were nominated for Parliament and from which they addressed the electors. [2] the proceedings at a parliamentary election. [3] political campaigning.
▷**HISTORY** C11: from Old Norse *hūsthing,* from *hūs* HOUSE + *thing* assembly

hustle ('hʌsəl) VERB [1] to shove or crowd (someone) roughly. [2] to move or cause to move hurriedly or furtively: *he hustled her out of sight.* [3] (*tr*) to deal with or cause to proceed hurriedly: *to hustle legislation through.* [4] *Slang* to earn or obtain (something) forcefully. [5] *US and Canadian slang* (of procurers and prostitutes) to solicit. ◆ NOUN [6] an instance of hustling. [7] undue activity. [8] a disco dance of the 1970s.
▷**HISTORY** C17: from Dutch *husselen* to shake, from Middle Dutch *hutsen*
▸ **'hustler** NOUN

hustle up VERB (*tr*) *Informal, chiefly US and Canadian* to prepare quickly.

hut (hʌt) NOUN [1] a small house or shelter, usually made of wood or metal. [2] **the.** *Austral* (on a sheep or cattle station) accommodation for the shearers, stockmen, etc. [3] *NZ* a shelter for mountaineers, skiers, etc. ◆ VERB [4] to furnish with or live in a hut.
▷**HISTORY** C17: from French *hutte,* of Germanic origin; related to Old High German *hutta* a crude dwelling
▸ **'hut,like** ADJECTIVE

hutch (hʌtʃ) NOUN [1] a cage, usually of wood and wire mesh, for small animals. [2] *Informal, derogatory* a small house. [3] a cart for carrying ore. [4] a trough, esp one used for kneading dough or (in mining) for washing ore. ◆ VERB [5] (*tr*) to store or keep in or as if in a hutch.
▷**HISTORY** C14 *hucche,* from Old French *huche,* from Medieval Latin *hutica,* of obscure origin

hutchie ('hʌtʃɪ) NOUN *Austral* a groundsheet draped over an upright stick, used as a temporary shelter.
▷**HISTORY** C20: from HUTCH

hut circle NOUN *Archaeol* a circle of earth or stones representing the site of a prehistoric hut.

hutment ('hʌtmənt) NOUN *Chiefly military* a number or group of huts.

Hutterite ('hʌtə,raɪt) NOUN a member of an Anabaptist Christian sect founded in Moravia, branches of which established farming communities in western Canada and the northwest US.
▷**HISTORY** C19: after Jacob *Hutter* (died 1536), Moravian Anabaptist

Hutu ('huː,tuː) NOUN, *plural* **-tu** *or* **-tus.** a member of a Negroid people of Rwanda and Burundi.

hutzpah ('xʊtspə) NOUN a variant spelling of **chutzpah.**

Huygens' eyepiece NOUN *Physics* a telescope eyepiece consisting of two planoconvex lenses separated by a distance equal to half the sum of their focal lengths, which are in the ratio of three to one, and oriented so that their curved surfaces face the incident light.
▷**HISTORY** C19: named after Christiaan *Huygens* (1629–95), Dutch physicist

huzzah (hə'zɑː) INTERJECTION, NOUN, VERB an archaic word for **hurrah.**
▷**HISTORY** C16: of unknown origin

HV *or* **h.v.** ABBREVIATION FOR high voltage.

HW *or* **h.w.** ABBREVIATION FOR: [1] **high water.** [2] *Cricket* **hit wicket.**

hwan (hwɑːn, wɑːn) NOUN another name for **won**[2] (senses 1, 2).
▷**HISTORY** Korean

HWM ABBREVIATION FOR **high-water mark.**

hwyl ('huːɪl) NOUN emotional fervour, as in the recitation of poetry.
▷**HISTORY** C19: Welsh

hyacinth ('haɪəsɪnθ) NOUN [1] any liliaceous plant of the Mediterranean genus *Hyacinthus,* esp any cultivated variety of *H. orientalis,* having a thick flower stalk bearing white, blue, or pink fragrant flowers. [2] the flower or bulb of such a plant. [3] any similar or related plant, such as the grape hyacinth. [4] Also called: **jacinth.** a red or reddish-brown transparent variety of the mineral zircon, used as a gemstone. [5] *Greek myth* a flower which sprang from the blood of the dead Hyacinthus. [6] any of the varying colours of the hyacinth flower or stone.

▷HISTORY C16: from Latin *hyacinthus,* from Greek *huakinthos*
▸**hyacinthine** (ˌhaɪəˈsɪnθaɪn) ADJECTIVE

Hyacinthus (ˌhaɪəˈsɪnθəs) NOUN *Greek myth* a youth beloved of Apollo and inadvertently killed by him. At the spot where the youth died, Apollo caused a flower to grow.

Hyades[1] (ˈhaɪəˌdiːz) *or* **Hyads** (ˈhaɪædz) PLURAL NOUN an open cluster of stars in the constellation Taurus. Compare **Pleiades.**
▷HISTORY C16: via Latin from Greek *huades,* perhaps from *huein* to rain

Hyades[2] (ˈhaɪəˌdiːz) PLURAL NOUN *Greek myth* seven nymphs, daughters of Atlas, whom Zeus placed among the stars after death.

hyaena (haɪˈiːnə) NOUN a variant spelling of **hyena.**
▸**hyˈaenic** ADJECTIVE

hyalin (ˈhaɪəlɪn) NOUN glassy translucent substance, such as occurs in certain degenerative skin conditions or in hyaline cartilage.

hyaline (ˈhaɪəlɪn) ADJECTIVE 1 *Biology* clear and translucent, with no fibres or granules. 2 *Archaic* transparent. ◆ NOUN 3 *Archaic* a glassy transparent surface.
▷HISTORY C17: from Late Latin *hyalinus,* from Greek *hualinos* of glass, from *hualos* glass

hyaline cartilage NOUN a common type of cartilage with a translucent matrix containing little fibrous tissue.

hyalite (ˈhaɪəˌlaɪt) NOUN a clear and colourless variety of opal in globular form.

hyalo- *or before a vowel* **hyal-** COMBINING FORM of, relating to, or resembling glass: *hyaloplasm.*
▷HISTORY from Greek *hualos* glass

hyaloid (ˈhaɪəˌlɔɪd) ADJECTIVE *Anatomy, zoology* clear and transparent; glassy; hyaline.
▷HISTORY C19: from Greek *hualoeidēs*

hyaloid membrane NOUN the delicate transparent membrane enclosing the vitreous humour of the eye.

hyaloplasm (ˈhaɪələʊˌplæzəm) NOUN the clear nongranular constituent of cell cytoplasm.
▸ˌ**hyaloˈplasmic** ADJECTIVE

hyaluronic acid (ˌhaɪəlʊˈrɒnɪk) NOUN a viscous polysaccharide with important lubricating properties, present, for example, in the synovial fluid in joints.
▷HISTORY C20: HYALO- + Greek *ouron* urine + -IC
▸ˌ**hyaluˈronic** ADJECTIVE

hyaluronidase (ˌhaɪəlʊˈrɒnɪˌdeɪs, -ˌdeɪz) NOUN an enzyme that breaks down hyaluronic acid, thus decreasing the viscosity of the medium containing the acid.
▷HISTORY C20: HYALO- + Greek *ouron* urine + -ID[3] + -ASE

hybrid (ˈhaɪbrɪd) NOUN 1 an animal or plant resulting from a cross between genetically unlike individuals. Hybrids between different species are usually sterile. 2 anything of mixed ancestry. 3 a word, part of which is derived from one language and part from another, such as *monolingual,* which has a prefix of Greek origin and a root of Latin origin. ◆ ADJECTIVE 4 denoting or being a hybrid; of mixed origin. 5 *Physics* (of an electromagnetic wave) having components of both electric and magnetic field vectors in the direction of propagation. 6 *Electronics* **a** (of a circuit) consisting of transistors and valves. **b** (of an integrated circuit) consisting of one or more fully integrated circuits and other components, attached to a ceramic substrate. Compare **monolithic** (sense 3).
▷HISTORY C17: from Latin *hibrida* offspring of a mixed union (human or animal)
▸ˈ**hybridism** NOUN ▸**hyˈbridity** NOUN

hybrid antibody NOUN a synthetic antibody that is able to combine with two different antigens.

hybrid bill NOUN (in Parliament) a public bill to which the standing orders for private business apply; a bill having a general application as well as affecting certain private interests.

hybrid computer NOUN a computer that uses both analogue and digital techniques.

hybridize *or* **hybridise** (ˈhaɪbrɪˌdaɪz) VERB to produce or cause to produce hybrids; crossbreed.
▸ˈ**hybridˌizable** *or* ˈ**hybridˌisable** ADJECTIVE ▸ˌ**hybridiˈzation** *or* ˌ**hybridiˈsation** NOUN ▸ˈ**hybridˌizer** *or* ˈ**hybridˌiser** NOUN

hybridoma (ˌhaɪbrəˈdəʊmə) NOUN a hybrid cell formed by the fusion of two different types of cell, esp one capable of producing antibodies, but of limited lifespan, fused with an immortal tumour cell.
▷HISTORY C20: from HYBRID + -OMA

hybrid rock NOUN an igneous rock formed by molten magma incorporating pre-existing rock through which it passes.

hybrid vigour NOUN *Biology* the increased size, strength, etc., of a hybrid as compared to either of its parents. Also called: **heterosis.**

hybris (ˈhaɪbrɪs) NOUN a variant of **hubris.**
▸**hyˈbristic** ADJECTIVE

hydantoin (haɪˈdæntəʊɪn) NOUN a colourless odourless crystalline compound present in beet molasses: used in the manufacture of pharmaceuticals and synthetic resins. Formula: $C_3H_4N_2O_2$.
▷HISTORY C20: from HYD(ROGEN + *all*)*antoin* product occurring in allantoic fluid

hydathode (ˈhaɪdəˌθəʊd) NOUN a pore in plants, esp on the leaves, specialized for excreting water.
▷HISTORY C19: from Greek, from *hudor* water + *hodos* way

hydatid (ˈhaɪdətɪd) NOUN 1 a large bladder containing encysted larvae of the tapeworm *Echinococcus:* causes serious disease in man. 2 a sterile fluid-filled cyst produced in man and animals during infestation by *Echinococcus* larval forms. Also called: **hydatid cyst.**
▷HISTORY C17: from Greek *hudatis* watery vesicle, from *hudōr, hudat-* water

Hyde (haɪd) NOUN a town in NW England, in Tameside unitary authority, Greater Manchester; textiles, footwear, engineering. Pop.: 30 666 (1991).

Hyde Park NOUN a park in W central London: popular for open-air meetings.

Hyderabad (ˈhaɪdərəˌbɑːd, -ˌbæd, ˈhaɪdrə-) NOUN 1 a city in S central India, capital of Andhra Pradesh state and capital of former Hyderabad state; university (1918). Pop.: 3 145 939 (1991). 2 a former state of S India: divided in 1956 between the states of Andhra Pradesh, Mysore, and Maharashtra. 3 a city in SW Pakistan, on the River Indus: seat of the University of Sind (1947). Pop.: 1 151 271 (1998).

hydnocarpate (ˌhɪdnəʊˈkɑːpeɪt) NOUN any salt or ester of hydnocarpic acid.

hydnocarpic acid (ˌhɪdnəʊˈkɑːpɪk) NOUN a cyclic fatty acid occurring in the form of its glycerides in chaulmoogra oil. Formula: $C_{16}H_{28}O_2$.
▷HISTORY C20: from Greek *hudnon* truffle + *karpos* fruit + -IC

hydr- COMBINING FORM a variant of **hydro-** before a vowel.

hydra (ˈhaɪdrə) NOUN, *plural* **-dras, -drae** (-driː). 1 any solitary freshwater hydroid coelenterate of the genus *Hydra,* in which the body is a slender polyp with tentacles around the mouth. 2 a persistent trouble or evil: *the hydra of the Irish problem.*
▷HISTORY C16: from Latin, from Greek *hudra* water serpent; compare OTTER

Hydra[1] (ˈhaɪdrə) NOUN *Greek myth* a monster with nine heads, each of which, when struck off, was replaced by two new ones.

Hydra[2] (ˈhaɪdrə) NOUN, *Latin genitive* **Hydrae** (ˈhaɪdriː). a very long faint constellation lying mainly in the S hemisphere and extending from near Virgo to Cancer.

hydracid (haɪˈdræsɪd) NOUN an acid, such as hydrochloric acid, that does not contain oxygen.

hydragogue (ˈhaɪdrəˌgɒg) NOUN *Med* any purgative that causes evacuation of water from the bowels.

hydrangea (haɪˈdreɪndʒə) NOUN any shrub or tree of the Asian and American genus *Hydrangea,* cultivated for their large clusters of white, pink, or blue flowers: family *Hydrangeaceae.*
▷HISTORY C18: from New Latin, from Greek *hudōr* water + *angeion* vessel: probably from the cup-shaped fruit

hydrant (ˈhaɪdrənt) NOUN an outlet from a water main, usually consisting of an upright pipe with a valve attached, from which water can be tapped for fighting fires. See also **fire hydrant.**
▷HISTORY C19: from HYDRO- + -ANT

hydranth (ˈhaɪdrænθ) NOUN a polyp in a colony of hydrozoan coelenterates that is specialized for feeding rather than reproduction.
▷HISTORY C19: from HYDRA + Greek *anthos* flower

hydrargyria (ˌhaɪdrɑːˈdʒaɪrɪə) *or* **hydrargyrism** (haɪˈdrɑːdʒɪrɪzəm) NOUN *Med* mercury poisoning.
▷HISTORY C17: see HYDRARGYRUM

hydrargyrum (haɪˈdrɑːdʒɪrəm) NOUN an obsolete name for **mercury** (sense 1).
▷HISTORY C16: from New Latin, from Latin *hydrargyrus* from Greek *hydrarguros,* from HYDRO- + *arguros* silver
▸**hydrargyric** (ˌhaɪdrɑːˈdʒɪərɪk) ADJECTIVE

hydrastine (haɪˈdræstiːn, -tɪn) NOUN a white poisonous alkaloid extracted from the roots of the goldenseal: has been used in medicine (in the form of one of its water-soluble salts) to contract the uterus and arrest haemorrhage. Formula: $C_{21}H_{21}NO_6$.
▷HISTORY C19: from HYDRAST(IS) + -INE[2]

hydrastinine (haɪˈdræstɪˌniːn) NOUN a colourless crystalline water-soluble compound whose pharmacological action resembles that of hydrastine. Formula: $C_{11}H_{13}NO_3$.

hydrastis (haɪˈdræstɪs) NOUN any ranunculaceous plant of the genus *Hydrastis,* of Japan and E North America, such as goldenseal, having showy foliage and ornamental red fruits.
▷HISTORY C18: New Latin, from Greek HYDRO- + *-astis,* of unknown origin

hydrate (ˈhaɪdreɪt) NOUN 1 a chemical compound containing water that is chemically combined with a substance and can usually be expelled without changing the constitution of the substance. 2 a chemical compound that can dissociate reversibly into water and another compound. For example sulphuric acid (H_2SO_4) dissociates into sulphur trioxide (SO_3) and water (H_2O). 3 (*not in technical usage*) a chemical compound, such as a carbohydrate, that contains hydrogen and oxygen atoms in the ratio two to one. ◆ VERB 4 to undergo or cause to undergo treatment or impregnation with water.
▷HISTORY C19: from HYDRO- + -ATE[1]
▸**hyˈdration** NOUN ▸ˈ**hydrator** NOUN

hydrated (ˈhaɪdreɪtɪd) ADJECTIVE (of a compound) chemically bonded to water molecules.

hydraulic (haɪˈdrɒlɪk) ADJECTIVE 1 operated by pressure transmitted through a pipe by a liquid, such as water or oil. 2 of, concerned with, or employing liquids in motion. 3 of or concerned with hydraulics. 4 hardening under water: *hydraulic cement.*
▷HISTORY C17: from Latin *hydraulicus* of a water organ, from Greek *hudraulikos,* from *hudraulos* water organ, from HYDRO- + *aulos* pipe, reed instrument
▸**hyˈdraulically** ADVERB

hydraulic brake NOUN a type of brake, used in motor vehicles, in which the braking force is transmitted from the brake pedal to the brakes by a liquid under pressure.

hydraulic coupling NOUN another name for **torque converter.**

hydraulic press NOUN a press that utilizes liquid pressure to enable a small force applied to a small piston to produce a large force on a larger piston. The small piston moves through a proportionately greater distance than the larger.

hydraulic ram NOUN 1 any large device involving the displacement of a piston or plunger driven by fluid pressure. 2 a form of water pump utilizing the kinetic energy of running water to provide static pressure to raise water to a reservoir higher than the source.

hydraulics (haɪˈdrɒlɪks) NOUN (*functioning as singular*) another name for **fluid mechanics.**

hydraulic suspension NOUN a system of motor-vehicle suspension using hydraulic members, often with hydraulic compensation between front and rear systems (**hydroelastic suspension**).

hydrazide (ˈhaɪdrəˌzaɪd) NOUN any of a class of chemical compounds that result when hydrogen in hydrazine or any of its derivatives is replaced by an acid radical.

hydrazine (ˈhaɪdrəˌziːn, -zɪn) NOUN a colourless basic liquid made from sodium hypochlorite and

ammonia: a strong reducing agent, used chiefly as a rocket fuel. Formula: N_2H_4.
▷HISTORY C19: from HYDRO- + AZO- + -INE[2]

hydrazoic acid (ˌhaɪdrəˈzəʊɪk) NOUN a colourless highly explosive liquid. Formula: HN_3. See also **azide.**

hydria (ˈhaɪdrɪə) NOUN (in ancient Greece and Rome) a large water jar.
▷HISTORY C19: from Latin, from Greek *hudria,* from *hudōr* water

hydric (ˈhaɪdrɪk) ADJECTIVE 1 of or containing hydrogen. 2 containing or using moisture.

hydride (ˈhaɪdraɪd) NOUN any compound of hydrogen with another element, including ionic compounds such as sodium hydride (NaH), covalent compounds such as borane (B_2H_6), and the transition metal hydrides formed when certain metals, such as palladium, absorb hydrogen.

hydrilla (haɪˈdrɪlə) NOUN any aquatic plant of the Eurasian genus *Hydrilla,* growing underwater and forming large masses: used as an oxygenator in aquaria and pools. It was introduced in the S US where it has become a serious problem, choking fish and hindering navigation.
▷HISTORY C20: New Latin, probably from HYDRA

hydriodic acid (ˌhaɪdrɪˈɒdɪk) NOUN the colourless or pale yellow aqueous solution of hydrogen iodide: a strong acid.
▷HISTORY C19: from HYDRO- + IODIC

hydro[1] (ˈhaɪdrəʊ) NOUN, *plural* **-dros.** *Brit* (esp formerly) a hotel or resort, often near a spa, offering facilities for hydropathic treatment.

hydro[2] (ˈhaɪdrəʊ) ADJECTIVE 1 short for **hydroelectric.** ◆ NOUN 2 a Canadian name for **electricity** as supplied to a residence, business, institution, etc.

hydro- *or sometimes before a vowel* **hydr-** COMBINING FORM 1 indicating or denoting water, liquid, or fluid: *hydrolysis; hydrodynamics.* 2 indicating the presence of hydrogen in a chemical compound: *hydrochloric acid.* 3 indicating a hydroid: *hydrozoan.*
▷HISTORY from Greek *hudōr* water

hydroacoustics (ˌhaɪdrəʊəˈkuːstɪks) NOUN (*functioning as singular*) *Physics* the study of sound travelling through water.

hydrobromic acid (ˌhaɪdrəʊˈbrəʊmɪk) NOUN the colourless or faintly yellow aqueous solution of hydrogen bromide: a strong acid.

hydrocarbon (ˌhaɪdrəʊˈkɑːbən) NOUN any organic compound containing only carbon and hydrogen, such as the alkanes, alkenes, alkynes, terpenes, and arenes.

hydrocele (ˈhaɪdrəʊˌsiːl) NOUN an abnormal collection of fluid in any saclike space, esp around the testicles.
▷HISTORY C16: from HYDRO- + -CELE

hydrocellulose (ˌhaɪdrəʊˈseljʊˌləʊs, -ˌləʊz) NOUN a gelatinous material consisting of hydrated cellulose, made by treating cellulose with water, acids, or alkalis: used in making paper, viscose rayon, and mercerized cotton.

hydrocephalus (ˌhaɪdrəʊˈsɛfələs) *or* **hydrocephaly** (ˌhaɪdrəʊˈsɛfəlɪ) NOUN accumulation of cerebrospinal fluid within the ventricles of the brain because its normal outlet has been blocked by congenital malformation or disease. In infancy it usually results in great enlargement of the head. Nontechnical name: **water on the brain.**
▸**hydrocephalic** (ˌhaɪdrəʊsɛˈfælɪk) *or* ˌ**hydroˈcephaloid** *or* ˌ**hydroˈcephalous** ADJECTIVE

hydrochloric acid (ˌhaɪdrəˈklɒrɪk) NOUN the colourless or slightly yellow aqueous solution of hydrogen chloride: a strong acid used in many industrial and laboratory processes. Formerly called: **muriatic acid.**

hydrochloride (ˌhaɪdrəˈklɔːraɪd) NOUN a quaternary salt formed by the addition of hydrochloric acid to an organic base, such as aniline hydrochloride, $[C_6H_5NH_3]^+Cl^-$.

hydrocoral (ˌhaɪdrəˈkɒrəl) *or* **hydrocoralline** NOUN any hydrozoan coelenterate of the order *Milleporina* (or *Hydrocorallinae*), which includes the millepores.
▷HISTORY C20: from HYDRO- + CORAL

hydrocortisone (ˌhaɪdrəʊˈkɔːtɪˌzəʊn) NOUN the principal glucocorticoid secreted by the adrenal cortex; 17-hydroxycorticosterone. The synthesized form is used mainly in treating rheumatic, allergic, and inflammatory disorders. Formula: $C_{21}H_{30}O_5$. Also called: **cortisol.**

hydrocyanic acid (ˌhaɪdrəʊsaɪˈænɪk) NOUN another name for **hydrogen cyanide,** esp when in aqueous solution

hydrodynamic (ˌhaɪdrəʊdaɪˈnæmɪk, -dɪ-) *or* **hydrodynamical** ADJECTIVE 1 of or concerned with the mechanical properties of fluids. 2 of or concerned with hydrodynamics.
▸ˌ**hydrodyˈnamically** ADVERB

hydrodynamics (ˌhaɪdrəʊdaɪˈnæmɪks, -dɪ-) NOUN 1 (*functioning as singular*) the branch of science concerned with the mechanical properties of fluids, esp liquids. Also called: **hydromechanics.** See also **hydrokinetics, hydrostatics.** 2 another name for **hydrokinetics.**

hydroelastic suspension (ˌhaɪdrəʊɪˈlæstɪk) NOUN See **hydraulic suspension.**

hydroelectric (ˌhaɪdrəʊɪˈlɛktrɪk) ADJECTIVE 1 generated by the pressure of falling water: *hydroelectric power.* 2 of or concerned with the generation of electricity by water pressure: *a hydroelectric scheme.*
▸**hydroelectricity** (ˌhaɪdrəʊɪlɛkˈtrɪsɪtɪ, -ˌiːlɛk-) NOUN

hydrofluoric acid (ˌhaɪdrəʊfluːˈɒrɪk) NOUN the colourless aqueous solution of hydrogen fluoride: a strong acid that attacks glass.

hydrofoil (ˈhaɪdrəˌfɔɪl) NOUN 1 a fast light vessel the hull of which is raised out of the water on one or more pairs of fixed vanes. 2 any of these vanes.

hydroforming (ˈhaɪdrəʊˌfɔːmɪŋ) NOUN *Chem* 1 the catalytic reforming of petroleum to increase the proportion of aromatic and branched-chain hydrocarbons. 2 *Engineering* a forming process in which a metal component is shaped by a metal punch forced against a die, consisting of a flexible bag containing a fluid.

hydrogel (ˈhaɪdrəˌdʒɛl) NOUN a gel in which the liquid constituent is water.

hydrogen (ˈhaɪdrɪdʒən) NOUN **a** a flammable colourless gas that is the lightest and most abundant element in the universe. It occurs mainly in water and in most organic compounds and is used in the production of ammonia and other chemicals, in the hydrogenation of fats and oils, and in welding. Symbol: H; atomic no.: 1; atomic wt.: 1.00794; valency: 1; density: 0.08988 kg/m^3; melting pt.: –259.34°C; boiling pt.: –252.87°C. See also **deuterium, tritium. b** (*as modifier*): *hydrogen bomb.*
▷HISTORY C18: from French *hydrogène,* from HYDRO- + -GEN; so called because its combustion produces water

hydrogenate (ˈhaɪdrədʒɪˌneɪt, haɪˈdrɒdʒɪˌneɪt), **hydrogenize,** *or* **hydrogenise** (ˈhaɪdrədʒɪˌnaɪz, haɪˈdrɒdʒɪˌnaɪz) VERB to undergo or cause to undergo a reaction with hydrogen: *to hydrogenate ethylene.*
▸ˌ**hydrogenˈation** *or* ˌ**hydrogeniˈzation** *or* ˌ**hydrogeniˈsation** NOUN ▸ˈ**hydrogenˌator** NOUN

hydrogen bomb NOUN a type of bomb in which energy is released by fusion of hydrogen nuclei to give helium nuclei. The energy required to initiate the fusion is provided by the detonation of an atomic bomb, which is surrounded by a hydrogen-containing substance such as lithium deuteride. Also called: **H-bomb.** See also **fusion bomb.**

hydrogen bond NOUN a weak chemical bond between an electronegative atom, such as fluorine, oxygen, or nitrogen, and a hydrogen atom bound to another electronegative atom. Hydrogen bonds are responsible for the properties of water and many biological molecules.

hydrogen bromide NOUN 1 a colourless pungent gas used in organic synthesis. Formula: HBr. 2 an aqueous solution of hydrogen bromide; hydrobromic acid.

hydrogen carbonate NOUN another name for **bicarbonate.**

hydrogen chloride NOUN 1 a colourless pungent corrosive gas obtained by the action of sulphuric acid on sodium chloride: used in making vinyl chloride and other organic chemicals. Formula: HCl. 2 an aqueous solution of hydrogen chloride; hydrochloric acid.

hydrogen cyanide NOUN a colourless poisonous liquid with a faint odour of bitter almonds, usually made by a catalysed reaction between ammonia, oxygen, and methane. It forms prussic acid in aqueous solution and is used for making plastics and dyes and as a war gas. Formula: HCN. Also called: **hydrocyanic acid.**

hydrogen embrittlement (ɪmˈbrɪtəlmənt) NOUN *Engineering* the weakening of metal by the sorption of hydrogen during a pickling process, such as that used in plating.

hydrogen fluoride NOUN 1 a colourless poisonous corrosive gas or liquid made by reaction between calcium fluoride and sulphuric acid: used as a fluorinating agent and catalyst. Formula: HF. 2 an aqueous solution of hydrogen fluoride; hydrofluoric acid.

hydrogen iodide NOUN 1 a colourless poisonous corrosive gas obtained by a catalysed reaction between hydrogen and iodine vapour: used in making iodides. Formula: HI. 2 an aqueous solution of this gas; hydriodic acid.

hydrogen ion NOUN 1 an ionized hydrogen atom, occurring in plasmas and in aqueous solutions of acids, in which it is solvated by one or more water molecules; proton. Formula: H^+. 2 an ionized hydrogen molecule; hydrogen molecular ion. Formula: H_2^+.

hydrogenize *or* **hydrogenise** (ˈhaɪdrədʒɪˌnaɪz, haɪˈdrɒdʒɪˌnaɪz) VERB variants of **hydrogenate.**
▸ˌ**hydrogeniˈzation** *or* ˌ**hydrogeniˈsation** NOUN

hydrogenolysis (ˌhaɪdrəʊdʒɪˈnɒlɪsɪs) NOUN a chemical reaction in which a compound is decomposed by hydrogen.

hydrogenous (haɪˈdrɒdʒɪnəs) ADJECTIVE of or containing hydrogen.

hydrogen peroxide NOUN a colourless oily unstable liquid, usually used in aqueous solution. It is a strong oxidizing agent used as a bleach for textiles, wood pulp, hair, etc., and as an oxidizer in rocket fuels. Formula: H_2O_2.

hydrogen sulphate NOUN another name for **bisulphate.**

hydrogen sulphide NOUN a colourless poisonous soluble flammable gas with an odour of rotten eggs: used as a reagent in chemical analysis. Formula: H_2S. Also called: **sulphuretted hydrogen.**

hydrogen sulphite NOUN another name for **bisulphite.**

hydrogen tartrate NOUN another name for **bitartrate.**

hydrogeology (ˌhaɪdrədʒɪˈɒlədʒɪ) NOUN the branch of geology dealing with the waters below the earth's surface and with the geological aspects of surface waters.
▸ˌ**hydrogeoˈlogical** ADJECTIVE ▸ˌ**hydrogeˈologist** NOUN

hydrograph (ˈhaɪdrəˌɡrɑːf, -ˌɡræf) NOUN a graph showing the seasonal variation in the level of a body of water, from which its velocity and discharge can be calculated.

hydrographic (ˌhaɪdrəˈɡræfɪk) ADJECTIVE of or relating to hydrographics.
▸ˌ**hydroˈgraphical** ADJECTIVE ▸ˌ**hydroˈgraphically** ADVERB

hydrography (haɪˈdrɒɡrəfɪ) NOUN 1 the study, surveying, and mapping of the oceans, seas, and rivers. Compare **hydrology.** 2 the oceans, seas, and rivers as represented on a chart.
▸**hyˈdrographer** NOUN

hydroid (ˈhaɪdrɔɪd) ADJECTIVE 1 of or relating to the *Hydroida,* an order of colonial hydrozoan coelenterates that have the polyp phase dominant. 2 (of coelenterate colonies or individuals) having or consisting of hydra-like polyps. ◆ NOUN 3 a hydroid colony or individual.
▷HISTORY C19: from HYDRA + -OID

hydrokinetic (ˌhaɪdrəʊkɪˈnɛtɪk, -kaɪ-) *or* **hydrokinetical** ADJECTIVE 1 of or concerned with fluids that are in motion. 2 of or concerned with hydrokinetics.

hydrokinetics (ˌhaɪdrəʊkɪˈnɛtɪks, -kaɪ-) NOUN (*functioning as singular*) the branch of science concerned with the mechanical behaviour and properties of fluids in motion, esp of liquids. Also called: **hydrodynamics.**

hydrolase (ˈhaɪdrəˌleɪz) NOUN an enzyme, such as an esterase, that controls hydrolysis.

hydrologic cycle NOUN another name for **water cycle.**

hydrology (haɪˈdrɒlədʒɪ) NOUN the study of the distribution, conservation, use, etc., of the water of the earth and its atmosphere, particularly at the land surface.
▸**hydrologic** (ˌhaɪdrəˈlɒdʒɪk) *or* **ˌhydroˈlogical** ADJECTIVE ▸**ˌhydroˈlogically** ADVERB ▸**hyˈdrologist** NOUN

hydrolysate (haɪˈdrɒlɪˌseɪt) NOUN a substance or mixture produced by hydrolysis.
▷HISTORY C20: from HYDROLYSIS + -ATE[1]

hydrolyse *or US* **hydrolyze** (ˈhaɪdrəˌlaɪz) VERB to subject to or undergo hydrolysis.
▸**ˈhydroˌlysable** *or US* **ˈhydroˌlyzable** ADJECTIVE ▸**ˌhydrolyˈsation** *or US* **ˌhydrolyˈzation** NOUN ▸**ˈhydroˌlyser** *or US* **ˈhydroˌlyzer** NOUN

hydrolysis (haɪˈdrɒlɪsɪs) NOUN a chemical reaction in which a compound reacts with water to produce other compounds.

hydrolyte (ˈhaɪdrəˌlaɪt) NOUN a substance subjected to hydrolysis.

hydrolytic (ˌhaɪdrəˈlɪtɪk) ADJECTIVE of, concerned with, producing, or produced by hydrolysis: *hydrolytic enzymes.*

hydromagnetics (ˌhaɪdrəʊmægˈnɛtɪks) NOUN another name for **magnetohydrodynamics.**
▸**ˌhydromagˈnetic** ADJECTIVE

hydromancy (ˈhaɪdrəʊˌmænsɪ) NOUN divination by water.
▸**ˈhydroˌmancer** NOUN ▸**ˌhydroˈmantic** ADJECTIVE

hydromechanics (ˌhaɪdrəʊmɪˈkænɪks) NOUN another name for **hydrodynamics.**
▸**ˌhydromeˈchanical** ADJECTIVE

hydromedusa (ˌhaɪdrəʊmɪˈdjuːsə) NOUN, *plural* **-sas** *or* **-sae** (-siː). the medusa form of hydrozoan coelenterates.
▸**ˌhydromeˈdusan** ADJECTIVE

hydromel (ˈhaɪdrəʊˌmɛl) NOUN *Archaic* another word for **mead** (the drink).
▷HISTORY C15: from Latin, from Greek *hudromeli,* from HYDRO- + *meli* honey

hydrometallurgy (ˌhaɪdrəʊˈmɛtᵊˌlɜːdʒɪ, -mɛˈtælədʒɪ) NOUN a technique for the recovery of a metal from an aqueous medium in which the metal or the gangue is preferentially dissolved.
▸**ˌhydroˌmetalˈlurgical** ADJECTIVE

hydrometeor (ˌhaɪdrəʊˈmiːtɪə) NOUN any weather condition produced by water or water vapour in the atmosphere, such as rain, snow, or cloud.
▸**ˌhydroˌmeteoroˈlogical** ADJECTIVE ▸**ˌhydroˌmeteorˈology** NOUN

hydrometer (haɪˈdrɒmɪtə) NOUN an instrument for measuring the relative density of a liquid, usually consisting of a sealed graduated tube with a weighted bulb on one end, the relative density being indicated by the length of the unsubmerged stem.
▸**hydrometric** (ˌhaɪdrəʊˈmɛtrɪk) *or* **ˌhydroˈmetrical** ADJECTIVE ▸**ˌhydroˈmetrically** ADVERB ▸**hyˈdrometry** NOUN

hydronaut (ˈhaɪdrəʊˌnɔːt) NOUN *US navy* a person trained to operate deep submergence vessels.
▷HISTORY C20: from Greek, from HYDRO- + *-naut,* as in *aeronaut, astronaut*

hydronium ion (haɪˈdrəʊnɪəm) NOUN *Chem* another name for **hydroxonium ion.**
▷HISTORY C20: from HYDRO- + (AMM)ONIUM

hydropathy (haɪˈdrɒpəθɪ) NOUN a pseudoscientific method of treating disease by the use of large quantities of water both internally and externally. Also called: **water cure.** Compare **hydrotherapy.**
▸**hydropathic** (ˌhaɪdrəʊˈpæθɪk) *or* **ˌhydroˈpathical** ADJECTIVE ▸**hyˈdropathist** *or* **ˈhydroˌpath** NOUN

hydrophane (ˈhaɪdrəʊˌfeɪn) NOUN a white partially opaque variety of opal that becomes translucent in water.
▸**hydrophanous** (haɪˈdrɒfənəs) ADJECTIVE

hydrophilic (ˌhaɪdrəʊˈfɪlɪk) ADJECTIVE *Chem* tending to dissolve in, mix with, or be wetted by water: *a hydrophilic colloid.* Compare **hydrophobic.**
▸**ˈhydroˌphile** NOUN

hydrophilous (haɪˈdrɒfɪləs) ADJECTIVE *Botany* growing in or pollinated by water.
▸**hyˈdrophily** NOUN

hydrophobia (ˌhaɪdrəˈfəʊbɪə) NOUN [1] another name for **rabies.** [2] a fear of drinking fluids, esp that of a person with rabies, because of painful spasms when trying to swallow. Compare **aquaphobia.**

hydrophobic (ˌhaɪdrəˈfəʊbɪk) ADJECTIVE [1] of or relating to hydrophobia. [2] *Chem* tending not to dissolve in, mix with, or be wetted by water: *a hydrophobic colloid.* Compare **hydrophilic.**

hydrophone (ˈhaɪdrəˌfəʊn) NOUN an electroacoustic transducer that converts sound or ultrasonic waves travelling through water into electrical oscillations.

hydrophyte (ˈhaɪdrəʊˌfaɪt) NOUN a plant that grows only in water or very moist soil.
▸**hydrophytic** (ˌhaɪdrəʊˈfɪtɪk) ADJECTIVE

hydroplane (ˈhaɪdrəʊˌpleɪn) NOUN [1] a motorboat equipped with hydrofoils or with a shaped bottom that raises its hull out of the water at high speeds. [2] an attachment to an aircraft to enable it to glide along the surface of water. [3] another name (esp US) for a **seaplane.** [4] a horizontal vane on the hull of a submarine for controlling its vertical motion. ◆ VERB [5] (*intr*) (of a boat) to rise out of the water in the manner of a hydroplane.

hydroponics (ˌhaɪdrəʊˈpɒnɪks) NOUN (*functioning as singular*) a method of cultivating plants by growing them in gravel, etc., through which water containing dissolved inorganic nutrient salts is pumped. Also called: **aquiculture.**
▷HISTORY C20: from HYDRO- + (GEO)PONICS
▸**ˌhydroˈponic** ADJECTIVE ▸**ˌhydroˈponically** ADVERB

hydropower (ˈhaɪdrəʊˌpaʊə) NOUN hydroelectric power.

hydroquinone (ˌhaɪdrəʊkwɪˈnəʊn) *or* **hydroquinol** (ˌhaɪdrəʊˈkwɪnɒl) NOUN a white crystalline soluble phenol used as a photographic developer; 1,4-dihydroxybenzene. Formula: $C_6H_4(OH)_2$. Also called: **quinol.**

hydroscope (ˈhaɪdrəˌskəʊp) NOUN any instrument for making observations of underwater objects.
▸**hydroscopic** (ˌhaɪdrəˈskɒpɪk) *or* **ˌhydroˈscopical** ADJECTIVE

hydrosere (ˈhaɪdrəʊsɪə) NOUN a sere that begins in an aquatic environment.

hydroski (ˈhaɪdrəʊˌskiː) NOUN a hydrofoil used on some seaplanes to provide extra lift when taking off.

hydrosol (ˈhaɪdrəˌsɒl) NOUN *Chem* a sol that has water as its liquid phase.

hydrosome (ˈhaɪdrəˌsəʊm) *or* **hydrosoma** (ˌhaɪdrəˈsəʊmə) NOUN *Zoology* the body of a colonial hydrozoan.
▷HISTORY C19: from *hydro-,* from HYDRA + -SOME[3]

hydrosphere (ˈhaɪdrəˌsfɪə) NOUN the watery part of the earth's surface, including oceans, lakes, water vapour in the atmosphere, etc.
▸**ˌhydroˈspheric** ADJECTIVE

hydrostat (ˈhaɪdrəʊˌstæt) NOUN a device that detects the presence of water as a prevention against drying out, overflow, etc., esp one used as a warning in a steam boiler.

hydrostatic (ˌhaɪdrəʊˈstætɪk) *or* **hydrostatical** ADJECTIVE [1] of or concerned with fluids that are not in motion: *hydrostatic pressure.* [2] of or concerned with hydrostatics.
▸**ˌhydroˈstatically** ADVERB

hydrostatic balance NOUN a balance for finding the weight of an object submerged in water in order to determine the upthrust on it and thus determine its relative density.

hydrostatics (ˌhaɪdrəʊˈstætɪks) NOUN (*functioning as singular*) the branch of science concerned with the mechanical properties and behaviour of fluids that are not in motion. See also **hydrodynamics.**

hydrosulphate (ˌhaɪdrəʊˈsʌlfeɪt) NOUN any quaternary acid salt formed by addition of an organic base to sulphuric acid, such as aniline hydrosulphate, $C_6H_5NH_3HSO_4$.

hydrosulphide (ˌhaɪdrəʊˈsʌlfaɪd) NOUN any salt derived from hydrogen sulphide by replacing one of its hydrogen atoms with a metal atom. Technical name: **hydrogen sulphide.**

hydrosulphite (ˌhaɪdrəʊˈsʌlfaɪt) NOUN another name (not in technical usage) for **dithionite.**
▷HISTORY C20: from HYDROSULPH(UROUS) + -ITE[2]

hydrosulphurous acid (ˌhaɪdrəʊˈsʌlfərəs) NOUN another name (not in technical usage) for **dithionous acid.**

hydrotaxis (ˌhaɪdrəʊˈtæksɪs) NOUN the directional movement of an organism or cell in response to the stimulus of water.
▸**ˌhydroˈtactic** ADJECTIVE

hydrotherapeutics (ˌhaɪdrəʊˌθɛrəˈpjuːtɪks) NOUN (*functioning as singular*) the branch of medical science concerned with hydrotherapy.
▸**ˌhydroˌtheraˈpeutic** ADJECTIVE

hydrotherapy (ˌhaɪdrəʊˈθɛrəpɪ) NOUN *Med* the treatment of certain diseases by the external use of water, esp by exercising in water in order to mobilize stiff joints or strengthen weakened muscles. Also called: **water cure.** Compare **hydropathy.**
▸**hydrotherapic** (ˌhaɪdrəʊθɪˈræpɪk) ADJECTIVE ▸**ˌhydroˈtherapist** NOUN

hydrothermal (ˌhaɪdrəʊˈθɜːməl) ADJECTIVE of or relating to the action of water under conditions of high temperature, esp in forming rocks and minerals.
▸**ˌhydroˈthermally** ADVERB

hydrothorax (ˌhaɪdrəʊˈθɔːræks) NOUN *Pathol* an accumulation of fluid in one or both pleural cavities, often resulting from disease of the heart or kidneys.
▸**hydrothoracic** (ˌhaɪdrəʊθɔːˈræsɪk) ADJECTIVE

hydrotropism (haɪˈdrɒtrəˌpɪzəm) NOUN the directional growth of plants in response to the stimulus of water.
▸**hydrotropic** (ˌhaɪdrəʊˈtrɒpɪk) ADJECTIVE ▸**ˌhydroˈtropically** ADVERB

hydrous (ˈhaɪdrəs) ADJECTIVE [1] containing water. [2] (of a chemical compound) combined with water molecules: *hydrous copper sulphate,* $CuSO_4.5H_2O$.

hydrovane (ˈhaɪdrəʊˌveɪn) NOUN a vane on a seaplane conferring stability on water (a sponson) or facilitating take off (a hydrofoil).

hydroxide (haɪˈdrɒksaɪd) NOUN [1] a base or alkali containing the ion OH^-. [2] any compound containing an -OH group.

hydroxonium ion (ˌhaɪdrɒkˈsəʊnɪəm) NOUN a positive ion, H_3O^+, formed by the attachment of a proton to a water molecule: occurs in solutions of acids and behaves like a hydrogen ion. Also called: **hydronium ion.**

hydroxy (haɪˈdrɒksɪ) ADJECTIVE (of a chemical compound) containing one or more hydroxyl groups.
▷HISTORY C19: HYDRO- + OXY(GEN)

hydroxy- COMBINING FORM (in chemical compounds) indicating the presence of one or more hydroxyl groups or ions.
▷HISTORY from HYDRO- + OXY(GEN)

hydroxy acid NOUN [1] any acid, such as sulphuric acid, containing hydroxyl groups in its molecules. [2] any of a class of carboxylic acids that contain both a hydroxyl group and a carboxyl group in their molecules.

hydroxyl (haɪˈdrɒksɪl) NOUN (*modifier*) of, consisting of, or containing the monovalent group -OH or the ion OH^-: *a hydroxyl group or radical.*
▸**ˌhydroxˈylic** ADJECTIVE

hydroxylamine (haɪˌdrɒksɪləˈmiːn, -ˈæmɪn, -ˈsaɪləˌmiːn) NOUN a colourless crystalline compound that explodes when heated: a reducing agent. Formula: NH_2OH.

hydroxyproline (haɪˌdrɒksɪˈprəʊliːn, -lɪn) NOUN an amino acid occurring in some proteins, esp collagen. Formula: $(OH)C_4H_7N(COOH)$.

hydroxytryptamine (haɪˌdrɒksɪˈtrɪptəmiːn) NOUN 5-hydroxytryptamine: another name for **serotonin.** Abbreviation: **5HT.**

hydrozoan (ˌhaɪdrəʊˈzəʊən) NOUN [1] any colonial or solitary coelenterate of the class *Hydrozoa,* which includes the hydra, Portuguese man-of-war, and the sertularians. ◆ ADJECTIVE [2] of, relating to, or belonging to the *Hydrozoa.*

Hydrus (ˈhaɪdrəs) NOUN, *Latin genitive* **Hydri** (ˈhaɪdraɪ). a constellation near the S celestial pole lying close to Eridanus and Tucana and containing part of the Small Magellanic cloud.
▷HISTORY C17: from Latin, from Greek *hudros* water serpent, from *hudōr* water

hyena *or* **hyaena** (haɪˈiːnə) NOUN any of several long-legged carnivorous doglike mammals of the genera *Hyaena* and *Crocuta,* such as *C. crocuta* (**spotted** or **laughing hyena**), of Africa and S Asia:

family *Hyaenidae,* order *Carnivora* (carnivores). See also **strandwolf.**
▷HISTORY C16: from Medieval Latin, from Latin *hyaena,* from Greek *huaina,* from *hus* hog
▸**hy'enic** *or* **hy'aenic** ADJECTIVE

hyetal ('haɪɪt^{ə}l) ADJECTIVE of or relating to rain, rainfall, or rainy regions.
▷HISTORY C19: from Greek *huetos* rain + -AL[1]

hyeto- *or before a vowel* **hyet-** COMBINING FORM indicating rain.
▷HISTORY from Greek *huetos*

hyetograph ('haɪɪtəˌgrɑːf, -ˌgræf) NOUN 1 a chart showing the distribution of rainfall of a particular area, usually throughout a year. 2 a self-recording rain gauge.

hyetography (ˌhaɪɪ'tɒgrəfɪ) NOUN the study of the distribution and recording of rainfall.
▸**hyetographic** (ˌhaɪɪtə'græfɪk) *or* **ˌhyeto'graphical** ADJECTIVE ▸**ˌhyeto'graphically** ADVERB

Hygeia (haɪ'dʒiːə) NOUN the Greek goddess of health.
▸**Hy'geian** ADJECTIVE

hygiene ('haɪdʒiːn) NOUN 1 Also called: **hygienics.** the science concerned with the maintenance of health. 2 clean or healthy practices or thinking: *personal hygiene.*
▷HISTORY C18: from New Latin *hygiēna,* from Greek *hugieinē,* from *hugieinos* healthful, from *hugiēs* healthy

hygienic (haɪ'dʒiːnɪk) ADJECTIVE promoting health or cleanliness; sanitary.
▸**hy'gienically** ADVERB

hygienics (haɪ'dʒiːnɪks) NOUN (*functioning as singular*) another word for **hygiene** (sense 1).

hygienist ('haɪdʒiːnɪst), **hygeist,** *or* **hygieist** ('haɪdʒiːɪst) NOUN a person skilled in the practice of hygiene. See also **dental hygienist.**

hygristor (haɪ'grɪstə) NOUN an electronic component the resistance of which varies with humidity.
▷HISTORY C20: from HYGRO- + (RES)ISTOR

hygro- *or before a vowel* **hygr-** COMBINING FORM indicating moisture: *hygrometer.*
▷HISTORY from Greek *hugros* wet

hygrograph ('haɪgrəˌgrɑːf, -ˌgræf) NOUN an automatic hygrometer that produces a graphic record of the humidity of the air.

hygroma (haɪ'grəʊmə) *or* **hydroma** (haɪˌdrəʊmə) NOUN *Pathol* a swelling in the soft tissue that occurs over a joint, usually caused by repeated injury.
▷HISTORY C19: from HYGRO- + -OMA

hygrometer (haɪ'grɒmɪtə) NOUN any of various instruments for measuring humidity.
▸**hygrometric** (ˌhaɪgrə'mɛtrɪk) ADJECTIVE ▸**ˌhygro'metrically** ADVERB ▸**hy'grometry** NOUN

hygrophilous (haɪ'grɒfɪləs) ADJECTIVE (of a plant) growing in moist places.
▸**hygrophile** ('haɪgrəʊˌfaɪl) NOUN

hygrophyte ('haɪgrəˌfaɪt) NOUN any plant that grows in wet or waterlogged soil.
▸**hygrophytic** (ˌhaɪgrə'fɪtɪk) ADJECTIVE

hygroscope ('haɪgrəˌskəʊp) NOUN any device that indicates the humidity of the air without necessarily measuring it.

hygroscopic (ˌhaɪgrə'skɒpɪk) ADJECTIVE (of a substance) tending to absorb water from the air.
▸**ˌhygro'scopically** ADVERB ▸**hygroscopicity** (ˌhaɪgrəskəʊ'pɪsɪtɪ) NOUN

hygrostat ('haɪgrəˌstæt) NOUN another name for **humidistat.**

hying ('haɪɪŋ) VERB a present participle of **hie.**

Hyksos ('hɪksɒs) NOUN, *plural* **-sos.** a member of a nomadic Asian people, probably Semites, who controlled Egypt from 1720 B.C. until 1560 B.C.
▷HISTORY from Greek *Huksōs* name of ruling dynasty in Egypt, from Egyptian *hq's'sw* ruler of the lands of the nomads

hyla ('haɪlə) NOUN any tree frog of the genus *Hyla,* such as *H. leucophyllata* (**white-spotted hyla**) of tropical America.
▷HISTORY C19: from New Latin, from Greek *hulē* forest, wood

hylo- *or before a vowel* **hyl-** COMBINING FORM 1 indicating matter (as distinguished from spirit): *hylozoism.* 2 indicating wood: *hylophagous.*
▷HISTORY from Greek *hulē* wood

hylomorphism (ˌhaɪlə'mɔːfɪzəm) NOUN the philosophical doctrine that identifies matter with the first cause of the universe.

hylophagous (haɪ'lɒfəgəs) ADJECTIVE (esp of insects) feeding on wood.
▷HISTORY C19: from Greek *hulophagos,* from *hulē* wood + *phagein* to devour

hylotheism (ˌhaɪlə'θiːɪzəm) NOUN the doctrine that God is identical to matter.

hylozoism (ˌhaɪlə'zəʊɪzəm) NOUN the philosophical doctrine that life is one of the properties of matter.
▷HISTORY C17: HYLO- + Greek *zōē* life
▸**ˌhylo'zoic** ADJECTIVE ▸**ˌhylo'zoist** NOUN ▸**ˌhylozo'istic** ADJECTIVE ▸**ˌhylozo'istically** ADVERB

hymen ('haɪmɛn) NOUN *Anatomy* a fold of mucous membrane that partly covers the entrance to the vagina and is usually ruptured when sexual intercourse takes place for the first time.
▷HISTORY C17: from Greek: membrane
▸**'hymenal** ADJECTIVE

Hymen ('haɪmɛn) NOUN the Greek and Roman god of marriage.

hymeneal (ˌhaɪmɛ'niːəl) ADJECTIVE 1 *Chiefly poetic* of or relating to marriage. ◆ NOUN 2 a wedding song or poem.

hymenium (haɪ'miːnɪəm) NOUN, *plural* **-nia** (-nɪə) *or* **-niums.** (in basidiomycetous and ascomycetous fungi) a layer of cells some of which produce the spores.

hymenophore (haɪ'miːnəʊˌfɔː) NOUN *Botany* the fruiting body of some basidiomycetous fungi.
▷HISTORY from HYMENIUM + -PHORE

hymenopteran (ˌhaɪmɪ'nɒptərən) *or* **hymenopteron** NOUN, *plural* **-terans** *or* **-tera** (-tərə), *or* **-terons.** any hymenopterous insect.

hymenopterous (ˌhaɪmɪ'nɒptərəs) *or* **hymenopteran** ADJECTIVE of, relating to, or belonging to the *Hymenoptera,* an order of insects, including bees, wasps, ants, and sawflies, having two pairs of membranous wings and an ovipositor specialized for stinging, sawing, or piercing.
▷HISTORY C19: from Greek *humenopteros* membrane wing; see HYMEN, -PTEROUS

Hymettus (haɪ'mɛtəs) NOUN a mountain in SE Greece, in Attica east of Athens: famous for its marble and for honey. Height: 1032 m (3386 ft.). Modern Greek name: **Imittós.**

hymn (hɪm) NOUN 1 a Christian song of praise sung to God or a saint. 2 a similar song praising other gods, a nation, etc. ◆ VERB 3 to express (praises, thanks, etc.) by singing hymns.
▷HISTORY C13: from Latin *hymnus,* from Greek *humnos*
▸**hymnic** ('hɪmnɪk) ADJECTIVE ▸**'hymnˌlike** ADJECTIVE

hymnal ('hɪmn^{ə}l) NOUN 1 a book of hymns. ◆ ADJECTIVE 2 of, relating to, or characteristic of hymns.

hymn book NOUN a book containing the words and music of hymns.

hymnist ('hɪmnɪst), **hymnodist** ('hɪmnədɪst), *or* **hymnographer** (hɪm'nɒgrəfə) NOUN a person who composes hymns.

hymnody ('hɪmnədɪ) NOUN 1 the composition or singing of hymns. 2 hymns collectively. Also called: **hymnology.**
▷HISTORY C18: from Medieval Latin *hymnōdia,* from Greek *humnōidia,* from *humnōidein* to chant a hymn, from HYMN + *aeidein* to sing
▸**hymnodical** (hɪm'nɒdɪk^{ə}l) ADJECTIVE

hymnology (hɪm'nɒlədʒɪ) NOUN 1 the study of hymn composition. 2 another word for **hymnody.**
▸**hymnologic** (ˌhɪmnə'lɒdʒɪk) *or* **ˌhymno'logical** ADJECTIVE ▸**hym'nologist** NOUN

hyoid ('haɪɔɪd) ADJECTIVE *also* **hyoidal, hyoidean.** 1 of or relating to the hyoid bone. ◆ NOUN *also* **hyoid bone.** 2 the horseshoe-shaped bone that lies at the base of the tongue and above the thyroid cartilage. 3 a corresponding bone or group of bones in other vertebrates.
▷HISTORY C19: from New Latin *hyoïdes,* from Greek *huoeidēs* having the shape of the letter UPSILON, from *hu* upsilon + -OID

hyoscine ('haɪəˌsiːn) NOUN another name for **scopolamine.**
▷HISTORY C19: from HYOSC(YAMUS) + -INE[2]

hyoscyamine (ˌhaɪə'saɪəˌmiːn, -mɪn) NOUN a poisonous alkaloid occurring in henbane and related plants: an optically active isomer of atropine, used in medicine in a similar way. Formula: $C_{17}H_{23}NO_3$.

hyoscyamus (ˌhaɪə'saɪəməs) NOUN any plant of the solanaceous genus *Hyoscyamus,* of Europe, Asia, and N Africa, including henbane.
▷HISTORY C18: from New Latin, from Greek *huoskuamos,* from *hus* pig + *kuamos* bean; the plant was thought to be poisonous to pigs

hyp. ABBREVIATION FOR hypotenuse. 3 hypothetical.

hyp- PREFIX a variant of **hypo-** before a vowel: *hypabyssal.*

hypabyssal (ˌhɪpə'bɪs^{ə}l) ADJECTIVE (of igneous rocks) derived from magma that has solidified at shallow depth in the form of dykes, sills, etc.
▷HISTORY C19: from HYP- + ABYSSAL

hypaesthesia *or US* **hypesthesia** (ˌhɪpiːs'θiːzɪə, ˌhaɪ-) NOUN *Pathol* a reduced sensibility to touch.
▸**hypaesthesic** *or US* **hypesthesic** (ˌhɪpiːs'θiːsɪk, ˌhaɪ-) ADJECTIVE

hypaethral *or US* **hypethral** (hɪ'piːθrəl, haɪ-) ADJECTIVE (esp of a classical temple) having no roof.
▷HISTORY C18: from Latin *hypaethrus* uncovered, from Greek *hupaithros,* from HYPO- + *aithros* clear sky

hypalgesia (ˌhaɪpæl'dʒiːzɪə, -sɪə) NOUN *Pathol* diminished sensitivity to pain.
▸**ˌhypal'gesic** ADJECTIVE

hypallage (haɪ'pæləˌdʒiː) NOUN *Rhetoric* a figure of speech in which the natural relations of two words in a statement are interchanged, as in *the fire spread the wind.*
▷HISTORY C16: via Late Latin from Greek *hupallagē* interchange, from HYPO- + *allassein* to exchange

hypanthium (haɪ'pænθɪəm) NOUN, *plural* **-thia** (-θɪə). *Botany* the cup-shaped or flat receptacle of perigynous or epigynous flowers.
▷HISTORY C19: from New Latin, from HYPO- + Greek *anthion* a little flower, from *anthos* flower
▸**hy'panthial** ADJECTIVE

hype[1] (haɪp) *Slang* ◆ NOUN 1 a hypodermic needle or injection. ◆ VERB 2 (*intr; usually foll by up*) to inject oneself with a drug. 3 (*tr*) to stimulate artificially or excite.
▷HISTORY C20: shortened from HYPODERMIC

hype[2] (haɪp) NOUN 1 a deception or racket. 2 intensive or exaggerated publicity or sales promotion: *media hype.* 3 the person or thing so publicized. ◆ VERB (*tr*) 4 to market or promote (a product) using exaggerated or intensive publicity. 5 to falsify or rig (something). 6 (in the pop-music business) to buy (copies of a particular record) in such quantity as to increase its ratings in the charts.
▷HISTORY C20: of unknown origin
▸**'hyper** NOUN ▸**'hyping** NOUN

hyped up ADJECTIVE *Slang* stimulated or excited by or as if by the effect of a stimulating drug.

hyper ('haɪpə) ADJECTIVE *Informal* overactive; overexcited.
▷HISTORY C20: probably independent use of HYPER-

hyper- PREFIX 1 above, over, or in excess: *hypercritical.* 2 (in medicine) denoting an abnormal excess: *hyperacidity.* 3 indicating that a chemical compound contains a greater than usual amount of an element: *hyperoxide.*
▷HISTORY from Greek *huper* over

hyperaccumulator (ˌhaɪpərə'kjuːmjʊˌleɪtə) NOUN a plant that absorbs toxins, such as heavy metals, to a greater concentration than that in the soil in which it is growing.

hyperacidity (ˌhaɪpərə'sɪdɪtɪ) NOUN excess acidity of the gastrointestinal tract, esp the stomach, producing a burning sensation.
▸**ˌhyper'acid** ADJECTIVE

hyperactive (ˌhaɪpər'æktɪv) ADJECTIVE abnormally active.
▸**ˌhyper'action** NOUN ▸**ˌhyperac'tivity** NOUN

hyperaemia *or US* **hyperemia** (ˌhaɪpər'iːmɪə) NOUN *Pathol* an excessive amount of blood in an organ or part.
▸**ˌhyper'aemic** *or US* **ˌhyper'emic** ADJECTIVE

hyperaesthesia *or US* **hyperesthesia** (ˌhaɪpəriːs'θiːzɪə) NOUN *Pathol* increased sensitivity of

any of the sense organs, esp of the skin to cold, heat, pain, etc.
▸**hyperaesthetic** *or US* **hyperesthetic** (ˌhaɪpəriːsˈθɛtɪk) ADJECTIVE

hyperbaric (ˌhaɪpəˈbærɪk) ADJECTIVE of, concerned with, or operating at pressures higher than normal.

hyperbaton (haɪˈpɜːbəˌtɒn) NOUN *Rhetoric* a figure of speech in which the normal order of words is reversed, as in *cheese I love*.
▹HISTORY C16: via Latin from Greek, literally: an overstepping, from HYPER- + *bainein* to step

hyperbola (haɪˈpɜːbələ) NOUN, *plural* **-las, -le** (-ˌliː). a conic section formed by a plane that cuts both bases of a cone; it consists of two branches asymptotic to two intersecting fixed lines and has two foci. Standard equation: $x^2/a^2 - y^2/b^2 = 1$ where $2a$ is the distance between the two intersections with the x-axis and $b = a\sqrt{(e^2 - 1)}$, where e is the eccentricity.
▹HISTORY C17: from Greek *huperbolē*, literally: excess, extravagance, from HYPER- + *ballein* to throw

hyperbole (haɪˈpɜːbəlɪ) NOUN a deliberate exaggeration used for effect: *he embraced her a thousand times*.
▹HISTORY C16: from Greek: from HYPER- + *bolē* a throw, from *ballein* to throw
▸**hyˈperbolism** NOUN

hyperbolic (ˌhaɪpəˈbɒlɪk) *or* **hyperbolical** ADJECTIVE 1 of or relating to a hyperbola. 2 *Rhetoric* of or relating to a hyperbole.
▸**ˌhyperˈbolically** ADVERB

hyperbolic function NOUN any of a group of functions of an angle expressed as a relationship between the distances of a point on a hyperbola to the origin and to the coordinate axes. The group includes sinh (**hyperbolic sine**), cosh (**hyperbolic cosine**), tanh (**hyperbolic tangent**), sech (**hyperbolic secant**), cosech (**hyperbolic cosecant**), and coth (**hyperbolic cotangent**).

hyperbolize *or* **hyperbolise** (haɪˈpɜːbəˌlaɪz) VERB to express (something) by means of hyperbole.

hyperboloid (haɪˈpɜːbəˌlɔɪd) NOUN a geometric surface consisting of one sheet, or of two sheets separated by a finite distance, whose sections parallel to the three coordinate planes are hyperbolas or ellipses. Equations $x^2/a^2 + y^2/b^2 - z^2/c^2 = 1$ (one sheet) or $x^2/a^2 - y^2/b^2 - z^2/c^2 = 1$ (two sheets) where *a, b,* and *c* are constants.

Hyperborean (ˌhaɪpəˈbɔːrɪən) NOUN 1 *Greek myth* one of a people believed to have lived beyond the North Wind in a sunny land. 2 an inhabitant of the extreme north. ◆ ADJECTIVE 3 (*sometimes not capital*) of or relating to the extreme north. 4 of or relating to the Hyperboreans.
▹HISTORY C16: from Latin *hyperboreus*, from Greek *huperboreos*, from HYPER- + *Boreas* the north wind

hypercapnia (ˌhaɪpəˈkæpnɪə) NOUN an excess of carbon dioxide in the blood. Also: **hypercarbia.**
▹HISTORY from HYPER- + Greek *kapnos* smoke
▸**ˌhyperˈcapnic** ADJECTIVE

hypercatalectic (ˌhaɪpəˌkætəˈlɛktɪk) ADJECTIVE *Prosody* (of a line of verse) having extra syllables after the last foot.

hypercharge (ˈhaɪpəˌtʃɑːdʒ) NOUN a property of baryons that is used to account for the absence of certain strong interaction decays.

hypercholesterolaemia *or US* **hypercholesterolemia** (ˌhaɪpəkəˌlɛstərɒlˈiːmɪə) NOUN the condition of having a high concentration of cholesterol in the blood. See **hyperlipidaemia.**

hypercorrect (ˌhaɪpəkəˈrɛkt) ADJECTIVE 1 excessively correct or fastidious. 2 resulting from or characterized by hypercorrection.
▸**ˌhypercorˈrectness** NOUN

hypercorrection (ˌhaɪpəkəˈrɛkʃən) NOUN a mistaken correction to text or speech made through a desire to avoid nonstandard pronunciation or grammar: *"between you and I" is a hypercorrection of "between you and me".*

hypercritical (ˌhaɪpəˈkrɪtɪkᵊl) ADJECTIVE excessively or severely critical; carping; captious.
▸**ˌhyperˈcritic** NOUN ▸**ˌhyperˈcritically** ADVERB
▸**ˌhyperˈcritiˌcism** NOUN

hypercube (ˈhaɪpəˌkjuːb) NOUN *Maths* a figure in a space of four or more dimensions having all its sides equal and all its angles right angles.

hyperdulia (ˌhaɪpədjuˈlɪə) NOUN *RC Church* special veneration accorded to the Virgin Mary. Compare **dulia, latria.**
▹HISTORY C16: from Latin HYPER- + Medieval Latin *dulia* service
▸**ˌhyperˈdulic** *or* **ˌhyperˈdulical** ADJECTIVE

hyperemia (ˌhaɪpərˈiːmɪə) NOUN *Pathol* the usual US spelling of **hyperaemia.**
▸**ˌhyperˈemic** ADJECTIVE

hyperesthesia (ˌhaɪpəriːsˈθiːzɪə) NOUN *Pathol* the usual US spelling of **hyperaesthesia.**
▸**ˌhyperesˈthetic** ADJECTIVE

hypereutectic (ˌhaɪpəjuːˈtɛktɪk) *or* **hypereutectoid** ADJECTIVE (of a mixture or alloy with two components) containing more of the minor component than a eutectic mixture. Compare **hypoeutectic.**

hyperextension (ˌhaɪpərɪkˈstɛnʃən) NOUN extension of an arm or leg beyond its normal limits.

hyperfine structure (ˈhaɪpəˌfaɪn) NOUN the splitting of a spectral line of an atom or molecule into two or more closely spaced components as a result of interaction of the electrons with the magnetic moments of the nuclei. Compare **fine structure.** See also **Zeeman effect.**

hyperfocal distance (ˌhaɪpəˈfəʊkᵊl) NOUN the distance from a camera lens to the point beyond which all objects appear sharp and clearly defined.

hypergamy (haɪˈpɜːgəmɪ) NOUN 1 *Anthropol* a custom that forbids a woman to marry a man of lower social status. 2 any marriage with a partner of higher social status.
▹HISTORY C19: from HYPER- + -GAMY
▸**ˌhyperˈgamous** ADJECTIVE

hyperglycaemia *or US* **hyperglycemia** (ˌhaɪpəglaɪˈsiːmɪə) NOUN *Pathol* an abnormally large amount of sugar in the blood.
▹HISTORY C20: from HYPER- + GLYCO- + -AEMIA
▸**ˌhyperglyˈcaemic** *or US* **ˌhyperglyˈcemic** ADJECTIVE

hypergolic (ˌhaɪpəˈgɒlɪk) ADJECTIVE (of a rocket fuel) able to ignite spontaneously on contact with an oxidizer.
▹HISTORY C20: from German *Hypergol* (perhaps from HYP(ER-) + ERG[1] + -OL[2]) + -IC

hypericum (haɪˈpɛrɪkəm) NOUN any herbaceous plant or shrub of the temperate genus *Hypericum*: family *Hypericaceae*. See **rose of Sharon** (sense 1), **Saint John's wort.**
▹HISTORY C16: via Latin from Greek *hupereikon*, from HYPER- + *ereikē* heath

hyperinflation (ˌhaɪpəɪnˈfleɪʃən) NOUN extremely high inflation, usually over 50 per cent per month, often involving social disorder. Also called: **galloping inflation.**

hyperinsulinism (ˌhaɪpərˈɪnsjʊlɪˌnɪzəm) NOUN *Pathol* an excessive amount of insulin in the blood, producing hypoglycaemia, caused by oversecretion of insulin by the pancreas or overdosage of insulin in treating diabetes. See **insulin reaction.**

Hyperion[1] (haɪˈpɪərɪən) NOUN *Greek myth* a Titan, son of Uranus and Gaea, father of Helios (sun), Selene (moon), and Eos (dawn).

Hyperion[2] (haɪˈpɪərɪən) NOUN an irregular-shaped outer satellite of the planet Saturn that tumbles chaotically.

hyperkeratosis (ˌhaɪpəˌkɛrəˈtəʊsɪs) NOUN *Pathol* overgrowth and thickening of the outer layer of the skin.
▸**hyperkeratotic** (ˌhaɪpəˌkɛrəˈtɒtɪk) ADJECTIVE

hyperkinesia (ˌhaɪpəkɪˈniːzɪə, -kaɪ-) *or* **hyperkinesis** (ˌhaɪpəkɪˈniːsɪs, -kaɪ-) NOUN *Pathol* 1 excessive movement, as in a muscle spasm. 2 extreme overactivity in children.
▹HISTORY C20: from HYPER- + *-kinesia* from Greek *kinēsis* movement, from *kinein* to move
▸**hyperkinetic** (ˌhaɪpəkɪˈnɛtɪk, -kaɪ-) ADJECTIVE

hyperlink (ˈhɒɪpəˌlɪŋk) NOUN 1 a word, phrase, picture, icon, etc., in a computer document on which a user may click to move to another part of the document or to another document. ◆ VERB 2 (*tr*) to link (files) in this way. ◆ Often shortened to **link.**

hyperlipidaemia *or US* **hyperlipidemia** (ˌhaɪpəˌlɪpɪˈdiːmɪə) NOUN an abnormally high level of lipids, esp cholesterol, in the blood, predisposing to atherosclerosis and other arterial diseases.

hypermania (ˌhaɪpəˈmeɪnɪə) NOUN *Psychol* a condition of extreme mania.

hypermarket (ˈhaɪpəˌmɑːkɪt) NOUN *Brit* a huge self-service store, usually built on the outskirts of a town.
▹HISTORY C20: translation of French *hypermarché*

hypermedia (ˈhaɪpəˌmiːdɪə) NOUN computer software and hardware that allows users to interact with text, graphics, sound, and video, each of which can be accessed from within any of the others. Compare **hypertext.**

hypermeter (haɪˈpɜːmɪtə) NOUN *Prosody* a verse line containing one or more additional syllables.
▸**hypermetric** (ˌhaɪpəˈmɛtrɪk) *or* **ˌhyperˈmetrical** ADJECTIVE

hypermetropia (ˌhaɪpəmɪˈtrəʊpɪə) *or* **hypermetropy** (ˌhaɪpəˈmɛtrəpɪ) NOUN *Pathol* variants of **hyperopia.**
▹HISTORY C19: from Greek *hupermetros* beyond measure (from HYPER- + *metron* measure) + -OPIA
▸**hypermetropic** (ˌhaɪpəmɪˈtrɒpɪk) *or* **ˌhypermeˈtropical** ADJECTIVE

hypermnesia (ˌhaɪpəmˈniːzɪə) NOUN *Psychol* an unusually good ability to remember, found in some mental disorders and possibly in hypnosis.
▹HISTORY C20: New Latin, from HYPER- + *-mnesia*, formed on the model of AMNESIA

hypermodern school (ˌhaɪpəˈmɒdən) NOUN a name given by S. G. Tartakower to a style of chess typified by Richard Reti and A. I. Nimzowitsch and characterized by control of the centre from the flanks.

hypernym (ˈhaɪpəˌnɪm) NOUN another name for **superordinate** (sense 3).
▹HISTORY C20: from HYPER- + Greek *onoma* name

hyperon (ˈhaɪpəˌrɒn) NOUN *Physics* any baryon that is not a nucleon.
▹HISTORY C20: from HYPER- + -ON

hyperopia (ˌhaɪpəˈrəʊpɪə) NOUN inability to see near objects clearly because the images received by the eye are focused behind the retina; long-sightedness. Also called: **hypermetropia, hypermetropy.** Compare **myopia, presbyopia.**
▸**hyperopic** (ˌhaɪpəˈrɒpɪk)

hyperorexia (ˌhaɪpərɒˈrɛksɪə) NOUN compulsive overeating.
▹HISTORY C20: from HYPER- + Greek *orexis* appetite

hyperosmia (ˌhaɪpəˈrɒzmɪə) NOUN an abnormally acute sense of smell.
▹HISTORY C20: from HYPER- + Greek *osmē* odour

hyperostosis (ˌhaɪpərɒˈstəʊsɪs) NOUN, *plural* **-ses** (-siːz). *Pathol* 1 an abnormal enlargement of the outer layer of a bone. 2 a bony growth arising from the root of a tooth or from the surface of a bone.
▸**hyperostotic** (ˌhaɪpərɒˈstɒtɪk) ADJECTIVE

hyperparasite (ˌhaɪpəˈpærəˌsaɪt) NOUN an organism that is parasitic on another parasite.

hyperphagia (ˌhaɪpəˈfeɪdʒɪə) NOUN *Psychol* compulsive overeating over a prolonged period.

hyperphysical (ˌhaɪpəˈfɪzɪkᵊl) ADJECTIVE beyond the physical; supernatural or immaterial.
▸**ˌhyperˈphysically** ADVERB

hyperpituitarism (ˌhaɪpəpɪˈtjuːɪtəˌrɪzəm) NOUN *Pathol* overactivity of the pituitary gland, sometimes resulting in acromegaly or gigantism.
▸**ˌhyperpiˈtuitary** ADJECTIVE

hyperplane (ˈhaɪpəˌpleɪn) NOUN *Maths* a higher dimensional analogue of a plane in three dimensions. It can be represented by one linear equation.

hyperplasia (ˌhaɪpəˈpleɪzɪə) NOUN enlargement of a bodily organ or part resulting from an increase in the total number of cells. Compare **hypertrophy.**
▸**hyperplastic** (ˌhaɪpəˈplæstɪk) ADJECTIVE

hyperploid (ˈhaɪpəˌplɔɪd) ADJECTIVE *Biology* having or relating to a chromosome number that exceeds an exact multiple of the haploid number.
▸**ˈhyperˌploidy** NOUN

hyperpnoea *or US* **hyperpnea** (ˌhaɪpəpˈniːə, ˌhaɪpəˈniːə) NOUN an increase in the breathing rate or in the depth of breathing, as after strenuous exercise.
▹HISTORY C20: from New Latin, from HYPER- + Greek *pnoia* breath, from *pnein* to breathe

hyperpower (ˈhaɪpəˌpaʊə) NOUN 1 an extremely

powerful state that dominates all other states in every sphere of activity. 2 the power wielded by such a state.

hyperprosexia (ˌhaɪpəprɒˈsɛksɪə) NOUN *Psychol* a condition in which the whole attention is occupied by one object or idea to the exclusion of others.
▷HISTORY C20: from HYPER- + Greek *prosexein* to heed

hyperpyrexia (ˌhaɪpəpaɪˈrɛksɪə) NOUN *Pathol* an extremely high fever, with a temperature of 41°C (106°F) or above. Also called: **hyperthermia, hyperthermy.**
▸**hyperpyretic** (ˌhaɪpəpaɪˈrɛtɪk) *or* ˌ**hyperpyˈrexial** ADJECTIVE

hyperreal (ˌhaɪpəˈrɪəl) ADJECTIVE 1 involving or characterized by particularly realistic graphic representation. 2 distorting or exaggerating reality. 3 pertaining to or creating a hyperreality. ◆ NOUN 4 **the hyperreal.** that which constitutes hyperreality. 5 short for **hyperreal number.**

hyperrealism (ˌhaɪpəˈrɪəlɪzəm) NOUN another word for **photorealism.**
▸ˌ**hyperˈrealist** NOUN, ADJECTIVE ▸ˌ**hyperˌrealˈistic** ADJECTIVE

hyperreality (ˌhaɪpərɪˈælɪtɪ) NOUN, *plural* **-ties.** an image or simulation, or an aggregate of images and simulations, that either distorts the reality it purports to depict or does not in fact depict anything with a real existence at all, but which nonetheless comes to constitute reality.

hyperreal number NOUN any of the set of numbers formed by the addition of infinite numbers and infinitesimal numbers to the set of real numbers.

hypersensitive (ˌhaɪpəˈsɛnsɪtɪv) ADJECTIVE 1 having unduly vulnerable feelings. 2 abnormally sensitive to an allergen, a drug, or other agent.
▸ˌ**hyperˈsensitiveness** *or* ˌ**hyperˌsensiˈtivity** NOUN

hypersensitize *or* **hypersensitise** (ˌhaɪpəˈsɛnsɪˌtaɪz) VERB (*tr*) to treat (a photographic emulsion), usually after manufacture and shortly before exposure, to increase its speed.
▸ˌ**hyperˌsensitiˈzation** *or* ˌ**hyperˌsensitiˈsation** NOUN

hypersonic (ˌhaɪpəˈsɒnɪk) ADJECTIVE concerned with or having a velocity of at least five times that of sound in the same medium under the same conditions.
▸ˌ**hyperˈsonics** NOUN

hyperspace (ˌhaɪpəˈspeɪs) NOUN 1 *Maths* space having more than three dimensions: often used to describe a multi-dimensional environment. 2 (in science fiction) a theoretical dimension within which conventional space-time relationship does not apply.
▸**hyperspatial** (ˌhaɪpəˈspeɪʃəl) ADJECTIVE

hypersthene (ˈhaɪpəˌsθiːn) NOUN a green, brown, or black pyroxene mineral consisting of magnesium iron silicate in orthorhombic crystalline form. Formula: $(Mg,Fe)_2Si_2O_6$.
▷HISTORY C19: from HYPER- + Greek *sthenos* strength
▸**hypersthenic** (ˌhaɪpəˈsθɛnɪk) ADJECTIVE

hypertension (ˌhaɪpəˈtɛnʃən) NOUN *Pathol* abnormally high blood pressure.
▸**hypertensive** (ˌhaɪpəˈtɛnsɪv) ADJECTIVE, NOUN

hypertext (ˈhaɪpəˌtɛkst) NOUN computer software and hardware that allows users to create, store, and view text and move between related items easily and in a nonsequential way; a word or phrase can be selected to link users to another part of the same document or to a different document.

hypertext markup language NOUN the full name for **HTML.**

hyperthermia (ˌhaɪpəˈθɜːmɪə) *or* **hyperthermy** (ˌhaɪpəˈθɜːmɪ) NOUN *Pathol* variants of **hyperpyrexia.**
▸ˌ**hyperˈthermal** ADJECTIVE

hyperthermophile (ˌhaɪpəˈθɜːməʊˌfaɪl) NOUN an organism, esp a bacterium, that lives at high temperatures (above 80°C), found in some hot springs.
▷HISTORY C20: from HYPER- + THERMOPHILE

hyperthymia (ˌhaɪpəˈθaɪmɪə) NOUN excessive emotionalism.
▷HISTORY C20: from HYPER- + Greek *thymos* spirit

hyperthyroidism (ˌhaɪpəˈθaɪrɔɪˌdɪzəm) NOUN overproduction of thyroid hormone by the thyroid gland, causing nervousness, insomnia, sweating, palpitation, and sensitivity to heat. Also called: **thyrotoxicosis.** See **exophthalmic goitre.**
▸ˌ**hyperˈthyroid** ADJECTIVE, NOUN

hypertonic (ˌhaɪpəˈtɒnɪk) ADJECTIVE 1 (esp of muscles) being in a state of abnormally high tension. 2 (of a solution) having a higher osmotic pressure than that of a specified, generally physiological, solution. Compare **hypotonic, isotonic.**
▸**hypertonicity** (ˌhaɪpətəʊˈnɪsɪtɪ) NOUN

hypertrophy (haɪˈpɜːtrəfɪ) NOUN, *plural* **-phies.** 1 enlargement of an organ or part resulting from an increase in the size of the cells. Compare **atrophy, hyperplasia.** ◆ VERB **-phies, -phying, -phied.** 2 to undergo or cause to undergo this condition.
▸**hypertrophic** (ˌhaɪpəˈtrɒfɪk) ADJECTIVE

hyperventilate (ˌhaɪpəˈvɛntɪleɪt) VERB (*intr*) to breathe in an abnormally deep, long, and rapid manner, sometimes resulting in cramp and dizziness.

hyperventilation (ˌhaɪpəˌvɛntɪˈleɪʃən) NOUN an increase in the depth, duration, and rate of breathing, sometimes resulting in cramp and dizziness.

hypervitaminosis (ˌhaɪpəˌvɪtəmɪˈnəʊsɪs, -ˌvaɪ-) NOUN *Pathol* the condition resulting from the chronic excessive intake of vitamins.
▷HISTORY C20: from HYPER- + VITAMIN + -OSIS

hypester (ˈhaɪpstə) NOUN a person or organization that gives an idea or product intense publicity in order to promote it.

hypesthesia (ˌhɪpiːsˈθiːzɪə, ˌhaɪ-) NOUN the usual US spelling of **hypaesthesia.**
▸**hypesthesic** (ˌhɪpiːsˈθiːsɪk, ˌhaɪ-) ADJECTIVE

hypethral (hɪˈpiːθrəl, haɪ-) ADJECTIVE the usual US spelling of **hypaethral.**

hypha (ˈhaɪfə) NOUN, *plural* **-phae** (-fiː). any of the filaments that constitute the body (mycelium) of a fungus.
▷HISTORY C19: from New Latin, from Greek *huphē* web
▸ˈ**hyphal** ADJECTIVE

hyphen (ˈhaɪfᵊn) NOUN 1 the punctuation mark (-), used to separate the parts of some compound words, to link the words of a phrase, and between syllables of a word split between two consecutive lines of writing or printing. ◆ VERB 2 (*tr*) another word for **hyphenate.**
▷HISTORY C17: from Late Latin (meaning: the combining of two words), from Greek *huphen* (adv) together, from HYPO- + *heis* one

hyphenate (ˈhaɪfᵊˌneɪt) *or* **hyphen** VERB (*tr*) to separate (syllables, words, etc.) with a hyphen.
▸ˌ**hyphenˈation** NOUN

hyphenated (ˈhaɪfᵊˌneɪtɪd) ADJECTIVE 1 containing or linked with a hyphen. 2 *Chiefly US* having a nationality denoted by a hyphenated word, as in *American-Irish.* 3 *Chiefly US* denoting something, such as a professional career, that consists of two elements, as in *singer-songwriter.*

hyphen help NOUN a word processing function that assists the operator to identify automatically those words that can be hyphenated at the end of a line of text.

hypnagogic *or* **hypnogogic** (ˌhɪpnəˈgɒdʒɪk) ADJECTIVE *Psychol* of or relating to the state just before one is fully asleep. See also **hypnagogic image, hypnopompic.**
▷HISTORY C19: from French *hypnagogique;* see HYPNO-, -AGOGIC

hypnagogic image NOUN *Psychol* an image experienced by a person just before falling asleep, which often resembles a hallucination.

hypno- *or before a vowel* **hypn-** COMBINING FORM 1 indicating sleep: *hypnophobia.* 2 relating to hypnosis: *hypnotherapy.*
▷HISTORY from Greek *hupnos* sleep

hypnoanalysis (ˌhɪpnəʊəˈnælɪsɪs) NOUN *Psychol* psychoanalysis conducted on a hypnotized person.
▸**hypnoanalytic** (ˌhɪpnəʊˌænəˈlɪtɪk) ADJECTIVE

hypnogenesis (ˌhɪpnəʊˈdʒɛnɪsɪs) NOUN *Psychol* the induction of sleep or hypnosis.
▸**hypnogenetic** (ˌhɪpnəʊdʒɪˈnɛtɪk) ADJECTIVE
▸ˌ**hypnogeˈnetically** ADVERB

hypnoid[1] (ˈhɪpˌnɔɪd) *or* **hypnoidal** (hɪpˈnɔɪdᵊl) ADJECTIVE *Psychol* of or relating to a state resembling sleep or hypnosis.

hypnoid[2] (ˈhɪpˌnɔɪd) ADJECTIVE resembling a moss, specifically a moss of the genus *Hypnum.*
▷HISTORY from New Latin *hypnum,* from Greek *hupnon* a type of lichen, + -OID

hypnology (hɪpˈnɒlədʒɪ) NOUN *Psychol* the study of sleep and hypnosis.
▸**hypnologic** (ˌhɪpnəˈlɒdʒɪk) *or* ˌ**hypnoˈlogical** ADJECTIVE
▸**hypˈnologist** NOUN

hypnopaedia (ˌhɪpnəʊˈpiːdɪə) NOUN the learning of lessons heard during sleep.
▷HISTORY C20: from HYPNO- + Greek *paideia* education

hypnopompic (ˌhɪpnəʊˈpɒmpɪk) ADJECTIVE *Psychol* relating to the state existing between sleep and full waking, characterized by the persistence of dreamlike imagery. See also **hypnagogic.**
▷HISTORY C20: from HYPNO- + Greek *pompē* a sending forth, escort + -IC; see POMP

Hypnos (ˈhɪpnɒs) NOUN *Greek myth* the god of sleep. Roman counterpart: **Somnus.** Compare **Morpheus.**
▷HISTORY Greek: sleep

hypnosis (hɪpˈnəʊsɪs) NOUN, *plural* **-ses** (-siːz). an artificially induced state of relaxation and concentration in which deeper parts of the mind become more accessible: used clinically to reduce reaction to pain, to encourage free association, etc. See also **autohypnosis.**

hypnotherapy (ˌhɪpnəʊˈθɛrəpɪ) NOUN the use of hypnosis in the treatment of emotional and psychogenic problems.
▸ˌ**hypnoˈtherapist** NOUN

hypnotic (hɪpˈnɒtɪk) ADJECTIVE 1 of, relating to, or producing hypnosis or sleep. 2 (of a person) susceptible to hypnotism. ◆ NOUN 3 a drug or agent that induces sleep. 4 a person susceptible to hypnosis.
▷HISTORY C17: from Late Latin *hypnōticus,* from Greek *hupnōtikos,* from *hupnoun* to put to sleep, from *hupnos* sleep
▸**hypˈnotically** ADVERB

hypnotism (ˈhɪpnəˌtɪzəm) NOUN 1 the scientific study and practice of hypnosis. 2 the process of inducing hypnosis.

hypnotist (ˈhɪpnətɪst) NOUN a person skilled in the theory and practice of hypnosis.

hypnotize *or* **hypnotise** (ˈhɪpnəˌtaɪz) VERB (*tr*) 1 to induce hypnosis in (a person). 2 to charm or beguile; fascinate.
▸ˈ**hypnoˌtizable** *or* ˈ**hypnoˌtisable** ADJECTIVE
▸ˌ**hypnoˌtizaˈbility** *or* ˌ**hypnoˌtisaˈbility** NOUN
▸ˌ**hypnotiˈzation** *or* ˌ**hypnotiˈsation** NOUN ▸ˈ**hypnoˌtizer** *or* ˈ**hypnoˌtiser** NOUN

hypo[1] (ˈhaɪpəʊ) NOUN another name for **sodium thiosulphate,** esp when used as a fixer in photographic developing
▷HISTORY C19: shortened from HYPOSULPHITE

hypo[2] (ˈhaɪpəʊ) NOUN, *plural* **-pos.** *Informal* short for **hypodermic syringe.**

hypo- *or before a vowel* **hyp-** PREFIX 1 under, beneath, or below: *hypodermic.* 2 lower; at a lower point: *hypogastrium.* 3 less than: *hypoploid.* 4 (in medicine) denoting a deficiency or an abnormally low level: *hypothyroid; hypoglycaemia.* 5 incomplete or partial: *hypoplasia.* 6 indicating that a chemical compound contains an element in a lower oxidation state than usual: *hypochlorous acid.*
▷HISTORY from Greek, from *hupo* under

Hypo- PREFIX indicating a plagal mode in music: *Hypodorian.*
▷HISTORY from Greek: beneath (it lies a fourth below the corresponding authentic mode)

hypoacidity (ˌhaɪpəʊəˈsɪdɪtɪ) NOUN *Med* abnormally low acidity, as of the contents of the stomach.

hypoallergenic (ˈhaɪpəʊˌæləˈdʒɛnɪk) ADJECTIVE (of cosmetics, earrings, etc.) not likely to cause an allergic reaction.

hypoblast (ˈhaɪpəˌblæst) NOUN 1 Also called: **endoblast.** *Embryol* the inner layer of an embryo at an early stage of development that becomes the endoderm at gastrulation. 2 a less common name for **endoderm.**
▸ˌ**hypoˈblastic** ADJECTIVE

hypocaust (ˈhaɪpəˌkɔːst) NOUN an ancient Roman heating system in which hot air circulated under the floor and between double walls.
▷HISTORY C17: from Latin *hypocaustum,* from Greek *hupokauston* room heated from below, from

hupokaiein to light a fire beneath, from HYPO- + *kaiein* to burn

hypocentre ('haɪpəʊˌsɛntə) NOUN [1] Also called: **ground zero**. the point on the ground immediately below the centre of explosion of a nuclear bomb in the atmosphere. [2] another term for **focus** (sense 6).

hypochlorite (ˌhaɪpə'klɔːraɪt) NOUN any salt or ester of hypochlorous acid.

hypochlorous acid (ˌhaɪpə'klɔːrəs) NOUN an unstable acid known only in solution and in the form of its salts, formed when chlorine dissolves in water: a strong oxidizing and bleaching agent. Formula: HOCl.

hypochondria (ˌhaɪpə'kɒndrɪə) NOUN chronic abnormal anxiety concerning the state of one's health, even in the absence of any evidence of disease on medicalexamination. Also called: **hypochondriasis** (ˌhaɪpəʊkɒn'draɪəsɪs).
▷HISTORY C18: from Late Latin: the abdomen, supposedly the seat of melancholy, from Greek *hupokhondria*, from *hupokhondrios* of the upper abdomen, from HYPO- + *khondros* cartilage

hypochondriac (ˌhaɪpə'kɒndrɪˌæk) NOUN [1] a person suffering from hypochondria. ◆ ADJECTIVE *also* **hypochondriacal** (ˌhaɪpəkɒn'draɪək^{ə}l). [2] relating to or suffering from hypochondria. [3] *Anatomy* of or relating to the hypochondrium.
▸ˌ**hypochon'driacally** ADVERB

hypochondrium (ˌhaɪpə'kɒndrɪəm) NOUN, *plural* **-dria** (-drɪə). *Anatomy* the upper region of the abdomen on each side of the epigastrium, just below the lowest ribs.
▷HISTORY C17: from New Latin, from Greek *hupokhondrion; see* HYPOCHONDRIA

hypocorism (haɪ'pɒkəˌrɪzəm) NOUN [1] a pet name, esp one using a diminutive affix: *"Sally" is a hypocorism for "Sarah"*. [2] another word for **euphemism** (sense 1).
▷HISTORY C19: from Greek *hupokorisma*, from *hupokorizesthai* to use pet names, from *hypo-* beneath + *korizesthai*, from *korē* girl, *koros* boy
▸**hypocoristic** (ˌhaɪpəkɔː'rɪstɪk) ADJECTIVE
▸ˌ**hypoco'ristically** ADVERB

hypocotyl (ˌhaɪpə'kɒtɪl) NOUN the part of an embryo plant between the cotyledons and the radicle.
▷HISTORY C19: from HYPO- + COTYL(EDON)
▸ˌ**hypo'cotylous** ADJECTIVE

hypocrisy (hɪ'pɒkrəsɪ) NOUN, *plural* **-sies**. [1] the practice of professing standards, beliefs, etc., contrary to one's real character or actual behaviour, esp the pretence of virtue and piety. [2] an act or instance of this.

hypocrite ('hɪpəkrɪt) NOUN a person who pretends to be what he is not.
▷HISTORY C13: from Old French *ipocrite*, via Late Latin, from Greek *hupokritēs* one who plays a part, from *hupokrinein* to feign, from *krinein* to judge
▸ˌ**hypo'critical** ADJECTIVE ▸ˌ**hypo'critically** ADVERB

hypocrystalline (ˌhaɪpəʊ'krɪstəˌlaɪn) ADJECTIVE (of igneous rocks) having both glass and crystalline components. Former word **hemicrystalline**. Compare **holocrystalline**.

hypocycloid (ˌhaɪpə'saɪklɔɪd) NOUN a curve described by a point on the circumference of a circle as the circle rolls around the inside of a fixed coplanar circle. Compare **epicycloid, cycloid** (sense 4).
▸ˌ**hypocy'cloidal** ADJECTIVE

hypoderm ('haɪpəˌdɜːm) NOUN a variant of **hypodermis**.
▸ˌ**hypo'dermal** ADJECTIVE

hypodermic (ˌhaɪpə'dɜːmɪk) ADJECTIVE [1] of or relating to the region of the skin beneath the epidermis. [2] injected beneath the skin. ◆ NOUN [3] a hypodermic syringe or needle. [4] a hypodermic injection.
▸ˌ**hypo'dermically** ADVERB

hypodermic syringe NOUN *Med* a type of syringe consisting of a hollow cylinder, usually of glass or plastic, a tightly fitting piston, and a hollow needle (**hypodermic needle**), used for withdrawing blood samples, injecting medicine, etc.

hypodermis (ˌhaɪpə'dɜːmɪs) *or* **hypoderm** NOUN [1] *Botany* a layer of thick-walled supportive or water-storing cells beneath the epidermis in some plants. [2] *Zoology* the epidermis of arthropods, annelids, etc., which secretes and is covered by a cuticle.
▷HISTORY C19: from HYPO- + EPIDERMIS

Hypodorian (ˌhaɪpə'dɔːrɪən) ADJECTIVE *Music* denoting a plagal mode represented by the ascending diatonic scale from A to A. Compare **Dorian** (sense 3). See **Hypo-**.

hypoeutectic (ˌhaɪpəʊjuː'tɛktɪk) *or* **hypoeutectoid** ADJECTIVE (of a mixture or alloy with two components) containing less of the minor component than a eutectic mixture. Compare **hypereutectic**.

hypogastrium (ˌhaɪpə'gæstrɪəm) NOUN, *plural* **-tria** (-trɪə). *Anatomy* the lower front central region of the abdomen, below the navel.
▷HISTORY C17: from New Latin, from Greek *hupogastrion*, from HYPO- + *gastrion*, diminutive of *gastēr* stomach
▸ˌ**hypo'gastric** ADJECTIVE

hypogeal (ˌhaɪpə'dʒiːəl) *or* **hypogeous** ADJECTIVE [1] occurring or living below the surface of the ground. [2] *Botany* of or relating to seed germination in which the cotyledons remain below the ground, because of the growth of the epicotyl.
▷HISTORY C19: from Latin *hypogēus*, from Greek *hupogeios*, from HYPO- + *gē* earth

hypogene ('haɪpəˌdʒiːn) ADJECTIVE formed, taking place, or originating beneath the surface of the earth. Compare **epigene**.
▸**hypogenic** (ˌhaɪpə'dʒɛnɪk) ADJECTIVE

hypogenous (haɪ'pɒdʒɪnəs) ADJECTIVE *Botany* produced or growing on the undersurface, esp (of fern spores) growing on the undersurface of the leaves.

hypogeous (ˌhaɪpə'dʒiːəs) ADJECTIVE another word for **hypogeal**.

hypogeum (ˌhaɪpə'dʒiːəm) NOUN, *plural* **-gea** (-'dʒiːə). an underground vault, esp one used for burials.
▷HISTORY C18: from Latin, from Greek *hupogeion*; see HYPOGEAL

hypoglossal (ˌhaɪpə'glɒs^{ə}l) ADJECTIVE [1] situated beneath the tongue. ◆ NOUN [2] short for **hypoglossal nerve**.

hypoglossal nerve NOUN the twelfth cranial nerve, which supplies the muscles of the tongue.

hypoglycaemia *or US* **hypoglycemia** (ˌhaɪpəʊglaɪ'siːmɪə) NOUN *Pathol* an abnormally small amount of sugar in the blood.
▷HISTORY C20: from HYPO- + GLYCO- + -AEMIA
▸ˌ**hypogly'caemic** *or US* ˌ**hypogly'cemic** ADJECTIVE

hypognathous (haɪ'pɒgnəθəs) ADJECTIVE [1] having a lower jaw that protrudes beyond the upper jaw. [2] (of insects) having downturned mouthparts.
▸**hy'pognathism** NOUN

hypogynous (haɪ'pɒdʒɪnəs) ADJECTIVE [1] (of a flower) having the gynoecium situated above the other floral parts, as in the buttercup. [2] of or relating to the parts of a flower arranged in this way.
▸**hy'pogyny** NOUN

hypoid gear ('haɪpɔɪd) NOUN a gear having a tooth form generated by a hypocycloidal curve; used extensively in motor vehicle transmissions to withstand a high surface loading.
▷HISTORY C20: *hypoid*, shortened from HYPOCYCLOID

hypolimnion (ˌhaɪpəʊ'lɪmnɪən) NOUN the lower and colder layer of water in a lake.
▷HISTORY C20: from HYPO- + Greek *limnion*, diminutive of *limnē* lake

Hypolydian (ˌhaɪpə'lɪdɪən) ADJECTIVE *Music* denoting a plagal mode represented by the diatonic scale from D to D. Compare **Lydian** (sense 2). See **Hypo-**.

hypomagnesaemia *or US* **hypomagnesemia** (ˌhaɪpəʊˌmægnə'siːmɪə) NOUN *Vet science* too little magnesium in the blood, particularly in cattle, in which it is also known as **lactation tetany**.

hypomania (ˌhaɪpəʊ'meɪnɪə) NOUN *Psychiatry* an abnormal condition of extreme excitement, milder than mania but characterized by great optimism and overactivity and often by reckless spending of money.
▸**hypomanic** (ˌhaɪpəʊ'mænɪk) ADJECTIVE

hyponasty ('haɪpəˌnæstɪ) NOUN increased growth of the lower surface of a plant part, resulting in an upward bending of the part. Compare **epinasty**.
▸ˌ**hypo'nastic** ADJECTIVE ▸ˌ**hypo'nastically** ADVERB

hyponatraemia (ˌhaɪpɒnə'triːmɪə) NOUN a condition in which there is a low concentration of sodium in the blood. Also called: **water intoxication**.
▷HISTORY C20: from HYPO- + Latin *natrium* sodium + -AEMIA

hyponitrite (ˌhaɪpə'naɪtraɪt) NOUN any salt or ester of hyponitrous acid.

hyponitrous acid (ˌhaɪpə'naɪtrəs) NOUN a white soluble unstable crystalline acid: an oxidizing and reducing agent. Formula: $H_2N_2O_2$.

hyponym ('haɪpəʊnɪm) NOUN a word whose meaning is included in that of another word: *'scarlet', 'vermilion', and 'crimson' are hyponyms of 'red'*. Compare **superordinate** (sense 3), **synonym, antonym**.
▷HISTORY C20: from HYPO- + Greek *onoma* name
▸**hyponymy** (haɪ'pɒnəmɪ) NOUN

hypophosphate (ˌhaɪpə'fɒsfeɪt) NOUN any salt or ester of hypophosphoric acid.

hypophosphite (ˌhaɪpə'fɒsfaɪt) NOUN any salt of hypophosphorous acid.

hypophosphoric acid (ˌhaɪpəfɒs'fɒrɪk) NOUN a crystalline odourless deliquescent solid: a tetrabasic acid produced by the slow oxidation of phosphorus in moist air. Formula: $H_4P_2O_6$.

hypophosphorous acid (ˌhaɪpə'fɒsfərəs) NOUN a colourless or yellowish oily liquid or white deliquescent solid: a monobasic acid and a reducing agent. Formula: H_3PO_2.

hypophyge (haɪ'pɒfɪdʒɪ) NOUN *Architect* another name for **apophyge**.

hypophysis (haɪ'pɒfɪsɪs) NOUN, *plural* **-ses** (-ˌsiːz). the technical name for **pituitary gland**.
▷HISTORY C18: from Greek: outgrowth, from HYPO- + *phuein* to grow
▸**hypophyseal** *or* **hypophysial** (ˌhaɪpə'fɪzɪəl, haɪˌpɒfɪ'sɪəl) ADJECTIVE

hypopituitarism (ˌhaɪpəpɪ'tjuːɪtəˌrɪzəm) NOUN *Pathol* underactivity of the pituitary gland.
▸ˌ**hypopi'tuitary** ADJECTIVE

hypoplasia (ˌhaɪpəʊ'pleɪzɪə) *or* **hypoplasty** ('haɪpəʊˌplæstɪ) NOUN *Pathol* incomplete development of an organ or part.
▸**hypoplastic** (ˌhaɪpəʊ'plæstɪk) ADJECTIVE

hypoploid ('haɪpəˌplɔɪd) ADJECTIVE having or designating a chromosome number that is less than a multiple of the haploid number.
▸'**hypoˌploidy** NOUN

hypopnoea *or US* **hypopnea** (haɪ'pɒpnɪə, ˌhaɪpə'niːə) NOUN *Pathol* abnormally shallow breathing, usually accompanied by a decrease in the breathing rate.
▷HISTORY C20: New Latin, from HYPO- + Greek *pnoia* breath, from *pnein* to breathe

hyposensitize *or* **hyposensitise** (ˌhaɪpəʊ'sɛnsɪˌtaɪz) VERB (*tr*) to desensitize; render less sensitive.
▸ˌ**hypoˌsensiti'zation** *or* ˌ**hypoˌsensiti'sation** NOUN

hypospadias (ˌhaɪpə'speɪdɪəs) NOUN *Pathol* a congenital condition in which the opening of the urethra is situated on the underside of the penis instead of at its tip.
▷HISTORY C19: from Greek *hypospadias* man with hypospadia, from HYPO- + *spadias*, prob. from *spadōn* eunuch

hypostasis (haɪ'pɒstəsɪs) NOUN, *plural* **-ses** (-ˌsiːz). [1] *Metaphysics* the essential nature of a substance as opposed to its attributes. [2] *Christianity* **a** any of the three persons of the Godhead, together constituting the Trinity. **b** the one person of Christ in which the divine and human natures are united. [3] the accumulation of blood in an organ or part, under the influence of gravity as the result of poor circulation. [4] another name for **epistasis** (sense 3).
▷HISTORY C16: from Late Latin: substance, from Greek *hupostasis* foundation, from *huphistasthai* to stand under, from HYPO- + *histanai* to cause to stand
▸**hypostatic** (ˌhaɪpə'stætɪk) *or* ˌ**hypo'statical** ADJECTIVE
▸ˌ**hypo'statically** ADVERB

hypostasize *or* **hypostasise** (haɪ'pɒstəˌsaɪz) VERB another word for **hypostatize**.
▸**hyˌpostasi'zation** *or* **hyˌpostasi'sation** NOUN

hypostatize *or* **hypostatise** (haɪ'pɒstəˌtaɪz)

VERB *(tr)* [1] to regard or treat as real. [2] to embody or personify.
▸**hy,postati'zation** *or* **hy,postati'sation** NOUN

hyposthenia (ˌhaɪpɒs'θiːnɪə) NOUN *Pathol* a weakened condition; lack of strength.
▷HISTORY C19: from HYPO- + Greek *sthenos* strength
▸**hyposthenic** (ˌhaɪpɒs'θɛnɪk) ADJECTIVE

hypostyle ('haɪpəʊˌstaɪl) ADJECTIVE [1] having a roof supported by columns. ◆ NOUN [2] a building constructed in this way.

hyposulphite (ˌhaɪpə'sʌlfaɪt) NOUN [1] another name for **sodium thiosulphate**, esp when used as a photographic fixer. Often shortened to **hypo.** [2] another name for **dithionite.**

hyposulphurous acid (ˌhaɪpə'sʌlfərəs) NOUN another name for **dithionous acid.**

hypotaxis (ˌhaɪpəʊ'tæksɪs) NOUN *Grammar* the subordination of one clause to another by a conjunction. Compare **parataxis.**
▸**hypotactic** (ˌhaɪpəʊ'tæktɪk) ADJECTIVE

hypotension (ˌhaɪpəʊ'tɛnʃən) NOUN *Pathol* abnormally low blood pressure.
▸**hypotensive** (ˌhaɪpəʊ'tɛnsɪv) ADJECTIVE

hypotenuse (haɪ'pɒtɪˌnjuːz) NOUN the side in a right-angled triangle that is opposite the right angle. Abbreviation: **hyp.**
▷HISTORY C16: from Latin *hypotēnūsa,* from Greek *hupoteinousa grammē* subtending line, from *hupoteinein* to subtend, from HYPO- + *teinein* to stretch

hypothalamus (ˌhaɪpə'θæləməs) NOUN, *plural* **-mi** (-ˌmaɪ). a neural control centre at the base of the brain, concerned with hunger, thirst, satiety, and other autonomic functions.
▸**hypothalamic** (ˌhaɪpəθə'læmɪk) ADJECTIVE

hypothec (haɪ'pɒθɪk) NOUN *Roman and Scots law* a charge on property in favour of a creditor.
▷HISTORY C16: from Late Latin *hypotheca* a security, from Greek *hupothēkē* deposit, pledge, from *hupotithenai* to deposit as a security, place under, from HYPO- + *tithenai* to place

hypotheca (ˌhaɪpəʊ'θiːkə) NOUN, *plural* **-cae** (-siː). the inner and younger layer of the cell wall of a diatom. Compare **epitheca.**
▷HISTORY from HYPO- + THECA

hypothecate (haɪ'pɒθɪˌkeɪt) VERB [1] *(tr) Law* to pledge (personal property or a ship) as security for a debt without transferring possession or title. [2] to allocate the revenue raised by a tax for a specified purpose. See also **bottomry.**
▷HISTORY C17: *hypothēcātus,* past participle of *hypothēcāre;* see HYPOTHEC, -ATE[1]
▸**hy,pothe'cation** NOUN ▸**hy'pothe,cator** NOUN

hypothermal (ˌhaɪpəʊ'θɜːməl) ADJECTIVE [1] of, relating to, or characterized by hypothermia. **Also.** hypothermic: [2] (of rocks and minerals) formed at great depth under conditions of high temperature.

hypothermia (ˌhaɪpəʊ'θɜːmɪə) NOUN [1] *Pathol* an abnormally low body temperature, as induced in the elderly by exposure to cold weather. [2] *Med* the intentional reduction of normal body temperature, as by ice packs, to reduce the patient's metabolic rate: performed esp in heart and brain surgery.

hypothesis (haɪ'pɒθɪsɪs) NOUN, *plural* **-ses** (-ˌsiːz). [1] a suggested explanation for a group of facts or phenomena, either accepted as a basis for further verification (**working hypothesis**) or accepted as likely to be true. Compare **theory** (sense 5). [2] an assumption used in an argument without its being endorsed; a supposition. [3] an unproved theory; a conjecture.
▷HISTORY C16: from Greek, from *hupotithenai* to propose, suppose, literally: put under; see HYPO-, THESIS
▸**hy'pothesist** NOUN

hypothesis testing NOUN *Statistics* the theory, methods, and practice of testing a hypothesis concerning the parameters of a population distribution (the **null hypothesis**) against another (the **alternative hypothesis**) which will be accepted only if its probability exceeds a predetermined significance level, generally on the basis of statistics derived from random sampling from the given population. Compare **statistical inference.**

hypothesize *or* **hypothesise** (haɪ'pɒθɪˌsaɪz) VERB to form or assume as a hypothesis.
▸**hy'pothe,sizer** *or* **hy'pothe,siser** NOUN

hypothetical (ˌhaɪpə'θɛtɪk[ə]l) *or* **hypothetic** ADJECTIVE [1] having the nature of a hypothesis. [2] assumed or thought to exist. [3] *Logic* another word for **conditional** (sense 4). [4] existing only as an idea or concept: *a time machine is a hypothetical device.*
▸**ˌhypo'thetically** ADVERB

hypothetical imperative NOUN (esp in the moral philosophy of Kant) any conditional rule of action, concerned with means and ends rather than with duty for its own sake. Compare **categorical imperative.**

hypothetico-deductive (ˌhaɪpə'θɛtɪkəʊdɪ'dʌktɪv) ADJECTIVE pertaining to or governed by the supposed method of scientific progress whereby a general hypothesis is tested by deducing predictions that may be experimentally tested. When such a prediction is falsified the theory is rejected and a new hypothesis is required.

hypothymia (haɪpə'θaɪmɪə) [1] a state of depression. [2] a diminished emotional response.
▷HISTORY C20: from HYPO- + Greek *thymos* spirit

hypothyroidism (ˌhaɪpəʊ'θaɪrɔɪˌdɪzəm) NOUN *Pathol* [1] insufficient production of thyroid hormones by the thyroid gland. [2] any disorder, such as cretinism or myxoedema, resulting from this.
▸**ˌhypo'thyroid** NOUN, ADJECTIVE

hypotonic (ˌhaɪpə'tɒnɪk) ADJECTIVE [1] *Pathol* (of muscles) lacking normal tone or tension. [2] (of a solution) having a lower osmotic pressure than that of a specified, generally physiological, solution. Compare **hypertonic, isotonic.**
▸**hypotonicity** (ˌhaɪpətə'nɪsɪtɪ) NOUN

hypoxanthine (ˌhaɪpə'zænθiːn, -θɪn) NOUN a white or colourless crystalline compound that is a breakdown product of nucleoproteins. Formula: $C_5H_4N_4O$.

hypoxia (haɪ'pɒksɪə) NOUN deficiency in the amount of oxygen delivered to the body tissues.
▷HISTORY C20: from HYPO- + OXY-[2] +-IA
▸**hypoxic** (haɪ'pɒksɪk) ADJECTIVE

hypso- *or before a vowel* **hyps-** COMBINING FORM indicating height: *hypsometry.*
▷HISTORY from Greek *hupsos*

hypsochromic (ˌhɪpsə'krəʊmɪk) ADJECTIVE *Chem* denoting or relating to a shift to a shorter wavelength in the absorption spectrum of a compound.
▸**'hypso,chrome** NOUN

hypsography (hɪp'sɒgrəfɪ) NOUN [1] the study and mapping of the earth's topography above sea level. [2] topography or relief, or a map showing this. [3] another name for **hypsometry.**
▸**hypsographic** (ˌhɪpsə'græfɪk) *or* **ˌhypso'graphical** ADJECTIVE

hypsometer (hɪp'sɒmɪtə) NOUN [1] an instrument for measuring altitudes by determining the boiling point of water at a given altitude. [2] any instrument used to calculate the heights of trees by triangulation.

hypsometry (hɪp'sɒmɪtrɪ) NOUN (in mapping) the establishment of height above sea level. Also called: **hypsography.**
▸**hypsometric** (ˌhɪpsə'mɛtrɪk) *or* **ˌhypso'metrical** ADJECTIVE ▸**ˌhypso'metrically** ADVERB ▸**hyp'sometrist** NOUN

hyracoid ('haɪrəˌkɔɪd) ADJECTIVE [1] of, relating to, or belonging to the mammalian order *Hyracoidea,* which contains the hyraxes. ◆ NOUN [2] a hyrax.
▸**ˌhyra'coidean** ADJECTIVE, NOUN

hyrax ('haɪræks) NOUN, *plural* **hyraxes** *or* **hyraces** ('haɪrəˌsiːz). any agile herbivorous mammal of the family *Procaviidae* and order *Hyracoidea,* of Africa and SW Asia, such as *Procavia capensis* (**rock hyrax**). They resemble rodents but have feet with hooflike toes. Also called: **dassie.**
▷HISTORY C19: from New Latin, from Greek *hurax* shrewmouse; probably related to Latin *sōrex*

Hyrcania (hɜː'keɪnɪə) NOUN an ancient district of Asia, southeast of the Caspian Sea.
▸**Hyr'canian** ADJECTIVE

Hyrcanian (hɜː'keɪnɪən) ADJECTIVE of or relating to Hyrcania, an ancient district of Asia.

hyson ('haɪs[ə]n) NOUN a Chinese green tea, the early crop of which is known as **young hyson** and the inferior leaves as **hyson skin.**
▷HISTORY C18: from Chinese (Cantonese) *hei-ch'un* bright spring

hyssop ('hɪsəp) NOUN [1] a widely cultivated Asian plant, *Hyssopus officinalis,* with spikes of small blue flowers and aromatic leaves, used as a condiment and in perfumery and folk medicine: family *Lamiaceae* (labiates). [2] any of several similar or related plants such as the hedge hyssop. [3] a Biblical plant, used for sprinkling in the ritual practices of the Hebrews.
▷HISTORY Old English *ysope,* from Latin *hyssōpus,* from Greek *hussōpos,* of Semitic origin; compare Hebrew *ēzōv*

hysterectomize *or* **hysterectomise** (ˌhɪstə'rɛktəˌmaɪz) VERB *(tr)* to perform a hysterectomy on (someone).

hysterectomy (ˌhɪstə'rɛktəmɪ) NOUN, *plural* **-mies.** surgical removal of the uterus.

hysteresis (ˌhɪstə'riːsɪs) NOUN *Physics* the lag in a variable property of a system with respect to the effect producing it as this effect varies, esp the phenomenon in which the magnetic flux density of a ferromagnetic material lags behind the changing external magnetic field strength.
▷HISTORY C19: from Greek *husterēsis* coming late, from *husteros* coming after
▸**hysteretic** (ˌhɪstə'rɛtɪk) ADJECTIVE ▸**ˌhyster'etically** ADVERB

hysteresis loop NOUN a closed curve showing the variation of the magnetic flux density of a ferromagnetic material with the external magnetic field producing it, when this field is changed through a complete cycle.

hysteria (hɪ'stɪərɪə) NOUN [1] a mental disorder characterized by emotional outbursts, susceptibility to autosuggestion, and, often, symptoms such as paralysis that mimic the effects of physical disorders. ◆ See also **conversion disorder.** [2] any frenzied emotional state, esp of laughter or crying.
▷HISTORY C19: from New Latin, from Latin *hystericus* HYSTERIC

hysteric (hɪ'stɛrɪk) NOUN [1] a hysterical person. ◆ ADJECTIVE [2] hysterical. ◆ See also **hysterics.**
▷HISTORY C17: from Latin *hystericus* literally: of the womb, from Greek *husterikos,* from *hustera* the womb; from the belief that hysteria in women originated in disorders of the womb

hysterical (hɪ'stɛrɪk[ə]l) *or* **hysteric** ADJECTIVE [1] of or suggesting hysteria: *hysterical cries.* [2] suffering from hysteria. [3] *Informal* wildly funny.
▸**hys'terically** ADVERB

hysterics (hɪ'stɛrɪks) NOUN *(functioning as plural or singular)* [1] an attack of hysteria. [2] *Informal* wild uncontrollable bursts of laughter.

hystero- *or before a vowel* **hyster-** COMBINING FORM [1] indicating the uterus: *hysterotomy.* [2] hysteria: *hysterogenic.*
▷HISTORY from Greek *hustera* womb

hysterogenic (ˌhɪstərə'dʒɛnɪk) ADJECTIVE inducing hysteria.
▷HISTORY C20: from HYSTERIA + -GENIC
▸**hysterogeny** (ˌhɪstə'rɒdʒənɪ) NOUN

hysteroid ('hɪstəˌrɔɪd) *or* **hysteroidal** ADJECTIVE resembling hysteria.

hysteron proteron ('hɪstəˌrɒn 'prɒtəˌrɒn) NOUN [1] *Logic* a fallacious argument in which the proposition to be proved is assumed as a premise. [2] *Rhetoric* a figure of speech in which the normal order of two sentences, clauses, etc., is reversed, as in *bred and born* (*for born and bred*).
▷HISTORY C16: from Late Latin, from Greek *husteron proteron* the latter (placed as) former

hysterotomy (ˌhɪstə'rɒtəmɪ) NOUN, *plural* **-mies.** surgical incision into the uterus.

hystricomorph (hɪ'straɪkəʊˌmɔːf) NOUN [1] any rodent of the suborder *Hystricomorpha,* which includes porcupines, cavies, agoutis, and chinchillas. ◆ ADJECTIVE *also* **hystricomorphic** (hɪˌstraɪkəʊ'mɔːfɪk). [2] of, relating to, or belonging to the *Hystricomorpha.*
▷HISTORY C19: from Latin *hystrix* porcupine, from Greek *hustrix*

Hz SYMBOL FOR hertz.

Ii

i *or* **I** (aɪ) NOUN, *plural* **i's, I's,** *or* **Is.** [1] the ninth letter and third vowel of the modern English alphabet. [2] any of several speech sounds represented by this letter, in English as in *bite* or *hit*. [3] **a** something shaped like an I. **b** (*in combination*): *an I-beam*. [4] **dot the i's and cross the t's.** to pay meticulous attention to detail.

i SYMBOL FOR the imaginary number √–1. Also called: **j**.

I[1] (aɪ) PRONOUN (*subjective*) refers to the speaker or writer.
▷HISTORY C12: reduced form of Old English *ic*; compare Old Saxon *ik*, Old High German *ih*, Sanskrit *ahám*

I[2] SYMBOL FOR: [1] *Chem* iodine. [2] *Physics* current. [3] *Physics* isospin. [4] *Logic* a particular affirmative categorial statement, such as *some men are married*, often symbolized as **SiP**. Compare **A, E, O**[1]. ◆ [5] THE ROMAN NUMERAL FOR one. See **Roman numerals.** ◆ [6] INTERNATIONAL CAR REGISTRATION FOR Italy.
▷HISTORY (for sense 4) from Latin *(aff)i(rmo)* I affirm

I. ABBREVIATION FOR: [1] International. [2] Island *or* Isle.

-i SUFFIX FORMING ADJECTIVES of or relating to a region or people, esp of the Middle East: *Iraqi*; *Bangladeshi*.
▷HISTORY from an adjectival suffix in Semitic and in Indo-Iranian languages

-i- CONNECTIVE VOWEL used between elements in a compound word: *cuneiform*; *coniferous*. Compare **-o-**.
▷HISTORY from Latin, stem vowel of nouns and adjectives in combination

Ia. *or* **IA** ABBREVIATION FOR Iowa.

-ia SUFFIX FORMING NOUNS [1] occurring in place names: *Albania*; *Columbia*. [2] occurring in names of diseases and pathological disorders: *pneumonia*; *aphasia*. [3] occurring in words denoting condition or quality: *utopia*. [4] occurring in names of botanical genera: *acacia*; *poinsettia*. [5] occurring in names of zoological classes: *Reptilia*. [6] occurring in collective nouns borrowed from Latin: *marginalia*; *memorabilia*; *regalia*.
▷HISTORY (for senses 1–4) New Latin, from Latin and Greek, suffix of feminine nouns; (for senses 5–6) from Latin, neuter plural suffix

IAA ABBREVIATION FOR **indoleacetic acid.**

IAAF ABBREVIATION FOR International Amateur Athletic Federation.

IAEA ABBREVIATION FOR International Atomic Energy Agency.

IAF ABBREVIATION FOR Indian Air Force.

-ial SUFFIX FORMING ADJECTIVES of; relating to; connected with: *managerial*.
▷HISTORY from Latin *-iālis*, adjective suffix; compare -AL[1]

iamb (ˈaɪæm, ˈaɪæmb) *or* **iambus** (aɪˈæmbəs) NOUN, *plural* **iambs, iambi** (aɪˈæmbaɪ) *or* **iambuses.** *Prosody* [1] a metrical foot consisting of two syllables, a short one followed by a long one (⏑–). [2] a line of verse of such feet.
▷HISTORY C19 *iamb*, from C16 *iambus*, from Latin, from Greek *iambos*

iambic (aɪˈæmbɪk) *Prosody* ◆ ADJECTIVE [1] of, relating to, consisting of, or using an iamb or iambs. [2] (in Greek literature) denoting a type of satirical verse written in iambs. ◆ NOUN [3] a metrical foot, line, or stanza of verse consisting of iambs. [4] a type of ancient Greek satirical verse written in iambs.
▸**i'ambically** ADVERB

-ian SUFFIX a variant of **-an**: *Etonian*; *Johnsonian*.
▷HISTORY from Latin *-iānus*

-iana SUFFIX FORMING NOUNS a variant of **-ana.**

IAP ABBREVIATION FOR Internet access provider: a company that provides organizations or individuals with access to the Internet.

Iapetus (aɪˈæpɪtəs) NOUN a large outer satellite of the planet Saturn.

IARU ABBREVIATION FOR International Amateur Radio Union.

IAS *Aeronautics* ABBREVIATION FOR indicated air speed.

Iaşi (*Romanian* ˈiaʃj) NOUN a city in NE Romania: capital of Moldavia (1565–1859); university (1860). Pop.: 348 399 (1997 est.). German name: **Jassy.**

-iasis *or* **-asis** NOUN COMBINING FORM (in medicine) indicating a diseased condition: *psoriasis*. Compare **-osis** (sense 2).
▷HISTORY from New Latin, from Greek, suffix of action

IATA (aɪˈɑːtə, iːˈɑːtə) NOUN ACRONYM FOR International Air Transport Association.

iatric (aɪˈætrɪk) *or* **iatrical** ADJECTIVE relating to medicine or physicians; medical.
▷HISTORY C19: from Greek *iatrikos* of healing, from *iasthai* to heal

-iatrics NOUN COMBINING FORM indicating medical care or treatment: *paediatrics*. Compare **-iatry.**
▷HISTORY from IATRIC

iatrogenic (aɪˌætrəʊˈdʒɛnɪk) ADJECTIVE [1] *Med* (of an illness or symptoms) induced in a patient as the result of a physician's words or actions, esp as a consequence of taking a drug prescribed by the physician. [2] *Social welfare* (of a problem) induced by the means of treating a problem but ascribed to the continuing natural development of the problem being treated.
▸**iatrogenicity** (aɪˌætrəʊdʒɜːˈnɪsɪtɪ) NOUN

-iatry NOUN COMBINING FORM indicating healing or medical treatment: *psychiatry*. Compare **-iatrics.**
▷HISTORY from New Latin *-iatria*, from Greek *iatreia* the healing art, from *iatros* healer, physician
▸**-iatric** ADJECTIVE COMBINING FORM

ib. See **ibid.**

IBA (in Britain) ABBREVIATION FOR Independent Broadcasting Authority.

Ibadan (ɪˈbædᵊn) NOUN a city in SW Nigeria, capital of Oyo state: university (1948). Pop.: 1 432 000 (1996 est.).

Ibagué (*Spanish* iβaˈɣe) NOUN a city in W central Colombia. Pop.: 393 664 (1999 est.).

I-beam NOUN a rolled steel joist or a girder with a cross section in the form of a capital letter *I*. Compare **H-beam.**

Iberia (aɪˈbɪərɪə) NOUN [1] the Iberian Peninsula. [2] an ancient region in central Asia, south of the Caucasus corresponding approximately to present-day Georgia.

Iberian (aɪˈbɪərɪən) NOUN [1] a member of a group of ancient Caucasoid peoples who inhabited the Iberian Peninsula in preclassical and classical times. See also **Celtiberian.** [2] a native or inhabitant of the Iberian Peninsula; a Spaniard or Portuguese. [3] a native or inhabitant of ancient Iberia in the Caucasus. ◆ ADJECTIVE [4] denoting, or relating to the pre-Roman peoples of the Iberian Peninsula or of Caucasian Iberia. [5] of or relating to the Iberian Peninsula, its inhabitants, or any of their languages.

Iberian Peninsula NOUN a peninsula of SW Europe, occupied by Spain and Portugal.

iberis (aɪˈbɪərɪs) NOUN any plant of the annual or perennial Eurasian genus *Iberis*, 12 to 25 cm (6–12 in.) in height, with white or purple flowers. *I. amara* and *I. umbellata* are the garden candytuft. Family *Brassicaceae* (crucifers).
▷HISTORY New Latin, from *Iberia* Spain, where many species are common

Ibero- (ˈaɪbərəʊ) COMBINING FORM indicating Iberia or Iberian: *Ibero-Caucasian*.

ibex (ˈaɪbɛks) NOUN, *plural* **ibexes, ibices** (ˈɪbɪˌsiːz, ˈaɪ-) *or* **ibex.** any of three wild goats, *Capra ibex*, *C. caucasica*, or *C. pyrenaica*, of mountainous regions of Europe, Asia, and North Africa, having large backward-curving horns.
▷HISTORY C17: from Latin: chamois

IBF ABBREVIATION FOR International Boxing Federation.

Ibibio (ɪˈbɪbɪəʊ) NOUN [1] (*plural* **-os** *or* **-o**) a member of a Negroid people of SE Nigeria, living esp in and around Calabar. [2] Also called: **Efik.** the language of this people.

ibid. *or* **ib.** (in annotations, bibliographies, etc., when referring to a book, article, chapter, or page previously cited) ABBREVIATION FOR ibidem.
▷HISTORY Latin: in the same place

ibis (ˈaɪbɪs) NOUN, *plural* **ibises** *or* **ibis.** any of various wading birds of the family *Threskiornithidae*, such as *Threskiornis aethiopica* (**sacred ibis**), that occur in warm regions and have a long thin down-curved bill: order *Ciconiiformes* (herons, storks, etc.). Compare **wood ibis.**
▷HISTORY C14: via Latin from Greek, from Egyptian *hby*

Ibiza *or* **Iviza** (*Spanish* iˈβiθa) NOUN [1] a Spanish island in the W Mediterranean, one of the Balearic Islands: hilly, with a rugged coast; tourism. Pop.: 45 000 (latest est.). Area: 541 sq. km (209 sq. miles). [2] the capital of Ibiza, a port on the south of the island. Pop.: 16 000 (latest est.).

Ibizan hound (ɪˈbiːθən) NOUN a tall slender short-haired breed of hound with large erect ears and a coat of white, chestnut, or tan, or of a combination of these colours.

-ible SUFFIX FORMING ADJECTIVES a variant of **-able.**
▸**-ibly** SUFFIX FORMING ADVERBS ▸**-ibility** SUFFIX FORMING NOUNS

Ibo *or* **Igbo** (ˈiːbəʊ) NOUN [1] (*plural* **-bos** *or* **-bo**) a member of a Negroid people of W Africa, living chiefly in S Nigeria. [2] the language of this people, belonging to the Kwa branch of the Niger-Congo family: one of the chief literary and cultural languages of S Nigeria.

IBRD ABBREVIATION FOR International Bank for Reconstruction and Development (the World Bank).

ibuprofen (aɪˈbjuːprəʊfən) NOUN a drug, isobutylphenylpropionic acid, that relieves pain and reduces inflammation: used to treat arthritis and muscular strains. Formula: $C_{13}H_{18}O_2$.

IC ABBREVIATION FOR: [1] internal-combustion. [2] *Electronics* **integrated circuit.** [3] *Text messaging* I see. [4] (in transformational grammar) **immediate constituent.** [5] *Astrology* Imum Coeli: the point on the ecliptic lying directly opposite the Midheaven.

i/c ABBREVIATION FOR in charge (of).

-ic SUFFIX FORMING ADJECTIVES [1] of, relating to, or resembling: *allergic*; *Germanic*; *periodic*. See also **-ical.** [2] (in chemistry) indicating that an element is chemically combined in the higher of two possible valence states: *ferric*; *stannic*. Compare **-ous** (sense 2).
▷HISTORY from Latin *-icus* or Greek *-ikos*; *-ic* also occurs in nouns that represent a substantive use of adjectives (*magic*) and in nouns borrowed directly from Latin or Greek (*critic, music*)

Içá (ˈiːsɑː; *Portuguese* iˈsa) NOUN the Brazilian part of the **Putumayo River.**

ICA ABBREVIATION FOR: [1] (in Britain) Institute of Contemporary Arts. [2] International Cooperation Administration.

-ical SUFFIX FORMING ADJECTIVES a variant of **-ic**, but in some words having a less literal application than corresponding adjectives ending in *-ic*: *economical*; *fanatical*.
▷HISTORY from Latin *-icālis*
▸**-ically** SUFFIX FORMING ADVERBS

ICAO ABBREVIATION FOR International Civil Aviation Organization.

Icaria (aɪˈkɛərɪə, ɪ-) NOUN a Greek island in the Aegean Sea, in the Southern Sporades group. Area: 256 sq. km (99 sq. miles). Modern Greek name: **Ikaría.** Also called: **Nikaria.**

Icarian[1] (aɪˈkɛərɪən, ɪ-) ADJECTIVE of or relating to Icarus.

Icarian[2] (aɪ'kɛərɪən, ɪ-) ADJECTIVE [1] of or relating to Icaria or its inhabitants. ◆ NOUN [2] an inhabitant of Icaria.

Icarian Sea NOUN the part of the Aegean Sea between the islands of Patmos and Leros and the coast of Asia Minor, where, according to legend, Icarus fell into the sea.

Icarus ('ɪkərəs, 'aɪ-) NOUN *Greek myth* the son of Daedalus, with whom he escaped from Crete, flying with wings made of wax and feathers. Heedless of his father's warning he flew too near the sun, causing the wax to melt, and fell into the Aegean and drowned.

ICBM ABBREVIATION FOR intercontinental ballistic missile: a missile with a range greater than 5500 km.

ICC ABBREVIATION FOR International Cricket Council.

ice (aɪs) NOUN [1] water in the solid state, formed by freezing liquid water. Related adjective: **glacial.** [2] a portion of ice cream. [3] *Slang* a diamond or diamonds. [4] the field of play in ice hockey. [5] *Slang* a concentrated and highly potent form of methamphetamine with dangerous side effects. [6] **break the ice. a** to relieve shyness, etc., esp between strangers. **b** to be the first of a group to do something. [7] **cut no ice.** *Informal* to fail to make an impression. [8] **on ice.** in abeyance; pending. [9] **on thin ice.** unsafe or unsafely; vulnerable or vulnerably. [10] **the Ice.** *NZ informal* Antarctica. ◆ VERB [11] (often foll by *up, over,* etc.) to form or cause to form ice; freeze. [12] (*tr*) to mix with ice or chill (a drink, etc.). [13] (*tr*) to cover (a cake, etc.) with icing. [14] (*tr*) *US slang* to kill.
▷HISTORY Old English *īs;* compare Old High German *īs,* Old Norse *īss*
▸ **'iceless** ADJECTIVE ▸ **'ice,like** ADJECTIVE

ICE (in Britain) ABBREVIATION FOR Institution of Civil Engineers.

Ice. ABBREVIATION FOR Iceland(ic).

ice age NOUN another name for **glacial period.**

ice axe NOUN a light axe used by mountaineers for cutting footholds in snow or ice, to provide an anchor point, or to control a slide on snow; it has a spiked tip and a head consisting of a pick and an adze.

ice bag NOUN [1] a waterproof bag used as an ice pack. [2] a strong bag, usually made of canvas and equipped with two handles, used for carrying blocks of ice.

ice beer NOUN a beer that is chilled after brewing so that any water is turned to ice and then removed.

iceberg ('aɪsbɜːg) NOUN [1] a large mass of ice floating in the sea, esp a mass that has broken off a polar glacier. [2] **tip of the iceberg.** the small visible part of something, esp a problem or difficulty, that is much larger. [3] *Slang, chiefly US* a person considered to have a cold or reserved manner.
▷HISTORY C18: probably part translation of Middle Dutch *ijsberg* ice mountain; compare Norwegian *isberg*

iceberg lettuce NOUN a type of lettuce with very crisp pale leaves tightly enfolded.

Ice Blacks PLURAL NOUN **the.** the international ice hockey team of New Zealand.

iceblink ('aɪs,blɪŋk) NOUN [1] Also called: **blink.** a yellowish-white reflected glare in the sky over an ice field. [2] a coastal ice cliff.

ice block NOUN *Scot, Austral, and NZ* a flavoured frozen water ice: in Australia and New Zealand, sometimes on a stick.

iceboat ('aɪs,bəʊt) NOUN another name for **icebreaker** (sense 1) or **ice yacht.**

icebound ('aɪs,baʊnd) ADJECTIVE covered or made immobile by ice; frozen in: *an icebound ship.*

icebox ('aɪs,bɒks) NOUN [1] a compartment in a refrigerator for storing or making ice. [2] an insulated cabinet packed with ice for storing food.

icebreaker ('aɪs,breɪkə) NOUN [1] Also called: **iceboat.** a vessel with a reinforced bow for breaking up the ice in bodies of water to keep channels open for navigation. [2] any tool or device for breaking ice into smaller pieces. [3] something intended to relieve mutual shyness at a gathering of strangers.

ice bridge NOUN *Canadian* a body of ice that forms across the width of a river and is strong enough to bear traffic.

icecap ('aɪs,kæp) NOUN a thick mass of glacial ice and snow that permanently covers an area of land, such as either of the polar regions or the peak of a mountain.

ice cream NOUN a kind of sweetened frozen liquid, properly made from cream and egg yolks but often made from milk or a custard base, flavoured in various ways.

ice-cream cone *or* **cornet** NOUN [1] a conical edible wafer for holding ice cream. [2] such a cone containing ice cream.

ice-cream soda NOUN *Chiefly US* ice cream served in a tall glass of carbonated water and a little milk, usually flavoured in various ways.

iced (aɪst) ADJECTIVE [1] covered, coated, or chilled with ice. [2] covered with icing: *iced cakes.*

ice dance NOUN any of a number of dances, mostly based on ballroom dancing, performed by a couple skating on ice.
▸ **ice dancer** NOUN ▸ **ice dancing** NOUN

icefall ('aɪs,fɔːl) NOUN a very steep part of a glacier that has deep crevasses and resembles a frozen waterfall.

ice field NOUN [1] a very large flat expanse of ice floating in the sea; large ice floe. [2] a large mass of ice permanently covering an extensive area of land.

ice fish NOUN any percoid fish of the family *Chaenichthyidae,* of Antarctic seas, having a semitransparent scaleless body.

ice floe NOUN a sheet of ice, of variable size, floating in the sea. See also **ice field** (sense 1).

ice foot NOUN a narrow belt of ice permanently attached to the coast in polar regions.

ice hockey NOUN a game played on ice by two opposing teams of six players each, who wear skates and try to propel a flat puck into their opponents' goal with long sticks having an offset flat blade at the end.

ice house NOUN a building for storing ice.

Içel (iː'tʃɛl) NOUN another name for **Mersin.**

Iceland ('aɪslənd) NOUN an island republic in the N Atlantic, regarded as part of Europe: settled by Norsemen, who established a legislative assembly in 930; under Danish rule (1380–1918); gained independence in 1918 and became a republic in 1944; contains large areas of glaciers, snowfields, and lava beds with many volcanoes and hot springs (the chief source of domestic heat); inhabited chiefly along the SW coast. The economy is based largely on fishing and tourism. Official language: Icelandic. Official religion: Evangelical Lutheran. Currency: krona. Capital: Reykjavik. Pop.: 284 000 (2001 est.). Area: 102 828 sq. km (39 702 sq. miles).

Iceland agate NOUN another name for **obsidian.**

Icelander ('aɪs,lændə, 'aɪsləndə) NOUN a native, citizen, or inhabitant of Iceland.

Icelandic (aɪs'lændɪk) ADJECTIVE [1] of, relating to, or characteristic of Iceland, its people, or their language. ◆ NOUN [2] the official language of Iceland, belonging to the North Germanic branch of the Indo-European family. See also **Old Icelandic.**

Iceland moss NOUN a lichen, *Cetraria islandica,* of arctic regions and N Europe, with brownish edible fronds.

Iceland poppy NOUN any of various widely cultivated arctic poppies, esp *Papaver nudicaule,* with white or yellow nodding flowers.

Iceland spar NOUN a pure transparent variety of calcite with double-refracting crystals used in making polarizing microscopes.

ice lolly NOUN *Brit informal* an ice cream or water ice on a stick. Also called: **lolly.** US and Canadian equivalent (trademark): **Popsicle.**

ice machine NOUN a machine that automatically produces ice for use in drinks, etc.

ice maiden NOUN a beautiful but aloof woman.

ice man NOUN *Chiefly US* a man who sells or delivers ice.

ice needle NOUN *Meteorol* one of many needle-like ice crystals that form cirrus clouds in clear cold weather.

Iceni (aɪ'siːnaɪ) PLURAL NOUN an ancient British tribe that rebelled against the Romans in 61 A.D. under Queen Boudicca.

ice pack NOUN [1] a bag or folded cloth containing ice, applied to a part of the body, esp the head, to cool, reduce swelling, etc. [2] another name for **pack ice.** [3] a sachet containing a gel that can be frozen or heated and that retains its temperature for an extended period of time, used esp in cool bags.

ice pick NOUN a pointed tool used for breaking ice.

ice plant NOUN a low-growing plant, *Mesembryanthemum* (or *Cryophytum*) *crystallinum,* of southern Africa, with fleshy leaves covered with icelike hairs and pink or white rayed flowers: family *Aizoaceae.*

ice point NOUN the temperature at which a mixture of ice and water are in equilibrium at a pressure of one atmosphere. It is 0° on the Celsius scale and 32° on the Fahrenheit scale. Compare **steam point.**

ice screw NOUN *Mountaineering* a screwed tubular or solid steel rod with a ring at one end for inserting into ice as an anchor point.

ice sheet NOUN a thick layer of ice covering a large area of land for a long time, esp those in Antarctica and Greenland.

ice shelf NOUN a thick mass of ice that is permanently attached to the land but projects into and floats on the sea.

ice show NOUN any entertainment performed by ice-skaters.

ice skate NOUN [1] a boot having a steel blade fitted to the sole to enable the wearer to glide swiftly over ice. [2] the steel blade on such a boot or shoe. ◆ VERB **ice-skate.** [3] (*intr*) to glide swiftly over ice on ice skates.
▸ **'ice-,skater** NOUN

ice station NOUN a scientific research station in polar regions, where ice movement, weather, and environmental conditions are monitored.

ice storm NOUN *Chiefly US* a storm of freezing rain that deposits a glaze of ice on the ground.

ice water NOUN [1] water formed from ice. [2] Also called: **iced water.** drinking water cooled by refrigeration or the addition of ice.

icewine ('aɪswaɪn) NOUN *Canadian* a dessert wine made from grapes that have frozen before being harvested.

ice yacht NOUN a sailing craft having a cross-shaped frame with a cockpit and runners for travelling over ice. Also called: **iceboat.**

ICFTU ABBREVIATION FOR International Confederation of Free Trade Unions.

Ichang *or* **I-ch'ang** ('iː'tʃæŋ) NOUN a variant transliteration of the Chinese name of **Yichang.**

I.Chem.E. ABBREVIATION FOR Institution of Chemical Engineers.

I Ching ('iː 'tʃɪŋ) NOUN an ancient Chinese book of divination and a source of Confucian and Taoist philosophy. Answers to questions and advice may be obtained by referring to the text accompanying one of 64 hexagrams, selected at random. Also called: **Book of Changes.**

ich-laut ('ɪç,laʊt, 'ɪk-) NOUN (*sometimes capital*) *Phonetics* the voiceless palatal fricative sound that is written as *ch* in German *ich,* often allophonic with the achlaut. See also **ach-laut.**
▷HISTORY from German, from *ich* I + *Laut* sound

ichneumon (ɪk'njuːmən) NOUN a mongoose, *Herpestes ichneumon,* of Africa and S Europe, having greyish-brown speckled fur.
▷HISTORY C16: via Latin from Greek, literally: tracker, hunter, from *ikhneuein* to track, from *ikhnos* a footprint; so named from the animal's alleged ability to locate the eggs of crocodiles

ichneumon fly *or* **wasp** NOUN any hymenopterous insect of the family *Ichneumonidae,* whose larvae are parasitic in caterpillars and other insect larvae.

ichnite ('ɪknaɪt) *or* **ichnolite** ('ɪknə,laɪt) NOUN a less common name for **trace fossil.**
▷HISTORY C19: from Greek *ikhnos* footprint, track + -ITE[1]

ichnofossil ('ɪknəʊ,fɒsəl) NOUN another name for **trace fossil.**

▷HISTORY C19: from Greek *ikhnos* footprint, track + -ITE[1]

ichnography (ɪk'nɒgrəfɪ) NOUN [1] the art of drawing ground plans. [2] the ground plan of a building, factory, etc.
▷HISTORY C16: from Latin *ichnographia*, from Greek *ikhnographia*, from *ikhnos* trace, track
▸**ichnographic** (ˌɪknə'græfɪk) *or* **ˌichno'graphical** ADJECTIVE ▸**ˌichno'graphically** ADVERB

ichnology (ɪk'nɒlədʒɪ) NOUN the study of trace fossils.
▷HISTORY C19: from Greek *ikhnos* footprint, track
▸**ichnological** (ˌɪknə'lɒdʒɪkəl) ADJECTIVE

ichor ('aɪkɔː) NOUN [1] *Greek myth* the fluid said to flow in the veins of the gods. [2] *Pathol* a foul-smelling watery discharge from a wound or ulcer.
▷HISTORY C17: from Greek *ikhōr*, of obscure origin
▸**'ichorous** ADJECTIVE

ichth. ABBREVIATION FOR ichthyology.

ichthyic ('ɪkθɪɪk) ADJECTIVE of, relating to, or characteristic of fishes.
▷HISTORY C19: from Greek, from *ikhthus* fish

ichthyo- *or before a vowel* **ichthy-** COMBINING FORM indicating or relating to fishes: *ichthyology*.
▷HISTORY from Latin, from Greek *ikhthus* fish

ichthyoid ('ɪkθɪˌɔɪd) ADJECTIVE *also* **ichthyoidal.** [1] resembling a fish. ♦ NOUN [2] a fishlike vertebrate.

ichthyolite ('ɪkθɪəˌlaɪt) NOUN *Rare* any fossil fish.
▸**ichthyolitic** (ˌɪkθɪə'lɪtɪk) ADJECTIVE

ichthyology (ˌɪkθɪ'ɒlədʒɪ) NOUN the study of the physiology, history, economic importance, etc., of fishes.
▸**ichthyologic** (ˌɪkθɪə'lɒdʒɪk) *or* **ˌichthyo'logical** ADJECTIVE ▸**ˌichthyo'logically** ADVERB ▸**ˌichthy'ologist** NOUN

ichthyophagous (ˌɪkθɪ'ɒfəgəs) ADJECTIVE feeding on fish.
▸**ichthyophagy** (ˌɪkθɪ'ɒfədʒɪ) NOUN

ichthyornis (ˌɪkθɪ'ɔːnɪs) NOUN an extinct Cretaceous sea bird of the genus *Ichthyornis*, thought to have resembled a tern.
▷HISTORY C19: New Latin, from ICHTHY- + Greek *ornis* bird

ichthyosaur ('ɪkθɪəˌsɔː) *or* **ichthyosaurus** (ˌɪkθɪə'sɔːrəs) NOUN, *plural* **-saurs, -sauruses,** *or* **-sauri** (-'sɔːraɪ). any extinct marine Mesozoic reptile of the order *Ichthyosauria*, which had a porpoise-like body with dorsal and tail fins and paddle-like limbs. See also **plesiosaur.**

ichthyosis (ˌɪkθɪ'əʊsɪs) NOUN a congenital disease in which the skin is coarse, dry, and scaly. Also called: **xeroderma.** Nontechnical name: **fishskin disease.**
▸**ichthyotic** (ˌɪkθɪ'ɒtɪk) ADJECTIVE

ICI ABBREVIATION FOR Imperial Chemical Industries.

-ician SUFFIX FORMING NOUNS indicating a person skilled or involved in a subject or activity: *physician; beautician*.
▷HISTORY from French *-icien*; see -IC, -IAN

icicle ('aɪsɪkəl) NOUN a hanging spike of ice formed by the freezing of dripping water.
▷HISTORY C14: from ICE + *ickel*, from Old English *gicel* icicle, related to Old Norse *jökull* large piece of ice, glacier
▸**'icicled** ADJECTIVE

icily ('aɪsɪlɪ) ADVERB in an icy or reserved manner.

iciness ('aɪsɪnɪs) NOUN [1] the condition of being icy or very cold. [2] a manner that is cold or reserved; aloofness.

icing ('aɪsɪŋ) NOUN [1] Also called (esp US and Canadian): **frosting.** a sugar preparation, variously flavoured and coloured, for coating and decorating cakes, biscuits, etc. [2] the formation of ice, as on a ship or aircraft, due to the freezing of moisture in the atmosphere. [3] any unexpected extra or bonus (esp in **icing on the cake**).

icing sugar NOUN *Brit* a very finely ground sugar used for icings, confections, etc. US term: **confectioners' sugar.**

ICJ ABBREVIATION FOR **International Court of Justice.**

ickle ('ɪkəl) ADJECTIVE *Brit informal* an ironically childish word for **little.**

icky ('ɪkɪ) ADJECTIVE **ickier, ickiest.** [1] sticky. [2] excessively sentimental or emotional.
▸**'ickiness** NOUN

icon *or* **ikon** ('aɪkɒn) NOUN [1] a representation of Christ, the Virgin Mary, or a saint, esp one painted in oil on a wooden panel, depicted in a traditional Byzantine style and venerated in the Eastern Church. [2] an image, picture, representation, etc. [3] a symbol resembling or analogous to the thing it represents. [4] a person regarded as a sex symbol or as a symbol of a belief or cultural movement. [5] a pictorial representation of a facility available on a computer system, that enables the facility to be activated by means of a screen cursor rather than by a textual instruction.
▷HISTORY C16: from Latin, from Greek *eikōn* image, from *eikenai* to be like

iconic (aɪ'kɒnɪk) *or* **iconical** ADJECTIVE [1] relating to, resembling, or having the character of an icon. [2] (of memorial sculptures, esp those depicting athletes of ancient Greece) having a fixed conventional style.

iconic memory NOUN *Psychol* the temporary persistence of visual impressions after the stimulus has been removed. Compare **echoic memory.**

Iconium (aɪ'kəʊnɪəm) NOUN the ancient name for **Konya.**

icono- *or before a vowel* **icon-** COMBINING FORM indicating an image or likeness: *iconology*.
▷HISTORY from Greek: ICON

iconoclasm (aɪ'kɒnəˌklæzəm) NOUN the acts or beliefs of an iconoclast.

iconoclast (aɪ'kɒnəˌklæst) NOUN [1] a person who attacks established or traditional concepts, principles, laws, etc. [2] **a** a destroyer of religious images or sacred objects. **b** an adherent of the heretical movement within the Greek Orthodox Church from 725 to 842 A.D., which aimed at the destruction of icons and religious images.
▷HISTORY C16: from Late Latin *iconoclastes*, from Late Greek *eikonoklastes*, from *eikōn* icon + *klastēs* breaker
▸**iˌcono'clastic** ADJECTIVE ▸**iˌcono'clastically** ADVERB

iconography (ˌaɪkɒ'nɒgrəfɪ) NOUN, *plural* **-phies.** [1] **a** the symbols used in a work of art or art movement. **b** the conventional significance attached to such symbols. [2] a collection of pictures of a particular subject, such as Christ. [3] the representation of the subjects of icons or portraits, esp on coins.
▸**ˌico'nographer** NOUN ▸**iconographic** (aɪˌkɒnə'græfɪk) *or* **iˌcono'graphical** ADJECTIVE

iconolatry (ˌaɪkɒ'nɒlətrɪ) NOUN the worship or adoration of icons as idols.
▸**ˌico'nolater** NOUN ▸**ˌico'nolatrous** ADJECTIVE

iconology (ˌaɪkɒ'nɒlədʒɪ) NOUN [1] the study or field of art history concerning icons. [2] icons collectively. [3] the symbolic representation or symbolism of icons.
▸**iconological** (aɪˌkɒnə'lɒdʒɪkəl) ADJECTIVE ▸**ˌico'nologist** NOUN

iconomatic (aɪˌkɒnə'mætɪk) ADJECTIVE employing pictures to represent not objects themselves but the sound of their names.
▷HISTORY C19: from Greek, from *eikon* image + *onoma* name
▸**iconomaticism** (aɪˌkɒnə'mætɪˌsɪzəm) NOUN

iconoscope (aɪ'kɒnəˌskəʊp) NOUN a television camera tube in which an electron beam scans a photoemissive surface, converting an optical image into electrical pulses.

iconostasis (ˌaɪkəʊ'nɒstəsɪs) *or* **iconostas** (aɪ'kɒnəˌstæs) NOUN, *plural* **iconostases** (ˌaɪkəʊ'nɒstəˌsiːz, aɪ'kɒnəˌstæsɪz). *Eastern Church* a screen with doors and icons set in tiers, which separates the bema (sanctuary) from the nave.
▷HISTORY C19: Church Latin, from Late Greek *eikonostasion* shrine, literally: area where images are placed, from ICONO- + *histanai* to stand

icosahedron (ˌaɪkəsə'hiːdrən) NOUN, *plural* **-drons** *or* **-dra** (-drə). a solid figure having 20 faces. The faces of a **regular icosahedron** are equilateral triangles.
▷HISTORY C16: from Greek *eikosaedron*, from *eikosi* twenty + *-edron* -HEDRON
▸**ˌicosa'hedral** ADJECTIVE

icositetrahedron (ˌaɪkəsɪˌtetrə'hiːdrən) NOUN, *plural* **-drons** *or* **-dra** (-drə). a solid figure having 24 trapezoid faces, as occurring in some crystals.

ICS ABBREVIATION FOR Indian Civil Service.

-ics SUFFIX FORMING NOUNS (*functioning as singular*) [1] indicating a science, art, or matters relating to a particular subject: *aeronautics; politics*. [2] indicating certain activities or practices: *acrobatics*.
▷HISTORY plural of *-ic*, representing Latin *-ica*, from Greek *-ika*, as in *mathēmatika* mathematics

ICSH ABBREVIATION FOR **interstitial-cell-stimulating hormone.**

ICT ABBREVIATION FOR Information and Communications Technology.

icterus ('ɪktərəs) NOUN [1] *Pathol* another name for **jaundice.** [2] a yellowing of plant leaves, caused by excessive cold or moisture.
▷HISTORY C18: from Latin: yellow bird, the sight of which reputedly cured jaundice, from Greek *ikteros*
▸**icteric** (ɪk'terɪk) ADJECTIVE

ictus ('ɪktəs) NOUN, *plural* **-tuses** *or* **-tus.** [1] *Prosody* metrical or rhythmic stress in verse feet, as contrasted with the stress accent on words. [2] *Med* a sudden attack or stroke.
▷HISTORY C18: from Latin *icere* to strike
▸**'ictal** ADJECTIVE

ICTZ ABBREVIATION FOR Intertropical Convergence Zone.

ICU ABBREVIATION FOR: [1] intensive care unit. [2] *Text messaging* I see you.

icy ('aɪsɪ) ADJECTIVE **icier, iciest.** [1] made of, covered with, or containing ice. [2] resembling ice. [3] freezing or very cold. [4] cold or reserved in manner; aloof.

icy pole NOUN the Austral name for an **ice lolly.**

id[1] (ɪd) NOUN *Psychoanal* the mass of primitive instincts and energies in the unconscious mind that, modified by the ego and the superego, underlies all psychic activity.
▷HISTORY C20: New Latin, from Latin: it; used to render German *Es*

id[2] THE INTERNET DOMAIN NAME FOR Indonesia.

ID ABBREVIATION FOR: [1] Idaho. [2] identification (document). [3] Also: **i.d.** inside diameter. [4] Intelligence Department. [5] Also: **i.d.** intradermal.

id. ABBREVIATION FOR idem.

Id. ABBREVIATION FOR Idaho.

I'd (aɪd) CONTRACTION OF I had *or* I would.

-id[1] SUFFIX FORMING NOUNS [1] indicating the names of meteor showers that appear to radiate from a specified constellation: *Orionids* (from Orion). [2] indicating a particle, body, or structure of a specified kind: *energid*.
▷HISTORY from Latin *-id-*, *-is*, from Greek, feminine suffix of origin

-id[2] SUFFIX FORMING NOUNS AND ADJECTIVES [1] indicating members of a zoological family: *cyprinid*. [2] indicating members of a dynasty: *Seleucid; Fatimid*.
▷HISTORY from New Latin *-idae* or *-ida*, from Greek *-idēs* suffix indicating offspring

-id[3] SUFFIX FORMING NOUNS a variant of **-ide.**

Ida ('aɪdə) NOUN **Mount.** [1] a mountain in central Crete: the highest on the island; in ancient times associated with the worship of Zeus. Height: 2456 m (8057 ft). Modern Greek name: **Idhi.** [2] a mountain in NW Turkey, southeast of the site of ancient Troy. Height: 1767 m (5797 ft.). Turkish name: **Kaz Daği.**

IDA ABBREVIATION FOR **International Development Association.**

Ida. ABBREVIATION FOR Idaho.

-idae SUFFIX FORMING NOUNS indicating names of zoological families: *Felidae; Hominidae*.
▷HISTORY New Latin, from Latin, from Greek *-idai*, suffix indicating offspring

Idaho ('aɪdəˌhəʊ) NOUN a state of the northwestern US: consists chiefly of ranges of the Rocky Mountains, with the Snake River basin in the south; important for agriculture (**Idaho potatoes**), livestock, and silver-mining. Capital: Boise. Pop.: 1 293 953 (2000). Area: 216 413 sq. km (83 557 sq. miles). Abbreviations: **Id., Ida.,** (with zip code) **ID.**

Idahoan ('aɪdəˌhəʊən) NOUN [1] a native or inhabitant of Idaho. ♦ ADJECTIVE [2] of or relating to Idaho or its inhabitants.

IDASA (ɪ'dɑːzə) NOUN ACRONYM FOR Institute for a Democratic South Africa.

IDB *Chiefly South African* ABBREVIATION FOR illicit diamond buying.

IDC ABBREVIATION FOR **industrial development certificate.**

ID card NOUN a card or document that serves to identify a person, or to prove his age, membership, etc.

IDD ABBREVIATION FOR international direct dialling.

IDDM ABBREVIATION FOR insulin-dependent diabetes mellitus; a form of diabetes in which patients have little or no ability to produce insulin and are therefore entirely dependent on insulin injections.

ide (aɪd) NOUN another name for the **silver orfe.** See **orfe.**
▷HISTORY C19: from New Latin *idus,* from Swedish *id*

-ide *or* **-id** SUFFIX FORMING NOUNS [1] *(added to the combining form of the nonmetallic or electronegative elements)* indicating a binary compound: *sodium chloride.* [2] indicating an organic compound derived from another: *acetanilide.* [3] indicating one of a class of compounds or elements: *peptide; lanthanide.*
▷HISTORY from German *-id,* from French *oxide* OXIDE, based on the suffix of *acide* ACID

idea (aɪˈdɪə) NOUN [1] any content of the mind, esp the conscious mind. [2] the thought of something: *the very idea appals me.* [3] a mental representation of something: *she's got a good idea of the layout of the factory.* [4] the characterization of something in general terms; concept: *the idea of a square circle is self-contradictory.* [5] an individual's conception of something: *his idea of honesty is not the same as yours and mine.* [6] the belief that something is the case: *he has the idea that what he's doing is right.* [7] a scheme, intention, plan, etc.: *here's my idea for the sales campaign.* [8] a vague notion or indication; inkling: *he had no idea of what life would be like in Africa.* [9] significance or purpose: *the idea of the game is to discover the murderer.* [10] *Philosophy* **a** a private mental object, regarded as the immediate object of thought or perception. **b** a Platonic Idea or Form. [11] *Music* a thematic phrase or figure; motif. [12] *Obsolete* a mental image. [13] **get ideas.** to become ambitious, restless, etc. [14] **not one's idea of.** not what one regards as (hard work, a holiday, etc.). [15] **that's an idea.** that is worth considering. [16] **the very idea!** that is preposterous, unreasonable, etc.
▷HISTORY C16: via Late Latin from Greek: model, pattern, notion, from *idein* to see
▸**iˈdealess** ADJECTIVE

> **Language note** It is usually considered correct to say that someone has *the idea of doing* something, rather than *the idea to do* it: *he had the idea of taking* (not *the idea to take) a short holiday.*

Idea (aɪˈdɪə) NOUN another name for **Form.**

idea hamster *or* **ideas hamster** NOUN *Slang* a person who is employed as a source of new ideas.

ideal (aɪˈdɪəl) NOUN [1] a conception of something that is perfect, esp that which one seeks to attain. [2] a person or thing considered to represent perfection: *he's her ideal.* [3] something existing only as an idea. [4] a pattern or model, esp of ethical behaviour. ◆ ADJECTIVE [5] conforming to an ideal. [6] of, involving, or existing in the form of an idea. [7] *Philosophy* **a** of or relating to a highly desirable and possible state of affairs. **b** of or relating to idealism.
▸**ideality** (ˌaɪdɪˈælɪtɪ) NOUN ▸**iˈdeally** ADVERB ▸**iˈdealness** NOUN

ideal crystal NOUN *Chem* a crystal in which there are no defects or impurities.

ideal element NOUN any element added to a mathematical theory in order to eliminate special cases. The ideal element i = √–1 allows all algebraic equations to be solved and the point at infinity (**ideal point**) ensures that any two lines in projective geometry intersect.

ideal gas NOUN a hypothetical gas which obeys Boyle's law exactly at all temperatures and pressures, and which has internal energy that depends only upon the temperature. Measurements upon real gases are extrapolated to zero pressure to obtain results in agreement with theories relating to an ideal gas, especially in thermometry. Also called: **perfect gas.**

idealism (aɪˈdɪəˌlɪzəm) NOUN [1] belief in or pursuance of ideals. [2] the tendency to represent things in their ideal forms, rather than as they are. [3] any of a group of philosophical doctrines that share the monistic view that material objects and the external world do not exist in reality independently of the human mind but are variously creations of the mind or constructs of ideas. Compare **materialism** (sense 2), **dualism** (sense 2).
▸**iˈdealist** NOUN ▸**iˌdealˈistic** ADJECTIVE ▸**iˌdealˈistically** ADVERB

idealization *or* **idealisation** (aɪˌdɪəlaɪˈzeɪʃən) NOUN [1] the representation of something as ideal. [2] a conception of something that dwells on its advantages and ignores its deficiencies. [3] a general theoretical account of natural phenomena that ignores features that are difficult to accommodate within a theory.

idealize *or* **idealise** (aɪˈdɪəˌlaɪz) VERB [1] to consider or represent (something) as ideal. [2] *(tr)* to portray as ideal; glorify. [3] *(intr)* to form an ideal or ideals.
▸**iˈdealˌizer** *or* **iˈdealˌiser** NOUN

ideas of reference PLURAL NOUN a schizophrenic symptom in which the patient thinks that things completely disconnected from him are influencing him or conveying messages to him.

ideate (ˈaɪdɪˌeɪt) VERB *(tr)* to form or have an idea of; to imagine or conceive.
▷HISTORY C17: from Medieval Latin *ideat-* formed as an idea, from *ideare,* from Greek *idea* model, pattern, notion

ideatum (ˌaɪdɪˈeɪtəm) NOUN, *plural* **-ata** (-ˈeɪtə). *Philosophy* the objective reality with which human ideas are supposed to correspond.
▷HISTORY C18: New Latin, from Latin: IDEA

idée fixe *French* (ide fiks) NOUN, *plural* ***idées fixes*** (ide fiks). a fixed idea; obsession.

idée reçue *French* (ide rəsy) NOUN, *plural* ***idées reçues*** (ide rəsy). a generally held opinion or concept.
▷HISTORY literally: received idea

idem *Latin* (ˈaɪdɛm, ˈɪdɛm) the same: used to refer to an article, chapter, etc., previously cited.

idempotent (ˈaɪdəmˌpəʊtənt, ˈɪd-) ADJECTIVE *Maths* (of a matrix, transformation, etc.) not changed in value following multiplication by itself.
▷HISTORY C20: from Latin *idem* same + POTENT[1]

ident (ˈaɪdɛnt) NOUN a short visual image employed between television programmes that works as a logo to locate the viewer to the channel.

identic (aɪˈdɛntɪk) ADJECTIVE [1] *Diplomacy* (esp of opinions expressed by two or more governments) having the same wording or intention regarding another power: *identic notes.* [2] an obsolete word for **identical.**

identical (aɪˈdɛntɪkᵊl) ADJECTIVE [1] Also called: **numerically identical.** being one and the same individual: *Cicero and Tully are identical.* [2] Also called: **quantitatively identical.** exactly alike, equal, or agreeing. [3] designating either or both of a pair of twins of the same sex who developed from a single fertilized ovum that split into two. Compare **fraternal** (sense 3).
▸**iˈdentically** ADVERB ▸**iˈdenticalness** NOUN

identical proposition NOUN *Logic* a necessary truth, esp a categorial identity, such as *whatever is triangular has three sides.*

identification (aɪˌdɛntɪfɪˈkeɪʃən) NOUN [1] the act of identifying or the state of being identified. [2] **a** something that identifies a person or thing. **b** *(as modifier)*: *an identification card.* [3] *Psychol* **a** the process of recognizing specific objects as the result of remembering. **b** the process by which one incorporates aspects of another person's personality. **c** the transferring of a response from one situation to another because the two bear similar features. See also **generalization** (sense 3).

identification parade NOUN a group of persons including one suspected of having committed a crime assembled for the purpose of discovering whether a witness can identify the suspect.

identifier (aɪˈdɛntɪˌfaɪə) NOUN a person or thing that establishes the identity of someone or something.

identify (aɪˈdɛntɪˌfaɪ) VERB **-fies, -fying, -fied.** *(mainly tr)* [1] to prove or recognize as being a certain person or thing; determine the identity of. [2] to consider as the same or equivalent. [3] *(also intr; often foll by with)* to consider (oneself) as similar to another. [4] to determine the taxonomic classification of (a plant or animal). [5] *(intr; usually foll by with) Psychol* to engage in identification.
▸**iˈdentiˌfiable** ADJECTIVE ▸**iˈdentiˌfiably** ADVERB

Identikit (aɪˈdɛntɪˌkɪt) NOUN *Trademark* [1] **a** a set of transparencies of various typical facial characteristics that can be superimposed on one another to build up, on the basis of a description, a picture of a person sought by the police. **b** *(as modifier)*: *an Identikit picture.* [2] *(modifier)* artificially created by copying different elements in an attempt to form a whole: *an identikit pop group.*

identity (aɪˈdɛntɪtɪ) NOUN, *plural* **-ties.** [1] the state of having unique identifying characteristics held by no other person or thing. [2] the individual characteristics by which a person or thing is recognized. [3] Also called: **numerical identity.** the property of being one and the same individual: *his loss of memory did not affect his identity.* [4] Also called: **qualitative identity.** the state of being the same in nature, quality, etc.: *they were linked by the identity of their tastes.* [5] the state of being the same as a person or thing described or claimed: *the identity of the stolen goods has not yet been established.* [6] identification of oneself as: *moving to London destroyed his Welsh identity.* [7] *Logic* **a** that relation that holds only between any entity and itself. **b** an assertion that that relation holds, as *Cicero is Tully.* [8] *Maths* **a** an equation that is valid for all values of its variables, as in $(x - y)(x + y) = x^2 - y^2$. Often denoted by the symbol ≡. **b** Also called: **identity element.** a member of a set that when operating on another member, *x,* produces that member *x:* the identity for multiplication of numbers is 1 since $x.1 = 1.x = x$. See also **inverse** (sense 2b). [9] *Austral and NZ informal* a well-known person, esp in a specified locality; figure (esp in the phrase **an old identity**).
▷HISTORY C16: from Late Latin *identitās,* from Latin *idem* the same

identity card NOUN a card that establishes a person's identity, esp one issued to all members of the population in wartime, to the staff of an organization, etc.

identity theft NOUN the crime of setting up and using bank accounts and credit facilities fraudulently in another person's name without his or her knowledge.

identity theory NOUN *Philosophy* a form of materialism which holds mental states to be identical with certain states of the brain and so to have no separate existence, but regards this identity as contingent so that mentalistic and physicalistic language are not held to be synonymous. See also **anomalous monism, materialism** (sense 2).

ideo- COMBINING FORM of or indicating idea or ideas: *ideology.*
▷HISTORY from French *idéo-,* from Greek *idea* IDEA

ideogram (ˈɪdɪəʊˌgræm) *or* **ideograph** (ˈɪdɪəʊˌgrɑːf, -ˌgræf) NOUN [1] a sign or symbol, used in such writing systems as those of China or Japan, that directly represents a concept, idea, or thing rather than a word or set of words for it. [2] any graphic sign or symbol, such as %, @, &, etc.

ideography (ˌɪdɪˈɒgrəfɪ) NOUN the use of ideograms to communicate ideas.

ideologist (ˌaɪdɪˈɒlədʒɪst) NOUN [1] a person who supports a particular ideology, esp a political theorist. [2] a person who studies an ideology or ideologies. [3] a theorist or visionary. ◆ Also called: **ideologue** (ˈaɪdɪəˌlɒg).

ideology (ˌaɪdɪˈɒlədʒɪ) NOUN, *plural* **-gies.** [1] a body of ideas that reflects the beliefs and interests of a nation, political system, etc. and underlies political action. [2] *Philosophy, sociol* the set of beliefs by which a group or society orders reality so as to render it intelligible. [3] speculation that is imaginary or visionary. [4] the study of the nature and origin of ideas.
▸**ideological** (ˌaɪdɪəˈlɒdʒɪkᵊl) *or* **ˌideoˈlogic** ADJECTIVE ▸**ˌideoˈlogically** ADVERB

ideomotor (ˌaɪdɪəˈməʊtə) ADJECTIVE *Physiol* designating automatic muscular movements stimulated by ideas, as in absent-minded acts.

ides (aɪdz) NOUN *(functioning as singular)* (in the Roman calendar) the 15th day in March, May, July, and October and the 13th day of each other month. See also **calends, nones.**

▷**HISTORY** C15: from Old French, from Latin *īdūs* (plural), of uncertain origin

id est *Latin* ('ɪd 'ɛst) the full form of **i.e.**

Idhi ('iðɪ) NOUN a transliteration of the Modern Greek name for (Mount) **Ida** (sense 1).

idio- COMBINING FORM indicating peculiarity, isolation, or that which pertains to an individual person or thing: *idiolect*.
▷**HISTORY** from Greek *idios* private, separate

idioblast ('ɪdɪəʊˌblæst) NOUN a plant cell that differs from those around it in the same tissue.
▸ˌ**idio'blastic** ADJECTIVE

idiocy ('ɪdɪəsɪ) NOUN, *plural* **-cies.** 1 (*not in technical usage*) severe mental retardation. 2 foolishness or senselessness; stupidity. 3 a foolish act or remark.

idioglossia (ˌɪdɪəʊ'glɒsɪə) NOUN 1 a private language, as invented by a child or between two children, esp twins. 2 a pathological condition in which a person's speech is so severely distorted that it is unintelligible.
▷**HISTORY** C19: from Greek *idios* private, separate + *glossa* tongue

idiogram ('ɪdɪəʊˌgræm) NOUN another name for **karyogram.**

idiographic (ˌɪdɪəʊ'græfɪk) ADJECTIVE *Psychol* of or relating to the study of individuals. Compare **nomothetic.**

idiolect ('ɪdɪəˌlɛkt) NOUN the variety or form of a language used by an individual.
▸ˌ**idio'lectal** *or* ˌ**idio'lectic** ADJECTIVE

idiom ('ɪdɪəm) NOUN 1 a group of words whose meaning cannot be predicted from the meanings of the constituent words, as for example (*It was raining*) *cats and dogs*. 2 linguistic usage that is grammatical and natural to native speakers of a language. 3 the characteristic vocabulary or usage of a specific human group or subject. 4 the characteristic artistic style of an individual, school, period, etc.
▷**HISTORY** C16: from Latin *idiōma* peculiarity of language, from Greek; see IDIO-
▸**idiomatic** (ˌɪdɪə'mætɪk) *or* ˌ**idio'matical** ADJECTIVE
▸ˌ**idio'matically** ADVERB ▸ˌ**idio'maticalness** NOUN

idiomorphic (ˌɪdɪəʊ'mɔːfɪk) ADJECTIVE (of minerals) occurring naturally in the form of well-developed crystals.
▸ˌ**idio'morphically** ADVERB ▸ˌ**idio'morphism** NOUN

idiopathy (ˌɪdɪ'ɒpəθɪ) NOUN, *plural* **-thies.** any disease of unknown cause.
▸**idiopathic** (ˌɪdɪəʊ'pæθɪk) ADJECTIVE

idiophone ('ɪdɪəˌfəʊn) NOUN *Music* a percussion instrument, such as a cymbal or xylophone, made of naturally sonorous material.
▸**idiophonic** (ˌɪdɪə'fɒnɪk) ADJECTIVE

idioplasm ('ɪdɪəʊˌplæzəm) NOUN another name for **germ plasm.**
▸ˌ**idio'plasmic** *or* **idioplasmatic** (ˌɪdɪəʊplæz'mætɪk) ADJECTIVE

idiosyncrasy (ˌɪdɪəʊ'sɪŋkrəsɪ) NOUN, *plural* **-sies.** 1 a tendency, type of behaviour, mannerism, etc., of a specific person; quirk. 2 the composite physical or psychological make-up of a specific person. 3 an abnormal reaction of an individual to specific foods, drugs, or other agents.
▷**HISTORY** C17: from Greek *idiosunkrasia*, from IDIO- + *sunkrasis* mixture, temperament, from *sun-* SYN- + *kerannunai* to mingle

idiosyncratic (ˌɪdɪəʊsɪŋ'krætɪk) ADJECTIVE of or relating to idiosyncrasy; characteristic of a specific person.
▸ˌ**idiosyn'cratically** ADVERB

idiot ('ɪdɪət) NOUN 1 a person with severe mental retardation. 2 a foolish or senseless person.
▷**HISTORY** C13: from Latin *idiōta* ignorant person, from Greek *idiōtēs* private person, one who lacks professional knowledge, ignoramus; see IDIO-

idiot board NOUN a slang name for **Autocue.**

idiot box NOUN *Slang* a television set.

idiotic (ˌɪdɪ'ɒtɪk) ADJECTIVE of or resembling an idiot; foolish; senseless.
▸ˌ**idi'otically** ADVERB ▸ˌ**idi'oticalness** NOUN

idiotism ('ɪdɪəˌtɪzəm) NOUN 1 an archaic word for **idiocy.** 2 an obsolete word for **idiom.**

idiot savant ('iːdjəʊ sæ'vɑ̃, 'ɪdɪət 'sævənt) NOUN, *plural* **idiots savants** ('iːdjəʊ sæ'vɑ̃) *or* **idiot savants.** a person with learning difficulties who performs brilliantly at some specialized intellectual task, such as giving the day of the week for any calendar date past or present.
▷**HISTORY** C19: from French: knowledgeable idiot

idiot strings PLURAL NOUN *Canadian informal* strings attached to children's mittens to prevent the wearer from losing them.

idiot tape NOUN *Printing* an input tape for a typesetting machine that contains text only, the typographical instructions being supplied by the typesetting machine itself.

idle ('aɪdᵊl) ADJECTIVE 1 unemployed or unoccupied; inactive. 2 not operating or being used. 3 (of money) not being used to earn interest or dividends. 4 not wanting to work; lazy. 5 (*usually prenominal*) frivolous or trivial: *idle pleasures*. 6 ineffective or powerless; fruitless; vain. 7 without basis; unfounded. ◆ VERB 8 (when *tr*, often foll by *away*) to waste or pass (time) fruitlessly or inactively: *he idled the hours away*. 9 (*intr*) to loiter or move aimlessly. 10 (*intr*) (of a shaft, engine, etc.) to turn without doing useful work. 11 (*intr*) Also (Brit): **tick over.** (of an engine) to run at low speed with the transmission disengaged. 12 (*tr*) *US and Canadian* to cause to be inactive or unemployed.
▷**HISTORY** Old English *īdel*; compare Old High German *ītal* empty, vain
▸'**idleness** NOUN ▸'**idly** ADVERB

idle pulley *or* **idler pulley** NOUN a freely rotating trolley used to control the tension or direction of a belt. Also called: **idler.**

idler ('aɪdlə) NOUN 1 a person who idles. 2 another name for **idle pulley** or **idle wheel.** 3 *Nautical* a ship's crew member, such as a carpenter, sailmaker, etc., whose duties do not include standing regular watches.

idler shaft NOUN a shaft carrying one or more gearwheels that idles between a driver shaft and a driven shaft, usually to reverse the direction of rotation or provide different spacing of gearwheels, esp in a gearbox.

idle time NOUN *Commerce* time during which a machine or a worker could be working but is not, as when one job has been completed and tooling or materials for the next are not complete or available. Compare **downtime.**

idle wheel NOUN a gearwheel interposed between two others to transmit torque without changing the direction of rotation to the velocity ratio. Also called: **idler.**

IDN ABBREVIATION FOR in Dei nomine. Also: **IND.**
▷**HISTORY** Latin: in the name of God

Ido ('iːdəʊ) NOUN an artificial language; a modification of Esperanto.
▷**HISTORY** C20: offspring, from Greek *-id* daughter of

idocrase ('aɪdəˌkreɪs, 'ɪd-) NOUN another name for **vesuvianite.**
▷**HISTORY** C19: from French, from Greek *eidos* form + *krasis* a mingling

idol ('aɪdᵊl) NOUN 1 a material object, esp a carved image, that is worshipped as a god. 2 *Christianity, judaism* any being (other than the one God) to which divine honour is paid. 3 a person who is revered, admired, or highly loved.
▷**HISTORY** C13: from Late Latin *īdōlum*, from Latin: image, from Greek *eidōlon*, from *eidos* shape, form

idolatrize *or* **idolatrise** (aɪ'dɒləˌtraɪz) VERB 1 (*tr*) a less common word for **idolize.** 2 (*intr*) to indulge in the worship of idols.
▸**i'dolaˌtrizer** *or* **i'dolaˌtriser** NOUN

idolatry (aɪ'dɒlətrɪ) NOUN 1 the worship of idols. 2 great devotion or reverence.
▸**i'dolater** NOUN *or* **i'dolatress** ◆ FEMININE NOUN
▸**i'dolatrous** ADJECTIVE ▸**i'dolatrously** ADVERB
▸**i'dolatrousness** NOUN

idolize *or* **idolise** ('aɪdəˌlaɪz) VERB 1 (*tr*) to admire or revere greatly. 2 (*tr*) to worship as an idol. 3 (*intr*) to worship idols.
▸**i'dolism,** ˌ**idoli'zation,** *or* ˌ**idoli'sation** NOUN ▸'**idolist,** '**idolˌizer,** *or* '**idolˌiser** NOUN

idolum (ɪ'dəʊlʊm) NOUN 1 a mental picture; idea. 2 a false idea, fallacy.
▷**HISTORY** C17: from Latin: IDOL

Idomeneus (aɪ'dɒmɪˌnjuːs) NOUN *Greek myth* a king of Crete who fought on the Greek side in the Trojan War.

IDP ABBREVIATION FOR integrated data processing.

Id-ul-Adha ('iːdʊlˌɑːdə) NOUN a variant spelling of **Eid-ul-Adha.**

Id-ul-Fitr ('iːdʊlˌfiːtə) NOUN a variant spelling of **Eid-ul-Fitr.**

Idun ('iːdʊn) *or* **Ithunn** NOUN *Norse myth* the goddess of spring who guarded the apples that kept the gods eternally young; wife of Bragi.

idyll *or sometimes US* **idyl** ('ɪdɪl) NOUN 1 a poem or prose work describing an idealized rural life, pastoral scenes, etc. 2 any simple narrative or descriptive piece in poetry or prose. 3 a charming or picturesque scene or event. 4 a piece of music with a calm or pastoral character.
▷**HISTORY** C17: from Latin *Tdyllium*, from Greek *eidullion*, from *eidos* shape, (literary) form

idyllic (ɪ'dɪlɪk, aɪ-) ADJECTIVE 1 of or relating to an idyll. 2 charming; picturesque.
▸**i'dyllically** ADVERB

idyllist *or US* **idylist** ('ɪdɪlɪst) NOUN a writer of idylls.

ie THE INTERNET DOMAIN NAME FOR Ireland.

IE ABBREVIATION FOR Indo-European (languages).

i.e. ABBREVIATION FOR id est.
▷**HISTORY** Latin: that is (to say); in other words

-ie SUFFIX FORMING NOUNS a variant of **-y**[2].

IEA ABBREVIATION FOR International Energy Agency.

iechyd da (ˌjækiː'dɑː; *Welsh* 'jɛxəd dɑː) INTERJECTION *Welsh* a drinking toast; good health; cheers.
▷**HISTORY** Welsh: good health

IEE ABBREVIATION FOR Institution of Electrical Engineers.

Ieper ('iːpər) NOUN the Flemish name for **Ypres.**

-ier SUFFIX FORMING NOUNS a variant of **-eer:** *brigadier*.
▷**HISTORY** from Old English *-ere* -ER[1] or (in some words) from Old French *-ier*, from Latin *-ārius* -ARY

if (ɪf) CONJUNCTION (*subordinating*) 1 in case that, or on condition that: *if you try hard it might work*; *if he were poor, would you marry him?* 2 used to introduce an indirect question. In this sense, *if* approaches the meaning of *whether*. 3 even though: *an attractive if awkward girl*. 4 **a** used to introduce expressions of desire, with *only*: *if I had only known*. **b** used to introduce exclamations of surprise, dismay, etc.: *if this doesn't top everything!* 5 **as if.** as it would be if; as though: *he treats me as if I were junior to him*. ◆ NOUN 6 an uncertainty or doubt: *the big if is whether our plan will work at all*. 7 a condition or stipulation: *I won't have any ifs or buts*.
▷**HISTORY** Old English *gif*; related to Old Saxon *ef* if, Old High German *iba* whether, if

IF *or* **i.f.** *Electronics* ABBREVIATION FOR **intermediate frequency.**

IFA ABBREVIATION FOR independent financial adviser.

IFAD ABBREVIATION FOR International Fund for Agricultural Development.

IFC ABBREVIATION FOR **International Finance Corporation.**

Ife ('iːfɪ) NOUN a town in W central Nigeria: one of the largest and oldest Yoruba towns; university (1961); centre of the cocoa trade. Pop.: 296 800 (1996 est.).

-iferous SUFFIX FORMING ADJECTIVES containing or yielding: *carboniferous*.

iff (ɪf) CONJUNCTION *Logic* a shortened form of *if and only if*: it indicates that the two sentences so connected are necessary and sufficient conditions for one another. Usually *iff* is used for equivalence in the metalanguage, rather than as the biconditional in the object language.

IFF *Military* ABBREVIATION FOR Identification, Friend or Foe: a system using radar transmissions to which equipment carried by friendly forces automatically responds with a precoded signal.

iffy ('ɪfɪ) ADJECTIVE **iffier, iffiest.** *Informal* uncertain or subject to contingency: *this scheme sounds a bit iffy*.
▷**HISTORY** C20: from IF + -Y[1]

Ifni (*Spanish* 'ifni) NOUN a former Spanish province in S Morocco, on the Atlantic: returned to Morocco in 1969.

IFP ABBREVIATION FOR Inkatha Freedom Party.

IFR *Aeronautics* ABBREVIATION FOR instrument flying regulations.

IFS ABBREVIATION FOR Irish Free State (now called Republic of Ireland).

iftar *or* **Iftar** ('ɪftɑː) NOUN the meal eaten by Muslims to break their fast after sunset every day during Ramadan.
▷HISTORY from Arabic *iftar* the breaking of the fast; compare ID-UL-FITR

-ify SUFFIX FORMING VERBS a variant of **-fy**: *intensify*.
▸**-ification** SUFFIX FORMING NOUNS

IG ABBREVIATION FOR: [1] Indo-Germanic (languages). [2] Inspector General.

Igbo ('iːbəʊ) NOUN, *plural* **-bo** *or* **-bos**. a variant spelling of **Ibo**.

IGBP ABBREVIATION FOR International Geosphere-Biosphere Programme.

IGC ABBREVIATION FOR inter-governmental conference (esp in the European Union).

Igdrasil ('ɪgdrəsɪl) NOUN a variant spelling of **Yggdrasil**.

IGFET ('ɪgfɛt) NOUN insulated-gate field-effect transistor; a type of field-effect transistor having one or more semiconductor gate electrodes. Compare **JFET**.

igloo *or* **iglu** ('ɪgluː) NOUN, *plural* **-loos** *or* **-lus**. [1] a dome-shaped Eskimo house, usually built of blocks of solid snow. [2] a hollow made by a seal in the snow over its breathing hole in the ice.
▷HISTORY C19: from Eskimo *igdlu* house

IGM *Chess* ABBREVIATION FOR **International Grandmaster**.

igneous ('ɪgnɪəs) ADJECTIVE [1] (of rocks) derived by solidification of magma or molten lava emplaced on or below the earth's surface. Compare **sedimentary, metamorphic** (sense 2). [2] of or relating to fire.
▷HISTORY C17: from Latin *igneus* fiery, from *ignis* fire

ignescent (ɪg'nɛsᵊnt) ADJECTIVE [1] giving off sparks when struck, as a flint. [2] capable of bursting into flame. ◆ NOUN [3] an ignescent substance.
▷HISTORY C19: from Latin *ignescere* to become inflamed

ignimbrite ('ɪgnɪm,braɪt) NOUN a rock formed by the deposition at high temperature and the consolidation of a nuée ardente or other type of ash flow, being a complicated mixture of volcanic materials welded together by heat, hot gases, and pressure. Also called: **welded tuft**. See **tuft**.
▷HISTORY C20: from Latin *ign(is)* fire + *imbr(is)*, *imber* shower of rain + -ITE[1]

ignis fatuus ('ɪgnɪs 'fætjʊəs) NOUN, *plural* **ignes fatui** ('ɪgniːz 'fætjʊ,aɪ). another name for **will-o'-the-wisp**.
▷HISTORY C16: from Medieval Latin, literally: foolish fire

ignite (ɪg'naɪt) VERB [1] to catch fire or set fire to; burn or cause to burn. [2] (*tr*) *Chem* to heat strongly. [3] (*tr*) to stimulate or provoke: *the case has ignited a nationwide debate*.
▷HISTORY C17: from Latin *ignīre* to set alight, from *ignis* fire
▸**ig'nitable** *or* **ig'nitible** ADJECTIVE ▸**ig,nita'bility** *or* **ig,niti'bility** NOUN

igniter (ɪg'naɪtə) NOUN [1] a person or thing that ignites. [2] a fuse to fire explosive charges. [3] an electrical device for lighting a gas turbine. [4] a subsidiary electrode in an ignitron.

ignition (ɪg'nɪʃən) NOUN [1] the act or process of initiating combustion. [2] the process of igniting the fuel in an internal-combustion engine. [3] (usually preceded by *the*) the devices used to ignite the fuel in an internal-combustion engine.

ignition coil NOUN an induction coil that supplies the high voltage to the sparking plugs of an internal-combustion engine.

ignition key NOUN the key used in a motor vehicle to turn the switch that connects the battery to the ignition system and other electrical devices.

ignitron (ɪg'naɪtrɒn, 'ɪgnɪ,trɒn) NOUN a mercury-arc rectifier controlled by a subsidiary electrode, the igniter, partially immersed in a mercury cathode. A current passed between igniter and cathode forms a hot spot sufficient to strike an arc between cathode and anode.
▷HISTORY C20: from IGNITER + ELECTRON

ignoble (ɪg'nəʊbᵊl) ADJECTIVE [1] dishonourable; base; despicable. [2] of low birth or origins; humble; common. [3] of low quality; inferior. [4] *Falconry* **a** designating short-winged hawks that capture their quarry by swiftness and adroitness of flight. Compare **noble** (sense 7). **b** designating quarry which is inferior or unworthy of pursuit by a particular species of hawk or falcon.
▷HISTORY C16: from Latin *ignōbilis*, from IN-[1] + Old Latin *gnōbilis* NOBLE
▸**,igno'bility** *or* **ig'nobleness** NOUN ▸**ig'nobly** ADVERB

ignominy ('ɪgnə,mɪnɪ) NOUN, *plural* **-minies**. [1] disgrace or public shame; dishonour. [2] a cause of disgrace; a shameful act.
▷HISTORY C16: from Latin *ignōminia* disgrace, from *ig-* (see IN-[2]) + *nōmen* name, reputation
▸**,igno'minious** ADJECTIVE ▸**,igno'miniously** ADVERB
▸**,igno'miniousness** NOUN

ignoramus (,ɪgnə'reɪməs) NOUN, *plural* **-muses**. an ignorant person; fool.
▷HISTORY C16: from legal Latin, literally: we have no knowledge of, from Latin *ignōrāre* to be ignorant of; see IGNORE; modern usage originated from the use of *Ignoramus* as the name of an unlettered lawyer in a play by G. Ruggle, 17th-century English dramatist

ignorance ('ɪgnərəns) NOUN lack of knowledge, information, or education; the state of being ignorant.

ignorant ('ɪgnərənt) ADJECTIVE [1] lacking in knowledge or education; unenlightened. [2] (*postpositive; often foll by of*) lacking in awareness or knowledge (of): *ignorant of the law*. [3] resulting from or showing lack of knowledge or awareness: *an ignorant remark*.
▸**'ignorantly** ADVERB

ignoratio elenchi (,ɪgnə'reɪʃɪəʊ ɪ'lɛŋkaɪ) NOUN *Logic* [1] a purported refutation of a proposition that does not in fact prove it false but merely establishes a related but strictly irrelevant proposition. [2] the fallacy of arguing in this way.
▷HISTORY Latin: an ignorance of proof, translating Greek *elenchou agnoia*

ignore (ɪg'nɔː) VERB (*tr*) [1] to fail or refuse to notice; disregard. ◆ NOUN [2] *Austral informal* disregard: *to treat someone with ignore*.
▷HISTORY C17: from Latin *ignōrāre* not to know, from *ignārus* ignorant of, from *i-* IN-[1] + *gnārus* knowing; related to Latin *noscere* to know
▸**ig'norable** ADJECTIVE ▸**ig'norer** NOUN

ignotum per ignotius *Latin* (ɪg'nəʊtʊm pər ɪg'nəʊtɪʊs) NOUN an explanation that is obscurer than the thing to be explained.
▷HISTORY literally: the unknown by means of the more unknown

Igorot (,ɪgə'rəʊt, ,iːgə-) *or* **Igorrote** (,ɪgə'rəʊtɪ, ,iːgə-) NOUN, *plural* **-rot, -rots** *or* **-rote, -rotes**. a member of a Negrito people of the mountains of N Luzon in the Philippines: noted as early exponents of mining.

Igraine (ɪ'greɪn) *or* **Ygerne** NOUN the mother of King Arthur.

Iguaçú *or* **Iguassú** (*Portuguese* igua'su) NOUN a river in SE South America, rising in S Brazil and flowing west to join the Paraná River, forming part of the border between Brazil and Argentina. Length: 1200 km (745 miles).

Iguaçú Falls NOUN a waterfall on the border between Brazil and Argentina, on the Iguaçú River: divided into hundreds of separate falls by forested rocky islands. Width: about 4 km (2.5 miles). Height: 82 m (269 ft.).

iguana (ɪ'gwɑːnə) NOUN [1] either of two large tropical American arboreal herbivorous lizards of the genus *Iguana*, esp *I. iguana* (**common iguana**), having a greyish-green body with a row of spines along the back: family *Iguanidae*. [2] Also called: **iguanid** (ɪ'gwɑːnɪd). any other lizard of the tropical American family *Iguanidae*. [3] another name for **leguaan**.
▷HISTORY C16: from Spanish, from Arawak *iwana*
▸**i'guanian** NOUN, ADJECTIVE

iguanodon (ɪ'gwɑːnə,dɒn) NOUN a massive herbivorous long-tailed bipedal dinosaur of the genus *Iguanodon*, common in Europe and N Africa in Jurassic and Cretaceous times: suborder *Ornithopoda* (ornithopods).
▷HISTORY C19: New Latin, from IGUANA + Greek *odōn* tooth

IGY ABBREVIATION FOR **International Geophysical Year**.

IHC (in New Zealand) ABBREVIATION FOR Intellectually Handicapped Children.

ihram (ɪ'rɑːm) NOUN the customary white robes worn by Muslim pilgrims to Mecca, symbolizing a sacred or consecrated state.
▷HISTORY C18: from Arabic *ihrām*, from *harama* he forbade

IHS the first three letters of the name Jesus in Greek (ΙΗΣΟΥΣ), often used as a Christian emblem.

iid *Statistics* ABBREVIATION FOR independent identically distributed (of random variables).

IJC (in the US and Canada) ABBREVIATION FOR **International Joint Commission**.

IJssel *or* **Yssel** ('aɪsᵊl; *Dutch* 'ɛisəl) NOUN a river in the central Netherlands: a distributary of the Rhine, flowing north to the IJsselmeer. Length: 116 km (72 miles).

IJsselmeer *or* **Ysselmeer** (*Dutch* ɛisəl'meːr) NOUN a shallow lake in the NW Netherlands; formed from the S part of the Zuider Zee by the construction of the **IJsselmeer Dam** in 1932; salt water gradually replaced by fresh water from the IJssel River; fisheries (formerly marine fish, now esp eels). Area: (before reclamation) 3690 sq. km (1425 sq. miles). Estimated final area: 1243 sq. km (480 sq. miles). English name: **Ijssel Lake**.

ikan ('iːkan) NOUN (in Malaysia) fish used esp in names of cooked dishes: *assam ikan*.
▷HISTORY from Malay

Ikaría (ika'ria) NOUN a transliteration of the Modern Greek name for **Icaria**.

ikat ('aɪkæt) NOUN a method of creating patterns in fabric by tie-dyeing the yarn before weaving.
▷HISTORY C20: from Malay, literally: to tie, bind

IKBS ABBREVIATION FOR **intelligent knowledge-based system**.

ikebana (,iːkə'bɑːnə) NOUN the Japanese decorative art of flower arrangement.

Ikeja (ɪ'keɪjə) NOUN a town in SW Nigeria, capital of Lagos state: residential and industrial suburb of Lagos. Pop.: 63 870 (latest est.).

Ikey ('aɪkɪ) NOUN *South African informal* a student at the University of Cape Town, esp one representing the University in a sport.
▷HISTORY from the name *Isaac*

ikon ('aɪkɒn) NOUN a variant spelling of **icon**.

il THE INTERNET DOMAIN NAME FOR Israel.

IL ABBREVIATION FOR: [1] Illinois. ◆ [2] INTERNATIONAL CAR REGISTRATION FOR Israel.

il- PREFIX variant of **in-**[1] and **in-**[2] before *l*.

ilang-ilang ('iːlæŋ'iːlæŋ) NOUN a variant spelling of **ylang-ylang**.

-ile SUFFIX FORMING ADJECTIVES AND NOUNS indicating capability, liability, or a relationship with something: *agile*; *fragile*; *juvenile*.
▷HISTORY via French from Latin or directly from Latin *-ilis*

ILEA ('ɪlɪə) NOUN (formerly) ◆ ACRONYM FOR Inner London Education Authority.

ileac ('ɪlɪ,æk) *or* **ileal** ('ɪlɪəl) ADJECTIVE [1] *Anatomy* of or relating to the ileum. [2] *Pathol* of or relating to ileus.

Île-de-France (*French* ildəfrɑ̃s) NOUN [1] a region of N France, in the Paris Basin: part of the duchy of France in the 10th century. [2] a former name (1715–1810) for **Mauritius**.

Île du Diable (il dy djɑblə) NOUN the French name for **Devil's Island**.

ileitis (,ɪlɪ'aɪtɪs) NOUN inflammation of the ileum.

ileo- *or before a vowel* **ile-** COMBINING FORM indicating the ileum: *ileostomy*.

ileostomy (,ɪlɪ'ɒstəmɪ) NOUN, *plural* **-mies**. the surgical formation of a permanent opening through the abdominal wall into the ileum.

Îles Comores (il kɔmɔr) PLURAL NOUN the French name for the **Comoros**.

Îles du Salut (il dy saly) PLURAL NOUN the French name for the **Safety Islands**.

Ilesha (ɪ'leɪʃə) NOUN a town in W Nigeria. Pop.: 378 400 (1996 est.).

Îles Mascareignes (il maskarɛɲ) PLURAL NOUN the French name for the **Mascarene Islands**.

Îles sous le Vent (il su lə vɑ̃) PLURAL NOUN the French name for the **Leeward Islands** (sense 3).

ileum ('ɪlɪəm) NOUN [1] the part of the small

intestine between the jejunum and the caecum. 2 the corresponding part in insects.
▷HISTORY C17: New Latin, from Latin *īlium, īleum* flank, groin, of obscure origin

ileus (ˈɪlɪəs) NOUN obstruction of the intestine, esp the ileum, by mechanical occlusion or as the result of distension of the bowel following loss of muscular action.
▷HISTORY C18: from Latin *īleos* severe colic, from Greek *eileos* a rolling, twisting, from *eilein* to roll

ilex (ˈaɪlɛks) NOUN 1 any of various trees or shrubs of the widely distributed genus *Ilex*, such as the holly and inkberry: family *Aquifoliaceae*. 2 another name for the **holm oak**.
▷HISTORY C16: from Latin

ilia (ˈɪlɪə) NOUN the plural of **ilium**.

Ilia (ˈɪlɪə) NOUN (in Roman legend) the daughter of Aeneas and Lavinia, who, according to some traditions, was the mother of Romulus and Remus. See also **Rhea Silvia**.

Ilía (iˈlia) NOUN a transliteration of the Modern Greek name for **Elia**[1].

iliac (ˈɪlɪˌæk) ADJECTIVE *Anatomy* of or relating to the ilium.

Iliad (ˈɪlɪəd) NOUN a Greek epic poem describing the siege of Troy, attributed to Homer (c. 800 B.C.) and probably composed before 700 B.C.
▸**Iliadic** (ˌɪlɪˈædɪk) ADJECTIVE

Iliamna (ˌɪlɪˈæmnə) NOUN 1 a lake in SW Alaska: the largest lake in Alaska. Length: about 130 km (80 miles). Width: 40 km (25 miles). 2 a volcano in SW Alaska, northwest of Iliamna Lake. Height: 3076 m (10 092 ft.).

Iligan (ɪˈliːgən) NOUN a city in the Philippines, a port on the N coast of Mindanao. Pop.: 209 639 (1994 est.).

Ilion (ˈɪlɪən) NOUN a transliteration of the Greek name for ancient **Troy**.

ilium (ˈɪlɪəm) NOUN, *plural* **-ia** (-ɪə). the uppermost and widest of the three sections of the hipbone.

Ilium (ˈɪlɪəm) NOUN the Latin name for ancient **Troy**.

ilk[1] (ɪlk) NOUN 1 a type; class; sort (esp in the phrase **of that, his, her,** etc., **ilk**): *people of that ilk should not be allowed here.* 2 **of that ilk.** *Scot* of the place of the same name: used to indicate that the person named is proprietor or laird of the place named: *Moncrieff of that ilk.*
▷HISTORY Old English *ilca* the same family, same kind; related to Gothic *is* he, Latin *is,* Old English *gelīc* like

> **Language note** Although the use of *ilk* in the sense of sense 1 is sometimes condemned as being the result of a misunderstanding of the original Scottish expression *of that ilk,* it is nevertheless well established and generally acceptable.

ilk[2] (ɪlk) *or* **ilka** (ˈɪlkə) DETERMINER *Scot* each; every.
▷HISTORY Old English *ǣlc* each (+ A[1])

Ilkeston (ˈɪlkɪstən) NOUN a town in N central England, in SE Derbyshire. Pop.: 35 134 (1991).

Ilkley (ˈɪlklɪ) NOUN a town in N England, in Bradford unitary authority, West Yorkshire: nearby is **Ilkley Moor** (to the south). Pop.: 13 530 (1991).

ill (ɪl) ADJECTIVE **worse, worst.** 1 (*usually postpositive*) not in good health; sick. 2 characterized by or intending evil, harm, etc.; hostile: *ill deeds.* 3 causing or resulting in pain, harm, adversity, etc.: *ill effects.* 4 ascribing or imputing evil to something referred to: *ill repute.* 5 promising an unfavourable outcome; unpropitious: *an ill omen.* 6 harsh; lacking kindness: *ill will.* 7 not up to an acceptable standard; faulty: *ill manners.* 8 **ill at ease.** unable to relax; uncomfortable. ◆ NOUN 9 evil or harm: *to wish a person ill.* 10 a mild disease. 11 misfortune; trouble. ◆ ADVERB 12 badly: *the title ill befits him.* 13 with difficulty; hardly: *he can ill afford the money.* 14 not rightly: *she ill deserves such good fortune.*
▷HISTORY C11 (in the sense: evil): from Old Norse *illr* bad

Ill. ABBREVIATION FOR Illinois.

I'll (aɪl) CONTRACTION OF I will *or* I shall.

ill-advised ADJECTIVE 1 acting without reasonable care or thought: *you would be ill-advised to sell your house now.* 2 badly thought out; not or insufficiently considered: *an ill-advised plan of action.*
▸ˌ**ill-adˈvisedly** ADVERB

ill-affected ADJECTIVE (often foll by *towards*) not well disposed; disaffected.

Illampu (*Spanish* iˈʎampu) NOUN one of the two peaks of Mount **Sorata**.

ill-assorted ADJECTIVE badly matched; incompatible.

illation (ɪˈleɪʃən) NOUN a rare word for **inference**.
▷HISTORY C16: from Late Latin *illātiō* a bringing in, from Latin *illātus* brought in, from *inferre* to bring in, from IN-[2] + *ferre* to bear, carry

illative (ɪˈleɪtɪv) ADJECTIVE 1 of or relating to illation; inferential. 2 *Grammar* denoting a word or morpheme used to signal inference, for example *so* or *therefore.* 3 (in the grammar of Finnish and other languages) denoting a case of nouns expressing a relation of motion or direction, usually translated by the English prepositions *into* or *towards.* Compare **elative** (sense 1). ◆ NOUN 4 *Grammar* **a** the illative case. **b** an illative word or speech element.
▷HISTORY C16: from Late Latin *illātīvus* inferring, concluding
▸**ilˈlatively** ADVERB

Illawarra (ˌɪləˈwɒrə) NOUN 1 a coastal district of E Australia, in S New South Wales. Pop.: 342 700 (1991). 2 an Australian breed of shorthorn dairy cattle noted for its high milk yield and ability to survive on poor pastures.

ill-behaved ADJECTIVE poorly behaved; lacking good manners.

ill-bred ADJECTIVE badly brought up; lacking good manners.
▸ˌ**ill-ˈbreeding** NOUN

ill-considered ADJECTIVE done without due consideration; not thought out: *an ill-considered decision.*

ill-defined ADJECTIVE imperfectly defined; having no clear outline.

ill-disposed ADJECTIVE (often foll by *towards*) not kindly disposed.

Ille-et-Vilaine (*French* ilevilɛn) NOUN a department of NW France, in E Brittany. Capital: Rennes. Pop.: 867 533 (1999). Area: 6992 sq. km (2727 sq. miles).

illegal (ɪˈliːgᵊl) ADJECTIVE 1 forbidden by law; unlawful; illicit. 2 unauthorized or prohibited by a code of official or accepted rules. ◆ NOUN 3 a person who has entered or attempted to enter a country illegally.
▸**ilˈlegally** ADVERB ▸**illeˈgality** NOUN

illegalize *or* **illegalise** (ɪˈliːgəˌlaɪz) VERB (*tr*) to make illegal.
▸**ilˌlegaliˈzation** *or* **ilˌlegaliˈsation** NOUN

illegible (ɪˈlɛdʒɪbᵊl) ADJECTIVE unable to be read or deciphered.
▸**ilˌlegiˈbility** *or* **ilˈlegibleness** NOUN ▸**ilˈlegibly** ADVERB

illegitimate (ˌɪlɪˈdʒɪtɪmɪt) ADJECTIVE 1 born of parents who were not married to each other at the time of birth; bastard. 2 forbidden by law; illegal; unlawful. 3 contrary to logic; incorrectly reasoned. ◆ NOUN 4 an illegitimate person; bastard.
▸ˌ**illeˈgitimacy** *or* ˌ**illeˈgitimateness** NOUN ▸ˌ**illeˈgitimately** ADVERB

ill-fated ADJECTIVE doomed or unlucky: *an ill-fated marriage.*

ill-favoured *or US* **ill-favored** ADJECTIVE 1 unattractive or repulsive in appearance; ugly. 2 offensive, disagreeable, or objectionable.
▸ˌ**ill-ˈfavouredly** *or US* ˌ**ill-ˈfavoredly** ADVERB
▸ˌ**ill-ˈfavouredness** *or US* ˌ**ill-ˈfavoredness** NOUN

ill feeling NOUN hostile feeling; animosity.

ill-founded ADJECTIVE not founded on true or reliable premises; unsubstantiated: *an ill-founded rumour.*

ill-gotten ADJECTIVE obtained dishonestly or illegally (esp in the phrase **ill-gotten gains**).

ill humour NOUN a disagreeable or sullen mood; bad temper.
▸ˌ**ill-ˈhumoured** ADJECTIVE ▸ˌ**ill-ˈhumouredly** ADVERB

illiberal (ɪˈlɪbərəl) ADJECTIVE 1 narrow-minded; prejudiced; bigoted; intolerant. 2 not generous; mean. 3 lacking in culture or refinement.
▸**ilˌliberˈality, ilˈliberalness,** *or* **ilˈliberalism** NOUN
▸**ilˈliberally** ADVERB

illicit (ɪˈlɪsɪt) ADJECTIVE 1 another word for **illegal**. 2 not allowed or approved by common custom, rule, or standard: *illicit sexual relations.*
▸**ilˈlicitly** ADVERB ▸**illicitness** NOUN

Illimani (*Spanish* iʎiˈmani) NOUN a mountain in W Bolivia, in the Andes near La Paz. Height: 6882 m (22 580 ft.).

illimitable (ɪˈlɪmɪtəbᵊl) ADJECTIVE limitless; boundless.
▸**ilˌlimitaˈbility** *or* **ilˈlimitableness** NOUN ▸**ilˈlimitably** ADVERB

illinium (ɪˈlɪnɪəm) NOUN *Chem* the former name for **promethium**.
▷HISTORY C20: New Latin, from ILLINOIS + -IUM

Illinois (ˌɪlɪˈnɔɪ) NOUN 1 a state of the N central US, in the Midwest: consists of level prairie crossed by the Illinois and Kaskaskia Rivers; mainly agricultural. Capital: Springfield. Pop.: 12 419 293 (2000). Area: 144 858 sq. km (55 930 sq. miles). Abbreviations: **Ill.,** (with zip code) **IL**. 2 a river in Illinois, flowing SW to the Mississippi. Length: 439 km (273 miles).

Illinoisan (ˌɪlɪˈnɔɪən), **Illinoian** (ˌɪlɪˈnɔɪən), *or* **Illinoisian** (ˌɪlɪˈnɔɪzɪən) NOUN 1 a native or inhabitant of Illinois. ◆ ADJECTIVE 2 of or relating to Illinois or its inhabitants.

illiquid (ɪˈlɪkwɪd) ADJECTIVE 1 (of an asset) not easily convertible into cash. 2 (of an enterprise, organization, etc.) deficient in liquid assets.

illite (ˈɪlaɪt) NOUN a clay mineral of the mica group, found in shales and mudstones. Crystal structure: monoclinic. Formula: $K_{1-1.5}Al_4(Si_{6.5-7}Al_{1-1.5}O_{20})(OH)_4$.
▷HISTORY C20: named after ILLINOIS, where it was first found

illiterate (ɪˈlɪtərɪt) ADJECTIVE 1 unable to read and write. 2 violating accepted standards in reading and writing: *an illiterate scrawl.* 3 uneducated, ignorant, or uncultured: *scientifically illiterate.* ◆ NOUN 4 an illiterate person.
▸**ilˈliteracy** *or* **ilˈliterateness** NOUN ▸**ilˈliterately** ADVERB

ill-judged ADJECTIVE rash; ill-advised.

ill-mannered ADJECTIVE having bad manners; rude; impolite.
▸ˌ**ill-ˈmanneredly** ADVERB

ill-natured ADJECTIVE naturally unpleasant and mean.
▸ˌ**ill-ˈnaturedly** ADVERB ▸ˌ**ill-ˈnaturedness** NOUN

illness (ˈɪlnɪs) NOUN 1 a disease or indisposition; sickness. 2 a state of ill health. 3 *Obsolete* wickedness.

illocution (ˌɪləˈkjuːʃən) NOUN *Philosophy* an act performed by a speaker by virtue of uttering certain words, as for example the acts of promising or of threatening. Also called: **illocutionary act**. See also **performative**. Compare **perlocution**.
▷HISTORY C20: from IL- + LOCUTION
▸ˌ**illoˈcutionary** ADJECTIVE

illogic (ɪˈlɒdʒɪk) NOUN reasoning characterized by lack of logic; illogicality.

illogical (ɪˈlɒdʒɪkᵊl) ADJECTIVE 1 characterized by lack of logic; senseless or unreasonable. 2 disregarding logical principles.
▸**illogicality** (ɪˌlɒdʒɪˈkælɪtɪ) *or* **ilˈlogicalness** NOUN
▸**ilˈlogically** ADVERB

ill-omened ADJECTIVE doomed to be unlucky; ill-fated.

ill-sorted ADJECTIVE badly arranged or matched; ill-assorted.

ill-starred ADJECTIVE unlucky; unfortunate; ill-fated.

ill temper NOUN bad temper; irritability.

ill-tempered ADJECTIVE showing bad temper; irritable.
▸ˌ**ill-ˈtemperedly** ADVERB

ill-timed ADJECTIVE occurring at or planned for an unsuitable time.

ill-treat VERB (*tr*) to behave cruelly or harshly towards; misuse; maltreat.
▸ˌ**ill-ˈtreatment** NOUN

illude (ɪˈluːd) VERB *Literary* to trick or deceive.
▷HISTORY C15: from Latin *illūdere* to sport with, from *lūdus* game

illume (ɪˈluːm) VERB (*tr*) a poetic word for **illuminate**.

▷HISTORY C17: shortened from ILLUMINE

illuminance (ɪˈluːmɪnəns) NOUN the luminous flux incident on unit area of a surface. It is measured in lux. Symbol: E^{v}. Sometimes called: **illumination.** Compare **irradiance.**

illuminant (ɪˈluːmɪnənt) NOUN [1] something that provides or gives off light. ◆ ADJECTIVE [2] giving off light; illuminating.

illuminate VERB (ɪˈluːmɪˌneɪt) [1] (*tr*) to throw light in or into; light up: *to illuminate a room.* [2] (*tr*) to make easily understood; clarify. [3] to adorn, decorate, or be decorated with lights. [4] (*tr*) to decorate (a letter, page, etc.) by the application of colours, gold, or silver. [5] (*intr*) to become lighted up. ◆ ADJECTIVE (ɪˈluːmɪnɪt, -ˌneɪt) [6] *Archaic* made clear or bright with light; illuminated. ◆ NOUN (ɪˈluːmɪnɪt, -ˌneɪt) [7] a person who has or claims to have special enlightenment.
▷HISTORY C16: from Latin *illūmināre* to light up, from *lūmen* light
▸**ilˈluminative** ADJECTIVE ▸**ilˈlumiˌnator** NOUN

illuminati (ɪˌluːmɪˈnɑːtiː) PLURAL NOUN, *singular* **-to** (-təʊ). a group of persons claiming exceptional enlightenment on some subject, esp religion.
▷HISTORY C16: from Latin, literally: the enlightened ones, from *illūmināre* to ILLUMINATE

Illuminati (ɪˌluːmɪˈnɑːtiː) PLURAL NOUN, *singular* **-to** (-təʊ). [1] any of several groups of illuminati, esp in 18th-century France. [2] a group of religious enthusiasts of 16th-century Spain who were persecuted by the Inquisition. [3] a masonic sect founded in Bavaria in 1778 claiming that the illuminating grace of Christ resided in it alone. [4] a rare name for the Rosicrucians.

illuminating (ɪˈluːmɪˌneɪtɪŋ) ADJECTIVE serving to inform or clarify; instructive.
▸**ilˈlumiˌnatingly** ADVERB

illumination (ɪˌluːmɪˈneɪʃən) NOUN [1] the act of illuminating or the state of being illuminated. [2] a source of light. [3] (*often plural*) *Chiefly Brit* a light or lights, esp coloured lights, used as decoration in streets, parks, etc. [4] spiritual or intellectual enlightenment; insight or understanding. [5] the act of making understood; clarification. [6] decoration in colours, gold, or silver used on some manuscripts or printed works. [7] *Physics* another name (not in technical usage) for **illuminance.**
▸**ilˌlumiˈnational** ADJECTIVE

illumine (ɪˈluːmɪn) VERB a literary word for **illuminate.**
▷HISTORY C14: from Latin *illūmināre* to make light; see ILLUMINATE
▸**ilˈluminable** ADJECTIVE

illuminism (ɪˈluːmɪˌnɪzəm) NOUN [1] belief in and advocation of special enlightenment. [2] the tenets and principles of the Illuminati or of any of several religious or political movements initiated by them.
▸**ilˈluminist** NOUN

ill-use VERB (ˈɪlˈjuːz) [1] to use badly or cruelly; abuse; maltreat. ◆ NOUN (ˈɪlˈjuːs) *also* **ill-usage.** [2] harsh or cruel treatment; abuse.

illusion (ɪˈluːʒən) NOUN [1] a false appearance or deceptive impression of reality: *the mirror gives an illusion of depth.* [2] a false or misleading perception or belief; delusion: *he has the illusion that he is really clever.* [3] *Psychol* a perception that is not true to reality, having been altered subjectively in some way in the mind of the perceiver. See also **hallucination.** [4] a very fine gauze or tulle used for trimmings, veils, etc.
▷HISTORY C14: from Latin *illūsiō* deceit, from *illūdere;* see ILLUDE
▸**ilˈlusionary** *or* **ilˈlusional** ADJECTIVE ▸**ilˈlusioned** ADJECTIVE

illusionism (ɪˈluːʒəˌnɪzəm) NOUN [1] *Philosophy* the doctrine that the external world exists only in illusory sense perceptions. [2] the use of highly illusory effects in art or decoration, esp the use of perspective in painting to create an impression of three-dimensional reality.

illusionist (ɪˈluːʒənɪst) NOUN [1] a person given to illusions; visionary; dreamer. [2] *Philosophy* a person who believes in illusionism. [3] an artist who practises illusionism. [4] a conjuror; magician.
▸**ilˌlusionˈistic** ADJECTIVE

illusory (ɪˈluːsərɪ) *or* **illusive** (ɪˈluːsɪv) ADJECTIVE producing, produced by, or based on illusion; deceptive or unreal.
▸**ilˈlusorily** *or* **ilˈlusively** ADVERB ▸**ilˈlusoriness** *or* **ilˈlusiveness** NOUN

> **Language note** *Illusive* is sometimes wrongly used where *elusive* is meant: *they fought hard, but victory remained elusive* (not *illusive*).

illust. *or* **illus.** ABBREVIATION FOR: [1] illustrated. [2] illustration.

illustrate (ˈɪləˌstreɪt) VERB [1] to clarify or explain by use of examples, analogy, etc. [2] (*tr*) to be an example or demonstration of. [3] (*tr*) to explain or decorate (a book, text, etc.) with pictures. [4] (*tr*) an archaic word for **enlighten.**
▷HISTORY C16: from Latin *illustrāre* to make light, explain, from *lustrāre* to purify, brighten; see LUSTRUM
▸**ˈillusˌtratable** ADJECTIVE ▸**ˈillusˌtrative** ADJECTIVE
▸**ˈillusˌtratively** ADVERB ▸**ˈillusˌtrator** NOUN

illustration (ˌɪləˈstreɪʃən) NOUN [1] pictorial matter used to explain or decorate a text. [2] an example or demonstration: *an illustration of his ability.* [3] the act of illustrating or the state of being illustrated.
▸**ˌillusˈtrational** ADJECTIVE

illustrious (ɪˈlʌstrɪəs) ADJECTIVE [1] of great renown; famous and distinguished. [2] glorious or great: *illustrious deeds.* [3] *Obsolete* shining.
▷HISTORY C16: from Latin *illustris* bright, distinguished, famous, from *illustrāre* to make light; see ILLUSTRATE
▸**ilˈlustriously** ADVERB ▸**ilˈlustriousness** NOUN

illuviation (ɪˌluːvɪˈeɪʃən) NOUN the process by which a material (**illuvium**), which includes colloids and mineral salts, is washed down from one layer of soil to a lower layer.
▷HISTORY C20: from Latin *illuviēs* dirt, mud, from IL- + *-luviēs,* from *lavere* to wash
▸**ilˈluvial** ADJECTIVE

ill will NOUN hostile feeling; enmity; antagonism.

Illyria (ɪˈlɪərɪə) NOUN an ancient region of uncertain boundaries on the E shore of the Adriatic Sea, including parts of present-day Croatia, Montenegro, and Albania.

Illyrian (ɪˈlɪərɪən) NOUN [1] a member of the group of related Indo-European peoples who occupied Illyria from the late third millennium to the early first millennium B.C. [2] the extinct and almost unrecorded language of these peoples: of uncertain relationship within the Indo-European family, but thought by some to be the ancestor of modern Albanian. ◆ ADJECTIVE [3] of, characteristic of, or relating to Illyria, its people, or their language.

Illyricum (ɪˈlɪrɪkəm) NOUN a Roman province founded after 168 B.C., based on the coastal area of Illyria.

Ilmen (ˈɪlmən) NOUN **Lake.** a lake in NW Russia, in the Novgorod Region: drains through the Volkhov River into Lake Ladoga. Area: between 780 sq. km (300 sq. miles) and 2200 sq. km (850 sq. miles), according to the season.

ilmenite (ˈɪlmɪˌnaɪt) NOUN a black mineral found in igneous rocks as layered deposits and in veins. It is the chief source of titanium. Composition: iron titanium oxide. Formula: $FeTiO_3$. Crystal structure: hexagonal (rhombohedral).
▷HISTORY C19: from *Ilmen,* mountain range in the southern Urals, Russia, + -ITE[1]

ILO ABBREVIATION FOR **International Labour Organisation.**

Iloilo (ˌiːləʊˈiːləʊ) NOUN a port in the W central Philippines, on SE Panay Island. Pop.: 365 820 (2000).

Ilorin (ɪˈlɒrɪn) NOUN a city in W Nigeria, capital of Kwara state: agricultural trade centre. Pop.: 475 800 (1996 est.).

ILR (in Britain) ABBREVIATION FOR Independent Local Radio.

ILS *Aeronautics* ABBREVIATION FOR instrument landing system.

ILU *Text messaging* ABBREVIATION FOR I love you.

im THE INTERNET DOMAIN NAME FOR Isle of Man.

IM ABBREVIATION FOR: [1] Also: **i.m.** intramuscular. [2] *Chess* **International Master.**

I'm (aɪm) CONTRACTION OF I am.

im- PREFIX a variant of **in-**[1] and **in-**[2] before *b, m,* and *p.*

image (ˈɪmɪdʒ) NOUN [1] a representation or likeness of a person or thing, esp in sculpture. [2] an optically formed reproduction of an object, such as one formed by a lens or mirror. [3] a person or thing that resembles another closely; double or copy. [4] a mental representation or picture; idea produced by the imagination. [5] the personality presented to the public by a person, organization, etc.: *a criminal charge is not good for a politician's image.* See also **corporate image.** [6] the pattern of light that is focused on to the retina of the eye. [7] *Psychol* the mental experience of something that is not immediately present to the senses, often involving memory. See also **imagery, body image, hypnagogic image.** [8] a personification of a specified quality; epitome: *the image of good breeding.* [9] a mental picture or association of ideas evoked in a literary work, esp in poetry. [10] a figure of speech, such as a simile or metaphor. [11] *Maths* **a** (of a point) the value of a function, f(*x*), corresponding to the point *x*. **b** the range of a function. [12] an obsolete word for **apparition.** ◆ VERB (*tr*) [13] to picture in the mind; imagine. [14] to make or reflect an image of. [15] *Computing* to project or display on a screen or visual display unit. [16] to portray or describe. [17] to be an example or epitome of; typify.
▷HISTORY C13: from Old French *imagene,* from Latin *imāgō* copy, representation; related to Latin *imitārī* to IMITATE
▸**ˈimageable** ADJECTIVE ▸**ˈimageless** ADJECTIVE

image converter *or* **tube** NOUN a device for producing a visual image formed by other electromagnetic radiation such as infrared or ultraviolet radiation or X-rays.

image enhancement NOUN a method of improving the definition of a video picture by a computer program, which reduces the lowest grey values to black and the highest to white: used for pictures from microscopes, surveillance cameras, and scanners.

image intensifier *or* **tube** NOUN any of various devices for amplifying the intensity of an optical image, sometimes used in conjunction with an image converter.

image orthicon NOUN a television camera tube in which electrons, emitted from a photoemissive surface in proportion to the intensity of the incident light, are focused onto the target causing secondary emission of electrons.

image printer NOUN *Computing* a printer which uses optical technology to produce an image of a complete page from digital input.

image processing NOUN the manipulation or modification of a digitized image, esp in order to enhance its quality.

imagery (ˈɪmɪdʒrɪ, -dʒərɪ) NOUN, *plural* **-ries.** [1] figurative or descriptive language in a literary work. [2] images collectively. [3] *Psychol* **a** the materials or general processes of the imagination. **b** the characteristic kind of mental images formed by a particular individual. See also **image** (sense 7), **imagination** (sense 1). [4] *Military* the presentation of objects reproduced photographically (by infrared or electronic means) as prints or electronic displays.

image tube NOUN another name for **image converter** or **image intensifier.**

imaginal (ɪˈmædʒɪnᵊl) ADJECTIVE [1] of, relating to, or resembling an imago. [2] of or relating to an image.

imaginary (ɪˈmædʒɪnərɪ, -dʒɪnrɪ) ADJECTIVE [1] existing in the imagination; unreal; illusory. [2] *Maths* involving or containing imaginary numbers. The imaginary part of a complex number, *z,* is usually written Im*z*.
▸**imˈaginarily** ADVERB ▸**imˈaginariness** NOUN

imaginary number NOUN any complex number of the form i*b*, where $i = \sqrt{-1}$.

imaginary part NOUN the coefficient *b* in a complex number $a + ib$, where $i = \sqrt{-1}$.

imagination (ɪˌmædʒɪˈneɪʃən) NOUN [1] the faculty or action of producing ideas, esp mental images of what is not present or has not been experienced. [2] mental creative ability. [3] the ability to deal resourcefully with unexpected or unusual problems, circumstances, etc. [4] (in romantic literary criticism, esp that of S. T. Coleridge) a creative act of perception that joins

passive and active elements in thinking and imposes unity on the poetic material. Compare **fancy** (sense 9).
▸**imˌagiˈnational** ADJECTIVE

imaginative (ɪˈmædʒɪnətɪv) ADJECTIVE 1 produced by or indicative of a vivid or creative imagination: *an imaginative story*. 2 having a vivid imagination.
▸**imˈaginatively** ADVERB ▸**imˈaginativeness** NOUN

imagine (ɪˈmædʒɪn) VERB 1 (*when tr, may take a clause as object*) to form a mental image of. 2 (*when tr, may take a clause as object*) to think, believe, or guess. 3 (*tr; takes a clause as object*) to suppose; assume: *I imagine he'll come*. 4 (*tr; takes a clause as object*) to believe or assume without foundation: *he imagines he knows the whole story*. 5 an archaic word for **plot**[1]. ◆ SENTENCE SUBSTITUTE 6 Also: **imagine that!** an exclamation of surprise.
▷HISTORY C14: from Latin *imāginārī* to fancy, picture mentally, from *imāgō* likeness; see IMAGE
▸**imˈaginable** ADJECTIVE ▸**imˈaginably** ADVERB ▸**imˈaginer** NOUN

imagism (ˈɪmɪˌdʒɪzəm) NOUN a poetic movement in England and America between 1912 and 1917, initiated chiefly by Ezra Pound, the US poet, translator, and critic (1885–1972), advocating the use of ordinary speech and the precise presentation of images.
▸**ˈimagist** NOUN, ADJECTIVE ▸**ˌimagˈistic** ADJECTIVE ▸**ˌimagˈistically** ADVERB

imago (ɪˈmeɪɡəʊ) NOUN, *plural* **imagoes** *or* **imagines** (ɪˈmædʒəˌniːz). 1 an adult sexually mature insect produced after metamorphosis. 2 *Psychoanal* an idealized image of another person, usually a parent, acquired in childhood and carried in the unconscious in later life.
▷HISTORY C18: New Latin, from Latin: likeness; see IMAGE

imam (ɪˈmɑːm) *or* **imaum** (ɪˈmɑːm, ɪˈmɔːm) NOUN *Islam* 1 a leader of congregational prayer in a mosque. 2 a caliph, as leader of a Muslim community. 3 an honorific title applied to eminent doctors of Islam, such as the founders of the orthodox schools. 4 any of a succession of either seven or twelve religious leaders of the Shiites, regarded by their followers as divinely inspired.
▷HISTORY C17: from Arabic: leader, from *amma* he guided

imamate (ɪˈmɑːmeɪt) NOUN *Islam* 1 the region or territory governed by an imam. 2 the office, rank, or period of office of an imam.

IMarE ABBREVIATION FOR Institute of Marine Engineers.

imaret (ɪˈmɑːrɛt) NOUN (in Turkey) a hospice for pilgrims or travellers.
▷HISTORY C17: from Turkish, from Arabic *ʿimārah* hospice, building, from *amara* he built

IMAX (ˈaɪmæks) NOUN *Trademark* a process of film projection using a giant screen on which an image approximately ten times larger than standard is projected.
▷HISTORY C20: from IMAGE + MAXIMUM

imbalance (ɪmˈbæləns) NOUN a lack of balance, as in emphasis, proportion, etc.: *the political imbalance of the programme*.

imbecile (ˈɪmbɪˌsiːl, -ˌsaɪl) NOUN 1 *Psychol* a person of very low intelligence (IQ of 25 to 50), usually capable only of guarding himself against danger and of performing simple mechanical tasks under supervision. 2 *Informal* an extremely stupid person; dolt. ◆ ADJECTIVE *also* **imbecilic** (ˌɪmbɪˈsɪlɪk). 3 of or like an imbecile; mentally deficient; feeble-minded. 4 stupid or senseless: *an imbecile thing to do*.
▷HISTORY C16: from Latin *imbēcillus* feeble (physically or mentally)
▸**ˈimbeˌcilely** *or* **ˌimbeˈcilically** ADVERB ▸**ˌimbeˈcility** NOUN

imbed (ɪmˈbɛd) VERB **-beds, -bedding, -bedded**. a less common spelling of **embed**.

imbibe (ɪmˈbaɪb) VERB 1 to drink (esp alcoholic drinks). 2 *Literary* to take in or assimilate (ideas, facts, etc.): *to imbibe the spirit of the Renaissance*. 3 (*tr*) to take in as if by drinking: *to imbibe fresh air*. 4 to absorb or cause to absorb liquid or moisture; assimilate or saturate.
▷HISTORY C14: from Latin *imbibere*, from *bibere* to drink
▸**imˈbiber** NOUN

imbibition (ˌɪmbɪˈbɪʃən) NOUN 1 *Chem* the absorption or adsorption of a liquid by a gel or solid. 2 *Photog* the absorption of dyes by gelatine, used in some colour printing processes. 3 *Obsolete* the act of imbibing.

imbizo (ɪmˈbiːzɒ) NOUN, *plural* **-zos**. *South African* a meeting, esp a gathering of the Zulu people called by the king or a traditional leader.
▷HISTORY from Zulu *biza* to call or summon

Imbolc *or* **Imbolg** (ˈɪmbəlk, ˈɪmbəʊlk, ˈɪmməlk) an ancient Celtic festival associated with the goddess Brigit, held on Feb. 1 or 2 to mark the beginning of spring. It is also celebrated by modern pagans.
▷HISTORY C15: from Old Irish *oimelc* ewe's milk

imbricate ADJECTIVE (ˈɪmbrɪkɪt, -ˌkeɪt) *also* **imbricated.** 1 *Architect* relating to or having tiles, shingles, or slates that overlap. 2 *Botany* (of leaves, scales, etc.) overlapping each other. ◆ VERB (ˈɪmbrɪˌkeɪt) 3 (*tr*) to decorate with a repeating pattern resembling scales or overlapping tiles.
▷HISTORY C17: from Latin *imbricāre* to cover with overlapping tiles, from *imbrex* pantile
▸**ˈimbricately** ADVERB ▸**ˌimbriˈcation** NOUN

imbroglio (ɪmˈbrəʊlɪˌəʊ) NOUN, *plural* **-glios.** 1 a confused or perplexing political or interpersonal situation. 2 *Obsolete* a confused heap; jumble.
▷HISTORY C18: from Italian, from *imbrogliare* to confuse, EMBROIL

Imbros (ˈɪmbrəs) NOUN a Turkish island in the NE Aegean Sea, west of the Gallipoli Peninsula: occupied by Greece (1912–14) and Britain (1914–23). Area: 280 sq. km (108 sq. miles). Turkish name: **Imroz.**

imbrue *or* **embrue** (ɪmˈbruː) VERB **-brues, -bruing, -brued**. (*tr*) *Rare* 1 to stain, esp with blood. 2 to permeate or impregnate.
▷HISTORY C15: from Old French *embreuver*, from Latin *imbibere* IMBIBE
▸**imˈbruement** *or* **emˈbruement** NOUN

imbue (ɪmˈbjuː) VERB **-bues, -buing, -bued**. (*tr;* usually foll by *with*) 1 to instil or inspire (with ideals, principles, etc.): *his sermons were imbued with the spirit of the Reformation*. 2 *Rare* to soak, esp with moisture, dye, etc.
▷HISTORY C16: from Latin *imbuere* to stain, accustom
▸**imˈbuement** NOUN

IMCO ABBREVIATION FOR Intergovernmental Maritime Consultative Organization: the department of the United Nations concerned with international maritime safety, antipollution regulations, etc.

IMechE ABBREVIATION FOR Institution of Mechanical Engineers.

IMF ABBREVIATION FOR **International Monetary Fund.**

IMHO *Text messaging* ABBREVIATION FOR in my humble *or* honest opinion.

imidazole (ˌɪmɪdˈæzəʊl, -ɪdəˈzəʊl) NOUN 1 Also called: **glyoxaline, iminazole.** a white crystalline basic heterocyclic compound; 1,3-diazole. Formula: $C_3H_4N_2$. 2 any substituted derivative of this compound.
▷HISTORY C19: from IMIDE + AZOLE

imide (ˈɪmaɪd) NOUN any of a class of organic compounds whose molecules contain the divalent group -CONHCO-.
▷HISTORY C19: alteration of AMIDE
▸**imidic** (ɪˈmɪdɪk) ADJECTIVE

imine (ɪˈmiːn, ˈɪmiːn) NOUN any of a class of organic compounds in which a nitrogen atom is bound to one hydrogen atom and to two alkyl or aryl groups. They contain the divalent group NH.
▷HISTORY C19: alteration of AMINE

IMinE ABBREVIATION FOR Institution of Mining Engineers.

iminourea (ɪˌmiːnəʊjʊəˈrɪə) NOUN another name for **guanidine.**

imipramine (ɪˈmɪprəˌmiːn) NOUN a tricyclic antidepressant drug. Formula: $C_{19}H_{24}N_2$.
▷HISTORY C20: from IMI(DE) + PR(OPYL) + AMINE

imitate (ˈɪmɪˌteɪt) VERB (*tr*) 1 to try to follow the manner, style, character, etc., of or take as a model: *many writers imitated the language of Shakespeare*. 2 to pretend to be or to impersonate, esp for humour; mimic. 3 to make a copy or reproduction of; duplicate; counterfeit. 4 to make or be like; resemble or simulate: *her achievements in politics imitated her earlier successes in business*.
▷HISTORY C16: from Latin *imitārī*; see IMAGE
▸**ˈimitable** ADJECTIVE ▸**ˌimitaˈbility** *or* **ˈimitableness** NOUN ▸**ˈimiˌtator** NOUN

imitation (ˌɪmɪˈteɪʃən) NOUN 1 the act, practice, or art of imitating; mimicry. 2 an instance or product of imitating, such as a copy of the manner of a person; impression. 3 **a** a copy or reproduction of a genuine article; counterfeit. **b** (*as modifier*): *imitation jewellery*. 4 (in contrapuntal or polyphonic music) the repetition of a phrase or figure in one part after its appearance in another, as in a fugue. 5 a literary composition that adapts the style of an older work to the writer's own purposes.
▸**ˌimiˈtational** ADJECTIVE

imitative (ˈɪmɪtətɪv) ADJECTIVE 1 imitating or tending to imitate or copy. 2 characterized by imitation. 3 copying or reproducing the features of an original, esp in an inferior manner: *imitative painting*. 4 another word for **onomatopoeic.**
▸**ˈimitatively** ADVERB ▸**ˈimitativeness** NOUN

Imittós (ˌimiˈtɔs) NOUN a transliteration of the Modern Greek name for **Hymettus.**

immaculate (ɪˈmækjʊlɪt) ADJECTIVE 1 completely clean; extremely tidy: *his clothes were immaculate*. 2 completely flawless, etc.: *an immaculate rendering of the symphony*. 3 morally pure; free from sin or corruption. 4 *Biology* of only one colour, with no spots or markings.
▷HISTORY C15: from Latin *immaculātus*, from IM- (not) + *macula* blemish
▸**imˈmaculacy** *or* **imˈmaculateness** NOUN ▸**imˈmaculately** ADVERB

Immaculate Conception NOUN *Christian theol, RC Church* the doctrine that the Virgin Mary was conceived without any stain of original sin.

immanent (ˈɪmənənt) ADJECTIVE 1 existing, operating, or remaining within; inherent. 2 of or relating to the pantheistic conception of God, as being present throughout the universe. Compare **transcendent** (sense 3).
▷HISTORY C16: from Latin *immanēre* to remain in, from IM- (in) + *manēre* to stay
▸**ˈimmanence** *or* **ˈimmanency** NOUN ▸**ˈimmanently** ADVERB

immanentism (ˈɪmənənˌtɪzəm) NOUN belief in the immanence of God.
▸**ˈimmanentist** NOUN

Immanuel *or* **Emmanuel** (ɪˈmænjʊəl) NOUN *Bible* the child whose birth was foretold by Isaiah (Isaiah 7:14) and who in Christian tradition is identified with Jesus.
▷HISTORY from Hebrew *ʿimmānūʾel*, literally: God with us

immaterial (ˌɪməˈtɪərɪəl) ADJECTIVE 1 of no real importance; inconsequential. 2 not formed of matter; incorporeal; spiritual.
▸**ˌimmaˌteriˈality** *or* **ˌimmaˈterialness** NOUN ▸**ˌimmaˈterially** ADVERB

immaterialism (ˌɪməˈtɪərɪəˌlɪzəm) NOUN *Philosophy* 1 the doctrine that the material world exists only in the mind. 2 the doctrine that only immaterial substances or spiritual beings exist. See also **idealism** (sense 3).
▸**ˌimmaˈterialist** NOUN

immaterialize *or* **immaterialise** (ˌɪməˈtɪərɪəˌlaɪz) VERB (*tr*) to make immaterial.

immature (ˌɪməˈtjʊə, -ˈtʃʊə) ADJECTIVE 1 not fully grown or developed. 2 deficient in maturity; lacking wisdom, insight, emotional stability, etc. 3 *Geography* a less common term for **youthful** (sense 4).
▸**ˌimmaˈturity** *or* **ˌimmaˈtureness** NOUN ▸**ˌimmaˈturely** ADVERB

immeasurable (ɪˈmɛʒərəbᵊl) ADJECTIVE incapable of being measured, esp by virtue of great size; limitless.
▸**imˌmeasuraˈbility** *or* **imˈmeasurableness** NOUN ▸**imˈmeasurably** ADVERB

immediate (ɪˈmiːdɪət) ADJECTIVE (*usually prenominal*) 1 taking place or accomplished without delay: *an immediate reaction*. 2 closest or most direct in effect or relationship: *the immediate cause of his downfall*. 3 having no intervening medium; direct in effect: *an immediate influence*. 4 contiguous in space, time, or relationship: *our immediate neighbour*. 5 present; current: *the immediate problem is food*. 6 *Philosophy* of or relating to an object or concept that is directly known or

intuited. 7 *Logic* (of an inference) deriving its conclusion from a single premise, esp by conversion or obversion of a categorial statement.
▷HISTORY C16: from Medieval Latin *immediātus,* from Latin IM- (not) + *mediāre* to be in the middle; see MEDIATE
▸**im'mediacy** *or* **im'mediateness** NOUN

immediate annuity NOUN an annuity that starts less than a year after its purchase. Compare **deferred annuity.**

immediate constituent NOUN a constituent of a linguistic construction at the first step in an analysis; for example, the immediate constituents of a sentence are the subject and the predicate.

immediately (ɪ'mi:dɪətlɪ) ADVERB 1 without delay or intervention; at once; instantly: *it happened immediately.* 2 very closely or directly: *this immediately concerns you.* 3 near or close by: *he's somewhere immediately in this area.* ◆ CONJUNCTION 4 (*subordinating*) *Chiefly Brit* at the same time as; as soon as: *immediately he opened the door, there was a gust of wind.*

immedicable (ɪ'mɛdɪkəbᵊl) ADJECTIVE (of wounds) unresponsive to treatment.
▸**im'medicableness** NOUN ▸**im'medicably** ADVERB

Immelmann turn *or* **Immelmann** ('ɪməlˌmɑ:n, -mən) NOUN an aircraft manoeuvre used to gain height while reversing the direction of flight. It consists of a half loop followed by a half roll.
▷HISTORY C20: named after Max *Immelmann* (1890–1916), German aviator

immemorial (ˌɪmɪ'mɔ:rɪəl) ADJECTIVE originating in the distant past; ancient (postpositive in the phrase **time immemorial**).
▷HISTORY C17: from Medieval Latin *immemoriālis,* from Latin IM- (not) + *memoria* MEMORY
▸ˌ**imme'morially** ADVERB

immense (ɪ'mɛns) ADJECTIVE 1 unusually large; huge; vast. 2 without limits; immeasurable. 3 *Informal* very good; excellent.
▷HISTORY C15: from Latin *immensus,* literally: unmeasured, from IM- (not) + *mensus* measured, from *mētīrī* to measure
▸**im'mensely** ADVERB ▸**im'menseness** NOUN

immensity (ɪ'mɛnsɪtɪ) NOUN, *plural* **-ties.** 1 the state or quality of being immense; vastness; enormity. 2 enormous expanse, distance, or volume: *the immensity of space.* 3 *Informal* a huge amount: *an immensity of wealth.*

immensurable (ɪ'mɛnʃərəbᵊl) ADJECTIVE a less common word for **immeasurable.**

immerge (ɪ'mɜ:dʒ) VERB an archaic word for **immerse.**
▷HISTORY C17: from Latin *immergere* to IMMERSE
▸**im'mergence** NOUN

immerse (ɪ'mɜ:s) VERB (*tr*) 1 (often foll by *in*) to plunge or dip into liquid. 2 (*often passive;* often foll by *in*) to involve deeply; engross: *to immerse oneself in a problem.* 3 to baptize by immersion.
▷HISTORY C17: from Latin *immergere,* from IM- (in) + *mergere* to dip
▸**im'mersible** ADJECTIVE

immersed (ɪ'mɜ:st) ADJECTIVE 1 sunk or submerged. 2 (of plants) growing completely submerged in water. 3 (of a plant or animal organ) embedded in another organ or part. 4 involved deeply; engrossed.

immerser (ɪ'mɜ:sə) NOUN an informal term for **immersion heater.**

immersion (ɪ'mɜ:ʃən) NOUN 1 a form of baptism in which part or the whole of a person's body is submerged in the water. 2 Also called: **ingress.** *Astronomy* the disappearance of a celestial body prior to an eclipse or occultation. 3 the act of immersing or state of being immersed.

immersion heater NOUN an electrical device, usually thermostatically controlled, for heating the liquid in which it is immersed, esp as a fixture in a domestic hot-water tank.

immersionism (ɪ'mɜ:ʃəˌnɪzəm) NOUN the doctrine that immersion is the only true and valid form of Christian baptism.
▸**im'mersionist** NOUN

immersive (ɪ'mɜ:sɪv) ADJECTIVE providing information or stimulation for a number of senses, not only sight and sound: *immersive television sets.*

immesh (ɪ'mɛʃ) VERB a variant of **enmesh.**

immethodical (ˌɪmɪ'θɒdɪkᵊl) ADJECTIVE lacking in method or planning; disorganized.
▸ˌ**imme'thodically** ADVERB ▸ˌ**imme'thodicalness** NOUN

immigrant ('ɪmɪgrənt) NOUN 1 **a** a person who immigrates. Compare **emigrant. b** (*as modifier*): *an immigrant community.* 2 *Brit* a person who has been settled in a country of which he is not a native for less than ten years. 3 an animal or plant that lives or grows in a region to which it has recently migrated.

immigrate ('ɪmɪˌgreɪt) VERB 1 (*intr*) to come to a place or country of which one is not a native in order to settle there. Compare **emigrate.** 2 (*intr*) (of an animal or plant) to migrate to a new geographical area. 3 (*tr*) to introduce or bring in as an immigrant.
▷HISTORY C17: from Latin *immigrāre* to go into, from IM- + *migrāre* to move
▸'**immiˌgratory** ADJECTIVE ▸'**immiˌgrator** NOUN

immigration (ˌɪmɪ'greɪʃən) NOUN 1 the movement of non-native people into a country in order to settle there. 2 the part of a port, airport, etc. where government employees examine the passports, visas, etc. of foreign nationals entering the country.
▸ˌ**immi'grational** ADJECTIVE

imminent ('ɪmɪnənt) ADJECTIVE 1 liable to happen soon; impending. 2 *Obsolete* jutting out or overhanging.
▷HISTORY C16: from Latin *imminēre* to project over, from IM- (in) + *-minēre* to project; related to *mons* mountain
▸'**imminence** *or* '**imminentness** NOUN ▸'**imminently** ADVERB

Immingham ('ɪmɪŋəm) NOUN a port in NE England, in North East Lincolnshire unitary authority, Lincolnshire: docks opened in 1912, principally for the exporting of coal; now handles chiefly bulk materials, esp imported iron ore. Pop.: 12 278 (1991).

immingle (ɪ'mɪŋgᵊl) VERB *Archaic* to blend or mix together; intermingle.

immiscible (ɪ'mɪsɪbᵊl) ADJECTIVE (of two or more liquids) incapable of being mixed to form a homogeneous substance: *oil and water are immiscible.*
▸**imˌmisci'bility** NOUN ▸**im'miscibly** ADVERB

immitigable (ɪ'mɪtɪgəbᵊl) ADJECTIVE *Rare* unable to be mitigated; relentless; unappeasable.
▸**im'mitigably** ADVERB ▸**imˌmitiga'bility** NOUN

immix (ɪ'mɪks) VERB (*tr*) *Archaic* to mix in; commix.
▸**im'mixture** NOUN

immobile (ɪ'məʊbaɪl) ADJECTIVE 1 not moving; motionless. 2 not able to move or be moved; fixed.
▸**immobility** (ˌɪməʊ'bɪlɪtɪ) NOUN

immobilism (ɪ'məʊbɪˌlɪzəm) NOUN a political policy characterized by inertia and antipathy to change.

immobilize *or* **immobilise** (ɪ'məʊbɪˌlaɪz) VERB (*tr*) 1 to make or become immobile: *to immobilize a car.* 2 *Finance* **a** to remove (specie) from circulation and hold it as a reserve. **b** to convert (circulating capital) into fixed capital.
▸**imˌmobili'zation** *or* **imˌmobili'sation** NOUN ▸**im'mobiˌlizer** *or* **im'mobiˌliser** NOUN

immoderate (ɪ'mɒdərɪt, ɪ'mɒdrɪt) ADJECTIVE 1 lacking in moderation; excessive: *immoderate demands.* 2 *Obsolete* venial; intemperate: *immoderate habits.*
▸**im'moderately** ADVERB ▸**imˌmoder'ation** *or* **im'moderateness** NOUN

immodest (ɪ'mɒdɪst) ADJECTIVE 1 indecent, esp with regard to sexual propriety; improper. 2 bold, impudent, or shameless.
▸**im'modestly** ADVERB ▸**im'modesty** NOUN

immolate ('ɪməʊˌleɪt) VERB (*tr*) 1 to kill or offer as a sacrifice, esp by fire. 2 *Literary* to sacrifice (something highly valued).
▷HISTORY C16: from Latin *immolāre* to sprinkle an offering with sacrificial meal, sacrifice, from IM- (in) + *mola* spelt grain; see MILL[1]
▸ˌ**immo'lation** NOUN ▸'**immoˌlator** NOUN

immoral (ɪ'mɒrəl) ADJECTIVE 1 transgressing accepted moral rules; corrupt. 2 sexually dissolute; profligate or promiscuous. 3 unscrupulous or unethical: *immoral trading.* 4 tending to corrupt or resulting from corruption: *an immoral film; immoral earnings.*
▸**im'morally** ADVERB

immoralist (ɪ'mɒrəlɪst) NOUN a person who advocates or practises immorality.

immorality (ˌɪmə'rælɪtɪ) NOUN, *plural* **-ties.** 1 the quality, character, or state of being immoral. 2 immoral behaviour, esp in sexual matters; licentiousness; profligacy or promiscuity. 3 an immoral act.

immortal (ɪ'mɔ:tᵊl) ADJECTIVE 1 not subject to death or decay; having perpetual life. 2 having everlasting fame; remembered throughout time. 3 everlasting; perpetual; constant. 4 of or relating to immortal beings or concepts. ◆ NOUN 5 an immortal being. 6 (*often plural*) a person who is remembered enduringly, esp an author: *Dante is one of the immortals.*
▸ˌ**immor'tality** NOUN ▸**im'mortally** ADVERB

immortalize *or* **immortalise** (ɪ'mɔ:təˌlaɪz) VERB (*tr*) 1 to give everlasting fame to, as by treating in a literary work: *Macbeth was immortalized by Shakespeare.* 2 to give immortality to. 3 *Biology* to cause (cells) to reproduce indefinitely.
▸**imˌmortali'zation** *or* **imˌmortali'sation** NOUN
▸**im'mortalˌizer** *or* **im'mortalˌiser** NOUN

Immortals (ɪ'mɔ:tᵊlz) PLURAL NOUN 1 (*sometimes not capital*) the gods of ancient Greece and Rome. 2 (in ancient Persia) the royal bodyguard or a larger elite unit of 10 000 men. 3 the members of the French Academy.

immortelle (ˌɪmɔ:'tɛl) NOUN any of various plants, mostly of the family *Asteraceae* (composites), that retain their colour when dried, esp *Xeranthemum annuum.* Also called: **everlasting, everlasting flower.**
▷HISTORY C19: from French (*fleur*) *immortelle* everlasting (flower)

immotile (ɪ'məʊtaɪl) ADJECTIVE (esp of living organisms or their parts) not capable of moving spontaneously and independently.
▸**immotility** (ˌɪməʊ'tɪlɪtɪ) NOUN

immovable *or* **immoveable** (ɪ'mu:vəbᵊl) ADJECTIVE 1 unable to move or be moved; fixed; immobile. 2 unable to be diverted from one's intentions; steadfast. 3 unaffected by feeling; impassive. 4 unchanging; unalterable. 5 (of feasts, holidays, etc.) occurring on the same date every year. 6 *Law* **a** (of property) not liable to be removed; fixed. **b** of or relating to immoveables. Compare **movable.**
▸**imˌmova'bility, imˌmovea'bility** *or* **im'movableness, im'moveableness** NOUN ▸**im'movably** *or* **im'moveably** ADVERB

immoveables (ɪ'mu:vəbᵊlz) PLURAL NOUN (in most foreign legal systems) real property.

immune (ɪ'mju:n) ADJECTIVE 1 protected against a specific disease by inoculation or as the result of innate or acquired resistance. 2 relating to or conferring immunity: *an immune body.* See **antibody.** 3 (*usually postpositive;* foll by *to*) unsusceptible (to) or secure (against): *immune to inflation.* 4 exempt from obligation, penalty, etc. ◆ NOUN 5 an immune person or animal.
▷HISTORY C15: from Latin *immūnis* exempt from a public service, from IM- (not) + *mūnus* duty

immune complex *or* **immunocomplex** ('ɪmjʊnəʊˌkɒmplɛks) NOUN a complex formed between an antibody and an antigen.

immune response NOUN the reaction of an organism's body to foreign materials (antigens), including the production of antibodies.

immunity (ɪ'mju:nɪtɪ) NOUN, *plural* **-ties.** 1 the ability of an organism to resist disease, either through the activities of specialized blood cells or antibodies produced by them in response to natural exposure or inoculation (**active immunity**) or by the injection of antiserum or the transfer of antibodies from a mother to her baby via the placenta or breast milk (**passive immunity**). See also **acquired immunity, natural immunity.** 2 freedom from obligation or duty, esp exemption from tax, duty, legal liability, etc. 3 any special privilege granting immunity. 4 the exemption of ecclesiastical persons or property from various civil obligations or liabilities.

immunize *or* **immunise** ('ɪmjʊˌnaɪz) VERB to make immune, esp by inoculation.

▸ˌ**immuniˈzation** *or* ˌ**immuniˈsation** NOUN ▸ˈ**immuˌnizer** *or* ˈ**immuˌniser** NOUN

immuno- *or before a vowel* **immun-** COMBINING FORM indicating immunity or immune: *immunology*.

immunoassay (ˌɪmjʊnəʊˈæseɪ) NOUN *Immunol* a technique of identifying a substance by its ability to bind to an antibody.
▸ˌ**immunoˈassayist** NOUN

immunochemistry (ˌɪmjʊnəʊˈkɛmɪstrɪ) NOUN [1] the study of the chemical reactions of immunity. [2] a method for the detection and localization of proteins and other cellular components using antibodies that specifically label the materials.

immunocompetence (ˌɪmjʊnəʊˈkɒmpɪtəns) NOUN the capacity of the immune system to carry out its function of distinguishing alien from endogenous material; ability of the body to resist disease.

immunocompromised (ˌɪmjʊnəʊˈkɒmprəmaɪzd) ADJECTIVE having an impaired immune system and therefore incapable of an effective immune response, usually as a result of disease, such as AIDS, that damages the immune system.

immunocytochemistry (ˌɪmjʊnəʊˌsaɪtəʊˈkɛmɪstrɪ) NOUN the use of immunochemistry to study cells.

immunodeficiency (ˌɪmjʊnəʊdɪˈfɪʃənsɪ) NOUN a deficiency in or breakdown of a person's immune system.

immunoelectrophoresis (ˌɪmjʊnəʊɪˌlɛktrəʊfəˈriːsɪs) NOUN a technique for identifying the antigens in a blood serum, which are separated into fractions by electrophoresis.

immunofluorescence (ˌɪmjʊnəʊflʊəˈrɛsəns) NOUN a method used to determine the location of antibodies or antigens in which the antibodies or antigens are labelled with a fluorescent dye.

immunogen (ɪˈmjuːnəʊdʒən) NOUN [1] any substance that evokes an immune response. [2] any substance that stimulates immunity.

immunogenetics (ˌɪmjʊnəʊdʒɪˈnɛtɪks) NOUN (*functioning as singular*) the study of the relationship between immunity and genetics.
▸ˌ**immunogeˈnetic** *or* ˌ**immunogeˈnetical** ADJECTIVE

immunogenic (ˌɪmjʊnəʊˈdʒɛnɪk) ADJECTIVE causing or producing immunity or an immune response.
▸ˌ**immunoˈgenically** ADVERB

immunoglobulin (ˌɪmjʊnəʊˈglɒbjʊlɪn) NOUN any of five classes of proteins, all of which show antibody activity. The most abundant ones are **immunoglobulin G** (**IgG**) and **immunoglobulin A** (**IgA**).

immunohistochemistry (ˌɪmjʊnəʊˌhɪstəʊˈkɛmɪstrɪ) NOUN the use of immunochemistry to study tissues.

immunological tolerance NOUN the absence of antibody production in response to the presence of antigens, usually as a result of previous exposure to the antigens.

immunology (ˌɪmjʊˈnɒlədʒɪ) NOUN the branch of biological science concerned with the study of immunity.
▸**immunologic** (ˌɪmjʊnəˈlɒdʒɪk) *or* ˌ**immunoˈlogical** ADJECTIVE ▸ˌ**immunoˈlogically** ADVERB ▸ˌ**immuˈnologist** NOUN

immunoreaction (ɪˌmjuːnəʊrɪˈækʃən) NOUN the reaction between an antigen and its antibody.

immunosuppression (ˌɪmjʊnəʊsəˈprɛʃən) NOUN medical suppression of the body's immune system, esp in order to reduce the likelihood of rejection of a transplanted organ.

immunosuppressive (ˌɪmjʊnəʊsəˈprɛsɪv) NOUN [1] any drug used for immunosuppression. ◆ ADJECTIVE [2] of or relating to such a drug.
▸ˌ**immunosupˈpressant** NOUN, ADJECTIVE

immunotherapy (ˌɪmjʊnəʊˈθɛrəpɪ) NOUN *Med* the treatment of disease by stimulating the body's production of antibodies.
▸**immunotherapeutic** (ˌɪmjʊnəʊˌθɛrəˈpjuːtɪk) ADJECTIVE

immure (ɪˈmjʊə) VERB (*tr*) [1] *Archaic or literary* to enclose within or as if within walls; imprison. [2] to shut (oneself) away from society. [3] *Obsolete* to build into or enclose within a wall.
▷HISTORY C16: from Medieval Latin *immūrāre*, from Latin IM- (in) + *mūrus* a wall
▸**imˈmurement** NOUN

immutable (ɪˈmjuːtəbəl) ADJECTIVE unchanging through time; unalterable; ageless: *immutable laws*.
▸**imˌmutaˈbility** *or* **imˈmutableness** NOUN ▸**imˈmutably** ADVERB

IMNSHO *Text messaging* ABBREVIATION FOR in my not so humble opinion.

Imo (ˈiːməʊ) NOUN a state of SE Nigeria, formed in 1976 from part of East-Central State. Capital: Owerri. Pop.: 2 779 028 (1995 est.). Area: 5530 sq. km (2135 sq. miles).

IMO ◆ ABBREVIATION FOR: [1] *Text messaging* in my opinion. [2] International Maritime Organization.

imp (ɪmp) NOUN [1] a small demon or devil; mischievous sprite. [2] a mischievous child. ◆ VERB [3] (*tr*) *Falconry* to insert (new feathers) into the stumps of broken feathers in order to repair the wing of a hawk or falcon.
▷HISTORY Old English *impa* bud, graft, hence offspring, child, from *impian* to graft, ultimately from Greek *emphutos* implanted, from *emphuein* to implant, from *phuein* to plant

imp. ABBREVIATION FOR: [1] imperative. [2] imperfect. [3] imperial. [4] imprimatur.

Imp. ABBREVIATION FOR: [1] Imperator. [2] Imperatrix. [3] Imperial.
▷HISTORY (for sense 1) Latin: Emperor; (for sense 2) Latin: Empress

impact NOUN (ˈɪmpækt) [1] the act of one body, object, etc., striking another; collision. [2] the force with which one thing hits another or with which two objects collide. [3] the impression made by an idea, cultural movement, social group, etc.: *the impact of the Renaissance on Medieval Europe*. ◆ VERB (ɪmˈpækt) [4] to drive or press (an object) firmly into (another object, thing, etc.) or (of two objects) to be driven or pressed firmly together. [5] to have an impact or strong effect (on).
▷HISTORY C18: from Latin *impactus* pushed against, fastened on, from *impingere* to thrust at, from *pangere* to drive in
▸**imˈpaction** NOUN

impact adhesive NOUN a glue designed to give adhesion when two coated surfaces are pressed together.

impacted (ɪmˈpæktɪd) ADJECTIVE [1] (of a tooth) unable to erupt, esp because of being wedged against another tooth below the gum. [2] (of a fracture) having the jagged broken ends wedged into each other.

impactive (ɪmˈpæktɪv) ADJECTIVE [1] of or relating to a physical impact. [2] making a strong impression.

impact printer NOUN any printing device in which the printing surface strikes the paper, such as a traditional typewriter or a line printer. See also **non-impact printer.**

impair (ɪmˈpɛə) VERB (*tr*) to reduce or weaken in strength, quality, etc.: *his hearing was impaired by an accident*.
▷HISTORY C14: from Old French *empeirer* to make worse, from Late Latin *pējorāre*, from Latin *pejor* worse; see PEJORATIVE
▸**imˈpairable** ADJECTIVE ▸**imˈpairer** NOUN ▸**imˈpairment** NOUN

impala (ɪmˈpɑːlə) NOUN, *plural* **-las** *or* **-la**. an antelope, *Aepyceros melampus*, of southern and eastern Africa, having lyre-shaped horns and able to move with enormous leaps when disturbed.
▷HISTORY from Zulu

impale *or* **empale** (ɪmˈpeɪl) VERB (*tr*) [1] (often foll by *on, upon*, or *with*) to pierce with a sharp instrument: *they impaled his severed head on a spear*. [2] *Archaic* to enclose with pales or fencing; fence in. [3] *Heraldry* to charge (a shield) with two coats of arms placed side by side.
▷HISTORY C16: from Medieval Latin *impālāre*, from Latin IM- (in) + *pālus* PALE[2]
▸**imˈpalement** *or* **emˈpalement** NOUN ▸**imˈpaler** *or* **emˈpaler** NOUN

impalpable (ɪmˈpælpəbᵊl) ADJECTIVE [1] imperceptible, esp to the touch: *impalpable shadows*. [2] difficult to understand; abstruse.
▸**imˌpalpaˈbility** NOUN ▸**imˈpalpably** ADVERB

impanation (ˌɪmpæˈneɪʃən) NOUN *Christianity* the embodiment of Christ in the consecrated bread and wine of the Eucharist.
▷HISTORY C16: from Medieval Latin *impanātiō*, from *impanātus* embodied in bread, from Latin IM- (in) + *panis* bread

impanel (ɪmˈpænᵊl) VERB **-els, -elling, -elled** *or US* **-els, -eling, -eled.** a variant spelling (esp US) of **empanel.**
▸**imˈpanelment** NOUN

imparadise (ɪmˈpærədaɪs) VERB (*tr*) [1] to make blissfully happy; enrapture. [2] to make into or like paradise.

imparipinnate (ˌɪmpærɪˈpɪneɪt, -ˈpɪnɪt) ADJECTIVE (of pinnate leaves) having a terminal unpaired leaflet. Compare **paripinnate.**

imparisyllabic (ɪmˌpærsɪˈlæbɪk) ADJECTIVE (of a noun or verb in inflected languages) having inflected forms with different numbers of syllables. Compare **parisyllabic.**

imparity (ɪmˈpærɪtɪ) NOUN, *plural* **-ties**. a less common word for **disparity** (sense 1).
▷HISTORY C16: from Late Latin *imparitās*, from Latin *impar* unequal

impart (ɪmˈpɑːt) VERB (*tr*) [1] to communicate (information); relate. [2] to give or bestow (something, esp an abstract quality): *to impart wisdom*.
▷HISTORY C15: from Old French *impartir*, from Latin *impertīre*, from IM- (in) + *partīre* to share, from *pars* part
▸**imˈpartable** ADJECTIVE ▸ˌ**imparˈtation** *or* **imˈpartment** NOUN ▸**imˈparter** NOUN

impartial (ɪmˈpɑːʃəl) ADJECTIVE not prejudiced towards or against any particular side or party; fair; unbiased.
▸**imˌpartiˈality** *or* **imˈpartialness** NOUN ▸**imˈpartially** ADVERB

impartible (ɪmˈpɑːtəbᵊl) ADJECTIVE [1] *Law* (of land, an estate, etc.) incapable of partition; indivisible. [2] capable of being imparted.
▸**imˌpartiˈbility** NOUN ▸**imˈpartibly** ADVERB

impassable (ɪmˈpɑːsəbᵊl) ADJECTIVE (of terrain, roads, etc.) not able to be travelled through or over.
▸**imˌpassaˈbility** *or* **imˈpassableness** NOUN ▸**imˈpassably** ADVERB

impasse (æmˈpɑːs, ˈæmpɑːs, ɪmˈpɑːs, ˈɪmpɑːs) NOUN a situation in which progress is blocked; an insurmountable difficulty; stalemate; deadlock.
▷HISTORY C19: from French; see IM-, PASS

impassible (ɪmˈpæsəbᵊl) ADJECTIVE *Rare* [1] not susceptible to pain or injury. [2] impassive or unmoved.
▸**imˌpassiˈbility** *or* **imˈpassibleness** NOUN ▸**imˈpassibly** ADVERB

impassion (ɪmˈpæʃən) VERB (*tr*) to arouse the passions of; inflame.

impassioned (ɪmˈpæʃənd) ADJECTIVE filled with passion; fiery; inflamed: *an impassioned appeal*.
▸**imˈpassionedly** ADVERB ▸**imˈpassionedness** NOUN

impassive (ɪmˈpæsɪv) ADJECTIVE [1] not revealing or affected by emotion; reserved. [2] calm; serene; imperturbable. [3] *Rare* unconscious or insensible.
▸**imˈpassively** ADVERB ▸**imˈpassiveness** *or* **impassivity** (ˌɪmpæˈsɪvɪtɪ) NOUN

impaste (ɪmˈpeɪst) VERB (*tr*) to apply paint thickly to.
▷HISTORY C16: from Italian *impastare*, from *pasta* PASTE[1]
▸**impastation** (ˌɪmpæsˈteɪʃən) NOUN

impasto (ɪmˈpæstəʊ) NOUN [1] paint applied thickly, so that brush and palette knife marks are evident. [2] the technique of applying paint in this way.
▷HISTORY C18: from Italian, from *impastare*; see IMPASTE

impatience (ɪmˈpeɪʃəns) NOUN [1] lack of patience; intolerance of or irritability with anything that impedes or delays. [2] restless desire for change and excitement.

impatiens (ɪmˈpeɪʃɪˌɛnz) NOUN, *plural* **-ens**. any balsaminaceous plant of the genus *Impatiens*, such as balsam, touch-me-not, busy Lizzie, and policeman's helmet.
▷HISTORY C18: New Latin from Latin: impatient; from the fact that the ripe pods burst open when touched

impatient (ɪmˈpeɪʃənt) ADJECTIVE [1] lacking patience; easily irritated at delay, opposition, etc. [2] exhibiting lack of patience: *an impatient retort*. [3]

(*postpositive;* foll by *of*) intolerant (of) or indignant (at): *impatient of indecision.* 4 (*postpositive;* often foll by *for*) restlessly eager (for something or to do something).
▸**im'patiently** ADVERB

impeach (ɪm'piːtʃ) VERB (*tr*) 1 *Criminal law* to bring a charge or accusation against. 2 *Brit criminal law* to accuse of a crime, esp of treason or some other offence against the state. 3 *Chiefly US* to charge (a public official) with an offence committed in office. 4 to challenge or question (a person's honesty, integrity, etc.).
▷HISTORY C14: from Old French *empeechier,* from Late Latin *impedicāre* to entangle, catch, from Latin IM- (in) + *pedica* a fetter, from *pēs* foot
▸**im'peacher** NOUN

impeachable (ɪm'piːtʃəbᵊl) ADJECTIVE 1 capable of being impeached or accused. 2 (of an offence) making a person liable to impeachment.
▸**im,peacha'bility** NOUN

impeachment (ɪm'piːtʃmənt) NOUN 1 *Rare* (in England) committal by the House of Commons, esp of a minister of the Crown, for trial by the House of Lords. The last instance occurred in 1805. 2 (in the US) a proceeding brought against a federal government official. 3 an accusation or charge. 4 *Obsolete* discredit; reproach.

impearl (ɪm'pɜːl) VERB (*tr*) *Archaic or poetic* 1 to adorn with pearls. 2 to form into pearl-like shapes or drops.

impeccable (ɪm'pɛkəbᵊl) ADJECTIVE 1 without flaw or error; faultless: *an impeccable record.* 2 *Rare* incapable of sinning.
▷HISTORY C16: from Late Latin *impeccābilis* sinless, from Latin IM- (not) + *peccāre* to sin
▸**im,pecca'bility** NOUN ▸**im'peccably** ADVERB

impeccant (ɪm'pɛkənt) ADJECTIVE not sinning; free from sin.
▷HISTORY C18: from IM- (not) + Latin *peccant-,* from *peccāre* to sin
▸**im'peccancy** NOUN

impecunious (,ɪmpɪ'kjuːnɪəs) ADJECTIVE without money; penniless.
▷HISTORY C16: from IM- (not) + *-pecunious,* from Latin *pecūniōsus* wealthy, from *pecūnia* money
▸**,impe'cuniously** ADVERB ▸**,impe'cuniousness** *or* **impecuniosity** (,ɪmpɪkjuːnɪ'ɒsɪtɪ) NOUN

impedance (ɪm'piːdᵊns) NOUN 1 a measure of the opposition to the flow of an alternating current equal to the square root of the sum of the squares of the resistance and the reactance, expressed in ohms. Symbol: *Z.* 2 a component that offers impedance. 3 Also called: **acoustic impedance.** the ratio of the sound pressure in a medium to the rate of alternating flow of the medium through a specified surface due to the sound wave. Symbol: Z_a. 4 Also called: **mechanical impedance.** the ratio of the mechanical force, acting in the direction of motion, to the velocity of the resulting vibration. Symbol: Z_m.

impede (ɪm'piːd) VERB (*tr*) to restrict or retard in action, progress, etc.; hinder; obstruct.
▷HISTORY C17: from Latin *impedīre* to hinder, literally: shackle the feet, from *pēs* foot
▸**im'peder** NOUN ▸**im'pedingly** ADVERB

impediment (ɪm'pɛdɪmənt) NOUN 1 a hindrance or obstruction. 2 a physical defect, esp one of speech, such as a stammer. 3 (*plural* **-ments** *or* **-menta** (-'mɛntə)) *Law* an obstruction to the making of a contract, esp a contract of marriage by reason of closeness of blood or affinity.
▸**im,pedi'mental** *or* **im,pedi'mentary** ADJECTIVE

impedimenta (ɪm,pɛdɪ'mɛntə) PLURAL NOUN 1 the baggage and equipment carried by an army. 2 any objects or circumstances that impede progress. 3 a plural of **impediment** (sense 3).
▷HISTORY C16: from Latin, plural of *impedīmentum* hindrance; see IMPEDE

impedor (ɪm'piːdə) NOUN *Physics* a component, such as an inductor or resistor, that offers impedance.

impel (ɪm'pɛl) VERB **-pels, -pelling, -pelled.** (*tr*) 1 to urge or force (a person) to an action; constrain or motivate. 2 to push, drive, or force into motion.
▷HISTORY C15: from Latin *impellere* to push against, drive forward, from IM- (in) + *pellere* to drive, push, strike
▸**im'pellent** NOUN, ADJECTIVE

impeller (ɪm'pɛlə) NOUN 1 the vaned rotating disc of a centrifugal pump, compressor, etc. 2 a compressor or centrifugal pump having such an impeller.

impend (ɪm'pɛnd) VERB (*intr*) 1 (esp of something threatening) to be about to happen; be imminent. 2 (foll by *over*) *Rare* to be suspended; hang.
▷HISTORY C16: from Latin *impendēre* to overhang, from *pendēre* to hang
▸**im'pendence** *or* **im'pendency** NOUN

impending (ɪm'pɛndɪŋ) ADJECTIVE about to happen; imminent.

impenetrable (ɪm'pɛnɪtrəbᵊl) ADJECTIVE 1 incapable of being pierced through or penetrated: *an impenetrable forest.* 2 incapable of being understood; incomprehensible: *impenetrable jargon.* 3 incapable of being seen through: *impenetrable gloom.* 4 not susceptible to ideas, influence, etc.: *impenetrable ignorance.* 5 *Physics* (of a body) incapable of occupying the same space as another body.
▸**im,penetra'bility** *or* **im'penetrableness** NOUN
▸**im'penetrably** ADVERB

impenitent (ɪm'pɛnɪtənt) ADJECTIVE not sorry or penitent; unrepentant.
▸**im'penitence, im'penitency,** *or* **im'penitentness** NOUN
▸**im'penitently** ADVERB

impennate (ɪm'pɛneɪt) ADJECTIVE *Rare* (of birds) lacking true functional wings or feathers.

imperative (ɪm'pɛrətɪv) ADJECTIVE 1 extremely urgent or important; essential. 2 peremptory or authoritative: *an imperative tone of voice.* 3 Also: **imperatival** (ɪm,pɛrə'taɪvᵊl). *Grammar* denoting a mood of verbs used in giving orders, making requests, etc. In English the verb root without any inflections is the usual form, as for example *leave* in *Leave me alone.* ◆ NOUN 4 something that is urgent or essential. 5 an order or command. 6 *Grammar* **a** the imperative mood. **b** a verb in this mood.
▷HISTORY C16: from Late Latin *imperātīvus,* from Latin *imperāre* to command
▸**im'peratively** ADVERB ▸**im'perativeness** NOUN

imperator (,ɪmpə'rɑːtɔː) NOUN 1 **a** (in imperial Rome) a title of the emperor. **b** (in republican Rome) a temporary title of honour bestowed upon a victorious general. 2 a less common word for **emperor.**
▷HISTORY C16: from Latin: commander, from *imperāre* to command
▸**imperatorial** (ɪm,pɛrə'tɔːrɪəl) ADJECTIVE
▸**im,pera'torially** ADVERB ▸**,impe'rator,ship** NOUN

imperceptible (,ɪmpə'sɛptɪbᵊl) ADJECTIVE too slight, subtle, gradual, etc., to be perceived.
▸**,imper,cepti'bility** *or* **,imper'ceptibleness** NOUN
▸**,imper'ceptibly** ADVERB

imperceptive (,ɪmpə'sɛptɪv) ADJECTIVE *also* **impercipient** (,ɪmpə'sɪpɪənt). lacking in perception; obtuse.
▸**,imper'ception** NOUN ▸**,imper'ceptively** ADVERB
▸**,impercep'tivity, ,imper'ceptiveness,** *or* **,imper'cipience** NOUN

imperf. ABBREVIATION FOR: 1 Also: **impf.** imperfect. 2 (of stamps) imperforate.

imperfect (ɪm'pɜːfɪkt) ADJECTIVE 1 exhibiting or characterized by faults, mistakes, etc.; defective. 2 not complete or finished; deficient. 3 *Botany* **a** (of flowers) lacking functional stamens or pistils. **b** (of fungi) not undergoing sexual reproduction. 4 *Grammar* denoting a tense of verbs used most commonly in describing continuous or repeated past actions or events, as for example *was walking* as opposed to *walked.* 5 *Law* (of a trust, an obligation, etc.) lacking some necessary formality to make effective or binding; incomplete; legally unenforceable. See also **executory** (sense 1). 6 *Music* **a** (of a cadence) proceeding to the dominant from the tonic, subdominant, or any chord other than the dominant. **b** of or relating to all intervals other than the fourth, fifth, and octave. Compare **perfect** (sense 9). ◆ NOUN 7 *Grammar* **a** the imperfect tense. **b** a verb in this tense.
▸**im'perfectly** ADVERB ▸**im'perfectness** NOUN

imperfect competition NOUN *Economics* the market situation that exists when one or more of the necessary conditions for perfect competition do not hold.

imperfection (,ɪmpə'fɛkʃən) NOUN 1 the condition or quality of being imperfect. 2 a fault or defect.

imperfective (,ɪmpə'fɛktɪv) *Grammar* ◆ ADJECTIVE 1 denoting an aspect of the verb in some languages, including English, used to indicate that the action is in progress without regard to its completion. Compare **perfective.** ◆ NOUN 2 **a** the imperfective aspect of a verb. **b** a verb in this aspect.
▸**,imper'fectively** ADVERB

imperforate (ɪm'pɜːfərɪt, -,reɪt) ADJECTIVE 1 not perforated. 2 (of a postage stamp) not provided with perforation or any other means of separation. Abbreviation: **imperf.** Compare **perforate.** 3 *Anatomy* (of a bodily part, such as the anus) without the normal opening.
▸**im,perfo'ration** NOUN

imperia (ɪm'pɪərɪə) NOUN the plural of **imperium.**

imperial (ɪm'pɪərɪəl) ADJECTIVE 1 of or relating to an empire, emperor, or empress. 2 characteristic of or befitting an emperor; majestic; commanding. 3 characteristic of or exercising supreme authority; imperious. 4 (esp of products and commodities) of a superior size or quality. 5 (*usually prenominal*) (of weights, measures, etc.) conforming to standards or definitions legally established in Britain: *an imperial gallon.* ◆ NOUN 6 any of various book sizes, esp 7½ by 11 inches (**imperial octavo**) or (chiefly Brit.) 11 by 15 inches (**imperial quarto**). 7 a size of writing or printing paper, 23 by 31 inches (US and Canadian) or 22 by 30 inches (Brit.). 8 (formerly) a Russian gold coin originally worth ten roubles. 9 *US* **a** the top of a carriage, such as a diligence. **b** a luggage case carried there. 10 *Architect* a dome that has a point at the top. 11 a small tufted beard popularized by the emperor Napoleon III. 12 a member of an imperial family, esp an emperor or empress. 13 a red deer having antlers with fourteen points.
▷HISTORY C14: from Late Latin *imperiālis,* from Latin *imperium* command, authority, empire
▸**im'perially** ADVERB ▸**im'perialness** NOUN

Imperial (ɪm'pɪərɪəl) ADJECTIVE 1 (*sometimes not capital*) of or relating to a specified empire, such as the British Empire. ◆ NOUN 2 a supporter or soldier of the Holy Roman Empire.

imperial gallon NOUN a formal name for **gallon** (sense 1).

imperialism (ɪm'pɪərɪə,lɪzəm) NOUN 1 the policy or practice of extending a state's rule over other territories. 2 an instance or policy of aggressive behaviour by one state against another. 3 the extension or attempted extension of authority, influence, power, etc., by any person, country, institution, etc.: *cultural imperialism.* 4 a system of imperial government or rule by an emperor. 5 the spirit, character, authority, etc., of an empire. 6 advocacy of or support for any form of imperialism.
▸**im'perialist** ADJECTIVE, NOUN ▸**im,perial'istic** ADJECTIVE
▸**im,perial'istically** ADVERB

Imperial War Museum NOUN a museum in London, founded in 1920, containing material related to military operations involving British and Commonwealth forces since 1914.

imperil (ɪm'pɛrɪl) VERB **-rils, -rilling, -rilled** *or US* **-rils, -riling, -riled** (*tr*) to place in danger or jeopardy; endanger.
▸**im'perilment** NOUN

imperious (ɪm'pɪərɪəs) ADJECTIVE 1 domineering; arrogant; overbearing. 2 *Rare* urgent; imperative.
▷HISTORY C16: from Latin *imperiōsus* from *imperium* command, power
▸**im'periously** ADVERB ▸**im'periousness** NOUN

imperishable (ɪm'pɛrɪʃəbᵊl) ADJECTIVE 1 not subject to decay or deterioration: *imperishable goods.* 2 not likely to be forgotten: *imperishable truths.*
▸**im,perisha'bility** *or* **im'perishableness** NOUN
▸**im'perishably** ADVERB

imperium (ɪm'pɪərɪəm) NOUN, *plural* **-ria** (-rɪə). 1 (in ancient Rome) the supreme power, held esp by consuls and emperors, to command and administer in military, judicial, and civil affairs. 2 the right to command; supreme power. 3 a less common word for **empire.**
▷HISTORY C17: from Latin: command, empire, from *imperāre* to command; see EMPEROR

impermanent (ɪm'pɜːmənənt) ADJECTIVE not permanent; fleeting; transitory.

▸**im'permanence** *or* **im'permanency** NOUN
▸**im'permanently** ADVERB

impermeable (ɪm'pɜːmɪəbᵊl) ADJECTIVE (of a substance) not allowing the passage of a fluid through interstices; not permeable.
▸**im,permea'bility** *or* **im'permeableness** NOUN
▸**im'permeably** ADVERB

impermissible (,ɪmpə'mɪsɪbᵊl) ADJECTIVE not permissible; not allowed.
▸**,imper,missi'bility** NOUN ▸**,imper'missibly** ADVERB

imperscriptible (,ɪmpə'skrɪptɪbᵊl) ADJECTIVE not supported by written authority.
▷HISTORY C19: from IM- (not) + Latin *perscribere* to write down

impersonal (ɪm'pɜːsənᵊl) ADJECTIVE [1] without reference to any individual person; objective: *an impersonal assessment.* [2] devoid of human warmth or sympathy; cold: *an impersonal manner.* [3] not having human characteristics: *an impersonal God.* [4] *Grammar* (of a verb) having no logical subject. Usually in English the pronoun *it* is used in such cases as a grammatical subject, as for example in *It is raining.* [5] *Grammar* (of a pronoun) not denoting a person.
▸**im,person'ality** NOUN ▸**im'personally** ADVERB

impersonalize *or* **impersonalise** (ɪm'pɜːsənə,laɪz) VERB (*tr*) to make impersonal, esp to rid of such human characteristics as sympathy, warmth, etc.; dehumanize.
▸**im,personali'zation** *or* **im,personali'sation** NOUN

impersonate (ɪm'pɜːsə,neɪt) VERB (*tr*) [1] to pretend to be (another person). [2] to imitate the character, mannerisms, etc., of (another person). [3] *Rare* to play the part or character of. [4] an archaic word for **personify.**
▸**im,person'ation** NOUN ▸**im'person,ator** NOUN

impertinence (ɪm'pɜːtɪnəns) *or* **impertinency** NOUN [1] disrespectful behaviour or language; rudeness; insolence. [2] an impertinent act, gesture, etc. [3] *Rare* lack of pertinence; irrelevance; inappropriateness.

impertinent (ɪm'pɜːtɪnənt) ADJECTIVE [1] rude; insolent; impudent. [2] irrelevant or inappropriate.
▷HISTORY C14: from Latin *impertinēns* not belonging, from Latin IM- (not) + *pertinēre* to be relevant; see PERTAIN
▸**im'pertinently** ADVERB

imperturbable (,ɪmpɜː'tɜːbəbᵊl) ADJECTIVE not easily perturbed; calm; unruffled.
▸**,imper,turba'bility** *or* **,imper'turbableness** NOUN
▸**,imper'turbably** ADVERB ▸**imperturbation** (,ɪmpɜːtɜː'beɪʃən) NOUN

impervious (ɪm'pɜːvɪəs) *or* **imperviable** ADJECTIVE [1] not able to be penetrated, as by water, light, etc.; impermeable. [2] (*often postpositive;* foll by *to*) not able to be influenced (by) or not receptive (to): *impervious to argument.*
▸**im'perviously** ADVERB ▸**im'perviousness** NOUN

impetigo (,ɪmpɪ'taɪgəʊ) NOUN a contagious bacterial skin disease characterized by the formation of pustules that develop into yellowish crusty sores.
▷HISTORY C16: from Latin: scabby eruption, from *impetere* to assail; see IMPETUS; for form, compare VERTIGO
▸**impetiginous** (,ɪmpɪ'tɪdʒɪnəs) ADJECTIVE

impetrate ('ɪmpɪ,treɪt) VERB (*tr*) [1] to supplicate or entreat for, esp by prayer. [2] to obtain by prayer.
▷HISTORY C16: from Latin *impetrāre* to procure by entreaty, from -*petrāre*, from *patrāre* to bring to pass, of uncertain origin; perhaps related to Latin *pater* a father
▸**,impe'tration** NOUN ▸**'impetrative** ADJECTIVE
▸**'impe,trator** NOUN

impetuous (ɪm'pɛtjʊəs) ADJECTIVE [1] liable to act without consideration; rash; impulsive. [2] resulting from or characterized by rashness or haste. [3] *Poetic* moving with great force or violence; rushing: *the impetuous stream hurtled down the valley.*
▷HISTORY C14: from Late Latin *impetuōsus* violent; see IMPETUS
▸**im'petuously** ADVERB ▸**im'petuousness** *or* **impetuosity** (ɪm,pɛtjʊ'ɒsɪtɪ) NOUN

impetus ('ɪmpɪtəs) NOUN, *plural* **-tuses.** [1] an impelling movement or force; incentive or impulse; stimulus. [2] *Physics* the force that sets a body in motion or that tends to resist changes in a body's motion.
▷HISTORY C17: from Latin: attack, from *impetere* to assail, from IM- (in) + *petere* to make for, seek out

imp. gal. *or* **imp. gall.** ABBREVIATION FOR imperial gallon.

Imphal (ɪm'fɑːl, 'ɪmfəl) NOUN a city in NE India, capital of Manipur Territory, on the Manipur River: formerly the seat of the Manipur kings: site of a major Anglo-Indian victory over the Japanese (1944), which was a turning point in the British recovery of Burma (now called Myanmar). Pop.: 198 535 (1991).

impi ('ɪmpɪ) NOUN, *plural* **-pi** *or* **-pies.** a group of Bantu warriors.
▷HISTORY C19: Nguni: regiment, army

impiety (ɪm'paɪɪtɪ) NOUN, *plural* **-ties.** [1] lack of reverence or proper respect for a god. [2] any lack of proper respect. [3] an impious act.

impinge (ɪm'pɪndʒ) VERB [1] (*intr;* usually foll by *on* or *upon*) to encroach or infringe; trespass: *to impinge on someone's time.* [2] (*intr;* usually foll by *on, against,* or *upon*) to collide (with); strike.
▷HISTORY C16: from Latin *impingere* to drive at, dash against, from *pangere* to fasten, drive in
▸**im'pingement** NOUN ▸**im'pinger** NOUN

impingement attack NOUN *Metallurgy* a form of corrosion of metals caused by erosion of the oxide layer by a moving fluid in which there are suspended particles or air bubbles.

impious ('ɪmpɪəs) ADJECTIVE [1] lacking piety or reverence for a god; ungodly. [2] lacking respect; undutiful.
▸**'impiously** ADVERB ▸**'impiousness** NOUN

impish ('ɪmpɪʃ) ADJECTIVE of or resembling an imp; mischievous.
▸**'impishly** ADVERB ▸**'impishness** NOUN

implacable (ɪm'plækəbᵊl) ADJECTIVE [1] incapable of being placated or pacified; unappeasable. [2] inflexible; intractable.
▸**im,placa'bility** *or* **im'placableness** NOUN ▸**im'placably** ADVERB

implacental (,ɪmplə'sɛntᵊl) ADJECTIVE another word for **aplacental.**

implant VERB (ɪm'plɑːnt) (*tr*) [1] to establish firmly; inculcate; instil: *to implant sound moral principles.* [2] to plant or embed; infix; entrench. [3] *Surgery* **a** to graft (a tissue) into the body. **b** to insert (a radioactive substance, hormone, etc.) into the tissues. ◆ NOUN ('ɪm,plɑːnt) [4] anything implanted, esp surgically, such as a tissue graft or hormone.
▸**im'planter** NOUN

implantation (,ɪmplɑːn'teɪʃən) NOUN [1] the act of implanting or the state of being implanted. [2] Also called: **nidation.** the attachment of the blastocyst of a mammalian embryo to the wall of the uterus of the mother.

implausible (ɪm'plɔːzəbᵊl) ADJECTIVE not plausible; provoking disbelief; unlikely.
▸**im,plausi'bility** *or* **im'plausibleness** NOUN ▸**im'plausibly** ADVERB

implead (ɪm'pliːd) VERB (*tr*) *Law, rare* [1] **a** to sue or prosecute. **b** to bring an action against. [2] to accuse.
▷HISTORY C13: from Anglo-French *empleder;* see IM-, PLEAD
▸**im'pleadable** ADJECTIVE ▸**im'pleader** NOUN

implement NOUN ('ɪmplɪmənt) [1] a piece of equipment; tool or utensil: *gardening implements.* [2] something used to achieve a purpose; agent. ◆ VERB ('ɪmplɪ,mɛnt) (*tr*) [3] to carry out; put into action; perform: *to implement a plan.* [4] *Archaic* to complete, satisfy, or fulfil.
▷HISTORY C17: from Late Latin *implēmentum,* literally: a filling up, from Latin *implēre* to fill up, satisfy, fulfil
▸**,imple'mental** ADJECTIVE ▸**,implemen'tation** NOUN
▸**'imple,menter** *or* **'imple,mentor** NOUN

implicate ('ɪmplɪ,keɪt) VERB (*tr*) [1] to show to be involved, esp in a crime. [2] to involve as a necessary inference; imply: *his protest implicated censure by the authorities.* [3] to affect intimately: *this news implicates my decision.* [4] *Rare* to intertwine or entangle.
▷HISTORY C16: from Latin *implicāre* to involve, from IM- + *plicāre* to fold
▸**implicative** (ɪm'plɪkətɪv) ADJECTIVE ▸**im'plicatively** ADVERB

implication (,ɪmplɪ'keɪʃən) NOUN [1] the act of implicating or the state of being implicated. [2] something that is implied; suggestion: *the implication of your silence is that you're bored.* [3] *Logic* **a** the operator that forms a sentence from two given sentences and corresponds to the English *if* … then …. **b** a sentence so formed. Usually written p→q or p⊃q, where p,q are the component sentences, it is true except when p (the antecedent) is true and q (the consequent) is false. **c** the relation between such sentences.
▸**,impli'cational** ADJECTIVE

implicature (ɪm'plɪkətʃə) NOUN *Logic, philosophy* [1] a proposition inferred from the circumstances of utterances of another proposition rather than from its literal meaning, as when an academic referee writes *the candidate's handwriting is excellent* to convey that he has nothing relevant to commend. [2] the relation between the uttered and the inferred statement.

implicit (ɪm'plɪsɪt) ADJECTIVE [1] not explicit; implied; indirect: *there was implicit criticism in his voice.* [2] absolute and unreserved; unquestioning: *you have implicit trust in him.* [3] (*when postpositive,* foll by *in*) contained or inherent: *to bring out the anger implicit in the argument.* [4] *Maths* (of a function) having an equation of the form $f(x,y) = 0$, in which y cannot be directly expressed in terms of x, as in $xy + x^2 + y^3x^2 = 0$. Compare **explicit**[1] (sense 4). [5] *Obsolete* intertwined.
▷HISTORY C16: from Latin *implicitus,* variant of *implicātus* interwoven; see IMPLICATE
▸**im'plicitly** ADVERB ▸**im'plicitness** *or* **im'plicity** NOUN

implied (ɪm'plaɪd) ADJECTIVE hinted at or suggested; not directly expressed: *an implied criticism.*
▸**impliedly** (ɪm'plaɪɪdlɪ) ADVERB

implode (ɪm'pləʊd) VERB [1] to collapse or cause to collapse inwards in a violent manner as a result of external pressure: *the vacuum flask imploded.* [2] (*tr*) to pronounce (a consonant) with or by implosion. ◆ Compare **explode.**
▷HISTORY C19: from IM- + (EX)PLODE

implore (ɪm'plɔː) VERB (*tr*) [1] to beg or ask (someone) earnestly (to do something); plead with; beseech. [2] to ask earnestly or piteously for; supplicate; beg: *to implore someone's mercy.*
▷HISTORY C16: from Latin *implōrāre,* from IM- + *plōrāre* to bewail
▸**,implo'ration** NOUN ▸**im'ploratory** ADJECTIVE ▸**im'plorer** NOUN ▸**im'ploringly** ADVERB

implosion (ɪm'pləʊʒən) NOUN [1] the act or process of imploding: *the implosion of a light bulb.* [2] *Phonetics* the suction or inhalation of breath employed in the pronunciation of an ingressive consonant.

implosive (ɪm'pləʊsɪv) ADJECTIVE [1] pronounced by or with implosion. ◆ NOUN [2] an implosive consonant.
▸**im'plosively** ADVERB

imply (ɪm'plaɪ) VERB **-plies, -plying, -plied.** (*tr; may take a clause as object*) [1] to express or indicate by a hint; suggest: *what are you implying by that remark?* [2] to suggest or involve as a necessary consequence. [3] *Logic* to enable (a conclusion) to be inferred. [4] *Obsolete* to entangle or enfold.
▷HISTORY C14: from Old French *emplier,* from Latin *implicāre* to involve; see IMPLICATE

> **Language note** See at **infer.**

impolder (ɪm'pəʊldə) *or* **empolder** VERB *Rare* to make into a polder; reclaim (land) from the sea.
▷HISTORY C19: from Dutch *inpolderen,* see IN-[2], POLDER

impolicy (ɪm'pɒlɪsɪ) NOUN, *plural* **-cies.** the act or an instance of being unjudicious or impolitic.

impolite (,ɪmpə'laɪt) ADJECTIVE discourteous; rude; uncivil.
▸**,impo'litely** ADVERB ▸**,impo'liteness** NOUN

impolitic (ɪm'pɒlɪtɪk) ADJECTIVE not politic or expedient; unwise.
▸**im'politicly** ADVERB ▸**im'politicness** NOUN

imponderabilia (ɪm,pɒndərə'bɪlɪə) PLURAL NOUN imponderables.
▷HISTORY C20: New Latin

imponderable (ɪm'pɒndərəbᵊl, -drəbᵊl) ADJECTIVE [1] unable to be weighed or assessed. ◆ NOUN [2] something difficult or impossible to assess.

▸im,pondera'bility *or* im'ponderableness NOUN
▸im'ponderably ADVERB

imponent (ɪm'pəʊnənt) NOUN a person who imposes a duty, etc.

import VERB (ɪm'pɔ:t, 'ɪmpɔ:t) [1] to buy or bring in (goods or services) from a foreign country. Compare **export**. [2] *(tr)* to bring in from an outside source: *to import foreign words into the language.* [3] *Rare* to signify or be significant; mean; convey: *to import doom.* ◆ NOUN ('ɪmpɔ:t) [4] *(often plural)* **a** goods (**visible imports**) or services (**invisible imports**) that are bought from foreign countries. **b** *(as modifier)*: *an import licence.* [5] significance or importance: *a man of great import.* [6] meaning or signification. [7] *Canadian informal* a sportsman or -woman who is not native to the country in which he or she plays.
▷HISTORY C15: from Latin *importāre* to carry in, from IM- + *portāre* to carry
▸im'portable ADJECTIVE ▸im,porta'bility NOUN ▸im'porter NOUN

importance (ɪm'pɔ:tᵊns) NOUN [1] the state of being important; significance. [2] social status; standing; esteem: *a man of importance.* [3] *Obsolete* **a** meaning or signification. **b** an important matter. **c** importunity.

important (ɪm'pɔ:tᵊnt) ADJECTIVE [1] of great significance or value; outstanding: *Voltaire is an important writer.* [2] of social significance; notable; eminent; esteemed: *an important man in the town.* [3] *(when postpositive,* usually foll by *to)* specially relevant or of great concern (to); valued highly (by): *your wishes are important to me.* [4] an obsolete word for **importunate**.
▷HISTORY C16: from Old Italian *importante,* from Medieval Latin *importāre* to signify, be of consequence, from Latin: to carry in; see IMPORT
▸im'portantly ADVERB

> **Language note** The use of *more importantly* as in *more importantly, the local council is opposed to this proposal* has become very common, but many people still prefer to use *more important.*

importation (,ɪmpɔ:'teɪʃən) NOUN [1] the act, business, or process of importing goods or services. [2] an imported product or service.

importunate (ɪm'pɔ:tjʊnɪt) ADJECTIVE [1] persistent or demanding; insistent. [2] *Rare* troublesome; annoying.
▸im'portunately ADVERB ▸im'portunateness NOUN

importune (ɪm'pɔ:tju:n) VERB *(tr)* [1] to harass with persistent requests; demand of (someone) insistently. [2] to beg for persistently; request with insistence. [3] *Obsolete* **a** to anger or annoy. **b** to force; impel.
▷HISTORY C16: from Latin *importūnus* tiresome, from *im-* IN-[1] + *-portūnus* as in *opportūnus* OPPORTUNE
▸im'portuner NOUN ▸,impor'tunity *or* im'portunacy NOUN

impose (ɪm'pəʊz) VERB (usually foll by *on* or *upon*) [1] *(tr)* to establish as something to be obeyed or complied with; enforce: *to impose a tax on the people.* [2] to force (oneself, one's presence, etc.) on another or others; obtrude. [3] *(intr)* to take advantage, as of a person or quality: *to impose on someone's kindness.* [4] *(tr) Printing* to arrange pages so that after printing and folding the pages will be in the correct order. [5] *(tr)* to pass off deceptively; foist: *to impose a hoax on someone.* [6] *(tr)* (of a bishop or priest) to lay (the hands) on the head of a candidate for certain sacraments.
▷HISTORY C15: from Old French *imposer,* from Latin *impōnere* to place upon, from *pōnere* to place, set
▸im'posable ADJECTIVE ▸im'poser NOUN

imposing (ɪm'pəʊzɪŋ) ADJECTIVE grand or impressive: *an imposing building.*
▸im'posingly ADVERB ▸im'posingness NOUN

imposing stone *or* **table** NOUN *Printing* a flat hard surface upon which pages printed from hot metal are imposed.

imposition (,ɪmpə'zɪʃən) NOUN [1] the act of imposing. [2] something that is imposed unfairly on someone. [3] (in Britain) a task set as a school punishment. [4] the arrangement of pages for printing so that the finished work will have its pages in the correct order.

impossibility (ɪm,pɒsə'bɪlɪtɪ, ,ɪmpɒs-) NOUN, *plural* **-ties.** [1] the state or quality of being impossible. [2] something that is impossible.

impossible (ɪm'pɒsəbᵊl) ADJECTIVE [1] incapable of being done, undertaken, or experienced. [2] incapable of occurring or happening. [3] absurd or inconceivable; unreasonable: *it's impossible to think of him as a bishop.* [4] *Informal* intolerable; outrageous: *those children are impossible.*
▸im'possibleness NOUN ▸im'possibly ADVERB

impossible figure NOUN a picture of an object that at first sight looks three-dimensional but cannot be a two-dimensional projection of a real three-dimensional object, for example a picture of a staircase that re-enters itself while appearing to ascend continuously. Also called: **Escher figure**.

impost¹ ('ɪmpəʊst) NOUN [1] a tax, esp a customs duty. [2] *Horse racing* the specific weight that a particular horse must carry in a handicap race. ◆ VERB [3] *(tr) US* to classify (imported goods) according to the duty payable on them.
▷HISTORY C16: from Medieval Latin *impostus* tax, from Latin *impositus* imposed; see IMPOSE
▸'imposter NOUN

impost² ('ɪmpəʊst) NOUN *Architect* a member at the top of a wall, pier, or column that supports an arch, esp one that has a projecting moulding.
▷HISTORY C17: from French *imposte,* from Latin *impositus* placed upon; see IMPOSE

impostor *or* **imposter** (ɪm'pɒstə) NOUN a person who deceives others, esp by assuming a false identity; charlatan.
▷HISTORY C16: from Late Latin: deceiver; see IMPOSE

impostume (ɪm'pɒstju:m) *or* **imposthume** (ɪm'pɒsθu:m) NOUN an archaic word for **abscess**.
▷HISTORY C15: from Old French *empostume,* from Late Latin *apostēma,* from Greek, literally: separation (of pus), from *aphistanai* to remove, from *histanai* to stand

imposture (ɪm'pɒstʃə) NOUN the act or an instance of deceiving others, esp by assuming a false identity.
▷HISTORY C16: from French, from Late Latin *impostūra,* from Latin *impōnere;* see IMPOSE
▸impostrous (ɪm'pɒstrəs), impostorous (ɪm'pɒstərəs), *or* im'posturous ADJECTIVE

impotent ('ɪmpətənt) ADJECTIVE [1] *(when postpositive, often takes an infinitive)* lacking sufficient strength; powerless. [2] (esp of males) unable to perform sexual intercourse. See **erectile impotence.** [3] *Obsolete* lacking self-control; unrestrained.
▸'impotence, 'impotency, *or* 'impotentness NOUN
▸'impotently ADVERB

impound (ɪm'paʊnd) VERB *(tr)* [1] to confine (stray animals, illegally parked cars, etc.) in a pound. [2] **a** to seize (chattels, etc.) by legal right. **b** to take possession of (a document, evidence, etc.) and hold in legal custody. [3] to collect (water) in a reservoir or dam, as for irrigation. [4] to seize or appropriate.
▸im'poundable ADJECTIVE ▸im'poundage *or* im'poundment NOUN ▸im'pounder NOUN

impoverish (ɪm'pɒvərɪʃ) VERB *(tr)* [1] to make poor or diminish the quality of: *to impoverish society by cutting the grant to the arts.* [2] to deprive (soil, etc.) of fertility.
▷HISTORY C15: from Old French *empovrir,* from *povre* POOR
▸im'poverisher NOUN ▸im'poverishment NOUN

impower (ɪm'paʊə) VERB a less common spelling of **empower.**

impracticable (ɪm'præktɪkəbᵊl) ADJECTIVE [1] incapable of being put into practice or accomplished; not feasible. [2] unsuitable for a desired use; unfit. [3] an archaic word for **intractable.**
▸im,practica'bility *or* im'practicableness NOUN
▸im'practicably ADVERB

impractical (ɪm'præktɪkᵊl) ADJECTIVE [1] not practical or workable: *an impractical solution.* [2] not given to practical matters or gifted with practical skills: *he is intelligent but too impractical for commercial work.*
▸im,practi'cality *or* im'practicalness NOUN
▸im'practically ADVERB

imprecate ('ɪmprɪ,keɪt) VERB [1] *(intr)* to swear, curse, or blaspheme. [2] *(tr)* to invoke or bring down (evil, a curse, etc.): *to imprecate disaster on the ship.* [3] *(tr)* to put a curse on.
▷HISTORY C17: from Latin *imprecārī* to invoke, from *im-* IN-[2] + *precārī* to PRAY
▸'impre,catory ADJECTIVE

imprecation (,ɪmprɪ'keɪʃən) NOUN [1] the act of imprecating. [2] a malediction; curse.

imprecise (,ɪmprɪ'saɪs) ADJECTIVE not precise; inexact or inaccurate.
▸,impre'cisely ADVERB ▸imprecision (,ɪmprɪ'sɪʒən) *or* ,impre'ciseness NOUN

impredicative (,ɪmprə'dɪkətɪv) ADJECTIVE *Logic* (of a definition) given in terms that require quantification over a range that includes that which is to be defined, as *having all the properties of a great general* where one of the properties as ascribed must be that property itself. Compare **predicative** (sense 2).

impregnable¹ (ɪm'prɛgnəbᵊl) ADJECTIVE [1] unable to be broken into or taken by force: *an impregnable castle.* [2] unable to be shaken or overcome: *impregnable self-confidence.* [3] incapable of being refuted: *an impregnable argument.*
▷HISTORY C15 *imprenable,* from Old French, from IM- (not) + *prenable* able to be taken, from *prendre* to take
▸im,pregna'bility *or* im'pregnableness NOUN
▸im'pregnably ADVERB

impregnable² (ɪm'prɛgnəbᵊl) *or* **impregnatable** (,ɪmprɛg'neɪtəbᵊl) ADJECTIVE able to be impregnated; fertile.

impregnate VERB ('ɪmprɛg,neɪt) *(tr)* [1] to saturate, soak, or infuse: *to impregnate a cloth with detergent.* [2] to imbue or permeate; pervade. [3] to cause to conceive; make pregnant. [4] to fertilize (an ovum). [5] to make (land, soil, etc.) fruitful. ◆ ADJECTIVE (ɪm'prɛgnɪt, -,neɪt) [6] pregnant or fertilized.
▷HISTORY C17: from Late Latin *impraegnāre* to make pregnant, from Latin *im-* IN-[2] + *praegnans* PREGNANT
▸,impreg'nation NOUN ▸im'pregnator NOUN

impresa (ɪm'preɪzə) *or* **imprese** (ɪm'pri:z) NOUN an emblem or device, usually a motto, as on a coat of arms.
▷HISTORY C16: from Italian, literally: undertaking, hence deed of chivalry, motto, from *imprendere* to undertake; see EMPRISE

impresario (,ɪmprə'sɑ:rɪ,əʊ) NOUN, *plural* **-sarios.** [1] a producer or sponsor of public entertainments, esp musical or theatrical ones. [2] the director or manager of an opera, ballet, or other performing company.
▷HISTORY C18: from Italian, literally: one who undertakes; see IMPRESA

imprescriptible (,ɪmprɪ'skrɪptəbᵊl) ADJECTIVE *Law* immune or exempt from prescription.
▸,impre,scripti'bility NOUN ▸,impre'scriptibly ADVERB

impress¹ VERB (ɪm'prɛs) *(tr)* [1] to make an impression on; have a strong, lasting, or favourable effect on: *I am impressed by your work.* [2] to produce (an imprint, etc.) by pressure in or on (something): *to impress a seal in wax; to impress wax with a seal.* [3] (often foll by *on*) to stress (something to a person); urge; emphasize: *to impress the danger of a situation on someone.* [4] to exert pressure on; press. [5] *Electronics* to apply (a voltage) to a circuit or device. ◆ NOUN ('ɪmprɛs) [6] the act or an instance of impressing. [7] a mark, imprint, or effect produced by impressing.
▷HISTORY C14: from Latin *imprimere* to press into, imprint, from *premere* to PRESS[1]
▸im'presser NOUN ▸im'pressible ADJECTIVE

impress² VERB (ɪm'prɛs) [1] to commandeer or coerce (men or things) into government service; press-gang. ◆ NOUN ('ɪmprɛs) [2] the act of commandeering or coercing into government service; impressment.
▷HISTORY C16: see *im-* IN-[2], PRESS[2]

impression (ɪm'prɛʃən) NOUN [1] an effect produced in the mind by a stimulus; sensation: *he gave the impression of wanting to help.* [2] an imprint or mark produced by pressing: *he left the impression of his finger in the mud.* [3] a vague idea, consciousness, or belief: *I had the impression we had met before.* [4] a strong, favourable, or remarkable effect: *he made an impression on the managers.* [5] the act of impressing or the state of being impressed. [6] *Printing* **a** the act, process, or result of printing from type, plates, etc. **b** one of a number of printings of a publication printed from the same setting of type with no or few alterations. Compare **edition** (sense 2). **c** the total number of copies of a publication printed at one time. [7] *Dentistry* an imprint of the teeth and gums, esp in wax or plaster, for use in

preparing crowns, inlays, or dentures. 8 an imitation or impersonation: *he did a funny impression of the politician.*
▸**im'pressional** ADJECTIVE ▸**im'pressionally** ADVERB

impressionable (ɪm'prɛʃənəbᵊl, -'prɛʃnə-) ADJECTIVE easily influenced or characterized by susceptibility to influence: *an impressionable child; an impressionable age.*
▸**im,pressiona'bility** *or* **im'pressionableness** NOUN

impressionism (ɪm'prɛʃə,nɪzəm) NOUN 1 *(often capital)* a movement in French painting, developed in the 1870s chiefly by Monet, Renoir, Pissarro, and Sisley, having the aim of objectively recording experience by a system of fleeting impressions, esp of natural light effects. 2 the technique in art, literature, or music of conveying experience by capturing fleeting impressions of reality or of mood.

impressionist (ɪm'prɛʃənɪst) NOUN 1 *(usually capital)* any of the French painters of the late 19th century who were exponents of impressionism. 2 *(sometimes capital)* any artist, composer, or writer who uses impressionism. 3 an entertainer who impersonates famous people. ◆ ADJECTIVE 4 *(often capital)* denoting, of, or relating to impressionism or the exponents of this style.
▸**im,pression'istic** ADJECTIVE

impressive (ɪm'prɛsɪv) ADJECTIVE capable of impressing, esp by size, magnificence, etc.; awe-inspiring; commanding.
▸**im'pressively** ADVERB ▸**im'pressiveness** NOUN

impressment (ɪm'prɛsmənt) NOUN the commandeering or conscription of things or men into government service.

impressure (ɪm'prɛʃə) NOUN an archaic word for **impression.**
▷HISTORY C17: see IMPRESS[1], -URE; formed on the model of PRESSURE

imprest (ɪm'prɛst) NOUN 1 a fund of cash from which a department or other unit pays incidental expenses, topped up periodically from central funds. 2 *Chiefly Brit* an advance from government funds for the performance of some public business or service. 3 *Brit* (formerly) an advance payment of wages to a sailor or soldier.
▷HISTORY C16: probably from Italian *imprestare* to lend, from Latin *in-* towards + *praestāre* to pay, from *praestō* at hand; see PRESTO

imprimatur (,ɪmprɪ'meɪtə, -'mɑː-) NOUN 1 *RC Church* a licence granted by a bishop certifying the Church's approval of a book to be published. 2 sanction, authority, or approval, esp for something to be printed.
▷HISTORY C17: New Latin, literally: let it be printed

imprimis (ɪm'praɪmɪs) ADVERB *Archaic* in the first place.
▷HISTORY C15: from Latin phrase *in prīmīs*, literally: among the first things

imprint NOUN ('ɪmprɪnt) 1 a mark or impression produced by pressure, printing, or stamping. 2 a characteristic mark or indication; stamp: *the imprint of great sadness on his face.* 3 the publisher's name and address, usually with the date of publication, in a book, pamphlet, etc. 4 the printer's name and address on any printed matter. ◆ VERB (ɪm'prɪnt) 5 to produce (a mark, impression, etc.) on (a surface) by pressure, printing, or stamping: *to imprint a seal on wax; to imprint wax with a seal.* 6 to establish firmly; impress; stamp: *to imprint the details on one's mind.* 7 (of young animals) to undergo the process of imprinting.
▸**im'printer** NOUN

imprinting (ɪm'prɪntɪŋ) NOUN the development through exceptionally fast learning in young animals of recognition of and attraction to members of their own species or to surrogates.

imprison (ɪm'prɪzən) VERB *(tr)* to confine in or as if in prison.
▸**im'prisoner** NOUN ▸**im'prisonment** NOUN

improbable (ɪm'prɒbəbᵊl) ADJECTIVE not likely or probable; doubtful; unlikely.
▸**im,proba'bility** *or* **im'probableness** NOUN ▸**im'probably** ADVERB

improbity (ɪm'prəʊbɪtɪ) NOUN, *plural* **-ties.** dishonesty, wickedness, or unscrupulousness.

impromptu (ɪm'prɒmptjuː) ADJECTIVE 1 unrehearsed; spontaneous; extempore. 2 produced or done without care or planning; improvised. ◆ ADVERB 3 in a spontaneous or improvised way: *he spoke impromptu.* ◆ NOUN 4 something that is impromptu. 5 a short piece of instrumental music, sometimes improvisatory in character.
▷HISTORY C17: from French, from Latin *in promptū* in readiness, from *promptus* (adjective) ready, PROMPT

improper (ɪm'prɒpə) ADJECTIVE 1 lacking propriety; not seemly or fitting. 2 unsuitable for a certain use or occasion; inappropriate: *an improper use for a tool.* 3 irregular or abnormal.
▸**im'properly** ADVERB ▸**im'properness** NOUN

improper fraction NOUN a fraction in which the numerator has a greater absolute value or degree than the denominator, as 7/6 or $(x^2 + 3)/(x + 1)$.

improper integral NOUN a definite integral having one or both limits infinite or having an integrand that becomes infinite within the limits of integration.

impropriate VERB (ɪm'prəʊprɪ,eɪt) 1 *(tr)* to transfer (property, rights, etc.) from the Church into lay hands. ◆ ADJECTIVE (ɪm'prəʊprɪɪt, -,eɪt) 2 transferred in this way.
▷HISTORY C16: from Medieval Latin *impropriāre* to make one's own, from Latin *im-* IN-[2] + *propriāre* to APPROPRIATE
▸**im,propri'ation** NOUN ▸**im'propri,ator** NOUN

impropriety (,ɪmprə'praɪɪtɪ) NOUN, *plural* **-ties.** 1 lack of propriety; indecency; indecorum. 2 an improper act or use. 3 the state of being improper.

improv ('ɪmprɒv) NOUN improvisational comedy.

improve (ɪm'pruːv) VERB 1 to make or become better in quality; ameliorate. 2 *(tr)* to make (buildings, land, etc.) more valuable by additions or betterment. 3 *(intr; usually foll by on or upon)* to achieve a better standard or quality in comparison (with): *to improve on last year's crop.* ◆ NOUN 4 **on the improve.** *Austral informal* improving.
▷HISTORY C16: from Anglo-French *emprouer* to turn to profit, from *en prou* into profit, from *prou* profit, from Late Latin *prōde* beneficial, from Latin *prōdesse* to be advantageous, from PRO-[1] + *esse* to be
▸**im'provable** ADJECTIVE ▸**im,prova'bility** *or* **im'provableness** NOUN ▸**im'provably** ADVERB ▸**im'prover** NOUN ▸**im'provingly** ADVERB

improvement (ɪm'pruːvmənt) NOUN 1 the act of improving or the state of being improved. 2 something that improves, esp an addition or alteration. 3 alteration of the structure, fixtures, fittings, or decor of a building without changing its function. Compare **conversion** (sense 9). 4 *(usually plural) Austral and NZ* a building or other works on a piece of land, adding to its value.

improvident (ɪm'prɒvɪdənt) ADJECTIVE 1 not provident; thriftless, imprudent, or prodigal. 2 heedless or incautious; rash.
▸**im'providence** NOUN ▸**im'providently** ADVERB

improvisation (,ɪmprəvaɪ'zeɪʃən) NOUN 1 the act or an instance of improvising. 2 a product of improvising; something improvised.
▸**,improvi'sational** *or* **improvisatory** (,ɪmprə'vaɪzətərɪ, -'vɪz-, ,ɪmprəvaɪ'zeɪtərɪ, -trɪ) ADJECTIVE

improvise ('ɪmprə,vaɪz) VERB 1 to perform or make quickly from materials and sources available, without previous planning. 2 to perform (a poem, play, piece of music, etc.), composing as one goes along.
▷HISTORY C19: from French, from Italian *improvvisare*, from Latin *imprōvīsus* unforeseen, from IM- (not) + *prōvīsus*, from *prōvidēre* to foresee; see PROVIDE
▸**'impro,viser** NOUN

imprudent (ɪm'pruːdᵊnt) ADJECTIVE not prudent; rash, heedless, or indiscreet.
▸**im'prudence** NOUN ▸**im'prudently** ADVERB

impudence ('ɪmpjʊdəns) *or* **impudency** NOUN 1 the quality of being impudent. 2 an impudent act or statement.
▷HISTORY C14: from Latin *impudēns* shameless, from IM- (not) + *pudēns* modest; see PUDENCY

impudent ('ɪmpjʊdənt) ADJECTIVE 1 mischievous, impertinent, or disrespectful. 2 an obsolete word for **immodest.**
▸**'impudently** ADVERB ▸**'impudentness** NOUN

impudicity (,ɪmpjʊ'dɪsɪtɪ) NOUN *Rare* immodesty.
▷HISTORY C16: from Old French *impudicite*, from Latin *impudīcus* shameless, from IN-[1] + *pudīcus* modest, virtuous

impugn (ɪm'pjuːn) VERB *(tr)* to challenge or attack as false; assail; criticize.
▷HISTORY C14: from Old French *impugner*, from Latin *impugnāre* to fight against, attack, from IM- + *pugnāre* to fight
▸**im'pugnable** ADJECTIVE ▸**impugnation** (,ɪmpʌg'neɪʃən) *or* **im'pugnment** NOUN ▸**im'pugner** NOUN

impuissant (ɪm'pjuːɪsᵊnt, ɪm'pwiː-) ADJECTIVE powerless, ineffectual, feeble, or impotent.
▷HISTORY C17: from French: powerless
▸**im'puissance** NOUN

impulse ('ɪmpʌls) NOUN 1 an impelling force or motion; thrust; impetus. 2 a sudden desire, whim, or inclination: *I bought it on an impulse.* 3 an instinctive drive; urge. 4 tendency; current; trend. 5 *Physics* **a** the product of the average magnitude of a force acting on a body and the time for which it acts. **b** the change in the momentum of a body as a result of a force acting upon it for a short period of time. 6 *Physiol* See **nerve impulse.** 7 *Electronics* a less common word for **pulse**[1] (sense 2). 8 **on impulse.** spontaneously or impulsively.
▷HISTORY C17: from Latin *impulsus* a pushing against, incitement, from *impellere* to strike against; see IMPEL

impulse buying NOUN the buying of retail merchandise prompted by a whim on seeing the product displayed.
▸**impulse buyer** NOUN

impulse turbine NOUN a turbine in which the expansion of the fluid, often steam, is completed in a static nozzle, the torque being produced by the change in momentum of the fluid impinging on curved rotor blades. Compare **reaction turbine.**

impulsion (ɪm'pʌlʃən) NOUN 1 the act of impelling or the state of being impelled. 2 motion produced by an impulse; propulsion. 3 a driving force; compulsion.

impulsive (ɪm'pʌlsɪv) ADJECTIVE 1 characterized by actions based on sudden desires, whims, or inclinations rather than careful thought: *an impulsive man.* 2 based on emotional impulses or whims; spontaneous: *an impulsive kiss.* 3 forceful, inciting, or impelling. 4 (of physical forces) acting for a short time; not continuous. 5 (of a sound) brief, loud, and having a wide frequency range.
▸**im'pulsively** ADVERB ▸**im'pulsiveness** NOUN

impundulu (ɪm'pʊn,dʊlʊ) NOUN *South African* a mythical bird associated with witchcraft, frequently manifested as the secretary bird.
▷HISTORY from Nguni *mpundulu*

impunity (ɪm'pjuːnɪtɪ) NOUN, *plural* **-ties.** 1 exemption or immunity from punishment or recrimination. 2 exemption or immunity from unpleasant consequences: *a successful career marked by impunity from early mistakes.* 3 **with impunity. a** with no unpleasant consequences. **b** with no care or heed for such consequences.
▷HISTORY C16: from Latin *impūnitās* freedom from punishment, from *impūnis* unpunished, from IM- (not) + *poena* punishment

impure (ɪm'pjʊə) ADJECTIVE 1 not pure; combined with something else; tainted or sullied. 2 (in certain religions) **a** (of persons) ritually unclean and as such debarred from certain religious ceremonies. **b** (of foodstuffs, vessels, etc.) debarred from certain religious uses. 3 (of a colour) mixed with another colour or with black or white. 4 of more than one origin or style, as of architecture or other design.
▸**im'purely** ADVERB ▸**im'pureness** NOUN

impurity (ɪm'pjʊərɪtɪ) NOUN, *plural* **-ties.** 1 the quality of being impure. 2 an impure thing, constituent, or element: *impurities in the water.* 3 *Electronics* a small quantity of an element added to a pure semiconductor crystal to control its electrical conductivity. See also **acceptor** (sense 2), **donor** (sense 5).

imputable (ɪm'pjuːtəbᵊl) ADJECTIVE capable of being imputed; attributable; ascribable.
▸**im,puta'bility** *or* **im'putableness** NOUN ▸**im'putably** ADVERB

imputation system NOUN a former taxation system in which some, or all, of the corporation tax on a company was treated as a tax credit on account of the income tax paid by its shareholders on their dividends; discontinued from 1999. See also **advance corporation tax.**

impute (ɪm'pjuːt) VERB *(tr)* 1 to attribute or

ascribe (something dishonest or dishonourable, esp a criminal offence) to a person. 2 to attribute to a source or cause: *I impute your success to nepotism.* 3 *Commerce* to give (a notional value) to goods or services when the real value is unknown.
▷HISTORY C14: from Latin *imputāre,* from IM- + *putāre* to think, calculate
▸ˌ**impu'tation** NOUN ▸**im'putative** ADJECTIVE ▸**im'puter** NOUN

Imroz ('imrɔz) NOUN the Turkish name for **Imbros.**

IMS ABBREVIATION FOR Indian Medical Service.

IMunE ABBREVIATION FOR Institution of Municipal Engineers.

in[1] (ɪn) PREPOSITION 1 inside; within: *no smoking in the auditorium.* 2 at a place where there is: *lying in the shade; walking in the rain.* 3 indicating a state, situation, or condition: *in a deep sleep; standing in silence.* 4 before or when (a period of time) has elapsed: *come back in one year.* 5 using (a language, etc.) as a means of communication: *written in code.* 6 concerned or involved with, esp as an occupation: *in journalism.* 7 while or by performing the action of; as a consequence of or by means of: *in crossing the street he was run over.* 8 used to indicate goal or purpose: *in honour of the president.* 9 (used of certain animals) about to give birth to; pregnant with (specified offspring): *in foal; in calf.* 10 a variant of **into**: *she fell in the water; he tore the paper in two.* 11 **have it in one.** (often foll by an infinitive) to have the ability (to do something). 12 **in it.** *Austral informal* joining in; taking part. 13 **in that** *or* **in so far as.** (*conjunction*) because or to the extent that; inasmuch as: *I regret my remark in that it upset you.* 14 **nothing, very little, quite a bit,** etc., **in it.** no, a great, etc., difference or interval between two things. ◆ ADVERB (*particle*) 15 in or into a particular place; inward or indoors: *come in; bring him in.* 16 so as to achieve office, power, or authority: *the Conservatives got in at the last election.* 17 so as to enclose: *block in; cover in a hole.* 18 (in certain games) so as to take one's turn or one's team's turn at a certain aspect of the play; taking one's innings: *you have to get the other side out before you go in.* 19 *Brit* (of a fire) alight: *do you keep the fire in all night?* 20 (*in combination*) indicating an activity or gathering, esp one organized to protest against something: *teach-in; work-in.* 21 **in at.** present at (the beginning, end, etc.). 22 **in between.** between. 23 **in for.** about to be affected by (something, esp something unpleasant): *you're in for a shock.* 24 **in on.** acquainted with or sharing in: *I was in on all his plans.* 25 **in with.** associated with; friendly with; regarded highly by. 26 **have (got) it in for.** *Informal* to wish or intend harm towards. ◆ ADJECTIVE 27 (*stressed*) fashionable; modish: *the in thing to do.* 28 *NZ* competing: *you've got to be in to win.* ◆ NOUN 29 **ins and outs.** intricacies or complications; details: *the ins and outs of a computer system.*
▷HISTORY Old English; compare Old High German *in,* Welsh *yn,* Old Norse *ī,* Latin *in,* Greek *en*

in[2] THE INTERNET DOMAIN NAME FOR India.

In THE CHEMICAL SYMBOL FOR indium.

IN ABBREVIATION FOR Indiana.

in. ABBREVIATION FOR inch(es).

in-[1], **il-, im-,** *or* **ir-** PREFIX not; non-: *incredible; insincere; illegal; imperfect; irregular.* Compare **un-**[1].
▷HISTORY from Latin *in-;* related to *ne-, nōn* not

in-[2], **il-, im-,** *or* **ir-** PREFIX 1 in; into; towards; within; on: *infiltrate; immigrate.* 2 having an intensive or causative function: *inflame; imperil.*
▷HISTORY from IN (preposition, adverb)

-in SUFFIX FORMING NOUNS 1 indicating a neutral organic compound, including proteins, glucosides, and glycerides: *insulin; digitoxin; tripalmitin.* 2 indicating an enzyme in certain nonsystematic names: *pepsin.* 3 indicating a pharmaceutical substance: *penicillin; riboflavin; aspirin.* 4 indicating a chemical substance in certain nonsystematic names: *coumarin.*
▷HISTORY from New Latin *-ina;* compare -INE[2]

inability (ˌɪnə'bɪlɪtɪ) NOUN lack of ability or means; incapacity.

in absentia *Latin* (ɪn æb'sentɪə) ADVERB in the absence of (someone indicated): *he was condemned in absentia.*

inaccessible (ˌɪnæk'sɛsəbəl) ADJECTIVE not accessible; unapproachable.
▸ˌ**inacˌcessi'bility** *or* ˌ**inac'cessibleness** NOUN
▸ˌ**inac'cessibly** ADVERB

inaccuracy (ɪn'ækjʊrəsɪ) NOUN, *plural* **-cies.** 1 lack of accuracy; imprecision. 2 an error, a mistake, or a slip.

inaccurate (ɪn'ækjʊrɪt) ADJECTIVE not accurate; imprecise, inexact, or erroneous.
▸**in'accurately** ADVERB ▸**in'accurateness** NOUN

inaction (ɪn'ækʃən) NOUN lack of action; idleness; inertia.

inactivate (ɪn'æktɪˌveɪt) VERB (*tr*) to render inactive.
▸**inˌacti'vation** NOUN

inactive (ɪn'æktɪv) ADJECTIVE 1 idle or inert; not active. 2 sluggish, passive, or indolent. 3 *Military* of or relating to persons or equipment not in active service. 4 *Chem* (of a substance) having little or no reactivity. 5 (of an element, isotope, etc.) having little or no radioactivity.
▸**in'actively** ADVERB ▸ˌ**inac'tivity** *or* **in'activeness** NOUN

inadequate (ɪn'ædɪkwɪt) ADJECTIVE 1 not adequate; insufficient. 2 not capable or competent; lacking.
▸**in'adequacy** NOUN ▸**in'adequately** ADVERB

inadmissible (ˌɪnəd'mɪsəbəl) ADJECTIVE not admissible or allowable.
▸ˌ**inadˌmissi'bility** NOUN ▸ˌ**inad'missibly** ADVERB

inadvertence (ˌɪnəd'vɜːtəns) *or* **inadvertency** NOUN 1 lack of attention; heedlessness. 2 an instance or an effect of being inadvertent; oversight; slip.

inadvertent (ˌɪnəd'vɜːtənt) ADJECTIVE 1 failing to act carefully or considerately; inattentive. 2 resulting from heedless action; unintentional.
▸ˌ**inad'vertently** ADVERB

inadvisable (ˌɪnəd'vaɪzəbəl) ADJECTIVE 1 not advisable; not recommended. 2 unwise; imprudent.
▸ˌ**inadˌvisa'bility** *or* ˌ**inad'visableness** NOUN ▸ˌ**inad'visably** ADVERB

-inae SUFFIX FORMING PLURAL PROPER NOUNS occurring in names of zoological subfamilies: *Felinae.*
▷HISTORY New Latin, from Latin, feminine plural of *-īnus* -INE[1]

in aeternum *Latin* (ɪn iː'tɜːnəm) ADVERB forever; eternally.

inalienable (ɪn'eɪljənəbəl) ADJECTIVE not able to be transferred to another; not alienable: *the inalienable rights of the citizen.*
▸**inˌaliena'bility** *or* **in'alienableness** NOUN ▸**in'alienably** ADVERB

inalterable (ɪn'ɔːltərəbəl) ADJECTIVE not alterable; unalterable.
▸**inˌaltera'bility** *or* **in'alterableness** NOUN ▸**in'alterably** ADVERB

inamorata (ɪnˌæmə'rɑːtə, ˌɪnæmə-) NOUN, *plural* **-tas.** a woman with whom one is in love; a female lover.
▷HISTORY C17: see INAMORATO

inamorato (ɪnˌæmə'rɑːtəʊ, ˌɪnæmə-) NOUN, *plural* **-tos** *or* **-ti** (-tiː). a man with whom one is in love; a male lover.
▷HISTORY C16: from Italian *innamorato, innamorata,* from *innamorare* to cause to fall in love, from *amore* love, from Latin *amor*

in-and-in ADJECTIVE (of breeding) carried out repeatedly among closely related individuals of the same species to eliminate or intensify certain characteristics.

inane (ɪ'neɪn) ADJECTIVE senseless, unimaginative, or empty; unintelligent: *inane remarks.*
▷HISTORY C17: from Latin *inānis* empty
▸**in'anely** ADVERB

inanga ('iːnʌŋə) NOUN another name for the New Zealand **whitebait** (sense 2).
▷HISTORY Maori

inanimate (ɪn'ænɪmɪt) ADJECTIVE 1 lacking the qualities or features of living beings; not animate: *inanimate objects.* 2 lacking any sign of life or consciousness; appearing dead. 3 lacking vitality; spiritless; dull.
▸**in'animately** ADVERB ▸**in'animateness** *or* **inanimation** (ɪnˌænɪ'meɪʃən) NOUN

inanition (ˌɪnə'nɪʃən) NOUN 1 exhaustion resulting from lack of food. 2 mental, social, or spiritual weakness or lassitude.
▷HISTORY C14: from Late Latin *inānītio* emptiness, from Latin *inānis* empty; see INANE

inanity (ɪ'nænɪtɪ) NOUN, *plural* **-ties.** 1 lack of intelligence or imagination; senselessness; silliness. 2 a senseless action, remark, etc. 3 an archaic word for **emptiness.**

inappellable (ˌɪnə'pɛləbəl) ADJECTIVE incapable of being appealed against, as a court decision; unchallengeable.
▷HISTORY C19: from IN-[1] + Latin *appellāre* to APPEAL

inappetence (ɪn'æpɪtəns) *or* **inappetency** NOUN *Rare* lack of appetite or desire.
▸**in'appetent** ADJECTIVE

inapplicable (ɪn'æplɪkəbəl, ˌɪnə'plɪk-) ADJECTIVE not applicable or suitable; irrelevant.
▸**inˌapplica'bility** *or* **in'applicableness** NOUN
▸**in'applicably** ADVERB

inapposite (ɪn'æpəzɪt) ADJECTIVE not appropriate or pertinent; unsuitable.
▸**in'appositely** ADVERB ▸**in'appositeness** NOUN

inappreciable (ˌɪnə'priːʃəbəl) ADJECTIVE 1 incapable of being appreciated. 2 imperceptible; negligible.
▸ˌ**inap'preciably** ADVERB

inappreciative (ˌɪnə'priːʃətɪv) ADJECTIVE lacking appreciation; unappreciative.
▸ˌ**inap'preciatively** ADVERB ▸ˌ**inapˌpreci'ation** *or* ˌ**inap'preciativeness** NOUN

inapprehensive (ˌɪnæprɪ'hɛnsɪv) ADJECTIVE 1 not perceiving or feeling fear or anxiety; untroubled. 2 *Rare* unable to understand; imperceptive.
▸ˌ**inappre'hensively** ADVERB ▸ˌ**inappre'hensiveness** NOUN

inapproachable (ˌɪnə'prəʊtʃəbəl) ADJECTIVE not accessible; unapproachable; unfriendly.
▸ˌ**inapˌproacha'bility** NOUN ▸ˌ**inap'proachably** ADVERB

inappropriate (ˌɪnə'prəʊprɪɪt) ADJECTIVE not fitting or appropriate; unsuitable or untimely.
▸ˌ**inap'propriately** ADVERB ▸ˌ**inap'propriateness** NOUN

inapt (ɪn'æpt) ADJECTIVE 1 not apt or fitting; inappropriate. 2 lacking skill; inept.
▸**in'aptiˌtude** *or* **in'aptness** NOUN ▸**in'aptly** ADVERB

inarch (ɪn'ɑːtʃ) VERB (*tr*) to graft (a plant) by uniting stock and scion while both are still growing independently.

inarticulate (ˌɪnɑː'tɪkjʊlɪt) ADJECTIVE 1 unable to express oneself fluently or clearly; incoherent. 2 (of speech, language, etc.) unclear or incomprehensible; unintelligible: *inarticulate grunts.* 3 unable to speak; dumb. 4 unable to be expressed; unvoiced: *inarticulate suffering.* 5 *Biology* having no joints, segments, or articulation.
▸ˌ**inar'ticulately** ADVERB ▸ˌ**inar'ticulateness** *or* ˌ**inar'ticulacy** NOUN

inartificial (ˌɪnɑːtɪ'fɪʃəl) ADJECTIVE *Archaic* 1 not artificial; real; natural. 2 inartistic.
▸ˌ**inarti'ficially** ADVERB

inartistic (ˌɪnɑː'tɪstɪk) ADJECTIVE lacking in artistic skill, appreciation, etc.; Philistine.
▸ˌ**inar'tistically** ADVERB

inasmuch as (ˌɪnəz'mʌtʃ) CONJUNCTION (*subordinating*) 1 in view of the fact that; seeing that; since. 2 to the extent or degree that; in so far as.

inattentive (ˌɪnə'tɛntɪv) ADJECTIVE not paying attention; heedless; negligent.
▸ˌ**inat'tention** *or* ˌ**inat'tentiveness** NOUN ▸ˌ**inat'tentively** ADVERB

inaudible (ɪn'ɔːdəbəl) ADJECTIVE not loud enough to be heard; not audible.
▸**inˌaudi'bility** *or* **in'audibleness** NOUN ▸**in'audibly** ADVERB

inaugural (ɪn'ɔːgjʊrəl) ADJECTIVE 1 characterizing or relating to an inauguration. ◆ NOUN 2 a speech made at an inauguration, esp by a president of the US.

inaugurate (ɪn'ɔːgjʊˌreɪt) VERB (*tr*) 1 to commence officially or formally; initiate. 2 to place in office formally and ceremonially; induct. 3 to open ceremonially; dedicate formally: *to inaugurate a factory.*
▷HISTORY C17: from Latin *inaugurāre,* literally: to take omens, practise augury, hence to install in office after taking auguries; see IN-[2], AUGUR
▸**inˌaugu'ration** NOUN ▸**in'auguˌrator** NOUN ▸**inauguratory** (ɪn'ɔːgjʊrətərɪ, -trɪ) ADJECTIVE

Inauguration Day NOUN the day on which the

inauguration of a president of the US takes place, Jan. 20.

inauspicious (ˌɪnɔːˈspɪʃəs) ADJECTIVE not auspicious; unlucky.
▸ **ˌinausˈpiciously** ADVERB ▸ **ˌinausˈpiciousness** NOUN

inbd ABBREVIATION FOR inboard (on an aircraft, a boat, etc.).

inbeing (ˈɪnˌbiːɪŋ) NOUN [1] existence in something else; inherence. [2] basic and inward nature; essence.

in-between ADJECTIVE [1] intermediate: *he's at the in-between stage, neither a child nor an adult.* ◆ NOUN [2] an intermediate person or thing.

in-betweener NOUN an intermediate person or thing.

inboard (ˈɪnˌbɔːd) ADJECTIVE [1] (esp of a boat's motor or engine) situated within the hull. Compare **outboard** (sense 1). [2] situated between the wing tip of an aircraft and its fuselage: *an inboard engine.* ◆ ADVERB [3] towards the centre line of or within a vessel, aircraft, etc.

in-bond shop NOUN *Caribbean* a duty-free shop.

inborn (ˈɪnˈbɔːn) ADJECTIVE existing from birth; congenital; innate.

inbound (ˈɪnˌbaʊnd) ADJECTIVE coming in; inward bound: *an inbound ship.*

inbreathe (ɪnˈbriːð) VERB (*tr*) *Rare* to infuse or imbue.

inbred (ˈɪnˈbrɛd) ADJECTIVE [1] produced as a result of inbreeding. [2] deeply ingrained; innate: *inbred good manners.*

inbreed (ˈɪnˈbriːd) VERB **-breeds, -breeding, -bred.** [1] to breed from unions between closely related individuals, esp over several generations. [2] (*tr*) to develop within; engender.
▸ **ˈinˈbreeding** NOUN, ADJECTIVE

in-built ADJECTIVE built-in, integral.

inby (ɪnˈbaɪ) ADVERB [1] *Scot* into the house or an inner room; inside; within. [2] *Scot and Northern English dialect* towards or near the house. ◆ ADJECTIVE [3] *Scot and Northern English dialect* located near or nearest to the house: *the inby field.*
▷HISTORY C18: from IN (adv) + BY (adv)

inc. ABBREVIATION FOR: [1] included. [2] including.

Inc. *or* **inc.** (esp after the names of US business organizations) ABBREVIATION FOR incorporated. Brit equivalent: **Ltd.**

Inca (ˈɪŋkə) NOUN, *plural* **-ca** *or* **-cas.** [1] a member of a South American Indian people whose great empire centred on Peru lasted from about 1100 A.D. to the Spanish conquest in the early 1530s and is famed for its complex culture. [2] the ruler or king of this empire or any member of his family. [3] the language of the Incas. See also **Quechua.**
▷HISTORY C16: from Spanish, from Quechua *inka* king
▸ **ˈIncan** ADJECTIVE

incalculable (ɪnˈkælkjʊləbᵊl) ADJECTIVE beyond calculation; unable to be predicted or determined.
▸ **inˌcalculaˈbility** *or* **inˈcalculableness** NOUN
▸ **inˈcalculably** ADVERB

incalescent (ˌɪnkəˈlɛsᵊnt) ADJECTIVE *Chem* increasing in temperature.
▷HISTORY C17: from Latin *incalescere,* from IN-² + *calescere* to grow warm, from *calēre* to be warm
▸ **ˌincaˈlescence** NOUN

in camera (ɪn ˈkæmərə) ADVERB, ADJECTIVE [1] in a private or secret session; not in public. [2] *Law* (formerly) **a** in the privacy of a judge's chambers. **b** in a court not open to the public. Official name for sense 2: **in chambers.**
▷HISTORY Latin: in the chamber

incandesce (ˌɪnkænˈdɛs) VERB (*intr*) to exhibit incandescence.

incandescence (ˌɪnkænˈdɛsəns) *or* **incandescency** NOUN [1] the emission of light by a body as a consequence of raising its temperature. Compare **luminescence.** [2] the light produced by raising the temperature of a body.

incandescent (ˌɪnkænˈdɛsᵊnt) ADJECTIVE [1] emitting light as a result of being heated to a high temperature; red-hot or white-hot. [2] *Informal* extremely angry; raging.
▷HISTORY C18: from Latin *incandescere* to become hot, glow, from IN-² + *candescere* to grow bright, from *candēre* to be white; see CANDID
▸ **ˌincanˈdescently** ADVERB

incandescent lamp NOUN a source of light that contains a heated solid, such as an electrically heated filament.

incantation (ˌɪnkænˈteɪʃən) NOUN [1] ritual recitation of magic words or sounds. [2] the formulaic words or sounds used; a magic spell.
▷HISTORY C14: from Late Latin *incantātiō* an enchanting, from *incantāre* to repeat magic formulas, from Latin, from IN-² + *cantāre* to sing; see ENCHANT
▸ **ˌincanˈtational** ADJECTIVE

incantatory (ɪnˈkæntətərɪ, -trɪ) ADJECTIVE relating to or having the characteristics of an incantation.

incapable (ɪnˈkeɪpəbᵊl) ADJECTIVE [1] (when *postpositive,* often foll by *of*) not capable (of); lacking the ability (to). [2] powerless or helpless, as through injury or intoxication. [3] (*postpositive;* foll by *of*) not susceptible (to); not admitting (of): *a problem incapable of solution.*
▸ **inˌcapaˈbility** *or* **inˈcapableness** NOUN ▸ **inˈcapably** ADVERB

incapacitant (ˌɪnkəˈpæsɪtənt) NOUN a substance that can temporarily incapacitate a person, used esp as a weapon in chemical warfare.

incapacitate (ˌɪnkəˈpæsɪˌteɪt) VERB (*tr*) [1] to deprive of power, strength, or capacity; disable. [2] to deprive of legal capacity or eligibility.
▸ **ˌincaˌpaciˈtation** NOUN

incapacity (ˌɪnkəˈpæsɪtɪ) NOUN, *plural* **-ties.** [1] lack of power, strength, or capacity; inability. [2] *Law* **a** legal disqualification or ineligibility. **b** a circumstance causing this.

incapacity benefit NOUN (in Britain) a regular government payment made to people who are unable to work for an extended period through disability.

Incaparina (ɪnˌkæpəˈriːnə) NOUN a cheap high-protein food made of cottonseed, sorghum flours, maize, yeast, etc., used, esp in Latin America, to prevent protein-deficiency diseases.
▷HISTORY C20: from *Institute of Nutrition in Central America and Panama* + (F)ARINA

incapsulate (ɪnˈkæpsjʊˌleɪt) VERB a less common spelling of **encapsulate.**
▸ **inˌcapsuˈlation** NOUN

in-car ADJECTIVE installed or provided within a car: *an in-car hi-fi system.*

incarcerate (ɪnˈkɑːsəˌreɪt) VERB (*tr*) to confine or imprison.
▷HISTORY C16: from Medieval Latin *incarcerāre,* from Latin IN-² + *carcer* prison
▸ **inˌcarcerˈation** NOUN ▸ **inˈcarcerˌator** NOUN

incardinate (ɪnˈkɑːdɪˌneɪt) VERB (*tr*) *RC Church* to transfer (a cleric) to the jurisdiction of a new bishop.
▷HISTORY C17: from Late Latin *incardināre,* from IN-² + *cardinālis* CARDINAL

incardination (ɪnˌkɑːdɪˈneɪʃən) NOUN [1] the official acceptance by one diocese of a clergyman from another diocese. [2] the promotion of a clergyman to the status of a cardinal.

incarnadine (ɪnˈkɑːnəˌdaɪn) *Archaic or literary* ◆ VERB [1] (*tr*) to tinge or stain with red. ◆ ADJECTIVE [2] of a pinkish or reddish colour similar to that of flesh or blood.
▷HISTORY C16: from French *incarnadin* flesh-coloured, from Italian, from Late Latin *incarnātus* made flesh, INCARNATE

incarnate ADJECTIVE (ɪnˈkɑːnɪt, -neɪt) (*usually immediately postpositive*) [1] possessing bodily form, esp the human form: *a devil incarnate.* [2] personified or typified: *stupidity incarnate.* [3] (esp of plant parts) flesh-coloured or pink. ◆ VERB (ɪnˈkɑːneɪt) (*tr*) [4] to give a bodily or concrete form to. [5] to be representative or typical of.
▷HISTORY C14: from Late Latin *incarnāre* to make flesh, from Latin IN-² + *carō* flesh

incarnation (ˌɪnkɑːˈneɪʃən) NOUN [1] the act of manifesting or state of being manifested in bodily form, esp human form. [2] a bodily form assumed by a god, etc. [3] a person or thing that typifies or represents some quality, idea, etc.: *the weasel is the incarnation of ferocity.*

Incarnation (ˌɪnkɑːˈneɪʃən) NOUN [1] *Christian theol* the assuming of a human body by the Son of God. [2] *Christianity* the presence of God on Earth in the person of Jesus.

incarvillea (ˌɪnkɑːˈvɪlɪə) NOUN any plant of the genus *Incarvillea,* native to China, of which some species are grown as garden or greenhouse plants for their large usually carmine-coloured trumpet-shaped flowers, esp *I. delavayi:* family *Bignoniaceae.*
▷HISTORY named after Pierre *d'Incarville* (1706–57), French missionary

incase (ɪnˈkeɪs) VERB a variant spelling of **encase.**
▸ **inˈcasement** NOUN

incautious (ɪnˈkɔːʃəs) ADJECTIVE not careful or cautious.
▸ **inˈcautiously** ADVERB ▸ **inˈcautiousness** *or* **inˈcaution** NOUN

incendiarism (ɪnˈsɛndɪəˌrɪzəm) NOUN [1] the act or practice of illegal burning; arson. [2] (esp formerly) the creation of civil strife or violence for political reasons.

incendiary (ɪnˈsɛndɪərɪ) ADJECTIVE [1] of or relating to the illegal burning of property, goods, etc. [2] tending to create strife, violence, etc.; inflammatory. [3] (of a substance) capable of catching fire, causing fires, or burning readily. ◆ NOUN, *plural* **-aries.** [4] a person who illegally sets fire to property, goods, etc.; arsonist. [5] (esp formerly) a person who stirs up civil strife, violence, etc., for political reasons; agitator. [6] Also called: **incendiary bomb.** a bomb that is designed to start fires. [7] an incendiary substance, such as phosphorus.
▷HISTORY C17: from Latin *incendiārius* setting alight, from *incendium* fire, from *incendere* to kindle

incense¹ (ˈɪnsɛns) NOUN [1] any of various aromatic substances burnt for their fragrant odour, esp in religious ceremonies. [2] the odour or smoke so produced. [3] any pleasant fragrant odour; aroma. [4] *Rare* homage or adulation. ◆ VERB [5] to burn incense in honour of (a deity). [6] (*tr*) to perfume or fumigate with incense.
▷HISTORY C13: from Old French *encens,* from Church Latin *incensum,* from Latin *incendere* to kindle
▸ **ˌincenˈsation** NOUN

incense² (ɪnˈsɛns) VERB (*tr*) to enrage greatly.
▷HISTORY C15: from Latin *incensus* set on fire, from *incendere* to kindle
▸ **inˈcensement** NOUN

incensory (ˈɪnsɛnsərɪ) NOUN, *plural* **-ries.** a less common name for a **censer.**
▷HISTORY C17: from Medieval Latin *incensorium*

incentive (ɪnˈsɛntɪv) NOUN [1] a motivating influence; stimulus. [2] **a** an additional payment made to employees as a means of increasing production. **b** (*as modifier*): *an incentive scheme.* ◆ ADJECTIVE [3] serving to incite to action.
▷HISTORY C15: from Late Latin *incentīvus* (adj), from Latin: striking up, setting the tune, from *incinere* to sing, from IN-² + *canere* to sing
▸ **inˈcentively** ADVERB

incentivize *or* **incentivise** (ɪnˈsɛntɪˌvaɪz) VERB (*tr*) **a** to provide (someone) with a good reason for wanting to do something: *why not incentivize companies to relocate?* **b** to promote (something) with a particular incentive: *an incentivized share option scheme.*

incept (ɪnˈsɛpt) VERB (*tr*) [1] (of organisms) to ingest (food). [2] *Brit* (formerly) to take a master's or doctor's degree at a university. ◆ NOUN [3] *Botany* a rudimentary organ.
▷HISTORY C19: from Latin *inceptus* begun, attempted, from *incipere* to begin, take in hand, from IN-² + *capere* to take
▸ **inˈceptor** NOUN

inception (ɪnˈsɛpʃən) NOUN the beginning, as of a project or undertaking.

inceptive (ɪnˈsɛptɪv) ADJECTIVE [1] beginning; incipient; initial. [2] Also called: **inchoative.** *Grammar* denoting an aspect of verbs in some languages used to indicate the beginning of an action. ◆ NOUN [3] *Grammar* **a** the inceptive aspect of verbs. **b** a verb in this aspect.
▸ **inˈceptively** ADVERB

incertitude (ɪnˈsɜːtɪˌtjuːd) NOUN [1] uncertainty; doubt. [2] a state of mental or emotional insecurity.

incessant (ɪnˈsɛsᵊnt) ADJECTIVE not ceasing; continual.
▷HISTORY C16: from Late Latin *incessāns,* from Latin IN-¹ + *cessāre* to CEASE

▸**in'cessancy** *or* **in'cessantness** NOUN ▸**in'cessantly** ADVERB

incest ('ɪnsɛst) NOUN sexual intercourse between two persons commonly regarded as too closely related to marry.
▷HISTORY C13: from Latin *incestus* incest (from adjective: impure, defiled), from IN-[1] + *castus* CHASTE

incestuous (ɪn'sɛstjʊəs) ADJECTIVE [1] relating to or involving incest: *an incestuous union.* [2] guilty of incest. [3] *Obsolete* resulting from incest: *an incestuous bastard.* [4] resembling incest in excessive or claustrophobic intimacy.
▸**in'cestuously** ADVERB ▸**in'cestuousness** NOUN

inch¹ (ɪntʃ) NOUN [1] a unit of length equal to one twelfth of a foot or 0.0254 metre. [2] *Meteorol* **a** an amount of precipitation that would cover a surface with water one inch deep: *five inches of rain fell in January.* **b** a unit of pressure equal to a mercury column one inch high in a barometer. [3] a very small distance, degree, or amount. [4] **every inch.** in every way; completely: *he was every inch an aristocrat.* [5] **inch by inch.** gradually; little by little. [6] **within an inch of.** very close to. ◆ VERB [7] to move or be moved very slowly or in very small steps: *the car inched forward.* [8] (*tr; foll by out*) to defeat (someone) by a very small margin.
▷HISTORY Old English *ynce,* from Latin *uncia* twelfth part; see OUNCE[1]

inch² (ɪntʃ) NOUN *Scot and Irish* a small island.
▷HISTORY C15: from Gaelic *innis* island; compare Welsh *ynys*

inchmeal ('ɪntʃˌmiːl) ADVERB gradually; inch by inch or little by little.
▷HISTORY C16: from INCH[1] + *-mele,* from Old English *mælum* quantity taken at one time; compare PIECEMEAL

inchoate ADJECTIVE (ɪn'kəʊeɪt, -'kəʊɪt) [1] just beginning; incipient. [2] undeveloped; immature; rudimentary. [3] (of a legal document, promissory note, etc.) in an uncompleted state; not yet made specific or valid. ◆ VERB (ɪn'kəʊeɪt) (*tr*) [4] to begin.
▷HISTORY C16: from Latin *incohāre* to make a beginning, literally: to hitch up, from IN-[2] + *cohum* yokestrap
▸**in'choately** ADVERB ▸**in'choateness** NOUN ▸ˌ**incho'ation** NOUN ▸**inchoative** (ɪn'kəʊətɪv) ADJECTIVE

Inchon *or* **Incheon** ('ɪn'tʃɒn) NOUN a port in W South Korea, on the Yellow Sea: the chief port for Seoul: site of a major strategic amphibious assault by UN troops, liberating Seoul (Sept. 15, 1950). Pop.: 2 307 618 (1995). Former name: **Chemulpo.**

inchworm ('ɪntʃˌwɜːm) NOUN another name for a **measuring worm.**

incidence ('ɪnsɪdəns) NOUN [1] degree, extent, or frequency of occurrence; amount: *a high incidence of death from pneumonia.* [2] the act or manner of impinging on or affecting by proximity or influence. [3] *Physics* the arrival of a beam of light or particles at a surface. See also **angle of incidence.** [4] *Geometry* the partial coincidence of two configurations, such as a point that lies on a circle.

incident ('ɪnsɪdənt) NOUN [1] a distinct or definite occurrence; event. [2] a minor, subsidiary, or related event or action. [3] a relatively insignificant event that might have serious consequences, esp in international politics. [4] a public disturbance: *the police had reports of an incident outside a pub.* ◆ ADJECTIVE [5] (*postpositive;* foll by *to*) related (to) or dependent (on). [6] (when *postpositive,* often foll by *to*) having a subsidiary or minor relationship (with). [7] (esp of a beam of light or particles) arriving at or striking a surface: *incident electrons.*
▷HISTORY C15: from Medieval Latin *incidens* an event, from Latin *incidere,* literally: to fall into, hence befall, happen, from IN-[2] + *cadere* to fall

incidental (ˌɪnsɪ'dɛntᵊl) ADJECTIVE [1] happening in connection with or resulting from something more important; casual or fortuitous. [2] (*postpositive;* foll by *to*) found in connection (with); related (to). [3] (*postpositive;* foll by *upon*) caused (by). [4] occasional or minor: *incidental expenses.* ◆ NOUN [5] (*often plural*) an incidental or minor expense, event, or action.
▸ˌ**inci'dentalness** NOUN

incidentally (ˌɪnsɪ'dɛntəlɪ) ADVERB [1] as a subordinate or chance occurrence. [2] (*sentence modifier*) by the way.

incidental music NOUN background music for a film, television programme, etc.

incinerate (ɪn'sɪnəˌreɪt) VERB to burn up completely; reduce to ashes.
▷HISTORY C16: from Medieval Latin *incinerāre,* from Latin IN-[2] + *cinis* ashes
▸**inˌciner'ation** NOUN

incinerator (ɪn'sɪnəˌreɪtə) NOUN a furnace or apparatus for incinerating something, esp refuse.

incipient (ɪn'sɪpɪənt) ADJECTIVE just starting to be or happen; beginning.
▷HISTORY C17: from Latin *incipiēns,* from *incipere* to begin, take in hand, from IN-[2] + *capere* to take
▸**in'cipience** *or* **in'cipiency** NOUN ▸**in'cipiently** ADVERB

incipit *Latin* ('ɪnkɪpɪt) here begins: used as an introductory word at the beginning of some medieval manuscripts.

incise (ɪn'saɪz) VERB (*tr*) to produce (lines, a design, etc.) by cutting into the surface of (something) with a sharp tool.
▷HISTORY C16: from Latin *incīdere* to cut into, from IN-[2] + *caedere* to cut

incised (ɪn'saɪzd) ADJECTIVE [1] cut into or engraved: *an incised surface.* [2] made by cutting or engraving: *an incised design.* [3] (of a wound) cleanly cut, as with a surgical knife. [4] having margins that are sharply and deeply indented: *an incised leaf.*

incisiform (ɪn'saɪzɪˌfɔːm) ADJECTIVE *Zoology* having the shape of an incisor tooth.

incision (ɪn'sɪʒən) NOUN [1] the act of incising. [2] a cut, gash, or notch. [3] a cut made with a knife during a surgical operation. [4] any indentation in an incised leaf. [5] *Rare* incisiveness.

incisive (ɪn'saɪsɪv) ADJECTIVE [1] keen, penetrating, or acute. [2] biting or sarcastic; mordant: *an incisive remark.* [3] having a sharp cutting edge: *incisive teeth.*
▸**in'cisively** ADVERB ▸**in'cisiveness** NOUN

incisor (ɪn'saɪzə) NOUN a chisel-edged tooth at the front of the mouth. In man there are four in each jaw.

incisure (ɪn'saɪʒə) NOUN *Anatomy* an incision or notch in an organ or part.
▸**in'cisural** ADJECTIVE

incite (ɪn'saɪt) VERB (*tr*) to stir up or provoke to action.
▷HISTORY C15: from Latin *incitāre,* from IN-[2] + *citāre* to excite
▸ˌ**inci'tation** NOUN ▸**in'citement** NOUN ▸**in'citer** NOUN ▸**in'citingly** ADVERB

incivility (ɪnsɪ'vɪlɪtɪ) NOUN, *plural* **-ties.** [1] lack of civility or courtesy; rudeness. [2] an impolite or uncivil act or remark.

incl. ABBREVIATION FOR: [1] including. [2] inclusive.

inclement (ɪn'klɛmənt) ADJECTIVE [1] (of weather) stormy, severe, or tempestuous. [2] harsh, severe, or merciless.
▸**in'clemency** *or* **in'clementness** NOUN ▸**in'clemently** ADVERB

inclinable (ɪn'klaɪnəbᵊl) ADJECTIVE [1] (*postpositive;* usually foll by *to*) having an inclination or tendency (to); disposed (to). [2] capable of being inclined.

inclination (ˌɪnklɪ'neɪʃən) NOUN [1] (often foll by *for, to, towards,* or an infinitive) a particular disposition, esp a liking or preference; tendency: *I've no inclination for such dull work.* [2] the degree of deviation from a particular plane, esp a horizontal or vertical plane. [3] a sloping or slanting surface; incline. [4] the act of inclining or the state of being inclined. [5] the act of bowing or nodding the head. [6] *Maths* **a** the angle between a line on a graph and the positive limb of the *x*-axis. **b** the smaller dihedral angle between one plane and another. [7] *Astronomy* the angle between the plane of the orbit of a planet or comet and another plane, usually that of the ecliptic. [8] *Physics* another name for **dip** (sense 28).
▸ˌ**incli'national** ADJECTIVE

incline VERB (ɪn'klaɪn) [1] to deviate or cause to deviate from a particular plane, esp a vertical or horizontal plane; slope or slant. [2] (when *tr,* may take an infinitive) to be disposed or cause to be disposed (towards some attitude or to do something): *he inclines towards levity; that does not incline me to think that you are right.* [3] to bend or lower (part of the body, esp the head), as in a bow or in order to listen. [4] **incline one's ear.** to listen favourably (to). ◆ NOUN ('ɪnklaɪn, ɪn'klaɪn) [5] an inclined surface or slope; gradient. [6] short for **inclined railway.**
▷HISTORY C13: from Latin *inclīnāre* to cause to lean, from *clīnāre* to bend; see LEAN[1]
▸**in'cliner** NOUN

inclined (ɪn'klaɪnd) ADJECTIVE [1] (*postpositive;* often foll by *to*) having a disposition; tending. [2] sloping or slanting.

inclined plane NOUN a plane whose angle to the horizontal is less than a right angle.

inclined railway NOUN *Chiefly US* a cable railway used on particularly steep inclines unsuitable for normal adhesion locomotives.

inclinometer (ˌɪnklɪ'nɒmɪtə) NOUN [1] an aircraft instrument for indicating the angle that an aircraft makes with the horizontal. [2] another name for **dip circle.**

inclose (ɪn'kləʊz) VERB a less common spelling of **enclose.**
▸**in'closable** ADJECTIVE ▸**in'closer** NOUN ▸**in'closure** NOUN

include (ɪn'kluːd) VERB (*tr*) [1] to have as contents or part of the contents; be made up of or contain. [2] to add as part of something else; put in as part of a set, group, or category. [3] to contain as a secondary or minor ingredient or element.
▷HISTORY C15 (in the sense: to enclose): from Latin *inclūdere* to enclose, from IN-[2] + *claudere* to close
▸**in'cludable** *or* **in'cludible** ADJECTIVE

included (ɪn'kluːdɪd) ADJECTIVE (of the stamens or pistils of a flower) not protruding beyond the corolla.
▸**in'cludedness** NOUN

include out VERB (*tr, adverb*) *Informal* to exclude: *you can include me out of that deal.*

inclusion (ɪn'kluːʒən) NOUN [1] the act of including or the state of being included. [2] something included. [3] *Geology* a solid fragment, liquid globule, or pocket of gas enclosed in a mineral or rock. [4] *Maths* **a** the relation between two sets that obtains when all the members of the first are members of the second. Symbol: $X \subseteq Y$. **b strict** *or* **proper inclusion.** the relation that obtains between two sets when the first includes the second but not vice versa. Symbol: $X \subset Y$. [5] *Engineering* a foreign particle in a metal, such as a particle of metal oxide.

inclusion body NOUN *Pathol* any of the small particles found in the nucleus and cytoplasm of cells infected with certain viruses.

inclusive (ɪn'kluːsɪv) ADJECTIVE [1] (*postpositive;* foll by *of*) considered together (with): *capital inclusive of profit.* [2] (*postpositive*) including the limits specified: *Monday to Friday inclusive is five days.* [3] comprehensive. [4] not excluding any particular groups of people: *an inclusive society.* [5] *Logic* (of a disjunction) true if at least one of its component propositions is true. Compare **exclusive** (sense 10).
▸**in'clusively** ADVERB ▸**in'clusiveness** NOUN

inclusive language NOUN language that avoids the use of certain expressions or words that might be considered to exclude particular groups of people, esp gender-specific words, such as "man", "mankind", and masculine pronouns, the use of which might be considered to exclude women.

inclusive or NOUN *Logic* the connective that gives the value *true* to a disjunction if either or both of the disjuncts are true. Also called: **inclusive disjunction.** Compare **exclusive or.**

inclusivity (ˌɪnkluː'sɪvɪtɪ) NOUN the fact or policy of not excluding members or participants on the grounds of gender, race, class, sexuality, disability, etc.

incoercible (ˌɪnkəʊ'ɜːsəbᵊl) ADJECTIVE [1] unable to be coerced or compelled. [2] (of a gas) not capable of being liquefied by pressure alone.

incog. ABBREVIATION FOR incognito.

incogitable (ɪn'kɒdʒɪtəbᵊl) ADJECTIVE *Rare* not to be contemplated; unthinkable.
▸**inˌcogita'bility** NOUN

incogitant (ɪn'kɒdʒɪtənt) ADJECTIVE *Rare* thoughtless.
▷HISTORY C17: from Latin *incōgitāns,* from IN-[1] + *cōgitāre* to think

incognito (ˌɪnkɒg'niːtəʊ, ɪn'kɒgnɪtəʊ) ADVERB, ADJECTIVE (*postpositive*) [1] under an assumed name or appearance; in disguise. ◆ NOUN, *plural* **-tos.** [2] a

ɪncognito. 3 the assumed name or ɜuch a person.
ᴋʏ C17: from Italian, from Latin *incognitus* ..iown, from IN-[1] + *cognitus* known

ɪncognizant (ɪnˈkɒgnɪzənt) ADJECTIVE (*when postpositive,* often foll by *of*) unaware (of).
▸**inˈcognizance** NOUN

incoherent (ˌɪnkəʊˈhɪərənt) ADJECTIVE 1 lacking in clarity or organization; disordered. 2 unable to express oneself clearly; inarticulate. 3 *Physics* (of two or more waves) having the same frequency but not the same phase: *incoherent light.*
▸**ˌincoˈherence, ˌincoˈherency,** *or* **ˌincoˈherentness** NOUN
▸**ˌincoˈherently** ADVERB

incombustible (ˌɪnkəmˈbʌstəbᵊl) ADJECTIVE 1 not capable of being burnt; fireproof. ◆ NOUN 2 an incombustible object or material.
▸**ˌincomˌbustiˈbility** *or* **ˌincomˈbustibleness** NOUN
▸**ˌincomˈbustibly** ADVERB

income (ˈɪnkʌm, ˈɪnkəm) NOUN 1 the amount of monetary or other returns, either earned or unearned, accruing over a given period of time. 2 receipts; revenue. 3 *Rare* an inflow or influx.
▷HISTORY C13 (in the sense: arrival, entrance): from Old English *incumen* a coming in

income bond NOUN a bond that pays interest at a rate in direct proportion to the issuer's earnings.

income group NOUN a group in a given population having incomes within a certain range.

incomer (ˈɪnkʌmə) NOUN a person who comes to live in a place in which he was not born.

incomes policy NOUN See **prices and incomes policy.**

income support NOUN (in Britain, formerly) a social security payment for people on very low incomes.

income tax NOUN a personal tax, usually progressive, levied on annual income subject to certain deductions.

incoming (ˈɪnˌkʌmɪŋ) ADJECTIVE 1 coming in; entering. 2 about to come into office; succeeding. 3 (of interest, dividends, etc.) being received; accruing. ◆ NOUN 4 the act of coming in; entrance. 5 (*usually plural*) income or revenue.

incommensurable (ˌɪnkəˈmɛnʃərəbᵊl) ADJECTIVE 1 incapable of being judged, measured, or considered comparatively. 2 (*postpositive;* foll by *with*) not in accordance; incommensurate. 3 *Maths* **a** (of two numbers) having an irrational ratio. **b** not having units of the same dimension. **c** unrelated to another measurement by integral multiples. ◆ NOUN 4 something incommensurable.
▸**ˌincomˌmensuraˈbility** *or* **ˌincomˈmensurableness** NOUN
▸**ˌincomˈmensurably** ADVERB

incommensurate (ˌɪnkəˈmɛnʃərɪt) ADJECTIVE 1 (when *postpositive,* often foll by *with*) not commensurate; disproportionate. 2 incommensurable.
▸**ˌincomˈmensurately** ADVERB ▸**ˌincomˈmensurateness** NOUN

incommode (ˌɪnkəˈməʊd) VERB (*tr*) to bother, disturb, or inconvenience.
▷HISTORY C16: from Latin *incommodāre* to be troublesome, from *incommodus* inconvenient, from IN-[1] + *commodus* convenient; see COMMODE

incommodious (ˌɪnkəˈməʊdɪəs) ADJECTIVE 1 insufficiently spacious; cramped. 2 troublesome or inconvenient.
▸**ˌincomˈmodiously** ADVERB ▸**ˌincomˈmodiousness** NOUN

incommodity (ˌɪnkəˈmɒdɪtɪ) NOUN, *plural* **-ties.** a less common word for **inconvenience.**

incommunicable (ˌɪnkəˈmju:nɪkəbᵊl) ADJECTIVE 1 incapable of being communicated. 2 an obsolete word for **incommunicative.**
▸**ˌincomˌmunicaˈbility** *or* **ˌincomˈmunicableness** NOUN
▸**ˌincomˈmunicably** ADVERB

incommunicado (ˌɪnkəˌmju:nɪˈkɑ:dəʊ) ADVERB, ADJECTIVE (*postpositive*) deprived of communication with other people, as while in solitary confinement.
▷HISTORY C19: from Spanish *incomunicado,* from *incomunicar* to deprive of communication; see IN-[1], COMMUNICATE

incommunicative (ˌɪnkəˈmju:nɪkətɪv) ADJECTIVE tending not to communicate with others; taciturn.
▸**ˌincomˈmunicatively** ADVERB ▸**ˌincomˈmunicativeness** NOUN

incommutable (ˌɪnkəˈmju:təbᵊl) ADJECTIVE incapable of being commuted; unalterable.
▸**ˌincomˌmutaˈbility** *or* **ˌincomˈmutableness** NOUN
▸**ˌincomˈmutably** ADVERB

incomparable (ɪnˈkɒmpərəbᵊl, -prəbᵊl) ADJECTIVE 1 beyond or above comparison; matchless; unequalled. 2 lacking a basis for comparison; not having qualities or features that can be compared.
▸**inˌcomparaˈbility** *or* **inˈcomparableness** NOUN
▸**inˈcomparably** ADVERB

incompatible (ˌɪnkəmˈpætəbᵊl) ADJECTIVE 1 incapable of living or existing together in peace or harmony; conflicting or antagonistic. 2 opposed in nature or quality; inconsistent. 3 (of an office, position, etc.) only able to be held by one person at a time. 4 *Med* (esp of two drugs or two types of blood) incapable of being combined or used together; antagonistic. 5 *Logic* (of two propositions) unable to be both true at the same time. 6 (of plants) **a** not capable of forming successful grafts. **b** incapable of fertilizing each other. 7 *Maths* another word for **inconsistent** (sense 4). ◆ NOUN 8 (*often plural*) a person or thing that is incompatible with another.
▸**ˌincomˌpatiˈbility** *or* **ˌincomˈpatibleness** NOUN
▸**ˌincomˈpatibly** ADVERB

incompetent (ɪnˈkɒmpɪtənt) ADJECTIVE 1 not possessing the necessary ability, skill, etc. to do or carry out a task; incapable. 2 marked by lack of ability, skill, etc. 3 *Law* not legally qualified: *an incompetent witness.* 4 (of rock strata, folds, etc.) yielding readily to pressure so as to undergo structural deformation. ◆ NOUN 5 an incompetent person.
▸**inˈcompetence** *or* **inˈcompetency** NOUN ▸**inˈcompetently** ADVERB

incomplete (ˌɪnkəmˈpli:t) ADJECTIVE 1 not complete or finished. 2 not completely developed; imperfect. 3 *Logic* **a** (of a formal theory) not so constructed that the addition of a non-theorem to the axioms renders it inconsistent. **b** (of an expression) not having a reference of its own but requiring completion by another expression.
▸**ˌincomˈpletely** ADVERB ▸**ˌincomˈpleteness** *or* **ˌincomˈpletion** NOUN

incompliant (ˌɪnkəmˈplaɪənt) ADJECTIVE not compliant; unyielding or inflexible.
▸**ˌincomˈpliance** *or* **ˌincomˈpliancy** NOUN ▸**ˌincomˈpliantly** ADVERB

incomprehensible (ˌɪnkɒmprɪˈhɛnsəbᵊl, ɪnˌkɒm-) ADJECTIVE 1 incapable of being understood; unintelligible. 2 *Archaic* limitless; boundless.
▸**ˌincompreˌhensiˈbility** *or* **ˌincompreˈhensibleness** NOUN
▸**ˌincompreˈhensibly** ADVERB

incomprehension (ˌɪnkɒmprɪˈhɛnʃən, ɪnˌkɒm-) NOUN inability or failure to comprehend; lack of understanding.

incomprehensive (ˌɪnkɒmprɪˈhɛnsɪv, ɪnˌkɒm-) ADJECTIVE not comprehensive; limited in range or scope.
▸**ˌincompreˈhensively** ADVERB ▸**ˌincompreˈhensiveness** NOUN

incompressible (ˌɪnkəmˈprɛsəbᵊl) ADJECTIVE incapable of being compressed or condensed.
▸**ˌincomˌpressiˈbility** *or* **ˌincomˈpressibleness** NOUN
▸**ˌincomˈpressibly** ADVERB

incomputable (ˌɪnkəmˈpju:təbᵊl) ADJECTIVE incapable of being computed; incalculable.
▸**ˌincomˌputaˈbility** NOUN ▸**ˌincomˈputably** ADVERB

inconceivable (ˌɪnkənˈsi:vəbᵊl) ADJECTIVE incapable of being conceived, imagined, or considered.
▸**ˌinconˌceivaˈbility** *or* **ˌinconˈceivableness** NOUN
▸**ˌinconˈceivably** ADVERB

inconclusive (ˌɪnkənˈklu:sɪv) ADJECTIVE not conclusive or decisive; not finally settled; indeterminate.
▸**ˌinconˈclusively** ADVERB ▸**ˌinconˈclusiveness** NOUN

incondensable *or* **incondensible** (ˌɪnkənˈdɛnsəbᵊl) ADJECTIVE incapable of being condensed.
▸**ˌinconˌdensaˈbility** *or* **ˌinconˌdensiˈbility** NOUN

incondite (ɪnˈkɒndɪt, -daɪt) ADJECTIVE *Rare* 1 poorly constructed or composed. 2 rough or crude.
▷HISTORY C17: from Latin *inconditus,* from IN-[1] + *conditus,* from *condere* to put together
▸**inˈconditely** ADVERB

inconformity (ˌɪnkənˈfɔ:mɪtɪ) NOUN lack of conformity; irregularity.

incongruity (ˌɪnkɒŋˈgru:ɪtɪ) NOUN, *plural* **-ties.** 1 something incongruous. 2 the state or quality of being incongruous.

incongruous (ɪnˈkɒŋgrʊəs) *or* **incongruent** ADJECTIVE 1 (when *postpositive,* foll by *with* or *to*) incompatible with (what is suitable); inappropriate. 2 containing disparate or discordant elements or parts.
▸**inˈcongruously** *or* **inˈcongruently** ADVERB
▸**inˈcongruousness** *or* **inˈcongruence** NOUN

inconnu (ˈɪnkənu:) NOUN a North American freshwater food and game fish, *Stenodus leucichthys,* related to the salmon.
▷HISTORY C19: from French, literally: unknown

inconsecutive (ˌɪnkənˈsɛkjʊtɪv) ADJECTIVE not consecutive; not in sequence.
▸**ˌinconˈsecutively** ADVERB ▸**ˌinconˈsecutiveness** NOUN

inconsequential (ˌɪnkɒnsɪˈkwɛnʃəl, ɪnˌkɒn-) *or* **inconsequent** (ɪnˈkɒnsɪkwənt) ADJECTIVE 1 not following logically as a consequence. 2 trivial or insignificant. 3 not in a logical sequence; haphazard.
▸**ˌinconseˌquentiˈality, ˌinconseˈquentialness, inˈconsequence,** *or* **inˈconsequentness** NOUN
▸**ˌinconseˈquentially** *or* **inˈconsequently** ADVERB

inconsiderable (ˌɪnkənˈsɪdərəbᵊl) ADJECTIVE 1 relatively small. 2 not worthy of consideration; insignificant.
▸**ˌinconˈsiderableness** NOUN ▸**ˌinconˈsiderably** ADVERB

inconsiderate (ˌɪnkənˈsɪdərɪt) ADJECTIVE 1 lacking in care or thought for others; heedless; thoughtless. 2 *Rare* insufficiently considered.
▸**ˌinconˈsiderately** ADVERB ▸**ˌinconˈsiderateness** *or* **ˌinconˌsiderˈation** NOUN

inconsistency (ˌɪnkənˈsɪstənsɪ) NOUN, *plural* **-cies.** 1 lack of consistency or agreement; incompatibility. 2 an inconsistent feature or quality. 3 *Logic* **a** the property of being inconsistent. **b** a self-contradictory proposition.

inconsistent (ˌɪnkənˈsɪstənt) ADJECTIVE 1 lacking in consistency, agreement, or compatibility; at variance. 2 containing contradictory elements. 3 irregular or fickle in behaviour or mood. 4 Also: **incompatible.** *Maths* (of two or more equations) not having one common set of values of the variables: $x + 2y = 5$ and $x + 2y = 6$ are inconsistent. 5 *Logic* (of a set of propositions) enabling an explicit contradiction to be validly derived.
▸**ˌinconˈsistently** ADVERB

inconsolable (ˌɪnkənˈsəʊləbᵊl) ADJECTIVE incapable of being consoled or comforted; disconsolate.
▸**ˌinconˌsolaˈbility** *or* **ˌinconˈsolableness** NOUN
▸**ˌinconˈsolably** ADVERB

inconsonant (ɪnˈkɒnsənənt) ADJECTIVE lacking in harmony or compatibility; discordant.
▸**inˈconsonance** NOUN ▸**inˈconsonantly** ADVERB

inconspicuous (ˌɪnkənˈspɪkjʊəs) ADJECTIVE not easily noticed or seen; not prominent or striking.
▸**ˌinconˈspicuously** ADVERB ▸**ˌinconˈspicuousness** NOUN

inconstant (ɪnˈkɒnstənt) ADJECTIVE 1 not constant; variable. 2 fickle.
▸**inˈconstancy** NOUN ▸**inˈconstantly** ADVERB

inconsumable (ˌɪnkənˈsju:məbᵊl) ADJECTIVE 1 incapable of being consumed or used up. 2 *Economics* providing an economic service without being consumed, as currency.
▸**ˌinconˈsumably** ADVERB

incontestable (ˌɪnkənˈtɛstəbᵊl) ADJECTIVE incapable of being contested or disputed.
▸**ˌinconˌtestaˈbility** *or* **ˌinconˈtestableness** NOUN
▸**ˌinconˈtestably** ADVERB

incontinent[1] (ɪnˈkɒntɪnənt) ADJECTIVE 1 lacking in restraint or control, esp sexually. 2 relating to or exhibiting involuntary urination or defecation. 3 (foll by *of*) having little or no control (over). 4 unrestrained; uncontrolled.
▷HISTORY C14: from Old French, from Latin *incontinens,* from IN-[1] + *continere* to hold, restrain
▸**inˈcontinence** *or* **inˈcontinency** NOUN ▸**inˈcontinently** ADVERB

incontinent[2] (ɪnˈkɒntɪnənt) *or* **incontinently** ADVERB obsolete words for **immediately.**
▷HISTORY C15: from Late Latin *in continentī tempore,*

literally: in continuous time, that is, with no interval

incontrollable (ˌɪnkənˈtrəʊləbᵊl) ADJECTIVE a less common word for **uncontrollable.**
▸ ˌinconˈtrollably ADVERB

incontrovertible (ˌɪnkɒntrəˈvɜːtəbᵊl, ɪnˌkɒn-) ADJECTIVE incapable of being contradicted or disputed; undeniable.
▸ ˌincontroˌvertiˈbility or ˌincontroˈvertibleness NOUN
▸ ˌincontroˈvertibly ADVERB

inconvenience (ˌɪnkənˈviːnjəns, -ˈviːnɪəns) NOUN 1 the state or quality of being inconvenient. 2 something inconvenient; a hindrance, trouble, or difficulty. ◆ VERB 3 (*tr*) to cause inconvenience to; trouble or harass.

inconvenient (ˌɪnkənˈviːnjənt, -ˈviːnɪənt) ADJECTIVE not convenient; troublesome, awkward, or difficult.
▸ ˌinconˈveniently ADVERB

inconvertible (ˌɪnkənˈvɜːtəbᵊl) ADJECTIVE 1 incapable of being converted or changed. 2 (of paper currency) **a** not redeemable for gold or silver specie. **b** not exchangeable for another currency.
▸ ˌinconˌvertiˈbility or ˌinconˈvertibleness NOUN
▸ ˌinconˈvertibly ADVERB

inconvincible (ˌɪnkənˈvɪnsəbᵊl) ADJECTIVE refusing or not able to be convinced.
▸ ˌinconˌvinciˈbility or ˌinconˈvincibleness NOUN
▸ ˌinconˈvincibly ADVERB

incoordinate (ˌɪnkəʊˈɔːdɪnɪt) ADJECTIVE 1 not coordinate; unequal in rank, order, or importance. 2 uncoordinated.

incoordination (ˌɪnkəʊˌɔːdɪˈneɪʃən) NOUN 1 lack of coordination or organization. 2 *Pathol* a lack of muscular control when making a voluntary movement.

incorporable (ɪnˈkɔːpərəbᵊl) ADJECTIVE capable of being incorporated or included.

incorporate[1] VERB (ɪnˈkɔːpəˌreɪt) 1 to include or be included as a part or member of a united whole. 2 to form or cause to form a united whole or mass; merge or blend. 3 to form (individuals, an unincorporated enterprise, etc.) into a corporation or other organization with a separate legal identity from that of its owners or members. ◆ ADJECTIVE (ɪnˈkɔːpərɪt, -prɪt) 4 combined into a whole; incorporated. 5 formed into or constituted as a corporation.
▷HISTORY C14 (in the sense: put into the body of something else): from Late Latin *incorporāre* to embody, from Latin IN-[2] + *corpus* body
▸ inˈcorporative ADJECTIVE ▸ inˌcorpoˈration NOUN

incorporate[2] (ɪnˈkɔːpərɪt, -prɪt) ADJECTIVE an archaic word for **incorporeal.**
▷HISTORY C16: from Late Latin *incorporātus,* from Latin IN-[1] + *corporātus* furnished with a body

incorporated (ɪnˈkɔːpəˌreɪtɪd) ADJECTIVE 1 united or combined into a whole. 2 organized as a legal corporation, esp in commerce. Abbreviation: **Inc** or **inc.**
▸ inˈcorpoˌratedness NOUN

incorporating (ɪnˈkɔːpəˌreɪtɪŋ) ADJECTIVE *Linguistics* another word for **polysynthetic.**

incorporator (ɪnˈkɔːpəˌreɪtə) NOUN 1 a person who incorporates. 2 *US commerce* **a** any of the signatories of a certificate of incorporation. **b** any of the original members of a corporation.

incorporeal (ˌɪnkɔːˈpɔːrɪəl) ADJECTIVE 1 without material form, body, or substance. 2 spiritual or metaphysical. 3 *Law* having no material existence but existing by reason of its annexation of something material, such as an easement, touchline, copyright, etc.: *an incorporeal hereditament.*
▸ ˌincorˈporeally ADVERB ▸ incorporeity (ɪnˌkɔːpəˈriːɪtɪ) or ˌincorˌporeˈality NOUN

incorrect (ˌɪnkəˈrɛkt) ADJECTIVE 1 false; wrong: *an incorrect calculation.* 2 not fitting or proper: *incorrect behaviour.*
▸ ˌincorˈrectly ADVERB ▸ ˌincorˈrectness NOUN

incorrigible (ɪnˈkɒrɪdʒəbᵊl) ADJECTIVE 1 beyond correction, reform, or alteration. 2 firmly rooted; ineradicable. 3 *Philosophy* (of a belief) having the property that whoever honestly believes it cannot be mistaken. Compare **defeasible.** ◆ NOUN 4 a person or animal that is incorrigible.
▸ inˌcorrigiˈbility or inˈcorrigibleness NOUN ▸ inˈcorrigibly ADVERB

incorrupt (ˌɪnkəˈrʌpt) ADJECTIVE 1 free from corruption; pure. 2 free from decay; fresh or untainted. 3 (of a manuscript, text, etc.) relatively free from error or alteration.
▸ ˌincorˈruptly ADVERB ▸ ˌincorˈruption or ˌincorˈruptness NOUN

incorruptible (ˌɪnkəˈrʌptəbᵊl) ADJECTIVE 1 incapable of being corrupted; honest; just. 2 not subject to decay or decomposition.
▸ ˌincorˌruptiˈbility or ˌincorˈruptibleness NOUN
▸ ˌincorˈruptibly ADVERB

Incoterms (ˈɪnkəʊˌtɜːmz) NOUN a glossary of terms used in international commerce and trade, published by the International Chamber of Commerce.

incrassate ADJECTIVE (ɪnˈkræsɪt, -eɪt) also **incrassated.** 1 *Biology* thickened or swollen: *incrassate cell walls.* 2 *Obsolete* fattened or swollen. ◆ VERB (ɪnˈkræseɪt) 3 *Obsolete* to make or become thicker.
▷HISTORY C17: from Late Latin *incrassāre,* from Latin *crassus* thick, dense
▸ ˌincrasˈsation NOUN

increase VERB (ɪnˈkriːs) 1 to make or become greater in size, degree, frequency, etc.; grow or expand. ◆ NOUN (ˈɪnkriːs) 2 the act of increasing; augmentation. 3 the amount by which something increases. 4 **on the increase.** increasing, esp becoming more frequent.
▷HISTORY C14: from Old French *encreistre,* from Latin *incrēscere,* from IN-[2] + *crēscere* to grow
▸ inˈcreasable ADJECTIVE ▸ increasedly (ɪnˈkriːsɪdlɪ) or inˈcreasingly ADVERB ▸ inˈcreaser NOUN

increate (ˌɪnkrɪˈeɪt, ˈɪnkrɪˌeɪt) ADJECTIVE *Archaic, poetic* (esp of gods) never having been created.
▸ ˌincreˈately ADVERB

incredible (ɪnˈkrɛdəbᵊl) ADJECTIVE 1 beyond belief or understanding; unbelievable. 2 *Informal* marvellous; amazing.
▸ inˌcrediˈbility or inˈcredibleness NOUN ▸ inˈcredibly ADVERB

incredulity (ˌɪnkrɪˈdjuːlɪtɪ) NOUN lack of belief; scepticism.

incredulous (ɪnˈkrɛdjʊləs) ADJECTIVE (often foll by *of*) not prepared or willing to believe (something); unbelieving.
▸ inˈcredulously ADVERB ▸ inˈcredulousness NOUN

increment (ˈɪnkrɪmənt) NOUN 1 an increase or addition, esp one of a series. 2 the act of increasing; augmentation. 3 *Maths* a small positive or negative change in a variable or function. Symbol: Δ, as in Δx or Δf.
▷HISTORY C15: from Latin *incrēmentum* growth, INCREASE

incremental (ˌɪnkrɪˈmɛntᵊl) ADJECTIVE of, relating to, using, or rising by increments.

incremental plotter NOUN a device that plots graphs on paper from computer-generated instructions. See also **microfilm plotter.**

incremental recorder NOUN *Computing* a device for recording data as it is generated, usually on paper tape or magnetic tape, and feeding it into a computer.

increscent (ɪnˈkrɛsᵊnt) ADJECTIVE (esp of the moon) increasing in size; waxing.
▷HISTORY C16: from Latin *incrēscēns*

incretion (ɪnˈkriːʃən) NOUN *Physiol* 1 direct secretion into the bloodstream, esp of a hormone from an endocrine gland. 2 the substance so secreted.
▷HISTORY C20: from IN-[2] + (SE)CRETION
▸ inˈcretionary or incretory (ˈɪnkrɪtərɪ, -trɪ) ADJECTIVE

incriminate (ɪnˈkrɪmɪˌneɪt) VERB (*tr*) 1 to imply or suggest the guilt or error of (someone). 2 to charge with a crime or fault.
▷HISTORY C18: from Late Latin *incrīmināre* to accuse, from Latin *crīmen* accusation; see CRIME
▸ inˌcrimiˈnation NOUN ▸ inˈcrimiˌnator NOUN
▸ inˈcriminatory ADJECTIVE

incross (ˈɪnkrɒs) NOUN 1 a plant or animal produced by continued inbreeding. ◆ VERB 2 to inbreed or produce by inbreeding.

incrust (ɪnˈkrʌst) VERB a variant spelling of **encrust.**
▸ inˈcrustant NOUN, ADJECTIVE ▸ ˌincrusˈtation NOUN

incubate (ˈɪnkjʊˌbeɪt) VERB 1 (of birds) to supply (eggs) with heat for their development, esp by sitting on them. 2 to cause (eggs, embryos, bacteria, etc.) to develop, esp in an incubator or culture medium. 3 (*intr*) (of eggs, embryos, bacteria, etc.) to develop in favourable conditions, esp in an incubator. 4 (*intr*) (of disease germs) to remain inactive in an animal or human before causing disease. 5 to develop or cause to develop gradually; foment or be fomented.
▷HISTORY C18: from Latin *incubāre* to lie upon, hatch, from IN-[2] + *cubāre* to lie down
▸ ˌincuˈbation NOUN ▸ ˌincuˈbational ADJECTIVE
▸ ˈincuˌbative or ˈincuˌbatory ADJECTIVE

incubation period NOUN *Med* the time between exposure to an infectious disease and the appearance of the first signs or symptoms. Sometimes shortened to **incubation.**

incubator (ˈɪnkjʊˌbeɪtə) NOUN 1 *Med* an enclosed transparent boxlike apparatus for housing prematurely born babies under optimum conditions until they are strong enough to survive in the normal environment. 2 a container kept at a constant temperature in which birds' eggs can be artificially hatched or bacterial cultures grown. 3 a person, animal, or thing that incubates. 4 a commercial property, divided into small work units, which provides equipment and support to new businesses.

incubous (ˈɪnkjʊbəs) ADJECTIVE (of a liverwort) having the leaves arranged so that the upper margin of each leaf lies above the lower margin of the next leaf along. Compare **succubous.**
▷HISTORY C19: from Latin *incubare* INCUBATE

incubus (ˈɪnkjʊbəs) NOUN, *plural* **-bi** (-ˌbaɪ) or **-buses.** 1 a demon believed in folklore to lie upon sleeping persons, esp to have sexual intercourse with sleeping women. Compare **succubus.** 2 something that oppresses, worries, or disturbs greatly, esp a nightmare or obsession.
▷HISTORY C14: from Late Latin, from *incubāre* to lie upon; see INCUBATE

incudes (ɪnˈkjuːdiːz) NOUN the plural of **incus.**

inculcate (ˈɪnkʌlˌkeɪt, ɪnˈkʌlkeɪt) VERB (*tr*) to instil by forceful or insistent repetition.
▷HISTORY C16: from Latin *inculcāre* to tread upon, ram down, from IN-[2] + *calcāre* to trample, from *calx* heel
▸ ˌinculˈcation NOUN ▸ ˈinculˌcator NOUN

inculpable (ɪnˈkʌlpəbᵊl) ADJECTIVE incapable of being blamed or accused; guiltless.
▸ inˌculpaˈbility or inˈculpableness NOUN ▸ inˈculpably ADVERB

inculpate (ˈɪnkʌlˌpeɪt, ɪnˈkʌlpeɪt) VERB (*tr*) to incriminate; cause blame to be imputed to.
▷HISTORY C18: from Late Latin *inculpāre,* from Latin *culpāre* to blame, from *culpa* fault, blame
▸ ˌinculˈpation NOUN ▸ inculpative (ɪnˈkʌlpətɪv) or inculpatory (ɪnˈkʌlpətərɪ, -trɪ) ADJECTIVE

incult (ɪnˈkʌlt) ADJECTIVE *Rare* 1 (of land) uncultivated; untilled; naturally wild. 2 lacking refinement and culture.
▷HISTORY C16: from Latin *incultus,* from IN-[1] + *colere* to till

incumbency (ɪnˈkʌmbənsɪ) NOUN, *plural* **-cies.** 1 the state or quality of being incumbent. 2 the office, duty, or tenure of an incumbent.

incumbent (ɪnˈkʌmbənt) ADJECTIVE 1 *Formal* (often *postpositive* and foll by *on* or *upon* and an infinitive) morally binding or necessary; obligatory: *it is incumbent on me to attend.* 2 (usually *postpositive* and foll by *on*) resting or lying (on). ◆ NOUN 3 a person who holds an office, esp a clergyman holding a benefice.
▷HISTORY C16: from Latin *incumbere* to lie upon, devote one's attention to, from IN-[2] + *-cumbere,* related to Latin *cubāre* to lie down
▸ inˈcumbently ADVERB

incumber (ɪnˈkʌmbə) VERB a less common spelling of **encumber.**
▸ inˈcumberingly ADVERB ▸ inˈcumbrance NOUN

incunabula (ˌɪnkjʊˈnæbjʊlə) PLURAL NOUN, *singular* **-lum** (-ləm) 1 any book printed before 1500. 2 the infancy or earliest stages of something; beginnings.
▷HISTORY C19: from Latin, originally: swaddling clothes, hence beginnings, from IN-[2] + *cūnābula* cradle
▸ ˌincuˈnabular ADJECTIVE

incur (ɪnˈkɜː) VERB **-curs, -curring, -curred.** (*tr*) 1 to

make oneself subject to (something undesirable); bring upon oneself. [2] to run into or encounter.
▷HISTORY C16: from Latin *incurrere* to run into, from *currere* to run
▸**in'currable** ADJECTIVE

incurable (ɪn'kjʊərəbᵊl) ADJECTIVE [1] (esp of a disease) not curable; unresponsive to treatment. ◆ NOUN [2] a person having an incurable disease.
▸**in,cura'bility** *or* **in'curableness** NOUN ▸**in'curably** ADVERB

incurious (ɪn'kjʊərɪəs) ADJECTIVE not curious; indifferent or uninterested.
▸**incuriosity** (ɪn,kjʊərɪ'ɒsɪtɪ) *or* **in'curiousness** NOUN ▸**in'curiously** ADVERB

incurrence (ɪn'kʌrəns) NOUN the act or state of incurring.

incurrent (ɪn'kʌrənt) ADJECTIVE [1] (of anatomical ducts, tubes, channels, etc.) having an inward flow. [2] flowing or running in an inward direction.
▷HISTORY C16: from Latin *incurrēns* running into; see INCUR

incursion (ɪn'kɜːʃən) NOUN [1] a sudden invasion, attack, or raid. [2] the act of running or leaking into; penetration.
▷HISTORY C15: from Latin *incursiō* onset, attack, from *incurrere* to run into; see INCUR
▸**incursive** (ɪn'kɜːsɪv) ADJECTIVE

incurvate VERB ('ɪnkɜː,veɪt) *also* **incurve** (ɪn'kɜːv). [1] to curve or cause to curve inwards. ◆ ADJECTIVE (ɪn'kɜːvɪt, -veɪt) [2] curved inwards.
▷HISTORY C16: from Latin *incurvāre* (*vb*)
▸**,incur'vation** NOUN ▸**incurvature** (ɪn'kɜːvətʃə) NOUN

incus ('ɪŋkəs) NOUN, *plural* **incudes** (ɪn'kjuːdiːz). the central of the three small bones in the middle ear of mammals. Nontechnical name: **anvil.** Compare **malleus, stapes.**
▷HISTORY C17: from Latin: anvil, from *incūdere* to forge
▸**incudate** ('ɪŋkju,deɪt) *or* **incudal** ('ɪŋkjudᵊl) ADJECTIVE

incuse (ɪn'kjuːz) NOUN [1] a design stamped or hammered onto a coin. ◆ VERB [2] to impress (a design) in a coin or to impress (a coin) with a design by hammering or stamping. ◆ ADJECTIVE [3] stamped or hammered onto a coin.
▷HISTORY C19: from Latin *incūsus* hammered; see INCUS

Ind (ɪnd) NOUN [1] a poetic name for **India.** [2] an obsolete name for the **Indies.**

IND [1] Also: **IDN.** ABBREVIATION FOR in nomine Dei. ◆ [2] INTERNATIONAL CAR REGISTRATION FOR India.
▷HISTORY (for sense 1) Latin: in the name of God

Ind. ABBREVIATION FOR: [1] Independent. [2] India. [3] Indian. [4] Indiana.

indaba (ɪn'dɑːbə) NOUN [1] *Anthropol, history* (among Bantu peoples of southern Africa) a meeting to discuss a serious topic. [2] *South African informal* a matter of concern or for discussion.
▷HISTORY C19: from Zulu: topic

indamine ('ɪndə,miːn, -mɪn) NOUN [1] an organic base used in the production of the dye safranine. Formula: $NH_2C_6H_4N{:}C_6H_4{:}NH$. [2] any of a class of organic bases with a similar structure to this compound. Their salts are unstable blue and green dyes.
▷HISTORY C20: from INDIGO + AMINE

indebted (ɪn'detɪd) ADJECTIVE (*postpositive*) [1] owing gratitude for help, favours, etc; obligated. [2] owing money.

indebtedness (ɪn'detɪdnɪs) NOUN [1] the state of being indebted. [2] the total of a person's debts.

indecency (ɪn'diːsənsɪ) NOUN, *plural* **-cies.** [1] the state or quality of being indecent. [2] an indecent act, etc.

indecent (ɪn'diːsᵊnt) ADJECTIVE [1] offensive to standards of decency, esp in sexual matters. [2] unseemly or improper (esp in the phrase **indecent haste**).
▸**in'decently** ADVERB

indecent assault NOUN the act of taking indecent liberties with a person without his or her consent.

indecent exposure NOUN the offence of indecently exposing parts of one's body in public, esp the genitals.

indeciduous (,ɪndɪ'sɪdjʊəs) ADJECTIVE [1] (of leaves) not deciduous. [2] a less common term for **evergreen** (sense 1).

indecipherable (,ɪndɪ'saɪfərəbᵊl, -frəbᵊl) ADJECTIVE not decipherable; illegible.
▸**,inde,ciphera'bility** *or* **,inde'cipherableness** NOUN ▸**,inde'cipherably** ADVERB

indecisive (,ɪndɪ'saɪsɪv) ADJECTIVE [1] (of a person) vacillating; irresolute. [2] not decisive or conclusive.
▸**,inde'cision** *or* **,inde'cisiveness** NOUN ▸**,inde'cisively** ADVERB

indeclinable (,ɪndɪ'klaɪnəbᵊl) ADJECTIVE (of a noun or pronoun) having only one form; not declined for case or number.
▸**,inde'clinableness** NOUN ▸**,inde'clinably** ADVERB

indecorous (ɪn'dekərəs) ADJECTIVE improper or ungraceful; unseemly.
▸**in'decorously** ADVERB ▸**in'decorousness** NOUN

indecorum (,ɪndɪ'kɔːrəm) NOUN indecorous behaviour or speech; unseemliness.

indeed (ɪn'diːd) SENTENCE CONNECTOR [1] certainly; actually: *indeed, it may never happen.* ◆ ADVERB [2] (intensifier): *that is indeed amazing.* [3] or rather; what is more: *a comfortable, indeed wealthy family.* ◆ INTERJECTION [4] an expression of doubt, surprise, etc.

indef. ABBREVIATION FOR indefinite.

indefatigable (,ɪndɪ'fætɪgəbᵊl) ADJECTIVE unable to be tired out; unflagging.
▷HISTORY C16: from Latin *indēfatīgābilis,* from IN-[1] + *dēfatīgāre,* from *fatīgāre* to tire
▸**,inde,fatiga'bility** *or* **,inde'fatigableness** NOUN ▸**,inde'fatigably** ADVERB

indefeasible (,ɪndɪ'fiːzəbᵊl) ADJECTIVE *Law* not liable to be annulled or forfeited.
▸**,inde,feasi'bility** *or* **,inde'feasibleness** NOUN ▸**,inde'feasibly** ADVERB

indefectible (,ɪndɪ'fektɪbᵊl) ADJECTIVE [1] not subject to decay or failure. [2] flawless.
▸**,inde,fecti'bility** NOUN ▸**,inde'fectibly** ADVERB

indefensible (,ɪndɪ'fensəbᵊl) ADJECTIVE [1] not justifiable or excusable. [2] capable of being disagreed with; untenable. [3] incapable of defence against attack.
▸**,inde,fensi'bility** *or* **,inde'fensibleness** NOUN ▸**,inde'fensibly** ADVERB

indefinable (,ɪndɪ'faɪnəbᵊl) ADJECTIVE incapable of being defined or analysed: *there was an indefinable sense of terror.*
▸**,inde'finableness** NOUN ▸**,inde'finably** ADVERB

indefinite (ɪn'defɪnɪt) ADJECTIVE [1] not certain or determined; unsettled. [2] without exact limits; indeterminate: *an indefinite number.* [3] vague, evasive, or unclear. [4] Also: **indeterminate.** *Botany* **a** too numerous to count: *indefinite stamens.* **b** capable of continued growth at the tip of the stem, which does not terminate in a flower: *an indefinite inflorescence.*
▸**in'definiteness** NOUN

indefinite article NOUN *Grammar* a determiner that expresses nonspecificity of reference, such as *a, an,* or *some.* Compare **definite article.**

indefinite integral NOUN *Maths* **a** any function whose derivative is the given function, as x^2, $x^2 + 3$, $x^2 – 5$, etc. of $2x$. **b** the schema representing all such functions, here $x^2 + k$. **c** the symbolic representation of this as a function of the given function, written $\int f(x)dx$ where $f(x)$ is the given function. **d** the symbol $\int$.

indefinitely (ɪn'defɪnɪtlɪ) ADVERB without any limit of time or number.

indefinite pronoun NOUN *Grammar* a pronoun having no specific referent, such as *someone, anybody,* or *nothing.*

indehiscent (,ɪndɪ'hɪsᵊnt) ADJECTIVE (of fruits) not dehiscent; not opening to release seeds.
▸**,inde'hiscence** NOUN

indelible (ɪn'delɪbᵊl) ADJECTIVE [1] incapable of being erased or obliterated. [2] making indelible marks: *indelible ink.*
▷HISTORY C16: from Latin *indēlēbilis* indestructible, from IN-[1] + *delēre* to destroy
▸**in,deli'bility** *or* **in'delibleness** NOUN ▸**in'delibly** ADVERB

indelicate (ɪn'delɪkɪt) ADJECTIVE [1] coarse, crude, or rough. [2] offensive, embarrassing, or tasteless.
▸**in'delicacy** *or* **in'delicateness** NOUN ▸**in'delicately** ADVERB

indemnify (ɪn'demnɪ,faɪ) VERB **-fies, -fying, -fied.** (*tr*) [1] to secure against future loss, damage, or liability; give security for; insure. [2] to compensate for loss, injury, expense, etc.; reimburse.
▸**in,demnifi'cation** NOUN ▸**in'demni,fier** NOUN

indemnity (ɪn'demnɪtɪ) NOUN, *plural* **-ties.** [1] compensation for loss or damage; reimbursement. [2] protection or insurance against future loss or damage. [3] legal exemption from penalties or liabilities incurred through one's acts or defaults. [4] (in Canada) the salary paid to a member of Parliament or of a legislature. [5] **act of indemnity.** an act of Parliament granting exemption to public officers from technical penalties that they may have been compelled to incur.
▷HISTORY C15: from Late Latin *indemnitās,* from *indemnis* uninjured, from Latin IN-[1] + *damnum* damage

indemonstrable (,ɪndɪ'mɒnstrəbᵊl) ADJECTIVE incapable of being demonstrated or proved.
▸**,inde,monstra'bility** NOUN ▸**,inde'monstrably** ADVERB

indene ('ɪndiːn) NOUN a colourless liquid hydrocarbon extracted from petroleum and coal tar and used in making synthetic resins. Formula: C_9H_8.
▷HISTORY C20: from INDOLE + -ENE

indent[1] VERB (ɪn'dent) (*mainly tr*) [1] to place (written or printed matter, etc.) in from the margin, as at the beginning of a paragraph. [2] to cut or tear (a document, esp a contract or deed in duplicate) so that the irregular lines may be matched to confirm its authenticity. [3] *Chiefly Brit* (in foreign trade) to place an order for (foreign goods), usually through an agent. [4] (when *intr,* foll by *for, on,* or *upon*) *Chiefly Brit* to make an order on (a source or supply) or for (something). [5] to notch (an edge, border, etc.); make jagged. [6] to bind (an apprentice, etc.) by indenture. ◆ NOUN ('ɪn,dent) [7] *Chiefly Brit* (in foreign trade) an order for foreign merchandise, esp one placed with an agent. [8] *Chiefly Brit* an official order for goods. [9] (in the late 18th-century US) a certificate issued by federal and state governments for the principal or interest due on the public debt. [10] another word for **indenture.** [11] another word for **indentation** (sense 4).
▷HISTORY C14: from Old French *endenter,* from EN-[1] + *dent* tooth, from Latin *dēns*
▸**in'denter** *or* **in'dentor** NOUN

indent[2] VERB (ɪn'dent) [1] (*tr*) to make a dent or depression in. ◆ NOUN ('ɪn,dent) [2] a dent or depression.
▷HISTORY C15: from IN-[2] + DENT[1]

indentation (,ɪnden'teɪʃən) NOUN [1] a hollowed, notched, or cut place, as on an edge or on a coastline. [2] a series of hollows, notches, or cuts. [3] the act of indenting or the condition of being indented. [4] Also called: **indention, indent.** the leaving of space or the amount of space left between a margin and the start of an indented line.

indention (ɪn'denʃən) NOUN another word for **indentation** (sense 4).

indenture (ɪn'dentʃə) NOUN [1] any deed, contract, or sealed agreement between two or more parties. [2] (formerly) a deed drawn up in duplicate, each part having correspondingly indented edges for identification and security. [3] (*often plural*) a contract between an apprentice and his master. [4] a formal or official list or certificate authenticated for use as a voucher, etc. [5] a less common word for **indentation.** ◆ VERB [6] (*intr*) to enter into an agreement by indenture. [7] (*tr*) to bind (an apprentice, servant, etc.) by indenture. [8] (*tr*) *Obsolete* to indent or wrinkle.
▸**in'denture,ship** NOUN

independence (,ɪndɪ'pendəns) NOUN the state or quality of being independent. Also called: **independency.**

Independence (,ɪndɪ'pendəns) NOUN a city in W Missouri, near Kansas City: starting point for the Santa Fe, Oregon, and California Trails (1831–44). Pop.: 113 288 (2000).

Independence Day NOUN the official name for the **Fourth of July.**

independency (,ɪndɪ'pendənsɪ) NOUN, *plural* **-cies.** [1] a territory or state free from the control of any other power. [2] another word for **independence.**

Independency (,ɪndɪ'pendənsɪ) NOUN (esp in the Congregational Church) the principle upholding the independence of each local church or congregation.

independent (,ɪndɪ'pendənt) ADJECTIVE [1] free from control in action, judgment, etc.;

autonomous. 2 not dependent on anything else for function, validity, etc.; separate: *two independent units make up this sofa.* 3 not reliant on the support, esp financial support, of others. 4 capable of acting for oneself or on one's own: *a very independent little girl.* 5 providing a large unearned sum towards one's support (esp in the phrases **independent income, independent means**). 6 living on an unearned income. 7 *Maths* (of a system of equations) not linearly dependent. See also **independent variable.** 8 *Statistics* **a** (of two or more variables) distributed so that the value taken by one variable will have no effect on that taken by another or others. **b** (of two or more events) such that the probability of all occurring equals the product of their individual probabilities. Compare **statistical dependence.** 9 *Logic* (of a set of propositions) **a** not validly derivable from one another, so that if the propositions are the axioms of some theory none can be dispensed with. **b** not logically related, so that in no case can the truth value of one be inferred from those of the others. ◆ NOUN 10 an independent person or thing. 11 a person who is not affiliated to or who acts independently of a political party.
▸**ˌindeˈpendently** ADVERB

Independent (ˌɪndɪˈpɛndənt) NOUN 1 (in England) a member of the Congregational Church. ◆ ADJECTIVE 2 of or relating to Independency.

independent clause NOUN *Grammar* a main or coordinate clause. Compare **dependent clause.**

independent school NOUN 1 (in Britain) a school that is neither financed nor controlled by the government or local authorities. 2 (in Australia) a school that is not part of the state system.

independent variable NOUN 1 Also called: **argument.** a variable in a mathematical equation or statement whose value determines that of the dependent variable: in $y = f(x)$, x is the independent variable. 2 *Statistics* Also called: **predictor.** the variable which an experimenter deliberately manipulates in order to observe its relationship with some other quantity, or which defines the distinct conditions in an experiment. See also **experimental condition.**

in-depth ADJECTIVE carefully worked out, detailed and thorough: *an in-depth study.*

indescribable (ˌɪndɪˈskraɪbəbᵊl) ADJECTIVE beyond description; too intense, extreme, etc., for words.
▸**ˌindeˌscribaˈbility** *or* **ˌindeˈscribableness** NOUN
▸**ˌindeˈscribably** ADVERB

indestructible (ˌɪndɪˈstrʌktəbᵊl) ADJECTIVE incapable of being destroyed; very durable.
▸**ˌindeˌstructiˈbility** *or* **ˌindeˈstructibleness** NOUN
▸**ˌindeˈstructibly** ADVERB

indeterminable (ˌɪndɪˈtɜːmɪnəbᵊl) ADJECTIVE 1 incapable of being ascertained. 2 incapable of being settled.
▸**ˌindeˈterminableness** NOUN ▸**ˌindeˈterminably** ADVERB

indeterminacy principle (ˌɪndɪˈtɜːmɪnəsɪ) NOUN another name for **uncertainty principle.**

indeterminate (ˌɪndɪˈtɜːmɪnɪt) ADJECTIVE 1 uncertain in extent, amount, or nature. 2 not definite; inconclusive: *an indeterminate reply.* 3 unable to be predicted, calculated, or deduced. 4 *Physics* (of an effect) not obeying the law of causality; noncausal. 5 *Maths* **a** having no numerical meaning, as 0/0. **b** (of an equation) having more than one variable and an unlimited number of solutions. 6 *Botany* another word for **indefinite** (sense 4). 7 (of a structure, framework, etc.) comprising forces that cannot be fully analysed, esp by vector analysis.
▸**ˌindeˈterminacy, ˌindeˌtermiˈnation,** *or* **ˌindeˈterminateness** NOUN ▸**ˌindeˈterminately** ADVERB

indeterminate sentence NOUN *Law* a prison sentence the length of which depends on the prisoner's conduct.

indeterminism (ˌɪndɪˈtɜːmɪˌnɪzəm) NOUN the philosophical doctrine that behaviour is not entirely determined by motives.
▸**ˌindeˈterminist** NOUN, ADJECTIVE ▸**ˌindeˌterminˈistic** ADJECTIVE

index (ˈɪndɛks) NOUN, *plural* **-dexes** *or* **-dices** (-dɪˌsiːz). 1 an alphabetical list of persons, places, subjects, etc., mentioned in the text of a printed work, usually at the back, and indicating where in the work they are referred to. 2 See **thumb index.** 3 *Library science* a systematic list of book titles or author's names, giving cross-references and the location of each book; catalogue. 4 an indication, sign, or token. 5 a pointer, needle, or other indicator, as on an instrument. 6 *Maths* **a** another name for **exponent** (sense 4). **b** a number or variable placed as a superscript to the left of a radical sign indicating by its value the root to be extracted, as in $\sqrt[3]{8} = 2$. **c** a subscript or superscript to the right of a variable to express a set of variables, as in using x_i for x_1, x_2, x_3, etc. 7 a numerical scale by means of which variables, such as levels of the cost of living, can be compared with each other or with some base number. 8 a number or ratio indicating a specific characteristic, property, etc.: *refractive index.* 9 Also called: **fist.** a printer's mark (☛) used to indicate notes, paragraphs, etc. 10 *Obsolete* a table of contents or preface. ◆ VERB (*tr*) 11 to put an index in (a book). 12 to enter (a word, item, etc.) in an index. 13 to point out; indicate. 14 to index-link. 15 to move (a machine or a workpiece held in a machine tool) so that one particular operation will be repeated at certain defined intervals.
▷**HISTORY** C16: from Latin: pointer, hence forefinger, title, index, from *indicāre* to disclose, show; see INDICATE
▸**ˈindexer** NOUN ▸**ˈindexless** ADJECTIVE

indexation (ˌɪndɛkˈseɪʃən) *or* **index-linking** NOUN the act of making wages, interest rates, etc., index-linked.

index case NOUN *Med* the first case of a disease, or the primary case referred to in a report.

index finger NOUN the finger next to the thumb. Also called: **forefinger.**

index fossil NOUN a fossil species that characterizes and is used to delimit a geological zone. Also called: **zone fossil.**

index futures PLURAL NOUN a form of financial futures based on projected movement of a share price index, such as the Financial Times Stock Exchange 100 Share Index.

indexical (ɪnˈdɛksɪkᵊl) ADJECTIVE 1 arranged as or relating to an index or indexes. ◆ NOUN 2 *Logic, linguistics* a term whose reference depends on the context of utterance, such as *I, you, here, now,* or *tomorrow.* Also: **deictic.**

indexing head NOUN a circular plate mounted to rotate on its centre, inscribed with concentric circles, each accurately divided, the dimensions being marked by drilled holes. The plate can be moved round with a workpiece to facilitate the accurate location of holes or other machining operations on the workpiece.

Index Librorum Prohibitorum *Latin* (ˈɪndɛks laɪˈbrɔːrʊm prəʊˌhɪbɪˈtɔːrʊm) NOUN *RC Church* (formerly) an official list of proscribed books. Often called: **the Index.**
▷**HISTORY** C17, literally: list of forbidden books

index-linked ADJECTIVE (of wages, interest rates, etc.) directly related to the cost-of-living index and rising or falling accordingly.

index number NOUN *Statistics* a statistic indicating the relative change occurring in each successive period of time in the price, volume, or value of a commodity or in a general economic variable, such as the price level, national income, or gross output, with reference to a previous base period conventionally given the number 100.

Index of Industrial Production NOUN (in Britain) an index produced by the Central Statistical Office showing changes in the production of the primary British industries.

index of refraction NOUN another name for **refractive index.**

India (ˈɪndɪə) NOUN 1 a republic in S Asia: history dates from the Indus Valley civilization (3rd millennium B.C.); came under British supremacy in 1763 and passed to the British Crown in 1858; nationalist movement arose under Gandhi (1869–1948); Indian subcontinent divided into Pakistan (Muslim) and India (Hindu) in 1947; became a republic within the Commonwealth in 1950. It consists chiefly of the Himalayas, rising over 7500 m (25 000 ft.) in the extreme north, the Ganges plain in the north, the Thar Desert in the northwest, the Chota Nagpur plateau in the northeast, and the Deccan Plateau in the south. Official and administrative languages: Hindi and English; each state has its own language. Religion: Hindu majority, Muslim minority. Currency: rupee. Capital: New Delhi. Pop.: 1 029 991 000 (2001 est.). Area: 3 268 100 sq. km (1 261 813 sq. miles). Hindi name: **Bharat.** 2 *Communications* a code word for the letter *i.*

Indiaman (ˈɪndɪəmən) NOUN, *plural* **-men.** (formerly) a large merchant ship engaged in trade with India.

Indian (ˈɪndɪən) NOUN 1 a native, citizen, or inhabitant of the Republic of India. 2 an American Indian. 3 (*not in scholarly usage*) any of the languages of the American Indians. ◆ ADJECTIVE 4 of, relating to, or characteristic of India, its inhabitants, or any of their languages. 5 of, relating to, or characteristic of the American Indians or any of their languages.

Indiana (ˌɪndɪˈænə) NOUN a state of the N central US, in the Midwest: consists of an undulating plain, with sand dunes and lakes in the north and limestone caves in the south. Capital: Indianapolis. Pop.: 6 080 485 (2000). Area: 93 491 sq. km (36 097 sq. miles). Abbreviations: **Ind.,** (with zip code) **IN.**

Indian agent NOUN an official who represents the US or Canadian government to a group of North American Indians.

Indianapolis (ˌɪndɪəˈnæpəlɪs) NOUN a city in central Indiana: the state capital. Pop.: 791 926 (2000).

Indian bread NOUN another name for **corn bread.**

Indian cholera NOUN another name for **cholera.**

Indian club NOUN a bottle-shaped club, usually used in pairs by gymnasts, jugglers, etc.

Indian corn NOUN another name for **maize** (sense 1).

Indian Desert NOUN another name for the **Thar Desert.**

Indian Empire NOUN British India and the Indian states under indirect British control, which gained independence as India and Pakistan in 1947.

Indian file NOUN another term for **single file.**

Indian giver NOUN *US and Canadian offensive* a person who asks for the return of a present he has given.
▸**Indian giving** NOUN

Indian hemp NOUN 1 another name for **hemp,** esp the variety *Cannabis indica,* from which several narcotic drugs are obtained 2 Also called: **dogbane.** a perennial American apocynaceous plant, *Apocynum cannabinum,* whose fibre was formerly used by the Indians to make rope.

Indianian (ˌɪndɪˈænɪən) NOUN 1 a native or inhabitant of Indiana. ◆ ADJECTIVE 2 of or relating to Indiana or its inhabitants.

Indian ink *or esp US and Canadian* **India ink** NOUN 1 a black pigment made from a mixture of lampblack and a binding agent such as gelatine or glue: usually formed into solid cakes and sticks. 2 a black liquid ink made from this pigment. ◆ Also called: **China ink, Chinese ink.**

Indian liquorice NOUN a woody leguminous climbing plant, *Abrus precatorius,* native to tropical Asia and naturalized elsewhere, having scarlet black-spotted poisonous seeds, used as beads, and roots used as a substitute for liquorice. Also called: **jequirity.**

Indian list NOUN *Informal* (in Canada) a list of persons to whom spirits may not be sold. Also called: **interdict list.**

Indian mallow NOUN a tall malvaceous weedy North American plant, *Abutilon theophrasti,* with small yellow flowers and large velvety leaves.

Indian meal NOUN another name for **corn meal.**

Indian millet NOUN another name for **durra.**

Indian mulberry NOUN a small rubiaceous tree, *Morinda citrifolia,* of SE Asia and Australasia, with rounded yellow fruits: yields red and yellow dyes.

Indian Mutiny NOUN a revolt of Indian troops (1857–59) that led to the transfer of the administration of India from the East India Company to the British Crown.

Indian National Congress NOUN the official name for **Congress** (the political party).

Indian Ocean NOUN an ocean bordered by Africa

in the west, Asia in the north, and Australia in the east and merging with the Antarctic Ocean in the south. Average depth: 3900 m (13 000 ft.). Greatest depth (off the Sunda Islands): 7450 m (24 442 ft.). Area: about 73 556 000 sq. km (28 400 000 sq. miles).

Indian pipe NOUN a white or pinkish saprophytic woodland plant, *Monotropa uniflora,* of the N hemisphere, with a solitary nodding flower resembling a pipe: family *Monotropaceae.*

Indian red NOUN [1] a red pigment containing ferric oxide, used in paints and cosmetics and produced by oxidizing iron salts. [2] a type of red soil containing ferric oxide, found in S Asia and used as a pigment and metal polish.

Indian reserve *or* **reservation** NOUN See **reservation** (sense 4).

Indian rice NOUN [1] an annual erect aquatic North American grass, *Zizania aquatica,* with edible purplish-black grain. [2] the grain of this plant. ◆ Also called: **wild rice.**

Indian rope-trick NOUN the supposed Indian feat of climbing an unsupported rope.

Indian sign NOUN *US* a magic spell designed to place the victim in one's power or bring him bad luck.

Indian States and Agencies PLURAL NOUN another name for the **Native States.**

Indian summer NOUN [1] a period of unusually settled warm weather after the end of summer proper. [2] a period of ease and tranquillity or of renewed productivity towards the end of a person's life or of an epoch. ◆ See also **Saint Martin's summer.**
▷HISTORY originally US: probably so named because it was first noted in regions occupied by American Indians

Indian sweater NOUN another name for **Cowichan sweater.**

Indian Territory NOUN the territory established in the early 19th century in present-day Oklahoma, where Indians were forced to settle by the US government. The last remnant was integrated into the new state of Oklahoma in 1907.

Indian tobacco NOUN a poisonous North American campanulaceous plant, *Lobelia inflata,* with small pale blue flowers and rounded inflated seed capsules.

India paper NOUN [1] a thin soft opaque printing paper made in the Orient. [2] another name (not in technical usage) for **Bible paper.**

India print NOUN a colourful cotton fabric, with a block-printed pattern, made in India.

India rubber NOUN another name for **rubber**[1] (sense 1).

Indic ('ɪndɪk) ADJECTIVE [1] denoting, belonging to, or relating to a branch of Indo-European consisting of the Indo-European languages of India, including Sanskrit, Hindi and Urdu, Punjabi, Gujerati, Bengali, and Sinhalese. ◆ NOUN [2] this group of languages. ◆ Also: **Indo-Aryan.**

indic. ABBREVIATION FOR: [1] indicating. [2] indicative. [3] indicator.

indican ('ɪndɪkən) NOUN a compound secreted in the urine, usually in the form of its potassium salt; indoxylsulphuric acid. Formula: $C_8H_6NOSO_2OH$.
▷HISTORY C19: from Latin *indicum* INDIGO + -AN

indicant ('ɪndɪkənt) NOUN something that indicates.

indicate ('ɪndɪˌkeɪt) VERB (*tr*) [1] (*may take a clause as object*) to be or give a sign or symptom of; imply: *cold hands indicate a warm heart.* [2] to point out or show. [3] (*may take a clause as object*) to state briefly; suggest: *he indicated what his feelings were.* [4] (of instruments) to show a reading of: *the speedometer indicated 50 miles per hour.* [5] (*usually passive*) to recommend or require: *surgery seems to be indicated for this patient.*
▷HISTORY C17: from Latin *indicāre* to point out, from IN-[2] + *dicāre* to proclaim; compare INDEX
▸'**indiˌcatable** ADJECTIVE ▸**indicatory** (ɪn'dɪkətərɪ, -trɪ) ADJECTIVE

indicated horsepower NOUN the power output of a piston engine calculated from the mean effective pressure in the cylinder as derived from an indicator diagram and the speed of the engine in revolutions per minute.

indication (ˌɪndɪ'keɪʃən) NOUN [1] something that serves to indicate or suggest; sign: *an indication of foul play.* [2] the degree or quantity represented on a measuring instrument or device. [3] the action of indicating. [4] something that is indicated as advisable, necessary, or expedient.

indicative (ɪn'dɪkətɪv) ADJECTIVE [1] (*usually postpositive;* foll by *of*) serving as a sign; suggestive: *indicative of trouble ahead.* [2] *Grammar* denoting a mood of verbs used chiefly to make statements. Compare **subjunctive** (sense 1). ◆ NOUN [3] *Grammar* **a** the indicative mood. **b** a verb in the indicative mood. ◆ Abbreviation: **indic.**
▸**in'dicatively** ADVERB

indicator ('ɪndɪˌkeɪtə) NOUN [1] something that provides an indication, esp of trends. See **economic indicator.** [2] a device to attract attention, such as the pointer of a gauge or a warning lamp. [3] an instrument that displays certain operating conditions in a machine, such as a gauge showing temperature, speed, pressure, etc. [4] **a** a device that records or registers something, such as the movements of a lift, or that shows information, such as arrival and departure times of trains. **b** (*as modifier*): *indicator light.* [5] Also called: **blinker.** a device for indicating that a motor vehicle is about to turn left or right, esp two pairs of lights that flash when operated or a pair of trafficators. [6] Also called: **dial gauge.** a delicate measuring instrument used to determine small differences in the height of mechanical components. It consists of a spring-loaded plunger that operates a pointer moving over a circular scale. [7] *Chem* **a** a substance used in titrations to indicate the completion of a chemical reaction, usually by a change of colour. **b** a substance, such as litmus, that indicates the presence of an acid or alkali. [8] Also called: **indicator species.** *Ecology* **a** a plant or animal species that thrives only under particular environmental conditions and therefore indicates these conditions where it is found. **b** a species of plant or animal whose well-being confirms the well-being of other species in the area.

indicator diagram NOUN a graphical or other representation of the cyclic variations of pressure and volume within the cylinder of a reciprocating engine obtained by using an indicator.

indices ('ɪndɪˌsiːz) NOUN a plural of **index.**

indicia (ɪn'dɪʃɪə) PLURAL NOUN, *singular or* **-cium** (-ʃɪəm) distinguishing markings or signs; indications.
▷HISTORY C17: from Latin, plural of *indicium* a notice, from INDEX
▸**in'dicial** ADJECTIVE

indicolite ('ɪndɪkəˌlaɪt) *or* **indigolite** NOUN a form of tourmaline ranging in colour from pale blue to blue-black.
▷HISTORY C19: from Spanish *indico* INDIGO + -LITE

indict (ɪn'daɪt) VERB (*tr*) to charge (a person) with crime, esp formally in writing; accuse.
▷HISTORY C14: alteration of *enditen* to INDITE
▸ˌ**indict'ee** NOUN ▸**in'dicter** *or* **in'dictor** NOUN

> **Language note** See at **indite.**

indictable (ɪn'daɪtəb^{ə}l) ADJECTIVE *Criminal law* [1] (of a person) liable to be indicted. [2] (of a crime) that makes a person liable to be indicted.
▸**in'dictably** ADVERB

indiction (ɪn'dɪkʃən) NOUN (in the Roman Empire and later in various medieval kingdoms) [1] a recurring fiscal period of 15 years, often used as a unit for dating events. [2] a particular year in this period or the number assigned it. [3] (from the reign of Constantine the Great) **a** a valuation of property made every 15 years as a basis for taxation. **b** the tax based on this valuation.
▷HISTORY C14: from Latin *indictiō* declaration, announcement of a tax; see INDITE
▸**in'dictional** ADJECTIVE

indictment (ɪn'daɪtmənt) NOUN *Criminal law* [1] a formal written charge of crime formerly referred to and presented on oath by a grand jury. [2] any formal accusation of crime. [3] *Scot* a charge of crime brought at the instance of the Lord Advocate. [4] the act of indicting or the state of being indicted.

indie ('ɪndɪ) NOUN *Informal* **a** an independent film or record company. **b** (*as modifier*): *an indie producer; the indie charts.*

Indies ('ɪndɪz) NOUN **the.** [1] the territories of S and SE Asia included in the East Indies, India, and Indochina. [2] See **East Indies.** [3] See **West Indies.**

indifference (ɪn'dɪfrəns, -fərəns) NOUN [1] the fact or state of being indifferent; lack of care or concern. [2] lack of quality; mediocrity. [3] lack of importance; insignificance. [4] See **principle of indifference.**

indifferent (ɪn'dɪfrənt, -fərənt) ADJECTIVE [1] (often foll by *to*) showing no care or concern; uninterested: *he was indifferent to my pleas.* [2] unimportant; immaterial. [3] **a** of only average or moderate size, extent, quality, etc. **b** not at all good; poor. [4] showing or having no preferences; impartial. [5] *Biology* **a** (of cells or tissues) not differentiated or specialized. **b** (of a species) not found in any particular community.
▷HISTORY C14: from Latin *indifferēns* making no distinction
▸**in'differently** ADVERB

indifferentism (ɪn'dɪfrənˌtɪzəm, -fərən-) NOUN systematic indifference, esp in matters of religion.
▸**in'differentist** NOUN

indigene ('ɪndɪˌdʒiːn) *or* **indigen** ('ɪndɪdʒən) NOUN an indigenous person, animal, or thing; native.

indigenous (ɪn'dɪdʒɪnəs) ADJECTIVE (when *postpositive,* foll by *to*) [1] originating or occurring naturally (in a country, region, etc.); native. [2] innate (to); inherent (in).
▷HISTORY C17: from Latin *indigenus,* from *indigena* indigene, from *indi-* in + *gignere* to beget
▸**in'digenously** ADVERB ▸**in'digenousness** *or* **indigenity** (ˌɪndɪ'dʒɛnɪtɪ) NOUN

indigent ('ɪndɪdʒənt) ADJECTIVE [1] so poor as to lack even necessities; very needy. [2] (usually foll by *of*) *Archaic* lacking (in) or destitute (of). ◆ NOUN [3] an impoverished person.
▷HISTORY C14: from Latin *indigēre* to need, from *egēre* to lack
▸'**indigence** NOUN ▸'**indigently** ADVERB

indigested (ˌɪndɪ'dʒɛstɪd) ADJECTIVE *Archaic* undigested.

indigestible (ˌɪndɪ'dʒɛstəb^{ə}l) ADJECTIVE [1] incapable of being digested or difficult to digest. [2] difficult to understand or absorb mentally: *an indigestible book.*
▸ˌ**indiˌgesti'bility** *or* ˌ**indi'gestibleness** NOUN
▸ˌ**indi'gestibly** ADVERB

indigestion (ˌɪndɪ'dʒɛstʃən) NOUN difficulty in digesting food, accompanied by abdominal pain, heartburn, and belching. Technical name: **dyspepsia.**

indigestive (ˌɪndɪ'dʒɛstɪv) ADJECTIVE relating to or suffering from indigestion; dyspeptic.

indign (ɪn'daɪn) ADJECTIVE *Obsolete or poetic* [1] undeserving; unworthy. [2] unseemly; disgraceful. [3] not deserved.
▷HISTORY C15: from Old French *indigne,* from Latin *indignus* unworthy, from IN-[1] + *dignus* worthy; see DIGNITY

indignant (ɪn'dɪgnənt) ADJECTIVE feeling or showing indignation.
▷HISTORY C16: from Latin *indignārī* to be displeased with
▸**in'dignantly** ADVERB

indignation (ˌɪndɪg'neɪʃən) NOUN anger or scorn aroused by something felt to be unfair, unworthy, or wrong.

indignity (ɪn'dɪgnɪtɪ) NOUN, *plural* **-ties.** [1] injury to one's self-esteem or dignity; humiliation. [2] *Obsolete* disgrace or disgraceful character or conduct.

indigo ('ɪndɪˌgəʊ) NOUN, *plural* **-gos** *or* **-goes.** [1] Also called: **indigotin.** a blue vat dye originally obtained from plants but now made synthetically. [2] any of various tropical plants of the leguminous genus *Indigofera,* such as the anil, that yield this dye. Compare **wild indigo.** [3] **a** any of a group of colours that have the same blue-violet hue; a spectral colour. **b** (*as adjective*): *an indigo carpet.*
▷HISTORY C16: from Spanish *indico,* via Latin from Greek *Indikos* of India
▸**indigotic** (ˌɪndɪ'gɒtɪk) ADJECTIVE

indigo blue NOUN, ADJECTIVE (**indigo-blue** *when*

prenominal) the full name for **indigo** (the colour and the dye).

indigo bunting, bird, *or* **finch** NOUN a North American bunting, *Passerina cyanea,* the male of which is bright blue and the female brown.

indigoid (ˈɪndɪˌɡɔɪd) ADJECTIVE 1 of, concerned with, or resembling indigo or its blue colour. ◆ NOUN 2 any of a number of synthetic dyes or pigments related in chemical structure to indigo.

indigolite (ˈɪndɪɡəˌlaɪt) NOUN a variant spelling of **indicolite.**

indigo snake NOUN a dark-blue nonvenomous North American colubrid snake, *Drymarchon corais couperi.*

indigotin (ɪnˈdɪɡətɪn, ˌɪndɪˈɡəʊ-) NOUN another name for **indigo** (the dye).
▷HISTORY C19: from INDIGO + -IN

indirect (ˌɪndɪˈrɛkt) ADJECTIVE 1 deviating from a direct course or line; roundabout; circuitous. 2 not coming as a direct effect or consequence; secondary: *indirect benefits.* 3 not straightforward, open, or fair; devious or evasive: *an indirect insult.* 4 (of a title or an inheritance) not inherited in an unbroken line of succession from father to son.
▸**ˌindiˈrectly** ADVERB ▸**ˌindiˈrectness** NOUN

indirect costs PLURAL NOUN another name for **overheads.**

indirection (ˌɪndɪˈrɛkʃən) NOUN 1 indirect procedure, courses, or methods. 2 lack of direction or purpose; aimlessness. 3 indirect dealing; deceit.

indirect labour NOUN *Commerce* work done in administration and sales rather than in the manufacturing of a product. Compare **direct labour** (sense 1).

indirect lighting NOUN reflected or diffused light from a concealed source.

indirect object NOUN *Grammar* a noun, pronoun, or noun phrase indicating the recipient or beneficiary of the action of a verb and its direct object, as *John* in the sentence *I bought John a newspaper.* Compare **direct object.**

indirect proof NOUN *Logic, maths* proof of a conclusion by showing its negation to be self-contradictory; reductio ad absurdum. Compare **direct** (sense 17).

indirect question NOUN a question reported in indirect speech, as in *She asked why you came.* Compare **direct question.**

indirect speech *or esp US* **indirect discourse** NOUN the reporting of something said or written by conveying what was meant rather than repeating the exact words, as in the sentence *He asked me whether I would go* as opposed to *He asked me, "Will you go?".* Also called: **reported speech.**

indirect tax NOUN a tax levied on goods or services rather than on individuals or companies. Compare **direct tax.**
▸**indirect taxation** NOUN

indiscernible (ˌɪndɪˈsɜːnəbəl) ADJECTIVE 1 incapable of being discerned. 2 scarcely discernible or perceptible.
▸**ˌindisˈcernibleness** *or* **ˌindiscerniˈbility** NOUN
▸**ˌindisˈcernibly** ADVERB

indiscipline (ɪnˈdɪsɪplɪn) NOUN lack of discipline.

indiscreet (ˌɪndɪˈskriːt) ADJECTIVE not discreet; imprudent or tactless.
▸**ˌindisˈcreetly** ADVERB ▸**ˌindisˈcreetness** NOUN

indiscrete (ˌɪndɪˈskriːt) ADJECTIVE not divisible or divided into parts.
▸**ˌindisˈcretely** ADVERB ▸**ˌindisˈcreteness** NOUN

indiscretion (ˌɪndɪˈskrɛʃən) NOUN 1 the characteristic or state of being indiscreet. 2 an indiscreet act, remark, etc.
▸**ˌindisˈcretionary** ADJECTIVE

indiscriminate (ˌɪndɪˈskrɪmɪnɪt) ADJECTIVE 1 lacking discrimination or careful choice; random or promiscuous. 2 jumbled; confused.
▸**ˌindisˈcriminately** ADVERB ▸**ˌindisˈcriminateness** NOUN
▸**ˌindisˌcrimiˈnation** NOUN

indispensable (ˌɪndɪˈspɛnsəbəl) ADJECTIVE 1 absolutely necessary; essential. 2 not to be disregarded or escaped: *an indispensable role.* ◆ NOUN 3 an indispensable person or thing.
▸**ˌindisˌpensaˈbility** *or* **ˌindisˈpensableness** NOUN
▸**ˌindisˈpensably** ADVERB

indispose (ˌɪndɪˈspəʊz) VERB (*tr*) 1 to make unwilling or opposed; disincline. 2 to cause to feel ill. 3 to make unfit (for something or to do something).

indisposed (ˌɪndɪˈspəʊzd) ADJECTIVE 1 sick or ill. 2 unwilling.
▷HISTORY C15: from Latin *indispositus* disordered
▸**indisposition** (ˌɪndɪspəˈzɪʃən) NOUN

indisputable (ˌɪndɪˈspjuːtəbəl) ADJECTIVE beyond doubt; not open to question.
▸**ˌindisˌputaˈbility** *or* **ˌindisˈputableness** NOUN
▸**ˌindisˈputably** ADVERB

indissoluble (ˌɪndɪˈsɒljʊbəl) ADJECTIVE incapable of being dissolved or broken; permanent.
▸**ˌindisˌsoluˈbility** *or* **ˌindisˈsolubleness** NOUN
▸**ˌindisˈsolubly** ADVERB

indistinct (ˌɪndɪˈstɪŋkt) ADJECTIVE incapable of being clearly distinguished, as by the eyes, ears, or mind; not distinct.
▸**ˌindisˈtinctly** ADVERB ▸**ˌindisˈtinctness** NOUN

indistinctive (ˌɪndɪˈstɪŋktɪv) ADJECTIVE 1 without distinctive qualities. 2 unable to make distinctions; undiscriminating.
▸**ˌindisˈtinctively** ADVERB ▸**ˌindisˈtinctiveness** NOUN

indistinguishable (ˌɪndɪˈstɪŋɡwɪʃəbəl) ADJECTIVE 1 (*often postpositive; foll by from*) identical or very similar (to): *twins indistinguishable from one another.* 2 not easily perceptible; indiscernible.
▸**ˌindisˌtinguishaˈbility** *or* **ˌindisˈtinguishableness** NOUN
▸**ˌindisˈtinguishably** ADVERB

indite (ɪnˈdaɪt) VERB (*tr*) 1 *Archaic* to write. 2 *Obsolete* to dictate.
▷HISTORY C14: from Old French *enditer,* from Latin *indīcere* to declare, from IN-[2] + *dīcere* to say
▸**inˈditement** NOUN ▸**inˈditer** NOUN

> **Language note** *Indite* and *inditement* are sometimes wrongly used where *indict* and *indictment* are meant: *he was indicted* (not *indited*) *for fraud.*

indium (ˈɪndɪəm) NOUN a rare soft silvery metallic element associated with zinc ores: used in alloys, electronics, and electroplating. Symbol: In; atomic no.: 49; atomic wt.: 114.82; valency: 1, 2, or 3; relative density: 7.31; melting pt.: 156.63°C; boiling pt.: 2073°C.
▷HISTORY C19: New Latin, from INDIGO + -IUM

indiv. *or* **individ.** ABBREVIATION FOR individual.

indivertible (ˌɪndɪˈvɜːtɪbəl) ADJECTIVE incapable of being diverted or turned aside.
▸**ˌindiˈvertibly** ADVERB

individual (ˌɪndɪˈvɪdjʊəl) ADJECTIVE 1 of, relating to, characteristic of, or meant for a single person or thing. 2 separate or distinct, esp from others of its kind; particular: *please mark the individual pages.* 3 characterized by unusual and striking qualities; distinctive. 4 *Obsolete* indivisible; inseparable. ◆ NOUN 5 a single person, esp when regarded as distinct from others. 6 *Biology* **a** a single animal or plant, esp as distinct from a species. **b** a single member of a compound organism or colony. 7 *Logic* **a** Also called: **particular.** an object as opposed to a property or class. **b** an element of the domain of discourse of a theory.
▷HISTORY C15: from Medieval Latin *indīviduālis,* from Latin *indīviduus*indivisible, from IN-[1] + *dīviduus* divisible, from *dīvidere* to DIVIDE
▸**ˌindiˈvidually** ADVERB

individualism (ˌɪndɪˈvɪdjʊəˌlɪzəm) NOUN 1 the action or principle of asserting one's independence and individuality; egoism. 2 an individual quirk or peculiarity. 3 another word for **laissez faire** (sense 1). 4 *Philosophy* the doctrine that only individual things exist and that therefore classes or properties have no reality. Compare **Platonism, realism** (sense 5).

individualist (ˌɪndɪˈvɪdjʊəlɪst) NOUN 1 a person who shows independence and individuality in his behaviour, opinions, or actions. 2 an advocate of individualism.
▸**ˌindiˌvidualˈistic** ADJECTIVE ▸**ˌindiˌvidualˈistically** ADVERB

individuality (ˌɪndɪˌvɪdjʊˈælɪtɪ) NOUN, *plural* **-ties.** 1 distinctive or unique character or personality: *a work of great individuality.* 2 the qualities that distinguish one person or thing from another; identity. 3 the state or quality of being a separate entity; discreteness.

individualize *or* **individualise** (ˌɪndɪˈvɪdjʊəˌlaɪz) VERB (*tr*) 1 to make or mark as individual or distinctive in character. 2 to consider or treat individually; particularize. 3 to make or modify so as to meet the special requirements of a person.
▸**ˌindiˌvidualiˈzation** *or* **ˌindiˌvidualiˈsation** NOUN
▸**ˌindiˈvidualˌizer** *or* **ˌindiˈvidualˌiser** NOUN

individuate (ˌɪndɪˈvɪdjʊˌeɪt) VERB (*tr*) 1 to give individuality or an individual form to. 2 to distinguish from others of the same species or group; individualize.
▸**ˌindiˈviduˌator** NOUN

individuation (ˌɪndɪˌvɪdjʊˈeɪʃən) NOUN 1 the act or process of individuating. 2 (in the psychology of Jung) the process by which the wholeness of the individual is established through the integration of consciousness and the collective unconscious. 3 *Zoology* the development of separate but mutually interdependent units, as in the development of zooids forming a colony.

indivisible (ˌɪndɪˈvɪzəbəl) ADJECTIVE 1 unable to be divided. 2 *Maths* leaving a remainder when divided by a given number: *8 is indivisible by 3.*
▸**ˌindiˌvisiˈbility** *or* **ˌindiˈvisibleness** NOUN ▸**ˌindiˈvisibly** ADVERB

Indo- (ˈɪndəʊ-) COMBINING FORM denoting India or Indian: *Indo-European.*

Indo-Aryan ADJECTIVE 1 another word for **Indic** (sense 1). ◆ NOUN 2 another name for **Indic** (sense 2). 3 a native speaker of an Indo-Aryan language.

Indo-Canadian NOUN 1 a Canadian of Indian descent. ◆ ADJECTIVE 2 of or relating to Canadians of Indian descent.

Indochina *or* **Indo-China** (ˌɪndəʊˈtʃaɪnə) NOUN 1 Also called: **Farther India.** a peninsula in SE Asia, between India and China: consists of Myanmar, Thailand, Laos, Cambodia, Vietnam, and Malaysia. 2 the former French colonial possessions of Cochin China, Annam, Tonkin, Laos, and Cambodia.

Indochinese *or* **Indo-Chinese** (ˌɪndəʊtʃaɪˈniːz) ADJECTIVE 1 of or relating to Indochina or its inhabitants. ◆ NOUN, *plural* **-nese.** 2 a native or inhabitant of Indochina.

indocile (ɪnˈdəʊsaɪl) ADJECTIVE difficult to discipline or instruct.
▸**indocility** (ˌɪndəʊˈsɪlɪtɪ) NOUN

indoctrinate (ɪnˈdɒktrɪˌneɪt) VERB (*tr*) 1 to teach (a person or group of people) systematically to accept doctrines, esp uncritically. 2 *Rare* to impart learning to; instruct.
▸**inˌdoctriˈnation** NOUN ▸**inˈdoctriˌnator** NOUN

Indo-European ADJECTIVE 1 denoting, belonging to, or relating to a family of languages that includes English and many other culturally and politically important languages of the world: a characteristic feature, esp of the older languages such as Latin, Greek, and Sanskrit, is inflection showing gender, number, and case. 2 denoting or relating to the hypothetical parent language of this family, primitive Indo-European. 3 denoting, belonging to, or relating to any of the peoples speaking these languages. ◆ NOUN 4 the Indo-European family of languages. 5 Also called: **primitive Indo-European, Proto-Indo-European.** the reconstructed hypothetical parent language of this family. 6 a member of the prehistoric people who spoke this language. 7 a descendant of this people or a native speaker of an Indo-European language.

Indo-Germanic ADJECTIVE, NOUN *Obsolete* another term for **Indo-European.**

Indo-Hittite NOUN the Indo-European family of languages: used by scholars who regard Hittite not as a branch of Indo-European but as a related language.

Indo-Iranian ADJECTIVE 1 of or relating to the Indic and Iranian branches of the Indo-European family of languages. ◆ NOUN 2 this group of languages, sometimes considered as forming a single branch of Indo-European.

indole (ˈɪndəʊl) *or* **indol** (ˈɪndəʊl, -dɒl) NOUN a white or yellowish crystalline heterocyclic compound extracted from coal tar and used in perfumery, medicine, and as a flavouring agent; 1-benzopyrrole. Formula: C_8H_7N.
▷HISTORY C19: from IND(IGO) + -OLE[1]

indoleacetic acid (ˌɪndəʊləˈsiːtɪk, -ˈsɛtɪk) NOUN

an auxin that causes elongation of the cells of plant stems. Formula: $C_{10}H_9NO_2$. Abbreviation: **IAA.**

indolebutyric acid (ˌɪndəʊlbjuːˈtɪrɪk) NOUN a synthetic auxin used for stimulating plant growth and root formation. Formula: $C_{12}H_{13}NO_2$.

indolent (ˈɪndələnt) ADJECTIVE [1] disliking work or effort; lazy; idle. [2] *Pathol* causing little pain: *an indolent tumour.* [3] (esp of a painless ulcer) slow to heal.
▷HISTORY C17: from Latin *indolēns* not feeling pain, from IN-[1] + *dolēns,* from *dolēre* to grieve, cause distress
▸ˈ**indolence** NOUN ▸ˈ**indolently** ADVERB

Indologist (ɪnˈdɒlədʒɪst) NOUN a student of Indian literature, history, philosophy, etc.
▸**Inˈdology** NOUN

indomethacin (ˌɪndəʊˈmɛθəsɪn) NOUN a drug administered orally to relieve pain, fever, and inflammation, esp in rheumatoid arthritis. Formula: $C_{19}H_{16}ClNO_4$.
▷HISTORY C20: from INDOLE + METH- + ACETIC ACID + -IN

indomitable (ɪnˈdɒmɪtəbᵊl) ADJECTIVE (of courage, pride, etc.) difficult or impossible to defeat or subdue.
▷HISTORY C17: from Late Latin *indomitābilis,* from Latin *indomitus* untamable, from IN-[1] + *domitus* subdued, from *domāre* to tame
▸**inˌdomitaˈbility** *or* **inˈdomitableness** NOUN ▸**inˈdomitably** ADVERB

Indonesia (ˌɪndəʊˈniːzɪə) NOUN a republic in SE Asia, in the Malay Archipelago, consisting of the main islands of Sumatra, Java and Madura, Bali, Sulawesi (Celebes), Lombok, Sumbawa, Flores, the Moluccas, part of Timor, part of Borneo (Kalimantan), Irian Jaya, and over 3000 small islands in the Indian and Pacific Oceans: became the Dutch East Indies in 1798; declared independence in 1945; became a republic in 1950; East Timor (illegally annexed in 1975) became independent in 2002; Official language: Bahasa Indonesia. Religion: Muslim majority. Currency: rupiah. Capital: Jakarta. Pop.: 212 195 000 (2001 est). Area: 1 919 317 sq. km (741 052 sq. miles). Former names (1798–1945): **Dutch East Indies, Netherlands East Indies.**

Indonesian (ˌɪndəʊˈniːzɪən) ADJECTIVE [1] of or relating to Indonesia, its people, or their language. ◆ NOUN [2] a native or inhabitant of Indonesia. [3] another name for **Bahasa Indonesia.**

indoor (ˈɪnˌdɔː) ADJECTIVE (*prenominal*) of, situated in, or appropriate to the inside of a house or other building: *an indoor tennis court; indoor amusements.*

indoors (ˌɪnˈdɔːz) ADVERB, ADJECTIVE (*postpositive*) inside or into a house or other building.

Indo-Pacific ADJECTIVE [1] of or relating to the region of the Indian and W Pacific Oceans off the coast of SE Asia. ◆ NOUN [2] a hypothetical family of languages relating the languages of New Guinea other than Malayo-Polynesian. Tentative affiliations with Malayo-Polynesian or Australian languages have been suggested.

indophenol (ˌɪndəʊˈfiːnɒl) NOUN [1] a derivative of quinonimine. Formula: $HOC_6H_4NC_6H_4O$. [2] any of a class of derivatives of this compound, esp one of the blue or green dyes that are used for wool and cotton.
▷HISTORY C19: from INDIGO + PHENOL

Indore (ɪnˈdɔː) NOUN [1] a city in central India, in W Madhya Pradesh. Pop.: 1 091 674 (1991). [2] a former state of central India: became part of Madhya Bharat in 1948, which in turn became part of Madhya Pradesh in 1956.

indorse (ɪnˈdɔːs) VERB a variant spelling of **endorse.**
▸**inˈdorsable** ADJECTIVE ▸**inˈdorsement** NOUN ▸**inˈdorser** *or* **inˈdorsor** NOUN

indorsee (ˌɪndɔːˈsiː, ɪnˈdɔːsiː) NOUN a variant of **endorsee.**

indoxyl (ɪnˈdɒksɪl) NOUN a yellow water-soluble crystalline compound occurring in woad as its glucoside and in urine as its ester. Formula: C_8H_7NO. See also **indican.**
▷HISTORY C19: from INDIGO + HYDROXYL

Indra (ˈɪndrə) NOUN *Hinduism* the most celebrated god of the Rig-Veda, governing the weather and dispensing rain.

indraught *or US* **indraft** (ˈɪnˌdrɑːft) NOUN [1] the act of drawing or pulling in. [2] an inward flow, esp of air.

indrawn (ˌɪnˈdrɔːn) ADJECTIVE [1] drawn or pulled in. [2] inward-looking or introspective.

Indre (*French* ɛ̃drə) NOUN a department of central France in the Centre region. Capital: Châteauroux. Pop.: 231 139 (1999). Area: 6906 sq. km (2693 sq. miles).

Indre-et-Loire (*French* ɛ̃drelwar) NOUN a department of W central France in the Centre region: contains many famous châteaux along the Loire. Capital: Tours. Pop.: 554 003 (1999). Area: 6158 sq. km (2402 sq. miles).

indris (ˈɪndrɪs) *or* **indri** (ˈɪndrɪ) NOUN, *plural* **-dris.** [1] a large Madagascan arboreal lemuroid primate, *Indri indri,* with thick silky fur patterned in black, white, and fawn: family *Indriidae.* [2] **woolly indris.** a related nocturnal Madagascan animal, *Avahi laniger,* with thick grey-brown fur and a long tail.
▷HISTORY C19: from French: lemur, from Malagasy *indry!* look! mistaken for the animal's name

indubitable (ɪnˈdjuːbɪtəbᵊl) ADJECTIVE incapable of being doubted; unquestionable.
▷HISTORY C18: from Latin *indubitābilis,* from IN-[1] + *dubitāre* to doubt
▸**inˌdubitaˈbility** *or* **inˈdubitableness** NOUN

indubitably (ɪnˈdjuːbɪtəblɪ) ADVERB without doubt; certainly.

induce (ɪnˈdjuːs) VERB (*tr*) [1] (often foll by an infinitive) to persuade or use influence on. [2] to cause or bring about. [3] *Med* to initiate or hasten (labour), as by administering a drug to stimulate uterine contractions. [4] *Logic, obsolete* to assert or establish (a general proposition, hypothesis, etc.) by induction. [5] to produce (an electromotive force or electrical current) by induction. [6] to transmit (magnetism) by induction.
▷HISTORY C14: from Latin *indūcere* to lead in, from *dūcere* to lead
▸**inˈducer** NOUN ▸**inˈducible** ADJECTIVE

induced drag NOUN the former name for **trailing vortex drag.**

inducement (ɪnˈdjuːsmənt) NOUN [1] the act of inducing. [2] a means of inducing; persuasion; incentive. [3] *Law* (in pleading) the introductory part that leads up to and explains the matter in dispute.

induct (ɪnˈdʌkt) VERB (*tr*) [1] to bring in formally or install in an office, place, etc.; invest. [2] (foll by *to* or *into*) to initiate in knowledge (of). [3] *US* to enlist for military service; conscript. [4] *Physics* another word for **induce** (senses 5, 6).
▷HISTORY C14: from Latin *inductus* led in, past participle of *indūcere* to introduce; see INDUCE

inductance (ɪnˈdʌktəns) NOUN [1] Also called: **induction.** the property of an electric circuit as a result of which an electromotive force is created by a change of current in the same circuit (see **self-inductance**) or in a neighbouring circuit (see **mutual inductance**). It is usually measured in henries. Symbol: *L.* [2] another name for **inductor.**

inductee (ˌɪndʌkˈtiː) NOUN *US* a military conscript.

inductile (ɪnˈdʌktaɪl) ADJECTIVE not ductile, pliant, or yielding.
▸**inductility** (ˌɪndʌkˈtɪlɪtɪ) NOUN

induction (ɪnˈdʌkʃən) NOUN [1] the act of inducting or state of being inducted. [2] the act of inducing. [3] (in an internal-combustion engine) the part of the action of a piston by which mixed air and fuel are drawn from the carburettor to the cylinder. [4] *Logic* **a** a process of reasoning, used esp in science, by which a general conclusion is drawn from a set of premises, based mainly on experience or experimental evidence. The conclusion goes beyond the information contained in the premises, and does not follow necessarily from them. Thus an inductive argument may be highly probable, yet lead from true premises to a false conclusion. **b** a conclusion reached by this process of reasoning. Compare **deduction** (sense 4). [5] the process by which electrical or magnetic properties are transferred, without physical contact, from one circuit or body to another. See also **inductance.** [6] *Biology* the effect of one tissue, esp an embryonic tissue, on the development of an adjacent tissue. [7] *Biochem* the process by which synthesis of an enzyme is stimulated by the presence of its substrate. [8] *Maths, logic* **a** a method of proving a proposition that all integers have a property, by first proving that 1 has the property and then that if the integer *n* has it so has *n + 1.* **b** the application of recursive rules. [9] **a** a formal introduction or entry into an office or position. **b** (*as modifier*): *induction course; induction period.* [10] *US* the formal enlistment of a civilian into military service. [11] an archaic word for **preface.**
▸**inˈductional** ADJECTIVE

induction coil NOUN a transformer for producing a high voltage from a low voltage. It consists of a cylindrical primary winding of few turns, a concentric secondary winding of many turns, and often a common soft-iron core. Sometimes shortened to: **coil.**

induction hardening NOUN a process in which the outer surface of a metal component is rapidly heated by means of induced eddy currents. After rapid cooling the resulting phase transformations produce a hard wear-resistant skin.

induction heating NOUN the heating of a conducting material as a result of the electric currents induced in it by an externally applied alternating magnetic field.

induction loop system NOUN a system enabling partially deaf people to hear dialogue and sound in theatres, cinemas, etc., consisting of a loop of wire placed round the perimeter of a designated area. This emits an electromagnetic signal which is picked up by a hearing aid. Often shortened to **induction loop.**

induction motor NOUN a type of brushless electric motor in which an alternating supply fed to the windings of the stator creates a magnetic field that induces a current in the windings of the rotor. Rotation of the rotor results from the interaction of the magnetic field created by the rotor current with the field of the stator.

inductive (ɪnˈdʌktɪv) ADJECTIVE [1] relating to, involving, or operated by electrical or magnetic induction: *an inductive reactance.* [2] *Logic, maths* of, relating to, or using induction: *inductive reasoning.* [3] serving to induce or cause. [4] a rare word for **introductory.** [5] *Biology* producing a reaction within an organism, esp induction in embryonic tissue.
▸**inˈductively** ADVERB ▸**inˈductiveness** NOUN

inductor (ɪnˈdʌktə) NOUN [1] a person or thing that inducts. [2] a component, such as a coil, in an electrical circuit the main function of which is to produce inductance.

indue (ɪnˈdjuː) VERB **-dues, -duing, -dued.** a variant spelling of **endue.**

indulge (ɪnˈdʌldʒ) VERB [1] (when *intr,* often foll by *in*) to yield to or gratify (a whim or desire for): *to indulge a desire for new clothes; to indulge in new clothes.* [2] (*tr*) to yield to the wishes of; pamper: *to indulge a child.* [3] (*tr*) to allow oneself the pleasure of something: *at Christmas he liked to indulge himself.* [4] (*tr*) *Commerce* to allow (a debtor) an extension of time for payment of (a bill, etc.). [5] (*intr*) *Informal* to take alcoholic drink, esp to excess.
▷HISTORY C17: from Latin *indulgēre* to concede, from *-dulgēre,* probably related to Greek *dolikhos* long, Gothic *tulgus* firm
▸**inˈdulger** NOUN ▸**inˈdulgingly** ADVERB

indulgence (ɪnˈdʌldʒəns) NOUN [1] the act of indulging or state of being indulgent. [2] a pleasure, habit, etc., indulged in; extravagance: *fur coats are an indulgence.* [3] liberal or tolerant treatment. [4] something granted as a favour or privilege. [5] *RC Church* a remission of the temporal punishment for sin after its guilt has been forgiven. [6] *Commerce* an extension of time granted as a favour for payment of a debt or as fulfilment of some other obligation. [7] Also called: **Declaration of Indulgence.** a royal grant during the reigns of Charles II and James II of England giving Nonconformists and Roman Catholics a measure of religious freedom. ◆ VERB (*tr*) [8] *RC Church* to designate as providing indulgence: *indulgenced prayers.*

indulgent (ɪnˈdʌldʒənt) ADJECTIVE showing or characterized by indulgence.
▸**inˈdulgently** ADVERB

induline (ˈɪndjʊˌlaɪn) *or* **indulin** (ˈɪndjʊlɪn) NOUN any of a class of blue dyes obtained from aniline and aminoazobenzene.
▷HISTORY C19: from INDIGO + -ULE + -INE[2]

indult (ɪnˈdʌlt) NOUN *RC Church* a faculty granted

by the Holy See allowing a specific deviation from the Church's common law.
▷HISTORY C16: from Church Latin *indultum* a privilege, from Latin *indulgēre* to INDULGE

indumentum (ɪndjʊ'mɛntəm) NOUN, *plural* **-ta** (-tə) *or* **-tums.** an outer covering, such as hairs or down on a plant or leaf, feathers, fur, etc.
▷HISTORY C19: Latin, literally: garment

induna (ɪn'du:nə) NOUN (in South Africa) a Black African overseer in a factory, mine, etc.
▷HISTORY C20: from Zulu *nduna* an official

induplicate (ɪn'dju:plɪkɪt, -ˌkeɪt) *or* **induplicated** ADJECTIVE (of the parts of a bud) bent or folded inwards with the edges touching but not overlapping.
▸**inˌdupliˈcation** NOUN

indurate *Rare* ◆ VERB ('ɪndjʊˌreɪt) [1] to make or become hard or callous. [2] to make or become hardy. ◆ ADJECTIVE ('ɪndjʊrɪt) [3] hardened, callous, or unfeeling.
▷HISTORY C16: from Latin *indūrāre* to make hard; see ENDURE
▸**ˌinduˈration** NOUN ▸**ˈinduˌrative** ADJECTIVE

Indus[1] ('ɪndəs) NOUN a faint constellation in the S hemisphere lying between Telescopium and Tucano.

Indus[2] ('ɪndəs) NOUN a river in S Asia, rising in SW Tibet in the Kailas Range of the Himalayas and flowing northwest through Kashmir, then southwest across Pakistan to the Arabian Sea: important throughout history, esp for the Indus Civilization (about 3000 to 1500 B.C.), and for irrigation. Length: about 2900 km (1800 miles).

indusium (ɪn'dju:zɪəm) NOUN, *plural* **-sia** (-zɪə). [1] a membranous outgrowth on the undersurface of fern leaves that covers and protects the developing sporangia. [2] an enveloping membrane, such as the amnion.
▷HISTORY C18: New Latin, from Latin: tunic, from *induere* to put on
▸**inˈdusial** ADJECTIVE

industrial (ɪn'dʌstrɪəl) ADJECTIVE [1] of, relating to, derived from, or characteristic of industry. [2] employed in industry: *the industrial workforce.* [3] relating to or concerned with workers in industry: *industrial conditions.* [4] used in industry: *industrial chemicals.*
▸**inˈdustrially** ADVERB

industrial action NOUN *Brit* any action, such as a strike or go-slow, taken by employees in industry to protest against working conditions, redundancies, etc.

industrial archaeology NOUN the study of past industrial machines, works, etc.
▸**industrial archaeologist** NOUN

industrial democracy NOUN control of an organization by the people who work for it, esp by workers holding positions on its board of directors.

industrial design NOUN the art or practice of designing any object for manufacture.
▸**industrial designer** NOUN

industrial development certificate NOUN (in Britain) a certificate issued by the Department of the Environment to an industrial organization wishing to build or extend a factory, which has to accompany an application for planning permission. Abbreviation: **IDC.**

industrial diamond NOUN a small often synthetic diamond, valueless as a gemstone, used in cutting tools, abrasives, etc.

industrial disease NOUN any disease to which workers in a particular industry are prone.

industrial espionage NOUN attempting to obtain trade secrets by dishonest means, as by telephone- or computer-tapping, infiltration of a competitor's workforce, etc.

industrial estate NOUN *Brit* another name for **trading estate.** US equivalent: **industrial park.**

industrialism (ɪn'dʌstrɪəˌlɪzəm) NOUN an organization of society characterized by large-scale mechanized manufacturing industry rather than trade, farming, etc.

industrialist (ɪn'dʌstrɪəlɪst) NOUN a person who has a substantial interest in the ownership or control of industrial enterprise.

industrialize *or* **industrialise** (ɪn'dʌstrɪəˌlaɪz) VERB [1] (*tr*) to develop industry on an extensive scale in (a country, region, etc.). [2] (*intr*) (of a country, region, etc.) to undergo the development of industry on an extensive scale.
▸**inˌdustrialiˈzation** *or* **inˌdustrialiˈsation** NOUN

industrial medicine NOUN the study and practice of the health care of employees of large organizations, including measures to prevent accidents, industrial diseases, and stress in the workforce and to monitor the health of executives.

industrial melanism NOUN See **melanism** (sense 1).

industrial misconduct NOUN behaviour by an employee that is considered to be negligent or irregular to such an extent that disciplinary action may be taken, usually by agreement between management and the employee's representatives.

industrial psychology NOUN the scientific study of human behaviour and cognitive processes in relation to the working environment.

industrial relations NOUN [1] (*functioning as plural*) those aspects of collective relations between management and workers' representatives which are normally covered by collective bargaining. [2] (*functioning as singular*) the management of relations between the employers or managers of an enterprise and their employees.

Industrial Revolution NOUN **the.** the transformation in the 18th and 19th centuries of first Britain and then other W European countries and the US into industrial nations.

industrials (ɪn'dʌstrɪəlz) PLURAL NOUN stocks, shares, and bonds of industrial enterprises.

industrial-strength ADJECTIVE *Chiefly humorous* extremely strong or powerful: *industrial-strength tea.*

industrial tribunal NOUN (in Northern Ireland and formerly elsewhere in the UK) a tribunal that rules on disputes between employers and employees regarding unfair dismissal, redundancy, etc.

industrial union NOUN a labour organization in which all workers in a given industry are eligible for membership. Compare **craft union.**

Industrial Workers of the World NOUN **the.** an international revolutionary federation of industrial unions founded in Chicago in 1905: banned in the US in 1949. Abbreviation: **IWW.** See also **Wobbly.**

industrious (ɪn'dʌstrɪəs) ADJECTIVE [1] hard-working, diligent, or assiduous. [2] an obsolete word for **skilful.**
▸**inˈdustriously** ADVERB ▸**inˈdustriousness** NOUN

industry ('ɪndəstrɪ) NOUN, *plural* **-tries.** [1] organized economic activity concerned with manufacture, extraction and processing of raw materials, or construction. [2] a branch of commercial enterprise concerned with the output of a specified product or service: *the steel industry.* [3] **a** industrial ownership and management interests collectively, as contrasted with labour interests. **b** manufacturing enterprise collectively, as opposed to agriculture. [4] diligence; assiduity.
▷HISTORY C15: from Latin *industria* diligence, from *industrius* active, of uncertain origin

industrywide ('ɪndəstrɪˌwaɪd) ADVERB, ADJECTIVE covering or available to all parts of an industry.

indwell (ɪn'dwɛl) VERB **-dwells, -dwelling, -dwelt.** [1] (*tr*) (of a spirit, principle, etc.) to inhabit; suffuse. [2] (*intr*) to dwell; exist.
▸**inˈdweller** NOUN

Indy Car racing ('ɪndɪ) NOUN a US form of professional motor racing around banked oval tracks.
▷HISTORY C20: named after the *Indianapolis 500* motor race

-ine[1] SUFFIX FORMING ADJECTIVES [1] of, relating to, or belonging to: *saturnine.* [2] consisting of or resembling: *crystalline.*
▷HISTORY from Latin *-īnus,* from Greek *-inos*

-ine[2] SUFFIX FORMING NOUNS [1] indicating a halogen: *chlorine.* [2] indicating a nitrogenous organic compound, including amino acids, alkaloids, and certain other bases: *alanine; nicotine; purine.* [3] Also: **-in.** indicating a chemical substance in certain nonsystematic names: *glycerine.* [4] indicating a mixture of hydrocarbons: *benzine.* [5] an obsolete equivalent of **-yne.**
▷HISTORY via French from Latin *-ina* (from *-inus*) and Greek *-inē*

inearth (ɪn'ɜ:θ) VERB (*tr*) a poetic word for **bury.**

inebriant (ɪn'i:brɪənt) ADJECTIVE [1] causing intoxication, esp drunkenness. ◆ NOUN [2] something that inebriates.

inebriate VERB (ɪn'i:brɪˌeɪt) (*tr*) [1] to make drunk; intoxicate. [2] to arouse emotionally; make excited. ◆ NOUN (ɪn'i:brɪɪt) [3] a person who is drunk, esp habitually. ◆ ADJECTIVE (ɪn'i:brɪɪt) *also* **inebriated.** [4] drunk, esp habitually.
▷HISTORY C15: from Latin *inēbriāre,* from IN-[2] + *ēbriāre* to intoxicate, from *ēbrius* drunk
▸**inˌebriˈation** NOUN ▸**inebriety** (ˌɪnɪ'braɪɪtɪ) NOUN

inedible (ɪn'ɛdɪbᵊl) ADJECTIVE not fit to be eaten; uneatable.
▸**inˌediˈbility** NOUN

inedited (ɪn'ɛdɪtɪd) ADJECTIVE [1] not edited. [2] not published.

ineducable (ɪn'ɛdjʊkəbᵊl) ADJECTIVE incapable of being educated, esp on account of mental retardation.
▸**inˌeducaˈbility** NOUN

ineffable (ɪn'ɛfəbᵊl) ADJECTIVE [1] too great or intense to be expressed in words; unutterable. [2] too sacred to be uttered. [3] indescribable; indefinable.
▷HISTORY C15: from Latin *ineffābilis* unutterable, from IN-[1] + *effābilis,* from *effārī* to utter, from *fārī* to speak
▸**inˌeffaˈbility** *or* **inˈeffableness** NOUN ▸**inˈeffably** ADVERB

ineffaceable (ˌɪnɪ'feɪsəbᵊl) ADJECTIVE incapable of being effaced; indelible.
▸**ˌinefˌfaceaˈbility** NOUN ▸**ˌinefˈfaceably** ADVERB

ineffective (ˌɪnɪ'fɛktɪv) ADJECTIVE [1] having no effect. [2] incompetent or inefficient.
▸**ˌinefˈfectively** ADVERB ▸**ˌinefˈfectiveness** NOUN

ineffectual (ˌɪnɪ'fɛktʃʊəl) ADJECTIVE [1] having no effect or an inadequate effect. [2] lacking in power or forcefulness; impotent: *an ineffectual ruler.*
▸**ˌinefˌfectuˈality** *or* **ˌinefˈfectualness** NOUN ▸**ˌinefˈfectually** ADVERB

inefficacious (ˌɪnɛfɪ'keɪʃəs) ADJECTIVE failing to produce the desired effect.
▸**ˌineffiˈcaciously** ADVERB ▸**inefficacy** (ɪn'ɛfɪkəsɪ), **ˌineffiˈcaciousness,** *or* **inefficacity** (ˌɪnɛfɪ'kæsɪtɪ) NOUN

inefficient (ˌɪnɪ'fɪʃənt) ADJECTIVE [1] unable to perform a task or function to the best advantage; wasteful or incompetent. [2] unable to produce the desired result.
▸**ˌinefˈficiency** NOUN ▸**ˌinefˈficiently** ADVERB

inelastic (ˌɪnɪ'læstɪk) ADJECTIVE [1] not elastic; not resilient. [2] *Physics* (of collisions) involving an overall decrease in translational kinetic energy.
▸**ineˈlastically** ADVERB ▸**inelasticity** (ˌɪnɪlæs'tɪsɪtɪ) NOUN

inelegant (ɪn'ɛlɪgənt) ADJECTIVE [1] lacking in elegance or refinement; unpolished or graceless. [2] coarse or crude.
▸**inˈelegance** *or* **inˈelegancy** NOUN ▸**inˈelegantly** ADVERB

ineligible (ɪn'ɛlɪdʒəbᵊl) ADJECTIVE [1] (often foll by *for* or an infinitive) not fit or qualified: *ineligible for a grant; ineligible to vote.* ◆ NOUN [2] an ineligible person.
▸**inˌeligiˈbility** *or* **inˈeligibleness** NOUN ▸**inˈeligibly** ADVERB

ineloquent (ɪn'ɛləkwənt) ADJECTIVE lacking eloquence or fluency of expression.
▸**inˈeloquence** NOUN ▸**inˈeloquently** ADVERB

ineluctable (ˌɪnɪ'lʌktəbᵊl) ADJECTIVE (esp of fate) incapable of being avoided; inescapable.
▷HISTORY C17: from Latin *inēluctābilis,* from IN-[1] + *ēluctārī* to escape, from *luctārī* to struggle
▸**ˌineˌluctaˈbility** NOUN ▸**ˌineˈluctably** ADVERB

ineludible (ˌɪnɪ'lu:dəbᵊl) ADJECTIVE a rare word for **inescapable.**
▸**ˌineˌludiˈbility** NOUN ▸**ˌineˈludibly** ADVERB

inept (ɪn'ɛpt) ADJECTIVE [1] awkward, clumsy, or incompetent. [2] not suitable, appropriate, or fitting; out of place.
▷HISTORY C17: from Latin *ineptus,* from IN-[1] + *aptus* fitting, suitable
▸**inˈeptiˌtude** NOUN ▸**inˈeptly** ADVERB ▸**inˈeptness** NOUN

inequable (ɪn'ɛkwəbᵊl) ADJECTIVE uneven; not uniform.

inequality (ˌɪnɪ'kwɒlɪtɪ) NOUN, *plural* **-ties.** [1] the state or quality of being unequal; disparity. [2] an instance of disparity. [3] lack of smoothness or regularity. [4] social or economic disparity. [5] *Maths* **a** a statement indicating that the value of one quantity or expression is not equal to another, as in $x \neq y$. **b** a relationship between real numbers involving inequality: *x* may be greater than *y*, denoted by $x > y$, or less than *y*, denoted by $x < y$. [6] *Astronomy* a departure from uniform orbital motion.

inequitable (ɪnˈɛkwɪtəbᵊl) ADJECTIVE not equitable; unjust or unfair.
▸ **inˈequitableness** NOUN ▸ **inˈequitably** ADVERB

inequity (ɪnˈɛkwɪtɪ) NOUN, *plural* **-ties.** [1] lack of equity; injustice; unfairness. [2] an unjust or unfair act, sentence, etc.

ineradicable (ˌɪnɪˈrædɪkəbᵊl) ADJECTIVE not able to be removed or rooted out; inextirpable: *an ineradicable disease.*
▸ **ˌineˈradicableness** NOUN ▸ **ˌineˈradicably** ADVERB

inerrable (ɪnˈɛrəbᵊl) *or* **inerrant** (ɪnˈɛrənt) ADJECTIVE less common words for **infallible.**
▸ **inˌerraˈbility, inˈerrableness,** *or* **inˈerrancy** NOUN
▸ **inˈerrably** ADVERB

inert (ɪnˈɜːt) ADJECTIVE [1] having no inherent ability to move or to resist motion. [2] inactive, lazy, or sluggish. [3] having only a limited ability to react chemically; unreactive.
▹ **HISTORY** C17: from Latin *iners* unskilled, from IN-[1] + *ars* skill; see ART[1]
▸ **inˈertly** ADVERB ▸ **inˈertness** NOUN

inert gas NOUN [1] Also called: **noble gas, rare gas, argonon.** any of the unreactive gaseous elements helium, neon, argon, krypton, xenon, and radon. [2] (loosely) any gas, such as carbon dioxide, that is nonoxidizing.

inertia (ɪnˈɜːʃə, -ʃɪə) NOUN [1] the state of being inert; disinclination to move or act. [2] *Physics* **a** the tendency of a body to preserve its state of rest or uniform motion unless acted upon by an external force. **b** an analogous property of other physical quantities that resist change: *thermal inertia.*
▸ **inˈertial** ADJECTIVE

inertia force NOUN an imaginary force supposed to act upon an accelerated body, equal in magnitude and opposite in direction to the resultant of the real forces.

inertial force NOUN an imaginary force which an accelerated observer postulates so that he can use the equations appropriate to an inertial observer. See also **Coriolis force.**

inertial fusion *or* **inertial confinement fusion** NOUN *Physics* a type of nuclear fusion in which the inertia of matter enables it to fuse by impact, as by pulses of laser radiation or high-energy charged particles, rather than by high temperature.

inertial guidance *or* **navigation** NOUN a method of controlling the flight path of a missile by instruments contained within it. Velocities or distances covered, computed from the acceleration measured by these instruments, are compared with stored data and used to control the speed and direction of the missile. Compare **celestial guidance, terrestrial guidance.**

inertial mass NOUN the mass of a body as determined by its momentum, as opposed to gravitational mass. The acceleration of a falling body is inversely proportional to its inertial mass but directly proportional to its gravitational mass: as all falling bodies have the same constant acceleration the two types of mass must be equal.

inertial observer NOUN a hypothetical observer who is not accelerated with respect to an inertial system. Newton's laws of motion and the special theory of relativity apply to the measurements which would be made by such observers.

inertial system NOUN a frame of reference within which bodies are not accelerated unless acted upon by external forces. Also called: **inertial reference frame.**

inertia-reel seat belt NOUN a type of car seat belt in which the belt is free to unwind from a metal drum except when the drum locks as a result of rapid deceleration.

inertia selling NOUN (in Britain) the illegal practice of sending unrequested goods to householders followed by a bill for the price of the goods if they do not return them.

inescapable (ˌɪnɪˈskeɪpəbᵊl) ADJECTIVE incapable of being escaped or avoided.
▸ **ˌinesˈcapably** ADVERB

inescutcheon (ˌɪnɪˈskʌtʃən) NOUN *Heraldry* a small shield-shaped charge in the centre of a shield.

in esse (ɪn ˈɛsɪ) ADJECTIVE actually existing. Compare **in posse.**
▹ **HISTORY** Latin, literally: in being

inessential (ˌɪnɪˈsɛnʃəl) ADJECTIVE [1] not necessary. ◆ NOUN [2] anything that is not essential.
▸ **ˌinesˌsentiˈality** NOUN

inessive (ɪnˈɛsɪv) ADJECTIVE [1] (in the grammar of Finnish and related languages) denoting a case of nouns, etc., used when indicating the location of the referent. ◆ NOUN [2] the inessive case.
▹ **HISTORY** C20: from Latin *inesse* to be in

inestimable (ɪnˈɛstɪməbᵊl) ADJECTIVE [1] not able to be estimated; immeasurable. [2] of immeasurable value.
▸ **inˌestimaˈbility** *or* **inˈestimableness** NOUN ▸ **inˈestimably** ADVERB

inevitable (ɪnˈɛvɪtəbᵊl) ADJECTIVE [1] unavoidable. [2] sure to happen; certain. ◆ NOUN [3] (often preceded by *the*) something that is unavoidable.
▹ **HISTORY** C15: from Latin *inēvītābilis,* from IN-[1] + *ēvītābilis,* from *ēvītāre* to shun, from *vītāre* to avoid
▸ **inˌevitaˈbility** *or* **inˈevitableness** NOUN ▸ **inˈevitably** ADVERB

inexact (ˌɪnɪɡˈzækt) ADJECTIVE not exact or accurate.
▸ **ˌinexˈactiˌtude** *or* **ˌinexˈactness** NOUN ▸ **ˌinexˈactly** ADVERB

inexcusable (ˌɪnɪkˈskjuːzəbᵊl) ADJECTIVE not able to be excused or justified.
▸ **ˌinexˌcusaˈbility** *or* **ˌinexˈcusableness** NOUN
▸ **ˌinexˈcusably** ADVERB

inexhaustible (ˌɪnɪɡˈzɔːstəbᵊl) ADJECTIVE [1] incapable of being used up; endless: *inexhaustible patience.* [2] incapable or apparently incapable of becoming tired; tireless.
▸ **ˌinexˌhaustiˈbility** *or* **ˌinexˈhaustibleness** NOUN
▸ **ˌinexˈhaustibly** ADVERB

inexistent (ˌɪnɪɡˈzɪstənt) ADJECTIVE a rare word for **nonexistent.**
▸ **ˌinexˈistence** *or* **ˌinexˈistency** NOUN

inexorable (ɪnˈɛksərəbᵊl) ADJECTIVE [1] not able to be moved by entreaty or persuasion. [2] relentless.
▹ **HISTORY** C16: from Latin *inexōrābilis,* from IN-[1] + *exōrābilis,* from *exōrāre* to prevail upon, from *ōrāre* to pray
▸ **inˌexoraˈbility** *or* **inˈexorableness** NOUN ▸ **inˈexorably** ADVERB

inexpedient (ˌɪnɪkˈspiːdɪənt) ADJECTIVE not suitable, advisable, or judicious.
▸ **ˌinexˈpedience** *or* **ˌinexˈpediency** NOUN ▸ **ˌinexˈpediently** ADVERB

inexpensive (ˌɪnɪkˈspɛnsɪv) ADJECTIVE not expensive; cheap.
▸ **ˌinexˈpensively** ADVERB ▸ **ˌinexˈpensiveness** NOUN

inexperience (ˌɪnɪkˈspɪərɪəns) NOUN lack of experience or of the knowledge and understanding derived from experience.
▸ **ˌinexˈperienced** ADJECTIVE

inexpert (ɪnˈɛkspɜːt) ADJECTIVE not expert; unskilled or unskilful; inept.
▸ **inˈexpertly** ADVERB ▸ **inˈexpertness** NOUN

inexpiable (ɪnˈɛkspɪəbᵊl) ADJECTIVE [1] incapable of being expiated; unpardonable. [2] *Archaic* implacable.
▸ **inˈexpiableness** NOUN ▸ **inˈexpiably** ADVERB

inexplicable (ˌɪnɪkˈsplɪkəbᵊl, ɪnˈɛksplɪkəbᵊl) *or* **inexplainable** ADJECTIVE not capable of explanation; unexplainable.
▸ **ˌinexplicaˈbility, ˌinexˈplicableness, ˌinexˌplainaˈbility,** *or* **ˌinexˈplainableness** NOUN ▸ **ˌinexˈplicably** *or* **ˌinexˈplainably** ADVERB

inexplicit (ˌɪnɪkˈsplɪsɪt) ADJECTIVE not explicit, clear, or precise; vague.
▸ **ˌinexˈplicitly** ADVERB ▸ **ˌinexˈplicitness** NOUN

inexpressible (ˌɪnɪkˈsprɛsəbᵊl) ADJECTIVE too great, etc., to be expressed or uttered; indescribable.
▸ **ˌinexˌpressiˈbility** *or* **ˌinexˈpressibleness** NOUN
▸ **ˌinexˈpressibly** ADVERB

inexpressive (ˌɪnɪkˈsprɛsɪv) ADJECTIVE [1] lacking in expression: *an inexpressive face.* [2] an archaic word for **inexpressible.**
▸ **ˌinexˈpressively** ADVERB ▸ **ˌinexˈpressiveness** NOUN

inexpugnable (ˌɪnɪkˈspʌɡnəbᵊl) ADJECTIVE a rare word for **impregnable[1].**
▸ **ˌinexˌpugnaˈbility** *or* **ˌinexˈpugnableness** NOUN
▸ **ˌinexˈpugnably** ADVERB

inexpungible (ˌɪnɪksˈpʌndʒɪbᵊl) ADJECTIVE incapable of being expunged.

inextensible (ˌɪnɪkˈstɛnsəbᵊl) ADJECTIVE not capable of extension.
▸ **ˌinexˌtensiˈbility** NOUN

in extenso *Latin* (ɪn ɪkˈstɛnsəʊ) ADVERB at full length.

inextinguishable (ˌɪnɪkˈstɪŋɡwɪʃəbᵊl) ADJECTIVE not able to be extinguished, quenched, or put to an end.
▸ **ˌinexˈtinguishableness** NOUN ▸ **ˌinexˈtinguishably** ADVERB

inextirpable (ˌɪnɪkˈstɜːpəbᵊl) ADJECTIVE not able to be extirpated; ineradicable.
▸ **ˌinexˈtirpableness** NOUN

in extremis *Latin* (ɪn ɪkˈstriːmɪs) ADVERB [1] in extremity; in dire straits. [2] at the point of death.
▹ **HISTORY** literally: in the furthest reaches

inextricable (ˌɪnɛksˈtrɪkəbᵊl) ADJECTIVE [1] not able to be escaped from: *an inextricable dilemma.* [2] not able to be disentangled, etc.: *an inextricable knot.* [3] extremely involved or intricate.
▸ **ˌinextricaˈbility** *or* **ˌinexˈtricableness** NOUN
▸ **ˌinexˈtricably** ADVERB

INF ABBREVIATION FOR intermediate-range nuclear forces: land-based missiles and aircraft with a range between 500 and 5000 km.

inf. ABBREVIATION FOR [1] infinitive. [2] infra.
▹ **HISTORY** Latin: below; after; later

infallibilism (ɪnˈfælɪbᵊˌlɪzəm) NOUN *RC Church* the principle of papal infallibility.
▸ **inˈfallibilist** NOUN

infallible (ɪnˈfæləbᵊl) ADJECTIVE [1] not fallible; not liable to error. [2] not liable to failure; certain; sure: *an infallible cure.* [3] completely dependable or trustworthy. ◆ NOUN [4] a person or thing that is incapable of error or failure.
▸ **inˌfalliˈbility** *or* **inˈfallibleness** NOUN ▸ **inˈfallibly** ADVERB

infamize *or* **infamise** (ˈɪnfəˌmaɪz) VERB (*tr*) to make infamous.

infamous (ˈɪnfəməs) ADJECTIVE [1] having a bad reputation; notorious. [2] causing or deserving a bad reputation; shocking: *infamous conduct.* [3] *Criminal law.* (formerly) **a** (of a person) deprived of certain rights of citizenship on conviction of certain offences. **b** (of a crime or punishment) entailing such deprivation.
▸ **ˈinfamously** ADVERB ▸ **ˈinfamousness** NOUN

infamy (ˈɪnfəmɪ) NOUN, *plural* **-mies.** [1] the state or condition of being infamous. [2] an infamous act or event.
▹ **HISTORY** C15: from Latin *infāmis* of evil repute, from IN-[1] + *fāma* FAME

infancy (ˈɪnfənsɪ) NOUN, *plural* **-cies.** [1] the state or period of being an infant; childhood. [2] an early stage of growth or development. [3] infants collectively. [4] the period of life prior to attaining legal majority (reached at 21 under common law, at 18 by statute); minority nonage.

infant (ˈɪnfənt) NOUN [1] a child at the earliest stage of its life; baby. [2] *Law* another word for **minor** (sense 10). [3] *Brit* a young schoolchild, usually under the age of seven. [4] a person who is beginning or inexperienced in an activity. [5] (*modifier*) **a** of or relating to young children or infancy. **b** designed or intended for young children. ◆ ADJECTIVE [6] in an early stage of development; nascent: *an infant science or industry.* [7] *Law* of or relating to the legal status of infancy.
▹ **HISTORY** C14: from Latin *infāns,* literally: speechless, from IN-[1] + *fārī* to speak
▸ **ˈinfantˌhood** NOUN

infanta (ɪnˈfæntə) NOUN (formerly) [1] a daughter of a king of Spain or Portugal. [2] the wife of an infante.
▹ **HISTORY** C17: from Spanish or Portuguese, feminine of INFANTE

infante (ɪnˈfæntɪ) NOUN (formerly) a son of a king of Spain or Portugal, esp one not heir to the throne.
▹ **HISTORY** C16: from Spanish or Portuguese, literally: INFANT

infanticide (ɪnˈfæntɪˌsaɪd) NOUN [1] the killing of an infant. [2] the practice of killing newborn

infants, still prevalent in some primitive tribes. 3 a person who kills an infant.
▸in,fanti'cidal ADJECTIVE

infantile ('ɪnfən,taɪl) ADJECTIVE 1 like a child in action or behaviour; childishly immature; puerile. 2 of, relating to, or characteristic of infants or infancy. 3 in an early stage of development.
▸**infantility** (,ɪnfən'tɪlɪtɪ) NOUN

infantile paralysis NOUN a former name for **poliomyelitis.**

infantilism (ɪn'fæntɪ,lɪzəm) NOUN 1 *Psychol* **a** a condition in which an older child or adult is mentally or physically undeveloped. **b** isolated instances of infantile behaviour in mature persons. 2 childish speech; baby talk.

infantivore (ɪn'fæntɪ,vɔː) NOUN a person or animal that eats children.
▷HISTORY C20: from Latin *infāns,* literally: speechless, from IN-[1] + *fārī* to speak + *vorāre* to consume

infant prodigy NOUN an exceptionally talented child.

infantry ('ɪnfəntrɪ) NOUN, *plural* **-tries. a** soldiers or units of soldiers who fight on foot with small arms. **b** (*as modifier*): *an infantry unit.* Abbreviations: **Inf., inf.**
▷HISTORY C16: from Italian *infanteria,* from *infante* boy, foot soldier; see INFANT

infantryman ('ɪnfəntrɪmən) NOUN, *plural* **-men.** a soldier belonging to the infantry.

infant school NOUN (in England and Wales) a school for children aged between 5 and 7. Compare **junior school.**

infarct (ɪn'fɑːkt) NOUN a localized area of dead tissue (necrosis) resulting from obstruction of the blood supply to that part, esp by an embolus. Also called: **infarction.**
▷HISTORY C19: via New Latin from Latin *infarctus* stuffed into, from *farcīre* to stuff
▸**in'farcted** ADJECTIVE

infarction (ɪn'fɑːkʃən) NOUN 1 the formation or development of an infarct. 2 another word for **infarct.**

infatuate VERB (ɪn'fætjʊ,eɪt) (*tr*) 1 to inspire or fill with foolish, shallow, or extravagant passion. 2 to cause to act foolishly. ◆ ADJECTIVE (ɪn'fætjʊɪt, -,eɪt) 3 an archaic word for **infatuated.** ◆ NOUN (ɪn'fætjʊɪt, -,eɪt) 4 *Literary* a person who is infatuated.
▷HISTORY C16: from Latin *infatuāre,* from IN-[2] + *fatuus* FATUOUS

infatuated (ɪn'fætjʊ,eɪtɪd) ADJECTIVE (often foll by *with*) possessed by a foolish or extravagant passion, esp for another person.
▸**in'fatu,atedly** ADVERB

infatuation (ɪn,fætjʊ'eɪʃən) NOUN 1 the act of infatuating or state of being infatuated. 2 foolish or extravagant passion. 3 an object of foolish or extravagant passion.

infeasible (ɪn'fiːzəb[ə]l) ADJECTIVE a less common word for **impracticable.**
▸**in,feasi'bility** *or* **in'feasibleness** NOUN

infect (ɪn'fɛkt) VERB (*mainly tr*) 1 to cause infection in; contaminate (an organism, wound, etc.) with pathogenic microorganisms. 2 (*also intr*) to affect with a communicable disease. 3 to taint, pollute, or contaminate. 4 to affect, esp adversely, as if by contagion. 5 *Computing* to affect with a computer virus. 6 *Chiefly international law* to taint with crime or illegality; expose to penalty or subject to forfeiture. ◆ ADJECTIVE 7 *Archaic* contaminated or polluted with or as if with a disease; infected.
▷HISTORY C14: from Latin *inficere* to dip into, stain, from *facere* to make
▸**in'fector** *or* **in'fecter** NOUN

infection (ɪn'fɛkʃən) NOUN 1 invasion of the body by pathogenic microorganisms. 2 the resulting condition in the tissues. 3 an infectious disease. 4 the act of infecting or state of being infected. 5 an agent or influence that infects. 6 persuasion or corruption, as by ideas, perverse influences, etc.

infectious (ɪn'fɛkʃəs) ADJECTIVE 1 (of a disease) capable of being transmitted. Compare **contagious.** 2 (of a disease) caused by microorganisms, such as bacteria, viruses, or protozoa. 3 causing or transmitting infection. 4 tending or apt to spread, as from one person to another: *infectious mirth.* 5 *International law* **a** tainting or capable of tainting with illegality. **b** rendering liable to seizure or forfeiture.
▸**in'fectiously** ADVERB ▸**in'fectiousness** NOUN

infectious canine hepatitis NOUN *Vet science* a disease of dogs caused by an adenovirus and characterized by signs of liver disease.

infectious hepatitis NOUN any form of hepatitis caused by viruses. See **hepatitis A, hepatitis B.**

infectious mononucleosis NOUN an acute infectious disease, caused by Epstein-Barr virus, characterized by fever, sore throat, swollen and painful lymph nodes, and abnormal lymphocytes in the blood. Also called: **glandular fever.**

infective (ɪn'fɛktɪv) ADJECTIVE 1 capable of causing infection. 2 a less common word for **infectious.**
▸**in'fectively** ADVERB ▸**in'fectiveness** *or* **,infec'tivity** NOUN

infecund (ɪn'fiːkənd) ADJECTIVE a less common word for **infertile.**
▸**infecundity** (,ɪnfɪ'kʌndɪtɪ) NOUN

infelicitous (,ɪnfɪ'lɪsɪtəs) ADJECTIVE 1 not felicitous; unfortunate. 2 inappropriate or unsuitable.
▸**,infe'licitously** ADVERB

infelicity (,ɪnfɪ'lɪsɪtɪ) NOUN, *plural* **-ties.** 1 the state or quality of being unhappy or unfortunate. 2 an instance of bad luck or mischance; misfortune. 3 something, esp a remark or expression, that is inapt or inappropriate.

infer (ɪn'fɜː) VERB **-fers, -ferring, -ferred.** (when *tr, may take a clause as object*) 1 to conclude (a state of affairs, supposition, etc.) by reasoning from evidence; deduce. 2 (*tr*) to have or lead to as a necessary or logical consequence; indicate. 3 (*tr*) to hint or imply.
▷HISTORY C16: from Latin *inferre* to bring into, from *ferre* to bear, carry
▸**in'ferable, in'ferible,** *or* **in'ferrable, in'ferrible** ADJECTIVE
▸**in'ferably** ADVERB ▸**in'ferrer** NOUN

> **Language note** The use of *infer* to mean *imply* is common in both speech and writing, but is regarded by many people as incorrect.

inference ('ɪnfərəns, -frəns) NOUN 1 the act or process of inferring. 2 an inferred conclusion, deduction, etc. 3 any process of reasoning from premises to a conclusion. 4 *Logic* the specific mode of reasoning used. See also **deduction** (sense 4), **induction** (sense 4).

inferencing ('ɪnfərənsɪŋ) NOUN *Psycholinguistics* the practice of inferring the meaning of an unfamiliar word or expression from the meaning of familiar words occurring with it in a context together with one's knowledge of or beliefs about the world.

inferential (,ɪnfə'rɛnʃəl) ADJECTIVE of, relating to, or derived from inference.
▸**,infer'entially** ADVERB

inferential statistics NOUN (*functioning as singular*) another name for **statistical inference.**

inferior (ɪn'fɪərɪə) ADJECTIVE 1 lower in value or quality. 2 lower in rank, position, or status; subordinate. 3 not of the best; mediocre; commonplace. 4 lower in position; situated beneath. 5 (of a plant ovary) enclosed by and fused with the receptacle so that it is situated below the other floral parts. 6 *Astronomy* **a** orbiting or occurring between the sun and the earth: *an inferior planet; inferior conjunction.* **b** lying below the horizon. 7 *Printing* (of a character) printed at the foot of an ordinary character, as the 2 in H_2O. ◆ NOUN 8 an inferior person. 9 *Printing* an inferior character.
▷HISTORY C15: from Latin: lower, from *inferus* low
▸**inferiority** (ɪn,fɪərɪ'ɒrɪtɪ) NOUN ▸**in'feriorly** ADVERB

inferior court NOUN 1 a court of limited jurisdiction. 2 any court other than the Supreme Court of Judicature.

inferiority complex NOUN *Psychiatry* a disorder arising from the conflict between the desire to be noticed and the fear of being humiliated, characterized by aggressiveness or withdrawal into oneself.

inferior planet NOUN either of the planets Mercury and Venus, whose orbits lie inside that of the earth.

infernal (ɪn'fɜːn[ə]l) ADJECTIVE 1 of or relating to an underworld of the dead. 2 deserving hell or befitting its occupants; diabolic; fiendish. 3 *Informal* irritating; confounded.
▷HISTORY C14: from Late Latin *infernālis,* from *infernus* hell, from Latin (adjective): lower, hellish; related to Latin *inferus* low
▸**,infer'nality** NOUN ▸**in'fernally** ADVERB

infernal machine NOUN *Archaic* a usually disguised explosive device or booby trap.

inferno (ɪn'fɜːnəʊ) NOUN, *plural* **-nos.** 1 (*sometimes capital;* usually preceded by *the*) hell; the infernal region. 2 any place or state resembling hell, esp a conflagration.
▷HISTORY C19: from Italian, from Late Latin *infernus* hell

infertile (ɪn'fɜːtaɪl) ADJECTIVE 1 not capable of producing offspring; sterile. 2 (of land) not productive; barren.
▸**in'fertilely** ADVERB ▸**infertility** (,ɪnfə'tɪlɪtɪ) NOUN

infest (ɪn'fɛst) VERB (*tr*) 1 to inhabit or overrun in dangerously or unpleasantly large numbers. 2 (of parasites such as lice) to invade and live on or in (a host).
▷HISTORY C15: from Latin *infestāre* to molest, from *infestus* hostile
▸**,infes'tation** NOUN ▸**in'fester** NOUN

infeudation (,ɪnfjʊ'deɪʃən) NOUN 1 (in feudal society) **a** the act of putting a vassal in possession of a fief. **b** the deed conferring such possession. **c** the consequent relationship of lord and vassal. 2 the granting of tithes to laymen.

infibulate (ɪn'fɪbjʊ,leɪt) VERB (*tr*) to enclose (esp the genitals, to prevent sexual intercourse) with a clasp.
▷HISTORY C17: from Latin *infībulāre,* from IN-[2] + *fībula* clasp, FIBULA
▸**in,fibu'lation** NOUN

infidel ('ɪnfɪd[ə]l) NOUN 1 a person who has no religious belief; unbeliever. ◆ ADJECTIVE 2 rejecting a specific religion, esp Christianity or Islam. 3 of, characteristic of, or relating to unbelievers or unbelief.
▷HISTORY C15: from Medieval Latin *infidēlis,* from Latin (adjective): unfaithful, from IN-[1] + *fidēlis* faithful; see FEAL

infidelity (,ɪnfɪ'dɛlɪtɪ) NOUN, *plural* **-ties.** 1 lack of faith or constancy, esp sexual faithfulness. 2 lack of religious faith; disbelief. 3 an act or instance of disloyalty.

infield ('ɪn,fiːld) NOUN 1 *Cricket* the area of the field near the pitch. Compare **outfield.** 2 *Baseball* **a** the area of the playing field enclosed by the base lines and extending beyond them towards the outfield. **b** the positions of the first baseman, second baseman, shortstop, third baseman, and sometimes the pitcher, collectively. Compare **outfield.** 3 *Agriculture* **a** the part of a farm nearest to the farm buildings. **b** land from which crops are regularly taken.

infielder ('ɪn,fiːldə) *or* **infieldsman** ('ɪnfiːldzmən) NOUN a player positioned in the infield.

infighting ('ɪn,faɪtɪŋ) NOUN 1 *Boxing* combat at close quarters in which proper blows are inhibited and the fighters try to wear down each other's strength. 2 intense competition, as between members of the same organization, esp when kept secret from outsiders.
▸**'in,fighter** NOUN

infill ('ɪnfɪl) *or* **infilling** ('ɪnfɪlɪŋ) NOUN 1 the act of filling or closing gaps, etc., in something, such as a row of buildings. 2 material used to fill a cavity, gap, hole, etc. 3 an acrylic gel application that fills in the gap between a false nail and the root of the real nail, which is created as the real nail grows.

infiltrate ('ɪnfɪl,treɪt) VERB 1 to undergo or cause to undergo the process in which a fluid passes into the pores or interstices of a solid; permeate. 2 *Military* to pass undetected through (an enemy-held line or position). 3 to gain or cause to gain entrance or access surreptitiously: *they infiltrated the party structure.* ◆ NOUN 4 something that infiltrates. 5 *Pathol* any substance that passes into and accumulates within cells, tissues, or organs. 6 *Pathol* a local anaesthetic solution injected into the tissues to cause local anaesthesia.
▷HISTORY C18: from IN-[2] + FILTRATE

▸ˌ**infil'tration** NOUN ▸'**infilˌtrative** ADJECTIVE ▸'**infilˌtrator** NOUN

infimum ('ɪnfɪməm) NOUN, *plural* **-ma** (-mə). the greatest lower bound.

infin. ABBREVIATION FOR infinitive.

infinite ('ɪnfɪnɪt) ADJECTIVE [1] **a** having no limits or boundaries in time, space, extent, or magnitude. **b** (*as noun; preceded by the*): *the infinite.* [2] extremely or immeasurably great or numerous: *infinite wealth.* [3] all-embracing, absolute, or total: *God's infinite wisdom.* [4] *Maths* **a** having an unlimited number of digits, factors, terms, members, etc.: *an infinite series.* **b** (of a set) able to be put in a one-to-one correspondence with part of itself. **c** (of an integral) having infinity as one or both limits of integration. Compare **finite** (sense 2).
▸'**infinitely** ADVERB ▸'**infiniteness** NOUN

infinitesimal (ˌɪnfɪnɪ'tɛsɪməl) ADJECTIVE [1] infinitely or immeasurably small. [2] *Maths* of, relating to, or involving a small change in the value of a variable that approaches zero as a limit. ◆ NOUN [3] *Maths* an infinitesimal quantity.
▸ˌ**infini'tesimally** ADVERB

infinitesimal calculus NOUN another name for **calculus** (sense 1).

infinitive (ɪn'fɪnɪtɪv) NOUN *Grammar* a form of the verb not inflected for grammatical categories such as tense and person and used without an overt subject. In English, the infinitive usually consists of the word *to* followed by the verb.
▸**infinitival** (ˌɪnfɪnɪ'taɪvᵊl) ADJECTIVE ▸**in'finitively** *or* ˌ**infini'tivally** ADVERB

infinitive marker NOUN *Grammar* a word or affix occurring with the verb stem in the infinitive, such as *to* in *to make.*

infinitude (ɪn'fɪnɪˌtjuːd) NOUN [1] the state or quality of being infinite. [2] an infinite extent, quantity, degree, etc.

infinity (ɪn'fɪnɪtɪ) NOUN, *plural* **-ties.** [1] the state or quality of being infinite. [2] endless time, space, or quantity. [3] an infinitely or indefinitely great number or amount. [4] *Optics, photog* a point that is far enough away from a lens, mirror, etc., for the light emitted by it to fall in parallel rays on the surface of the lens, etc. [5] *Physics* a dimension or quantity of sufficient size to be unaffected by finite variations. [6] *Maths* the concept of a value greater than any finite numerical value. [7] a distant ideal point at which two parallel lines are assumed to meet. ◆ Symbol (for senses 4–7): ∞.

infirm (ɪn'fɜːm) ADJECTIVE [1] **a** weak in health or body, esp from old age. **b** (*as collective noun; preceded by the*): *the infirm.* [2] lacking moral certainty; indecisive or irresolute. [3] not stable, sound, or secure: *an infirm structure; an infirm claim.* [4] *Law* (of a law, custom, etc.) lacking legal force; invalid.
▸**in'firmly** ADVERB ▸**in'firmness** NOUN

infirmary (ɪn'fɜːmərɪ) NOUN, *plural* **-ries.** a place for the treatment of the sick or injured; dispensary; hospital.

infirmity (ɪn'fɜːmɪtɪ) NOUN, *plural* **-ties.** [1] the state or quality of being infirm. [2] physical weakness or debility; frailty. [3] a moral flaw or failing.

infix VERB (ɪn'fɪks, 'ɪnˌfɪks) [1] (*tr*) to fix firmly in. [2] (*tr*) to instil or inculcate. [3] *Grammar* to insert (an affix) or (of an affix) to be inserted into the middle of a word. ◆ NOUN ('ɪnˌfɪks) [4] *Grammar* an affix inserted into the middle of a word.
▸ˌ**infix'ation** *or* **infixion** (ɪn'fɪkʃən) NOUN

in flagrante delicto (ɪn flə'græntɪ dɪ'lɪktəʊ) ADVERB *Chiefly law* while committing the offence; red-handed. Also: **flagrante delicto.**
▷HISTORY Latin, literally: with the crime still blazing

inflame (ɪn'fleɪm) VERB [1] to arouse or become aroused to violent emotion. [2] (*tr*) to increase or intensify; aggravate. [3] to produce inflammation in (a tissue, organ, or part) or (of a tissue, etc.) to become inflamed. [4] to set or be set on fire; kindle. [5] (*tr*) to cause to redden.
▸**in'flamer** NOUN ▸**in'flamingly** ADVERB

inflammable (ɪn'flæməbᵊl) ADJECTIVE [1] liable to catch fire; flammable. [2] readily aroused to anger or passion. ◆ NOUN [3] something that is liable to catch fire.
▸**inˌflamma'bility** *or* **in'flammableness** NOUN
▸**in'flammably** ADVERB

Language note See at **flammable.**

inflammation (ˌɪnflə'meɪʃən) NOUN [1] the reaction of living tissue to injury or infection, characterized by heat, redness, swelling, and pain. [2] the act of inflaming or the state of being inflamed.

inflammatory (ɪn'flæmətərɪ, -trɪ) ADJECTIVE [1] characterized by or caused by inflammation. [2] tending to arouse violence, strong emotion, etc.
▸**in'flammatorily** ADVERB

inflatable (ɪn'fleɪtəbᵊl) NOUN [1] any of various large air-filled objects made of strong plastic or rubber, used for children to play on at fairs, carnivals, etc. ◆ ADJECTIVE [2] capable of being inflated.

inflate (ɪn'fleɪt) VERB [1] to expand or cause to expand by filling with gas or air. [2] (*tr*) to cause to increase excessively; puff up; swell: *to inflate one's opinion of oneself.* [3] (*tr*) to cause inflation of (prices, money, etc.). [4] (*tr*) to raise in spirits; elate. [5] (*intr*) to undergo economic inflation.
▷HISTORY C16: from Latin *inflāre* to blow into, from *flāre* to blow
▸**in'flatedly** ADVERB ▸**in'flatedness** NOUN ▸**in'flater** *or* **in'flator** NOUN

inflation (ɪn'fleɪʃən) NOUN [1] the act of inflating or state of being inflated. [2] *Economics* a progressive increase in the general level of prices brought about by an expansion in demand or the money supply (**demand-pull inflation**) or by autonomous increases in costs (**cost-push inflation**). Compare **deflation.** [3] *Informal* the rate of increase of prices.

inflationary (ɪn'fleɪʃənərɪ) ADJECTIVE of, relating to, causing, or characterized by inflation: *inflationary wage claims.*

inflationary gap NOUN the excess of total spending in an economy over the value, at current prices, of the output it can produce.

inflationary spiral NOUN the situation in which price and income increases may each induce further rises in the other.

inflationary universe NOUN a variation of the cosmological big-bang theory in which the early stage of the evolution of the universe is postulated to include a period of accelerated expansion.

inflationism (ɪn'fleɪʃəˌnɪzəm) NOUN the advocacy or policy of inflation through expansion of the supply of money and credit.
▸**in'flationist** NOUN, ADJECTIVE

inflect (ɪn'flɛkt) VERB [1] (*Grammar*) to change (the form of a word) or (of a word) to change in form by inflection. [2] (*tr*) to change (the voice) in tone or pitch; modulate. [3] (*tr*) to cause to deviate from a straight or normal line or course; bend.
▷HISTORY C15: from Latin *inflectere* to curve round, alter, from *flectere* to bend
▸**in'flectedness** NOUN ▸**in'flective** ADJECTIVE ▸**in'flector** NOUN

inflection *or* **inflexion** (ɪn'flɛkʃən) NOUN [1] modulation of the voice. [2] *Grammar* a change in the form of a word, usually modification or affixation, signalling change in such grammatical functions as tense, voice, mood, person, gender, number, or case. [3] an angle or bend. [4] the act of inflecting or the state of being inflected. [5] *Maths* a change in curvature from concave to convex or vice versa. See also **point of inflection.**
▸**in'flectional** *or* **in'flexional** ADJECTIVE ▸**in'flectionally** *or* **in'flexionally** ADVERB ▸**in'flectionless** *or* **in'flexionless** ADJECTIVE

inflexed (ɪn'flɛkst) ADJECTIVE *Biology* curved or bent inwards and downwards towards the axis: *inflexed leaves.*

inflexible (ɪn'flɛksəbᵊl) ADJECTIVE [1] not flexible; rigid; stiff. [2] obstinate; unyielding. [3] without variation; unalterable; fixed.
▷HISTORY C14: from Latin *inflexibilis;* see INFLECT
▸**inˌflexi'bility** *or* **in'flexibleness** NOUN ▸**in'flexibly** ADVERB

inflict (ɪn'flɪkt) VERB (*tr*) [1] (often foll by *on* or *upon*) to impose (something unwelcome, such as pain, oneself, etc.). [2] *Rare* to cause to suffer; afflict (with). [3] to deal out (blows, lashes, etc.).
▷HISTORY C16: from Latin *inflīgere* to strike (something) against, dash against, from *flīgere* to strike
▸**in'flictable** ADJECTIVE ▸**in'flicter** *or* **in'flictor** NOUN
▸**in'fliction** NOUN ▸**in'flictive** ADJECTIVE

in-flight ADJECTIVE provided during flight in an aircraft: *in-flight meals.*

inflorescence (ˌɪnflɔː'rɛsəns) NOUN [1] the part of a plant that consists of the flower-bearing stalks. [2] the arrangement of the flowers on the stalks. [3] the process of flowering; blossoming.
▷HISTORY C16: from New Latin *inflōrēscentia,* from Late Latin *inflōrescere* to blossom, from *flōrescere* to bloom
▸ˌ**inflo'rescent** ADJECTIVE

inflow ('ɪnˌfləʊ) NOUN [1] something, such as a liquid or gas, that flows in. [2] the amount or rate of flowing in. [3] Also called: **inflowing.** the act of flowing in; influx.

influence ('ɪnflʊəns) NOUN [1] an effect of one person or thing on another. [2] the power of a person or thing to have such an effect. [3] power or sway resulting from ability, wealth, position, etc. [4] a person or thing having influence. [5] *Astrology* an ethereal fluid or occult power regarded as emanating from the stars and affecting a person's actions, future, etc. [6] **under the influence.** *Informal* drunk. ◆ VERB (*tr*) [7] to persuade or induce. [8] to have an effect upon (actions, events, etc.); affect.
▷HISTORY C14: from Medieval Latin *influentia* emanation of power from the stars, from Latin *influere* to flow into, from *fluere* to flow
▸'**influenceable** ADJECTIVE ▸'**influencer** NOUN

influent ('ɪnflʊənt) ADJECTIVE *also* **inflowing.** [1] flowing in. ◆ NOUN [2] something flowing in, esp a tributary. [3] *Ecology* an organism that has a major effect on the nature of its community.

influential (ˌɪnflʊ'ɛnʃəl) ADJECTIVE having or exerting influence.
▸ˌ**influ'entially** ADVERB

influenza (ˌɪnflʊ'ɛnzə) NOUN a highly contagious and often epidemic viral disease characterized by fever, prostration, muscular aches and pains, and inflammation of the respiratory passages. Also called: **grippe.** Informal name: **flu.**
▷HISTORY C18: from Italian, literally: INFLUENCE, hence, incursion, epidemic (first applied to influenza in 1743)
▸ˌ**influ'enzal** ADJECTIVE

influx ('ɪnˌflʌks) NOUN [1] the arrival or entry of many people or things. [2] the act of flowing in; inflow. [3] the mouth of a stream or river.
▷HISTORY C17: from Late Latin *influxus,* from *influere;* see INFLUENCE

info¹ ('ɪnfəʊ) NOUN *Informal* short for **information.**

info² AN INTERNET DOMAIN NAME FOR an information provider.

infold (ɪn'fəʊld) VERB a variant spelling of **enfold.**
▸**in'folder** NOUN ▸**in'foldment** NOUN

infomercial (ˌɪnfə'mɜːʃəl) NOUN a short film, usually for television, which advertises a product or service in an informative way.
▷HISTORY C20: from INFO + (COM)MERCIAL

infopreneurial (ˌɪnfəʊprə'nɜːrɪəl) ADJECTIVE of or relating to the manufacture or sales of electronic office or factory equipment designed to distribute information: *an infopreneurial industry.*
▷HISTORY C20: INFO(RMATION) + (ENTRE)PRENEUR + -IAL

inform¹ (ɪn'fɔːm) VERB [1] (*tr; often foll by of or about*) to give information to; tell. [2] (*tr; often foll by of or about*) to make conversant (with). [3] (*intr; often foll by against or on*) to give information regarding criminals, as to the police, etc. [4] to give form to. [5] to impart some essential or formative characteristic to. [6] (*tr*) to animate or inspire. [7] (*tr*) *Obsolete* **a** to train or educate. **b** to report.
▷HISTORY C14: from Latin *informāre* to give form to, describe, from *formāre* to FORM
▸**in'formable** ADJECTIVE ▸**informedly** (ɪn'fɔːmɪdlɪ) ADVERB
▸**in'formingly** ADVERB

inform² (ɪn'fɔːm) ADJECTIVE *Archaic* without shape; unformed.
▷HISTORY C16: from Latin *informis* from IN-¹ + *forma* shape

informal (ɪn'fɔːməl) ADJECTIVE [1] not of a formal, official, or stiffly conventional nature: *an informal luncheon.* [2] appropriate to everyday life or use:

informal clothes. 3 denoting or characterized by idiom, vocabulary, etc., appropriate to everyday conversational language rather than to formal written language. 4 denoting a second-person pronoun in some languages used when the addressee is regarded as a friend or social inferior: *In French the pronoun "tu" is informal, while "vous" is formal.*
▸**in'formally** ADVERB

informality (ˌɪnfɔːˈmælɪtɪ) NOUN, *plural* **-ties.** 1 the condition or quality of being informal. 2 an informal act.

informal settlement NOUN *South African euphemistic* a squatter camp.

informal vote NOUN *Austral and NZ* an invalid vote or ballot.

informant (ɪnˈfɔːmənt) NOUN a person who gives information about a thing, a subject being studied, etc.

informatics (ˌɪnfəˈmætɪks) NOUN (*functioning as singular*) another term for **information science.**

information (ˌɪnfəˈmeɪʃən) NOUN 1 knowledge acquired through experience or study. 2 knowledge of specific and timely events or situations; news. 3 the act of informing or the condition of being informed. 4 **a** an office, agency, etc., providing information. **b** (*as modifier*): *information service.* 5 **a** a charge or complaint made before justices of the peace, usually on oath, to institute summary criminal proceedings. **b** a complaint filed on behalf of the Crown, usually by the attorney general. 6 *Computing* **a** the meaning given to data by the way in which it is interpreted. **b** another word for **data** (sense 2). 7 **too much information.** *Informal* I don't want to hear any more.
▸ˌ**infor'mational** ADJECTIVE

information age NOUN a time when large amounts of information are widely available to many people, largely through computer technology.

information processing NOUN *Computing* the combined processing of numerical data, graphics, text, etc.

information question NOUN another term for **WH question.**

information retrieval NOUN *Computing* the process of recovering specific information from stored data.

information science NOUN the science of the collection, evaluation, organization, and dissemination of information, often employing computers.

information superhighway NOUN 1 the concept of a worldwide network of computers capable of transferring all types of digital information at high speed. 2 another name for the **Internet.** ◆ Also called: **information highway.**

information technology NOUN the technology of the production, storage, and communication of information using computers and microelectronics. Abbreviation: **IT.**

information theory NOUN a collection of mathematical theories, based on statistics, concerned with methods of coding, transmitting, storing, retrieving, and decoding information.

information warfare NOUN the use of electronic communciations and the Internet to disrupt a country's telecommunications, power supply, transport system, etc.

informative (ɪnˈfɔːmətɪv) *or* **informatory** ADJECTIVE providing information; instructive.
▸**in'formatively** ADVERB ▸**in'formativeness** NOUN

informed (ɪnˈfɔːmd) ADJECTIVE 1 having much knowledge or education; learned or cultured. 2 based on information: *an informed judgment.*

informer (ɪnˈfɔːmə) NOUN 1 a person who informs against someone, esp a criminal. 2 a person who provides information: *he was the President's financial informer.*

infotainment (ˌɪnfəʊˈteɪnmənt) NOUN (in television) the practice of presenting serious or instructive subjects in a style designed primarily to be entertaining.
▷HISTORY C20: from INFO + (ENTER)TAINMENT

infra *Latin* (ˈɪnfrə) ADVERB (esp in textual annotation) below; further on.

infra- PREFIX below; beneath; after: *infrasonic; infralapsarian.*
▷HISTORY from Latin *infrā*

infracostal (ˌɪnfrəˈkɒstᵊl) ADJECTIVE *Anatomy* situated beneath the ribs.

infract (ɪnˈfrækt) VERB (*tr*) to violate or break (a law, an agreement, etc.).
▷HISTORY C18: from Latin *infractus* broken off, from *infringere;* see INFRINGE
▸**in'fraction** NOUN ▸**in'fractor** NOUN

infra dig (ˈɪnfrə ˈdɪɡ) ADJECTIVE (*postpositive*) *Informal* beneath one's dignity.
▷HISTORY C19: from Latin phrase *infrā dignitātem*

infralapsarian (ˌɪnfrəlæpˈsɛərɪən) NOUN *Christian theol, chiefly Calvinist* a person who believes that foreknowledge of the Fall preceded God's decree of who was predestined to salvation and who was not. Compare **supralapsarian.**
▷HISTORY C18: from INFRA- + *lapsarian* (see SUPRALAPSARIAN)
▸ˌ**infralap'sarianism** NOUN

infrangible (ɪnˈfrændʒɪbᵊl) ADJECTIVE 1 incapable of being broken. 2 not capable of being violated or infringed.
▷HISTORY C16: from Late Latin *infrangibilis,* from Latin IN-[1] + *frangere* to break
▸**in,frangi'bility** *or* **in'frangibleness** NOUN ▸**in'frangibly** ADVERB

infrared (ˌɪnfrəˈrɛd) NOUN 1 the part of the electromagnetic spectrum with a longer wavelength than light but a shorter wavelength than radio waves; radiation with wavelength between 0.8 micrometres and 1 millimetre. ◆ ADJECTIVE 2 of, relating to, using, or consisting of radiation lying within the infrared: *infrared radiation.*

infrared astronomy NOUN the study of radiations from space in the infrared region of the electromagnetic spectrum.

infrared photography NOUN photography using film with an emulsion that is sensitive to infrared light, enabling it to be used in misty weather, in darkened interiors, or at night. It has applications in aerial surveys, the detection of forgeries, etc.

infrasound (ˈɪnfrəˌsaʊnd) NOUN soundlike waves having a frequency below the audible range, that is, below about 16Hz.
▸**infrasonic** (ˌɪnfrəˈsɒnɪk) ADJECTIVE

infraspecific (ˌɪnfrəspəˈsɪfɪk) ADJECTIVE *Biology* occurring within or affecting all members of a species: *infraspecific variation.*

infrastructure (ˈɪnfrəˌstrʌktʃə) NOUN 1 the basic structure of an organization, system, etc. 2 the stock of fixed capital equipment in a country, including factories, roads, schools, etc., considered as a determinant of economic growth.

infrequent (ɪnˈfriːkwənt) ADJECTIVE rarely happening or present; only occasional.
▸**in'frequency** *or* **in'frequence** NOUN ▸**in'frequently** ADVERB

infringe (ɪnˈfrɪndʒ) VERB 1 (*tr*) to violate or break (a law, an agreement, etc.). 2 (*intr;* foll by *on* or *upon*) to encroach or trespass.
▷HISTORY C16: from Latin *infringere* to break off, from *frangere* to break
▸**in'fringement** NOUN ▸**in'fringer** NOUN

infulae (ˈɪnfjʊliː) PLURAL NOUN, *singular* **-la** (-lə). the two ribbons hanging from the back of a bishop's mitre.
▷HISTORY C17: from Latin, plural of *infula,* woollen fillet worn on forehead by ancient Romans during religious rites

infundibular (ˌɪnfʌnˈdɪbjʊlə) ADJECTIVE funnel-shaped.
▷HISTORY C18: from INFUNDIBULUM

infundibuliform (ˌɪnfʌnˈdɪbjʊlɪˌfɔːm) ADJECTIVE (of plant parts) shaped like a funnel.

infundibulum (ˌɪnfʌnˈdɪbjʊləm) NOUN, *plural* **-la** (-lə). *Anatomy* any funnel-shaped part, esp the stalk connecting the pituitary gland to the base of the brain.
▷HISTORY C18: from Latin: funnel, from *infundere* to INFUSE
▸ˌ**infun'dibulate** ADJECTIVE

infuriate VERB (ɪnˈfjʊərɪˌeɪt) 1 (*tr*) to anger; annoy. ◆ ADJECTIVE (ɪnˈfjʊərɪɪt) 2 *Archaic* furious; infuriated.
▷HISTORY C17: from Medieval Latin *infuriāre* (vb); see IN-[2], FURY
▸**in'furiately** ADVERB ▸**in'furi,ating** ADJECTIVE
▸**in'furiatingly** ADVERB ▸**in,furi'ation** NOUN

infuscate (ɪnˈfʌskeɪt) *or* **infuscated** ADJECTIVE (esp of the wings of an insect) tinged with brown.
▷HISTORY C17: from Latin *infuscāre* to darken, from *fuscus* dark

infuse (ɪnˈfjuːz) VERB 1 (*tr;* often foll by *into*) to instil or inculcate. 2 (*tr;* foll by *with*) to inspire; emotionally charge. 3 to soak or be soaked in order to extract flavour or other properties. 4 *Rare* (foll by *into*) to pour.
▷HISTORY C15: from Latin *infundere* to pour into

infuser (ɪnˈfjuːzə) NOUN any device used to make an infusion, esp a tea maker.

infusible[1] (ɪnˈfjuːzəbᵊl) ADJECTIVE not fusible; not easily melted; having a high melting point.
▷HISTORY C16: from IN-[1] + FUSIBLE
▸**in,fusi'bility** *or* **in'fusibleness** NOUN

infusible[2] (ɪnˈfjuːzəbᵊl) ADJECTIVE capable of being infused.
▷HISTORY C17: from INFUSE + -IBLE
▸**in,fusi'bility** *or* **in'fusibleness** NOUN

infusion (ɪnˈfjuːʒən) NOUN 1 the act of infusing. 2 something infused. 3 an extract obtained by soaking. 4 *Med* introduction of a liquid, such as a saline solution, into a vein or the subcutaneous tissues of the body.
▸**infusive** (ɪnˈfjuːsɪv) ADJECTIVE

infusionism (ɪnˈfjuːʒəˌnɪzəm) NOUN *Christian theol* the doctrine that at the birth of each individual a pre-existing soul is implanted in his body, to remain there for the duration of his earthly life.
▸**in'fusionist** NOUN, ADJECTIVE

infusorial earth (ˌɪnfjʊˈzɔːrɪəl) NOUN another name for **diatomaceous earth.** See **diatomite.**

infusorian (ˌɪnfjʊˈzɔːrɪən) NOUN *Obsolete* 1 any of the microscopic organisms, such as protozoans and rotifers, found in infusions of organic material. 2 any member of the subclass *Ciliata* (see **ciliate** (sense 3)). ◆ ADJECTIVE 3 of or relating to infusorians.
▷HISTORY C18: from New Latin *Infusoria* former class name; see INFUSE
▸ˌ**infu'sorial** ADJECTIVE

-ing[1] SUFFIX FORMING NOUNS 1 (*from verbs*) the action of, process of, result of, or something connected with the verb: *coming; meeting; a wedding; winnings.* 2 (*from other nouns*) something used in, consisting of, involving, etc.: *tubing; soldiering.* 3 (*from other parts of speech*): *an outing.*
▷HISTORY Old English *-ing, -ung*

-ing[2] SUFFIX 1 forming the present participle of verbs: *walking; believing.* 2 forming participial adjectives: *a growing boy; a sinking ship.* 3 forming adjectives not derived from verbs: *swashbuckling.*
▷HISTORY Middle English *-ing, -inde,* from Old English *-ende*

-ing[3] SUFFIX FORMING NOUNS a person or thing having a certain quality or being of a certain kind: *sweeting; whiting.*
▷HISTORY Old English *-ing;* related to Old Norse *-ingr*

ingather (ɪnˈɡæðə) VERB (*tr*) to gather together or in (a harvest).
▸**in'gatherer** NOUN

ingeminate (ɪnˈdʒɛmɪˌneɪt) VERB (*tr*) *Rare* to repeat; reiterate.
▷HISTORY C16: from Latin *ingemināre* to redouble, from IN-[2] + *gemināre* to GEMINATE
▸**in,gemi'nation** NOUN

ingenerate[1] (ɪnˈdʒɛnərɪt) ADJECTIVE *Rare* inherent, intrinsic, or innate.
▷HISTORY C17: from Late Latin *ingenerātus* not generated; see IN-[1], GENERATE

ingenerate[2] (ɪnˈdʒɛnəˌreɪt) VERB (*tr*) *Archaic* to produce within; engender.
▷HISTORY C16: from Latin *ingenerāre;* see IN-[2], GENERATE
▸**in,gener'ation** NOUN

ingenious (ɪnˈdʒiːnjəs, -nɪəs) ADJECTIVE 1 possessing or done with ingenuity; skilful or clever. 2 *Obsolete* having great intelligence; displaying genius.
▷HISTORY C15: from Latin *ingeniōsus,* from *ingenium* natural ability; see ENGINE
▸**in'geniously** ADVERB ▸**in'geniousness** NOUN

ingénue (ˌænʒeɪˈnjuː; *French* ɛ̃ʒeny) NOUN an artless, innocent, or inexperienced girl or young woman.
▷HISTORY C19: from French, feminine of *ingénu* INGENUOUS

ingenuity (ˌɪndʒɪˈnjuːɪtɪ) NOUN, *plural* **-ties**. 1 inventive talent; cleverness. 2 an ingenious device, act, etc. 3 *Archaic* frankness; candour.
▷HISTORY C16: from Latin *ingenuitās* a freeborn condition, outlook consistent with such a condition, from *ingenuus* native, freeborn (see INGENUOUS); meaning influenced by INGENIOUS

ingenuous (ɪnˈdʒɛnjʊəs) ADJECTIVE 1 naive, artless, or innocent. 2 candid; frank; straightforward.
▷HISTORY C16: from Latin *ingenuus* freeborn, worthy of a freeman, virtuous, from IN-[2] + *-genuus*, from *gignere* to beget
▸**inˈgenuously** ADVERB ▸**inˈgenuousness** NOUN

ingest (ɪnˈdʒɛst) VERB (*tr*) 1 to take (food or liquid) into the body. 2 (of a jet engine) to suck in (an object, a bird, etc.).
▷HISTORY C17: from Latin *ingerere* to put into, from IN-[2] + *gerere* to carry; see GEST
▸**inˈgestible** ADJECTIVE ▸**inˈgestion** NOUN ▸**inˈgestive** ADJECTIVE

ingesta (ɪnˈdʒɛstə) PLURAL NOUN nourishment taken into the body through the mouth.

ingle (ˈɪŋgᵊl) NOUN *Archaic or dialect* a fire in a room or a fireplace.
▷HISTORY C16: probably from Scots Gaelic *aingeal* fire

Ingleborough (ˈɪŋgᵊlbərə, -brə) NOUN a mountain in N England, in North Yorkshire: potholes. Height: 723 m (2373 ft.).

inglenook (ˈɪŋgᵊlˌnʊk) NOUN *Brit* a corner by a fireplace; chimney corner.

inglorious (ɪnˈglɔːrɪəs) ADJECTIVE 1 without courage or glory; dishonourable, shameful, or disgraceful. 2 unknown or obscure.
▸**inˈgloriously** ADVERB ▸**inˈgloriousness** NOUN

ingo (ˈɪŋgəʊ) NOUN *Scot* a reveal. Also: **ingoing.**

ingoing (ˈɪnˌgəʊɪŋ) ADJECTIVE 1 coming or going in; entering. ♦ NOUN 2 (*often plural*) *English law* the sum paid by a new tenant for fixtures left behind by the outgoing tenant. 3 *Scot* another word for **ingo.**

Ingolstadt (*German* ˈɪŋgɔlʃtat) NOUN a city in S central Germany, in Bavaria on the River Danube: oil-refining. Pop.: 114 500 (1999 est.).

ingot (ˈɪŋgət) NOUN 1 a piece of cast metal obtained from a mould in a form suitable for storage, transporting, and further use. ♦ VERB 2 (*tr*) to shape (metal) into ingots.
▷HISTORY C14: perhaps from IN-[2] + Old English *goten*, past participle of *geotan* to pour

ingot iron NOUN a type of steel containing a small amount of carbon and very small quantities of other elements.

ingraft (ɪnˈgrɑːft) VERB a variant spelling of **engraft.**
▸**inˈgraftment** *or* **ˌingrafˈtation** NOUN

ingrain *or* **engrain** VERB (ɪnˈgreɪn) (*tr*) 1 to impress deeply on the mind or nature; instil. 2 *Archaic* to dye into the fibre of (a fabric). ♦ ADJECTIVE (ˈɪnˌgreɪn) 3 variants of **ingrained.** 4 (of woven or knitted articles, esp rugs and carpets) made of dyed yarn or of fibre that is dyed before being spun into yarn. ♦ NOUN (ˈɪnˌgreɪn) 5 **a** a carpet made from ingrained yarn. **b** such yarn.
▷HISTORY C18: from the phrase *dyed in grain* dyed with kermes through the fibre

ingrained *or* **engrained** (ɪnˈgreɪnd) ADJECTIVE 1 deeply impressed or instilled: *his fears are deeply ingrained.* 2 (*prenominal*) complete or inveterate; utter: *an ingrained fool.* 3 (esp of dirt) worked into or through the fibre, grain, pores, etc.
▸**ingrainedly** *or* **engrainedly** (ɪnˈgreɪnɪdlɪ) ADVERB
▸**inˈgrainedness** *or* **enˈgrainedness** NOUN

ingrate (ˈɪngreɪt, ɪnˈgreɪt) *Archaic* ♦ NOUN 1 an ungrateful person. ♦ ADJECTIVE 2 ungrateful.
▷HISTORY C14: from Latin *ingrātus* (adj), from IN-[1] + *grātus* GRATEFUL
▸**ˈingrately** ADVERB

ingratiate (ɪnˈgreɪʃɪˌeɪt) VERB (*tr; often foll by with*) to place (oneself) purposely in the favour (of another).
▷HISTORY C17: from Latin, from IN-[2] + *grātia* grace, favour
▸**inˈgratiˌating** *or* **inˈgratiatory** ADJECTIVE ▸**inˈgratiˌatingly** ADVERB ▸**inˌgratiˈation** NOUN

ingratitude (ɪnˈgrætɪˌtjuːd) NOUN lack of gratitude; ungratefulness; thanklessness.

ingravescent (ˌɪngrəˈvɛsᵊnt) ADJECTIVE *Rare* (esp of a disease) becoming more severe.
▷HISTORY C19: from Latin *ingravescere* to become heavier, from *gravescere* to grow heavy, from *gravis* heavy
▸**ˌingraˈvescence** NOUN

ingredient (ɪnˈgriːdɪənt) NOUN a component of a mixture, compound, etc., esp in cooking.
▷HISTORY C15: from Latin *ingrediēns* going into, from *ingredī* to enter; see INGRESS

ingress (ˈɪngrɛs) NOUN 1 the act of going or coming in; an entering. 2 a way in; entrance. 3 the right or permission to enter. 4 *Astronomy* another name for **immersion** (sense 2).
▷HISTORY C15: from Latin *ingressus*, from *ingredī* to go in, from *gradī* to step, go
▸**ingression** (ɪnˈgrɛʃən) NOUN

ingressive (ɪnˈgrɛsɪv) ADJECTIVE 1 of or concerning ingress. 2 (of a speech sound) pronounced with an inhalation rather than exhalation of breath. ♦ NOUN 3 an ingressive speech sound, such as a Zulu click.
▸**inˈgressiveness** NOUN

in-group NOUN *Sociol* a highly cohesive and relatively closed social group characterized by the preferential treatment reserved for its members and the strength of loyalty between them. Compare **out-group.**

ingrowing (ˈɪnˌgrəʊɪŋ) ADJECTIVE 1 (esp of a toenail) growing abnormally into the flesh. 2 growing within or into.

ingrown (ˈɪnˌgrəʊn, ɪnˈgrəʊn) ADJECTIVE 1 (esp of a toenail) grown abnormally into the flesh; covered by adjacent tissues. 2 grown within; native; innate. 3 excessively concerned with oneself, one's own particular group, etc. 4 ingrained.

ingrowth (ˈɪnˌgrəʊθ) NOUN 1 the act of growing inwards: *the ingrowth of a toenail.* 2 something that grows inwards.

inguinal (ˈɪŋgwɪnᵊl) ADJECTIVE *Anatomy* of or relating to the groin.
▷HISTORY C17: from Latin *inguinālis*, from *inguen* groin

ingulf (ɪnˈgʌlf) VERB a variant spelling of **engulf.**
▸**inˈgulfment** NOUN

ingurgitate (ɪnˈgɜːdʒɪˌteɪt) VERB to swallow (food) with greed or in excess; gorge.
▷HISTORY C16: from Latin *ingurgitāre* to flood, from IN-[2] + *gurges* abyss
▸**inˌgurgiˈtation** NOUN

Ingush (ɪŋˈguːʃ) NOUN, *plural* **-gushes** *or* **-gush.** a member of a people of S central Russia, speaking a Circassian language and chiefly inhabiting the Ingush Republic.

Ingush Republic NOUN a constituent republic of S Russia: part of the Checheno-Ingush Autonomous Republic from 1936 until 1992. Capital: Nazran. Also called: **Ingushetia** (ˌɪŋguːˈʃɛtɪə).

inhabit (ɪnˈhæbɪt) VERB **-its, -iting, -ited.** 1 (*tr*) to live or dwell in; occupy. 2 (*intr*) *Archaic* to abide or dwell.
▷HISTORY C14: from Latin *inhabitāre*, from *habitāre* to dwell
▸**inˈhabitable** ADJECTIVE ▸**inˌhabitaˈbility** NOUN
▸**inˌhabiˈtation** NOUN

inhabitant (ɪnˈhæbɪtənt) NOUN a person or animal that is a permanent resident of a particular place or region.
▸**inˈhabitancy** *or* **inˈhabitance** NOUN

inhalant (ɪnˈheɪlənt) ADJECTIVE 1 (esp of a volatile medicinal formulation) inhaled for its soothing or therapeutic effect. 2 inhaling. ♦ NOUN 3 an inhalant medicinal formulation.

inhalation (ˌɪnhəˈleɪʃən) NOUN 1 the act of inhaling; breathing in of air or other vapours. 2 an inhalant formulation.

inhalator (ˈɪnhəˌleɪtə) NOUN another name for **nebulizer.**

inhale (ɪnˈheɪl) VERB to draw (breath) into the lungs; breathe in.
▷HISTORY C18: from IN-[2] + Latin *halāre* to breathe

inhaler (ɪnˈheɪlə) NOUN 1 a device for breathing in therapeutic vapours through the nose or mouth, esp one for relieving nasal congestion or asthma. 2 a person who inhales.

Inhambane (ˌɪnjəmˈbɑːnə) NOUN a port in SE Mozambique on an inlet of the Mozambique Channel (**Inhambane Bay**). Pop.: 64 274 (latest est.).

inharmonious (ˌɪnhɑːˈməʊnɪəs) ADJECTIVE 1 Also: **inharmonic** (ˌɪnhɑːˈmɒnɪk). lacking harmony; discordant. 2 lacking accord or agreement.
▸**ˌinharˈmoniously** ADVERB ▸**ˌinharˈmoniousness** NOUN

inhaul (ˈɪnˌhɔːl) *or* **inhauler** NOUN *Nautical* a line for hauling in a sail.

inhere (ɪnˈhɪə) VERB (*intr;* foll by *in*) to be an inseparable part (of).
▷HISTORY C16: from Latin *inhaerēre* to stick in, from *haerēre* to stick

inherence (ɪnˈhɪərəns, -ˈhɛr-) *or* **inherency** NOUN 1 the state or condition of being inherent. 2 *Metaphysics* the relation of attributes, elements, etc., to the subject of which they are predicated, esp if they are its essential constituents.

inherent (ɪnˈhɪərənt, -ˈhɛr-) ADJECTIVE existing as an inseparable part; intrinsic.
▸**inˈherently** ADVERB

inherit (ɪnˈhɛrɪt) VERB **-its, -iting, -ited.** 1 to receive (property, a right, title, etc.) by succession or under a will. 2 (*intr*) to succeed as heir. 3 (*tr*) to possess (a characteristic) through genetic transmission. 4 (*tr*) to receive (a position, attitude, property, etc.) from a predecessor.
▷HISTORY C14: from Old French *enheriter*, from Late Latin *inhērēditāre* to appoint an heir, from Latin *hērēs* HEIR
▸**inˈherited** ADJECTIVE ▸**inˈheritor** NOUN ▸**inˈheritress** *or* **inˈheritrix** FEMININE NOUN

inheritable (ɪnˈhɛrɪtəbᵊl) ADJECTIVE 1 capable of being transmitted by heredity from one generation to a later one. 2 capable of being inherited. 3 *Rare* capable of inheriting; having the right to inherit.
▸**inˌheritaˈbility** *or* **inˈheritableness** NOUN ▸**inˈheritably** ADVERB

inheritance (ɪnˈhɛrɪtəns) NOUN 1 *Law* **a** hereditary succession to an estate, title, etc. **b** the right of an heir to succeed to property on the death of an ancestor. **c** something that may legally be transmitted to an heir. 2 the act of inheriting. 3 something inherited; heritage. 4 the derivation of characteristics of one generation from an earlier one by heredity. 5 *Obsolete* hereditary rights.

inheritance tax NOUN 1 (in Britain) a tax introduced in 1986 to replace capital transfer tax, consisting of a percentage levied on that part of an inheritance exceeding a specified allowance, and scaled charges on gifts made within seven years of death. 2 (in the US) a state tax imposed on an inheritance according to its size and the relationship of the beneficiary to the deceased.

inhesion (ɪnˈhiːʒən) NOUN a less common word for **inherence** (sense 1).
▷HISTORY C17: from Late Latin *inhaesiō*, from *inhaerēre* to INHERE

inhibit (ɪnˈhɪbɪt) VERB **-its, -iting, -ited** (*tr*) 1 to restrain or hinder (an impulse, a desire, etc.). 2 to prohibit; forbid. 3 to stop, prevent, or decrease the rate of (a chemical reaction). 4 *Electronics* **a** to prevent the occurrence of (a particular signal) in a circuit. **b** to prevent the performance of (a particular operation).
▷HISTORY C15: from Latin *inhibēre* to restrain, from IN-[2] + *habēre* to have
▸**inˈhibitable** ADJECTIVE ▸**inˈhibitive** *or* **inˈhibitory** ADJECTIVE

inhibition (ˌɪnɪˈbɪʃən, ˌɪnhɪ-) NOUN 1 the act of inhibiting or the condition of being inhibited. 2 *Psychol* **a** a mental state or condition in which the varieties of expression and behaviour of an individual become restricted. **b** the weakening of a learned response usually as a result of extinction or because of the presence of a distracting stimulus. **c** (in psychoanalytical theory) the unconscious restraining of an impulse. See also **repression.** 3 the process of stopping or retarding a chemical reaction. 4 *Physiol* the suppression of the function or action of an organ or part, as by stimulation of its nerve supply. 5 *Church of England* an episcopal order suspending an incumbent.

inhibitor (ɪnˈhɪbɪtə) NOUN 1 Also called: **inhibiter.**

a person or thing that inhibits. [2] Also called: **anticatalyst.** a substance that retards or stops a chemical reaction. Compare **catalyst.** [3] *Biochem* **a** a substance that inhibits the action of an enzyme. **b** a substance that inhibits a metabolic or physiological process: *a plant growth inhibitor.* [4] any impurity in a solid that prevents luminescence. [5] an inert substance added to some rocket fuels to inhibit ignition on certain surfaces.

inhomogeneous (ɪnˌhəʊməˈdʒiːnɪəs, -ˌhɒm-) ADJECTIVE not homogeneous or uniform.
▸**inhomogeneity** (ɪnˌhəʊmədʒɪˈniːɪtɪ, -ˌhɒm-) NOUN

inhospitable (ɪnˈhɒspɪtəb^{ə}l, ˌɪnhɒˈspɪt-) ADJECTIVE [1] not hospitable; unfriendly. [2] (of a region, an environment, etc.) lacking a favourable climate, terrain, etc.
▸**inˈhospitableness** NOUN ▸**inˈhospitably** ADVERB

inhospitality (ˌɪnhɒspɪˈtælɪtɪ, ɪnˌhɒs-) NOUN the state or attitude of being inhospitable or unwelcoming.

in-house ADJECTIVE, ADVERB within an organization or group: *an in-house job; the job was done in-house.*

inhuman (ɪnˈhjuːmən) ADJECTIVE [1] Also: **inhumane** (ˌɪnhjuːˈmeɪn). lacking humane feelings, such as sympathy, understanding, etc.; cruel; brutal. [2] not human.
▸**ˌinhuˈmanely** ADVERB ▸**inˈhumanly** ADVERB
▸**inˈhumanness** NOUN

inhumanity (ˌɪnhjuːˈmænɪtɪ) NOUN, *plural* **-ties.** [1] lack of humane qualities. [2] an inhumane act, decision, etc.

inhume (ɪnˈhjuːm) VERB (*tr*) to inter; bury.
▷HISTORY C17: from Latin *inhumāre,* from IN-^{2} + *humus* ground
▸**ˌinhuˈmation** NOUN ▸**inˈhumer** NOUN

inimical (ɪˈnɪmɪk^{ə}l) ADJECTIVE [1] adverse or unfavourable. [2] not friendly; hostile.
▷HISTORY C17: from Late Latin *inimīcālis,* from *inimīcus,* from IN-^{1} + *amīcus* friendly; see ENEMY
▸**inˈimically** ADVERB ▸**inˈimicalness** *or* **inˌimiˈcality** NOUN

inimitable (ɪˈnɪmɪtəb^{ə}l) ADJECTIVE incapable of being duplicated or imitated; unique.
▸**inˌimitaˈbility** *or* **inˈimitableness** NOUN ▸**inˈimitably** ADVERB

inion (ˈɪnɪən) NOUN *Anatomy* the most prominent point at the back of the head, used as a point of measurement in craniometry.
▷HISTORY C19: from Greek: back of the head

iniquity (ɪˈnɪkwɪtɪ) NOUN, *plural* **-ties.** [1] lack of justice or righteousness; wickedness; injustice. [2] a wicked act; sin.
▷HISTORY C14: from Latin *inīquitās,* from *inīquus* unfair, from IN-^{1} + *aequus* even, level; see EQUAL
▸**inˈiquitous** ADJECTIVE ▸**inˈiquitously** ADVERB
▸**inˈiquitousness** NOUN

initial (ɪˈnɪʃəl) ADJECTIVE [1] of, at, or concerning the beginning. ◆ NOUN [2] the first letter of a word, esp a person's name. [3] *Printing* a large sometimes highly decorated letter set at the beginning of a chapter or work. [4] *Botany* a cell from which tissues and organs develop by division and differentiation; a meristematic cell. ◆ VERB **-tials, -tialling, -tialled** *or US* **-tials, -tialing, -tialed.** [5] (*tr*) to sign with one's initials, esp to indicate approval; endorse.
▷HISTORY C16: from Latin *initiālis* of the beginning, from *initium* beginning, literally: an entering upon, from *inīre* to go in, from IN-^{2} + *īre* to go
▸**inˈitialer** *or* **inˈitialler** NOUN ▸**inˈitially** ADVERB

initialize *or* **initialise** (ɪˈnɪʃəˌlaɪz) VERB (*tr*) to assign an initial value to (a variable or storage location) in a computer program.
▸**inˌitialiˈzation** *or* **inˌitialiˈsation** NOUN

initiate VERB (ɪˈnɪʃɪˌeɪt) (*tr*) [1] to begin or originate. [2] to accept (new members) into an organization such as a club, through often secret ceremonies. [3] to teach fundamentals to: *she initiated him into the ballet.* ◆ ADJECTIVE (ɪˈnɪʃɪɪt, -ˌeɪt) [4] initiated; begun. ◆ NOUN (ɪˈnɪʃɪɪt, -ˌeɪt) [5] a person who has been initiated, esp recently. [6] a beginner; novice.
▷HISTORY C17: from Latin *initiāre* (vb), from *initium;* see INITIAL

initiation (ɪˌnɪʃɪˈeɪʃən) NOUN [1] the act of initiating or the condition of being initiated. [2] the often secret ceremony initiating new members into an organization.

initiative (ɪˈnɪʃɪətɪv, -ˈnɪʃətɪv) NOUN [1] the first step or action of a matter; commencing move: *he took the initiative; a peace initiative.* [2] the right or power to begin or initiate something: *he has the initiative.* [3] the ability or attitude required to begin or initiate something. [4] *Government* **a** the right or power to introduce legislation, etc., in a legislative body. **b** the procedure by which citizens originate legislation, as in many American states and Switzerland. [5] **on one's own initiative.** without being prompted. ◆ ADJECTIVE [6] of or concerning initiation or serving to initiate; initiatory.
▸**inˈitiatively** ADVERB

initiator (ɪˈnɪʃɪˌeɪtə) NOUN [1] a person or thing that initiates. [2] *Chem* a substance that starts a chain reaction. [3] *Chem* an explosive used in detonators.
▸**inˈitiˌatress** *or* **inˈitiˌatrix** FEMININE NOUN

initiatory (ɪˈnɪʃɪətərɪ) ADJECTIVE of or concerning initiation or serving to initiate; initiative.

inject (ɪnˈdʒɛkt) VERB (*tr*) [1] *Med* to introduce (a fluid) into (the body of a person or animal) by means of a syringe or similar instrument. [2] (foll by *into*) to introduce (a new aspect or element): *to inject humour into a scene.* [3] to interject (a comment, idea, etc.). [4] to place (a rocket, satellite, etc.) in orbit.
▷HISTORY C17: from Latin *injicere* to throw in, from *jacere* to throw
▸**inˈjectable** ADJECTIVE

injection (ɪnˈdʒɛkʃən) NOUN [1] fluid injected into the body, esp for medicinal purposes. [2] something injected. [3] the act of injecting. [4] **a** the act or process of introducing fluid under pressure, such as fuel into the combustion chamber of an engine. **b** (*as modifier*): *injection moulding.* [5] *Maths* a function or mapping for which $f(x) = f(y)$ only if $x = y$. See also **surjection, bijection.**
▸**inˈjective** ADJECTIVE

injector (ɪnˈdʒɛktə) NOUN [1] a person or thing that injects. [2] a device for spraying fuel into the combustion chamber of an internal-combustion engine. [3] a device for forcing water into a steam boiler. Also called: **inspirator.**

injera (ɪnˈdʒɪərə) NOUN a white Ethiopian flatbread, similar to a crepe.
▷HISTORY Amharic

injudicious (ˌɪndʒuˈdɪʃəs) ADJECTIVE not discreet; imprudent.
▸**ˌinjuˈdiciously** ADVERB ▸**ˌinjuˈdiciousness** NOUN

Injun (ˈɪndʒən) NOUN [1] *US* an informal or dialect word for (American) **Indian.** [2] **honest Injun.** (*interjection*) *Slang* genuinely; really.

injunct (ɪnˈdʒʌŋkt) VERB (*tr*) to issue a legal injunction against (a person).
▷HISTORY C19: from Late Latin *injunctiō;* see ENJOIN

injunction (ɪnˈdʒʌŋkʃən) NOUN [1] *Law* an instruction or order issued by a court to a party to an action, esp to refrain from some act, such as causing a nuisance. [2] a command, admonition, etc. [3] the act of enjoining.
▷HISTORY C16: from Late Latin *injunctiō,* from Latin *injungere* to ENJOIN
▸**inˈjunctive** ADJECTIVE ▸**inˈjunctively** ADVERB

injure (ˈɪndʒə) VERB (*tr*) [1] to cause physical or mental harm or suffering to; hurt or wound. [2] to offend, esp by an injustice.
▷HISTORY C16: back formation from INJURY
▸**ˈinjurable** ADJECTIVE ▸**ˈinjured** ADJECTIVE ▸**ˈinjurer** NOUN

injurious (ɪnˈdʒʊərɪəs) ADJECTIVE [1] causing damage or harm; deleterious; hurtful. [2] abusive, slanderous, or libellous.
▸**inˈjuriously** ADVERB ▸**inˈjuriousness** NOUN

injury (ˈɪndʒərɪ) NOUN, *plural* **-ries.** [1] physical damage or hurt. [2] a specific instance of this: *a leg injury.* [3] harm done to a reputation. [4] *Law* a violation or infringement of another person's rights that causes him harm and is actionable at law. [5] an obsolete word for **insult.**
▷HISTORY C14: from Latin *injūria* injustice, wrong, from *injūriōsus* acting unfairly, wrongful, from IN-^{1} + *jūs* right

injury time NOUN *Sport* extra playing time added on to compensate for time spent attending to injured players during the match. Also called: **stoppage time.**

injustice (ɪnˈdʒʌstɪs) NOUN [1] the condition or practice of being unjust or unfair. [2] an unjust act.

ink (ɪŋk) NOUN [1] a fluid or paste used for printing, writing, and drawing. [2] a dark brown fluid ejected into the water for self-concealment by an octopus or related mollusc from a gland (**ink sac**) near the anus. ◆ VERB (*tr*) [3] to mark with ink. [4] to coat (a printing surface) with ink. ◆ See also **ink in, ink up.**
▷HISTORY C13: from Old French *enque,* from Late Latin *encaustum* a purplish-red ink, from Greek *enkauston* purple ink, from *enkaustos* burnt in, from *enkaiein* to burn in; see EN-^{2}, CAUSTIC
▸**ˈinker** NOUN

Inkatha (ɪnˈkɑːtə) NOUN a South African Zulu organization founded by Chief Mangosouthu Buthelezi in 1975 as a paramilitary group seeking nonracial democracy; won four seats in South Africa's first nonracial elections in 1994.
▷HISTORY C20: Zulu name for the grass coil used by Zulu women carrying loads on their heads, the many strands of which provide its strength and cohesion

inkberry (ˈɪŋkˌbɛrɪ) NOUN, *plural* **-ries.** [1] a North American holly tree, *Ilex glabra,* with black berry-like fruits. [2] another name for the **pokeweed.** [3] the fruit of either of these plants.

inkblot (ˈɪŋkˌblɒt) NOUN *Psychol* an abstract patch of ink, one of ten commonly used in the Rorschach test.

ink-cap NOUN any of several saprotrophic agaricaceous fungi of the genus *Coprinus,* whose caps disintegrate into a black inky fluid after the spores mature. It includes the **shaggy ink-cap** (*Coprinus comatus*), also called **lawyer's wig,** a distinctive fungus having a white cylindrical cap covered with shaggy white or brownish scales.

Inkerman (ˈɪŋkəmən; *Russian* inkɪrˈman) NOUN a village in the Ukraine, in the S Crimea east of Sevastopol: scene of a battle during the Crimean War in which British and French forces defeated the Russians (1854).

inkhorn (ˈɪŋkˌhɔːn) NOUN (formerly) a small portable container for ink, usually made from horn.

inkhorn term NOUN an affectedly learned and obscure borrowing from another language, esp Greek or Latin.

ink in VERB (*adverb*) [1] (*tr*) to use ink to go over pencil lines in (a drawing). [2] to apply ink to (a printing surface) in preparing to print from it. [3] to arrange or confirm definitely.

ink jet NOUN a method of printing using streams of electrically charged ink.

inkle (ˈɪŋk^{ə}l) NOUN [1] a kind of linen tape used for trimmings. [2] the thread or yarn from which this tape is woven.
▷HISTORY C16: of unknown origin

inkling (ˈɪŋklɪŋ) NOUN a slight intimation or suggestion; suspicion.
▷HISTORY C14: probably from *inclen* to hint at; related to Old English *inca*

inkstand (ˈɪŋkˌstænd) NOUN a stand or tray on which are kept writing implements and containers for ink.

ink up VERB (*adverb*) to apply ink to (a printing machine) in preparing it for operation.

inkwell (ˈɪŋkˌwɛl) NOUN a small container for pen ink, often let into the surface of a desk.

inky (ˈɪŋkɪ) ADJECTIVE **inkier, inkiest.** [1] resembling ink, esp in colour; dark or black. [2] of, containing, or stained with ink: *inky fingers.*
▸**ˈinkiness** NOUN

inky smudge NOUN *Austral slang* a judge.
▷HISTORY rhyming slang

INLA ABBREVIATION FOR Irish National Liberation Army; a Republican paramilitary organization in Ireland.

inlace (ɪnˈleɪs) VERB a variant spelling of **enlace.**

inlaid (ˈɪnˌleɪd, ɪnˈleɪd) ADJECTIVE [1] set in the surface, as a design in wood. [2] having such a design or inlay: *an inlaid table.*

inland ADJECTIVE (ˈɪnlənd) [1] of, concerning, or located in the interior of a country or region away from a sea or border. [2] *Chiefly Brit* operating within a country or region; domestic; not foreign. ◆ NOUN (ˈɪnˌlænd, -lənd) [3] the interior of a country or region. ◆ ADVERB (ˈɪnˌlænd, -lənd) [4] towards or into the interior of a country or region.
▸**ˈinlander** NOUN

inland bill NOUN a bill of exchange that is both drawn and made payable in the same country. Compare **foreign bill.**

Inland Revenue NOUN (in Britain and New Zealand) a government board that administers and collects major direct taxes, such as income tax, corporation tax, and capital gains tax. Abbreviation: **IR.**

Inland Sea NOUN a sea in SW Japan, between the islands of Honshu, Shikoku, and Kyushu. Japanese name: **Seto Naikai.**

in-law NOUN [1] a relative by marriage. ◆ ADJECTIVE [2] *(postpositive; in combination)* related by marriage: *a father-in-law.*
▷HISTORY C19: back formation from *father-in-law,* etc.

inlay VERB (ɪn'leɪ) **-lays, -laying, -laid.** *(tr)* [1] to decorate (an article, esp of furniture, or a surface) by inserting pieces of wood, ivory, etc., into prepared slots in the surface. ◆ NOUN ('ɪn,leɪ) [2] *Dentistry* a filling, made of gold, porcelain, etc., inserted into a cavity and held in position by cement. [3] decoration made by inlaying. [4] an inlaid article, surface, etc.
▸**'in,laid** ADJECTIVE ▸**'in,layer** NOUN

inlet NOUN ('ɪn,lɛt) [1] a narrow inland opening of the coastline. [2] an entrance or opening. [3] the act of letting someone or something in. [4] something let in or inserted. [5] **a** a passage, valve, or part through which a substance, esp a fluid, enters a device or machine. **b** *(as modifier)*: *an inlet valve.* ◆ VERB (ɪn'lɛt) **-lets, -letting, -let.** [6] *(tr)* to insert or inlay.

inlier ('ɪn,laɪə) NOUN an outcrop of rocks that is entirely surrounded by younger rocks.

in-line ADJECTIVE [1] denoting a linked sequence of manufacturing processes. [2] denoting an internal-combustion engine having its cylinders arranged in a line.

in-line skate NOUN another name for **Rollerblade.**

in loc. cit. (in textual annotation) ABBREVIATION FOR in loco citato.
▷HISTORY Latin: in the place cited

in loco parentis *Latin* (ɪn 'ləʊkəʊ pə'rɛntɪs) in place of a parent: said of a person acting in a parental capacity.

inly ('ɪnlɪ) ADVERB *Poetic* inwardly; intimately.

inlying ('ɪn,laɪɪŋ) ADJECTIVE situated within or inside.

inmate ('ɪn,meɪt) NOUN [1] a person who is confined to an institution such as a prison or hospital. See also **resident** (sense 2). [2] *Obsolete* a person who lives with others in a house.

in medias res *Latin* (ɪn 'mi:dɪ,æs 'reɪs) in or into the middle of events or a narrative.
▷HISTORY literally: into the midst of things, taken from a passage in Horace's *Ars Poetica*

in mem. ABBREVIATION FOR in memoriam.

in memoriam (ɪn mɪ'mɔ:rɪəm) in memory of; as a memorial to: used in obituaries, epitaphs, etc.
▷HISTORY Latin

inmesh (ɪn'mɛʃ) VERB a variant spelling of **enmesh.**

inmigrant ('ɪn,maɪgrənt) ADJECTIVE [1] coming in from another area of the same country: *an inmigrant worker.* ◆ NOUN [2] an inmigrant person or animal.

inmost ('ɪn,məʊst) ADJECTIVE another word for **innermost.**

inn (ɪn) NOUN [1] a pub or small hotel providing food and accommodation. [2] (formerly, in England) a college or hall of residence for students, esp of law, now only in the names of such institutions as the b.
▷HISTORY Old English; compare Old Norse *inni* inn, house, place of refuge

Inn (ɪn) NOUN a river in central Europe, rising in Switzerland in Graubünden and flowing northeast through Austria and Bavaria to join the River Danube at Passau: forms part of the border between Austria and Germany. Length: 514 km (319 miles).

innards ('ɪnədz) PLURAL NOUN *Informal* [1] the internal organs of the body, esp the viscera. [2] the interior parts or components of anything, esp the working parts.
▷HISTORY C19: colloquial variant of *inwards*

innate (ɪ'neɪt, 'ɪneɪt) ADJECTIVE [1] existing in a person or animal from birth; congenital; inborn. [2] being an essential part of the character of a person or thing. [3] instinctive; not learned: *innate capacities.* [4] *Botany* (of anthers) joined to the filament by the base only. [5] (in rationalist philosophy) (of ideas) present in the mind before any experience and knowable by pure reason.
▷HISTORY C15: from Latin, from *innascī* to be born in, from *nascī* to be born
▸**in'nately** ADVERB ▸**in'nateness** NOUN

innate releasing mechanism NOUN *Psychol* the process by which a stimulus evokes a response when the connection between the two is inborn. Abbreviation: **IRM.**

inner ('ɪnə) ADJECTIVE *(prenominal)* [1] being or located further inside: *an inner room.* [2] happening or occurring inside: *inner movement.* [3] relating to the soul, mind, spirit, etc.: *inner feelings.* [4] more profound or obscure; less apparent: *the inner meaning.* [5] exclusive or private: *inner regions of the party.* [6] *Chem* (of a compound) having a cyclic structure formed or apparently formed by reaction of one functional group in a molecule with another group in the same molecule: *an inner ester.* ◆ NOUN [7] Also called: **red.** *Archery* **a** the red innermost ring on a target. **b** a shot which hits this ring.
▸**'innerly** ADVERB ▸**'innerness** NOUN

inner bar NOUN *Brit* all Queen's or King's Counsel collectively.

inner child NOUN *Psychol* the part of the psyche believed to retain feelings as they were experienced in childhood.

inner city NOUN **a** the parts of a city in or near its centre, esp when they are associated with poverty, unemployment, substandard housing, etc. **b** *(as modifier)*: *inner-city schools.*

inner-directed ADJECTIVE guided by one's own conscience and values rather than external pressures to conform. Compare **other-directed.**
▸**'inner-di'rection** NOUN

inner ear NOUN another name for **internal ear, labyrinth.**

Inner Hebrides PLURAL NOUN See **Hebrides.**

Inner Light *or* **Word** NOUN *Quakerism* the presence and inner working of God in the soul acting as a guiding spirit that is superior even to Scripture and unites man to Christ.

inner man NOUN [1] a man's mind, soul, or nature. [2] *Jocular* the stomach or appetite.

Inner Mongolia NOUN an autonomous region of NE China: consists chiefly of the Mongolian plateau, with the Gobi Desert in the north and the Great Wall of China in the south. Capital: Hohhot. Pop.: 23 760 000 (2000 est.). Area: 1 177 500 sq. km (459 225 sq. miles).

innermost ('ɪnə,məʊst) ADJECTIVE [1] being or located furthest within; central. [2] intimate; private: *innermost beliefs.*

inner planet NOUN any of the planets Mercury, Venus, earth, and Mars, whose orbits lie inside the asteroid belt.

inner space NOUN [1] the environment beneath the surface of the sea. [2] the human mind regarded as being as unknown or as unfathomable as space.

Inner Temple NOUN (in England) one of the four legal societies in London that together form the Inns of Court.

inner tube NOUN an inflatable rubber tube that fits inside a pneumatic tyre casing.

inner-tubing NOUN the sport of floating on rivers, rapids, etc. using a large inflated inner tube as a buoyancy device.

innervate ('ɪnɜ:,veɪt) VERB *(tr)* [1] to supply nerves to (a bodily organ or part). [2] to stimulate (a bodily organ or part) with nerve impulses.
▸**,inner'vation** NOUN

innerve (ɪ'nɜ:v) VERB *(tr)* to supply with nervous energy; stimulate.

inner woman NOUN [1] a woman's mind, soul, or nature. [2] *Jocular* the stomach or appetite.

inning ('ɪnɪŋ) NOUN [1] *Baseball* a division of the game consisting of a turn at bat and a turn in the field for each side. [2] *Archaic* the reclamation of land from the sea.
▷HISTORY Old English *innung* a going in, from *innian* to go in

innings ('ɪnɪŋz) NOUN [1] *(functioning as singular) Cricket* **a** the batting turn of a player or team. **b** the runs scored during such a turn. [2] *(sometimes singular)* a period of opportunity or action. [3] *(functioning as plural)* land reclaimed from the sea.

Inniskilling (,ɪnɪs'kɪlɪŋ) NOUN the former name of **Enniskillen.**

innkeeper ('ɪn,ki:pə) NOUN an owner or manager of an inn.

innocence ('ɪnəsəns) NOUN the quality or state of being innocent. Archaic word: **innocency** ('ɪnəsənsɪ).
▷HISTORY C14: from Latin *innocentia* harmlessness, from *innocēns* doing no harm, blameless, from IN-[1] + *nocēns* harming, from *nocēre* to hurt, harm; see NOXIOUS

innocent ('ɪnəsənt) ADJECTIVE [1] not corrupted or tainted with evil or unpleasant emotion; sinless; pure. [2] not guilty of a particular crime; blameless. [3] *(postpositive; foll by of)* free (of); lacking: *innocent of all knowledge of history.* [4] **a** harmless or innocuous: *an innocent game.* **b** not cancerous: *an innocent tumour.* [5] credulous, naive, or artless. [6] simple-minded; slow-witted. ◆ NOUN [7] an innocent person, esp a young child or an ingenuous adult. [8] a simple-minded person; simpleton.
▸**'innocently** ADVERB

innocuous (ɪ'nɒkjʊəs) ADJECTIVE having little or no adverse or harmful effect; harmless.
▷HISTORY C16: from Latin *innocuus* harmless, from IN-[1] + *nocēre* to harm
▸**in'nocuously** ADVERB ▸**in'nocuousness** *or* **innocuity** (,ɪnə'kju:ɪtɪ) NOUN

innominate (ɪ'nɒmɪnɪt) ADJECTIVE [1] having no name; nameless. [2] a less common word for **anonymous.**

innominate bone NOUN either of the two bones that form the sides of the pelvis, consisting of three fused components, the ilium, ischium, and pubis. Nontechnical name: **hipbone.**

in nomine (ɪn 'nɒmɪ,neɪ, -,ni:) NOUN *Music* any of several pieces of music of the 16th or 17th centuries for keyboard or for a consort of viols, based on a cantus firmus derived from the Vespers antiphon *Gloria tibi Trinitas.*
▷HISTORY from Latin *in nomine Jesu* in the name of Jesus, the first words of an introit for which this type of music was originally composed

innovate ('ɪnə,veɪt) VERB to invent or begin to apply (methods, ideas, etc.).
▷HISTORY C16: from Latin *innovāre* to renew, from IN-[2] + *novāre* to make new, from *novus* new
▸**'inno,vative, 'inno,vatory** ADJECTIVE ▸**'inno,vator** NOUN

innovation (,ɪnə'veɪʃən) NOUN [1] something newly introduced, such as a new method or device. [2] the act of innovating.
▸**,inno'vational** ADJECTIVE ▸**,inno'vationist** NOUN

innovative ('ɪnə,veɪtɪv) ADJECTIVE using or showing new methods, ideas, etc.

innoxious (ɪ'nɒkʃəs) ADJECTIVE not noxious; harmless.
▸**in'noxiously** ADVERB ▸**in'noxiousness** NOUN

Innsbruck ('ɪnzbrʊk) NOUN a city in W Austria, on the River Inn at the foot of the Brenner Pass: tourist centre. Pop.: 113 826 (2001).

Inns of Court PLURAL NOUN (in England) the four private unincorporated societies in London that function as a law school and have the exclusive privilege of calling candidates to the English bar. See **Lincoln's Inn, Inner Temple, Middle Temple, Gray's Inn.**

Innu ('ɪnu:) NOUN [1] a member of an Algonquian people living in Labrador and northern Quebec. [2] the Algonquian language of this people.

innuendo (,ɪnjʊ'ɛndəʊ) NOUN, *plural* **-dos** *or* **-does.** [1] an indirect or subtle reference, esp one made maliciously or indicating criticism or disapproval; insinuation. [2] *Law* (in pleading) a word introducing an explanatory phrase, usually in parenthesis. [3] *Law* (in an action for defamation) **a** an explanation of the construction put upon words alleged to be defamatory where the defamatory meaning is not apparent. **b** the words thus explained.
▷HISTORY C17: from Latin, literally: by hinting, from *innuendum,* gerund of *innuere* to convey by a nod, from IN-[2] + *nuere* to nod

Innuit ('ɪnju:ɪt) NOUN a variant spelling of **Inuit.**

innumerable (ɪ'nju:mərəbᵊl, ɪ'nju:mrəbᵊl) *or* **innumerous** ADJECTIVE so many as to be uncountable; extremely numerous.

▸**in,numera'bility** *or* **in'numerableness** NOUN
▸**in'numerably** ADVERB

innumerate (ɪ'njuːmərɪt) ADJECTIVE [1] having neither knowledge nor understanding of mathematics or science. ◆ NOUN [2] an innumerate person.
▸**in'numeracy** NOUN

innutrition (ˌɪnjuː'trɪʃən) NOUN lack or absence of nutrition. Compare **malnutrition**.
▸**ˌinnu'tritious** ADJECTIVE

inobservance (ˌɪnəb'zɜːvəns) NOUN [1] heedlessness. [2] lack of compliance with or adherence to a law, religious duty, etc.
▸**ˌinob'servant** ADJECTIVE ▸**ˌinob'servantly** ADVERB

inoculable (ɪ'nɒkjʊləb[ə]l) ADJECTIVE capable of being inoculated.
▸**in,ocula'bility** NOUN

inoculate (ɪ'nɒkjʊˌleɪt) VERB [1] to introduce (the causative agent of a disease) into the body of (a person or animal), in order to induce immunity. [2] (*tr*) to introduce (microorganisms, esp bacteria) into (a culture medium). [3] (*tr*) to cause to be influenced or imbued, as with ideas or opinions.
▷HISTORY C15: from Latin *inoculāre* to implant, from IN-[2] + *oculus* eye, bud
▸**in,ocu'lation** NOUN ▸**in'oculative** ADJECTIVE ▸**in'ocu,lator** NOUN

inoculum (ɪ'nɒkjʊləm) *or* **inoculant** NOUN, *plural* **-la** (-lə) *or* **-lants**. *Med* the substance used in giving an inoculation.
▷HISTORY C20: New Latin; see INOCULATE

inodorous (ɪn'əʊdərəs) ADJECTIVE odourless; having no odour.

in-off NOUN *Billiards, snooker* a shot that goes into a pocket after striking another ball.

inoffensive (ˌɪnə'fensɪv) ADJECTIVE [1] not giving offence; unobjectionable. [2] not unpleasant, poisonous, or harmful.
▸**ˌinof'fensively** ADVERB ▸**ˌinof'fensiveness** NOUN

inofficious (ˌɪnə'fɪʃəs) ADJECTIVE contrary to moral obligation, as the disinheritance of a child by his parents: *an inofficious will.*
▸**ˌinof'ficiously** ADVERB ▸**ˌinof'ficiousness** NOUN

inoperable (ɪn'ɒpərəb[ə]l, -'ɒprə-) ADJECTIVE [1] incapable of being implemented or operated; unworkable. [2] *Surgery* not suitable for operation without risk, esp (of a malignant tumour) because metastasis has rendered surgery useless.
▸**in,opera'bility** *or* **in'operableness** NOUN ▸**in'operably** ADVERB

inoperative (ɪn'ɒpərətɪv, -'ɒprə-) ADJECTIVE [1] not operating. [2] useless or ineffective.
▸**in'operativeness** NOUN

inopportune (ɪn'ɒpəˌtjuːn) ADJECTIVE not opportune; inappropriate or badly timed.
▸**in'oppor,tunely** ADVERB ▸**in'oppor,tuneness** *or* **in,oppor'tunity** NOUN

inordinate (ɪn'ɔːdɪnɪt) ADJECTIVE [1] exceeding normal limits; immoderate. [2] unrestrained, as in behaviour or emotion; intemperate. [3] irregular or disordered.
▷HISTORY C14: from Latin *inordinātus* disordered, from IN-[1] + *ordināre* to put in order
▸**in'ordinacy** *or* **in'ordinateness** NOUN ▸**in'ordinately** ADVERB

inorg. ABBREVIATION FOR inorganic.

inorganic (ˌɪnɔː'gænɪk) ADJECTIVE [1] not having the structure or characteristics of living organisms; not organic. [2] relating to or denoting chemical compounds that do not contain carbon. Compare **organic** (sense 4). [3] not having a system, structure, or ordered relation of parts; amorphous. [4] not resulting from or produced by growth; artificial. [5] *Linguistics* denoting or relating to a sound or letter introduced into the pronunciation or spelling of a word at some point in its history.
▸**ˌinor'ganically** ADVERB

inorganic chemistry NOUN the branch of chemistry concerned with the elements and all their compounds except those containing carbon. Some simple carbon compounds, such as oxides, carbonates, etc., are treated as inorganic. Compare **organic chemistry**.

inosculate (ɪn'ɒskjʊˌleɪt) VERB [1] *Physiol* (of small blood vessels) to communicate by anastomosis. [2] to unite or be united so as to be continuous; blend. [3] to intertwine or cause to intertwine.
▷HISTORY C17: from IN-[2] + Latin *ōsculāre* to equip with an opening, from *ōsculum,* diminutive of *ōs* mouth
▸**in,oscu'lation** NOUN

inositol (ɪ'nəʊsɪˌtɒl) NOUN a cyclic alcohol, one isomer of which (*i*-inositol) is present in yeast and is a growth factor for some organisms; cyclohexanehexol. Formula: $C_6H_{12}O_6$.
▷HISTORY C19: from Greek *in-, is* sinew + -OSE[2] + -ITE[1] + -OL[1]

inotropic (ˌɪnə'trɒpɪk, ˌaɪnə-) ADJECTIVE affecting or controlling the contraction of muscles, esp those of the heart: *inotropic drugs.*
▷HISTORY C20: from Greek, from *is* (stem *in-*) tendon + -TROPIC

inpatient ('ɪnˌpeɪʃənt) NOUN a hospital patient who occupies a bed for at least one night in the course of treatment, examination, or observation. Compare **outpatient**.

in perpetuum *Latin* (ɪn pɜː'pɛtjʊəm) ADVERB for ever.

in personam (ɪn pɜː'səʊnæm) ADJECTIVE *Law* (of a judicial act) directed against a specific person or persons. Compare **in rem**.
▷HISTORY Latin

in petto (ɪn 'pɛtəʊ) ADJECTIVE *RC Church* not disclosed: used of the names of cardinals designate.
▷HISTORY Italian, literally: in the breast

in posse (ɪn 'pɒsɪ) ADJECTIVE possible; potential. Compare **in esse**.
▷HISTORY Latin, literally: in possibility

in propria persona *Latin* (ɪn 'prəʊprɪə pɜː'səʊnə) ADVERB *Chiefly law* in person; personally.

input ('ɪnˌpʊt) NOUN [1] the act of putting in. [2] that which is put in. [3] (*often plural*) a resource required for industrial production, such as capital goods, labour services, raw materials, etc. [4] *Electronics* **a** the signal or current fed into a component or circuit. **b** the terminals, or some other point, to which the signal is applied. [5] *Computing* the data fed into a computer from a peripheral device. [6] (*modifier*) of or relating to electronic, computer, or other input: *input program.* ◆ VERB [7] (*tr*) to insert (data) into a computer.

input device NOUN *Computing* a peripheral device that accepts data and feeds it into a computer.

input/output NOUN *Computing* [1] the data or information that is passed into or out of a computer. Abbreviation: **I/O**. [2] (*modifier*) concerned with or relating to such passage of data or information.

input-output analysis NOUN *Economics* an analysis of production relationships between the industries of an economy involving a study of each industry's inputs and outputs, esp as used in social accounting.

inqilab ('ɪnkɪˌlɑːb) NOUN (in India, Pakistan, etc.) revolution (esp in the phrase **inqilab zindabad** long live the revolution).
▷HISTORY Urdu

inquest ('ɪnˌkwest) NOUN [1] an inquiry into the cause of an unexplained, sudden, or violent death, or as to whether or not property constitutes treasure trove, held by a coroner, in certain cases with a jury. [2] *Informal* any inquiry or investigation.
▷HISTORY C13: from Medieval Latin *inquēsta,* from Latin IN-[2] + *quaesītus* investigation, from *quaerere* to examine

inquietude (ɪn'kwaɪɪˌtjuːd) NOUN restlessness, uneasiness, or anxiety.
▸**inquiet** (ɪn'kwaɪət) ADJECTIVE ▸**in'quietly** ADVERB

inquiline ('ɪnkwɪˌlaɪn) NOUN [1] an animal that lives in close association with another animal without harming it. See also **commensal** (sense 1). ◆ ADJECTIVE [2] of or living as an inquiline.
▷HISTORY C17: from Latin *inquilīnus* lodger, from IN-[2] + *colere* to dwell
▸**inquilinism** ('ɪnkwɪlɪˌnɪzəm) *or* **inquilinity** (ˌɪnkwɪ'lɪnɪtɪ) NOUN ▸**inquilinous** (ˌɪnkwɪ'laɪnəs) ADJECTIVE

inquire *or* **enquire** (ɪn'kwaɪə) VERB [1] **a** to seek information; ask: *she inquired his age; she inquired about rates of pay.* **b** (foll by *of*) to ask (a person) for information: *I'll inquire of my aunt when she is coming.* [2] (*intr;* often foll by *into*) to make a search or investigation.
▷HISTORY C13: from Latin *inquīrere* from IN-[2] + *quaerere* to seek
▸**in'quirer** *or* **en'quirer** NOUN

inquiring (ɪn'kwaɪərɪŋ) ADJECTIVE seeking or tending to seek answers, information, etc.: *an inquiring mind.*
▸**in'quiringly** ADVERB

inquiry *or* **enquiry** (ɪn'kwaɪərɪ) NOUN, *plural* **-ries**. [1] a request for information; a question. [2] an investigation, esp a formal one conducted into a matter of public concern by a body constituted for that purpose by a government, local authority, or other organization.

inquisition (ˌɪnkwɪ'zɪʃən) NOUN [1] the act of inquiring deeply or searchingly; investigation. [2] a deep or searching inquiry, esp a ruthless official investigation of individuals in order to suppress revolt or root out the unorthodox. [3] an official inquiry, esp one held by a jury before an officer of the Crown. [4] another word for **inquest** (sense 2).
▷HISTORY C14: from legal Latin *inquīsītiō,* from *inquīrere* to seek for; see INQUIRE
▸**ˌinqui'sitional** ADJECTIVE ▸**ˌinqui'sitionist** NOUN

Inquisition (ˌɪnkwɪ'zɪʃən) NOUN *History* a judicial institution of the Roman Catholic Church (1232–1820) founded to discover and suppress heresy. See also **Spanish Inquisition**.

inquisitive (ɪn'kwɪzɪtɪv) ADJECTIVE [1] excessively curious, esp about the affairs of others; prying. [2] eager to learn; inquiring.
▸**in'quisitively** ADVERB ▸**in'quisitiveness** NOUN

inquisitor (ɪn'kwɪzɪtə) NOUN [1] a person who inquires, esp deeply, searchingly, or ruthlessly. [2] (*often capital*) an official of the ecclesiastical court of the Inquisition.

Inquisitor-General NOUN, *plural* **Inquisitors-General**. the head of the Spanish court of Inquisition.

inquisitorial (ɪnˌkwɪzɪ'tɔːrɪəl) ADJECTIVE [1] of, relating to, or resembling inquisition or an inquisitor. [2] offensively curious; prying. [3] *Law* denoting criminal procedure in which one party is both prosecutor and judge, or in which the trial is held in secret. Compare **accusatorial** (sense 2).
▸**in,quisi'torially** ADVERB ▸**in,quisi'torialness** NOUN

inquorate (ɪn'kwɔːreɪt) ADJECTIVE *Brit* not consisting of or being a quorum: *this meeting is inquorate.*

in re (ɪn 'reɪ) PREPOSITION in the matter of: used esp in bankruptcy proceedings.
▷HISTORY C17: from Latin

in rem (ɪn 'rɛm) ADJECTIVE *Law* (of a judicial act) directed against property rather than against a specific person. Compare **in personam**.
▷HISTORY Latin, literally: against the matter

in rerum natura *Latin* (ɪn 'rɛərʊm næ'tʊərə) in the nature of things.

INRI ABBREVIATION FOR Iesus Nazarenus Rex Iudaeorum (the inscription placed over Christ's head during the Crucifixion).
▷HISTORY Latin: Jesus of Nazareth, King of the Jews

inroad ('ɪnˌrəʊd) NOUN [1] an invasion or hostile attack; raid or incursion. [2] an encroachment or intrusion.

inrush ('ɪnˌrʌʃ) NOUN a sudden usually overwhelming inward flow or rush; influx.
▸**'in,rushing** NOUN, ADJECTIVE

INS ABBREVIATION FOR International News Service.

ins. ABBREVIATION FOR inches.

insalivate (ɪn'sælɪˌveɪt) VERB (*tr*) to mix (food) with saliva during mastication.
▸**in,sali'vation** NOUN

insalubrious (ˌɪnsə'luːbrɪəs) ADJECTIVE not salubrious; unpleasant, unhealthy, or sordid.
▸**ˌinsa'lubriously** ADVERB ▸**insalubrity** (ˌɪnsə'luːbrɪtɪ) NOUN

insane (ɪn'seɪn) ADJECTIVE [1] **a** mentally deranged; crazy; of unsound mind. **b** (*as collective noun;* preceded by *the*): *the insane.* [2] characteristic of a person of unsound mind: *an insane stare.* [3] irresponsible; very foolish; stupid.
▸**in'sanely** ADVERB ▸**in'saneness** NOUN

insanitary (ɪn'sænɪtərɪ, -trɪ) ADJECTIVE not sanitary; dirty or infected.
▸**in'sanitariness** *or* **in,sani'tation** NOUN

insanity (ɪn'sænɪtɪ) NOUN, *plural* **-ties**. [1] relatively permanent disorder of the mind; state or condition of being insane. [2] *Law* a defect of reason as a result of mental illness, such that a defendant does not know what he or she is doing or that it is wrong. [3] utter folly; stupidity.

insatiable (ɪnˈseɪʃəb^{ə}l, -ʃɪə-) *or* **insatiate** (ɪnˈseɪʃɪɪt) ADJECTIVE not able to be satisfied or satiated; greedy or unappeasable.
▸**in,satia'bility, in'satiableness,** *or* **in'satiateness** NOUN ▸**in'satiably** *or* **in'satiately** ADVERB

inscape (ˈɪnskeɪp) NOUN the essential inner nature of a person, an object, etc.
▷HISTORY C19: from IN-^{2} + *-scape,* as in LANDSCAPE; coined by Gerard Manley *Hopkins* (1844–89), British poet and Jesuit priest

inscribe (ɪnˈskraɪb) VERB *(tr)* [1] to make, carve, or engrave (writing, letters, a design, etc.) on (a surface such as wood, stone, or paper). [2] to enter (a name) on a list or in a register. [3] to sign one's name on (a book, photograph, etc.) before presentation to another person. [4] to draw (a geometric construction such as a circle, polygon, etc.) inside another construction so that the two are in contact but do not intersect. Compare **circumscribe** (sense 3).
▷HISTORY C16: from Latin *inscrībere;* see INSCRIPTION
▸**in'scribable** ADJECTIVE ▸**in'scribableness** NOUN ▸**in'scriber** NOUN

inscription (ɪnˈskrɪpʃən) NOUN [1] something inscribed, esp words carved or engraved on a coin, tomb, etc. [2] a signature or brief dedication in a book or on a work of art. [3] the act of inscribing. [4] *Philosophy, linguistics* an element of written language, esp a sentence. Compare **utterance**^{1} (sense 3).
▷HISTORY C14: from Latin *inscriptiō* a writing upon, from *inscrībere* to write upon, from IN-^{2} + *scrībere* to write
▸**in'scriptional** *or* **in'scriptive** ADJECTIVE ▸**in'scriptively** ADVERB

inscrutable (ɪnˈskruːtəb^{ə}l) ADJECTIVE incomprehensible; mysterious or enigmatic.
▷HISTORY C15: from Late Latin *inscrūtābilis,* from Latin IN-^{1} + *scrūtārī* to examine
▸**in,scruta'bility** *or* **in'scrutableness** NOUN ▸**in'scrutably** ADVERB

insect (ˈɪnsɛkt) NOUN [1] any small air-breathing arthropod of the class *Insecta,* having a body divided into head, thorax, and abdomen, three pairs of legs, and (in most species) two pairs of wings. Insects comprise about five sixths of all known animal species, with a total of over one million named species. Related adjective: **entomic.** [2] (loosely) any similar invertebrate, such as a spider, tick, or centipede. [3] a contemptible, loathsome, or insignificant person.
▷HISTORY C17: from Latin *insectum* (animal that has been) cut into, insect, from *insecāre,* from IN-^{2} + *secāre* to cut; translation of Greek *entomon* insect
▸**in'sectean, in'sectan,** *or* **in'sectile** ADJECTIVE ▸**'insect-,like** ADJECTIVE

insectarium (,ɪnsɛkˈtɛərɪəm) *or* **insectary** (ɪnˈsɛktərɪ) NOUN, *plural* **-tariums, -taria** (-ˈtɛərɪə) *or* **-taries.** a place where living insects are kept, bred, and studied.

insecticide (ɪnˈsɛktɪ,saɪd) NOUN a substance used to destroy insect pests.
▸**in,secti'cidal** ADJECTIVE

insectivore (ɪnˈsɛktɪ,vɔː) NOUN [1] any placental mammal of the order *Insectivora,* being typically small, with simple teeth, and feeding on invertebrates. The group includes shrews, moles, and hedgehogs. [2] any animal or plant that derives nourishment from insects.

insectivorous (,ɪnsɛkˈtɪvərəs) ADJECTIVE [1] feeding on or adapted for feeding on insects: *insectivorous plants.* [2] of or relating to the order *Insectivora.*

insectivorous bat NOUN any bat of the suborder *Microchiroptera,* typically having large ears and feeding on insects. The group includes common bats (*Myotis* species), vampire bats, etc. Compare **fruit bat.**

insecure (,ɪnsɪˈkjʊə) ADJECTIVE [1] anxious or afraid; not confident or certain. [2] not adequately protected: *an insecure fortress.* [3] unstable or shaky.
▸**,inse'curely** ADVERB ▸**,inse'cureness** NOUN ▸**,inse'curity** NOUN

inselberg (ˈɪnz^{ə}l,bɜːg) NOUN an isolated rocky hill rising abruptly from a flat plain.
▷HISTORY from German, from *Insel* island + *Berg* mountain

inseminate (ɪnˈsɛmɪ,neɪt) VERB *(tr)* [1] to impregnate (a female) with semen. [2] to introduce (ideas or attitudes) into the mind of (a person or group).
▷HISTORY C17: from Latin *insēmināre,* from IN-^{2} + *sēmināre* to sow, from *sēmen* seed
▸**in,semi'nation** NOUN ▸**in'semi,nator** NOUN

insensate (ɪnˈsɛnseɪt, -sɪt) ADJECTIVE [1] lacking sensation or consciousness. [2] insensitive; unfeeling. [3] foolish; senseless.
▸**in'sensately** ADVERB ▸**in'sensateness** NOUN

insensible (ɪnˈsɛnsəb^{ə}l) ADJECTIVE [1] lacking sensation or consciousness. [2] (foll by *of* or *to*) unaware (of) or indifferent (to): *insensible to suffering.* [3] thoughtless or callous. [4] a less common word for **imperceptible.**
▸**in,sensi'bility** *or* **in'sensibleness** NOUN ▸**in'sensibly** ADVERB

insensitive (ɪnˈsɛnsɪtɪv) ADJECTIVE [1] lacking sensitivity; unfeeling. [2] lacking physical sensation. [3] *(postpositive;* foll by *to)* not sensitive (to) or affected (by): *insensitive to radiation.*
▸**in'sensitively** ADVERB ▸**in'sensitiveness** *or* **in,sensi'tivity** NOUN

insentient (ɪnˈsɛnʃɪənt) ADJECTIVE *Rare* lacking consciousness or senses; inanimate.
▸**in'sentience** *or* **in'sentiency** NOUN

inseparable (ɪnˈsɛpərəb^{ə}l, -ˈsɛprə-) ADJECTIVE incapable of being separated or divided.
▸**in,separa'bility** *or* **in'separableness** NOUN ▸**in'separably** ADVERB

insert VERB (ɪnˈsɜːt) *(tr)* [1] to put in or between; introduce. [2] to introduce, as into text, such as a newspaper; interpolate. ◆ NOUN (ˈɪnsɜːt) [3] something inserted. [4] **a** a folded section placed in another for binding in with a book. **b** a printed sheet, esp one bearing advertising, placed loose between the leaves of a book, periodical, etc. [5] another word for **cut-in** (sense 6).
▷HISTORY C16: from Latin *inserere* to plant in, ingraft, from IN-^{2} + *serere* to join
▸**in'sertable** ADJECTIVE ▸**in'serter** NOUN

inserted (ɪnˈsɜːtɪd) ADJECTIVE [1] *Anatomy* (of a muscle) attached to the bone that it moves. [2] *Botany* (of parts of a plant) growing from another part, as stamens from the corolla.

insertion (ɪnˈsɜːʃən) NOUN [1] the act of inserting or something that is inserted. [2] a word, sentence, correction, etc., inserted into text, such as a newspaper. [3] a strip of lace, embroidery, etc., between two pieces of material. [4] *Anatomy* the point or manner of attachment of a muscle to the bone that it moves. [5] *Botany* the manner or point of attachment of one part to another.
▸**in'sertional** ADJECTIVE

insertion element *or* **sequence** NOUN *Genetics* a section of DNA that is capable of becoming inserted into another chromosome. See **transposon.**

in-service ADJECTIVE denoting training that is given to employees during the course of employment: *an in-service course.*

insessorial (,ɪnsɛˈsɔːrɪəl) ADJECTIVE [1] (of feet or claws) adapted for perching. [2] (of birds) having insessorial feet.
▷HISTORY C19: from New Latin *Insessōrēs* birds that perch, from Latin: perchers, from *insidēre* to sit upon, from *sedēre* to sit

inset VERB (ɪnˈsɛt) **-sets, -setting, -set.** [1] *(tr)* to set or place in or within; insert. ◆ NOUN (ˈɪn,sɛt) [2] something inserted. [3] *Printing* **a** a small map or diagram set within the borders of a larger one. **b** another name for **insert** (sense 4). [4] a piece of fabric inserted into a garment, as to shape it or for decoration. [5] a flowing in, as of the tide.
▸**'in,setter** NOUN

inshallah (ɪnˈʃælə) SENTENCE SUBSTITUTE *Islam* if Allah wills it.
▷HISTORY C19: from Arabic

inshore (ˈɪnˈʃɔː) ADJECTIVE [1] in or on the water, but close to the shore: *inshore weather.* ◆ ADVERB, ADJECTIVE [2] towards the shore from the water: *an inshore wind; we swam inshore.*

inshrine (ɪnˈʃraɪn) VERB a variant spelling of **enshrine.**

inside NOUN (ˈɪnˈsaɪd) [1] the interior; inner or enclosed part or surface. [2] the side of a path away from the road or adjacent to a wall. [3] *(also plural) Informal* the internal organs of the body, esp the stomach and bowels. [4] **inside of.** in a period of time less than; within. [5] **inside out.** with the inside facing outwards. [6] **know (something) inside out.** to know thoroughly or perfectly. ◆ PREPOSITION (,ɪnˈsaɪd) [7] in or to the interior of; within or to within; on the inside of. ◆ ADJECTIVE (ˈɪn,saɪd) [8] on or of an interior; on the inside: *an inside door.* [9] *(prenominal)* arranged or provided by someone within an organization or building, esp illicitly: *the raid was an inside job; inside information.* ◆ ADVERB (,ɪnˈsaɪd) [10] within or to within a thing or place; indoors. [11] by nature; fundamentally: *inside, he's a good chap.* [12] *Slang* in or into prison.

Language note See at **outside.**

inside forward NOUN *Soccer* (esp formerly) one of two players (the **inside right** and the **inside left**) having mainly midfield and attacking roles.

inside job NOUN *Informal* a crime committed with the assistance of someone associated with the victim, such as a person employed on the premises burgled.

inside lane NOUN *Athletics* the inside, and therefore the shortest, route around a circular or oval multi-lane running track.

insider (,ɪnˈsaɪdə) NOUN [1] a member of a specified group. [2] a person with access to exclusive information.

insider dealing *or* **trading** NOUN dealing in company securities on a recognized stock exchange, with a view to making a profit or avoiding a loss, by a person who has confidential information about the securities that, if generally known, would affect their price. Its practice by those connected with a company is illegal.
▸**insider dealer** *or* **trader** NOUN

inside track NOUN [1] the inner and therefore shorter side of a racecourse. [2] *Informal* a position of advantage: *the local man has the inside track in this contest.*

insidious (ɪnˈsɪdɪəs) ADJECTIVE [1] stealthy, subtle, cunning, or treacherous. [2] working in a subtle or apparently innocuous way, but nevertheless deadly: *an insidious illness.*
▷HISTORY C16: from Latin *insidiōsus* cunning, from *insidiae* an ambush, from *insidēre* to sit in; see INSESSORIAL
▸**in'sidiously** ADVERB ▸**in'sidiousness** NOUN

insight (ˈɪn,saɪt) NOUN [1] the ability to perceive clearly or deeply; penetration. [2] a penetrating and often sudden understanding, as of a complex situation or problem. [3] *Psychol* **a** the capacity for understanding one's own or another's mental processes. **b** the immediate understanding of the significance of an event or action. [4] *Psychiatry* the ability to understand one's own problems, sometimes used to distinguish between psychotic and neurotic disorders.
▸**'in,sightful** ADJECTIVE

insignia (ɪnˈsɪgnɪə) NOUN, *plural* **-nias** *or* **-nia.** [1] a badge or emblem of membership, office, or dignity. [2] a distinguishing sign or mark. ◆ Also called (rare): **insigne** (ɪnˈsɪgniː).
▷HISTORY C17: from Latin: marks, badges, from *insignis* distinguished by a mark, prominent, from IN-^{2} + *signum* mark

insignificant (,ɪnsɪgˈnɪfɪkənt) ADJECTIVE [1] having little or no importance; trifling. [2] almost or relatively meaningless. [3] small or inadequate: *an insignificant wage.* [4] not distinctive in character, etc.
▸**,insig'nificance** *or* **,insig'nificancy** NOUN ▸**,insig'nificantly** ADVERB

insincere (,ɪnsɪnˈsɪə) ADJECTIVE lacking sincerity; hypocritical.
▸**,insin'cerely** ADVERB ▸**insincerity** (,ɪnsɪnˈsɛrɪtɪ) NOUN

insinuate (ɪnˈsɪnjʊ,eɪt) VERB [1] *(may take a clause as object)* to suggest by indirect allusion, hints, innuendo, etc. [2] *(tr)* to introduce subtly or

deviously. [3] (*tr*) to cause (someone, esp oneself) to be accepted by gradual approaches or manoeuvres.
▷**HISTORY** C16: from Latin *insinuāre* to wind one's way into, from IN-[2] + *sinus* curve
▸**in'sinuative** *or* **in'sinuatory** ADJECTIVE ▸**in'sinu,ator** NOUN

insinuation (ɪn,sɪnjʊ'eɪʃən) NOUN [1] an indirect or devious hint or suggestion. [2] the act or practice of insinuating.

insipid (ɪn'sɪpɪd) ADJECTIVE [1] lacking spirit; boring. [2] lacking taste; unpalatable.
▷**HISTORY** C17: from Latin *insipidus*, from IN-[1] + *sapidus* full of flavour, SAPID
▸**,insi'pidity** *or* **in'sipidness** NOUN ▸**in'sipidly** ADVERB

insipience (ɪn'sɪpɪəns) NOUN *Archaic* lack of wisdom.
▷**HISTORY** C15: from Latin *insipientia*, from IN-[1] + *sapientia* wisdom; see SAPIENT
▸**in'sipient** ADJECTIVE ▸**in'sipiently** ADVERB

insist (ɪn'sɪst) VERB (when *tr., takes a clause as object;* when *intr.,* usually foll. by *on* or *upon*) [1] to make a determined demand (for): *he insisted that his rights be respected; he insisted on his rights.* [2] to express a convinced belief (in) or assertion (of): *he insisted that she was mad; he insisted on her madness.*
▷**HISTORY** C16: from Latin *insistere* to stand upon, urge, from IN-[2] + *sistere* to stand
▸**in'sister** NOUN ▸**in'sistingly** ADVERB

insistent (ɪn'sɪstənt) ADJECTIVE [1] making continual and persistent demands. [2] demanding notice or attention; compelling: *the insistent cry of a bird.*
▸**in'sistence** *or* **in'sistency** NOUN ▸**in'sistently** ADVERB

in situ *Latin* (ɪn 'sɪtjuː) ADVERB, ADJECTIVE (*postpositive*) [1] in the natural, original, or appropriate position. [2] *Pathol* (esp of a cancerous growth or tumour) not seen to be spreading from a localized position.

insnare (ɪn'snɛə) VERB a less common spelling of **ensnare**.
▸**in'snarement** NOUN ▸**in'snarer** NOUN

insobriety (,ɪnsəʊ'braɪɪtɪ) NOUN lack of sobriety; intemperance.

in so far as *or* **insofar as** (,ɪnsəʊ'fɑː) ADVERB to the degree or extent that.

insolate ('ɪnsəʊ,leɪt) VERB (*tr*) to expose to sunlight, as for bleaching.
▷**HISTORY** C17: from Latin *insōlāre* to place in the sun, from IN-[2] + *sōl* sun

insolation (,ɪnsəʊ'leɪʃən) NOUN [1] the quantity of solar radiation falling upon a body or planet, esp per unit area. [2] exposure to the sun's rays. [3] former name for **sunstroke**.

insole ('ɪn,səʊl) NOUN [1] the inner sole of a shoe or boot. [2] a loose additional inner sole used to give extra warmth, comfort, etc.

insolent ('ɪnsələnt) ADJECTIVE offensive, impudent, or disrespectful.
▷**HISTORY** C14: from Latin *insolens*, from IN-[1] + *solēre* to be accustomed
▸**'insolence** NOUN ▸**'insolently** ADVERB

insoluble (ɪn'sɒljʊbᵊl) ADJECTIVE [1] incapable of being dissolved; incapable of forming a solution, esp in water. [2] incapable of being solved.
▸**in,solu'bility** *or* **in'solubleness** NOUN ▸**in'solubly** ADVERB

insolvable (ɪn'sɒlvəbᵊl) ADJECTIVE another word for **insoluble** (sense 2).
▸**in,solva'bility** NOUN ▸**in'solvably** ADVERB

insolvency provision NOUN *Brit* the right of employees of a firm that goes bankrupt or into receivership to receive money owed to them as wages, etc.

insolvent (ɪn'sɒlvənt) ADJECTIVE [1] (of a person, company, etc.) having insufficient assets to meet debts and liabilities; bankrupt. [2] of or relating to bankrupts or bankruptcy. ◆ NOUN [3] a person who is insolvent; bankrupt.
▸**in'solvency** NOUN

insomnia (ɪn'sɒmnɪə) NOUN chronic inability to fall asleep or to enjoy uninterrupted sleep. Related adjective: **agrypnotic**.
▷**HISTORY** C18: from Latin, from *insomnis* sleepless, from *somnus* sleep
▸**in'somnious** ADJECTIVE

insomniac (ɪn'sɒmnɪ,æk) ADJECTIVE [1] exhibiting or causing insomnia. ◆ NOUN [2] a person experiencing insomnia.

insomuch (,ɪnsəʊ'mʌtʃ) ADVERB [1] (foll by *as* or *that*) to such an extent or degree. [2] (foll by *as*) because of the fact (that); inasmuch (as).

insouciant (ɪn'suːsɪənt) ADJECTIVE carefree or unconcerned; light-hearted.
▷**HISTORY** C19: from French, from IN-[1] + *souciant* worrying, from *soucier* to trouble, from Latin *sollicitāre;* compare SOLICITOUS
▸**in'souciance** NOUN ▸**in'souciantly** ADVERB

insoul (ɪn'səʊl) VERB (*tr*) a variant of **ensoul**.

inspan (ɪn'spæn) VERB **-spans, -spanning, -spanned**. (*tr*) *Chiefly South African* to harness (animals) to (a vehicle); yoke.
▷**HISTORY** C19: from Afrikaans, from Middle Dutch *inspannen*, from *spannen* to stretch, yoke; see SPAN[1]

inspect (ɪn'spɛkt) VERB (*tr*) [1] to examine closely, esp for faults or errors. [2] to scrutinize officially (a document, military personnel on ceremonial parade, etc.).
▷**HISTORY** C17: from Latin *inspicere*, from *specere* to look
▸**in'spectable** ADJECTIVE ▸**in'spectingly** ADVERB
▸**in'spection** NOUN ▸**in'spectional** ADJECTIVE ▸**in'spective** ADJECTIVE

inspection chamber NOUN a more formal name for **manhole** (sense 1).

inspection pit NOUN a hole in the floor of a garage etc. from which the underside of a vehicle can be examined and serviced.

inspector (ɪn'spɛktə) NOUN [1] a person who inspects, esp an official who examines for compliance with regulations, standards, etc. [2] a police officer ranking below a superintendent or chief inspector and above a sergeant.
▸**in'spectoral** *or* **inspectorial** (,ɪnspɛk'tɔːrɪəl) ADJECTIVE
▸**in'spector,ship** NOUN

inspectorate (ɪn'spɛktərɪt) NOUN [1] the office, rank, or duties of an inspector. [2] a body of inspectors. [3] a district under an inspector.

inspector general NOUN, *plural* **inspectors general**. [1] the head of an inspectorate or inspection system; an officer with wide investigative powers. [2] a staff officer of the military, air, or naval service with the responsibility of conducting inspections and investigations.

inspector of taxes NOUN an official of the Inland Revenue whose work is to assess individuals' income tax liability.

insphere (ɪn'sfɪə) VERB a variant spelling of **ensphere**.

inspiration (,ɪnspɪ'reɪʃən) NOUN [1] stimulation or arousal of the mind, feelings, etc., to special or unusual activity or creativity. [2] the state or quality of being so stimulated or aroused. [3] someone or something that causes this state. [4] an idea or action resulting from such a state. [5] the act or process of inhaling; breathing in.

inspirational (,ɪnspɪ'reɪʃənᵊl) ADJECTIVE [1] of, relating to, or tending to arouse inspiration; inspiring. [2] resulting from inspiration; inspired.
▸**,inspi'rationally** ADVERB

inspirator ('ɪnspɪ,reɪtə) NOUN a device for drawing in or injecting a vapour, liquid, etc. Also called: **injector**.

inspiratory (ɪn'spaɪərətərɪ, -trɪ) ADJECTIVE of or relating to inhalation or the drawing in of air.

inspire (ɪn'spaɪə) VERB [1] to exert a stimulating or beneficial effect upon (a person); animate or invigorate. [2] (*tr; foll by* with *or* to; *may take an infinitive*) to arouse (with a particular emotion or to a particular action); stir. [3] (*tr*) to prompt or instigate; give rise to: *her beauty inspired his love.* [4] (*tr; often passive*) to guide or arouse by divine influence or inspiration. [5] to take or draw (air, gas, etc.) into the lungs; inhale. [6] (*tr*) *Archaic* **a** to breathe into or upon. **b** to breathe life into.
▷**HISTORY** C14 (in the sense: to breathe upon, blow into): from Latin *inspīrāre*, from *spīrāre* to breathe
▸**in'spirable** ADJECTIVE ▸**in'spirative** ADJECTIVE ▸**in'spirer** NOUN ▸**in'spiringly** ADVERB

inspired (ɪn'spaɪəd) ADJECTIVE [1] aroused or guided by or as if aroused or guided by divine inspiration: *an inspired performance; she was like one inspired.* [2] extremely accurate or apt but based on intuition rather than knowledge or logical deduction: *an inspired guess.*

inspirit (ɪn'spɪrɪt) VERB (*tr*) to fill with vigour; inspire.
▸**in'spiriter** NOUN ▸**in'spiritingly** ADVERB ▸**in'spiritment** NOUN

inspissate (ɪn'spɪseɪt) VERB *Archaic* to thicken, as by evaporation.
▷**HISTORY** C17: from Late Latin *inspissātus* thickened, from Latin *spissāre* to thicken, from *spissus* thick
▸**,inspis'sation** NOUN ▸**'inspis,sator** NOUN

Inst. ABBREVIATION FOR: [1] Institute. [2] Institution.

instability (,ɪnstə'bɪlɪtɪ) NOUN, *plural* **-ties**. [1] lack of stability or steadiness. [2] tendency to variable or unpredictable behaviour. [3] *Physics* a fast growing disturbance or wave in a plasma.

instable (ɪn'steɪbᵊl) ADJECTIVE a less common word for **unstable**.

install *or* **instal** (ɪn'stɔːl) VERB **-stalls, -stalling, -stalled** *or* **-stals, -stalling, -stalled**. (*tr*) [1] to place (machinery, equipment, etc.) in position and connect and adjust for use. [2] to transfer (computer software) from a distribution file to a permanent location on disk, and prepare it for its particular environment and application. [3] to put in a position, rank, etc. [4] to settle (a person, esp oneself) in a position or state: *she installed herself in an armchair.*
▷**HISTORY** C16: from Medieval Latin *installāre*, from IN-[2] + *stallum* STALL[1]
▸**in'staller** NOUN

installant (ɪn'stɔːlənt) NOUN **a** a person who installs another in an office, etc. **b** (*as modifier*): *an installant bishop.*

installation (,ɪnstə'leɪʃən) NOUN [1] the act of installing or the state of being installed. [2] a large device, system, or piece of equipment that has been installed. [3] a military establishment usually serving in a support role. [4] an art exhibit often involving video or moving parts where the relation of the parts to the whole is important to the interpretation of the piece.

installment plan *or esp Canadian* **instalment plan** NOUN the US and Canadian name for **hire-purchase**.

instalment[1] *or US* **installment** (ɪn'stɔːlmənt) NOUN [1] one of the portions, usually equal, into which a debt is divided for payment at specified intervals over a fixed period. [2] a portion of something that is issued, broadcast, or published in parts, such as a serial in a magazine.
▷**HISTORY** C18: from obsolete *estallment*, probably from Old French *estaler* to fix, hence to agree rate of payment, from *estal* something fixed, place, from Old High German *stal* STALL[1]

instalment[2] *or US* **installment** (ɪn'stɔːlmənt) NOUN another word for **installation** (sense 1).

instance ('ɪnstəns) NOUN [1] a case or particular example. [2] **for instance**. for or as an example. [3] a specified stage in proceedings; step (in the phrases **in the first, second,** etc., **instance**). [4] urgent request or demand (esp in the phrase **at the instance of**). [5] *Logic* **a** an expression derived from another by instantiation. **b** See **substitution** (sense 4b). [6] *Archaic* motive or reason. ◆ VERB (*tr*) [7] to cite as an example.
▷**HISTORY** C14 (in the sense: case, example): from Medieval Latin *instantia* example, (in the sense: urgency) from Latin: a being close upon, presence, from *instāns* pressing upon, urgent; see INSTANT

instancy ('ɪnstənsɪ) NOUN *Rare* [1] the quality of being urgent or imminent. [2] instantaneousness; immediateness.

instant ('ɪnstənt) NOUN [1] a very brief time; moment. [2] a particular moment or point in time: *at the same instant.* [3] **on the instant**. immediately; without delay. ◆ ADJECTIVE [4] immediate; instantaneous. [5] (esp of foods) prepared or designed for preparation with very little time and effort: *instant coffee.* [6] urgent or imperative. [7] (*postpositive*) *Rare except when abbreviated in formal correspondence* **a** of the present month: *a letter of the 7th instant.* Abbreviation: **inst.** Compare **proximo, ultimo. b** currently under consideration. ◆ ADVERB [8] a poetic word for **instantly**.
▷**HISTORY** C15: from Latin *instāns*, from *instāre* to be present, press closely, from IN-[2] + *stāre* to stand

instantaneous (,ɪnstən'teɪnɪəs) ADJECTIVE [1] occurring with almost no delay; immediate. [2] happening or completed within a moment: *instantaneous death.* [3] *Maths* **a** occurring at or

associated with a particular instant. **b** equal to the limit of the average value of a given variable as the time interval over which the variable is considered approaches zero: *instantaneous velocity*.
▸ˌ**instanˈtaneously** ADVERB ▸ˌ**instanˈtaneousness** *or* **instantaneity** (ɪnˌstæntəˈniːɪtɪ) NOUN

instanter (ɪnˈstæntə) ADVERB *Law* without delay; (in connection with pleading) the same day or within 24 hours.
▷HISTORY C17: from Latin: urgently, from *instans* INSTANT

instantiate (ɪnˈstænʃɪˌeɪt) VERB (*tr*) to represent by an instance.
▷HISTORY C20: from Latin *instantia* (see INSTANCE) + -ATE[1]

instantiation (ɪnˌstænʃɪˈeɪʃən) NOUN 1 the act or an instance of instantiating. 2 the representation of (an abstraction) by a concrete example. 3 *Logic* **a** the process of deriving an individual statement from a general one by replacing the variable with a name or other referring expression. **b** the valid inference of an instance from a universally quantified statement, as *David is rational* from *all men are rational*. **c** a statement so derived.

instantly (ˈɪnstəntlɪ) ADVERB 1 immediately; at once. 2 *Archaic* urgently or insistently.

instant replay NOUN another name for **action replay.**

instar (ˈɪnstɑː) NOUN the stage in the development of an insect between any two moults.
▷HISTORY C19: New Latin from Latin: image

instate (ɪnˈsteɪt) VERB (*tr*) to place in a position or office; install.
▸**inˈstatement** NOUN

instauration (ˌɪnstɔːˈreɪʃən) NOUN *Rare* restoration or renewal.
▷HISTORY C17: from Latin *instaurātiō*, from *instaurāre* to renew
▸ˈ**instauˌrator** NOUN

instead (ɪnˈstɛd) ADVERB 1 as a replacement, substitute, or alternative. 2 **instead of.** (*preposition*) in place of or as an alternative to.
▷HISTORY C13: from phrase *in stead* in place

instep (ˈɪnˌstɛp) NOUN 1 the middle section of the human foot, forming the arch between the ankle and toes. 2 the part of a shoe, stocking, etc., covering this.
▷HISTORY C16: probably from IN-[2] + STEP

instigate (ˈɪnstɪˌɡeɪt) VERB (*tr*) 1 to bring about, as by incitement or urging: *to instigate rebellion*. 2 to urge on to some drastic or inadvisable action.
▷HISTORY C16: from Latin *instīgāre* to stimulate, incite; compare Greek *stizein* to prick
▸ˈ**instiˌgatingly** ADVERB ▸ˌ**instiˈgation** NOUN ▸ˈ**instiˌgative** ADJECTIVE ▸ˈ**instiˌgator** NOUN

instil *or US* **instill** (ɪnˈstɪl) VERB **-stils** *or* **-stills, -stilling, -stilled.** (*tr*) 1 to introduce gradually; implant or infuse. 2 *Rare* to pour in or inject in drops.
▷HISTORY C16: from Latin *instillāre* to pour in a drop at a time, from *stillāre* to drip
▸**inˈstiller** NOUN ▸**inˈstilment,** *US* **inˈstillment,** *or* ˌ**instilˈlation** NOUN

instinct (ˈɪnstɪŋkt) NOUN 1 the innate capacity of an animal to respond to a given stimulus in a relatively fixed way. 2 inborn intuitive power. 3 a natural and apparently innate aptitude. ◆ ADJECTIVE (ɪnˈstɪŋkt) 4 *Rare* (*postpositive; often foll by with*) **a** animated or impelled (by). **b** imbued or infused (with).
▷HISTORY C15: from Latin *instinctus* roused, from *instinguere* to incite; compare INSTIGATE

instinctive (ɪnˈstɪŋktɪv) *or* **instinctual** ADJECTIVE 1 of, relating to, or resulting from instinct. 2 conditioned so as to appear innate: *an instinctive movement in driving*.
▸**inˈstinctively** *or* **inˈstinctually** ADVERB

institute (ˈɪnstɪˌtjuːt) VERB (*tr*) 1 to organize; establish. 2 to initiate: *to institute a practice*. 3 to establish in a position or office; induct. 4 (foll by *in* or *into*) to install (a clergyman) in a church. ◆ NOUN 5 an organization founded for particular work, such as education, promotion of the arts, or scientific research. 6 the building where such an organization is situated. 7 something instituted, esp a rule, custom, or precedent.
▷HISTORY C16: from Latin *instituere*, from *statuere* to place, stand
▸ˈ**instiˌtutor** *or* ˈ**instiˌtuter** NOUN

institutes (ˈɪnstɪˌtjuːts) PLURAL NOUN a digest or summary, esp of laws.

Institutes (ˈɪnstɪˌtjuːts) PLURAL NOUN 1 an introduction to legal study in ancient Rome, compiled by order of Justinian and divided into four books forming part of the Corpus Juris Civilis. 2 short for **Institutes of the Christian Religion**, the book by Calvin, completed in 1536 and constituting the basic statement of the Reformed faith, that repudiates papal authority and postulates the doctrines of justification by faith alone and predestination.

institution (ˌɪnstɪˈtjuːʃən) NOUN 1 the act of instituting. 2 an organization or establishment founded for a specific purpose, such as a hospital, church, company, or college. 3 the building where such an organization is situated. 4 an established custom, law, or relationship in a society or community. 5 Also called: **institutional investor.** a large organization, such as an insurance company, bank, or pension fund, that has substantial sums to invest on a stock exchange. 6 *Informal* a constant feature or practice: *Jones' drink at the bar was an institution*. 7 the appointment or admission of an incumbent to an ecclesiastical office or pastoral charge. 8 *Christian theol* the creation of a sacrament by Christ, esp the Eucharist.
▸ˌ**instiˈtutionary** ADJECTIVE

institutional (ˌɪnstɪˈtjuːʃənᵊl) ADJECTIVE 1 of, relating to, or characteristic of institutions. 2 dull, routine, and uniform: *institutional meals*. 3 relating to principles or institutes, esp of law.
▸ˌ**instiˈtutionally** ADVERB

institutionalism (ˌɪnstɪˈtjuːʃənəˌlɪzəm) NOUN the system of or belief in institutions.
▸ˌ**instiˈtutionalist** NOUN

institutionalize *or* **institutionalise** (ˌɪnstɪˈtjuːʃənəˌlaɪz) VERB 1 (*tr; often passive*) to subject to the deleterious effects of confinement in an institution: *a mental patient who was institutionalized into boredom and apathy*. 2 (*tr*) to place in an institution. 3 to make or become an institution.
▸ˌ**instiˌtutionaliˈzation** *or* ˌ**instiˌtutionaliˈsation** NOUN

institutive (ˈɪnstɪˌtjuːtɪv) ADJECTIVE 1 concerned with instituting and establishing. 2 established by custom or law.
▸ˈ**instiˌtutively** ADVERB

in-store ADJECTIVE available or taking place within a supermarket or other large shop: *in-store banking facilities*.

instruct (ɪnˈstrʌkt) VERB (*tr*) 1 to direct to do something; order. 2 to teach (someone) how to do (something). 3 to furnish with information; apprise. 4 *Law, chiefly Brit* **a** (esp of a client to his solicitor or a solicitor to a barrister) to give relevant facts or information to. **b** to authorize (a barrister or solicitor) to conduct a case on a person's behalf: *to instruct counsel*.
▷HISTORY C15: from Latin *instruere* to construct, set in order, equip, teach, from *struere* to build
▸**inˈstructible** ADJECTIVE

instruction (ɪnˈstrʌkʃən) NOUN 1 a direction; order. 2 the process or act of imparting knowledge; teaching; education. 3 *Computing* a part of a program consisting of a coded command to the computer to perform a specified function.
▸**inˈstructional** ADJECTIVE

instructions (ɪnˈstrʌkʃənz) PLURAL NOUN 1 directions, orders, or recommended rules for guidance, use, etc. 2 *Law* the facts and details relating to a case given by a client to his solicitor or by a solicitor to a barrister with directions to conduct the case: *to take instructions*.

instructive (ɪnˈstrʌktɪv) ADJECTIVE serving to instruct or enlighten; conveying information.
▸**inˈstructively** ADVERB ▸**inˈstructiveness** NOUN

instructor (ɪnˈstrʌktə) NOUN 1 someone who instructs; teacher. 2 *US and Canadian* a university teacher ranking below assistant professor.
▸**inˈstructorˌship** NOUN ▸**instructress** (ɪnˈstrʌktrɪs) FEMININE NOUN

instrument NOUN (ˈɪnstrəmənt) 1 a mechanical implement or tool, esp one used for precision work: *surgical instrument*. 2 *Music* any of various contrivances or mechanisms that can be played to produce musical tones or sounds. 3 an important factor or agency in something: *her evidence was an instrument in his arrest*. 4 *Informal* a person used by another to gain an end; dupe; tool. 5 a measuring device, such as a pressure gauge or ammeter. 6 **a** a device or system for use in navigation or control, esp of aircraft. **b** (*as modifier*): *instrument landing*. 7 a formal legal document. ◆ VERB (ˈɪnstrəˌmɛnt) (*tr*) 8 another word for **orchestrate** (sense 1). 9 to equip with instruments.
▷HISTORY C13: from Latin *instrūmentum* tool, equipment, from *instruere* to erect, furnish; see INSTRUCT

instrumental (ˌɪnstrəˈmɛntᵊl) ADJECTIVE 1 serving as a means or influence; helpful. 2 of, relating to, or characterized by an instrument or instruments. 3 played by or composed for musical instruments. 4 *Grammar* denoting a case of nouns, etc., in certain inflected languages, indicating the instrument used in performing an action, usually translated into English using the prepositions *with* or *by means of*. ◆ NOUN 5 a piece of music composed for instruments rather than for voices. 6 *Grammar* **a** the instrumental case. **b** a word or speech element in the instrumental case.
▸ˌ**instrumenˈtality** NOUN ▸ˌ**instruˈmentally** ADVERB

instrumentalism (ˌɪnstrəˈmɛntəˌlɪzəm) NOUN 1 a system of pragmatic philosophy holding that ideas are instruments, that they should guide our actions and can change the world, and that their value consists not in their truth but in their success. 2 an antirealist philosophy of science that holds that theories are not true or false but are merely tools for deriving predictions from observational data.

instrumentalist (ˌɪnstrəˈmɛntəlɪst) NOUN 1 a person who plays a musical instrument. 2 *Philosophy* a person who believes in the doctrines of instrumentalism. ◆ ADJECTIVE 3 of or relating to instrumentalism.

instrumental learning NOUN *Psychol* a method of training in which the reinforcement is made contingent on the occurrence of the response. Compare **classical conditioning.**

instrumentation (ˌɪnstrəmɛnˈteɪʃən) NOUN 1 the instruments specified in a musical score or arrangement. 2 another word for **orchestration.** 3 the study of the characteristics of musical instruments. 4 the use of instruments or tools. 5 means; agency.

instrument flying NOUN the navigation of an aircraft by the use of instruments only.

instrument landing NOUN an aircraft landing relying only upon instruments and ground radio devices, usually made when visibility is very poor.

instrument panel *or* **board** NOUN 1 a panel on which instruments are mounted, as on a car. See also **dashboard.** 2 an array of instruments, gauges, etc., mounted to display the condition or performance of a machine or process.

insubordinate (ˌɪnsəˈbɔːdɪnɪt) ADJECTIVE 1 not submissive to authority; disobedient or rebellious. 2 not in a subordinate position or rank. ◆ NOUN 3 an insubordinate person.
▸ˌ**insubˈordinately** ADVERB ▸ˌ**insubˌordiˈnation** NOUN

insubstantial (ˌɪnsəbˈstænʃəl) ADJECTIVE 1 not substantial; flimsy, tenuous, or slight. 2 imaginary; unreal.
▸ˌ**insubˌstantiˈality** NOUN ▸ˌ**insubˈstantially** ADVERB

insufferable (ɪnˈsʌfərəbᵊl) ADJECTIVE intolerable; unendurable.
▸**inˈsufferableness** NOUN ▸**inˈsufferably** ADVERB

insufficiency (ˌɪnsəˈfɪʃənsɪ) NOUN 1 Also called: **insufficience.** the state of being insufficient. 2 *Pathol* failure in the functioning of an organ, tissue, etc.: *cardiac insufficiency*.

insufficient (ˌɪnsəˈfɪʃənt) ADJECTIVE not sufficient; inadequate or deficient.
▸ˌ**insufˈficiently** ADVERB

insufflate (ˈɪnsʌˌfleɪt) VERB 1 (*tr*) to breathe or blow (something) into (a room, area, etc.). 2 *Med* to blow (air, medicated powder, etc.) into the lungs or into a body cavity. 3 (*tr*) to breathe or blow upon (someone or something) as a ritual or sacramental act, esp so as to symbolize the influence of the Holy Spirit.
▸ˌ**insufˈflation** NOUN ▸ˈ**insufˌflator** NOUN

insula (ˈɪnsjʊlə) NOUN, *plural* **-lae** (-ˌliː). a pyramid-shaped area of the brain within each

cerebral hemisphere beneath parts of the frontal and temporal lobes. Also called: **island of Reil.**
▷**HISTORY** Latin, literally: island

insular (ˈɪnsjʊlə) ADJECTIVE 1 of, relating to, or resembling an island. 2 remote, detached, or aloof. 3 illiberal or narrow-minded. 4 isolated or separated.
▷**HISTORY** C17: from Late Latin *insulāris,* from Latin *insula* island, ISLE
▸**ˈinsularism** *or* **insularity** (ˌɪnsjʊˈlærɪtɪ) NOUN ▸**ˈinsularly** ADVERB

insulate (ˈɪnsjʊˌleɪt) VERB *(tr)* 1 to prevent or reduce the transmission of electricity, heat, or sound to or from (a body, device, or region) by surrounding with a nonconducting material. 2 to isolate or detach.
▷**HISTORY** C16: from Late Latin *insulātus:* made into an island

insulating tape NOUN *Brit* adhesive tape, impregnated with a moisture-repelling substance, used to insulate exposed electrical conductors. US and Canadian name: **friction tape.**

insulation (ˌɪnsjʊˈleɪʃən) NOUN 1 Also called: **insulant** (ˈɪnsjʊlənt). material used to insulate a body, device, or region. 2 the act or process of insulating.

insulator (ˈɪnsjʊˌleɪtə) NOUN any material or device that insulates, esp a material with a very low electrical conductivity or thermal conductivity or something made of such a material.

insulin (ˈɪnsjʊlɪn) NOUN a protein hormone, secreted in the pancreas by the islets of Langerhans, that controls the concentration of glucose in the blood. Insulin deficiency results in diabetes mellitus.
▷**HISTORY** C20: from New Latin *insula* islet (of the pancreas) + -IN

insulin reaction *or* **shock** NOUN the condition in a diabetic resulting from an overdose of insulin, causing a sharp drop in the blood sugar level with tremor, profuse sweating, and convulsions. See also **hyperinsulinism.**

insult VERB (ɪnˈsʌlt) *(tr)* 1 to treat, mention, or speak to rudely; offend; affront. 2 *Obsolete* to assault; attack. ◆ NOUN (ˈɪnsʌlt) 3 an offensive or contemptuous remark or action; affront; slight. 4 a person or thing producing the effect of an affront: *some television is an insult to intelligence.* 5 *Med* an injury or trauma. 6 **add insult to injury.** to make an unfair or unacceptable situation even worse.
▷**HISTORY** C16: from Latin *insultāre* to jump upon, from IN-[2] + *saltāre* to jump
▸**inˈsulter** NOUN

insuperable (ɪnˈsuːpərəbᵊl, -prəbᵊl, -ˈsjuː-) ADJECTIVE incapable of being overcome; insurmountable.
▸**inˌsuperaˈbility** *or* **inˈsuperableness** NOUN ▸**inˈsuperably** ADVERB

insupportable (ˌɪnsəˈpɔːtəbᵊl) ADJECTIVE 1 incapable of being endured; intolerable; insufferable. 2 incapable of being supported or justified; indefensible.
▸**ˌinsupˈportableness** NOUN ▸**ˌinsupˈportably** ADVERB

insuppressible (ˌɪnsəˈprɛsəbᵊl) ADJECTIVE incapable of being suppressed, overcome, or muffled: *an insuppressible giggle.*
▸**ˌinsupˈpressibly** ADVERB

insurable interest NOUN *Law* a financial or other interest in the life or property covered by an insurance contract, without which the contract cannot be enforced.

insurance (ɪnˈʃʊərəns, -ˈʃɔː-) NOUN 1 **a** the act, system, or business of providing financial protection for property, life, health, etc., against specified contingencies, such as death, loss, or damage, and involving payment of regular premiums in return for a policy guaranteeing such protection. **b** the state of having such protection. **c** Also called: **insurance policy.** the policy providing such protection. **d** the pecuniary amount of such protection. **e** the premium payable in return for such protection. **f** *(as modifier)*: *insurance agent; insurance broker; insurance company.* 2 a means of protecting or safeguarding against risk or injury.

insure (ɪnˈʃʊə, -ˈʃɔː-) VERB 1 (often foll by *against*) to guarantee or protect (against risk, loss, etc.): *we insured against disappointment by making an early reservation.* 2 (often foll by *against*) to issue (a person) with an insurance policy or take out an insurance policy (on): *his house was heavily insured against fire; after all his car accidents the company refuses to insure him again.* 3 another word (esp US) for **ensure** (senses 1, 2). ◆ Also (rare) (for senses 1, 2): **ensure.**
▸**inˈsurable** ADJECTIVE ▸**inˌsuraˈbility** NOUN

insured (ɪnˈʃʊəd, -ˈʃɔːd) ADJECTIVE 1 covered by insurance: *an insured risk.* ◆ NOUN 2 the person, persons, or organization covered by an insurance policy.

insurer (ɪnˈʃʊərə, -ˈʃɔː-) NOUN 1 a person or company offering insurance policies in return for premiums. 2 a person or thing that insures.

insurgence (ɪnˈsɜːdʒəns) NOUN rebellion, uprising, or riot.

insurgent (ɪnˈsɜːdʒənt) ADJECTIVE 1 rebellious or in revolt, as against a government in power or the civil authorities. ◆ NOUN 2 a person who takes part in an uprising or rebellion; insurrectionist. 3 *International law* a person or group that rises in revolt against an established government or authority but whose conduct does not amount to belligerency.
▷**HISTORY** C18: from Latin *insurgēns* rising upon or against, from *insurgere* to rise up, from *surgere* to rise
▸**inˈsurgency** NOUN

insurmountable (ˌɪnsəˈmaʊntəbᵊl) ADJECTIVE incapable of being overcome; insuperable.
▸**ˌinsurˌmountaˈbility** *or* **ˌinsurˈmountableness** NOUN ▸**ˌinsurˈmountably** ADVERB

insurrection (ˌɪnsəˈrɛkʃən) NOUN the act or an instance of rebelling against a government in power or the civil authorities; insurgency.
▷**HISTORY** C15: from Late Latin *insurrectiō,* from *insurgere* to rise up
▸**ˌinsurˈrectional** ADJECTIVE ▸**ˌinsurˈrectionary** NOUN, ADJECTIVE ▸**ˌinsurˈrectionism** NOUN ▸**ˌinsurˈrectionist** NOUN, ADJECTIVE

insusceptible (ˌɪnsəˈsɛptəbᵊl) ADJECTIVE (when *postpositive,* usually foll by *to*) not capable of being affected (by); not susceptible (to).
▸**ˌinsusˌceptiˈbility** NOUN ▸**ˌinsusˈceptibly** ADVERB

inswing (ˈɪnˌswɪŋ) NOUN *Cricket* the movement of a bowled ball from off to leg through the air. Compare **outswing.**

inswinger (ˈɪnˌswɪŋə) NOUN 1 *Cricket* a ball bowled so as to move from off to leg through the air. 2 *Soccer* a ball kicked, esp from a corner, so as to move through the air in a curve towards the goal or the centre.

int AN INTERNET DOMAIN NAME FOR an international organization.

intact (ɪnˈtækt) ADJECTIVE untouched or unimpaired; left complete or perfect.
▷**HISTORY** C15: from Latin *intactus* not touched, from *tangere* to touch
▸**inˈtactness** NOUN

intaglio (ɪnˈtɑːlɪˌəʊ) NOUN, *plural* **-lios** *or* **-li** (-ljiː). 1 a seal, gem, etc., ornamented with a sunken or incised design, as opposed to a design in relief. Compare **cameo.** 2 the art or process of incised carving. 3 a design, figure, or ornamentation carved, engraved, or etched into the surface of the material used. 4 any of various printing techniques using an etched or engraved plate. The whole plate is smeared with ink, the surface wiped clean, and the ink in the recesses then transferred to the paper or other material. 5 an incised die used to make a design in relief.
▷**HISTORY** C17: from Italian, from *intagliare* to engrave, from *tagliare* to cut, from Late Latin *tāliāre;* see TAILOR
▸**intagliated** (ɪnˈtɑːlɪˌeɪtɪd) ADJECTIVE

intake (ˈɪnˌteɪk) NOUN 1 a thing or a quantity taken in: *an intake of students.* 2 the act of taking in. 3 the opening through which fluid enters a duct or channel, esp the air inlet of a jet engine. 4 a ventilation shaft in a mine. 5 a contraction or narrowing: *an intake in a garment.*

intangible (ɪnˈtændʒɪbᵊl) ADJECTIVE 1 incapable of being perceived by touch; impalpable. 2 imprecise or unclear to the mind: *intangible ideas.* 3 (of property or a business asset) saleable though not possessing intrinsic productive value. ◆ NOUN 4 something that is intangible.
▸**inˌtangiˈbility** *or* **inˈtangibleness** NOUN ▸**inˈtangibly** ADVERB

intarsia (ɪnˈtɑːsɪə) *or* **tarsia** NOUN 1 a decorative or pictorial mosaic of inlaid wood or sometimes ivory of a style developed in the Italian Renaissance and used esp on wooden wall panels. 2 the art or practice of making such mosaics. 3 (in knitting) an individually worked motif.
▷**HISTORY** C19: changed from Italian *intarsio*

integer (ˈɪntɪdʒə) NOUN 1 any rational number that can be expressed as the sum or difference of a finite number of units, being a member of the set ...–3, –2, –1, 0, 1, 2, 3.... 2 an individual entity or whole unit.
▷**HISTORY** C16: from Latin: untouched, entire, from *tangere* to touch

integral ADJECTIVE (ˈɪntɪgrəl, ɪnˈtɛgrəl) 1 (often foll by *to*) being an essential part (of); intrinsic (to). 2 intact; entire. 3 formed of constituent parts; united. 4 *Maths* **a** of or involving an integral. **b** involving or being an integer. ◆ NOUN (ˈɪntɪgrəl) 5 *Maths* the limit of an increasingly large number of increasingly smaller quantities, related to the function that is being integrated (the integrand). The independent variables may be confined within certain limits (**definite integral**) or unconfined (**indefinite integral**). Symbol: ∫. 6 a complete thing; whole.
▸**integrality** (ˌɪntɪˈgrælɪtɪ) NOUN ▸**ˈintegrally** ADVERB

integral calculus NOUN the branch of calculus concerned with the determination of integrals and their application to the solution of differential equations, the determination of areas and volumes, etc. Compare **differential calculus.**

integrand (ˈɪntɪˌgrænd) NOUN a mathematical function to be integrated.
▷**HISTORY** C19: from Latin: to be integrated

integrant (ˈɪntəgrənt) ADJECTIVE 1 part of a whole; integral; constituent. ◆ NOUN 2 an integrant thing or part.

integrate VERB (ˈɪntɪˌgreɪt) 1 to make or be made into a whole; incorporate or be incorporated. 2 *(tr)* to designate (a school, park, etc.) for use by all races or groups; desegregate. 3 to amalgamate or mix (a racial or religious group) with an existing community. 4 *Maths* to perform an integration on (a quantity, expression, etc.). ◆ ADJECTIVE (ˈɪntɪgrɪt) 5 made up of parts; integrated.
▷**HISTORY** C17: from Latin *integrāre;* see INTEGER
▸**integrable** (ˈɪntəgrəbᵊl) ADJECTIVE ▸**ˌintegraˈbility** NOUN ▸**ˈinteˌgrative** ADJECTIVE

integrated (ˈɪntɪˌgreɪtɪd) ADJECTIVE 1 characterized by integration. 2 denoting a works which combines various processes normally carried out at different locations: *an integrated steelworks.* 3 *Biology* denoting a virus the DNA of which is incorporated into the chromosomes of the host cell.

integrated circuit NOUN a very small electronic circuit consisting of an assembly of elements made from a chip of semiconducting material, such as crystalline silicon. Abbreviation: **IC.**

integrated school NOUN (in New Zealand) a private or church school that has joined the state school system.

integration (ˌɪntɪˈgreɪʃən) NOUN 1 the act of combining or adding parts to make a unified whole. 2 the act of amalgamating a racial or religious group with an existing community. 3 the combination of previously racially segregated social facilities into a nonsegregated system. 4 *Psychol* organization into a unified pattern, esp of different aspects of the personality into a hierarchical system of functions. 5 the assimilation of nutritive material by the body during the process of anabolism. 6 *Maths* an operation used in calculus in which the integral of a function or variable is determined; the inverse of differentiation.
▸**ˌinteˈgrationist** NOUN

integrative bargaining (ˈɪntɪˌgreɪtɪv) NOUN *Industrial relations* a type of bargaining in which all parties involved recognize that there are common problems requiring mutual resolution.

integrator (ˈɪntɪˌgreɪtə) NOUN 1 a person or thing that integrates, esp a mechanical instrument that determines the value of a definite integral, as the area under a curve. See also **planimeter.** 2 *Computing* **a** an arithmetic component with two input variables, *x* and *y*, whose output variable *z* is proportional to the integral of *y* with respect to *x*. **b** an arithmetic component whose output variable is proportional to the integral of the input variable with respect to elapsed time.

integrity (ɪnˈtɛgrɪtɪ) NOUN 1 adherence to moral principles; honesty. 2 the quality of being unimpaired; soundness. 3 unity; wholeness.
▷HISTORY C15: from Latin *integritās;* see INTEGER

integument (ɪnˈtɛgjʊmənt) NOUN 1 the protective layer around an ovule that becomes the seed coat. 2 the outer protective layer or covering of an animal, such as skin or a cuticle.
▷HISTORY C17: from Latin *integumentum,* from *tegere* to cover
▸**in,tegu'mental** *or* **in,tegu'mentary** ADJECTIVE

intellect (ˈɪntɪˌlɛkt) NOUN 1 the capacity for understanding, thinking, and reasoning, as distinct from feeling or wishing. 2 a mind or intelligence, esp a brilliant one: *his intellect is wasted on that job.* 3 *Informal* a person possessing a brilliant mind; brain. 4 those possessing the greatest mental power: *the intellect of a nation.*
▷HISTORY C14: from Latin *intellectus* comprehension, intellect, from *intellegere* to understand; see INTELLIGENCE
▸**,intel'lective** ADJECTIVE ▸**,intel'lectively** ADVERB

intellection (ˌɪntɪˈlɛkʃən) NOUN 1 mental activity; thought. 2 an idea or thought.

intellectual (ˌɪntɪˈlɛktʃʊəl) ADJECTIVE 1 of or relating to the intellect, as opposed to the emotions. 2 appealing to or characteristic of people with a developed intellect: *intellectual literature.* 3 expressing or enjoying mental activity. ◆ NOUN 4 a person who enjoys mental activity and has highly developed tastes in art, literature, etc. 5 a person who uses or works with his intellect. 6 a highly intelligent person.
▸**,intel,lectu'ality** *or* **,intel'lectualness** NOUN
▸**,intel'lectually** ADVERB

intellectualism (ˌɪntɪˈlɛktʃʊəˌlɪzəm) NOUN 1 development and exercise of the intellect. 2 the placing of excessive value on the intellect, esp with disregard for the emotions. 3 *Philosophy* **a** the doctrine that reason is the ultimate criterion of knowledge. **b** the doctrine that deliberate action is consequent on a process of conscious or subconscious reasoning.
▸**,intel'lectualist** NOUN, ADJECTIVE ▸**,intel,lectual'istic** ADJECTIVE ▸**,intel,lectual'istically** ADVERB

intellectualize *or* **intellectualise** (ˌɪntɪˈlɛktʃʊəˌlaɪz) VERB 1 to make or become intellectual. 2 (*tr*) to treat or consider in an intellectual way; rationalize.
▸**,intel,lectuali'zation** *or* **,intel,lectuali'sation** NOUN
▸**,intel'lectual,izer** *or* **,intel'lectual,iser** NOUN

intellectual property NOUN an intangible asset, such as a copyright or patent.

intelligence (ɪnˈtɛlɪdʒəns) NOUN 1 the capacity for understanding; ability to perceive and comprehend meaning. 2 good mental capacity: *a person of intelligence.* 3 *Old-fashioned* news; information. 4 military information about enemies, spies, etc. 5 a group or department that gathers or deals with such information. 6 (*often capital*) an intelligent being, esp one that is not embodied. 7 (*modifier*) of or relating to intelligence: *an intelligence network.*
▷HISTORY C14: from Latin *intellegentia,* from *intellegere* to discern, comprehend, literally: choose between, from INTER- + *legere* to choose
▸**in,telli'gential** ADJECTIVE

intelligence quotient NOUN a measure of the intelligence of an individual derived from results obtained from specially designed tests. The quotient is traditionally derived by dividing an individual's mental age by his chronological age and multiplying the result by 100. Abbreviation: **IQ**.

intelligencer (ɪnˈtɛlɪdʒənsə) NOUN *Archaic* an informant or spy.

intelligence test NOUN any of a number of tests designed to measure a person's mental skills. See also **Binet-Simon scale.**

intelligent (ɪnˈtɛlɪdʒənt) ADJECTIVE 1 having or indicating intelligence. 2 having high intelligence; clever. 3 indicating high intelligence; perceptive: *an intelligent guess.* 4 guided by reason; rational. 5 (of computerized functions) able to modify action in the light of ongoing events. 6 (*postpositive; foll by of*) *Archaic* having knowledge or information: *they were intelligent of his whereabouts.*
▸**in'telligently** ADVERB

intelligent card NOUN another name for **smart card.**

intelligent knowledge-based system NOUN a computer system in which the properties of a database and an expert system are combined to enable the system to store and process data and make deductions from stored data. Abbreviation: **IKBS.**

intelligentsia (ɪnˌtɛlɪˈdʒɛntsɪə) NOUN (usually preceded by *the*) the educated or intellectual people in a society or community.
▷HISTORY C20: from Russian *intelligentsiya,* from Latin *intellegentia* INTELLIGENCE

intelligent terminal NOUN a computer operating terminal that can carry out some data processing, as well as sending data to and receiving it from a central processor.

intelligible (ɪnˈtɛlɪdʒəbᵊl) ADJECTIVE 1 able to be understood; comprehensible. 2 *Philosophy* **a** capable of being apprehended by the mind or intellect alone. **b** (in metaphysical systems such as those of Plato or Kant) denoting that metaphysical realm which is accessible to the intellect as opposed to the world of mere phenomena accessible to the senses.
▷HISTORY C14: from Latin *intellegibilis;* see INTELLECT
▸**in,telligi'bility** *or* **in'telligibleness** NOUN ▸**in'telligibly** ADVERB

Intelsat (ˈɪntɛlˌsæt) NOUN any of the series of communications satellites operated by the International Telecommunications Satellite Consortium.

intemerate (ɪnˈtɛmərɪt) ADJECTIVE *Rare* not defiled; pure; unsullied.
▷HISTORY C15: from Latin *intemerātus* undefiled, pure, from IN-[1] + *temerāre* to darken, violate, from *temere* rashly
▸**in'temerately** ADVERB ▸**in'temerateness** NOUN

intemperate (ɪnˈtɛmpərɪt, -prɪt) ADJECTIVE 1 consuming alcoholic drink habitually or to excess. 2 indulging bodily appetites to excess; immoderate. 3 unrestrained: *intemperate rage.* 4 extreme or severe: *an intemperate climate.*
▸**in'temperance** *or* **in'temperateness** NOUN
▸**in'temperately** ADVERB

intend (ɪnˈtɛnd) VERB 1 (*may take a clause as object*) to propose or plan (something or to do something); have in mind; mean. 2 (*tr; often foll by for*) to design or destine (for a certain purpose, person, etc.): *that shot was intended for the President.* 3 (*tr*) to mean to express or indicate: *what do his words intend?* 4 (*intr*) to have a purpose as specified; mean: *he intends well.* 5 (*tr*) *Archaic* to direct or turn (the attention, eyes, etc.).
▷HISTORY C14: from Latin *intendere* to stretch forth, give one's attention to, from *tendere* to stretch
▸**in'tender** NOUN

intendance (ɪnˈtɛndəns) NOUN 1 any of various public departments, esp in France. 2 a less common word for **superintendence.**

intendancy (ɪnˈtɛndənsɪ) NOUN 1 the position or work of an intendant. 2 intendants collectively. 3 *History* the district or area administered by an intendant.

intendant (ɪnˈtɛndənt) NOUN 1 *History* a provincial or colonial official of France, Spain, or Portugal. 2 a senior administrator in some countries, esp in Latin America. 3 a superintendent or manager.

intended (ɪnˈtɛndɪd) ADJECTIVE 1 planned or future. ◆ NOUN 2 *Informal* a person whom one is to marry; fiancé or fiancée.

intendment (ɪnˈtɛndmənt) NOUN 1 the meaning of something as fixed or understood by the law. 2 *Obsolete* intention, design, or purpose.

intenerate (ɪnˈtɛnəˌreɪt) VERB (*tr*) *Rare* to soften or make tender.
▷HISTORY C16: from IN-[2] + Latin *tener* delicate, TENDER[1]
▸**in,tener'ation** NOUN

intense (ɪnˈtɛns) ADJECTIVE 1 of extreme force, strength, degree, or amount: *intense heat.* 2 characterized by deep or forceful feelings: *an intense person.*
▷HISTORY C14: from Latin *intensus* stretched, from *intendere* to stretch out; see INTEND
▸**in'tensely** ADVERB ▸**in'tenseness** NOUN

> **Language note** *Intense* is sometimes wrongly used where *intensive* is meant: *the land is under intensive* (not *intense*) *cultivation. Intensely* is sometimes wrongly used where *intently* is meant: *he listened intently* (not *intensely*).

intensifier (ɪnˈtɛnsɪˌfaɪə) NOUN 1 a person or thing that intensifies. 2 a word, esp an adjective or adverb, that has little semantic content of its own but that serves to intensify the meaning of the word or phrase that it modifies: *awfully* and *up* are intensifiers in the phrases *awfully sorry* and *cluttered up.* 3 a substance, esp one containing silver or uranium, used to increase the density of a photographic film or plate. Compare **reducer** (sense 1).

intensify (ɪnˈtɛnsɪˌfaɪ) VERB **-fies, -fying, -fied.** 1 to make or become intense or more intense. 2 (*tr*) to increase the density of (a photographic film or plate).
▸**in,tensifi'cation** NOUN

intension (ɪnˈtɛnʃən) NOUN 1 *Logic* **a** the set of characteristics or properties by which the referent or referents of a given word are determined: thus, the intension of *marsupial* is the set containing the characteristics *suckling its young* and *having a pouch.* Compare **extension** (sense 11a). **b** See **subjective intension.** 2 a rare word for **intensity, determination,** or **intensification.**

intensional (ɪnˈtɛnʃənᵊl) ADJECTIVE *Logic* (of a predicate) incapable of explanation solely in terms of the set of objects to which it is applicable; requiring explanation in terms of meaning or understanding. Compare **extensional.** See also **opaque context, Electra paradox.**
▸**in'tensionally** ADVERB

intensional object NOUN *Logic, philosophy* the object of a propositional attitude that may or may not exist, as in *Robert is dreaming of the pot of gold at the end of the rainbow.* This must be an intensional (or opaque) context, for otherwise, since there is no pot of gold, Robert would be dreaming of nothing.

intensity (ɪnˈtɛnsɪtɪ) NOUN, *plural* **-ties.** 1 the state or quality of being intense. 2 extreme force, degree, or amount. 3 *Physics* **a** a measure of field strength or of the energy transmitted by radiation. See **radiant intensity, luminous intensity. b** (of sound in a specified direction) the average rate of flow of sound energy, usually in watts, for one period through unit area at right angles to the specified direction. Symbol: *I.* 4 Also called: **earthquake intensity.** *Geology* a measure of the size of an earthquake based on observation of the effects of the shock at the earth's surface. Specified on the Mercalli scale. See **Mercalli scale, Richter scale.**

intensive (ɪnˈtɛnsɪv) ADJECTIVE 1 involving the maximum use of land, time, or some other resource: *intensive agriculture; an intensive course.* 2 (*usually in combination*) using one factor of production proportionately more than others, as specified: *capital-intensive; labour-intensive.* 3 *Agriculture* involving or farmed using large amounts of capital or labour to increase production from a particular area. Compare **extensive** (sense 3). 4 denoting or relating to a grammatical intensifier. 5 denoting or belonging to a class of pronouns used to emphasize a noun or personal pronoun, such as *himself* in the sentence *John himself did it.* In English, intensive pronouns are identical in form with reflexive pronouns. 6 of or relating to intension. 7 *Physics* of or relating to a local property, measurement, etc., that is independent of the extent of the system. Compare **extensive** (sense 4). ◆ NOUN 8 an intensifier or intensive pronoun or grammatical construction.
▸**in'tensively** ADVERB ▸**in'tensiveness** NOUN

intensive care NOUN extensive and continuous care and treatment provided for an acutely ill patient, usually in a specially designated section (**intensive care unit**) of a hospital.

intent (ɪnˈtɛnt) NOUN 1 something that is intended; aim; purpose; design. 2 the act of

intending. [3] *Law* the will or purpose with which one does an act. [4] implicit meaning; connotation. [5] **to all intents and purposes.** for all practical purposes; virtually. ◆ ADJECTIVE [6] firmly fixed; determined; concentrated: *an intent look.* [7] (*postpositive;* usually foll by *on* or *upon*) having the fixed intention (of); directing one's mind or energy (to): *intent on committing a crime.*
▷HISTORY C13 (in the sense: intention): from Late Latin *intentus* aim, intent, from Latin: a stretching out; see INTEND
▸**in'tently** ADVERB ▸**in'tentness** NOUN

intention (ɪn'tɛnʃən) NOUN [1] a purpose or goal; aim: *it is his intention to reform.* [2] *Law* the resolve or design with which a person does or refrains from doing an act, a necessary ingredient of certain offences. [3] *Med* a natural healing process, as by **first intention**, in which the edges of a wound cling together with no tissue between, or by **second intention**, in which the wound edges adhere with granulation tissue. [4] (*usually plural*) design or purpose with respect to a proposal of marriage (esp in the phrase **honourable intentions**). [5] an archaic word for **meaning** or **intentness.**

intentional (ɪn'tɛnʃənᵊl) ADJECTIVE [1] performed by or expressing intention; deliberate. [2] of or relating to intention or purpose. [3] *Philosophy* **a** of or relating to the capacity of the mind to refer to different kinds of objects. **b** (of an object) existing only as the object of some mental attitude rather than in reality, as *a unicorn* in *she hopes to meet a unicorn.* See also **intensional.**
▸**in,tention'ality** NOUN ▸**in'tentionally** ADVERB

inter (ɪn'tɜː) VERB **-ters, -terring, -terred.** (*tr*) to place (a body) in the earth; bury, esp with funeral rites.
▷HISTORY C14: from Old French *enterrer,* from Latin IN-[2] + *terra* earth

inter. ABBREVIATION FOR intermediate.

inter- PREFIX [1] between or among: *international.* [2] together, mutually, or reciprocally: *interdependent; interchange.*
▷HISTORY from Latin

Interact ('ɪntər,ækt) NOUN *Canadian* a system of electronic bank payments or withdrawals.

interact (,ɪntər'ækt) VERB (*intr*) to act on or in close relation with each other.

interaction (,ɪntər'ækʃən) NOUN [1] a mutual or reciprocal action or influence. [2] *Physics* the transfer of energy between elementary particles, between a particle and a field, or between fields. See **strong interaction, electromagnetic interaction, fundamental interaction, gravitational interaction, weak interaction, electroweak interaction.**
▸**,inter'actional** ADJECTIVE

interactionism (,ɪntər'ækʃə,nɪzəm) NOUN *Philosophy* the dualistic doctrine that holds that mind and body have a causal effect upon one another, as when pricking one's finger (physical) causes pain (mental), or an embarrassing memory (mental) causes one to blush (physical). Compare **parallelism** (sense 3).

interactive (,ɪntər'æktɪv) ADJECTIVE [1] allowing or relating to continuous two-way transfer of information between a user and the central point of a communication system, such as a computer or television. [2] (of two or more persons, forces, etc.) acting upon or in close relation with each other; interacting.
▸**,interac'tivity** NOUN

interactive engineering NOUN another name for **concurrent engineering.**

interactive video NOUN a computer-optical disk system that displays still or moving video images as determined by computer program and user needs.

inter alia *Latin* ('ɪntər 'eɪlɪə) ADVERB among other things.

inter alios *Latin* ('ɪntər 'eɪlɪəʊs) ADVERB among other people.

interatomic (,ɪntərə'tɒmɪk) ADJECTIVE existing or occurring between or among atoms. Compare **intra-atomic.**

interbank (ɪntə'bæŋk) ADJECTIVE conducted between or involving two or more banks.

interbedded (,ɪntə'bɛdɪd) ADJECTIVE *Geology* occurring between beds, esp (of lava flows or sills) occurring between strata of a different origin or character.

interbrain ('ɪntə,breɪn) NOUN *Anatomy* a nontechnical word for **diencephalon.**

interbreed (,ɪntə'briːd) VERB **-breeds, -breeding, -bred.** [1] (*intr*) to breed within a single family or strain so as to produce particular characteristics in the offspring. [2] another term for **crossbreed** (sense 1).

interbroker dealer (,ɪntə'brəʊkə) NOUN *Stock Exchange* a specialist who matches the needs of different market makers and facilitates dealings between them.

intercalary (ɪn'tɜːkələrɪ) ADJECTIVE [1] (of a day, month, etc.) inserted in the calendar. [2] (of a particular year) having one or more days inserted. [3] inserted, introduced, or interpolated. [4] *Botany* growing between the upper branches and the lower branches or bracts on a stem.
▷HISTORY C17: from Latin *intercalārius;* see INTERCALATE
▸**in'tercalarily** ADVERB

intercalate (ɪn'tɜːkə,leɪt) VERB (*tr*) [1] to insert (one or more days) into the calendar. [2] to interpolate or insert.
▷HISTORY C17: from Latin *intercalāre* to insert, proclaim that a day has been inserted, from INTER- + *calāre* to proclaim
▸**in,terca'lation** NOUN ▸**in'tercalative** ADJECTIVE

intercede (,ɪntə'siːd) VERB (*intr*) [1] (often foll by *in*) to come between parties or act as mediator or advocate: *to intercede in the strike.* [2] *Roman history* (of a tribune or other magistrate) to interpose a veto.
▷HISTORY C16: from Latin *intercēdere* to intervene, from INTER- + *cēdere* to move
▸**,inter'ceder** NOUN

intercellular (,ɪntə'sɛljʊlə) ADJECTIVE *Biology* between or among cells: *intercellular fluid.*

intercensal (,ɪntə'sɛnsəl) ADJECTIVE (of population figures, etc.) estimated at a time between official censuses.
▷HISTORY C19: from INTER- + *censal,* irregularly formed from CENSUS

intercept VERB (,ɪntə'sɛpt) (*tr*) [1] to stop, deflect, or seize on the way from one place to another; prevent from arriving or proceeding. [2] *Sport* to seize or cut off (a pass) on its way from one opponent to another. [3] *Maths* to cut off, mark off, or bound (some part of a line, curve, plane, or surface). ◆ NOUN ('ɪntə,sɛpt) [4] *Maths* **a** a point at which two figures intersect. **b** the distance from the origin to the point at which a line, curve, or surface cuts a coordinate axis. **c** an intercepted segment. [5] *Sport, US and Canadian* the act of intercepting an opponent's pass.
▷HISTORY C16: from Latin *intercipere* to seize before arrival, from INTER- + *capere* to take
▸**,inter'ception** NOUN ▸**,inter'ceptive** ADJECTIVE

interceptor *or* **intercepter** (,ɪntə'sɛptə) NOUN [1] a person or thing that intercepts. [2] a fast highly manoeuvrable fighter aircraft used to intercept enemy aircraft.

intercession (,ɪntə'sɛʃən) NOUN [1] the act or an instance of interceding. [2] the act of interceding or offering petitionary prayer to God on behalf of others. [3] such petitionary prayer. [4] *Roman history* the interposing of a veto by a tribune or other magistrate.
▷HISTORY C16: from Latin *intercessio;* see INTERCEDE
▸**,inter'cessional** *or* **,inter'cessory** ADJECTIVE
▸**,inter'cessor** NOUN ▸**,interces'sorial** ADJECTIVE

interchange VERB (,ɪntə'tʃeɪndʒ) [1] to change places or cause to change places; alternate; exchange; switch. ◆ NOUN ('ɪntə,tʃeɪndʒ) [2] the act of interchanging; exchange or alternation. [3] a motorway junction of interconnecting roads and bridges designed to prevent streams of traffic crossing one another.
▸**,inter'changeable** ADJECTIVE ▸**,inter,changea'bility** *or* **,inter'changeableness** NOUN ▸**,inter'changeably** ADVERB

Intercity (,ɪntə'sɪtɪ) ADJECTIVE *Trademark* (in Britain) denoting a fast train or passenger rail service, esp between main towns.

interclavicle (,ɪntə'klævɪkᵊl) NOUN a membrane bone between and beneath the clavicles, present in some fossil amphibians, all reptiles except snakes, and monotremes.
▸**interclavicular** (,ɪntəklə'vɪkjʊlə) ADJECTIVE

interclub (ɪntə'klʌb) ADJECTIVE of, relating to, or conducted between two or more clubs.

intercollegiate (,ɪntəkə'liːdʒɪɪt) ADJECTIVE of, relating to, or conducted between two or more colleges or universities.

intercolumniation (,ɪntəkə,lʌmnɪ'eɪʃən) NOUN *Architect* [1] the horizontal distance between two adjacent columns. [2] the system of spacing for a set of columns.
▷HISTORY C17: from Latin *intercolumnium* space between two columns
▸**,interco'lumnar** ADJECTIVE

intercom ('ɪntə,kɒm) NOUN *Informal* an internal telephone system for communicating within a building, an aircraft, etc.
▷HISTORY C20: short for *intercommunication*

intercommunicate (,ɪntəkə'mjuːnɪ,keɪt) VERB (*intr*) [1] to communicate mutually. [2] to interconnect, as two rooms.
▸**,intercom'municable** ADJECTIVE ▸**,intercom,munica'bility** NOUN ▸**,intercom,muni'cation** NOUN
▸**,intercom'municative** ADJECTIVE ▸**,intercom'muni,cator** NOUN

intercommunion (,ɪntəkə'mjuːnjən) NOUN association between Churches, involving esp mutual reception of Holy Communion.

intercompany (,ɪntə'kʌmpənɪ) ADJECTIVE conducted between or involving two or more companies.

interconnect (,ɪntəkə'nɛkt) VERB (*intr;* often foll by *with*) [1] to relate well: *people I really interconnect with.* [2] to be meaningfully or complexly related or joined: *these three strands of thought interconnect.* ◆ NOUN [3] **a** a device that connects things. **b** (*as modifier*): *interconnect cable.*
▸**,intercon'nection** NOUN

intercontinental (,ɪntə,kɒntɪ'nɛntᵊl) ADJECTIVE relating to travel, commerce, relations, etc., between continents.

intercontinental ballistic missile NOUN a missile that follows a ballistic trajectory and has the range to carry a nuclear bomb over 5500 km. Abbreviation: **ICBM.**

interconversion (,ɪntəkən'vɜːʃən) NOUN a process in which two things are each converted into the other, often as the result of chemical or physical activity.

intercooler (,ɪntə'kuːlə) NOUN a heat exchanger used in a supercharger or turbocharger.

intercostal (,ɪntə'kɒstᵊl) ADJECTIVE *Anatomy* between the ribs: *intercostal muscles.*
▷HISTORY C16: via New Latin from Latin INTER- + *costa* rib

intercounty (,ɪntə'kaʊntɪ) ADJECTIVE conducted between or involving two or more counties: *intercounty football.*

intercourse ('ɪntə,kɔːs) NOUN [1] communication or exchange between individuals; mutual dealings. [2] See **sexual intercourse.**
▷HISTORY C15: from Medieval Latin *intercursus* business, from Latin *intercurrere* to run between, from *currere* to run

intercrop (,ɪntə'krɒp) NOUN [1] a crop grown between the rows of another crop. ◆ VERB **-crops, -cropping, -cropped.** [2] to grow (one crop) between the rows of (another).

intercross (,ɪntə'krɒs) VERB, NOUN another word for **crossbreed.**

intercurrent (,ɪntə'kʌrənt) ADJECTIVE [1] occurring during or in between; intervening. [2] *Pathol* (of a disease) occurring during the course of another disease.
▸**,inter'currence** NOUN ▸**,inter'currently** ADVERB

intercut (,ɪntə'kʌt) VERB **-cuts, -cutting, -cut.** *Films* another word for **crosscut.**

interdental (,ɪntə'dɛntᵊl) ADJECTIVE [1] situated between teeth. [2] *Phonetics* (of a consonant) pronounced with the tip of the tongue lying between the upper and lower front teeth, as for the *th* sounds in English *thin* and *then.*
▸**,inter'dentally** ADVERB

interdepartmental (,ɪntə,diːpɑːt'mɛntᵊl) ADJECTIVE of, relating to, or conducted between two or more departments.

interdependence (,ɪntədɪ'pɛndəns) NOUN

dependence between two or more people, groups, or things: *the interdependence of economies.*
▸ ˌinterdeˈpendency NOUN

interdependent (ˌɪntədɪˈpɛndənt) ADJECTIVE relating to two or more people or things dependent on each other.

interdict NOUN (ˈɪntəˌdɪkt, -ˌdaɪt) 1 *RC Church* the exclusion of a person or all persons in a particular place from certain sacraments and other benefits, although not from communion. 2 *Civil law* any order made by a court or official prohibiting an act. 3 *Scots law* an order having the effect of an injunction. 4 *Roman history* **a** an order of a praetor commanding or forbidding an act. **b** the procedure by which this order was sought. ◆ VERB (ˌɪntəˈdɪkt, -ˈdaɪt) *(tr)* 5 to place under legal or ecclesiastical sanction; prohibit; forbid. 6 *Military* to destroy (an enemy's lines of communication) by firepower.
▷HISTORY C13: from Latin *interdictum* prohibition, from *interdīcere* to forbid, from INTER- + *dīcere* to say
▸ ˌinterˈdictive *or* ˌinterˈdictory ADJECTIVE ▸ ˌinterˈdictively ADVERB ▸ ˌinterˈdictor NOUN

interdiction (ˌɪntəˈdɪkʃən) NOUN 1 the act of interdicting or state of being interdicted. 2 an interdict.

interdict list NOUN another name for **Indian list**.

interdigitate (ˌɪntəˈdɪdʒɪˌteɪt) VERB *(intr)* to interlock like the fingers of clasped hands.
▷HISTORY C19: from INTER- + Latin *digitus* (see DIGIT) + -ATE[1]

interdisciplinary (ˌɪntəˈdɪsɪˌplɪnərɪ) ADJECTIVE involving two or more academic disciplines.

interest (ˈɪntrɪst, -tərɪst) NOUN 1 the sense of curiosity about or concern with something or someone: *an interest in butterflies.* 2 the power of stimulating such a sense: *to have great interest.* 3 the quality of such stimulation. 4 something in which one is interested; a hobby or pursuit. 5 *(often plural)* benefit; advantage: *in one's own interest.* 6 *(often plural)* **a** a right, share, or claim, esp in a business or property. **b** the business, property, etc., in which a person has such concern. 7 **a** a charge for the use of credit or borrowed money. **b** such a charge expressed as a percentage per time unit of the sum borrowed or used. 8 *(often plural)* a section of a community, etc., whose members have common aims: *we must not offend the landed interest.* 9 **declare an interest.** to make known one's connection, esp a prejudicial connection, with an affair. ◆ VERB *(tr)* 10 to arouse or excite the curiosity or concern of. 11 to cause to become involved in something; concern.
▷HISTORY C15: from Latin: it concerns, from *interesse;* from INTER- + *esse* to be

interested (ˈɪntrɪstɪd, -tərɪs-) ADJECTIVE 1 showing or having interest. 2 *(usually prenominal)* personally involved or implicated: *the interested parties met to discuss the business.*
▸ ˈinterestedly ADVERB ▸ ˈinterestedness NOUN

interesting (ˈɪntrɪstɪŋ, -tərɪs-) ADJECTIVE inspiring interest; absorbing.
▸ ˈinterestingly ADVERB ▸ ˈinterestingness NOUN

interest-rate futures PLURAL NOUN financial futures based on projected movements of interest rates.

interface NOUN (ˈɪntəˌfeɪs) 1 *Chem* a surface that forms the boundary between two bodies, liquids, or chemical phases. 2 a common point or boundary between two things, subjects, etc. 3 an electrical circuit linking one device, esp a computer, with another. ◆ VERB (ˌɪntəˈfeɪs) 4 *(tr)* to design or adapt the input and output configurations of (two electronic devices) so that they may work together compatibly. 5 to be or become an interface (with). 6 to be or become interactive (with).
▸ interfacial (ˌɪntəˈfeɪʃəl) ADJECTIVE ▸ ˌinterˈfacially ADVERB

interfacing (ˈɪntəˌfeɪsɪŋ) NOUN 1 a piece of fabric sewn beneath the facing of a garment, usually at the inside of the neck, armholes, etc., to give shape and firmness. 2 another name for **interlining**.

interfascicular (ˌɪntəfəˈsɪkjʊlə) ADJECTIVE *Botany* between the vascular bundles of the stem: *interfascicular cambium.*

interfere (ˌɪntəˈfɪə) VERB *(intr)* 1 (often foll by *in*) to interpose, esp meddlesomely or unwarrantedly; intervene. 2 (often foll by *with*) to come between or in opposition; hinder; obstruct. 3 (foll by *with*) *Euphemistic* to assault sexually. 4 to strike one against the other, as a horse's legs. 5 *Physics* to cause or produce interference.
▷HISTORY C16: from Old French *s'entreferir* to collide, from *entre-* INTER- + *ferir* to strike, from Latin *ferīre*
▸ ˌinterˈferer NOUN ▸ ˌinterˈfering ADJECTIVE ▸ ˌinterˈferingly ADVERB

interference (ˌɪntəˈfɪərəns) NOUN 1 the act or an instance of interfering. 2 *Physics* the process in which two or more coherent waves combine to form a resultant wave in which the displacement at any point is the vector sum of the displacements of the individual waves. If the individual waves converge the resultant is a system of fringes. Two waves of equal or nearly equal intensity moving in opposite directions combine to form a standing wave. 3 Also called: **radio interference.** any undesired signal that tends to interfere with the reception of radio waves. 4 *Aeronautics* the effect on the flow pattern around a body of objects in the vicinity.
▸ interferential (ˌɪntəfəˈrɛnʃəl) ADJECTIVE

interference fit NOUN *Engineering* a match between the size and shape of two parts, such that force is required for assembly as one part is slightly larger than the other.

interferometer (ˌɪntəfəˈrɒmɪtə) NOUN 1 *Physics* any acoustic, optical, or microwave instrument that uses interference patterns or fringes to make accurate measurements of wavelength, wave velocity, distance, etc. 2 *Astronomy* a radio or optical array consisting of two or more telescopes separated by a known distance and connected so that the radiation from a source in space undergoes interference, enabling the source to be imaged or the position of the source to be accurately determined.
▸ interferometric (ˌɪntəˌfɛrəˈmetrɪk) ADJECTIVE ▸ ˌinterˌferoˈmetrically ADVERB ▸ ˌinterferˈometry NOUN

interferon (ˌɪntəˈfɪərɒn) NOUN *Biochem* any of a family of proteins made by cells in response to virus infection that prevent the growth of the virus. Some interferons can prevent cell growth and have been tested for use in cancer therapy.
▷HISTORY C20: from INTERFERE + -ON

interfertile (ˌɪntəˈfɜːtaɪl) ADJECTIVE (of plants and animals) able to interbreed.
▸ ˌinterferˈtility NOUN

interfile (ˌɪntəˈfaɪl) VERB *(tr)* 1 to place (one or more items) among other items in a file or arrangement. 2 to combine (two or more sets of items) in one file or arrangement.

interflow (ˌɪntəˈfləʊ) VERB *(intr)* to flow together; merge.

interfluent (ɪnˈtɜːflʊənt) ADJECTIVE flowing together; merging.
▷HISTORY C17: from Latin *interfluere,* from INTER- + *fluere* to flow

interfluve (ˈɪntəˌfluːv) NOUN a ridge or area of land dividing two river valleys.
▷HISTORY C20: back formation from *interfluvial,* from INTER- + Latin *fluvius* river
▸ ˌinterˈfluvial ADJECTIVE

interfuse (ˌɪntəˈfjuːz) VERB 1 to diffuse or mix throughout or become so diffused or mixed; intermingle. 2 to blend or fuse or become blended or fused.
▸ ˌinterˈfusion NOUN

intergalactic (ˌɪntəgəˈlæktɪk) ADJECTIVE of, relating to, or existing between two or more galaxies: *the dark clouds of intergalactic space.*

intergenerational mobility (ˌɪntəˌdʒɛnəˈreɪʃənəl) NOUN *Sociol* movement within or between social classes and occupations, the change occurring from one generation to the next. Compare **intragenerational mobility**.

interglacial (ˌɪntəˈgleɪsɪəl, -ʃəl) ADJECTIVE 1 occurring or formed between periods of glacial action. ◆ NOUN 2 a period of comparatively warm climate between two glaciations, esp of the Pleistocene epoch.

intergovernmental (ˌɪntəˌgʌvənˈmɛntəl) ADJECTIVE conducted between or involving two or more governments: *an intergovernmental conference.*

intergrade VERB (ˌɪntəˈgreɪd) 1 *(intr)* (esp of biological species, etc.) to merge one into another. ◆ NOUN (ˈɪntəˌgreɪd) 2 an intermediate stage or form.
▸ ˌintergraˈdation NOUN ▸ ˌintergraˈdational ADJECTIVE ▸ ˌinterˈgradient ADJECTIVE

interim (ˈɪntərɪm) ADJECTIVE 1 *(prenominal)* temporary, provisional, or intervening: *interim measures to deal with the emergency.* ◆ NOUN 2 (usually preceded by *the*) the intervening time; the meantime (esp in the phrase **in the interim**). ◆ ADVERB 3 *Rare* meantime.
▷HISTORY C16: from Latin: meanwhile

Interim (ˈɪntərɪm) NOUN any of three provisional arrangements made during the Reformation by the German emperor and Diet to regulate religious differences between Roman Catholics and Protestants.

Interim Standard Atmosphere NOUN an agreed theoretical description of the atmosphere for altitudes between 50 and 80 km, pending refinement by further measurements. See **International Standard Atmosphere.**

interior (ɪnˈtɪərɪə) NOUN 1 a part, surface, or region that is inside or on the inside: *the interior of Africa.* 2 inner character or nature. 3 a film or scene shot inside a building, studio, etc. 4 a picture of the inside of a room or building, as in a painting or stage design. 5 the inside of a building or room, with respect to design and decoration. ◆ ADJECTIVE 6 of, situated on, or suitable for the inside; inner. 7 coming or acting from within; internal. 8 of or involving a nation's domestic affairs; internal. 9 (esp of one's spiritual or mental life) secret or private; not observable.
▷HISTORY C15: from Latin (adj), comparative of *inter* within
▸ inˈteriorly ADVERB

Interior (ɪnˈtɪərɪə) NOUN *(in titles;* usually preceded by *the)* the domestic or internal affairs of any of certain countries: *Department of the Interior.*

interior angle NOUN 1 an angle of a polygon contained between two adjacent sides. 2 any of the four angles made by a transversal that lie inside the region between the two intersected lines.

interior decoration NOUN 1 the colours, furniture, etc., of the interior of a house, etc. 2 Also called: **interior design.** the art or business of an interior decorator.

interior decorator NOUN 1 Also called: **interior designer.** a person whose profession is the planning of the decoration and furnishings of the interior of houses, shops, etc. 2 a person whose profession is the painting and wallpapering of houses.

interiorize *or* **interiorise** (ɪnˈtɪərɪəˌraɪz) VERB *(tr)* another word for **internalize**.

interior monologue NOUN a literary attempt to present the mental processes of a character before they are formed into regular patterns of speech or logical sequence. See also **stream of consciousness.**

interior-sprung ADJECTIVE (esp of a mattress) containing springs.

interj. ABBREVIATION FOR interjection.

interjacent (ˌɪntəˈdʒeɪsənt) ADJECTIVE located in between; intervening.
▷HISTORY C16: from Latin *interjacent-,* from *interjacēre,* from INTER- + *jacēre* to lie

interject (ˌɪntəˈdʒɛkt) VERB *(tr)* 1 to interpose abruptly or sharply; interrupt with; throw in: *she interjected clever remarks.* 2 *Archaic* to come between; interpose.
▷HISTORY C16: from Latin *interjicere* to place between, from *jacere* to throw
▸ ˌinterˈjector NOUN

interjection (ˌɪntəˈdʒɛkʃən) NOUN 1 a word or remark expressing emotion; exclamation. 2 the act of interjecting. 3 a word or phrase that is characteristically used in syntactic isolation and that usually expresses sudden emotion; expletive. Abbreviation: **interj.**
▸ ˌinterˈjectional, ˌinterˈjectory, *or* ˌinterˈjectural ADJECTIVE ▸ ˌinterˈjectionally ADVERB

interlace (ˌɪntəˈleɪs) VERB 1 to join together (patterns, fingers, etc.) by crossing, as if woven; intertwine. 2 *(tr)* to mingle or blend in an intricate way. 3 *(tr;* usually foll by *with)* to change the pattern of; diversify; intersperse: *to interlace a speech with humour.*

▸**interlacedly** (ˌɪntəˈleɪsɪdlɪ) ADVERB ▸ˌ**interˈlacement** NOUN

interlaced scanning NOUN a system of scanning a television picture, first along the even-numbered lines, then along the odd-numbered lines, in one complete scan.

Interlaken (ˈɪntəˌlɑːkən) NOUN a town and resort in central Switzerland, situated between Lakes Brienz and Thun on the River Aar. Pop.: 4900 (latest est.).

interlaminate (ˌɪntəˈlæmɪˌneɪt) VERB (*tr*) to place, stick, or insert (a sheet, layer, etc.) between (other layers).
▸ˌ**interˈlaminar** ADJECTIVE ▸ˌ**interˌlamiˈnation** NOUN

interlap (ˌɪntəˈlæp) VERB **-laps, -lapping, -lapped.** a less common word for **overlap.**

interlard (ˌɪntəˈlɑːd) VERB (*tr*) [1] to scatter thickly in or between; intersperse: *to interlard one's writing with foreign phrases.* [2] to occur frequently in; be scattered in or through: *foreign phrases interlard his writings.*

interlay VERB (ˌɪntəˈleɪ) **-lays, -laying, -laid** (-ˈleɪd). [1] (*tr*) to insert (layers) between; interpose: *to interlay gold among the silver; to interlay the silver with gold.* ◆ NOUN (ˈɪntəˌleɪ) [2] material, such as paper, placed between a printing plate and its base, either all over in order to bring it up to type height, or in places in order to achieve the correct printing pressure all over the plate.

interleaf (ˈɪntəˌliːf) NOUN, *plural* **-leaves.** a blank leaf inserted between the leaves of a book.

interleave (ˌɪntəˈliːv) VERB (*tr*) [1] (often foll by *with*) to intersperse (with), esp alternately, as the illustrations in a book (with protective leaves). [2] to provide (a book) with blank leaves for notes, etc., or to protect illustrations.

interleukin (ˌɪntəˈluːkɪn) NOUN a substance extracted from white blood cells that stimulates their activity against infection and may be used to combat some forms of cancer.

interlibrary loan (ˌɪntəˈlaɪbrərɪ) NOUN [1] a system by which libraries borrow publications from other libraries. [2] **a** an instance of such borrowing. **b** a publication so borrowed.

interline[1] (ˌɪntəˈlaɪn) *or* **interlineate** (ˌɪntəˈlɪnɪˌeɪt) VERB (*tr*) to write or print (matter) between the lines of (a text, book, etc.).
▸ˈ**interˌlining** *or* ˌ**interˌlineˈation** NOUN

interline[2] (ˌɪntəˈlaɪn) VERB (*tr*) to provide (a part of a garment, such as a collar or cuff) with a second lining, esp of stiffened material.
▸ˈ**interˌliner** NOUN

interlinear (ˌɪntəˈlɪnɪə) *or* **interlineal** ADJECTIVE [1] written or printed between lines of text. [2] written or printed with the text in different languages or versions on alternate lines.
▸ˌ**interˈlinearly** *or* ˌ**interˈlineally** ADVERB

interlinear spacing ADVERB, NOUN See **leading**[2].

interlingua (ˌɪntəˈlɪŋgwə) NOUN [1] (*usually capital*) an artificial language based on words common to English and the Romance languages. [2] any artificial language used to represent the meaning of natural languages, as for purposes of machine translation.
▷HISTORY C20: from Italian, from INTER- + *lingua* language

interlining (ˈɪntəˌlaɪnɪŋ) NOUN the material used to interline parts of garments, now often made of reinforced paper.

interlock VERB (ˌɪntəˈlɒk) [1] to join or be joined firmly, as by a mutual interconnection of parts. ◆ NOUN (ˈɪntəˌlɒk) [2] the act of interlocking or the state of being interlocked. [3] a device, esp one operated electromechanically, used in a logic circuit or electrical safety system to prevent an activity being initiated unless preceded by certain events. [4] a closely knitted fabric. ◆ ADJECTIVE (ˈɪntəˌlɒk) [5] (of fabric) closely knitted.
▸ˈ**interˌlocker** NOUN

interlocking directorates PLURAL NOUN boards of directors of different companies having sufficient members in common to ensure that the companies involved are under the same control.

interlocution (ˌɪntəlɒˈkjuːʃən) NOUN conversation, discussion, or dialogue.

interlocutor (ˌɪntəˈlɒkjʊtə) NOUN [1] a person who takes part in a conversation. [2] Also called: **middleman.** the man in the centre of a troupe of minstrels who engages the others in talk or acts as announcer. [3] *Scots Law* a decree by a judge.
▸ˌ**interˈlocutress**, ˌ**interˈlocutrice**, *or* ˌ**interˈlocutrix** FEMININE NOUN

interlocutory (ˌɪntəˈlɒkjʊtərɪ, -trɪ) ADJECTIVE [1] *Law* pronounced during the course of proceedings; provisional: *an interlocutory injunction.* [2] interposed, as into a conversation, narrative, etc. [3] of, relating to, or characteristic of dialogue.
▸ˌ**interˈlocutorily** ADVERB

interloper (ˈɪntəˌləʊpə) NOUN [1] an intruder. [2] a person who introduces himself into professional or social circles where he does not belong. [3] a person who interferes in matters that are not his concern. [4] a person who trades unlawfully.
▷HISTORY C17: from INTER- + *loper*, from Middle Dutch *loopen* to leap

interlude (ˈɪntəˌluːd) NOUN [1] a period of time or different activity between longer periods, processes, or events; episode or interval. [2] *Theatre* a short dramatic piece played separately or as part of a longer entertainment, common in 16th-century England. [3] a brief piece of music, dance, etc., given between the sections of another performance.
▷HISTORY C14: from Medieval Latin *interlūdium,* from Latin INTER- + *lūdus* play

interlunation (ˌɪntəluˈneɪʃən) NOUN the period between the old and new moons during which the moon is invisible. See **new moon.**
▸ˌ**interˈlunar** ADJECTIVE

intermarry (ˌɪntəˈmærɪ) VERB **-ries, -rying, -ried.** (*intr*) [1] (of different groups, races, religions, creeds, etc.) to become connected by marriage. [2] to marry within one's own family, clan, group, etc.
▸ˌ**interˈmarriage** NOUN

intermeddle (ˌɪntəˈmɛdᵊl) VERB (*intr*) *Rare* another word for **meddle.**
▷HISTORY C14 *entremedle,* from Anglo-Norman *entremedler,* from Old French; see INTER- + MEDDLE

intermediary (ˌɪntəˈmiːdɪərɪ) NOUN, *plural* **-aries.** [1] a person who acts as a mediator or agent between parties. [2] something that acts as a medium or means. [3] an intermediate state or period. ◆ ADJECTIVE [4] acting as an intermediary. [5] situated, acting, or coming between; intermediate.

intermediate ADJECTIVE (ˌɪntəˈmiːdɪɪt) [1] occurring or situated between two points, extremes, places, etc.; in between. [2] (of a class, course, etc.) suitable for learners with some degree of skill or competence. [3] *Physics* (of a neutron) having an energy between 100 and 100 000 electronvolts. [4] *Geology* (of such igneous rocks as syenite) containing between 55 and 66 per cent silica. ◆ NOUN (ˌɪntəˈmiːdɪɪt) [5] something intermediate. [6] a substance formed during one of the stages of a chemical process before the desired product is obtained. ◆ VERB (ˌɪntəˈmiːdɪˌeɪt) [7] (*intr*) to act as an intermediary or mediator.
▷HISTORY C17: from Medieval Latin *intermediāre* to intervene, from Latin INTER- + *medius* middle
▸ˌ**interˈmediacy** *or* ˌ**interˈmediateness** NOUN
▸ˌ**interˈmediately** ADVERB ▸ˌ**interˌmediˈation** NOUN
▸ˌ**interˈmediˌator** NOUN

intermediate-acting ADJECTIVE (of a drug) intermediate in its effects between long- and short-acting drugs. Compare **long-acting, short-acting.**

intermediate frequency NOUN *Electronics* the frequency to which the signal carrier frequency is changed in a superheterodyne receiver and at which most of the amplification takes place.

intermediate host NOUN an animal that acts as host to a parasite that has not yet become sexually mature.

intermediate-level waste NOUN radioactive waste material, such as reactor and processing-plant components, that is solidified before being mixed with concrete and stored in steel drums in deep mines or beneath the seabed in concrete chambers. Compare **high-level waste, low-level waste.**

intermediate range ballistic missile NOUN a missile that follows a ballistic trajectory with a medium range, normally of the order of 750–1500 miles. Abbreviation: **IRBM.**

intermediate school NOUN *NZ* a school for children aged between 11 and 13.

intermediate technology NOUN technology which combines sophisticated ideas with cheap and readily available materials, especially for use in developing countries.

intermediate treatment NOUN *Social welfare* a form of child care for young people in trouble that involves neither custody nor punishment and provides opportunities to learn constructive patterns of behaviour to replace potentially criminal ones.

intermediate vector boson NOUN *Physics* a hypothetical particle believed to mediate the weak interaction between elementary particles.

interment (ɪnˈtɜːmənt) NOUN burial, esp with ceremonial rites.

intermezzo (ˌɪntəˈmɛtsəʊ) NOUN, *plural* **-zos** *or* **-zi** (-tsiː). [1] a short piece of instrumental music composed for performance between the acts or scenes of an opera, drama, etc. [2] an instrumental piece either inserted between two longer movements in an extended composition or intended for independent performance. [3] another name for **interlude** (sense 3).
▷HISTORY C19: from Italian, from Late Latin *intermedium* interval; see INTERMEDIATE

intermigration (ˌɪntəmaɪˈgreɪʃən) NOUN migration between two groups of people, animals, etc., resulting in an exchange of habitat.

interminable (ɪnˈtɜːmɪnəbᵊl) ADJECTIVE endless or seemingly endless because of monotony or tiresome length.
▸**inˌterminaˈbility** *or* **inˈterminableness** NOUN
▸**inˈterminably** ADVERB

intermingle (ˌɪntəˈmɪŋgᵊl) VERB to mix or cause to mix or mingle together.

intermission (ˌɪntəˈmɪʃən) NOUN [1] an interval, as between parts of a film. [2] a period between events or activities; pause. [3] the act of intermitting or the state of being intermitted.
▷HISTORY C16: from Latin *intermissiō,* from *intermittere* to leave off, INTERMIT
▸ˌ**interˈmissive** ADJECTIVE

intermit (ˌɪntəˈmɪt) VERB **-mits, -mitting, -mitted.** to suspend (activity) or (of activity) to be suspended temporarily or at intervals.
▷HISTORY C16: from Latin *intermittere* to leave off, from INTER- + *mittere* to send
▸ˌ**interˈmittingly** ADVERB ▸ˌ**interˈmittor** NOUN

intermittent (ˌɪntəˈmɪtᵊnt) ADJECTIVE occurring occasionally or at regular or irregular intervals; periodic.
▸ˌ**interˈmittence** *or* ˌ**interˈmittency** NOUN ▸ˌ**interˈmittently** ADVERB

intermittent claudication NOUN *Pathol* pain and cramp in the calf muscles, aggravated by walking and caused by an insufficient supply of blood.

intermittent fever NOUN any fever, such as malaria, characterized by intervals of periodic remission.

intermixture (ˌɪntəˈmɪkstʃə) NOUN [1] the act of intermixing or state of being intermixed. [2] another word for **mixture.** [3] an additional constituent or ingredient.

intermodal (ˌɪntəˈməʊdᵊl) ADJECTIVE [1] (of a transport system) using different modes of conveyance in conjunction, such as ships, aircraft, road vehicles, etc. [2] (of a container) able to be carried by different modes of conveyance without being unpacked. [3] *Psychol* denoting an interaction between different senses.

intermodulation (ˈɪntəˌmɒdjuˈleɪʃən) NOUN *Electronics* **a** interaction between two signals in electronic apparatus such that each affects the amplitude of the other. **b** (*as modifier*): *intermodulation distortion.*

intermolecular (ˌɪntəməˈlɛkjʊlə) ADJECTIVE occurring among or between molecules.

intermontane (ˌɪntəmɒnˈteɪn) ADJECTIVE occurring or situated between mountain ranges: *an intermontane basin.*

intern VERB [1] (ɪnˈtɜːn) (*tr*) to detain or confine (foreign or enemy citizens, ships, etc.), esp during wartime. [2] (ˈɪntɜːn) (*intr*) *Chiefly US* to serve or train as an intern. ◆ NOUN (ˈɪntɜːn) [3] another word for **internee.** [4] Also: **interne.** the approximate US and Canadian equivalent of a British **house officer.** [5] *Chiefly US* a student teacher. [6] *Chiefly US* a student or recent graduate receiving practical training in a

working environment. ◆ ADJECTIVE (ɪn'tɜːn) 7 an archaic word for **internal.**
▷HISTORY C19: from Latin *internus* internal

internal (ɪn'tɜːnᵊl) ADJECTIVE 1 of, situated on, or suitable for the inside; inner. 2 coming or acting from within; interior. 3 involving the spiritual or mental life; subjective. 4 of or involving a nation's domestic as opposed to foreign affairs. 5 *Education* denoting assessment by examiners who are employed at the candidate's place of study. 6 situated within, affecting, or relating to the inside of the body. ◆ NOUN 7 a medical examination of the vagina, uterus, or rectum.
▷HISTORY C16: from Medieval Latin *internālis,* from Late Latin *internus* inward
▸ ˌ**inter'nality** *or* **in'ternalness** NOUN ▸ **in'ternally** ADVERB

internal-combustion engine NOUN a heat engine in which heat is supplied by burning the fuel in the working fluid (usually air).

internal ear NOUN the part of the ear that consists of the cochlea, vestibule, and semicircular canals. Also called: **inner ear, labyrinth.**

internal energy NOUN the thermodynamic property of a system that changes by an amount equal to the work done on the system when it suffers an adiabatic change. It is the sum of the kinetic and potential energies of its constituent atoms, molecules, etc. Symbol: *U or E.*

internalize *or* **internalise** (ɪn'tɜːnəˌlaɪz) VERB (*tr*) *Psychol, sociol* to make internal, esp to incorporate within oneself (values, attitudes, etc.) through learning or socialization. Compare **introject.** Also: **interiorize.**
▸ **inˌternali'zation** *or* **inˌternali'sation** NOUN

internal market NOUN a system in which goods and services are sold by the provider to a range of purchasers within the same organization, who compete to establish the price of the product.

internal medicine NOUN the branch of medical science concerned with the diagnosis and nonsurgical treatment of disorders of the internal structures of the body.

internal rate of return NOUN an interest rate giving a net present value of zero when applied to the expected cash flow of a project. Its value, compared to the cost of the capital involved, is used to determine the project's viability.

internal resistance NOUN *Physics* the resistance of a cell, accumulator, etc., usually given as $(E-V)/I$, where E is the emf of the cell, and V the potential difference between terminals when it is delivering a current I.

internal revenue NOUN *US* government income derived from taxes, etc., within the country.

internal rhyme NOUN *Prosody* rhyme that occurs between words within a verse line.

internal secretion NOUN *Physiol* a secretion, esp a hormone, that is absorbed directly into the blood.

international (ˌɪntə'næʃənᵊl) ADJECTIVE 1 of, concerning, or involving two or more nations or nationalities. 2 established by, controlling, or legislating for several nations: *an international court; international fishing rights.* 3 available for use by all nations: *international waters.* ◆ NOUN 4 *Sport* **a** a contest between two national teams. **b** a member of these teams.
▸ ˌ**interˌnation'ality** NOUN ▸ ˌ**inter'nationally** ADVERB

International (ˌɪntə'næʃənᵊl) NOUN 1 any of several international socialist organizations. See **Comintern, First International, Labour and Socialist International, Second International, Socialist International, Trotskyist International, Vienna Union.** 2 a member of any of these organizations.

International Atomic Time NOUN the scientific standard of time based on the SI unit, the second, used by means of atomic clocks and satellites to synchronize the time standards of the major nations. Abbreviation: **TAI.**

International Bank for Reconstruction and Development NOUN the official name for the **World Bank.** Abbreviation: **IBRD.**

International Brigade NOUN a military force that fought on the Republican side in the Spanish Civil War, consisting of volunteers (predominantly socialists and communists) from many countries.

international candle NOUN a former international unit of luminous intensity, originally defined in terms of a standard candle and later in terms of a pentane-burning lamp. It has now been replaced by the candela.

International Court of Justice NOUN a court established in the Hague to settle disputes brought by nations that are parties to the Statute of the Court. Also called: **World Court.**

International Criminal Police Organization NOUN See **Interpol.**

International Date Line NOUN the line approximately following the 180° meridian from Greenwich on the east side of which the date is one day earlier than on the west. Also called: **date line.**

International Development Association NOUN an organization set up in 1960 to provide low-interest loans to developing countries. It is part of the World Bank Group. Abbreviation: **IDA.**

Internationale (ˌɪntənæʃə'nɑːl) NOUN **the.** a revolutionary socialist hymn, first sung in 1871 in France.
▷HISTORY C19: shortened from French *chanson internationale* international song

International Finance Corporation NOUN an organization that invests directly in private companies and makes or guarantees loans to private investors. It is affiliated to the World Bank and is part of the World Bank Group. Abbreviation: **IFC.**

International Geophysical Year NOUN the 18-month period from July 1, 1957, to Dec. 31, 1958, during which a number of nations agreed to cooperate in a geophysical research programme. Abbreviation: **IGY.**

International Gothic NOUN a style in art during the late 14th and early 15th centuries characterized by elegant stylization of illuminated manuscripts, mosaics, stained glass, etc., and by increased interest in secular themes. Major contributors were Simone Martini, Giotto, and Pisanello.

International Grandmaster NOUN *Chess* See **grandmaster** (sense 2).

internationalism (ˌɪntə'næʃənəˌlɪzəm) NOUN 1 the ideal or practice of cooperation and understanding between nations. 2 the state or quality of being international.

internationalist (ˌɪntə'næʃənəlɪst) NOUN 1 an advocate of internationalism. 2 a person versed in international law. 3 (*capital*) a member of an International.

internationalize *or* **internationalise** (ˌɪntə'næʃənəˌlaɪz) VERB (*tr*) 1 to make international. 2 to put under international control.
▸ ˌ**interˌnationali'zation** *or* ˌ**interˌnationali'sation** NOUN

International Joint Commission NOUN a joint US–Canadian federal government agency set up in 1909 to oversee the management of shared water resources (esp the Great Lakes–St Lawrence River system).

International Labour Organisation NOUN a special agency of the United Nations responsible for research and recommendations in the field of labour conditions and practices: founded in 1919 in affiliation to the League of Nations. Abbreviation: **ILO.**

international law NOUN the body of rules generally recognized by civilized nations as governing their conduct towards each other and towards each other's subjects.

International Master NOUN *Chess* the second highest title awarded by the FIDE to a player: won by obtaining a certain number of points during specific international chess tournaments. Often shortened to **master.** Compare **grandmaster** (sense 2).

International Modernism NOUN See **International Style.**

International Monetary Fund NOUN an international financial institution organized in 1945 to promote international trade by increasing the exchange stability of the major currencies. A fund is maintained out of which member nations with temporary balance-of-payments deficits may make withdrawals. Abbreviation: **IMF.**

international Morse code NOUN the full name for **Morse code.**

international nautical mile NOUN the full name for **nautical mile** (sense 1).

International Phonetic Alphabet NOUN a series of signs and letters propagated by the Association Phonétique Internationale for the representation of human speech sounds. It is based on the Roman alphabet but supplemented by modified signs or symbols from other writing systems, and is usually employed in its revised form of 1951. Abbreviation: **IPA.**

international pitch NOUN *Music* the frequency of 435 hertz assigned to the A above middle C, widely used until 1939. See **pitch**[1] (sense 28b).

International Practical Temperature Scale NOUN a temperature scale adopted by international agreement in 1968, and revised in 1990, based on thermodynamic temperature and using experimental values to define 16 fixed points. The lowest is the triple point of an equilibrium mixture of orthohydrogen and parahydrogen (–259.34°C) and the highest the freezing point of copper (1084.62°C).

international screw thread NOUN *Engineering* a metric system for screw threads relating the pitch to the diameter.

international sea and swell scale NOUN another name for the **Douglas scale.**

International Standard Atmosphere NOUN a theoretical vertical distribution of the physical properties of the atmosphere up to an altitude of 50 km established by international agreement. It permits the standardization of aircraft instruments and performance of all types of flying vehicles.

International Style *or* **Modernism** NOUN a 20th-century architectural style characterized by undecorated rectilinear forms and the use of glass, steel, and reinforced concrete.

International Telecommunications Union NOUN a special agency of the United Nations, founded in 1947, that is responsible for the international allocation and registration of frequencies for communications and the regulation of telegraph, telephone, and radio services: originally established in 1865 as the International Telegraph Union.

international telegram NOUN a telemessage sent from the UK to a foreign country.

interne ('ɪntɜːn) NOUN a variant spelling of **intern** (sense 4).

internecine (ˌɪntə'niːsaɪn) ADJECTIVE 1 mutually destructive or ruinous; maiming both or all sides: *internecine war.* 2 of or relating to slaughter or carnage; bloody. 3 of or involving conflict within a group or organization.
▷HISTORY C17: from Latin *internecīnus,* from *internecāre* to destroy, from *necāre* to kill

internee (ˌɪntɜː'niː) NOUN a person who is interned, esp an enemy citizen in wartime or a terrorism suspect.

Internet ('ɪntəˌnɛt) NOUN **the.** (*sometimes not capital*) the single worldwide computer network that interconnects other computer networks, on which end-user services, such as World Wide Web sites or data archives, are located, enabling data and other information to be exchanged. Also called: **the Net.**

Internet access provider NOUN See **IAP.**

Internet service provider NOUN See **ISP.**

interneuron (ˌɪntə'njʊərɒn) NOUN *Physiol* any neuron that connects afferent and efferent neurons in a reflex arc. Also called: **internuncial neuron.**

internist ('ɪntɜːnɪst, ɪn'tɜːnɪst) NOUN *Chiefly US* a physician who specializes in internal medicine.

internment (ɪn'tɜːnmənt) NOUN **a** the act of interning or state of being interned, esp of enemy citizens in wartime or of terrorism suspects. **b** (*as modifier*): *an internment camp.*

internode ('ɪntəˌnəʊd) NOUN 1 the part of a plant stem between two nodes. 2 the part of a nerve fibre between two nodes of Ranvier.
▸ ˌ**inter'nodal** ADJECTIVE

internship ('ɪntɜːnʃɪp) NOUN *Chiefly US and Canadian* the position of being an intern or the period during which a person is an intern.

internuncial (ˌɪntə'nʌnʃəl) ADJECTIVE 1 *Physiol* (esp of neurons) interconnecting. See **internode.** 2 of, relating to, or emanating from a papal internuncio.

internuncio (ˌɪntə'nʌnʃɪˌəʊ) NOUN, *plural* **-cios.** 1

an ambassador of the pope ranking immediately below a nuncio. 2 a messenger, agent, or go-between.
▷HISTORY C17: from Italian *internunzio,* from Latin *internuntius,* from INTER- + *nuntius* messenger

interoceptor (ˌɪntərəʊˈsɛptə) NOUN *Physiol* a sensory receptor of an internal organ (excluding the muscles). Compare **exteroceptor, proprioceptor.**
▷HISTORY C20: from INTER(IOR) + (RE)CEPTOR
▸ˌ**intero'ceptive** ADJECTIVE

interosculate (ˌɪntərˈɒskjʊˌleɪt) VERB *(intr) Biology* (of two different species or groups of organisms) to share certain characteristics.
▸ˌ**interˌoscu'lation** NOUN

interpage (ˌɪntəˈpeɪdʒ) VERB *(tr)* 1 to print (matter) on intervening pages. 2 to insert (intervening pages) into a book.

interpellant (ˌɪntəˈpɛlənt) ADJECTIVE 1 causing an interpellation. ◆ NOUN 2 a deputy who interpellates.

interpellate (ɪnˈtɜːpɛˌleɪt) VERB *(tr) Parliamentary procedure* (in European legislatures) to question (a member of the government) on a point of government policy, often interrupting the business of the day.
▷HISTORY C16: from Latin *interpellāre* to disturb, from INTER- + *pellere* to push
▸**inˌterpel'lation** NOUN ▸**in'terpelˌlator** NOUN

interpenetrate (ˌɪntəˈpɛnɪˌtreɪt) VERB 1 to penetrate (something) thoroughly; pervade. 2 to penetrate each other or one another mutually.
▸ˌ**inter'penetrable** ADJECTIVE ▸ˌ**inter'penetrant** ADJECTIVE ▸ˌ**interˌpene'tration** NOUN ▸ˌ**inter'penetrative** ADJECTIVE ▸ˌ**inter'penetratively** ADVERB

interpersonal (ˌɪntəˈpɜːsənᵊl) ADJECTIVE between persons; involving personal relationships.

interphase (ˈɪntəˌfeɪz) NOUN *Biology* the period between two successive divisions of a cell.

interphone (ˈɪntəˌfəʊn) NOUN a telephone system for linking different rooms within a building, ship, etc.

interplanetary (ˌɪntəˈplænɪtərɪ, -trɪ) ADJECTIVE of, relating to, or existing between planets.

interplay (ˈɪntəˌpleɪ) NOUN reciprocal and mutual action and reaction, as in circumstances, events, or personal relations.

interplead (ˌɪntəˈpliːd) VERB **-pleads, -pleading; -pleaded, -plead** (-ˈplɛd) *or* **-pled.** *(intr) Law* to institute interpleader proceedings.

interpleader (ˌɪntəˈpliːdə) NOUN *Law* 1 a process by which a person holding money or property claimed by two or more parties and having no interest in it himself can require the claimants to litigate with each other to determine the issue. 2 a person who interpleads.

Interpol (ˈɪntəˌpɒl) NOUN ACRONYM FOR International Criminal Police Organization, an association of over 100 national police forces, devoted chiefly to fighting international crime.

interpolate (ɪnˈtɜːpəˌleɪt) VERB 1 to insert or introduce (a comment, passage, etc.) into (a conversation, text, etc.). 2 to falsify or alter (a text, manuscript, etc.) by the later addition of (material, esp spurious or valueless passages). 3 *(intr)* to make additions, interruptions, or insertions. 4 *Maths* to estimate (a value of a function) between the values already known or determined. Compare **extrapolate** (sense 1).
▷HISTORY C17: from Latin *interpolāre* to give a new appearance to, from INTER- + *polīre* to POLISH
▸**in'terpoˌlater** *or* **in'terpoˌlator** NOUN ▸**in'terpolative** ADJECTIVE

interpolation (ɪnˌtɜːpəˈleɪʃən) NOUN 1 the act of interpolating or the state of being interpolated. 2 something interpolated.

interpose (ˌɪntəˈpəʊz) VERB 1 to put or place between or among other things. 2 to introduce (comments, questions, etc.) into a speech or conversation; interject. 3 to exert or use power, influence, or action in order to alter or intervene in (a situation).
▷HISTORY C16: from Old French *interposer,* from Latin *interpōnere,* from INTER- + *pōnere* to put
▸ˌ**inter'posable** ADJECTIVE ▸ˌ**inter'posal** NOUN ▸ˌ**inter'poser** NOUN

interposition (ˌɪntəpəˈzɪʃən) NOUN 1 something interposed. 2 the act of interposing or the state of being interposed.

interpret (ɪnˈtɜːprɪt) VERB 1 *(tr)* to clarify or explain the meaning of; elucidate. 2 *(tr)* to construe the significance or intention of: *to interpret a smile as an invitation.* 3 *(tr)* to convey or represent the spirit or meaning of (a poem, song, etc.) in performance. 4 *(intr)* to act as an interpreter; translate orally.
▷HISTORY C14: from Latin *interpretārī,* from *interpres* negotiator, one who explains, from INTER- + *-pres,* probably related to *pretium* PRICE
▸**in'terpretable** ADJECTIVE ▸**inˌterpreta'bility** *or* **in'terpretableness** NOUN ▸**in'terpretably** ADVERB

interpretation (ɪnˌtɜːprɪˈteɪʃən) NOUN 1 the act or process of interpreting or explaining; elucidation. 2 the result of interpreting; an explanation. 3 a particular view of an artistic work, esp as expressed by stylistic individuality in its performance. 4 explanation, as of the environment, a historical site, etc., provided by the use of original objects, personal experience, visual display material, etc. 5 *Logic* an allocation of significance to the terms of a purely formal system, by specifying ranges for the variables, denotations for the individual constants, etc.; a function from the formal language to such elements of a possible world.
▸**inˌterpre'tational** ADJECTIVE

interpretative (ɪnˈtɜːprɪtətɪv) *or* **interpretive** (ɪnˈtɜːprɪtɪv) ADJECTIVE of, involving, or providing interpretation; expository.
▸**in'terpretatively** *or* **in'terpretively** ADVERB

interpretive centre NOUN (at a place of interest, such as a country park, historical site, etc.) a building or group of buildings that provides interpretation of the place of interest through a variety of media, such as video displays and exhibitions of material, and, often, includes facilities such as refreshment rooms and gift shops. Also called: **visitor centre.**

interpretive semantics NOUN *(functioning as singular)* a school of semantic theory based on the doctrine that the rules that relate sentences to their meanings form an autonomous system, separate from the rules that determine what is grammatical in a language. Compare **generative semantics.**

interprovincial (ˌɪntəprəˈvɪnʃəl) ADJECTIVE conducted between or involving two or more provinces.

interquartile range (ˌɪntəˈkwɔːtaɪl) NOUN *Statistics* the difference between the value of a variable below which lie 25 per cent of the population, and that below which lie 75 per cent: a measure of the spread of the distribution.

interracial (ˌɪntəˈreɪʃəl) ADJECTIVE conducted, involving, or existing between different races or ethnic groups.

interradial (ˌɪntəˈreɪdɪəl) ADJECTIVE situated between two radii or rays, esp between the radii of a sea urchin or similar animal.
▸ˌ**inter'radially** ADVERB

interregional (ˌɪntəˈriːdʒənᵊl) ADJECTIVE of, relating to, or conducted between two or more regions.

interregnum (ˌɪntəˈrɛgnəm) NOUN, *plural* **-nums** *or* **-na** (-nə). 1 an interval between two reigns, governments, incumbencies, etc. 2 any period in which a state lacks a ruler, government, etc. 3 a period of absence of some control, authority, etc. 4 a gap in a continuity.
▷HISTORY C16: from Latin, from INTER- + *regnum* REIGN
▸ˌ**inter'regnal** ADJECTIVE

interrelate (ˌɪntərɪˈleɪt) VERB to place in or come into a mutual or reciprocal relationship.
▸ˌ**interre'lation** NOUN ▸ˌ**interre'lationˌship** NOUN

interreligious (ˌɪntərɪˈlɪdʒəs) ADJECTIVE conducted, involving, or existing between two or more religious groups or movements.

interrex (ˌɪntəˈrɛks) NOUN, *plural* **interreges** (ˌɪntəˈriːdʒiːz). a person who governs during an interregnum; provisional ruler.
▷HISTORY C16: from Latin, from INTER- + *rēx* king

interrogate (ɪnˈtɛrəˌgeɪt) VERB to ask questions (of), esp to question (a witness in court, spy, etc.) closely.
▷HISTORY C15: from Latin *interrogāre* to question, examine, from *rogāre* to ask
▸**in'terroˌgatingly** ADVERB

interrogation (ɪnˌtɛrəˈgeɪʃən) NOUN 1 the technique, practice, or an instance of interrogating. 2 a question or query. 3 *Telecomm* the transmission of one or more triggering pulses to a transponder.
▸**inˌterro'gational** ADJECTIVE

interrogation mark NOUN a less common term for **question mark.**

interrogative (ˌɪntəˈrɒgətɪv) ADJECTIVE 1 asking or having the nature of a question. 2 denoting a form or construction used in asking a question. 3 denoting or belonging to a class of words, such as *which* and *whom,* that are determiners, adjectives, or pronouns and serve to question which individual referent or referents are intended. Compare **demonstrative, relative.** ◆ NOUN 4 an interrogative word, phrase, sentence, or construction. 5 a question mark.
▸ˌ**inter'rogatively** ADVERB

interrogator (ɪnˈtɛrəˌgeɪtə) NOUN 1 a person who interrogates. 2 a radio or radar transmitter used to send interrogating signals.

interrogatories (ˌɪntəˈrɒgətərɪz, -trɪz) PLURAL NOUN *Law* written questions asked by one party to a suit, to which the other party has to give written answers under oath.

interrogatory (ˌɪntəˈrɒgətərɪ, -trɪ) ADJECTIVE 1 expressing or involving a question. ◆ NOUN, *plural* **-tories.** 2 a question or interrogation.
▸ˌ**inter'rogatorily** ADVERB

interrupt (ˌɪntəˈrʌpt) VERB 1 to break the continuity of (an action, event, etc.) or hinder (a person) by intrusion. 2 *(tr)* to cease to perform (some action). 3 *(tr)* to obstruct (a view). 4 to prevent or disturb (a conversation, discussion, etc.) by questions, interjections, or comment. ◆ NOUN 5 the signal to initiate the stopping of the running of one computer program in order to run another, after which the running of the original program is usually continued.
▷HISTORY C15: from Latin *interrumpere,* from INTER- + *rumpere* to break
▸ˌ**inter'ruptible** ADJECTIVE ▸ˌ**inter'ruptive** ADJECTIVE ▸ˌ**inter'ruptively** ADVERB

interrupted (ˌɪntəˈrʌptɪd) ADJECTIVE 1 broken, discontinued, or hindered. 2 (of plant organs, esp leaves) not evenly spaced along an axis. 3 Also: **deceptive.** *Music* (of a cadence) progressing from the dominant chord to any other, such as the subdominant or submediant.
▸ˌ**inter'ruptedly** ADVERB

interrupted screw NOUN a screw with a slot or slots cut into the thread, esp one used in the breech of some guns permitting both engagement and release of the block by a partial turn of the screw.

interrupter *or* **interruptor** (ˌɪntəˈrʌptə) NOUN 1 a person or thing that interrupts. 2 an electromechanical device for opening and closing an electric circuit.

interruption (ˌɪntəˈrʌpʃən) NOUN 1 something that interrupts, such as a comment, question, or action. 2 an interval or intermission. 3 the act of interrupting or the state of being interrupted.

interscholastic (ˌɪntəskəˈlæstɪk) ADJECTIVE 1 (of sports events, competitions, etc.) occurring between two or more schools. 2 representative of various schools.

inter se *Latin* (ˈɪntə ˈseɪ) ADVERB among or between themselves.

intersect (ˌɪntəˈsɛkt) VERB 1 to divide, cut, or mark off by passing through or across. 2 (esp of roads) to cross (each other). 3 *Maths* (often foll by *with*) to have one or more points in common (with another configuration).
▷HISTORY C17: from Latin *intersecāre* to divide, from INTER- + *secāre* to cut

intersection (ˌɪntəˈsɛkʃən, ˈɪntəˌsɛk-) NOUN 1 a point at which things intersect, esp a road junction. 2 the act of intersecting or the state of being intersected. 3 *Maths* **a** a point or set of points common to two or more geometric configurations. **b** Also called: **product.** the set of elements that are common to two sets. **c** the operation that yields that set from a pair of given sets. Symbol: $\cap$, as in $A \cap B$.
▸ˌ**inter'sectional** ADJECTIVE

intersex ('ɪntəˌsɛks) NOUN *Zoology* an individual with characteristics intermediate between those of a male and a female. Compare **gynandromorph, hermaphrodite** (sense 1).

intersexual (ˌɪntə'sɛksjʊəl) ADJECTIVE [1] occurring or existing between the sexes. [2] relating to or being an intersex.
▸ **ˌinterˌsexu'ality** *or* **ˌinter'sexualism** NOUN
▸ **ˌinter'sexually** ADVERB

interspace VERB (ˌɪntə'speɪs) [1] (*tr*) to make or occupy a space between. ◆ NOUN ('ɪntəˌspeɪs) [2] space between or among things.
▸ **interspatial** (ˌɪntə'speɪʃəl) ADJECTIVE ▸ **ˌinter'spatially** ADVERB

interspecific (ˌɪntəspə'sɪfɪk) ADJECTIVE hybridized from, relating to, or occurring between different species: *interspecific competition.*

intersperse (ˌɪntə'spɜːs) VERB (*tr*) [1] to scatter or distribute among, between, or on. [2] to diversify (something) with other things scattered here and there.
▷HISTORY C16: from Latin *interspargere,* from INTER- + *spargere* to sprinkle
▸ **interspersedly** (ˌɪntə'spɜːsɪdlɪ) ADVERB ▸ **interspersion** (ˌɪntə'spɜːʃən) *or* **ˌinter'spersal** NOUN

interstadial (ˌɪntə'steɪdɪəl) ADJECTIVE, NOUN another word for **interglacial.**
▷HISTORY C20: from New Latin, from INTER- + *stadium* stage

interstate ('ɪntəˌsteɪt) ADJECTIVE [1] between or involving two or more of the states of the US, Australia, etc. ◆ ADVERB [2] *Austral* to or into another state.

interstellar (ˌɪntə'stɛlə) ADJECTIVE conducted, or existing between two or more stars.

interstellar medium NOUN the matter occurring between the stars of our Galaxy, largely in the spiral arms, and consisting mainly of huge clouds of ionized, neutral, or molecular hydrogen. Abbreviation: **ISM.**

interstice (ɪn'tɜːstɪs) NOUN (*usually plural*) [1] a minute opening or crevice between things. [2] *Physics* the space between adjacent atoms in a crystal lattice.
▷HISTORY C17: from Latin *interstitium* interval, from *intersistere,* from INTER- + *sistere* to stand

interstitial (ˌɪntə'stɪʃəl) ADJECTIVE [1] of or relating to an interstice or interstices. [2] *Physics* forming or occurring in an interstice: *an interstitial atom.* [3] *Chem* containing interstitial atoms or ions: *an interstitial compound.* [4] *Anatomy, zoology* occurring in the spaces between organs, tissues, etc.: *interstitial cells.* ◆ NOUN [5] *Chem* an atom or ion situated in the interstices of a crystal lattice.
▸ **ˌinter'stitially** ADVERB

interstitial-cell-stimulating hormone NOUN another name for **luteinizing hormone.**

interstratify (ˌɪntə'strætɪˌfaɪ) VERB **-fies, -fying, -fied.** (*tr; usually passive*) to arrange (a series of rock strata) in alternating beds.
▸ **ˌinterˌstratifi'cation** NOUN

intertexture (ˌɪntə'tɛkstʃə) NOUN [1] the act or process of interweaving or the condition of having been interwoven. [2] something that has been interwoven.

intertidal (ˌɪntə'taɪdᵊl) ADJECTIVE of or relating to the zone of the shore between the high-water mark and low-water mark.

intertribal (ˌɪntə'traɪbəl) ADJECTIVE conducted between or involving two or more tribes.

intertrigo (ˌɪntə'traɪgəʊ) NOUN chafing between two moist closely opposed skin surfaces, as under the breasts or at the armpit.
▷HISTORY C18: from INTER- + *-trigo,* from Latin *terere* to rub

Intertropical Convergence Zone (ˌɪntə'trɒpɪkᵊl) NOUN *Meteorol* the zone of deep convection and heavy rainfall in the tropics, esp along or near the equator. Abbreviation: **ITCZ.**

intertwine (ˌɪntə'twaɪn) VERB to unite or be united by twisting or twining together. Also: **intertwist.**
▸ **ˌinter'twinement** NOUN ▸ **ˌinter'twiningly** ADVERB

interval ('ɪntəvəl) NOUN [1] the period of time marked off by or between two events, instants, etc. [2] the distance between two points, objects, etc. [3] a pause or interlude, as between periods of intense activity. [4] *Brit* a short period between parts of a play, concert, film, etc.; intermission. [5] *Music* the difference of pitch between two notes, either sounded simultaneously (**harmonic interval**) or in succession as in a musical part (**melodic interval**). An interval is calculated by counting the (inclusive) number of notes of the diatonic scale between the two notes: *the interval between C and G is a fifth.* [6] the ratio of the frequencies of two sounds. [7] *Maths* the set containing all real numbers or points between two given numbers or points, called the endpoints. A **closed interval** includes the endpoints, but an **open interval** does not. [8] **at intervals. a** occasionally or intermittently. **b** with spaces between.
▷HISTORY C13: from Latin *intervallum,* literally: space between two palisades, from INTER- + *vallum* palisade, rampart
▸ **intervallic** (ˌɪntə'vælɪk) ADJECTIVE

interval estimate NOUN *Statistics* an interval within which the true value of a parameter of a population is stated to lie with a predetermined probability on the basis of sampling statistics. Compare **point estimate.**

intervalometer (ˌɪntəvə'lɒmɪtə) NOUN an automatic device used to trigger an operation at regular intervals, esp such a device operating the shutter of a camera.

interval scale NOUN *Statistics* a scale of measurement of data according to which the differences between values can be quantified in absolute but not relative terms and for which any zero is merely arbitrary: for instance, dates are measured on an interval scale since differences can be measured in years, but no sense can be given to a ratio of times. Compare **ordinal scale, ratio scale, nominal scale.**

interval signal NOUN a characteristic snatch of music, chimes, etc., transmitted as an identifying signal by a radio station between programme items.

interval training NOUN a method of athletic training using alternate sprinting and jogging. Also called: **fartlek.**

intervarsity (ˌɪntə'vɑːsɪtɪ) ADJECTIVE conducted, involving, or existing between two or more universities.

intervene (ˌɪntə'viːn) VERB (*intr*) [1] (often foll by *in*) to take a decisive or intrusive role (in) in order to modify or determine events or their outcome. [2] (foll by *in* or *between*) to come or be (among or between). [3] (of a period of time) to occur between events or points in time. [4] (of an event) to disturb or hinder a course of action. [5] *Economics* to take action to affect the market forces of an economy, esp to maintain the stability of a currency. [6] *Law* to interpose and become a party to a legal action between others, esp in order to protect one's interests.
▷HISTORY C16: from Latin *intervenīre* to come between, from INTER- + *venīre* to come
▸ **ˌinter'vener** *or* **ˌinter'venor** NOUN

intervening variable (ˌɪntə'viːnɪŋ) NOUN *Psychol* a hypothetical variable postulated to account for the way in which a set of independent variables control a set of dependent variables.

intervention (ˌɪntə'vɛnʃən) NOUN [1] the act of intervening. [2] any interference in the affairs of others, esp by one state in the affairs of another. [3] *Economics* the action of a central bank in supporting the international value of a currency by buying large quantities of the currency to keep the price up. [4] *Commerce* the action of the EU in buying up surplus produce when the market price drops to a certain value.
▸ **ˌinter'ventional** ADJECTIVE

interventional radiology NOUN an application of radiology that enables minimally invasive surgery to be performed with the aid of simultaneous radiological imaging of the field of operation within the body.

interventionist (ˌɪntə'vɛnʃənɪst) ADJECTIVE [1] of, relating to, or advocating intervention, esp in the affairs of a foreign country. ◆ NOUN [2] an interventionist person or state.
▸ **ˌinter'ventionism** NOUN

intervention price NOUN *Commerce* the price at which the EU intervenes to buy surplus produce.

intervertebral disc (ˌɪntə'vɜːtəbrəl) NOUN any of the cartilaginous discs between individual vertebrae, acting as shock absorbers.

interview ('ɪntəˌvjuː) NOUN [1] a conversation with or questioning of a person, usually conducted for television, radio, or a newspaper. [2] a formal discussion, esp one in which an employer assesses an applicant for a job. ◆ VERB [3] to conduct an interview with (someone). [4] (*intr*) to be interviewed, esp for a job: *he interviewed well and was given the position.*
▷HISTORY C16: from Old French *entrevue;* see INTER-, VIEW
▸ **ˌinterview'ee** NOUN ▸ **'interˌviewer** NOUN

inter vivos *Latin* ('ɪntə 'viːvɒs) ADJECTIVE *Law* between living people: *an inter vivos gift.*

intervocalic (ˌɪntəvəʊ'kælɪk) ADJECTIVE pronounced or situated between vowels.
▸ **ˌintervo'calically** ADVERB

interwar (ˌɪntə'wɔː) ADJECTIVE of or happening in the period between World War I and World War II.

interweave (ˌɪntə'wiːv) VERB **-weaves, -weaving, -wove** *or* **-weaved; -woven, -wove,** *or* **-weaved.** to weave, blend, or twine together; intertwine. Also: **interwork.**
▸ **ˌinter'weavement** NOUN ▸ **'interˌweaver** NOUN

intestate (ɪn'tɛsteɪt, -tɪt) ADJECTIVE [1] **a** (of a person) not having made a will. **b** (of property) not disposed of by will. ◆ NOUN [2] a person who dies without having made a will. ◆ Compare **testate.**
▷HISTORY C14: from Latin *intestātus,* from IN-[1] + *testātus,* from *testārī* to bear witness, make a will, from *testis* a witness
▸ **in'testacy** NOUN

intestinal flora NOUN microorganisms that normally inhabit the lumen of the intestinal tract.

intestine (ɪn'tɛstɪn) NOUN (*usually plural*) the part of the alimentary canal between the stomach and the anus. See **large intestine, small intestine.** Related adjective: **alvine.**
▷HISTORY C16: from Latin *intestīnum* gut, from *intestīnus* internal, from *intus* within
▸ **intestinal** (ɪn'tɛstɪnᵊl, ˌɪntɛs'taɪnᵊl) ADJECTIVE
▸ **in'testinally** ADVERB

inti ('ɪntɪ) NOUN a former monetary unit of Peru.
▷HISTORY C20: from Quechua

intifada (ˌɪntɪ'fɑːdə) NOUN the Palestinian uprising against Israel in the West Bank and Gaza Strip that started at the end of 1987.
▷HISTORY C20: Arabic, literally: uprising

intima ('ɪntɪmə) NOUN, *plural* **-mae** (-ˌmiː). *Anatomy, zoology* the innermost layer of an organ or part, esp of a blood vessel.
▷HISTORY C19: from Latin, feminine of *intimus* innermost; see INTIMATE[1]
▸ **'intimal** ADJECTIVE

intimacy ('ɪntɪməsɪ) NOUN, *plural* **-cies.** [1] close or warm friendship or understanding; personal relationship. [2] (*often plural*) *Euphemistic* sexual relations.

intimate[1] ('ɪntɪmɪt) ADJECTIVE [1] characterized by a close or warm personal relationship: *an intimate friend.* [2] deeply personal, private, or secret. [3] (*often postpositive;* foll by *with*) *Euphemistic* having sexual relations (with). [4] **a** (*postpositive;* foll by *with*) having a deep or unusual knowledge (of). **b** (of knowledge) deep; extensive. [5] having a friendly, warm, or informal atmosphere: *an intimate nightclub.* [6] of or relating to the essential part or nature of something; intrinsic. [7] denoting the informal second person of verbs and pronouns in French and other languages. ◆ NOUN [8] a close friend.
▷HISTORY C17: from Latin *intimus* very close friend, from (adj): innermost, deepest, from *intus* within
▸ **'intimately** ADVERB ▸ **'intimateness** NOUN

intimate[2] ('ɪntɪˌmeɪt) VERB (*tr; may take a clause as object*) [1] to hint; suggest. [2] to proclaim; make known.
▷HISTORY C16: from Late Latin *intimāre* to proclaim, from Latin *intimus* innermost
▸ **'intiˌmater** NOUN

intimation (ˌɪntɪ'meɪʃən) NOUN [1] a hint or suggestion. [2] *Rare* an announcement or notice.

intimidate (ɪn'tɪmɪˌdeɪt) VERB (*tr*) [1] to make timid or frightened; scare. [2] to discourage, restrain, or silence illegally or unscrupulously, as by threats or blackmail.

▷HISTORY C17: from Medieval Latin *intimidāre,* from Latin IN-[2] + *timidus* fearful, from *timor* fear
▸**in'timi,dating** ADJECTIVE ▸**in,timi'dation** NOUN
▸**in'timi,dator** NOUN

intinction (ɪn'tɪŋkʃən) NOUN *Christianity* the practice of dipping the Eucharistic bread into the wine at Holy Communion.
▷HISTORY C16: from Late Latin *intinctiō* a dipping in, from Latin *intingere* to dip in, from *tingere* to dip

intine ('ɪntɪn, -tiːn, -taɪn) NOUN the inner wall of a pollen grain or a spore. Compare **exine.**
▷HISTORY C19: from Latin *intimus* innermost + -INE[1]

intitule (ɪn'tɪtjuːl) VERB (*tr*) *Parliamentary procedure* (in Britain) to entitle (an Act).
▷HISTORY C15: from Old French *intituler,* from Latin *titulus* TITLE

intl ABBREVIATION FOR international.

into ('ɪntuː; *unstressed* 'ɪntə) PREPOSITION 1 to the interior or inner parts of: *to look into a case.* 2 to the middle or midst of so as to be surrounded by: *into the water; into the bushes.* 3 against; up against: *he drove into a wall.* 4 used to indicate the result of a transformation or change: *he changed into a monster.* 5 *Maths* used to indicate a dividend: *three into six is two.* 6 *Informal* interested or enthusiastically involved in: *I'm really into Freud these days.*

intolerable (ɪn'tɒlərəbᵊl) ADJECTIVE 1 more than can be tolerated or endured; insufferable. 2 *Informal* extremely irritating or annoying.
▸**in,tolera'bility** *or* **in'tolerableness** NOUN ▸**in'tolerably** ADVERB

intolerant (ɪn'tɒlərənt) ADJECTIVE 1 lacking respect for practices and beliefs other than one's own. 2 (*postpositive;* foll by *of*) not able or willing to tolerate or endure: *intolerant of noise.*
▸**in'tolerance** NOUN ▸**in'tolerantly** ADVERB

intonate ('ɪntəʊ,neɪt) VERB (*tr*) 1 to pronounce or articulate (continuous connected speech) with a characteristic rise and fall of the voice. 2 a less common word for **intone.**

intonation (,ɪntəʊ'neɪʃən) NOUN 1 the sound pattern of phrases and sentences produced by pitch variation in the voice. 2 the act or manner of intoning. 3 an intoned, chanted, or monotonous utterance; incantation. 4 *Music* the opening of a piece of plainsong, sung by a soloist. 5 *Music* **a** the correct or accurate pitching of intervals. **b** the capacity to play or sing in tune. See also **just intonation.**
▸,**into'national** ADJECTIVE

intonation pattern *or* **contour** NOUN *Linguistics* a characteristic series of musical pitch levels that serves to distinguish between questions, statements, and other types of utterance in a language.

intone (ɪn'təʊn) VERB 1 to utter, recite, or sing (a chant, prayer, etc.) in a monotonous or incantatory tone. 2 (*intr*) to speak with a particular or characteristic intonation or tone. 3 to sing (the opening phrase of a psalm, etc.) in plainsong.
▷HISTORY C15: from Medieval Latin *intonare,* from IN-[2] + TONE
▸**in'toner** NOUN

intorsion (ɪn'tɔːʃən) NOUN *Botany* a spiral twisting in plant stems or other parts.

in toto *Latin* (ɪn 'təʊtəʊ) ADVERB totally; entirely; completely.

intoxicant (ɪn'tɒksɪkənt) NOUN 1 anything that causes intoxication. ◆ ADJECTIVE 2 causing intoxication.

intoxicate (ɪn'tɒksɪ,keɪt) VERB (*tr*) 1 (of an alcoholic drink) to produce in (a person) a state ranging from euphoria to stupor, usually accompanied by loss of inhibitions and control; make drunk; inebriate. 2 to stimulate, excite, or elate so as to overwhelm. 3 (of a drug) to poison.
▷HISTORY C16: from Medieval Latin, from *intoxicāre* to poison, from Latin *toxicum* poison; see TOXIC
▸**in'toxicable** ADJECTIVE ▸**in'toxi,cative** ADJECTIVE
▸**in'toxi,cator** NOUN

intoxicating (ɪn'tɒksɪ,keɪtɪŋ) ADJECTIVE 1 (of an alcoholic drink) producing in a person a state ranging from euphoria to stupor, usually accompanied by loss of inhibitions and control; inebriating. 2 stimulating, exciting, or producing great elation.
▸**in'toxi,catingly** ADVERB

intoxication (ɪn,tɒksɪ'keɪʃən) NOUN 1 drunkenness; inebriation. 2 great elation. 3 the act of intoxicating. 4 poisoning.

intr. ABBREVIATION FOR intransitive.

intra- PREFIX within; inside: *intravenous.*
▷HISTORY from Latin *intrā* on the inside, within; see INTERIOR

intra-atomic (,ɪntrəə'tɒmɪk) ADJECTIVE existing or occurring within an atom or atoms. Compare **interatomic.**

intracapsular (,ɪntrə'kæpsjʊlə) ADJECTIVE *Anatomy* within a capsule, esp within the capsule of a joint.

intracardiac (,ɪntrə'kɑːdɪ,æk) ADJECTIVE within the heart.

intracellular (,ɪntrə'sɛljʊlə) ADJECTIVE *Biology* situated or occurring inside a cell or cells.
▸,**intra'cellularly** ADVERB

Intracoastal Waterway (,ɪntrə'kəʊstᵊl) NOUN short for **Atlantic Intracoastal Waterway.**

intracranial (,ɪntrə'kreɪnɪəl) ADJECTIVE within the skull.

intractable (ɪn'træktəbᵊl) ADJECTIVE 1 difficult to influence or direct: *an intractable disposition.* 2 (of a problem, illness, etc.) difficult to solve, alleviate, or cure. 3 difficult to shape or mould, esp with the hands.
▸**in,tracta'bility** *or* **in'tractableness** NOUN ▸**in'tractably** ADVERB

intracutaneous (,ɪntrəkjuː'teɪnɪəs) ADJECTIVE *Anatomy* within the skin. Also: **intradermal.**
▸,**intracu'taneously** ADVERB

intradermal (,ɪntrə'dɜːməl) *or* **intradermic** ADJECTIVE *Anatomy* other words for **intracutaneous.** Abbreviation (esp of an injection): **ID, i.d.**
▸,**intra'dermally** *or* ,**intra'dermically** ADVERB

intrados (ɪn'treɪdɒs) NOUN, *plural* **-dos** *or* **-doses.** *Architect* the inner curve or surface of an arch or vault. Compare **extrados.**
▷HISTORY C18: from French, from INTRA- + *dos* back, from Latin *dorsum*

intrafascicular (,ɪntrəfə'sɪkjʊlə) ADJECTIVE *Botany* between the xylem and phloem elements of a vascular bundle: *intrafascicular cambium.*

intragenerational mobility (,ɪntrə,dʒɛnə'reɪʃənᵊl) NOUN *Sociol* movement within or between social classes and occupations, the change occurring within an individual's lifetime. Compare **intergenerational mobility.**

intramolecular (,ɪntrəmə'lɛkjʊlə) ADJECTIVE occurring within a molecule or molecules.

intramural (,ɪntrə'mjʊərəl) ADJECTIVE 1 *Education chiefly US and Canadian* operating within or involving those in a single establishment. 2 *Anatomy* within the walls of a cavity or hollow organ.
▸,**intra'murally** ADVERB

intramuscular (,ɪntrə'mʌskjʊlə) ADJECTIVE *Anatomy* within a muscle: *an intramuscular injection.* Abbreviation (esp of an injection): **IM, i.m.**
▸,**intra'muscularly** ADVERB

intranational (,ɪntrə'næʃənᵊl) ADJECTIVE within one nation.

intranet ('ɪntrə,nɛt) NOUN *Computing* an internal network that makes use of Internet technology.
▷HISTORY C20: from INTRA- + NET[1] (sense 8), modelled on INTERNET

intrans. ABBREVIATION FOR intransitive.

intransigent (ɪn'trænsɪdʒənt) ADJECTIVE 1 not willing to compromise; obstinately maintaining an attitude. ◆ NOUN *also* **in'transigentist.** 2 an intransigent person, esp in politics.
▷HISTORY C19: from Spanish *los intransigentes* the uncompromising (ones), a name adopted by certain political extremists, from IN-[1] + *transigir* to compromise, from Latin *transigere* to settle; see TRANSACT
▸**in'transigence** *or* **in'transigency** NOUN ▸**in'transigently** ADVERB

intransitive (ɪn'trænsɪtɪv) ADJECTIVE 1 **a** denoting a verb when it does not require a direct object. **b** denoting a verb that customarily does not require a direct object: *"to faint" is an intransitive verb.* **c** (*as noun*) a verb in either of these categories. 2 denoting an adjective or noun that does not require any particular noun phrase as a referent. 3 *Logic, maths* (of a relation) having the property that if it holds between one argument and a second, and between the second and a third, it must fail to hold between the first and the third: *"being the mother of" is an intransitive relation.* ◆ Compare **transitive, pseudo-intransitive.**
▸**in'transitively** ADVERB ▸**in,transi'tivity** *or* **in'transitiveness** NOUN

intranuclear (,ɪntrə'njuːklɪə) ADJECTIVE situated or occurring within a nucleus.

intraocular (,ɪntrə'ɒkjʊlə) ADJECTIVE *Anatomy* within an eyeball.

intrapartum (,ɪntrə'pɑːtəm) ADJECTIVE *Med* of or relating to childbirth or delivery: *intrapartum care.*
▷HISTORY C20: New Latin, from INTRA- + *partum,* from *partus* birth

intrapreneur (,ɪntrəprə'nɜː) NOUN a person who while remaining within a larger organization uses entrepreneurial skills to develop a new product or line of business as a subsidiary of the organization.
▷HISTORY C20: from INTRA- + (ENTRE)PRENEUR

intraspecific (,ɪntrəspə'sɪfɪk) ADJECTIVE relating to or occurring between members of the same species: *intraspecific competition.*

intrastate (,ɪntrə'steɪt) ADJECTIVE *Chiefly US* of, relating to, or confined within a single state, esp a state of the US.

intratelluric (,ɪntrətə'ljʊərɪk) ADJECTIVE 1 (of rocks and their constituents, processes, etc.) formed or occurring below the surface of the earth. 2 denoting crystals formed at depth before magma erupted at the earth's surface. 3 denoting the period during which crystallization took place.

intrauterine (,ɪntrə'juːtəraɪn) ADJECTIVE within the womb.

intrauterine device NOUN a metal or plastic device, in the shape of a loop, coil, or ring, inserted into the uterus to prevent conception. Abbreviation: **IUD.**

intravasation (ɪn,trævə'seɪʃən) NOUN the passage of extraneous material, such as pus, into a blood or lymph vessel. Compare **extravasation.**

intravenous (,ɪntrə'viːnəs) ADJECTIVE *Anatomy* within a vein: *an intravenous injection.* Abbreviations (esp of an injection): **IV, i.v.**
▸,**intra'venously** ADVERB

in-tray NOUN a tray for incoming papers requiring attention.

intrazonal soil (,ɪntrə'zəʊnᵊl) NOUN a soil that has a well-developed profile determined by relief, parent material, age, etc.

intreat (ɪn'triːt) VERB an archaic spelling of **entreat.**
▸**in'treatingly** ADVERB ▸**in'treatment** NOUN

intrench (ɪn'trɛntʃ) VERB a less common spelling of **entrench.**
▸**in'trencher** NOUN ▸**in'trenchment** NOUN

intrepid (ɪn'trɛpɪd) ADJECTIVE fearless; daring; bold.
▷HISTORY C17: from Latin *intrepidus,* from IN-[1] + *trepidus* fearful, timid
▸,**intre'pidity** *or* **in'trepidness** NOUN ▸**in'trepidly** ADVERB

intricate ('ɪntrɪkɪt) ADJECTIVE 1 difficult to understand; obscure; complex; puzzling. 2 entangled or involved: *intricate patterns.*
▷HISTORY C15: from Latin *intrīcāre* to entangle, perplex, from IN-[2] + *trīcae* trifles, perplexities
▸'**intricacy** *or* '**intricateness** NOUN ▸'**intricately** ADVERB

intrigant *or* **intriguant** ('ɪntrɪgənt; *French* ɛ̃trigɑ̃) NOUN *Archaic* a person who intrigues; intriguer.

intrigue VERB (ɪn'triːg) **-trigues, -triguing, -trigued.** 1 (*tr*) to make interested or curious: *I'm intrigued by this case, Watson.* 2 (*intr*) to make secret plots or employ underhand methods; conspire. 3 (*intr; often foll by with*) to carry on a clandestine love affair. ◆ NOUN (ɪn'triːg, 'ɪntriːg) 4 the act or an instance of secret plotting, etc. 5 a clandestine love affair. 6 the quality of arousing interest or curiosity; beguilement.
▷HISTORY C17: from French *intriguer,* from Italian *intrigare,* from Latin *intrīcāre;* see INTRICATE
▸**in'triguer** NOUN

intriguing (ɪn'triːgɪŋ) ADJECTIVE arousing great interest or curiosity: *an intriguing mystery.*
▸**in'triguingly** ADVERB

intrinsic (ɪn'trɪnsɪk) *or* **intrinsical** ADJECTIVE 1 of or relating to the essential nature of a thing; inherent. 2 *Anatomy* situated within or peculiar to a part: *intrinsic muscles.*
▷HISTORY C15: from Late Latin *intrinsecus* from Latin, inwardly, from *intrā* within + *secus* alongside; related to *sequī* to follow
▸in'trinsically ADVERB

intrinsic factor NOUN *Biochem* a glycoprotein, secreted by the stomach, the presence of which is necessary for the absorption of cyanocobalamin (vitamin B_{12}) in the intestine.

intrinsic semiconductor NOUN an almost pure semiconductor to which no impurities have been added and in which the electron and hole densities are equal at thermal equilibrium. Also called: **i-type semiconductor.**

intro ('ɪntrəʊ) NOUN, *plural* **-tros.** *Informal* short for **introduction.**

intro. *or* **introd.** ABBREVIATION FOR: 1 introduction. 2 introductory.

intro- PREFIX in, into, or inward: *introvert.*
▷HISTORY from Latin *intrō* towards the inside, inwardly, within

introduce (ˌɪntrə'dju:s) VERB *(tr)* 1 (often foll by *to*) to present (someone) by name (to another person) or (two or more people to each other). 2 (foll by *to*) to cause to experience for the first time: *to introduce a visitor to beer.* 3 to present for consideration or approval, esp before a legislative body: *to introduce a draft bill.* 4 to bring in; establish: *to introduce decimal currency.* 5 to present (a radio or television programme, etc.) verbally. 6 (foll by *with*) to start: *he introduced his talk with some music.* 7 (often foll by *into*) to insert or inject: *he introduced the needle into his arm.* 8 to place (members of a species of plant or animal) in a new environment with the intention of producing a resident breeding population.
▷HISTORY C16: from Latin *intrōdūcere* to bring inside, from INTRO- + *dūcere* to lead
▸ˌintro'ducer NOUN ▸ˌintro'ducible ADJECTIVE

introduction (ˌɪntrə'dʌkʃən) NOUN 1 the act of introducing or fact of being introduced. 2 a presentation of one person to another or others. 3 a means of presenting a person to another person, group, etc., such as a letter of introduction or reference. 4 a preliminary part, as of a book, speech, etc. 5 *Music* **a** an instrumental passage preceding the entry of a soloist, choir, etc. **b** an opening passage in a movement or composition that precedes the main material. 6 something that has been or is introduced, esp something that is not native to an area, country, etc. 7 a basic or elementary work of instruction, reference, etc. 8 *Logic* (qualified by the name of an operation) a syntactic rule specifying the conditions under which a formula or statement containing the specified operator may be derived from others: *conjunction-introduction; negation-introduction.*

introductory (ˌɪntrə'dʌktərɪ, -trɪ) ADJECTIVE serving as an introduction; preliminary; prefatory.
▸ˌintro'ductorily ADVERB ▸ˌintro'ductoriness NOUN

introgression (ˌɪntrə'grɛʃən) NOUN the introduction of genes from the gene pool of one species into that of another during hybridization.

introit ('ɪntrɔɪt) NOUN *RC Church, Church of England* a short prayer said or sung as the celebrant is entering the sanctuary to celebrate Mass or Holy Communion.
▷HISTORY C15: from Church Latin *introitus* introit, from Latin: entrance, from *introīre* to go in, from INTRO- + *īre* to go
▸in'troital ADJECTIVE

introject (ˌɪntrə'dʒɛkt) VERB *Psychol* 1 *(intr)* (esp of a child) to incorporate ideas of others, or (in fantasy) of objects. 2 to turn (feelings for another) towards oneself. ◆ Compare **project.** See also **internalize.**

introjection (ˌɪntrə'dʒɛkʃən) NOUN *Psychol* the act or process of introjecting.
▷HISTORY C20: from INTRO- + (PRO)JECTION
▸ˌintro'jective ADJECTIVE

intromission (ˌɪntrə'mɪʃən) NOUN a less common word for **insertion** or **introduction.**
▸ˌintro'missive ADJECTIVE

intromit (ˌɪntrə'mɪt) VERB **-mits, -mitting, -mitted.** *(tr) Rare* to enter or insert or allow to enter or be inserted.
▷HISTORY C15: from Latin *intrōmittere* to send in, from INTRO- + *mittere* to send
▸ˌintro'missible ADJECTIVE ▸ˌintroˌmissi'bility NOUN
▸ˌintro'mittent ADJECTIVE ▸ˌintro'mitter NOUN

intron ('ɪntrɒn) NOUN *Biochem* a stretch of DNA that interrupts a gene and does not contribute to the specification of a protein. Compare **exon**[2].
▷HISTORY C20: from *intr(agenic) (regi)on*

introrse (ɪn'trɔ:s) ADJECTIVE *Botany* turned inwards or towards the axis, as anthers that shed their pollen towards the centre of the flower.
▷HISTORY C19: from Latin *introrsus,* contraction of *intrōversus,* from INTRO- + *versus* turned, from *vertere* to turn
▸in'trorsely ADVERB

introspect (ˌɪntrə'spɛkt) VERB *(intr)* to examine and analyse one's own thoughts and feelings.

introspection (ˌɪntrə'spɛkʃən) NOUN the examination of one's own thoughts, impressions, and feelings, esp for long periods.
▷HISTORY C17: from Latin *intrōspicere* to look within, from INTRO- + *specere* to look
▸ˌintro'spectional *or* ˌintro'spective ADJECTIVE
▸ˌintro'spectionist NOUN ▸ˌintro'spectively ADVERB
▸ˌintro'spectiveness NOUN

introversion (ˌɪntrə'vɜ:ʃən) NOUN 1 *Psychol* the directing of interest inwards towards one's own thoughts and feelings rather than towards the external world or making social contacts. 2 *Pathol* the turning inside out of a hollow organ or part. ◆ Compare **extroversion.**
▸ˌintro'versive *or* ˌintro'vertive ADJECTIVE

introvert NOUN ('ɪntrəˌvɜ:t) 1 *Psychol* a person prone to introversion. ◆ ADJECTIVE ('ɪntrəˌvɜ:t) 2 Also: **introverted.** characterized by introversion. ◆ VERB (ˌɪntrə'vɜ:t) 3 *(tr) Pathol* to turn (a hollow organ or part) inside out. ◆ Compare **extrovert.**
▷HISTORY C17: see INTRO-, INVERT

intrude (ɪn'tru:d) VERB 1 (often foll by *into, on,* or *upon*) to put forward or interpose (oneself, one's views, something) abruptly or without invitation. 2 *Geology* to force or thrust (rock material, esp molten magma) or (of rock material) to be thrust between solid rocks.
▷HISTORY C16: from Latin *intrūdere* to thrust in, from IN-[2] + *trūdere* to thrust
▸in'trudingly ADVERB

intruder (ɪn'tru:də) NOUN a person who enters a building, grounds, etc., without permission.

intrusion (ɪn'tru:ʒən) NOUN 1 the act or an instance of intruding; an unwelcome visit, interjection, etc.: *an intrusion on one's privacy.* 2 **a** the movement of magma from within the earth's crust into spaces in the overlying strata to form igneous rock. **b** any igneous rock formed in this way. 3 *Property law* an unlawful entry onto land by a stranger after determination of a particular estate of freehold and before the remainderman or reversioner has made entry.
▸in'trusional ADJECTIVE

intrusive (ɪn'tru:sɪv) ADJECTIVE 1 characterized by intrusion or tending to intrude. 2 (of igneous rocks) formed by intrusion. Compare **extrusive** (sense 2). 3 *Phonetics* relating to or denoting a speech sound that is introduced into a word or piece of connected speech for a phonetic rather than a historical or grammatical reason, such as the (r) often pronounced between *idea* and *of* in *the idea of it.*
▸in'trusively ADVERB ▸in'trusiveness NOUN

intrust (ɪn'trʌst) VERB a less common spelling of **entrust.**
▸in'trustment NOUN

intubate ('ɪntjʊˌbeɪt) VERB *(tr) Med* to insert a tube or cannula into (a hollow organ); cannulate.
▸ˌintu'bation NOUN

INTUC ('ɪntʌk) NOUN ACRONYM FOR Indian National Trade Union Congress.

intuit (ɪn'tju:ɪt) VERB to know or discover by intuition.
▸in'tuitable ADJECTIVE

intuition (ˌɪntjʊ'ɪʃən) NOUN 1 knowledge or belief obtained neither by reason nor by perception. 2 instinctive knowledge or belief. 3 a hunch or unjustified belief. 4 *Philosophy* immediate knowledge of a proposition or object such as Kant's account of our knowledge of sensible objects. 5 the supposed faculty or process by which we obtain any of these.
▷HISTORY C15: from Late Latin *intuitiō* a contemplation, from Latin *intuērī* to gaze upon, from *tuērī* to look at
▸ˌintu'itional ADJECTIVE ▸ˌintu'itionally ADVERB

intuitionism (ˌɪntjʊ'ɪʃəˌnɪzəm) *or* **intuitionalism** NOUN 1 (in ethics) **a** the doctrine that there are moral truths discoverable by intuition. **b** the doctrine that there is no single principle by which to resolve conflicts between intuited moral rules. ◆ See also **deontological.** 2 *Philosophy* the theory that general terms are used of a variety of objects in accordance with perceived similarities. Compare **nominalism, Platonism.** 3 *Logic* the doctrine that logical axioms rest on prior intuitions concerning time, negation, and provability. 4 **a** the theory that mathematics cannot intelligibly comprehend the properties of infinite sets, and that only what can be shown to be provable can be justifiably asserted. **b** the reconstruction of mathematics or logic in accordance with this view. ◆ Compare **formalism, logicism, finitism.** 5 the doctrine that knowledge, esp of the external world, is acquired by intuition.
▸ˌintu'itionist *or* ˌintu'itionalist NOUN

intuitive (ɪn'tju:ɪtɪv) ADJECTIVE 1 resulting from intuition: *an intuitive awareness.* 2 of, characterized by, or involving intuition.
▸in'tuitively ADVERB ▸in'tuitiveness NOUN

intumesce (ˌɪntjʊ'mɛs) VERB *(intr)* to swell or become swollen; undergo intumescence.
▷HISTORY C18: from Latin *intumescere,* from *tumescere* to begin to swell, from *tumēre* to swell

intumescence (ˌɪntjʊ'mɛsəns) *or* **intumescency** NOUN 1 *Pathol* a swelling up, as with blood or other fluid. 2 *Pathol* a swollen organ or part. 3 *Chem* the swelling of certain substances on heating, often accompanied by the escape of water vapour.
▸ˌintu'mescent ADJECTIVE

intussuscept (ˌɪntəssə'sɛpt) VERB *(tr; usually passive) Pathol* to turn or fold (an organ or a part) inwards; invaginate.
▸ˌintussus'ceptive ADJECTIVE

intussusception (ˌɪntəssə'sɛpʃən) NOUN 1 *Pathol* invagination of a tubular organ or part, esp the telescoping of one section of the intestinal tract into a lower section, causing obstruction. 2 *Biology* growth in the surface area of a cell by the deposition of new material between the existing components of the cell wall. Compare **apposition** (sense 3).
▷HISTORY C18: from Latin *intus* within + *susceptiō* a taking up

intwine (ɪn'twaɪn) VERB a less common spelling of **entwine.**
▸in'twinement NOUN

Inuit *or* **Innuit** ('ɪnju:ɪt) NOUN, *plural* **-it** *or* **-its.** an Eskimo of N America or Greenland, as distinguished from one from Asia or the Aleutian Islands: the general name for an Eskimo in Canada. Compare **Yupik.**
▷HISTORY from Eskimo *inuit* the people, pl of *inuk* a man

Inuk (ɪ'nʊk) NOUN a member of any Inuit people.
▷HISTORY from Eskimo *inuk* man

inukshuk (ɪ'nʊkʃʊk) NOUN, *plural* **inukshuks** *or* **inukshuit** (ɪ'nʊkʃju:ɪt). a stone used by the Inuit to mark a location.
▷HISTORY from Inuktitut, literally: something in the shape of a man

Inuktitut (ɪ'nʊktɪˌtʊt) NOUN *Canadian* the language of the Inuit; Eskimo.
▷HISTORY from Eskimo *inuk* man + *titut* speech

inulin ('ɪnjʊlɪn) NOUN a fructose polysaccharide present in the tubers and rhizomes of some plants. Formula: $(C_6H_{10}O_5)_n$.
▷HISTORY C19: from Latin *inula* elecampane + -IN

inunction (ɪn'ʌŋkʃən) NOUN 1 the application of an ointment to the skin, esp by rubbing. 2 the ointment so used. 3 the act of anointing; anointment.
▷HISTORY C15: from Latin *inunguere* to anoint, from *unguere;* see UNCTION

inundate ('ɪnʌnˌdeɪt) VERB *(tr)* 1 to cover completely with water; overflow; flood; swamp. 2

to overwhelm, as if with a flood: *to be inundated with requests.*
▷HISTORY C17: from Latin *inundāre* to flood, from *unda* wave
▸**'inundant** *or* **in'undatory** ADJECTIVE ▸**,inun'dation** NOUN ▸**'inun,dator** NOUN

inurbane (,ɪnɜː'beɪn) ADJECTIVE *Rare* not urbane; lacking in courtesy or polish.
▸**inurbanity** (,ɪnɜː'bænɪtɪ) NOUN ▸**,inur'banely** ADVERB

inure *or* **enure** (ɪ'njʊə) VERB 1 (*tr; often passive;* often foll by *to*) to cause to accept or become hardened to; habituate. 2 (*intr*) (esp of a law, etc.) to come into operation; take effect.
▷HISTORY C15 *enuren* to accustom, from *ure* use, from Old French *euvre* custom, work, from Latin *opera* works, plural of *opus*
▸**inuredness** *or* **enuredness** (ɪ'njʊərɪdnɪs) NOUN
▸**in'urement** *or* **en'urement** NOUN

inurn (ɪn'ɜːn) VERB (*tr*) 1 to place (esp cremated ashes) in an urn. 2 a less common word for **inter**.
▸**in'urnment** NOUN

in utero *Latin* (ɪn 'juːtə,rəʊ) ADVERB within the womb.

inutile (ɪn'juːtaɪl) ADJECTIVE *Rare* useless; unprofitable.
▸**in'utilely** ADVERB ▸**inutility** (,ɪnjuː'tɪlɪtɪ) NOUN

in vacuo *Latin* (ɪn 'vækjʊ,əʊ) ADVERB 1 in a vacuum. 2 in isolation; without reference to facts or evidence.

invade (ɪn'veɪd) VERB 1 to enter (a country, territory, etc.) by military force. 2 (*tr*) to occupy in large numbers; overrun; infest. 3 (*tr*) to trespass or encroach upon (privacy, etc.). 4 (*tr*) to enter and spread throughout, esp harmfully; pervade. 5 (of plants, esp weeds) to become established in (a place to which they are not native).
▷HISTORY C15: from Latin *invādere*, from *vādere* to go
▸**in'vadable** ADJECTIVE ▸**in'vader** NOUN

invaginate VERB (ɪn'vædʒɪ,neɪt) 1 *Pathol* to push one section of (a tubular organ or part) back into itself so that it becomes ensheathed; intussuscept. 2 (*intr*) (of the outer layer of an organism or part) to undergo invagination. ◆ ADJECTIVE (ɪn'vædʒɪnɪt, -,neɪt) 3 (of an organ or part) folded back upon itself.
▷HISTORY C19: from Medieval Latin *invāgīnāre*, from Latin IN-[2] + *vāgīna* sheath
▸**in'vaginable** ADJECTIVE

invagination (ɪn,vædʒɪ'neɪʃən) NOUN 1 *Pathol* the process of invaginating or the condition of being invaginated; intussusception. 2 *Pathol* an invaginated organ or part. 3 an infolding of the outer layer of cells of an organism or part of an organism so as to form a pocket in the surface, as in the embryonic development of a gastrula from a blastula.

invalid[1] ('ɪnvə,liːd, -lɪd) NOUN 1 **a** a person suffering from disablement or chronic ill health. **b** (*as modifier*): *an invalid chair.* ◆ ADJECTIVE 2 suffering from or disabled by injury, sickness, etc. ◆ VERB (*tr*) 3 to cause to become an invalid; disable. 4 (usually foll by *out; often passive*) *Chiefly Brit* to require (a member of the armed forces) to retire from active service through wounds or illness.
▷HISTORY C17: from Latin *invalidus* infirm, from IN-[1] + *validus* strong
▸**,inva'lidity** NOUN

invalid[2] (ɪn'vælɪd) ADJECTIVE 1 not valid; having no cogency or legal force. 2 *Logic* (of an argument) having a conclusion that does not follow from the premises: it may be false when the premises are all true; not valid.
▷HISTORY C16: from Medieval Latin *invalidus* without legal force; see INVALID[1]
▸**invalidity** (,ɪnvə'lɪdɪtɪ) *or* **in'validness** NOUN ▸**in'validly** ADVERB

invalidate (ɪn'vælɪ,deɪt) VERB (*tr*) 1 to render weak or ineffective, as an argument. 2 to take away the legal force or effectiveness of; annul, as a contract.
▸**in,vali'dation** NOUN ▸**in'vali,dator** NOUN

invalidism ('ɪnvəlɪ,dɪzəm) NOUN 1 the state of being an invalid, esp by reason of ill health. 2 a state of being abnormally preoccupied with one's physical health.

invalidity benefit NOUN (formerly, in the British National Insurance scheme) a weekly payment to a person who had been off work through illness for more than six months: replaced by **incapacity benefit** in 1995. Abbreviation: **IVB.**

invaluable (ɪn'væljʊəbəl) ADJECTIVE having great value that is impossible to calculate; priceless.
▸**in'valuableness** NOUN ▸**in'valuably** ADVERB

Invar (ɪn'vɑː) NOUN *Trademark* an alloy containing iron (63.8 per cent), nickel (36 per cent), and carbon (0.2 per cent). It has a very low coefficient of expansion and is used for the balance springs of watches, etc.
▷HISTORY C20: shortened from INVARIABLE

invariable (ɪn'veərɪəbəl) ADJECTIVE 1 not subject to alteration; unchanging. ◆ NOUN 2 a mathematical quantity having an unchanging value; a constant.
▸**in,varia'bility** *or* **in'variableness** NOUN

invariably (ɪn'veərɪəblɪ) ADVERB always; without exception.

invariant (ɪn'veərɪənt) NOUN 1 *Maths* an entity, quantity, etc., that is unaltered by a particular transformation of coordinates: *a point in space, rather than its coordinates, is an invariant.* ◆ ADJECTIVE 2 *Maths* (of a relationship or a property of a function, configuration, or equation) unaltered by a particular transformation of coordinates. 3 a rare word for **invariable.**
▸**in'variance** *or* **in'variancy** NOUN

invasion (ɪn'veɪʒən) NOUN 1 the act of invading with armed forces. 2 any encroachment or intrusion: *an invasion of rats.* 3 the onset or advent of something harmful, esp of a disease. 4 *Pathol* the spread of cancer from its point of origin into surrounding tissues. 5 the movement of plants to a new area or to an area to which they are not native.

invasive (ɪn'veɪsɪv) ADJECTIVE 1 of or relating to an invasion, intrusion, etc. 2 relating to or denoting cancer at the stage at which it has spread from its site of origin to other tissues. 3 (of surgery) involving making a relatively large incision in the body to gain access to the target of the surgery, as opposed to making a small incision or gaining access endoscopically through a natural orifice.

invective (ɪn'vɛktɪv) NOUN 1 vehement accusation or denunciation, esp of a bitterly abusive or sarcastic kind. ◆ ADJECTIVE 2 characterized by or using abusive language, bitter sarcasm, etc.
▷HISTORY C15: from Late Latin *invectīvus* reproachful, scolding, from Latin *invectus* carried in; see INVEIGH
▸**in'vectively** ADVERB ▸**in'vectiveness** NOUN

inveigh (ɪn'veɪ) VERB (*intr;* foll by *against*) to speak with violent or invective language; rail.
▷HISTORY C15: from Latin *invehī*, literally: to be carried in, hence, assail physically or verbally, from IN-[2] + *vehī* to be carried, ride
▸**in'veigher** NOUN

inveigle (ɪn'viːgəl, -'veɪ-) VERB (*tr;* often foll by *into* or an infinitive) to lead (someone into a situation) or persuade (to do something) by cleverness or trickery; cajole: *to inveigle customers into spending more.*
▷HISTORY C15: from Old French *avogler* to blind, deceive, from *avogle* blind, from Medieval Latin *ab oculis* without eyes
▸**in'veiglement** NOUN ▸**in'veigler** NOUN

invent (ɪn'vɛnt) VERB 1 to create or devise (new ideas, machines, etc.). 2 to make up (falsehoods); fabricate.
▷HISTORY C15: from Latin *invenīre* to find, come upon, from IN-[2] + *venīre* to come
▸**in'ventible** *or* **in'ventable** ADJECTIVE

invention (ɪn'vɛnʃən) NOUN 1 the act or process of inventing. 2 something that is invented. 3 *Patent law* the discovery or production of some new or improved process or machine that is both useful and is not obvious to persons skilled in the particular field. 4 creative power or ability; inventive skill. 5 *Euphemistic* a fabrication; lie. 6 (in traditional rhetoric) one of the five steps in preparing a speech or discourse: the process of finding suitable topics on which to talk or write. 7 *Music* a short piece consisting of two or three parts usually in imitative counterpoint. 8 *Sociol* the creation of a new cultural pattern or trait.
▸**in'ventional** ADJECTIVE ▸**in'ventionless** ADJECTIVE

inventive (ɪn'vɛntɪv) ADJECTIVE 1 skilled or quick at contriving; ingenious; resourceful. 2 characterized by inventive skill: *an inventive programme of work.* 3 of or relating to invention.
▸**in'ventively** ADVERB ▸**in'ventiveness** NOUN

inventor (ɪn'vɛntə) NOUN a person who invents, esp as a profession.
▸**in'ventress** FEMININE NOUN

inventory ('ɪnvəntərɪ, -trɪ) NOUN 1 a detailed list of articles, goods, property, etc. 2 (*often plural*) *Accounting, chiefly US* **a** the amount or value of a firm's current assets that consist of raw materials, work in progress, and finished goods; stock. **b** such assets individually. ◆ VERB **-tories, -torying, -toried.** 3 (*tr*) to enter (items) in an inventory; make a list of.
▷HISTORY C16: from Medieval Latin *inventōrium;* see INVENT
▸**'inventoriable** ADJECTIVE ▸**,inven'torial** ADJECTIVE
▸**,inven'torially** ADVERB

inveracity (,ɪnvə'ræsɪtɪ) NOUN, *plural* **-ties.** *Formal or euphemistic* 1 lying; untruthfulness. 2 an untruth; lie.

Inveraray (,ɪnvə'rɛərɪ) NOUN a town in W Scotland, in Argyll and Bute: Inveraray Castle is the seat of the Dukes of Argyll. Pop.: 512 (1991).

Invercargill (,ɪnvə'kɑːgɪl) NOUN a city in New Zealand, on South Island: regional trading centre for sheep and agricultural products. Pop.: 51 600 (1995 est.).

Inverclyde (,ɪnvə'klaɪd) NOUN a council area of W central Scotland: created in 1996 from part of Strathclyde region. Administrative centre: Greenock. Pop.: 84 203 (2001). Area: 162 sq. km (63 sq. miles).

Inverness (,ɪnvə'nɛs) NOUN 1 a city in N Scotland, administrative centre of Highland: tourism and specialized engineering. Pop.: 41 234 (1991). 2 (*sometimes not capital*) an overcoat with a removable cape.

Inverness-shire (,ɪnvə'nɛs,ʃɪə, -ʃə) NOUN (until 1975) a county of NW Scotland, now part of Highland.

inverse (ɪn'vɜːs, 'ɪnvɜːs) ADJECTIVE 1 opposite or contrary in effect, sequence, direction, etc. 2 *Maths* **a** (of a relationship) containing two variables such that an increase in one results in a decrease in the other: *the volume of a gas is in inverse ratio to its pressure.* **b** (of an element) operating on a specified member of a set to produce the identity of the set: *the additive inverse element of x is –x, the multiplicative inverse element of x is 1/x.* 3 (*usually prenominal*) upside-down; inverted: *in an inverse position.* ◆ NOUN 4 *Maths* **a** another name for **reciprocal** (sense 7). **b** an inverse element. 5 *Logic* a categorial proposition derived from another by changing both the proposition and its subject from affirmative to negative, or vice versa, as *all immortals are angels* from *no mortals are angels.*
▷HISTORY C17: from Latin *inversus*, from *invertere* to INVERT
▸**in'versely** ADVERB

inverse square law NOUN any natural law in which the magnitude of a physical quantity varies inversely with the square of the distance from its source.

inversion (ɪn'vɜːʃən) NOUN 1 the act of inverting or state of being inverted. 2 something inverted, esp a reversal of order, mutual functions, etc.: *an inversion of their previous relationship.* 3 Also called: **anastrophe.** *Rhetoric* the reversal of a normal order of words. 4 *Chem* **a** the conversion of a dextrorotatory solution of sucrose into a laevorotatory solution of glucose and fructose by hydrolysis. **b** any similar reaction in which the optical properties of the reactants are opposite to those of the products. 5 *Music* **a** the process or result of transposing the notes of a chord (esp a triad) such that the root, originally in the bass, is placed in an upper part. When the bass note is the third of the triad, the resulting chord is the **first inversion;** when it is the fifth, the resulting chord is the **second inversion.** See also **root position. b** (in counterpoint) the modification of a melody or part in which all ascending intervals are replaced by corresponding descending intervals and vice versa. **c** the modification of an interval in which the

higher note becomes the lower or the lower one the higher. See **complement** (sense 8). [6] *Pathol* abnormal positioning of an organ or part, as in being upside down or turned inside out. [7] *Psychiatry* **a** the adoption of the role or characteristics of the opposite sex. **b** another word for **homosexuality.** [8] *Meteorol* an abnormal condition in which the layer of air next to the earth's surface is cooler than an overlying layer. [9] *Anatomy, phonetics* another word for **retroflexion** (sense 2). [10] *Computing* an operation by which each digit of a binary number is changed to the alternative digit, as *10110* to *01001.* [11] *Genetics* a type of chromosomal mutation in which a section of a chromosome, and hence the order of its genes, is reversed. [12] *Logic* the process of deriving the inverse of a categorial proposition. [13] *Maths* a transformation that takes a point *P* to a point *P′* such that *OP•OP′* = a^2, where *a* is a constant and *P* and *P′* lie on a straight line through a fixed point *O* and on the same side of it.
▸**in'versive** ADJECTIVE

invert VERB (ɪn'vɜːt) [1] to turn or cause to turn upside down or inside out. [2] (*tr*) to reverse in effect, sequence, direction, etc. [3] (*tr*) *Phonetics* **a** to turn (the tip of the tongue) up and back. **b** to pronounce (a speech sound) by retroflexion. [4] *Logic* to form the inverse of a categorial proposition. ◆ NOUN ('ɪnvɜːt) [5] *Psychiatry* **a** a person who adopts the role of the opposite sex. **b** another word for **homosexual.** [6] *Architect* **a** the lower inner surface of a drain, sewer, etc. Compare **soffit** (sense 2). **b** an arch that is concave upwards, esp one used in foundations.
▷HISTORY C16: from Latin *invertere,* from IN-[2] + *vertere* to turn
▸**in'vertible** ADJECTIVE ▸**in,verti'bility** NOUN

invertase (ɪn'vɜːteɪz) NOUN an enzyme, occurring in the intestinal juice of animals and in yeasts, that hydrolyses sucrose to glucose and fructose. Also called: **saccharase.**

invertebrate (ɪn'vɜːtɪbrɪt, -ˌbreɪt) NOUN [1] any animal lacking a backbone, including all species not classified as vertebrates. ◆ ADJECTIVE *also* **in'vertebral.** [2] of, relating to, or designating invertebrates.

inverted comma NOUN another term for **quotation mark.**

inverted mordent NOUN *Music* a melodic ornament consisting of the rapid single or double alternation of a principal note with a note one degree higher. Also called: **upper mordent.** See also **pralltriller.**

inverted pleat NOUN *Dressmaking* a box pleat reversed so that the fullness of the material is turned inwards.

inverted snob NOUN a person who scorns the conventions or attitudes of his own class or social group by attempting to identify with people of a supposedly lower class.

inverter *or* **invertor** (ɪn'vɜːtə) NOUN [1] any device for converting a direct current into an alternating current. [2] *Computing* another name for **NOT circuit.**

invert sugar ('ɪnvɜːt) NOUN a mixture of fructose and glucose obtained by the inversion of sucrose.

invest (ɪn'vest) VERB [1] (often foll by *in*) to lay out (money or capital in an enterprise, esp by purchasing shares) with the expectation of profit. [2] (*tr; often foll by in*) to devote (effort, resources, etc., to a project). [3] (*tr; often foll by in* or *with*) *Archaic or ceremonial* to clothe or adorn (in some garment, esp the robes of an office): *to invest a king in the insignia of an emperor.* [4] (*tr; often foll by in*) to install formally or ceremoniously (in an official position, rank, etc.). [5] (*tr; foll by in* or *with*) to place (power, authority, etc., in) or provide (with power or authority): *to invest new rights in the monarchy.* [6] (*tr; usually passive;* foll by *in* or *with*) to provide or endow (a person with qualities, characteristics, etc.): *he was invested with great common sense.* [7] (*tr;* foll by *with*) *Usually poetic* to cover or adorn, as if with a coat or garment: *when spring invests the trees with leaves.* [8] (*tr*) *Rare* to surround with military forces; besiege. [9] (*intr;* foll by *in*) *Informal* to purchase; buy.
▷HISTORY C16: from Medieval Latin *investīre* to clothe, from Latin, from *vestīre,* from *vestis* a garment
▸**in'vestable** *or* **in'vestible** ADJECTIVE ▸**in'vestor** NOUN

investigate (ɪn'vɛstɪˌgeɪt) VERB to inquire into (a situation or problem, esp a crime or death) thoroughly; examine systematically, esp in order to discover the truth.
▷HISTORY C16: from Latin *investīgāre* to search after, from IN-[2] + *vestīgium* track; see VESTIGE
▸**in'vestigable** ADJECTIVE ▸**in'vestigative** *or* **in'vestigatory** ADJECTIVE

investigation (ɪnˌvɛstɪ'geɪʃən) NOUN the act or process of investigating; a careful search or examination in order to discover facts, etc.
▸**in,vesti'gational** ADJECTIVE

investigator (ɪn'vɛstɪˌgeɪtə) NOUN a person who investigates, such as a private detective.

investiture (ɪn'vɛstɪtʃə) NOUN [1] the act of presenting with a title or with the robes and insignia of an office or rank. [2] (in feudal society) the formal bestowal of the possessory right to a fief or other benefice. [3] a less common word for **investment** (sense 7).
▸**in'vestitive** ADJECTIVE

investment (ɪn'vɛstmənt) NOUN [1] **a** the act of investing money. **b** the amount invested. **c** an enterprise, asset, etc., in which money is or can be invested. [2] **a** the act of investing effort, resources, etc. **b** the amount invested. [3] *Economics* the amount by which the stock of capital (plant, machinery, materials, etc.) in an enterprise or economy changes. [4] *Biology* the outer layer or covering of an organ, part, or organism. [5] a less common word for **investiture** (sense 1). [6] the act of investing or state of being invested, as with an official robe, a specific quality, etc. [7] *Rare* the act of besieging with military forces, works, etc.

investment analyst NOUN a specialist in forecasting the prices of stocks and shares.

investment bond NOUN a single-premium life-assurance policy in which a fixed sum is invested in an asset-backed fund.

investment trust NOUN a financial enterprise that invests its subscribed capital in securities for its investors' benefit.

inveterate (ɪn'vɛtərɪt) ADJECTIVE [1] long established, esp so as to be deep-rooted or ingrained: *an inveterate feeling of hostility.* [2] (*prenominal*) settled or confirmed in a habit or practice, esp a bad one; hardened: *an inveterate smoker.* [3] *Obsolete* full of hatred; hostile.
▷HISTORY C16: from Latin *inveterātus* of long standing, from *inveterāre* to make old, from IN-[2] + *vetus* old
▸**in'veteracy** *or* **in'veterateness** NOUN ▸**in'veterately** ADVERB

inviable (ɪn'vaɪəbᵊl) ADJECTIVE not viable, esp financially; not able to survive: *an inviable company.*
▸**in,via'bility** *or* **in'viableness** NOUN ▸**in'viably** ADVERB

invidious (ɪn'vɪdɪəs) ADJECTIVE [1] incurring or tending to arouse resentment, unpopularity, etc.: *an invidious task.* [2] (of comparisons or distinctions) unfairly or offensively discriminating. [3] *Obsolete* grudging; envious.
▷HISTORY C17: from Latin *invidiōsus* full of envy, from *invidia* ENVY
▸**in'vidiously** ADVERB ▸**in'vidiousness** NOUN

invigilate (ɪn'vɪdʒɪˌleɪt) VERB (*intr*) [1] *Brit* to watch examination candidates, esp to prevent cheating. US word: **proctor.** [2] *Archaic* to keep watch.
▷HISTORY C16: from Latin *invigilāre* to watch over, from IN-[2] + *vigilāre* to keep watch; see VIGIL
▸**in,vigi'lation** NOUN ▸**in'vigi,lator** NOUN

invigorate (ɪn'vɪgəˌreɪt) VERB (*tr*) to give vitality and vigour to; animate; brace; refresh: *to be invigorated by fresh air.*
▷HISTORY C17: from IN-[2] + Latin *vigor* VIGOUR
▸**in'vigor,atingly** ADVERB ▸**in,vigor'ation** NOUN
▸**in'vigorative** ADJECTIVE ▸**in'vigoratively** ADVERB
▸**in'vigor,ator** NOUN

invincible (ɪn'vɪnsəbᵊl) ADJECTIVE [1] incapable of being defeated; unconquerable. [2] unable to be overcome; insuperable: *invincible prejudices.*
▷HISTORY C15: from Late Latin *invincibilis,* from Latin IN-[1] + *vincere* to conquer
▸**in,vinci'bility** *or* **in'vincibleness** NOUN ▸**in'vincibly** ADVERB

in vino veritas *Latin* (ɪn 'viːnəʊ 'vɛrɪˌtæs) in wine there is truth; people speak the truth when they are drunk.

inviolable (ɪn'vaɪələbᵊl) ADJECTIVE that must not or cannot be transgressed, dishonoured, or broken; to be kept sacred: *an inviolable oath.*
▸**in,viola'bility** *or* **in'violableness** NOUN ▸**in'violably** ADVERB

inviolate (ɪn'vaɪəlɪt, -ˌleɪt) ADJECTIVE [1] free from violation, injury, disturbance, etc. [2] a less common word for **inviolable.**
▸**in'violacy** *or* **in'violateness** NOUN ▸**in'violately** ADVERB

invisible (ɪn'vɪzəbᵊl) ADJECTIVE [1] not visible; not able to be perceived by the eye: *invisible rays.* [2] concealed from sight; hidden. [3] not easily seen or noticed: *invisible mending.* [4] kept hidden from public view; secret; clandestine. [5] *Economics* of or relating to services rather than goods in relation to the invisible balance: *invisible earnings.* ◆ NOUN [6] *Economics* an invisible item of trade; service.
▸**in,visi'bility** *or* **in'visibleness** NOUN ▸**in'visibly** ADVERB

invisible balance NOUN *Economics* the difference in value between total exports of services plus payment of property incomes from abroad and total imports of services plus payment abroad of property incomes. Compare **balance of trade.**

invisible ink NOUN a liquid used for writing that does not become visible until it has been treated with chemicals, heat, ultraviolet light, etc.

invitation (ˌɪnvɪ'teɪʃən) NOUN [1] **a** the act of inviting, such as an offer of entertainment or hospitality. **b** (*as modifier*): *an invitation dance; an invitation race.* [2] the act of enticing or attracting; allurement.

invitatory (ɪn'vaɪtətərɪ, -trɪ) ADJECTIVE [1] serving as or conveying an invitation. ◆ NOUN, *plural* **-tories.** [2] any of various invitations to prayer, such as Psalm 95 in a religious service.

invite VERB (ɪn'vaɪt) (*tr*) [1] to ask (a person or persons) in a friendly or polite way (to do something, attend an event, etc.): *he invited them to dinner.* [2] to make a request for, esp publicly or formally: *to invite applications.* [3] to bring on or provoke; give occasion for: *you invite disaster by your actions.* [4] to welcome or tempt. ◆ NOUN ('ɪnvaɪt) [5] an informal word for **invitation.**
▷HISTORY C16: from Latin *invītāre* to invite, entertain, from IN-[2] + *-vītāre,* probably related to Greek *hiesthai* to be desirous of
▸**in'viter** NOUN

inviting (ɪn'vaɪtɪŋ) ADJECTIVE tempting; alluring; attractive.
▸**in'vitingly** ADVERB ▸**in'vitingness** NOUN

in vitro (ɪn 'viːtrəʊ) ADVERB, ADJECTIVE (of biological processes or reactions) made to occur outside the living organism in an artificial environment, such as a culture medium.
▷HISTORY New Latin, literally: in glass

in vitro fertilization NOUN a technique enabling some women who are unable to conceive to bear children. Egg cells removed from a woman's ovary are fertilized by sperm in vitro; some of the resulting fertilized egg cells are incubated until the blastocyst stage, which are then implanted into her uterus. Abbreviation: **IVF.**

in vivo (ɪn 'viːvəʊ) ADVERB, ADJECTIVE (of biological processes or experiments) occurring or carried out in the living organism.
▷HISTORY New Latin, literally: in a living (thing)

invocate ('ɪnvəˌkeɪt) VERB an archaic word for **invoke.**
▸**invocative** (ɪn'vɒkətɪv) ADJECTIVE ▸**'invo,cator** NOUN

invocation (ˌɪnvə'keɪʃən) NOUN [1] the act of invoking or calling upon some agent for assistance. [2] a prayer asking God for help, forgiveness, etc., esp as part of a religious service. [3] an appeal for inspiration and guidance from a Muse or deity at the beginning of a poem. [4] **a** the act of summoning a spirit or demon from another world by ritual incantation or magic. **b** the incantation used in this act.
▸**,invo'cational** ADJECTIVE ▸**invocatory** (ɪn'vɒkətərɪ, -trɪ) ADJECTIVE

invoice ('ɪnvɔɪs) NOUN [1] a document issued by a seller to a buyer listing the goods or services supplied and stating the sum of money due. ◆ VERB [2] (*tr*) **a** to present (a customer) with an invoice. **b** to list (merchandise sold) on an invoice.
▷HISTORY C16: from earlier *invoyes,* from Old French *envois,* plural of *envoi* message; see ENVOY[1]

invoke (ɪn'vəʊk) VERB (*tr*) [1] to call upon (an

agent, esp God or another deity) for help, inspiration, etc. 2 to put (a law, penalty, etc.) into use: *the union invoked the dispute procedure.* 3 to appeal to (an outside agent or authority) for confirmation, corroboration, etc. 4 to implore or beg (help, etc.). 5 to summon (a spirit, demon, etc.); conjure up.
▷HISTORY C15: from Latin *invocāre* to call upon, appeal to, from *vocāre* to call
▸**in'vocable** ADJECTIVE ▸**in'voker** NOUN

> **Language note** *Invoke* is sometimes wrongly used where *evoke* is meant: *this proposal evoked* (not *invoked*) *a strong reaction.*

involucel (ɪn'vɒljʊˌsɛl) *or* **involucellum** (ɪnˌvɒljʊ'sɛləm) NOUN, *plural* **-cels** *or* **-cella** (-'sɛlə). a ring of bracts at the base of the florets of a compound umbel.
▷HISTORY C19: from New Latin *involūcellum* a little cover; see INVOLUCRE
▸**inˌvolu'cellate** *or* **inˌvolu'cellated** ADJECTIVE

involucre ('ɪnvəˌluːkə) *or* **involucrum** (ˌɪnvə'luːkrəm) NOUN, *plural* **-cres** *or* **-cra** (-krə). a ring of bracts at the base of an inflorescence in such plants as the composites.
▷HISTORY C16 (in the sense: envelope): from New Latin *involucrum,* from Latin: wrapper, from *involvere* to wrap; see INVOLVE
▸**ˌinvo'lucral** ADJECTIVE ▸**ˌinvo'lucrate** ADJECTIVE

involuntary (ɪn'vɒləntərɪ, -trɪ) ADJECTIVE 1 carried out without one's conscious wishes; not voluntary; unintentional. 2 *Physiol* (esp of a movement or muscle) performed or acting without conscious control.
▸**in'voluntarily** ADVERB ▸**in'voluntariness** NOUN

involute ADJECTIVE ('ɪnvəˌluːt) *also* **involuted.** 1 complex, intricate, or involved. 2 *Botany* (esp of petals, leaves, etc., in bud) having margins that are rolled inwards. 3 (of certain shells) closely coiled so that the axis is obscured. ◆ NOUN ('ɪnvəˌluːt) 4 *Geometry* the curve described by the free end of a thread as it is wound around another curve, the **evolute**, such that its normals are tangential to the evolute. ◆ VERB (ˌɪnvə'luːt) 5 (*intr*) to become involute.
▷HISTORY C17: from Latin *involūtus,* from *involvere;* see INVOLVE
▸**'invoˌlutely** ADVERB ▸**ˌinvo'lutedly** ADVERB

involute gear NOUN a gear tooth form that is generated by involute geometry.

involution (ˌɪnvə'luːʃən) NOUN 1 the act of involving or complicating or the state of being involved or complicated. 2 something involved or complicated. 3 *Zoology* degeneration or structural deformation. 4 *Biology* an involute formation or structure. 5 *Physiol* reduction in size of an organ or part, as of the uterus following childbirth or as a result of ageing. 6 an algebraic operation in which a number, variable, expression etc., is raised to a specified power. Compare **evolution** (sense 5). 7 *Grammar* an involved construction, such as one in which the subject is separated from the predicate by an additional clause.
▸**ˌinvo'lutional** ADJECTIVE

involve (ɪn'vɒlv) VERB (*tr*) 1 to include or contain as a necessary part: *the task involves hard work.* 2 to have an effect on; spread to: *the investigation involved many innocent people.* 3 (*often passive;* usually foll by *in* or *with*) to concern or associate significantly: *many people were involved in the crime.* 4 (*often passive*) to make complicated; tangle: *the situation was further involved by her disappearance.* 5 *Rare, often poetic* to wrap or surround. 6 *Maths, obsolete* to raise to a specified power.
▷HISTORY C14: from Latin *involvere* to roll in, surround, from IN-^{2} + *volvere* to roll
▸**in'volvement** NOUN ▸**in'volver** NOUN

involved (ɪn'vɒlvd) ADJECTIVE 1 complicated; difficult to comprehend: *an involved literary style.* 2 (*usually postpositive*) concerned or implicated: *one of the men involved.* 3 (*postpositive;* foll by *with*) *Euphemistic* having sexual relations: *she was involved with a number of men.*

invulnerable (ɪn'vʌlnərəbᵊl, -'vʌlnrəbᵊl) ADJECTIVE 1 incapable of being wounded, hurt, damaged, etc., either physically or emotionally. 2 incapable of being damaged or captured: *an invulnerable fortress.*
▸**inˌvulnera'bility** *or* **in'vulnerableness** NOUN
▸**in'vulnerably** ADVERB

invultuation (ɪnˌvʌltʃʊ'eɪʃən) NOUN the use of or the act of making images of people, animals, etc., for witchcraft.
▷HISTORY C19: from Medieval Latin *invultuāre* to make a likeness, from IN-^{2} + *vultus* likeness

inward ('ɪnwəd) ADJECTIVE 1 going or directed towards the middle of or into something. 2 situated within; inside. 3 of, relating to, or existing in the mind or spirit: *inward meditation.* 4 of one's own country or a specific country: *inward investment.* ◆ ADVERB 5 a variant of **inwards** (sense 1). ◆ NOUN 6 the inward part; inside.
▸**'inwardness** NOUN

inwardly ('ɪnwədlɪ) ADVERB 1 within the private thoughts or feelings; secretly: *inwardly troubled, he kept smiling.* 2 not aloud: *to laugh inwardly.* 3 with reference to the inside or inner part; internally. 4 *Archaic* intimately; essentially: *the most inwardly concerned of the plotters.*

inwards ADVERB ('ɪnwədz) *also* **inward.** 1 towards the interior or middle of something. 2 in, into, or towards the mind or spirit. ◆ PLURAL NOUN ('ɪnədz) 3 a variant spelling of **innards.**

inweave (ɪn'wiːv) VERB **-weaves, -weaving, -wove** *or* **-weaved; -woven** *or* **-weaved.** (*tr*) to weave together into or as if into a design, fabric, etc.; interweave.

inwrap (ɪn'ræp) VERB **-wraps, -wrapping, -wrapped.** a less common spelling of **enwrap.**

inwrought (ˌɪn'rɔːt) ADJECTIVE 1 worked or woven into material, esp decoratively. 2 *Rare* blended with other things.

in-your-face ADJECTIVE *Slang* aggressive and confrontational: *provocative in-your-face activism.*

io THE INTERNET DOMAIN NAME FOR British Indian Ocean Territory.

Io[1] ('aɪəʊ) NOUN *Greek myth* a maiden loved by Zeus and turned into a white heifer by either Zeus or Hera.

Io[2] ('aɪəʊ) NOUN the innermost of the four Galilean satellites of Jupiter, displaying intense volcanic activity. Diameter: 3640 km; orbital radius: 422 000 km.

Io[3] THE CHEMICAL SYMBOL FOR ionium.

I/O ABBREVIATION FOR input/output.

Ioánnina (*Greek* jɔ'anina) *or* **Yanina** NOUN a city in NW Greece: belonged to the Serbs (1349–1430) and then the Turks (until 1913); seat of Ali Pasha, the "Lion of Janina", from 1788 to 1822. Pop.: 56 496 (1991 est.). Serbian name: **Janina.**

IOC ABBREVIATION FOR International Olympic Committee.

iodate ('aɪəˌdeɪt) NOUN 1 a salt of iodic acid. ◆ VERB 2 (*tr*) another word for **iodize.**
▸**ˌio'dation** NOUN

iodic (aɪ'ɒdɪk) ADJECTIVE of or containing iodine, esp in the pentavalent state.

iodic acid NOUN a colourless or pale yellow soluble crystalline substance that forms acidic aqueous solutions. Used as a reagent and disinfectant. Formula: HIO_3.

iodide ('aɪəˌdaɪd) NOUN 1 a salt of hydriodic acid, containing the iodide ion, I^-. 2 a compound containing an iodine atom, such as methyl iodide, CH_3I.

iodine ('aɪəˌdiːn) NOUN a bluish-black element of the halogen group that sublimates into a violet irritating gas. Its compounds are used in medicine and photography and in dyes. The radioisotope **iodine-131** (**radioiodine**), with a half-life of 8 days, is used in the diagnosis and treatment of thyroid disease. Symbol: I; atomic no.: 53; atomic wt.: 126.90447; valency: 1, 3, 5, or 7; relative density: 4.93; melting pt.: 113.5°C; boiling pt.: 184.35°C.
▷HISTORY C19: from French *iode,* from Greek *iōdēs* rust-coloured, but taken to mean violet-coloured, through a mistaken derivation from *ion* violet

iodism ('aɪəˌdɪzəm) NOUN poisoning induced by ingestion of iodine or its compounds.

iodize *or* **iodise** ('aɪəˌdaɪz) VERB (*tr*) to treat or react with iodine or an iodine compound. Also: **iodate.**
▸**ˌiodi'zation** *or* **ˌiodi'sation** NOUN ▸**'ioˌdizer** *or* **'ioˌdiser** NOUN

iodo- *or before a vowel* **iod-** COMBINING FORM indicating iodine: *iodoform; iodism.*

iodoform (aɪ'ɒdəˌfɔːm) NOUN a yellow crystalline insoluble volatile solid with a penetrating sweet odour made by heating alcohol with iodine and an alkali: used as an antiseptic. Formula: CHI_3. Systematic name: **triiodomethane.**

iodometry (ˌaɪə'dɒmɪtrɪ) NOUN *Chem* a procedure used in volumetric analysis for determining the quantity of substance present that contains, liberates, or reacts with iodine.
▸**iodometric** (ˌaɪədəʊ'mɛtrɪk) *or* **ˌiodo'metrical** ADJECTIVE
▸**ˌiodo'metrically** ADVERB

iodopsin (ˌaɪə'dɒpsɪn) NOUN a violet light-sensitive pigment in the cones of the retina of the eye that is responsible for colour vision. Also called: **visual violet.** See also **rhodopsin.**

iodous (aɪ'ɒdəs) ADJECTIVE 1 of or containing iodine, esp in the trivalent state. 2 concerned with or resembling iodine.

iolite ('aɪəˌlaɪt) NOUN another name for **cordierite.**
▷HISTORY C19: from Greek *ion* a violet + -LITE

IOM ABBREVIATION FOR Isle of Man.

Io moth NOUN an American saturniid moth, *Automeris io,* bright yellow with a blue-and-pink eyelike spot on each of the hind wings.
▷HISTORY C19: after Io (who was tormented by a gadfly), referring to the sting of the larva

ion ('aɪən, -ɒn) NOUN an electrically charged atom or group of atoms formed by the loss or gain of one or more electrons. See also **cation, anion.**
▷HISTORY C19: from Greek, literally: going, from *ienai* to go

-ion SUFFIX FORMING NOUNS indicating an action, process, or state: *creation; objection.* Compare **-ation, -tion.**
▷HISTORY from Latin *-iōn-, -io*

Iona (aɪ'əʊnə) NOUN an island off the W coast of Scotland, in the Inner Hebrides: site of St Columba's monastery (founded in 563) and an important early centre of Christianity. Area: 854 ha (2112 acres).

IONARC ABBREVIATION FOR Indian Ocean National Association for Regional Cooperation.

ion engine NOUN a type of rocket engine in which thrust is obtained by the electrostatic acceleration of charged positive ions. Compare **plasma engine.**

ion exchange NOUN the process in which ions are exchanged between a solution and an insoluble solid, usually a resin. It is used to soften water, to separate radioactive isotopes, and to purify certain industrial chemicals.

Ionia (aɪ'əʊnɪə) NOUN an ancient region of W central Asia Minor, including adjacent Aegean islands: colonized by Greeks in about 1100 B.C.

Ionian (aɪ'əʊnɪən) NOUN 1 a member of a Hellenic people who settled in Attica in about 1100 B.C. and later colonized the islands and E coast of the Aegean Sea. ◆ ADJECTIVE 2 of or relating to this people or their dialect of Ancient Greek; Ionic. 3 of or relating to Ionia. 4 *Music* relating to or denoting an authentic mode represented by the ascending natural diatonic scale from C to C and forming the basis of the modern major key. See also **Hypo-.**

Ionian Islands PLURAL NOUN a group of Greek islands in the Ionian Sea, consisting of Corfu, Cephalonia, Zante, Levkas, Ithaca, Cythera, and Paxos: ceded to Greece in 1864. Pop.: 214 274 (2001). Area: 2307 sq. km (891 sq. miles).

Ionian Sea NOUN the part of the Mediterranean Sea between SE Italy, E Sicily, and Greece.

ionic (aɪ'ɒnɪk) ADJECTIVE of, relating to, or occurring in the form of ions.

Ionic (aɪ'ɒnɪk) ADJECTIVE 1 of, denoting, or relating to one of the five classical orders of architecture, characterized by fluted columns and capitals with scroll-like ornaments. See also **Doric, Composite, Tuscan, Corinthian.** 2 of or relating to Ionia, its inhabitants, or their dialect of Ancient Greek. 3 *Prosody* of, relating to, designating, or employing Ionics in verse. ◆ NOUN 4 one of four chief dialects of Ancient Greek; the dialect spoken in Ionia. Compare **Aeolic, Arcadic, Doric.** See also **Attic**

(sense 3). [5] (in classical prosody) a type of metrical foot having either two long followed by two short syllables (**greater Ionic**), or two short followed by two long syllables (**lesser Ionic**).

ionic bond NOUN another name for **electrovalent bond.**

ion implantation NOUN a technique used in the manufacture of semiconductor devices in which impurities are implanted by means of beams of electrically accelerated ions.

ionium (aɪˈəʊnɪəm) NOUN *Obsolete* a naturally occurring radioisotope of thorium with a mass number of 230. Symbol: Io.
▷HISTORY C20: from New Latin, from ION + -IUM

ionization *or* **ionisation** (ˌaɪənaɪˈzeɪʃən) NOUN **a** the formation of ions as a result of a chemical reaction, high temperature, electrical discharge, particle collisions, or radiation. **b** (*as modifier*): *ionization temperature; ionization current.*

ionization chamber NOUN a device for detecting and measuring ionizing radiation, consisting of a tube containing a low pressure gas and two electrodes between which a high voltage is maintained. The current between the electrodes is a function of the intensity of the radiation.

ionization potential NOUN the energy usually required to remove an electron from an atom, molecule, or radical, usually measured in electronvolts. Symbol: *I*. Compare **electron affinity.**

ionize *or* **ionise** (ˈaɪəˌnaɪz) VERB to change or become changed into ions.
▸ˈ**ion**ˌ**izable** *or* ˈ**ion**ˌ**isable** ADJECTIVE

ionizer *or* **ioniser** (ˈaɪəˌnaɪzə) NOUN a person or thing that ionizes, esp an electrical device used within a room to refresh its atmosphere by restoring negative ions.

ionizing radiation NOUN electromagnetic or corpuscular radiation that is able to cause ionization.

ionone (ˈaɪəˌnəʊn) NOUN [1] a yellowish liquid mixture of two isomers with an odour of violets, extracted from certain plants and used in perfumery. [2] either of these two isomers. Formula: $C_{13}H_{20}O$.

ionopause (aɪˈɒnəˌpɔːz) NOUN the transitional zone in the atmosphere between the ionosphere and the exosphere, about 644 km (400 miles) from the earth's surface.

ionophore (aɪˈɒnəˌfɔː) NOUN a chemical compound capable of forming a complex with an ion and transporting it through a biological membrane.
▷HISTORY C20: from ION + -O- + -PHORE

ionosphere (aɪˈɒnəˌsfɪə) NOUN a region of the earth's atmosphere, extending from about 60 kilometres to 1000 km above the earth's surface, in which there is a high concentration of free electrons formed as a result of ionizing radiation entering the atmosphere from space. See also **D region, E region, F region.**
▸**ionospheric** (aɪˌɒnəˈsferɪk) ADJECTIVE

ionospheric wave NOUN another name for **sky wave.**

ionotropy (ˌaɪəˈnɒtrəpɪ) NOUN *Chem* the reversible interconversion of a pair of organic isomers as a result of the migration of an ionic part of the molecule.

ion rocket NOUN a rocket propelled by an ion engine.

iontophoresis (aɪˌɒntəʊfəˈriːsɪs) NOUN *Biochem* a technique for studying neurotransmitters in the brain by the application of experimental solutions to the tissues through fine glass electrodes.
▷HISTORY C20: from Greek *iont-, ion,* from *ienai* to go + -PHORESIS

IOOF ABBREVIATION FOR Independent Order of Oddfellows.

iota (aɪˈəʊtə) NOUN [1] the ninth letter in the Greek alphabet (Ι, ι), a vowel or semivowel, transliterated as *i* or *j*. [2] (*usually used with a negative*) a very small amount; jot (esp in the phrase **not one** *or* **an iota**).
▷HISTORY C16: via Latin from Greek, of Semitic origin; see JOT

iotacism (aɪˈəʊtəˌsɪzəm) NOUN a tendency of vowels and diphthongs, esp in Modern Greek, to acquire the pronunciation of the vowel iota (iː).

IOU NOUN a written promise or reminder to pay a debt.
▷HISTORY C17: representing *I owe you*

-ious SUFFIX FORMING ADJECTIVES FROM NOUNS characterized by or full of: *ambitious; religious; suspicious.* Compare **-eous.**
▷HISTORY from Latin *-ius* and *-iōsus* full of

IOW ABBREVIATION FOR: [1] Isle of Wight. [2] *Text messaging* in other words.

Iowa (ˈaɪəʊə) NOUN a state of the N central US, in the Midwest: consists of rolling plains crossed by many rivers, with the Missouri forming the western border and the Mississippi the eastern. Capital: Des Moines. Pop.: 2 926 324 (2000). Area: 144 887 sq. km (55 941 sq. miles). Abbreviations: **Ia.,** (with zip code) **IA.**

Iowan (ˈaɪəʊən) NOUN [1] a native or inhabitant of Iowa. ◆ ADJECTIVE [2] of or relating to Iowa or its inhabitants.

IP ABBREVIATION FOR Internet protocol: a code used to label packets of data sent across the Internet, identifying both the sending and the receiving computers.

IPA ABBREVIATION FOR International Phonetic Alphabet.

IPCC ABBREVIATION FOR Intergovernmental Panel on Climate Change.

ipecacuanha (ˌɪpɪˌkækjʊˈænə) *or* **ipecac** (ˈɪpɪˌkæk) NOUN [1] a low-growing South American rubiaceous shrub, *Cephaelis ipecacuanha.* [2] a drug prepared from the dried roots of this plant, used as a purgative and emetic.
▷HISTORY C18: from Portuguese, from Tupi *ipekaaguéne,* from *ipeh* low + *kaa* leaves + *guéne* vomit

Iphigenia (ˌɪfɪdʒɪˈnaɪə) NOUN *Greek myth* the daughter of Agamemnon, taken by him to be sacrificed to Artemis, who saved her life and made her a priestess.

I-pin (ɪˈpɪn) NOUN a variant transliteration of the Chinese name for **Yibin.**

IPO ABBREVIATION FOR: [1] independent publicly owned company. ◆ [2] *Stock Exchange* initial public offering.

Ipoh (ˈiːpəʊ) NOUN a city in Malaysia, capital of Perak state: tin-mining centre. Pop.: 382 633 (1991).

ipomoea (ˌɪpəˈmɪə, ˌaɪ-) NOUN [1] any tropical or subtropical convolvulaceous plant of the genus *Ipomoea,* such as the morning-glory, sweet potato, and jalap, having trumpet-shaped flowers. [2] the dried root of a Mexican species, *I. orizabensis,* which yields a cathartic resin.
▷HISTORY C18: New Latin, from Greek *ips* worm + *homoios* like

ippon (ˈɪpɒn) NOUN *Judo, karate* a winning point awarded in a sparring competition for a perfectly executed technique.
▷HISTORY C20: Japanese, literally: one point

Ipsambul (ˌɪpsæmˈbuːl) NOUN another name for **Abu Simbel.**

ipse dixit *Latin* (ˈɪpseɪ ˈdɪksɪt) NOUN an arbitrary and unsupported assertion.
▷HISTORY C16, literally: he himself said it

ipsilateral (ˌɪpsɪˈlætərəl) ADJECTIVE on or affecting the same side of the body.
▷HISTORY C20: irregularly formed from Latin *ipse* self + LATERAL

ipsissima verba *Latin* (ɪpˈsɪsɪmə ˈvɜːbə) PLURAL NOUN the very words; verbatim.

ipso facto (ˈɪpsəʊ ˈfæktəʊ) ADVERB by that very fact or act: *ipso facto his guilt was apparent.*
▷HISTORY from Latin

ipso jure (ˈɪpsəʊ ˈjʊərɪ) ADVERB by the law itself; by operation of law.
▷HISTORY from Latin

Ipsus (ˈɪpsəs) NOUN an ancient town in Asia Minor, in S Phrygia: site of a decisive battle (301 B.C.) in the Wars of the Diadochi in which Lysimachus and Seleucus defeated Antigonus and Demetrius.

Ipswich (ˈɪpswɪtʃ) NOUN a town in E England, administrative centre of Suffolk, a port at the head of the Orwell estuary: financial services, telecommunications. Pop.: 130 157 (1991).

iq THE INTERNET DOMAIN NAME FOR Iraq.

IQ ABBREVIATION FOR intelligence quotient.

i.q. ABBREVIATION FOR idem quod.

▷HISTORY Latin: the same as

Iqaluit (ɪˈkælʊɪt) NOUN a town in N Canada, capital of Nunavut. Pop: 3700 (1999 est.). Former name: **Frobisher Bay.**

ir THE INTERNET DOMAIN NAME FOR Iran.

Ir THE CHEMICAL SYMBOL FOR iridium.

IR ABBREVIATION FOR: [1] infrared. [2] (in Britain) Inland Revenue. ◆ [3] INTERNATIONAL CAR REGISTRATION FOR Iran.

Ir. ABBREVIATION FOR: [1] Ireland. [2] Irish.

ir- PREFIX a variant of **in-**[1] and **in-**[2] before *r.*

IRA ABBREVIATION FOR **Irish Republican Army.**

iracund (ˈaɪərəˌkʌnd) ADJECTIVE *Rare* easily angered.
▷HISTORY C19: from Latin *īrācundus,* from *īra* anger
▸ˌ**ira**ˈ**cundity** NOUN

irade (ɪˈrɑːdɛ) NOUN a written edict of a Muslim ruler.
▷HISTORY C19: from Turkish: will, desire, from Arabic *irādah*

Iráklion (*Greek* iˈrakliɔn) NOUN a port in Greece, in N Crete: former capital of Crete (until 1841); ruled by Venetians (13th–17th centuries). Pop.: 117 167 (1991). Italian name: **Candia.** Also called: **Heraklion, Herakleion.**

Iran (ɪˈrɑːn) NOUN a republic in SW Asia, between the Caspian Sea and the Persian Gulf: consists chiefly of a high central desert plateau almost completely surrounded by mountains, a semitropical fertile region along the Caspian coast, and a hot and dry area beside the Persian Gulf. Oil is the most important export. Official language: Farsi (Persian). Official religion: Muslim majority. Currency: rial. Capital: Tehran. Pop.: 63 442 000 (2001 est.). Area: 1 647 050 sq. km (635 932 sq. miles). Former name (until 1935): **Persia.** Official name: **Islamic Republic of Iran.** See also **Persian Empire.**

Iranian (ɪˈreɪnɪən) NOUN [1] a native, citizen, or inhabitant of Iran. [2] a branch of the Indo-European family of languages, divided into **West Iranian** (including Old Persian, Pahlavi, modern Persian, Kurdish, Baluchi, and Tajik) and **East Iranian** (including Avestan, Sogdian, Pashto, and Ossetic). [3] the modern Persian language. ◆ ADJECTIVE [4] relating to, denoting, or characteristic of Iran, its inhabitants, or their language; Persian. [5] belonging to the Iranian branch of Indo-European.

Iran-Iraq War NOUN the war (1980–88) fought by Iran and Iraq, following the Iraqi invasion of disputed border territory in Iran. It ended indecisively with no important gains on either side: Iraq subsequently (1990) conceded the disputed territory. Also called: **Gulf War.**

Iraq (ɪˈrɑːk) NOUN a republic in SW Asia, on the Persian Gulf: coextensive with ancient Mesopotamia; became a British mandate in 1920, independent in 1932, and a republic in 1958. The Iraqi invasion of Kuwait (1990) led to their defeat in the first Gulf War (1991) by US-led UN forces. Refusal to destroy their weapons of mass destruction resulted in Iraq's defeat in the second Gulf War (2003) by a coalition of US and UK forces. Iraq consists chiefly of the mountains of Kurdistan in the northeast, part of the Syrian Desert, and the lower basin of the Rivers Tigris and Euphrates. Oil is the major export. Official language: Arabic; Kurdish is official in the Kurdish Autonomous Region only. Official religion: Muslim. Currency: dinar. Capital: Baghdad. Pop.: 23 332 000 (2001 est.). Area: 438 446 sq. km (169 284 sq. miles).

Iraqi (ɪˈrɑːkɪ) ADJECTIVE [1] of or relating to Iraq or its inhabitants. ◆ NOUN [2] a native or inhabitant of Iraq.

IRAS ABBREVIATION FOR Infrared Astronomical Satellite, a pioneering international earth-orbiting satellite that during 1983 made an all-sky survey at infrared wavelengths.

irascible (ɪˈræsɪbᵊl) ADJECTIVE [1] easily angered; irritable. [2] showing irritability: *an irascible action.*
▷HISTORY C16: from Late Latin *īrascibilis,* from Latin *īra* anger
▸**i**ˌ**rasci**ˈ**bility** *or* **i**ˈ**rascibleness** NOUN ▸**i**ˈ**rascibly** ADVERB

irate (aɪˈreɪt) ADJECTIVE [1] incensed with anger; furious. [2] marked by extreme anger: *an irate letter.*
▷HISTORY C19: from Latin *īrātus* enraged, from *īrascī* to be angry
▸**i**ˈ**rately** ADVERB

Irbid (ˈɪrbɪd) NOUN a town in NW Jordan. Pop.: 208 201 (1994).

Irbil (ˈɪəbɪl) NOUN a variant of **Erbil**.

IRBM ABBREVIATION FOR **intermediate range ballistic missile**.

IRC ABBREVIATION FOR: [1] International Red Cross. [2] International Red Crescent.

IRD (in New Zealand) ABBREVIATION FOR Inland Revenue Department.

ire (aɪə) NOUN *Literary* anger; wrath.
▷HISTORY C13: from Old French, from Latin *īra*
▸ˈ**ireful** ADJECTIVE ▸ˈ**irefully** ADVERB ▸ˈ**irefulness** NOUN
▸ˈ**ireless** ADJECTIVE

Ire. ABBREVIATION FOR Ireland.

Ireland (ˈaɪələnd) NOUN [1] an island off NW Europe: part of the British Isles, separated from Britain by the North Channel, the Irish Sea, and St George's Channel; contains large areas of peat bog, with mountains that rise over 900 m (3000 ft.) in the southwest and several large lakes. It was conquered by England in the 16th and early 17th centuries and ruled as a dependency until 1801, when it was united with Great Britain until its division in 1921 into the Irish Free State and Northern Ireland. Latin name: **Hibernia**. [2] **Republic of Ireland**. Also called: **Irish Republic, Southern Ireland**. a republic in NW Europe occupying most of Ireland: established as the Irish Free State (a British dominion) in 1921 and declared a republic in 1949; joined the European Community (now the European Union) in 1973. Official languages: Irish (Gaelic) and English. Currency: euro. Capital: Dublin. Pop.: 3 823 000 (2001 est.). Area: 70 285 sq. km (27 137 sq.miles). Gaelic name: **Eire**. ◆ See also **Northern Ireland**.

irenic, eirenic (aɪˈriːnɪk, -ˈrɛn-), **irenical,** *or* **eirenical** ADJECTIVE tending to conciliate or promote peace.
▷HISTORY C19: from Greek *eirēnikos,* from *eirēnē* peace
▸**iˈrenically** *or* **eiˈrenically** ADVERB

irenicon (aɪˈriːnɪˌkɒn) NOUN a variant spelling of **eirenicon**.

irenics (aɪˈriːnɪks, -ˈrɛn-) NOUN (*functioning as singular*) that branch of theology that is concerned with unity between Christian sects and denominations.

Irian Barat (ˈɪərɪən ˈbærɑːt) NOUN the former Indonesian name for **Irian Jaya**.

Irian Jaya NOUN the W part of the island of New Guinea: formerly under Dutch rule, becoming a province of Indonesia in 1963. Capital: Jayapura. Pop.: 2 165 300 (1999 est.). Area: 416 990 sq. km (161 000 sq. miles). Former names (until 1963): **Dutch New Guinea, Netherlands New Guinea**. English name: **West Irian**.

iridaceous (ˌɪrɪˈdeɪʃəs, ˌaɪ-) ADJECTIVE of, relating to, or belonging to the *Iridaceae,* a family of monocotyledonous plants, including iris, crocus, and gladiolus, having swordlike leaves and showy flowers.

iridectomy (ˌɪrɪˈdɛktəmɪ, ˌaɪ-) NOUN, *plural* **-mies**. surgical removal of part of the iris.

iridescent (ˌɪrɪˈdɛsᵊnt) ADJECTIVE displaying a spectrum of colours that shimmer and change due to interference and scattering as the observer's position changes.
▷HISTORY C18: from IRIDO- + -ESCENT
▸ˌ**iriˈdescence** NOUN ▸ˌ**iriˈdescently** ADVERB

iridic (aɪˈrɪdɪk, ɪˈrɪd-) ADJECTIVE [1] of or containing iridium, esp in the tetravalent state. [2] of or relating to the iris of the eye.

iridium (aɪˈrɪdɪəm, ɪˈrɪd-) NOUN a very hard inert yellowish-white transition element that is the most corrosion-resistant metal known. It occurs in platinum ores and is used as an alloy with platinum. Symbol: Ir; atomic no.: 77; atomic wt.: 192.22; valency: 3 or 4; relative density: 22.42; melting pt.: 2447°C; boiling pt.: 4428°C.
▷HISTORY C19: New Latin, from IRIDO- + -IUM; from its colourful appearance when dissolving in certain acids

irido- *or before a vowel* **irid-** COMBINING FORM [1] denoting the iris of the eye or the genus of plants: *iridectomy; iridaceous.* [2] denoting a rainbow: *iridescent.*
▷HISTORY from Latin *irid-,* IRIS

iridocyte (ˈɪrɪdəʊˌsaɪt) NOUN *Zoology* a guanine-containing cell in the skin of fish and some cephalopods, giving these animals their iridescence.

iridology (ˌɪrɪˈdɒlədʒɪ) NOUN a technique used in complementary medicine to diagnose illness by studying a patient's eyes.
▷HISTORY C20: from Latin IRIDO- + OLOGY
▸ˌ**iriˈdologist** NOUN

iridosmine (ˌɪrɪˈdɒsmaɪn, ˌaɪrɪ-) *or* **iridosmium** NOUN other names for **osmiridium**.
▷HISTORY C19: from IRIDO- + OSM(IUM) + INE-²

iridotomy (ˌɪrɪˈdɒtəmɪ, ˌaɪrɪ-) NOUN, *plural* **-mies**. surgical incision into the iris, esp to create an artificial pupil.

iris (ˈaɪrɪs) NOUN, *plural* **irises** *or* **irides** (ˈaɪrɪˌdiːz, ˈɪrɪ-). [1] the coloured muscular diaphragm that surrounds and controls the size of the pupil. [2] Also called: **fleur-de-lys**. any plant of the iridaceous genus *Iris,* having brightly coloured flowers composed of three petals and three drooping sepals. See also **flag²**, **orris¹**, **stinking iris**. [3] Also called: **rainbow quartz**. a form of quartz that reflects light polychromatically from internal fractures. [4] a rare or poetic word for **rainbow**. [5] something resembling a rainbow; iridescence. [6] short for **iris diaphragm**.
▷HISTORY C14: from Latin: rainbow, iris (flower), crystal, from Greek

Iris (ˈaɪrɪs) NOUN the goddess of the rainbow along which she travelled to earth as a messenger of the gods.

iris diaphragm NOUN an adjustable diaphragm that regulates the amount of light entering an optical instrument, esp a camera. It usually consists of a number of thin metal leaves arranged so that they open out into an approximately circular aperture. Sometimes shortened to: **iris**.

Irish (ˈaɪrɪʃ) ADJECTIVE [1] of, relating to, or characteristic of Ireland, its people, their Celtic language, or their dialect of English. [2] *Informal, offensive* ludicrous or illogical. ◆ NOUN [3] **the Irish**. (*functioning as plural*) the natives or inhabitants of Ireland. [4] another name for **Irish Gaelic**.

Irish bull NOUN a ludicrously illogical statement. See also **bull²**.

Irish coffee NOUN hot coffee mixed with Irish whiskey and topped with double cream.

Irish elk NOUN an extinct Eurasian giant deer of the Pleistocene genus *Megaloceros,* which had antlers up to 4 metres across.

Irish Free State NOUN a former name for the (Republic of) **Ireland** (1921–37).

Irish Gaelic NOUN the Goidelic language of the Celts of Ireland, now spoken mainly along the west coast; an official language of the Republic of Ireland since 1921.

Irishism (ˈaɪrɪˌʃɪzəm) NOUN an Irish custom or idiom.

Irishman (ˈaɪrɪʃmən) NOUN, *plural* **-men**. a male native, citizen, or inhabitant of Ireland or a male descendant of someone Irish.

Irish moss NOUN another name for **carrageen**.

Irish potato NOUN *Chiefly US* another name for the **potato**.

Irish Republic NOUN See **Ireland¹** (sense 2).

Irish Republican Army NOUN a militant organization of Irish nationalists founded with the aim of striving for a united independent Ireland by means of guerrilla warfare. Abbreviation: **IRA**.

Irish Sea NOUN an arm of the North Atlantic Ocean between Great Britain and Ireland.

Irish setter NOUN a breed of setter developed in Ireland, having a flat soft brownish-red coat. Also called: **red setter**.

Irish stew NOUN a white stew made of mutton, lamb, or beef, with potatoes, onions, etc.

Irish terrier NOUN a breed of terrier with a wiry wheaten or reddish coat.

Irish water spaniel NOUN a breed of dog used to hunt duck and having a dense coat of a purplish-liver colour that falls in tight ringlets covering the whole body except for the face and tail.

Irish whiskey NOUN any of the whiskeys made in Ireland, usually from malt and subject to three distillations.

Irish wolfhound NOUN a very large breed of hound with a rough thick coat.

Irishwoman (ˈaɪrɪʃwʊmən) NOUN, *plural* **-women**. a female native, citizen, or inhabitant of Ireland or a female descendant of someone Irish.

iritis (aɪˈraɪtɪs) NOUN inflammation of the iris of the eye.
▸**iritic** (aɪˈrɪtɪk) ADJECTIVE

irk (ɜːk) VERB (*tr*) to irritate, vex, or annoy.
▷HISTORY C13 *irken* to grow weary; probably related to Old Norse *yrkja* to work

irksome (ˈɜːksəm) ADJECTIVE causing vexation, annoyance, or boredom; troublesome or tedious.
▸ˈ**irksomely** ADVERB ▸ˈ**irksomeness** NOUN

IRL ABBREVIATION FOR: [1] *Text messaging* in real life. ◆ [2] INTERNATIONAL CAR REGISTRATION FOR Republic of Ireland.

IRM ABBREVIATION FOR **innate releasing mechanism**.

IRO ABBREVIATION FOR: [1] (in Britain) Inland Revenue Office. [2] International Refugee Organization.

iroko (ɪˈrəʊkəʊ) NOUN, *plural* **-kos**. [1] a tropical African hardwood tree of the genus *Chlorophora*. [2] the hard reddish-brown wood of this tree.
▷HISTORY C19: from Yoruba

iron (ˈaɪən) NOUN [1] **a** a malleable ductile silvery-white ferromagnetic metallic element occurring principally in haematite and magnetite. It is widely used for structural and engineering purposes. See also **steel, cast iron, wrought iron, pig iron**. Symbol: Fe; atomic no.: 26; atomic wt.: 55.847; valency: 2,3,4, or 6; relative density: 7.874; melting pt.: 1538°C; boiling pt.: 2862°C. Related adjectives: **ferric, ferrous**. Related prefix: **ferro-**. **b** (*as modifier*): *iron railings.* [2] any of certain tools or implements made of iron or steel, esp for use when hot: *a grappling iron; a soldering iron.* [3] an appliance for pressing fabrics using dry heat or steam, esp a small electrically heated device with a handle and a weighted flat bottom. [4] any of various golf clubs with narrow metal heads, numbered from 1 to 9 according to the slant of the face, used esp for approach shots: *a No. 6 iron.* [5] an informal word for **harpoon** (sense 1). [6] *US slang* a splintlike support for a malformed leg. [7] great hardness, strength, or resolve: *a will of iron.* [8] *Astronomy* short for **iron meteorite**. [9] See **shooting iron**. [10] **strike while the iron is hot**. to act at an opportune moment. ◆ ADJECTIVE [11] very hard, immovable, or implacable: *iron determination.* [12] very strong; extremely robust: *an iron constitution.* [13] cruel or unyielding: *he ruled with an iron hand.* [14] **an iron fist**. a cruel and unyielding attitude or approach. See also **velvet** (sense 6). ◆ VERB [15] to smooth (clothes or fabric) by removing (creases or wrinkles) using a heated iron; press. [16] (*tr*) to furnish or clothe with iron. [17] (*tr*) *Rare* to place (a prisoner) in irons. ◆ See also **iron out, irons**.
▷HISTORY Old English *īren;* related to Old High German *īsan,* Old Norse *jārn;* compare Old Irish *īarn*
▸ˈ**ironer** NOUN ▸ˈ**ironless** ADJECTIVE ▸ˈ**ironˌlike** ADJECTIVE

iron age NOUN *Classical myth* the last and worst age in the history of the world.

Iron Age NOUN **a** the period following the Bronze Age characterized by the extremely rapid spread of iron tools and weapons, which began in the Middle East about 1100 B.C. **b** (*as modifier*): *an Iron-Age weapon.*

ironbark (ˈaɪənˌbɑːk) NOUN any of several Australian eucalyptus trees that have hard rough bark.

ironbound (ˈaɪənˌbaʊnd) ADJECTIVE [1] bound with iron. [2] unyielding; inflexible. [3] (of a coast) rocky; rugged.

ironclad ADJECTIVE (ˌaɪənˈklæd) [1] covered or protected with iron: *an ironclad warship.* [2] inflexible; rigid: *an ironclad rule.* [3] not able to be assailed or contradicted: *an ironclad argument.* ◆ NOUN (ˈaɪənˌklæd) [4] a large wooden 19th-century warship with armoured plating.

Iron Cross NOUN the highest decoration for bravery awarded to the German armed forces in wartime: instituted in 1813.

Iron Curtain NOUN **a** (formerly) the guarded

border between the countries of the Soviet bloc and the rest of Europe. **b** (*as modifier*): *Iron Curtain countries*.

Iron Gate *or* **Iron Gates** NOUN a gorge of the River Danube on the border between Romania and Serbia and Montenegro. Length: 3 km (2 miles). Romanian name: **Porțile de Fier.**

iron glance NOUN another name for **haematite.**

iron grey NOUN **a** a neutral or dark grey colour. **b** (*as adjective*): *iron-grey hair*.

Iron Guard NOUN a Romanian fascist party that ceased to exist after World War II.

iron hand NOUN harsh or rigorous control; overbearing or autocratic force: *he ruled with an iron hand*.

iron horse NOUN *Archaic* a steam-driven railway locomotive.

ironic (aɪˈrɒnɪk) *or* **ironical** ADJECTIVE of, characterized by, or using irony.
▸ **iˈronicalness** NOUN

ironically (aɪˈrɒnɪkəlɪ) ADVERB [1] (*sentence modifier*) it is ironic that: *ironically, McCoist has never scored against Rangers*. [2] in an ironic manner: *I laughed ironically*.

ironing (ˈaɪənɪŋ) NOUN [1] the act of ironing washed clothes. [2] clothes that are to be or that have been ironed.

ironing board NOUN a board, usually on legs, with a suitable covering on which to iron clothes.

ironize *or* **ironise** (ˈaɪrəˌnaɪz) VERB [1] (*intr*) to use or indulge in irony. [2] (*tr*) to make ironic or use ironically.
▸ **ˈironist** NOUN

iron lung NOUN [1] an airtight metal cylinder enclosing the entire body up to the neck and providing artificial respiration when the respiratory muscles are paralysed, as by poliomyelitis. [2] *Irish informal* a gas container used in dispensing beer.

iron maiden NOUN a medieval instrument of torture, consisting of a hinged case (often shaped in the form of a woman) lined with iron spikes, which was forcibly closed on the victim.

iron man NOUN *Austral* an event at a surf carnival in which contestants compete at swimming, surfing, running, etc.

ironmaster (ˈaɪənˌmɑːstə) NOUN *Brit* a manufacturer of iron, esp (formerly) the owner of an ironworks.

iron meteorite NOUN a meteorite that is composed mainly of iron and nickel.

ironmonger (ˈaɪənˌmʌŋgə) NOUN *Brit* a dealer in metal utensils, hardware, locks, etc. US and Canadian equivalent: **hardware dealer.**
▸ **ˈironˌmongery** NOUN

iron out VERB (*tr, adverb*) [1] to smooth, using a heated iron. [2] to put right or settle (a problem or difficulty) as a result of negotiations or discussions. [3] *Austral informal* to knock unconscious.

iron pan NOUN *Geology* a hard layer of precipitated iron salts often found below the surface of sands and gravels.

iron pyrites (ˈpaɪraɪts) NOUN another name for **pyrite.**

iron rations PLURAL NOUN emergency food supplies, esp for military personnel in action. See also **C ration, K ration, MRE.**

irons (ˈaɪənz) PLURAL NOUN [1] fetters or chains (often in the phrase **in** *or* **into irons**). [2] **in irons.** *Nautical* (of a sailing vessel) headed directly into the wind without steerageway. [3] **have several irons in the fire.** to be involved in many projects, activities, etc.

ironsides (ˈaɪənˌsaɪdz) NOUN [1] a person with great stamina or resistance. [2] an ironclad ship. [3] (*often capital*) (in the English Civil War) **a** the cavalry regiment trained and commanded by Oliver Cromwell. **b** Cromwell's entire army.

iron sights PLURAL NOUN conventional non-telescopic sights on a rifle.

ironstone (ˈaɪənˌstəʊn) NOUN [1] any rock consisting mainly of an iron-bearing ore. [2] Also called: **ironstone china.** a tough durable earthenware.

ironware (ˈaɪənˌwɛə) NOUN domestic articles made of iron.

ironwood (ˈaɪənˌwʊd) NOUN [1] any of various betulaceous trees, such as hornbeam, that have very hard wood. [2] a Californian rosaceous tree, *Lyonothamnus floribundus*, with very hard wood. [3] any of various other trees with hard wood, such as the mopani. [4] the wood of any of these trees.

ironwork (ˈaɪənˌwɜːk) NOUN [1] work done in iron, esp decorative work. [2] the craft or practice of working in iron. ◆ See also **ironworks.**

ironworker (ˈaɪənˌwɜːkə) NOUN [1] a person who works in an ironworks. [2] a person who makes articles of iron.

ironworks (ˈaɪənˌwɜːks) NOUN (*sometimes functioning as singular*) a building in which iron is smelted, cast, or wrought.

irony[1] (ˈaɪrənɪ) NOUN, *plural* **-nies.** [1] the humorous or mildly sarcastic use of words to imply the opposite of what they normally mean. [2] an instance of this, used to draw attention to some incongruity or irrationality. [3] incongruity between what is expected to be and what actually is, or a situation or result showing such incongruity. [4] See **dramatic irony.** [5] *Philosophy* See **Socratic irony.**
▷ **HISTORY** C16: from Latin *ironia*, from Greek *eirōneia*, from *eirōn* dissembler, from *eirein* to speak

irony[2] (ˈaɪənɪ) ADJECTIVE of, resembling, or containing iron.

Iroquoian (ˌɪrəˈkwɔɪən) NOUN [1] a family of North American Indian languages including Cherokee, Mohawk, Seneca, Oneida, and Onondaga: probably related to Siouan. ◆ ADJECTIVE [2] of or relating to the Iroquois, their culture, or their languages.

Iroquois (ˈɪrəˌkwɔɪ, -ˌkwɔɪz) NOUN, *plural* **-quois.** [1] a member of any of a group of North American Indian peoples formerly living between the Hudson River and the St Lawrence and Lake Erie. See also **Five Nations, Six Nations.** [2] any of the Iroquoian languages. ◆ ADJECTIVE [3] of or relating to the Iroquois, their language, or their culture.

IRQ INTERNATIONAL CAR REGISTRATION FOR Iraq.

irradiance (ɪˈreɪdɪəns) NOUN the radiant flux incident on unit area of a surface. It is measured in watts per square metre. Symbol: E_e. Also called: **irradiation.** Compare **illuminance.**

irradiant (ɪˈreɪdɪənt) ADJECTIVE radiating light; shining brightly.

irradiate (ɪˈreɪdɪˌeɪt) VERB [1] (*tr*) *Physics* to subject to or treat with light or other electromagnetic radiation or with beams of particles. [2] (*tr*) to expose (food) to electromagnetic radiation to kill bacteria and retard deterioration. [3] (*tr*) to make clear or bright intellectually or spiritually; illumine. [4] a less common word for **radiate** (sense 1). [5] (*intr*) *Obsolete* to become radiant.
▸ **irˈradiative** ADJECTIVE ▸ **irˈradiˌator** NOUN

irradiation (ɪˌreɪdɪˈeɪʃən) NOUN [1] the act or process of irradiating or the state of being irradiated. [2] the apparent enlargement of a brightly lit object when it is viewed against a dark background. [3] a shaft of light; beam or ray. [4] *Med* **a** the therapeutic or diagnostic use of radiation, esp X-rays. **b** exposure of a patient to such radiation. [5] another name for **radiation** or **irradiance.**

irrational (ɪˈræʃənəl) ADJECTIVE [1] inconsistent with reason or logic; illogical; absurd. [2] incapable of reasoning. [3] *Maths* **a** not rational. **b** (*as noun*): *an irrational*. [4] *Prosody* (in Greek or Latin verse) **a** of or relating to a metrical irregularity, usually the occurrence of a long syllable instead of a short one. **b** denoting a metrical foot where such an irregularity occurs.
▸ **irˈrationally** ADVERB ▸ **irˈrationalness** NOUN

irrationality (ɪˌræʃəˈnælɪtɪ) *or* **irrationalism** NOUN [1] the state or quality of being irrational. [2] irrational thought, action, or behaviour.

irrational number NOUN any real number that cannot be expressed as the ratio of two integers, such as π.

Irrawaddy (ˌɪrəˈwɒdɪ) NOUN the main river in Myanmar, rising in the north in two headstreams and flowing south through the whole length of Myanmar, to enter the Andaman Sea by nine main mouths. Length: 2100 km (1300 miles).

irreclaimable (ˌɪrɪˈkleɪməbəl) ADJECTIVE not able to be reclaimed.
▸ **ˌirreˌclaimaˈbility** *or* **ˌirreˈclaimableness** NOUN
▸ **ˌirreˈclaimably** ADVERB

irreconcilable (ɪˈrɛkənˌsaɪləbəl, ɪˌrɛkənˈsaɪ-) ADJECTIVE [1] not able to be reconciled; uncompromisingly conflicting; incompatible. ◆ NOUN [2] a person or thing that is implacably hostile or uncompromisingly opposed. [3] (*usually plural*) one of various principles, ideas, etc., that are incapable of being brought into agreement.
▸ **irˌreconˌcilaˈbility** *or* **irˈreconˌcilableness** NOUN
▸ **irˈreconˌcilably** ADVERB

irrecoverable (ˌɪrɪˈkʌvərəbəl, -ˈkʌvrə-) ADJECTIVE [1] not able to be recovered or regained. [2] not able to be remedied or rectified.
▸ **ˌirreˈcoverableness** NOUN ▸ **ˌirreˈcoverably** ADVERB

irrecusable (ˌɪrɪˈkjuːzəbəl) ADJECTIVE not able to be rejected or challenged, as evidence, etc.
▸ **ˌirreˈcusably** ADVERB

irredeemable (ˌɪrɪˈdiːməbəl) ADJECTIVE [1] (of bonds, debentures, shares, etc.) without a date of redemption of capital; incapable of being bought back directly or paid off. [2] (of paper money) not convertible into specie. [3] (of a sinner) not able to be saved or reformed. [4] (of a loss) not able to be recovered; irretrievable. [5] not able to be improved or rectified; irreparable.
▸ **ˌirreˌdeemaˈbility** *or* **ˌirreˈdeemableness** NOUN
▸ **ˌirreˈdeemably** ADVERB

irredentist (ˌɪrɪˈdɛntɪst) NOUN [1] a person who favours the acquisition of territory that once was part of his country or is considered to have been. ◆ ADJECTIVE [2] of, relating to, or advocating this belief.
▷ **HISTORY** C19: from Italian *irredentista*, from the phrase *Italia irredenta*, literally: Italy unredeemed, from *ir-* IN-[1] + *redento* redeemed, from Latin *redemptus* bought back; see REDEEM
▸ **ˌirreˈdentism** NOUN

Irredentist (ˌɪrɪˈdɛntɪst) NOUN (*sometimes not capital*) a member of an Italian association prominent in 1878 that sought to recover for Italy certain neighbouring regions (***Italia irredenta***) with a predominantly Italian population that were under foreign control.

irreducible (ˌɪrɪˈdjuːsɪbəl) ADJECTIVE [1] not able to be reduced or lessened. [2] not able to be brought to a simpler or reduced form. [3] *Maths* **a** (of a polynomial) unable to be factorized into polynomials of lower degree, as $(x^2 + 1)$. **b** (of a radical) incapable of being reduced to a rational expression, as $\sqrt{(x + 1)}$.
▸ **ˌirreˌduciˈbility** *or* **ˌirreˈducibleness** NOUN ▸ **ˌirreˈducibly** ADVERB

irreflexive (ˌɪrɪˈflɛksɪv) ADJECTIVE *Logic* (of a relation) failing to hold between each member of its domain and itself: *'... is distinct from ...' is irreflexive*. Compare **reflexive** (sense 4), **nonreflexive.**

irrefragable (ɪˈrɛfrəgəbəl) ADJECTIVE not able to be denied or refuted; indisputable.
▷ **HISTORY** C16: from Late Latin *irrefrāgābilis*, from Latin IR- + *refrāgārī* to resist, thwart
▸ **irˌrefragaˈbility** *or* **irˈrefragableness** NOUN ▸ **irˈrefragably** ADVERB

irrefrangible (ˌɪrɪˈfrændʒəbəl) ADJECTIVE [1] not to be broken or transgressed; inviolable. [2] *Physics* incapable of being refracted.
▸ **ˌirreˌfrangiˈbility** *or* **ˌirreˈfrangibleness** NOUN
▸ **ˌirreˈfrangibly** ADVERB

irrefutable (ɪˈrɛfjʊtəbəl, ˌɪrɪˈfjuːtəbəl) ADJECTIVE impossible to deny or disprove; incontrovertible.
▸ **irˌrefutaˈbility** *or* **irˈrefutableness** NOUN ▸ **irˈrefutably** ADVERB

irreg. ABBREVIATION FOR irregular(ly).

irregular (ɪˈrɛgjʊlə) ADJECTIVE [1] lacking uniformity or symmetry; uneven in shape, position, arrangement, etc. [2] not occurring at expected or equal intervals: *an irregular pulse*. [3] differing from the normal or accepted practice or routine. [4] not according to established standards of behaviour; unconventional. [5] (of the formation, inflections, or derivations of a word) not following the usual pattern of formation in a language, as English plurals ending other than in *-s* or *-es*. [6] of or relating to guerrillas or volunteers not belonging to regular forces: *irregular troops*. [7] (of flowers) having any of their parts, esp petals, differing in size, shape, etc.; asymmetric. [8] *US* (of merchandise) not up to the manufacturer's standards or specifications; flawed; imperfect. ◆ NOUN [9] a soldier not in a regular army. [10] (*often*

plural) US imperfect or flawed merchandise. Compare **second**[1] (sense 15).
▸**ir'regularly** ADVERB

irregularity (ɪˌrɛgjʊ'lærɪtɪ) NOUN, *plural* **-ties.** 1 the state or quality of being irregular. 2 something irregular, such as a bump in a smooth surface. 3 a breach of a convention or normal procedure.

irrelative (ɪ'rɛlətɪv) ADJECTIVE 1 unrelated. 2 a rare word for **irrelevant.**
▸**ir'relatively** ADVERB ▸**ir'relativeness** NOUN

irrelevant (ɪ'rɛləvənt) ADJECTIVE not relating or pertinent to the matter at hand; not important.
▸**ir'relevance** *or* **ir'relevancy** NOUN ▸**ir'relevantly** ADVERB

irrelievable (ˌɪrɪ'li:vəbᵊl) ADJECTIVE not able to be relieved.

irreligion (ˌɪrɪ'lɪdʒən) NOUN 1 lack of religious faith. 2 indifference or opposition to religion.
▸ˌ**irre'ligionist** NOUN

irreligious (ˌɪrɪ'lɪdʒəs) ADJECTIVE lacking in, indifferent to, or opposed to religious faith.
▸ˌ**irre'ligiously** ADVERB ▸ˌ**irre'ligiousness** NOUN

irremeable (ɪ'rɛmɪəbᵊl, ɪ'ri:-) ADJECTIVE *Archaic or poetic* affording no possibility of return.
▷**HISTORY** C16: from Latin *irremeābilis,* from IR- + *remeāre* to return, from RE- + *meāre* to go
▸**ir'remeably** ADVERB

irremediable (ˌɪrɪ'mi:dɪəbᵊl) ADJECTIVE not able to be remedied; incurable or irreparable.
▸ˌ**irre'mediableness** NOUN ▸ˌ**irre'mediably** ADVERB

irremissible (ˌɪrɪ'mɪsəbᵊl) ADJECTIVE 1 unpardonable; inexcusable. 2 that must be done, as through duty or obligation.
▸ˌ**irreˌmissi'bility** *or* ˌ**irre'missibleness** NOUN
▸ˌ**irre'missibly** ADVERB

irremovable (ˌɪrɪ'mu:vəbᵊl) ADJECTIVE not able to be removed.
▸ˌ**irreˌmova'bility** *or* ˌ**irre'movableness** NOUN
▸ˌ**irre'movably** ADVERB

irreparable (ɪ'rɛpərəbᵊl, ɪ'rɛprəbᵊl) ADJECTIVE not able to be repaired or remedied; beyond repair.
▸**irˌrepara'bility** *or* **ir'reparableness** NOUN ▸**ir'reparably** ADVERB

irrepealable (ˌɪrɪ'pi:ləbᵊl) ADJECTIVE not able to be repealed.
▸ˌ**irreˌpeala'bility** *or* ˌ**irre'pealableness** NOUN
▸ˌ**irre'pealably** ADVERB

irreplaceable (ˌɪrɪ'pleɪsəbᵊl) ADJECTIVE not able to be replaced: *an irreplaceable antique.*
▸ˌ**irre'placeably** ADVERB

irrepleviable (ˌɪrɪ'plɛvɪəbᵊl) *or* **irreplevisable** (ˌɪrɪ'plɛvɪzəbᵊl) ADJECTIVE *Law, archaic* not able to be replevied.
▷**HISTORY** C16: see *ir-* IN-[1], REPLEVIN

irrepressible (ˌɪrɪ'prɛsəbᵊl) ADJECTIVE not capable of being repressed, controlled, or restrained.
▸ˌ**irreˌpressi'bility** *or* ˌ**irre'pressibleness** NOUN
▸ˌ**irre'pressibly** ADVERB

irreproachable (ˌɪrɪ'prəʊtʃəbᵊl) ADJECTIVE not deserving reproach; blameless.
▸ˌ**irreˌproacha'bility** *or* ˌ**irre'proachableness** NOUN
▸ˌ**irre'proachably** ADVERB

irresistible (ˌɪrɪ'zɪstəbᵊl) ADJECTIVE 1 not able to be resisted or refused; overpowering: *an irresistible impulse.* 2 very fascinating or alluring: *an irresistible woman.*
▸ˌ**irreˌsisti'bility** *or* ˌ**irre'sistibleness** NOUN ▸ˌ**irre'sistibly** ADVERB

irresoluble (ɪ'rɛzəljubᵊl) ADJECTIVE 1 a less common word for **insoluble.** 2 *Archaic* not capable of being relieved.
▸**irˌresolu'bility** NOUN ▸**ir'resolubly** ADVERB

irresolute (ɪ'rɛzəˌlu:t) ADJECTIVE lacking resolution; wavering; hesitating.
▸**ir'resoˌlutely** ADVERB ▸**ir'resoˌluteness** *or* **irˌreso'lution** NOUN

irresolvable (ˌɪrɪ'zɒlvəbᵊl) ADJECTIVE 1 not able to be resolved into parts or elements. 2 not able to be solved; insoluble.
▸ˌ**irreˌsolva'bility** *or* ˌ**irre'solvableness** NOUN
▸ˌ**irre'solvably** ADVERB

irrespective (ˌɪrɪ'spɛktɪv) ADJECTIVE 1 **irrespective of.** (*preposition*) without taking account of; regardless of. ◆ ADVERB 2 *Informal* regardless; without due consideration: *he carried on with his plan irrespective.*
▸ˌ**irre'spectively** ADVERB

irrespirable (ɪ'rɛspɪrəbᵊl, ˌɪrɪ'spaɪərəbᵊl) ADJECTIVE not fit for breathing or incapable of being breathed.

irresponsible (ˌɪrɪ'spɒnsəbᵊl) ADJECTIVE 1 not showing or done with due care for the consequences of one's actions or attitudes; reckless. 2 not capable of bearing responsibility. 3 *Archaic* not answerable to a higher authority for one's actions.
▸ˌ**irreˌsponsi'bility** *or* ˌ**irre'sponsibleness** NOUN
▸ˌ**irre'sponsibly** ADVERB

irresponsive (ˌɪrɪ'spɒnsɪv) ADJECTIVE not responsive.
▸ˌ**irre'sponsively** ADVERB ▸ˌ**irre'sponsiveness** NOUN

irretentive (ˌɪrɪ'tɛntɪv) ADJECTIVE not retentive.
▸ˌ**irre'tentiveness** NOUN

irretrievable (ˌɪrɪ'tri:vəbᵊl) ADJECTIVE not able to be retrieved, recovered, or repaired.
▸ˌ**irreˌtrieva'bility** *or* ˌ**irre'trievableness** NOUN
▸ˌ**irre'trievably** ADVERB

irreverence (ɪ'rɛvərəns, ɪ'rɛvrəns) NOUN 1 lack of due respect or veneration; disrespect. 2 a disrespectful remark or act.

irreverent (ɪ'rɛvərənt, ɪ'rɛvrənt) *or* **irreverential** (ɪˌrɛvə'rɛnʃəl) ADJECTIVE without due respect or veneration; disrespectful; flippant.
▸**ir'reverently** ADVERB

irreversible (ˌɪrɪ'vɜ:səbᵊl) ADJECTIVE 1 not able to be reversed: *the irreversible flow of time.* 2 not able to be revoked or repealed; irrevocable. 3 *Chem, physics* capable of changing or producing a change in one direction only: *an irreversible reaction.* 4 *Thermodynamics* (of a change, process, etc.) occurring through a number of intermediate states that are not all in thermodynamic equilibrium.
▸ˌ**irreˌversi'bility** *or* ˌ**irre'versibleness** NOUN ▸ˌ**irre'versibly** ADVERB

irrevocable (ɪ'rɛvəkəbᵊl) ADJECTIVE not able to be revoked, changed, or undone; unalterable.
▸**irˌrevoca'bility** *or* **ir'revocableness** NOUN ▸**ir'revocably** ADVERB

irrigate ('ɪrɪˌgeɪt) VERB 1 to supply (land) with water by means of artificial canals, ditches, etc., esp to promote the growth of food crops. 2 *Med* to bathe or wash out a bodily part, cavity, or wound. 3 (*tr*) to make fertile, fresh, or vital by or as if by watering.
▷**HISTORY** C17: from Latin *irrigāre,* from *rigāre* to moisten, conduct water
▸'**irrigable** ADJECTIVE ▸ˌ**irri'gation** NOUN ▸ˌ**irri'gational** *or* '**irriˌgative** ADJECTIVE ▸'**irriˌgator** NOUN

irriguous (ɪ'rɪgjʊəs) ADJECTIVE *Archaic or poetic* well-watered; watery.
▷**HISTORY** C17: from Latin *irriguus* supplied with water, from *riguus* watered; see IRRIGATE

irritable ('ɪrɪtəbᵊl) ADJECTIVE 1 quickly irritated; easily annoyed; peevish. 2 (of all living organisms) capable of responding to such stimuli as heat, light, and touch. 3 *Pathol* abnormally sensitive.
▸ˌ**irrita'bility** NOUN ▸'**irritableness** NOUN ▸'**irritably** ADVERB

irritable bowel syndrome NOUN *Med* a chronic condition of recurring abdominal pain with constipation or diarrhoea or both.

irritant ('ɪrɪtənt) ADJECTIVE 1 causing irritation; irritating. ◆ NOUN 2 something irritant.
▸'**irritancy** NOUN

irritate ('ɪrɪˌteɪt) VERB 1 to annoy or anger (someone). 2 (*tr*) *Biology* to stimulate (an organism or part) to respond in a characteristic manner. 3 (*tr*) *Pathol* to cause (a bodily organ or part) to become excessively stimulated, resulting in inflammation, tenderness, etc.
▷**HISTORY** C16: from Latin *irrītāre* to provoke, exasperate
▸'**irriˌtator** NOUN

irritation (ˌɪrɪ'teɪʃən) NOUN 1 something that irritates. 2 the act of irritating or the condition of being irritated.
▸'**irriˌtative** ADJECTIVE

irrupt (ɪ'rʌpt) VERB (*intr*) 1 to enter forcibly or suddenly. 2 (of a plant or animal population) to enter a region suddenly and in very large numbers. 3 (of a population) to increase suddenly and greatly.
▷**HISTORY** C19: from Latin *irrumpere* to rush into, invade, from *rumpere* to break, burst
▸**ir'ruption** NOUN

irruptive (ɪ'rʌptɪv) ADJECTIVE 1 irrupting or tending to irrupt. 2 of, involving, or causing irruption. 3 *Obsolete* (of igneous rocks) intrusive.
▸**ir'ruptively** ADVERB

IRS (in the US) ABBREVIATION FOR Internal Revenue Service.

Irtysh *or* **Irtish** (ɪə'tɪʃ) NOUN a river in central Asia, rising in China in the Altai Mountains and flowing west through Kazakhstan, then northwest into Russia to join the Ob River as its chief tributary. Length: 4444 km (2760 miles).

Irvine ('ɜ:vɪn) NOUN a town on the W coast of Scotland, the administrative centre of North Ayrshire: designated a new town in 1966. Pop.: 32 988 (1991).

IRW *Text messaging* ABBREVIATION FOR in the real world.

is[1] (ɪz) VERB (used with *he, she, it,* and with singular nouns) a form of the present tense (indicative mood) of **be.**
▷**HISTORY** Old English; compare Old Norse *es,* German *ist,* Latin *est,* Greek *esti*

is[2] THE INTERNET DOMAIN NAME FOR Iceland.

IS INTERNATIONAL CAR REGISTRATION FOR Iceland.
▷**HISTORY** Icelandic *Ísland*

Is. ABBREVIATION FOR: 1 Also: **Isa.** *Bible* Isaiah. 2 Island(s) *or* Isle(s).

is- COMBINING FORM variant of **iso-** before a vowel: *isentropic.*

ISA[1] *Aeronautics* ABBREVIATION FOR: 1 **International Standard Atmosphere.** 2 **Interim Standard Atmosphere.**

ISA[2] ('aɪsə) NOUN ACRONYM FOR individual savings account: a tax-free savings scheme introduced in Britain in 1999.

Isaac ('aɪzək) NOUN an Old Testament patriarch, the son of Abraham and Sarah and father of Jacob and Esau (Genesis 17; 21–27).

Isabella[1] (ˌɪzə'bɛlə) *or* **Isabel** ('ɪzəˌbɛl) NOUN **a** a greyish-yellow colour. **b** Also: **Isabelline** (ˌɪzə'bɛli:n). (*as adjective*): *an Isabella mohair coat.*
▷**HISTORY** C17: from the name *Isabella;* original reference uncertain

isagoge ('aɪsəˌgəʊdʒɪ, ˌaɪsə'gəʊ-) NOUN an academic introduction to a specialized subject field or area of research.
▷**HISTORY** C17: from Latin, from Greek *eisagōgē,* from *eisagein* to introduce, from *eis-* into + *agein* to lead

isagogics (ˌaɪsə'gɒdʒɪks) NOUN (*usually functioning as singular*) introductory studies, esp in the history of the Bible.
▸ˌ**isa'gogic** ADJECTIVE

Isaiah (aɪ'zaɪə) NOUN *Old Testament* 1 the first of the major Hebrew prophets, who lived in the 8th century B.C. 2 the book of his and others' prophecies.

isallobar (aɪ'sæləˌbɑ:) NOUN *Meteorol* a line on a map running through places experiencing equal pressure changes.

Isar ('i:zɑ:) NOUN a river in central Europe, rising in W Austria and flowing generally northeast through S Germany into the Danube. Length: over 260 km (160 miles).

isatin ('aɪsətɪn) *or* **isatine** ('aɪsəˌti:n) NOUN a yellowish-red crystalline compound soluble in hot water, used for the preparation of vat dyes. Formula: $C_8H_5NO_2$.
▷**HISTORY** C19: from Latin *isatis* woad + -IN
▸ˌ**isa'tinic** ADJECTIVE

Isauria (aɪ'sɔ:rɪə) NOUN an ancient district of S central Asia Minor, chiefly on the N slopes of the W Taurus Mountains.
▸**I'saurian** ADJECTIVE, NOUN

Isaurian (aɪ'sɔ:rɪən) ADJECTIVE 1 of or relating to Isauria, an ancient district of S central Asia Minor, or its inhabitants. ◆ NOUN 2 a native or inhabitant of Isauria.

ISBN ABBREVIATION FOR International Standard Book Number.

Iscariot (ɪ'skærɪət) NOUN See **Judas** (Iscariot).

ischaemia *or* **ischemia** (ɪ'ski:mɪə) NOUN *Pathol* an inadequate supply of blood to an organ or part, as from an obstructed blood flow.
▷**HISTORY** C19: from Greek *iskhein* to restrict, + -EMIA
▸**ischaemic** *or* **ischemic** (ɪ'skemɪk) ADJECTIVE

Ischia ('i:skjɑ:, 'ɪskɪə) NOUN a volcanic island in the

Tyrrhenian Sea, at the N end of the Bay of Naples. Area: 47 sq. km (18 sq. miles).

ischium (ˈɪskɪəm) NOUN, *plural* **-chia** (-kɪə). one of the three sections of the hipbone, situated below the ilium.
▷HISTORY C17: from Latin: hip joint, from Greek *iskhion*
▸ **ˈischial** ADJECTIVE

ISD ABBREVIATION FOR international subscriber dialling.

ISDN ABBREVIATION FOR integrated services digital network: a rapid telecommunications network, combining data transfer and telephony.

-ise SUFFIX FORMING VERBS a variant of **-ize**.

> **Language note** See at **-ize**.

isentropic (ˌaɪsɛnˈtrɒpɪk) ADJECTIVE having or taking place at constant entropy.

Isère (*French* izɛr) NOUN 1 a department of SE France, in Rhône-Alpes region. Capital: Grenoble. Pop.: 1 094 006 (1999). Area: 7904 sq. km (3083 sq. miles). 2 a river in SE France, rising in the Graian Alps and flowing west and southwest to join the River Rhône near Valence. Length: 290 km (180 miles).

Iseult, Yseult (ɪˈsuːlt), *or* **Isolde** (ɪˈzəʊldə) NOUN (in Arthurian legend) 1 an Irish princess wed to Mark, king of Cornwall, but in love with his knight Tristan. 2 (in another account) the daughter of the king of Brittany, married to Tristan.

Isfahan (ˌɪsfəˈhɑːn) *or* **Eşfahān** NOUN a city in central Iran: the second largest city in the country; capital of Persia in the 11th century and from 1598 to 1722. Pop.: 1 266 765 (1996). Ancient name: **Aspadana** (ˌæspəˈdɑːnə).

-ish SUFFIX FORMING ADJECTIVES 1 of or belonging to a nationality or group: *Scottish*. 2 *Often derogatory* having the manner or qualities of; resembling: *slavish; prudish; boyish*. 3 somewhat; approximately: *yellowish; sevenish*. 4 concerned or preoccupied with: *bookish*.
▷HISTORY Old English *-isc*; related to German *-isch*, Greek *-iskos*

Ishmael (ˈɪʃmeɪəl) NOUN 1 the son of Abraham and Hagar, Sarah's handmaid: the ancestor of 12 Arabian tribes (Genesis 21:8–21; 25:12–18). 2 a bandit chieftain, who defied the Babylonian conquerors of Judah and assassinated the governor appointed by Nebuchadnezzar (II Kings 25:25; Jeremiah 40:13–41:18). 3 *Rare* an outcast.

Ishmaelite (ˈɪʃmeɪəˌlaɪt) NOUN 1 a supposed descendant of Ishmael; a member of a desert people of Old Testament times. 2 *Rare* an outcast.
▸ **ˈIshmaelˌitism** NOUN

Ishtar (ˈɪʃtɑː) NOUN the principal goddess of the Babylonians and Assyrians; divinity of love, fertility, and war.

isinglass (ˈaɪzɪŋˌglɑːs) NOUN a gelatine made from the air bladders of freshwater fish, used as a clarifying agent and adhesive.

Isis[1] (ˈaɪsɪs) NOUN the local name for the River Thames at Oxford.

Isis[2] (ˈaɪsɪs) NOUN an ancient Egyptian fertility goddess, depicted as a woman with a cow's horns, between which was the disc of the sun; wife and sister of Osiris.

Isl. ABBREVIATION FOR: 1 Island. 2 Isle.

Islam (ˈɪzlɑːm) NOUN 1 Also called: **Islamism** (ɪzˈlɑːmɪzəm, ˈɪzləmɪzəm). the religion of Muslims, having the Koran as its sacred scripture and teaching that there is only one God and that Mohammed is his prophet; Mohammedanism. 2 **a** Muslims collectively and their civilization. **b** the countries where the Muslim religion is predominant.
▷HISTORY C19: from Arabic: surrender (to God), from *aslama* to surrender
▸ **Isˈlamic** ADJECTIVE

Islamabad (ɪzˈlɑːməˌbɑːd) NOUN the capital of Pakistan, in the north on the Potwar Plateau: site chosen in 1959; surrounded by the Capital Territory of Islamabad for 909 sq. km (351 sq. miles). Pop.: 524 500 (1998).

Islamist (ˈɪzləmɪst) ADJECTIVE 1 supporting or advocating Islamic fundamentalism. ◆ NOUN 2 a supporter or advocate of Islamic fundamentalism.

Islamize *or* **Islamise** (ˈɪzləˌmaɪz) VERB (*tr*) to convert or subject to the influence of Islam.
▸ **ˌIslamiˈzation** *or* **ˌIslamiˈsation** NOUN

Islamophobia (ˌɪzlɑːməˈfəʊbɪə) NOUN hatred or fear of Muslims or of their politics or culture.
▸ **ˌIslamoˈphobic** ADJECTIVE

island (ˈaɪlənd) NOUN 1 a mass of land that is surrounded by water and is smaller than a continent. 2 See **traffic island.** 3 *Anatomy* a part, structure, or group of cells distinct in constitution from its immediate surroundings. ◆ Related adjective: **insular.** ◆ VERB (*tr*) *Rare* 4 to cause to become an island. 5 to intersperse with islands. 6 to place on an island; insulate; isolate.
▷HISTORY Old English *īgland*, from *īg* island + LAND; *s* inserted through influence of ISLE
▸ **ˈisland-ˌlike** ADJECTIVE

island arc NOUN an arc-shaped chain of islands, such as the Aleutian Islands or the Japanese Islands, usually lying at the edge of a Benioff zone, indicating volcanic activity where the oceanic lithosphere is descending into the earth's interior.

islander (ˈaɪləndə) NOUN 1 a native or inhabitant of an island. 2 (*capital*) *NZ* a native or inhabitant of the Pacific Islands.

island of Reil (raɪl) NOUN another name for **insula.**
▷HISTORY after Johann *Reil* (died 1813), German physician

Islands (ˈaɪləndz) PLURAL NOUN **the.** *NZ* the islands of the South Pacific.

islands council NOUN (in Scotland since 1975) any of the three divisions (Orkney, Shetland, and the Western Isles) into which the Scottish islands are divided for purposes of local government. See also **region** (sense 6).

Islands of the Blessed PLURAL NOUN *Greek myth* lands where the souls of heroes and good men were taken after death. Also called: **Hesperides.**

island universe NOUN a former name for **galaxy.**

Islay (ˈaɪlə, ˈaɪleɪ) NOUN an island off the W coast of Scotland: the southernmost of the Inner Hebrides; separated from the island of Jura by the **Sound of Islay**. Pop.: 3500 (latest est.). Area: 606 sq. km (234 sq. miles).

isle (aɪl) NOUN *Poetic except when cap. and part of place name* an island, esp a small one.
▷HISTORY C13: from Old French *isle*, from Latin *insula* island

Isle of Dogs NOUN See (Isle of) **Dogs.**

Isle of Man NOUN See (Isle of) **Man.**

Isle of Pines NOUN the former name of the (Isle of) **Youth.**

Isle of Sheppey NOUN See (Isle of) **Sheppey.**

Isle of Wight NOUN See (Isle of) **Wight.**

Isle of Youth NOUN See (Isle of) **Youth.**

Isle Royale (ˈrɔɪəl) NOUN an island in the northeast US, in NW Lake Superior: forms, with over 100 surrounding islands, **Isle Royale National Park.** Area: 541 sq. km (209 sq. miles).

islet (ˈaɪlɪt) NOUN a small island.
▷HISTORY C16: from Old French *islette*; see ISLE

islets of Langerhans *or* **islands of Langerhans** (ˈlæŋəˌhæns) PLURAL NOUN small groups of endocrine cells in the pancreas that secrete the hormones insulin and glucagon.
▷HISTORY C19: named after Paul *Langerhans* (1847–88), German physician

Islington (ˈɪzlɪŋtən) NOUN a borough of N Greater London. Pop.: 175 787 (2001). Area: 16 sq. km (6 sq. miles).

islomania (ˌaɪləˈmeɪnɪə) NOUN an obsessional enthusiasm or partiality for islands.

ism (ˈɪzəm) NOUN *Informal, often derogatory* an unspecified doctrine, system, or practice.

ISM ABBREVIATION FOR **interstellar medium.**

-ism SUFFIX FORMING NOUNS 1 indicating an action, process, or result: *criticism; terrorism*. 2 indicating a state or condition: *paganism*. 3 indicating a doctrine, system, or body of principles and practices: *Leninism; spiritualism*. 4 indicating behaviour or a characteristic quality: *heroism*. 5 indicating a characteristic usage, esp of a language: *colloquialism; Scotticism*. 6 indicating prejudice on the basis specified: *sexism; ageism*.
▷HISTORY from Old French *-isme*, from Latin *-ismus*, from Greek *-ismos*

Ismaili *or* **Isma'ili** (ˌɪzmɑːˈiːlɪ) NOUN *Islam* 1 a Shiah sect whose adherents believe that Ismail, son of the sixth imam, was the rightful seventh imam. 2 (*plural* **-lis**) Also called: **Ismailian** (ˌɪzmɑːˈɪliːən). a member of this sect.

isna *or* **isnae** (ˈɪznɪ) VERB *Scot* is not.

isn't (ˈɪzᵊnt) VERB CONTRACTION OF is not.

ISO NOUN International Organization for Standardization.
▷HISTORY from Greek *isos* equal; often wrongly thought to be an abbreviation for *International Standards Organization*

iso- *or before a vowel* **is-** COMBINING FORM 1 equal or identical: *isomagnetic*. 2 indicating that a chemical compound is an isomer of a specified compound: *isobutane; isocyanic acid*.
▷HISTORY from Greek *isos* equal

isoagglutination (ˌaɪsəʊəˌgluːtɪˈneɪʃən) NOUN the agglutination of red blood cells of an organism by the blood serum of another organism of the same species.
▸ **ˌisoagˈglutinative** ADJECTIVE

isoagglutinin (ˌaɪsəʊəˈgluːtɪnɪn) NOUN an antibody that causes agglutination of red blood cells in animals of the same species from which it was derived.

isoamyl acetate (ˌaɪsəʊˈæmɪl) NOUN a colourless volatile compound used as a solvent for cellulose lacquers and as a flavouring. Formula: $(CH_3)_2CHCH_2CH_2OOCCH_3$.

isoantigen (ˌaɪsəʊˈæntɪdʒən) NOUN *Immunol* an antigen that stimulates antibody production in different members of the same species.

isobar (ˈaɪsəʊˌbɑː) NOUN 1 a line on a map connecting places of equal atmospheric pressure, usually reduced to sea level for purposes of comparison, at a given time or period. 2 *Physics* any of two or more atoms that have the same mass number but different atomic numbers: *tin-115 and indium-115 are isobars*. Compare **isotope.**
▷HISTORY C19: from Greek *isobarēs* of equal weight, from ISO- + *baros* weight
▸ **ˈisobarˌism** NOUN

isobaric (ˌaɪsəʊˈbærɪk) ADJECTIVE 1 Also: **isopiestic.** having equal atmospheric pressure. 2 of or relating to isobars.

isobaric spin NOUN See **isospin.**

isobath (ˈaɪsəʊˌbæθ) NOUN a line on a map connecting points of equal underwater depth.
▷HISTORY C19: from Greek *isobathēs* of equal depth, from ISO- + *bathos* depth
▸ **ˌisoˈbathic** ADJECTIVE

isobilateral (ˌaɪsəʊbaɪˈlætərəl) ADJECTIVE *Botany* (esp of a leaf) capable of being divided into symmetrical halves along two different planes.

isocheim *or* **isochime** (ˈaɪsəʊˌkaɪm) NOUN a line on a map connecting places with the same mean winter temperature.
▷HISTORY C19: from ISO- + Greek *kheima* winter weather
▸ **ˌisoˈcheimal, ˌisoˈcheimenal,** *or* **ˌisoˈchimal** ADJECTIVE

isochor *or* **isochore** (ˈaɪsəʊˌkɔː) NOUN a line on a graph showing the variation of the temperature of a fluid with its pressure, when the volume is kept constant.
▷HISTORY C19: from ISO- + Greek *khōros* place, space
▸ **ˌisoˈchoric** ADJECTIVE

isochromatic (ˌaɪsəʊkrəʊˈmætɪk) ADJECTIVE 1 **a** having the same colour. **b** of uniform colour. 2 *Photog* (of an early type of emulsion) sensitive to green light in addition to blue light but not to red light.

isochron (ˈaɪsəʊˌkrɒn) NOUN 1 a line on an isotope ratio diagram denoting a suite of rock or mineral samples all formed at the same time. The slope of the line is related to the age of the rock or mineral suite. 2 a line or curve on a geological map or cross section (esp of oceanic crust) connecting points of identical age.

isochronal (aɪˈsɒkrənᵊl) *or* **isochronous** ADJECTIVE 1 having the same duration; equal in

time. [2] occurring at equal time intervals; having a uniform period of vibration or oscillation.
▷**HISTORY** C17: from New Latin *isochronus,* from Greek *isokhronos,* from ISO- + *khronos* time
▸**i'sochronally** *or* **i'sochronously** ADVERB ▸**i'sochro,nism** NOUN

isochrone ('aɪsəʊ,krəʊn) NOUN a line on a map or diagram connecting places from which it takes the same time to travel to a certain point.

isochronize *or* **isochronise** (aɪ'sɒkrə,naɪz) VERB (*tr*) to make isochronal.

isochroous (aɪ'sɒkrəʊəs) ADJECTIVE of uniform colour.

isoclinal (,aɪsəʊ'klaɪnᵊl) *or* **isoclinic** (,aɪsəʊ'klɪnɪk) ADJECTIVE [1] sloping in the same direction and at the same angle. [2] *Geology* (of folds) having limbs that are parallel to each other. ◆ NOUN [3] Also called: **isocline, isoclinal line.** an imaginary line connecting points on the earth's surface having equal angles of dip.

isocline ('aɪsəʊ,klaɪn) NOUN [1] a series of rock strata with isoclinal folds. [2] another name for **isoclinal** (sense 3).

isocracy (aɪ'sɒkrəsɪ) NOUN, *plural* **-cies.** [1] a form of government in which all people have equal powers. [2] equality of political power.
▸**isocratic** (,aɪsəʊ'krætɪk) ADJECTIVE

isocyanic acid (,aɪsəʊsaɪ'ænɪk) NOUN a hypothetical acid known only in the form of its compounds. Formula: HNCO.

isocyanide (,aɪsəʊ'saɪə,naɪd) NOUN any salt or ester of isocyanic acid. Also called: **carbylamine, isonitrile.**

isodiametric (,aɪsəʊ,daɪə'mɛtrɪk) ADJECTIVE [1] having diameters of the same length. [2] (of a crystal) having three equal axes. [3] (of a cell or similar body) having a similar diameter in all planes.

isodiaphere (,aɪsəʊ'daɪə,fɪə) NOUN one of two or more nuclides in which the difference between the number of neutrons and the number of protons is the same: *a nuclide that has emitted an alpha particle, and its decay product, are isodiapheres.*

isodimorphism (,aɪsəʊdaɪ'mɔːfɪzəm) NOUN a property of a dimorphous substance such that it is isomorphous with another dimorphous substance in both its forms.
▸**,isodi'morphous** *or* **,isodi'morphic** ADJECTIVE

isodose ('aɪsəʊ,dəʊs) NOUN *Med* a dose of radiation applied to a part of the body in radiotherapy that is equal to the dose applied to a different part.

isodynamic (,aɪsəʊdaɪ'næmɪk) ADJECTIVE *Physics* [1] having equal force or strength. [2] of or relating to an imaginary line on the earth's surface connecting points of equal horizontal magnetic intensity.

isoelectric (,aɪsəʊɪ'lɛktrɪk) ADJECTIVE having the same electric potential.

isoelectric point NOUN *Biochem* the pH value at which the net electric charge of a molecule, such as a protein or amino acid, is zero.

isoelectronic (,aɪsəʊɪlɛk'trɒnɪk) ADJECTIVE (of atoms, radicals, or ions) having an equal number of electrons or a similar configuration of electrons.

isoenzyme (,aɪsəʊ'ɛnzaɪm) NOUN another name for **isozyme.**
▸**isoenzymic** (,aɪsəʊɛn'zaɪmɪk, -'zɪm-) ADJECTIVE

isogamete (,aɪsəʊgæ'miːt) NOUN a gamete that is similar in size and form to the one with which it unites in fertilization. Compare **heterogamete.**
▸**isogametic** (,aɪsəʊgæ'mɛtɪk) ADJECTIVE

isogamy (aɪ'sɒgəmɪ) NOUN (in some algae and fungi) sexual fusion of gametes of similar size and form. Compare **heterogamy** (sense 1).
▸**i'sogamous** ADJECTIVE

isogenous (aɪ'sɒdʒɪnəs) ADJECTIVE *Biology* [1] of similar origin, as parts derived from the same embryonic tissue. [2] Also: **isogenic** (,aɪsəʊ'dʒɛnɪk). genetically uniform.
▸**i'sogeny** NOUN

isogeotherm (,aɪsəʊ'dʒiːəʊ,θɜːm) NOUN an imaginary line below the surface of the earth connecting points of equal temperature.
▸**,iso,geo'thermal** *or* **,iso,geo'thermic** ADJECTIVE

isogloss ('aɪsəʊ,glɒs) NOUN a line drawn on a map around the area in which a linguistic feature is to be found, such as a particular pronunciation of a given word.
▸**,iso'glossal** *or* **,iso'glottic** ADJECTIVE

isogon ('aɪsəʊ,gɒn) NOUN an equiangular polygon.

isogonic (,aɪsəʊ'gɒnɪk) *or* **isogonal** (aɪ'sɒgənᵊl) ADJECTIVE [1] *Maths* having, making, or involving equal angles. ◆ NOUN [2] Also called: **isogonic line, isogonal line, isogone.** *Physics* an imaginary line connecting points on the earth's surface having equal magnetic declination.

isogram ('aɪsəʊ,græm) NOUN another name for **isopleth.**

isohel ('aɪsəʊ,hɛl) NOUN a line on a map connecting places with an equal period of sunshine.
▷**HISTORY** C20: from ISO- + Greek *hēlios* sun

isohydric (,aɪsəʊ'haɪdrɪk) ADJECTIVE *Chem* having the same acidity or hydrogen-ion concentration.

isohyet (,aɪsəʊ'haɪɪt) NOUN a line on a map connecting places having equal rainfall.
▷**HISTORY** C19: from ISO- + *-hyet,* from Greek *huetos* rain

isolate VERB ('aɪsə,leɪt) (*tr*) [1] to place apart; cause to be alone. [2] *Med* to quarantine (a person or animal) having or suspected of having a contagious disease. [3] to obtain (a compound) in an uncombined form. [4] to obtain pure cultures of (bacteria, esp those causing a particular disease). [5] *Electronics* to prevent interaction between (circuits, components, etc.); insulate. ◆ NOUN ('aɪsəlɪt) [6] an isolated person or group.
▷**HISTORY** C19: back formation from *isolated,* via Italian from Latin *insulātus,* literally: made into an island; see INSULATE
▸**'isolable** ADJECTIVE ▸**,isola'bility** NOUN ▸**'iso,lator** NOUN

isolated pawn NOUN *Chess* a pawn without pawns of the same colour on neighbouring files.

isolating ('aɪsə,leɪtɪŋ) ADJECTIVE *Linguistics* another word for **analytic.**

isolation (,aɪsə'leɪʃən) NOUN [1] the act of isolating or the condition of being isolated. [2] (of a country, party, etc.) nonparticipation in or withdrawal from international politics. [3] *Med* **a** social separation of a person who has or is suspected of having a contagious disease. Compare **quarantine. b** (*as modifier*): *an isolation hospital.* [4] *Sociol* a lack of contact between persons, groups, or whole societies. [5] *Social psychol* the failure of an individual to maintain contact with others or genuine communication where interaction with others persists. [6] **in isolation.** without regard to context, similar matters, etc.

isolationism (,aɪsə'leɪʃə,nɪzəm) NOUN [1] a policy of nonparticipation in or withdrawal from international affairs. [2] an attitude favouring such a policy.
▸**,iso'lationist** NOUN, ADJECTIVE

isolative ('aɪsə,leɪtɪv, 'aɪsələtɪv) ADJECTIVE [1] (of a sound change) occurring in all linguistic environments, as the change of Middle English /iː/ to Modern English /aɪ/, as in *time.* Compare **combinative** (sense 2). [2] of, relating to, or concerned with isolation.

Isolde (ɪ'zɒldə) NOUN the German name of **Iseult.**

isolecithal (,aɪsəʊ'lɛsɪθəl) ADJECTIVE (of the ova of mammals and certain other vertebrates) having an evenly distributed yolk. Compare **heterolecithal.**

isoleucine (,aɪsəʊ'luːsiːn, -sɪn) NOUN an essential amino acid that occurs in proteins and is formed by protein hydrolysis.

isolex ('aɪsə,lɛks) NOUN *Linguistics* an isogloss marking off the area in which a particular item of vocabulary is found.
▷**HISTORY** C20: from ISO(GLOSS) + Greek *lex(is)* word

isoline ('aɪsəʊ,laɪn) NOUN another term for **isopleth.**

isologous (aɪ'sɒləgəs) ADJECTIVE (of two or more organic compounds) having a similar structure but containing different atoms of the same valency.
▷**HISTORY** C19: from ISO- + (HOMO)LOGOUS
▸**isologue** ('aɪsəʊ,lɒg) NOUN

isomagnetic (,aɪsəʊmæg'nɛtɪk) ADJECTIVE [1] having equal magnetic induction or force. ◆ NOUN [2] Also called: **isomagnetic line.** an imaginary line connecting points on the earth's surface having equal magnetic intensity.

isomer ('aɪsəmə) NOUN [1] *Chem* a compound that exhibits isomerism with one or more other compounds. [2] *Physics* a nuclide that exhibits isomerism with one or more other nuclides.
▸**isomeric** (,aɪsə'mɛrɪk) ADJECTIVE

isomerase (aɪ'sɒmə,reɪs) NOUN any enzyme that catalyses the conversion of one isomeric form of a compound to another.

isomerism (aɪ'sɒmə,rɪzəm) NOUN [1] the existence of two or more compounds having the same molecular formula but a different arrangement of atoms within the molecule. See also **stereoisomerism, optical isomerism.** [2] the existence of two or more nuclides having the same atomic numbers and mass numbers but different energy states.

isomerize *or* **isomerise** (aɪ'sɒmə,raɪz) VERB *Chem* to change or cause to change from one isomer to another.
▸**i,someri'zation** *or* **i,someri'sation** NOUN

isomerous (aɪ'sɒmərəs) ADJECTIVE [1] having an equal number of parts or markings. [2] (of flowers) having floral whorls with the same number of parts. Compare **anisomerous.**

isometric (,aɪsəʊ'mɛtrɪk) ADJECTIVE *also* **isometrical.** [1] having equal dimensions or measurements. [2] *Physiol* of or relating to muscular contraction that does not produce shortening of the muscle. [3] (of a crystal or system of crystallization) having three mutually perpendicular equal axes. [4] *Crystallog* another word for **cubic** (sense 4). [5] *Prosody* having or made up of regular feet. [6] (of a method of projecting a drawing in three dimensions) having the three axes equally inclined and all lines drawn to scale. ◆ NOUN [7] Also called: **isometric drawing.** a drawing made in this way. [8] Also called: **isometric line.** a line on a graph showing variations of pressure with temperature at constant volume.
▷**HISTORY** C19: from Greek *isometria* (see ISO- + -METRY) + -IC
▸**,iso'metrically** ADVERB

isometrics (,aɪsəʊ'mɛtrɪks) NOUN (*functioning as singular*) physical exercise involving isometric contraction of muscles.

isometropia (,aɪsəʊmɪ'trəʊpɪə) NOUN *Ophthalmol* equal refraction of the two eyes.
▷**HISTORY** from Greek *isometros* of equal measure + -OPIA

isometry (aɪ'sɒmɪtrɪ) NOUN [1] *Maths* rigid motion of a plane or space such that the distance between any two points before and after this motion is unaltered. [2] equality of height above sea level.

isomorph ('aɪsəʊ,mɔːf) NOUN a substance or organism that exhibits isomorphism.

isomorphic (,aɪsəʊ'mɔːfɪk) *or* **isomorphous** (,aɪsəʊ'mɔːfəs) ADJECTIVE exhibiting isomorphism.

isomorphism (,aɪsəʊ'mɔːfɪzəm) NOUN [1] *Biology* similarity of form, as in different generations of the same life cycle. [2] *Chem* the existence of two or more substances of different composition in a similar crystalline form. [3] *Maths* a one-to-one correspondence between the elements of two or more sets, such as those of Arabic and Roman numerals, and between the sums or products of the elements of one of these sets and those of the equivalent elements of the other set or sets.

isoniazid (,aɪsəʊ'naɪəzɪd) NOUN a soluble colourless crystalline compound used to treat tuberculosis. Formula: $C_6H_7N_3O$.
▷**HISTORY** C20 *isoni(cotinic acid hydr)azid(e)*

isonome ('aɪsəʊ,nəʊm) NOUN *Botany* a line on a chart connecting points of equal abundance values of a plant species sampled in different sections of an area. Isonomes of different species from the same area are compared in studies of plant distribution.
▷**HISTORY** C20: from ISO- + Greek *nomos* rule, law

isonomy (aɪ'sɒnəmɪ) NOUN [1] the equality before the law of the citizens of a state. [2] the equality of civil or political rights.
▸**isonomic** (,aɪsəʊ'nɒmɪk) *or* **i'sonomous** ADJECTIVE

isooctane (,aɪsəʊ'ɒkteɪn) NOUN a colourless liquid alkane hydrocarbon produced from petroleum and used in standardizing petrol. Formula: $(CH_3)_3CCH_2CH(CH_3)_2$. See also **octane number.**

isopach ('aɪsəʊ,pæk) *or* **isopachyte** (,aɪsəʊ'pækaɪt) NOUN *Geology* a line on a map connecting points below which a particular rock stratum has the same thickness.

▷HISTORY C20: from ISO- + Greek *pakhus* thick, *pakhutēs* thickness

isophone (ˈaɪsəˌfəʊn) NOUN *Linguistics* an isogloss marking off an area in which a particular feature of pronunciation is found.
▷HISTORY C20: from *iso-* (as in ISOGLOSS) + *-phone* (as in PHONEME)

isophote (ˈaɪsəˌfəʊt) NOUN *Astronomy* a line on a diagram or image of a galaxy, nebula, or other celestial object joining points of equal surface brightness.

isopiestic (ˌaɪsəʊpaɪˈɛstɪk) ADJECTIVE a line on a map connecting places with equal ground water pressure.
▷HISTORY C19: from ISO- + Greek *piestos* compressible, from *piezein* to press
▸ˌ**isopiˈestically** ADVERB

isopleth (ˈaɪsəʊˌplɛθ) NOUN a line on a map connecting places registering the same amount or ratio of some geographical or meteorological phenomenon or phenomena. Also called: **isogram, isoline.**
▷HISTORY C20: from Greek *isoplēthēs* equal in number, from ISO- + *plēthos* multitude, great number

isopod (ˈaɪsəʊˌpɒd) NOUN [1] any crustacean of the order *Isopoda,* including woodlice and pill bugs, in which the body is flattened dorsoventrally. ◆ ADJECTIVE [2] of, relating to, or belonging to the *Isopoda.*
▸**isopodan** (aɪˈsɒpədən) *or* **iˈsopodous** ADJECTIVE

isoprene (ˈaɪsəʊˌpriːn) NOUN a colourless volatile liquid with a penetrating odour: used in making synthetic rubbers. Formula: CH_2:CHC(CH_3):CH_2. Systematic name: **methylbuta-1,3-diene.**
▷HISTORY C20: from ISO- + PR(OPYL) + -ENE

isopropyl (ˌaɪsəʊˈprəʊpɪl) NOUN (*modifier*) of, consisting of, or containing the group of atoms $(CH_3)_2CH$-, derived from propane: *an isopropyl group or radical.*

isopycnal (ˌaɪsəʊˈpɪknəl) *or* **isopycnic** (-ˈpɪknɪk) NOUN a line on a map connecting points of equal atmospheric density.
▷HISTORY C19: from ISO- + Greek *puknos* thick

ISO rating NOUN *Photog* a classification of film speed in which a doubling of the ISO number represents a doubling in sensitivity; for example, ISO 400 film requires half the exposure of ISO 200 under the same conditions. The system uses identical numbers to the obsolete ASA rating.
▷HISTORY C20: from *I*nternational *S*tandards *O*rganization

isorhythmic (ˌaɪsəˈrɪðmɪk) ADJECTIVE *Music* (of medieval motets) having a cantus firmus that is repeated according to a strict system of internal reiterated note values.

isosceles (aɪˈsɒsɪˌliːz) ADJECTIVE [1] (of a triangle) having two sides of equal length. [2] (of a trapezium) having the two nonparallel sides of equal length.
▷HISTORY C16: from Late Latin, from Greek *isoskelēs,* from ISO- + *skelos* leg

isoseismal (ˌaɪsəʊˈsaɪzməl) ADJECTIVE [1] of or relating to equal intensity of earthquake shock. ◆ NOUN [2] a line on a map connecting points at which earthquake shocks are of equal intensity. ◆ Also: **isoseismic.**

isosmotic (ˌaɪsɒzˈmɒtɪk) ADJECTIVE another word for **isotonic** (sense 3).

isospin (ˈaɪsəʊˌspɪn) NOUN an internal quantum number used in the classification of elementary particles. Particles which have very similar properties except for those associated with their charge are regarded as forms of the same fundamental particle with different components of the isospin in a certain direction in an imaginary space. Also called: **isobaric spin, isotopic spin.**

isospondylous (ˌaɪsəˈspɒndᵊləs) ADJECTIVE of, relating to, or belonging to the *Isospondyli* (or *Clupeiformes*), an order of soft-finned teleost fishes that includes the herring, salmon, trout, and pike.
▷HISTORY C20: from ISO- + Greek *spondulos* vertebra

isostasy (aɪˈsɒstəsɪ) NOUN the state of balance, or equilibrium, which sections of the earth's lithosphere (whether continental or oceanic) are thought ultimately to achieve when the vertical forces upon them remain unchanged. The lithosphere floats upon the semifluid asthenosphere below. If a section of lithosphere is loaded, as by ice, it will slowly subside to a new equilibrium position; if a section of lithosphere is reduced in mass, as by erosion, it will slowly rise to a new equilibrium position.
▷HISTORY C19: ISO- + *-stasy,* from Greek *stasis* a standing
▸**isostatic** (ˌaɪsəʊˈstætɪk) ADJECTIVE

isostemonous (ˌaɪsəʊˈstiːmənəs, -ˈstɛm-) ADJECTIVE *Botany* (of a flower) having the stamens arranged in a single whorl and equal to the number of petals.
▷HISTORY C19: from ISO- + Greek *-stemonus* relating to a STAMEN

isosteric (ˌaɪsəʊˈstɛrɪk) ADJECTIVE (of two different molecules) having the same number of atoms and the same number and configuration of valency electrons, as carbon dioxide and nitrous oxide.

isotach (ˈaɪsəʊˌtæk) NOUN a line on a map connecting points of equal wind speed.
▷HISTORY from ISO- + Greek *takhos* speed

isotactic (ˌaɪsəʊˈtæktɪk) ADJECTIVE *Chem* (of a stereospecific polymer) having identical steric configurations of the groups on each asymmetric carbon atom on the chain. Compare **syndiotactic.**

isoteniscope (ˌaɪsəʊˈtɛnɪˌskəʊp) NOUN *Chem* an instrument used to measure vapour pressure.
▷HISTORY C20: from ISO- + TEN(SION) + -I- + -SCOPE

isothere (ˈaɪsəʊˌθɪə) NOUN a line on a map linking places with the same mean summer temperature. Compare **isocheim.**
▷HISTORY C19: from ISO- + Greek *theros* summer
▸**isotheral** (aɪˈsɒθərəl) ADJECTIVE

isotherm (ˈaɪsəʊˌθɜːm) NOUN [1] a line on a map linking places of equal temperature. [2] *Physics* a curve on a graph that connects points of equal temperature. ◆ Also called: **isothermal, isothermal line.**

isothermal (ˌaɪsəʊˈθɜːməl) ADJECTIVE [1] (of a process or change) taking place at constant temperature. [2] of or relating to an isotherm. ◆ NOUN [3] another word for **isotherm.**
▸ˌ**isoˈthermally** ADVERB

isotone (ˈaɪsəˌtəʊn) NOUN one of two or more atoms of different atomic number that contain the same number of neutrons.

isotonic (ˌaɪsəʊˈtɒnɪk) ADJECTIVE [1] *Physiol* (of two or more muscles) having equal tension. [2] (of a drink) designed to replace the fluid and salts lost from the body during strenuous exercise. [3] Also: **isosmotic.** (of two solutions) having the same osmotic pressure, commonly having physiological osmotic pressure. Compare **hypertonic, hypotonic.** [4] *Music* of, relating to, or characterized by the equal intervals of the well-tempered scale: *isotonic tuning.*
▸**isotonicity** (ˌaɪsəʊtəʊˈnɪsɪtɪ) NOUN

isotope (ˈaɪsəˌtəʊp) NOUN one of two or more atoms with the same atomic number that contain different numbers of neutrons.
▷HISTORY C20: from ISO- + Greek *topos* place
▸**isotopic** (ˌaɪsəˈtɒpɪk) ADJECTIVE ▸ˌ**isoˈtopically** ADVERB
▸**isotopy** (aɪˈsɒtəpɪ) NOUN

isotope geology NOUN the study and application of stable and radioactive isotopes to geological processes and their time scales.

isotopic spin NOUN See **isospin.**

isotretinoin (ˌaɪsəʊtrəˈtɪnəʊɪn) NOUN a drug related to vitamin A, used to treat severe acne that has failed to respond to other treatment.

isotron (ˈaɪsəˌtrɒn) NOUN *Physics* a device for separating small quantities of isotopes by ionizing them and separating the ions by a mass spectrometer.
▷HISTORY C20: from ISOTOPE + -TRON

isotropic (ˌaɪsəʊˈtrɒpɪk) *or* **isotropous** (aɪˈsɒtrəpəs) ADJECTIVE [1] having uniform physical properties in all directions. [2] *Biology* not having predetermined axes: *isotropic eggs.*
▸ˌ**isoˈtropically** ADVERB ▸**iˈsotropy** NOUN

isozyme (ˈaɪsəʊˌzaɪm) NOUN any of a set of structural variants of an enzyme occurring in different tissues in a single species. Also called: **isoenzyme.**
▷HISTORY from ISO- + (EN)ZYME
▸**isozymic** (ˌaɪsəʊˈzaɪmɪk, -ˈzɪm-) ADJECTIVE

ISP ABBREVIATION FOR Internet service provider, a business providing its customers with connection to the Internet and other related services.

ispaghula (ˌɪspəˈguːlə) NOUN dietary fibre derived from the seed husks of *Plantago orata* and used as a thickener or stabilizer in the food industry.

I-spy NOUN a game in which one player specifies the initial letter of the name of an object that he can see, which the other players then try to guess.

Israel (ˈɪzreɪəl, -rɪəl) NOUN [1] a republic in SW Asia, on the Mediterranean Sea: established in 1948, in the former British mandate of Palestine, as a primarily Jewish state; 8 disputes with Arab neighbours (who did not recognize the state of Israel), erupted into full-scale wars in 1948, 1956, 1967 (the Six Day War), and 1973 (the Yom Kippur War). In 1993 Israel agreed to grant autonomous status to the Gaza Strip and the West Bank, according to the terms of a peace agreement with the P.L.O. Official languages: Hebrew and Arabic. Religion: Jewish majority, Muslim and Christian minorities. Currency: shekel. Capital: Jerusalem (international recognition withheld as East Jerusalem was annexed (1967) by Israel: UN recognized capital: Tel Aviv). Pop.: 6 258 000 (2001 est). Area (including Golan Heights and East Jerusalem): 21 946 sq. km (8473 sq. miles). [2] **a** the ancient kingdom of the 12 Hebrew tribes at the SE end of the Mediterranean. **b** the kingdom in the N part of this region formed by the ten northern tribes of Israel in the 10th century B.C. and destroyed by the Assyrians in 721 B.C. [3] *Informal* the Jewish community throughout the world.

Israeli (ɪzˈreɪlɪ) NOUN, *plural* **-lis** *or* **-li.** [1] a citizen or inhabitant of the state of Israel. ◆ ADJECTIVE [2] of, relating to, or characteristic of the state of Israel or its inhabitants.

Israelite (ˈɪzrɪəˌlaɪt, -rə-) NOUN [1] *Bible* a member of the ethnic group claiming descent from Jacob; a Hebrew. [2] *Bible* a citizen of the kingdom of Israel (922 to 721B.C.) as opposed to Judah. [3] a member of any of various Christian sects who regard themselves as God's chosen people. [4] an archaic word for a **Jew.**

Israfil (ˈɪzrəˌfiːl), **Israfel** (ˈɪzrəˌfɛl), *or* **Israfeel** (ˈɪzrəˌfiːl) NOUN *Koran* the archangel who will sound the trumpet on the Day of Judgment, heralding the end of the world.

Issachar (ˈɪsəˌkɑː) NOUN *Old Testament* [1] the fifth son of Jacob by his wife Leah (Genesis 30:17–18). [2] the tribe descended from this patriarch. [3] the territory of this tribe.

ISSN ABBREVIATION FOR International Standard Serial Number.

ISSP ABBREVIATION FOR Intensive Supervision and Surveillance Programme: a method of dealing with persistent young offenders involving electronic tagging and making a digital photograph of the subject available for recognition by CCTV surveillance cameras.

issuable (ˈɪʃjʊəbᵊl) ADJECTIVE [1] capable of issuing or being issued. [2] *Chiefly law* open to debate or litigation. [3] authorized to be issued.
▸ˈ**issuably** ADVERB

issuance (ˈɪʃjʊəns) NOUN the act of issuing.

issuant (ˈɪʃjʊənt) ADJECTIVE *Heraldry* emerging or issuing.

issue (ˈɪʃjuː) NOUN [1] the act of sending or giving out something; supply; delivery. [2] something issued; an edition of stamps, a magazine, etc. [3] the number of identical items, such as banknotes or shares in a company, that become available at a particular time. [4] the act of emerging; outflow; discharge. [5] something flowing out, such as a river. [6] a place of outflow; outlet. [7] the descendants of a person; offspring; progeny. [8] a topic of interest or discussion. [9] an important subject requiring a decision. [10] an outcome or consequence; result. [11] *Pathol* **a** a suppurating sore. **b** discharge from a wound. [12] *Law* the matter remaining in dispute between the parties to an action after the pleadings. [13] the yield from or profits arising out of land or other property. [14] *Military* the allocation of items of government stores, such as food, clothing, and ammunition. [15] *Library science* **a** the system for recording current loans. **b** the number of books loaned in a specified period. [16] *Obsolete* an act, deed, or proceeding. [17]

at issue. **a** under discussion. **b** in disagreement. 18 **force the issue.** to compel decision on some matter. 19 **join issue.** **a** to join in controversy. **b** to submit an issue for adjudication. 20 **take issue.** to disagree. ◆ VERB **-sues, -suing, -sued.** 21 to come forth or emerge or cause to come forth or emerge. 22 to publish or deliver (a newspaper, magazine, etc.). 23 (*tr*) to make known or announce. 24 (*intr*) to originate or proceed. 25 (*intr*) to be a consequence; result. 26 (*intr; foll by in*) to end or terminate. 27 (*tr*) **a** to give out or allocate (equipment, a certificate, etc.) officially to someone. **b** (foll by *with*) to supply officially (with).
▷HISTORY C13: from Old French *eissue* way out, from *eissir* to go out, from Latin *exīre*, from EX-[1] + *īre* to go
▸'**issueless** ADJECTIVE ▸'**issuer** NOUN

issue price NOUN *Stock Exchange* the price at which a new issue of shares is offered to the public.

issuing house NOUN *Brit* a financial institution that engages in finding capital for established companies or for private firms wishing to convert to public companies, by issuing shares on their behalf.

Issus ('ɪsəs) NOUN an ancient town in S Asia Minor, in Cilicia north of present-day Iskenderun: scene of a battle (333 B.C.) in which Alexander the Great defeated the Persians.

-ist SUFFIX 1 (*forming nouns*) a person who performs a certain action or is concerned with something specified: *motorist; soloist.* 2 (*forming nouns*) a person who practises in a specific field: *physicist; typist.* 3 (*forming nouns and adjectives*) a person who advocates a particular doctrine, system, etc., or relating to such a person or the doctrine advocated: *socialist.* 4 (*forming nouns and adjectives*) a person characterized by a specified trait, tendency, etc., or relating to such a person or trait: *purist.* 5 (*forming nouns and adjectives*) a person who is prejudiced on the basis specified: *sexist; ageist.*
▷HISTORY via Old French from Latin *-ista, -istēs,* from Greek *-istēs*

-ista COMBINING FORM indicating a supporter or follower of someone or something: *fashionista; Portillista.*
▷HISTORY C20: back formation from SANDINISTA

istana (iː'stana) NOUN (in Malaysia) a royal palace.
▷HISTORY from Malay

Istanbul (ˌɪstæn'buːl) NOUN a port in NW Turkey, on the western (European) shore of the Bosporus: the largest city in Turkey; founded in about 660 B.C. by Greeks; refounded by Constantine the Great in 330 A.D. as the capital of the Eastern Roman Empire; taken by the Turks in 1453 and remained capital of the Ottoman Empire until 1922; industrial centre for shipbuilding, textiles, etc. Pop.: 8 260 438 (1997). Ancient name: **Byzantium.** Former name (330–1926): **Constantinople.**

Isth. *or* **isth.** ABBREVIATION FOR isthmus.

isthmian ('ɪsθmɪən) ADJECTIVE relating to or situated in an isthmus.

Isthmian ('ɪsθmɪən) ADJECTIVE relating to or situated in the Isthmus of Corinth or the Isthmus of Panama.

Isthmian Games NOUN a Panhellenic festival celebrated every other year in ancient Corinth.

isthmus ('ɪsməs) NOUN, *plural* **-muses** *or* **-mi** (-maɪ). 1 a narrow strip of land connecting two relatively large land areas. 2 *Anatomy* **a** a narrow band of tissue connecting two larger parts of a structure. **b** a narrow passage connecting two cavities.
▷HISTORY C16: from Latin, from Greek *isthmos*
▸'**isthmoid** ADJECTIVE

-istic SUFFIX FORMING ADJECTIVES equivalent to a combination of **-ist** and **-ic** but in some words having a less specific or literal application and sometimes a mildly pejorative force, as compared with corresponding adjectives ending in **-ist**: *communistic; impressionistic.*
▷HISTORY from Latin *-isticus,* from Greek *istikos*

istle ('ɪstlɪ) *or* **ixtle** NOUN a fibre obtained from various tropical American agave and yucca trees used in making carpets, cord, etc.
▷HISTORY C19: from Mexican Spanish *ixtle,* from Nahuatl *ichtli*

Istria ('ɪstrɪə) NOUN a peninsula in the N Adriatic Sea: passed from Italy to Yugoslavia (except for Trieste) in 1947 and to Croatia in 1991.
▸'**Istrian** NOUN, ADJECTIVE

Istrian ('ɪstrɪən) ADJECTIVE 1 of or relating to Istria, a peninsula in the N Adriatic Sea, or its inhabitants. ◆ NOUN 2 a native or inhabitant of Istria.

it[1] (ɪt) PRONOUN (*subjective or objective*) 1 refers to a nonhuman, animal, plant, or inanimate thing, or sometimes to a small baby: *it looks dangerous; give it a bone.* 2 refers to an unspecified or implied antecedent or to a previous or understood clause, phrase, etc.: *it is impossible; I knew it.* 3 used to represent human life or experience either in totality or in respect of the present situation: *how's it going?; I've had it; to brazen it out.* 4 used as a formal subject (or object), referring to a following clause, phrase, or word: *it helps to know the truth; I consider it dangerous to go on.* 5 used in the nominative as the formal grammatical subject of impersonal verbs. When *it* functions absolutely in such sentences, not referring to any previous or following clause or phrase, the context is nearly always a description of the environment or of some physical sensation: *it is raining; it hurts.* 6 (used as complement with *be*) *Informal* the crucial or ultimate point: *the steering failed and I thought that was it.* ◆ NOUN 7 (in children's games) the player whose turn it is to try to touch another. Compare **he**[1] (sense 5b). 8 *Informal* **a** sexual intercourse. **b** sex appeal. 9 *Informal* a desirable quality or ability: *he's really got it.*
▷HISTORY Old English *hit*

it[2] THE INTERNET DOMAIN NAME FOR Italy.

IT ABBREVIATION FOR information technology.

It. ABBREVIATION FOR: 1 Italian. 2 Italy.

ITA (in Britain) ABBREVIATION FOR Independent Television Authority: now superseded by the IBA.

i.t.a. *or* **ITA** ABBREVIATION FOR initial teaching alphabet, a partly phonetic alphabet used to teach reading.

itacolumite (ˌɪtə'kɒljʊˌmaɪt) NOUN a fine-grained micaceous sandstone that occurs in thin flexible slabs.
▷HISTORY C19: named after *Itacolumi* mountain in Brazil where it is found

itaconic acid (ˌɪtə'kɒnɪk) NOUN a white colourless crystalline carboxylic acid obtained by the fermentation of carbohydrates and used in the manufacture of synthetic resins. Formula: CH_2:C(COOH)CH_2COOH.

ital. ABBREVIATION FOR italic.

Ital. ABBREVIATION FOR: 1 Italian. 2 Italy.

Italia (i'taːlja) NOUN the Italian name for **Italy.**

Italia irredenta *Italian* (irre'denta) NOUN See **Irredentist.**

Italian (ɪ'tæljən) NOUN 1 the official language of Italy and one of the official languages of Switzerland: the native language of approximately 60 million people. It belongs to the Romance group of the Indo-European family, and there is a considerable diversity of dialects. 2 a native, citizen, or inhabitant of Italy, or a descendant of one. 3 See **Italian vermouth.** ◆ ADJECTIVE 4 relating to, denoting, or characteristic of Italy, its inhabitants, or their language.

Italianate (ɪ'tæljənɪt, -ˌneɪt) *or* **Italianesque** (ɪˌtæljə'nɛsk) ADJECTIVE Italian in style or character.

Italian East Africa NOUN a former Italian territory in E Africa, formed in 1936 from the possessions of Eritrea, Italian Somaliland, and Ethiopia: taken by British forces in 1941.

Italian greyhound NOUN a breed of dog like a miniature greyhound.

Italianism (ɪ'tæljəˌnɪzəm) *or* **Italicism** (ɪ'tælɪˌsɪzəm) NOUN 1 an Italian custom or style. 2 Italian quality or life, or the cult of either.

Italianize *or* **Italianise** (ɪ'tæljəˌnaɪz) VERB to make or become Italian or like an Italian person or thing.
▸**Iˌtalianiˈzation** *or* **Iˌtalianiˈsation** NOUN

Italian sixth NOUN (in musical harmony) an augmented sixth chord characterized by having a major third and an augmented sixth above the root.

Italian Somaliland NOUN a former Italian colony in E Africa, united with British Somaliland in 1960 to form the independent republic of Somalia.

Italian sonnet NOUN another term for **Petrarchan sonnet.**

Italian spinone (spɪ'nəʊnɪ) NOUN, *plural* **-ni** (-niː). a strongly-built gun dog with a wiry white coat and pendulous ears.
▷HISTORY C20: Italian

Italian vermouth NOUN sweet vermouth.

italic (ɪ'tælɪk) ADJECTIVE 1 Also: **Italian.** of, relating to, or denoting a style of handwriting with the letters slanting to the right. ◆ NOUN 2 a style of printing type modelled on this, chiefly used to indicate emphasis, a foreign word, etc. Compare **roman**[1]. 3 (*often plural*) italic type or print.
▷HISTORY C16 (after an edition of Virgil (1501) printed in Venice and dedicated to Italy): from Latin *Italicus* of Italy, from Greek *Italikos*

Italic (ɪ'tælɪk) NOUN 1 a branch of the Indo-European family of languages that includes many of the ancient languages of Italy, such as Venetic and the Osco-Umbrian group, Latin, which displaced them, and the Romance languages. ◆ ADJECTIVE 2 denoting, relating to, or belonging to this group of languages, esp the extinct ones.

italicize *or* **italicise** (ɪ'tælɪˌsaɪz) VERB 1 to print (textual matter) in italic type. 2 (*tr*) to underline (letters, words, etc.) with a single line to indicate italics.
▸**iˌtaliciˈzation** *or* **iˌtaliciˈsation** NOUN

Italo- (ɪ'tæləʊ-) COMBINING FORM indicating Italy or Italian: *Italophobia; Italo-German.*

Italy ('ɪtəlɪ) NOUN a republic in S Europe, occupying a peninsula in the Mediterranean between the Tyrrhenian and the Adriatic Seas, with the islands of Sardinia and Sicily to the west: first united under the Romans but became fragmented into numerous political units in the Middle Ages; united kingdom proclaimed in 1861; under the dictatorship of Mussolini (1922–43); became a republic in 1946; a member of the European Union. It is generally mountainous, with the Alps in the north and the Apennines running the length of the peninsula. Official language: Italian. Religion: Roman Catholic majority. Currency: euro. Capital: Rome. Pop.: 57 892 000 (2001 est.) Area: 301 247 sq. km (116 312 sq. miles). Italian name: **Italia.**

Itar Tass (ɪ'tɑː tæs) NOUN a news agency serving Russia, eastern Europe, and central Asia, created in 1992 to replace the former Soviet news agency Tass.
▷HISTORY Information Telegraph Agency of Russia, Telegraph Agency of Sovereign States

ITC (in Britain) ABBREVIATION FOR Independent Television Commission.

itch (ɪtʃ) NOUN 1 an irritation or tickling sensation of the skin causing a desire to scratch. 2 a restless desire. 3 any skin disorder, such as scabies, characterized by intense itching. ◆ VERB 4 (*intr*) to feel or produce an irritating or tickling sensation. 5 (*intr*) to have a restless desire (to do something). 6 *Not standard* to scratch (the skin). 7 **itching palm.** a grasping nature; avarice. 8 **have itchy feet.** to be restless; have a desire to travel.
▷HISTORY Old English *gīccean* to itch, of Germanic origin
▸'**itchy** ADJECTIVE ▸'**itchiness** NOUN

itch mite NOUN any mite of the family *Sarcoptidae,* all of which are skin parasites, esp *Sarcoptes scabei,* which causes scabies.

-ite[1] SUFFIX FORMING NOUNS 1 a native or inhabitant of: *Israelite.* 2 a follower or advocate of; a member or supporter of a group: *Luddite; labourite.* 3 (in biology) indicating a division of a body or organ: *somite.* 4 indicating a mineral or rock: *nephrite; peridotite.* 5 indicating a commercial product: *vulcanite.*
▷HISTORY via Latin *-ita* from Greek *-itēs* or directly from Greek

-ite[2] SUFFIX FORMING NOUNS indicating a salt or ester of an acid having a name ending in *-ous*: *a nitrite is a salt of nitrous acid.*
▷HISTORY from French, arbitrary alteration of -ATE[1]

item NOUN ('aɪtəm) 1 a thing or unit, esp included in a list or collection. 2 *Book-keeping* an entry in an account. 3 a piece of information, detail, or note: *a news item.* 4 *Informal* two people having a romantic or sexual relationship. ◆ VERB ('aɪtəm) 5

(*tr*) an archaic word for **itemize.** ◆ ADVERB ('aɪtɛm) 6 likewise; also.
▷HISTORY C14 (adv) from Latin: in like manner

itemize *or* **itemise** ('aɪtəˌmaɪz) VERB (*tr*) to put on a list or make a list of.
▸ˌ**itemi'zation** *or* ˌ**itemi'sation** NOUN

item veto NOUN (in the US) the power of a state governor to veto items in bills without vetoing the entire measure.

Iténez (i'teneθ) NOUN the Spanish name for the **Guaporé.**

iterate ('ɪtəˌreɪt) VERB (*tr*) to say or do again; repeat.
▷HISTORY C16: from Latin *iterāre,* from *iterum* again
▸'**iterant** ADJECTIVE ▸ˌ**iter'ation** *or* '**iterance** NOUN

iterative ('ɪtərətɪv) ADJECTIVE 1 repetitious or frequent. 2 *Maths, logic* another word for **recursive.** 3 *Grammar* another word for **frequentative.**
▸'**iteratively** ADVERB ▸'**iterativeness** NOUN

iteroparous ('ɪtərəʊˌpærəs) ADJECTIVE 1 Also: **polycarpic.** (of a plant) producing flowers and fruit more than once (usually many times) before dying. 2 (of an animal) producing offspring more than once during its lifetime.
▸'**iteroˌparity** NOUN

It girl NOUN a rich, usually attractive, young woman who spends most of her time shopping or socializing.
▷HISTORY C20: from IT, in the sense: sex appeal

Ithaca ('ɪθəkə) NOUN a Greek island in the Ionian Sea, the smallest of the Ionian Islands: regarded as the home of Homer's Odysseus. Area: 93 sq. km (36 sq. miles). Modern Greek name: **Itháki** (i'θaki).

Ithacan ('ɪθəkən) ADJECTIVE 1 of or relating to the Greek island of Ithaca or its inhabitants. ◆ NOUN 2 a native or inhabitant of Ithaca.

ither ('ɪðər) DETERMINER a Scot word for **other.**

Ithunn ('i:ðʊn) NOUN a variant of **Idun.**

ithyphallic (ˌɪθɪ'fælɪk) ADJECTIVE 1 *Prosody* (in classical verse) of or relating to the usual metre in hymns to Bacchus. 2 of or relating to the phallus carried in the ancient festivals of Bacchus. 3 (of sculpture and graphic art) having or showing an erect penis. ◆ NOUN 4 *Prosody* a poem in ithyphallic metre.
▷HISTORY C17: from Late Latin, from Greek *ithuphallikos,* from *ithuphallos* erect phallus, from *ithus* straight + *phallos* PHALLUS

itinerancy (ɪ'tɪnərənsɪ, aɪ-) *or* **itineracy** NOUN 1 the act of itinerating. 2 *Chiefly Methodist Church* the system of appointing a minister to a circuit of churches or chapels. 3 itinerants collectively.

itinerant (ɪ'tɪnərənt, aɪ-) ADJECTIVE 1 itinerating. 2 working for a short time in various places, esp as a casual labourer. ◆ NOUN 3 an itinerant worker or other person.
▷HISTORY C16: from Late Latin *itinerārī* to travel, from *iter* a journey
▸**i'tinerantly** ADVERB

itinerary (aɪ'tɪnərərɪ, ɪ-) NOUN, *plural* **-aries.** 1 a plan or line of travel; route. 2 a record of a journey. 3 a guidebook for travellers. ◆ ADJECTIVE 4 of or relating to travel or routes of travel. 5 a less common word for **itinerant.**

itinerate (aɪ'tɪnəˌreɪt, ɪ-) VERB (*intr*) to travel from place to place.
▸**iˌtiner'ation** NOUN

-itious SUFFIX FORMING ADJECTIVES having the nature of; characterized by: *nutritious; suppositious.*
▷HISTORY from Latin *-icius, -itious*

-itis SUFFIX FORMING NOUNS 1 indicating inflammation of a specified part: *tonsillitis.* 2 *Informal* indicating a preoccupation with or imaginary condition of illness caused by: *computeritis; telephonitis.*
▷HISTORY New Latin, from Greek, feminine of *-itēs* belonging to; see -ITE¹

it'll ('ɪtᵊl) CONTRACTION OF it will *or* it shall.

ITN (in Britain) ABBREVIATION FOR Independent Television News.

ITO ABBREVIATION FOR International Trade Organization.

-itol SUFFIX FORMING NOUNS indicating that certain chemical compounds are polyhydric alcohols: *inisitol; sorbitol.*
▷HISTORY from -ITE² + -OL¹

its (ɪts) DETERMINER **a** of, belonging to, or associated in some way with it: *its left rear wheel.* **b** (*as pronoun*): *each town claims its is the best.*

it's (ɪts) CONTRACTION OF it is *or* it has.

itself (ɪt'sɛlf) PRONOUN 1 **a** the reflexive form of **it. b** (intensifier): *even the money itself won't convince me.* 2 (*preceded by a copula*) its normal or usual self: *my cat isn't itself today.*

itsy-bitsy ('ɪtsɪ'bɪtsɪ) *or* **itty-bitty** ('ɪtɪ'bɪtɪ) ADJECTIVE *Informal* very small; tiny.
▷HISTORY C20: baby talk alteration of *little bit*

ITU ABBREVIATION FOR: 1 Intensive Therapy Unit. 2 **International Telecommunications Union.**

ITV (in Britain) ABBREVIATION FOR Independent Television.

-ity SUFFIX FORMING NOUNS indicating state or condition: *technicality.*
▷HISTORY from Old French *-ite,* from Latin *-itās*

i-type semiconductor NOUN another name for **intrinsic semiconductor.**

IU ABBREVIATION FOR: 1 immunizing unit. 2 international unit.

IU(C)D ABBREVIATION FOR **intrauterine (contraceptive) device.**

Iulus (aɪ'ju:ləs) NOUN 1 *Roman myth* another name for **Ascanius.** 2 *Roman myth* the son of Ascanius, founder of the Julian gens or clan.

-ium *or sometimes* **-um** SUFFIX FORMING NOUNS 1 indicating a metallic element: *platinum; barium.* 2 (in chemistry) indicating groups forming positive ions: *ammonium chloride; hydroxonium ion.* 3 indicating a biological structure: *syncytium.*
▷HISTORY New Latin, from Latin, from Greek *-ion,* diminutive suffix

IUS ABBREVIATION FOR intrauterine system; a hormonal contraceptive coil, such as Mirena, that carries a supply of progestogen, which is released in small amounts over a period of three to five years.

i.v. *or* **IV** intravenous(ly).

I've (aɪv) CONTRACTION OF I have.

-ive SUFFIX 1 (*forming adjectives*) indicating a tendency, inclination, character, or quality: *divisive; prohibitive; festive; massive.* 2 (*forming nouns of adjectival origin*): *detective; expletive.*
▷HISTORY from Latin *-īvus*

ivermectin (ˌaɪvə'mɛktɪn) NOUN a drug that kills parasitic nematode worms, mites, and insects. It is used to treat a variety of parasitic infections in domestic animals and onchocerciasis in humans.

IVF ABBREVIATION FOR **in vitro fertilization.**

ivied ('aɪvɪd) ADJECTIVE covered with ivy.

Iviza (*Spanish* i'βiθa) NOUN a variant spelling of **Ibiza.**

Ivorian (aɪ'vɔ:rɪən) NOUN 1 a native or inhabitant of the Côte d'Ivoire. ◆ ADJECTIVE 2 of or relating to the Côte d'Ivoire or its inhabitants.

ivories ('aɪvərɪz, -vrɪz) PLURAL NOUN *Slang* 1 the keys of a piano. 2 another word for **teeth.** 3 another word for **dice.**

ivory ('aɪvərɪ, -vrɪ) NOUN, *plural* **-ries.** 1 **a** a hard smooth creamy white variety of dentine that makes up a major part of the tusks of elephants, walruses, and similar animals. **b** (*as modifier*): *ivory ornaments.* 2 a tusk made of ivory. 3 **a** a yellowish-white colour; cream. **b** (*as adjective*): *ivory shoes.* 4 a substance resembling elephant tusk. 5 an ornament, etc., made of ivory. 6 **black ivory.** *Obsolete* Black slaves collectively. ◆ See also **ivories.**
▷HISTORY C13: from Old French *ivurie,* from Latin *evoreus* made of ivory, from *ebur* ivory; related to Greek *elephas* ivory, ELEPHANT
▸'**ivory-ˌlike** ADJECTIVE

ivory black NOUN a black pigment obtained by grinding charred scraps of ivory in oil.

Ivory Coast NOUN **the.** the former name (until 1986) of **Côte d'Ivoire.**

ivory gull NOUN a white gull, *Pagophila* (or *Larus*) *eburneus,* mostly confined to arctic regions.

ivory nut NOUN 1 the seed of the ivory palm, which contains an ivory-like substance used to make buttons, etc. 2 any similar seed from other palms. ◆ Also called: **vegetable ivory.**

ivory palm NOUN a low-growing South American palm tree, *Phytelephas macrocarpa,* that yields the ivory nut.

ivory tower ('taʊə) NOUN **a** seclusion or remoteness of attitude regarding real problems, everyday life, etc. **b** (*as modifier*): *ivory-tower aestheticism.*
▸ˌ**ivory-'towered** ADJECTIVE

ivorywood ('aɪvərɪˌwʊd) NOUN 1 the yellowish-white wood of an Australian tree, *Siphonodon australe,* used for engraving, inlaying, and turnery. 2 the tree itself: family *Celastraceae.*

IVR ABBREVIATION FOR International Vehicle Registration.

ivy ('aɪvɪ) NOUN, *plural* **ivies.** 1 any woody climbing or trailing araliaceous plant of the Old World genus *Hedera,* esp *H. helix,* having lobed evergreen leaves and black berry-like fruits. 2 any of various other climbing or creeping plants, such as Boston ivy, poison ivy, and ground ivy.
▷HISTORY Old English *īfig;* related to Old High German *ebah,* perhaps to Greek *iphuon* a plant
▸'**ivy-ˌlike** ADJECTIVE

Ivy League NOUN *US* **a the.** a group of eight universities (Brown, Columbia, Cornell, Dartmouth College, Harvard, Princeton, the University of Pennsylvania, and Yale) that have similar academic and social prestige in the US to Oxford and Cambridge in Britain. **b** (*as modifier*): *an Ivy-League education.*

IWC ABBREVIATION FOR International Whaling Commission.

iwi ('i:wɪ:) NOUN *NZ* a Maori tribe.
▷HISTORY Maori, literally: bone(s)

iwis *or* **ywis** (ɪ'wɪs) ADVERB an archaic word for **certainly.**
▷HISTORY C12: from Old English *gewiss* certain

Iwo Jima ('dʒi:mə) NOUN an island in the W Pacific, about 1100 km (700 miles) south of Japan: one of the Volcano Islands; scene of prolonged fighting between US and Japanese forces until taken by the US in 1945; returned to Japan in 1968. Area: 20 sq. km (8 sq. miles).

IWW ABBREVIATION FOR **Industrial Workers of the World.**

ixia ('ɪksɪə) NOUN any plant of the iridaceous genus *Ixia,* of southern Africa, having showy ornamental funnel-shaped flowers.
▷HISTORY C18: New Latin from Greek *ixos* mistletoe, birdlime prepared from mistletoe berries

Ixion (ɪk'saɪən) NOUN *Greek myth* a Thessalian king punished by Zeus for his love of Hera by being bound to a perpetually revolving wheel.
▸**Ixionian** (ˌɪksɪ'əʊnɪən) ADJECTIVE

ixtle ('ɪkstlɪ, 'ɪst-) NOUN a variant of **istle.**

Iyar *or* **Iyyar** (i'jar) NOUN (in the Jewish calendar) the second month of the year according to biblical reckoning and the eighth month of the civil year, usually falling within April and May.
▷HISTORY from Hebrew

IYKWIMAITYD *Text messaging* ABBREVIATION FOR if you know what I mean and I think you do.

izard ('ɪzəd) NOUN (esp in the Pyrenees) another name for **chamois.**

-ize *or* **-ise** SUFFIX FORMING VERBS 1 to cause to become, resemble, or agree with: *legalize.* 2 to become; change into: *crystallize.* 3 to affect in a specified way; subject to: *hypnotize.* 4 to act according to some practice, principle, policy, etc.: *economize.*
▷HISTORY from Old French *-iser,* from Late Latin *-izāre,* from Greek *-izein*

> **Language note** In Britain and the US *-ize* is the preferred ending for many verbs, but *-ise* is equally acceptable in British English. Certain words (chiefly those not formed by adding the suffix to an existing word) are, however, always spelt with *-ise* in both Britain and the US: *advertise, revise.*

izzard ('ɪzəd) NOUN *Archaic* the letter *Z.*
▷HISTORY C18: from earlier *ezed,* probably from Old French *et zède,* literally: and zed

izzat ('ɪzət) NOUN *Islam* honour or prestige.
▷HISTORY Urdu, from Arabic *'izzah* glory

Jj

j *or* **J** (dʒeɪ) NOUN, *plural* **j's, J's** *or* **Js.** [1] the tenth letter and seventh consonant of the modern English alphabet. [2] a speech sound represented by this letter, in English usually a voiced palato-alveolar affricate, as in *jam.*

j SYMBOL FOR: [1] *Maths* the unit vector along the *y*-axis. [2] *Obsolete* the imaginary number √–1. Also called: **i.**

J SYMBOL FOR: [1] *Cards* jack. [2] joule(s). [3] current density. ◆ [4] INTERNATIONAL CAR REGISTRATION FOR Japan.

ja (jɑː) SENTENCE SUBSTITUTE *South African* yes.
▷**HISTORY** from Afrikaans

JA ABBREVIATION FOR: [1] Also: **J/A.** *Banking* joint account. [2] Judge Advocate. ◆ [3] INTERNATIONAL CAR REGISTRATION FOR Jamaica.

jaap (jɑːp) NOUN *South African, offensive* a simpleton or country bumpkin.
▷**HISTORY** from Afrikaans

jab (dʒæb) VERB **jabs, jabbing, jabbed.** [1] to poke or thrust sharply. [2] to strike with a quick short blow or blows. ◆ NOUN [3] a sharp poke or stab. [4] a quick short blow, esp (in boxing) a straight punch with the leading hand. [5] *Informal* an injection: *polio jabs.*
▷**HISTORY** C19: originally Scottish variant of JOB
▸ **'jabbingly** ADVERB

Jabalpur *or* **Jubbulpore** (ˌdʒʌbəl'pʊə) NOUN a city in central India, in central Madhya Pradesh. Pop.: 741 927 (1991).

jabber ('dʒæbə) VERB [1] to speak or say rapidly, incoherently, and without making sense; chatter. ◆ NOUN [2] such talk.
▷**HISTORY** C15: of imitative origin; compare GIBBER[1]
▸ **'jabberer** NOUN

jabberwocky ('dʒæbəˌwɒkɪ) NOUN, *plural* **-wockies.** nonsense verse.
▷**HISTORY** C19: coined by Lewis Carroll as the title of a poem in *Through the Looking Glass* (1871)

jabiru ('dʒæbɪˌruː) NOUN [1] a large white tropical American stork, *Jabiru mycteria,* with a dark naked head and a dark bill. [2] Also called: **black-necked stork, policeman bird.** a large Australian stork, *Xenorhyncus asiaticus,* having a white plumage, dark green back and tail, and red legs. [3] another name for **saddlebill.** [4] (*not in ornithological usage*) another name for **wood ibis.**
▷**HISTORY** C18: via Portuguese from Tupi-Guarani

jaborandi (ˌdʒæbə'rændɪ) NOUN [1] any of several tropical American rutaceous shrubs of the genus *Pilocarpus,* esp *P. jaborandi.* [2] the dried leaves of any of these plants, used to induce sweating.
▷**HISTORY** C19: from Portuguese, from Tupi-Guarani *yaborandí*

jabot ('ʒæbəʊ) NOUN a frill or ruffle on the breast or throat of a garment, originally to hide the closure of a shirt.
▷**HISTORY** C19: from French: bird's crop, jabot; compare Old French *gave* throat

jacamar ('dʒækəˌmɑː) NOUN any bird of the tropical American family *Galbulidae,* having an iridescent plumage and feeding on insects: order *Piciformes* (woodpeckers, etc.).
▷**HISTORY** C19: from French, from Tupi *jacamá-ciri*

jaçana (ˌʒɑːsə'nɑː, ˌdʒæ-) NOUN any bird of the family *Jacanidae,* of tropical and subtropical marshy regions, having long legs and very long toes that enable walking on floating plants: order *Charadriiformes.* Also called: **lily-trotter.**
▷**HISTORY** C18: from Portuguese *jaçanã,* from Tupi-Guarani *jasaná*

jacaranda (ˌdʒækə'rændə) NOUN [1] any bignoniaceous tree of the tropical American genus *Jacaranda,* having fernlike leaves and pale purple flowers and widely cultivated in temperate areas of Australia. [2] the fragrant ornamental wood of any of these trees. [3] any of several related or similar trees or their wood.
▷**HISTORY** C18: from Portuguese, from Tupi-Guarani *yacarandá*

jacaré ('dʒækəreɪ) NOUN another name for **cayman.**
▷**HISTORY** C18: from Portuguese, from Tupi *jacaré*

jacinth ('dʒæsɪnθ) NOUN another name for **hyacinth** (sense 4).
▷**HISTORY** C13: from Medieval Latin *jacinthus,* from Latin *hyacinthus* plant, precious stone; see HYACINTH

jack[1] (dʒæk) NOUN [1] a man or fellow. [2] a sailor. [3] the male of certain animals, esp of the ass or donkey. [4] a mechanical or hydraulic device for exerting a large force, esp to raise a heavy weight such as a motor vehicle. [5] any of several mechanical devices that replace manpower, such as a contrivance for rotating meat on a spit. [6] one of four playing cards in a pack, one for each suit, bearing the picture of a young prince; knave. [7] *Bowls* a small usually white bowl at which the players aim with their own bowls. [8] *Electrical engineering* a female socket with two or more terminals designed to receive a male plug (**jack plug**) that either makes or breaks the circuit or circuits. [9] a flag, esp a small flag flown at the bow of a ship indicating the ship's nationality. Compare **Union Jack.** [10] *Nautical* either of a pair of crosstrees at the head of a topgallant mast used as standoffs for the royal shrouds. [11] a part of the action of a harpsichord, consisting of a fork-shaped device on the end of a pivoted lever on which a plectrum is mounted. [12] any of various tropical and subtropical carangid fishes, esp those of the genus *Caranx,* such as *C. hippos* (**crevalle jack**). [13] Also called: **jackstone.** one of the pieces used in the game of jacks. [14] short for **applejack, bootjack, jackass, jackfish, jack rabbit,** and **lumberjack.** [15] *US* a slang word for **money.** [16] **every man jack.** everyone without exception. ◆ ADJECTIVE [17] **jack of.** *Austral, slang* tired or fed up with (something). ◆ VERB (*tr*) [18] to lift or push (an object) with a jack. [19] Also: **jacklight.** *US and Canadian* to hunt (fish or game) by seeking them out or dazzling them with a flashlight. ◆ See also **jack in, jacks, jack up.**
▷**HISTORY** C16 *jakke,* variant of *Jankin,* diminutive of *John*

jack[2] *or* **jak** (dʒæk) NOUN short for **jackfruit** or **jakfruit.**
▷**HISTORY** C17: from Portuguese *jaca;* see JACKFRUIT

jack[3] (dʒæk) NOUN [1] a short sleeveless coat of armour of the Middle Ages, consisting usually of a canvas base with metal plates. [2] *Archaic* a drinking vessel, often of leather.
▷**HISTORY** C14: from Old French *jaque,* of uncertain origin

Jack (dʒæk) NOUN **I'm all right, Jack.** *Brit informal* **a** a remark indicating smug and complacent selfishness. **b** (*as modifier*): *an "I'm all right, Jack" attitude.*

jackal ('dʒækɔːl) NOUN [1] any of several African or S Asian canine mammals of the genus *Canis,* closely related to the dog, having long legs and pointed ears and muzzle: predators and carrion-eaters. [2] a person who does menial tasks for another. [3] a villain, esp a swindler.
▷**HISTORY** C17: from Turkish *chakāl,* from Persian *shagāl,* from Sanskrit *sṛgāla*

jackanapes ('dʒækəˌneɪps) NOUN [1] a conceited impertinent person. [2] a mischievous child. [3] *Archaic* a monkey.
▷**HISTORY** C16: variant of *Jakken-apes,* literally: Jack of the ape, nickname of William de la Pole (1396–1450), first Duke of Suffolk, whose badge showed an ape's ball and chain

jackass ('dʒækˌæs) NOUN [1] a male donkey. [2] a stupid person; fool. [3] **laughing jackass.** another name for **kookaburra.**
▷**HISTORY** C18: from JACK[1] (male) + ASS[1]

jack bean NOUN a tropical American leguminous plant, *Canavalia ensiformis,* that has clusters of purple flowers and long pods and is grown in the southern US for forage.

jackboot ('dʒækˌbuːt) NOUN [1] an all-leather military boot, extending up to or above the knee. [2] **a** arbitrary, cruel, and authoritarian rule or behaviour. **b** (*as modifier*): *jackboot tactics.*
▸ **'jackˌbooted** ADJECTIVE

jack-by-the-hedge NOUN another name for **garlic mustard.**

jackdaw ('dʒækˌdɔː) NOUN a large common Eurasian passerine bird, *Corvus monedula,* in which the plumage is black and dark grey: noted for its thieving habits: family *Corvidae* (crows).
▷**HISTORY** C16: from JACK[1] + DAW

Jackeen (dʒæ'kiːn) NOUN *Irish* a slick self-assertive lower-class Dubliner.
▷**HISTORY** C19: from proper name *Jack* + *-een,* Irish diminutive suffix, from Irish Gaelic *-ín*

jackeroo *or* **jackaroo** (ˌdʒækə'ruː) NOUN, *plural* **-roos.** *Austral informal* a young male management trainee on a sheep or cattle station.
▷**HISTORY** C19: from JACK[1] + (KANG)AROO

jacket ('dʒækɪt) NOUN [1] a short coat, esp one that is hip-length and has a front opening and sleeves. [2] something that resembles this or is designed to be worn around the upper part of the body: *a life jacket.* [3] any exterior covering or casing, such as the insulating cover of a boiler. [4] the part of the cylinder block of an internal-combustion engine that encloses the coolant. [5] See **dust jacket.** [6] **a** the skin of a baked potato. **b** (*as modifier*): *jacket potatoes.* [7] a metal casing used in certain types of ammunition. [8] *US* a cover to protect a gramophone record. Brit name: **sleeve.** [9] *Chiefly US* a folder or envelope to hold documents. ◆ VERB [10] (*tr*) to put a jacket on (someone or something).
▷**HISTORY** C15: from Old French *jaquet* short jacket, from *jacque* peasant, from proper name *Jacques* James
▸ **'jacketed** ADJECTIVE ▸ **'jacket-ˌlike** ADJECTIVE

jackfish ('dʒækˌfɪʃ) NOUN, *plural* **-fish** *or* **-fishes.** a popular name for **pike** (the fish), esp when small.

Jack Frost NOUN a personification of frost or winter.

jackfruit *or* **jakfruit** ('dʒækˌfruːt) NOUN [1] a tropical Asian moraceous tree, *Artocarpus heterophyllus.* [2] the edible fruit of this tree, which resembles breadfruit and can weigh up to 27 kilograms (60 pounds). ◆ Sometimes shortened to: **jack** *or* **jak.**
▷**HISTORY** C19: from Portuguese *jaca,* from Malayalam *cakka*

Jack-go-to-bed-at-noon NOUN another name for **goatsbeard** (sense 1).

jackhammer ('dʒækˌhæmə) NOUN a hand-held hammer drill, driven by compressed air, for drilling rocks, etc.

Jackie *or* **Jacky** ('dʒækɪ) NOUN, *plural* **Jackies.** *Austral, offensive slang* [1] a native Australian. [2] native Australians collectively. [3] **sit up like Jackie.** to sit bolt upright, esp cheekily.

jack in VERB (*tr, adverb*) *Slang* to abandon or leave (an attempt or enterprise).

jack-in-office NOUN a self-important petty official.

jack-in-the-box NOUN, *plural* **jack-in-the-boxes** *or* **jacks-in-the-box.** a toy consisting of a figure on a compressed spring in a box, which springs out when the lid is opened.

jack-in-the-green NOUN (in England, formerly) a man who wore or supported a leaf-covered wooden framework while dancing in May-Day celebrations.

jack-in-the-pulpit NOUN [1] an E North American aroid plant, *Arisaema triphyllum,* having a leaflike spathe partly arched over a clublike spadix. [2] *Brit* another name for **cuckoopint.**

Jack Ketch (ketʃ) NOUN *Brit, archaic* a hangman.

▷HISTORY C18: after *John Ketch* (died 1686), public executioner in England

jackknife ('dʒækˌnaɪf) NOUN, *plural* **-knives.** 1 a knife with the blade pivoted to fold into a recess in the handle. 2 a former name for a type of dive in which the diver bends at the waist in midair, with his legs straight and his hands touching his feet, finally straightening out and entering the water headfirst: forward pike dive. ◆ VERB (*intr*) 3 (of an articulated lorry) to go out of control in such a way that the trailer swings round at an angle to the cab. 4 to make a jackknife dive.

jack ladder NOUN another name for **Jacob's ladder** (sense 2).

jack of all trades NOUN, *plural* **jacks of all trades.** a person who undertakes many different kinds of work.

jack-o'-lantern NOUN 1 a lantern made from a hollowed pumpkin, which has holes cut in it to represent a human face. 2 a will-o'-the-wisp or similar phenomenon.

jack pine NOUN a coniferous tree, *Pinus banksiana*, of North America, having paired needle-like leaves and small cones that remain on the branches for many years: family *Pinaceae*.

jack plane NOUN a carpenter's plane, usually with a wooden body, used for rough planing of timber.

jackpot ('dʒækˌpɒt) NOUN 1 any large prize, kitty, or accumulated stake that may be won in gambling, such as a pool in poker that accumulates until the betting is opened with a pair of jacks or higher. 2 **hit the jackpot. a** to win a jackpot. **b** *Informal* to achieve great success, esp through luck.
▷HISTORY C20: probably from JACK[1] (playing card) + POT[1]

jack rabbit NOUN any of various W North American hares, such as *Lepus townsendi* (**white-tailed jack rabbit**), having long hind legs and large ears.
▷HISTORY C19: shortened from *jackass-rabbit*, referring to its long ears

jack rafter NOUN a short rafter used in a hip roof.

Jack Robinson NOUN **before you could** (*or* **can**) **say Jack Robinson.** extremely quickly or suddenly.

Jack Russell NOUN a small short-legged terrier having a white coat with tan, black, or lemon markings: there are rough- and smooth-haired varieties. Also called: **Jack Russell terrier.**
▷HISTORY named after John *Russell* (1795–1883), English clergyman who developed the breed

jacks (dʒæks) NOUN (*functioning as singular*) a game in which bone, metal, or plastic pieces (**jackstones**) are thrown and then picked up in various groups between bounces or throws of a small ball. Sometimes called: **knucklebones.**
▷HISTORY C19: shortened from *jackstones*, variant of *checkstones* pebbles

jackscrew ('dʒækˌskruː) NOUN another name for **screw jack.**

jackshaft ('dʒækˌʃɑːft) NOUN a short length of shafting that transmits power from an engine or motor to a machine.

jacksie *or* **jacksy** ('dʒæksɪ) NOUN *Brit, slang* the buttocks or anus. Also called: **jaxie** *or* **jaxy.**
▷HISTORY C19: probably from JACK[1]

jacksmelt ('dʒækˌsmɛlt) NOUN, *plural* **-smelts** *or* **-smelt.** a marine teleost food fish, *Atherinopsis californiensis*, of American coastal waters of the North Pacific: family *Atherinidae* (silversides).

jacksnipe ('dʒækˌsnaɪp) NOUN, *plural* **-snipe** *or* **-snipes.** 1 a small Eurasian short-billed snipe, *Lymnocryptes minima*. 2 any of various similar birds, such as the pectoral sandpiper.

Jackson ('dʒæksən) NOUN a city in and state capital of Mississippi, on the Pearl River. Pop.: 184 256 (2000).

Jacksonian (dʒæk'səʊnɪən) ADJECTIVE of or relating to a person surnamed Jackson, esp Andrew Jackson, the US president, general, and lawyer (1767–1845).

Jacksonville ('dʒæksənˌvɪl) NOUN a port in NE Florida: the leading commercial centre of the southeast. Pop.: 735 617 (2000).

jackstay ('dʒækˌsteɪ) NOUN *Nautical* 1 a metal rod, wire rope, or wooden batten to which an edge of a sail is fastened along a yard. 2 a support for the parrel of a yard.

jackstraws ('dʒækˌstrɔːz) NOUN (*functioning as singular*) another name for **spillikins.**

Jack Tar NOUN *Now chiefly literary* a sailor.

Jack-the-lad NOUN *Slang* a young man who is regarded as a brash, loud show-off.

Jack-the-rags NOUN *South Wales, dialect* a rag-and-bone man.

jack towel NOUN another name for **roller towel.**

jack up VERB (*adverb*) 1 (*tr*) to increase (prices, salaries, etc.). 2 (*tr*) to raise an object, such as a car, with or as with a jack. 3 (*intr*) *Slang* to inject oneself with a drug, usually heroin. 4 (*intr*) *Austral informal* to refuse to comply; rebel, esp collectively. 5 *NZ informal* to initiate, organize, or procure.

Jacky ('dʒækɪ) NOUN See **Jackie.**

Jacky Howe NOUN *Austral informal* (formerly) a sleeveless flannel shirt worn by shearers.
▷HISTORY C19: named after *Jacky Howe* (1855–1922) who was the world champion shearer in 1892

Jacob ('dʒeɪkəb) NOUN 1 *Old Testament* the son of Isaac, twin brother of Esau, and father of the twelve patriarchs of Israel. 2 Also called: **Jacob sheep.** any of an ancient breed of sheep having a fleece with dark brown patches and two or four horns.
▷HISTORY sense 2 in allusion to Genesis 30:40

Jacobean (ˌdʒækə'bɪən) ADJECTIVE 1 *History* characteristic of or relating to James I (1566–1625) of England or to the period of his rule (1603–25). 2 of or relating to the style of furniture current at this time, characterized by the use of dark brown carved oak. 3 denoting, relating to, or having the style of architecture used in England during this period, characterized by a combination of late Gothic and Palladian motifs. ◆ NOUN 4 any writer or other person who lived in the reign of James I.
▷HISTORY C18: from New Latin *jacōbaeus*, from *Jacōbus* James

Jacobian (dʒə'kəʊbɪən) *or* **Jacobian determinant** NOUN *Maths* a function from *n* equations in *n* variables whose value at any point is the *n x n* determinant of the partial derivatives of those equations evaluated at that point.
▷HISTORY named after Karl Gustav Jacob *Jacobi* (1804–51), German mathematician.

Jacobin ('dʒækəbɪn) NOUN 1 a member of the most radical club founded during the French Revolution, which overthrew the Girondists in 1793 and, led by Maximilien Robespierre (1758–94), instituted the Reign of Terror. 2 a leftist or extreme political radical. 3 a French Dominican friar. 4 (*sometimes not capital*) a variety of fancy pigeon with a hood of feathers swept up over and around the head. ◆ ADJECTIVE 5 of, characteristic of, or relating to the Jacobins or their policies.
▷HISTORY C14: from Old French, from Medieval Latin *Jacōbīnus*, from Late Latin *Jacōbus* James; applied to the Dominicans, from the proximity of the church of *St Jacques* (St James) to their first convent in Paris; the political club originally met in the convent in 1789
▸ˌ**Jaco'binic** *or* ˌ**Jaco'binical** ADJECTIVE ▸ˌ**Jaco'binically** ADVERB ▸'**Jacobinism** NOUN

Jacobite ('dʒækəˌbaɪt) NOUN 1 *Brit history* an adherent of James II (1633–1701, king of England, Ireland, and, as James VII, of Scotland, 1685–88) after his overthrow in 1688, or of his descendants in their attempts to regain the throne. 2 a member of the Monophysite Church of Syria, which became a schismatic church in 451 A.D.
▷HISTORY C17: from Late Latin *Jacōbus* James + -ITE[1]
▸**Jacobitic** (ˌdʒækə'bɪtɪk) ADJECTIVE ▸'**Jacoˌbitism** NOUN

Jacobite Rebellion NOUN **the.** *Brit history* 1 the unsuccessful Jacobite rising of 1715 led by James Francis Edward Stuart. 2 the last Jacobite rising (1745-46) led by Charles Edward Stuart, the Young Pretender, which after initial successes was crushed at Culloden.

Jacob sheep NOUN See **Jacob** (sense 2).

Jacob's ladder NOUN 1 *Old Testament* the ladder reaching up to heaven that Jacob saw in a dream (Genesis 28:12–17). 2 Also called: **jack ladder.** a ladder made of wooden or metal steps supported by ropes or chains. 3 a North American polemoniaceous plant, *Polemonium caeruleum*, with blue flowers and a ladder-like arrangement of leaves. 4 any of several similar or related plants.

Jacob's staff NOUN a medieval instrument for measuring heights and distances.

jacobus (dʒə'kəʊbəs) NOUN, *plural* **-buses.** an English gold coin minted in the reign of James I.
▷HISTORY C17: from Late Latin: James

jaconet ('dʒækənɪt) NOUN a light cotton fabric used for clothing, bandages, etc.
▷HISTORY C18: from Urdu *jagannāthī*, from *Jagannāthpūrī*, India, where it was originally made

Jacquard ('dʒækɑːd, dʒə'kɑːd; *French* ʒakar) NOUN 1 Also called: **Jacquard weave.** a fabric in which the design is incorporated into the weave instead of being printed or dyed on. 2 Also called: **Jacquard loom.** the loom that produces this fabric.
▷HISTORY C19: named after Joseph M. *Jacquard* (1752–1834), French inventor

Jacquerie *French* (ʒakri) NOUN the revolt of the N French peasants against the nobility in 1358.
▷HISTORY C16: from Old French: the peasantry, from *jacque* a peasant, from *Jacques* James, from Late Latin *Jacōbus*

jactation (dʒæk'teɪʃən) NOUN 1 *Rare* the act of boasting. 2 *Pathol* another word for **jactitation** (sense 3).
▷HISTORY C16: from Latin *jactātiō* bragging, from *jactāre* to flourish, from *jacere* to throw

jactitation (ˌdʒæktɪ'teɪʃən) NOUN 1 the act of boasting. 2 a false boast or claim that tends to harm another person, esp a false assertion that one is married to another, formerly actionable at law. 3 Also called: **jactation.** *Pathol* restless tossing in bed, characteristic of severe fevers and certain mental disorders.
▷HISTORY C17: from Medieval Latin *jactitātiō*, from Latin *jacitāre* to utter publicly, from *jactitāre* to toss about; see JACTATION

Jacuzzi (dʒə'kuːzɪ) NOUN, *plural* **-zis.** 1 *Trademark* a system of underwater jets that keep the water in a bath or pool constantly agitated. 2 (*sometimes not capital*) a bath or pool equipped with this.
▷HISTORY C20: named after Candido and Roy *Jacuzzi*, who developed and marketed it

jade[1] (dʒeɪd) NOUN 1 **a** a semiprecious stone consisting of either jadeite or nephrite. It varies in colour from white to green and is used for making ornaments and jewellery. **b** (*as modifier*): *jade ornaments*. 2 the green colour of jade.
▷HISTORY C18: from French, from Italian *giada*, from obsolete Spanish *piedra de ijada* colic stone (literally: stone of the flank, because it was believed to cure renal colic); *ijada*, from Vulgar Latin *īliata* (unattested) flanks, from Latin *īlia*, plural of *īlium;* see ILEUM
▸'**jadeˌlike** ADJECTIVE

jade[2] (dʒeɪd) NOUN 1 an old overworked horse; nag; hack. 2 *Derogatory or facetious* a woman considered to be ill-tempered or disreputable. ◆ VERB 3 to exhaust or make exhausted from work or use.
▷HISTORY C14: of unknown origin
▸'**jadish** ADJECTIVE ▸'**jadishly** ADVERB ▸'**jadishness** NOUN

jaded ('dʒeɪdɪd) ADJECTIVE 1 exhausted or dissipated. 2 satiated.
▸'**jadedly** ADVERB ▸'**jadedness** NOUN

jade green NOUN, ADJECTIVE **a** a colour varying from yellowish-green to bluish-green. **b** (*as adjective*): *a jade-green carpet*.

jadeite ('dʒeɪdaɪt) NOUN a usually green or white mineral of the clinopyroxene group, found in igneous and metamorphic rocks. It is used as a gemstone (jade). Composition: sodium aluminium silicate. Formula: $NaAlSi_2O_6$. Crystal structure: monoclinic.

Jadotville (*French* ʒadovil) NOUN the former name of **Likasi.**

j'adoube *French* (ʒadub) INTERJECTION *Chess* an expression of an intention to touch a piece in order to adjust its placement rather than to make a move.
▷HISTORY literally: I adjust

jaeger ('jeɪgə) NOUN 1 *Military* a marksman in certain units of the German or Austrian armies. 2 a member of a light or mountain infantry unit in some European armies. 3 *US and Canadian* any of several skuas of the genus *Stercorarius*. 4 *Rare* a hunter or hunter's attendant. ◆ Also (for senses 1, 2, 4): **jager, jäger.**
▷HISTORY C18: from German *Jäger* hunter, from *jagen* to hunt; see YACHT

Jael ('dʒeɪəl) NOUN *Old Testament* the woman who killed Sisera when he took refuge in her tent (Judges 4:17–21).

Jaén (xa'en) NOUN a city in S Spain. Pop.: 107 184 (1998 est.).

jafa ('dʒæfə) NOUN *NZ, slang* an offensive name for a person from Auckland.
▷**HISTORY** from *j(ust) a(nother) f(ucking) A(ucklander)*

Jaffa ('dʒæfə, 'dʒɑː-) NOUN [1] a port in W Israel, on the Mediterranean: incorporated into Tel Aviv in 1950; an old Canaanite city. Biblical name: **Joppa.** Hebrew name: **Yafo.** [2] a large variety of orange, having a thick skin.

Jaffna ('dʒæfnə) NOUN a port in N Sri Lanka: for many centuries the capital of a Tamil kingdom. Pop.: 145 600 (1997 est.).

jag[1] *or* **jagg** (dʒæg) VERB **jags, jagging, jagged.** [1] *(tr)* to cut unevenly; make jagged. [2] *Austral* to catch (fish) by impaling them on an unbaited hook. ◆ NOUN, VERB [3] *Scot* an informal word for **jab** (senses 3, 5). ◆ NOUN [4] a jagged notch or projection.
▷**HISTORY** C14: of unknown origin

jag[2] (dʒæg) NOUN *Slang* [1] **a** intoxication from drugs or alcohol. **b** a bout of drinking or drug taking. [2] a period of uncontrolled activity: *a crying jag.*
▷**HISTORY** of unknown origin

Jag (dʒæg) NOUN *Informal* a Jaguar car: often understood as a symbol of affluence.

JAG ABBREVIATION FOR Judge Advocate General.

jaga ('dʒaga) (in Malaysia) NOUN [1] a guard; sentry. ◆ VERB [2] *(tr)* to guard or watch: *jaga the door.*
▷**HISTORY** from Malay

Jagannath, Jagganath ('dʒʌgəˌnɑːt, -ˌnɔːt), *or* **Jagannatha** (ˌdʒʌgə'nɑːθə) NOUN *Hinduism* other names for **Juggernaut.**

jäger ('jeɪgə) NOUN See **jaeger.**

jagged ('dʒægɪd) ADJECTIVE having sharp projecting notches; ragged; serrate.
▸ **'jaggedly** ADVERB ▸ **'jaggedness** NOUN

jaggery, jaggary, *or* **jagghery** ('dʒægərɪ) NOUN a coarse brown sugar made in the East Indies from the sap of the date palm.
▷**HISTORY** C16: from Hindi *jāgrī*; compare Sanskrit *śárkarā* gritty substance, sugar

jaggy ('dʒægɪ) ADJECTIVE **-gier, -giest.** [1] a less common word for **jagged.** [2] *Scot* prickly.

jaguar ('dʒægjʊə) NOUN a large feline mammal, *Panthera onca,* of S North America, Central America, and N South America, similar to the leopard but with a shorter tail and larger spots on its coat.
▷**HISTORY** C17: from Portuguese, from Tupi *jaguara,* Guarani *yaguara*

jaguarondi (ˌdʒægwə'rɒndɪ) *or* **jaguarundi** (ˌdʒægwə'rʌndɪ) NOUN, *plural* **-dis.** a feline mammal, *Felis yagouaroundi,* of Central and South America, with a reddish or grey coat, short legs, and a long tail. See also **eyra.**
▷**HISTORY** C19: via Portuguese from Tupi

Jahveh ('jɑːveɪ) *or* **Jahweh** ('jɑːweɪ) NOUN variant of **Yahweh.**

Jahvist ('jɑːvɪst) *or* **Jahwist** ('jɑːwɪst) NOUN variant of **Yahwist.**

Jahwism ('jɑːwɪz(ə)m) *or* **Jahvism** ('jɑːvɪzəm) NOUN variants of **Yahwism** or **Yahvism.**
▸ **Jah'wistic** *or* **Jah'vistic** ADJECTIVE

jai (dʒæ) NOUN *Indian* victory (to).
▷**HISTORY** Hindi *jaya* victory

jai alai ('haɪ 'laɪ, 'haɪ əˌlaɪ, ˌhaɪ ə'laɪ) NOUN a version of pelota played by two or four players.
▷**HISTORY** via Spanish from Basque, from *jai* game, festival + *alai* merry

Jai Hind ('dʒæ 'hɪnd) victory to India: a political slogan and a form of greeting in Hindi.
▷**HISTORY** Hindi, from *jaya* victory + *Hind* India

jail *or* **gaol** (dʒeɪl) NOUN [1] a place for the confinement of persons convicted and sentenced to imprisonment or of persons awaiting trial to whom bail is not granted. [2] **get out of jail (free).** *Informal* to get out of a difficult situation. ◆ VERB [3] *(tr)* to confine in prison.
▷**HISTORY** C13: from Old French *jaiole* cage, from Vulgar Latin *caveola* (unattested), from Latin *cavea* enclosure; see CAGE: the two spellings derive from the forms of the word that developed in two different areas of France, and the spelling *gaol* represents a pronunciation in use until the 17th century
▸ **'jailless** *or* **'gaolless** ADJECTIVE ▸ **'jail-like** *or* **'gaol-like** ADJECTIVE

jailbait ('dʒeɪlˌbeɪt) NOUN *Slang* a young woman, or young women collectively, considered sexually attractive but below the age of consent.

jailbird *or* **gaolbird** ('dʒeɪlˌbɜːd) NOUN a person who is or has been confined to jail, esp repeatedly; convict.

jailbreak *or* **gaolbreak** ('dʒeɪlˌbreɪk) NOUN an escape from jail.

jail delivery NOUN [1] forcible and illegal liberation of prisoners from jail. [2] *English law* (formerly) a commission issued to assize judges when they come to a circuit town authorizing them to try all prisoners and release those acquitted.

jailer, jailor, *or* **gaoler** ('dʒeɪlə) NOUN a person in charge of prisoners in a jail.

jail fever NOUN a former name for **typhus,** once a common disease in jails

jailhouse ('dʒeɪlˌhaʊs) NOUN *Southern US* a jail; prison.

Jain (dʒaɪn) *or* **Jaina** ('dʒaɪnə) NOUN [1] an adherent of Jainism. [2] one of the saints believed to be the founders of Jainism. ◆ ADJECTIVE [3] of or relating to Jainism or the Jains.
▷**HISTORY** C19: from Hindi *jaina* saint, literally: overcomer, from Sanskrit

Jainism ('dʒaɪˌnɪzəm) NOUN an ancient Hindu religion, which has its own scriptures and believes that the material world is eternal, progressing endlessly in a series of vast cycles.
▸ **'Jainist** NOUN, ADJECTIVE

Jaipur (dʒaɪ'pʊə) NOUN a city of great beauty in N India, capital of Rajasthan state: University of Rajasthan (1947). Pop.: 1 458 183 (1991).

Jakarta *or* **Djakarta** (dʒə'kɑːtə) NOUN the capital of Indonesia, in N West Java: founded in 1619 and ruled by the Dutch until 1945; the chief trading centre of the East in the 17th century; University of Indonesia (1947). Pop.: 9 160 500 (1995 est.). Former name (until 1949): **Batavia.**

jake (dʒeɪk) ADJECTIVE *Austral and NZ, slang* [1] satisfactory; all right. [2] **she's jake.** everything is under control.
▷**HISTORY** probably from the name *Jake*

jakes (dʒeɪks) NOUN [1] an archaic slang word for **lavatory.** [2] *Southwestern English, dialect* human excrement.
▷**HISTORY** C16: probably from French *Jacques* James

Jalandhar ('dʒælænˌdɑː) NOUN a city in NW India, in central Punjab. Pop.: 509 510 (1991).

jalap *or* **jalop** ('dʒæləp) NOUN [1] a Mexican convolvulaceous plant, *Exogonium* (or *Ipomoea*) *purga.* [2] any of several similar or related plants. [3] the dried and powdered root of any of these plants, used as a purgative. [4] the resin obtained from any of these plants.
▷**HISTORY** C17: from French, from Mexican Spanish *jalapa,* short for *purga de Jalapa* purgative of Jalapa
▸ **jalapic** (dʒə'læpɪk) ADJECTIVE

Jalapa (*Spanish* xa'lapa) NOUN a city in E central Mexico, capital of Veracruz State, at an altitude of 1427 m (4681 ft.): resort. Pop.: 375 000 (2000 est.).

jalapeño (dʒælə'piːnəʊ; *Spanish* xala'penjo) NOUN a very hot type of green chilli pepper, used esp in Mexican cookery. Also: **jalapeño pepper.**
▷**HISTORY** Mexican Spanish

Jalisco (*Spanish* xa'lisko) NOUN a state of W Mexico, on the Pacific: crossed by the Sierra Madre; valuable mineral resources. Capital: Guadalajara. Pop.: 6 321 278 (2000). Area: 80 137 sq. km (30 934 sq. miles).

jalopy *or* **jaloppy** (dʒə'lɒpɪ) NOUN, *plural* **-lopies** *or* **-loppies.** *Informal* a dilapidated old car.
▷**HISTORY** C20: of unknown origin

jalouse (dʒə'luːz) VERB *Scot* to suspect; infer.
▷**HISTORY** C19: from French *jalouser* to be jealous of

jalousie ('ʒælʊˌziː) NOUN [1] a window blind or shutter constructed from angled slats of wood, plastic, etc. [2] a window made of similarly angled slats of glass.
▷**HISTORY** C19: from Old French *gelosie* latticework screen, literally: JEALOUSY, perhaps because one can look through the screen without being seen

jam[1] (dʒæm) VERB **jams, jamming, jammed.** [1] *(tr)* to cram or wedge into or against something: *to jam paper into an incinerator.* [2] *(tr)* to crowd or pack: *cars jammed the roads.* [3] to make or become stuck or locked: *the switch has jammed.* [4] *(tr; often foll by on)* to activate suddenly (esp in the phrase **jam on the brakes**). [5] *(tr)* to block; congest: *to jam the drain with rubbish.* [6] *(tr)* to crush, bruise, or squeeze; smash. [7] *Radio* to prevent the clear reception of (radio communications or radar signals) by transmitting other signals on the same frequency. [8] *(intr) Slang* to play in a jam session. ◆ NOUN [9] a crowd or congestion in a confined space: *a traffic jam.* [10] the act of jamming or the state of being jammed. [11] *Informal* a difficult situation; predicament: *to help a friend out of a jam.* [12] See **jam session.**
▷**HISTORY** C18: probably of imitative origin; compare CHAMP[1]
▸ **'jammer** NOUN

jam[2] (dʒæm) NOUN [1] a preserve containing fruit, which has been boiled with sugar until the mixture sets. [2] *Slang* something desirable: *you want jam on it.* [3] **jam today.** the principle of living for the moment.
▷**HISTORY** C18: perhaps from JAM[1] (the act of squeezing)

Jam. ABBREVIATION FOR: [1] Jamaica. [2] *Bible* James.

Jamaica (dʒə'meɪkə) NOUN an island and state in the Caribbean: colonized by the Spanish from 1494 onwards, large numbers of Black slaves being imported; captured by the British in 1655 and established as a colony in 1866; gained full independence in 1962; a member of the Commonwealth. Exports: chiefly bauxite and alumina, sugar, and bananas. Official language: English. Religion: Protestant majority. Currency: Jamaican dollar. Capital: Kingston. Pop.: 2 624 000 (2001 est.). Area: 10 992 sq. km (4244 sq. miles).

Jamaican (dʒə'meɪkən) ADJECTIVE [1] of or relating to Jamaica or its inhabitants. ◆ NOUN [2] a native or inhabitant of Jamaica.

Jamaican ebony NOUN another name for **cocuswood.**

Jamaica pepper NOUN another name for **allspice.**

Jamaica rum NOUN a highly flavoured rum produced in Jamaica.

jamb *or* **jambe** (dʒæm) NOUN [1] a vertical side member of a doorframe, window frame, or lining. [2] a vertical inside face of an opening in a wall.
▷**HISTORY** C14: from Old French *jambe* leg, jamb, from Late Latin *gamba* hoof, hock, from Greek *kampē* joint

jambalaya (ˌdʒʌmbə'laɪə) NOUN a Creole dish made of shrimps, ham, rice, onions, etc.
▷**HISTORY** C19: from Louisiana French, from Provençal *jambalaia* chicken and rice stew

jambeau ('dʒæmbəʊ), **jambart** ('dʒæmbɑːt), *or* **jamber** ('dʒæmbə) NOUN, *plural* **-beaux** (-bəʊz), **-barts** *or* **-bers.** *(often plural)* other words for **greave.**
▷**HISTORY** C14: from Anglo-French, from *jambe* leg; see JAMB

Jambi *or* **Djambi** ('dʒæmbɪ) NOUN a port in W Indonesia, in SE Sumatra on the Hari River. Pop.: 410 400 (1995 est.). Also called: **Telanaipura.**

jambo ('dʒambɔ) SENTENCE SUBSTITUTE an E African salutation.
▷**HISTORY** C20: from Swahili

jamboree (ˌdʒæmbə'riː) NOUN [1] a large and often international gathering of Scouts. [2] a party or spree.
▷**HISTORY** C19: of uncertain origin

James (dʒeɪmz) NOUN *New Testament* an epistle traditionally ascribed to James, a brother or close relative of Jesus (in full **The Epistle of James**).

James Bay NOUN the S arm of Hudson Bay, in central Canada. Area: 108 780 sq. km (42 000 sq. miles).

James-Lange theory ('dʒeɪmz'lɑːŋgə) NOUN *Psychol* a theory that emotions are caused by bodily sensations; for example, we are sad because we weep.
▷**HISTORY** named after William *James* (1842–1910), US philosopher and psychologist + Carl *Lange* (1834–1900), Danish psychologist

Jameson Raid ('dʒeɪms(ə)n) NOUN an expedition into the Transvaal in 1895 led by Sir Leander Starr

Jameson (1853–1917) in an unsuccessful attempt to topple its Boer regime.

Jamestown (ˈdʒeɪmzˌtaʊn) NOUN a ruined village in E Virginia, on **Jamestown Island** (a peninsula in the James River): the first permanent settlement by the English in America (1607); capital of Virginia (1607–98); abandoned in 1699.

jamming (ˈdʒæmɪŋ) NOUN *Mountaineering* a rock-climbing technique in which holds are got by wedging the hands and feet in suitable cracks.

Jammu (ˈdʒʌmuː) NOUN a city in N India, winter capital of the state of Jammu and Kashmir. Pop.: 206 135 (1991).

Jammu and Kashmir NOUN the official name for the part of **Kashmir** under Indian control.

jammy (ˈdʒæmɪ) ADJECTIVE **-mier, -miest.** 1 covered with or tasting like jam. 2 *Brit, slang* lucky: *jammy so-and-sos!*

Jamnagar (ˌdʒæmnəˈgɑː) NOUN a city in India, in Gujarat: noted for its palaces and temples: cement, pottery, textiles. Pop.: 341 637 (1991).

jam-packed ADJECTIVE crowded, packed, or filled to capacity.

jampan (ˈdʒæmˌpæn) NOUN a type of sedan chair used in India.
▷**HISTORY** C19: from Bengali *jhāmpān*

jam session NOUN *Slang* an unrehearsed or improvised jazz or rock performance.
▷**HISTORY** C20: probably from JAM[1]

Jamshedpur (ˌdʒʌmʃedˈpʊə) NOUN a city in NE India, in Jharkand: large iron and steel works (1907–11); a major industrial centre. Pop.: 478 950 (1991).

Jamshid *or* **Jamshyd** (dʒæmˈʃiːd) NOUN *Persian myth* a ruler of the peris who was punished for bragging that he was immortal by being changed into human form. He then became a great king of Persia. See also **peri.**

Jan. ABBREVIATION FOR January.

Jana Sangh (ˈdʒʌnə ˈsʌŋ) NOUN a political party in India.
▷**HISTORY** Hindi, literally: people's party

Janata (ˈdʒʌnətɑː) NOUN 1 (in India) the general public; the people. 2 a political party in India: founded in 1976 and came to power in 1977.
▷**HISTORY** Hindi

Jandal (ˈdʒændᵊl) NOUN *Trademark NZ* a type of sandal with a strip of material between the big toe and the other toes and over the foot.

jane (dʒeɪn) NOUN *Slang, chiefly US* a girl or woman.

Janeite (ˈdʒeɪˌnaɪt) NOUN a devotee of the works of Jane Austen (1775–1817), English novelist.

Jane's (dʒeɪnz) NOUN any of several periodical publications such as *Fighting Ships* and *All the World's Aircraft*.
▷**HISTORY** C20: named after Frederick Thomas *Jane* (1865–1916), British naval writer and artist

jangle (ˈdʒæŋgᵊl) VERB 1 to sound or cause to sound discordantly, harshly, or unpleasantly: *the telephone jangled.* 2 (*tr*) to produce a jarring effect on: *the accident jangled his nerves.* 3 an archaic word for **wrangle.** ◆ NOUN 4 a harsh, unpleasant ringing noise. 5 an argument or quarrel.
▷**HISTORY** C13: from Old French *jangler,* of Germanic origin; compare Middle Dutch *jangelen* to whine, complain
▸ˈ**jangler** NOUN

Janiculum (dʒəˈnɪkjʊləm) NOUN a hill in Rome across the River Tiber from the Seven Hills.

Janina (ˈjaniːna) NOUN the Serbian name for **Ioánnina.**

janissary (ˈdʒænɪsərɪ) *or* **janizary** (ˈdʒænɪzərɪ) NOUN, *plural* **-saries** *or* **-zaries.** an infantryman in the Turkish army, originally a member of the sovereign's personal guard, from the 14th to the early 19th century.
▷**HISTORY** C16: from French *janissaire,* from Italian *giannizzero,* from Turkish *yeniçeri,* from *yeni* new + *çeri* soldiery

janitor (ˈdʒænɪtə) NOUN 1 *Scot, US, and Canadian* the caretaker of a building, esp a school. 2 *Chiefly US and Canadian* a person employed to clean and maintain a building, esp the public areas in a block of flats or office building; porter.
▷**HISTORY** C17: from Latin: doorkeeper, from *jānua* door, entrance, from *jānus* covered way (compare JANUS[1]); related to Latin *īre* to go
▸**janitorial** (ˌdʒænɪˈtɔːrɪəl) ADJECTIVE ▸ˈ**janitress** FEMININE NOUN

Jan Mayen (ˈjæn ˈmaɪən) NOUN an island in the Arctic Ocean, between Greenland and N Norway: volcanic, with large glaciers; former site of Dutch whaling stations; annexed to Norway in 1929. Area: 373 sq. km (144 sq. miles).

janny (ˈdʒænɪ) NOUN, *plural* **-nies.** *Scot informal* a janitor.

janola (ˌdʒəˈnəʊlə) NOUN *Trademark NZ* household bleach.

Jansenism (ˈdʒænsəˌnɪzəm) NOUN 1 *RC Church* the doctrine of the Dutch Roman Catholic theologian Cornelis Jansen (1585–1638), and his disciples, who maintained that salvation was limited to those subject to a supernatural determinism, the rest being destined to perdition. 2 the religious movement arising from these doctrines.
▸ˈ**Jansenist** NOUN, ADJECTIVE ▸ˌ**Jansen**ˈ**istic** *or* ˈ**Jansen**ˌ**istical** ADJECTIVE

jansky (ˈdʒænskɪ) NOUN, *plural* **-skys.** a unit of flux density equal to 10^{-26} W m^{-2} Hz^{-1}, used predominantly in radio and infrared astronomy. Symbol: Jy.
▷**HISTORY** C20: named after Karl Guthe *Jansky* (1905–50), US electrical engineer

January (ˈdʒænjʊərɪ) NOUN, *plural* **-aries.** the first month of the year, consisting of 31 days.
▷**HISTORY** C14: from Latin *Jānuārius,* from adjective: (month) of JANUS[1]

Janus[1] (ˈdʒeɪnəs) NOUN the Roman god of doorways, passages, and bridges. In art he is depicted with two heads facing opposite ways.
▷**HISTORY** C16: from Latin, from *jānus* archway

Janus[2] (ˈdʒeɪnəs) NOUN a small inner satellite of Saturn.

Janus-faced ADJECTIVE two-faced; hypocritical; deceitful.

Jap (dʒæp) NOUN, ADJECTIVE *Informal, often derogatory* short for **Japanese.**

JAP ABBREVIATION FOR *US, slang* **Jewish American Princess.**

Jap. ABBREVIATION FOR Japan(ese).

japan (dʒəˈpæn) NOUN 1 a glossy durable black lacquer originally from the Orient, used on wood, metal, etc. 2 work decorated and varnished in the Japanese manner. 3 a liquid used as a paint drier. ◆ ADJECTIVE 4 relating to or varnished with japan. ◆ VERB **-pans, -panning, -panned.** 5 (*tr*) to lacquer with japan or any similar varnish.

Japan (dʒəˈpæn) NOUN an archipelago and empire in E Asia, extending for 3200 km (2000 miles) between the Sea of Japan and the Pacific and consisting of the main islands of Hokkaido, Honshu, Shikoku, and Kyushu and over 3000 smaller islands: feudalism abolished in 1871, followed by industrialization and expansion of territories, esp during World Wars I and II, when most of SE Asia came under Japanese control; dogma of the emperor's divinity abolished in 1946 under a new democratic constitution; rapid economic growth has made Japan the most industrialized nation in the Far East. Official language: Japanese. Religion: Shintoist majority, large Buddhist minority. Currency: yen. Capital: Tokyo. Pop.: 127 100 000 (2001 est.). Area: 369 660 sq. km (142 726 sq. miles). Japanese names: **Nippon, Nihon.**

Japan Current NOUN a warm ocean current flowing northeastwards off the E coast of Japan towards the North Pacific. Also called: **Kuroshio.**

Japanese (ˌdʒæpəˈniːz) ADJECTIVE 1 of, relating to, or characteristic of Japan, its people, or their language. ◆ NOUN 2 (*plural* **-nese**) a native or inhabitant of Japan or a descendant of one. 3 the official language of Japan: the native language of approximately 100 million people: considered by some scholars to be part of the Altaic family of languages.

Japanese andromeda NOUN an ericaceous Japanese shrub, *Pieris japonica,* with drooping clusters of small bell-shaped white flowers.

Japanese beetle NOUN a scarabaeid beetle, *Popillia japonica,* that eats the leaves and fruits of various plants: accidentally introduced into the US from Japan.

Japanese cedar NOUN another name for **cryptomeria.**

Japanese Chin NOUN a small compact dog of a Japanese breed with a long straight silky coat in black and white or red and white and feathered ears, legs, feet, and tail.

Japanese ivy NOUN another name for **Virginia creeper** (sense 2).

Japanese lantern NOUN another name for **Chinese lantern** (sense 1).

Japanese persimmon NOUN an Asian persimmon tree, *Diospyros kaki,* with red or orange edible fruit. Also called: **kaki.**

Japanese river fever NOUN another name for **scrub typhus.**

Japanese slippers PLURAL NOUN (in Malaysia) casual sandals; flip-flops.

Japanese stranglehold NOUN a wrestling hold in which an opponent's wrists are pulled to cross his arms in front of his own neck and exert pressure on his windpipe.

Japanese umbrella pine NOUN a single aberrant species of pine, *Sciadopitys verticillata,* in which the leaves are fused in pairs and the crown is spire-shaped.

Japanglish (dʒəˈpæŋlɪʃ) NOUN another name for **Japlish.**

Japan wax *or* **tallow** NOUN a yellow wax obtained from the berries of plants of the genus *Rhus.* It is used in making matches, soaps, candles, and polishes.

jape (dʒeɪp) NOUN 1 a jest or joke. ◆ VERB 2 to joke or jest (about).
▷**HISTORY** C14: perhaps from Old French *japper* to bark, yap, of imitative origin
▸ˈ**japer** NOUN ▸ˈ**japery** NOUN ▸ˈ**japingly** ADVERB

Japheth (ˈdʒeɪfeθ) NOUN *Old Testament* the second son of Noah, traditionally regarded as the ancestor of a number of non-Semitic nations (Genesis 10:1–5).

Japhetic (dʒeɪˈfɛtɪk) ADJECTIVE denoting a discredited grouping of languages that postulated a relationship between Basque, Etruscan, and Georgian among others.
▷**HISTORY** C19: from New Latin *Japheti* descendants of JAPHETH + -IC

Japlish (ˈdʒæplɪʃ) NOUN the adoption and adaptation of English words into the Japanese language. Also called: **Japanglish.**
▷**HISTORY** C20: from a blend of JAPANESE + ENGLISH

japonica (dʒəˈpɒnɪkə) NOUN 1 Also called: **Japanese quince, flowering quince.** a Japanese rosaceous shrub, *Chaenomeles japonica,* cultivated for its red flowers and yellowish fruit. 2 another name for the **camellia.**
▷**HISTORY** C19: from New Latin, feminine of *japonicus* Japanese, from *Japonia* JAPAN

Japurá (*Portuguese* ʒapuˈra) NOUN a river in NW South America, rising in SW Colombia and flowing southeast across Colombia and Brazil to join the Amazon near Tefé: known as the Caquetá in Colombia. Length: about 2800 km (1750 miles). Spanish name: **Yapurá.**

jar[1] (dʒɑː) NOUN 1 a wide-mouthed container that is usually cylindrical, made of glass or earthenware, and without handles. 2 Also: **jarful.** the contents or quantity contained in a jar. 3 *Brit informal* a glass of alcoholic drink, esp beer: *to have a jar with someone.* 4 *Obsolete* a measure of electrical capacitance.
▷**HISTORY** C16: from Old French *jarre,* from Old Provençal *jarra,* from Arabic *jarrah* large earthen vessel

jar[2] (dʒɑː) VERB **jars, jarring, jarred.** 1 to vibrate or cause to vibrate. 2 to make or cause to make a harsh discordant sound. 3 (often foll by *on*) to have a disturbing or painful effect (on the nerves, mind, etc.). 4 (*intr*) to disagree; clash. ◆ NOUN 5 a jolt or shock. 6 a harsh discordant sound.
▷**HISTORY** C16: probably of imitative origin; compare Old English *cearran* to creak
▸ˈ**jarring** ADJECTIVE ▸ˈ**jarringly** ADVERB

jar[3] (dʒɑː) NOUN **on a** (*or* **the**) **jar.** (of a door) slightly open; ajar.

▷**HISTORY** C17 (in the sense: turn): from earlier *char,* from Old English *cierran* to turn; see AJAR[1]

jardinière (ˌʒɑːdɪˈnjɛə) NOUN [1] an ornamental pot or trough for plants. [2] a garnish of fresh vegetables, cooked, diced, and served around a dish of meat.
▷**HISTORY** C19: from French, feminine of *jardinier* gardener, from *jardin* GARDEN

jargon[1] (ˈdʒɑːɡən) NOUN [1] specialized language concerned with a particular subject, culture, or profession. [2] language characterized by pretentious syntax, vocabulary, or meaning. [3] gibberish. [4] another word for **pidgin.** ◆ VERB [5] *(intr)* to use or speak in jargon.
▷**HISTORY** C14: from Old French, perhaps of imitative origin; see GARGLE

jargon[2] (ˈdʒɑːɡɒn) *or* **jargoon** (dʒɑːˈɡuːn) NOUN *Mineralogy, rare* a golden yellow, smoky, or colourless variety of zircon.
▷**HISTORY** C18: from French, from Italian *giargone,* ultimately from Persian *zargūn* of the golden colour; see ZIRCON

jargonize *or* **jargonise** (ˈdʒɑːɡəˌnaɪz) VERB [1] *(tr)* to translate into jargon. [2] *(intr)* to talk in jargon.
▸ **ˌjargoniˈzation** *or* **ˌjargoniˈsation** NOUN

jarl (jɑːl) NOUN *Medieval history* a Scandinavian chieftain or noble.
▷**HISTORY** C19: from Old Norse; see EARL
▸ **ˈjarldom** NOUN

Jarlsberg (ˈjɑːlzbɜːɡ) NOUN *Trademark* a hard mild-tasting yellow-coloured cheese with holes in it.
▷**HISTORY** C20: after *Jarlsberg,* Norway, where it originated

jarosite (ˈdʒærəˌsaɪt) NOUN a yellow to brown secondary mineral consisting of basic hydrated sulphate of iron and potassium in masses or hexagonal crystals. Formula: $KFe_3(SO_4)_2(OH)_6$.
▷**HISTORY** C19: from *Barranco Jaroso,* in Almeria, Spain + -ITE[1]

jarp (dʒɑːp) *or* **jaup** (dʒɔːp) VERB *(tr) Northeast English, dialect* to strike or smash, esp to break the shell of (an egg) at Easter.
▷**HISTORY** from Scottish *jaup, jawp* to dash or splash like water: perhaps of imitative origin

jarrah (ˈdʒærə) NOUN a widely planted Australian eucalyptus tree, *Eucalyptus marginata,* that yields a valuable timber.
▷**HISTORY** from a native Australian language

Jarrow (ˈdʒærəʊ) NOUN a port in NE England, in South Tyneside unitary authority, Tyne and Wear: ruined monastery where the Venerable Bede lived and died; its unemployed marched on London in the 1930s; shipyards, oil installations, iron and steel works. Pop.: 29 325 (1991 est.).

jarvey *or* **jarvie** (ˈdʒɑːvɪ) NOUN *Brit informal obsolete* a hackney coachman.
▷**HISTORY** C19: from *Jarvey,* familiar form of personal name *Jarvis*

Jas. ABBREVIATION FOR James.

jasmine (ˈdʒæsmɪn, ˈdʒæz-) NOUN [1] Also called: **jessamine.** any oleaceous shrub or climbing plant of the tropical and subtropical genus *Jasminum,* esp *J. officinalis:* widely cultivated for their white, yellow, or red fragrant flowers, which are used in making perfume and in flavouring tea. See also **winter jasmine.** [2] any of several other shrubs with fragrant flowers, such as the Cape jasmine, yellow jasmine, and frangipani (**red jasmine**). [3] a light to moderate yellow colour.
▷**HISTORY** C16: from Old French *jasmin,* from Arabic *yāsamīn,* from Persian *yāsmīn*

Jason (ˈdʒeɪsᵊn) NOUN *Greek myth* the hero who led the Argonauts in quest of the Golden Fleece. He became the husband of Medea, whom he later abandoned for Glauce.

jaspé (ˈdʒæspeɪ) ADJECTIVE resembling jasper; variegated.
▷**HISTORY** C19: from French, from *jasper* to marble

jasper (ˈdʒæspə) NOUN [1] an opaque impure microcrystalline form of quartz, red, yellow, brown, or dark green in colour, used as a gemstone and for ornamental decoration. [2] Also called: **jasper ware.** a dense hard stoneware, invented in 1775 by Wedgwood, capable of being stained throughout its substance with metallic oxides and used as background for applied classical decoration.
▷**HISTORY** C14: from Old French *jaspe,* from Latin *jaspis,* from Greek *iaspis,* of Semitic origin; related to Assyrian *ashpū,* Arabic *yashb,* Hebrew *yāshpheh*

Jasper National Park (ˈdʒæspə) NOUN a national park in SW Canada, in W Alberta in the Rockies: wildlife sanctuary. Area: 10 900 sq. km (4200 sq. miles).

Jassy (ˈjasi) NOUN the German name for **Iaşi.**

Jat (dʒɑːt) NOUN, *plural* **Jat** *or* **Jats.** a member of an Indo-European people widely dispersed throughout N India.

Jataka Tales (ˈdʒɑːtəkə) PLURAL NOUN a body of literature comprising accounts of previous lives of the Buddha.

jato (ˈdʒeɪtəʊ) NOUN, *plural* **-tos.** *Aeronautics* jet-assisted takeoff.
▷**HISTORY** C20 *j(et-)a(ssisted) t(ake)o(ff)*

jaundice (ˈdʒɔːndɪs) NOUN [1] Also called: **icterus.** yellowing of the skin and whites of the eyes due to the abnormal presence of bile pigments in the blood, as in hepatitis. [2] a mental state of bitterness, jealousy, and ill humour resulting in distorted judgment. ◆ VERB [3] to distort (the judgment, etc.) adversely: *jealousy had jaundiced his mind.* [4] to affect with or as if with jaundice.
▷**HISTORY** C14: from Old French *jaunisse,* from *jaune* yellow, from Latin *galbinus* yellowish, from *galbus*
▸ **ˈjaundiced** ADJECTIVE

jaunt (dʒɔːnt) NOUN [1] a short pleasurable excursion; outing. ◆ VERB [2] *(intr)* to go on such an excursion.
▷**HISTORY** C16: of unknown origin
▸ **ˈjauntingly** ADVERB

jaunting car *or* **jaunty car** NOUN a light two-wheeled one-horse car, formerly widely used in Ireland.

jaunty (ˈdʒɔːntɪ) ADJECTIVE **-tier, -tiest.** [1] sprightly, self-confident, and cheerful; brisk: *a jaunty step.* [2] smart; trim: *a jaunty hat.*
▷**HISTORY** C17: from French *gentil* noble; see GENTEEL
▸ **ˈjauntily** ADVERB ▸ **ˈjauntiness** NOUN

Java[1] (ˈdʒɑːvə) NOUN an island of Indonesia, south of Borneo, from which it is separated by the **Java Sea:** politically the most important island of Indonesia; it consists chiefly of active volcanic mountains and is densely forested. It came under Dutch control in 1596 and became part of Indonesia in 1949. It is one of the most densely populated areas in the world. Capital: Jakarta. Pop. (with Madura): 121 193 000 (1999 est.). Area: 132 174 sq. km (51 032 sq. miles).

Java[2] (ˈdʒɑːvə) NOUN *Trademark* a programming language especially applicable to the World Wide Web.
▷**HISTORY** C20: named after *Java* coffee, said to be consumed in large quantities by the language's creators

Java man NOUN a type of primitive man, *Homo erectus* (formerly called *Pithecanthropus erectus*), that lived in the middle Palaeolithic Age in Java. Also called: **Trinil man.**

Javan (ˈdʒɑːvən) ADJECTIVE [1] of or relating to Java or its inhabitants. ◆ NOUN [2] a native or inhabitant of Java.

Javanese (ˌdʒɑːvəˈniːz) ADJECTIVE [1] of, relating to, or characteristic of Java, its people, or the Javanese language. ◆ NOUN [2] *(plural* **-nese***)* a native or inhabitant of Java. [3] a Malayo-Polynesian language of Central and Eastern Java.

Javari *or* **Javary** (*Portuguese* ʒavaˈri) NOUN a river in South America, flowing northeast as part of the border between Peru and Brazil to join the Amazon. Length: about 1050 km (650 miles). Spanish name: **Yavarí.**

Java sparrow NOUN a small grey-and-pink finchlike Indonesian weaverbird, *Padda oryzivora:* a popular cage bird.

javelin (ˈdʒævlɪn) NOUN [1] a long pointed spear thrown as a weapon or in competitive field events. [2] **the javelin.** the event or sport of throwing the javelin.
▷**HISTORY** C16: from Old French *javeline,* variant of *javelot,* of Celtic origin

javelin fish NOUN a fish of the genus *Pomadasys* of semitropical Australian seas with a long spine on its anal fin.

Javel water *or* **Javelle water** (ˈdʒævᵊl, dʒəˈvɛl) NOUN [1] an aqueous solution containing sodium hypochlorite and some sodium chloride, used as a bleach and disinfectant. [2] Also called: **eau de Javelle.** a similar solution made from potassium carbonate and chlorine.
▷**HISTORY** C19: partial translation of French *eau de Javel,* from *Javel,* formerly a town, now part of Paris

jaw (dʒɔː) NOUN [1] the part of the skull of a vertebrate that frames the mouth and holds the teeth. In higher vertebrates it consists of the **upper jaw** (maxilla) fused to the cranium and the **lower jaw** (mandible). Related adjectives: **gnathal, gnathic.** [2] the corresponding part of an invertebrate, esp an insect. [3] a pair or either of a pair of hinged or sliding components of a machine or tool designed to grip an object. [4] *Slang* **a** impudent talk; cheek. **b** idle conversation; chat. **c** moralizing talk; a lecture. ◆ VERB [5] *(intr) Slang* **a** to talk idly; chat; gossip. **b** to lecture. ◆ See also **jaws.**
▷**HISTORY** C14: probably from Old French *joue* cheek; related to Italian *gota* cheek
▸ **ˈjawˌlike** ADJECTIVE

Jawan (dʒəˈwɑːn) NOUN (in India) [1] a soldier. [2] a young man.
▷**HISTORY** Urdu: young man

jawbone (ˈdʒɔːˌbəʊn) NOUN [1] a nontechnical name for **mandible** or (less commonly) **maxilla** ◆ VERB [2] *US* to try to persuade or bring pressure to bear (on) by virtue of one's high office or position, esp in urging compliance with official policy.

jawbreaker (ˈdʒɔːˌbreɪkə) NOUN [1] Also called: **jawcrusher.** a device having hinged jaws for crushing rocks and ores. [2] *Informal* a word that is hard to pronounce.
▸ **ˈjawˌbreaking** ADJECTIVE ▸ **ˈjawˌbreakingly** ADVERB

jaw-dropping ADJECTIVE *Informal* amazing.
▸ **ˈjaw-ˌdroppingly** ADVERB

ja well no fine SENTENCE SUBSTITUTE *South African* used to indicate reluctant acceptance.

jaws (dʒɔːz) PLURAL NOUN [1] the narrow opening of some confined place such as a gorge. [2] **the jaws.** a dangerously close position: *the jaws of death.*

jaws of life PLURAL NOUN *(functioning as singular)* powerful shears used for cutting a vehicle open after a collision.

Jaxartes (dʒækˈsɑːtiːz) NOUN the ancient name for **Syr Darya.**

jay (dʒeɪ) NOUN [1] any of various passerine birds of the family *Corvidae* (crows), esp the Eurasian *Garrulus glandarius,* with a pinkish-brown body, blue-and-black wings, and a black-and-white crest. See also **blue jay.** [2] a foolish or gullible person.
▷**HISTORY** C13: from Old French *jai,* from Late Latin *gāius,* perhaps from proper name *Gāius*

Jaya (ˈdʒɑːjə) *or* **Djaja** NOUN **Mount** a mountain in E Indonesia, in Irian Jaya in the Sudirman Range: the highest mountain in New Guinea. Height: 5039 m (16 532 ft.). Former names: (Mount) **Carstensz, Sukarno Peak.**

Jayapura (ˌdʒɑːjɑːˈpʊərə) *or* **Djajapura** NOUN a port in NE Indonesia, capital of Irian Jaya, on the N coast. Pop.: 180 400 (1995 est.). Former names: **Sukarnapura, Kotabaru, Hollandia.**

Jaycee (ˈdʒeɪˈsiː) NOUN *Austral, NZ, US, and Canadian* a young person who belongs to a junior chamber of commerce.
▷**HISTORY** C20: from the initials of *J*(unior) *C*(hamber), short for *United States Junior Chamber of Commerce*

Jay's Treaty (dʒeɪ) NOUN a treaty between the United States and Great Britain that settled outstanding disputes, negotiated by John Jay (1745–1829) in 1794.

jaywalk (ˈdʒeɪˌwɔːk) VERB *(intr)* to cross or walk in a street recklessly or illegally.
▷**HISTORY** C20: from JAY (sense 2)
▸ **ˈjayˌwalker** NOUN ▸ **ˈjayˌwalking** NOUN

jazz (dʒæz) NOUN [1] **a** a kind of music of African-American origin, characterized by syncopated rhythms, solo and group improvisation, and a variety of harmonic idioms and instrumental techniques. It exists in a number of styles. Compare **blues.** See also **bebop, bop, Dixieland, free** (sense 7), **hard bop, harmolodics, mainstream** (sense 2), **modern jazz. New Orleans jazz, swing** (sense 28), **trad. b** *(as modifier)*: *a jazz band.* **c** *(in combination)*: *a jazzman.* [2] *Informal* enthusiasm or liveliness. [3] *Slang* rigmarole;

paraphernalia: *legal papers and all that jazz.* 4 *African-American slang, obsolete* sexual intercourse. ◆ VERB 5 *(intr)* to play or dance to jazz music. 6 *African-American slang, obsolete* to have sexual intercourse with (a person).
▷HISTORY C20: of unknown origin
▸ 'jazzer NOUN

jazz age NOUN *(often capitals)* **the.** (esp in the US) the period between the end of World War I and the beginning of the Depression during which jazz became popular.
▷HISTORY C20: popularized by F. Scott Fitzgerald (1896–1940) US novelist and short-story writer, who called a collection of his short stories *Tales of the Jazz Age* (1922)

jazz mag NOUN *Brit slang* a pornographic magazine.

jazz up VERB *(tr, adverb) Informal* 1 to imbue (a piece of music) with jazz qualities, esp by improvisation or a quicker tempo. 2 to make more lively, gaudy, or appealing.

jazzy ('dʒæzɪ) ADJECTIVE **jazzier, jazziest.** *Informal* 1 of, characteristic of, or resembling jazz music. 2 gaudy or flashy: *a jazzy car.*
▸ 'jazzily ADVERB ▸ 'jazziness NOUN

JC ABBREVIATION FOR jurisconsult.

JCB NOUN *Trademark* a type of construction machine with a hydraulically operated shovel on the front and an excavator arm on the back.
▷HISTORY named from the initials of *J*(oseph) *C*(yril) *B*(amford) (born 1916), its English manufacturer

JCD ABBREVIATION FOR: 1 Doctor of Canon Law. [Latin *Juris Canonici Doctor*] 2 Doctor of Civil Law.
▷HISTORY Latin *Juris Civilis Doctor*

JCL *Computing* ABBREVIATION FOR Job Control Language.

JCR ABBREVIATION FOR junior common room.

JCS ABBREVIATION FOR Joint Chiefs of Staff.

JD ABBREVIATION FOR: 1 Doctor of Laws. [Latin *Jurum Doctor*] 2 juvenile delinquent.

je THE INTERNET DOMAIN NAME FOR Jersey.

jealous ('dʒɛləs) ADJECTIVE 1 suspicious or fearful of being displaced by a rival: *a jealous lover.* 2 (often *postpositive* and foll by *of*) resentful (of) or vindictive (towards), esp through envy: *a child jealous of his brother.* 3 (often *postpositive* and foll by *of*) possessive and watchful in the maintenance or protection (of): *jealous of one's reputation.* 4 characterized by or resulting from jealousy. 5 *Obsolete except in biblical use* demanding exclusive loyalty: *a jealous God.* 6 an obsolete word for **zealous.**
▷HISTORY C13: from Old French *gelos,* from Medieval Latin *zēlōsus,* from Late Latin *zēlus* emulation, jealousy, from Greek *zēlos* ZEAL
▸ 'jealously ADVERB ▸ 'jealousness NOUN

jealousy ('dʒɛləsɪ) NOUN, *plural* **-ousies.** the state or quality of being jealous.

jean (dʒiːn) NOUN a tough twill-weave cotton fabric used for hard-wearing trousers, overalls, etc. See also **jeans.**
▷HISTORY C16: short for *jean fustian,* from *Gene* GENOA

jeans (dʒiːnz) PLURAL NOUN informal trousers for casual wear, made esp of denim or corduroy.
▷HISTORY plural of JEAN

jebel *or* **djebel** ('dʒɛbᵊl) NOUN a hill or mountain in an Arab country.

Jebel Musa ('dʒɛbᵊl 'muːsə) NOUN a mountain in NW Morocco, near the Strait of Gibraltar: one of the Pillars of Hercules. Height: 850 m (2790 ft.).

Jedda ('dʒɛdə) NOUN another name for **Jidda.**

jeelie *or* **jeely** ('dʒiːlɪ) NOUN *Scot* jelly or jam.

Jeep (dʒiːp) NOUN *Trademark* a small military road vehicle with four-wheel drive.
▷HISTORY C20: probably from the initials *GP,* for *general purpose* (*vehicle*)

jeepers *or* **jeepers creepers** ('dʒiːpəz 'kriːpəz) INTERJECTION *US and Canadian, slang* a mild exclamation of surprise.
▷HISTORY C20: euphemism for *Jesus*

jeer (dʒɪə) VERB 1 (often foll by *at*) to laugh or scoff (at a person or thing); mock. ◆ NOUN 2 a remark or cry of derision; gibe; taunt.
▷HISTORY C16: of unknown origin
▸ 'jeerer NOUN ▸ 'jeering ADJECTIVE, NOUN ▸ 'jeeringly ADVERB

Jeevesian ('dʒiːvzɪən) ADJECTIVE of, relating to, or like the butler Jeeves in the fiction of the English-born US writer P.G. Wodehouse (1881–1975), a master of tact, euphemism, and ingenuity.

jefe (*Spanish* 'xefe) NOUN (in Spanish-speaking countries) a military or political leader.
▷HISTORY Spanish, from French *chef* CHIEF

jeff (dʒɛf) VERB *(tr) Austral, slang* 1 to downsize or close down (an organization). 2 to reduce (staff numbers) or dismiss (an employee). 3 to spoil or destroy ruthlessly. ◆ Also called: **kennett.**
▷HISTORY C20: named after *Jeff* Kennett, former governer of the state of Victoria, Australia

Jefferson City NOUN a city in central Missouri, the state capital, on the Missouri River. Pop.: 35 481 (1990).

jehad (dʒɪ'hæd) NOUN a variant spelling of **jihad.**

Jehol (dʒə'hɒl) NOUN 1 a former province of NE China, north of the Great Wall: divided among Hebei, Liaoning, and Inner Mongolia in 1956. Area: 192 380 sq. km (74 278 sq. miles). 2 a region of NE China, in Hebei and Liaoning provinces: mountainous.

Jehoshaphat (dʒɪ'hɒʃəˌfæt, -'hɒs-) NOUN *Old Testament* 1 the king of Judah (?873–?849 B.C.) (I Kings 22:41–50). 2 the site of Jehovah's apocalyptic judgment upon the nations (Joel 4:14).

Jehovah (dʒɪ'həʊvə) NOUN *Old Testament* the personal name of God, revealed to Moses on Mount Horeb (Exodus 3).
▷HISTORY C16: from Medieval Latin, from Hebrew YHVH: the original vocalization was considered too sacred to be pronounced and the vowels of Eloah (God) were therefore substituted in the Masoretic text, whence Yetto Vah

Jehovah's Witness NOUN a member of a Christian Church of American origin, the followers of which believe that the end of the present world system of government is near, that all other Churches and religions are false or evil, that all war is unlawful, and that the civil law must be resisted whenever it conflicts with their Church's own religious principles.

Jehovist (dʒɪ'həʊvɪst) NOUN 1 another name for the **Yahwist.** 2 a person who maintains that the name YHVH in the Hebrew text of the Old Testament was originally pronounced *Jehovah.* ◆ ADJECTIVE 3 of or relating to the Yahwist source of the Pentateuch.
▸ Je'hovism NOUN ▸ Jehovistic (ˌdʒiːhəʊ'vɪstɪk) ADJECTIVE

Jehu ('dʒiːhjuː) NOUN 1 *Old Testament* the king of Israel (?842–?815 B.C.); the slayer of Jezebel (II Kings 9:11–30). 2 a fast driver, esp one who is reckless (from the phrase **to drive like Jehu.** II Kings 9:20).

jejune (dʒɪ'dʒuːn) ADJECTIVE 1 simple; naive; unsophisticated. 2 insipid; dull; dry. 3 lacking nourishment; insubstantial or barren.
▷HISTORY C17: from Latin *jējūnus* hungry, empty
▸ je'junely ADVERB ▸ je'juneness *or* je'junity NOUN

jejunostomy (dʒɪdʒuː'nɒstəmɪ) NOUN the surgical formation of an opening from the jejunum to the surface of the body, through which food may be introduced.

jejunum (dʒɪ'dʒuːnəm) NOUN the part of the small intestine between the duodenum and the ileum.
▷HISTORY C16: from Latin, from *jējūnus* empty; from the belief that the jejunum is empty after death
▸ je'junal ADJECTIVE

Jekyll and Hyde ('dʒɛkᵊl, haɪd) NOUN **a** a person with two distinct personalities, one good, the other evil. **b** *(as modifier)*: *a Jekyll-and-Hyde personality.*
▷HISTORY C19: after the principal character of Robert Louis Stevenson's novel *The Strange Case of Dr Jekyll and Mr Hyde* (1886)

jell *or* **gel** (dʒɛl) VERB **jells, jelling, jelled** *or* **gels, gelling, gelled.** 1 to make or become gelatinous; congeal. 2 *(intr)* to assume definite form: *his ideas have jelled.* ◆ NOUN 3 *US* an informal word for **jelly.**
▷HISTORY C19: back formation from JELLY[1]

jellaba *or* **jellabah** ('dʒɛləbə) NOUN variant spellings of **djellaba.**
▷HISTORY from Arabic *jallabah*

jellied ('dʒɛlɪd) ADJECTIVE 1 congealed into jelly, esp by cooling. 2 containing, set in, or coated with jelly.

jellies ('dʒɛlɪz) PLURAL NOUN 1 *Brit, slang* gelatine capsules of temazepam, dissolved and injected as a recreational drug. 2 Also called: **jelly shoes.** shoes made from brightly coloured transparent plastic.
▷HISTORY C20: shortened from GELATINE

jellify ('dʒɛlɪˌfaɪ) VERB **-fies, -fying, -fied.** to make into or become jelly.
▸ ˌjellifi'cation NOUN

Jell-o ('dʒɛləʊ) NOUN *Trademark* (in US and Canada) jelly.

jelly[1] ('dʒɛlɪ) NOUN, *plural* **-lies.** 1 a fruit-flavoured clear dessert set with gelatine. US and Canadian trademark: **Jell-o.** 2 a preserve made from the juice of fruit boiled with sugar and used as jam. 3 a savoury food preparation set with gelatine or with a strong gelatinous stock and having a soft elastic consistency: *calf's-foot jelly.* 4 anything having the consistency of jelly. 5 *Informal* a coloured gelatine filter that can be fitted in front of a stage or studio light. ◆ VERB **-lies, -lying, -lied.** 6 to jellify.
▷HISTORY C14: from Old French *gelee* frost, jelly, from *geler* to set hard, from Latin *gelāre,* from *gelu* frost
▸ 'jelly-ˌlike ADJECTIVE

jelly[2] ('dʒɛlɪ) NOUN *Brit* a slang name for **gelignite.**

jelly baby NOUN *Brit* a small sweet made from a gelatinous substance formed to resemble a baby in shape.

jelly bag NOUN a muslin bag used to strain off the juice from the fruit in making jelly (the preserve).

jellybean ('dʒɛlɪˌbiːn) NOUN a bean-shaped sweet with a brightly coloured coating around a gelatinous filling.

jellyfish ('dʒɛlɪˌfɪʃ) NOUN, *plural* **-fish** *or* **-fishes.** 1 any marine medusoid coelenterate of the class *Scyphozoa,* having a gelatinous umbrella-shaped body with trailing tentacles. 2 any other medusoid coelenterate. 3 *Informal* a weak indecisive person.

jelly fungus NOUN a member of any of three orders (*Auriculariales, Tremellales,* and *Dacrymycetales*) of basidiomycetous fungi that grow on trees and have a jelly-like consistency when wet. They include the conspicuous **yellow brain fungus** (*Tremella mesenterica*), the black **witch's butter** (*Exidia plana*), and the pinky-red **jew's-ear** (*Auricularia auricula-judae*).

jelly mould NOUN 1 a mould made of glass, copper, etc., used to make a jelly in a decorative shape. 2 the NZ term for **jelly fungus.**

jelutong ('dʒɛləˌtɒŋ) NOUN 1 a Malaysian apocynaceous tree of the genus *Dyera,* esp *D. costulata.* 2 the latex obtained from this tree, used in the manufacture of chewing gum. 3 the wood of this tree.
▷HISTORY C19: from Malay

jemadar ('dʒɛməˌdɑː) NOUN 1 a native junior officer belonging to a locally raised regiment serving as mercenaries in India, esp with the British Army (until 1947). 2 an officer in the Indian police.
▷HISTORY C18: from Urdu *jama 'dār,* from Persian *jama 'at* body of men + *dār* having

Jemappes (*French* ʒəmap) NOUN a town in SW Belgium, in Hainaut province west of Mons: scene of a battle (1792) during the French Revolutionary Wars, in which the French defeated the Austrians. Pop.: 18 100 (latest est.).

jembe ('dʒɛmbɛ) NOUN *E African* a hoe.
▷HISTORY C19: from Swahili

jemmy ('dʒɛmɪ) *or US* **jimmy** NOUN, *plural* **-mies.** 1 a short steel crowbar used, esp by burglars, for forcing doors and windows. ◆ VERB **-mies, -mying, -mied.** 2 *(tr)* to prise (something) open with a jemmy.
▷HISTORY C19: from the pet name for *James*

Jena (*German* 'jeːna) NOUN a city in E central Germany, in Thuringia: university (1558), at which Hegel and Schiller taught; site of the battle (1806) in which Napoleon Bonaparte defeated the Prussians; optical and precision instrument industry. Pop.: 101 061 (1996 est.).

je ne sais quoi *French* (ʒənsɛkwa) NOUN an indefinable quality, esp of personality.
▷HISTORY literally: I don't know what

jennet, genet, *or* **gennet** ('dʒɛnɪt) NOUN [1] Also called: **jenny.** a female donkey or ass. [2] a small Spanish riding horse.
▷HISTORY C15: from Old French *genet,* from Catalan *ginet,* horse of the type used by the *Zenete,* from Arabic *Zanātah* the Zenete, a Moorish people renowned for their horsemanship

jenny ('dʒɛnɪ) NOUN, *plural* **-nies.** [1] a hand-operated machine for turning up the edge of a piece of sheet metal in preparation for making a joint. [2] the female of certain animals or birds, esp a donkey, ass, or wren. [3] short for **spinning jenny.** [4] *Billiards, snooker* an in-off. See **long jenny, short jenny.**
▷HISTORY C17: from the name *Jenny,* diminutive of *Jane*

jeopardize *or* **jeopardise** ('dʒɛpəˌdaɪz) VERB (*tr*) [1] to risk; hazard: *he jeopardized his job by being persistently unpunctual.* [2] to put in danger; imperil.

jeopardy ('dʒɛpədɪ) NOUN (usually preceded by *in*) [1] danger of injury, loss, death, etc.; risk; peril; hazard: *his health was in jeopardy.* [2] *Law* danger of being convicted and punished for a criminal offence. See also **double jeopardy.**
▷HISTORY C14: from Old French *jeu parti,* literally: divided game, hence uncertain issue, from *jeu* game, from Latin *jocus* joke, game + *partir* to divide, from Latin *partīrī*

Jephthah ('dʒɛfθə) NOUN *Old Testament* a judge of Israel, who sacrificed his daughter in fulfilment of a vow (Judges 11:12–40). Douay spelling: **Jephte** ('dʒɛftə).

jequirity *or* **jequerity** (dʒɪ'kwɪrɪtɪ) NOUN, *plural* **-ties.** [1] other names for **Indian liquorice.** [2] the seed of the Indian liquorice.
▷HISTORY C19: from Portuguese *jequiriti,* from Tupi-Guarani *jekiriti*

Jer. *Bible* ABBREVIATION FOR Jeremiah.

Jerba ('dʒɜːbə) NOUN a variant spelling of **Djerba.**

jerbil ('dʒɜːbɪl) NOUN a variant spelling of **gerbil.**

jerboa (dʒɜː'bəʊə) NOUN any small nocturnal burrowing rodent of the family *Dipodidae,* inhabiting dry regions of Asia and N Africa, having pale sandy fur, large ears, and long hind legs specialized for jumping.
▷HISTORY C17: from New Latin, from Arabic *yarbū'*

jeremiad (ˌdʒɛrɪ'maɪəd) NOUN a long mournful lamentation or complaint.

Jeremiah (ˌdʒɛrɪ'maɪə) NOUN [1] *Old Testament* **a** a major prophet of Judah from about 626 to 587 B.C. **b** the book containing his oracles. [2] a person who habitually prophesies doom or denounces contemporary society.

jerepigo (ˌdʒɛrə'piːgəʊ) NOUN *South African* a usually red heavy dessert wine.
▷HISTORY from Portuguese *geropiga*

Jerez (*Spanish* xe'rɛθ) NOUN a town in SW Spain: famous for the making of sherry. Pop.: 181 602 (1998 est.). Official name: **Jerez de la Frontera** (xe'rɛð ðe la frɔn'tera). Former name: **Xeres.**

Jericho ('dʒɛrɪˌkəʊ) NOUN a village in the West Bank near the N end of the Dead Sea, 251 m (825 ft.) below sea level: on the site of an ancient city, the first place to be taken by the Israelites under Joshua after entering the Promised Land in the 14th century B.C. (Joshua 6).

jerid (dʒə'riːd) NOUN a wooden javelin used in Muslim countries in military displays on horseback. Also: **jereed** *or* **jerreed.**

jerk[1] (dʒɜːk) VERB [1] to move or cause to move with an irregular or spasmodic motion. [2] to throw, twist, pull, or push (something) abruptly or spasmodically. [3] (*tr;* often foll by *out*) to utter (words, sounds, etc.) in a spasmodic, abrupt, or breathless manner. ◆ NOUN [4] an abrupt or spasmodic movement. [5] an irregular jolting motion: *the car moved with a jerk.* [6] (*plural*) Also called: **physical jerks.** *Brit informal* physical exercises. [7] (*plural*) *US* a slang word for **chorea.** [8] *Slang, chiefly US and Canadian* a person regarded with contempt, esp a stupid or ignorant person.
▷HISTORY C16: probably variant of *yerk* to pull stitches tight in making a shoe; compare Old English *gearcian* to make ready
▸ **'jerker** NOUN ▸ **'jerking** ADJECTIVE, NOUN

jerk[2] (dʒɜːk) VERB (*tr*) [1] to preserve (venison, beef, etc.) by cutting into thin strips and curing by drying in the sun. ◆ NOUN [2] Also called: **jerky.** jerked meat, esp beef.
▷HISTORY C18: back formation from *jerky,* from CHARQUI

jerkin ('dʒɜːkɪn) NOUN [1] a sleeveless and collarless short jacket worn by men or women. [2] a man's sleeveless and collarless fitted jacket, often made of leather, worn in the 16th and 17th centuries.
▷HISTORY C16: of unknown origin

jerk off *or US* **jack off** VERB (*adverb often reflexive*) *Slang* (of a male) to masturbate.

> **Language note** This word was formerly considered to be taboo, and it was labelled as such in previous editions of *Collins English Dictionary.* However, it has now become acceptable in speech, although some older or more conservative people may object to its use.

jerkwater ('dʒɜːkˌwɔːtə) ADJECTIVE *US and Canadian, slang* inferior and insignificant: *a jerkwater town.*
▷HISTORY C19: originally referring to railway locomotives for which water was taken on in buckets from streams along the route

jerky[1] ('dʒɜːkɪ) ADJECTIVE **jerkier, jerkiest.** characterized by jerks; spasmodic.
▸ **'jerkily** ADVERB ▸ **'jerkiness** NOUN

jerky[2] ('dʒɜːkɪ) NOUN another word for **jerk**[2] (sense 2).

jeroboam (ˌdʒɛrə'bəʊəm) NOUN a wine bottle holding the equivalent of four normal bottles (approximately 104 ounces). Also called: **double-magnum.**
▷HISTORY C19: humorous allusion to JEROBOAM (sense 1), described as a "mighty man of valour" (I Kings 11:28) who "made Israel to sin" (I Kings 14:16)

Jeroboam (ˌdʒɛrə'bəʊəm) NOUN *Old Testament* [1] the first king of the northern kingdom of Israel (?922–?901 B.C.). [2] king of the northern kingdom of Israel (?786–?746 B.C.).

jerreed (dʒə'riːd) NOUN a variant spelling of **jerid.**

jerry ('dʒɛrɪ) NOUN, *plural* **-ries.** [1] *Brit* an informal word for **chamber pot.** [2] short for **jeroboam.**

Jerry ('dʒɛrɪ) NOUN, *plural* **-ries.** *Brit, slang* [1] a German, esp a German soldier. [2] the Germans collectively: *Jerry didn't send his bombers out last night.*

jerry-build VERB **-builds, -building, -built.** (*tr*) to build (houses, flats, etc.) badly using cheap materials.
▸ **'jerry-ˌbuilder** NOUN

jerry can NOUN a flat-sided can with a capacity of between 4.5 and 5 gallons used for storing or transporting liquids, esp motor fuel: originally a German design adopted by the British Army during World War II.
▷HISTORY C20: from JERRY

jersey ('dʒɜːzɪ) NOUN [1] a knitted garment covering the upper part of the body. [2] **a** a machine-knitted slightly elastic cloth of wool, silk, nylon, etc., used for clothing. **b** (*as modifier*): *a jersey suit.* [3] a football shirt.
▷HISTORY C16: from JERSEY, from the woollen sweaters traditionally worn by the fishermen

Jersey ('dʒɜːzɪ) NOUN [1] an island in the English Channel, the largest of the Channel Islands: forms, with two other islands, the bailiwick of Jersey; colonized from Normandy in the 11th century and still officially French-speaking; noted for finance, market gardening, dairy farming, and tourism. Capital: St Helier. Pop.: 89 400 (2001 est.). Area: 116 sq. km (45 sq. miles). [2] a breed of dairy cattle producing milk with a high butterfat content, originating from the island of Jersey.

Jersey City NOUN an industrial city in NE New Jersey, opposite Manhattan on a peninsula between the Hudson and Hackensack Rivers: part of the Port of New York; site of one of the greatest railway terminals in the world. Pop.: 240 055 (2000).

Jerusalem (dʒə'ruːsələm) NOUN [1] the de facto capital of Israel (recognition of this has been withheld by the United Nations), situated in the Judaean hills: became capital of the Hebrew kingdom after its capture by David around 1000 B.C.; destroyed by Nebuchadnezzar of Babylon in 586 B.C.; taken by the Romans in 63 B.C.; devastated in 70 A.D. and 135 A.D. during the Jewish rebellions against Rome; fell to the Arabs in 637 and to the Seljuk Turks in 1071; ruled by Crusaders from 1099 to 1187 and by the Egyptians and Turks until conquered by the British (1917); centre of the British mandate of Palestine from 1920 to 1948, when the Arabs took the old city and the Jews held the new city; unified after the Six Day War (1967) under the Israelis; the holy city of Jews, Christians, and Muslims. Pop.: 633 700 (1999 est.). [2] **a the New Jerusalem.** *Christianity* Heaven. **b** any ideal city.

Jerusalem artichoke NOUN [1] a North American sunflower, *Helianthus tuberosus,* widely cultivated for its underground edible tubers. [2] the tuber of this plant, which is cooked and eaten as a vegetable. ◆ See also **artichoke** (senses 1, 2).
▷HISTORY C17: by folk etymology from Italian *girasole articiocco;* see GIRASOL

Jerusalem cherry NOUN a small South American solanaceous shrub, *Solanum pseudo-capsicum,* cultivated as a house plant for its white flowers and inedible reddish cherry-like fruit.

Jerusalem cross NOUN a cross the equal arms of which end in a bar. Also called: **cross potent.**

Jerusalem oak NOUN a weedy North American chenopodiaceous plant, *Chenopodium botrys,* that has lobed leaves and smells of turpentine.

Jerusalem syndrome NOUN a delusive condition affecting some visitors to Jerusalem in which the sufferer identifies with a major figure from his or her religious background.

Jervis Bay ('dʒɑːvɪs) NOUN an inlet of the Pacific in SE Australia, on the coast of S New South Wales: part of the Australian Capital Territory: site of the Royal Australian Naval College.

jess (dʒɛs) *Falconry* ◆ NOUN [1] a short leather strap, one end of which is permanently attached to the leg of a hawk or falcon while the other can be attached to a leash. ◆ VERB [2] (*tr*) to put jesses on (a hawk or falcon).
▷HISTORY C14: from Old French *ges,* from Latin *jactus* a throw, from *jacere* to throw
▸ **jessed** ADJECTIVE

jessamine ('dʒɛsəmɪn) NOUN another name for **jasmine** (sense 1).

Jesse ('dʒɛsɪ) NOUN *Old Testament* the father of David (I Samuel 16).

Jesselton ('dʒɛsəltən) NOUN the former name of **Kota Kinabalu.**

Jesse window NOUN a window in a church with a representation of Christ's descent from Jesse, usually in the form of a genealogical tree.

jessie ('dʒɛsɪ) NOUN *Slang* an effeminate, weak, or cowardly boy or man.

jest (dʒɛst) NOUN [1] something done or said for amusement; joke. [2] a frivolous mood or attitude; playfulness; fun: *to act in jest.* [3] a jeer or taunt. [4] an object of derision; laughing stock; butt. ◆ VERB [5] to act or speak in an amusing, teasing, or frivolous way; joke. [6] to make fun of (a person or thing); scoff or mock.
▷HISTORY C13: variant of GEST
▸ **'jestful** ADJECTIVE ▸ **'jesting** ADJECTIVE, NOUN ▸ **'jestingly** ADVERB

jester ('dʒɛstə) NOUN a professional clown employed by a king or nobleman, esp at courts during the Middle Ages.

Jesuit ('dʒɛzjʊɪt) NOUN [1] a member of a Roman Catholic religious order (the **Society of Jesus**) founded by the Spanish ecclesiastic Saint Ignatius Loyola (1491–1556) in 1534 with the aims of defending the papacy and Catholicism against the Reformation and to undertake missionary work among the heathen. [2] (*sometimes not capital*) *Informal, offensive* a person given to subtle and equivocating arguments; casuist.
▷HISTORY C16: from New Latin *Jēsuita,* from Late Latin *Jēsus* + *-ita* -ITE[1]
▸ **ˌJesu'itic** *or* **ˌJesu'itical** ADJECTIVE ▸ **ˌJesu'itically** ADVERB

Jesuitism ('dʒɛzjʊɪˌtɪzəm) *or* **Jesuitry** NOUN [1] theology or practices of the Jesuits. [2] *Informal offensive* subtle and equivocating arguments; casuistry.

Jesus ('dʒiːzəs) INTERJECTION *also* **Jesus wept.** *Taboo slang* used to express intense surprise, dismay, etc.
▷HISTORY from Jesus (?4 B.C.–?29 A.D.), founder of Christianity

Jesus freak NOUN *Informal* a member of any of various Christian groups that combine a hippy communal way of life with zealous evangelicalism.

jet¹ (dʒɛt) NOUN 1 a thin stream of liquid or gas forced out of a small aperture or nozzle. 2 an outlet or nozzle for emitting such a stream. 3 a jet-propelled aircraft. 4 *Astronomy* a long thin feature extending from an active galaxy and usually observed at radio wavelengths. ◆ VERB **jets, jetting, jetted.** 5 to issue or cause to issue in a jet: *water jetted from the hose; he jetted them with water.* 6 to transport or be transported by jet aircraft.
▷HISTORY C16: from Old French *jeter* to throw, from Latin *jactāre* to toss about, frequentative of *jacere* to throw

jet² (dʒɛt) NOUN **a** a hard black variety of coal that takes a brilliant polish and is used for jewellery, ornaments, etc. **b** (*as modifier*): *jet earrings.*
▷HISTORY C14: from Old French *jaiet,* from Latin *gagātēs,* from Greek *lithos gagatēs* stone of *Gagai,* a town in Lycia, Asia Minor

JET (dʒɛt) NOUN ACRONYM FOR Joint European Torus; a tokamak plasma-containment device at Culham, Oxfordshire, for research into energy production by nuclear fusion.

jet black NOUN **a** a deep black colour. **b** (*as adjective*): *jet-black hair.*

jet boat NOUN *NZ* a power boat that is powered and steered by a jet of water under pressure.

jet condenser NOUN a steam condenser in which steam is condensed by jets of water.

jeté (ʒəˈteɪ) NOUN *Ballet* a step in which the dancer springs from one leg and lands on the other.
▷HISTORY French, literally: thrown, from *jeter;* see JET¹

jet engine NOUN a gas turbine, esp one fitted to an aircraft.

jetfoil (ˈdʒɛtˌfɔɪl) NOUN a type of hydrofoil that is propelled by water jets.
▷HISTORY C20: from a blend of JET¹ + (HYDRO)FOIL

Jethro (ˈdʒɛθrəʊ) NOUN *Old Testament* a Midianite priest, the father-in-law of Moses (Exodus 3:1; 4:18).

jet lag NOUN a general feeling of fatigue and disorientation often experienced by travellers by jet aircraft who cross several time zones in relatively few hours.

jetliner (ˈdʒɛtˌlaɪnə) NOUN a commercial airliner powered by jet engines.

jet pipe NOUN the duct attached to the rear of a gas turbine through which the exhaust gases are discharged, esp one fitted to an aircraft engine.

jet plane NOUN an aircraft powered by one or more jet engines.

jetport (ˈdʒɛtˌpɔːt) NOUN *Obsolete* an airport for jet planes.

jet-propelled ADJECTIVE 1 driven by jet propulsion. 2 *Informal* very fast.

jet propulsion NOUN 1 propulsion by means of a jet of fluid. 2 propulsion by means of a gas turbine, esp when the exhaust gases provide the propulsive thrust.

jetsam *or* **jetsom** (ˈdʒɛtsəm) NOUN 1 that portion of the equipment or cargo of a vessel thrown overboard to lighten her, as during a storm. Compare **flotsam** (sense 1), **lagan.** 2 another word for **flotsam** (sense 2).
▷HISTORY C16: shortened from JETTISON

jet set NOUN **a** a rich and fashionable social set the members of which travel widely for pleasure. **b** (*as modifier*): *jet-set travellers.*
▸ˈ**jet-ˌsetter** NOUN ▸ˈ**jet-ˌsetting** ADJECTIVE

Jet Ski NOUN 1 *Trademark* a small self-propelled vehicle for one person resembling a scooter, which skims across water on a flat keel, and is steered by means of handlebars. ◆ VERB **jet-ski, -skis, -skiing, -skied** *or* **-skiʼd.** (*intr; usually not capital*) 2 to ride a Jet Ski.
▸**Jet Skier** NOUN ▸**Jet Skiing** NOUN

jet stream NOUN 1 *Meteorol* a narrow belt of high-altitude winds (about 12 000 metres high) moving east at high speeds and having an important effect on frontogenesis. 2 the jet of exhaust gases produced by a gas turbine, rocket motor, etc.

jettison (ˈdʒɛtɪsᵊn, -zᵊn) VERB (*tr*) **-sons, -soning, -soned** 1 to throw away; abandon: *to jettison old clothes.* 2 to throw overboard. ◆ NOUN 3 another word for **jetsam** (sense 1).
▷HISTORY C15: from Old French *getaison,* ultimately from Latin *jactātiō* a tossing about; see JACTATION

jetton (ˈdʒɛtᵊn) NOUN a counter or token, esp a chip used in such gambling games as roulette.
▷HISTORY C18: from French *jeton,* from *jeter* to cast up (accounts); see JET¹

jetty¹ (ˈdʒɛtɪ) NOUN, *plural* **-ties.** 1 a structure built from a shore out into the water to direct currents or protect a harbour. 2 a landing pier; dock.
▷HISTORY C15: from Old French *jetee* projecting part, literally: something thrown out, from *jeter* to throw; see JET¹

jetty² (ˈdʒɛtɪ) ADJECTIVE of or resembling jet, esp in colour or polish.
▸ˈ**jettiness** NOUN

jeu d'esprit *French* (ʒø dɛspri) NOUN, *plural* ***jeux d'esprit*** (ʒø dɛspri). a light-hearted display of wit or cleverness, esp in literature.
▷HISTORY literally: play of spirit

jeunesse dorée *French* (ʒœnɛs dɔre) NOUN rich and fashionable young people.
▷HISTORY literally: gilded youth

Jew (dʒuː) NOUN 1 a member of the Semitic people who are notionally descended from the ancient Israelites, are spread throughout the world, and are linked by loose cultural or religious ties. 2 a person whose religion is Judaism. ◆ See also **Hebrew, Israeli, Israelite.**
▷HISTORY C12: from Old French *juiu,* from Latin *jūdaeus,* from Greek *ioudaios,* from Hebrew *yehūdī,* from *yehūdāh* JUDAH

Jew-baiting NOUN active persecution or harassment of Jews.
▸ˈ**Jew-ˌbaiter** NOUN

jewel (ˈdʒuːəl) NOUN 1 a precious or semiprecious stone; gem. 2 a person or thing resembling a jewel in preciousness, brilliance, etc. 3 a gemstone, often synthetically produced, used as a bearing in a watch. 4 a piece of jewellery. 5 an ornamental glass boss, sometimes faceted, used in stained glasswork. 6 **jewel in the crown.** the most valuable, esteemed, or successful person or thing of a number: *who will be the jewel in the crown of English soccer?* ◆ VERB **-els, -elling, -elled** *or US* **-els, -eling, -eled.** 7 (*tr*) to fit or decorate with a jewel or jewels.
▷HISTORY C13: from Old French *jouel,* perhaps from *jeu* game, from Latin *jocus*
▸ˈ**jewelled** *or US* ˈ**jeweled** ADJECTIVE ▸ˈ**jewel-ˌlike** ADJECTIVE

jewel case *or* **box** NOUN 1 a box, usually ornamental, in which jewels are kept. 2 a plastic case for a compact disc.

jewelfish (ˈdʒuːəlˌfɪʃ) NOUN, *plural* **-fish** *or* **-fishes.** an African cichlid, *Hemichromis bimaculatus*: a beautifully coloured and popular aquarium fish.

jeweller *or US* **jeweler** (ˈdʒuːələ) NOUN a person whose business is the cutting, polishing, or setting of gemstones or the making, repairing, or selling of jewellery.

jeweller's rouge NOUN a finely powdered form of ferric oxide used as a metal polish. Also called: **crocus.** See also **colcothar.**

jewellery *or US* **jewelry** (ˈdʒuːəlrɪ) NOUN 1 objects that are worn for personal adornment, such as bracelets, rings, necklaces, etc., considered collectively. 2 the art or business of a jeweller.

Jewess (ˈdʒuːɪs) NOUN *Offensive* a Jewish girl or woman.

jewfish (ˈdʒuːˌfɪʃ) NOUN, *plural* **-fish** *or* **-fishes.** 1 any of various large dark serranid fishes, such as *Mycteroperca bonaci,* of warm or tropical seas. 2 *Austral* any of various marine sciaenid food and game fish, esp the mulloway. 3 *Austral* a large food fish of W Australian waters *Glaucosoma hebraicum.*
▷HISTORY C17: of uncertain origin

jewie (ˈdʒuːɪ) NOUN *Austral informal* a jewfish.

Jewish (ˈdʒuːɪʃ) ADJECTIVE 1 of, relating to, or characteristic of Jews. ◆ NOUN 2 a less common word for **Yiddish.**
▸ˈ**Jewishly** ADVERB ▸ˈ**Jewishness** NOUN

Jewish American Princess NOUN *US, slang* an American Jewish girl of a prosperous family, regarded as being typically pampered and spoilt. Abbreviation: **JAP.**

Jewish Autonomous Region NOUN an administrative division of SE Russia, in E Siberia: colonized by Jews in 1928; largely agricultural. Capital: Birobidzhan. Pop.: 216 000 (1995 est.). Area: 36 000 sq. km (13 895 sq. miles). Also called: **Birobidzhan, Birobijan.**

Jewish calendar NOUN the lunisolar calendar used by the Jews, in which time is reckoned from 3761 B.C.: regarded as the year of the Creation. The months, Nisan, Iyar, Sivan, Tammuz, Av, Elul, Tishri, Cheshvan, Kislev, Tevet, Shevat, and Adar, have either 29 or 30 days. Originally a new month was declared when the new moon was sighted in Jerusalem, but when this became impossible, a complex formula was devised to keep Rosh Chodesh near to the new moon. In addition, to keep the harvest festivals in the right seasons, there is a Metonic cycle of 14 years, in five of which an additional month is added after Shevat (see **Adar**). The year according to biblical reckoning begins with Nisan, and the civil year begins with Tishri; the years are numbered from Tishri. Also called: **Hebrew calendar.**

jew lizard NOUN another name for **bearded dragon.**

Jewry (ˈdʒʊərɪ) NOUN, *plural* **-ries.** 1 **a** Jews collectively. **b** the Jewish religion or culture. 2 *Archaic* (sometimes found in street names in England) a quarter of a town inhabited by Jews. 3 **the.** (in some anti-semitic literature) the Jews conceived of as an organized force seeking world domination. 4 *Archaic* the land of Judaea.

jew's-ear NOUN See **jelly fungus.**

jew's-harp NOUN a musical instrument consisting of a small lyre-shaped metal frame held between the teeth, with a steel tongue plucked with the finger. Changes in pitch are produced by varying the size of the mouth cavities.

Jezebel (ˈdʒɛzəˌbɛl, -bᵊl) NOUN 1 *Old Testament* the wife of Ahab, king of Israel: she fostered the worship of Baal and tried to destroy the prophets of Israel (I Kings 18:4–13); she was killed by Jehu (II Kings 9:29–37). 2 (*sometimes not capital*) a shameless or scheming woman.

Jezreel (ˈdʒɛzrɪəl) NOUN **Plain of.** another name for **Esdraelon.**
▸ˈ**Jezreelˌite** NOUN

Jezreelite (ˈdʒɛzrɪəlˌaɪts) NOUN a native or inhabitant of Jezreel.

JFET (ˈdʒeɪfɛt) NOUN ACRONYM FOR junction field-effect transistor; a type of field-effect transistor in which the semiconductor gate region or regions form one or more p-n junctions with the conduction channel. Compare **IGFET.**

Jhansi (ˈdʒɑːnsɪ) NOUN a city in central India, in SW Uttar Pradesh: scene of a mutiny against the British in 1857. Pop.: 300 850 (1991).

Jharkand (ˈdʒɑːkʌnd) NOUN a state of NE India, created in 2000 from the S part of Bihar: consists of part of the Chota Nagpur plateau; mineral extraction, including coal and mica. Capital: Ranchi. Pop.: 26 909 428 (2001). Area: 74 677 sq. km (28 833 sq. miles).

jhatka (ˈdʒætkə) NOUN the slaughter of animals for food according to Sikh law.
▷HISTORY Punjabi

Jhelum (ˈdʒiːləm) NOUN a river in Pakistan and Kashmir, rising in W central Kashmir and flowing northwest through the Vale of Kashmir, then southwest into N West Punjab to join the Chenab River: important for irrigation, having the Mangla Dam (Pakistan), completed in 1967. Length: about 720 km (450 miles).

JHVH *or* **JHWH** *Old Testament* variants of **YHVH.**

-ji (-dziː) *Indian* a suffix placed after a person's name or title as a mark of respect.
▷HISTORY Hindi

Jiangsu (ˈdʒjæŋˈsuː) *or* **Kiangsu** NOUN a province of E China, on the Yellow Sea: consists mostly of the marshy delta of the Yangtze River, with some of China's largest cities and most densely populated areas. Capital: Nanjing. Pop.: 74 380 000 (2000 est.). Area: 102 200 sq. km (39 860 sq. miles).

Jiangxi (ˈdʒjæŋˈʃiː) *or* **Kiangsi** NOUN a province of SE central China, in the basins of the Kan River and the Poyang Lake: mineral resources include coal and tungsten. Capital: Nanchang. Pop.: 41 400 000 (2000 est.). Area: 164 800 sq. km (64 300 sq. miles).

Jiazhou ('dʒjæ'dʒəʊ) *or* **Kiaochow** NOUN a territory of NE China, in SE Shandong province, surrounding **Jiazhou Bay** (an inlet of the Yellow Sea): leased to Germany from 1898 to 1914. Area: about 520 sq. km (200 sq. miles).

jib[1] (dʒɪb) NOUN [1] *Nautical* any triangular sail set forward of the foremast of a vessel. [2] **cut of someone's jib.** someone's manner, behaviour, style, etc. [3] *Obsolete* **a** the lower lip, usually when it protrudes forwards in a grimace. **b** the face or nose.
▷HISTORY C17: of unknown origin

jib[2] (dʒɪb) VERB **jibs, jibbing, jibbed.** (*intr*) *Chiefly Brit* [1] (often foll by *at*) to be reluctant (to); hold back (from); balk (at). [2] (of an animal) to stop short and refuse to go forwards: *the horse jibbed at the jump.* [3] *Nautical* variant of **gybe.**
▷HISTORY C19: of unknown origin
▸'**jibber** NOUN

jib[3] (dʒɪb) NOUN the projecting arm of a crane or the boom of a derrick, esp one that is pivoted to enable it to be raised or lowered.
▷HISTORY C18: probably based on GIBBET

jib[4] (dʒɪb) NOUN (*often plural*) *South Wales, dialect* a contortion of the face; a face: *stop making jibs.*
▷HISTORY special use of JIB[1] (in the sense: lower lip, face)

jibbons ('dʒɪbənz) PLURAL NOUN *Southwest Brit, dialect* spring onions.
▷HISTORY from Norman French *chiboule,* variant of French *ciboule* onion, ultimately from Latin *capulla* an onion patch, from *caepa* an onion

jib boom NOUN *Nautical* a spar forming an extension of the bowsprit.

jibe[1] (dʒaɪb), **jib,** *or* **jibb** (dʒɪb) VERB, NOUN *Nautical* variants of **gybe.**

jibe[2] (dʒaɪb) VERB a variant spelling of **gibe.**
▸'**jiber** NOUN ▸'**jibingly** ADVERB

jibe[3] (dʒaɪb) VERB (*intr*) *Informal* to agree; accord; harmonize.
▷HISTORY C19: of unknown origin

jib-headed ADJECTIVE *Nautical* [1] (of a sail) pointed at the top or head. [2] (of a sailing vessel or rig) having sails that are triangular.

Jibouti *or* **Jibuti** (dʒɪ'bu:tɪ) NOUN variant spellings of **Djibouti.**

jicama (dʒɪ'kɑ:mə; *Spanish* xɪkama) NOUN a pale brown turnip with crisp sweet flesh, originating in Mexico.
▷HISTORY C17: from Mexican Spanish *jícama,* from Nahuatl *xicama*

JICTAR ('dʒɪktɑ:) NOUN ACRONYM FOR Joint Industry Committee for Television Advertising Research.

Jidda ('dʒɪdə) *or* **Jedda** NOUN a port in W Saudi Arabia, on the Red Sea: the diplomatic capital of the country; the port of entry for Mecca, 80 km (50 miles) east. Pop.: 2 046 000 (1991 est.).

jiffy ('dʒɪfɪ) *or* **jiff** (dʒɪf) NOUN, *plural* **jiffies** *or* **jiffs.** *Informal* a very short time: *wait a jiffy.*
▷HISTORY C18: of unknown origin

Jiffy bag NOUN *Trademark* a thickly padded but light envelope in which articles such as books are placed for protection in the post.

jig (dʒɪg) NOUN [1] any of several old rustic kicking and leaping dances. [2] a piece of music composed for or in the rhythm of this dance, usually in six-eight time. [3] a mechanical device designed to hold and locate a component during machining and to guide the cutting tool. [4] *Angling* any of various spinning lures that wobble when drawn through the water. [5] Also called: **jigger.** *Mining* a device for separating ore or coal from waste material by agitation in water. [6] *Obsolete* a joke or prank. ◆ VERB **jigs, jigging, jigged.** [7] to dance (a jig). [8] to jerk or cause to jerk up and down rapidly. [9] (often foll by *up*) to fit or be fitted in a jig. [10] (*tr*) to drill or cut (a workpiece) in a jig. [11] *Mining* to separate ore or coal from waste material using a jig. [12] (*intr*) to produce or manufacture a jig. [13] *Austral, slang* to play truant from school.
▷HISTORY C16 (originally: a dance or the music for it; applied to various modern devices because of the verbal sense: to jerk up and down rapidly): of unknown origin

Jigawa (ˌdʒɪ'gɑ:wə) NOUN a state of N Nigeria. Capital: Dutse. Pop.: 3 164 134 (1995 est.). Area (including Kano state): 43 285 sq. km (16 712 sq. miles).

jigger[1] ('dʒɪgə) NOUN [1] a person or thing that jigs. [2] *Golf* an iron, now obsolete, with a thin blade, used for hitting long shots from a bare lie. [3] any of a number of mechanical devices having a vibratory or jerking motion. [4] a light lifting tackle used on ships. [5] a small glass, esp for whisky, with a capacity of about one and a half ounces. [6] *NZ* a light hand- or power-propelled vehicle used on railway lines. [7] *Engineering* a type of hydraulic lift in which a hydraulic ram operates the lift through a block and tackle which increases the length of the stroke. [8] *Canadian* a device used when setting a gill net beneath ice. [9] *Mining* another word for **jig** (sense 5). [10] *Nautical* short for **jiggermast.** [11] *Billiards* another word for **bridge**[1] (sense 10). [12] *US and Canadian informal* a device or thing the name of which is unknown or temporarily forgotten. [13] *Liverpool, dialect* an alleyway.

jigger[2] *or* **jigger flea** ('dʒɪgə) NOUN other names for the **chigoe** (sense 1).

jiggered ('dʒɪgəd) ADJECTIVE (*postpositive*) [1] *Informal* damned; blowed: *I'm jiggered if he'll get away with it.* [2] (sometimes foll by *up*) *Scot and northern English, dialect* tired out.
▷HISTORY C19: probably euphemism for *buggered;* see BUGGER

jiggermast ('dʒɪgəˌmɑ:st) NOUN *Nautical* any small mast on a sailing vessel, esp the mizzenmast of a yawl. Sometimes shortened to: **jigger.**

jiggery-pokery ('dʒɪgərɪ'pəʊkərɪ) NOUN *Informal, chiefly Brit* dishonest or deceitful behaviour or business; trickery.
▷HISTORY C19: from Scottish dialect *joukery-pawkery*

jiggle ('dʒɪgəl) VERB [1] to move or cause to move up and down or to and fro with a short jerky motion: *to jiggle the door handle.* ◆ NOUN [2] a short jerky motion.
▷HISTORY C19: frequentative of JIG; compare JOGGLE
▸'**jiggly** ADJECTIVE

jiggy ('dʒɪgɪ) ADJECTIVE **get jiggy with.** *Slang* to have sexual relations with.

jigsaw ('dʒɪgˌsɔ:) NOUN [1] a mechanical saw with a fine steel blade for cutting intricate curves in sheets of material. [2] See **jigsaw puzzle.**
▷HISTORY C19: from JIG (to jerk up and down rapidly) + SAW[1]

jigsaw puzzle NOUN a puzzle in which the player has to reassemble a picture that has been mounted on a wooden or cardboard base and cut into a large number of irregularly shaped interlocking pieces.

jihad *or* **jehad** (dʒɪ'hæd) NOUN [1] *Islam* a holy war against infidels undertaken by Muslims in defence of the Islamic faith. [2] *Islam* the personal struggle of the individual believer against evil and persecution. [3] *Rare* a crusade in support of a cause.
▷HISTORY C19: from Arabic *jihād* a conflict

jilbab (dʒɪl'bɑ:b) NOUN [1] a long robe worn by Muslim women.
▷HISTORY from Arabic

Jilin ('dʒi:'lɪn) *or* **Kirin** NOUN [1] a province of NE China, in central Manchuria. Capital: Changchun. Pop.: 27 280 000 (2000 est.). Area: 187 000 sq. km (72 930 sq. miles). [2] Also called: **Chi-lin** ('tʃi:'lɪn). a river port in NE China, in N central Jilin province on the Songhua River. Pop.: 1 165 418 (1999 est.).

jill (dʒɪl) NOUN *Dialect* a variant spelling of **gill**[4] (sense 2).

jillaroo (ˌdʒɪlə'ru:) NOUN, *plural* **-roos.** *Austral informal* a female jackeroo.

jillion ('dʒɪljən) NOUN *Informal* an extremely large number or amount: *jillions of pounds.*
▷HISTORY C20: fanciful coinage based on MILLION, BILLION, etc.
▸'**jillionth** ADJECTIVE

Jilolo (dʒaɪ'ləʊləʊ) NOUN a variant spelling of **Djailolo.** See **Halmahera.**

Jilong ('dʒi:'lʊŋ) NOUN the Pinyin transliteration of the Chinese name for **Chilung.**

jilt (dʒɪlt) VERB [1] (*tr*) to leave or reject (a lover), esp without previous warning: *she was jilted at the altar.* ◆ NOUN [2] a woman who jilts a lover.
▷HISTORY C17: from dialect *jillet* flighty girl, diminutive of proper name *Gill*
▸'**jilter** NOUN

jim crow ('dʒɪm 'krəʊ) NOUN (*often capitals*) *US* [1] **a** the policy or practice of segregating Blacks. **b** (*as modifier*): *jim-crow laws.* [2] **a** a derogatory term for a Black person. **b** (*as modifier*): *a jim-crow saloon.* [3] an implement for bending iron bars or rails. [4] a crowbar fitted with a claw.
▷HISTORY C19: from *Jim Crow,* name of song used as the basis of an act by Thomas Rice (1808–60), American entertainer
▸'**jim-'crowism** NOUN

jimjams ('dʒɪmˌdʒæmz) PLURAL NOUN [1] a slang word for **delirium tremens.** [2] a state of nervous tension, excitement, or anxiety. [3] *Informal* pyjamas.
▷HISTORY C19: whimsical formation based on JAM[1]

jimmy ('dʒɪmɪ) NOUN, *plural* **-mies,** VERB **-mies, -mying, -mied.** the US word for **jemmy.**

Jimmy ('dʒɪmɪ) NOUN *Central Scot, urban dialect* an informal term of address to a male stranger.

Jimmy Woodser (ˌdʒɪmɪ 'wʊdzə) NOUN *Austral informal* [1] a man who drinks by himself. [2] a drink taken alone.

jimson weed ('dʒɪmsən) NOUN the US and Canadian name for **thorn apple** (sense 1).
▷HISTORY C17: from earlier *Jamestown weed,* from *Jamestown,* Virginia

Jinan ('dʒi:'næn), **Chinan,** *or* **Tsinan** NOUN an industrial city in NE China, capital of Shandong province; probably over 3000 years old. Pop.: 1 713 036 (1999 est.).

Jingdezhen ('dʒɪŋ'dɛdʒɛn), **Fowliang,** *or* **Fou-liang** NOUN a city in SE China, in NE Jiangxi province east of Lake Poyang: famous for its porcelain industry, established in the sixth century. Pop.: 315 036 (1999 est.).

jingle ('dʒɪŋgəl) VERB [1] to ring or cause to ring lightly and repeatedly. [2] (*intr*) to sound in a manner suggestive of jingling: *a jingling verse.* ◆ NOUN [3] a sound of metal jingling: *the jingle of the keys.* [4] a catchy and rhythmic verse, song, etc., esp one used in advertising.
▷HISTORY C16: probably of imitative origin; compare Dutch *jengelen*
▸'**jingler** NOUN ▸'**jingly** ADJECTIVE

jingo ('dʒɪŋgəʊ) NOUN, *plural* **-goes.** [1] a loud and bellicose patriot; chauvinist. [2] jingoism. [3] **by jingo.** an exclamation of surprise.
▷HISTORY C17: originally perhaps a euphemism for *Jesus;* applied to bellicose patriots after the use of *by Jingo!* in the refrain of a 19th-century music-hall song
▸'**jingoish** ADJECTIVE

jingoism ('dʒɪŋgəʊˌɪzəm) NOUN the belligerent spirit or foreign policy of jingoes; chauvinism.
▸'**jingoist** NOUN, ADJECTIVE ▸ˌ**jingo'istic** ADJECTIVE ▸ˌ**jingo'istically** ADVERB

Jinja ('dʒɪndʒə) NOUN a town in Uganda, on the N shore of Lake Victoria. Pop.: 60 979 (1991).

Jinjiang ('dʒɪn'dʒjæŋ), **Chinkiang,** *or* **Cheng-chiang** NOUN a port in E China, in S Jiangsu at the confluence of the Yangtze River and the Grand Canal. Pop.: 136 204 (1999 est.).

jink (dʒɪŋk) VERB [1] to move swiftly or jerkily or make a quick turn in order to dodge or elude. ◆ NOUN [2] a jinking movement.
▷HISTORY C18: of Scottish origin, imitative of swift movement

jinker ('dʒɪŋkə) NOUN *Austral* a vehicle for transporting timber, consisting of a tractor and two sets of wheels for supporting the logs.
▷HISTORY of unknown origin

jinks (dʒɪŋks) PLURAL NOUN boisterous or mischievous play (esp in the phrase **high jinks**).
▷HISTORY C18: of unknown origin

jinn (dʒɪn) NOUN (*often functioning as singular*) the plural of **jinni.**

jinni, jinnee, djinni, *or* **djinny** (dʒɪ'ni:, 'dʒɪnɪ) NOUN, *plural* **jinn** *or* **djinn** (dʒɪn). a being or spirit in Muslim belief who could assume human or animal form and influence man by supernatural powers.
▷HISTORY C17: from Arabic

jinrikisha, jinricksha, jinrickshaw, *or* **jinriksha** (dʒɪn'rɪkʃɔ:, -ʃə) NOUN other names for **rickshaw.**
▷HISTORY C19: from Japanese, from *jin* man + *riki* power + *sha* carriage

jinx (dʒɪŋks) NOUN [1] an unlucky or malevolent force, person, or thing. ◆ VERB [2] (*tr*) to be or put a jinx on.
▷HISTORY C20: perhaps from New Latin *Jynx* genus name of the wryneck, from Greek *iunx* wryneck, the name of a bird used in magic

Jinzhou (ˈdʒɪnˈdʒəʊ), **Chin-Chou**, *or* **Chin-chow** NOUN a city in NE China, in SW Liaoning province. Pop.: 596 860 (1990 est.). Former name (1913–47): **Chin-hsien.**

jipijapa (ˌhiːpiːˈhɑːpɑː) NOUN a palmlike plant, *Carludovica palmata,* of central and South America, whose fanlike leaves are bleached for making panama hats: family *Cyclanthaceae.*
▷HISTORY American Spanish, after *Jipijapa,* Ecuador

jism (ˈdʒɪzəm) *or* **jissom** (ˈdʒɪsəm) NOUN *Taboo* informal words for **semen.**
▷HISTORY of unknown origin

JIT ABBREVIATION FOR **just-in-time.**

jitney (ˈdʒɪtnɪ) NOUN *US, now rare* [1] a small bus that carries passengers for a low price, originally five cents. [2] *Slang* a nickel; five cents.
▷HISTORY C20: of unknown origin

jitter (ˈdʒɪtə) *Informal* ◆ VERB [1] (*intr*) to be anxious or nervous. ◆ NOUN [2] **the jitters.** nervousness and anxiety. [3] *Electronics* small rapid variations in the amplitude or timing of a waveform arising from fluctuations in the voltage supply, mechanical vibrations, etc.
▷HISTORY C20: of unknown origin

jitterbug (ˈdʒɪtəˌbʌg) NOUN [1] a fast jerky American dance, usually to a jazz accompaniment, that was popular in the 1940s. [2] a person who dances the jitterbug. [3] a highly nervous or excitable person. ◆ VERB **-bugs, -bugging, -bugged.** [4] (*intr*) to perform such a dance.

jittery (ˈdʒɪtərɪ) ADJECTIVE *Informal* nervous and anxious.
▸ˈ**jitteriness** NOUN

jiujitsu *or* **jiujutsu** (dʒuːˈdʒɪtsuː) NOUN variant spellings of **jujitsu.**

jive (dʒaɪv) NOUN [1] a style of lively and jerky dance performed to jazz and, later, to rock and roll, popular esp in the 1940s and 1950s. [2] Also called: **jive talk.** a variety of American slang spoken chiefly by Blacks, esp jazz musicians. [3] **a** *Slang, chiefly US* deliberately misleading or deceptive talk. **b** (*as modifier*): *jive talk.* ◆ VERB [4] (*intr*) to dance the jive. [5] *Slang, chiefly US* to mislead; tell lies (to).
▷HISTORY C20: of unknown origin
▸ˈ**jiver** NOUN

jizz (dʒɪz) NOUN a term for the total combination of characteristics that serve to identify a particular species of bird or plant.
▷HISTORY origin obscure

JJ. ABBREVIATION FOR: [1] Judges. [2] Justices.

jm THE INTERNET DOMAIN NAME FOR Jamaica.

jnd ABBREVIATION FOR just noticeable difference.

Jnr ABBREVIATION FOR junior.

jo[1] *or* **joe** (dʒəʊ) NOUN, *plural* **joes.** a Scot word for **sweetheart.**
▷HISTORY C16: alteration of JOY

jo[2] THE INTERNET DOMAIN NAME FOR Jordan.

Joab (ˈdʒəʊæb) NOUN *Old Testament* the successful commander of King David's forces and the slayer of Abner and Absalom (II Samuel 2:18–23; 3:24–27; 18:14–15).

joannes (dʒəʊˈæniːz) NOUN, *plural* **-nes.** a variant of **johannes.**

João Pessoa (*Portuguese* ˈʒuəum peˈsoa) NOUN a port in NE Brazil, capital of Paraíba state. Pop.: 594 922 (2000).

job (dʒɒb) NOUN [1] an individual piece of work or task. [2] an occupation; post of employment. [3] an object worked on or a result produced from working. [4] a duty or responsibility: *her job was to cook the dinner.* [5] *Informal* a difficult task or problem: *I had a job to contact him.* [6] a state of affairs: *make the best of a bad job; it's a good job I saw you.* [7] *Informal* a damaging piece of work: *he really did a job on that.* [8] *Informal* a crime, esp a robbery or burglary. [9] *Informal* an article or specimen: *the new car was a nice little job.* [10] an instance of jobbery. [11] *Computing* a unit of work for a computer consisting of a single complete task submitted by a user. [12] **jobs for the boys.** appointments given to or created for allies or favourites. [13] **on the job. a** actively engaged in one's employment. **b** *Brit, taboo* engaged in sexual intercourse. [14] **just the job.** exactly what was required. ◆ VERB **jobs, jobbing, jobbed.** [15] (*intr*) to work by the piece or at casual jobs. [16] to make a private profit out of (a public office, etc.). [17] (*intr; usually foll by in*) **a** to buy and sell (goods or services) as a middleman: *he jobs in government surplus.* **b** *Brit* to buy and sell stocks and shares as a stockjobber: *he jobs in blue chips.* [18] (*tr;* often foll by *out*) to apportion (a contract, work, etc.) among several contractors, workers, etc.
▷HISTORY C16: of uncertain origin

Job (dʒəʊb) NOUN [1] *Old Testament* **a** a Jewish patriarch, who maintained his faith in God in spite of the afflictions sent by God to test him. **b** the book containing Job's pleas to God under these afflictions, attempted explanations of them by his friends, and God's reply to him. [2] any person who withstands great suffering without despairing.

job analysis NOUN the analysis of the contents of a job in order to provide a job description for such purposes as fitting the job into a grading structure or matching individual capabilities to job requirements.

jobber (ˈdʒɒbə) NOUN [1] *Brit* short for **stockjobber** (sense 1). [2] a person who jobs.

jobbery (ˈdʒɒbərɪ) NOUN the practice of making private profit out of a public office; corruption or graft.

jobbing (ˈdʒɒbɪŋ) ADJECTIVE working on occasional jobs or by the piece rather than in a regular job: *a jobbing gardener.*

jobbing printer NOUN one who prints mainly commercial and display work rather than books or newspapers.

Jobcentre (ˈdʒɒbˌsɛntə) NOUN *Brit* any of a number of government offices having premises usually situated in or near the main shopping area of a town in which people seeking jobs can consult displayed advertisements in informal surroundings.

Jobclub (ˈdʒɒbˌklʌb) NOUN a group of unemployed people organized through a Jobcentre, which meets every day and is given advice on job seeking to increase its members' chances of finding employment.

Job Corps (dʒɒb) NOUN *US* a Federal organization established in 1964 to train unemployed youths in order to make it easier for them to find work.

job description NOUN a detailed written account, agreed between management and worker, of all the duties and responsibilities which together make up a particular job.

job enlargement NOUN a widening of the range of tasks performed by an employee in order to provide variety in the activities undertaken.

job evaluation NOUN the analysis of the relationship between jobs in an organization: often used as a basis for a wages structure.

jobless (ˈdʒɒblɪs) ADJECTIVE **a** unemployed. **b** (*as collective noun; preceded by the*): *the jobless.*
▸ˈ**joblessness** NOUN

job lot NOUN [1] a miscellaneous collection of articles sold as a lot. [2] a collection of cheap or trivial items.

job rotation NOUN the practice of transferring an employee from one work station or activity to another during the working day in order to add variety to a job: often used in assembly line work.

job satisfaction NOUN the extent to which a person's hopes, desires, and expectations about the employment he is engaged in are fulfilled.

Job's comforter NOUN a person who, while purporting to give sympathy, succeeds only in adding to distress.

jobseeker's allowance (ˈdʒɒbˌsiːkəz) NOUN (in Britain) a National Insurance or social security payment for unemployed people; replaced unemployment benefit in 1996. Abbreviation: **JSA.**

job sharing NOUN the division of a job between two or more people such that each covers the same job for complementary parts of the day or week.
▸**job sharer** NOUN

Job's-tears NOUN [1] (*functioning as singular*) a tropical Asian grass, *Coix lacryma-jobi,* cultivated for its white beadlike modified leaves, which contain edible seeds. [2] (*functioning as plural*) the beadlike structures of this plant, used as rosary or ornamental beads.

jobsworth (ˈdʒɒbzˌwɜːθ) NOUN *Informal* a person in a position of minor authority who invokes the letter of the law in order to avoid any action requiring initiative, cooperation, etc.
▷HISTORY C20: from *it's more than my job's worth to ...*

Joburg (ˈdʒəʊˌbɜːg) NOUN *Informal* Johannesburg. See also **Josi.**

Jocasta (dʒəʊˈkæstə) NOUN *Greek myth* a queen of Thebes, the wife of Laius, who married Oedipus without either of them knowing he was her son.

jock (dʒɒk) NOUN [1] *Informal* short for **disc jockey.** [2] *Informal* short for **jockstrap.** [3] *US informal* an athlete. [4] *NZ, Mining* a pointed bar of steel inserted into the wheel of a mine vehicle and used for emergency braking.

Jock (dʒɒk) NOUN a slang word or term of address for a Scot.

jockey (ˈdʒɒkɪ) NOUN [1] a person who rides horses in races, esp as a profession or for hire. ◆ VERB [2] **a** (*tr*) to ride (a horse) in a race. **b** (*intr*) to ride as a jockey. [3] (*intr;* often foll by *for*) to try to obtain an advantage by manoeuvring, esp literally in a race or metaphorically, as in a struggle for power (esp in the phrase **jockey for position**). [4] to trick or cheat (a person).
▷HISTORY C16 (in the sense: lad): from name *Jock* + -EY

jockey cap NOUN a cap with a long peak projecting from the forehead.

Jockey Club NOUN *Brit* the governing body that regulates and controls horse-racing both on the flat and over jumps.

jocko (ˈdʒɒkəʊ) NOUN, *plural* **-os.** a W African name for **chimpanzee.**
▷HISTORY C19: from French, based on Bantu *ngeko*

jockstrap (ˈdʒɒkˌstræp) NOUN an elasticated belt with a pouch worn by men, esp athletes, to support the genitals. Also called: **athletic support.**
▷HISTORY C20: from slang *jock* penis + STRAP

jocose (dʒəˈkəʊs) ADJECTIVE characterized by humour; merry.
▷HISTORY C17: from Latin *jocōsus* given to jesting, from *jocus* JOKE
▸**joˈcosely** ADVERB ▸**joˈcoseness** *or* **jocosity** (dʒəˈkɒsɪtɪ) NOUN

jocular (ˈdʒɒkjʊlə) ADJECTIVE [1] characterized by joking and good humour. [2] meant lightly or humorously; facetious.
▷HISTORY C17: from Latin *joculāris,* from *joculus* little JOKE
▸**jocularity** (ˌdʒɒkjʊˈlærɪtɪ) NOUN ▸ˈ**jocularly** ADVERB

jocund (ˈdʒɒkənd) ADJECTIVE of a humorous temperament; merry.
▷HISTORY C14: from Late Latin *jocundus,* from Latin *jūcundus* pleasant, from *juvāre* to please
▸**jocundity** (dʒəʊˈkʌndɪtɪ) *or* ˈ**jocundness** NOUN
▸ˈ**jocundly** ADVERB

Jodhpur (ˌdʒɒdˈpʊə) NOUN [1] a former state of NW India, one of the W Rajputana states: now part of Rajasthan. [2] a walled city in NW India, in W Rajasthan: university (1962). Pop.: 666 279 (1991).

Jodhpuri (ˈdʒɒdpʊrɪ) ADJECTIVE of or relating to Jodhpur or its inhabitants.

Jodhpuri coat NOUN a coat worn by men in India, similar to but shorter than a sherwani.
▷HISTORY named after JODHPUR

jodhpurs (ˈdʒɒdpəz) PLURAL NOUN [1] riding breeches, loose-fitting around the hips and tight-fitting from the thighs to the ankles. [2] Also called: **jodhpur boots.** ankle-length leather riding boots.
▷HISTORY C19: from the town JODHPUR

Jodo (ˈdʒəʊˌdəʊ) NOUN a Japanese Buddhist sect teaching salvation through faith in Buddha.
▷HISTORY from Japanese

Jodrell Bank (ˈdʒɒdrəl) NOUN an astronomical observatory in NW England, in Cheshire: radio telescope with a steerable parabolic dish, 75 m (250 ft.) in diameter.

Joe (dʒəʊ) NOUN (*sometimes not capital*) *Slang* [1] *US and Canadian* a man or fellow. [2] *US* a GI; soldier.

Joe Blake NOUN *Austral* [1] *Rhyming slang* a snake. [2] **the Joe Blakes.** the DT's.

Joe Bloggs (blɒgz) NOUN *Brit, slang* an average or typical man. US, Canadian, and Austral equivalent: **Joe Blow.** See also **Joe Six-Pack.**

Joel (ˈdʒəʊəl) NOUN *Old Testament* [1] a Hebrew prophet. [2] the book containing his oracles.

Joe Public NOUN *Slang* the general public.

joe-pye weed (ˈdʒəʊˈpaɪ) NOUN *US and Canadian* any of several North American plants of the genus *Eupatorium*, esp *E. purpureum*, having pale purplish clusters of flower heads lacking rays: family *Asteraceae* (composites).
▷HISTORY C19: of unknown origin

joes (dʒəʊz) PLURAL NOUN *Austral informal* **the.** a fit of depression.
▷HISTORY short for *the Joe Blakes*

Joe Six-Pack (ˈsɪks,pæk) NOUN *US, slang* an average or typical man.

Joe Soap NOUN [1] *Brit, slang* a person who is regarded as unintelligent and imposed upon as a stooge or scapegoat. [2] the NZ term for **Joe Bloggs.**

joey (ˈdʒəʊɪ) NOUN *Austral informal* [1] a young kangaroo or possum. [2] a young animal or child.
▷HISTORY C19: from a native Australian language

Joey Hooker (ˈdʒəʊɪ ˈhʊkə) NOUN another name for **gallant soldier** (a plant).

jog¹ (dʒɒg) VERB **jogs, jogging, jogged.** [1] (*intr*) to run or move slowly or at a jog trot, esp for physical exercise. [2] (*intr;* foll by *on* or *along*) to continue in a plodding way. [3] (*tr*) to jar or nudge slightly; shake lightly. [4] (*tr*) to remind; stimulate: *please jog my memory.* [5] (*tr*) *Printing* to even up the edges of (a stack of paper); square up. ◆ NOUN [6] the act of jogging. [7] a slight jar or nudge. [8] a jogging motion; trot.
▷HISTORY C14: probably variant of *shog* to shake, influenced by dialect *jot* to jolt

jog² (dʒɒg) NOUN *US and Canadian* [1] a sharp protruding point in a surface; jag. [2] a sudden change in course or direction.
▷HISTORY C18: probably variant of JAG¹

jogger (ˈdʒɒgə) NOUN [1] a person who runs at a jog trot over some distance for exercise, usually regularly. [2] *NZ* a cart with rubber-tyred wheels used on a farm.

jogger's nipple NOUN *Informal* painful inflammation of the nipple, caused by friction with a garment when running for long distances.

jogging (ˈdʒɒgɪŋ) NOUN running at a slow regular pace usually over a long distance as part of an exercise routine.

joggle (ˈdʒɒgᵊl) VERB [1] to shake or move (someone or something) with a slightly jolting motion. [2] (*tr*) to join or fasten (two pieces of building material) by means of a joggle. ◆ NOUN [3] the act of joggling. [4] a slight irregular shake; jolt. [5] a joint between two pieces of building material by means of a projection on one piece that fits into a notch in the other; dowel. [6] a shoulder designed to take the thrust of a strut or brace.
▷HISTORY C16: frequentative of JOG¹
▸ˈ**joggler** NOUN

joggle post NOUN a post or beam consisting of two timbers joined to each other by joggles.

Jogjakarta (ˌdʒəʊgjɑːˈkɑːtɑː, ˌdʒɒg-) NOUN a variant spelling of **Yogyakarta.**

jog trot NOUN [1] an easy bouncy gait, esp of a horse, midway between a walk and a trot. [2] a monotonous or regular way of living or doing something. ◆ VERB **jog-trot, -trots, -trotting, -trotted.** [3] (*intr*) to move at a jog trot.

johannes (dʒəʊˈhæniːz) *or* **joannes** NOUN, *plural* **-nes.** a Portuguese gold coin minted in the early 18th century.
▷HISTORY C18: after *Joannes* (King John V) of Portugal, whose name was inscribed on the coin

Johannesburg (dʒəʊˈhænɪsˌbɜːg) NOUN a city in N South Africa, in Gauteng province: South Africa's largest city and chief industrial centre; grew with the establishment in 1886 of the gold-mining industry; University of Witwatersrand (1922). Pop.: 1 480 530 (1996).

john (dʒɒn) NOUN [1] *Chiefly US and Canadian* a slang word for **lavatory** (sense 1). [2] *Slang, chiefly US* a prostitute's client. [3] *Austral, slang* short for **John Hop.**
▷HISTORY C20: special use of the proper name

John Barleycorn NOUN *Usually humorous* the personification of alcoholic drink, esp of malt spirits.

John Birch Society NOUN *US Politics* a fanatical right-wing association organized along semisecret lines to fight Communism.
▷HISTORY C20: named after *John Birch* (killed by Chinese communists 1945), American USAF captain whom its members regarded as the first cold-war casualty

John Bull NOUN [1] a personification of England or the English people. [2] a typical Englishman.
▷HISTORY C18: name of a character intended to be representative of the English nation in *The History of John Bull* (1712) by John Arbuthnot
▸**John Bullish** ADJECTIVE ▸**John Bullishness** NOUN ▸**John Bullism** NOUN

John Doe NOUN See **Doe.**

John Dory (ˈdɔːrɪ) NOUN [1] a European dory (the fish), *Zeus faber,* having a deep compressed body, spiny dorsal fins, and massive mobile jaws. [2] *Austral* a related fish, *Zeus australis*, which is a valued food fish of Australia.
▷HISTORY C18: from proper name *John* + DORY¹; on the model of DOE

Johne's disease (ˈjəʊnəz) NOUN an infectious disease of ruminants characterized by chronic inflammation of the bowel and caused by *Mycobacterium paratuberculosis*, a bacterium that can be transmitted in milk.
▷HISTORY C20: named after H. A. *Johne* (1839–1910), German veterinary surgeon

John Hancock NOUN *US and Canadian informal* a person's signature: *put your John Hancock on this form.* Also called: **John Henry.**
▷HISTORY after *John Hancock* (1737–93), American statesman, from his clear and legible signature on the American Declaration of Independence

John Hop NOUN *Austral, slang* a policeman.
▷HISTORY rhyming slang for COP¹

johnny (ˈdʒɒnɪ) NOUN, *plural* **-nies.** *Brit* [1] (*often capital*) *Informal* a man or boy; chap. [2] a slang word for **condom.**

johnny cake *or* **johnny-cake** NOUN [1] *US* a type of thin flat corn bread baked on a griddle. [2] *Austral* a thin cake of flour and water paste cooked in the ashes of a fire or in a pan.

Johnny Canuck (ˈdʒɒnɪ kəˈnʌk) NOUN *Canadian* [1] an informal name for a **Canadian.** [2] a personification of Canada.

Johnny-come-lately NOUN, *plural* **Johnny-come-latelies** *or* **Johnnies-come-lately.** a brash newcomer, novice, or recruit.

Johnny-jump-up NOUN *US and Canadian* any of several violaceous plants, esp the wild pansy.
▷HISTORY C19: so called from its quick growth

Johnny raw NOUN *Slang* a novice; new recruit.

Johnny Reb NOUN *US informal* (in the American Civil War) a Confederate soldier.
▷HISTORY C19: from REBEL (n)

John o'Groats (əˈgrəʊts) NOUN a village at the northeasternmost tip of the Scottish mainland: considered to be the northernmost point of the mainland of Great Britain although Dunnet Head, slightly to the west, lies further north. See also **Land's End.**

Johnson grass NOUN a persistent perennial Mediterranean grass, *Sorghum halepense,* cultivated for hay and pasture in the US where it also grows as a weed. See also **sorghum.**
▷HISTORY C19: named after William *Johnson* (died 1859), American agriculturalist who introduced it

Johnsonian (dʒɒnˈsəʊnɪən) ADJECTIVE of, relating to, or characteristic of the British lexicographer, critic, poet, and conversationalist Samuel *Johnson* (1709–84), his works, or his style of writing.

John Thomas NOUN a slang name for **penis.**

Johore (dʒəʊˈhɔː) NOUN a state of Malaysia, on the S Malay Peninsula: mostly forested, with large swamps; bauxite- and iron-mining. Capital: Johore Bahru. Pop.: 2 565 701 (2000). Area: 18 984 sq. km (7330 sq. miles).

Johore Bahru (ˈbɑːruː) NOUN a city in S Malaysia, capital of Johore state: important trading centre, situated at the sole crossing point of **Johore Strait** (between Malaya and Singapore Island). Pop.: 328 646 (1991).

joie de vivre *French* (ʒwa də vivrə) NOUN joy of living; enjoyment of life; ebullience.

join (dʒɔɪn) VERB [1] to come or bring together; connect. [2] to become a member of (a club, organization, etc.). [3] (*intr; often foll by with*) to become associated or allied. [4] (*intr;* usually foll by *in*) to take part. [5] (*tr*) to meet (someone) as a companion. [6] (*tr*) to become part of; take a place in or with. [7] (*tr*) to unite (two people) in marriage. [8] (*tr*) *Geometry* to connect with a straight line or a curve. [9] (*tr*) an informal word for **adjoin.** [10] **join battle.** to start fighting. [11] **join duty.** *Indian* to report for work after a period of leave or a strike. [12] **join hands. a** to hold one's own hands together. **b** (of two people) to hold each other's hands. **c** (usually foll by *with*) to work together in an enterprise or task. ◆ NOUN [13] a joint; seam. [14] the act of joining. [15] *Maths* another name for **union** (sense 9). ◆ See also **join up.**
▷HISTORY C13: from Old French *joindre* from Latin *jungere* to yoke
▸ˈ**joinable** ADJECTIVE

joinder (ˈdʒɔɪndə) NOUN [1] the act of joining, esp in legal contexts. [2] *Law* **a** (in pleading) the stage at which the parties join issue (**joinder of issue**). **b** the joining of two or more persons as coplaintiffs or codefendants (**joinder of parties**). **c** the joining of two or more causes in one suit.
▷HISTORY C17: from French *joindre* to JOIN

joined-up ADJECTIVE [1] with all departments or sections communicating efficiently with each other and acting together purposefully and effectively: *joined-up government.* [2] **a** focusing on or producing an integrated and coherent result, strategy, etc.: *joined-up thinking.* **b** forming an integrated and coherent whole: *joined-up policies.*

joiner (ˈdʒɔɪnə) NOUN [1] *Chiefly Brit* a person trained and skilled in making finished woodwork, such as windows, doors, and stairs. [2] a person or thing that joins. [3] *Informal* a person who joins many clubs, causes, etc.

joinery (ˈdʒɔɪnərɪ) NOUN [1] the skill or craft of a joiner. [2] work made by a joiner.

joint (dʒɔɪnt) NOUN [1] a junction of two or more parts or objects. [2] the part or space between two such junctions. [3] *Anatomy* the junction between two or more bones, usually formed of connective tissue and cartilage. [4] the point of connection between movable parts in invertebrates, esp insects and other arthropods. Related adjective: **articular.** [5] the part of a plant stem from which a branch or leaf grows. [6] one of the parts into which a carcass of meat is cut by the butcher, esp for roasting. [7] *Geology* a crack in a rock along which no displacement has occurred. [8] *Slang* **a** a disreputable establishment, such as a bar or nightclub. **b** *Often facetious* a dwelling or meeting place. [9] *Slang* a cannabis cigarette. [10] **out of joint. a** dislocated. **b** out of order or disorganized. [11] **put someone's nose out of joint.** See **nose** (sense 18). ◆ ADJECTIVE [12] shared by or belonging to two or more: *joint property.* [13] created by combined effort. [14] sharing with others or with one another: *joint rulers.* [15] *Law* (of persons) combined in ownership or obligation; regarded as a single entity in law. ◆ VERB (*tr*) [16] to provide with or fasten by a joint or joints. [17] to plane the edge of (a board, etc.) into the correct shape for a joint. [18] to cut or divide (meat, fowl, etc.) into joints or at a joint.
▸ˈ**jointly** ADVERB

joint account NOUN a bank account registered in the name of two or more persons, any of whom may make deposits and withdrawals.

joint consultation NOUN a formal system of communication between the management of an organization and the employees' representatives used prior to taking decisions affecting the workforce, usually effected through a joint consultative committee.

joint density function NOUN *Statistics* a function of two or more random variables from which can be obtained a single probability that all the variables in the function will take specified values or fall within specified intervals.

jointed (ˈdʒɔɪntɪd) ADJECTIVE [1] **a** having a joint or joints. **b** (*in combination*): *large-jointed*. [2] (of a plant stem or similar part) marked with constrictions, at which the stem breaks into separate portions.
▸ **ˈjointedly** ADVERB ▸ **ˈjointedness** NOUN

jointer (ˈdʒɔɪntə) NOUN [1] a tool for pointing mortar joints, as in brickwork. [2] Also called: **jointing plane.** a long plane for shaping the edges of planks so that they can be fitted together. [3] a person or thing that makes joints.

joint resolution NOUN *US* a resolution passed by both houses of a bicameral legislature, signed by the chief executive and legally binding.

jointress (ˈdʒɔɪntrɪs) NOUN *Law* a woman entitled to a jointure.

joint stock NOUN capital funds held in common and usually divided into shares between the owners.

joint-stock company NOUN [1] *Brit* a business enterprise characterized by its separate legal existence and the sharing of ownership between shareholders, whose liability is limited. [2] *US* a business enterprise whose owners are issued shares of transferable stock but do not enjoy limited liability.

jointure (ˈdʒɔɪntʃə) NOUN [1] *Law* **a** a provision made by a husband for his wife by settling property upon her at marriage for her use after his death. **b** the property so settled. [2] *Obsolete* the act of joining or the condition of being joined.
▷ **HISTORY** C14: from Old French, from Latin *junctūra* a joining

jointworm (ˈdʒɔɪntˌwɜːm) NOUN *US* the larva of chalcid flies of the genus *Harmolita*, esp *H. tritici*, which form galls on the stems of cereal plants.

join up VERB (*adverb*) [1] (*intr*) to become a member of a military or other organization; enlist. [2] (often foll by *with*) to unite or connect.

joist (dʒɔɪst) NOUN [1] a beam made of timber, steel, or reinforced concrete, used in the construction of floors, roofs, etc. See also **rolled-steel joist.** ◆ VERB [2] (*tr*) to construct (a floor, roof, etc.) with joists.
▷ **HISTORY** C14: from Old French *giste* beam supporting a bridge, from Vulgar Latin *jacitum* (unattested) support, from *jacēre* to lie

jojoba (həʊˈhəʊbə) NOUN a shrub or small tree of SW North America, *Simmondsia californica*, that has edible seeds containing a valuable oil used in cosmetics.
▷ **HISTORY** Mexican Spanish

joke (dʒəʊk) NOUN [1] a humorous anecdote. [2] something that is said or done for fun; prank. [3] a ridiculous or humorous circumstance. [4] a person or thing inspiring ridicule or amusement; butt. [5] a matter to be joked about or ignored. [6] **joking apart.** seriously: said to recall a discussion to seriousness after there has been joking. [7] **no joke.** something very serious. ◆ VERB [8] (*intr*) to tell jokes. [9] (*intr*) to speak or act facetiously or in fun. [10] to make fun of (someone); tease; kid.
▷ **HISTORY** C17: from Latin *jocus* a jest
▸ **ˈjokingly** ADVERB

joker (ˈdʒəʊkə) NOUN [1] a person who jokes, esp in an obnoxious manner. [2] *Slang, often derogatory* a person: *who does that joker think he is?* [3] an extra playing card in a pack, which in many card games can substitute for or rank above any other card. [4] *Chiefly US* a clause or phrase inserted in a legislative bill in order to make the bill inoperative or to alter its apparent effect.

jokey *or* **joky** (ˈdʒəʊkɪ) ADJECTIVE **jokier, jokiest.** intended as a joke; full of jokes.

Jokjakarta (ˌdʒəʊkjɑːˈkɑːtɑː, ˌdʒɒk-) NOUN a variant spelling of **Yogyakarta.**

jol (dʒɒl) *South African, slang* ◆ NOUN [1] a party. ◆ VERB **jolling, jolled.** [2] (*intr*) to have a good time.

jolie laide *French* (ʒɔli lɛd) NOUN, *plural* ***jolies laides*** (ʒɔli lɛd). a woman whose ugliness forms her chief fascination.
▷ **HISTORY** literally: pretty (attractive) ugly woman

jollification (ˌdʒɒlɪfɪˈkeɪʃən) NOUN a merry festivity.

jollify (ˈdʒɒlɪˌfaɪ) VERB **-fies, -fying, -fied.** to be or cause to be jolly.

jollities (ˈdʒɒlɪtɪz) PLURAL NOUN *Brit* a party or celebration.

jollity (ˈdʒɒlɪtɪ) NOUN, *plural* **-ties.** the condition of being jolly.

jollop (ˈdʒɒləp) NOUN *Brit informal* a cream or unguent.
▷ **HISTORY** C20: from French *jalap*, from Spanish *jalapa*, from *purga de Jalapa* purge of Jalapa, Jalapa being a city in Mexico

jolly (ˈdʒɒlɪ) ADJECTIVE **-lier, -liest.** [1] full of good humour; jovial. [2] having or provoking gaiety and merrymaking; festive. [3] greatly enjoyable; pleasing. ◆ ADVERB [4] *Brit* (intensifier): *you're jolly nice.* ◆ VERB **-lies, -lying, -lied.** (*tr*) *Informal* [5] (often foll by *up* or *along*) to try to make or keep (someone) cheerful. [6] to make goodnatured fun of. ◆ NOUN [7] *Informal, chiefly Brit* a festivity or celebration. [8] *Informal, chiefly Brit* a trip, esp one made for pleasure by a public official or committee at public expense. [9] *Brit, slang* a Royal Marine.
▷ **HISTORY** C14: from Old French *jolif*, probably from Old Norse *jōl* YULE
▸ **ˈjolliness** NOUN

jolly boat NOUN [1] a small boat used as a utility tender for a vessel. [2] a small sailing boat used for pleasure.
▷ **HISTORY** C18: *jolly* probably from Danish *jolle* YAWL[1]

Jolly Jumper NOUN *Trademark, Canadian* a type of fixed sprung baby harness in which an infant may be placed and allowed to bounce up and down for exercise.

Jolly Roger NOUN the traditional pirate flag, consisting of a white skull and crossbones on a black field.

Jolo (həʊˈləʊ) NOUN an island in the SW Philippines: the main island of the Sulu Archipelago. Pop.: 360 590 (latest est.). Area: 893 sq. km (345 sq. miles).

jolt (dʒəʊlt) VERB (*tr*) [1] to bump against with a jarring blow; jostle. [2] to move in a jolting manner. [3] to surprise or shock. ◆ NOUN [4] a sudden jar or blow. [5] an emotional shock.
▷ **HISTORY** C16: probably blend of dialect *jot* to jerk and dialect *joll* to bump
▸ **ˈjolter** NOUN ▸ **ˈjoltingly** ADVERB ▸ **ˈjolty** ADJECTIVE

Jon. *Bible* ABBREVIATION FOR Jonah.

Jonah (ˈdʒəʊnə) *or* **Jonas** (ˈdʒəʊnəs) NOUN [1] *Old Testament* **a** a Hebrew prophet who, having been thrown overboard from a ship in which he was fleeing from God, was swallowed by a great fish and vomited onto dry land. **b** the book in which his adventures are recounted. [2] a person believed to bring bad luck to those around him; a jinx.
▸ **ˌJonahˈesque** ADJECTIVE

Jonathan[1] (ˈdʒɒnəθən) NOUN a variety of red apple that ripens in early autumn.
▷ **HISTORY** C19: named after *Jonathan* Hasbrouk (died 1846), American jurist

Jonathan[2] NOUN *Old Testament* the son of Saul and David's close friend, who was killed in battle (I Samuel 31; II Samuel 1:19–26).

jong (jɒŋ) NOUN *South African informal* a friend, often used in direct address.
▷ **HISTORY** from Afrikaans

jongleur (*French* ʒɔ̃glœr) NOUN (in medieval France) an itinerant minstrel.
▷ **HISTORY** C18: from Old French *jogleour*, from Latin *joculātor* joker, jester; see JUGGLE

Jönköping (*Swedish* ˈjœntçøːpiŋ) NOUN a city in S Sweden, on the S shore of Lake Vättern: scene of the conclusion of peace between Sweden and Denmark in 1809. Pop.: 116 344 (2004 est.).

jonnock (ˈdʒɒnək) *or* **jannock** (ˈdʒænək) *Dialect* ◆ ADJECTIVE [1] (*usually postpositive*) genuine; real. ◆ ADVERB [2] honestly; truly; genuinely.
▷ **HISTORY** of uncertain origin

jonquil (ˈdʒɒŋkwɪl) NOUN [1] a Eurasian amaryllidaceous plant, *Narcissus jonquilla* with long fragrant yellow or white short-tubed flowers. [2] any of various other small daffodil-like plants.
▷ **HISTORY** C17: from French *jonquille*, from Spanish *junquillo*, diminutive of *junco* reed; see JUNCO

jook (dʒʊk) *or* **chook** *Caribbean informal* ◆ VERB [1] (*tr*) to poke or puncture (the skin). ◆ NOUN [2] a jab or the resulting wound.
▷ **HISTORY** C20: of uncertain origin

Joppa (ˈdʒɒpə) NOUN the biblical name of **Jaffa**, the port from which Jonah embarked (Jonah 1:3)

Jordan (ˈdʒɔːdᵊn) NOUN [1] a kingdom in SW Asia: coextensive with the biblical Moab, Gilead, and Edom; made a League of Nations mandate and emirate under British control in 1922 and became an independent kingdom in 1946; territories west of the River Jordan and the Jordanian part of Jerusalem (intended to be part of an autonomous Palestine) were occupied by Israel after the war of 1967. It contains part of the Great Rift Valley and consists mostly of desert. Official language: Arabic. Official religion: (Sunni) Muslim. Currency: dinar. Capital: Amman. Pop.: 5 132 000 (2001 est.). Area: 89 185 sq. km (34 434 sq. miles). Official name: **Hashemite Kingdom of Jordan.** Former name (1922–49): **Trans-Jordan.** [2] the chief and only perennial river of Israel and Jordan, rising in several headstreams in Syria and Lebanon, and flowing south through the Sea of Galilee to the Dead Sea: occupies the N end of the Great Rift Valley system and lies mostly below sea level. Length: over 320 km (200 miles).

Jordan almond NOUN [1] a large variety of Spanish almond used in confectionery. [2] a sugar-coated almond.
▷ **HISTORY** C15: by folk etymology from earlier *jardyne almaund*, literally: garden almond, from Old French *jardin* GARDEN

Jordanian (dʒɔːˈdeɪnɪən) ADJECTIVE [1] of or relating to Jordan or its inhabitants. ◆ NOUN [2] a native or inhabitant of Jordan.

jorum (ˈdʒɔːrəm) NOUN a large drinking bowl or vessel or its contents: *a jorum of punch.*
▷ **HISTORY** C18: probably named after *Jorum*, who brought vessels of silver, gold, and brass to King David (II Samuel 8:10)

Jos (dʒɒs) NOUN a city in central Nigeria, capital of Plateau state on the **Jos Plateau:** major centre of the tin-mining industry. Pop.: 206 300 (1996 est.).

joseph (ˈdʒəʊzɪf) NOUN a woman's floor-length riding coat with a small cape, worn esp in the 18th century.
▷ **HISTORY** perhaps from the story of Joseph and his long coat (Genesis 37:3)

Joseph Bonaparte Gulf NOUN an inlet of the Timor Sea in N Australia. Width: 360 km (225 miles).

Joseph of Arimathea (ˌærɪməˈθɪːə) NOUN **Saint.** *New Testament* a wealthy member of the Sanhedrin, who obtained the body of Jesus after the Crucifixion and laid it in his own tomb (Matthew 27:57–60). Feast day: Mar. 17 or July 31.

Josephson effect (ˈdʒəʊzɪfsən) NOUN *Physics* any one of the phenomena which occur when an electric current passes through a very thin insulating layer between two superconducting substances. The applications include the very precise standardization of the volt.
▷ **HISTORY** C20: named after Brian David *Josephson* (born 1940), English physicist; shared the Nobel prize for physics in 1973

josh (dʒɒʃ) *Slang* ◆ VERB [1] to tease (someone) in a bantering way. ◆ NOUN [2] a teasing or bantering joke.
▷ **HISTORY** C19: perhaps from JOKE, influenced by BOSH[1]
▸ **ˈjosher** NOUN

Josh. *Bible* ABBREVIATION FOR Joshua.

Joshua (ˈdʒɒʃʊə) NOUN *Old Testament* [1] Moses' successor, who led the Israelites in the conquest of Canaan. [2] the book recounting his deeds. Douay spelling: **Josue** (ˈdʒɒsjuːɪ).

Joshua tree NOUN a treelike desert yucca plant, *Yucca brevifolia*, of the southwestern US, with sword-shaped leaves and greenish-white flowers.
▷ **HISTORY** named after the prophet *Joshua*, alluding to the extended branches of the tree

Josi (ˈdʒəʊsɪ) NOUN *South African informal* Johannesburg. See also **Joburg.**

Josiah (dʒəʊˈsaɪə) NOUN died ?609 B.C., king of Judah (?640–?609). After the discovery of a book of law (probably Deuteronomy) in the Temple he began a programme of religious reform. Douay spelling: **Josias** (dʒəʊˈsaɪəs).

joss (dʒɒs) NOUN a Chinese deity worshipped in the form of an idol.
▷ **HISTORY** C18: from pidgin English, from Portuguese *deos* god, from Latin *deus*

josser (ˈdʒɒsə) NOUN *Slang* [1] *Brit* a simpleton; fool. [2] *Brit* a fellow; chap. [3] *Austral* a clergyman.
▷ **HISTORY** C19: from JOSS + -ER[1]

joss house NOUN a Chinese temple or shrine where an idol or idols are worshipped.

joss stick NOUN a stick of dried perfumed paste, giving off a fragrant odour when burnt as incense.

jostle ('dʒɒsəl) VERB [1] to bump or push (someone) roughly. [2] to come or bring into contact. [3] to force (one's way) by pushing. ◆ NOUN [4] the act of jostling. [5] a rough bump or push.
▷HISTORY C14: see JOUST
▸'**jostlement** NOUN ▸'**jostler** NOUN

jot (dʒɒt) VERB **jots, jotting, jotted.** [1] (*tr; usually foll by down*) to write a brief note of. ◆ NOUN [2] (*used with a negative*) a little bit (in phrases such as **not to care** (*or* **give**) **a jot**).
▷HISTORY C16: from Latin *jota,* from Greek *iōta,* of Semitic origin; see IOTA

jota (*Spanish* 'ɔxta) NOUN a Spanish dance with castanets in fast triple time, usually to a guitar and voice accompaniment.
▷HISTORY Spanish, probably modification of Old Spanish *sota,* from *sotar* to dance, from Latin *saltāre*

jotter ('dʒɒtə) NOUN a small notebook.

jotting ('dʒɒtɪŋ) NOUN something jotted down.

Jotun *or* **Jotunn** ('jɔːtʊn) NOUN *Norse myth* any of a race of giants.
▷HISTORY from Old Norse *jötunn* giant; related to EAT

Jotunheim *or* **Jotunnheim** ('jɔːtʊnˌheɪm) NOUN *Norse myth* the home of the giants in the northeast of Asgard.
▷HISTORY from Old Norse, from *jötunn* giant + *heimr* world, HOME

joual (ʒwɑːl) NOUN nonstandard Canadian French dialect, esp as associated with ill-educated speakers.
▷HISTORY from the pronunciation in this dialect of French *cheval* horse

jougs (dʒʊgz) PLURAL NOUN *Scot history* an iron ring, fastened by a chain to a wall, post, or tree, in which an offender was held by the neck: common in Scotland from the 16th to 18th century.
▷HISTORY C16: probably from French *joug* yoke

jouk (dʒʊk) *Scot* ◆ VERB [1] to duck or dodge. ◆ NOUN [2] a sudden evasive movement.
▷HISTORY C16: of uncertain origin

joule (dʒuːl) NOUN the derived SI unit of work or energy; the work done when the point of application of a force of 1 newton is displaced through a distance of 1 metre in the direction of the force. 1 joule is equivalent to 1 watt-second, 10^7 ergs, 0.2390 calories, or 0.738 foot-pound. Symbol: J.
▷HISTORY C19: named after James Prescott *Joule* (1818–89), English physicist

Joule effect NOUN *Physics* [1] the production of heat as the result of a current flowing through a conductor. Also called: **Joule heating.** See **Joule's law.** [2] an increase in length of certain ferromagnetic materials when longitudinally magnetized.
▷HISTORY C20: named after James Prescott *Joule* (1818–89), English physicist

Joule's law NOUN [1] *Physics* the principle that the heat produced by an electric current is equal to the product of the resistance of the conductor, the square of the current, and the time for which it flows. [2] *Thermodynamics* the principle that at constant temperature the internal energy of an ideal gas is independent of volume. Real gases change their internal energy with volume as a result of intermolecular forces.
▷HISTORY C19: named after James Prescott *Joule* (1818–89), English physicist

Joule-Thomson effect NOUN a change in temperature of a thermally insulated gas when it is forced through a small hole or a porous material. For each gas there is a temperature of inversion above which the change is positive and below which it is negative. Also called: **Joule-Kelvin effect.**
▷HISTORY C20: named after James Prescott *Joule* (1818–89), English physicist, and Sir William *Thomson,* 1st Baron Kelvin (1824–1907), British physicist

jounce (dʒaʊns) VERB [1] to shake or jolt or cause to shake or jolt; bounce. ◆ NOUN [2] a jolting movement; shake; bump.
▷HISTORY C15: probably a blend of dialect *joll* to bump + BOUNCE

journal ('dʒɜːnəl) NOUN [1] a newspaper or periodical. [2] a book in which a daily record of happenings, etc., is kept. [3] an official record of the proceedings of a legislative body. [4] *Book-keeping* **a** one of several books in which transactions are initially recorded to facilitate subsequent entry in the ledger. **b** another name for **daybook.** [5] the part of a shaft or axle in contact with or enclosed by a bearing. [6] a plain cylindrical bearing to support a shaft or axle.
▷HISTORY C14: from Old French: daily, from Latin *diurnālis;* see DIURNAL

journal box NOUN *Machinery* a case enclosing or supporting a journal, often used as a means of retaining the lubricant.

journalese (ˌdʒɜːnəˈliːz) NOUN *Derogatory* a superficial cliché-ridden style of writing regarded as typical of newspapers.

journalism ('dʒɜːnəˌlɪzəm) NOUN [1] the profession or practice of reporting about, photographing, or editing news stories for one of the mass media. [2] newspapers and magazines collectively; the press. [3] the material published in a newspaper, magazine, etc.: *this is badly written journalism.* [4] news reports presented factually without analysis.

journalist ('dʒɜːnəlɪst) NOUN [1] a person whose occupation is journalism. [2] a person who keeps a journal.

journalistic (ˌdʒɜːnəˈlɪstɪk) ADJECTIVE of, relating to, or characteristic of journalism or journalists.
▸ˌ**journal'istically** ADVERB

journalize *or* **journalise** ('dʒɜːnəˌlaɪz) VERB to record (daily events) in a journal.
▸ˌ**journali'zation** *or* ˌ**journali'sation** NOUN ▸'**journal**ˌ**izer** *or* '**journal**ˌ**iser** NOUN

journey ('dʒɜːnɪ) NOUN [1] a travelling from one place to another; trip or voyage. [2] **a** the distance travelled in a journey. **b** the time taken to make a journey. ◆ VERB [3] (*intr*) to make a journey.
▷HISTORY C13: from Old French *journee* a day, a day's travelling, from Latin *diurnum* day's portion; see DIURNAL
▸'**journeyer** NOUN

journeyman ('dʒɜːnɪmən) NOUN, *plural* **-men.** [1] a craftsman, artisan, etc., who is qualified to work at his trade in the employment of another. [2] a competent workman. [3] (formerly) a worker hired on a daily wage.
▷HISTORY C15: from JOURNEY (in obsolete sense: a day's work) + MAN

journeywork ('dʒɜːnɪˌwɜːk) NOUN *Rare* [1] necessary, routine, and menial work. [2] the work of a journeyman.

journo ('dʒɜːnəʊ) NOUN, *plural* **journos.** a journalist.

joust (dʒaʊst) *History* ◆ NOUN [1] a combat between two mounted knights tilting against each other with lances. A tournament consisted of a series of such engagements. ◆ VERB [2] (*intr; often foll by against* or *with*) to encounter or engage in such a tournament: *he jousted with five opponents.*
▷HISTORY C13: from Old French *jouste,* from *jouster* to fight on horseback, from Vulgar Latin *juxtāre* (unattested) to come together, from Latin *juxtā* close
▸'**jouster** NOUN

j'ouvert ('ʒuːvɛət) NOUN *Chiefly Caribbean* the eve of Mardi gras; the Monday morning on which the festivities begin.
▷HISTORY from French *jour ouvert* the day having been opened

Jove (dʒəʊv) NOUN [1] another name for **Jupiter**[1]. [2] **by Jove.** an exclamation of surprise or excitement.
▷HISTORY C14: from Old Latin *Jovis* Jupiter

jovial ('dʒəʊvɪəl) ADJECTIVE having or expressing convivial humour; jolly.
▷HISTORY C16: from Latin *joviālis* of (the planet) Jupiter, considered by astrologers to foster good humour
▸ˌ**jovi'ality** *or* '**jovialness** NOUN ▸'**jovially** ADVERB

Jovian ('dʒəʊvɪən) ADJECTIVE [1] of or relating to the god Jove (Jupiter). [2] of, occurring on, or relating to the planet Jupiter. [3] of or relating to the giant planets Jupiter, Saturn, Uranus, and Neptune: *the Jovian planets.*
▷HISTORY C16: from Old Latin *Jovis* Jupiter

jowl[1] (dʒaʊl) NOUN [1] the jaw, esp the lower one. [2] (*often plural*) a cheek, esp a prominent one. [3] **cheek by jowl.** See **cheek** (sense 7).
▷HISTORY Old English *ceafl* jaw; related to Middle High German *kivel,* Old Norse *kjaptr*
▸**jowled** ADJECTIVE

jowl[2] (dʒaʊl) NOUN [1] fatty flesh hanging from the lower jaw. [2] a similar fleshy part in animals, such as the wattle of a fowl or the dewlap of a bull.
▷HISTORY Old English *ceole* throat; compare Old High German *kela*

joy (dʒɔɪ) NOUN [1] a deep feeling or condition of happiness or contentment. [2] something causing such a feeling; a source of happiness. [3] an outward show of pleasure or delight; rejoicing. [4] *Brit informal* success; satisfaction: *I went to the bank for a loan, but got no joy.* ◆ VERB [5] (*intr*) to feel joy. [6] (*tr*) *Obsolete* to make joyful; gladden.
▷HISTORY C13: from Old French *joie,* from Latin *gaudium* joy, from *gaudēre* to be glad

joyance ('dʒɔɪəns) NOUN *Archaic* a joyous feeling or festivity.

Joycean ('dʒɔɪsɪən) ADJECTIVE [1] of, relating to, or like, the Irish novelist and short-story writer James Joyce (1882–1941) or his works. ◆ NOUN [2] a student or admirer of Joyce or his works.

joyful ('dʒɔɪfʊl) ADJECTIVE [1] full of joy; elated. [2] expressing or producing joy: *a joyful look; a joyful occasion.*
▸'**joyfully** ADVERB ▸'**joyfulness** NOUN

joyless ('dʒɔɪlɪs) ADJECTIVE having or producing no joy or pleasure.
▸'**joylessly** ADVERB ▸'**joylessness** NOUN

joyous ('dʒɔɪəs) ADJECTIVE [1] having a happy nature or mood. [2] joyful.
▸'**joyously** ADVERB ▸'**joyousness** NOUN

joypop ('dʒɔɪˌpɒp) VERB **-pops, -popping, -popped.** (*intr*) *Slang* to take addictive drugs occasionally without becoming addicted.

joyride NOUN [1] a ride taken for pleasure in a car, esp in a stolen car driven recklessly. ◆ VERB **joy-ride, -rides, -riding, -rode, -ridden.** [2] (*intr*) to take such a ride.
▸'**joy**ˌ**rider** NOUN ▸'**joy**ˌ**riding** NOUN

joystick ('dʒɔɪˌstɪk) NOUN [1] *Informal* the control stick of an aircraft or of any of various machines. [2] *Computing* a lever by means of which the display on a screen may be controlled, used esp for games, flight simulators, etc.

jp THE INTERNET DOMAIN NAME FOR Japan.

JP ABBREVIATION FOR Justice of the Peace.

JPEG ('dʒeɪˌpɛg) NOUN *Computing* a standard file format for compressing pictures by disposing of redundant pixels.
▷HISTORY C20: technique devised by the *J(oint) P(hotographic) E(xperts) G(roup)*

J/psi particle NOUN a type of elementary particle (meson) thought to be formed from charmed quarks. See **charm**[1] (sense 7).

Jr *or* **jr** ABBREVIATION FOR junior.

JSA (in Britain) ABBREVIATION FOR **jobseeker's allowance.**

JSD ABBREVIATION FOR Doctor of Juristic Science.

jt ABBREVIATION FOR joint.

Juan de Fuca ('dʒuːən dɪ 'fjuːkə; *Spanish* xwan de 'fuka) NOUN **Strait of.** a strait between Vancouver Island (Canada) and NW Washington (US). Length: about 129 km (80 miles). Width: about 24 km (15 miles).

Juan Fernández Islands ('dʒuːən fəˈnændɛz; *Spanish* xwan ferˈnandeθ) PLURAL NOUN a group of three islands in the S Pacific Ocean, administered by Chile: volcanic and wooded. Area: about 180 sq. km (70 sq. miles).

Juárez (*Spanish* 'xwareθ) NOUN short for **Ciudad Juárez.**

juba ('dʒuːbə) NOUN a lively African-American dance developed in the southern US.
▷HISTORY C19: of Zulu origin

Juba ('dʒuːbə) NOUN a river in NE Africa, rising in S central Ethiopia and flowing south across Somalia to the Indian Ocean: the chief river of Somalia. Length: about 1660 km (1030 miles).

Jubal ('dʒuːbəl) NOUN *Old Testament* the alleged inventor of musical instruments (Genesis 4:21).

jubbah ('dʒʊbə) NOUN a long loose outer garment with wide sleeves, worn by Muslim men and women, esp in India.
▷HISTORY C16: from Arabic

Jubbulpore (ˌdʒʌbᵊlˈpʊə) NOUN a variant spelling of **Jabalpur.**

jube¹ (ˈdʒuːbɪ) NOUN [1] a gallery or loft over the rood screen in a church or cathedral. [2] another name for **rood screen.**

▷HISTORY C18: from French *jubé,* from opening words of Medieval Latin prayer *Jube, Domine, benedicere* Bid, Lord, a blessing; probably from the deacon's standing by the rood screen or in the rood loft to pronounce this prayer

jube² (dʒuːb) NOUN *Austral and NZ informal* any jelly-like sweet.

▷HISTORY C20: shortened from JUJUBE

jubilant (ˈdʒuːbɪlənt) ADJECTIVE feeling or expressing great joy.

▷HISTORY C17: from Latin *jūbilāns* shouting for joy, from *jūbilāre* to give a joyful cry, from *jūbilum* a shout, wild cry

▸ˈ**jubilance** *or* ˈ**jubilancy** NOUN ▸ˈ**jubilantly** ADVERB

jubilate (ˈdʒuːbɪˌleɪt) VERB (*intr*) [1] to have or express great joy; rejoice. [2] to celebrate a jubilee.

▷HISTORY C17: from Latin *jūbilāre* to raise a shout of joy; see JUBILANT

Jubilate (ˌdʒuːbɪˈlɑːtɪ) NOUN [1] *RC Church, Church of England* the 100th psalm used as a canticle in the liturgy. [2] a musical setting of this psalm.

▷HISTORY from the opening word (*Jubilate* make a joyful noise) of the Vulgate version

jubilation (ˌdʒuːbɪˈleɪʃən) NOUN a feeling of great joy and celebration.

jubilee (ˈdʒuːbɪˌliː, ˌdʒuːbɪˈliː) NOUN [1] a time or season for rejoicing. [2] a special anniversary, esp a 25th or 50th one. [3] *RC Church* a specially appointed period, now ordinarily every 25th year, in which special indulgences are granted. [4] *Old Testament* a year that was to be observed every 50th year, during which Hebrew slaves were to be liberated, alienated property was to be restored, etc. [5] a less common word for **jubilation.**

▷HISTORY C14: from Old French *jubile,* from Late Latin *jubilaeus,* from Late Greek *iōbēlaios,* from Hebrew *yōbhēl* ram's horn, used for the proclamation of the year of jubilee; influenced by Latin *jūbilāre* to shout for joy

JUD ABBREVIATION FOR Doctor of Canon and Civil Law.

▷HISTORY Latin *Juris Utriusque Doctor*

Jud. *Bible* ◆ ABBREVIATION FOR: [1] Also: **Judg.** Judges. [2] Judith.

Judaea *or* **Judea** (dʒuːˈdɪə) NOUN the S division of ancient Palestine, succeeding the kingdom of Judah: a Roman province during the time of Christ.

Judaean *or* **Judean** (dʒuːˈdɪən) ADJECTIVE [1] of or relating to Judaea, the S division of ancient Palestine, or its inhabitants. ◆ NOUN [2] a native or inhabitant of Judaea.

Judaeo- *or US* **Judeo-** (dʒuːˈdeɪəʊ-, dʒuːˈdiːəʊ-) COMBINING FORM relating to Judaism: *Judaeo-Christian.*

Judaeo-German NOUN another name for **Yiddish.**

Judaeo-Spanish NOUN another name for **Ladino.**

Judah (ˈdʒuːdə) NOUN *Old Testament* [1] the fourth son of Jacob, one of whose descendants was to be the Messiah (Genesis 29:35; 49:8–12). [2] the tribe descended from him. [3] the tribal territory of his descendants which became the nucleus of David's kingdom and, after the kingdom had been divided into Israel and Judah, the southern kingdom of Judah, with Jerusalem as its centre. Douay spelling: **Juda.**

Judaic (dʒuːˈdeɪɪk) *or* **Judaical** ADJECTIVE [1] of or relating to the Jews or Judaism. [2] a less common word for **Jewish.**

▸**Juˈdaically** ADVERB

Judaica (dʒuːˈdeɪɪkə) PLURAL NOUN [1] the literature, customs, culture, etc., of the Jews. [2] books or artefacts of Jewish interest, esp as a collection.

▷HISTORY Latin, literally: Jewish matters

Judaism (ˈdʒuːdeɪˌɪzəm) NOUN [1] the religion of the Jews, based on the Old Testament and the Talmud and having as its central point a belief in the one God as transcendent creator of all things and the source of all righteousness. [2] the religious and cultural traditions, customs, attitudes, and way of life of the Jews.

▸ˌ**Judaˈistic** ADJECTIVE

Judaize *or* **Judaise** (ˈdʒʊdeɪˌaɪz) VERB [1] to conform or bring into conformity with Judaism. [2] (*tr*) to convert to Judaism. [3] (*tr*) to imbue with Jewish principles.

▸ˌ**Judaiˈzation** *or* ˌ**Judaiˈsation** NOUN ▸ˈ**Judaˌizer** *or* ˈ**Judaˌiser** NOUN

judas (ˈdʒuːdəs) NOUN (*sometimes capital*) a peephole or a very small window in a door. Also called: **judas window, judas hole.**

▷HISTORY C19: after *Judas Iscariot*

Judas (ˈdʒuːdəs) NOUN [1] *New Testament* the apostle who betrayed Jesus to his enemies for 30 pieces of silver (Luke 22:3–6, 47–48). Full name: **Judas Iscariot.** [2] a person who betrays a friend; traitor. [3] a brother or relative of James and also of Jesus (Matthew 13:55). This figure, Thaddaeus, and Jude were probably identical. ◆ ADJECTIVE [4] denoting an animal or bird used to lure others of its kind or lead them to slaughter.

Judas tree NOUN small Eurasian leguminous tree, *Cercis siliquastrum,* with pinkish-purple flowers that bloom before the leaves appear: popularly thought to be the tree on which Judas hanged himself. See also **redbud.**

judder (ˈdʒʌdə) *Informal, chiefly Brit* ◆ VERB [1] (*intr*) to shake or vibrate. ◆ NOUN [2] abnormal vibration in a mechanical system, esp due to grabbing between friction surfaces, as in the clutch of a motor vehicle. [3] a juddering motion.

▷HISTORY probably blend of JAR² + SHUDDER

judder bar NOUN a NZ name for **sleeping policeman.**

Jude (dʒuːd) NOUN [1] a book of the New Testament (in full **The Epistle of Jude**). [2] **Saint.** Also called: **Judas.** the author of this, stated to be the brother of James (Jude 1) and almost certainly identical with Thaddaeus (Matthew 10:2–4). Feast day: Oct. 28 or June 19.

Judea (dʒuːˈdɪə) NOUN a variant spelling of **Judaea.**

Judezmo (dʒʊˈdɛzməʊ) NOUN another name for **Ladino.**

▷HISTORY from Ladino: Jewish

judge (dʒʌdʒ) NOUN [1] a public official with authority to hear cases in a court of law and pronounce judgment upon them. Compare **magistrate, justice** (senses 5, 6). Related adjective: **judicial.** [2] a person who is appointed to determine the result of contests or competitions. [3] a person qualified to comment critically: *a good judge of antiques.* [4] a leader of the peoples of Israel from Joshua's death to the accession of Saul. ◆ VERB [5] to hear and decide upon (a case at law). [6] (*tr*) to pass judgment on; sentence. [7] (when *tr, may take a clause as object or an infinitive*) to decide or deem (something) after inquiry or deliberation. [8] to determine the result of (a contest or competition). [9] to appraise (something) critically. [10] (*tr; takes a clause as object*) to believe (something) to be the case; suspect.

▷HISTORY C14: from Old French *jugier,* from Latin *jūdicāre* to pass judgment, from *jūdex* a judge

▸ˈ**judgeable** ADJECTIVE ▸ˈ**judgeless** ADJECTIVE ▸ˈ**judgeˌlike** ADJECTIVE ▸ˈ**judger** NOUN ▸ˈ**judgingly** ADVERB

judge advocate NOUN, *plural* **judge advocates.** an officer who superintends proceedings at a military court martial.

judge advocate general NOUN, *plural* **judge advocates general** *or* **judge advocate generals.** the civil adviser to the Crown on matters relating to courts martial and on military law generally.

judge-made ADJECTIVE based on a judge's interpretation or decision (esp in the phrase **judge-made law**).

Judges (ˈdʒʌdʒɪz) NOUN (*functioning as singular*) the book of the Old Testament recounting the history of Israel under the warrior champions and national leaders known as judges from the death of Joshua to the birth of Samuel.

judgeship (ˈdʒʌdʒˌʃɪp) NOUN the position, office, or function of a judge.

judges' rules PLURAL NOUN (in English law, formerly) a set of rules, not legally binding, governing the behaviour of police towards suspects, as in administering a caution to a person under arrest.

judgment *or* **judgement** (ˈdʒʌdʒmənt) NOUN [1] the faculty of being able to make critical distinctions and achieve a balanced viewpoint; discernment. [2] **a** the decision or verdict pronounced by a court of law. **b** an obligation arising as a result of such a decision or verdict, such as a debt. **c** the document recording such a decision or verdict. **d** (*as modifier*): *a judgment debtor.* [3] the formal decision of one or more judges at a contest or competition. [4] a particular decision or opinion formed in a case in dispute or doubt. [5] an estimation: *a good judgment of distance.* [6] criticism or censure. [7] *Logic* **a** the act of establishing a relation between two or more terms, esp as an affirmation or denial. **b** the expression of such a relation. [8] **against one's better judgment.** contrary to a more appropriate or preferred course of action. [9] **sit in judgment. a** to preside as judge. **b** to assume the position of critic. [10] **in someone's judgment.** in someone's opinion.

Judgment (ˈdʒʌdʒmənt) NOUN [1] the estimate by God of the ultimate worthiness or unworthiness of the individual (the **Particular Judgment**) or of all mankind (the **General Judgment** or **Last Judgment**). [2] God's subsequent decision determining the final destinies of all individuals.

judgmental *or* **judgemental** (dʒʌdʒˈmɛntᵊl) ADJECTIVE of or denoting an attitude in which judgments about other people's conduct are made.

Judgment Day NOUN the occasion of the Last (or General) Judgment by God at the end of the world. Also called: **Day of Judgment.** See **Last Judgment.**

judicable (ˈdʒuːdɪkəbᵊl) ADJECTIVE capable of being judged, esp in a court of law.

judicative (ˈdʒuːdɪkətɪv) ADJECTIVE [1] having the function of trying causes. [2] competent to judge and pass sentence.

judicator (ˈdʒuːdɪˌkeɪtə) NOUN a person who acts as a judge.

judicatory (ˈdʒuːdɪkətərɪ) ADJECTIVE [1] of or relating to the administration of justice. ◆ NOUN [2] a court of law. [3] the administration of justice.

▸ˌ**judicaˈtorial** ADJECTIVE

judicature (ˈdʒuːdɪkətʃə) NOUN [1] the administration of justice. [2] the office, function, or power of a judge. [3] the extent of authority of a court or judge. [4] a body of judges or persons exercising judicial authority; judiciary. [5] a court of justice or such courts collectively.

judicial (dʒuːˈdɪʃəl) ADJECTIVE [1] of or relating to the administration of justice. [2] of or relating to judgment in a court of law or to a judge exercising this function. [3] inclined to pass judgment; discriminating. [4] allowed or enforced by a court of law: *a decree of judicial separation.* [5] having qualities appropriate to a judge. [6] giving or seeking judgment, esp determining or seeking determination of a contested issue.

▷HISTORY C14: from Latin *jūdiciālis* belonging to the law courts, from *jūdicium* judgment, from *jūdex* a judge

▸**juˈdicially** ADVERB

Judicial Committee of the Privy Council NOUN the highest appellate court for Britain's dependencies and for some dominions of the Commonwealth.

judicial separation NOUN *Family law* a court decree requiring a man and wife to cease cohabiting but not dissolving the marriage. See also **a mensa et thoro.** Compare **divorce.**

judiciary (dʒuːˈdɪʃɪərɪ, -ˈdɪʃərɪ) ADJECTIVE [1] of or relating to courts of law, judgment, or judges. ◆ NOUN, *plural* **-aries.** [2] the branch of the central authority in a state concerned with the administration of justice. Compare **executive** (sense 2), **legislature.** [3] the system of courts in a country. [4] the judges collectively; bench.

judicious (dʒuːˈdɪʃəs) ADJECTIVE having or proceeding from good judgment.

▸**juˈdiciously** ADVERB ▸**juˈdiciousness** NOUN

Judith (ˈdʒuːdɪθ) NOUN [1] the heroine of one of the books of the Apocrypha, who saved her native town by decapitating Holofernes. [2] the book recounting this episode.

judo (ˈdʒuːdəʊ) NOUN **a** the modern sport derived from jujitsu, in which the object is to throw, hold to the ground, or otherwise force an opponent to submit, using the minimum of physical effort. **b** (*as modifier*): *a judo throw.*

▷HISTORY Japanese, from *jū* gentleness + *dō* way

▸ˈ**judoist** NOUN

judogi (dʒʊ'dəʊgɪ) NOUN a white two-piece cotton costume worn during judo contests.
▷HISTORY from Japanese

judoka ('dʒu:dəʊ,kæ) NOUN a competitor or expert in judo.
▷HISTORY Japanese; see JUDO

Judy ('dʒu:dɪ) NOUN, *plural* **-dies.** [1] the wife of Punch in the children's puppet show *Punch and Judy*. See **Punch.** [2] (*often not capital*) *Brit, slang* a girl or woman.

jug (dʒʌg) NOUN [1] a vessel for holding or pouring liquids, usually having a handle and a spout or lip. US equivalent: **pitcher.** [2] *Austral and NZ* such a vessel used as a kettle: *an electric jug.* [3] *US* a large vessel with a narrow mouth. [4] Also called: **jugful.** the amount of liquid held by a jug. [5] *Brit informal* a glass of alcoholic drink, esp beer. [6] a slang word for **jail.** ◆ VERB **jugs, jugging, jugged.** [7] to stew or boil (meat, esp hare) in an earthenware container. [8] (*tr*) *Slang* to put in jail.
▷HISTORY C16: probably from *Jug,* nickname from girl's name *Joan*

jugal ('dʒu:gᵊl) ADJECTIVE [1] of or relating to the zygomatic bone. ◆ NOUN [2] Also called: **jugal bone.** other names for **zygomatic bone.**
▷HISTORY C16: from Latin *jugālis* of a yoke, from *jugum* a yoke

jugate ('dʒu:geɪt, -gɪt) ADJECTIVE (esp of compound leaves) having parts arranged in pairs.
▷HISTORY C19: from New Latin *jugātus* (unattested), from Latin *jugum* a yoke

jug band NOUN a small group playing folk or jazz music, using empty jugs that are played by blowing across their openings to produce bass notes.

Jugendstil *German* ('ju:gəntʃti:l) NOUN another name for **Art Nouveau.**
▷HISTORY from *Jugend* literally: youth, name of illustrated periodical that first appeared in 1896, + *Stil* STYLE

jugged hare NOUN a stew of hare cooked in an earthenware pot or casserole.

juggernaut ('dʒʌgə,nɔ:t) NOUN [1] any terrible force, esp one that destroys or that demands complete self-sacrifice. [2] *Brit* a very large lorry for transporting goods by road, esp one that travels throughout Europe.

Juggernaut ('dʒʌgə,nɔ:t) NOUN *Hinduism* [1] a crude idol of Krishna worshipped at Puri and throughout Orissa and Bengal. At an annual festival the idol is wheeled through the town on a gigantic chariot and devotees are supposed to have formerly thrown themselves under the wheels. [2] a form of Krishna miraculously raised by Brahma from the state of a crude idol to that of a living god.
▷HISTORY C17: from Hindi *Jagannath,* from Sanskrit *Jagannātha* lord of the world (that is, Vishnu, chief of the Hindu gods), from *jagat* world + *nātha* lord

juggins ('dʒʌgɪnz) NOUN *Brit informal* a silly person; simpleton.
▷HISTORY C19: special use of the surname *Juggins*

juggle ('dʒʌgᵊl) VERB [1] to throw and catch (several objects) continuously so that most are in the air all the time, as an entertainment. [2] to arrange or manipulate (facts, figures, etc.) so as to give a false or misleading picture. [3] (*tr*) to keep (several activities) in progress, esp with difficulty. ◆ NOUN [4] an act of juggling.
▷HISTORY C14: from Old French *jogler* to perform as a jester, from Latin *joculārī* to jest, from *jocus* a jest
▸'**jugglery** NOUN

juggler ('dʒʌglə) NOUN [1] a person who juggles, esp a professional entertainer. [2] a person who fraudulently manipulates facts or figures.

juglandaceous (,dʒu:glæn'deɪʃəs) ADJECTIVE of, relating to, or belonging to the *Juglandaceae,* a family of trees that includes walnut and hickory.
▷HISTORY C19: via New Latin from Latin *juglans* walnut, from *ju-,* shortened from *Jovi-* of Jupiter + *glans* acorn

Jugoslav ('ju:gəʊ,slɑ:v) *or* **Jugoslavian** (,ju:gəʊ'slɑ:vɪən) ADJECTIVE, NOUN a variant spelling of **Yugoslav** or **Yugoslavian.**

Jugoslavia (,ju:gəʊ'slɑ:vɪə) NOUN a variant spelling of **Yugoslavia.**

jugular ('dʒʌgjʊlə) ADJECTIVE [1] of, relating to, or situated near the throat or neck. [2] of, having, or denoting pelvic fins situated in front of the pectoral fins: *a jugular fish.* ◆ NOUN [3] short for **jugular vein.** [4] **go for the jugular.** to make a savage and destructive attack on an enemy's weakest point.
▷HISTORY C16: from Late Latin *jugulāris,* from Latin *jugulum* throat

jugular vein NOUN any of three large veins of the neck that return blood to the heart from the head and face.

jugulate ('dʒʌgjʊ,leɪt) VERB (*tr*) *Rare* to check (a disease) by extreme measures or remedies.
▷HISTORY C17 (in the obsolete sense: kill by cutting the throat of): from Latin *jugulāre,* from *jugulum* throat, from *jugum* yoke
▸,**jugu'lation** NOUN

jugum ('dʒu:gəm) NOUN [1] a small process at the base of each forewing in certain insects by which the forewings are united to the hindwings during flight. [2] *Botany* a pair of opposite leaflets.
▷HISTORY C19: from Latin, literally: YOKE

Jugurthine War (dʒu:'gɜ:θaɪn) NOUN an unsuccessful war waged against the Romans (112–105 B.C.) by Jugurtha, king of Numidia (died 104).

juice (dʒu:s) NOUN [1] any liquid that occurs naturally in or is secreted by plant or animal tissue: *the juice of an orange; digestive juices.* [2] *Informal* **a** fuel for an engine, esp petrol. **b** electricity. **c** alcoholic drink. [3] **a** vigour or vitality. **b** essence or fundamental nature. [4] **stew in one's own juice.** See **stew**[1] (sense 10). ◆ VERB [5] to extract juice from (fruits or vegetables) in order to drink.
▷HISTORY C13: from Old French *jus,* from Latin
▸'**juiceless** ADJECTIVE

juicer NOUN a kitchen appliance, usually operated by electricity, for extracting juice from fruits and vegetables. Also called: **juice extractor.**

juice up VERB (*tr, adverb*) [1] *US, slang* to make lively: *to juice up a party.* [2] (*often passive*) to cause to be drunk: *he got juiced up on Scotch last night.*

juicy ('dʒu:sɪ) ADJECTIVE **juicier, juiciest.** [1] full of juice. [2] provocatively interesting; spicy: *juicy gossip.* [3] *Slang* voluptuous or seductive: *she's a juicy bit.* [4] *Chiefly US and Canadian* profitable: *a juicy contract.*
▸'**juicily** ADVERB ▸'**juiciness** NOUN

Juiz de Fora (*Portuguese* ʒu'iʃ di 'fɔra) NOUN a city in SE Brazil, in Minas Gerais state on the Rio de Janeiro–Belo Horizonte railway: textiles. Pop.: 443 359 (2000).

jujitsu, jujutsu, *or* **jiujutsu** (dʒu:'dʒɪtsu:) NOUN the traditional Japanese system of unarmed self-defence perfected by the samurai. See also **judo.**
▷HISTORY C19: from Japanese, from *jū* gentleness + *jutsu* art

juju ('dʒu:dʒu:) NOUN [1] an object superstitiously revered by certain W African peoples and used as a charm or fetish. [2] the power associated with a juju. [3] a taboo effected by a juju. [4] any process in which a mystery is exploited to confuse people.
▷HISTORY C19: probably from Hausa *djudju* evil spirit, fetish
▸'**jujuism** NOUN ▸'**jujuist** NOUN

jujube ('dʒu:dʒu:b) NOUN [1] any of several Old World spiny rhamnaceous trees of the genus *Ziziphus,* esp *Z. jujuba,* that have small yellowish flowers and dark red edible fruits. See also **Christ's-thorn.** [2] the fruit of any of these trees. [3] a chewy sweet made of flavoured gelatine and sometimes medicated to soothe sore throats. ◆ Also called (for senses 1, 2): **Chinese date.**
▷HISTORY C14: from Medieval Latin *jujuba,* modification of Latin *zīzyphum,* from Greek *zizuphon*

jukebox ('dʒu:k,bɒks) NOUN a coin-operated machine, usually found in pubs, clubs, etc., that contains records, CDs, or videos, which are played when selected by a customer.
▷HISTORY C20: from Gullah *juke* bawdy (as in *juke house* brothel) + BOX[1]

jukskei ('jʊk,skeɪ) NOUN *South African* a game in which a peg is thrown over a fixed distance at a stake driven into the ground.
▷HISTORY from Afrikaans *juk* yoke + *skei* pin

Jul. ABBREVIATION FOR July.

julep ('dʒu:lɪp) NOUN [1] a sweet drink, variously prepared and sometimes medicated. [2] *Chiefly US* short for **mint julep.**
▷HISTORY C14: from Old French, from Arabic *julāb,* from Persian *gulāb* rose water, from *gul* rose + *āb* water

Julian Alps PLURAL NOUN a mountain range in Slovenia: an E range of the Alps.

Julian calendar NOUN the calendar introduced by Julius Caesar in 46 B.C., identical to the present calendar in all but two aspects: the beginning of the year was not fixed on Jan. 1 and leap years occurred every fourth year and in every centenary year. Compare **Gregorian calendar.**

julienne (,dʒu:lɪ'en) ADJECTIVE [1] (of vegetables) cut into thin shreds. ◆ NOUN [2] a clear consommé to which a mixture of such vegetables has been added.
▷HISTORY French, from name *Jules, Julien,* or *Julienne*

Juliet (dʒu:lɪ'ɛt) NOUN *Communications* a code word for the letter *j*.

Juliet cap ('dʒu:lɪət) NOUN a close-fitting decorative cap, worn esp by brides.
▷HISTORY C20: after the heroine of Shakespeare's *Romeo and Juliet* (1594)

Jullundur ('dʒʌləndə) NOUN the former name of **Jalandhar.**

July (dʒu:'laɪ, dʒə-, dʒʊ-) NOUN, *plural* **-lies.** the seventh month of the year, consisting of 31 days.
▷HISTORY C13: from Anglo-French *julie,* from Latin *Jūlius,* after Gaius Julius Caesar (100–44 B.C.), Roman statesman in whose honour it was named

Jumada (dʒu'mɑ:də) NOUN either the fifth or the sixth month of the Muslim year, known respectively as **Jumada I** and **Jumada II.**
▷HISTORY Arabic

jumar ('dʒu:mə) NOUN *Mountaineering* [1] Also called: **jumar clamp.** a clamp with a handle that can move freely up a rope on which it is clipped but locks when downward pressure is applied. ◆ VERB (*intr*) [2] to climb (up a fixed rope) using jumars.
▷HISTORY C20: Swiss name

jumble ('dʒʌmbᵊl) VERB [1] to mingle (objects, papers, etc.) in a state of disorder. [2] (*tr; usually passive*) to remember in a confused form; muddle. ◆ NOUN [3] a disordered mass, state, etc. [4] *Brit* articles donated for a jumble sale. [5] Also called: **jumbal.** a small thin cake, usually ring-shaped.
▷HISTORY C16: of uncertain origin
▸'**jumbler** NOUN ▸'**jumbly** ADJECTIVE

jumble sale NOUN a sale of miscellaneous articles, usually cheap and predominantly secondhand, in aid of charity. US and Canadian equivalent: **rummage sale.**

jumbo ('dʒʌmbəʊ) NOUN, *plural* **-bos.** [1] *Informal* **a** a very large person or thing. **b** (*as modifier*): *a jumbo box of detergent.* [2] See **jumbo jet.**
▷HISTORY C19: after the name of a famous elephant exhibited by P. T. Barnum, from Swahili *jumbe* chief

jumboize *or* **jumboise** ('dʒʌmbəʊ,aɪz) VERB (*tr*) to extend (a ship, esp a tanker) by cutting out the middle part and inserting a new larger part between the original bow and stern.
▷HISTORY C20: from JUMBO + -IZE

jumbo jet NOUN *Informal* a type of large jet-propelled airliner that carries several hundred passengers.

jumbuck ('dʒʌm,bʌk) NOUN *Austral, archaic* an informal word for **sheep.**
▷HISTORY C19: from a native Australian language

Jumna ('dʒʌmnə) NOUN a river in N India, rising in Uttaranchal in the Himalayas and flowing south and southeast to join the Ganges just below Allahabad (a confluence held sacred by Hindus). Length: 1385 km (860 miles).

jump (dʒʌmp) VERB [1] (*intr*) to leap or spring clear of the ground or other surface by using the muscles in the legs and feet. [2] (*tr*) to leap over or clear (an obstacle): *to jump a gap.* [3] (*tr*) to cause to leap over an obstacle: *to jump a horse over a hedge.* [4] (*intr*) to move or proceed hastily (into, onto, out of, etc.): *she jumped into a taxi and was off.* [5] (*tr*) *Informal* to board so as to travel illegally on: *he jumped the train as it was leaving.* [6] (*intr*) to parachute from an aircraft. [7] (*intr*) to jerk or start, as with astonishment, surprise, etc.: *she jumped when she heard the explosion.* [8] to rise or cause to rise suddenly or abruptly. [9] to pass or skip over (intervening objects or matter): *she jumped a few lines and then continued reading.* [10] (*intr*) to change from one thing to another, esp from one subject to

another. [11] (*tr*) to drill by means of a jumper. [12] (*intr*) (of a film) **a** to have sections of a continuous sequence omitted, as through faulty cutting. **b** to flicker, as through faulty alignment of the film. [13] (*tr*) *US* to promote in rank, esp unexpectedly or to a higher rank than expected. [14] (*tr*) to start (a car) using jump leads. [15] *Draughts* to capture (an opponent's piece) by moving one of one's own pieces over it to an unoccupied square. [16] (*intr*) *Bridge* to bid in response to one's partner at a higher level than is necessary, to indicate a strong hand. [17] (*tr*) to come off (a track, rail, etc.): *the locomotive jumped the rails.* [18] (*intr*) (of the stylus of a record player) to be jerked out of the groove. [19] (*intr*) *Slang* to be lively: *the party was jumping when I arrived.* [20] (*tr*) *Informal* to attack without warning: *thieves jumped the old man as he walked through the park.* [21] (*tr*) *Informal* (of a driver or a motor vehicle) to pass through (a red traffic light) or move away from (traffic lights) before they change to green. [22] (*tr*) *Brit, slang* (of a man) to have sexual intercourse with. [23] **jump bail.** to forfeit one's bail by failing to appear in court, esp by absconding. [24] **jump down someone's throat.** *Informal* to address or reply to someone with unexpected sharpness. [25] **jump ship.** to desert, esp to leave a ship in which one is legally bound to serve. [26] **jump the queue.** See **queue-jump.** [27] **jump to it.** *Informal* to begin something quickly and efficiently. ◆ NOUN [28] an act or instance of jumping. [29] a space, distance, or obstacle to be jumped or that has been jumped. [30] a descent by parachute from an aircraft. [31] *Sport* any of several contests involving a jump: *the high jump.* [32] a sudden rise: *the jump in prices last month.* [33] a sudden or abrupt transition. [34] a sudden jerk or involuntary muscular spasm, esp as a reaction of surprise. [35] a step or degree: *one jump ahead.* [36] *Draughts* a move that captures an opponent's piece by jumping over it. [37] *Films* **a** a break in continuity in the normal sequence of shots. **b** (*as modifier*): *a jump cut.* [38] *Computing* another name for **branch** (sense 7). [39] *Brit, slang* an act of sexual intercourse. [40] **on the jump.** *Informal, chiefly US and Canadian* **a** in a hurry. **b** busy and energetic. [41] **take a running jump.** *Brit informal* a contemptuous expression of dismissal. ◆ See also **jump at, jump-off, jump on, jump-up.**
▷**HISTORY** C16: probably of imitative origin; compare Swedish *gumpa* to jump
▸ **ˈjumpable** ADJECTIVE ▸ **ˈjumpingly** ADVERB

jump at VERB (*intr, preposition*) to be glad to accept: *I would jump at the chance of going.*

jump ball NOUN *Basketball* a ball thrown high by the referee between two opposing players to put it in play, as after a stoppage in which no foul or violation was committed.

jump bid NOUN *Bridge* a bid by the responder at a higher level than is necessary.

jumped-up ADJECTIVE *Informal* suddenly risen in significance, esp when appearing arrogant.

jumper[1] (ˈdʒʌmpə) NOUN [1] *Chiefly Brit* a knitted or crocheted garment covering the upper part of the body. [2] the US and Canadian term for **pinafore dress.**
▷**HISTORY** C19: from obsolete *jump* man's loose jacket, variant of *jupe,* from Old French, from Arabic *jubbah* long cloth coat

jumper[2] (ˈdʒʌmpə) NOUN [1] a boring tool that works by repeated impact, such as a steel bit in a hammer drill used in boring rock. [2] Also called: **jumper cable, jumper lead.** a short length of wire used to make a connection, usually temporarily, between terminals or to bypass a component. [3] a type of sled with a high crosspiece. [4] a person or animal that jumps. [5] *Irish, derogatory slang* a person who changes religion; a convert.

jumping bean NOUN a seed of any of several Mexican euphorbiaceous plants, esp species of *Sebastiania,* that contains a moth caterpillar whose movements cause it to jerk about.

jumping gene NOUN a fragment of nucleic acid, such as a plasmid or a transposon, that can become incorporated into the DNA of a cell.

jumping jack NOUN [1] a firework having a long narrow tube filled with gunpowder, folded like an accordion so that when lit it burns with small explosions causing it to jump along the ground. [2] a toy figure of a man with jointed limbs that can be moved by pulling attached strings.

jumping mouse NOUN any long-tailed small mouselike rodent of the family *Zapodidae,* of North America, E Asia, and N and E Europe, having long hind legs specialized for leaping.

jumping-off place *or* **point** NOUN [1] a starting point, as in an enterprise. [2] a final or extreme condition. [3] *Canadian* a place where one leaves civilization to go into the wilderness. [4] *US* a very remote spot.

jumping spider NOUN any spider of the family *Salticidae,* esp *Attulus saltator,* that catch their prey by hunting and can jump considerable distances.

jump jet NOUN a fixed-wing jet aircraft that is capable of landing and taking off vertically.

jump jockey NOUN *Brit* a jockey who rides in steeplechases, as opposed to one who rides in flat races.

jump leads (li:dz) PLURAL NOUN two heavy cables fitted with crocodile clips used to start a motor vehicle with a discharged battery by connecting the battery to an external battery. US and Canadian name: **jumper cables.**

jump-off NOUN [1] an extra round in a showjumping contest when two or more horses are equal first, the fastest round deciding the winner. ◆ VERB **jump off.** [2] (*intr, adverb*) to begin or engage in a jump-off.

jump on VERB (*intr, preposition*) *Informal* to reprimand or attack suddenly and forcefully.

jump seat NOUN [1] a folding seat for temporary use, as on the flight deck of some aircraft for an additional crew member. [2] *Brit* a folding seat in a motor vehicle such as in a London taxi.

jump shot NOUN *Basketball* a shot at the basket made by a player releasing the ball at the highest point of a leap.

jump-start VERB [1] to start the engine of (a car) by pushing or rolling it and then engaging the gears or (of a car) to start in this way. ◆ NOUN [2] the act of starting a car in this way. ◆ Also (Brit): **bump-start.**

jump suit NOUN a one-piece garment of combined trousers and jacket or shirt.

jump-up NOUN [1] (in the Caribbean) an occasion of mass dancing and merrymaking, as in a carnival. ◆ VERB **jump up.** (*intr, adverb*) [2] to stand up quickly and suddenly. [3] (in the Caribbean) to take part in a jump-up.

jumpy (ˈdʒʌmpɪ) ADJECTIVE **jumpier, jumpiest.** [1] nervous or apprehensive. [2] moving jerkily or fitfully.
▸ **ˈjumpily** ADVERB ▸ **ˈjumpiness** NOUN

Jun. ABBREVIATION FOR: [1] June. [2] Also: **jun.** junior.

Junagadh (ˌdʒu:nəˈgæd) NOUN a town in India, in Gujarat: noted for its Buddhist caves and temples. Pop.: 130 484 (1991).

junc. ABBREVIATION FOR junction.

juncaceous (dʒʌŋˈkeɪʃəs) ADJECTIVE of, relating to, or belonging to the *Juncaceae,* a family of grasslike plants with small brown flowers: includes the rushes and woodrushes. Compare **cyperaceous.**
▷**HISTORY** C19: via New Latin from Latin *juncus* a rush

junco (ˈdʒʌŋkəʊ) NOUN, *plural* **-cos** *or* **-coes.** any North American bunting of the genus *Junco,* having a greyish plumage with white outer tail feathers.
▷**HISTORY** C18: from Spanish: a rush, a marsh bird, from Latin *juncus* rush

junction (ˈdʒʌŋkʃən) NOUN [1] a place where several routes, lines, or roads meet, link, or cross each other: *a railway junction.* [2] a point on a motorway where traffic may leave or join it. [3] *Electronics* **a** a contact between two different metals or other materials: *a thermocouple junction.* **b** a transition region between regions of differing electrical properties in a semiconductor: *a p-n junction.* [4] a connection between two or more conductors or sections of transmission lines. [5] the act of joining or the state of being joined.
▷**HISTORY** C18: from Latin *junctiō* a joining, from *junctus* joined, from *jungere* to join
▸ **ˈjunctional** ADJECTIVE

junction box NOUN an earthed enclosure within which wires or cables can be safely connected.

junction transistor NOUN a bipolar transistor consisting of two p-n junctions combined to form either an n-p-n or a p-n-p transistor, having the three electrodes, the emitter, base, and collector.

juncture (ˈdʒʌŋktʃə) NOUN [1] a point in time, esp a critical one (often in the phrase **at this juncture**). [2] *Linguistics* **a** a pause in speech or a feature of pronunciation that introduces, accompanies, or replaces a pause. **b** the set of phonological features signalling a division between words, such as those that distinguish *a name* from *an aim.* [3] a less common word for **junction.**

Jundiaí (*Portuguese* ʒundiaˈi) NOUN an industrial city in SE Brazil, in São Paulo state. Pop.: 299 669 (2000).

June (dʒu:n) NOUN the sixth month of the year, consisting of 30 days.
▷**HISTORY** Old English *iunius,* from Latin *junius,* probably from *Junius* name of Roman gens

Juneau (ˈdʒu:nəʊ) NOUN a port in SE Alaska: state capital. Pop.: 26 751 (1990).

Juneberry (ˈdʒu:nˌbɛrɪ) NOUN, *plural* **-ries.** another name for **serviceberry** (senses 1, 2).

June bug *or* **beetle** NOUN any of various large brown North American scarabaeid beetles that are common in late spring and early summer, esp any of the genus *Polyphylla.* Also called: **May beetle, May bug.**

Jungfrau (*German* ˈjʊŋfrau) NOUN a mountain in S Switzerland, in the Bernese Alps south of Interlaken. Height: 4158 m (13 642 ft.).

Junggar Pendi (ˈdʒʊŋˈgɛər ˈpɛnˈdi:), **Dzungaria,** *or* **Zungaria** NOUN an arid region of W China, in N Xinjiang Uygur between the Altai Mountains and the Tian Shan.

Jungian (ˈjʊŋɪən) ADJECTIVE of, following, or relating to the Swiss psychologist Carl Gustav Jung (1875–1961), his system of psychoanalysis, or to analytical psychology.

jungle (ˈdʒʌŋgəl) NOUN [1] an equatorial forest area with luxuriant vegetation, often almost impenetrable. [2] any dense or tangled thicket or growth. [3] a place of intense competition or ruthless struggle for survival: *the concrete jungle.* [4] a type of fast electronic dance music, originating in the early 1990s, which combines elements of techno and ragga. [5] *US, slang* (esp in the Depression) a gathering place for the unemployed, etc.
▷**HISTORY** C18: from Hindi *jangal,* from Sanskrit *jāngala* wilderness
▸ **ˈjungly** ADJECTIVE

jungle fever NOUN a serious malarial fever occurring in the East Indies.

jungle fowl NOUN [1] any small gallinaceous bird of the genus *Gallus,* of S and SE Asia, the males of which have an arched tail and a combed and wattled head: family *Phasianidae* (pheasants). *G. gallus* (**red jungle fowl**) is thought to be the ancestor of the domestic fowl. [2] *Austral* any of several megapodes, esp *Megapodius freycinet.*

jungle gym NOUN a climbing frame for young children.
▷**HISTORY** from a trademark

jungle juice NOUN a slang name for alcoholic liquor, esp home-made liquor.

junior (ˈdʒu:njə) ADJECTIVE [1] lower in rank or length of service; subordinate. [2] younger in years: *junior citizens.* [3] of or relating to youth or childhood: *junior pastimes.* [4] *Brit* of or relating to schoolchildren between the ages of 7 and 11 approximately. [5] *US* of, relating to, or designating the third year of a four-year course at college or high school. ◆ NOUN [6] *Law* (in England) any barrister below the rank of Queen's Counsel. [7] a junior person. [8] *Brit* a junior schoolchild. [9] *US* a junior student.
▷**HISTORY** C17: from Latin: younger, from *juvenis* young

Junior (ˈdʒu:njə) ADJECTIVE being the younger: usually used after a name to distinguish the son from the father with the same first name or names: *Charles Parker, Junior.* Abbreviations: **Jnr, Jr, Jun, Junr.**

junior college NOUN *US and Canadian* [1] an educational establishment providing a two-year course that either terminates with an associate degree or is the equivalent of the freshman and sophomore years of a four-year undergraduate course. [2] the junior section of a college or university.

junior common room NOUN (in certain universities and colleges) a common room for the use of students. Compare **senior common room, middle common room.**

junior lightweight NOUN **a** a professional boxer weighing 126–130 pounds (57–59 kg). **b** (*as modifier*): *a junior-lightweight bout.*

junior middleweight NOUN **a** a professional boxer weighing 147–154 pounds (66.5–70 kg). **b** (*as modifier*): *the junior-middleweight championship.* Compare **light middleweight.**

junior school NOUN (in England and Wales) a school for children aged between 7 and 11. Compare **infant school.**

junior technician NOUN a rank in the RAF senior to aircraftman: comparable to that of private in the army.

junior welterweight NOUN **a** a professional boxer weighing 135–140 pounds (61–63.5 kg). **b** (*as modifier*): *a junior-welterweight fight.* Compare **light welterweight.**

juniper ('dʒuːnɪpə) NOUN [1] any coniferous shrub or small tree of the genus *Juniperus,* of the N hemisphere, having purple berry-like cones. The cones of *J. communis* (**common** or **dwarf juniper**) are used as a flavouring in making gin. See also **red cedar** (sense 1). [2] any of various similar trees, grown mainly as ornamentals. [3] *Old Testament* one of the trees used in the building of Solomon's temple (I Kings 6:15, 34) and for shipbuilding (Ezekiel 27:5).
▷HISTORY C14: from Latin *jūniperus,* of obscure origin

junk[1] (dʒʌŋk) NOUN [1] discarded or secondhand objects, etc., collectively. [2] *Informal* **a** rubbish generally. **b** nonsense: *the play was absolute junk.* [3] *Slang* any narcotic drug, esp heroin. ◆ VERB [4] (*tr*) *Informal* to discard as junk; scrap.
▷HISTORY C15 *jonke* old useless rope

junk[2] (dʒʌŋk) NOUN a sailing vessel used in Chinese waters and characterized by a very high poop, flat bottom, and square sails supported by battens.
▷HISTORY C17: from Portuguese *junco,* from Javanese *jon;* related to Dutch *jonk*

junk bond NOUN *Finance* a security that offers a high yield but often involves a high risk of default.

junk DNA NOUN DNA that consists of repeated sequences of nucleotide and has no apparent function.

Junker ('jʊŋkə) NOUN [1] *History* any of the aristocratic landowners of Prussia who were devoted to maintaining their identity and extensive social and political privileges. [2] an arrogant, narrow-minded, and tyrannical German army officer or official. [3] (formerly) a young German nobleman.
▷HISTORY C16: from German, from Old High German *junchērro* young lord, from *junc* young + *hērro* master, lord
▸ **'Junkerdom** NOUN ▸ **'Junkerism** NOUN

junket ('dʒʌŋkɪt) NOUN [1] an excursion, esp one made for pleasure at public expense by a public official or committee. [2] a sweet dessert made of flavoured milk set to a curd with rennet. [3] a feast or festive occasion. ◆ VERB [4] (*intr*) (of a public official, committee, etc.) to go on a junket. [5] to have or entertain with a feast or festive gathering.
▷HISTORY C14 (in the sense: rush basket, hence custard served on rushes): from Old French (dialect) *jonquette,* from *jonc* rush, from Latin *juncus* reed
▸ **'junketer** *or* **'junketter** *or* **ˌjunke'teer** NOUN

junk food NOUN food that is low in nutritional value, often highly processed or ready-prepared, and eaten instead of or in addition to well-balanced meals.

junkie *or* **junky** ('dʒʌŋkɪ) NOUN, *plural* **junkies.** an informal word for **drug addict,** esp one who injects heroin into himself

junk mail NOUN untargeted mail advertising goods or services.

junkman ('dʒʌŋkˌmæn) NOUN, *plural* **-men.** the US and Canadian term for **rag-and-bone man.**

junk shop NOUN [1] a shop selling miscellaneous secondhand goods. [2] *Derogatory* a shop selling antiques.

junkyard ('dʒʌŋkˌjɑːd) NOUN a place where junk is stored or collected for sale.

Juno[1] ('dʒuːnəʊ) NOUN [1] (in Roman tradition) the queen of the Olympian gods. Greek counterpart: **Hera.** [2] a woman of stately bearing and regal beauty.

Juno[2] ('dʒuːnəʊ) NOUN *Astronomy* the fourth largest known asteroid (approximate diameter 240 kilometres) and one of the four brightest.

Junoesque (ˌdʒuːnəʊ'ɛsk) ADJECTIVE having stately bearing and regal beauty like the goddess Juno.

Junr *or* **junr** ABBREVIATION FOR junior.

junta ('dʒʊntə, 'dʒʌn-; *chiefly US* 'hʊntə) NOUN [1] a group of military officers holding the power in a country, esp after a coup d'état. [2] Also called: **junto.** a small group of men; cabal, faction, or clique. [3] a legislative or executive council in some parts of Latin America.
▷HISTORY C17: from Spanish: council, from Latin *junctus* joined, from *jungere* to JOIN

junto ('dʒʊntəʊ, 'dʒʌn-) NOUN, *plural* **-tos.** a variant of **junta** (sense 2).
▷HISTORY C17: variant of JUNTA

Jupiter[1] ('dʒuːpɪtə) NOUN (in Roman tradition) the king and ruler of the Olympian gods. Greek counterpart: **Zeus.**

Jupiter[2] ('dʒuːpɪtə) NOUN the largest of the planets and the fifth from the sun. It has 16 satellites and is surrounded by a transient planar ring system consisting of dust particles. Mean distance from sun: 778 million km; period of revolution around sun: 11.86 years; period of axial rotation: 9.83 hours; diameter and mass: 11.2 and 317.9 times that of earth respectively. See **Galilean satellite.**

jupon ('ʒuːpɒn) NOUN a short close-fitting sleeveless padded garment, used in the late 14th and early 15th centuries with armour. Also called: **gipon.**
▷HISTORY C15: from Old French, from Old French *jupe;* see JUMPER[1]

jura ('dʒʊərə) NOUN the plural of **jus.**

Jura ('dʒʊərə) NOUN [1] a department of E France, in Franche-Comté region. Capital: Lons-le-Saunier. Pop.: 250 857 (1999). Area: 5055 sq. km (1971 sq. miles). [2] a canton of Switzerland, bordering the French frontier: formed in 1979 from part of Bern. Capital: Delémont. Pop.: 68 800 (2000 est.). Area: 838 sq. km (323 sq. miles). [3] an island off the W coast of Scotland, in the Inner Hebrides, separated from the mainland by the **Sound of Jura.** Pop. (with Colonsay): 250 (latest est.). Area: 381 sq. km (147 sq.miles). [4] a mountain range in W central Europe, between the Rivers Rhine and Rhône: mostly in E France, extending into W Switzerland. [5] a range of mountains in the NE quadrant of the moon lying on the N border of the Mare Imbrium.

jural ('dʒʊərəl) ADJECTIVE [1] of or relating to law or to the administration of justice. [2] of or relating to rights and obligations.
▷HISTORY C17: from Latin *iūs* law + -AL[1]
▸ **'jurally** ADVERB

Jurassic (dʒʊ'ræsɪk) ADJECTIVE [1] of, denoting, or formed in the second period of the Mesozoic era, between the Triassic and Cretaceous periods, lasting for 55 million years during which dinosaurs and ammonites flourished. ◆ NOUN [2] **the.** the Jurassic period or rock system.
▷HISTORY C19: from French *jurassique,* after the JURA (Mountains)

jurat ('dʒʊəræt) NOUN [1] *Law* a statement at the foot of an affidavit, naming the parties, stating when, where, and before whom it was sworn, etc. [2] (in England) a municipal officer of the Cinque Ports, having a similar position to that of an alderman. [3] (in France and the Channel Islands) a magistrate.
▷HISTORY C16: from Medieval Latin *jūrātus* one who has been sworn, from Latin *jūrāre* to swear

juratory ('dʒʊərətərɪ, -trɪ) ADJECTIVE *Law* of, relating to, or expressed in an oath.

JurD ABBREVIATION FOR Doctor of Law.
▷HISTORY Latin *Juris Doctor*

jurel (huː'rɛl) NOUN any of several carangid food fishes of the genus *Caranx,* of warm American Atlantic waters.
▷HISTORY C18: from Spanish, from Catalan *sorell,* from Late Latin *saurus* horse mackerel, from Greek *sauros* lizard

juridical (dʒʊ'rɪdɪkᵊl) *or* **juridic** ADJECTIVE of or relating to law, to the administration of justice, or to the office or function of a judge; legal.
▷HISTORY C16: from Latin *jūridicus,* from *iūs* law + *dicere* to say
▸ **ju'ridically** ADVERB

juridical days PLURAL NOUN *Law* days on which the courts are in session. Compare **dies non.**

jurisconsult (ˌdʒʊərɪs'kɒnsʌlt) NOUN [1] a person qualified to advise on legal matters. [2] a master of jurisprudence.
▷HISTORY C17: from Latin *jūris consultus;* see JUS, CONSULT

jurisdiction (ˌdʒʊərɪs'dɪkʃən) NOUN [1] the right or power to administer justice and to apply laws. [2] the exercise or extent of such right or power. [3] power or authority in general.
▷HISTORY C13: from Latin *jūrisdictiō* administration of justice; see JUS, DICTION
▸ **ˌjuris'dictional** ADJECTIVE ▸ **ˌjuris'dictionally** ADVERB
▸ **ˌjuris'dictive** ADJECTIVE

jurisprudence (ˌdʒʊərɪs'pruːdᵊns) NOUN [1] the science or philosophy of law. [2] a system or body of law. [3] a branch of law: *medical jurisprudence.*
▷HISTORY C17: from Latin *jūris prūdentia;* see JUS, PRUDENCE
▸ **jurisprudential** (ˌdʒʊərɪspruː'dɛnʃəl) ADJECTIVE
▸ **ˌjurispru'dentially** ADVERB

jurisprudent (ˌdʒʊərɪs'pruːdᵊnt) ADJECTIVE [1] skilled in jurisprudence or versed in the principles of law. ◆ NOUN [2] a jurisprudent person.

jurist ('dʒʊərɪst) NOUN [1] a person versed in the science of law, esp Roman or civil law. [2] a writer on legal subjects. [3] a student or graduate of law. [4] (in the US) a lawyer.
▷HISTORY C15: from French *juriste,* from Medieval Latin *jūrista;* see JUS

juristic (dʒʊ'rɪstɪk) *or* **juristical** ADJECTIVE [1] of or relating to jurists. [2] of, relating to, or characteristic of the study of law or the legal profession.
▸ **ju'ristically** ADVERB

juristic act NOUN [1] a proceeding designed to have a legal effect. [2] an act by an individual aimed at altering, terminating, or otherwise affecting a legal right.

juror ('dʒʊərə) NOUN [1] a member of a jury. [2] a person whose name is included on a panel from which a jury is selected. [3] a person who takes an oath.
▷HISTORY C14: from Anglo-French *jurour,* from Old French *jurer* to take an oath, from Latin *jūrāre*

Juruá (*Portuguese* ʒu'rua) NOUN a river in South America, rising in E central Peru and flowing northeast across NW Brazil to join the Amazon. Length: 1900 km (1200 miles).

jury[1] ('dʒʊərɪ) NOUN, *plural* **-ries.** [1] a group of, usually twelve, people sworn to deliver a true verdict according to the evidence upon a case presented in a court of law. See also **grand jury, petit jury.** [2] a body of persons appointed to judge a competition and award prizes. [3] **the jury is still out.** *Informal* it has not yet been decided or agreed on.
▷HISTORY C14: from Old French *juree,* from *jurer* to swear; see JUROR

jury[2] ('dʒʊərɪ) ADJECTIVE *Chiefly nautical* (*in combination*) makeshift: *jury-rigged.*
▷HISTORY C17: of unknown origin

jury box NOUN an enclosure where the jury sit in court.

juryman ('dʒʊərɪmən) NOUN, *plural* **-men.** a member of a jury, esp a man.

jury process NOUN the writ used to summon jurors.

jury-rigged ADJECTIVE *Chiefly nautical* set up in a makeshift manner, usually as a result of the loss of regular gear.

jurywoman ('dʒʊərɪwʊmən) NOUN, *plural* **-women.** a female member of a jury.

jus[1] (dʒʌs) NOUN, *plural* **jura** ('dʒʊərə). *Law* [1] a right, power, or authority. [2] law in the abstract or as a system, as distinguished from specific enactments.
▷HISTORY Latin: law

jus[2] (ʒuː; *French* ʒy) NOUN a sauce.
▷HISTORY French: literally, juice

jus canonicum (kə'nɒnɪkəm) NOUN canon law.
▷HISTORY from Latin

jus civile (sɪ'viːlɪ) NOUN [1] the civil law of the Roman state. [2] the body of law derived from the

principles of this law. Compare **jus gentium, jus naturale.**
▷**HISTORY** from Latin

jus divinum (dɪˈviːnəm) NOUN divine law.
▷**HISTORY** from Latin

jus gentium (ˈdʒɛntɪəm) NOUN *Roman law* those rules of law common to all nations.
▷**HISTORY** from Latin

jus naturale (ˌnætjʊˈreɪlɪ) NOUN *Roman law* 1 (originally) a system of law based on fundamental ideas of right and wrong; natural law. 2 (in later usage) another term for **jus gentium.**
▷**HISTORY** from Latin

jus sanguinis (ˈsæŋgwɪnɪs) NOUN *Law* the principle that a person's nationality at birth is the same as that of his natural parents. Compare **jus soli.**
▷**HISTORY** Latin, literally: law of blood

jussive (ˈdʒʌsɪv) ADJECTIVE *Grammar* another word for **imperative** (sense 3).
▷**HISTORY** C19: from Latin *jūssus* ordered, from *jubēre* to command

jus soli (ˈsəʊlaɪ) NOUN *Law* the principle that a person's nationality at birth is determined by the territory within which he was born. Compare **jus sanguinis.**
▷**HISTORY** from Latin, literally: law of soil

just ADJECTIVE (dʒʌst) 1 **a** fair or impartial in action or judgment. **b** (*as collective noun; preceded by the*): *the just.* 2 conforming to high moral standards; honest. 3 consistent with justice: *a just action.* 4 rightly applied or given; deserved: *a just reward.* 5 legally valid; lawful: *a just inheritance.* 6 well-founded; reasonable: *just criticism.* 7 correct, accurate, or true: *a just account.* ◆ ADVERB (dʒʌst; *unstressed* dʒəst) 8 used with forms of *have* to indicate an action performed in the very recent past: *I have just closed the door.* 9 at this very instant: *he's just coming in to land.* 10 no more than; merely; only: *just an ordinary car.* 11 exactly; precisely: *that's just what I mean.* 12 by a small margin; barely: *he just got there in time.* 13 (intensifier): *it's just wonderful to see you.* 14 *Informal* indeed; with a vengeance: *isn't it just.* 15 **just about.** **a** at the point of starting (to do something). **b** very nearly; almost: *I've just about had enough.* 16 **just a moment, second,** *or* **minute.** an expression requesting the hearer to wait or pause for a brief period of time. 17 **just now.** **a** a very short time ago. **b** at this moment. **c** *South African informal* in a little while. 18 **just on.** having reached exactly: *it's just on five o'clock.* 19 **just so.** **a** an expression of complete agreement or of unwillingness to dissent. **b** arranged with precision.
▷**HISTORY** C14: from Latin *jūstus* righteous, from *jūs* justice
▸ **ˈjustly** ADVERB ▸ **ˈjustness** NOUN

> **Language note** The use of *just* with *exactly* (*it's just exactly what they want*) is redundant and should be avoided: *it's exactly what they want.*

justice (ˈdʒʌstɪs) NOUN 1 the quality or fact of being just. 2 *Ethics* **a** the principle of fairness that like cases should be treated alike. **b** a particular distribution of benefits and burdens fairly in accordance with a particular conception of what are to count as like cases. **c** the principle that punishment should be proportionate to the offence. 3 the administration of law according to prescribed and accepted principles. 4 conformity to the law; legal validity. 5 a judge of the Supreme Court of Judicature. 6 short for **justice of the peace.** 7 good reason (esp in the phrase **with justice**): *he was disgusted by their behaviour, and with justice.* 8 **do justice to.** **a** to show to full advantage: *the picture did justice to her beauty.* **b** to show full appreciation of by action: *he did justice to the meal.* **c** to treat or judge fairly. 9 **do oneself justice.** to make full use of one's abilities. 10 **bring to justice.** to capture, try, and usually punish (a criminal, an outlaw, etc.).
▷**HISTORY** C12: from Old French, from Latin *jūstitia,* from *justus* JUST

justice court NOUN an inferior court presided over by a justice of the peace.

justice of the peace NOUN 1 (in Britain) a lay magistrate, appointed by the crown or acting *ex officio,* whose function is to preserve the peace in his area, try summarily such cases as are within his jurisdiction, and perform miscellaneous administrative duties. 2 (in Australia and New Zealand) a person authorised to administer oaths, attest instruments, and take declarations.

justice of the peace court NOUN (in Scotland, formerly) a court with limited criminal jurisdiction held by justices of the peace in counties: replaced in 1975 by the **district court.**

justiceship (ˈdʒʌstɪsˌʃɪp) NOUN the rank or office of a justice.

justiciable (dʒʌˈstɪʃɪəb^{ə}l) ADJECTIVE 1 capable of being determined by a court of law. 2 liable to be brought before a court for trial; subject to jurisdiction.
▸ **jusˌticiaˈbility** NOUN

justiciar (dʒʌˈstɪʃɪˌɑː) NOUN *English legal history* the chief political and legal officer from the time of William I to that of Henry III, who deputized for the king in his absence and presided over the kings' courts. Also called: **justiciary.**
▸ **jusˈticiarˌship** NOUN

justiciary (dʒʌˈstɪʃɪərɪ) ADJECTIVE 1 of or relating to the administration of justice. ◆ NOUN, *plural* **-aries.** 2 an officer or administrator of justice; judge. 3 another word for **justiciar.**

justifiable (ˈdʒʌstɪˌfaɪəb^{ə}l) ADJECTIVE capable of being justified; understandable.
▸ **ˌjustiˌfiaˈbility** *or* **ˈjustiˌfiableness** NOUN ▸ **ˈjustiˌfiably** ADVERB

justifiable homicide NOUN lawful killing, as in self-defence or to prevent a crime.

justification (ˌdʒʌstɪfɪˈkeɪʃən) NOUN 1 reasonable grounds for complaint, defence, etc. 2 the act of justifying; proof, vindication, or exculpation. 3 *Theol* **a** the act of justifying. **b** the process of being justified or the condition of having been justified. 4 Also called: **justification by faith.** *Protestant theol* the doctrine that God vindicates only those who repent and believe in Jesus. 5 *Printing, computing* the process of adjusting interword spacing in text or data so that both right and left margins are straight. 6 *Computing* the process of moving data right or left so that the first or last character occurs in a predefined position.

justificatory (ˈdʒʌstɪfɪˌkeɪtərɪ, -trɪ) *or* **justificative** (ˈdʒʌstɪfɪˌkeɪtɪv) ADJECTIVE serving as justification or capable of justifying; vindicatory.

justify (ˈdʒʌstɪˌfaɪ) VERB **-fies, -fying, -fied.** (*mainly tr*) 1 (*often passive*) to prove or see to be just or valid; vindicate: *he was certainly justified in taking the money.* 2 to show to be reasonable; warrant or substantiate: *his behaviour justifies our suspicion.* 3 to declare or show to be free from blame or guilt; absolve. 4 *Law* **a** to show good reason in court for (some action taken). **b** to show adequate grounds for doing (that with which a person is charged): *to justify a libel.* 5 (*also intr*) *Printing, computing* to adjust the spaces between words in (a line of type or data) so that it is of the required length or (of a line of type or data) to fit exactly. 6 **a** *Protestant theol* to account or declare righteous by the imputation of Christ's merits to the sinner. **b** *RC theol* to change from sinfulness to righteousness by the transforming effects of grace. 7 (*also intr*) *Law* to prove (a person) to have sufficient means to act as surety, etc., or (of a person) to qualify to provide bail or surety.
▷**HISTORY** C14: from Old French *justifier,* from Latin *justificāre,* from *jūstus* JUST + *facere* to make
▸ **ˈjustiˌfier** NOUN

Justinian Code NOUN a compilation of Roman imperial law made by order of Justinian I, forming part of the **Corpus Juris Civilis.**

just-in-time ADJECTIVE denoting or relating to an industrial method in which waste of resources is eliminated or reduced by producing production-line components, etc., as they are required, rather than holding large stocks. Abbreviation: **JIT.**

just intonation NOUN a form of tuning employing the pitch intervals of the untempered natural scale, sometimes employed in the playing of the violin, cello, etc.

justle (ˈdʒʌs^{ə}l) VERB a less common word for **jostle.**

just noticeable difference NOUN *Psychol* another name for **difference threshold.** Abbreviation: **jnd.**

jut (dʒʌt) VERB **juts, jutting, jutted.** 1 (*intr;* often foll by *out*) to stick out or overhang beyond the surface or main part; protrude or project. ◆ NOUN 2 something that juts out.
▷**HISTORY** C16: variant of JET[1]
▸ **ˈjutting** ADJECTIVE

jute (dʒuːt) NOUN 1 either of two Old World tropical yellow-flowered herbaceous plants, *Corchorus capsularis* or *C. olitorius,* cultivated for their strong fibre: family *Tiliaceae.* 2 this fibre, used in making sacks, rope, etc.
▷**HISTORY** C18: from Bengali *jhuto,* from Sanskrit *jūta* braid of hair, matted hair

Jute (dʒuːt) NOUN a member of one of various Germanic tribes, some of whom invaded England in the 6th century A.D., settling in Kent.

Jutish (ˈdʒuːtɪʃ) ADJECTIVE 1 of or relating to the Jutes. ◆ NOUN 2 another name for **Kentish.**

Jutland (ˈdʒʌtlənd) NOUN a peninsula of N Europe: forms the continental portion of Denmark and geographically includes the N part of the German province of Schleswig-Holstein, while politically it includes only the mainland of Denmark and the islands north of Limfjorden; a major but inconclusive naval battle was fought off its NW coast in 1916 between the British and German fleets. Danish name: **Jylland.**

Jutlander (ˈdʒʌtləndə) NOUN a native or inhabitant of Jutland.

juvenal (ˈdʒuːvɪn^{ə}l) ADJECTIVE *Ornithol* a variant spelling (esp US) of **juvenile** (sense 4).

juvenescence (ˌdʒuːvɪˈnɛsəns) NOUN 1 youth or immaturity. 2 the act or process of growing from childhood to youth. 3 restoration of youth; rejuvenation.

juvenescent (ˌdʒuːvɪˈnɛs^{ə}nt) ADJECTIVE becoming or being young or youthful.
▷**HISTORY** C19: from Latin *juvenēscere* to grow up, regain strength, from *juvenis* youthful

juvenile (ˈdʒuːvɪˌnaɪl) ADJECTIVE 1 young, youthful, or immature. 2 suitable or designed for young people: *juvenile pastimes.* 3 (of animals or plants) not yet fully mature. 4 of or denoting young birds that have developed their first plumage of adult feathers. 5 *Geology* occurring at the earth's surface for the first time; new: *juvenile water; juvenile gases.* ◆ NOUN 6 a juvenile person, animal, or plant. 7 an actor who performs youthful roles. 8 a book intended for young readers.
▷**HISTORY** C17: from Latin *juvenīlis* youthful, from *juvenis* young
▸ **ˈjuveˌnilely** ADVERB ▸ **ˈjuveˌnileness** NOUN

juvenile court NOUN the former name for **youth court.**

juvenile delinquency NOUN antisocial or criminal conduct by juvenile delinquents.

juvenile delinquent NOUN a child or young person guilty of some offence, act of vandalism, or antisocial behaviour or whose conduct is beyond parental control and who may be brought before a juvenile court.

juvenile hormone NOUN a hormone, secreted by insects from a pair of glands behind the brain, that promotes the growth of larval characteristics and inhibits metamorphosis.

juvenilia (ˌdʒuːvɪˈnɪlɪə) PLURAL NOUN works of art, literature, or music produced in youth or adolescence, before the artist, author, or composer has formed a mature style.
▷**HISTORY** C17: from Latin, literally: youthful things; see JUVENILE

juvenility (ˌdʒuːvɪˈnɪlɪtɪ) NOUN, *plural* **-ties.** 1 the quality or condition of being juvenile, esp of being immature. 2 (*often plural*) a juvenile act or manner. 3 juveniles collectively.

juxtapose (ˌdʒʌkstəˈpəʊz) VERB (*tr*) to place close together or side by side.
▷**HISTORY** C19: back formation from *juxtaposition,* from Latin *juxta* next to + POSITION
▸ **ˌjuxtapoˈsition** NOUN ▸ **ˌjuxtapoˈsitional** ADJECTIVE

JWV ABBREVIATION FOR Jewish War Veterans.

Jylland (ˈjylan) NOUN the Danish name for **Jutland.**

Kk

k *or* **K** (keɪ) NOUN, *plural* **k's, K's** *or* **Ks.** [1] the 11th letter and 8th consonant of the modern English alphabet. [2] a speech sound represented by this letter, usually a voiceless velar stop, as in *kitten.* [3] See **five Ks.**

k SYMBOL FOR: [1] kilo(s). [2] *Maths* the unit vector along the z-axis.

K SYMBOL FOR: [1] kelvin(s). [2] *Chess* king. [3] *Chem* potassium. [4] *Physics* kaon. [5] *Currency* **a** kina. **b** kip. **c** kopeck. **d** kwacha. **e** kyat. [6] one thousand. [7] *Computing* **a** a unit of 1024 words, bits, or bytes. **b** (not in technical usage) 1000. ◆ [8] INTERNATIONAL CAR REGISTRATION FOR Cambodia.
▷**HISTORY** (for sense 3) from New Latin *kalium;* (for sense 6) from KILO-; (for sense 8) from *Kampuchea*

K *or* **K.** ABBREVIATION FOR Köchel: indicating the serial number in the catalogue (1862) of the works of Mozart made by Ludwig von Köchel (1800–1877).

K2 NOUN a mountain in the Karakoram Range on the Kashmir-Xinjiang Uygur AR border: the second highest mountain in the world. Height: 8611 m (28 250 ft.). Also called: **Godwin Austen, Dapsang.**

ka (kɑː) NOUN (in ancient Egypt) an attendant spirit supposedly dwelling as a vital force in a man or statue.
▷**HISTORY** from Egyptian

Kaaba *or* **Caaba** (ˈkɑːbə) NOUN a cube-shaped building in Mecca, the most sacred Muslim pilgrim shrine, into which is built the black stone believed to have been given by Gabriel to Abraham. Muslims turn in its direction when praying.
▷**HISTORY** from Arabic *ka'bah,* from *ka'b* cube

kaal (ˈkɑːl) *or* **kaal gat** (ˈkɑːl gæt) ADJECTIVE *South African informal* naked.
▷**HISTORY** from Afrikaans, literally: bare (arsed)

kab (kæb) NOUN a variant spelling of **cab**[2].

kabaddi (kəˈbɑːdɪ) NOUN a game played between two teams of seven players, in which individuals take turns to chase and try to touch members of the opposing team without being captured by them.
▷**HISTORY** Tamil

kabaka (kaˈbaka) NOUN any of the former rulers of the Baganda people of S Uganda.
▷**HISTORY** C19: from Luganda

Kabalega Falls (ˌkɑːbəˈleɪgə) PLURAL NOUN rapids on the lower Victoria Nile, about 35 km (22 miles) east of Lake Albert, where the Nile drops 120 m (400 ft.).

kabaragoya (kəˌbɑːrəˈgəʊjə) NOUN a very large monitor lizard, *Varanus salvator,* of SE Asia: it grows to a length of three metres. Also called: **Malayan monitor.**
▷**HISTORY** perhaps Tagalog

Kabardian (kəˈbɑːdɪən) NOUN [1] a member of a Circassian people of the North West Caucasus. [2] the Eastern dialect of the Circassian language. Compare **Adygei.**

Kabardino-Balkar Republic (ˌkæbəˈdiːnəʊˌbælkə) NOUN a constituent republic of S Russia, on the N side of the Caucasus Mountains. Capital: Nalchik. Pop.: 792 000 (2000 est.). Area: 12 500 sq. km (4825 sq. miles). Also called: **Kabardino-Balkaria** (kæbəˌdiːnəʊbælˈkɑːrɪə).

kabbala *or* **kabala** (kəˈbɑːlə) NOUN variant spellings of **cabbala.**
▸**kabbalism** *or* **kabalism** (ˈkæbəˌlɪzəm) NOUN ▸**ˈkabbalist** *or* **ˈkabalist** NOUN ▸**ˌkabbaˈlistic** *or* **ˌkabaˈlistic** ADJECTIVE

kabeljou (ˈkɑːbəlˌjəʊ) NOUN *South African* a large marine sciaenid fish, *Argyrosomus hololepidotus,* that is an important food fish of South African waters.
▷**HISTORY** C18: from Afrikaans, from Dutch, cod

Kabinett (ˌkæbɪˈnet) NOUN a dry, usually white, wine produced in Germany, made from mature grapes with no added sugar.
▷**HISTORY** C20: from German, literally: cabinet

Kabloona (kəˈbluːnə) NOUN (in Canada) a person who is not of Inuit ancestry, esp a White person.
▷**HISTORY** from Inuktituk

kabob (kəˈbɒb) NOUN another name for **kebab.**

kabuki (kæˈbuːkɪ) NOUN a form of Japanese drama based on popular legends and characterized by elaborate costumes, stylized acting, and the use of male actors for all roles. See also **No**[1].
▷**HISTORY** Japanese, from *ka* singing + *bu* dancing + *ki* art

Kabul (kəˈbʊl, ˈkɔːbᵊl) NOUN [1] the capital of Afghanistan, in the northeast of the country at an altitude of 1800 m (5900 ft.) on the **Kabul River:** over 3000 years old, with a strategic position commanding passes through the Hindu Kush and main routes to the Khyber Pass; destroyed and rebuilt many times; capital of the Mogul Empire from 1504 until 1738 and of Afghanistan from 1773; university (1932). Pop.: 700 000 (1993 est.). [2] a river in Afghanistan and Pakistan, rising in the Hindu Kush and flowing east into the Indus at Attock, Pakistan. Length: 700 km (435 miles).

Kabyle (kəˈbaɪl) NOUN [1] (*plural* **-byles** *or* **-byle**) a member of a Berber people inhabiting the E Atlas Mountains in Tunisia and Algeria. [2] the dialect of Berber spoken by this people.
▷**HISTORY** C19: from Arabic *qabā'il,* plural of *qabīlah* tribe

kachang puteh (ˈkatʃaŋ puːˈteɪ) NOUN (in Malaysia) roasted or fried nuts or beans.
▷**HISTORY** from Malay, literally: white beans

Kachera (kʌˈtʃeɪrə) *or* **Kacha** (ˈkʌtʃə) NOUN short trousers traditionally worn by Sikhs as a symbol of their religious and cultural loyalty: originally worn for ease of horse riding. See also **five Ks.**
▷**HISTORY** Punjabi

kachina (kəˈtʃiːnə) NOUN any of the supernatural beings believed by the Hopi Indians to be the ancestors of living humans.
▷**HISTORY** from Hopi *qačina* supernatural

kadaitcha (kəˈdaɪtʃə) NOUN a variant spelling of **kurdaitcha.**

Kaddish (ˈkædɪʃ) NOUN, *plural* **Kaddishim** (kæˈdɪʃɪm). *Judaism* [1] an ancient Jewish liturgical prayer largely written in Aramaic and used in various forms to separate sections of the liturgy. Mourners have the right to recite some of these in public prayer during the year after, and on the anniversary of, a death. [2] **say Kaddish.** to be a mourner.
▷**HISTORY** C17: from Aramaic *qaddīsh* holy

kadi (ˈkɑːdɪ, ˈkeɪdɪ) NOUN, *plural* **-dis.** a variant spelling of **cadi.**

Kaduna (kəˈduːnə) NOUN [1] a state of N Nigeria. Capital: Kaduna. Pop.: 4 438 007 (1995 est.). Area: 46 053 sq. km (17 781 sq. miles). Former name (until 1976): **North-Central State.** [2] a city in N central Nigeria, capital of Kaduna state on the **Kaduna River** (a principal tributary of the Niger). Pop.: 342 200 (1996 est.).

Kaesŏng (ˌkeɪˈsɒŋ) NOUN a city in SW North Korea: former capital of Korea (938–1392). Pop.: 120 000 (latest est.).

Kaffir *or* **Kafir** (ˈkæfə) NOUN, *plural* **-firs** *or* **-fir.** [1] *Offensive* **a** (in southern Africa) any Black African. **b** (*as modifier*): *Kaffir farming.* [2] a former name for the **Xhosa** language. [3] *Offensive* (among Muslims) a non-Muslim or infidel.
▷**HISTORY** C19: from Arabic *kāfir* infidel, from *kafara* to deny, refuse to believe

kaffir beer NOUN *South African* beer made from sorghum (kaffir corn) or millet.

kaffirboom (ˈkæfəˌbʊəm) NOUN *South African* a deciduous flowering tree, *Erythrina caffra,* having large clusters of brilliant orange or scarlet flowers.
▷**HISTORY** from KAFFIR + Afrikaans *boom* tree

kaffir corn *or sometimes US* **kafir corn** NOUN a Southern African variety of sorghum, cultivated in dry regions for its grain and as fodder. Sometimes shortened to: **kaffir,** (US) **kafir.**

kaffiyeh (kæˈfiːjə) NOUN a variant of **keffiyeh.**

Kaffraria (kæˈfrɛərɪə) NOUN a former region of S central South Africa: inhabited chiefly by the Kaffirs; British Kaffraria was a crown colony established in 1853 in the southwest of the region and annexed to Cape Colony in 1865.

Kaffrarian (kæˈfrɛərɪən) ADJECTIVE [1] of or relating to Kaffraria, a former region of S central South Africa, or its inhabitants. ◆ NOUN [2] a native or inhabitant of Kaffraria.

Kafir (ˈkæfə) NOUN, *plural* **-irs** *or* **-ir.** [1] another name for the **Nuri.** [2] a variant spelling of **Kaffir.**
▷**HISTORY** C19: from Arabic; see KAFFIR

Kafiristan (ˌkæfɪrɪˈstɑːn) NOUN the former name of **Nuristan.**

Kafkaesque (ˌkæfkəˈɛsk) ADJECTIVE reminiscent of the nightmarish dehumanized world portrayed in the novels of Franz Kafka, the Czech novelist (1883–1924).

kaftan *or* **caftan** (ˈkæftæn, -ˌtɑːn) NOUN [1] a long coatlike garment, usually worn with a belt and made of rich fabric, worn in the East. [2] an imitation of this, worn, esp by women, in the West, consisting of a loose dress with long wide sleeves.
▷**HISTORY** C16: from Turkish *qaftān*

Kagera (kæˈgɛrə) NOUN a river in E Africa, rising in headstreams on the border between Tanzania and Rwanda and flowing east to Lake Victoria: the most remote headstream of the Nile and largest tributary of Lake Victoria. Length: about 480 km (300 miles).

Kagoshima (ˌkægɒˈʃiːmə) NOUN a port in SW Japan, on S Kyushu. Pop.: 546 294 (1995).

kagoul *or* **kagoule** (kəˈguːl) NOUN variant spellings of **cagoule.**

kagu (ˈkɑːguː) NOUN a crested nocturnal bird, *Rhynochetos jubatus,* with a red bill and greyish plumage: occurs only in New Caledonia and is nearly extinct: family *Rhynochetidae,* order *Gruiformes* (cranes, rails, etc.).
▷**HISTORY** native name in New Caledonia

kahawai (ˈkɑːhəˌwaɪ) NOUN a large food and game fish of Australian and New Zealand coastal waters, *Arripis trutta,* that is greenish grey to silvery underneath and spotted with brown: resembles a salmon but is in fact a marine perch. Also called: **Australian salmon.**
▷**HISTORY** Maori

kahikatea (ˌkaɪkəˈtɪə) NOUN a tall New Zealand coniferous tree, *Podocarpus dacrydioides,* valued for its timber and resin. Also called: **white pine.**
▷**HISTORY** Maori

kai (kaɪ) NOUN *NZ* food.
▷**HISTORY** Maori, from Melanesian pidgin *kaikai*

kaiak (ˈkaɪæk) NOUN a variant of **kayak.**

Kaieteur Falls (ˌkaɪəˈtʊə) PLURAL NOUN a waterfall in Guyana, on the Potaro River. Height: 226 m (741 ft.). Width: about 107 m (350 ft.).

kaif (kaɪf) NOUN a variant of **kif.**

Kaifeng (ˈkaɪˈfɛŋ) NOUN a city in E China, in N Henan on the Yellow River: one of the oldest cities in China and its capital (as Pien-liang) from 907 to 1126. Pop.: 569 300 (1999 est.).

kaik (kaɪk) NOUN *NZ* the South Island dialect word for **kainga.**

kail (keɪl) NOUN a variant spelling of **kale.**

kailyard (ˈkeɪlˌjɑːd) NOUN a variant spelling of **kaleyard.**

kai moana (məʊˈænə) NOUN *NZ* seafood.
▷**HISTORY** Maori, from KAI + *moana* sea

kain (keɪn) NOUN *History* a variant spelling of **cain.**

kainga (ˈkaɪŋə) NOUN (in New Zealand) a Maori village or small settlement. Also called (on South Island): **kaik.**
▷**HISTORY** Maori

kainite (ˈkaɪnaɪt) NOUN a white mineral consisting of potassium chloride and magnesium sulphate: a fertilizer and source of potassium salts. Formula: $KCl.MgSO_4.3H_2O$.

▷HISTORY C19: from German *Kainit,* from Greek *kainos* new + -ITE[1]

kainogenesis (ˌkaɪnəʊˈdʒɛnɪsɪs) NOUN another name for **caenogenesis.**
▸**kainogenetic** (ˌkaɪnəʊdʒəˈnɛtɪk) ADJECTIVE
▸ˌ**kainogeˈnetically** ADVERB

Kairouan (*French* kɛrwɑ̃), **Kairwan,** *or* **Qairwan** (kaɪəˈwɑːn) NOUN a city in NE Tunisia: one of the holy cities of Islam; pilgrimage and trading centre. Pop.: 102 600 (1994).

Kaiser (ˈkaɪzə) NOUN (*sometimes not capital*) *History* [1] any German emperor, esp Wilhelm II (1888–1918). [2] *Obsolete* any Austro-Hungarian emperor.
▷HISTORY C16: from German, ultimately from Latin *Caesar* emperor, from the cognomen of Gaius Julius Caesar (100–44 B.C.), Roman general, statesman, and historian
▸ˈ**kaiserdom** *or* ˈ**kaiserism** NOUN

Kaiserslautern (*German* kaizərsˈlautərn) NOUN a city in W Germany, in S Rhineland-Palatinate. Pop.: 100 300 (1999 est.).

kaizen *Japanese* (kaɪˈzɛn) NOUN a philosophy of continuous improvement of working practices that underlies total quality management and just-in-time business techniques.
▷HISTORY literally: improvement

kak (ˈkʌk) NOUN *South African, taboo* [1] faeces. [2] rubbish.
▷HISTORY Afrikaans

kaka (ˈkɑːkə) NOUN a New Zealand parrot, *Nestor meridionalis,* with a long compressed bill.
▷HISTORY C18: from Maori, perhaps imitative of its call

kaka beak NOUN an evergreen climbing shrub, *Clianthus puniceus,* having pinnate leaves and clusters of bright red flowers in the shape of a parrot's beak. It is native to New Zealand but now rare except in cultivation. Also called: **red kowhai.**

kakapo (ˈkɑːkəˌpəʊ) NOUN, *plural* **-pos.** a ground-living nocturnal parrot, *Strigops habroptilus,* of New Zealand, resembling an owl.
▷HISTORY C19: from Maori, literally: night kaka

kakemono (ˌkækɪˈməʊnəʊ) NOUN, *plural* **-nos.** a Japanese paper or silk wall hanging, usually long and narrow, with a picture or inscription on it and a roller at the bottom.
▷HISTORY C19: from Japanese, from *kake* hanging + *mono* thing

kaki (ˈkɑːkɪ) NOUN, *plural* **kakis.** another name for **Japanese persimmon.**
▷HISTORY Japanese

kala-azar (ˌkɑːləəˈzɑː) NOUN a tropical infectious disease caused by the protozoan *Leishmania donovani* in the liver, spleen, etc., characterized by fever and weight loss; visceral leishmaniasis.
▷HISTORY from Assamese *kālā* black + *āzār* disease

Kalahari (ˌkæləˈhɑːrɪ) NOUN **the.** an extensive arid plateau of South Africa, Namibia, and Botswana. Area: 260 000 sq. km (100 000 sq. miles). Also called: **Kalahari Desert.**

kalamata olive *or* **calamata olive** (ˌkæləˈmɑːtə) NOUN an aubergine-coloured Greek olive.
▷HISTORY Greek

Kalamazoo (ˌkæləməˈzuː) NOUN a city in SW Michigan, midway between Detroit and Chicago: aircraft, missile parts. Pop.: 77 145 (2000).

kalanchoe (ˌkælənˈkəʊɪ) NOUN any plant of the tropical succulent genus *Kalanchoe,* grown as pot plants for their small brightly coloured flowers, sometimes scented, and their dark shiny leaves: family *Crassulaceae.*
▷HISTORY New Latin, from the Chinese name of one of the species

Kalashnikov (ˌkəˈlæʃnɪˌkɒf) NOUN a Russian-made automatic rifle. See also **AK-47.**
▷HISTORY C20: named after Mikhail *Kalashnikov* (born 1919), its designer

Kalat *or* **Khelat** (kəˈlɑːt) NOUN a region of SW Pakistan, in S Baluchistan: formerly a princely state ruled by the Khan of Kalat, which joined Pakistan in 1948.

kale[1] *or* **kail** (keɪl) NOUN [1] a cultivated variety of cabbage, *Brassica oleracea acephala,* with crinkled leaves: used as a potherb. See also **collard.** [2] *Scot* a cabbage. [3] *US, slang* money. ◆ Compare (for senses 1, 2) **sea kale.**
▷HISTORY Old English *cāl;* see COLE

kale[2] (keɪl) NOUN *Northern English dialect* a queue.

kaleidoscope (kəˈlaɪdəˌskəʊp) NOUN [1] an optical toy for producing symmetrical patterns by multiple reflections in inclined mirrors enclosed in a tube. Loose pieces of coloured glass, paper, etc., are placed between transparent plates at the far end of the tube, which is rotated to change the pattern. [2] any complex pattern of frequently changing shapes and colours. [3] a complicated set of circumstances.
▷HISTORY C19: from Greek *kalos* beautiful + *eidos* form + -SCOPE
▸**kaleidoscopic** (kəˌlaɪdəˈskɒpɪk) ADJECTIVE
▸**kaˌleidoˈscopically** ADVERB

kalends (ˈkælɪndz) PLURAL NOUN a variant spelling of **calends.**

Kalevala (ˌkɑːləˈvɑːlə; *Finnish* ˈkɑlɛvɑlɑ) NOUN *Finnish legend* [1] the land of the hero Kaleva, who performed legendary exploits. [2] the Finnish national epic in which these exploits are recounted, compiled by Elias Lönnrot from folk poetry in 1835 to 1849.
▷HISTORY Finnish, from *kaleva* of a hero + *-la* dwelling place, home

kaleyard *or* **kailyard** (ˈkeɪlˌjɑːd; *Scot* -ˌjard) NOUN *Scot* a vegetable garden.
▷HISTORY C19: literally: cabbage garden

kaleyard school *or* **kailyard school** NOUN a group of writers who depicted the sentimental and homely aspects of life in the Scottish Lowlands from about 1880 to 1914. The best known contributor to the school was J. M. Barrie.

Kalgan (ˈkɑːlˈgɑːn) NOUN a former name of **Zhangjiakou.**

Kalgoorlie (kælˈgʊəlɪ) NOUN a city in Western Australia, adjoining the town of Boulder: a centre of the Coolgardie gold rushes of the early 1890s; declining gold resources superseded by the discovery of nickel ore in 1966. Pop.: 26 079 (including Boulder) (1991).

kali (ˈkælɪ, ˈkeɪ-) NOUN another name for **saltwort[1].**

Kali (ˈkɑːlɪ) NOUN the Hindu goddess of destruction, consort of Siva. Her cult was characterized by savagery and cannibalism.

kalian (kælˈjɑːn) NOUN another name for **hookah.**
▷HISTORY C19: from Persian, from Arabic *qalyān*

kalif (ˈkeɪlɪf, ˈkæl-) NOUN a variant spelling of **caliph.**

Kalimantan (ˌkælɪˈmæntən) NOUN the Indonesian name for Borneo: applied to the Indonesian part of the island only, excluding the Malaysian states of Sabah and Sarawak and the sultanate of Brunei. Pop.: 11 396 100 (1999 est.).

Kalinin (*Russian* kaˈlinin) NOUN the former name (until 1991) of **Tver.**

Kaliningrad (*Russian* kəlininˈgrat) NOUN a port in W Russia, on the Pregolya River: severely damaged in World War II as the chief German naval base on the Baltic; ceded to the Soviet Union in 1945 and is now Russia's chief Baltic naval base. Pop.: 427 200 (1999 est.). Former name (until 1946): **Königsberg.**

Kalisz (*Polish* ˈkaliʃ) NOUN a town in central Poland, on an island in the Prosna River: textile industry. Pop.: 106 641 (1999 est.). Ancient name: **Calissia** (kəˈlɪsɪə).

Kaliyuga (ˌkɑːlɪˈjuːgə) NOUN (in Hindu mythology) the fourth (present) age of the world, characterized by total decadence.

Kalmar (*Swedish* ˈkalmar) NOUN a port in SE Sweden, partly on the mainland and partly on a small island in the **Sound of Kalmar** opposite Öland: scene of the signing of the Union of Kalmar, which united Sweden, Denmark, and Norway into a single monarchy (1397–1523). Pop.: 58 070 (1994).

kalmia (ˈkælmɪə) NOUN any evergreen ericaceous shrub of the North American genus *Kalmia,* having showy clusters of white or pink flowers. See also **mountain laurel.**
▷HISTORY C18: named after Peter *Kalm* (1715–79), Swedish botanist and pupil of Linnaeus

Kalmuck (ˈkælmʌk) *or* **Kalmyk** (ˈkælmɪk) NOUN [1] (*plural* **-mucks, -muck** *or* **-myks, -myk**) a member of a Mongoloid people of Buddhist tradition, who migrated from W China in the 17th century. [2] the language of this people, belonging to the Mongolic branch of the Altaic family.

Kalmuck Republic *or* **Kalmyk Republic** NOUN a constituent republic of S Russia, on the Caspian Sea: became subject to Russia in 1646. Capital: Elista. Pop.: 316 000 (2000 est.). Area: 76 100 sq. km (29 382 sq. miles). Also called: **Kalmykia.**

kalong (ˈkɑːlɒŋ) NOUN any fruit bat of the genus *Pteropus;* a flying fox.
▷HISTORY Javanese

kalpa (ˈkælpə) NOUN (in Hindu cosmology) a period in which the universe experiences a cycle of creation and destruction.
▷HISTORY C18: Sanskrit

kalpak (ˈkælpæk) NOUN a variant spelling of **calpac.**

kalsomine (ˈkælsəˌmaɪn, -mɪn) NOUN, VERB a variant of **calcimine.**

Kaluga (*Russian* kaˈlugə) NOUN a city in central Russia, on the Oka River. Pop.: 342 400 (1999 est.).

Kama[1] (*Russian* ˈkamə) NOUN a river in central Russia, rising in the Ural Mountains and flowing to the River Volga, of which it is the largest tributary. Length: 2030 km (1260 miles).

Kama[2] (ˈkɑːmə) NOUN the Hindu god of love.
▷HISTORY from Sanskrit

kamacite (ˈkæməˌsaɪt) NOUN an alloy of iron and nickel, occurring in meteorites.
▷HISTORY C19: from (obsolete) German *Kamacit,* from Greek *kamax* shaft, pole + -ITE[1]

Kamakura (ˌkæməˈkʊərə) NOUN a city in central Japan, on S Honshu: famous for its Great Buddha (Daibutsu), a 13th-century bronze, 15 m (49 ft.) high. Pop.: 170 319 (1995 est.).

kamala (kəˈmɑːlə, ˈkæmələ) NOUN [1] an East Indian euphorbiaceous tree, *Mallotus philippinensis.* [2] a powder obtained from the seed capsules of this tree, used as a dye and formerly as a worm powder.
▷HISTORY C19: from Sanskrit, probably of Dravidian origin; compare Kanarese *kōmale*

Kama Sutra (ˌkɑːmə ˈsuːtrə) NOUN **the.** an ancient Hindu text on erotic pleasure and other topics.
▷HISTORY Sanskrit: book on love, from *kāma* love + *sūtra* thread

Kamchatka (*Russian* kamˈtʃatkə) NOUN a peninsula in E Russia, between the Sea of Okhotsk and the Bering Sea. Length: about 1200 km (750 miles).

Kamchatkan (*Russian* kamˈtʃatkən) ADJECTIVE [1] of or relating to Kamchatka, a peninsula in E Russia, or its inhabitants. ◆ NOUN [2] a native or inhabitant of Kamchatka.

kame (keɪm) NOUN an irregular mound or ridge of gravel, sand, etc., deposited by water derived from melting glaciers.
▷HISTORY C19: Scottish and northern English variant of COMB

kameez (kəˈmiːz) NOUN a long tunic worn in the Indian subcontinent, often with shalwar.
▷HISTORY Urdu *kamis,* from Arabic *qamīs*

Kamensk-Uralski (*Russian* ˈkamɪnskuˈraljskij) NOUN an industrial city in S Russia. Pop.: 192 000 (1999 est.).

Kamerad *German* (kaməˈraːt; *English* ˈkæməˌrɑːd) SENTENCE SUBSTITUTE a shout of surrender, used by German soldiers.
▷HISTORY German: COMRADE

Kamerun (ˈkaməruːn) NOUN the German name for **Cameroon.**

Kamet (ˈkɑːmɛt, ˈkʌmeɪt) NOUN a mountain in N India, in Uttar Pradesh in the Himalayas. Height: 7756 m (25 447 ft.).

kami (ˈkɑːmɪ) NOUN, *plural* **-mi.** a divine being or spiritual force in Shinto.
▷HISTORY C18: from Japanese: god, lord

kamik (ˈkɑːmɪk) NOUN *Canadian* a traditional Inuit boot made of caribou hide or sealskin.
▷HISTORY from Inuktitut

kamikaze (ˌkæmɪˈkɑːzɪ) NOUN (*often capital*) [1] (in World War II) one of a group of Japanese pilots who performed suicidal missions by crashing their aircraft, loaded with explosives, into an enemy target, esp a ship. [2] an aircraft used for such a mission. [3] (*modifier*) (of an action) undertaken or (of a person) undertaking an action in the knowledge that it will result in the death of the person performing it in order that maximum damage may be inflicted on an enemy: *a kamikaze attack; a kamikaze bomber.* [4] (*modifier*) extremely foolhardy and possibly self-defeating: *kamikaze pricing.*

▷HISTORY C20: from Japanese, from *kami* divine + *kaze* wind, referring to the winds that, according to Japanese tradition, destroyed a Mongol invasion fleet in 1281

Kamilaroi (ˈkæmələrɔɪ) NOUN an Australian Aboriginal language formerly used in NW New South Wales.

Kamloops trout (ˈkæmˌluːps) NOUN *Canadian* a variety of rainbow trout found in Canadian lakes.

Kampala (kæmˈpɑːlə) NOUN the capital and largest city of Uganda, in Central region on Lake Victoria: Makerere University (1961). Pop.: 1 154 000 (1999 est.).

kampong (ˈkæmpɒŋ, kæmˈpɒŋ) NOUN (in Malaysia) a village.
▷HISTORY C19: from Malay

Kampuchea (ˌkæmpuˈtʃɪə) NOUN the name of **Cambodia** from 1976 until 1989.

Kampuchean (ˌkæmpuˈtʃɪən) ADJECTIVE [1] of or relating to Kampuchea, a former name for Cambodia, or its inhabitants. ◆ NOUN [2] a native or inhabitant of Kampuchea.

kamseen (kæmˈsiːn) *or* **kamsin** (ˈkæmsɪn) NOUN variants of **khamsin**.

Kan. ABBREVIATION FOR Kansas.

kana (ˈkɑːnə) NOUN the Japanese syllabary, which consists of two written varieties. See **hiragana, katakana**.
▷HISTORY C18: from Japanese, literally: borrowed or provisional letters; compare KANJI, which are regarded as real letters

Kanak (kəˈnæk) NOUN a native or inhabitant of New Caledonia who seeks independence from France.
▷HISTORY C20: from Hawaiian: man

Kanaka (kəˈnækə, ˈkænəkə) NOUN [1] (esp in Hawaii) a native Hawaiian. [2] (*often not capital*) *Austral* any native of the South Pacific islands, esp (formerly) one abducted to work in Australia.
▷HISTORY C19: from Hawaiian: man, human being

kanamycin (ˌkænəˈmaɪsɪn) NOUN an aminoglycoside antibiotic obtained from the soil bacterium *Streptomyces kanamyceticus*, used in the treatment of various infections, esp those caused by Gram-negative bacteria. Formula: $C_{18}H_{36}N_4O_{11}$.
▷HISTORY C20: from New Latin *kanamyceticus*

Kananga (kəˈnæŋgə) NOUN a city in the SW Democratic Republic of Congo (formerly Zaïre): a commercial centre on the railway from Lubumbashi to Port Francqui. Pop.: 393 030 (1994 est.). Former name (until 1966): **Luluabourg**.

Kanara *or* **Canara** (kəˈnɑːrə) NOUN a region of SW India, in Karnataka on the Deccan Plateau and the W Coast. Area: about 155 000 sq. km (60 000 sq. miles).

Kanarese *or* **Canarese** (ˌkænəˈriːz) NOUN [1] *plural* **-rese** a member of a people of S India living chiefly in Kanara. [2] the language of this people; Kannada.

Kanazawa (ˌkænəˈzɑːwə) NOUN a port in central Japan, on W Honshu: textile and porcelain industries. Pop.: 453 977 (1995).

kanban *Japanese* (ˈkænbæn) NOUN [1] a just-in-time manufacturing process in which the movements of materials through a process are recorded on specially designed cards. [2] any of the cards used for ordering materials in such a system.
▷HISTORY literally: advertisement hoarding

Kanchenjunga (ˌkæntʃənˈdʒʌŋgə) NOUN a variant spelling of **Kangchenjunga**.

Kanchipuram (kɑːnˈtʃiːpərəm) NOUN a city in SE India, in Tamil Nadu: a sacred Hindu town known as "the Benares of the South"; textile industries. Pop.: 144 955 (1991).

Kandahar (ˌkændəˈhɑː) NOUN a city in S Afghanistan: an important trading centre, built by Ahmad Shah Durrani (1724–73) as his capital on the site of several former cities. Pop.: 237 500 (1990 est.).

Kandy (ˈkændɪ) NOUN a city in central Sri Lanka: capital of the kingdom of Kandy from 1480 until 1815, when occupied by the British; sacred Buddhist temple; University of Sri Lanka. Pop.: 150 532 (1997 est.).

kanga *or* **khanga** (ˈkɑːŋgɑː) NOUN a piece of gaily decorated thin cotton cloth used as a garment by women in E Africa.
▷HISTORY from Swahili

kangaroo (ˌkæŋgəˈruː) NOUN, *plural* **-roos.** [1] any large herbivorous marsupial of the genus *Macropus* and related genera, of Australia and New Guinea, having large powerful hind legs, used for leaping, and a long thick tail: family *Macropodidae*. See also **rat kangaroo, tree kangaroo.** [2] (*usually plural*) *Stock Exchange* an Australian share, esp in mining, land, or a tobacco company. ◆ VERB **-roos, -rooing, -rooed.** [3] *Informal* (of a car) to move forward or to cause (a car) to move forward with short sudden jerks, as a result of improper use of the clutch.
▷HISTORY C18: probably from a native Australian language
▸ **ˌkangaˈroo-ˌlike** ADJECTIVE

kangaroo closure NOUN *Parliamentary procedure* a form of closure in which the chairman or speaker selects certain amendments for discussion and excludes others. Compare **guillotine** (sense 4).

kangaroo court NOUN an irregular court, esp one set up by prisoners in a jail or by strikers to judge strikebreakers.

kangaroo dog NOUN an Australian breed of large rough-haired dog that resembles a greyhound and is bred to hunt kangaroos.

kangaroo grass NOUN a tall widespread Australian grass, *Themeda australis,* which is highly palatable to cattle and is used for fodder.

Kangaroo Island NOUN an island in the Indian Ocean, off South Australia. Area: 4350 sq. km (1680 sq. miles).

kangaroo paw NOUN any plant of the Australian genus *Anigozanthos,* resembling a kangaroo's paw, esp the red-and-green flowered *A. manglesii,* which is the floral emblem of Western Australia: family *Haemodoraceae*.

kangaroo rat NOUN [1] any small leaping rodent of the genus *Dipodomys,* related to the squirrels and inhabiting desert regions of North America, having a stocky body and very long hind legs and tails: family *Heteromyidae*. [2] Also called: **kangaroo mouse.** any of several leaping murine rodents of the Australian genus *Notomys*.

kangaroo vine NOUN See **cissus.**

Kangchenjunga, Kanchenjunga (ˌkæntʃənˈdʒʌŋgə), *or* **Kinchinjunga** NOUN a mountain on the border between Nepal and Sikkim, in the Himalayas: the third highest mountain in the world. Height: 8598 m (28 208 ft.).

Kangha (ˈkʌŋhə) NOUN the comb traditionally worn by Sikhs as a symbol of their religious and cultural loyalty: originally worn to keep the hair clean. See also **five Ks.**
▷HISTORY Punjabi *kanghā*

KaNgwane (ˌkɑːᵊŋˈgwɑːneɪ) NOUN (formerly) a Bantu homeland in South Africa; replaced in 1994. Capital: Schoemansdal. Former name: **Swazi Territory.**

kanji (ˈkændʒɪ, ˈkɑːn-) NOUN, *plural* **-ji** *or* **-jis.** [1] a Japanese writing system using characters mainly derived from Chinese ideograms. [2] a character in this system.
▷HISTORY Japanese, from Chinese *han* Chinese + *zi* character

Kannada (ˈkɑːnədə, ˈkæn-) NOUN a language of S India belonging to the Dravidian family of languages: the state language of Karnataka, also spoken in Madras and Maharashtra. Also called: **Kanarese.**

Kannon (kɑnon) NOUN the Japanese name for **Kuan Yin.**

Kano (ˈkɑːnəʊ, ˈkeɪnəʊ) NOUN [1] a state of N Nigeria: consists of wooded savanna in the south and scrub vegetation in the north. Capital: Kano. Pop.: 6 297 165 (1995 est.). Area: 20 131 sq. km (7773 sq. miles). [2] a city in N Nigeria, capital of Kano state: transport and market centre. Pop.: 674 100 (1996 est.).

Kanpur (kɑːnˈpʊə) NOUN an industrial city in NE India, in S Uttar Pradesh on the River Ganges: scene of the massacre by Nana Sahib of British soldiers and European families and his later defeat by British forces in 1857. Pop.: 1 874 409 (1991). Former name: **Cawnpore.**

Kansan (ˈkænzən) NOUN [1] a native or inhabitant of Kansas. ◆ ADJECTIVE [2] of or relating to Kansas or its inhabitants.

Kansas (ˈkænzəs) NOUN a state of the central US: consists of undulating prairie, drained chiefly by the Arkansas, Kansas, and Missouri Rivers; mainly agricultural. Capital: Topeka. Pop.: 2 688 418 (2000). Area: 213 096 sq. km (82 277 sq. miles). Abbreviations: **Kan., Kans.,** (with zip code) **KS.**

Kansas City NOUN [1] a city in W Missouri, at the confluence of the Missouri and Kansas Rivers: important centre of livestock and meat-packing industry. Pop.: 441 545 (2000). [2] a city in NE Kansas, adjacent to Kansas City, Missouri. Pop.: 146 866 (2000).

Kansu (ˈkænˈsuː) NOUN a variant transliteration of the Chinese name for **Gansu.**

kantar (kænˈtɑː) NOUN a unit of weight used in E Mediterranean countries, equivalent to 100 pounds or 45 kilograms but varying from place to place.
▷HISTORY C16: from Arabic *qinṭār,* from Late Greek *kentēnarion* weight of a hundred pounds, from Late Latin *centēnārium,* from *centum* hundred

Kantian (ˈkæntɪən) ADJECTIVE (of a philosophical theory) derived from or analogous to a position of the German idealist philosopher Immanuel Kant (1724–1804), esp his doctrines that there are synthetic a priori propositions which order our experience but are not derived from it, that metaphysical conclusions can be inferred from the nature of possible experience, that duty is to be done for its own sake and not as a means to any other end, and that there is a world of things-in-themselves to be distinguished from mere phenomena. See also **transcendental argument, transcendental idealism, categorical imperative, noumenon.**
▸ **ˈKantianˌism** *or* **ˈKantism** NOUN

KANU (ˈkɑːnuː) NOUN ACRONYM FOR Kenya African National Union.

kanzu (ˈkænzʊ) NOUN a long garment, usually white, with long sleeves, worn by E African men.
▷HISTORY C20: from Swahili

Kaohsiung, Kao-hsiung (ˈkaʊˈʃjʊŋ), *or* **Gaoxiong** NOUN a port in SW Taiwan, on the South China Sea: the chief port of the island. Pop.: 1 475 505 (2000 est.). Japanese name: **Takao.**

Kaolack (ˈkɑːəʊˌlæk, ˈkaʊlæk) NOUN a port in SW Senegal, on the Saloum River. Pop.: 200 000 (1998 est.).

kaoliang (ˌkeɪəʊlɪˈæŋ) NOUN any of various E Asian varieties of the sorghum *Sorghum vulgare*.
▷HISTORY from Chinese *kao* tall + *liang* grain

kaolin *or* **kaoline** (ˈkeɪəlɪn) NOUN a fine white clay used for the manufacture of hard-paste porcelain and bone china and in medicine as a poultice and gastrointestinal absorbent. Also called: **china clay, china stone.**
▷HISTORY C18: from French, from Chinese *Kaoling* Chinese mountain where supplies for Europe were first obtained, from *kao* high + *ling* hill
▸ **ˌkaoˈlinic** ADJECTIVE

kaolinite (ˈkeɪəlɪˌnaɪt) NOUN a white or grey clay mineral consisting of hydrated aluminium silicate in triclinic crystalline form, the main constituent of kaolin. Formula: $Al_2Si_2O_5(OH)_4$.

kaon (ˈkeɪɒn) NOUN a meson that has a positive or negative charge and a rest mass of about 966 electron masses, or no charge and a rest mass of 974 electron masses. Also called: **K-meson.**
▷HISTORY C20: *ka* representing the letter *k* + (MES)ON

kapa haka (ˈkɑːpə ˈhɑːkə) SENTENCE SUBSTITUTE *NZ* good! well done!
▷HISTORY Maori

ka pai (ˌkə ˈpaɪ) NOUN *NZ* the traditional Maori performing arts, often performed competitively.
▷HISTORY Maori, literally: traditional dance performed by groups in a line

kapellmeister (kæˈpɛlˌmaɪstə) NOUN, *plural* **-ter.** a variant spelling of **capellmeister.**

Kapfenberg (*German* ˈkapfənbɛrk) NOUN an industrial town in E Austria, in Styria. Pop.: 23 490 (1991).

kaph (kɔːf, kɑːf; *Hebrew* kaf) NOUN the 11th letter of the Hebrew alphabet (כ or, at the end of a word, ך) transliterated as *k* or, when final, *kh*.
▷HISTORY Hebrew, literally: palm of the hand

kapok (ˈkeɪpɒk) NOUN a silky fibre obtained from

the hairs covering the seeds of a tropical bombacaceous tree, *Ceiba pentandra* (**kapok tree** or **silk-cotton tree**): used for stuffing pillows, etc., and for sound insulation. Also called: **silk cotton.**
▷HISTORY C18: from Malay

Kaposi's sarcoma (kæ'pəʊsɪz) NOUN a form of skin cancer found in Africans and more recently in victims of AIDS.
▷HISTORY C20: named after Moritz Kohn *Kaposi* (1837–1902), Austrian dermatologist who first described the sores that characterize the disease

kappa ('kæpə) NOUN the tenth letter in the Greek alphabet (Κ, κ), a consonant, transliterated as *c* or *k*.
▷HISTORY Greek, of Semitic origin

kaput (kæ'pʊt) ADJECTIVE (*postpositive*) *Informal* ruined, broken, or not functioning.
▷HISTORY C20: from German *kaputt* done for, from French *être capot* to have made no tricks (literally: to be hoodwinked), from *capot* hooded cloak

Kara ('kʌrə) NOUN the steel bangle traditionally worn by Sikhs as a symbol of their religious and cultural loyalty, symbolizing unity with God: originally worn as a wristguard by swordsmen. See also **five Ks.**
▷HISTORY Punjabi *karā*

karabiner (ˌkærə'biːnə) NOUN *Mountaineering* a metal clip with a spring for attaching to a piton, belay, etc. Also called: **snaplink, krab.**
▷HISTORY shortened from German *Karabinerhaken,* literally: carbine hook, that is, one used to attach carbines to a belt

Karachai-Cherkess Republic (kərʌ'tʃaɪtʃɛə'kɛs) *or* **Karachayevo-Cherkess Republic** (kərʌ'tʃaɪɛvəʊtʃɛə'kɛs) NOUN a constituent republic of W Russia, on the N side of the Caucasus Mountains. Capital: Cherkessk. Pop.: 435 000 (2000 est.). Area: 14 100 sq. km (5440 sq. miles). Also called: **Karachai-Cherkessia** (kærəˌtʃaɪtʃɛə'kɛsɪə).

Karachi (kə'rɑːtʃɪ) NOUN a port in S Pakistan, on the Arabian Sea: capital of Pakistan (1947–60); university (1950); chief port: commercial and industrial centre. Pop.: 9 269 265 (1998).

Karafuto (ˌkɑːrɑː'fuːtɔ) NOUN transliteration of the Japanese name for **Sakhalin.**

Karaganda (*Russian* kərəgan'da) NOUN a city in E central Kazakhstan, founded in 1857: a major coal-mining and industrial centre. Pop.: 436 900 (1999). Also called: **Qaraghandy.**

Karaite ('kɛərəˌaɪt) NOUN [1] a member of a Jewish sect originating in the 8th century A.D., which rejected the Talmud, favoured strict adherence to and a literal interpretation of the Bible, and attempted to deduce a code of life from it. ◆ ADJECTIVE [2] of, relating to, or designating the Karaite sect.
▷HISTORY C18: from Hebrew *qārāīm* members of the sect, scripturalists, from *qārā* to read

Kara-Kalpak (kə'rɑːkəl'pɑːk) NOUN [1] (*plural* **-paks** *or* **-pak**) a member of a Mongoloid people of central Asia. [2] the language of this people, belonging to the Turkic branch of the Altaic family.

Kara-Kalpak Autonomous Republic (kə'rɑːkəl'pɑːk) NOUN an administrative division in NW Uzbekistan, on the Aral Sea: came under Russian rule by stages from 1873 until Uzbekistan became independent in 1991. Capital: Nukus. Pop.: 1 343 000 (1993 est.). Area: 165 600 sq. km (63 900 sq. miles). Also called: **Kara-Kalpakia** (kə'rɑːkəl'pɑːkɪə), **Kara-Kalpakstan** (kə'rɑːkəlˌpɑːkˌstæn, -'stɑːn).

karakia (ˌkɑːrə'kiːə) NOUN *NZ* a prayer.
▷HISTORY Maori

Karakoram *or* **Karakorum** (ˌkærə'kɔːrəm) NOUN a mountain system in N Kashmir, extending for about 480 km (300 miles) from northwest to southeast: contains the second highest peak in the world (K2); crossed by several high passes, notably the **Karakoram Pass** 5575 m (18 290 ft.).

Karakorum (ˌkærə'kɔːrəm) NOUN a ruined city in Mongolia: founded in 1220 by Ghenghis Khan; destroyed by Kublai Khan when his brother rebelled against him, after Kublai Khan had moved his capital to Peking (now Beijing).

karakul *or* **caracul** ('kærəkᵊl) NOUN [1] a breed of sheep of central Asia having coarse black, grey, or brown hair: the lambs have soft curled usually black hair. [2] the fur prepared from these lambs. ◆ See also **Persian lamb.**
▷HISTORY C19: from Russian, from the name of a region in Bukhara where the sheep originated

Kara Kum (*Russian* kəra 'kum) NOUN a desert in Turkmenistan, covering most of the country: extensive areas now irrigated. Area: about 300 000 sq. km (120 000 sq. miles).

karanga (kə'ræŋə) NOUN *NZ* a call or chant of welcome, sung by a female elder.
▷HISTORY Maori

karaoke (ˌkɑːrə'əʊkɪ) NOUN **a** an entertainment of Japanese origin in which people take it in turns to sing well-known songs over a prerecorded backing tape. **b** (*as modifier*): *a karaoke bar.*
▷HISTORY from Japanese, from *kara* empty + *ōkesutora* orchestra

Kara Sea ('kɑːrə) NOUN a shallow arm of the Arctic Ocean off the N coast of Russia: ice-free for about three months of the year.

karat ('kærət) NOUN the usual US and Canadian spelling of **carat** (sense 2).

karate (kə'rɑːtɪ) NOUN **a** a traditional Japanese system of unarmed combat, employing smashes, chops, kicks, etc., made with the hands, feet, elbows, or legs. **b** (*as modifier*): *karate chop.*
▷HISTORY Japanese, literally: empty hand, from *kara* empty + *te* hand

karateka (kə'rɑːtɪˌkæ) NOUN a competitor or expert in karate.
▷HISTORY Japanese; see KARATE

Karbala ('kɑːbələ) *or* **Kerbela** NOUN a town in central Iraq: the chief holy city of Iraq and centre of Shiah Muslim pilgrimage; burial place of Mohammed's grandson Husain. Pop.: 296 705 (latest est.).

Karelia (kə'riːlɪə; *Russian* ka'reljə) NOUN [1] a region of NE Europe, formerly in Finland but annexed in several stages by the former Soviet Union: corresponds roughly to the Karelian Republic in Russia. [2] another name for the **Karelian Republic.**

Karelian (kə'riːlɪən) ADJECTIVE [1] of or relating to Karelia, its people, or their language. ◆ NOUN [2] a native or inhabitant of Karelia. [3] the dialect of Finnish spoken in Karelia.

Karelian Isthmus NOUN a strip of land, now in Russia, between the Gulf of Finland and Lake Ladoga: annexed by the former Soviet Union after the Russo-Finnish War (1939–40).

Karelian Republic NOUN a constituent republic of NW Russia between the White Sea and Lakes Onega and Ladoga. Capital: Petrozavodsk. Pop.: 766 000 (2000 est.). Area: 172 400 sq. km (66 560 sq. miles). Also called: **Karelia.**

Karen (kə'rɛn) NOUN [1] (*plural* **-rens** *or* **-ren**) a member of a Thai people of Myanmar. [2] the language of this people, probably related to Thai and belonging to the Sino-Tibetan family.

Kariba (kə'riːbə) NOUN **Lake.** a lake on the Zambia-Zimbabwe border, created by the building of the **Kariba Dam** across the Zambezi for hydroelectric power. Length: 282 km (175 miles).

Karitane (ˌkærɪ'tɑːnɪ) NOUN short for **Karitane nurse.**

Karitane hospital NOUN *NZ* a hospital for young babies and their mothers.
▷HISTORY from *Karitane,* a town on South Island, New Zealand, headquarters of the PLUNKET SOCIETY

Karitane nurse NOUN *NZ* a nurse trained in the care of young babies and their mothers according to the principles of the Plunket Society. Often shortened to: **Karitane.**

Karl-Marx-Stadt (*German* karl'marksʃtat) NOUN the former name (1953–90) of **Chemnitz.**

Karlovy Vary (*Czech* 'karlɔvi 'vari) NOUN a city in the W Czech Republic, at the confluence of the Tepla and Ohře Rivers: warm mineral springs. Pop.: 56 290 (1991). German name: **Karlsbad** *or* **Carlsbad** ('karlsbaːt).

Karlskrona ('kɑːlsˌkrəʊnə) NOUN a port in S Sweden: Sweden's main naval base since 1680. Pop.: 60 642 (1994).

Karlsruhe (*German* 'karlsruːə) NOUN a city in SW Germany, in Baden-Württemberg: capital of the former Baden state. Pop.: 276 700 (1999 est.).

karma ('kɑːmə) NOUN [1] *Hinduism, Buddhism* the principle of retributive justice determining a person's state of life and the state of his reincarnations as the effect of his past deeds. [2] *Theosophy* the doctrine of inevitable consequence. [3] destiny or fate.
▷HISTORY C19: from Sanskrit: action, effect, from *karoti* he does
▸'**karmic** ADJECTIVE

Kármán vortex street ('kɑːmən) NOUN a regular stream of vortices shed from a body placed in a fluid stream: investigated by Kármán who advanced a formula for the frequency of the shed vortices in terms of the stream velocity and the dimensions of the body. See also **vortex street.**
▷HISTORY named after Theodore Von *Kármán* (1881–1963), Hungarian-born engineer

Karmapa ('kɑːməpə) *or* **Karmapa Lama** NOUN the head of the Kagyupa, Karma Kagyu or Black Hat sect of Tibetan Buddhism, third in importance in the hierarchy of lamas.

Karnak ('kɑːnæk) NOUN a village in E Egypt, on the Nile: site of the N part of the ruins of ancient Thebes.

Karnataka (kə'nɑːtəkə) NOUN a state of S India, on the Arabian Sea: consists of a narrow coastal plain rising to the South Deccan plateau; mainly agricultural. Capital: Bangalore. Pop.: 52 733 958 (2001). Area: 191 791 sq. km (74 051 sq. miles). Former name (1956–73): **Mysore.**

Karnatak music (kə'nɑːtək) NOUN the classical music of South India.

Kärnten ('kɛrntən) NOUN the German name for **Carinthia.**

Karoo *or* **Karroo** (kə'ruː) NOUN, *plural* **-roos.** (*often not capital*) [1] any of several high arid plateaus in South Africa, esp the **Central Karoo** and the **Little Karoo.** The highveld, north of the Central Karoo, is sometimes called the **Northern Karoo.** [2] a period or rock system in Southern Africa equivalent to the period or system extending from the Upper Carboniferous to the Lower Jurassic: divided into **Lower** and **Upper Karoo.** ◆ ADJECTIVE [3] of, denoting, or formed in the Karoo period.
▷HISTORY C18: from Afrikaans *karo,* probably from Khoikhoi *garo* desert

karoshi (ka'rəʊʃɪ) NOUN (in Japan) death caused by overwork.
▷HISTORY from Japanese *ka* excess + *ro* labour + *shi* death

kaross (kə'rɒs) NOUN a garment of skins worn by indigenous peoples in southern Africa.
▷HISTORY C18: from Afrikaans *karos,* perhaps from Dutch *kuras,* from French *cuirasse* CUIRASS

karri ('kɑːrɪ) NOUN, *plural* **-ris.** [1] an Australian eucalyptus tree, *Eucalyptus diversifolia.* [2] the durable wood of this tree, used esp for construction.
▷HISTORY from a native Australian language

karst (kɑːst) NOUN (*modifier*) denoting the characteristic scenery of a limestone region, including underground streams, gorges, etc.
▷HISTORY C19: German, from *Karst,* limestone plateau near Trieste
▸'**karstic** ADJECTIVE

kart (kɑːt) NOUN a light low-framed vehicle with small wheels and engine used for recreational racing. Also called: **go-cart, go-kart.**

karyo- *or* **caryo-** COMBINING FORM indicating the nucleus of a cell: *karyogamy.*
▷HISTORY from New Latin, from Greek *karuon* kernel, nut

karyogamy (ˌkærɪ'ɒgəmɪ) NOUN *Biology* the fusion of two gametic nuclei during fertilization.
▸**karyogamic** (ˌkærɪə'gæmɪk) ADJECTIVE

karyogram ('kærɪəʊˌgræm) NOUN a diagram or photograph of the chromosomes of a cell, arranged in homologous pairs and in a numbered sequence. Also called: **idiogram.**

karyokinesis (ˌkærɪəʊkɪ'niːsɪs, -kaɪ-) NOUN the division of a cell nucleus in mitosis or meiosis.
▷HISTORY C19: from KARYO- + Greek *kinēsis* movement
▸**karyokinetic** (ˌkærɪəʊkɪ'nɛtɪk, -kaɪ-) ADJECTIVE

karyology (ˌkærɪ'ɒlədʒɪ) NOUN the study of cell nuclei, esp with reference to the number and shape of the chromosomes.
▸ˌ**kary'ologist** NOUN

karyolymph ('kærɪəʊˌlɪmf) NOUN the liquid portion of the nucleus of a cell.

karyolysis (ˌkærɪˈɒlɪsɪs) NOUN *Cytology* the disintegration of a cell nucleus, which occurs on death of the cell.
▷HISTORY C20: from Greek, from *karyon* a nut + -LYSIS
▸**karyolytic** (ˌkærɪəˈlɪtɪk) ADJECTIVE

karyoplasm (ˈkærɪəʊˌplæzəm) NOUN another name for **nucleoplasm.**
▸ˌ**karyoˈplasmic** ADJECTIVE

karyosome (ˈkærɪəʊˌsəʊm) NOUN 1 any of the dense aggregates of chromatin in the nucleus of a cell. 2 the nucleus of a cell.

karyotin (ˌkærɪˈəʊtɪn) NOUN a less common word for **chromatin.**
▷HISTORY from KARYO- + (CHROMA)TIN

karyotype (ˈkærɪəˌtaɪp) NOUN 1 the appearance of the chromosomes in a somatic cell of an individual or species, with reference to their number, size, shape, etc. ◆ VERB (*tr*) 2 to determine the karyotype of (a cell).
▸**karyotypic** (ˌkærɪəˈtɪpɪk) *or* ˌ**karyoˈtypical** ADJECTIVE

Kasai (kɑːˈsaɪ) NOUN a river in southwestern Africa, rising in central Angola and flowing east then north as part of the border between Angola and the Democratic Republic of Congo (formerly Zaïre), continuing northwest through the Democratic Republic of Congo to the River Congo. Length: 2154 km (1338 miles).

kasbah *or* **casbah** (ˈkæzbɑː) NOUN (*sometimes capital*) 1 the citadel of any of various North African cities. 2 the quarter in which a kasbah is located. Compare **medina.**
▷HISTORY from Arabic *qaṣba* citadel

kasha (ˈkɑːʃə) NOUN a dish originating in Eastern Europe, consisting of boiled or baked buckwheat.
▷HISTORY from Russian

kasher *Hebrew* (ˈkɑːʃə) VERB (*tr*) *Judaism* to make fit for use; render kosher: for instance, to remove excess blood from (meat) by the prescribed process of washing and salting, or to remove all trace of previous nonkosher substances from (a utensil) by heating, immersion, etc. See also **kosher.**
▷HISTORY see KOSHER

Kashi (ˈkɑːˈʃiː) *or* **Kashgar** (ˈkɑːʃˈgɑː) NOUN an oasis city in W China, in W Xinjiang Uygur AR. Pop.: 205 056 (1999 est.).

kashmir (ˈkæʃmɪə) NOUN a variant spelling of **cashmere.**

Kashmir (kæʃˈmɪə) NOUN a region of SW central Asia: from the 16th century ruled by the Moguls, Afghanis, Sikhs, and British successively; since 1947 disputed between India, Pakistan, and China; 84 000 sq. km (33 000 sq. miles) in the northwest are held by Pakistan and known as Azad Kashmir (Free Kashmir); 42 735 sq. km (16 496 sq. miles) in the east are held by China; the remainder was in 1956 officially incorporated into India as the state of Jammu and Kashmir; traversed by the Himalaya and Karakoram mountain ranges and the Rivers Jhelum and Indus; a fruit-growing and cattle-grazing region, with a woollen industry. Capitals: (Azad Kashmir) Muzaffarabad; (Jammu and Kashmir) Srinagar (summer), Jammu (winter).

Kashmir goat NOUN a Himalayan breed of goat having an undercoat of silky wool from which cashmere wool is obtained.

Kashmiri (kæʃˈmɪərɪ) ADJECTIVE 1 of or relating to Kashmir, its people, or their language. ◆ NOUN 2 (*plural* **-miris** *or* **-miri**) a member of the people of Kashmir. 3 the state language of Kashmir, belonging to the Dardic group of the Indo-European family of languages.

Kashmirian (kæʃˈmɪərɪən) ADJECTIVE 1 of or relating to Kashmir, its people, or their language. ◆ NOUN 2 a member of the people of Kashmir.

kashruth *or* ***kashrut*** *Hebrew* (kaʃˈruːt) NOUN 1 the condition of being fit for ritual use in general. 2 the system of dietary laws which require ritual slaughter, the removal of excess blood from meat, and the complete separation of milk and meat, and prohibit such foods as pork and shellfish. ◆ See also **kosher** (sense 1).
▷HISTORY literally: appropriateness, fitness

Kassa (ˈkɔʃʃɔ) NOUN the Hungarian name for **Košice.**

Kassala (kəˈsɑːlə) NOUN a city in the E Sudan: founded as a fort by the Egyptians in 1834. Pop.: 234 270 (1993).

Kassel *or* **Cassel** (*German* ˈkasəl) NOUN a city in central Germany, in Hesse; capital of Westphalia (1807–13) and of the Prussian province of Hesse-Nassau (1866–1945). Pop.: 196 700 (1999 est.).

Kastrop-Rauxel (*German* ˈkastrɔpˈrauksəl) NOUN a variant spelling of **Castrop-Rauxel.**

kat (kæt, kɑːt) NOUN a variant spelling of **khat.**

kata (ˈkætə) NOUN an exercise consisting of a sequence of the specific movements of a martial art, used in training and designed to show skill in technique.
▷HISTORY C20: Japanese, literally: shape, pattern

kata- PREFIX a variant of **cata-.**

katabasis (kəˈtæbəsɪs) NOUN, *plural* **-ses** (-ˌsiːz). 1 the retreat of the Greek mercenaries of Cyrus the Younger, after his death at Cunaxa, from the Euphrates to the Black Sea in 401–400 B.C. under the leadership of Xenophon: recounted in his *Anabasis.* Compare **anabasis.** 2 *Literary* a retreat.
▷HISTORY C19: from Greek: a going down, from *katabainein* to go down

katabatic (ˌkætəˈbætɪk) ADJECTIVE (of winds) blowing downhill through having become denser with cooling, esp at night when heat is lost from the earth's surface. Compare **anabatic.**

katabolism (kəˈtæbəˌlɪzəm) NOUN a variant spelling of **catabolism.**
▸**katabolic** (ˌkætəˈbɒlɪk) ADJECTIVE ▸ˌ**kataˈbolically** ADVERB

katakana (ˌkɑːtəˈkɑːnə) NOUN one of the two systems of syllabic writing employed for the representation of Japanese, based on Chinese ideograms. It is used mainly for foreign or foreign-derived words.
▷HISTORY Japanese, from *kata* side + KANA

Katanga (kəˈtæŋgə) NOUN the former name (until 1972) of **Shaba.**

Katar (kæˈtɑː) NOUN a variant spelling of **Qatar.**

Katari (kæˈtɑːrɪ) ADJECTIVE, NOUN a variant spelling of **Qatari.**

Kathak (ˈkʌtək) NOUN a form of N Indian classical dancing that tells a story.
▷HISTORY Bengali: narrator, from Sanskrit *kathayati* he tells

Kathakali (ˌkɑːθəˈkɑːlɪ) NOUN, *plural* **-lis.** a form of dance drama of S India using mime and based on Hindu literature.
▷HISTORY from Malayalam, from *katha* story + *kali* play

Katharevusa *or* **Katharevousa** (ˌkɑːθəˈrɛvəˌsɑː) NOUN a literary style of Modern Greek, derived from the Attic dialect of Ancient Greek and including many archaic features. Compare **Demotic.**

katharometer (ˌkæθəˈrɒmɪtə) NOUN *Chem* an instrument used for the analysis of gases by measurement of thermal conductivity.

Kathiawar (ˌkætɪəˈwɑː) NOUN a large peninsula of W India, in Gujarat between the Gulf of Kutch and the Gulf of Cambay. Area: about 60 690 sq. km (23 430 sq. miles).

katipo (ˈkætɪˌpəʊ, ˈkɑːd-) NOUN, *plural* **-pos.** a small venomous spider, *Latrodectus katipo,* of New Zealand, commonly black with a red or orange stripe on the abdomen.
▷HISTORY Maori

Katmai (ˈkætmaɪ) NOUN **Mount.** a volcano in SW Alaska, in the Aleutian Range: erupted in 1912 forming the Valley of Ten Thousand Smokes, a region with numerous fumaroles; established as **Katmai National Monument,** 10 917 sq. km (4215 sq. miles), in 1918. Height: 2100 m (7000 ft.). Depth of crater: 1130 m (3700 ft.). Width of crater: about 4 km (2.5 miles).

Katmandu *or* **Kathmandu** (ˌkætmænˈduː) NOUN the capital of Nepal, in the east at the confluence of the Baghmati and Vishnumati Rivers. Pop.: 701 499 (2000 est.).

Katowice (*Polish* katɔˈvitsɛ) NOUN an industrial city in S Poland. Pop.: 345 934 (1999 est.). Former name (1953–56): **Stalinogrod.**

Katrine (ˈkætrɪn) NOUN **Loch.** a lake in central Scotland, east of Loch Lomond: noted for its associations with Sir Walter Scott's *Lady of the Lake.* Length: about 13 km (8 miles).

Katsina (kætˈsiːnə) NOUN a city in N Nigeria, in Kaduna state: a major intellectual and cultural centre of the Hausa people (16th–18th centuries). Pop.: 206 500 (1996 est.).

Kattegat *or* **Cattegat** (ˈkætɪˌgæt) NOUN a strait between Denmark and Sweden: linked by the Sound, the Great Belt, and the Little Belt with the Baltic Sea and by the Skagerrak with the North Sea.

katydid (ˈkeɪtɪˌdɪd) NOUN any typically green long-horned grasshopper of the genus *Microcentrum* and related genera, living among the foliage of trees in North America.
▷HISTORY C18: of imitative origin

katzenjammer (ˈkætsənˌdʒæmə) NOUN *Chiefly US* 1 a confused uproar. 2 a hangover.
▷HISTORY German, literally: hangover, from *Katzen* cats + *jammer* misery, wailing

Kauai (kɑːˈwɑːiː) NOUN a volcanic island in NW Hawaii, northwest of Oahu. Chief town: Lihue. Pop.: 50 947 (1990). Area: 1433 sq. km (553 sq. miles).

kaumatua (kaʊˈmɑːtuːə) NOUN *NZ* a senior member of a tribe; elder.
▷HISTORY Maori

Kaunas (ˈkaʊnəs) NOUN a city in central Lithuania at the confluence of the Neman and Viliya Rivers: ceded by Poland to Russia in 1795; became the provisional capital of Lithuania (1920–40); incorporated into the Soviet Union 1944–91; university (1922). Pop.: 412 614 (2000 est.). Russian name: **Kovno.**

kaupapa (kaʊˈpɑːpə) NOUN *NZ* a strategy, policy, or cause.
▷HISTORY Maori

Kaur (ˈkaʊr) NOUN a title assumed by a Sikh woman when she becomes a full member of the community.
▷HISTORY from Punjabi, literally: princess

kauri (ˈkaʊrɪ) NOUN, *plural* **-ris.** 1 a New Zealand coniferous tree, *Agathis australis,* with oval leaves and round cones: family *Araucariaceae.* 2 the wood or resin of this tree.
▷HISTORY C19: Maori

kauri gum NOUN a hard resin from the kauri tree, found usually as a fossil in the soil where an extinct tree once grew: used chiefly in making varnishes.

kava (ˈkɑːvə) NOUN 1 a Polynesian shrub, *Piper methysticum:* family *Piperaceae.* 2 a drink prepared from the aromatic roots of this shrub.
▷HISTORY C18: from Polynesian (Tongan): bitter

Kavála (kəˈvælə; *Greek* kaˈvala) NOUN a port in E Greece, in Macedonia East and Thrace region on the **Bay of Kavála** an important Macedonian fortress of the Byzantine empire; ceded to Greece by Turkey after the Balkan War (1912–13). Pop.: 58 576 (1991). Ancient name: **Neapolis.**

Kaveri (ˈkɔːvərɪ) NOUN a variant spelling of **Cauvery.**

Kavir Desert (kæˈvɪə) NOUN another name for the **Dasht-i-Kavir.**

kawa (ˈkɑːwə) NOUN *NZ* protocol or etiquette, particularly in a Maori tribal meeting place.
▷HISTORY Maori

kawakawa (ˈkɑːwəˌkɑːwə) NOUN an aromatic shrub or small tree of New Zealand, *Macropiper excelsum:* held to be sacred by the Maoris. Also called: **peppertree.**
▷HISTORY Maori

Kawasaki (ˌkɑːwəˈsɑːkɪ) NOUN an industrial port in central Japan, on SE Honshu, between Tokyo and Yokohama. Pop.: 1 202 811 (1995).

Kawasaki's disease (ˌkæwəˈsækɪ) NOUN a disease of children that causes a rash, fever, and swelling of the lymph nodes and often damages the heart muscle.
▷HISTORY C20: named after T. *Kawasaki,* Japanese physician who first described it

Kay (keɪ) NOUN **Sir.** (in Arthurian legend) the braggart foster brother and steward of King Arthur.

kayak *or* **kaiak** (ˈkaɪæk) NOUN 1 a small light canoe-like boat used by Eskimos, consisting of a light frame covered with watertight animal skins. 2 a fibreglass or canvas-covered canoe of similar design.
▷HISTORY C18: from Eskimo (Greenland dialect)

kayo *or* **KO** (ˈkeɪˈəʊ) NOUN, *plural* **kayos**, VERB **kayoes** *or* **kayos, kayoing, kayoed**. *Boxing, slang* another term for **knockout** or **knock out**.
▷HISTORY C20: from the initial letters of *knock out*

Kayseri (ˌkaɪseˈriː; *Turkish* ˈkaiseri) NOUN a city in central Turkey: trading centre since ancient times as the chief city of Cappadocia. Pop.: 498 233 (1997). Ancient name: **Caesarea Mazaca**.

kazachok (ˌkɑːzəˈtʃɒk) NOUN a Russian folk dance in which the performer executes high kicks from a squatting position.
▷HISTORY Russian

Kazakh *or* **Kazak** (kəˈzɑːk, kɑː-) NOUN 1 (*plural* **-zakhs** *or* **-zaks**) a member of a traditionally Muslim Mongoloid people of Kazakhstan. 2 the language of this people, belonging to the Turkic branch of the Altaic family.

Kazakhstan *or* **Kazakstan** (ˌkɑːzɑːkˈstæn, -ˈstɑːn) NOUN a republic in central Asia: conquered by Mongols in the 13th century; came under Russian control in the 18th and 19th centuries; was a Soviet republic from 1936 until it gained independence in 1991. It has rich mineral deposits and agriculture is important. Official language: Kazakh. Religion: nonreligious, Muslim, and Christian. Official currency: tenge. Capital: Akmola. Pop.: 14 868 000 (2001 est.). Area: 2 715 100 sq. km (1 048 030 sq. miles).

Kazan (kəˈzæn, -ˈzɑːn; *Russian* kaˈzanj) NOUN a city in W Russia, capital of the Tatar Autonomous Republic on the River Volga: capital of an independent khanate in the 15th century; university (1804); a major industrial centre. Pop.: 1 100 800 (1999 est.).

Kazan Retto (kɑːˈzɑːn ˈrɛtəʊ) NOUN transliteration of the Japanese name for the **Volcano Islands**.

Kazbek (kɑːzˈbɛk) NOUN **Mount**. an extinct volcano in N Georgia in the central Caucasus Mountains. Height: 5047 m (16 558 ft.).

Kaz Daği (ˈkɑz ˈdɑj) NOUN the Turkish name for (Mount) **Ida** (sense 2).

kazoo (kəˈzuː) NOUN, *plural* **-zoos**. a cigar-shaped musical instrument of metal or plastic with a membranous diaphragm of thin paper that vibrates with a nasal sound when the player hums into it.
▷HISTORY C20: probably imitative of the sound produced

kb ABBREVIATION FOR kilobar.

KB ABBREVIATION FOR: 1 (in Britain) King's Bench. 2 (in Britain) Knight Bachelor. 3 *Computing* kilobyte. ◆ 4 *Chess* SYMBOL FOR king's bishop.

KBE ABBREVIATION FOR Knight (Commander of the Order) of the British Empire.

KBP *Chess* SYMBOL FOR king's bishop's pawn.

kbyte *Computing* ABBREVIATION FOR kilobyte.

kc ABBREVIATION FOR kilocycle.

KC (in Britain) ABBREVIATION FOR: 1 King's Counsel. 2 Kennel Club.

kcal ABBREVIATION FOR kilocalorie.

KCB ABBREVIATION FOR Knight Commander of the Bath (a Brit. title).

KCMG ABBREVIATION FOR Knight Commander (of the Order) of St Michael and St George (a Brit title).

Kčs. ABBREVIATION FOR koruna.
▷HISTORY Czech *koruna československá*

KCVO ABBREVIATION FOR Knight Commander of the Royal Victorian Order (a Brit title).

KD *or* **k.d.** *Commerce* ABBREVIATION FOR knocked down: indicating furniture, machinery, etc., in separate parts.

ke THE INTERNET DOMAIN NAME FOR Kenya.

KE ABBREVIATION FOR **kinetic energy**.

kea (ˈkeɪə) NOUN a large New Zealand parrot, *Nestor notabilis*, with brownish-green plumage.
▷HISTORY C19: from Maori, imitative of its call

Kéa (ˈkɛa) NOUN transliteration of the Modern Greek name for **Keos**.

kebab (kəˈbæb) NOUN a dish consisting of small pieces of meat, tomatoes, onions, etc., threaded onto skewers and grilled, generally over charcoal. Also called: **shish kebab, kabob, cabob**.
▷HISTORY C17: via Urdu from Arabic *kabāb* roast meat

Kechua (ˈkɛtʃwə) NOUN a variant of **Quechua**.

keck[1] (kɛk) VERB (*intr*) *Chiefly US* 1 to retch or feel nausea. 2 to feel or express disgust.
▷HISTORY C17: of imitative origin

keck[2] (kɛk) NOUN another name for **cow parsnip** and **cow parsley**.
▷HISTORY C17: from KEX, which was mistaken as a plural (as if *kecks*)

kecks *or* **keks** (kɛks) PLURAL NOUN *Northern English dialect* trousers.
▷HISTORY C19: from obsolete *kicks* breeches

Kecskemét (*Hungarian* ˈkɛtʃkɛmeːt) NOUN a city in central Hungary: vineyards and fruit farms. Pop.: 105 606 (2000 est.).

ked (kɛd) NOUN See **sheep ked**.
▷HISTORY C16: of unknown origin

Kedah (ˈkɛdə) NOUN a state of NW Malaysia: under Thai control until it came under the British in 1909; the chief exports are rice, tin, and rubber. Capital: Alor Star. Pop.: 1 572 107 (2000 est.). Area: 9425 sq. km (3639 sq. miles).

keddah (ˈkɛdə) NOUN a variant spelling of **kheda**.

kedge (kɛdʒ) *Nautical* ◆ VERB 1 to draw (a vessel) along by hauling in on the cable of a light anchor that has been dropped at some distance from it, or (of a vessel) to be drawn in this fashion. ◆ NOUN 2 a light anchor, used esp for kedging.
▷HISTORY C15: from *caggen* to fasten

kedgeree (ˌkɛdʒəˈriː) NOUN *Chiefly Brit* a dish consisting of rice, cooked flaked fish, and hard-boiled eggs.
▷HISTORY C17: from Hindi *khicarī*, from Sanskrit *khiccā*, of obscure origin

Kediri (kɪˈdɪərɪ) NOUN a city in Indonesia, in E Java: commercial centre. Pop.: 261 300 (1995 est.).

Kedleston Hall (ˈkɛdəlstən) NOUN a mansion near Derby in Derbyshire: rebuilt (1759–65) for the Curzon family by Matthew Brettingham, James Paine, and Robert Adam.

Kedron (ˈkɛdrɒn) *or* **Kidron** NOUN *Bible* a ravine under the eastern wall of Jerusalem.

keef (kiːf) NOUN a variant spelling of **kif**.

keek (kiːk) NOUN, VERB a Scot word for **peep**.
▷HISTORY C18: probably from Middle Dutch *kīken* to look

keel[1] (kiːl) NOUN 1 one of the main longitudinal structural members of a vessel to which the frames are fastened and that may extend into the water to provide lateral stability. 2 **on an even keel**. well-balanced; steady. 3 any structure corresponding to or resembling the keel of a ship, such as the central member along the bottom of an aircraft fuselage. 4 *Biology* a ridgelike part; carina. 5 a poetic word for **ship**. ◆ VERB 6 to capsize. ◆ See also **keel over**.
▷HISTORY C14: from Old Norse *kjölr;* related to Middle Dutch *kiel*, KEEL[2]
▸ˈ**keel-less** ADJECTIVE

keel[2] (kiːl) NOUN *Eastern English dialect* 1 a flat-bottomed vessel, esp one used for carrying coal. 2 a measure of coal equal to about 21 tons.
▷HISTORY C14 *kele*, from Middle Dutch *kiel;* compare Old English *cēol* ship

keel[3] (kiːl) NOUN 1 red ochre stain used for marking sheep, timber, etc. ◆ VERB (*tr*) 2 to mark with this stain.
▷HISTORY Old English *cēlan*, from *cōl* COOL

keel[4] (kiːl) VERB an archaic word for **cool**.
▷HISTORY C15: probably from Scottish Gaelic *cīl*

keel[5] (kiːl) NOUN a fatal disease of young ducks, characterized by intestinal bleeding caused by Salmonella bacteria.
▷HISTORY C19: from KEEL[1]; see KEEL OVER

keelage (ˈkiːlɪdʒ) NOUN a fee charged by certain ports to allow a ship to dock.

keel arch NOUN another name for **ogee arch**.

keelboat (ˈkiːlˌbəʊt) NOUN a river boat with a shallow draught and a keel, used for freight and moved by towing, punting, or rowing.

keelhaul (ˈkiːlˌhɔːl) VERB (*tr*) 1 to drag (a person) by a rope from one side of a vessel to the other through the water under the keel. 2 to rebuke harshly.
▷HISTORY C17: from Dutch *kielhalen;* see KEEL[1], HAUL

keelie (ˈkiːlɪ) NOUN *Scot* 1 a kestrel. 2 an urban ruffian; lower-class town or city dweller, esp Glaswegian.
▷HISTORY C19: of uncertain origin

Keeling Islands (ˈkiːlɪŋ) PLURAL NOUN another name for the **Cocos Islands**.

keel over VERB (*adverb*) 1 to turn upside down; capsize. 2 (*intr*) *Informal* to collapse suddenly.

keelson (ˈkɛlsən, ˈkiːl-) *or* **kelson** NOUN a longitudinal beam fastened to the keel of a vessel for strength and stiffness.
▷HISTORY C17: probably from Low German *kielswin*, keel swine, ultimately of Scandinavian origin

Keelung (ˈkiːˈlʊŋ) NOUN another name for **Chilung**.

keen[1] (kiːn) ADJECTIVE 1 eager or enthusiastic. 2 (*postpositive; foll by on*) fond (of); devoted (to): *keen on a girl; keen on golf*. 3 intellectually acute: *a keen wit*. 4 (of sight, smell, hearing, etc.) capable of recognizing fine distinctions. 5 having a sharp cutting edge or point. 6 extremely cold and penetrating: *a keen wind*. 7 intense or strong: *a keen desire*. 8 *Chiefly Brit* extremely low so as to be competitive: *keen prices*. 9 *Slang, chiefly US and Canadian* very good.
▷HISTORY Old English *cēne;* related to Old High German *kuoni* brave, Old Norse *koenn* wise; see CAN[1], KNOW
▸ˈ**keenly** ADVERB ▸ˈ**keenness** NOUN

keen[2] (kiːn) VERB (*intr*) 1 to lament the dead. ◆ NOUN 2 a dirge or lament for the dead.
▷HISTORY C19: from Irish Gaelic *caoine*, from Old Irish *coīnim* I wail
▸ˈ**keener** NOUN

keener (ˈkiːnə) NOUN *Canadian informal* a person, esp a student, who is keen, enthusiastic, or zealous.

keep (kiːp) VERB **keeps, keeping, kept** (kɛpt). 1 (*tr*) to have or retain possession of. 2 (*tr*) to have temporary possession or charge of: *keep my watch for me during the game*. 3 (*tr*) to store in a customary place: *I keep my books in the desk*. 4 to remain or cause to remain in a specified state or condition: *keep the dog quiet; keep ready*. 5 to continue or cause to continue: *keep the beat; keep in step*. 6 (*tr*) to have or take charge or care of: *keep the shop for me till I return*. 7 (*tr*) to look after or maintain for use, pleasure, etc.: *to keep chickens; keep two cars*. 8 (*tr*) to provide for the upkeep or livelihood of. 9 (*tr*) to support financially, esp in return for sexual favours: *he keeps a mistress in the country*. 10 to confine or detain or be confined or detained. 11 to withhold or reserve or admit of withholding or reserving: *your news will keep till later*. 12 (*tr*) to refrain from divulging or violating: *to keep a secret; keep one's word*. 13 to preserve or admit of preservation. 14 (*tr; sometimes foll by up*) to observe with due rites or ceremonies: *to keep Christmas*. 15 (*tr*) to maintain by writing regular records in: *to keep a diary*. 16 (when *intr*, foll by *in, on, to*, etc.) to stay in, on, or at (a place or position): *please keep your seats; keep to the path*. 17 (*tr*) to associate with (esp in the phrase **keep bad company**). 18 (*tr*) to maintain in existence: *to keep court in the palace*. 19 (*tr*) *Chiefly Brit* to have habitually in stock: *this shop keeps all kinds of wool*. 20 **how are you keeping?** how are you? 21 **keep tabs on**. *Informal* to keep a watchful eye on. 22 **keep track of**. See **track** (sense 15). 23 **keep time**. See **time** (sense 42). 24 **keep wicket**. to play as wicketkeeper in the game of cricket. 25 **you can keep it**. *Informal* I have no interest in what you are offering. ◆ NOUN 26 living or support: *he must work for his keep*. 27 *Archaic* charge or care. 28 Also called: **dungeon, donjon**. the main tower within the walls of a medieval castle or fortress. 29 *Informal* **a** completely; permanently. **b** for the winner or possessor to keep permanently. ◆ See also **keep at, keep away, keep back, keep down, keep from, keep in, keep off, keep on, keep out, keep to, keep under, keep up**.
▷HISTORY Old English *cēpan* to observe; compare Old Saxon *kapōn* to look, Old Norse *kōpa* to stare

keep at VERB (*preposition*) 1 (*intr*) to persevere with or persist in. 2 (*tr*) to constrain (a person) to continue doing (a task).

keep away VERB (*adverb; often foll by from*) 1 to refrain or prevent from coming (near). 2 to stop using, touching, etc.

keep back VERB (*adverb; often foll by from*) 1 (*tr*) to refuse to reveal or disclose. 2 to prevent, be prevented, or refrain from advancing, entering, etc.

keep down VERB (*adverb, mainly tr*) 1 to repress; hold in submission. 2 to restrain or control: *he had difficulty keeping his anger down*. 3 to cause not to increase or rise: *prices were kept down for six months.* [4] (*intr*) not to show oneself to one's opponents; lie low. [5] to cause (food) to stay in the stomach; not vomit.

keeper ('ki:pə) NOUN [1] a person in charge of animals, esp in a zoo. [2] a person in charge of a museum, collection, or section of a museum. [3] a person in charge of other people, such as a warder in a jail. [4] See **goalkeeper, wicketkeeper, gamekeeper.** [5] a person who keeps something. [6] a device, such as a clip, for keeping something in place. [7] a soft iron or steel bar placed across the poles of a permanent magnet to close the magnetic circuit when it is not in use.
▸ **'keeperless** ADJECTIVE ▸ **'keeper,ship** NOUN

keeper ring NOUN another name for **guard ring.**

keep fit NOUN **a** exercises designed to promote physical fitness if performed regularly. **b** (*as modifier*): *keep-fit classes.*

keep from VERB (*preposition*) [1] (*foll by a gerund*) to prevent or restrain (oneself or another); refrain or cause to refrain. [2] (*tr*) to protect or preserve from.

keep in VERB (*mainly adverb*) [1] (*intr; also preposition*) to stay indoors. [2] (*tr*) to restrain (an emotion); repress. [3] (*tr*) to detain (a schoolchild) after hours as a punishment. [4] (of a fire) to stay alight or to cause (a fire) to stay alight. [5] (*tr, prep*) to allow a constant supply of: *her prize money kept her in new clothes for a year.* [6] **keep in with.** to maintain good relations with.

keeping ('ki:pɪŋ) NOUN [1] conformity or harmony (esp in the phrases **in** *or* **out of keeping**). [2] charge or care: *valuables in the keeping of a bank.*

keepnet ('ki:p,nɛt) NOUN a cylindrical net strung on wire hoops and sealed at one end, suspended in water by anglers to keep alive the fish they have caught.

keep off VERB [1] to stay or cause to stay at a distance (from). [2] (*preposition*) not to eat or drink or prevent from eating or drinking. [3] (*preposition*) to avoid or cause to avoid (a topic). [4] (*intr, adverb*) not to start: *the rain kept off all day.*

keep on VERB (*adverb*) [1] to continue or persist in (doing something): *keep on running.* [2] (*tr*) to continue to wear. [3] (*tr*) to continue to employ: *the firm kept on only ten men.* [4] (*intr; foll by about*) to persist in talking (about). [5] (*intr; foll by at*) to nag (a person).

keep out VERB (*adverb*) [1] to remain or cause to remain outside. [2] **keep out of. a** to remain or cause to remain unexposed to: *keep out of the sun.* **b** to avoid or cause to avoid: *the boss is in an angry mood, so keep out of her way.*

keepsake ('ki:p,seɪk) NOUN a gift that evokes memories of a person or event with which it is associated.

keep to VERB (*preposition*) [1] to adhere to or stand by or cause to adhere to or stand by: *to keep to a promise.* [2] to confine or be confined to. [3] **keep to oneself. a** (*intr*) to avoid the society of others. **b** (*tr*) to refrain from sharing or disclosing. [4] **keep oneself to oneself.** to avoid the society of others.

keep under VERB [1] to remain or cause to remain below (a surface). [2] (*tr, adverb*) to cause to remain unconscious. [3] (*tr, adverb*) to hold in submission.

keep up VERB (*adverb*) [1] (*tr*) to maintain (prices, one's morale) at the present level. [2] (*intr*) to maintain a pace or rate set by another. [3] (*intr; often foll by with*) to remain informed: *to keep up with technological developments.* [4] (*tr*) to maintain in good condition. [5] (*tr*) to hinder (a person) from going to bed at night: *the excitement kept the children up well past their bedtime.* [6] **keep it up.** to continue a good performance. [7] **keep one's chin up.** to keep cheerful under difficult circumstances. [8] **keep one's end up.** to maintain one's stance or position against opposition or misfortune. [9] **keep up with.** to remain in contact with, esp by letter. [10] **keep up with (the Joneses).** *Informal* to compete with (one's neighbours) in material possessions, etc.

keepy-uppy (,ki:pɪ'ʌpɪ) NOUN *Soccer* the act or an instance of keeping a ball off the ground by bouncing it repeatedly on a foot, knee, or head.

keeshond ('keɪs,hɒnd, 'ki:s-) NOUN, *plural* **-honds** *or* **-honden** (-,hɒndᵊn). a breed of dog of the spitz type with a shaggy greyish coat and tightly curled tail, originating in Holland.

▷**HISTORY** C20: from Dutch, probably from *Kees* nickname for *Cornelis* Cornelius, from Latin + *hond* HOUND[1]

Keewatin (ki:'weɪtɪn) NOUN a former administrative district of the Northwest Territories of Canada stretching from the district of Mackenzie to Hudson Bay; became part of Nunavut in 1999: mostly tundra.

kef (kɛf) NOUN a variant of **kif.**

keffiyeh (kɛ'fi:jə), **kaffiyeh,** *or* **kufiyah** NOUN a cotton headdress worn by Arabs.
▷**HISTORY** C19: from Arabic, perhaps from Late Latin *cofea* COIF

Keflavík ('kɛflə,vɪk) NOUN a port in SW Iceland: Nato airbase, fishing. Pop.: 7627 (1994).

keftedes (kɛf'tɛðɛs) NOUN a Greek dish of meatballs cooked with herbs and onions.
▷**HISTORY** C20: from Modern Greek

keg (kɛg) NOUN [1] a small barrel with a capacity of between five and ten gallons. [2] *Brit* **a** an aluminium container in which beer is transported and stored. **b** Also called: **keg beer.** beer kept in a keg: it is infused with gas and served under pressure.
▷**HISTORY** C17: variant of Middle English *kag,* of Scandinavian origin; related to Old Norse *kaggi* cask

Kegel exercises ('kɛgəl) PLURAL NOUN exercises for rehabilitating the pelvic-floor muscles of women suffering stress incontinence, esp after childbirth. Also called: **pelvic-floor exercises.**
▷**HISTORY** C20: named after A. H. *Kegel,* US gynaecologist

kegler ('kɛglə) *or* **kegeler** ('kɛgələ) NOUN *Informal, chiefly US* a participant in a game of tenpin bowling.
▷**HISTORY** from German, from *Kegel* pin, from Old High German *kegil* peg

Keighley ('ki:θlɪ) NOUN a town in N England, in Bradford unitary authority, West Yorkshire, on the River Aire: textile industry. Pop.: 49 567 (1991).

Keijo (,keɪ'dʒəʊ) NOUN transliteration of the Japanese name for **Seoul.**

keister *or* **keester** ('ki:stə) NOUN *Slang, chiefly US* [1] the rump; buttocks. [2] a suitcase, trunk, or box.
▷**HISTORY** C20: of uncertain origin

keitloa ('kaɪtləʊə, 'keɪt-) NOUN a southern African variety of the black two-horned rhinoceros, *Diceros bicornis.*
▷**HISTORY** C19: from Tswana *khetlwa*

keks (kɛks) PLURAL NOUN a variant spelling of **kecks.**

Kekulé formula ('kɛkjə,leɪ) NOUN a representation of the benzene molecule as six carbon atoms at the corners of a regular hexagon with alternate double and single bonds joining them and with one hydrogen atom bound to each carbon atom. See **benzene ring.**
▷**HISTORY** C19: named after Friedrich August *Kekulé* von Stradonitz (1829–96), German chemist

Kekulé structure NOUN the structure of many molecules, notably benzene, suggested by Friedrich August *Kekulé* von Stradonitz (1829–96), the German chemist.

Kelantan (kɛ'læntən, kɪ,læn'tæn) NOUN a state of NE Malaysia: under Thai control until it came under the British in 1909; produces rice and rubber. Capital: Kota Bharu. Pop.: 1 289 199 (2000 est.). Area: 14 930 sq. km (5765 sq. miles).

Kells (kɛlz) NOUN a town in the Republic of Ireland, in Co. Meath: *The Book of Kells,* an illuminated manuscript of the Gospels, was produced at the monastery here in the 8th century. Pop.: 2187 (1991).

Kelly ('kɛlɪ) NOUN **(as) game as Ned Kelly.** See **game**[1] (sense 25).
▷**HISTORY** from Ned *Kelly* (1855–80), Australian horse and cattle thief and bushranger: captured by the police and hanged

Kelmscott Manor ('kɛlmz,kɒt) NOUN a Tudor house near Lechlade in Oxfordshire: home (1871–96) of William Morris.

keloid *or* **cheloid** ('ki:lɔɪd) NOUN *Pathol* a hard smooth pinkish raised growth of scar tissue at the site of an injury, tending to occur more frequently in dark-skinned races.
▷**HISTORY** C19: from Greek *khēlē* claw
▸ **ke'loidal** *or* **che'loidal** ADJECTIVE

kelp (kɛlp) NOUN [1] any large brown seaweed, esp any in the order *Laminariales.* [2] the ash of such seaweed, used as a source of iodine and potash.
▷**HISTORY** C14: of unknown origin

kelpie[1] *or* **kelpy** ('kɛlpɪ) NOUN, *plural* **-pies.** an Australian breed of sheepdog, originally developed from Scottish collies, having a smooth coat of various colours and erect ears.
▷**HISTORY** named after a particular specimen of the breed, c. 1870

kelpie[2] ('kɛlpɪ) NOUN (in Scottish folklore) a water spirit in the form of a horse that drowned its riders.
▷**HISTORY** C18: probably related to Scottish Gaelic *cailpeach* heifer, of obscure origin

kelson ('kɛlsən) NOUN a variant of **keelson.**

kelt (kɛlt) NOUN a salmon that has recently spawned and is usually in poor condition.
▷**HISTORY** C14: of unknown origin

Kelt (kɛlt) NOUN a variant of **Celt.**
▸ **'Keltic** ADJECTIVE ▸ **'Keltically** ADVERB ▸ **'Kelti,cism** NOUN ▸ **'Kelticist** *or* **'Keltist** NOUN

kelter ('kɛltə) NOUN a variant of **kilter.**

kelvin ('kɛlvɪn) NOUN the basic SI unit of thermodynamic temperature; the fraction 1/273.16 of the thermodynamic temperature of the triple point of water. Symbol: K.

Kelvin scale NOUN a thermodynamic temperature scale based upon the efficiencies of ideal heat engines. The zero of the scale is absolute zero. Originally the degree was equal to that on the Celsius scale but it is now defined so that the triple point of water is exactly 273.16 kelvins. The International Practical Temperature Scale (1968, revised 1990) realizes the Kelvin scale over a wide range of temperatures. Compare **Rankine scale.**

kelyphitic rim (,kɛlɪ'fɪtɪk) NOUN *Geology* a mineral shell enclosing another mineral in an igneous rock, formed by reaction of the interned mineral with the surrounding rock.
▷**HISTORY** C19: from Greek *keluphos* pod + *-itic;* see -ITE[1]

Kemalism (kɛ'mɑ:lɪzəm) NOUN the theory and form of government associated with Kemal Atatürk, the Turkish general and statesman (1881–1938), who founded the Turkish republic and westernized and secularized the country.
▸ **Ke'malist** NOUN, ADJECTIVE

kembla ('kɛmblə) NOUN *Austral, slang* small change.
▷**HISTORY** from rhyming slang *Kembla Grange*

Kemerovo (*Russian* 'kjemɪrəvə) NOUN a city in S Russia: a major coal-mining centre of the Kuznetsk Basin, with important chemical plants. Pop.: 496 300 (1999 est.). Former name (until 1932): **Shcheglovsk.**

kemp (kɛmp) NOUN a coarse hair or strand of hair, esp one in a fleece that resists dyeing.
▷**HISTORY** C14: from Old Norse *kampr* beard, moustache
▸ **'kempy** ADJECTIVE

kempt (kɛmpt) ADJECTIVE (of hair) tidy; combed. See also **unkempt.**
▷**HISTORY** C20: back formation from *unkempt;* originally past participle of dialect *kemb* to COMB

ken (kɛn) NOUN [1] range of knowledge or perception (esp in the phrases **beyond** *or* **in one's ken**). ◆ VERB **kens, kenning, kenned** *or* **kent** (kɛnt). [2] *Scot and northern English dialect* to know. [3] *Scot and northern English dialect* to understand; perceive. [4] (*tr*) *Archaic* to see.
▷**HISTORY** Old English *cennan;* related to Old Norse *kenna* to perceive, Old High German *kennen* to make known; see CAN[1]

Ken. ABBREVIATION FOR Kentucky.

kenaf (kə'næf) NOUN another name for **ambary.**
▷**HISTORY** from Persian

Kendal ('kɛndᵊl) NOUN a town in NW England, in Cumbria: a gateway town to the Lake District, with an ancient woollen industry. Pop.: 25 461 (1991).

Kendal green NOUN [1] a green woollen cloth, formerly worn by foresters. [2] the colour of this cloth, produced by a dye obtained from the woad plant. See also **dyer's-greenweed.**
▷**HISTORY** C14: from *Kendal,* where it originated

kendo ('kɛndəʊ) NOUN the Japanese art of fencing with pliable bamboo staves or, sometimes, real swords: strict conventions are observed.
▷**HISTORY** from Japanese

Kenilworth ('kenɪl,wɜːθ) NOUN a town in central England, in Warwickshire: ruined 12th-century castle, subject of Sir Walter Scott's novel *Kenilworth*. Pop.: 21 623 (1991).

Kénitra (*French* kenitra) NOUN another name for **Mina Hassan Tani**.

Kennedy ('kenɪdɪ) NOUN **Cape**. a former name (1963–73) of (Cape) **Canaveral**.

kennel[1] ('kenᵊl) NOUN [1] a hutlike shelter for a dog. US name: **doghouse**. [2] (*usually plural*) an establishment where dogs are bred, trained, boarded, etc. [3] the lair of a fox or other animal. [4] a ramshackle house; hovel. [5] a pack of hounds. ◆ VERB **-nels, -nelling, -nelled** *or US* **-nels, -neling, -neled**. [6] to put or go into a kennel; keep or stay in a kennel.
▷HISTORY C14: from Old French *chenil*, from Vulgar Latin *canīle* (unattested), from Latin *canis* dog

kennel[2] ('kenᵊl) NOUN *Archaic* an open sewer or street gutter.
▷HISTORY C16: variant of *cannel* CHANNEL[1]

Kennelly-Heaviside layer NOUN See **E region**.

kennett ('kenɪt) VERB (*tr*) *Austral, slang* **another word for**. jeff

kenning ('kenɪŋ) NOUN a conventional metaphoric name for something, esp in Old Norse and Old English poetry, such as Old English *bānhūs* (bone house) for "body".
▷HISTORY C14: from Old Norse, from *kenna;* see KEN

Kenny method *or* **treatment** ('kenɪ) NOUN a method of treating poliomyelitis by applying hot moist packs to the affected muscles alternated by passive and later active movement of the muscles.
▷HISTORY C20: named after Sister Elizabeth *Kenny*, 1886–1952, Australian nurse who developed it

keno, keeno, kino, *or* **quino** ('kiːno) NOUN *US and Canadian* a game of chance similar to bingo.
▷HISTORY C19: of unknown origin

kenogenesis (,kiːnəʊ'dʒenɪsɪs) NOUN a secondary US spelling of **caenogenesis**.
▸**kenogenetic** (,kiːnəʊdʒə'netɪk) ADJECTIVE
▸**,kenoge'netically** ADVERB

kenosis (kɪ'nəʊsɪs) NOUN *Christianity* Christ's voluntary renunciation of certain divine attributes, in order to identify himself with mankind (Philippians 2:6–7).
▷HISTORY C19: from Greek: an emptying, from *kenoun* to empty from *kenos* empty
▸**kenotic** (kɪ'nɒtɪk) ADJECTIVE, NOUN

Kensington and Chelsea ('kenzɪŋtən) NOUN a borough of Greater London, on the River Thames: **Kensington Palace** (17th century) and gardens. Pop.: 158 922 (2001). Area: 12 sq. km (5 sq. miles).

kenspeckle ('ken,spekᵊl) ADJECTIVE *Scot* easily seen or recognized.
▷HISTORY C18: from dialect *kenspeck*, of Scandinavian origin; compare Old Norse *kennispecki* power of recognition; related to KEN

kent (kent) VERB a past tense and past participle of **ken**.

Kent (kent) NOUN a county of SE England, on the English Channel: the first part of Great Britain to be colonized by the Romans; one of the seven kingdoms of Anglo-Saxon England until absorbed by Wessex in the 9th century A.D. Apart from the Downs it is mostly low-lying and agricultural, specializing in fruit and hops. The Medway towns (Rochester and Gillingham) became an independent unitary authority in 1998. Administrative centre: Maidstone. Pop. (excluding Medway): 1 329 653 (2001). Area (excluding Medway): 3526 sq. km (1361 sq. miles).

kente ('kentɪ) NOUN [1] Also called: **kente cloth**. a brightly coloured handwoven cloth of Ghana, usually with some gold thread. [2] the toga made of this cloth.
▷HISTORY from a Ghanaian language, possibly Akan

kentia ('kentɪə) NOUN a plant name formerly used to include palms now allotted to several different genera and still used commercially to denote the feather palm genus *Howea*, native to Lord Howe Island, popular as greenhouse or house plants for their decorative arching foliage: family *Palmaceae*.
▷HISTORY named after William *Kent* (died 1828), British botanist

Kentish ('kentɪʃ) ADJECTIVE [1] of or relating to Kent. ◆ NOUN [2] Also called: **Jutish**. the dialect of Old and Middle English spoken in Kent. See also **Anglian, West Saxon**.

Kentish glory NOUN a moth, *Endromis versicolora*, common in north and central Europe, having brown variegated front wings and, in the male, orange hindwings.

kentledge ('kentlɪdʒ) NOUN *Nautical* scrap metal used as ballast in a vessel.
▷HISTORY C17: perhaps from Old French *quintelage* ballast, from *quintal* hundredweight, ultimately from Arabic *qintār;* see KANTAR

Kentuckian (ken'tʌkɪən) NOUN [1] a native or inhabitant of Kentucky. ◆ ADJECTIVE [2] of or relating to Kentucky or its inhabitants.

Kentucky (ken'tʌkɪ) NOUN [1] a state of the S central US: consists of an undulating plain in the west, the Bluegrass region in the centre, the Tennessee and Ohio River basins in the southwest, and the Appalachians in the east. Capital: Frankfort. Pop.: 4 041 769 (2000). Area: 102 693 sq. km (39 650 sq. miles). Abbreviations: **Ken, Ky,** (with zip code) **KY**. [2] a river in central Kentucky, rising in the Cumberland Mountains and flowing northwest to the Ohio River. Length: 417 km (259 miles).

Kentucky bluegrass NOUN a Eurasian grass, *Poa pratensis*, grown for forage and naturalized throughout North America.

Kentucky coffee tree NOUN a North American leguminous tree, *Gymnocladus dioica*, whose seeds, in brown curved pulpy pods, were formerly used as a coffee substitute.

Kentucky Derby NOUN a race for three-year-old horses run annually since 1875 at Louisville, Kentucky.

Kenwood House ('kenwʊd) NOUN a 17th-century mansion on Hampstead Heath in London: remodelled and decorated by Robert Adam: contains the Iveagh bequest, a noted art collection.

Kenya ('kenjə, 'kiːnjə) NOUN [1] a republic in E Africa, on the Indian Ocean: became a British protectorate in 1895 and a colony in 1920; gained independence in 1963 and is a member of the Commonwealth. Tea and coffee constitute about a third of the total exports. Official languages: Swahili and English. Religions: Christian majority, animist minority. Currency: shilling. Capital: Nairobi. Pop.: 30 766 000 (2001 est.). Area: 582 647 sq. km (224 960 sq. miles). [2] **Mount**. an extinct volcano in central Kenya: the second highest mountain in Africa; girth at 2400 m (8000 ft.) is about 150 km (95 miles). The regions above 3200 m (10 500 ft.) constitute **Mount Kenya National Park**. Height: 5200 m (17 058 ft.).

Kenyan ('kenjən, 'kiːnjən) ADJECTIVE [1] of or relating to Kenya or its inhabitants. ◆ NOUN [2] a native or inhabitant of Kenya.

Keos ('keɪɒs) NOUN an island in the Aegean Sea, in the NW Cyclades. Pop.: 1700 (latest est.). Area: 174 sq. km (67 sq. miles). Italian name: **Zea**. Modern Greek name: **Kéa**.

kep (kep) VERB **keps, kepping, keppit** ('kepɪt). (*tr*) *Scot and N English dialect* to catch.
▷HISTORY from KEEP (in obsolete sense: to put oneself in the way of)

Kephallinía (,kefali'nia; *English* ,kefə'liːnɪə) NOUN transliteration of the Modern Greek name for **Cephalonia**.

kepi ('keɪpiː) NOUN, *plural* **kepis**. a military cap with a circular top and a horizontal peak.
▷HISTORY C19: from French *képi*, from German (Swiss dialect) *käppi* a little cap, from *kappe* CAP

Kepler ('keplə) NOUN a small crater in the NW quadrant of the moon, centre of a large bright ray system.

Kepler's laws PLURAL NOUN three laws of planetary motion published by Johannes Kepler between 1609 and 1619. The first states that the orbit of a planet describes an ellipse with the sun at one focus. The second states that, during one orbit, the straight line joining the sun and a planet sweeps out equal areas in equal times. The third states that the squares of the periods of any two planets are proportional to the cubes of their orbital major axes.

kept (kept) VERB [1] the past tense and past participle of **keep**. [2] **kept woman**. *Censorious* a woman maintained by a man as his mistress.

Kerala ('kerələ, kə'rɑːlə) NOUN a state of SW India, on the Arabian Sea: formed in 1956, it includes the former state of Travancore-Cochin; has the highest population density of any Indian state. Capital: Trivandrum. Pop.: 31 838 619 (2001). Area: 38 863 sq. km (15 005 sq. miles).

keramic (kɪ'ræmɪk) ADJECTIVE a rare variant of **ceramic**.

keramics (kɪ'ræmɪks) NOUN a rare variant of **ceramics**.

keratin ('kerətɪn) *or* **ceratin** NOUN a fibrous protein that occurs in the outer layer of the skin and in hair, nails, feathers, hooves, etc.

keratinize *or* **keratinise** (kɪ'rætɪ,naɪz, 'kerətɪ-) VERB to become or cause to become impregnated with keratin.
▸**ke,ratini'zation** *or* **ke,ratini'sation** NOUN

keratitis (,kerə'taɪtɪs) NOUN inflammation of the cornea.

kerato- *or before a vowel* **kerat-** COMBINING FORM [1] indicating horn or a horny substance: *keratin; keratogenous*. [2] indicating the cornea: *keratoplasty*.
▷HISTORY from Greek *kerat-, keras* horn

keratogenous (,kerə'tɒdʒɪnəs) ADJECTIVE developing or causing the growth of horny tissue.

keratoid ('kerə,tɔɪd) ADJECTIVE resembling horn; horny.

keratoplasty ('kerətəʊ,plæstɪ) NOUN, *plural* **-ties**. plastic surgery of the cornea, esp involving corneal grafting.
▸**,kerato'plastic** ADJECTIVE

keratose ('kerə,təʊs, -,təʊz) ADJECTIVE (esp of certain sponges) having a horny skeleton.

keratosis (,kerə'təʊsɪs) NOUN *Pathol* [1] any skin condition marked by a horny growth, such as a wart. [2] a horny growth.

keratotomy (,kerə'tɒtəmɪ) NOUN surgical incision of the cornea.

kerb *or US and Canadian* **curb** (kɜːb) NOUN [1] a line of stone or concrete forming an edge between a pavement and a roadway, so that the pavement is some 15 cm above the level of the road. ◆ VERB [2] (*tr*) to provide with or enclose with a kerb.
▷HISTORY C17: from Old French *courbe* bent, from Latin *curvus;* see CURVE

kerbaya ('kerbaja) NOUN a blouse worn by Malay women.
▷HISTORY from Malay

kerb crawling NOUN the act of driving slowly along the edge of the pavement seeking to entice someone into the car for sexual purposes.
▸**kerb crawler** NOUN

kerb drill NOUN a pedestrian's procedure for crossing a road safely, esp as taught to children.

Kerbela ('kɜːbələ) NOUN a variant of **Karbala**.

kerbing *or US and Canadian* **curbing** ('kɜːbɪŋ) NOUN [1] material used for a kerb. [2] a less common word for **kerb** (sense 1).

kerb market NOUN *Stock Exchange* [1] an after-hours street market. [2] a street market dealing in unquoted securities.

kerbside ('kɜːb,saɪd) NOUN **a** the edge of a pavement where it drops to the level of the road. **b** *as modifier*: *kerbside rubbish collections*.

kerbstone *or US and Canadian* **curbstone** ('kɜːb,stəʊn) NOUN one of a series of stones that form a kerb.

kerb weight NOUN the weight of a motor car without occupants, luggage, etc.

Kerch (*Russian* kjertʃ) NOUN a port in the S Ukraine on the **Kerch Peninsula** and the **Strait of Kerch** (linking the Black Sea with the Sea of Azov): founded as a Greek colony in the 6th century B.C.; ceded to Russia in 1774; iron-mining, steel production, and fishing. Pop.: 167 400 (1998 est.).

kerchief ('kɜːtʃɪf) NOUN a piece of cloth worn tied over the head or around the neck.
▷HISTORY C13: from Old French *cuevrechef*, from *covrir* to COVER + *chef* head; see CHIEF
▸**'kerchiefed** ADJECTIVE

kerel ADJECTIVE ('kerəl), NOUN *South African* a chap or fellow.
▷HISTORY C19: Afrikaans

kerf (kɜːf) NOUN the cut made by a saw, an axe, etc.
▷HISTORY Old English *cyrf* a cutting; related to Old English *ceorfan* to CARVE

kerfuffle, carfuffle, *or* **kurfuffle** (kəˈfʌfᵊl) NOUN [1] *Informal, chiefly Brit* commotion; disorder; agitation. ◆ VERB [2] (*tr*) *Scot* to put into disorder or disarray; ruffle or disarrange.
▷HISTORY from Scottish *curfuffle, carfuffle,* from Scottish Gaelic *car* twist, turn + *fuffle* to disarrange

Kerguelen (ˈkɜːgɪlɪn) NOUN an archipelago in the S Indian Ocean: consists of one large volcanic island (Kerguelen or Desolation Island) and 300 small islands; part of the French Southern and Antarctic Territories.

Kerkrade (*Dutch* ˈkɛrkraːdə) NOUN a town in the SE Netherlands, in Limburg: one of the oldest coal-mining centres in Europe. Pop.: 52 848 (1994).

kerky (ˈkɜːkɪ) ADJECTIVE **kerkier, kerkiest.** *Midland English dialect* stupid.

Kérkyra (ˈkɛrkira) NOUN transliteration of the Modern Greek name for **Corfu.**

kerma (ˈkɜːmə) NOUN *Physics* the quotient of the sum of the initial kinetic energies of all the charged particles liberated by indirectly ionizing radiation in a volume element of a material divided by the mass of the volume element. The SI unit is the gray.
▷HISTORY C20: *k*(inetic) *e*(nergy) *r*(eleased per unit) *ma*(ss)

Kerman (kəˈmɑːn) NOUN a city in SE Iran: carpet-making centre. Pop.: 384 991 (1996).

Kermanshah (ˌkɜːmænˈʃɑː) NOUN the former name (until 1987) of **Bakhtaran.**

kermes (ˈkɜːmɪz) NOUN [1] the dried bodies of female scale insects of the genus *Kermes,* esp *K. ilices* of Europe and W Asia, used as a red dyestuff. [2] a small evergreen Eurasian oak tree, *Quercus coccifera,* with prickly leaves resembling holly: the host plant of kermes scale insects.
▷HISTORY C16: from French *kermès,* from Arabic *qirmiz,* from Sanskrit *krmija-* red dye, literally: produced by a worm, from *krmi* worm + *ja-* produced

kermis *or* **kirmess** (ˈkɜːmɪs) NOUN [1] (formerly, esp in Holland and Northern Germany) an annual country festival or carnival. [2] *US and Canadian* a similar event, esp one held to collect money for charity.
▷HISTORY C16: from Middle Dutch *kercmisse,* from *kerc* church + *misse* MASS; originally a festival held to celebrate the dedication of a church

kern¹ *or* **kerne** (kɜːn) NOUN [1] the part of the character on a piece of printer's type that projects beyond the body. ◆ VERB [2] (*tr*) to furnish (a typeface) with a kern.
▷HISTORY C17: from French *carne* corner of type, projecting angle, ultimately from Latin *cardō* hinge

kern² (kɜːn) NOUN [1] a lightly armed foot soldier in medieval Ireland or Scotland. [2] a troop of such soldiers. [3] *Archaic* a loutish peasant.
▷HISTORY C14: from Middle Irish *cethern* band of foot soldiers, from *cath* battle

kern³ (kɜːn) NOUN *Engineering* the central area of a wall, column, etc., through which all compressive forces pass.
▷HISTORY from German *Kern* core, heart

kernel (ˈkɜːnᵊl) NOUN [1] the edible central part of a seed, nut, or fruit within the shell or stone. [2] the grain of a cereal, esp wheat, consisting of the seed in a hard husk. [3] the central or essential part of something. ◆ VERB **-nels, -nelling, -nelled** *or US* **-nels, -neling, -neled.** [4] (*intr*) *Rare* to form kernels.
▷HISTORY Old English *cyrnel* a little seed, from *corn* seed; see CORN¹
▸ˈ**kernel-less** ADJECTIVE

kerning ADJECTIVE (ˈkɜːnɪŋ), NOUN *Printing* the adjustment of space between the letters of words to improve the appearance of text matter.

kernite (ˈkɜːnaɪt) NOUN a light soft colourless or white mineral consisting of a hydrated sodium borate in monoclinic crystalline form: an important source of borax and other boron compounds. Formula: $Na_2B_4O_7.4H_2O$.
▷HISTORY C20: from *Kern* County, California, where it was found + -ITE¹

kernmantel rope (ˈkɜːnˌmæntᵊl) NOUN *Mountaineering* a rope made of many straight nylon fibres within a plaited sheath; used for its tensile strength, freedom from twisting, and elasticity.
▷HISTORY C20: from German *Kernmantel,* from *Kern* core + *Mantel* coat, casing

kero (ˈkɛrəʊ) NOUN *Austral and NZ* short for **kerosene.**

kerogen (ˈkɛrədʒən) NOUN the solid organic material found in some rocks, such as oil shales, that produces hydrocarbons similar to petroleum when heated.
▷HISTORY C20: from Greek *kēro(s)* wax + -GEN

kerosene *or* **kerosine** (ˈkɛrəˌsiːn) NOUN [1] another name (esp US and Canadian) for **paraffin.** [2] the general name for paraffin as a fuel for jet aircraft.
▷HISTORY C19: from Greek *kēros* wax + -ENE

> **Language note** The spelling *kerosine* is now the preferred form in technical and industrial usage.

Kerr effect NOUN [1] Also called: **electro-optical effect.** the production of double refraction in certain transparent substances by the application of a strong electric field. [2] Also called: **magneto-optical effect.** a slight elliptical polarization of plane polarized light when reflected from one of the poles of a strong magnet.
▷HISTORY C19: named after John *Kerr* (1824–1907), Scottish physicist

Kerry (ˈkɛrɪ) NOUN [1] a county of SW Republic of Ireland, in W Munster province: mostly mountainous (including the highest peaks in Ireland), with a deeply indented coast and many offshore islands. County town: Tralee. Pop.: 126 130 (1996). Area: 4701 sq. km (1815 sq. miles). [2] a small black breed of dairy cattle, originally from Kerry.

Kerry blue terrier NOUN an Irish breed of terrier with a soft silky wavy coat of a silvery-grey or smoky blue colour.

Kerry Hill NOUN a breed of sturdy sheep having black-and-white markings on the head and legs and a dense fleece, originating from Powys, on the English-Welsh borders.

kersey (ˈkɜːzɪ) NOUN [1] a smooth woollen cloth used for overcoats, etc. [2] a twilled woollen cloth with a cotton warp.
▷HISTORY C14: probably from *Kersey,* village in Suffolk

kerseymere (ˈkɜːzɪˌmɪə) NOUN a fine soft woollen cloth of twill weave.
▷HISTORY C18: from KERSEY + (CASSI)MERE

kerygma (ˌkeˈriːgmə) NOUN *Christianity* the essential news of Jesus, as preached by the early Christians to elicit faith rather than to educate or instruct.
▷HISTORY from Greek: preaching, proclamation

Kesh (keɪʃ) NOUN the beard and uncut hair, covered by the turban, traditionally worn by Sikhs as a symbol of their religious and cultural loyalty, symbolizing the natural life. See also **five Ks.**
▷HISTORY Punjabi *keś*

Kesteven (ˈkɛstɪvᵊn, kɛˈstiːvᵊn) NOUN **Parts of.** an area in E England constituting a former administrative division of Lincolnshire.

kestrel (ˈkɛstrəl) NOUN any of several small falcons, esp the European *Falco tinnunculus,* that tend to hover against the wind and feed on small mammals on the ground.
▷HISTORY C15: changed from Old French *cresserele,* from *cressele* rattle, from Vulgar Latin *crepicella* (unattested), from Latin *crepitāre* to crackle, from *crepāre* to rustle

Keswick (ˈkɛzɪk) NOUN a market town in NW England, in Cumbria in the Lake District: tourist centre. Pop.: 4836 (1991).

ketamine (ˈkɛtəmiːn) NOUN a drug, chemically related to PCP, that is used in medicine as a general anaesthetic, being administered by injection; cyclohexylamine.

ketch (kɛtʃ) NOUN a two-masted sailing vessel, fore-and-aft rigged, with a tall mainmast and a mizzen stepped forward of the rudderpost. Compare **yawl¹** (sense 1).
▷HISTORY C15 *cache,* probably from *cacchen* to hunt; see CATCH

ketchup (ˈkɛtʃəp), **catchup,** *or* **catsup** NOUN any of various piquant sauces containing vinegar: *tomato ketchup.*
▷HISTORY C18: from Chinese (Amoy) *kōetsiap* brine of pickled fish, from *kōe* seafood + *tsiap* sauce

ketene (ˈkiːtiːn, ˈkɛt-) NOUN a colourless irritating toxic gas used as an acetylating agent in organic synthesis. Formula: CH_2:CO. Also called: **ethonone.**

keto- *or before a vowel* **ket-** COMBINING FORM indicating that a chemical compound is a ketone or is derived from a ketone: *ketose; ketoxime.*

keto-enol tautomerism (ˈkiːtəʊˈiːnɒl) NOUN *Chem* tautomerism in which the tautomers are an enol and a keto form. The change occurs by transfer of a hydrogen atom within the molecule.

keto form (ˈkiːtəʊ) NOUN the form of tautomeric compounds when they are ketones rather than enols. See **keto-enol tautomerism.**

ketogenic (ˌkiːtəʊˈdʒɛnɪk) ADJECTIVE *Med* forming or able to stimulate the production of ketone bodies: *a ketogenic diet.*

ketonaemia *or US* **ketonemia** (ˌkiːtəʊˈniːmɪə) NOUN *Pathol* an excess of ketone bodies in the blood.

ketone (ˈkiːtəʊn) NOUN any of a class of compounds with the general formula R′COR, where R and R′ are alkyl or aryl groups. See also **acetone.**
▷HISTORY C19: from German *Keton,* from *Aketon* ACETONE
▸**ketonic** (kɪˈtɒnɪk) ADJECTIVE

ketone body NOUN *Biochem* any of three compounds (acetoacetic acid, 3-hydroxybutanoic acid, and acetone) produced when fatty acids are broken down in the liver to provide a source of energy. Excess ketone bodies are present in the blood and urine of people unable to use glucose as an energy source, as in diabetes and starvation. Also called: **acetone body.**

ketone group NOUN *Chem* the functional group of ketones: a carbonyl group attached to the carbon atoms of two other organic groups.

ketonuria (ˌkiːtəʊˈnjʊərɪə, ˌkiːtə-) NOUN *Pathol* the presence of ketone bodies in the urine. Also called: **acetonuria.**

ketose (ˈkiːtəʊz) NOUN any monosaccharide that contains a ketone group.

ketosis (kɪˈtəʊsɪs) NOUN *Pathol* a high concentration of ketone bodies in the blood. Also called: **acetonaemia.**

ketoxime (kiːˈtɒksiːm) NOUN an oxime formed by reaction between hydroxylamine and a ketone.

Kettering (ˈkɛtərɪŋ) NOUN a town in central England, in Northamptonshire: footwear industry. Pop.: 47 186 (1991).

kettle (ˈkɛtᵊl) NOUN [1] a metal or plastic container with a handle and spout for boiling water. [2] any of various metal containers for heating liquids, cooking fish, etc. [3] a large metal vessel designed to withstand high temperatures, used in various industrial processes such as refining and brewing. [4] short for **kettle hole.**
▷HISTORY C13: from Old Norse *ketill;* related to Old English *cietel* kettle, Old High German *kezzil;* all ultimately from Latin *catillus* a little pot, from *catīnus* pot

kettledrum (ˈkɛtᵊlˌdrʌm) NOUN a percussion instrument of definite pitch, consisting of a hollow bowl-like hemisphere covered with a skin or membrane, supported on a tripod or stand. The pitch may be adjusted by means of screws or pedals, which alter the tension of the skin.
▸ˈ**kettle,drummer** NOUN

kettle hole NOUN a round hollow formed by the melting of a mass of buried ice. Often shortened to: **kettle.**

kettle of fish NOUN [1] a situation; state of affairs (often used ironically in the phrase **a pretty** or **fine kettle of fish**). [2] case; matter for consideration: *that's quite a different kettle of fish.*

ketubah (kətuˈbaː) NOUN *Judaism* the contract that states the obligations within Jewish marriage.
▷HISTORY from Hebrew, literally: document

keV ABBREVIATION FOR kilo-electronvolt.

kevel (ˈkɛvᵊl) NOUN [1] *Nautical* a strong bitt or bollard for securing heavy hawsers. [2] *Building trades* a hammer having an edged end and a pointed end, used for breaking and rough-shaping stone.
▷HISTORY C14: from Old Northern French *keville,* from Latin *clāvicula* a little key, from *clāvis* key

Kevlar ('kɛvˌlɑː) NOUN *Trademark* a synthetic fibre, consisting of long-chain polyamides, having high tensile strength and temperate resistance.

Kew (kjuː) NOUN part of the Greater London borough of Richmond-upon-Thames, on the River Thames: famous for **Kew Gardens** (the Royal Botanic Gardens), established in 1759 and given to the nation in 1841.

kewl (kuːl) ADJECTIVE *Informal* a nonstandard variant spelling of **cool** (sense 11).

Kewpie Doll ('kjuːpɪ) NOUN *US and Canadian* 1 *Trademark* a doll having rosy cheeks and a curl of hair on its head. 2 *(often not capitals)* any brightly coloured doll, commonly given as a prize at carnivals.
▷HISTORY C20 *kewpie*, perhaps from *Cupid*

kex (kɛks) NOUN 1 any of several large hollow-stemmed umbelliferous plants, such as cow parsnip and chervil. 2 the dried stalks of any of these plants.
▷HISTORY C14: of obscure origin

key[1] (kiː) NOUN 1 a metal instrument, usually of a specifically contoured shape, that is made to fit a lock and, when rotated, operates the lock's mechanism. 2 any instrument that is rotated to operate a valve, clock winding mechanism, etc. 3 a small metal peg or wedge inserted into keyways. 4 any of a set of levers operating a typewriter, computer, etc. 5 any of the visible parts of the lever mechanism of a musical keyboard instrument that when depressed set in motion the action that causes the instrument to sound. 6 **a** Also called: **tonality.** any of the 24 major and minor diatonic scales considered as a corpus of notes upon which a piece of music draws for its tonal framework. **b** the main tonal centre in an extended composition: *a symphony in the key of F major.* **c** the tonic of a major or minor scale. **d** See **tuning key.** 7 something that is crucial in providing an explanation or interpretation: *the key to adult behaviour lies in childhood.* 8 a means of achieving a desired end: *the key to happiness.* 9 a means of access or control: *Gibraltar is the key to the Mediterranean.* 10 a list of explanations of symbols, codes, etc. 11 a text that explains or gives information about a work of literature, art, or music. 12 Also called: **key move.** the correct initial move in the solution of a set problem. 13 *Biology* a systematic list of taxonomic characteristics, used to identify animals or plants. 14 *Photog, painting* the dominant tonal value and colour intensity of a picture. See also **low-key** (sense 3), **high-key.** 15 *Electrical engineering* **a** a hand-operated device for opening or closing a circuit or for switching circuits. **b** a hand-operated switch that is pressed to transmit coded signals, esp Morse code. 16 the grooving or scratching of a surface or the application of a rough coat of plaster, etc., to provide a bond for a subsequent finish. 17 pitch: *he spoke in a low key.* 18 a characteristic mood or style: *a poem in a melancholic key.* 19 level of intensity: *she worked herself up to a high key.* 20 *Railways* a wooden wedge placed between a rail and a chair to keep the rail firmly in place. 21 a wedge for tightening a joint or for splitting stone or timber. 22 short for **keystone** (sense 1). 23 *Botany* any dry winged fruit, esp that of the ash. 24 *(modifier)* of great importance: *a key issue.* 25 *(modifier) Photog* determining the tonal value of a photograph: *flesh colour is an important key tone.* ◆ VERB *(mainly tr)* 26 (foll by *to*) to harmonize (with): *to key one's actions to the prevailing mood.* 27 to adjust or fasten with a key or some similar device. 28 to provide with a key or keys. 29 to scratch the paintwork of (a car) with a key. 30 (often foll by *up*) to locate the position of (a piece of copy, artwork, etc.) on a layout by the use of symbols. 31 *(also intr)* another word for **keyboard** (sense 3). 32 to include a distinguishing device in (an advertisement, etc.), so that responses to it can be identified. 33 to provide a keystone for (an arch). ◆ See also **key in, key up.**
▷HISTORY Old English *cǣg;* related to Old Frisian *kēi,* Middle Low German *keie* spear
▸**'keyless** ADJECTIVE

key[2] (kiː) NOUN a variant spelling of **cay.**

keyboard ('kiːˌbɔːd) NOUN 1 **a** a complete set of keys, usually hand-operated, as on a piano, organ, typewriter, or typesetting machine. **b** *(as modifier): a keyboard instrument.* 2 *(often plural)* a musical instrument, esp an electronic one, played by means of a keyboard. ◆ VERB 3 to set (a text) in type, onto magnetic tape, or into some other medium, by using a keyboard machine.
▸**'keyˌboarder** NOUN

keyboardist ('kiːˌbɔːdɪst) NOUN a person who plays a keyboard instrument, esp an electronic musical instrument.

key fruit NOUN another name for **samara.**

key grip NOUN *Chiefly US* the person in charge of moving and setting up camera tracks and scenery in a film or television studio. See also **grip**[1] (sense 11).

keyhole ('kiːˌhəʊl) NOUN 1 an aperture in a door or a lock case through which a key may be passed to engage the lock mechanism. 2 any small aperture resembling a keyhole in shape or function. 3 a transient column of vapour or plasma formed during the welding or cutting of materials, using high energy beams, such as lasers.

keyhole surgery NOUN surgery carried out through a very small incision.

key in VERB *(tr, adverb)* to enter (information or instructions) in a computer or other device by means of a keyboard or keypad.

key light NOUN *Television, theatre, photog* the main stage or studio light that gives the required overall intensity of illumination.

key-man assurance NOUN an assurance policy taken out, esp by a small company, on the life of a senior executive whose death would create a serious loss.

key money NOUN a fee payment required from a new tenant of a house or flat before he moves in.

Keynesian (keɪnzɪən) ADJECTIVE 1 of or relating to the theories of John Maynard Keynes, 1st Baron Keynes, the English economist (1883–1946). 2 a follower or admirer of Keynes.
▸**'Keynesianˌism** NOUN

keynote ('kiːˌnəʊt) NOUN 1 **a** a central or determining principle in a speech, literary work, etc. **b** *(as modifier): a keynote speech.* 2 the note upon which a scale or key is based; tonic. ◆ VERB *(tr)* 3 to deliver a keynote address to (a political convention, etc.). 4 to outline (political issues, policy, etc.) in or as in a keynote address.

keypad ('kiːˌpæd) NOUN 1 a small keyboard with push buttons, as on a pocket calculator, remote control unit for a television, etc. 2 *Computing* a data input device consisting of a limited number of keys, each with nominated functions.

key punch NOUN 1 Also called: **card punch.** a device having a keyboard that is operated manually to transfer data onto punched cards, paper tape, etc. ◆ VERB **key-punch.** 2 to transfer (data) onto punched cards, paper tape, etc., by using a key punch.

keys (kiːz) INTERJECTION *Scot, dialect* a children's cry for truce or respite from the rules of a game.
▷HISTORY origin uncertain

key signature NOUN *Music* a group of sharps or flats appearing at the beginning of each stave line to indicate the key in which a piece, section, etc., is to be performed.

key stage NOUN *Brit Education* any one of four broad age-group divisions (5–7; 7–11; 11–14; 14–16) to which each level of the National Curriculum applies.

keystone ('kiːˌstəʊn) NOUN 1 Also called: **headstone, quoin.** the central stone at the top of an arch or the top stone of a dome or vault. 2 something that is necessary to connect or support a number of other related things.

keystroke ('kiːˌstrəʊk) NOUN a single operation of the mechanism of a typewriter or keyboard-operated typesetting machine by the action of a key.

key up VERB *(tr, adverb)* to raise the intensity, excitement, tension, etc., of.

keyway ('kiːˌweɪ) NOUN a longitudinal slot cut into a component to accept a key that engages with a similar slot on a mating component to prevent relative motion of the two components.

keyword ('kiːˌwɜːd) NOUN 1 a word used as a key to a code. 2 any significant word or phrase, esp a word used to describe the contents of a document.

key worker NOUN a social or mental health worker assigned to an individual case or patient.

kg[1] 1 ABBREVIATION FOR keg. ◆ 2 SYMBOL FOR kilogram.

kg[2] THE INTERNET DOMAIN NAME FOR Kyrgyzstan.

KG ABBREVIATION FOR Knight of the Order of the Garter (a Brit title).

KGB ABBREV the former Soviet secret police, founded in 1954. Compare **GRU.**
▷HISTORY from Russian *Komitet Gosudarstvennoi Bezopasnosti* State Security Committee

kh THE INTERNET DOMAIN NAME FOR Cambodia.

Khabarovsk *(Russian* xaˈbarəfsk) NOUN a port in E Russia, on the Amur River: it was the administrative centre of the whole Soviet Far Eastern territory until 1938; a major industrial centre. Pop.: 614 000 (1999 est.).

khaddar ('kɑːdə) *or* **khadi** ('kɑːdɪ) NOUN a cotton cloth of plain weave, produced in India.
▷HISTORY from Hindi *khādar*

Khakass Republic (kəˈkæs) NOUN a constituent republic of S central Russia, in the Krasnoyarsk Territory: formed in 1930. Capital: Abakan. Pop.: 581 000 (2000 est.). Area: 61 900 sq. km (23 855 sq. miles). Also called: **Khakassia** (kəˈkæsɪə; *Russian* xəˈkasɪjə).

khaki ('kɑːkɪ) NOUN, *plural* **-kis.** 1 **a** a dull yellowish-brown colour. **b** *(as adjective): a khaki background.* 2 **a** a hard-wearing fabric of this colour, used esp for military uniforms. **b** *(as modifier): a khaki jacket.*
▷HISTORY C19: from Urdu, from Persian: dusty, from *khāk* dust

khaki election NOUN *Brit* a general election held during or immediately after a war, esp one in which the war has an effect on how people vote.
▷HISTORY C20: first used of the 1900 general election, during which the conduct of the Boer war was an election issue

khalif ('keɪlɪf, 'kæl-) NOUN a variant spelling of **caliph.**

Khalkha ('kælkə) NOUN the dialect of Mongolian that is the official language of Mongolia.

Khalkidíki (xalkiðiˈki) NOUN transliteration of the Modern Greek name for **Chalcidice.**

Khalkís (xalˈkis) NOUN transliteration of the Modern Greek name for **Chalcis.**

Khalsa ('kælsə) NOUN an order of the Sikh religion, founded (1699) by Guru Gobind Singh. Members vow to wear the five Ks, to eat only ritually killed meat, and to refrain from committing adultery or cutting their hair.

khamsin ('kæmsɪn, kæmˈsiːn), **kamseen,** *or* **kamsin** NOUN a hot southerly wind blowing from about March to May, esp in Egypt.
▷HISTORY C17: from Arabic, literally: fifty

khan[1] (kɑːn) NOUN 1 **a** (formerly) a title borne by medieval Chinese emperors and Mongol and Turkic rulers: usually added to a name: *Kublai Khan.* **b** such a ruler. 2 a title of respect borne by important personages in Afghanistan and central Asia.
▷HISTORY C14: from Old French *caan,* from Medieval Latin *caanus,* from Turkish *khān,* contraction of *khāqān* ruler

khan[2] (kɑːn) NOUN an inn in Turkey, certain Arab countries, etc.; caravanserai.
▷HISTORY C14: via Arabic from Persian

khanate ('kɑːneɪt, 'kæn-) NOUN 1 the territory ruled by a khan. 2 the position or rank of a khan.

khanda ('kʌndə) NOUN a double-edged sword that appears as the emblem on the Sikh flag and is used in the Amrit ceremony to stir the amrit.

khanga ('kæŋgə) NOUN a variant spelling of **kanga.**

Khaniá (xaˈnja) NOUN transliteration of the Modern Greek name for **Chania.**

kharif (kəˈriːf) NOUN (in Pakistan, India, etc.) a crop that is harvested at the beginning of winter. Compare **rabi.**
▷HISTORY Urdu, ultimately from Arabic *kharafa* to gather

Kharkov *(Russian* ˈxarjkəf) NOUN a city in the E Ukraine: capital of the Ukrainian Soviet Socialist Republic (1917–34); university (1805). Pop.: 1 521 400 (1998 est.).

Khartoum *or* **Khartum** (kɑːˈtuːm) NOUN the capital of the Sudan, at the junction of the Blue and the White Nile: with adjoining Khartoum North and Omdurman, the largest conurbation in the country; destroyed by the Mahdists in 1885 when General Gordon was killed; seat of the Anglo-Egyptian government of the Sudan until 1954, then capital of the new republic. Pop.: 924 505 (1993).

khat *or* **kat** (kæt, kɑːt) NOUN [1] a white-flowered evergreen shrub, *Catha edulis,* of Africa and Arabia, whose leaves have narcotic properties. [2] the leaves of this shrub, chewed or prepared as a drink.
▷HISTORY C19: from Arabic *qāt*

khayal (kəˈjɑːl) NOUN a kind of Indian classical vocal music.
▷HISTORY Urdu: literally: thought, imagination

khazi (ˈkɑːzɪ) NOUN *Slang* a lavatory; toilet.
▷HISTORY C19: from *casa, case* a brothel, from Italian *casa* a house; modern spelling probably influenced by KHAKI

kheda, khedah, *or* **keddah** (ˈkɛdə) NOUN (in India, Myanmar, etc.) an enclosure into which wild elephants are driven to be captured.
▷HISTORY from Hindi

khedive (kɪˈdiːv) NOUN the viceroy of Egypt under Ottoman suzerainty (1867–1914).
▷HISTORY C19: from French *khédive,* from Turkish *hidiv,* from Persian *khidīw* prince
▸**kheˈdival** *or* **kheˈdivial** ADJECTIVE ▸**kheˈdivate** *or* **kheˈdiviate** NOUN

Khelat (kəˈlɑːt) NOUN a variant spelling of **Kalat.**

Kherson (*Russian* xɪrˈsɔn) NOUN a port in the S Ukraine on the Dnieper River near the Black Sea: shipyards. Pop.: 358 700 (1998 est.).

Khingan Mountains (ˈʃɪŋˈɑːn) PLURAL NOUN a mountain system of NE China, in W Manchuria. Highest peak: 2034 m (6673 ft.).

Khíos (ˈçiɔs) NOUN transliteration of the Modern Greek name for **Chios.**

Khirbet Qumran (ˈkɪəbɛt ˈkʊmrɑːn) NOUN an archaeological site in NW Jordan, near the NW shore of the Dead Sea: includes the caves where the Dead Sea Scrolls were found.

Khiva (*Russian* xiˈva) NOUN a former khanate of W Asia, on the Amu Darya River: divided between the former Uzbek and Turkmen Soviet Socialist Republics in 1924.

Khmer (kmɛə, kmɜː) NOUN [1] a member of a people of Cambodia, noted for a civilization that flourished from about 800 A.D. to about 1370, remarkable for its architecture. [2] the language of this people, belonging to the Mon-Khmer family: the official language of Cambodia. ◆ ADJECTIVE [3] of or relating to this people or their language.
▸**ˈKhmerian** ADJECTIVE

Khmer Republic NOUN the former official name (1970–76) of **Cambodia.**

Khmer Rouge (ruːʒ) NOUN the Kampuchean communist party, which seized power (1975) in a civil war: in exile since 1979, dispersed in 1999.

Khoikhoi (kɔɪˈkɔɪ, xɔɪˈxɔɪ) NOUN [1] a member of a race of people of Southern Africa, of short stature and a dark yellowish-brown complexion, who formerly occupied the region near the Cape of Good Hope and are now almost extinct. [2] any of the languages of this people, belonging to the Khoisan family.

Khoisan (ˈkɔɪsɑːn, kɔɪˈsɑːn) NOUN [1] a family of languages spoken in southern Africa by the Khoikhoi and Bushmen and by two small groups in Tanzania. A characteristic phonological feature of these languages is the use of suction stops (clicks). ◆ ADJECTIVE [2] denoting, relating to, or belonging to this family of languages.

Khojent, Khodzhent (*Russian* xadˈʒɛnt), *or* **Khujand** (*Russian* xuˈʃænd) NOUN a town in Tajikistan on the Syr Darya River: one of the oldest towns in central Asia; textile industries. Pop.: 163 000 (1998 est.). Former name (1936–91): **Leninabad.**

Khotan (ˈkəʊˈtɑːn) NOUN another name for **Hotan.**

Khujand (*Russian* xuˈʃænd) NOUN a variant spelling of **Khojent.**

Khulna (ˈkʊlnɑː) NOUN a city in S Bangladesh. Pop.: 731 000 (1991).

khurta (ˈkuətə) NOUN a variant spelling of **kurta.**

khuskhus (ˈkʊskʊs) NOUN an aromatic perennial Indian grass, *Vetiveria zizanioides* (or *Andropogon squarrosus*), whose roots are woven into mats, fans, and baskets.
▷HISTORY Hindi

Khyber Pass (ˈkaɪbə) NOUN a narrow pass over the Safed Koh Range between Afghanistan and Pakistan, over which came the Persian, Greek, Tatar, Mogul, and Afghan invasions of India; scene of bitter fighting between the British and Afghans (1838–42, 1878–80). Length: about 53 km (33 miles). Highest point: 1072 m (3518 ft.).

kHz SYMBOL FOR kilohertz.

ki THE INTERNET DOMAIN NAME FOR Kiribati.

kiaat (ˈkiːɑːt) NOUN [1] a tropical African leguminous tree, *Pterocarpus angolensis.* [2] the wood of this tree, used for furniture, floors, etc.
▷HISTORY C19: Afrikaans, from Dutch, probably from Malay *kaju* wood

kia kaha (ˌkɪə ˈkɑːhə) SENTENCE SUBSTITUTE *NZ* be strong!
▷HISTORY Maori

kiang (kɪˈæŋ) NOUN a variety of the wild ass, *Equus hemionus,* that occurs in Tibet and surrounding regions. Compare **onager.**
▷HISTORY C19: from Tibetan *rkyan*

Kiangsi (ˈkjæŋˈsiː) NOUN a variant transliteration of the Chinese name for **Jiangxi.**

Kiangsu (ˈkjæŋˈsuː) NOUN a variant transliteration of the Chinese name for **Jiangsu.**

Kiaochow (ˈkjaʊˈtʃaʊ) NOUN a variant transliteration of the Chinese name for **Jiazhou.**

kia ora (ˌkɪə ˈɔːrə) SENTENCE SUBSTITUTE *NZ* greetings! good luck!
▷HISTORY Maori, literally: be well!

kibble¹ (ˈkɪb^{ə}l) NOUN *Brit* a bucket used in wells or in mining for hoisting.
▷HISTORY C17: from German *Kübel;* related to Old English *cyfel,* ultimately from Medieval Latin *cuppa* CUP

kibble² (ˈkɪb^{ə}l) VERB [1] (*tr*) to grind into small pieces. ◆ NOUN [2] *US and Canadian* ground meal formed into pellets and used as pet food.
▷HISTORY C18: of unknown origin

kibbutz (kɪˈbʊts) NOUN, *plural* **kibbutzim** (ˌkɪbʊtˈsiːm). a collective agricultural settlement in modern Israel, owned and administered communally by its members and on which children are reared collectively.
▷HISTORY C20: from Modern Hebrew *qibbūs:* gathering, from Hebrew *qibbūtz*

kibe (kaɪb) NOUN a chilblain, esp an ulcerated one on the heel.
▷HISTORY C14: probably from Welsh *cibi,* of obscure origin

kibi- (ˈkɪbɪ) PREFIX *Computing* denoting 2^{10}: *kibibyte.* Symbol: Ki.
▷HISTORY C20: from KI(LO-) + BI(NARY)

kibitka (kɪˈbɪtkə) NOUN [1] (in Russia) a covered sledge or wagon. [2] a felt tent used among the Tatars of central Asia. [3] a Tatar family.
▷HISTORY C18: Russian, from Tatar *kibits*

kibitz (ˈkɪbɪts) VERB (*intr*) *US and Canadian informal* to interfere or offer unwanted advice, esp as a spectator at a card game.
▷HISTORY C20: from Yiddish *kibitzen,* from German *kiebitzen* to be an onlooker, from *Kiebitz* busybody, literally: plover
▸**ˈkibitzer** NOUN

kiblah *or* **kibla** (ˈkɪblɑː) NOUN *Islam* the direction of Mecca, to which Muslims turn in prayer, indicated in mosques by a niche (mihrab) in the wall.
▷HISTORY C18: from Arabic *qiblah* that which is placed opposite; related to *qabala* to be opposite

kibosh *or* **kybosh** (ˈkaɪˌbɒʃ) *Slang* ◆ NOUN [1] **put the kibosh on.** to put a stop to; prevent from continuing; halt. ◆ VERB [2] (*tr*) to put a stop to.
▷HISTORY C19: of unknown origin

kick (kɪk) VERB [1] (*tr*) to drive or impel with the foot. [2] (*tr*) to hit with the foot or feet. [3] (*intr*) to strike out or thrash about with the feet, as in fighting or swimming. [4] (*intr*) to raise a leg high, as in dancing. [5] (of a gun, etc.) to recoil or strike in recoiling when fired. [6] (*tr*) *Rugby* **a** to make (a conversion or a drop goal) by means of a kick. **b** to score (a goal) by means of a kicked conversion. [7] (*tr*) *Soccer* to score (a goal) by a kick. [8] (*intr*) *Cricket* (of a ball) to rear up sharply. [9] (*intr; sometimes foll by against*) *Informal* to object or resist. [10] (*intr*) *Informal* to be active and in good health (esp in the phrase **alive and kicking**). [11] *Informal* to change gear in (a car, esp a racing car): *he kicked into third and passed the bigger car.* [12] (*tr*) *Informal* to free oneself of (an addiction, etc.): *to kick heroin; to kick the habit.* [13] **kick against the pricks.** See **prick** (sense 20). [14] **kick into touch. a** *Rugby, soccer* to kick the ball out of the playing area and into touch. See **touch** (sense 15). **b** *Informal* to take some temporizing action so that a problem is shelved or a decision postponed. [15] **kick one's heels.** to wait or be kept waiting. [16] **kick over the traces.** See **trace²** (sense 3). [17] **kick the bucket.** *Slang* to die. [18] **kick up one's heels.** *Informal* to enjoy oneself without inhibition. ◆ NOUN [19] a thrust or blow with the foot. [20] any of certain rhythmic leg movements used in swimming. [21] the recoil of a gun or other firearm. [22] *Informal* a stimulating or exciting quality or effect (esp in the phrases **get a kick out of** or **for kicks**). [23] *Informal* the sudden stimulating or intoxicating effect of strong alcoholic drink or certain drugs. [24] *Informal* power or force. [25] *Slang* a temporary enthusiasm: *he's on a new kick every week.* [26] **kick in the pants.** *Slang* **a** a reprimand or scolding designed to produce greater effort, enthusiasm, etc., in the person receiving it. **b** a setback or disappointment. [27] **kick in the teeth.** *Slang* a humiliating rebuff. ◆ See also **kick about, kickback, kick in, kick off, kick out, kick up, kick upstairs.**
▷HISTORY C14 *kiken,* perhaps of Scandinavian origin
▸**ˈkickable** ADJECTIVE

kick about *or* **around** VERB (*mainly adverb*) *Informal* [1] (*tr*) to treat harshly. [2] (*tr*) to discuss (ideas, etc.) informally. [3] (*intr*) to wander aimlessly. [4] (*intr*) to lie neglected or forgotten. [5] (*intr; also preposition*) to be present in (some place).

kick ass *Slang* ◆ VERB (*intr*) [1] to be impressive, esp in a forceful way: *pop music that kicks ass.* ◆ ADJECTIVE **kick-ass.** [2] forceful, aggressive, and impressive.

kickback (ˈkɪkˌbæk) NOUN [1] a strong reaction. [2] part of an income paid to a person having influence over the size or payment of the income, esp by some illegal arrangement. ◆ VERB **kick back.** (*adverb*) [3] (*intr*) to have a strong reaction. [4] (*intr*) (esp of a gun) to recoil. [5] to pay a kickback to (someone).

kick boxing NOUN a martial art that resembles boxing but permits blows with the feet as well as punches.

kickdown (ˈkɪkˌdaʊn) NOUN a method of changing gear in a car with automatic transmission, by fully depressing the accelerator.

kicker (ˈkɪkə) NOUN [1] a person or thing that kicks. [2] *Sport* a player in a rugby or occasionally a soccer team whose task is to attempt to kick conversions, penalty goals, etc. [3] *US and Canadian, slang* a hidden and disadvantageous factor, such as a clause in a contract. [4] *Informal* any light outboard motor for propelling a boat.

kick in VERB (*adverb*) [1] (*intr*) to start or become activated. [2] (*tr*) *Chiefly Austral and NZ informal* to contribute.

kick off VERB (*intr, adverb*) [1] to start play in a game of football by kicking the ball from the centre of the field. [2] *Informal* to commence a discussion, job, etc. ◆ NOUN **kickoff.** [3] **a** a place kick from the centre of the field in a game of football. **b** the time at which the first such kick is due to take place: *kickoff is at 2.30 p.m.* [4] *Informal* **a** the beginning of something. **b for a kickoff.** to begin with.

kick on VERB (*adverb*) *Informal* to continue.

kick out VERB (*tr, adverb*) *Informal* to eject or dismiss.

kick pleat NOUN a back pleat at the hem of a straight skirt to allow the wearer greater ease in walking.

kickshaw (ˈkɪkˌʃɔː) *or* **kickshaws** NOUN [1] a valueless trinket. [2] *Archaic* a small elaborate or exotic delicacy.
▷HISTORY C16: back formation from *kickshaws,* by folk etymology from French *quelque chose* something

kicksorter (ˈkɪkˌsɔːtə) NOUN *Physics* a multichannel pulse-height analyser used esp to distinguish between isotopes by sorting their characteristic pulses (kicks).

kickstand ('kɪkˌstænd) NOUN a short metal bar attached to and pivoting on the bottom of the frame of a motorcycle or bicycle, which when kicked into a vertical position holds the stationary vehicle upright.

kick-start ('kɪkˌstɑːt) VERB *(tr)* [1] to start (a motorcycle engine) by means of a pedal that is kicked downwards. [2] *Informal* to make (something) active, functional, or productive again. ◆ NOUN [3] an action or event resulting in the reactivation of something.
▸ **'kick-ˌstarter** NOUN

kick turn NOUN *Skiing* a standing turn performed by swivelling each ski separately through 180°.

kick up VERB *(adverb)* [1] *Informal* to cause (trouble, a fuss, etc.). [2] **kick up bobsy-die.** See **bobsy-die.**

kick upstairs VERB *(tr, adverb) Informal* to promote to a nominally higher but effectively powerless position.

kid¹ (kɪd) NOUN [1] the young of a goat or of a related animal, such as an antelope. [2] soft smooth leather made from the hide of a kid. [3] *Informal* **a** a young person; child. **b** *(modifier)* younger or being still a child: *kid brother; kid sister.* [4] **our kid.** *Liverpool dialect* my younger brother or sister. ◆ VERB **kids, kidding, kidded.** [5] (of a goat) to give birth to (young).
▷HISTORY C12: of Scandinavian origin; compare Old Norse *kith,* Shetland Islands *kidi* lamb
▸ **'kiddishness** NOUN ▸ **'kidˌlike** ADJECTIVE

kid² (kɪd) VERB **kids, kidding, kidded.** (sometimes foll by *on* or *along*) *Informal* [1] *(tr)* to tease or deceive for fun. [2] *(intr)* to behave or speak deceptively for fun. [3] *(tr)* to delude or fool (oneself) into believing (something): *don't kid yourself that no-one else knows.*
▷HISTORY C19: probably from KID¹
▸ **'kidder** NOUN ▸ **'kiddingly** ADVERB

kid³ (kɪd) NOUN a small wooden tub.
▷HISTORY C18: probably variant of KIT¹ (in the sense: barrel)

kidder ('kɪdə) NOUN [1] a person who kids. [2] *Northern English dialect* a brother or friend.

Kidderminster ('kɪdəˌmɪnstə) NOUN [1] a town in W central England, in N Worcestershire on the River Stour: carpet industry. Pop.: 54 644 (1991 est.). [2] a type of ingrain reversible carpet originally made at Kidderminster.

kiddle ('kɪdᵊl) NOUN *Brit, archaic* a device, esp a barrier constructed of nets and stakes, for catching fish in a river or in the sea.
▷HISTORY C13: from Anglo-French, from Old French *quidel,* of obscure origin

Kiddush ('kɪdəʃ; *Hebrew* kɪ'duʃ) NOUN *Judaism* [1] a special blessing said before a meal on sabbaths and festivals, usually including the blessing for wine or bread. [2] a reception usually for the congregants after a service at which drinks and snacks are served and this grace is said.
▷HISTORY from Hebrew *qiddūsh* sanctification

kiddy *or* **kiddie** ('kɪdɪ) NOUN, *plural* **-dies.** *Informal* an affectionate word for **child.**

kid glove NOUN [1] a glove made of kidskin. [2] **handle with kid gloves.** to treat with great tact or caution. ◆ ADJECTIVE **kidglove.** [3] overdelicate or overrefined. [4] diplomatic; tactful: *a kidglove approach.*

kidnap ('kɪdnæp) VERB **-naps, -napping, -napped** *or US* **-naps, -naping, -naped** *(tr)* to carry off and hold (a person), usually for ransom.
▷HISTORY C17: KID¹ + obsolete *nap* to steal; see NAB
▸ **'kidnapper** *or US* **'kidnaper** NOUN ▸ **'kidnapping** *or US* **'kidnaping** NOUN

kidney ('kɪdnɪ) NOUN [1] either of two bean-shaped organs at the back of the abdominal cavity in man, one on each side of the spinal column. They maintain water and electrolyte balance and filter waste products from the blood, which are excreted as urine. Related adjectives: **nephritic, renal.** [2] the corresponding organ in other animals. [3] the kidneys of certain animals used as food. [4] class, type, or disposition (esp in the phrases **of the same** or **a different kidney**).
▷HISTORY C14: of uncertain origin
▸ **'kidneyˌlike** ADJECTIVE

kidney bean NOUN [1] any of certain bean plants having kidney-shaped seeds, esp the French bean and scarlet runner. [2] the seed of any of these beans.

kidney machine NOUN another name for **artificial kidney.** See **haemodialysis.**

kidney ore NOUN *Geology* a form of hematite that occurs in kidney-shaped masses.

kidney-shaped ADJECTIVE shaped like an oval with an inward curve at one side.

kidney stone NOUN [1] *Pathol* a hard mass formed in the kidney, usually composed of oxalates, phosphates, and carbonates. Also called: **renal calculus.** [2] *Mineralogy* another name for **nephrite.**

kidney vetch NOUN a silky leguminous perennial plant, *Anthyllis vulneraria,* of Europe and N Africa, with yellow or orange flowers. Also called: **ladies' fingers.**

kidology (kɪ'dɒlədʒɪ) NOUN *Brit informal* the art or practice of bluffing or deception.
▷HISTORY C20: from KID² + OLOGY

kid-on ADJECTIVE *Brit informal* artificial; make-believe.

Kidron ('kiːdrən) NOUN a variant of **Kedron.**

kidskin ('kɪdˌskɪn) NOUN a soft smooth leather made from the hide of a young goat. Often shortened to: **kid.**

kids' stuff NOUN *Slang* [1] something considered fit only for children. [2] something considered simple or easy.

kidstakes ('kɪdˌsteɪks) PLURAL NOUN *Austral informal* pretence; nonsense: *cut the kidstakes!*

kidult ('kɪdʌlt) *Informal* ◆ NOUN [1] an adult who is interested in forms of entertainment such as computer games, television programmes, etc. that are intended for children. ◆ ADJECTIVE [2] aimed at or suitable for kidults, or both children and adults.
▷HISTORY C20: from KID¹ + (AD)ult

kief (kiːf) NOUN a variant spelling of **kif.**

kiekie ('kɪəˌkɪə, 'kiːˌkiː) NOUN a climbing bush plant, *Freycinetia banksii,* of New Zealand, having elongated leaves and edible berries.
▷HISTORY Maori

Kiel (kiːl) NOUN a port in N Germany, capital of Schleswig-Holstein state, on the **Kiel Canal** (connecting the North Sea with the Baltic): joined the Hanseatic League in 1284; became part of Denmark in 1773 and passed to Prussia in 1866; an important naval base in World Wars I and II; shipbuilding and engineering industries. Pop.: 235 500 (1999 est.).

Kielce (*Polish* 'kjɛltsɛ) NOUN an industrial city in S Poland. Pop.: 212 383 (1999 est.).

kier (kɪə) NOUN a vat in which cloth is bleached.
▷HISTORY C16: from Old Norse *ker* tub; related to Old High German *kar*

Kierkegaardian (ˌkɪəkə'gɑːdɪən) ADJECTIVE of or relating to Søren Aabye Kierkegaard, the Danish philosopher and theologian (1813–55), whose theories anticipated existentialism.

kieselguhr ('kiːzᵊlˌguə) NOUN an unconsolidated form of **diatomite.**
▷HISTORY C19: from German *Kieselgur,* from *Kiesel* flint, pebble + *Gur* loose earthy deposit

kieserite ('kiːzəˌraɪt) NOUN a white mineral consisting of hydrated magnesium sulphate. Formula: $MgSO_4.H_2O$.
▷HISTORY C19: named after Dietrich G. Kieser (died 1862), German physician; see -ITE¹

Kiev ('kiːɛf; *Russian* 'kijɪf) NOUN the capital of the Ukraine, on the Dnieper River: formed the first Russian state by the late 9th century; university (1834). Pop.: 2 620 900 (1998 est.).

kif (kɪf, kiːf), **kaif, keef, kef,** *or* **kief** NOUN [1] another name for **marijuana.** [2] any drug or agent that when smoked is capable of producing a euphoric condition. [3] the euphoric condition produced by smoking marijuana.
▷HISTORY C20: from Arabic *kayf* pleasure

Kigali (kɪ'gɑːlɪ) NOUN the capital of Rwanda, in the central part. Pop.: 256 000 (1996 est.).

Kigoma-Ujiji (kɪ'gəumə uː'dʒiːdʒɪ) NOUN a city in W Tanzania, on the shore of Lake Tanganyika; formed by the merger of the towns of Kigoma and Ujiji in the 1960s.

kike (kaɪk) NOUN *US and Canadian, slang* an offensive word for **Jew.**
▷HISTORY C20: probably variant of *kiki,* reduplication of *-ki,* common name-ending among Jews from Slavic countries

Kikládhes (ki'klaðɛs) NOUN transliteration of the Modern Greek name for **Cyclades.**

kikoi ('kiːkɔɪ) NOUN (in E Africa) **a** a piece of cotton cloth with coloured bands, worn wrapped around the body. **b** *(as modifier): kikoi material.*
▷HISTORY C20: from Swahili

kikumon ('kɪkuːˌmɒn) NOUN the chrysanthemum emblem of the imperial family of Japan.
▷HISTORY Japanese

Kikuyu (kɪ'kuːjuː) NOUN [1] *(plural* **-yus** *or* **-yu)** a member of a Negroid people of E Africa, living chiefly in Kenya on the high foothills around Mount Kenya. [2] the language of this people, belonging to the Bantu group of the Niger-Congo family.

Kilauea (ˌkiːlɑːuː'eɪə) NOUN a crater on the E side of Mauna Loa volcano, on SE Hawaii Island: the world's largest active crater. Height: 1247 m (4090 ft.). Width: 3 km (2 miles).

Kildare (kɪl'dɛə) NOUN a county of E Republic of Ireland, in Leinster province: mostly low-lying and fertile. County town: Naas. Pop.: 134 992 (1996). Area: 1694 sq. km (654 sq. miles).

kilderkin ('kɪldəkɪn) NOUN [1] an obsolete unit of liquid capacity equal to 16 or 18 Imperial gallons or of dry capacity equal to 16 or 18 wine gallons. [2] a cask capable of holding a kilderkin.
▷HISTORY C14: from Middle Dutch *kindekijn,* from *kintal* hundredweight, from Medieval Latin *quintale;* see KENTLEDGE

kiley ('kaɪlɪ) NOUN a variant spelling of **kylie.**

kilim (kɪ'liːm, 'kiːlɪːm) NOUN a pileless woven rug of intricate design made in the Middle East.
▷HISTORY C19: from Turkish, from Persian *kilīm*

Kilimanjaro (ˌkɪlɪmən'dʒɑːrəu) NOUN a volcanic massif in N Tanzania: the highest peak in Africa; extends from east to west for 80 km (50 miles). Height: 5895 m (19 340 ft.).

Kilkenny (kɪl'kɛnɪ) NOUN [1] a county of SE Republic of Ireland, in Leinster province: mostly agricultural. County town: Kilkenny. Pop.: 75 336 (1996). Area: 2062 sq. km (796 sq. miles). [2] a market town in SE Republic of Ireland, county town of Co. Kilkenny: capital of the ancient kingdom of Ossory. Pop.: 9500 (latest est.).

kill¹ (kɪl) VERB *(mainly tr)* [1] *(also intr;* when *tr,* sometimes foll by *off)* to cause the death of (a person or animal). [2] to put an end to; destroy: *to kill someone's interest.* [3] to make (time) pass quickly, esp while waiting for something. [4] to deaden (sound). [5] *Informal* to tire out; exhaust: *the effort killed him.* [6] *Informal* to cause to suffer pain or discomfort: *my shoes are killing me.* [7] *Informal* to cancel, cut, or delete: *to kill three lines of text.* [8] *Informal* to quash, defeat, or veto: *the bill was killed in the House of Lords.* [9] *Informal* to switch off; stop: *to kill a motor.* [10] *(also intr) Informal* to overcome with attraction, laughter, surprise, etc.: *she was dressed to kill; his gags kill me.* [11] *Slang* to consume (alcoholic drink) entirely: *he killed three bottles of rum.* [12] *Sport* to hit (a ball) so hard or so accurately that the opponent cannot return it. [13] *Soccer* to bring (a moving ball) under control; trap. [14] **kill oneself.** *Informal* to overexert oneself: *don't kill yourself.* [15] **kill two birds with one stone.** to achieve two results with one action. ◆ NOUN [16] the act of causing death, esp at the end of a hunt, bullfight, etc. [17] the animal or animals killed during a hunt. [18] *NZ* the seasonal tally of stock slaughtered at a freezing works. [19] the destruction of a battleship, tank, etc. [20] **in at the kill.** present at the end or climax of some undertaking.
▷HISTORY C13 *cullen;* perhaps related to Old English *cwellan* to kill; compare German (Westphalian dialect) *küllen;* see QUELL

kill² (kɪl) NOUN *US* a channel, stream, or river (chiefly as part of place names).
▷HISTORY C17: from Middle Dutch *kille;* compare Old Norse *kīll* small bay, creek

Killarney (kɪ'lɑːnɪ) NOUN a town in SW Republic of Ireland, in Co. Kerry: a tourist centre near the **Lakes of Killarney.** Pop.: 7250 (1991).

killdeer ('kɪlˌdɪə) NOUN, *plural* **-deer** *or* **-deers.** a large brown-and-white North American plover, *Charadrius vociferus,* with two black breast bands and a noisy cry.

▷HISTORY C18: of imitative origin

killer ('kɪlə) NOUN 1 **a** a person or animal that kills, esp habitually. **b** (*as modifier*): *a killer shark.* 2 something, esp a task or activity, that is particularly taxing or exhausting. 3 *Austral and NZ* an animal selected to be slaughtered for food.

killer application NOUN a highly innovative, very powerful, or extremely useful computer application, esp one sufficiently important as to justify purchase of the equipment or software.

killer bee NOUN an African honeybee, or one of its hybrids originating in Brazil, that is extremely aggressive when disturbed.

killer cell NOUN a type of white blood cell that is able to kill cells, such as cancer cells and cells infected with viruses.

killer whale NOUN a predatory black-and-white toothed whale, *Orcinus orca,* with a large erect dorsal fin, most common in cold seas: family *Delphinidae.* Also called: **killer, grampus, orc.**

killick ('kɪlɪk) *or* **killock** ('kɪlək) NOUN *Nautical* a small anchor, esp one made of a heavy stone.
▷HISTORY C17: of unknown origin

Killiecrankie (ˌkɪlɪ'kræŋkɪ) NOUN a pass in central Scotland, in the Grampians: scene of a battle (1689) in which the Jacobites defeated William III's forces but lost their leader, Viscount Dundee.

killifish ('kɪlɪˌfɪʃ) NOUN, *plural* **-fish** *or* **-fishes.** any of various chiefly American minnow-like cyprinodont fishes of the genus *Fundulus* and related genera, of fresh and brackish waters: used as aquarium fishes, to control mosquitoes, and as anglers' bait.
▷HISTORY C19: see KILL[2], FISH

killikinick (ˌkɪlɪkɪ'nɪk) NOUN a variant of **kinnikinnick.**

killing ('kɪlɪŋ) ADJECTIVE 1 *Informal* very tiring; exhausting: *a killing pace.* 2 *Informal* extremely funny; hilarious. 3 causing death; fatal. ◆ NOUN 4 the act of causing death; slaying. 5 *Informal* a sudden stroke of success, usually financial, as in speculations on the stock market (esp in the phrase **make a killing**).
▸'**killingly** ADVERB

killjoy ('kɪlˌdʒɔɪ) NOUN a person who spoils other people's pleasure.

kill-time NOUN **a** an occupation that passes the time. **b** (*as modifier*): *kill-time pursuits.*

Kilmarnock (kɪl'mɑːnək) NOUN a town in SW Scotland, the administrative centre of East Ayrshire: associations with Robert Burns; engineering and textile industries; whisky blending. Pop.: 44 307 (1991).

kiln (kɪln) NOUN 1 a large oven for burning, drying, or processing something, such as porcelain or bricks. ◆ VERB 2 (*tr*) to fire or process in a kiln.
▷HISTORY Old English *cylen,* from Late Latin *culīna* kitchen, from Latin *coquere* to COOK

Kilner jar ('kɪlnə) NOUN *Trademark* a glass preserving jar with an airtight lid, used for bottling fruit or vegetables.

kilo[1] ('kiːləʊ) NOUN, *plural* **kilos.** short for **kilogram** or **kilometre.**

kilo[2] ('kiːləʊ) NOUN *Communications* a code word for the letter *k.*

kilo- PREFIX 1 denoting 10^3 (1000): *kilometre.* Symbol: k. 2 (in computer technology) denoting 2^{10} (1024): *kilobyte:* in computer usage, *kilo-* is restricted to sizes of storage (e.g. *kilobit*) when it means 1024; in other computer contexts it retains its usual meaning of 1000.
▷HISTORY from French, from Greek *khilioi* thousand

kilobyte ('kɪləˌbaɪt) NOUN *Computing* 1024 bytes. Abbreviations: **KB, kbyte.** See also **kilo-** (sense 2).

kilocalorie ('kɪləʊˌkælərɪ) NOUN another name for **Calorie.**

kilocycle ('kɪləʊˌsaɪkᵊl) NOUN short for kilocycle per second: a former unit of frequency equal to 1 kilohertz.

kilogram ('kɪləʊˌɡræm) NOUN 1 one thousand grams. 2 the basic SI unit of mass, equal to the mass of the international prototype held by the *Bureau International des Poids et Mesures.* One kilogram is equivalent to 2.204 62 pounds. Symbol: kg.

kilogram calorie NOUN another name for **Calorie.**

kilohertz ('kɪləʊˌhɜːts) NOUN one thousand hertz; one thousand cycles per second. Symbol: kHz.

kilometre *or US* **kilometer** ('kɪləˌmiːtə, kɪ'lɒmɪtə) NOUN one thousand metres, equal to 0.621371 miles. Symbol: km.
▸**kilometric** (ˌkɪləʊ'metrɪk) *or* ˌ**kilo'metrical** ADJECTIVE

kiloton ('kɪləʊˌtʌn) NOUN 1 one thousand tons. 2 an explosive power, esp of a nuclear weapon, equal to the power of 1000 tons of TNT. Abbreviation: **kt.**

kilovolt ('kɪləʊˌvəʊlt) NOUN one thousand volts. Symbol: kV.

kilowatt ('kɪləʊˌwɒt) NOUN one thousand watts. Symbol: kW.

kilowatt-hour NOUN a unit of energy equal to the work done by a power of 1000 watts in one hour. Symbol: kWh.

kilt (kɪlt) NOUN 1 a knee-length pleated skirt, esp one in tartan, as worn by men in Highland dress. ◆ VERB (*tr*) 2 to tuck (the skirt) up around one's body. 3 to put pleats in (cloth, a skirt, etc.).
▷HISTORY C18: of Scandinavian origin; compare Danish *kilte* to tuck up, Old Swedish *kilta* lap
▸'**kilted** ADJECTIVE ▸'**kilt,like** ADJECTIVE

kilter ('kɪltə) *or* **kelter** NOUN working order or alignment (esp in the phrases **off kilter, out of kilter**).
▷HISTORY C17: origin unknown

Kilung ('kiː'lʊŋ) NOUN another name for **Chilung.**

Kimberley ('kɪmbəlɪ) NOUN 1 a city in central South Africa, in Northern Cape province: besieged (1899–1900) for 126 days during the Boer War; diamond-mining and -marketing centre, with heavy engineering works. Pop.: 170 432 (1996). 2 Also called: **the Kimberleys.** a plateau region of NW Australia, in N Western Australia: consists of rugged mountains surrounded by grassland. Area: about 360 000 sq. km (140 000 sq. miles).

kimberlite ('kɪmbəˌlaɪt) NOUN an intrusive igneous rock generated at great depth in the earth's mantle and consisting largely of olivine and phlogopite. It often contains diamonds.
▷HISTORY C19: from KIMBERLEY + -ITE[1]

kimono (kɪ'məʊnəʊ) NOUN, *plural* **-nos.** 1 a loose sashed ankle-length garment with wide sleeves, worn in Japan. 2 any garment copied from this.
▷HISTORY C19: from Japanese: clothing, from *kiru* to wear + *mono* thing
▸**ki'monoed** ADJECTIVE

kin (kɪn) NOUN 1 a person's relatives collectively; kindred. 2 a class or group with similar characteristics. 3 See **next of kin.** ◆ ADJECTIVE 4 (*postpositive*) related by blood. 5 a less common word for **akin.**
▷HISTORY Old English *cyn;* related to Old Norse *kyn* family, Old High German *kind* child, Latin *genus* kind

-kin SUFFIX FORMING NOUNS small: *lambkin.*
▷HISTORY from Middle Dutch, of West Germanic origin; compare German *-chen*

kina ('kiːnə) NOUN the standard monetary unit of Papua New Guinea, divided into 100 toea.
▷HISTORY from a Papuan language

Kinabalu (ˌkɪnəbə'luː) NOUN a mountain in Malaysia, on N Borneo in central Sabah: the highest peak in Borneo. Height: 4125 m (13 533 ft.).

kinaesthesia (ˌkɪnɪs'θiːzɪə, ˌkaɪn-), **kinaesthesis,** *or US* **kinesthesia, kinesthesis** NOUN the sensation by which bodily position, weight, muscle tension, and movement are perceived. Also called: **muscle sense.**
▷HISTORY C19: from New Latin, from Greek *kinein* to move + AESTHESIA
▸**kinaesthetic** *or US* **kinesthetic** (ˌkɪnɪs'θɛtɪk, ˌkaɪn-) ADJECTIVE

kinase ('kaɪneɪz, 'kɪn-) NOUN 1 any enzyme that can convert an inactive zymogen to the corresponding enzyme. 2 any enzyme that brings about the phosphorylation of a molecule.
▷HISTORY C20: from KIN(ETIC) + -ASE

Kincardineshire (kɪn'kɑːdɪnˌʃɪə, -ʃə) NOUN a former county of E Scotland: became part of Grampian region in 1975 and part of Aberdeenshire in 1996. Also called: **the Mearns.**

Kinchinjunga (ˌkɪntʃɪn'dʒʌŋɡə) NOUN a variant of **Kangchenjunga.**

kincob ('kɪŋkɒb) NOUN a fine silk fabric embroidered with threads of gold or silver, of a kind made in India.
▷HISTORY C18: from Urdu *kimkhāb*

kind[1] (kaɪnd) ADJECTIVE 1 having a friendly or generous nature or attitude. 2 helpful to others or to another: *a kind deed.* 3 considerate or humane. 4 cordial; courteous (esp in the phrase **kind regards**). 5 pleasant; agreeable; mild: *a kind climate.* 6 *Informal* beneficial or not harmful: *a detergent that is kind to the hands.* 7 *Archaic* loving.
▷HISTORY Old English *gecynde* natural, native; see KIND[2]

kind[2] (kaɪnd) NOUN 1 a class or group having characteristics in common; sort; type: *two of a kind; what kind of creature?* 2 an instance or example of a class or group, esp a rudimentary one: *heating of a kind.* 3 essential nature or character: *the difference is one of kind rather than degree.* 4 *Archaic* gender or sex. 5 *Archaic* nature; the natural order. 6 **in kind. a** (of payment) in goods or produce rather than in money. **b** with something of the same sort: *to return an insult in kind.* 7 **kind of.** (*adverb*) *Informal* somewhat; rather: *kind of tired.*
▷HISTORY Old English *gecynd* nature; compare Old English *cyn* KIN, Gothic *kuni* race, Old High German *kikunt,* Latin *gens*

Language note The mixture of plural and singular constructions, although often used informally with *kind* and *sort,* should be avoided in serious writing: *children enjoy those kinds* (not *those kind*) *of stories; these sorts* (not *these sort*) *of distinctions are becoming blurred.*

kindergarten ('kɪndəˌɡɑːtᵊn) NOUN a class or small school for young children, usually between the ages of four and six to prepare them for primary education. Often shortened (in Australia) to **kinder** or (in Australia and New Zealand) to **kindy** or **kindie.**
▷HISTORY C19: from German, literally: children's garden
▸'**kinder,gartener** NOUN

kind-hearted ADJECTIVE characterized by kindness; sympathetic.
▸ˌ**kind-'heartedly** ADVERB ▸ˌ**kind-'heartedness** NOUN

kindle ('kɪndᵊl) VERB 1 to set alight or start to burn. 2 to arouse or be aroused: *the project kindled his interest.* 3 to make or become bright.
▷HISTORY C12: from Old Norse *kynda,* influenced by Old Norse *kyndill* candle
▸'**kindler** NOUN

kindless ('kaɪndlɪs) ADJECTIVE *Archaic* 1 heartless. 2 against nature; unnatural.
▸'**kindlessly** ADVERB

kindling ('kɪndlɪŋ) NOUN material for starting a fire, such as dry wood, straw, etc.

kindly ('kaɪndlɪ) ADJECTIVE **-lier, -liest.** 1 having a sympathetic or warm-hearted nature. 2 motivated by warm and sympathetic feelings: *a kindly act.* 3 pleasant, mild, or agreeable: *a kindly climate.* 4 *Archaic* natural; normal. ◆ ADVERB 5 in a considerate or humane way. 6 with tolerance or forbearance: *he kindly forgave my rudeness.* 7 cordially; pleasantly: *he greeted us kindly.* 8 please (often used to express impatience or formality): *will you kindly behave yourself!* 9 *Archaic* in accordance with nature; appropriately. 10 to react favourably.
▸'**kindliness** NOUN

kindness ('kaɪndnɪs) NOUN 1 the practice or quality of being kind. 2 a kind, considerate, or helpful act.

kindred ('kɪndrɪd) ADJECTIVE 1 having similar or common qualities, origin, etc. 2 related by blood or marriage. 3 **kindred spirit.** a person with whom one has something in common. ◆ NOUN 4 relationship by blood. 5 similarity in character. 6 a person's relatives collectively.
▷HISTORY C12 *kinred,* from KIN + *-red,* from Old English *rǣden* rule, from *rǣdan* to rule
▸'**kindredness** *or* '**kindred,ship** NOUN

kindy *or* **kindie** ('kɪndɪ) NOUN *Austral and NZ informal* short for **kindergarten.**

kine (kaɪn) NOUN (*functioning as plural*) an archaic word for **cows** or **cattle.**
▷HISTORY Old English *cȳna* of cows, from *cū* COW[1]

kinematics (ˌkɪnɪ'mætɪks, ˌkaɪ-) NOUN (*functioning as singular*) the study of the motion of bodies without reference to mass or force. Compare **dynamics** (sense 1).

▷HISTORY C19: from Greek *kinēma* movement; see CINEMA, -ICS
▸ˌkine'matic ADJECTIVE ▸ˌkine'matically ADVERB

kinematic viscosity NOUN a measure of the resistance to flow of a fluid, equal to its absolute viscosity divided by its density. Symbol: ν.

kinematograph (ˌkɪnɪ'mætəˌgrɑːf, ˌkaɪnɪ-, -ˌgræf) NOUN a variant of **cinematograph**.
▸**kinematographer** (ˌkɪnəmə'tɒgrəfə) NOUN
▸**kinematographic** (ˌkɪnɪˌmætə'græfɪk, ˌkaɪnɪ-) ADJECTIVE ▸ˌ**kinema'tography** NOUN

kinescope ('kɪnəskəʊp) NOUN the US name for **television tube.**

kinesics (kɪ'niːsɪks) NOUN *(functioning as singular)* the study of the role of body movements, such as winking, shrugging, etc., in communication.

kinesiology (kɪˌniːsɪ'ɒlədʒɪ) NOUN the study of the mechanics and anatomy of human muscles.

kinesis (kɪ'niːsɪs, kaɪ-) NOUN *Biology* the nondirectional movement of an organism or cell in response to a stimulus, the rate of movement being dependent on the strength of the stimulus.

kinesthesia (ˌkɪnɪs'θiːzɪə, ˌkaɪn-) *or* **kinesthesis** NOUN the usual US spelling of **kinaesthesia.**

kinetheodolite (ˌkɪnəθɪ'ɒdəˌlaɪt) NOUN a type of theodolite containing a cine camera instead of a telescope and giving continuous film of a moving target together with a record of its altitude and azimuth: used in tracking a missile, satellite, etc.

kinetic (kɪ'nɛtɪk, kaɪ-) ADJECTIVE relating to, characterized by, or caused by motion.
▷HISTORY C19: from Greek *kinētikos,* from *kinein* to move
▸**ki'netically** ADVERB

kinetic art NOUN art, esp sculpture, that moves or has moving parts.

kinetic energy NOUN the energy of motion of a body, equal to the work it would do if it were brought to rest. The **translational kinetic energy** depends on motion through space, and for a rigid body of constant mass is equal to the product of half the mass times the square of the speed. The **rotational kinetic energy** depends on rotation about an axis, and for a body of constant moment of inertia is equal to the product of half the moment of inertia times the square of the angular velocity. In relativistic physics kinetic energy is equal to the product of the increase of mass caused by motion times the square of the speed of light. The SI unit is the joule but the electronvolt is often used in atomic physics. Symbol: E_k, *K, or T.* Abbreviation: **KE.**

kinetics (kɪ'nɛtɪks, kaɪ-) NOUN *(functioning as singular)* [1] another name for **dynamics** (sense 2). [2] the branch of mechanics, including both dynamics and kinematics, concerned with the study of bodies in motion. [3] the branch of dynamics that excludes the study of bodies at rest. [4] the branch of chemistry concerned with the rates of chemical reactions.

kinetic theory NOUN **the.** a theory of gases postulating that they consist of particles of negligible size moving at random and undergoing elastic collisions. In full: **kinetic theory of gases.**

kinetoplast (kɪ'nɛtəˌplæst, -'niː-, -ˌplɑːst) NOUN a small granular cell body close to the nucleus in some flagellate protozoans. Also called: **kinetonucleus** (kɪˌnɛtəʊ'njuːklɪəs).
▷HISTORY C20: from Greek; see KINETIC, -PLAST

kinfolk ('kɪnˌfəʊk) PLURAL NOUN *Chiefly US and Canadian* another word for **kinsfolk.**

king (kɪŋ) NOUN [1] a male sovereign prince who is the official ruler of an independent state; monarch. Related adjectives: **royal, regal, monarchical.** [2] **a** a ruler or chief: *king of the fairies.* **b** *(in combination)*: *the pirate king.* [3] **a** a person, animal, or thing considered as the best or most important of its kind. **b** *(as modifier)*: *a king bull.* [4] any of four playing cards in a pack, one for each suit, bearing the picture of a king. [5] the most important chess piece, although theoretically the weakest, being able to move only one square at a time in any direction. See also **check** (sense 30), **checkmate.** [6] *Draughts* a piece that has moved entirely across the board and has been crowned, after which it may move backwards as well as forwards. [7] **king of kings. a** God. **b** a title of any of various oriental monarchs. ◆ VERB *(tr)* [8] to make (someone) a king. [9] **king it.** to act in a superior fashion.
▷HISTORY Old English *cyning;* related to Old High German *kunig* king, Danish *konge*
▸'**king,hood** NOUN ▸'**kingless** ADJECTIVE ▸'**king,like** ADJECTIVE

kingbird ('kɪŋˌbɜːd) NOUN any of several large American flycatchers of the genus *Tyrannus,* esp *T. tyrannus* (**eastern kingbird** *or* **bee martin**).

kingbolt ('kɪŋˌbəʊlt) *or* **king rod** NOUN **a** the pivot bolt that connects the body of a horse-drawn carriage to the front axle and provides the steering joint. **b** a similar bolt placed between a railway carriage and the bogies.

King Charles spaniel NOUN [1] a toy breed of spaniel with a short turned-up nose and a domed skull. [2] **cavalier King Charles spaniel.** a similar breed that is slightly larger and has a longer nose.
▷HISTORY C17: named after Charles II of England, who popularized the breed

king cobra NOUN a very large venomous tropical Asian elapid snake, *Ophiophagus hannah,* that feeds on snakes and other reptiles and extends its neck into a hood when alarmed. Also called: **hamadryad.**

King Country NOUN **the.** an area in the centre of North Island, New Zealand: home of the King Movement, a nineteenth-century Maori separatist movement.

king crab NOUN another name for the **horseshoe crab.**

kingcraft ('kɪŋˌkrɑːft) NOUN *Archaic* the art of ruling as a king, esp by diplomacy and cunning.

kingcup ('kɪŋˌkʌp) NOUN *Brit* any of several yellow-flowered ranunculaceous plants, esp the marsh marigold.

kingdom ('kɪŋdəm) NOUN [1] a territory, state, people, or community ruled or reigned over by a king or queen. [2] any of the three groups into which natural objects may be divided: the animal, plant, and mineral kingdoms. [3] *Biology* any of the major categories into which living organisms of the domain *Eukarya* are classified. Modern systems recognize four kingdoms: *Protoctista* (algae, protozoans, etc.), *Fungi, Plantae,* and *Animalia.* ◆ See also **domain** (sense 12). [4] *Theol* the eternal sovereignty of God. [5] an area of activity, esp mental activity, considered as being the province of something specified: *the kingdom of the mind.*
▸'**kingdomless** ADJECTIVE

kingdom come NOUN [1] the next world; life after death. [2] *Informal* the end of the world (esp in the phrase **until kingdom come**). [3] *Informal* unconsciousness or death.

kingfish ('kɪŋˌfɪʃ) NOUN, *plural* **-fish** *or* **-fishes.** [1] any marine sciaenid food and game fish of the genus *Menticirrhus,* occurring in warm American Atlantic coastal waters. [2] another name for **opah** (the fish). [3] any of various other large food fishes, esp the Spanish mackerel.

kingfisher ('kɪŋˌfɪʃə) NOUN any coraciiform bird of the family *Alcedinidae,* esp the Eurasian *Alcedo atthis,* which has a greenish-blue and orange plumage. Kingfishers have a large head, short tail, and long sharp bill and tend to live near open water and feed on fish.
▷HISTORY C15: originally *king's fisher*

king-hit *Austral informal* ◆ NOUN [1] a knockout blow, esp an unfair one. ◆ VERB **-hits, -hitting, -hit.** *(tr)* [2] to deliver a knockout blow to.

King James Version *or* **Bible** NOUN **the.** another name for the **Authorized Version.**

kingklip ('kɪŋˌklɪp) NOUN *South African* an edible eel-like marine fish.

kinglet ('kɪŋlɪt) NOUN [1] *Often derogatory* the king of a small or insignificant territory. [2] *US and Canadian* any of various small warblers of the genus *Regulus,* having a black-edged yellow crown: family *Muscicapidae.*

kingly ('kɪŋlɪ) ADJECTIVE **-lier, -liest.** [1] appropriate to a king; majestic. [2] royal. ◆ ADVERB [3] *Poetic or archaic* in a manner appropriate to a king.
▸'**kingliness** NOUN

kingmaker ('kɪŋˌmeɪkə) NOUN a person who has control over appointments to positions of authority.

king-of-arms NOUN, *plural* **kings-of-arms.** [1] the highest rank of heraldic officer, itself divided into the ranks of Garter, Clarenceaux, and Norroy and Ulster. In Scotland the first is Lyon. [2] a person holding this rank.

king of the castle NOUN *Chiefly Brit* [1] a children's game in which each child attempts to stand alone on a mound, sandcastle, etc., by pushing other children off it. [2] *Informal* a person who is in a commanding or superior position.

king of the herrings NOUN another name for **oarfish** or **rabbitfish** (sense 1).

king penguin NOUN a large penguin, *Aptenodytes patagonica,* found on islands bordering the Antarctic Circle.

kingpin ('kɪŋˌpɪn) NOUN [1] the most important person in an organization. [2] the crucial or most important feature of a theory, argument, etc. [3] Also called (Brit): **swivel pin.** a pivot pin that provides a steering joint in a motor vehicle by securing the stub axle to the axle beam. [4] *Tenpin bowling* the front pin in the triangular arrangement of the ten pins. [5] (in ninepins) the central pin in the diamond pattern of the nine pins.

king post NOUN a vertical post connecting the apex of a triangular roof truss to the tie beam. Also called: **joggle post.** Compare **queen post.**

king prawn NOUN any of several large prawns of the genus *Penaeus,* which are fished commercially in Australian waters.

Kings (kɪŋz) NOUN *(functioning as singular) Old Testament* (in versions based on the Hebrew, including the Authorized Version) either of the two books called **I** and **II Kings** recounting the histories of the kings of Judah and Israel.

king salmon NOUN another name for **Chinook salmon.**

King's Bench NOUN (when the sovereign is male) another name for **Queen's Bench Division.**

King's Counsel NOUN (when the sovereign is male) another name for **Queen's Counsel.**

King's English NOUN (esp when the British sovereign is male) standard Southern British English.

king's evidence NOUN (when the sovereign is male) another name for **queen's evidence.**

king's evil NOUN **the.** *Pathol* a former name for **scrofula.**
▷HISTORY C14: from the belief that the king's touch would heal scrofula

king's highway NOUN (in Britain, esp when the sovereign is male) any public road or right of way.

kingship ('kɪŋʃɪp) NOUN [1] the position or authority of a king. [2] the skill or practice of ruling as a king.

king-size *or* **king-sized** ADJECTIVE larger or longer than a standard size.

King's Lynn ('kɪŋz 'lɪn) NOUN a market town in E England, in Norfolk on the estuary of the Great Ouse near the Wash: a leading port in the Middle Ages. Pop.: 41 281 (1991). Also called: **Lynn, Lynn Regis.**

king snake NOUN any nonvenomous North American colubrid snake of the genus *Lampropeltis,* feeding on other snakes, small mammals, etc.

king's peace NOUN [1] (in early medieval England) the protection secured by the king for particular people or places. [2] (in medieval England) the general peace secured to the entire realm by the law administered in the king's name.

King's proctor NOUN (in England when the sovereign is male) an official empowered to intervene in divorce and certain other cases when it is alleged that facts are being suppressed.

King's Regulations PLURAL NOUN (in Britain and the Commonwealth when the sovereign is male) the code of conduct for members of the armed forces that deals with discipline, aspects of military law, etc.

King's Scout NOUN (in Britain and the Commonwealth when the sovereign is male) another name for **Queen's Scout.** US equivalent: **Eagle Scout.**

king's shilling *or when the sovereign was female* **queen's shilling** NOUN [1] (until 1879) a shilling paid to new recruits to the British army. [2] **take the king's shilling.** *Brit, archaic* to enlist in the army.

King's speech NOUN (in Britain and the Commonwealth when the sovereign is male) another name for the **speech from the throne.**

Kingston ('kɪŋstən) NOUN 1 the capital and chief port of Jamaica, on the SE coast: University of the West Indies. Pop.: 103 771 (1991). 2 a port in SE Canada, in SE Ontario: the chief naval base of Lake Ontario and a large industrial centre; university (1841). Pop.: 56 597 (1991). 3 short for **Kingston upon Thames.**

Kingston upon Hull NOUN 1 the official name of **Hull**[1]. 2 a unitary authority in NE England, in the East Riding of Yorkshire: formerly (1974–96) part of the county of Humberside. Pop.: 243 595 (2001). Area: 71 sq. km (27 sq. miles).

Kingston upon Thames NOUN a borough of SW Greater London, on the River Thames: formed in 1965 by the amalgamation of several former boroughs of Surrey; administrative centre of Surrey. Pop.: 147 295 (2001). Area: 38 sq. km (15 sq. miles).

Kingstown ('kɪŋzˌtaʊn) NOUN the capital of St Vincent and the Grenadines: a port and resort. Pop.: 16 175 (1999 est.).

Kingwana (kɪŋ'wɑːnə) NOUN a language of the Democratic Republic of Congo (formerly Zaïre) in W Africa, closely related to Swahili and used as a lingua franca.

kingwood ('kɪŋˌwʊd) NOUN 1 the hard fine-grained violet-tinted wood of a Brazilian leguminous tree, *Dalbergia cearensis,* used in cabinetwork. 2 the tree yielding this wood.

kinin ('kaɪnɪn) NOUN 1 any of a group of polypeptides in the blood that cause dilation of the blood vessels and make smooth muscles contract. 2 another name for **cytokinin.**
▷HISTORY C20: from Greek *kin(ēma)* motion + -IN

kink (kɪŋk) NOUN 1 a sharp twist or bend in a wire, rope, hair, etc., esp one caused when it is pulled tight. 2 a crick in the neck or similar muscular spasm. 3 a flaw or minor difficulty in some undertaking or project. 4 a flaw or idiosyncrasy of personality; quirk. 5 *Brit informal* a sexual deviation. 6 *US* a clever or unusual idea. ◆ VERB 7 to form or cause to form a kink.
▷HISTORY C17: from Dutch: a curl in a rope; compare Middle Low German *kinke* kink, Old Norse *kinka* to nod

kinkajou ('kɪŋkəˌdʒuː) NOUN 1 Also called: **honey bear, potto.** an arboreal fruit-eating mammal, *Potos flavus,* of Central and South America, with a long prehensile tail: family *Procyonidae* (raccoons), order *Carnivora* (carnivores). 2 another name for **potto** (sense 1).
▷HISTORY C18: from French *quincajou,* from Algonquian; related to Ojibwa *gwĭngwâage* wolverine

kinky ('kɪŋkɪ) ADJECTIVE **kinkier, kinkiest.** 1 *Slang* given to unusual, abnormal, or deviant sexual practices. 2 *Informal* exhibiting unusual idiosyncrasies of personality; quirky; eccentric. 3 *Informal* attractive or provocative in a bizarre way: *kinky clothes.* 4 tangled or tightly looped, as a wire or rope. 5 tightly curled, as hair.
▸ **'kinkily** ADVERB ▸ **'kinkiness** NOUN

kinnikinnick, kinnikinic (ˌkɪnɪkɪ'nɪk), *or* **killikinick** NOUN 1 the dried leaves and bark of certain plants, sometimes with tobacco added, formerly smoked by some North American Indians. 2 any of the plants used for such a preparation, such as the sumach *Rhus glabra.*
▷HISTORY C18: from Algonquian, literally: that which is mixed; related to Natick *kinukkinuk* mixture

kino ('kiːnəʊ) NOUN a dark red resin obtained from various tropical plants, esp an Indian leguminous tree, *Pterocarpus marsupium,* used as an astringent and in tanning. Also called: **kino gum.**
▷HISTORY C18: of West African origin; related to Mandingo *keno*

Kinross-shire (kɪn'rɒsˌʃɪə, -ʃə) NOUN a former county of E central Scotland: became part of Tayside region in 1975 and part of Perth and Kinross in 1996.

kin selection NOUN *Biology* natural selection resulting from altruistic behaviour by animals towards members of the same species, esp their offspring or other relatives.

kinsfolk ('kɪnzˌfəʊk) PLURAL NOUN one's family or relatives.

Kinshasa (kɪn'ʃɑːzə, -'ʃɑːsə) NOUN the capital of the Democratic Republic of Congo (formerly Zaïre), on the River Congo opposite Brazzaville: became capital of the Belgian Congo in 1929 and of Zaïre in 1960; university (1954). Pop.: 4 655 313 (1994 est.). Former name (until 1966): **Léopoldville.**

kinship ('kɪnʃɪp) NOUN 1 blood relationship. 2 the state of having common characteristics or a common origin.

kinsman ('kɪnzmən) NOUN, *plural* **-men.** 1 a blood relation or a relation by marriage. 2 a member of the same race, tribe, or ethnic stock.
▸ **'kinsˌwoman** FEMININE NOUN

kiosk ('kiːɒsk) NOUN 1 a small sometimes movable booth from which cigarettes, newspapers, light refreshments, etc., are sold. 2 *Chiefly Brit* a telephone box. 3 *Chiefly US* a thick post on which advertisements are posted. 4 (in Turkey, Iran, etc., esp formerly) a light open-sided pavilion.
▷HISTORY C17: from French *kiosque* bandstand, from Turkish *kösk,* from Persian *kūshk* pavilion

Kioto (kɪ'əʊtəʊ, 'kjəʊ-) NOUN a variant spelling of **Kyoto.**

kip[1] (kɪp) *Slang* ◆ NOUN 1 *Brit* sleep or slumber: *to get some kip.* 2 *Brit* a bed or lodging. 3 *Obsolete (except Irish)* a brothel. ◆ VERB **kips, kipping, kipped.** *(intr)* 4 *Brit* to sleep or take a nap. 5 *Brit* (foll by *down*) to prepare for sleep.
▷HISTORY C18: of uncertain origin; apparently related to Danish *kippe* common alehouse

kip[2] (kɪp) *or* **kipskin** ('kɪpˌskɪn) NOUN the hide of a young animal, esp a calf or lamb.
▷HISTORY C16: from Middle Dutch *kipp;* related to Middle Low German *kip,* Old Norse *kippa* bundle

kip[3] (kɪp) NOUN a unit of weight equal to one thousand pounds.
▷HISTORY C20: from KI(LO)[1] + P(OUND)[2]

kip[4] (kɪp) NOUN the standard monetary unit of Laos, divided into 100 at.
▷HISTORY from Thai

kip[5] (kɪp) NOUN *Austral* a small board used to spin the coins in two-up.
▷HISTORY C19: from KEP

kippa (ki'pa) NOUN *Judaism* a skullcap worn by orthodox male Jews at all times and by others for prayer, esp a crocheted one worn by those with a specifically religious Zionist affiliation.

kipper[1] ('kɪpə) NOUN 1 a fish, esp a herring, that has been cleaned, salted, and smoked. 2 a male salmon during the spawning season. 3 *Austral, archaic derogatory slang* an Englishman. ◆ VERB 4 *(tr)* to cure (a fish, esp a herring) by salting and smoking.
▷HISTORY Old English *cypera,* perhaps from *coper* COPPER[1]; referring to its colour

kipper[2] ('kɪpə) NOUN a native Australian youth who has completed an initiation rite.
▷HISTORY from a native Australian language

kippered ('kɪpəd) ADJECTIVE 1 (of fish, esp herring) having been cleaned, salted, and smoked. 2 *Slang* utterly defeated or outwitted.

Kipp's apparatus (kɪps) NOUN a laboratory apparatus for producing a gas, usually hydrogen sulphide, by the action of a liquid on a solid without heating.
▷HISTORY C19: named after Petrus Jacobus *Kipp* (1808–84), Dutch chemist

kir (kɜː, kɪr) NOUN a drink made from dry white wine and cassis.
▷HISTORY named after Canon F. *Kir* (1876–1968), mayor of Dijon, who is said to have invented it

kirby grip ('kɜːbɪ) NOUN *Brit* a hairgrip consisting of a piece of metal bent over to form a tight clip and having the upper part ridged to prevent it slipping on the hair.
▷HISTORY from *Kerbigrip,* trademark for the original such hairgrip

Kirchhoff's laws PLURAL NOUN two laws describing the flow of currents in electric circuits. The first states that the algebraic sum of all the electric currents meeting at any point in a circuit is zero. The second states that in a closed loop of a circuit the algebraic sum of the products of the resistances and the currents flowing through them is equal to the algebraic sum of all the electromotive forces acting in the loop.
▷HISTORY C19: after G. R. *Kirchhoff* (1824–87), German physicist

Kirghiz *or* **Kirgiz** ('kɜːgɪz) NOUN a variant spelling of **Kyrgyz.**

Kirghizia *or* **Kirgizia** (kɜː'gɪzɪə) NOUN the former Russian name for **Kyrgyzstan.**

Kirghiz Steppe NOUN a variant spelling of **Kyrgyz Steppe.**

Kiribati (ˌkɪrɪ'bætɪ) NOUN an independent republic in the W Pacific: comprises 33 islands including Banaba (Ocean Island), the Gilbert and Phoenix Islands, and eight of the Line Islands; part of the British colony of the Gilbert and Ellice Islands until 1975; became self-governing in 1977 and gained full independence in 1979 as the Republic of Kiribati; a member of the Commonwealth. Official languages: English, I-Kiribati (Gilbertese) is widely spoken. Religion: Christian majority. Currency: Australian dollar. Capital: Bairiki islet, in Tarawa atoll. Pop.: 94 000 (2001 est.). Area: 684 sq. km (264 sq. miles).

kirigami (ˌkɪrɪ'gɑːmɪ) NOUN the art, originally Japanese, of folding and cutting paper into decorative shapes. Compare **origami.**
▷HISTORY C20: from Japanese

Kirin ('kiː'rɪn) NOUN a variant transliteration of the Chinese name for **Jilin.**

Kiritimati ('kɪrɪtɪ'mɑːtɪ) NOUN an island in the central Pacific, in Kiribati: one of the Line Islands; the largest atoll in the world. Pop.: 3225 (1995). Former name: **Christmas Island.**

kirk (kɜːk; *Scot* kɪrk) NOUN 1 a Scot word for **church.** 2 a Scottish church.
▷HISTORY C12: from Old Norse *kirkja,* from Old English *cirice* CHURCH

Kirk (kɜːk; *Scot* kɪrk) NOUN **the.** *Informal* the Presbyterian Church of Scotland.

Kirkby ('kɜːbɪ) NOUN a town in NW England, in Knowsley unitary authority, Merseyside. Pop.: 43 017 (1991).

Kirkcaldy (kɜː'kɔːdɪ) NOUN a port in E Scotland, in SE Fife on the Firth of Forth. Pop.: 47 155 (1991).

Kirkcudbrightshire (kɜː'kuːbrɪˌʃɪə, -ʃə) NOUN a former county of SW Scotland, part of Dumfries and Galloway since 1975.

Kirklees (ˌkɜːk'liːz) NOUN a unitary authority in N England, in West Yorkshire. Pop.: 388 576 (2001). Area: 410 sq. km (158 sq. miles).

kirkman ('kɜːkmən, 'kɪrk-) NOUN, *plural* **-men.** *Scot* 1 a member or strong upholder of the Kirk. 2 a churchman; clergyman.

Kirkpatrick (kɜːk'pætrɪk) NOUN **Mount.** a mountain in Antarctica, in S Victoria Land in the Queen Alexandra Range. Height: 4528 m (14 856 ft.).

kirk session NOUN the lowest court of the Presbyterian Church.

Kirkuk (kɜː'kʊk, 'kɜːkʊk) NOUN a city in NE Iraq: centre of a rich oilfield with pipelines to the Mediterranean. Pop.: 418 625 (latest est.).

Kirkwall ('kɜːkˌwɔːl) NOUN a town on the N coast of Mainland in the Orkney Islands: administrative centre of the island authority of Orkney: cathedral built by Norsemen (begun in 1137). Pop.: 6469 (1991).

Kirlian photography ('kɜːlɪən) NOUN a process that is said to record directly on photographic film the field radiation of electricity emitted by an object to which an electric charge has been applied.
▷HISTORY C20: named after Semyan D. and Valentina K. *Kirlian,* Russian researchers who described the process

Kirman (kɪə'mɑːn) NOUN, *plural* **-mans.** a Persian carpet or rug.
▷HISTORY named after KERMAN, Iran

kirmess ('kɜːmɪs) NOUN a variant spelling of **kermis.**

Kirov (*Russian* 'kirəf) NOUN a city in NW Russia, on the Vyatka River: an early trading centre; engineering industries. Pop.: 466 100 (1995 est.). Former name (1780–1934): **Vyatka.**

Kirovabad (*Russian* kirəva'bat) NOUN See **Gandzha.**

Kirovograd (*Russian* kirəva'grat) NOUN a city in the S central Ukraine on the Ingul River:

manufacturing centre of a rich agricultural area. Pop.: 270 200 (1999 est.). Former names: **Yelisavetgrad** (until 1924), **Zinovievsk** (1924–36).

Kirpan (kɪr'pɑ:n) NOUN the short sword traditionally carried by Sikhs as a symbol of their religious and cultural loyalty, symbolizing protection for the weak. See also **five Ks.**
▷HISTORY Punjabi *kirpān*

Kirsch (kɪəʃ) *or* **Kirschwasser** ('kɪəʃˌvɑ:sə) NOUN a brandy distilled from cherries, made chiefly in the Black Forest in Germany and in the Jura and Vosges districts of France.
▷HISTORY German *Kirschwasser* cherry water

kirtan ('kɪrtɑn) NOUN *Hinduism* devotional singing, usually accompanied by musical instruments.
▷HISTORY from Sanskrit *kīrtanam* praise, eulogy

kirtle ('kɜ:tᵊl) NOUN *Archaic* [1] a woman's skirt or dress. [2] a man's coat.
▷HISTORY Old English *cyrtel,* probably from *cyrtan* to shorten, ultimately from Latin *curtus* cut short

Kiruna (*Swedish* 'ki:runa) NOUN a town in N Sweden: iron-mining centre. Pop.: 26 150 (1990).

Kirundi (kɪ'rʊndɪ) NOUN the official language of Burundi, belonging to the Bantu group of the Niger-Congo family and closely related to Rwanda.

Kisangani (ˌkɪsæŋ'gɑ:nɪ) NOUN a city in the N Democratic Republic of Congo (formerly Zaïre), at the head of navigation of the River Congo below Stanley Falls: Université Libre du Congo (1963). Pop.: 417 517 (1994 est.). Former name (until 1966): **Stanleyville.**

kish (kɪʃ) NOUN *Metallurgy* graphite formed on the surface of molten iron that contains a large amount of carbon.
▷HISTORY C19: perhaps changed from German *Kies* gravel; related to Old High German *kisil* pebble

Kishinev (*Russian* kiʃi'njɔf) NOUN the capital of Moldova on the Byk River: manufacturing centre of a rich agricultural region; university (1945). Pop.: 655 000 (1999 est.). Romanian name: **Chişinău.**

kishke ('kɪʃkə) NOUN a beef or fowl intestine or skin stuffed with flour, onion, etc., and boiled and roasted.
▷HISTORY Yiddish: gut, probably from Russian *kishka*

Kislev (ki'slev) NOUN (in the Jewish calendar) the ninth month of the year according to biblical reckoning and the third month of the civil year, usually falling within November and December.
▷HISTORY from Hebrew

Kismayu (kɪs'mɑ:ju:) NOUN another name for **Chisimaio.**

kismet ('kɪzmɛt, 'kɪs-) NOUN [1] *Islam* the will of Allah. [2] fate or destiny.
▷HISTORY C19: from Turkish, from Persian *qismat,* from Arabic *qasama* he divided

kiss (kɪs) VERB [1] (*tr*) to touch with the lips or press the lips against as an expression of love, greeting, respect, etc. [2] (*intr*) to join lips with another person in an act of love or desire. [3] to touch (each other) lightly: *their hands kissed.* [4] *Billiards* (of balls) to touch (each other) lightly while moving. ◆ NOUN [5] the act of kissing; a caress with the lips. Related adjective: **oscular.** [6] a light touch. [7] a small light sweet or cake, such as one made chiefly of egg white and sugar: *coffee kisses.* ◆ See also **kiss off.**
▷HISTORY Old English *cyssan,* from *coss;* compare Old High German *kussen,* Old Norse *kyssa*
▸'**kissable** ADJECTIVE

KISS *Text messaging* ABBREVIATION FOR keep it simple, stupid.

kissagram ('kɪsəˌgræm) NOUN a greetings service in which a person is employed to present greetings by kissing the person celebrating.
▷HISTORY C20: blend of *kiss* and *telegram*

kiss-and-tell MODIFIER denoting the practice of publicizing one's former sexual relationship with a celebrity, esp in the tabloid press: *a kiss-and-tell interview.*

kiss curl NOUN *Brit* a circular curl of hair pressed flat against the cheek or forehead. US and Canadian term: **spit curl.**

kissel ('kɪsᵊl) NOUN a Russian dessert of sweetened fruit purée thickened with arrowroot.
▷HISTORY from Russian *kisel*

kisser ('kɪsə) NOUN [1] a person who kisses, esp in a way specified: *a good kisser.* [2] a slang word for **mouth** or **face.**

kissing bug NOUN a North American assassin bug, *Melanolestes picipes,* with a painful bite, usually attacking the lips or cheeks of man.

kissing gate NOUN a gate set in a U- or V-shaped enclosure, allowing only one person to pass through at a time.

kiss of death NOUN an act or relationship that has fatal or disastrous consequences.
▷HISTORY from Judas' kiss that betrayed Jesus in the garden of Gethsemane (Mark 14:44–45)

kiss off *Slang, chiefly US and Canadian* ◆ VERB [1] (*tr, adverb*) to ignore or dismiss rudely and abruptly. ◆ NOUN **kiss-off.** [2] a rude and abrupt dismissal.

kiss of life NOUN **the.** [1] mouth-to mouth or mouth-to-nose resuscitation in which a person blows gently into the mouth or nose of an unconscious person, allowing the lungs to deflate after each blow. [2] something that revitalizes or reinvigorates.

kissy ('kɪsɪ) *or* **kissy-kissy** ADJECTIVE *Informal* showing exaggerated affection, esp by frequent touching or kissing.

kist¹ (kɪst) NOUN *Scot and northern English dialect* a large chest or coffer.
▷HISTORY C14: from Old Norse *kista;* see CHEST

kist² (kɪst) NOUN *Archaeol* a variant spelling of **cist².**

kist³ (kɪst) NOUN *South African* a large wooden chest in which linen is stored, esp one used to store a bride's trousseau.
▷HISTORY from Afrikaans, from Dutch: CHEST

Kistna ('kɪstnə) NOUN another name for the (River) **Krishna.**

Kisumu (kɪ'su:mu:) NOUN a port in W Kenya, in Nyanza province on the NE shore of Lake Victoria: fishing and trading centre. Pop.: 201 100 (1991 est.).

kit¹ (kɪt) NOUN [1] a set of tools, supplies, construction materials, etc., for use together or for a purpose: *a first-aid kit; a model aircraft kit.* [2] the case or container for such a set. [3] **a** a set of pieces of equipment ready to be assembled. **b** (*as modifier*): *kit furniture.* [4] **a** clothing and other personal effects, esp those of a traveller or soldier: *safari kit; battle kit.* **b** *Informal* clothing in general (esp in the phrase **get one's kit off**). [5] *NZ* a flax basket. [6] **the whole kit** *or* **kit and caboodle.** *Informal* everything or everybody. ◆ See also **kit out.**
▷HISTORY C14: from Middle Dutch *kitte* tankard

kit² (kɪt) NOUN a kind of small violin, now obsolete, used esp by dancing masters in the 17th–18th centuries.
▷HISTORY C16: of unknown origin

kit³ (kɪt) NOUN [1] an informal or diminutive name for **kitten.** [2] a cub of various small mammals, such as the ferret or fox.
▷HISTORY C16: by shortening

kit⁴ (kɪt) NOUN *NZ* a plaited flax basket.
▷HISTORY from Maori *kete*

KIT *Text messaging* ABBREVIATION FOR keep in touch.

Kitakyushu (ˌki:tə'kju:ʃu:) NOUN a port in Japan, on N Kyushu: formed in 1963 by the amalgamation of the cities of Wakamatsu, Yahata, Tobata, Kokura, and Moji; one of Japan's largest industrial centres. Pop.: 1 019 562 (1995).

kitbag ('kɪtˌbæg) NOUN a canvas or other bag for a serviceman's kit.

kitchen ('kɪtʃɪn) NOUN **a** a room or part of a building equipped for preparing and cooking food. **b** (*as modifier*): *a kitchen table.*
▷HISTORY Old English *cycene,* ultimately from Late Latin *coquīna,* from Latin *coquere* to COOK; see KILN

kitchenalia (ˌkɪtʃɪ'neɪlɪə) NOUN cooking equipment and other items found in a kitchen.

kitchen cabinet NOUN a group of unofficial advisers to a political leader, esp when considered to be more influential than the official cabinet.

Kitchener ('kɪtʃɪnə) NOUN an industrial town in SE Canada, in S Ontario: founded in 1806 as Dutch Sand Hills, it was renamed Berlin in 1830 and Kitchener in 1916. Pop.: 178 420 (1996).

kitchenette *or* **kitchenet** (ˌkɪtʃɪ'nɛt) NOUN a small kitchen or part of another room equipped for use as a kitchen.

kitchen garden NOUN a garden where vegetables and sometimes also fruit are grown.
▸**kitchen gardener** NOUN

kitchen kaffir NOUN a derogatory term for **Fanagalo.**

kitchen midden NOUN *Archaeol* the site of a large mound of domestic refuse marking a prehistoric settlement: usually including bones, potsherds, seashells, etc.

kitchen police PLURAL NOUN *US* soldiers who have been detailed to work in the kitchen, esp as a punishment. Abbreviation: **KP.**

kitchen sink NOUN [1] a sink in a kitchen for washing dishes, vegetables, etc. [2] **everything but the kitchen sink.** everything that can be conceived of. [3] (*modifier*) denoting a type of drama or painting of the 1950s depicting the sordid aspects of domestic reality.

kitchen tea NOUN *Austral and NZ* a party held before a wedding to which female guests bring items of kitchen equipment as wedding presents.

kitchenware ('kɪtʃɪnˌwɛə) NOUN pots and pans, knives, forks, spoons, and other utensils used in the kitchen.

kite¹ (kaɪt) NOUN [1] a light frame covered with a thin material flown in the wind at the end of a length of string. [2] *Brit, slang* an aeroplane. [3] (*plural*) *Nautical* any of various light sails set in addition to the working sails of a vessel. [4] any diurnal bird of prey of the genera *Milvus, Elanus,* etc., typically having a long forked tail and long broad wings and usually preying on small mammals and insects: family *Accipitridae* (hawks, etc.). [5] *Archaic* a person who preys on others. [6] *Commerce* a negotiable paper drawn without any actual transaction or assets and designed to obtain money on credit, give an impression of affluence, etc. [7] **fly a kite.** See **fly¹** (sense 14). [8] **high as a kite.** See **high** (sense 30). ◆ VERB [9] to issue (fictitious papers) to obtain credit or money. [10] (*tr*) *US and Canadian* to write (a cheque) in anticipation of sufficient funds to cover it. [11] (*intr*) to soar and glide.
▷HISTORY Old English *cȳta;* related to Middle High German *küze* owl, Old Norse *kȳta* to quarrel
▸'**kiter** NOUN

kite² (kəɪt) NOUN a variant spelling of **kyte.**

kite fighting NOUN (in Malaysia) a game in which one player attempts to cut the string of his opponent's kite with the string of his own. See also **glass string.**

kite flying NOUN *Commerce* the practice of drawing cheques on deposits which are already committed, assuming that the delay in clearing the cheque will allow time to replenish the account. Also called: **kiting.**

Kitemark NOUN *Brit* the official mark of quality and reliability, in the form of a kite, on articles approved by the British Standards Institution.

kitenge (ki:'tɛŋge) NOUN *E African* **a** a thick cotton cloth measuring 114 × 213 cm (45 × 84 inches), used in making garments. **b** (*as modifier*): *a kitenge dress.*
▷HISTORY C20: from Swahili

kitesurfing ('kaɪtˌsɜ:fɪŋ) NOUN the sport of sailing standing up on a surfboard while being pulled along by a large kite.

kit fox NOUN another name for **swift fox.**

kith (kɪθ) NOUN one's friends and acquaintances (esp in the phrase **kith and kin**).
▷HISTORY Old English *cȳthth,* from *cūth;* see UNCOUTH

kithara ('kɪθərə) NOUN a variant of **cithara.**

Kíthira ('kiθira) NOUN transliteration of the Modern Greek name for **Cythera.**

kit out *or* **up** VERB **kits, kitting, kitted.** [1] (*tr, adverb*) *Chiefly Brit* to provide with (a kit of personal effects and necessities). [2] to provide with (an outfit of clothes).

kitsch (kɪtʃ) NOUN **a** tawdry, vulgarized, or pretentious art, literature, etc., usually with popular or sentimental appeal. **b** (*as modifier*): *a kitsch plaster bust of Beethoven.*
▷HISTORY C20: from German
▸'**kitschy** ADJECTIVE

kitschness ('kɪtʃnɪs) NOUN the quality of being

tawdry, vulgarized, or pretentious, and usually with popular or sentimental appeal.

kittel ADJECTIVE ('ki:tɛl), NOUN a white garment used as a shroud or worn by traditional Jews on Yom Kippur.
▷HISTORY from German *Kittel* smock

kitten ('kɪtᵊn) NOUN [1] a young cat. [2] **have kittens.** Also: **have a canary.** *Brit informal* to react with disapproval, anxiety, etc.: *she had kittens when she got the bill.* US equivalent: **have a cow.** ◆ VERB [3] (of cats) to give birth to (young).
▷HISTORY C14: from Old Northern French *caton,* from CAT[1]; probably influenced by Middle English *kiteling*
▸ **'kitten-ˌlike** ADJECTIVE

kitten heel NOUN [1] a low stiletto heel on a woman's shoe. [2] a woman's shoe with a low stiletto heel.

kittenish ('kɪtᵊnɪʃ) ADJECTIVE [1] like a kitten; lively. [2] (of a woman) flirtatious, esp coyly flirtatious.
▸ **'kittenishly** ADVERB ▸ **'kittenishness** NOUN

kitten moth NOUN any of three prominent moths, notably the **poplar kitten** (*Furcula bifida*), that have larvae like those of the related puss moth.

kittiwake ('kɪtɪˌweɪk) NOUN either of two oceanic gulls of the genus *Rissa,* esp *R. tridactyla,* having a white plumage with pale grey black-tipped wings and a square-cut tail.
▷HISTORY C17: of imitative origin

kittle ('kɪtᵊl) *Scot* ◆ ADJECTIVE [1] capricious and unpredictable. ◆ VERB [2] to be troublesome or puzzling to (someone). [3] to tickle.
▷HISTORY C16: probably from Old Norse *kitla* to TICKLE

kitty[1] ('kɪtɪ) NOUN, *plural* **-ties.** a diminutive or affectionate name for a **kitten** or **cat**[1].
▷HISTORY C18: see KIT[3]

kitty[2] ('kɪtɪ) NOUN, *plural* **-ties.** [1] the pool of bets in certain gambling games. [2] any shared fund of money, etc. [3] (in bowls) the jack.
▷HISTORY C19: see KIT[1]

kitty-cornered ADJECTIVE a variant of **cater-cornered.**

Kitty Hawk ('kɪtɪ hɔːk) NOUN a village in NE North Carolina, near Kill Devil Hill, where the Wright brothers made the first aeroplane flight in the US (1903).

Kitwe ('kɪtweɪ) NOUN a city in N Zambia: commercial centre of the Copper Belt. Pop.: 338 207 (1990).

Kitzbühel ('kɪtsbuəl) NOUN a town in W Austria, in the Tirol: centre for winter sports. Pop.: 8223 (1991).

Kiushu ('kjuːʃuː) NOUN a variant spelling of **Kyushu.**

kiva ('kiːvə) NOUN a large underground or partly underground room in a Pueblo Indian village, used chiefly for religious ceremonies.
▷HISTORY from Hopi

Kivu ('kiːvuː) NOUN **Lake.** a lake in central Africa, between the Democratic Republic of Congo (formerly Zaïre) and Rwanda at an altitude of 1460 m (4790 ft.). Area: 2698 sq. km (1042 sq. miles). Depth: (maximum) 475 m (1558 ft.).

Kiwanis (kɪ'wɑːnɪs) NOUN a North American organization of men's clubs founded in 1915 to promote community service.
▷HISTORY C20: alleged to be from an American Indian language: to make oneself known
▸ **Ki'wanian** NOUN

kiwi ('kiːwiː) NOUN, *plural* **kiwis.** [1] any nocturnal flightless New Zealand bird of the genus *Apteryx,* having a long beak, stout legs, and weakly barbed feathers: order *Apterygiformes* (see **ratite**). [2] short for **kiwi fruit.** [3] *Informal except in New Zealand* a New Zealander.
▷HISTORY C19: from Maori, of imitative origin

Kiwiana (ˌkiːwɪ'ɑːnə) PLURAL NOUN *Austral and NZ* collectable objects, ornaments, etc., esp dating from the 1950s or 1960s, relating to the history or popular culture of New Zealand.

Kiwi Ferns PLURAL NOUN **the.** the women's international Rugby League football team of New Zealand.

kiwi fruit NOUN the edible oval fruit of the kiwi plant, *Actinidia chinensis,* a climbing plant native to Asia but grown extensively in New Zealand; it has a brown fuzzy skin and pale green flesh. Also called: **Chinese gooseberry.**

Kiwis ('kiːwiːz) PLURAL NOUN **the.** the international Rugby League football team of New Zealand.

kiwisports ('kiːwiːˌspɔːts) PLURAL NOUN *NZ (functioning as singular)* a fitness programme developed for schools, involving a selection of sports such as rounders, cricket, and netball.

Kizil Irmak (kɪ'zɪl ɪə'mɑːk) NOUN a river in Turkey, rising in the Kizil Dag and flowing southwest, northwest, and northeast to the Black Sea: the longest river in Asia Minor. Length: about 1150 km (715 miles). Ancient name: **Halys** ('heɪlɪs).

KKK ABBREVIATION FOR **Ku Klux Klan.**

KKt *Chess* SYMBOL FOR king's knight.

KKtP *Chess* SYMBOL FOR king's knight's pawn.

kl SYMBOL FOR kilolitre.

Klagenfurt (*German* 'klaːgənfʊrt) NOUN a city in S Austria, capital of Carinthia province: tourist centre. Pop.: 89 415 (1991).

Klaipeda (*Russian* 'klajpɪdə) NOUN a port in Lithuania on the Baltic: shipbuilding and fish canning. Pop.: 202 484 (2000 est.). German name: **Memel.**

Klan (klæn) NOUN (usually preceded by *the*) short for **Ku Klux Klan.**
▸ **'Klanism** NOUN

klangfarbe ('klɑːŋˌfɑːbə) NOUN (*often capital*) instrumental timbre or tone colour.
▷HISTORY German: tone colour

Klansman ('klænzmən) NOUN, *plural* **-men.** a member of the Ku Klux Klan.

Klausenburg ('klauzənbʊrk) NOUN the German name for **Cluj.**

klaxon *or* **claxon** ('klæksᵊn) NOUN a type of loud horn formerly used on motor vehicles.
▷HISTORY C20: former trademark, from the name of the manufacturing company

Klebs-Löffler bacillus ('klɛbz'lʌflə; *German* 'kleːps'lœflər) NOUN a rodlike Gram-positive bacterium, *Corynebacterium diphtheriae,* that causes diphtheria: family *Corynebacteriaceae.*
▷HISTORY C19: named after Edwin *Klebs* (1834–1913) and Friedrich A. J. *Löffler* (1852–1915), German bacteriologists

Kleenex ('kliːnɛks) NOUN, *plural* **-ex** *or* **-exes.** *Trademark* a kind of soft paper tissue, used esp as a handkerchief.

Klein bottle (klaɪn) NOUN *Maths* a surface formed by inserting the smaller end of an open tapered tube through the surface of the tube and making this end contiguous with the other end.
▷HISTORY named after Felix *Klein* (1849–1925) German mathematician

kleinhuisie ('kleɪn'heɪsɪ) NOUN *South African* an outside lavatory.
▷HISTORY C20: Afrikaans: literally, little house

klepht (klɛft) NOUN any of the Greeks who fled to the mountains after the 15th-century Turkish conquest of Greece and whose descendants survived as brigands into the 19th century.
▷HISTORY C19: from Modern Greek *klephtēs,* from Greek *kleptēs* thief
▸ **'klephtic** ADJECTIVE

kleptocratic (ˌklɛptəʊ'krætɪk) ADJECTIVE (of a government, state, etc.) characterized by corruption amongst those in power.

kleptomania (ˌklɛptəʊ'meɪnɪə) NOUN *Psychol* a strong impulse to steal, esp when there is no obvious motivation.
▷HISTORY C19: *klepto-* from Greek *kleptēs* thief, from *kleptein* to steal + -MANIA
▸ **ˌklepto'maniˌac** NOUN

kletterschuh ('klɛtəʃuː) NOUN, *plural* **kletterschuhe** ('klɛtəˌʃuːə). a lightweight climbing boot with a canvas or suede upper and Vibram (originally felt or cord) sole. Also called: **klett.**
▷HISTORY C20: from German: climbing shoe

klezmer ('klɛzmə) NOUN [1] a Jewish folk musician, usually a member of a small band. [2] Also called: **klezmer music.** the music performed by such a band.
▷HISTORY Yiddish

klieg light (kliːg) NOUN an intense carbon-arc light used for illumination in producing films.
▷HISTORY C20: named after John H. *Kliegl* (1869–1959) and his brother Anton (1872–1927), German-born American inventors in the field of lighting

klipspringer ('klɪpˌsprɪŋə) NOUN a small agile antelope, *Oreotragus oreotragus,* inhabiting rocky regions of Africa south of the Sahara.
▷HISTORY C18: from Afrikaans, from Dutch *klip* rock (see CLIFF) + *springer,* from *springen* to SPRING

Klondike ('klɒndaɪk) NOUN [1] a region of NW Canada, in the Yukon in the basin of the Klondike River: site of rich gold deposits, discovered in 1896 but largely exhausted by 1910. Area: about 2100 sq. km (800 sq. miles). [2] a river in NW Canada, rising in the Yukon and flowing west to the Yukon River. Length: about 145 km (90 miles).

klondyker *or* **klondiker** ('klɒnˌdaɪkə) NOUN *Brit* an East European factory ship.
▷HISTORY C20: from the gold miners who took part in the 19th-century gold rush to the KLONDIKE

klong (klɒŋ) NOUN a type of canal in Thailand.
▷HISTORY from Thai

kloof (kluːf) NOUN a mountain pass or gorge in southern Africa.
▷HISTORY C18: from Afrikaans, from Middle Dutch *clove* a cleft; see CLEAVE[1]

klootchman ('kluːtʃmən) NOUN, *plural* **-mans** *or* **-men.** *Northwestern Canadian* an Indian woman; squaw. Also called: **klootch, klooch.**
▷HISTORY C19: from Chinook Jargon, from Nootka *hlotssma* woman, wife

klutz (klʌts) NOUN *US and Canadian, slang* a clumsy or stupid person.
▷HISTORY from German *Klotz* dolt; compare CLOT
▸ **'klutzy** ADJECTIVE

klystron ('klɪstrɒn, 'klaɪ-) NOUN an electron tube for the amplification or generation of microwaves by means of velocity modulation.
▷HISTORY C20 *klys-,* from Greek *klus-, kluzein* to wash over, break over + -TRON

km[1] SYMBOL FOR kilometre.

km[2] THE INTERNET DOMAIN NAME FOR Comoros.

K-meson NOUN another name for **kaon.**

kn[1] ABBREVIATION FOR: [1] *Nautical* knot. [2] krona. [3] krone.

kn[2] THE INTERNET DOMAIN NAME FOR Saint Kitts and Nevis.

KN *Chess* SYMBOL FOR king's knight.

knack (næk) NOUN [1] a skilful, ingenious, or resourceful way of doing something. [2] a particular talent or aptitude, esp an intuitive one.
▷HISTORY C14: probably variant of *knak* sharp knock, rap, of imitative origin

knacked (nækd) ADJECTIVE *Brit informal* broken or worn out.
▷HISTORY C20: from KNACKERED

knacker ('nækə) *Brit* ◆ NOUN [1] a person who buys up old horses for slaughter. [2] a person who buys up old buildings and breaks them up for scrap. [3] (*usually plural*) *Slang* another word for **testicle.** [4] *Irish, slang* a despicable person. ◆ VERB [5] (*tr; usually passive*) *Slang* to exhaust; tire.
▷HISTORY C16: probably from *nacker* saddler, probably of Scandinavian origin; compare Old Norse *hnakkur* saddle

knackered ('nækəd) *Brit, slang* ◆ ADJECTIVE [1] exhausted; tired out. [2] worn out; no longer working, esp after long or hard use.

knacker's yard NOUN *Brit* [1] a slaughterhouse for horses. [2] *Informal* destruction because of being beyond all usefulness (esp in the phrase **ready for the knacker's yard**).

knackwurst *or* **knockwurst** ('nɒkˌwɜːst) NOUN a short fat highly seasoned sausage.
▷HISTORY German, from *knacken* to make a cracking sound + *Wurst* sausage

knag (næg) NOUN [1] a knot in wood. [2] a wooden peg.
▷HISTORY C15: perhaps from Low German *knagge*

knap[1] (næp) NOUN *Dialect* the crest of a hill.
▷HISTORY Old English *cnæpp* top; compare Old Norse *knappr* knob

knap[2] (næp) VERB **knaps, knapping, knapped.** (*tr*) *Dialect* to hit, hammer, or chip.
▷HISTORY C15 (in the sense: to strike with a sharp

sound): of imitative origin; compare Dutch *knappen* to crack
▸ **'knapper** NOUN

knapping hammer NOUN a hammer used for breaking and shaping stones.

knapsack ('næpˌsæk) NOUN a canvas or leather bag carried strapped on the back or shoulder.
▷HISTORY C17: from Low German *knappsack,* probably from *knappen* to bite, snap + *sack* bag; related to Dutch *knapzak;* see SACK[1]

knapweed ('næpˌwi:d) NOUN any of several plants of the genus *Centaurea,* having purplish thistle-like flowers: family *Asteraceae* (composites). See also **centaury** (sense 2), **hardheads.**
▷HISTORY C15 *knopwed;* see KNOP, WEED[1]

knar (nɑ:) NOUN a variant of **knur.**
▷HISTORY C14 *knarre* rough stone, knot on a tree; related to Low German *knarre*
▸ **knarred** *or* **'knarry** ADJECTIVE

knave (neɪv) NOUN [1] *Archaic* a dishonest man; rogue. [2] another word for **jack** (the playing card). [3] *Obsolete* a male servant.
▷HISTORY Old English *cnafa;* related to Old High German *knabo* boy
▸ **'knavish** ADJECTIVE ▸ **'knavishly** ADVERB ▸ **'knavishness** NOUN

knavery ('neɪvərɪ) NOUN, *plural* **-eries.** [1] a deceitful or dishonest act. [2] dishonest conduct; trickery.

knawel ('nɔ:əl) NOUN any of several Old World caryophyllaceous plants of the genus *Scleranthus,* having heads of minute petal-less flowers.
▷HISTORY C16: from German *Knauel,* literally: ball of yarn, from Old High German *kliuwa* ball

knead (ni:d) VERB *(tr)* [1] to work and press (a soft substance, such as bread dough) into a uniform mixture with the hands. [2] to squeeze, massage, or press with the hands. [3] to make by kneading.
▷HISTORY Old English *cnedan;* related to Old Saxon *knedan,* Old Norse *knotha*
▸ **'kneader** NOUN

Knebworth House ('nɛbwɜ:θ) NOUN a Tudor mansion in Knebworth in Hertfordshire: home of Sir Edward Bulwer-Lytton; decorated (1843) in the Gothic style.

knee (ni:) NOUN [1] the joint of the human leg connecting the tibia and fibula with the femur and protected in front by the patella. Technical name: **genu.** Related adjective: **genicular.** [2] **a** the area surrounding and above this joint. **b** *(modifier)* reaching or covering the knee: *knee breeches; knee socks.* [3] a corresponding or similar part in other vertebrates. [4] the part of a garment that covers the knee. [5] the upper surface of a seated person's thigh: *the child sat on her mother's knee.* [6] anything resembling a knee in action, such as a device pivoted to allow one member angular movement in relation to another. [7] anything resembling a knee in shape, such as an angular bend in a pipe. [8] any of the hollow rounded protuberances that project upwards from the roots of the swamp cypress: thought to aid respiration in waterlogged soil. [9] **bend** *or* **bow the knee.** to kneel or submit. [10] **bring someone to his knees.** to force someone into submission. [11] **bring something to its knees.** to cause something to be in a weakened or impoverished state. ◆ VERB **knees, kneeing, kneed.** [12] *(tr)* to strike, nudge, or push with the knee.
▷HISTORY Old English *cnēow;* compare Old High German *kneo,* Old Norse *knē,* Latin *genu*

kneecap ('ni:ˌkæp) NOUN [1] *Anatomy* a nontechnical name for **patella.** [2] another word for **poleyn.** ◆ VERB **-caps, -capping, -capped.** *(tr)* [3] (esp of certain terrorist groups) to shoot (a person) in the kneecap, esp as an act of retaliation.

knee-deep ADJECTIVE [1] so deep as to reach or cover the knees: *knee-deep mud.* [2] *(postpositive;* often foll by *in)* **a** sunk or covered to the knees: *knee-deep in sand.* **b** immersed; deeply involved: *knee-deep in work.*

knee drop NOUN a wrestling attack in which a wrestler lifts his opponent and drops him onto his bent knee.

knee-high ADJECTIVE [1] another word for **knee-deep** (sense 1). [2] as high as the knee: *a knee-high child.*

kneehole ('ni:ˌhəʊl) NOUN **a** a space for the knees, esp under a desk. **b** *(as modifier): a kneehole desk.*

knee jerk NOUN [1] *Physiol* Also called: **patellar reflex.** an outward reflex kick of the lower leg caused by a sharp tap on the quadriceps tendon just below the patella. ◆ MODIFIER **kneejerk.** [2] made or occurring as a predictable and automatic response, without thought: *kneejerk support.*

kneel (ni:l) VERB **kneels, kneeling, knelt** *or* **kneeled.** [1] *(intr)* to rest, fall, or support oneself on one's knees. ◆ NOUN [2] the act or position of kneeling.
▷HISTORY Old English *cnēowlian;* see KNEE
▸ **'kneeler** NOUN

knee-length ADJECTIVE reaching to the knee: *a knee-length skirt; knee-length boots.*

kneepad ('ni:ˌpæd) NOUN any of several types of protective covering for the knees. Also called: **kneecap.**

kneepan ('ni:ˌpæn) NOUN *Anatomy* another word for **patella.**

knee spavin NOUN *Vet science* chronic inflammation of the carpal joint of a horse.

knees-up NOUN, *plural* **knees-ups.** [1] a boisterous dance involving the raising of alternate knees. [2] a lively noisy party or celebration, esp one with dancing.
▷HISTORY C20: from the song "Knees up Mother Brown" to which the dance is performed

knee-trembling ADJECTIVE *Informal* very exciting.

kneidel ('kneɪdəl, 'knaɪ-) NOUN (in Jewish cookery) a small dumpling, usually served in chicken soup.
▷HISTORY from Yiddish

knell (nɛl) NOUN [1] the sound of a bell rung to announce a death or a funeral. [2] something that precipitates or indicates death or destruction. ◆ VERB [3] *(intr)* to ring a knell. [4] *(tr)* to proclaim or announce by or as if by a tolling bell.
▷HISTORY Old English *cnyll;* related to Middle High German *knüllen* to strike, Dutch *knallen* to bang

knelt (nɛlt) VERB a past tense and past participle of **kneel.**

Knesset *or* **Knesseth** ('knɛsɪt) NOUN the unicameral parliament of Israel.
▷HISTORY Hebrew, literally: gathering

knew (nju:) VERB the past tense of **know.**

Knickerbocker ('nɪkəˌbɒkə) NOUN *US* [1] a descendant of the original Dutch settlers of New York. [2] an inhabitant of New York.
▷HISTORY C19: named after Diedrich *Knickerbocker,* fictitious Dutchman alleged to be the author of Washington Irving's *History of New York* (1809)

knickerbocker glory NOUN a rich confection consisting of layers of ice cream, jelly, cream, and fruit served in a tall glass.

knickerbockers ('nɪkəˌbɒkəz) PLURAL NOUN baggy breeches fastened with a band at the knee or above the ankle. Also called (US): **knickers.**
▷HISTORY C19: regarded as the traditional dress of the Dutch settlers in America; see KNICKERBOCKER

knickers ('nɪkəz) PLURAL NOUN [1] an undergarment for women covering the lower trunk and sometimes the thighs and having separate legs or leg-holes. [2] a US variant of **knickerbockers.** [3] **get one's knickers in a twist.** *Slang* to become agitated, flustered, or upset.
▷HISTORY C19: contraction of KNICKERBOCKERS

knick-knack *or* **nick-nack** ('nɪkˌnæk) NOUN [1] a cheap ornament; trinket. [2] an ornamental article of furniture, dress, etc.
▷HISTORY C17: by reduplication from *knack,* in obsolete sense: toy
▸ **'knick-ˌknackery** *or* **'nick-ˌnackery** NOUN

knickpoint *or esp US* **nickpoint** ('nɪkˌpɔɪnt) NOUN a break in the slope of a river profile caused by renewed erosion by a rejuvenated river.
▷HISTORY C20: partial translation of German *Knickpunkt,* from *knicken* to bend + *Punkt* POINT

knife (naɪf) NOUN, *plural* **knives** (naɪvz). [1] a cutting instrument consisting of a sharp-edged often pointed blade of metal fitted into a handle or onto a machine. [2] a similar instrument used as a weapon. [3] **have one's knife in someone.** to have a grudge against or victimize someone. [4] **twist the knife.** to make a bad situation worse in a deliberately malicious way. [5] **the knives are out for (someone).** *Brit* people are determined to harm or put a stop to (someone): *the knives are out for Stevens.* [6] **under the knife.** undergoing a surgical operation. ◆ VERB *(tr)* [7] to cut, stab, or kill with a knife. [8] to betray, injure, or depose in an underhand way.
▷HISTORY Old English *cnīf;* related to Old Norse *knīfr,* Middle Low German *knīf*
▸ **'knifeˌlike** ADJECTIVE ▸ **'knifer** NOUN

knife edge NOUN [1] the sharp cutting edge of a knife. [2] any sharp edge. [3] a sharp-edged wedge of hard material on which the beam of a balance pivots or about which a pendulum is suspended. [4] a critical point in the development of a situation, process of making a decision, etc.

knife grinder NOUN a person who makes and sharpens knives, esp an itinerant one.

knife pleat NOUN a single pleat turned in one direction.

knife-point NOUN [1] the tip of a knife blade. [2] **at knife-point.** under threat of being stabbed.

kniferest ('naɪfˌrɛst) NOUN a support on which a carving knife or carving fork is placed at the table.

knife switch NOUN an electric switch in which a flat metal blade, hinged at one end, is pushed between fixed contacts.

knight (naɪt) NOUN [1] (in medieval Europe) **a** (originally) a person who served his lord as a mounted and heavily armed soldier. **b** (later) a gentleman invested by a king or other lord with the military and social standing of this rank. [2] (in modern times) a person invested by a sovereign with a nonhereditary rank and dignity usually in recognition of personal services, achievements, etc. A British knight bears the title *Sir* placed before his name, as in *Sir Winston Churchill.* [3] a chess piece, usually shaped like a horse's head, that moves either two squares horizontally and one square vertically or one square horizontally and two squares vertically. [4] a heroic champion of a lady or of a cause or principle. [5] a member of the Roman class of the equites. ◆ VERB [6] *(tr)* to make (a person) a knight; dub.
▷HISTORY Old English *cniht* servant; related to Old High German *kneht* boy

knight bachelor NOUN, *plural* **knights bachelors** *or* **knights bachelor.** [1] a person who has been knighted but who does not belong to any of the orders of knights. [2] another name for a **bachelor** (sense 3).

knight banneret NOUN, *plural* **knights bannerets.** another name for a **banneret.**

knight errant NOUN, *plural* **knights errant.** (esp in medieval romance) a knight who wanders in search of deeds of courage, chivalry, etc.

knight errantry NOUN [1] the practices of a knight errant. [2] quixotic behaviour or practices.

knighthead ('naɪtˌhɛd) NOUN *Nautical* either of a pair of vertical supports for each side of the bowsprit.
▷HISTORY C18: originally decorated with carvings of knights' heads

knighthood ('naɪthʊd) NOUN [1] the order, dignity, or rank of a knight. [2] the qualities of a knight; knightliness. [3] knights collectively.

knightly ('naɪtlɪ) ADJECTIVE of, relating to, resembling, or befitting a knight.
▸ **'knightliness** NOUN

knight marshal NOUN another name for **marshal** (sense 5).

knight of the road NOUN *Informal or facetious* [1] a tramp. [2] a commercial traveller. [3] a lorry driver. [4] *Obsolete* a highwayman.

Knights Hospitallers NOUN [1] Also called: **Knights of St John of Jerusalem.** a military religious order founded about the time of the first crusade (1096–99) among European crusaders. It took its name from a hospital and hostel in Jerusalem. Full name: **Knights of the Hospital of St John of Jerusalem.** [2] See **Hospitaller.**

Knights of St. Columba NOUN an international, semi-secret fraternal and charitable order for Catholic laymen, which originated in New Haven, Connecticut in 1882 (the **Knights of Columbus**).

Knights of the Round Table NOUN (in Arthurian legend) an order of knights created by King Arthur.

Knight Templar NOUN, *plural* **Knights Templars** *or* **Knights Templar.** another term for **Templar.**

kniphofia (nɪ'fəʊfɪə) NOUN any plant of the perennial southern African genus *Kniphofia,* some species of which are cultivated for their conical spikes of bright red or yellow drooping tubular flowers: family *Liliaceae.* Also called: **red-hot poker.**
▷HISTORY named after J. H. *Kniphof* (1704–1763), German doctor and botanist

knish (knɪʃ) NOUN a piece of dough stuffed with potato, meat, or some other filling and baked or fried.
▷HISTORY Yiddish, from Russian *knysh* cake; compare Polish *knysz*

knit (nɪt) VERB **knits, knitting, knitted** *or* **knit.** 1 to make (a garment, etc.) by looping and entwining (yarn, esp wool) by hand by means of long eyeless needles (**knitting needles**) or by machine (**knitting machine**). 2 to join or be joined together closely. 3 to draw (the brows) together or (of the brows) to come together, as in frowning or concentrating. 4 (of a broken bone) to join together; heal. ◆ NOUN 5 **a** a fabric or garment made by knitting. **b** (*in combination*): *a heavy knit.*
▷HISTORY Old English *cnyttan* to tie in; related to Middle Low German *knütten* to knot together; see KNOT[1]
▸'**knittable** ADJECTIVE ▸'**knitter** NOUN

knitting ('nɪtɪŋ) NOUN **a** knitted work or the process of producing it. **b** (*as modifier*): *a knitting machine.*

knitwear ('nɪt,wɛə) NOUN knitted clothes, esp sweaters.

knives (naɪvz) NOUN the plural of **knife.**

knob (nɒb) NOUN 1 a rounded projection from a surface, such as a lump on a tree trunk. 2 a handle of a door, drawer, etc., esp one that is rounded. 3 a round hill or knoll or morainic ridge. 4 *Brit, taboo* a slang word for **penis.** 5 **and the same to you with (brass) knobs on.** *Brit informal* the same to you but even more so. ◆ VERB **knobs, knobbing, knobbed.** 6 (*tr*) to supply or ornament with knobs. 7 (*intr*) to form into a knob; bulge. 8 *Brit, taboo* to have sexual intercourse with (someone).
▷HISTORY C14: from Middle Low German *knobbe* knot in wood; see KNOP
▸'**knobby** ADJECTIVE ▸'**knob,like** ADJECTIVE

knobbly ('nɒblɪ) ADJECTIVE **-blier, -bliest.** having or covered with small knobs; bumpy.

knobby (nɒbɪ) ADJECTIVE **-bier, -biest.** having or covered with small knobs; knobbly.

knobhead ('nɒb,hɛd) NOUN *Derogatory, slang* a stupid person.

knobkerrie ('nɒb,kɛrɪ) *or* **knobstick** ('nɒb,stɪk) NOUN a stick with a round knob at the end, used as a club or missile by South African tribesmen.
▷HISTORY C19: from Afrikaans *knopkierie,* from *knop* knob, from Middle Dutch *cnoppe* + *kierie* stick, from Khoikhoi *kīrri*

knock (nɒk) VERB 1 (*tr*) to give a blow or push to; strike. 2 (*intr*) to rap sharply with the knuckles, a hard object, etc., esp to capture attention: *to knock at the door.* 3 (*tr*) to make or force by striking: *to knock a hole in the wall.* 4 (*intr; usually foll by against*) to collide (with). 5 (*tr*) to bring into a certain condition by hitting or pushing: *to knock someone unconscious.* 6 (*tr*) *Informal* to criticize adversely; belittle: *to knock someone's work.* 7 (*intr*) Also: **pink.** (of an internal-combustion engine) to emit a characteristic metallic noise as a result of faulty combustion. 8 (*intr*) (of a bearing, esp one in an engine) to emit a regular characteristic sound as a result of wear. 9 *Brit, slang* to have sexual intercourse with (a person). 10 **knock (a person) into the middle of next week.** *Informal* to hit (a person) with a very heavy blow. 11 **knock one's head against.** to have a violent or unpleasant encounter with (adverse facts or circumstances). 12 **knock on the head. a** to daze or kill (a person) by striking on the head. **b** effectively to prevent the further development of (a plan). ◆ NOUN 13 **a** a blow, push, or rap: *he gave the table a knock.* **b** the sound so caused. 14 the sound of knocking in an engine or bearing. 15 *Informal* a misfortune, rebuff, or setback. 16 *Informal* unfavourable criticism. 17 *Informal* (in cricket) an innings or a spell of batting. ◆ See also **knock about, knock back, knock down, knock off, knock-on, knockout, knock up.**
▷HISTORY Old English *cnocian,* of imitative origin; related to Old Norse *knoka* to hit

knock about *or* **around** VERB 1 (*intr, adverb*) to wander about aimlessly. 2 (*intr, preposition*) to travel about, esp as resulting in varied or exotic experience: *he's knocked about the world a bit.* 3 (*intr, adverb; foll by with*) to associate: *to knock about with a gang.* 4 (*tr, adverb*) to treat brutally: *he knocks his wife about.* 5 (*tr, adverb*) to consider or discuss informally: *to knock an idea about.* ◆ NOUN **knockabout.** 6 a sailing vessel, usually sloop-rigged, without a bowsprit and with a single jib. ◆ ADJECTIVE **knockabout.** 7 rough; boisterous: *knockabout farce.*

knock back VERB (*tr, adverb*) 1 *Informal* to drink, esp quickly. 2 *Informal* to cost. 3 *Slang* to reject or refuse: *you cannot possibly knock back such an offer.* 4 *Slang* to come as an unpleasant surprise to; disconcert. ◆ NOUN **knock-back.** 5 *Slang* a refusal or rejection. 6 *Prison slang* failure to obtain parole.

knock down VERB (*tr, adverb*) 1 to strike to the ground with a blow, as in boxing. 2 (in auctions) to declare (an article) sold, as by striking a blow with a gavel. 3 to demolish. 4 to dismantle, for ease of transport. 5 *Informal* to reduce (a price, etc.). 6 *Austral, slang* to spend (a cheque). 7 *Austral, slang* to drink. ◆ ADJECTIVE **knockdown.** (*prenominal*) 8 overwhelming; powerful: *a knockdown blow.* 9 *Chiefly Brit* cheap: *I got the table at a knockdown price.* 10 easily dismantled: *knockdown furniture.* ◆ NOUN **knockdown.** 11 *US and Austral, slang* an introduction: *will you give me a knockdown to her?*

knocker ('nɒkə) NOUN 1 an object, usually ornamental and made of metal, attached to a door by a hinge and used for knocking. 2 *Informal* a person who finds fault or disparages. 3 (*usually plural*) *Slang* a female breast. 4 a person or thing that knocks. 5 **on the knocker.** *Austral and NZ informal* promptly; at once: *you pay on the knocker here.*

knock-for-knock ADJECTIVE designating an agreement between vehicle insurers that in the event of an accident each will pay for the damage to the vehicle insured with him without attempting to establish blame for the accident.

knocking copy NOUN advertising or publicity material designed to denigrate a competing product.

knocking-shop NOUN *Brit* a slang word for **brothel.**

knock-knee NOUN a condition in which the legs are bent inwards causing the knees to touch when standing. Technical name: **genu valgum.**
▸,**knock-'kneed** ADJECTIVE

knock off VERB (*mainly adverb*) 1 (*intr, also preposition*) *Informal* to finish work: *we knocked off an hour early.* 2 (*tr*) *Informal* to make or do hastily or easily: *to knock off a novel in a week.* 3 (*tr; also preposition*) *Informal* to reduce the price of (an article) by (a stated amount). 4 (*tr*) *Slang* to kill. 5 (*tr*) *Slang* to rob or steal: *to knock off a bank; to knock off a watch.* 6 (*tr*) *Slang* to stop doing something, used as a command: *knock it off!* 7 (*tr*) *Slang* to have sexual intercourse with; to seduce.

knock-on ADJECTIVE 1 resulting inevitably but indirectly from another event or circumstance: *the works closed with the direct loss of 3000 jobs and many more from the knock-on effect on the area.* ◆ NOUN 2 *Rugby* the infringement of playing the ball forward with the hand or arm. ◆ VERB **knock on.** (*adverb*) 3 *Rugby* to play (the ball) forward with the hand or arm.

knockout ('nɒk,aʊt) NOUN 1 the act of rendering unconscious. 2 a blow that renders an opponent unconscious. 3 **a** a competition in which competitors are eliminated progressively. **b** (*as modifier*): *a knockout contest.* 4 a series of absurd invented games, esp obstacle races, involving physical effort or skill. 5 *Informal* a person or thing that is overwhelmingly impressive or attractive: *she's a knockout.* ◆ VERB **knock out.** (*tr, adverb*) 6 to render unconscious, esp by a blow. 7 *Boxing* to defeat (an opponent) by a knockout. 8 to destroy, damage, or injure badly. 9 to eliminate, esp in a knockout competition. 10 *Informal* to overwhelm or amaze, esp with admiration or favourable reaction: *I was knocked out by that new song.* 11 to remove the ashes from (one's pipe) by tapping.

knockout drops PLURAL NOUN *Slang* a drug secretly put into someone's drink to cause stupefaction. See also **Mickey Finn.**

knock up VERB (*adverb, mainly tr*) 1 Also: **knock together.** *Informal* to assemble quickly; improvise: *to knock up a set of shelves.* 2 *Brit informal* to waken; rouse: *to knock someone up early.* 3 *Slang* to make pregnant. 4 *Brit informal* to exhaust: *the heavy work knocked him up.* 5 *Cricket* to score (runs). 6 (*intr*) *Tennis, squash, badminton* to practise or hit the ball about informally, esp before a match. ◆ NOUN **knock-up.** 7 a practice session at tennis, squash, or a similar game.

knockwurst ('nɒk,wɜːst) NOUN a variant spelling of **knackwurst.**

Knole (nəʊl) NOUN a mansion in Sevenoaks in Kent: built (1454) for Thomas Bourchier, Archbishop of Canterbury; later granted to the Sackville family, who made major alterations (1603–08).

knoll[1] (nəʊl) NOUN a small rounded hill.
▷HISTORY Old English *cnoll;* compare Old Norse *knollr* hilltop
▸'**knolly** ADJECTIVE

knoll[2] (nəʊl) NOUN, VERB an archaic or dialect word for **knell.**
▸'**knoller** NOUN

knop (nɒp) NOUN *Archaic* a knob, esp an ornamental one.
▷HISTORY C14: from Germanic; compare Middle Dutch *cnoppe* bud, Old High German *knopf*

Knossos *or* **Cnossus** ('nɒsəs, 'knɒs-) NOUN a ruined city in N central Crete: remains of the Minoan Bronze Age civilization.

knot[1] (nɒt) NOUN 1 any of various fastenings formed by looping and tying a piece of rope, cord, etc., in upon itself, to another piece of rope, or to another object. 2 a prescribed method of tying a particular knot. 3 a tangle, as in hair or string. 4 a decorative bow or fastening, as of ribbon or braid. 5 a small cluster or huddled group. 6 a tie or bond: *the marriage knot.* 7 a difficult problem. 8 a protuberance or lump of plant tissues, such as that occurring on the trunks of certain trees. 9 **a** a hard mass of wood at the point where a branch joins the trunk of a tree. **b** a cross section of this, usually roundish and cross-grained, visible in a piece of timber. 10 a sensation of constriction, caused by tension or nervousness: *his stomach was tying itself in knots.* 11 **a** *Pathol* a lump of vessels or fibres formed in a part, as in a muscle. **b** *Anatomy* a protuberance on an organ or part. 12 a unit of speed used by nautical vessels and aircraft, being one nautical mile (about 1.15 statute miles or 1.85 km) per hour. 13 one of a number of equally spaced knots on a log line used to indicate the speed of a ship in nautical miles per hour. 14 **at a rate of knots.** very fast. 15 **tie (someone) in knots.** to completely perplex or confuse (someone). 16 **tie the knot.** *Informal* to get married. ◆ VERB **knots, knotting, knotted.** 17 (*tr*) to tie or fasten in a knot. 18 to form or cause to form into a knot. 19 (*tr*) to ravel or entangle or become ravelled or entangled. 20 (*tr*) to make (an article or a design) by tying thread in an interlaced pattern of ornamental knots, as in macramé.
▷HISTORY Old English *cnotta;* related to Old High German *knoto,* Old Norse *knūtr*
▸'**knotter** NOUN ▸'**knotless** ADJECTIVE ▸'**knot,like** ADJECTIVE

knot[2] (nɒt) NOUN a small northern sandpiper, *Calidris canutus,* with a short bill and grey plumage.
▷HISTORY C15: of unknown origin

knot garden NOUN (esp formerly) a formal garden of intricate design.

knotgrass ('nɒt,grɑːs) NOUN 1 Also called: **allseed.** a polygonaceous weedy plant, *Polygonum aviculare,* whose small green flowers produce numerous seeds. 2 any of several related plants.

knothole ('nɒt,həʊl) NOUN a hole in a piece of wood where a knot has been.

knotted ('nɒtɪd) ADJECTIVE 1 (of wood, rope, etc.) having knots. 2 **get knotted!** *Brit, slang* used as a response to express disapproval or rejection.

knotting ('nɒtɪŋ) NOUN 1 a sealer applied over knots in new wood before priming to prevent resin from exuding. 2 (esp formerly) a kind of decorative knotted fancywork.

knotty ('nɒtɪ) ADJECTIVE **-tier, -tiest.** 1 (of wood,

rope, etc.) full of or characterized by knots. 2 extremely difficult or intricate.
▸ 'knottily ADVERB ▸ 'knottiness NOUN

knotweed ('nɒt,wiːd) NOUN any of several polygonaceous plants of the genus *Polygonum*, having small flowers and jointed stems.

knotwork ('nɒt,wɜːk) NOUN ornamentation consisting of a mass of intertwined and knotted cords.

knout (naʊt) NOUN a stout whip used formerly in Russia as an instrument of punishment.
▷HISTORY C17: from Russian *knut*, of Scandinavian origin; compare Old Norse *knūtr* knot

know (nəʊ) VERB **knows, knowing, knew** (njuː), **known** (nəʊn). (*mainly tr*) 1 (*also intr; may take a clause as object*) to be or feel certain of the truth or accuracy of (a fact, etc.). 2 to be acquainted or familiar with: *she's known him five years*. 3 to have a familiarity or grasp of, as through study or experience: *he knows French*. 4 (*also intr; may take a clause as object*) to understand, be aware of, or perceive (facts, etc.): *he knows the answer now*. 5 (foll by *how*) to be sure or aware of (how to be or do something). 6 to experience, esp deeply: *to know poverty*. 7 to be intelligent, informed, or sensible enough (to do something): *she knew not to go home yet*. 8 (*may take a clause as object*) to be able to distinguish or discriminate. 9 *Archaic* to have sexual intercourse with. 10 **I know what.** I have an idea. 11 **know what's what.** to know how one thing or things in general work. 12 **you know.** *Informal* a parenthetical filler phrase used to make a pause in speaking or add slight emphasis to a statement. 13 **you never know.** things are uncertain. ◆ NOUN 14 **in the know.** *Informal* aware or informed.
▷HISTORY Old English *gecnāwan;* related to Old Norse *knā* I can, Latin *noscere* to come to know
▸ 'knowable ADJECTIVE ▸ 'knower NOUN

know-all NOUN *Informal, disparaging* a person who pretends or appears to know a great deal.

know-how NOUN *Informal* 1 ingenuity, aptitude, or skill; knack. 2 commercial and saleable knowledge of how to do a particular thing; experience.

knowing ('nəʊɪŋ) ADJECTIVE 1 suggesting secret information or knowledge. 2 wise, shrewd, or clever. 3 deliberate; intentional. ◆ NOUN 4 **there is no knowing.** one cannot tell.
▸ 'knowingly ADVERB ▸ 'knowingness NOUN

knowledge ('nɒlɪdʒ) NOUN 1 the facts, feelings or experiences known by a person or group of people. 2 the state of knowing. 3 awareness, consciousness, or familiarity gained by experience or learning. 4 erudition or informed learning. 5 specific information about a subject. 6 sexual intercourse (obsolete except in the legal phrase **carnal knowledge**). 7 **come to one's knowledge.** to become known to one. 8 **to my knowledge. a** as I understand it. **b** as I know. 9 **grow out of one's knowledge.** *Irish* to behave in a presumptuous or conceited manner.

knowledgeable *or* **knowledgable** ('nɒlɪdʒəbᵊl) ADJECTIVE possessing or indicating much knowledge.
▸ 'knowledgeableness *or* 'knowledgableness NOUN
▸ 'knowledgeably *or* 'knowledgably ADVERB

knowledge economy NOUN an economy in which information services are dominant as an area of growth.

knowledge worker NOUN a person employed to produce or analyse ideas and information.

known (nəʊn) VERB 1 the past participle of **know**. ◆ ADJECTIVE 2 specified and identified: *a known criminal*. ◆ NOUN 3 a fact or entity known.

know-nothing NOUN *Informal, disparaging* an ignorant person.

Knowsley ('nəʊzlɪ) NOUN a unitary authority of NW England, in Merseyside. Pop.: 150 468 (2001). Area: 97 sq. km (38 sq. miles).

Knoxville ('nɒksvɪl) NOUN an industrial city in E Tennessee, on the Tennessee River: state capital (1796–1812; 1817–19). Pop.: 173 890 (2000).

KNP *Chess* SYMBOL FOR king's knight's pawn.

Knt ABBREVIATION FOR Knight.

knuckle ('nʌkᵊl) NOUN 1 a joint of a finger, esp that connecting a finger to the hand. 2 a joint of veal, pork, etc., consisting of the part of the leg below the knee joint, often used in making stews or stock. 3 the cylindrical portion of a hinge through which the pin passes. 4 an angle joint between two members of a structure. 5 **near the knuckle.** *Informal* approaching indecency. ◆ VERB 6 (*tr*) to rub or press with the knuckles. 7 (*intr*) to keep the knuckles on the ground while shooting a marble. ◆ See also **knuckle down, knuckle under.**
▷HISTORY C14: related to Middle High German *knöchel*, Middle Low German *knoke* bone, Dutch *knok*
▸ 'knuckly ADJECTIVE

knucklebone ('nʌkᵊl,bəʊn) NOUN any bone forming part of a knuckle or knuckle joint.

knucklebones ('nʌkᵊl,bəʊnz) NOUN (*functioning as singular*) a less common name for **jacks** (the game).

knuckle down VERB (*intr, adverb*) *Informal* to apply oneself diligently: *to knuckle down to some work*.

knuckle-duster NOUN (*often plural*) a metal bar fitted over the knuckles, often with holes for the fingers, for inflicting injury by a blow with the fist.

knucklehead ('nʌkᵊl,hɛd) NOUN *Informal* fool; idiot.
▸ 'knuckle,headed ADJECTIVE

knuckle joint NOUN 1 any of the joints of the fingers. 2 *Mechanical engineering* a hinged joint between two rods, often a ball and socket joint.

knuckle under VERB (*intr, adverb*) to give way under pressure or authority; yield.

knur, knurr (nɜː), *or* **knar** NOUN a knot or protuberance in a tree trunk or in wood.
▷HISTORY C16 *knor;* related to Middle High German *knorre* knot; compare KNAR

knurl *or* **nurl** (nɜːl) VERB (*tr*) 1 to impress with a series of fine ridges or serrations. ◆ NOUN 2 a small ridge, esp one of a series providing a rough surface that can be gripped.
▷HISTORY C17: probably from KNUR

knurly ('nɜːlɪ) ADJECTIVE **knurlier, knurliest.** a rare word for **gnarled.**

KO *or* **k.o.** ('keɪ'əʊ) VERB **KO's, KO'ing, KO'd; k.o.'s, k.o.'ing, k.o.'d,** NOUN, *plural* **KO's** *or* **k.o.'s.** a slang term for **knock out** or **knockout.**

koa ('kəʊə) NOUN 1 a Hawaiian leguminous tree, *Acacia koa*, yielding a hard wood. 2 the reddish wood of this tree, used esp for furniture.
▷HISTORY C19: from Hawaiian

koala *or* **koala bear** (kəʊ'ɑːlə) NOUN a slow-moving Australian arboreal marsupial, *Phascolarctus cinereus*, having dense greyish fur and feeding on eucalyptus leaves and bark. Also called (Austral): **native bear.**
▷HISTORY from a native Australian language

koan ('kəʊæn) NOUN (in Zen Buddhism) a problem or riddle that admits no logical solution.
▷HISTORY from Japanese

kob (kɒb) NOUN any of several species of African antelope, esp *Kobus kob:* similar to waterbucks.
▷HISTORY C20: from a Niger-Congo language; compare Wolof *koba*, Fulani *kōba*

Kobarid ('kəʊbə,riːd; *Serbo-Croat* 'kɔba,rid) NOUN a village in Slovenia on the Isonzo River: part of Italy until 1947; scene of the defeat of the Italians by Austro-German forces (1917). Italian name: **Caporetto.**

Kobe ('kəʊbɪ) NOUN a port in S Japan, on S Honshu on Osaka Bay: formed in 1889 by the amalgamation of Hyogo and Kobe; a major industrial complex, producing ships, steel, and rubber goods. Pop.: 1 423 830 (1995).

Kobe beef NOUN a grade of beef from cattle raised in Kobe, Japan, which is extremely tender and full-flavoured as a result of the cattle being massaged with sake and fed a special diet including large quantities of beer.

København (købən'haun) NOUN the Danish name for **Copenhagen.**

Koblenz *or* **Coblenz** (*German* 'koːblɛnts) NOUN a city in W central Germany, in the Rhineland-Palatinate at the confluence of the Rivers Moselle and Rhine: ruled by the archbishop-electors of Trier from 1018 until occupied by the French in 1794; passed to Prussia in 1815, becoming capital of the Rhine Province (1824–1945) and of the Rhineland-Palatinate (1946–50); wine trade centre. Pop.: 108 700 (1999 est.). Latin name: **Confluentes** (,kɒnflʊ'ɛntiːz).

kobold ('kɒbəʊld) NOUN *German myth* 1 a mischievous household sprite. 2 a spirit that haunts subterranean places, such as mines.
▷HISTORY C19: from German; see COBALT

Köchel (*German* 'kœçəl) NOUN See **K.**

Kochi (kəʊ'tʃiː) NOUN a port in SW Japan, on central Shikoku on Urado Bay. Pop.: 322 077 (1995 est.).

kochia ('kəʊkɪə) NOUN any plant of the widely distributed annual genus *Kochia*, esp *K. Scoparia trichophila*, grown for its foliage, which turns dark red in the late summer: family *Chenopodiaceae*. Also called: **burning bush, summer cypress.**
▷HISTORY named after W. D. J. *Koch* (1771–1849), German botanist

Kodiak ('kəʊdɪ,æk) NOUN an island in S Alaska, in the Gulf of Alaska: site of the first European settlement in Alaska, made by Russians in 1784. Pop.: 13 309 (1990). Area: 8974 sq. km (3465 sq. miles).

Kodiak bear *or* **Kodiak** NOUN a large variety of the brown bear, *Ursus arctos*, inhabiting the west coast of Alaska and neighbouring islands, esp Kodiak.

Kodok ('kəʊdɒk) NOUN the modern name for **Fashoda.**

koeksister ('kʊk,sɪstə) NOUN *South African* a plaited doughnut deep-fried and soaked in syrup.
▷HISTORY Afrikaans, but possibly of Malay origin

koel ('kəʊəl) NOUN any of several parasitic cuckoos of the genus *Eudynamys*, esp *E. scolopacea*, of S and SE Asia and Australia.
▷HISTORY C19: from Hindi, from Sanskrit *kokila*

kofta ('kɒftə) NOUN an Indian dish of seasoned minced meat shaped into small balls and cooked.
▷HISTORY Urdu

koftgar ('kɒftgɑː) NOUN (in India) a person skilled in the art of inlaying steel with gold (**koftgari**).
▷HISTORY C19: Urdu

Kofu ('kəʊfuː) NOUN a city in central Japan, on S Honshu: textiles. Pop.: 201 123 (1995 est.).

Kogi ('kəʊgɪ) NOUN a state of W Nigeria. Capital: Lokoja. Pop.: 2 346 946 (1995 est.).

koha ('kəʊhə) NOUN *NZ* a gift or donation, esp of cash.
▷HISTORY Maori

kohanga reo (kɔː'hɑːŋɑː 'reɪəʊ) NOUN *NZ* an infant class in which the lessons are conducted in Maori.
▷HISTORY Maori, literally: language nest

Koheleth (kəʊ'hɛlɪθ) NOUN *Old Testament* Ecclesiastes or its author, traditionally believed to be Solomon.
▷HISTORY from Hebrew *qōheleth*

Kohen *or* **Cohen** (kɒ'hɛn, kəɪn) NOUN *Judaism* a member of the priestly family of the Tribe of Levi, descended from Aaron, who has certain ritual privileges in the synagogue service.
▷HISTORY from Hebrew, literally: priest

Kohima ('kəʊhɪ,mɑː) NOUN a city in NE India, capital of Nagaland, near the Burmese border: centre of fierce fighting in World War II, when it was surrounded by the Japanese but not captured (1944). Pop.: 21 545 (latest est.).

Koh-i-noor, Kohinor, *or* **Kohinur** (,kəʊɪ'nʊə) NOUN a very large oval Indian diamond, part of the British crown jewels since 1849, weighing 108.8 carats.
▷HISTORY C19: from Persian *Kōh-i-nūr*, literally: mountain of light, from *kōh* mountain + Arabic *nūr* light

kohl (kəʊl) NOUN a cosmetic powder used, originally esp in Muslim and Asian countries, to darken the area around the eyes. It is usually powdered antimony sulphide.
▷HISTORY C18: from Arabic *kohl;* see ALCOHOL

kohlrabi (kəʊl'rɑːbɪ) NOUN, *plural* **-bies.** a cultivated variety of cabbage, *Brassica oleracea caulorapa* (or *gongylodes*), whose thickened stem is eaten as a vegetable. Also called: **turnip cabbage.**
▷HISTORY C19: from German, from Italian *cavoli rape* (plural), from *cavolo* cabbage (from Latin *caulis*) + *rapa* turnip (from Latin); influenced by German *Kohl* cabbage

Kohoutek (kəˈhuːtɛk) NOUN a comet of almost parabolic orbit that reached its closest approach to the sun in Dec. 1973.
▷HISTORY C20: named after Luboš *Kohoutek,* Czech astronomer working in Germany who discovered it in March 1973

koi (kɔɪ) NOUN any of various ornamental forms of the common carp.
▷HISTORY Japanese

koine (ˈkɔɪniː) NOUN a common language among speakers of different languages; lingua franca.
▷HISTORY from Greek *koinē dialektos* common language

Koine (ˈkɔɪniː) NOUN (*sometimes not capital*) **the**. the Ancient Greek dialect that was the lingua franca of the empire of Alexander the Great and was widely used throughout the E Mediterranean area in Roman times.

kokako (ˈkəʊˌkɑːkəʊ) NOUN, *plural* **-kos**. a dark grey long-tailed wattled crow of New Zealand, *Callaeas cinerea*.
▷HISTORY Maori

Kokand (*Russian* kaˈkant) NOUN a city in NE Uzbekistan, in the Fergana valley. Pop.: 184 000 (1998 est.).

kokanee (kəʊˈkænɪ) NOUN a landlocked salmon, *Oncorhynchus nerka kennerlyi,* of lakes in W North America: a variety of sockeye.
▷HISTORY probably from *Kokanee* Creek, in SE British Columbia

kokobeh (ˈkʌkʌbɛ) ADJECTIVE (of certain fruit) having a rough skin: *kokobeh breadfruit.*
▷HISTORY from Twi: leprosy

Koko Nor (ˈkəʊˈkəʊ ˈnɔː) *or* **Kuku Nor** NOUN a lake in W China, in Qinghai province in the NE Tibetan Highlands at an altitude of about 3000 m (10 000 ft.): the largest lake in China. Area: about 4100 sq. km (1600 sq. miles). Chinese name: **Qinghai.**

Kokura (ˌkəʊkəˈrɑː) NOUN a former city in SW Japan, on N Kyushu: merged with adjacent townships in 1963 to form the new city of **Kitakyushu.**

kola (ˈkəʊlə) NOUN a variant spelling of **cola.**

kola nut NOUN a variant spelling of **cola nut.**

Kola Peninsula (ˈkəʊlə) NOUN a peninsula in NW Russia, between the Barents and White Seas: forms most of the Murmansk region. Area: about 130 000 sq. km (50 000 sq. miles).

Kolar Gold Fields (kəʊˈlɑː) NOUN a city in S India, in SE Karnataka: a major gold-mining centre since 1881. Pop.: 83 219 (1991 est.).

Kolding (*Danish* ˈkɔlɛŋ) NOUN a port in Denmark, in E Jutland at the head of **Kolding Fjord** (an inlet of the Little Belt). Pop.: 59 558 (1995).

Kolhapur (ˌkəʊlhɑːˈpʊə) NOUN a city in W India, in S Maharashtra: university (1963). Pop.: 406 370 (1991).

kolinsky (kəˈlɪnskɪ) NOUN, *plural* **-skies.** 1 any of various Asian minks, esp *Mustela sibirica* of Siberia. 2 the rich tawny fur of this animal.
▷HISTORY C19: from Russian *kolinski* of *Kola:* see KOLA PENINSULA

Kolkata (ˈkolkɑːtə) NOUN the official name of **Calcutta.**

kolkhoz, kolkhos (kɒlˈhɔːz; *Russian* kalˈxɔs), *or* **kolkoz** (kɒlˈkɔːz) NOUN a Russian collective farm.
▷HISTORY C20: from Russian, short for *kollektivnoe khozyaistvo* collective farm

Kolmar (ˈkɔlmar) NOUN the German name for **Colmar.**

Köln (kœln) NOUN the German name for **Cologne.**

Kol Nidre (kɔːl ˈnɪdreɪ; *Hebrew* kɔl niːˈdre) NOUN *Judaism* 1 the evening service with which Yom Kippur begins. 2 the opening prayer of that service, declaring null in advance any purely religious vows one may come to make in the coming year.
▷HISTORY Aramaic *kōl nidhrē* all the vows; the prayer's opening words

kolo (ˈkəʊləʊ) NOUN, *plural* **-los.** 1 a Serbian folk dance in which a circle of people dance slowly around one or more dancers in the centre. 2 a piece of music composed for or in the rhythm of this dance.
▷HISTORY Serbo-Croat, from Old Slavonic: wheel; related to Old English *hwēol* WHEEL

Kolomna (*Russian* kaˈlɔmnə) NOUN a city in the W central Russia, at the confluence of the Moskva and Oka Rivers: railway engineering centre. Pop.: 151 500 (1999 est.).

Kolozsvár (ˈkoloʒvaːr) NOUN the Hungarian name for **Cluj.**

Kolyma (*Russian* kəliˈma) NOUN a river in NE Russia, rising in the Kolyma Mountains north of the Sea of Okhotsk and flowing generally north to the East Siberian Sea. Length: 2600 km (1615 miles).

Kolyma Range NOUN a mountain range in NE Russia, in NE Siberia, extending about 1100 km (700 miles) between the Kolyma River and the Sea of Okhotsk. Highest peak: 1862 m (6109 ft.).

Komati (kəˈmɑːtɪ, ˈkəʊmətɪ) NOUN a river in southern Africa, rising in E South Africa and flowing east through Swaziland and Mozambique to the Indian Ocean at Delagoa Bay. Length: about 800 km (500 miles).

komatik (ˈkəʊmætɪk) NOUN a sledge having wooden runners and crossbars bound with rawhide, used by Eskimos.
▷HISTORY C20: from Eskimo (Labrador)

kombu (ˈkɒmbuː) *or* **konbu** NOUN a dark brown seaweed of the genus *Laminaria* (class Phaeophyceae) the leaves of which are dried and used esp in Japanese cookery.
▷HISTORY C19: Japanese

Komi (ˈkəʊmɪ) NOUN 1 (*plural* **Komi** *or* **Komis**) a member of a Finno-Ugric people living chiefly in the Komi Republic, in the NW Urals. 2 the Finno-Ugric language of this people; Zyrian.

Komi Republic (ˈkəʊmɪ) NOUN a constituent republic of NW Russia: annexed by the princes of Moscow in the 14th century. Capital: Syktyvkar. Pop.: 1 135 000 (2000 est.). Area: 415 900 sq. km (160 540 sq. miles).

Kommunarsk (*Russian* kəmuˈnarsk) NOUN the former name (until 1992) of **Alchevsk.**

Kommunizma Peak (*Russian* kəmuˈnjizmə) NOUN a mountain in SE Tajikistan in the Pamirs: the highest mountain in the former Soviet Union. Height: 7495 m (24 590 ft.). Former name: **Stalin Peak.**

Komodo dragon *or* **lizard** (kəˈməʊdəʊ) NOUN the largest monitor lizard, *Varanus komodoensis,* of Komodo and other East Indian islands: grows to a length of 3 m (about 10 ft.) and a weight of 135 kilograms (about 300 lbs.).

komondor (ˈkɒmənˌdɔː) NOUN a large powerful dog of an ancient Hungarian breed, originally used for sheep herding. It has a very long white coat that hangs in woolly or matted locks.

Komsomol (ˌkɒmsəˈmɒl, ˈkɒmsəˌmɒl; *Russian* kəmsaˈmɔl) NOUN (formerly) the youth association of the Soviet Union for 14- to 26-year-olds.
▷HISTORY C20: from Russian, from *Kom(munisticheski) So(yuz) Mol(odezhi)* Communist Union of Youth

Komsomolsk (*Russian* kəmsaˈmɔljsk) NOUN an industrial city in W Russia, on the Amur River: built by members of the Komsomol (Communist youth league) in 1932. Pop.: 295 100 (1999 est.).

Konakry *or* **Konakri** (*French* kɔnakri) NOUN variant spellings of **Conakry.**

konbu (ˈkɒnbuː) NOUN a variant of **kombu.**
▷HISTORY C19: Japanese

kondo (ˈkɒndəʊ) NOUN, *plural* **-dos.** (in Uganda) a thief or armed robber.
▷HISTORY C20: from Luganda

koneke (ˈkɒnˌɛkɪ) NOUN *NZ* a farm vehicle with runners in front and wheels at the rear.
▷HISTORY Maori

Kongo (ˈkɒŋgəʊ) NOUN 1 (*plural* **-gos** *or* **-go**) a member of a Negroid people of Africa living in the tropical forests of the Democratic Republic of Congo (formerly Zaïre), Congo Brazzaville, and Angola. 2 the language of this people, belonging to the Bantu group of the Niger-Congo family.

kongoni (kɒŋˈgəʊnɪ) NOUN, *plural* **-ni.** an E African hartebeest, *Alcelaphus buselaphus.* See **hartebeest** (sense 1).
▷HISTORY Swahili

Kongur Shan (ˈkʊŋgʊə ˈʃæn), **Kungur,** *or* **Qungur** NOUN a mountain in China, in W Xinjiang Uygur: the highest peak in the Pamirs. Height: 7719 m (25 325 ft.).

Königgrätz (køːnɪçˈgrɛːts) NOUN the German name for **Hradec Králové.**

Königsberg (ˈkɜːnɪgzˌbɜːg; *German* ˈkøːnɪçsbɛrk) NOUN the former name (until 1946) of **Kaliningrad.**

Königshütte (ˈkøːnɪçshytə) NOUN the German name for **Chorzów.**

konimeter (kəʊˈnɪmɪtə) NOUN a device for measuring airborne dust concentration in which samples are obtained by sucking the air through a hole and allowing it to pass over a glass plate coated with grease on which the particles collect.
▷HISTORY C20: from Greek *konia* dust + -METER

koniology *or* **coniology** (ˌkəʊnɪˈɒlədʒɪ) NOUN the study of atmospheric dust and its effects.
▷HISTORY C20: from Greek *konia* dust + -LOGY

Konstanz (ˈkɔnstants) NOUN the German name for **Constance.**

Konya *or* **Konia** (ˈkɔːnjɑː) NOUN a city in SW central Turkey: in ancient times a Phrygian city and capital of Lycaonia. Pop.: 623 333 (1997). Ancient name: **Iconium.**

koodoo (ˈkuːduː) NOUN a variant spelling of **kudu.**

kook (kuːk) NOUN *US and Canadian informal* an eccentric, crazy, or foolish person.
▷HISTORY C20: probably from CUCKOO

kookaburra (ˈkʊkəˌbʌrə) NOUN 1 a large arboreal Australian kingfisher, *Dacelo novaeguineae* (or *gigas*), with a cackling cry. Also called: **laughing jackass.** 2 a related smaller bird, *D. Leachii,* of tropical Australia and New Guinea. Also called: **blue-winged kookaburra.**
▷HISTORY C19: from a native Australian language

kooky *or* **kookie** (ˈkuːkɪ) ADJECTIVE **kookier, kookiest.** *Informal* crazy, eccentric, or foolish.

koori (ˈkʊərɪ) NOUN, *plural* **-ries.** a native Australian.
▷HISTORY C19: from a native Australian language

Kootenay *or* **Kootenai** (ˈkuːtᵊniː, ˈkuːtneɪ) NOUN a river in W North America, rising in SE British Columbia and flowing south into NW Montana, then north into Idaho before re-entering British Columbia, broadening into **Kootenay Lake,** then flowing to the Columbia River. Length: 655 km (407 miles).

kop (kɒp) NOUN a prominent isolated hill or mountain in southern Africa. See **inselberg.**
▷HISTORY from Afrikaans: head, hence high part; compare German *Kopf* head; see COP[2]

kopeck, kopek, *or* **copeck** (ˈkəʊpɛk) NOUN a monetary unit of Russia and Belarus worth one hundredth of a rouble: coins are still used as tokens for coin-operated machinery although the kopeck itself is virtually valueless.
▷HISTORY Russian *kopeika,* from *kopye* lance; so called because of the representation of Tsar Ivan IV on the coin with a lance in his hand

Kopeisk *or* **Kopeysk** (*Russian* kaˈpjejsk) NOUN a city in SW central Russia, in Chelyabinsk province: lignite mining. Pop.: 78 300 (1991 est.). Former name: **Kopi** (ˈkɔpi).

koph *or* **qoph** (kɒf) NOUN the 19th letter in the Hebrew alphabet (ק) transliterated as *q,* and pronounced as a velar or uvular stop.
▷HISTORY from Hebrew *qoph;* see QOPH

kopiyka (ˈkəʊpɪkə) NOUN a monetary unit of Ukraine, worth one hundredth of a hryvna.

kopje *or* **koppie** (ˈkɒpɪ) NOUN a small isolated hill.
▷HISTORY C19: from Afrikaans *koppie,* from Dutch *kopje,* literally: a little head, from *kop* head; see KOP

koppa (ˈkɒpə) NOUN a consonantal letter in the Greek alphabet pronounced like kappa (K) with the point of articulation further back in the throat. It became obsolete in classical (Attic) Greek orthography, but was passed on to the Romans who incorporated it into their alphabet as Q.
▷HISTORY Greek, of Semitic origin

kora (ˈkɔːrə) NOUN a West African instrument with twenty-one strings, combining features of the harp and the lute.

Koran (kɔːˈrɑːn) NOUN the sacred book of Islam, believed by Muslims to be the infallible word of God dictated to Mohammed through the medium of the angel Gabriel. Also: **Qur'an.**

▷**HISTORY** C17: from Arabic *qur'ān* reading, book; related to *qara'a* to read, recite
▸**Ko'ranic** ADJECTIVE

Korat cat ('kɔːræt) NOUN a rare type of cat originating in Thailand that has a blue-grey coat and, in the adult, brilliant green eyes.
▷**HISTORY** named after the *Korat* Plateau in Thailand

Korçë (*Albanian* 'kortʃə) NOUN a market town in SE Albania. Pop.: 67 100 (1991 est.).

Kordofan (ˌkɔːdəʊ'fæn) NOUN a region of the central Sudan: consists of a plateau with rugged uplands (the Nuba Mountains). Area: 380 548 sq. km (146 930 sq. miles).

Kordofanian (ˌkɔːdəʊ'feɪnɪən) NOUN 1 a group of languages spoken in the Kordofan and Nuba Hills of the S Sudan: classed as an independent family, probably distantly related to Niger-Congo. ◆ ADJECTIVE 2 denoting, relating to, or belonging to this group of languages. 3 of or relating to Kordofan.

Korea (kə'riːə) NOUN a former country in E Asia, now divided into two separate countries, North Korea and South Korea. Korea occupied the peninsula between the Sea of Japan and the Yellow Sea: an isolated vassal of Manchu China for three centuries until the opening of ports to Japanese trade in 1876; gained independence in 1895; annexed to Japan in 1910 and divided in 1945 into two occupation zones (Russian in the north, American in the south), which became North Korea and South Korea in 1948. Japanese name (1910–45): **Chosen**. See **North Korea, South Korea**.

Korean (kə'riːən) ADJECTIVE 1 of or relating to Korea, its people, or their language. ◆ NOUN 2 a native or inhabitant of Korea. 3 the official language of North and South Korea, considered by some scholars to be part of the Altaic family of languages.

Korean War NOUN the war (1950–53) fought between North Korea, aided by Communist China, and South Korea, supported by the US and other members of the UN.

Korea Strait NOUN a strait between South Korea and SW Japan, linking the Sea of Japan with the East China Sea.

korero ('kɒrərɔː) NOUN, *plural* **-ros**. a talk or discussion; meeting.
▷**HISTORY** Maori

korfball ('kɔːfˌbɔːl) NOUN a game similar to basketball, in which each team consists of six men and six women.
▷**HISTORY** C20: from Dutch *korfbal* basketball

Kórinthos ('kɔrinθɔs) NOUN transliteration of the Modern Greek name for **Corinth**.

korma *or* **qorma** ('kɔːmə) NOUN any of a variety of Indian dishes consisting of meat or vegetables braised with water, stock, yogurt, or cream.
▷**HISTORY** from Urdu

Korsakoffian (ˌkɔːsə'kɒfɪən) ADJECTIVE 1 relating to or suffering from Korsakoff's psychosis. ◆ NOUN 2 a person suffering from Korsakoff's psychosis.

Korsakoff's psychosis *or* **syndrome** ('kɔːsəkɒfs) NOUN a mental illness involving severe confusion and inability to retain recent memories, usually caused by alcoholism.
▷**HISTORY** C19: named after Sergei *Korsakoff* (1854–1900), Russian neuropsychiatrist, who described it

Kortrijk ('kɔrtrεik) NOUN the Flemish name for **Courtrai**.

koru ('kɒruː) NOUN *NZ* a stylized curved pattern used esp in carving.
▷**HISTORY** Maori

koruna (kɒ'ruːnə) NOUN the standard monetary unit of the Czech Republic and Slovakia, divided into 100 hellers.

kos (kəʊs) NOUN, *plural* **kos**. an Indian unit of distance having different values in different localities. It is usually between 1 and 3 miles or 1 and 5 kilometres. Also called: **coss**.
▷**HISTORY** from Hindi *kōs*

Kos *or* **Cos** (kɒs) NOUN an island in the SE Aegean Sea, in the Greek Dodecanese Islands: separated from SW Turkey by the **Kos Channel**; settled in ancient times by Dorians and became famous for literature and medicine. Pop.: 21 000 (latest est.). Area: 282 sq. km (109 sq. miles).

Kosciusko (ˌkɒsɪ'ʌskəʊ) NOUN **Mount**. a mountain in Australia, in SE New South Wales in the Australian Alps: the highest peak in Australia. Height: 2230 m (7316 ft.).

kosher ('kəʊʃə) ADJECTIVE 1 *Judaism* conforming to religious law; fit for use: esp, (of food) prepared in accordance with the dietary laws. See also **kasher, kashruth**. 2 *Informal* **a** genuine or authentic. **b** legitimate or proper.
▷**HISTORY** C19: from Yiddish, from Hebrew *kāshēr* right, proper

Košice (*Czech* 'kɔʃitsε) NOUN a city in E Slovakia: passed from Hungary to Czechoslovakia in 1920 and to Slovakia in 1993. Pop.: 241 874 (2000 est.). Hungarian name: **Kassa**.

Kosovo (*Serbo-Croat* 'kɔsɔvɔ) NOUN an autonomous province of Serbia and Montenegro, in SW Serbia: chiefly Albanian in population since the 13th century, it declared independence in 1990; Serb suppression of separatists escalated to a policy of ethnic cleansing in 1998, provoking NATO airstrikes against Serbia in 1999: now under UN administration: mainly a plateau. Capital: Priština. Pop.: 2 227 742 (1997 est.). Area: 10 887 sq. km (4203 sq. miles). Full name: **Kosovo-Metohija** (*Serbo-Croat* 'kɔsɔvɔmεˌtɔhija).

Kostroma (*Russian* kəstra'ma) NOUN a city in W central Russia, on the River Volga: fought over bitterly by Novgorod, Tver, and Moscow, until annexed by Moscow in 1329; textile centre. Pop.: 289 300 (1999 est.).

Kota *or* **Kotah** ('kəʊtə) NOUN a city in NW India, in Rajasthan on the Chambal River: textile industry. Pop.: 537 371 (1991).

Kotabaru ('kəʊtə'bɑːruː) NOUN a former name of **Jayapura**.

Kota Bharu *or* **Bahru** ('kəʊtə 'bɑːruː) NOUN a port in NE Peninsular Malaysia: capital of Kelantan state on the delta of the Kelantan River. Pop.: 219 713 (1991).

Kota Kinabalu ('kəʊtə ˌkɪnəbə'luː) NOUN a port in Malaysia, capital of Sabah state on the South China Sea: exports timber and rubber. Pop.: 208 484 (1991). Former name: **Jesselton**.

koto ('kəʊtəʊ) NOUN, *plural* **kotos**. a Japanese stringed instrument, consisting of a rectangular wooden body over which are stretched silk strings, which are plucked with plectrums or a nail-like device.
▷**HISTORY** Japanese

kotuku ('kəʊtʊkuː) NOUN, *plural* **-ku**. the white heron, *Egretta alba,* having brilliant white plumage, black legs and yellow eyes and bill.
▷**HISTORY** Maori

koulibiaca *or* **coulibiaca** (ˌkəʊlɪ'bjɑːkə) NOUN a Russian baked dish consisting of flaked fish mixed with semolina encased in pastry.
▷**HISTORY** from Russian

koumis ('kuːmɪs) NOUN a variant spelling of **kumiss**.

kouprey ('kuːpreɪ) NOUN a large wild member of the cattle tribe, *Box sauveli,* of SE Asia, having a blackish-brown body and white legs: an endangered species.
▷**HISTORY** C20: from French, from a Cambodian native name, from Pali *gō* cow + Khmer *brai* forest

Kovno ('kɔvnə) NOUN transliteration of the Russian name for **Kaunas**.

Kovrov (*Russian* kav'rɔf) NOUN a city in W central Russia, on the Klyazma River: textiles and heavy engineering. Pop.: 161 200 (1999 est.).

Kowaiti (kəʊ'weɪtɪ) ADJECTIVE, NOUN a variant of **Kuwaiti**.

Koweit (kəʊ'weɪt) NOUN a variant of **Kuwait**.

kowhai ('kəʊwaɪ, 'kəʊfaɪ) NOUN *NZ* a small leguminous tree, *Sophora tetraptera,* of New Zealand and Chile, with clusters of yellow flowers.
▷**HISTORY** C19: from Maori

Kowloon ('kaʊ'luːn) NOUN 1 a peninsula of SE China, opposite Hong Kong Island: part of the former British colony of Hong Kong. Area: 10 sq. km (3.75 sq. miles). 2 a port in Hong Kong, on Kowloon Peninsula. Pop.: 2 025 800 (2001).

kowtow (ˌkaʊ'taʊ) VERB (*intr*) 1 to touch the forehead to the ground as a sign of deference: a former Chinese custom. 2 (often foll by *to*) to be servile or obsequious (towards). ◆ NOUN 3 the act of kowtowing.
▷**HISTORY** C19: from Chinese *k'o t'ou,* from *k'o* to strike, knock + *t'ou* head
▸ˌ**kow'tower** NOUN

Kozhikode (ˌkəʊʒɪ'kəʊd) NOUN a port in SW India, in W Kerala on the Malabar coast: important European trading post (1511–1765): formerly calico-manufacturing. Pop.: 420 000 (1991). Former name: **Calicut**.

kp THE INTERNET DOMAIN NAME FOR Democratic Republic of Korea.

KP ABBREVIATION FOR: 1 Knight (of the Order) of St Patrick. 2 *US Military* **kitchen police**. ◆ 3 *Chess* SYMBOL FOR king's pawn.

kph ABBREVIATION FOR kilometres per hour.

kr THE INTERNET DOMAIN NAME FOR Republic of Korea.

Kr 1 *Currency* SYMBOL FOR **a** krona. **b** krone. ◆ 2 THE CHEMICAL SYMBOL FOR krypton.

KR *Chess* SYMBOL FOR king's rook.

kr. ABBREVIATION FOR: 1 krona. 2 krone.

Kra (krɑː) NOUN **Isthmus of**. an isthmus of SW Thailand, between the Bay of Bengal and the Gulf of Siam: the narrowest part of the Malay Peninsula. Width: about 56 km (35 miles).

kraal (krɑːl) *South African* ◆ NOUN 1 a hut village in southern Africa, esp one surrounded by a stockade. 2 an enclosure for livestock. ◆ ADJECTIVE 3 denoting or relating to the tribal aspects of the Black African way of life. ◆ VERB 4 (*tr*) to enclose (livestock) in a kraal.
▷**HISTORY** C18: from Afrikaans, from Portuguese *curral* pen; see CORRAL

kraft (krɑːft) NOUN strong wrapping paper, made from pulp processed with a sulphate solution.
▷**HISTORY** from German: force

Kragujevac (*Serbo-Croat* 'kragujεvats) NOUN a town in E central Serbia and Montenegro, in Serbia; capital of Serbia (1818–39); automobile industry. Pop.: 154 489 (2000 est.).

krait (kraɪt) NOUN any nonaggressive brightly coloured venomous elapid snake of the genus *Bungarus,* of S and SE Asia.
▷**HISTORY** C19: from Hindi *karait,* of obscure origin

Krakatoa (ˌkrɑːkə'təʊə, ˌkrækə'təʊə) *or* **Krakatau** (ˌkrɑːkə'taʊ, ˌkrækə'taʊ) NOUN a volcanic island in Indonesia, in the Sunda Strait between Java and Sumatra: partially destroyed by its eruption in 1883, the greatest in recorded history. Further eruptions 44 years later formed a new island, **Anak Krakatau** ("Child of Krakatau"). Also called: **Rakata**.

Krakau ('kraːkau) NOUN the German name for **Cracow**.

kraken ('krɑːkən) NOUN a legendary sea monster of gigantic size believed to dwell off the coast of Norway.
▷**HISTORY** C18: from Norwegian, of obscure origin

Kraków ('krakuf) NOUN the Polish name for **Cracow**.

Kramatorsk (*Russian* krəma'tɔrsk) NOUN a city in the E Ukraine: a major industrial centre of the Donets Basin. Pop.: 190 800 (1998 est.).

krameria (krə'mɪərɪə) NOUN another name for **rhatany** (plant or drug).
▷**HISTORY** C18: New Latin, named (by Linnaeus) after J. G. H. *Kramer,* an Austrian botanist

Kranj (kraːnj) NOUN the Slovene name for **Carniola**.

krans (krɑːns) NOUN *South African* a sheer rock face; precipice.
▷**HISTORY** C18: from Afrikaans

Krasnodar (*Russian* krəsna'dar) NOUN an industrial city in SW Russia, on the Kuban River. Pop.: 643 400 (1999 est.). Former name (until 1920): **Yekaterinodar**.

Krasnoyarsk (*Russian* krəsna'jarsk) NOUN a city in E central Russia, on the Yenisei River: the country's largest hydroelectric power station is nearby. Pop.: 877 800 (1999 est.).

K ration NOUN a small package containing emergency rations used by US and Allied forces in the field in World War II.
▷**HISTORY** C20: *K,* from the initial of the surname of Ancel *Keys* (born 1904), US physiologist who instigated it

Kraut (kraut) NOUN, ADJECTIVE *Slang* a derogatory word for **German**.
▷**HISTORY** from German (*Sauer*)*kraut,* literally: (pickled) cabbage

Krav Maga (kræv 'mægə) NOUN a form of exercise based on unarmed combat movements developed by the Israeli armed forces.

Krebs cycle NOUN a stage of tissue respiration: a series of biochemical reactions occurring in mitochondria in the presence of oxygen by which acetate, derived from the breakdown of foodstuffs, is converted to carbon dioxide and water, with the release of energy. Also called: **citric acid cycle, tricarboxylic acid cycle.**
▷HISTORY C20: named after Hans Adolf *Krebs* (1900–81), German-born British biochemist

Krefeld ('kreɪfɛld; *German* 'kre:fɛlt) NOUN a city in Germany, in W North Rhine-Westphalia: textile industries. Pop.: 242 800 (1999 est.).

Kremenchug (*Russian* krɪmɪn'tʃuk) NOUN an industrial city in the E central Ukraine on the Dnieper River. Pop.: 240 700 (1998 est.).

kremlin ('krɛmlɪn) NOUN the citadel of any Russian city.
▷HISTORY C17: from obsolete German *Kremelin,* from Russian *kreml*

Kremlin ('krɛmlɪn) NOUN [1] the 12th-century citadel in Moscow, containing the former Imperial Palace, three Cathedrals, and the offices of the Russian government. [2] (formerly) the central government of the Soviet Union.

Kremlinology (ˌkrɛmlɪn'ɒlədʒɪ) NOUN (formerly) the study and analysis of the policies and practices of the Soviet government.
▸**ˌKremlin'ologist** NOUN

Krems (*German* krɛms) NOUN a town in NE Austria, in Lower Austria on the River Danube. Pop.: 22 830 (1991).

kreplach ('krɛplɑ:k, -lɑ:x) PLURAL NOUN small filled dough casings usually served in soup.
▷HISTORY C20: from Yiddish

kreutzer *or* **kreuzer** ('krɔɪtsə) NOUN any of various former copper and silver coins of Germany or Austria.
▷HISTORY C16: from German *Kreuzer,* from *Kreuz* cross, from Latin *crux;* referring to the cross originally stamped upon such coins

kriegspiel ('kri:gˌspi:l) NOUN [1] (*sometimes capital*) a form of war game in which symbols representing military formations are moved about on maps. [2] a variation of chess in which each player has his own board and men and does not see his opponent's board and men. The moves are regulated by an umpire on a third board out of sight of both players.
▷HISTORY C19: from German *Kriegsspiel* war game

Kriemhild ('kri:mhɪlt) *or* **Kriemhilde** ('kri:mˌhɪldə) NOUN (in the *Nibelungenlied*) the wife of Siegfried. She corresponds to Gudrun in Norse mythology.

krill (krɪl) NOUN, *plural* **krill.** any small shrimplike marine crustacean of the order *Euphausiacea*: the principal food of whalebone whales.
▷HISTORY C20: from Norwegian *kril* young fish

krimmer *or* **crimmer** ('krɪmə) NOUN a tightly curled light grey fur obtained from the skins of lambs from the Crimean region.
▷HISTORY C20: from German, from *Krim* CRIMEA

Krio ('kri:əʊ) NOUN [1] the English-based creole widely used as a lingua franca in Sierra Leone. Its principal language of admixture is Yoruba. [2] (*plural* **-os**) a native speaker of Krio. [3] (*modifier*) of or relating to the Krio language or Krios: *Krio poetry.*
▷HISTORY alteration of CREOLE

Kriol ('krɪɒl) NOUN a creole language used by Aboriginal communities in the northern regions of Australia, developed from Northern Territory pidgin.

kris (krɪs) NOUN a Malayan and Indonesian stabbing or slashing knife with a scalloped edge. Also called: **crease, creese.**
▷HISTORY C16: from Malay *kris*

Krishna[1] ('krɪʃnə) NOUN a river in S India, rising in the Western Ghats and flowing generally southeast to the Bay of Bengal. Length: 1300 km (800 miles). Also called: **Kistna.**

Krishna[2] ('krɪʃnə) NOUN *Hinduism* the most celebrated of the Hindu deities, whose life story is told in the *Mahabharata*.
▷HISTORY via Hindi from Sanskrit, literally: dark, black
▸**'Krishnaism** NOUN

Kriss Kringle (ˌkrɪs 'krɪŋgᵊl) NOUN *Chiefly US* another name for **Santa Claus.**

▷HISTORY changed from German *Christkindl* little Christ child, from CHRIST+ *Kindl,* from *Kind* child

Kristiania (ˌkrɪstɪ'ɑ:nɪə) NOUN a former name (1877–1924) of **Oslo.**

Kristiansand *or* **Christiansand** ('krɪstjənˌsænd; *Norwegian* kristian'san) NOUN a port in S Norway, on the Skagerrak: shipbuilding. Pop.: 65 543 (1990).

Kristianstad ('krɪstjənˌstɑ:d; *Swedish* kri'ʃanstɑ:d) NOUN a town in S Sweden: founded in 1614 as a Danish fortress, it was finally acquired by Sweden in 1678. Pop.: 73 543 (1994).

Kríti ('kriti) NOUN transliteration of the Modern Greek name for **Crete.**

Krivoy Rog (*Russian* kri'vɔj 'rɔk) NOUN a city in the SE Ukraine: founded in the 17th century by Cossacks; iron-mining centre; iron- and steelworks. Pop.: 715 400 (1998 est.).

KRL ABBREVIATION FOR knowledge representation language (in artificial intelligence).

kromesky (krə'mɛskɪ) NOUN, *plural* **-kies.** a croquette consisting of a piece of bacon wrapped round minced meat or fish.
▷HISTORY C19: from Russian *kromochka,* diminutive of *kroma* slice of bread

krona ('krəʊnə) NOUN, *plural* **kronor** ('krəʊnə). the standard monetary unit of Sweden, divided into 100 öre.

króna ('krəʊnə) NOUN, *plural* **-nur** (-nə). the standard monetary unit of Iceland, divided into 100 aurar.

krone[1] ('krəʊnə) NOUN, *plural* **-ner** (-nə). [1] the standard monetary unit of Denmark, the Faeroe Islands, and Greenland, divided into 100 øre. [2] the standard monetary unit of Norway, divided into 100 øre.
▷HISTORY C19: from Danish or Norwegian, from Middle Low German *krōne,* ultimately from Latin *corōna* CROWN

krone[2] ('krəʊnə) NOUN, *plural* **-nen** (-nən). [1] a former German gold coin worth ten marks. [2] a former Austrian monetary unit.
▷HISTORY C19: from German, literally: crown; see KRONE[1]

Kronecker delta ('krɒnɪkə) NOUN *Maths* a function of two variables, *i* and *j*, that has a value of zero unless $i = j$, when it has a value of unity. Symbol: δ_{ij}.
▷HISTORY named after Leopold *Kronecker* (1823–91), German mathematician

Kronos ('krəʊnɒs) NOUN a variant of **Cronus.**

Kronstadt NOUN [1] (*Russian* kran'ʃtat) a port in NW Russia, on Kotlin island in the Gulf of Finland: naval base. Pop.: 44 400 (1994 est.). [2] ('kro:nʃtat) the German name for **Braşov.**

kroon (kru:n) NOUN, *plural* **kroons** *or* **krooni** ('kru:nɪ). the standard monetary unit of Estonia, divided into 100 senti.
▷HISTORY Estonian *kron,* from German *Krone* KRONE[2]

KRP *Chess* SYMBOL FOR king's rook's pawn.

Kruger National Park NOUN a wildlife sanctuary in NE South Africa: the world's largest game reserve. Area: over 21 700 sq. km (8400 sq. miles).

Krugerrand ('kru:gəˌrænd) NOUN a South African coin used for investment only and containing 1 troy ounce of gold.
▷HISTORY C20: from Stephanus Johannes Paulus *Kruger* (1825–1904), Boer statesman + RAND[1]

Krugersdorp ('kru:gəzˌdɔ:p) NOUN a city in NE South Africa, on the Witwatersrand, at an altitude of 1722 m (5650 ft.): a gold-, manganese-, and uranium-mining centre. Pop. (urban area): 203 168 (1996).

kruller ('krʌlə) NOUN a variant spelling of **cruller.**

krummholz ('krʊmˌhəʊlts) NOUN *Botany* another name for **elfin forest, woodland.**
▷HISTORY C20: from German *krumm* bent + *Holz* wood

krummhorn ('krʌmˌhɔ:n) NOUN a variant spelling of **crumhorn.**

Krušné Hory ('krʊʃnɛ 'hɔrɪ) NOUN the Czech name for the **Erzgebirge.**

Krym *or* **Krim** (krɪm) NOUN transliteration of the Russian name for **Crimea.**

krypton ('krɪptɒn) NOUN an inert gaseous element occurring in trace amounts in air and used in fluorescent lights and lasers. Symbol: Kr; atomic no.: 36; atomic wt.: 83.80; valency: 0; density: 3.733 kg/m^3; melting pt.: –157.37°C; boiling pt.: –153.23±0.10°C.
▷HISTORY C19: from Greek, from *kruptos* hidden; see CRYPT

krytron ('kraɪtrɒn) NOUN *Electronics* a type of fast electronic gas-discharge switch, used as a trigger in nuclear weapons.

KS [1] ABBREVIATION FOR Kansas. ◆ [2] INTERNATIONAL CAR REGISTRATION FOR Kyrgyzstan.

Kshatriya ('kʃætrɪə) NOUN a member of the second of the four main Hindu castes, the warrior caste.
▷HISTORY C18: from Sanskrit, from *kshatra* rule

KStJ ABBREVIATION FOR Knight of the Order of St John.

kt ABBREVIATION FOR: [1] karat. [2] *Nautical* knot.

Kt [1] Also: **Knt.** ABBREVIATION FOR knight. ◆ [2] Also: **N.** *Chess* SYMBOL FOR knight.

KT ABBREVIATION FOR: [1] Knight of the Order of the Thistle (a Brit title). [2] Knight Templar.

K/T boundary NOUN *Geology* **a** Cretaceous/Tertiary boundary: the time zone comprising the end of the Cretaceous and the beginning of the Tertiary periods. **b** (*as modifier*): *K/T boundary sediments.*
▷HISTORY C20 *K* and *T*, symbols for Cretaceous and Tertiary, respectively

Kuala Lumpur ('kwɑ:lə 'lʊmpʊə, -pə) NOUN a city in Malaysia, in the SW Malay Peninsula: formerly (until 1999) the capital of Malaysia; became capital of the Federated Malay States in 1895, and of Malaysia in 1963; capital of Selangor state from 1880 to 1973, when it was made a federal territory. Pop.: 1 145 075 (1991).

Kuan Yin *or* **Kwan Yin** (kwan jɪn) NOUN a female Chinese Bodhisattva of compassion, regarded as the protector of women and children and patron of sailors. Japanese name: **Kannon.**
▷HISTORY from Chinese: one who hears the sounds of the world

Kuban (*Russian* ku'banj) NOUN a river in SW Russia, rising in the Caucasus Mountains and flowing north and northwest to the Sea of Azov. Length: 906 km (563 miles).

Kuch Bihar ('ku:tʃ bɪ'hɑ:) NOUN a variant spelling of **Cooch Behar.**

kuchen ('ku:xən) NOUN a breadlike cake containing apple, nuts, and sugar, originating from Germany.
▷HISTORY German: CAKE

Kuching ('ku:tʃɪŋ) NOUN a port in E Malaysia, capital of Sarawak state, on the Sarawak River 24 km (15 miles) from its mouth. Pop.: 147 729 (1991).

kudlik ('ku:dlɪk) NOUN *Canadian* an Inuit soapstone seal-oil lamp.
▷HISTORY Inuktitut

kudos ('kju:dɒs) NOUN (*functioning as singular*) acclaim, glory, or prestige.
▷HISTORY C18: from Greek

kudu *or* **koodoo** ('ku:du:) NOUN either of two spiral-horned antelopes, *Tragelaphus strepsiceros* (**greater kudu**) or *T. imberbis* (**lesser kudu**), which inhabit the bush of Africa.
▷HISTORY C18: from Afrikaans *koedoe,* probably from Khoi

kudzu ('kʊdzu:) NOUN a hairy leguminous climbing plant, *Pueraria thunbergiana,* of China and Japan, with trifoliate leaves and purple fragrant flowers.
▷HISTORY from Japanese *kuzu*

kueh ('kɔeɪ) NOUN (*functioning as singular or plural*) (in Malaysia) any cake of Malay, Chinese, or Indian origin.
▷HISTORY from Malay

Kuenlun ('kʊn'lʊn) NOUN a variant spelling of **Kunlun.**

Kufic *or* **Cufic** ('ku:fɪk, 'kju:-) ADJECTIVE [1] of, relating to, or denoting an early form of the Arabic alphabet employed in making copies of the Koran. ◆ NOUN [2] the script formed by the letters of this alphabet.

kufiyah (kʊ'fi:jə) NOUN a variant of **keffiyeh.**

kuia ('ku:jə) NOUN *NZ* a Maori female elder or elderly woman.
▷HISTORY Maori

Kuibyshev *or* **Kuybyshev** (*Russian* 'kujbɪʃəf) NOUN the former name (until 1991) of **Samara.**

Kuiper belt ('kɪpə) NOUN a region of the solar system beyond the orbit of Neptune, some 30–1000 astronomical units from the sun, containing up to one thousand million icy planetesimals or comet nuclei. See also **Oort cloud.**
▷HISTORY C20: named after G. P. *Kuiper* (1905–73), Dutch American astronomer, who proposed it in 1951

Ku Klux Klan ('kuː 'klʌks 'klæn) NOUN 1 a secret organization of White Southerners formed after the US Civil War to fight Black emancipation and Northern domination. 2 a secret organization of White Protestant Americans, mainly in the South, who use violence against Blacks, Jews, and other minority groups.
▷HISTORY C19 *Ku Klux,* probably based on Greek *kuklos* CIRCLE + *Klan* CLAN
▸**Ku Kluxer** *or* **Ku Klux Klanner** NOUN ▸**Ku Kluxism** NOUN

kukri ('kʊkrɪ) NOUN, *plural* **-ris.** a knife with a curved blade that broadens towards the point, esp as used by Gurkhas.
▷HISTORY from Hindi

Kuku Nor ('kuː'kuː 'nɔː) NOUN a variant of **Koko Nor.**

kula ('kuːlə) NOUN a ceremonial gift exchange practised among a group of islanders in the W Pacific, used to establish relations between islands.
▷HISTORY of Melanesian origin

kulak ('kuːlæk) NOUN (in Russia after 1906) a member of the class of peasants who became proprietors of their own farms. After the October Revolution the kulaks opposed collectivization of land, but in 1929 Stalin initiated their liquidation.
▷HISTORY C19: from Russian: fist, hence, tightfisted person; related to Turkish *kol* arm

kulan ('kuːˌlɑːn) NOUN the Asiatic wild ass of the Russian steppes, probably a variety of kiang or onager.
▷HISTORY C18: from Kirghiz

kulfi ('kʊlfɪ) NOUN an Indian dessert made by freezing milk which has been concentrated by boiling away some of the water in it, and flavoured with nuts and cardamom seeds.

Kultur (kʊl'tʊə) NOUN (often used ironically) German civilization, esp as characterized by authoritarianism and earnestness.
▷HISTORY German, from Latin *cultūra* CULTURE

Kulturkampf (kʊl'tʊəˌkæmpf, 'kʊltə-) NOUN the struggle of the Prussian state against the Roman Catholic Church (1872–87), which took the form of laws designed to bring education, marriage, etc., under the control of the state.
▷HISTORY German: culture struggle

Kulun ('kuː'luːn) NOUN the Chinese name for **Ulan Bator.**

Kum (kʊm) NOUN a variant spelling of **Qom.**

Kumamoto (ˌkʊmə'məʊtəʊ) NOUN a city in SW Japan, on W central Kyushu: Kumamoto Medical University (1949). Pop.: 650 322 (1995).

kumara *or* **kumera** ('kuːmərə) NOUN the NZ name for **sweet potato.**
▷HISTORY Maori

Kumasi (kuː'mæsɪ) NOUN a city in S Ghana: seat of Ashanti kings since 1663; university (1961); market town for a cocoa-producing region. Pop.: 578 000 (1998 est.).

Kumayri (*Russian* ˌkʊmaɪ'rɪ) NOUN a city in NW Armenia: textile centre. Pop.: 120 000 (1995 est.). Former names: **Aleksandropol** (1840–1924), **Leninakan** (1924–91).

kumbaloi (ˌkʊmbə'lɔɪ) PLURAL NOUN another name for **worry beads.**
▷HISTORY C20: Modern Greek

Kumbh Mela (ˌkʊm 'meɪlə, ˌkʊm mə'lɑː) NOUN a Hindu festival held once every twelve years in one of four sacred sites, where bathing for purification from sin is considered especially efficacious.
▷HISTORY from Hindi, literally: pitcher festival or Aquarius festival, from Sanskrit *kumbha* pot, Aquarius + *melā* assembly

kumiss, koumiss, koumis, *or* **koumyss** ('kuːmɪs) NOUN a drink made from fermented mare's or other milk, drunk by certain Asian tribes, esp in Russia or used for dietetic and medicinal purposes.
▷HISTORY C17: from Russian *kumys,* from Kazan Tatar *kumyz*

kumite ('kuːmɪˌteɪ) NOUN *Martial Arts* freestyle sparring or fighting.
▷HISTORY C20: Japanese, literally: sparring

kümmel ('kʊməl; *German* 'kyməl) NOUN a German liqueur flavoured with aniseed and cumin.
▷HISTORY C19: from German *Kümmel,* from Old High German *kumil,* probably variant of *kumin* CUMIN

kummerbund ('kʌməˌbʌnd) NOUN a variant spelling of **cummerbund.**

Kumon ('kuːmɔːn) *or* **Kumon Method** NOUN **a** a method of teaching mathematics, reading, and languages in which students start at a level of work at which they have a firm grasp of facts and concepts and then, working at their own pace in an individualized study programme of problem-solving on worksheets, progress by small steps to more advanced levels of knowledge. **b** (*as modifier*): *Kumon mathematics.*
▷HISTORY C20: named after its founder, Toru *Kumon* (1914–95), a Japanese mathematics teacher

kumquat *or* **cumquat** ('kʌmkwɒt) NOUN 1 any of several small Chinese trees of the rutaceous genus *Fortunella.* 2 the small round orange fruit of such a tree, with a sweet rind, used in preserves and confections.
▷HISTORY C17: from Chinese (Cantonese) *kam kwat,* representing Mandarin Chinese *chin chü* golden orange

kuna ('kuːnə) *plural* **-ne** (-nɪ) NOUN the standard monetary unit of Croatia, divided into 100 lipa.

kundalini ('kʊndəˌliːnɪ) NOUN (*sometimes capital*) (in yoga) the life force that resides at the base of the spine.

kung fu ('kʌŋ 'fuː) NOUN a Chinese martial art combining principles of karate and judo.
▷HISTORY from Chinese: martial art

Kungur ('kʊŋgʊə) NOUN a variant transliteration of the Chinese name for **Kongur Shan.**

Kunlun ('kʊn'lʊn), **Kuenlun,** *or* **Kwenlun** NOUN a mountain range in China, between the Tibetan plateau and the Tarim Basin, extending over 1600 km (1000 miles) east from the Pamirs: the largest mountain system of Asia. Highest peak: Ulugh Muztagh, 7723 m (25 338 ft.).

Kunming *or* **K'un-ming** ('kʊn'mɪŋ) NOUN a city in SW China, capital of Yunnan province, near Lake Tien: important during World War II as a Chinese military centre, American air base, and transport terminus for the Burma Road; Yunnan University (1934). Pop.: 1 350 640 (1999 est.).

kunzite ('kʊntsaɪt) NOUN a pink-coloured transparent variety of the mineral spodumene: a gemstone.
▷HISTORY C20: named after George F. *Kunz* (1856–1932), US gem expert

Kuomintang ('kwəʊ'mɪn'tæŋ) NOUN the political party founded by Sun Yat-sen in 1911 and dominant in China from 1928 until 1949 under the leadership of Chiang Kai-shek. Since then it has been the official ruling party of Taiwan.
▷HISTORY C20: from Chinese (Mandarin): National People's Party, from *kuo* nation + *min* people + *tang* party

Kuopio (*Finnish* 'kwɔpjɔ) NOUN a city in S central Finland. Pop.: 83 955 (1994).

Kura (kʊ'rɑː) NOUN a river in W Asia, rising in NE Turkey and flowing across Georgia and Azerbaijan to the Caspian Sea. Length: 1515 km (941 miles).

kurchatovium (ˌkɜːtʃə'təʊvɪəm) NOUN another name for **rutherfordium,** esp as used in the former Soviet Union
▷HISTORY C20: from Russian, named after I. V. *Kurchatov* (1903–60), Soviet physicist

Kurd (kɜːd) NOUN a member of a nomadic people living chiefly in E Turkey, N Iraq, and W Iran.

kurdaitcha (kə'daɪtʃə) NOUN (in certain Central Australian Aboriginal tribes) the man with the mission of avenging the death of a tribesman. Also: **kadaitcha.**

kurdaitcha shoes PLURAL NOUN (in certain Central Australian Aboriginal tribes) the emu-feather shoes worn by the kurdaitcha on his mission so that his footsteps may not be traced. Also: **kadaitcha shoes.**

Kurdish ('kɜːdɪʃ) NOUN 1 the language of the Kurds, belonging to the West Iranian branch of the Indo-European family. ◆ ADJECTIVE 2 of or relating to the Kurds or their language.

Kurdistan, Kurdestan, *or* **Kordestan** (ˌkɜːdɪ'stɑːn) NOUN a large plateau and mountainous region, between the Caspian Sea and the Black Sea, south of the Caucasus. Area: over 29 000 sq. km (74 000 sq. miles).

Kure (kuː'reɪ) NOUN a port in SW Japan, on SW Honshu: a naval base; shipyards. Pop.: 209 477 (1995 est.).

Kurgan (*Russian* kur'gan) NOUN a city in W Russia, on the Tobol River: industrial centre for an agricultural region. Pop.: 367 200 (1999 est.).

kuri ('kuːrɪ) NOUN, *plural* **-ris.** *NZ* a mongrel dog. Also called: **goorie.**
▷HISTORY Maori

Kuril Islands *or* **Kurile Islands** (kʊ'riːl) PLURAL NOUN a chain of 56 volcanic islands off the NE coast of Asia, extending for 1200 km (750 miles) from the S tip of the Kamchatka Peninsula to NE Hokkaido. Area: 14 990 sq. km (6020 sq. miles). Japanese name: **Chishima.**

Kurland ('kʊələnd) NOUN a variant spelling of **Courland.**

Kuroshio (kə'rəʊʃɪˌəʊ) NOUN another name for **Japan Current.**

kurrajong *or* **currajong** ('kʌrəˌdʒɒŋ) NOUN any of various Australian trees or shrubs, esp *Brachychiton populneum,* a sterculiaceous tree that yields a tough durable fibre.
▷HISTORY C19: from a native Australian language

kursaal ('kɜːzᵊl) NOUN 1 a public room at a health resort. 2 an amusement park at a seaside or other resort.
▷HISTORY from German, literally: cure room

Kursk (*Russian* kursk) NOUN a city in W Russia: industrial centre of an agricultural region: scene of a major Soviet victory (1943). Pop.: 445 400 (1999 est.).

kurta *or* **khurta** ('kʊətə) NOUN a long loose garment like a shirt without a collar worn in India.
▷HISTORY Hindi

kurtosis (kə'təʊsɪs) NOUN *Statistics* a measure of the concentration of a distribution around its mean, esp the statistic $B_2 = m_4/m_2^2$ where m_2 and m_4 are respectively the second and fourth moment of the distribution around the mean. In a normal distribution $B_2 = 3$. See also **platykurtic, mesokurtic, leptokurtic.** Compare **skewness.**
▷HISTORY from Greek: curvature, from *kurtos* arched

kuru ('kʊruː) NOUN a degenerative disease of the nervous system, restricted to certain tribes in New Guinea, marked by loss of muscular control and thought to be caused by a slow virus.
▷HISTORY C20: from a native name

kuruş (kʊ'ruːʃ) NOUN, *plural* **-ruş.** a Turkish monetary unit worth one hundredth of a lira. Also called: **piastre.**
▷HISTORY from Turkish

Kurzeme ('kʊrzɛmɛ) NOUN the Latvian name for **Courland.**

Kush (kʌʃ, kʊʃ) NOUN a variant spelling of **Cush.**

Kuskokwim ('kʌskəˌkwɪm) NOUN a river in SW Alaska, rising in the Alaska Range and flowing generally southwest to **Kuskokwim Bay** an inlet of the Bering Sea. Length: about 970 km (600 miles).

Kutaisi (*Russian* kuta'isi) NOUN an industrial city in W Georgia on the Rioni River: one of the oldest towns of the Caucasus. Pop.: 240 000 (1997 est.).

Kutch *or* **Cutch** (kʌtʃ) NOUN 1 a former state of W India, on the **Gulf of Kutch** (an inlet of the Arabian Sea): part of Gujarat state since 1960. 2 **Rann of.** an extensive salt waste in W central India, and S Pakistan: consists of the Great Rann in the north and the Little Rann in the southeast; seasonal alternation between marsh and desert; some saltworks. In 1968 an international tribunal awarded about 10 per cent of the border area to Pakistan. Area: 23 000 sq. km (9000 sq. miles).

kutu ('kuːtuː) NOUN *NZ* a slang word for **body louse** (see **louse** (sense 1)). Also called: **cootie.**
▷HISTORY Maori

Kuwait (kʊ'weɪt) *or* **Koweit** NOUN 1 a state on the NW coast of the Persian Gulf: came under British protection in 1899 and gained independence in 1961; invaded by Iraq in 1990; liberated by

US-led UN forces 1991 in the first Gulf War: mainly desert. The economy is dependent on oil. Official language: Arabic. Official religion: Muslim. Currency: dinar. Capital: Kuwait. Pop.: 2 275 000 (2001 est.). Area: 24 280 sq. km (9375 sq. miles). [2] the capital of Kuwait: a port on the Persian Gulf. Pop.: 28 859 (1995).

Kuwaiti (kʊˈweɪtɪ) *or* **Koweiti** ADJECTIVE [1] of or relating to Kuwait or its inhabitants. ◆ NOUN [2] a native or inhabitant of Kuwait.

Kuznetsk Basin (*Russian* kuzˈnjetsk) *or* **Kuzbass** (*Russian* kuzˈbas) NOUN a region of S Russia, in the Kemerovo Region of W Siberia: the richest coalfield in the country, with reserves of iron ore. Chief industrial centre: Novokuznetsk. Area: about 69 900 sq. km (27 000 sq. miles).

kV ABBREVIATION FOR kilovolt.

KV ABBREVIATION FOR Köchel Verzeichnis. See **K.**
▷HISTORY German, literally: Köchel catalogue

Kvaløy (*Norwegian* ˈkvaːlœj) NOUN two islands in the Arctic Ocean, off the N coast of Norway: **North Kvaløy,** 329 sq. km (127 sq. miles), and **South Kvaløy,** 735 sq. km (284 sq. miles).

kvass, kvas, *or* **quass** (kvɑːs) NOUN an alcoholic drink of low strength made in Russia and E Europe from cereals and stale bread.
▷HISTORY C16: from Russian *kvas;* related to Old Slavic *kvasŭ* yeast, Latin *cāseus* cheese

kvetch (kvɛtʃ) VERB (*intr*) *Slang, chiefly US* to complain or grumble, esp incessantly.
▷HISTORY C20: from Yiddish *kvetshn,* literally: to squeeze, press

kvetchy (ˈkvɛtʃɪ) ADJECTIVE *Slang, chiefly US* tending to grumble or complain; complaining.
▸ˈ**kvetchily** ADVERB ▸ˈ**kvetchiness** NOUN

kw THE INTERNET DOMAIN NAME FOR Kuwait.

kW ABBREVIATION FOR kilowatt.

Kwa (kwɑː) NOUN [1] a group of languages, now generally regarded as a branch of the Niger-Congo family, spoken in an area of W Africa extending from the Ivory Coast to E Nigeria and including Akan, Ewe, Yoruba, and Ibo. ◆ ADJECTIVE [2] relating to or belonging to this group of languages.

kwacha (ˈkwɑːtʃɑː) NOUN [1] the standard monetary unit of Zambia, divided into 100 ngwee. [2] the standard monetary unit of Malawi, divided into 100 tambala.
▷HISTORY from a native word in Zambia

kwaito (ˈkwaɪˌtəʊ) NOUN a type of South African pop music with lyrics spoken over an instrumental backing.
▷HISTORY C20: from *Amakwaito*, a gang in Sophiatown, South Africa, in the 1950s

Kwajalein (ˈkwɑːdʒəˌleɪn) NOUN an atoll in the W Pacific, in the W Marshall Islands, in the central part of the Ralik Chain. Length: about 125 km (78 miles).

Kwakiutl (ˌkwɑːkɪˈuːtᵊl) NOUN [1] (*plural* **-utl** *or* **-utls**) a member of a North American Indian people of N Vancouver Island and the adjacent mainland. [2] the language of this people, belonging to the Wakashan family.

Kwangchow (ˈkwæŋˈtʃaʊ) NOUN a variant transliteration of the Chinese name for **Canton.**

Kwangchowan (ˈkwæŋˈtʃaʊˈwɑːn) NOUN a territory of SE China, in SW Kwantung province: leased to France as part of French Indochina from 1898 to 1945. Area: 842 sq. km (325 sq. miles).

Kwangju (ˈkwæŋˈdʒuː) NOUN a city in SW South Korea: an important military base during the Korean War; cotton textile industry. Pop.: 1 257 504 (1995).

Kwangsi-Chuang Autonomous Region (ˈkwæŋˈsiːˈtʃwæŋ) NOUN a variant transliteration of the Chinese name for **Guangxi Zhuang Autonomous Region.**

Kwangtung (ˈkwæŋˈtʊŋ) NOUN a variant transliteration of the Chinese name for **Guangdong.**

Kwantung Leased Territory (ˌkwænˈtʊŋ) NOUN a strategic territory of NE China, at the S tip of the Liaotung Peninsula of Manchuria: leased forcibly by Russia in 1898; taken over by Japan in 1905; occupied by the Soviet Union in 1945 and subsequently returned to China on the condition of shared administration; made part of Liaoning province by China in 1954. Area: about 3400 sq. km (1300 sq. miles). Also called: **Kuan-tung.**

kwanza (ˈkwænzə) NOUN the standard monetary unit of Angola, divided into 100 lwei.
▷HISTORY from a Bantu language

Kwanzaa (ˈkwænzɑː) NOUN a seven-day festival beginning on Dec. 26 when African-Americans celebrate family, community, and culture.
▷HISTORY C20: from Swahili (*matunda ya*) *kwanza* first (fruits)

Kwara (ˈkwɑːrə) NOUN a state of W Nigeria: mainly wooded savanna. Capital: Ilorin. Pop.: 1 751 464 (1995 est.). Area: 36 825 sq. km (14 218 sq. miles).

kwashiorkor (ˌkwæʃɪˈɔːkə) NOUN severe malnutrition of infants and young children, esp soon after weaning, resulting from dietary deficiency of protein.
▷HISTORY C20: from a native word in Ghana

KwaZulu (kwɑːˈzuːluː) NOUN (formerly) a Bantu homeland in South Africa, in Natal: abolished in 1993 and became part of the new province of KwaZulu/Natal in 1994. Capital: Ulundi.

KwaZulu/Natal (kwɑːˌzuːluːnəˈtæl, -ˈtɑːl) NOUN a province of NE South Africa; replaced the former province of Natal in 1994: service industries. Capital: Pietermaritzburg. Pop.: 8 924 643 (1999 est.). Area: 92 180 sq. km (35 591 sq. miles).

Kwedien (kwɪˈdiːn) NOUN a young African boy, esp one who has not yet undergone the rites of initiation.
▷HISTORY from Xhosa *inKwenkwe* boy

Kweichow *or* **Kueichou** (ˈkweɪˈtʃaʊ) NOUN a variant transliteration of the Chinese name for **Guizhou.**

Kweilin *or* **Kuei-lin** (ˈkweɪˈlɪn) NOUN a variant transliteration of the Chinese name for **Guilin.**

Kweisui (ˈkweɪˈsweɪ) NOUN the former name of **Hohhot.**

Kweiyang *or* **Kuei-yang** (ˈkweɪˈjæŋ) NOUN a variant transliteration of the Chinese name for **Guiyang.**

kwela (ˈkweɪlə, ˈkwɛlə) NOUN a type of pop music popular among the Black communities of South Africa.
▷HISTORY C20: said to be from Zulu or Xhosa: jump up

kWh ABBREVIATION FOR kilowatt-hour.

KWIC (kwɪk) NOUN ACRONYM FOR key word in context (esp in the phrase **KWIC index**).

KWOC (kwɒk) NOUN ACRONYM FOR key word out of context.

KWT INTERNATIONAL CAR REGISTRATION FOR Kuwait.

ky THE INTERNET DOMAIN NAME FOR Cayman Islands.

Ky. *or* **KY** ABBREVIATION FOR Kentucky.

kyanite (ˈkaɪəˌnaɪt) NOUN a grey, green, or blue mineral consisting of aluminium silicate in triclinic crystalline form. It occurs in metamorphic rocks and is used as a refractory. Formula AL_2SiO_5.
▸**kyanitic** (ˌkaɪəˈnɪtɪk) ADJECTIVE

kyanize *or* **kyanise** (ˈkaɪəˌnaɪz) VERB (*tr*) to treat (timber) with corrosive sublimate to make it resistant to decay.
▷HISTORY C19: after J. H. *Kyan* (died 1850), English inventor of the process
▸ˌ**kyaniˈzation** *or* ˌ**kyaniˈsation** NOUN

kyat (kɪˈɑːt) NOUN the standard monetary unit of Myanmar, divided into 100 pyas.
▷HISTORY from Burmese

kybo (ˈkaɪˌbəʊ) NOUN *Austral, slang* a temporary lavatory constructed for use when camping.
▷HISTORY said to be an acronym for *k*(*eep*) *y*(*our*) *b*(*owels*) *o*(*pen*)

kybosh (ˈkaɪˌbɒʃ) a variant spelling of **kibosh.**

kye (kaɪ) NOUN (*functioning as plural*) a Scottish and Northern English variant of **kine.**

kyle (kaɪl) NOUN *Scot* (esp in place names) a narrow strait or channel: *Kyle of Lochalsh.*
▷HISTORY C16: from Gaelic *caol,* from *caol* narrow

kylie *or* **kiley** (ˈkaɪlɪ) NOUN *Austral* a boomerang that is flat on one side and convex on the other.
▷HISTORY C19: from a native Australian language

kylin (ˈkiːˈlɪn) NOUN (in Chinese art) a mythical animal of composite form.
▷HISTORY C19: from Chinese *ch'i-lin,* literally: male-female

kylix *or* **cylix** (ˈkaɪlɪks, ˈkɪl-) NOUN, *plural* **-likes** (-lɪˌkiːz). a shallow two-handled drinking vessel used in ancient Greece.
▷HISTORY C19: from Greek *kulix* cup; compare CHALICE

kyloe (ˈkaɪləʊ) NOUN a breed of small long-horned long-haired beef cattle from NW Scotland.
▷HISTORY C19: of uncertain origin

kymograph (ˈkaɪməˌgrɑːf, -ˌgræf) *or* **cymograph** NOUN [1] *Med* a rotatable drum for holding paper on which a tracking stylus continuously records variations in blood pressure, respiratory movements, etc. [2] *Phonetics* this device as applied to the measurement of variations in the muscular action of the articulatory organs. [3] an instrument for recording the angular oscillations of an aircraft in flight.
▷HISTORY C20: from Greek *kuma* wave + -GRAPH
▸ˌ**kymoˈgraphic** *or* ˌ**cymoˈgraphic** ADJECTIVE

Kymric (ˈkɪmrɪk) NOUN, ADJECTIVE a variant spelling of **Cymric.**

Kymry (ˈkɪmrɪ) PLURAL NOUN a variant spelling of **Cymry.**

Kyongsong (ˈkjɔːŋˈsɔːŋ) NOUN another name for **Seoul.**

Kyoto *or* **Kioto** (kɪˈəʊtəʊ, ˈkjəʊ-) NOUN a city in central Japan, on S Honshu: the capital of Japan from 794 to 1868; cultural centre, with two universities (1875, 1897). Pop.: 1 463 601 (1995).

kype (kaɪp) NOUN the hook on the lower jaw of a mature male salmon.
▷HISTORY from Scot *kip, kipp* anything beaked or hooked; perhaps related to Low German *kippe* point, tip

kyphosis (kaɪˈfəʊsɪs) NOUN *Pathol* backward curvature of the thoracic spine, of congenital origin or resulting from injury or disease; hunchback. See also **Pott's disease.** Compare **lordosis, scoliosis.**
▷HISTORY C19: from New Latin, from Greek *kuphōsis,* from *kuphos* humpbacked
▸**kyphotic** (kaɪˈfɒtɪk) ADJECTIVE

Kyrgyz (ˈkɪəgɪz), **Kirghiz,** *or* **Kirgiz** NOUN [1] (*plural* **-gyz, -ghiz** *or* **-giz**) a member of a Mongoloid people of central Asia, inhabiting Kyrgyzstan and a vast area of central Siberia. [2] the language of this people, belonging to the Turkic branch of the Altaic family.

Kyrgyzstan (ˈkɪəgɪzˌstɑːn, -ˌstæn), **Kirghizstan,** *or* **Kirgizstan** NOUN a republic in central Asia: came under Russian rule in the 19th century, became a Soviet republic in 1936 and gained independence in 1991; it has deposits of minerals, oil, and gas. Official languages: Kyrgyz and Russian. Religion: nonreligious, Muslim. Currency: som. Capital: Bishkek. Pop.: 4 934 000 (2001 est.). Area: 198 500 sq. km (76 460 sq. miles).

Kyrgyz Steppe NOUN a vast steppe region in central Kazakhstan. Also called: **the Steppes.**

Kyrie eleison (ˈkɪrɪɪ əˈleɪsᵊn) NOUN [1] a formal invocation used in the liturgies of the Roman Catholic, Greek Orthodox, and Anglican Churches. [2] a musical setting of this. Often shortened to: **Kyrie.**
▷HISTORY C14: via Late Latin from Late Greek *kurie, eleēson* Lord, have mercy

kyte *or* **kite** (kəɪt) NOUN *Scot* the belly.
▷HISTORY C16: of uncertain origin

Kythera (ˈkɪθɪrə) NOUN a variant spelling of **Cythera.**

kyu (kjuː) NOUN *Judo* [1] one of the five student grades for inexperienced competitors. [2] a student in the kyu grades. Compare **dan**[2].
▷HISTORY from Japanese

Kyushu *or* **Kiushu** (ˈkjuːʃuː) NOUN an island of SW Japan: the southernmost of Japan's four main islands, with over 300 surrounding small islands; coalfield and chemical industries. Chief cities: Fukuoka, Kitakyushu, and Nagasaki. Pop.: 13 446 000 (2001 est.). Area: 35 659 sq. km (13 768 sq. miles).

Kyzyl Kum (*Russian* kiˈzil ˈkum) NOUN a desert in Kazakhstan and Uzbekistan.

kz THE INTERNET DOMAIN NAME FOR Kazakhstan.

KZ INTERNATIONAL CAR REGISTRATION FOR Kazakhstan.

KZN (in South Africa) ABBREVIATION FOR KwaZulu/Natal.

Ll

l *or* **L** (ɛl) NOUN, *plural* **l's, L's** *or* **Ls.** [1] the 12th letter and ninth consonant of the modern English alphabet. [2] a speech sound represented by this letter, usually a lateral, as in *label.* [3] **a** something shaped like an L. **b** (*in combination*): *an L-shaped room.*

l SYMBOL FOR: [1] litre. [2] *Physics* lepton number.

L SYMBOL FOR: [1] ell (unit). [2] lambert(s). [3] large. [4] Latin. [5] (on British motor vehicles) learner driver. [6] *Physics* length. [7] live. [8] *Currency* **a** Usually written **£**. pound. **b** lempira. **c** lek. **d** leu. **e** lire. [9] *Aeronautics* lift. [10] *Electronics* inductor (in circuit diagrams). [11] *Physics* latent heat. [12] *Physics* self-inductance. [13] *Chem* the Avogadro constant. ◆ [14] THE ROMAN NUMERAL FOR 50. See **Roman numerals.** ◆ [15] INTERNATIONAL CAR REGISTRATION FOR Luxembourg.
▷**HISTORY** (for sense 8a) Latin *libra*

L. *or* **l.** ABBREVIATION FOR: [1] lake. [2] left. [3] length.

L8R (ˈleɪtə) *Text messaging* ABBREVIATION FOR later.

la[1] (lɑː) NOUN *Music* a variant spelling of **lah.**

la[2] (lɔː) INTERJECTION an exclamation of surprise or emphasis.
▷**HISTORY** Old English *lā* LO

la[3] THE INTERNET DOMAIN NAME FOR Lao People's Democratic Republic.

La THE CHEMICAL SYMBOL FOR lanthanum.

LA ABBREVIATION FOR: [1] Legislative Assembly. [2] Library Association. [3] local agent. [4] Los Angeles. [5] Louisiana.

La. ABBREVIATION FOR Louisiana.

laager *or* **lager** (ˈlɑːɡə) NOUN [1] (in Africa) a camp, esp one defended by a circular formation of wagons. [2] *Military* a place where armoured vehicles are parked. ◆ VERB [3] to form (wagons) into a laager. [4] (*tr*) to park (armoured vehicles) in a laager.
▷**HISTORY** C19: from Afrikaans *lager,* via German from Old High German *legar* bed, lair

Laaland (*Danish* ˈlɔlan) NOUN a variant spelling of **Lolland.**

lab (læb) NOUN *Informal* short for: [1] laboratory. [2] Labrador retriever.

lab. ABBREVIATION FOR: [1] laboratory. [2] labour.

Lab. ABBREVIATION FOR: [1] *Politics* Labour. [2] Labrador.

Laban (ˈleɪbᵊn) NOUN *Old Testament* the father-in-law of Jacob, father of Leah and Rachel (Genesis 29:16).

labarum (ˈlæbərəm) NOUN, *plural* **-ra** (-rə). [1] a standard or banner carried in Christian religious processions. [2] the military standard bearing a Christian monogram used by Constantine the Great.
▷**HISTORY** C17: from Late Latin, of obscure origin

labdanum (ˈlæbdənəm) *or* **ladanum** NOUN a dark resinous juice obtained from various rockroses of the genus *Cistus,* used in perfumery and in the manufacture of fumigants and medicinal plasters.
▷**HISTORY** C16: Latin, from Greek *ladanon,* from *lēdon* rockrose, from Semitic

Labe (ˈlabɛ) NOUN the Czech name for the (River) **Elbe.**

labefaction (ˌlæbɪˈfækʃən) *or* **labefactation** (ˌlæbɪfækˈteɪʃən) NOUN *Rare* deterioration; weakening.
▷**HISTORY** C17: from Late Latin *labefactiō,* from Latin *labefacere* shake, from *lābī* to fall + *facere* to make

label (ˈleɪbᵊl) NOUN [1] a piece of paper, card, or other material attached to an object to identify it or give instructions or details concerning its ownership, use, nature, destination, etc.; tag. [2] a brief descriptive phrase or term given to a person, group, school of thought, etc.: *the label "Romantic" is applied to many different kinds of poetry.* [3] a word or phrase heading a piece of text to indicate or summarize its contents. [4] a trademark or company or brand name on certain goods, esp on gramophone records. [5] another name for **dripstone** (sense 2). [6] *Heraldry* a charge consisting of a horizontal line across the chief of a shield with three or more pendants: the charge of an eldest son. [7] *Computing* a group of characters, such as a number or a word, appended to a particular statement in a program to allow its unique identification. [8] *Chem* a radioactive element used in a compound to trace the mechanism of a chemical reaction. ◆ VERB **-bels, -belling, -belled** *or US* **-bels, -beling, -beled.** (*tr*) [9] to fasten a label to. [10] to mark with a label. [11] to describe or classify in a word or phrase: *to label someone a liar.* [12] to make (one or more atoms in a compound) radioactive, for use in determining the mechanism of a reaction.
▷**HISTORY** C14: from Old French, from Germanic; compare Old High German *lappa* rag
▸ˈ**labeller** NOUN

labellist (ˈleɪbəlɪst) NOUN *NZ informal* a person who wears only clothes with fashionable brand names.

labellum (ləˈbɛləm) NOUN, *plural* **-la** (-lə). [1] the part of the corolla of certain plants, esp orchids, that forms a distinct, often lobed, lip. [2] a lobe at the tip of the proboscis of a fly.
▷**HISTORY** C19: New Latin, diminutive of Latin *labrum* lip
▸**la**ˈ**belloid** ADJECTIVE

labia (ˈleɪbɪə) NOUN the plural of **labium.**

labial (ˈleɪbɪəl) ADJECTIVE [1] of, relating to, or near lips or labia. [2] *Music* producing sounds by the action of an air stream over a narrow liplike fissure, as in a flue pipe of an organ. [3] *Phonetics* relating to a speech sound whose articulation involves movement or use of the lips: *a labial click.* ◆ NOUN [4] Also called: **labial pipe.** *Music* an organ pipe with a liplike fissure. [5] *Phonetics* a speech sound such as English *p* or *m,* whose articulation involves movement or use of the lips.
▷**HISTORY** C16: from Medieval Latin *labiālis,* from Latin *labium* lip
▸ˌ**labi**ˈ**ality** NOUN ▸ˈ**labially** ADVERB

labialize *or* **labialise** (ˈleɪbɪəˌlaɪz) VERB (*tr*) *Phonetics* to pronounce with articulation involving rounded lips, such as for (k) before a close back vowel (uː) as in English *cool.*
▸ˈ**labialˌism** *or* ˌ**labiali**ˈ**zation** *or* ˌ**labiali**ˈ**sation** NOUN

labia majora (məˈdʒɔːrə) PLURAL NOUN the two elongated outer folds of skin in human females surrounding the vaginal orifice.
▷**HISTORY** C18: New Latin: greater lips

labia minora (mɪˈnɔːrə) PLURAL NOUN the two small inner folds of skin in human females forming the margins of the vaginal orifice.
▷**HISTORY** C18: New Latin: smaller lips

labiate (ˈleɪbɪˌeɪt, -ɪt) NOUN [1] any plant of the family *Lamiaceae* (formerly *Labiatae*), having square stems, aromatic leaves, and a two-lipped corolla: includes mint, thyme, sage, rosemary, etc. ◆ ADJECTIVE [2] of, relating to, or belonging to the family *Lamiaceae.*
▷**HISTORY** C18: from New Latin *labiātus,* from Latin *labium* lip

labile (ˈleɪbɪl) ADJECTIVE [1] *Chem* (of a compound) prone to chemical change. [2] liable to change or move.
▷**HISTORY** C15: via Late Latin *lābilis,* from Latin *lābī* to slide, slip
▸**lability** (ləˈbɪlɪtɪ) NOUN

labio- *or before a vowel* **labi-** COMBINING FORM relating to or formed by the lips and (another organ or part): *labiodental.*
▷**HISTORY** from Latin *labium* lip

labiodental (ˌleɪbɪəʊˈdɛntᵊl) *Phonetics* ◆ ADJECTIVE [1] pronounced by bringing the bottom lip into contact or near contact with the upper teeth, as for the fricative (f) in English *fat, puff.* ◆ NOUN [2] a labiodental consonant.

labionasal (ˌleɪbɪəʊˈneɪzᵊl) *Phonetics* ◆ ADJECTIVE [1] pronounced by making a complete closure of the air passage at the lips and lowering the soft palate allowing air to escape through the nasal cavity. ◆ NOUN [2] a labionasal consonant, such as *m.*

labiovelar (ˌleɪbɪəʊˈviːlə) *Phonetics* ◆ ADJECTIVE [1] relating to or denoting a speech sound pronounced with simultaneous articulation at the soft palate and the lips. ◆ NOUN [2] a labiovelar speech sound, such as some pronunciations of the consonant spelt *q* in English.

labium (ˈleɪbɪəm) NOUN, *plural* **-bia** (-bɪə). [1] a lip or liplike structure. [2] any one of the four lip-shaped folds of the female vulva. See **labia majora, labia minora.** [3] the fused pair of appendages forming the lower lip of insects. [4] the lower lip of the corolla of labiate flowers.
▷**HISTORY** C16: New Latin, from Latin: lip

lablab (ˈlæbˌlæb) NOUN [1] a twining leguminous plant, *Dolichos lablab* (or *Lablab niger*), of tropical Africa but widely cultivated. [2] the edible pod or bean of this plant.
▷**HISTORY** from Arabic

labor (ˈleɪbə) VERB, NOUN the US spelling of **labour.**

laboratory (ləˈbɒrətərɪ, -trɪ; *US* ˈlæbrəˌtɔːrɪ) NOUN, *plural* **-ries.** [1] **a** a building or room equipped for conducting scientific research or for teaching practical science. **b** (*as modifier*): *laboratory equipment.* [2] a place where chemicals or medicines are manufactured. ◆ Often shortened to: **lab.** See also **language laboratory.**
▷**HISTORY** C17: from Medieval Latin *labōrātōrium* workshop, from Latin *labōrāre* to LABOUR

Labor Day NOUN [1] (in the US and Canada) a public holiday in honour of labour, held on the first Monday in September. [2] (in Australia) a public holiday observed on different days in different states.

laborious (ləˈbɔːrɪəs) ADJECTIVE [1] involving great exertion or long effort. [2] given to working hard. [3] (of literary style, etc.) not fluent.
▸**la**ˈ**boriously** ADVERB ▸**la**ˈ**boriousness** NOUN

Labor Party NOUN one of the chief political parties of Australia, generally supporting the interests of organized labour.

labour *or US* **labor** (ˈleɪbə) NOUN [1] productive work, esp physical toil done for wages. [2] **a** the people, class, or workers involved in this, esp in contrast to management, capital, etc. **b** (*as modifier*): *a labour dispute; labour relations.* [3] **a** difficult or arduous work or effort. **b** (*in combination*): *labour-saving.* [4] a particular job or task, esp of a difficult nature. [5] **a** the process or effort of childbirth or the time during which this takes place. **b** (*as modifier*): *labour pains.* [6] **labour of love.** something done for pleasure rather than gain. ◆ VERB [7] (*intr*) to perform labour; work. [8] (*intr; foll by for,* etc.) to strive or work hard (for something). [9] (*intr;* usually foll by *under*) to be burdened (by) or be at a disadvantage (because of): *to labour under a misapprehension.* [10] (*intr*) to make one's way with difficulty. [11] (*tr*) to deal with or treat too persistently: *to labour a point.* [12] (*intr*) (of a woman) to be in labour. [13] (*intr*) (of a ship) to pitch and toss.
▷**HISTORY** C13: via Old French from Latin *labor;* perhaps related to *lābī* to fall
▸ˈ**labouringly** *or US* ˈ**laboringly** ADVERB

Labour and Socialist International NOUN **the.** an international association of socialist parties formed in Hamburg in 1923: destroyed by World War II. Also called: **Second International.**

labour camp NOUN [1] a penal colony involving forced labour. [2] a camp for migratory labourers.

Labour Day NOUN a public holiday in many countries in honour of labour, usually held on May 1. See also **Labor Day.**

laboured *or US* **labored** ('leɪbəd) ADJECTIVE [1] (of breathing) performed with difficulty. [2] showing effort; contrived; lacking grace or fluency.
▸ **'labouredly** *or US* **'laboredly** ADVERB ▸ **'labouredness** *or US* **'laboredness** NOUN

labourer *or US* **laborer** ('leɪbərə) NOUN a person engaged in physical work, esp of an unskilled kind.

labour exchange NOUN *Brit* a former name for **employment office.**

labour-intensive ADJECTIVE of or denoting a task, organization, industry, etc., in which a high proportion of the costs are due to wages, salaries, etc.

labourism *or US* **laborism** ('leɪbəˌrɪzəm) NOUN [1] the dominance of the working classes. [2] a political, social, or economic system that favours such dominance. [3] support for workers' rights.

labourist *or US* **laborist** ('leɪbərɪst) NOUN [1] a person who supports workers' rights. [2] a supporter of labourism.

Labourite ('leɪbəˌraɪt) NOUN an adherent of the Labour Party.

labour law NOUN those areas of law which appertain to the relationship between employers and employees and between employers and trade unions.

Labour Party NOUN [1] a British political party, formed in 1900 as an amalgam of various trade unions and socialist groups, generally supporting the interests of organized labour and advocating democratic socialism and social equality. [2] any similar party in any of various other countries.

labour relations PLURAL NOUN **a** collective relations between the management of an organization and its employees or employees' representatives. **b** a set of such relations in a wider context, such as in an industry, or in a national economy.

labra ('leɪbrə, 'læb-) NOUN the plural of **labrum.**

Labrador ('læbrəˌdɔː) NOUN [1] Also called: **Labrador-Ungava.** a large peninsula of NE Canada, on the Atlantic, the Gulf of St. Lawrence, Hudson Strait, and Hudson Bay: contains most of the province of Quebec and the mainland part of Newfoundland; geologically part of the Canadian Shield. Area: 1 619 000 sq. km (625 000 sq. miles). [2] Also called: **Coast of Labrador.** a region of NE Canada, on the Atlantic and consisting of the mainland part of Newfoundland province. [3] (*often not capital*) short for **Labrador retriever.**

Labrador Current NOUN a cold ocean current flowing southwards off the coast of Labrador and meeting the warm Gulf Stream, causing dense fogs off Newfoundland.

labradorescent (ˌlæbrədɔːˈrɛsənt) ADJECTIVE (of minerals) displaying a brilliant play of colours, as that shown by some forms of labradorite.

labradorite (ˌlæbrəˈdɔːraɪt) NOUN a blue, green, or reddish-brown feldspar mineral of the plagioclase series: used as a decorative stone. Formula: $CaAl_2Si_2O_8.NaAlSi_3O_8$.
▷**HISTORY** C18: named after LABRADOR, where it was found; see -ITE[1]

Labrador retriever NOUN a powerfully-built variety of retriever with a short dense usually black or golden-brown coat. Often shortened to: **Labrador,** (informal) **lab.**

Labrador tea NOUN [1] either of two arctic evergreen ericaceous shrubs, *Ledum groenlandicum* or *L. palustre* var. *decumbens.* [2] (in Canada) an infusion brewed from the leaves of either of these plants.

labret ('leɪbrɛt) NOUN a piece of bone, shell, etc.; inserted into the lip as an ornament by certain peoples.
▷**HISTORY** C19: from Latin *labrum* lip

labroid ('læbrɔɪd, 'leɪ-) *or* **labrid** ('læbrɪd) NOUN [1] any percoid fish of the family *Labridae* (wrasses). ◆ ADJECTIVE [2] of or relating to the *Labridae.*
▷**HISTORY** C19: from New Latin *Labroidea,* from Latin *lābrus* a fish, from *labrum* lip

labrum ('leɪbrəm, 'læb-) NOUN, *plural* **-bra** (-brə). a lip or liplike part, such as the cuticular plate forming the upper lip of insects.
▷**HISTORY** C19: New Latin, from Latin

Labuan (ləˈbuːən) NOUN an island in Malaysia, off the NW coast of Borneo: part of the Straits Settlements until 1946, when transferred to North Borneo. Chief town: Victoria. Area: 98 sq. km (38 sq. miles).

laburnum (ləˈbɜːnəm) NOUN any leguminous tree or shrub of the Eurasian genus *Laburnum,* having clusters of yellow drooping flowers: all parts of the plant are poisonous.
▷**HISTORY** C16: New Latin, from Latin

labyrinth ('læbərɪnθ) NOUN [1] a mazelike network of tunnels, chambers, or paths, either natural or man-made. Compare **maze** (sense 1). [2] any complex or confusing system of streets, passages, etc. [3] a complex or intricate situation. [4] **a** any system of interconnecting cavities, esp those comprising the internal ear. **b** another name for **internal ear.** [5] *Electronics* an enclosure behind a high-performance loudspeaker, consisting of a series of air chambers designed to absorb unwanted sound waves.
▷**HISTORY** C16: via Latin from Greek *laburinthos,* of obscure origin

Labyrinth ('læbərɪnθ) NOUN *Greek myth* a huge maze constructed for King Minos in Crete by Daedalus to contain the Minotaur.

labyrinth fish NOUN any tropical freshwater spiny-finned fish of the family *Anabantidae* of SE Asia and Africa, having a lunglike respiratory organ. See also **anabantid.**

labyrinthine (ˌlæbəˈrɪnθaɪn), **labyrinthian** (ˌlæbəˈrɪnθɪən), *or* **labyrinthic** (ˌlæbəˈrɪnθɪk) ADJECTIVE [1] of or relating to a labyrinth. [2] resembling a labyrinth in complexity.
▸ **ˌlabyˈrinthically** ADVERB

labyrinthitis (ˌlæbərɪnˈθaɪtɪs) NOUN inflammation of the inner ear, causing loss of balance, vertigo, and vomiting. Also called: **otitis interna.**

labyrinthodont (ˌlæbəˈrɪnθəˌdɒnt) NOUN any primitive amphibian of the order *Labyrinthodontia,* of late Devonian to Triassic times, having teeth with much-folded dentine.
▷**HISTORY** C19: from Greek *laburinthos* LABYRINTH + -ODONT

lac[1] (læk) NOUN a resinous substance secreted by certain lac insects, used in the manufacture of shellac.
▷**HISTORY** C16: from Dutch *lak* or French *laque,* from Hindi *lākh* resin, ultimately from Sanskrit *lākshā*

lac[2] (lɑːk) NOUN a variant spelling of **lakh.**

LAC *Brit* ABBREVIATION FOR **leading aircraftman.**

Laccadive, Minicoy, and Amindivi Islands ('lækədɪv, 'mɪnɪˌkɔɪ, ˌʌmənˈdiːviː) PLURAL NOUN the former name (until 1973) of the **Lakshadweep Islands.**

laccolith ('lækəlɪθ) *or* **laccolite** ('lækəˌlaɪt) NOUN a dome-shaped body of igneous rock between two layers of older sedimentary rock: formed by the intrusion of magma, forcing the overlying strata into the shape of a dome.
▷**HISTORY** C19: from Greek *lakkos* cistern + -LITH
▸ **ˌlaccoˈlithic** *or* **laccolitic** (ˌlækəˈlɪtɪk) ADJECTIVE

lace (leɪs) NOUN [1] a delicate decorative fabric made from cotton, silk, etc., woven in an open web of different symmetrical patterns and figures. [2] a cord or string drawn through holes or eyelets or around hooks to fasten a shoe or garment. [3] ornamental braid often used on military uniforms, etc. [4] a dash of spirits added to a beverage. ◆ VERB [5] to fasten (shoes, etc.) with a lace. [6] (*tr*) to draw (a cord or thread) through holes, eyes, etc., as when tying shoes. [7] (*tr*) to compress the waist of (someone), as with a corset. [8] (*tr*) to add a small amount of alcohol or drugs to (food or drink). [9] (*tr; usually passive* and foll by *with*) to streak or mark with lines or colours: *the sky was laced with red.* [10] (*tr*) to intertwine; interlace. [11] (*tr*) *Informal* to give a sound beating to. ◆ See also **lace into, lace up.**
▷**HISTORY** C13 *las,* from Old French *laz,* from Latin *laqueus* noose
▸ **'laceˌlike** ADJECTIVE ▸ **'lacer** NOUN

lacebark ('leɪsbɑːk) NOUN another name for **ribbonwood.**

lace bug NOUN a small bug of the family *Tingidae,* having a delicate pattern in the wing venation. They are plant feeders and include the **thistle lace bugs** (*Tingis cardui* and *T. ampliata*) and the **rhododendron bug** (*Stephanitis rhododendri*).

Lacedaemon (ˌlæsɪˈdiːmən) NOUN another name for **Sparta** or **Laconia.**

Lacedaemonian (ˌlæsɪdɪˈməʊnɪən) ADJECTIVE, NOUN another word for **Spartan.**

lace into VERB (*intr, preposition*) to attack violently, either verbally or physically.

lacerant ('læsərənt) ADJECTIVE painfully distressing; harrowing.

lacerate VERB ('læsəˌreɪt) (*tr*) [1] to tear (the flesh, etc.) jaggedly. [2] to hurt or harrow (the feelings, etc.). ◆ ADJECTIVE ('læsəˌreɪt, -rɪt) [3] having edges that are jagged or torn; lacerated: *lacerate leaves.*
▷**HISTORY** C16: from Latin *lacerāre* to tear, from *lacer* mangled
▸ **'lacerable** ADJECTIVE ▸ **ˌlaceraˈbility** NOUN ▸ **ˌlacerˈation** NOUN ▸ **'lacerative** ADJECTIVE

Lacerta (ləˈsɜːtə) NOUN, *Latin genitive* **Lacertae** (ləˈsɜːtiː). a small faint constellation in the N hemisphere, part of which is crossed by the Milky Way, lying between Cygnus and Andromeda.
▷**HISTORY** Latin: lizard

lacertilian (ˌlæsəˈtɪlɪən) NOUN *also* **lacertian** (ləˈsɜːʃən). [1] any reptile of the suborder *Lacertilia* (lizards). ◆ ADJECTIVE [2] of, relating to, or belonging to the *Lacertilia.*
▷**HISTORY** C19: New Latin, from Latin *lacerta* lizard

lace up VERB [1] (*tr, adverb*) to tighten or fasten (clothes or footwear) with laces. ◆ ADJECTIVE **lace-up.** [2] (of footwear) to be fastened with laces. ◆ NOUN **lace-up.** [3] a lace-up shoe or boot.

lacewing ('leɪsˌwɪŋ) NOUN any of various neuropterous insects, esp any of the families *Chrysopidae* (**green lacewings**) and *Hemerobiidae* (**brown lacewings**), having lacy wings and preying on aphids and similar pests.

laches ('lætʃɪz) NOUN *Law* negligence or unreasonable delay in pursuing a legal remedy.
▷**HISTORY** C14 *lachesse,* via Old French *lasche* slack, from Latin *laxus* LAX

Lachesis ('lækɪsɪs) NOUN *Greek myth* one of the three Fates.
▷**HISTORY** via Latin from Greek, from *lakhesis* destiny, from *lakhein* to befall by lot

Lachlan ('lɒklən) NOUN a river in SE Australia, rising in central New South Wales and flowing northwest then southwest to the Murrumbidgee River. Length: about 1450 km (900 miles).
▷**HISTORY** named after *Lachlan* Macquarie, governor of New South Wales (1809–21)

lachryma Christi ('lækrəmə 'krɪstɪ) NOUN a red or white wine from the bay of Naples in S Italy.
▷**HISTORY** C17: from Latin: Christ's tear

lachrymal ('lækrɪməl) ADJECTIVE a variant spelling of **lacrimal.**

lachrymator ('lækrɪˌmeɪtə) NOUN a variant spelling of **lacrimator.**

lachrymatory ('lækrɪmətərɪ, -trɪ) NOUN, *plural* **-ries.** [1] a small vessel found in ancient tombs, formerly thought to hold the tears of mourners. ◆ ADJECTIVE [2] a variant spelling of **lacrimatory.**

lachrymose ('lækrɪˌməʊs, -ˌməʊz) ADJECTIVE [1] given to weeping; tearful. [2] mournful; sad.
▷**HISTORY** C17: from Latin *lacrimōsus,* from *lacrima* a tear
▸ **'lachryˌmosely** ADVERB ▸ **lachrymosity** (ˌlækrɪˈmɒsɪtɪ) NOUN

lacing ('leɪsɪŋ) NOUN [1] *Chiefly Brit* a course of bricks, stone, etc., for strengthening a rubble or flint wall. [2] another word for **lace** (senses 2, 3). [3] *Informal* a severe beating (esp in the phrase **give someone a lacing**).

laciniate (ləˈsɪnɪˌeɪt, -ɪt) *or* **laciniated** ADJECTIVE [1] *Biology* jagged: *a laciniate leaf.* [2] having a fringe.
▷**HISTORY** C17: from Latin *lacinia* flap
▸ **laˌciniˈation** NOUN

lac insect (læk) NOUN any of various homopterous insects of the family *Lacciferidae,* esp *Laccifer lacca* of India, the females of which secrete lac.

lack (læk) NOUN [1] an insufficiency, shortage, or absence of something required or desired. [2] something that is required but is absent or in short supply. ◆ VERB [3] (when *intr,* often foll by *in* or *for*) to be deficient (in) or have need (of): *to lack purpose.*
▷**HISTORY** C12: related to Middle Dutch *laken* to be wanting

lackadaisical (ˌlækəˈdeɪzɪkᵊl) ADJECTIVE [1] lacking vitality and purpose. [2] lazy or idle, esp in a dreamy way.
▷HISTORY C18: from earlier *lackadaisy,* extended form of LACKADAY
▸ˌ**lackaˈdaisically** ADVERB ▸ˌ**lackaˈdaisicalness** NOUN

lackaday (ˈlækəˌdeɪ) INTERJECTION *Archaic* another word for **alas.**
▷HISTORY C17: from *alack the day*

lacker (ˈlækə) NOUN a variant spelling of **lacquer.**

lackey (ˈlækɪ) NOUN [1] a servile follower; hanger-on. [2] a liveried male servant or valet. [3] a person who is treated like a servant. ◆ VERB [4] (when *intr,* often foll by *for*) to act as a lackey (to). ◆ Also (rare): **lacquey.**
▷HISTORY C16: via French *laquais,* from Old French, perhaps from Catalan *lacayo, alacayo;* perhaps related to ALCALDE

lackey moth NOUN a bombycid moth, *Malacosoma neustria,* whose brightly striped larvae live at first in a communal web often on fruit trees, of which they may become a pest.

lacklustre *or US* **lackluster** (ˈlækˌlʌstə) ADJECTIVE lacking force, brilliance, or vitality.

Laconia (ləˈkəʊnɪə) NOUN an ancient country of S Greece, in the SE Peloponnese, of which Sparta was the capital: corresponds to the present-day department of Lakonia.

Laconian (ləˈkəʊnɪən) NOUN [1] a native or inhabitant of Laconia, the ancient Greek country of which Sparta was the capital. ◆ ADJECTIVE [2] of or relating to Laconia or its inhabitants.

laconic (ləˈkɒnɪk) *or* **laconical** ADJECTIVE (of a person's speech) using few words; terse.
▷HISTORY C16: via Latin from Greek *Lakōnikos,* from *Lakōn* Laconian, Spartan; referring to the Spartans' terseness of speech
▸**laˈconically** ADVERB

laconism (ˈlækəˌnɪzəm) *or* **laconicism** (ləˈkɒnɪˌsɪzəm) NOUN *Rare* [1] economy of expression. [2] a terse saying.

La Coruña (*Spanish* la koˈruɲa) NOUN a port in NW Spain, on the Atlantic: point of departure for the Spanish Armada (1588); site of the defeat of the French by the British under Sir John Moore in the Peninsular War (1809). Pop.: 243 134 (1998 est.). English name: **Corunna.**

lacquer (ˈlækə) NOUN [1] a hard glossy coating made by dissolving cellulose derivatives or natural resins in a volatile solvent. [2] a black resinous substance, obtained from certain trees, used to give a hard glossy finish to wooden furniture. [3] **lacquer tree.** Also called: **varnish tree.** an E Asian anacardiaceous tree, *Rhus verniciflua,* whose stem yields a toxic exudation from which black lacquer is obtained. [4] Also called: **hair lacquer.** a mixture of shellac and alcohol for spraying onto the hair to hold a style in place. [5] *Art* decorative objects coated with such lacquer, often inlaid. ◆ VERB (*tr*) [6] to apply lacquer to.
▷HISTORY C16: from obsolete French *lacre* sealing wax, from Portuguese *laca* LAC[1]
▸ˈ**lacquerer** NOUN

lacrimal, lachrymal, *or* **lacrymal** (ˈlækrɪməl) ADJECTIVE of or relating to tears or to the glands that secrete tears.
▷HISTORY C16: from Medieval Latin *lachrymālis,* from Latin *lacrima* a tear

lacrimal duct NOUN a short tube in the inner corner of the eyelid through which tears drain into the nose. Nontechnical name: **tear duct.**

lacrimal gland NOUN the compound gland that secretes tears and lubricates the surface of the eye and the conjunctiva of the eyelid.

lacrimation (ˌlækrɪˈmeɪʃən) NOUN the secretion of tears.

lacrimator, lachrymator, *or* **lacrymator** (ˈlækrɪˌmeɪtə) NOUN a substance causing an increase in the flow of tears. See **tear gas.**

lacrimatory, lachrymatory, *or* **lacrymatory** (ˈlækrɪmətərɪ, -trɪ) ADJECTIVE of, causing, or producing tears.

lacrosse (ləˈkrɒs) NOUN a ball game invented by American Indians, now played by two teams who try to propel a ball into each other's goal by means of long-handled hooked sticks that are loosely strung with a kind of netted pouch.
▷HISTORY C19: Canadian French: the hooked stick, crosier

lactalbumin (lækˈtælbjʊmɪn) NOUN a protein occurring in milk that contains all the amino acids essential to man. See also **caseinogen.**
▷HISTORY C19: from LACTO- + ALBUMIN

lactam (ˈlæktæm) NOUN *Chem* any of a group of inner amides, derived from amino acids, having the characteristic group -CONH-.
▷HISTORY C20: from LACT(ONE) + AM(IDE)

lactase (ˈlækteɪs, -teɪz) NOUN any of a group of enzymes that hydrolyse lactose to glucose and galactose.
▷HISTORY C20: from LACTO- + -ASE

lactate[1] (ˈlækteɪt) NOUN an ester or salt of lactic acid.
▷HISTORY C18: from LACTO- + -ATE[1]

lactate[2] (ˈlækteɪt) VERB (*intr*) (of mammals) to produce or secrete milk.

lactation (lækˈteɪʃən) NOUN [1] the secretion of milk from the mammary glands after parturition. [2] the period during which milk is secreted.
▸**lacˈtational** ADJECTIVE ▸**lacˈtationally** ADVERB

lactation tetany NOUN *Vet science* another name for **hypomagnesaemia.**

lacteal (ˈlæktɪəl) ADJECTIVE [1] of, relating to, or resembling milk. [2] (of lymphatic vessels) conveying or containing chyle. ◆ NOUN [3] any of the lymphatic vessels conveying chyle from the small intestine to the thoracic duct.
▷HISTORY C17: from Latin *lacteus* of milk, from *lac* milk
▸ˈ**lacteally** ADVERB

lactescent (lækˈtɛsᵊnt) ADJECTIVE [1] (of plants and certain insects) secreting a milky fluid. [2] milky or becoming milky.
▷HISTORY C18: from Latin *lactescēns,* from *lactescere* to become milky, from *lact-, lac* milk
▸**lacˈtescence** NOUN

lactic (ˈlæktɪk) ADJECTIVE relating to or derived from milk.
▷HISTORY C18: from Latin *lact-, lac* milk

lactic acid NOUN a colourless syrupy carboxylic acid found in sour milk and many fruits and used as a preservative (**E270**) for foodstuffs, such as soft margarine, and for making pharmaceuticals and adhesives. Formula: $CH_3CH(OH)COOH$. Systematic name: **2-hydroxypropanoic acid.**

lactiferous (lækˈtɪfərəs) ADJECTIVE [1] producing, conveying, or secreting milk or a milky fluid: *lactiferous ducts.* [2] *Botany* containing latex; laticiferous.
▷HISTORY C17: from Latin *lactifer,* from *lact-, lac* milk
▸**lacˈtiferousness** NOUN

lacto- *or before a vowel* **lact-** COMBINING FORM indicating milk: *lactobacillus.*
▷HISTORY from Latin *lact-, lac* milk

lactobacillus (ˌlæktəʊbəˈsɪləs) NOUN, *plural* **-li** (-laɪ). any Gram-positive rod-shaped bacterium of the genus *Lactobacillus,* which ferments carbohydrates to lactic acid, for example in the souring of milk: family *Lactobacillaceae.*

lactoflavin (ˌlæktəʊˈfleɪvɪn) NOUN a less common name for **riboflavin.**

lactogenic (ˌlæktəˈdʒɛnɪk) ADJECTIVE inducing lactation: *lactogenic hormone.* See also **prolactin.**

lactoglobulin (ˌlæktəʊˈglɒbjʊlɪn) NOUN *Biochem* any of a number of globular proteins found in milk.

lactometer (lækˈtɒmɪtə) NOUN a hydrometer used to measure the relative density of milk and thus determine its quality. Also called: **galactometer.**

lactone (ˈlæktəʊn) NOUN any of a class of organic compounds formed from hydroxy acids and containing the group -C(CO)OC-, where the carbon atoms are part of a ring.
▸**lactonic** (lækˈtɒnɪk) ADJECTIVE

lactoprotein (ˌlæktəʊˈprəʊtiːn) NOUN any protein, such as lactalbumin or caseinogen, that is present in milk.

lactoscope (ˈlæktəˌskəʊp) NOUN an instrument for measuring the amount of cream in milk.

lactose (ˈlæktəʊs, -təʊz) NOUN a white crystalline disaccharide occurring in milk and used in the manufacture of pharmaceuticals and baby foods. Formula: $C_{12}H_{22}O_{11}$. Also called: **milk sugar.**

lactosuria (ˌlæktəʊˈsjʊərɪə) NOUN *Med* the presence of lactose in the urine.

lacto-vegetarian NOUN a vegetarian whose diet includes dairy produce and eggs.

La Cumbre (lə ˈkuːmbreɪ) NOUN another name for the **Uspallata Pass.**

lacuna (ləˈkjuːnə) NOUN, *plural* **-nae** (-niː) *or* **-nas.** [1] a gap or space, esp in a book or manuscript. [2] *Biology* a cavity or depression, such as any of the spaces in the matrix of bone. [3] another name for **coffer** (sense 3).
▷HISTORY C17: from Latin *lacūna* pool, cavity, from *lacus* lake
▸**laˈcunose** *or* **laˈcunal** *or* **laˈcunary** ADJECTIVE ▸**lacunosity** (ˌlækjʊˈnɒsɪtɪ) NOUN

lacunar (ləˈkjuːnə) NOUN, *plural* **lacunars** *or* **lacunaria** (ˌlækjʊˈnɛərɪə). [1] Also called: **lequear.** a ceiling, soffit, or vault having coffers. [2] another name for **coffer** (sense 3). ◆ ADJECTIVE [3] of, relating to, or containing a lacuna or lacunas.
▷HISTORY C17: from Latin *lacūnar* panelled ceiling, from *lacūna* cavity; see LACUNA

lacustrine (ləˈkʌstraɪn) ADJECTIVE [1] of or relating to lakes. [2] living or growing in or on the shores of a lake.
▷HISTORY C19: from Italian *lacustre,* from Latin *lacus* lake

LACW *Brit* ABBREVIATION FOR leading aircraftwoman.

lacy (ˈleɪsɪ) ADJECTIVE **lacier, laciest.** made of or resembling lace.
▸ˈ**lacily** ADVERB ▸ˈ**laciness** NOUN

lad (læd) NOUN [1] a boy or young man. [2] *Informal* a familiar form of address for any male. [3] a lively or dashing man or youth (esp in the phrase **a bit of a lad**). [4] a young man whose behaviour is characteristic of male adolescents, esp in being rowdy, macho, or immature. [5] *Brit* a boy or man who looks after horses.
▷HISTORY C13 *ladde;* perhaps of Scandinavian origin

ladanum (ˈlædənəm) NOUN another name for **labdanum.**

ladder (ˈlædə) NOUN [1] a portable framework of wood, metal, rope, etc., in the form of two long parallel members connected by several parallel rungs or steps fixed to them at right angles, for climbing up or down. [2] any hierarchy conceived of as having a series of ascending stages, levels, etc.: *the social ladder.* [3] **a** anything resembling a ladder. **b** (*as modifier*): *ladder stitch.* [4] Also called: **run.** *Chiefly Brit* a line of connected stitches that have come undone in knitted material, esp stockings. [5] See **ladder tournament.** ◆ VERB [6] *Chiefly Brit* to cause a line of interconnected stitches in (stockings, etc.) to undo, as by snagging, or (of a stocking) to come undone in this way.
▷HISTORY Old English *hlǣder;* related to Old High German *leitara*

ladder back NOUN a type of chair in which the back is constructed of horizontal slats between two uprights.

ladder tournament NOUN a tournament in a sport or game in which each contestant in a list attempts to defeat and displace the contestant above him. Also called: **ladder.**

laddie (ˈlædɪ) NOUN *Chiefly Scot* a familiar term for a male, esp a young man; lad.

laddish (ˈlædɪʃ) ADJECTIVE *Informal, usually derogatory* characteristic of male adolescents or young men, esp by being rowdy, macho, or immature: *laddish behaviour.*
▸ˈ**laddishˌness** NOUN

lade[1] (leɪd) VERB **lades, lading, laded, laden** (ˈleɪdᵊn) *or* **laded.** [1] to put cargo or freight on board (a ship, etc.) or (of a ship, etc.) to take on cargo or freight. [2] (*tr; usually passive* and foll by *with*) to burden or oppress. [3] (*tr; usually passive* and foll by *with*) to fill or load. [4] to remove (liquid) with or as if with a ladle.
▷HISTORY Old English *hladen* to load; related to Dutch *laden*
▸ˈ**lader** NOUN

lade[2] (led, leɪd) NOUN *Scot* a watercourse, esp a millstream.
▷HISTORY of uncertain origin

laden (ˈleɪdᵊn) VERB [1] a past participle of **lade[1]**. ◆

ADJECTIVE [2] weighed down with a load; loaded. [3] encumbered; burdened.

ladette (ˌlæd'ɛt) NOUN *Informal* a young woman whose social behaviour is similar to that of male adolescents or young men.

la-di-da, lah-di-dah, *or* **la-de-da** (ˌlɑːdiː'dɑː) ADJECTIVE [1] *Informal* affecting exaggeratedly genteel manners or speech. ◆ NOUN [2] a la-di-da person.
▷HISTORY C19: mockingly imitative of affected speech

ladies *or* **ladies' room** NOUN (*functioning as singular*) *Informal* a women's public lavatory.

ladies' fingers NOUN (*functioning as singular or plural*) another name for **kidney vetch** or **okra.**

ladies' gallery NOUN (formerly, in Britain) [1] a gallery in the old House of Commons set aside for women spectators. [2] a portion of the strangers' gallery of the new House of Commons similarly reserved.

ladies' man *or* **lady's man** NOUN a man who is fond of, attentive to, and successful with women.

ladies'-tresses NOUN (*functioning as singular or plural*) a variant spelling of **lady's-tresses.**

Ladin (læ'diːn) NOUN a Rhaetian dialect spoken in parts of South Tyrol. Compare **Friulian, Romansch.**
▷HISTORY C19: from Italian *ladino,* from Latin *latīnus* Latin

lading ('leɪdɪŋ) NOUN a load; cargo; freight.

ladino (lə'diːnəʊ) NOUN, *plural* **-nos.** an Italian variety of white clover grown as a forage crop in North America.
▷HISTORY C20: perhaps from Italian *ladino* (see LADIN), referring to a person or thing from the Italian-speaking area of Switzerland, where the clover is grown

Ladino (lə'diːnəʊ) NOUN a language of Sephardic Jews, based on Spanish with some Hebrew elements and usually written in Hebrew characters. Also called: **Judaeo-Spanish, Judezmo.**
▷HISTORY from Spanish: Latin

ladle ('leɪdᵊl) NOUN [1] a long-handled spoon having a deep bowl for serving or transferring liquids: *a soup ladle.* [2] a large bucket-shaped container for transferring molten metal. ◆ VERB [3] (*tr*) to lift or serve out with or as if with a ladle.
▷HISTORY Old English *hlædel,* from *hladan* to draw out
▸ **'ladle,ful** NOUN

ladle out VERB (*tr, adverb*) *Informal* to distribute (money, gifts, etc.) generously.

lad lit NOUN **a** fiction about young men and their emotional and personal lives. **b** (*as modifier*): *lad-lit novels.*

lad mag NOUN a magazine aimed at or appealing to men, focusing on fashion, gadgets, and often featuring scantily dressed women.

Ladoga (*Russian* 'ladəgə) NOUN **Lake.** a lake in NW Russia, in the SW Karelian Republic: the largest lake in Europe; drains through the River Neva into the Gulf of Finland. Area: about 18 000 sq. km (7000 sq. miles). Russian name: **Ladozhskoye Ozero** ('ladəʃskəjə 'ɔzɪrə).

Ladrone Islands (lə'drəʊn) PLURAL NOUN the former name (1521–1668) of the **Mariana Islands.**

lad's love NOUN another name for **southernwood.**

lady ('leɪdɪ) NOUN, *plural* **-dies.** [1] a woman regarded as having the characteristics of a good family and high social position; female counterpart of **gentleman** (sense 1). [2] **a** a polite name for a woman. **b** (*as modifier*): *a lady doctor.* [3] an informal name for **wife.** [4] **lady of the house.** the female head of the household. [5] *History* a woman with proprietary rights and authority, as over a manor. Compare **lord** (sense 3).
▷HISTORY Old English *hlǣfdīge,* from *hlāf* bread + *dīge* kneader, related to *dāh* dough

Lady ('leɪdɪ) NOUN, *plural* **-dies.** [1] (in Britain) a title of honour borne by various classes of women of the peerage. [2] **my lady.** a term of address to holders of the title Lady, used esp by servants. [3] **Our Lady.** a title of the Virgin Mary. [4] *Archaic* an allegorical prefix for the personifications of certain qualities: *Lady Luck.* [5] *Chiefly Brit* the term of address by which certain positions of respect are prefaced when held by women: *Lady Chairman.*

ladybird ('leɪdɪˌbɜːd) NOUN any of various small brightly coloured beetles of the family *Coccinellidae,* such as *Adalia bipunctata* (**two-spotted ladybird**), which has red elytra marked with black spots. Usual US and Canadian name: **ladybug.**
▷HISTORY C18: named after Our *Lady,* the Virgin Mary

lady bountiful NOUN an ostentatiously charitable woman.
▷HISTORY after a character in George Farquhar's play *The Beaux' Stratagem* (1707)

ladyboy ('leɪdɪˌbɔɪ) NOUN *Informal* a transvestite or transsexual, esp one from the Far East.

Lady Chapel NOUN a chapel within a church or cathedral, dedicated to the Virgin Mary.

Lady Day NOUN March 25, the feast of the Annunciation of the Virgin Mary; one of the four quarter days in England, Wales and Ireland. Also called: **Annunciation Day.**

lady fern NOUN a large, graceful, but variable fern, *Athyrium filix-femina,* with bipinnate fronds, commonly found on damp acid soils in woods and on hillsides.

ladyfinger ('leɪdɪˌfɪŋgə) *or* **lady's finger** NOUN a small finger-shaped sponge cake.

ladyfy *or* **ladify** ('leɪdɪˌfaɪ) VERB **-fies, -fying, -fied.** (*tr*) to make a lady of (someone).

lady-in-waiting NOUN, *plural* **ladies-in-waiting.** a lady of a royal household who attends a queen or princess.

lady-killer NOUN *Informal* a man who is, or thinks he is, irresistibly fascinating to women.
▸ **'lady-ˌkilling** NOUN, ADJECTIVE

ladylike ('leɪdɪˌlaɪk) ADJECTIVE [1] like or befitting a lady in manners and bearing; refined and fastidious. [2] *Derogatory* (of a man) effeminate.
▸ **'lady,likeness** NOUN

ladylove ('leɪdɪˌlʌv) NOUN *Now rare* a beloved woman.

Lady Luck NOUN the personification of fortune or chance.

Lady Macbeth strategy NOUN *Informal* a strategy in a takeover battle in which a third party makes a bid acceptable to the target company, appearing to act as a white knight but subsequently joining forces with the original (unwelcome) bidder.
▷HISTORY C20: after *Lady Macbeth* in Shakespeare's *Macbeth* (1605)

lady mayoress NOUN *Brit* the wife of a lord mayor.

Lady Muck NOUN *Informal, usually derogatory* an ordinary woman behaving or being treated as if she were aristocratic. See also **Lord Muck.**

Lady of the Lake NOUN (in Arthurian legend) a mysterious supernatural being sometimes identified with **Vivian.**

lady orchid NOUN a tall graceful orchid, *Orchis purpurea,* with faintly scented purple-brown and green flowers with a pinkish or white lip.
▷HISTORY C19: named from a fancied resemblance to a lady in regency dress and bonnet

lady's bedstraw NOUN a Eurasian rubiaceous plant, *Galium verum,* with clusters of small yellow flowers.

lady's finger NOUN another name for **bhindi.**

Ladyship ('leɪdɪʃɪp) NOUN (preceded by *your* or *her*) a title used to address or refer to any peeress except a duchess.

lady's maid NOUN a personal servant to a woman, esp in matters of dress and toilet.

lady's man NOUN a variant spelling of **ladies' man.**

lady's mantle NOUN any of various rosaceous plants of the N temperate genus *Alchemilla,* having small green flowers.

Ladysmith ('leɪdɪˌsmɪθ) NOUN a city in E South Africa: besieged by Boers for four months (1899–1900) during the Boer War. Pop.: 56 600 (latest est.).

lady's-slipper NOUN any of various orchids of the Eurasian genus *Cypripedium,* esp *C. calceolus,* having reddish or purple flowers. See also **moccasin flower, cypripedium.**

lady's-smock NOUN a N temperate plant, *Cardamine pratensis,* with white or rose-pink flowers: family *Brassicaceae* (crucifers). Also called: **cuckooflower.**

lady's-thumb NOUN the usual US name for **red shank** (the plant).

lady's-tresses *or* **ladies'-tresses** NOUN (*functioning as singular or plural*) any of various orchids of the genera *Spiranthes* or *Goodyera,* having spikes of small white fragrant flowers.

Laertes (leɪ'ɜːtiːz) NOUN *Greek myth* the father of Odysseus.

laetrile ('leɪəˌtraɪl) NOUN an extract of peach stones, containing amygdalin, sold as a cure for cancer but judged useless and possibly dangerous by medical scientists.
▷HISTORY C20: from LAEVOROTATORY + NITRILE

laevo- *or US* **levo-** COMBINING FORM [1] on or towards the left: *laevorotatory.* [2] (in chemistry) denoting a laevorotatory compound: *laevulose.*
▷HISTORY from Latin *laevus* left

laevogyrate (ˌliːvəʊ'dʒaɪreɪt) ADJECTIVE another word for **laevorotatory.**

laevorotation (ˌliːvəʊrəʊ'teɪʃən) NOUN [1] a rotation to the left. [2] an anticlockwise rotation of the plane of polarization of plane-polarized light as a result of its passage through a crystal, liquid, or solution. ◆ Compare **dextrorotation.**

laevorotatory (ˌliːvəʊ'rəʊtətərɪ, -trɪ) *or* **laevorotary** ADJECTIVE of, having, or causing laevorotation. Also: **laevogyrate.**

laevulin ('lɛvjʊlɪn) NOUN a polysaccharide occurring in the tubers of certain helianthus plants.
▷HISTORY C19: from LAEVULOSE + -IN

laevulose ('lɛvjʊˌləʊs, -ˌləʊz) NOUN another name for **fructose.**
▷HISTORY C19: from LAEVO- + -ULE + -OSE²

Laffer curve ('læfə) NOUN *Economics* a curve on a graph showing government tax revenue plotted against percentage tax rates. It has been used to show that a cut in a high tax rate can increase government revenue.
▷HISTORY C20: named after Arthur *Laffer* (born 1940), US economist

LAFTA ('læftə) NOUN ACRONYM FOR Latin American Free Trade Area, the name before 1981 of the Latin American Integration Association. See **LAIA.**

lag¹ (læg) VERB **lags, lagging, lagged.** (*intr*) [1] (often foll by *behind*) to hang (back) or fall (behind) in movement, progress, development, etc. [2] to fall away in strength or intensity. [3] to determine an order of play in certain games, as by rolling marbles towards a line or, in billiards, hitting cue balls up the table against the top cushion in an attempt to bring them back close to the headrail. ◆ NOUN [4] the act or state of slowing down or falling behind. [5] the interval of time between two events, esp between an action and its effect. [6] an act of lagging in a game, such as billiards.
▷HISTORY C16: of obscure origin

lag² (læg) *Slang* ◆ NOUN [1] a convict or ex-convict (esp in the phrase **old lag**). [2] a term of imprisonment. ◆ VERB **lags, lagging, lagged.** [3] (*tr*) to arrest or put in prison.
▷HISTORY C19: of unknown origin

lag³ (læg) VERB **lags, lagging, lagged.** [1] (*tr*) to cover (a pipe, cylinder, etc.) with lagging to prevent loss of heat. ◆ NOUN [2] the insulating casing of a steam cylinder, boiler, etc.; lagging. [3] a stave or lath.
▷HISTORY C17: of Scandinavian origin; related to Swedish *lagg* stave

lagan ('lægᵊn) *or* **ligan** ('laɪgᵊn) NOUN goods or wreckage on the sea bed, sometimes attached to a buoy to permit recovery. Compare **flotsam, jetsam.**
▷HISTORY C16: from Old French *lagan,* probably of Germanic origin; compare Old Norse *lögn* dragnet

Lag b'Omer *Hebrew* (lag bə'ɔmɛr; *English* læg 'bəʊmə) NOUN a Jewish holiday celebrated on the 18th day of Iyar.
▷HISTORY Hebrew, literally: 33rd (day) of the Omer

lag correlation NOUN *Statistics* another name for **cross-correlation.**

lagena (lə'dʒiːnə) NOUN [1] a bottle with a narrow neck. [2] an outgrowth of the sacculus in the ear of fishes and amphibians, thought to be homologous to the cochlea of mammals.
▷HISTORY C19: Latin, a flask, from Greek *lagēnos*

lager¹ ('lɑːgə) NOUN a light-bodied effervescent

beer, fermented in a closed vessel using yeasts that sink to the bottom of the brew. Compare **ale**.
▷HISTORY C19: from German *Lagerbier* beer for storing, from *Lager* storehouse

lager² (ˈlɑːgə) NOUN a variant spelling of **laager**.

lagered-up *or* **lagered** (ˈlɑːgəd) ADJECTIVE *Brit informal* intoxicated, esp after drinking lager.

lager lout NOUN a rowdy or aggressive young drunk male.

lager top *or* **lager tops** NOUN *Brit* a pint or half-pint of lager with a dash of lemonade.

laggard (ˈlægəd) NOUN [1] a person who lags behind. [2] a dawdler or straggler. ◆ ADJECTIVE [3] *Rare* sluggish, slow, or dawdling.
▸ˈ**laggardly** ADVERB ▸ˈ**laggardness** NOUN

lagging (ˈlægɪŋ) NOUN [1] insulating material wrapped around pipes, boilers, etc., or laid in a roof loft, to prevent loss of heat. [2] the act or process of applying lagging. [3] a wooden frame used to support an arch during construction.

lagniappe *or* **lagnappe** (lænˈjæp, ˈlænjæp) NOUN *US* [1] a small gift, esp one given to a customer who makes a purchase. [2] something given or obtained as a gratuity or bonus.
▷HISTORY C19: Louisiana French, from American Spanish *la ñapa,* from Quechua *yápa* addition

lagomorph (ˈlægəʊˌmɔːf) NOUN any placental mammal of the order *Lagomorpha,* having two pairs of upper incisors specialized for gnawing: includes pikas, rabbits, and hares.
▷HISTORY C19: via New Latin from Greek *lagōs* hare; see -MORPH
▸ˌ**lagoˈmorphic** *or* ˌ**lagoˈmorphous** ADJECTIVE

lagoon (ləˈguːn) NOUN [1] a body of water cut off from the open sea by coral reefs or sand bars. [2] any small body of water, esp one adjoining a larger one. ◆ Also (rare): **lagune**.
▷HISTORY C17: from Italian *laguna,* from Latin *lacūna* pool; see LACUNA

Lagoon Islands PLURAL NOUN a former name of **Tuvalu**.

Lagos (ˈleɪgɒs) NOUN [1] the former capital and chief port of Nigeria, on the Bight of Benin: first settled in the sixteenth century; a slave market until the nineteenth century; ceded to Britain (1861); university (1962). Pop.: 1 484 000 (1995 est.). [2] a state of SW Nigeria. Capital: Ikeja. Pop.: 6 357 253 (1995 est.). Area: 3345 sq. km (1292 sq. miles).

Lagrangian point NOUN *Astronomy* one of five points in the plane of revolution of two bodies in orbit around their common centre of gravity, at which a third body of negligible mass can remain in equilibrium with respect to the other two bodies.
▷HISTORY named after Comte Joseph Louis *Lagrange* (1736–1813), French mathematician and astronomer

La Granja (*Spanish* la ˈgraŋxa) NOUN another name for **San Ildefonso**.

lag screw NOUN a woodscrew with a square head.
▷HISTORY from LAG³; the screw was originally used to fasten barrel staves

Lagting *or* **Lagthing** (ˈlɑːgtɪŋ) NOUN the upper chamber of the Norwegian parliament. See also **Storting, Odelsting**.
▷HISTORY Norwegian, from *lag* law + *ting* parliament

La Guaira *or* **La Guayra** (*Spanish* la ˈgwaira) NOUN the chief seaport of Venezuela, on the Caribbean. Pop.: 26 669 (1990 est.).

lah (lɑː) NOUN *Music* (in tonic sol-fa) the sixth note of any major scale; submediant.
▷HISTORY C14: see GAMUT

lahar (ˈlɑːhɑː) NOUN a landslide of volcanic debris mixed with water down the sides of a volcano, usually precipitated by heavy rainfall.
▷HISTORY C20: from Javanese: lava

lah-di-dah (ˌlɑːdiːˈdɑː) ADJECTIVE, NOUN *Informal* a variant spelling of **la-di-da**.

Lahnda (ˈlɑːndə) NOUN a language or group of dialects of Pakistan, belonging to the Indic branch of the Indo-European family and closely related to Punjabi.

La Hogue (*French* la ɔg) NOUN a roadstead off the NW coast of France: scene of the defeat of the French by the Dutch and English fleet (1692).

Lahore (ləˈhɔː) NOUN [1] a city in NE Pakistan: capital of the former province of West Pakistan (1955–70); University of the Punjab (1882). Pop.: 5 063 499 (1998). [2] a variety of large domestic fancy pigeon having a black-and-white plumage.

Lahti (*Finnish* ˈlɑhti) NOUN a town in S Finland: site of the main Finnish radio and television stations; furniture industry. Pop.: 94 706 (1994).

LAIA ABBREVIATION FOR Latin American Integration Association (before 1981, known as the Latin American Free Trade Area). An economic group, its members are Argentina, Bolivia, Brazil, Chile, Colombia, Ecuador, Mexico, Paraguay, Peru, Uruguay, and Venezuela.

Laibach (ˈlaibax) NOUN the German name for **Ljubljana**.

laic (ˈleɪɪk) ADJECTIVE *also* **laical**. [1] of or involving the laity; secular. ◆ NOUN [2] a rare word for **layman**.
▷HISTORY C15: from Late Latin *lāicus* LAY³
▸ˈ**laically** ADVERB ▸ˈ**laicism** NOUN

laicize *or* **laicise** (ˈleɪɪˌsaɪz) VERB (*tr*) to withdraw clerical or ecclesiastical character or status from (an institution, building, etc.).
▸ˌ**laiciˈzation** *or* ˌ**laiciˈsation** NOUN

laid (leɪd) VERB the past tense and past participle of **lay¹**.

laid-back ADJECTIVE *Informal* relaxed in style, character, or behaviour; easy-going and unhurried.

laid paper NOUN paper with a regular mesh impressed upon it by the dandy roller on a paper-making machine. Compare **wove paper**.

laik (leɪk) VERB *Northern English dialect* [1] (when *intr,* often foll by *about*) to play (a game, etc.). [2] (*intr*) to be on holiday, esp to take a day off work. [3] (*intr*) to be unemployed.
▷HISTORY C14: *leiken,* from Old Norse *leika;* related to Old English *lacan* to manoeuvre; compare LARK²

Lailat-ul-Qadr (ˌleɪlætʊlˈkɑːdə) NOUN a night of study and prayer observed annually by Muslims to mark the communication of the Koran: it usually follows the 27th day of Ramadan.
▷HISTORY from Arabic: night of determination

lain (leɪn) VERB the past participle of **lie²**.

Laingian (ˈlæŋɪən) ADJECTIVE [1] of or based on the theory of Scottish psychiatrist R. D. Laing (1927–89) that mental illnesses are understandable as natural responses to stress in family and social situations. ◆ NOUN [2] a follower or adherent of Laing's teaching.

laipse (leɪps) *Northern and Midland English dialect* ◆ VERB (*tr*) [1] to beat soundly. [2] to defeat totally.

lair¹ (lɛə) NOUN [1] the resting place of a wild animal. [2] *Informal* a place of seclusion or hiding. [3] an enclosure or shed for farm animals. [4] *Scot* the ground for a grave in a cemetery. ◆ VERB [5] (*intr*) (esp of a wild animal) to retreat to or rest in a lair. [6] (*tr*) to drive or place (an animal) in a lair.
▷HISTORY Old English *leger;* related to LIE² and Old High German *leger* bed

lair² (ler) NOUN, VERB a Scot word for **mire**.
▷HISTORY from Old Norse *leir* mud

lair³ (lɛə) *Austral, slang* ◆ NOUN [1] a flashy man who shows off. ◆ VERB [2] (*intr;* foll by *up* or *around*) to behave or dress like a lair.
▷HISTORY perhaps from LEER

lairage (ˈlɛərɪdʒ) NOUN accommodation for farm animals, esp at docks or markets.

laird (lɛəd; *Scot* lerd) NOUN *Scot* a landowner, esp of a large estate.
▷HISTORY C15: Scottish variant of LORD

lairy (ˈlɛərɪ) ADJECTIVE **lairier, lairiest**. gaudy or flashy.
▷HISTORY C20: from LEERY

laissez aller *or* ***laisser aller*** *French* (lese ale) NOUN lack of constraint; freedom.
▷HISTORY literally: let go

laissez faire *or* **laisser faire** (ˌleseɪ ˈfɛə; *French* lese fɛr) NOUN [1] **a** Also called: **individualism**. the doctrine of unrestricted freedom in commerce, esp for private interests. **b** (*as modifier*): *a laissez-faire economy*. [2] indifference or noninterference, esp in the affairs of others.
▷HISTORY French, literally: let (them) act
▸ˌ**laissez-ˈfaireism** *or* ˌ**laisser-ˈfaireism** NOUN

laissez passer *or* ***laisser passer*** *French* (lese pase) NOUN a document granting unrestricted access or movement to its holder.
▷HISTORY literally: let pass

laity (ˈleɪɪtɪ) NOUN [1] laymen, as distinguished from clergymen. [2] all people not of a specific occupation.
▷HISTORY C16: from LAY³

Laius (ˈlaɪəs) NOUN *Greek myth* a king of Thebes, killed by his son Oedipus, who did not know of their relationship.

lake¹ (leɪk) NOUN [1] an expanse of water entirely surrounded by land and unconnected to the sea except by rivers or streams. Related adjective: **lacustrine**. [2] anything resembling this. [3] a surplus of a liquid commodity: *a wine lake*.
▷HISTORY C13: *lac,* via Old French from Latin *lacus* basin

lake² (leɪk) NOUN [1] a bright pigment used in textile dyeing and printing inks, produced by the combination of an organic colouring matter with an inorganic compound, usually a metallic salt, oxide, or hydroxide. See also **mordant**. [2] a red dye obtained by combining a metallic compound with cochineal.
▷HISTORY C17: variant of LAC¹

Lake District NOUN a region of lakes and mountains in NW England, in Cumbria: includes England's largest lake (Windermere) and highest mountain (Scafell Pike); national park; literary associations (the Lake Poets); tourist region. Also called: **Lakeland**.

lake dwelling NOUN a dwelling, esp in prehistoric villages, constructed on platforms supported by wooden piles driven into the bottom of a lake.
▸**lake dweller** NOUN

lake herring NOUN [1] another name for **cisco**. [2] another name for **powan**.

Lakeland (ˈleɪkˌlænd) NOUN [1] another name for the **Lake District**. ◆ ADJECTIVE [2] of or relating to the Lake District.

Lakeland terrier NOUN a wire-haired breed of terrier, originally from the Lake District and used for hunting.

Lake of the Woods NOUN a lake in N central North America, mostly in W Northern Ontario, Canada: fed chiefly by the Rainy River; drains into Lake Winnipeg by the Winnipeg River; many islands; tourist region. Area: 3846 sq. km (1485 sq. miles).

Lake Poets PLURAL NOUN the English poets Wordsworth, Coleridge, and Southey, who lived in and drew inspiration from the Lake District at the beginning of the 19th century.

laker (ˈleɪkə) NOUN a cargo vessel used on lakes.

Lake Success NOUN a village in SE New York State, on W Long Island: headquarters of the United Nations Security Council from 1946 to 1951. Pop.: 2450 (1990 est.).

lakh *or* **lac** (lɑːk) NOUN (in India and Pakistan) the number 100 000, esp when referring to this sum of rupees.
▷HISTORY C17: from Hindi *lākh,* ultimately from Sanskrit *lakshā* a sign

laksa (ˈlæksa) NOUN (in Malaysia) a dish of Chinese origin consisting of rice noodles served in curry or hot soup.
▷HISTORY from Malay: ten thousand

Lakshadweep Islands (lækˈʃædwiːp) PLURAL NOUN a group of 26 coral islands and reefs in the Arabian Sea, off the SW coast of India: a union territory of India since 1956. Administrative centre: Kavaratti Island. Pop.: 60 595 (2001). Area: 28 sq. km (11 sq. miles). Former name (until 1973): **Laccadive, Minicoy, and Amindivi Islands**.

Lakshmi (ˈlɑːkʃmɪ) NOUN *Hinduism* the goddess of wealth and prosperity, and the consort of the god Vishnu.
▷HISTORY from Sanskrit *Lākṣmī,* literally: wealth, splendour

laky (ˈleɪkɪ) ADJECTIVE **lakier, lakiest**. of the reddish colour of the pigment lake.

Lala (ˈlɑːlɑː) NOUN a title or form of address, equivalent to *Mr,* used in India.
▷HISTORY Hindi

La-La land (ˈlɑːˌlɑː) NOUN *Slang* [1] a nickname for

Los Angeles. 2 (*not capitals*) a place that is remote from reality.
▷HISTORY C20: reduplication of the initials LA

lalang (ˈlɑːlɑːŋ) NOUN a coarse weedy Malaysian grass, *Imperata arundinacea*.
▷HISTORY Malay

lalapalooza (ˌlɒləpəˈluːzə) NOUN a variant spelling of **lollapalooza**.

-lalia COMBINING FORM indicating a speech defect or abnormality: *coprolalia; echolalia*.
▷HISTORY New Latin, from Greek *lalia* chatter, from *lalein* to babble

La Línea (*Spanish* la ˈlinea) NOUN a town in SW Spain, on the Bay of Gibraltar. Pop.: 57 000 (latest est.). Official name: **La Línea de la Concepción** (ðe la ˌkonθepˈθjon).

Lallans (ˈlælənz) *or* **Lallan** (ˈlælən) NOUN 1 a literary version of the variety of English spoken and written in the Lowlands of Scotland. 2 (*modifier*) of or relating to the Lowlands of Scotland or their dialects.
▷HISTORY Scottish variant of LOWLANDS

lallation (læˈleɪʃən) NOUN *Phonetics* a defect of speech consisting of the pronunciation of (r) as (l).
▷HISTORY C17: from Latin *lallāre* to sing lullaby, of imitative origin

lallygag (ˈlælɪˌɡæɡ) *or* **lollygag** VERB **-gags, -gagging, -gagged.** (*intr*) *US* to loiter aimlessly.
▷HISTORY C20: of unknown origin

lam[1] (læm) VERB **lams, lamming, lammed.** *Slang* 1 (*tr*) to thrash or beat. 2 (*intr; usually foll by* into *or* out) to make a sweeping stroke or blow.
▷HISTORY C16: from Scandinavian; related to Old Norse *lemja*

lam[2] (læm) *US and Canadian, slang* ◆ NOUN 1 a sudden flight or escape, esp to avoid arrest. 2 **on the lam. a** making an escape. **b** in hiding. ◆ VERB **lams, lamming, lammed.** 3 (*intr*) to escape or flee.
▷HISTORY C19: perhaps from LAM[1] (hence, to be off)

Lam. *Bible* ABBREVIATION FOR Lamentations.

lama (ˈlɑːmə) NOUN a priest or monk of Lamaism.
▷HISTORY C17: from Tibetan *blama*

Lamaism (ˈlɑːməˌɪzəm) NOUN the Mahayana form of Buddhism of Tibet and Mongolia. See also **Dalai Lama.**
▸**ˈLamaist** NOUN, ADJECTIVE ▸**ˌLamaˈistic** ADJECTIVE

La Mancha (*Spanish* la ˈmantʃa) NOUN a plateau of central Spain, between the mountains of Toledo and the hills of Cuenca: traditionally associated with episodes in *Don Quixote*. Average height: 600 m (2000 ft.).

La Manche (*French* la mɑ̃ʃ) NOUN See **Manche** (sense 2).

Lamarckian (lɑːˈmɑːkɪən) ADJECTIVE 1 of or relating to Jean Baptiste Pierre Antoine de Monet, Chevalier de Lamarck (1744–1829), the French naturalist. ◆ NOUN 2 a supporter of Lamarckism.

Lamarckism (lɑːˈmɑːkɪzəm) NOUN the theory of organic evolution proposed by Jean Baptiste Pierre Antoine de Monet, Chevalier de Lamarck (1744–1829), the French naturalist, based on the principle that characteristics of an organism modified during its lifetime are inheritable. See also **acquired characteristic, Neo-Lamarckism.**

lamasery (ˈlɑːməsərɪ) NOUN, *plural* **-series.** a monastery of lamas.
▷HISTORY C19: from French *lamaserie*, from LAMA + French *-serie*, from Persian *serāī* palace

lamb (læm) NOUN 1 the young of a sheep. 2 the meat of a young sheep. 3 a person, esp a child, who is innocent, meek, good, etc. 4 a person easily deceived. 5 **like a lamb to the slaughter. a** without resistance. **b** innocently. ◆ VERB 6 (*intr*) Also: **lamb down.** (of a ewe) to give birth. 7 (*tr; used in the passive*) (of a lamb) to be born. 8 (*intr*) (of a shepherd) to tend the ewes and newborn lambs at lambing time. ◆ See also **lamb down.**
▷HISTORY Old English *lamb*, from Germanic; compare German *Lamm*, Old High German and Old Norse *lamb*
▸**ˈlambˌlike** ADJECTIVE

Lamb (læm) NOUN **the.** a title given to Christ in the New Testament.

lambada (læmˈbɑːdə) NOUN 1 an erotic dance, originating in Brazil, performed by two people who hold each other closely and gyrate their hips in synchronized movements. 2 the music that accompanies the lambada, combining salsa, calypso, and reggae.
▷HISTORY C20: from Portuguese, literally: the snapping of a whip

Lambaréné (*French* lɑ̃barene) NOUN a town in W Gabon on the Ogooué River: site of the hospital built by Albert Schweitzer, who died and was buried there (1965). Pop.: 50 000 (latest est.).

lambast (læmˈbæst) *or* **lambaste** (læmˈbeɪst) VERB (*tr*) 1 to beat or whip severely. 2 to reprimand or scold.
▷HISTORY C17: perhaps from LAM[1] + BASTE[3]

lambda (ˈlæmdə) NOUN the 11th letter of the Greek alphabet (Λ, λ), a consonant transliterated as *l*.
▷HISTORY C14: from Greek, from Semitic; related to LAMED

lambda calculus NOUN *Logic, computing* a formalized description of functions and the way in which they combine, developed by Alonzo Church and used in the theory of certain high-level programming languages.
▷HISTORY C20: from the use of the symbol *lambda* (λ) to represent the mathematical functions

lambdacism (ˈlæmdəˌsɪzəm) NOUN *Phonetics* 1 excessive use or idiosyncratic pronunciation of *l*. 2 another word for **lallation.**
▷HISTORY C17: from Late Latin *labdacismus*, from Greek

lambdoid (ˈlæmdɔɪd) *or* **lambdoidal** ADJECTIVE 1 having the shape of the Greek letter lambda. 2 of or denoting the suture near the back of the skull between the occipital and parietal bones.
▷HISTORY C16: via French from Greek *lambdoeidēs*

lamb down VERB (*adverb*) 1 (*intr*) another term for **lamb** (sense 6). 2 (*tr*) *Austral informal* to persuade (someone) to spend all his money.

lambent (ˈlæmbənt) ADJECTIVE 1 (esp of a flame) flickering softly over a surface. 2 glowing with soft radiance. 3 (of wit or humour) light or brilliant.
▷HISTORY C17: from the present participle of Latin *lambere* to lick
▸**ˈlambency** NOUN ▸**ˈlambently** ADVERB

lambert (ˈlæmbət) NOUN the cgs unit of illumination, equal to 1 lumen per square centimetre. Symbol: L.
▷HISTORY named after J. H. *Lambert* (1728–77), German mathematician and physicist

Lambeth (ˈlæmbəθ) NOUN 1 a borough of S Greater London, on the Thames: contains **Lambeth Palace** (the London residence of the Archbishop of Canterbury). Pop.: 266 170 (2001). Area: 27 sq. km (11 sq. miles). 2 the Archbishop of Canterbury in his official capacity.

Lambeth Conference NOUN the decennial conference of Anglican bishops, begun in 1867. See also **Lambeth Quadrilateral.**

Lambeth Quadrilateral NOUN the four essentials agreed upon at the Lambeth Conference of 1888 for a United Christian Church, namely, the Holy Scriptures, the Apostles' Creed, the sacraments of baptism and Holy Communion, and the historic episcopate.

Lambeth walk NOUN *Chiefly Brit* a line dance popular in the 1930s.

lambing (ˈlæmɪŋ) NOUN 1 **a** the birth of lambs. **b** (*as modifier*): *lambing time.* 2 the shepherd's work of tending the ewes and newborn lambs at this time.

lambkin (ˈlæmkɪn) *or* **lambie** NOUN 1 a small or young lamb. 2 a term of affection for a small endearing child.

Lamb of God NOUN a title given to Christ in the New Testament, probably with reference to his sacrificial death.

lambrequin (ˈlæmbrɪkɪn, ˈlæmbə-) NOUN 1 an ornamental hanging covering the edge of a shelf or the upper part of a window or door. 2 **a** a border pattern giving a draped effect, used on ceramics, etc. **b** (*as modifier*): *a lambrequin pattern.* 3 (*often plural*) a scarf worn over a helmet. 4 *Heraldry* another name for **mantling.**
▷HISTORY C18: from French, from Dutch *lamperkin* (unattested), diminutive of *lamper* veil

lamb's ears NOUN (*functioning as singular*) a perennial herb, *Stachys lanata*, planted for its foliage, which is covered with white woolly down; the purplish or striped flowers are small. Also called: **lamb's tongue,** (Scot) **lamb's lugs.**

lamb's fry NOUN 1 *Brit* lamb's offal, esp lamb's testicles, as food. 2 *Austral and NZ* lamb's liver as food.

Lamb shift NOUN the small difference in energy between two states of the hydrogen atom detected by Willis Eugene Lamb (born 1913), the US physicist.

lambskin (ˈlæmˌskɪn) NOUN 1 the skin of a lamb, esp with the wool still on. 2 **a** a material or garment prepared from this skin. **b** (*as modifier*): *a lambskin coat.* 3 a cotton or woollen fabric resembling this skin.

lamb's lettuce NOUN another name for **corn salad.**

lamb's-quarters NOUN, *plural* **lamb's-quarters.** a US name for **fat hen.**

lamb's tails PLURAL NOUN the pendulous catkins of the hazel tree.

lamb's wool NOUN **a** a fine soft wool obtained from a lamb at its first shearing. **b** (*as modifier*): *lamb's-wool jumpers.*

LAMDA (ˈlæmdə) NOUN ACRONYM FOR London Academy of Music and Dramatic Art.

lame[1] (leɪm) ADJECTIVE 1 disabled or crippled in the legs or feet. 2 painful or weak: *a lame back.* 3 weak; unconvincing: *a lame excuse.* 4 not effective or enthusiastic: *a lame try.* 5 *US, slang* conventional or uninspiring. ◆ VERB 6 (*tr*) to make lame.
▷HISTORY Old English *lama*; related to Old Norse *lami*, German *lahm*
▸**ˈlamely** ADVERB ▸**ˈlameness** NOUN

lame[2] (leɪm) NOUN one of the overlapping metal plates used in armour after about 1330; splint.
▷HISTORY C16: via Old French from Latin *lāmina* a thin plate, LAMINA

lamé (ˈlɑːmeɪ) NOUN **a** a fabric of silk, cotton, or wool interwoven with threads of metal. **b** (*as modifier*): *a gold lamé gown.*
▷HISTORY from French, from Old French *lame* gold or silver thread, thin plate, from Latin *lāmina* thin plate

lamebrain (ˈleɪmˌbreɪn) NOUN *Informal* a stupid or slow-witted person.

lamed (ˈlɑːmɪd; *Hebrew* ˈlamɛd) NOUN the 12th letter in the Hebrew alphabet (ל), transliterated as *l*. Also: **lamedh** (ˈlamɛd).
▷HISTORY from Hebrew, literally: ox goad (from its shape)

lame duck NOUN 1 a person or thing that is disabled or ineffectual. 2 *Stock Exchange* a speculator who cannot discharge his liabilities. 3 a company with a large workforce and high prestige that is unable to meet foreign competition without government support. 4 *US* **a** an elected official or body of officials remaining in office in the interval between the election and inauguration of a successor. **b** (*as modifier*): *a lame-duck president.* 5 (*modifier*) *US* designating a term of office after which the officeholder will not run for re-election.

lamella (ləˈmɛlə) NOUN, *plural* **-lae** (-liː) *or* **-las.** 1 a thin layer, plate, or membrane, esp any of the calcified layers of which bone is formed. 2 *Botany* **a** any of the spore-bearing gills of a mushroom. **b** any of the membranes in a chloroplast. **c** Also called: **middle lamella.** a layer of pectin cementing together adjacent cells. 3 one of a number of timber, metal, or concrete members connected along a pattern of intersecting diagonal lines to form a framed vaulted roof structure. 4 any thin sheet of material or thin layer in a fluid.
▷HISTORY C17: New Latin, from Latin, diminutive of *lāmina* thin plate
▸**laˈmellar** *or* **lamellate** (ˈlæmɪˌleɪt, -lɪt, ləˈmɛleɪt, -lɪt) *or* **lamellose** (ləˈmɛləʊs, ˈlæmɪˌləʊs) ADJECTIVE ▸**laˈmellarly** *or* **ˈlamellately** ADVERB ▸**ˈlamelˌlated** ADJECTIVE ▸**ˌlamelˈlation** NOUN ▸**lamellosity** (ˌlæməˈlɒsɪtɪ) NOUN

lamelli- COMBINING FORM indicating lamella or lamellae: *lamellibranch.*

lamellibranch (ləˈmɛlɪˌbræŋk) NOUN, ADJECTIVE another word for **bivalve** (senses 1, 2).
▷HISTORY C19: from New Latin *lamellibranchia* plate-gilled (animals); see LAMELLA, BRANCHIA
▸**laˌmelliˈbranchiate** ADJECTIVE, NOUN

lamellicorn (ləˈmɛlɪˌkɔːn) NOUN 1 any beetle of

the superfamily *Lamellicornia,* having flattened terminal plates to the antennae: includes the scarabs and stag beetles. ◆ ADJECTIVE [2] of, relating to, or belonging to the *Lamellicornia.* [3] designating antennae with platelike terminal segments.
▷HISTORY C19: from New Latin *Lamellicornia* plate-horned (animals)

lamelliform (ləˈmɛlɪˌfɔːm) ADJECTIVE shaped like a lamella; platelike: *lamelliform antennae.*

lamellirostral (ləˌmɛlɪˈrɒstrəl) *or* **lamellirostrate** (ləˌmɛlɪˈrɒstreɪt) ADJECTIVE (of ducks, geese, etc.) having a bill fringed with thin plates on the inner edge for straining water from food.
▷HISTORY C19: from New Latin *lāmellirostris,* from LAMELLA + *rostrum* beak

lament (ləˈmɛnt) VERB [1] to feel or express sorrow, remorse, or regret (for or over). ◆ NOUN [2] an expression of sorrow. [3] a poem or song in which a death is lamented.
▷HISTORY C16: from Latin *lāmentum*
▸**laˈmenter** NOUN ▸**laˈmentingly** ADVERB

lamentable (ˈlæməntəbᵊl) ADJECTIVE [1] wretched, deplorable, or distressing. [2] an archaic word for **mournful.**
▸**ˈlamentableness** NOUN ▸**ˈlamentably** ADVERB

lamentation (ˌlæmɛnˈteɪʃən) NOUN [1] a lament; expression of sorrow. [2] the act of lamenting.

Lamentations (ˌlæmɛnˈteɪʃənz) NOUN (*functioning as singular*) [1] a book of the Old Testament, traditionally ascribed to the prophet Jeremiah, lamenting the destruction of Jerusalem. [2] a musical setting of these poems.

lamented (ləˈmɛntɪd) ADJECTIVE grieved for or regretted (often in the phrase **late lamented**): *our late lamented employer.*
▸**laˈmentedly** ADVERB

lamia (ˈleɪmɪə) NOUN, *plural* **-mias** *or* **-miae** (-mɪˌiː). [1] *Classical myth* one of a class of female monsters depicted with a snake's body and a woman's head and breasts. [2] a vampire or sorceress.
▷HISTORY C14: via Latin from Greek *Lamia*

lamina (ˈlæmɪnə) NOUN, *plural* **-nae** (-ˌniː) *or* **-nas.** [1] a thin plate or layer, esp of bone or mineral. [2] *Botany* the flat blade of a leaf, petal, or thallus.
▷HISTORY C17: New Latin, from Latin: thin plate
▸**ˈlaminar** *or* **laminose** (ˈlæmɪˌnəʊs, -ˌnəʊz) ADJECTIVE

laminar flow NOUN nonturbulent motion of a fluid in which parallel layers have different velocities relative to each other. Compare **turbulent flow.** See also **streamline flow.**

laminaria (ˌlæmɪˈnɛərɪə) NOUN any brown seaweed of the genus *Laminaria,* having large fluted leathery fronds.
▷HISTORY C19: genus name formed from Latin *lamina* plate

laminarin (ˌlæmɪˈnɑːrɪn) NOUN a carbohydrate, consisting of repeated glucose units, that is the main storage product of brown algae.
▷HISTORY C20: from LAMINAR(IA) + -IN

laminate VERB (ˈlæmɪˌneɪt) [1] (*tr*) to make (material in sheet form) by bonding together two or more thin sheets. [2] to split or be split into thin sheets. [3] (*tr*) to beat, form, or press (material, esp metal) into thin sheets. [4] (*tr*) to cover or overlay with a thin sheet of material. ◆ NOUN (ˈlæmɪˌneɪt, -nɪt) [5] a material made by bonding together two or more sheets. ◆ ADJECTIVE (ˈlæmɪˌneɪt, -nɪt) [6] having or composed of lamina; laminated.
▷HISTORY C17: from New Latin *lāminātus* plated
▸**laminable** (ˈlæmɪnəbᵊl) ADJECTIVE ▸**ˈlamiˌnator** NOUN

laminated (ˈlæmɪˌneɪtɪd) ADJECTIVE [1] composed of thin sheets (of plastic, wood, etc.) superimposed and bonded together by synthetic resins, usually under heat and pressure. [2] covered with a thin protective layer of plastic or synthetic resin. [3] another word for **laminate** (sense 6).

lamination (ˌlæmɪˈneɪʃən) NOUN [1] the act of laminating or the state of being laminated. [2] a layered structure. [3] a layer; lamina. [4] one of a set of iron plates forming the core of an electrical transformer. [5] *Geology* laminar stratification, typically shown by shales.

laminectomy (ˌlæmɪˈnɛktəmɪ) NOUN, *plural* **-mies.** surgical incision into the backbone to gain access to the spinal cord. Also called: **rachiotomy.**

lamington (ˈlæmɪŋtən) NOUN *Austral and NZ* a cube of sponge cake coated in chocolate and dried coconut.
▷HISTORY C20 (in the earlier sense: a homburg hat): named after Baron *Lamington,* governor of Queensland (1896–1901)

laminitis (ˌlæmɪˈnaɪtɪs) NOUN inflammation of the laminated tissue structure to which the hoof is attached, esp in horses and cattle. Also called: **founder.**
▷HISTORY C19: from New Latin, from LAMINA + -ITIS

Lammas (ˈlæməs) NOUN [1] *RC Church* Aug. 1, held as a feast, commemorating St. Peter's miraculous deliverance from prison. [2] Also called: **Lammas Day.** the same day formerly observed in England as a harvest festival. In Scotland Lammas is a quarter day.
▷HISTORY Old English *hlāfmæsse* loaf mass

Lammastide (ˈlæməsˌtaɪd) NOUN *Archaic* the season of Lammas.

lammergeier *or* **lammergeyer** (ˈlæməˌgaɪə) NOUN a rare vulture, *Gypaetus barbatus,* of S Europe, Africa, and Asia, with dark wings, a pale breast, and black feathers around the bill: family *Accipitridae* (hawks). Also called: **bearded vulture.**
▷HISTORY C19: from German *Lämmergeier,* from *Lämmer* lambs + *Geier* vulture

lamp (læmp) NOUN [1] **a** any of a number of devices that produce illumination: *an electric lamp; a gas lamp; an oil lamp.* **b** (*in combination*): *lampshade.* [2] a device for holding one or more electric light bulbs: *a table lamp.* [3] a vessel in which a liquid fuel is burned to supply illumination. [4] any of a variety of devices that produce radiation, esp for therapeutic purposes: *an ultraviolet lamp.*
▷HISTORY C13 *lampe,* via Old French from Latin *lampas,* from Greek, from *lampein* to shine

lampas[1] (ˈlæmpəs) *or* **lampers** (ˈlæmpəz) NOUN a swelling of the mucous membrane of the hard palate of horses.
▷HISTORY C16: from Old French; origin obscure

lampas[2] (ˈlæmpəs) NOUN an ornate damask-like cloth of cotton or silk and cotton, used in upholstery.
▷HISTORY C14 (a kind of crepe): probably from Middle Dutch *lampers*

lampblack (ˈlæmpˌblæk) NOUN a finely divided form of almost pure carbon produced by the incomplete combustion of organic compounds, such as natural gas, used in making carbon electrodes and dynamo brushes and as a pigment.

lamp chimney NOUN a glass tube that surrounds the wick in an oil lamp.

Lampedusa (ˌlæmpɪˈdjuːzə) NOUN an island in the Mediterranean, between Malta and Tunisia. Area: about 21 sq. km (8 sq. miles).

lamper eel (ˈlæmpə) NOUN another name for **lamprey.**
▷HISTORY C19 *lamper,* variant of LAMPREY

lampern (ˈlæmpən) NOUN a migratory European lamprey, *Lampetra fluviatilis,* that spawns in rivers. Also called: **river lamprey.**
▷HISTORY C14 *laumprun,* from Old French, from *lampreie* LAMPREY

lampion (ˈlæmpɪən) NOUN an oil-burning lamp.
▷HISTORY C19: from French via Italian *lampione,* from Old French *lampe* LAMP

lamplighter (ˈlæmpˌlaɪtə) NOUN [1] (formerly) a person who lit and extinguished street lamps, esp gas ones. [2] *Chiefly US and Canadian* any of various devices used to light lamps.

lampoon (læmˈpuːn) NOUN [1] a satire in prose or verse ridiculing a person, literary work, etc. ◆ VERB [2] (*tr*) to attack or satirize in a lampoon.
▷HISTORY C17: from French *lampon,* perhaps from *lampons* let us drink (frequently used as a refrain in poems)
▸**lamˈpooner** *or* **lamˈpoonist** NOUN ▸**lamˈpoonery** NOUN

lamppost (ˈlæmpˌpəʊst) NOUN a post supporting a lamp, esp in a street.

lamprey (ˈlæmprɪ) NOUN any eel-like cyclostome vertebrate of the family *Petromyzonidae,* having a round sucking mouth for clinging to and feeding on the blood of other animals. Also called: **lamper eel.** See also **sea lamprey.**
▷HISTORY C13: from Old French *lamproie,* from Late Latin *lamprēda;* origin obscure

lamprophyre (ˈlæmprəˌfaɪə) NOUN any of a group of basic igneous rocks consisting of feldspathoids and ferromagnesian minerals, esp biotite: occurring as dykes and minor intrusions.
▷HISTORY C19: from Greek *lampros* bright + *-phyre,* from PORPHYRY

lamp shell NOUN another name for a **brachiopod.**
▷HISTORY C19: from its likeness in shape to an ancient Roman oil lamp

lamp standard NOUN a tall metal or concrete post supporting a street lamp.

LAN ABBREVIATION FOR **local area network.**

lanai (lɑːˈnɑːɪ, ləˈnaɪ) NOUN a Hawaiian word for **veranda.**

Lanai (lɑːˈnɑːɪ, ləˈnaɪ) NOUN an island in central Hawaii, west of Maui Island. Pop.: 2426 (1990). Area: 363 sq. km. (140 sq. miles).

Lanarkshire (ˈlænəkˌʃɪə, -ʃə) NOUN a historical county of S Scotland: became part of Strathclyde region in 1975; since 1996 administered by the council areas of North Lanarkshire, South Lanarkshire, and Glasgow.

lanate (ˈleɪneɪt) *or* **lanose** (ˈleɪnəʊs, -nəʊz) ADJECTIVE *Biology* having or consisting of a woolly covering of hairs.
▷HISTORY C18: from Latin *lānātus,* from *lāna* wool

Lancashire (ˈlæŋkəˌʃɪə, -ʃə) NOUN [1] a county of NW England, on the Irish Sea: became a county palatine in 1351 and a duchy attached to the Crown; much reduced in size after the 1974 boundary changes, losing the Furness district to Cumbria and much of the south to Greater Manchester, Merseyside, and Cheshire: Blackburn with Darwen and Blackpool became independent unitary authorities in 1998. It was traditionally a cotton textiles manufacturing region. Administrative centre: Preston. Pop. (excluding unitary authorities): 1 134 974 (2001). Area (excluding unitary authorities): 2889 sq. km (1115 sq. miles). Abbreviation: **Lancs.** [2] a mild whitish-coloured cheese with a crumbly texture.

Lancashire heeler NOUN a small sturdy dog of a breed with a short thick black or liver-coloured coat with tan markings, often used for herding cattle.

Lancaster (ˈlæŋkəstə) NOUN a city in NW England, former county town of Lancashire, on the River Lune: castle (built on the site of a Roman camp); university (1964). Pop.: 44 497 (1991).

Lancastrian (læŋˈkæstrɪən) NOUN [1] a native or resident of Lancashire or Lancaster. [2] an adherent of the house of Lancaster in the Wars of the Roses. Compare **Yorkist.** ◆ ADJECTIVE [3] of or relating to Lancashire or Lancaster. [4] of or relating to the house of Lancaster.

lance (lɑːns) NOUN [1] a long weapon with a pointed head used by horsemen to unhorse or injure an opponent. [2] a similar weapon used for hunting, whaling, etc. [3] *Surgery* another name for **lancet.** [4] short for **sand lance** (another name for **sand eel**). ◆ VERB (*tr*) [5] to pierce (an abscess or boil) with a lancet to drain off pus. [6] to pierce with or as if with a lance.
▷HISTORY C13 *launce,* from Old French *lance,* from Latin *lancea*

lance corporal NOUN a noncommissioned officer of the lowest rank in the British Army.

lancejack (ˈlɑːnsˌdʒæk) NOUN *Brit military, slang* a lance corporal.

lancelet (ˈlɑːnslɪt) NOUN any of several marine animals of the genus *Branchiostoma* (formerly *Amphioxus*), esp *B. lanceolatus,* that are closely related to the vertebrates: subphylum *Cephalochordata* (cephalochordates). Also called: **amphioxus.**
▷HISTORY C19: referring to the slender shape

Lancelot (ˈlɑːnslət) NOUN (in Arthurian legend) one of the Knights of the Round Table; the lover of Queen Guinevere.

lanceolate (ˈlɑːnsɪəˌleɪt, -lɪt) ADJECTIVE narrow and tapering to a point at each end: *lanceolate leaves.*
▷HISTORY C18: from Late Latin *lanceolātus,* from *lanceola* small LANCE

lancer (ˈlɑːnsə) NOUN [1] (formerly) a cavalryman armed with a lance. [2] **a** a member of a regiment retaining such a title. **b** (*plural; capital when part of a name*) *the 21st Lancers.* ◆ See also **lancers.**

lance rest NOUN [1] a hinged bracket on the breastplate of a medieval horseman on which the lance was rested in a charge. 2 a similar structure on a knight's saddle.

lancers ('lɑːnsəz) NOUN *(functioning as singular)* 1 a quadrille for eight or sixteen couples. 2 a piece of music composed for this dance.

lance sergeant NOUN a corporal acting as a sergeant, usually on a temporary basis and without additional pay.

lancet ('lɑːnsɪt) NOUN 1 Also called: **lance.** a pointed surgical knife with two sharp edges. 2 short for **lancet arch** or **lancet window.**
▷HISTORY C15 *lancette,* from Old French: small LANCE

lancet arch NOUN a narrow acutely pointed arch having two centres of equal radii. Sometimes shortened to: **lancet.** Also called: **acute arch, Gothic arch, pointed arch, ogive.**

lanceted ('lɑːnsɪtɪd) ADJECTIVE *Architect* having one or more lancet arches or windows.

lancet fish NOUN either of two deep-sea teleost fishes, *Alepisaurus ferox* or *A. borealis,* having a long body with a long sail-like dorsal fin: family *Alepisauridae.*

lancet window NOUN a narrow window having a lancet arch. Sometimes shortened to: **lancet.**

lancewood ('lɑːnsˌwʊd) NOUN 1 any of various tropical trees, esp *Oxandra lanceolata,* yielding a tough elastic wood: family *Annonaceae.* 2 the wood of any of these trees.

Lanchow *or* **Lan-chou** ('læn'tʃaʊ) NOUN a variant transliteration of the Chinese name for **Lanzhou.**

lancinate ('lɑːnsɪˌneɪt) ADJECTIVE (esp of pain) sharp or cutting.
▷HISTORY C17: from Latin *lancinātus* pierced, rent; related to *lacer* mangled
▸ **ˌlanciˈnation** NOUN

Lancs (læŋks) ABBREVIATION FOR Lancashire.

land (lænd) NOUN 1 the solid part of the surface of the earth as distinct from seas, lakes, etc. Related adjective: **terrestrial.** 2 **a** ground, esp with reference to its use, quality, etc. **b** *(in combination)*: *land-grabber.* 3 rural or agricultural areas as contrasted with urban ones. 4 farming as an occupation or way of life. 5 *Law* **a** any tract of ground capable of being owned as property, together with any buildings on it, extending above and below the surface. **b** any hereditament, tenement, or other interest; realty. 6 **a** a country, region, or area. **b** the people of a country, etc. 7 a realm, sphere, or domain. 8 *Economics* the factor of production consisting of all natural resources. 9 the unindented part of a grooved surface, esp one of the ridges inside a rifle bore. 10 **how the land lies.** the prevailing conditions or state of affairs. ◆ VERB 11 to transfer (something) or go from a ship or boat to the shore: *land the cargo.* 12 *(intr)* to come to or touch shore. 13 to come down or bring (something) down to earth after a flight or jump. 14 to come or bring to some point, condition, or state. 15 *(tr) Angling* to retrieve (a hooked fish) from the water. 16 *(tr) Informal* to win or obtain: *to land a job.* 17 *(tr) Informal* to deliver (a blow). ◆ See also **lands, land up, land with.**
▷HISTORY Old English; compare Old Norse, Gothic *land,* Old High German *lant*
▸ **'landless** ADJECTIVE ▸ **'landlessness** NOUN

Land *German* (lant) NOUN, *plural* ***Länder*** ('lɛndər). **a** any of the federal states of Germany. **b** any of the provinces of Austria.

land agent NOUN 1 a person who administers a landed estate and its tenancies. 2 a person who acts as an agent for the sale of land.
▸ **land agency** NOUN

landammann ('lændəmən) NOUN *(sometimes capital)* the chairman of the governing council in any of several Swiss cantons.
▷HISTORY C18: Swiss German, from *Land* country + *Ammann,* from *Amt* office + *Mann* MAN

landau ('lændɔː) NOUN a four-wheeled carriage, usually horse-drawn, with two folding hoods that meet over the middle of the passenger compartment.
▷HISTORY C18: named after *Landau* (a town in Bavaria), where it was first made

landaulet *or* **landaulette** (ˌlændɔː'lɛt) NOUN 1 a small landau. 2 *US* an early type of car with a folding hood over the passenger seats and an open driver's seat.

land bank NOUN a bank that issues banknotes on the security of property.

land bridge NOUN (in zoogeography) a connecting tract of land between two continents, enabling animals to pass from one continent to the other.

land crab NOUN any of various crabs, esp of the tropical family *Gecarcinidae,* that are adapted to a partly terrestrial life.

Landdrost ('lændrɒst) NOUN *South African history* the chief magistrate of a district.
▷HISTORY C18: Afrikaans, from Dutch *land* country + *drost* sheriff, bailiff

landed ('lændɪd) ADJECTIVE 1 owning land: *landed gentry.* 2 consisting of or including land: *a landed estate.*

landed immigrant NOUN *Canadian* a former term for **permanent resident.**

lander ('lændə) NOUN a spacecraft designed to land on a planet or other body. Compare **orbiter.**

Landes *(French* lɑ̃d) NOUN 1 a department of SW France, in Aquitaine region. Capital: Mont-de-Marsan. Pop.: 327 334 (1999). Area: 9364 sq. km (3652 sq. miles). 2 a region of SW France, on the Bay of Biscay: occupies most of the Landes department and parts of Gironde and Lot-et-Garonne; consists chiefly of the most extensive forest in France. Area: 14 000 sq. km (5400 sq. miles).

Landeshauptmann ('lɑːndɪsˌhaʊptmən) NOUN the head of government in an Austrian state.
▷HISTORY C20: from German, from *Land* country + *Hauptmann* leader

landfall ('lændˌfɔːl) NOUN 1 the act of sighting or nearing land, esp from the sea. 2 the land sighted or neared.

landfill ('lændˌfɪl) NOUN **a** disposal of waste material by burying it under layers of earth. **b** *(as modifier)*: *landfill sites.*

land forces PLURAL NOUN armed forces serving on land.

landform ('lændˌfɔːm) NOUN *Geology* any natural feature of the earth's surface, such as valleys and mountains.

land girl NOUN a girl or woman who does farm work, esp in wartime.

landgrab ('lændˌgræb) NOUN *Informal* a sudden attempt to establish ownership of or copyright on something in advance of competitors.
▷HISTORY C20: from the competition to stake claims to available land in 19th-century America

land grant NOUN 1 *US and Canadian* a grant of public land to a college, railway, etc. 2 *(modifier) US* designating a state university established with such a grant.

landgrave ('lændˌgreɪv) NOUN *German history* 1 (from the 13th century to 1806) a count who ruled over a specified territory. 2 (after 1806) the title of any of various sovereign princes in central Germany.
▷HISTORY C16: via German, from Middle High German *lantgrāve,* from *lant* land + *grāve* count

landgraviate (lænd'greɪvɪɪt, -ˌeɪt) *or* **landgravate** ('lændgrəˌveɪt) NOUN the domain or position of a landgrave or landgravine.

landgravine ('lændgrəˌviːn) NOUN 1 the wife or widow of a landgrave. 2 a woman who held the rank of landgrave.

land-holder NOUN a person who owns or occupies land.
▸ **'land-ˌholding** ADJECTIVE, NOUN

landing ('lændɪŋ) NOUN 1 **a** the act of coming to land, esp after a flight or sea voyage. **b** *(as modifier)*: *landing place.* 2 a place of disembarkation. 3 the floor area at the top of a flight of stairs or between two flights of stairs.

landing beacon NOUN a radio transmitter that emits a landing beam.

landing beam NOUN a radio beam transmitted from a landing field to enable aircraft to make an instrument landing.

landing craft NOUN *Military* any small vessel designed for the landing of troops and equipment on beaches.

landing field NOUN an area of land on which aircraft land and from which they take off.

landing gear NOUN another name for **undercarriage** (sense 1).

landing net NOUN *Angling* a loose long-handled net on a triangular frame for lifting hooked fish from the water.

landing speed NOUN the minimum air speed at which an aircraft lands safely.

landing stage NOUN a platform used for landing goods and passengers from a vessel.

landing strip NOUN another name for **airstrip.**

landlady ('lændˌleɪdɪ) NOUN, *plural* **-dies.** 1 a woman who owns and leases property. 2 a landlord's wife. 3 a woman who owns or runs a lodging house, pub, etc.

ländler *(German* 'lɛntlər) NOUN 1 an Austrian country dance in which couples spin and clap. 2 a piece of music composed for or in the rhythm of this dance, in three-four time.
▷HISTORY German, from dialect *Landl* Upper Austria

land line NOUN a telecommunications wire or cable laid over land.

landlocked ('lændˌlɒkt) ADJECTIVE 1 (of a country) completely surrounded by land. 2 (esp of lakes) completely or almost completely surrounded by land. 3 (esp of certain salmon) living in fresh water that is permanently isolated from the sea.

landloper ('lændˌləʊpə) NOUN *Scot* a vagabond or vagrant.
▷HISTORY C16: from Dutch, from LAND + *loopen* to run, LEAP

landlord ('lændˌlɔːd) NOUN 1 a man who owns and leases property. 2 a man who owns or runs a lodging house, pub, etc. 3 *Brit, archaic* the lord of an estate.

landlordism ('lændlɔːˌdɪzəm) NOUN the system by which land under private ownership is rented for a fixed sum to tenants.

landlubber ('lændˌlʌbə) NOUN *Nautical* any person having no experience at sea.
▷HISTORY C18: LAND + LUBBER

landmark ('lændˌmɑːk) NOUN 1 a prominent or well-known object in or feature of a particular landscape. 2 an important or unique decision, event, fact, discovery, etc. 3 a boundary marker or signpost.

landmass ('lændˌmæs) NOUN a large continuous area of land, as opposed to seas or islands.

land mine NOUN *Military* an explosive charge placed in the ground, usually detonated by stepping or driving on it.

land office NOUN *US and Canadian* an office that administers the sale of public land.

land-office business NOUN *US and Canadian informal* a booming or thriving business.

land of milk and honey NOUN 1 *Old Testament* the land of natural fertility promised to the Israelites by God (Ezekiel 20:6). 2 any fertile land, state, etc.

land of Nod NOUN 1 *Old Testament* a region to the east of Eden to which Cain went after he had killed Abel (Genesis 4:14). 2 an imaginary land of sleep.

Land of the Midnight Sun NOUN 1 any land north of the Arctic Circle, which has continuous daylight throughout the short summer, esp N parts of Norway, Sweden, and Finland. 2 an informal name for **Lapland.**

landowner ('lændˌəʊnə) NOUN a person who owns land.
▸ **'landˌownerˌship** NOUN ▸ **'landˌowning** NOUN, ADJECTIVE

L & P *NZ* ABBREVIATION FOR Lemon and Paeroa: a soda water drink, originally from the town of Paeroa.

land-poor ADJECTIVE owning much unprofitable land and lacking the money to maintain its fertility or improve it.

landrace ('lændˌreɪs) NOUN 1 *Chiefly Brit* a white very long-bodied lop-eared breed of pork pig. 2 a breed of Finnish sheep known for multiple births. 3 *Botany* an ancient or primitive cultivated variety of a crop plant.
▷HISTORY from Danish, literally: land race

land rail NOUN another name for **corncrake**.

land reform NOUN the redistributing of large agricultural holdings among the landless.

Landrost ('lændrɒst) NOUN a variant spelling of **Landdrost**.

lands (lændz) PLURAL NOUN [1] holdings in land. [2] *South African* the part of a farm on which crops are grown.

landscape ('lænd,skeɪp) NOUN [1] an extensive area of land regarded as being visually distinct: *ugly slagheaps dominated the landscape*. [2] a painting, drawing, photograph, etc., depicting natural scenery. [3] **a** the genre including such pictures. **b** (*as modifier*): *landscape painter*. [4] the distinctive features of a given area of intellectual activity, regarded as an integrated whole: *the landscape of the European imagination*. ◆ ADJECTIVE [5] *Printing* **a** (of a publication or an illustration in a publication) of greater width than height. Compare **portrait** (sense 3). **b** (of a page) carrying an illustration or table printed at right angles to the normal text. ◆ VERB [6] (*tr*) to improve the natural features of (a garden, park, etc.), as by creating contoured features and planting trees. [7] (*intr*) to work as a landscape gardener.
▷HISTORY C16 *landskip* (originally a term in painting), from Middle Dutch *lantscap* region; related to Old English *landscipe* tract of land, Old High German *lantscaf* region

landscape gardening NOUN the art of laying out grounds in imitation of natural scenery. Also called: **landscape architecture**.
▸**landscape gardener** NOUN

landscapist ('lænd,skeɪpɪst) NOUN a painter of landscapes.

Land's End NOUN a granite headland in SW England, on the SW coast of Cornwall: the westernmost point of England.

landshark ('lænd,ʃɑːk) NOUN *Informal* a person who makes inordinate profits by buying and selling land.

Landshut (*German* 'lantshuːt) NOUN a city in SE Germany, in Bavaria: Trausnitz castle (13th century); manufacturing centre for machinery and chemicals. Pop.: 59 670 (1991).

landside ('lænd,saɪd) NOUN [1] the part of an airport farthest from the aircraft, the boundary of which is the security check, customs, passport control, etc. Compare **airside**. [2] the part of a plough that slides along the face of the furrow wall on the opposite side to the mouldboard.

landsknecht ('læntskə,nɛkt) NOUN a mercenary foot soldier in late 15th-, 16th-, and 17th-century Europe, esp a German pikeman.
▷HISTORY German, literally: landknight

landslide ('lænd,slaɪd) NOUN [1] Also called: **landslip**. **a** the sliding of a large mass of rock material, soil, etc., down the side of a mountain or cliff. **b** the material dislodged in this way. [2] **a** an overwhelming electoral victory. **b** (*as modifier*): *a landslide win*.

Landsmål ('lɑːntsmoːl) NOUN another name for **Nynorsk**.

landsman[1] ('lændzmən) NOUN, *plural* **-men**. [1] a person who works or lives on land, as distinguished from a seaman. [2] a person with no experience at sea.

landsman[2] ('lændzmən) NOUN, *plural* **-men**. a Jewish compatriot from the same area of origin as another.
▷HISTORY from Yiddish

Landsturm *German* ('lantʃturm) NOUN (in German-speaking countries) [1] a reserve force; militia. [2] a general levy in wartime.
▷HISTORY C19: literally: landstorm; originally a summons to arms by means of storm-warning bells

Landtag ('lɑːnt,tɑːk) NOUN [1] the legislative assembly of each state in present-day Germany and Austria. [2] the estates of principalities in medieval and modern Germany. [3] the assembly of numerous states in 19th-century Germany.
▷HISTORY C16: German: land assembly

land tax NOUN (formerly) a tax payable annually by virtue of ownership of land, abolished in Britain in 1963.

land up VERB (*adverb, usually intr*) to arrive or cause to arrive at a final point: *after a summer in Europe, he suddenly landed up at home*.

landwaiter ('lænd,weɪtə) NOUN an officer of the Custom House.

landward ('lændwəd) ADJECTIVE [1] lying, facing, or moving towards land. [2] in the direction of the land. ◆ ADVERB [3] a variant of **landwards**.

landwards ('lændwədz) *or* **landward** ADVERB towards land.

land with VERB (*tr, preposition*) to give to, so as to put in difficulties; cause to be burdened with: *why did you land me with this extra work?*

lane[1] (leɪn) NOUN [1] **a** a narrow road or way between buildings, hedges, fences, etc. **b** (*capital as part of a street name*): *Drury Lane*. [2] **a** any of the parallel strips into which the carriageway of a major road or motorway is divided. **b** any narrow well-defined route or course for ships or aircraft. [3] one of the parallel strips into which a running track or swimming bath is divided for races. [4] the long strip of wooden flooring down which balls are bowled in a bowling alley.
▷HISTORY Old English *lane, lanu*, of Germanic origin; related to Middle Dutch *lāne* lane

lane[2] (leɪn) ADJECTIVE *Scot, dialect* [1] lone or alone. [2] (**on**) **one's lane**. on one's own.

lang (læŋ) ADJECTIVE a Scot word for **long**.

langar ('lʌngaː) NOUN *Sikhism* **a** the dining hall in a gurdwara. **b** the food served, given to all regardless of caste or religion as a gesture of equality.
▷HISTORY Punjabi

Langerhans islets ('læŋə,hæns) *or* **islands** NOUN *Anatomy* See **islets of Langerhans**.

langlauf ('lɑːŋ,lauf) NOUN cross-country skiing.
▷HISTORY German, literally: long run
▸**langläufer** ('lɑːŋ,lɔɪfə) NOUN

Langobard ('læŋgə,bɑːd) NOUN a less common name for a **Lombard**.
▷HISTORY C18: from Late Latin *Langobardicus* Lombard

Langobardic (,læŋgə'bɑːdɪk) NOUN [1] the language of the ancient Lombards: a dialect of Old High German. ◆ ADJECTIVE [2] of or relating to the Lombards or their language.

langouste ('lɒŋguːst, lɒŋ'guːst) NOUN another name for the **spiny lobster**.
▷HISTORY French, from Old Provençal *langosta*, perhaps from Latin *lōcusta* lobster, locust

langoustine (,lɒŋguːs'tiːn) NOUN a large prawn or small lobster.
▷HISTORY from French, diminutive of LANGOUSTE

langrage ('læŋgrɪdʒ), **langrel** ('læŋgrəl), *or* **langridge** NOUN shot consisting of scrap iron packed into a case, formerly used in naval warfare.
▷HISTORY C18: of unknown origin

Langres Plateau (*French* lɑ̃grə) NOUN a calcareous plateau of E France north of Dijon between the Seine and the Saône, reaching over 580 m (1900 ft.): forms a watershed between rivers flowing to the Mediterranean and to the English Channel.

langsyne (,læŋ'saɪn, -'zaɪn) *Scot* ◆ ADVERB [1] long ago; long since. ◆ NOUN [2] times long past, esp those fondly remembered. See also **auld lang syne**.
▷HISTORY C16: Scottish: long since

language ('læŋgwɪdʒ) NOUN [1] a system for the expression of thoughts, feelings, etc., by the use of spoken sounds or conventional symbols. [2] the faculty for the use of such systems, which is a distinguishing characteristic of man as compared with other animals. [3] the language of a particular nation or people: *the French language*. [4] any other systematic or nonsystematic means of communicating, such as gesture or animal sounds: *the language of love*. [5] the specialized vocabulary used by a particular group: *medical language*. [6] a particular manner or style of verbal expression: *your language is disgusting*. [7] *Computing* See **programming language**. [8] **speak the same language**. to communicate with understanding because of common background, values, etc.
▷HISTORY C13: from Old French *langage*, ultimately from Latin *lingua* tongue

language laboratory NOUN a room equipped with tape recorders, etc., for learning foreign languages.

language school NOUN a school for the teaching of a foreign language or languages.

langue (lɑːŋg) NOUN *Linguistics* language considered as an abstract system or a social institution, being the common possession of a speech community. Compare **parole** (sense 5).
▷HISTORY C19: from French: language

langue de chat ('lɑːŋ də 'ʃɑː) NOUN [1] a flat sweet finger-shaped biscuit. [2] a piece of chocolate having the same shape.
▷HISTORY French: cat's tongue

Languedoc (*French* lɑ̃gdɔk) NOUN [1] a former province of S France, lying between the foothills of the Pyrenees and the River Rhône: formed around the countship of Toulouse in the 13th century; important production of bulk wines. [2] a wine from this region.

langue d'oc *French* (lɑ̃g dɔk) NOUN the group of medieval French dialects spoken in S France: often regarded as including Provençal. Compare ***langue d'oïl***.
▷HISTORY literally: language of *oc* (the Provençal form for *yes*), ultimately from Latin *hoc* this

Languedoc-Roussillon (*French* lɑ̃gdɔkrusijɔ̃) NOUN a region of S France, on the Gulf of Lions: consists of the departments of Lozère, Gard, Hérault, Aude, and Pyrénées-Orientales; mainly mountainous with a coastal plain.

langue d'oïl *French* (lɑ̃g dɔj) NOUN the group of medieval French dialects spoken in France north of the Loire; the medieval basis of modern French.
▷HISTORY literally: language of *oïl* (the northern form for *yes*), ultimately from Latin *hoc ille (fecit)* this he (did)

languet ('læŋgwɛt) NOUN *Rare* anything resembling a tongue in shape or function.
▷HISTORY C15: from Old French *languette*, diminutive of *langue* tongue

languid ('læŋgwɪd) ADJECTIVE [1] without energy or spirit. [2] without interest or enthusiasm. [3] sluggish; inactive.
▷HISTORY C16: from Latin *languidus*, from *languēre* to languish
▸'**languidly** ADVERB ▸'**languidness** NOUN

languish ('læŋgwɪʃ) VERB (*intr*) [1] to lose or diminish in strength or energy. [2] (often foll by *for*) to be listless with desire; pine. [3] to suffer deprivation, hardship, or neglect: *to languish in prison*. [4] to put on a tender, nostalgic, or melancholic expression.
▷HISTORY C14 *languishen*, from Old French *languiss-*, stem of *languir*, ultimately from Latin *languēre*
▸'**languishing** ADJECTIVE ▸'**languishingly** ADVERB
▸'**languishment** NOUN

languor ('læŋgə) NOUN [1] physical or mental laziness or weariness. [2] a feeling of dreaminess and relaxation. [3] oppressive silence or stillness.
▷HISTORY C14 *langour*, via Old French from Latin *languor*, from *languēre* to languish; the modern spelling is directly from Latin

languorous ('læŋgərəs) ADJECTIVE [1] characterized by or producing languor. [2] another word for **languid**.
▸'**languorously** ADVERB ▸'**languorousness** NOUN

langur (lʌŋ'guə) NOUN any of various agile arboreal Old World monkeys of the genus *Presbytis* and related genera, of S and SE Asia having a slender body, long tail and hands, and long hair surrounding the face.
▷HISTORY Hindi, perhaps related to Sanskrit *lāngūla* tailed

laniard ('lænjəd) NOUN a variant spelling of **lanyard**.

laniary ('lænɪərɪ) ADJECTIVE [1] (esp of canine teeth) adapted for tearing. ◆ NOUN, *plural* **-aries**. [2] a tooth adapted for tearing.
▷HISTORY C19: from Latin *lanius* butcher, from *laniāre* to tear

laniferous (lə'nɪfərəs) *or* **lanigerous** (lə'nɪdʒərəs) ADJECTIVE *Biology* bearing wool or fleecy hairs resembling wool.
▷HISTORY C17: from Latin *lānifer*, from *lāna* wool

La Niña (læ 'niːnjə) NOUN *Meteorol* a cooling of the eastern tropical Pacific, occurring in certain years.
▷HISTORY C20: from Spanish: The Little Girl, to distinguish it from El Niño

lank (læŋk) ADJECTIVE [1] long and limp. [2] thin or gaunt.
▷HISTORY Old English *hlanc* loose
▸'**lankly** ADVERB ▸'**lankness** NOUN

lanky ('læŋkɪ) ADJECTIVE **lankier, lankiest**. tall, thin, and loose-jointed.
▸'**lankily** ADVERB ▸'**lankiness** NOUN

lanner ('lænə) NOUN [1] a large falcon, *Falco biarmicus*, of Mediterranean regions, N Africa, and S Asia. [2] *Falconry* the female of this falcon. Compare **lanneret**.
▷HISTORY C15: from Old French (*faucon*) *lanier* cowardly (falcon), from Latin *lanārius* wool worker, coward; referring to its sluggish flight and timid nature

lanneret ('lænəˌrɛt) NOUN the male or tercel of the lanner falcon.
▷HISTORY C15: diminutive of LANNER

lanolin ('lænəlɪn) *or* **lanoline** ('lænəlɪn, -ˌliːn) NOUN a yellowish viscous substance extracted from wool, consisting of a mixture of esters of fatty acids: used in some ointments. Also called: **wool fat**.
▷HISTORY C19: via German from Latin *lāna* wool + *oleum* oil; see -IN
▸**lanolated** ('lænəˌleɪtɪd) ADJECTIVE

lanose ('leɪnəʊs, -nəʊz) ADJECTIVE another word for **lanate**.
▷HISTORY C19: from Latin *lānosus*
▸**lanosity** (leɪ'nɒsɪtɪ) NOUN

Lansing ('lænsɪŋ) NOUN a city in S Michigan, on the Grand River: the state capital. Pop.: 119 128 (2000).

Lansker line ('lænskə) NOUN (in Pembrokeshire) the linguistic and ethnic division between the Welsh-speaking north and the English-speaking south.
▷HISTORY C19: from Pembrokeshire dialect *lansker* boundary

lansquenet ('lænskəˌnɛt) NOUN [1] a gambling game of chance. [2] an archaic spelling of **landsknecht**.
▷HISTORY from French

lantana (læn'teɪnə, -'tɑː-) NOUN any verbenaceous shrub or herbaceous plant of the tropical American genus *Lantana*, esp *L. camara*, having spikes or umbels of yellow or orange flowers. It has been widely introduced and is regarded as a troublesome weed in some places.
▷HISTORY C18: New Latin, from Italian dialect *lantana* wayfaring tree

lantern ('læntən) NOUN [1] a light with a transparent or translucent protective case. [2] a structure on top of a dome or roof having openings or windows to admit light or air. [3] the upper part of a lighthouse that houses the light. [4] *Photog* short for **magic lantern**.
▷HISTORY C13: from Latin *lanterna*, from Greek *lamptēr* lamp, from *lampein* to shine

lantern fish NOUN any small deep-sea teleost fish of the family *Myctophidae*, having a series of luminescent spots along the body.

lantern fly NOUN any of various tropical insects of the homopterous family *Fulgoridae*, many species of which have a snoutlike process formerly thought to emit light.

lantern jaw NOUN (when *plural*, refers to upper and lower jaw; when *singular* usually to lower jaw) a long hollow jaw that gives the face a drawn appearance.

lantern-jawed ADJECTIVE having a long hollow jaw that gives the face a drawn appearance.

lantern pinion *or* **wheel** NOUN a type of gearwheel, now used only in clocks, consisting of two parallel circular discs connected by a number of pins running parallel to the axis.

lantern slide NOUN (formerly) a photographic slide for projection, used in a magic lantern.

lanthanide ('lænθəˌnaɪd) *or* **lanthanon** ('lænθəˌnɒn) NOUN any element of the lanthanide series. Also called: **rare earth, rare-earth element**.
▷HISTORY C19: from LANTHANUM + -IDE

lanthanide series NOUN a class of 15 chemically related elements with atomic numbers from 57 (lanthanum) to 71 (lutetium).

lanthanum ('lænθənəm) NOUN a silvery-white ductile metallic element of the lanthanide series, occurring principally in bastnaesite and monazite: used in pyrophoric alloys, electronic devices, and in glass manufacture. Symbol: La; atomic no.: 57; atomic wt.: 138.9055; valency: 3; relative density: 6.145; melting pt.: 918°C; boiling pt.: 3464°C.
▷HISTORY C19: New Latin, from Greek *lanthanein* to lie unseen

lanthorn ('lænt,hɔːn, 'læntən) NOUN an archaic word for **lantern**.

lanugo (lə'njuːgəʊ) NOUN, *plural* **-gos**. a layer of fine hairs, esp the covering of the human fetus before birth.
▷HISTORY C17: from Latin: down, from *lāna* wool
▸**lanuginous** (lə'njuːdʒɪnəs) *or* **la'nugiˌnose** ADJECTIVE
▸**la'nuginousness** NOUN

Lanús (*Spanish* la'nus) NOUN a city in E Argentina: a S suburb of Buenos Aires. Pop.: 466 755 (1991).

lanyard *or* **laniard** ('lænjəd) NOUN [1] a cord worn around the neck, shoulder, etc., to hold something such as a whistle or knife. [2] a similar but merely decorative cord worn as part of a military uniform. [3] a cord with an attached hook used in firing certain types of cannon. [4] *Nautical* a line rove through deadeyes for extending or tightening standing rigging.
▷HISTORY C15 *lanyer*, from French *lanière*, from *lasne* strap, probably of Germanic origin

Lanzhou, Lanchow, *or* **Lan-chou** ('læn'dʒəʊ) NOUN a city in N China, capital of Gansu province, on the Yellow River: situated on the main route between China and the West. Pop.: 1 429 673 (1999 est.).

Lao ADJECTIVE, NOUN another name for **Laotian**.

LAO INTERNATIONAL CAR REGISTRATION FOR Laos.

Laoag (lɑː'wɑːg) NOUN a city in the N Philippines, on NW Luzon: trade centre for an agricultural region. Pop.: 84 000 (1990 est.).

Laocoon (leɪ'ɒkəʊˌɒn) NOUN *Greek myth* a priest of Apollo at Troy who warned the Trojans against the wooden horse left by the Greeks; killed with his twin sons by two sea serpents.

Laodicea (ˌleɪəʊdɪ'sɪə) NOUN the ancient name of several Greek cities in W Asia, notably of **Latakia**.

laodicean (ˌleɪəʊdɪ'sɪən) ADJECTIVE [1] lukewarm and indifferent, esp in religious matters. ◆ NOUN [2] a person having a lukewarm attitude towards religious matters.
▷HISTORY C17: referring to the early Christians of Laodicea (Revelation 3:14–16)

Laoighis ('liː) NOUN a variant spelling of **Laois**.

Laois ('liː) NOUN a county of central Republic of Ireland, in Leinster province: formerly boggy but largely reclaimed for agriculture. County town: Portlaoise. Pop.: 52 945 (1996). Area: 1719 sq. km (664 sq. miles). Also called: **Laoighis, Leix**. Former name: **Queen's County**.

Laomedon (leɪ'ɒmɪˌdɒn) NOUN *Greek myth* the founder and ruler of Troy, who cheated Apollo and Poseidon of their wage for constructing the city's walls; the father of Priam.

Laos (laʊz, laʊs) NOUN a republic in SE Asia: first united as the kingdom of Lan Xang ("million elephants") in 1353, after being a province of the Khmer Empire for about four centuries; made part of French Indochina in 1893 and gained independence in 1949; became a republic in 1975. It is generally forested and mountainous, with the Mekong River running almost the whole length of the W border. Official language: Laotian. Religion: Buddhist majority, tribal religions. Currency: kip. Capital: Vientiane. Pop.: 5 636 000 (2001 est.). Area: 236 800 sq. km (91 429 sq. miles). Official name: **People's Democratic Republic of Laos**.

Laotian ('laʊʃɪən) *or* **Lao** (laʊ) NOUN [1] (*plural* **Laotians, Lao** *or* **Laos**) a member of a Buddhist people of Laos and NE Thailand, related to the Thais. [2] the language of this people, closely related to Thai. ◆ ADJECTIVE [3] of or relating to this people or their language or to Laos.

lap¹ (læp) NOUN [1] the area formed by the upper surface of the thighs of a seated person. [2] Also called: **lapful**. the amount held in one's lap. [3] a protected place or environment: *in the lap of luxury*. [4] any of various hollow or depressed areas, such as a hollow in the land. [5] the part of one's clothing that covers the lap. [6] **drop in someone's lap**. give someone the responsibility of. [7] **in the lap of the gods**. beyond human control and power.
▷HISTORY Old English *læppa* flap; see LOBE, LAPPET, LOP²

lap² (læp) NOUN [1] one circuit of a racecourse or track. [2] a stage or part of a journey, race, etc. [3] **a** an overlapping part or projection. **b** the extent of overlap. [4] the length of material needed to go around an object. [5] a rotating disc coated with fine abrasive for polishing gemstones. [6] any device for holding a fine abrasive to polish materials. [7] *Metallurgy* a defect in rolled metals caused by the folding of a fin onto the surface. [8] a sheet or band of fibres, such as cotton, prepared for further processing. ◆ VERB **laps, lapping, lapped**. [9] (*tr*) to wrap or fold (around or over): *he lapped a bandage around his wrist*. [10] (*tr*) to enclose or envelop in: *he lapped his wrist in a bandage*. [11] to place or lie partly or completely over or project beyond. [12] (*tr; usually passive*) to envelop or surround with comfort, love, etc.: *lapped in luxury*. [13] (*intr*) to be folded. [14] (*tr*) to overtake (an opponent) in a race so as to be one or more circuits ahead. [15] (*tr*) to polish or cut (a workpiece, gemstone, etc.) with a fine abrasive, esp to hone (mating metal parts) against each other with an abrasive. [16] to form (fibres) into a sheet or band.
▷HISTORY C13 (in the sense: to wrap): probably from LAP¹
▸'**lapper** NOUN

lap³ (læp) VERB **laps, lapping, lapped**. [1] (of small waves) to wash against (a shore, boat, etc.), usually with light splashing sounds. [2] (often foll by *up*) (esp of animals) to scoop (a liquid) into the mouth with the tongue. ◆ NOUN [3] the act or sound of lapping. [4] a thin food for dogs or other animals. ◆ See also **lap up**.
▷HISTORY Old English *lapian*; related to Old High German *laffan*, Latin *lambere*, Greek *laptein*
▸'**lapper** NOUN

La Palma (*Spanish* la 'palma) NOUN an island in the N Atlantic, in the NW Canary Islands: administratively part of Spain. Chief town: Santa Cruz de la Palma. Pop.: 77 000 (latest est.). Area: 725 sq. km (280 sq. miles).

laparoscope ('læpərəˌskəʊp) NOUN a medical instrument consisting of a tube that is inserted through the abdominal wall and illuminated to enable a doctor to view the internal organs.
▷HISTORY C19 (applied to various instruments used to examine the abdomen) and C20 (in the specific modern sense): from Greek *lapara* (see LAPAROTOMY) + -SCOPE
▸ˌ**lapa'roscopy** NOUN

laparotomy (ˌlæpə'rɒtəmɪ) NOUN, *plural* **-mies**. [1] surgical incision through the abdominal wall, esp to investigate the cause of an abdominal disorder. [2] surgical incision into the loin.
▷HISTORY C19: from Greek *lapara* flank, from *laparos* soft + -TOMY

La Paz (læ 'pæz; *Spanish* la 'paθ) NOUN a city in W Bolivia, at an altitude of 3600 m (12 000 ft.): seat of government since 1898 (though Sucre is still the official capital); the country's largest city; founded in 1548 by the Spaniards; university (1830). Pop. (urban area): 1 000 899 (2000 est.).

lapboard ('læpˌbɔːd) NOUN a flat board that can be used on the lap as a makeshift table or desk.

lap-chart NOUN *Motor racing* a log of every lap covered by each car in a race, showing the exact position throughout.

lap dancing NOUN a form of entertainment in which scantily dressed women dance erotically for individual members of the audience.

lap dissolve NOUN *Films* the technique of allowing the end of one scene to overlap the beginning of the next scene by fading out the former while fading in the latter.

lapdog ('læpˌdɒg) NOUN [1] a pet dog small and docile enough to be cuddled in the lap. [2] *Informal* a person who attaches himself to someone in admiration or infatuation.

lapel (lə'pɛl) NOUN the continuation of the turned or folded back collar on a suit coat, jacket, etc.
▷HISTORY C18: from LAP¹
▸**la'pelled** ADJECTIVE

LaPerm (lə'pɜːm) NOUN a breed of medium-sized curly-haired cat with large ears.

lapheld ('læpˌhɛld) ADJECTIVE (esp of a personal

computer) small enough to be used on one's lap; portable.

lapidary ('læpɪdərɪ) NOUN, *plural* **-daries.** [1] a person whose business is to cut, polish, set, or deal in gemstones. ♦ ADJECTIVE [2] of or relating to gemstones or the work of a lapidary. [3] Also: **lapidarian** (ˌlæpɪ'deərɪən). engraved, cut, or inscribed in a stone or gemstone. [4] of sufficiently high quality to be engraved on a stone: *a lapidary inscription.*
▷HISTORY C14: from Latin *lapidārius,* from *lapid-, lapis* stone
▸**ˌlapi'darian** ADJECTIVE

lapidate ('læpɪˌdeɪt) VERB *(tr) Literary* [1] to pelt with stones. [2] to kill by stoning.
▷HISTORY C17: from Latin *lapidāre,* from *lapis* stone
▸**ˌlapi'dation** NOUN

lapidicolous (ˌlæpɪ'dɪkələs) ADJECTIVE *Zoology* living under stones.

lapidify (lə'pɪdɪˌfaɪ) VERB **-fies, -fying, -fied.** to change into stone.
▷HISTORY C17: from French *lapidifier,* from Medieval Latin *lapidificāre,* ultimately from Latin *lapis* stone
▸**laˌpidifi'cation** NOUN

lapillus (lə'pɪləs) NOUN, *plural* **-li** (-laɪ). a small piece of lava thrown from a volcano.
▷HISTORY C18: Latin: little stone

lapis lazuli *or* **lazuli** ('læpɪs) NOUN [1] a brilliant blue variety of the mineral lazurite, used as a gemstone. [2] the deep blue colour of lapis lazuli. ♦ Also called: **lapis.**
▷HISTORY C14: from Latin *lapis* stone + Medieval Latin *lazulī,* from *lazulum,* from Arabic *lāzaward,* from Persian *lāzhuward,* of obscure origin

Lapith ('læpɪθ) NOUN, *plural* **Lapithae** ('læpɪˌθiː) *or* **Lapiths.** *Greek myth* a member of a people in Thessaly who at the wedding of their king, Pirithoüs, fought the drunken centaurs.

lap joint NOUN a joint made by placing one member over another and fastening them together. Also called: **lapped joint.**
▸**'lap-ˌjointed** ADJECTIVE

Laplace operator (læ'plɑːs) NOUN *Maths* the operator $\partial^2/\partial x^2 + \partial^2/\partial y^2 + \partial^2/\partial z^2$. Symbol: ∇^2. Also called: **Laplacian** (lə'pleɪʃɪən).
▷HISTORY named after Pierre Simon, Marquis de *Laplace* (1749–1827), the French mathematician, physicist, and astronomer

Lapland ('læpˌlænd) NOUN an extensive region of N Europe, mainly within the Arctic Circle: consists of the N parts of Norway, Sweden, Finland, and the Kola Peninsula of the extreme NW of Russia. Also called (informal): **Land of the Midnight Sun.**

Laplander ('læpˌlændə) NOUN a native or inhabitant of Lapland.

La Plata (*Spanish* la 'plata) NOUN [1] a port in E Argentina, near the Río de la Plata estuary: founded in 1882 and modelled on Washington DC; university (1897). Pop.: 556 308 (1999 est.). [2] See (Río de la) **Plata.**

lap of honour NOUN a ceremonial circuit of a racing track, etc., by the winner of a race.

Lapp (læp) NOUN [1] a member of a nomadic people living chiefly in N Scandinavia and the Kola Peninsula of Russia. [2] the language of this people, belonging to the Finno-Ugric family. ♦ ADJECTIVE [3] of or relating to this people or their language.

> **Language note** The indigenous people of Lapland prefer to be called *Sami,* although *Lapp* is still in widespread use.

lappet ('læpɪt) NOUN [1] a small hanging flap or piece of lace, etc., such as one dangling from a headdress. [2] *Zoology* a lobelike hanging structure, such as the wattle on a bird's head.
▷HISTORY C16: from LAP[1] + -ET
▸**'lappeted** ADJECTIVE

lappet moth NOUN a large purple-brown hairy eggar moth, *Gastropacha quercifolia,* whose grey furry caterpillars have lappets on each flank.

Lappish ('læpɪʃ) ADJECTIVE [1] of or relating to the Lapps, a nomadic people living chiefly in N Scandinavia and the Kola Peninsula of Russia, or their language. ♦ NOUN [2] the language of this people, belonging to the Finno-Ugric family.

Lapsang Souchong ('læpsæŋ suː'ʃɒŋ) NOUN a large-leafed variety of China tea with a slightly smoky flavour.

lapse (læps) NOUN [1] a drop in standard of an isolated or temporary nature: *a lapse of justice.* [2] a break in occurrence, usage, etc.: *a lapse of five weeks between letters.* [3] a gradual decline or a drop to a lower degree, condition, or state: *a lapse from high office.* [4] a moral fall. [5] *Law* the termination of some right, interest, or privilege, as by neglecting to exercise it or through failure of some contingency. [6] *Insurance* the termination of coverage following a failure to pay the premiums. ♦ VERB *(intr)* [7] to drop in standard or fail to maintain a norm. [8] to decline gradually or fall in status, condition, etc. [9] to be discontinued, esp through negligence or other failure. [10] (usually foll by *into*) to drift or slide (into a condition): *to lapse into sleep.* [11] (often foll by *from*) to turn away (from beliefs or norms). [12] *Law* (of a devise or bequest) to become void, as on the beneficiary's predeceasing the testator. [13] (of time) to slip away.
▷HISTORY C15: from Latin *lāpsus* error, from *lābī* to glide
▸**'lapsable** *or* **'lapsible** ADJECTIVE ▸**lapsed** ADJECTIVE
▸**'lapser** NOUN

lapse rate NOUN the rate of change of any meteorological factor with altitude, esp atmospheric temperature, which usually decreases at a rate of 0.6°C per 100 metres (**environmental lapse rate**). Unsaturated air loses about 1°C per 100 m (**dry adiabatic lapse rate**), whereas saturated air loses an average 0.5°C per 100 m (**saturated adiabatic lapse rate**).

lapstrake ('læpˌstreɪk) *or* **lapstreak** ('læpˌstriːk) *Nautical* ♦ ADJECTIVE [1] another term for **clinker-built.** ♦ NOUN [2] a clinker-built boat.
▷HISTORY C18: from LAP[2] + STRAKE

lapsus ('læpsəs) NOUN, *plural* **-sus.** *Formal* a lapse or error.
▷HISTORY from Latin: LAPSE

lapsus linguae ('lɪŋgwiː) NOUN a slip of the tongue.
▷HISTORY Latin

Laptev Sea ('læptɪf) NOUN a shallow arm of the Arctic Ocean, along the N coast of Russia between the Taimyr Peninsula and the New Siberian Islands. Former name: **Nordenskjöld Sea.**

laptop ('læpˌtɒp) *or* **laptop computer** NOUN a personal computer that is small and light enough to be operated on the user's lap. Compare **palmtop computer.**

laptray ('læpˌtreɪ) NOUN a tray with a cushioned underside, designed to rest in a person's lap while supporting reading material, a meal eaten while watching television, etc.

lap up VERB *(tr, adverb)* [1] to eat or drink. [2] to relish or delight in: *he laps up old horror films.* [3] to believe or accept eagerly and uncritically: *he laps up tall stories.*

lapwing ('læpˌwɪŋ) NOUN any of several plovers of the genus *Vanellus,* esp *V. vanellus,* typically having a crested head, wattles, and spurs. Also called: **green plover, pewit, peewit.**
▷HISTORY C17: altered form of Old English *hlēapewince* plover, from *hlēapan* to LEAP + *wincian* to jerk, WINK[1]

lar[1] (lɑː) NOUN the singular of **lares.** See **lares and penates.**
▷HISTORY Latin

lar[2] (lɑː) NOUN *Northern English, dialect* a boy or young man.

LAR INTERNATIONAL CAR REGISTRATION FOR Libya(n Arab Republic).

larboard ('lɑːbəd) NOUN, ADJECTIVE *Nautical* a former word for **port[2].**
▷HISTORY C14 *laddeborde* (changed to *larboard* by association with *starboard*), from *laden* to load + *borde* BOARD

larceny ('lɑːsɪnɪ) NOUN, *plural* **-nies.** *Law* (formerly) a technical word for **theft.**
▷HISTORY C15: from Old French *larcin,* from Latin *lātrōcinium* robbery, from *latrō* robber
▸**'larcenist** *or* **'larcener** NOUN ▸**'larcenous** ADJECTIVE
▸**'larcenously** ADVERB

larch (lɑːtʃ) NOUN [1] any coniferous tree of the genus *Larix,* having deciduous needle-like leaves and egg-shaped cones: family *Pinaceae.* [2] the wood of any of these trees.
▷HISTORY C16: from German *Lärche,* ultimately from Latin *larix*

lard (lɑːd) NOUN [1] the rendered fat from a pig, esp from the abdomen, used in cooking. [2] *Informal* excess fat on a person's body. ♦ VERB *(tr)* [3] to prepare (lean meat, poultry, etc.) by inserting small strips of bacon or fat before cooking. [4] to cover or smear (foods) with lard. [5] to add extra material to (speech or writing); embellish.
▷HISTORY C15: via Old French from Latin *lāridum* bacon fat
▸**'lardˌlike** ADJECTIVE

larder ('lɑːdə) NOUN a room or cupboard, used as a store for food.
▷HISTORY C14: from Old French *lardier,* from LARD

larder beetle NOUN See **dermestid.**

lardon ('lɑːdᵊn) *or* **lardoon** (lɑː'duːn) NOUN a strip or cube of fat or bacon used in larding meat.
▷HISTORY C15: from Old French, from LARD

lard pig NOUN a large type of pig used principally for lard.

lardy ('lɑːdɪ) ADJECTIVE fat; obese.

lardy cake ('lɑːdɪ) NOUN *Brit* a rich sweet cake made of bread dough, lard, sugar, and dried fruit.

Laredo (lə'reɪdəʊ) NOUN a city in the US, in Texas, on the Mexican border: founded by the Spanish in 1755 on the Rio Grande. Pop.: 176 576 (2000).

lares and penates ('lɛəriːz, 'lɑː-) PLURAL NOUN [1] *Roman myth* **a** household gods. **b** statues of these gods kept in the home. [2] the valued possessions of a household.

large (lɑːdʒ) ADJECTIVE [1] having a relatively great size, quantity, extent, etc.; big. [2] of wide or broad scope, capacity, or range; comprehensive: *a large effect.* [3] having or showing great breadth of understanding: *a large heart.* [4] *Nautical* (of the wind) blowing from a favourable direction. [5] *Rare* overblown; pretentious. [6] generous. [7] *Obsolete* (of manners and speech) gross; rude. ♦ NOUN [8] **at large.** **a** (esp of a dangerous criminal or wild animal) free; not confined. **b** roaming freely, as in a foreign country. **c** as a whole; in general. **d** in full detail; exhaustively. **e ambassador-at-large.** See **ambassador** (sense 4). [9] **in (the) large.** as a totality or on a broad scale. ♦ ADVERB [10] *Nautical* with the wind blowing from a favourable direction. [11] **by and large. a** (*sentence modifier*) generally; as a rule: *by and large, the man is the breadwinner.* **b** *Nautical* towards and away from the wind. [12] **loom large.** to be very prominent or important.
▷HISTORY C12 (originally: generous): via Old French from Latin *largus* ample, abundant
▸**'largeness** NOUN

Large Black NOUN a heavy black breed of pig with long lop ears: used for crossbreeding.

large calorie NOUN another name for **Calorie.**

large-format ADJECTIVE of or relating to a camera with an image area of 5 inches by 4 inches or more.

large-handed ADJECTIVE generous; profuse.

large-hearted ADJECTIVE kind; sympathetic. Also: **large-souled.**

large intestine NOUN the part of the alimentary canal consisting of the caecum, colon, and rectum. It extracts moisture from food residues, which are later excreted as faeces. Compare **small intestine.**

large it VERB *(intr, pron) Brit, slang* to enjoy oneself or celebrate in an extravagant way.

largely ('lɑːdʒlɪ) ADVERB [1] principally; to a great extent. [2] on a large scale or in a large manner.

large-minded ADJECTIVE generous or liberal in attitudes.
▸**ˌlarge-'mindedly** ADVERB ▸**ˌlarge-'mindedness** NOUN

largemouth bass ('lɑːdʒˌmaʊθ 'bæs) NOUN a common North American freshwater black bass, *Micropterus salmoides:* a popular game fish.

Large Munsterlander ('mʊnstəˌlændə) NOUN a strongly built gun dog with a long dense black-and-white coat.

largen ('lɑːdʒən) VERB *(tr)* another word for **enlarge.**

large-scale ADJECTIVE [1] wide-ranging or extensive. [2] (of maps and models) constructed or drawn to a big scale.

large-scale integration NOUN *Electronics* the

process of integrating several thousand circuits on a single silicon chip. Abbreviation: **LSI**.

largesse *or* **largess** (lɑːˈdʒɛs) NOUN [1] the generous bestowal of gifts, favours, or money. [2] the things so bestowed. [3] generosity of spirit or attitude.
▷HISTORY C13: from Old French, from LARGE

large white NOUN [1] Also called: **cabbage white**. a large white butterfly, *Pieris brassicae*, with scanty black markings, the larvae of which feed on brassica leaves. [2] (*often capitals*) a white large-bodied breed of pig commonly kept for pork, bacon, and for fattening.

larghetto (lɑːˈɡɛtəʊ) *Music* ◆ ADJECTIVE, ADVERB [1] to be performed moderately slowly. ◆ NOUN, *plural* **-tos**. [2] a piece or passage to be performed in this way.
▷HISTORY Italian: diminutive of LARGO

largish (ˈlɑːdʒɪʃ) ADJECTIVE fairly large.

largo (ˈlɑːɡəʊ) *Music* ◆ ADJECTIVE, ADVERB [1] to be performed slowly and broadly. ◆ NOUN, *plural* **-gos**. [2] a piece or passage to be performed in this way.
▷HISTORY C17: from Italian, from Latin *largus* LARGE

lari *or* **laari** (lɑːrɪ) NOUN the standard monetary unit of Georgia, divided into 100 tetri.

Lariam (ˈlærɪæm) NOUN *Trademark* a brand of mefloquine, used in the treatment and prevention of malaria.

lariat (ˈlærɪət) NOUN *US and Canadian* [1] another word for **lasso**. [2] a rope for tethering animals.
▷HISTORY C19: from Spanish *la reata* the LASSO

larine (ˈlæraɪn, -rɪn) ADJECTIVE [1] of, relating to, or resembling a gull. [2] of, relating to, or belonging to the suborder *Lari*, which contains the gulls, terns, skuas, and skimmers.
▷HISTORY C20: via New Latin from *Larus* genus name, from Greek *laros* a kind of gull

Larisa *or* **Larissa** (ləˈrɪsə; *Greek* ˈlarisa) NOUN a city in E Greece, in E Thessaly: fortified by Justinian; annexed to Greece in 1881. Pop.: 113 426 (1991).

lark[1] (lɑːk) NOUN [1] any brown songbird of the predominantly Old World family *Alaudidae*, esp the skylark: noted for their singing. [2] short for **titlark** or **meadowlark**. [3] (*often capital*) any of various slender but powerful fancy pigeons, such as the **Coburg Lark**. [4] **up with the lark**. up early in the morning.
▷HISTORY Old English *lāwerce, lǣwerce*, of Germanic origin; related to German *Lerche*, Icelandic *lævirki*

lark[2] (lɑːk) *Informal* ◆ NOUN [1] a carefree adventure or frolic. [2] a harmless piece of mischief. [3] **what a lark!** how amusing! ◆ VERB (*intr*) [4] (often foll by *about*) to have a good time by frolicking. [5] to play a prank.
▷HISTORY C19: originally slang, perhaps related to LAIK
▸ˈ**larker** NOUN ▸ˈ**larkish** ADJECTIVE ▸ˈ**larkishness** NOUN

larkspur (ˈlɑːkˌspɜː) NOUN any of various ranunculaceous plants of the genus *Delphinium*, with spikes of blue, pink, or white irregular spurred flowers.
▷HISTORY C16: LARK[1] + SPUR

larky (ˈlɑːkɪ) ADJECTIVE **larkier, larkiest**. *Informal* frolicsome or mischievous.

Larmor precession (ˈlɑːmɔː) NOUN precession of the orbit of an electron in an atom that is subjected to a magnetic field.
▷HISTORY C20: named after Sir Joseph *Larmor* (1857–1942), British physicist

larn (lɑːn) VERB *Not standard* [1] *Facetious* to learn. [2] (*tr*) to teach (someone) a lesson: *that'll larn you!*
▷HISTORY C18: from a dialect form of LEARN

larnax (ˈlɑːnæks) NOUN *Archaeol* a coffin made of terracotta.
▷HISTORY from Greek; perhaps related to Late Greek *narnax* chest

Larne (lɒːn) NOUN a district of NE Northern Ireland, in Co. Antrim. Pop.: 30 832 (2001). Area: 336 sq. km (130 sq. miles).

larney (ˈlɑːnɪ) *South African* ◆ NOUN [1] a white person. [2] a rich person. ◆ ADJECTIVE [3] (of clothes) smart.
▷HISTORY C20: probably from an Indian language

La Rochelle (*French* la rɔʃɛl) NOUN a port in W France, on the Bay of Biscay: a Huguenot stronghold until its submission through famine to Richelieu's forces after a long siege (1627–28). Pop.: 71 094 (1990).

larrigan (ˈlærɪɡən) NOUN a knee-high oiled leather moccasin boot worn by trappers, etc.
▷HISTORY C19: of unknown origin

larrikin (ˈlærɪkɪn) NOUN *Austral and NZ, slang* **a** a mischievous person. **b** (*as modifier*): *a larrikin bloke*.
▷HISTORY C19: from English dialect: a mischievous youth

larrup (ˈlærəp) VERB (*tr*) *Dialect* to beat or flog.
▷HISTORY C19: of unknown origin
▸ˈ**larruper** NOUN

Larry (ˈlærɪ) NOUN *Brit, Austral, and NZ informal* (**as**) **happy as Larry**. extremely happy.
▷HISTORY of uncertain origin

larum (ˈlærəm) NOUN an archaic word for **alarm**.

larva (ˈlɑːvə) NOUN, *plural* **-vae** (-viː). an immature free-living form of many animals that develops into a different adult form by metamorphosis.
▷HISTORY C18: (C17 in the original Latin sense: ghost): New Latin
▸ˈ**larval** ADJECTIVE

larval therapy NOUN the use of maggots that feed on dead tissue to assist in the healing of serious wounds. An ancient practice, it has been revived in rare cases in which healing is hampered by the resistance of bacteria to antibiotics.

larvicide (ˈlɑːvɪˌsaɪd) NOUN a chemical used for killing larvae.
▸ˌ**larviˈcidal** ADJECTIVE

laryngeal (ˌlærɪnˈdʒiːəl, ləˈrɪndʒɪəl) *or* **laryngal** (ləˈrɪŋɡ[ə]l) ADJECTIVE [1] of or relating to the larynx. [2] *Phonetics* articulated at the larynx; glottal.
▷HISTORY C18: from New Latin *laryngeus* of the LARYNX
▸**larynˈgeally** ADVERB

laryngitis (ˌlærɪnˈdʒaɪtɪs) NOUN inflammation of the larynx.
▸**laryngitic** (ˌlærɪnˈdʒɪtɪk) ADJECTIVE

laryngo- *or before a vowel* **laryng-** COMBINING FORM indicating the larynx: *laryngoscope*.

laryngology (ˌlærɪŋˈɡɒlədʒɪ) NOUN the branch of medicine concerned with the larynx and its diseases.
▸**laryngological** (ləˌrɪŋɡəˈlɒdʒɪk[ə]l) *or* **laˌryngoˈlogic** ADJECTIVE ▸**laˌryngoˈlogically** ADVERB ▸ˌ**larynˈgologist** NOUN

laryngoscope (ləˈrɪŋɡəˌskəʊp) NOUN a medical instrument for examining the larynx.
▸**laryngoscopic** (ləˌrɪŋɡəˈskɒpɪk) ADJECTIVE ▸**laˌryngoˈscopically** ADVERB ▸**laryngoscopist** (ˌlærɪŋˈɡɒskəpɪst) NOUN ▸ˌ**larynˈgoscopy** NOUN

laryngotomy (ˌlærɪŋˈɡɒtəmɪ) NOUN, *plural* **-mies**. surgical incision into the larynx.

larynx (ˈlærɪŋks) NOUN, *plural* **larynges** (ləˈrɪndʒiːz). a cartilaginous and muscular hollow organ forming part of the air passage to the lungs: in higher vertebrates it contains the vocal cords.
▷HISTORY C16: from New Latin *larynx*, from Greek *larunx*

lasagne *or* **lasagna** (ləˈzænjə, -ˈsæn-) NOUN [1] a form of pasta consisting of wide flat sheets. [2] any of several dishes made from layers of lasagne and meat, cheese, etc.
▷HISTORY from Italian *lasagna*, from Latin *lasanum* cooking pot

La Salle (lə ˈsæl) NOUN a city in SE Canada, in Quebec: a S suburb of Montreal. Pop.: 73 804 (1991).

La Scala (la ˈskaːla) NOUN the chief opera house in Italy, in Milan (opened 1776).

lascar (ˈlæskə) NOUN a sailor from the East Indies.
▷HISTORY C17: from Urdu *lashkar* soldier, from Persian: the army

Lascaux (*French* lasko) NOUN the site of a cave in SW France, in the Dordogne: contains Palaeolithic wall drawings and paintings.

lascivious (ləˈsɪvɪəs) ADJECTIVE [1] lustful; lecherous. [2] exciting sexual desire.
▷HISTORY C15: from Late Latin *lascīviōsus*, from Latin *lascīvia* wantonness, from *lascīvus*
▸**lasˈciviously** ADVERB ▸**lasˈciviousness** NOUN

lase (leɪz) VERB (*intr*) (of a substance, such as carbon dioxide or ruby) to be capable of acting as a laser.

laser (ˈleɪzə) NOUN [1] a source of high-intensity optical, infrared, or ultraviolet radiation produced as a result of stimulated emission maintained within a solid, liquid, or gaseous medium. The photons involved in the emission process all have the same energy and phase so that the laser beam is monochromatic and coherent, allowing it to be brought to a fine focus. [2] any similar source producing a beam of any electromagnetic radiation, such as infrared or microwave radiation. See also **maser**.
▷HISTORY C20: from *l*ight *a*mplification by *s*timulated *e*mission of *r*adiation

laser card NOUN *Computing* another name for **smart card**.

laserdisc *or esp US* **laserdisk** (ˈleɪzəˌdɪsk) NOUN a disk similar in size to a long-playing record, on which data is stored in pits in a similar way to data storage on a compact disk, used esp for storing high-quality video.

laser printer NOUN a quiet high-quality computer printer that uses a laser beam shining on a photoconductive drum to produce characters, which are then transferred to paper.

laser ring gyro NOUN *Aeronautics* a system of aerial navigation in which rotation is sensed by the measuring of the frequency shift of laser light in a closed circuit in a horizontal plane.

laser treatment NOUN any of various medical and surgical techniques using lasers, such as the removal of small growths.

lash[1] (læʃ) NOUN [1] a sharp cutting blow from a whip or other flexible object: *twenty lashes was his punishment*. [2] the flexible end or ends of a whip. [3] a cutting or hurtful blow to the feelings, as one caused by ridicule or scolding. [4] a forceful beating or impact, as of wind, rain, or waves against something. [5] See **eyelash**. [6] **have a lash (at)**. *Austral and NZ informal* to make an attempt at or take part in (something). ◆ VERB (*tr*) [7] to hit (a person or thing) sharply with a whip, rope, etc., esp as a punishment. [8] (of rain, waves, etc.) to beat forcefully against. [9] to attack with words, ridicule, etc. [10] to flick or wave sharply to and fro: *the restless panther lashed his tail*. [11] to urge or drive with or as if with a whip: *to lash the audience into a violent mood*. ◆ See also **lash out**.
▷HISTORY C14: perhaps imitative
▸ˈ**lasher** NOUN ▸ˈ**lashingly** ADVERB

lash[2] (læʃ) VERB (*tr*) to bind or secure with rope, string, etc.
▷HISTORY C15: from Old French *lachier*, ultimately from Latin *laqueāre* to ensnare, from *laqueus* noose
▸ˈ**lasher** NOUN

lashed (laʃt) ADJECTIVE *Brit informal* intoxicated; drunk.

-lashed ADJECTIVE having eyelashes as specified: *long-lashed*.

lashing[1] (ˈlæʃɪŋ) NOUN [1] a whipping; flogging. [2] a scolding. [3] (*plural; usually foll by of*) *Brit informal* large amounts; lots.

lashing[2] (ˈlæʃɪŋ) NOUN rope, cord, etc., used for binding or securing.

Lashio (ˈlæʃɪˌəʊ) NOUN a town in NE central Myanmar: starting point of the Burma Road to Chongqing, China.

Lashkar (ˈlʌʃkə) NOUN a former city in N India, in Madhya Pradesh: capital of the former states of Gwalior and Madhya Bharat; now part of the city of Gwalior.

lash out VERB (*intr, adverb*) [1] to burst into or resort to verbal or physical attack. [2] *Brit informal* to be extravagant, as in spending.

lash-up (ˈlæʃˌʌp) NOUN **a** Also called: **hook-up**. a temporary connection of equipment for experimental or emergency use. **b** (*as modifier*): *lash-up equipment*.

lasket (ˈlæskɪt) NOUN a loop at the foot of a sail onto which an extra sail may be fastened.
▷HISTORY C18: perhaps an alteration of French *lacet* LATCHET, through the influence of GASKET

Las Palmas (*Spanish* las ˈpalmas) NOUN a port in the central Canary Islands, on NE Grand Canary: a major fuelling port on the major shipping route between Europe and South America. Pop.: 352 641 (1998 est.).

La Spezia (*Italian* la ˈspɛttsia) NOUN a port in NW

Italy, in Liguria, on the **Gulf of Spezia:** the chief naval base in Italy. Pop.: 100 458 (1992).

lass (læs) NOUN a girl or young woman.
▷HISTORY C13: origin uncertain

Lassa ('lɑ:sə) NOUN a variant spelling of **Lhasa.**

Lassa fever NOUN a serious viral disease of Central West Africa, characterized by high fever and muscular pains.
▷HISTORY named after *Lassa,* the village in Nigeria where it was first identified

Lassen Peak ('læsᵊn) NOUN a volcano in S California, in the S Cascade Range. An area of 416 sq. km (161 sq. miles) was established as **Lassen Volcanic National Park** in 1916. Height: 3187 m (10 457 ft.).

lassi ('læsɪ) NOUN a cold drink made with yoghurt or buttermilk and flavoured with sugar, salt, or a mild spice.
▷HISTORY from Hindi

lassie ('læsɪ) NOUN *Informal* a little lass; girl.

lassitude ('læsɪˌtju:d) NOUN physical or mental weariness.
▷HISTORY C16: from Latin *lassitūdō,* from *lassus* tired

lasso (læ'su:, 'læsəu) NOUN, *plural* **-sos** *or* **-soes.** [1] a long rope or thong with a running noose at one end, used (esp in America) for roping horses, cattle, etc.; lariat. ◆ VERB **-sos** *or* **-soes; -soing, -soed.** [2] (*tr*) to catch with or as if with a lasso.
▷HISTORY C19: from Spanish *lazo,* ultimately from Latin *laqueus* noose
▸**las'soer** NOUN

last¹ (lɑ:st) ADJECTIVE (*often prenominal*) [1] being, happening, or coming at the end or after all others: *the last horse in the race.* [2] being or occurring just before the present; most recent: *last Thursday.* [3] **last but not least.** coming last in order but nevertheless important. [4] **last but one.** next to last. [5] only remaining: *one's last cigarette.* [6] most extreme; utmost. [7] least suitable, appropriate, or likely: *he was the last person I would have chosen.* [8] (esp relating to the end of a person's life or of the world) **a** final or ultimate: *last rites.* **b** (*capital*): *the Last Judgment.* [9] (*postpositive*) *Liverpool, dialect* inferior, unpleasant, or contemptible: *this ale is last.* ◆ ADVERB [10] after all others; at or in the end: *he came last.* [11] **a** most recently: *he was last seen in the mountains.* **b** (*in combination*): *last-mentioned.* [12] (*sentence modifier*) as the last or latest item. ◆ NOUN [13] **the last. a** a person or thing that is last. **b** the final moment; end. [14] one's last moments before death. [15] the last thing a person can do (esp in the phrase **breathe one's last**). [16] the final appearance, mention, or occurrence: *we've seen the last of him.* [17] **at last.** in the end; finally. [18] **at long last.** finally, after difficulty, delay, or irritation.
▷HISTORY variant of Old English *latest, lætest,* superlative of LATE

> **Language note** Since *last* can mean either *after all others* or *most recent,* it is better to avoid using this word where ambiguity might arise as in *her last novel. Final* or *latest* should be used in such contexts to avoid ambiguity.

last² (lɑ:st) VERB [1] (when *intr,* often foll by *for*) to remain in being (for a length of time); continue: *his hatred lasted for several years.* [2] to be sufficient for the needs of (a person) for (a length of time): *it will last us until Friday.* [3] (when *intr,* often foll by *for*) to remain fresh, uninjured, or unaltered (for a certain time or duration): *he lasted for three hours underground.* ◆ See also **last out.**
▷HISTORY Old English *lǣstan;* related to Gothic *laistjan* to follow
▸**'laster** NOUN

last³ (lɑ:st) NOUN [1] the wooden or metal form on which a shoe or boot is fashioned or repaired. ◆ VERB [2] (*tr*) to fit (a shoe or boot) on a last.
▷HISTORY Old English *lǣste,* from *lāst* footprint; related to Old Norse *leistr* foot, Gothic *laists*
▸**'laster** NOUN

last⁴ (lɑ:st) NOUN a unit of weight or capacity having various values in different places and for different commodities. Commonly used values are 2 tons, 2000 pounds, 80 bushels, or 640 gallons.
▷HISTORY Old English *hlæst* load; related to *hladan* to LADE¹

last chance saloon NOUN [1] a place frequented by unsavoury or contemptible people. [2] a situation considered to be the last opportunity for success.

last-cyclic ADJECTIVE *Transformational grammar* denoting rules that apply only to main clauses. Compare **cyclic** (sense 6), **post-cyclic.**

last-ditch NOUN (*modifier*) made or done as a last desperate attempt or effort in the face of opposition.

last-gasp NOUN (*modifier*) done in desperation at the last minute: *a last-gasp attempt to save the talks.*

lasting ('lɑ:stɪŋ) ADJECTIVE [1] permanent or enduring. ◆ NOUN [2] a strong durable closely woven fabric used for shoe uppers, etc.
▸**'lastingly** ADVERB ▸**'lastingness** NOUN

Last Judgment NOUN **the.** the occasion, after the resurrection of the dead at the end of the world, when, according to biblical tradition, God will decree the final destinies of all men according to the good and evil in their earthly lives. Also called: **the Last Day, Doomsday, Judgment Day.**

lastly ('lɑ:stlɪ) ADVERB [1] at the end or at the last point. ◆ SENTENCE CONNECTOR [2] in the end; finally: *lastly, he put on his jacket.*

last-minute NOUN (*modifier*) given or done at the latest possible time: *last-minute preparations.*

last name NOUN another term for **surname** (sense 1).

last out VERB (*adverb*) [1] (*intr*) to be sufficient for one's needs: *how long will our supplies last out?* [2] (*tr*) to endure or survive: *some old people don't last out the winter.*

last post NOUN (in the British military services) [1] a bugle call that orders men to retire for sleep. [2] a similar call sounded at military funerals.

last quarter NOUN one of the four principal phases of the moon, occurring between full moon and new moon, when half the lighted surface is visible. Compare **first quarter.**

last rites PLURAL NOUN *Christianity* religious rites prescribed for those close to death.

last straw NOUN **the.** the final irritation or problem that stretches one's endurance or patience beyond the limit.
▷HISTORY from the proverb, "It is the last straw that breaks the camel's back"

Last Supper NOUN **the.** the meal eaten by Christ with his disciples on the night before his Crucifixion, during which he is believed to have instituted the Eucharist.

last thing ADVERB as the final action, esp before retiring to bed at night.

Las Vegas (læs 'veɪgəs) NOUN a city in SE Nevada: famous for luxury hotels and casinos. Pop.: 478 434 (2000).

lat. ABBREVIATION FOR latitude.

Lat. ABBREVIATION FOR Latin.

latah ('lɑ:tə) NOUN a psychological condition, observed esp in Malaysian cultures, in which an individual, after experiencing a shock, becomes anxious and suggestible, often imitating the actions of another person.
▷HISTORY C19: from Malay

Latakia *or* **Lattakia** (ˌlætə'ki:ə) NOUN the chief port of Syria, in the northwest: tobacco industry. Pop.: 306 535 (1994 est.). Latin name: **Laodicea ad Mare.**

Latam ('læt'æm) NOUN, ADJECTIVE short for **Latin America** or **Latin American.**

latch (lætʃ) NOUN [1] a fastening for a gate or door that consists of a bar that may be slid or lowered into a groove, hole, etc. [2] a spring-loaded door lock that can be opened by a key from outside. [3] Also called: **latch circuit.** *Electronics* a logic circuit that transfers the input states to the output states when signalled, the output thereafter remaining insensitive to changes in input status until signalled again. ◆ VERB [4] to fasten, fit, or be fitted with or as if with a latch.
▷HISTORY Old English *læccan* to seize, of Germanic origin; related to Greek *lazesthai*

latchet ('lætʃɪt) NOUN *Archaic* a shoe fastening, such as a thong or lace.
▷HISTORY C14: from Old French *lachet,* from *las* LACE

latchkey ('lætʃˌki:) NOUN [1] a key for an outside door or gate, esp one that lifts a latch. [2] **a** a supposed freedom from restrictions. **b** (*as modifier*): *a latchkey existence.*

latchkey child NOUN a child who has to let himself in at home on returning from school, as his parents are out at work.

latch on VERB (*intr, adverb; often foll by to*) *Informal* [1] to attach oneself (to): *to latch on to a new acquaintance.* [2] to understand: *he suddenly latched on to what they were up to.* [3] *US and Canadian* to obtain; get.

latchstring ('lætʃˌstrɪŋ) NOUN a length of string fastened to a latch and passed through a hole in the door so that it can be opened from the other side.

late (leɪt) ADJECTIVE [1] occurring or arriving after the correct or expected time: *the train was late.* [2] (*prenominal*) occurring, scheduled for, or being at a relatively advanced time: *a late marriage.* [3] (*prenominal*) towards or near the end: *the late evening.* [4] at an advanced time in the evening or at night: *it was late.* [5] (*prenominal*) occurring or being just previous to the present time: *his late remarks on industry.* [6] (*prenominal*) having died, esp recently: *my late grandfather.* [7] (*prenominal*) just preceding the present or existing person or thing; former: *the late manager of this firm.* [8] **of late.** recently; lately. ◆ ADVERB [9] after the correct or expected time: *he arrived late.* [10] at a relatively advanced age: *she married late.* [11] recently; lately: *as late as yesterday he was selling books.* [12] **late hours.** rising and going to bed later than is usual. [13] **late in the day. a** at a late or advanced stage. **b** too late.
▷HISTORY Old English *læt;* related to Old Norse *latr,* Gothic *lats*
▸**'lateness** NOUN

> **Language note** Since *late* can mean *deceased,* many people think it is better to avoid using this word to refer to the person who held a post or position before its present holder: *the previous* (not *the late*) *editor of The Times.*

latecomer ('leɪtˌkʌmə) NOUN a person or thing that comes late.

lated ('leɪtɪd) ADJECTIVE an archaic word for **belated.**

lateen (lə'ti:n) ADJECTIVE *Nautical* denoting a rig with a triangular sail (**lateen sail**) bent to a yard hoisted to the head of a low mast, used esp in the Mediterranean.
▷HISTORY C18: from French *voile latine* Latin sail

lateenrigged (lə'ti:nˌrɪgd) ADJECTIVE *Nautical* rigged with a lateen sail.

Late Greek NOUN the Greek language from about the 3rd to the 8th centuries A.D. Compare **Medieval Greek, Koine.**

Late Latin NOUN the form of written Latin used from the 3rd to the 7th centuries A.D. See also **Biblical Latin, Medieval Latin.**

lately ('leɪtlɪ) ADVERB in recent times; of late.

latency period NOUN *Psychoanal* a period according to Freud, from the age of about five to puberty, when sexual interest is diminished.

La Tène (læ 'tɛn) ADJECTIVE of or relating to a Celtic culture in Europe from about the 5th to the 1st centuries B.C., characterized by a distinctive type of curvilinear decoration. See also **Hallstatt.**
▷HISTORY C20: from *La Tène,* a part of Lake Neuchâtel, Switzerland, where remains of this culture were first discovered

latent ('leɪtᵊnt) ADJECTIVE [1] potential but not obvious or explicit. [2] (of buds, spores, etc.) dormant. [3] *Pathol* (esp of an infectious disease) not yet revealed or manifest. [4] (of a virus) inactive in the host cell, its nucleic acid being integrated into, and replicated with, the host cell's DNA. [5] *Psychoanal* relating to that part of a dream expressive of repressed desires: *latent content.* Compare **manifest** (sense 2).
▷HISTORY C17: from Latin *latēnt-,* from *latens* present participle of *latēre* to lie hidden
▸**'latency** NOUN ▸**'latently** ADVERB

latent heat NOUN (*no longer in technical usage*) the heat evolved or absorbed by unit mass (**specific latent heat**) or unit amount of substance (**molar latent heat**) when it changes phase without change of temperature.

latent image NOUN *Photog* the invisible image produced by the action of light, etc., on silver halide crystals suspended in the emulsion of a photographic material. It becomes visible after development.

latent learning NOUN *Psychol* learning mediated neither by reward nor by the expectation of reward.

latent period NOUN [1] the incubation period of an infectious disease, before symptoms appear. [2] another name for **latent time.**

latent time NOUN *Psychol* the time from the onset of a stimulus to that of the response. Also called: **latency, reaction time.**

later ('leɪtə) ADJECTIVE, ADVERB [1] the comparative of **late.** ◆ ADVERB [2] afterwards; subsequently. [3] **see you later.** an expression of farewell. [4] **sooner or later.** eventually; inevitably.

lateral ('lætərəl) ADJECTIVE [1] of or relating to the side or sides: *a lateral blow.* [2] *Phonetics* (of a speech sound like *l*) pronounced with the tip of the tongue touching the centre of the alveolar ridge, leaving space on one or both sides for the passage of the airstream. ◆ NOUN [3] a lateral object, part, passage, or movement. [4] *Phonetics* a lateral speech sound.
▷HISTORY C17: from Latin *laterālis,* from *latus* side
▸'**laterally** ADVERB

laterality (ˌlætə'rælɪtɪ) NOUN *Psychol* the difference in the mental functions controlled by the left and right cerebral hemispheres of the brain.

lateral line system NOUN a system of sensory organs in fishes and aquatic amphibians consisting of a series of cells on the head and along the sides of the body that detect pressure changes and vibrations.

lateral thinking NOUN a way of solving problems by rejecting traditional methods and employing unorthodox and apparently illogical means.

Lateran ('lætərən) NOUN **the.** [1] Also called: **Lateran palace.** a palace in Rome, formerly the official residence of the popes. [2] any of five ecumenical councils held in this palace between 1123 and 1512. [3] the basilica of Saint John Lateran, the cathedral church of Rome.
▷HISTORY from Latin: the district is named after the ancient Roman family *Plautii Laterani*

laterigrade ('lætərɪˌgreɪd) ADJECTIVE *Zoology* (of some crabs) having a gait characterized by sideways movement.

laterite ('lætəˌraɪt) NOUN any of a group of deposits consisting of residual insoluble deposits of ferric and aluminium oxides: formed by weathering of rocks in tropical regions.
▷HISTORY C19: from Latin *later* brick, tile
▸**lateritic** (ˌlætə'rɪtɪk) ADJECTIVE

lateroversion (ˌlætərəʊ'vɜːʃən) NOUN abnormal lateral displacement of a bodily organ or part, esp of the uterus.
▷HISTORY C20: from LATERAL + *-version,* from Latin *versiō* a turning

latest ('leɪtɪst) ADJECTIVE, ADVERB [1] the superlative of **late.** ◆ ADJECTIVE [2] most recent, modern, or new: *the latest fashions.* ◆ NOUN [3] **at the latest.** no later than the time specified. [4] **the latest.** *Informal* the most recent fashion or development.

late-star type NOUN *Astronomy* any star with a surface temperature below that of the sun, of spectral type K, M, C, or S. Compare: **early-type star.**

latex ('leɪteks) NOUN, *plural* **latexes** *or* **latices** ('lætɪˌsiːz). [1] a whitish milky fluid containing protein, starch, alkaloids, etc., that is produced by many plants. Latex from the rubber tree is used in the manufacture of rubber. [2] a suspension of synthetic rubber or plastic in water, used in the manufacture of synthetic rubber products, etc.
▷HISTORY C19: New Latin, from Latin: liquid, fluid

lath (lɑːθ) NOUN, *plural* **laths** (lɑːðz, lɑːθs). [1] one of several thin narrow strips of wood used to provide a supporting framework for plaster, tiles, etc. [2] expanded sheet metal, wire mesh, etc., used to provide backing for plaster or rendering. [3] any thin strip of wood. ◆ VERB [4] *(tr)* to attach laths to (a ceiling, roof, floor, etc.).
▷HISTORY Old English *lætt;* related to Dutch *lat,* Old High German *latta*
▸'**lath**ˌ**like** ADJECTIVE

lathe[1] (leɪð) NOUN [1] a machine for shaping, boring, facing, or cutting a screw thread in metal, wood, etc., in which the workpiece is turned about a horizontal axis against a fixed tool. ◆ VERB [2] *(tr)* to shape, bore, or cut a screw thread in or on (a workpiece) on a lathe.
▷HISTORY perhaps C15 *lath* a support, of Scandinavian origin; compare Old Danish *lad* lathe, Old English *hlæd* heap

lathe[2] (leɪð) NOUN *Brit history* any of the former administrative divisions of Kent.
▷HISTORY Old English *læth* district

lather ('lɑːðə, 'læ-) NOUN [1] foam or froth formed by the action of soap or a detergent in water. [2] foam formed by other liquid, such as the sweat of a horse. [3] *Informal* a state of agitation or excitement. ◆ VERB [4] to coat or become coated with lather. [5] *(intr)* to form a lather.
▷HISTORY Old English *lēathor* soap; related to Old Norse *lauthr* foam
▸'**lathery** ADJECTIVE

lathi ('lɑːtɪ) NOUN a long heavy wooden stick used as a weapon in India, esp by the police.
▷HISTORY Hindi

lathy ('lɑːθɪ) ADJECTIVE **lathier, lathiest.** resembling a lath, esp in being tall and thin.

lathyrism ('læθərɪzəm) NOUN a neurological disease often resulting in weakness and paralysis of the legs: caused by eating the pealike seeds of the leguminous plant *Lathyrus sativus.*

latices ('lætɪˌsiːz) NOUN a plural of **latex.**

laticifer (lə'tɪsɪfə) NOUN *Botany* a cell or group of cells in a plant that contains latex.
▷HISTORY C19: from New Latin *latic-* LATEX + -FER
▸**laticiferous** (ˌlætɪ'sɪfərəs) ADJECTIVE

latifundium (ˌlætɪ'fʌndɪəm) NOUN, *plural* **-dia** (-dɪə). a large agricultural estate, esp one worked by slaves in ancient Rome.
▷HISTORY C17: from Latin *lātus* broad + *fundus* farm, estate

latimeria (ˌlætɪ'mɪərɪə) NOUN any coelacanth fish of the genus *Latimeria.*
▷HISTORY C20: named after Marjorie Courtenay-*Latimer* (born 1902), South African museum curator

Latin ('lætɪn) NOUN [1] the language of ancient Rome and the Roman Empire and of the educated in medieval Europe, which achieved its classical form during the 1st century B.C. Having originally been the language of Latium, belonging to the Italic branch of the Indo-European family, it later formed the basis of the Romance group. See **Late Latin, Low Latin, Medieval Latin, New Latin, Old Latin.** See also **Romance.** [2] a member of any of those peoples whose languages are derived from Latin. [3] an inhabitant of ancient Latium. ◆ ADJECTIVE [4] of or relating to the Latin language, the ancient Latins, or Latium. [5] characteristic of or relating to those peoples in Europe and Latin America whose languages are derived from Latin. [6] of or relating to the Roman Catholic Church. [7] denoting or relating to the Roman alphabet.
▷HISTORY Old English *latin* and *læden* Latin, language, from Latin *Latīnus* of Latium

Latina (*Italian* la'tiːna) NOUN a city in W central Italy, in Lazio: built as a planned town in 1932 on reclaimed land of the Pontine Marshes. Pop.: 114 099 (2000 est.). Former name (until 1947): **Littoria.**

Latin alphabet NOUN another term for **Roman alphabet.**

Latin America NOUN those areas of America whose official languages are Spanish and Portuguese, derived from Latin: South America, Central America, Mexico, and certain islands in the Caribbean.

Latin American NOUN [1] a native or inhabitant of Latin America. ◆ ADJECTIVE [2] of or relating to Latin America or its inhabitants.

Latinate ('lætɪˌneɪt) ADJECTIVE (of writing, vocabulary, etc.) imitative of or derived from Latin.

Latin Church NOUN the Roman Catholic Church.

Latin cross NOUN a cross the lowest arm of which is longer than the other three.

Latinism ('lætɪˌnɪzəm) NOUN a word, idiom, or phrase borrowed from Latin.

Latinist ('lætɪnɪst) NOUN a person who studies or is proficient in Latin.

Latinity (lə'tɪnɪtɪ) NOUN [1] facility in the use of Latin. [2] Latin style, esp in literature.

Latinize *or* **Latinise** ('lætɪˌnaɪz) VERB *(tr)* [1] to translate into Latin or Latinisms. [2] to transliterate into the Latin alphabet. [3] to cause to acquire Latin style or customs. [4] to bring Roman Catholic influence to bear upon (the form of religious ceremonies, etc.).
▸ˌ**Latini'zation** *or* ˌ**Latini'sation** NOUN ▸'**Latin**ˌ**izer** *or* '**Latin**ˌ**iser** NOUN

Latino (læ'tiːnəʊ) NOUN, *plural* **-nos.** *US* an inhabitant of the US who is of Latin American origin.
▸**La'tina** FEMININE NOUN

Latin Quarter NOUN an area of Paris, on the S bank of the River Seine: contains the city's main educational establishments; centre for students and artists.

Latin square NOUN (in statistical analysis) one of a set of square arrays of *n* rows and columns, esp as used in statistics and studied in combinatorial analysis, built up from *n* different symbols so that no symbol occurs more than once in any row or column.

latish ('leɪtɪʃ) ADJECTIVE rather late.

latitude ('lætɪˌtjuːd) NOUN [1] **a** an angular distance in degrees north or south of the equator (latitude 0°), equal to the angle subtended at the centre of the globe by the meridian between the equator and the point in question. **b** *(often plural)* a region considered with regard to its distance from the equator. See **longitude** (sense 1). [2] scope for freedom of action, thought, etc.; freedom from restriction: *his parents gave him a great deal of latitude.* [3] *Photog* the range of exposure over which a photographic emulsion gives an acceptable negative. [4] *Astronomy* See **celestial latitude.**
▷HISTORY C14: from Latin *lātitūdō,* from *lātus* broad
▸ˌ**lati'tudinal** ADJECTIVE ▸ˌ**lati'tudinally** ADVERB

latitudinarian (ˌlætɪˌtjuːdɪ'nɛərɪən) ADJECTIVE [1] permitting or marked by freedom of attitude or behaviour, esp in religious matters. [2] *(sometimes capital)* of or relating to a school of thought within the Church of England in the 17th century that minimized the importance of divine authority in matters of doctrine and stressed the importance of reason and personal judgment. ◆ NOUN [3] a person with latitudinarian views.
▷HISTORY C17: from Latin *lātitūdō* breadth, LATITUDE, influenced in form by TRINITARIAN
▸ˌ**lati**ˌ**tudi'narianism** NOUN

Latium ('leɪʃɪəm) NOUN an ancient territory in W central Italy, in modern Lazio, on the Tyrrhenian Sea: inhabited by the Latin people from the 10th century B.C. until dominated by Rome (4th century B.C.). Italian name: **Lazio.**

Latona (lə'təʊnə) NOUN the Roman name of **Leto.**

La Trappe (*French* la trap) NOUN a monastery in NW France, in the village of Soligny-la-Trappe northeast of Alençon: founded in about 1140, site of the Trappist reform of Cistercian order in 1664.

latria (lə'traɪə) NOUN *RC Church, theol* the adoration that may be offered to God alone.
▷HISTORY C16: via Latin from Greek *latreia* worship

latrine (lə'triːn) NOUN a lavatory, as in a barracks, camp, etc.
▷HISTORY C17: from French, from Latin *lātrīna,* shortened form of *lavātrīna* bath, from *lavāre* to wash

-latry NOUN COMBINING FORM indicating worship of or excessive veneration of: *idolatry; Mariolatry.*
▷HISTORY from Greek *-latria,* from *latreia* worship
▸**-latrous** ADJECTIVE COMBINING FORM

lats (læts) NOUN, *plural* **lati** ('læti:). the standard monetary unit of Latvia, divided into 100 santimi.

latte ('læteɪ, 'lɑːteɪ) NOUN coffee made with hot milk.
▷HISTORY C20: from Italian *(caffè e) latte* (coffee and) milk

latten ('lætᵊn) NOUN metal or alloy, esp brass, made in thin sheets.
▷HISTORY C14: from Old French *laton,* of unknown origin

latter ('lætə) ADJECTIVE *(prenominal)* [1] **a** denoting the second or second mentioned of two: distinguished from *former.* **b** *(as noun; functioning as singular or plural)*: *the latter is not important.* [2] near or nearer the end: *the latter part of a film.* 3 more advanced in time or sequence; later.

> **Language note** *The latter* should only be used to refer to the second of two items: *many people choose to go by hovercraft rather than use the ferry, but I prefer the latter.* The last of three or more items can be referred to as *the last-named.*

latter-day ADJECTIVE present-day; modern.

Latter-day Saint NOUN a more formal name for a **Mormon.**

latterly (ˈlætəlɪ) ADVERB recently; lately.

lattermost (ˈlætəˌməʊst) ADJECTIVE a less common word for **last**[1].

lattice (ˈlætɪs) NOUN 1 Also called: **latticework.** an open framework of strips of wood, metal, etc., arranged to form an ornamental pattern. 2 **a** a gate, screen, etc., formed of such a framework. **b** (*as modifier*): *a lattice window.* 3 something, such as a decorative or heraldic device, resembling such a framework. 4 an array of objects or points in a periodic pattern in two or three dimensions, esp an array of atoms, ions, etc., in a crystal or an array of points indicating their positions in space. See also **Bravais lattice.** ♦ VERB 5 to make, adorn, or supply with a lattice or lattices.
▷HISTORY C14: from Old French *lattis,* from *latte* LATH
▸ˈ**latticed** ADJECTIVE

lattice energy NOUN *Chem* the energy required to separate the ions of a crystal to an infinite distance, usually expressed in joules per mole.

latus rectum (ˈlɑːtəs ˈrɛktəm) NOUN, *plural* **latera recta** (ˈlætərə ˈrɛktə). *Geometry* a chord that passes through the focus of a conic and is perpendicular to the major axis.
▷HISTORY C18: New Latin: straight side

Latvia (ˈlætvɪə) NOUN a republic in NE Europe, on the Gulf of Riga and the Baltic Sea: ruled by Poland, Sweden, and Russia since the 13th century, Latvia was independent from 1919 until 1940 and was a Soviet republic (1940–91), gaining its independence after conflict with Soviet forces; it is mostly forested. Official language: Latvian. Religion: nonreligious, Christian. Currency: lats. Capital: Riga. Pop.: 2 358 000 (2001 est.). Area: 63 700 sq. km (25 590 sq. miles).

Latvian (ˈlætvɪən) ADJECTIVE 1 of or relating to Latvia, its people, or their language. ♦ NOUN 2 Also called: **Lettish.** the official language of Latvia: closely related to Lithuanian and belonging to the Baltic branch of the Indo-European family. 3 a native or inhabitant of Latvia.

laud (lɔːd) *Literary* ♦ VERB 1 (*tr*) to praise or glorify. ♦ NOUN 2 praise or glorification.
▷HISTORY C14: vb from Latin *laudāre;* n from *laudēs,* pl of Latin *laus* praise
▸ˈ**lauder** NOUN

laudable (ˈlɔːdəbᵊl) ADJECTIVE deserving or worthy of praise; admirable; commendable.
▸ˈ**laudableness** *or* ˌ**laudaˈbility** NOUN ▸ˈ**laudably** ADVERB

laudanum (ˈlɔːdᵊnəm) NOUN 1 a tincture of opium. 2 (formerly) any medicine of which opium was the main ingredient.
▷HISTORY C16: New Latin, name chosen by Paracelsus for a preparation probably containing opium, perhaps based on LABDANUM

laudation (lɔːˈdeɪʃən) NOUN a formal word for **praise.**

laudatory (ˈlɔːdətərɪ, -trɪ) *or* **laudative** ADJECTIVE expressing or containing praise; eulogistic.

Laudian (ˈlɔːdɪən) ADJECTIVE *Church of England* of or relating to the High-Church standards set up for the Church of England by William Laud (1573–1645), English archbishop of Canterbury (1633–45).

lauds (lɔːdz) NOUN (*functioning as singular or plural*) *Chiefly RC Church* the traditional morning prayer of the Western Church, constituting with matins the first of the seven canonical hours.
▷HISTORY C14: see LAUD

laugh (lɑːf) VERB 1 (*intr*) to express or manifest emotion, esp mirth or amusement, typically by expelling air from the lungs in short bursts to produce an inarticulate voiced noise, with the mouth open. 2 (*intr*) (esp of certain mammals or birds) to make a noise resembling a laugh. 3 (*tr*) to utter or express with laughter: *he laughed his derision at the play.* 4 (*tr*) to bring or force (someone, esp oneself) into a certain condition by laughter: *he laughed himself sick.* 5 (*intr;* foll by *at*) to make fun (of); jeer (at). 6 (*intr;* foll by *over*) to read or discuss something with laughter. 7 **don't make me laugh.** *Informal* I don't believe you for a moment. 8 **laugh all the way to the bank.** *Informal* to be unashamedly pleased at making a lot of money. 9 **laugh in a person's face.** to show open contempt or defiance towards a person. 10 **laugh like a drain.** *Informal* to laugh loudly and coarsely. 11 **laugh up one's sleeve.** to laugh or have grounds for amusement, self-satisfaction, etc., secretly. 12 **laugh on the other side of one's face.** to show sudden disappointment or shame after appearing cheerful or confident. 13 **be laughing.** *Informal* to be in a favourable situation. ♦ NOUN 14 the act or an instance of laughing. 15 a manner of laughter. 16 *Informal* a person or thing that causes laughter: *that holiday was a laugh.* 17 **the last laugh.** the final success in an argument, situation, etc., after previous defeat. ♦ See also **laugh away, laugh down, laugh off.**
▷HISTORY Old English *læhan, hliehhen;* related to Gothic *hlahjan,* Dutch *lachen*
▸ˈ**laugher** NOUN ▸ˈ**laughing** NOUN, ADJECTIVE ▸ˈ**laughingly** ADVERB

laughable (ˈlɑːfəbᵊl) ADJECTIVE 1 producing scorn; ludicrous: *he offered me a laughable sum for the picture.* 2 arousing laughter.
▸ˈ**laughableness** NOUN ▸ˈ**laughably** ADVERB

laugh away VERB (*tr, adverb*) 1 to dismiss or dispel (something unpleasant) by laughter. 2 to make (time) pass pleasantly by jesting.

laugh down VERB (*tr, adverb*) to silence by laughing contemptuously.

laughing gas NOUN another name for **nitrous oxide.**

laughing hyena NOUN another name for the **spotted hyena** (see **hyena**).

laughing jackass NOUN another name for the **kookaburra** (sense 1).

laughing stock NOUN an object of humiliating ridicule: *his mistakes have made him a laughing stock.*

laugh off VERB (*tr, adverb*) to treat or dismiss lightly, esp with stoicism: *he laughed off his injuries.*

laughter (ˈlɑːftə) NOUN 1 the action of or noise produced by laughing. 2 the experience or manifestation of mirth, amusement, scorn, or joy.
▷HISTORY Old English *hleahtor;* related to Old Norse *hlātr*

launce (lɑːns) NOUN another name for the **sand eel.**

Launceston (ˈlɔːnsəstən) NOUN a city in Australia, the chief port of the island state of Tasmania on the Tamar River, 64 km (40 miles) from Bass Strait. Pop.: 93 347 (1991).

launch[1] (lɔːntʃ) VERB 1 to move (a vessel) into the water. 2 to move (a newly built vessel) into the water for the first time. 3 (*tr*) **a** to start off or set in motion: *to launch a scheme.* **b** to put (a new product) on the market. 4 (*tr*) to propel with force. 5 to involve (oneself) totally and enthusiastically: *to launch oneself into work.* 6 (*tr*) to set (a missile, spacecraft, etc.) into motion. 7 (*tr*) to catapult (an aircraft), as from the deck of an aircraft carrier. 8 (*intr;* foll by *into*) to start talking or writing (about): *he launched into a story.* 9 (*intr;* usually foll by *out*) to start (out) on a fresh course. 10 (*intr;* usually foll by *out*) *Informal* to spend a lot of money. ♦ NOUN 11 an act or instance of launching.
▷HISTORY C14: from Anglo-French *lancher,* from Late Latin *lanceāre* to use a lance, hence, to set in motion. See LANCE

launch[2] (lɔːntʃ) NOUN 1 a motor driven boat used chiefly as a transport boat. 2 the largest of the boats of a man-of-war.
▷HISTORY C17: via Spanish *lancha* and Portuguese from Malay *lancharan* boat, from *lanchar* speed

launcher (ˈlɔːntʃə) NOUN any installation, vehicle, or other device for launching rockets, missiles, or other projectiles.

launch pad *or* **launching pad** NOUN 1 a platform from which a spacecraft, rocket, etc., is launched. 2 an effective starting point for a career, enterprise, or campaign.

launch shoe *or* **launching shoe** NOUN an attachment to an aircraft from which a missile is launched.

launch vehicle *or* **launching vehicle** NOUN 1 a rocket, without its payload, used to launch a spacecraft. 2 another name for **booster** (sense 2).

launch window NOUN the limited period during which a spacecraft can be launched on a particular mission.

launder (ˈlɔːndə) VERB 1 to wash, sometimes starch, and often also iron (clothes, linen, etc.). 2 (*intr*) to be capable of being laundered without shrinking, fading, etc. 3 (*tr*) to process (something acquired illegally) to make it appear respectable, esp to process illegally acquired funds through a legitimate business or to send them to a foreign bank for subsequent transfer to a home bank. ♦ NOUN 4 a water trough, esp one used for washing ore in mining.
▷HISTORY C14 (n, meaning: a person who washes linen): changed from *lavender* washerwoman, from Old French *lavandiere,* ultimately from Latin *lavāre* to wash
▸ˈ**launderer** NOUN

Launderette (ˌlɔːndəˈrɛt, lɔːnˈdrɛt) NOUN *Trademark, Brit and NZ* a commercial establishment where clothes can be washed and dried, using coin-operated machines. Also called (US, Canadian, and NZ): **Laundromat.**

laundress (ˈlɔːndrɪs) NOUN a woman who launders clothes, sheets, etc., for a living.

laundrette (lɔːnˈdrɛt) NOUN a variant of **Launderette.**

Laundromat (ˈlɔːndrəˌmæt) NOUN *Trademark* a US, Canadian, and NZ name for **Launderette.**

laundry (ˈlɔːndrɪ) NOUN, *plural* **-dries.** 1 a place where clothes and linen are washed and ironed. 2 the clothes or linen washed and ironed. 3 the act of laundering.
▷HISTORY C16: changed from C14 *lavendry;* see LAUNDER

laundryman (ˈlɔːndrɪmən) NOUN, *plural* **-men.** 1 a man who collects or delivers laundry. 2 a man who works in a laundry.

laundrywoman (ˈlɔːndrɪwʊmən) NOUN, *plural* **-women.** 1 a woman who collects or delivers laundry. 2 a woman who works in a laundry.

lauraceous (lɔːˈreɪʃəs) ADJECTIVE of, relating to, or belonging to the *Lauraceae,* a family of aromatic trees and shrubs having leathery leaves: includes the laurels and avocado.

Laurasia (lɔːˈreɪʃə) NOUN one of the two ancient supercontinents produced by the first split of the even larger supercontinent Pangaea about 200 million years ago, comprising what are now North America, Greenland, Europe, and Asia (excluding India). See also **Gondwanaland, Pangaea.**
▷HISTORY C20: from New Latin *Laur(entia)* (referring to the ancient N American landmass, from *Laurentian* strata of the Canadian Shield) + *(Eur)asia*

laureate (ˈlɔːrɪɪt) ADJECTIVE (*usually immediately postpositive*) 1 *Literary* crowned with laurel leaves as a sign of honour. 2 *Archaic* made of laurel. ♦ NOUN 3 short for **poet laureate.** 4 a person honoured with an award for art or science: *a Nobel laureate.* 5 *Rare* a person honoured with the laurel crown or wreath.
▷HISTORY C14: from Latin *laureātus,* from *laurea* LAUREL
▸ˈ**laureateˌship** NOUN ▸**laureation** (ˌlɔːrɪˈeɪʃən) NOUN

laurel (ˈlɒrəl) NOUN 1 Also called: **bay, true laurel.** any lauraceous tree of the genus *Laurus,* such as the bay tree (see **bay**[4]) and *L. canariensis,* of the Canary Islands and Azores. 2 any lauraceous plant. 3 short for **cherry laurel** or **mountain laurel.** 4 **spurge laurel.** a European thymelaeaceous evergreen shrub, *Daphne laureola,* with glossy leaves and small green flowers. 5 **spotted** or **Japan laurel.** an evergreen cornaceous shrub, *Aucuba japonica,* of S and SE Asia, the female of which has yellow-spotted leaves. 6 (*plural*) a wreath of true laurel, worn on the head as an emblem of victory or honour in classical times. 7 (*plural*) honour, distinction, or fame. 8 **look to one's laurels.** to be on guard against one's rivals. 9 **rest on one's laurels.** to be satisfied with distinction won by past achievements and cease to strive for further achievements. ♦ VERB **-rels, -relling, -relled** *or US* **-rels, -reling, -reled.** 10 (*tr*) to crown with laurels.

▷**HISTORY** C13 *lorer,* from Old French *lorier* laurel tree, ultimately from Latin *laurus*

Laurentian (lɔːˈrɛnʃən) ADJECTIVE 1 Also: **Lawrentian.** of or resembling the style of D. H. Lawrence (1885–1930), the British novelist, poet, and short-story writer, or T. E. *Lawrence* "of Arabia" (1885–1935), the British soldier and writer. 2 of, relating to, or situated near the St Lawrence River.

Laurentian Mountains PLURAL NOUN a range of low mountains in E Canada, in Quebec between the St Lawrence River and Hudson Bay. Highest point: 1191 m (3905 ft.). Also called: **Laurentides** (ˈlɔːrənˌtaɪdz).

Laurentian Shield NOUN another name for the **Canadian Shield.** Also called: **Laurentian Plateau.**

lauric acid (ˈlɔːrɪk, ˈlɒ-) NOUN another name for **dodecanoic acid.**
▷**HISTORY** C19: from Latin *laurus* laurel; from its occurrence in the berries of the laurel (*Laurus nobilis*)

laurustinus (ˌlɔːrəˈstaɪnəs) NOUN a Mediterranean caprifoliaceous shrub, *Viburnum tinus,* with glossy evergreen leaves and white or pink fragrant flowers.
▷**HISTORY** C17: from New Latin, from Latin *laurus* laurel

lauryl alcohol (ˈlɔːrɪl, ˈlɒ-) NOUN a water-insoluble crystalline solid used in the manufacture of detergents; 1-dodecanol. Formula: $CH_3(CH_2)_{10}CH_2OH$.
▷**HISTORY** C20: from LAUR(IC ACID) + -YL

Lausanne (ləʊˈzæn; *French* lozan) NOUN a city in W Switzerland, capital of Vaud canton, on Lake Geneva; cultural and commercial centre; university (1537). Pop.: 114 161 (1999 est.).

lav (læv) NOUN *Brit informal* short for **lavatory.**

lava (ˈlɑːvə) NOUN 1 magma emanating from volcanoes and other vents. 2 any extrusive igneous rock formed by the cooling and solidification of molten lava.
▷**HISTORY** C18: from Italian (Neapolitan dialect), from Latin *lavāre* to wash

lavabo (ləˈveɪbəʊ) NOUN, *plural* **-boes** *or* **-bos.** *Chiefly RC Church* 1 **a** the ritual washing of the celebrant's hands after the offertory at Mass. **b** (*as modifier*): *lavabo basin; lavabo towel.* 2 another name for **washbasin.** 3 a trough for washing in a convent or monastery.
▷**HISTORY** C19: from Latin: I shall wash, the opening of Psalm 26:6

lavage (ˈlævɪdʒ, læˈvɑːʒ) NOUN *Med* the washing out of a hollow organ by flushing with water.
▷**HISTORY** C19: via French, from Latin *lavāre* to wash

Laval (ləˈvæl) NOUN a city in SE Canada, in Quebec: a NW suburb of Montreal. Pop.: 330 343 (1996).

lava lamp NOUN a decorative type of lamp in which a luminous viscous material moves in constantly changing shapes.
▷**HISTORY** C20: from the resemblance of the shapes to molten lava in water

lava-lava NOUN a draped skirtlike garment of printed cotton or calico worn by Polynesians.
▷**HISTORY** Samoan

lavatera (ˌlævəˈtɪərə) NOUN any plant of the genus *Lavatera,* closely resembling mallow and grown for their purple, white, or rose-coloured flowers: family *Malvaceae.*
▷**HISTORY** named after the two brothers *Lavater,* 18th-century Swiss doctors and naturalists

lavation (læˈveɪʃən) NOUN *Formal or literary* the act or process of washing.
▷**HISTORY** C17: from Latin *lavātio,* from *lavāre* to wash
▸ **laˈvational** ADJECTIVE

lavatorial (ˌlævəˈtɔːrɪəl) ADJECTIVE 1 of or in the style of decoration supposed to typify public lavatories: *white lavatorial tiling.* 2 characterized by excessive mention of lavatories and the excretory functions; vulgar or scatological: *lavatorial humour.*

lavatory (ˈlævətərɪ, -trɪ) NOUN, *plural* **-ries.** 1 Also called: **toilet, water closet, WC. a** a sanitary installation for receiving and disposing of urine and faeces, consisting of a bowl fitted with a water-flushing device and connected to a drain. **b** a room containing such an installation. 2 the washing place in a convent or monastic establishment.
▷**HISTORY** C14: from Late Latin *lavātōrium,* from Latin *lavāre* to wash

lavatory paper NOUN *Brit* another name for **toilet paper.**

lave (leɪv) VERB an archaic word for **wash.**
▷**HISTORY** Old English *lafian,* perhaps from Latin *lavāre* to wash

lavender (ˈlævəndə) NOUN 1 any of various perennial shrubs or herbaceous plants of the genus *Lavandula,* esp *L. vera,* cultivated for its mauve or blue flowers and as the source of a fragrant oil (**oil of lavender**): family *Lamiaceae* (labiates). See also **spike lavender.** Compare **sea lavender.** 2 the dried parts of *L. vera,* used to perfume clothes. 3 **a** a pale or light bluish-purple to a very pale violet colour. **b** (*as adjective*): *lavender socks.* 4 perfume scented with lavender.
▷**HISTORY** C13: *lavendre,* via French from Medieval Latin *lavendula,* of obscure origin

lavender bag NOUN a small fabric bag filled with dried lavender flowers and placed amongst clothes or linen to scent them.

lavender water NOUN a perfume made of essential oils of lavender and alcohol.

laver[1] (ˈleɪvə) NOUN 1 *Old Testament* a large basin of water used by the priests for ritual ablutions. 2 the font or the water of baptism.
▷**HISTORY** C14: from Old French *laveoir,* from Late Latin *lavātōrium* washing place

laver[2] (ˈlɑːvə) NOUN any of several seaweeds of the genus *Porphyra* and related genera, with edible fronds: phylum *Rhodophyta* (red algae).
▷**HISTORY** C16: from Latin

laver bread (ˈlɑːvə) NOUN laver seaweed fried as a breakfast food; popular in Wales.

laverock (ˈlævərək; *Scot also* ˈlevərək, ˈlevrək) NOUN a Scot and northern English dialect word for **skylark** (bird).
▷**HISTORY** Old English *lǣwerce* LARK[1]

lavish (ˈlævɪʃ) ADJECTIVE 1 prolific, abundant, or profuse. 2 generous; unstinting; liberal. 3 extravagant; prodigal; wasteful: *lavish expenditure.* ◆ VERB 4 (*tr*) to give, expend, or apply abundantly, generously, or in profusion.
▷**HISTORY** C15: adj use of *lavas* profusion, from Old French *lavasse* torrent, from Latin *lavāre* to wash
▸ **ˈlavisher** NOUN ▸ **ˈlavishly** ADVERB ▸ **ˈlavishment** NOUN ▸ **ˈlavishness** NOUN

lavolta (ləˈvɒltə) NOUN another word for **volta.**
▷**HISTORY** C16: from Italian *la volta* the turn; see VOLTA

law[1] (lɔː) NOUN 1 a rule or set of rules, enforceable by the courts, regulating the government of a state, the relationship between the organs of government and the subjects of the state, and the relationship or conduct of subjects towards each other. 2 **a** a rule or body of rules made by the legislature. See **statute law. b** a rule or body of rules made by a municipal or other authority. See **bylaw.** 3 **a** the condition and control enforced by such rules. **b** (*in combination*): *lawcourt.* 4 a rule of conduct: *a law of etiquette.* 5 one of a set of rules governing a particular field of activity: *the laws of tennis.* 6 **the law. a** the legal or judicial system. **b** the profession or practice of law. **c** *Informal* the police or a policeman. 7 a binding force or statement: *his word is law.* 8 Also called: **law of nature.** a generalization based on a recurring fact or event. 9 the science or knowledge of law; jurisprudence. 10 the principles originating and formerly applied only in courts of common law. Compare **equity** (sense 3). 11 a general principle, formula, or rule describing a phenomenon in mathematics, science, philosophy, etc.: *the laws of thermodynamics.* 12 *Judaism* (*capital;* preceded by *the*) **a** short for **Law of Moses. b** the English term for **Torah.** ◆ See also **Oral Law, Written Law.** 13 **a law unto itself** (**oneself,** etc.). a person or thing that is outside established laws. 14 **go to law.** to resort to legal proceedings on some matter. 15 **lay down the law.** to speak in an authoritative or dogmatic manner. 16 **reading** (**of**) **the Law.** *Judaism* that part of the morning service on Sabbaths, festivals, and Mondays and Thursdays during which a passage is read from the Torah scrolls. 17 **take the law into one's own hands.** to ignore or bypass the law when redressing a grievance. ◆ Related adjectives **judicial, jural, juridical, legal.**
▷**HISTORY** Old English *lagu,* from Scandinavian; compare Icelandic *lög* (pl) things laid down, law

law[2] (lɔː) NOUN *Scot* a hill, esp one rounded in shape.
▷**HISTORY** Old English *hlǣw*

law[3] (lɔː) ADJECTIVE a Scot word for **low**[1].

law-abiding ADJECTIVE adhering more or less strictly to the laws: *a law-abiding citizen.*
▸ **ˈlaw-aˌbidingness** NOUN

law agent NOUN (in Scotland) a solicitor holding a certificate from the Law Society of Scotland and thereby entitled to appear for a client in any Sheriff Court.

law-and-order NOUN (*modifier*) favouring or advocating strong measures to suppress crime and violence: *a law-and-order candidate.*

lawbreaker (ˈlɔːˌbreɪkə) NOUN 1 a person who breaks the law. 2 *Informal* something that does not conform with legal standards or requirements.
▸ **ˈlawˌbreaking** NOUN, ADJECTIVE

law centre NOUN *Brit* an office, usually staffed by professional volunteers, at which free legal advice and information are provided to the general public.

Law French NOUN a set of Anglo-Norman terms used in English laws and law books.

lawful (ˈlɔːfʊl) ADJECTIVE allowed, recognized, or sanctioned by law; legal.
▸ **ˈlawfully** ADVERB ▸ **ˈlawfulness** NOUN

lawgiver (ˈlɔːˌgɪvə) NOUN 1 the giver of a code of laws. 2 Also called: **lawmaker.** a maker of laws.
▸ **ˈlawˌgiving** NOUN, ADJECTIVE

lawin *or* **lawing** (ˈlɔːɪn) NOUN *Scot* a bill or reckoning.
▷**HISTORY** C16: from Old Norse *lag* market price

lawks (lɔːks) INTERJECTION *Brit* an expression of surprise or dismay.
▷**HISTORY** C18: variant of *Lord!,* probably influenced in form by ALACK

lawless (ˈlɔːlɪs) ADJECTIVE 1 without law. 2 disobedient to the law. 3 contrary to or heedless of the law. 4 uncontrolled; unbridled: *lawless rage.*
▸ **ˈlawlessly** ADVERB ▸ **ˈlawlessness** NOUN

Law Lords PLURAL NOUN (in Britain) members of the House of Lords who sit as the highest court of appeal, although in theory the full House of Lords has this role.

lawman (ˈlɔːmən) NOUN, *plural* **-men.** *Chiefly US* an officer of the law, such as a policeman or sheriff.

law merchant NOUN *Mercantile law* the body of rules and principles determining the rights and obligations of the parties to commercial transactions; commercial law.

lawn[1] (lɔːn) NOUN 1 a flat and usually level area of mown and cultivated grass. 2 an archaic or dialect word for **glade.**
▷**HISTORY** C16: changed form of C14 *launde,* from Old French *lande,* of Celtic origin; compare Breton *lann* heath; related to LAND
▸ **ˈlawny** ADJECTIVE

lawn[2] (lɔːn) NOUN a fine linen or cotton fabric, used for clothing.
▷**HISTORY** C15: probably from *Laon,* a town in France where linen was made
▸ **ˈlawny** ADJECTIVE

lawn mower NOUN a hand-operated or power-operated machine with rotary blades for cutting grass on lawns.

lawn mower racing NOUN the sport of racing modified versions of the type of lawn mower that has a seated driver.

lawn tennis NOUN 1 tennis played on a grass court. 2 the formal name for **tennis.**

law of averages NOUN (popularly) the expectation that a possible event is bound to occur regularly with a frequency approximating to its probability, as in the (actually false) example: *after five heads in a row the law of averages makes tails the better bet.* Compare **law of large numbers.**

law of effect NOUN *Psychol* another name for **Thorndike's Law.**

law of large numbers NOUN the fundamental statistical result that the average of a sequence of n identically distributed independent random variables tends to their common mean as n tends to infinity, whence the frequency of the occurrence of an event in *n* independent repetitions of an experiment tends to its probability.

Law of Moses NOUN [1] the first five books of the Old Testament; Pentateuch. [2] *Judaism* a law or body of laws derived from the Torah in accordance with interpretations (the Oral Law) traditionally believed to have been given to Moses on Mount Sinai together with the Written Law.

law of nations NOUN another term for **international law.**

law of nature NOUN [1] an empirical truth of great generality, conceived of as a physical (but not a logical) necessity, and consequently licensing counterfactual conditionals. [2] a system of morality conceived of as grounded in reason. See **natural law** (sense 2), **nomological** (sense 2). [3] See **law** (sense 8).

law of supply and demand NOUN the theory that prices are determined by the interaction of supply and demand: an increase in supply will lower prices if not accompanied by increased demand, and an increase in demand will raise prices unless accompanied by increased supply.

law of the jungle NOUN a state of ruthless competition or self-interest.

law of thermodynamics NOUN [1] any of three principles governing the relationships between different forms of energy. The **first law of thermodynamics** (law of conservation of energy) states that the change in the internal energy of a system is equal to the sum of the heat added to the system and the work done on it. The **second law of thermodynamics** states that heat cannot be transferred from a colder to a hotter body within a system without net changes occurring in other bodies within that system; in any irreversible process, entropy always increases. The **third law of thermodynamics** (Nernst heat theorem) states that it is impossible to reduce the temperature of a system to absolute zero in a finite number of steps. [2] Also called: **zeroth law of thermodynamics.** the principle that if two bodies are each in thermal equilibrium with a third body then the first two bodies are in thermal equilibrium with each other.

lawrencium (lɒˈrɛnsɪəm, lɔ:-) NOUN a transuranic element artificially produced from californium. Symbol: Lr; atomic no.: 103; half-life of most stable isotope, ^{256}Lr: 35 seconds; valency: 3.
▷HISTORY C20: named after Ernest Orlando Lawrence (1901–58), US physicist

Lawrentian (lɔːˈrɛnʃən) ADJECTIVE relating to or characteristic of D(avid) H(erbert) Lawrence (1885-1930), the British novelist, poet, and short-story writer.

Law Society NOUN (in England or Scotland) the professional body of solicitors, established in 1825 and entrusted with the registration of solicitors (requiring the passing of certain examinations) and the regulation of professional conduct.

law stationer NOUN [1] a stationer selling articles used by lawyers. [2] *Brit* a person who makes handwritten copies of legal documents.

lawsuit (ˈlɔːˌsuːt, -ˌsjuːt) NOUN a proceeding in a court of law brought by one party against another, esp a civil action.

law term NOUN [1] an expression or word used in law. [2] any of various periods of time appointed for the sitting of law courts.

lawyer (ˈlɔːjə, ˈlɔɪə) NOUN [1] a member of the legal profession, esp a solicitor. See also **advocate, barrister, solicitor.** [2] a popular name for **burbot** (a fish).
▷HISTORY C14: from LAW[1]

lawyer's wig NOUN another name for the **shaggy ink-cap:** see **ink-cap.**

lawyer vine NOUN *Austral* any of various kinds of entangling and thorny vegetation, such as the rattan palm, esp in tropical areas. Also called: **lawyer cane, lawyer palm.**

lax (læks) ADJECTIVE [1] lacking firmness; not strict. [2] lacking precision or definition. [3] not taut. [4] *Phonetics* (of a speech sound) pronounced with little muscular effort and consequently having relatively imprecise accuracy of articulation and little temporal duration. In English the vowel *i* in *bit* is lax. [5] (of flower clusters) having loosely arranged parts.
▷HISTORY C14 (originally used with reference to the bowels): from Latin *laxus* loose
▸ˈ**laxly** ADVERB ▸ˈ**laxity** *or* ˈ**laxness** NOUN

laxation (lækˈseɪʃən) NOUN [1] the act of making lax or the state of being lax. [2] *Physiol* another word for **defecation.**
▷HISTORY C14: from Latin *laxātio,* from *laxāre* to slacken

laxative (ˈlæksətɪv) NOUN [1] an agent stimulating evacuation of faeces. ◆ ADJECTIVE [2] stimulating evacuation of faeces.
▷HISTORY C14 (originally: relaxing): from Medieval Latin *laxātīvus,* from Latin *laxāre* to loosen

lay[1] (leɪ) VERB **lays, laying, laid** (leɪd). (*mainly tr*) [1] to put in a low or horizontal position; cause to lie: *to lay a cover on a bed.* [2] to place, put, or be in a particular state or position: *he laid his finger on his lips.* [3] (*intr*) *Dialect or not standard* to be in a horizontal position; lie: *he often lays in bed all the morning.* [4] (sometimes foll by *down*) to establish as a basis: *to lay a foundation for discussion.* [5] to place or dispose in the proper position: *to lay a carpet.* [6] to arrange (a table) for eating a meal. [7] to prepare (a fire) for lighting by arranging fuel in the grate. [8] (*also intr*) (of birds, esp the domestic hen) to produce (eggs). [9] to present or put forward: *he laid his case before the magistrate.* [10] to impute or attribute: *all the blame was laid on him.* [11] to arrange, devise, or prepare: *to lay a trap.* [12] to place, set, or locate: *the scene is laid in London.* [13] to apply on or as if on a surface: *to lay a coat of paint.* [14] to impose as a penalty or burden: *to lay a fine.* [15] to make (a bet) with (someone): *I lay you five to one on Prince.* [16] to cause to settle: *to lay the dust.* [17] to allay; suppress: *to lay a rumour.* [18] to bring down forcefully: *to lay a whip on someone's back.* [19] *Slang* to have sexual intercourse with. [20] to press down or make smooth: *to lay the nap of cloth.* [21] to cut (small trunks or branches of shrubs or trees) halfway through and bend them diagonally to form a hedge: *to lay a hedge.* [22] to arrange and twist together (strands) in order to form (a rope, cable, etc.). [23] *Military* to apply settings of elevation and training to (a weapon) prior to firing. [24] (foll by *on*) *Hunting* to put (hounds or other dogs) onto a scent. [25] another word for **inlay.** [26] (*intr; often foll by to or out*) *Dialect or informal* to plan, scheme, or devise. [27] (*intr*) *Nautical* to move or go, esp into a specified position or direction: *to lay close to the wind.* [28] **lay aboard.** *Nautical* (formerly) to move alongside a warship to board it. [29] **lay a course. a** *Nautical* to sail on a planned course without tacking. **b** to plan an action. [30] **lay bare.** to reveal or explain: *he laid bare his plans.* [31] **lay hands on.** See **hands** (sense 12). [32] **lay hold of.** to seize or grasp. [33] **lay oneself open.** to make oneself vulnerable (to criticism, attack, etc.): *by making such a statement he laid himself open to accusations of favouritism.* [34] **lay open.** to reveal or disclose. [35] **lay siege to.** to besiege (a city, etc.). ◆ NOUN [36] the manner or position in which something lies or is placed. [37] *Taboo slang* **a** an act of sexual intercourse. **b** a sexual partner. [38] a portion of the catch or the profits from a whaling or fishing expedition. [39] the amount or direction of hoist in the strands of a rope. ◆ See also **layabout, lay aside, lay away, lay-by, lay down, lay in, lay into, lay off, lay on, lay out, lay over, lay to, lay up.**
▷HISTORY Old English *lecgan;* related to Gothic *lagjan,* Old Norse *leggja*

> **Language note** In careful English, the verb *lay* is used with an object and *lie* without one: *the soldier laid down his arms; the Queen laid a wreath; the book was lying on the table; he was lying on the floor.* In informal English, *lay* is frequently used for *lie: the book was laying on the table.* All careful writers and speakers observe the distinction even in informal contexts.

lay[2] (leɪ) VERB the past tense of **lie**[2].

lay[3] (leɪ) ADJECTIVE [1] of, involving, or belonging to people who are not clergy. [2] nonprofessional or nonspecialist; amateur.
▷HISTORY C14: from Old French *lai,* from Late Latin *lāicus,* ultimately from Greek *laos* people

lay[4] (leɪ) NOUN [1] a ballad or short narrative poem, esp one intended to be sung. [2] a song or melody.
▷HISTORY C13: from Old French *lai,* perhaps of Germanic origin

layabout (ˈleɪəˌbaʊt) NOUN [1] a lazy person; loafer. ◆ VERB **lay about.** [2] (*preposition,* usually *intr* or *reflexive*) *Old-fashioned* to hit out with violent and repeated blows in all directions.

lay analyst NOUN a person without medical qualifications who practises psychoanalysis.

lay aside VERB (*tr, adverb*) [1] to abandon or reject. [2] to store or reserve for future use.

lay away VERB (*tr, adverb*) [1] to store or reserve for future use. [2] to reserve (merchandise) for future delivery, while payments are being made.

layback (ˈleɪˌbæk) NOUN *Mountaineering* a technique for climbing cracks by pulling on one side of the crack with the hands and pressing on the other with the feet.

lay brother NOUN a man who has taken the vows of a religious order but is not ordained and not bound to divine office.

lay-by NOUN [1] *Brit* a place for drivers to stop at the side of a main road. [2] *Nautical* an anchorage in a narrow waterway, away from the channel. [3] a small railway siding where rolling stock may be stored or parked. [4] *Austral and NZ* a system of payment whereby a buyer pays a deposit on an article, which is reserved for him until he has paid the full price. ◆ VERB **lay by.** (*adverb*) [5] (*tr*) to set aside or save for future needs. [6] Also: **lay to.** to cause (a sailing vessel) to stop in open water or (of a sailing vessel) to stop.

lay days PLURAL NOUN [1] *Commerce* the number of days permitted for the loading or unloading of a ship without payment of demurrage. [2] *Nautical* the time during which a ship is kept from sailing because of loading, bad weather, etc.

laydeez (ˈleɪdiːz) PLURAL NOUN *Informal* a jocular spelling of ladies, as pronounced in a mid-Atlantic accent.

lay down VERB (*tr, adverb*) [1] to place on the ground, etc. [2] to relinquish or discard: *to lay down one's life.* [3] to formulate (a rule, principle, etc.). [4] to build or begin to build: *the railway was laid down as far as Manchester.* [5] to record (plans) on paper. [6] to convert (land) into pasture. [7] to store or stock: *to lay down wine.* [8] *Informal* to wager or bet. [9] (*tr, adverb*) *Informal* to record (tracks) in a studio.

layer (ˈleɪə) NOUN [1] a thickness of some homogeneous substance, such as a stratum or a coating on a surface. [2] one of four or more levels of vegetation defined in ecological studies: the ground or moss layer, the field or herb layer, the shrub layer, and one or more tree layers. [3] a laying hen. [4] *Horticulture* **a** a shoot or branch rooted during layering. **b** a plant produced as a result of layering. ◆ VERB [5] to form or make a layer of (something). [6] to take root or cause to take root by layering.
▷HISTORY C14 *leyer, legger,* from LAY[1] + -ER[1]

layer cake NOUN a cake made in layers with a filling.

layering (ˈleɪərɪŋ) NOUN [1] *Horticulture* a method of propagation that induces a shoot or branch to take root while it is still attached to the parent plant. [2] *Geology* the banded appearance of certain igneous and metamorphic rocks, each band being of a different mineral composition.

layette (leɪˈɛt) NOUN a complete set of articles, including clothing, bedclothes, and other accessories, for a newborn baby.
▷HISTORY C19: from French, from Old French, from *laie,* from Middle Dutch *laege* box

lay figure NOUN [1] an artist's jointed dummy, used in place of a live model, esp for studying effects of drapery. [2] a person considered to be subservient or unimportant.
▷HISTORY C18: from obsolete *layman,* from Dutch *leeman,* literally: joint-man

lay in VERB (*tr, adverb*) to accumulate and store: *we must lay in food for the party.*

laying on of hands NOUN (in Christian ordination, confirmation, faith healing, etc.) the act of laying hands on a person's head to confer spiritual blessing.

lay into VERB (*intr, preposition*) *Informal* [1] to attack forcefully. [2] to berate severely.

layman (ˈleɪmən) NOUN, *plural* **-men.** [1] a man who is not a member of the clergy. [2] a person who does not have specialized or professional knowledge of a subject: *science for the layman.*

lay off VERB [1] (*tr, adverb*) to suspend (workers) from employment with the intention of re-employing them at a later date: *the firm had to lay off 100 men.* [2] (*intr*) *Informal* to leave (a person, thing, or activity) alone: *lay off me, will you!* [3] (*tr, adverb*) to mark off the boundaries of. [4] (*tr, adverb*) *Soccer* to pass or deflect (the ball) to a team-mate, esp one in a more advantageous position. [5] *Gambling* another term for **hedge** (sense 10). ◆ NOUN **lay-off.** [6] the act of suspending employees. [7] a period of imposed unemployment.

lay on VERB (*tr, adverb*) [1] to provide or supply: *to lay on entertainment.* [2] *Brit* to install: *to lay on electricity.* [3] **lay it on.** *Informal* **a** to exaggerate, esp when flattering. **b** to charge an exorbitant price. **c** to punish or strike harshly.

lay out VERB (*tr, adverb*) [1] to arrange or spread out. [2] to prepare (a corpse) for burial or cremation. [3] to plan or contrive. [4] *Informal* to spend (money), esp lavishly. [5] *Informal* to knock unconscious. [6] *Informal* to exert (oneself) or put (oneself) to an effort: *he laid himself out to please us.* ◆ NOUN **layout.** [7] the arrangement or plan of something, such as a building. [8] the arrangement of written material, photographs, or other artwork on an advertisement or page in a book, newspaper, etc. [9] a preliminary plan indicating this. [10] a drawing showing the relative disposition of parts in a machine, etc. [11] the act of laying out. [12] something laid out. [13] the formation of cards on the table in various games, esp in patience. [14] *Informal, chiefly US* a residence or establishment, esp a large one.

lay over *US and Canadian* ◆ VERB (*adverb*) [1] (*tr*) to postpone for future action. [2] (*intr*) to make a temporary stop in a journey. ◆ NOUN **layover.** [3] a break in a journey, esp in waiting for a connection.

lay person *or* **layperson** NOUN, *plural* **lay persons** *or* **laypersons; lay people** *or* **laypeople** [1] a person who is not a member of the clergy. [2] a person who does not have specialized or professional knowledge of a subject: *a lay person's guide to conveyancing.*

lay reader NOUN [1] *Church of England* a person licensed by a bishop to conduct religious services other than the Eucharist. [2] *RC Church* a layman chosen from among the congregation to read the epistle at Mass and sometimes other prayers.

layshaft ('leɪˌʃɑːft) NOUN an auxiliary shaft in a gearbox, running parallel to the main shaft, to and from which drive is transferred to enable varying ratios to be obtained.

lay sister NOUN a woman who has taken the vows of a religious order but is not ordained and not bound to divine office.

lay to VERB (*intr, adverb*) *Nautical* [1] to bring a vessel into a haven. [2] another term for **heave to.**

lay up VERB (*tr, adverb*) [1] to store or reserve for future use. [2] (*usually passive*) *Informal* to incapacitate or confine through illness.

laywoman ('leɪwʊmən) NOUN, *plural* **-women.** [1] a woman who is not a member of the clergy. [2] a woman who does not have specialized or professional knowledge of a subject: *a guide for the laywoman.*

lazar ('læzə) NOUN an archaic word for **leper.**
▷HISTORY C14: via Old French and Medieval Latin, after LAZARUS
▸'**lazar-ˌlike** ADJECTIVE

lazaretto (ˌlæzə'rɛtəʊ), **lazaret,** *or* **lazarette** (ˌlæzə'rɛt) NOUN, *plural* **-rettos, -rets** *or* **-rettes.** [1] Also called: **glory hole.** *Nautical* a small locker at the stern of a boat or a storeroom between decks of a ship. [2] Also called: **lazar house, pesthouse.** (formerly) a hospital for persons with infectious diseases, esp leprosy.
▷HISTORY C16: Italian, from *lazzaro* LAZAR

Lazarus ('læzərəs) NOUN *New Testament* [1] the brother of Mary and Martha, whom Jesus restored to life (John 11–12). [2] the beggar who lay at the gate of the rich man Dives in Jesus' parable (Luke 16:19–31).

laze (leɪz) VERB [1] (*intr*) to be indolent or lazy. [2] (*tr;* often foll by *away*) to spend (time) in indolence. ◆ NOUN [3] the act or an instance of idling.
▷HISTORY C16: back formation from LAZY

Lazio ('lattsjo) NOUN [1] a region of W central Italy, on the Tyrrhenian Sea: includes the plain of the lower Tiber, the reclaimed Pontine Marshes, and Campagna. Capital: Rome. Pop.: 5 264 077 (2000 est.). [2] the Italian name for **Latium.**

lazuli ('læzjʊˌlaɪ) NOUN short for **lapis lazuli.**

lazulite ('læzjʊˌlaɪt) NOUN a blue mineral, consisting of hydrated magnesium iron phosphate, occurring in metamorphic rocks. Formula: $(Mg,Fe)Al_2(PO_4)_2(OH)_2$.
▷HISTORY C19: from Medieval Latin *lāzulum* azure, LAPIS LAZULI

lazurite ('læzjʊˌraɪt) NOUN a rare blue mineral consisting of a sodium–calcium–aluminium silicate and sulphide: used as the gemstone lapis lazuli. Formula: $(Na,Ca)_8(AlSiO_4)_6(SO_4,S,Cl)_2$.
▷HISTORY C19: from Medieval Latin *lāzur* LAPIS LAZULI

lazy ('leɪzɪ) ADJECTIVE **lazier, laziest.** [1] not inclined to work or exertion. [2] conducive to or causing indolence. [3] moving in a languid or sluggish manner: *a lazy river.* [4] (of a brand letter or mark on livestock) shown as lying on its side.
▷HISTORY C16: origin uncertain
▸'**lazily** ADVERB ▸'**laziness** NOUN

lazy bed NOUN (in parts of Scotland and Ireland, formerly) a patch in which potatoes were cultivated by laying them on the surface and covering them with kelp and with soil from a trench on either side of the bed.

lazybones ('leɪzɪˌbəʊnz) NOUN *Informal* a lazy person.

lazy daisy stitch NOUN an embroidery stitch consisting of a long chain stitch, usually used in making flower patterns.

lazy Susan NOUN a revolving tray, often divided into sections, for holding condiments, etc.

lazy tongs PLURAL NOUN a set of tongs with extensible arms to allow objects to be grasped or handled at a distance.

lb[1] ABBREVIATION FOR: [1] *Cricket* leg bye. [2] Also: **lb.** pound (weight).
▷HISTORY Latin: *libra*

lb[2] THE INTERNET DOMAIN NAME FOR Lebanon.

LB INTERNATIONAL CAR REGISTRATION FOR Liberia.

LBD *Informal* ABBREVIATION FOR little black dress.

lbf ABBREVIATION FOR pound force. See **pound**[2] (sense 4).

LBO ABBREVIATION FOR **leveraged buyout.**

lb tr *or* **lb t** ABBREVIATION FOR troy pound. See **pound** (sense 2).

LBV ABBREVIATION FOR Late Bottled Vintage: applied to port wine that has been matured in casks for six years and is then ready for drinking.

lbw *Cricket* ABBREVIATION FOR leg before wicket.

lc[1] ABBREVIATION FOR: [1] left centre (of a stage, etc.). [2] loco citato. [Latin: in the place cited] [3] *Printing* lower case.

lc[2] THE INTERNET DOMAIN NAME FOR Saint Lucia.

LC (in the US) ABBREVIATION FOR Library of Congress.

L/C, l/c, *or* **lc** ABBREVIATION FOR letter of credit.

lcd *or* **LCD** ABBREVIATION FOR lowest common denominator.

LCD ABBREVIATION FOR **liquid-crystal display.**

l'chaim (lə'xɑjim) INTERJECTION, NOUN a variant spelling of **lechaim.**

LCJ *Brit* ABBREVIATION FOR **Lord Chief Justice.**

LCL *or* **lcl** *Commerce* ABBREVIATION FOR less than carload lot.

lcm *or* **LCM** ABBREVIATION FOR lowest common multiple.

L/Cpl ABBREVIATION FOR lance corporal.

ld ABBREVIATION FOR load.

Ld ABBREVIATION FOR Lord (title).

LD ABBREVIATION FOR: [1] lethal dosage: usually used with a subscript numeral showing what percentage of a test group of animals dies as a result of either being given a substance being tested on them or being exposed to ionizing radiation, esp in the median lethal dose: LD_{50}. [2] Low Dutch.

L-D converter NOUN *Metallurgy* a vessel in which steel is made from pig iron by blowing oxygen into the molten metal through a water-cooled tube.
▷HISTORY C20: L(inz)-D(onawitz), from the Austrian towns of *Linz* and *Donawitz,* where the process was first used successfully

Ldg ABBREVIATION FOR leading: *Ldg seaman.*

LDL ABBREVIATION FOR **low-density lipoprotein.**

L-dopa (ɛl'dəʊpə) NOUN a substance occurring naturally in the body and used to treat Parkinson's disease. Formula: $C_9H_{11}NO_4$. Also called: **levodopa.**
▷HISTORY C20: from *L-d(ihydr)o(xy)p(henyl)a(lanine)*

LDR *Text messaging* ABBREVIATION FOR long distance relationship.

L-driver NOUN *Brit* a learner-driver: a person who is learning to drive, has not yet passed the official driving test, and must be accompanied by a qualified driver and display L-plates on the car.

LDS ABBREVIATION FOR: [1] Latter-day Saints. [2] laus Deo semper. [Latin: praise be to God for ever] [3] (in Britain) Licentiate in Dental Surgery.

LE ABBREVIATION FOR **lupus erythematosus.**

-le SUFFIX FORMING VERBS denoting repeated or continuous action, often of a diminutive nature: *twiddle; wriggle; wrestle.*
▷HISTORY from Middle English *-len,* Old English *-lian,* with similar significance

lea[1] (liː) NOUN [1] *Poetic* a meadow or field. [2] land that has been sown with grass seed.
▷HISTORY Old English *lēah;* related to German dialect *loh* thicket

lea[2] (liː) NOUN [1] a unit for measuring lengths of yarn, usually taken as 80 yards for wool, 120 yards for cotton and silk, and 300 yards for linen. [2] a measure of yarn expressed as the length per unit weight, usually the number of leas per pound.
▷HISTORY C14: of uncertain origin

LEA (in Britain) ABBREVIATION FOR Local Education Authority.

leach[1] (liːtʃ) VERB [1] to remove or be removed from a substance by a percolating liquid. [2] to lose or cause to lose soluble substances by the action of a percolating liquid. [3] another word for **percolate** (senses 1, 2). ◆ NOUN [4] the act or process of leaching. [5] a substance that is leached or the constituents removed by leaching. [6] a porous vessel for leaching.
▷HISTORY C17: variant of obsolete *letch* to wet, perhaps from Old English *leccan* to water; related to LEAK
▸'**leacher** NOUN

leach[2] (liːtʃ) NOUN a variant spelling of **leech**[2].

leachate ('liːtʃeɪt) NOUN water that carries salts dissolved out of materials through which it has percolated, esp polluted water from a refuse tip.

lead[1] (liːd) VERB **leads, leading, led** (lɛd). [1] to show the way to (an individual or a group) by going with or ahead: *lead the party into the garden.* [2] to guide or be guided by holding, pulling, etc.: *he led the horse by its reins.* [3] (*tr*) to cause to act, feel, think, or behave in a certain way; induce; influence: *he led me to believe that he would go.* [4] (*tr*) to phrase a question to (a witness) that tends to suggest the desired answer. [5] (when *intr,* foll by *to*) (of a road, route, etc.) to serve as the means of reaching a place. [6] (*tr*) to go ahead so as to indicate (esp in the phrase **lead the way**). [7] to guide, control, or direct: *to lead an army.* [8] (*tr*) to direct the course of or conduct (water, a rope or wire, etc.) along or as if along a channel. [9] to initiate the action of (something); have the principal part in (something): *to lead a discussion.* [10] to go at the head of or have the top position in (something): *he leads his class in geography.* [11] (*intr;* foll by *with*) to have as the first or principal item: *the newspaper led with the royal birth.* [12] *Music* **a** *Brit* to play first violin in (an orchestra). **b** (*intr*) (of an instrument or voice) to be assigned an important entry in a piece of music. [13] to direct and guide (one's partner) in a dance. [14] (*tr*) **a** to pass or spend: *I lead a miserable life.* **b** to cause to pass a life of a particular kind: *to lead a person a dog's life.* [15] (*intr;* foll by *to*) to tend (to) or result (in): *this will only lead to misery.* [16] to initiate a round of cards by putting down (the first card) or to have the right to do this: *she led a diamond.* [17] (*tr*) to aim at a point in front of (a moving target) in shooting, etc., in order to allow for the time of flight. [18] (*intr*) *Boxing* to make an offensive blow, esp as one's habitual attacking punch: *southpaws lead with their right.* [19] **lead astray.** to mislead so as to cause error or wrongdoing. [20] **lead by the nose.** See **nose** (sense 12). ◆ NOUN [21] **a** the first, foremost, or most prominent place. **b** (*as modifier*): *lead singer.* [22] example, precedence, or

leadership: *the class followed the teacher's lead.* 23 an advance or advantage held over others: *the runner had a lead of twenty yards.* 24 anything that guides or directs; indication; clue. 25 another name for **leash.** 26 the act or prerogative of playing the first card in a round of cards or the card so played. 27 the principal role in a play, film, etc., or the person playing such a role. 28 **a** the principal news story in a newspaper: *the scandal was the lead in the papers.* **b** the opening paragraph of a news story. **c** (*as modifier*): *lead story.* 29 *Music* an important entry assigned to one part usually at the beginning of a movement or section. 30 a wire, cable, or other conductor for making an electrical connection. 31 *Boxing* **a** one's habitual attacking punch. **b** a blow made with this. 32 *Nautical* the direction in which a rope runs. 33 a deposit of metal or ore; lode. 34 the firing of a gun, missile, etc., ahead of a moving target to correct for the time of flight of the projectile. ◆ See also **lead off, lead on, lead up to.**
▷HISTORY Old English *lǣdan;* related to *līthan* to travel, Old High German *līdan* to go

lead² (lɛd) NOUN 1 a heavy toxic bluish-white metallic element that is highly malleable: occurs principally as galena and used in alloys, accumulators, cable sheaths, paints, and as a radiation shield. Symbol: Pb; atomic no.: 82; atomic wt.: 207.2; valency: 2 or 4; relative density: 11.35; melting pt.: 327.502°C; boiling pt.: 1750°C. Related adjectives: **plumbic, plumbeous, plumbous.** 2 a lead weight suspended on a line used to take soundings of the depth of water. 3 **swing the lead.** to malinger or make up excuses. 4 lead weights or shot, as used in cartridges, fishing lines, etc. 5 a thin grooved strip of lead for holding small panes of glass or pieces of stained glass. 6 (*plural*) **a** thin sheets or strips of lead used as a roof covering. **b** a flat or low-pitched roof covered with such sheets. 7 *Printing* a thin strip of type metal used for spacing between lines of hot-metal type. Compare **reglet** (sense 2). 8 **a** graphite or a mixture containing graphite, clay, etc., used for drawing. **b** a thin stick of this material, esp the core of a pencil. 9 (*modifier*) of, consisting of, relating to, or containing lead. 10 **go down like a lead balloon.** See **balloon** (sense 9). ◆ VERB (*tr*) 11 to fill or treat with lead. 12 to surround, cover, or secure with lead or leads. 13 *Printing* to space (type) by use of leads.
▷HISTORY Old English; related to Dutch *lood,* German *Lot*
▸ **'leadless** ADJECTIVE ▸ **'leady** ADJECTIVE

lead acetate (lɛd) NOUN a white crystalline toxic solid used in dyeing cotton and in making varnishes and enamels. Formula: $Pb(CH_3CO)_2$. Systematic name: **lead(II) acetate.** Also called: **sugar of lead.**

lead arsenate (lɛd) NOUN a white insoluble toxic crystalline powder used as an insecticide and fungicide. Formula: $Pb_3(AsO_4)_2$.

Leadbeater's cockatoo ('lɛd,biːtəs) NOUN another name for **Major Mitchell.**
▷HISTORY named after Benjamin *Leadbeater,* 19th-century British natural historian

lead chromate (lɛd) NOUN *Chem* a yellow solid used as a pigment, as in chrome yellow. Formula: $PbCrO_4$.

lead colic (lɛd) NOUN a symptom of lead poisoning characterized by intense abdominal pain. Also called: **painter's colic.**

leaded ('lɛdɪd) ADJECTIVE 1 (of windows) composed of small panes of glass held in place by thin grooved strips of lead: *leaded lights.* 2 (of petrol) containing tetraethyl lead in order to improve combustion.

leaden ('lɛdᵊn) ADJECTIVE 1 heavy and inert. 2 laboured or sluggish: *leaden steps.* 3 gloomy, spiritless, or lifeless. 4 made partly or wholly of lead. 5 of a dull greyish colour: *a leaden sky.*
▸ **'leadenly** ADVERB ▸ **'leadenness** NOUN

leader ('liːdə) NOUN 1 a person who rules, guides, or inspires others; head. 2 *Music* **a** Also called (esp US and Canadian): **concertmaster.** the principal first violinist of an orchestra, who plays solo parts, and acts as the conductor's deputy and spokesman for the orchestra. **b** *US* a conductor or director of an orchestra or chorus. 3 **a** the first man on a climbing rope. **b** the leading horse or dog in a team. 4 *Chiefly US and Canadian* an article offered at a sufficiently low price to attract customers. See also **loss leader.** 5 a statistic or index that gives an advance indication of the state of the economy. 6 *Chiefly Brit* Also called: **leading article.** the leading editorial in a newspaper. 7 *Angling* another word for **trace²** (sense 2) or **cast** (sense 32a). 8 *Nautical* another term for **fairlead.** 9 a strip of blank film or tape used to facilitate threading a projector, developing machine, etc., and to aid identification. 10 (*plural*) *Printing* rows of dots or hyphens used to guide the reader's eye across a page, as in a table of contents. 11 *Botany* any of the long slender shoots that grow from the stem or branch of a tree: usually removed during pruning. 12 *Brit* a member of the Government having primary authority in initiating legislative business (esp in the phrases **Leader of the House of Commons** and **Leader of the House of Lords**). 13 the senior barrister, usually a Queen's Counsel, in charge of the conduct of a case. Compare **junior** (sense 6).
▸ **'leaderless** ADJECTIVE

leaderboard ('liːdə,bɔːd) NOUN a board displaying the names and current scores of the leading competitors, esp in a golf tournament.

leadership ('liːdəʃɪp) NOUN 1 the position or function of a leader. 2 the period during which a person occupies the position of leader: *during her leadership very little was achieved.* 3 **a** the ability to lead. **b** (*as modifier*): *leadership qualities.* 4 the leaders as a group of a party, union, etc.: *the union leadership is now very reactionary.*

lead glass (lɛd) NOUN glass that contains lead oxide as a flux.

lead-in ('liːd,ɪn) NOUN 1 **a** an introduction to a subject. **b** (*as modifier*): *a lead-in announcement.* 2 the connection between a radio transmitter, receiver, etc., and the aerial or transmission line.

leading¹ ('liːdɪŋ) ADJECTIVE 1 guiding, directing, or influencing. 2 (*prenominal*) principal or primary. 3 in the first position: *the leading car in the procession.* 4 *Maths* (of a coefficient) associated with the term of highest degree in a polynomial containing one variable: *in $5x^2 + 2x + 3$, 5 is the leading coefficient.*
▸ **'leadingly** ADVERB

leading² ('lɛdɪŋ) NOUN *Printing* the spacing between lines of photocomposed or digitized type. Also called: **interlinear spacing.**

leading aircraftman ('liːdɪŋ) NOUN *Brit Air Force* the rank above aircraftman.
▸ **leading aircraftwoman** FEMININE NOUN

leading article ('liːdɪŋ) NOUN *Journalism* 1 another term for **leader** (sense 6). 2 *Chiefly US* the article given most prominence in a magazine or newspaper.

leading dog NOUN *NZ* a dog trained to lead a flock of sheep to prevent them breaking or stampeding.

leading edge ('liːdɪŋ) NOUN 1 the forward edge of a propeller blade, aerofoil, or wing. Compare **trailing edge.** 2 *Electrical engineering* the part of a pulse signal that has an increasing amplitude. ◆ MODIFIER **leading-edge.** 3 advanced; foremost: *leading-edge technology.*

leading light ('liːdɪŋ) NOUN 1 an important or outstanding person, esp in an organization or cause. 2 *Nautical* a less common term for **range light.**

leading man ('liːdɪŋ) NOUN a man who plays the main part in a film, play, etc.
▸ **leading lady** FEMININE NOUN

leading note ('liːdɪŋ) NOUN *Music* 1 another word for **subtonic.** 2 (esp in cadences) a note, usually the subtonic of a scale, that tends most naturally to resolve to the note lying one semitone above it.

leading question ('liːdɪŋ) NOUN a question phrased in a manner that tends to suggest the desired answer, such as *What do you think of the horrible effects of pollution?*

leading rating NOUN a rank in the Royal Navy comparable but junior to that of a corporal in the army.

leading reins *or US and Canadian* **leading strings** ('liːdɪŋ) PLURAL NOUN 1 straps or a harness and strap used to assist and control a child who is learning to walk. 2 excessive guidance or restraint.

lead line (lɛd) NOUN *Nautical* a length of line for swinging a lead, marked at various points to indicate multiples of fathoms.

lead monoxide (lɛd) NOUN a poisonous insoluble oxide of lead existing in red and yellow forms: used in making glass, glazes, and cements, and as a pigment. Formula: PbO. Systematic name: **lead(II) oxide.** Also called: **litharge, plumbous oxide.**

lead off (liːd) VERB (*adverb*) 1 to initiate the action of (something); begin. ◆ NOUN **lead-off.** 2 an initial move or action. 3 a person or thing that begins something.

lead on (liːd) VERB (*tr, adverb*) to lure or entice, esp into trouble or wrongdoing.

lead pencil (lɛd) NOUN a pencil in which the writing material is a thin stick of a graphite compound.

lead poisoning (lɛd) NOUN 1 Also called: **plumbism, saturnism.** acute or chronic poisoning by lead or its salts, characterized by abdominal pain, vomiting, convulsions, and coma. 2 *US, slang* death or injury resulting from being shot with bullets.

lead screw (liːd) NOUN a threaded rod that drives the tool carriage in a lathe when screw cutting, etc.

leadsman ('lɛdzmən) NOUN, *plural* **-men.** *Nautical* a sailor who takes soundings with a lead line.

lead tetraethyl (lɛd) NOUN another name for **tetraethyl lead.**

lead time (liːd) NOUN 1 *Manufacturing* the time between the design of a product and its production. 2 *Commerce* the time from the placing of an order to the delivery of the goods.

lead up to (liːd) VERB (*intr, adverb + preposition*) 1 to act as a preliminary or introduction to. 2 to approach (a topic) gradually or cautiously.

leadwort ('lɛd,wɜːt) NOUN any shrub of the plumbaginaceous genus *Plumbago,* of tropical and subtropical regions, with red, blue, or white flowers.

leaf (liːf) NOUN, *plural* **leaves** (liːvz). 1 the main organ of photosynthesis and transpiration in higher plants, usually consisting of a flat green blade attached to the stem directly or by a stalk. Related adjectives: **foliar, foliate.** 2 foliage collectively. 3 **in leaf.** (of shrubs, trees, etc.) having a full complement of foliage leaves. 4 one of the sheets of paper in a book. 5 a hinged, sliding, or detachable part, such as an extension to a table. 6 metal in the form of a very thin flexible sheet: *gold leaf.* 7 a foil or thin strip of metal in a composite material; lamina. 8 short for **leaf spring.** 9 the inner or outer wall of a cavity wall. 10 a crop that is harvested in the form of leaves. 11 a metal strip forming one of the laminations in a leaf spring. 12 a slang word for **marijuana.** 13 **take a leaf out of** (*or* **from**) **someone's book.** to imitate someone, esp in one particular course of action. 14 **turn over a new leaf.** to begin a new and improved course of behaviour. ◆ VERB 15 (when *intr,* usually foll by *through*) to turn (through pages, sheets, etc.) cursorily. 16 (*intr*) (of plants) to produce leaves.
▷HISTORY Old English; related to Gothic *laufs,* Icelandic *lauf*
▸ **'leafless** ADJECTIVE ▸ **'leaflessness** NOUN ▸ **'leaf,like** ADJECTIVE

leafage ('liːfɪdʒ) NOUN a less common word for **foliage.**

leaf beet NOUN another name for **chard.**

leaf beetle NOUN any of a large family of beetles (*Chrysomelidae*) that includes more than 25,000 species, mostly leaf feeders and mostly brightly coloured, with a metallic sheen. It includes the notorious **Colorado beetle,** the **bloody-nosed beetle** and the **flea beetles** (*Phyllotreta* species) which attack young cabbage plants.

leaf-climber NOUN a plant that climbs by using leaves specialized as tendrils.

leafcutter ant ('liːf,kʌtə) NOUN any of various South American ants of the genus *Atta* that cut pieces of leaves and use them as fertilizer for the fungus on which they feed.

leafcutter bee NOUN any of various solitary bees of the genus *Megachile* that nest in soil or rotten wood, constructing the cells in which they lay their eggs from pieces of leaf.

leaf fat NOUN the dense fat that accumulates in

layers around the kidneys of certain animals, esp pigs.

leaf gap NOUN *Botany* a region of parenchyma cells in the vascular tissue of flowering plants and some ferns, situated above a leaf trace.

leaf-hopper NOUN any homopterous insect of the family *Cicadellidae,* including various pests of crops.

leaf insect NOUN any of various mostly tropical Asian insects of the genus *Phyllium* and related genera, having a flattened leaflike body: order *Phasmida.* See also **stick insect.**

leaf-lard NOUN lard prepared from the leaf fat of a pig.

leaflet ('li:flɪt) NOUN 1 a printed and usually folded sheet of paper for distribution, usually free and containing advertising material or information about a political party, charity, etc. 2 any of the subdivisions of a compound leaf such as a fern leaf. 3 (loosely) any small leaf or leaflike part. ◆ VERB 4 to distribute printed leaflets (to): *they leafleted every flat in the area.*
▸ '**leafleter** NOUN

leaf miner NOUN 1 any of various insect larvae that bore into and feed on leaf tissue, esp the larva of dipterous flies of the genus *Philophylla* (family *Trypetidae*) and the caterpillar of moths of the family *Gracillariidae.* 2 the adult insect of any of these larvae.

leaf monkey NOUN another name for **langur.**

leaf mould NOUN 1 a nitrogen-rich material consisting of decayed leaves, etc., used as a fertilizer. 2 any of various fungus diseases affecting the leaves of certain plants.

leaf sheath NOUN *Botany* the basal part of a grass leaf that encircles the stem.

leaf sight NOUN a folding rear sight on certain rifles.

leaf spot NOUN any of various plant diseases, usually caused by fungi: characterized by dark lesions on the leaves.

leaf spring NOUN 1 one of a number of metal strips bracketed together in length to form a compound spring. 2 the compound spring so formed.

leafstalk ('li:fˌstɔ:k) NOUN the stalk attaching a leaf to a stem or branch. Technical name: **petiole.**

leaf trace NOUN *Botany* a vascular bundle connecting the vascular tissue of the stem with that of a leaf.

leafy ('li:fɪ) ADJECTIVE **leafier, leafiest.** 1 covered with or having leaves. 2 resembling a leaf or leaves.
▸ '**leafiness** NOUN

league[1] (li:g) NOUN 1 an association or union of persons, nations, etc., formed to promote the interests of its members. 2 an association of sporting clubs that organizes matches between member teams of a similar standard. 3 a class, category, or level: *he is not in the same league.* 4 **in league (with).** working or planning together with. 5 (*modifier*) of, involving, or belonging to a league: *a league game; a league table.* ◆ VERB **leagues, leaguing, leagued.** 6 to form or be formed into a league.
▹HISTORY C15: from Old French *ligue,* from Italian *liga,* ultimately from Latin *ligāre* to bind

league[2] (li:g) NOUN an obsolete unit of distance of varying length. It is commonly equal to 3 miles.
▹HISTORY C14 *leuge,* from Late Latin *leuga, leuca,* of Celtic origin

league football NOUN 1 Also called: **league.** *Chiefly Austral* rugby league football. 2 *Austral* an Australian Rules competition conducted within a league rather than a football association.

League of Nations NOUN an international association of states founded in 1920 with the aim of preserving world peace: dissolved in 1946.

leaguer[1] ('li:gə) NOUN *Archaic* 1 an encampment, esp of besiegers. 2 the siege itself.
▹HISTORY C16: from Dutch *leger* siege; related to LAIR[1]

leaguer[2] ('li:gə) NOUN *Chiefly US and Canadian* a member of a league.

league table NOUN *Brit* 1 a tabulated comparison of clubs or teams competing in a sporting league. 2 a set of statistics used to compare the performance of a number of individuals, groups, or institutions: *a league table of examination results.*

Leah ('lɪə) NOUN *Old Testament* the first wife of Jacob and elder sister of Rachel, his second wife (Genesis 29).

leak (li:k) NOUN 1 **a** a crack, hole, etc., that allows the accidental escape or entrance of fluid, light, etc. **b** such escaping or entering fluid, light, etc. 2 **spring a leak.** to develop a leak. 3 something resembling this in effect: *a leak in the defence system.* 4 the loss of current from an electrical conductor because of faulty insulation, etc. 5 a disclosure, often intentional, of secret information. 6 the act or an instance of leaking. 7 a slang word for **urination.** ◆ VERB 8 to enter or escape or allow to enter or escape through a crack, hole, etc. 9 (when *intr,* often foll by *out*) to disclose (secret information), often intentionally, or (of secret information) to be disclosed. 10 (*intr*) a slang word for **urinate.**
▹HISTORY C15: from Scandinavian; compare Old Norse *leka* to drip
▸ '**leaker** NOUN

leakage ('li:kɪdʒ) NOUN 1 the act or an instance of leaking. 2 something that escapes or enters by a leak. 3 *Commerce* an allowance made for partial loss (of stock, etc.) due to leaking. 4 *Physics* **a** an undesired flow of electric current, neutrons, etc. **b** (*as modifier*): *leakage current.*

leaky ('li:kɪ) ADJECTIVE **leakier, leakiest.** leaking or tending to leak.
▸ '**leakiness** NOUN

leal (li:l) ADJECTIVE *Scot* loyal; faithful.
▹HISTORY C13: from Old French *leial,* from Latin *lēgālis* LEGAL; related to LOYAL
▸ '**leally** ADVERB ▸ **lealty** ('li:əltɪ) NOUN

Leamington Spa ('lɛmɪŋtən) NOUN a town in central England, in central Warwickshire: saline springs. Pop.: 55 396 (1991). Official name: **Royal Leamington Spa.**

lean[1] (li:n) VERB **leans, leaning; leaned** *or* **leant.** 1 (foll by *against, on,* or *upon*) to rest or cause to rest against a support. 2 to incline or cause to incline from a vertical position. 3 (*intr;* foll by *to* or *towards*) to have or express a tendency or leaning. 4 **lean over backwards.** *Informal* to make a special effort, esp in order to please. ◆ NOUN 5 the condition of inclining from a vertical position. ◆ See also **lean on.**
▹HISTORY Old English *hleonian, hlinian;* related to Old High German *hlinēn,* Latin *clīnāre* to INCLINE

lean[2] (li:n) ADJECTIVE 1 (esp of a person or an animal) having no surplus flesh or bulk; not fat or plump. 2 not bulky or full. 3 (of meat) having little or no fat. 4 not rich, abundant, or satisfying. 5 (of a mixture of fuel and air) containing insufficient fuel and too much air: *a lean mixture.* 6 (of printer's type) having a thin appearance. 7 (of a paint) containing relatively little oil. 8 (of an ore) not having a high mineral content. 9 (of concrete) made with a small amount of cement. ◆ NOUN 10 the part of meat that contains little or no fat.
▹HISTORY Old English *hlǣne,* of Germanic origin
▸ '**leanly** ADVERB ▸ '**leanness** NOUN

lean-burn ADJECTIVE (esp of an internal-combustion engine) designed to use a lean mixture of fuel and air in order to reduce petrol consumption and exhaust emissions.

Leander (lɪ'ændə) NOUN (in Greek legend) a youth of Abydos, who drowned in the Hellespont in a storm on one of his nightly visits to Hero, his beloved. See also **Hero**[1].

leaning ('li:nɪŋ) NOUN a tendency or inclination.

lean on VERB (*intr, preposition*) 1 Also: **lean upon.** to depend on for advice, support, etc. 2 *Informal* to exert pressure on (someone), as by threats or intimidation.

leant (lɛnt) VERB a past tense and past participle of **lean**[1].

lean-to NOUN, *plural* **-tos.** 1 a roof that has a single slope with its upper edge adjoining a wall or building. 2 a shed or outbuilding with such a roof.

leap (li:p) VERB **leaps, leaping; leapt** *or* **leaped.** 1 (*intr*) to jump suddenly from one place to another. 2 (*intr;* often foll by *at*) to move or react quickly. 3 (*tr*) to jump over. 4 to come into prominence rapidly: *the thought leapt into his mind.* 5 (*tr*) to cause (an animal, esp a horse) to jump a barrier. ◆ NOUN 6 the act of jumping. 7 a spot from which a leap was or may be made. 8 the distance of a leap. 9 an abrupt change or increase. 10 Also called (US and Canadian): **skip.** *Music* a relatively large melodic interval, esp in a solo part. 11 **a leap in the dark.** an action performed without knowledge of the consequences. 12 **by leaps and bounds.** with unexpectedly rapid progress.
▹HISTORY Old English *hlēapan;* related to Gothic *hlaupan,* German *laufen*
▸ '**leaper** NOUN

leapfrog ('li:pˌfrɒg) NOUN 1 a children's game in which each player in turn leaps over the others' bent backs, leaning on them with the hands and spreading the legs wide. ◆ VERB **-frogs, -frogging, -frogged.** 2 **a** (*intr*) to play leapfrog. **b** (*tr*) to leap in this way over (something). 3 to advance or cause to advance by jumps or stages.

leap second NOUN a second added to or removed from a scale for reckoning time on one particular occasion, to synchronize it with another scale.

leapt (lɛpt, li:pt) VERB a past tense and past participle of **leap.**

leap year NOUN a calendar year of 366 days, February 29 (**leap day**) being the additional day, that occurs every four years (those whose number is divisible by four) except for century years whose number is not divisible by 400. It offsets the difference between the length of the solar year (365.2422 days) and the calendar year of 365 days.

lea-rig ('li:ˌrɪg) NOUN *Scot* a ridge of unploughed land.
▹HISTORY Old English *lǣghrycg*

learn (lɜ:n) VERB **learns, learning; learned** (lɜ:nd) *or* **learnt.** 1 (when *tr, may take a clause as object*) to gain knowledge of (something) or acquire skill in (some art or practice). 2 (*tr*) to commit to memory. 3 (*tr*) to gain by experience, example, etc. 4 (*intr;* often foll by *of* or *about*) to become informed; know. 5 *Not standard* to teach.
▹HISTORY Old English *leornian;* related to Old High German *lirnen*
▸ '**learnable** ADJECTIVE ▸ '**learner** NOUN

learned ('lɜ:nɪd) ADJECTIVE 1 having great knowledge or erudition. 2 involving or characterized by scholarship. 3 (*prenominal*) a title applied in referring to a member of the legal profession, esp to a barrister: *my learned friend.*
▸ '**learnedly** ADVERB ▸ '**learnedness** NOUN

learned helplessness NOUN the act of giving up trying as a result of consistent failure to be rewarded in life, thought to be a cause of depression.

learner's chain NOUN *NZ* an inexperienced team of slaughtermen working in a freezing works.

learning ('lɜ:nɪŋ) NOUN 1 knowledge gained by study; instruction or scholarship. 2 the act of gaining knowledge. 3 *Psychol* any relatively permanent change in behaviour that occurs as a direct result of experience.

learning curve NOUN a graphical representation of progress in learning: *I'm still only half way up the learning curve.*

learnt (lɜ:nt) VERB a past tense and past participle of **learn.**

leary ADJECTIVE **learier, leariest** *Southwest English dialect* empty.

lease[1] (li:s) NOUN 1 a contract by which property is conveyed to a person for a specified period, usually for rent. 2 the instrument by which such property is conveyed. 3 the period of time for which it is conveyed. 4 a prospect of renewed health, happiness, etc.: *a new lease of life.* ◆ VERB (*tr*) 5 to grant possession of (land, buildings, etc.) by lease. 6 to take a lease of (property); hold under a lease.
▹HISTORY C15: via Anglo-French from Old French *lais* (n), from *laissier* to let go, from Latin *laxāre* to loosen
▸ '**leasable** ADJECTIVE ▸ '**leaser** NOUN

lease[2] (li:z) NOUN *Dialect* open pasture or common.
▹HISTORY Old English *lǣs;* perhaps related to Old Norse *lāth* property

leaseback ('li:sˌbæk) NOUN a property transaction in which the buyer leases the property to the seller.

leasehold (ˈliːsˌhəʊld) NOUN 1 land or property held under a lease. 2 the tenure by which such property is held. 3 (*modifier*) held under a lease.

leaseholder (ˈliːsˌhəʊldə) NOUN 1 a person in possession of leasehold property. 2 a tenant under a lease.

leash (liːʃ) NOUN 1 a line or rope used to walk or control a dog or other animal; lead. 2 something resembling this in function: *he kept a tight leash on his emotions.* 3 *Hunting* three of the same kind of animal, usually hounds, foxes, or hares. 4 **straining at the leash.** eagerly impatient to begin something. ◆ VERB 5 (*tr*) to control or secure by or as if by a leash.
▷HISTORY C13: from Old French *laisse,* from *laissier* to loose (hence, to let a dog run on a leash), ultimately from Latin *laxus* LAX

least (liːst) DETERMINER 1 **a the.** the superlative of **little**: *you have the least talent of anyone.* **b** (*as pronoun; functioning as singular*): *least isn't necessarily worst.* 2 **at least. a** if nothing else: *you should at least try.* **b** at the least. 3 **at the least.** Also: **at least.** at the minimum: *at the least you should earn a hundred pounds.* 4 **in the least.** (*usually used with a negative*) in the slightest degree; at all: *I don't mind in the least.* ◆ ADVERB 5 **the least.** superlative of **little**: *they travel the least of all.* ◆ ADJECTIVE 6 of very little importance or rank.
▷HISTORY Old English *lǣst,* superlative of *lǣssa* LESS

least common denominator NOUN another name for **lowest common denominator.**

least common multiple NOUN another name for **lowest common multiple.**

least squares NOUN a method for determining the best value of an unknown quantity relating one or more sets of observations or measurements, esp to find a curve that best fits a set of data. It states that the sum of the squares of the deviations of the experimentally determined value from its optimum value should be a minimum.

leastways (ˈliːstˌweɪz) *or US and Canadian* **leastwise** ADVERB *Informal* at least; anyway; at any rate.

leat (liːt) NOUN *Brit* a trench or ditch that conveys water to a mill wheel.
▷HISTORY Old English *-gelǣt* (as in *wætergelǣt* water channel), from LET[1]

leather (ˈlɛðə) NOUN 1 **a** a material consisting of the skin of an animal made smooth and flexible by tanning, removing the hair, etc. **b** (*as modifier*): *leather goods.* Related adjectives: **coriaceous, leathern.** 2 (*plural*) leather clothes, esp as worn by motorcyclists. 3 the flap of a dog's ear. ◆ VERB (*tr*) 4 to cover with leather. 5 to whip with or as if with a leather strap.
▷HISTORY Old English *lether-* (in compound words); related to Old High German *leder,* Old Norse *lethr-*

leatherback (ˈlɛðəˌbæk) NOUN a large turtle, *Dermochelys coriacea,* of warm and tropical seas, having a ridged leathery carapace: family *Dermochelidae.* Also called (in Britain): **leathery turtle.**

leather beetle NOUN See **dermestid.**

leatherette (ˌlɛðəˈrɛt) NOUN an imitation leather made from paper, cloth, etc.

leatherhead (ˈlɛðəˌhɛd) NOUN another name for **friarbird.**

Leatherhead (ˈlɛðəˌhɛd) NOUN a town in S England, in Surrey. Pop.: 42 903 (1991).

leatherjacket (ˈlɛðəˌdʒækɪt) NOUN 1 any of various tropical carangid fishes of the genera *Oligoplites* and *Scomberoides,* having a leathery skin. 2 any of various brightly coloured tropical triggerfishes of the genus *Monacanthus* and related genera. 3 the greyish-brown tough-skinned larva of certain craneflies, esp of the genus *Tipula,* which destroy the roots of grasses, etc.

leathern (ˈlɛðən) ADJECTIVE *Archaic* made of or resembling leather.

leatherneck (ˈlɛðəˌnɛk) NOUN *Slang* a member of the US Marine Corps.
▷HISTORY from the custom of facing the neckband of their uniform with leather

leatherwood (ˈlɛðəˌwʊd) NOUN 1 Also called: **wicopy.** a North American thymelaeaceous shrub, *Dirca palustris,* with pale yellow flowers and tough flexible branches. 2 any of various Australian shrubs of the family *Cunoniaceae.*

leathery (ˈlɛðərɪ) ADJECTIVE having the appearance or texture of leather, esp in toughness.
▸ˈ**leatheriness** NOUN

leave[1] (liːv) VERB **leaves, leaving, left.** (*mainly tr*) 1 (*also intr*) to go or depart (from a person or place). 2 to cause to remain behind, often by mistake, in a place: *he often leaves his keys in his coat.* 3 to cause to be or remain in a specified state: *paying the bill left him penniless.* 4 to renounce or abandon: *to leave a political movement.* 5 to refrain from consuming or doing something: *the things we have left undone.* 6 to result in; cause: *childhood problems often leave emotional scars.* 7 to allow to be or remain subject to another person or thing: *leave the past to look after itself.* 8 to entrust or commit: *leave the shopping to her.* 9 to submit in place of one's personal appearance: *will you leave your name and address?* 10 to pass in a specified direction: *flying out of the country, we left the cliffs on our left.* 11 to be survived by (members of one's family): *he leaves a wife and two children.* 12 to bequeath or devise: *he left his investments to his children.* 13 (*tr*) to have as a remainder: *37 – 14 leaves 23.* 14 *Not standard* to permit; let. 15 **leave be.** *Informal* to leave undisturbed. 16 **leave go** *or* **hold of.** *Not standard* to stop holding. 17 **leave it at that.** *Informal* to take a matter no further. 18 **leave much to be desired.** to be very unsatisfactory. 19 **leave (someone) alone. a** Also: **let alone.** See **let**[1] (sense 7). **b** to permit to stay or be alone. 20 **leave someone to himself.** not to control or direct someone. ◆ See also **leave behind, leave off, leave out.**
▷HISTORY Old English *lǣfan;* related to *belīfan* to be left as a remainder
▸ˈ**leaver** NOUN

leave[2] (liːv) NOUN 1 permission to do something: *he was granted leave to speak.* 2 **by** *or* **with your leave.** with your permission. 3 permission to be absent, as from a place of work or duty: *leave of absence.* 4 the duration of such absence: *ten days' leave.* 5 a farewell or departure (esp in the phrase **take (one's) leave**). 6 **on leave.** officially excused from work or duty. 7 **take leave (of).** to say farewell (to). 8 **take leave of one's senses.** to go mad or become irrational.
▷HISTORY Old English *lēaf;* related to *alȳfan* to permit, Middle High German *loube* permission

leave[3] (liːv) VERB **leaves, leaving, leaved.** (*intr*) to produce or grow leaves.

leave behind VERB (*tr*) 1 (*adverb*) to forget or neglect to bring or take. 2 to cause to remain as a result or sign of something: *the storm left a trail of damage behind.* 3 to pass: *once the wind came up, we soon left the land behind us.*

leaved (liːvd) ADJECTIVE **a** having a leaf or leaves; leafed. **b** (*in combination*): *a five-leaved stem.*

leaven (ˈlɛvᵊn) NOUN *also* **leavening.** 1 any substance that produces fermentation in dough or batter, such as yeast, and causes it to rise. 2 a piece of such a substance kept to ferment a new batch of dough. 3 an agency or influence that produces a gradual change. ◆ VERB (*tr*) 4 to cause fermentation in (dough or batter). 5 to pervade, causing a gradual change, esp with some moderating or enlivening influence.
▷HISTORY C14: via Old French ultimately from Latin *levāmen* relief, (hence, raising agent, leaven), from *levāre* to raise

Leavenworth (ˈlɛvᵊnˌwɜːθ, -wəθ) NOUN a city in NE Kansas, on the Missouri River: the state's oldest city, founded in 1854 by proslavery settlers from Missouri. Pop.: 38 495 (1990).

leave of absence NOUN 1 permission to be absent from work or duty. 2 the period of absence.

leave off VERB 1 (*intr*) to stop; cease. 2 (*tr, adverb*) to stop wearing or using.

leave out VERB (*tr, adverb*) 1 to cause to remain in the open: *you can leave your car out tonight.* 2 to omit or exclude.

leaves (liːvz) NOUN the plural of **leaf.**

leave-taking NOUN the act of departing; a farewell.

leavings (ˈliːvɪŋz) PLURAL NOUN something remaining, such as food on a plate, residue, refuse, etc.

Leavisite (ˈliːvɪsˌaɪt) ADJECTIVE 1 of or relating to F(rank) R(aymond) Leavis, the English literary critic (1895–1978). ◆ NOUN 2 a follower or admirer of Leavis.

Lebanese (ˌlɛbəˈniːz) ADJECTIVE 1 of or relating to Lebanon or its inhabitants. ◆ NOUN 2 a native or inhabitant of Lebanon.

Lebanon (ˈlɛbənən) NOUN (sometimes preceded by *the*) a republic in W Asia, on the Mediterranean: an important centre of the Phoenician civilization in the third millennium B.C.; part of the Ottoman Empire from 1516 until 1919; gained independence in 1941 (effective by 1945). Official language: Arabic; French and English are also widely spoken. Religion: Muslim and Christian. Currency: Lebanese pound. Capital: Beirut. Pop.: 3 628 000 (2001 est.). Area: 10 400 sq. km (4015 sq. miles).

Lebanon Mountains PLURAL NOUN a mountain range in central Lebanon, extending across the whole country parallel with the Mediterranean coast. Highest peak: 3104 m (10 184 ft.). Arabic name: **Jebel Liban** (ˈdʒɛbᵊl ˈliːbɑːn).

leben (ˈlɛbᵊn) NOUN a semiliquid food made from curdled milk in N Africa and the Levant.
▷HISTORY C17: from Arabic *laban*

Lebensraum (ˈleɪbənzˌraʊm) NOUN territory claimed by a nation or state on the grounds that it is necessary for survival or growth.
▷HISTORY German, literally: living space

lebkuchen (ˈleɪbˌkuːkən) NOUN, *plural* **-chen.** a biscuit, originating from Germany, usually containing honey, spices, etc.
▷HISTORY German: literally, loaf cake

Lebowa (ləˈbəʊə) NOUN a former Bantu homeland in NE South Africa, consisting of three separate territories with several smaller exclaves: abolished in 1993.

LEC (lɛk) NOUN ACRONYM FOR Local Enterprise Company. See **Training Agency.**

Le Cateau (*French* lə kato) NOUN a town in NE France: site (August 26, 1914) of the largest British battle since Waterloo, which led to the disruption of the German attack on the Allies. Pop.: 9205 (latest est.).

Lecce (*Italian* ˈlettʃe) NOUN a walled city in SE Italy, in Puglia: Greek and Roman remains. Pop.: 100 046 (1996 est.).

leccy (ˈlɛkɪ) NOUN *Brit informal* electricity.

lech *or* **letch** (lɛtʃ) *Informal* ◆ VERB 1 (*intr;* usually foll by *after*) to behave lecherously (towards); lust (after). ◆ NOUN 2 a lecherous act or indulgence.
▷HISTORY C19: back formation from LECHER

Lech (lɛk; *German* lɛç) NOUN a river in central Europe, rising in SW Austria and flowing generally north through S Germany to the River Danube. Length: 285 km (177 miles).

lechaim, lehaim, *or* **l'chaim** (ləˈxɑjim) *Judaism* ◆ INTERJECTION 1 a drinking toast. ◆ NOUN 2 a small drink with which to toast something or someone.
▷HISTORY from Hebrew, literally: to life

Le Chatelier's principle (lə ʃæˈtɛljeɪz) NOUN *Chem* the principle that if a system in chemical equilibrium is subjected to a disturbance it tends to change in a way that opposes this disturbance.
▷HISTORY C19: named after H. L. *Le Chatelier* (1850–1936), French chemist

lecher (ˈlɛtʃə) NOUN a promiscuous or lewd man.
▷HISTORY C12: from Old French *lecheor* lecher, from *lechier* to lick, of Germanic origin; compare Old High German *leccōn* to lick

lecherous (ˈlɛtʃərəs) ADJECTIVE characterized by or inciting lechery.
▸ˈ**lecherously** ADVERB

lechery (ˈlɛtʃərɪ) NOUN, *plural* **-eries.** unrestrained and promiscuous sexuality.

lecithin (ˈlɛsɪθɪn) NOUN *Biochem* any of a group of phospholipids that are found in many plant and animal tissues, esp egg yolk: used in making candles, cosmetics, and inks, and as an emulsifier and stabilizer in foods (**E322**). Systematic name: **phosphatidylcholine.**
▷HISTORY C19: from Greek *lekithos* egg yolk

lecithinase (ləˈsɪθɪˌneɪs) NOUN any of a group of enzymes that remove the fatty-acid residue from lecithins: present in the venom of many snakes.

Leclanché cell (ləˈklɑːnʃeɪ) NOUN *Electrical engineering* a primary cell with a carbon anode, surrounded by crushed carbon and manganese dioxide in a porous container, immersed in an electrolyte of aqueous ammonium chloride into

which the zinc cathode dips. The common dry battery is a form of Leclanché cell.
▷**HISTORY** C19: named after Georges *Leclanché* (1839–82), French engineer

Le Creusot (*French* lə krøzo) NOUN a town in E central France: metal, machinery, and armaments industries. Pop.: 33 275 (latest est.).

lectern (ˈlɛktən) NOUN [1] a reading desk or support in a church. [2] any similar desk or support.
▷**HISTORY** C14: from Old French *lettrun,* from Late Latin *lectrum,* ultimately from *legere* to read

lectin (ˈlɛktɪn) NOUN a type of protein possessing high affinity for a specific sugar; lectins are often highly toxic.
▷**HISTORY** C20: from Latin *lectus,* past participle of *legere* to select + -IN

lection (ˈlɛkʃən) NOUN a variant reading of a passage in a particular copy or edition of a text.
▷**HISTORY** C16: from Latin *lectio* a reading, from *legere* to read, select

lectionary (ˈlɛkʃənərɪ) NOUN, *plural* **-aries.** a book containing readings appointed to be read at divine services.
▷**HISTORY** C15: from Church Latin *lectiōnārium,* from *lectio* LECTION

lector (ˈlɛktɔː) NOUN [1] a lecturer or reader in certain universities. [2] *RC Church* **a** a person appointed to read lessons at certain services. **b** (in convents or monastic establishments) a member of the community appointed to read aloud during meals.
▷**HISTORY** C15: from Latin, from *legere* to read
▸**lectorate** (ˈlɛktərɪt) *or* ˈ**lector**ˌ**ship** NOUN

lecture (ˈlɛktʃə) NOUN [1] a discourse on a particular subject given or read to an audience. [2] the text of such a discourse. [3] a method of teaching by formal discourse. [4] a lengthy reprimand or scolding. ◆ VERB [5] to give or read a lecture (to an audience or class). [6] (*tr*) to reprimand at length.
▷**HISTORY** C14: from Medieval Latin *lectūra* reading, from *legere* to read

lecturer (ˈlɛktʃərə) NOUN [1] a person who lectures. [2] a teacher in higher education without professorial status.

lectureship (ˈlɛktʃəˌʃɪp) NOUN [1] the office or position of lecturer. [2] an endowment financing a series of lectures.

lecythus (ˈlɛsɪθəs) NOUN, *plural* **-thi** (-θaɪ). (in ancient Greece) a vase with a narrow neck.
▷**HISTORY** from Greek *lēkuthos*

led (lɛd) VERB the past tense and past participle of **lead**[1].

LED *Electronics* ABBREVIATION FOR **light-emitting diode.**

Leda[1] (ˈliːdə) NOUN *Greek myth* a queen of Sparta who was the mother of Helen and Pollux by Zeus, who visited her in the form of a swan.

Leda[2] (ˈliːdə) NOUN *Astronomy* a small satellite of Jupiter in an intermediate orbit.

LED display NOUN a flat-screen device in which an array of light-emitting diodes can be selectively activated to display numerical and alphabetical information, used esp in pocket calculators, digital timepieces, measuring instruments, and in some microcomputers.

lederhosen (ˈleɪdəˌhəʊzᵊn) PLURAL NOUN leather shorts with H-shaped braces, worn by men in Austria, Bavaria, etc.
▷**HISTORY** German: leather trousers

ledge (lɛdʒ) NOUN [1] a narrow horizontal surface resembling a shelf and projecting from a wall, window, etc. [2] a layer of rock that contains an ore; vein. [3] a ridge of rock that lies beneath the surface of the sea. [4] a narrow shelflike rock projection on a cliff or mountain.
▷**HISTORY** C14 *legge,* perhaps from *leggen* to LAY[1]
▸ˈ**ledgy** *or* **ledged** ADJECTIVE

ledger (ˈlɛdʒə) NOUN [1] *Book-keeping* the principal book in which the commercial transactions of a company are recorded. [2] a flat horizontal slab of stone. [3] a horizontal scaffold pole fixed to two upright poles for supporting the outer ends of putlogs. [4] *Angling* **a** a wire trace that allows the weight to rest on the bottom and the bait to float freely. **b** (*as modifier*): *ledger tackle.* ◆ VERB [5] (*intr*) *Angling* to fish using a ledger.
▷**HISTORY** C15 *legger* book retained in a specific place, probably from *leggen* to LAY[1]

ledger board NOUN [1] a timber board forming the top rail of a fence or balustrade. [2] Also called: **ribbon strip.** a timber board fixed horizontally to studding to support floor joists.

ledger line NOUN [1] *Music* a short line placed above or below the staff to accommodate notes representing pitches above or below the staff. [2] *Angling* a line using ledger tackle.

lee (liː) NOUN [1] a sheltered part or side; the side away from the direction from which the wind is blowing. [2] **by the lee.** *Nautical* so that the wind is blowing on the wrong side of the sail. [3] **under the lee.** *Nautical* towards the lee. ◆ ADJECTIVE [4] (*prenominal*) *Nautical* on, at, or towards the side or part away from the wind: *on a lee shore.* Compare **weather** (sense 5).
▷**HISTORY** Old English *hlēow* shelter; related to Old Norse *hle*

Lee (liː) NOUN a river in SW Republic of Ireland, flowing east into Cork Harbour. Length: about 80 km (50 miles).

leeboard (ˈliːˌbɔːd) NOUN *Nautical* one of a pair of large adjustable paddle-like boards that may be lowered along the lee side to reduce sideways drift or leeway.

leech[1] (liːtʃ) NOUN [1] any annelid worm of the class *Hirudinea,* which have a sucker at each end of the body and feed on the blood or tissues of other animals. See also **horseleech, medicinal leech.** [2] a person who clings to or preys on another person. [3] **a** an archaic word for **physician. b** (*in combination*): *leechcraft.* [4] **cling like a leech.** to cling or adhere persistently to something. ◆ VERB [5] (*tr*) to use leeches to suck the blood of (a person), as a method of medical treatment.
▷**HISTORY** Old English *lǣce, lœce;* related to Middle Dutch *lieke*
▸ˈ**leech**ˌ**like** ADJECTIVE

leech[2] *or* **leach** (liːtʃ) NOUN *Nautical* the after edge of a fore-and-aft sail or either of the vertical edges of a squaresail.
▷**HISTORY** C15: of Germanic origin; compare Dutch *lijk*

Leeds (liːdz) NOUN [1] a city in N England, in Leeds unitary authority, West Yorkshire on the River Aire: linked with Liverpool and Goole by canals; a former centre of the clothing industry; two universities (1904, 1992). Pop.: 424 194 (1991). [2] a unitary authority in N England, in West Yorkshire. Pop.: 715 404 (2001). Area 562 sq. km (217 sq. miles).

Leeds Castle NOUN a castle near Maidstone in Kent: the home of several medieval queens of England.

leek (liːk) NOUN [1] Also called: **scallion.** an alliaceous plant, *Allium porrum,* with a slender white bulb, cylindrical stem, and broad flat overlapping leaves: used in cooking. [2] any of several related species, such as *A. ampeloprasum* (wild leek). [3] a leek, or a representation of one, as a national emblem of Wales.
▷**HISTORY** Old English *lēac;* related to Old Norse *laukr,* Old High German *louh*

leer (lɪə) VERB [1] (*intr*) to give an oblique, sneering, or suggestive look or grin. ◆ NOUN [2] such a look.
▷**HISTORY** C16: perhaps verbal use of obsolete *leer* cheek, from Old English *hlēor*
▸ˈ**leering** ADJECTIVE, NOUN ▸ˈ**leeringly** ADVERB

leery *or* **leary** (ˈlɪərɪ) ADJECTIVE **leerier, leeriest** *or* **learier, leariest.** [1] *Now chiefly dialect* knowing or sly. [2] *Slang* (foll by *of*) suspicious or wary. [3] *Slang* rowdy or boisterous.
▷**HISTORY** C18: perhaps from obsolete sense (to look askance) of LEER
▸ˈ**leeriness** *or* ˈ**leariness** NOUN

lees (liːz) PLURAL NOUN the sediment from an alcoholic drink.
▷**HISTORY** C14: plural of obsolete *lee,* from Old French, probably from Celtic; compare Irish *lige* bed

leet[1] (liːt) NOUN *English history* [1] Also called: **court-leet.** a special kind of manorial court that some lords were entitled to hold. [2] the jurisdiction of this court.
▷**HISTORY** C15: from Anglo-French, of unknown origin

leet[2] (liːt) NOUN *Scot* a list of candidates for an office.
▷**HISTORY** C15: perhaps from Anglo-French *litte,* variant of LIST[1]

Leeuwarden (*Dutch* ˈleːwardə) NOUN a city in the N Netherlands, capital of Friesland province. Pop.: 87 464 (1994).

leeward (ˈliːwəd; *Nautical* ˈluːəd) *Chiefly nautical* ◆ ADJECTIVE [1] of, in, or moving to the quarter towards which the wind blows. ◆ NOUN [2] the point or quarter towards which the wind blows. [3] the side towards the lee. ◆ ADVERB [4] towards the lee. ◆ Compare **windward.**

Leeward Islands (ˈliːwəd) PLURAL NOUN [1] a group of islands in the Caribbean, in the N Lesser Antilles between Puerto Rico and Martinique. [2] a former British colony in the E Caribbean (1871–1956), consisting of Antigua, Barbuda, Redonda, Saint Kitts, Nevis, Anguilla, Montserrat, and the British Virgin Islands. [3] a group of islands in the S Pacific, in French Polynesia in the W Society Archipelago: Huahiné, Raiatéa, Tahaa, Bora-Bora, and Maupiti. Pop.: 26 838 (1996). French name: **Îles sous le Vent.**

lee wave NOUN *Meteorol* a stationary wave sometimes formed in an air stream on the leeward side of a hill or mountain range.

leeway (ˈliːˌweɪ) NOUN [1] room for free movement within limits, as in action or expenditure. [2] sideways drift of a boat or aircraft.

Lefkoşa (lefˈkoʃə) NOUN the Turkish name for **Nicosia.**

left[1] (lɛft) ADJECTIVE [1] (*usually prenominal*) of or designating the side of something or someone that faces west when the front is turned towards the north. [2] (*usually prenominal*) worn on a left hand, foot, etc. [3] (*sometimes capital*) of or relating to the political or intellectual left. [4] (*sometimes capital*) radical or progressive, esp as compared to less radical or progressive groups, persons, etc. ◆ ADVERB [5] on or in the direction of the left. ◆ NOUN [6] a left side, direction, position, area, or part. Related adjectives: **sinister, sinistral.** [7] (*often capital*) the supporters or advocates of varying degrees of social, political, or economic change, reform, or revolution designed to promote the greater freedom, power, welfare, or comfort of the common people. [8] **to the left.** radical in the methods, principles, etc., employed in striving to achieve such change. [9] *Boxing* **a** a blow with the left hand. **b** the left hand.
▷**HISTORY** Old English *left* idle, weak, variant of *lyft-* (in *lyftādl* palsy, literally: left-disease); related to Middle Dutch *lucht* left

left[2] (lɛft) VERB the past tense and past participle of **leave**[1].

Left Bank NOUN a district of Paris, on the S bank of the River Seine; frequented by artists, students, etc.

left brain NOUN **a** the left hemisphere of the human brain, which is believed to control linear and analytical thinking, decision-making, and language. **b** (*as modifier*): *a left-brain activity.*

left-field ADJECTIVE *Informal* regarded as being outside the mainstream; unconventional.
▷**HISTORY** C20: from baseball term *left field,* the area of the outfield to the batter's left, regarded as the scene of little action

left-footer NOUN *Informal* (esp in Ireland and Scotland) a Roman Catholic.
▷**HISTORY** C20: from the Northern Irish saying that farm workers in Eire use the left foot to push a spade when digging

left-hand ADJECTIVE (*prenominal*) [1] of, relating to, located on, or moving towards the left: *this car is left-hand drive; a left-hand bend.* [2] for use by the left hand; left-handed.

left-handed ADJECTIVE [1] using the left hand with greater ease than the right. [2] performed with the left hand. [3] designed or adapted for use by the left hand. [4] worn on the left hand. [5] awkward or clumsy. [6] ironically ambiguous: *a left-handed compliment.* [7] turning from right to left; anticlockwise. [8] *Law* another term for **morganatic.** ◆ ADVERB [9] with the left hand.
▸ˌ**left-**ˈ**handedly** ADVERB ▸ˌ**left-**ˈ**handedness** NOUN

left-hander NOUN [1] a blow with the left hand. [2] a left-handed person.

leftist (ˈlɛftɪst) ADJECTIVE 1 of, tending towards, or relating to the political left or its principles. ◆ NOUN 2 a person who supports or belongs to the political left.
▸ **ˈleftism** NOUN

left-luggage office NOUN *Brit* a place at a railway station, airport, etc., where luggage may be left for a small charge with an attendant for safekeeping. US and Canadian name: **checkroom.**

leftover (ˈlɛftˌəʊvə) NOUN 1 (*often plural*) an unused portion or remnant, as of material or of cooked food. ◆ ADJECTIVE 2 left as an unused portion or remnant.

leftward (ˈlɛftwəd) ADJECTIVE 1 on or towards the left. ◆ ADVERB 2 a variant of **leftwards.**

leftwards (ˈlɛftwədz) *or* **leftward** ADVERB towards or on the left.

left wing NOUN 1 (*often capital*) the leftist faction of an assembly, party, group, etc.; the radical or progressive wing. 2 the units of an army situated on the left of a battle position. 3 *Sport* **a** the left-hand side of the field of play from the point of view of either team facing its opponents' goal. **b** a player positioned in this area in certain games. ◆ ADJECTIVE **left-wing.** 4 of, belonging to, or relating to the political left wing.
▸ **ˌleft-ˈwinger** NOUN

lefty (ˈlɛftɪ) NOUN, *plural* **lefties.** *Informal* 1 a left-winger. 2 *Chiefly US and Canadian* a left-handed person.

leg (lɛg) NOUN 1 **a** either of the two lower limbs, including the bones and fleshy covering of the femur, tibia, fibula, and patella. **b** (*as modifier*): *leg guard; leg rest.* Related adjective: **crural.** 2 any similar or analogous structure in animals that is used for locomotion or support. 3 this part of an animal, esp the thigh, used for food: *leg of lamb.* 4 something similar to a leg in appearance or function, such as one of the four supporting members of a chair. 5 a branch, limb, or part of a forked or jointed object. 6 the part of a garment that covers the leg. 7 a section or part of a journey or course. 8 a single stage, lap, length, etc., in a relay race. 9 either one of two races on which a cumulative bet has been placed. 10 either the opposite or adjacent side of a right-angled triangle. 11 *Nautical* **a** the distance travelled without tacking. **b** (in yacht racing) the course between any two marks. 12 one of a series of games, matches, or parts of games. 13 *Cricket* **a** the side of the field to the left of a right-handed batsman as he faces the bowler. **b** (*as modifier*): *a leg slip; leg stump.* 14 **give (someone) a leg up. a** to help (someone) to climb an obstacle by pushing upwards. **b** to help (someone) to advance. 15 **have legs.** *Informal* to be successful or show the potential to succeed. 16 **not have a leg to stand on.** to have no reasonable or logical basis for an opinion or argument. 17 **on his, its, etc., last legs.** (of a person or thing) worn out; exhausted. 18 **pull (someone's) leg.** *Informal* to tease, fool, or make fun of (someone). 19 **shake a leg.** *Informal* **a** to hurry up: usually used in the imperative. **b** to dance. 20 **show a leg.** *Informal* to get up in the morning. 21 **stretch one's legs.** See **stretch** (sense 17). ◆ VERB **legs, legging, legged.** 22 (*tr*) *Obsolete* to propel (a canal boat) through a tunnel by lying on one's back and walking one's feet along the tunnel roof. 23 **leg it.** *Informal* to walk, run, or hurry.
▹ HISTORY C13: from Old Norse *leggr,* of obscure origin
▸ **ˈlegˌlike** ADJECTIVE

leg. ABBREVIATION FOR legato.

legacy (ˈlɛgəsɪ) NOUN, *plural* **-cies.** 1 a gift by will, esp of money or personal property. 2 something handed down or received from an ancestor or predecessor. 3 (*modifier*) surviving computer systems, hardware, or software: *legacy network; legacy application.*
▹ HISTORY C14 (meaning: office of a legate), C15 (meaning: bequest): from Medieval Latin *lēgātia* commission; see LEGATE

legal (ˈliːgᵊl) ADJECTIVE 1 established by or founded upon law; lawful. 2 of or relating to law. 3 recognized, enforceable, or having a remedy at law rather than in equity. 4 relating to or characteristic of the profession of law.
▹ HISTORY C16: from Latin *lēgālis,* from *lēx* law
▸ **ˈlegally** ADVERB

legal aid NOUN a means-tested benefit in the form of financial assistance for persons to meet the cost of advice and representation in legal proceedings.

legal cap NOUN *US* ruled writing paper, about 8 by 13½ inches with the fold at the top, for use by lawyers.

legalese (ˌliːgəˈliːz) NOUN the conventional language in which legal documents, etc., are written.

legal holiday NOUN *US* any of several weekdays which are observed as national holidays. Also called (Canadian): **statutory holiday.** Brit equivalent: **bank holiday.**

legalism (ˈliːgəˌlɪzəm) NOUN strict adherence to the law, esp the stressing of the letter of the law rather than its spirit.
▸ **ˈlegalist** NOUN, ADJECTIVE

legalistic (ˌliːgəˈlɪstɪk) ADJECTIVE of, relating to, or exhibiting strict adherence to the law, esp to the letter of the law rather than its spirit.
▸ **ˌlegalˈistically** ADVERB

legality (lɪˈgælɪtɪ) NOUN, *plural* **-ties.** 1 the state or quality of being legal or lawful. 2 adherence to legal principles.

legalize *or* **legalise** (ˈliːgəˌlaɪz) VERB (*tr*) 1 to make lawful or legal. 2 to confirm or validate (something previously unlawful).
▸ **ˌlegaliˈzation** *or* **ˌlegaliˈsation** NOUN

legal medicine NOUN another name for **forensic medicine.**

legal positivism NOUN another name for **positivism** (sense 2).

legal separation NOUN another term (esp US) for **judicial separation.**

legal tender NOUN currency in specified denominations that a creditor must by law accept in redemption of a debt.

Legaspi (lɛˈgæspɪ) NOUN a port in the Philippines, on SE Luzon on the Gulf of Albay. Pop.: 125 128 (1994 est.).

legate (ˈlɛgɪt) NOUN 1 a messenger, envoy, or delegate. 2 *RC Church* an emissary to a foreign state representing the Pope.
▹ HISTORY Old English, via Old French from Latin *lēgātus* deputy, from *lēgāre* to delegate; related to *lēx* law
▸ **ˈlegateˌship** NOUN ▸ **legatine** (ˈlɛgəˌtaɪn) ADJECTIVE

legatee (ˌlɛgəˈtiː) NOUN a person to whom a legacy is bequeathed. Compare **devisee.**

legation (lɪˈgeɪʃən) NOUN 1 a diplomatic mission headed by a minister. 2 the official residence and office of a diplomatic minister. 3 the act of sending forth a diplomatic envoy. 4 the mission or business of a diplomatic envoy. 5 the rank or office of a legate.
▹ HISTORY C15: from Latin *lēgātiō,* from *lēgātus* LEGATE
▸ **leˈgationary** ADJECTIVE

legato (lɪˈgɑːtəʊ) *Music* ◆ ADJECTIVE, ADVERB 1 to be performed smoothly and connectedly. ◆ NOUN, *plural* **-tos.** 2 **a** a style of playing in which no perceptible gaps are left between notes. **b** (*as modifier*): *a legato passage.*
▹ HISTORY C19: from Italian, literally: bound

legator (ˌlɛgəˈtɔː) NOUN a person who gives a legacy or makes a bequest.
▹ HISTORY C17: from Latin, from *lēgāre* to bequeath; see LEGATE
▸ **ˌlegaˈtorial** ADJECTIVE

leg before wicket NOUN *Cricket* a manner of dismissal on the grounds that a batsman has been struck on the leg by a bowled ball that otherwise would have hit the wicket. Abbreviation: **lbw.**

leg break NOUN *Cricket* a bowled ball that spins from leg to off on pitching.

leg bye NOUN *Cricket* a run scored after the ball has hit the batsman's leg or some other part of his body, except his hand, without touching the bat. Abbreviation: **lb.**

Legco (ˈlɛgkəʊ) NOUN the Legislative Council of Hong Kong.

legend (ˈlɛdʒənd) NOUN 1 a popular story handed down from earlier times whose truth has not been ascertained. 2 a group of such stories: *the Arthurian legend.* 3 a modern story that has taken on the characteristics of a traditional legendary tale. 4 a person whose fame or notoriety makes him a source of exaggerated or romanticized tales or exploits. 5 an inscription or title, as on a coin or beneath a coat of arms. 6 explanatory matter accompanying a table, map, chart, etc. 7 **a** a story of the life of a saint. **b** a collection of such stories.
▹ HISTORY C14 (in the sense: a saint's life or a collection of saints' lives): from Medieval Latin *legenda* passages to be read, from Latin *legere* to read
▸ **ˈlegendry** NOUN

legendary (ˈlɛdʒəndərɪ, -drɪ) ADJECTIVE 1 of or relating to legend. 2 celebrated or described in a legend or legends. 3 very famous or notorious.

legerdemain (ˌlɛdʒədəˈmeɪn) NOUN 1 another name for **sleight of hand.** 2 cunning deception or trickery.
▹ HISTORY C15: from Old French: light of hand
▸ **ˌlegerdeˈmainist** NOUN

leger line (ˈlɛdʒə) NOUN a variant spelling of **ledger line.**

leges (ˈliːdʒiːz) NOUN the plural of **lex.**

legged (ˈlɛgɪd, lɛgd) ADJECTIVE **a** having a leg or legs. **b** (*in combination*): *three-legged; long-legged.*

leggings (ˈlɛgɪŋz) PLURAL NOUN 1 an extra outer covering for the lower legs. 2 close-fitting trousers worn by women and children.
▸ **ˈlegginged** ADJECTIVE

leggy (ˈlɛgɪ) ADJECTIVE **-gier, -giest.** 1 having unusually long legs. 2 (of a woman) having long and shapely legs. 3 (of a plant) having an unusually long and weak stem.
▸ **ˈlegginess** NOUN

leghorn (ˈlɛgˌhɔːn) NOUN 1 a type of Italian wheat straw that is woven into hats. 2 any hat made from this straw when plaited.
▹ HISTORY C19: named after LEGHORN (Livorno)

Leghorn NOUN 1 (ˈlɛgˌhɔːn) the English name for **Livorno.** 2 (lɛˈgɔːn) a breed of domestic fowl laying white eggs.

legible (ˈlɛdʒəbᵊl) ADJECTIVE 1 (of handwriting, print, etc.) able to be read or deciphered. 2 able to be discovered; discernible.
▹ HISTORY C14: from Late Latin *legibilis,* from Latin *legere* to read
▸ **ˌlegiˈbility** *or* **ˈlegibleness** NOUN ▸ **ˈlegibly** ADVERB

legion (ˈliːdʒən) NOUN 1 a military unit of the ancient Roman army made up of infantry with supporting cavalry, numbering some three to six thousand men. 2 any large military force: *the French Foreign Legion.* 3 (*usually capital*) an association of ex-servicemen: *the British Legion.* 4 (*often plural*) any very large number, esp of people. ◆ ADJECTIVE 5 (*usually postpositive*) very large or numerous.
▹ HISTORY C13: from Old French, from Latin *legio,* from *legere* to choose

legionary (ˈliːdʒənərɪ) ADJECTIVE 1 of or relating to a legion. ◆ NOUN, *plural* **-aries.** 2 a soldier belonging to a legion.

legionary ant NOUN another name for the **army ant.**

legionnaire (ˌliːdʒəˈnɛə) NOUN (*often capital*) a member of certain military forces or associations, such as the French Foreign Legion or the British Legion.

legionnaire's *or* **legionnaires' disease** NOUN a serious, sometimes fatal, infection, caused by the bacterium *Legionella pneumophila,* which has symptoms similar to those of pneumonia: believed to be spread by inhalation of contaminated water vapour from showers and air-conditioning plants.
▹ HISTORY C20: after the outbreak at a meeting of the American Legion at Philadelphia in 1976

Legion of Honour NOUN an order for civil or military merit instituted by Napoleon in France in 1802. French name: **Légion d'honneur** (leʒjɔ̃ dɔnœr).

legislate (ˈlɛdʒɪsˌleɪt) VERB 1 (*intr*) to make or pass laws. 2 (*tr*) to bring into effect by legislation.
▹ HISTORY C18: back formation from LEGISLATOR

legislation (ˌlɛdʒɪsˈleɪʃən) NOUN 1 the act or process of making laws; enactment. 2 the laws so made.

legislative (ˈlɛdʒɪslətɪv) ADJECTIVE 1 of or relating to legislation. 2 having the power or function of legislating: *a legislative assembly.* 3 of or relating to a legislature. ◆ NOUN 4 *Rare* another word for **legislature.**

▸ **'legislatively** ADVERB

legislative assembly NOUN (*often capitals*) [1] the bicameral legislature in 28 states of the US. [2] the lower chamber of the bicameral state legislatures in several Commonwealth countries, such as Australia. [3] the unicameral legislature in most Canadian provinces. [4] any assembly with legislative powers.

legislative council NOUN (*often capitals*) [1] the upper chamber of certain bicameral legislatures, such as those of the Indian and Australian states. [2] the unicameral legislature of certain colonies or dependent territories. [3] (in the US) a committee composed of members of both chambers of a state legislature, that meets to discuss problems, construct a legislative programme, etc.

legislator ('lɛdʒɪsˌleɪtə) NOUN [1] a person concerned with the making or enactment of laws. [2] a member of a legislature.
▷ HISTORY C17: from Latin *lēgis lātor,* from *lēx* law + *lātor* from *lātus,* past participle of *ferre* to bring
▸ **'legisˌlatorˌship** NOUN ▸ **'legisˌlatress** FEMININE NOUN

legislatorial (ˌlɛdʒɪslə'tɔːrɪəl) ADJECTIVE of or relating to a legislator or legislature.

legislature ('lɛdʒɪsˌleɪtʃə) NOUN a body of persons vested with power to make, amend, and repeal laws. Compare **executive, judiciary.**

legist ('liːdʒɪst) NOUN a person versed in the law.
▷ HISTORY C15: from Medieval Latin *lēgista,* from *lēx* law

legit (lɪ'dʒɪt) *Slang* ◆ ADJECTIVE [1] short for **legitimate.** ◆ NOUN [2] legitimate or professionally respectable drama.

legitimate ADJECTIVE (lɪ'dʒɪtɪmɪt) [1] born in lawful wedlock; enjoying full filial rights. [2] conforming to established standards of usage, behaviour, etc. [3] based on correct or acceptable principles of reasoning. [4] reasonable, sensible, or valid: *a legitimate question.* [5] authorized, sanctioned by, or in accordance with law. [6] of, relating to, or ruling by hereditary right: *a legitimate monarch.* [7] of or relating to a body of famous long-established plays as distinct from films, television, vaudeville, etc.: *the legitimate theatre.* ◆ VERB (lɪ'dʒɪtɪˌmeɪt) [8] (*tr*) to make, pronounce, or show to be legitimate.
▷ HISTORY C15: from Medieval Latin *lēgitimātus* made legal, from *lēx* law
▸ **le'gitimacy** *or* **le'gitimateness** NOUN ▸ **le'gitimately** ADVERB ▸ **leˌgiti'mation** NOUN

legitimist (lɪ'dʒɪtɪmɪst) NOUN [1] a monarchist who supports the rule of a legitimate dynasty or of its senior branch. [2] (formerly) a supporter of the elder line of the Bourbon family in France. [3] a supporter of legitimate authority. ◆ ADJECTIVE *also* **legitimistic.** [4] of or relating to legitimists.
▸ **le'gitimism** NOUN

legitimize, legitimise (lɪ'dʒɪtɪˌmaɪz), **legitimatize,** *or* **legitimatise** (lɪ'dʒɪtɪməˌtaɪz) VERB (*tr*) to make legitimate; legalize.
▸ **leˌgitimi'zation** *or* **leˌgitimi'sation** *or* **leˌgitimati'zation** *or* **leˌgitimati'sation** NOUN

legless ('lɛglɪs) ADJECTIVE [1] without legs. [2] *Informal* very drunk.

legman ('lɛgmən) NOUN, *plural* **-men.** *Chiefly US and Canadian* [1] a newsman who reports on news stories from the scene of action or original source. [2] a person employed to run errands, collect information, etc., outside an office.

Legnica (*Polish* lɛg'nitsa) NOUN an industrial town in SW Poland. Pop.: 109 335 (1999 est.). German name: **Liegnitz.**

Lego ('lɛgəʊ) NOUN *Trademark* a construction toy consisting of plastic bricks and other standardized components that fit together with studs.
▷ HISTORY C20: from Danish *leg godt* play well

leg-of-mutton *or* **leg-o'-mutton** NOUN (*modifier*) (of a sail, sleeve, etc.) tapering sharply or having a triangular profile.

leg-pull NOUN *Brit informal* a practical joke or mild deception.

legroom ('lɛgˌruːm) NOUN room to move one's legs comfortably, as in a car.

leg rope *Austral and NZ* ◆ NOUN [1] a rope used to secure an animal by its hind leg. ◆ VERB **leg-rope.** (*tr*) [2] to restrain (an animal) by a leg rope.

leguaan ('lɛgjʊən, 'lɛgʊˌɑːn) NOUN *South African* a large amphibious monitor lizard of the genus *Varanus,* esp *V. niloticus* (the **water leguaan**), which can grow up to 2 or 3 m. Also called: **iguana.**
▷ HISTORY C19: Dutch, from French *l'iguane* the iguana

legume ('lɛgjuːm, lɪ'gjuːm) NOUN [1] the long dry dehiscent fruit produced by leguminous plants; a pod. [2] any table vegetable of the family *Fabaceae* (formerly *Leguminosae*), esp beans or peas. [3] any leguminous plant.
▷ HISTORY C17: from French *légume,* from Latin *legūmen* bean, from *legere* to pick (a crop)

legumin (lɪ'gjuːmɪn) NOUN a protein obtained mainly from the seeds of leguminous plants.
▷ HISTORY C19: from LEGUME

leguminous (lɪ'gjuːmɪnəs) ADJECTIVE of, relating to, or belonging to the *Fabaceae* (formerly *Leguminosae*), a family of flowering plants having pods (or legumes) as fruits and root nodules enabling storage of nitrogen-rich material: includes peas, beans, clover, gorse, acacia, and carob.
▷ HISTORY C17: from Latin *legūmen;* see LEGUME

legwarmer ('lɛgˌwɔːmə) NOUN one of a pair of garments resembling stockings without feet, usually knitted and brightly coloured, often worn over jeans, tights, etc. or during exercise.

legwork ('lɛgˌwɜːk) NOUN *Informal* work that involves travelling on foot or as if on foot.

lehaim (lə'xɑjim) INTERJECTION, NOUN a variant spelling of **lechaim.**

Le Havre (lə 'hɑːvrə; *French* lə ɑvrə) NOUN a port in N France, on the English Channel at the mouth of the River Seine: transatlantic trade; oil refining. Pop.: 190 651 (1999).

lehr (lɪə) NOUN a long tunnel-shaped oven used for annealing glass.
▷ HISTORY from German: pattern, model

lei[1] (leɪ) NOUN (in Hawaii) a garland of flowers, worn around the neck.
▷ HISTORY from Hawaiian

lei[2] (leɪ) NOUN the plural of **leu.**

Leibnizian *or* **Leibnitzian** (laɪb'nɪtsɪən) ADJECTIVE of or relating to Baron Gottfried Wilhelm von Leibnitz, the German rationalist philosopher and mathematician (1646–1716).

Leibniz Mountains ('laɪbnɪts) PLURAL NOUN a mountain range on the SW limb of the moon, containing the highest peaks (10 000 metres) on the moon.

Leibniz's law NOUN *Logic, philosophy* [1] the principle that two expressions satisfy exactly the same predicates if and only if they both refer to the same subject. [2] the weaker principle that if $a=b$ whatever is true of a is true of b.
▷ HISTORY named after Gottfried Wilhelm von *Leibnitz* (1646–1716), German philosopher and mathematician

Leibniz's rule NOUN *Maths* a rule for finding a derivative of the product of two functions. For a first derivative it is $d(uv)/dx = u dv/dx + v du/dx$.

Leicester ('lɛstə) NOUN [1] a city in central England, in Leicester unitary authority, on the River Soar: administrative centre of Leicestershire: Roman remains and a ruined Norman castle; two universities (1957, 1992); light engineering, hosiery, and footwear industries. Pop.: 293 400 (1994 est.). [2] a unitary authority in central England, in Leicestershire. Pop.: 279 923 (2001). Area: 73 sq. km (28 sq. miles). [3] short for **Leicestershire.** [4] a breed of sheep with long wool, originally from Leicestershire. [5] a fairly mild dark orange whole-milk cheese, similar to Cheddar.

Leicestershire ('lɛstəˌʃɪə, -ʃə) NOUN a county of central England: absorbed the small historical county of Rutland in 1974; Rutland and Leicester city became independent unitary authorities in 1997: largely agricultural. Administrative centre: Leicester. Pop. (excluding Leicester city): 609 579 (2001). Area (excluding Leicester city): 2084 sq. km (804 sq. miles). Shortened form: **Leicester.** Abbreviation: **Leics.**

Leics ABBREVIATION FOR Leicestershire.

Leiden *or* **Leyden** ('laɪdᵊn; *Dutch* 'lɛidə) NOUN a city in the W Netherlands, in South Holland province: residence of the Pilgrim Fathers for 11 years before they sailed for America in 1620; university (1575). Pop.: 117 389 (1999 est.).

Leigh (liː) NOUN a town in NW England, in Wigan unitary authority, Greater Manchester: engineering industries. Pop.: 43 150 (1991).

Leinster ('lɛnstə) NOUN a province of E and SE Republic of Ireland: it consists of the counties of Carlow, Dublin, Kildare, Kilkenny, Laois, Longford, Louth, Meath, Offaly, Westmeath, Wexford, and Wicklow. Pop.: 1 924 702 (1996). Area: 19 632 sq. km (7580 sq. miles).

Leipzig ('laɪpsɪg; *German* 'laiptsɪç) NOUN a city in E central Germany, in Saxony: famous fairs, begun about 1170; publishing and music centre; university (1409); scene of a decisive defeat for Napoleon Bonaparte in 1813. Pop.: 490 000 (1999 est.).

Leiria (*Portuguese* lei'riə) NOUN a city in central Portugal: site of the first printing press in Portugal (1466). Pop.: 96 585 (latest est.).

leishmania (liːʃ'meɪnɪə) NOUN any parasitic flagellate protozoan of the genus *Leishmania*: infects humans and animals and causes diseases ranging from skin lesions to potentially fatal organ damage.
▷ HISTORY C20: New Latin, named after Sir W.B. *Leishman* (1865–1926), Scottish bacteriologist

leishmaniasis (ˌliːʃmə'naɪəsɪs) *or* **leishmaniosis** (liːʃˌmeɪnɪ'əʊsɪs, -ˌmæn-) NOUN any disease, such as kala-azar, caused by protozoa of the genus *Leishmania.*

leister ('liːstə) NOUN [1] a spear with three or more prongs for spearing fish, esp salmon. ◆ VERB [2] (*tr*) to spear (a fish) with a leister.
▷ HISTORY C16: from Scandinavian; related to Old Norse *ljōstr,* from *ljōsta* to stab

leisure ('lɛʒə; *US also* 'liːʒər) NOUN [1] **a** time or opportunity for ease, relaxation, etc. **b** (*as modifier*): *leisure activities.* [2] ease or leisureliness. [3] **at leisure. a** having free time for ease, relaxation, etc. **b** not occupied or engaged. **c** without hurrying. [4] **at one's leisure.** when one has free time.
▷ HISTORY C14: from Old French *leisir;* ultimately from Latin *licēre* to be allowed

leisure centre NOUN a building designed to provide facilities for a range of leisure pursuits, such as a sports hall, café, and meeting rooms.

leisured ('lɛʒəd) ADJECTIVE [1] (*usually prenominal*) having much leisure, as through unearned wealth: *the leisured classes.* [2] unhurried or relaxed: *in a leisured manner.*

leisurely ('lɛʒəlɪ) ADJECTIVE [1] unhurried; relaxed. ◆ ADVERB [2] without haste; in a relaxed way.
▸ **'leisureliness** NOUN

leisure sickness NOUN a medical condition in which people who have been working become ill with symptoms such as fatigue or muscular pains at a weekend or while on holiday.

Leith (liːθ) NOUN a port in SE Scotland, on the Firth of Forth: part of Edinburgh since 1920.

leitmotif *or* **leitmotiv** ('laɪtməʊˌtiːf) NOUN [1] *Music* a recurring short melodic phrase or theme used, esp in Wagnerian music dramas, to suggest a character, thing, etc. [2] an often repeated word, phrase, image, or theme in a literary work.
▷ HISTORY C19: from German *leitmotiv* leading motif

Leitrim ('liːtrɪm) NOUN a county of N Republic of Ireland in Connacht province, on Donegal Bay: agricultural. County town: Carrick-on-Shannon. Pop.: 25 057 (1996). Area: 1525 sq. km (589 sq. miles).

Leix (liːʃ) NOUN another name for **Laois.**

Leizhou ('leɪ'dʒəʊ) *or* **Luichow Peninsula** NOUN a peninsula of SE China, in SW Guangdong province, separated from Hainan Island by Hainan Strait.

lek[1] (lɛk) NOUN [1] a small area in which birds of certain species, notably the black grouse, gather for sexual display and courtship. [2] the act or practice of so gathering.
▷ HISTORY C19: perhaps from dialect *lake* (vb) from Old English *lácan* to frolic, fight, or perhaps from Swedish *leka* to play

lek[2] (lɛk) NOUN the standard monetary unit of Albania, divided into 100 qindarka.
▷ HISTORY from Albanian

lekgotla (lɛ'xʊtlə) *or* **kgotla** ('xʊtlə) NOUN *South African* a meeting place for village assemblies, court cases, and meetings of village leaders.
▷ HISTORY from Sotho and Tswana *lekgotla* courtyard or court

lekker ('lɛkə) ADJECTIVE *South African, slang* [1] pleasing or enjoyable. [2] tasty.
▷HISTORY C20: Afrikaans, from Dutch

LEM (lɛm) NOUN ACRONYM FOR lunar excursion module.

leman ('lɛmən, 'li:-) NOUN *Archaic* [1] a beloved; sweetheart. [2] a lover or mistress.
▷HISTORY C13 *lemman, leofman,* from *leof* dear, LIEF + MAN

Léman (lemɑ̃) NOUN **Lac.** the French name for (Lake) **Geneva.**

Le Mans (*French* lə mɑ̃) NOUN a city in NW France: scene of the first experiments in motoring and flying; annual motor race. Pop.: 146 405 (1999).

Lemberg ('lɛmbɛrk) NOUN the German name for **Lviv.**

lemma[1] ('lɛmə) NOUN, *plural* **-mas** *or* **-mata** (-mətə). [1] a subsidiary proposition, proved for use in the proof of another proposition. [2] *Linguistics* a word considered as its citation form together with all the inflected forms. For example, the lemma *go* consists of *go* together with *goes, going, went,* and *gone.* [3] an argument or theme, esp when used as the subject or title of a composition.
▷HISTORY C16 (meaning: proposition), C17 (meaning: title, theme): via Latin from Greek: premise, from *lambanein* to take (for granted)

lemma[2] ('lɛmə) NOUN, *plural* **-mas** *or* **-mata** (-mətə). the outer of two bracts surrounding each floret in a grass spikelet. ◆ Compare **palea.**
▷HISTORY C19: from Greek: rind, from *lepein* to peel

lemmatize *or* **lemmatise** ('lɛmə,taɪz) VERB (*tr*) *Linguistics* to group together the inflected forms of (a word) for analysis as a single item.
▸ **,lemmati'zation** *or* **,lemmati'sation** NOUN

lemming ('lɛmɪŋ) NOUN [1] any of various volelike rodents of the genus *Lemmus* and related genera, of northern and arctic regions of Europe, Asia, and North America: family *Cricetidae.* The Scandinavian variety, *Lemmus lemmus,* migrates periodically when its population reaches a peak. [2] a member of any large group following an unthinking course towards mass destruction.
▷HISTORY C17: from Norwegian; related to Latin *lātrāre* to bark
▸ **'lemming-,like** ADJECTIVE

Lemnian ('lɛmnɪən) ADJECTIVE [1] of or relating to the Greek island of Lemnos or its inhabitants. ◆ NOUN [2] a native or inhabitant of Lemnos.

lemniscate ('lɛmnɪskɪt) NOUN a closed plane curve consisting of two symmetrical loops meeting at a node. Equation: $(x^2 + y^2)^2 = a^2(x^2 - y^2)$, where a is the greatest distance from the curve to the origin. The symbol for infinity (∞) is an example.

lemniscus (lɛm'nɪskəs) NOUN, *plural* **-nisci** (-'nɪsaɪ, -'nɪski:). *Anatomy* a technical name for **fillet** (sense 9).
▷HISTORY C19: New Latin, from Latin, from Greek *lēmniskos* ribbon

Lemnos ('lɛmnɒs) NOUN a Greek island in the N Aegean Sea: famous for its medicinal earth (**Lemnian seal**). Chief town: Kastron. Pop.: 16 000 (latest est.). Area: 477 sq. km (184 sq. miles). Modern Greek name: **Límnos.**

lemon ('lɛmən) NOUN [1] a small Asian evergreen tree, *Citrus limon,* widely cultivated in warm and tropical regions, having pale green glossy leaves and edible fruits. Related adjectives: **citric, citrine, citrous.** [2] **a** the yellow oval fruit of this tree, having juicy acidic flesh rich in vitamin C. **b** (*as modifier*): *a lemon jelly.* [3] Also called: **lemon yellow. a** a greenish-yellow or strong yellow colour. **b** (*as adjective*): *lemon wallpaper.* [4] a distinctive tart flavour made from or in imitation of the lemon. [5] *Slang* a person or thing considered to be useless or defective.
▷HISTORY C14: from Medieval Latin *lemōn-,* from Arabic *laymūn*
▸ **'lemonish** ADJECTIVE ▸ **'lemon-,like** ADJECTIVE

lemonade (,lɛmə'neɪd) NOUN a drink made from lemon juice, sugar, and water or from carbonated water, citric acid, etc.

lemon balm NOUN the full name of **balm** (sense 5).

lemon cheese *or* **curd** NOUN a soft paste made from lemons, sugar, eggs, and butter, used as a spread or filling.

lemon drop NOUN a lemon-flavoured boiled sweet.

lemon fish NOUN another name for **cobia.**

lemon geranium NOUN a cultivated geraniaceous plant, *Pelargonium limoneum,* with lemon-scented leaves.

lemon grass NOUN a perennial grass, *Cymbopogon citratus,* with a large flower spike: used in cooking and grown in tropical regions as the source of an aromatic oil (**lemon grass oil**).

lemon sole NOUN a European flatfish, *Microstomus kitt,* with a variegated brown body: highly valued as a food fish: family *Pleuronectidae.*

lemon squash NOUN *Brit* a drink made from a sweetened lemon concentrate and water.

lemon squeezer NOUN [1] any of various devices for extracting the juice from citrus fruit. [2] *NZ informal* a peaked hat with four indentations worn by the army on ceremonial occasions.

lemon verbena NOUN a tropical American verbenaceous shrub, *Lippia citriodora,* with slender lemon-scented leaves yielding an oil used in perfumery.

lemonwood ('lɛmən,wʊd) NOUN a small tree, *Pittosporum eugenioides,* of New Zealand having a white bark and lemon-scented flowers.

lemony ('lɛmənɪ) ADJECTIVE [1] having or resembling the taste or colour of a lemon. [2] *Austral, slang* angry or irritable.

lempira (lɛm'pɪərə) NOUN the standard monetary unit of Honduras, divided into 100 centavos.
▷HISTORY American Spanish, after *Lempira,* Indian chief who opposed the Spanish

lemur ('li:mə) NOUN [1] any Madagascan prosimian primate of the family *Lemuridae,* such as *Lemur catta* (the **ring-tailed lemur**). They are typically arboreal, having foxy faces and long tails. [2] any similar or closely related animal, such as a loris or indris.
▷HISTORY C18: New Latin, adapted from Latin *lemurēs* ghosts; so named by Linnaeus for its ghost-like face and nocturnal habits
▸ **'lemur-,like** ADJECTIVE

lemures ('lɛmjʊ,ri:z) PLURAL NOUN *Roman myth* the spirits of the dead.
▷HISTORY Latin: see LEMUR

lemuroid ('lɛmjʊ,rɔɪd) *or* **lemurine** ('lɛmjʊ,raɪn, -rɪn) ADJECTIVE [1] of, relating to, or belonging to the superfamily *Lemuroidea,* which includes the lemurs and indrises. [2] resembling or closely related to a lemur. ◆ NOUN [3] an animal that resembles or is closely related to a lemur.

Lena ('li:nə; *Russian* 'ljɛnə) NOUN a river in Russia, rising in S Siberia and flowing generally north through the Sakha Republic to the Laptev Sea by an extensive delta: the longest river in Russia. Length: 4271 km (2653 miles).

lend (lɛnd) VERB **lends, lending, lent** (lɛnt). [1] (*tr*) to permit the use of (something) with the expectation of return of the same or an equivalent. [2] to provide (money) temporarily, often at interest. [3] (*intr*) to provide loans, esp as a profession. [4] (*tr*) to impart or contribute (something, esp some abstract quality): *her presence lent beauty.* [5] (*tr*) to provide, esp in order to assist or support: *he lent his skill to the company.* [6] **lend an ear.** to listen. [7] **lend itself.** to possess the right characteristics or qualities for: *the novel lends itself to serialization.* [8] **lend oneself.** to give support, cooperation, etc.
▷HISTORY C15 *lende* (originally the past tense), from Old English *lǣnan,* from *lǣn* LOAN[1]; related to Icelandic *lāna,* Old High German *lēhanōn*
▸ **'lender** NOUN

lender of last resort NOUN the central bank of a country with authority for controlling its banking system.

lending library NOUN [1] Also called (esp US): **circulating library.** the department of a public library providing books for use outside the building. [2] a small commercial library.

lend-lease NOUN (during World War II) the system organized by the US in 1941 by which equipment and services were provided for countries fighting Germany.

length (lɛŋkθ, lɛŋθ) NOUN [1] the linear extent or measurement of something from end to end, usually being the longest dimension or, for something fixed, the longest horizontal dimension. [2] the extent of something from beginning to end, measured in some more or less regular units or intervals: *the book was 600 pages in length.* [3] a specified distance, esp between two positions or locations: *the length of a race.* [4] a period of time, as between specified limits or moments. [5] something of a specified, average, or known size or extent measured in one dimension, often used as a unit of measurement: *a length of cloth.* [6] a piece or section of something narrow and long: *a length of tubing.* [7] the quality, state, or fact of being long rather than short. [8] (*usually plural*) the amount of trouble taken in pursuing or achieving something (esp in the phrase **to great lengths**). [9] (*often plural*) the extreme or limit of action (in phrases such as **to any length(s), to what length(s) would someone go,** etc.). [10] *Prosody, phonetics* the metrical quantity or temporal duration of a vowel or syllable. [11] the distance from one end of a rectangular swimming bath to the other. Compare **width** (sense 4). [12] *Prosody* the quality of a vowel, whether stressed or unstressed, that distinguishes it from another vowel of similar articulatory characteristics. Thus (i:) in English *beat* is of greater length than (ɪ) in English *bit.* [13] *Cricket* the distance from the batsman at which the ball pitches. [14] *Bridge* a holding of four or more cards in a suit. [15] *NZ informal* the general idea; the main purpose. [16] **at length. a** in depth; fully. **b** eventually. **c** for a long time; interminably.
▷HISTORY Old English *lengthu;* related to Middle Dutch *lengede,* Old Norse *lengd*

lengthen ('lɛŋkθən, 'lɛŋθən) VERB to make or become longer.
▸ **'lengthener** NOUN

lengthman ('lɛŋkθmən, 'lɛŋθ-) NOUN, *plural* **-men.** a person whose job it is to maintain a particular length of road or railway line.

lengthways ('lɛŋkθ,weɪz, 'lɛŋθ-) *or* **lengthwise** ADVERB, ADJECTIVE in, according to, or along the direction of length.

lengthy ('lɛŋkθɪ, 'lɛŋθɪ) ADJECTIVE **lengthier, lengthiest.** of relatively great or tiresome extent or duration.
▸ **'lengthily** ADVERB ▸ **'lengthiness** NOUN

lenient ('li:nɪənt) ADJECTIVE [1] showing or characterized by mercy or tolerance. [2] *Archaic* caressing or soothing.
▷HISTORY C17: from Latin *lēnīre* to soothe, from *lēnis* soft
▸ **'leniency** *or* **'lenience** NOUN ▸ **'leniently** ADVERB

Leninabad (*Russian* lɪnina'bat) NOUN the former name (1937–91) of **Khojent.**

Leninakan (*Russian* lɪnina'kan) NOUN the former name (1925–91) of **Kumayri.**

Leningrad ('lɛnɪn,græd; *Russian* lɪnin'grat) NOUN the former name (1937–91) of **Saint Petersburg.**

Leninism ('lɛnɪ,nɪzəm) NOUN [1] the political and economic theories of Vladimir Ilyich Lenin (original surname *Ulyanov;* 1870–1924) the Russian statesman and Marxist theoretician. [2] another name for **Marxism-Leninism.**
▸ **'Leninist** *or* **'Leninite** NOUN, ADJECTIVE

Lenin Peak NOUN a mountain in Tajikistan; the highest peak in the Trans Alai Range. Height: 7134 m (23 406 ft.).

lenis ('li:nɪs) *Phonetics* ◆ ADJECTIVE [1] (of a consonant) articulated with weak muscular tension. ◆ NOUN, *plural* **lenes** ('li:ni:z). [2] a consonant, such as English *b* or *v,* pronounced with weak muscular force. ◆ Compare **fortis.**
▷HISTORY C19: from Latin: gentle

lenitive ('lɛnɪtɪv) ADJECTIVE [1] soothing or alleviating pain or distress. ◆ NOUN [2] *Obsolete* a lenitive drug.
▷HISTORY C16: from Medieval Latin *lēnītīvus,* from Latin *lēnīre* to soothe

lenity ('lɛnɪtɪ) NOUN, *plural* **-ties.** the state or quality of being lenient.
▷HISTORY C16: from Latin *lēnitās* gentleness, from *lēnis* soft

leno ('li:nəʊ) NOUN, *plural* **-nos.** [1] (in textiles) a weave in which the warp yarns are twisted together in pairs between the weft or filling yarns. [2] a fabric of this weave.
▷HISTORY C19: probably from French *linon* lawn, from *lin* flax, from Latin *līnum.* See LINEN

lens (lɛnz) NOUN [1] a piece of glass or other transparent material, used to converge or diverge

transmitted light and form optical images. 2 Also called: **compound lens.** a combination of such lenses for forming images or concentrating a beam of light. 3 a device that diverges or converges a beam of electromagnetic radiation, sound, or particles. See **electron lens.** 4 *Anatomy* See **crystalline lens.** ◆ Related adjective **lenticular.**
▷HISTORY C17: from Latin *lēns* lentil, referring to the similarity of a lens to the shape of a lentil

Lens (lenz; *French* lɑ̃) NOUN an industrial town in N France, in the Pas de Calais department; badly damaged in both World Wars. Pop. (town): 35 278 (1990), with a conurbation of 323 174 (1990).

lens hood NOUN *Photog* an extension piece fixed to a camera lens to shield it from a direct light source.

lent (lɛnt) VERB the past tense and past participle of **lend.**

Lent (lɛnt) NOUN 1 *Christianity* the period of forty weekdays lasting from Ash Wednesday to Holy Saturday, observed as a time of penance and fasting commemorating Jesus' fasting in the wilderness. 2 (*modifier*) falling within or associated with the season before Easter: *Lent observance.* 3 (*plural*) (at Cambridge University) Lent term boat races.
▷HISTORY Old English *lencten, lengten* spring, literally: lengthening (of hours of daylight)

lentamente (ˌlɛntəˈmɛntɪ) ADVERB *Music* to be played slowly.
▷HISTORY C18: Italian, from LENTO

lenten (ˈlɛntən) ADJECTIVE 1 (*often capital*) of or relating to Lent. 2 *Archaic or literary* spare, plain, or meagre: *lenten fare.* 3 *Archaic* cold, austere, or sombre: *a lenten lover.*

lentic (ˈlɛntɪk) ADJECTIVE *Ecology* of, relating to, or inhabiting still water: *a lentic fauna.* Compare **lotic.**
▷HISTORY C20: from Latin *lentus* slow

lenticel (ˈlɛntɪˌsɛl) NOUN any of numerous pores in the stem of a woody plant allowing exchange of gases between the plant and the exterior.
▷HISTORY C19: from New Latin *lenticella,* from Latin *lenticula* diminutive of *lēns* LENTIL
▸**lenticellate** (ˌlɛntɪˈsɛlɪt) ADJECTIVE

lenticle (ˈlɛntɪkᵊl) NOUN *Geology* a lens-shaped layer of mineral or rock embedded in a matrix of different constitution.

lenticular (lɛnˈtɪkjʊlə) *or* **lentiform** (ˈlɛntɪˌfɔːm) ADJECTIVE 1 Also: **lentoid** (ˈlɛntɔɪd). shaped like a biconvex lens. 2 of or concerned with a lens or lenses. 3 shaped like a lentil seed. 4 of or relating to a galaxy with a large central bulge, small disc, but no spiral arms, intermediate in shape between spiral and elliptical galaxies.
▷HISTORY C17: from Latin *lenticulāris* like a LENTIL

lentigo (lɛnˈtaɪgəʊ) NOUN, *plural* **lentigines** (lɛnˈtɪdʒɪˌniːz). a technical name for a **freckle.**
▷HISTORY C14: from Latin, from *lēns* LENTIL
▸**lenˈtiginous** *or* **lenˈtiginose** ADJECTIVE

lentil (ˈlɛntɪl) NOUN 1 a small annual leguminous plant, *Lens culinaris,* of the Mediterranean region and W Asia, having edible brownish convex seeds. 2 any of the seeds of this plant, which are cooked and eaten as a vegetable, in soups, etc.
▷HISTORY C13: from Old French *lentille,* from Latin *lenticula,* diminutive of *lēns* lentil

lentissimo (lɛnˈtɪsɪˌməʊ) ADJECTIVE, ADVERB *Music* to be played very slowly.
▷HISTORY Italian, superlative of *lento* slow

lentivirus (ˈlɛntɪˌvaɪrəs) NOUN any of a group of slowly acting viruses that includes the human immunodeficiency virus (HIV), which causes AIDS.
▷HISTORY C20: from Latin *lentus* slow + VIRUS

lent lily NOUN another name for the **daffodil.**

lento (ˈlɛntəʊ) *Music* ◆ ADJECTIVE, ADVERB 1 to be performed slowly. ◆ NOUN, *plural* **-tos.** 2 a movement or passage performed in this way.
▷HISTORY C18: Italian, from Latin *lentus* slow

Lent term NOUN the spring term at Cambridge University and some other educational establishments.

Lenz's law (ˈlɛntsɪz) NOUN *Physics* the principle that the direction of the current induced in a circuit by a changing magnetic field is such that the magnetic field produced by this current will oppose the original field.
▷HISTORY C19: named after H. F. E. *Lenz* (1804–65), German physicist

Leo[1] (ˈliːəʊ) NOUN a name for a lion, used in children's tales, fables, etc.
▷HISTORY from Latin: lion

Leo[2] (ˈliːəʊ) NOUN, *Latin genitive* **Leonis** (liːˈəʊnɪs). 1 *Astronomy* a zodiacal constellation in the N hemisphere, lying between Cancer and Virgo on the ecliptic, that contains the star Regulus and the radiant of the Leonid meteor shower. 2 *Astrology* **a** Also called: **the Lion.** the fifth sign of the zodiac, symbol ♌, having a fixed fire classification and ruled by the sun. The sun is in this sign between about July 23 and Aug. 22. **b** a person born during a period when the sun is in this sign. ◆ ADJECTIVE 3 *Astrology* born under or characteristic of Leo. ◆ Also (for senses 2b, 3): **Leonian** (liːˈəʊnɪən).

LEO ABBREVIATION FOR low earth orbit.

Leoben (*German* leˈoːbən) NOUN a city in E central Austria, in Styria on the Mur River: lignite mining. Pop.: 28 504 (1991).

Leo Minor NOUN a small faint constellation in the N hemisphere lying near Leo and Ursa Major.

León (*Spanish* leˈɔn) NOUN 1 a region and former kingdom of NW Spain, which united with Castile in 1230. 2 a city of NW Spain: capital of the kingdom of León (10th century). Pop.: 139 809 (1998 est.). 3 a city in central Mexico, in W Guanajuato state: commercial centre of a rich agricultural region. Pop.: 1 019 510 (2000 est.). Official name: **León de los Aldamas** (de los ˈaldamas). 4 a city in W Nicaragua: one of the oldest towns of Central America, founded in 1524; capital of Nicaragua until 1855; university (1812). Pop.: 123 865 (1995).

leone (liːˈəʊnɪ) NOUN the standard monetary unit of Sierra Leone, divided into 100 cents.
▷HISTORY C20: from SIERRA LEONE

Leonid (ˈliːənɪd) NOUN, *plural* **Leonids** *or* **Leonides** (lɪˈɒnɪˌdiːz). any member of a meteor shower that is usually insignificant, but more spectacular every 33 years, and occurs annually in mid-November, appearing to radiate from a point in the constellation Leo.
▷HISTORY C19: from New Latin *Leōnidēs,* from *leō* lion

leonine (ˈliːəˌnaɪn) ADJECTIVE of, characteristic of, or resembling a lion.
▷HISTORY C14: from Latin *leōnīnus,* from *leō* lion

Leonine (ˈliːəˌnaɪn) ADJECTIVE 1 connected with one of the popes called Leo: an epithet applied to. **a** a district of Rome on the right bank of the Tiber fortified by Pope Leo IV (**Leonine City**). **b** certain prayers in the Mass prescribed by Pope Leo XIII (1810–1903; pope 1878–1903). ◆ NOUN 2 Also called: **Leonine verse. a** a type of medieval hexameter or elegiac verse having internal rhyme. **b** a type of English verse with internal rhyme.

leontopodium (lɪˌɒntəˈpəʊdɪəm) NOUN any plant of the Eurasian alpine genus *Leontopodium,* esp *L. alpinum.* See **edelweiss.**
▷HISTORY New Latin, from Greek *leōn* lion + *podion,* diminutive of *pous* foot (from the shape of the flowers)

leopard (ˈlɛpəd) NOUN 1 Also called: **panther.** a large feline mammal, *Panthera pardus,* of forests of Africa and Asia, usually having a tawny yellow coat with black rosette-like spots. 2 any of several similar felines, such as the snow leopard and cheetah. 3 **clouded leopard.** a feline, *Neofelis nebulosa,* of SE Asia and Indonesia with a yellowish-brown coat marked with darker spots and blotches. 4 *Heraldry* a stylized leopard, painted as a lion with the face turned towards the front. 5 the pelt of a leopard.
▷HISTORY C13: from Old French *lepart,* from Late Latin *leōpardus,* from Late Greek *leópardos,* from *leōn* lion + *pardos* PARD[2] (the leopard was thought to be the result of cross-breeding)
▸**ˈleopardess** FEMININE NOUN

leopard lily NOUN a North American lily plant, *Lilium pardalinum,* cultivated for its large orange-red flowers, with brown-spotted petals and long stamens.

leopard moth NOUN a nocturnal European moth, *Zeuzera pyrina,* having white wings and body, both marked with black spots: family *Cossidae.*

leopard's-bane NOUN any of several Eurasian perennial plants of the genus *Doronicum,* esp *D. plantagineum,* having clusters of yellow flowers: family *Asteraceae* (composites).

Léopoldville (ˈlɪəpəʊldˌvɪl; *French* leɔpɔlvil) NOUN the former name (until 1966) of **Kinshasa.**

leotard (ˈlɪəˌtɑːd) NOUN 1 a tight-fitting garment covering the body from the shoulders down to the thighs and worn by acrobats, ballet dancers, etc. 2 (*plural*) *US and Canadian* another name for **tights** (sense 1b).
▷HISTORY C19: named after Jules *Léotard,* French acrobat

Lepanto NOUN 1 (lɪˈpæntəʊ) a port in W Greece, between the Gulfs of Corinth and Patras: scene of a naval battle (1571) in which the Turkish fleet was defeated by the fleets of the Holy League. Pop.: 8170 (latest est.). Greek name: **Návpaktos.** 2 **Gulf of.** another name for the (Gulf of) **Corinth.**

Lepaya (lɪˈpɑːjə) NOUN a variant spelling of **Liepāja.**

Lepcha (ˈlɛptʃə) NOUN 1 (*plural* **-cha** *or* **-chas**) a member of a Mongoloid people of Sikkim. 2 the language of this people, belonging to the Tibeto-Burman branch of the Sino-Tibetan family. ◆ ADJECTIVE 3 of or relating to this people or their language.

leper (ˈlɛpə) NOUN 1 a person who has leprosy. 2 a person who is ignored or despised.
▷HISTORY C14: via Late Latin from Greek *lepra,* noun use of *lepros* scaly, from *lepein* to peel

lepido- *or before a vowel* **lepid-** COMBINING FORM scale or scaly: *lepidopterous.*
▷HISTORY from Greek *lepis* scale; see LEPER

lepidolite (lɪˈpɪdəˌlaɪt, ˈlɛpɪdəˌlaɪt) NOUN a lilac, pink, or greyish mica consisting of a hydrous silicate of lithium, potassium, aluminium, and fluorine, containing rubidium as an impurity: a source of lithium and rubidium. Formula: $K_2Li_3Al_4Si_7O_{21}(OH,F)_3$.

lepidopteran (ˌlɛpɪˈdɒptərən) NOUN, *plural* **-terans** *or* **-tera** (-tərə). *also* **lepidopteron.** 1 any of numerous insects of the order *Lepidoptera,* typically having two pairs of wings covered with fragile scales, mouthparts specialized as a suctorial proboscis, and caterpillars as larvae: comprises the butterflies and moths. ◆ ADJECTIVE *also* **lepidopterous.** 2 of, relating to, or belonging to the order *Lepidoptera.*
▷HISTORY C19: from New Latin *lepidoptera,* from LEPIDO- + Greek *pteron* wing

lepidopterist (ˌlɛpɪˈdɒptərɪst) NOUN a person who studies or collects moths and butterflies.

lepidosiren (ˌlɛpɪdəʊˈsaɪərən) NOUN a South American lungfish, *Lepidosiren paradoxa,* having an eel-shaped body and whiplike paired fins.

lepidote (ˈlɛpɪˌdəʊt) ADJECTIVE *Biology* covered with scales, scaly leaves, or spots.
▷HISTORY C19: via New Latin *lepidōtus,* from Greek, from *lepis* scale

Lepontine Alps (lɪˈpɒntaɪn) PLURAL NOUN a range of the S central Alps, in S Switzerland and N Italy. Highest peak: Monte Leone, 3553 m (11 657 ft.).

leporid (ˈlɛpərɪd) ADJECTIVE 1 of, relating to, or belonging to the *Leporidae,* a family of lagomorph mammals having long ears and limbs and a short tail: includes rabbits and hares. ◆ NOUN 2 any animal belonging to the family *Leporidae.*
▷HISTORY C19: from Latin *lepus* hare

leporine (ˈlɛpəˌraɪn) ADJECTIVE of, relating to, or resembling a hare.
▷HISTORY C17: from Latin *leporīnus,* from *lepus* hare

LEPRA (ˈlɛprə) NOUN ACRONYM FOR Leprosy Relief Association.

leprechaun (ˈlɛprəˌkɔːn) NOUN (in Irish folklore) a mischievous elf, often believed to have a treasure hoard.
▷HISTORY C17: from Irish Gaelic *leipreachān,* from Middle Irish *lūchorpān,* from *lū* small + *corp* body, from Latin *corpus* body

leprosarium (ˌlɛprəˈsɛərɪəm) NOUN, *plural* **-ia** (-ɪə). a hospital or other centre for the treatment or care of lepers.
▷HISTORY C20: from Medieval Latin: see LEPER

leprose (ˈlɛprəʊs, -rəʊz) ADJECTIVE *Biology* having or denoting a whitish scurfy surface.

leprosy (ˈlɛprəsɪ) NOUN *Pathol* a chronic infectious disease occurring mainly in tropical and subtropical regions, characterized by the formation of painful inflamed nodules beneath the skin and disfigurement and wasting of affected parts, caused

by the bacillus *Mycobacterium leprae*. Also called: **Hansen's disease.**
▷HISTORY C16: from LEPROUS + -Y[3]

leprous ('lɛprəs) ADJECTIVE [1] having leprosy. [2] relating to or resembling leprosy. [3] *Biology* a less common word for **leprose.**
▷HISTORY C13: from Old French, from Late Latin *leprosus,* from *lepra* LEPER
▸'**leprously** ADVERB ▸'**leprousness** NOUN

-lepsy *or sometimes* **-lepsia** NOUN COMBINING FORM indicating a seizure or attack: *catalepsy.*
▷HISTORY from New Latin *-lepsia,* from Greek, from *lēpsis* a seizure, from *lambanein* to seize
▸**-leptic** ADJECTIVE COMBINING FORM

leptin ('lɛptɪn) NOUN a protein, produced by fat cells in the body, that acts on the brain to regulate the amount of additional fat laid down in the body.
▷HISTORY C20: from LEPTO- + -IN

lepto- *or before a vowel* **lept-** COMBINING FORM fine, slender, or slight: *leptosome.*
▷HISTORY from Greek *leptos* thin, literally: peeled, from *lepein* to peel

leptocephalic (ˌlɛptəʊsɪ'fælɪk) *or* **leptocephalous** (ˌlɛptəʊ'sɛfələs) ADJECTIVE having a narrow skull.

leptocephalus (ˌlɛptəʊ'sɛfələs) NOUN, *plural* **-li** (-ˌlaɪ). the slender transparent oceanic larva of eels of the genus *Anguilla* that migrates from its hatching ground in the Caribbean to European freshwater habitats.

leptocercal (ˌlɛptəʊ'sɜːk[ə]l) ADJECTIVE *Zoology* having a long thin tail.
▷HISTORY from LEPTO- + Greek *kerkos* tail

leptodactylous (ˌlɛptəʊ'dæktɪləs) ADJECTIVE *Zoology* having slender digits.

leptokurtic (ˌlɛptəʊ'kɜːtɪk) ADJECTIVE *Statistics* (of a distribution) having kurtosis B_2 greater than 3, more heavily concentrated about the mean than a normal distribution. Compare **platykurtic, mesokurtic.**
▷HISTORY C20: from LEPTO- + Greek *kurtos* arched, bulging + -IC

lepton[1] ('lɛptɒn) NOUN, *plural* **-ta** (-tə). [1] a former Greek monetary unit worth one hundredth of a drachma. [2] a small coin of ancient Greece.
▷HISTORY from Greek *lepton* (*nomisma*) small (coin)

lepton[2] ('lɛptɒn) NOUN *Physics* any of a group of elementary particles and their antiparticles, such as an electron, muon, or neutrino, that participate in electromagnetic and weak interactions and have a half-integral spin.
▷HISTORY C20: from LEPTO- + -ON
▸**lep'tonic** ADJECTIVE

lepton number NOUN *Physics* a quantum number describing the behaviour of elementary particles, equal to the number of leptons present minus the number of antileptons. It is thought to be conserved in all processes. Symbol: l.

leptophyllous (ˌlɛptəʊ'fɪləs) ADJECTIVE (of plants) having long slender leaves.

leptorrhine ('lɛptərɪn) ADJECTIVE another word for **catarrhine** (sense 2).

leptosome ('lɛptəˌsəʊm) NOUN a person with a small bodily frame and a slender physique.
▸ˌ**lepto'somic** *or* **leptosomatic** (ˌlɛptəʊsə'mætɪk) ADJECTIVE

leptospirosis (ˌlɛptəʊspaɪ'rəʊsɪs) NOUN any of several infectious diseases caused by spirochaete bacteria of the genus *Leptospira,* transmitted to man by animals and characterized by jaundice, meningitis, and kidney failure. Also called: **Weil's disease.**
▷HISTORY C20: from New Latin *Leptospira* (LEPTO- + Greek *speira* coil + -OSIS)

leptosporangiate (ˌlɛptəʊspə'rændʒɪɪt) ADJECTIVE (of ferns) having each sporangium developing from a single cell, rather than from a group, and normally with specialized explosive spore dispersal. ◆ Compare **eusporangiate.**

leptotene ('lɛptəʊˌtiːn) NOUN the first stage of the prophase of meiosis during which the nuclear material becomes resolved into slender single-stranded chromosomes.
▷HISTORY C20: from LEPTO- + *-tene,* from Greek *tainia* band, filament

Lepus ('lɛpəs, 'liː-) NOUN, *Latin genitive* **Leporis** ('lɛpərɪs). a small constellation in the S hemisphere lying between Orion and Columba.
▷HISTORY New Latin, from Latin: hare

lequear (lə'kwɪə) NOUN another name for **lacunar** (sense 1).

Lérida (*Spanish* 'leriða) NOUN a city in NE Spain, in Catalonia: commercial centre of an agricultural region. Pop.: 112 207 (1998 est.).

Lerwick ('lɜːwɪk) NOUN a town in Shetland, administrative centre of the island authority of Shetland, on the island of Mainland: the most northerly town in the British Isles; knitwear, oil refining. Pop.: 7336 (1991 est.).

lesbian ('lɛzbɪən) NOUN [1] a female homosexual. ◆ ADJECTIVE [2] of or characteristic of lesbians.
▷HISTORY C19: from the homosexuality attributed to Sappho (6th century B.C.), poetess of Lesbos
▸'**lesbianism** NOUN

Lesbian ('lɛzbɪən) NOUN [1] a native or inhabitant of Lesbos. [2] the Aeolic dialect of Ancient Greek spoken in Lesbos. ◆ ADJECTIVE [3] of or relating to Lesbos. [4] of or relating to the poetry of Lesbos, esp that of Sappho.

Lesbos ('lɛzbɒs) NOUN an island in the E Aegean, off the NW coast of Turkey: a centre of lyric poetry, led by Alcaeus and Sappho (6th century B.C.); annexed to Greece in 1913. Chief town: Mytilene. Pop.: 105 082 (1991). Area: 1630 sq. km (630 sq. miles). Modern Greek name: **Lésvos.** Former name: **Mytilene.**

Les Cayes (leɪ 'keɪ; *French* le kaj) NOUN a port in SW Haiti, on the S Tiburon Peninsula. Pop.: 45 904 (1992). Also called: **Cayes.** Former name: **Aux Cayes.**

lese-majesty ('liːz'mædʒɪstɪ) NOUN [1] any of various offences committed against the sovereign power in a state; treason. [2] an attack on authority or position.
▷HISTORY C16: from French *lèse majesté,* from Latin *laesa mājestās* wounded majesty

lesion ('liːʒən) NOUN [1] any structural change in a bodily part resulting from injury or disease. [2] an injury or wound.
▷HISTORY C15: via Old French from Late Latin *laesiō* injury, from Latin *laedere* to hurt

Lesotho (lɪ'suːtuː, lə'səʊtəʊ) NOUN a kingdom in southern Africa, forming an enclave in the Republic of South Africa: annexed to British Cape Colony in 1871; made a protectorate in 1884; gained independence in 1966; a member of the Commonwealth. It is generally mountainous, with temperate grasslands throughout. Languages: Sesotho and English. Religion: Christian majority. Currency: loti. Capital: Maseru. Pop.: 2 177 000 (2001 est.). Area: 30 344 sq. km (11 716 sq. miles). Former name (1884–1966): **Basutoland.**

less (lɛs) DETERMINER [1] **a** the comparative of **little** (sense 1): *less sugar; less spirit than before.* **b** (*as pronoun; functioning as singular or plural*): *she has less than she needs; the less you eat, the less you want.* [2] (usually preceded by *no*) lower in rank or importance: *no less a man than the president; St. James the Less.* [3] **no less.** *Informal* used to indicate surprise or admiration, often sarcastic, at the preceding statement: *she says she's been to Italy, no less.* [4] **less of.** to a smaller extent or degree: *we see less of John these days; less of a success than I'd hoped.* ◆ ADVERB [5] the comparative of **little** (sense 1): *she walks less than she should; less quickly; less beautiful.* [6] **much** *or* **still less.** used to reinforce a negative: *we don't like it, still less enjoy it.* [7] **think less of.** to have a lower opinion of. ◆ PREPOSITION [8] subtracting; minus: *three weeks less a day.*
▷HISTORY Old English *lǣssa* (adj), *lǣs* (adv, n)

> **Language note** *Less* should not be confused with *fewer. Less* refers strictly only to quantity and not to number: *there is less water than before. Fewer* means smaller in number: *there are fewer people than before.*

-less SUFFIX FORMING ADJECTIVES [1] without; lacking: *speechless.* [2] not able to (do something) or not able to be (done, performed, etc.): *countless.*
▷HISTORY Old English *-lās,* from *lēas* lacking

lessee (lɛ'siː) NOUN a person to whom a lease is granted; a tenant under a lease.
▷HISTORY C15: via Anglo-French from Old French *lessé,* from *lesser* to LEASE[1]
▸**les'seeship** NOUN

lessen ('lɛs[ə]n) VERB [1] to make or become less. [2] (*tr*) to make little of.

lesser ('lɛsə) ADJECTIVE not as great in quantity, size, or worth.

Lesser Antilles PLURAL NOUN **the.** a group of islands in the Caribbean, including the Leeward Islands, the Windward Islands, Barbados, and the Netherlands Antilles. Also called: **Caribbees.**

lesser celandine NOUN a Eurasian ranunculaceous plant, *Ranunculus ficaria,* having yellow flowers and heart-shaped leaves. Also called: **pilewort.** Compare **greater celandine.**

lesser panda NOUN See **panda** (sense 2).

Lesser Sunda Islands PLURAL NOUN the former name of **Nusa Tenggara.**

lesson ('lɛs[ə]n) NOUN [1] **a** a unit, or single period of instruction in a subject; class: *an hour-long music lesson.* **b** the content of such a unit. [2] material assigned for individual study. [3] something from which useful knowledge or principles can be learned; example. [4] the principles, knowledge, etc., gained. [5] a reprimand or punishment intended to correct. [6] a portion of Scripture appointed to be read at divine service. ◆ VERB [7] (*tr*) *Rare* to censure or punish.
▷HISTORY C13: from Old French *leçon,* from Latin *lēctiō,* from *legere* to read

lessor ('lɛsɔː, lɛ'sɔː) NOUN a person who grants a lease of property.

lest (lɛst) CONJUNCTION (*subordinating;* takes *should* or a subjunctive verb) [1] so as to prevent any possibility that: *he fled the country lest he be captured and imprisoned.* [2] (*after verbs or phrases expressing fear, worry, anxiety, etc.*) for fear that; in case: *he was alarmed lest she should find out.*
▷HISTORY Old English *thē lǣste,* earlier *thȳ lǣs the,* literally: whereby less that

Lésvos ('lɛzvɔs) NOUN transliteration of the Modern Greek name for **Lesbos.**

let[1] (lɛt) VERB **lets, letting, let.** (*tr;* usually takes an infinitive without *to* or an implied infinitive) [1] to permit; allow: *she lets him roam around.* [2] (*imperative or dependent imperative*) **a** used as an auxiliary to express a request, proposal, or command, or to convey a warning or threat: *let's get on; just let me catch you here again!* **b** (in mathematical or philosophical discourse) used as an auxiliary to express an assumption or hypothesis: *let "a" equal "b".* **c** used as an auxiliary to express resigned acceptance of the inevitable: *let the worst happen.* [3] **a** to allow the occupation of (accommodation) in return for rent. **b** to assign (a contract for work). [4] to allow or cause the movement of (something) in a specified direction: *to let air out of a tyre.* [5] *Irish informal* to utter: *to let a cry.* [6] **let alone.** (*conjunction*) much less; not to mention: *I can't afford wine, let alone champagne.* [7] **let** *or* **leave alone** *or* **be.** to refrain from annoying or interfering with: *let the poor cat alone.* [8] **let go.** See **go**[1] (sense 59). [9] **let loose. a** to set free. **b** *Informal* to make (a sound or remark) suddenly: *he let loose a hollow laugh.* **c** *Informal* to discharge (rounds) from a gun or guns: *they let loose a couple of rounds of ammunition.* ◆ NOUN [10] *Brit* the act of letting property or accommodation: *the majority of new lets are covered by the rent regulations.* ◆ See also **let down, let in, let into, let off, let on, let out, let through, let up.**
▷HISTORY Old English *lǣtan* to permit; related to Gothic *lētan,* German *lassen*

let[2] (lɛt) NOUN [1] an impediment or obstruction (esp in the phrase **without let or hindrance**). [2] *Tennis, squash* **a** a minor infringement or obstruction of the ball, requiring a point to be replayed. **b** the point so replayed. ◆ VERB **lets, letting, letted** *or* **let.** [3] (*tr*) *Archaic* to hinder; impede.
▷HISTORY Old English *lettan* to hinder, from *læt* LATE; related to Old Norse *letja*

-let SUFFIX FORMING NOUNS [1] small or lesser: *booklet; starlet.* [2] an article of attire or ornament worn on a specified part of the body: *anklet.*
▷HISTORY from Old French *-elet,* from Latin *-āle,* neuter of adj suffix *-ālis* or from Latin *-ellus,* diminutive suffix

letch (lɛtʃ) VERB, NOUN a variant spelling of **lech.**
▷HISTORY C18: perhaps back formation from LECHER

Letchworth ('lɛtʃwəθ, -ˌwɜːθ) NOUN a town in SE England, in N Hertfordshire: the first garden city in

Great Britain (founded in 1903). Pop.: 31 418 (1991).

let down VERB (*tr, mainly adverb*) 1 (*also preposition*) to lower. 2 to fail to fulfil the expectations of (a person); disappoint. 3 to undo, shorten, and resew (the hem) so as to lengthen (a dress, skirt, etc.). 4 to untie (long hair that is bound up) and allow to fall loose. 5 to deflate: *to let down a tyre.* ◆ NOUN **letdown.** 6 a disappointment. 7 the gliding descent of an aircraft in preparation for landing. 8 the release of milk from the mammary glands following stimulation by the hormone oxytocin.

lethal ('li:θəl) ADJECTIVE 1 able to cause or causing death. 2 of or suggestive of death.
▷HISTORY C16: from Latin *lēthālis,* from *lētum* death
▸**lethality** (li:'θælɪtɪ) NOUN ▸**'lethally** ADVERB

lethal dose NOUN the amount of a drug or other agent that if administered to an animal or human will prove fatal. Abbreviation: **LD.** See also **median lethal dose.**

lethargy ('lɛθədʒɪ) NOUN, *plural* **-gies.** 1 sluggishness, slowness, or dullness. 2 an abnormal lack of energy, esp as the result of a disease.
▷HISTORY C14: from Late Latin *lēthargia,* from Greek *lēthargos* drowsy, from *lēthē* forgetfulness
▸**lethargic** (lɪ'θɑ:dʒɪk) *or* **le'thargical** ADJECTIVE
▸**le'thargically** ADVERB

Lethbridge ('lɛθbrɪdʒ) NOUN a city in Canada, in S Alberta: coal-mining. Pop.: 60 974 (1991).

Lethe ('li:θɪ) NOUN 1 *Greek myth* a river in Hades that caused forgetfulness in those who drank its waters. 2 forgetfulness.
▷HISTORY C16: via Latin from Greek, from *lēthē* oblivion
▸**Lethean** (lɪ'θi:ən) ADJECTIVE

let in VERB (*tr, adverb*) 1 to allow to enter. 2 **let in for.** to involve (oneself or another) in (something more than is expected): *he let himself in for a lot of extra work.* 3 **let in on.** to allow (someone) to know about or participate in.

let into VERB (*tr, preposition*) 1 to allow to enter. 2 to put into the surface of: *to let a pipe into the wall.* 3 to allow (someone) to share (a secret).

Leto ('li:təʊ) NOUN the mother by Zeus of Apollo and Artemis. Roman name: **Latona.**

let off VERB (*tr, mainly adverb*) 1 (*also preposition*) to allow to disembark or leave. 2 to explode or fire (a bomb, gun, etc.). 3 (*also preposition*) to excuse from (work or other responsibilities): *I'll let you off for a week.* 4 to allow to get away without the expected punishment, work, etc. 5 to let (accommodation) in portions. 6 to release (liquid, air, etc.). 7 **let off steam.** See **steam** (sense 6). 8 **let (someone) off with.** to give (a light punishment) to (someone).

let on VERB (*adverb; when tr, takes a clause as object*) *Informal* 1 to allow (something, such as a secret) to be known; reveal: *he never let on that he was married.* 2 (*tr*) to cause or encourage to be believed; pretend.

let out VERB (*adverb, mainly tr*) 1 to give vent to; emit: *to let out a howl.* 2 to allow to go or run free; release. 3 (*may take a clause as object*) to reveal (a secret). 4 to make available to tenants, hirers, or contractors. 5 to permit to flow out: *to let air out of the tyres.* 6 to make (a garment) larger, as by unpicking (the seams) and sewing nearer the outer edge. ◆ NOUN **let-out.** 7 a chance to escape.

LETS (lɛts) NOUN ACRONYM FOR Local Exchange and Trading System: an economic system in which members of a community exchange goods and services using a cashless local currency.

let's (lɛts) CONTRACTION OF let us: used to express a suggestion, command, etc., by the speaker to himself and his hearers.

Lett (lɛt) NOUN another name for a **Latvian.**

letter ('lɛtə) NOUN 1 any of a set of conventional symbols used in writing or printing a language, each symbol being associated with a group of phonetic values in the language; character of the alphabet. 2 a written or printed communication addressed to a person, company, etc., usually sent by post in an envelope. Related adjective: **epistolary.** 3 (often preceded by *the*) the strict legalistic or pedantic interpretation of the meaning of an agreement, document, etc.; exact wording as distinct from actual intention (esp in the phrase **the letter of the law**). Compare **spirit**[1] (sense 10). 4 *Printing, archaic* a style of typeface: *a fancy letter.* 5 **to the letter. a** following the literal interpretation or wording exactly. **b** attending to every detail. ◆ VERB 6 to write or mark letters on (a sign, etc.), esp by hand. 7 (*tr*) to set down or print using letters. ◆ See also **letters.**
▷HISTORY C13: from Old French *lettre,* from Latin *littera* letter of the alphabet
▸**'letterer** NOUN

letter bomb NOUN a thin explosive device inside an envelope, detonated when the envelope is opened.

letter box NOUN *Chiefly Brit* 1 **a** a slot, usually covered with a hinged flap, through which letters, etc. are delivered to a building. **b** a private box into which letters, etc., are delivered. 2 Also called: **postbox.** a public box into which letters, etc., are put for collection and delivery.

letterboxing ('lɛtə,bɒksɪŋ) NOUN a method of formatting film that enables all of a wide-screen film to be transmitted on a television screen, resulting in a blank strip of screen above and below the picture.

letter card NOUN 1 a card, usually one on which the postage is prepaid, that is sealed by being folded in half so that its gummed edges come into contact with each other. 2 a long card consisting of a number of postcard views, with space for writing a letter on the backs, that is folded like a concertina for posting.

lettered ('lɛtəd) ADJECTIVE 1 well educated in literature, the arts, etc. 2 literate. 3 of or characterized by learning or culture. 4 printed or marked with letters.

letterhead ('lɛtə,hɛd) NOUN a sheet of paper printed with one's address, name, etc., for writing a letter on.

letter-high ADJECTIVE another term for **type-high.**

lettering ('lɛtərɪŋ) NOUN 1 the act, art, or technique of inscribing letters on to something. 2 the letters so inscribed.

letter of advice NOUN a commercial letter giving a specific notification, such as the consignment of goods.

letter of attorney NOUN a less common term for **power of attorney.**

letter of credit NOUN 1 a letter issued by a bank entitling the bearer to draw funds up to a specified maximum from that bank or its agencies. 2 a letter addressed by a bank instructing the addressee to allow the person named to draw a specified sum on the credit of the addressor bank.

letter of intent NOUN a letter indicating that the writer has the serious intention of doing something, such as signing a contract in the circumstances specified. It does not constitute either a promise or a contract.

letter of introduction NOUN a letter given by one person to another, as an introduction to a third party.

letter of marque *or* **letters of marque** NOUN 1 a licence granted by a state to a private citizen to arm a ship and seize merchant vessels of another nation. 2 a similar licence issued by a nation allowing a private citizen to seize goods or citizens of another nation. ◆ Also called: **letter of marque and reprisal.**

letter-perfect ADJECTIVE another term (esp in the US) for **word-perfect.**

letterpress ('lɛtə,prɛs) NOUN 1 **a** a method of printing in which ink is transferred from raised surfaces to paper by pressure; relief printing. **b** matter so printed. 2 text matter as distinct from illustrations.

letter-quality printing NOUN *Computing* high-quality output in printed form from a printer linked to a word processor. Compare **draft-quality printing.**

letters ('lɛtəz) NOUN (*functioning as plural or singular*) 1 literary knowledge, ability, or learning: *a man of letters.* 2 literary culture in general. 3 an official title, degree, etc., indicated by an abbreviation: *letters after one's name.*

letterset ('lɛtə,sɛt) NOUN a method of rotary printing in which ink is transferred from raised surfaces to paper via a rubber-covered cylinder.
▷HISTORY C20: from LETTER(PRESS) + (OFF)SET

letters of administration PLURAL NOUN *Law* a formal document nominating a specified person to take over, administer, and dispose of an estate when there is no executor to carry out the testator's will.

letters of credence *or* **letters credential** PLURAL NOUN a formal document accrediting a diplomatic officer to a foreign court or government.

letters patent PLURAL NOUN See **patent** (sense 1).

let through VERB (*tr*) to allow to pass (through): *the invalid was let through to the front of the queue.*

Lettish ('lɛtɪʃ) NOUN, ADJECTIVE another word for **Latvian.**

lettre de cachet *French* (lɛtrə də kaʃɛ) NOUN, *plural* **lettres de cachet** (lɛtrə də kaʃɛ). *French history* a letter under the sovereign's seal, often authorizing imprisonment without trial.
▷HISTORY literally: letter with a seal

lettuce ('lɛtɪs) NOUN 1 any of various plants of the genus *Lactuca,* esp *L. sativa,* which is cultivated in many varieties for its large edible leaves: family *Asteraceae* (composites). 2 the leaves of any of these varieties, which are eaten in salads. 3 any of various plants that resemble true lettuce, such as lamb's lettuce and sea lettuce.
▷HISTORY C13: probably from Old French *laitues,* pl of *laitue,* from Latin *lactūca,* from *lac-* milk, because of its milky juice

let up VERB (*intr, adverb*) 1 to diminish, slacken, or stop. 2 (foll by *on*) *Informal* to be less harsh (towards someone). ◆ NOUN **let-up.** 3 *Informal* a lessening or abatement.

leu ('leɪu:) NOUN, *plural* **lei** (leɪ). the standard monetary unit of Romania and Moldova, divided into 100 bani.
▷HISTORY from Romanian: lion

Leucas ('lu:kəs) NOUN a variant spelling of **Leukas.**

leucine ('lu:si:n) *or* **leucin** ('lu:sɪn) NOUN an essential amino acid found in many proteins.

leucite ('lu:saɪt) NOUN a grey or white mineral consisting of potassium aluminium silicate: a source of potash for fertilizers and of aluminium. Formula: $KAlSi_2O_6$.
▸**leucitic** (lu:'sɪtɪk) ADJECTIVE

leuco-, leuko-, *or before a vowel* **leuc-, leuk-** COMBINING FORM white or lacking colour: *leucocyte; leucorrhoea; leukaemia.*
▷HISTORY from Greek *leukos* white

leuco base ('lu:kəʊ) NOUN a colourless compound formed by reducing a dye so that the original dye can be regenerated by oxidation.

leucoblast *or esp US* **leukoblast** ('lu:kəʊ,blɑ:st) NOUN an immature leucocyte.

leucocratic (,lu:kə'krætɪk) ADJECTIVE (of igneous rocks) light-coloured because of a low content of ferromagnesian minerals.
▷HISTORY C20: from German *leukokrat,* from LEUCO- + Greek *kratein* to rule

leucocyte *or esp US* **leukocyte** ('lu:kə,saɪt) NOUN any of the various large unpigmented cells in the blood of vertebrates. Also called: **white blood cell, white (blood) corpuscle.** See also **lymphocyte, granulocyte, monocyte.**
▸**leucocytic** *or (esp US)* **leukocytic** (,lu:kə'sɪtɪk) ADJECTIVE

leucocytosis *or esp US* **leukocytosis** (,lu:kəʊsaɪ'təʊsɪs) NOUN a gross increase in the number of white blood cells in the blood, usually as a response to an infection.
▸**leucocytotic** *or (esp US)* **leukocytotic** (,lu:kəʊsaɪ'tɒtɪk) ADJECTIVE

leucodepleted ('lu:kəʊdɪ,pli:tɪd) ADJECTIVE of or denoting blood from which the white cells have been removed.

leucoderma *or esp US* **leukoderma** (,lu:kəʊ'dɜ:mə) NOUN any area of skin that is white from congenital (**albinism**; see **albino**) or acquired absence or loss of melanin pigmentation. Also called: **vitiligo.**
▸**,leuco'dermal** *or* **,leuco'dermic** *or (esp US)* **,leuko'dermal** *or* **,leuko'dermic** ADJECTIVE

leucoma (luːˈkəʊmə) NOUN *Pathol* a white opaque scar of the cornea.

leucomaine (ˈluːkəˌmeɪn) NOUN *Biochem* any of a group of toxic amines produced during animal metabolism.
▷HISTORY C20: from LEUCO- + *-maine,* as in *ptomaine*

leucopenia *or esp US* **leukopenia** (ˌluːkəʊˈpiːnɪə) NOUN *Pathol* an abnormal reduction in the number of white blood cells in the blood, characteristic of certain diseases.
▷HISTORY C19: from LEUCO- + Greek *penia* poverty
▸ˌ**leucoˈpenic** *or (esp US)* ˌ**leukoˈpenic** ADJECTIVE

leucoplast (ˈluːkəˌplæst) *or* **leucoplastid** NOUN any of the small colourless bodies occurring in the cytoplasm of plant cells and used for storing food material, esp starch.

leucopoiesis *or esp US* **leukopoiesis** (ˌluːkəʊpɔɪˈiːsɪs) NOUN *Physiol* formation of leucocytes in the body. Also called: **leucocytopoiesis.** ▸**leucopoietic** *or (esp US)* **leukopoietic** (ˌluːkəʊpɔɪˈɛtɪk) ADJECTIVE

leucorrhoea *or esp US* **leukorrhea** (ˌluːkəˈriːə) NOUN *Pathol* a white or yellowish discharge of mucous material from the vagina, often an indication of infection.
▸ˌ**leucorˈrhoeal** *or (esp US)* ˌ**leukorˈrheal** ADJECTIVE

leucotomy (luːˈkɒtəmɪ) NOUN the surgical operation of cutting some of the nerve fibres in the frontal lobes of the brain for treating intractable mental disorders. See also **lobotomy.**
▷HISTORY C20: from LEUCO- (with reference to the white brain tissue) + -TOMY

Leuctra (ˈluːktrə) NOUN an ancient town in Greece southwest of Thebes in Boeotia: site of a victory of Thebes over Sparta (371 B.C.), which marked the end of Spartan military supremacy in Greece.

leukaemia *or esp US* **leukemia** (luːˈkiːmɪə) NOUN an acute or chronic disease characterized by a gross proliferation of leucocytes, which crowd into the bone marrow, spleen, lymph nodes, etc., and suppress the blood-forming apparatus.
▷HISTORY C19: from LEUCO- + Greek *haima* blood

Leukas *or* **Leucas** (ˈluːkəs) NOUN another name for **Levkás.**

leuko- COMBINING FORM a variant of **leuco-.**

leukotriene (ˌluːkəʊˈtraɪiːn) NOUN one of a class of products of metabolic conversion of arachidonic acid; the active constituents of slow-reacting substance, responsible for bronchial constriction, contraction of smooth muscle, and inflammatory processes.
▷HISTORY C20: from *leukocyte,* in which they were discovered + *triene* from the conjugated triene unit that they contain

Leuven (ˈløːvə) NOUN the Flemish name for **Louvain.**

lev (lɛf) NOUN, *plural* **leva** (ˈlɛvə). the standard monetary unit of Bulgaria, divided into 100 stotinki.
▷HISTORY from Bulgarian: lion

Lev. *Bible* ABBREVIATION FOR Leviticus.

Levalloisian (ˌlɛvəˈlɔɪzɪən) *or* **Levallois** (ləˈvælwɑː) ADJECTIVE of or relating to a Lower Palaeolithic culture in W Europe, characterized by a method of flaking flint tools so that one side of the core is flat and the other domed.

levant[1] (lɪˈvænt) NOUN a type of leather made from the skins of goats, sheep, or seals, having a pattern of irregular creases.
▷HISTORY C19: shortened from *Levant morocco* (type of leather)

levant[2] (lɪˈvænt) VERB *(intr) Brit* to bolt or abscond, esp to avoid paying debts.
▷HISTORY C18: perhaps from Spanish *levantar (el campo)* to break (camp)

Levant (lɪˈvænt) NOUN **the.** a former name for the area of the E Mediterranean now occupied by Lebanon, Syria, and Israel.
▷HISTORY C15: from Old French, from the present participle of *lever* to raise (referring to the rising of the sun in the east), from Latin *levāre*

levanter[1] (lɪˈvæntə) NOUN *(sometimes capital)* 1 an easterly wind in the W Mediterranean area, esp in the late summer. 2 an inhabitant of the Levant.

levanter[2] (lɪˈvæntə) NOUN *Brit* a person who bolts or absconds.

levantine (ˈlɛvənˌtaɪn) NOUN a cloth of twilled silk.

Levantine (ˈlɛvənˌtaɪn) ADJECTIVE 1 of or relating to the Levant. ◆ NOUN 2 (esp formerly) an inhabitant of the Levant.

levator (lɪˈveɪtə, -tɔː) NOUN 1 *Anatomy* any of various muscles that raise a part of the body. 2 *Surgery* an instrument for elevating a part or structure.
▷HISTORY C17: New Latin, from Latin *levāre* to raise

levee[1] (ˈlɛvɪ) NOUN *US* 1 an embankment alongside a river, produced naturally by sedimentation or constructed by man to prevent flooding. 2 an embankment that surrounds a field that is to be irrigated. 3 a landing place on a river; quay.
▷HISTORY C18: from French, from Medieval Latin *levāta,* from Latin *levāre* to raise

levee[2] (ˈlɛvɪ, ˈlɛveɪ) NOUN 1 a formal reception held by a sovereign just after rising from bed. 2 (in Britain) a public court reception for men, held in the early afternoon.
▷HISTORY C17: from French, variant of *lever* a rising, from Latin *levāre* to raise

level (ˈlɛvᵊl) ADJECTIVE 1 on a horizontal plane. 2 having a surface of completely equal height. 3 being of the same height as something else. 4 (of quantities to be measured, as in recipes) even with the top of the cup, spoon, etc. 5 equal to or even with (something or someone else). 6 not having or showing inconsistency or irregularities. 7 Also: **level-headed.** even-tempered; steady. ◆ VERB **-els, -elling, -elled** *or US* **-els, -eling, -eled.** 8 *(tr; sometimes foll by off)* to make (a surface) horizontal, level, or even. 9 to make (two or more people or things) equal, as in position or status. 10 *(tr)* to raze to the ground. 11 *(tr)* to knock (a person) down by or as if by a blow. 12 *(tr)* to direct (a gaze, criticism, etc.) emphatically at someone. 13 *(intr; often foll by with) Informal* to be straightforward and frank. 14 *(intr; foll by off or out)* to manoeuvre an aircraft into a horizontal flight path after a dive, climb, or glide. 15 (often foll by *at*) to aim (a weapon) horizontally. 16 *Surveying* to determine the elevation of a section of (land), sighting through a levelling instrument to a staff at successive pairs or points. ◆ NOUN 17 a horizontal datum line or plane. 18 a device, such as a spirit level, for determining whether a surface is horizontal. 19 a surveying instrument consisting basically of a telescope with a spirit level attached, used for measuring relative heights of land. See **Abney level, dumpy level.** 20 a reading of the difference in elevation of two points taken with such an instrument. 21 position or status in a scale of values. 22 amount or degree of progress; stage. 23 a specified vertical position; altitude. 24 a horizontal line or plane with respect to which measurement of elevation is based: *sea level.* 25 a flat even surface or area of land. 26 a horizontal passage or drift in a mine. 27 any of the successive layers of material that have been deposited with the passage of time to build up and raise the height of the land surface. 28 *Physics* the ratio of the magnitude of a physical quantity to an arbitrary magnitude: *sound-pressure level.* 29 **do one's level best.** to make every possible effort; try one's utmost. 30 **find one's level.** to find one's most suitable place socially, professionally, etc. 31 **on a level.** on the same horizontal plane as another. 32 **on the level.** *Informal* sincere, honest, or genuine.
▷HISTORY C14: from Old French *livel,* from Vulgar Latin *lībellum* (unattested), from Latin *lībella,* diminutive of *lībra* scales
▸ˈ**levelly** ADVERB ▸ˈ**levelness** NOUN

level crossing NOUN *Brit* a point at which a railway and a road cross, esp one with barriers that close the road when a train is scheduled to pass. US and Canadian name: **grade crossing.**

level descriptor (dɪˈskrɪptə) NOUN *Brit, education* one of a set of criteria used to assess the performance of a pupil in a particular subject.

level-headed ADJECTIVE even-tempered, balanced, and reliable; steady.
▸ˌ**level-ˈheadedly** ADVERB ▸ˌ**level-ˈheadedness** NOUN

leveller *or US* **leveler** (ˈlɛvələ) NOUN 1 a person or thing that levels. 2 a person who works for the abolition of inequalities.

Levellers (ˈlɛvələz) NOUN **the.** *English history* a radical group on the Parliamentarian side during the Civil War that advocated republicanism, freedom of worship, etc.

levelling screw NOUN a screw, often one of three, for adjusting the level of an apparatus.

level of attainment NOUN *Brit, education* one of ten groupings, each with its own attainment criteria based on pupil age and ability, within which a pupil is assessed.

level pegging *Brit informal* ◆ NOUN 1 equality between two contestants. ◆ ADJECTIVE 2 (of two contestants) equal.

level playing field NOUN a situation in which none of the competing parties has an advantage at the outset of a competitive activity.

Leven (ˈliːvᵊn) NOUN **Loch.** 1 a lake in E central Scotland: one of the shallowest of Scottish lochs, with seven islands, on one of which Mary, Queen of Scots was imprisoned (1567–8). Length: 6 km (3.7 miles). Width: 4 km (2.5 miles). 2 a sea loch in W Scotland, extending for about 14 km (9 miles) east from Loch Linnhe.

lever (ˈliːvə) NOUN 1 a rigid bar pivoted about a fulcrum, used to transfer a force to a load and usually to provide a mechanical advantage. 2 any of a number of mechanical devices employing this principle. 3 a means of exerting pressure in order to accomplish something; strategic aid. ◆ VERB 4 to prise or move (an object) with a lever.
▷HISTORY C13: from Old French *leveour,* from *lever* to raise, from Latin *levāre,* from *levis* light
▸ˈ**lever-ˌlike** ADJECTIVE

leverage (ˈliːvərɪdʒ, -vrɪdʒ) NOUN 1 the action of a lever. 2 the mechanical advantage gained by employing a lever. 3 power to accomplish something; strategic advantage. 4 the enhanced power available to a large company: *the supermarket chains have greater leverage than single-outlet enterprises.* 5 US word for **gearing** (sense 3). 6 the use made by a company of its limited assets to guarantee the substantial loans required to finance its business.

leveraged buyout (ˈliːvərɪdʒd) NOUN a takeover bid in which a small company makes use of its limited assets, and those of the usually larger target company, to raise the loans required to finance the takeover. Abbreviation: **LBO.**

leveret (ˈlɛvərɪt, -vrɪt) NOUN a young hare, esp one less than one year old.
▷HISTORY C15: from Norman French *levrete,* diminutive of *levre,* from Latin *lepus* hare

Leverkusen (*German* ˈleːvərˌkuːzən) NOUN a town in NW Germany, in North Rhine-Westphalia on the Rhine: chemical industries. Pop.: 161 100 (1999 est.).

Levi[1] (ˈliːvaɪ) NOUN 1 *Old Testament* **a** the third son of Jacob and Leah and the ancestor of the tribe of Levi (Genesis 29:34). **b** the priestly tribe descended from this patriarch (Numbers 18:21–24). 2 *New Testament* another name for **Matthew** (the apostle).

Levi[2] (ˈliːvaɪ; *Hebrew* ˈlevi) *or* **Levite** (ˈliːvaɪt) NOUN *Judaism* a descendant of the tribe of Levi who has certain privileges in the synagogue service.

leviable (ˈlɛvɪəbᵊl) ADJECTIVE 1 (of taxes, tariffs, etc.) liable to be levied. 2 (of goods, etc.) liable to bear a levy; taxable.

leviathan (lɪˈvaɪəθən) NOUN 1 *Bible* a monstrous beast, esp a sea monster. 2 any huge or powerful thing.
▷HISTORY C14: from Late Latin, ultimately from Hebrew *liwyāthān,* of obscure origin

levigate (ˈlɛvɪˌgeɪt) VERB *Chem* 1 *(tr)* to grind into a fine powder or a smooth paste. 2 to form or cause to form a homogeneous mixture, as in the production of gels. 3 *(tr)* to suspend (fine particles) by grinding in a liquid, esp as a method of separating fine from coarse particles. ◆ ADJECTIVE 4 *Botany* having a smooth polished surface; glabrous.
▷HISTORY C17: from Latin *lēvigāre,* from *lēvis* smooth
▸ˌ**leviˈgation** NOUN ▸ˈ**leviˌgator** NOUN

levin (ˈlɛvɪn) NOUN an archaic word for **lightning.**
▷HISTORY C13: probably from Scandinavian; compare Danish *lygnild*

levirate (ˈlɛvɪrɪt) NOUN the practice, required by Old Testament law, of marrying the widow of one's brother.
▷HISTORY C18: from Latin *lēvir* a husband's brother

▸leviratic (ˌlɛvɪˈrætɪk) *or* ˌleviˈratical ADJECTIVE

Levi's (ˈliːvaɪz) PLURAL NOUN *Trademark* jeans, usually blue and made of denim.

levitate (ˈlɛvɪˌteɪt) VERB [1] to rise or cause to rise and float in the air, without visible agency, attributed, esp formerly, to supernatural causes. [2] *(tr) Med* to support (a patient) on a cushion of air in the treatment of severe burns.
▷HISTORY C17: from Latin *levis* light + *-tate*, as in *gravitate*
▸ˌleviˈtation NOUN ▸ˈleviˌtator NOUN

Levite (ˈliːvaɪt) NOUN [1] *Old Testament* a member of the priestly tribe of Levi. [2] *Judaism* another word for **Levi**[2].

Levitical (lɪˈvɪtɪkᵊl) *or* **Levitic** ADJECTIVE [1] of or relating to the Levites. [2] of or relating to the book of Leviticus containing moral precepts and many of the laws concerning the Temple ritual and construction.
▸Leˈvitically ADVERB

Leviticus (lɪˈvɪtɪkəs) NOUN *Old Testament* the third book of the Old Testament, containing Levitical law and ritual precepts.

levity (ˈlɛvɪtɪ) NOUN, *plural* **-ties**. [1] inappropriate lack of seriousness. [2] fickleness or instability. [3] *Archaic* lightness in weight.
▷HISTORY C16: from Latin *levitās* lightness, from *levis* light

Levkás (lɛfˈkæs), **Leukas,** *or* **Leucas** NOUN a Greek island in the Ionian Sea, in the Ionian Islands. Pop.: 22 000 (latest est.). Area: 295 sq. km (114 sq. miles). Italian name: **Santa Maura.**

Levkosia (lɛfˈkəʊsɪə) *or* **Leukosia** NOUN the Greek name for **Nicosia.**

levo- COMBINING FORM a US variant of **laevo-.**
▷HISTORY from Latin *laevus* left, on the left

levodopa (ˌliːvəʊˈdəʊpə) NOUN another name for **L-dopa.**

levy (ˈlɛvɪ) VERB **levies, levying, levied.** *(tr)* [1] to impose and collect (a tax, tariff, fine, etc.). [2] to conscript troops for service. [3] to seize or attach (property) in accordance with the judgment of a court. ◆ NOUN, *plural* **levies.** [4] **a** the act of imposing and collecting a tax, tariff, etc. **b** the money so raised. [5] **a** the conscription of troops for service. **b** a person conscripted in this way.
▷HISTORY C15: from Old French *levée* a raising, from *lever*, from Latin *levāre* to raise
▸ˈlevier NOUN

levy en masse (ˈlɛvɪ ɒn ˈmæs) NOUN the conscription of the civilian population in large numbers in the face of impending invasion. Also called: **levée en masse** *(French* ləve ɑ̃ mas).

lewd (luːd) ADJECTIVE [1] characterized by or intended to excite crude sexual desire; obscene. [2] *Obsolete* **a** wicked. **b** ignorant.
▷HISTORY C14: from Old English *lǣwde* lay, ignorant; see LAY[3]
▸ˈlewdly ADVERB ▸ˈlewdness NOUN

Lewes (ˈluːɪs) NOUN a market town in S England, administrative centre of East Sussex, on the River Ouse: site of a battle (1264) in which Henry III was defeated by Simon de Montfort. Pop.: 15 376 (1991).

lewis (ˈluːɪs) *or* **lewisson** NOUN a lifting device for heavy stone or concrete blocks consisting of a number of curved pieces of metal or wedges fitting into a dovetailed recess cut into the block.
▷HISTORY C18: perhaps from the name of the inventor

Lewis (ˈluːɪs) NOUN the N part of the island of Lewis with Harris, in the Outer Hebrides. Area: 1634 sq. km (631 sq. miles).

Lewis acid NOUN a substance capable of accepting a pair of electrons from a base to form a covalent bond. Compare **Lewis base.**
▷HISTORY C20: named after G. N. *Lewis* (1875–1946), US chemist

Lewis base NOUN a substance capable of donating a pair of electrons to an acid to form a covalent bond. Compare **Lewis acid.**
▷HISTORY C20: named after G. N. *Lewis* (1875–1946), US chemist

Lewis gun NOUN a light air-cooled drum-fed gas-operated machine gun used chiefly in World War I.
▷HISTORY C20: named after I. N. *Lewis* (1858–1931), US soldier

Lewisham (ˈluːɪʃəm) NOUN a borough of S Greater London, on the River Thames. Pop.: 248 924 (2001). Area: 35 sq. km (13 sq. miles).

lewisite (ˈluːɪˌsaɪt) NOUN a colourless oily poisonous liquid with an odour resembling that of geraniums, having a powerful vesicant action and used as a war gas; 1-chloro-2-dichloroarsinoethene. Formula: $ClCH{:}CHAsCl_2$.
▷HISTORY C20: named after W. L. *Lewis* (1878–1943), US chemist

Lewis with Harris *or* **Lewis and Harris** NOUN an island in the Outer Hebrides, separated from the NW coast of Scotland by the Minch: consists of Lewis in the north and Harris in the south; many lakes and peat moors; economy based chiefly on the Harris tweed industry, with some fishing. Chief town: Stornoway. Pop.: 23 500 (latest est.). Area: 2134 sq. km (824 sq. miles).

Lewy bodies (ˈluːɪ) PLURAL NOUN abnormal proteins that occur in the nerve cells of the cerebral cortex and the basal ganglia, causing Parkinson's disease and dementia.
▷HISTORY C20: named after F. H. *Lewy* (1885–1950), German neurologist

lex (lɛks) NOUN, *plural* **leges** (ˈliːdʒiːz). [1] a system or body of laws. [2] a particular specified law.
▷HISTORY Latin

lexeme (ˈlɛksiːm) NOUN *Linguistics* a minimal meaningful unit of language, the meaning of which cannot be understood from that of its component morphemes. *Take off* (in the senses to mimic, to become airborne, etc.) is a lexeme, as well as the independent morphemes *take* and *off*.
▷HISTORY C20: from LEX(ICON) + -EME

lexical (ˈlɛksɪkᵊl) ADJECTIVE [1] of or relating to items of vocabulary in a language. [2] of or relating to a lexicon.
▸lexicality (ˌlɛksɪˈkælɪtɪ) NOUN ▸ˈlexically ADVERB

lexical decision task NOUN *Psychol* an experimental task in which subjects have to decide as fast as possible whether a given letter string is a word.

lexical insertion NOUN *Generative grammar* the process in which actual morphemes of a language are substituted either for semantic material or for place-fillers in the course of a derivation of a sentence.

lexicalize *or* **lexicalise** (ˈlɛksɪkəˌlaɪz) VERB *Linguistics* to form (a word or lexeme) or (of a word or lexeme) to be formed from constituent morphemes, words, or lexemes, as to form *cannot* from *can* and *not*.
▸ˌlexicaliˈzation *or* ˌlexicaliˈsation NOUN

lexical meaning NOUN the meaning of a word in relation to the physical world or to abstract concepts, without reference to any sentence in which the word may occur. Compare **grammatical meaning, content word.**

lexical order NOUN the arrangement of a set of items in accordance with a recursive algorithm, such as the entries in a dictionary whose order depends on their first letter unless these are the same in which case it is the second which decides, and so on.

lexicog. ABBREVIATION FOR: [1] lexicographical. [2] lexicography.

lexicography (ˌlɛksɪˈkɒgrəfɪ) NOUN the process or profession of writing or compiling dictionaries.
▸ˌlexiˈcographer NOUN ▸lexicographic (ˌlɛksɪkəˈgræfɪk) *or* ˌlexicoˈgraphical ADJECTIVE ▸ˌlexicoˈgraphically ADVERB

lexicology (ˌlɛksɪˈkɒlədʒɪ) NOUN the study of the overall structure and history of the vocabulary of a language.
▸lexicological (ˌlɛksɪkəˈlɒdʒɪkᵊl) ADJECTIVE
▸ˌlexicoˈlogically ADVERB ▸ˌlexiˈcologist NOUN

lexicon (ˈlɛksɪkən) NOUN [1] a dictionary, esp one of an ancient language such as Greek or Hebrew. [2] a list of terms relating to a particular subject. [3] the vocabulary of a language or of an individual. [4] *Linguistics* the set of all the morphemes of a language.
▷HISTORY C17: New Latin, from Greek *lexikon*, n use of *lexikos* relating to words, from Greek *lexis* word, from *legein* to speak

lexicostatistics (ˌlɛksɪkəʊstəˈtɪstɪks) NOUN *(functioning as singular)* the statistical study of the vocabulary of a language, with special attention to the historical links with other languages. See also **glottochronology.**

lexigram (ˈlɛksɪˌgræm) NOUN a figure or symbol that represents a word.
▷HISTORY C20: from Greek *lexis* word + -GRAM

lexigraphy (lɛkˈsɪgrəfɪ) NOUN a system of writing in which each word is represented by a sign.
▷HISTORY C19: from Greek *lexis* word + -GRAPHY

Lexington (ˈlɛksɪŋtən) NOUN [1] a city in NE central Kentucky, in the bluegrass region: major centre for horse-breeding. Pop.: 260 512 (2000). [2] a city in Massachusetts, northwest of Boston: site of the first action (1775) of the War of American Independence. Pop.: 28 974 (1990).

lexis (ˈlɛksɪs) NOUN the totality of vocabulary items in a language, including all forms having lexical meaning or grammatical function.
▷HISTORY C20: from Greek *lexis* word

lex loci (ˈləʊsaɪ, -kiː) NOUN the law of the place.
▷HISTORY from Latin

lex non scripta (nɒn ˈskrɪptə) NOUN the unwritten law; common law.
▷HISTORY from Latin

lex scripta NOUN the written law; statute law.
▷HISTORY from Latin

lex talionis (ˌtælɪˈəʊnɪs) NOUN the law of revenge or retaliation.
▷HISTORY C16: New Latin

ley (leɪ, liː) NOUN [1] arable land put down to grass; grassland or pastureland. [2] Also called: **ley line.** a line joining two prominent points in the landscape, thought to be the line of a prehistoric track.
▷HISTORY C14: variant of LEA[1]

Leyden (ˈlaɪdᵊn; *Dutch* ˈlɛidə) NOUN a variant spelling of **Leiden.**

Leyden jar NOUN *Physics* an early type of capacitor consisting of a glass jar with the lower part of the inside and outside coated with tin foil.
▷HISTORY C18: first made in Leiden

ley farming NOUN the alternation at intervals of several years of crop growing and grassland pasture.

Leyland cypress (ˈleɪlənd) a fast-growing cypress, *Cupressocyparis leylandii*, that is a hybrid produced by crossing the macrocarpa with the Nootka cypress (*Chamaecyparis nootkatensis*): widely grown for hedging. Also called: **Leylandii, Leylandi.**
▷HISTORY C19: named after C. J. *Leyland* (1849–1926), British horticulturalist

leylandii (leɪˈlændɪaɪ) *or* **leylandi** (-ˈlændɪ) NOUN other names for **Leyland cypress.**

Leyte (ˈleɪteɪ) NOUN an island in the central Philippines, in the Visayan Islands. Chief town: Tacloban. Pop.: 1 362 050 (1990). Area: 7215 sq. km (2786 sq. miles).

Leyte Gulf NOUN an inlet of the Pacific in the E Philippines, east of Leyte and south of Samar: scene of a battle (Oct. 23–26, 1944) during World War II, in which the Americans defeated almost the entire Japanese navy, thereby ensuring ultimate Allied victory.

lezzie (ˈlɛzɪ) *or* **lezza** (ˈlɛzə) NOUN *Slang* a lesbian.

LF *Radio* ABBREVIATION FOR **low frequency.**

LG ABBREVIATION FOR Low German.

lg. *or* **lge** ABBREVIATION FOR large.

lgth ABBREVIATION FOR length.

LGV (in Britain) ABBREVIATION FOR large goods vehicle.

lh *or* **LH** ABBREVIATION FOR left hand.

LH ABBREVIATION FOR **luteinizing hormone.**

Lhasa *or* **Lassa** (ˈlɑːsə) NOUN a city in SW China, capital of Tibet AR, at an altitude of 3606 m (11 830 ft.): for centuries the sacred city of Lamaism and residence of the Dalai Lamas from the 17th century until 1950; known as the Forbidden City because it was closed to Westerners until the beginning of the 20th century; annexed by China in 1951. The Dalai Lama fled after an unsuccessful revolt against Chinese rule in 1959. Pop.: 121 568 (1999 est.).

Lhasa apso (ˈlɑːsə ˈæpsəʊ) NOUN, *plural* **Lhasa apsos.** a small dog of a Tibetan breed having a long straight dense coat, often gold or greyish, and a well-feathered tail carried curled over its back.
▷HISTORY Tibetan

lhd ABBREVIATION FOR left-hand drive.

LH-RH ABBREVIATION FOR **luteinizing hormone-releasing hormone.**

li[1] (li:) NOUN a Chinese unit of length, approximately equal to 590 yards.
▷HISTORY from Chinese

li[2] THE INTERNET DOMAIN NAME FOR Liechtenstein.

Li THE CHEMICAL SYMBOL FOR lithium.

LI ABBREVIATION FOR: 1 Long Island. 2 Light Infantry.

liabilities (ˌlaɪəˈbɪlɪtɪz) PLURAL NOUN *Accounting* business obligations incurred but not discharged and entered as claims on the assets shown on the balance sheet. Compare **assets** (sense 1).

liability (ˌlaɪəˈbɪlɪtɪ) NOUN, *plural* **-ties.** 1 the state of being liable. 2 a financial obligation. 3 a hindrance or disadvantage. 4 likelihood or probability.

liable (ˈlaɪəbᵊl) ADJECTIVE (*postpositive*) 1 legally obliged or responsible; answerable. 2 susceptible or exposed; subject. 3 probable, likely, or capable: *it's liable to happen soon.*
▷HISTORY C15: perhaps via Anglo-French, from Old French *lier* to bind, from Latin *ligāre*
▸ˈ**liableness** NOUN

> **Language note** The use of *liable to* to mean *likely to* was formerly considered incorrect, but is now acceptable.

liaise (lɪˈeɪz) VERB (*intr;* usually foll by *with*) to communicate and maintain contact (with).
▷HISTORY C20: back formation from LIAISON

liaison (lɪˈeɪzɒn) NOUN 1 communication and contact between groups or units. 2 (*modifier*) of or relating to liaison between groups or units: *a liaison officer.* 3 a secretive or adulterous sexual relationship. 4 the relationship between military units necessary to ensure unity of purpose. 5 (in the phonology of several languages, esp French) the pronunciation of a normally silent consonant at the end of a word immediately before another word commencing with a vowel, in such a way that the consonant is taken over as the initial sound of the following word. Liaison is seen between French *ils* (il) and *ont* (ɔ̃), to give *ils ont* (il zɔ̃). 6 any thickening for soups, sauces, etc., such as egg yolks or cream.
▷HISTORY C17: via French from Old French, from *lier* to bind, from Latin *ligāre*

liaison officer NOUN 1 a person who liaises between groups or units. 2 *NZ* a university official who oversees the operation of the accrediting system in schools.

Liákoura (ˈljakura) NOUN transliteration of the Modern Greek name for (Mount) **Parnassus.**

liana (lɪˈɑːnə) *or* **liane** (lɪˈɑːn) NOUN any of various woody climbing plants mainly of tropical forests.
▷HISTORY C19: changed from earlier *liane* (through influence of French *lier* to bind), from French, of obscure origin
▸**liˈanoid** ADJECTIVE

Lianyungang (ˈljænˈjʊŋˈgæŋ), **Sinhailien,** *or* **Hsin-hai-lien** NOUN a city in E China, near the coast of Jiangsu. Pop.: 447 918 (1997 est.).

Liao (ljaʊ) NOUN a river in NE China, rising in SE Inner Mongolia and flowing northeast then southwest to the Gulf of Liaodong. Length: about 1100 km (700 miles).

Liaodong (ˈljaʊˈdʊŋ) *or* **Liaotung** (ˈljaʊˈtʊŋ) NOUN 1 a peninsula of NE China, in S Manchuria extending south into the Yellow Sea: forms the S part of Liaoning province. 2 **Gulf of.** the N part of the Gulf of Chihli, west of the peninsula of Liaodong.

Liaoning (ˈljaʊˈnɪŋ) NOUN a province of NE China, in S Manchuria. Capital: Shenyang. Pop.: 42 380 000 (2000 est.). Area: 150 000 sq. km (58 500 sq. miles).

Liaoyang (ˈljaʊˈjæŋ) NOUN a city in NE China, in S Manchuria, in Liaoning province: a regional capital in the early dynasties. Pop.: 570 483 (1999 est.).

liar (ˈlaɪə) NOUN a person who has lied or lies repeatedly.

liard (lɪˈɑːd) NOUN a former small coin of various European countries.
▷HISTORY C16: after G. *Liard,* French minter

Liard (ˈliːɑːd, liːˈɑːd, -ˈɑː) NOUN a river in W Canada, rising in the SE Yukon and flowing east and then northwest to the Mackenzie River. Length: 885 km (550 miles).

liar paradox NOUN *Logic* the paradox that *this statement is false* is true only if it is false and false only if it is true: attributed to Epimenides the Cretan in the form *all Cretans are liars.*

Lias (ˈlaɪəs) NOUN the lowest series of rocks of the Jurassic system.
▷HISTORY C15 (referring to a kind of limestone), C19 (geological sense) from Old French *liois,* perhaps from *lie* lees, dregs, so called from its appearance
▸**Liassic** (laɪˈæsɪk) ADJECTIVE

liatris (laɪˈætrɪs) NOUN See **blazing star** (sense 2).
▷HISTORY C18: New Latin, of uncertain origin

lib (lɪb) NOUN *Informal, sometimes derogatory* short for **liberation** (sense 2).

lib. 1 librarian. 2 library.

Lib. ABBREVIATION FOR Liberal.

libation (laɪˈbeɪʃən) NOUN 1 **a** the pouring out of wine, etc., in honour of a deity. **b** the liquid so poured out. 2 *Usually facetious* an alcoholic drink.
▷HISTORY C14: from Latin *lībātiō,* from *lībāre* to pour an offering of drink
▸**liˈbational** *or* **liˈbationary** ADJECTIVE

Libau (ˈliːbaʊ) NOUN the German name for **Liepāja.**

Libava (lɪˈbavə) NOUN transliteration of the Russian name for **Liepāja.**

Lib Dem ABBREVIATION FOR *Politics* Liberal Democrat.

libeccio (lɪˈbɛtʃɪəʊ) *or* **libecchio** (lɪˈbɛkɪəʊ) NOUN a strong westerly or southwesterly wind blowing onto the W coast of Corsica.
▷HISTORY Italian, via Latin, from Greek *libs*

libel (ˈlaɪbᵊl) NOUN 1 *Law* **a** the publication of defamatory matter in permanent form, as by a written or printed statement, picture, etc. **b** the act of publishing such matter. 2 any defamatory or unflattering representation or statement. 3 *Ecclesiastical law* a claimant's written statement of claim. 4 *Scots law* the formal statement of a charge. ♦ VERB **-bels, -belling, -belled** *or US* **-bels, -beling, -beled.** (*tr*) 5 *Law* to make or publish a defamatory statement or representation about (a person). 6 to misrepresent injuriously. 7 *Ecclesiastical law* to bring an action against (a person) in the ecclesiastical courts.
▷HISTORY C13 (in the sense: written statement), hence C14 legal sense: a plaintiff's statement, via Old French from Latin *libellus* a little book, from *liber* a book
▸ˈ**libeller** *or* ˈ**libelist** NOUN ▸ˈ**libellous** *or* ˈ**libelous** ADJECTIVE

libellant *or US* **libelant** (ˈlaɪbᵊlənt) NOUN 1 a party who brings an action in the ecclesiastical courts by presenting a libel. 2 a person who publishes a libel.

libellee *or US* **libelee** (ˌlaɪbᵊˈliː) NOUN a person against whom a libel has been filed in an ecclesiastical court.

liber (ˈlaɪbə) NOUN a rare name for **phloem.**
▷HISTORY C18: from Latin, in original sense: tree bark

liberal (ˈlɪbərəl, ˈlɪbrəl) ADJECTIVE 1 relating to or having social and political views that favour progress and reform. 2 relating to or having policies or views advocating individual freedom. 3 giving and generous in temperament or behaviour. 4 tolerant of other people. 5 abundant; lavish: *a liberal helping of cream.* 6 not strict; free: *a liberal translation.* 7 of or relating to an education that aims to develop general cultural interests and intellectual ability. ♦ NOUN 8 a person who has liberal ideas or opinions.
▷HISTORY C14: from Latin *līberālis* of freedom, from *līber* free
▸ˈ**liberally** ADVERB ▸ˈ**liberalness** NOUN

Liberal (ˈlɪbərəl, ˈlɪbrəl) NOUN 1 a member or supporter of a Liberal Party or Liberal Democrat party. ♦ ADJECTIVE 2 of or relating to a Liberal Party.

liberal arts PLURAL NOUN the fine arts, humanities, sociology, languages, and literature. Often shortened to: **arts.**

Liberal Democrat NOUN a member or supporter of the Liberal Democrats.

Liberal Democrats PLURAL NOUN (in Britain) a political party with centrist policies; established in 1988 as the Social and Liberal Democrats when the Liberal Party merged with the Social Democratic Party; renamed Liberal Democrats in 1989.

liberal elite NOUN the group of people in a society who are considered as having a high level of education and liberal ideas.

liberalism (ˈlɪbərəˌlɪzəm, ˈlɪbrə-) NOUN 1 liberal opinions, practices, or politics. 2 a movement in modern Protestantism that rejects biblical authority.
▸ˈ**liberalist** NOUN, ADJECTIVE ▸ˌ**liberalˈistic** ADJECTIVE

liberality (ˌlɪbəˈrælɪtɪ) NOUN, *plural* **-ties.** 1 generosity; bounty. 2 the quality or condition of being liberal.

liberalize *or* **liberalise** (ˈlɪbərəˌlaɪz, ˈlɪbrə-) VERB to make or become liberal.
▸ˌ**liberaliˈzation** *or* ˌ**liberaliˈsation** NOUN ▸ˈ**liberalˌizer** *or* ˈ**liberalˌiser** NOUN

Liberal Party NOUN 1 one of the former major political parties in Britain; in 1988 merged with the Social Democratic Party to form the Social and Liberal Democrats; renamed the Liberal Democrats in 1989. 2 one of the major political parties in Australia, a conservative party, generally opposed to the Labor Party. 3 one of the major political parties in Canada, generally representing viewpoints between those of the Progressive Conservative Party and the New Democratic Party. 4 any other party supporting liberal policies.

liberal studies NOUN (*functioning as singular*) *Brit* a supplementary arts course for those specializing in scientific, technical, or professional studies.

Liberal Unionist NOUN a Liberal who opposed Gladstone's policy of Irish Home Rule in 1886 and after.
▸**Liberal Unionism** NOUN

liberate (ˈlɪbəˌreɪt) VERB (*tr*) 1 to give liberty to; make free. 2 to release (something, esp a gas) from chemical combination during a chemical reaction. 3 to release from occupation or subjugation by a foreign power. 4 to free from social prejudices or injustices. 5 *Euphemistic or facetious* to steal.
▸ˈ**liberˌator** NOUN

liberated (ˈlɪbəˌreɪtɪd) ADJECTIVE 1 given liberty; freed; released. 2 released from occupation or subjugation by a foreign power. 3 (esp in feminist theory) not bound by traditional sexual and social roles.

liberation (ˌlɪbəˈreɪʃən) NOUN 1 a liberating or being liberated. 2 the seeking of equal status or just treatment for or on behalf of any group believed to be discriminated against: *women's liberation; animal liberation.*
▸ˌ**liberˈationist** NOUN, ADJECTIVE

liberation theology NOUN the belief that Christianity involves not only faith in the teachings of the Church but also a commitment to change social and political conditions from within in societies in which it is considered exploitation and oppression exist.

Liberec (*Czech* ˈlibɛrɛts) NOUN a city in the N Czech Republic, on the Neisse River: a centre of the German Sudeten movement in 1938. Pop.: 100 604 (1996 est.). German name: **Reichenberg.**

Liber Extra (ˈlaɪbər ˈɛkstrə) NOUN See **Decretals.**
▷HISTORY Latin: book of additional (decretals)

Liberia (laɪˈbɪərɪə) NOUN a republic in W Africa, on the Atlantic: originated in 1822 as a home for freed Afro-American slaves, with land purchased by the American Colonization Society; republic declared in 1847; exports are predominantly rubber and iron ore. Official language: English. Religion: Christian majority, also animist. Currency: dollar. Capital: Monrovia. Pop.: 3 226 000 (2001 est.). Area: 111 400 sq. km (43 000 sq. miles).

Liberian (laɪˈbɪərɪən) ADJECTIVE 1 of or relating to Liberia or its inhabitants. ♦ NOUN 2 a native or inhabitant of Liberia.

libero (ˈliːbero) NOUN another name for **sweeper** (sense 3).

libertarian (ˌlɪbəˈtɛərɪən) NOUN 1 a believer in freedom of thought, expression, etc. 2 *Philosophy* a believer in the doctrine of free will. Compare

determinism. ◆ ADJECTIVE [3] of, relating to, or characteristic of a libertarian.
▷HISTORY C18: from LIBERTY
▸ˌ**liberˈtarianism** NOUN

liberticide (lɪˈbɜːtɪˌsaɪd) NOUN [1] a destroyer of freedom. [2] the destruction of freedom.
▸**liˌbertiˈcidal** ADJECTIVE

libertine (ˈlɪbəˌtiːn, -ˌtaɪn) NOUN [1] a morally dissolute person. ◆ ADJECTIVE [2] morally dissolute.
▷HISTORY C14 (in the sense: freedman, dissolute person): from Latin *lībertīnus* freedman, from *lībertus* freed, from *līber* free
▸ˈ**liberˌtinage** *or* ˈ**libertinˌism** NOUN

liberty (ˈlɪbətɪ) NOUN, *plural* **-ties.** [1] the power of choosing, thinking, and acting for oneself; freedom from control or restriction. [2] the right or privilege of access to a particular place; freedom. [3] (*often plural*) a social action regarded as being familiar, forward, or improper. [4] (*often plural*) an action that is unauthorized or unwarranted in the circumstances: *he took liberties with the translation.* [5] **a** authorized leave granted to a sailor. **b** (*as modifier*): *liberty man; liberty boat.* [6] **at liberty.** free, unoccupied, or unrestricted. [7] **take liberties (with).** to be overfamiliar or overpresumptuous. [8] **take the liberty (of** *or* **to).** to venture or presume (to do something).
▷HISTORY C14: from Old French *liberté,* from Latin *lībertās,* from *līber* free

Liberty bodice NOUN *Trademark* a sleeveless vest-like undergarment made from thick cotton and covering the upper part of the body, formerly worn esp by young children.

liberty cap NOUN [1] a cap of soft felt worn as a symbol of liberty, esp during the French Revolution, from the practice in ancient Rome of giving a freed slave such a cap. [2] a poisonous hallucinogenic basidiomycetous fungus, *Psilocybe semilanceata,* yellowish-brown with a distinctive pointed cap, found in groups in grassland.

liberty hall NOUN (*sometimes capitals*) *Informal* a place or condition of complete liberty.

liberty horse NOUN (in a circus) a riderless horse that performs movements to verbal commands.

Liberty Island NOUN a small island in upper New York Bay: site of the Statue of Liberty. Area: 5 hectares (12 acres). Former name (until 1956): **Bedloe's Island.**

liberty ship NOUN a supply ship of World War II.

Libia (ˈliːbja) NOUN the Italian name for **Libya.**

libidinous (lɪˈbɪdɪnəs) ADJECTIVE [1] characterized by excessive sexual desire. [2] of or relating to the libido.
▸**liˈbidinously** ADVERB ▸**liˈbidinousness** NOUN

libido (lɪˈbiːdəʊ) NOUN, *plural* **-dos.** [1] *Psychoanal* psychic energy emanating from the id. [2] sexual urge or desire.
▷HISTORY C20 (in psychoanalysis): from Latin: desire
▸**libidinal** (lɪˈbɪdɪnᵊl) ADJECTIVE ▸**liˈbidinally** ADVERB

libra (ˈlaɪbrə) NOUN, *plural* **-brae** (-briː). an ancient Roman unit of weight corresponding to 1 pound, but equal to about 12 ounces.
▷HISTORY C14: from Latin, literally: scales

Libra (ˈliːbrə) NOUN, *Latin genitive* **Librae** (ˈliːbriː). [1] *Astronomy* a small faint zodiacal constellation in the S hemisphere, lying between Virgo and Scorpius on the ecliptic. [2] *Astrology* **a** Also called: **the Scales, the Balance.** the seventh sign of the zodiac, symbol ♎, having a cardinal air classification and ruled by the planet Venus. The sun is in this sign between about Sept. 23 and Oct. 22. **b** a person born under this sign. ◆ ADJECTIVE [3] *Astrology* born under or characteristic of Libra. ◆ Also (for senses 2b, 3): **Libran** (ˈlɪbrən).

librarian (laɪˈbrɛərɪən) NOUN a person in charge of or assisting in a library.

librarianship (lɪˈbrɛərɪənʃɪp, laɪ-) NOUN the professional administration of library resources and services. Also called: **library science.**

library (ˈlaɪbrərɪ) NOUN, *plural* **-braries.** [1] a room or set of rooms where books and other literary materials are kept. [2] a collection of literary materials, films, CDs, children's toys, etc., kept for borrowing or reference. [3] the building or institution that houses such a collection: *a public library.* [4] a set of books published as a series, often in a similar format. [5] *Computing* a collection of standard programs and subroutines for immediate use, usually stored on disk or some other storage device. [6] a collection of specific items for reference or checking against: *a library of genetic material.*
▷HISTORY C14: from Old French *librairie,* from Medieval Latin *librāris,* n use of Latin *librārius* relating to books, from *liber* book

library edition NOUN an edition of a book having a superior quality of paper, binding, etc.

librate (ˈlaɪbreɪt) VERB (*intr*) [1] to oscillate or waver. [2] to hover or be balanced.
▷HISTORY C17: from Latin *librātus,* from *librāre* to balance
▸**libratory** (ˈlaɪbrətərɪ, -trɪ) ADJECTIVE

libration (laɪˈbreɪʃən) NOUN [1] the act or an instance of oscillating. [2] a real or apparent oscillation of the moon enabling approximately 59 per cent of the surface to be visible from the earth over a period of time.
▸**liˈbrational** ADJECTIVE

librettist (lɪˈbrɛtɪst) NOUN the author of a libretto.

libretto (lɪˈbrɛtəʊ) NOUN, *plural* **-tos** *or* **-ti** (-tiː). a text written for and set to music in an opera, etc.
▷HISTORY C18: from Italian, diminutive of *libro* book

Libreville (*French* librəvil) NOUN the capital of Gabon, in the west on the estuary of the Gabon River: founded as a French trading post in 1843 and expanded with the settlement of freed slaves in 1848. Pop.: 362 386 (1993).

libriform (ˈlaɪbrɪˌfɔːm) ADJECTIVE (of a fibre of woody tissue) elongated and having a pitted thickened cell wall.

Librium (ˈlɪbrɪəm) NOUN *Trademark* a brand of the drug chlordiazepoxide. See also **benzodiazepine.**

Libya (ˈlɪbɪə) NOUN a republic in N Africa, on the Mediterranean: became an Italian colony in 1912; divided after World War II into Tripolitania and Cyrenaica (under British administration) and Fezzan (under French); gained independence in 1951; monarchy overthrown by a military junta in 1969. It consists almost wholly of desert and is a major exporter of oil. Official language: Arabic. Official religion: (Sunni) Muslim. Currency: Libyan dinar. Capital: Tripoli. Pop.: 5 241 000 (2001 est.). Area: 1 760 000 sq. km (680 000 sq. miles). Official name: **Al-Jumhuria al-Arabia allibya**

Libyan (ˈlɪbɪən) ADJECTIVE [1] of or relating to Libya, its people, or its language. ◆ NOUN [2] a native or inhabitant of Libya. [3] the extinct Hamitic language of ancient Libya.

Libyan Desert NOUN a desert in N Africa, in E Libya, W Egypt, and the NW Sudan: the NE part of the Sahara.

lice (laɪs) NOUN the plural of **louse.**

licence *or US* **license** (ˈlaɪsəns) NOUN [1] a certificate, tag, document, etc., giving official permission to do something. [2] formal permission or exemption. [3] liberty of action or thought; freedom. [4] intentional disregard of or deviation from conventional rules to achieve a certain effect: *poetic licence.* [5] excessive freedom. [6] licentiousness.
▷HISTORY C14: via Old French and Medieval Latin *licentia* permission, from Latin: freedom, from *licet* it is allowed

license (ˈlaɪsəns) VERB (*tr*) [1] to grant or give a licence for (something, such as the sale of alcohol). [2] to give permission to or for.
▸ˈ**licensable** ADJECTIVE ▸ˈ**licenser** *or* ˈ**licensor** NOUN

licensed aircraft engineer NOUN the official name for **ground engineer.**

licensee (ˌlaɪsənˈsiː) NOUN a person who holds a licence, esp one to sell alcoholic drink.

license plate *or Canadian* **licence plate** NOUN the US and Canadian term for **numberplate.**

licentiate (laɪˈsɛnʃɪɪt) NOUN [1] a person who has received a formal attestation of professional competence to practise a certain profession or teach a certain skill or subject. [2] a degree between that of bachelor and doctor awarded now only by certain chiefly European universities. [3] a person who holds this degree. [4] *Chiefly Presbyterian Church* a person holding a licence to preach.
▷HISTORY C15: from Medieval Latin *licentiātus,* from *licentiāre* to permit
▸**liˈcentiateˌship** NOUN ▸**liˌcentiˈation** NOUN

licentious (laɪˈsɛnʃəs) ADJECTIVE [1] sexually unrestrained or promiscuous. [2] *Now rare* showing disregard for convention.
▷HISTORY C16: from Latin *licentiōsus* capricious, from *licentia* LICENCE
▸**liˈcentiously** ADVERB ▸**liˈcentiousness** NOUN

lichee (ˌlaɪˈtʃiː) NOUN a variant spelling of **litchi.**

lichen (ˈlaɪkən, ˈlɪtʃən) NOUN [1] an organism that is formed by the symbiotic association of a fungus and an alga or cyanobacterium and occurs as crusty patches or bushy growths on tree trunks, bare ground, etc. Lichens are now classified as a phylum of fungi (*Mycophycophyta*). [2] *Pathol* any of various eruptive disorders of the skin.
▷HISTORY C17: via Latin from Greek *leikhēn,* from *leikhein* to lick
▸ˈ**lichened** ADJECTIVE ▸ˈ**lichen-ˌlike** ADJECTIVE
▸ˈ**lichenˌoid** ADJECTIVE ▸ˈ**lichenous** *or* ˈ**lichenˌose** ADJECTIVE

lichenin (ˈlaɪkənɪn) NOUN a complex polysaccharide occurring in certain species of mosses.

lichenology (ˌlaɪkəˈnɒlədʒɪ, ˌlɪ-) NOUN the study of the structure, physiology, and ecology of lichens.

Lichfield (ˈlɪtʃˌfiːld) NOUN a city in central England, in SE Staffordshire: cathedral with three spires (13th-14th century); birthplace of Samuel Johnson, during whose lifetime the **Lichfield Group** (a literary circle) flourished. Pop.: 28 666 (1991).

lich gate (lɪtʃ) NOUN a variant spelling of **lych gate.**

lichi (ˌlaɪˈtʃiː) NOUN a variant spelling of **litchi.**

licht (lɪxt) NOUN, ADJECTIVE, VERB a Scot word for **light**[1] and **light**[2].

licit (ˈlɪsɪt) ADJECTIVE a less common word for **lawful.**
▷HISTORY C15: from Latin *licitus* permitted, from *licēre* to be permitted
▸ˈ**licitly** ADVERB ▸ˈ**licitness** NOUN

lick (lɪk) VERB [1] (*tr*) to pass the tongue over, esp in order to taste or consume. [2] to flicker or move lightly over or round (something): *the flames licked around the door.* [3] (*tr*) *Informal* **a** to defeat or vanquish. **b** to flog or thrash. **c** to be or do much better than. [4] **lick into shape.** to put into a satisfactory condition: from the former belief that bear cubs were born formless and had to be licked into shape by their mother. [5] **lick one's lips.** to anticipate or recall something with glee or relish. [6] **lick one's wounds.** to retire after a defeat or setback in order to husband one's resources. [7] **lick the boots of.** See **boot**[1] (sense 14). ◆ NOUN [8] an instance of passing the tongue over something. [9] a small amount: *a lick of paint.* [10] Also called: **salt lick.** a block of compressed salt or chemical matter provided for domestic animals to lick for medicinal and nutritional purposes. [11] a place to which animals go to lick exposed natural deposits of salt. [12] *Informal* a hit; blow. [13] *Slang* a short musical phrase, usually on one instrument. [14] *Informal* speed; rate of movement: *he was going at quite a lick when he hit it.* [15] **a lick and a promise.** something hastily done, esp a hurried wash.
▷HISTORY Old English *liccian;* related to Old High German *leckon,* Latin *lingere,* Greek *leikhein*
▸ˈ**licker** NOUN

lick-alike ADJECTIVE *Irish informal* very similar: *he and his father are lick-alike.*

lickerish *or* **liquorish** (ˈlɪkərɪʃ) ADJECTIVE *Archaic* [1] lecherous or lustful. [2] greedy; gluttonous. [3] appetizing or tempting.
▷HISTORY C16: changed from C13 *lickerous,* via Norman French from Old French *lechereus* lecherous; see LECHER
▸ˈ**lickerishly** *or* ˈ**liquorishly** ADVERB ▸ˈ**lickerishness** *or* ˈ**liquorishness** NOUN

lickety-split (ˈlɪkɪtɪˈsplɪt) ADVERB *US and Canadian informal* very quickly; speedily.
▷HISTORY C19: from LICK + SPLIT

licking (ˈlɪkɪŋ) NOUN *Informal* [1] a beating. [2] a defeat.

lickspittle (ˈlɪkˌspɪtᵊl) NOUN a flattering or servile person.

licorice (ˈlɪkərɪs) NOUN the usual US and Canadian spelling of **liquorice.**

lictor (ˈlɪktə) NOUN one of a group of ancient Roman officials, usually bearing fasces, who attended magistrates, etc.

▷**HISTORY** C16 *lictor,* C14 *littour,* from Latin *ligāre* to bind

lid (lɪd) NOUN [1] a cover, usually removable or hinged, for a receptacle: *a saucepan lid; a desk lid.* [2] short for **eyelid.** [3] *Botany* another name for **operculum** (sense 2). [4] *Slang* short for **skidlid.** [5] *US, dated slang* a quantity of marijuana, usually an ounce. [6] **dip one's lid.** *Austral informal* to raise one's hat as a greeting, etc. [7] **flip one's lid.** *Slang* to become crazy or angry. [8] **put the lid on.** *Informal* **a** *Brit* to be the final blow to. **b** to curb, prevent, or discourage. [9] **take the lid off.** *Informal* to make startling or spectacular revelations about.
▷**HISTORY** Old English *hlid;* related to Old Friesian *hlid,* Old High German *hlit* cover
▸**'lidded** ADJECTIVE

Lidice (*Czech* 'lidjtsɛ) NOUN a mining village in the Czech Republic: destroyed by the Germans in 1942 in reprisal for the assassination of Reinhard Heydrich; rebuilt as a national memorial.

lidless ('lɪdlɪs) ADJECTIVE [1] having no lid or top. [2] (of animals) having no eyelids. [3] *Archaic* vigilant and watchful.

lido ('liːdəʊ) NOUN, *plural* **-dos.** *Brit* a public place of recreation, including a pool for swimming or water sports.
▷**HISTORY** C20: after the *Lido,* island bathing beach near Venice, from Latin *litus* shore

lidocaine ('laɪdəˌkeɪn) NOUN a powerful local anaesthetic administered by injection, or topically to mucous membranes. Formula: $C_{14}H_{22}N_2O.HCl.H_2O$. Also called: **lignocaine.**
▷**HISTORY** C20: from (ACETANI)LID(E) + *-caine* on the model of *cocaine*

lie[1] (laɪ) VERB **lies, lying, lied.** [1] (*intr*) to speak untruthfully with intent to mislead or deceive. [2] (*intr*) to convey a false impression or practise deception: *the camera does not lie.* ◆ NOUN [3] an untrue or deceptive statement deliberately used to mislead. [4] something that is deliberately intended to deceive. [5] **give the lie to. a** to disprove. **b** to accuse of lying. ◆ Related adjective **mendacious.**
▷**HISTORY** Old English *lyge* (n), *lēogan* (vb); related to Old High German *liogan,* Gothic *liugan*

lie[2] (laɪ) VERB **lies, lying, lay** (leɪ), **lain** (leɪn). (*intr*) [1] (often foll by *down*) to place oneself or be in a prostrate position, horizontal to the ground. [2] to be situated, esp on a horizontal surface: *the pencil is lying on the desk; India lies to the south of Russia.* [3] to be buried: *here lies Jane Brown.* [4] (*copula*) to be and remain (in a particular state or condition): *to lie dormant.* [5] to stretch or extend: *the city lies before us.* [6] (usually foll by *on* or *upon*) to rest or weigh: *my sins lie heavily on my mind.* [7] (usually foll by *in*) to exist or consist inherently: *strength lies in unity.* [8] (foll by *with*) **a** to be or rest (with): *the ultimate decision lies with you.* **b** *Archaic* to have sexual intercourse (with). [9] (of an action, claim, appeal, etc.) to subsist; be maintainable or admissible. [10] *Archaic* to stay temporarily. [11] **lie in state.** See **state** (sense 13). [12] **lie low. a** to keep or be concealed or quiet. **b** to wait for a favourable opportunity. ◆ NOUN [13] the manner, place, or style in which something is situated. [14] the hiding place or lair of an animal. [15] *Golf* **a** the position of the ball after a shot: *a bad lie.* **b** the angle made by the shaft of the club before the upswing. [16] **lie of the land. a** the topography of the land. **b** the way in which a situation is developing or people are behaving. ◆ See also **lie down, lie in, lie to, lie up.**
▷**HISTORY** Old English *licgan* akin to Old High German *ligen* to lie, Latin *lectus* bed

Language note See at **lay**[1].

Liebfraumilch ('liːbfraʊˌmɪlk; *German* 'liːpfraumɪlç) *or* **Liebfrauenmilch** (*German* liːp'frauənmɪlç) NOUN a white table wine from the Rhine vineyards.
▷**HISTORY** German: from *Liebfrau* the Virgin Mary + *Milch* milk; after *Liebfrauenstift* convent in Worms where the wine was originally made

Liebig condenser (*German* 'liːbɪç) NOUN *Chem* a laboratory condenser consisting of a glass tube surrounded by a glass envelope through which cooling water flows.
▷**HISTORY** named after Justus, Baron von *Liebig* (1803–73), German chemist

Liechtenstein ('lɪktənˌstaɪn; *German* 'lɪçtənʃtain) NOUN a small mountainous principality in central Europe on the Rhine: formed in 1719 by the uniting of the lordships of Schellenburg and Vaduz, which had been purchased by the Austrian family of Liechtenstein; customs union formed with Switzerland in 1924. Official language: German. Religion: Roman Catholic majority. Currency: Swiss franc. Capital: Vaduz. Pop.: 33 000 (2001 est.). Area: 160 sq. km (62 sq. miles).

Liechtensteiner ('lɪktənˌstaɪnə) NOUN [1] a native or inhabitant of Liechtenstein. ◆ ADJECTIVE [2] of or relating to Liechtenstein or its inhabitants.

lied (liːd; *German* liːt) NOUN, *plural* **lieder** ('liːdə; *German* 'liːdər). *Music* any of various musical settings for solo voice and piano of a romantic or lyrical poem, for which composers such as Schubert, Schumann, and Wolf are famous.
▷**HISTORY** from German: song

lie detector NOUN a polygraph used esp by a police interrogator to detect false or devious answers to questions, a sudden change in one or more involuntary physiological responses being considered a manifestation of guilt, fear, etc. See **polygraph** (sense 1), **galvanic skin response.**

lie down VERB (*intr, adverb*) [1] to place oneself or be in a prostrate position in order to rest or sleep. [2] to accept without protest or opposition (esp in the phrases **lie down under, take something lying down**). ◆ NOUN **lie-down.** [3] a rest.

lief (liːf) ADVERB [1] *Now rare* gladly; willingly: *I'd as lief go today as tomorrow.* ◆ ADJECTIVE [2] *Archaic* **a** ready; glad. **b** dear; beloved.
▷**HISTORY** Old English *leof;* related to *lufu* love

liege (liːdʒ) ADJECTIVE [1] (of a lord) owed feudal allegiance (esp in the phrase **liege lord**). [2] (of a vassal or servant) owing feudal allegiance: *a liege subject.* [3] of or relating to the relationship or bond between liege lord and liegeman: *liege homage.* [4] faithful; loyal. ◆ NOUN [5] a liege lord. [6] a liegeman or true subject.
▷**HISTORY** C13: from Old French *lige,* from Medieval Latin *līticus,* from *lītus, laetus* serf, of Germanic origin

Liège (lɪ'eɪʒ; *French* ljɛʒ) NOUN [1] a province of E Belgium: formerly a principality of the Holy Roman Empire, much larger than the present-day province. Pop.: 1 019 442 (2000 est.). Area: 3877 sq. km (1497 sq. miles). [2] a city in E Belgium, capital of Liège province: the largest French-speaking city in Belgium; river port and industrial centre. Pop.: 185 638 (2000 est.). ◆ Flemish name: **Luik.**

liegeman ('liːdʒˌmæn) NOUN, *plural* **-men.** [1] (formerly) the subject of a sovereign or feudal lord; vassal. [2] a loyal follower.

Liegnitz ('liːgnɪts) NOUN the German name for **Legnica.**

lie in VERB (*intr, adverb*) [1] to remain in bed late in the morning. [2] to be confined in childbirth. ◆ NOUN **lie-in.** [3] a long stay in bed in the morning.

lien ('liːən, liːn) NOUN *Law* a right to retain possession of another's property pending discharge of a debt.
▷**HISTORY** C16: via Old French from Latin *ligāmen* bond, from *ligāre* to bind

lienal ('laɪənᵊl) ADJECTIVE of or relating to the spleen.
▷**HISTORY** C19: from Latin *lien* SPLEEN

lientery ('laɪəntərɪ, -trɪ) NOUN *Pathol* the passage of undigested food in the faeces.
▷**HISTORY** C16: from French, from Medieval Latin, from Greek *leienteria,* from *leios* smooth + *enteron* intestine
▸**ˌlien'teric** ADJECTIVE

Liepāja *or* **Lepaya** (lɪ'pɑːjə) NOUN a port in W Latvia on the Baltic Sea; founded by the Teutonic Knights in 1263: a naval and industrial centre, with a fishing fleet. Pop.: 100 271 (1995 est.). Russian name: **Libava.** German name: **Libau.**

lierne (lɪ'ɜːn) NOUN *Architect* a short secondary rib that connects the intersections of the primary ribs, esp as used in Gothic vaulting.
▷**HISTORY** C19: from French, perhaps related to *lier* to bind

Liestal (*German* 'liːstaːl) NOUN a city in NW Switzerland, capital of Basel-Land demicanton. Pop.: 12 160 (latest est.).

lie to VERB (*intr, adverb*) *Nautical* (of a vessel) to be hove to with little or no swinging.

Lietuva (lɪə'tuːvə) NOUN the Lithuanian name for **Lithuania.**

lieu (ljuː, luː) NOUN stead; place (esp in the phrases **in lieu, in lieu of**).
▷**HISTORY** C13: from Old French, ultimately from Latin *locus* place

lie up VERB (*intr, adverb*) [1] to go into or stay in one's room or bed, as through illness. [2] to be out of commission or use: *my car has been lying up for months.*

Lieut ABBREVIATION FOR lieutenant. Also: **Lt.**

lieutenant (lɛf'tɛnənt; *US* luː'tɛnənt) NOUN [1] a military officer holding commissioned rank immediately junior to a captain. [2] a naval officer holding commissioned rank immediately junior to a lieutenant commander. [3] *US* an officer in a police or fire department ranking immediately junior to a captain. [4] a person who holds an office in subordination to or in place of a superior.
▷**HISTORY** C14: from Old French, literally: place-holding
▸**lieu'tenancy** NOUN

lieutenant colonel NOUN an officer holding commissioned rank immediately junior to a colonel in certain armies, air forces, and marine corps.

lieutenant commander NOUN an officer holding commissioned rank in certain navies immediately junior to a commander.

lieutenant general NOUN an officer holding commissioned rank in certain armies, air forces, and marine corps immediately junior to a general.

lieutenant governor NOUN [1] a deputy governor. [2] (in the US) an elected official who acts as deputy to a state governor and succeeds him if he dies. [3] **lieutenant-governor.** (in Canada) the representative of the Crown in a province: appointed by the federal government acting for the Crown.

life (laɪf) NOUN, *plural* **lives** (laɪvz). [1] the state or quality that distinguishes living beings or organisms from dead ones and from inorganic matter, characterized chiefly by metabolism, growth, and the ability to reproduce and respond to stimuli. Related adjectives: **animate, vital.** [2] the period between birth and death. [3] a living person or being: *to save a life.* [4] the time between birth and the present time. [5] **a** the remainder or extent of one's life. **b** (*as modifier*): *a life sentence; life membership; life subscription; life work.* [6] short for **life imprisonment.** [7] the amount of time that something is active or functioning: *the life of a battery.* [8] a present condition, state, or mode of existence: *my life is very dull here.* [9] **a** a biography. **b** (*as modifier*): *a life story.* [10] **a** a characteristic state or mode of existence: *town life.* **b** (*as modifier*): *life style.* [11] the sum or course of human events and activities. [12] liveliness or high spirits: *full of life.* [13] a source of strength, animation, or vitality: *he was the life of the show.* [14] all living things, taken as a whole: *there is no life on Mars; plant life.* [15] sparkle, as of wines. [16] strong or high flavour, as of fresh food. [17] (*modifier*) *Arts* drawn or taken from a living model: *life drawing; a life mask.* [18] *Physics* another name for **lifetime.** [19] (in certain games) one of a number of opportunities of participation. [20] **as large as life.** *Informal* real and living. [21] **larger than life.** in an exaggerated form. [22] **come to life. a** to become animate or conscious. **b** to be realistically portrayed or represented. [23] **for dear life.** urgently or with extreme vigour or desperation. [24] **for the life of me (him, her,** etc.). though trying desperately. [25] **go for your life.** *Austral and NZ informal* an expression of encouragement. [26] **a matter of life and death.** a matter of extreme urgency. [27] **not on your life.** *Informal* certainly not. [28] **the life and soul.** *Informal* a person regarded as the main source of merriment and liveliness: *the life and soul of the party.* [29] **the life of Riley.** *Informal* an easy life. [30] **to the life.** (of a copy or image) resembling the original exactly. [31] **to save (one's) life.** *Informal* in spite of all considerations or attempts: *he couldn't play football to save his life.* [32] **the time of one's life.** a memorably enjoyable time. [33] **true to life.** faithful to reality.
▷**HISTORY** Old English *līf;* related to Old High German *lib,* Old Norse *līf* life, body

life assurance NOUN a form of insurance

providing for the payment of a specified sum to a named beneficiary on the death of the policyholder. Also called: **life insurance.**

life belt NOUN a ring filled with buoyant material or air, used to keep a person afloat when in danger of drowning.

lifeblood (ˈlaɪfˌblʌd) NOUN 1 the blood, considered as vital to sustain life. 2 the essential or animating force.

lifeboat (ˈlaɪfˌbəʊt) NOUN 1 a boat, propelled by oars or a motor, used for rescuing people at sea, escaping from a sinking ship, etc. 2 *Informal* a fund set up by the dealers in a market to rescue any member who may become insolvent as a result of a collapse in market prices.

life buoy NOUN any of various kinds of buoyant device for keeping people afloat in an emergency.

life coach NOUN a person whose job is to improve the quality of his or her client's life, by offering advice on professional and personal matters, such as career, health, personal relationships, etc.

life cycle NOUN the series of changes occurring in an animal or plant between one development stage and the identical stage in the next generation.

life estate NOUN property that may be held only for the extent of the holder's lifetime.

life expectancy NOUN the statistically determined average number of years of life remaining after a specified age for a given group of individuals. Also called: **expectation of life.**

life form NOUN 1 *Biology* the characteristic overall form and structure of a mature organism on the basis of which it can be classified. 2 any living creature. 3 (in science fiction) an alien.

lifeguard (ˈlaɪfˌgɑːd) NOUN a person present at a beach or pool to guard people against the risk of drowning. Also called: **life-saver.**

Life Guards PLURAL NOUN (in Britain) a cavalry regiment forming part of the Household Brigade, who wear scarlet jackets and white plumes in their helmets.

life history NOUN 1 the series of changes undergone by an organism between fertilization of the egg and death. 2 the series of events that make up a person's life.

life imprisonment NOUN (in Britain) an indeterminate sentence always given for murder and as a maximum sentence in several other crimes. There is no remission, although the Home Secretary may order the prisoner's release on licence.

life instinct NOUN *Psychoanal* the instinct for reproduction and self-preservation.

life insurance NOUN another name for **life assurance.**

life interest NOUN interest (esp from property) that is payable to a person during his life but ceases with his death.

life jacket NOUN an inflatable sleeveless jacket worn to keep a person afloat when in danger of drowning.

lifeless (ˈlaɪflɪs) ADJECTIVE 1 without life; inanimate; dead. 2 not sustaining living organisms. 3 having no vitality or animation. 4 unconscious.
▸ **ˈlifelessly** ADVERB ▸ **ˈlifelessness** NOUN

life lesson NOUN something from which useful knowledge or principles can be learned.

lifelike (ˈlaɪfˌlaɪk) ADJECTIVE closely resembling or representing life.
▸ **ˈlifeˌlikeness** NOUN

lifeline (ˈlaɪfˌlaɪn) NOUN 1 a line thrown or fired aboard a vessel for hauling in a hawser for a breeches buoy. 2 any rope or line attached to a vessel or trailed from it for the safety of passengers, crew, swimmers, etc. 3 a line by which a deep-sea diver is raised or lowered. 4 a vital line of access or communication.

lifelong (ˈlaɪfˌlɒŋ) ADJECTIVE lasting for or as if for a lifetime.

lifelong learning NOUN the provision or use of both formal and informal learning opportunities throughout people's lives in order to foster the continuous development and improvement of the knowledge and skills needed for employment and personal fulfilment.

life mask NOUN a cast taken from the face of a living person, usually using plaster of Paris.

life partner NOUN either member of a couple in a long-term relationship.

life peer NOUN *Brit* a peer whose title lapses at his death.

life preserver NOUN 1 *Brit* a club or bludgeon, esp one kept for self-defence. 2 *US and Canadian* a life belt or life jacket.

lifer (ˈlaɪfə) NOUN *Informal* a prisoner sentenced to life imprisonment.

life raft NOUN a raft for emergency use at sea.

life-saver NOUN 1 the saver of a person's life. 2 another name for **lifeguard.** 3 *Informal* a person or thing that gives help in time of need.

life-saving ADJECTIVE 1 acting to save a person's life. 2 *Informal* giving help in time of need. ◆ NOUN 3 the practice or techniques of saving people's lives.

life science NOUN any one of the branches of science concerned with the structure and behaviour of living organisms, such as biology, botany, zoology, physiology, or biochemistry. Compare **physical science.** See also **social science.**

life-size *or* **life-sized** ADJECTIVE representing actual size.

life space NOUN *Psychol* a spatial representation of all the forces that control a person's behaviour.

life span NOUN the period of time during which a human being, animal, machine, etc., may be expected to live or function under normal conditions.

lifestyle (ˈlaɪfˌstaɪl) NOUN 1 a set of attitudes, habits, or possessions associated with a particular person or group. 2 such attitudes, etc., regarded as fashionable or desirable. 3 *NZ* **a** a luxurious semirural manner of living. **b** (*as modifier*): *a lifestyle property.* ◆ ADJECTIVE 4 suggestive of a fashionable or desirable lifestyle: *a lifestyle café.* 5 (of a drug) designed to treat problems, such as impotence or excess weight, which affect a person's quality of life rather than their health.

lifestyle block NOUN *NZ* a semi-rural property comprising a house and land for small-scale farming.

lifestyle business NOUN a small business in which the owners are more anxious to pursue interests that reflect their lifestyle than to make more than a comfortable living.

lifestyle guru NOUN a person hired to give someone advice on various aspects of his or her life, work, and relationships.

lifestyler (ˈlaɪfˌstaɪlə) NOUN *Informal* a person who adopts a particular lifestyle: *new lifestyler; vampire lifestyler.*

life-support ADJECTIVE of or providing the equipment required to sustain human life in an unnatural environment, such as in space, or in severe illness or disability.

life table NOUN another name for **mortality table.**

lifetime (ˈlaɪfˌtaɪm) NOUN 1 **a** the length of time a person or animal is alive. **b** (*as modifier*): *a lifetime supply.* 2 the length of time that something functions, is useful, etc. 3 *Physics* the average time of existence of an unstable or reactive entity, such as a nucleus, excited state, elementary particle, etc.; mean life.

Liffey (ˈlɪfɪ) NOUN a river in E Republic of Ireland, rising in the Wicklow Mountains and flowing west, then northeast through Dublin into Dublin Bay. Length: 80 km (50 miles).

Lifford (ˈlɪfərd) NOUN the county town of Donegal, Republic of Ireland; market town. Pop.: 1460 (latest est.).

LIFO (ˈlaɪfəʊ) ACRONYM FOR last in, first out (as an accounting principle in sorting stock). Compare **FIFO.**

lift[1] (lɪft) VERB 1 to rise or cause to rise upwards from the ground or another support to a higher place: *to lift a sack.* 2 to move or cause to move upwards: *to lift one's eyes.* 3 (*tr*) to take hold of in order to carry or remove: *to lift something down from a shelf.* 4 (*tr*) to raise in status, spirituality, estimation, etc.: *his position lifted him from the common crowd.* 5 (*tr*) to revoke or rescind: *to lift tax restrictions.* 6 to make or become audible or louder: *to lift one's voice in song.* 7 (*tr*) to take (plants or underground crops) out of the ground for transplanting or harvesting. 8 (*intr*) to disappear by lifting or as if by lifting: *the fog lifted.* 9 to transport in a vehicle. 10 (*tr*) *Informal* to take unlawfully or dishonourably; steal. 11 (*tr*) *Informal* to make dishonest use of (another person's idea, writing, etc.); plagiarize. 12 (*tr*) *Slang* to arrest. 13 (*tr*) to perform a face-lift on. 14 (*tr*) *US and Canadian* to pay off (a mortgage, etc.). ◆ NOUN 15 the act or an instance of lifting. 16 the power or force available or used for lifting. 17 **a** *Brit* a platform, compartment, or cage raised or lowered in a vertical shaft to transport persons or goods in a building. US and Canadian word: **elevator. b** See **chairlift, ski lift.** 18 the distance or degree to which something is lifted. 19 a usually free ride as a passenger in a car or other vehicle. 20 a rise in the height of the ground. 21 a rise in morale or feeling of cheerfulness usually caused by some specific thing or event. 22 the force required to lift an object. 23 a layer of the heel of a shoe, etc., or a detachable pad inside the shoe to give the wearer added height. 24 aid; help. 25 *Mining* **a** the thickness of ore extracted in one operation. **b** a set of pumps used in a mine. 26 **a** the component of the aerodynamic forces acting on a wing, etc., at right angles to the airflow. **b** the upward force exerted by the gas in a balloon, airship, etc. 27 See **airlift** (sense 1).
▹ **HISTORY** C13: from Scandinavian; related to Old Norse *lypta,* Old English *lyft* sky; compare LOFT
▸ **ˈliftable** ADJECTIVE ▸ **ˈlifter** NOUN

lift[2] (lɪft) NOUN *Scot* the sky.
▹ **HISTORY** Old English *lyft*

liftboy (ˈlɪftˌbɔɪ) *or* **liftman** NOUN, *plural* **-boys** *or* **-men.** a person who operates a lift, esp in large public or commercial buildings and hotels.

lifting body NOUN a wingless aircraft or spacecraft that derives its aerodynamic lift from the shape of its body.

liftoff (ˈlɪftˌɒf) NOUN 1 the initial movement or ascent of a rocket from its launch pad. 2 the instant at which this occurs. ◆ VERB **lift off.** 3 (*intr, adverb*) (of a rocket) to leave its launch pad.

lift pump NOUN a pump that raises a fluid to a higher level. It usually consists of a piston and vertical cylinder with flap or ball valves in both piston and cylinder base. Compare **force pump.**

lig (lɪg) *Brit, slang* ◆ NOUN 1 (esp in the entertainment industry and the media) a function at which free entertainment and refreshments are available. ◆ VERB **ligs, ligging, ligged.** 2 (*intr*) to attend such a function in order to take advantage of free entertainment and refreshments; freeload.
▹ **HISTORY** C20: origin uncertain
▸ **ˈligger** NOUN ▸ **ˈligging** NOUN

ligament (ˈlɪgəmənt) NOUN 1 *Anatomy* any one of the bands or sheets of tough fibrous connective tissue that restrict movement in joints, connect various bones or cartilages, support muscles, etc. 2 any physical or abstract connection or bond.
▹ **HISTORY** C14: from Medieval Latin *ligāmentum,* from Latin (in the sense: bandage), from *ligāre* to bind

ligamentous (ˌlɪgəˈmɛntəs), **ligamental,** *or* **ligamentary** ADJECTIVE relating to or shaped like a ligament.

ligan (ˈlaɪgən) NOUN a variant of **lagan.**

ligand (ˈlɪgənd, ˈlaɪ-) NOUN *Chem* an atom, molecule, radical, or ion forming a complex with a central atom.
▹ **HISTORY** C20: from Latin *ligandum,* gerund of *ligāre* to bind

ligase (ˈlaɪˌgeɪz) NOUN any of a class of enzymes that catalyse the formation of covalent bonds and are important in the synthesis and repair of biological molecules, such as DNA.

ligate (ˈlaɪgeɪt) VERB (*tr*) to tie up or constrict (something) with a ligature.
▹ **HISTORY** C16: from Latin *ligātus,* from *ligāre* to bind
▸ **liˈgation** NOUN ▸ **ligative** (ˈlɪgətɪv) ADJECTIVE

ligature (ˈlɪgətʃə, -ˌtʃʊə) NOUN 1 the act of binding or tying up. 2 something used to bind. 3 a link, bond, or tie. 4 *Surgery* a thread or wire for tying around a vessel, duct, etc., as for constricting the flow of blood to a part. 5 *Printing* a character of

two or more joined letters, such as, fi, fl, ffi, ffl. 6 *Music* **a** a slur or the group of notes connected by it. **b** (in plainsong notation) a symbol indicating two or more notes grouped together. ◆ VERB 7 (*tr*) to bind with a ligature; ligate.
▷HISTORY C14: from Late Latin *ligātūra*, ultimately from Latin *ligāre* to bind

liger (ˈlaɪgə) NOUN the hybrid offspring of a female tiger and a male lion.

light[1] (laɪt) NOUN 1 the medium of illumination that makes sight possible. 2 Also called: **visible radiation.** electromagnetic radiation that is capable of causing a visual sensation and has wavelengths from about 380 to about 780 nanometres. 3 (*not in technical usage*) electromagnetic radiation that has a wavelength outside this range, esp ultraviolet radiation: *ultraviolet light.* 4 the sensation experienced when electromagnetic radiation within the visible spectrum falls on the retina of the eye. Related prefix: **photo-.** 5 anything that illuminates, such as a lamp or candle. 6 See **traffic light.** 7 a particular quality or type of light: *a good light for reading.* 8 **a** illumination from the sun during the day; daylight. **b** the time this appears; daybreak; dawn. 9 anything that allows the entrance of light, such as a window or compartment of a window. 10 the condition of being visible or known (esp in the phrases **bring** *or* **come to light**). 11 an aspect or view: *he saw it in a different light.* 12 mental understanding or spiritual insight. 13 a person considered to be an authority or leader. 14 brightness of countenance, esp a sparkle in the eyes. 15 **a** the act of igniting or kindling something, such as a cigarette. **b** something that ignites or kindles, esp in a specified manner, such as a spark or flame. **c** something used for igniting or kindling, such as a match. 16 See **lighthouse.** 17 **a** the effect of illumination on objects or scenes, as created in a picture. **b** an area of brightness in a picture, as opposed to shade. 18 a poetic or archaic word for **eyesight.** 19 the answer to a clue in a crossword. 20 **in (the) light of.** in view of; taking into account; considering. 21 **light at the end of the tunnel.** hope for the ending of a difficult or unpleasant situation. 22 **out like a light.** quickly asleep or unconscious. 23 **see the light. a** to gain sudden insight into or understanding of something. **b** to experience a religious conversion. 24 **see the light (of day). a** to come into being. **b** to come to public notice. 25 **shed** (*or* **throw**) **light on.** to clarify or supply additional information on. 26 **stand in a person's light.** to stand so as to obscure a person's vision. 27 **strike a light. a** (*verb*) to ignite something, esp a match, by friction. **b** (*interjection*) *Brit* an exclamation of surprise. ◆ ADJECTIVE 28 full of light; well-lighted. 29 (of a colour) reflecting or transmitting a large amount of light: *light yellow.* Compare **medium** (sense 2), **dark** (sense 2). 30 *Phonetics* relating to or denoting an (l) pronounced with front vowel resonance; clear: *the French "l" is much lighter than that of English.* Compare **dark** (sense 9). ◆ VERB **lights, lighting, lighted** *or* **lit** (lɪt). 31 to ignite or cause to ignite. 32 (often foll by *up*) to illuminate or cause to illuminate. 33 to make or become cheerful or animated. 34 (*tr*) to guide or lead by light. ◆ See also **lights**[1], **light up.**
▷HISTORY Old English *lēoht;* related to Old High German *lioht,* Gothic *liuhath,* Latin *lux*
▸ˈ**lightish** ADJECTIVE ▸ˈ**lightless** ADJECTIVE

light[2] (laɪt) ADJECTIVE 1 not heavy; weighing relatively little. 2 having relatively low density: *magnesium is a light metal.* 3 lacking sufficient weight; not agreeing with standard or official weights. 4 not great in degree, intensity, or number: *light rain; a light eater.* 5 without burdens, difficulties, or problems; easily borne or done: *a light heart; light work.* 6 graceful, agile, or deft: *light fingers.* 7 not bulky or clumsy. 8 not serious or profound; entertaining: *light verse.* 9 without importance or consequence; insignificant: *no light matter.* 10 frivolous or capricious. 11 loose in morals. 12 dizzy or unclear: *a light head.* 13 (of bread, cake, etc.) spongy or well leavened. 14 easily digested: *a light meal.* 15 relatively low in alcoholic content: *a light wine.* 16 (of a soil) having a crumbly texture. 17 (of a vessel, lorry, etc.) **a** designed to carry light loads. **b** not loaded. 18 carrying light arms or equipment: *light infantry.* 19 (of an industry) engaged in the production of small consumer goods using light machinery. Compare **heavy** (sense 10). 20 *Aeronautics* (of an aircraft) having a maximum take-off weight less than 5670 kilograms (12 500 pounds). 21 *Chem* (of an oil fraction obtained from coal tar) having a boiling range between about 100° and 210°C. 22 (of a railway) having a narrow gauge, or in some cases a standard gauge with speed or load restrictions not applied to a main line. 23 *Bridge* **a** (of a bid) made on insufficient values. **b** (of a player) having failed to take sufficient tricks to make his contract. 24 *Phonetics, prosody* (of a syllable, vowel, etc.) unaccented or weakly stressed; short. Compare **heavy** (sense 13). See also **light**[1] (sense 30). 25 *Phonetics* the least of three levels of stress in an utterance, in such languages as English. 26 **light on.** *Informal* lacking a sufficient quantity of (something). 27 **make light of.** to treat as insignificant or trifling. ◆ ADVERB 28 a less common word for **lightly.** 29 with little equipment, baggage, etc.: *to travel light.* ◆ VERB **lights, lighting, lighted** *or* **lit** (lɪt). (*intr*) 30 (esp of birds) to settle or land after flight. 31 to get down from a horse, vehicle, etc. 32 (foll by *on* or *upon*) to come upon unexpectedly. 33 to strike or fall on: *the choice lighted on me.* ◆ See also **light into, light out, lights**[2].
▷HISTORY Old English *lēoht;* related to Dutch *licht,* Gothic *leihts*
▸ˈ**lightish** ADJECTIVE ▸ˈ**lightly** ADVERB ▸ˈ**lightness** NOUN

Light (laɪt) NOUN 1 God regarded as a source of illuminating grace and strength. 2 *Quakerism* short for **Inner Light.**

light air NOUN very light air movement of force one on the Beaufort scale.

light box NOUN a light source contained in a box and covered with a diffuser, used for viewing photographic transparencies, negatives, etc.

light breeze NOUN a very light wind of force two on the Beaufort scale.

light bulb NOUN a glass bulb containing a gas, such as argon or nitrogen, at low pressure and enclosing a thin metal filament that emits light when an electric current is passed through it. Sometimes shortened to: **bulb.**

light bulb moment NOUN *Informal* a moment of sudden inspiration, revelation, or recognition.
▷HISTORY C20: from the cartoon image of a light bulb lighting up above a character's head when he or she has an idea

light cannon NOUN a particularly powerful torch, spotlight, or searchlight.

light-emitting diode NOUN a diode of semiconductor material, such as gallium arsenide, that emits light when a forward bias is applied, the colour depending on the semiconductor material: used as off/on indicators. Abbreviation: **LED.**

lighten[1] (ˈlaɪtᵊn) VERB 1 to become or make light. 2 (*intr*) to shine; glow. 3 (*intr*) (of lightning) to flash. 4 (*tr*) an archaic word for **enlighten.**

lighten[2] (ˈlaɪtᵊn) VERB 1 to make or become less heavy. 2 to make or become less burdensome or oppressive; mitigate. 3 to make or become more cheerful or lively.

light engine NOUN a railway locomotive in motion without drawing any carriages or wagons. US equivalent: **wildcat.**

lightening (ˈlaɪtᵊnɪŋ) NOUN *Obstetrics* the sensation, experienced by many women late in pregnancy when the head of the fetus enters the pelvis, of a reduction in pressure on the diaphragm, making it easier to breathe.

lighter[1] (ˈlaɪtə) NOUN 1 a small portable device for providing a naked flame or red-hot filament to light cigarettes, etc. 2 a person or thing that ignites something.

lighter[2] (ˈlaɪtə) NOUN a flat-bottomed barge used for transporting cargo, esp in loading or unloading a ship.
▷HISTORY C15: probably from Middle Dutch; compare C16 Dutch *lichter*

lighterage (ˈlaɪtərɪdʒ) NOUN 1 the conveyance or loading and unloading of cargo by means of a lighter. 2 the charge for this service.

lighter than air ADJECTIVE (**lighter-than-air** when prenominal) 1 having a lower density than that of air. 2 of or relating to an aircraft, such as a balloon or airship, that depends on buoyancy for support in the air.

light face NOUN 1 *Printing* a weight of type characterized by light thin lines. Compare **bold face.** ◆ ADJECTIVE *also* **light-faced.** 2 (of type) having this weight.

light-fast ADJECTIVE (of a dye or dyed article) unaffected by light.

light-fingered ADJECTIVE having nimble or agile fingers, esp for thieving or picking pockets.
▸ˌ**light-ˈfingeredness** NOUN

light flyweight NOUN **a** an amateur boxer weighing not more than 48 kg (106 pounds). **b** (*as modifier*): *a light-flyweight fight.*

light-footed ADJECTIVE having a light or nimble tread.
▸ˌ**light-ˈfootedly** ADVERB ▸ˌ**light-ˈfootedness** NOUN

light-headed ADJECTIVE 1 frivolous in disposition or behaviour. 2 giddy; feeling faint or slightly delirious.
▸ˌ**light-ˈheadedly** ADVERB ▸ˌ**light-ˈheadedness** NOUN

light-hearted ADJECTIVE cheerful or carefree in mood or disposition.
▸ˌ**light-ˈheartedly** ADVERB ▸ˌ**light-ˈheartedness** NOUN

light heavyweight NOUN 1 Also called (in Britain): **cruiserweight. a** a professional boxer weighing 160–175 pounds (72.5–79.5 kg). **b** an amateur boxer weighing 75–81 kg (165–179 pounds). **c** (*as modifier*): *a light-heavyweight bout.* 2 a wrestler in a similar weight category (usually 192–214 pounds (87–97 kg)).

light horse NOUN lightly armed and highly mobile cavalry.
▸ˌ**light-ˈhorseman** NOUN

lighthouse (ˈlaɪtˌhaʊs) NOUN a fixed structure in the form of a tower equipped with a light visible to mariners for warning them of obstructions, for marking harbour entrances, etc.

lighting (ˈlaɪtɪŋ) NOUN 1 the act or quality of illumination or ignition. 2 the apparatus for supplying artificial light effects to a stage, film, or television set. 3 the distribution of light on an object or figure, as in painting, photography, etc.

lighting cameraman NOUN *Films* the person who designs and supervises the lighting of scenes to be filmed.

lighting-up time NOUN the time when vehicles are required by law to have their lights switched on.

light into VERB (*intr, preposition*) *Informal* to assail physically or verbally.

light meter NOUN another name for **exposure meter.**

light middleweight NOUN **a** an amateur boxer weighing 67–71 kg (148–157 pounds). **b** (*as modifier*): *a light-middleweight bout.* Compare **junior middleweight.**

light music NOUN music for popular entertainment.

lightness (ˈlaɪtnɪs) NOUN the attribute of an object or colour that enables an observer to judge the extent to which the object or colour reflects or transmits incident light. See also **colour.**

lightning (ˈlaɪtnɪŋ) NOUN 1 a flash of light in the sky, occurring during a thunderstorm and caused by a discharge of electricity, either between clouds or between a cloud and the earth. Related adjectives: **fulgurous, fulminous.** 2 (*modifier*) fast and sudden: *a lightning raid.*
▷HISTORY C14: variant of *lightening*

lightning arrester NOUN a device that protects electrical equipment, such as an aerial, from an excessive voltage resulting from a lightning discharge or other accidental electric surge, by discharging it to earth.

lightning bug NOUN *US and Canadian* another name for the **firefly.**

lightning chess NOUN rapid chess in which either each move has a fixed time allowed (usually 10 seconds) or each player is allotted a fixed time (often 5 minutes) for all his moves. US name: **rapid transit chess.**

lightning conductor *or* **rod** NOUN a metal strip terminating in a series of sharp points, attached to the highest part of a building, etc., to discharge the electric field before it can reach a dangerous level and cause a lightning strike.

lightning stroke NOUN 1 a discharge of

lightning between a cloud and the earth, esp one that causes damage. [2] *Vet science* sudden death due to being struck by lightning, esp of cattle, horses or sheep.

light opera NOUN another term for **operetta**.

light out VERB *(intr, adverb) Informal* to depart quickly, as if being chased.

light pen NOUN *Computing* **a** a rodlike device which, when applied to the screen of a cathode-ray tube, can detect the time of passage of the illuminated spot across that point thus enabling a computer to determine the position on the screen being pointed at. **b** a penlike device, used to read bar codes, that emits light and determines the intensity of that light as reflected from a small area of an adjacent surface.

light pollution NOUN the glow from street and domestic lighting that obscures the night sky and hinders the observation of faint stars.

light rail NOUN a transport system using small trains or trams, often serving parts of a large metropolitan area.

light reaction NOUN *Botany* the stage of photosynthesis during which light energy is absorbed by chlorophyll and transformed into chemical energy stored in ATP. Compare **dark reaction**.

lights[1] (laɪts) PLURAL NOUN a person's ideas, knowledge, or understanding: *he did it according to his lights.*

lights[2] (laɪts) PLURAL NOUN the lungs, esp of sheep, bullocks, and pigs, used for feeding pets and occasionally in human food.
▷**HISTORY** C13: plural noun use of LIGHT[2], referring to the light weight of the lungs

light-sensitive ADJECTIVE *Physics* (of a surface) having a photoelectric property, such as the ability to generate a current, change its electrical resistance, etc., when exposed to light.

lightship (ˈlaɪtˌʃɪp) NOUN a ship equipped as a lighthouse and moored where a fixed structure would prove impracticable.

light show NOUN a kaleidoscopic display of moving lights, etc., projected onto a screen, esp during pop concerts.

lightsome[1] (ˈlaɪtsəm) ADJECTIVE *Archaic or poetic* [1] lighthearted. [2] airy or buoyant. [3] not serious; frivolous.
▸**ˈlightsomely** ADVERB ▸**ˈlightsomeness** NOUN

lightsome[2] (ˈlaɪtsəm) ADJECTIVE *Archaic or poetic* [1] producing or reflecting light. [2] full of or flooded with light.

lights out NOUN [1] the time when those resident at an institution, such as soldiers in barracks or children at a boarding school, are expected to retire to bed. [2] a fanfare or other signal indicating or signifying this.

light table NOUN *Printing* a translucent surface of ground glass or a similar substance, illuminated from below and used for the examination of positive or negative film, and for the make-up of photocomposed pages.

light trap NOUN any mechanical arrangement that allows some form of movement to take place while excluding light, such as a light-proof door or the lips of a film cassette.

light up VERB *(adverb)* [1] to light a cigarette, pipe, etc. [2] to illuminate or cause to illuminate. [3] to make or become cheerful or animated.

light water NOUN a name for water (H_2O), as distinct from heavy water.

lightweight (ˈlaɪtˌweɪt) ADJECTIVE [1] of a relatively light weight. [2] not serious; trivial. ◆ NOUN [3] a person or animal of a relatively light weight. [4] **a** a professional boxer weighing 130–135 pounds (59–61 kg). **b** an amateur boxer weighing 57–60 kg (126–132 pounds). **c** *(as modifier)*: *the lightweight contender.* [5] a wrestler in a similar weight category (usually 115–126 pounds (52–57 kg)). [6] *Informal* a person of little importance or influence.

light welterweight NOUN **a** an amateur boxer weighing 60–63.5 kg (132–140 pounds). **b** *(as modifier)*: *the light welterweight champion.* Compare **junior welterweight**.

light year NOUN a unit of distance used in astronomy, equal to the distance travelled by light in one year, i.e. 9.4607×10^{12} kilometres or 0.3066 parsecs.

lignaloes (laɪˈnæləʊz, lɪg-) NOUN *(functioning as singular)* another name for **eaglewood** (sense 2).
▷**HISTORY** C14 *ligne aloes,* from Medieval Latin *lignum aloēs* wood of the aloe

ligneous (ˈlɪgnɪəs) ADJECTIVE of or resembling wood.
▷**HISTORY** C17: from Latin *ligneus,* from *lignum* wood

ligni-, ligno-, *or before a vowel* **lign-** COMBINING FORM indicating wood: *lignocellulose.*
▷**HISTORY** from Latin *lignum* wood

lignicolous (lɪgˈnɪkələs) *or* **lignicole** (ˈlɪgnɪˌkəʊl) ADJECTIVE growing or living on or in wood.
▷**HISTORY** C19: LIGNI- + -COLOUS

ligniform (ˈlɪgnɪˌfɔːm) ADJECTIVE having the appearance of wood.

lignify (ˈlɪgnɪˌfaɪ) VERB **-fies, -fying, -fied.** *Botany* to make or become woody as a result of the deposition of lignin in the cell walls.
▸**ˌlignifiˈcation** NOUN

lignin (ˈlɪgnɪn) NOUN a complex polymer occurring in certain plant cell walls making the plant rigid.

lignite (ˈlɪgnaɪt) NOUN a brown carbonaceous sedimentary rock with woody texture that consists of accumulated layers of partially decomposed vegetation: used as a fuel. Fixed carbon content: 46–60 per cent; calorific value: 1.28×10^7 to 1.93×10^7 J/kg (5500 to 8300 Btu/lb). Also called: **brown coal.**
▸**lignitic** (lɪgˈnɪtɪk) ADJECTIVE

lignivorous (lɪgˈnɪvərəs) ADJECTIVE (of animals) feeding on wood.

lignocaine (ˈlɪgnəˌkeɪn) NOUN another name for **lidocaine.**
▷**HISTORY** C20: from LIGNO- + *caine,* on the model of *cocaine*

lignocellulose (ˌlɪgnəʊˈsɛljʊˌləʊs, -ˌləʊz) NOUN a compound of lignin and cellulose that occurs in the walls of xylem cells in woody tissue.

lignum (ˈlɪgnəm) NOUN *Austral* another name for **polygonum.**

lignum vitae (ˈvaɪtɪ) NOUN [1] either of two zygophyllaceous tropical American trees, *Guaiacum officinale* or *G. sanctum,* having blue or purple flowers. [2] the heavy resinous wood of either of these trees, which is used in machine bearings, casters, etc.: formerly thought to have medicinal properties. ◆ See also **guaiacum.**
▷**HISTORY** New Latin, from Late Latin, literally: wood of life

ligroin (ˈlɪgrəʊɪn) NOUN a volatile fraction of petroleum containing aliphatic hydrocarbons of the paraffin series. It has an approximate boiling point range of 70°–130°C and is used as a solvent.
▷**HISTORY** origin unknown

ligula (ˈlɪgjʊlə) NOUN, *plural* **-lae** (-ˌliː) *or* **-las.** [1] *Entomol* the terminal part of the labium of an insect consisting of paired lobes. [2] a variant spelling of **ligule.**
▷**HISTORY** C18: New Latin; see LIGULE
▸**ˈligular** ADJECTIVE ▸**ˈliguˌloid** ADJECTIVE

ligulate (ˈlɪgjʊlɪt, -ˌleɪt) ADJECTIVE [1] having the shape of a strap. [2] *Biology* of, relating to, or having a ligule or ligula.

ligule (ˈlɪgjuːl) *or* **ligula** NOUN [1] a membranous outgrowth at the junction between the leaf blade and sheath in many grasses and sedges. [2] a strap-shaped corolla, such as that of a ray floret in the daisy.
▷**HISTORY** C19: via French, from Latin *ligula* strap, variant of *lingula,* from *lingua* tongue

ligure (ˈlɪgjʊə) NOUN *Old Testament* any of the 12 precious stones used in the breastplates of high priests.
▷**HISTORY** C14: from Late Latin *ligūrius,* from Late Greek *ligurion*

Liguria (lɪˈgjʊərɪə) NOUN a region of NW Italy, on the **Ligurian Sea** (an arm of the Mediterranean): the third smallest of the regions of Italy. Pop.: 1 625 870 (2000 est.). Area: 5410 sq. km (2089 sq. miles).

Ligurian (lɪˈgjʊərɪən) ADJECTIVE [1] of or relating to Liguria, a region of NW Italy, or its inhabitants. ◆ NOUN [2] a native or inhabitant of Liguria.

likable *or* **likeable** (ˈlaɪkəbᵊl) ADJECTIVE easy to like; pleasing.
▸**ˈlikableness** *or* **ˈlikeableness** NOUN

Likasi (lɪˈkɑːsɪ) NOUN a city in the S Democratic Republic of Congo (formerly Zaïre): a centre of copper and cobalt production. Pop.: 299 118 (1994 est.). Former name: **Jadotville.**

like[1] (laɪk) ADJECTIVE [1] *(prenominal)* similar; resembling. ◆ PREPOSITION [2] similar to; similarly to; in the manner of: *acting like a maniac; he's so like his father.* [3] used correlatively to express similarity in certain proverbs: *like mother, like daughter.* [4] such as: *there are lots of ways you might amuse yourself — like taking a long walk, for instance.* ◆ ADVERB [5] a dialect word for **likely.** [6] *Not standard* as it were: often used as a parenthetic filler: *there was this policeman just staring at us, like.* ◆ CONJUNCTION [7] *Not standard* as though; as if: *you look like you've just seen a ghost.* [8] in the same way as; in the same way that: *she doesn't dance like you do.* ◆ NOUN [9] the equal or counterpart of a person or thing, esp one respected or prized: *compare like with like; her like will never be seen again.* [10] **the like.** similar things: *dogs, foxes, and the like.* [11] **the likes** (*or* **like**) **of.** people or things similar to (someone or something specified): *we don't want the likes of you around here.*
▷**HISTORY** shortened from Old English *gelīc;* compare Old Norse *glīkr* and *līkr* like

> **Language note** The use of *like* to mean *such as* was formerly thought to be undesirable in formal writing, but has now become acceptable. It was also thought that *as* rather than *like* should be used to mean *in the same way that,* but now both *as* and *like* are acceptable: *they hunt and catch fish as/like their ancestors used to.* The use of *look like* and *seem like* before a clause, although very common, is thought by many people to be incorrect or non-standard: *it looks as though he won't come* (not *it looks like he won't come*).

like[2] (laɪk) VERB [1] *(tr)* to find (something) enjoyable or agreeable or find it enjoyable or agreeable (to do something): *he likes boxing; he likes to hear music.* [2] *(tr)* to be fond of. [3] *(tr)* to prefer or wish (to do something): *we would like you to go.* [4] *(tr)* to feel towards; consider; regard: *how did she like it?* [5] *(intr)* to feel disposed or inclined; choose; wish. [6] *(tr) Archaic* to please; agree with: *it likes me not to go.* ◆ NOUN [7] *(usually plural)* a favourable feeling, desire, preference, etc. (esp in the phrase **likes and dislikes**).
▷**HISTORY** Old English *līcian;* related to Old Norse *līka,* Dutch *lijken*

-like SUFFIX FORMING ADJECTIVES [1] resembling or similar to: *lifelike; springlike.* [2] having the characteristics of: *childlike; ladylike.*
▷**HISTORY** from LIKE[1] (prep)

likelihood (ˈlaɪklɪˌhʊd) *or* **likeliness** NOUN [1] the condition of being
or probable; probability. [2] something that is probable. [3] *Statistics* the probability of a given sample being randomly drawn regarded as a function of the parameters of the population. The likelihood ratio is the ratio of this to the maximized likelihood. See also **maximum likelihood.**

likely (ˈlaɪklɪ) ADJECTIVE [1] (usually foll by an infinitive) tending or inclined; apt: *likely to rain.* [2] probable: *a likely result.* [3] believable or feasible; plausible. [4] appropriate for a purpose or activity. [5] having good possibilities of success: *a likely candidate.* [6] *Dialect, chiefly US* attractive, agreeable, or enjoyable: *her likely ways won her many friends.* ◆ ADVERB [7] probably or presumably. [8] **as likely as not.** very probably.
▷**HISTORY** C14: from Old Norse *līkligr*

> **Language note** *Likely* as an adverb is preceded by another, intensifying adverb, as in *it will very likely rain* or *it will most likely rain.* Its use without an intensifier, as in *it will likely rain* is regarded as unacceptable by most users of British English, though it is common in colloquial US English.

like-minded ADJECTIVE agreeing in opinions, goals, etc.
▸**ˌlike-ˈmindedly** ADVERB ▸**ˌlike-ˈmindedness** NOUN

liken ('laɪkən) VERB (*tr*) to see or represent as the same or similar; compare.
▷HISTORY C14: from LIKE[1] (adjective)

likeness ('laɪknɪs) NOUN 1 the condition of being alike; similarity. 2 a painted, carved, moulded, or graphic image of a person or thing. 3 an imitative appearance; semblance.

likewise ('laɪk,waɪz) ADVERB 1 in addition; moreover; also. 2 in like manner; similarly.

liking ('laɪkɪŋ) NOUN 1 the feeling of a person who likes; fondness. 2 a preference, inclination, or pleasure.

likuta (li:'ku:tɑ:) NOUN, *plural* **makuta** (mɑ:'ku:tɑ:). (formerly) a coin used in Zaïre.
▷HISTORY C20: from Congolese

lilac ('laɪlək) NOUN 1 Also called: **syringa.** any of various Eurasian oleaceous shrubs or small trees of the genus *Syringa,* esp *S. vulgaris* (**common lilac**) which has large sprays of purple or white fragrant flowers. 2 **French lilac.** another name for **goat's-rue** (sense 1). 3 **a** a light or moderate purple colour, sometimes with a bluish or reddish tinge. **b** (*as adjective*): *a lilac carpet.*
▷HISTORY C17: via French from Spanish, from Arabic *līlak,* changed from Persian *nīlak* bluish, from *nīl* blue

lilangeni ('lɪlɑ:ŋ,geɪnɪ) NOUN, *plural* **emalangeni** ('ɛmɑ:lɑ:ŋ,geɪnɪ). the standard monetary unit of Swaziland, divided into 100 cents.

liliaceous (,lɪlɪ'eɪʃəs) ADJECTIVE of, relating to, or belonging to the *Liliaceae,* a family of plants having showy flowers and a bulb or bulblike organ: includes the lily, tulip, and bluebell.
▷HISTORY C18: from Late Latin *līliāceus,* from *līlium* lily

Lilith ('lɪlɪθ) NOUN 1 (in the Old Testament and in Jewish folklore) a female demon, who attacks children. 2 (in Talmudic literature) Adam's first wife. 3 a witch notorious in medieval demonology.

Lille (*French* lil) NOUN an industrial city in N France: the medieval capital of Flanders; forms with Roubaix and Tourcoing one of the largest conurbations in France. Pop.: 182 228 (1999).

Lille Bælt ('lilə 'bɛld) NOUN the Danish name for the **Little Belt.**

Lilliputian (,lɪlɪ'pju:ʃɪən) NOUN 1 a tiny person or being. ◆ ADJECTIVE 2 tiny; very small. 3 petty or trivial.
▷HISTORY C18: from *Lilliput,* an imaginary country of tiny inhabitants in Swift's *Gulliver's Travels* (1726)

lilly-pilly ('lɪlɪ,pɪlɪ) NOUN *Austral* a tall myrtaceous tree, *Acmena smithii,* having dark green leaves, spikes of feathery flowers, and white to purplish edible berries.
▷HISTORY C19: of uncertain origin

Lilo ('laɪləʊ) NOUN, *plural* **-los.** *Trademark* a type of inflatable plastic or rubber mattress.

Lilongwe (lɪ'lɒŋwɪ) NOUN the capital of Malawi, in the central part west of Lake Malawi. Pop.: 435 964 (1998 est.).

lilt (lɪlt) NOUN 1 (in music) a jaunty rhythm. 2 a buoyant motion. ◆ VERB (*intr*) 3 (of a melody) to have a lilt. 4 to move in a buoyant manner.
▷HISTORY C14 *lulten,* origin obscure
▸**'lilting** ADJECTIVE

lily ('lɪlɪ) NOUN, *plural* **lilies.** 1 any liliaceous perennial plant of the N temperate genus *Lilium,* such as the Turk's-cap lily and tiger lily, having scaly bulbs and showy typically pendulous flowers. 2 the bulb or flower of any of these plants. 3 any of various similar or related plants, such as the water lily, plantain lily, and day lily.
▷HISTORY Old English, from Latin *līlium;* related to Greek *leirion* lily
▸**'lily-,like** ADJECTIVE

lily iron NOUN a harpoon, the head of which is detachable.
▷HISTORY C19: from the shape of its shaft, which resembles lily leaves

lily-livered ADJECTIVE cowardly; timid.

lily of the valley NOUN, *plural* **lilies of the valley.** a small liliaceous plant, *Convallaria majalis,* of Eurasia and North America cultivated as a garden plant, having two long oval leaves and spikes of white bell-shaped flowers.

lily pad NOUN any of the floating leaves of a water lily.

lily-trotter NOUN another name for **jaçana.**

lily-white ADJECTIVE 1 of a pure white: *lily-white skin.* 2 *Informal* pure; irreproachable. 3 *US informal* **a** discriminating against Blacks: *a lily-white club.* **b** racially segregated.

Lima ('li:mə) NOUN 1 the capital of Peru, near the Pacific coast on the Rímac River: the centre of Spanish colonization in South America; university founded in 1551 (the oldest in South America); an industrial centre with a port at nearby Callao. Pop. (city): 316 322 (1998 est.), with a conurbation of 6 022 213 (1995). 2 *Communications* a code word for the letter *L.*

lima bean ('laɪmə, 'li:-) NOUN 1 any of several varieties of the bean plant, *Phaseolus lunatus* (or *P. limensis*), native to tropical America but cultivated in the US for its flat pods containing pale green edible seeds. 2 the seed of such a plant. ◆ See also **butter bean.**
▷HISTORY C19: named after LIMA

limacine ('lɪmə,saɪn, -sɪn, 'laɪ-) ADJECTIVE 1 of, or relating to slugs, esp those of the genus *Limax.* 2 Also: **limaciform** (lɪ'mæsɪ,fɔ:m). resembling a slug.
▷HISTORY C19: from New Latin, from Latin *līmax,* from *līmus* mud

limaçon ('lɪmə,sɒn) NOUN a heart-shaped curve generated by a point lying on a line at a fixed distance from the intersection of the line with a fixed circle, the line rotating about a point on the circumference of the circle.
▷HISTORY French, literally: snail (so named by Pascal)

Limassol ('lɪmə,sɒl) NOUN a port in S Cyprus: trading centre. Pop.: 152 900 (1998 est.). Ancient name: **Lemessus** (lə'mɛsəs).

Limavady (,lɪmə'vædɪ) NOUN a district of N Northern Ireland, in Co. Londonderry. Pop.: 32 422 (2001). Area: 586 sq. km (226 sq. miles).

limb[1] (lɪm) NOUN 1 an arm or leg, or the analogous part on an animal, such as a wing. 2 any of the main branches of a tree. 3 a branching or projecting section or member; extension. 4 a person or thing considered to be a member, part, or agent of a larger group or thing. 5 *Chiefly Brit* a mischievous child (esp in **limb of Satan** *or* **limb of the devil**). 6 **out on a limb. a** in a precarious or questionable position. **b** *Brit* isolated, esp because of unpopular opinions. ◆ VERB 7 (*tr*) a rare word for **dismember.**
▷HISTORY Old English *lim;* related to Old Norse *limr*
▸**limbed** ADJECTIVE ▸**'limbless** ADJECTIVE

limb[2] (lɪm) NOUN 1 the edge of the apparent disc of the sun, a moon, or a planet. 2 a graduated arc attached to instruments, such as the sextant, used for measuring angles. 3 *Botany* **a** the expanded upper part of a bell-shaped corolla. **b** the expanded part of a leaf, petal, or sepal. 4 either of the two halves of a bow. 5 Also called: **fold limb.** either of the sides of a geological fold.
▷HISTORY C15: from Latin *limbus* edge

limbate ('lɪmbeɪt) ADJECTIVE *Biology* having an edge or border of a different colour from the rest: *limbate flowers.*
▷HISTORY C19: from Late Latin *limbātus* bordered, from LIMBUS

limbed (lɪmd) ADJECTIVE **a** having limbs. **b** (*in combination*): *short-limbed; strong-limbed.*

limber[1] ('lɪmbə) ADJECTIVE 1 capable of being easily bent or flexed; pliant. 2 able to move or bend freely; agile.
▷HISTORY C16: origin uncertain
▸**'limberly** ADVERB ▸**'limberness** NOUN

limber[2] ('lɪmbə) NOUN 1 part of a gun carriage, often containing ammunition, consisting of an axle, pole, and two wheels, that is attached to the rear of an item of equipment, esp field artillery. ◆ VERB 2 (usually foll by *up*) to attach the limber (to a gun, etc.).
▷HISTORY C15 *lymour* shaft of a gun carriage, origin uncertain

limber[3] ('lɪmbə) NOUN (*often plural*) *Nautical* (in the bilge of a vessel) a fore-and-aft channel through a series of holes in the frames (**limber holes**) where water collects and can be pumped out.
▷HISTORY C17: probably changed from French *lumière* hole (literally: light)

limber up VERB (*adverb*) 1 (*intr*) (esp in sports) to exercise in order to be limber and agile. 2 (*tr*) to make flexible.

limbic system ('lɪmbɪk) NOUN the part of the brain bordering on the corpus callosum: concerned with basic emotion, hunger, and sex.
▷HISTORY C19 *limbic,* from French *limbique,* from *limbe* limbus, from New Latin *limbus,* from Latin: border

limbo[1] ('lɪmbəʊ) NOUN, *plural* **-bos.** 1 (*often capital*) *Christianity* the supposed abode of infants dying without baptism and the just who died before Christ. 2 an imaginary place for lost, forgotten, or unwanted persons or things. 3 an unknown intermediate place or condition between two extremes: *in limbo.* 4 a prison or confinement.
▷HISTORY C14: from Medieval Latin *in limbo* on the border (of hell)

limbo[2] ('lɪmbəʊ) NOUN, *plural* **-bos.** a Caribbean dance in which dancers pass, while leaning backwards, under a bar.
▷HISTORY C20: origin uncertain

Limbourg (lɛ̃bur) NOUN the French name for **Limburg** (sense 3).

Limburg ('lɪmbɜ:g; *Dutch* 'lɪmbyrx) NOUN 1 a medieval duchy of W Europe: divided between the Netherlands and Belgium in 1839. 2 a province of the SE Netherlands: contains a coalfield and industrial centres. Capital: Maastricht. Pop.: 1 141 200 (2000 est.). Area: 2253 sq. km (809 sq. miles). 3 a province of NE Belgium: contains the industrial regions of the Kempen coalfield. Capital: Hassett. Pop.: 1 019 442 (2000 est.). Area: 2422 sq. km (935 sq. miles). French name: **Limbourg.**

Limburger ('lɪmbɜ:gə) NOUN a semihard white cheese of very strong smell and flavour. Also called: **Limburg cheese.**

limbus ('lɪmbəs) NOUN, *plural* **-bi** (-baɪ). *Anatomy* the edge or border of any of various structures or parts.
▷HISTORY C15: from Latin: edge
▸**'limbic** ADJECTIVE

lime[1] (laɪm) NOUN 1 short for **quicklime, birdlime, slaked lime.** 2 *Agriculture* any of certain calcium compounds, esp calcium hydroxide, spread as a dressing on lime-deficient land. ◆ VERB (*tr*) 3 to spread (twigs, etc.) with birdlime. 4 to spread a calcium compound upon (land) to improve plant growth. 5 to catch (animals, esp birds) with or as if with birdlime. 6 to whitewash or cover (a wall, ceiling, etc.) with a mixture of lime and water (**limewash**).
▷HISTORY Old English *līm;* related to Icelandic *līm* glue, Latin *līmus* slime

lime[2] (laɪm) NOUN 1 a small Asian citrus tree, *Citrus aurantifolia,* with stiff sharp spines and small round or oval greenish fruits. 2 **a** the fruit of this tree, having acid fleshy pulp rich in vitamin C. **b** (*as modifier*): *lime juice.* ◆ ADJECTIVE 3 having the flavour of lime fruit.
▷HISTORY C17: from French, from Provençal, from Arabic *līmah*

lime[3] (laɪm) NOUN any linden tree, such as *Tilia europaea,* planted in many varieties for ornament.
▷HISTORY C17: changed from obsolete *line,* from Old English *lind* LINDEN

lime[4] (laɪm) VERB (*intr*) *Caribbean, slang* (of young people) to sit or stand around on the pavement.
▷HISTORY of unknown origin

limeade (,laɪm'eɪd) NOUN a drink made from sweetened lime juice and plain or carbonated water.

lime burner NOUN a person whose job it is to burn limestone to make lime.

lime green NOUN **a** a moderate greenish-yellow colour. **b** (*as adjective*): *a lime-green dress.*

limekiln ('laɪm,kɪln) NOUN a kiln in which calcium carbonate is calcined to produce quicklime.

limelight ('laɪm,laɪt) NOUN 1 **the.** a position of public attention or notice (esp in the phrase **in the limelight**). 2 **a** a type of lamp, formerly used in stage lighting, in which light is produced by heating lime to white heat. **b** Also called: **calcium light.** brilliant white light produced in this way.
▸**'lime,lighter** NOUN

limen ('laɪmɛn) NOUN, *plural* **limens** *or* **limina** ('lɪmɪnə). *Psychol* another term for **threshold** (sense 4). See also **liminal.**

▷HISTORY C19: from Latin

lime pit NOUN (in tanning) a pit containing lime in which hides are placed to remove the hair.

limerick ('lɪmərɪk) NOUN a form of comic verse consisting of five anapaestic lines of which the first, second, and fifth have three metrical feet and rhyme together and the third and fourth have two metrical feet and rhyme together.
▷HISTORY C19: allegedly from *will you come up to Limerick?,* a refrain sung between nonsense verses at a party

Limerick ('lɪmərɪk) NOUN [1] a county of SW Republic of Ireland, in N Munster province: consists chiefly of an undulating plain with rich pasture and mountains in the south. County town: Limerick. Pop.: 165 042 (1996). Area: 2686 sq. km (1037 sq. miles). [2] a port in SW Republic of Ireland, county town of Limerick, at the head of the Shannon estuary. Pop.: 52 039 (1996).

limes ('laɪmiːz) NOUN, *plural* **limites** ('lɪmɪˌtiːz). the fortified boundary of the Roman Empire.
▷HISTORY from Latin

limescale ('laɪmskeɪl) NOUN a flaky deposit left in containers such as kettles by the action of heat on water containing calcium salts. Often shortened to: **scale.**
▷HISTORY from LIME[1] (sense 1) + SCALE[1] (sense 3)

limestone ('laɪmˌstəʊn) NOUN a sedimentary rock consisting mainly of calcium carbonate, deposited as the calcareous remains of marine animals or chemically precipitated from the sea: used as a building stone and in the manufacture of cement, lime, etc.

limestone pavement NOUN *Geology* a horizontal surface of exposed limestone in which the joints have been enlarged, cutting the surface into roughly rectangular blocks. See also **clint, grike.**

limewater ('laɪmˌwɔːtə) NOUN [1] a clear colourless solution of calcium hydroxide in water, formerly used in medicine as an antacid. [2] water that contains dissolved lime or calcium salts, esp calcium carbonate or calcium sulphate.

limey ('laɪmɪ) *US and Canadian, slang* ◆ NOUN [1] a British person. [2] a British sailor or ship. ◆ ADJECTIVE [3] British.
▷HISTORY abbreviated from C19 *lime-juicer,* because British sailors were required to drink lime juice as a protection against scurvy

limicoline (laɪ'mɪkəˌlaɪn, -lɪn) ADJECTIVE of, relating to, or belonging to the *Charadrii,* a suborder of birds containing the plovers, sandpipers, snipes, oystercatchers, avocets, etc.
▷HISTORY C19: from New Latin *Limicolae* former name of order, from Latin *līmus* mud + *colere* to inhabit

limicolous (laɪ'mɪkələs) ADJECTIVE (of certain animals) living in mud or muddy regions.

liminal ('lɪmɪn[ə]l) ADJECTIVE *Psychol* relating to the point (or threshold) beyond which a sensation becomes too faint to be experienced.
▷HISTORY C19: from Latin *līmen* threshold

limit ('lɪmɪt) NOUN [1] (*sometimes plural*) the ultimate extent, degree, or amount of something: *the limit of endurance.* [2] (*often plural*) the boundary or edge of a specific area: *the city limits.* [3] (*often plural*) the area of premises within specific boundaries. [4] the largest quantity or amount allowed. [5] *Maths* **a** a value to which a function f(x) approaches as closely as desired as the independent variable approaches a specified value (x = a) or approaches infinity. **b** a value to which a sequence a_n approaches arbitrarily close as n approaches infinity. **c** the limit of a sequence of partial sums of a convergent infinite series: *the limit of* 1 + ½ + ¼ + ⅛ + … *is 2.* [6] *Maths* one of the two specified values between which a definite integral is evaluated. [7] **the limit.** *Informal* a person or thing that is intolerably exasperating. [8] **off limits. a** out of bounds. **b** forbidden to do or use: *smoking was off limits everywhere.* [9] **within limits.** to a certain or limited extent: *I approve of it within limits.* ◆ VERB (*tr*) **-its, -iting, -ited** [10] to restrict or confine, as to area, extent, time, etc. [11] *Law* to agree, fix, or assign specifically.
▷HISTORY C14: from Latin *līmes* boundary
▸'**limitable** ADJECTIVE ▸'**limitableness** NOUN ▸'**limitless** ADJECTIVE ▸'**limitlessly** ADVERB ▸'**limitlessness** NOUN

limitarian (ˌlɪmɪ'tɛərɪən) NOUN *Christianity* a person who regards salvation as limited to only a part of mankind.

limitary ('lɪmɪtərɪ, -trɪ) ADJECTIVE [1] of, involving, or serving as a limit. [2] restricted or limited.

limitation (ˌlɪmɪ'teɪʃən) NOUN [1] something that limits a quality or achievement. [2] the act of limiting or the condition of being limited. [3] *Law* a certain period of time, legally defined, within which an action, claim, etc., must be commenced. [4] *Property law* a restriction upon the duration or extent of an estate.

limited ('lɪmɪtɪd) ADJECTIVE [1] having a limit; restricted; confined. [2] without fullness or scope; narrow. [3] (of governing powers, sovereignty, etc.) restricted or checked, by or as if by a constitution, laws, or an assembly: *limited government.* [4] *US and Canadian* (of a train) stopping only at certain stations and having only a set number of cars for passengers. [5] *Chiefly Brit* (of a business enterprise) owned by shareholders whose liability for the enterprise's debts is restricted. ◆ NOUN [6] *US and Canadian* a limited train, bus, etc.
▸'**limitedly** ADVERB ▸'**limitedness** NOUN

limited company NOUN *Brit* a company whose owners enjoy limited liability for the company's debts and losses.

limited edition NOUN an edition of something such as a book, plate, etc., that is limited to a specified number.

limited liability NOUN *Brit* liability restricted to the unpaid portion (if any) of the par value of the shares of a limited company. It is a feature of share ownership.

limited monarchy NOUN another term for **constitutional monarchy.**

limited war NOUN a war in which the belligerents do not seek the total destruction of the enemy, esp one in which nuclear weapons are deliberately not used.

limiter ('lɪmɪtə) NOUN an electronic circuit that produces an output signal whose positive or negative amplitude, or both, is limited to some predetermined value above which the peaks become flattened. Also called: **clipper.**

limit man NOUN (in a handicap sport or game) the competitor with the maximum handicap.

limit point NOUN *Maths* (of a set) a point that is the limit of a sequence of points in the set. Also called: **accumulation point.**

limitrophe ('lɪmɪˌtrəʊf) ADJECTIVE (of a country or region) on or near a frontier.
▷HISTORY C19: via French from Late Latin *limitrophus,* from *limit-* LIMIT + Greek *-trophus* supporting; originally referring to borderland that supported frontier troops

limit-state design NOUN a design criterion specifying that with acceptable probabilities a structure will not reach a limit state in which it either is unfit for the use for which it was designed (unavailability limit state) or fails (ultimate limit state).

limivorous (lɪ'mɪvərəs) ADJECTIVE (of certain invertebrate animals) feeding on mud.
▷HISTORY C19: from Latin *līmus* mud + -VOROUS

limn (lɪm) VERB (*tr*) [1] to represent in drawing or painting. [2] *Archaic* to describe in words. [3] an obsolete word for **illuminate.**
▷HISTORY C15: from Old French *enluminer* to illumine (a manuscript) from Latin *inlūmināre* to brighten, from *lūmen* light
▸**limner** ('lɪmnə) NOUN

limnetic (lɪm'nɛtɪk) ADJECTIVE of, relating to, or inhabiting the open water of lakes down to the depth of light penetration: *the limnetic zone.*
▷HISTORY C20: from Greek *limnē* pool

limnology (lɪm'nɒlədʒɪ) NOUN the study of bodies of fresh water with reference to their plant and animal life, physical properties, geographical features, etc.
▷HISTORY C20: from Greek *limnē* lake
▸**limnological** (ˌlɪmnə'lɒdʒɪk[ə]l) *or* ˌ**limno'logic** ADJECTIVE ▸ˌ**limno'logically** ADVERB ▸**lim'nologist** NOUN

limnophilous (lɪm'nɒfɪləs) ADJECTIVE (of animals) living in lakes or freshwater marshes.

Límnos ('limnɔs) NOUN transliteration of the Modern Greek name for **Lemnos.**

limo ('lɪməʊ) NOUN, *plural* **-mos.** *Informal* short for **limousine.**

Limoges (lɪ'məʊʒ; *French* limɔʒ) NOUN a city in S central France, on the Vienne River: a centre of the porcelain industry since the 18th century. Pop.: 133 960 (1990).

limonene ('lɪməˌniːn) NOUN a liquid optically active terpene with a lemon-like odour, found in lemon, orange, peppermint, and other essential oils and used as a wetting agent and in the manufacture of resins. Formula: $C_{10}H_{16}$.
▷HISTORY C19: from New Latin *limonum* lemon

limonite ('laɪməˌnaɪt) NOUN a common brown, black, or yellow amorphous secondary mineral that consists of hydrated ferric oxides and is a source of iron. Formula: $FeO(OH).nH_2O$.
▷HISTORY C19: probably from Greek *leimōn,* translation of earlier German name, *Wiesenerz* meadow ore
▸**limonitic** (ˌlaɪmə'nɪtɪk) ADJECTIVE

Limousin[1] (*French* limuzɛ̃) NOUN a region and former province of W central France, in the W part of the Massif Central.

Limousin[2] ('lɪmʊˌzɛ̃) NOUN a breed of fairly large yellowish-to-reddish-gold beef cattle originally from France.

limousine ('lɪməˌziːn, ˌlɪmə'ziːn) NOUN [1] any large and luxurious car, esp one that has a glass division between the driver and passengers. [2] a former type of car in which the roof covering the rear seats projected over the driver's compartment.
▷HISTORY C20: from French, literally: cloak (originally one worn by shepherds in *Limousin*), hence later applied to the car

limp[1] (lɪmp) VERB (*intr*) [1] to walk with an uneven step, esp with a weak or injured leg. [2] to advance in a labouring or faltering manner. ◆ NOUN [3] an uneven walk or progress.
▷HISTORY C16: probably a back formation from obsolete *limphalt* lame, from Old English *lempheait;* related to Middle High German *limpfen* to limp
▸'**limper** NOUN ▸'**limping** ADJECTIVE, NOUN ▸'**limpingly** ADVERB

limp[2] (lɪmp) ADJECTIVE [1] not firm or stiff. [2] not energetic or vital. [3] (of the binding of a book) not stiffened with boards.
▷HISTORY C18: probably of Scandinavian origin; related to Icelandic *limpa* looseness
▸'**limply** ADVERB ▸'**limpness** NOUN

limpet ('lɪmpɪt) NOUN [1] any of numerous marine gastropods, such as *Patella vulgata* (**common limpet**) and *Fissurella* (or *Diodora*) *apertura* (**keyhole limpet**), that have a conical shell and are found clinging to rocks. [2] any of various similar freshwater gastropods, such as *Ancylus fluviatilis* (**river limpet**). [3] (*modifier*) relating to or denoting certain weapons that are attached to their targets by magnetic or adhesive properties and resist removal: *limpet mines.* [4] a small open caisson shaped to fit against a dock wall, used mainly in repair work.
▷HISTORY Old English *lempedu,* from Latin *lepas,* from Greek

limpid ('lɪmpɪd) ADJECTIVE [1] clear or transparent. [2] (esp of writings, style, etc.) free from obscurity. [3] calm; peaceful.
▷HISTORY C17: from French *limpide,* from Latin *limpidus* clear
▸**lim'pidity** *or* '**limpidness** NOUN ▸'**limpidly** ADVERB

limpkin ('lɪmpkɪn) NOUN a rail-like wading bird, *Aramus guarauna,* of tropical American marshes, having dark brown plumage with white markings and a wailing cry: order *Gruiformes* (cranes, rails, etc.). Also called: **courlan.**
▷HISTORY C19: named from its awkward gait

Limpopo (lɪm'pəʊpəʊ) NOUN [1] a province of NE South Africa, comprising the N part of the former province of Transvaal: agriculture and service industries. Capital: Polokwane (formerly Pietersburg). Pop.: 5 337 267 (1999 est.). Area: 123 910 sq. km (47 842 sq. miles). Former name (1994–2002): **Northern Province.** [2] a river in SE Africa, rising in E South Africa and flowing northeast, then southeast as the border between South Africa and Zimbabwe and through Mozambique to the Indian Ocean. Length: 1770 km (1100 miles).

limp-wristed ADJECTIVE ineffectual; effete.

limulus ('lɪmjʊləs) NOUN, *plural* **-li** (-ˌlaɪ). any

horseshoe crab of the genus *Limulus,* esp *L. polyphemus*.
▷**HISTORY** C19: from New Latin (name of genus), from Latin *līmus* sidelong

limy¹ (ˈlaɪmɪ) ADJECTIVE **limier, limiest.** [1] of, like, or smeared with birdlime. [2] containing or characterized by the presence of lime.
▸**ˈliminess** NOUN

limy² (ˈlaɪmɪ) ADJECTIVE **limier, limiest.** of or tasting of lime (the fruit).

linac (ˈlɪnæk) NOUN short for **linear accelerator.**

linage *or* **lineage** (ˈlaɪnɪdʒ) NOUN [1] the number of lines in a piece of written or printed matter. [2] payment for written material calculated according to the number of lines. [3] a less common word for **alignment.**

linalool (lɪˈnæləʊˌɒl, ˈlɪnəˌluːl) *or* **linalol** (ˈlɪnəˌlɒl) NOUN an optically active colourless fragrant liquid found in many essential oils and used in perfumery. Formula: $C_{10}H_{18}O$.
▷**HISTORY** from LIGNALOES + -OL¹

Linares (*Spanish* liˈnares) NOUN a city in S Spain: site of Scipio Africanus' defeat of the Carthaginians (208 B.C.); lead mines. Pop.: 57 210 (1991).

linchpin *or* **lynchpin** (ˈlɪntʃˌpɪn) NOUN [1] a pin placed transversely through an axle to keep a wheel in position. [2] a person or thing regarded as an essential or coordinating element: *the linchpin of the company*.
▷**HISTORY** C14 *lynspin,* from Old English *lynis*

Lincoln (ˈlɪŋkən) NOUN [1] a city in E central England, administrative centre of Lincolnshire: an important ecclesiastical and commercial centre in the Middle Ages; Roman ruins, a castle (founded by William the Conqueror) and a famous cathedral (begun in 1086). Pop.: 80 281 (1991). Latin name: **Lindum** (ˈlɪndəm). [2] a city in SE Nebraska: state capital; University of Nebraska (1869). Pop.: 225 581 (2000). [3] short for **Lincolnshire.** [4] a breed of long-woolled sheep, originally from Lincolnshire.

Lincoln Center NOUN a centre for the performing arts in New York City, including theatres, a library, and a school. Official name: **Lincoln Center for the Performing Arts.**

Lincoln green NOUN, ADJECTIVE [1] **a** a yellowish-green or brownish-green colour. **b** (*as adjective*): *a Lincoln-green suit*. [2] a cloth of this colour.
▷**HISTORY** C16: so named after a green fabric formerly made at LINCOLN, England

Lincolnshire (ˈlɪŋkənˌʃɪə, -ʃə) NOUN a county of E England, on the North Sea and the Wash: mostly low-lying and fertile, with fenland around the Wash and hills (the **Lincoln Wolds**) in the east; one of the main agricultural counties of Great Britain: the geographical and ceremonial county includes the unitary authorities of North Lincolnshire and North East Lincolnshire (both part of Humberside county from 1974 to 1996). Administrative centre: Lincoln. Pop. (excluding unitary authorities): 646 646 (2001). Area (excluding unitary authorities): 5880 sq. km (2270 sq. miles). Abbreviation: **Lincs.**

Lincoln's Inn NOUN one of the four legal societies in London which together form the Inns of Court.

lincrusta (lɪnˈkrʌstə) NOUN a type of wallpaper having a hard embossed surface.
▷**HISTORY** C19: from Latin *linum* flax + *crusta* rind

Lincs (lɪŋks) ABBREVIATION FOR Lincolnshire.

linctus (ˈlɪŋktəs) NOUN, *plural* **-tuses.** a syrupy medicinal formulation taken to relieve coughs and sore throats.
▷**HISTORY** C17 (in the sense: medicine to be licked with the tongue): from Latin, past participle of *lingere* to lick

lindane (ˈlɪndeɪn) NOUN a white poisonous crystalline powder with a slight musty odour: used as an insecticide, weedkiller, and, in low concentrations, in treating scabies; 1,2,3,4,5,6-hexachlorocyclohexane. Formula: $C_6H_6Cl_6$.
▷**HISTORY** C20: named after T. van der *Linden,* Dutch chemist

linden (ˈlɪndən) NOUN any of various tiliaceous deciduous trees of the N temperate genus *Tilia,* having heart-shaped leaves and small fragrant yellowish flowers: cultivated for timber and as shade trees. See also **lime³, basswood.**
▷**HISTORY** C16: n use of obsolete adj *linden,* from Old English *linde* lime tree

Lindesnes (ˈlɪndɪsˌnɛs) NOUN a cape at the S tip of Norway, projecting into the North Sea. Also called: **the Naze.**

Lindisfarne (ˈlɪndɪsˌfɑːn) NOUN another name for **Holy Island.**

Lindsey (ˈlɪndzɪ) NOUN **Parts of.** an area in E England constituting a former administrative division of Lincolnshire.

line¹ (laɪn) NOUN [1] a narrow continuous mark, as one made by a pencil, pen, or brush across a surface. [2] such a mark cut into or raised from a surface. [3] a thin indented mark or wrinkle. [4] a straight or curved continuous trace having no breadth that is produced by a moving point. [5] *Maths* **a** any straight one-dimensional geometrical element whose identity is determined by two points. A **line segment** lies between any two points on a line. **b** a set of points (x, y) that satisfies the equation $y = mx + c$, where m is the gradient and c is the intercept with the y-axis. [6] a border or boundary: *the county line*. [7] *Sport* **a** a white or coloured band indicating a boundary or division on a field, track, etc. **b** a mark or imaginary mark at which a race begins or ends. [8] *American football* **a** See **line of scrimmage. b** the players arranged in a row on either side of the line of scrimmage at the start of each play. [9] a specified point of change or limit: *the dividing line between sanity and madness*. [10] **a** the edge or contour of a shape, as in sculpture or architecture, or a mark on a painting, drawing, etc., defining or suggesting this. **b** the sum or type of such contours or marks, characteristic of a style or design: *the line of a draughtsman; the line of a building*. [11] anything long, flexible, and thin, such as a wire or string: *a washing line; a fishing line*. [12] a telephone connection: *a direct line to New York*. [13] **a** a conducting wire, cable, or circuit for making connections between pieces of electrical apparatus, such as a cable for electric-power transmission, telecommunications, etc. **b** (*as modifier*): *the line voltage*. [14] a system of travel or transportation, esp over agreed routes: *a shipping line*. [15] a company operating such a system. [16] a route between two points on a railway. [17] *Chiefly Brit* **a** a railway track, including the roadbed, sleepers, etc. **b** one of the rails of such a track. [18] *NZ* a roadway usually in a rural area. [19] a course or direction of movement or advance: *the line of flight of a bullet*. [20] a course or method of action, behaviour, etc.: *take a new line with him*. [21] a policy or prescribed course of action or way of thinking (often in the phrases **bring** *or* **come into line**). [22] a field of study, interest, occupation, trade, or profession: *this book is in your line*. [23] alignment; true (esp in the phrases **in line, out of line**). [24] one kind of product or article: *a nice line in hats*. [25] *NZ* a collection of bales of wool all of the one type. [26] a row of persons or things: *a line of cakes on the conveyor belt*. [27] a chronological or ancestral series, esp of people: *a line of prime ministers*. [28] a row of words printed or written across a page or column. [29] a unit of verse consisting of the number of feet appropriate to the metre being used and written or printed with the words in a single row. [30] a short letter; note: *just a line to say thank you*. [31] a piece of useful information or hint about something: *give me a line on his work*. [32] one of a number of narrow horizontal bands forming a television picture. [33] *Physics* a narrow band in an electromagnetic spectrum, resulting from a transition in an atom, ion, or molecule of a gas or plasma. [34] *Music* **a** any of the five horizontal marks that make up the stave. Compare **space** (sense 10). **b** the musical part or melody notated on one such set. **c** a discernible shape formed by sequences of notes or musical sounds: *a meandering melodic line*. **d** (in polyphonic music) a set of staves that are held together with a bracket or brace. [35] a unit of magnetic flux equal to 1 maxwell. [36] a defensive or fortified position, esp one that marks the most forward position in war or a national boundary: *the front line*. [37] **line ahead** *or* **line abreast.** a formation adopted by a naval unit for manoeuvring. [38] a formation adopted by a body or a number of military units when drawn up abreast. [39] the combatant forces of certain armies and navies, excluding supporting arms. [40] *Fencing* one of four divisions of the target on a fencer's body, considered as areas to which specific attacks are made. [41] the scent left by a fox. [42] **a** the equator (esp in the phrase **crossing the line**). **b** any circle or arc on the terrestrial or celestial sphere. [43] the amount of insurance written by an underwriter for a particular risk. [44] a US and Canadian word for **queue.** [45] *Slang* a portion of a powdered drug for snorting. [46] *Slang* something said for effect, esp to solicit for money, sex, etc.: *he gave me his usual line*. [47] **above the line. a** *Accounting* denoting entries above a horizontal line on a profit and loss account, separating those that establish the profit or loss from those that show how the profit is distributed. **b** denoting revenue transactions rather than capital transactions in a nation's accounts. **c** *Marketing* expenditure on media advertising through an agency, rather than internally arranged advertising, such as direct mail, free samples, etc. **d** *Bridge* denoting bonus points, marked above the horizontal line on the score card. [48] **below the line. a** *Accounting* denoting entries below a horizontal line on a profit and loss account, separating those that establish the profit or loss from those that show how the profit is distributed. **b** denoting capital transactions rather than revenue transactions in a nation's accounts. **c** *Marketing* denoting expenditure on advertising by other means than the traditional media, such as the provision of free gifts, special displays, direct mailshots, etc. **d** *Bridge* denoting points scored towards game and rubber, marked below the horizontal line on the score card. [49] **all along the line. a** at every stage in a series. **b** in every detail. [50] **do a line (with).** *Irish and Austral informal* to associate (with a person of the opposite sex) regularly; go out (with): *he is doing a line with her*. [51] **draw the line (at).** to reasonably object (to) or set a limit (on): *her father draws the line at her coming in after midnight*. [52] **get a line on.** *Informal* to obtain information about. [53] **hold the line. a** to keep a telephone line open. **b** *Football* to prevent the opponents from taking the ball forward. **c** (of soldiers) to keep formation, as when under fire. [54] **in line for.** in the running for; a candidate for: *he's in line for a directorship*. [55] **in line with.** conforming to. [56] **in the line of duty.** as a necessary and usually undesired part of the performance of one's responsibilities. [57] **lay** *or* **put on the line. a** to pay money. **b** to speak frankly and directly. **c** to risk (one's career, reputation, etc.) on something. [58] **shoot a line.** *Informal* to try to create a false image, as by boasting or exaggerating. [59] **step out of line.** to fail to conform to expected standards, attitudes, etc. [60] **toe the line.** to conform to expected standards, attitudes, etc. ◆ VERB [61] (*tr*) to mark with a line or lines. [62] (*tr*) to draw or represent with a line or lines. [63] (*tr*) to be or put as a border to: *tulips lined the lawns*. [64] to place in or form a row, series, or alignment. ◆ See also **lines, line-up.**
▷**HISTORY** C13: partly from Old French *ligne,* ultimately from Latin *līnea,* n use of *līneus* flaxen, from *līnum* flax; partly from Old English *līn,* ultimately also from Latin *līnum* flax
▸**ˈlinable** *or* **ˈlineable** ADJECTIVE ▸**lined** ADJECTIVE
▸**ˈlineˌlike** ADJECTIVE ▸**ˈliny** *or* **ˈliney** ADJECTIVE

line² (laɪn) VERB (*tr*) [1] to attach an inside covering to (a garment, curtain, etc.), as for protection, to hide the seaming, or so that it should hang well. [2] to cover or fit the inside of: *to line the walls with books*. [3] to fill plentifully: *a purse lined with money*. [4] to reinforce the back of (a book) with fabric, paper, etc.
▷**HISTORY** C14: ultimately from Latin *līnum* flax, since linings were often made of linen

lineage¹ (ˈlɪnɪɪdʒ) NOUN [1] direct descent from an ancestor, esp a line of descendants from one ancestor. [2] a less common word for **derivation.**
▷**HISTORY** C14: from Old French *lignage,* from Latin *līnea* LINE¹

lineage² (ˈlaɪnɪdʒ) NOUN a variant spelling of **linage.**

lineal (ˈlɪnɪəl) ADJECTIVE [1] being in a direct line of descent from an ancestor. [2] of, involving, or derived from direct descent. [3] a less common word for **linear.**
▷**HISTORY** C14: via Old French from Late Latin *līneālis,* from Latin *līnea* LINE¹
▸**ˈlineally** ADVERB

lineament (ˈlɪnɪəmənt) NOUN (*often plural*) [1] a

facial outline or feature. [2] a distinctive characteristic or feature. [3] *Geology* any long natural feature on the surface of the earth, such as a fault, esp as revealed by aerial photography.
▷HISTORY C15: from Latin: line, from *līneāre* to draw a line
▸**lineamental** (ˌlɪnɪəˈmentᵊl) ADJECTIVE

linear (ˈlɪnɪə) ADJECTIVE [1] of, in, along, or relating to a line. [2] of or relating to length. [3] resembling, represented by, or consisting of a line or lines. [4] having one dimension. [5] designating a style in the arts, esp painting, that obtains its effects through line rather than colour or light and in which the edges of forms and planes are sharply defined. Compare **painterly.** [6] *Maths* of or relating to the first degree: *a linear equation.* [7] narrow and having parallel edges: *a linear leaf.* [8] *Electronics* **a** (of a circuit, etc.) having an output that is directly proportional to input: *linear amplifier.* **b** having components arranged in a line.
▷HISTORY C17: from Latin *līneāris* of or by means of lines
▸**linearity** (ˌlɪnɪˈærɪtɪ) NOUN ▸ˈ**linearly** ADVERB

Linear A NOUN a hitherto undeciphered script, partly syllabic and partly ideographic, found on tablets and pottery in Crete and dating mainly from the 15th century B.C.

linear accelerator NOUN an accelerator in which charged particles are accelerated along a linear path by potential differences applied to a number of electrodes along their path. Sometimes shortened to: **linac.**

Linear B NOUN an ancient system of writing, apparently a modified form of Linear A, found on clay tablets and jars of the second millennium B.C. The earliest excavated examples, dating from about 1400, came from Knossos, in Crete, but all the later finds are at Pylos and Mycenae on the Greek mainland, dating from the 14th–12th centuries. The script is generally accepted as being an early representation of Mycenaean Greek.

linear equation NOUN a polynomial equation of the first degree, such as $x + y = 7$.

linear measure NOUN a unit or system of units for the measurement of length. Also called: **long measure.**

linear motor NOUN a form of electric motor in which the stator and the rotor are linear and parallel. It can be used to drive a train, one part of the motor being in the locomotive, the other in the track.

linear perspective NOUN the branch of perspective in which the apparent size and shape of objects and their position with respect to foreground and background are established by actual or suggested lines converging on the horizon.

linear programming NOUN *Maths* a technique used in economics, etc., for determining the maximum or minimum of a linear function of non-negative variables subject to constraints expressed as linear equalities or inequalities.

linear space NOUN *Maths* another name for **vector space.**

lineate (ˈlɪnɪɪt, -ˌeɪt) *or* **lineated** ADJECTIVE marked with lines; streaked.
▷HISTORY C17: from Latin *līneātus* drawn with lines

lineation (ˌlɪnɪˈeɪʃən) NOUN [1] the act of marking with lines. [2] an arrangement of or division into lines. [3] an outline or contour. [4] any linear arrangement involving rocks or minerals, such as a parallel arrangement of elongated mineral grains.

linebacker (ˈlaɪnˌbækə) NOUN a defensive player in American or Canadian football who is positioned just behind the line of scrimmage.

line block NOUN a letterpress printing block made by a photoengraving process without the use of a screen.

line breeding NOUN selective inbreeding that produces individuals possessing one or more of the favourable characteristics of their common ancestor.

line call NOUN *Tennis* the judgment of the umpire or linesman as to whether the ball has landed in or out of court.

linecaster (ˈlaɪnˌkɑːstə) NOUN a typesetting machine that casts metal type in lines.

line composition NOUN *Printing* type produced on a linecaster.

line dancing NOUN a form of dancing performed by rows of people to country and western music.

line drawing NOUN a drawing made with lines only, gradations in tone being provided by the spacing and thickness of the lines.

line-engraving NOUN [1] the art or process of hand-engraving in intaglio and copper plate. [2] a plate so engraved. [3] a print taken from such a plate.
▸ˈ**line-enˌgraver** NOUN

Line Islands PLURAL NOUN a group of coral islands in the central Pacific, including Tabuaeran, Teraina, and Kiritimati: part of Kiribati, with Palmyra and Jarvis administered by the US.

lineman (ˈlaɪnmən) NOUN, *plural* **-men.** [1] another name for **platelayer.** [2] a person who does the chaining, taping, or marking of points for a surveyor. [3] *Austral and NZ* (formerly) the member of a beach life-saving team who controlled the line used to help drowning swimmers and surfers. [4] *American football* a member of the row of players who start each down positioned on either side of the line of scrimmage. [5] *US and Canadian* another word for **linesman** (sense 2).

line management NOUN *Commerce* those managers in an organization who are responsible for the main activity or product of the organization, as distinct from those, such as transport, accounting, or personnel, who provide services to the line management.
▸**line manager** NOUN

linen (ˈlɪnɪn) NOUN [1] **a** a hard-wearing fabric woven from the spun fibres of flax. **b** (*as modifier*): *a linen tablecloth.* [2] yarn or thread spun from flax fibre. [3] clothes, sheets, tablecloths, etc., made from linen cloth or from a substitute such as cotton. [4] See **linen paper.**
▷HISTORY Old English *linnen,* ultimately from Latin *līnum* flax, LINE[2]

linen paper NOUN paper made from flax fibres or having a similar texture.

line of battle NOUN a formation adopted by a military or naval force when preparing for action.

line of credit NOUN *US and Canadian* another name for **credit line.**

line of fire NOUN the flight path of a missile discharged or to be discharged from a firearm.

line of force NOUN an imaginary line representing a field of force, such as an electric or magnetic field, such that the tangent at any point is the direction of the field vector at that point.

line of scrimmage NOUN *American football* an imaginary line, parallel to the goal lines, on which the ball is placed at the start of a down and on either side of which the offense and defense line up.

line of sight NOUN [1] the straight line along which an observer looks or a beam of radiation travels. [2] *Ophthalmol* another term for **line of vision.**

line of vision NOUN *Ophthalmol* a straight line extending from the fovea centralis of the eye to an object on which the eye is focused. Also called: **line of sight.**

lineolate (ˈlɪnɪəˌleɪt) *or* **lineolated** ADJECTIVE *Biology* marked with very fine parallel lines.
▷HISTORY C19: from Latin *līneola,* diminutive of *līnea* LINE[1]

line-out NOUN *Rugby Union* the method of restarting play when the ball goes into touch, the forwards forming two parallel lines at right angles to the touchline and jumping for the ball when it is thrown in.

line printer NOUN an electromechanical device that prints a line of characters at a time rather than a character at a time, at speeds from about 200 to 3000 lines per minute: used in printing and in computer systems.

liner[1] (ˈlaɪnə) NOUN [1] a passenger ship or aircraft, esp one that is part of a commercial fleet. [2] See **freightliner.** [3] Also called: **eye liner.** a cosmetic used to outline the eyes, consisting of a liquid or cake mixed with water and applied by brush or a grease pencil. [4] a person or thing that uses lines, esp in drawing or copying.

liner[2] (ˈlaɪnə) NOUN [1] a material used as a lining. [2] a person who supplies or fits linings. [3] *Engineering* a sleeve, usually of a metal that will withstand wear or corrosion, fixed inside or outside a structural component or vessel: *cylinder liner.*

liner notes PLURAL NOUN the US name for **sleeve notes.**

lines (laɪnz) PLURAL NOUN [1] general appearance or outline: *a car with fine lines.* [2] a plan of procedure or construction: *built on traditional lines.* [3] **a** the spoken words of a theatrical presentation. **b** the words of a particular role: *he forgot his lines.* [4] *Informal, chiefly Brit* a marriage certificate: *marriage lines.* [5] luck, fate, or fortune (esp in the phrase **hard lines**). [6] **a** rows of tents, buildings, temporary stabling, etc., in a military camp: *transport lines.* **b** a defensive position, row of trenches, or other fortification: *we broke through the enemy lines.* [7] **a** a school punishment of writing the same sentence or phrase out a specified number of times. **b** the phrases or sentences so written out: *a hundred lines.* [8] **read between the lines.** to understand or find an implicit meaning in addition to the obvious one.

linesman (ˈlaɪnzmən) NOUN, *plural* **-men.** [1] an official who helps the referee or umpire in various sports, esp by indicating when the ball has gone out of play. [2] *Chiefly Brit* a person who installs, maintains, or repairs telephone or electric-power lines. US and Canadian name: **lineman.**

line squall NOUN a squall or series of squalls along a cold front.

line-up NOUN [1] a row or arrangement of people or things assembled for a particular purpose: *the line-up for the football match.* [2] the members of such a row or arrangement. [3] an identity parade. ◆ VERB **line up.** (*adverb*) [4] to form, put into, or organize a line-up. [5] (*tr*) to produce, organize, and assemble: *they lined up some questions.* [6] (*tr*) to align.

ling[1] (lɪŋ) NOUN, *plural* **ling** *or* **lings.** [1] any of several gadoid food fishes of the northern coastal genus *Molva,* esp *M. molva,* having an elongated body with long fins. [2] another name for **burbot** (a fish).
▷HISTORY C13: probably from Low German; related to LONG[1]

ling[2] (lɪŋ) NOUN another name for **heather** (sense 1).
▷HISTORY C14: from Old Norse *lyng*
▸ˈ**lingy** ADJECTIVE

ling. ABBREVIATION FOR linguistics.

-ling[1] SUFFIX FORMING NOUNS [1] *Often disparaging* a person or thing belonging to or associated with the group, activity, or quality specified: *nestling; underling.* [2] used as a diminutive: *duckling.*
▷HISTORY Old English *-ling,* of Germanic origin; related to Icelandic *-lingr,* Gothic *-lings*

-ling[2] SUFFIX FORMING ADVERBS in a specified condition, manner, or direction: *darkling; sideling.*
▷HISTORY Old English *-ling,* adverbial suffix

lingam (ˈlɪŋgəm) *or* **linga** (ˈlɪŋgə) NOUN [1] (in Sanskrit grammar) the masculine gender. [2] **a** the Hindu phallic image of the god Siva. **b** the penis.
▷HISTORY C18: from Sanskrit

Lingayen Gulf (ˈlɪŋgɑːˈjen) NOUN a large inlet of the South China Sea in the Philippines, on the NW coast of Luzon: site of the Japanese landing in the 1941 invasion.

lingcod (ˈlɪŋˌkɒd) NOUN, *plural* **-cod** *or* **-cods.** any scorpaenoid food fish of the family *Ophiodontidae,* esp *Ophiodon elongatus,* of the N Pacific Ocean.

linger (ˈlɪŋgə) VERB (*mainly intr*) [1] to delay or prolong departure. [2] to go in a slow or leisurely manner; saunter. [3] to remain just alive for some time prior to death. [4] to persist or continue, esp in the mind. [5] to be slow to act; dither; procrastinate.
▷HISTORY C13 (northern dialect) *lengeren* to dwell, from *lengen* to prolong, from Old English *lengan;* related to Old Norse *lengja;* see LONG[1]
▸ˈ**lingerer** NOUN ▸ˈ**lingering** ADJECTIVE ▸ˈ**lingeringly** ADVERB

lingerie (ˈlænʒərɪ) NOUN [1] women's underwear and nightwear. [2] *Archaic* linen goods collectively.
▷HISTORY C19: from French, from *linge,* from Latin *līneus* linen, from *līnum* flax

lingo (ˈlɪŋgəʊ) NOUN, *plural* **-goes.** *Informal* any foreign or unfamiliar language, jargon, etc.

▷HISTORY C17: perhaps from LINGUA FRANCA; compare Portuguese *lingoa* tongue

lingua ('lɪŋgwə) NOUN, *plural* **-guae** (-gwi:). *Anatomy* 1 the technical name for **tongue.** 2 any tongue-like structure.
▷HISTORY C17: Latin

lingua franca ('fræŋkə) NOUN, *plural* **lingua francas** *or* **linguae francae** ('frænsi:). 1 a language used for communication among people of different mother tongues. 2 a hybrid language containing elements from several different languages used in this way. 3 any system of communication providing mutual understanding.
▷HISTORY C17: Italian, literally: Frankish tongue

Lingua Franca NOUN a particular lingua franca spoken from the time of the Crusades to the 18th century in the ports of the Mediterranean, based on Italian, Spanish, French, Arabic, Greek, and Turkish.

lingual ('lɪŋgwəl) ADJECTIVE 1 *Anatomy* of or relating to the tongue or a part or structure resembling a tongue. 2 **a** *Rare* of or relating to language or languages. **b** (*in combination*): *polylingual.* 3 articulated with the tongue. ◆ NOUN 4 a lingual consonant, such as Scots (r).
▸ **'lingually** ADVERB

linguiform ('lɪŋgwɪ,fɔ:m) ADJECTIVE shaped like a tongue.

linguine *or* **linguini** (lɪŋ'gwi:nɪ) NOUN a kind of pasta in the shape of thin flat strands.
▷HISTORY from Italian: small tongues

linguist ('lɪŋgwɪst) NOUN 1 a person who has the capacity to learn and speak foreign languages. 2 a person who studies linguistics. 3 *West African, esp Ghanaian* the spokesman for a chief.
▷HISTORY C16: from Latin *lingua* tongue

linguistic (lɪŋ'gwɪstɪk) ADJECTIVE 1 of or relating to language. 2 of or relating to linguistics.
▸ **lin'guistically** ADVERB

linguistic atlas NOUN an atlas showing the distribution of distinctive linguistic features of languages or dialects.

linguistic borrowing NOUN another name for **loan word.**

linguistic geography NOUN the study of the distribution of dialectal speech elements.
▸ **linguistic geographer** NOUN

linguistic philosophy NOUN the approach to philosophy common in the mid 20th century that tends to see philosophical problems as arising from inappropriate theoretical use of language and therefore as being resolved by detailed attention to the common use of expressions.

linguistics (lɪŋ'gwɪstɪks) NOUN (*functioning as singular*) the scientific study of language. See also **historical linguistics, descriptive linguistics.**

lingulate ('lɪŋgjʊ,leɪt) *or* **lingulated** ADJECTIVE shaped like a tongue: *a lingulate leaf.*
▷HISTORY C19: from Latin *lingulātus*

linhay ('lɪnɪ) NOUN *Dialect* a farm building with an open front.
▷HISTORY C17: of unknown origin

liniment ('lɪnɪmənt) NOUN a medicated liquid, usually containing alcohol, camphor, and an oil, applied to the skin to relieve pain, stiffness, etc.
▷HISTORY C15: from Late Latin *linīmentum,* from *linere* to smear, anoint

linin ('laɪnɪn) NOUN the network of viscous material in the nucleus of a cell that connects the chromatin granules.
▷HISTORY C19: from Latin *līnum* flax + -IN

lining ('laɪnɪŋ) NOUN 1 **a** material used to line a garment, curtain, etc. **b** (*as modifier*): *lining satin.* 2 a material, such as mull or brown paper, used to strengthen the back of a book. 3 *Civil engineering* a layer of concrete, brick, or timber, etc., used in canals to prevent them leaking or in tunnels or shafts to prevent them falling in. 4 any material used as an interior covering.

link[1] (lɪŋk) NOUN 1 any of the separate rings, loops, or pieces that connect or make up a chain. 2 something that resembles such a ring, loop, or piece. 3 a road, rail, air, or sea connection, as between two main routes. 4 a connecting part or episode. 5 a connecting piece in a mechanism, often having pivoted ends. 6 Also called: **radio link.** a system of transmitters and receivers that connect two locations by means of radio and television signals. 7 a unit of length equal to one hundredth of a chain. 1 link of a Gunter's chain is equal to 7.92 inches, and of an engineer's chain to 1 foot. 8 *Computing* short for **hyperlink.** 9 **weak link.** an unreliable person or thing within an organization or system. ◆ VERB 10 (often foll by *up*) to connect or be connected with or as if with links. 11 (*tr*) to connect by association, etc.
▷HISTORY C14: from Scandinavian; compare Old Norse *hlekkr* link
▸ **'linkable** ADJECTIVE

link[2] (lɪŋk) NOUN (formerly) a torch used to light dark streets.
▷HISTORY C16: perhaps from Latin *lychnus,* from Greek *lukhnos* lamp

linkage ('lɪŋkɪdʒ) NOUN 1 the act of linking or the state of being linked. 2 a system of interconnected levers or rods for transmitting or regulating the motion of a mechanism. 3 *Electronics* the product of the total number of lines of magnetic flux and the number of turns in a coil or circuit through which they pass. 4 *Genetics* the occurrence of two genes close together on the same chromosome so that they are unlikely to be separated during crossing over and tend to be inherited as a single unit. 5 the fact of linking separate but related issues in the course of political negotiations.

linkboy ('lɪŋk,bɔɪ) *or* **linkman** NOUN, *plural* **-boys** *or* **-men.** (formerly) a boy who carried a torch for pedestrians in dark streets.

linked list NOUN *Computing* a list in which each item contains both data and a pointer to one or both neighbouring items, thus eliminating the need for the data items to be ordered in memory.

linker ('lɪŋkə) NOUN 1 *Computing* a program that adjusts two or more machine-language program segments so that they may be simultaneously loaded and executed as a unit. 2 (in systemic grammar) a word that links one word, phrase, sentence, or clause to another; a co-ordinating conjunction or a sentence connector. Compare **binder** (sense 11).

linkman ('lɪŋkmən) NOUN, *plural* **-men.** 1 a presenter of a television or radio programme, esp a sports transmission, consisting of a number of outside broadcasts from different locations. 2 another word for **linkboy.**

link motion NOUN a mechanism controlling the valves of a steam engine, consisting of a slotted link terminating in a pair of eccentrics.

Linköping (*Swedish* 'lintçø:piŋ) NOUN a city in S Sweden: a political and ecclesiastical centre in the Middle Ages; engineering industry. Pop.: 132 500 (2000 est.).

links (lɪŋks) PLURAL NOUN 1 **a** short for **golf links. b** (*as modifier*): *a links course.* 2 *Chiefly Scot* undulating sandy ground near the shore.
▷HISTORY Old English *hlincas* plural of *hlinc* ridge

Link trainer NOUN *Trademark* a ground-training device for training pilots and aircrew in the use of flight instruments. Compare **flight simulator.**
▷HISTORY named after E. A. *Link* (1904–81), its US inventor

linkup ('lɪŋk,ʌp) NOUN 1 the establishing of a connection or union between objects, groups, organizations, etc. 2 the connection or union established.

linkwork ('lɪŋk,wɜ:k) NOUN 1 something made up of links. 2 a mechanism consisting of a series of links to impart or control motion; linkage.

Linlithgow (lɪn'lɪθgəʊ) NOUN 1 a town in SE Scotland, in West Lothian: ruined palace, residence of Scottish kings and birthplace of Mary, Queen of Scots. Pop.: 11 866 (1991). 2 the former name of **West Lothian.**

linn (lɪn) NOUN *Chiefly Scot* 1 a waterfall or a pool at the foot of it. 2 a ravine or precipice.
▷HISTORY C16: probably from a confusion of two words, Scottish Gaelic *linne* pool and Old English *hlynn* torrent

Linnean *or* **Linnaean** (lɪ'ni:ən, -'neɪ-) ADJECTIVE 1 of or relating to Carolus Linnaeus (original name *Carl von Linné*; 1707–78), the Swedish botanist who established the binomial system of biological nomenclature. 2 relating to the system of classification of plants and animals using binomial nomenclature.

linnet ('lɪnɪt) NOUN 1 a brownish Old World finch, *Acanthis cannabina*: the male has a red breast and forehead. 2 Also called: **house finch.** a similar and related North American bird, *Carpodacus mexicanus.*
▷HISTORY C16: from Old French *linotte,* ultimately from Latin *līnum* flax (because the bird feeds on flaxseeds)

linney ('lɪnɪ) NOUN *Southwest English, dialect* a lean-to shed.

Linnhe ('lɪnɪ) NOUN **Loch.** a sea loch of W Scotland, at the SW end of the Great Glen. Length: about 32 km (20 miles).

lino ('laɪnəʊ) NOUN short for **linoleum.**

linocut ('laɪnəʊ,kʌt) NOUN 1 a design cut in relief on linoleum mounted on a wooden block. 2 a print made from such a design.

linoleate (lɪ'nəʊlɪ,eɪt) NOUN an ester or salt of linoleic acid.

linoleic acid (,lɪnəʊ'li:ɪk) NOUN a colourless oily essential fatty acid found in many natural oils, such as linseed: used in the manufacture of soaps, emulsifiers, and driers. Formula: $C_{18}H_{32}O_2$.
▷HISTORY C19: from Latin *līnum* flax + OLEIC ACID; so named because it is found in linseed oil

linolenic acid (,lɪnəʊ'lenɪk, -'li:-) NOUN a colourless unsaturated essential fatty acid found in drying oils, such as linseed oil, and used in making paints and synthetic resins; 9,12,15-octadecatrienoic acid. Formula: $C_{18}H_{30}O_2$. Also called: **alpha-linolenic acid.**

linoleum (lɪ'nəʊlɪəm) NOUN a sheet material made of hessian, jute, etc., coated under pressure and heat with a mixture of powdered cork, linseed oil, rosin, and pigment, used as a floor covering. Often shortened to: **lino.**
▷HISTORY C19: from Latin *līnum* flax + *oleum* oil

lino tile NOUN a tile made of linoleum or a similar substance, used as a floor covering.

Linotype ('laɪnəʊ,taɪp) NOUN 1 *Trademark* a typesetting machine, operated by a keyboard, that casts an entire line on one solid slug of metal. 2 type produced by such a machine.

linsang ('lɪnsæŋ) NOUN any of several forest-dwelling viverrine mammals, *Poiana richardsoni* of W Africa or either of the two species of *Prionodon* of S Asia: closely related to the genets, having a very long tail and a spotted or banded coat of thick fur.
▷HISTORY C19: Malay

linseed ('lɪn,si:d) NOUN another name for **flaxseed.**
▷HISTORY Old English *līnsǣd,* from *līn* flax + *sǣd* seed

linseed oil NOUN a yellow oil extracted from seeds of the flax plant. It has great drying qualities and is used in making oil paints, printer's ink, linoleum, etc.

linsey-woolsey ('lɪnzɪ'wʊlzɪ) NOUN 1 a thin rough fabric of linen warp and coarse wool or cotton filling. 2 a strange nonsensical mixture or confusion.
▷HISTORY C15: probably from *Lindsey,* Suffolk village where the fabric was first made + WOOL (with rhyming suffix *-sey*)

linstock ('lɪn,stɒk) NOUN a long staff holding a lighted match, formerly used to fire a cannon.
▷HISTORY C16: from Dutch *lontstok,* from *lont* match + *stok* stick

lint (lɪnt) NOUN 1 an absorbent cotton or linen fabric with the nap raised on one side, used to dress wounds, etc. 2 shreds of fibre, yarn, etc. 3 *Chiefly US* staple fibre for making cotton yarn.
▷HISTORY C14: probably from Latin *linteus* made of linen, from *līnum* flax
▸ **'linty** ADJECTIVE

lintel ('lɪntᵊl) NOUN a horizontal beam, as over a door or window.
▷HISTORY C14: via Old French probably from Late Latin *līmitāris* (unattested) of the boundary, influenced in meaning by *līminaris* of the threshold

linter ('lɪntə) NOUN 1 a machine for stripping the short fibres of ginned cotton seeds. 2 (*plural*) the fibres so removed.

lintie ('lɪntɪ) NOUN a Scot word for **linnet** (sense 1).

lintwhite ('lɪnt,waɪt) NOUN *Archaic or poetic, chiefly Scot* the linnet.
▷HISTORY Old English *līnetwige,* probably from *līn*

flax + *-twige,* perhaps related to Old High German *zwigon* to pluck

linum ('laɪnəm) NOUN any plant of the annual or perennial genus *Linum,* of temperate regions, esp *L. grandiflorum,* from N Africa, cultivated for its showy red or blue flowers: family *Linaceae*. See also **flax.**
▷HISTORY Latin, from Greek *linon* flax

Linux ('laɪnʌks) NOUN a nonproprietary computer operating system suitable for use on personal computers.

Linz¹ (lɪnts) NOUN a port in N Austria, capital of Upper Austria, on the River Danube: cultural centre; steelworks. Pop.: 186 298 (2001). Latin name: **Lentia** ('lɛntɪə, 'lɛnsɪə).

Linz² NOUN ACRONYM FOR Land Information New Zealand; the official body responsible for land registration, mapping, and surveying in New Zealand.

lion ('laɪən) NOUN 1 a large gregarious predatory feline mammal, *Panthera leo,* of open country in parts of Africa and India, having a tawny yellow coat and, in the male, a shaggy mane. Related adjective: **leonine.** 2 a conventionalized lion, the principal beast used as an emblem in heraldry. It has become the national emblem of Great Britain. 3 a courageous, strong, or bellicose person. 4 a celebrity or idol who attracts much publicity and a large following. 5 **beard the lion in his den.** to approach a feared or influential person, esp in order to ask a favour. 6 **the lion's share.** the largest portion.
▷HISTORY Old English *līo, lēo* (Middle English *lioun,* from Anglo-French *liun*), both from Latin *leo,* Greek *leōn*

Lion ('laɪən) NOUN **the.** the constellation Leo, the fifth sign of the zodiac.

lioness ('laɪənɪs) NOUN a female lion.

lionfish ('laɪən,fɪʃ) NOUN, *plural* **-fish** *or* **-fishes.** any of various scorpion fishes of the tropical Pacific genus *Pterois,* having a striped body and elongated spiny fins.

lion-hearted ADJECTIVE very brave; courageous.
▸ **'lion-,heartedly** ADVERB ▸ **'lion,heartedness** NOUN

lionize *or* **lionise** ('laɪə,naɪz) VERB (*tr*) to treat as or make into a celebrity.
▸ **,lioni'zation** *or* **,lioni'sation** NOUN ▸ **'lion,izer** *or* **'lion,iser** NOUN

Lions ('laɪənz) NOUN **Gulf of.** a wide bay of the Mediterranean off the S coast of France, between the Spanish border and Toulon. French name: **Golfe du Lion** (gɔlf dy ljɔ̃).

Lions Club NOUN any of the local clubs that form the International Association of Lions Clubs, formed in the US in 1917 to foster local and international good relations and service to the community.

lip (lɪp) NOUN 1 *Anatomy* **a** either of the two fleshy folds surrounding the mouth, playing an important role in the production of speech sounds, retaining food in the mouth, etc. Related adjective: **labial. b** (*as modifier*): *lip salve.* 2 the corresponding part in animals, esp mammals. 3 any structure resembling a lip, such as the rim of a crater, the margin of a gastropod shell, etc. 4 a nontechnical word for **labium** and **labellum** (sense 1). 5 *Slang* impudent talk or backchat. 6 the embouchure and control in the lips needed to blow wind and brass instruments. 7 **bite one's lip. a** to stifle one's feelings. **b** to be annoyed or irritated. 8 **button (up) one's lip.** *Slang* to stop talking: often imperative. 9 **keep a stiff upper lip.** to maintain one's courage or composure during a time of trouble without giving way to or revealing one's emotions. 10 **lick** *or* **smack one's lips.** to anticipate or recall something with glee or relish. ◆ VERB **lips, lipping, lipped.** 11 (*tr*) to touch with the lip or lips. 12 (*tr*) to form or be a lip or lips for. 13 (*tr*) *Rare* to murmur or whisper. 14 (*intr*) to use the lips in playing a wind instrument. ◆ See also **lip out.**
▷HISTORY Old English *lippa;* related to Old High German *leffur,* Norwegian *lepe,* Latin *labium*
▸ **'lipless** ADJECTIVE ▸ **'lip,like** ADJECTIVE

lip- COMBINING FORM a variant of **lipo-** before a vowel.

lipa ('li:pə) NOUN, *plural* **lipa.** a monetary unit of Croatia worth one hundredth of a kuna.

lipaemia *or US* **lipemia** (lɪ'pi:mɪə) NOUN *Pathol* an abnormally large amount of fat in the blood.
▷HISTORY from Greek *lipos* fat + -AEMIA

Lipari Islands ('lɪpərɪ) PLURAL NOUN a group of volcanic islands under Italian administration off the N coast of Sicily: remains that form a continuous record from Neolithic times. Chief town: Lipari. Pop.: 10 300 (latest est.). Area: 114 sq. km (44 sq. miles). Also called: **Aeolian Islands.** Italian name: **Isole Eolie** ('i:zole e'ɔ:lje).

lipase ('laɪpeɪs, 'lɪpeɪs) NOUN any of a group of fat-digesting enzymes produced in the stomach, pancreas, and liver and also occurring widely in the seeds of plants.
▷HISTORY C19: from Greek *lipos* fat + -ASE

Lipetsk (*Russian* 'lipɪtsk) NOUN a city in central Russia, on the Voronezh River: steelworks. Pop.: 521 600 (1999 est.).

lip gloss NOUN a cosmetic preparation applied to the lips to give a sheen.

lipid *or* **lipide** ('laɪpɪd, 'lɪpɪd) NOUN *Biochem* any of a large group of organic compounds that are esters of fatty acids (**simple lipids**, such as fats and waxes) or closely related substances (**compound lipids**, such as phospholipids): usually insoluble in water but soluble in alcohol and other organic solvents. They are important structural materials in living organisms. Former name: **lipoid.**
▷HISTORY C20: from French *lipide,* from Greek *lipos* fat

Lipizzaner (,lɪpɪt'sɑ:nə) NOUN a breed of riding and carriage horse used by the Spanish Riding School in Vienna and nearly always grey in colour.
▷HISTORY German, after *Lipizza,* near Trieste, where these horses were bred

lip microphone NOUN a microphone designed and shaped to be held close to the mouth, for use in noisy environments.

lipo- *or before a vowel* **lip-** COMBINING FORM fat or fatty: *lipoprotein.*
▷HISTORY from Greek *lipos* fat

lipodystrophy (,lɪpəʊ'dɪstrəfɪ) NOUN any condition resulting in bodily loss or redistribution of fat tissue.

lipogenesis (,lɪpəʊ'dʒɛnɪsɪs) ADJECTIVE *Biochem* the synthesis of fatty acids in the body from glucose and other substrates.

lipogram ('lɪpəʊ,græm) NOUN a piece of writing from which all words containing a particular letter have been deliberately omitted.

lipography (lɪ'pɒgrəfɪ) NOUN the accidental omission of words or letters in writing.
▷HISTORY C19: from Greek *lip-,* stem of *leipein* to omit + -GRAPHY

lipoic acid NOUN *Biochem* a sulphur-containing fatty acid, regarded as an element of the vitamin B complex, minute amounts of which are required for carbohydrate metabolism.

lipoid ('lɪpɔɪd, 'laɪ-) ADJECTIVE *also* **lipoidal.** 1 resembling fat; fatty. ◆ NOUN 2 a fatlike substance, such as wax. 3 *Biochem* a former name for **lipid.**

lipolysis (lɪ'pɒlɪsɪs) NOUN *Chem* the hydrolysis of fats resulting in the production of carboxylic acids and glycerol.
▸ **lipolytic** (,lɪpəʊ'lɪtɪk) ADJECTIVE

lipoma (lɪ'pəʊmə) NOUN, *plural* **-mas** *or* **-mata** (-mətə). *Pathol* a benign tumour composed of fatty tissue.
▷HISTORY C19: New Latin
▸ **lipomatous** (lɪ'pɒmətəs) ADJECTIVE

lipophilic (,lɪpəʊ'fɪlɪk) *or* **lipotropic** (,lɪpəʊ'trɒpɪk, ,laɪ-) ADJECTIVE *Chem* having an affinity for lipids.

lipoplast ('lɪpəʊ,plɑ:st) *or* **lipidoplast** ('lɪpɪdəʊ,plɑ:st) NOUN *Botany* a small particle in plant cytoplasm, esp that of seeds, in which fat is stored.

lipopolysaccharide (,lɪpəʊ,pɒlɪ'sækə,raɪd) NOUN a molecule, consisting of lipid and polysaccharide components, that is the main constituent of the cell walls of Gram-negative bacteria.

lipoprotein (,lɪpəʊ'prəʊti:n, ,laɪ-) NOUN any of a group of proteins to which a lipid molecule is attached, important in the transport of lipids in the bloodstream. They exist in two main forms: high-density lipoproteins and low-density lipoproteins. See also **low-density lipoprotein.**

liposome ('lɪpəʊ,səʊm) NOUN a particle formed by lipids, consisting of a double layer similar to a natural biological membrane, enclosing an aqueous compartment.

liposuck ('lɪpəʊ,sʌk) VERB (*tr*) *Informal* to subject to liposuction: *she's already had her thighs liposucked.*

liposuction ('lɪpəʊ,sʌkʃən) NOUN a cosmetic surgical operation in which subcutaneous fat is removed from the body by suction.

lipotropic (,lɪpəʊ'trɒpɪk) ADJECTIVE *Biochem* (of a substance) increasing the utilization of fat by the tissues.

lip out VERB (*intr, adverb*) *Golf* (of a ball) to reach the edge of the hole without dropping in.

Lippe ('lɪpə) NOUN 1 a former state of NW Germany, now part of the German state of North Rhine-Westphalia: part of West Germany until 1990. 2 a river in NW Germany, flowing west to the Rhine. Length: about 240 km (150 miles).

-lipped ADJECTIVE having a lip or lips as specified: *tight-lipped.*

Lippizaner (,lɪpɪt'zɑ:nə) NOUN a variant spelling of **Lipizzaner.**

lippy¹ ('lɪpɪ) ADJECTIVE *Informal* **-pier, -piest** insolent or cheeky.

lippy² ('lɪpɪ) NOUN *Informal* lipstick.

lip-read ('lɪp,ri:d) VERB **-reads, -reading, -read** (-'rɛd). to interpret (words) by lip-reading.

lip-reading NOUN a method used by deaf people to comprehend spoken words by interpreting movements of the speaker's lips. Also called: **speech-reading.**
▸ **'lip-,reader** NOUN

lip service NOUN insincere support or respect expressed but not put into practice.

lipstick ('lɪp,stɪk) NOUN a cosmetic for colouring the lips, usually in the form of a stick.

lip-synch *or* **lip-sync** ('lɪp,sɪŋk) VERB to mouth (prerecorded words) on television or film.

lipuria (lɪ'pjʊərɪə) NOUN *Pathol* the presence of fat in the urine.

liq. ABBREVIATION FOR liquid.

liquate ('laɪkweɪt) VERB (*tr;* often foll by *out*) to separate one component of (an alloy, impure metal, or ore) by heating so that the more fusible part melts.
▷HISTORY C17: from Latin *liquāre* to dissolve
▸ **li'quation** NOUN

liquefacient (,lɪkwɪ'feɪʃənt) NOUN 1 a substance that liquefies or causes liquefaction. ◆ ADJECTIVE 2 becoming or causing to become liquid.
▷HISTORY C19: from Latin *liquefacere* to make LIQUID

liquefied natural gas NOUN a mixture of various gases, esp methane, liquefied under pressure for transportation and used as an engine fuel. Abbreviation: **LNG.**

liquefied petroleum gas NOUN a mixture of various petroleum gases, esp propane and butane, stored as a liquid under pressure and used as an engine fuel. See also **bottled gas.** Abbreviation: **LPG** *or* **LP gas.**

liquefy ('lɪkwɪ,faɪ) VERB **-fies, -fying, -fied.** (esp of a gas) to become or cause to become liquid.
▷HISTORY C15: via Old French from Latin *liquefacere* to make liquid
▸ **liquefaction** (,lɪkwɪ'fækʃən) NOUN ▸ **,lique'factive** ADJECTIVE ▸ **'lique,fiable** ADJECTIVE ▸ **'lique,fier** NOUN

liquesce (lɪ'kwɛs) VERB (*intr*) to become liquid.

liquescent (lɪ'kwɛsᵊnt) ADJECTIVE (of a solid or gas) becoming or tending to become liquid.
▷HISTORY C18: from Latin *liquescere*
▸ **li'quescence** *or* **li'quescency** NOUN

liqueur (lɪ'kjʊə; *French* likœr) NOUN 1 **a** any of several highly flavoured sweetened spirits such as kirsch or cointreau, intended to be drunk after a meal. **b** (*as modifier*): *liqueur glass.* 2 a small hollow chocolate sweet containing liqueur.
▷HISTORY C18: from French; see LIQUOR

liquid ('lɪkwɪd) NOUN 1 a substance in a physical state in which it does not resist change of shape but does resist change of size. Compare **gas** (sense 1), **solid** (sense 1). 2 a substance that is a liquid at room temperature and atmospheric pressure. 3 *Phonetics* a frictionless continuant, esp (l) or (r). ◆ ADJECTIVE 4 of, concerned with, or being a liquid or having the characteristic state of liquids: *liquid wax.* 5 shining, transparent, or brilliant. 6 flowing, fluent, or smooth. 7 (of assets) in the form of money or easily convertible into money.

▷HISTORY C14: via Old French from Latin *liquidus,* from *liquēre* to be fluid
▸ **ˈliquidly** ADVERB ▸ **ˈliquidness** NOUN

liquid air NOUN air that has been liquefied by cooling. It is a pale blue and consists mainly of liquid oxygen (boiling pt.: –182.9°C) and liquid nitrogen (boiling pt.: –195.7°C): used in the production of pure oxygen, nitrogen, and the inert gases, and as a refrigerant.

liquidambar (ˌlɪkwɪdˈæmbə) NOUN [1] any deciduous tree of the hamamelidaceous genus *Liquidambar,* of Asia and North and Central America, with star-shaped leaves, and exuding a yellow aromatic balsam. See also **sweet gum.** [2] the balsam of this tree, used in medicine. See also **storax** (sense 3).
▷HISTORY C16: New Latin, from Latin *liquidus* liquid + Medieval Latin *ambar* AMBER

liquidate (ˈlɪkwɪˌdeɪt) VERB [1] **a** to settle or pay off (a debt, claim, etc.). **b** to determine by litigation or agreement the amount of (damages, indebtedness, etc.). [2] **a** to terminate the operations of (a commercial firm, bankrupt estate, etc.) by assessment of liabilities and appropriation of assets for their settlement. **b** (of a commercial firm, etc.) to terminate operations in this manner. [3] *(tr)* to convert (assets) into cash. [4] *(tr)* to eliminate or kill.

liquidation (ˌlɪkwɪˈdeɪʃən) NOUN [1] **a** the process of terminating the affairs of a business firm, etc., by realizing its assets to discharge its liabilities. **b** the state of a business firm, etc., having its affairs so terminated (esp in the phrase **to go into liquidation**). [2] destruction; elimination.

liquidator (ˈlɪkwɪˌdeɪtə) NOUN a person assigned to supervise the liquidation of a business concern and whose legal authorization, rights, and duties differ according to whether the liquidation is compulsory or voluntary.

liquid crystal NOUN a liquid that has some crystalline characteristics, such as the presence of different optical properties in different directions; a substance in a mesomorphic state. See also **smectic, nematic.**

liquid-crystal display NOUN a flat-screen display in which an array of liquid-crystal elements can be selectively activated to generate an image, an electric field applied to each element altering its optical properties; it is used, for example, in portable computers, digital watches, and calculators. Abbreviation: **LCD.**

liquid ecstasy NOUN another name for **GHB.**

liquid fire NOUN inflammable petroleum or other liquid used as a weapon of war in flamethrowers, etc.

liquid glass NOUN another name for **water glass.**

liquidity (lɪˈkwɪdɪtɪ) NOUN [1] the possession of sufficient liquid assets to discharge current liabilities. [2] the state or quality of being liquid.

liquidity preference NOUN *Economics* the desire to hold money rather than other assets, in Keynsian theory based on motives of transactions, precaution, and speculation.

liquidity ratio NOUN [1] the ratio of those assets that can easily be exchanged for money to the total assets of a bank or other financial institution. Also called: **liquid assets ratio.** [2] the ratio of a company's liquid assets to its current liabilities, used as a measure of its solvency. [3] another name for **cash ratio.**

liquidize *or* **liquidise** (ˈlɪkwɪˌdaɪz) VERB [1] to make or become liquid; liquefy. [2] *(tr)* to pulverize (food) in a liquidizer so as to produce a fluid.

liquidizer *or* **liquidiser** (ˈlɪkwɪˌdaɪzə) NOUN a kitchen appliance with blades for cutting and puréeing vegetables, blending liquids, etc. Also called: **blender.**

liquid measure NOUN a unit or system of units for measuring volumes of liquids or their containers.

liquid oxygen NOUN the clear pale blue liquid state of oxygen produced by liquefying air and allowing the nitrogen to evaporate: used in rocket fuels. Also called: **lox.**

liquid paraffin NOUN a colourless almost tasteless oily liquid obtained by petroleum distillation and used as a laxative. Also called (esp US and Canadian): **mineral oil.**

liquor (ˈlɪkə) NOUN [1] any alcoholic drink, esp spirits, or such drinks collectively. [2] any liquid substance, esp that in which food has been cooked. [3] *Pharmacol* a solution of a pure substance in water. [4] *Brewing* warm water added to malt to form wort. [5] **in liquor.** drunk; intoxicated. ◆ VERB [6] *Brewing* to steep (malt) in warm water to form wort; mash.
▷HISTORY C13: via Old French from Latin, from *liquēre* to be liquid

liquorice *or US and Canadian* **licorice** (ˈlɪkərɪs, -ərɪʃ) NOUN [1] a perennial Mediterranean leguminous shrub, *Glycyrrhiza glabra,* having spikes of pale blue flowers and flat red-brown pods. [2] the dried root of this plant, used as a laxative and in confectionery. [3] a sweet having a liquorice flavour.
▷HISTORY C13: via Anglo-Norman and Old French from Late Latin *liquirītia,* from Latin *glycyrrhīza,* from Greek *glukurrhiza,* from *glukus* sweet + *rhiza* root

liquorish (ˈlɪkərɪʃ) ADJECTIVE [1] a variant spelling of **lickerish.** [2] *Brit* a variant of **liquorice.**
▸ **ˈliquorishly** ADVERB ▸ **ˈliquorishness** NOUN

liquor store NOUN *US and Canadian* See **package store.**

liquor up VERB *(adverb) US and Canadian, slang* to become or cause to become drunk.

lira (ˈlɪərə; *Italian* ˈliːra) NOUN, *plural* **lire** (ˈlɪərɪ; *Italian* ˈliːre) *or* **liras.** [1] the former standard monetary unit of Italy, San Marino, and the Vatican City, divided into 100 centesimi; replaced by the euro in 2002. [2] Also called: **pound.** the standard monetary unit of Turkey, divided into 100 kuruş. [3] the standard monetary unit of Malta, divided into 100 cents or 1000 mils.
▷HISTORY Italian, from Latin *lībra* pound

liriodendron (ˌlɪrɪəʊˈdɛndrən) NOUN, *plural* **-drons** *or* **-dra** (-drə). either of the two deciduous trees of the magnoliaceous genus *Liriodendron,* the tulip trees of North America or China.
▷HISTORY C18: New Latin, from Greek *leiron* lily + *dendron* tree

liripipe (ˈlɪrɪˌpaɪp) *or* **liripoop** (ˈlɪrɪˌpuːp) NOUN the tip of a graduate's hood.
▷HISTORY C14: Medieval Latin *liripipium,* origin obscure

Lisbon (ˈlɪzbən) NOUN the capital and chief port of Portugal, in the southwest on the Tagus estuary: became capital in 1256; subject to earthquakes and severely damaged in 1755; university (1911). Pop. (urban area): 3 754 000 (2001). Portuguese name: **Lisboa** (liʒˈboə).

Lisburn (ˈlɪzbɜːn) NOUN [1] a city in Northern Ireland in Lisburn district, Co. Antrim, noted for its linen industry: headquarters of the British Army in Northern Ireland. Pop.: 42 110 (1991). [2] a district of S Northern Ireland, in Co. Antrim and Co. Down. Pop.: 108 694 (2001). Area: 446 sq. km (172 sq. miles).

Lisieux (*French* lizjø) NOUN a town in NW France: Roman Catholic pilgrimage centre, for its shrine of St Thérèse, who lived there. Pop.: 24 506 (1990).

lisle (laɪl) NOUN **a** a strong fine cotton thread or fabric. **b** *(as modifier)*: *lisle stockings.*
▷HISTORY C19: named after *Lisle* (now Lille), town in France where this type of thread was originally manufactured

lisp (lɪsp) NOUN [1] the articulation of *s* and *z* like or nearly like the *th* sounds in English *thin* and *then* respectively. [2] the habit or speech defect of pronouncing *s* and *z* in this manner. [3] the sound of a lisp in pronunciation. ◆ VERB [4] to use a lisp in the pronunciation of (speech). [5] to speak or pronounce imperfectly or haltingly.
▷HISTORY Old English *āwlispian,* from *wlisp* lisping (adj), of imitative origin; related to Old High German *lispen*
▸ **ˈlisper** NOUN ▸ **ˈlisping** ADJECTIVE, NOUN ▸ **ˈlispingly** ADVERB

LISP (lɪsp) NOUN a high-level computer-programming language suitable for work in artificial intelligence.
▷HISTORY C20: from *lis(t) p(rocessing)*

lis pendens (lɪs ˈpɛndɛnz) NOUN [1] a suit pending in a court that concerns the title to land. [2] a notice filed to warn interested persons of such a suit.
▷HISTORY Latin: pending lawsuit

Lissajous figure (ˈliːsəˌʒuː, ˌliːsəˈʒuː) NOUN a curve traced out by a point that undergoes two simple harmonic motions in mutually perpendicular directions. The shape of these curves is characteristic of the relative phases and frequencies of the motion; they are used to determine the frequencies and phases of alternating voltages.
▷HISTORY C19: named after Jules A. *Lissajous* (1822–80), French physicist

lissom *or* **lissome** (ˈlɪsəm) ADJECTIVE [1] supple in the limbs or body; lithe; flexible. [2] agile; nimble.
▷HISTORY C19: variant of LITHESOME
▸ **ˈlissomly** *or* **ˈlissomely** ADVERB ▸ **ˈlissomness** *or* **ˈlissomeness** NOUN

list[1] (lɪst) NOUN [1] an item-by-item record of names or things, usually written or printed one under the other. [2] *Computing* a linearly ordered data structure. [3] **be on the danger list.** to be in a critical medical or physical condition. ◆ VERB [4] *(tr)* to make a list of. [5] *(tr)* to include in a list. [6] *(tr)* *Brit* to declare to be a listed building. [7] *(tr)* *Stock Exchange* to obtain an official quotation for (a security) so that it may be traded on the recognized market. [8] an archaic word for **enlist.**
▷HISTORY C17: from French, ultimately related to LIST[2]; compare Italian *lista* list of names (earlier: border, strip, as of paper), Old High German *līsta* border
▸ **ˈlistable** ADJECTIVE

list[2] (lɪst) NOUN [1] a border or edging strip, esp of cloth. [2] a less common word for **selvage.** [3] a strip of bark, sapwood, etc., trimmed from a board or plank. [4] another word for **fillet** (sense 8). [5] a strip, band, ridge or furrow. [6] *Agriculture* a ridge in ploughed land formed by throwing two furrows together. ◆ VERB *(tr)* [7] to border with or as if with a list or lists. [8] *Agriculture* to plough (land) so as to form lists. [9] to cut a list from (a board, plank, etc.). ◆ See also **lists.**
▷HISTORY Old English *līst;* related to Old High German *līsta*

list[3] (lɪst) VERB [1] (esp of ships) to lean over or cause to lean over to one side. ◆ NOUN [2] the act or an instance of leaning to one side.
▷HISTORY C17: origin unknown

list[4] (lɪst) *Archaic* ◆ VERB [1] to be pleasing to (a person). [2] *(tr)* to desire or choose. ◆ NOUN [3] a liking or desire.
▷HISTORY Old English *lystan;* related to Old High German *lusten* and Gothic *lūston* to desire

list[5] (lɪst) VERB an archaic or poetic word for **listen.**
▷HISTORY Old English *hlystan;* related to Old Norse *hlusta*

listed building NOUN (in Britain) a building officially recognized as having special historical or architectural interest and therefore protected from demolition or alteration.

listed company NOUN *Stock Exchange* a company whose shares are quoted on the main market of the London Stock Exchange.

listed security NOUN *Stock Exchange* a security that is quoted on the main market of the London Stock Exchange and appears in its *Official List of Securities*. Compare **Third Market, unlisted securities market.**

listel (ˈlɪstᵊl) NOUN another name for **fillet** (sense 8).
▷HISTORY C16: via French from Italian *listello,* diminutive of *lista* band, LIST[2]

listen (ˈlɪsᵊn) VERB *(intr)* [1] to concentrate on hearing something. [2] to take heed; pay attention: *I told you many times but you wouldn't listen.*
▷HISTORY Old English *hlysnan;* related to Old High German *lūstrēn*
▸ **ˈlistener** NOUN

listenable (ˈlɪsᵊnəbᵊl) ADJECTIVE easy or pleasant to listen to.
▸ **ˌlistenaˈbility** NOUN

listen in VERB *(intr, adverb;* often foll by *to)* [1] to listen to the radio. [2] to intercept radio communications. [3] to listen but not contribute (to a discussion), esp surreptitiously.

listening post NOUN [1] *Military* a forward position set up to obtain early warning of enemy movement. Abbreviation: **LP.** [2] any strategic position or place for obtaining information about another country or area.

lister ('lɪstə) NOUN *US and Canadian agriculture* a plough with a double mouldboard designed to throw soil to either side of a central furrow. Also called: **lister plough, middlebreaker, middle buster.**
▷HISTORY C19: from LIST[2]

listeria (lɪs'tɪərɪə) NOUN any rodlike Gram-positive bacterium of the genus *Listeria*, esp *L. monocytogenes*, the cause of listeriosis.
▷HISTORY C20: named after Joseph, 1st Baron *Lister* (1827–1912), British surgeon
▸**lis'terial** ADJECTIVE

listeriosis (lɪˌstɪərɪ'əʊsɪs) NOUN a serious form of food poisoning, caused by bacteria of the genus *Listeria*. Its symptoms can include meningitis and in pregnant women it may cause damage to the fetus.

Listerism ('lɪstəˌrɪzəm) NOUN *Surgery* the use of or theory of using antiseptic techniques.

listing ('lɪstɪŋ) NOUN 1 a list or an entry in a list. 2 *Computing* a printed copy of a program or file in a form that can be read by humans. 3 a place on the Official List of Securities of the London Stock Exchange obtained by a company that has fulfilled the listing requirements and whose shares are quoted on the main market. 4 (*plural*) lists of concerts, films, and other events printed in newspapers or magazines, showing details, such as times and venues.

listless ('lɪstlɪs) ADJECTIVE disinclined for any effort or exertion; lacking vigour, enthusiasm, or energy.
▷HISTORY C15: from *list* desire + -LESS
▸**'listlessly** ADVERB ▸**'listlessness** NOUN

list price NOUN the selling price of merchandise as quoted in a catalogue or advertisement.

list renting NOUN the practice of renting a list of potential customers to a direct-mail seller of goods or to the fundraisers of a charity.

lists (lɪsts) PLURAL NOUN 1 *History* **a** the enclosed field of combat at a tournament. **b** the barriers enclosing the field at a tournament. 2 any arena or scene of conflict, controversy, etc. 3 **enter the lists.** to engage in a conflict, controversy, etc.
▷HISTORY C14: plural of LIST[2] (border, boundary)

listserv (ˌlɪst'sɜːv) NOUN a service on the Internet that provides an electronic mailing to subscribers with similar interests.

lit (lɪt) VERB 1 a past tense and past participle of **light[1]**. 2 an alternative past tense and past participle of **light[2]**.

lit. ABBREVIATION FOR: 1 literal(ly). 2 literary. 3 literature.

litany ('lɪtənɪ) NOUN, *plural* **-nies.** 1 *Christianity* **a** a form of prayer consisting of a series of invocations, each followed by an unvarying response. **b the Litany.** the general supplication in this form included in the Book of Common Prayer. 2 any long or tedious speech or recital.
▷HISTORY C13: via Old French from Medieval Latin *litanīa* from Late Greek *litaneia* prayer, ultimately from Greek *litē* entreaty

litas ('liːtɑːs) NOUN, *plural* **litai** ('liːteɪ). the standard monetary unit of Lithuania, divided into 100 centai.

litchi, lichee, lichi, *or* **lychee** (ˌlaɪ'tʃiː) NOUN 1 a Chinese sapindaceous tree, *Litchi chinensis*, cultivated for its round edible fruits. 2 the fruit of this tree, which has a whitish juicy edible aril.
▷HISTORY C16: from Cantonese *lai chi*

lite (laɪt) ADJECTIVE 1 (of food and drink) containing few calories or little alcohol or fat. 2 denoting a more restrained or less extreme version of a person or thing: *reggae lite*.
▷HISTORY C20: variant spelling of LIGHT[2]

-lite NOUN COMBINING FORM (in names of minerals) stone: *chrysolite*. Compare **-lith.**
▷HISTORY from French *-lite* or *-lithe*, from Greek *lithos* stone

liter ('liːtə) NOUN the US spelling of **litre.**

literacy ('lɪtərəsɪ) NOUN 1 the ability to read and write. 2 the ability to use language proficiently.

literae humaniores ('lɪtəˌriː hjuːˌmænɪ'ɔːriːz) NOUN (at Oxford University) the faculty concerned with Greek and Latin literature, ancient history, and philosophy; classics.
▷HISTORY Latin, literally: the more humane letters

literal ('lɪtərəl) ADJECTIVE 1 in exact accordance with or limited to the primary or explicit meaning of a word or text. 2 word for word. 3 dull, factual, or prosaic. 4 consisting of, concerning, or indicated by letters. 5 true; actual. 6 *Maths* containing or using coefficients and constants represented by letters: $ax^2 + b$ is a literal expression. Compare **numerical** (sense 3a). ◆ NOUN 7 Also called: **literal error.** a misprint or misspelling in a text.
▷HISTORY C14: from Late Latin *litterālis* concerning letters, from Latin *littera* LETTER
▸**'literalness** *or* **literality** (ˌlɪtə'rælɪtɪ) NOUN

literalism ('lɪtərəˌlɪzəm) NOUN 1 the disposition to take words and statements in their literal sense. 2 literal or realistic portrayal in art or literature.
▸**'literalist** NOUN ▸**ˌliteral'istic** ADJECTIVE ▸**ˌliteral'istically** ADVERB

literally ('lɪtərəlɪ) ADVERB 1 in a literal manner. 2 (intensifier): *there were literally thousands of people*.

> **Language note** The use of *literally* as an intensifier is common, esp in informal contexts. In some cases, it provides emphasis without adding to the meaning: *the house was literally only five minutes walk away*. Often, however, its use results in absurdity: *the news was literally an eye-opener to me*. It is therefore best avoided in formal contexts.

literary ('lɪtərərɪ, 'lɪtrərɪ) ADJECTIVE 1 of, relating to, concerned with, or characteristic of literature or scholarly writing: *a literary discussion*; *a literary style*. 2 versed in or knowledgeable about literature: *a literary man*. 3 (of a word) formal; not colloquial.
▷HISTORY C17: from Latin *litterārius* concerning reading and writing. See LETTER
▸**'literarily** ADVERB ▸**'literariness** NOUN

literary agent NOUN a person who manages the business affairs of an author.
▸**literary agency** NOUN

literate ('lɪtərɪt) ADJECTIVE 1 able to read and write. 2 educated; learned. 3 used to words rather than numbers as a means of expression. Compare **numerate.** ◆ NOUN 4 a literate person.
▷HISTORY C15: from Latin *litterātus* learned. See LETTER
▸**'literately** ADVERB

literati (ˌlɪtə'rɑːtiː) PLURAL NOUN literary or scholarly people.
▷HISTORY C17: from Latin

literatim (ˌlɪtə'rɑːtɪm) ADVERB letter for letter.
▷HISTORY C17: from Medieval Latin, from Latin *littera* LETTER

literation (ˌlɪtə'reɪʃən) NOUN the use of letters to represent sounds or words.

literator ('lɪtəˌreɪtə) NOUN another word for **littérateur.**
▷HISTORY C18: from Latin, from *littera* letter

literature ('lɪtərɪtʃə, 'lɪtrɪ-) NOUN 1 written material such as poetry, novels, essays, etc., esp works of imagination characterized by excellence of style and expression and by themes of general or enduring interest. 2 the body of written work of a particular culture or people: *Scandinavian literature*. 3 written or printed matter of a particular type or on a particular subject: *scientific literature*; *the literature of the violin*. 4 printed material giving a particular type of information: *sales literature*. 5 the art or profession of a writer. 6 *Obsolete* learning.
▷HISTORY C14: from Latin *litterātūra* writing; see LETTER

Lith. ABBREVIATION FOR Lithuania(n).

-lith NOUN COMBINING FORM indicating stone or rock: *megalith*. Compare **-lite.**
▷HISTORY from Greek *lithos* stone

litharge ('lɪθɑːdʒ) NOUN another name for **lead monoxide.**
▷HISTORY C14: via Old French from Latin *lithargyrus*, from Greek, from *lithos* stone + *arguros* silver

lithe (laɪð) ADJECTIVE flexible or supple.
▷HISTORY Old English (in the sense: gentle; C15: supple); related to Old High German *lindi* soft, Latin *lentus* slow
▸**'lithely** ADVERB ▸**'litheness** NOUN

lithesome ('laɪðsəm) ADJECTIVE a less common word for **lissom.**
▷HISTORY C18: from LITHE + -SOME[1]

lithia ('lɪθɪə) NOUN 1 another name for **lithium oxide.** 2 lithium present in mineral waters as lithium salts.
▷HISTORY C19: New Latin, ultimately from Greek *lithos* stone

lithiasis (lɪ'θaɪəsɪs) NOUN *Pathol* the formation of a calculus.
▷HISTORY C17: New Latin; see LITHO-, -IASIS

lithia water NOUN a natural or artificial mineral water that contains lithium salts.

lithic ('lɪθɪk) ADJECTIVE 1 of, relating to, or composed of stone. 2 containing abundant fragments of previously formed rock: *a lithic sandstone*. 3 *Pathol* of or relating to a calculus or calculi, esp one in the urinary bladder. 4 of or containing lithium.
▷HISTORY C18: from Greek *lithikos* stony

-lithic ADJECTIVE COMBINING FORM (in anthropology) relating to the use of stone implements in a specified cultural period: *Neolithic*.
▷HISTORY from Greek *lithikos*, from *lithos* stone

lithification (ˌlɪθɪfɪ'keɪʃən) NOUN the consolidation of a loosely deposited sediment into a hard sedimentary rock.

lithium ('lɪθɪəm) NOUN a soft silvery element of the alkali metal series: the lightest known metal, used as an alloy hardener, as a reducing agent, and in batteries. Symbol: Li; atomic no.: 3; atomic wt.: 6.941; valency: 1; relative density: 0.534; melting pt.: 180.6°C; boiling pt.: 1342°C.
▷HISTORY C19: New Latin, from LITHO- + -IUM

lithium carbonate NOUN a white crystalline solid used in the treatment of manic-depressive illness and mania. Formula: Li_2CO_3. Lithium citrate is also sometimes used for this purpose.

lithium citrate NOUN a white crystalline solid sometimes used in the treatment of manic-depressive illness and mania. Formula: $Li_3C_6H_5O_7$.

lithium oxide NOUN a white crystalline compound. It absorbs carbon dioxide and water vapour.

litho ('laɪθəʊ) NOUN, *plural* **-thos,** ADJECTIVE, ADVERB short for **lithography, lithograph, lithographic** or **lithographically.**

litho- *or before a vowel* **lith-** COMBINING FORM stone: *lithograph*.
▷HISTORY from Latin, from Greek, from *lithos* stone

lithogenous (lɪ'θɒdʒɪnəs) ADJECTIVE (of animals, esp certain corals) rock-building.

lithograph ('lɪθəˌgrɑːf, -ˌgræf) NOUN 1 a print made by lithography. ◆ VERB 2 (*tr*) to reproduce (pictures, text, etc.) by lithography.
▸**lithographic** (ˌlɪθə'græfɪk) *or* ˌ**litho'graphical** ADJECTIVE ▸ˌ**litho'graphically** ADVERB

lithography (lɪ'θɒgrəfɪ) NOUN a method of printing from a metal or stone surface on which the printing areas are not raised but made ink-receptive while the non-image areas are made ink-repellent.
▷HISTORY C18: from New Latin *lithographia*, from LITHO- + -GRAPHY
▸**li'thographer** NOUN

lithoid ('lɪθɔɪd) *or* **lithoidal** (lɪ'θɔɪdᵊl) ADJECTIVE resembling stone or rock.
▷HISTORY C19: from Greek *lithoeidēs*, from *lithos* stone

lithology (lɪ'θɒlədʒɪ) NOUN 1 the physical characteristics of a rock, including colour, composition, and texture. 2 the study of rocks.
▸**lithologic** (ˌlɪθə'lɒdʒɪk) *or* ˌ**litho'logical** ADJECTIVE ▸ˌ**litho'logically** ADVERB ▸**li'thologist** NOUN

lithomarge ('lɪθəˌmɑːdʒ) NOUN a smooth compact type of kaolin: white or reddish and often mottled.
▷HISTORY C18: from New Latin *lithomarga* from LITHO- + Latin *marga* marl

lithometeor (ˌlɪθə'miːtɪə) NOUN a mass of solid particles, such as dust, sand, etc., falling through the atmosphere.

lithophyte ('lɪθəˌfaɪt) NOUN 1 a plant that grows on rocky or stony ground. 2 an organism, such as a coral, that is partly composed of stony material.
▸**lithophytic** (ˌlɪθə'fɪtɪk) ADJECTIVE

lithopone ('lɪθəˌpəʊn) NOUN a white pigment consisting of a mixture of zinc sulphide, zinc oxide, and barium sulphate.

▷HISTORY C20: from LITHO- + Greek *ponos* work

lithosol ('lɪθəˌsɒl) NOUN *Chiefly US* a type of azonal soil consisting chiefly of unweathered or partly weathered rock fragments, usually found on steep slopes.
▷HISTORY C20: from LITHO- + Latin *solum* soil

lithosphere ('lɪθəˌsfɪə) NOUN the rigid outer layer of the earth, having an average thickness of about 75 km and comprising the earth's crust and the solid part of the mantle above the asthenosphere.

lithostatic another name for **geostatic.**

lithotomy (lɪ'θɒtəmɪ) NOUN, *plural* **-mies.** the surgical removal of a calculus, esp one in the urinary bladder.
▷HISTORY C18: via Late Latin from Greek, from LITHO- + -TOMY
▸**lithotomic** (ˌlɪθə'tɒmɪk) *or* ˌ**litho'tomical** ADJECTIVE
▸**li'thotomist** NOUN

lithotripsy ('lɪθəʊˌtrɪpsɪ) NOUN the use of ultrasound, often generated by a lithotripter, to pulverize kidney stones and gallstones *in situ.*
▷HISTORY C20: from LITHO- + Greek *thruptein* to crush

lithotripter ('lɪθəˌtrɪptə) NOUN a machine that pulverizes kidney stones by ultrasound as an alternative to their surgical removal.

lithotrity (lɪ'θɒtrɪtɪ) NOUN, *plural* **-ties.** *Surgery* the crushing of a calculus in the bladder by means of an instrument (**lithotrite**) so that it can be expelled by urinating.
▷HISTORY C19: from LITHO- + Latin *trītus,* from *terere* to crush

Lithuania (ˌlɪθju'eɪnɪə) NOUN a republic in NE Europe, on the Baltic Sea: a grand duchy in medieval times; united with Poland in 1569; occupied by Russia in 1795 and by Germany during World War I; independent Lithuania formed in 1918, but occupied by Soviet troops in 1919 and then by Poland; became a Soviet republic in 1940; unilaterally declared independence from the Soviet Union in 1990; recognized as independent in 1991. Official language: Lithuanian. Religion: Roman Catholic majority. Currency: litas. Capital: Vilnius. Pop.: 3 691 000 (2001 est.). Area: 65 200 sq. km (25 174 sq. miles). Also called: **Lithuanian Republic.** Lithuanian name: **Lietuva.**

Lithuanian (ˌlɪθju'eɪnɪən) ADJECTIVE 1 of, relating to, or characteristic of Lithuania, its people, or their language. ♦ NOUN 2 the official language of Lithuania: belonging to the Baltic branch of the Indo-European family. 3 a native or inhabitant of Lithuania.

litigable ('lɪtɪgəbᵊl) ADJECTIVE *Law* that may be the subject of litigation.

litigant ('lɪtɪgənt) NOUN 1 a party to a lawsuit. ♦ ADJECTIVE 2 engaged in litigation.

litigate ('lɪtɪˌgeɪt) VERB 1 to bring or contest (a claim, action, etc.) in a lawsuit. 2 (*intr*) to engage in legal proceedings.
▷HISTORY C17: from Latin *lītigāre,* from *līt-,* stem of *līs* lawsuit + *agere* to carry on
▸'**litiˌgator** NOUN

litigation (ˌlɪtɪ'geɪʃən) NOUN 1 the act or process of bringing or contesting a legal action in court. 2 a judicial proceeding or contest.

litigation friend NOUN *Law* a person acting on behalf of an infant or other person under legal disability. Former name: **next friend.**

litigious (lɪ'tɪdʒəs) ADJECTIVE 1 excessively ready to go to law. 2 of or relating to litigation. 3 inclined to dispute or disagree.
▷HISTORY C14: from Latin *lītigiōsus* quarrelsome, from *lītigium* strife
▸**li'tigiously** ADVERB ▸**li'tigiousness** NOUN

litmus ('lɪtməs) NOUN a soluble powder obtained from certain lichens. It turns red under acid conditions and blue under basic conditions and is used as an indicator.
▷HISTORY C16: perhaps from Scandinavian; compare Old Norse *litmosi,* from *litr* dye + *mosi* moss

litmus test NOUN 1 a test to establish the acidity or alkalinity of a mixture. 2 a critical indication of future success or failure.

litotes ('laɪtəʊˌtiːz) NOUN, *plural* **-tes.** understatement for rhetorical effect, esp when achieved by using negation with a term in place of using an antonym of that term, as in "She was not a little upset" for "She was extremely upset.".
▷HISTORY C17: from Greek, from *litos* small

litre *or US* **liter** ('liːtə) NOUN 1 one cubic decimetre. 2 (formerly) the volume occupied by 1 kilogram of pure water at 4°C and 760 millimetres of mercury. This is equivalent to 1.000 028 cubic decimetres or about 1.76 pints.
▷HISTORY C19: from French, from Medieval Latin *litra,* from Greek: a unit of weight

LittB *or* **LitB** ABBREVIATION FOR Bachelor of Letters *or* Bachelor of Literature.
▷HISTORY Latin: *Litterarum Baccalaureus*

LittD *or* **LitD** ABBREVIATION FOR Doctor of Letters *or* Doctor of Literature.
▷HISTORY Latin: *Litterarum Doctor*

litter ('lɪtə) NOUN 1 **a** small refuse or waste materials carelessly dropped, esp in public places. **b** (*as modifier*): *litter bin.* 2 a disordered or untidy condition or a collection of objects in this condition. 3 a group of offspring produced at one birth by a mammal such as a sow. 4 a layer of partly decomposed leaves, twigs, etc., on the ground in a wood or forest. 5 straw, hay, or similar material used as bedding, protection, etc., by animals or plants. 6 See **cat litter.** 7 a means of conveying people, esp sick or wounded people, consisting of a light bed or seat held between parallel sticks. ♦ VERB 8 to make (a place) untidy by strewing (refuse). 9 to scatter (objects, etc.) about or (of objects) to lie around or upon (anything) in an untidy fashion. 10 (of pigs, cats, etc.) to give birth to (offspring). 11 (*tr*) to provide (an animal or plant) with straw or hay for bedding, protection, etc.
▷HISTORY C13 (in the sense: bed): via Anglo-French, ultimately from Latin *lectus* bed

littérateur (ˌlɪtərə'tɜː; *French* literatœr) NOUN an author, esp a professional writer.
▷HISTORY C19: from French from Latin *litterātor* a grammarian

litter lout *or US and Canadian* **litterbug** ('lɪtəˌbʌg) NOUN *Slang* a person who tends to drop refuse in public places.

little ('lɪtᵊl) DETERMINER 1 (often preceded by *a*) **a** a small quantity, extent, or duration of: *the little hope there is left; very little milk.* **b** (*as pronoun*): *save a little for me.* 2 not much: *little damage was done.* 3 **make little of.** See **make of** (sense 3). 4 **not a little. a** very. **b** a lot. 5 **quite a little.** a considerable amount. 6 **think little of.** to have a low opinion of. ♦ ADJECTIVE 7 of small or less than average size. 8 young: *a little boy; our little ones.* 9 endearingly familiar; dear: *my husband's little ways.* 10 contemptible, mean, or disagreeable: *your filthy little mind.* 11 (of a region or district) resembling another country or town in miniature: *little Venice.* 12 **little game.** a person's secret intention or business: *so that's his little game!* 13 **no little.** considerable. ♦ ADVERB 14 (usually preceded by *a*) in a small amount; to a small extent or degree; not a lot: *to laugh a little.* 15 (*used preceding a verb*) not at all, or hardly: *he little realized his fate.* 16 not much or often: *we go there very little now.* 17 **little by little.** by small degrees. ♦ See also **less, lesser, least, littler, littlest.**
▷HISTORY Old English *lȳtel;* related to *lȳr* few, Old High German *luzzil*

Little America NOUN the chief US base in the Antarctic, on the Ross Ice Shelf: first established by Richard Byrd (1928); used for polar exploration.

Little Bear NOUN **the.** the English name for **Ursa Minor.**

Little Belt NOUN a strait in Denmark, between Jutland and Funen Island, linking the Kattegat with the Baltic. Length: about 48 km (30 miles). Width: up to 29 km (18 miles). Danish name: **Lille Bælt.**

Little Bighorn NOUN a river in the W central US, rising in N Wyoming and flowing north to the Bighorn River. Its banks were the scene of the defeat (1876) and killing of General Custer and his command by Indians.

Little Corporal NOUN **the.** a nickname of Napoleon Bonaparte.

Little Diomede NOUN the smaller of the two Diomede Islands in the Bering Strait: administered by the US. Area: about 10 sq. km (4 sq. miles).

Little Dipper NOUN **the.** a US and Canadian name for **Ursa Minor.**

Little Dog NOUN **the.** the English name for **Canis Minor.**

little end NOUN *Brit* 1 Also called (in vertical engines): **top end.** the smaller end of a connecting rod in an internal-combustion engine or reciprocating pump. Compare **big end.** 2 the bearing surface between the smaller end of a connecting rod and the gudgeon pin.

Little Englander ('ɪŋgləndə) NOUN 1 (esp in the 19th century) a person opposed to the extension of the British Empire. 2 *Brit informal* a person who perceives most foreign influences on Britain's culture and institutions as damaging or insidious.

little grebe NOUN a small brownish European diving bird, *Podiceps ruficollis,* frequenting lakes, family *Podicipitidae* (grebes).

little hours PLURAL NOUN *RC Church* the canonical hours of prime, terce, sext, and nones in the divine office.

Little John NOUN one of Robin Hood's companions, noted for his great size and strength.

little lion dog NOUN another name for **Lowchen.**

little magazine NOUN a literary magazine that features experimental or other writing of interest to a limited number of readers.

little man NOUN 1 a man of no importance or significance. 2 *Brit* a tradesman or artisan operating on a small scale.

little office NOUN *RC Church* a series of psalms and prayers similar to the divine office but shorter.

little owl NOUN a small Old World owl, *Athene noctua,* having a speckled brown plumage and flattish head.

little people *or* **folk** PLURAL NOUN *Folklore* small supernatural beings, such as elves, pixies, or leprechauns.

littler ('lɪtlə) DETERMINER *Not standard* the comparative of **little.**

Little Rock NOUN a city in central Arkansas, on the Arkansas River: state capital. Pop.: 183 133 (2000).

Little Russia NOUN a region of the former SW Soviet Union, consisting chiefly of the Ukraine.

Little Russian NOUN, ADJECTIVE a former word for **Ukrainian.**

little slam NOUN *Bridge* the winning of all tricks except one by one side, or the contract to do so. Also called: **small slam.**

littlest ('lɪtlɪst) DETERMINER *Not standard* the superlative of **little.**

Little St Bernard Pass NOUN a pass over the Savoy Alps, between Bourg-Saint-Maurice, France, and La Thuile, Italy: 11th-century hospice. Height: 2187 m (7177 ft.).

little theatre NOUN *Theatre, chiefly US and Canadian* experimental or avant-garde drama, usually amateur, originating from a theatrical movement of the 1920s.

little woman NOUN **the.** *Brit, old-fashioned* a facetious term for **wife.**

littlie ('lɪtlɪ) NOUN *Austral informal* a young child.

littoral ('lɪtərəl) ADJECTIVE 1 of or relating to the shore of a sea, lake, or ocean. 2 *Biology* inhabiting the shore of a sea or lake or the shallow waters near the shore: *littoral fauna.* ♦ NOUN 3 a coastal or shore region.
▷HISTORY C17: from Late Latin *littorālis,* from *lītorālis,* from *lītus* shore

Littoria (*Italian* lit'tɔːrja) NOUN the former name (until 1947) of **Latina.**

lit up ADJECTIVE *Slang* 1 drunk. 2 drugged, esp on heroin.

liturgical (lɪ'tɜːdʒɪkᵊl) *or* **liturgic** ADJECTIVE 1 of or relating to public worship. 2 of or relating to the liturgy.
▸**li'turgically** ADVERB

liturgics (lɪ'tɜːdʒɪks) NOUN (*functioning as singular*) the study of liturgies. Also called: **liturgiology** (lɪˌtɜːdʒɪ'ɒlədʒɪ).

liturgist ('lɪtədʒɪst) NOUN a student or composer of liturgical forms.
▸'**liturgism** NOUN ▸ˌ**litur'gistic** ADJECTIVE

liturgy ('lɪtədʒɪ) NOUN, *plural* **-gies.** 1 the forms of public services officially prescribed by a Church. 2 (*often capital*) Also called: **Divine Liturgy.** *Chiefly*

Eastern Churches the Eucharistic celebration. 3 a particular order or form of public service laid down by a Church.
▷**HISTORY** C16: via Medieval Latin, from Greek *leitourgia,* from *leitourgos* minister, from *leit-* people + *ergon* work

livable *or* **liveable** (ˈlɪvəbᵊl) ADJECTIVE 1 (of a room, house, etc.) suitable for living in. 2 worth living; tolerable. 3 (foll by *with*) pleasant to live (with).
▸ **ˈlivableness** *or* **ˈliveableness** *or* **ˌlivaˈbility** *or* **ˌliveaˈbility** NOUN

live¹ (lɪv) VERB (*mainly intr*) 1 to show the characteristics of life; be alive. 2 to remain alive or in existence. 3 to exist in a specified way: *to live poorly.* 4 (usually foll by *in* or *at*) to reside or dwell: *to live in London.* 5 (often foll by *on*) to continue or last: *the pain still lives in her memory.* 6 (usually foll by *by*) to order one's life (according to a certain philosophy, religion, etc.). 7 (foll by *on, upon,* or *by*) to support one's style of life; subsist: *to live by writing.* 8 (foll by *with*) to endure the effects (of a crime, mistake, etc.). 9 (foll by *through*) to experience and survive: *he lived through the war.* 10 (*tr*) to pass or spend (one's life, etc.). 11 to enjoy life to the full: *he knows how to live.* 12 (*tr*) to put into practice in one's daily life; express: *he lives religion every day.* 13 **live and let live.** to refrain from interfering in others' lives; to be tolerant. 14 **where one lives.** *US informal* in one's sensitive or defenceless position. ◆ See also **live down, live in, live out, live together, live up, live with.**
▷**HISTORY** Old English *libban, lifian;* related to Old High German *libēn,* Old Norse *lifa*

live² (laɪv) ADJECTIVE 1 (*prenominal*) showing the characteristics of life. 2 (*usually prenominal*) of, relating to, or abounding in life: *the live weight of an animal.* 3 (*usually prenominal*) of current interest; controversial: *a live issue.* 4 actual: *a real live cowboy.* 5 *Informal* full of life and energy. 6 (of a coal, ember, etc.) glowing or burning. 7 (esp of a volcano) not extinct. 8 loaded or capable of exploding: *a live bomb.* 9 *Radio, television* transmitted or present at the time of performance, rather than being a recording: *a live show.* 10 (of a record) **a** recorded in concert. **b** recorded in one studio take, without overdubs or splicing. 11 connected to a source of electric power: *a live circuit.* 12 (esp of a colour or tone) brilliant or splendid. 13 acoustically reverberant: *a live studio.* 14 *Sport* (of a ball) in play. 15 (of rocks, ores, etc.) not quarried or mined; native. 16 being in a state of motion or transmitting power; positively connected to a driving member. 17 *Printing* **a** (of copy) not yet having been set into type. **b** (of type that has been set) still in use. ◆ ADVERB 18 during, at, or in the form of a live performance: *the show went out live.*
▷**HISTORY** C16: from *on live* ALIVE

live axle NOUN an axle which rotates with the wheel; driving axle.

live-bearer NOUN a fish, esp a cyprinodont, that gives birth to living young.

live birth NOUN the birth of a living child. Compare **stillbirth.**

live centre (laɪv) NOUN a conically pointed rod mounted in the headstock of a lathe that locates and turns with the workpiece. Compare **dead centre** (sense 2).

-lived (-lɪvd) ADJECTIVE having or having had a life as specified: *short-lived.*

lived-in ADJECTIVE having a comfortable, natural, or homely appearance, as if subject to regular use or habitation.

livedo (lɪˈviːdəʊ) NOUN, *plural* **livedos.** *Med* a reddish discoloured patch on the skin.
▷**HISTORY** from Latin

live down (lɪv) VERB (*tr, adverb*) to withstand the effects of (a crime, mistake, etc.) by waiting until others forget or forgive it.

live in (lɪv) VERB (*intr, adverb*) 1 (of an employee, as in a hospital or hotel) to dwell at one's place of employment. ◆ ADJECTIVE **live-in.** 2 living in the place at which one works: *a live-in maid.* 3 living with someone else in that person's home: *a live-in lover.*

livelihood (ˈlaɪvlɪˌhʊd) NOUN occupation or employment.

live load (laɪv) NOUN a variable weight on a structure, such as moving traffic on a bridge. Also called: **superload.** Compare **dead load.**

livelong (ˈlɪvˌlɒŋ) ADJECTIVE *Chiefly poetic* 1 (of time) long or seemingly long, esp in a tedious way (esp in the phrase **all the livelong day**). 2 whole; entire. ◆ NOUN 3 *Brit* another name for **orpine.**

lively (ˈlaɪvlɪ) ADJECTIVE **-lier, -liest.** 1 full of life or vigour. 2 vivacious or animated, esp when in company. 3 busy; eventful. 4 characterized by mental or emotional intensity; vivid. 5 having a striking effect on the mind or senses. 6 refreshing: *a lively breeze.* 7 springy or bouncy or encouraging springiness: *a lively ball.* 8 (of a boat or ship) readily responsive to the helm. ◆ ADVERB *also* **ˈlivelily.** 9 in a brisk manner: *step lively.* 10 **look lively.** (*interjection*) make haste.
▸ **ˈliveliness** NOUN

liven (ˈlaɪvᵊn) VERB (usually foll by *up*) to make or become lively; enliven.
▸ **ˈlivener** NOUN

live oak (laɪv) NOUN a hard-wooded evergreen oak, *Quercus virginianus,* of S North America: used for shipbuilding.

live out (lɪv) VERB (*intr, adverb*) (of an employee, as in a hospital or hotel) to dwell away from one's place of employment.

liver¹ (ˈlɪvə) NOUN 1 a multilobed highly vascular reddish-brown glandular organ occupying most of the upper right part of the human abdominal cavity immediately below the diaphragm. It secretes bile, stores glycogen, detoxifies certain poisons, and plays an important part in the metabolism of carbohydrates, proteins, and fat, helping to maintain a correct balance of nutrients. Related adjective: **hepatic.** 2 the corresponding organ in animals. 3 the liver of certain animals used as food. 4 a reddish-brown colour, sometimes with a greyish tinge.
▷**HISTORY** Old English *lifer;* related to Old High German *lebrav,* Old Norse *lefr,* Greek *liparos* fat
▸ **ˈliverless** ADJECTIVE

liver² (ˈlɪvə) NOUN a person who lives in a specified way: *a fast liver.*

liver extract NOUN an extract of raw mammalian liver containing vitamin B_{12}: sometimes used to treat pernicious anaemia.

liver fluke NOUN any of various parasitic flatworms, esp *Fasciola hepatica,* that inhabit the bile ducts of sheep, cattle, etc., and have a complex life cycle: class *Digenea.* See also **trematode.**

liveried (ˈlɪvərɪd) ADJECTIVE (esp of servants or footmen) wearing livery.

liverish (ˈlɪvərɪʃ) ADJECTIVE 1 *Informal* having a disorder of the liver. 2 disagreeable; peevish.
▸ **ˈliverishness** NOUN

liver of sulphur NOUN a mixture of potassium sulphides used as a fungicide and insecticide and in the treatment of skin diseases.

liver opal NOUN a form of opal having a reddish-brown coloration. Also called: **menilite.**

Liverpool (ˈlɪvəˌpuːl) NOUN 1 a city in NW England, in Liverpool unitary authority, Merseyside, on the Mersey estuary: second largest seaport in Great Britain; developed chiefly in the 17th century with the industrialization of S Lancashire; Liverpool University (1881) and John Moore's University (1992). Pop.: 474 000 (1994 est.). 2 a unitary authority in NW England, in Merseyside. Pop.: 439 476 (2001). Area: 113 sq. km (44 sq miles).

Liverpudlian (ˌlɪvəˈpʌdlɪən) NOUN 1 a native or inhabitant of Liverpool. ◆ ADJECTIVE 2 of or relating to Liverpool.
▷**HISTORY** C19: from LIVERPOOL, with humorous alteration of *pool* to *puddle*

liver salts PLURAL NOUN a preparation of mineral salts used to treat indigestion.

liver sausage *or esp US* **liverwurst** (ˈlɪvəˌwɜːst) NOUN a sausage made of or containing liver.

liverwort (ˈlɪvəˌwɜːt) NOUN any bryophyte plant of the phylum *Hepatophyta,* growing in wet places and resembling green seaweeds or leafy mosses. See also **scale moss.**
▷**HISTORY** late Old English *liferwyrt*

livery¹ (ˈlɪvərɪ) NOUN, *plural* **-eries.** 1 the identifying uniform, badge, etc., of a member of a guild or one of the servants of a feudal lord. 2 a uniform worn by some menservants and chauffeurs. 3 an individual or group that wears such a uniform. 4 distinctive dress or outward appearance. 5 **a** the stabling, keeping, or hiring out of horses for money. **b** (*as modifier*): *a livery horse.* 6 **at livery.** being kept in a livery stable. 7 *Legal history* an ancient method of conveying freehold land.
▷**HISTORY** C14: via Anglo-French from Old French *livrée* allocation, from *livrer* to hand over, from Latin *līberāre* to set free

livery² (ˈlɪvərɪ) ADJECTIVE 1 of or resembling liver. 2 another word for **liverish.**

livery company NOUN *Brit* one of the chartered companies of the City of London originating from the craft guilds.

liveryman (ˈlɪvərɪmən) NOUN, *plural* **-men.** 1 *Brit* a member of a livery company. 2 a worker in a livery stable.

livery stable NOUN a stable where horses are accommodated and from which they may be hired out.

lives (laɪvz) NOUN the plural of **life.**

live steam (laɪv) NOUN steam supplied directly from a boiler at full pressure, before it has performed any work.

livestock (ˈlaɪvˌstɒk) NOUN (*functioning as singular or plural*) cattle, horses, poultry, and similar animals kept for domestic use but not as pets, esp on a farm or ranch.

live together (lɪv) VERB (*intr, adverb*) (esp of an unmarried couple) to dwell in the same house or flat; cohabit.

live trap (laɪv) NOUN 1 a box constructed to trap an animal without injuring it. ◆ VERB **livetrap, -traps, -trapping, -trapped.** 2 (*tr*) to catch (an animal) in such a box.

live up (lɪv) VERB 1 (*intr, adverb; foll by to*) to fulfil (an expectation, obligation, principle, etc.). 2 **live it up.** *Informal* to enjoy oneself, esp flamboyantly.

liveware (ˈlaɪvˌwɛə) NOUN the programmers, systems analysts, operating staff, and other personnel working in a computer system. Compare **hardware** (sense 2), **software.**

live wire (laɪv) NOUN 1 *Informal* an energetic or enterprising person. 2 a wire carrying an electric current.

live with (lɪv) VERB (*tr, preposition*) to dwell with (a person to whom one is not married).

liveyer *or* **liveyere** (ˈlɪvjə) NOUN *Canadian* (in Newfoundland) a full-time resident.
▷**HISTORY** altered from LIVER, a dweller

livid (ˈlɪvɪd) ADJECTIVE 1 (of the skin) discoloured, as from a bruise or contusion. 2 of a greyish tinge or colour: *livid pink.* 3 *Informal* angry or furious.
▷**HISTORY** C17: via French from Latin *līvidus,* from *līvēre* to be black and blue
▸ **ˈlividly** ADVERB ▸ **ˈlividness** *or* **liˈvidity** NOUN

living (ˈlɪvɪŋ) ADJECTIVE 1 **a** possessing life; not dead. **b** (*as collective noun* preceded by *the*): *the living.* 2 having the characteristics of life (used esp to distinguish organisms from nonliving matter). 3 currently in use or valid: *living language.* 4 seeming to be real: *a living image.* 5 (of animals or plants) existing in the present age; extant. Compare **extinct** (sense 1). 6 *Geology* another word for **live²** (sense 15). 7 presented by actors before a live audience: *living theatre.* 8 (*prenominal*) (intensifier): *the living daylights.* ◆ NOUN 9 the condition of being alive. 10 the manner in which one conducts one's life: *fast living.* 11 the means, esp the financial means, whereby one lives. 12 *Church of England* another term for **benefice.** 13 (*modifier*) of, involving, or characteristic of everyday life: *living area.* 14 (*modifier*) of or involving those now alive (esp in the phrase **living memory**).

living death NOUN a life or lengthy experience of constant misery.

living fossil NOUN an animal or plant, such as the coelacanth and ginkgo, belonging to a group most of whose members are extinct.

living history NOUN any of various activities involving the re-enactment of historical events or the recreation of living conditions of the past.

living picture NOUN another term for **tableau vivant.**

living room NOUN a room in a private house or

flat used for relaxation and entertainment of guests.

Livingston (ˈlɪvɪŋstən) NOUN a town in SE Scotland, the administrative centre of West Lothian: founded as a new town in 1962. Pop.: 41 647 (1991).

Livingstone daisy NOUN a gardener's name for various species of *Mesembryanthemum,* especially *M. criniflorum,* grown as garden annuals (though several are perennial) for their brightly coloured showy flowers: family *Aizoaceae.*
▷HISTORY C20: of unknown origin

living wage NOUN a wage adequate to permit a wage earner to live and support a family in reasonable comfort.

living will NOUN a document stating that if its author becomes terminally ill, his or her life should not be prolonged by artificial means, such as a life-support machine.

Livonia (lɪˈvəʊnɪə) NOUN [1] a former Russian province on the Baltic, north of Lithuania: became Russian in 1721; divided between Estonia and Latvia in 1918. [2] a city in SE Michigan, west of Detroit. Pop.: 100 545 (2000).

Livonian (lɪˈvəʊnɪən) ADJECTIVE [1] of or relating to Livonia, a former Russian Baltic province, or its inhabitants. ◆ NOUN [2] a native or inhabitant of Livonia.

Livorno (*Italian* liˈvorno) NOUN a port in W central Italy, in Tuscany on the Ligurian Sea: shipyards; oil-refining. Pop.: 161 673 (2000 est.). English name: **Leghorn.**

livraison *French* (livrɛzɔ̃) NOUN *Rare* one of the numbers of a book published in parts.
▷HISTORY literally: delivery (of goods)

livre (ˈliːvrə; *French* livrə) NOUN a former French unit of money of account, equal to 1 pound of silver.
▷HISTORY C16: via Old French from Latin *lībra* the Roman pound

lixiviate (lɪkˈsɪvɪˌeɪt) VERB (*tr*) *Chem* a less common word for **leach**[1] (senses 1, 2).
▷HISTORY C17: from LIXIVIUM
▸**lixˈivial** ADJECTIVE ▸**lixˌiviˈation** NOUN

lixivium (lɪkˈsɪvɪəm) NOUN, *plural* **-iums** *or* **-ia** (-ɪə). [1] the alkaline solution obtained by leaching wood ash with water; lye. [2] any solution obtained by leaching.
▷HISTORY C17: from Late Latin, from *lix* lye

lizard (ˈlɪzəd) NOUN [1] any reptile of the suborder *Lacertilia* (or *Sauria*), esp those of the family *Lacertidae* (Old World lizards), typically having an elongated body, four limbs, and a long tail: includes the geckos, iguanas, chameleons, monitors, and slow worms. Related adjectives: **lacertilian, saurian.** [2] **a** leather made from the skin of such an animal. **b** (*as modifier*): *a lizard handbag.*
▷HISTORY C14: via Old French from Latin *lacerta*

Lizard (ˈlɪzəd) NOUN **the.** a promontory in SW England, in SW Cornwall: the southernmost point in Great Britain. Also called: **Lizard Head, Lizard Peninsula.**

lizard fish NOUN any small teleost fish of the family *Synodontidae,* having a slender body and a lizard-like head and living at the bottom of warm seas.

lizard orchid NOUN a European orchid, *Himantoglossum hircinum,* rare in Britain, having a spike of grey-green flowers smelling of goats.

LJ *Brit* ABBREVIATION FOR Lord Justice.

Ljubljana (luːˈbljɑːnə) NOUN the capital of Slovenia: capital of Illyria (1816–49); part of Yugoslavia (1918–91); university (1595). Pop.: 270 986 (2000 est.). German name: **Laibach.**

lk THE INTERNET DOMAIN NAME FOR Sri Lanka.

LL ABBREVIATION FOR: [1] Late Latin. [2] Low Latin. [3] Lord Lieutenant.

ll. ABBREVIATION FOR lines (of written matter).

llama (ˈlɑːmə) NOUN [1] a domesticated South American cud-chewing mammal, *Lama glama* (or *L. peruana*), that is used as a beast of burden and is valued for its hair, flesh, and hide: family *Camelidae* (camels). [2] the cloth made from the wool of this animal. [3] any other animal of the genus *Lama.* See **alpaca**[1]**, guanaco.**
▷HISTORY C17: via Spanish from Quechua

Llandaff (ˈlændəf, -dæf) *or* **Llandaf** (*Welsh* hlanˈdav) NOUN a town in SE Wales, now a suburb of Cardiff; the oldest bishopric in Wales (6th century).

Llandudno (lænˈdɪdnəʊ; *Welsh* hlanˈdɪdnɔ) NOUN a town and resort in NW Wales, in Conwy county borough on the Irish Sea. Pop.: 14 576 (1991).

Llanelli *or* **Llanelly** (θlæˈnɛθlɪ; *Welsh* hlaˈnɛhliː) NOUN an industrial town in S Wales, in SE Carmarthenshire on an inlet of Carmarthen Bay. Pop.: 44 953 (1991).

Llanfairpwllgwyngyll (*Welsh* hlanˌvaɪrpʊhl-ˈgwɪŋgɪhl), **Llanfairpwll,** *or* **Llanfair P. G.** NOUN a village in NW Wales, in SE Anglesey: reputed to be the longest place name in Great Britain when unabbreviated; means: St. Mary's Church in the hollow of the white hazel near the rapid whirlpool of Llandysilio of the red cave. Full name: **Llanfairpwllgwyngyllgogerychwyrndrobwll-llantysiliogogogoch** (*Welsh* hlanˈvaɪrpʊhlˈgwɪŋgɪhl-gɔˈgɛraxwɪrnˈdrɔbʊhlˈhlantəˈsɪljɔˈgɔgɔˈgɔx).

Llangollen (*Welsh* hlanˈgɒhlɛn) NOUN a town in NE Wales, in Denbighshire on the River Dee: International Musical Eisteddfod held annually since 1946. Pop.: 3267 (1991).

llano (ˈlɑːnəʊ; *Spanish* ˈʎano) NOUN, *plural* **-nos** (-nəʊz; *Spanish* -nɔs). an extensive grassy treeless plain, esp in South America.
▷HISTORY C17: Spanish, from Latin *plānum* level ground

Llano Estacado (ˈlɑːnəʊ ˌɛstəˈkɑːdəʊ) NOUN the S part of the Great Plains of the US, extending over W Texas and E New Mexico: oil and natural gas resources. Chief towns: Lubbock and Amarillo. Area: 83 700 sq. km (30 000 sq. miles). Also called: **Staked Plain.**

LLB ABBREVIATION FOR Bachelor of Laws.
▷HISTORY Latin: *Legum Baccalaureus*

LLD ABBREVIATION FOR Doctor of Laws.
▷HISTORY Latin: *Legum Doctor*

Lleyn Peninsula (*Welsh* hliːn) NOUN a peninsula in NW Wales between Cardigan Bay and Caernarvon Bay.

LLM ABBREVIATION FOR Master of Laws.
▷HISTORY Latin: *Legum Magister*

Lloyd's (lɔɪdz) NOUN an association of London underwriters, set up in the late 17th century. Originally concerned exclusively with marine insurance and a shipping information service, it now subscribes a variety of insurance policies and publishes a daily list (**Lloyd's List**) of shipping data and news.
▷HISTORY C17: named after Edward *Lloyd* (died ?1726) at whose coffee house in London the underwriters originally carried on their business

Lloyd's Register NOUN [1] a society formed in 1760 by a group of merchants operating at Lloyd's coffee house to draw up rules concerning the construction of merchant ships. [2] an annual publication giving details of all ships that have been built according to the various classifications established by this society. ◆ In full: **Lloyd's Register of Shipping.**

lm SYMBOL FOR lumen.

LMS (in Britain) ABBREVIATION FOR local management of schools: the system of making each school responsible for controlling its total budget, after the budget has been calculated by the Local Education Authority.

LMVD (in New Zealand) ABBREVIATION FOR Licensed Motor Vehicle Dealer.

ln ABBREVIATION FOR (natural) logarithm.

LNG ABBREVIATION FOR **liquefied natural gas.**

lo (ləʊ) INTERJECTION look! see! (now often in the phrase **lo and behold**).
▷HISTORY Old English *lā*

LO *Text messaging* ABBREVIATION FOR hello.

loach (ləʊtʃ) NOUN any carplike freshwater cyprinoid fish of the family *Cobitidae,* of Eurasia and Africa, having a long narrow body with barbels around the mouth.
▷HISTORY C14: from Old French *loche,* of obscure origin

load (ləʊd) NOUN [1] something to be borne or conveyed; weight. [2] **a** the usual amount borne or conveyed. **b** (*in combination*): *a carload.* [3] something that weighs down, oppresses, or burdens: *that's a load off my mind.* [4] a single charge of a firearm. [5] the weight that is carried by a structure. See also **dead load, live load.** [6] *Electrical engineering, electronics* **a** a device that receives or dissipates the power from an amplifier, oscillator, generator, or some other source of signals. **b** the power delivered by a machine, generator, circuit, etc. [7] the force acting on a component in a mechanism or structure. [8] the resistance overcome by an engine or motor when it is driving a machine, etc. [9] an external force applied to a component or mechanism. [10] **a load of.** *Informal* a quantity of: *a load of nonsense.* [11] **get a load of.** *Informal* pay attention to. [12] **have a load on.** *US and Canadian, slang* to be intoxicated. [13] **shoot one's load.** *Slang* (of a man) to ejaculate at orgasm. ◆ VERB (*mainly tr*) [14] (*also intr*) to place or receive (cargo, goods, etc.) upon (a ship, lorry, etc.). [15] to burden or oppress. [16] to supply or beset (someone) with in abundance or overwhelmingly: *they loaded her with gifts.* [17] to cause to be biased: *to load a question.* [18] (*also intr*) to put an ammunition charge into (a firearm). [19] *Photog* to position (a film, cartridge, or plate) in (a camera). [20] to weight or bias (a roulette wheel, dice, etc.). [21] *Insurance* to increase (a premium) to cover expenses, etc. [22] to draw power from (an electrical device, such as a generator). [23] to add material of high atomic number to (concrete) to increase its effectiveness as a radiation shield. [24] to increase the power output of (an electric circuit). [25] to increase the work required from (an engine or motor). [26] to apply force to (a mechanism or component). [27] *Computing* to transfer (a program) to a memory. [28] **load the dice. a** to add weights to dice in order to bias them. **b** to arrange to have a favourable or unfavourable position. ◆ See also **loads.**
▷HISTORY Old English *lād* course; in meaning, influenced by LADE[1]; related to LEAD[1]

load displacement NOUN *Nautical* the total weight of a cargo vessel loaded so that its waterline reaches the summer load line.

loaded (ˈləʊdɪd) ADJECTIVE [1] carrying a load. [2] (of dice, a roulette wheel, etc.) weighted or otherwise biased. [3] (of a question or statement) containing a hidden trap or implication. [4] charged with ammunition. [5] (of concrete) containing heavy metals, esp iron or lead, for use in making radiation shields. [6] *Slang* wealthy. [7] (*postpositive*) *Slang, chiefly US and Canadian* **a** drunk. **b** drugged; influenced by drugs.

loader (ˈləʊdə) NOUN [1] a person who loads a gun or other firearm. [2] (*in combination*) designating a firearm or machine loaded in a particular way: *breech-loader; top-loader.* [3] *Computing* a system program that takes a program in a form close to machine code and places it into a memory for execution.

load factor NOUN [1] the ratio of the average electric load to the peak load over a period of time. [2] *Aeronautics* **a** the ratio of a given external load to the weight of an aircraft. **b** the actual payload carried by an aircraft as a percentage of its maximum payload.

loading (ˈləʊdɪŋ) NOUN [1] a load or burden; weight. [2] the addition of an inductance to electrical equipment, such as a transmission line or aerial, to improve its performance. See **loading coil.** [3] an addition to an insurance premium to cover expenses, provide a safer profit margin, etc. [4] the ratio of the gross weight of an aircraft to its engine power (**power loading**), wing area (**wing loading**), or some other parameter, or of the gross weight of a helicopter to its rotor disc area (**disc loading**). [5] *Psychol* the correlation of a factor, such as a personality trait, with a performance score derived from a psychological test. [6] material, such as china clay or size, added to paper, textiles, or similar materials to produce a smooth surface, increase weight, etc. [7] *Austral and NZ* a payment made in addition to a basic wage or salary to reward special skills, compensate for unfavourable conditions, etc.

loading coil NOUN an inductance coil inserted at regular intervals and in series with the conductors of a transmission line in order to improve its characteristics.

load line NOUN *Nautical* a pattern of lines painted

on the hull of a ship, approximately midway between the bow and the stern, indicating the various levels that the waterline should reach if the ship is properly loaded under given circumstances.

load-lugger NOUN a motor vehicle that is capable of carrying a load rather than, or as well as, passengers.

loads (ləʊdz) *Informal* ◆ PLURAL NOUN [1] (often foll by *of*) a lot: *loads to eat.* ◆ ADVERB [2] (intensifier): *loads better; thanks loads.*

load shedding NOUN the act or practice of temporarily reducing the supply of electricity to an area to avoid overloading the generators.

loadspace ('ləʊdˌspeɪs) NOUN the area in a motor vehicle where a load can be carried.

loadstar ('ləʊdˌstɑː) NOUN a variant spelling of **lodestar.**

loadstone ('ləʊdˌstəʊn) NOUN a variant spelling of **lodestone.**

loaf[1] (ləʊf) NOUN, *plural* **loaves** (ləʊvz). [1] a shaped mass of baked bread. [2] any shaped or moulded mass of food, such as cooked meat. [3] *Slang* the head; sense: *use your loaf!*
▷HISTORY Old English *hlāf;* related to Old High German *hleib* bread, Old Norse *hleifr,* Latin *lībum* cake

loaf[2] (ləʊf) VERB [1] (*intr*) to loiter or lounge around in an idle way. [2] (*tr;* foll by *away*) to spend (time) idly: *he loafed away his life.*
▷HISTORY C19: perhaps back formation from LOAFER

loafer ('ləʊfə) NOUN [1] a person who avoids work; idler. [2] a moccasin-like shoe for casual wear.
▷HISTORY C19: perhaps from German *Landläufer* vagabond

loaf sugar NOUN (esp formerly) [1] a large conical mass of hard refined sugar; sugar loaf. [2] small cube-shaped lumps of this, the form in which it was often sold.

loam (ləʊm) NOUN [1] rich soil consisting of a mixture of sand, clay, and decaying organic material. [2] a paste of clay and sand used for making moulds in a foundry, plastering walls, etc. ◆ VERB [3] (*tr*) to cover, treat, or fill with loam.
▷HISTORY Old English *lām;* related to Old Swedish *lēmo* clay, Old High German *leimo*
▸ **'loamy** ADJECTIVE ▸ **'loaminess** NOUN

loan[1] (ləʊn) NOUN [1] the act of lending: *the loan of a car.* [2] **a** property lent, esp money lent at interest for a period of time. **b** (*as modifier*): *loan holder.* [3] the adoption by speakers of one language of a form current in another language. [4] short for **loan word.** [5] **on loan. a** lent out; borrowed. **b** (esp of personnel) transferred from a regular post to a temporary one elsewhere. ◆ VERB [6] to lend (something, esp money).
▷HISTORY C13 *loon, lan,* from Old Norse *lān;* related to Old English *lǣn* loan; compare German *Lehen* fief, *Lohn* wages
▸ **'loanable** ADJECTIVE ▸ **'loaner** NOUN

loan[2] (ləʊn) *or* **loaning** ('ləʊnɪŋ) NOUN *Scot and northern English, dialect* [1] a lane. [2] a place where cows are milked.
▷HISTORY Old English *lone,* variant of LANE[1]

loanback ('ləʊnˌbæk) NOUN [1] a facility offered by some life-assurance companies in which an individual can borrow from his pension fund. ◆ VERB **loan back.** [2] to make use of this facility.

loan collection NOUN a number of works of art lent by their owners for a temporary public exhibition.

Loan Council NOUN (in Australia) a statutory body that controls borrowing by the states.

Loanda (ləʊ'ændə) NOUN a variant spelling of **Luanda.**

loan shark NOUN *Informal* a person who lends funds at illegal or exorbitant rates of interest.

loan translation NOUN the adoption by one language of a phrase or compound word whose components are literal translations of the components of a corresponding phrase or compound in a foreign language: *English "superman" is a loan translation from German "Übermensch.".* Also called: **calque.**

loan word NOUN a word adopted, often with some modification of its form, from one language into another.

loath *or* **loth** (ləʊθ) ADJECTIVE [1] (usually foll by *to*) reluctant or unwilling. [2] **nothing loath.** willing.
▷HISTORY Old English *lāth* (in the sense: hostile); related to Old Norse *leithr*
▸ **'loathness** *or* **'lothness** NOUN

loathe (ləʊð) VERB (*tr*) to feel strong hatred or disgust for.
▷HISTORY Old English *lāthiān,* from LOATH
▸ **'loather** NOUN

loathing ('ləʊðɪŋ) NOUN abhorrence; disgust.
▸ **'loathingly** ADVERB

loathly[1] ('ləʊθlɪ) ADVERB with reluctance; unwillingly.

loathly[2] ('ləʊðlɪ) ADJECTIVE an archaic word for **loathsome.**

loathsome ('ləʊðsəm) ADJECTIVE causing loathing; abhorrent.
▸ **'loathsomely** ADVERB ▸ **'loathsomeness** NOUN

loaves (ləʊvz) NOUN the plural of **loaf**[1].

lob[1] (lɒb) *Sport* ◆ NOUN [1] a ball struck in a high arc. [2] *Cricket* a ball bowled in a slow high arc. ◆ VERB **lobs, lobbing, lobbed.** [3] to hit or kick (a ball) in a high arc. [4] *Informal* to throw, esp in a high arc.
▷HISTORY C14: probably of Low German origin, originally in the sense: something dangling; compare Middle Low German *lobbe* hanging lower lip, Old English *loppe* spider

lob[2] (lɒb) NOUN short for **lobworm.**
▷HISTORY C17 (in the sense: pendulous object): related to LOB[1]

lobar ('ləʊbə) ADJECTIVE of, relating to, or affecting a lobe.

lobate ('ləʊbeɪt) *or* **lobated** ADJECTIVE [1] having or resembling lobes. [2] (of birds) having separate toes that are each fringed with a weblike lobe.
▸ **'lobately** ADVERB

lobby ('lɒbɪ) NOUN, *plural* **-bies.** [1] a room or corridor used as an entrance hall, vestibule, etc. [2] *Chiefly Brit* a hall in a legislative building used for meetings between the legislators and members of the public. [3] Also called: **division lobby.** *Chiefly Brit* one of two corridors in a legislative building in which members vote. [4] a group of persons who attempt to influence legislators on behalf of a particular interest. ◆ VERB **-bies, -bying, -bied.** [5] to attempt to influence (legislators, etc.) in the formulation of policy. [6] (*intr*) to act in the manner of a lobbyist. [7] (*tr*) to apply pressure or influence for the passage of (a bill, etc.).
▷HISTORY C16: from Medieval Latin *lobia* portico, from Old High German *lauba* arbor, from *laub* leaf
▸ **'lobbyer** NOUN

lobbyist ('lɒbɪɪst) NOUN a person employed by a particular interest to lobby.
▸ **'lobbyˌism** NOUN

lobe (ləʊb) NOUN [1] any rounded projection forming part of a larger structure. [2] any of the subdivisions of a bodily organ or part, delineated by shape or connective tissue. [3] short for **ear lobe.** [4] any of the loops that form part of the graphic representation in cylindrical coordinates of the radiation pattern of a transmitting aerial. Compare **radiation pattern.** [5] any of the parts, not entirely separate from each other, into which a flattened plant part, such as a leaf, is divided.
▷HISTORY C16: from Late Latin *lobus,* from Greek *lobos* lobe of the ear or of the liver

lobectomy (ləʊ'bɛktəmɪ) NOUN, *plural* **-mies.** surgical removal of a lobe from any organ or gland in the body, esp removal of tissue from the frontal lobe of the brain in an attempt to alleviate mental disorder.

lobelia (ləʊ'biːlɪə) NOUN any plant of the campanulaceous genus *Lobelia,* having red, blue, white, or yellow five-lobed flowers with the three lower lobes forming a lip.
▷HISTORY C18: from New Latin, named after Matthias de *Lobel* (1538–1616), Flemish botanist

lobeline ('ləʊbəˌliːn) NOUN a crystalline alkaloid extracted from the seeds of the Indian tobacco plant, used as a smoking deterrent and respiratory stimulant.
▷HISTORY C19: from LOBELIA

Lobito (*Portuguese* lu'βitu) NOUN the chief port in Angola, in the west on **Lobito Bay:** terminus of the railway through Benguela to Mozambique. Pop.: 70 000 (latest est.).

loblolly ('lɒbˌlɒlɪ) NOUN, *plural* **-lies.** [1] a southern US pine tree, *Pinus taeda,* with bright red-brown bark, green needle-like leaves, and reddish-brown cones. [2] *Nautical* a thick gruel. [3] *US, dialect* a mire; mudhole.
▷HISTORY C16: perhaps from dialect *lob* to boil + obsolete dialect *lolly* thick soup

loblolly boy *or* **man** NOUN *Brit, naval* (formerly) a boy or man acting as a medical orderly on board ship.
▷HISTORY C18: from LOBLOLLY sense 2, applied to a ship's doctor's medicines

lobo ('ləʊbəʊ) NOUN, *plural* **-bos.** *Western US* another name for **timber wolf.**
▷HISTORY Spanish, from Latin *lupus* wolf

lobola *or* **lobolo** (lɔː'bɔːlə, lə'bəʊ-) NOUN (in southern Africa) an African custom by which a bridegroom's family makes a payment in cattle or cash to the bride's family shortly before the marriage.
▷HISTORY from Nguni *ukulobola* to give the bride price

lobotomized *or* **lobotomised** (ləʊ'bɒtəmaɪzd) ADJECTIVE *Informal* apathetic, sluggish, and zombie-like.
▷HISTORY C20: from *lobotomize* (chiefly US) to perform a lobotomy on

lobotomy (ləʊ'bɒtəmɪ) NOUN, *plural* **-mies.** [1] surgical incision into a lobe of any organ. [2] Also called: **prefrontal leucotomy.** surgical interruption of one or more nerve tracts in the frontal lobe of the brain: used in the treatment of intractable mental disorders.
▷HISTORY C20: from LOBE + -TOMY

lobscouse ('lɒbˌskaʊs) NOUN a sailor's stew of meat, vegetables, and hardtack.
▷HISTORY C18: perhaps from dialect *lob* to boil + *scouse,* broth; compare LOBLOLLY

lobster ('lɒbstə) NOUN, *plural* **-sters** *or* **-ster.** [1] any of several large marine decapod crustaceans of the genus *Homarus,* esp *H. vulgaris,* occurring on rocky shores and having the first pair of limbs modified as large pincers. [2] any of several similar crustaceans, esp the spiny lobster. [3] the flesh of any of these crustaceans, eaten as a delicacy.
▷HISTORY Old English *loppestre,* from *loppe* spider

lobster moth NOUN a large sombre-hued prominent moth, *Stauropus fagi,* that when at rest resembles dead leaves. The modified thoracic legs of the larva, carried curled over its body, look like a lobster's claw.

lobster Newburg ('njuːbɜːg) NOUN lobster cooked in a rich cream sauce flavoured with sherry.

lobster pot *or* **trap** NOUN a round basket or trap made of open slats used to catch lobsters.

lobster thermidor ('θɜːmɪˌdɔː) NOUN a dish of cooked lobster, replaced in its shell with a creamy cheese sauce.

lobule ('lɒbjuːl) NOUN a small lobe or a subdivision of a lobe.
▷HISTORY C17: from New Latin *lobulus,* from Late Latin *lobus* LOBE
▸ **lobular** ('lɒbjʊlə) *or* **lobulate** ('lɒbjʊlɪt) *or* **'lobuˌlated** *or* **'lobulose** ADJECTIVE ▸ **ˌlobu'lation** NOUN

lobworm ('lɒbˌwɜːm) NOUN [1] another name for **lugworm.** Sometimes shortened to: **lob.** [2] a large earthworm used as bait in fishing.
▷HISTORY C17: from obsolete *lob* lump + WORM

local ('ləʊkᵊl) ADJECTIVE [1] characteristic of or associated with a particular locality or area. [2] of, concerned with, or relating to a particular place or point in space. [3] *Med* of, affecting, or confined to a limited area or part. Compare **general** (sense 10), **systemic** (sense 2). [4] (of a train, bus, etc.) stopping at all stations or stops. ◆ NOUN [5] a train, bus, etc., that stops at all stations or stops. [6] an inhabitant of a specified locality. [7] *Brit, informal* a pub close to one's home or place of work. [8] *Med* short for **local anaesthetic.** [9] *US and Canadian* an item of local interest in a newspaper. [10] *US and Canadian* a local or regional branch of an association. [11] *Canadian* a telephone extension.
▷HISTORY C15: via Old French from Late Latin *locālis,* from Latin *locus* place, LOCUS
▸ **'localness** NOUN

local anaesthetic NOUN *Med* a drug that produces local anaesthesia. Often shortened to: **local.** See **anaesthesia** (sense 2).

local area network NOUN *Computing* the linking of a number of different devices by cable within a system. Abbreviation: **LAN**.

local authority NOUN *Brit and NZ* the governing body of a county, district, etc. US equivalent: **local government**.

local colour NOUN the characteristic features or atmosphere of a place or time.

locale (ləʊ'kɑːl) NOUN a place or area, esp with reference to events connected with it.
▷HISTORY C18: from French *local* (n use of adj); see LOCAL

local examinations PLURAL NOUN any of various examinations, such as the GCE, set by university boards and conducted in local centres, schools, etc.

local government NOUN [1] government of the affairs of counties, towns, etc., by locally elected political bodies. [2] the US equivalent of **local authority**.

Local Group NOUN *Astronomy* the cluster of galaxies to which our galaxy and the Andromeda Galaxy belong.

localism ('ləʊkəˌlɪzəm) NOUN [1] a pronunciation, phrase, etc., peculiar to a particular locality. [2] another word for **provincialism**.
▸ **'localist** NOUN ▸ **ˌlocal'istic** ADJECTIVE

locality (ləʊ'kælɪtɪ) NOUN, *plural* **-ties**. [1] a neighbourhood or area. [2] the site or scene of an event. [3] the fact or condition of having a location or position in space.

localize *or* **localise** ('ləʊkəˌlaɪz) VERB [1] to make or become local in attitude, behaviour, etc. [2] (*tr*) to restrict or confine (something) to a particular area or part. [3] (*tr*) to assign or ascribe to a particular region.
▸ **'localˌizable** *or* **'localˌisable** ADJECTIVE ▸ **ˌlocali'zation** *or* **ˌlocali'sation** NOUN ▸ **'localˌizer** *or* **'localˌiser** NOUN

local loan NOUN (in Britain) a loan issued by a local government authority.

locally ('ləʊkəlɪ) ADVERB within a particular area or place.

local option NOUN (esp in Scotland, New Zealand, and the US) the privilege of a municipality, county, etc., to determine by referendum whether a particular activity, esp the sale of liquor, shall be permitted there.

local oscillator NOUN *Electronics* the oscillator in a superheterodyne receiver whose output frequency is mixed with the incoming modulated radio-frequency carrier signal to produce the required intermediate frequency.

local sign NOUN *Physiol* the information from a receptor in the eye or the skin signifying respectively a direction in space or a given point on the body.

local time NOUN the time in a particular region or area expressed with reference to the meridian passing through it.

Locarno (*Italian* lo'karno) NOUN a town in S Switzerland, in Ticino canton at the N end of Lake Maggiore: tourist resort. Pop.: 14 150 (1990 est.).

Locarno Pact (ləʊ'kɑːnəʊ) NOUN a series of treaties, concluded in Locarno, Switzerland in 1925, between Germany, France, Belgium, the United Kingdom, Italy, Poland, and Czechoslovakia. The principal treaty, between Germany, France, and Belgium, concerned the maintenance of their existing frontiers, settlement of disputes by arbitration without resort to force, and the demilitarization of the Rhineland. This treaty was guaranteed by the United Kingdom and Italy but was violated when Germany occupied the Rhineland in 1936. Also called: **Treaties of Locarno**.

locate (ləʊ'keɪt) VERB [1] (*tr*) to discover the position, situation, or whereabouts of; find. [2] (*tr; often passive*) to situate or place: *located on the edge of the city*. [3] (*intr*) to become established or settled.
▸ **lo'catable** ADJECTIVE ▸ **lo'cater** NOUN

location (ləʊ'keɪʃən) NOUN [1] a site or position; situation. [2] the act or process of locating or the state of being located. [3] a place outside a studio where filming is done: *shot on location*. [4] (in South Africa) **a** a Black African or Coloured township, usually located near a small town. See also **township** (sense 4). **b** (formerly) an African tribal reserve. [5] *Computing* a position in a memory capable of holding a unit of information, such as a word, and identified by its address. [6] *Roman and Scots law* the letting out on hire of a chattel or of personal services.
▷HISTORY C16: from Latin *locātiō*, from *locāre* to place

locative ('lɒkətɪv) *Grammar* ◆ ADJECTIVE [1] (of a word or phrase) indicating place or direction. [2] denoting a case of nouns, etc., that refers to the place at which the action described by the verb occurs. ◆ NOUN [3] **a** the locative case. **b** a word or speech element in this case.
▷HISTORY C19: LOCATE + -IVE, on the model of *vocative*

loc. cit. (in textual annotation) ABBREVIATION FOR loco citato.

loch (lɒx, lɒk) NOUN [1] a Scot word for **lake**[1]. [2] Also called: **sea loch**. a long narrow bay or arm of the sea in Scotland.
▷HISTORY C14: from Gaelic

lochan ('lɒxən, 'lɒkᵊn) NOUN *Scot* a small inland loch.
▷HISTORY C18: Gaelic, diminutive of LOCH

lochia ('lɒkɪə) NOUN a vaginal discharge of cellular debris, mucus, and blood following childbirth.
▷HISTORY C17: New Latin from Greek *lokhia*, from *lokhios*, from *lokhos* childbirth
▸ **'lochial** ADJECTIVE

loci ('ləʊsaɪ) NOUN the plural of **locus**.

lock[1] (lɒk) NOUN [1] a device fitted to a gate, door, drawer, lid, etc., to keep it firmly closed and often to prevent access by unauthorized persons. [2] a similar device attached to a machine, vehicle, etc., to prevent use by unauthorized persons: *a steering lock*. [3] **a** a section of a canal or river that may be closed off by gates to control the water level and the raising and lowering of vessels that pass through it. **b** (*as modifier*): *a lock gate*. [4] the jamming, fastening, or locking together of parts. [5] *Brit* the extent to which a vehicle's front wheels will turn to the right or left: *this car has a good lock*. [6] a mechanism that detonates the charge of a gun. [7] *US and Canadian informal* a person or thing that is certain to win or to succeed: *she is a lock for the Academy Award*. [8] **lock, stock, and barrel**. completely; entirely. [9] any wrestling hold in which a wrestler seizes a part of his opponent's body and twists it or otherwise exerts pressure upon it. [10] Also called: **lock forward**. *Rugby* either of two players who make up the second line of the scrum and apply weight to the forwards in the front line. [11] a gas bubble in a hydraulic system or a liquid bubble in a pneumatic system that stops or interferes with the fluid flow in a pipe, capillary, etc.: *an air lock*. ◆ VERB [12] to fasten (a door, gate, etc.) or (of a door, etc.) to become fastened with a lock, bolt, etc., so as to prevent entry or exit. [13] (*tr*) to secure (a building) by locking all doors, windows, etc. [14] to fix or become fixed together securely or inextricably. [15] to become or cause to become rigid or immovable: *the front wheels of the car locked*. [16] (when *tr, often passive*) to clasp or entangle (someone or each other) in a struggle or embrace. [17] (*tr*) to furnish (a canal) with locks. [18] (*tr*) to move (a vessel) through a system of locks. [20] **lock horns**. (esp of two equally matched opponents) to become engaged in argument or battle. [21] **lock the stable door after the horse has bolted** *or* **been stolen**. to take precautions after harm has been done. ◆ See also **lock on to, lock out, lock up**.
▷HISTORY Old English *loc*; related to Old Norse *lok*
▸ **'lockable** ADJECTIVE

lock[2] (lɒk) NOUN [1] a strand, curl, or cluster of hair. [2] a tuft or wisp of wool, cotton, etc. [3] (*plural*) *Chiefly literary* hair, esp when curly or fine.
▷HISTORY Old English *loc*; related to Old Frisian *lok*, Old Norse *lokkr* lock of wool

lockage ('lɒkɪdʒ) NOUN [1] a system of locks in a canal. [2] passage through a lock or the fee charged for such passage.

locked-in syndrome NOUN a condition in which a person is conscious but unable to move any part of the body except the eyes: results from damage to the brainstem.

locker ('lɒkə) NOUN [1] **a** a small compartment or drawer that may be locked, as one of several in a gymnasium, etc., for clothes and valuables. **b** (*as modifier*): *a locker room*. [2] a person or thing that locks. [3] *US and Canadian* a refrigerated compartment for keeping frozen foods, esp one rented in an establishment.

Lockerbie ('lɒkəbɪ) NOUN a town in SW Scotland, in Dumfries and Galloway: scene (1988) of the UK's worst air disaster when a jumbo jet was brought down by a terrorist bomb, killing 270 people, including eleven residents of the town.

locket ('lɒkɪt) NOUN a small ornamental case, usually on a necklace or chain, that holds a picture, keepsake, etc.
▷HISTORY C17: from French *loquet* latch, diminutive of *loc* LOCK[1]

lockfast ('lɒkˌfɑːst) ADJECTIVE *Scot* securely fastened with a lock.

lock-in NOUN an illegal session of selling alcohol in a bar after the time when it should, by law, be closed.

lockjaw ('lɒkˌdʒɔː) NOUN *Pathol* a nontechnical name for **trismus** and (often) **tetanus**.

locknut ('lɒkˌnʌt) NOUN [1] a supplementary nut screwed down upon a primary nut to prevent it from shaking loose. [2] a threaded nut having a feature, such as a nylon insert, to prevent it from shaking loose.

lock on to VERB (*intr, adverb + preposition*) (of a radar beam) to automatically follow (a target).

lock out VERB (*tr, adverb*) [1] to prevent from entering by locking a door. [2] to prevent (employees) from working during an industrial dispute, as by closing a factory. ◆ NOUN **lockout**. [3] the closing of a place of employment by an employer, in order to bring pressure on employees to agree to terms.

locksmith ('lɒkˌsmɪθ) NOUN a person who makes or repairs locks.
▸ **'lockˌsmithery** *or* **'lockˌsmithing** NOUN

lock step NOUN a method of marching in step such that the men follow one another as closely as possible.

lock stitch NOUN a sewing-machine stitch in which the top thread interlocks with the bobbin thread.

lock up VERB (*adverb*) [1] (*tr*) Also: **lock in, lock away**. to imprison or confine. [2] to lock or secure the doors, windows, etc., of (a building). [3] (*tr*) to keep or store securely: *secrets locked up in history*. [4] (*tr*) to invest (funds) so that conversion into cash is difficult. [5] *Printing* to secure (type, etc.) in a chase or in the bed of the printing machine by tightening the quoins. ◆ NOUN **lockup**. [6] the action or time of locking up. [7] a jail or block of cells. [8] *Brit* a small shop with no attached quarters for the owner or shopkeeper. [9] *Brit* a garage or storage place separate from the main premises. [10] *Stock Exchange* an investment that is intended to be held for a relatively long period. [11] *Printing* the pages of type held in a chase by the positioning of quoins. ◆ ADJECTIVE [12] **lock-up**. *Brit and NZ* (of premises) without living accommodation: *a lock-up shop*.

Lockwood home ('lɒkˌwʊd) NOUN *Trademark, NZ* a house built of timber planks that lock together without the use of nails.

loco[1] ('ləʊkəʊ) NOUN *Informal* short for **locomotive**.

loco[2] ('ləʊkəʊ) ADJECTIVE [1] *Slang, chiefly US* insane. [2] (of an animal) affected with loco disease. ◆ NOUN, *plural* **-cos**. [3] short for **locoweed**. ◆ VERB (*tr*) [4] to poison with locoweed. [5] *US, slang* to make insane.
▷HISTORY C19: via Mexican Spanish from Spanish: crazy

loco[3] ('ləʊkəʊ) ADJECTIVE denoting a price for goods, esp goods to be exported, that are in a place specified or known, the buyer being responsible for all transport charges from that place: *loco Bristol*; *a loco price*.
▷HISTORY C20: from Latin *locō* from a place

loco citato ('lɒkəʊ sɪ'tɑːtəʊ) in the place or passage quoted. Abbreviations: **loc. cit, lc.**
▷HISTORY Latin: in the place cited

loco disease *or* **poisoning** NOUN a disease of cattle, sheep, and horses characterized by paralysis and faulty vision, caused by ingestion of locoweed.

locoism ('ləʊkəʊˌɪzəm) NOUN another word for **loco disease**.

locoman ('ləʊkəʊmən) NOUN, *plural* **-men**. *Brit informal* a railwayman, esp an engine-driver.

locomotion (ˌləukəˈməuʃən) NOUN the act, fact, ability, or power of moving.
▷HISTORY C17: from Latin *locō* from a place, ablative of *locus* place + MOTION

locomotive (ˌləukəˈməutɪv) NOUN 1 **a** Also called: **locomotive engine.** a self-propelled engine driven by steam, electricity, or diesel power and used for drawing trains along railway tracks. **b** (*as modifier*): *a locomotive shed; a locomotive works.* ◆ ADJECTIVE 2 of or relating to locomotion. 3 moving or able to move, as by self-propulsion.
▸ **ˌlocoˈmotively** ADVERB ▸ **ˌlocoˈmotiveness** NOUN

locomotor (ˌləukəˈməutə) ADJECTIVE of or relating to locomotion.
▷HISTORY C19: from Latin *locō* from a place, ablative of *locus* place + MOTOR (mover)

locomotor ataxia NOUN *Pathol* another name for **tabes dorsalis.**

locoweed (ˈləukəuˌwiːd) NOUN any of several perennial leguminous plants of the genera *Oxytropis* and *Astragalus* of W North America that cause loco disease in horses, cattle, and sheep.

Locrian *or* **Lokrian** (ˈləukrɪən, ˈlɒk-) ADJECTIVE 1 of or relating to Locris, an ancient region of central Greece, or its inhabitants. ◆ NOUN 2 a native or inhabitant of Locris.

Locris *or* **Lokris** (ˈləukrɪs, ˈlɒk-) NOUN an ancient region of central Greece.

locular (ˈlɒkjulə) *or* **loculate** (ˈlɒkjuˌleɪt, -lɪt) ADJECTIVE *Biology* divided into compartments by septa: *the locular ovary of a plant.*
▷HISTORY C19: from New Latin *loculāris* kept in boxes
▸ **ˌlocuˈlation** NOUN

locule (ˈlɒkjuːl) *or* **loculus** (ˈlɒkjuləs) NOUN, *plural* **locules** *or* **loculi** (ˈlɒkjuˌlaɪ). 1 *Botany* any of the chambers of an ovary or anther. 2 *Biology* any small cavity or chamber.
▷HISTORY C19: New Latin, from Latin: compartment, from *locus* place

locum tenens (ˈləukəm ˈtiːnɛnz) NOUN, *plural* **locum tenentes** (təˈnɛntiːz). *Chiefly Brit* a person who stands in temporarily for another member of the same profession, esp for a physician, chemist, or clergyman. Often shortened to: **locum.**
▷HISTORY C17: Medieval Latin: (someone) holding the place (of another)

locus (ˈləukəs) NOUN, *plural* **loci** (ˈləusaɪ). 1 (in many legal phrases) a place or area, esp the place where something occurred. 2 *Maths* a set of points whose location satisfies or is determined by one or more specified conditions: *the locus of points equidistant from a given point is a circle.* 3 *Genetics* the position of a particular gene on a chromosome.
▷HISTORY C18: Latin

locus classicus (ˈklæsɪkəs) NOUN, *plural* **loci classici** (ˈklæsɪˌsaɪ). an authoritative and often quoted passage from a standard work.
▷HISTORY Latin: classical place

locus sigilli (sɪˈdʒɪlaɪ) NOUN, *plural* **loci sigilli.** the place to which the seal is affixed on legal documents, etc.
▷HISTORY Latin

locus standi (ˈstændaɪ) NOUN *Law* the right of a party to appear and be heard before a court.
▷HISTORY from Latin: a place for standing

locust (ˈləukəst) NOUN 1 any of numerous orthopterous insects of the genera *Locusta, Melanoplus,* etc., such as *L. migratoria,* of warm and tropical regions of the Old World, which travel in vast swarms, stripping large areas of vegetation. See also **grasshopper** (sense 1). Compare **seventeen-year locust.** 2 Also called: **locust tree, false acacia.** a North American leguminous tree, *Robinia pseudoacacia,* having prickly branches, hanging clusters of white fragrant flowers, and reddish-brown seed pods. 3 the yellowish durable wood of this tree. 4 any of several similar trees, such as the honey locust and carob.
▷HISTORY C13 (the insect): from Latin *locusta* locust; applied to the tree (C17) because the pods resemble locusts
▸ **ˈlocust-ˌlike** ADJECTIVE

locust bird NOUN any of various pratincoles, esp *Glareola nordmanni* (**black-winged pratincole**), that feed on locusts.

locution (ləuˈkjuːʃən) NOUN 1 a word, phrase, or expression. 2 manner or style of speech or expression.
▷HISTORY C15: from Latin *locūtiō* an utterance, from *loquī* to speak
▸ **loˈcutionary** ADJECTIVE

locutionary act NOUN the act of uttering a sentence considered only as such. Compare **illocution, perlocution.**

Lod (lɒd) NOUN a town in central Israel, southeast of Tel Aviv: Israel's chief airport. Pop.: 42 000 (latest est.). Also called: **Lydda.**

lode (ləud) NOUN 1 a deposit of valuable ore occurring between definite limits in the surrounding rock; vein. 2 a deposit of metallic ore filling a fissure in the surrounding rock.
▷HISTORY Old English *lād* course. Compare LOAD

loden (ˈləudᵊn) NOUN 1 a thick heavy waterproof woollen cloth with a short pile, used to make garments, esp coats. 2 a dark bluish-green colour, in which the cloth is often made.
▷HISTORY German, from Old High German *lodo* thick cloth, perhaps related to Old English *lotha* cloak

lodestar *or* **loadstar** (ˈləudˌstɑː) NOUN 1 a star, esp the North Star, used in navigation or astronomy as a point of reference. 2 something that serves as a guide or model.
▷HISTORY C14: literally, guiding star. See LODE

lodestone *or* **loadstone** (ˈləudˌstəun) NOUN 1 **a** a rock that consists of pure or nearly pure magnetite and thus is naturally magnetic. **b** a piece of such rock, which can be used as a magnet and which was formerly used as a primitive compass. 2 a person or thing regarded as a focus of attraction.
▷HISTORY C16: literally: guiding stone

lodge (lɒdʒ) NOUN 1 *Chiefly Brit* a small house at the entrance to the grounds of a country mansion, usually occupied by a gatekeeper or gardener. 2 a house or cabin used occasionally, as for some seasonal activity. 3 *US and Canadian* a central building in a resort, camp, or park. 4 (*capital when part of a name*) a large house or hotel. 5 a room for the use of porters in a university, college, etc. 6 a local branch or chapter of certain societies. 7 the building used as the meeting place of such a society. 8 the dwelling place of certain animals, esp the dome-shaped den constructed by beavers. 9 a hut or tent of certain North American Indian peoples. 10 (at Cambridge University) the residence of the head of a college. ◆ VERB 11 to provide or be provided with accommodation or shelter, esp rented accommodation. 12 to live temporarily, esp in rented accommodation. 13 to implant, embed, or fix or be implanted, embedded, or fixed. 14 (*tr*) to deposit or leave for safety, storage, etc. 15 (*tr*) to bring (a charge or accusation) against someone. 16 (*tr; often foll by in or with*) to place (authority, power, etc.) in the control (of someone). 17 (*intr; often foll by in*) *Archaic* to exist or be present (in). 18 (*tr*) (of wind, rain, etc.) to beat down (crops).
▷HISTORY C15: from Old French *loge,* perhaps from Old High German *louba* porch
▸ **ˈlodgeable** ADJECTIVE

Lodge (lɒdʒ) NOUN **the.** the official Canberra residence of the Australian Prime Minister.

lodger (ˈlɒdʒə) NOUN a person who pays rent in return for accommodation in someone else's house.

lodging (ˈlɒdʒɪŋ) NOUN 1 a temporary residence. 2 (*sometimes plural*) sleeping accommodation. 3 (*sometimes plural*) (at Oxford University) the residence of the head of a college. ◆ See also **lodgings.**

lodging house NOUN a private home providing accommodation and meals for lodgers.

lodgings (ˈlɒdʒɪŋz) PLURAL NOUN a rented room or rooms in which to live, esp in another person's house.

lodging turn NOUN a period of work or duty, esp among railway workers, which involves sleeping away from home.

lodgment *or* **lodgement** (ˈlɒdʒmənt) NOUN 1 the act of lodging or the state of being lodged. 2 a blockage or accumulation. 3 a small area gained and held in enemy territory.

Lodi (*Italian* ˈlɔːdi) NOUN a town in N Italy, in Lombardy: scene of Napoleon's defeat of the Austrians in 1796. Pop.: 42 277 (1993 est.).

lodicule (ˈlɒdɪˌkjuːl) NOUN any of two or three minute scales at the base of the ovary in grass flowers that represent the corolla.
▷HISTORY C19: from Latin *lōdīcula,* diminutive of *lōdix* blanket

Łódź (*Polish* wudʒ) NOUN a city in central Poland: the country's second largest city; major centre of the textile industry; university (1945). Pop.: 806 728 (1999 est.).

loerie (ˈlaurɪ) NOUN a variant of **lourie.**

loess (ˈləuɪs; *German* lœs) NOUN a light-coloured fine-grained accumulation of clay and silt particles that have been deposited by the wind.
▷HISTORY C19: from German *Löss,* from Swiss German dialect *lösch* loose
▸ **loessial** (ləuˈɛsɪəl) *or* **loˈessal** ADJECTIVE

lo-fi (ˈləuˈfaɪ) *or* **low-fi** ADJECTIVE *Informal* (of sound reproduction) of or giving an impression of poor quality.
▷HISTORY C20: modelled on HI-FI

Lofoten and Vesterålen (*Norwegian* ˈluːfutən, ˈvɛstəroːlən) PLURAL NOUN a group of islands off the NW coast of Norway, within the Arctic Circle. Largest island: Hinny. Pop.: 66 600 (latest est.). Area: about 5130 sq. km (1980 sq. miles).

loft (lɒft) NOUN 1 the space inside a roof. 2 a gallery, esp one for the choir in a church. 3 a room over a stable used to store hay. 4 an upper storey of a warehouse or factory, esp when converted into living space. 5 a raised house or coop in which pigeons are kept. 6 *Sport* **a** (in golf) the angle from the vertical made by the club face to give elevation to a ball. **b** elevation imparted to a ball. **c** a lofting stroke or shot. ◆ VERB (*tr*) 7 *Sport* to strike or kick (a ball) high in the air. 8 to store or place in a loft. 9 to lay out a full-scale working drawing of (the lines of a vessel's hull).
▷HISTORY Late Old English, from Old Norse *lopt* air, ceiling; compare Old Danish and Old High German *loft* (German *Luft* air)

loftsman (ˈlɒftsmən) NOUN, *plural* **-men.** a person who reproduces in actual size a draughtsman's design for a ship or an aircraft, working on the floor of a building (**mould loft**) with a large floor area.

lofty (ˈlɒftɪ) ADJECTIVE **loftier, loftiest.** 1 of majestic or imposing height. 2 exalted or noble in character or nature. 3 haughty or supercilious. 4 elevated, eminent, or superior.
▸ **ˈloftily** ADVERB ▸ **ˈloftiness** NOUN

log[1] (lɒg) NOUN 1 **a** a section of the trunk or a main branch of a tree, when stripped of branches. **b** (*modifier*) constructed out of logs: *a log cabin.* 2 **a** a detailed record of a voyage of a ship or aircraft. **b** a record of the hours flown by pilots and aircrews. **c** a book in which these records are made; logbook. 3 a written record of information about transmissions kept by radio stations, amateur radio operators, etc. 4 **a** a device consisting of a float with an attached line, formerly used to measure the speed of a ship. See also **chip log.** **b heave the log.** to determine a ship's speed with such a device. 5 *Austral* a claim for better pay and conditions presented by a trade union to an employer. 6 **like a log.** without stirring or being disturbed (in the phrase **sleep like a log**). ◆ VERB **logs, logging, logged.** 7 (*tr*) to fell the trees of (a forest, area, etc.) for timber. 8 (*tr*) to saw logs from (trees). 9 (*intr*) to work at the felling of timber. 10 (*tr*) to enter (a distance, event, etc.) in a logbook or log. 11 (*tr*) to record the punishment received by (a sailor) in a logbook. 12 (*tr*) to travel (a specified distance or time) or move at (a specified speed).
▷HISTORY C14: origin obscure

log[2] (lɒg) NOUN short for **logarithm.**

-log COMBINING FORM a US variant of **-logue.**

logagraphia (ˌlɒgəˈgræfɪə) NOUN *Med* inability to express ideas in writing.

logan[1] (ˈləugən) *or* **logan-stone** NOUN other names for **rocking stone.**
▷HISTORY C18: from *logging-stone,* from dialect *log* to rock

logan[2] (ˈləugən) NOUN *Canadian* another name for **bogan** (a backwater).

Logan (ˈləugən) NOUN **Mount.** a mountain in NW Canada, in SW Yukon in the St. Elias Range: the highest peak in Canada and the second highest in North America. Height: 6050 m (19 850 ft.).

loganberry ('ləʊgənbərɪ, -brɪ) NOUN, *plural* **-ries.** [1] a trailing prickly hybrid rosaceous plant, *Rubus loganobaccus*, cultivated for its edible fruit: probably a hybrid between an American blackberry and a raspberry. [2] **a** the purplish-red acid fruit of this plant. **b** (*as modifier*): *loganberry pie.*
▷HISTORY C19: named after James H. *Logan* (1841–1928), American judge and horticulturist who first grew it (1881)

loganiaceous (ləʊˌgeɪnɪ'eɪʃəs) ADJECTIVE of, relating to, or belonging to the *Loganiaceae*, a tropical and subtropical family of plants that includes nux vomica, pinkroot, and gelsemium.
▷HISTORY C19: from New Latin *Logania*, named after James *Logan* (1674–1751) Irish-American botanist

logaoedic (ˌlɒgə'iːdɪk) (in classical prosody) ADJECTIVE [1] of or relating to verse in which mixed metres are combined within a single line to give the effect of prose. ◆ NOUN [2] a line or verse of this kind.
▷HISTORY C19: via Late Latin from Greek *logaoidikos*, from *logos* speech + *aoidē* poetry

logarithm ('lɒgəˌrɪðəm) NOUN the exponent indicating the power to which a fixed number, the base, must be raised to obtain a given number or variable. It is used esp to simplify multiplication and division: if $a^x = M$, then the logarithm of *M* to the base *a* (written $\log_a M$) is *x*. Often shortened to: **log.** See also **common logarithm, natural logarithm.**
▷HISTORY C17: from New Latin *logarithmus*, coined 1614 by John Napier (1550–1617), Scottish mathematician who invented them, from Greek, *logos* ratio, reckoning + *arithmos* number

logarithmic (ˌlɒgə'rɪðmɪk) *or* **logarithmical** ADJECTIVE [1] of, relating to, using, or containing logarithms of a number or variable. [2] consisting of, relating to, or using points or lines whose distances from a fixed point or line are proportional to the logarithms of numbers. ◆ Abbreviation: **log.**
▸ˌ**loga'rithmically** ADVERB

logarithmic function NOUN **a** the mathematical function $y = \log x$. **b** a function that can be expressed in terms of this function.

logbook ('lɒgˌbʊk) NOUN [1] a book containing the official record of trips made by a ship or aircraft; log. [2] *Brit* (formerly) a document listing the registration, manufacture, ownership and previous owners, etc., of a motor vehicle. Compare **registration document.**

log chip NOUN *Nautical* the chip of a chip log.

loge (ləʊʒ) NOUN [1] a small enclosure or box in a theatre or opera house. [2] the upper section in a theatre or cinema.
▷HISTORY C18: French; see LODGE

logger ('lɒgə) NOUN [1] another word for **lumberjack.** [2] a tractor or crane for handling logs.

loggerhead ('lɒgəˌhɛd) NOUN [1] Also called: **loggerhead turtle.** a large-headed turtle, *Caretta caretta*, occurring in most seas: family *Chelonidae*. [2] **loggerhead shrike.** a North American shrike, *Lanius ludovicianus*, having a grey head and body, black-and-white wings and tail, and black facial stripe. [3] a tool consisting of a large metal sphere attached to a long handle, used for warming liquids, melting tar, etc. [4] a strong round upright post in a whaleboat for belaying the line of a harpoon. [5] *Archaic or dialect* a blockhead; dunce. [6] **at loggerheads.** engaged in dispute or confrontation.
▷HISTORY C16: probably from dialect *logger* wooden block + HEAD
▸'**logger,headed** ADJECTIVE

loggia ('lɒdʒə, 'lɒdʒɪə) NOUN, *plural* **-gias** *or* **-gie** (-dʒɛ). [1] a covered area on the side of a building, esp one that serves as a porch. [2] an open balcony in a theatre.
▷HISTORY C17: Italian, from French *loge*. See LODGE

logging ('lɒgɪŋ) NOUN the work of felling, trimming, and transporting timber.

logia ('lɒgɪə) NOUN [1] a supposed collection of the sayings of Christ held to have been drawn upon by the writers of the gospels. [2] the plural of **logion.**

logic ('lɒdʒɪk) NOUN [1] the branch of philosophy concerned with analysing the patterns of reasoning by which a conclusion is properly drawn from a set of premises, without reference to meaning or context. See also **formal logic, deduction** (sense 4), **induction** (sense 4). [2] any particular formal system in which are defined axioms and rules of inference. Compare **formal system, formal language.** [3] the system and principles of reasoning used in a specific field of study. [4] a particular method of argument or reasoning. [5] force or effectiveness in argument or dispute. [6] reasoned thought or argument, as distinguished from irrationality. [7] the relationship and interdependence of a series of events, facts, etc. [8] **chop logic.** to use excessively subtle or involved logic or argument. [9] *Electronics, computing* **a** the principles underlying the units in a computer system that perform arithmetical and logical operations. See also **logic circuit. b** (*as modifier*): *a logic element.*
▷HISTORY C14: from Old French *logique* from Medieval Latin *logica* (neuter plural, treated in Medieval Latin as feminine singular), from Greek *logikos* concerning speech or reasoning

logical ('lɒdʒɪkᵊl) ADJECTIVE [1] relating to, used in, or characteristic of logic. [2] using, according to, or deduced from the principles of logic: *a logical conclusion.* [3] capable of or characterized by clear or valid reasoning. [4] reasonable or necessary because of facts, events, etc.: *the logical candidate.* [5] *Computing* of, performed by, used in, or relating to the logic circuits in a computer.
▸ˌ**logi'cality** *or* '**logicalness** NOUN ▸'**logically** ADVERB

logical atomism NOUN the philosophical theory of Bertrand Russell, the British philosopher (1872–1970), and the early Ludwig Wittgenstein, the Austrian-born British philosopher (1889–1951), which held that all meaningful expressions must be analysable into atomic elements which refer directly to atomic elements of the real world.

logical consequence NOUN the relation that obtains between the conclusion and the premises of a formally valid argument.

logical constant NOUN one of the connectives of a given system of formal logic, esp those of the sentential calculus, *not, and, or,* and *if ... then ....*

logical form NOUN the syntactic structure that may be shared by different expressions as abstracted from their content and articulated by the logical constants of a particular logical system, esp the structure of an argument by virtue of which it can be shown to be formally valid. Thus *John is tall and thin, so John is tall* has the same logical form as *London is large and dirty, so London is large,* namely *P & Q, so P.*

logically possible ADJECTIVE capable of being described without self-contradiction.

logical operation NOUN *Computing* an operation involving the use of logical functions, such as *and* or *or,* that are applied to the input signals of a particular logic circuit.

logical positivism NOUN a philosophical theory that holds to be meaningful only those propositions that can be analysed by the tools of logic into elementary propositions that are either tautological or are empirically verifiable. It therefore rejects metaphysics, theology, and sometimes ethics as meaningless.

logical sum NOUN another name for **disjunction** (sense 3).

logical truth NOUN [1] another term for **tautology** (sense 2). [2] the property of being logically tautologous.

logic array NOUN *Computing* an integrated circuit consisting of interconnected logic gates.

logic bomb NOUN *Computing* an unauthorized program that is inserted into a computer system; when activated it interferes with the operation of the computer.

logic cell NOUN a logic circuit forming part of a chip.

logic circuit NOUN an electronic circuit used in computers to perform a logical operation on its two or more input signals. There are six basic circuits, the AND, NOT, NAND, OR, NOR, and exclusive OR circuits, which can be combined into more complex circuits.

logician (lɒ'dʒɪʃən) NOUN a person who specializes in or is skilled at logic.

logicism ('lɒdʒɪˌsɪzəm) NOUN the philosophical theory that all of mathematics can be deduced from logic. Compare **intuitionism, formalism.**

logic level NOUN the voltage level representing one or zero in an electronic logic circuit.

logic programming NOUN the study or implementation of computer programs capable of discovering or checking proofs of formal expressions or segments.

Logie ('ləʊgɪ) NOUN (in Australia) one of the awards made annually for outstanding television performances.
▷HISTORY C20: after (John) *Logie* Baird (1888–1946), the Scottish inventor of the television

log in *Computing* ◆ VERB [1] Also: **log on.** to enter (an identification number, password, etc.) from a remote terminal to gain access to a multiaccess system. ◆ NOUN [2] Also: **login.** the process by which a computer user logs in.

logion ('lɒgɪˌɒn) NOUN, *plural* **logia** ('lɒgɪə). a saying of Christ regarded as authentic. See also **logia.**
▷HISTORY C16: from Greek: a saying, oracle, from *logos* word

logistic¹ (lɒ'dʒɪstɪk) NOUN [1] an uninterpreted calculus or system of symbolic logic. Compare **formal language.** ◆ ADJECTIVE [2] *Maths* (of a curve) having an equation of the form $y = k/(1 + e^{a+bx})$, where *b* is less than zero. [3] *Rare* of, relating to, or skilled in arithmetical calculations.
▷HISTORY C17: via French, from Late Latin *logisticus* of calculation, from Greek *logistikos* rational, from *logos* word, reason

logistic² (lɒ'dʒɪstɪk) *or* **logistical** ADJECTIVE of or relating to logistics.
▸**lo'gistically** ADVERB

logistics (lɒ'dʒɪstɪks) NOUN (*functioning as singular or plural*) [1] the science of the movement, supplying, and maintenance of military forces in the field. [2] the management of materials flow through an organization, from raw materials through to finished goods. [3] the detailed planning and organization of any large complex operation.
▷HISTORY C19: from French *logistique*, from *loger* to LODGE
▸**lo'gistically** ADVERB ▸**logistician** (ˌlɒdʒɪ'stɪʃən) NOUN

log jam NOUN *Chiefly US and Canadian* [1] blockage caused by the crowding together of a number of logs floating in a river. [2] a deadlock; standstill.

loglog ('lɒglɒg) NOUN the logarithm of a logarithm (in equations, etc.).

logo ('ləʊgəʊ, 'lɒg-) NOUN, *plural* **-os.** short for **logotype** (sense 2).

logo- COMBINING FORM indicating word or speech: *logogram.*
▷HISTORY from Greek; see LOGOS

log of wood NOUN *NZ* **the.** an informal name for **Ranfurly Shield.**

logogram ('lɒgəˌgræm) *or* **logograph** ('lɒgəˌgrɑːf, -ˌgræf) NOUN a single symbol representing an entire morpheme, word, or phrase, as for example the symbol (%) meaning *per cent.*
▸**logogrammatic** (ˌlɒgəgrə'mætɪk) *or* **logographic** (ˌlɒgə'græfɪk) *or* ˌ**logo'graphical** ADJECTIVE
▸ˌ**logogram'matically** *or* ˌ**logo'graphically** ADVERB

logography (lɒ'gɒgrəfɪ) NOUN (formerly) a method of longhand reporting.
▸**lo'gographer** NOUN

logogriph ('lɒgəʊˌgrɪf) NOUN a word puzzle, esp one based on recombination of the letters of a word.
▷HISTORY C16: via French from LOGO- + Greek *grīphos* puzzle
▸ˌ**logo'griphic** ADJECTIVE

logomachy (lɒ'gɒməkɪ) NOUN, *plural* **-chies.** argument about words or the meaning of words.
▷HISTORY C16: from Greek *logomakhia*, from *logos* word + *makhē* battle
▸**lo'gomachist** NOUN

logopaedics *or US* **logopedics** (ˌlɒgə'piːdɪks) NOUN (*functioning as singular*) another name for **speech therapy.**
▸ˌ**logo'paedic** *or US* ˌ**logo'pedic** ADJECTIVE

logorrhoea *or esp US* **logorrhea** (ˌlɒgə'rɪə) NOUN excessive, uncontrollable, or incoherent talkativeness.

logos ('lɒgɒs) NOUN *Philosophy* reason or the rational principle expressed in words and things, argument, or justification; esp personified as the source of order in the universe.

▷HISTORY C16: from Greek: word, reason, discourse, from *legein* to speak

Logos ('lɒgɒs) NOUN *Christian theol* the divine Word; the second person of the Trinity incarnate in the person of Jesus.

logotype ('lɒgəʊ,taɪp) NOUN [1] *Printing* a piece of type with several uncombined characters cast on it. [2] Also called: **logo.** a trademark, company emblem, or similar device.
▸'**logo,typy** NOUN

log out *Computing* ◆ VERB [1] Also: **log off.** to disconnect a remote terminal from a multiaccess system by entering (an identification number, password, etc.). ◆ NOUN [2] Also: **logout.** the process by which a computer user logs out.

logroll ('lɒg,rəʊl) VERB *Chiefly US* to use logrolling in order to procure the passage of (legislation).
▸'**log,roller** NOUN

logrolling ('lɒg,rəʊlɪŋ) NOUN [1] *US* the practice of undemocratic agreements between politicians involving mutual favours, the trading of votes, etc. [2] another name for **birling.** See **birl**[1].

Logroño (*Spanish* lo'ɣroɲo) NOUN a walled city in N Spain, on the Ebro River: trading centre of an agricultural region noted for its wine. Pop.: 125 617 (1998 est.).

-logue *or US* **-log** NOUN COMBINING FORM indicating speech or discourse of a particular kind: *travelogue; monologue.*
▷HISTORY from French, from Greek *-logos*

logway ('lɒg,weɪ) NOUN another name for **gangway** (sense 4).

logwood ('lɒg,wʊd) NOUN [1] a leguminous tree, *Haematoxylon campechianum,* of the Caribbean and Central America. [2] the heavy reddish-brown wood of this tree, yielding the dye haematoxylin. See also **haematoxylon.**

logy ('ləʊgɪ) ADJECTIVE **logier, logiest.** *Chiefly US* dull or listless.
▷HISTORY C19: perhaps from Dutch *log* heavy
▸'**loginess** NOUN

-logy NOUN COMBINING FORM [1] indicating the science or study of: *musicology.* [2] indicating writing, discourse, or body of writings: *trilogy; phraseology; martyrology.*
▷HISTORY from Latin *-logia,* from Greek, from *logos* word; see LOGOS
▸**-logical** *or* **-logic** ADJECTIVE COMBINING FORM ▸**-logist** NOUN COMBINING FORM

lohan ('ləʊ'hɑ:n) NOUN (*sometimes capital*) another word for **arhat.**

Lohengrin ('ləʊɪŋgrɪn) NOUN (in German legend) a son of Parzival and knight of the Holy Grail.

loin (lɔɪn) NOUN [1] Also called: **lumbus.** *Anatomy* the part of the lower back and sides between the pelvis and the ribs. Related adjective: **lumbar.** [2] a cut of meat from this part of an animal. ◆ See also **loins.**
▷HISTORY C14: from Old French *loigne,* perhaps from Vulgar Latin *lumbra* (unattested), from Latin *lumbus* loin

loincloth ('lɔɪn,klɒθ) NOUN a piece of cloth worn round the loins. Also called: **breechcloth.**

loins (lɔɪnz) PLURAL NOUN [1] the hips and the inner surface of the legs where they join the trunk of the body; crotch. [2] **a** *Euphemistic* the reproductive organs. **b** *Chiefly literary* the womb.

Loire (*French* lwar) NOUN [1] a department of E central France, in Rhône-Alpes region. Capital: St. Étienne. Pop.: 728 524 (1999). Area: 4799 sq. km (1872 sq. miles). [2] a river in France, rising in the Massif Central and flowing north and west in a wide curve to the Bay of Biscay: the longest river in France. Its valley is famous for its wines and châteaux. Length: 1020 km (634 miles). Ancient name: **Liger.**

Loire-Atlantique (*French* lwaratlɑ̃tik) NOUN a department of W France, in Pays de la Loire region. Capital: Nantes. Pop.: 1 134 266 (1999). Area: 6980 sq. km (2722 sq. miles).

Loiret (*French* lwarɛ) NOUN a department of central France, in Centre region. Capital: Orléans. Pop.: 618 126 (1999). Area: 6812 sq. km (2657 sq. miles).

Loir-et-Cher (*French* lwareʃɛr) NOUN a department of N central France, in Centre region. Capital: Blois. Pop.: 314 968 (1999). Area: 6422 sq. km (2505 sq. miles).

loiter ('lɔɪtə) VERB (*intr*) to stand or act aimlessly or idly.
▷HISTORY C14: perhaps from Middle Dutch *löteren* to wobble: perhaps related to Old English *lūtian* to lurk
▸'**loiterer** NOUN ▸'**loitering** NOUN, ADJECTIVE

Loki ('ləʊkɪ) NOUN *Norse myth* the god of mischief and destruction.

Lok Sabha ('ləʊk 'sʌbə) NOUN the lower chamber of India's Parliament. Compare **Rajya Sabha.**
▷HISTORY Hindi, from *lok* people + *sabha* assembly

LOL *Text messaging* ABBREVIATION FOR laughing out loud.

Lolita (,lɒ'li:tə) NOUN a sexually precocious young girl.
▷HISTORY C20: after the character in Nabokov's novel *Lolita* (1955)

loll (lɒl) VERB [1] (*intr*) to lie, lean, or lounge in a lazy or relaxed manner. [2] to hang or allow to hang loosely. ◆ NOUN [3] an act or instance of lolling.
▷HISTORY C14: perhaps imitative; perhaps related to Middle Dutch *lollen* to doze
▸'**loller** NOUN ▸'**lolling** ADJECTIVE

Lolland *or* **Laaland** (*Danish* 'lɔlan) NOUN an island of Denmark in the Baltic Sea, south of Sjælland. Pop.: 80 500 (latest est.). Area: 1240 sq. km (480 sq. miles).

lollapalooza (,lɒləpə'lu:zə) *or* **lalapalooza** NOUN *US, slang* something excellent.
▷HISTORY origin unknown

Lollard ('lɒləd) NOUN *English history* a follower of John Wycliffe during the 14th, 15th, and 16th centuries.
▷HISTORY C14: from Middle Dutch; mutterer, from *lollen* to mumble (prayers)
▸'**Lollardy** *or* '**Lollardry** *or* '**Lollardism** NOUN

lollipop ('lɒlɪ,pɒp) NOUN [1] a boiled sweet or toffee stuck on a small wooden stick. [2] *Brit* another word for **ice lolly.**
▷HISTORY C18: perhaps from Northern English dialect *lolly* the tongue (compare LOLL) + POP[1]

lollipop man *or* **lady** NOUN (in Britain) a person wearing a white coat and carrying a pole bearing a circular warning sign who stops traffic to allow children travelling to or from school to cross a road safely. Official name: **school crossing patrol.**

lollop ('lɒləp) VERB (*intr*) *Chiefly Brit* [1] to walk or run with a clumsy or relaxed bouncing movement. [2] a less common word for **lounge.**
▷HISTORY C18: probably from LOLL + *-op* as in GALLOP, to emphasize the contrast in meaning

lollo rosso ('lɒləʊ 'rɒsəʊ) NOUN a variety of lettuce originating in Italy, having curly red-tipped leaves and a slightly bitter taste.

lolly ('lɒlɪ) NOUN, *plural* **-lies.** [1] an informal word for **lollipop.** [2] *Brit* short for **ice lolly.** [3] *Brit, Austral, and NZ* a slang word for **money.** [4] *Austral and NZ informal* a sweet, esp a boiled one. [5] **do the** (*or* **one's**) **lolly.** *Austral informal* to lose one's temper.
▷HISTORY shortened from LOLLIPOP

lollygag ('lɒlɪ,gæg) VERB **-gags, -gagging, -gagged.** (*intr*) a variant of **lallygag.**

lolly water NOUN *Austral and NZ informal* any of various coloured soft drinks.

Lombard ('lɒmbəd, -bɑ:d, 'lʌm-) NOUN [1] a native or inhabitant of Lombardy. [2] Also called: **Langobard.** a member of an ancient Germanic people who settled in N Italy after 568 A.D. ◆ ADJECTIVE *also* **Lombardic.** [3] of or relating to Lombardy or the Lombards.

Lombard Street NOUN the British financial and banking world.
▷HISTORY C16: from a street in London once occupied by Lombard bankers

Lombardy ('lɒmbədɪ, 'lʌm-) NOUN a region of N central Italy, bordering on the Alps: dominated by prosperous lordships and city-states during the Middle Ages; later ruled by Spain and then by Austria before becoming part of Italy in 1859; intensively cultivated and in parts highly industrialized. Pop.: 9 065 440 (2000 est.). Area: 23 804 sq. km (9284 sq. miles). Italian name: **Lombardia** (,lombar'di:a).

Lombardy poplar NOUN an Italian poplar tree, *Populus nigra italica,* with upwardly pointing branches giving it a columnar shape.

Lombok ('lɒmbɒk) NOUN an island of Indonesia, in the Nusa Tenggara Islands east of Java: came under Dutch rule in 1894; important biologically as being transitional between Asian and Australian in flora and fauna, the line of demarcation beginning at **Lombok Strait** (a channel between Lombok and Bali, connecting the Flores Sea with the Indian Ocean). Chief town: Mataram. Pop.: 2 500 000 (1991). Area: 4730 sq. km (1826 sq. miles).

Lombrosian (lɒm'brəʊzɪən) ADJECTIVE of or relating to the doctrine propounded by the Italian criminologist Cesare Lombroso (1836–1909) that criminals are a product of hereditary and atavistic factors and can be classified as a definite abnormal type.

Lomé (*French* lɔme) NOUN the capital and chief port of Togo, on the Bight of Benin. Pop.: 790 000 (1999 est.).

loment ('ləʊmɛnt) *or* **lomentum** (ləʊ'mɛntəm) NOUN, *plural* **-ments** *or* **-menta** (-'mɛntə). the pod of certain leguminous plants, constricted between each seed and breaking into one-seeded portions when ripe.
▷HISTORY C19: from Latin *lomentum* bean meal
▸**lomentaceous** (,ləʊmən'teɪʃəs) ADJECTIVE

Lomond ('ləʊmənd) NOUN [1] **Loch.** a lake in W Scotland, north of Glasgow: the largest Scottish lake; designated a national park in 2002. Length: about 38 km (24 miles). Width: up to 8 km (5 miles). [2] See **Ben Lomond.**

London ('lʌndən) NOUN [1] the capital of the United Kingdom, a port in S England on the River Thames near its estuary on the North Sea: consists of the **City** (the financial quarter), the **West End** (the entertainment and major shopping centre), the **East End** (the industrial and former dock area), and extensive suburbs. Latin name: **Londinium.** See also **City.** [2] **Greater.** the administrative area of London, consisting of the City of London and 32 boroughs (13 Inner London boroughs and 19 Outer London boroughs): formed in 1965 from the City, parts of Surrey, Kent, Essex, and Hertfordshire, and almost all of Middlesex: a Mayor of London and a London Assembly took office in 2000. Pop.: 7 172 036 (2001). Area: 1579 sq. km (610 sq. miles). [3] a city in SE Canada, in SE Ontario on the Thames River: University of Western Ontario (1878). Pop.: 325 646 (1996).

Londonderry ('lʌndən,dɛrɪ) *or* **Derry** NOUN [1] a historical county of NW Northern Ireland, on the Atlantic: in 1973 replaced for administrative purposes by the districts of Coleraine, Derry, Limavady, and Magherafelt. Area: 2108 sq. km (814 sq. miles). [2] a port in N Northern Ireland, second city of Northern Ireland: given to the City of London in 1613 to be colonized by Londoners; besieged by James II's forces (1688–89). Pop.: 72 334 (1991). ◆ See also **Derry.**

Londoner ('lʌndənə) NOUN a native or inhabitant of London.

London pride NOUN a saxifragaceous plant, a hybrid between *Saxifraga spathularis* and *S. umbrosa,* having a basal rosette of leaves and pinkish-white flowers.

Londrina (*Portuguese* lon'drina) NOUN a city in S Brazil, in Paraná: centre of a coffee-growing area. Pop.: 433 264 (2000).

lone (ləʊn) ADJECTIVE (*prenominal*) [1] unaccompanied; solitary. [2] single or isolated: *a lone house.* [3] a literary word for **lonely.** [4] unmarried or widowed.
▷HISTORY C14: from the mistaken division of ALONE into *a lone*
▸'**loneness** NOUN

lone hand NOUN [1] (in card games such as euchre) an independent player or hand played without a partner. [2] **play a lone hand.** to operate without assistance.

lonely ('ləʊnlɪ) ADJECTIVE **-lier, -liest.** [1] unhappy as a result of being without the companionship of others: *a lonely man.* [2] causing or resulting from the state of being alone: *a lonely existence.* [3] isolated, unfrequented, or desolate. [4] without companions; solitary.
▸'**loneliness** NOUN

lonely hearts ADJECTIVE (*often capitals*) of or for people who wish to meet a congenial companion or marriage partner: *a lonely hearts advertisement.*

lone pair NOUN *Chem* a pair of valency electrons of opposite spin that are not shared between the atoms in a molecule and are responsible for the formation of coordinate bonds.

loner (ˈləʊnə) NOUN *Informal* a person or animal who avoids the company of others or prefers to be alone.

lonesome (ˈləʊnsəm) ADJECTIVE 1 *Chiefly US and Canadian* another word for **lonely.** ◆ NOUN 2 **on** *or* **US by one's lonesome.** *Informal* on one's own.
▸ˈ**lonesomely** ADVERB ▸ˈ**lonesomeness** NOUN

lone wolf NOUN a person who prefers to be alone.

long[1] (lɒŋ) ADJECTIVE 1 having relatively great extent in space on a horizontal plane. 2 having relatively great duration in time. 3 **a** (*postpositive*) of a specified number of units in extent or duration: *three hours long.* **b** (*in combination*): *a two-foot-long line.* 4 having or consisting of a relatively large number of items or parts: *a long list.* 5 having greater than the average or expected range: *a long memory.* 6 being the longer or longest of alternatives: *the long way to the bank.* 7 having more than the average or usual quantity, extent, or duration: *a long match.* 8 seeming to occupy a greater time than is really so: *she spent a long afternoon waiting in the departure lounge.* 9 intense or thorough (esp in the phrase **a long look**). 10 (of drinks) containing a large quantity of nonalcoholic beverage. 11 (of a garment) reaching to the wearer's ankles. 12 *Informal* (foll by *on*) plentifully supplied or endowed (with): *long on good ideas.* 13 *Phonetics* (of a speech sound, esp a vowel) **a** of relatively considerable duration. **b** classified as long, as distinguished from the quality of other vowels. **c** (in popular usage) denoting the qualities of the five English vowels in such words as *mate, mete, mite, moat, moot,* and *mute.* 14 from end to end; lengthwise. 15 unlikely to win, happen, succeed, etc.: *a long chance.* 16 *Prosody* **a** denoting a vowel of relatively great duration or (esp in classical verse) followed by more than one consonant. **b** denoting a syllable containing such a vowel. **c** (in verse that is not quantitative) carrying the emphasis or ictus. 17 *Finance* having or characterized by large holdings of securities or commodities in anticipation of rising prices: *a long position.* 18 *Cricket* (of a fielding position) near the boundary: *long leg.* 19 *Informal* (of people) tall and slender. 20 **in the long run.** See **run** (sense 82). 21 **long in the tooth.** *Informal* old or ageing. ◆ ADVERB 22 for a certain time or period: *how long will it last?* 23 for or during an extensive period of time: *long into the next year.* 24 at a distant time; quite a bit of time: *long before I met you; long ago.* 25 *Finance* into a position with more security or commodity holdings than are required by sale contracts and therefore dependent on rising prices for profit: *to go long.* 26 **as** (*or* **so**) **long as. a** for or during just the length of time that. **b** inasmuch as; since. **c** provided that; if. 27 **no longer.** not any more; formerly but not now. ◆ NOUN 28 a long time (esp in the phrase **for long**). 29 a relatively long thing, such as a signal in Morse code. 30 a clothing size for tall people, esp in trousers. 31 *Phonetics* a long vowel or syllable. 32 *Finance* a person with large holdings of a security or commodity in expectation of a rise in its price; bull. 33 *Music* a note common in medieval music but now obsolete, having the time value of two breves. 34 **before long.** soon. 35 **the long and the short of it.** the essential points or facts. ◆ See also **longs.**
▷HISTORY Old English *lang;* related to Old High German *lang,* Old Norse *langr,* Latin *longus*

long[2] (lɒŋ) VERB (*intr;* foll by *for* or an infinitive) to have a strong desire.
▷HISTORY Old English *langian;* related to LONG[1]

long[3] (lɒŋ) VERB (*intr*) *Archaic* to belong, appertain, or be appropriate.
▷HISTORY Old English *langian* to belong, from *gelang* at hand, belonging to; compare ALONG

long. ABBREVIATION FOR longitude.

long- ADVERB (*in combination*) for or lasting a long time: *long-awaited; long-established; long-lasting.*

long-acting ADJECTIVE (of a drug) slowly effective after initial dosage, but maintaining its effects over a long period of time, being slowly absorbed and persisting in the tissues before being excreted. Compare **intermediate-acting, short-acting.**

longan (ˈlɒŋgən) *or* **lungan** NOUN 1 a sapindaceous tree, *Euphoria longan,* of tropical and subtropical Asia, with small yellowish-white flowers and small edible fruits. 2 the fruit of this tree, which is similar to but smaller than the litchi, having white juicy pulp and a single seed.
▷HISTORY C18: from Chinese *lung yen* dragon's eye

long-and-short work NOUN *Architect* the alternation in masonry of vertical and horizontal blocks of stone.

longanimity (ˌlɒŋgəˈnɪmɪtɪ) NOUN *Now rare* patience or forbearance.
▷HISTORY C15: from Late Latin *longanimitās,* from *longanimis* forbearing, from *longus* long + *animus* mind, soul
▸**longanimous** (lɒŋˈgænɪməs) ADJECTIVE

long arm NOUN *Informal* 1 power, esp far-reaching power: *the long arm of the law.* 2 **make a long arm.** to reach out for something, as from a sitting position.

Long Beach NOUN a city in SW California, on San Pedro Bay: resort and naval base; oil-refining. Pop.: 461 522 (2000).

Longbenton (ˌlɒŋˈbentən) NOUN a town in N England, in North Tyneside unitary authority, Tyne and Wear. Pop.: 34 630 (1991).

longboat (ˈlɒŋˌbəʊt) NOUN 1 the largest boat carried aboard a commercial sailing vessel. 2 another term for **longship.**

longbow (ˈlɒŋˌbəʊ) NOUN a large powerful hand-drawn bow, esp as used in medieval England.

longcase clock (ˈlɒŋˌkeɪs) NOUN another name for **grandfather clock.**

long-chain ADJECTIVE *Chem* having a relatively long chain of atoms in the molecule.

longcloth (ˈlɒŋˌklɒθ) NOUN 1 a fine plain-weave cotton cloth made in long strips. 2 *US* a light soft muslin.

long-coats PLURAL NOUN dress-like garments formerly worn by a baby. Archaic name: **long clothes.**

long-dated ADJECTIVE (of a gilt-edged security) having more than 15 years to run before redemption. Compare **medium-dated, short-dated.**

long-day ADJECTIVE (of certain plants) able to mature and flower only if exposed to long periods of daylight (more than 12 hours), each followed by a shorter period of darkness. Compare **short-day.**

long-distance NOUN 1 (*modifier*) covering relatively long distances: *a long-distance driver.* 2 (*modifier*) (of telephone calls, lines, etc.) connecting points a relatively long way apart. 3 *Chiefly US and Canadian* a long-distance telephone call. 4 a long-distance telephone system or its operator. ◆ ADVERB 5 by a long-distance telephone line: *he phoned long-distance.*

long-drawn-out ADJECTIVE over-prolonged or extended.

longe (lʌndʒ, lɒndʒ) NOUN an older variant of **lunge**[2].
▷HISTORY C17: via Old French from Latin *longus* LONG[1]

long-eared owl NOUN a slender European owl, *Asio otus,* with long ear tufts: most common in coniferous forests.

Long Eaton (ˈiːtᵊn) NOUN a town in N central England, in SE Derbyshire. Pop.: 44 826 (1991).

longeron (ˈlɒndʒərən) NOUN a main longitudinal structural member of an aircraft.
▷HISTORY C20: from French: side support, ultimately from Latin *longus* LONG[1]

longevity (lɒnˈdʒevɪtɪ) NOUN 1 long life. 2 relatively long duration of employment, service, etc.
▷HISTORY C17: from Late Latin *longaevitās,* from Latin *longaevus* long-lived, from *longus* LONG[1] + *aevum* age
▸**longevous** (lɒnˈdʒiːvəs) ADJECTIVE

long face NOUN a disappointed, solemn, or miserable facial expression.
▸ˌ**long-ˈfaced** ADJECTIVE

long finger NOUN **put (something) on the long finger.** *Irish* to postpone (something) for a long time.

Longford (ˈlɒŋfəd) NOUN 1 a county of N Republic of Ireland, in Leinster province. County town: Longford. Pop.: 30 166 (1996). Area: 1043 sq. km (403 sq. miles). 2 a town in N Republic of Ireland, county town of Co. Longford. Pop.: 6800 (1995 est.).

longhand (ˈlɒŋˌhænd) NOUN ordinary handwriting, in which letters, words, etc., are set down in full, as opposed to shorthand or to typing.

long haul NOUN 1 a journey over a long distance, esp one involving the transport of goods. 2 a lengthy job.

long-headed ADJECTIVE astute; shrewd; sagacious.
▸ˌ**long-ˈheadedly** ADVERB ▸ˌ**long-ˈheadedness** NOUN

long hop NOUN *Cricket* a short-pitched ball, which can easily be hit.

longhorn (ˈlɒŋˌhɔːn) NOUN 1 Also called: **Texas longhorn.** a long-horned breed of beef cattle, usually red or variegated, formerly common in SW US. 2 a now rare British breed of beef cattle with long curved horns.

long-horned beetle NOUN another name for **longicorn beetle** (see **longicorn** (sense 1)).

long house NOUN 1 a long communal dwelling of the Iroquois and other North American Indian peoples. It often served as a council house as well. 2 a long dwelling found in other parts of the world, such as Borneo.

long hundredweight NOUN the full name for **hundredweight** (sense 1).

longicorn (ˈlɒndʒɪˌkɔːn) NOUN 1 Also called: **longicorn beetle, long-horned beetle.** any beetle of the family *Cerambycidae,* having a long narrow body, long legs, and long antennae. ◆ ADJECTIVE 2 *Zoology* having or designating long antennae.
▷HISTORY C19: from New Latin *longicornis* long-horned

longing (ˈlɒŋɪŋ) NOUN 1 a prolonged unfulfilled desire or need. ◆ ADJECTIVE 2 having or showing desire or need: *a longing look.*
▸ˈ**longingly** ADVERB

longipennate (ˌlɒndʒɪˈpeneɪt) ADJECTIVE (of birds) having long slender wings or feathers.

longirostral (ˌlɒndʒɪˈrɒstrəl) ADJECTIVE (of birds) having a long beak.

longish (ˈlɒŋɪʃ) ADJECTIVE rather long.

Long Island NOUN an island in SE New York State, separated from the S shore of Connecticut by **Long Island Sound** (an arm of the Atlantic): contains the New York City boroughs of Brooklyn and Queens in the west, many resorts (notably Coney Island), and two large airports (La Guardia and John F. Kennedy). Area: 4462 sq. km (1723 sq. miles).

longitude (ˈlɒndʒɪˌtjuːd, ˈlɒŋg-) NOUN 1 distance in degrees east or west of the prime meridian at 0° measured by the angle between the plane of the prime meridian and that of the meridian through the point in question, or by the corresponding time difference. See **latitude** (sense 1). 2 *Astronomy* short for **celestial longitude.**
▷HISTORY C14: from Latin *longitūdō* length, from *longus* LONG[1]

longitudinal (ˌlɒndʒɪˈtjuːdɪnᵊl, ˌlɒŋg-) ADJECTIVE 1 of or relating to longitude or length. 2 placed or extended lengthways. Compare **transverse** (sense 1). 3 *Psychol* (of a study of behaviour) carried on over a protracted period of time.
▸ˌ**longiˈtudinally** ADVERB

longitudinal wave NOUN a wave that is propagated in the same direction as the displacement of the transmitting medium. Compare **transverse wave.**

long jenny NOUN *Billiards* an in-off up the cushion into a far pocket. Compare **short jenny.**
▷HISTORY from *Jenny,* pet form of *Janet*

long johns PLURAL NOUN *Informal* underpants with long legs.

long jump NOUN an athletic contest in which competitors try to cover the farthest distance possible with a running jump from a fixed board or mark. US and Canadian equivalent: **broad jump.**
▸**long jumping** NOUN

longleaf pine (ˈlɒŋˌliːf) NOUN a North American pine tree, *Pinus palustris,* with long needle-like leaves and orange-brown bark: the most important timber tree of the southeastern US.

long lease NOUN (in England and Wales) a lease, originally for a period of over 21 years, on a whole house of low rent and ratable value, which is the occupants' only or main residence. The leaseholder is entitled to buy the freehold, claim an extension of 50 years, or become a statutory tenant.

Longleat House ('lɒŋliːt) NOUN an Elizabethan mansion near Warminster in Wiltshire, built (from 1568) by Robert Smythson for Sir John Thynne; the grounds, landscaped by Capability Brown, now contain a famous safari park.

long leg NOUN *Cricket* **a** a fielding position on the leg side near the boundary almost directly behind the batsman's wicket. **b** a fielder in this position.

long-legged ('lɒŋˌlɛgd, -ˌlɛgɪd) ADJECTIVE 1 having long legs. 2 *Informal* (of a person or animal) able to run fast.

long list *Chiefly Brit* ◆ NOUN 1 a list of suitable applicants for a job, post, etc., from which a short list will be selected. ◆ VERB **long-list.** 2 (*tr*) to put (someone) on a long list.

long-lived ADJECTIVE having long life, existence, or currency.
▸ ˌ**long-'livedness** NOUN

Long March NOUN **the.** a journey of about 10 000 km (6000 miles) undertaken (1934–35) by some 100 000 Chinese Communists when they were forced out of their base in Kiangsi in SE China. They made their way to Shensi in NW China; only about 8000 survived the rigours of the journey.

long mark NOUN another name for **macron.**

long measure NOUN another name for **linear measure.**

long metre NOUN a stanzaic form consisting of four octosyllabic lines, used esp for hymns.

long moss NOUN another name for **Spanish moss.**

Longobard ('lɒŋgəˌbɑːd) NOUN, *plural* **-bards** *or* **-bardi** (-ˌbɑːdɪ). a rare name for an ancient **Lombard.**
▸ ˌ**Longo'bardian** *or* ˌ**Longo'bardic** ADJECTIVE

long-off NOUN *Cricket* **a** a fielding position on the off side near the boundary almost directly behind the bowler. **b** a fielder in this position.

long-on NOUN *Cricket* **a** a fielding position on the leg side near the boundary almost directly behind the bowler. **b** a fielder in this position.

Long Parliament NOUN *English history* 1 the Parliament summoned by Charles I that assembled on Nov. 3, 1640, was expelled by Cromwell in 1653, and was finally dissolved in 1660. See also **Rump Parliament.** 2 the Cavalier Parliament of 1661–79. 3 the Parliament called in Henry IV's reign that met from March 1 to Dec. 22, 1406.

long pig NOUN *Obsolete* human flesh eaten by cannibals.
▷HISTORY translation of a Maori and Polynesian term

long-playing ADJECTIVE of or relating to an LP (long-playing record).

long primer NOUN (formerly) a size of printer's type, approximately equal to 10 point.

long purse NOUN *Informal* wealth; riches.

long-range ADJECTIVE 1 of or extending into the future: *a long-range weather forecast.* 2 (of vehicles, aircraft, etc.) capable of covering great distances without refuelling. 3 (of weapons) made to be fired at a distant target.

longs (lɒŋz) PLURAL NOUN 1 full-length trousers. 2 long-dated gilt-edged securities. 3 *Finance* unsold securities or commodities held in anticipation of rising prices.

long *s* NOUN a lower-case *s*, printed ſ, formerly used in handwriting and printing. Also called: **long ess.**

longship ('lɒŋˌʃɪp) NOUN a narrow open vessel with oars and a square sail, used esp by the Vikings during medieval times.

longshore ('lɒŋˌʃɔː) ADJECTIVE situated on, relating to, or along the shore.
▷HISTORY C19: shortened form of *alongshore*

longshore drift NOUN the process whereby beach material is gradually shifted laterally as a result of waves meeting the shore at an oblique angle.

longshoreman ('lɒŋˌʃɔːmən) NOUN, *plural* **-men.** a US and Canadian word for **docker**[1].

long shot NOUN 1 a competitor, as in a race, considered to be unlikely to win. 2 a bet against heavy odds. 3 an undertaking, guess, or possibility with little chance of success. 4 *Films, television* a shot where the camera is or appears to be distant from the object to be photographed. 5 **by a long shot.** by any means: *he still hasn't finished by a long shot.*

long-sighted ADJECTIVE 1 related to or suffering from hyperopia. 2 able to see distant objects in focus. 3 having foresight.
▸ ˌ**long-'sightedly** ADVERB ▸ ˌ**long-'sightedness** NOUN

Longs Peak NOUN a mountain in N Colorado, in the Front Range of the Rockies: the highest peak in the Rocky Mountain National Park. Height: 4345 m (14 255 ft.).

longspur ('lɒŋˌspɜː) NOUN any of various Arctic and North American buntings of the genera *Calcarius* and *Rhyncophanes,* all of which have a long claw on the hind toe.

long-standing ADJECTIVE existing or in effect for a long time.

long-suffering ADJECTIVE 1 enduring pain, unhappiness, etc., without complaint. ◆ NOUN *also* **long-sufferance.** 2 long and patient endurance.
▸ ˌ**long-'sufferingly** ADVERB

long suit NOUN 1 **a** the longest suit in a hand of cards. **b** a holding of four or more cards of a suit. 2 *Informal* an outstanding advantage, personal quality, or talent.

long-tailed tit NOUN a small European songbird, *Aegithalos caudatus,* with a black, white, and pink plumage and a very long tail: family *Paridae* (tits).

long-term ADJECTIVE 1 lasting, staying, or extending over a long time: *long-term prospects.* 2 *Finance* maturing after a long period of time: *a long-term bond.*

long-termism NOUN the tendency to focus attention on long-term gains.

long-term memory NOUN *Psychol* that section of the memory storage system in which experiences are stored on a semipermanent basis. Compare **short-term memory.**

longtime ('lɒŋˌtaɪm) ADJECTIVE of long standing.

long tin NOUN *Brit* a tall long loaf of bread.

long tom NOUN 1 a long swivel cannon formerly used in naval warfare. 2 a long-range land gun. 3 an army slang name for **cannon** (sense 1).

long ton NOUN the full name for **ton**[1] (sense 1).

Longueuil (lɒŋ'geɪl; *French* lɔ̃gœj) NOUN a city in SE Canada, in S Quebec: a suburb of Montreal. Pop.: 127 977 (1996).

longueur (*French* lɔ̃gœr) NOUN a period of boredom or dullness.
▷HISTORY literally: length

long vacation NOUN the long period of holiday in the summer during which universities, law courts, etc., are closed.

long view NOUN the consideration of events or circumstances likely to occur in the future.

long wave NOUN **a** a radio wave with a wavelength greater than 1000 metres. **b** (*as modifier*): *a long-wave broadcast.*

longways ('lɒŋˌweɪz) *or US and Canadian* **longwise** ('lɒŋˌwaɪz) ADVERB another word for **lengthways.**

long weekend NOUN a weekend holiday extended by a day or days on either side.

long white lop-eared NOUN a former name for **British lop.**

long-winded ADJECTIVE 1 tiresomely long. 2 capable of energetic activity without becoming short of breath.
▸ ˌ**long-'windedly** ADVERB ▸ ˌ**long-'windedness** NOUN

long-wire aerial NOUN a travelling-wave aerial consisting of one or more conductors, the length of which usually exceeds several wavelengths.

Longyearbyen ('lɒŋjɪəˌbjen) NOUN a village on Spitsbergen island, administrative centre of the Svalbard archipelago: coal-mining.

lonicera (lɒ'nɪsərə) NOUN See **honeysuckle.**

Lonk (lɒŋk) NOUN a breed of large mountain sheep having horns in both male and female, a trim even fleece, and black face and legs, found only in Lancashire and Derbyshire, England.
▷HISTORY possibly from a local Lancashire pronunciation of *Lancs*

Lonsdale Belt ('lɒnzˌdeɪl) NOUN (in Britain) a belt conferred as a trophy on professional boxing champions, in various weight categories: if a champion wins it three times it becomes his personal property.
▷HISTORY named after Hugh Cecil Lowther, 5th Earl of *Lonsdale* (1857–1944), who presented the first one

Lons-le-Saunier (*French* lɔ̃ləsonje) NOUN a town in E France: saline springs; manufactures sparkling wines. Pop. (conurbation): 210 140 (1990).

loo[1] (luː) NOUN, *plural* **loos.** *Brit* an informal word for **lavatory** (sense 1).
▷HISTORY C20: perhaps from French *lieux d'aisance* water closet

loo[2] (luː) NOUN, *plural* **loos.** 1 a gambling card game. 2 a stake used in this game.
▷HISTORY C17: shortened form of *lanterloo,* via Dutch from French *lanterelu,* originally a meaningless word from the refrain of a popular song

loo[3] (luː) VERB a variant spelling of **lou.**

looby ('luːbɪ) NOUN, *plural* **-bies.** a foolish or stupid person.
▷HISTORY C14: of unknown origin

loofah ('luːfə) NOUN 1 the fibrous interior of the fruit of the dishcloth gourd, which is dried, bleached, and used as a bath sponge or for scrubbing. 2 another name for **dishcloth gourd.** ◆ Also called (esp US): **loofa, luffa.**
▷HISTORY C19: from New Latin *luffa,* from Arabic *lūf*

look (lʊk) VERB (*mainly intr*) 1 (often foll by *at*) to direct the eyes (towards): *to look at the sea.* 2 (often foll by *at*) to direct one's attention (towards): *let's look at the circumstances.* 3 (often foll by *to*) to turn one's interests or expectations (towards): *to look to the future.* 4 (*copula*) to give the impression of being by appearance to the eye or mind; seem: *that looks interesting.* 5 to face in a particular direction: *the house looks north.* 6 to expect, hope, or plan (to do something): *I look to hear from you soon; he's looking to get rich.* 7 (foll by *for*) **a** to search or seek: *I looked for you everywhere.* **b** to cherish the expectation (of); hope (for): *I look for success.* 8 (foll by *to*) **a** to be mindful (of): *to look to the promise one has made.* **b** to have recourse (to): *look to your swords, men!* 9 to be a pointer or sign: *these early inventions looked towards the development of industry.* 10 (foll by *into*) to carry out an investigation: *to look into a mystery.* 11 (*tr*) to direct a look at (someone) in a specified way: *she looked her rival up and down.* 12 (*tr*) to accord in appearance with (something): *to look one's age.* 13 **look alive** *or* **lively.** hurry up; get busy. 14 **look daggers.** See **dagger** (sense 4). 15 **look here.** an expression used to attract someone's attention, add emphasis to a statement, etc. 16 **look sharp** *or* **smart.** (*imperative*) to hurry up; make haste. 17 **not look at.** to refuse to consider: *they won't even look at my offer of £5000.* 18 **not much to look at.** unattractive; plain. ◆ NOUN 19 the act or an instance of looking: *a look of despair.* 20 a view or sight (of something): *let's have a look.* 21 (*often plural*) appearance to the eye or mind; aspect: *the look of innocence; I don't like the looks of this place.* 22 style; fashion: *the new look for summer.* ◆ SENTENCE CONNECTOR 23 an expression demanding attention or showing annoyance, determination, etc.: *look, I've had enough of this.* ◆ See also **look after, look back, look down, look forward to, look-in, look on, lookout, look over, look through, look up.**
▷HISTORY Old English *lōcian;* related to Middle Dutch *læken,* Old High German *luogen* to look out

> **Language note** See at **like.**

look after VERB (*intr, preposition*) 1 to take care of; be responsible for: *she looked after the child while I was out.* 2 to follow with the eyes: *he looked after the girl thoughtfully.*

lookalike ('lʊkəˌlaɪk) NOUN **a** a person, esp a celebrity, or thing that is the double of another. **b** (*as modifier*): *a lookalike Minister; a lookalike newspaper.*

look back VERB (*intr, adverb*) 1 to cast one's mind to the past. 2 **to never look back.** to become increasingly successful: *after his book was published, he never looked back.* 3 *Chiefly Brit* to pay another visit later.

look down VERB [1] (*intr, adverb; foll by on or upon*) to express or show contempt or disdain (for). [2] **look down one's nose at.** *Informal* to be contemptuous or disdainful of.

looker (ˈlʊkə) NOUN *Informal* [1] a person who looks. [2] a very attractive person, esp a woman or girl.

look forward to VERB (*intr, adverb + preposition*) to wait or hope for, esp with pleasure.

lookie-likie NOUN *Informal* a lookalike.

look-in *Informal* ◆ NOUN [1] a chance to be chosen, participate, etc. [2] a short visit. ◆ VERB **look in.** [3] (*intr, adverb; often foll by on*) to pay a short visit.

looking glass NOUN [1] a mirror, esp a ladies' dressing mirror. ◆ MODIFIER **looking-glass.** [2] with normal or familiar circumstances reversed; topsy-turvy: *a looking-glass world.*
▷HISTORY sense 2 in allusion to Lewis Carroll's *Through the Looking-Glass*

lookism (ˈlʊkɪzəm) NOUN discrimination against a person on the grounds of physical appearance.
▸ˈ**lookist** ADJECTIVE

look on VERB (*intr*) [1] (*adverb*) to be a spectator at an event or incident. [2] (*preposition*) Also: **look upon.** to consider or regard: *she looked on the whole affair as a joke; he looks on his mother-in-law with disapproval.*
▸ˌ**looker-ˈon** NOUN

lookout (ˈlʊkˌaʊt) NOUN [1] the act of keeping watch against danger, etc. [2] a person or persons instructed or employed to keep such a watch, esp on a ship. [3] a strategic point from which a watch is kept. [4] *Informal* worry or concern: *that's his lookout.* [5] *Chiefly Brit* outlook, chances, or view. ◆ VERB **look out.** (*adverb, mainly intr*) [6] to heed one's behaviour; be careful: *look out for the children's health.* [7] to be on the watch: *look out for my mother at the station.* [8] (*tr*) to search for and find: *I'll look out some curtains for your new house.* [9] (foll by *on* or *over*) to face in a particular direction: *the house looks out over the moor.*

look over VERB [1] (*intr, preposition*) to inspect by making a tour of (a factory, house, etc.): *we looked over the country house.* [2] (*tr, adverb*) to examine (a document, letter, etc.): *please look the papers over quickly.* ◆ NOUN **lookover.** [3] an inspection: often, specifically, a brief or cursory one.

look-see NOUN *Informal* a brief inspection or look.

look through VERB [1] (*intr, preposition* or *tr, adverb*) to examine, esp cursorily: *he looked through his notes before the lecture.* [2] (*intr, preposition*) to ignore (a person) deliberately: *whenever he meets his ex-girlfriend, she looks straight through him.*

look up VERB (*adverb*) [1] (*tr*) to discover (something required to be known) by resorting to a work of reference, such as a dictionary. [2] (*intr*) to increase, as in quality or value: *things are looking up.* [3] (*intr; foll by to*) to have respect (for): *I've always wanted a girlfriend I could look up to.* [4] (*tr*) to visit or make contact with (a person): *I'll look you up when I'm in town.*

loom¹ (luːm) NOUN [1] an apparatus, worked by hand or mechanically (**power loom**), for weaving yarn into a textile. [2] the middle portion of an oar, which acts as a fulcrum swivelling in the rowlock.
▷HISTORY C13 (meaning any kind of tool): variant of Old English *gelōma* tool; compare HEIRLOOM

loom² (luːm) VERB (*intr*) [1] to come into view indistinctly with an enlarged and often threatening aspect. [2] (of an event) to seem ominously close. [3] (often foll by *over*) (of large objects) to dominate or overhang. ◆ NOUN [4] a rising appearance, as of something far away.
▷HISTORY C16: perhaps from East Frisian *lomen* to move slowly

loom³ (luːm) NOUN *Archaic or dialect* [1] another name for **diver** (the bird). [2] any of various other birds, esp the guillemot.
▷HISTORY C17: from Old Norse *lomr*

loo mask NOUN a half-mask worn during the 18th century for masquerades, etc. Also called: **loup.**
▷HISTORY C17 *loo,* from French *loup,* literally: wolf, from Latin *lupus*

loom-state ADJECTIVE (of a woven cotton fabric) not yet dyed.

loon¹ (luːn) NOUN the US and Canadian name for **diver** (the bird).
▷HISTORY C17: of Scandinavian origin; related to Old Norse *lōmr*

loon² (luːn) NOUN [1] *Informal* a simple-minded or stupid person. [2] *Northeast Scot, dialect* a lad. [3] *Archaic* a person of low rank or occupation (esp in the phrase **lord and loon**).
▷HISTORY C15: origin obscure

loonie (ˈluːnɪ) NOUN *Canadian, slang* **a** a Canadian dollar coin with a loon bird on one of its faces. **b** the Canadian currency.

loony, looney, *or* **luny** (ˈluːnɪ) *Slang* ◆ ADJECTIVE **loonier, looniest** *or* **lunier, luniest.** [1] lunatic; insane. [2] foolish or ridiculous. ◆ NOUN, *plural* **loonies, looneys,** *or* **lunies.** [3] a foolish or insane person.
▸ˈ**looniness** *or* ˈ**luniness** NOUN

loony bin NOUN *Slang* a mental hospital or asylum.

loop¹ (luːp) NOUN [1] the round or oval shape formed by a line, string, etc., that curves around to cross itself. [2] any round or oval-shaped thing that is closed or nearly closed. [3] a piece of material, such as string, curved round and fastened to form a ring or handle for carrying by. [4] an intrauterine contraceptive device in the shape of a loop. [5] *Electronics* **a** a closed electric or magnetic circuit through which a signal can circulate. **b** short for **loop aerial.** [6] a flight manoeuvre in which an aircraft flies one complete circle in the vertical plane. [7] Also called: **loop line.** *Chiefly Brit* a railway branch line which leaves the main line and rejoins it after a short distance. [8] *Maths, physics* a closed curve on a graph: *hysteresis loop.* [9] another name for **antinode.** [10] *Anatomy* **a** the most common basic pattern of the human fingerprint, formed by several sharply rising U-shaped ridges. Compare **arch¹** (sense 4b). **b** a bend in a tubular structure, such as the U-shaped curve in a kidney tubule (**Henle's loop** or **loop of Henle**). [11] *Computing* a series of instructions in a program, performed repeatedly until some specified condition is satisfied. [12] *Skating* a jump in which the skater takes off from a back outside edge, makes one, two, or three turns in the air, and lands on the same back outside edge. [13] a group of people to whom information is circulated (esp in the phrases **in** *or* **out of the loop**). ◆ VERB [14] (*tr*) to make a loop in or of (a line, string, etc.). [15] (*tr*) to fasten or encircle with a loop or something like a loop. [16] Also: **loop the loop.** to cause (an aircraft) to perform a loop or (of an aircraft) to perform a loop. [17] (*intr*) to move in loops or in a path like a loop.
▷HISTORY C14: *loupe,* origin unknown

loop² (luːp) NOUN an archaic word for **loophole.**
▷HISTORY C14: perhaps related to Middle Dutch *lupen* to watch, peer

loop aerial NOUN an aerial that consists of one or more coils of wire wound on a frame. Maximum radiation or reception is in the plane of the loop, the minimum occurring at right angles to it. Sometimes shortened to: **loop.** Also called: **frame aerial.**

loop diuretic NOUN *Med* any of a group of diuretics, including frusemide, that act by inhibiting resorption of salts from Henle's loop of the kidney tubule.

looper (ˈluːpə) NOUN [1] a person or thing that loops or makes loops. [2] another name for a **measuring worm.**

loophole (ˈluːpˌhəʊl) NOUN [1] an ambiguity, omission, etc., as in a law, by which one can avoid a penalty or responsibility. [2] a small gap or hole in a wall, esp one in a fortified wall. ◆ VERB [3] (*tr*) to provide with loopholes.
▷HISTORY C16: from LOOP² + HOLE

loop knot NOUN a knot that leaves a loop extending from it.

loopy (ˈluːpɪ) ADJECTIVE **loopier, loopiest.** [1] full of loops; curly or twisted. [2] *Informal* slightly mad, crazy, or stupid.

loose (luːs) ADJECTIVE [1] free or released from confinement or restraint. [2] not close, compact, or tight in structure or arrangement. [3] not fitted or fitting closely: *loose clothing is cooler.* [4] not bundled, packaged, fastened, or put in a container: *loose nails.* [5] inexact; imprecise: *a loose translation.* [6] (of funds, cash, etc.) not allocated or locked away; readily available. [7] **a** (esp of women) promiscuous or easy. **b** (of attitudes, ways of life, etc.) immoral or dissolute. [8] lacking a sense of responsibility or propriety: *loose talk.* [9] **a** (of the bowels) emptying easily, esp excessively; lax. **b** (of a cough) accompanied by phlegm, mucus, etc. [10] (of a dye or dyed article) fading as a result of washing; not fast. [11] *Informal, chiefly US and Canadian* very relaxed; easy. ◆ NOUN [12] **the loose.** *Rugby* the part of play when the forwards close round the ball in a ruck or loose scrum. See **scrum.** [13] **on the loose. a** free from confinement or restraint. **b** *Informal* on a spree. ◆ ADVERB [14] **a** in a loose manner; loosely. **b** (*in combination*): *loose-fitting.* [15] **hang loose.** *Informal, chiefly US* to behave in a relaxed, easy fashion. ◆ VERB [16] (*tr*) to set free or release, as from confinement, restraint, or obligation. [17] (*tr*) to unfasten or untie. [18] to make or become less strict, tight, firmly attached, compact, etc. [19] (when *intr,* often foll by *off*) to let fly (a bullet, arrow, or other missile).
▷HISTORY C13 (in the sense: not bound): from Old Norse *lauss* free; related to Old English *lēas* free from, -LESS
▸ˈ**loosely** ADVERB ▸ˈ**looseness** NOUN

loosebox (ˈluːsˌbɒks) NOUN an enclosed and covered stall with a door in which an animal can be confined.

loose cannon NOUN a person or thing that appears to be beyond control and is potentially a source of unintentional damage.

loose change NOUN money in the form of coins suitable for small expenditures.

loose cover NOUN a fitted but easily removable cloth cover for a chair, sofa, etc. US and Canadian name: **slipcover.**

loose end NOUN [1] a detail that is left unsettled, unexplained, or incomplete. [2] **at a loose end.** without purpose or occupation.

loose head NOUN *Rugby* the prop on the hooker's left in the front row of a scrum. Compare **tight head.**

loose-jointed ADJECTIVE [1] supple and easy in movement. [2] loosely built; with ill-fitting joints.
▸ˌ**loose-ˈjointedness** NOUN

loose-leaf ADJECTIVE [1] (of a binder, album, etc.) capable of being opened to allow removal and addition of pages. ◆ NOUN [2] a serial publication published in loose leaves and kept in such a binder.

loose-limbed ADJECTIVE (of a person) having supple limbs.

loose metal NOUN *NZ* shingle on a road.

loosen (ˈluːsᵊn) VERB [1] to make or become less tight, fixed, etc. [2] (often foll by *up*) to make or become less firm, compact, or rigid. [3] (*tr*) to untie. [4] (*tr*) to let loose; set free. [5] (often foll by *up*) to make or become less strict, severe, etc. [6] (*tr*) to rid or relieve (the bowels) of constipation.
▷HISTORY C14: from LOOSE
▸ˈ**loosener** NOUN

loose order NOUN *Military* a formation in which soldiers, units, etc., are widely separated from each other.

loose smut NOUN a disease of cereal grasses caused by smut fungi of the genus *Ustilago,* in which powdery spore masses replace the host tissue.

loosestrife (ˈluːsˌstraɪf) NOUN [1] any of various primulaceous plants of the genus *Lysimachia,* esp the yellow-flowered *L. vulgaris* (**yellow loosestrife**). See also **moneywort.** [2] **purple loosestrife.** a purple-flowered lythraceous marsh plant, *Lythrum salicaria.* [3] any of several similar or related plants, such as the primulaceous plant *Naumburgia thyrsiflora* (**tufted loosestrife**).
▷HISTORY C16: LOOSE + STRIFE, an erroneous translation of Latin *lysimachia,* as if from Greek *lusimakhos* ending strife, instead of from the name of the supposed discoverer, *Lusimakhos*

loose-tongued ADJECTIVE careless or irresponsible in talking.

loosies (ˈluːsɪz) PLURAL NOUN *Northern English informal* cigarettes sold individually.

loosing *or* **lowsening** (ˈluːsɪŋ, -zɪŋ, ˈlɔɪ-) NOUN *Yorkshire, dialect* a celebration of one's 21st birthday.

loot (luːt) NOUN [1] goods stolen during pillaging, as in wartime, during riots, etc. [2] goods, money, etc., obtained illegally. [3] *Informal* money or wealth. [4] the act of looting or plundering. ◆ VERB [5] to pillage (a city, settlement, etc.) during war or

riots. [6] to steal (money or goods), esp during pillaging.
▷**HISTORY** C19: from Hindi *lūt*
▸'**looter** NOUN

lop[1] (lɒp) VERB **lops, lopping, lopped.** (*tr*; usually foll by *off*) [1] to sever (parts) from a tree, body, etc., esp with swift strokes. [2] to cut out or eliminate from as excessive. ◆ NOUN [3] a part or parts lopped off, as from a tree.
▷**HISTORY** C15 *loppe* branches cut off; compare LOB[1]
▸'**lopper** NOUN

lop[2] (lɒp) VERB **lops, lopping, lopped.** [1] to hang or allow to hang loosely. [2] (*intr*) to slouch about or move awkwardly. [3] (*intr*) a less common word for **lope.**
▷**HISTORY** C16: perhaps related to LOP[1]; compare LOB[1]

lop[3] (lɒp) NOUN *Northern English, dialect* a flea.
▷**HISTORY** probably from Old Norse *hloppa* (unattested) flea, from *hlaupa* to LEAP

lope (ləʊp) VERB [1] (*intr*) (of a person) to move or run with a long swinging stride. [2] (*intr*) (of four-legged animals) to run with a regular bounding movement. [3] to cause (a horse) to canter with a long easy stride or (of a horse) to canter in this manner. ◆ NOUN [4] a long steady gait or stride.
▷**HISTORY** C15: from Old Norse *hlaupa* to LEAP; compare Middle Dutch *lopen* to run
▸'**loper** NOUN

lop-eared ADJECTIVE (of animals) having ears that droop.

lopho- COMBINING FORM indicating a crested or tufted part: *lophophore.*
▷**HISTORY** from Greek *lophos* crest

lophobranch ('ləʊfəˌbræŋk) NOUN [1] any teleost fish of the suborder *Lophobranchii,* having the gills arranged in rounded tufts: includes the pipefishes and sea horses. ◆ ADJECTIVE [2] of, relating to, or belonging to the *Lophobranchii.*
▸**lophobranchiate** (ˌləʊfə'bræŋkɪɪt, -ˌeɪt) ADJECTIVE

lophophore ('ləʊfəˌfɔː) NOUN a circle or horseshoe of ciliated tentacles surrounding the mouth and used for the capture of food in minute sessile animals of the phyla *Brachiopoda, Phoronida,* and *Ectoprocta.*
▸'**lopho'phorate** ADJECTIVE

lopolith ('lɒpəlɪθ) NOUN a saucer- or lens-shaped body of intrusive igneous rock, formed by the penetration of magma between the beds or layers of existing rock and subsequent subsidence beneath the intrusion. Compare **laccolith.**
▷**HISTORY** C20: from Greek *lopas* dish + -LITH

loppy ('lɒpɪ) NOUN *Austral informal* a man employed to do maintenance tasks on a ranch.

lopsided (ˌlɒp'saɪdɪd) ADJECTIVE [1] leaning or inclined to one side. [2] greater in weight, height, or size on one side.
▸ˌ**lop'sidedly** ADVERB ▸ˌ**lop'sidedness** NOUN

loq. ABBREVIATION FOR loquitur.

loquacious (lɒ'kweɪʃəs) ADJECTIVE characterized by or showing a tendency to talk a great deal.
▷**HISTORY** C17: from Latin *loquāx* from *loquī* to speak
▸**lo'quaciously** ADVERB ▸**loquacity** (lɒ'kwæsɪtɪ) *or* **lo'quaciousness** NOUN

loquat ('ləʊkwɒt, -kwæt) NOUN [1] an ornamental evergreen rosaceous tree, *Eriobotrya japonica,* of China and Japan, having reddish woolly branches, white flowers, and small yellow edible plumlike fruits. [2] the fruit of this tree. ◆ Also called: **Japan plum.**
▷**HISTORY** C19: from Chinese (Cantonese) *lō kwat,* literally: rush orange

loquitur *Latin* ('lɒkwɪtə) he (or she) speaks: used, esp formerly, as a stage direction. Usually abbreviated to: **loq.**

lor (lɔː) INTERJECTION *Not standard* an exclamation of surprise or dismay.
▷**HISTORY** from LORD (interj)

loran ('lɔːrən) NOUN a radio navigation system operating over long distances. Synchronized pulses are transmitted from widely spaced radio stations to aircraft or shipping, the time of arrival of the pulses being used to determine position.
▷**HISTORY** C20: *lo(ng-)ra(nge) n(avigation)*

Lorca (*Spanish* 'lɔrka) NOUN a town in SE Spain, on the Guadalentín River. Pop.: 66 940 (1991).

lord (lɔːd) NOUN [1] a person who has power or authority over others, such as a monarch or master. [2] a male member of the nobility, esp in Britain. [3] (in medieval Europe) a feudal superior, esp the master of a manor. Compare **lady** (sense 5). [4] a husband considered as head of the household (archaic except in the facetious phrase **lord and master**). [5] *Astrology* a planet having a dominating influence. [6] **my lord.** a respectful form of address used to a judge, bishop, or nobleman. ◆ VERB [7] (*tr*) *Now rare* to make a lord of (a person). [8] to act in a superior manner towards (esp in the phrase **lord it over**).
▷**HISTORY** Old English *hlāford* bread keeper; see LOAF[1], WARD
▸'**lordless** ADJECTIVE ▸'**lord,like** ADJECTIVE

Lord (lɔːd) NOUN [1] a title given to God or Jesus Christ. [2] *Brit* **a** a title given to men of high birth, specifically to an earl, marquess, baron, or viscount. **b** a courtesy title given to the younger sons of a duke or marquess. **c** the ceremonial title of certain high officials or of a bishop or archbishop: *Lord Mayor; Lord of Appeal; Law Lord; Lord Bishop of Durham.* ◆ INTERJECTION [3] (*sometimes not capital*) an exclamation of dismay, surprise, etc.: *Good Lord!; Lord only knows!*

Lord Advocate NOUN (in Scotland) the chief law officer of the Crown: he acts as public prosecutor and is in charge of the administration of criminal justice.

Lord Chamberlain NOUN (in Britain) the chief official of the royal household.

Lord Chancellor NOUN *Brit government* the cabinet minister who is head of the judiciary in England and Wales and Speaker of the House of Lords.

Lord Chief Justice NOUN the judge who is second only to the Lord Chancellor in the English legal hierarchy; president of one division of the High Court of Justice.

Lord High Chancellor NOUN another name for the **Lord Chancellor.**

Lord Howe Island (haʊ) NOUN an island in the Tasman Sea, southeast of Australia: part of New South Wales. Area: 17 sq. km (6 sq. miles). Pop.: 300 (latest est.).

lording ('lɔːdɪŋ) NOUN [1] *Archaic* a gentleman; lord: used in the plural as a form of address. [2] an obsolete word for **lordling.**
▷**HISTORY** Old English *hlāfording,* from *hlāford* LORD + -ING[3], suffix indicating descent

Lord Justice of Appeal NOUN an ordinary judge of the Court of Appeal.

Lord Lieutenant NOUN [1] (in Britain) the representative of the Crown in a county. [2] (formerly) the British viceroy in Ireland.

lordling ('lɔːdlɪŋ) NOUN *Now rare* a young lord.

lordly ('lɔːdlɪ) ADJECTIVE **-lier, -liest.** [1] haughty; arrogant; proud. [2] of or befitting a lord. ◆ ADVERB [3] *Archaic* in the manner of a lord.
▸'**lordliness** NOUN

Lord Mayor NOUN the mayor in the City of London and in certain other important boroughs and large cities.

Lord Muck NOUN *Informal* an ordinary man behaving or being treated as if he were aristocratic. See also **Lady Muck.**

Lord of Appeal NOUN *Brit* one of several judges appointed to assist the House of Lords in hearing appeals.

Lord of Hosts NOUN Jehovah or God when regarded as having the angelic forces at his command.

Lord of Misrule NOUN (formerly, in England) a person appointed master of revels at a Christmas celebration.

Lord of the Flies NOUN a name for **Beelzebub.**
▷**HISTORY** translation of Hebrew: see BEELZEBUB

lordosis (lɔː'dəʊsɪs) NOUN [1] *Pathol* forward curvature of the lumbar spine: congenital or caused by trauma or disease. Nontechnical name: **hollow-back.** Compare **kyphosis, scoliosis.** [2] *Zoology* concave arching of the back occurring in many female animals during sexual stimulation.
▷**HISTORY** C18: New Latin from Greek *lordōsis,* from *lordos* bent backwards
▸**lordotic** (lɔː'dɒtɪk) ADJECTIVE

Lord President of the Council NOUN (in Britain) the cabinet minister who presides at meetings of the Privy Council.

Lord Privy Seal NOUN (in Britain) the senior cabinet minister without official duties.

Lord Protector NOUN See **Protector.**

Lord Provost NOUN the provost of one of the five major Scottish cities (Edinburgh, Glasgow, Aberdeen, Dundee, and Perth).

Lords (lɔːdz) NOUN **the.** short for **House of Lords.**

Lord's (lɔːdz) NOUN a cricket ground in N London; headquarters of the MCC.

lords-and-ladies NOUN (*functioning as singular*) another name for **cuckoopint.**

Lord's Day NOUN **the.** the Christian Sabbath; Sunday.

lordship ('lɔːdʃɪp) NOUN the position or authority of a lord.

Lordship ('lɔːdʃɪp) NOUN (preceded by *Your* or *His*) *Brit* a title used to address or refer to a bishop, a judge of the high court, or any peer except a duke.

Lordship of the Isles NOUN an overlordship of the Western Isles of Scotland and adjacent lands instituted in 1266 when Magnus of Norway ceded the Hebrides, the Isle of Man, and Kintyre to the King of Scotland, and claimed by the chiefs of Clan Dougall and later by those of Clan Donald. The title was forfeited to James IV in 1493 and is now held by the eldest son of the sovereign.
▸**Lord of the Isles** NOUN

Lord's Prayer NOUN **the.** the prayer taught by Jesus Christ to his disciples, as in Matthew 6:9–13, Luke 11:2–4. Also called: **Our Father,** (esp Latin version) **Paternoster.**

Lords Spiritual PLURAL NOUN the two Anglican archbishops and 24 most senior bishops of England and Wales who sit as members of the House of Lords.

Lord's Supper NOUN **the.** another term for **Holy Communion** (I Corinthians 11:20).

Lord's table NOUN **the.** *Chiefly Protestantism* [1] Holy Communion. [2] another name for **altar.**

Lords Temporal PLURAL NOUN **the.** (in Britain) peers other than bishops in their capacity as members of the House of Lords.

lordy ('lɔːdɪ) INTERJECTION *Chiefly US and Canadian* an exclamation of surprise or dismay.

lore[1] (lɔː) NOUN [1] collective knowledge or wisdom on a particular subject, esp of a traditional nature. [2] knowledge or learning. [3] *Archaic* teaching, or something that is taught.
▷**HISTORY** Old English *lār;* related to *leornian* to LEARN

lore[2] (lɔː) NOUN [1] the surface of the head of a bird between the eyes and the base of the bill. [2] the corresponding area in a snake or fish.
▷**HISTORY** C19: from New Latin *lōrum,* from Latin: strap

Lorelei ('lɒrəˌlaɪ) NOUN (in German legend) a siren, said to dwell on a rock at the edge of the Rhine south of Koblenz, who lures boatmen to destruction.
▷**HISTORY** C19: from German *Lurlei* name of the rock; from a poem by Clemens Brentano (1778–1842)

Lorentz-Fitzgerald contraction NOUN the supposed contraction of a body in the direction of its motion through the ether, postulated to explain the result of the Michelson-Morley experiment. The special theory of relativity denies that any such real change can occur in a body as a result of uniform motion but shows that an observer moving with respect to the body will determine an apparent change given by a formula similar to that of Lorentz and Fitzgerald.
▷**HISTORY** C20: named after Hendrik Antoon *Lorentz* (1853–1928), Dutch physicist, and G. F. *Fitzgerald* (1851–1901), Irish physicist

Lorentz transformation NOUN a set of equations relating the coordinates of space and time used by two hypothetical observers in uniform relative motion. According to the special theory of

relativity the laws of physics are invariant under this transformation.
▷**HISTORY** C20: named after Hendrik Antoon *Lorentz* (1853–1928), Dutch physicist

lorgnette (lɔːˈnjet) NOUN a pair of spectacles or opera glasses mounted on a handle.
▷**HISTORY** C19: from French, from *lorgner* to squint, from Old French *lorgne* squinting

lorgnon (*French* lɔrɲɔ̃) NOUN 1 a monocle or pair of spectacles. 2 another word for **lorgnette.**
▷**HISTORY** C19: from French, from *lorgner;* see LORGNETTE

lorica (lɒˈraɪkə) NOUN, *plural* **-cae** (-siː, -kiː). 1 the hard outer covering of rotifers, ciliate protozoans, and similar organisms. 2 an ancient Roman cuirass of leather or metal.
▷**HISTORY** C18: from New Latin, from Latin: leather cuirass; related to *lōrum* thong
▸**loricate** (ˈlɒrɪˌkeɪt) *or* **ˈloriˌcated** ADJECTIVE

Lorient (*French* lɔrjɑ̃) NOUN a port in W France, on the Bay of Biscay. Pop.: 59 437 (1990).

lorikeet (ˈlɒrɪˌkiːt, ˌlɒrɪˈkiːt) NOUN any of various small lories, such as *Glossopsitta versicolor* (**varied lorikeet**) or *Trichoglossus moluccanus* (**rainbow lorikeet**).
▷**HISTORY** C18: from LORY + *-keet,* as in PARAKEET

lorimer (ˈlɒrɪmə) *or* **loriner** (ˈlɒrɪnə) NOUN *Brit* (formerly) a person who made bits, spurs, and other small metal objects.
▷**HISTORY** C15: from Old French, from *lorain* harness strap, ultimately from Latin *lōrum* strap

loris (ˈlɔːrɪs) NOUN, *plural* **-ris.** any of several omnivorous nocturnal slow-moving prosimian primates of the family *Lorisidae,* of S and SE Asia, esp *Loris tardigradus* (**slow loris**) and *Nycticebus coucang* (**slender loris**), having vestigial digits and no tails.
▷**HISTORY** C18: from French; of uncertain origin

lorn (lɔːn) ADJECTIVE *Poetic* forsaken or wretched.
▷**HISTORY** Old English *loren,* past participle of *-lēosan* to lose
▸**ˈlornness** NOUN

Lorraine (lɒˈreɪn; *French* lɔrɛn) NOUN 1 a region and former province of E France; ceded to Germany in 1871 after the Franco-Prussian war and regained by France in 1919; rich iron-ore deposits. German name: **Lothringen.** 2 **Kingdom of.** an early medieval kingdom on the Meuse, Moselle, and Rhine rivers: later a duchy. 3 a former duchy in E France, once the S half of this kingdom.

Lorraine cross NOUN See **cross of Lorraine.**

lorry (ˈlɒrɪ) NOUN, *plural* **-ries.** 1 a large motor vehicle designed to carry heavy loads, esp one with a flat platform. US and Canadian name: **truck.** See also **articulated lorry.** 2 **off the back of a lorry.** *Brit informal* a phrase used humorously to imply that something has been dishonestly acquired: *it fell off the back of a lorry.* 3 any of various vehicles with a flat load-carrying surface, esp one designed to run on rails.
▷**HISTORY** C19: perhaps related to northern English dialect *lurry* to pull, tug

lory (ˈlɔːrɪ) NOUN, *plural* **-ries.** any of various small brightly coloured parrots of Australia and Indonesia, having a brush-tipped tongue with which to feed on nectar and pollen.
▷**HISTORY** C17: via Dutch from Malay *lūrī,* variant of *nūrī*

Los Alamos (lɒs ˈæləmɒs) NOUN a town in the US, in New Mexico: the first atomic bomb was developed here. Pop.: 11 455 (1990).

Los Angeles (lɒs ˈændʒɪˌliːz) NOUN a city in SW California, on the Pacific: the second largest city in the US, having absorbed many adjacent townships; industrial centre and port, with several universities. Pop.: 3 694 820 (2000). Abbreviation: **LA.**

lose (luːz) VERB **loses, losing, lost.** (*mainly tr*) 1 to part with or come to be without, as through theft, accident, negligence, etc. 2 to fail to keep or maintain: *to lose one's balance.* 3 to suffer the loss or deprivation of: *to lose a parent.* 4 to cease to have or possess. 5 to fail to get or make use of: *to lose a chance.* 6 (*also intr*) to fail to gain or win (a contest, game, etc.): *to lose the match.* 7 to fail to see, hear, perceive, or understand: *I lost the gist of his speech.* 8 to waste: *to lose money gambling.* 9 to wander from so as to be unable to find: *to lose one's way.* 10 to cause the loss of: *his delay lost him the battle.* 11 to allow to go astray or out of sight: *we lost him in the crowd.* 12 (*usually passive*) to absorb or engross: *he was lost in contemplation.* 13 (*usually passive*) to cause the death or destruction of: *two men were lost in the attack.* 14 to outdistance or elude: *he soon lost his pursuers.* 15 (*intr*) to decrease or depreciate in value or effectiveness: *poetry always loses in translation.* 16 (*also intr*) (of a timepiece) to run slow (by a specified amount): *the clock loses ten minutes every day.* 17 (of a physician) to fail to sustain the life of (a patient). 18 (of a woman) to fail to give birth to (a viable baby), esp as the result of a miscarriage. 19 *Motor racing, slang* to lose control of (the car), as on a bend: *he lost it going into Woodcote.* 20 **lose it.** *Slang* to lose control of oneself or one's temper.
▷**HISTORY** Old English *losian* to perish; related to Old English *-lēosan* as in *forlēosan* to forfeit. Compare LOOSE
▸**ˈlosable** ADJECTIVE ▸**ˈlosableness** NOUN

losel (ˈləʊzᵊl) *Archaic or dialect* ◆ NOUN 1 a worthless person. ◆ ADJECTIVE 2 (of a person) worthless, useless, or wasteful.
▷**HISTORY** C14: from *losen,* from the past participle of LOSE

lose out VERB *Informal* 1 (*intr, adverb*) to be defeated or unsuccessful. 2 **lose out on.** to fail to secure or make use of: *we lost out on the sale.*

loser (ˈluːzə) NOUN 1 a person or thing that loses. 2 a person or thing that seems destined to be taken advantage of, fail, etc.: *a born loser.* 3 *Bridge* a card that will not take a trick.

losing (ˈluːzɪŋ) ADJECTIVE unprofitable; failing: *the business was a losing concern.*

losings (ˈluːzɪŋz) PLURAL NOUN losses, esp money lost in gambling.

loss (lɒs) NOUN 1 the act or an instance of losing. 2 the disadvantage or deprivation resulting from losing: *a loss of reputation.* 3 the person, thing, or amount lost: *a large loss.* 4 (*plural*) military personnel lost by death or capture. 5 (*sometimes plural*) the amount by which the costs of a business transaction or operation exceed its revenue. 6 a measure of the power lost in an electrical system expressed as the ratio of or difference between the input power and the output power. 7 *Insurance* **a** an occurrence of something that has been insured against, thus giving rise to a claim by a policyholder. **b** the amount of the resulting claim. 8 **at a loss. a** uncertain what to do; bewildered. **b** rendered helpless (for lack of something): *at a loss for words.* **c** at less than the cost of buying, producing, or maintaining (something): *the business ran at a loss for several years.*
▷**HISTORY** C14: noun probably formed from *lost,* past participle of *losen* to perish, from Old English *lōsian* to be destroyed, from *los* destruction

loss adjuster NOUN *Insurance* a person qualified to adjust losses incurred through fire, explosion, accident, theft, natural disaster, etc., to agree the loss and the compensation to be paid.

loss leader NOUN an article offered below cost in the hope that customers attracted by it will buy other goods.

lossmaker (ˈlɒsˌmeɪkə) NOUN *Brit* an organization, industry, or enterprise that consistently fails to make a profit.

lossmaking (ˈlɒsˌmeɪkɪŋ) ADJECTIVE *Brit* unprofitable; losing money.

loss ratio NOUN the ratio of the annual losses sustained to the premiums received by an insurance company.

lossy (ˈlɒsɪ) ADJECTIVE (of a dielectric material, transmission line, etc.) designed to have a high attenuation; dissipating energy: *lossy line.*
▷**HISTORY** C20: from LOSS

lost (lɒst) ADJECTIVE 1 unable to be found or recovered. 2 unable to find one's way or ascertain one's whereabouts. 3 confused, bewildered, or helpless: *he is lost in discussions of theory.* 4 (sometimes foll by *on*) not utilized, noticed, or taken advantage of (by): *rational arguments are lost on her.* 5 no longer possessed or existing because of defeat, misfortune, or the passage of time: *a lost art.* 6 destroyed physically: *the lost platoon.* 7 (foll by *to*) no longer available or open (to). 8 (foll by *to*) insensible or impervious (to a sense of shame, justice, etc.). 9 (foll by *in*) engrossed (in): *he was lost in his book.* 10 morally fallen: *a lost woman.* 11 damned: *a lost soul.* 12 **get lost.** (*usually imperative*) *Informal* go away and stay away.

lost cause NOUN a cause with no chance of success.

Lost Generation NOUN (*sometimes not capitals*) 1 the large number of talented young men killed in World War I. 2 the generation of writers, esp American authors such as Scott Fitzgerald and Hemingway, active after World War I.

lost tribes PLURAL NOUN **the.** *Old Testament* the ten tribes deported from the N kingdom of Israel in 721 B.C. and believed never to have returned to Palestine.

lot (lɒt) PRONOUN 1 (*functioning as singular or plural; preceded by a*) a great number or quantity: *a lot to do; a lot of people; a lot of trouble.* ◆ NOUN 2 a collection of objects, items, or people: *a nice lot of youngsters.* 3 portion in life; destiny; fortune: *it falls to my lot to be poor.* 4 any object, such as a straw or slip of paper, drawn from others at random to make a selection or choice (esp in the phrase **draw** *or* **cast lots**). 5 the use of lots in making a selection or choice (esp in the phrase **by lot**). 6 an assigned or apportioned share. 7 an item or set of items for sale in an auction. 8 *Chiefly US and Canadian* an area of land: *a parking lot.* 9 *US and Canadian* a piece of land with fixed boundaries. 10 *Chiefly US and Canadian* a film studio and the site on which it is located. 11 **a bad lot.** an unpleasant or disreputable person. 12 **cast** *or* **throw in one's lot with.** to join with voluntarily and share the fortunes of. 13 **the lot.** the entire amount or number. ◆ ADVERB (preceded by *a*) *Informal* 14 to a considerable extent, degree, or amount; very much: *to delay a lot.* 15 a great deal of the time or often: *to sing madrigals a lot.* ◆ VERB **lots, lotting, lotted.** 16 to draw lots for (something). 17 (*tr*) to divide (land, etc.) into lots. 18 (*tr*) another word for **allot.** ◆ See also **lots.**
▷**HISTORY** Old English *hlot;* related to Old High German *lug* portion of land, Old Norse *hlutr* lot, share

Lot[1] (lɒt) NOUN 1 a department of S central France, in Midi-Pyrénées region. Capital: Cahors. Pop.: 160 197 (1999). Area: 5226 sq. km (2038 sq. miles). 2 a river in S France, rising in the Cevennes and flowing west into the Garonne River. Length: about 483 km (300 miles).

Lot[2] (lɒt) NOUN *Old Testament* Abraham's nephew: he escaped the destruction of Sodom, but his wife was changed into a pillar of salt for looking back as they fled (Genesis 19).

lota *or* **lotah** (ˈləʊtə) NOUN a globular water container, usually of brass, used in India, Myanmar, etc.
▷**HISTORY** C19: from Hindi *lotā*

lo tech NOUN, ADJECTIVE a variant spelling of **low tech.**

Lot-et-Garonne (*French* lɔtegarɔn) NOUN a department of SW France, in Aquitaine. Capital: Agen. Pop.: 305 380 (1999). Area: 5385 sq. km (2100 sq. miles).

loth (ləʊθ) ADJECTIVE a variant spelling of **loath.**
▸**ˈlothness** NOUN

Lothario (ləʊˈθɑːrɪˌəʊ) NOUN, *plural* **-os.** (*sometimes not capital*) a rake, libertine, or seducer.
▷**HISTORY** C18: after a seducer in Nicholas Rowe's tragedy *The Fair Penitent* (1703)

Lothian Region (ˈləʊðɪən) NOUN a former local government region in SE central Scotland, formed in 1975 from East Lothian, most of Midlothian, and West Lothian; replaced in 1996 by the council areas of East Lothian, Midlothian, West Lothian, and Edinburgh.

Lothians (ˈləʊðɪənz) PLURAL NOUN **the.** three historic counties of SE central Scotland (now council areas): East Lothian, West Lothian, and Midlothian (including Edinburgh).

Lothringen (ˈloːtrɪŋən) NOUN the German name for **Lorraine.**

loti (ˈləʊtɪ, ˈluːtɪ) NOUN, *plural* **maloti** (məˈləʊtɪ, -ˈluːtɪ). the standard monetary unit of Lesotho, divided into 100 lisente.

lotic (ˈləʊtɪk) ADJECTIVE *Ecology* of, relating to, or designating natural communities living in rapidly flowing water. Compare **lentic.**

▷HISTORY C20: from Latin *lotus*, a past participle of *lavāre* to wash

lotion ('ləʊʃən) NOUN a liquid preparation having a soothing, cleansing, or antiseptic action, applied to the skin, eyes, etc.
▷HISTORY C14: via Old French from Latin *lōtiō* a washing, from *lōtus* past participle of *lavāre* to wash

lots (lɒts) *Informal* ◆ PLURAL NOUN [1] (often foll by *of*) great numbers or quantities: *lots of people; to eat lots.* ◆ ADVERB [2] a great deal. [3] (intensifier): *the journey is lots quicker by train.*

lottery ('lɒtərɪ) NOUN, *plural* **-teries.** [1] a method of raising money by selling numbered tickets and giving a proportion of the money raised to holders of numbers drawn at random. [2] a similar method of raising money in which players select a small group of numbers out of a larger group printed on a ticket. If a player's selection matches some or all of the numbers drawn at random the player wins a proportion of the prize fund. [3] an activity or endeavour the success of which is regarded as a matter of fate or luck.
▷HISTORY C16: from Old French *loterie*, from Middle Dutch *loterije*. See LOT

lotto ('lɒtəʊ) NOUN [1] Also called: **housey-housey.** a children's game in which numbered discs, counters, etc., are drawn at random and called out, while the players cover the corresponding numbers on cards, the winner being the first to cover all the numbers, a particular row, etc. Compare **bingo.** [2] a lottery.
▷HISTORY C18: from Italian, from Old French *lot*, from Germanic. See LOT

lotus ('ləʊtəs) NOUN [1] (in Greek mythology) a fruit that induces forgetfulness and a dreamy languor in those who eat it. [2] the plant bearing this fruit, thought to be the jujube, the date, or any of various other plants. [3] any of several water lilies of tropical Africa and Asia, esp the **white lotus** (*Nymphaea lotus*), which was regarded as sacred in ancient Egypt. [4] a similar plant, *Nelumbo nucifera*, which is the sacred lotus of India, China, and Tibet and also sacred in Egypt: family *Nelumbonaceae*. [5] a representation of such a plant, common in Hindu, Buddhist, and ancient Egyptian carving and decorative art. [6] any leguminous plant of the genus *Lotus*, of the Old World and North America, having yellow, pink, or white pealike flowers. ◆ Also called (rare): **lotos.**
▷HISTORY C16: via Latin from Greek *lōtos*, from Semitic; related to Hebrew *lōt* myrrh

lotus-eater NOUN *Greek myth* one of a people encountered by Odysseus in North Africa who lived in indolent forgetfulness, drugged by the fruit of the legendary lotus.

lotus position NOUN a seated cross-legged position used in yoga, meditation, etc.

Lotus Sutra NOUN a central scripture of Mahayana Buddhism, emphasizing that anyone can attain enlightenment.

lou *or* **loo** (lu:) VERB a Scot word for **love.**

louche (lu:ʃ) ADJECTIVE shifty or disreputable.
▷HISTORY C19: from French, literally: squinting

loud (laʊd) ADJECTIVE [1] (of sound) relatively great in volume: *a loud shout.* [2] making or able to make sounds of relatively great volume: *a loud voice.* [3] clamorous, insistent, and emphatic: *loud protests.* [4] (of colours, designs, etc.) offensive or obtrusive to look at. [5] characterized by noisy, vulgar, and offensive behaviour. ◆ ADVERB [6] in a loud manner. [7] **out loud.** audibly, as distinct from silently.
▷HISTORY Old English *hlūd*; related to Old Swedish *hlūd*, German *laut*
▸ **'loudly** ADVERB ▸ **'loudness** NOUN

louden ('laʊdᵊn) VERB to make or become louder.

loud-hailer NOUN a portable loudspeaker having a built-in amplifier and microphone. Also called (US and Canadian): **bullhorn.**

loudish ('laʊdɪʃ) ADJECTIVE fairly loud; somewhat loud.

loudmouth ('laʊd,maʊθ) NOUN *Informal* [1] a person who brags or talks too loudly. [2] a person who is gossipy or tactless.
▸ **loudmouthed** ('laʊd,maʊðd, -,maʊθt) ADJECTIVE

loudspeaker (,laʊd'spi:kə) NOUN a device for converting audio-frequency signals into the equivalent sound waves by means of a vibrating conical diaphragm. Sometimes shortened to: **speaker.** Also called: **reproducer.**

loudspeaker van NOUN a motor vehicle carrying a public address system. US and Canadian name: **sound truck.**

Lou Gehrig's disease (lu: 'gɛrɪg) NOUN another name for **amyotrophic lateral sclerosis.**
▷HISTORY C20: named after *Lou Gehrig* (1903–41), US baseball player who suffered from it

lough (lɒx, lɒk) NOUN [1] an Irish word for **lake**¹. [2] a long narrow bay or arm of the sea in Ireland. ◆ Compare **loch.**
▷HISTORY C14: from Irish *loch* lake

Loughborough ('lʌfbərə, -brə) NOUN a town in central England, in N Leicestershire: university (1966). Pop.: 46 867 (1991).

louis ('lu:ɪ; *French* lwi) NOUN, *plural* **louis** ('lu:ɪz; *French* lwi). short for **louis d'or.**

Louisbourg ('lu:ɪs,bɜ:g) NOUN a fortress in Canada, in Nova Scotia on SE Cape Breton Island: founded in 1713 by the French and strongly fortified (1720–40); captured by the British (1758) and demolished; reconstructed as a historic site.

louis d'or (,lu:ɪ 'dɔ:; *French* lwi dɔr) NOUN, *plural* **louis d'or** (,lu:ɪz 'dɔ:; *French* lwi dɔr). [1] a former French gold coin worth 20 francs. [2] an old French coin minted in the reign of Louis XIII. ◆ Often shortened to: **louis.**
▷HISTORY C17: from French: golden louis, named after Louis XIII

Louisiana (lu:,i:zɪ'ænə) NOUN a state of the southern US, on the Gulf of Mexico: originally a French colony; bought by the US in 1803 as part of the Louisiana Purchase; chiefly low-lying. Capital: Baton Rouge. Pop.: 4 468 976 (2000). Area: 116 368 sq. km (44 930 sq. miles). Abbreviations: **La,** (with zip code) **LA.**

Louisiana Purchase NOUN the large region of North America sold by Napoleon I to the US in 1803 for 15 million dollars: consists of the W part of the Mississippi basin. Area: about 2 292 150 sq. km (885 000 sq. miles).

Louis Quatorze (kə'tɔ:z) ADJECTIVE of or relating to the baroque style of furniture, decoration, and architecture of the time of Louis XIV of France (1638–1715; king 1643–1715) and characterized by massive forms and heavy ornamentation.

Louis Quinze (kænz) ADJECTIVE of or relating to the rococo style of the furniture, decoration, and architecture of the time of Louis XV of France (1710–74; king 1715–74).

Louis Seize (sɛz) ADJECTIVE of or relating to the style of furniture, decoration, and architecture of the time of Louis XVI of France (1754–93; king 1774–92), belonging to the late French rococo and early neoclassicism.

Louis Treize (trɛz) ADJECTIVE of or relating to the style of furniture, decoration, and architecture of the time of Louis XIII of France (1601–43; king 1610–43), with rich decorative features based on classical models.

Louisville ('lu:ɪ,vɪl) NOUN a port in N Kentucky, on the Ohio River: site of the annual Kentucky Derby; university (1837). Pop.: 256 231 (2000).

lounge (laʊndʒ) VERB [1] (*intr;* often foll by *about* or *around*) to sit, lie, walk, or stand in a relaxed manner. [2] to pass (time) lazily or idly. ◆ NOUN [3] **a** a communal room in a hotel, ship, theatre, etc., used for waiting or relaxing in. **b** (*as modifier*): *lounge chair.* [4] *Chiefly Brit* a living room in a private house. [5] Also called: **lounge bar, saloon bar.** *Brit* a more expensive bar in a pub or hotel. [6] *Chiefly US and Canadian* **a** an expensive bar, esp in a hotel. **b** short for **cocktail lounge.** [7] a sofa or couch, esp one with a headrest and no back. [8] the act or an instance of lounging.
▷HISTORY C16: origin unknown

lounge lizard NOUN *Informal* an idle frequenter of places where rich or prominent people gather.

lounger ('laʊndʒə) NOUN [1] a comfortable sometimes adjustable couch or extending chair designed for someone to relax on. [2] a loose comfortable leisure garment. [3] a person who lounges.

lounge suit NOUN the customary suit of matching jacket and trousers worn by men for the normal business day.

loup¹ (lu:) NOUN another name for **loo mask.**
▷HISTORY C19: from French, from Latin *lupus* wolf

loup² *or* **lowp** (laʊp) VERB, NOUN a Scot word for **leap.**

loupe (lu:p) NOUN a magnifying glass used by jewellers, horologists, etc.
▷HISTORY C20: from French (formerly an imperfect precious stone), from Old French, of obscure origin

louping ill ('laʊpɪŋ, 'ləʊ-) NOUN a viral disease of sheep causing muscular twitching and partial paralysis: transmitted by the bite of an infected tick (*Ixodes ricinus*).
▷HISTORY C18 *louping*, from LOUP²

lour *or* **lower** (laʊə) VERB (*intr*) [1] (esp of the sky, weather, etc.) to be overcast, dark, and menacing. [2] to scowl or frown. ◆ NOUN [3] a menacing scowl or appearance.
▷HISTORY C13 *louren* to scowl; compare German *lauern* to lurk
▸ **'louring** *or* **'lowering** ADJECTIVE ▸ **'louringly** *or* **'loweringly** ADVERB

Lourdes (*French* lurd) NOUN a town in SW France: a leading place of pilgrimage for Roman Catholics after a peasant girl, Bernadette Soubirous, had visions of the Virgin Mary in 1858. Pop.: 17 100 (1995 est.).

Lourenço Marques (lə'rɛnsəʊ 'mɑ:k, 'mɑ:ks; *Portuguese* lo'rẽsu 'markɪʃ) NOUN the former name (until 1975) of **Maputo.**

lourie *or* **loerie** ('laʊrɪ) NOUN *South African* any of several species of touraco: louries are divided into two groups, the arboreal species having a mainly green plumage and crimson wings and the species which inhabits the more open savanna areas having a plain grey plumage.
▷HISTORY from Malay *luri*

louse (laʊs) NOUN, *plural* **lice** (laɪs). [1] any wingless bloodsucking insect of the order *Anoplura:* includes *Pediculus capitis* (**head louse**), *Pediculus corporis* (**body louse**), and the crab louse, all of which infest man. Related adjective: **pedicular.** [2] **biting** *or* **bird louse.** any wingless insect of the order *Mallophaga*, such as the chicken louse: external parasites of birds and mammals with biting mouthparts. [3] any of various similar but unrelated insects, such as the plant louse and book louse. [4] (*plural* **louses**) *Slang* an unpleasant or mean person. ◆ VERB (*tr*) [5] to remove lice from. [6] (foll by *up*) *Slang* to ruin or spoil.
▷HISTORY Old English *lūs*; related to Old High German, Old Norse *lūs*

louser ('laʊzər) NOUN *Irish, slang* a mean nasty person.
▷HISTORY C20: from *louse (up)* + -ER¹

lousewort ('laʊs,wɜ:t) NOUN any of various N temperate scrophulariaceous plants of the genus *Pedicularis*, having spikes of white, yellow, or mauve flowers. See also **betony** (sense 3).

lousy ('laʊzɪ) ADJECTIVE **lousier, lousiest.** [1] *Slang* very mean or unpleasant: *a lousy thing to do.* [2] *Slang* inferior or bad: *this is a lousy film.* [3] infested with lice. [4] (foll by *with*) *Slang* **a** provided with an excessive amount (of): *he's lousy with money.* **b** full of or teeming with.
▸ **'lousily** ADVERB ▸ **'lousiness** NOUN

lout¹ (laʊt) NOUN a crude or oafish person; boor.
▷HISTORY C16: perhaps from LOUT²

lout² (laʊt) VERB (*intr*) *Archaic* to bow or stoop.
▷HISTORY Old English *lūtan*; related to Old Norse *lūta*

Louth (laʊθ) NOUN a county of NE Republic of Ireland, in Leinster province on the Irish Sea: the smallest of the counties. County town: Dundalk. Pop.: 92 166 (1996). Area: 821 sq. km (317 sq. miles).

loutish ('laʊtɪʃ) ADJECTIVE characteristic of a lout; unpleasant and uncouth.
▸ **'loutishly** ADVERB ▸ **'loutishness** NOUN

Louvain (*French* luvɛ̃) NOUN a town in central Belgium, in Flemish Brabant province: capital of the duchy of Brabant (11th–15th centuries) and centre of the cloth trade; university (1426). Pop.: 87 165 (1995 est.). Flemish name: **Leuven.**

louvar ('lu:vɑ:) NOUN a large silvery whalelike scombroid fish, *Luvarus imperialis*, that occurs in most tropical and temperate seas and feeds on plankton: family *Luvaridae*.

▷**HISTORY** from Italian (Calabrian and Sicilian dialect) *lùvaru,* perhaps from Latin *ruber* red

louvre *or US* **louver** ('luːvə) NOUN 1 **a** any of a set of horizontal parallel slats in a door or window, sloping outwards to throw off rain and admit air. **b** Also called: **louvre boards.** the slats together with the frame supporting them. 2 *Architect* a lantern or turret that allows smoke to escape.
▷**HISTORY** C14: from Old French *lovier,* of obscure origin

Louvre (*French* luvrə) NOUN the national museum and art gallery of France, in Paris: formerly a royal palace, begun in 1546; used for its present purpose since 1793.

louvred *or US* **louvered** ('luːvəd) ADJECTIVE (of a window, door, etc.) having louvres.

lovable *or* **loveable** ('lʌvəb^{ə}l) ADJECTIVE attracting or deserving affection.
▸ **ˌlova'bility** *or* **ˌlovea'bility** *or* **'lovableness** *or* **'loveableness** NOUN ▸ **'lovably** *or* **'loveably** ADVERB

lovage ('lʌvɪdʒ) NOUN 1 a European umbelliferous plant, *Levisticum officinale,* with greenish-white flowers and aromatic fruits, which are used for flavouring food. 2 **Scotch lovage.** a similar and related plant, *Ligusticum scoticum,* of N Europe.
▷**HISTORY** C14 *loveache,* from Old French *luvesche,* from Late Latin *levisticum,* from Latin *ligusticum,* literally: Ligurian (plant)

lovat ('lʌvət) NOUN a yellowish-green or bluish-green mixture, esp in tweeds or woollens.
▷**HISTORY** named after *Lovat,* Inverness-shire

love (lʌv) VERB 1 (*tr*) to have a great attachment to and affection for. 2 (*tr*) to have passionate desire, longing, and feelings for. 3 (*tr*) to like or desire (to do something) very much. 4 (*tr*) to make love to. 5 (*intr*) to be in love. ◆ NOUN 6 **a** an intense emotion of affection, warmth, fondness, and regard towards a person or thing. **b** (*as modifier*): *love song; love story.* 7 a deep feeling of sexual attraction and desire. 8 wholehearted liking for or pleasure in something. 9 *Christianity* **a** God's benevolent attitude towards man. **b** man's attitude of reverent devotion towards God. 10 Also: **my love.** a beloved person: used esp as an endearment. 11 *Brit informal* a term of address, esp but not necessarily for a person regarded as likable. 12 (in tennis, squash, etc.) a score of zero. 13 **fall in love.** to become in love. 14 **for love.** without payment. 15 **for love or money.** (*used with a negative*) in any circumstances: *I wouldn't eat a snail for love or money.* 16 **for the love of.** for the sake of. 17 **in love.** in a state of strong emotional attachment and usually sexual attraction. 18 **make love (to). a** to have sexual intercourse (with). **b** *Now archaic* to engage in courtship (with). ◆ Related adjective **amatory.**
▷**HISTORY** Old English *lufu;* related to Old High German *luba;* compare also Latin *libēre* (originally *lubēre*) to please

love affair NOUN 1 a romantic or sexual relationship, esp a temporary one, between two people. 2 a great enthusiasm or liking for something: *a love affair with ballet.*

love apple NOUN an archaic name for **tomato.**

lovebird ('lʌvˌbɜːd) NOUN 1 any of several small African parrots of the genus *Agapornis,* often kept as cage birds. 2 another name for **budgerigar.** 3 *Informal* a lover: *the lovebirds are in the garden.*

lovebite ('lʌvˌbaɪt) NOUN a temporary red mark left on a person's skin by a partner's biting or sucking it during lovemaking.

love child NOUN *Euphemistic* an illegitimate child; bastard.

loved-up ADJECTIVE *Slang* experiencing feelings of love, through or as if through taking a drug, esp the drug ecstasy.

love feast NOUN 1 Also called: **agape.** (among the early Christians) a religious meal eaten with others as a sign of mutual love and fellowship. 2 a ritual meal modelled upon this.

love game NOUN *Tennis* a game in which the loser has a score of zero.

love handles PLURAL NOUN *Informal* folds of excess fat on either side of the waist.

love-in NOUN a gathering at which people express feelings of love, friendship, or physical attraction towards each other.

love-in-a-mist NOUN an erect S European ranunculaceous plant, *Nigella damascena,* cultivated as a garden plant, having finely cut leaves and white or pale blue flowers. See also **fennelflower.**

love-in-idleness NOUN another name for the **wild pansy.**

love knot NOUN a stylized bow, usually of ribbon, symbolizing the bond between two lovers. Also called: **lover's knot.**

loveless ('lʌvlɪs) ADJECTIVE 1 without love: *a loveless marriage.* 2 receiving or giving no love.
▸ **'lovelessly** ADVERB ▸ **'lovelessness** NOUN

love letter NOUN 1 a letter or note written by someone to his or her sweetheart or lover. 2 (in Malaysia) a type of biscuit, made from eggs and rice flour and rolled into a cylinder.

love-lies-bleeding NOUN any of several amaranthaceous plants of the genus *Amaranthus,* esp *A. caudatus,* having drooping spikes of small red flowers.

love life NOUN the part of a person's life consisting of his or her sexual relationships.

lovelock ('lʌvˌlɒk) NOUN a long lock of hair worn on the forehead.

lovelorn ('lʌvˌlɔːn) ADJECTIVE miserable because of unrequited love or unhappiness in love.
▸ **'loveˌlornness** NOUN

lovely ('lʌvlɪ) ADJECTIVE **-lier, -liest.** 1 very attractive or beautiful. 2 highly pleasing or enjoyable: *a lovely time.* 3 loving and attentive. 4 inspiring love; lovable. ◆ NOUN, *plural* **-lies.** 5 *Slang* a lovely woman.
▸ **'loveliness** NOUN

lovemaking ('lʌvˌmeɪkɪŋ) NOUN 1 sexual play and activity between lovers, esp including sexual intercourse. 2 an archaic word for **courtship.**

love match NOUN a betrothal or marriage based on mutual love rather than any other considerations.

love nest NOUN a place suitable for or used for making love.

love potion NOUN any drink supposed to arouse sexual love in the one who drinks it.

lover ('lʌvə) NOUN 1 a person, now esp a man, who has an extramarital or premarital sexual relationship with another person. 2 (*often plural*) either of the two people involved in a love affair. 3 **a** someone who loves a specified person or thing: *a lover of music.* **b** (*in combination*): *a music-lover; a cat-lover.*

love seat NOUN a small upholstered sofa for two people.

love set NOUN *Tennis* a set in which the loser has a score of zero.

lovesick ('lʌvˌsɪk) ADJECTIVE pining or languishing because of love.
▸ **'loveˌsickness** NOUN

lovey ('lʌvɪ) NOUN *Brit informal* another word for **love** (sense 11).

lovey-dovey ADJECTIVE making an excessive or ostentatious display of affection.

loving ('lʌvɪŋ) ADJECTIVE feeling, showing, or indicating love and affection.
▸ **'lovingly** ADVERB ▸ **'lovingness** NOUN

loving cup NOUN 1 a large vessel, usually two-handled, out of which people drink in turn at a banquet. 2 a similar cup awarded to the winner of a competition.

low^{1} (ləʊ) ADJECTIVE 1 having a relatively small distance from base to top; not tall or high: *a low hill; a low building.* 2 **a** situated at a relatively short distance above the ground, sea level, the horizon, or other reference position: *low cloud.* **b** (*in combination*): *low-lying.* 3 **a** involving or containing a relatively small amount of something: *a low supply.* **b** (*in combination*): *low-pressure.* 4 **a** having little value or quality. **b** (*in combination*): *low-grade.* 5 of less than the usual or expected height, depth, or degree: *low temperature.* 6 **a** (of numbers) small. **b** (of measurements) expressed in small numbers. 7 unfavourable: *a low opinion.* 8 not advanced in evolution: *a low form of plant life.* 9 deep: *a low obeisance.* 10 coarse or vulgar: *a low conversation.* 11 **a** inferior in culture or status. **b** (*in combination*): *low-class.* 12 in a physically or mentally depressed or weakened state. 13 designed so as to reveal the wearer's neck and part of the bosom: *a low neckline.* 14 with a hushed tone; quiet or soft: *a low whisper.* 15 of relatively small price or monetary value: *low cost.* 16 *Music* relating to or characterized by a relatively low pitch. 17 (of latitudes) situated not far north or south of the equator. 18 having little or no money. 19 abject or servile. 20 *Phonetics* of, relating to, or denoting a vowel whose articulation is produced by moving the back of the tongue away from the soft palate or the blade away from the hard palate, such as for the *a* in English *father.* Compare **high** (sense 22). 21 (of a gear) providing a relatively low forward speed for a given engine speed. 22 (*usually capital*) of or relating to the Low Church. ◆ ADVERB 23 in a low position, level, degree, intensity, etc.: *to bring someone low.* 24 at a low pitch; deep: *to sing low.* 25 at a low price; cheaply: *to buy low.* 26 **lay low. a** to cause to fall by a blow. **b** to overcome, defeat or destroy. 27 **lie low. a** to keep or be concealed or quiet. **b** to wait for a favourable opportunity. ◆ NOUN 28 a low position, level, or degree: *an all-time low.* 29 an area of relatively low atmospheric pressure, esp a depression. 30 *Electronics* the voltage level in a logic circuit corresponding to logical zero. Compare **high** (sense 40).
▷**HISTORY** C12 *lāh,* from Old Norse *lāgr;* related to Old Frisian *lēch* low, Dutch *laag*
▸ **'lowness** NOUN

low^{2} (ləʊ) NOUN *also* **lowing.** 1 the sound uttered by cattle; moo. ◆ VERB 2 to make or express by a low or moo.
▷**HISTORY** Old English *hlōwan;* related to Dutch *loeien,* Old Saxon *hlōian*

low-alcohol ADJECTIVE (of beer or wine) containing only a small amount of alcohol. Compare **alcohol-free.**

lowan ('ləʊən) NOUN *Austral* another name for **mallee fowl.**

Low Archipelago NOUN another name for the **Tuamotu Archipelago.**

lowball ('ləʊˌbɔːl) NOUN 1 a game of poker in which the player with the lowest hand wins. 2 **a** a very low estimate or offer. **b** (*as modifier*): *a lowball bid.* ◆ VERB (*tr*) 3 to make a very low estimate or offer for (a service, product, company, etc.).

lowborn (ˌləʊ'bɔːn) *or* **lowbred** (ˌləʊ'brɛd) ADJECTIVE *Now rare* of ignoble or common parentage; not royal or noble.

lowboy ('ləʊˌbɔɪ) NOUN *US and Canadian* a table fitted with drawers.

lowbrow ('ləʊˌbraʊ) *Disparaging* ◆ NOUN 1 a person who has uncultivated or nonintellectual tastes. ◆ ADJECTIVE *also* **lowbrowed.** 2 of or characteristic of such a person.
▸ **'lowˌbrowism** NOUN

low camp NOUN an unsophisticated form of **camp** (the style).

low-carbon steel NOUN *Engineering* steel containing between 0.04 and 0.25 per cent carbon.

Lowchen (ˌlaʊ'tʃɛn) NOUN a small dog of a breed with a long wavy coat, often having the hindquarters and tail clipped to resemble a lion. Also called: **little lion dog.**
▷**HISTORY** from German *Löwchen* little lion

Low Church NOUN 1 the school of thought in the Church of England stressing evangelical beliefs and practices. Compare **Broad Church, High Church.** ◆ ADJECTIVE **Low-Church.** 2 of or relating to this school.
▸ **ˌLow-'Churchman** NOUN

low comedy NOUN comedy characterized by slapstick and physical action.
▸ **low comedian** NOUN

low-context ADJECTIVE tending to communicate by electronic methods such as e-mail, rather than in person. Compare **high-context.**

Low Countries PLURAL NOUN the lowland region of W Europe, on the North Sea: consists of Belgium, Luxembourg, and the Netherlands.

low-density lipoprotein NOUN a lipoprotein that is the form in which cholesterol is transported in the bloodstream to the cells and tissues of the body. High levels of low-density lipoprotein in the blood are associated with atheroma. Abbreviation: **LDL.**

low-down *Informal* ◆ ADJECTIVE 1 mean,

underhand, or despicable. ◆ NOUN **lowdown.** [2] information, esp secret or true information.

lower¹ ('ləʊə) ADJECTIVE [1] being below one or more other things: *the lower shelf; the lower animals.* [2] reduced in amount or value: *a lower price.* [3] *Maths* (of a limit or bound) less than or equal to one or more numbers or variables. [4] (*sometimes capital*) *Geology* denoting the early part or division of a period, system, formation, etc.: *Lower Silurian.* ◆ VERB [5] (*tr*) to cause to become low or on a lower level; bring, put, or cause to move down. [6] (*tr*) to reduce or bring down in estimation, dignity, value, etc.: *to lower oneself.* [7] to reduce or be reduced: *to lower one's confidence.* [8] (*tr*) to make quieter: *to lower the radio.* [9] (*tr*) to reduce the pitch of. [10] (*tr*) *Phonetics* to modify the articulation of (a vowel) by bringing the tongue further away from the roof of the mouth. [11] (*intr*) to diminish or become less. ▷HISTORY C12 (comparative of LOW¹); C17 (vb) ▸ **'lowerable** ADJECTIVE

lower² ('laʊə) VERB a variant spelling of **lour.**

Lower Austria NOUN a state of NE Austria: the largest Austrian province, containing most of the Vienna basin. Capital: Sankt Pölten. Pop.: 1 549 640 (2001). Area: 19 170 sq. km (7476 sq. miles). German name: **Niederösterreich.**

Lower California NOUN a mountainous peninsula of NW Mexico, between the Pacific and the Gulf of California: administratively divided into the states of Baja California and Baja California Sur. Spanish name: **Baja California.**

Lower Canada NOUN (from 1791 to 1841) the official name of the S region of the present-day province of Quebec. Compare **Upper Canada.**

lower case NOUN [1] a compositor's type case, in which the small letters are kept. ◆ ADJECTIVE **lower-case.** [2] of or relating to small letters. ◆ VERB **lower-case.** [3] (*tr*) to print with lower-case letters.

lower chamber NOUN another name for a **lower house.**

lower class NOUN [1] the social stratum having the lowest position in the social hierarchy. Compare **middle class, upper class, working class.** ◆ ADJECTIVE **lower-class.** [2] of or relating to the lower class. [3] inferior or vulgar.

lowerclassman (ˌləʊə'klɑːsmən) NOUN, *plural* **-men.** *US* a freshman or sophomore. Also called: **underclassman.**

lower criticism NOUN textual criticism, esp the study of the extant manuscripts of the Scriptures in order to establish the original text. Compare **higher criticism.**

lower deck NOUN [1] the deck of a ship situated immediately above the hold. [2] *Informal* the petty officers and seamen of a ship collectively.

Lower Egypt NOUN one of the two main administrative districts of Egypt: consists of the Nile Delta.

lower house NOUN one of the two houses of a bicameral legislature: usually the larger and more representative house. Also called: **lower chamber.** Compare **upper house.**

Lower Hutt (hʌt) NOUN an industrial town in New Zealand on the S coast of North Island. Pop.: 62 900 (latest est.).

Lower Lakes PLURAL NOUN *Chiefly Canadian* Lakes Erie and Ontario.

lower mordent NOUN another term for **mordent.**

lowermost ('ləʊəˌməʊst) ADJECTIVE lowest.

Lower Palaeolithic NOUN [1] the earliest of the three sections of the Palaeolithic, beginning about 3 million years ago and ending about 70 000 B.C. with the emergence of Neanderthal man. ◆ ADJECTIVE [2] of or relating to this period.

lower regions PLURAL NOUN (usually preceded by *the*) hell.

Lower Saxony NOUN a state of N Germany, on the North Sea and including the E Frisian Islands; formerly in West Germany: a leading European producer of petroleum. Capital: Hanover. Pop.: 7 898 800 (2000 est.). Area: 47 408 sq. km (18 489 sq. miles). German name: **Niedersachsen.**

lower school NOUN the younger pupils in a secondary school, usually those in the first three or four year groups.

lower world NOUN [1] the earth as opposed to heaven or the spiritual world. [2] another name for **hell.**

lowest common denominator NOUN the smallest integer or polynomial that is exactly divisible by each denominator of a set of fractions. Abbreviations: **LCD, lcd.** Also called: **least common denominator.**

lowest common multiple NOUN the smallest number or quantity that is exactly divisible by each member of a set of numbers or quantities. Abbreviations: **LCM, lcm.** Also called: **least common multiple.**

Lowestoft ('ləʊstɒft) NOUN a fishing port and resort in E England, in NE Suffolk on the North Sea. Pop.: 62 907 (1991).

low explosive NOUN an explosive of relatively low power, as used in firearms.

low-fi ('ləʊ'faɪ) ADJECTIVE *Informal* a variant spelling of **lo-fi.**

low frequency NOUN a radio-frequency band or a frequency lying between 300 and 30 kilohertz. Abbreviation: **LF.**

Low German NOUN a language of N Germany, spoken esp in rural areas: more closely related to Dutch than to standard High German. Also called: **Plattdeutsch.** Abbreviation: **LG.** See also **German, High German.**

low-key *or* **low-keyed** ADJECTIVE [1] having a low intensity or tone. [2] restrained, subdued, or understated. [3] (of a photograph, painting, etc.) having a predominance of dark grey tones or dark colours with few highlights. Compare **high-key.**

lowland ('ləʊlənd) NOUN [1] relatively low ground. [2] (*often plural*) a low generally flat region. ◆ ADJECTIVE [3] of or relating to a lowland or lowlands. ▸ **'lowlander** NOUN

Lowland ('ləʊlənd) ADJECTIVE of or relating to the Lowlands of Scotland or the dialect of English spoken there.

Lowlands ('ləʊləndz) PLURAL NOUN **the.** a low generally flat region of central Scotland, around the Forth and Clyde valleys, separating the Southern Uplands from the Highlands. ▸ **'Lowlander** NOUN

Low Latin NOUN any form or dialect of Latin other than the classical, such as Vulgar or Medieval Latin.

low-level language NOUN a computer programming language that is closer to machine language than to human language. Compare **high-level language.**

low-level waste NOUN waste material contaminated by traces of radioactivity that can be disposed of in steel drums in concrete-lined trenches but not (since 1983) in the sea. Compare **high-level waste, intermediate-level waste.**

lowlife ('ləʊˌlaɪf) NOUN, *plural* **-lifes.** *Slang* **a** a member or members of the underworld. **b** (*as modifier*): *his lowlife friends.*

lowlight ('ləʊˌlaɪt) NOUN [1] an unenjoyable or unpleasant part of an event. [2] (*usually plural*) a streak of darker colour artificially applied to the hair.

low-loader NOUN a road or rail vehicle for heavy loads with a low platform for ease of access.

lowly ('ləʊlɪ) *Now rare* ◆ ADJECTIVE **-lier, -liest.** [1] humble or low in position, rank, status, etc. [2] full of humility; meek. [3] simple, unpretentious, or plain. ◆ ADVERB [4] in a low or lowly manner. ▸ **'lowliness** NOUN

Low Mass NOUN a Mass that has a simplified ceremonial form and is spoken rather than sung. Compare **High Mass.**

low-minded ADJECTIVE having a vulgar or crude mind and character. ▸ **ˌlow-'mindedly** ADVERB ▸ **ˌlow-'mindedness** NOUN

low-necked ADJECTIVE (of a woman's garment) having a low neckline.

lowp (laʊp) VERB, NOUN *Scot* a variant spelling of **loup².**

low-pass filter NOUN *Electronics* a filter that transmits all frequencies below a specified value, substantially attenuating frequencies above this value. Compare **high-pass filter, band-pass filter.**

low-pitched ADJECTIVE [1] pitched low in tone. [2] (of a roof) having sides with a shallow slope.

low-pressure ADJECTIVE [1] having, using, or involving a pressure below normal: *a low-pressure gas.* [2] relaxed or calm.

low profile NOUN [1] **a** a position or attitude characterized by a deliberate avoidance of prominence or publicity. **b** (*as modifier*): *a low-profile approach.* ◆ ADJECTIVE **low-profile.** [2] (of a tyre) wide in relation to its height. ◆ Compare **high profile.**

low relief NOUN another term for **bas-relief.**

low-rent ADJECTIVE *Informal* cheap and inferior: *low-rent films.*

low-rise ADJECTIVE [1] of or relating to a building having only a few storeys. Compare **high-rise.** ◆ NOUN [2] such a building.

lowry *or* **lowrie** ('laʊrɪ) NOUN another name for **lory.**

lowse (lauz, laʊs) *Scot* ◆ ADJECTIVE [1] loose. ◆ VERB [2] (*tr*) to release; loose. [3] (*intr*) to finish work. [4] **lowsing time.** the time at which work or school finishes; knocking-off time. ▷HISTORY a Scot variant of LOOSE

low-spirited ADJECTIVE depressed, dejected, or miserable. ▸ **ˌlow-'spiritedly** ADVERB ▸ **ˌlow-'spiritedness** NOUN

Low Sunday NOUN the Sunday after Easter. ▷HISTORY probably so named because of its relative unimportance in contrast with Easter Sunday

low tech NOUN [1] short for **low technology.** [2] a style of interior design using items associated with low technology. ◆ ADJECTIVE **low-tech.** [3] of or using low technology. [4] of or in the interior design style. ◆ Compare **hi tech.**

low technology NOUN simple unsophisticated technology, often that used for centuries, that is limited to the production of basic necessities.

low-tension ADJECTIVE subjected to, carrying, or capable of operating at a low voltage. Abbreviation: **LT.**

low tide NOUN [1] the tide when it is at its lowest level or the time at which it reaches this. [2] a lowest point.

lowveld ('ləʊˌfɛlt, -ˌvɛlt) NOUN **the.** another name for **bushveld.**

low-velocity zone NOUN a layer or zone in the earth in which the velocity of seismic waves is slightly lower than in the layers above and below. The asthenosphere is thought to be such a zone. See **asthenosphere.**

low water NOUN [1] another name for **low tide** (sense 1). [2] the state of any stretch of water at its lowest level. [3] a situation of difficulty or point of least success, excellence, etc.

low-water mark NOUN [1] the level reached by seawater at low tide or by other stretches of water at their lowest level. [2] the lowest point or level; nadir.

lox¹ (lɒks) NOUN a kind of smoked salmon. ▷HISTORY C19: from Yiddish *laks,* from Middle High German *lahs* salmon

lox² (lɒks) NOUN short for **liquid oxygen,** esp when used as an oxidizer for rocket fuels

loxodromic (ˌlɒksə'drɒmɪk) *or* **loxodromical** ADJECTIVE of or relating to rhumb lines or to map projections on which rhumb lines appear straight, as on a Mercator projection. ▷HISTORY C17: from Greek *loxos* oblique + *dromikos* relating to a course ▸ **ˌloxo'dromically** ADVERB

loxodromics (ˌlɒksə'drɒmɪks) *or* **loxodromy** (lɒk'sɒdrəmɪ) NOUN (*functioning as singular*) the technique of navigating using rhumb lines.

loy (lɔɪ) NOUN *Irish* a narrow spade with a single footrest. ▷HISTORY C18: from Irish Gaelic *láí*

loya jirga (ˌlɔɪə 'dʒɜːgə) NOUN (*often with capitals*) an assembly of regional leaders and tribal chiefs in Afghanistan. ▷HISTORY from Pashto, literally: grand assembly

loyal ('lɔɪəl) ADJECTIVE [1] having or showing continuing allegiance. [2] faithful to one's country, government, etc. [3] of or expressing loyalty. ▷HISTORY C16: from Old French *loial, leial,* from Latin *lēgālis* LEGAL ▸ **'loyally** ADVERB ▸ **'loyalness** NOUN

loyalist ('lɔɪəlɪst) NOUN a patriotic supporter of his sovereign or government. ▸ **'loyalism** NOUN

Loyalist (ˈlɔɪəlɪst) NOUN 1 (in Northern Ireland) any of the Protestants wishing to retain Ulster's link with Britain. 2 (in North America) an American colonist who supported Britain during the War of American Independence. 3 (during the Spanish Civil War) a supporter of the republican government.

loyalty (ˈlɔɪəltɪ) NOUN, *plural* **-ties.** 1 the state or quality of being loyal. 2 (*often plural*) a feeling of allegiance.

loyalty card NOUN a swipe card issued by a supermarket or chain store to a customer, used to record credit points awarded for money spent in the store.

Loyang (ˈləʊˈjæŋ) NOUN a variant transliteration of the Chinese name for **Luoyang.**

lozenge (ˈlɒzɪndʒ) NOUN 1 Also called: **pastille, troche.** *Med* a medicated tablet held in the mouth until it has dissolved. 2 *Geometry* another name for **rhombus.** 3 *Heraldry* a diamond-shaped charge.
▷HISTORY C14: from Old French *losange*, of Gaulish origin; compare Vulgar Latin *lausa* flat stone

lozenged (ˈlɒzɪndʒd) ADJECTIVE decorated with lozenges.

lozengy (ˈlɒzɪndʒɪ) ADJECTIVE (*usually postpositive*) *Heraldry* divided by diagonal lines to form a lattice.

Lozère (*French* lɔzɛr) NOUN a department of S central France, in Languedoc-Roussillon region. Capital: Mende. Pop.: 73 509 (1999). Area: 5180 sq. km (2020 sq. miles).

Lozi (ˈləʊzɪ) NOUN the language of the Barotse people of Zambia, belonging to the Bantu group of the Niger-Congo family.

LP[1] NOUN 1 **a** a long-playing gramophone record: usually one 12 inches (30 cm) or 10 inches (25 cm) in diameter, designed to rotate at 33⅓ revolutions per minute. Compare **EP. b** (*as modifier*): *an LP sleeve.* 2 long play: a slow-recording facility on a VCR which allows twice the length of material to be recorded on a tape from that of standard play.

LP[2] ABBREVIATION FOR: 1 (in Britain) **Lord Provost.** 2 Also: **lp.** low pressure.

L/P *Printing* ABBREVIATION FOR letterpress.

LPG ABBREVIATION FOR **liquefied petroleum gas.**

L-plate NOUN *Brit* a white rectangle with an "L" sign fixed to the back and front of a motor vehicle; a red "L" sign is used to show that a driver using it is a learner who has not passed the driving test; a green "L" sign may be displayed by new drivers for up to a year after passing the driving test.

LPO ABBREVIATION FOR London Philharmonic Orchestra.

L'pool ABBREVIATION FOR Liverpool.

LPS (in Britain) ABBREVIATION FOR **Lord Privy Seal.**

lr THE INTERNET DOMAIN NAME FOR Liberia.

Lr THE CHEMICAL SYMBOL FOR lawrencium.

LRSC ABBREVIATION FOR Licentiate of the Royal Society of Chemistry.

LRT (in the US and Canada) ABBREVIATION FOR: 1 light-rail transit. 2 light-rapid transit.

ls[1] (on a document) the place of the seal.
▷HISTORY from Latin *locus sigilli*

ls[2] THE INTERNET DOMAIN NAME FOR Lesotho.

LS INTERNATIONAL CAR REGISTRATION FOR Lesotho.

LSD NOUN lysergic acid diethylamide; a crystalline compound prepared from lysergic acid, used in experimental medicine and taken illegally as a hallucinogenic drug. Informal name (as an illegal hallucinogen): **acid.**

L.S.D., £.s.d., *or* **l.s.d.** (in Britain, esp formerly) ABBREVIATION FOR librae, solidi, denarii.
▷HISTORY Latin: pounds, shillings, pence

LSE ABBREVIATION FOR London School of Economics.

LSI *Electronics* ABBREVIATION FOR large scale integration.

LSO ABBREVIATION FOR London Symphony Orchestra.

LSZ (in New Zealand) ABBREVIATION FOR limited speed zone.

lt[1] ABBREVIATION FOR: 1 long ton. 2 (esp in the US) local time.

lt[2] THE INTERNET DOMAIN NAME FOR Lithuania.

Lt ABBREVIATION FOR Lieutenant.

LT 1 ABBREVIATION FOR low-tension. ◆ 2 INTERNATIONAL CAR REGISTRATION FOR Lithuania.

LTA ABBREVIATION FOR Lawn Tennis Association.

Lt Cdr ABBREVIATION FOR lieutenant commander.

Lt Col ABBREVIATION FOR lieutenant colonel.

Ltd *or* **ltd** (esp after the names of British business organizations) ABBREVIATION FOR limited (liability). US equivalent: **Inc.**

Lt Gen ABBREVIATION FOR lieutenant general.

Lt Gov ABBREVIATION FOR lieutenant governor.

LTNS *Text messaging* ABBREVIATION FOR long time no see.

LTR ABBREVIATION FOR long-term relationship: used in lonely hearts columns and personal advertisements.

LTSA (in New Zealand) ABBREVIATION FOR Land Transport Safety Authority.

Lu THE CHEMICAL SYMBOL FOR lutetium.

lu THE INTERNET DOMAIN NAME FOR Luxembourg.

LU *Physics* ABBREVIATION FOR loudness unit.

luach (ˈlʊɑx) NOUN *Judaism* a calendar that shows the dates of festivals and, usually, the times of start and finish of the Sabbath.

Lualaba (ˌluːəˈlɑːbə) NOUN a river in the SE Democratic Republic of Congo (formerly Zaïre), rising in Shaba province and flowing north as the W headstream of the River Congo. Length: about 1800 km (1100 miles).

Luanda *or* **Loanda** (lʊˈændə) NOUN the capital of Angola, a port in the west, on the Atlantic: founded in 1576, it became a centre of the slave trade to Brazil in the 17th and 18th centuries; oil refining. Pop.: 2 255 000 (1999 est.). Official name: **São Paulo de Loanda.**

Luang Prabang (luːˈæŋ prɑːˈbæŋ) NOUN a market town in N Laos, on the Mekong River: residence of the monarch of Laos (1946–75). Pop.: 59 800 (1995 est.).

luau (luːˈaʊ, ˈluːaʊ) NOUN 1 a feast of Hawaiian food. 2 a dish of taro leaves usually prepared with coconut cream and octopus or chicken.
▷HISTORY from Hawaiian *lu'au*

Luba (ˈluːbə) NOUN 1 (*plural* **Luba**) a member of a Negroid people of Africa living chiefly in the S Democratic Republic of Congo (formerly Zaïre). 2 Also called: **Tshiluba.** the language of this people, belonging to the Bantu group of the Niger-Congo family.

lubber (ˈlʌbə) NOUN 1 a big, awkward, or stupid person. 2 short for **landlubber.**
▷HISTORY C14 *lobre*, probably from Scandinavian. See LOB[1]
▸ **ˈlubberly** ADJECTIVE, ADVERB ▸ **ˈlubberliness** NOUN

lubber line NOUN a mark on a ship's compass that designates the fore-and-aft axis of the vessel. Also called: **lubber's line.**

lubber's hole NOUN *Nautical* a hole in a top or platform on a mast through which a sailor can climb.

Lübeck (*German* ˈlyːbɛk) NOUN a port in N Germany, in Schleswig-Holstein on the Baltic: the leading member of the Hanseatic League, and a major European commercial centre until the 15th century. Pop.: 213 800 (1999 est.).

Lublin (*Polish* ˈlublin) NOUN an industrial city in E Poland: provisional seat of the government in 1918 and 1944. Pop.: 356 251 (1999 est.). Russian name: **Lyublin.**

lubra (ˈluːbrə) NOUN *Austral* an Aboriginal woman.
▷HISTORY C19: from a native Australian language

lubricant (ˈluːbrɪkənt) NOUN 1 a lubricating substance, such as oil. ◆ ADJECTIVE 2 serving to lubricate.
▷HISTORY C19: from Latin *lūbricāns*, present participle of *lūbricāre*. See LUBRICATE

lubricate (ˈluːbrɪˌkeɪt) VERB 1 (*tr*) to cover or treat with an oily or greasy substance so as to lessen friction. 2 (*tr*) to make greasy, slippery, or smooth. 3 (*intr*) to act as a lubricant.
▷HISTORY C17: from Latin *lūbricāre*, from *lūbricus* slippery
▸ **ˌlubriˈcation** NOUN ▸ **ˌlubriˈcational** ADJECTIVE
▸ **ˈlubriˌcative** ADJECTIVE

lubricator (ˈluːbrɪˌkeɪtə) NOUN 1 a person or thing that lubricates. 2 a device for applying lubricant.

lubricious (luːˈbrɪʃəs) *or* **lubricous** (ˈluːbrɪkəs) ADJECTIVE 1 *Formal or literary* lewd, lascivious. 2 *Rare* oily or slippery.
▷HISTORY C16: from Latin *lūbricus*
▸ **luˈbriciously** *or* **ˈlubricously** ADVERB

lubricity (luːˈbrɪsɪtɪ) NOUN 1 *Formal or literary* lewdness or salaciousness. 2 *Rare* smoothness or slipperiness. 3 capacity to lubricate.
▷HISTORY C15 (lewdness), C17 (slipperiness): from Old French *lubricité*, from Medieval Latin *lubricitās*, from Latin, from *lūbricus* slippery

lubritorium (ˌluːbrɪˈtɔːrɪəm) NOUN, *plural* **-ria** (-rɪə). *Chiefly US* a place, as in a service station, for the lubrication of motor vehicles.
▷HISTORY C20: from LUBRICATE + *-orium*, as in *sanatorium*

Lubumbashi (ˌluːbʊmˈbæʃɪ) NOUN a city in the S Democratic Republic of Congo (formerly Zaïre): founded in 1910 as a copper-mining centre; university (1955). Pop.: 851 381 (1994 est.). Former name (until 1966): **Elisabethville.**

Lucan (ˈluːkən) ADJECTIVE of or relating to St. Luke, a fellow worker of Paul and a physician (Colossians 4:14), or St. Luke's gospel.

Lucania (luːˈkeɪnɪə) NOUN the Latin name for **Basilicata.**

lucarne (luːˈkɑːn) NOUN a type of dormer window.
▷HISTORY C16: from French, from Provençal *lucana*, of obscure origin

Lucca (*Italian* ˈlukka) NOUN a city in NW Italy, in Tuscany: centre of a rich agricultural region, noted for the production of olive oil. Pop.: 86 676 (1990 est.). Ancient name: **Luca** (ˈluːkə).

luce (luːs) NOUN another name for the **pike** (the fish).
▷HISTORY C14: from Old French *lus*, from Late Latin *lūcius* pike

lucent (ˈluːsᵊnt) ADJECTIVE brilliant, shining, or translucent.
▷HISTORY C16: from Latin *lūcēns*, present participle of *lūcēre* to shine
▸ **ˈlucently** ADVERB

lucerne (luːˈsɜːn) NOUN *Brit* another name for **alfalfa.**

Lucerne (luːˈsɜːn; *French* lysɛrn) NOUN 1 a canton in central Switzerland, northwest of Lake Lucerne: joined the Swiss Confederacy in 1332. Pop.: 345 400 (2000 est.). Area: 1494 sq. km (577 sq. miles). 2 a city in central Switzerland, capital of Lucerne canton, on Lake Lucerne: tourist centre. Pop.: 60 600 (latest est.). 3 **Lake.** a lake in central Switzerland: fed and drained chiefly by the River Reuss. Area: 115 sq. km (44 sq. miles). German name: **Vierwaldstättersee.** ◆ German name (for senses 1 and 2): **Luzern.**

lucid (ˈluːsɪd) ADJECTIVE 1 readily understood; clear. 2 shining or glowing. 3 *Psychiatry* of or relating to a period of normality between periods of insane or irresponsible behaviour.
▷HISTORY C16: from Latin *lūcidus* full of light, from *lūx* light
▸ **luˈcidity** *or* **ˈlucidness** NOUN ▸ **ˈlucidly** ADVERB

lucifer (ˈluːsɪfə) NOUN a friction match: originally a trade name for a match manufactured in England in the 19th century.

Lucifer (ˈluːsɪfə) NOUN 1 the leader of the rebellion of the angels: usually identified with Satan. 2 the planet Venus when it rises as the morning star.
▷HISTORY Old English, from Latin *Lūcifer*, light-bearer, from *lūx* light + *ferre* to bear

luciferin (luːˈsɪfərɪn) NOUN *Biochem* a substance occurring in bioluminescent organisms, such as glow-worms and fireflies. It undergoes an enzyme-catalysed oxidation and emits light on decaying to its ground state.
▷HISTORY C20: from Latin *lucifer* (literally: light-bearer) + -IN

luciferous (luːˈsɪfərəs) ADJECTIVE *Rare* bringing or giving light.

lucifugous (luːˈsɪfjʊgəs) ADJECTIVE avoiding light.
▷HISTORY C17: from Latin *lucifugus*, from *lux* (genitive *lūcis*) light + *fugere* to flee + -OUS

Lucina (luːˈsaɪnə) NOUN *Roman myth* a title or name given to Juno as goddess of childbirth.

▷HISTORY C14: from Latin *lūcīnus* bringing to the light, from *lūx* light

luck (lʌk) NOUN [1] events that are beyond control and seem subject to chance; fortune. [2] success or good fortune. [3] something considered to bring good luck. [4] **down on one's luck.** having little or no good luck to the point of suffering hardships. [5] **no such luck.** *Informal* unfortunately not. [6] **try one's luck.** to attempt something that is uncertain. ◆ See also **luck out**.
▷HISTORY C15: from Middle Dutch *luc;* related to Middle High German *gelücke,* late Old Norse *lukka, lykka*

luckless ('lʌklɪs) ADJECTIVE having no luck; unlucky.
▸'**lucklessly** ADVERB ▸'**lucklessness** NOUN

Lucknow ('lʌknaʊ) NOUN a city in N India, capital of Uttar Pradesh: capital of Oudh (1775–1856); the British residency was besieged (1857) during the Indian Mutiny. Pop.: 1 619 115 (1991).

luck out VERB (*intr, adverb*) to have good fortune; be lucky: *the US economy lucked out for most of the decade.*

luckpenny ('lʌk,pɛnɪ) NOUN, *plural* **-nies.** *Brit* [1] a coin kept for luck. [2] a small amount of money returned for luck by a seller to a customer.

lucky ('lʌkɪ) ADJECTIVE **luckier, luckiest.** [1] having or bringing good fortune. [2] happening by chance, esp as desired.
▸'**luckily** ADVERB ▸'**luckiness** NOUN

Lucky Country NOUN *Austral, slang* a jocular name for **Australia.**

lucky dip NOUN *Brit* [1] a barrel or box filled with sawdust and small prizes for which children search. [2] *Informal* an undertaking of uncertain outcome.

lucrative ('lu:krətɪv) ADJECTIVE producing a profit; profitable; remunerative.
▷HISTORY C15: from Old French *lucratif;* see LUCRE
▸'**lucratively** ADVERB ▸'**lucrativeness** NOUN

lucre ('lu:kə) NOUN *Usually facetious* money or wealth (esp in the phrase **filthy lucre**).
▷HISTORY C14: from Latin *lūcrum* gain; related to Old English *lēan* reward, German *Lohn* wages

Lucretia (lu:'kri:ʃɪə) NOUN (in Roman legend) a Roman woman who killed herself after being raped by a son of Tarquin the Proud.

lucubrate ('lu:kjʊ,breɪt) VERB (*intr*) to write or study, esp at night.
▷HISTORY C17: from Latin *lūcubrāre* to work by lamplight
▸'**lucu,brator** NOUN

lucubration (,lu:kjʊ'breɪʃən) NOUN [1] laborious study, esp at night. [2] (*often plural*) a solemn literary work.

luculent ('lu:kjʊlənt) ADJECTIVE *Rare* [1] easily understood; lucid. [2] bright or shining; glowing.
▷HISTORY C15: from Latin *lūculentus* full of light, from *lūx* light
▸'**luculently** ADVERB

Lucullan (lu:'kʌlən), **Lucullean,** *or* **Lucullian** (,lu:kʌ'lɪən) ADJECTIVE luxurious or sumptuous.
▷HISTORY named after Lucius Licinius *Lucullus,* the Roman general and consul (?110–56 B.C.), famous for his luxurious banquets

lud (lʌd) *Brit* ◆ NOUN [1] lord (in the phrase **my lud, m'lud**): used when addressing a judge in court. ◆ INTERJECTION [2] *Archaic* an exclamation of dismay or surprise.

Luddite ('lʌdaɪt) NOUN *English history* [1] any of the textile workers opposed to mechanization who rioted and organized machine-breaking between 1811 and 1816. [2] any opponent of industrial change or innovation. ◆ ADJECTIVE [3] of or relating to the Luddites.
▷HISTORY C19: alleged to be named after Ned *Ludd,* an 18th-century Leicestershire workman, who destroyed industrial machinery
▸'**Luddism** NOUN

luderick ('lu:dərɪk) NOUN an estuarine and rock fish, *Girella tricuspidata,* of Australia, usually black or dark brown in colour: a kind of blackfish. Also called: **black bream.**
▷HISTORY C19: from a native Australian language

ludic ('lu:dɪk) ADJECTIVE *Literary* playful.
▷HISTORY C20: from French *ludique,* from Latin *lūdus* game

ludicrous ('lu:dɪkrəs) ADJECTIVE absurd or incongruous to the point of provoking ridicule or laughter.
▷HISTORY C17: from Latin *lūdicrus* done in sport, from *lūdus* game; related to *lūdere* to play
▸'**ludicrously** ADVERB ▸'**ludicrousness** NOUN

Ludlow[1] ('lʌdləʊ) NOUN *Trademark* a machine for casting type from matrices set by hand, used esp for headlines.

Ludlow[2] ('lʌdləʊ) NOUN a market town in W central England, in Shropshire: castle (11th–16th century). Pop.: 9040 (1991).

ludo ('lu:dəʊ) NOUN *Brit* a simple board game in which players advance counters by throwing dice.
▷HISTORY C19: from Latin: I play

lues ('lu:i:z) NOUN, *plural* **lues.** *Rare* [1] any venereal disease. [2] a pestilence.
▷HISTORY C17: from New Latin, from Latin: calamity
▸**luetic** (lu:'ɛtɪk) ADJECTIVE ▸**lu'etically** ADVERB

luff (lʌf) NOUN [1] *Nautical* the leading edge of a fore-and-aft sail. ◆ NOUN [2] tackle consisting of a single and a double, block for use with rope having a large diameter. ◆ VERB [3] *Nautical* to head (a sailing vessel) into the wind so that her sails flap. [4] (*intr*) *Nautical* (of a sail) to flap when the wind is blowing equally on both sides. [5] to move the jib of (a crane) or raise or lower the boom of (a derrick) in order to shift a load.
▷HISTORY C13 (in the sense: steering gear): from Old French *lof,* perhaps from Middle Dutch *loef* peg of a tiller; compare Old High German *laffa* palm of hand, oar blade, Russian *lapa* paw

luffa ('lʌfə) NOUN [1] any tropical climbing plant of the cucurbitaceous genus *Luffa,* esp the dishcloth gourd. [2] *US* another name for **loofah.**

Luftwaffe *German* ('lʊftvafə) NOUN the German Air Force.
▷HISTORY C20: German, literally: air weapon

lug[1] (lʌg) VERB **lugs, lugging, lugged.** [1] to carry or drag (something heavy) with great effort. [2] (*tr*) to introduce (an irrelevant topic) into a conversation or discussion. [3] (*tr*) (of a sailing vessel) to carry too much (sail) for the amount of wind blowing. ◆ NOUN [4] the act or an instance of lugging.
▷HISTORY C14: probably from Scandinavian; apparently related to Norwegian *lugge* to pull by the hair

lug[2] (lʌg) NOUN [1] a projecting piece by which something is connected, supported, or lifted. [2] Also called: **tug.** a leather loop used in harness for various purposes. [3] a box or basket for vegetables or fruit with a capacity of 28 to 40 pounds. [4] *Scot and northern English, dialect* another word for **ear**[1]. [5] *Slang* a man, esp a stupid or awkward one.
▷HISTORY C15 (Scots dialect) *lugge* ear, perhaps related to LUG[1] (in the sense: to pull by the ear)

lug[3] (lʌg) NOUN *Nautical* short for **lugsail.**

lug[4] (lʌg) NOUN short for **lugworm.**
▷HISTORY C16: origin uncertain

Luganda (lu:'gændə, -'gɑ:ndə) NOUN the language of the Buganda, spoken chiefly in Uganda, belonging to the Bantu group of the Niger-Congo family.

Lugano (lʊ'gɑ:nəʊ) NOUN a town in S Switzerland, on Lake Lugano: a financial centre and tourist resort. Pop.: 26 800 (1995 est.).

luge (lu:ʒ) NOUN [1] a racing toboggan on which riders lie on their backs, descending feet first. ◆ VERB [2] (*intr*) to ride on a luge.
▷HISTORY C20: from French

Luger ('lu:gə) NOUN *Trademark* a German 9 mm calibre automatic pistol.
▷HISTORY C20: named after George *Luger* (1849–1923), German gun designer

luggage ('lʌgɪdʒ) NOUN suitcases, trunks, etc., containing personal belongings for a journey; baggage.
▷HISTORY C16: perhaps from LUG[1], influenced in form by BAGGAGE

luggage van NOUN *Brit* a railway carriage used to transport passengers' luggage, bicycles, etc. US and Canadian name: **baggage car.**

lugger ('lʌgə) NOUN *Nautical* a small working boat rigged with a lugsail.
▷HISTORY C18: from LUGSAIL

Lughnasadh ('lu:nasa) NOUN an ancient Celtic festival held on Aug. 1. It is also celebrated by modern pagans. Also called: **Lammas.**
▷HISTORY from Old Irish

lughole ('lʌg,həʊl) NOUN *Brit* an informal word for **ear**[1]. See also **lug**[2] (sense 4).

Lugo (*Spanish* 'luɣo) NOUN a city in NW Spain: Roman walls; Romanesque cathedral. Pop.: 86 658 (1991). Latin name: **Lucus Augusti** ('lu:kəs aʊ'gʊ:sti:, ɔ:'gʌsti:).

lugsail ('lʌgsəl) *or* **lug** (lʌg) NOUN *Nautical* a four-sided sail bent and hoisted on a yard.
▷HISTORY C17: perhaps from Middle English (now dialect) *lugge* pole, or from *lugge* ear

lug screw NOUN a small screw without a head.

lugubrious (lʊ'gu:brɪəs) ADJECTIVE excessively mournful; doleful.
▷HISTORY C17: from Latin *lūgubris* mournful, from *lūgēre* to grieve
▸**lu'gubriously** ADVERB ▸**lu'gubriousness** NOUN

lugworm ('lʌg,wɜ:m) NOUN any polychaete worm of the genus *Arenicola,* living in burrows on sandy shores and having tufted gills: much used as bait by fishermen. Sometimes shortened to: **lug.** Also called: **lobworm.**
▷HISTORY C17: of uncertain origin

lug wrench NOUN a spanner with a lug or lugs projecting from its jaws to engage the component to be rotated.

Luik (lœik) NOUN the Flemish name for **Liège.**

Luke (lu:k) NOUN *New Testament* [1] **Saint.** a fellow worker of Paul and a physician (Colossians 4:14). Feast day: Oct 18. [2] the third Gospel, traditionally ascribed to Luke. Related adjective: **Lucan.**

lukewarm (,lu:k'wɔ:m) ADJECTIVE [1] (esp of water) moderately warm; tepid. [2] having or expressing little enthusiasm or conviction.
▷HISTORY C14 *luke* probably from Old English *hlēow* warm; compare German *lauwarm*
▸,**luke'warmly** ADVERB ▸,**luke'warmness** NOUN

lull (lʌl) VERB [1] to soothe (a person or animal) by soft sounds or motions (esp in the phrase **lull to sleep**). [2] to calm (someone or someone's fears, suspicions, etc.), esp by deception. ◆ NOUN [3] a short period of calm or diminished activity.
▷HISTORY C14: possibly imitative of crooning sounds; related to Middle Low German *lollen* to soothe, Middle Dutch *lollen* to talk drowsily, mumble
▸'**lulling** ADJECTIVE

lullaby ('lʌlə,baɪ) NOUN, *plural* **-bies.** [1] a quiet song to lull a child to sleep. [2] the music for such a song. ◆ VERB **-bies, -bying, -bied.** [3] (*tr*) to quiet or soothe with or as if with a lullaby.
▷HISTORY C16: perhaps a blend of LULL + GOODBYE

lulu ('lu:lu:) NOUN *Slang* a person or thing considered to be outstanding in size, appearance, etc.
▷HISTORY C19: probably from the nickname for *Louise*

lum (lʌm) NOUN *Scot* a chimney.
▷HISTORY C17: of obscure origin

luma (lʊ:mə) NOUN a monetary unit of Armenia worth one hundredth of a dram.

lumbago (lʌm'beɪgəʊ) NOUN pain in the lower back; backache affecting the lumbar region.
▷HISTORY C17: from Late Latin *lumbāgo,* from Latin *lumbus* loin

lumbar ('lʌmbə) ADJECTIVE of, near, or relating to the part of the body between the lowest ribs and the hipbones.
▷HISTORY C17: from New Latin *lumbāris,* from Latin *lumbus* loin

lumbar puncture NOUN *Med* insertion of a hollow needle into the lower region of the spinal cord to withdraw cerebrospinal fluid, introduce drugs, etc.

lumber[1] ('lʌmbə) NOUN [1] *Chiefly US and Canadian* **a** logs; sawn timber. **b** cut timber, esp when sawn and dressed ready for use in joinery, carpentry, etc. **c** (*as modifier*): *the lumber trade.* [2] *Brit* **a** useless household articles that are stored away. **b** (*as modifier*): *lumber room.* ◆ VERB [3] (*tr*) to pile together in a disorderly manner. [4] (*tr*) to fill up or encumber with useless household articles. [5] *Chiefly US and Canadian* to convert (the trees) of (a forest) into marketable timber. [6] (*tr*) *Brit informal*

to burden with something unpleasant, tedious, etc. [7] (*tr*) *Austral* to arrest; imprison.
▷HISTORY C17: perhaps from a noun use of LUMBER[2]
▸ '**lumberer** NOUN

lumber[2] ('lʌmbə) VERB (*intr*) [1] to move awkwardly. [2] an obsolete word for **rumble.**
▷HISTORY C14 *lomeren; perhaps related to lome* LAME[1], Swedish dialect *loma* to move ponderously

lumbering[1] ('lʌmbərɪŋ) NOUN *Chiefly US and Canadian* the business or trade of cutting, transporting, preparing, or selling timber.

lumbering[2] ('lʌmbərɪŋ) ADJECTIVE [1] awkward in movement. [2] moving with a rumbling sound.
▸ '**lumberingly** ADVERB ▸ '**lumberingness** NOUN

lumberjack ('lʌmbəˌdʒæk) NOUN (esp in North America) a person whose work involves felling trees, transporting the timber, etc.
▷HISTORY C19: from LUMBER[1] + JACK[1] (man)

lumberjacket ('lʌmbəˌdʒækɪt) NOUN a boldly coloured, usually checked jacket in warm cloth, as worn by lumberjacks. US name: **lumberjack.**

lumberyard ('lʌmbəˌjɑːd) NOUN the US and Canadian word for **timberyard.**

lumbricalis (ˌlʌmbrɪ'keɪlɪs) NOUN *Anatomy* any of the four wormlike muscles in the hand or foot.
▷HISTORY C18: New Latin, from Latin *lumbrīcus* worm
▸**lumbrical** ('lʌmbrɪkᵊl) ADJECTIVE

lumbricoid ('lʌmbrɪˌkɔɪd) ADJECTIVE [1] *Anatomy* designating any part or structure resembling a worm. [2] of, relating to, or resembling an earthworm.
▷HISTORY C19: from New Latin *lumbricoides,* from Latin *lumbrīcus* worm

lumen ('luːmɪn) NOUN, *plural* **-mens** *or* **-mina** (-mɪnə). [1] the derived SI unit of luminous flux; the flux emitted in a solid angle of 1 steradian by a point source having a uniform intensity of 1 candela. Symbol: lm. [2] *Anatomy* a passage, duct, or cavity in a tubular organ. [3] a cavity within a plant cell enclosed by the cell walls.
▷HISTORY C19: New Latin, from Latin: light, aperture
▸ '**lumenal** *or* '**luminal** ADJECTIVE

lum-hat (ˌlʌm'hæt) NOUN *Scot* a top hat.
▷HISTORY C19: from LUM

luminance ('luːmɪnəns) NOUN [1] a state or quality of radiating or reflecting light. [2] a measure (in candelas per square metre) of the brightness of a point on a surface that is radiating or reflecting light. It is the luminous intensity in a given direction of a small element of surface area divided by the orthogonal projection of this area onto a plane at right angles to the direction. Symbol: *L.*
▷HISTORY C19: from Latin *lūmen* light

luminary ('luːmɪnərɪ) NOUN, *plural* **-naries.** [1] a person who enlightens or influences others. [2] a famous person. [3] *Literary* something, such as the sun or moon, that gives off light. ◆ ADJECTIVE [4] of, involving, or characterized by light or enlightenment.
▷HISTORY C15: via Old French, from Latin *lūmināre* lamp, from *lūmen* light

luminesce (ˌluːmɪ'nɛs) VERB (*intr*) to exhibit luminescence.
▷HISTORY back formation from LUMINESCENT

luminescence (ˌluːmɪ'nɛsəns) NOUN *Physics* **a** the emission of light at low temperatures by any process other than incandescence, such as phosphorescence or chemiluminescence. **b** the light emitted by such a process.
▷HISTORY C19: from Latin *lūmen* light
▸ ˌ**lumi'nescent** ADJECTIVE

luminosity (ˌluːmɪ'nɒsɪtɪ) NOUN, *plural* **-ties.** [1] the condition of being luminous. [2] something that is luminous. [3] *Astronomy* a measure of the radiant power emitted by a star. [4] *Physics* the attribute of an object or colour enabling the extent to which an object emits light to be observed. Former name: **brightness.** See also **colour.**

luminous ('luːmɪnəs) ADJECTIVE [1] radiating or reflecting light; shining; glowing: *luminous colours.* [2] (*not in technical use*) exhibiting luminescence: *luminous paint.* [3] full of light; well-lit. [4] (of a physical quantity in photometry) evaluated according to the visual sensation produced in an observer rather than by absolute energy measurements: *luminous flux; luminous intensity.* Compare **radiant.** [5] easily understood; lucid; clear. [6] enlightening or wise.
▷HISTORY C15: from Latin *lūminōsus* full of light, from *lūmen* light
▸ '**luminously** ADVERB ▸ '**luminousness** NOUN

luminous efficacy NOUN [1] the quotient of the luminous flux of a radiation and its corresponding radiant flux. Symbol: *K.* [2] the quotient of the luminous flux emitted by a source of radiation and the power it consumes. It is measured in lumens per watt. Symbol: η_v, Φ_v.

luminous efficiency NOUN the efficiency of polychromatic radiation in producing a visual sensation. It is the radiant flux weighed according to the spectral luminous efficiencies of its constituent wavelengths divided by the corresponding radiant flux. Symbol: *V.*

luminous energy NOUN energy emitted or propagated in the form of light; the product of a luminous flux and its duration, measured in lumen seconds. Symbol: Q_v.

luminous exitance NOUN the ability of a surface to emit light expressed as the luminous flux per unit area at a specified point on the surface. Symbol: M_v.

luminous flux NOUN a measure of the rate of flow of luminous energy, evaluated according to its ability to produce a visual sensation. For a monochromatic light it is the radiant flux multiplied by the spectral luminous efficiency of the light. It is measured in lumens. Symbol: Φ_v.

luminous intensity NOUN a measure of the amount of light that a point source radiates in a given direction. It is expressed by the luminous flux leaving the source in that direction per unit of solid angle. Symbol: I_v.

lumisterol (luː'mɪstəˌrɒl) NOUN *Biochem* a steroid compound produced when ergosterol is exposed to ultraviolet radiation. Formula: $C_{28}H_{44}O$.
▷HISTORY C20: from Latin *lumin-, lūmen* light + STEROL

lumme *or* **lummy** ('lʌmɪ) INTERJECTION *Brit* an exclamation of surprise or dismay.
▷HISTORY C19: alteration of *Lord love me*

lummox ('lʌməks) NOUN *Informal* a clumsy or stupid person.
▷HISTORY C19: origin unknown

lump[1] (lʌmp) NOUN [1] a small solid mass without definite shape. [2] *Pathol* any small swelling or tumour. [3] a collection of things; aggregate. [4] *Informal* an awkward, heavy, or stupid person. [5] (*plural*) *US informal* punishment, defeat, or reverses: *he took his lumps.* [6] **the lump.** *Brit* **a** self-employed workers in the building trade considered collectively, esp with reference to tax and national insurance evasion. **b** (*as modifier*): *lump labour.* [7] (*modifier*) in the form of a lump or lumps: *lump sugar.* [8] **a lump in one's throat.** a tight dry feeling in one's throat, usually caused by great emotion. ◆ VERB [9] (*tr; often foll by together*) to collect into a mass or group. [10] (*intr*) to grow into lumps or become lumpy. [11] (*tr*) to consider as a single group, often without justification. [12] (*tr*) to make or cause lumps in or on. [13] (*intr; often foll by along*) to move or proceed in a heavy manner.
▷HISTORY C13: probably related to early Dutch *lompe* piece, Scandinavian dialect *lump* block, Middle High German *lumpe* rag

lump[2] (lʌmp) VERB (*tr*) *Informal* to tolerate or put up with; endure (in the phrase **lump it**).
▷HISTORY C16: origin uncertain

lumpectomy (lʌm'pɛktəmɪ) NOUN, *plural* **-mies.** the surgical removal of a tumour in a breast.
▷HISTORY C20: from LUMP[1] + -ECTOMY

lumpen ('lʌmpᵊn) ADJECTIVE *Informal* stupid or unthinking.
▷HISTORY from German *Lump* vagabond, influenced in meaning by *Lumpen* rag, as in LUMPENPROLETARIAT

lumpenproletariat (ˌlʌmpənˌprəʊlɪ'tɛərɪət) NOUN (esp in Marxist theory) the amorphous urban social group below the proletariat, consisting of criminals, tramps, etc.
▷HISTORY German, literally: ragged proletariat

lumper ('lʌmpə) NOUN *US* a stevedore; docker.

lumpfish ('lʌmpˌfɪʃ) NOUN, *plural* **-fish** *or* **-fishes.** [1] a North Atlantic scorpaenoid fish, *Cyclopterus lumpus,* having a globular body covered with tubercles, pelvic fins fused into a sucker, and an edible roe: family *Cyclopteridae.* [2] any other fish of the family *Cyclopteridae.* ◆ Also called: **lumpsucker.**
▷HISTORY C16: *lump* (now obsolete) lumpfish, from Middle Dutch *lumpe,* perhaps related to LUMP[1]

lump hammer NOUN a heavy hammer used for driving stakes or breaking stone.

lumpish ('lʌmpɪʃ) ADJECTIVE [1] resembling a lump. [2] stupid, clumsy, or heavy.
▸ '**lumpishly** ADVERB ▸ '**lumpishness** NOUN

lumpsucker ('lʌmpˌsʌkə) NOUN See **lumpfish.**

lump sum NOUN a relatively large sum of money, paid at one time, esp in cash.

lumpy ('lʌmpɪ) ADJECTIVE **lumpier, lumpiest.** [1] full of or having lumps. [2] (esp of the sea) rough. [3] (of a person) heavy or bulky.
▸ '**lumpily** ADVERB ▸ '**lumpiness** NOUN

lumpy jaw NOUN *Vet science* a nontechnical name for **actinomycosis.**

Luna[1] ('luːnə) NOUN [1] the alchemical name for **silver.** [2] the Roman goddess of the moon. Greek counterpart: **Selene.**
▷HISTORY from Latin: moon

Luna[2] ('luːnə) *or* **Lunik** ('luːnɪk) NOUN any of a series of Soviet lunar space-probes, one of which, **Luna 9**, made the first soft landing on the moon (1966).

lunacy ('luːnəsɪ) NOUN, *plural* **-cies.** [1] (formerly) any severe mental illness. [2] foolishness or a foolish act.

luna moth NOUN a large American saturniid moth, *Tropaea* (or *Actias*) *luna,* having light green wings with a yellow crescent-shaped marking on each forewing.
▷HISTORY C19: so named from the markings on its wings

lunar ('luːnə) ADJECTIVE [1] of or relating to the moon. [2] occurring on, used on, or designed to land on the surface of the moon: *lunar module.* [3] relating to, caused by, or measured by the position or orbital motion of the moon. [4] of or containing silver.
▷HISTORY C17: from Latin *lūnāris,* from *lūna* the moon

lunar caustic NOUN silver nitrate fused into sticks, which were formerly used in cauterizing.

lunar eclipse NOUN See **eclipse** (sense 1).

lunarian (luː'nɛərɪən) NOUN [1] an archaic word for **selenographer.** [2] *Myth* an inhabitant of the moon.

lunar module NOUN the module used to carry two of the three astronauts on an Apollo spacecraft to the surface of the moon and back to the spacecraft.

lunar month NOUN another name for **synodic month.** See **month** (sense 6).

lunar year NOUN See **year** (sense 6).

lunate ('luːneɪt) ADJECTIVE *also* **lunated.** [1] *Anatomy, botany* shaped like a crescent. ◆ NOUN [2] a crescent-shaped bone forming part of the wrist.
▷HISTORY C18: from Latin *lūnātus* crescent-shaped, from *lūnāre,* from *lūna* moon

lunatic ('luːnətɪk) ADJECTIVE *also or rarely* **lunatical** (luː'nætɪkᵊl). [1] an archaic word for **insane.** [2] foolish; eccentric; crazy. ◆ NOUN [3] a person who is insane.
▷HISTORY C13 (adjective) via Old French from Late Latin *lūnāticus* crazy, moonstruck, from Latin *lūna* moon
▸ **lu'natically** ADVERB

lunatic asylum NOUN another name, usually regarded as offensive, for **mental home.**

lunatic fringe NOUN the members of a society or group who adopt or support views regarded as extreme or fanatical.

lunation (luː'neɪʃən) NOUN another name for **synodic month.** See **month** (sense 6).

lunch (lʌntʃ) NOUN [1] a meal eaten during the middle of the day. [2] *Caribbean* (among older people) mid-afternoon tea. ◆ VERB [3] (*intr*) to eat lunch. [4] (*tr*) to provide or buy lunch for.
▷HISTORY C16: probably short form of LUNCHEON
▸ '**luncher** NOUN

lunchbox ('lʌntʃˌbɒks) NOUN [1] a container for

carrying a packed lunch. [2] *Brit and Austral, humorous* a man's genitals.

luncheon ('lʌntʃən) NOUN a lunch, esp a formal one.
▷HISTORY C16: probably variant of *nuncheon,* from Middle English *noneschench,* from *none* NOON + *schench* drink

luncheon club NOUN [1] *Social welfare* (in Britain) an arrangement or organization for serving hot midday meals for a small charge to old people in clubs or daycentres. [2] a society or group of people who meet regularly for an organized lunch: *a ladies' luncheon club.*

luncheonette (ˌlʌntʃə'nɛt) NOUN *US and Canadian* a café or small informal restaurant where light meals and snacks are served.

luncheon meat NOUN a ground mixture of meat (often pork) and cereal, usually tinned.

luncheon voucher NOUN a voucher worth a specified amount issued to employees and redeemable at a restaurant for food. Abbreviation: **LV.** US equivalent: **meal ticket.**

lunch hour NOUN [1] Also called: **lunch break.** a break in the middle of the working day, usually of one hour, during which lunch may be eaten. [2] Also called: **lunch time.** the time at which lunch is usually eaten.

lunchroom ('lʌntʃˌruːm, -ˌrʊm) NOUN *US and Canadian* a room where lunch is served or where students, employees, etc., may eat lunches they bring.

Lundy ('lʌndɪ) NOUN an island in SW England, in Devon, in the Bristol Channel: now a bird sanctuary. Pop.: 50 (latest est.).

Lundy's Lane ('lʌndɪz) NOUN the site, near Niagara Falls, of a major battle (1814) in the War of 1812, in which British and Canadian forces defeated the Americans.

lune[1] (luːn) NOUN [1] **a** a section of the surface of a sphere enclosed between two semicircles that intersect at opposite points on the sphere. **b** a crescent-shaped figure formed on a plane surface by the intersection of the arcs of two circles. [2] something shaped like a crescent. [3] *RC Church* another word for **lunette** (sense 6).
▷HISTORY C18: from Latin *lūna* moon

lune[2] (luːn) NOUN *Falconry* a leash for hawks or falcons.
▷HISTORY C14 *loigne,* from Old French, from Medieval Latin *longia, longea,* from Latin *longus* LONG[1]

lunette (luː'nɛt) NOUN [1] anything that is shaped like a crescent. [2] an oval or circular opening to admit light in a dome. [3] a semicircular panel containing a window, mural, or sculpture. [4] a ring attached to a vehicle, into which a hook is inserted so that it can be towed. [5] a type of fortification like a detached bastion. [6] Also called: **lune.** *RC Church* a case fitted with a bracket to hold the consecrated host.
▷HISTORY C16: from French: crescent, from *lune* moon, from Latin *lūna*

lung (lʌŋ) NOUN [1] either one of a pair of spongy saclike respiratory organs within the thorax of higher vertebrates, which oxygenate the blood and remove its carbon dioxide. [2] any similar or analogous organ in other vertebrates or in invertebrates. [3] **at the top of one's lungs.** in one's loudest voice; yelling. ◆ Related adjectives **pneumonic, pulmonary, pulmonic.**
▷HISTORY Old English *lungen;* related to Old High German *lungun* lung. Compare LIGHTS[2]

lungan ('lʌŋgən) NOUN another name for **longan.**

lunge[1] (lʌndʒ) NOUN [1] a sudden forward motion. [2] *Fencing* a thrust made by advancing the front foot and straightening the back leg, extending the sword arm forwards. ◆ VERB [3] to move or cause to move with a lunge. [4] *(intr) Fencing* to make a lunge.
▷HISTORY C18: shortened form of obsolete C17 *allonge,* from French *allonger* to stretch out (one's arm), from Late Latin *ēlongāre* to lengthen. Compare ELONGATE
▸'**lunger** NOUN

lunge[2] (lʌndʒ) NOUN [1] a rope used in training or exercising a horse. ◆ VERB [2] to exercise or train (a horse) on a lunge.
▷HISTORY C17: from Old French *longe,* shortened from *allonge,* ultimately from Latin *longus* LONG[1]; related to LUNGE[1]

lungfish ('lʌŋˌfɪʃ) NOUN, *plural* **-fish** *or* **-fishes.** any freshwater bony fish of the subclass *Dipnoi,* having an air-breathing lung, fleshy paired fins, and an elongated body. The only living species are those of the genera *Lepidosiren* of South America, *Protopterus* of Africa, and *Neoceratodus* of Australia.

lungi *or* **lungee** ('lʊŋgiː) NOUN a long piece of cotton cloth worn as a loincloth, sash, or turban by Indian men or as a skirt.
▷HISTORY C17: Hindi, from Persian

lungworm ('lʌŋˌwɜːm) NOUN [1] any parasitic nematode worm of the family *Metastrongylidae,* occurring in the lungs of mammals, esp *Metastrongylus apri* which infects pigs. [2] any of certain other nematodes that are parasitic in the lungs.

lungwort ('lʌŋˌwɜːt) NOUN [1] any of several Eurasian plants of the boraginaceous genus *Pulmonaria,* esp *P. officinalis,* which has spotted leaves and clusters of blue or purple flowers: formerly used to treat lung diseases. [2] any of various boraginaceous plants of the N temperate genus *Mertensia,* such as *Mertensia maritima* (sea lungwort), having drooping clusters of tubular usually blue flowers.

Lunik ('luːnɪk) NOUN another name for **Luna**[2].

lunisolar (ˌluːnɪ'səʊlə) ADJECTIVE resulting from, relating to, or based on the combined gravitational attraction of the sun and moon.
▷HISTORY C17: from Latin *lūna* moon + SOLAR

lunitidal (ˌluːnɪ'taɪdᵊl) ADJECTIVE of or relating to tidal phenomena as produced by the moon.
▷HISTORY C19: from Latin *lūna* moon + TIDAL

lunitidal interval NOUN the difference in time between the moon crossing a meridian and the following high tide at that meridian.

lunk (lʌŋk) NOUN an awkward, heavy, or stupid person.

lunula ('luːnjʊlə) *or* **lunule** ('luːnjuːl) NOUN, *plural* **-nulae** (-njʊˌliː) *or* **-nules.** the white crescent-shaped area at the base of the human fingernail. Nontechnical name: **half-moon.**
▷HISTORY C16: from Latin: small moon, from *lūna*

lunulate ('luːnjʊˌleɪt) *or* **lunulated** ADJECTIVE [1] having markings shaped like crescents: *lunulate patterns on an insect.* [2] Also: **lunular.** shaped like a crescent.

Luo (lə'wəʊ, 'luːəʊ) NOUN [1] *(plural* **Luo** *or* **Luos)** a member of a cattle-herding Nilotic people living chiefly east of Lake Victoria in Kenya. [2] the language of this people, belonging to the Nilotic group of the Nilo-Saharan family.

Lupercalia (ˌluːpɜː'keɪlɪə) NOUN, *plural* **-lia** *or* **-lias.** an ancient Roman festival of fertility, celebrated annually on Feb. 15. See also **Saint Valentine's Day.**
▷HISTORY Latin, from *Lupercālis* belonging to *Lupercus,* a Roman god of the flocks
▸ˌ**Luper'calian** ADJECTIVE

lupin *or US* **lupine** ('luːpɪn) NOUN any leguminous plant of the genus *Lupinus,* of North America, Europe, and Africa, with large spikes of brightly coloured flowers and flattened pods.
▷HISTORY C14: from Latin *lupīnus* wolfish (see LUPINE); from the belief that the plant ravenously exhausted the soil

lupine ('luːpaɪn) ADJECTIVE of, relating to, or resembling a wolf.
▷HISTORY C17: from Latin *lupīnus,* from *lupus* wolf

lupulin ('luːpjʊlɪn) NOUN a resinous powder extracted from the female flowers of the hop plant and used as a sedative.
▷HISTORY C19: from New Latin *lupulus,* diminutive of *lupus* the hop plant

lupus ('luːpəs) NOUN any of various ulcerative skin diseases.
▷HISTORY C16: via Medieval Latin from Latin: wolf; said to be so called because it rapidly eats away the affected part

> **Language note** In current usage the word *lupus* alone is generally understood to signify lupus vulgaris, lupus erythematosus being normally referred to in full or by the abbreviation LE.

Lupus ('luːpəs) NOUN, *Latin genitive* **Lupi** ('luːpaɪ). a constellation in the S hemisphere lying between Centaurus and Ara.

lupus erythematosus (ˌɛrɪˌθiːmə'təʊsəs) NOUN either of two inflammatory diseases of the connective tissue. **Discoid lupus erythematosus** is characterized by a scaly rash over the cheeks and bridge of the nose; **disseminated** or **systemic lupus erythematosus** affects the joints, lungs, kidneys, or skin. Abbreviation: **LE.**

lupus vulgaris (vʌl'gɛərɪs) NOUN tuberculosis of the skin, esp of the face, with the formation of raised translucent nodules. Sometimes shortened to: **lupus.**

lur *or* **lure** (lʊə) NOUN, *plural* **lures** ('lʊərɪz). a large bronze musical horn found in Danish peat bogs and probably dating to the Bronze Age.
▷HISTORY from Danish (and Swedish and Norwegian) *lur,* from Old Norse *lūthr* trumpet

lurch[1] (lɜːtʃ) VERB *(intr)* [1] to lean or pitch suddenly to one side. [2] to stagger or sway. ◆ NOUN [3] the act or an instance of lurching.
▷HISTORY C19: origin unknown
▸'**lurching** ADJECTIVE

lurch[2] (lɜːtʃ) NOUN [1] **leave (someone) in the lurch.** to desert (someone) in trouble. [2] *Cribbage* the state of a losing player with less than 30 points at the end of a game (esp in the phrase **in the lurch**).
▷HISTORY C16: from French *lourche* a game similar to backgammon, apparently from *lourche* (adj) deceived, probably of Germanic origin

lurch[3] (lɜːtʃ) VERB *(intr) Archaic or dialect* to prowl or steal about suspiciously.
▷HISTORY C15: perhaps a variant of LURK

lurcher ('lɜːtʃə) NOUN [1] a crossbred hunting dog, usually a greyhound cross with a collie, esp one trained to hunt silently. [2] *Archaic* a person who prowls or lurks.
▷HISTORY C16: from LURCH[3]

lurdan ('lɜːdᵊn) *Archaic* ◆ NOUN [1] a stupid or dull person. ◆ ADJECTIVE [2] dull or stupid.
▷HISTORY C14: from Old French *lourdin,* Old French *lourd* heavy, from Latin *lūridus* LURID

lure (lʊə) VERB *(tr)* [1] (sometimes foll by *away* or *into*) to tempt or attract by the promise of some type of reward. [2] *Falconry* to entice (a hawk or falcon) from the air to the falconer by a lure. ◆ NOUN [3] a person or thing that lures. [4] *Angling* any of various types of brightly-coloured artificial spinning baits, usually consisting of a plastic or metal body mounted with hooks and trimmed with feathers, etc. See **jig, plug, spoon.** [5] *Falconry* a feathered decoy to which small pieces of meat can be attached and which is equipped with a long thong.
▷HISTORY C14: from Old French *loirre* falconer's lure, from Germanic; related to Old English *lathian* to invite
▸'**lurer** NOUN

Lurex ('lʊərɛks) NOUN *Trademark* [1] a thin metallic thread coated with plastic. [2] fabric containing such thread, which gives it a glittering appearance.

lurgy ('lɜːgɪ) NOUN, *plural* **-gies.** *Facetious* any undetermined illness.

lurid ('lʊərɪd) ADJECTIVE [1] vivid in shocking detail; sensational. [2] horrible in savagery or violence. [3] pallid in colour; wan. [4] glowing with an unnatural glare.
▷HISTORY C17: from Latin *lūridus* pale yellow; probably related to *lūtum* a yellow vegetable dye
▸'**luridly** ADVERB ▸'**luridness** NOUN

lurk (lɜːk) VERB *(intr)* [1] to move stealthily or be concealed, esp for evil purposes. [2] to be present in an unobtrusive way; go unnoticed. ◆ NOUN [3] to read messages posted on an electronic network without contributing messages oneself. [4] *Austral and NZ, slang* a scheme or stratagem for success.
▷HISTORY C13: probably frequentative of LOUR; compare Middle Dutch *loeren* to lie in wait
▸'**lurker** NOUN

lurking ('lɜːkɪŋ) ADJECTIVE [1] lingering and persistent, though unsuspected or unacknowledged: *a lurking suspicion.* [2] dimly perceived: *a lurking shape half concealed in the shadows.*

Lusaka (luː'zɑːkə, -'sɑːkə) NOUN the capital of Zambia, in the southeast at an altitude of 1280 m (4200 ft.): became capital of Northern Rhodesia in

1932 and of Zambia in 1964; University of Zambia (1966). Pop.: 982 362 (1990).

Lusatia (luːˈseɪʃɪə) NOUN a region of central Europe, lying between the upper reaches of the Elbe and Oder Rivers: now mostly in E Germany, extending into SW Poland; inhabited chiefly by Sorbs.

Lusatian (luːˈseɪʃɪən) ADJECTIVE [1] of or relating to Lusatia, its people, or their language. ◆ NOUN [2] a native or inhabitant of Lusatia; a Sorb. [3] the Sorbian language.

luscious (ˈlʌʃəs) ADJECTIVE [1] extremely pleasurable, esp to the taste or smell. [2] very attractive. [3] *Archaic* cloying.
▷HISTORY C15 *lucius, licius,* perhaps a shortened form of DELICIOUS
▸ **ˈlusciously** ADVERB ▸ **ˈlusciousness** NOUN

luser (ˈluːzə) NOUN *Facetious* a user of a computer system, as considered by a systems administator or other member of a technical support team.
▷HISTORY C20: a blend of LOSER + USER

lush[1] (lʌʃ) ADJECTIVE [1] (of vegetation) abounding in lavish growth. [2] (esp of fruits) succulent and fleshy. [3] luxurious, elaborate, or opulent.
▷HISTORY C15: probably from Old French *lasche* lax, lazy, from Latin *laxus* loose; perhaps related to Old English *læc,* Old Norse *lakr* weak, German *lasch* loose
▸ **ˈlushly** ADVERB ▸ **ˈlushness** NOUN

lush[2] (lʌʃ) *Slang* ◆ NOUN [1] a heavy drinker, esp an alcoholic. [2] alcoholic drink. ◆ VERB [3] *US and Canadian* to drink (alcohol) to excess.
▷HISTORY C19: origin unknown

Lusitania (ˌluːsɪˈteɪnɪə) NOUN an ancient region of the W Iberian Peninsula: a Roman province from 27 B.C. to the late 4th century A.D.; corresponds to most of present-day Portugal and the Spanish provinces of Salamanca and Cáceres.

Lusitanian (ˌluːsɪˈteɪnɪən) ADJECTIVE [1] *Chiefly poetic* of or relating to Lusitania or Portugal. [2] *Biology* denoting flora or fauna characteristically found only in the warm, moist, west-facing coastal regions of Portugal, Spain, France, and the west and southwest coasts of Great Britain and Ireland.

Luso- COMBINING FORM indicating Portugal or Portuguese.
▷HISTORY from Portuguese *lusitano,* from Latin, from LUSITANIA

lust (lʌst) NOUN [1] a strong desire for sexual gratification. [2] a strong desire or drive. ◆ VERB [3] (*intr;* often foll by *after* or *for*) to have a lust (for).
▷HISTORY Old English; related to Old High German *lust* desire, Old Norse *losti* sexual desire, Latin *lascīvus* playful, wanton, lustful. Compare LISTLESS

lustful (ˈlʌstfʊl) ADJECTIVE [1] driven by lust. [2] *Archaic* vigorous or lusty.
▸ **ˈlustfully** ADVERB ▸ **ˈlustfulness** NOUN

lustral (ˈlʌstrəl) ADJECTIVE [1] of or relating to a ceremony of purification. [2] taking place at intervals of five years; quinquennial.
▷HISTORY C16: from Latin *lūstrālis* adj from LUSTRUM

lustrate (ˈlʌstreɪt) VERB (*tr*) to purify by means of religious rituals or ceremonies.
▷HISTORY C17: from Latin *lūstrāre* to brighten
▸ **lusˈtration** NOUN ▸ **lustrative** (ˈlʌstrətɪv) ADJECTIVE

lustre *or US* **luster** (ˈlʌstə) NOUN [1] reflected light; sheen; gloss. [2] radiance or brilliance of light. [3] great splendour of accomplishment, beauty, etc. [4] a substance used to polish or put a gloss on a surface. [5] a vase or chandelier from which hang cut-glass drops. [6] a drop-shaped piece of cut glass or crystal used as a decoration on a chandelier, vase, etc. [7] **a** a shiny metallic surface on some pottery and porcelain. **b** (*as modifier*): *lustre decoration.* [8] *Mineralogy* the way in which light is reflected from the surface of a mineral. It is one of the properties by which minerals are defined. ◆ VERB [9] to make, be, or become lustrous.
▷HISTORY C16: from Old French, from Old Italian *lustro,* from Latin *lustrāre* to make bright; related to LUSTRUM
▸ **ˈlustreless** *or US* **ˈlusterless** ADJECTIVE ▸ **ˈlustrous** ADJECTIVE

lustreware *or US* **lusterware** (ˈlʌstəˌwɛə) NOUN pottery or porcelain ware with lustre decoration.

lustring (ˈlʌstrɪŋ) *or* **lutestring** (ˈluːtˌstrɪŋ) NOUN a glossy silk cloth, formerly used for clothing, upholstery, etc.
▷HISTORY C17: from Italian *lustrino,* from *lustro* LUSTRE

lustrum (ˈlʌstrəm) *or* **lustre** NOUN, *plural* **-trums** *or* **-tra** (-trə). a period of five years.
▷HISTORY C16: from Latin: ceremony of purification, from *lustrāre* to brighten, purify

lusty (ˈlʌstɪ) ADJECTIVE **lustier, lustiest.** [1] having or characterized by robust health. [2] strong or invigorating: *a lusty brew.* [3] lustful.
▸ **ˈlustily** ADVERB ▸ **ˈlustiness** NOUN

lusus naturae (ˈluːsʊs næˈtʊəriː) NOUN a freak, mutant, or monster.
▷HISTORY C17: Latin: whim of nature

lutanist (ˈluːtənɪst) NOUN a variant spelling of **lutenist.**

lute[1] (luːt) NOUN an ancient plucked stringed instrument, consisting of a long fingerboard with frets and gut strings, and a body shaped like a sliced pear.
▷HISTORY C14: from Old French *lut,* via Old Provençal from Arabic *al ʽūd,* literally: the wood

lute[2] (luːt) NOUN [1] Also called: **luting.** a mixture of cement and clay used to seal the joints between pipes, etc. [2] *Dentistry* a thin layer of cement used to fix a crown or inlay in place on a tooth. ◆ VERB [3] (*tr*) to seal (a joint or surface) with lute.
▷HISTORY C14: via Old French ultimately from Latin *lutum* clay

luteal (ˈluːtɪəl) ADJECTIVE relating to or characterized by the development of the corpus luteum: *the luteal phase of the oestrous cycle.*
▷HISTORY C20: from Latin *lūteus* yellow, relating to *lūtum* a yellow weed

lutein (ˈluːtɪɪn) NOUN a xanthophyll pigment, occurring in plants, that has a light-absorbing function in photosynthesis.
▷HISTORY C20: from Latin *lūteus* yellow + -IN

luteinizing hormone (ˈluːtɪɪˌnaɪzɪŋ) NOUN a gonadotrophic hormone secreted by the anterior lobe of the pituitary gland. In female vertebrates it stimulates ovulation, and in mammals it also induces the conversion of the ruptured follicle into the corpus luteum. In male vertebrates it promotes maturation of the interstitial cells of the testes and stimulates androgen secretion. Abbreviation: **LH.** Also called: **interstitial cell-stimulating hormone.** See also **follicle-stimulating hormone, prolactin.**
▷HISTORY C19: from Latin *lūteum* egg yolk, from *lūteus* yellow

luteinizing hormone-releasing hormone NOUN a hypothalamic peptide that stimulates the pituitary gland to release luteinizing hormone. Abbreviation: **LH-RH.**

lutenist, lutanist (ˈluːtənɪst) *or US and Canadian (sometimes)* **lutist** (ˈluːtɪst) NOUN a person who plays the lute.
▷HISTORY C17: from Medieval Latin *lūtānista,* from *lūtāna,* apparently from Old French *lut* LUTE[1]

luteolin (ˈluːtɪəlɪn) NOUN a yellow crystalline compound found, in the form of its glycoside, in many plants. Formula: $C_{15}H_{10}O_6$.
▷HISTORY C19: via French from New Latin *reseda lūteola,* dyer's rocket, from which this substance is obtained; *lūteola* from Latin *lūteus* yellow

luteotrophin (ˌluːtɪəʊˈtrəʊfɪn), **luteotrophic hormone,** *or esp US* **luteotropin, luteotropic hormone** NOUN other names for **prolactin.**

luteous (ˈluːtɪəs) ADJECTIVE of a light to moderate greenish-yellow colour.
▷HISTORY C17: from Latin *lūteus* yellow

lutestring (ˈluːtˌstrɪŋ) NOUN *Textiles* a variant of **lustring.**

Lutetia *or* **Lutetia Parisiorum** (luːˈtiːʃə pəˌrɪzɪˈɔːrəm) NOUN an ancient name for **Paris** (the French city).

lutetium *or* **lutecium** (luˈtiːʃɪəm) NOUN a silvery-white metallic element of the lanthanide series, occurring in monazite and used as a catalyst in cracking, alkylation, and polymerization. Symbol: Lu; atomic no.: 71; atomic wt.: 174.967; valency: 3; relative density: 9.841; melting pt.: 1663°C; boiling pt.: 3402°C.
▷HISTORY C19: New Latin, from Latin *Lūtētia* ancient name of Paris, home of G. Urbain (1872–1938), French chemist, who discovered it

Luth. ABBREVIATION FOR Lutheran.

Lutheran (ˈluːθərən) NOUN [1] a follower of Martin Luther (1483–1546), the German leader of the Protestant Reformation, or a member of a Lutheran Church. ◆ ADJECTIVE [2] of or relating to Luther or his doctrines, the most important being justification by faith alone, consubstantiation, and the authority of the Bible. [3] of or denoting any Protestant Church that follows Luther's doctrines.
▸ **ˈLutheranism** NOUN

Lutherism (ˈluːθərɪzəm) NOUN the religious doctrines of Martin Luther, the German leader of the Protestant Reformation (1483–1546).

luthern (ˈluːθən) NOUN another name for **dormer.**
▷HISTORY C17: probably from LUCARNE, perhaps influenced by LUTHERAN

Lutine bell (ˈluːtiːn, luːˈtiːn) NOUN a bell, taken from the ship *Lutine,* kept at Lloyd's in London and rung before important announcements, esp the loss of a vessel.

luting (ˈluːtɪŋ) NOUN [1] another name for **lute**[2] (sense 1). [2] Also called: **luting paste.** a strip of pastry placed around the dish to seal the lid of a pie.

lutist (ˈluːtɪst) NOUN [1] *US and Canadian* another word for **lutenist.** [2] a person who makes lutes.

lutite (ˈluːtaɪt) NOUN another name for **pelite.**
▷HISTORY C20: from Latin *lutum* mud + -ITE[1]

Luton (ˈluːtᵊn) NOUN [1] a town in SE central England, in Luton unitary authority, S Bedfordshire: airport; motor-vehicle industries; university (1993). Pop.: 171 671 (1991). [2] a unitary authority in SE central England, in Bedfordshire. Pop.: 184 390 (2001). Area: 43 sq. km (17 sq. miles).

Luton Hoo (huː) NOUN a mansion near Luton in Bedfordshire: built (1766–67) for the 3rd Earl of Bute by Robert Adam; rebuilt in the 19th century: houses the Wernher Collection of tapestries, porcelain, and paintings.

lutz (luːts) NOUN *Skating* a jump in which the skater takes off from the back outside edge of one skate, makes one, two, or three turns in the air, and lands on the back outside edge of the other skate.
▷HISTORY C20: of uncertain origin

Lützen (*German* ˈlytsən) NOUN a town near Leipzig in E Germany, in Saxony; site of a battle (1632) in the Thirty Years' War in which the army of the Holy Roman Empire under Wallenstein was defeated by the Swedes under Gustavus Adolphus, who died in the battle.

LUV *Text messaging* ABBREVIATION FOR love.

luvvie *or* **luvvy** (ˈlʌvɪ) NOUN, *plural* **-vies.** *Facetious* a person who is involved in the acting profession or the theatre, esp one with a tendency to affectation.
▷HISTORY C20: from LOVEY

lux (lʌks) NOUN, *plural* **lux.** the derived SI unit of illumination equal to a luminous flux of 1 lumen per square metre. 1 lux is equivalent to 0.0929 foot-candle. Symbol: lx.
▷HISTORY C19: from Latin: light

Lux. ABBREVIATION FOR Luxembourg.

luxate (ˈlʌkseɪt) VERB (*tr*) *Pathol* to put (a shoulder, knee, etc.) out of joint; dislocate.
▷HISTORY C17: from Latin *luxāre* to displace, from *luxus* dislocated; related to Greek *loxos* oblique
▸ **luxˈation** NOUN

luxe (lʌks, lʊks; *French* lyks) NOUN See **de luxe.**
▷HISTORY C16: from French from Latin *luxus* extravagance, LUXURY

Luxembourg (ˈlʌksəmˌbɜːg; *French* lyksɑ̃bur) NOUN [1] a grand duchy in W Europe: formed the Benelux customs union with Belgium and the Netherlands in 1948 and is now a member of the European Union. Languages: French, German, and Luxemburgish. Religion: Roman Catholic majority. Currency: euro. Capital: Luxembourg. Pop.: 444 000 (2001 est.). Area: 2586 sq. km (999 sq. miles). [2] the capital of Luxembourg, on the Alzette River: an industrial centre. Pop.: 79 800 (1999 est.). [3] a province in SE Belgium, in the Ardennes. Capital: Arlon. Pop.: 246 820 (2000 est.). Area: 4416 sq. km (1705 sq. miles).

Luxembourger (ˈlʌksəmˌbɜːgə) NOUN a native or inhabitant of Luxembourg.

Luxor (ˈlʌksɔː) NOUN a town in S Egypt, on the River Nile: the southern part of the site of ancient Thebes; many ruins and tombs, notably the temple built by Amenhotep III (about 1411–1375 B.C.). Pop.: 360 503 (1996).

luxulianite *or* **luxullianite** (lʌk'suːljəˌnaɪt) NOUN a rare variety of granite containing tourmaline embedded in quartz and feldspar.
▷HISTORY C19: named after *Luxulyan*, a village in Cornwall near which it was first found

luxuriant (lʌg'zjʊərɪənt) ADJECTIVE **1** rich and abundant; lush. **2** very elaborate or ornate. **3** extremely productive or fertile.
▷HISTORY C16: from Latin *luxuriāns*, present participle of *luxuriāre* to abound to excess
▸**lux'uriance** NOUN ▸**lux'uriantly** ADVERB

> **Language note** See at **luxurious**.

luxuriate (lʌg'zjʊərɪˌeɪt) VERB (*intr*) **1** (foll by *in*) to take voluptuous pleasure; revel. **2** to flourish extensively or profusely. **3** to live in a sumptuous way.
▷HISTORY C17: from Latin *luxuriāre*
▸**luxˌuri'ation** NOUN

luxurious (lʌg'zjʊərɪəs) ADJECTIVE **1** characterized by luxury. **2** enjoying or devoted to luxury. **3** an archaic word for **lecherous**.
▷HISTORY C14: via Old French from Latin *luxuriōsus* excessive
▸**lux'uriously** ADVERB ▸**lux'uriousness** NOUN

> **Language note** *Luxurious* is sometimes wrongly used where *luxuriant* is meant: *he had a luxuriant* (not *luxurious*) *moustache; the walls were covered with a luxuriant growth of wisteria.*

luxury ('lʌkʃərɪ) NOUN, *plural* **-ries**. **1** indulgence in and enjoyment of rich, comfortable, and sumptuous living. **2** (*sometimes plural*) something that is considered an indulgence rather than a necessity. **3** something pleasant and satisfying: *the luxury of independence*. **4** (*modifier*) relating to, indicating, or supplying luxury: *a luxury liner*.
▷HISTORY C14 (in the sense: lechery): via Old French from Latin *luxuria* excess, from *luxus* extravagance

Luzern (lu'tsɛrn) NOUN the German name for **Lucerne**.

Luzon (luː'zɒn) NOUN the main and largest island of the Philippines, in the N part of the archipelago, separated from the other islands by the Sibuyan Sea: important agriculturally, producing most of the country's rice, with large forests and rich mineral resources; industrial centres at Manila and Batangas. Capital: Quezon City. Pop.: 32 558 000 (1995 est.). Area: 108 378 sq. km (41 845 sq. miles).

lv THE INTERNET DOMAIN NAME FOR Latvia.

Lv *Currency* ABBREVIATION FOR lev(a).

LV **1** (in Britain) ABBREVIATION FOR luncheon voucher. ◆ **2** INTERNATIONAL CAR REGISTRATION FOR Latvia.

LVAD ABBREVIATION FOR left ventricular assist device; an implanted device that boosts the output of the heart on a short-term basis; for example in people awaiting heart transplants.

Lviv (lvif) NOUN an industrial city in the W Ukraine: it has belonged to Poland (1340–1772; 1919–39), Austria (1772–1918), Germany (1939–45), and the Soviet Union (1945–91); Ukrainian cultural centre, with a university (1661). Pop.: 793 700 (1998 est.). Russian name: **Lviv**. Polish name: **Lwów**. German name: **Lemberg**.

Lvov (*Russian* ljvɔf) NOUN the Russian name for **Lviv**.

LVP ABBREVIATION FOR least valuable player.

Lw THE FORMER CHEMICAL SYMBOL FOR lawrencium (now superseded by **Lr**).

LW ABBREVIATION FOR: **1** *Radio* long wave. **2** low water.

lwl *or* **LWL** ABBREVIATION FOR length waterline; the length of a vessel at the waterline, taken at the centre axis.

LWM *or* **lwm** ABBREVIATION FOR low water mark.

Lwów (lvuf) NOUN the Polish name for **Lviv**.

lx *Physics* SYMBOL FOR lux.

LXX SYMBOL FOR Septuagint.

ly THE INTERNET DOMAIN NAME FOR Libyan Arab Jamahiriya.

-ly[1] SUFFIX FORMING ADJECTIVES **1** having the nature or qualities of: *brotherly; godly*. **2** occurring at certain intervals; every: *daily; yearly*.
▷HISTORY Old English *-lic*

-ly[2] SUFFIX FORMING ADVERBS in a certain manner; to a certain degree: *quickly; recently; chiefly*.
▷HISTORY Old English *-lice*, from *-lic* -LY[1]

lyase ('laɪeɪz) NOUN any enzyme that catalyses the separation of two parts of a molecule by the formation of a double bond between them.
▷HISTORY C20: from Greek *lusis* a loosening + -ASE

lycanthrope ('laɪkənˌθrəʊp, laɪ'kænθrəʊp) NOUN **1** a werewolf. **2** *Psychiatry* a person who believes that he is a wolf.
▷HISTORY C17: via New Latin, from Greek *lukanthrōpos*, from *lukos* wolf + *anthrōpos* man

lycanthropy (laɪ'kænθrəpɪ) NOUN **1** the supposed magical transformation of a person into a wolf. **2** *Psychiatry* a delusion in which a person believes that he is a wolf.
▷HISTORY C16: from Greek *lukānthropía*, from *lukos* wolf + *anthrōpos* man
▸**lycanthropic** (ˌlaɪkən'θrɒpɪk) ADJECTIVE

Lycaon (laɪ'keɪɒn) NOUN *Greek myth* a king of Arcadia said to have offered Zeus a plate of human flesh to learn whether the god was omniscient.

lycée *French* ('lise; *English* 'liːseɪ) NOUN, *plural* ***lycées*** (lise; *English* 'liːseɪz). a secondary school.
▷HISTORY C19: French, from Latin: LYCEUM

lyceum (laɪ'sɪəm) NOUN (now chiefly in the names of buildings) **1** a public building for concerts, lectures, etc. **2** *US* a cultural organization responsible for presenting concerts, lectures, etc. **3** another word for **lycée**.

Lyceum (laɪ'sɪəm) NOUN **the**. **1** a school and sports ground of ancient Athens: site of Aristotle's discussions with his pupils. **2** the Aristotelian school of philosophy.
▷HISTORY from Greek *Lukeion*, named after a temple nearby dedicated to *Apollo Lukeios*, an epithet of unknown origin

lychee (ˌlaɪ'tʃiː) NOUN a variant spelling of **litchi**.

lych gate *or* **lich gate** (lɪtʃ) NOUN a roofed gate to a churchyard, formerly used during funerals as a temporary shelter for the bier.
▷HISTORY C15: *lich*, from Old English *līc* corpse

lychnis ('lɪknɪs) NOUN any caryophyllaceous plant of the genus *Lychnis*, having red, pink, or white five-petalled flowers. See also **ragged robin**.
▷HISTORY C17: New Latin, via Latin, from Greek *lukhnis* a red flower; related to *lukhnos* lamp

Lycia ('lɪsɪə) NOUN an ancient region on the coast of SW Asia Minor: a Persian, Rhodian, and Roman province.

Lycian ('lɪsɪən) ADJECTIVE **1** of or relating to ancient Lycia, its inhabitants, or their language. ◆ NOUN **2** an inhabitant of Lycia. **3** the extinct language of the Lycians, belonging to the Anatolian group or family.

lycopene ('laɪkəˌpiːn) NOUN an acyclic carotenoid occuring in tomatoes and some other ripe fruit as a red pigment. As an antioxidant its consumption can reduce the risk of some cancers.

lycopod ('laɪkəˌpɒd) NOUN another name for a **club moss**, esp one of the genus *Lycopodium*

lycopodium (ˌlaɪkə'pəʊdɪəm) NOUN any club moss of the genus *Lycopodium*, resembling moss but having vascular tissue and spore-bearing cones: family *Lycopodiaceae*. See also **ground pine** (sense 2).
▷HISTORY C18: New Latin, from Greek, from *lukos* wolf + *pous* foot

Lycra ('laɪkrə) NOUN *Trademark* a type of synthetic elastic fabric and fibre used for tight-fitting garments, such as swimming costumes.

Lydda ('lɪdə) NOUN another name for **Lod**.

lyddite ('lɪdaɪt) NOUN **1** an explosive consisting chiefly of fused picric acid. **2** a dense black variety of chert, formerly used as a touchstone.
▷HISTORY C19: (sense 1) named after *Lydd*, a town in Kent near which the first tests were made

Lydia ('lɪdɪə) NOUN an ancient region on the coast of W Asia Minor: a powerful kingdom in the century and a half before the Persian conquest (546 B.C.). Chief town: Sardis.

Lydian ('lɪdɪən) ADJECTIVE **1** of or relating to ancient Lydia, its inhabitants, or their language. **2** *Music* of or relating to an authentic mode represented by the ascending natural diatonic scale from F to F. See also **Hypo-**. Compare **Hypolydian**. ◆ NOUN **3** an inhabitant of Lydia. **4** the extinct language of the Lydians, thought to belong to the Anatolian group or family.

lye (laɪ) NOUN **1** any solution obtained by leaching, such as the caustic solution obtained by leaching wood ash. **2** a concentrated solution of sodium hydroxide or potassium hydroxide.
▷HISTORY Old English *lēag*; related to Middle Dutch *lōghe*, Old Norse *laug* bath, Latin *lavāre* to wash

lying[1] ('laɪɪŋ) VERB the present participle and gerund of **lie**[1].

lying[2] ('laɪɪŋ) VERB the present participle and gerund of **lie**[2].

lying-in NOUN, *plural* **lyings-in**. **a** confinement in childbirth. **b** (*as modifier*): *a lying-in hospital*.

lyke-wake ('laɪkˌweɪk) NOUN *Brit* a watch held over a dead person, often with festivities.
▷HISTORY C16: perhaps from Old Norse; see LYCH GATE, WAKE[1]

Lyme disease (laɪm) NOUN a disease of domestic animals and humans, caused by the spirochaete *Borrelia burghdorferi* and transmitted by ticks, and variously affecting the joints, heart, and brain.
▷HISTORY C20: named after *Lyme*, Connecticut, the town where it was first identified in humans

lyme grass (laɪm) NOUN a N temperate perennial dune grass, *Elymus arenarius*, with a creeping stem and rough bluish leaves.
▷HISTORY C18: probably a respelling (influenced by its genus name, *Elymus*) of LIME[1], referring to its stabilizing effect (like lime in mortar)

Lyme Regis (laɪm 'riːdʒɪs) NOUN a resort in S England, in Dorset, on the English Channel: noted for finds of prehistoric fossils. Pop.: 3851 (1991).

Lymington ('lɪmɪŋtən) NOUN a market town in S England, in SW Hampshire, on the Solent: yachting centre and holiday resort. Pop.: 13 508 (1991).

lymph (lɪmf) NOUN the almost colourless fluid, containing chiefly white blood cells, that is collected from the tissues of the body and transported in the lymphatic system.
▷HISTORY C17: from Latin *lympha* water, from earlier *limpa* influenced in form by Greek *numphē* nymph

lymphadenitis (lɪmˌfædɪ'naɪtɪs, ˌlɪmfæd-) NOUN inflammation of a lymph node.
▷HISTORY C19: New Latin. See LYMPH, ADENITIS

lymphadenopathy (lɪmˌfædɪ'nɒpəθɪ, ˌlɪmfæd-) NOUN a swelling of the lymph nodes, usually caused by inflammation associated with a viral infection such as rubella.

lymphangial (lɪm'fændʒɪəl) ADJECTIVE of or relating to a lymphatic vessel.

lymphangitis (ˌlɪmfæn'dʒaɪtɪs) NOUN, *plural* **-gitides** (-'dʒɪtɪˌdiːz). inflammation of one or more of the lymphatic vessels.
▷HISTORY C19: see LYMPH, ANGIO-, -ITIS
▸**lymphangitic** (ˌlɪmfæn'dʒɪtɪk) ADJECTIVE

lymphatic (lɪm'fætɪk) ADJECTIVE **1** of, relating to, or containing lymph: *the lymphatic vessels*. **2** of or relating to the lymphatic system. **3** sluggish or lacking vigour. ◆ NOUN **4** a lymphatic vessel.
▷HISTORY C17 (meaning: mad): from Latin *lymphāticus*. Original meaning perhaps arose from a confusion between *nymph* and LYMPH; compare Greek *numphaleptos* frenzied
▸**lym'phatically** ADVERB

lymphatic system NOUN an extensive network of capillary vessels that transports the interstitial fluid of the body as lymph to the venous blood circulation.

lymphatic tissue NOUN tissue, such as the lymph nodes, tonsils, spleen, and thymus, that produces lymphocytes. Also called: **lymphoid tissue**.

lymph cell NOUN another name for **lymphocyte**.

lymph gland NOUN a former name for **lymph node**.

lymph node NOUN any of numerous bean-shaped masses of tissue, situated along the course of lymphatic vessels, that help to protect against infection by killing bacteria and neutralizing toxins and are the source of lymphocytes.

lympho- *or before a vowel* **lymph-** COMBINING FORM indicating lymph or the lymphatic system: *lymphogranuloma.*

lymphoblast ('lɪmfəʊˌblɑːst) NOUN an abnormal cell consisting of a large nucleus and small cytoplasm that was once thought to be an immature lymphocyte and is now associated with a type of leukaemia (**lymphoblastic leukaemia**).
▸**lymphoblastic** (ˌlɪmfəʊ'blæstɪk) ADJECTIVE

lymphocyte ('lɪmfəʊˌsaɪt) NOUN a type of white blood cell formed in lymphoid tissue. See also **B-lymphocyte, T-lymphocyte.**
▸**lymphocytic** (ˌlɪmfəʊ'sɪtɪk) ADJECTIVE

lymphocytopenia (ˌlɪmfəʊˌsaɪtəʊ'piːnɪə) NOUN *Pathol* an abnormally low level of lymphocytes in the blood. Also called: **lymphopenia.**

lymphocytosis (ˌlɪmfəʊsaɪ'təʊsɪs) NOUN an abnormally large number of lymphocytes in the blood: often found in diseases such as glandular fever and smallpox.
▸**lymphocytotic** (ˌlɪmfəʊsaɪ'tɒtɪk) ADJECTIVE

lymphoid ('lɪmfɔɪd) ADJECTIVE of or resembling lymph, or relating to the lymphatic system.

lymphoid tissue NOUN another name for **lymphatic tissue.**

lymphokine ('lɪmfəʊˌkaɪn) NOUN *Immunol* a protein, released by lymphocytes, that affects other cells involved in the immune response.

lymphoma (lɪm'fəʊmə) NOUN, *plural* **-mata** (-mətə) *or* **-mas.** any form of cancer of the lymph nodes. Also called: **lymphosarcoma** (ˌlɪmfəʊsɑː'kəʊmə).
▸**lym'phomatous** *or* **lym'phomaˌtoid** ADJECTIVE

lymphopoiesis (ˌlɪmfəʊpɔɪ'iːsɪs) NOUN, *plural* **-ses** (-siːz). the formation of lymphatic tissue or lymphocytes.
▸**lymphopoietic** (ˌlɪmfəʊpɔɪ'ɛtɪk) ADJECTIVE

lyncean (lɪn'siːən) ADJECTIVE [1] of or resembling a lynx. [2] *Rare* having keen sight.
▹HISTORY C17: probably via Latin, from Greek *Lunkeios* concerning *Lunkeos,* an Argonaut renowned for his sharpsightedness, from *lunx* lynx

lynch (lɪntʃ) VERB *(tr)* (of a mob) to punish (a person) for some supposed offence by hanging without a trial.
▹HISTORY probably after Charles *Lynch* (1736–96), Virginia justice of the peace, who presided over extralegal trials of Tories during the American War of Independence
▸**'lyncher** NOUN ▸**'lynching** NOUN

lynchet ('lɪntʃɪt) NOUN a terrace or ridge formed in prehistoric or medieval times by ploughing a hillside.
▹HISTORY Old English *hlinc* ridge

lynch law NOUN the practice of condemning and punishing a person by mob action without a proper trial.

Lynn (lɪn) NOUN another name for **King's Lynn.** Also called: **Lynn Regis** ('riːdʒɪs).

lynx (lɪŋks) NOUN, *plural* **lynxes** *or* **lynx.** [1] a feline mammal, *Felis lynx* (or *canadensis*), of Europe and North America, with grey-brown mottled fur, tufted ears, and a short tail. Related adjective: **lyncean.** [2] the fur of this animal. [3] **bay lynx.** another name for **bobcat.** [4] **desert lynx.** another name for **caracal.** [5] Also called: **Polish lynx.** a large fancy pigeon from Poland, with spangled or laced markings.
▹HISTORY C14: via Latin from Greek *lunx;* related to Old English *lox,* German *Luchs*
▸**'lynxˌlike** ADJECTIVE

Lynx (lɪŋks) NOUN, *Latin genitive* **Lyncis** ('lɪnsɪs). a faint constellation in the N hemisphere lying between Ursa Major and Cancer.

lynx-eyed ADJECTIVE having keen sight.

lyo- COMBINING FORM indicating dispersion or dissolution: *lyophilic; lyophilize; lyophobic.*
▹HISTORY from Greek *luein* to loose

lyolysis (laɪ'ɒlɪsɪs) NOUN *Chem* the formation of an acid and a base from the interaction of a salt with a solvent.

Lyon (*French* ljɔ̃) NOUN a city in SE central France, capital of Rhône department, at the confluence of the Rivers Rhône and Saône: the third largest city in France; a major industrial centre and river port. Pop.: 445 257 (1999). English name: **Lyons** ('laɪənz). Ancient name: **Lugdunum** (lʊg'duːnəm).

Lyon King of Arms ('laɪən) NOUN the chief herald of Scotland. Also called: **Lord Lyon.**
▹HISTORY C14: archaic spelling of LION, referring to the figure on the royal shield

Lyonnais (*French* ljɔnɛ) NOUN a former province of E central France, on the Rivers Rhône and Saône: occupied by the present-day departments of Rhône and Loire. Chief town: Lyon.

lyonnaise (ˌlaɪə'neɪz; *French* ljɔnɛz) ADJECTIVE (of food) cooked or garnished with onions, usually fried.

Lyonnesse (ˌlaɪə'nɛs) NOUN (in Arthurian legend) the mythical birthplace of Sir Tristram, situated in SW England and believed to have been submerged by the sea.

lyophilic (ˌlaɪəʊ'fɪlɪk) ADJECTIVE *Chem* (of a colloid) having a dispersed phase with a high affinity for the continuous phase: *a lyophilic sol.* Compare **lyophobic.**

lyophilize *or* **lyophilise** (laɪ'ɒfɪˌlaɪz) VERB *(tr)* to dry (blood, serum, tissue, etc.) by freezing in a high vacuum; freeze dry.

lyophobic (ˌlaɪəʊ'fəʊbɪk) ADJECTIVE *Chem* (of a colloid) having a dispersed phase with little or no affinity for the continuous phase: *a lyophobic sol.* Compare **lyophilic.**

lyosorption (ˌlaɪəʊ'sɔːpʃən) NOUN *Chem* the adsorption of a liquid on a solid surface, esp of a solvent on suspended particles.

Lyra ('laɪərə) NOUN, *Latin genitive* **Lyrae** ('laɪəriː). a small constellation in the N hemisphere lying near Cygnus and Draco and containing the star Vega, an eclipsing binary (**Beta Lyrae**), a planetary nebula (the **Ring Nebula**), and a variable star, **RR Lyrae.**

lyrate ('laɪərɪt) *or* **lyrated** ADJECTIVE [1] shaped like a lyre. [2] (of leaves) having a large terminal lobe and smaller lateral lobes.
▹HISTORY C18: from New Latin *lyrātus,* Latin from *lyra* LYRE
▸**'lyrately** ADVERB

lyra viol ('lɑɪərə) NOUN a lutelike musical instrument popular in the 16th and 17th centuries: the forerunner of the mandolin.

lyre (laɪə) NOUN [1] an ancient Greek stringed instrument consisting of a resonating tortoise shell to which a crossbar was attached by two projecting arms. It was plucked with a plectrum and used for accompanying songs. [2] any ancient instrument of similar design. [3] a medieval bowed instrument of the violin family.
▹HISTORY C13: via Old French from Latin *lyra,* from Greek *lura*

lyrebird ('laɪəˌbɜːd) NOUN either of two pheasant-like Australian birds, *Menura superba* and *M. alberti,* constituting the family *Menuridae:* during courtship displays, the male spreads its tail into the shape of a lyre.

lyric ('lɪrɪk) ADJECTIVE [1] (of poetry) **a** expressing the writer's personal feelings and thoughts. **b** having the form and manner of a song. [2] of or relating to such poetry. [3] (of a singing voice) having a light quality and tone. [4] intended for singing, esp (in classical Greece) to the accompaniment of the lyre. ◆ NOUN [5] a short poem of songlike quality. [6] *(plural)* the words of a popular song. ◆ Also (for senses 1–3): **lyrical.**
▹HISTORY C16: from Latin *lyricus,* from Greek *lurikos,* from *lura* LYRE
▸**'lyrically** ADVERB ▸**'lyricalness** NOUN

lyrical ('lɪrɪkᵊl) ADJECTIVE [1] another word for **lyric** (senses 1–3). [2] enthusiastic; effusive (esp in the phrase **to wax lyrical**).

lyricism ('lɪrɪˌsɪzəm) NOUN [1] the quality or style of lyric poetry. [2] emotional or enthusiastic outpouring.

lyricist ('lɪrɪsɪst) NOUN [1] a person who writes the words for a song, opera, or musical play. [2] Also called: **lyrist.** a lyric poet.

lyrism ('lɪrɪzəm) NOUN [1] the art or technique of playing the lyre. [2] a less common word for **lyricism.**

lyrist NOUN [1] ('laɪərɪst) a person who plays the lyre. [2] ('lɪrɪst) another word for **lyricist** (sense 2).

lys- COMBINING FORM a variant of **lyso-** before a vowel.

lyse (laɪs, laɪz) VERB to undergo or cause to undergo lysis.

Lysenkoism (lɪ'sɛŋkəʊˌɪzəm) NOUN a form of Neo-Lamarckism advocated by Trofim Denisovich Lysenko, the Russian biologist and geneticist (1898–1976), emphasizing the importance of the inheritance of acquired characteristics.

lysergic acid (lɪ'sɜːdʒɪk, laɪ-) NOUN a crystalline compound with a polycyclic molecular structure: used in medical research. Formula $C_{16}H_{16}N_2O_2$.
▹HISTORY C20: from (HYDRO)LYS(IS) + ERG(OT) + -IC

lysergic acid diethylamide (daɪˌɛθɪl'eɪmaɪd, -ˌiːθaɪl-) NOUN See **LSD.**

lysimeter (laɪ'sɪmɪtə) NOUN an instrument for determining solubility, esp the amount of water-soluble matter in soil.
▹HISTORY C20: from *lysi-* (variant of LYSO-) + -METER

lysin ('laɪsɪn) NOUN any of a group of antibodies or other agents that cause dissolution of cells against which they are directed.

lysine ('laɪsiːn, -sɪn) NOUN an essential amino acid that occurs in proteins.

lysis ('laɪsɪs) NOUN, *plural* **-ses** (-siːz). [1] the destruction or dissolution of cells by the action of a particular lysin. [2] *Med* the gradual reduction in severity of the symptoms of a disease.
▹HISTORY C19: New Latin, from Greek, from *luein* to release

-lysis NOUN COMBINING FORM indicating a loosening, decomposition, or breaking down: *electrolysis; paralysis.*
▹HISTORY from Greek, from *lusis* a loosening; see LYSIS

Lysithea (laɪ'sɪθɪə) NOUN *Astronomy* a small satellite of Jupiter in an intermediate orbit.

lyso- *or before a vowel* **lys-** COMBINING FORM indicating a dissolving or loosening: *lysozyme.*
▹HISTORY from Greek *lusis* a loosening

lysogeny (laɪ'sɒdʒənɪ) NOUN the biological process in which a bacterium is infected by a bacteriophage that integrates its DNA into that of the host such that the host is not destroyed.
▸**lysogenic** (ˌlaɪsəʊ'dʒɛnɪk) ADJECTIVE

Lysol ('laɪsɒl) NOUN *Trademark* a solution containing a mixture of cresols in water, used as an antiseptic and disinfectant.

lysosome ('laɪsəˌsəʊm) NOUN any of numerous small particles, containing digestive enzymes, that are present in the cytoplasm of most cells.
▸**ˌlyso'somal** ADJECTIVE

lysozyme ('laɪsəˌzaɪm) NOUN an enzyme occurring in tears, certain body tissues, and egg white: destroys bacteria by hydrolysing polysaccharides in their cell walls.
▹HISTORY C20: from LYSO- + (EN)ZYME

lyssa ('lɪsə) NOUN *Pathol* a less common word for **rabies.**

-lyte NOUN COMBINING FORM indicating a substance that can be decomposed or broken down: *electrolyte.*
▹HISTORY from Greek *lutos* soluble, from *luein* to loose

Lytham Saint Anne's ('lɪðəm sənt 'ænz) NOUN, *usually abbreviated to* **Lytham St Anne's.** a resort in NW England, in Lancashire on the Irish Sea. Pop.: 40 866 (1991).

lythraceous (lɪ'θreɪʃəs, laɪ'θreɪ-) ADJECTIVE of, relating to, or belonging to the *Lythraceae,* a mostly tropical American family of herbaceous plants, shrubs, and trees that includes purple loosestrife and crape myrtle.
▹HISTORY C19: from New Latin *Lythrum* type genus, from Greek *luthron* blood, from the red flowers

lytic ('lɪtɪk) ADJECTIVE [1] relating to, causing, or resulting from lysis. [2] of or relating to a lysin.
▹HISTORY C19: Greek *lutikos* capable of loosing

-lytic ADJECTIVE COMBINING FORM indicating a loosening or dissolving: *paralytic.*
▹HISTORY from Greek, from *lusis;* see -LYSIS

lytta ('lɪtə) NOUN, *plural* **-tas** *or* **-tae** (-tiː). a rodlike mass of cartilage beneath the tongue in the dog and other carnivores.
▹HISTORY C17: New Latin, from Greek *lussa* madness; in dogs, it was believed to be a cause of rabies

Lyublin ('ljublɪn) NOUN transliteration of the Russian name for **Lublin.**

Mm

m *or* **M** (ɛm) NOUN, *plural* **m's, M's** *or* **Ms.** [1] the 13th letter and tenth consonant of the modern English alphabet. [2] a speech sound represented by this letter, usually a bilabial nasal, as in *mat.*

m SYMBOL FOR: [1] metre(s). [2] mile(s). [3] milli-. [4] minute(s).

M SYMBOL FOR: [1] mach. [2] medium (size). [3] mega-. [4] *Currency* mark(s). [5] million. [6] *Astronomy* Messier catalogue; a catalogue published in 1784, in which 103 nebulae and clusters are listed using a numerical system: *M13 is the globular cluster in Hercules.* [7] Middle. [8] *Physics* modulus. [9] (in Britain) motorway: *the M1 runs from London to Leeds.* [10] (in Australia) **a** mature audience (used to describe a category of film certified as suitable for viewing by anyone over the age of 15). **b** (*as modifier*): *an M film.* [11] *Logic* the middle term of a syllogism. [12] *Physics* mutual inductance. [13] *Chem* molar. ◆ [14] THE ROMAN NUMERAL FOR 1000. See **Roman numerals.** ◆ [15] INTERNATIONAL CAR REGISTRATION FOR Malta.

M8 *Text messaging* ABBREVIATION FOR mate.

m. ABBREVIATION FOR: [1] *Cricket* maiden (over). [2] male. [3] mare. [4] married. [5] masculine.

M. ABBREVIATION FOR: [1] Majesty. [2] (in titles) Member. [3] million. [4] (*plural* **MM.** *or* **MM**) Also: **M** (*French*) Monsieur. [French equivalent of *Mr*] [5] mountain.

m- PREFIX short for **meta-** (sense 4).

M'- PREFIX a variant of **Mac-**.

'm CONTRACTION OF: [1] (*verb*) am. [2] (*noun*) madam: *yes'm.*

M0 SYMBOL FOR the amount of money in circulation in notes and coin, plus the banks' till money and the banks' balances at the Bank of England. Informal name: **narrow money.**

M1 SYMBOL FOR the amount of money in circulation in notes, coin, current accounts, and deposit accounts transferable by cheque.

M-1 rifle NOUN a semiautomatic .30 calibre rifle: the basic infantry weapon of the US Army in World War II and the Korean War. Also called: **Garand rifle.**

M2 SYMBOL FOR the amount of money in circulation in notes and coin plus non-interest-bearing bank deposits, building-society deposits, and National Savings accounts.

M3 SYMBOL FOR the amount of money in circulation given by M1 plus all private-sector bank deposits and certificates of deposit. Former symbol: £M3 (sterling M3).

M3c SYMBOL FOR the amount of money in circulation given by M3 plus foreign currency bank deposits. Former symbol: M3. Informal name: **broad money.**

M4 SYMBOL FOR the amount of money in circulation given by M1 plus most private-sector bank deposits and holdings of money-market instruments. Also called: **PSL1.**

M5 SYMBOL FOR the amount of money in circulation given by M4 plus building-society deposits. Also called: **PSL2.**

ma[1] (mɑː) NOUN an informal word for **mother**[1].

ma[2] THE INTERNET DOMAIN NAME FOR Morocco.

MA ABBREVIATION FOR: [1] Massachusetts. [2] Master of Arts. [3] *Psychol* **mental age.** [4] Military Academy. ◆ [5] INTERNATIONAL CAR REGISTRATION FOR Morocco.
▷**HISTORY** (for sense 5) from French *Maroc*

ma'am (mæm, mɑːm; *unstressed* məm) NOUN short for **madam**: used as a title of respect, esp for female royalty.

maar (mɑː) NOUN, *plural* **maars** *or* **maare** (ˈmɑːrə). (*sometimes capital*) a coneless volcanic crater that has been formed by a single explosion.
▷**HISTORY** C19: from German

Maarianhamina (ˈmɑːrianhɑminɑ) NOUN the Finnish name for **Mariehamn.**

Ma'ariv *Hebrew* (mɑɑˈriv; *Yiddish* ˈmɑriv) NOUN *Judaism* the evening service.

maas (mɑːs) NOUN *South African* thick soured milk.
▷**HISTORY** from Nguni *amasi* milk

Maas (mɑːs) NOUN the Dutch name for the **Meuse.**

Maastricht *or* **Maestricht** (ˈmɑːstrɪxt; *Dutch* maːˈstrɪxt) NOUN a city in the SE Netherlands near the Belgian and German borders: capital of Limburg province, on the River Maas (Meuse); a European Community treaty (**Maastricht Treaty**) was signed here in 1992, setting out the terms for the creation of the European Union. Pop.: 121 479 (1999 est.).

Mab (mæb) NOUN (in English and Irish folklore) a fairy queen said to create and control men's dreams.

mabela (mɑːˈbɛlə) NOUN *South African* ground kaffir corn used for making porridge.
▷**HISTORY** from Zulu *amabele* kaffir corn

Mabinogion (ˌmæbɪˈnɒgɪən) NOUN **the.** a collection of Welsh tales based on old Celtic legends and mythology in which magic and the supernatural play a large part.
▷**HISTORY** from Welsh *mabinogi* instruction for young bards

mac *or* **mack** (mæk) NOUN *Brit informal* short for **mackintosh** (senses 1, 3).

Mac (mæk) NOUN *Chiefly US and Canadian* an informal term of address to a man.
▷**HISTORY** C20: abstracted from MAC-, prefix of Scottish surnames

MAC ABBREVIATION FOR multiplexed analogue component: a transmission coding system for colour television using satellite broadcasting.

Mac. ABBREVIATION FOR Maccabees (books of the Apocrypha).

Mac-, Mc-, *or* **M'-** PREFIX (in surnames of Scottish or Irish Gaelic origin) son of: *MacDonald; MacNeice.*
▷**HISTORY** from Goidelic *mac* son of; compare Welsh *mab,* Cornish *mab*

macabre (məˈkɑːbə, -brə) ADJECTIVE [1] gruesome; ghastly; grim. [2] resembling or associated with the danse macabre.
▷**HISTORY** C15: from Old French *danse macabre* dance of death, probably from *macabé* relating to the Maccabees, who were associated with death because of the doctrines and prayers for the dead in II Macc. (12:43–46)
▸**maˈcabrely** ADVERB

macaco (məˈkɑːkəʊ, -ˈkeɪ-) NOUN, *plural* **-cos.** any of various lemurs, esp *Lemur macaco,* the males of which are usually black and the females brown.
▷**HISTORY** C18: from French *mococo,* of unknown origin

macadam (məˈkædəm) NOUN a road surface made of compressed layers of small broken stones, esp one that is bound together with tar or asphalt.
▷**HISTORY** C19: named after John *McAdam* (1756–1836), Scottish engineer, the inventor

macadamia (ˌmækəˈdeɪmɪə) NOUN [1] any tree of the Australian proteaceous genus *Macadamia,* esp *M. ternifolia,* having clusters of small white flowers and edible nutlike seeds. [2] **macadamia nut.** the seed of this tree.
▷**HISTORY** C19: New Latin, named after John *Macadam* (1827–65), Australian chemist

macadamize *or* **macadamise** (məˈkædəˌmaɪz) VERB (*tr*) to construct or surface (a road) with macadam.
▸**macˌadamiˈzation** *or* **macˌadamiˈsation** NOUN
▸**macˈadamˌizer** *or* **macˈadamˌiser** NOUN

Macao (məˈkaʊ) NOUN a special administrative region of S China, across the estuary of the Zhu Jiang from Hong Kong: chief centre of European trade with China in the 18th century; attained partial autonomy in 1976; formerly (until 1999) a Portuguese overseas province; transit trade with China; tourism and financial services. Pop.: 445 000 (2001 est.). Area: 16 sq. km (6 sq. miles). Portuguese name: **Macáu.**

Macapá (*Portuguese* makaˈpa) NOUN a town in NE Brazil, capital of the federal territory of Amapá, on the Canal do Norte of the Amazon delta. Pop. (urban area): 270 077 (2000).

macaque (məˈkɑːk) NOUN any of various Old World monkeys of the genus *Macaca,* inhabiting wooded or rocky regions of Asia and Africa. Typically the tail is short or absent and cheek pouches are present.
▷**HISTORY** C17: from French, from Portuguese *macaco,* from Fiot (a W African language) *makaku,* from *kaku* monkey

macaroni *or* **maccaroni** (ˌmækəˈrəʊnɪ) NOUN, *plural* **-nis** *or* **-nies.** [1] pasta tubes made from wheat flour. [2] (in 18th-century Britain) a dandy who affected foreign manners and style.
▷**HISTORY** C16: from Italian (Neapolitan dialect) *maccarone,* probably from Greek *makaria* food made from barley

macaronic (ˌmækəˈrɒnɪk) ADJECTIVE [1] (of verse) characterized by a mixture of vernacular words jumbled together with Latin words or Latinized words or with words from one or more other foreign languages. ◆ NOUN [2] (*often plural*) macaronic verse.
▷**HISTORY** C17: from New Latin *macarōnicus,* literally: resembling macaroni (in lack of sophistication); see MACARONI
▸**ˌmacaˈronically** ADVERB

macaroni cheese NOUN a dish of macaroni with a cheese sauce.

macaroon (ˌmækəˈruːn) NOUN a kind of sweet biscuit made of ground almonds, sugar, and egg whites.
▷**HISTORY** C17: via French *macaron* from Italian *maccarone* MACARONI

Macassar (məˈkæsə) NOUN a variant spelling of **Makasar.**

Macassar oil NOUN an oily preparation formerly put on the hair to make it smooth and shiny.
▷**HISTORY** C19: so called because its ingredients were originally claimed to have come from MAKASAR

Macáu (məˈkau) NOUN the Portuguese name for **Macao.**

macaw (məˈkɔː) NOUN any large tropical American parrot of the genera *Ara* and *Anodorhynchus,* having a long tail and brilliant plumage.
▷**HISTORY** C17: from Portuguese *macau,* of unknown origin

Macc. ABBREVIATION FOR Maccabees (books of the Apocrypha).

Maccabean (ˌmækəˈbiːən) ADJECTIVE of or relating to the Maccabees or to Judas Maccabaeus, the Jewish leader of a revolt (166–161 B.C.) against Seleucid oppression.

Maccabees (ˈmækəˌbiːz) NOUN any of four books of Jewish history, including the last two of the Apocrypha.
▷**HISTORY** from the *Maccabees,* a Jewish family of patriots who freed Judaea from Seleucid oppression (168–142 B.C.)

maccaboy, maccoboy (ˈmækəˌbɔɪ), *or* **maccabaw** (ˈmækəˌbɔː) NOUN a dark rose-scented snuff.
▷**HISTORY** C18: from French *macouba,* from the name of the district of Martinique where it is made

maccaroni (ˌmækəˈrəʊnɪ) NOUN, *plural* **-nis** *or* **-nies.** a variant spelling of **macaroni.**

McCarthyism (məˈkɑːθɪˌɪzəm) NOUN *Chiefly US* [1] the practice of making unsubstantiated accusations of disloyalty or Communist leanings. [2] the use of unsupported accusations for any purpose.
▷**HISTORY** C20: after Joseph Raymond *McCarthy* (1908–57), US Republican senator, who led (1950–54) the notorious investigations of alleged Communist infiltration into the US government

▸**Mc'Carthyite** NOUN, ADJECTIVE

macchiato (ˌmækɪ'ɑːtəʊ) NOUN, *plural* **-tos.** espresso coffee served with a dash of hot or cold milk.
▷HISTORY Italian, literally: stained

Macclesfield ('mækᵊlzˌfiːld) NOUN a market town in NW England, in Cheshire: former centre of the silk industry; pharmaceuticals, services. Pop.: 50 270 (1991).

McCoy (mə'kɔɪ) NOUN *Slang* the genuine person or thing (esp in the phrase **the real McCoy**).
▷HISTORY C20: perhaps after Kid *McCoy,* professional name of Norman Selby (1873–1940), American boxer, who was called "the real McCoy" to distinguish him from another boxer of that name

Macdonnell Ranges (mək'dɒnəl) PLURAL NOUN a mountain system of central Australia, in S central Northern Territory, extending about 160 km (100 miles) east and west of Alice Springs. Highest peak: Mount Ziel, 1510 m (4955 ft.).

mace[1] (meɪs) NOUN 1 a club, usually having a spiked metal head, used esp in the Middle Ages. 2 a ceremonial staff of office carried by certain officials. 3 See **macebearer.** 4 an early form of billiard cue.
▷HISTORY C13: from Old French, probably from Vulgar Latin *mattea* (unattested); apparently related to Latin *mateola* mallet

mace[2] (meɪs) NOUN a spice made from the dried aril round the nutmeg seed.
▷HISTORY C14: formed as a singular from Old French *macis* (wrongly assumed to be plural), from Latin *macir* an oriental spice

Mace (meɪs) *US* ◆ NOUN 1 *Trademark* a liquid causing tears and nausea, used as a spray for riot control, etc. ◆ VERB 2 *(tr; sometimes not capital)* to use Mace on.

macebearer ('meɪsˌbɛərə) NOUN a person who carries a mace in processions or ceremonies.

Maced. ABBREVIATION FOR Macedonia(n).

macedoine (ˌmæsɪ'dwɑːn) NOUN 1 a hot or cold mixture of diced vegetables. 2 a mixture of fruit served in a syrup or in jelly. 3 any mixture; medley.
▷HISTORY C19: from French, literally: Macedonian, alluding to the mixture of nationalities in Macedonia

Macedon ('mæsɪˌdɒn) *or* **Macedonia** NOUN a region of the S Balkans, now divided among Greece, Bulgaria, and Macedonia (Former Yugoslav Republic of Macedonia). As a kingdom in the ancient world it achieved prominence under Philip II (359–336 B.C.) and his son Alexander the Great.

Macedonia (ˌmæsɪ'dəʊnɪə) NOUN 1 a country in SE Europe, comprising the NW half of ancient Macedon: it became part of the kingdom of Serbs, Croats, and Slovenes (subsequently Yugoslavia) in 1913; it declared independence in 1992, but Greece objected to the use of the historical name Macedonia; in 1993 it was recognized by the UN under its current official name. Official language: Macedonian. Religion: Christian majority, Muslim, nonreligious, and Jewish minorities. Currency: denar. Capital: Skopje. Pop.: 2 046 000 (2001 est.). Area: 25 713 sq. km (10 028 sq. miles). Serbian name: **Makedonija.** Official name: **Former Yugoslav Republic of Macedonia** (FYROM). 2 an area of N Greece, comprising the regions of Macedonia Central, Macedonia West, and part of Macedonia East and Thrace. Modern Greek name: **Makedhonia.** 3 a district of SW Bulgaria, now occupied by Blagoevgrad province. Area: 6465 sq. km (2496 sq. miles).

Macedonian (ˌmæsɪ'dəʊnɪən) ADJECTIVE 1 of or relating to Macedonia, its inhabitants, or any of their languages or dialects. ◆ NOUN 2 a native or inhabitant of Macedonia. 3 the language of the Former Yugoslav Republic of Macedonia, belonging to the south Slavonic branch of the Indo-European family. 4 an extinct language spoken in ancient Macedonia.

Maceió (mase'jɔ) NOUN a port in NE Brazil, capital of Alagôas state, on the Atlantic. Pop.: 794 894 (2000).

macer ('meɪsə) NOUN a macebearer, esp (in Scotland) an official who acts as usher in a court of law.
▷HISTORY C14: from Old French *massier,* from *masse* MACE[1]

maceral ('mæsərəl) NOUN *Geology* any of the organic units that constitute coal: equivalent to any of the mineral constituents of a rock.
▷HISTORY C20: from Latin *mācerāre* to MACERATE

macerate ('mæsəˌreɪt) VERB 1 to soften or separate or be softened or separated as a result of soaking. 2 to break up or cause to break up by soaking: *macerated peaches.* 3 to become or cause to become thin.
▷HISTORY C16: from Latin *mācerāre* to soften
▸'**macerˌater** *or* '**macerˌator** NOUN ▸'**macerative** ADJECTIVE ▸ˌ**macer'ation** NOUN

Macgillicuddy's Reeks (məˌgɪlɪˌkʌdɪz 'riːks) PLURAL NOUN a range of mountains in SW Republic of Ireland in Kerry: includes Ireland's highest mountain (Carrantuohill).

MacGuffin (mə'gʌfɪn) NOUN an object or event in a book or a film that serves as the impetus for the plot.
▷HISTORY C20: coined (c. 1935) by Sir Alfred Joseph Hitchcock (1899–1980), English film director

Mach (mæk) NOUN short for **Mach number.**

machair ('mæxər) NOUN *Scot* (in the western Highlands of Scotland) a strip of sandy, grassy, often lime-rich land just above the high-water mark at a sandy shore: used as grazing or arable land.
▷HISTORY C17: from Scottish Gaelic

machan (mə'tʃɑːn) NOUN (in India) a raised platform used in tiger hunting.
▷HISTORY C19: from Hindi

macher *Yiddish* ('mɑxər) NOUN an important or influential person: often used ironically.
▷HISTORY Yiddish, from German, literally: doer

machete (mə'ʃɛtɪ, -'tʃeɪ-) *or* **matchet** NOUN a broad heavy knife used for cutting or as a weapon, esp in parts of Central and South America.
▷HISTORY C16 *macheto,* from Spanish *machete,* from *macho* club, perhaps from Vulgar Latin *mattea* (unattested) club

Machiavellian *or* **Machiavelian** (ˌmækɪə'vɛlɪən) ADJECTIVE *(sometimes not capital)* 1 of or relating to the alleged political principles of Niccolò Machiavelli (1469–1527), Florentine statesman and political philosopher; cunning, amoral, and opportunist. ◆ NOUN 2 a cunning, amoral, and opportunist person, esp a politician.
▸ˌ**Machia'vellianism** *or* ˌ**Machia'vellism** NOUN
▸ˌ**Machia'vellist** ADJECTIVE, NOUN

machicolate (mə'tʃɪkəʊˌleɪt) VERB *(tr)* to construct machicolations at the top of (a wall).
▷HISTORY C18: from Old French *machicoller,* ultimately from Provençal *machacol,* from *macar* to crush + *col* neck

machicolation (məˌtʃɪkəʊ'leɪʃən) NOUN 1 (esp in medieval castles) a projecting gallery or parapet supported on corbels having openings through which missiles could be dropped. 2 any such opening.

machinate ('mækɪˌneɪt, 'mæʃ-) VERB *(usually tr)* to contrive, plan, or devise (schemes, plots, etc.).
▷HISTORY C17: from Latin *māchinārī* to plan, from *māchina* MACHINE
▸'**machiˌnator** NOUN

machination (ˌmækɪ'neɪʃən, ˌmæʃ-) NOUN 1 an intrigue, plot, or scheme. 2 the act of devising plots or schemes.

machine (mə'ʃiːn) NOUN 1 an assembly of interconnected components arranged to transmit or modify force in order to perform useful work. 2 Also called: **simple machine.** a device for altering the magnitude or direction of a force, esp a lever, screw, wedge, or pulley. 3 a mechanically operated device or means of transport, such as a car, aircraft, etc. 4 any mechanical or electrical device that automatically performs tasks or assists in performing tasks. 5 **a** *(modifier)* denoting a firearm that is fully automatic as distinguished from semiautomatic. **b** *(in combination)*: *machine pistol; machine gun.* 6 any intricate structure or agency: *the war machine.* 7 a mechanically efficient, rigid, or obedient person. 8 an organized body of people that controls activities, policies, etc. 9 (esp in the classical theatre) a device such as a pulley to provide spectacular entrances and exits for supernatural characters. 10 an event, etc., introduced into a literary work for special effect. ◆ VERB 11 *(tr)* to shape, cut, or remove (excess material) from (a workpiece) using a machine tool. 12 to use a machine to carry out a process on (something).
▷HISTORY C16: via French from Latin *māchina* machine, engine, from Doric Greek *makhana* pulley; related to *makhos* device, contrivance
▸**ma'chinable** *or* **ma'chineable** ADJECTIVE ▸**maˌchina'bility** NOUN ▸**ma'chineless** ADJECTIVE ▸**ma'chine-ˌlike** ADJECTIVE

machine bolt NOUN a fastening bolt with a machine-cut thread.

machine code *or* **language** NOUN instructions for the processing of data in a binary, octal, or hexadecimal code that can be understood and executed by a computer.

machine gun NOUN 1 **a** a rapid-firing automatic gun, usually mounted, from which small-arms ammunition is discharged. **b** *(as modifier)*: *machine-gun fire.* ◆ VERB **machine-gun, -guns, -gunning, -gunned.** 2 *(tr)* to shoot or fire at with a machine gun.
▸**machine gunner** NOUN

machine head NOUN a metal peg-and-gear mechanism for tuning a string on an instrument such as a guitar.

machine intelligence NOUN *Brit, now rare* another term for **artificial intelligence.**

machine learning NOUN a branch of artificial intelligence in which a computer generates rules underlying or based on raw data that has been fed into it.

machine moulding NOUN *Engineering* the process of making moulds and cores for castings by mechanical means, usually by compacting the moulding sand by vibration instead of by ramming down.

machine readable ADJECTIVE (of data) in a form in which it can be fed into a computer.

machinery (mə'ʃiːnərɪ) NOUN, *plural* **-eries.** 1 machines, machine parts, or machine systems collectively. 2 a particular machine system or set of machines. 3 a system similar to a machine: *the machinery of government.* 4 literary devices used for effect in epic poetry.

machine screw NOUN a fastening screw with a machine-cut thread throughout the length of its shank.

machine shop NOUN a workshop in which machine tools are operated.

machine tool NOUN a power-driven machine, such as a lathe, miller, or grinder, that is used for cutting, shaping, and finishing metals or other materials.
▸**ma'chine-ˌtooled** ADJECTIVE

machine translation NOUN the production of text in one natural language from that in another by means of computer procedures.

machinist (mə'ʃiːnɪst) NOUN 1 a person who operates machines to cut or process materials. 2 a maker or repairer of machines.

machismo (mæ'kɪzməʊ, -'tʃɪz-) NOUN exaggerated masculine pride.
▷HISTORY Mexican Spanish, from Spanish *macho* male, from Latin *masculus* MASCULINE

Machmeter ('mækˌmiːtə) NOUN an instrument for measuring the Mach number of an aircraft in flight.

Mach number NOUN *(often not capital)* the ratio of the speed of a body in a particular medium to the speed of sound in that medium. Mach number 1 corresponds to the speed of sound. Often shortened to: **Mach.**
▷HISTORY C19: named after Ernst *Mach* (1838–1916), Austrian physicist and philosopher

macho ('mætʃəʊ) ADJECTIVE 1 denoting or exhibiting pride in characteristics believed to be typically masculine, such as physical strength, sexual appetite, etc. ◆ NOUN, *plural* **machos.** 2 a man who displays such characteristics.
▷HISTORY C20: from Spanish: male; see MACHISMO

machree (mə'kriː) ADJECTIVE *(postpositive) Irish* my dear: *mother machree.*
▷HISTORY from Irish *mo croidhe*

machtpolitik ('mɑːxtˌpɒlɪtiːk) NOUN power politics.
▷HISTORY from German

Machu Picchu (ˈmɑːtʃuː ˈpiːktʃuː) NOUN a ruined Incan city in S Peru.

machzor** or **mahzor *Hebrew* (maxˈzɔr; *English* mɑːkˈzɔː) NOUN, *plural* **-zorim** (-zɔˈriːm; *English* -zəˈriːm). a Jewish prayer book containing prescribed holiday rituals.
▷HISTORY literally: cycle

Macías Nguema (məˈsiːəs əŋˈgweɪmə) NOUN the former name (until 1979) of **Bioko**.

macintosh (ˈmækɪnˌtɒʃ) NOUN a variant spelling of **mackintosh**.

McIntosh (ˈmækɪnˌtɒʃ) *or* **McIntosh red** NOUN a Canadian variety of red-skinned eating apple.
▷HISTORY C19: named after John *McIntosh* (1777–c. 1845), US-born Canadian farmer on whose property the variety was first found growing wild

mack[1] (mæk) NOUN *Brit informal* a variant spelling of **mac**, short for **mackintosh** (senses 1, 3).

mack[2] (mæk) NOUN *Slang* a pimp.
▷HISTORY C19: shortened from obsolete *mackerel*, from Old French, of uncertain origin

Mackay (məˈkaɪ) NOUN a port in E Australia, in Queensland: artificial harbour. Pop.: 55 772 (1993).

Mackem (ˈmækəm) *Brit* ◆ NOUN 1 a person who comes from or lives in the Sunderland and Wearside area. 2 the dialect spoken by these people. ◆ ADJECTIVE 3 of or relating to these people or their dialect.

Mackenzie (məˈkɛnzɪ) NOUN a river in NW Canada, in the Northwest Territories and Nunavut, flowing northwest from Great Slave Lake to the Beaufort Sea: the longest river in Canada; navigable in summer. Length: 1770 km (1100 miles).

mackerel (ˈmækrəl) NOUN, *plural* **-rel** *or* **-rels.** 1 a spiny-finned food fish, *Scomber scombrus*, occurring in northern coastal regions of the Atlantic and in the Mediterranean: family *Scombridae*. It has a deeply forked tail and a greenish-blue body marked with wavy dark bands on the back. Compare **Spanish mackerel** (sense 1). 2 any of various other fishes of the family *Scombridae*, such as *Scomber colias* (**Spanish mackerel**) and *S. japonicus* (**Pacific mackerel**). ◆ Compare **horse mackerel.**
▷HISTORY C13: from Anglo-French, from Old French *maquerel*, of unknown origin

mackerel breeze NOUN a strong breeze.
▷HISTORY C18: so named because the ruffling of the water by the wind aids mackerel fishing

mackerel shark NOUN another name for **porbeagle.**

mackerel sky NOUN a sky patterned with cirrocumulus or small altocumulus clouds.
▷HISTORY from the similarity to the pattern on a mackerel's back

Mackinac (ˈmækɪˌnɔː, -ˌnæk) NOUN a wooded island in N Michigan, in the **Straits of Mackinac** (a channel between the lower and upper peninsulas of Michigan): an ancient Indian burial ground; state park. Length: 5 km (3 miles).

Mackinaw coat (ˈmækɪˌnɔː) NOUN *Chiefly US and Canadian* a thick short double-breasted plaid coat. Also called: **mackinaw.**
▷HISTORY C19: named after *Mackinaw*, variant of MACKINAC

McKinley (məˈkɪnlɪ) NOUN **Mount.** a mountain in S central Alaska, in the Alaska Range: the highest peak in North America. Height: 6194 m (20 320 ft.).

mackintosh *or* **macintosh** (ˈmækɪnˌtɒʃ) NOUN 1 a waterproof raincoat made of rubberized cloth. 2 such cloth. 3 any raincoat.
▷HISTORY C19: named after Charles *Macintosh* (1760–1843), who invented it

mackle[1] (ˈmækəl) *or* **macule** (ˈmækjuːl) NOUN *Printing* a double or blurred impression caused by shifting paper or type.
▷HISTORY C16: via French from Latin *macula* spot, stain

mackle[2] (ˈmækəl) VERB **mackles, mackled, mackling.** (*tr*) *Midland English dialect* to mend hurriedly or in a makeshift way.

Maclaurin's series (məˈklɔːrɪnz) NOUN *Maths* an infinite sum giving the value of a function f(*x*) in terms of the derivatives of the function evaluated at zero: $f(x) = f(0) + (f'(0)x)/1! + (f''(0)x^2)/2! + \ldots$ Also called: **Maclaurin series.**
▷HISTORY C18: named after Colin *Maclaurin* (1698–1746), British mathematician who formulated it

macle (ˈmækəl) NOUN another name for **chiastolite** and **twin** (sense 3).
▷HISTORY C19: via French from Latin *macula* spot, stain

Mcmurdo Sound (məkˈmɜːdəʊ) NOUN an inlet of the Ross Sea in Antarctica, north of Victoria Land.

McNaughten Rules *or* **McNaghten Rules** (məkˈnɔːtən) PLURAL NOUN (in English law) a set of rules established by the case of Regina v. McNaughten (1843) by which legal proof of insanity in the commission of a crime depends upon whether or not the accused can show either that he did not know what he was doing or that he is incapable of realizing that what he was doing was wrong.

Macon (ˈmeɪkən) NOUN a city in the US, in central Georgia, on the Ocmulgee River. Pop.: 97 255 (2000).

Mâcon (*French* mɑkɔ̃) NOUN 1 a city in E central France, in the Saône valley: a centre of the wine-producing region of lower Burgundy. Pop.: 39 700 (1995 est.). 2 a red or white wine from the Mâcon area, heavier than the other burgundies.

Macquarie (məˈkwɒrɪ) NOUN 1 an Australian island in the Pacific, SE of Tasmania: noted for its species of albatross and penguin. Area: about 168 sq. km (65 sq. miles). 2 a river in SE Australia, in E central New South Wales, rising in the Blue Mountains and flowing NW to the Darling. Length: about 1200 km (750 miles).

macramé (məˈkrɑːmɪ) NOUN a type of ornamental work made by knotting and weaving coarse thread into a pattern.
▷HISTORY C19: via French and Italian from Turkish *makrama* towel, from Arabic *migramah* striped cloth

macrencephaly (ˌmækrənˈsɛfəlɪ) *or less commonly* **macrencephalia** (ˌmækrənsɪˈfeɪlɪə) NOUN the condition of having an abnormally large brain.

macro (ˈmækrəʊ) NOUN, *plural* **macros.** 1 a macro lens. 2 Also: **macro instruction.** a single computer instruction that initiates a set of instructions to perform a specific task.

macro- *or before a vowel* **macr-** COMBINING FORM 1 large, long, or great in size or duration: *macroscopic.* 2 (in pathology) indicating abnormal enlargement or overdevelopment: *macrocyte.* Compare **micro-** (sense 5). 3 producing larger than life images: *macrophotography.*
▷HISTORY from Greek *makros* large; compare Latin *macer* MEAGRE

macrobiotic (ˌmækrəʊbaɪˈɒtɪk) ADJECTIVE 1 of or relating to macrobiotics. 2 of a diet comprising only food conforming to the principles of macrobiotics.

macrobiotics (ˌmækrəʊbaɪˈɒtɪks) NOUN (*functioning as singular*) a dietary system in which foods are classified according to the principles of Yin and Yang. It advocates diets of whole grains and vegetables grown without chemical additives.
▷HISTORY C20: from MACRO- + Greek *biotos* life + -ICS

macrocarpa (ˌmækrəʊˈkɑːpə) NOUN a large coniferous tree of New Zealand, *Cupressus macrocarpa*, used for shelter belts on farms and for rough timber. Also called: **Monterey cypress.**
▷HISTORY C19: from New Latin, from Greek MACRO- + *karpos* fruit

macrocephaly (ˌmækrəʊˈsɛfəlɪ) *or less commonly* **macrocephalia** (ˌmækrəʊsɪˈfeɪlɪə) NOUN the condition of having an abnormally large head or skull.
▸**macrocephalic** (ˌmækrəʊsɪˈfælɪk) *or* ˌ**macro**ˈ**cephalous** ADJECTIVE

macroclimate (ˈmækrəʊˌklaɪmɪt) NOUN the prevailing climate of a large area.
▸**macroclimatic** (ˌmækrəʊklaɪˈmætɪk) ADJECTIVE
▸ˌ**macrocli**ˈ**matically** ADVERB

macrocosm (ˈmækrəˌkɒzəm) NOUN 1 a complex structure, such as the universe or society, regarded as an entirety, as opposed to microcosms, which have a similar structure and are contained within it. 2 any complex entity regarded as a complete system in itself. ◆ Compare **microcosm.**
▷HISTORY C16: via French and Latin from Greek *makros kosmos* great world
▸ˌ**macro**ˈ**cosmic** ADJECTIVE ▸ˌ**macro**ˈ**cosmically** ADVERB

macrocyst (ˈmækrəʊˌsɪst) NOUN 1 an unusually large cyst. 2 (in slime moulds) an encysted resting protoplasmic mass. See **plasmodium** (sense 1).

macrocyte (ˈmækrəʊˌsaɪt) NOUN *Pathol* an abnormally large red blood cell, over 10 µm in diameter.
▸**macrocytic** (ˌmækrəʊˈsɪtɪk) ADJECTIVE

macrocytosis (ˌmækrəʊsaɪˈtəʊsɪs) NOUN *Pathol* the presence in the blood of macrocytes.

macroeconomics (ˌmækrəʊˌiːkəˈnɒmɪks, -ˌɛk-) NOUN (*functioning as singular*) the branch of economics concerned with aggregates, such as national income, consumption, and investment. Compare **microeconomics.**
▸ˌ**macro**ˌ**eco**ˈ**nomic** ADJECTIVE

macroevolution (ˌmækrəʊˌiːvəˈluːʃən) NOUN *Biology* the evolution of large taxonomic groups such as genera and families.
▸ˌ**macro**ˌ**evo**ˈ**lutionary** ADJECTIVE

macrogamete (ˌmækrəʊˈgæmiːt) *or* **megagamete** (ˌmɛgəˈgæmiːt) NOUN the larger and apparently female of two gametes in conjugating protozoans. Compare **microgamete.**

macroglia (ˌmækrəʊˈglɪə) NOUN one of the two types of non-nervous tissue (glia) found in the central nervous system: includes astrocytes. Compare **microglia.**

macroglobulin (ˌmækrəʊˈglɒbjʊlɪn) NOUN *Immunol* 1 an immunoglobulin of unusually high relative molecular mass, observed in the blood in some diseases. 2 Also called: **immunoglobulin M.** the normal form of this immunoglobulin.

macrograph (ˈmækrəʊˌgrɑːf, -ˌgræf) NOUN a photograph, drawing, etc., in which an object appears as large as or several times larger than the original.
▸**macrographic** (ˌmækrəʊˈgræfɪk) ADJECTIVE

macro lens NOUN a camera lens used for close-up photography (2–10 cm).

macrolepidoptera (ˌmækrəʊˌlɛpɪˈdɒptərə) PLURAL NOUN a collector's name for that part of the lepidoptera that comprises the butterflies and the larger moths (noctuids, geometrids, bombycids, springtails, etc.): a term without taxonomic significance. Compare **microlepidoptera.**

macromere (ˈmækrəʊˌmɪə) NOUN *Embryol* any of the large yolk-filled cells formed by unequal cleavage of a fertilized ovum.

macromolecule (ˌmækrəʊˈmɒlɪˌkjuːl) NOUN any very large molecule, such as a protein or synthetic polymer.
▸**macromolecular** (ˌmækrəʊməˈlɛkjʊlə) ADJECTIVE

macron (ˈmækrɒn) NOUN a diacritical mark (¯) placed over a letter, used in prosody, in the orthography of some languages, and in several types of phonetic respelling systems, to represent a long vowel.
▷HISTORY C19: from Greek *makron* something long, from *makros* long

macronucleus (ˌmækrəʊˈnjuːklɪəs) NOUN, *plural* **-clei** (-klɪˌaɪ). the larger of the two nuclei in ciliated protozoans. Compare **micronucleus.**

macronutrient (ˌmækrəʊˈnjuːtrɪənt) NOUN any substance, such as carbon, hydrogen, or oxygen, that is required in large amounts for healthy growth and development.

macrophage (ˈmækrəʊˌfeɪdʒ) NOUN any large phagocytic cell occurring in the blood, lymph, and connective tissue of vertebrates. See also **histiocyte.**
▸**macrophagic** (ˌmækrəʊˈfædʒɪk) ADJECTIVE

macrophagous (məˈkrɒfəgəs) ADJECTIVE *Zoology* (of an animal) feeding on relatively large particles of food.

macrophotography (ˌmækrəʊfəˈtɒgrəfɪ) NOUN extremely close-up photography in which the image on the film is as large as, or larger than, the object.

macrophysics (ˌmækrəʊˈfɪzɪks) NOUN (*functioning as singular*) the branch of physics concerned with macroscopic systems and objects.

macropsia (məˈkrɒpsɪə) NOUN the condition of seeing everything in the field of view as larger than it really is, which can occur in diseases of the retina or in some brain disorders.

macropterous (məˈkrɒptərəs) ADJECTIVE (of certain animals, esp some types of ant) having large wings.

macroscopic (ˌməkrəʊˈskɒpɪk) ADJECTIVE 1 large enough to be visible to the naked eye. Compare **microscopic.** 2 comprehensive; concerned with large units. 3 *Physics* capable of being described by the statistical properties of a large number of parts. ◆ Also: **megascopic.**
▷HISTORY C19: see MACRO-, -SCOPIC
▸ˌ**macroˈscopically** ADVERB

macrosociology (ˌmækrəʊˌsəʊsɪˈɒlədʒɪ) NOUN the branch of sociology concerned with the study of human societies on a wide scale.
▸ˌ**macroˌsocioˈlogical** ADJECTIVE

macrosporangium (ˌmækrəʊspɔːˈrændʒɪəm) NOUN, *plural* **-gia** (-dʒɪə). another name for **megasporangium.**

macrospore (ˈmækrəʊˌspɔː) NOUN another name for **megaspore** (sense 1).

macrotous (məˈkrəʊtəs) ADJECTIVE *Zoology* having large ears.
▷HISTORY from MACRO- + Greek *ous* ear

macruran (məˈkrʊərən) NOUN 1 any decapod crustacean of the group (formerly suborder) *Macrura,* which includes the lobsters, prawns, and crayfish. ◆ ADJECTIVE *also* **macrurous, macrural, macruroid.** 2 of, relating to, or belonging to the *Macrura.*
▷HISTORY C19: via New Latin, from Greek *makros* long + *oura* tail

macula (ˈmækjʊlə) *or* **macule** (ˈmækjuːl) NOUN, *plural* **-ulae** (-jʊˌliː) *or* **-ules.** *Anatomy* 1 a small spot or area of distinct colour, esp the macula lutea. 2 any small discoloured spot or blemish on the skin, such as a freckle.
▷HISTORY C14: from Latin
▸ˈ**macular** ADJECTIVE

macula lutea (ˈluːtɪə) NOUN, *plural* **maculae luteae** (ˈluːtɪˌiː). a small yellowish oval-shaped spot, rich in cones, near the centre of the retina of the eye, where vision is especially sharp. See also **fovea centralis.**
▷HISTORY New Latin, literally: yellow spot

macular degeneration NOUN pathological changes in the macula lutea, resulting in loss of central vision: a common cause of blindness in the elderly.

maculate *Archaic or literary* ◆ VERB (ˈmækjʊˌleɪt) 1 (*tr*) to spot, stain, or pollute. ◆ ADJECTIVE (ˈmækjʊlɪt) 2 spotted or polluted.
▷HISTORY C15: from Latin *maculāre* to stain

maculation (ˌmækjʊˈleɪʃən) NOUN 1 a pattern of spots, as on certain animals and plants. 2 *Archaic* the act of maculating or the state of being maculated.

macule (ˈmækjuːl) NOUN 1 *Anatomy* another name for **macula.** 2 *Printing* another name for **mackle.**
▷HISTORY C15: from Latin *macula* spot

Macumba (*Portuguese* maˈkumba) NOUN a religious cult in Brazil that combines Christian and voodoo elements.

mad (mæd) ADJECTIVE **madder, maddest.** 1 mentally deranged; insane. 2 senseless; foolish: *a mad idea.* 3 (often foll by *at*) *Informal* angry; resentful. 4 (foll by *about, on,* or *over;* often postpositive) wildly enthusiastic (about) or fond (of): *mad about football; football-mad.* 5 extremely excited or confused; frantic: *a mad rush.* 6 temporarily overpowered by violent reactions, emotions, etc.: *mad with grief.* 7 (of animals) **a** unusually ferocious: *a mad buffalo.* **b** afflicted with rabies. 8 **like mad.** *Informal* with great energy, enthusiasm, or haste; wildly. 9 **mad as a hatter.** crazily eccentric. ◆ VERB **mads, madding, madded.** 10 *Archaic* to make or become mad; act or cause to act as if mad.
▷HISTORY Old English *gemǣded,* past participle of *gemǣdan* to render insane; related to *gemād* insane, and to Old High German *gimeit* silly, crazy, Old Norse *meitha* to hurt, damage
▸ˈ**maddish** ADJECTIVE

MAD (mæd) NOUN *US* ACRONYM FOR mutual assured destruction: a theory of nuclear deterrence whereby each side in a conflict has the capacity to destroy the other in retaliation for a nuclear attack.

madafu (maˈdafuː) NOUN *E African* coconut milk.
▷HISTORY C19: from Swahili

Madag. ABBREVIATION FOR Madagascar.

Madagascan (ˌmædəˈgæskən) ADJECTIVE 1 of or relating to Madagascar or its inhabitants. ◆ NOUN 2 a native or inhabitant of Madagascar.

Madagascar (ˌmædəˈgæskə) NOUN an island republic in the Indian Ocean, off the E coast of Africa: made a French protectorate in 1895; became autonomous in 1958 and fully independent in 1960; contains unique flora and fauna. Languages: Malagasy and French. Religions: animist and Christian. Currency: franc. Capital: Antananarivo. Pop.: 15 983 000 (2001 est.). Area: 587 041 sq. km (266 657 sq. miles). Official name (since 1975): **Democratic Republic of Madagascar.** Former name (1958–75): **Malagasy Republic.**
▸ˌ**Madaˈgascan** NOUN, ADJECTIVE

Madagascar aquamarine NOUN a form of blue beryl from Madagascar, used as a gemstone.

madam (ˈmædəm) NOUN, *plural* **madams** *or for sense 1* **mesdames** (ˈmeɪˌdæm). 1 a polite term of address for a woman, esp one considered to be of relatively high social status. 2 a woman who runs a brothel. 3 *Brit informal* a precocious or pompous little girl. 4 *South African informal* **the.** the lady of the house.
▷HISTORY C13: from Old French *ma dame* my lady

madame (ˈmædəm; *French* madam) NOUN, *plural* **mesdames** (ˈmeɪˌdæm; *French* medam). a married Frenchwoman: usually used as a title equivalent to *Mrs,* and sometimes extended to older unmarried women to show respect and to women of other nationalities.
▷HISTORY C17: from French. See MADAM

madcap (ˈmædˌkæp) ADJECTIVE 1 impulsive, reckless, or lively. ◆ NOUN 2 an impulsive, reckless, or lively person.
▷HISTORY C16: from MAD + *cap* (in the figurative sense: head)

mad cow disease NOUN an informal name for **BSE.**

madden (ˈmædᵊn) VERB to make or become mad or angry.

maddening (ˈmædᵊnɪŋ) ADJECTIVE 1 serving to send mad. 2 extremely annoying; exasperating.
▸ˈ**maddeningly** ADVERB ▸ˈ**maddeningness** NOUN

madder[1] (ˈmædə) NOUN 1 any of several rubiaceous plants of the genus *Rubia,* esp the Eurasian *R. tinctoria,* which has small yellow flowers and a red fleshy root. 2 the root of this plant. 3 a dark reddish-purple dye formerly obtained by fermentation of this root; identical to the synthetic dye, alizarin. 4 a red lake obtained from alizarin and an inorganic base; used as a pigment in inks and paints.
▷HISTORY Old English *mædere;* related to Middle Dutch *mēde,* Old Norse *mathra*

madder[2] (ˈmædə) ADJECTIVE the comparative of **mad.**

madding (ˈmædɪŋ) ADJECTIVE *Archaic* 1 acting or behaving as if mad: *the madding crowd.* 2 making mad; maddening.
▸ˈ**maddingly** ADVERB

made (meɪd) VERB 1 the past tense and past participle of **make**[1]. ◆ ADJECTIVE 2 artificially produced. 3 (*in combination*) produced or shaped as specified: *handmade.* 4 **get** *or* **have it made.** *Informal* to be assured of success. 5 **made of money.** very rich.

made dish NOUN *Cookery* a dish consisting of a number of different ingredients cooked together.

Madeira (məˈdɪərə; *Portuguese* məˈðəirə) NOUN 1 a group of volcanic islands in the N Atlantic, west of Morocco: constitutes the Portuguese administrative district of Funchal; consists of the chief island, Madeira, Pôrto Santo, and the uninhabited Deserta and Selvagen Islands; gained partial autonomy in 1976. Capital: Funchal. Pop.: 242 603 (2001). Area: 797 sq. km (311 sq. miles). 2 a river in W Brazil, flowing northeast to the Amazon below Manaus. Length: 3241 km (2013 miles). 3 a rich strong fortified white wine made on Madeira.

Madeira cake NOUN a kind of rich sponge cake.

madeleine (ˈmædəlɪn, -ˌleɪn) NOUN a small fancy sponge cake.
▷HISTORY C19: perhaps after *Madeleine* Paulmier, French pastry cook

mademoiselle (ˌmædmwəˈzɛl; *French* madmwazɛl) NOUN, *plural* **mesdemoiselles** (ˌmeɪdmwəˈzɛl; *French* medmwazɛl). 1 a young unmarried French girl or woman: usually used as a title equivalent to *Miss.* 2 a French teacher or governess.
▷HISTORY C15: French, from *ma* my + *demoiselle* DAMSEL

made-up ADJECTIVE 1 invented; fictional: *a made-up story.* 2 wearing make-up: *a well made-up woman.* 3 put together; assembled. 4 (of a road) surfaced with tarmac, concrete, etc.

madhouse (ˈmædˌhaʊs) NOUN *Informal* 1 a mental hospital or asylum. 2 a state of uproar or confusion.

Madhya Bharat (ˈmʌdjə ˈbɑːrət) NOUN a former state of central India: part of Madhya Pradesh since 1956.

Madhya Pradesh (ˈmʌdjə prɑːˈdɛʃ) NOUN a state of central India, situated on the Deccan Plateau: rich in mineral resources, with several industrial cities: formerly the largest Indian state, it lost much of the SE to the new state of Chhattisgarh in 2000. Capital: Bhopal. Pop.: 60 385 118 (2001). Area: 308 332 sq. km (119 016 sq. miles).

Madiba (məˈdiːbə) NOUN *South African* a title of respect for Nelson Mandela, deriving from his Xhosa clan name.

madison (ˈmædɪsᵊn) NOUN a type of cycle relay race.
▷HISTORY C20: from *Madison Square Gardens* in New York City, early venue for such races

Madison (ˈmædɪsᵊn) NOUN a city in the US, in S central Wisconsin, on an isthmus between Lakes Mendota and Monona: the state capital. Pop.: 208 054 (2000).

Madison Avenue NOUN a street in New York City: a centre of American advertising and public-relations firms and a symbol of their attitudes and methods.

madly (ˈmædlɪ) ADVERB 1 in an insane or foolish manner. 2 with great speed and energy. 3 *Informal* extremely or excessively: *I love you madly.*

madman (ˈmædmən) NOUN, *plural* **-men.** a man who is insane, esp one who behaves violently; lunatic.

madness (ˈmædnɪs) NOUN 1 insanity; lunacy. 2 extreme anger, excitement, or foolishness. 3 a nontechnical word for **rabies.**

Madonna (məˈdɒnə) NOUN 1 *Chiefly RC Church* a designation of the Virgin Mary. 2 (*sometimes not capital*) a picture or statue of the Virgin Mary.
▷HISTORY C16: Italian, from *ma* my + *donna* lady

Madonna lily NOUN a perennial widely cultivated Mediterranean lily plant, *Lilium candidum,* with white trumpet-shaped flowers. Also called: **Annunciation lily.**

madras (ˈmædrəs, məˈdræs, -ˈdrɑːs) NOUN 1 **a** a strong fine cotton or silk fabric, usually with a woven stripe. **b** (*as modifier*): *madras cotton.* 2 something made of this, esp a scarf. 3 a medium-hot curry: *chicken madras.*
▷HISTORY C19: so named because the material originated in the MADRAS area

Madras (məˈdrɑːs, -ˈdræs) NOUN 1 a port in SE India, capital of Tamil Nadu, on the Bay of Bengal: founded in 1639 by the English East India Company as **Fort St George;** traditional burial place of St Thomas; university (1857). Pop. (city): 3 841 396 (1991), with a conurbation of 5 421 985 (1991). Official name: **Chennai.** 2 the former name (until 1968) for the state of **Tamil Nadu.**

madrasah, madrasa (məˈdræsə, ˈmɑːdræsə), *or* **medrese** (məˈdrɛseɪ) NOUN *Islam* an educational institution, particularly for Islamic religious instruction.
▷HISTORY from Arabic, literally: place of learning

Madre de Dios (*Spanish* ˈmaðre ðe ˈðiɔs) NOUN a river in NE South America, rising in SE Peru and flowing northeast to the Beni River in N Bolivia. Length: about 965 km (600 miles).

madrepore (ˌmædrɪˈpɔː) NOUN any coral of the genus *Madrepora,* many of which occur in tropical seas and form large coral reefs: order *Zoantharia.*
▷HISTORY C18: via French from Italian *madrepora* mother-stone, from *madre* mother + *-pora,* from Latin *porus* or Greek *poros* calcareous stone, stalactite
▸ˌ**madreˈporal** *or* **madreporic** (ˌmædrɪˈpɒrɪk) *or* **madreporitic** (ˌmædrɪpəˈrɪtɪk) *or* ˌ**madreˈporian** ADJECTIVE

Madrid (məˈdrɪd) NOUN the capital of Spain,

situated centrally in New Castile: the highest European capital, at an altitude of about 700 m (2300 ft.); a Moorish fortress in the 10th century, captured by Castile in 1083 and made capital of Spain in 1561; university (1836). Pop.: 2 881 506 (1998 est.).

madrigal ('mædrɪgᵊl) NOUN [1] *Music* a type of 16th- or 17th-century part song for unaccompanied voices with an amatory or pastoral text. Compare **glee** (sense 2). [2] a 14th-century Italian song, related to a pastoral stanzaic verse form.
▷HISTORY C16: from Italian, from Medieval Latin *mātricāle* primitive, apparently from Latin *mātrīcālis* of the womb, from *matrīx* womb
▸ **'madrigal,esque** ADJECTIVE ▸ **madrigalian** (ˌmædrɪ'gælɪən, -'geɪ-) ADJECTIVE ▸ **'madrigalist** NOUN

madrilène ('mædrɪˌlɛn, -ˌleɪn; *French* madrilɛn) NOUN a cold consommé flavoured with tomato juice.
▷HISTORY shortened from French (*consommé*) *madrilène* from Spanish *madrileño* of Madrid

madroña (mə'drəʊnjə), **madroño** (mə'drəʊnjəʊ), *or* **madrone** (mə'drəʊnə) NOUN, *plural* **-ñas, -ños,** *or* **-nes**. an ericaceous North American evergreen tree or shrub, *Arbutus menziesii*, with white flowers and red berry-like fruits. See also **strawberry tree.**
▷HISTORY C19: from Spanish

Madura (mə'dʊərə) NOUN an island in Indonesia, off the NE coast of Java: extensive forests and saline springs. Capital: Pamekasan. Area: 5472 sq. km (2113 sq. miles).

Madurai ('mædjʊˌraɪ) NOUN a city in S India, in S Tamil Nadu: centre of Dravidian culture for over 2000 years; cotton industry. Pop.: 940 989 (1991). Former name: **Madura.**

Madurese (ˌmædjʊə'ri:z) ADJECTIVE [1] of or relating to the Indonesian island of Madura or its inhabitants. ◆ NOUN, *plural* **-ese**. [2] a native or inhabitant of Madura.

maduro (mə'dʊərəʊ) ADJECTIVE [1] (of cigars) dark and strong. ◆ NOUN, *plural* **-ros**. [2] a cigar of this type.
▷HISTORY Spanish, literally: ripe, from Latin *mātūrus* ripe, MATURE

madwoman ('mædwʊmən) NOUN, *plural* **-women**. a woman who is insane, esp one who behaves violently; lunatic.

madwort ('mædˌwɜ:t) NOUN [1] a low-growing Eurasian boraginaceous plant, *Asperugo procumbens*, with small blue flowers. [2] any of certain other plants, such as alyssum.
▷HISTORY C16: once alleged to be a cure for madness

madzoon (mɑ:d'zu:n) NOUN a variant of **matzoon.**

Maeander (mi:'ændə) NOUN ancient name of the river **Menderes** (sense 1). Also spelt: **Meander.**

Maebashi ('mɑ:e'bɑ:ʃi:) NOUN a city in central Japan, on central Honshu: centre of sericulture and silk-spinning; university (1949). Pop.: 284 780 (1995).

Maecenas (mi:'si:næs) NOUN a wealthy patron of the arts.
▷HISTORY from Gaius *Maecenas* (?70–8 B.C.), Roman statesman and patron of Horace and Virgil

maelstrom ('meɪlstrəʊm) NOUN [1] a large powerful whirlpool. [2] any turbulent confusion.
▷HISTORY C17: from obsolete Dutch *maelstroom*, from *malen* to grind, whirl round + *stroom* STREAM

Maelstrom ('meɪlstrəʊm) NOUN a strong tidal current in a restricted channel in the Lofoten Islands off the NW coast of Norway.

maenad *or* **menad** ('mi:næd) NOUN [1] *Classical myth* a woman participant in the orgiastic rites of Dionysus; bacchante. [2] a frenzied woman.
▷HISTORY C16: from Latin *Maenas*, from Greek *mainas* madwoman
▸ **mae'nadic** ADJECTIVE ▸ **mae'nadically** ADVERB
▸ **'maenadism** NOUN

maestoso (maɪ'stəʊsəʊ) *Music* ◆ ADJECTIVE, ADVERB [1] to be performed majestically. ◆ NOUN, *plural* **-tos**. [2] a piece or passage directed to be played in this way.
▷HISTORY C18: Italian: majestic, from Latin *māiestās* MAJESTY

Maestricht ('mɑ:strɪxt; *Dutch* ma:'strɪxt) NOUN an obsolete spelling of **Maastricht.**

maestro ('maɪstrəʊ) NOUN, *plural* **-tri** (-trɪ) *or* **-tros**. [1] a distinguished music teacher, conductor, or musician. [2] any man regarded as the master of an art: often used as a term of address. [3] See **maestro di cappella.**
▷HISTORY C18: Italian: master

maestro di cappella (dɪ kə'pɛlə) NOUN a person in charge of an orchestra, esp a private one attached to the palace of a prince in Italy during the baroque period. See **kapellmeister.**
▷HISTORY Italian: master of the chapel

mae west (meɪ) NOUN *Slang* an inflatable life jacket, esp as issued to the US armed forces for emergency use.
▷HISTORY C20: after *Mae West*, 1892–1980, American actress, renowned for her generous bust

Maewo (mɑ:'eɪwəʊ) NOUN an almost uninhabited island in Vanuatu. Also called: **Aurora.**

MAF (mæf) NOUN (in New Zealand) ACRONYM FOR Ministry of Agriculture and Forestry.

Mafeking ('mæfɪˌkɪŋ) NOUN the former name (until 1980) of **Mafikeng.**

MAFF (mæf) NOUN (formerly, in Britain) ACRONYM FOR Ministry of Agriculture, Fisheries, and Food.

maffick ('mæfɪk) VERB (*intr*) *Brit, archaic* to celebrate extravagantly and publicly.
▷HISTORY C20: back formation from *Mafeking* (now Mafikeng), from the rejoicings at the relief of the siege there in 1900
▸ **'mafficker** NOUN

Mafia *or* **Maffia** ('mæfɪə) NOUN [1] **the.** an international secret organization founded in Sicily, probably in opposition to tyranny. It developed into a criminal organization and in the late 19th century was carried to the US by Italian immigrants. [2] any group considered to resemble the Mafia. See also **Black Hand, Camorra, Cosa Nostra.**
▷HISTORY C19: from Sicilian dialect of Italian, literally hostility to the law, boldness, perhaps from Arabic *mahyah* bragging

Mafikeng ('mæfɪˌkɛŋ) NOUN a town in N South Africa: besieged by the Boers for 217 days (1899–1900) during the second Boer War: administrative headquarters of the British protectorate of Bechuanaland until 1965, although outside its borders. Pop.: 7000 (latest est.). Former name (until 1980): **Mafeking.**

mafioso (ˌmæfɪ'əʊsəʊ; *Italian* mafi'oso) NOUN, *plural* **-sos** *or* **-si** (*Italian* -si). a person belonging to the Mafia.

mafted ('mæftɪd) ADJECTIVE *Northern English dialect* suffering under oppressive heat.

maftir ('mɑftɪr) NOUN *Judaism* [1] the final section of the weekly Torah reading. [2] the person to whom it is read, who also reads the Haftarah.

mag¹ (mæg) NOUN *Informal* See **magazine.**

mag² (mæg) *Informal, now chiefly Austral* ◆ VERB **mags, magging, magged**. (*intr*) [1] to talk; chatter. ◆ NOUN [2] talk; chatter.
▷HISTORY C18: from *Mag*, see MAGPIE

mag. ABBREVIATION FOR: [1] magazine. [2] magnitude.

magainin (mə'geɪnɪn) NOUN any of a series of related substances with antibacterial properties, derived from the skins of frogs.
▷HISTORY C20: from Hebrew *magain* a shield

Magallanes (*Spanish* maɣa'ʎanes) NOUN the former name of **Punta Arenas.**

magalogue *or US* **magalog** ('magəˌlɒg) NOUN a combination of a magazine and a catalogue.
▷HISTORY C20: from MAG(AZINE) + (CAT)ALOGUE

magazine (ˌmægə'zi:n) NOUN [1] a periodical paperback publication containing articles, fiction, photographs, etc. [2] a metal box or drum holding several cartridges used in some kinds of automatic firearms; it is removed and replaced when empty. [3] a building or compartment for storing weapons, explosives, military provisions, etc. [4] a stock of ammunition. [5] a device for continuously recharging a handling system, stove, or boiler with solid fuel. [6] *Photog* another name for **cartridge** (sense 5). [7] a rack for automatically feeding a number of slides through a projector. [8] a TV or radio programme made up of a series of short nonfiction items.
▷HISTORY C16: via French *magasin* from Italian *magazzino*, from Arabic *makhāzin*, plural of *makhzan* storehouse, from *khazana* to store away

magdalen ('mægdəlɪn) *or* **magdalene** ('mægdəˌli:n, ˌmægdə'li:nɪ) NOUN [1] *Literary* a reformed prostitute. [2] *Rare* a reformatory for prostitutes.
▷HISTORY from MARY MAGDALENE

Magdalena (ˌmægdə'leɪnə, -'li:-; *Spanish* maɣða'lena) NOUN a river in SW Colombia, rising on the E slopes of the Andes and flowing north to the Caribbean near Barranquilla. Length: 1540 km (956 miles).

Magdalena Bay NOUN an inlet of the Pacific on the coast of NW Mexico, in Lower California.

Magdalene ('mægdəˌli:n, ˌmægdə'li:nɪ) NOUN See **Mary Magdalene.**

Magdalenian (ˌmægdə'li:nɪən) ADJECTIVE [1] of or relating to the latest Palaeolithic culture in Europe, which ended about 10 000 years ago. ◆ NOUN [2] the Magdalenian culture.
▷HISTORY C19: from French *magdalénien*, after *La Madeleine*, village in Dordogne, France, near which artefacts of the culture were found

Magdeburg ('mægdəˌbɜ:g; *German* 'makdəburk) NOUN an industrial city and port in central Germany, on the River Elbe, capital of Saxony-Anhalt: a leading member of the Hanseatic League, whose local laws, the **Magdeburg Laws** were adopted by many European cities. Pop.: 238 000 (1999 est.).

mage (meɪdʒ) NOUN an archaic word for **magician.**
▷HISTORY C14: from MAGUS

Magellan (mə'gɛlən) NOUN **Strait of.** a strait between the mainland of S South America and Tierra del Fuego, linking the S Pacific with the S Atlantic. Length: 600 km (370 miles). Width: up to 32 km (20 miles).

Magellanic Cloud (ˌmægɪ'lænɪk) NOUN either of two small irregular galaxies, the **Large Magellanic Cloud** (Nubecula Major) and the **Small Magellanic Cloud** (Nubecula Minor), lying near the S celestial pole; they are probably satellites of the Galaxy. Distances: 163 000 light years (Large), 196 000 light years (Small).

Magen David *or* **Mogen David** ('mɔ:gən 'deɪvɪd) NOUN *Judaism* another name for the **Star of David.**
▷HISTORY C20: from Hebrew *māghēn Dāwīdh* shield of David; David (about 1000–962 B.C.) was the second king of the Hebrews, and was responsible for uniting Israel as a kingdom

magenta (mə'dʒɛntə) NOUN [1] **a** a deep purplish red that is the complementary colour of green and, with yellow and cyan, forms a set of primary colours. **b** (*as adjective*): *a magenta filter.* [2] another name for **fuchsin.**
▷HISTORY C19: named after *Magenta*, Italy, alluding to the blood shed in a battle there (1859)

maggie ('mægɪ) NOUN *Slang* a magpie.

Maggiore (ˌmædʒɪ'ɔ:rɪ; *Italian* mad'dʒore) NOUN **Lake.** a lake in N Italy and S Switzerland, in the S Lepontine Alps.

maggot ('mægət) NOUN [1] the soft limbless larva of dipterous insects, esp the housefly and blowfly, occurring in decaying organic matter. [2] *Rare* a fancy or whim.
▷HISTORY C14: from earlier *mathek;* related to Old Norse *mathkr* worm, Old English *matha*, Old High German *mado* grub

maggoty ('mægətɪ) ADJECTIVE [1] relating to, resembling, or ridden with maggots. [2] *Slang* very drunk. [3] *Austral, slang* annoyed, angry.

Magherafelt ('mæhərəˌfɛlt) NOUN a district of N Northern Ireland, in Co. Londonderry. Pop.: 39 780 (2001). Area: 572 sq. km (221 sq. miles).

Maghreb *or* **Maghrib** ('mʌgrəb) NOUN NW Africa, including Morocco, Algeria, Tunisia, and sometimes Libya.
▷HISTORY from Arabic, literally: the West

Maghrebi *or* **Maghribi** ('mʌgrəbɪ) ADJECTIVE [1] of or relating to the Maghreb region of NW Africa or its inhabitants. ◆ NOUN [2] a native or inhabitant of the Maghreb.

magi ('meɪdʒaɪ) PLURAL NOUN, *singular* **magus** ('meɪgəs). [1] the Zoroastrian priests of the ancient Medes and Persians. [2] **the three magi.** the wise men from the East who came to do homage to the infant Jesus (Matthew 2:1–12) and traditionally called Caspar, Melchior, and Balthazar.

▸**magian** ('meɪdʒɪən) ADJECTIVE

magic ('mædʒɪk) NOUN 1 the art that, by use of spells, supposedly invokes supernatural powers to influence events; sorcery. 2 the practice of this art. 3 the practice of illusory tricks to entertain other people; conjuring. 4 any mysterious or extraordinary quality or power: *the magic of springtime.* 5 **like magic.** very quickly. ◆ ADJECTIVE *also* **magical.** 6 of or relating to magic: *a magic spell.* 7 possessing or considered to possess mysterious powers: *a magic wand.* 8 unaccountably enchanting: *magic beauty.* 9 *Informal* wonderful; marvellous; exciting. ◆ VERB **-ics, -icking, -icked.** (*tr*) 10 to transform or produce by or as if by magic. 11 (foll by *away*) to cause to disappear by or as if by magic.
▷HISTORY C14: via Old French *magique,* from Greek *magikē* witchcraft, from *magos* MAGUS
▸**'magical** ADJECTIVE ▸**'magically** ADVERB

magic bullet NOUN *Informal* any therapeutic agent, esp one in the early stages of development, reputed to be very effective in treating a condition, such as a malignant tumour, by specifically targeting the diseased tissue.

magic carpet NOUN (in fairy stories) a carpet capable of transporting people through the air.

Magic Circle NOUN 1 the British association of magicians, traditionally forbidden to reveal any of the secrets of their art. 2 (*not capitals*) a group of influential people involved in a conspiracy.

magic eye NOUN a miniature cathode-ray tube in some radio receivers, on the screen of which a pattern is displayed in order to assist tuning.

magician (mə'dʒɪʃən) NOUN 1 another term for **conjuror.** 2 a person who practises magic. 3 a person who has extraordinary skill, influence, or qualities.

magic lantern NOUN an early type of slide projector. Sometimes shortened to: **lantern.**

magic mushroom NOUN *Informal* any of various types of fungi that contain a hallucinogenic substance, esp *Psilocybe mexicana,* which contains psilocybin.

magic number NOUN 1 *Physics* any of the numbers 2, 8, 20, 28, 50, 82, and 126. Nuclides with these numbers of nucleons appear to have greater stability than other nuclides. 2 *Chem* a number of atoms that is particularly stable in certain types of compound that have clusters of the same type of atom.

magic realism *or* **magical realism** NOUN a style of painting or writing that depicts images or scenes of surreal fantasy in a representational or realistic way.
▸**magic realist** *or* **magical realist** NOUN

magic square NOUN a square array of rows of integers arranged so that the sum of the integers is the same when taken vertically, horizontally, or diagonally.

magilp (mə'gɪlp) NOUN *Arts* a variant spelling of **megilp.**

Maginot line ('mæʒɪˌnəʊ; *French* maʒino) NOUN 1 a line of fortifications built by France to defend its border with Germany prior to World War II; it proved ineffective against the German invasion. 2 any line of defence in which blind confidence is placed.
▷HISTORY named after André *Maginot* (1877–1932), French minister of war when the fortifications were begun in 1929

magisterial (ˌmædʒɪ'stɪərɪəl) ADJECTIVE 1 commanding; authoritative. 2 domineering; dictatorial. 3 of or relating to a teacher or person of similar status. 4 of or relating to a magistrate.
▷HISTORY C17: from Late Latin *magisteriālis,* from *magister* master
▸**ˌmagis'terially** ADVERB ▸**ˌmagis'terialness** NOUN

magisterium (ˌmædʒɪ'stɪərɪəm) NOUN the teaching authority or function of the Roman Catholic Church.
▷HISTORY C19: see MAGISTERY

magistery ('mædʒɪstərɪ, -trɪ) NOUN, *plural* **-teries.** *Alchemy* 1 an agency or substance, such as the philosopher's stone, believed to transmute other substances. 2 any substance capable of healing.
▷HISTORY C16: from Medieval Latin *magisterium,* from Latin: mastery, from *magister* master

magistracy ('mædʒɪstrəsɪ) *or* **magistrature** ('mædʒɪstrəˌtjʊə) NOUN, *plural* **-cies** *or* **-tures.** 1 the office or function of a magistrate. 2 magistrates collectively. 3 the district under the jurisdiction of a magistrate.

magistral (mə'dʒɪstrəl) ADJECTIVE 1 of, relating to, or characteristic of a master. 2 *Pharmacol, obsolete* made up according to a special prescription. Compare **officinal.** 3 *Fortifications* determining the location of other fortifications: *the magistral line.* ◆ NOUN 4 a fortification in a determining position.
▷HISTORY C16: from Latin *magistrālis* concerning a master, from *magister* master
▸**magistrality** (ˌmædʒɪ'strælɪtɪ) NOUN ▸**magistratically** (ˌmædʒɪ'strætɪkəlɪ) ADVERB

magistrate ('mædʒɪˌstreɪt, -strɪt) NOUN 1 a public officer concerned with the administration of law. Related adjective: **magisterial.** 2 another name for **justice of the peace.** 3 *NZ* the former name for **district court judge.**
▷HISTORY C17: from Latin *magistrātus,* from *magister* master
▸**'magisˌtrateship** NOUN

magistrates' court NOUN (in England) a court of summary jurisdiction held before two or more justices of the peace or a stipendiary magistrate to deal with minor crimes, certain civil actions, and preliminary hearings.

Maglemosian *or* **Maglemosean** (ˌmæglə'məʊzɪən) NOUN 1 the first Mesolithic culture of N Europe, dating from 8000 B.C. to about 5000 B.C.: important for the rare wooden objects that have been preserved, such as dugout canoes. ◆ ADJECTIVE 2 designating or relating to this culture.
▷HISTORY C20: named after the site at *Maglemose,* Denmark, where the culture was first classified

maglev ('mægˌlɛv) NOUN a type of high-speed train that runs on magnets supported by a magnetic field generated around the track.
▷HISTORY C20: from *mag(netic) lev(itation)*

magma ('mægmə) NOUN, *plural* **-mas** *or* **-mata** (-mətə). 1 a paste or suspension consisting of a finely divided solid dispersed in a liquid. 2 hot molten rock, usually formed in the earth's upper mantle, some of which finds its way into the crust and onto the earth's surface, where it solidifies to form igneous rock.
▷HISTORY C15, from Latin: dregs (of an ointment), from Greek: salve made by kneading, from *massein* to knead
▸**magmatic** (mæg'mætɪk) ADJECTIVE ▸**'magmatism** NOUN

magma chamber NOUN a reservoir of magma in the earth's crust where the magma may reside temporarily on its way from the upper mantle to the earth's surface.

Magna Carta *or* **Magna Charta** ('mægnə 'kɑːtə) NOUN *English history* the charter granted by King John at Runnymede in 1215, recognizing the rights and privileges of the barons, church, and freemen.
▷HISTORY Medieval Latin: great charter

magna cum laude ('mægnə kʊm 'laʊdeɪ) *Chiefly US* with great praise: the second of three designations for above-average achievement in examinations. Compare **cum laude, summa cum laude.**
▷HISTORY Latin

Magna Graecia ('mægnə 'griːʃɪə) NOUN (in the ancient world) S Italy, where numerous colonies were founded by Greek cities.
▷HISTORY Latin: Great Greece

magnanimity (ˌmægnə'nɪmɪtɪ) NOUN, *plural* **-ties.** generosity.
▷HISTORY C14: via Old French from Latin *magnanimitās,* from *magnus* great + *animus* soul

magnanimous (mæg'nænɪməs) ADJECTIVE generous and noble.
▷HISTORY C16: from Latin *magnanimus* great-souled
▸**mag'nanimously** ADVERB ▸**mag'nanimousness** NOUN

magnate ('mægneɪt, -nɪt) NOUN 1 a person of power and rank in any sphere, esp in industry. 2 *History* a great nobleman. 3 (formerly) a member of the upper chamber in certain European parliaments, as in Hungary.
▷HISTORY C15: back formation from earlier *magnates* from Late Latin: great men, plural of *magnās,* from Latin *magnus* great
▸**'magnateˌship** NOUN

magnesia (mæg'niːʃə) NOUN another name for **magnesium oxide.**
▷HISTORY C14: via Medieval Latin from Greek *Magnēsia,* of *Magnēs* ancient mineral-rich region
▸**mag'nesian** *or* **magnesic** (mæg'niːsɪk) *or* **mag'nesial** ADJECTIVE

magnesite ('mægnɪˌsaɪt) NOUN a white, colourless, or lightly tinted mineral consisting of naturally occurring magnesium carbonate in hexagonal crystalline form: a source of magnesium and also used in the manufacture of refractory bricks. Formula: $MgCO_3$.
▷HISTORY C19: from MAGNESIUM + -ITE[1]

magnesium (mæg'niːzɪəm) NOUN a light silvery-white metallic element of the alkaline earth series that burns with an intense white flame, occurring principally in magnesite, dolomite, and carnallite: used in light structural alloys, flashbulbs, flares, and fireworks. Symbol: Mg; atomic no.: 12; atomic wt.: 24.3050; valency: 2; relative density: 1.738; melting pt.: 650°C; boiling pt.: 1090°C.
▷HISTORY C19: New Latin, from MAGNESIA

magnesium oxide NOUN a white tasteless substance occurring naturally as periclase: used as an antacid and laxative and in refractory materials, such as crucibles and fire bricks. Formula: MgO. Also called: **magnesia.**

magnet ('mægnɪt) NOUN 1 a body that can attract certain substances, such as iron or steel, as a result of a magnetic field; a piece of ferromagnetic substance. See also **electromagnet.** 2 a person or thing that exerts a great attraction.
▷HISTORY C15: via Latin from Greek *magnēs,* shortened from *ho Magnēs lithos* the Magnesian stone. See MAGNESIA

magnetar ('mægnɪtɑː) NOUN a type of neutron star that has a very intense magnetic field, over 1000 times greater than that of a pulsar.
▷HISTORY C20: from MAGNET(IC) (ST)AR, on the model of QUASAR

magnetic (mæg'nɛtɪk) ADJECTIVE 1 of, producing, or operated by means of magnetism. 2 of or concerned with a magnet. 3 of or concerned with the magnetism of the earth: *the magnetic equator.* 4 capable of being magnetized. 5 exerting a powerful attraction: *a magnetic personality.*
▸**mag'netically** ADVERB

magnetic bottle NOUN a configuration of magnetic fields for containing plasma.

magnetic bubble NOUN *Physics* a small round magnetic domain induced by a magnetic field in a thin film of magnetic material, used in certain types of computer memories.

magnetic character reader NOUN a device that automatically scans and interprets characters printed with magnetic ink. It operates by the process of **magnetic character recognition.**

magnetic compass NOUN a compass containing a magnetic needle pivoted in a horizontal plane, that indicates the direction of magnetic north at points on the earth's surface.

magnetic confinement NOUN another name for **containment** (sense 3).

magnetic constant NOUN the permeability of free space, which has the value $4\pi \times 10^{-7}$henry per metre. Symbol: M_0. Also called: **absolute permeability.**

magnetic course NOUN an aircraft's course in relation to the magnetic north. Also called: **magnetic heading.**

magnetic declination NOUN the angle that a compass needle makes with the direction of the geographical north pole at any given point on the earth's surface. Also called: **declination, magnetic variation.**

magnetic dip *or* **inclination** NOUN another name for **dip** (sense 28).

magnetic dipole moment NOUN a measure of the magnetic strength of a magnet or current-carrying coil, expressed as the torque per unit magnetic-flux density produced when the magnet or coil is set with its axis perpendicular to the magnetic field. Symbol: *m, j.* Also called: **magnetic moment.** Compare **electromagnetic moment.**

magnetic disk NOUN *Computing* another name for **disk** (sense 2).

magnetic epoch NOUN *Geology* a geologically long period of time during which the magnetic field of the earth retains the same polarity. The magnetic field may reverse during such a period for a geologically short period of time (a **magnetic event**).

magnetic equator NOUN an imaginary line on the earth's surface, near the equator, at all points on which there is no magnetic dip. Also called: **aclinic line.**

magnetic field NOUN a field of force surrounding a permanent magnet or a moving charged particle, in which another permanent magnet or moving charge experiences a force. Compare **electric field.**

magnetic flux NOUN a measure of the strength of a magnetic field over a given area perpendicular to it, equal to the product of the area and the magnetic flux density through it. Symbol: ϕ.

magnetic flux density NOUN a measure of the strength of a magnetic field at a given point, expressed by the force per unit length on a conductor carrying unit current at that point. Symbol: *B*. Also called: **magnetic induction.**

magnetic induction NOUN another name for **magnetic flux density.**

magnetic ink NOUN ink containing particles of a magnetic material used for printing characters for magnetic character recognition.

magnetic ink character recognition NOUN the process of reading characters printed in magnetic ink. Abbreviation: **MICR.**

magnetic lens NOUN a set of magnets, esp electromagnets, used to focus or defocus a beam of charged particles in an electron microscope, particle accelerator, or similar device.

magnetic meridian NOUN a continuous imaginary line around the surface of the earth passing through both magnetic poles.

magnetic mine NOUN a mine designed to activate when a magnetic field such as that generated by the metal of a ship's hull is detected.

magnetic mirror NOUN *Physics* a configuration of magnetic fields used to confine charged particles, as in a magnetic bottle.

magnetic moment NOUN short for **magnetic dipole moment** or **electromagnetic moment.**

magnetic monopole NOUN another name for **monopole** (sense 2).

magnetic needle NOUN a slender magnetized rod used in certain instruments, such as the magnetic compass, for indicating the direction of a magnetic field.

magnetic north NOUN the direction in which a compass needle points, at an angle (the declination) from the direction of true (geographic) north.

magnetic particle inspection NOUN *Engineering* a method of testing for cracks and other defects in a magnetic material, such as steel, by covering it with a magnetic powder and magnetizing it: any variation in the concentration of the powder indicates a flaw in the material.

magnetic pick-up NOUN a type of record player pick-up in which the stylus moves an iron core in a coil, causing a changing magnetic field that produces the current.

magnetic pole NOUN [1] either of two regions in a magnet where the magnetic induction is concentrated. [2] either of two variable points on the earth's surface towards which a magnetic needle points, where the lines of force of the earth's magnetic field are vertical.

magnetic resonance NOUN the response by atoms, molecules, or nuclei subjected to a magnetic field to radio waves or other forms of energy: used in medicine for scanning. See **magnetic resonance imaging, magnetic resonance angiography.**

magnetic resonance angiography NOUN a form of magnetic resonance imaging in which either the injection of a magnetic resonance contrast agent or the movement of the blood provides information of value in diagnosis. Abbreviation: **MRA.**

magnetic resonance imaging NOUN a noninvasive medical diagnostic technique in which the absorption and transmission of high-frequency radio waves are analysed as they irradiate the hydrogen atoms in water molecules and other tissue components placed in a strong magnetic field. This computerized analysis provides a powerful aid to the diagnosis and treatment planning of many diseases, including cancer. Abbreviation: **MRI.**

magnetics (mæg'nɛtɪks) NOUN (*functioning as singular*) the branch of physics concerned with magnetism.

magnetic storm NOUN a sudden severe disturbance of the earth's magnetic field, caused by emission of charged particles from the sun.

magnetic stripe NOUN (across the back of various types of cheque card, credit card, etc.) a dark stripe of magnetic material consisting of several tracks onto which information may be coded and which may be read or written to electronically.

magnetic tape NOUN a long narrow plastic or metal strip coated or impregnated with a ferromagnetic material such as iron oxide, used to record sound or video signals or to store information in computers. Sometimes (informal) shortened to: **mag tape.**

magnetic tape unit *or* **drive** NOUN a computer device that moves reels of magnetic tape past read-write heads so that data can be transferred to or from the computer.

magnetic variation NOUN another name for **magnetic declination.**

magnetism ('mægnɪˌtɪzəm) NOUN [1] the property of attraction displayed by magnets. [2] any of a class of phenomena in which a field of force is caused by a moving electric charge. See also **electromagnetism, ferromagnetism, diamagnetism, paramagnetism.** [3] the branch of physics concerned with magnetic phenomena. [4] powerful attraction.
▸**'magnetist** NOUN

magnetite ('mægnɪˌtaɪt) NOUN a black magnetic mineral, found in igneous and metamorphic rocks and as a separate deposit. It is a source of iron. Composition: iron oxide. Formula: Fe_3O_4. Crystal structure: cubic.
▸**magnetitic** (ˌmægnɪ'tɪtɪk) ADJECTIVE

magnetize *or* **magnetise** ('mægnɪˌtaɪz) VERB (*tr*) [1] to make (a substance or object) magnetic. [2] to attract strongly. [3] an obsolete word for **mesmerize.**
▸**ˌmagnet'izable** *or* **ˌmagnet'isable** ADJECTIVE
▸**ˌmagneti'zation** *or* **ˌmagneti'sation** NOUN ▸**'magnetˌizer** *or* **'magnetˌiser** NOUN

magneto (mæg'niːtəʊ) NOUN, *plural* **-tos.** a small electric generator in which the magnetic field is produced by a permanent magnet, esp one for providing the spark in an internal-combustion engine.
▷HISTORY C19: short for *magnetoelectric generator*

magneto- COMBINING FORM indicating magnetism or magnetic properties: *magnetosphere.*

magnetochemistry (mægˌniːtəʊ'kɛmɪstrɪ) NOUN the branch of chemistry concerned with the relationship between magnetic and chemical properties.
▸**magˌneto'chemical** ADJECTIVE

magnetoelectricity (mægˌniːtəʊɪlɛk'trɪsɪtɪ) NOUN electricity produced by the action of magnetic fields.
▸**magˌnetoe'lectric** *or* **magˌnetoe'lectrical** ADJECTIVE

magnetograph (mæg'niːtəʊˌgrɑːf, -ˌgræf) NOUN a recording magnetometer, usually used for studying variations in the earth's magnetic field.

magnetohydrodynamics (mægˌniːtəʊˌhaɪdrəʊdaɪ'næmɪks) NOUN (*functioning as singular*) [1] the study of the behaviour of conducting fluids, such as liquid metals or plasmas, in magnetic fields. [2] the generation of electricity by subjecting a plasma to a magnetic field and collecting the deflected free electrons. ♦ Abbreviation: **MHD.**
▸**magˌnetoˌhydrody'namic** ADJECTIVE

magnetometer (ˌmægnɪ'tɒmɪtə) NOUN any instrument for measuring the intensity or direction of a magnetic field, esp the earth's field.
▸**magnetometric** (ˌmægnɪtəʊ'mɛtrɪk) ADJECTIVE
▸**ˌmagne'tometry** NOUN

magnetomotive (mægˌniːtəʊ'məʊtɪv) ADJECTIVE causing a magnetic flux.

magnetomotive force NOUN the agency producing a magnetic flux, considered analogous to the electromotive force in an electric circuit; equal to the circular integral of the magnetic field strength. Symbol: *F*.

magneton ('mægnɪˌtɒn, mæg'niːtɒn) NOUN [1] Also called: **Bohr magneton.** a unit of magnetic moment equal to $eh/4\pi m$ where *e* and *m* are the charge and mass of an electron and *h* is the Planck constant. It has the value $9.274\ 096 \times 10^{-24}$ joule per tesla. Symbol: β *or* m_B. [2] Also called: **nuclear magneton.** a similar unit equal to $\beta m/M$ where *M* is the mass of the proton.
▷HISTORY C20: from MAGNET + (ELECTR)ON

magnetosphere (mæg'niːtəʊˌsfɪə) NOUN the region surrounding a planet, such as the earth, in which the behaviour of charged particles is controlled by the planet's magnetic field.
▸**magnetospheric** (mægˌniːtəʊ'sfɛrɪk) ADJECTIVE

magnetostatics (mægˌniːtəʊ'stætɪks) NOUN (*functioning as singular*) *Physics* the study of steady-state magnetic fields.

magnetostriction (mægˌniːtəʊ'strɪkʃən) NOUN a change in dimensions of a ferromagnetic material that is subjected to a magnetic field.
▷HISTORY C19: from MAGNETO- + CONSTRICTION
▸**magˌneto'strictive** ADJECTIVE

magnetron ('mægnɪˌtrɒn) NOUN an electronic valve with two coaxial electrodes used with an applied magnetic field to generate high-power microwave oscillations, esp for use in radar.
▷HISTORY C20: from MAGNET + ELECTRON

magnet school NOUN a school that provides a focus on one subject area throughout its curriculum in order to attract, often from an early age, pupils who wish to specialize in this subject.

magnet steel NOUN *Engineering* steel used for the manufacture of permanent magnets, often having a high cobalt content and smaller amounts of nickel, aluminium, or copper.

magnific (mæg'nɪfɪk) *or* **magnifical** ADJECTIVE *Archaic* magnificent, grandiose, or pompous.
▷HISTORY C15: via Old French from Latin *magnificus* great in deeds, from *magnus* great + *facere* to do
▸**mag'nifically** ADVERB

Magnificat (mæg'nɪfɪˌkæt) NOUN *Christianity* the hymn of the Virgin Mary (Luke 1:46-55), used as a canticle.
▷HISTORY from the opening phrase in the Latin version, *Magnificat anima mea Dominum* (my soul doth magnify the Lord)

magnification (ˌmægnɪfɪ'keɪʃən) NOUN [1] the act of magnifying or the state of being magnified. [2] the degree to which something is magnified. [3] a copy, photograph, drawing, etc., of something magnified. [4] a measure of the ability of a lens or other optical instrument to magnify, expressed as the ratio of the size of the image to that of the object.

magnificence (mæg'nɪfɪsəns) NOUN the quality of being magnificent.
▷HISTORY C14: via French from Latin *magnificentia*

magnificent (mæg'nɪfɪsᵊnt) ADJECTIVE [1] splendid or impressive in appearance. [2] superb or very fine. [3] (esp of ideas) noble or elevated. [4] *Archaic* great or exalted in rank or action.
▷HISTORY C16: from Latin *magnificentior* more splendid; irregular comparative of *magnificus* great in deeds; see MAGNIFIC
▸**mag'nificently** ADVERB ▸**mag'nificentness** NOUN

magnifico (mæg'nɪfɪˌkəʊ) NOUN, *plural* **-coes.** a magnate; grandee.
▷HISTORY C16: Italian from Latin *magnificus*; see MAGNIFIC

magnify ('mægnɪˌfaɪ) VERB **-fies, -fying, -fied.** [1] to increase, cause to increase, or be increased in apparent size, as through the action of a lens, microscope, etc. [2] to exaggerate or become exaggerated in importance: *don't magnify your troubles.* [3] (*tr*) *Rare* to increase in actual size. [4] (*tr*) *Archaic* to glorify.
▷HISTORY C14: via Old French from Latin *magnificāre* to praise; see MAGNIFIC
▸**'magniˌfiable** ADJECTIVE

magnifying glass *or* **magnifier** NOUN a convex lens used to produce an enlarged image of an object.

magniloquent (mæg'nɪləkwənt) ADJECTIVE (of speech) lofty in style; grandiloquent.
▷HISTORY C17: from Latin *magnus* great + *loquī* to speak
▸**mag'niloquence** NOUN ▸**mag'niloquently** ADVERB

Magnitogorsk (*Russian* məgnita'gɔrsk) NOUN a city in central Russia, on the Ural River: founded in 1930 to exploit local magnetite ores; site of one of the world's largest, but outdated, metallurgical plants. Pop.: 428 100 (1999 est.).

magnitude ('mægnɪˌtjuːd) NOUN [1] relative importance or significance: *a problem of the first magnitude.* [2] relative size or extent: *the magnitude of the explosion.* [3] *Maths* a number assigned to a quantity, such as weight, and used as a basis of comparison for the measurement of similar quantities. [4] Also called: **apparent magnitude.** *Astronomy* the apparent brightness of a celestial body expressed on a numerical scale on which bright stars have a low value. Values are measured by eye (**visual magnitude**) or more accurately by photometric or photographic methods, and range from –26.7 (the sun), through 1.5 (Sirius), down to about +30. Each integral value represents a brightness 2.512 times greater than the next highest integral value. See also **absolute magnitude.** [5] Also called: **earthquake magnitude.** *Geology* a measure of the size of an earthquake based on the quantity of energy released: specified on the Richter scale. See **Richter scale.**
▷HISTORY C14: from Latin *magnitūdō* size, from *magnus* great
▸ˌ**magni'tudinous** ADJECTIVE

magnolia (mæg'nəʊlɪə) NOUN [1] any tree or shrub of the magnoliaceous genus *Magnolia* of Asia and North America: cultivated for their white, pink, purple, or yellow showy flowers. [2] the flower of any of these plants. [3] a very pale pinkish-white or purplish-white colour.
▷HISTORY C18: New Latin, named after Pierre *Magnol* (1638–1715), French botanist

magnoliaceous (mægˌnəʊlɪ'eɪʃəs) ADJECTIVE of, relating to, or belonging to the *Magnoliaceae,* a family of trees and shrubs, including magnolias and the tulip tree, having large showy flowers.

magnolia metal NOUN *Engineering* an alloy used for bearings, consisting largely of lead (up to 80 per cent) and antimony, with the addition of smaller quantities of iron and tin.

magnox ('mægnɒks) NOUN an alloy consisting mostly of magnesium with small amounts of aluminium and other metals, used in fuel elements of nuclear reactors.
▷HISTORY C20: from *mag(nesium) n(o) ox(idation)*

magnox reactor NOUN a nuclear reactor using carbon dioxide as the coolant, graphite as the moderator, and uranium cased in magnox as the fuel.

magnum ('mægnəm) NOUN, *plural* **-nums.** a wine bottle holding the equivalent of two normal bottles (approximately 52 fluid ounces).
▷HISTORY C18: from Latin: a big thing, from *magnus* large

magnum opus NOUN a great work of art or literature, esp the greatest single work of an artist.
▷HISTORY Latin

magnus hitch ('mægnəs) NOUN a knot similar to a clove hitch but having one more turn.
▷HISTORY C19 *magnus,* of unknown origin

Magog ('meɪgɒg) NOUN See **Gog and Magog.**

magot (mɑː'gəʊ, 'mægət) NOUN [1] a Chinese or Japanese figurine in a crouching position, usually grotesque. [2] a less common name for **Barbary ape.**
▷HISTORY C17: from French: grotesque figure, after the Biblical giant MAGOG

magpie ('mægˌpaɪ) NOUN [1] any of various passerine birds of the genus *Pica,* esp *P. pica,* having a black-and-white plumage, long tail, and a chattering call: family *Corvidae* (crows, etc.). [2] any of various similar birds of the Australian family *Cracticidae.* See also **butcherbird** (sense 2). [3] any of various other similar or related birds. [4] (*often capital*) a variety of domestic fancy pigeon typically having black-and-white markings. [5] *Brit* a person who hoards small objects. [6] a person who chatters. [7] **a** the outmost ring but one on a target. **b** a shot that hits this ring.
▷HISTORY C17: from *Mag* diminutive of *Margaret,* used to signify a chatterbox + PIE[2]

magpie goose NOUN a large black-and-white goose, *Anseranas semipalmata,* of N Australia and adjacent islands.

magpie lark NOUN a common black-and-white bird of Australia, *Grallina cyanoleuca,* that builds a mud nest. Also called: **peewee.**

magpie moth NOUN [1] a geometrid moth, *Abraxas grossulariata,* showing variable patterning in black on white or yellow, whose looper larvae attack currant and gooseberry bushes. The paler **clouded magpie** is *A. sylvata.* [2] **small magpie.** an unrelated micro, *Eurrhypara hortulata.*

MAgr ABBREVIATION FOR Master of Agriculture.

magsman ('mægzˌmæn) NOUN, *plural* **-men.** *Austral, slang* [1] a raconteur. [2] a confidence trickster.

mag tape NOUN *Informal* short for **magnetic tape.**

maguey ('mægweɪ) NOUN [1] any of various tropical American agave plants of the genera *Agave* or *Furcraea,* esp one that yields a fibre or is used in making an alcoholic beverage. [2] the fibre from any of these plants, used esp for rope.
▷HISTORY C16: Spanish, from Taino

magus ('meɪgəs) NOUN, *plural* **magi** ('meɪdʒaɪ). [1] a Zoroastrian priest. [2] an astrologer, sorcerer, or magician of ancient times.
▷HISTORY C14: from Latin, from Greek *magos,* from Old Persian *magus* magician

Magus ('meɪgəs) NOUN **Simon.** *New Testament* a sorcerer who tried to buy spiritual powers from the apostles (Acts 8:9-24).

Magyar ('mægjɑː) NOUN [1] (*plural* **-yars**) a member of the predominant ethnic group of Hungary, also found in NW Siberia. [2] the Hungarian language. ◆ ADJECTIVE [3] of or relating to the Magyars or their language. [4] *Sewing* of or relating to a style of sleeve cut in one piece with the bodice.

Magyarország ('mɔdjɔrorsaːg) NOUN the Hungarian name for **Hungary.**

Mahabharata (məˌhɑː'bɑːrətə), **Mahabharatam,** *or* **Mahabharatum** (məˌhɑː'bɑːrətəm) NOUN an epic Sanskrit poem of India, dealing chiefly with the struggle between two rival families. It contains many separate episodes, the most notable of which is the *Bhagavad-Gita.*
▷HISTORY Sanskrit, from *mahā* great + *bhārata* story

Mahajanga (ˌmæhə'dʒæŋgə) NOUN a port in NW Madagascar, on Bombetoka Bay. Pop.: 100 807 (1993). Former name: **Majunga.**

Mahalla el Kubra (mə'hɑːlə ɛl 'kuːbrə) NOUN a city in N Egypt, on the Nile delta: one of the largest diversified textile centres in Egypt. Pop.: 395 402 (1996).

Mahanadi (mə'hɑːnədɪ) NOUN a river in E India, rising in Chhattisgarh and flowing north, then south and east to the Bay of Bengal. Length: 885 km (550 miles).

maharajah *or* **maharaja** (ˌmɑːhə'rɑːdʒə) NOUN any of various Indian princes, esp any of the rulers of the former native states.
▷HISTORY C17: Hindi, from *mahā* great + RAJAH

maharani *or* **maharanee** (ˌmɑːhə'rɑːniː) NOUN [1] the wife of a maharajah. [2] a woman holding the rank of maharajah.
▷HISTORY C19: from Hindi, from *mahā* great + RANI

Maharashtra (ˌmɑːhə'ræʃtrə) NOUN a state of W central India, formed in 1960 from the Marathi-speaking S and E parts of former Bombay state: lies mainly on the Deccan plateau; mainly agricultural. Capital: Bombay. Pop.: 96 752 247 (1994 est.). Area: 307 690 sq. km (118 800 sq. miles).

maharishi (ˌmɑːhɑː'riːʃɪ, mə'hɑːriːʃɪ) NOUN *Hinduism* a Hindu teacher of religious and mystical knowledge.
▷HISTORY from Hindi, from *mahā* great + *rishi* sage, saint

mahatma (mə'hɑːtmə, -'hæt-) NOUN (*sometimes capital*) [1] *Hinduism* a Brahman sage. [2] *Theosophy* an adept or sage.
▷HISTORY C19: from Sanskrit *mahātman,* from *mahā* great + *ātman* soul
▸**ma'hatmaism** NOUN

Mahayana (ˌmɑːhə'jɑːnə) NOUN **a** a liberal Buddhist school of Tibet, China, and Japan, whose adherents aim to disseminate Buddhist doctrines, seeking enlightenment not for themselves alone, but for all sentient beings. **b** (*as modifier*): *Mahayana Buddhism.*
▷HISTORY from Sanskrit, from *mahā* great + *yāna* vehicle
▸ˌ**Maha'yanist** NOUN

Mahé (mɑː'heɪ) NOUN an island in the Indian Ocean, the chief island of the Seychelles. Capital: Victoria. Pop.: 67 338 (1997). Area: 147 sq. km (57 sq. miles).

mahewu (ma'hewʊ, -'xe-) NOUN (in South Africa) fermented liquid mealie-meal porridge, used as a stimulant, esp by Black Africans.
▷HISTORY from Xhosa *amarewu*

Mahican (mə'hiːkən) NOUN, *plural* **-cans** *or* **-can.** a variant of **Mohican.**

mah jong *or* **mah-jongg** (ˌmɑː'dʒɒŋ) NOUN a game of Chinese origin, usually played by four people, in which tiles bearing various designs are drawn and discarded until one player has an entire hand of winning combinations.
▷HISTORY from Chinese, literally: sparrows

mahlstick ('mɔːlˌstɪk) NOUN a variant spelling of **maulstick.**

mahogany (mə'hɒgənɪ) NOUN, *plural* **-nies.** [1] any of various tropical American trees of the meliaceous genus *Swietenia,* esp *S. mahagoni* and *S. macrophylla,* valued for their hard reddish-brown wood. [2] any of several trees with similar wood, such as African mahogany (genus *Khaya*) and Philippine mahogany (genus *Shorea*). [3] **a** the wood of any of these trees. See also **acajou** (sense 1). **b** (*as modifier*): *a mahogany table.* [4] a reddish-brown colour.
▷HISTORY C17: origin obscure

Mahometan (mə'hɒmɪtᵊn) NOUN, ADJECTIVE a former word for **Muslim.**
▸**Ma'hometanism** NOUN

mahonia (mə'həʊnɪə) NOUN any evergreen berberidaceous shrub of the Asian and American genus *Mahonia,* esp *M. aquifolium:* cultivated for their ornamental spiny divided leaves and clusters of small yellow flowers.
▷HISTORY C19: New Latin, named after Bernard *McMahon* (died 1816), American botanist

mahout (mə'haʊt) NOUN (in India and the East Indies) an elephant driver or keeper.
▷HISTORY C17: Hindi *mahāut,* from Sanskrit *mahāmātra* of great measure, originally a title

Mahratta (mə'rɑːtə) NOUN a variant spelling of **Maratha.**
▸**Mah'ratti** NOUN, ADJECTIVE

Mähren ('mɛːrən) NOUN the German name for **Moravia.**

mahseer ('mɑːsɪə) NOUN any of various large freshwater Indian cyprinid fishes, such as *Barbus tor.*
▷HISTORY from Hindi

mahzor *Hebrew* (max'zɔr; *English* mɑː'kzɔː) NOUN, *plural* ***-zorim*** (-zɔ'riːm; *English* -zə'riːm). a variant spelling of **machzor.**

Maia ('maɪə) NOUN *Greek myth* the eldest of the seven Pleiades, mother by Zeus of Hermes.

maid (meɪd) NOUN [1] *Archaic or literary* a young unmarried girl; maiden. [2] **a** a female servant. **b** (*in combination*): *a housemaid.* [3] a spinster.
▷HISTORY C12: shortened form of MAIDEN
▸'**maidish** ADJECTIVE ▸'**maidishness** NOUN

maidan (mæ'dɑːn) NOUN (in Pakistan, India, etc.) an open space used for meetings, sports, etc.
▷HISTORY Urdu, from Arabic

maiden ('meɪdᵊn) NOUN [1] *Archaic or literary* **a** a young unmarried girl, esp when a virgin. **b** (*as modifier*): *a maiden blush.* [2] *Horse racing* **a** a horse that has never won a race. **b** (*as modifier*): *a maiden race.* [3] *Cricket* See **maiden over.** [4] Also called: **clothes maiden.** *Northern English dialect* a frame on which clothes are hung to dry; clothes horse. [5] (*modifier*) of or relating to an older unmarried woman: *a maiden aunt.* [6] (*modifier*) of or involving an initial experience or attempt: *a maiden voyage; maiden speech.* [7] (*modifier*) (of a person or thing) untried; unused. [8] (*modifier*) (of a place) never trodden, penetrated, or captured.
▷HISTORY Old English *mægden;* related to Old High

German *magad,* Old Norse *mogr* young man, Old Irish *mug* slave
▸ **'maidenish** ADJECTIVE ▸ **'maiden-ˌlike** ADJECTIVE

maidenhair fern *or* **maidenhair** ('meɪdᵊnˌhɛə) NOUN any fern of the cosmopolitan genus *Adiantum,* esp *A. capillis-veneris,* having delicate fan-shaped fronds with small pale-green leaflets: family *Adiantaceae.*
▷HISTORY C15: so called from the hairlike appearance of its fine fronds

maidenhair tree NOUN another name for **ginkgo.**

maidenhead ('meɪdᵊnˌhɛd) NOUN 1 a nontechnical word for the **hymen.** 2 virginity; maidenhood.
▷HISTORY C13: from *maiden* + *-hed,* variant of -HOOD

Maidenhead ('meɪdᵊnˌhɛd) NOUN a town in S England, in Windsor and Maidenhead unitary authority, Berkshire, on the River Thames. Pop.: 59 605 (1991).

maidenhood ('meɪdᵊnˌhʊd) NOUN 1 the time during which a woman is a maiden or a virgin. 2 the condition of being a maiden or virgin.

maidenly ('meɪdᵊnlɪ) ADJECTIVE of or befitting a maiden.
▸ **'maidenliness** NOUN

maiden name NOUN a woman's surname before marriage.

maiden over NOUN *Cricket* an over in which no runs are scored.

maiden voyage NOUN *Nautical* the first voyage of a vessel.

Maid Marian NOUN 1 a character in morris dancing, played by a man dressed as a woman. 2 *Legend* the sweetheart of Robin Hood.

maid of all work NOUN 1 a maid who does all types of housework. 2 a general factotum.

maid of honour NOUN 1 *US and Canadian* the principal unmarried attendant of a bride. Compare **bridesmaid, matron of honour.** 2 *Brit* a small tart with an almond-flavoured filling. 3 an unmarried lady attending a queen or princess.

maidservant ('meɪdˌsɜːvənt) NOUN a female servant.

Maidstone ('meɪdstən, -ˌstəʊn) NOUN a town in SE England, administrative centre of Kent, on the River Medway. Pop.: 90 878 (1991).

Maiduguri (ˌmaɪdʊ'guːrɪ) NOUN a city in NE Nigeria, capital of Bornu State; agricultural trade centre. Pop.: 320 000 (1996 est.). Also called: **Yerwa-Maiduguri.**

maieutic (meɪ'juːtɪk) *or* **maieutical** ADJECTIVE *Philosophy* of or relating to the Socratic method of eliciting knowledge by a series of questions and answers.
▷HISTORY C17: from Greek *maieutikos* relating to midwifery (used figuratively by Socrates), from *maia* midwife

maigre ('meɪgə) ADJECTIVE *RC Church* 1 not containing flesh, and so permissible as food on days of religious abstinence: *maigre food.* 2 of or designating such a day.
▷HISTORY C17: from French: thin; see MEAGRE

maihem ('meɪhɛm) NOUN a variant spelling of **mayhem.**

maik (mek) NOUN *Scot* an old halfpenny. Also called: **meck.**
▷HISTORY of obscure origin

maiko ('maɪkəʊ) NOUN, *plural* **-ko** *or* **-kos.** an apprentice geisha.
▷HISTORY from Japanese, literally: dancer

Maikop (*Russian* maj'kɔp) NOUN a city in SW Russia, capital of the Adygei Republic: extensive oilfields to the southwest; mineral springs. Pop.: 167 000 (1999 est.).

mail¹ (meɪl) NOUN 1 Also called (esp Brit): **post.** letters, packages, etc., that are transported and delivered by the post office. 2 the postal system. 3 a single collection or delivery of mail. 4 a train, ship, or aircraft that carries mail. 5 short for **electronic mail.** 6 (*modifier*) of, involving, or used to convey mail: *a mail train.* ◆ VERB (*tr*) 7 *Chiefly US and Canadian* to send by mail. Usual Brit word: **post.** 8 to contact (a person) by electronic mail. 9 to send (a message, document, etc.) by electronic mail.
▷HISTORY C13: from Old French *male* bag, probably from Old High German *malha* wallet
▸ **ˌmaila'bility** NOUN ▸ **'mailable** ADJECTIVE

mail² (meɪl) NOUN 1 a type of flexible armour consisting of riveted metal rings or links. 2 the hard protective shell of such animals as the turtle and lobster. ◆ VERB 3 (*tr*) to clothe or arm with mail.
▷HISTORY C14: from Old French *maille* mesh, from Latin *macula* spot
▸ **'mail-less** ADJECTIVE

mail³ (meɪl) NOUN *Archaic, chiefly Scot* a monetary payment, esp of rent or taxes.
▷HISTORY Old English *māl* terms, from Old Norse *māl* agreement

mail⁴ (meɪl) NOUN *Austral informal* a rumour or report, esp a racing tip.

mailbag ('meɪlˌbæg), **mailsack,** *or sometimes US* **mailpouch** NOUN a large bag used for transporting or delivering mail.

mailbox ('meɪlˌbɒks) NOUN another name (esp US and Canadian) for **letter box.**

mailcoach ('meɪlˌkəʊtʃ) *or US and Canadian* **mailcar** NOUN a railway coach specially constructed for the transportation of mail.

mail drop NOUN *Chiefly US and Canadian* a receptacle or chute for mail.

mailer ('meɪlə) NOUN 1 a person who addresses or mails letters, etc. 2 *US and Canadian* a machine used for stamping and addressing mail. 3 *US and Canadian* a container for mailing things.

mailing list NOUN a register of names and addresses to which advertising matter, etc., is sent by post or electronic mail.

maillot (mæ'jəʊ) NOUN 1 tights worn for ballet, gymnastics, etc. 2 a woman's swimsuit. 3 a jersey.
▷HISTORY from French

mailman ('meɪlˌmæn) NOUN, *plural* **-men.** *Chiefly US and Canadian* another name for **postman.**

mail merging NOUN *Computing* a software facility that can produce a large number of personalized letters by combining a file containing a list of names and addresses with one containing a single standard document.

mail order NOUN 1 an order for merchandise sent by post. 2 **a** a system of buying and selling merchandise through the post. **b** (*as modifier*): *a mail-order firm.*

mailsack ('meɪlˌsæk) NOUN another name for a **mailbag.**

mailshot ('meɪlˌʃɒt) NOUN a circular, leaflet, or other advertising material sent by post, or the posting of such material to a large group of people at one time.

maim (meɪm) VERB (*tr*) 1 to mutilate, cripple, or disable a part of the body of (a person or animal). 2 to make defective. ◆ NOUN 3 *Obsolete* an injury or defect.
▷HISTORY C14: from Old French *mahaignier* to wound, probably of Germanic origin
▸ **maimedness** ('meɪmɪdnɪs) NOUN ▸ **'maimer** NOUN

mai mai ('maɪ maɪ) NOUN *NZ* a duck-shooter's shelter; hide.
▷HISTORY probably from Australian aboriginal *mia-mia* shelter

main¹ (meɪn) ADJECTIVE (*prenominal*) 1 chief or principal in rank, importance, size, etc. 2 sheer or utmost (esp in the phrase **by main force**). 3 *Nautical* of, relating to, or denoting any gear, such as a stay or sail, belonging to the mainmast. 4 *Obsolete* significant or important. ◆ NOUN 5 a principal pipe, conduit, duct, or line in a system used to distribute water, electricity, etc. 6 (*plural*) **a** the main distribution network for water, gas, or electricity. **b** (*as modifier*): *mains voltage.* 7 the chief or most important part or consideration. 8 great strength or force (now chiefly in the phrase (**with**) **might and main**). 9 *Literary* the open ocean. 10 *Archaic* short for **Spanish Main.** 11 *Archaic* short for **mainland.** 12 **in** (*or* **for**) **the main.** on the whole; for the most part.
▷HISTORY C13: from Old English *mægen* strength

main² (meɪn) NOUN 1 a throw of the dice in dice games. 2 a cockfighting contest. 3 a match in archery, boxing, etc.
▷HISTORY C16: of unknown origin

Main (meɪn; *German* main) NOUN a river in central and W Germany, flowing west through Würzburg and Frankfurt to the Rhine. Length: about 515 km (320 miles).

mainbrace ('meɪnˌbreɪs) NOUN *Nautical* a brace attached to the main yard.

main clause NOUN *Grammar* a clause that can stand alone as a sentence. Compare **subordinate clause.**

main course NOUN 1 the principal dish of a meal. 2 *Nautical* a square mainsail.

main deck NOUN the uppermost sheltered deck that runs the entire length of a vessel.

Maine (meɪn) NOUN a state of the northeastern US, on the Atlantic: chiefly hilly, with many lakes, rivers, and forests. Capital: Augusta. Pop.: 1 274 923 (2000). Area: 86 156 sq. km (33 265 sq. miles). Abbreviation: **Me,** (with zip code) **ME.**

Maine Coon NOUN a breed of large powerfully-built long-haired indigenous American cat.
▷HISTORY C20: so-called because it was first recognized as a specific breed in MAINE, and because it somewhat resembles a raccoon in appearance

Maine-et-Loire (*French* mɛnelwar) NOUN a department of W France, in Pays de la Loire region. Capital: Angers. Pop.: 732 942 (1999). Area: 7218 sq. km (2815 sq. miles).

mainframe ('meɪnˌfreɪm) NOUN 1 **a** a high-speed general-purpose computer, usually with a large store capacity. **b** (*as modifier*): *mainframe systems.* 2 the central processing unit of a computer.

mainland ('meɪnlənd) NOUN 1 the main part of a land mass as opposed to an island or peninsula. 2 **the mainland.** a particular landmass as viewed from a nearby island with which it has close links, such as Great Britain as viewed from Northern Ireland or continental Australia as viewed from Tasmania.
▸ **'mainlander** NOUN

Mainland ('meɪnlənd) NOUN 1 an island off N Scotland: the largest of the Shetland Islands. Chief town: Lerwick. Pop.: 17 596 (1991). Area: about 583 sq. km (225 sq. miles). 2 Also called: **Pomona.** an island off N Scotland: the largest of the Orkney Islands. Chief town: Kirkwall. Pop.: 15 128 (1991). Area: 492 sq. km (190 sq. miles). 3 **the Mainland.** *NZ* a South Islanders' name for **South Island.**

main line NOUN 1 *Railways* **a** the trunk route between two points, usually fed by branch lines. **b** (*as modifier*): *a main-line station.* 2 *US* a main road. ◆ VERB **mainline.** 3 (*intr*) *Slang* to inject a drug into a vein. ◆ ADJECTIVE **mainline.** 4 having an important position, esp having responsibility for the main areas of activity.
▸ **'mainˌliner** NOUN

mainly ('meɪnlɪ) ADVERB 1 for the most part; to the greatest extent; principally. 2 *Obsolete* strongly; very much.

main man NOUN *Slang, chiefly US* 1 one's best friend. 2 a boss or leader.

main market NOUN the market for trading in the listed securities of companies on the London Stock Exchange. Compare **Third Market, unlisted securities market.**

mainmast ('meɪnˌmɑːst) NOUN *Nautical* the chief mast of a sailing vessel with two or more masts, being the foremast of a yawl, ketch, or dandy and the second mast from the bow of most others.

main memory NOUN the central memory-storage facility in a computer.

main plane NOUN **a** one of the principal supporting surfaces of an aircraft, esp either of the wings. **b** both wings considered together.

mainsail ('meɪnˌseɪl; *Nautical* 'meɪnsᵊl) NOUN *Nautical* the largest and lowermost sail on the mainmast.

main sequence NOUN *Astronomy* **a** a diagonal band on the Hertzsprung Russell diagram containing about 90% of all known stars; stars evolve onto and then off the band during their lifetime. **b** (*as modifier*): *a main-sequence star.*

mainsheet ('meɪnˌʃiːt) NOUN *Nautical* the line used to control the angle of the mainsail to the wind.

mainspring ('meɪnˌsprɪŋ) NOUN 1 the principal power spring of a mechanism, esp in a watch or clock. 2 the chief cause or motive of something.

mainstay ('meɪnˌsteɪ) NOUN 1 *Nautical* the

forestay that braces the mainmast. [2] a chief support.

main store NOUN *Computing* another name for **memory** (sense 7).

mainstream ('meɪnˌstriːm) NOUN [1] **a** the main current (of a river, cultural trend, etc.): *in the mainstream of modern literature.* **b** (*as modifier*): *mainstream politics.* ◆ ADJECTIVE [2] of or relating to the style of jazz that lies between the traditional and the modern.

mainstream corporation tax NOUN (formerly in Britain) the balance of the corporation tax paid by a company for an accounting period after the advance corporation tax had been deducted.

mainstreeting ('meɪnˌstriːtɪŋ) NOUN *Canadian* the practice of a politician walking about the streets of a town or city to gain votes and greet supporters.

maintain (meɪn'teɪn) VERB (*tr*) [1] to continue or retain; keep in existence. [2] to keep in proper or good condition: *to maintain a building.* [3] to support a style of living: *the money maintained us for a month.* [4] (*takes a clause as object*) to state or assert: *he maintained that Talbot was wrong.* [5] to defend against contradiction; uphold: *she maintained her innocence.* [6] to defend against physical attack.
▷HISTORY C13: from Old French *maintenir,* ultimately from Latin *manū tenēre* to hold in the hand
▸**main'tainable** ADJECTIVE ▸**main'tainer** NOUN

maintained school NOUN a school financially supported by the state.

maintenance ('meɪntɪnəns) NOUN [1] the act of maintaining or the state of being maintained. [2] a means of support; livelihood. [3] (*modifier*) of or relating to the maintaining of buildings, machinery, etc.: *maintenance man.* [4] *Law* (formerly unlawful) the interference in a legal action by a person having no interest in it, as by providing funds to continue the action. See also **champerty.** [5] *Law* a provision ordered to be made by way of periodical payments or a lump sum, as after a divorce for a spouse. [6] *Computing* **a** the correction or prevention of faults in hardware by a programme of inspection and the replacement of parts. **b** the removal of existing faults and the modification of software in response to changes in specification or environment.
▷HISTORY C14: from Old French; see MAINTAIN

maintop ('meɪnˌtɒp) NOUN a top or platform at the head of the mainmast.

main-topmast NOUN *Nautical* the mast immediately above the mainmast.

maintopsail (ˌmeɪn'tɒpseɪl; *Nautical* ˌmeɪn'tɒpsᵊl) NOUN *Nautical* a topsail set on the mainmast.

main yard NOUN *Nautical* a yard for a square mainsail.

Mainz (*German* maints) NOUN a port in W Germany, capital of the Rhineland-Palatinate, at the confluence of the Main and Rhine: an archbishopric from about 780 until 1801; important in the 15th century for the development of printing (by Johann Gutenberg). Pop.: 185 600 (1999 est.). French name: **Mayence.**

maiolica (mə'jɒlɪkə) NOUN a variant of **majolica.**

maisonette *or* **maisonnette** (ˌmeɪzə'nɛt) NOUN self-contained living accommodation often occupying two floors of a larger house and having its own outside entrance.
▷HISTORY C19: from French, diminutive of *maison* house

maist (mest) DETERMINER a Scot word for **most.**

Maitland ('meɪtlənd) NOUN a town in SE Australia, in E New South Wales: industrial centre of an agricultural region. Pop.: 38 865 (latest est.).

maître d'hôtel (ˌmɛtrə dəʊ'tɛl; *French* mɛtrə dotɛl) NOUN, *plural* **maîtres d'hôtel.** [1] a head waiter or steward. [2] the manager or owner of a hotel.
▷HISTORY C16: from French: master of (the) hotel

maître d'hôtel butter NOUN melted butter mixed with parsley and lemon juice.

Maitreya (mi'treːjə) NOUN the future Buddha.
▷HISTORY Sanskrit

maize (meɪz) NOUN [1] Also called: **Indian corn. a** a tall annual grass, *Zea mays,* cultivated for its yellow edible grains, which develop on a spike. **b** the grain of this plant, used for food, fodder, and as a source of oil. Usual US and Canadian name: **corn.** See also **sweet corn.** [2] a yellow colour.
▷HISTORY C16: from Spanish *maíz,* from Taino *mahiz*

Maj. ABBREVIATION FOR Major.

majestic (mə'dʒɛstɪk) *or less commonly* **majestical** ADJECTIVE having or displaying majesty or great dignity; grand; lofty.
▸**ma'jestically** ADVERB

majesty ('mædʒɪstɪ) NOUN [1] great dignity of bearing; loftiness; grandeur. [2] supreme power or authority. [3] an archaic word for **royalty.**
▷HISTORY C13: from Old French, from Latin *mājestās;* related to Latin *major,* comparative of *magnus* great

Majesty ('mædʒɪstɪ) NOUN, *plural* **-ties.** (preceded by *Your, His, Her,* or *Their*) a title used to address or refer to a sovereign or the wife or widow of a sovereign.

Maj. Gen. ABBREVIATION FOR Major General.

Majlis ('mædʒlɪs) NOUN [1] the parliament of Iran. [2] (in various N African and Middle Eastern countries) an assembly; council.
▷HISTORY from Persian: assembly

majolica (mə'dʒɒlɪkə, mə'jɒl-) *or* **maiolica** NOUN a type of porous pottery glazed with bright metallic oxides that was originally imported into Italy via Majorca and was extensively made in Italy during the Renaissance.
▷HISTORY C16: from Italian, from Late Latin *Mājorica* Majorca

major ('meɪdʒə) NOUN [1] *Military* an officer immediately junior to a lieutenant colonel. [2] a person who is superior in a group or class. [3] a large or important company: *the oil majors.* [4] (often preceded by *the*) *Music* a major key, chord, mode, or scale. [5] *US, Canadian, Austral, and NZ* **a** the principal field of study of a student at a university, etc.: *his major is sociology.* **b** a student who is studying a particular subject as his principal field: *a sociology major.* [6] a person who has reached the age of legal majority. [7] *Logic* a major term or premise. [8] (*plural*) **the.** *US and Canadian* the major leagues. ◆ ADJECTIVE [9] larger in extent, number, etc.: *the major part.* [10] of greater importance or priority. [11] very serious or significant: *a major disaster.* [12] main, chief, or principal. [13] of, involving, or making up a majority. [14] *Music* **a** (of a scale or mode) having notes separated by the interval of a whole tone, except for the third and fourth degrees, and seventh and eighth degrees, which are separated by a semitone. **b** relating to or employing notes from the major scale: *a major key.* **c** (*postpositive*) denoting a specified key or scale as being major: *C major.* **d** denoting a chord or triad having a major third above the root. **e** (in jazz) denoting a major chord with a major seventh added above the root. [15] *Logic* constituting the major term or major premise of a syllogism. [16] *Chiefly US, Canadian, Austral, and NZ* of or relating to a student's principal field of study at a university, etc. [17] *Brit* the elder: used after a schoolboy's surname if he has one or more younger brothers in the same school: *Price major.* [18] of full legal age. [19] (*postpositive*) *Bell-ringing* of, relating to, or denoting a method rung on eight bells. ◆ VERB [20] (*intr;* usually foll by *in*) *US, Canadian, Austral, and NZ* to do one's principal study (in a particular subject): *to major in English literature.*
▷HISTORY C15 (adj): from Latin, comparative of *magnus* great; C17 (n, in military sense): from French, short for SERGEANT MAJOR
▸**'majorship** NOUN

major axis NOUN the longer or longest axis of an ellipse or ellipsoid.

Majorca (mə'jɔːkə, -'dʒɔː-) NOUN an island in the W Mediterranean: the largest of the Balearic Islands; tourism. Capital: Palma. Pop.: 605 510 (latest est.). Area: 3639 sq. km (1465 sq. miles). Spanish name: **Mallorca.**

major-domo (ˌmeɪdʒə'dəʊməʊ) NOUN, *plural* **-mos.** [1] the chief steward or butler of a great household. [2] *Facetious* a steward or butler.
▷HISTORY C16: from Spanish *mayordomo,* from Medieval Latin *mājor domūs* head of the household

majorette (ˌmeɪdʒə'rɛt) NOUN See **drum majorette.**

major general NOUN *Military* an officer immediately junior to a lieutenant general.
▸**'major-'generalship** *or* **'major-'generalcy** NOUN

major histocompatibility complex NOUN the full name for **MHC.**

majority (mə'dʒɒrɪtɪ) NOUN, *plural* **-ties.** [1] the greater number or part of something: *the majority of the constituents.* [2] (in an election) the number of votes or seats by which the strongest party or candidate beats the combined opposition or the runner-up. See **relative majority, absolute majority.** [3] the largest party or group that votes together in a legislative or deliberative assembly. [4] the time of reaching or state of having reached full legal age, when a person is held competent to manage his own affairs, exercise civil rights and duties, etc. [5] the rank, office, or commission of major. [6] *Euphemistic* the dead (esp in the phrases **join the majority, go** *or* **pass over to the majority**). [7] *Obsolete* the quality or state of being greater; superiority. [8] (*modifier*) of, involving, or being a majority: *a majority decision; a majority verdict.* [9] **in the majority.** forming or part of the greater number of something.
▷HISTORY C16: from Medieval Latin *mājoritās,* from MAJOR (adj)

> **Language note** *The majority of* can only refer to a number of things or people. When talking about an amount, *most of* should be used: *most of* (not *the majority of*) *the harvest was saved.*

majority carrier NOUN the entity responsible for carrying the greater part of the current in a semiconductor. In n-type semiconductors the majority carriers are electrons; in p-type semiconductors they are positively charged holes. Compare **minority carrier.**

major league NOUN *US and Canadian* a league of highest classification in baseball, football, hockey, etc.

majorly ('meɪdʒəlɪ) ADVERB *Slang, chiefly US and Canadian* very; really; extremely: *it was majorly important for us to do that.*

Major Mitchell ('mɪtʃəl) NOUN an Australian cockatoo, *Kakatoe leadbeateri,* with a white-and-pink plumage. Also called: **Leadbeater's cockatoo.**
▷HISTORY C19: named after *Major* (later Sir) Thomas *Mitchell* (1792–1855), Scots-born Australian explorer

major orders PLURAL NOUN *RC Church* the three higher degrees of holy orders: bishop, priest, and deacon.

major planet NOUN a planet of the solar system, as opposed to an asteroid (minor planet).

major premise NOUN *Logic* the premise of a syllogism containing the predicate of its conclusion.

major seventh chord NOUN a chord much used in modern music, esp jazz and pop, consisting of a major triad with an added major seventh above the root. Compare **minor seventh chord.** Often shortened to: **major seventh.**

major suit NOUN *Bridge* hearts or spades. Compare **minor suit.**

major term NOUN *Logic* the predicate of the conclusion of a syllogism, also occurring as the subject or predicate in the major premise.

Majunga (*French* maʒœ̃ga) NOUN the former name of **Mahajanga.**

majuscule ('mædʒəˌskjuːl) NOUN [1] a large letter, either capital or uncial, used in printing or writing. ◆ ADJECTIVE [2] relating to, printed, or written in such letters. Compare **minuscule.**
▷HISTORY C18: via French from Latin *mājusculus,* diminutive of *mājor* bigger, MAJOR
▸**majuscular** (mə'dʒʌskjʊlə) ADJECTIVE

mak (mæk) VERB a Scot word for **make¹.**

Makalu ('mʌkəˌluː) NOUN a massif in NE Nepal, on the border with Tibet in the Himalayas.

makar ('mækər) NOUN *Scot* a creative artist, esp a poet.
▷HISTORY a Scot variant of *maker*

Makasar, Makassar, *or* **Macassar** (mə'kæsə, -'kɑː-) NOUN another name for **Ujung Pandang.**

make¹ (meɪk) VERB **makes, making, made.** (*mainly tr*) [1] to bring into being by shaping, changing, or combining materials, ideas, etc.; form or fashion; create: *to make a chair from bits of wood; make a poem.*

2 to draw up, establish, or form: *to make a decision; make one's will.* 3 to cause to exist, bring about, or produce: *don't make a noise.* 4 to cause, compel, or induce: *please make him go away.* 5 to appoint or assign, as to a rank or position: *they made him chairman.* 6 to constitute: *one swallow doesn't make a summer.* 7 (*also intr*) to come or cause to come into a specified state or condition: *to make merry; make someone happy.* 8 (*copula*) to be or become through development: *he will make a good teacher.* 9 to cause or ensure the success of: *your news has made my day.* 10 to amount to: *twelve inches make a foot.* 11 to be part of or a member of: *did she make one of the party?* 12 to serve as or be suitable for: *that piece of cloth will make a coat.* 13 to prepare or put into a fit condition for use: *to make a bed.* 14 to be the essential element in or part of: *charm makes a good salesman.* 15 to carry out, effect, or do: *to make a gesture.* 16 (*intr; foll by to, as if to,* or *as though to*) to act with the intention or with a show of doing something: *they made to go out; he made as if to hit her.* 17 to use for a specified purpose: *I will make this town my base.* 18 to deliver or pronounce: *to make a speech.* 19 to judge, reckon, or give one's own opinion or information as to: *what time do you make it?* 20 to cause to seem or represent as being: *that furniture makes the room look dark.* 21 to earn, acquire, or win for oneself: *to make friends; make a fortune.* 22 to engage in: *make love not war.* 23 to traverse or cover (distance) by travelling: *we can make a hundred miles by nightfall.* 24 to arrive in time for: *he didn't make the first act of the play.* 25 *Cards* **a** to win a trick with (a specified card). **b** to shuffle (the cards). **c** *Bridge* to fulfil (a contract) by winning the necessary number of tricks. 26 *Cricket* to score (runs). 27 *Electronics* to close (a circuit) permitting a flow of current. Compare **break** (sense 44). 28 (*intr*) to increase in depth: *the water in the hold was making a foot a minute.* 29 (*intr*) (of hay) to dry and mature. 30 *Informal* to gain a place or position on or in: *to make the headlines; make the first team.* 31 *Informal* to achieve the rank of. 32 *Slang* to seduce. 33 **make a book.** to take bets on a race or other contest. 34 **make a day, night,** etc., **of it.** to cause an activity to last a day, night, etc. 35 **make do.** See **do**[1] (sense 37). 36 **make eyes at.** to flirt with or ogle. 37 **make good.** See **good** (sense 44). 38 **make heavy weather (of). a** *Nautical* to roll and pitch in heavy seas. **b** *Informal* to carry out with great difficulty or unnecessarily great effort. 39 **make it. a** *Informal* to be successful in doing something. **b** (foll by *with*) *Slang* to have sexual intercourse. **c** *Slang* to inject a narcotic drug. 40 **make like.** *Slang chiefly US and Canadian* to imitate. 41 **make love (to). a** to have sexual intercourse (with). **b** *Now archaic* to engage in courtship (with). 42 **make or break.** to bring success or ruin. 43 **make time.** See **time** (sense 45). 44 **make water. a** another term for **urinate. b** (of a boat, hull, etc.) to let in water. ◆ NOUN 45 brand, type, or style: *what make of car is that?* 46 the manner or way in which something is made. 47 disposition or character; make-up. 48 the act or process of making. 49 the amount or number made. 50 *Bridge* the contract to be played. 51 *Cards* a player's turn to shuffle. 52 **on the make. a** *Informal* out for profit or conquest. **b** *Slang* in search of a sexual partner. ◆ See also **make after, make away, make for, make of, make off, make out, make over, make-up, make with.**
▷HISTORY Old English *macian;* related to Old Frisian *makia* to construct, Dutch *maken,* German *machen* to make
▸**'makable** ADJECTIVE

make[2] (meɪk) NOUN *Archaic* 1 a peer or consort. 2 a mate or spouse.
▷HISTORY Old English *gemaca* mate; related to MATCH[1]
▸**'makeless** ADJECTIVE

make after VERB (*intr, preposition*) *Archaic* to set off in pursuit of; chase.

make away VERB (*intr, adverb*) 1 to depart in haste. 2 **make away with. a** to steal or abduct. **b** to kill, destroy, or get rid of.

make believe VERB 1 to pretend or enact a fantasy: *the children made believe they were doctors.* ◆ NOUN **make-believe.** 2 **a** a fantasy, pretence, or unreality. **b** (*as modifier*): *a make-believe world.* 3 a person who pretends.

Makedhonia (ˌmakɛðɔ'nia) NOUN transliteration of the Modern Greek name for **Macedonia** (sense 2).

makefast ('meɪkˌfɑːst) NOUN a strong support to which a vessel is secured.

make for VERB (*intr, preposition*) 1 to head towards, esp in haste. 2 to prepare to attack. 3 to help to bring about: *your cooperation will make for the success of our project.*

make of VERB (*tr, preposition*) 1 to interpret as the meaning of: *what do you make of this news?* 2 to produce or construct from: *houses made of brick.* 3 **make little, nothing,** etc., **of. a** not to understand. **b** to attribute little, no, etc., importance to. **c** to gain little or no benefit from. 4 **make much, a lot,** etc., **of. a** (*used with a negative*) to make sense of: *he couldn't make much of her babble.* **b** to give importance to. **c** to gain benefit from. **d** to pay flattering attention to: *the reporters made much of the film star.*

make off VERB 1 (*intr, adverb*) to go or run away in haste. 2 **make off with.** to steal or abduct.

make out VERB (*adverb*) 1 (*tr*) to discern or perceive: *can you make out that house in the distance?* 2 (*tr*) to understand or comprehend: *I can't make out this letter.* 3 (*tr*) to write out: *he made out a cheque.* 4 (*tr*) to attempt to establish or prove: *he made me out to be a liar.* 5 (*intr*) to pretend: *he made out that he could cook.* 6 (*intr*) to manage or fare: *how did you make out in the contest?* 7 (*intr;* often foll by *with*) *Informal, chiefly US and Canadian* to engage in necking or petting: *Alan is making out with Jane.*

make over VERB (*tr, adverb*) 1 to transfer the title or possession of (property, etc.). 2 to renovate or remodel: *she made over the dress to fit her sister.* ◆ NOUN **makeover** ('meɪkˌəʊvə). 3 a complete remodelling. 4 a series of alterations, including beauty treatments and new clothes, intended to make a noticeable improvement in a person's appearance.

maker ('meɪkə) NOUN 1 a person who makes (something); fabricator; constructor. 2 a person who executes a legal document, esp one who signs a promissory note. 3 *Archaic Scot* Also called (esp Scot): **makar.** a poet.

Maker ('meɪkə) NOUN 1 a title given to **God** (as Creator). 2 **(go to) meet one's Maker.** to die.

make-ready NOUN *Printing* the process of preparing the forme and the cylinder or platen packing to achieve the correct impression all over the forme.

makeshift ('meɪkˌʃɪft) ADJECTIVE 1 serving as a temporary or expedient means, esp during an emergency. ◆ NOUN 2 something serving in this capacity.

make-up NOUN 1 cosmetics, such as powder, lipstick, etc., applied to the face to improve its appearance. 2 **a** the cosmetics, false hair, etc., used by an actor to highlight his features or adapt his appearance. **b** the art or result of applying such cosmetics. 3 the manner of arrangement of the parts or qualities of someone or something. 4 the arrangement of type matter and illustrations on a page or in a book. 5 mental or physical constitution. ◆ VERB **make up.** (*adverb*) 6 (*tr*) to form or constitute: *these arguments make up the case for the defence.* 7 (*tr*) to devise, construct, or compose, sometimes with the intent to deceive: *to make up a song; to make up an excuse.* 8 (*tr*) to supply what is lacking or deficient in; complete: *these extra people will make up our total.* 9 (*tr*) to put in order, arrange, or prepare: *to make up a bed.* 10 (*intr;* foll by *for*) to compensate or atone (for): *his kindness now makes up for his rudeness yesterday.* 11 to settle (differences) amicably (often in the phrase **make it up**). 12 to apply cosmetics to (the face) to enhance one's appearance or so as to alter the appearance for a theatrical role. 13 to assemble (type and illustrations) into (columns or pages). 14 (*tr*) to surface (a road) with tarmac, concrete, etc. 15 (*tr*) **a** to set in order and balance (accounts). **b** to draw up (accounting statements). 16 **make up one's mind.** to decide (about something or to do something): *he made up his mind to take vengeance.* 17 **make up to.** *Informal* **a** to make friendly overtures to. **b** to flirt with.

makeweight ('meɪkˌweɪt) NOUN 1 something put on a scale to make up a required weight. 2 an unimportant person or thing added to make up a lack.

make with VERB (*intr, preposition*) *Slang, chiefly US* to proceed with the doing, showing, etc., of: *make with the music.*

Makeyevka (*Russian* ma'kjejɪfkə) NOUN a city in the SE Ukraine: coal-mining centre. Pop.: 394 800 (1998 est.).

Makhachkala (*Russian* məxətʃka'la) NOUN a port in SW Russia, capital of the Dagestan Republic, on the Caspian Sea: fishing fleet; oil refining. Pop.: 334 900 (1999 est.). Former name (until 1921): **Petrovsk.**

making ('meɪkɪŋ) NOUN 1 **a** the act of a person or thing that makes or the process of being made. **b** (*in combination*): *watchmaking.* 2 **be the making of.** to cause the success of. 3 **in the making.** in the process of becoming or being made: *a politician in the making.* 4 something made or the quantity of something made at one time. 5 make-up; composition.

makings ('meɪkɪŋz) PLURAL NOUN 1 potentials, qualities, or materials: *he had the makings of a leader.* 2 Also called: **rollings.** *Slang* the tobacco and cigarette paper used for rolling a cigarette. 3 profits; earnings.

Makkah *or* **Makah** ('mækə, -kɑː) NOUN transliteration of the Arabic name for **Mecca.**

mako[1] ('mɑːkəʊ) NOUN, *plural* **-kos.** 1 any shark of the genus *Isurus,* esp *I. glaucus* of Indo-Pacific and Australian seas: family *Isuridae.* 2 *NZ* the teeth of the mako worn as a decoration by early Maoris.
▷HISTORY from Maori

mako[2] ('mɑːkəʊ) *or* **mako-mako** ('mɑːkəʊˌmɑːkəʊ) NOUN, *plural* **-kos.** 1 Also called: **wineberry.** a small evergreen New Zealand tree, *Aristotelia serrata:* family *Elaeocarpaceae.* 2 *NZ* another name for the **bellbird,** *Anthornis melanura.*
▷HISTORY from Maori

Makurdi (mə'kɜːdɪ) NOUN a port in E central Nigeria, capital of Benue State on the Benue River: agricultural trade centre. Pop.: 123 100 (1996 est.).

makuta (mɑː'kuːtɑː) NOUN the plural of **likuta.**

MAL INTERNATIONAL CAR REGISTRATION FOR Malaysia.

Mal. ABBREVIATION FOR: 1 *Bible* Malachi. 2 Malay(an).

mal- COMBINING FORM bad or badly; wrong or wrongly; imperfect or defective: *maladjusted; malfunction.*
▷HISTORY Old French, from Latin *malus* bad, *male* badly

mala ('mɑːlaː) NOUN *Hinduism* a string of beads or knots, used in praying and meditating.

Malabar Coast *or* **Malabar** ('mæləˌbɑː) NOUN a region along the SW coast of India, extending from Goa to Cape Comorin: includes most of Kerala state.

Malabo (mə'lɑːbəʊ) NOUN the capital and chief port of Equatorial Guinea, on the island of Bioko in the Gulf of Guinea. Pop.: 58 040 (1991 est.). Former name (until 1973): **Santa Isabel.**

malabsorption (ˌmæləb'sɔːpʃən) NOUN a failure of absorption, esp by the small intestine in coeliac disease, cystic fibrosis, etc.

malacca *or* **malacca cane** (mə'lækə) NOUN 1 the stem of the rattan palm. 2 a walking stick made from this stem.

Malacca (mə'lækə) NOUN a state of SW Peninsular Malaysia: rubber plantations. Capital: Malacca. Pop.: 602 867 (2000). Area: 1650 sq. km (637 sq. miles).

Malachi ('mæləˌkaɪ) NOUN *Old Testament* 1 a Hebrew prophet of the 5th century B.C. 2 the book containing his oracles. Douay spelling: **Malachias** (ˌmælə'kaɪəs).

malachite ('mæləˌkaɪt) NOUN a bright green mineral, found in veins and in association with copper deposits. It is a source of copper and is used as an ornamental stone. Composition: hydrated copper carbonate. Formula: $Cu_2CO_3(OH)_2$. Crystal structure: monoclinic.
▷HISTORY C16: via Old French from Latin *molochītēs,* from Greek *molokhitis* mallow-green stone, from *molokhē* mallow

malacia (mə'leɪʃɪə) NOUN the pathological softening of an organ or tissue, such as bone.

malaco- *or before a vowel* **malac-** COMBINING FORM denoting softness: *malacology; malacostracan.*
▷HISTORY from Greek *malakos*

malacology (ˌmælə'kɒlədʒɪ) NOUN the branch of zoology concerned with the study of molluscs. ▸**malacological** (ˌmæləkə'lɒdʒɪkᵊl) ADJECTIVE ▸**ˌmala'cologist** NOUN

malacophily (ˌmælə'kɒfɪlɪ) NOUN *Botany* pollination of plants by snails. ▸**ˌmala'cophilous** ADJECTIVE

malacophyllous (ˌmælə'kɒfɪləs) ADJECTIVE (of plants living in dry regions) having fleshy leaves in which water is stored.

malacopterygian (ˌmæləˌkɒptə'rɪdʒɪən) ADJECTIVE 1 of, relating to, or belonging to the *Malacopterygii*, a group of teleost fishes, including herrings and salmon, having soft fin rays. ◆ NOUN 2 any malacopterygian fish; a soft-finned fish. ◆ Compare **acanthopterygian.**
▷HISTORY C19: from New Latin *Malacopterygii*, from MALACO- + Greek *pterux* wing, fin

malacostracan (ˌmælə'kɒstrəkᵊn) NOUN 1 any crustacean of the subclass or group *Malacostraca*, including lobsters, crabs, woodlice, sand hoppers, and opossum shrimps. ◆ ADJECTIVE *also* **malacostracous.** 2 of, relating to, or belonging to the *Malacostraca*.
▷HISTORY C19: from New Latin, from Greek *malakōstrakos*, from MALACO- + *ostrakon* shell

maladaptive (ˌmælə'dæptɪv) ADJECTIVE 1 unsuitably adapted or adapting poorly to (a situation, purpose, etc.). 2 not encouraging adaptation.
▸**ˌmala'dapted** ADJECTIVE ▸**ˌmala'daptively** ADVERB

maladdress (ˌmælə'drɛs) NOUN awkwardness; tactlessness.

maladjusted (ˌmælə'dʒʌstɪd) ADJECTIVE 1 *Psychol* suffering from maladjustment. 2 badly adjusted.

maladjustment (ˌmælə'dʒʌstmənt) NOUN 1 *Psychol* a failure to meet the demands of society, such as coping with problems and social relationships: usually reflected in emotional instability. 2 faulty or bad adjustment.

maladminister (ˌmæləd'mɪnɪstə) VERB (*tr*) to administer badly, inefficiently, or dishonestly.
▸**ˌmaladˌminis'tration** NOUN ▸**ˌmalad'minisˌtrator** NOUN

maladroit (ˌmælə'drɔɪt) ADJECTIVE 1 showing or characterized by clumsiness; not dexterous. 2 tactless and insensitive in behaviour or speech.
▷HISTORY C17: from French, from *mal* badly + ADROIT
▸**ˌmala'droitly** ADVERB ▸**ˌmala'droitness** NOUN

malady ('mælədɪ) NOUN, *plural* **-dies.** 1 any disease or illness. 2 any unhealthy, morbid, or desperate condition: *a malady of the spirit.*
▷HISTORY C13: from Old French, from Vulgar Latin *male habitus* (unattested) in poor condition, from Latin *male* badly + *habitus*, from *habēre* to have

mala fide ('mælə 'faɪdɪ) ADJECTIVE undertaken in bad faith.
▷HISTORY from Latin

Málaga ('mæləgə; *Spanish* 'malaɣa) NOUN 1 a port and resort in S Spain, in Andalusia on the Mediterranean. Pop.: 528 079 (1998 est.). 2 a sweet fortified dessert wine from Málaga.

Malagasy (ˌmælə'gæzɪ) NOUN 1 (*plural* **-gasy** *or* **-gasies**) a native or inhabitant of Madagascar. 2 the official language of Madagascar belonging to the Malayo-Polynesian family. ◆ ADJECTIVE 3 of or relating to Madagascar, its people, or their language.

Malagasy Republic NOUN the former name (1958–75) of **Madagascar.**

malagueña (ˌmælə'geɪnjə) NOUN a Spanish dance similar to the fandango.
▷HISTORY Spanish: of MÁLAGA

malaise (mæ'leɪz) NOUN 1 a feeling of unease or depression. 2 a mild sickness, not symptomatic of any disease or ailment. 3 a complex of problems affecting a country, economy, etc.: *Bulgaria's economic malaise.*
▷HISTORY C18: from Old French, from *mal* bad + *aise* EASE

malam ('mælæm, -əm) NOUN a variant spelling of **mallam.**

malamute *or* **malemute** ('mæləˌmu:t) NOUN an Alaskan sled dog of the spitz type, having a dense usually greyish coat.
▷HISTORY from the name of an Eskimo tribe

malanders, mallanders, *or* **mallenders** ('mæləndəz) PLURAL NOUN (*functioning as singular*) a disease of horses characterized by an eczematous inflammation behind the knee.
▷HISTORY C15: via Old French from Latin *malandria* sore on the neck of a horse

Malang ('mælæŋ) NOUN a city in S Indonesia, on E Java: commercial centre. Pop.: 763 400 (1995 est.).

malapert ('mæləˌpɜ:t) *Archaic or literary* ◆ ADJECTIVE 1 saucy or impudent. ◆ NOUN 2 a saucy or impudent person.
▷HISTORY C15: from Old French: unskilful (see MAL-, EXPERT); meaning in English influenced by *apert* frank, from Latin *apertus* open
▸**'malaˌpertly** ADVERB ▸**'malaˌpertness** NOUN

malapropism ('mæləprɒpˌɪzəm) NOUN 1 the unintentional misuse of a word by confusion with one of similar sound, esp when creating a ridiculous effect, as in *I am not under the affluence of alcohol.* 2 the habit of misusing words in this manner.
▷HISTORY C18: after Mrs *Malaprop* in Sheridan's play *The Rivals* (1775), a character who misused words, from MALAPROPOS
▸**'malaprop** *or* **ˌmala'propian** ADJECTIVE

malapropos (ˌmælæprə'pəʊ) ADJECTIVE 1 of an inappropriate or misapplied nature or kind. ◆ ADVERB 2 in an inappropriate way or manner. ◆ NOUN 3 something inopportune or inappropriate.
▷HISTORY C17: from French *mal à propos* not to the purpose

malar ('meɪlə) ADJECTIVE 1 of or relating to the cheek or cheekbone. ◆ NOUN 2 Also called: **malar bone.** another name for **zygomatic bone.**
▷HISTORY C18: from New Latin *mālāris*, from Latin *māla* jaw

Mälar ('meɪlə) NOUN **Lake.** a lake in S Sweden, extending 121 km (75 miles) west from Stockholm, where it joins with an inlet of the Baltic Sea (the **Saltsjön**). Area: 1140 sq. km (440 sq. miles). Swedish name: **Mälaren** ('melaren).

malaria (mə'lɛərɪə) NOUN an infectious disease characterized by recurring attacks of chills and fever, caused by the bite of an anopheles mosquito infected with any of four protozoans of the genus *Plasmodium* (*P. vivax, P. falciparum, P. malariae,* or *P. ovale*).
▷HISTORY C18: from Italian *mala aria* bad air, from the belief that the disease was caused by the unwholesome air in swampy districts
▸**ma'larial** *or* **ma'larian** *or* **ma'larious** ADJECTIVE

malariology (məˌlɛərɪ'ɒlədʒɪ) NOUN the study of malaria.
▸**maˌlari'ologist** NOUN

malarkey *or* **malarky** (mə'lɑ:kɪ) NOUN *Slang* nonsense; rubbish.
▷HISTORY C20: of unknown origin

malassimilation (ˌmæləˌsɪmɪ'leɪʃən) NOUN *Pathol* defective assimilation of nutrients.

malate ('mæleɪt, 'meɪ-) NOUN any salt or ester of malic acid.
▷HISTORY C18: from MALIC ACID

Malathion (ˌmælə'θaɪɒn) NOUN *Trademark* a yellow organophosphorus insecticide used as a dust or mist for the control of house flies and garden pests. Formula: $C_{10}H_{19}O_6PS_2$.
▷HISTORY C20: from (*diethyl*) MAL(EATE) + THIO- + -ON

Malatya (ˌmɑ:lɑ:'tjɑ:) NOUN a city in E central Turkey: nearby is the ruined Roman and medieval city of Melitene (Old Malatya). Pop.: 400 248 (1997).

Malawi (mə'lɑ:wɪ) NOUN 1 a republic in E central Africa: established as a British protectorate in 1891; became independent in 1964 and a republic, within the Commonwealth, in 1966; lies along the Great Rift Valley, with Lake Nyasa (Malawi) along the E border, the Nyika Plateau in the northwest, and the Shiré Highlands in the southeast. Official language: Chichewa; English and various other Bantu languages are also widely spoken. Religion: Christian majority, Muslim, and animist minorities. Currency: kwacha. Capital: Lilongwe. Pop.: 10 491 000 (2001 est.). Area: 118 484 sq. km (45 747 sq. miles). Former name: **Nyasaland.** 2 **Lake.** the Malawi name for (Lake) **Nyasa.**

Malawian (mə'lɑ:wɪən) ADJECTIVE 1 of or relating to Malawi or its inhabitants. ◆ NOUN 2 a native or inhabitant of Malawi.

Malay (mə'leɪ) NOUN 1 a member of a people living chiefly in Malaysia and Indonesia who are descendants of Mongoloid immigrants. 2 the language of this people, belonging to the Malayo-Polynesian family. ◆ ADJECTIVE 3 of or relating to the Malays or their language.

Malaya (mə'leɪə) NOUN 1 **States of the Federation of.** part of Malaysia, in the S Malay Peninsula, constituting Peninsular Malaysia: consists of the former Federated Malay States, the former Unfederated Malay States, and the former Straits Settlements. Capital: Kuala Lumpur. Pop.: 16 567 142 (2000). Area: 131 587 sq. km (50 806 sq. miles). 2 **Federation of.** a federation of the nine Malay States of the Malay Peninsula and two of the Straits Settlements (Malacca and Penang): formed in 1948: became part of the British Commonwealth in 1957 and joined Malaysia in 1963.

Malayalam *or* **Malayalaam** (ˌmælɪ'ɑ:ləm) NOUN a language of SW India, belonging to the Dravidian family and closely related to Tamil: the state language of Kerala.

Malayan (mə'leɪən) ADJECTIVE 1 of or relating to Malaya or its inhabitants. ◆ NOUN 2 a native or inhabitant of Malaya.

Malay Archipelago NOUN a group of islands in the Indian and Pacific Oceans, between SE Asia and Australia: the largest group of islands in the world; includes over 3000 Indonesian islands, about 7000 islands of the Philippines, and, sometimes, New Guinea.

Malayo-Polynesian NOUN 1 Also called: **Austronesian.** a family of languages extending from Madagascar to the central Pacific, including Malagasy, Malay, Indonesian, Tagalog, and Polynesian. See also **Austro-Asiatic.** ◆ ADJECTIVE 2 of or relating to this family of languages.

Malay Peninsula NOUN a peninsula of SE Asia, extending south from the Isthmus of Kra in Thailand to Cape Tanjong Piai in Malaysia: consists of SW Thailand and the states of Malaya (Peninsular Malaysia). Ancient name: **Chersonesus Aurea** (ˌkɜ:sə'ni:səs 'ɔ:rɪə).

Malaysia (mə'leɪzɪə) NOUN a federation in SE Asia (within the Commonwealth), consisting of **Peninsular Malaysia** on the Malay Peninsula, and **East Malaysia** (Sabah and Sarawak), occupying the N part of the island of Borneo: formed in 1963 as a federation of Malaya, Sarawak, Sabah, and Singapore (the latter seceded in 1965); densely forested and mostly mountainous. Official language: Malay; English and various Chinese and Indian minority languages are also spoken. Official religion: Muslim. Currency: ringgit. Capital: Putrajaya (the transfer of government from Kuala Lumpur is scheduled for completion by 2005). Pop.: 22 602 000 (2001 est.). Area: 333 403 sq. km (128 727 sq. miles).

Malaysian (mə'leɪzɪən) ADJECTIVE 1 of or relating to Malaysia or its inhabitants. ◆ NOUN 2 a native or inhabitant of Malaysia.

Malay States PLURAL NOUN the former states of the Malay Peninsula that, together with Penang and Malacca, formed the Union of Malaya (1946) and the Federation of Malaya (1948). Perak, Selangor, Negri Sembilan, and Pahang were established as the **Federated Malay States** by the British in 1895 and Perlis, Kedah, Kelantan, and Trengannu as the **Unfederated Malay States** in 1909 (joined by Johore in 1914).

malcontent ('mælkənˌtɛnt) ADJECTIVE 1 disgusted or discontented. ◆ NOUN 2 a person who is malcontent.
▷HISTORY C16: from Old French

mal de mer *French* (mal də mɛr) NOUN seasickness.

maldistribution (ˌmældɪstrɪ'bju:ʃən) NOUN faulty, unequal, or unfair distribution (as of wealth, business, etc.).

Maldives ('mɔ:ldaɪvz) PLURAL NOUN **Republic of.** a republic occupying an archipelago of 1087 coral islands in the Indian Ocean, southwest of Sri Lanka: came under British protection in 1887; became independent in 1965 and a republic in 1968; a member of the Commonwealth. Official language: Divehi. Official religion: (Sunni) Muslim. Currency: rufiyaa. Capital: Malé. Pop.: 275 000 (2001 est.).

Area: 298 sq. km (115 sq. miles). Also called: **Maldive Islands.**

Maldivian (mɔːlˈdɪvɪən) *or* **Maldivan** (ˈmɔːldaɪvᵊn, -dɪ-) ADJECTIVE 1 of or relating to the Maldives or their inhabitants. ◆ NOUN 2 a native or inhabitant of the Maldives.

Maldon (ˈmɔːldən) NOUN a market town in SE England, in Essex; scene of a battle (991) between the East Saxons and the victorious Danes, celebrated in *The Battle of Maldon,* an Old English poem. Pop.: 15 841 (1991).

male (meɪl) ADJECTIVE 1 of, relating to, or designating the sex producing gametes (spermatozoa) that can fertilize female gametes (ova). 2 of, relating to, or characteristic of a man; masculine. 3 for or composed of men or boys: *a male choir.* 4 (of gametes) capable of fertilizing an egg cell in sexual reproduction. 5 (of reproductive organs, such as a testis or stamen) capable of producing male gametes. 6 (of flowers) bearing stamens but lacking a functional pistil. 7 *Electronics, mechanical engineering* having a projecting part or parts that fit into a female counterpart: *a male plug.* ◆ NOUN 8 a male person, animal, or plant.
▷HISTORY C14: via Old French from Latin *masculus* MASCULINE
▸ **ˈmaleness** NOUN

Malé (ˈmɑːleɪ) NOUN the capital of the Republic of Maldives, on Malé Island in the centre of the island group. Pop.: 62 973 (1995 est.).

maleate (ˈmælɪˌeɪt) NOUN any salt or ester of maleic acid.
▷HISTORY C19: from MALE(IC ACID) + -ATE[1]

male chauvinism NOUN the belief, held or alleged to be held by certain men, that men are inherently superior to women.
▸ **male chauvinist** NOUN, ADJECTIVE

male chauvinist pig NOUN *Informal, derogatory* a man who exhibits male chauvinism. Abbreviation: **MCP.**

maledict (ˈmælɪdɪkt) VERB 1 (*tr*) *Literary* to utter a curse against. ◆ ADJECTIVE 2 *Archaic* cursed or detestable.

malediction (ˌmælɪˈdɪkʃən) NOUN 1 the utterance of a curse against someone or something. 2 slanderous accusation or comment.
▷HISTORY C15: from Latin *maledictiō* a reviling, from *male* ill + *dīcere* to speak
▸ **ˌmaleˈdictive** *or* **ˌmaleˈdictory** ADJECTIVE

malefactor (ˈmælɪˌfæktə) NOUN a criminal; wrongdoer.
▷HISTORY C15: via Old French from Latin, from *malefacere* to do evil
▸ **ˈmaleˌfaction** NOUN ▸ **ˈmaleˌfactress** FEMININE NOUN

male fern NOUN a fern, *Dryopteris filix-mas,* having scaly stalks and pinnate fronds with kidney-shaped spore-producing bodies on the underside: family *Polypodiaceae.*
▷HISTORY C16: so called because it was formerly believed to be the male of the lady fern

maleficent (məˈlefɪsənt) ADJECTIVE causing or capable of producing evil or mischief; harmful or baleful.
▷HISTORY C17: from Latin *maleficent-,* from *maleficus* wicked, prone to evil, from *malum* evil
▸ **maˈlefic** ADJECTIVE ▸ **maˈleficence** NOUN

maleic acid (məˈleɪɪk) NOUN a colourless soluble crystalline substance used to synthesize other compounds. Formula: HOOCCH:CHCOOH. Systematic name: ***cis*-butanedioic acid.**
▷HISTORY C19: from French *maléique,* altered form of *malique;* see MALIC ACID

male menopause NOUN a period in a man's later middle age in which he may experience an identity crisis as he feels age overtake his sexual powers.

malemute (ˈmæləˌmuːt) NOUN a variant spelling of **malamute.**

malevolent (məˈlevələnt) ADJECTIVE 1 wishing or appearing to wish evil to others; malicious. 2 *Astrology* having an evil influence.
▷HISTORY C16: from Latin *malevolens,* from *male* ill + *volens,* present participle of *velle* to wish
▸ **maˈlevolence** NOUN ▸ **maˈlevolently** ADVERB

malfeasance (mælˈfiːzᵊns) NOUN *Law* the doing of a wrongful or illegal act, esp by a public official. Compare **misfeasance, nonfeasance.**
▷HISTORY C17: from Old French *mal faisant,* from *mal* evil + *faisant* doing, from *faire* to do, from Latin *facere*
▸ **malˈfeasant** NOUN, ADJECTIVE

malformation (ˌmælfɔːˈmeɪʃən) NOUN 1 the condition of being faulty or abnormal in form or shape. 2 *Pathol* a deformity in the shape or structure of a part, esp when congenital.
▸ **malˈformed** ADJECTIVE

malfunction (mælˈfʌŋkʃən) VERB 1 (*intr*) to function imperfectly or irregularly or fail to function. ◆ NOUN 2 failure to function or defective functioning.

malgré lui *French* (malgre lɥi) ADVERB in spite of himself.

Mali (ˈmɑːlɪ) NOUN a landlocked republic in West Africa: conquered by the French by 1898 and incorporated (as French Sudan) into French West Africa; became independent in 1960; settled chiefly in the basins of the Rivers Senegal and Niger in the south. Official language: French. Religion: Muslim majority, also animist. Currency: franc. Capital: Bamako. Pop.: 11 009 000 (2001 est.). Area: 1 248 574 sq. km (482 077 sq. miles). Former name (1898–1959): **French Sudan.**

malibu board (ˈmælɪbuː) NOUN a lightweight surfboard, usually having a fin.
▷HISTORY C20: named after *Malibu* beach, California

malic acid (ˈmælɪk, ˈmeɪ-) NOUN a colourless crystalline compound occurring in apples and other fruits. Formula: $HOOCCH_2CH(OH)COOH$.
▷HISTORY C18 *malic,* via French *malique* from Latin *mālum* apple

malice (ˈmælɪs) NOUN 1 the desire to do harm or mischief. 2 evil intent. 3 *Law* the state of mind with which an act is committed and from which the intent to do wrong may be inferred. See also **malice aforethought.**
▷HISTORY C13: via Old French from Latin *malitia,* from *malus* evil

malice aforethought NOUN *Criminal law* 1 the predetermination to do an unlawful act, esp to kill or seriously injure. 2 the intent with which an unlawful killing is effected, which must be proved for the crime to constitute murder. See also **murder, manslaughter.**

malicious (məˈlɪʃəs) ADJECTIVE 1 characterized by malice. 2 motivated by wrongful, vicious, or mischievous purposes.
▸ **maˈliciously** ADVERB ▸ **maˈliciousness** NOUN

malign (məˈlaɪn) ADJECTIVE 1 evil in influence, intention, or effect. ◆ VERB 2 (*tr*) to slander or defame.
▷HISTORY C14: via Old French from Latin *malīgnus* spiteful, from *malus* evil
▸ **maˈligner** NOUN ▸ **maˈlignly** ADVERB

malignancy (məˈlɪɡnənsɪ) NOUN, *plural* **-cies.** 1 the state or quality of being malignant. 2 *Pathol* a cancerous growth.

malignant (məˈlɪɡnənt) ADJECTIVE 1 having or showing desire to harm others. 2 tending to cause great harm; injurious. 3 *Pathol* (of a tumour) uncontrollable or resistant to therapy; rapidly spreading. ◆ NOUN 4 *History* (in the English Civil War) a Parliamentarian term for a **royalist.**
▷HISTORY C16: from Late Latin *malīgnāre* to behave spitefully, from Latin *malīgnus* MALIGN
▸ **maˈlignantly** ADVERB

malignity (məˈlɪɡnɪtɪ) NOUN, *plural* **-ties.** 1 the condition or quality of being malign, malevolent, or deadly. 2 (*often plural*) a malign or malicious act or feeling.

malihini (ˌmɑːlɪˈhiːnɪ) NOUN, *plural* **-nis.** (in Hawaii) a foreigner or stranger.
▷HISTORY from Hawaiian

malimprinted (ˌmælɪmˈprɪntɪd) ADJECTIVE (of an animal or person) suffering from a defect in the behavioural process of imprinting, resulting in attraction to members of other species, fetishism, etc.
▸ **ˌmalimˈprinting** NOUN

malines (məˈliːn) NOUN 1 a type of silk net used in dressmaking. 2 another name for **Mechlin lace.**
▷HISTORY C19: from French *Malines* (Mechelen), where this lace was traditionally made

Malines (malin) NOUN the French name for **Mechelen.**

malinger (məˈlɪŋɡə) VERB (*intr*) to pretend or exaggerate illness, esp to avoid work.
▷HISTORY C19: from French *malingre* sickly, perhaps from *mal* badly + Old French *haingre* feeble
▸ **maˈlingerer** NOUN

Malinke (məˈlɪŋkɪ) *or* **Maninke** NOUN 1 (*plural* **-ke** *or* **-kes**) a member of a Negroid people of W Africa, living chiefly in Guinea and Mali, noted for their use of cowry shells as currency. 2 the language of this people, belonging to the Mande branch of the Niger-Congo family.

Maliseet (ˈmælɪˌsiːt) NOUN a member of a Native Canadian people of New Brunswick and E Quebec. 2 the Algonquian language of this people.
▷HISTORY from Micmac *malisiit* one speaking an incomprehensible language

malison (ˈmælɪzᵊn, -sᵊn) NOUN an archaic or poetic word for **curse.**
▷HISTORY C13: via Old French from Latin *maledictiō* MALEDICTION

malkin (ˈmɔːkɪn, ˈmɔːl-, ˈmæl-) NOUN 1 an archaic or dialect name for a **cat**[1]. Compare **grimalkin.** 2 a variant of **mawkin.**
▷HISTORY C13: diminutive of *Maud*

mall (mæl, mɔːl) NOUN 1 a shaded avenue, esp one that is open to the public. 2 *US, Canadian, Austral, and NZ* short for **shopping mall.**
▷HISTORY C17: after *The Mall,* in St James's Park, London. See PALL-MALL

mallam *or* **malam** (ˈmælæm, -əm) NOUN *W African* 1 (in Islamic W Africa) a man learned in Koranic studies. 2 (in N Nigeria) a title and form of address for a learned or educated man.
▷HISTORY C20: from Hausa

mallanders (ˈmæləndəz) NOUN a variant spelling of **malanders.**

mallard (ˈmælɑːd) NOUN, *plural* **-lard** *or* **-lards.** a duck, *Anas platyrhynchos,* common over most of the N hemisphere, the male of which has a dark green head and reddish-brown breast: the ancestor of all domestic breeds of duck.
▷HISTORY C14: from Old French *mallart,* perhaps from *maslart* (unattested); see MALE, -ARD

malleable (ˈmælɪəbᵊl) ADJECTIVE 1 (esp of metal) able to be worked, hammered, or shaped under pressure or blows without breaking. 2 able to be influenced; pliable or tractable.
▷HISTORY C14: via Old French from Medieval Latin *malleābilis,* from Latin *malleus* hammer
▸ **ˌmalleaˈbility** *or* (*less commonly*) **ˈmalleableness** NOUN
▸ **ˈmalleably** ADVERB

malleable iron NOUN 1 Also called: **malleable cast iron.** cast iron that has been toughened by gradual heating or slow cooling. 2 a less common name for **wrought iron.**

mallee (ˈmæliː) NOUN 1 any of several low shrubby eucalyptus trees that flourish in desert regions of Australia. 2 (usually preceded by *the*) *Austral informal* another name for the **bush** (sense 4). 3 See **mallee root.**
▷HISTORY C19: native Australian name

mallee fowl NOUN an Australian megapode, *Leipoa ocellata,* that allows its eggs to incubate naturally in a sandy mound.

mallee root NOUN *Austral* the rootstock (rhizome) of a mallee tree, often used as fuel.

mallemuck (ˈmælɪˌmʌk) NOUN any of various sea birds, such as the albatross, fulmar, or shearwater.
▷HISTORY C17: from Dutch *mallemok* from *mal* silly + *mok* gull

mallenders (ˈmæləndəz) NOUN a less common spelling of **malanders.**

malleolus (məˈliːələs) NOUN, *plural* **-li** (-ˌlaɪ). either of two rounded bony projections of the tibia and fibula on the sides of each ankle joint.
▷HISTORY C17: diminutive of Latin *malleus* hammer
▸ **malˈleolar** ADJECTIVE

mallet (ˈmælɪt) NOUN 1 a tool resembling a hammer but having a large head of wood, copper, lead, leather, etc., used for driving chisels, beating sheet metal, etc. 2 a long stick with a head like a hammer used to strike the ball in croquet or polo. 3 *Chiefly US* a very large powerful steam

locomotive with a conventional boiler but with two separate articulated engine units.
▷HISTORY C15: from Old French *maillet* wooden hammer, diminutive of *mail* MAUL (n)

malleus ('mælɪəs) NOUN, *plural* **-lei** (-lɪˌaɪ). the outermost and largest of the three small bones in the middle ear of mammals. Nontechnical name: **hammer**. See also **incus, stapes.**
▷HISTORY C17: from Latin: hammer

Mallorca (ma'ʎɔrka) NOUN the Spanish name for **Majorca.**

mallow ('mæləʊ) NOUN [1] any plant of the malvaceous genus *Malva,* esp *M. sylvestris* of Europe, having purple, pink, or white flowers. See also **dwarf mallow, musk mallow.** [2] any of various related plants, such as the marsh mallow, rose mallow, Indian mallow, and tree mallow.
▷HISTORY Old English *mealuwe,* from Latin *malva;* probably related to Greek *malakhē* mallow

mallowpuff ('mæləʊˌpʌf) NOUN *NZ* a white marshmallow on a biscuit base and covered with chocolate.

mallowpuff Maori NOUN *NZ informal, derogatory* a Maori who is considered to behave like a white person.

mall rat (mɔ:l) NOUN *Slang, chiefly US* a youngster who spends much of his or her time in shopping malls.

malm (mɑ:m) NOUN [1] a soft greyish limestone that crumbles easily. [2] a chalky soil formed from this limestone. [3] an artificial mixture of clay and chalk used to make bricks.
▷HISTORY Old English *mealm-* (in compound words); related to Old Norse *malmr* ore, Gothic *malma* sand

Malmédy (*French* malmedi) NOUN See **Eupen and Malmédy.**

Malmö ('mælməʊ; *Swedish* 'malmø:) NOUN a port in S Sweden, on the Sound: part of Denmark until 1658; industrial centre. Pop.: 257 574 (2000 est.).

malmsey ('mɑ:mzɪ) NOUN a sweet Madeira wine.
▷HISTORY C15: from Medieval Latin *Malmasia,* corruption of Greek *Monembasia,* Greek port from which the wine was shipped

malnourished (mæl'nʌrɪʃt) ADJECTIVE undernourished.

malnutrition (ˌmælnju:'trɪʃən) NOUN lack of adequate nutrition resulting from insufficient food, unbalanced diet, or defective assimilation.

malocclusion (ˌmælə'klu:ʒən) NOUN *Dentistry* a defect in the normal position of the upper and lower teeth when the mouth is closed, as from abnormal development of the jaw.
▸ˌ**maloc'cluded** ADJECTIVE

malodorous (mæl'əʊdərəs) ADJECTIVE having a bad smell.
▸**mal'odorously** ADVERB ▸**mal'odorousness** NOUN

malonic acid (mə'ləʊnɪk, -'lɒn-) NOUN another name for **propanedioic acid.**
▷HISTORY C19: from French *malonique,* altered form of *malique;* see MALIC ACID

malonylurea (ˌmælənɪlju'rɪə, -'jʊərɪə, -ni:l-) NOUN another name for **barbituric acid.**

maloti (mə'ləʊtɪ, -'lu:tɪ) NOUN the plural of **loti.**

malpighiaceous (mælˌpɪgɪ'eɪʃəs) ADJECTIVE of, relating to, or belonging to the *Malpighiaceae,* a family of tropical plants many of which are lianas.
▷HISTORY C19: from New Latin *Malpighia,* after Marcello *Malpighi* (1628–94), Italian physiologist

Malpighian (mæl'pɪgɪən) ADJECTIVE of or relating to Marcello Malpighi (1628–94), the Italian physiologist.

Malpighian corpuscle *or* **body** NOUN *Anatomy* an encapsulated cluster of capillaries at the end of each urine-secreting tubule of the kidney.

Malpighian layer NOUN *Anatomy* the innermost layer of the epidermis.

Malpighian tubules *or* **tubes** PLURAL NOUN organs of excretion in insects and many other arthropods: narrow tubules opening into the anterior part of the hindgut.

malposition (ˌmælpə'zɪʃən) NOUN abnormal position of a bodily part.
▸**malposed** (mæl'pəʊzd) ADJECTIVE

malpractice (mæl'præktɪs) NOUN [1] immoral, illegal, or unethical professional conduct or neglect of professional duty. [2] any instance of improper professional conduct.
▸**malpractitioner** (ˌmælpræk'tɪʃənə) NOUN

malt (mɔ:lt) NOUN [1] cereal grain, such as barley, that is kiln-dried after it has germinated by soaking in water. [2] See **malt liquor.** [3] short for **malt whisky.** ◆ VERB [4] to make into or become malt. [5] to make (something, esp liquor) with malt.
▷HISTORY Old English *mealt;* related to Dutch *mout,* Old Norse *malt;* see also MELT

Malta ('mɔ:ltə) NOUN a republic occupying the islands of Malta, Gozo, and Comino, in the Mediterranean south of Sicily: governed by the Knights Hospitallers from 1530 until Napoleon's conquest in 1798; French driven out, with British help, 1800; became British dependency 1814; suffered severely in World War II; became independent in 1964 and a republic in 1974; a member of the Commonwealth. Official languages: Maltese and English. Official religion: Roman Catholic. Currency: Maltese lira. Capital: Valletta. Pop.: 381 000 (2001 est.). Area: 316 sq. km (122 sq. miles).

Malta fever NOUN another name for **brucellosis.**

maltase ('mɔ:lteɪz) NOUN an enzyme that hydrolyses maltose and similar glucosides (α-glucosides) to glucose. Also called: **α-glucosidase.**
▷HISTORY C19: from MALT + -ASE

malted milk NOUN [1] a soluble powder made from dehydrated milk and malted cereals. [2] a drink made from this powder.

Maltese (mɔ:l'ti:z) ADJECTIVE [1] of or relating to Malta, its inhabitants, or their language. ◆ NOUN [2] (*plural* **-tese**) a native or inhabitant of Malta. [3] the official language of Malta, a form of Arabic with borrowings from Italian, etc. [4] a breed of toy dog having a very long straight silky white coat. [5] a domestic fancy pigeon having long legs and a long neck.

Maltese cross NOUN [1] a cross with triangular arms that taper towards the centre, sometimes having indented outer sides: formerly worn by the Knights of Malta. [2] (in a film projector) a cam mechanism of this shape that produces intermittent motion.

malt extract NOUN a sticky substance obtained from an infusion of malt.

maltha ('mælθə) NOUN [1] another name for **mineral tar.** [2] any of various naturally occurring mixtures of hydrocarbons, such as ozocerite.
▷HISTORY C15: via Latin from Greek: a mixture of wax and pitch

Malthusian (mæl'θju:zɪən) ADJECTIVE [1] of or relating to the theory of the English economist Thomas Robert Malthus (1766–1834) stating that increases in population tend to exceed increases in the means of subsistence and that therefore sexual restraint should be exercised. ◆ NOUN [2] a supporter of this theory.
▸**Mal'thusianism** NOUN

malting ('mɔ:ltɪŋ) NOUN a building in which malt is made or stored. Also called: **malt house.**

malt liquor NOUN any alcoholic drink brewed from malt.

maltose ('mɔ:ltəʊz) NOUN a disaccharide of glucose formed by the enzymic hydrolysis of starch: used in bacteriological culture media and as a nutrient in infant feeding. Formula: $C_{12}H_{22}O_{11}$.
▷HISTORY C19: from MALT + -OSE[2]

maltreat (mæl'tri:t) VERB (*tr*) to treat badly, cruelly, or inconsiderately.
▷HISTORY C18: from French *maltraiter*
▸**mal'treater** NOUN ▸**mal'treatment** NOUN

maltster ('mɔ:ltstə) NOUN a person who makes or deals in malt.

malt whisky NOUN whisky made from malted barley.

malty ('mɔ:ltɪ) ADJECTIVE **maltier, maltiest.** of, like, or containing malt.
▸'**maltiness** NOUN

Maluku (mɑ:'lu:ku:) NOUN the Indonesian name for the **Moluccas.**

malvaceous (mæl'veɪʃəs) ADJECTIVE of, relating to, or belonging to the *Malvaceae,* a family of plants that includes mallow, cotton, okra, althaea, and abutilon.
▷HISTORY C17: from Latin *malvāceus,* from *malva* MALLOW

malvasia (ˌmælvə'sɪə) NOUN [1] another word for **malmsey.** [2] the type of grape used to make malmsey.
▷HISTORY C19: from Italian, from Greek *Monembasia;* see MALMSEY
▸ˌ**malva'sian** ADJECTIVE

Malvern ('mɔ:lvən) NOUN a town and resort in W England, in S Worcestershire on the E slopes of the **Malvern Hills**: annual dramatic festival; mineral springs. Pop.: 31 537 (1991).

malversation (ˌmælvɜ:'seɪʃən) NOUN *Rare* professional or public misconduct.
▷HISTORY C16: from French, from *malverser* to behave badly, from Latin *male versārī*

Malvinas (*Spanish* mal'βinas) PLURAL NOUN **Islas** ('izlas). the Argentine name for the **Falkland Islands.**

malvoisie ('mælvɔɪzɪ, -və-) NOUN an amber dessert wine made in France, similar to malmsey.
▷HISTORY C14: via Old French from Italian *Malvasia,* from Greek *Monembasia;* see MALMSEY

malwa ('malwa) NOUN a Ugandan drink brewed from millet.
▷HISTORY from Rutooro, a language of W Uganda

mam (mæm) NOUN *Informal or dialect* another word for **mother**[1].

mama (mə'mɑ:) NOUN *Old-fashioned* an informal word for **mother**[1].

mamaguy ('mɑ:məˌgaɪ) *Caribbean* ◆ VERB [1] (*tr*) to deceive or tease, either in jest or by deceitful flattery. ◆ NOUN [2] an instance of such deception or flattery.
▷HISTORY from Spanish *mamar el gallo,* literally: to feed the cock

mamba ('mæmbə) NOUN any aggressive partly arboreal tropical African venomous elapid snake of the genus *Dendroaspis,* esp *D. angusticeps* (**green** and **black mambas**).
▷HISTORY from Zulu *im-amba*

mambo ('mæmbəʊ) NOUN, *plural* **-bos.** [1] a modern Latin American dance, resembling the rumba, derived from the ritual dance of voodoo. [2] a voodoo priestess. ◆ VERB **-bos, -boing, -boed.** [3] (*intr*) to perform this dance.
▷HISTORY American Spanish, probably from Haitian Creole: voodoo priestess

mamelon ('mæməlᵊn) NOUN a small rounded hillock.
▷HISTORY C19: from French: nipple

Mameluke, Mamaluke ('mæməˌlu:k), *or* **Mamluk** ('mæmlu:k) NOUN [1] a member of a military class, originally of Turkish slaves, ruling in Egypt from about 1250 to 1517 and remaining powerful until crushed in 1811. [2] (in Muslim countries) a slave.
▷HISTORY C16: via French, ultimately from Arabic *mamlūk* slave, from *malaka* to possess

mamey, mammee, *or* **mammee apple** (mæ'mi:) NOUN [1] a tropical American tree, *Mammea americana,* cultivated for its large edible fruits: family *Clusiaceae.* [2] the fruit of this tree, having yellow pulp and a red skin. [3] another name for the **marmalade tree.**
▷HISTORY C16: from Spanish *mamey,* from Haitian

mamilla *or US* **mammilla** (mæ'mɪlə) NOUN, *plural* **-lae** (-li:). [1] a nipple or teat. [2] any nipple-shaped part or prominence.
▷HISTORY C17: from Latin, diminutive of *mamma* breast
▸'**mamillary** *or (US)* '**mammillary** ADJECTIVE

mamillate ('mæmɪˌleɪt), **mamillated,** *or US* **mammillate, mammillated** ADJECTIVE having nipples or nipple-like protuberances.

mamma[1] NOUN *Chiefly US* [1] ('mɑ:mə, mə'mɑ:) Also: **momma.** another word for **mother**[1]. [2] ('mɑ:mə) *Informal* a buxom and voluptuous woman.
▷HISTORY C16: reduplication of childish syllable *ma;* compare Welsh *mam,* French *maman,* Russian *mama*

mamma[2] ('mæmə) NOUN, *plural* **-mae** (-mi:). [1] the milk-secreting organ of female mammals: the breast in women, the udder in cows, sheep, etc. [2] (*functioning as plural*) breast-shaped protuberances, esp from the base of cumulonimbus clouds.
▷HISTORY C17: from Latin: breast

mammal ('mæməl) NOUN any animal of the

Mammalia, a large class of warm-blooded vertebrates having mammary glands in the female, a thoracic diaphragm, and a four-chambered heart. The class includes the whales, carnivores, rodents, bats, primates, etc.
▷HISTORY C19: via New Latin from Latin *mamma* breast
▸**mammalian** (mæˈmeɪlɪən) ADJECTIVE, NOUN
▸**ˈmammal-ˌlike** ADJECTIVE

mammalogy (mæˈmælədʒɪ) NOUN the branch of zoology concerned with the study of mammals.
▸**mammalogical** (ˌmæməˈlɒdʒɪk^{ə}l) ADJECTIVE
▸**mamˈmalogist** NOUN

mammary (ˈmæmərɪ) ADJECTIVE of, relating to, or like a mamma or breast.

mammary gland NOUN any of the milk-producing glands in mammals. In higher mammals each gland consists of a network of tubes and cavities connected to the exterior by a nipple.

mammee (mæˈmiː) NOUN a variant spelling of **mamey.**

mammet (ˈmæmɪt) NOUN another word for **maumet.**

mammiferous (mæˈmɪfərəs) ADJECTIVE having breasts or mammae.

mammilla (mæˈmɪlə) NOUN, *plural* **-lae** (-liː). the US spelling of **mamilla.**
▸**ˈmammillary** ADJECTIVE

mammillate (ˈmæmɪˌleɪt) *or* **mammillated** ADJECTIVE the US spellings of **mamillate, mamillated.**

mammock (ˈmæmək) *Dialect* ◆ NOUN [1] a fragment. ◆ VERB [2] *(tr)* to tear or shred.
▷HISTORY C16: of unknown origin

mammography (mæˈmɒgrəfɪ) NOUN the technique of using X-rays to examine the breast in the early detection of cancer.
▸**ˈmammoˌgraph** *or* **ˈmammoˌgram** NOUN

mammon (ˈmæmən) NOUN [1] riches or wealth regarded as a source of evil and corruption. [2] avarice or greed.
▷HISTORY C14: via Late Latin from New Testament Greek *mammōnas,* from Aramaic *māmōnā* wealth
▸**ˈmammonish** ADJECTIVE ▸**ˈmammonism** NOUN
▸**ˈmammonist** *or* **ˈmammonite** NOUN ▸**ˌmammonˈistic** ADJECTIVE

Mammon (ˈmæmən) NOUN *New Testament* the personification of riches and greed in the form of a false god.

mammoth (ˈmæməθ) NOUN [1] any large extinct elephant of the Pleistocene genus *Mammuthus* (or *Elephas*), such as *M. primigenius* (**woolly mammoth**), having a hairy coat and long curved tusks. ◆ ADJECTIVE [2] of gigantic size or importance.
▷HISTORY C18: from Russian *mamot,* from Tatar *mamont,* perhaps from *mamma* earth, because of a belief that the animal made burrows

Mammoth Cave National Park NOUN a national park in W central Kentucky: established in 1941 to protect a system of limestone caverns.

mammy *or* **mammie** (ˈmæmɪ) NOUN, *plural* **-mies.** [1] a child's word for **mother**^{1}. [2] *Chiefly southern US* a Black woman employed as a nurse or servant to a White family.

mammy wagon NOUN a W African vehicle built on a lorry chassis, capable of carrying both passengers and goods.

Mamoré (*Spanish* mamoˈre) NOUN a river in central Bolivia, flowing north to the Beni River to form the Madeira River. Length: about 1500 km (930 miles).

mampara (mamˈpɑːrə) NOUN *South African informal* [1] a foolish person, idiot. [2] *Obsolete* an incompetent worker.
▷HISTORY of unknown origin

mampoer (məmˈpʊə) NOUN *South African* a home-distilled brandy made from peaches, prickly pears, etc.
▷HISTORY Afrikaans, possibly from Sotho *mampuru,* strong man

mamzer (ˈmɑmzə) NOUN [1] a Yiddish slang word for **bastard.** [2] *Judaism* a child of an incestuous or adulterous union.
▷HISTORY from Hebrew

man (mæn) NOUN, *plural* **men** (mɛn). [1] an adult male human being, as distinguished from a woman. [2] *(modifier)* male; masculine: *a man child.* [3] a human being regardless of sex or age, considered as a representative of mankind; a person. [4] *(sometimes capital)* human beings collectively; mankind: *the development of man.* [5] Also called: **modern man. a** a member of any of the living races of *Homo sapiens,* characterized by erect bipedal posture, a highly developed brain, and powers of articulate speech, abstract reasoning, and imagination. **b** any extinct member of the species *Homo sapiens,* such as Cro-Magnon man. [6] a member of any of the extinct species of the genus *Homo,* such as Java man, Heidelberg man, and Solo man. [7] an adult male human being with qualities associated with the male, such as courage or virility: *be a man.* [8] manly qualities or virtues: *the man in him was outraged.* [9] **a** a subordinate, servant, or employee contrasted with an employer or manager. **b** *(in combination)*: *the number of man-days required to complete a job.* [10] *(usually plural)* a member of the armed forces who does not hold commissioned, warrant, or noncommissioned rank (as in the phrase **officers and men**). [11] a member of a group, team, etc. [12] a husband, boyfriend, etc.: *man and wife.* [13] an expression used parenthetically to indicate an informal relationship between speaker and hearer. [14] a movable piece in various games, such as draughts. [15] *South African, slang* any person: used as a term of address. [16] a vassal of a feudal lord. [17] **as one man.** with unanimous action or response. [18] **be one's own man.** to be independent or free. [19] **he's your man.** he's the person needed (for a particular task, role, job, etc.). [20] **man and boy.** from childhood. [21] **sort out** *or* **separate the men from the boys.** to separate the experienced from the inexperienced. [22] **to a man. a** unanimously. **b** without exception: *they were slaughtered to a man.* ◆ INTERJECTION [23] *Informal* an exclamation or expletive, often indicating surprise or pleasure. ◆ VERB **mans, manning, manned.** *(tr)* [24] to provide with sufficient men for operation, defence, etc.: *to man a ship.* [25] to take one's place at or near in readiness for action. [26] *Falconry* to induce (a hawk or falcon) to endure the presence of and handling by man, esp strangers.
▷HISTORY Old English *mann;* related to Old Frisian *man,* Old High German *man,* Dutch *man,* Icelandic *mathr*
▸**ˈmanless** ADJECTIVE

Man^1 (mæn) NOUN **the.** *(sometimes not capital) US* [1] *Black slang* a White man or White men collectively, esp when in authority, in the police, or held in contempt. [2] *Slang* a drug peddler.

Man^2 (mæn) NOUN **Isle of.** an island in the British Isles, in the Irish Sea between Cumbria and Northern Ireland: a Crown possession with its own parliament, the Court of Tynwald; a dependency of Norway until 1266, when it came under Scottish rule; its own language, Manx, became extinct in the 19th century but has been revived. Capital: Douglas. Pop.: 73 500 (2001 est.). Area: 588 sq. km (227 sq. miles).

-man NOUN COMBINING FORM indicating a person who has a role, works in a place, or operates equipment as specified: *salesman, barman, cameraman.*

> **Language note** The use of words ending in *-man* is avoided as implying a male in job advertisements, where sexual discrimination is illegal, and in many other contexts where a term that is not gender-specific is available, such as *salesperson, barperson, camera operator.*

mana (ˈmɑːnə) NOUN *Anthropol* [1] (in Polynesia, Melanesia, etc.) a concept of a life force, believed to be seated in the head, and associated with high social status and ritual power. [2] any power achieved by ritual means; prestige; authority.
▷HISTORY from Polynesian

man about town NOUN a fashionable sophisticate, esp one in a big city.

manacle (ˈmænək^{ə}l) NOUN [1] *(usually plural)* a shackle, handcuff, or fetter, used to secure the hands of a prisoner, convict, etc. ◆ VERB *(tr)* [2] to put manacles on. [3] to confine or constrain.
▷HISTORY C14: via Old French from Latin *manicula,* diminutive of *manus* hand

Manado (məˈnɑːdəʊ) NOUN a variant of **Menado.**

manage (ˈmænɪdʒ) VERB *(mainly tr)* [1] *(also intr)* to be in charge (of); administer: *to manage one's affairs; to manage a shop.* [2] to succeed in being able (to do something) despite obstacles; contrive: *did you manage to go to sleep?* [3] to have room, time, etc., for: *can you manage dinner tomorrow?* [4] to exercise control or domination over, often in a tactful or guileful manner. [5] *(intr)* to contrive to carry on despite difficulties, esp financial ones: *he managed quite well on very little money.* [6] to wield or handle (a weapon). [7] *Rare* to be frugal in the use of. ◆ NOUN [8] an archaic word for **manège.**
▷HISTORY C16: from Italian *maneggiare* to control, train (esp horses), ultimately from Latin *manus* hand

manageable (ˈmænɪdʒəb^{ə}l) ADJECTIVE able to be managed or controlled.
▸**ˌmanageaˈbility** *or (less commonly)* **ˈmanageableness** NOUN ▸**ˈmanageably** ADVERB

managed bonds PLURAL NOUN investment in a combination of fixed interest securities, equities, gilts, and property, in which an investment manager, acting on a client's behalf, varies the amount invested in each according to the returns expected.

managed currency NOUN a currency that is subject to governmental control with respect to the amount in circulation and the rate of exchange with other currencies.

managed forest NOUN a sustainable forest in which usually at least one tree is planted for every tree felled.

management (ˈmænɪdʒmənt) NOUN [1] the members of the executive or administration of an organization or business. See also **line management, middle management, top management.** [2] managers or employers collectively. [3] the technique, practice, or science of managing, controlling or dealng with: *anger management.* [4] the skilful or resourceful use of materials, time, etc. [5] the specific treatment of a disease, disorder, etc.

management accounting NOUN another name for **cost accounting.**

management buyout NOUN the purchase of a company by its managers, usually with outside backing from a bank or other institution. Abbreviation: **MBO.**

management company NOUN a company that manages a unit trust.

management information system NOUN an arrangement of equipment and procedures, often computerized, that is designed to provide managers with information.

management union NOUN a union that represents managers in negotiations with their employers concerning terms and conditions of employment.

manager (ˈmænɪdʒə) NOUN [1] a person who directs or manages an organization, industry, shop, etc. [2] a person who controls the business affairs of an actor, entertainer, etc. [3] a person who controls the training of a sportsman or team. [4] a person who has a talent for managing efficiently. [5] *Law* a person appointed by a court to carry on a business during receivership. [6] (in Britain) a member of either House of Parliament appointed to arrange a matter in which both Houses are concerned. [7] a computer program that organizes a resource, such as a set of files or a database.
▸**ˈmanagerˌship** NOUN

manageress (ˌmænɪdʒəˈrɛs, ˈmænɪdʒəˌrɛs) NOUN a woman who is in charge of a shop, department, canteen, etc.

managerial (ˌmænɪˈdʒɪərɪəl) ADJECTIVE of or relating to a manager or to the functions, responsibilities, or position of management.
▸**ˌmanaˈgerially** ADVERB

managerialism (ˌmænɪˈdʒɪərɪəˌlɪzəm) NOUN the application of managerial techniques of businesses to the running of other organizations, such as the civil service or local authorities.
▸**ˌmanaˈgerialist** NOUN

managing (ˈmænɪdʒɪŋ) ADJECTIVE having administrative control or authority: *a managing director.*

Managua (məˈnægwə; *Spanish* maˈnaɣwa) NOUN [1] the capital of Nicaragua, on the S shore of Lake Managua: chosen as capital in 1857. Pop. (urban area): 1 195 000 (1995 est.). [2] **Lake.** a lake in W Nicaragua: drains into Lake Nicaragua by the Tipitapa River. Length: 61 km (38 miles). Width: about 26 km (16 miles).

manakin ('mænəkɪn) NOUN [1] any small South American passerine bird of the family *Pipridae,* having a colourful plumage, short bill, and elaborate courtship behaviour. [2] a variant of **manikin.**

Manama (məˈnɑːmə) NOUN the capital of Bahrain, at the N end of Bahrain Island: transit port. Pop.: 162 000 (1999 est.).

mana motuhake ('mɑːnə məʊtuːˈhɑːkɪ) NOUN *NZ* independence or autonomy.
▷HISTORY Maori

mañana *Spanish* (maˈɲana; *English* məˈnjɑːnə) NOUN, ADVERB **a** tomorrow. **b** some other and later time.

Manáos (*Portuguese* məˈnaus) NOUN a variant spelling of **Manaus.**

Manassas (məˈnæsəs) NOUN a town in NE Virginia, west of Alexandria: site of the victory of Confederate forces in the Battles of Bull Run, or First and Second Manassas (1861; 1862), during the American Civil War. Pop.: 27 957 (1990).

Manasseh (məˈnæsɪ) NOUN *Old Testament* [1] the elder son of Joseph (Genesis 41:51). [2] the Israelite tribe descended from him. [3] the territory of this tribe, in the upper Jordan valley. Douay spelling: **Manases** (məˈnæsiːz).

manat (mæˈnæt) NOUN [1] the standard monetary unit of Azerbaijan, divided into 100 gopik. [2] the standard monetary unit of Turkmenistan, divided into 100 tenesi.

man-at-arms NOUN, *plural* **men-at-arms.** a soldier, esp a heavily armed mounted soldier in medieval times.

manatee ('mænəˌtiː, ˌmænəˈtiː)) NOUN any sirenian mammal of the genus *Trichechus,* occurring in tropical coastal waters of America, the Caribbean, and Africa: family *Trichechidae.* They resemble whales and have a prehensile upper lip and a broad flattened tail.
▷HISTORY C16: via Spanish from Carib *manattouī*
▸ **'manaˌtoid** ADJECTIVE

Manaus *or* **Manáos** (*Portuguese* məˈnaus) NOUN a port in N Brazil, capital of Amazonas state, on the Rio Negro 19 km (12 miles) above its confluence with the Amazon: chief commercial centre of the Amazon basin. Pop. conurbation: 1 394 724 (2000).

Manc (mæŋk) NOUN, ADJECTIVE *Brit informal* short for **Mancunian.**

Manche (*French* mɑ̃ʃ) NOUN [1] a department of NW France, in Basse-Normandie region. Capital: St Lô. Pop.: 481 471 (1999). Area: 6412 sq. km (2501 sq. miles). [2] **La.** the French name for the **English Channel.**

manchester ('mæntʃɪstə) NOUN *Austral and NZ* [1] household linen or cotton goods, such as sheets and towels. [2] Also called: **manchester department.** a section of a store where such goods are sold.
▷HISTORY from MANCHESTER, England

Manchester ('mæntʃɪstə) NOUN [1] a city in NW England, in Manchester unitary authority, Greater Manchester: linked to the Mersey estuary by the **Manchester Ship Canal**: commercial, industrial, and cultural centre; formerly the centre of the cotton and textile trades; two universities. Pop.: 402 889 (1991). Latin name: **Man'cunium.** [2] a unitary authority in NW England, in Greater Manchester. Pop.: 392 819 (2001). Area: 116 sq. km (45 sq. miles).

Manchester terrier NOUN a small breed of terrier with a glossy black-and-tan coat. Also called (less commonly): **black-and-tan terrier.**

manchineel (ˌmæntʃɪˈniːl) NOUN a tropical American euphorbiaceous tree, *Hippomane mancinella,* having fruit and milky highly caustic poisonous sap, which causes skin blisters.
▷HISTORY C17: via French from Spanish MANZANILLA

Manchu (mænˈtʃuː) NOUN [1] (*plural* **-chus** *or* **-chu**) a member of a Mongoloid people of Manchuria who conquered China in the 17th century, establishing an imperial dynasty that lasted until 1912. [2] the language of this people, belonging to the Tungusic branch of the Altaic family. ◆ ADJECTIVE [3] Also: **Ching.** of or relating to the dynasty of the Manchus.
▷HISTORY from Manchu, literally: pure

Manchukuo *or* **Manchoukuo** ('mænˈtʃuːˈkwəʊ) NOUN a former state of E Asia (1932–45), consisting of the three provinces of old Manchuria and Jehol.

Manchuria (mænˈtʃʊərɪə) NOUN a region of NE China, historically the home of the Manchus, rulers of China from 1644 to 1912: includes part of the Inner Mongolian AR and the provinces of Heilongjiang, Jilin, and Liaoning. Area: about 1 300 000 sq. km (502 000 sq. miles).

Manchurian (mænˈtʃʊərɪən) ADJECTIVE [1] of or relating to Manchuria, a region of NE China, or its inhabitants. ◆ NOUN [2] a native or inhabitant of Manchuria.

manciple ('mænsɪpᵊl) NOUN a steward who buys provisions, esp in a college, Inn of Court, or monastery.
▷HISTORY C13: via Old French from Latin *mancipium* purchase, from *manceps* purchaser, from *manus* hand + *capere* to take

Mancunian (mæŋˈkjuːnɪən) NOUN [1] a native or inhabitant of Manchester. ◆ ADJECTIVE [2] of or relating to Manchester.
▷HISTORY from Medieval Latin *Mancunium* Manchester

-mancy NOUN COMBINING FORM indicating divination of a particular kind: *chiromancy.*
▷HISTORY from Old French *-mancie,* from Latin *-mantia,* from Greek *manteia* soothsaying
▸ **-mantic** ADJECTIVE COMBINING FORM

Mandaean *or* **Mandean** (mænˈdɪən) NOUN [1] a member of a Gnostic sect of Iraq. [2] the form of Aramaic used by this sect. ◆ ADJECTIVE [3] of or relating to this sect.
▷HISTORY C19: from Aramaic *mandaya* Gnostics, from *mandā* knowledge
▸ **Man'daeanism** *or* **Man'deanism** NOUN

mandala ('mændələ, mænˈdɑːlə) NOUN [1] *Hindu and Buddhist art* any of various designs symbolizing the universe, usually circular. [2] *Psychol* such a symbol expressing a person's striving for unity of the self.
▷HISTORY Sanskrit: circle

Mandalay (ˌmændəˈleɪ) NOUN a city in central Myanmar, on the Irrawaddy River: the second largest city in the country and former capital of Burma and of Upper Burma; Buddhist religious centre. Pop.: 677 000 (1995 est.).

mandamus (mænˈdeɪməs) NOUN, *plural* **-muses.** *Law* formerly a writ from, now an order of, a superior court commanding an inferior tribunal, public official, corporation, etc., to carry out a public duty.
▷HISTORY C16: Latin, literally: we command, from *mandāre* to command

mandarin ('mændərɪn) NOUN [1] (in the Chinese Empire) a member of any of the nine senior grades of the bureaucracy, entered by examinations. [2] a high-ranking official whose powers are extensive and thought to be outside political control. [3] a person of standing and influence, as in literary or intellectual circles. [4] **a** a small citrus tree, *Citrus nobilis,* cultivated for its edible fruit. **b** the fruit of this tree, resembling the tangerine.
▷HISTORY C16: from Portuguese *mandarim,* via Malay *menteri* from Sanskrit *mantrin* counsellor, from *mantra* counsel
▸ **'mandarinate** NOUN

Mandarin Chinese *or* **Mandarin** NOUN the official language of China since 1917; the form of Chinese spoken by about two thirds of the population and taught in schools throughout China. See also **Chinese, Pekingese.**

Mandarin collar NOUN a high stiff round collar.

mandarin duck NOUN an Asian duck, *Aix galericulata,* the male of which has a brightly coloured and patterned plumage and crest.

mandate NOUN ('mændeɪt, -dɪt) [1] an official or authoritative instruction or command. [2] *Politics* the support or commission given to a government and its policies or an elected representative and his policies through an electoral victory. [3] (*often capital*) Also called: **mandated territory.** (formerly) any of the territories under the trusteeship of the League of Nations administered by one of its member states. [4] **a** *Roman law* a contract by which one person commissions another to act for him gratuitously and the other accepts the commission. **b** *Contract law* a contract of bailment under which the party entrusted with goods undertakes to perform gratuitously some service in respect of such goods. **c** *Scots law* a contract by which a person is engaged to act in the management of the affairs of another. ◆ VERB ('mændeɪt) (*tr*) [5] *International law* to assign (territory) to a nation under a mandate. [6] to delegate authority to. [7] *Obsolete* to give a command to.
▷HISTORY C16: from Latin *mandātum* something commanded, from *mandāre* to command, perhaps from *manus* hand + *dāre* to give
▸ **'manˌdator** NOUN

mandatory ('mændətərɪ, -trɪ) ADJECTIVE [1] having the nature or powers of a mandate. [2] obligatory; compulsory. [3] (of a state) having received a mandate over some territory. ◆ NOUN, *plural* **-ries.** [4] Also called: **mandatary.** a person or state holding a mandate.
▸ **'mandatorily** ADVERB

Mande ('mɑːndeɪ) NOUN, *plural* **-de** *or* **-des.** [1] a group of African languages, a branch of the Niger-Congo family, spoken chiefly in Mali, Guinea, and Sierra Leone. ◆ ADJECTIVE [2] of or relating to this group of languages.

Mandelbrot set ('mændəlˌbrɒt) NOUN *Maths* a set of points in the complex plane that is self-replicating according to some predetermined rule such that the boundary of the set has fractal dimensions, used in the study of fractal geometry and in producing patterns in computer graphics.
▷HISTORY C20: after Benoît *Mandelbrot* (born 1924), French mathematician, born in Poland

mandi ('mʌndɪ) NOUN (in India) a big market.
▷HISTORY Hindi

mandible ('mændɪbᵊl) NOUN [1] the lower jawbone in vertebrates. See **jaw** (sense 1). [2] either of a pair of mouthparts in insects and other arthropods that are usually used for biting and crushing food. [3] *Ornithol* either the upper or the lower part of the bill, esp the lower part.
▷HISTORY C16: via Old French from Late Latin *mandibula* jaw, from *mandere* to chew
▸ **mandibular** (mænˈdɪbjʊlə) ADJECTIVE ▸ **mandibulate** (mænˈdɪbjʊlɪt, -ˌleɪt) NOUN, ADJECTIVE

mandibular disease NOUN *Vet science* another name for **shovel beak.**

Mandingo (mænˈdɪŋgəʊ) NOUN, *plural* **-gos** *or* **-goes.** a former name for **Mande** or **Malinke.**

mandir ('mʌndɪə) NOUN a Hindu or Jain temple.
▷HISTORY Hindi, from Sanskrit *mandira*

mandola ('mændələ) NOUN an early type of mandolin.
▷HISTORY from Italian

mandolin *or* **mandoline** (ˌmændəˈlɪn) NOUN a plucked stringed instrument related to the lute, having four pairs of strings tuned in ascending fifths stretched over a small light body with a fretted fingerboard. It is usually played with a plectrum, long notes being sustained by the tremolo.
▷HISTORY C18: via French from Italian *mandolino,* diminutive of *mandora* lute, ultimately from Greek *pandoura* musical instrument with three strings
▸ **ˌmando'linist** NOUN

mandorla (mænˈdɔːlə) NOUN (in painting, sculpture, etc.) an almond-shaped area of light, usually surrounding the resurrected Christ or the Virgin at the Assumption. Also called: **vesica.**
▷HISTORY from Italian, literally: almond, from Late Latin *amandula;* see ALMOND

mandrake ('mændreɪk) *or* **mandragora** (mænˈdrægərə) NOUN [1] a Eurasian solanaceous plant, *Mandragora officinarum,* with purplish flowers and a forked root. It was formerly thought to have magic powers and a narcotic was prepared from its root. [2] another name for the **May apple.**
▷HISTORY C14: probably via Middle Dutch from Latin *mandragoras* (whence Old English *mandragora*), from Greek. The form *mandrake* was probably adopted through folk etymology, because of the allegedly human appearance of the root and because *drake* (dragon) suggested magical powers

mandrel *or* **mandril** ('mændrəl) NOUN [1] a spindle on which a workpiece is supported during machining operations. [2] a shaft or arbor on which a machining tool is mounted. [3] the driving

spindle in the headstock of a lathe. 4 *Brit* a miner's pick.
▷HISTORY C16: perhaps related to French *mandrin* lathe

mandrill (ˈmændrɪl) NOUN an Old World monkey, *Mandrillus sphinx*, of W Africa. It has a short tail and brown hair, and the ridged muzzle, nose, and hindquarters are red and blue.
▷HISTORY C18: from MAN + DRILL[4]

manducate (ˈmændjʊˌkeɪt) VERB (*tr*) *Literary* to eat or chew.
▷HISTORY C17: from Latin *mandūcāre* to chew
▸**ˌmanduˈcation** NOUN ▸**ˌmanduˈcatory** ADJECTIVE

mane (meɪn) NOUN 1 the long coarse hair that grows from the crest of the neck in such mammals as the lion and horse. 2 long thick human hair.
▷HISTORY Old English *manu;* related to Old High German *mana,* Old Norse *mön,* and perhaps to Old English *mene* and Old High German *menni* necklace
▸**maned** ADJECTIVE ▸**ˈmaneless** ADJECTIVE

man-eater NOUN 1 an animal, such as a tiger, that has become accustomed to eating human flesh. 2 any of various sharks that feed on human flesh, esp the great white shark (*Carcharodon carcharias*). 3 a human cannibal. 4 *Informal* a woman with many lovers.

man-eating ADJECTIVE 1 eating human flesh. 2 *Informal* (of a woman) having many lovers.

manège *or* **manege** (mæˈneɪʒ) NOUN 1 the art of training horses and riders. Compare **dressage.** 2 a riding school.
▷HISTORY C17: via French from Italian *maneggio,* from *maneggiare* to MANAGE

manes (ˈmɑːneɪz; *Latin* ˈmɑːnɛs) PLURAL NOUN (*sometimes capital*) (in Roman legend) 1 the spirits of the dead, often revered as minor deities. 2 (*functioning as singular*) the shade of a dead person.
▷HISTORY C14: from Latin, probably: the good ones, from Old Latin *mānus* good

maneuver (məˈnuːvə) NOUN, VERB the usual US spelling of **manoeuvre.**
▸**maˈneuverable** ADJECTIVE ▸**maˌneuveraˈbility** NOUN
▸**maˈneuverer** NOUN ▸**maˈneuvering** NOUN

man Friday NOUN a loyal male servant or assistant.
▷HISTORY after the native in Daniel Defoe's novel *Robinson Crusoe* (1719)

manful (ˈmænfʊl) ADJECTIVE a less common word for **manly.**
▸**ˈmanfully** ADVERB ▸**ˈmanfulness** NOUN

manga (ˈmæŋgə) NOUN, *plural* **manga. a** a type of Japanese comic book with an adult theme. **b** (*as modifier*): *manga videos.*

mangabey (ˈmæŋgəˌbeɪ) NOUN any of several large agile arboreal Old World monkeys of the genus *Cercocebus,* of central Africa, having long limbs and tail and white upper eyelids.
▷HISTORY C18: after the name of a region in Madagascar

Mangalore (ˌmæŋgəˈlɔː) NOUN a port in S India, in Karnataka on the Malabar Coast. Pop.: 273 304 (1991).

manganate (ˈmæŋgəˌneɪt) NOUN a salt of manganic acid.

manganese (ˈmæŋgəˌniːz) NOUN a brittle greyish-white metallic element that exists in four allotropic forms, occurring principally in pyrolusite and rhodonite: used in making steel and ferromagnetic alloys. Symbol: Mn; atomic no.: 25; atomic wt.: 54.93805; valency: 1, 2 ,3, 4, 6, or 7; relative density: 7.21–7.44; melting pt.: 1246±3°C; boiling pt.: 2062°C.
▷HISTORY C17: via French from Italian *manganese,* probably altered form of Medieval Latin MAGNESIA

manganese bronze NOUN any of various alloys containing copper (55–60 per cent), zinc (35–42 per cent), and manganese (about 3.5 per cent).

manganese nodule NOUN *Geology* a small irregular concretion found on deep ocean floors having high concentrations of certain metals, esp manganese.

manganese steel NOUN any very hard steel containing manganese (11–14 per cent), used in dredger buckets, rock-crushers, railway points, etc.

manganic (mænˈgænɪk) ADJECTIVE of or containing manganese in the trivalent state.

manganic acid NOUN a hypothetical dibasic acid known only in solution and in the form of manganate salts. Formula: H_2MnO_4.

Manganin (ˈmæŋgənɪn) NOUN *Trademark* an alloy of copper containing manganese (13–18 per cent) and nickel (1–4 per cent): it has a high electrical resistance that does not vary greatly with temperature and is used in resistors.

manganite (ˈmæŋgəˌnaɪt) NOUN a blackish mineral consisting of basic manganese oxide in monoclinic crystalline form: a source of manganese. Formula: MnO(OH).

manganous (ˈmæŋgənəs, mænˈgænəs) ADJECTIVE of or containing manganese in the divalent state.

mange (meɪndʒ) NOUN an infectious disorder mainly affecting domestic animals, characterized by itching, formation of papules and vesicles, and loss of hair: caused by parasitic mites.
▷HISTORY C14: from Old French *mangeue* itch, literally: eating, from *mangier* to eat

mangelwurzel (ˈmæŋgəlˌwɜːzəl) *or* **mangoldwurzel** (ˈmæŋgəʊldˌwɜːzəl) NOUN a Eurasian variety of the beet plant, *Beta vulgaris,* cultivated as a cattle food, having a large yellowish root. Often shortened to: **mangel** *or* **mangold.**
▷HISTORY C18: from German *Mangoldwurzel,* from *Mangold* beet + *Wurzel* root

manger (ˈmeɪndʒə) NOUN 1 a trough or box in a stable, barn, etc., from which horses or cattle feed. 2 *Nautical* a basin-like construction in the bows of a vessel for catching water draining from an anchor rode or coming in through the hawseholes.
▷HISTORY C14: from Old French *maingeure* food trough, from *mangier* to eat, ultimately from Latin *mandūcāre* to chew

mangetout (ˈmɑ̃ʒˈtuː) NOUN a variety of garden pea in which the pod is also edible. Also called: **sugar pea.**
▷HISTORY C20: from French: eat all

mangey (ˈmeɪndʒɪ) ADJECTIVE **-gier, -giest.** a variant spelling of **mangy.**

mangle[1] (ˈmæŋgəl) VERB (*tr*) 1 to mutilate, disfigure, or destroy by cutting, crushing, or tearing. 2 to ruin, spoil, or mar.
▷HISTORY C14: from Norman French *mangler,* probably from Old French *mahaignier* to maim
▸**ˈmangler** NOUN ▸**ˈmangled** ADJECTIVE

mangle[2] (ˈmæŋgəl) NOUN 1 Also called: **wringer.** a machine for pressing or drying wet textiles, clothes, etc., consisting of two heavy rollers between which the cloth is passed. ◆ VERB (*tr*) 2 to press or dry in a mangle.
▷HISTORY C18: from Dutch *mangel,* ultimately from Late Latin *manganum.* See MANGONEL

mango (ˈmæŋgəʊ) NOUN, *plural* **-goes** *or* **-gos.** 1 a tropical Asian anacardiaceous evergreen tree, *Mangifera indica,* cultivated in the tropics for its fruit. 2 the ovoid edible fruit of this tree, having a smooth rind and sweet juicy orange-yellow flesh.
▷HISTORY C16: via Portuguese from Malay *mangā,* from Tamil *mānkāy* from *mān* mango tree + *kāy* fruit

mangonel (ˈmæŋgəˌnɛl) NOUN *History* a war engine for hurling stones.
▷HISTORY C13: via Old French from Medieval Latin *manganellus,* ultimately from Greek *manganon*

mangosteen (ˈmæŋgəʊˌstiːn) NOUN 1 an East Indian tree, *Garcinia mangostana,* with thick leathery leaves and edible fruit: family *Clusiaceae.* 2 the fruit of this tree, having a sweet juicy pulp and a hard skin.
▷HISTORY C16: from Malay *mangustan*

mangrove (ˈmæŋgrəʊv, ˈmæn-) NOUN 1 **a** any tropical evergreen tree or shrub of the genus *Rhizophora,* having stiltlike intertwining aerial roots and growing below the highest tide levels in estuaries and along coasts, forming dense thickets: family *Rhizophoraceae.* **b** (*as modifier*): *mangrove swamp.* 2 any of various similar trees or shrubs of the genus *Avicennia:* family *Avicenniaceae.*
▷HISTORY C17 *mangrow* (changed through influence of *grove*), from Portuguese *mangue,* ultimately from Taino

mangrove Jack NOUN a predatory food and game fish, *Lutjanus argentimaculatus,* of Australian rivers and tidal creeks dominated by mangroves.

mangulate (ˈmæŋgjʊˌleɪt) VERB (*tr*) *Austral, slang* to bend or twist out of shape; mangle.

mangy *or* **mangey** (ˈmeɪndʒɪ) ADJECTIVE **-gier, -giest.** 1 having or caused by mange: *a mangy dog.* 2 scruffy or shabby: *a mangy carpet.* 3 *Irish informal* stingy or miserly: *a mangy reward.*
▸**ˈmangily** ADVERB ▸**ˈmanginess** NOUN

manhandle (ˈmænˌhændəl, ˌmænˈhændəl) VERB (*tr*) 1 to handle or push (someone) about roughly. 2 to move or do by manpower rather than by machinery.
▷HISTORY C19: from MAN + HANDLE; sense 1 perhaps also influenced by Devon dialect *manangle* to mangle

Manhattan (mænˈhætən, mən-) NOUN 1 an island at the N end of New York Bay, between the Hudson, East, and Harlem Rivers: administratively (with adjacent islets) a borough of New York City; a major financial, commercial, and cultural centre. Pop.: 1 487 536 (1990). Area: 47 sq. km (22 sq. miles). 2 a mixed drink consisting of four parts whisky, one part vermouth, and a dash of bitters.

Manhattan Project NOUN (during World War II) the code name for the secret US project set up in 1942 to develop an atomic bomb.

manhole (ˈmænˌhəʊl) NOUN 1 Also called: **inspection chamber.** a shaft with a removable cover that leads down to a sewer or drain. 2 a hole, usually with a detachable cover, through which a man can enter a boiler, tank, etc.

manhood (ˈmænhʊd) NOUN 1 the state or quality of being a man or being manly. 2 men collectively. 3 the state of being human.

manhood suffrage NOUN the right of adult male citizens to vote.

man-hour NOUN a unit for measuring work in industry, equal to the work done by one man in one hour.

manhunt (ˈmænˌhʌnt) NOUN an organized search, usually by police, for a wanted man or fugitive.
▸**ˈmanˌhunter** NOUN

mania (ˈmeɪnɪə) NOUN 1 a mental disorder characterized by great excitement and occasionally violent behaviour. See also **manic-depressive.** 2 an obsessional enthusiasm or partiality.
▷HISTORY C14: via Late Latin from Greek: madness

-mania NOUN COMBINING FORM indicating extreme desire or pleasure of a specified kind or an abnormal excitement aroused by something: *kleptomania; nymphomania; pyromania.*
▷HISTORY from MANIA
▸**-maniac** NOUN AND ADJECTIVE COMBINING FORM

maniac (ˈmeɪnɪˌæk) NOUN 1 a wild disorderly person. 2 a person who has a great craving or enthusiasm for something: *a football maniac.* 3 *Psychiatry, obsolete* a person afflicted with mania.
▷HISTORY C17: from Late Latin *maniacus* belonging to madness, from Greek

maniacal (məˈnaɪəkəl) *or* **maniac** (ˈmeɪnɪæk) ADJECTIVE 1 affected with or characteristic of mania. 2 characteristic of or befitting a maniac: *maniacal laughter.*
▸**maˈniacally** ADVERB

manic (ˈmænɪk) ADJECTIVE 1 characterizing, denoting, or affected by mania. ◆ NOUN 2 a person afflicted with mania.
▷HISTORY C19: from Greek, from MANIA

manic-depressive *Psychiatry* ◆ ADJECTIVE 1 denoting a mental disorder characterized either by an alternation between extreme euphoria and deep depression (bipolar manic-depressive disorder or syndrome) or by depression on its own or (rarely) by elation on its own (unipolar disorder). ◆ NOUN 2 a person afflicted with this disorder. Compare **cyclothymia.**

Manichaean *or* **Manichean** (ˌmænɪˈkiːən) ADJECTIVE 1 of or relating to Manichaeism. 2 *Chiefly RC Church* involving a radical dualism. ◆ NOUN 3 an adherent of Manichaeism.

Manichaeism *or* **Manicheism** (ˈmænɪkiːˌɪzəm) NOUN 1 the system of religious doctrines, including elements of Gnosticism, Zoroastrianism, Christianity, Buddhism, etc., taught by the Persian prophet Mani (?216–?276 A.D.), based on a supposed primordial conflict between light and darkness or goodness and evil. 2 *Chiefly RC Church* any similar heretical philosophy involving a radical dualism.
▷HISTORY C14: from Late Latin *Manichaeus,* from Late Greek *Manikhaios* of Mani
▸**ˈManichee** NOUN

manicotti (ˌmænɪˈkɒtɪ) PLURAL NOUN large tubular noodles, usually stuffed with ricotta cheese and baked in a tomato sauce.
▷**HISTORY** Italian: sleeves, plural of *manicotto,* diminutive of *manica* sleeve

manicure (ˈmænɪˌkjʊə) NOUN [1] care of the hands and fingernails, involving shaping the nails, removing cuticles, etc. [2] another word for **manicurist.** ◆ VERB [3] to care for (the hands and fingernails) in this way. [4] (*tr*) to trim neatly.
▷**HISTORY** C19: from French, from Latin *manus* hand + *cūra* care

manicurist (ˈmænɪˌkjʊərɪst) NOUN a person who gives manicures, esp as a profession.

manifest (ˈmænɪˌfɛst) ADJECTIVE [1] easily noticed or perceived; obvious; plain. [2] *Psychoanal* of or relating to the ostensible elements of a dream: *manifest content.* Compare **latent** (sense 5). ◆ VERB [3] (*tr*) to show plainly; reveal or display: *to manifest great emotion.* [4] (*tr*) to prove beyond doubt. [5] (*intr*) (of a disembodied spirit) to appear in visible form. [6] (*tr*) to list in a ship's manifest. ◆ NOUN [7] a customs document containing particulars of a ship, its cargo, and its destination. [8] **a** a list of cargo, passengers, etc., on an aeroplane. **b** a list of railway trucks or their cargo. **c** *Chiefly US and Canadian* a fast freight train carrying perishables.
▷**HISTORY** C14: from Latin *manifestus* plain, literally: struck with the hand, from *manū* with the hand + *-festus* struck
▸**ˈmaniˌfestable** ADJECTIVE ▸**ˈmaniˌfestly** ADVERB
▸**ˈmaniˌfestness** NOUN

manifestation (ˌmænɪfɛˈsteɪʃən) NOUN [1] the act of demonstrating; display: *a manifestation of solidarity.* [2] the state of being manifested. [3] an indication or sign. [4] a public demonstration of feeling. [5] the materialization of a disembodied spirit.
▸**ˌmanifesˈtational** ADJECTIVE ▸**ˌmaniˈfestative** ADJECTIVE

Manifest Destiny NOUN (esp in the 19th-century US) the belief that the US was a chosen land that had been allotted the entire North American continent by God.

manifesto (ˌmænɪˈfɛstəʊ) NOUN, *plural* **-tos** *or* **-toes.** a public declaration of intent, policy, aims, etc., as issued by a political party, government, or movement.
▷**HISTORY** C17: from Italian, from *manifestare* to MANIFEST

manifold (ˈmænɪˌfəʊld) ADJECTIVE *Formal* [1] of several different kinds; multiple: *manifold reasons.* [2] having many different forms, features, or elements: *manifold breeds of dog.* ◆ NOUN [3] something having many varied parts, forms, or features. [4] a copy of a page, book, etc. [5] a chamber or pipe with a number of inlets or outlets used to collect or distribute a fluid. In an internal-combustion engine the **inlet manifold** carries the vaporized fuel from the carburettor to the inlet ports and the **exhaust manifold** carries the exhaust gases away. [6] *Maths* **a** a collection of objects or a set. **b** a topological space having specific properties. [7] (in the philosophy of Kant) the totality of the separate elements of sensation which are then organized by the active mind and conceptualized as a perception of an external object. ◆ VERB [8] (*tr*) to duplicate (a page, book, etc.). [9] to make manifold; multiply.
▷**HISTORY** Old English *manigfeald.* See MANY, -FOLD
▸**ˈmaniˌfolder** NOUN ▸**ˈmaniˌfoldly** ADVERB ▸**ˈmaniˌfoldness** NOUN

manikin, mannikin (ˈmænɪkɪn), *or formerly* **manakin** NOUN [1] a little man; dwarf or child. [2] **a** an anatomical model of the body or a part of the body, esp for use in medical or art instruction. **b** Also called: **phantom.** an anatomical model of a fully developed fetus, for use in teaching midwifery or obstetrics. [3] variant spellings of **mannequin.**
▷**HISTORY** C17: from Dutch *manneken,* diminutive of MAN

Manila (məˈnɪlə) NOUN [1] the chief port of the Philippines, on S Luzon on Manila Bay: capital of the republic until 1948 and from 1976; seat of the Far Eastern University and the University of Santo Tomas (1611). Pop.: 1 581 082 (2000), with a conurbation of 9 932 560 (2000). [2] a type of cigar made in this city. [3] (*often not capital*) short for **Manila hemp, Manila paper.**

Manila Bay NOUN an almost landlocked inlet of the South China Sea in the Philippines, in W Luzon: mostly forms Manila harbour. Area: 1994 sq. km (770 sq. miles).

Manila hemp *or* **Manilla hemp** NOUN a fibre obtained from the plant abaca, used for rope, paper, etc.

Manila paper *or* **Manilla paper** NOUN a strong usually brown paper made from Manila hemp or similar fibres.

Manila rope *or* **Manilla rope** NOUN rope of Manila hemp.

manilla (məˈnɪlə) NOUN an early form of currency in W Africa in the pattern of a small bracelet.
▷**HISTORY** from Spanish: bracelet, diminutive of *mano* hand, from Latin *manus*

manille (mæˈnɪl) NOUN (in ombre and quadrille) the second best trump.
▷**HISTORY** C17: from French, from Spanish *malilla,* diminutive of *mala* bad

Maninke (məˈnɪŋkə) NOUN, *plural* **-ke** *or* **-kes.** a variant of **Malinke.**

man in the moon NOUN [1] the moon when considered to resemble the face of a man. [2] (in folklore and nursery rhyme) a character dwelling in the moon.

man in the street NOUN the typical or ordinary person, esp as a hypothetical unit in statistics.

manioc (ˈmænɪˌɒk) *or* **manioca** (ˌmænɪˈəʊkə) NOUN another name for **cassava** (sense 1).
▷**HISTORY** C16: from Tupi *mandioca;* earlier form *manihot* from French, from Guarani *mandio*

maniple (ˈmænɪpᵊl) NOUN [1] (in ancient Rome) a unit of 120 to 200 foot soldiers. [2] *Christianity* an ornamental band formerly worn on the left arm by the celebrant at the Eucharist.
▷**HISTORY** C16: from Medieval Latin *manipulus* (the Eucharistic vestment), from Latin, literally: a handful, from *manus* hand

manipular (məˈnɪpjʊlə) ADJECTIVE [1] of or relating to an ancient Roman maniple. [2] of or relating to manipulation.

manipulate (məˈnɪpjʊˌleɪt) VERB [1] (*tr*) to handle or use, esp with some skill, in a process or action: *to manipulate a pair of scissors.* [2] to negotiate, control, or influence (something or someone) cleverly, skilfully, or deviously. [3] to falsify (a bill, accounts, etc.) for one's own advantage. [4] (in physiotherapy) to examine or treat manually, as in loosening a joint.
▷**HISTORY** C19: back formation from *manipulation,* from Latin *manipulus* handful
▸**manipulability** (məˌnɪpjʊləˈbɪlɪtɪ) NOUN
▸**maˈnipuˌlatable** *or* **maˈnipulable** ADJECTIVE
▸**maˌnipuˈlation** NOUN ▸**maˈnipulative** ADJECTIVE
▸**maˈnipulatively** ADVERB ▸**maˈnipuˌlator** NOUN
▸**maˈnipulatory** ADJECTIVE

Manipur (ˌmʌnɪˈpʊə) NOUN a state in NE India: largely densely forested mountains. Capital: Imphal. Pop.: 2 388 634 (2001). Area: 22 327 sq. km (8621 sq. miles).

Manisa (ˈmɑːnɪˌsɑː) NOUN a city in W Turkey: the Byzantine seat of government (1204–1313). Pop.: 201 340 (1997).

Manitoba (ˌmænɪˈtəʊbə) NOUN [1] a province of W Canada: consists of prairie in the southwest, with extensive forests in the north and tundra near Hudson Bay in the northeast. Capital: Winnipeg. Pop.: 1 150 200 (2001 est.). Area: 650 090 sq. km (251 000 sq. miles). Abbreviation: **MB.** [2] **Lake.** a lake in W Canada, in S Manitoba: fed by the outflow from Lake Winnipegosis; drains into Lake Winnipeg. Area: 4706 sq. km (1817 sq. miles).

Manitoba maple NOUN a Canadian fast-growing variety of maple.

Manitoban (ˌmænɪˈtəʊbən) NOUN [1] a native or inhabitant of Manitoba. ◆ ADJECTIVE [2] of or relating to Manitoba or its inhabitants.

manitou, manitu (ˈmænɪˌtuː), *or* **manito** (ˈmænɪˌtəʊ) NOUN, *plural* **-tous, -tus, -tos** *or* **-tou, -tu, -to.** (among the Algonquian Indians) a deified spirit or force.
▷**HISTORY** C17: from Algonquian; related to Ojibwa *manito* spirit

Manitoulin Island (ˌmænɪˈtuːlɪn) NOUN an island in N Lake Huron in Ontario: the largest freshwater island in the world. Length: 129 km (80 miles). Width: up to 48 km (30 miles).

Manizales (ˌmænɪˈzɑːlɛs; *Spanish* maniˈθales) NOUN a city in W Colombia, in the Cordillera Central of the Andes at an altitude of 2100 m (7000 ft.): commercial centre of a rich coffee-growing area. Pop.: 337 580 (1999 est.).

man jack NOUN *Informal* a single individual (in the phrases **every man jack, no man jack**).

mankind (ˌmænˈkaɪnd) NOUN [1] human beings collectively; humanity. [2] men collectively, as opposed to womankind.

> **Language note** Some people object to the use of *mankind* to refer to all human beings and prefer the term *humankind.*

manky (ˈmæŋkɪ) ADJECTIVE **mankier, mankiest.** *Slang* [1] worthless, rotten, or in bad taste. [2] dirty, filthy, or bad.
▷**HISTORY** via Polari from Italian *mancare* to be lacking

manlike (ˈmænˌlaɪk) ADJECTIVE resembling or befitting a man.

man lock NOUN *Civil engineering* an airlock that allows workmen to pass in and out of spaces with differing air pressures, esp one providing access to and from a tunnel, shaft, or caisson in which the air is compressed.

manly (ˈmænlɪ) ADJECTIVE **-lier, -liest.** [1] possessing qualities, such as vigour or courage, generally regarded as appropriate to or typical of a man; masculine. [2] characteristic of or befitting a man: *a manly sport.*
▸**ˈmanliness** NOUN

man-made ADJECTIVE made or produced by man; artificial.

man-mark VERB *Sport, Brit* (*tr*) to stay close to (a specific opponent) to hamper his or her play.

man-mountain NOUN *Informal* a man who is very tall and heavily built.

manna (ˈmænə) NOUN [1] *Old Testament* the miraculous food which sustained the Israelites in the wilderness (Exodus 16:14–36). [2] any spiritual or divine nourishment. [3] a windfall; an unexpected gift (esp in the phrase **manna from heaven**). [4] a sweet substance obtained from various plants, esp from an ash tree, *Fraxinus ornus* (**manna** or **flowering ash**) of S Europe, used as a mild laxative.
▷**HISTORY** Old English via Late Latin from Greek, from Hebrew *mān*

Mannar (məˈnɑː) NOUN **Gulf of.** the part of the Indian Ocean between SE India and the island of Sri Lanka: pearl fishing.

manned (mænd) ADJECTIVE [1] supplied or equipped with men, esp soldiers. [2] (of spacecraft, aircraft, etc.) having a human crew.

mannequin (ˈmænɪkɪn) NOUN [1] a woman who wears the clothes displayed at a fashion show; model. [2] a life-size dummy of the human body used to fit or display clothes. [3] *Arts* another name for **lay figure.**
▷**HISTORY** C18: via French from Dutch *manneken* MANIKIN

manner (ˈmænə) NOUN [1] a way of doing or being. [2] a person's bearing and behaviour: *she had a cool manner.* [3] the style or customary way of doing or accomplishing something: *sculpture in the Greek manner.* [4] type or kind: *what manner of man is this?* [5] mannered style, as in art; mannerism. [6] **by all manner of means.** certainly; of course. [7] **by no manner of means.** definitely not: *he was by no manner of means a cruel man.* [8] **in a manner of speaking.** in a way; so to speak. [9] **to the manner born.** naturally fitted to a specified role or activity. ◆ See also **manners.**
▷**HISTORY** C12: via Norman French from Old French *maniere,* from Vulgar Latin *manuāria* (unattested) a way of handling something, noun use of Latin *manuārius* belonging to the hand, from *manus* hand

mannered (ˈmænəd) ADJECTIVE [1] having idiosyncrasies or mannerisms; affected: *mannered gestures.* [2] of or having mannerisms of style, as in art or literature. [3] (*in combination*) having manners as specified: *ill-mannered.*

mannerism (ˈmænəˌrɪzəm) NOUN 1 a distinctive and individual gesture or trait; idiosyncrasy. 2 (*often capital*) a principally Italian movement in art and architecture between the High Renaissance and Baroque periods (1520–1600) that sought to represent an ideal of beauty rather than natural images of it, using characteristic distortion and exaggeration of human proportions, perspective, etc. 3 adherence to a distinctive or affected manner, esp in art or literature.
▸ **ˈmannerist** NOUN ▸ **ˌmannerˈistic** *or* **ˌmannerˈistical** ADJECTIVE ▸ **ˌmannerˈistically** ADVERB

mannerless (ˈmænəlɪs) ADJECTIVE having bad manners; boorish.
▸ **ˈmannerlessness** NOUN

mannerly (ˈmænəlɪ) ADJECTIVE 1 well-mannered; polite; courteous. ◆ ADVERB 2 *Now rare* with good manners; politely; courteously.
▸ **ˈmannerliness** NOUN

manners (ˈmænəz) PLURAL NOUN 1 social conduct: *he has the manners of a pig.* 2 a socially acceptable way of behaving.

Mannheim (ˈmænhaɪm; *German* ˈmanhaim) NOUN a city in SW Germany, in Baden-Württemberg at the confluence of the Rhine and Neckar: one of Europe's largest inland harbours; a cultural and musical centre. Pop.: 308 400 (1999 est.).

Mannheim School (ˈmænhaɪm) NOUN *Music* a group of musicians and composers connected with the court orchestra at Mannheim during the mid-18th century, who evolved the controlled orchestral crescendo as well as a largely homophonic musical style.

mannikin (ˈmænɪkɪn) NOUN a variant spelling of **manikin.**

mannish (ˈmænɪʃ) ADJECTIVE 1 (of a woman) having or displaying qualities regarded as typical of a man. 2 of or resembling a man.
▸ **ˈmannishly** ADVERB ▸ **ˈmannishness** NOUN

mannitol (ˈmænɪˌtɒl) *or* **mannite** (ˈmænaɪt) NOUN a white crystalline water-soluble sweet-tasting alcohol, found in plants and used in diet sweets and as a dietary supplement (**E421**). Formula: $C_6H_{14}O_6$.
▷ **HISTORY** from MANNOSE + -ITE[2] + -OL[1]
▸ **mannitic** (məˈnɪtɪk) ADJECTIVE

mannose (ˈmænəʊs, -nəʊz) NOUN a hexose sugar found in mannitol and many polysaccharides. Formula: $C_6H_{12}O_6$.
▷ **HISTORY** C20: from MANNA + -OSE[2]

Mann-Whitney test (ˈmænˈwɪtnɪ) NOUN a statistical test of the difference between the distributions of data collected in two experimental conditions applied to unmatched groups of subjects but comparing the distributions of the ranks of the scores. Also called: **Wilcoxon Mann-Whitney test.**

manoeuvre *or US* **maneuver** (məˈnuːvə) NOUN 1 a contrived, complicated, and possibly deceptive plan or action: *political manoeuvres.* 2 a movement or action requiring dexterity and skill. 3 **a** a tactic or movement of one or a number of military or naval units. **b** (*plural*) tactical exercises, usually on a large scale. 4 a planned movement of an aircraft in flight. 5 any change from the straight steady course of a ship. ◆ VERB 6 (*tr*) to contrive or accomplish with skill or cunning. 7 (*intr*) to manipulate situations, etc., in order to gain some end: *to manoeuvre for the leadership.* 8 (*intr*) to perform a manoeuvre or manoeuvres. 9 to move or deploy or be moved or deployed, as military units, etc.
▷ **HISTORY** C15: from French, from Medieval Latin *manuopera* manual work, from Latin *manū operāre* to work with the hand
▸ **maˈnoeuvrable** *or* (*US*) **maˈneuverable** ADJECTIVE ▸ **maˌnoeuvraˈbility** *or* (*US*) **maˌneuveraˈbility** NOUN ▸ **maˈnoeuvrer** *or* (*US*) **maˈneuverer** NOUN ▸ **maˈnoeuvring** *or* (*US*) **maˈneuvering** NOUN

man of God NOUN 1 a saint or prophet. 2 a clergyman.

man of straw NOUN 1 a person of little substance. 2 Also called: **straw man.** *Chiefly US* a person used as a cover for some dubious plan or enterprise; front man.

man-of-war *or* **man o' war** NOUN, *plural* **men-of-war, men o' war.** 1 a warship. 2 See **Portuguese man-of-war.**

man-of-war bird *or* **man-o'-war bird** NOUN another name for **frigate bird.**

manometer (məˈnɒmɪtə) NOUN an instrument for comparing pressures; typically a glass U-tube containing mercury, in which pressure is indicated by the difference in levels in the two arms of the tube.
▷ **HISTORY** C18: from French *manomètre,* from Greek *manos* sparse + *metron* measure
▸ **manometric** (ˌmænəʊˈmɛtrɪk) *or* **ˌmanoˈmetrical** ADJECTIVE ▸ **ˌmanoˈmetrically** ADVERB ▸ **maˈnometry** NOUN

manor (ˈmænə) NOUN 1 (in medieval Europe) the manor house of a lord and the lands attached to it. 2 (before 1776 in some North American colonies) a tract of land granted with rights of inheritance by royal charter. 3 a manor house. 4 a landed estate. 5 *Brit, slang* a geographical area of operation, esp of a local police force.
▷ **HISTORY** C13: from Old French *manoir* dwelling, from *maneir* to dwell, from Latin *manēre* to remain
▸ **manorial** (məˈnɔːrɪəl) ADJECTIVE

man orchid NOUN an orchid, *Aceras anthropophorum,* having greenish or reddish flowers in a loose spike, with a deeply lobed dark brown lip thought to resemble the silhouette of a man.

manor house NOUN (esp formerly) the house of the lord of a manor.

manoscopy (məˈnɒskəpɪ) NOUN *Chem* the measurement of the densities of gases.

manpower (ˈmænˌpaʊə) NOUN 1 power supplied by men. 2 a unit of power based on the rate at which a man can work; approximately 75 watts. 3 available or suitable power: *the manpower of a battalion.*

manpower planning NOUN a procedure used in organizations to balance future requirements for all levels of employee with the availability of such employees.

Manpower Services Commission NOUN *Brit* the former name of the **Training Agency.**

manqué *French* (mɑ̃ke; *English* ˈmɒŋkeɪ) ADJECTIVE (*postpositive*) unfulfilled; potential; would-be: *the manager is an actor manqué.*
▷ **HISTORY** C19: literally: having missed

Manresa (*Spanish* manˈrɛsa) NOUN a city in NE Spain: contains a cave used as the spiritual retreat of St Ignatius Loyola. Pop.: 65 610 (latest est.).

manrope (ˈmænˌrəʊp) NOUN *Nautical* a rope railing.

mansard (ˈmænsɑːd, -səd) NOUN 1 Also called: **mansard roof.** a roof having two slopes on both sides and both ends, the lower slopes being steeper than the upper. Compare **gambrel roof.** 2 an attic having such a roof.
▷ **HISTORY** C18: from French *mansarde,* after François *Mansart* (1598–1666), French architect

manse (mæns) NOUN (in certain religious denominations) the house provided for a minister.
▷ **HISTORY** C15: from Medieval Latin *mansus* dwelling, from the past participle of Latin *manēre* to stay

manservant (ˈmænˌsɜːvənt) NOUN, *plural* **menservants.** a male servant, esp a valet.

Mansfield (ˈmænsˌfiːld) NOUN a town in central England, in W Nottinghamshire: former coal-mining and cotton-textiles industries. Pop.: 71 858 (1991).

mansion (ˈmænʃən) NOUN 1 Also called: **mansion house.** a large and imposing house. 2 a less common word for **manor house.** 3 *Archaic* any residence. 4 *Brit* (*plural*) a block of flats. 5 *Astrology* any of 28 divisions of the zodiac each occupied on successive days by the moon.
▷ **HISTORY** C14: via Old French from Latin *mansio* a remaining, from *mansus;* see MANSE

Mansion House NOUN **the.** 1 the residence of the Lord Mayor of London. 2 the residence of the Lord Mayor of Dublin.

man-sized ADJECTIVE 1 of a size appropriate for or convenient for a man. 2 *Informal* big; large.

manslaughter (ˈmænˌslɔːtə) NOUN 1 *Law* the unlawful killing of one human being by another without malice aforethought. Compare **murder.** See also **homicide, malice aforethought.** 2 (loosely) the killing of a human being.

mansuetude (ˈmænswɪˌtjuːd) NOUN *Archaic* gentleness or mildness.
▷ **HISTORY** C14: from Latin *mansuētūdō,* from *mansuētus,* past participle of *mansuēscere* to make tame by handling, from *manus* hand + *suescēre* to train

Mansûra (mænˈsʊərə) NOUN See **El Mansûra.**

manta (ˈmæntə; *Spanish* ˈmanta) NOUN 1 Also called: **manta ray, devilfish, devil ray.** any large ray (fish) of the family *Mobulidae,* having very wide winglike pectoral fins and feeding on plankton. 2 a rough cotton cloth made in Spain and Spanish America. 3 a piece of this used as a blanket or shawl. 4 another word for **mantelet** (sense 2).
▷ **HISTORY** Spanish: cloak, from Vulgar Latin; see MANTLE. The manta ray is so called because it is caught in a trap resembling a blanket

manteau (ˈmæntəʊ; *French* mɑ̃to) NOUN, *plural* **-teaus** (-təʊz) *or* **-teaux** (*French* -to). a cloak or mantle.
▷ **HISTORY** C17: via French from Latin *mantellum* MANTLE

mantel *or less commonly* **mantle** (ˈmæntᵊl) NOUN 1 a wooden or stone frame around the opening of a fireplace, together with its decorative facing. 2 Also called: **mantel shelf.** a shelf above this frame.
▷ **HISTORY** C15: from French, variant of MANTLE

mantelet (ˈmæntᵊˌlɛt) *or* **mantlet** NOUN 1 a woman's short mantle, often lace-trimmed, worn in the mid-19th century. 2 a portable bulletproof screen or shelter.
▷ **HISTORY** C14: from Old French, diminutive of *mantel* MANTLE

mantelletta (ˌmæntɪˈlɛtə) NOUN *RC Church* a sleeveless knee-length vestment, worn by cardinals, bishops, etc.
▷ **HISTORY** Italian, from Old French *mantelet* or Medieval Latin *mantelletum,* diminutive of Latin *mantellum* MANTLE

mantelpiece (ˈmæntᵊlˌpiːs) NOUN 1 Also called: **mantel shelf, chimneypiece.** a shelf above a fireplace often forming part of the mantel. 2 another word for **mantel** (sense 1).

manteltree *or* **mantletree** (ˈmæntᵊlˌtriː) NOUN a beam made of stone or wood that forms the lintel over a fireplace.

mantic (ˈmæntɪk) ADJECTIVE 1 of or relating to divination and prophecy. 2 having divining or prophetic powers.
▷ **HISTORY** C19: from Greek *mantikos* prophetic, from *mantis* seer
▸ **ˈmantically** ADVERB

-mantic ADJECTIVE COMBINING FORM forming adjectives corresponding to nouns ending in **-mancy**: *necromantic.*

mantilla (mænˈtɪlə) NOUN 1 a woman's lace or silk scarf covering the shoulders and head, often worn over a comb in the hair, esp in Spain. 2 a similar covering for the shoulders only.
▷ **HISTORY** C18: Spanish, diminutive of *manta* cloak

Mantinea *or* **Mantineia** (ˌmæntɪˈneɪə) NOUN (in ancient Greece) a city in E Arcadia; site of several battles.

mantis (ˈmæntɪs) NOUN, *plural* **-tises** *or* **-tes** (-tiːz). any carnivorous typically green insect of the family *Mantidae,* of warm and tropical regions, having a long body and large eyes and resting with the first pair of legs raised as if in prayer: order *Dictyoptera.* Also called: **praying mantis.** See also **cockroach.**
▷ **HISTORY** C17: New Latin, from Greek: prophet, alluding to its praying posture

mantissa (mænˈtɪsə) NOUN the fractional part of a common logarithm representing the digits of the associated number but not its magnitude: *the mantissa of 2.4771 is .4771.* Compare **characteristic** (sense 2a).
▷ **HISTORY** C17: from Latin: something added, of Etruscan origin

mantis shrimp *or* **crab** NOUN any of various burrowing marine shrimplike crustaceans of the order *Stomatopoda* that have a pair of large grasping appendages: subclass *Malacostraca.* See also **squilla.**

mantle (ˈmæntᵊl) NOUN 1 *Archaic* a loose wrap or cloak. 2 such a garment regarded as a symbol of someone's power or authority: *he assumed his father's mantle.* 3 anything that covers completely or envelops: *a mantle of snow.* 4 a small dome-shaped or cylindrical mesh impregnated with cerium or thorium nitrates, used to increase illumination in a gas or oil lamp. 5 Also called:

pallium. *Zoology* **a** a protective layer of epidermis in molluscs that secretes a substance forming the shell. **b** a similar structure in brachiopods. [6] *Ornithol* the feathers of the folded wings and back, esp when these are of a different colour from the remaining feathers. [7] *Geology* the part of the earth between the crust and the core, accounting for more than 82% of the earth's volume (but only 68% of its mass) and thought to be composed largely of peridotite. See also **asthenosphere.** [8] a less common spelling of **mantel.** [9] *Anatomy* another word for **pallium** (sense 3). [10] a clay mould formed around a wax model which is subsequently melted out. ◆ VERB [11] (*tr*) to envelop or supply with a mantle. [12] to spread over or become spread over: *the trees were mantled with snow.* [13] (*tr*) (of the face, cheeks) to become suffused with blood; flush. [14] (*intr*) *Falconry* (of a hawk or falcon) to spread the wings and tail over food.
▷**HISTORY** C13: via Old French from Latin *mantellum,* diminutive of *mantum* cloak

mantling ('mæntlɪŋ) NOUN *Heraldry* the drapery or scrollwork around a shield.
▷**HISTORY** C16: from MANTLE

man-to-man ADJECTIVE characterized by directness or candour: *a man-to-man discussion.*

Mantoux test (mæn'tuː; *French* mɑ̃tu) NOUN *Med* a test for determining the presence of a tubercular infection by injecting tuberculin into the skin.
▷**HISTORY** C19: named after C. *Mantoux,* French physician (1877–1956)

Mantova ('mantova) NOUN the Italian name for **Mantua.**

mantra ('mæntrə, 'mʌn-) NOUN [1] *Hinduism* any of those parts of the Vedic literature which consist of the metrical psalms of praise. [2] *Hinduism, Buddhism* any sacred word or syllable used as an object of concentration and embodying some aspect of spiritual power.
▷**HISTORY** C19: from Sanskrit, literally: speech, instrument of thought, from *man* to think

mantrap ('mænˌtræp) NOUN a snare for catching people, esp trespassers.

mantua ('mæntjʊə) NOUN a loose gown of the 17th and 18th centuries, worn open in front to show the underskirt.
▷**HISTORY** C17: changed from MANTEAU, through the influence of MANTUA

Mantua ('mæntjʊə) NOUN a city in N Italy, in E Lombardy, surrounded by lakes: birthplace of Virgil. Pop.: 54 808 (1990). Italian name: **Mantova.**

manual ('mænjʊəl) ADJECTIVE [1] of or relating to a hand or hands. [2] operated or done by hand: *manual controls.* [3] physical, as opposed to mental or mechanical: *manual labour.* [4] by human labour rather than automatic or computer-aided means. [5] of, relating to, or resembling a manual. ◆ NOUN [6] a book, esp of instructions or information: *a car manual.* [7] *Music* one of the keyboards played by hand on an organ. [8] *Military* the prescribed drill with small arms.
▷**HISTORY** C15: via Old French from Latin *manuālis,* from *manus* hand
▶'**manually** ADVERB

manubrium (mə'njuːbrɪəm) NOUN, *plural* **-bria** (-brɪə) *or* **-briums.** [1] *Anatomy* any handle-shaped part, esp the upper part of the sternum. [2] *Zoology* the tubular mouth that hangs down from the centre of a coelenterate medusa such as a jellyfish.
▷**HISTORY** C17: from New Latin, from Latin: handle, from *manus* hand
▶**ma'nubrial** ADJECTIVE

manuf. *or* **manufac.** ABBREVIATION FOR: [1] manufacture. [2] manufactured.

manufactory (ˌmænjʊ'fæktərɪ, -trɪ) NOUN, *plural* **-ries.** an obsolete word for **factory.**
▷**HISTORY** C17: from obsolete *manufact;* see MANUFACTURE

manufacture (ˌmænjʊ'fæktʃə) VERB [1] to process or make (a product) from a raw material, esp as a large-scale operation using machinery. [2] (*tr*) to invent or concoct: *to manufacture an excuse.* ◆ NOUN [3] the production of goods, esp by industrial processes. [4] a manufactured product. [5] the creation or production of anything.
▷**HISTORY** C16: from obsolete *manufact* hand-made, from Late Latin *manūfactus,* from Latin *manus* hand + *facere* to make
▶ˌ**manu'facturable** ADJECTIVE ▶ˌ**manu'facturing** NOUN, ADJECTIVE

manufacturer (ˌmænjʊ'fæktʃərə) NOUN a person or business concern that manufactures goods or owns a factory.

manuhiri (ˌmɑːnuː'hiːrɪ) NOUN *NZ* [1] a visitor to a Maori marae. [2] a Maori term for a non-Maori person, seen as a guest in the country.
▷**HISTORY** Maori

manuka ('mɑːnuːkə) NOUN a New Zealand myrtaceous tree, *Leptospermum scoparium,* with strong elastic wood and aromatic leaves. Also called: **tea tree.**

Manukau ('mɑːnʊˌkaʊ) NOUN a city in New Zealand, on **Manukau Harbour** (an inlet of the Tasman Sea) near Auckland on NW North Island. Pop.: 281 800 (1999 est.).

manumit (ˌmænjʊ'mɪt) VERB **-mits, -mitting, -mitted.** (*tr*) to free from slavery, servitude, etc.; emancipate.
▷**HISTORY** C15: from Latin *manūmittere* to release, from *manū* from one's hand + *ēmittere* to send away
▶**manumission** (ˌmænjʊ'mɪʃən) NOUN ▶ˌ**manu'mitter** NOUN

manure (mə'njʊə) NOUN [1] animal excreta, usually with straw, used to fertilize land. [2] *Chiefly Brit* any material, esp chemical fertilizer, used to fertilize land. ◆ VERB [3] (*tr*) to spread manure upon (fields or soil).
▷**HISTORY** C14: from Medieval Latin *manuopera;* manual work; see MANOEUVRE
▶**ma'nurer** NOUN

manus ('meɪnəs) NOUN, *plural* **-nus.** [1] *Anatomy* the wrist and hand. [2] the corresponding part in other vertebrates. [3] *Roman law* the authority of a husband over his wife. [4] *English law* (formerly) an oath or the person taking an oath.
▷**HISTORY** C19: Latin: hand

Manu Samoa ('mænu) NOUN the international Rugby Union football team of Western Samoa.

manuscript ('mænjʊˌskrɪpt) NOUN [1] a book or other document written by hand. [2] the original handwritten or typed version of a book, article, etc., as submitted by an author for publication. [3] **a** handwriting, as opposed to printing. **b** (*as modifier*): *a manuscript document.*
▷**HISTORY** C16: from Medieval Latin *manūscriptus,* from Latin *manus* hand + *scribere* to write

Manx (mæŋks) ADJECTIVE [1] of, relating to, or characteristic of the Isle of Man, its inhabitants, their language, or their dialect of English. ◆ NOUN [2] a language of the Isle of Man, belonging to the N Celtic branch of the Indo-European family and closely related to Scottish Gaelic. [3] (*functioning as plural*) the people of the Isle of Man.
▷**HISTORY** C16: earlier *Maniske,* from Scandinavian, from *Mana* Isle of Man + *-iske* -ISH

Manx cat NOUN a short-haired tailless variety of cat, believed to originate on the Isle of Man.

Manxman ('mæŋksmən) *or feminine* **Manxwoman** ('mæŋkswʊmən) NOUN, *plural* **-men** *or* **-women.** a native or inhabitant of the Isle of Man.

Manx shearwater NOUN a European oceanic bird, *Puffinus puffinus,* with long slender wings and black-and-white plumage: family *Procellariidae* (shearwaters).

many ('mɛnɪ) DETERMINER [1] (sometimes preceded by *a great* or *a good*) **a** a large number of: *many coaches; many times.* **b** (*as pronoun; functioning as plural*): *many are seated already.* [2] (foll by *a, an,* or *another,* and a singular noun) each of a considerable number of: *many a man.* [3] (preceded by *as, too, that,* etc.) **a** a great number of: *as many apples as you like; too many clouds to see.* **b** (*as pronoun; functioning as plural*): *I have as many as you.* ◆ NOUN [4] **the many.** the majority of mankind, esp the common people: *the many are kept in ignorance while the few prosper.* Compare **few** (sense 7). ◆ See also **more, most.**
▷**HISTORY** Old English *manig;* related to Old Frisian *manich,* Middle Dutch *menech,* Old High German *manag*

many-one ADJECTIVE *Maths, logic* (of a function) associating a single element of a range with more than one member of the domain.

manyplies ('mɛnɪˌplaɪz) NOUN (*functioning as singular*) another name for **psalterium.**
▷**HISTORY** C18: from the large number of plies or folds of its membrane

many-sided ADJECTIVE having many sides, aspects, etc.: *a many-sided personality.*
▶ˌ**many-'sidedness** NOUN

many-valued logic NOUN **a** the study of logical systems in which the truth-values that a proposition may have are not restricted to two, representing only truth and falsity. **b** such a logical system.

manzanilla (ˌmænzə'nɪlə) NOUN a very dry pale sherry.
▷**HISTORY** C19: from Spanish: camomile (referring to its bouquet)

MAOI ABBREVIATION FOR **monoamine oxidase inhibitor.**

Maoism ('maʊɪzəm) NOUN [1] Marxism-Leninism as interpreted by Mao Tse-tung (1893–1976), the Chinese Marxist theoretician and statesman: distinguished by its theory of guerrilla warfare and its emphasis on the revolutionary potential of the peasantry. [2] adherence to or reverence for Mao Tse-tung and his teachings.
▶'**Maoist** NOUN, ADJECTIVE

Maori ('maʊrɪ) NOUN [1] (*plural* **-ri** *or* **-ris**) a member of the people living in New Zealand and the Cook Islands since before the arrival of European settlers. They are descended from Polynesian voyagers who migrated in successive waves from the ninth century onwards. [2] the language of this people, belonging to the Malayo-Polynesian family. ◆ ADJECTIVE [3] of or relating to this people or their language.

Maori Battalion NOUN the Maori unit of the 2nd New Zealand Expeditionary Force in World War II.

Maori bread NOUN *NZ* bread made with fermented potato yeast.

Maori bug NOUN a large shining black wingless cockroach of New Zealand, *Platyzosteria novae-zelandiae.*

Maori bunk NOUN *NZ* a raised sleeping platform.

Maori hen NOUN *NZ* another name for **weka.**

Maoriland ('maʊrɪˌlænd) NOUN an obsolete name for **New Zealand.**

Maorilander ('maʊrɪˌlændə) NOUN an obsolete name for a **New Zealander.**

Maori oven NOUN another name for **hangi** (sense 1).

Maori rat NOUN a small brown rat, *Rattus exulans,* native to New Zealand.

Maoritanga ('maʊrɪˌtʌŋə) NOUN *NZ* the Maori culture; Maori way of life.
▷**HISTORY** Maori

Maori warden NOUN a person appointed to exercise advisory and minor disciplinary powers in Maori communities.

Mao suit (maʊ) NOUN a simple style of clothing, traditionally made of cotton and commonly worn in Communist China, consisting of loose trousers and a straight jacket with a close-fitting stand-up collar.
▷**HISTORY** C20: named after *Mao* Tse-tung (1893–1976), Chinese Marxist theoretician and statesman, who popularized the style

map (mæp) NOUN [1] a diagrammatic representation of the earth's surface or part of it, showing the geographical distributions, positions, etc., of natural or artificial features such as roads, towns, relief, rainfall, etc. [2] a diagrammatic representation of the distribution of stars or of the surface of a celestial body: *a lunar map.* [3] a maplike drawing of anything. [4] *Maths* another name for **function** (sense 4). [5] a slang word for **face** (sense 1). [6] **off the map.** no longer important or in existence (esp in the phrase **wipe off the map**). [7] **put on the map.** to make (a town, company, etc.) well-known. ◆ VERB **maps, mapping, mapped.** (*tr*) [8] to make a map of. [9] *Maths* to represent or transform (a function, figure, set, etc.).
▷**HISTORY** C16: from Medieval Latin *mappa* (*mundi*) map (of the world), from Latin *mappa* cloth
▶'**mappable** ADJECTIVE ▶'**mapless** ADJECTIVE ▶'**mapper** NOUN

maple ('meɪpᵊl) NOUN [1] any tree or shrub of the N temperate genus *Acer,* having winged seeds borne in pairs and lobed leaves: family *Aceraceae.* [2] the hard close-grained wood of any of these trees, used for furniture and flooring. [3] the flavour of the sap of the sugar maple. ◆ See also **sugar maple, silver maple, Norway maple, sycamore.**

▷**HISTORY** C14: from Old English *mapel-*, as in *mapeltrēow* maple tree

Maple Leaf NOUN **the.** the national flag of Canada, consisting of a representation of a maple leaf in red on a white central panel with a vertical red bar on either side.

maple sugar NOUN *US and Canadian* sugar made from the sap of the sugar maple.

maple syrup NOUN a very sweet syrup made from the sap of the sugar maple.

map out VERB (*tr, adverb*) to plan or design: *to map out a route.*

mapping ('mæpɪŋ) NOUN *Maths* another name for **function** (sense 4).

map projection NOUN a means of representing or a representation of the globe or celestial sphere or part of it on a flat map, using a grid of lines of latitude and longitude.

Maputo (mə'pu:təʊ) NOUN the capital and chief port of Mozambique, in the south on Delagoa Bay: became capital in 1907; the nearest port to the Rand gold-mining and industrial region of South Africa. Pop.: 989 386 (1997). Former name (until 1975): **Lourenço Marques.**

maquette (mæ'kɛt) NOUN a sculptor's small preliminary model or sketch.
▷**HISTORY** C20: from French, from Italian *macchietta* a little sketch, from *macchia,* from *macchiare,* from Latin *maculāre* to stain, from *macula* spot, blemish

maquillage *French* (makijaʒ) NOUN 1 make-up; cosmetics. 2 the application of make-up.
▷**HISTORY** from *maquiller* to make up

maquis (mɑ:'ki:) NOUN, *plural* **-quis** (-'ki:). 1 shrubby mostly evergreen vegetation found in coastal regions of the Mediterranean: includes myrtles, heaths, arbutus, cork oak, and ilex. 2 (*often capital*) **a** the French underground movement that fought against the German occupying forces in World War II. **b** a member of this movement.
▷**HISTORY** C20: from French, from Italian *macchia* thicket, from Latin *macula* spot

mar (mɑ:) VERB **mars, marring, marred.** 1 (*tr*) to cause harm to; spoil or impair. ◆ NOUN 2 a disfiguring mark; blemish.
▷**HISTORY** Old English *merran;* compare Old Saxon *merrian* to hinder, Old Norse *merja* to bruise
▸**'marrer** NOUN

Mar. ABBREVIATION FOR March.

mara (mə'rɑ:) NOUN a harelike South American rodent, *Dolichotis patagonum,* inhabiting the pampas of Argentina: family *Caviidae* (cavies).
▷**HISTORY** from American Spanish *mará,* perhaps of Araucanian origin

marabi (ˌmɑ'rɑ:bɪ) NOUN *South African* a kind of music popular in townships in the 1930s.
▷**HISTORY** of uncertain origin, possibly from Sotho

marabou ('mærəˌbu:) NOUN 1 a large black-and-white African carrion-eating stork, *Leptoptilos crumeniferus,* with a very short naked neck and a straight heavy bill. See also **adjutant bird.** 2 a down feather of this bird, used to trim garments. 3 **a** a fine white raw silk. **b** fabric made of this.
▷**HISTORY** C19: from French, from Arabic *murābit* MARABOUT, so called because the stork is considered a holy bird in Islam

marabout ('mærəˌbu:) NOUN 1 a Muslim holy man or hermit of North Africa. 2 a shrine of the grave of a marabout.
▷**HISTORY** C17: via French and Portuguese *marabuto,* from Arabic *murābit*

marabunta ('mærəˌbʌntə) NOUN *Caribbean* 1 any of several social wasps. 2 *Slang* an ill-tempered woman.
▷**HISTORY** C19: perhaps of W African origin

maraca (mə'rækə) NOUN a percussion instrument, usually one of a pair, consisting of a gourd or plastic shell filled with dried seeds, pebbles, etc. It is used chiefly in Latin American music.
▷**HISTORY** C20: Brazilian Portuguese, from Tupi

Maracaibo (ˌmærə'kaɪbəʊ; *Spanish* mara'kaiβo) NOUN 1 a port in NW Venezuela, on the channel from Lake Maracaibo to the Gulf of Venezuela: the second largest city in the country; University of Zulia (1891); major oil centre. Pop.: 1 764 038 (2000 est.). 2 **Lake.** a lake in NW Venezuela, linked with the Gulf of Venezuela by a dredged channel: centre of the Venezuelan and South American oil industry. Area: about 13 000 sq. km (500 sq. miles).

Maracanda (ˌmærə'kændə) NOUN the ancient name for **Samarkand.**

Maracay (*Spanish* mara'kai) NOUN a city in N central Venezuela: developed greatly as the headquarters of Juan Vicente Gómez during his dictatorship; textile industries. Pop.: 459 007 (2000 est.).

marae (mə'raɪ) NOUN 1 *NZ* a traditional Maori tribal meeting place, originally one in the open air, now frequently a purpose-built building. 2 (in Polynesia) an open-air place of worship.
▷**HISTORY** Maori

maraging steel ('mɑ:ˌreɪdʒɪŋ) NOUN a strong low-carbon steel containing nickel and small amounts of titanium, aluminium, and niobium, produced by transforming to a martensitic structure and heating at 500°C.
▷**HISTORY** C20 *maraging,* from MAR(TENSITE) + *aging*

Marajó (*Portuguese* mara'ʒɔ) NOUN an island in N Brazil, at the mouth of the Amazon. Area: 38 610 sq. km (15 444 sq. miles).

Maranhão (*Portuguese* marə'ɲɜ̃u) NOUN a state of NE Brazil, on the Atlantic: forested and humid in the northwest, with high plateaus in the east and south. Capital: São Luís. Pop.: 5 638 381 (2000). Area: 328 666 sq. km (128 179 sq. miles).

Marañón (*Spanish* mara'ɲɔn) NOUN a river in NE Peru, rising in the Andes and flowing northwest into the Ucayali River, forming the Amazon. Length: about 1450 km (900 miles).

maranta (mə'ræntə) NOUN any plant of the tropical American rhizomatous genus *Maranta,* some species of which are grown as pot plants for their showy leaves in variegated shades of green: family *Marantaceae.*
▷**HISTORY** named after Bartolomea *Maranti,* died 1571, Venetian botanist

marari ('mɑ:rɑ:ri:) NOUN *NZ* a Maori name for **butterfish** (sense 2).

Maraş (mæ'ræʃ) NOUN a town in S Turkey: noted formerly for the manufacture of weapons but now for carpets and embroidery. Pop.: 303 594 (1997).

marasca (mə'ræskə) NOUN a European cherry tree, *Prunus cerasus marasca,* with red acid-tasting fruit from which maraschino is made.
▷**HISTORY** C19: from Italian, variant of *amarasca* from *amaro,* from Latin *amārus* bitter

maraschino (ˌmærə'ski:nəʊ, -'ʃi:nəʊ) NOUN a liqueur made from marasca cherries and flavoured with the kernels, having a taste like bitter almonds.
▷**HISTORY** C18: from Italian; see MARASCA

maraschino cherry NOUN a cherry preserved in maraschino or an imitation of this liqueur, used as a garnish.

marasmus (mə'ræzməs) NOUN *Pathol* general emaciation and wasting, esp of infants, thought to be associated with severe malnutrition or impaired utilization of nutrients.
▷**HISTORY** C17: from New Latin, from Greek *marasmos,* from *marainein* to waste
▸**ma'rasmic** ADJECTIVE

Maratha *or* **Mahratta** (mə'rɑ:tə) NOUN a member of a people of India living chiefly in Maharashtra.

Marathi *or* **Mahratti** (mə'rɑ:tɪ) ADJECTIVE 1 of or relating to Maharashtra state in India, its people, or their language. ◆ NOUN 2 the state language of Maharashtra, belonging to the Indic branch of the Indo-European family.

marathon ('mærəθən) NOUN 1 a race on foot of 26 miles 385 yards (42.195 kilometres): an event in the modern Olympics. 2 **a** any long or arduous task, assignment, etc. **b** (*as modifier*): *a marathon effort.*
▷**HISTORY** referring to the feat of the messenger who ran more than 20 miles from Marathon to Athens to bring the news of victory in 490 B.C.

Marathon ('mærəθən) NOUN a plain in Attica northeast of Athens: site of a victory of the Athenians and Plataeans over the Persians (490 B.C.).

marathon group NOUN (in psychotherapy) an encounter group that lasts for many hours or days.

maraud (mə'rɔ:d) VERB 1 to wander or raid in search of plunder. ◆ NOUN 2 an archaic word for **foray.**
▷**HISTORY** C18: from French *marauder* to prowl, from *maraud* vagabond
▸**ma'rauder** NOUN

marauding (mə'rɔ:dɪŋ) ADJECTIVE wandering or raiding in search of plunder or victims.

maravedi (ˌmærə'veɪdɪ) NOUN, *plural* **-dis.** any of various Spanish coins of copper or gold.
▷**HISTORY** C15: from Spanish, from Arabic *Murābitīn* (plural of *murābit* MARABOUT), the Moorish dynasty in Córdoba, 1087–1147

marble ('mɑ:bᵊl) NOUN 1 **a** a hard crystalline metamorphic rock resulting from the recrystallization of a limestone: takes a high polish and is used for building and sculpture. **b** (*as modifier*): *a marble bust.* Related adjective: **marmoreal.** 2 a block or work of art of marble. 3 a small round glass or stone ball used in playing marbles. 4 **make one's marble good.** *Austral and NZ informal* to succeed or do the right thing. 5 **pass in one's marble.** *Austral informal* to die. ◆ VERB 6 (*tr*) to mottle with variegated streaks in imitation of marble. ◆ ADJECTIVE 7 cold, hard, or unresponsive. 8 white like some kinds of marble. ◆ See also **marbles.**
▷**HISTORY** C12: via Old French from Latin *marmor,* from Greek *marmaros,* related to Greek *marmairein* to gleam
▸**'marbled** ADJECTIVE ▸**'marbler** NOUN ▸**'marbly** ADJECTIVE

marble cake NOUN a cake with a marbled appearance obtained by incompletely mixing dark and light mixtures.

marbled white NOUN any butterfly of the satyrid genus *Melanargia,* with panelled black-and-white wings, but technically a brown butterfly; found in grassland.

marbles ('mɑ:bᵊlz) NOUN 1 (*functioning as singular*) a game in which marbles are rolled at one another, similar to bowls. 2 (*functioning as plural*) *Informal* wits: *to lose one's marbles.*

marblewood ('mɑ:bᵊlˌwʊd) NOUN 1 a Malaysian tree, *Diospyros marmorata*: family *Ebenaceae.* 2 the distinctively marked wood of this tree, having black bands on a lighter background.

marbling ('mɑ:blɪŋ) NOUN 1 a mottled effect or pattern resembling marble. 2 such an effect obtained by transferring floating colours from a bath of gum solution. 3 the streaks of fat in meat.

Marburg ('mɑ:ˌbɜ:g; *German* 'ma:rbʊrk) NOUN 1 a city in W central Germany, in Hesse: famous for the religious debate between Luther and Zwingli in 1529; Europe's first Protestant university (1527). Pop.: 75 400 (1995 est.). 2 the German name for **Maribor.**

Marburg disease NOUN a severe, sometimes fatal, viral disease of the green monkey, which may be transmitted to humans. Symptoms include fever, vomiting, and internal bleeding. Also called: **green monkey disease.**

marc (mɑ:k; *French* mar) NOUN 1 the remains of grapes or other fruit that have been pressed for wine-making. 2 a brandy distilled from these.
▷**HISTORY** C17: from French, from Old French *marchier* to trample (grapes), MARCH[1]

marcasite ('mɑ:kəˌsaɪt) NOUN 1 a metallic pale yellow mineral consisting of iron sulphide in orthorhombic crystalline form used in jewellery. Formula: FeS_2. 2 a cut and polished form of steel or any white metal used for making jewellery.
▷**HISTORY** C15: from Medieval Latin *marcasīta,* from Arabic *marqashītā,* perhaps from Persian
▸**marcasitical** (ˌmɑ:kə'sɪtɪkᵊl) ADJECTIVE

marcato (mɑ:'kɑ:təʊ) *Music* ◆ ADJECTIVE 1 (of notes) heavily accented. ◆ ADVERB 2 with each note heavily accented.
▷**HISTORY** C19: from Italian: marked

marcel (mɑ:'sɛl) NOUN 1 Also called: **marcel wave.** a hairstyle characterized by repeated regular waves, popular in the 1920s. ◆ VERB **-cels, -celling, -celled.** 2 (*tr*) to make such waves in (the hair) with special hot irons.
▷**HISTORY** C20: after *Marcel* Grateau (1852–1936), French hairdresser
▸**mar'celler** NOUN

marcescent (mɑ:'sɛsənt) ADJECTIVE (of the parts of certain plants) remaining attached to the plant when withered.
▷**HISTORY** C18: from Latin *marcescere* to grow weak, from *marcēre* to wither
▸**mar'cescence** NOUN

march¹ (mɑːtʃ) VERB [1] (*intr*) to walk or proceed with stately or regular steps, usually in a procession or military formation. [2] (*tr*) to make (a person or group) proceed: *he marched his army to the town.* [3] (*tr*) to traverse or cover by marching: *to march a route.* ◆ NOUN [4] the act or an instance of marching. [5] a regular stride: *a slow march.* [6] a long or exhausting walk. [7] advance; progression (of time, etc.). [8] a distance or route covered by marching. [9] a piece of music, usually in four beats to the bar, having a strongly accented rhythm. [10] **steal a march on.** to gain an advantage over, esp by a secret or underhand enterprise.
▷HISTORY C16: from Old French *marchier* to tread, probably of Germanic origin; compare Old English *mearcian* to MARK¹
▸ **'marcher** NOUN

march² (mɑːtʃ) NOUN [1] Also called: **marchland.** a frontier, border, or boundary or the land lying along it, often of disputed ownership. ◆ VERB [2] (*intr; often foll by upon or with*) to share a common border (with).
▷HISTORY C13: from Old French *marche,* from Germanic; related to MARK¹

March¹ (mɑːtʃ) NOUN the third month of the year, consisting of 31 days.
▷HISTORY from Old French, from Latin *Martius* (month) of Mars

March² (març) NOUN the German name for the **Morava** (sense 1).

MArch ABBREVIATION FOR Master of Architecture.

March. ABBREVIATION FOR Marchioness.

march brown NOUN an angler's name for the dun and spinner of various mayflies or an artificial fly imitating one of these.

Marche (*French* marʃ) NOUN a former province of central France.

marcher ('mɑːtʃə) NOUN [1] an inhabitant of any of the Marches. [2] (formerly) **a** a lord governing and defending such a borderland. **b** (*as modifier*): *the marcher lords.*

Marches ('mɑːtʃɪz) NOUN **the.** [1] the border area between England and Wales or Scotland, both characterized by continual feuding (13th–16th centuries). [2] a region of central Italy. Capital: Ancona. Pop.: 1 460 989 (2000 est.). Area: 9692 sq. km (3780 sq. miles). Italian name: **Le Marche** (le 'marke). [3] any of various other border regions.

marchesa *Italian* (mar'keːza) NOUN, *plural* ***-se*** (-ze). (in Italy) the wife or widow of a marchese; marchioness.

marchese *Italian* (mar'keːze) NOUN, *plural* ***-si*** (-zi). (in Italy) a nobleman ranking below a prince and above a count; marquis.

Marcheshvan *Hebrew* (marxeʃ'van) NOUN another word for ***Cheshvan.***
▷HISTORY from Hebrew *mar* bitter (because it contains no festivals) + CHESHVAN

March hare NOUN a hare during its breeding season in March, noted for its wild and excitable behaviour (esp in the phrase **mad as a March hare**).

marching girl NOUN (*often plural*) *Austral and NZ* one of a team of girls dressed in fancy uniform who perform marching formations.

marching orders PLURAL NOUN [1] military orders, esp to infantry, giving instructions about a march, its destination, etc. [2] *Informal* notice of dismissal, esp from employment. [3] *Informal* the instruction to proceed with a task.

marchioness ('mɑːʃənɪs, ˌmɑːʃə'nɛs) NOUN [1] the wife or widow of a marquis. [2] a woman who holds the rank of marquis.
▷HISTORY C16: from Medieval Latin *marchionissa,* feminine of *marchiō* MARQUIS

marchland ('mɑːtʃˌlænd, -lənd) NOUN a less common word for **borderland** or **march².**

marchpane ('mɑːtʃˌpeɪn) NOUN an archaic word for **marzipan.**
▷HISTORY C15: from French

march past NOUN the marching of troops on parade past a person who is reviewing them.

Marcionism ('mɑːʃəˌnɪzəm) NOUN a Gnostic movement of the 2nd and 3rd centuries A.D.
▷HISTORY C16: after *Marcion* of Sinope, 2nd-century Gnostic

Marconi rig (mɑː'kəʊnɪ) NOUN *Nautical* a fore-and-aft sailing boat rig with triangular sails.
▷HISTORY C20: from Guglielmo *Marconi* (1874–1937), the Italian physicist who developed radiotelegraphy, from its resemblance to some types of radio aerial
▸ **Mar'coni-ˌrigged** ADJECTIVE

Mar del Plata (*Spanish* 'mar ðel 'plata) NOUN a city and resort in E Argentina, on the Atlantic: fishing port. Pop.: 579 483 (1999 est.).

Mardi Gras ('mɑːdɪ 'grɑː) NOUN the festival of Shrove Tuesday, celebrated in some cities with great revelry.
▷HISTORY French: fat Tuesday

Marduk ('mɑːdʊk) NOUN the chief god of the Babylonian pantheon.

mardy ('mɑːdɪ) ADJECTIVE *Dialect* [1] (of a child) spoilt. [2] irritable.
▷HISTORY from *marred,* past participle of MAR

mare¹ (mɛə) NOUN the adult female of a horse or zebra.
▷HISTORY C12: from Old English, of Germanic origin; related to Old High German *mariha,* Old Norse *merr* mare

mare² ('mɑːreɪ, -rɪ) NOUN, *plural* **maria** ('mɑːrɪə). [1] (*capital when part of a name*) any of a large number of huge dry plains on the surface of the moon, visible as dark markings and once thought to be seas: *Mare Imbrium* (*Sea of Showers*). [2] a similar area on the surface of Mars, such as *Mare Sirenum.*
▷HISTORY from Latin: sea

mare clausum ('mɑːreɪ 'klaʊsʊm) NOUN *Law* a sea coming under the jurisdiction of one nation and closed to all others. Compare **mare liberum.**
▷HISTORY Latin: closed sea

mare liberum ('mɑːreɪ 'liːbərʊm) NOUN *Law* a sea open to navigation by shipping of all nations. Compare **mare clausum.**
▷HISTORY Latin: free sea

maremma (mə'rɛmə) NOUN, *plural* **-me** (-miː). a marshy unhealthy region near the shore, esp in Italy.
▷HISTORY C19: from Italian, from Latin *maritima* MARITIME

maremma sheepdog NOUN a large strongly-built sheepdog of a breed with a long, slightly wavy, white coat.

Marengo¹ (mə'rɛŋgəʊ) ADJECTIVE (*postpositive*) browned in oil and cooked with tomatoes, mushrooms, garlic, wine, etc.: *chicken Marengo.*
▷HISTORY C19: after a dish prepared for Napoleon after the battle of Marengo

Marengo² (mə'rɛŋgəʊ; *Italian* ma'reŋgo) NOUN a village in NW Italy: site of a major battle in which Napoleon decisively defeated the Austrians (1800).

mare nostrum *Latin* ('mɑːreɪ 'nɒstrʊm) NOUN the Latin name for the **Mediterranean.**
▷HISTORY literally: our sea

mare's-nest NOUN [1] a discovery imagined to be important but proving worthless. [2] a disordered situation.

mare's-tail NOUN [1] a wisp of trailing cirrus cloud, often indicating high winds in the upper troposphere. [2] an erect cosmopolitan pond plant, *Hippuris vulgaris,* with minute flowers and crowded whorls of narrow leaves: family *Hippuridaceae.*

Mareva injunction (mə'riːvə) NOUN *Law* the former name for **freezing injunction.**
▷HISTORY C20: named after *Mareva Compañia Naviera SA,* the plaintiff in an early case (1975) in which such an order was made

marg (mɑːdʒ) NOUN *Brit informal* short for **margarine.**

margaric (mɑː'gærɪk) *or* **margaritic** ADJECTIVE of or resembling pearl.
▷HISTORY C19: from Greek *margaron* pearl

margaric acid NOUN another name for **heptadecanoic acid.**

margarine (ˌmɑːdʒə'riːn, ˌmɑːgə-) NOUN a substitute for butter, prepared from vegetable and animal fats by emulsifying them with water and adding small amounts of milk, salt, vitamins, colouring matter, etc.
▷HISTORY C19: from MARGARIC

margarita (ˌmɑːgə'riːtə) NOUN a mixed drink consisting of tequila and lemon juice.
▷HISTORY C20: from the woman's name

Margarita (ˌmɑːgə'riːtə) NOUN an island in the Caribbean, off the NE coast of Venezuela: pearl fishing. Capital: La Asunción.

margarite ('mɑːgəˌraɪt) NOUN [1] a pink pearly micaceous mineral consisting of hydrated calcium aluminium silicate. Formula: $CaAl_4Si_2O_{10}(OH)_2$. [2] an aggregate of minute beadlike masses occurring in some glassy igneous rocks.
▷HISTORY C19: via German from Greek *margaron* pearl

Margate ('mɑːgeɪt) NOUN a town and resort in SE England, in E Kent on the Isle of Thanet. Pop.: 56 734 (1991).

Margaux (*French* margo) NOUN a red wine produced in the region around the village of Margaux near Bordeaux.

margay ('mɑːˌgeɪ) NOUN a feline mammal, *Felis wiedi,* of Central and South America, having a dark-striped coat.
▷HISTORY C18: from French, from Tupi *mbaracaiá*

marge¹ (mɑːdʒ) NOUN *Brit informal* short for **margarine.**

marge² (mɑːdʒ) NOUN *Archaic* a margin.
▷HISTORY C16: from French

margin ('mɑːdʒɪn) NOUN [1] an edge or rim, and the area immediately adjacent to it; border. [2] the blank space surrounding the text on a page. [3] a vertical line on a page, esp one on the left-hand side, delineating this space. [4] an additional amount or one beyond the minimum necessary: *a margin of error.* [5] *Chiefly Austral* a payment made in addition to a basic wage, esp for special skill or responsibility. [6] a bound or limit. [7] the amount by which one thing differs from another: *a large margin separated the parties.* [8] *Commerce* the profit on a transaction. [9] *Economics* the minimum return below which an enterprise becomes unprofitable. [10] *Finance* **a** collateral deposited by a client with a broker as security. **b** the excess of the value of a loan's collateral over the value of the loan. ◆ Also (archaic): **margent** ('mɑːdʒənt). ◆ VERB (*tr*) [11] to provide with a margin; border. [12] *Finance* to deposit a margin upon.
▷HISTORY C14: from Latin *margō* border; related to MARCH², MARK¹

marginal ('mɑːdʒɪnᵊl) ADJECTIVE [1] of, in, on, or constituting a margin. [2] close to a limit, esp a lower limit: *marginal legal ability.* [3] not considered central or important; insignificant, minor, small. [4] *Economics* relating to goods or services produced and sold at the margin of profitability: *marginal cost.* [5] *Politics, chiefly Brit and NZ* of or designating a constituency in which elections tend to be won by small margins: *a marginal seat.* [6] designating agricultural land on the margin of cultivated zones. [7] *Economics* relating to a small change in something, such as total cost, revenue, or consumer satisfaction.
▸ **marginality** (ˌmɑːdʒɪ'nælɪtɪ) NOUN ▸ **'marginally** ADVERB

marginal costing NOUN a method of cost accounting and decision making used for internal reporting in which only marginal costs are charged to cost units and fixed costs are treated as a lump sum. Compare **absorption costing.**

marginalia (ˌmɑːdʒɪ'neɪlɪə) PLURAL NOUN notes in the margin of a book, manuscript, or letter.
▷HISTORY C19: New Latin, noun (neuter plural) from *margināli s* marginal

marginalize *or* **marginalise** ('mɑːdʒɪnᵊˌlaɪz) VERB (*tr*) to relegate to the fringes, out of the mainstream; make seem unimportant: *various economic assumptions marginalize women.*
▸ **ˌmarginali'zation** *or* **ˌmarginali'sation** NOUN

marginal probability NOUN *Statistics* (in a multivariate distribution) the probability of one variable taking a specific value irrespective of the values of the others.

marginate ('mɑːdʒɪˌneɪt) VERB [1] (*tr*) to provide with a margin or margins. ◆ ADJECTIVE [2] *Biology* having a margin of a distinct colour or form: *marginate leaves.*
▷HISTORY C18: from Latin *margināre*
▸ **ˌmargin'ation** NOUN

margravate ('mɑːgrəvɪt) *or* **margraviate** (mɑː'greɪvɪɪt) NOUN the domain of a margrave.

margrave ('mɑːˌgreɪv) NOUN a German nobleman

ranking above a count. Margraves were originally counts appointed to govern frontier provinces, but all had become princes of the Holy Roman Empire by the 12th century.
▷HISTORY C16: from Middle Dutch *markgrave,* literally: count of the MARCH^{2}

margravine ('mɑːgrəˌviːn) NOUN [1] the wife or widow of a margrave. [2] a woman who holds the rank of margrave.
▷HISTORY C17: from Middle Dutch, feminine of MARGRAVE

marguerite (ˌmɑːgə'riːt) NOUN [1] a cultivated garden plant, *Chrysanthemum frutescens,* whose flower heads have white or pale yellow rays around a yellow disc: family *Asteraceae* (composites). [2] any of various related plants with daisy-like flowers, esp *C. leucanthemum.*
▷HISTORY C19: from French: daisy, pearl, from Latin *margarīta,* from Greek *margaritēs,* from *margaron*

Marheshvan *or* ***Marcheshvan*** *Hebrew* (marxɛʃ'van) NOUN another word for ***Cheshvan.***

Mari ('mɑːrɪ) NOUN, *plural* **Mari** *or* **Maris.** another name for **Cheremiss.**

maria ('mɑːrɪə) NOUN the plural of **mare^{2}**.

mariachi (ˌmɑːrɪ'ɑːtʃɪ) NOUN a small ensemble of street musicians in Mexico.
▷HISTORY C20: from Mexican Spanish

mariage blanc *French* (marjaʒ blɑ̃) NOUN, *plural* ***mariages blancs*** (marjaʒ blɑ̃). unconsummated marriage.
▷HISTORY C20: literally: white marriage

mariage de convenance *French* (marjaʒ də kɔ̃vənɑ̃s) NOUN, *plural* ***mariages de convenance.*** another term for **marriage of convenience.**

Marian ('mɛərɪən) ADJECTIVE [1] of or relating to the Virgin Mary, the mother of Jesus. [2] of or relating to some other Mary, such as Mary Queen of Scots (1542–87; queen 1542–67) or Mary I of England (1516–58; queen 1553–58). ◆ NOUN [3] a person who has a special devotion to the Virgin Mary. [4] a supporter of some other Mary.

Mariana Islands (ˌmærɪ'ɑːnə) PLURAL NOUN a chain of volcanic and coral islands in the W Pacific, east of the Philippines and north of New Guinea: divided politically into Guam (a US unincorporated territory) and the islands north of Guam constituting the Commonwealth of the Northern Mariana Islands (a US commonwealth territory). Pop.: (Guam) 158 000 (2001 est.); (Northern Marianas) 73 400 (2001 est.). Area: 958 sq. km (370 sq. miles). Former name (1521–1668): **Ladrone Islands.**

Marianao (*Spanish* marja'nao) NOUN a city in NW Cuba, adjacent to W Havana city: the chief Cuban military base. Pop.: 133 015 (latest est.).

Marianne (*French* marjan) NOUN a female figure personifying the French republic after the Revolution (1789).

Mariánské Lázně (*Czech* 'marjanskɛː 'laːznjɛ) NOUN a town in the W Czech Republic: a fashionable spa in the 18th and 19th centuries. Pop.: 15 380 (1991). German name: **Marienbad.**

Maribor ('mærɪbɔː) NOUN an industrial city in N Slovenia on the Drava River: a flourishing Hapsburg trading centre in the 13th century; resort. Pop.: 134 289 (1996 est.). German name: **Marburg.**

mariculture ('mærɪˌkʌltʃə) NOUN the cultivation of marine plants and animals in their natural environment.
▷HISTORY C20: from Latin *mari-, mare* sea + CULTURE

Marie Byrd Land ('mɑːrɪ 'bɜːd) NOUN the former name of **Byrd Land.**

Marie Galante (*French* mari galɑ̃t) NOUN an island in the E Caribbean southeast of Guadeloupe, of which it is a dependency. Chief town: Grand Bourg. Pop.: 13 463 (1990). Area: 155 sq. km (60 sq. miles).

Mariehamn (mariə'hamn) NOUN a city in SW Finland, chief port of the Åland Islands. Pop.: 10 260 (1990). Finnish name: **Maarianhamina.**

Mari El Republic ('mɑːrɪ) NOUN a constituent republic of W central Russia, in the middle Volga basin. Capital: Yoshkar-Ola. Pop.: 759 000 (2000 est.). Area: 23 200 sq. km (8955 sq. miles).

Marienbad ('mærɪənˌbæd; *German* ma'riːənbaːt) NOUN the German name for **Mariánské Lázně.**

marigold ('mærɪˌgəʊld) NOUN [1] any of various tropical American plants of the genus *Tagetes,* esp *T. erecta* (**African marigold**) and *T. patula* (**French marigold**), cultivated for their yellow or orange flower heads and strongly scented foliage: family *Asteraceae* (composites). [2] any of various similar or related plants, such as the marsh marigold, pot marigold, bur marigold, and fig marigold.
▷HISTORY C14: from *Mary* (the Virgin) + GOLD

marigram ('mærɪˌgræm) NOUN a graphic record of the tide levels at a particular coastal station.
▷HISTORY from Latin *mare* sea + -GRAM

marigraph ('mærɪˌgræf, -ˌgrɑːf) NOUN a gauge for recording the levels of the tides.
▷HISTORY from Latin *mare* sea + -GRAPH

marijuana *or* **marihuana** (ˌmærɪ'hwɑːnə) NOUN [1] the dried leaves and flowers of the hemp plant, used for its euphoric effects, esp in the form of cigarettes. See also **cannabis.** [2] another name for **hemp** (the plant).
▷HISTORY C19: from Mexican Spanish

marimba (mə'rɪmbə) NOUN a Latin American percussion instrument consisting of a set of hardwood plates placed over tuned metal resonators, played with two soft-headed sticks in each hand.
▷HISTORY C18: of West African origin

marina (mə'riːnə) NOUN an elaborate docking facility for pleasure boats.
▷HISTORY C19: via Italian and Spanish from Latin: MARINE

marinade NOUN (ˌmærɪ'neɪd) [1] a spiced liquid mixture of oil, wine, vinegar, herbs, etc., in which meat or fish is soaked before cooking. [2] meat or fish soaked in this liquid. ◆ VERB ('mærɪˌneɪd) [3] a variant of **marinate.**
▷HISTORY C17: from French, from Spanish *marinada,* from *marinar* to pickle in brine, MARINATE

marinate ('mærɪˌneɪt) VERB to soak in marinade.
▷HISTORY C17: probably from Italian *marinato,* from *marinare* to pickle, ultimately from Latin *marīnus* MARINE
▸ **ˌmari'nation** NOUN

Marinduque (ˌmɑːrɪn'duːkeɪ) NOUN an island of the central Philippines, east of Mindoro: forms, with offshore islets, a province of the Philippines. Capital: Boac. Pop.: 173 715 (latest est.). Area: 960 sq. km (370 sq. miles).

marine (mə'riːn) ADJECTIVE (*usually prenominal*) [1] of, found in, or relating to the sea. [2] of or relating to shipping, navigation, etc. [3] of or relating to a body of seagoing troops: *marine corps.* [4] of or relating to a government department concerned with maritime affairs. [5] used or adapted for use at sea: *a marine camera.* ◆ NOUN [6] shipping and navigation in general: *the merchant marine.* [7] (*capital when part of a name*) a member of a marine corps or similar body. [8] a picture of a ship, seascape, etc. [9] **tell it to the marines.** *Informal* an expression of disbelief.
▷HISTORY C15: from Old French *marin,* from Latin *marīnus,* from *mare* sea

marine borer NOUN any mollusc or crustacean that lives usually in warm seas and destroys wood by boring into and eating it. The gribble and shipworm are the best known since they penetrate any wood in favourable water. See also **piddock.**

marine engineer NOUN an engineer responsible for all heavy machinery on a ship or an offshore structure.

marine insurance NOUN insurance covering damage to or loss of ship, passengers, or cargo caused by the sea.

mariner ('mærɪnə) NOUN a formal or literary word for **seaman.**
▷HISTORY C13: from Anglo-French, ultimately from Latin *marīnus* MARINE

Mariner ('mærɪnə) NOUN any of a series of US space probes launched between 1962 and 1971 that sent back photographs and information concerning the surface of Mars and Venus and also studied interplanetary matter.

marine railway NOUN another term for **slipway** (sense 2).

marine snow NOUN small particles of organic and biogenic marine sediment, including the remains of organisms, faecal matter, and the shells of planktonic organisms, that slowly drift down to the sea floor.

Mariolatry *or* **Maryolatry** (ˌmɛərɪ'ɒlətrɪ) NOUN *Derogatory* exaggerated veneration of the Virgin Mary.
▸ **ˌMari'olater** *or* **ˌMary'olater** NOUN ▸ **ˌMari'olatrous** *or* **ˌMary'olatrous** ADJECTIVE

Mariology *or* **Maryology** (ˌmɛərɪ'ɒlədʒɪ) NOUN *RC Church* the study of the traditions and doctrines concerning the Virgin Mary.
▸ **ˌMari'ologist** *or* **ˌMary'ologist** NOUN

marionette (ˌmærɪə'nɛt) NOUN an articulated puppet or doll whose jointed limbs are moved by strings.
▷HISTORY C17: from French, from *Marion,* diminutive of *Marie* Mary + -ETTE

mariposa (ˌmærɪ'pəʊzə, -sə) NOUN any of several liliaceous plants of the genus *Calochortus,* of the southwestern US and Mexico, having brightly coloured tulip-like flowers. Also called: **mariposa lily** *or* **tulip.**
▷HISTORY C19: from Spanish: butterfly; from the likeness of the blooms to butterflies

marish ('mærɪʃ) ADJECTIVE *Obsolete* marshy; swampy.
▷HISTORY C14: from Old French *marais* MARSH

Marist ('mɛərɪst) *RC Church* ◆ NOUN [1] a member of the Society of Mary, a religious congregation founded in 1824. [2] *NZ* a teacher or pupil in a school belonging to the Marist Order. ◆ ADJECTIVE [3] of a Marist.
▷HISTORY C19: from French *Mariste,* from *Marie* Mary (the virgin)

maritage ('mærɪtɪdʒ) NOUN *Feudal history* [1] the right of a lord to choose the spouses of his wards. [2] a sum paid to a lord in lieu of his exercising this right.
▷HISTORY C16: from Medieval Latin *marītāgium,* a Latinized form of French *mariage* marriage

marital ('mærɪt^{ə}l) ADJECTIVE [1] of or relating to marriage: *marital status.* [2] of or relating to a husband.
▷HISTORY C17: from Latin *marītālis,* from *marītus* married (adj), husband (n); related to *mās* male
▸ **'maritally** ADVERB

maritime ('mærɪˌtaɪm) ADJECTIVE [1] of or relating to navigation, shipping, etc.; seafaring. [2] of, relating to, near, or living near the sea. [3] (of a climate) having small temperature differences between summer and winter; equable.
▷HISTORY C16: from Latin *maritimus* from *mare* sea

Maritime Alps PLURAL NOUN a range of the W Alps in SE France and NW Italy. Highest peak: Argentera, 3297 m (10 817 ft.).

Maritime Command NOUN *Canadian* the naval branch of the Canadian armed forces.

Maritime Provinces *or* **Maritimes** PLURAL NOUN **the.** another name for the **Atlantic Provinces,** but often excluding Newfoundland

Maritimer ('mærɪˌtaɪmə) NOUN a native or inhabitant of the Maritime Provinces of Canada.

Maritsa (*Bulgarian* ma'ritsa) NOUN a river in S Europe, rising in S Bulgaria and flowing east into Turkey, then south from Edirne as part of the border between Turkey and Greece to the Aegean. Length: 483 km (300 miles). Turkish name: **Meriç.** Greek name: **Évros.**

Mariupol (*Russian* məri'upəlj) NOUN a port in SE Ukraine, on an estuary leading to the Sea of Azov. Pop.: 504 400 (1998 est.). Former name (1948–91): **Zhdanov.**

marjoram ('mɑːdʒərəm) NOUN [1] Also called: **sweet marjoram.** an aromatic Mediterranean plant, *Origanum* (or *Marjorana*) *hortensis,* with small pale purple flowers and sweet-scented leaves, used for seasoning food and in salads: family *Lamiaceae* (labiates). [2] Also called: **wild marjoram, pot marjoram, origan.** a similar and related European plant, *Origanum vulgare.* See also **oregano, origanum.**
▷HISTORY C14: via Old French *majorane,* from Medieval Latin *marjorana*

mark^{1} (mɑːk) NOUN [1] a visible impression, stain, etc., on a surface, such as a spot or scratch. [2] a sign, symbol, or other indication that distinguishes something: *an owner's mark.* [3] a cross or other symbol made instead of a signature. [4] a written or printed sign or symbol, as for punctuation: *a*

question mark. 5 a letter, number, or percentage used to grade academic work. 6 a thing that indicates position or directs; marker. 7 a desired or recognized standard: *he is not up to the mark.* 8 an indication of some quality, feature, or prowess: *he has the mark of an athlete.* 9 quality or importance; note: *a person of little mark.* 10 a target or goal. 11 impression or influence: *he left his mark on German literature.* 12 one of the temperature settings on a gas oven: *gas mark 5.* 13 (*often capital*) (in trade names) **a** model, brand, or type: *the car is a Mark 4.* **b** a variation on a particular model: *a Mark 3 Cortina.* 14 *Slang* a suitable victim, esp for swindling. 15 *Nautical* one of the intervals distinctively marked on a sounding lead. Compare **deep** (sense 21). 16 *Bowls* another name for the **jack.** 17 *Rugby Union* an action in which a player standing inside his own 22m line catches a forward kick by an opponent and shouts "mark", entitling himself to a free kick. 18 *Australian Rules football* a catch of the ball from a kick of at least 10 yards, after which a free kick is taken. 19 **the mark.** *Boxing* the middle of the stomach at or above the line made by the boxer's trunks. 20 (in medieval England and Germany) a piece of land held in common by the free men of a community. 21 an obsolete word for **frontier.** 22 *Statistics* See **class mark.** 23 **make one's mark.** to succeed or achieve recognition. 24 **on your mark** *or* **marks.** a command given to runners in a race to prepare themselves at the starting line. ◆ VERB 25 to make or receive (a visible impression, trace, or stain) on (a surface). 26 (*tr*) to characterize or distinguish: *his face was marked by anger.* 27 (often foll by *off* or *out*) to set boundaries or limits (on): *to mark out an area for negotiation.* 28 (*tr*) to select, designate, or doom by or as if by a mark: *to mark someone as a criminal.* 29 (*tr*) to put identifying or designating labels, stamps, etc., on, esp to indicate price: *to mark the book at one pound.* 30 (*tr*) to pay heed or attention to: *mark my words.* 31 to observe; notice. 32 to grade or evaluate (scholastic work): *she marks fairly.* 33 *Brit sport* to stay close to (an opponent) to hamper his or her play. 34 to keep (score) in some games. 35 **mark time. a** to move the feet alternately as in marching but without advancing. **b** to act in a mechanical and routine way. **c** to halt progress temporarily, while awaiting developments. ◆ INTERJECTION 36 *Rugby Union* the shout given by a player when calling for a mark. ◆ See also **markdown, mark-up.**
▷HISTORY Old English *mearc* mark; related to Old Norse *mörk* boundary land, Old High German *marha* boundary, Latin *margō* MARGIN

mark[2] (mɑːk) NOUN 1 See **Deutschmark, markka, Reichsmark, Ostmark.** 2 a former monetary unit and coin in England and Scotland worth two thirds of a pound sterling. 3 a silver coin of Germany until 1924.
▷HISTORY Old English *marc* unit of weight of precious metal, perhaps from the marks on metal bars; apparently of Germanic origin and related to MARK[1]

Mark (mɑːk) NOUN *New Testament* 1 one of the four Evangelists. Feast day: April 25. 2 the second Gospel, traditionally ascribed to him.

marka (ˈmɑːkə) NOUN a unit of currency introduced as an interim currency in Bosnia-Herzegovina; replaced by the euro in 2002.

markdown (ˈmɑːkˌdaʊn) NOUN 1 a price reduction. ◆ VERB **mark down.** 2 (*tr, adverb*) to reduce in price.

marked (mɑːkt) ADJECTIVE 1 obvious, evident, or noticeable. 2 singled out, esp for punishment, killing, etc.: *a marked man.* 3 *Linguistics* distinguished by a specific feature, as in phonology. For example, of the two phonemes /t/ and /d/, the /d/ is marked because it exhibits the feature of voice.
▸**markedly** (ˈmɑːkɪdlɪ) ADVERB ▸ˈ**markedness** NOUN

marker (ˈmɑːkə) NOUN 1 **a** something used for distinguishing or marking. **b** (*as modifier*): *a marker buoy.* 2 a person or thing that marks. 3 a person or object that keeps or shows scores in a game. 4 a trait, condition, gene, or substance that indicates the presence of, or a probable increased predisposition to, a medical or psychological disorder. Compare **biological marker, genetic marker, medical marker.**

market (ˈmɑːkɪt) NOUN 1 **a** an event or occasion, usually held at regular intervals, at which people meet for the purpose of buying and selling merchandise. **b** (*as modifier*): *market day.* 2 a place, such as an open space in a town, at which a market is held. 3 a shop that sells a particular merchandise: *an antique market.* 4 **the market.** business or trade in a commodity as specified: *the sugar market.* 5 the trading or selling opportunities provided by a particular group of people: *the foreign market.* 6 demand for a particular product or commodity: *there is no market for furs here.* 7 See **stock market.** 8 See **market price, market value.** 9 **at market.** at the current price. 10 **be in the market for.** to wish to buy or acquire. 11 **on the market.** available for purchase. 12 **play the market. a** to speculate on a stock exchange. **b** to act aggressively or unscrupulously in one's own commercial interests. 13 **seller's** (*or* **buyer's**) **market.** a market characterized by excess demand (or supply) and thus favourable to sellers (or buyers). ◆ VERB **-kets, -keting, -keted.** 14 (*tr*) to offer or produce for sale. 15 (*intr*) to buy or deal in a market.
▷HISTORY C12: from Latin *mercātus;* from *mercārī* to trade, from *merx* merchandise
▸ˈ**marketer** NOUN

marketable (ˈmɑːkɪtəb^{ə}l) ADJECTIVE 1 (of commodities, assets, etc.) **a** being in good demand; saleable. **b** suitable for sale. 2 of or relating to buying or selling on a market: *marketable value.*
▸ˌ**marketaˈbility** *or* ˈ**marketableness** NOUN ▸ˈ**marketably** ADVERB

marketeer (ˌmɑːkɪˈtɪə) NOUN 1 *Brit* a supporter of the European Union and of Britain's membership of it. 2 a marketer.

marketeer (ˌmɑːkəˈtɪə) NOUN a person employed in marketing.

market forces PLURAL NOUN the effect of supply and demand on trading within a free market.

market garden NOUN *Chiefly Brit* an establishment where fruit and vegetables are grown for sale.
▸**market gardener** NOUN

market gardening NOUN *Chiefly Brit* the business of growing fruit and vegetables on a commercial scale. Also called (in the US and Canada): **truck farming, trucking.**

marketing (ˈmɑːkɪtɪŋ) NOUN the provision of goods or services to meet customer or consumer needs.

marketing mix NOUN the variables, such as price, promotion, and service, managed by an organization to influence demand for a product or service.

marketing research *or* **market research** NOUN the study of influences upon customer and consumer behaviour and the analysis of market characteristics and trends.

market maker NOUN a dealer in securities on the London Stock Exchange who buys and sells as a principal and since 1986 can also deal with the public as a broker.

market order NOUN an instruction to a broker to sell or buy at the best price currently obtainable on the market.

marketplace (ˈmɑːkɪtˌpleɪs) NOUN 1 a place where a public market is held. 2 any centre where ideas, opinions, etc., are exchanged. 3 the commercial world of buying and selling.

market price NOUN the prevailing price, as determined by supply and demand, at which goods, services, etc., may be bought or sold.

market rent NOUN (in Britain) the rent chargeable for accommodation, allowing for the scarcity of that kind of property and the willingness of tenants to pay.

market research NOUN the study of influences upon customer and consumer behaviour and the analysis of market characteristics and trends.

market segment NOUN a part of a market identifiable as having particular customers with specific buying characteristics.

market segmentation NOUN the division of a market into identifiable groups, esp to improve the effectiveness of a marketing strategy.

market share NOUN the percentage of a total market, in terms of either value or volume, accounted for by the sales of a specific brand.

market-test VERB (*tr*) to put (a section of a public-sector enterprise) out to tender, often as a prelude to full-scale privatization.

market town NOUN *Chiefly Brit* a town that holds a market, esp an agricultural centre in a rural area.

market value NOUN the amount obtainable on the open market for the sale of property, financial assets, or goods and services. Compare **par value, book value.**

Markham (ˈmɑːkəm) NOUN **Mount.** a mountain in Antarctica, in Victoria Land. Height: 4350 m (14 272 ft.).

markhor (ˈmɑːkɔː) *or* **markhoor** (ˈmɑːkʊə) NOUN, *plural* **-khors, -khor** *or* **-khoors, -khoor.** a large wild Himalayan goat, *Capra falconeri,* with a reddish-brown coat and large spiralled horns.
▷HISTORY C19: from Persian, literally: snake-eater, from *mār* snake + *-khōr* eating

marking (ˈmɑːkɪŋ) NOUN 1 a mark or series of marks. 2 the arrangement of colours on an animal, plant, etc. 3 assessment and correction of school children's or students' written work by teaching staff.

marking ink NOUN indelible ink used for marking linen, clothes, etc.

markka (ˈmɑːkɑː, -kə) NOUN, *plural* **-kaa** (-kɑː). the former standard monetary unit of Finland, divided into 100 penniä; replaced by the euro in 2002.
▷HISTORY Finnish. See MARK[2]

Markov chain (ˈmɑːkɒf) NOUN *Statistics* a sequence of events the probability for each of which is dependent only on the event immediately preceding it.
▷HISTORY C20: named after Andrei *Markov* (1856–1922), Russian mathematician

marksman (ˈmɑːksmən) NOUN, *plural* **-men.** 1 a person skilled in shooting. 2 a serviceman selected for his skill in shooting, esp for a minor engagement. 3 a qualification awarded in certain armed services for skill in shooting.
▸ˈ**marksmanˌship** NOUN ▸ˈ**marksˌwoman** FEMININE NOUN

mark-up NOUN 1 a percentage or amount added to the cost of a commodity to provide the seller with a profit and to cover overheads, costs, etc. 2 **a** an increase in the price of a commodity. **b** the amount of this increase. ◆ VERB **mark up.** (*tr, adverb*) 3 to add a percentage for profit, overheads, etc., to the cost of (a commodity). 4 to increase the price of.

marl[1] (mɑːl) NOUN 1 a fine-grained sedimentary rock consisting of clay minerals, calcite or aragonite, and silt: used as a fertilizer. ◆ VERB 2 (*tr*) to fertilize (land) with marl.
▷HISTORY C14: via Old French, from Late Latin *margila,* diminutive of Latin *marga*
▸**marlacious** (mɑːˈleɪʃəs) *or* ˈ**marly** ADJECTIVE

marl[2] (mɑːl) VERB *Nautical* to seize (a rope) with marline, using a hitch at each turn.
▷HISTORY C15 *marlyn* to bind; related to Dutch *marlen* to tie, Old English *mārels* cable

Marlborough (ˈmɑːlbərə, -brə, ˈmɔːl-) NOUN a town in S England, in Wiltshire: besieged and captured by Royalists in the Civil War (1642); site of Marlborough College, a public school founded in 1843. Pop.: 6429 (1991).

marlin (ˈmɑːlɪn) NOUN, *plural* **-lin** *or* **-lins.** any of several large scombroid food and game fishes of the genera *Makaira, Istiompax,* and *Tetrapturus,* of warm and tropical seas, having a very long upper jaw: family *Istiophoridae.* Also called: **spearfish.**
▷HISTORY C20: from MARLINESPIKE; with allusion to the shape of the beak

marline, marlin (ˈmɑːlɪn), *or less commonly* **marling** (ˈmɑːlɪŋ) NOUN *Nautical* a light rope, usually tarred, made of two strands laid left-handed.
▷HISTORY C15: from Dutch *marlijn,* from *marren* to tie + *lijn* line

marlinespike, marlinspike (ˈmɑːlɪnˌspaɪk), *or less commonly* **marlingspike** (ˈmɑːlɪŋˌspaɪk) NOUN *Nautical* a pointed metal tool used as a fid, spike, and for various other purposes.

marlite (ˈmɑːlaɪt) *or* **marlstone** (ˈmɑːlˌstəʊn) NOUN a type of marl that contains clay and calcium carbonate and is resistant to the decomposing action of air.

marmalade (ˈmɑːməˌleɪd) NOUN 1 a preserve

made by boiling the pulp and rind of citrus fruits, esp oranges, with sugar. ◆ ADJECTIVE [2] (of cats) streaked orange or yellow and brown.
▷HISTORY C16: via French from Portuguese *marmelada,* from *marmelo* quince, from Latin, from Greek *melimēlon,* from *meli* honey + *mēlon* apple

marmalade tree NOUN a tropical American sapotaceous tree, *Calocarpum sapota,* with durable wood: its fruit is used to make preserves. Also called: **mamey.**

marmalize *or* **marmalise** (ˈmɑːməˌlaɪz) VERB (*tr*) *Slang* to beat soundly or defeat utterly; thrash.
▷HISTORY C20: a humorous coinage

Marmara *or* **Marmora** (ˈmɑːmərə) NOUN **Sea of.** a deep inland sea in NW Turkey, linked with the Black Sea by the Bosporus and with the Aegean by the Dardanelles: separates Turkey in Europe from Turkey in Asia. Area: 11 471 sq. km (4429 sq. miles). Ancient name: **Propontis.**

marmite (ˈmɑːmaɪt) NOUN [1] a large cooking pot. [2] soup cooked in such a pot. [3] an individual covered casserole for serving soup. [4] *US military* a container used to bring food to troops in the field.
▷HISTORY from French: pot

Marmite (ˈmɑːmaɪt) NOUN *Trademark, Brit* a yeast and vegetable extract used as a spread, flavouring, etc.

Marmolada (*Italian* marmoˈlaːda) NOUN a mountain in NE Italy: highest peak in the Dolomites. Height: 3342 m (10 965 ft.).

marmoreal (mɑːˈmɔːrɪəl) *or less commonly* **marmorean** ADJECTIVE of, relating to, or resembling marble: *a marmoreal complexion.*
▷HISTORY C18: from Latin *marmoreus,* from *marmor* marble
▸**marˈmoreally** ADVERB

marmoset (ˈmɑːməˌzɛt) NOUN [1] any small South American monkey of the genus *Callithrix* and related genera, having long hairy tails, clawed digits, and tufts of hair around the head and ears: family *Callithricidae.* [2] **pygmy marmoset.** a related form, *Cebuella pygmaea:* the smallest monkey, inhabiting tropical forests of the Amazon.
▷HISTORY C14: from Old French *marmouset* grotesque figure, of obscure origin

marmot (ˈmɑːmət) NOUN [1] any burrowing sciurine rodent of the genus *Marmota,* of Europe, Asia, and North America. They are heavily built, having short legs, a short furry tail, and coarse fur. [2] **prairie marmot.** another name for **prairie dog.**
▷HISTORY C17: from French *marmotte,* perhaps ultimately from Latin *mūr-* (stem of *mūs*) mouse + *montis* of the mountain

Marne (*French* marn) NOUN [1] a department of NE France, in Champagne-Ardenne region. Capital: Châlons-sur-Marne. Pop.: 565 229 (1999). Area: 8205 sq. km (3200 sq. miles). [2] a river in NE France, rising on the plateau of Langres and flowing north, then west to the River Seine, north of Paris: linked by canal with the Rivers Saône, Rhine, and Aisne; scene of two unsuccessful German offensives (1914, 1918) during World War I. Length: 525 km (326 miles).

Maroc (marɔk) NOUN the French name for **Morocco.**

marocain (ˈmærəˌkeɪn) NOUN [1] a fabric of ribbed crepe. [2] a garment made from this fabric.
▷HISTORY C20: from French *maroquin* Moroccan

Maronite (ˈmærəˌnaɪt) NOUN *Christianity* a member of a body of Uniats of Syrian origin, now living chiefly in Lebanon.
▷HISTORY C16: from Late Latin *Marōnīta,* after *Maro,* 5th-century Syrian monk

maroon[1] (məˈruːn) VERB (*tr*) [1] to leave ashore and abandon, esp on an island. [2] to isolate without resources. ◆ NOUN [3] a descendant of a group of runaway slaves living in the remoter areas of the Caribbean or Guyana. [4] *US and Canadian informal* a person who has been marooned, esp on an island.
▷HISTORY C17 (applied to fugitive slaves): from American Spanish *cimarrón* wild, literally: dwelling on peaks, from Spanish *cima* summit

maroon[2] (məˈruːn) NOUN [1] **a** a dark red to purplish-red colour. **b** (*as adjective*): *a maroon carpet.* [2] an exploding firework, esp one used as a warning signal.
▷HISTORY C18: from French, literally: chestnut, MARRON[1]

maroquin (ˌmærəˈkiːn, ˈmærəkɪn, -kwɪn) NOUN *Tanning* morocco leather.
▷HISTORY C16: from French: Moroccan

Maros (ˈmɔrɔʃ) NOUN the Hungarian name for the **Mureş.**

Marq. ABBREVIATION FOR Marquis.

marque (mɑːk) NOUN [1] a brand of product, esp of a car. [2] an emblem or nameplate used to identify a product, esp a car. [3] See **letter of marque.**
▷HISTORY from French, from *marquer* to MARK[1]

marquee (mɑːˈkiː) NOUN [1] a large tent used for entertainment, exhibition, etc. [2] Also called: **marquise.** *Chiefly US and Canadian* a canopy over the entrance to a theatre, hotel, etc. [3] (*modifier*) *Chiefly US and Canadian* celebrated or pre-eminent: *a marquee player.*
▷HISTORY C17 (originally an officer's tent): invented singular form of MARQUISE, erroneously taken to be plural

Marquesan (mɑːˈkeɪzᵊn, -sᵊn) ADJECTIVE [1] of or relating to the Marquesas Islands or their inhabitants. ◆ NOUN [2] a native or inhabitant of the Marquesas Islands.

Marquesas Islands (mɑːˈkeɪsæs) PLURAL NOUN a group of volcanic islands in the S Pacific, in French Polynesia. Pop.: 8064 (1996). Area: 1287 sq. km (497 sq. miles). French name: **Îles Marquises** (il markiz).

marquess (ˈmɑːkwɪs) NOUN [1] (in the British Isles) a nobleman ranking between a duke and an earl. [2] See **marquis.**

marquessate (ˈmɑːkwɪzɪt) NOUN (in the British Isles) the dignity, rank, or position of a marquess; marquisate.

marquetry *or* **marqueterie** (ˈmɑːkɪtrɪ) NOUN, *plural* **-quetries** *or* **-queteries.** a pattern of inlaid veneers of wood, brass, ivory, etc., fitted together to form a picture or design, used chiefly as ornamentation in furniture. Compare **parquetry.**
▷HISTORY C16: from Old French, from *marqueter* to inlay, from *marque* MARK[1]

marquis (ˈmɑːkwɪs, mɑːˈkiː; *French* marki) NOUN, *plural* **-quises** *or* **-quis.** (in various countries) a nobleman ranking above a count, corresponding to a British marquess. The title of marquis is often used in place of that of marquess.
▷HISTORY C14: from Old French *marchis,* literally: count of the march, from *marche* MARCH[2]

marquisate (ˈmɑːkwɪzɪt) NOUN [1] the rank or dignity of a marquis. [2] the domain of a marquis.

marquise (mɑːˈkiːz; *French* markiz) NOUN [1] (in various countries) another word for **marchioness.** [2] **a** a gemstone, esp a diamond, cut in a pointed oval shape and usually faceted. **b** a piece of jewellery, esp a ring, set with such a stone or with an oval cluster of stones. [3] another name for **marquee** (sense 2).
▷HISTORY C18: from French, feminine of MARQUIS

marquisette (ˌmɑːkɪˈzɛt, -kwɪ-) NOUN a leno-weave fabric of cotton, silk, etc.
▷HISTORY C20: from French, diminutive of MARQUISE

Marrakech *or* **Marrakesh** (məˈrækɛʃ, ˌmærəˈkɛʃ) NOUN a city in W central Morocco: several times capital of Morocco; tourist centre. Pop.: 621 914 (1994).

marram grass (ˈmærəm) NOUN any of several grasses of the genus *Ammophila,* esp *A. arenaria,* that grow on sandy shores and can withstand drying: often planted to stabilize sand dunes.
▷HISTORY C17 *marram,* from Old Norse *marálmr,* from *marr* sea + *hálmr* HAULM

Marrano (məˈrɑːnəʊ) NOUN, *plural* **-nos.** a Spanish or Portuguese Jew of the late Middle Ages who was converted to Christianity, esp one forcibly converted but secretly adhering to Judaism.
▷HISTORY from Spanish, literally: pig, with reference to the Jewish prohibition against eating pig meat

marri (ˈmærɪ) NOUN, *plural* **-ris.** a species of eucalyptus, *Eucalyptus calophylla,* of Western Australia, widely cultivated for its coloured flowers.
▷HISTORY C19: from a native Australian language

marriage (ˈmærɪdʒ) NOUN [1] the state or relationship of being husband and wife. [2] **a** the legal union or contract made by a man and woman to live as husband and wife. **b** (*as modifier*): *marriage licence; marriage certificate.* [3] the religious or legal ceremony formalizing this union; wedding. [4] a close or intimate union, relationship, etc.: *a marriage of ideas.* [5] (in certain card games, such as bezique, pinochle) the king and queen of the same suit. ◆ Related adjectives: **conjugal, marital, nuptial.**
▷HISTORY C13: from Old French; see MARRY[1], -AGE

marriageable (ˈmærɪdʒəbᵊl) ADJECTIVE (esp of women) suitable for marriage, usually with reference to age.
▸**ˌmarriageaˈbility** *or* **ˈmarriageableness** NOUN

marriage bureau NOUN an agency that provides introductions to single people seeking a marriage partner.

marriage guidance NOUN **a** advice given to couples who have problems in their married life. **b** (*as modifier*): *a marriage guidance counsellor.*

marriage of convenience NOUN a marriage based on expediency rather than on love.

married (ˈmærɪd) ADJECTIVE [1] having a husband or wife. [2] joined in marriage: *a married couple.* [3] of or involving marriage or married persons. [4] closely or intimately united. ◆ NOUN [5] (*usually plural*) a married person (esp in the phrase **young marrieds**).

marron[1] (ˈmærən; *French* marɔ̃) NOUN a large edible sweet chestnut.
▷HISTORY from French, of obscure origin

marron[2] (ˈmærən) NOUN a large freshwater crayfish of Western Australia, *Cherax tenuimanus.*
▷HISTORY from a native Australian language

marrons glacés *French* (marɔ̃ glase) PLURAL NOUN chestnuts cooked in syrup and glazed.

marrow[1] (ˈmærəʊ) NOUN [1] the fatty network of connective tissue that fills the cavities of bones. [2] the vital part; essence. [3] vitality. [4] rich food. [5] *Brit* short for **vegetable marrow.**
▷HISTORY Old English *mærg;* related to Old Frisian *merg,* Old Norse *mergr*
▸**ˈmarrowy** ADJECTIVE

marrow[2] (ˈmærəʊ, -rə) NOUN *Northeastern English dialect, chiefly Durham* a companion, esp a workmate.
▷HISTORY C15 *marwe* fellow worker, perhaps of Scandinavian origin; compare Icelandic *margr* friendly

marrowbone (ˈmærəʊˌbəʊn) NOUN **a** a bone containing edible marrow. **b** (*as modifier*): *marrowbone jelly.*

marrowbones (ˈmærəʊˌbəʊnz) PLURAL NOUN [1] *Facetious* the knees. [2] a rare word for **crossbones.**

marrow fat (ˈmærəʊˌfæt) *or* **marrow pea** NOUN [1] any of several varieties of pea plant that have large seeds. [2] the seed of such a plant.

marrow squash NOUN *US and Canadian* any of several oblong squashes that have a hard smooth rind, esp the vegetable marrow.

marry[1] (ˈmærɪ) VERB **-ries, -rying, -ried.** [1] to take (someone as one's husband or wife) in marriage. [2] (*tr*) to join or give in marriage. [3] (*tr*) to acquire (something) by marriage: *marry money.* [4] to unite closely or intimately. [5] (*tr;* sometimes foll by *up*) to fit together or align (two things); join. [6] (*tr*) *Nautical* **a** to match up (the strands) of unlaid ropes before splicing. **b** to seize (two ropes) together at intervals along their lengths. ◆ See also **marry up.**
▷HISTORY C13: from Old French *marier,* from Latin *marītāre,* from *marītus* married (man), perhaps from *mās* male
▸**ˈmarrier** NOUN

marry[2] (ˈmærɪ) INTERJECTION *Archaic* an exclamation of surprise, anger, etc.
▷HISTORY C14: euphemistic for the Virgin *Mary*

marry into VERB (*intr, preposition*) to become a member of (a family) by marriage.

marry off VERB (*tr, adverb*) to find a husband or wife for (a person, esp one's son or daughter).

marry up VERB (*adverb*) [1] (*tr*) to join. [2] (*intr*) to tally or correspond: *the reactor did not marry up to his expectations.* [3] (*intr*) to marry someone of a higher social class than oneself.

Mars[1] (mɑːz) NOUN the Roman god of war, the father of Romulus and Remus. Greek counterpart: **Ares.**

Mars[2] (mɑːz) NOUN [1] Also called: **the Red Planet.** the fourth planet from the sun, having a reddish-orange surface with numerous dark patches and two white polar caps. It has a thin atmosphere, mainly carbon dioxide, and low surface temperatures. Spacecraft encounters have revealed a history of volcanic activity and running surface water. The planet has two tiny satellites, Phobos and Deimos. Mean distance from sun: 228 million km; period of revolution around sun: 686.98 days; period of axial rotation: 24.6225 hours; diameter and mass: 53.2 and 10.7 per cent that of earth respectively. 2 the alchemical name for **iron**.

Marsala (mɑːˈsɑːlə) NOUN 1 a port in W Sicily: landing place of Garibaldi at the start of his Sicilian campaign (1860). Pop.: 80 760 (1990). 2 (*sometimes not capital*) a dark sweet dessert wine made in Sicily.

Marseillaise (ˌmɑːsəˈleɪz; *French* marsɛjez) NOUN **the.** the French national anthem. Words and music were composed in 1792 by C. J. Rouget de Lisle as a war song for the Rhine army of revolutionary France.
▷HISTORY C18: from French (*chanson*) *Marseillaise* song of Marseille (it was first sung in Paris by the battalion of Marseille)

marseille (mɑːˈseɪl) *or* **marseilles** (mɑːˈseɪlz) NOUN a strong cotton fabric with a raised pattern, used for bedspreads, etc.
▷HISTORY C18: from *Marseille quilting,* made in Marseille

Marseille (*French* marsɛj) NOUN a port in SE France, on the Gulf of Lions: second largest city in the country and a major port; founded in about 600 B.C. by Greeks from Phocaea; oil refining. Pop.: 797 486 (1999). Ancient name: **Massilia.** English name: **Marseilles** (mɑːˈseɪ, -ˈseɪlz).

marsh (mɑːʃ) NOUN low poorly drained land that is sometimes flooded and often lies at the edge of lakes, streams, etc. Related adjective: **paludal.** Compare **swamp** (sense 1).
▷HISTORY Old English *merisc;* related to German *Marsch,* Dutch *marsk;* related to MERE[2]
▸**ˈmarshˌlike** ADJECTIVE

marshal (ˈmɑːʃəl) NOUN 1 (in some armies and air forces) an officer of the highest rank. 2 (in England) an officer, usually a junior barrister, who accompanies a judge on circuit and performs miscellaneous secretarial duties. 3 (in the US) **a** a Federal court officer assigned to a judicial district whose functions are similar to those of a sheriff. **b** (in some states) the chief police or fire officer. 4 an officer who organizes or conducts ceremonies, parades, etc. 5 Also called: **knight marshal.** (formerly in England) an officer of the royal family or court, esp one in charge of protocol. 6 an obsolete word for **ostler.** ◆ VERB **-shals, -shalling, -shalled** *or US* **-shals, -shaling, -shaled.** (*tr*) 7 to arrange in order: *to marshal the facts.* 8 to assemble and organize (troops, vehicles, etc.) prior to onward movement. 9 to arrange (assets, mortgages, etc.) in order of priority. 10 to guide or lead, esp in a ceremonious way. 11 to combine (two or more coats of arms) on one shield.
▷HISTORY C13: from Old French *mareschal;* related to Old High German *marahscalc* groom, from *marah* horse + *scalc* servant
▸**ˈmarshalcy** *or* **ˈmarshalˌship** NOUN ▸**ˈmarshaller** *or* (*US*) **ˈmarshaler** NOUN

marshalling yard NOUN *Railways* a place or depot where railway wagons are shunted and made up into trains and where engines, carriages, etc., are kept when not in use.

Marshall Islands (ˈmɑːʃəl) PLURAL NOUN a republic, consisting of a group of 34 coral islands in the W central Pacific: administratively part of the Trust Territory of the Pacific Islands (1947–87); status of free association with the US from 1986; consists of two parallel chains, Ralik and Ratak. Official languages: Marshallese and English. Religion: Roman Catholic majority. Currency: US dollar. Capital: Majuro. Pop.: 52 300 (2001). Area: (land) 181 sq. km (70 sq. miles); (lagoon) 11 655 sq. km (4500 sq. miles).

Marshall Plan NOUN a programme of US economic aid for the reconstruction of post-World War II Europe (1948–52). Official name: **European Recovery Programme.**

Marshal of the Royal Air Force NOUN a rank in the Royal Air Force comparable to that of Field Marshal in the British army.

Marshalsea (ˈmɑːʃəlˌsiː) NOUN 1 (formerly in England) a court held before the knight marshal: abolished 1849. 2 a prison for debtors and others, situated in Southwark, London: abolished in 1842.
▷HISTORY C14: see MARSHAL, -CY

marsh andromeda NOUN a low-growing pink-flowered ericaceous evergreen shrub, *Andromeda polifolia,* that grows in peaty bogs of northern regions. Also called: **moorwort, bog rosemary.**

marshbuck (ˈmɑːʃˌbʌk) NOUN an antelope of the central African swamplands, *Strepsiceros spekei,* with spreading hoofs adapted to boggy ground; an important vector of the tsetse fly. Also called: **sitatunga.**

marsh elder NOUN any of several North American shrubs of the genus *Iva,* growing in salt marshes: family *Asteraceae* (composites). Compare **elder**[2].

marsh fern NOUN a fern of marshy woodlands, *Thelypteris palustris,* having pale green pinnate leaves and an underground rootstock.

marsh fever NOUN another name for **malaria.**

marsh gas NOUN a hydrocarbon gas largely composed of methane formed when organic material decays in the absence of air.

marsh harrier NOUN 1 a European harrier, *Circus aeruginosus,* that frequents marshy regions. 2 a US and Canadian name for **hen harrier.**

marsh hawk NOUN the usual US and Canadian name for the **hen harrier.**

marsh hen NOUN any bird that frequents marshes and swamps, esp a rail, coot, or gallinule.

marshland (ˈmɑːʃlənd) NOUN land consisting of marshes.

marshmallow (ˌmɑːʃˈmæləʊ) NOUN 1 a sweet of a spongy texture containing gum arabic or gelatine, sugar, etc. 2 a sweetened paste or confection made from the root of the marsh mallow.
▸**ˌmarshˈmallowy** ADJECTIVE

marsh mallow NOUN 1 a malvaceous plant, *Althaea officinalis,* that grows in salt marshes and has pale pink flowers. The roots yield a mucilage formerly used to make marshmallows. 2 *US and Canadian* another name for **rose mallow** (sense 1).

marsh marigold NOUN a yellow-flowered ranunculaceous plant, *Caltha palustris,* that grows in swampy places. Also called: **kingcup, May blobs,** and (US) **cowslip.**

marsh orchid NOUN any of various orchids of the genus *Dactylorhiza,* growing in damp places and having mostly purplish flowers.

marsh tit NOUN a small European songbird, *Parus palustris,* with a black head and greyish-brown body: family *Paridae* (tits).

marshwort (ˈmɑːʃˌwɜːt) NOUN a prostrate creeping aquatic perennial umbelliferous plant of the genus *Apium,* esp *A. inundatum,* having small white flowers: related to wild celery.

marshy (ˈmɑːʃɪ) ADJECTIVE **marshier, marshiest.** of, involving, or like a marsh.
▸**ˈmarshiness** NOUN

marsipobranch (ˈmɑːsɪpəʊˌbræŋk) NOUN, ADJECTIVE another word for **cyclostome.**
▷HISTORY C19: from New Latin *Marsipobranchia,* from Greek *marsipos* pouch + *branchia* gills

Marston Moor NOUN a flat low-lying area in NE England, west of York: scene of a battle (1644) in which the Parliamentarians defeated the Royalists.

marsupial (mɑːˈsjuːpɪəl, -ˈsuː-) NOUN 1 any mammal of the order *Marsupialia,* in which the young are born in an immature state and continue development in the marsupium. The order occurs mainly in Australia and South and Central America and includes the opossums, bandicoots, koala, wombats, and kangaroos. ◆ ADJECTIVE 2 of, relating to, or belonging to the *Marsupialia.* 3 of or relating to a marsupium.
▷HISTORY C17: see MARSUPIUM
▸**marsupialian** (mɑːˌsjuːpɪˈeɪlɪən, -ˌsuː-) *or* **marˈsupian** NOUN, ADJECTIVE

marsupial mole NOUN any molelike marsupial of the family *Notoryctidae.*

marsupial mouse NOUN any mouselike insectivorous marsupial of the subfamily *Phascogalinae:* family *Dasyuridae.*

marsupium (mɑːˈsjuːpɪəm, -ˈsuː-) NOUN, *plural* **-pia** (-pɪə). an external pouch in most female marsupials within which the newly born offspring are suckled and complete their development.
▷HISTORY C17: New Latin, from Latin: purse, from Greek *marsupion,* diminutive of *marsipos*

mart (mɑːt) NOUN a market or trading centre.
▷HISTORY C15: from Middle Dutch *mart* MARKET

Martaban (ˌmɑːtəˈbɑːn) NOUN **Gulf of.** an inlet of the Bay of Bengal in Myanmar.

martagon *or* **martagon lily** (ˈmɑːtəgən) NOUN a Eurasian lily plant, *Lilium martagon,* cultivated for its mottled purplish-red flowers with reflexed petals. Also called: **Turk's-cap lily.**
▷HISTORY C15: from French, from Turkish *martagān* a type of turban

martellato (ˌmɑːtəˈlɑːtəʊ) *or* **martellando** NOUN (in string playing) the practice of bowing the string with a succession of short sharp blows.
▷HISTORY Italian: hammered

Martello tower *or* **Martello** (mɑːˈtɛləʊ) NOUN a small circular tower for coastal defence, formerly much used in Europe.
▷HISTORY C18: after Cape *Mortella* in Corsica, where the British navy captured a tower of this type in 1794

marten (ˈmɑːtɪn) NOUN, *plural* **-tens** *or* **-ten.** 1 any of several agile arboreal musteline mammals of the genus *Martes,* of Europe, Asia, and North America, having bushy tails and golden brown to blackish fur. See also **pine marten.** 2 the highly valued fur of these animals, esp that of *M. americana.* ◆ See also **sable** (sense 1).
▷HISTORY C15: from Middle Dutch *martren,* from Old French (*peau*) *martrine* skin of a marten, from *martre,* probably of Germanic origin

martensite (ˈmɑːtɪnˌzaɪt) NOUN a constituent formed in steels by rapid quenching, consisting of a supersaturated solid solution of carbon in iron. It is formed by the breakdown of austenite when the rate of cooling is large enough to prevent pearlite forming.
▷HISTORY C20: named after Adolf *Martens* (died 1914), German metallurgist
▸**martensitic** (ˌmɑːtɪnˈzɪtɪk) ADJECTIVE

martial (ˈmɑːʃəl) ADJECTIVE of, relating to, or characteristic of war, soldiers, or the military life.
▷HISTORY C14: from Latin *martiālis* of MARS[1]
▸**ˈmartialism** NOUN ▸**ˈmartialist** NOUN ▸**ˈmartially** ADVERB
▸**ˈmartialness** NOUN

Martial (ˈmɑːʃəl) ADJECTIVE of or relating to Mars.

martial art NOUN any of various philosophies of self-defence and techniques of single combat, such as judo or karate, originating in the Far East.

martial law NOUN the rule of law established and maintained by the military in the absence of civil law.

Martian (ˈmɑːʃən) ADJECTIVE 1 of, occurring on, or relating to the planet Mars. ◆ NOUN 2 an inhabitant of Mars, esp in science fiction.

martin (ˈmɑːtɪn) NOUN any of various swallows of the genera *Progne, Delichon, Riparia,* etc., having a square or slightly forked tail. See also **house martin.**
▷HISTORY C15: perhaps from St *Martin* (??316–??397 A.D.), bishop of Tours, because the birds were believed to migrate at the time of Martinmas

martinet (ˌmɑːtɪˈnɛt) NOUN a person who maintains strict discipline, esp in a military force.
▷HISTORY C17: from French, from the name of General *Martinet,* drillmaster under Louis XIV
▸**ˌmartiˈnetish** ADJECTIVE ▸**ˌmartiˈnetism** NOUN

martingale (ˈmɑːtɪnˌgeɪl) NOUN 1 a strap from the reins to the girth of a horse preventing it from carrying its head too high. 2 any gambling system in which the stakes are raised, usually doubled, after each loss. 3 Also called: **martingale boom.** *Nautical* **a** a chain or cable running from a jib boom to the dolphin striker, serving to counteract strain. **b** another term for **dolphin striker.**
▷HISTORY C16: from French, of uncertain origin

Martini (mɑːˈtiːnɪ) NOUN, *plural* **-nis.** 1 *Trademark* an Italian vermouth. 2 a cocktail of gin and vermouth.
▷HISTORY C19 (sense 2): perhaps from the name of the inventor

Martinican (ˌmɑːtɪˈniːkən) ADJECTIVE 1 of or relating to the Caribbean island of Martinique or its inhabitants. ◆ NOUN 2 a native or inhabitant of Martinique.

Martinique (ˌmɑːtɪˈniːk) NOUN an island in the E Caribbean, in the Windward Islands of the Lesser

Antilles: administratively an overseas region of France. Capital: Fort-de-France. Pop.: 388 000 (2001 est.). Area: 1090 sq. km (420 sq. miles).

Martinmas ('mɑːtɪnməs) NOUN the feast of St Martin on Nov. 11; one of the four quarter days in Scotland.

martlet ('mɑːtlɪt) NOUN 1 an archaic name for a **martin.** 2 *Heraldry* a footless bird often found in coats of arms, standing for either a martin or a swallow.
▷HISTORY C16: from French *martelet,* variant of *martinet,* diminutive of MARTIN

martyr ('mɑːtə) NOUN 1 a person who suffers death rather than renounce his religious beliefs. 2 a person who suffers greatly or dies for a cause, belief, etc. 3 a person who suffers from poor health, misfortune, etc.: *he's a martyr to rheumatism.* 4 *Facetious or derogatory* a person who feigns suffering to gain sympathy, help, etc. ◆ VERB *also* **'martyr,ize, 'martyr,ise.** (*tr*) 5 to kill as a martyr. 6 to make a martyr of.
▷HISTORY Old English *martir,* from Church Latin *martyr,* from Late Greek *martur-, martus* witness
▸ **,martyri'zation** *or* **,martyri'sation** NOUN

martyrdom ('mɑːtədəm) NOUN 1 the sufferings or death of a martyr. 2 great suffering or torment.

martyrology (,mɑːtə'rɒlədʒɪ) NOUN, *plural* **-gies.** 1 an official list of martyrs. 2 *Christianity* the study of the lives of the martyrs. 3 a historical account of the lives of martyrs.
▸ **martyrological** (,mɑːtərə'lɒdʒɪkᵊl) *or* **,martyro'logic** ADJECTIVE ▸ **,martyr'ologist** NOUN

martyry ('mɑːtərɪ) NOUN, *plural* **-tyries.** a shrine or chapel erected in honour of a martyr.

MARV (mɑːv) NOUN ACRONYM FOR manoeuvrable re-entry vehicle: a missile that has one or more warheads that may be controlled so as to avoid enemy defences.

marvel ('mɑːvᵊl) VERB **-vels, -velling, -velled** *or US* **-vels, -veling, -veled.** 1 (when *intr*, often foll by *at* or *about;* when *tr, takes a clause as object*) to be filled with surprise or wonder. ◆ NOUN 2 something that causes wonder. 3 *Archaic* astonishment.
▷HISTORY C13: from Old French *merveille,* from Late Latin *mīrābilia,* from Latin *mīrābilis,* from *mīrārī* to wonder at

marvellous *or US* **marvelous** ('mɑːvᵊləs) ADJECTIVE 1 causing great wonder, surprise, etc.; extraordinary. 2 improbable or incredible. 3 excellent; splendid.
▸ **'marvellously** *or* (*US*) **'marvelously** ADVERB
▸ **'marvellousness** *or* (*US*) **'marvelousness** NOUN

marvel-of-Peru NOUN, *plural* **marvels-of-Peru.** another name for **four-o'clock** (the plant).
▷HISTORY C16: first found in Peru

Marxian ('mɑːksɪən) ADJECTIVE of or relating to Karl Marx (1818–83), the German founder of modern Communism, and his theories.
▸ **'Marxianism** NOUN

Marxism ('mɑːksɪzəm) NOUN the economic and political theory and practice originated by the German political philosophers Karl Marx (1818–83) and Friedrich Engels (1820–95), that holds that actions and human institutions are economically determined, that the class struggle is the basic agency of historical change, and that capitalism will ultimately be superseded by communism.

Marxism-Leninism NOUN the modification of Marxism by the Russian statesman and Marxist theoretician V. I. Lenin (1870–1924) stressing that imperialism is the highest form of capitalism.
▸ **'Marxist-'Leninist** NOUN, ADJECTIVE

Marxist ('mɑːksɪst) NOUN 1 a follower of Marxism. ◆ ADJECTIVE 2 (of an economic or political theory) analogous to or derived from the doctrines of Karl Marx (1818–83), the German founder of modern Communism. 3 of or relating to Marx, Marxism, or Marxists and their theories.

mary jane NOUN *US and Canadian* a slang term for **marijuana.**

Maryland ('mɛərɪ,lænd, 'mɛrɪlənd) NOUN a state of the eastern US, on the Atlantic: divided into two unequal parts by Chesapeake Bay: mostly low-lying, with the Alleghenies in the northwest. Capital: Annapolis. Pop.: 5 296 486 (2000 est.). Area: 31 864 sq. km (12 303 sq. miles). Abbreviations: **Md,** (with zip code) **MD.**

Mary Magdalene NOUN *New Testament* **Saint.** a woman of **Magdala** ('mægdələ) in Galilee whom Jesus cured of evil spirits (Luke 8:2) and who is often identified with the sinful woman of Luke 7:36–50. In Christian tradition she is usually taken to have been a prostitute. See **magdalen.** Feast day: July 22.

Maryolatry (,mɛərɪ'ɒlətrɪ) NOUN a variant spelling of **Mariolatry.**

Maryology (,mɛərɪ'ɒlədʒɪ) NOUN a variant spelling of **Mariology.**

marzipan ('mɑːzɪ,pæn) NOUN 1 a paste made from ground almonds, sugar, and egg whites, used to coat fruit cakes or moulded into sweets. Also called (esp formerly): **marchpane.** ◆ MODIFIER 2 *Informal* of or relating to the stratum of middle managers in a financial institution or other business: *marzipan layer job losses.*
▷HISTORY C19: via German from Italian *marzapane.* See MARCHPANE

mas (mɑːs) NOUN *Caribbean* 1 a carnival. 2 music played for a carnival, or a band playing this.
▷HISTORY C20: from MASQUERADE

-mas NOUN COMBINING FORM indicating a Christian festival: *Christmas; Michaelmas.*
▷HISTORY from MASS

Masada (mə'sɑːdə) NOUN an ancient mountaintop fortress in Israel, 400 m (1300 ft.) above the W shore of the Dead Sea: the last Jewish stronghold during a revolt in Judaea (66–73 A.D.). Besieged by the Romans for a year, almost all of the inhabitants killed themselves rather than surrender. The site is an Israeli national monument.

Masai ('mɑːsaɪ, mɑː'saɪ, 'mæsaɪ) NOUN 1 (*plural* **-sais** *or* **-sai**) a member of a Nilotic people, formerly noted as warriors, living chiefly in Kenya and Tanzania. 2 the language of this people, belonging to the Nilotic group of the Nilo-Saharan family.

Masakhane (,masa'kanɪ) SENTENCE SUBSTITUTE *South African* a political slogan of solidarity.
▷HISTORY C20: Nguni, literally: let us build together

masala (mɑː'sɑːlə) NOUN a mixture of spices ground into a paste, used in Indian cookery.
▷HISTORY from Urdu *masalah,* from Arabic *masalih* ingredients

Masan ('mɑː,sɑːn) NOUN a port in SE South Korea, on an inlet of the Korea Strait: first opened to foreign trade in 1899. Pop.: 441 358 (1995).

Masbate (mæs'bɑːtɪ) NOUN 1 an island in the central Philippines, between Negros and SE Luzon: agricultural, with resources of gold, copper, and manganese. Pop.: 599 355 (1990). Area: 4045 sq. km (1562 sq. miles). 2 the capital of this island, a port in the northeast. Pop.: 52 944 (1980).

masc. ABBREVIATION FOR masculine.

mascara (mæ'skɑːrə) NOUN a cosmetic substance for darkening, colouring, and thickening the eyelashes, applied with a brush or rod.
▷HISTORY C20: from Spanish: mask

Mascarene Islands (,mæskə'riːn) PLURAL NOUN a group of volcanic islands in the W Indian Ocean, east of Madagascar: consists of the islands of Réunion, Mauritius, and Rodrigues. French name: **Îles Mascareignes.**

mascarpone (,mæskə'pəʊnɪ) NOUN a soft Italian cream cheese.
▷HISTORY from Italian, from dialect (Lombardy) *mascherpa* ricotta

mascle ('mɑːskᵊl) NOUN *Heraldry* a charge consisting of a lozenge with a lozenge-shaped hole in the middle. Also called: **voided lozenge.**
▷HISTORY C14: from Old French *macle,* perhaps from Latin *macula* spot

mascon ('mæskɒn) NOUN any of several lunar regions of high gravity.
▷HISTORY C20: from MAS(S) + CON(CENTRATION)

mascot ('mæskət) NOUN a person, animal, or thing considered to bring good luck.
▷HISTORY C19: from French *mascotte,* from Provençal *mascotto* charm, from *masco* witch

masculine ('mæskjʊlɪn) ADJECTIVE 1 possessing qualities or characteristics considered typical of or appropriate to a man; manly. 2 unwomanly. 3 *Grammar* **a** denoting a gender of nouns, occurring in many inflected languages, that includes all kinds of referents as well as some male animate referents. **b** (*as noun*): *German "Weg" is a masculine.*
▷HISTORY C14: via French from Latin *masculīnus,* from *masculus* male, from *mās* a male
▸ **'masculinely** ADVERB ▸ **,mascu'linity** *or* (*less commonly*) **'masculineness** NOUN

masculine ending NOUN *Prosody* a stressed syllable at the end of a line of verse. Compare **feminine ending.**

masculine rhyme NOUN *Prosody* a rhyme between stressed monosyllables or between the final stressed syllables of polysyllabic words: *book, cook; collect, direct.* Compare **feminine rhyme.**

masculinist ('mæskjʊlɪnɪst) *or* **masculist** ('mæskjʊlɪst) NOUN 1 an advocate of the rights of men. ◆ ADJECTIVE 2 of, characterized by, or relating to men's rights.

masculinize *or* **masculinise** ('mæskjʊlɪn,aɪz) VERB to make or become masculine, esp to cause (a woman) to show male secondary sexual characteristics as a result of taking steroids.
▸ **,masculini'zation** *or* **,masculini'sation** NOUN

maser ('meɪzə) NOUN a device for amplifying microwaves, working on the same principle as a laser.
▷HISTORY C20: *m(icrowave) a(mplification by) s(timulated) e(mission of) r(adiation)*

Maseru (mə'sɛəruː) NOUN the capital of Lesotho, in the northwest near the W border with South Africa; established as capital of Basutoland in 1869. Pop.: 160 100 (1996 est.).

mash (mæʃ) NOUN 1 a soft pulpy mass or consistency. 2 *Agriculture* a feed of bran, meal, or malt mixed with water and fed to horses, cattle, or poultry. 3 (esp in brewing) a mixture of mashed malt grains and hot water, from which malt is extracted. 4 *Brit informal* mashed potatoes. 5 *Northern English dialect* a brew of tea. ◆ VERB (*tr*) 6 to beat or crush into a mash. 7 to steep (malt grains) in hot water in order to extract malt, esp for making malt liquors. 8 *Northern English dialect* to brew (tea). 9 *Archaic* to flirt with.
▷HISTORY Old English *mǣsc-* (in compound words); related to Middle Low German *mēsch*
▸ **mashed** ADJECTIVE ▸ **'masher** NOUN

MASH (mæʃ) NOUN (in the US) ACRONYM FOR Mobile Army Surgical Hospital.

Masham ('mæsəm) NOUN a crossbreed of large sheep having a black and white face and a long curly fleece: kept for lamb production.
▷HISTORY C20: named after *Masham,* town in N Yorkshire

Masharbrum *or* **Masherbrum** ('mʌʃə,brum) NOUN a mountain in N India, in N Kashmir in the Karakoram Range of the Himalayas. Height: 7822 m (25 660 ft.).

mashed (mæʃt) ADJECTIVE *Slang* intoxicated; drunk.

Mashhad (mæʃ'hæd) *or* **Meshed** NOUN a city in NE Iran: the holy city of Shi'ite Muslims; carpet manufacturing. Pop.: 1 887 405 (1996).

mashiach (mə'ʃiɑx) NOUN *Judaism* the messiah.
▷HISTORY Hebrew, literally: anointed; compare MESSIAH

mashie *or* **mashy** ('mæʃɪ) NOUN, *plural* **mashies.** *Golf* (formerly) a club, corresponding to the modern No. 5 or No. 6 iron, used for approach shots.
▷HISTORY C19: perhaps from French *massue* club, ultimately from Latin *mateola* mallet

Mashona (mə'ʃəʊnə) NOUN, *plural* **-na** *or* **-nas.** another name for the **Shona** (sense 1).

mashup ('mæʃʌp) NOUN a piece of recorded or live music in which a producer or DJ blends together two or more tracks, often of contrasting genres.
▷HISTORY C20: from MASH blend + UP

masjid *or* **musjid** ('mʌsdʒɪd) NOUN a mosque in an Arab country.
▷HISTORY Arabic; see MOSQUE

mask (mɑːsk) NOUN 1 any covering for the whole or a part of the face worn for amusement, protection, disguise, etc. 2 a fact, action, etc., that conceals something: *his talk was a mask for his ignorance.* 3 another name for **masquerade.** 4 a likeness of a face or head, either sculpted or moulded, such as a death mask. 5 an image of a face worn by an actor, esp in ancient Greek and Roman drama, in order to symbolize the character being portrayed. 6 a variant spelling of **masque.** 7

Surgery a sterile gauze covering for the nose and mouth worn esp during operations to minimize the spread of germs. 8 *Sport* a protective covering for the face worn for fencing, ice hockey, etc. 9 a carving in the form of a face or head, used as an ornament. 10 a natural land feature or artificial object which conceals troops, etc., from view. 11 a device placed over the nose and mouth to facilitate or prevent inhalation of a gas. 12 *Photog* a shield of paper, paint, etc., placed over an area of unexposed photographic surface to stop light falling on it. 13 *Electronics* a thin sheet of material from which a pattern has been cut, placed over a semiconductor chip so that an integrated circuit can be formed on the exposed areas. 14 *Computing* a bit pattern which, by convolution with a second pattern in a logical operation, can be used to isolate a specific subset of the second pattern for examination. 15 *Entomol* a large prehensile mouthpart (labium) of the dragonfly larva. 16 the face or head of an animal, such as a fox, or the dark coloration of the face of some animals, such as Siamese cats and certain dogs. 17 another word for **face pack.** 18 *Now rare* a person wearing a mask. ♦ VERB 19 to cover with or put on a mask. 20 (*tr*) to conceal; disguise: *to mask an odour.* 21 (*tr*) *Photog* to shield a particular area of (an unexposed photographic surface) in order to prevent or reduce the action of light there. 22 (*tr*) to shield a particular area of (a surface to be painted) with masking tape. 23 (*tr*) to cover (cooked food, esp meat) with a savoury sauce or glaze. 24 a Scot variant of **mash** (sense 8).
▷HISTORY C16: from Italian *maschera,* ultimately from Arabic *maskharah* clown, from *sakhira* mockery
▸**'mask,like** ADJECTIVE

maskanonge ('mæskə,nɒndʒ), **maskinonge** ('mæskɪ,nɒndʒ), *or* **maskalonge** ('mæskə,lɒndʒ) NOUN, *plural* **-nonges, -nonge** *or* **-longes, -longe**. variants of **muskellunge.**

masked (mɑːskt) ADJECTIVE 1 disguised or covered by or as if by a mask. 2 *Botany* another word for **personate^2.**

masked ball NOUN a ball at which masks are worn.

masker *or* **masquer** ('mɑːskə) NOUN a person who wears a mask or takes part in a masque.

masking ('mɑːskɪŋ) NOUN 1 the act or practice of masking. 2 *Psychol* the process by which a stimulus (usually visual or auditory) is obscured by the presence of another almost simultaneous stimulus.

masking tape NOUN an adhesive tape used to mask and protect surfaces surrounding an area to be painted.

masochism ('mæsə,kɪzəm) NOUN 1 *Psychiatry* an abnormal condition in which pleasure, esp sexual pleasure, is derived from pain or from humiliation, domination, etc., by another person. 2 *Psychoanal* the directing towards oneself of any destructive tendencies. 3 a tendency to take pleasure from one's own suffering. Compare **sadism.**
▷HISTORY C19: named after Leopold von Sacher *Masoch* (1836–95), Austrian novelist, who described it
▸**'masochist** NOUN, ADJECTIVE ▸**,maso'chistic** ADJECTIVE ▸**,maso'chistically** ADVERB

mason ('meɪsᵊn) NOUN 1 a person skilled in building with stone. 2 a person who dresses stone. ♦ VERB 3 (*tr*) to construct or strengthen with masonry.
▷HISTORY C13: from Old French *masson,* of Frankish origin; perhaps related to Old English *macian* to make

Mason ('meɪsᵊn) NOUN short for **Freemason.**

mason bee NOUN any bee of the family *Megachilidae* that builds a hard domelike nest of sand, clay, etc., held together with saliva.

Mason-Dixon Line *or* **Mason and Dixon Line** ('dɪksən) NOUN the state boundary between Maryland and Pennsylvania: surveyed between 1763 and 1767 by Charles Mason and Jeremiah Dixon; popularly regarded as the dividing line between North and South, esp between the free and the slave states before the American Civil War.

masonic (mə'sɒnɪk) ADJECTIVE 1 (*often capital*) of, characteristic of, or relating to Freemasons or Freemasonry. 2 of or relating to masons or masonry.
▸**ma'sonically** ADVERB

Masonite ('meɪsə,naɪt) NOUN *Austral and NZ, Trademark* a kind of dark brown hardboard used for partitions, lining, etc.

mason jar NOUN *US* an airtight glass jar for preserving food.
▷HISTORY C20: named after its US inventor, John L. *Mason* (1832–1902)

masonry ('meɪsənrɪ) NOUN, *plural* **-ries**. 1 the craft of a mason. 2 work that is built by a mason; stonework or brickwork. 3 (*often capital*) short for **Freemasonry.**

mason wasp NOUN a solitary wasp of the genus *Odynerus* that excavates its nest in sand or the mortar of old walls.

Masora, Masorah, Massora, *or* **Massorah** (mə'sɔːrə) NOUN 1 the text of the Hebrew Bible as officially revised by the Masoretes from the 6th to the 10th centuries A.D., with critical notes and commentary. 2 the collection of these notes, commentaries, etc.
▷HISTORY C17: from Hebrew: tradition

Masorete, Massorete ('mæsə,riːt), *or* **Masorite** ('mæsə,raɪt) NOUN 1 a member of the school of rabbis that produced the Masora. 2 a Hebrew scholar who is expert in the Masora.
▷HISTORY C16: from Hebrew *māsōreth* MASORA

Masoretic, Massoretic (,mæsə'retɪk), **Masoretical,** *or* **Massoretical** ADJECTIVE of or relating to the Masora, the Masoretes, or the system of textual criticism and explanation evolved by them.

Masqat ('mʌskət, -kæt) NOUN a transliteration of the Arabic name for **Muscat.**

masque *or* **mask** (mɑːsk) NOUN 1 a dramatic entertainment of the 16th to 17th centuries in England, consisting of pantomime, dancing, dialogue, and song, often performed at court. 2 the words and music written for a masque. 3 short for **masquerade.**
▷HISTORY C16: variant of MASK

masquer ('mɑːskə) NOUN a variant spelling of **masker.**

masquerade (,mæskə'reɪd) NOUN 1 a party or other gathering to which the guests wear masks and costumes. 2 the disguise worn at such a function. 3 a pretence or disguise. ♦ VERB (*intr*) 4 to participate in a masquerade; disguise oneself. 5 to dissemble.
▷HISTORY C16: from Spanish *mascarada,* from *mascara* MASK
▸**,masquer'ader** NOUN

mass (mæs) NOUN 1 a large coherent body of matter without a definite shape. 2 a collection of the component parts of something. 3 a large amount or number, such as a great body of people. 4 the main part or majority: *the mass of the people voted against the government's policy.* 5 **in the mass.** in the main; collectively. 6 the size of a body; bulk. 7 *Physics* a physical quantity expressing the amount of matter in a body. It is a measure of a body's resistance to changes in velocity (**inertial mass**) and also of the force experienced in a gravitational field (**gravitational mass**): according to the theory of relativity, inertial and gravitational masses are equal. 8 (in painting, drawing, etc.) an area of unified colour, shade, or intensity, usually denoting a solid form or plane. 9 *Pharmacol* a pastelike composition of drugs from which pills are made. 10 *Mining* an irregular deposit of ore not occurring in veins. 11 (*modifier*) done or occurring on a large scale: *mass hysteria; mass radiography.* 12 (*modifier*) consisting of a mass or large number, esp of people: *a mass meeting.* ♦ VERB 13 to form (people or things) or (of people or things) to join together into a mass: *the crowd massed outside the embassy.* ♦ See also **masses, mass in.**
▷HISTORY C14: from Old French *masse,* from Latin *massa* that which forms a lump, from Greek *maza* barley cake; perhaps related to Greek *massein* to knead
▸**massed** ADJECTIVE ▸**massedly** ('mæsɪdlɪ, 'mæstlɪ) ADVERB

Mass (mæs, mɑːs) NOUN 1 (in the Roman Catholic Church and certain Protestant Churches) the celebration of the Eucharist. See also **High Mass, Low Mass.** 2 a musical setting of those parts of the Eucharistic service sung by choir or congregation.
▷HISTORY Old English *mæsse,* from Church Latin *missa,* ultimately from Latin *mittere* to send away; perhaps derived from the concluding dismissal in the Roman Mass, *Ite, missa est,* Go, it is the dismissal

Mass. ABBREVIATION FOR Massachusetts.

Massa (*Italian* 'massa) NOUN a town in W Italy, in NW Tuscany. Pop.: 67 780 (1990).

Massachuset (,mæsə'tʃuːsɪt) *or* **Massachusetts** NOUN 1 (*plural* **-sets, -set** *or* **-setts**) a member of a North American Indian people formerly living around Massachusetts Bay. 2 the language of this people, belonging to the Algonquian family.
▷HISTORY probably from Algonquian, literally: at the big hill

Massachusetts (,mæsə'tʃuːsɪts) NOUN a state of the northeastern US, on the Atlantic: a centre of resistance to English colonial policy during the War of American Independence; consists of a coastal plain rising to mountains in the west. Capital: Boston. Pop.: 6 349 097 (2000 est.). Area: 20 269 sq. km (7826 sq. miles). Abbreviations: **Mass,** (with zip code) **MA.**

Massachusetts Bay NOUN an inlet of the Atlantic on the E coast of Massachusetts.

massacre ('mæsəkə) NOUN 1 the wanton or savage killing of large numbers of people, as in battle. 2 *Informal* an overwhelming defeat, as in a game. ♦ VERB (*tr*) 3 to kill indiscriminately or in large numbers. 4 *Informal* to defeat overwhelmingly.
▷HISTORY C16: from Old French, of unknown origin
▸**massacrer** ('mæsəkrə) NOUN

Massacre of the Innocents NOUN the slaughter of all the young male children of Bethlehem at Herod's command in an attempt to destroy Jesus (Matthew 2:16–18).

massage ('mæsɑːʒ, -sɑːdʒ) NOUN 1 the act of kneading, rubbing, etc., parts of the body to promote circulation, suppleness, or relaxation. ♦ VERB (*tr*) 2 to give a massage to. 3 to treat (stiffness, aches, etc.) by a massage. 4 to manipulate (statistics, data, etc.) so that they appear to support a particular interpretation or to be better than they are; doctor. 5 **massage (someone's) ego.** to boost (someone's) sense of self-esteem by flattery.
▷HISTORY C19: from French, from *masser* to rub; see MASS
▸**'massager** *or* **'massagist** NOUN

massage parlour NOUN 1 a business providing massage services. 2 *Euphemistic* a brothel.

massasauga (,mæsə'sɔːgə) NOUN a North American venomous snake, *Sistrurus catenatus,* that has a horny rattle at the end of the tail: family *Crotalidae* (pit vipers).
▷HISTORY C19: named after the *Missisauga* River, Ontario, Canada, where it was first found

Massawa *or* **Massaua** (mə'sɑːwə) NOUN a port in E central Eritrea, on the Red Sea: capital of Eritrea during Italian occupation, from 1885 until 1900. Pop.: 40 000 (1992).

mass defect NOUN *Physics* the amount by which the mass of a particular nucleus is less than the total mass of its constituent particles. See also **binding energy.**

massé *or* **massé shot** ('mæsɪ) NOUN *Billiards* a stroke made by hitting the cue ball off centre with the cue held nearly vertically, esp so as to make the ball move in a curve around another ball before hitting the object ball.
▷HISTORY C19: from French, from *masser* to hit from above with a hammer, from *masse* sledgehammer, from Old French *mace* MACE^1

massed practice NOUN *Psychol* learning with no intervals or short intervals between successive bouts of learning. Compare **distributed practice.**

mass-energy NOUN mass and energy considered as equivalent and interconvertible, according to the theory of relativity.

masses ('mæsɪz) PLURAL NOUN 1 (preceded by *the*) the body of common people. 2 (often foll by *of*) *Informal, chiefly Brit* great numbers or quantities: *masses of food.*

masseter (mæ'siːtə) NOUN *Anatomy* a muscle of the cheek used in moving the jaw, esp in chewing.

▷HISTORY C17: from New Latin from Greek *masētēr* one who chews, from *masāsthai* to chew
▸**masseteric** (ˌmæsɪˈtɛrɪk) ADJECTIVE

masseur (mæˈsɜː) NOUN a man who gives massages, esp as a profession.
▷HISTORY C19: from French *masser* to MASSAGE

masseuse (mæˈsɜːz) NOUN a woman who gives massages, esp as a profession.

massicot (ˈmæsɪˌkɒt) NOUN a yellow earthy secondary mineral consisting of lead oxide. Formula: PbO.
▷HISTORY C15: via French from Italian *marzacotto* ointment, perhaps from Arabic *shabb qubti* Egyptian alum

massif (ˈmæsiːf; *French* masif) NOUN [1] a geologically distinct mass of rock or a series of connected masses forming the peaks of a mountain range. [2] a topographically high part of the earth's crust that is bounded by faults and may be shifted by tectonic movements.
▷HISTORY C19: from French, noun use of *massif* MASSIVE

Massif Central (*French* masif sɑ̃tral) NOUN a mountainous plateau region of S central France, occupying about one sixth of the country: contains several extinct volcanic cones, notably Puy de Dôme, 1465 m (4806 ft.). Highest point: Puy de Sancy, 1886 m (6188 ft.). Area: about 85 000 sq. km (33 000 sq. miles).

mass in VERB (*adverb*) to fill or block in (the areas of unified colour, shade, etc.) in a painting or drawing.

massive (ˈmæsɪv) ADJECTIVE [1] (of objects) large in mass; bulky, heavy, and usually solid. [2] impressive or imposing in quality, degree, or scope: *massive grief*. [3] relatively intensive or large; considerable: *a massive dose*. [4] *Pathol* affecting a large area of the body: *a massive cancer*. [5] *Geology* **a** (of igneous rocks) having no stratification, cleavage, etc.; homogeneous. **b** (of sedimentary rocks) arranged in thick poorly defined strata. [6] *Mineralogy* without obvious crystalline structure. ◆ NOUN [7] *Slang* a group of friends or associates; gang: *the Staines massive*.
▷HISTORY C15: from French *massif*, from *masse* MASS
▸**ˈmassively** ADVERB ▸**ˈmassiveness** NOUN

mass leave NOUN (in India) leave taken by a large number of employees at the same time, as a form of protest.

mass-market ADJECTIVE of, for, or appealing to a large number of people; popular: *mass-market paperbacks*.

mass media PLURAL NOUN the means of communication that reach large numbers of people in a short time, such as television, newspapers, magazines, and radio.

mass noun NOUN a noun that refers to an extended substance rather than to each of a set of isolable objects, as, for example, *water* as opposed to *lake*. In English when used indefinitely they are characteristically preceded by *some* rather than *a* or *an;* they do not have normal plural forms. Compare **count noun.**

mass number NOUN the total number of neutrons and protons in the nucleus of a particular atom. Symbol: *A*. Also called: **nucleon number.**

mass observation NOUN *Chiefly Brit* (*sometimes capitals*) the study of the social habits of people through observation, interviews, etc.

Massorete (ˈmæsəˌriːt) NOUN a variant spelling of **Masorete.**

massotherapy (ˌmæsəʊˈθɛrəpɪ) NOUN medical treatment by massage.
▷HISTORY C20: from MASS(AGE) + THERAPY
▸**massotherapeutic** (ˌmæsəʊˌθɛrəˈpjuːtɪk) ADJECTIVE
▸**ˌmassoˈtherapist** NOUN

mass-produce VERB (*tr*) to manufacture (goods) to a standardized pattern on a large scale by means of extensive mechanization and division of labour.
▸**ˌmass-proˈduced** ADJECTIVE ▸**ˌmass-proˈducer** NOUN
▸**mass production** NOUN

mass ratio NOUN the ratio of the mass of a fully-fuelled rocket at liftoff to the mass of the rocket without fuel.

mass spectrograph NOUN a mass spectrometer that produces a photographic record of the mass spectrum.

mass spectrometer *or* **spectroscope** NOUN an analytical instrument in which ions, produced from a sample, are separated by electric or magnetic fields according to their ratios of charge to mass. A record is produced (**mass spectrum**) of the types of ion present and their relative amounts.

massy (ˈmæsɪ) ADJECTIVE **massier, massiest.** a literary word for **massive.**
▸**ˈmassiness** NOUN

mast[1] (mɑːst) NOUN [1] *Nautical* any vertical spar for supporting sails, rigging, flags, etc., above the deck of a vessel or any components of such a composite spar. [2] any sturdy upright pole used as a support. [3] Also called: **captain's mast.** *Nautical* a hearing conducted by the captain of a vessel into minor offences of the crew. [4] **before the mast.** *Nautical* as an apprentice seaman. ◆ VERB [5] (*tr*) *Nautical* to equip with a mast or masts.
▷HISTORY Old English *mæst;* related to Middle Dutch *mast* and Latin *mālus* pole
▸**ˈmastless** ADJECTIVE ▸**ˈmastˌlike** ADJECTIVE

mast[2] (mɑːst) NOUN the fruit of forest trees, such as beech, oak, etc., used as food for pigs.
▷HISTORY Old English *mæst;* related to Old High German *mast* food, and perhaps to MEAT

mast- COMBINING FORM a variant of **masto-** before a vowel.

mastaba *or* **mastabah** (ˈmæstəbə) NOUN a mudbrick superstructure above tombs in ancient Egypt from which the pyramid developed.
▷HISTORY from Arabic: bench

mast cell NOUN a type of granular basophil cell in connective tissue that releases heparin, histamine, and serotonin during inflammation and allergic reactions.
▷HISTORY C19: from MAST[2], on the model of German *Mastzelle*

mastectomy (mæˈstɛktəmɪ) NOUN, *plural* **-mies.** the surgical removal of a breast.

-masted ADJECTIVE (*in combination*) *Nautical* having a mast or masts of a specified kind or number: *three-masted; tall-masted*.

master (ˈmɑːstə) NOUN [1] the man in authority, such as the head of a household, the employer of servants, or the owner of slaves or animals. Related adjective: **magistral.** [2] **a** a person with exceptional skill at a certain thing: *a master of the violin*. **b** (*as modifier*): *a master thief*. [3] (*often capital*) a great artist, esp an anonymous but influential artist. [4] **a** a person who has complete control of a situation. **b** an abstract thing regarded as having power or influence: *they regarded fate as the master of their lives*. [5] **a** a workman or craftsman fully qualified to practise his trade and to train others in it. **b** (*as modifier*): *master carpenter*. [6] **a** an original copy, stencil, tape, etc., from which duplicates are made. **b** (*as modifier*): *master copy*. [7] a player of a game, esp chess or bridge, who has won a specified number of tournament games. [8] the principal of some colleges. [9] a highly regarded teacher or leader whose religion or philosophy is accepted by followers. [10] a graduate holding a master's degree. [11] the chief executive officer aboard a merchant ship. [12] a person presiding over a function, organization, or institution. [13] *Chiefly Brit* a male teacher. [14] an officer of the Supreme Court of Judicature subordinate to a judge. [15] the superior person or side in a contest. [16] a machine or device that operates to control a similar one. [17] (*often capital*) the heir apparent of a Scottish viscount or baron. [18] (*modifier*) overall or controlling: *master plan*. [19] (*modifier*) designating a device or mechanism that controls others: *master switch*. [20] (*modifier*) main; principal: *master bedroom*. [21] *South African informal* **the.** the man of the house. ◆ VERB (*tr*) [22] to become thoroughly proficient in: *to master the art of driving*. [23] to overcome; defeat: *to master your emotions*. [24] to rule or control as master.
▷HISTORY Old English *magister* teacher, from Latin; related to Latin *magis* more, to a greater extent
▸**ˈmasterdom** NOUN ▸**ˈmasterˌhood** NOUN ▸**ˈmasterless** ADJECTIVE ▸**ˈmastership** NOUN

Master (ˈmɑːstə) NOUN [1] a title of address placed before the first name or surname of a boy. [2] a respectful term of address, esp as used by disciples when addressing or referring to a religious teacher. [3] an archaic equivalent of **Mr.**

master aircrew NOUN a warrant rank in the Royal Air Force, equal to but before a warrant officer.

master-at-arms NOUN, *plural* **masters-at-arms.** the senior rating, of Chief Petty Officer rank, in a naval unit responsible for discipline, administration, and police duties.

master builder NOUN [1] a person skilled in the design and construction of buildings, esp before the foundation of the profession of architecture. [2] a self-employed builder who employs labour.

masterclass (ˈmɑːstəˌklɑːs) NOUN a session of tuition by an expert, esp a musician, for exceptional students, usually given in public or on television.

master corporal NOUN a noncommissioned officer in the Canadian forces senior to a corporal and junior to a sergeant.

master cylinder NOUN a large cylinder in a hydraulic system in which the working fluid is compressed by a piston enabling it to drive one or more slave cylinders. See also **slave cylinder.**

masterful (ˈmɑːstəfʊl) ADJECTIVE [1] having or showing mastery. [2] fond of playing the master; imperious. [3] masterly.
▸**ˈmasterfully** ADVERB ▸**ˈmasterfulness** NOUN

> **Language note** The use of *masterful* to mean masterly as in *a masterful performance*, although common, is considered incorrect by many people.

master key NOUN a key that opens all the locks of a set, the individual keys of which are not interchangeable. Also called: **pass key.**

masterly (ˈmɑːstəlɪ) ADJECTIVE of the skill befitting a master: *a masterly performance*.
▸**ˈmasterliness** NOUN

mastermind (ˈmɑːstəˌmaɪnd) VERB [1] (*tr*) to plan and direct (a complex undertaking): *he masterminded the robbery*. ◆ NOUN [2] a person of great intelligence or executive talent, esp one who directs an undertaking.

Master of Arts NOUN a degree, usually postgraduate and in a nonscientific subject, or the holder of this degree. Abbreviation: **MA.**

master of ceremonies NOUN a person who presides over a public ceremony, formal dinner, or entertainment, introducing the events, performers, etc. Abbreviation: **MC.**

master of foxhounds NOUN a person responsible for the maintenance of a pack of foxhounds and the associated staff, equipment, hunting arrangements, etc. Abbreviation: **MFH.**

Master of Science NOUN a postgraduate degree, usually in science, or the holder of this degree. Abbreviation: **MSc.**

Master of the Horse NOUN (in England) the third official of the royal household.

Master of the Queen's Music NOUN (in Britain when the sovereign is female) a court post dating from the reign of Charles I. It is an honorary title and normally held by an established English composer. Also called (when the sovereign is male): **Master of the King's Music.**

Master of the Rolls NOUN (in England) a judge of the court of appeal: the senior civil judge in the country and the Keeper of the Records at the Public Record Office.

masterpiece (ˈmɑːstəˌpiːs) *or less commonly* **masterwork** (ˈmɑːstəˌwɜːk) NOUN [1] an outstanding work, achievement, or performance. [2] the most outstanding piece of work of a creative artist, craftsman, etc.
▷HISTORY C17: compare Dutch *meesterstuk*, German *Meisterstück*, a sample of work submitted to a guild by a craftsman in order to qualify for the rank of master

master plan NOUN a comprehensive long-term strategy.

master race NOUN a race, nation, or group, such as the Germans or Nazis as viewed by Hitler, believed to be superior to other races. German name: **Herrenvolk.**

master sergeant NOUN a senior noncommissioned officer in the US Army, Air Force, and Marine Corps and certain other military forces, ranking immediately below the most senior noncommissioned rank.

mastersinger ('mɑːstəˌsɪŋə) NOUN an English spelling of **Meistersinger**.

masterstroke ('mɑːstəˌstrəʊk) NOUN an outstanding piece of strategy, skill, talent, etc.: *your idea is a masterstroke*.

master warrant officer NOUN a noncommissioned officer in the Canadian forces junior to a chief warrant officer.

mastery ('mɑːstərɪ) NOUN, *plural* **-teries**. 1 full command or understanding of a subject. 2 outstanding skill; expertise. 3 the power of command; control. 4 victory or superiority.

masthead ('mɑːstˌhɛd) NOUN 1 *Nautical* **a** the head of a mast. **b** (*as modifier*): *masthead sail*. 2 Also called: **flag**. the name of a newspaper or periodical, its proprietors, staff, etc., printed in large type at the top of the front page. ◆ VERB (*tr*) 3 to send (a sailor) to the masthead as a punishment. 4 to raise (a sail) to the masthead.

mastic ('mæstɪk) NOUN 1 an aromatic resin obtained from the mastic tree and used as an astringent and to make varnishes and lacquers. 2 **mastic tree.** **a** a small Mediterranean anacardiaceous evergreen tree, *Pistacia lentiscus,* that yields the resin mastic. **b** any of various similar trees, such as the pepper tree. 3 any of several sticky putty-like substances used as a filler, adhesive, or seal in wood, plaster, or masonry. 4 a liquor flavoured with mastic gum.
▷HISTORY C14: via Old French from Late Latin *mastichum,* from Latin, from Greek *mastikhē* resin used as chewing gum; from *mastikhan* to grind the teeth

masticate ('mæstɪˌkeɪt) VERB 1 to chew (food). 2 to reduce (materials such as rubber) to a pulp by crushing, grinding, or kneading.
▷HISTORY C17: from Late Latin *masticāre,* from Greek *mastikhan* to grind the teeth
▸ **'masticable** ADJECTIVE ▸ **ˌmasti'cation** NOUN
▸ **'mastiˌcator** NOUN

masticatory ('mæstɪkətərɪ, -trɪ) ADJECTIVE 1 of, relating to, or adapted to chewing. ◆ NOUN, *plural* **-tories**. 2 *Obsolete* a medicinal substance chewed to increase the secretion of saliva.

mastiff ('mæstɪf) NOUN an old breed of large powerful short-haired dog, usually fawn or brindle with a dark mask.
▷HISTORY C14: from Old French, ultimately from Latin *mansuētus* tame; see MANSUETUDE

mastigophoran (ˌmæstɪ'gɒfərən) NOUN *also* **mastigophore** ('mæstɪgəˌfɔː). 1 any protozoan having one or more flagella. ◆ ADJECTIVE *also* **mastigophorous.** 2 of or relating to flagellated protozoans. Also: **flagellate.**
▷HISTORY C19 *mastigophore* whip-bearer, from Greek *mastigophoros,* from *mastix* whip + *-phoros* -PHORE

mastitis (mæ'staɪtɪs) NOUN inflammation of a breast or an udder.

masto- *or before a vowel* **mast-** COMBINING FORM indicating the breast, mammary glands, or something resembling a breast or nipple: *mastodon; mastoid.*
▷HISTORY from Greek *mastos* breast

mastodon ('mæstəˌdɒn) NOUN any extinct elephant-like proboscidean mammal of the genus *Mammut* (or *Mastodon*), common in Pliocene times.
▷HISTORY C19: from New Latin, literally: breast-tooth, referring to the nipple-shaped projections on the teeth
▸ **ˌmasto'dontic** ADJECTIVE

mastoid ('mæstɔɪd) ADJECTIVE 1 shaped like a nipple or breast. 2 designating or relating to a nipple-like process of the temporal bone behind the ear. ◆ NOUN 3 the mastoid process. 4 *Informal* mastoiditis.

mastoidectomy (ˌmæstɔɪ'dɛktəmɪ) NOUN, *plural* **-mies**. surgical removal of the mastoid process.

mastoiditis (ˌmæstɔɪ'daɪtɪs) NOUN inflammation of the mastoid process.

masturbate ('mæstəˌbeɪt) VERB to stimulate the genital organs of (oneself or another) to achieve sexual pleasure.
▷HISTORY C19: from Latin *masturbārī,* of unknown origin; formerly thought to be derived from *manus* hand + *stuprāre* to defile
▸ **ˌmastur'bation** NOUN ▸ **'masturˌbator** NOUN

masturbatory ('mæstəˌbeɪtərɪ) ADJECTIVE involving, conducive to, or suggestive of masturbation.

Masuria (mə'sjʊərɪə) NOUN a region of NE Poland: until 1945 part of East Prussia: includes the **Masurian Lakes,** scene of Russian defeats by the Germans (1914, 1915) during World War I.

Masurian (mə'sjʊərɪən) ADJECTIVE 1 of or relating to Masuria, a region of NE Poland, or its inhabitants. ◆ NOUN 2 a native or inhabitant of Masuria.

masurium (mə'sʊərɪəm) NOUN the former name for **technetium.**
▷HISTORY C20: New Latin, after MASURIA, where it was discovered

mat¹ (mæt) NOUN 1 a thick flat piece of fabric used as a floor covering, a place to wipe one's shoes, etc. 2 a smaller pad of material used to protect a surface from the heat, scratches, etc., of an object placed upon it. 3 a large piece of thick padded material put on the floor as a surface for wrestling, judo, or gymnastic sports. 4 *NZ* a Maori cloak. 5 **go back to the mat.** *NZ* to abandon urban civilization. 6 any surface or mass that is densely interwoven or tangled: *a mat of grass and weeds.* 7 the solid part of a lace design. 8 **a** a heavy net of cable or rope laid over a blasting site to prevent the scatter of debris. **b** a heavy mesh of reinforcement in a concrete slab. **c** (esp US) a steel or concrete raft serving as a footing to support a post. 9 *Civil engineering* short for **mattress** (sense 3). ◆ VERB **mats, matting, matted.** 10 to tangle or weave or become tangled or woven into a dense mass. 11 (*tr*) to cover with a mat or mats.
▷HISTORY Old English *matte;* related to Old High German *matta*
▸ **'matless** ADJECTIVE

mat² (mæt) NOUN 1 a border of cardboard, cloth, etc., placed around a picture to act as a frame or as a contrast between picture and frame. 2 a surface, as on metal or paint. ◆ ADJECTIVE 3 having a dull, lustreless, or roughened surface. ◆ VERB **mats, matting, matted.** (*tr*) 4 to furnish (a picture) with a mat. 5 to give (a surface) a mat finish. ◆ Also (for senses 2, 3, 5): **matt.**
▷HISTORY C17: from French, literally: dead; see CHECKMATE

mat³ (mæt) NOUN *Printing informal* short for **matrix** (sense 5).

mat. ABBREVIATION FOR matinée.

Matabele (ˌmætə'biːlɪ, -'bɛlɪ) NOUN 1 (*plural* **-les** *or* **-le**) a member of a formerly warlike people of southern Africa, now living in Zimbabwe: driven out of the Transvaal by the Boers in 1837. Now known as: **Ndebele.** 2 the language of this people, belonging to the Bantu group of the Niger-Congo family.

Matabeleland (ˌmætə'biːlɪˌlænd, -'bɛlɪ-) NOUN a region of W Zimbabwe, between the Rivers Limpopo and Zambezi, comprises three provinces, Matabeleland North, Matabeleland South, and Bulawayo: rich gold deposits. Chief town: Bulawayo. Area: 181 605 sq. km (70 118 sq. miles).

Matadi (mə'tɑːdɪ) NOUN the chief port of the Democratic Republic of Congo (formerly Zaïre), in the west at the mouth of the River Congo. Pop.: 172 730 (1994 est.).

matador ('mætədɔː) NOUN 1 the principal bullfighter who is appointed to kill the bull. 2 (in some card games such as skat) one of the highest ranking cards. 3 a game played with dominoes in which the dots on adjacent halves must total seven.
▷HISTORY C17: from Spanish, from *matar* to kill

matagouri (ˌmætə'guːrɪ) NOUN, *plural* **-ris**. a thorny bush of New Zealand, *Discaria toumatou,* that forms thickets in open country. Also called: **wild Irishman.**
▷HISTORY from Maori *tumatakuru*

matai ('mɑːtaɪ) NOUN, *plural* **-tais**. a coniferous evergreen tree of New Zealand, *Podocarpus spicatus,* having a bluish bark and small linear leaves arranged in two rows: timber used for flooring and weatherboards. Also called: **black pine.**
▷HISTORY Maori

mata-mata ('mata'mata) NOUN (in Malaysia) a former name for **police.**
▷HISTORY from Malay, reduplicated plural of *mata* eye

Matamoros (ˌmætə'mɔːrəs; *Spanish* mata'morɔs) NOUN a port in NE Mexico, on the Río Grande: scene of bitter fighting during the US-Mexican War; centre of a cotton-growing area. Pop.: 370 000 (2000 est.).

Matanzas (mə'tænzəs; *Spanish* ma'tanθas) NOUN a port in W central Cuba: founded in 1693 and developed into the second city of Cuba in the mid-19th century; exports chiefly sugar. Pop.: 123 843 (1994 est.).

Matapan ('mætəˌpæn, ˌmætə'pæn) NOUN **Cape.** a cape in S Greece, at the S central tip of the Peloponnese: the southern point of the mainland of Greece. Modern Greek name: **Taínaron.**

match¹ (mætʃ) NOUN 1 a formal game or sports event in which people, teams, etc., compete to win. 2 a person or thing able to provide competition for another: *she's met her match in talking ability.* 3 a person or thing that resembles, harmonizes with, or is equivalent to another in a specified respect: *that coat is a good match for your hat.* 4 a person or thing that is an exact copy or equal of another. 5 **a** a partnership between a man and a woman, as in marriage. **b** an arrangement for such a partnership. 6 a person regarded as a possible partner, as in marriage. ◆ VERB (*mainly tr*) 7 to fit (parts) together: *to match the tongue and groove of boards.* 8 (*also intr;* sometimes foll by *up*) to resemble, harmonize with, correspond to, or equal (one another or something else): *the skirt matches your shoes well.* 9 (sometimes foll by *with* or *against*) to compare in order to determine which is the superior: *they matched wits.* 10 (often foll by *to* or *with*) to adapt so as to correspond with: *to match hope with reality.* 11 (often foll by *with* or *against*) to arrange a competition between. 12 to find a match for. 13 *Electronics* to connect (two circuits) so that their impedances are equal or are equalized by a coupling device, to produce a maximum transfer of energy.
▷HISTORY Old English *gemæcca* spouse; related to Old High German *gimmaha* wife, Old Norse *maki* mate
▸ **'matchable** ADJECTIVE ▸ **'matcher** NOUN ▸ **'matching** ADJECTIVE

match² (mætʃ) NOUN 1 a thin strip of wood or cardboard tipped with a chemical that ignites by friction when rubbed on a rough surface or a surface coated with a suitable chemical (see **safety match**). 2 a length of cord or wick impregnated with a chemical so that it burns slowly. It is used to fire cannons, explosives, etc.
▷HISTORY C14: from Old French *meiche,* perhaps from Latin *myxa* wick, from Greek *muxa* lamp nozzle

matchboard ('mætʃˌbɔːd) NOUN a long thin board with a tongue along one edge and a corresponding groove along the other, used with similar boards to line walls, ceilings, etc.

matchbox ('mætʃˌbɒks) NOUN a small box for holding matches.

matched-pairs design NOUN (*modifier*) *Statistics* (of an experiment) concerned with measuring the values of the dependent variables for pairs of subjects that have been matched to eliminate individual differences and that are respectively subjected to the control and the experimental condition. Compare **between-subjects design, within-subjects design.**

matched sample NOUN *Statistics* a sample in which the individuals selected for analysis share all properties except that under investigation.

matchet ('mætʃət) NOUN an earlier name for **machete.**

match-fit ADJECTIVE in good physical condition for competing in a match.

match-funding NOUN the stipulation set by a grant-providing body that the recipients of a grant raise a certain percentage of the money they require, generally a sum more or less equal to that of the sum of money being granted.

matchless ('mætʃlɪs) ADJECTIVE unequalled; incomparable; peerless.
▸ **'matchlessly** ADVERB ▸ **'matchlessness** NOUN

matchlock ('mætʃˌlɒk) NOUN 1 an obsolete type

of gunlock igniting the powder by means of a slow match. [2] a gun having such a lock.

matchmaker[1] ('mætʃˌmeɪkə) NOUN [1] a person who brings together suitable partners for marriage. [2] a person who arranges competitive matches.
▸ **'match,making** NOUN, ADJECTIVE

matchmaker[2] ('mætʃˌmeɪkə) NOUN a person who makes matches (for igniting).
▸ **'match,making** NOUN, ADJECTIVE

matchmark ('mætʃˌmɑːk) NOUN [1] a mark made on mating components of an engine, machine, etc., to ensure that the components are assembled in the correct relative positions. ◆ VERB [2] (*tr*) to stamp (an object) with matchmarks.

match play NOUN *Golf* **a** scoring according to the number of holes won and lost. **b** (*as modifier*): *a matchplay tournament.* ◆ Compare **Stableford, stroke play.**
▸ **match player** NOUN

match point NOUN [1] *Sport* the final point needed to win a match. [2] *Bridge* the unit used for scoring in tournaments.

matchstick ('mætʃˌstɪk) NOUN [1] the wooden part of a match. ◆ ADJECTIVE [2] made with or as if with matchsticks: *a matchstick model.* [3] (esp of figures drawn with single strokes) thin and straight: *matchstick men.*

matchup ('mætʃʌp) NOUN *US and Canadian* a sports match.

matchwood ('mætʃˌwʊd) NOUN [1] wood suitable for making matches. [2] splinters or fragments: *the bomb blew the house to matchwood.*

mate[1] (meɪt) NOUN [1] the sexual partner of an animal. [2] a marriage partner. [3] **a** *Informal, chiefly Brit, Austral, and NZ* a friend, usually of the same sex: often used between males in direct address. **b** (*in combination*) an associate, colleague, fellow sharer, etc.: *a classmate; a flatmate.* [4] one of a pair of matching items. [5] *Nautical* **a** short for **first mate. b** any officer below the master on a commercial ship. **c** a warrant officer's assistant on a ship. [6] (in some trades) an assistant: *a plumber's mate.* [7] *Archaic* a suitable associate. [8] **mate rates.** *Austral, slang* the reduced rate charged for work done for a friend. ◆ VERB [9] to pair (a male and female animal) or (of animals) to pair for reproduction. [10] to marry or join in marriage. [11] (*tr*) to join as a pair; match.
▷ **HISTORY** C14: from Middle Low German; related to Old English *gemetta* table-guest, from *mete* MEAT
▸ **'mateless** ADJECTIVE

mate[2] (meɪt) NOUN, VERB *Chess* See **checkmate.**

maté *or* **mate** ('mɑːteɪ, 'mæteɪ) NOUN [1] an evergreen tree, *Ilex paraguariensis,* cultivated in South America for its leaves, which contain caffeine: family *Aquifoliaceae.* [2] a stimulating milky beverage made from the dried leaves of this tree. ◆ Also called: **Paraguay tea, yerba, yerba maté.**
▷ **HISTORY** C18: from American Spanish (originally referring to the vessel in which the drink was brewed), from Quechua *máti* gourd

matelassé (mæt'læseɪ) ADJECTIVE (in textiles) having a raised design, as quilting; embossed.
▷ **HISTORY** C19: from French *matelasser* to quilt, from *matelas* MATTRESS

matelot, matlo, *or* **matlow** ('mætləʊ) NOUN *Slang, chiefly Brit* a sailor.
▷ **HISTORY** C20: from French

matelote *or* **matelotte** ('mætᵊˌləʊt; *French* matlɔt) NOUN fish served with a sauce of wine, onions, seasonings, and fish stock.
▷ **HISTORY** C18: from French, feminine of *matelot* sailor

mater ('meɪtə) NOUN *Brit, public school slang* a word for **mother**[1]: often used facetiously.
▷ **HISTORY** C16: from Latin

mater dolorosa (ˌdɒlə'rəʊsə) NOUN the Virgin Mary sorrowing for the dead Christ, esp as depicted in art.
▷ **HISTORY** Latin: sorrowful mother

materfamilias (ˌmeɪtəfə'mɪlɪˌæs) NOUN, *plural* **matresfamilias** (ˌmeɪtreɪzfə'mɪlɪˌæs). the mother of a family or the female head of a family.
▷ **HISTORY** C18: from Latin

material (mə'tɪərɪəl) NOUN [1] the substance of which a thing is made or composed; component or constituent matter: *raw material.* [2] facts, notes, etc., that a finished work may be based on or derived from: *enough material for a book.* [3] cloth or fabric. [4] a person who has qualities suitable for a given occupation, training, etc.: *that boy is not university material.* ◆ ADJECTIVE [5] of, relating to, or composed of physical substance; corporeal. [6] *Philosophy* composed of or relating to physical as opposed to mental or spiritual substance: *the material world.* [7] of, relating to, or affecting economic or physical wellbeing: *material ease.* [8] of or concerned with physical rather than spiritual interests. [9] of great import or consequence: *of material benefit to the workers.* [10] (often foll by *to*) relevant. [11] *Philosophy* of or relating to matter as opposed to form. [12] *Law* relevant to the issue before court: applied esp to facts or testimony of much significance: *a material witness.* ◆ See also **materials.**
▷ **HISTORY** C14: via French from Late Latin *māteriālis,* from Latin *māteria* MATTER
▸ **ma'terialness** NOUN

material implication NOUN *Logic* [1] the truth-functional connective that forms a compound sentence from two given sentences and assigns the value false to it only when its antecedent is true and its consequent false, without consideration of relevance; loosely corresponds to the English *if ... then.* [2] a compound sentence formed with this connective.

materialism (mə'tɪərɪəˌlɪzəm) NOUN [1] interest in and desire for money, possessions, etc., rather than spiritual or ethical values. [2] *Philosophy* the monist doctrine that matter is the only reality and that the mind, the emotions, etc., are merely functions of it. Compare **idealism** (sense 3), **dualism** (sense 2). See also **identity theory.** [3] *Ethics* the rejection of any religious or supernatural account of things.
▸ **ma'terialist** NOUN, ADJECTIVE ▸ **ma,terial'istic** ADJECTIVE
▸ **ma,terial'istically** ADVERB

materiality (məˌtɪərɪ'ælɪtɪ) NOUN [1] the state or quality of being physical or material. [2] substance; matter.

materialize *or* **materialise** (mə'tɪərɪəˌlaɪz) VERB [1] (*intr*) to become fact; actually happen: *our hopes never materialized.* [2] to invest or become invested with a physical shape or form. [3] to cause (a spirit, as of a dead person) to appear in material form or (of a spirit) to appear in such form. [4] (*intr*) to take shape; become tangible: *after hours of discussion, the project finally began to materialize.* [5] *Physics* to form (material particles) from energy, as in pair production.
▸ **ma,teriali'zation** *or* **ma,teriali'sation** NOUN
▸ **ma'terial,izer** *or* **ma'terial,iser** NOUN

materially (mə'tɪərɪəlɪ) ADVERB [1] to a significant extent; considerably: *his death alters the situation materially.* [2] with respect to material objects. [3] *Philosophy* with respect to substance as distinct from form.

material mode NOUN *Philosophy* the normal use of language that refers to extra-linguistic subjects without explicit mention of the words themselves. *Fido is a dog* is in the material mode, while *"Fido" is a dog's name* is in the formal mode. See also **use** (sense 18).

materials (mə'tɪərɪəlz) PLURAL NOUN the equipment necessary for a particular activity.

materia medica (mə'tɪərɪə 'medɪkə) NOUN [1] the branch of medical science concerned with the study of drugs used in the treatment of disease: includes pharmacology, clinical pharmacology, and the history and physical and chemical properties of drugs. [2] the drugs used in the treatment of disease.
▷ **HISTORY** C17: from Medieval Latin: medical matter

materiel *or* **matériel** (məˌtɪərɪ'ɛl) NOUN the materials and equipment of an organization, esp of a military force. Compare **personnel.**
▷ **HISTORY** C19: from French: MATERIAL

maternal (mə'tɜːnᵊl) ADJECTIVE [1] of, relating to, derived from, or characteristic of a mother. [2] related through the mother's side of the family: *his maternal uncle.*
▷ **HISTORY** C15: from Medieval Latin *māternālis,* from Latin *māternus,* from *māter* mother
▸ **ma'ternalism** NOUN ▸ **ma,ternal'istic** ADJECTIVE
▸ **ma'ternally** ADVERB

maternity (mə'tɜːnɪtɪ) NOUN [1] motherhood. [2] the characteristics associated with motherhood; motherliness. [3] (*modifier*) relating to pregnant women or women at the time of childbirth: *a maternity ward.*

maternity benefit NOUN (in the British National Insurance scheme) a payment (**maternity allowance**) made to a pregnant woman who usually works but does not qualify for statutory maternity pay, normally from 11 weeks before confinement for a period of 18 weeks; there is also a flat-rate benefit (**maternity grant**) for those on low incomes.

maternity leave NOUN a period of paid absence from work, in Britain currently six months, to which a woman is legally entitled during the months immediately before and after childbirth.

mateship ('meɪtʃɪp) NOUN *Austral* the comradeship of friends, usually male, viewed as an institution.

mate's rates PLURAL NOUN *NZ informal* preferential rates of payment offered to a friend.

matey *or* **maty** ('meɪtɪ) *Brit informal* ◆ ADJECTIVE [1] friendly or intimate; on good terms. ◆ NOUN [2] friend or fellow: usually used in direct address.
▸ **'mateyness** *or* **'matiness** NOUN

mat grass NOUN a widespread perennial European grass, *Nardus stricta,* with dense tufts of bristly leaves, characteristic of peaty moors.

math (mæθ) NOUN *US and Canadian informal* short for **mathematics.** Brit equivalent: **maths.**

math. *US and Canadian* ABBREVIATION FOR mathematics.

mathematical (ˌmæθə'mætɪkᵊl, ˌmæθ'mæt-) *or less commonly* **mathematic** ADJECTIVE [1] of, used in, or relating to mathematics. [2] characterized by or using the precision of mathematics; exact. [3] using, determined by, or in accordance with the principles of mathematics.
▸ **,mathe'matically** ADVERB

mathematical expectation NOUN *Statistics* another name for **expected value.**

mathematical logic NOUN symbolic logic, esp that branch concerned with the foundations of mathematics.

mathematical probability NOUN *Statistics* [1] the probability of an event consisting of *n* out of *m* possible equally likely occurrences, defined to be *n*/*m*. See also **principle of indifference.** [2] the study of such probabilities. ◆ Also called: **classical probability.**

mathematician (ˌmæθəmə'tɪʃən, ˌmæθmə-) NOUN an expert or specialist in mathematics.

mathematics (ˌmæθə'mætɪks, ˌmæθ'mæt-) NOUN [1] (*functioning as singular*) a group of related sciences, including algebra, geometry, and calculus, concerned with the study of number, quantity, shape, and space and their interrelationships by using a specialized notation. [2] (*functioning as singular or plural*) mathematical operations and processes involved in the solution of a problem or study of some scientific field.
▷ **HISTORY** C14 *mathematik* (n), via Latin from Greek (adj), from *mathēma* a science, *mathēmatikos* (adj); related to *manthanein* to learn

maths (mæθs) NOUN (*functioning as singular*) *Brit informal* short for **mathematics.** US and Canadian equivalent: **math.**

maths. *Brit* ABBREVIATION FOR mathematics.

Mathura ('mʌtʊərə, mʌ'θʊərə) NOUN a city in N India, in W Uttar Pradesh on the Jumna River: a place of Hindu pilgrimage, revered as the birthplace of Krishna. Pop.: 226 691 (1991). Former name: **Muttra.**

Matie ('mɑːtɪ) NOUN *South African informal* a student at the University of Stellenbosch, esp one representing the University in a sport.
▷ **HISTORY** perhaps from Afrikaans *tamatie* tomato, from the red colour of the rugby jersey

Matilda (mə'tɪldə) NOUN *Austral informal* [1] a bushman's swag. [2] **walk** *or* **waltz Matilda.** to travel the road carrying one's swag.
▷ **HISTORY** C20: from the Christian name

matin, mattin ('mætɪn), *or* **matinal** ADJECTIVE of or relating to matins.
▷ **HISTORY** C14: see MATINS

matinée ('mætɪˌneɪ) NOUN a daytime, esp afternoon, performance of a play, concert, etc.
▷ **HISTORY** C19: from French; see MATINS

matinée coat *or* **jacket** NOUN a short coat for a baby.

matinée idol NOUN (esp in the 1930s and 1940s) an actor popular as a romantic figure among women.

matins *or* **mattins** (ˈmætɪnz) NOUN (*functioning as singular or plural*) [1] **a** *Chiefly RC Church* the first of the seven canonical hours of prayer, originally observed at night but now often recited with lauds at daybreak. **b** the service of morning prayer in the Church of England. [2] *Literary* a morning song, esp of birds.
▷HISTORY C13: from Old French, ultimately from Latin *mātūtīnus* of the morning, from *Mātūta* goddess of dawn

matlo *or* **matlow** (ˈmætləʊ) NOUN variant spellings of **matelot.**

Matlock (ˈmætˌlɒk) NOUN a town in England, on the River Derwent, administrative centre of Derbyshire: mineral springs. Pop.: 14 680 (1991).

Mato Grosso *or* **Matto Grosso** (ˈmætəʊ ˈgrɒsəʊ; *Portuguese* ˈmatu ˈgrosu) NOUN [1] a high plateau of SW Brazil: forms the watershed separating the Amazon and Plata river systems. [2] a state of W central Brazil: mostly on the Mato Grosso Plateau, with the Amazon basin to the north; valuable mineral resources. Capital: Cuiabá. Pop.: 2 498 150 (2000). Area: 881 001 sq. km (340 083 sq. miles).

Mato Grosso do Sul (ˈdu: sul) NOUN a state of W central Brazil: formed in 1979 from part of Mato Grosso state. Capital: Campo Grande. Pop.: 2 075 275 (2000). Area: 350 548 sq. km (135 318 sq. miles).

matoke (maˈtɔkɛ) NOUN (in Uganda) the flesh of bananas, boiled and mashed as a food.
▷HISTORY C20: from Luganda

Matopo Hills (məˈtəʊpə) *or* **Matopos** PLURAL NOUN the granite hills south of Bulawayo, Zimbabwe, where Cecil Rhodes chose to be buried.

Matozinhos (*Portuguese* mətuˈziɲuʃ) NOUN a port in N Portugal, on the estuary of the Leça River north of Oporto: fishing industry. Pop.: 26 500 (latest est.).

matrass *or* **mattrass** (ˈmætrəs) NOUN *Chem, obsolete* a long-necked glass flask, used for distilling, dissolving substances, etc.
▷HISTORY C17: from French, perhaps related to Latin *mētiri* to measure

matri- COMBINING FORM mother or motherhood: *matriarchy*.
▷HISTORY from Latin *māter* mother

matriarch (ˈmeɪtrɪˌɑ:k) NOUN [1] a woman who dominates an organization, community, etc. [2] the female head of a tribe or family, esp in a matriarchy. [3] a very old or venerable woman.
▷HISTORY C17: from MATRI- + -ARCH, by false analogy with PATRIARCH
▸ˈ**matriˌarchal** *or* (*less commonly*) ˈ**matriˌarchic** ADJECTIVE
▸ˌ**matriˈarchalism** NOUN

matriarchate (ˈmeɪtrɪˌɑ:kɪt, -keɪt) NOUN *Rare* a family or people under female domination or government.

matriarchy (ˈmeɪtrɪˌɑ:kɪ) NOUN, *plural* **-chies.** [1] a form of social organization in which a female is head of the family or society, and descent and kinship are traced through the female line. [2] any society dominated by women.

matric (məˈtrɪk) NOUN *Brit and South African* short for **matriculation** (sense 2).

matrices (ˈmeɪtrɪˌsi:z, ˈmæ-) NOUN a plural of **matrix.**

matricide (ˈmætrɪˌsaɪd, ˈmeɪ-) NOUN [1] the act of killing one's own mother. [2] a person who kills his mother.
▷HISTORY C16: from Latin *mātrīcīdium* (the act), *mātrīcīda*(the agent). See MATRI-, -CIDE
▸ˌ**matriˈcidal** ADJECTIVE

matriclinous (ˌmætrɪˈklaɪnəs), **matroclinous,** *or* **matroclinal** ADJECTIVE (of an animal or plant) showing the characters of the female parent. Compare **patriclinous.**
▷HISTORY C20: from MATRI- + Greek *klīnein* to lean

matriculate VERB (məˈtrɪkjʊˌleɪt) [1] to enrol or be enrolled in an institution, esp a college or university. [2] (*intr*) to attain the academic standard required for a course at such an institution. ◆ NOUN (məˈtrɪkjʊlɪt) [3] Also called: **matriculant.** a person who has matriculated.
▷HISTORY C16: from Medieval Latin *mātrīculāre* to register, from *mātrīcula*, diminutive of *matrix* list, MATRIX
▸**maˈtricuˌlator** NOUN

matriculation (məˌtrɪkjʊˈleɪʃən) NOUN [1] the process of matriculating. [2] (in Britain, except Scotland) a former school examination, which was replaced by the General Certificate of Education (Ordinary Level), now superseded by the General Certificate of Secondary Education.

matrilineal (ˌmætrɪˈlɪnɪəl, ˌmeɪ-) ADJECTIVE relating to descent or kinship through the female line.
▸ˌ**matriˈlineally** ADVERB

matrilocal (ˈmætrɪˌləʊkᵊl, ˈmeɪ-) ADJECTIVE denoting, having, or relating to a marriage pattern in which the couple live with the wife's family.
▸**matrilocality** (ˌmætrɪləʊˈkælɪtɪ, ˌmeɪ-) NOUN
▸ˌ**matriˈlocally** ADVERB

matrimonial (ˌmætrɪˈməʊnɪəl) ADJECTIVE relating to marriage: *matrimonial troubles.*
▸ˌ**matriˈmonially** ADVERB

matrimony (ˈmætrɪmənɪ) NOUN, *plural* **-nies.** [1] the state or condition of being married. [2] the ceremony or sacrament of marriage. [3] **a** a card game in which the king and queen together are a winning combination. **b** such a combination.
▷HISTORY C14: via Norman French from Latin *mātrimōnium* wedlock, from *māter* mother

matrimony vine NOUN any of various shrubs of the solanaceous genus *Lycium,* cultivated for their purple flowers and colourful berries. Also called: **boxthorn.**

matrix (ˈmeɪtrɪks, ˈmæ-) NOUN, *plural* **matrices** (ˈmeɪtrɪˌsi:z, ˈmæ-) *or* **matrixes.** [1] a substance, situation, or environment in which something has its origin, takes form, or is enclosed. [2] *Anatomy* the thick tissue at the base of a nail from which a fingernail or toenail develops. [3] the intercellular substance of bone, cartilage, connective tissue, etc. [4] **a** the rock material in which fossils, pebbles, etc., are embedded. **b** the material in which a mineral is embedded; gangue. [5] *Printing* **a** a metal mould for casting type. **b** a papier-mâché or plastic mould impressed from the forme and used for stereotyping. Sometimes shortened to: **mat.** [6] (formerly) a mould used in the production of gramophone records. It is obtained by electrodeposition onto the master. [7] a bed of perforated material placed beneath a workpiece in a press or stamping machine against which the punch operates. [8] *Metallurgy* **a** the shaped cathode used in electroforming. **b** the metal constituting the major part of an alloy. **c** the soft metal in a plain bearing in which the hard particles of surface metal are embedded. [9] the main component of a composite material, such as the plastic in a fibre-reinforced plastic. [10] *Maths* a rectangular array of elements set out in rows and columns, used to facilitate the solution of problems, such as the transformation of coordinates. Usually indicated by parentheses: $\begin{pmatrix} a & b & c \\ d & e & f \end{pmatrix}$. Compare **determinant** (sense 3). [11] *Linguistics* the main clause of a complex sentence. [12] *Computing* a rectangular array of circuit elements usually used to generate one set of signals from another. [13] *Obsolete* the womb.
▷HISTORY C16: from Latin: womb, female animal used for breeding, from *māter* mother

matroclinous (ˌmætrəˈklaɪnəs) ADJECTIVE a variant of **matriclinous.**

matron (ˈmeɪtrən) NOUN [1] a married woman regarded as staid or dignified, esp a middle-aged woman with children. [2] a woman in charge of the domestic or medical arrangements in an institution, such as a boarding school. [3] *US* a wardress in a prison. [4] Official name: **nursing officer.** *Brit* the former name for the administrative head of the nursing staff in a hospital.
▷HISTORY C14: via Old French from Latin *mātrōna,* from *māter* mother
▸ˈ**matronal** ADJECTIVE ▸ˈ**matronˌhood** *or* ˈ**matronˌship** NOUN
▸ˈ**matron-ˌlike** ADJECTIVE

matronage (ˈmeɪtrənɪdʒ) NOUN [1] the state of being a matron. [2] supervision or care by a matron. [3] matrons collectively.

matronly (ˈmeɪtrənlɪ) ADJECTIVE of, characteristic of, or suitable for a matron; staid and dignified in a manner associated with a middle-aged, usually plump, woman.
▸ˈ**matronliness** NOUN

matron of honour NOUN, *plural* **matrons of honour.** [1] a married woman serving as chief attendant to a bride. Compare **bridesmaid, maid of honour.** [2] a married woman, usually a member of the nobility, who attends a queen or princess.

matronymic (ˌmætrəˈnɪmɪk) ADJECTIVE, NOUN a less common word for **metronymic.**

matryoshka, matryoshka doll, *or* **matrioshka** (ˌmætrɪˈɒʃkə) NOUN another word for **Russian doll.**
▷HISTORY C20: from Russian *matreshka* mother, highly respected lady

Matsu *or* **Mazu** (mætˈsu:) NOUN an island group in Formosa Strait, off the SE coast of mainland China: belongs to Taiwan. Pop.: 3145 (1990 est.). Area: 44 sq. km (17 sq. miles).

Matsuyama (ˌmætsʊˈjɑ:mə) NOUN a port in SW Japan, on NW Shikoku: textile and chemical industries; Ehime University (1949). Pop.: 460 870 (1995).

matt *or* **matte** (mæt) ADJECTIVE, NOUN, VERB variant spellings of **mat**[2] (senses 2, 3, 5).

Matt. *Bible* ABBREVIATION FOR Matthew.

mattamore (ˈmætəˌmɔ:) NOUN a subterranean storehouse or dwelling.
▷HISTORY C17: from French, from Arabic *matmūra,* from *tamara* to store, bury

matte[1] (mæt) NOUN an impure fused material consisting of metal sulphides produced during the smelting of a sulphide ore.
▷HISTORY C19: from French

matte[2] (mæt) NOUN *Films, television* a mask used to blank out part of an image so that another image can be superimposed.

matted (ˈmætɪd) ADJECTIVE [1] tangled into a thick mass: *matted hair.* [2] covered with or formed of matting.

matter (ˈmætə) NOUN [1] that which makes up something, esp a physical object; material. [2] substance that occupies space and has mass, as distinguished from substance that is mental, spiritual, etc. [3] substance of a specified type: *vegetable matter; reading matter.* [4] (sometimes foll by *of* or *for*) thing; affair; concern; question: *a matter of taste; several matters to attend to; no laughing matter.* [5] a quantity or amount: *a matter of a few pence.* [6] the content of written or verbal material as distinct from its style or form. [7] (*used with a negative*) importance; consequence. [8] *Philosophy* (in the writings of Aristotle and the Scholastics) that which is itself formless but can receive form and become substance. [9] *Philosophy* (in the Cartesian tradition) one of two basic modes of existence, the other being **mind:** matter being extended in space as well as time. [10] *Printing* **a** type set up, either standing or for use. **b** copy to be set in type. [11] a secretion or discharge, such as pus. [12] *Law* **a** something to be proved. **b** statements or allegations to be considered by a court. [13] **for that matter.** as regards that. [14] See **grey matter.** [15] **no matter. a** regardless of; irrespective of: *no matter what the excuse, you must not be late.* **b** (*sentence substitute*) it is unimportant. [16] **the matter.** wrong; the trouble: *there's nothing the matter.* ◆ VERB (*intr*) [17] to be of consequence or importance. [18] to form and discharge pus.
▷HISTORY C13 (n), C16 (vb): from Latin *māteria* cause, substance, esp wood, or a substance that produces something else; related to *māter* mother

Matterhorn (ˈmætəˌhɔ:n) NOUN a mountain on the border between Italy and Switzerland, in the Pennine Alps. Height: 4477 m (14 688 ft.). French name: **Mont Cervin.** Italian name: **Monte Cervino** (ˈmonte tʃerˈvi:no).

matter of course NOUN [1] an event or result that is natural or inevitable. ◆ ADJECTIVE **matter-of-course.** [2] (*usually postpositive*) occurring as a matter of course. [3] accepting things as inevitable or natural: *a matter-of-course attitude.*

matter of fact NOUN [1] a fact that is undeniably true. [2] *Law* a statement of facts the truth of which the court must determine on the basis of the evidence before it: contrasted with **matter of law.** [3] *Philosophy* a proposition that is amenable to empirical testing, as contrasted with the truths of logic or mathematics. [4] **as a matter of fact.** actually; in fact. ◆ ADJECTIVE **matter-of-fact.** [5] unimaginative or emotionless: *he gave a matter-of-fact account of the murder.*

matter of law NOUN *Law* an issue requiring the court's interpretation of the law or relevant principles of the law: contrasted with **matter of fact.**

matter of opinion NOUN a point open to question; a debatable statement.

matter waves PLURAL NOUN See **de Broglie waves.**

mattery ('mætərɪ) ADJECTIVE discharging pus.

Matthew ('mæθju:) NOUN *New Testament* [1] **Saint.** Also called: **Levi.** a tax collector of Capernaum called by Christ to be one of the 12 apostles (Matthew 9:9–13; 10:3). Feast day: Sept. 21 or Nov. 16. [2] the first Gospel, traditionally ascribed to him.

Matthew Walker ('wɔ:kə) NOUN a knot made at the end of a rope by unlaying the strands and passing them up through the loops formed in the next two strands.
▷HISTORY C19: probably named after the man who introduced it

mattify ('mætɪˌfaɪ) VERB **-fies, -fying, -fied.** (*tr*) to make (the skin of the face) less oily or shiny using cosmetics.
▷HISTORY C20: from MAT²

matting¹ ('mætɪŋ) NOUN [1] a coarsely woven fabric, usually made of a natural fibre such as straw or hemp and used as a floor covering, packing material, etc. [2] the act or process of making mats. [3] material for mats.

matting² ('mætɪŋ) NOUN [1] another word for **mat²** (sense 1). [2] the process of producing a mat finish.

mattins ('mætɪnz) NOUN a variant spelling of **matins.**

mattock ('mætək) NOUN a type of large pick that has one end of its blade shaped like an adze, used for loosening soil, cutting roots, etc.
▷HISTORY Old English *mattuc,* of unknown origin; related to Latin *mateola* club, mallet

Matto Grosso ('mætəʊ 'grɒsəʊ) NOUN a variant spelling of **Mato Grosso.**

mattoid ('mætɔɪd) NOUN *Rare* a person displaying eccentric behaviour and mental characteristics that approach the psychotic.
▷HISTORY C19: from Italian, from *matto* insane

mattrass ('mætrəs) NOUN a variant spelling of **matrass.**

mattress ('mætrɪs) NOUN [1] a large flat pad with a strong cover, filled with straw, foam rubber, etc., and often incorporating coiled springs, used as a bed or as part of a bed. [2] Also called: **Dutch mattress.** a woven mat of brushwood, poles, etc., used to protect an embankment, dyke, etc., from scour. [3] a concrete or steel raft or slab used as a foundation or footing. Sometimes shortened to: **mat.** [4] a network of reinforcing rods or expanded metal sheeting, used in reinforced concrete. [5] *Civil engineering* another name for **blinding** (sense 3).
▷HISTORY C13: via Old French from Italian *materasso,* from Arabic *almatrah* place where something is thrown

maturate ('mætjʊˌreɪt, 'mætʃʊ-) VERB [1] to mature or bring to maturity. [2] a less common word for **suppurate.**
▸**maturative** (mə'tjʊərətɪv, mə'tʃʊə-) ADJECTIVE

maturation (ˌmætjʊ'reɪʃən, ˌmætʃʊ-) NOUN [1] the process of maturing or ripening. [2] *Zoology* the development of ova and spermatozoa from precursor cells in the ovary and testis, involving meiosis. [3] a less common word for **suppuration.**
▸**ˌmatu'rational** ADJECTIVE

mature (mə'tjʊə, -'tʃʊə) ADJECTIVE [1] relatively advanced physically, mentally, emotionally, etc.; grown-up. [2] (of plans, theories, etc.) fully considered; perfected. [3] due or payable: *a mature debenture.* [4] *Biology* **a** fully developed or differentiated: *a mature cell.* **b** fully grown; adult: *a mature animal.* [5] (of fruit, wine, cheese, etc.) ripe or fully aged. [6] (of a river valley or land surface) in the middle stage of the cycle of erosion, characterized by meanders, maximum relief, etc. See also **youthful** (sense 4), **old** (sense 18). ◆ VERB [7] to make or become mature. [8] (*intr*) (of notes, bonds, etc.) to become due for payment or repayment.
▷HISTORY C15: from Latin *mātūrus* early, developed
▸**ma'turely** ADVERB ▸**ma'tureness** NOUN

mature student NOUN a student at a college or university who has passed the usual age for formal education.

maturity (mə'tjʊərɪtɪ, -'tʃʊə-) NOUN [1] the state or quality of being mature; full development. [2] *Finance* **a** the date upon which a bill of exchange, bond, note, etc., becomes due for repayment. **b** the state of a bill, note, etc., when due.

matutinal (ˌmætjʊ'taɪnᵊl) ADJECTIVE of, occurring in, or during the morning.
▷HISTORY C17: from Late Latin *mātūtīnālis,* from Latin *mātūtīnus,* from *Mātūta* goddess of the dawn
▸**ˌmatu'tinally** ADVERB

maty ('meɪtɪ) NOUN, *plural* **maties,** ADJECTIVE **matier, matiest.** a variant of **matey.**

matzo, matzoh ('mæt'səʊ), **matza,** *or* **matzah** ('mætsə) NOUN, *plural* **matzos, matzohs, matzas, matzahs,** *or* **matzoth** (*Hebrew* ma'tsɔt). a brittle very thin biscuit of unleavened bread, traditionally eaten during Passover.
▷HISTORY from Hebrew *matsāh*

matzoon (mɑ:t'su:n) *or* **madzoon** (mɑ:d'zu:n) NOUN a fermented milk product similar to yogurt.
▷HISTORY from Armenian *madzun*

Maubeuge (*French* mobøʒ) NOUN an industrial town in N France, near the border with Belgium. Pop.: 35 225 (1990).

mauby ('mɑ:bɪ, 'mɔ:-) NOUN, *plural* **-bies.** (in the E Caribbean) a bittersweet drink made from the bark of a rhamnaceous tree.
▷HISTORY C20: of uncertain origin

maud (mɔ:d) NOUN a shawl or rug of grey wool plaid formerly worn in Scotland.
▷HISTORY C18: of unknown origin

maudlin ('mɔ:dlɪn) ADJECTIVE foolishly tearful or sentimental, as when drunk.
▷HISTORY C17: from Middle English *Maudelen* Mary Magdalene, typically portrayed as a tearful penitent
▸**'maudlinism** NOUN ▸**'maudlinly** ADVERB ▸**'maudlinness** NOUN

maugre *or* **mauger** ('mɔ:gə) PREPOSITION *Obsolete* in spite of.
▷HISTORY C13 (meaning: ill will): from Old French *maugre,* literally: bad pleasure

Maui ('maʊɪ) NOUN a volcanic island in S central Hawaii: the second largest of the Hawaiian Islands. Pop.: 91 361 (1990). Area: 1885 sq. km (728 sq. miles).

maul (mɔ:l) VERB (*tr*) [1] to handle clumsily; paw. [2] to batter or lacerate. ◆ NOUN [3] a heavy two-handed hammer suitable for driving piles, wedges, etc. [4] *Rugby* a loose scrum that forms around a player who is holding the ball and on his feet.
▷HISTORY C13: from Old French *mail,* from Latin *malleus* hammer. See MALLET
▸**'mauler** NOUN

Maulana (mɔ:'lɑ:nɑ:) NOUN (in Pakistan, India, etc.) a title used for a scholar of Persian and Arabic.
▷HISTORY Urdu, from Arabic *mawlānā*

maulers ('mɔ:ləz) PLURAL NOUN *Brit, slang* the hands.

Maulmain (maʊl'meɪn) NOUN a variant spelling of **Moulmein.**

maulstick *or* **mahlstick** ('mɔ:lˌstɪk) NOUN a long stick used by artists to steady the hand holding the brush.
▷HISTORY C17: partial translation of Dutch *maalstok,* from obsolete *malen* to paint + *stok* STICK¹

Mau Mau ('maʊ ˌmaʊ) NOUN, *plural* **Mau Maus** *or* **Mau Mau.** [1] a secret political society consisting chiefly of Kikuyu tribesmen that was founded in 1952 to drive European settlers from Kenya by acts of terrorism. [2] *E African, slang* a Ugandan motorcycle policeman who directs traffic.

maumet ('mɔ:mɪt) *or* **mammet** ('mæmɪt) NOUN [1] *Obsolete* a false god; idol. [2] *English dialect* a figure dressed up, such as a guy or scarecrow.
▷HISTORY C13: from Old French *mahomet* idol, literally: the prophet *Mohammed,* from the belief that his image was worshipped
▸**'maumetry** NOUN

maun, man (mɑ:n, mɔ:n), *or* **mun** (mʌn) VERB a dialect word for **must¹.**
▷HISTORY C14: from Old Norse *man* must, will

Mauna Kea ('maʊnɑ: 'keɪɑ:) NOUN an extinct volcano in Hawaii, on N central Hawaii Island: the highest island mountain in the world. Height: 4206 m (13 799 ft.).

Mauna Loa ('maʊnɑ: 'ləʊɑ:) NOUN an active volcano in Hawaii, on S central Hawaii Island. Height: 4171 m (13 684 ft.).

maund (mɔ:nd) NOUN a unit of weight used in Asia, esp India, having different values in different localities. A common value in India is 82 pounds or 37 kilograms.
▷HISTORY C17: from Hindi *man,* from Sanskrit *manā*

maunder ('mɔ:ndə) VERB (*intr*) to move, talk, or act aimlessly or idly.
▷HISTORY C17: perhaps from obsolete *maunder* to beg, from Latin *mendīcāre;* see MENDICANT
▸**'maunderer** NOUN ▸**'maundering** ADJECTIVE

maundy ('mɔ:ndɪ) NOUN, *plural* **maundies.** *Christianity* the ceremonial washing of the feet of poor persons in commemoration of Jesus' washing of his disciples' feet (John 13:4–34) re-enacted in some churches on Maundy Thursday.
▷HISTORY C13: from Old French *mandé* something commanded, from Latin *mandatum* commandment, from the words of Christ: *Mandātum novum dō vōbīs* A new commandment give I unto you

Maundy money NOUN specially minted coins distributed by the British sovereign on Maundy Thursday.

Maundy Thursday NOUN *Christianity* the Thursday before Easter observed as a commemoration of the Last Supper.

maungy ('mɔ:ndʒɪ) ADJECTIVE **-gier, -giest.** *West Yorkshire dialect* (esp of a child) sulky, bad-tempered, or peevish.
▷HISTORY variant of MANGY, in extended sense: restless, dissatisfied

Mauretania (ˌmɒrɪ'teɪnɪə) NOUN an ancient region of N Africa, corresponding approximately to the N parts of modern Algeria and Morocco.

Mauretanian (ˌmɒrɪ'teɪnɪən) ADJECTIVE [1] of or relating to Mauretania, an ancient region of N Africa, or its inhabitants. ◆ NOUN [2] a native or inhabitant of Mauretania.

Maurist ('mɔːrɪst) NOUN a member of a congregation of French Benedictine monks founded in 1621 and noted for its scholarly work.
▷HISTORY C19: named after *St Maurus,* 6th-century disciple of St Benedict

Mauritania (ˌmɒrɪ'teɪnɪə) NOUN a republic in NW Africa, on the Atlantic: established as a French protectorate in 1903 and a colony in 1920; gained independence in 1960; lies in the Sahara; contains rich resources of iron ore. Official language: Arabic; Fulani, Soninke, Wolof, and French are also spoken. Official religion: Muslim. Currency: ouguiya. Capital: Nouakchott. Pop.: 2 591 000 (2001 est.). Area: 1 030 700 sq. km (398 000 sq. miles). Official name: **Islamic Republic of Mauritania.**

Mauritanian (ˌmɒrɪ'teɪnɪən) ADJECTIVE [1] of or relating to Mauritania, a republic in NW Africa, or its inhabitants. ◆ NOUN [2] a native or inhabitant of Mauritania.

Mauritian (mə'rɪʃən) ADJECTIVE [1] of or relating to the Indian Ocean island of Mauritius or its inhabitants. ◆ NOUN [2] a native or inhabitant of Mauritius.

Mauritius (mə'rɪʃəs) NOUN an island and state in the Indian Ocean, east of Madagascar: originally uninhabited, it was settled by the Dutch (1638–1710) then abandoned; taken by the French in 1715 and the British in 1810; became an independent member of the Commonwealth in 1968. It is economically dependent on sugar. Official language: English; a French creole is widely spoken. Religion: Hindu majority, large Christian minority. Currency: rupee. Capital: Port Louis. Pop.: 1 195 000 (2001 est.). Area: 1865 sq. km (720 sq. miles). Former name (1715–1810): **Île-de-France.**

Maurya ('maʊrjə) NOUN a dynasty (?321–?185 B.C.) that united most of the Indian subcontinent and presided over a great flowering of Indian civilization.

Mauser ('maʊzə) NOUN *Trademark* [1] a high-velocity magazine rifle. [2] a type of automatic pistol.
▷HISTORY C19: named after P. P. von *Mauser* (1838–1914), German firearms inventor

mausoleum (ˌmɔːsəˈlɪəm) NOUN, *plural* **-leums** *or* **-lea** (-ˈlɪə). a large stately tomb.
▷HISTORY C16: via Latin from Greek *mausōleion*, the tomb of *Mausolus*, king of Caria; built at Halicarnassus in the 4th century B.C.
▸ˌ**mauso'lean** ADJECTIVE

mauvaise foi *French* (movɛz fwa) NOUN (in the philosophy of Sartre) the expression usually rendered as *bad faith*: see **bad faith** (sense 2).

mauvais pas (ˈməʊvɛ ˈpɑː) NOUN, *plural* **mauvais pas** (-ˈpɑː, -ˈpɑːz). *Mountaineering* a place that presents a particular difficulty on a climb or walk.
▷HISTORY C19: from French: bad step

mauvais quart d'heure *French* (movɛ kar dœr) NOUN *Brit* a brief unpleasant experience.
▷HISTORY literally: (a) bad quarter of an hour

mauve (məʊv) NOUN [1] **a** any of various pale to moderate pinkish-purple or bluish-purple colours. **b** (*as adjective*): *a mauve flower.* [2] Also called: **Perkin's mauve, mauveine** (ˈməʊviːn, -vɪn). a reddish-purple aniline dye.
▷HISTORY C19: from French, from Latin *malva* MALLOW

maven *or* **mavin** (ˈmeɪvən) NOUN *US* an expert or connoisseur.
▷HISTORY C20: from Yiddish, from Hebrew *mevin* understanding

maverick (ˈmævərɪk) NOUN [1] (in US and Canadian cattle-raising regions) an unbranded animal, esp a stray calf. [2] **a** a person of independent or unorthodox views. **b** (*as modifier*): *a maverick politician.*
▷HISTORY C19: after Samuel A. *Maverick* (1803–70), Texas rancher, who did not brand his cattle

mavis (ˈmeɪvɪs) NOUN a popular name for the **song thrush.**
▷HISTORY C14: from Old French *mauvis* thrush; origin obscure

mavourneen *or* **mavournin** (məˈvʊəniːn) NOUN *Irish* my darling.
▷HISTORY C18: from Irish, from *mo* my + *muirnīn* love

maw (mɔː) NOUN [1] the mouth, throat, crop, or stomach of an animal, esp of a voracious animal. [2] *Informal* the mouth or stomach of a greedy person.
▷HISTORY Old English *maga;* related to Middle Dutch *maghe*, Old Norse *magi*

mawger (ˈmɔːgə) ADJECTIVE *Caribbean* (of persons or animals) thin or lean.
▷HISTORY from Dutch *mager* thin, MEAGRE

mawkin (ˈmɔːkɪn) NOUN [1] a variant of **malkin.** [2] *Brit, dialect* **a** a slovenly woman. **b** a scarecrow.

mawkish (ˈmɔːkɪʃ) ADJECTIVE [1] falsely sentimental, esp in a weak or maudlin way. [2] nauseating or insipid in flavour, smell, etc.
▷HISTORY C17: from obsolete *mawk* MAGGOT + -ISH
▸ˈ**mawkishly** ADVERB ▸ˈ**mawkishness** NOUN

max (mæks) NOUN *Informal* [1] the most significant, highest, furthest, or greatest thing. [2] **to the max.** to the ultimate extent. ◆ See also **max out.**

max. ABBREVIATION FOR maximum.

maxi (ˈmæksɪ) ADJECTIVE [1] **a** (of a garment) reaching the ankle. **b** (*as noun*): *she wore a maxi.* **c** (*in combination*): *a maxidress.* ◆ NOUN [2] a type of large racing yacht.
▷HISTORY C20: shortened from MAXIMUM

maxilla (mækˈsɪlə) NOUN, *plural* **-lae** (-liː). [1] the upper jawbone in vertebrates. See **jaw** (sense 1). [2] any member of one or two pairs of mouthparts in insects and other arthropods used as accessory jaws.
▷HISTORY C17: New Latin, from Latin: jaw
▸**maxillar** (mækˈsɪlə) *or* **max'illary** ADJECTIVE

maxilliped (mækˈsɪlɪˌpɛd) NOUN any member of three pairs of appendages in crustaceans, behind the maxillae: specialized for feeding.
▷HISTORY C19: *maxilli-*, from MAXILLA + -PED
▸**maxˌilli'pedary** ADJECTIVE

maxillofacial (mækˌsɪləʊˈfeɪʃəl, ˌmæksɪləʊ-) ADJECTIVE of, relating to, or affecting the upper jawbone and face: *maxillofacial surgery.*
▷HISTORY C20: from MAXILLA + -O- + FACIAL

maxim (ˈmæksɪm) NOUN a brief expression of a general truth, principle, or rule of conduct.
▷HISTORY C15: via French from Medieval Latin, from *maxima*, in the phrase *maxima prōpositio* basic axiom (literally: greatest proposition); see MAXIMUM

maxima (ˈmæksɪmə) NOUN a plural of **maximum.**

maximal (ˈmæksɪməl) ADJECTIVE [1] of, relating to, or achieving a maximum; being the greatest or best possible. [2] *Maths* (of a member of an ordered set) being preceded, in order, by all other members of the set.
▸ˈ**maximally** ADVERB

maximalist (ˈmæksɪməlɪst) NOUN a person who favours direct action to achieve all his goals and rejects compromise.

Maximalist (ˈmæksɪməlɪst) NOUN (in early 20th-century Russia) [1] a member of the radical faction of Social Revolutionaries that supported terrorism against the tsarist regime and advocated a short period of postrevolutionary working-class dictatorship. [2] a less common name for a **Bolshevik.** ◆ Compare **Minimalist.**
▷HISTORY C20: from French, a translation of Russian; see BOLSHEVIK

Maxim gun (ˈmæksɪm) NOUN an obsolete water-cooled machine gun having a single barrel and utilizing the recoil force of each shot to maintain automatic fire.
▷HISTORY C19: named after Sir Hiram Stevens *Maxim* (1840–1916), its US-born British inventor

maximin (ˈmæksɪˌmɪn) NOUN [1] *Maths* the highest of a set of minimum values. [2] (in game theory, etc.) the procedure of choosing the strategy that most benefits the least advantaged member of a group. Compare **minimax.**
▷HISTORY C20: from MAXI(MUM) + MIN(IMUM)

maximize *or* **maximise** (ˈmæksɪˌmaɪz) VERB [1] (*tr*) to make as high or great as possible; increase to a maximum. [2] *Maths* to find the maximum of (a function).
▸ˌ**maximi'zation** *or* ˌ**maximi'sation** *or* ˌ**maxi'mation** NOUN
▸ˈ**maxiˌmizer** *or* ˈ**maxiˌmiser** NOUN

maximum (ˈmæksɪməm) NOUN, *plural* **-mums** *or* **-ma** (-mə). [1] the greatest possible amount, degree, etc. [2] the highest value of a variable quantity. [3] *Maths* **a** a value of a function that is greater than any neighbouring value. **b** a stationary point on a curve at which the tangent changes from a positive value on the left of this point to a negative value on the right. Compare **minimum** (sense 4). **c** the largest number in a set. [4] *Astronomy* **a** the time at which the brightness of a variable star has its greatest value. **b** the magnitude of the star at that time. ◆ ADJECTIVE [5] of, being, or showing a maximum or maximums. Abbreviation: **max.**
▷HISTORY C18: from Latin: greatest (the neuter form used as noun), from *magnus* great

maximum likelihood NOUN *Statistics* [1] the probability of randomly drawing a given sample from a population maximized over the possible values of the population parameters. [2] the non-Bayesian rule that, given an experimental observation, one should utilize as point estimates of parameters of a distribution those values which give the highest conditional probability to that observation, irrespective of the prior probability assigned to the parameters.

maximum-minimum thermometer NOUN a thermometer that records the highest and lowest temperatures since it was last set.

maximus (ˈmæksɪməs) NOUN *Bell-ringing* a method rung on twelve bells.
▷HISTORY from Latin: superlative of *magnus* great

maxixe (məˈʃiːʃ, mækˈsiːks, məˈʃiːʃeɪ) NOUN a Brazilian dance in duple time, a precursor of the tango.
▷HISTORY from Brazilian Portuguese

max out VERB (*adverb*) *Informal* to reach or cause to reach the full extent or allowance: *the goal was to max out the customer's credit card.*

maxwell (ˈmækswəl) NOUN the cgs unit of magnetic flux equal to the flux through one square centimetre normal to a field of one gauss. It is equivalent to 10^{-8} weber. Symbol: Mx.
▷HISTORY C20: named after James Clerk *Maxwell* (1831–79), Scottish physicist

Maxwell equations (ˈmækswəl) PLURAL NOUN equations developed by James Clerk Maxwell (1831–79) upon which classical electromagnetic theory is based.

may[1] (meɪ) VERB, *past* **might.** (takes an infinitive without *to* or an implied infinitive, used as an auxiliary) [1] to indicate that permission is requested by or granted to someone: *he may go to the park tomorrow if he behaves himself.* [2] (often foll by *well*) to indicate possibility: *the rope may break; he may well be a spy.* [3] to indicate ability or capacity, esp in questions: *may I help you?* [4] to express a strong wish: *long may she reign.* [5] to indicate result or purpose: used only in clauses introduced by *that* or *so that*: *he writes so that the average reader may understand.* [6] another word for **might**[1]. [7] to express courtesy in a question: *whose child may this little girl be?* [8] **be that as it may.** in spite of that: a sentence connector conceding the possible truth of a previous statement and introducing an adversative clause: *be that as it may, I still think he should come.* [9] **come what may.** whatever happens. [10] **that's as may be.** (foll by a clause introduced by *but*) that may be so.
▷HISTORY Old English *mæg*, from *magan:* compare Old High German *mag*, Old Norse *mā*

Language note It was formerly considered correct to use *may* rather than *can* when referring to permission as in: *you may use the laboratory for your experiments*, but this use of *may* is now almost entirely restricted to polite questions such as *your analysis may have been more more credible if …* is generally regarded as incorrect, *might* being preferred: *your analysis might have been more credible if ….*

may[2] (meɪ) NOUN an archaic word for **maiden.**
▷HISTORY Old English *mæg;* related to Old High German *māg* kinsman, Old Norse *māgr* a relative by marriage

may[3] (meɪ) NOUN [1] Also: **may tree.** a Brit name for **hawthorn.** [2] short for **may blossom.**
▷HISTORY C16: from the month of MAY, when it flowers

May (meɪ) NOUN the fifth month of the year, consisting of 31 days.
▷HISTORY from Old French, from Latin *Maius*, probably from *Maia*, Roman goddess, identified with the Greek goddess MAIA

maya (ˈmaɪə, ˈmɑːjə, ˈmɑːjɑː) NOUN *Hinduism* illusion, esp the material world of the senses regarded as illusory.
▷HISTORY C19: from Sanskrit
▸ˈ**mayan** ADJECTIVE

Maya[1] (ˈmaɪə, ˈmɑːjə, ˈmɑːjɑː) NOUN the Hindu goddess of illusion, the personification of the idea that the material world is illusory.
▸ˈ**Mayan** ADJECTIVE

Maya[2] (ˈmaɪə) NOUN [1] (*plural* **-ya** *or* **-yas**) Also called: **Mayan.** a member of an American Indian people of Yucatan, Belize, and N Guatemala, having an ancient culture once characterized by outstanding achievements in architecture, astronomy, chronology, painting, and pottery. [2] the language of this people. See also **Mayan.**

Mayagüez (*Spanish* majaˈɣweθ) NOUN a port in W Puerto Rico; needlework industry. Pop.: 100 937 (1996 est.).

Mayan (ˈmaɪən) ADJECTIVE [1] of, relating to, or characteristic of the Maya or any of their languages. ◆ NOUN [2] a family of Central American Indian languages, including Maya, possibly a member of the Penutian phylum. [3] another name for a **Maya**[2].

May apple NOUN [1] an American berberidaceous plant, *Podophyllum peltatum*, with edible yellowish egg-shaped fruit. [2] the fruit of this plant.

maybe (ˈmeɪˌbiː) ADVERB [1] **a** perhaps. **b** (*as sentence modifier*): *maybe I'll come tomorrow.* ◆ SENTENCE SUBSTITUTE [2] possibly; neither yes nor no.

May beetle *or* **bug** NOUN another name for **cockchafer** and **June bug.**

May blobs NOUN (*functioning as singular*) another name for **marsh marigold.**

may blossom *or* **may** NOUN the blossom of the may tree or hawthorn.

Mayday (ˈmeɪˌdeɪ) NOUN the international radiotelephone distress signal.
▷HISTORY C20: phonetic spelling of French *m'aidez* help me

May Day NOUN **a** the first day of May, traditionally a celebration of the coming of spring: in some countries now observed as a holiday in honour of workers. **b** (*as modifier*): *May-Day celebrations.*

Mayence (majɑ̃s) NOUN the French name for **Mainz**.

Mayenne (*French* majɛn) NOUN a department of NW France, in Pays de la Loire region. Capital: Laval. Pop.: 285 338 (1999). Area: 5212 sq. km (2033 sq. miles).

mayest (ˈmeɪɪst) VERB a variant of **mayst**.

Mayfair (ˈmeɪˌfɛə) NOUN a fashionable district of west central London.

mayflower (ˈmeɪˌflaʊə) NOUN 1 any of various plants that bloom in May. 2 *US and Canadian* another name for **trailing arbutus**. 3 *Brit* another name for **hawthorn, cowslip** or **marsh marigold**.

Mayflower (ˈmeɪˌflaʊə) NOUN **the**. the ship in which the Pilgrim Fathers sailed from Plymouth to Massachusetts in 1620.

mayfly (ˈmeɪˌflaɪ) NOUN, *plural* **-flies**. 1 Also called: **dayfly**. any insect of the order *Ephemeroptera* (or *Ephemerida*). The short-lived adults, found near water, have long tail appendages and large transparent wings; the larvae are aquatic. 2 *Angling* an artificial fly resembling this.

mayhap (ˈmeɪˌhæp) ADVERB an archaic word for **perhaps**.
▷HISTORY C16: shortened from *it may hap*

mayhem *or* **maihem** (ˈmeɪhɛm) NOUN 1 *Law* the wilful and unlawful infliction of injury upon a person, esp (formerly) the injuring or removing of a limb rendering him less capable of defending himself against attack. 2 any violent destruction or confusion.
▷HISTORY C15: from Anglo-French *mahem* injury, from Germanic; related to Icelandic *meitha* to hurt. See MAIM

Maying (ˈmeɪɪŋ) NOUN the traditional celebration of May Day.

mayn't (ˈmeɪənt, meɪnt) VERB CONTRACTION OF may not.

Mayo (ˈmeɪəʊ) NOUN a county of NW Republic of Ireland, in NW Connacht province, on the Atlantic: has many offshore islands and several large lakes. County town: Castlebar. Pop.: 111 524 (1996). Area: 5397 sq. km (2084 sq. miles).

Mayon (mɑːˈjɔːn) NOUN a volcano in the Philippines, on SE Luzon: Height: 2421 m (7943 ft.).

mayonnaise (ˌmeɪəˈneɪz) NOUN a thick creamy sauce made from egg yolks, oil, and vinegar or lemon juice, eaten with salads, eggs, etc.
▷HISTORY C19: from French, perhaps from *Mahonnais* of *Mahón*, a port in Minorca

mayor (mɛə) NOUN the chairman and civic head of a municipal corporation in many countries. Scottish equivalent: **provost**.
▷HISTORY C13: from Old French *maire*, from Latin *maior* greater. See MAJOR
▸ˈ**mayoral** ADJECTIVE ▸ˈ**mayorˌship** NOUN

mayoralty (ˈmɛərəltɪ) NOUN, *plural* **-ties**. the office or term of office of a mayor.
▷HISTORY C14: from Old French *mairalté*

mayoress (ˈmɛərɪs) NOUN 1 *Chiefly Brit* the wife of a mayor. 2 a female mayor.

Mayotte (*French* majɔt) NOUN an island in the Indian Ocean, northwest of Madagascar; administered by France. Pop. (including Pamanzi): 159 000 (2001 est.). Area: 374 sq. km (146 sq. miles).

maypole (ˈmeɪˌpəʊl) NOUN a tall pole fixed upright in an open space during May-Day celebrations, around which people dance holding streamers attached at its head.

May queen NOUN a girl chosen, esp for her beauty, to preside over May-Day celebrations.

mayst (meɪst) *or* **mayest** VERB *Archaic or dialect* (used with the pronoun *thou* or its relative equivalent) a singular form of the present tense of **may**.

may tree NOUN a Brit name for **hawthorn**.

mayweed (ˈmeɪˌwiːd) NOUN 1 Also called: **dog fennel, stinking mayweed**. a widespread Eurasian weedy plant, *Anthemis cotula*, having evil-smelling leaves and daisy-like flower heads: family *Asteraceae* (composites). 2 **scentless mayweed**. a similar and related plant, *Matricaria maritima*, with scentless leaves.
▷HISTORY C16: changed from Old English *mægtha* mayweed + WEED[1]

mazard *or* **mazzard** (ˈmæzəd) NOUN 1 an obsolete word for the **head** or **skull**. 2 another word for **mazer**.
▷HISTORY C17: altered from MAZER

Mazatlán (*Spanish* maθaˈtlan) NOUN a port in W Mexico, in S Sinaloa on the Pacific: situated opposite the tip of the peninsula of Lower California, for which it is the chief link with the mainland. Pop.: 325 000 (2000 est.).

Mazdaism *or* **Mazdeism** (ˈmæzdəˌɪzəm) NOUN another word for **Zoroastrianism**.

maze (meɪz) NOUN 1 a complex network of paths or passages, esp one with high hedges in a garden, designed to puzzle those walking through it. Compare **labyrinth** (sense 1). 2 a similar system represented diagrammatically as a pattern of lines. 3 any confusing network of streets, pathways, etc.: *a maze of paths*. 4 a state of confusion. ◆ VERB 5 an archaic or dialect word for **amaze**.
▷HISTORY C13: see AMAZE
▸ˈ**mazeˌlike** ADJECTIVE ▸ˈ**mazement** NOUN

mazer (ˈmeɪzə), **mazard**, *or* **mazzard** (ˈmæzəd) NOUN *Obsolete* a large hardwood drinking bowl.
▷HISTORY C12: from Old French *masere*, of Germanic origin; compare Old Norse *mösurr* maple

mazey (ˈmeɪzɪ) ADJECTIVE **mazier, maziest**. *Northern English dialect* dizzy.

Mazu (ˈmæˈzuː) NOUN the Pinyin transliteration of the Chinese name for **Matsu**.

mazuma (məˈzuːmə) NOUN *Slang, chiefly US* money.
▷HISTORY C20: from Yiddish

mazurka *or* **mazourka** (məˈzɜːkə) NOUN 1 a Polish national dance in triple time. 2 a piece of music composed for this dance.
▷HISTORY C19: from Polish: (dance) of *Mazur* (Mazovia) province in Poland

mazy (ˈmeɪzɪ) ADJECTIVE **mazier, maziest**. of or like a maze; perplexing or confused.
▸ˈ**mazily** ADVERB ▸ˈ**maziness** NOUN

mazzard *or* **mazard** (ˈmæzəd) NOUN a wild sweet cherry tree, *Prunus avium*, often used as a grafting stock for cultivated cherries.
▷HISTORY C16: perhaps related to MAZER

mb SYMBOL FOR millibar.

Mb *Computing* ABBREVIATION FOR megabyte.

MB ABBREVIATION FOR: 1 Bachelor of Medicine. 2 maternity benefit. 3 (esp in postal addresses) Manitoba. 4 (in Canada) Medal of Bravery.

MBA ABBREVIATION FOR Master of Business Administration.

Mbabane (ᵊmbɑːˈbɑːnɪ) NOUN the capital of Swaziland, in the northwest: administrative and financial centre, with a large iron mine nearby. Pop.: 60 000 (1998 est.).

mbaqanga (ᵊmbɑːˈkæŋgə) NOUN a style of Black popular music of urban South Africa.
▷HISTORY C20: perhaps from Zulu *umbaqanga* mixture

MBE ABBREVIATION FOR Member of the Order of the British Empire (a Brit title).

mbira (ᵊmˈbiːrə) NOUN an African musical instrument consisting of tuned metal strips attached to a resonating box, which are plucked with the thumbs. Also called: **thumb piano**.
▷HISTORY Shona

MBO ABBREVIATION FOR management buyout.

Mbujimayi (ᵊmˈbuːdʒɪˌmaɪiː) NOUN a city in S Democratic Republic of Congo (formerly Zaïre): diamond mining. Pop.: 806 475 (1994 est.).

mbyte *Computing* ABBREVIATION FOR megabyte.

mc THE INTERNET DOMAIN NAME FOR Monaco.

MC ABBREVIATION FOR: 1 Master of Ceremonies. 2 *Astrology* Medium Coeli. [Latin: Midheaven.] 3 (in the US) Member of Congress. 4 (in Britain) Military Cross. ◆ 5 INTERNATIONAL CAR REGISTRATION FOR Monaco.

Mc- PREFIX a variant of **Mac-**. For names beginning with this prefix, see under **Mac-**.

MCB ABBREVIATION FOR miniature circuit breaker; a small trip switch operated by an overload and used to protect an electric circuit, esp a domestic circuit as an alternative to a fuse.

MCC (in Britain) ABBREVIATION FOR Marylebone Cricket Club.

MCG (in Australia) ABBREVIATION FOR Melbourne Cricket Ground.

MCh ABBREVIATION FOR Master of Surgery.
▷HISTORY Latin *Magister Chirurgiae*

McJob (məkˈdʒɒb) NOUN *Informal* a job that is poorly paid and menial.
▷HISTORY C20: a humorous corruption of *McDonald's*, a major American fast-food enterprise

MCom ABBREVIATION FOR Master of Commerce.

m-commerce (ˈɛmˌkɒmɜːs) NOUN business transactions conducted on the Internet using a mobile phone.
▷HISTORY C20: from *m-* mobile + COMMERCE

MCP *Informal* ABBREVIATION FOR male chauvinist pig.

MCPS ABBREVIATION FOR Mechanical Copyright Protection Society.

M.C.S. (in the US and Canada) ABBREVIATION FOR Master of Computer Science.

md THE INTERNET DOMAIN NAME FOR Moldova.

Md THE CHEMICAL SYMBOL FOR mendelevium.

MD ABBREVIATION FOR: 1 Doctor of Medicine. [from Latin *Medicinae Doctor*] 2 Maryland. 3 Medical Department. 4 mentally deficient. 5 Managing Director. ◆ 6 INTERNATIONAL CAR REGISTRATION FOR Moldova.

Md. ABBREVIATION FOR Maryland.

MDF ABBREVIATION FOR medium-density fibreboard: a wood-substitute material used in interior decoration.

MDMA ABBREVIATION FOR 3,4-methylenedioxymethamphetamine. Also called (informal): **ecstasy**.

MDR ABBREVIATION FOR multi-drug resistant: *MDR tuberculosis*.

MDS ABBREVIATION FOR Master of Dental Surgery.

me[1] (miː; *unstressed* mɪ) PRONOUN (*objective*) 1 refers to the speaker or writer: *that shocks me; he gave me the glass*. 2 *Chiefly US* a dialect word for **myself** when used as an indirect object: *I want to get me a car*. ◆ NOUN 3 *Informal* the personality of the speaker or writer or something that expresses it: *the real me comes out when I'm happy*.
▷HISTORY Old English *mē* (dative); compare Dutch, German *mir*, Latin *mē* (accusative), *mihi* (dative) having a job of my own

me[2] (miː) NOUN a variant spelling of **mi**.

Me THE CHEMICAL SYMBOL FOR the methyl group.

ME ABBREVIATION FOR: 1 Maine. 2 Marine Engineer. 3 Mechanical Engineer. 4 Methodist Episcopal. 5 Mining Engineer. 6 Middle English. 7 (in titles) Most Excellent. 8 **myalgic encephalopathy**.

Me. ABBREVIATION FOR Maine.

mea culpa *Latin* (ˈmeɪɑː ˈkʊlpɑː) an acknowledgment of guilt.
▷HISTORY literally: my fault

mead[1] (miːd) NOUN an alcoholic drink made by fermenting a solution of honey, often with spices added.
▷HISTORY Old English *meodu*; related to Old High German *metu*, Greek *methu*, Welsh *medd*

mead[2] (miːd) NOUN an archaic or poetic word for **meadow**.
▷HISTORY Old English *mǣd*

Mead (miːd) NOUN **Lake**. a reservoir in NW Arizona and SE Nevada, formed by the Hoover Dam across the Colorado River: one of the largest man-made lakes in the world. Area: 588 sq. km (227 sq. miles).

meadow (ˈmɛdəʊ) NOUN 1 an area of grassland, often used for hay or for grazing of animals. 2 a low-lying piece of grassland, often boggy and near a river.
▷HISTORY Old English *mǣdwe*, from *mǣd* MEAD[2]; related to *māwan* to MOW[1]
▸ˈ**meadowy** ADJECTIVE

meadow fescue NOUN an erect Eurasian perennial grass, *Festuca pratensis*, with lustrous leaves and stem bases surrounded by dark brown sheaths.

meadow grass NOUN a perennial grass, *Poa pratensis*, that has erect hairless leaves and grows in meadows and similar places in N temperate regions.

meadowlark (ˈmɛdəʊˌlɑːk) NOUN either of two

North American yellow-breasted songbirds, *Sturnella magna* (**eastern meadowlark**) or *S. neglecta* (**western meadowlark**): family *Icteridae* (American orioles).

meadow lily NOUN another name for **Canada lily.**

meadow mouse NOUN *US* another name for **vole**[1].

meadow mushroom NOUN a saprotrophic agaricaceous edible fungus, *Agaricus campestris,* having a white cap with pink or brown gills on the underside.

meadow pipit NOUN a common European songbird, *Anthus pratensis,* with a pale brown speckled plumage: family *Motacillidae* (pipits and wagtails).

meadow rue NOUN any ranunculaceous plant of the N temperate genus *Thalictrum,* esp *T. flavum,* having clusters of small yellowish-green, white, or purple flowers.

meadow saffron NOUN another name for **autumn crocus.**

meadowsweet (ˈmɛdəʊˌswiːt) NOUN 1 a Eurasian rosaceous plant, *Filipendula ulmaria,* with dense heads of small fragrant cream-coloured flowers. See also **dropwort** (sense 1). 2 any of several North American rosaceous plants of the genus *Spiraea,* having pyramid-shaped sprays of small flowers.

meagre *or US* **meager** (ˈmiːgə) ADJECTIVE 1 deficient in amount, quality, or extent. 2 thin or emaciated. 3 lacking in richness or strength.
▷HISTORY C14: from Old French *maigre,*from Latin *macer* lean, poor
▸ˈ**meagrely** *or* (*US*) ˈ**meagerly** ADVERB ▸ˈ**meagreness** *or* (*US*) ˈ**meagerness** NOUN

meal[1] (miːl) NOUN 1 **a** any of the regular occasions, such as breakfast, lunch, dinner, etc., when food is served and eaten. **b** (*in combination*): *mealtime.* Related adjective: **prandial.** 2 the food served and eaten. 3 **make a meal of.** *Informal* to perform (a task) with unnecessarily great effort.
▷HISTORY Old English *mǣl* measure, set time, meal; related to Old High German *māl* mealtime

meal[2] (miːl) NOUN 1 the edible part of a grain or pulse (excluding wheat) ground to a coarse powder, used chiefly as animal food. 2 *Scot* oatmeal. 3 *Chiefly US* maize flour.
▷HISTORY Old English *melu;* compare Dutch *meel,* Old High German *melo,* Old Norse *mjöl*
▸ˈ**meal-less** ADJECTIVE

mealie *or* **mielie** (ˈmiːlɪ) NOUN *South African* an ear of maize. See also **mealies.**
▷HISTORY C19: from Afrikaans *milie,* from Portuguese *milho,* from Latin *milium* millet

mealie meal *or* **mielie meal** NOUN *South African* finely ground maize.

mealie pap *or* **mielie pap** NOUN *South African* mealie porridge.
▷HISTORY Afrikaans

mealies *or* **mielies** (ˈmiːlɪz) NOUN (*functioning as singular*) a South African word for **maize.**

meal moth NOUN a small pyralid moth, *Pyralis farinalis,* whose larvae are an important pest of stored cereals. The **Indian meal moth** (*Plodia interpunctella*) and the **Mediterranean flour moth** (*Ephestia kuehniella*) are other pyralids with similar habits.

meals on wheels *or* **meals-on-wheels** NOUN (*functioning as singular*) *Social welfare, Brit* a service, usually subsidized, and run by a social services department or voluntary body, which delivers hot meals to elderly or housebound people who might otherwise be unable to have them.

meal ticket NOUN *Slang* a person, situation, etc., providing a source of livelihood or income.
▷HISTORY from original US sense of ticket entitling holder to a meal

mealworm (ˈmiːlˌwɜːm) NOUN the larva of various beetles of the genus *Tenebrio,* esp *T. molitor,* feeding on meal, flour, and similar stored foods: family *Tenebrionidae.*

mealy (ˈmiːlɪ) ADJECTIVE **mealier, mealiest.** 1 resembling meal; powdery. 2 containing or consisting of meal or grain. 3 sprinkled or covered with meal or similar granules. 4 (esp of horses) spotted; mottled. 5 pale in complexion. 6 short for **mealy-mouthed.**
▸ˈ**mealiness** NOUN

mealy bug NOUN any plant-eating homopterous insect of the genus *Pseudococcus* and related genera, coated with a powdery waxy secretion: some species are pests of citrus fruits and greenhouse plants: family *Pseudococcidae.*

mealy-mouthed ADJECTIVE hesitant or afraid to speak plainly; not outspoken.
▷HISTORY C16: from MEALY (in the sense: soft, soft-spoken)
▸ˌ**mealy-ˈmouthedness** NOUN

mean[1] (miːn) VERB **means, meaning, meant.** (*mainly tr*) 1 (*may take a clause as object or an infinitive*) to intend to convey or express. 2 (*may take a clause as object or an infinitive*) intend: *she didn't mean to hurt it.* 3 (*may take a clause as object*) to say or do in all seriousness: *the boss means what he says about strikes.* 4 (*often passive;* often foll by *for*) to destine or design (for a certain person or purpose): *she was meant for greater things.* 5 (*may take a clause as object*) to denote or connote; signify; represent: *examples help show exactly what a word means.* 6 (*may take a clause as object*) to produce; cause: *the weather will mean long traffic delays.* 7 (*may take a clause as object*) to foretell; portend: *those dark clouds mean rain.* 8 to have the importance of: *money means nothing to him.* 9 (*intr*) to have the intention of behaving or acting (esp in the phrases **mean well** *or* **mean ill**). 10 **mean business.** to be in earnest.
▷HISTORY Old English *mænan;* compare Old Saxon *mēnian* to intend, Dutch *meenen*

> **Language note** In standard English, *mean* should not be followed by *for* when expressing intention: *I didn't mean this to happen* (not *I didn't mean for this to happen*).

mean[2] (miːn) ADJECTIVE 1 *Chiefly Brit* miserly, ungenerous, or petty. 2 humble, obscure, or lowly: *he rose from mean origins to high office.* 3 despicable, ignoble, or callous: *a mean action.* 4 poor or shabby: *mean clothing; a mean abode.* 5 *Informal, chiefly US and Canadian* bad-tempered; vicious. 6 *Informal* ashamed: *he felt mean about not letting the children go to the zoo.* 7 *Informal chiefly US* unwell; in low spirits. 8 *Slang* excellent; skilful: *he plays a mean trombone.* 9 **no mean. a** of high quality: *no mean performer.* **b** difficult: *no mean feat.*
▷HISTORY C12: from Old English *gemǣne* common; related to Old High German *gimeini,* Latin *communis* common, at first with no pejorative sense
▸ˈ**meanly** ADVERB ▸ˈ**meanness** NOUN

mean[3] (miːn) NOUN 1 the middle point, state, or course between limits or extremes. 2 moderation. 3 *Maths* **a** the second and third terms of a proportion, as *b* and *c* in *a/b* = *c/d.* **b** another name for **average** (sense 2). See also **geometric mean.** 4 *Statistics* a statistic obtained by multiplying each possible value of a variable by its probability and then taking the sum or integral over the range of the variable. ◆ ADJECTIVE 5 intermediate or medium in size, quantity, etc. 6 occurring halfway between extremes or limits; average. ◆ See also **means.**
▷HISTORY C14: via Anglo-Norman from Old French *moien,* from Late Latin *mediānus* MEDIAN

meander (mɪˈændə) VERB (*intr*) 1 to follow a winding course. 2 to wander without definite aim or direction. ◆ NOUN 3 (*often plural*) a curve or bend, as in a river. 4 (*often plural*) a winding course or movement. 5 an ornamental pattern, esp as used in ancient Greek architecture.
▷HISTORY C16: from Latin *maeander,* from Greek *Maiandros* the River Maeander; see MENDERES (sense 1)
▸**meˈanderer** NOUN ▸**meˈandering** ADJECTIVE
▸**meˈanderingly** ADVERB ▸**meˈandrous** ADJECTIVE

Meander (miːˈændə) NOUN a variant spelling of **Maeander.**

mean deviation NOUN *Statistics* 1 the difference between an observed value of a variable and its mean. 2 Also called: **mean deviation from the mean** (*or* **median), average deviation.** a measure of dispersion derived by computing the mean of the absolute values of the differences between observed values of a variable and the variable's mean.

mean distance NOUN the average of the greatest and least distances of a celestial body from its primary.

mean free path NOUN the average distance travelled by a particle, atom, etc., between collisions.

meanie *or* **meany** (ˈmiːnɪ) NOUN, *plural* **meanies.** *Informal* 1 *Chiefly Brit* a miserly or stingy person. 2 *Chiefly US* a nasty ill-tempered person.

meaning (ˈmiːnɪŋ) NOUN 1 the sense or significance of a word, sentence, symbol, etc.; import; semantic or lexical content. 2 the purpose underlying or intended by speech, action, etc. 3 the inner, symbolic, or true interpretation, value, or message: *the meaning of a dream.* 4 valid content; efficacy: *a law with little or no meaning.* 5 *Philosophy* **a** the sense of an expression; its connotation. **b** the reference of an expression; its denotation. In recent philosophical writings meaning can be used in both the above senses. See also **sense** (sense 13). ◆ ADJECTIVE 6 expressive of some sense, intention, criticism, etc.: *a meaning look.* ◆ See also **well-meaning.**

meaningful (ˈmiːnɪŋfʊl) ADJECTIVE 1 having great meaning or validity. 2 eloquent, expressive: *a meaningful silence.*
▸ˈ**meaningfully** ADVERB ▸ˈ**meaningfulness** NOUN

meaningless (ˈmiːnɪŋlɪs) ADJECTIVE futile or empty of meaning.
▸ˈ**meaninglessly** ADVERB ▸ˈ**meaninglessness** NOUN

mean lethal dose NOUN another term for **median lethal dose.**

mean life NOUN *Physics* the average time of existence of an unstable or reactive entity, such as a nucleus, elementary particle, charge carrier, etc.; lifetime. It is equal to the half-life divided by 0.693 15. Symbol: τ.

means (miːnz) NOUN 1 (*functioning as singular or plural*) the medium, method, or instrument used to obtain a result or achieve an end: *a means of communication.* 2 (*functioning as plural*) resources or income. 3 (*functioning as plural*) considerable wealth or income: *a man of means.* 4 **by all means.** without hesitation or doubt; certainly: *come with us by all means.* 5 **by means of.** with the use or help of. 6 **by no manner of means.** definitely not: *he was by no manner of means a cruel man.* 7 **by no** (*or* **not by any**) **means.** on no account; in no way: *by no means come!*

mean sea level NOUN (in the UK) the sea level used by the Ordnance Survey as a datum level, determined at Newlyn in Cornwall. See **sea level.**

means of production PLURAL NOUN (in Marxist theory) the raw materials and means of labour (tools, machines, etc.) employed in the production process.

mean solar day NOUN the time between two successive passages of the mean sun across the meridian at noon. It is equal to 24 hours 3 minutes and 56.555 seconds of mean sidereal time.

means test NOUN a test involving the checking of a person's income to determine whether he qualifies for financial or social aid from a government. Compare **needs test.**
▸ˈ**means-tested** ADJECTIVE

mean sun NOUN an imaginary sun moving along the celestial equator at a constant rate and completing its annual course in the same time as the sun takes to move round the ecliptic at a varying rate. It is used in the measurement of mean solar time.

meant (mɛnt) VERB the past tense and past participle of **mean**[1].

mean time *or* **mean solar time** NOUN the time, at a particular place, measured in terms of the passage of the mean sun; the timescale is not precisely constant. See **mean solar day.**

meantime (ˈmiːnˌtaɪm) NOUN 1 the intervening time or period, as between events (esp in the phrase **in the meantime**). ◆ ADVERB 2 another word for **meanwhile.**

mean-tone tuning NOUN See **temperament** (sense 4).

meanwhile (ˈmiːnˌwaɪl) ADVERB 1 during the intervening time or period. 2 at the same time, esp in another place. ◆ NOUN 3 another word for **meantime.**

meany (ˈmiːnɪ) NOUN *Informal* a variant spelling of **meanie.**

Mearns (mɛənz) NOUN **the.** another name for **Kincardineshire.**

measled ('miːzəld) ADJECTIVE (of cattle, sheep, or pigs) infested with tapeworm larvae; measly.

measles ('miːzəlz) NOUN (*functioning as singular or plural*) 1 a highly contagious viral disease common in children, characterized by fever, profuse nasal discharge of mucus, conjunctivitis, and a rash of small red spots spreading from the forehead down to the limbs. Technical names: **morbilli, rubeola.** See also **German measles.** 2 a disease of cattle, sheep, and pigs, caused by infestation with tapeworm larvae.
▷HISTORY C14: from Middle Low German *masele* spot on the skin; influenced by Middle English *mesel* leper, from Latin *misellus,* diminutive of *miser* wretched

measly ('miːzlɪ) ADJECTIVE **-slier, -sliest.** 1 *Informal* meagre in quality or quantity. 2 (of meat) measled. 3 having or relating to measles.
▷HISTORY C17: see MEASLES

measurable ('mɛʒərəbᵊl, 'mɛʒrə-) ADJECTIVE able to be measured; perceptible or significant.
▸**ˌmeasura'bility** *or* **'measurableness** NOUN ▸**'measurably** ADVERB

measure ('mɛʒə) NOUN 1 the extent, quantity, amount, or degree of something, as determined by measurement or calculation. 2 a device for measuring distance, volume, etc., such as a graduated scale or container. 3 a system of measurement: *give the size in metric measure.* 4 a standard used in a system of measurements: *the international prototype kilogram is the measure of mass in SI units.* 5 a specific or standard amount of something: *a measure of grain; short measure; full measure.* 6 a basis or standard for comparison: *his work was the measure of all subsequent attempts.* 7 reasonable or permissible limit or bounds: *we must keep it within measure.* 8 degree or extent (often in phrases such as **in some measure, in a measure,** etc.): *they gave him a measure of freedom.* 9 (*often plural*) a particular action intended to achieve an effect: *they took measures to prevent his leaving.* 10 a legislative bill, act, or resolution: *to bring in a measure.* 11 *Music* another word for **bar**[1] (sense 15a). 12 *Prosody* poetic rhythm or cadence; metre. 13 a metrical foot. 14 *Poetic* a melody or tune. 15 the act of measuring; measurement. 16 *Archaic* a dance. 17 *Printing* the width of a page or column of type. 18 **for good measure.** as an extra precaution or beyond requirements. 19 **get the measure of** *or* **get someone's measure.** to assess the nature, character, quality, etc., of someone or something. 20 **made to measure.** (of clothes) made to fit an individual purchaser. ◆ VERB 21 (*tr;* often foll by *up*) to determine the size, amount, etc., of by measurement. 22 (*intr*) to make a measurement or measurements. 23 (*tr*) to estimate or determine: *I measured his strength to be greater than mine.* 24 (*tr*) to function as a measurement of: *the ohm measures electrical resistance.* 25 (*tr*) to bring into competition or conflict: *he measured his strength against that of his opponent.* 26 (*intr*) to be as specified in extent, amount, etc.: *the room measures six feet.* 27 (*tr*) to travel or move over as if measuring. 28 (*tr*) to adjust or choose: *he measured his approach to suit the character of his client.* 29 (*intr*) to allow or yield to measurement. ◆ See also **measure off, measure out, measures, measure up.**
▷HISTORY C13: from Old French, from Latin *mēnsūra* measure, from *mēnsus,* past participle of *mētīrī* to measure
▸**'measurer** NOUN

measured ('mɛʒəd) ADJECTIVE 1 determined by measurement. 2 slow, stately, or leisurely. 3 carefully considered; deliberate.
▸**'measuredly** ADVERB ▸**'measuredness** NOUN

measured daywork ('deɪˌwɜːk) NOUN a system of wage payment, usually determined by work-study techniques, whereby the wage of an employee is fixed on the understanding that a specific level of work performance will be maintained.

measureless ('mɛʒəlɪs) ADJECTIVE limitless, vast, or infinite.
▸**'measurelessly** ADVERB ▸**'measurelessness** NOUN

measurement ('mɛʒəmənt) NOUN 1 the act or process of measuring. 2 an amount, extent, or size determined by measuring. 3 a system of measures based on a particular standard.

measurement ton NOUN the full name for **ton**[1] (sense 5).

measure off *or* **out** VERB (*tr, adverb*) to determine the limits of; mark out: *to measure off an area.*

measure out VERB (*tr, adverb*) 1 to pour or dole out: *they measure out a pint of fluid.* 2 to administer; mete out: *they measured out harsh punishments.*

measures ('mɛʒəz) PLURAL NOUN rock strata that are characterized by a particular type of sediment or deposit: *coal measures.*

measure up VERB 1 (*adverb*) to determine the size of (something) by measurement. 2 **measure up to.** to fulfil (expectations, standards, etc.).

measuring jug NOUN a graduated jug used in cooking to measure ingredients.

measuring worm NOUN the larva of a geometrid moth: it has legs on its front and rear segments only and moves in a series of loops. Also called: **looper, inchworm.**

meat (miːt) NOUN 1 the flesh of mammals used as food, as distinguished from that of birds and fish. 2 anything edible, esp flesh with the texture of meat: *crab meat.* 3 food, as opposed to drink. 4 the essence or gist. 5 an archaic word for **meal**[1]. 6 **meat and drink.** a source of pleasure. 7 **have one's meat and one's manners.** *Irish informal* to lose nothing because one's offer is not accepted.
▷HISTORY Old English *mete;* related to Old High German *maz* food, Old Saxon *meti,* Gothic *mats*
▸**'meatless** ADJECTIVE

meataxe ('miːtˌæks) NOUN 1 a cleaver. 2 **mad as a meataxe.** *Austral and NZ informal* raving.

meatball ('miːtˌbɔːl) NOUN 1 minced beef, shaped into a ball before cooking. 2 *US and Canadian, slang* a stupid or boring person.

Meath (miːð, miːθ) NOUN a county of E Republic of Ireland, in Leinster province on the Irish Sea: formerly a kingdom much larger than the present county; livestock farming. County town: Trim. Pop.: 109 732 (1996). Area: 2338 sq. km (903 sq. miles).

meatspace ('miːtˌspeɪs) NOUN *Slang* the real physical world, as contrasted with the world of cyberspace.

meatus (mɪ'eɪtəs) NOUN, *plural* **-tuses** *or* **-tus.** *Anatomy* a natural opening or channel, such as the canal leading from the outer ear to the eardrum.
▷HISTORY C17: from Latin: passage, from *meāre* to pass

meaty ('miːtɪ) ADJECTIVE **meatier, meatiest.** 1 of, relating to, or full of meat: *a meaty stew.* 2 heavily built; fleshy or brawny. 3 full of import or interest: *a meaty discussion.* 4 *Judaism* another word for **fleishik.**
▸**'meatily** ADVERB ▸**'meatiness** NOUN

mebi- ('mɛbɪ) PREFIX *Computing* denoting 2^{20}: *mebibyte.* Symbol: Mi.
▷HISTORY C20: from ME(GA-) + BI(NARY)

MEC (in South Africa) ABBREVIATION FOR Member of the Executive Council.

mecamylamine (ˌmɛkə'mɪləˌmiːn) NOUN a ganglion-blocking drug administered orally to lower high blood pressure. Formula: $C_{11}H_{21}N$.
▷HISTORY C20: from ME(THYL) + *cam(phane)* (a former name of bornane) + -YL + AMINE

Mecca *or* **Mekka** ('mɛkə) NOUN 1 a city in W Saudi Arabia, joint capital (with Riyadh) of Saudi Arabia: birthplace of Mohammed; the holiest city of Islam, containing the Kaaba. Pop.: 965 697 (1992). Arabic name: **Makkah.** 2 (*sometimes not capital*) a place that attracts many visitors: *Athens is a Mecca for tourists.*

Meccano (mɪ'kɑːnəʊ) NOUN *Trademark* a construction set consisting of miniature metal or plastic parts from which mechanical models can be made.

mechanic (mɪ'kænɪk) NOUN 1 a person skilled in maintaining or operating machinery, motors, etc. 2 *Archaic* a common labourer.
▷HISTORY C14: from Latin *mēchanicus,* from Greek *mēkhanikos,* from *mēkhanē* MACHINE

mechanical (mɪ'kænɪkᵊl) ADJECTIVE 1 made, performed, or operated by or as if by a machine or machinery: *a mechanical process.* 2 concerned with machines or machinery. 3 relating to or controlled or operated by physical forces. 4 of or concerned with mechanics. 5 (of a gesture, etc.) automatic; lacking thought, feeling, etc. 6 *Philosophy* accounting for phenomena by physically determining forces. 7 (of paper, such as newsprint) made from pulp that has been mechanically ground and contains impurities. ◆ NOUN 8 *Printing* another name for **camera-ready copy.** 9 *Archaic* another word for **mechanic** (sense 2).
▸**me'chanicalism** NOUN ▸**me'chanically** ADVERB
▸**me'chanicalness** NOUN

mechanical advantage NOUN the ratio of the working force exerted by a mechanism to the applied effort.

mechanical drawing NOUN a drawing to scale of a machine, machine component, architectural plan, etc., from which dimensions can be taken for manufacture.

mechanical engineering NOUN the branch of engineering concerned with the design, construction, and operation of machines and machinery.
▸**mechanical engineer** NOUN

mechanical equivalent of heat NOUN *Physics* a factor for converting units of energy into heat units. It has the value 4.1868 joules per calorie. Symbol: *J.*

mechanical instrument NOUN a musical instrument, such as a barrel organ or music box, that plays a preselected piece of music by mechanical means.

mechanically recovered meat NOUN an amalgamation of the gristle, cartilage, and fat removed from animal carcasses, sometimes used in the manufacture of meat products such as sausages and hamburgers. Also called: **MRM.**

mechanician (ˌmɛkə'nɪʃən) *or* **mechanist** NOUN a person skilled in making machinery and tools; technician.

mechanics (mɪ'kænɪks) NOUN 1 (*functioning as singular*) the branch of science, divided into statics, dynamics, and kinematics, concerned with the equilibrium or motion of bodies in a particular frame of reference. See also **quantum mechanics, wave mechanics, statistical mechanics.** 2 (*functioning as singular*) the science of designing, constructing, and operating machines. 3 the working parts of a machine. 4 the technical aspects of something: *the mechanics of poetic style.*

mechanism ('mɛkəˌnɪzəm) NOUN 1 a system or structure of moving parts that performs some function, esp in a machine. 2 something resembling a machine in the arrangement and working of its parts: *the mechanism of the ear.* 3 any form of mechanical device or any part of such a device. 4 a process or technique, esp of execution: *the mechanism of novel writing.* 5 *Philosophy* **a** the doctrine that human action can be explained in purely physical terms, whether mechanical or biological. **b** the explanation of phenomena in causal rather than teleological or essentialist terms. **c** the view that the task of science is to seek such explanations. **d** strict determinism. ◆ Compare **dynamism, vitalism.** 6 *Psychoanal* **a** the ways in which psychological forces interact and operate. **b** a structure having an influence on the behaviour of a person, such as a defence mechanism.

mechanist ('mɛkənɪst) NOUN 1 a person who accepts a mechanistic philosophy. 2 another name for a **mechanician.**

mechanistic (ˌmɛkə'nɪstɪk) ADJECTIVE 1 *Philosophy* of or relating to the theory of mechanism. 2 *Maths* of or relating to mechanics.
▸**ˌmecha'nistically** ADVERB

mechanize *or* **mechanise** ('mɛkəˌnaɪz) VERB (*tr*) 1 to equip (a factory, industry, etc.) with machinery. 2 to make mechanical, automatic, or monotonous. 3 to equip (an army, etc.) with motorized or armoured vehicles.
▸**ˌmechani'zation** *or* **ˌmechani'sation** NOUN ▸**'mechaˌnizer** *or* **'mechaˌniser** NOUN

mechanoreceptor (ˌmɛkənəʊrɪ'sɛptə) NOUN *Physiol* a sensory receptor, as in the skin, that is sensitive to a mechanical stimulus, such as pressure.

mechanotherapy (ˌmɛkənəʊ'θɛrəpɪ) NOUN the treatment of disorders or injuries by means of mechanical devices, esp devices that provide exercise for bodily parts.

mechatronics (ˌmɛkə'trɒnɪks) NOUN (*functioning*

as singular) the combination of mechanical engineering, computing, and electronics, as used in the design and development of new manufacturing techniques.
▷HISTORY C20: from MECHA(NICS) + (ELEC)TRONICS

Mechelen ('mɛxələn) NOUN a city in N Belgium, in Antwerp province: capital of the Netherlands from 1507 to 1530; formerly famous for lace-making; now has an important vegetable market. Pop.: 75 718 (1995 est.). French name: **Malines.** English name: **Mechlin.**

Mechlin ('mɛklɪn) NOUN the English name for **Mechelen.**

Mechlin lace NOUN bobbin lace made at Mechlin, characterized by patterns outlined by a heavier flat thread. Also called: **malines.**

meck (mɛk) NOUN *Northeastern Scot dialect* a variant of **maik.**

Mecklenburg ('mɛklənˌbɜːg; *German* 'meːklənbʊrk) NOUN a historic region and former state of NE Germany, along the Baltic coast; now part of Mecklenburg-West Pomerania: formerly (1949–90) in East Germany.

Mecklenburg-West Pomerania (ˌpɒmə'reɪnɪə) NOUN a state of NE Germany, along the Baltic coast: consists of the former state of Mecklenburg and those parts of W Pomerania not incorporated into Poland after World War II: part of East Germany until 1990. Pop.: 1 789 300 (2000 est.).

MEcon ABBREVIATION FOR Master of Economics.

meconium (mɪ'kəʊnɪəm) NOUN [1] the dark green mucoid material that forms the first faeces of a newborn infant. [2] opium or the juice from the opium poppy.
▷HISTORY C17: from New Latin, from Latin: poppy juice (used also of infant's excrement because of similarity in colour), from Greek *mēkōneion,* from *mēkōn* poppy

meconopsis (ˌmɛkə'nɒpsɪs) NOUN any plant of the mostly Asiatic papaveraceous genus *Meconopsis,* esp *M. betonicifolia* (the Tibetan or blue poppy), grown for its showy sky-blue flowers. *M. cambrica* is the Welsh poppy.
▷HISTORY New Latin, from Greek *mēkōn* poppy + -OPSIS

Med (mɛd) NOUN **the.** *Informal* the Mediterranean region.

MEd ABBREVIATION FOR Master of Education.

med. ABBREVIATION FOR: [1] medical. [2] medicine. [3] medium.

médaillons (medaɪ'jɔ̃) PLURAL NOUN *Cookery* small round thin pieces of meat, fish, vegetables, etc. Also called: **medallions.**
▷HISTORY C20: French: medallions

medal ('mɛd^{ə}l) NOUN [1] a small flat piece of metal bearing an inscription or image, given as an award or commemoration of some outstanding action, event, etc. ◆ VERB **-als, -alling, -alled** *or US* **-als, -aling, -aled.** [2] *(tr)* to honour with a medal.
▷HISTORY C16: from French *médaille,* probably from Italian *medaglia,* ultimately from Latin *metallum* METAL
▸**medallic** (mɪ'dælɪk) ADJECTIVE

medallion (mɪ'dæljən) NOUN [1] a large medal. [2] an oval or circular decorative device resembling a medal, usually bearing a portrait or relief moulding, used in architecture and textile design.
▷HISTORY C17: from French, from Italian *medaglione,* from *medaglia* MEDAL

medallist *or US* **medalist** ('mɛd^{ə}lɪst) NOUN [1] a designer, maker, or collector of medals. [2] *Chiefly sport* a winner or recipient of a medal or medals.

Medal of Bravery NOUN a Canadian award for courage. Abbreviation: **MB.**

Medal of Honor NOUN the highest US military decoration, awarded by Congress for conspicuous bravery in action: instituted in 1861 (Navy), 1862 (Army).

medal play NOUN *Golf* another name for **stroke play.**

Medan ('mɛdɑːn) NOUN a city in Indonesia, in NE Sumatra: seat of the University of North Sumatra (1952) and the Indonesian Islam University (1952). Pop.: 1 909 700 (1995 est.).

meddle ('mɛd^{ə}l) VERB *(intr)* [1] (usually foll by *with*) to interfere officiously or annoyingly. [2] (usually foll by *in*) to involve oneself unwarrantedly: *to meddle in someone's private affairs.*
▷HISTORY C14: from Old French *medler,* ultimately from Latin *miscēre* to mix
▸**'meddler** NOUN ▸**'meddling** ADJECTIVE ▸**'meddlingly** ADVERB

meddlesome ('mɛd^{ə}lsəm) ADJECTIVE intrusive or meddling.
▸**'meddlesomely** ADVERB ▸**'meddlesomeness** NOUN

Mede (miːd) NOUN a member of an Indo-European people of West Iranian speech who established an empire in SW Asia in the 7th and 6th centuries B.C.
▸**'Median** NOUN, ADJECTIVE

Medea (mɪ'dɪə) NOUN *Greek myth* a princess of Colchis, who assisted Jason in obtaining the Golden Fleece from her father.

Medellín (*Spanish* meðe'ʎin) NOUN a city in W Colombia, at an altitude of 1554 m (5100 ft.): the second largest city in the country, with three universities; important coffee centre, with large textile mills; dominated by drug cartels in recent years. Pop.: 1 861 265 (1999 est.).

medevac ('mɛdɪˌvæk) NOUN [1] *Military* the evacuation of casualties from forward areas to the nearest hospital or base. [2] a helicopter used for transporting wounded or sick people to hospital. ◆ VERB **-vacs, -vacking, -vacked.** [3] *(tr)* to transport (a wounded or sick person) to hospital by medevac.
▷HISTORY C20: from *med(ical) evac(uation)*

medfly ('mɛdˌflaɪ) NOUN, *plural* **-fly** *or* **-flies.** another name for **Mediterranean fruit fly.**

media^{1} ('miːdɪə) NOUN [1] a plural of **medium.** [2] the means of communication that reach large numbers of people, such as television, newspapers, and radio. ◆ ADJECTIVE [3] of or relating to the mass media: *media hype.*

> **Language note** When *media* refers to the mass media, it is sometimes treated as a singular form, as in: *the media has shown great interest in these events.* Many people think this use is incorrect and that *media* should always be treated as a plural form: *the media have shown great interest in these events.*

media^{2} ('mɛdɪə) NOUN, *plural* **-diae** (-dɪˌiː). [1] the middle layer of the wall of a blood or lymph vessel. [2] one of the main veins in the wing of an insect. [3] *Phonetics* **a** a consonant whose articulation lies midway between that of a voiced and breathed speech sound. **b** a consonant pronounced with weak voice, as *c* in French *second.*
▷HISTORY C19: from Latin *medius* middle

Media ('miːdɪə) NOUN an ancient country of SW Asia, south of the Caspian Sea: inhabited by the Medes; overthrew the Assyrian Empire in 612 B.C. in alliance with Babylonia; conquered by Cyrus the Great in 550 B.C.; corresponds to present-day NW Iran.

mediacy ('miːdɪəsɪ) NOUN [1] the quality or state of being mediate. [2] a less common word for **mediation.**

mediad ('miːdɪæd) ADJECTIVE *Anatomy, zoology* situated near the median line or plane of an organism.

mediaeval (ˌmɛdɪ'iːv^{ə}l) ADJECTIVE a variant spelling of **medieval.**

media event NOUN an event that is staged for or exploited by the mass media, whose attention lends it an apparent importance.

mediagenic (ˌmiːdɪə'dʒɛnɪk) ADJECTIVE presenting an attractive or sympathetic image when portrayed in the media.

medial ('miːdɪəl) ADJECTIVE [1] of or situated in the middle. [2] ordinary or average in size. [3] *Maths* relating to an average. [4] another word for **median** (senses 1, 2, 3). [5] *Zoology* of or relating to a media. ◆ NOUN [6] *Phonetics* a speech sound between being fortis and lenis; media.
▷HISTORY C16: from Late Latin *mediālis,* from *medius* middle
▸**'medially** ADVERB

median ('miːdɪən) ADJECTIVE [1] of, relating to, situated in, or directed towards the middle. [2] *Biology* of or relating to the plane that divides an organism or organ into symmetrical parts. [3] *Statistics* of or relating to the median. ◆ NOUN [4] a middle point, plane, or part. [5] *Geometry* **a** a straight line joining one vertex of a triangle to the midpoint of the opposite side. See also **centroid. b** a straight line joining the midpoints of the nonparallel sides of a trapezium. [6] *Statistics* the middle value in a frequency distribution, below and above which lie values with equal total frequencies. [7] *Statistics* the middle number or average of the two middle numbers in an ordered sequence of numbers: *7 is the median of both 1, 7, 31 and 2, 5, 9, 16.* [8] the Canadian word for **central reserve.**
▷HISTORY C16: from Latin *mediānus,* from *medius* middle
▸**'medianly** ADVERB

median lethal dose *or* **mean lethal dose** NOUN [1] the amount of a drug or other substance that, when administered to a group of experimental animals, will kill 50 per cent of the group in a specified time. [2] the amount of ionizing radiation that will kill 50 per cent of a population in a specified time. ◆ Abbreviation: $\mathbf{LD_{50}}$.

median strip NOUN the US term for **central reserve.**

mediant ('miːdɪənt) NOUN *Music* **a** the third degree of a major or minor scale. **b** *(as modifier)*: *a mediant chord.*
▷HISTORY C18: from Italian *mediante,* from Late Latin *mediāre* to be in the middle

mediastinum (ˌmiːdɪə'staɪnəm) NOUN, *plural* **-na** (-nə). *Anatomy* [1] a membrane between two parts of an organ or cavity such as the pleural tissue between the two lungs. [2] the part of the thoracic cavity that lies between the lungs, containing the heart, trachea, etc.
▷HISTORY C16: from medical Latin, neuter of Medieval Latin *mediastīnus* median, from Latin: low grade of servant, from *medius* mean
▸**ˌmedias'tinal** ADJECTIVE

mediate VERB ('miːdɪˌeɪt) [1] *(intr;* usually foll by *between* or *in)* to intervene (between parties or in a dispute) in order to bring about agreement. [2] to bring about (an agreement). [3] to bring about (an agreement) between parties in a dispute. [4] to resolve (differences) by mediation. [5] *(intr)* to be in a middle or intermediate position. [6] *(tr)* to serve as a medium for causing (a result) or transferring (objects, information, etc.). ◆ ADJECTIVE ('miːdɪɪt) [7] occurring as a result of or dependent upon mediation. [8] a rare word for **intermediate.** [9] *Logic* (of an inference) having more than one premise, esp, being syllogistic in form.
▷HISTORY C16: from Late Latin *mediāre* to be in the middle
▸**'mediately** ADVERB ▸**'mediateness** NOUN ▸**'mediative** *or* **'mediatory** *or* **ˌmedia'torial** ADJECTIVE ▸**'mediˌator** NOUN ▸**ˌmedia'torially** ADVERB

mediation (ˌmiːdɪ'eɪʃən) NOUN [1] the act of mediating; intercession. [2] *International law* an attempt to reconcile disputed matters arising between states, esp by the friendly intervention of a neutral power. [3] a method of resolving an industrial dispute whereby a third party consults with those involved and recommends a solution which is not, however, binding on the parties.

mediatize *or* **mediatise** ('miːdɪəˌtaɪz) VERB *(tr)* to annex (a state) to another state, allowing the former ruler to retain his title and some authority.
▷HISTORY C19: from French *médiatiser;* see MEDIATE, -IZE
▸**ˌmediati'zation** *or* **ˌmediati'sation** NOUN

medic^{1} ('mɛdɪk) NOUN *Informal* a doctor, medical orderly, or medical student.
▷HISTORY C17: from MEDICAL

medic^{2} ('mɛdɪk) NOUN the usual US spelling of **medick.**

medicable ('mɛdɪkəb^{ə}l) ADJECTIVE potentially able to be treated or cured medically.
▸**'medicably** ADVERB

Medicaid ('mɛdɪˌkeɪd) NOUN *US* a health assistance programme financed by federal, state, and local taxes to help pay hospital and medical costs for persons of low income.
▷HISTORY C20: MEDIC(AL) + AID

medical ('mɛdɪk^{ə}l) ADJECTIVE [1] of or relating to the science of medicine or to the treatment of patients by drugs, etc., as opposed to surgery. [2] a

less common word for **medicinal.** ◆ NOUN [3] *Informal* a medical examination.
▷HISTORY C17: from Medieval Latin *medicālis,* from Latin *medicus* physician, surgeon, from *medērī* to heal
▸'**medically** ADVERB

medical audit NOUN a review of the professional standards of doctors, usually within a hospital, conducted by a medical committee.

medical certificate NOUN [1] a document stating the result of a satisfactory medical examination. [2] a doctor's certificate giving evidence of a person's unfitness for work.

medical examination NOUN an examination carried out to determine the physical fitness of an applicant for a job, life insurance, etc.

medical examiner NOUN [1] *Chiefly US* a medical expert, usually a physician, employed by a state or local government to determine the cause of sudden death in cases of suspected violence, suicide, etc. Compare **coroner.** [2] a physician who carries out medical examinations.

medical jurisprudence NOUN another name for **forensic medicine.**

medical marker NOUN [1] a trait, condition, etc. that indicates the presence of, or a probable increased predisposition towards, a medical or psychological disorder. [2] a pen or an inklike substance used in medicine, for example to mark on a surgical patient the places where incisions are to be made.

medicament (mɪˈdɪkəmənt, ˈmɛdɪ-) NOUN a medicine or remedy in a specified formulation.
▷HISTORY C16: via French from Latin *medicāmentum,* from *medicāre* to cure
▸**medicamental** (ˌmɛdɪkəˈmɛntᵊl) *or* ˌ**medicaˈmentary** ADJECTIVE

Medicare (ˈmɛdɪˌkɛə) NOUN [1] (in the US) a federally sponsored health insurance programme for persons of 65 or older. [2] (*often not capital*) (in Canada) a similar programme covering all citizens. [3] (in Australia) a government-controlled general health-insurance scheme.
▷HISTORY C20: MEDI(CAL) + CARE

medicate (ˈmɛdɪˌkeɪt) VERB (*tr*) [1] to cover or impregnate (a wound, etc.) with an ointment, cream, etc. [2] to treat (a patient) with a medicine. [3] to add a medication to (a bandage, shampoo, etc.).
▷HISTORY C17: from Latin *medicāre* to heal
▸ˈ**medicative** ADJECTIVE

medicated ADJECTIVE [1] (of a patient) having been treated with a medicine or drug. [2] (of a bandage, shampoo, etc.) containing medication.

medication (ˌmɛdɪˈkeɪʃən) NOUN [1] treatment with drugs or remedies. [2] a drug or remedy.

Medicean (ˌmɛdɪˈsiːən, -ˈtʃiː-) ADJECTIVE of or relating to the Medici, the Italian family of bankers, merchants, and rulers of Florence and Tuscany, prominent in Italian political and cultural history in the 15th, 16th, and 17th centuries.

medicinal (mɛˈdɪsɪnᵊl) ADJECTIVE [1] relating to or having therapeutic properties. ◆ NOUN [2] a medicinal substance.
▸**meˈdicinally** ADVERB

medicinal leech NOUN a large European freshwater leech, *Hirudo medicinalis,* formerly used in medical bloodletting.

medicine (ˈmɛdɪsɪn, ˈmɛdsɪn) NOUN [1] any drug or remedy for use in treating, preventing, or alleviating the symptoms of disease. [2] the science of preventing, diagnosing, alleviating, or curing disease. [3] any nonsurgical branch of medical science. [4] the practice or profession of medicine: *he's in medicine.* Related adjectives: **Aesculapian, iatric.** [5] something regarded by primitive people as having magical or remedial properties. [6] **take one's medicine.** to accept a deserved punishment. [7] **a taste** (*or* **dose**) **of one's own medicine.** an unpleasant experience in retaliation for and by similar methods to an unkind or aggressive act.
▷HISTORY C13: via Old French from Latin *medicīna* (*ars*) (art of) healing, from *medicus* doctor, from *medērī* to heal

medicine ball NOUN a heavy ball used for physical training.

medicine chest NOUN a small chest or cupboard for storing medicines, bandages, etc.

medicine lodge NOUN a wooden structure used for magical and religious ceremonies among certain North American Indian peoples.

medicine man NOUN (among certain peoples, esp North American Indians) a person believed to have supernatural powers of healing; a magician or sorcerer.

medicine shop NOUN (in Malaysia) a Chinese chemist's shop where traditional herbs are sold as well as modern drugs. It is not, however, a dispensary for prescribed medicines.

medicine wheel NOUN a Native American ceremonial tool representing a sacred circle.

medick *or US* **medic** (ˈmɛdɪk) NOUN any small leguminous plant of the genus *Medicago,* such as black medick or sickle medick, having yellow or purple flowers and trifoliate leaves.
▷HISTORY C15: from Latin *mēdica,* from Greek *mēdikē* (*poa*) Median (grass), a type of clover

medico (ˈmɛdɪˌkəʊ) NOUN, *plural* **-cos.** a doctor or medical student.
▷HISTORY C17: via Italian from Latin *medicus*

medico- COMBINING FORM medical: *medicolegal.*

medieval *or* **mediaeval** (ˌmɛdɪˈiːvᵊl) ADJECTIVE [1] of, relating to, or in the style of the Middle Ages. [2] *Informal* old-fashioned; primitive.
▷HISTORY C19: from New Latin *medium aevum* the middle age. See MEDIUM, AGE
▸ˌ**mediˈevally** *or* ˌ**mediˈaevally** ADVERB

Medieval Greek NOUN the Greek language from the 7th century A.D. to shortly after the sacking of Constantinople in 1204. Also called: **Middle Greek, Byzantine Greek.** Compare **Koine, Late Greek, Ancient Greek.**

medievalism *or* **mediaevalism** (ˌmɛdɪˈiːvəˌlɪzəm) NOUN [1] the beliefs, life, or style of the Middle Ages or devotion to those. [2] a belief, custom, or point of style copied or surviving from the Middle Ages.

medievalist *or* **mediaevalist** (ˌmɛdɪˈiːvəlɪst) NOUN a student or devotee of the Middle Ages.
▸ˌ**mediˌevalˈistic** *or* ˌ**mediˌaevalˈistic** ADJECTIVE

Medieval Latin NOUN the Latin language as used throughout Europe in the Middle Ages. It had many local forms incorporating Latinized words from other languages.

medina (meˈdiːnə) NOUN (*sometimes capital*) the ancient quarter of any of various North African cities. Compare **kasbah.**
▷HISTORY C20: Arabic, literally: town

Medina (meˈdiːnə) NOUN a city in W Saudi Arabia: the second most holy city of Islam (after Mecca), with the tomb of Mohammed; university (1960). Pop.: 608 295 (1992). Arabic name: **Al Madinah.** Ancient Arabic name: **Yathrib.**

mediocre (ˌmiːdɪˈəʊkə, ˈmiːdɪˌəʊkə) ADJECTIVE *Often derogatory* average or ordinary in quality: *a mediocre book.*
▷HISTORY C16: via French from Latin *mediocris* moderate, literally: halfway up the mountain, from *medius* middle + *ocris* stony mountain

mediocrity (ˌmiːdɪˈɒkrɪtɪ, ˌmɛd-) NOUN, *plural* **-ties.** [1] the state or quality of being mediocre. [2] a mediocre person or thing.

meditate (ˈmɛdɪˌteɪt) VERB [1] (*intr;* foll by *on* or *upon*) to think about something deeply. [2] (*intr*) to reflect deeply on spiritual matters, esp as a religious act. [3] (*tr*) to plan, consider, or think of doing (something).
▷HISTORY C16: from Latin *meditārī* to reflect upon
▸ˈ**meditative** ADJECTIVE ▸ˈ**meditatively** ADVERB
▸ˈ**meditativeness** NOUN ▸ˈ**mediˌtator** NOUN

meditation (ˌmɛdɪˈteɪʃən) NOUN [1] the act of meditating; contemplation; reflection. [2] contemplation of spiritual matters, esp as a religious practice.

Mediterranean (ˌmɛdɪtəˈreɪnɪən) NOUN [1] short for the **Mediterranean Sea.** [2] a native or inhabitant of a Mediterranean country. ◆ ADJECTIVE [3] of, relating to, situated or dwelling on or near the Mediterranean Sea. [4] denoting a postulated subdivision of the Caucasoid race, characterized by slender build and dark complexion. [5] *Meteorol* (of a climate) characterized by hot summers and relatively warm winters when most of the annual rainfall occurs. [6] (*often not capital*) *Obsolete* situated in the middle of a landmass; inland.
▷HISTORY C16: from Latin *mediterrāneus,* from *medius* middle + *-terrāneus,* from *terra* land, earth

Mediterranean fever NOUN another name for **brucellosis.**

Mediterranean fruit fly NOUN a species of dipterous fly, *Ceratitis capitata,* having marbled wings, whose maggots tunnel into fruits such as citrus, peach, and vine in the Mediterranean area, South Africa, and elsewhere: family *Trypetidae.* Also called: **medfly.**

Mediterranean Sea NOUN a large inland sea between S Europe, N Africa, and SW Asia: linked with the Atlantic by the Strait of Gibraltar, with the Red Sea by the Suez Canal, and with the Black Sea by the Dardanelles, Sea of Marmara, and Bosporus; many ancient civilizations developed around its shores. Greatest depth: 4770 m (15 900 ft.). Length: (west to east) over 3700 km (2300 miles). Greatest width: about 1368 km (850 miles). Area: (excluding the Black Sea) 2 512 300 sq. km (970 000 sq. miles). Ancient name: **Mare Internum.**

medium (ˈmiːdɪəm) ADJECTIVE [1] midway between extremes; average: *a medium size.* [2] (of a colour) reflecting or transmitting a moderate amount of light: *a medium red.* Compare **light**[1] (sense 29), **dark** (sense 2). ◆ NOUN, *plural* **-dia** (-dɪə) *or* **-diums.** [3] an intermediate or middle state, degree, or condition; mean: *the happy medium.* [4] an intervening substance or agency for transmitting or producing an effect; vehicle: *air is a medium for sound.* [5] a means or agency for communicating or diffusing information, news, etc., to the public: *television is a powerful medium.* [6] a person supposedly used as a spiritual intermediary between the dead and the living. [7] the substance in which specimens of animals and plants are preserved or displayed. [8] *Biology* short for **culture medium.** [9] the substance or surroundings in which an organism naturally lives or grows. [10] *Art* **a** the category of a work of art, as determined by its materials and methods of production: *the medium of wood engraving.* **b** the materials used in a work of art. [11] any solvent in which pigments are mixed and thinned. [12] any one of various sizes of writing or printing paper, esp 18½ by 23½ inches or 17½ by 22 inches (**small medium**). ◆ See also **mediums.**
▷HISTORY C16: from Latin: neuter singular of *medius* middle

Language note See at **media.**

medium-dated ADJECTIVE (of a gilt-edged security) having between five and fifteen years to run before redemption. Compare **long-dated, short-dated.**

medium frequency NOUN a radio-frequency band or radio frequency lying between 3000 and 300 kilohertz. Abbreviation: **MF.**

mediumistic (ˌmiːdɪəˈmɪstɪk) ADJECTIVE of or relating to a spiritual medium.

medium of exchange NOUN anything acceptable as a measure of value and a standard of exchange for goods and services in a particular country, region, etc.

medium-range ballistic missile NOUN a missile that can carry a nuclear weapon with a range of 800 to 2400 km. Abbreviation: **MRBM.**

mediums (ˈmiːdɪəmz) PLURAL NOUN medium-dated gilt-edged securities.

medium wave NOUN **a** a radio wave with a wavelength between 100 and 1000 metres. **b** (*as modifier*): *a medium-wave broadcast.*

medivac (ˈmɛdɪˌvæk) NOUN, VERB **-vacs, -vacking, -vacked.** a variant spelling of **medevac.**

medlar (ˈmɛdlə) NOUN [1] a small Eurasian rosaceous tree, *Mespilus germanica.* [2] the fruit of this tree, which resembles the crab apple and is not edible until it has begun to decay. [3] any of several other rosaceous trees or their fruits.
▷HISTORY C14: from Old French *medlier,* from Latin *mespilum* medlar fruit, from Greek *mespilon*

medley (ˈmɛdlɪ) NOUN [1] a mixture of various types or elements. [2] a musical composition consisting of various tunes arranged as a continuous whole. [3] Also called: **medley relay. a**

Swimming a race in which a different stroke is used for each length. **b** *Athletics* a relay race in which each leg has a different distance. [4] an archaic word for **melee.** ♦ ADJECTIVE [5] of, being, or relating to a mixture or variety.
▷HISTORY C14: from Old French *medlee,* from *medler* to mix, quarrel

Médoc (meɪ'dɒk, 'mɛdɒk; *French* medɔk) NOUN [1] a district of SW France, on the left bank of the Gironde estuary: famous vineyards. [2] a fine red wine from this district.

medrese (mə'drɛseɪ) NOUN a variant of **madrasah.**

medulla (mɪ'dʌlə) NOUN, *plural* **-las** *or* **-lae** (-liː). [1] *Anatomy* **a** the innermost part of an organ or structure. **b** short for **medulla oblongata.** [2] *Botany* another name for **pith** (sense 4).
▷HISTORY C17: from Latin: marrow, pith, probably from *medius* middle
▸**me'dullary** *or* **me'dullar** ADJECTIVE

medulla oblongata (ˌɒblɒŋ'gɑːtə) NOUN, *plural* **medulla oblongatas** *or* **medullae oblongatae** (mɪ'dʌliː ˌɒblɒŋ'gɑːtiː). the lower stalklike section of the brain, continuous with the spinal cord, containing control centres for the heart and lungs.
▷HISTORY C17: New Latin: oblong-shaped medulla

medullary ray NOUN any of the sheets of conducting tissue that run radially through the vascular tissue of some higher plants.

medullary sheath NOUN [1] *Anatomy* a myelin layer surrounding and insulating certain nerve fibres. [2] a layer of thick-walled cells surrounding the pith of the stems of some higher plants.

medullated ('mɛdəˌleɪtɪd, mɪ'dʌl-) ADJECTIVE [1] *Anatomy* encased in a myelin sheath. [2] having a medulla.

medulloblastoma (mɪˌdʌləʊblæs'təʊmə) NOUN a rapidly growing brain tumour that develops in children and is responsive to radiotherapy.

medusa (mɪ'djuːzə) NOUN, *plural* **-sas** *or* **-sae** (-ziː). [1] another name for **jellyfish** (senses 1, 2). [2] one of the two forms in which a coelenterate exists. It has a jelly-like umbrella-shaped body, is free swimming, and produces gametes. Also called: **medusoid, medusan.** Compare **polyp.**
▷HISTORY C18: from the likeness of its tentacles to the snaky locks of Medusa
▸**me'dusan** ADJECTIVE

Medusa (mɪ'djuːzə) NOUN *Greek myth* a mortal woman who was transformed by Athena into one of the three Gorgons. Her appearance was so hideous that those who looked directly at her were turned to stone. Perseus eventually slew her. See also **Pegasus**[1].
▸**Me'dusan** ADJECTIVE

medusoid (mɪ'djuːzɔɪd) ADJECTIVE [1] of, relating to, or resembling a medusa. ♦ NOUN [2] another name for **medusa** (sense 2).

Medway ('mɛdˌweɪ) NOUN [1] a river in SE England, flowing through Kent and the **Medway towns** (Rochester, Chatham, and Gillingham) to the Thames estuary. Length: 110 km (70 miles). [2] a unitary authority in SE England, in Kent. Pop.: 249 502 (2001). Area: 204 sq. km (79 sq. miles).

mee (miː) NOUN (in Malaysia) noodles or a dish containing noodles.
▷HISTORY from Chinese (Cantonese) *mien* noodles

Meech Lake Accord (miːtʃ) NOUN the agreement reached in 1987 at Meech Lake, Quebec, at a Canadian federal-provincial conference that accepted Quebec's conditions for signing the Constitution Act of 1982. The Accord lapsed when the legislatures of two provinces, Newfoundland and Quebec, failed to ratify it by the deadline of June 23, 1990.

meed (miːd) NOUN *Archaic* a recompense; reward.
▷HISTORY Old English: wages; compare Old High German *mēta* pay

meek (miːk) ADJECTIVE [1] patient, long-suffering, or submissive in disposition or nature; humble. [2] spineless or spiritless; compliant. [3] an obsolete word for **gentle.**
▷HISTORY C12: related to Old Norse *mjūkr* amenable; compare Welsh *mwytho* to soften
▸**'meekly** ADVERB ▸**'meekness** NOUN

meerkat ('mɪəˌkæt) NOUN any of several South African mongooses, esp *Suricata suricatta* (**slender-tailed meerkat** or **suricate**), which has a lemur-like face and four-toed feet.
▷HISTORY C19: from Dutch: sea-cat

meerschaum ('mɪəʃəm) NOUN [1] Also called: **sepiolite.** a white, yellowish, or pink compact earthy mineral consisting of hydrated magnesium silicate: used to make tobacco pipes and as a building stone. Formula: $Mg_2Si_3O_6(OH)_4$. [2] a tobacco pipe having a bowl made of this mineral.
▷HISTORY C18: German, literally: sea foam

Meerut ('mɪərət) NOUN an industrial city in N India, in W Uttar Pradesh: founded as a military base by the British in 1806 and scene of the first uprising (1857) of the Indian Mutiny. Pop.: 753 778 (1991).

meet[1] (miːt) VERB **meets, meeting, met.** [1] (sometimes foll by *up* or (*US*) *with*) to come together (with), either by design or by accident; encounter: *I met him unexpectedly; we met at the station.* [2] to come into or be in conjunction or contact with (something or each other): *the roads meet in the town; the sea meets the sky.* [3] (*tr*) to come to or be at the place of arrival of: *to meet a train.* [4] to make the acquaintance of or be introduced to (someone or each other): *have you two met?* [5] to gather in the company of (someone or each other): *the board of directors meets on Tuesday.* [6] to come into the presence of (someone or each other) as opponents: *Joe meets Fred in the boxing match.* [7] (*tr*) to cope with effectively; satisfy: *to meet someone's demands.* [8] (*tr*) to be apparent to (esp in the phrase **meet the eye**). [9] (*tr*) to return or counter: *to meet a blow with another.* [10] to agree with (someone or each other): *we met him on the price he suggested.* [11] (*tr;* sometimes foll by *with*) to experience; suffer: *he met his death in a road accident.* [12] to occur together: *courage and kindliness met in him.* [13] (*tr*) *Caribbean* to find (a person, situation, etc.) in a specified condition: *I met the door open.* [14] **meet and greet.** (of a celebrity, politician, etc.) to have a session of being introduced to and questioned by members of the public or journalists. ♦ NOUN [15] the assembly of hounds, huntsmen, etc., prior to a hunt. [16] a meeting, esp a sports meeting. [17] *US* the place where the paths of two railway trains meet or cross. [18] **meet-and-greet.** a session where a celebrity, etc., is introduced to or questioned by members of the public or journalists.
▷HISTORY Old English *mētan;* related to Old Norse *mǿta,* Old Saxon *mōtian*
▸**'meeter** NOUN

meet[2] (miːt) ADJECTIVE *Archaic* proper, fitting, or correct.
▷HISTORY C13: from variant of Old English *gemǣte;* related to Old High German *māza* suitability, Old Norse *mætr* valuable
▸**'meetly** ADVERB

meeting ('miːtɪŋ) NOUN [1] an act of coming together; encounter. [2] an assembly or gathering. [3] a conjunction or union. [4] a sporting competition, as of athletes, or of horse racing.

meeting house NOUN [1] the place in which certain religious groups, esp Quakers, hold their meetings for worship. [2] Also called: **wharepuni.** *NZ* a large Maori tribal hall.

meff (mɛf) NOUN *Northern English dialect* [1] a tramp. [2] a stupid or worthless person.

mefloquine ('mɛfləʊˌkwiːn) NOUN a synthetic drug administered orally to prevent or treat malaria.
▷HISTORY C20

meg (mɛg) NOUN *Informal* short for **megabyte.**

mega ('mɛgə) ADJECTIVE *Slang* extremely good, great, or successful.
▷HISTORY C20: probably independent use of MEGA-

mega- COMBINING FORM [1] denoting 10^6: *megawatt.* Symbol: M. [2] (in computer technology) denoting 2^{20} (1 048 576): *megabyte.* [3] large or great: *megalith.* [4] *Informal* great in importance or amount: *megastar.*
▷HISTORY from Greek *megas* huge, powerful

megabit ('mɛgəˌbɪt) NOUN *Computing* [1] one million bits. [2] 2^{20} bits.

megabuck ('mɛgəˌbʌk) NOUN *US and Canadian, slang* **a** a million dollars. **b** (*as modifier*): *a megabuck movie.*

megabyte ('mɛgəˌbaɪt) NOUN *Computing* 2^{20} or 1 048 576 bytes. Abbreviations: **MB, mbyte.** See also **mega-** (sense 2).

megacephaly (ˌmɛgə'sɛfəlɪ) *or* **megalocephaly** NOUN the condition of having an unusually large head or cranial capacity. It can be of congenital origin or result from an abnormal overgrowth of the facial bones. Compare **microcephaly.**
▸**megacephalic** (ˌmɛgəsɪ'fælɪk), ˌ**mega'cephalous** *or* ˌ**megaloce'phalic** *or* ˌ**megalo'cephalous** ADJECTIVE

megacity ('mɛgəˌsɪtɪ) NOUN, *plural* **-cities.** a city with over 10 million inhabitants.

megadeath ('mɛgəˌdɛθ) NOUN the death of a million people, esp in a nuclear war or attack.

megadose ('mɛgəˌdəʊs) NOUN a very large dose, as of a medicine, vitamin, etc.

Megaera (mɪ'dʒɪərə) NOUN *Greek myth* one of the three Furies; the others are Alecto and Tisiphone.

megafauna ('mɛgəˌfɔːnə) NOUN the component of the fauna of a region or period that comprises the larger terrestrial animals.

megaflop ('mɛgəˌflɒp) NOUN *Computing* a measure of processing speed, consisting of a million floating-point operations a second.
▷HISTORY C20: from MEGA- + *flo(ating) p(oint)*

megagamete (ˌmɛgə'gæmiːt) NOUN another name for **macrogamete.**

megahertz ('mɛgəˌhɜːts) NOUN, *plural* **-hertz.** one million hertz; one million cycles per second. Symbol: MHz. Former name: **megacycle.**

megalith ('mɛgəlɪθ) NOUN a stone of great size, esp one forming part of a prehistoric monument. See also **alignment** (sense 6), **circle** (sense 11).
▸ˌ**mega'lithic** ADJECTIVE

megalithic tomb NOUN a burial chamber constructed of large stones, either underground or covered by a mound and usually consisting of long transepted corridors (**gallery graves**) or of a distinct chamber and passage (**passage graves**). The tombs may date from the 4th millennium B.C.

megalo- *or before a vowel* **megal-** COMBINING FORM indicating greatness, or abnormal size: *megalopolis; megaloblast.*
▷HISTORY from Greek *megas* great

megaloblast ('mɛgələʊˌblɑːst) NOUN an abnormally large red blood cell precursor, present in certain types of anaemia.
▸**megaloblastic** (ˌmɛgələʊ'blæstɪk) ADJECTIVE

megaloblastic anaemia NOUN any anaemia, esp pernicious anaemia, characterized by the presence of megaloblasts in the blood or bone marrow.

megalocardia (ˌmɛgələʊ'kɑːdɪə) NOUN *Pathol* abnormal increase in the size of the heart. Also called: **cardiomegaly.**

megalocephaly (ˌmɛgələʊ'sɛfəlɪ) NOUN another word for **megacephaly.**

megalomania (ˌmɛgələʊ'meɪnɪə) NOUN [1] a mental illness characterized by delusions of grandeur, power, wealth, etc. [2] *Informal* a lust or craving for power.
▸ˌ**megalo'maniac** ADJECTIVE, NOUN ▸**megalomaniacal** (ˌmɛgələʊmə'naɪək[ə]l) ADJECTIVE

megalopolis (ˌmɛgə'lɒpəlɪs) NOUN an urban complex, usually comprising several large towns.
▷HISTORY C20: MEGALO- + Greek *polis* city
▸**megalopolitan** (ˌmɛgələ'pɒlɪt[ə]n) ADJECTIVE, NOUN

megalosaur ('mɛgələʊˌsɔː) NOUN any very large Jurassic or Cretaceous bipedal carnivorous dinosaur of the genus *Megalosaurus,* common in Europe: suborder *Theropoda* (theropods).
▷HISTORY C19: from New Latin *megalosaurus,* from MEGALO- + Greek *sauros* lizard
▸ˌ**megalo'saurian** ADJECTIVE, NOUN

megaphanerophyte (ˌmɛgə'fænərəʊˌfaɪt) NOUN *Botany* any tree with a height over 30 metres.

megaphone ('mɛgəˌfəʊn) NOUN a funnel-shaped instrument used to amplify the voice. See also **loud-hailer.**
▸**megaphonic** (ˌmɛgə'fɒnɪk) ADJECTIVE
▸ˌ**mega'phonically** ADVERB

megaphyll ('mɛgəfɪl) NOUN *Botany* the relatively large type of leaf produced by ferns and seed plants. Compare **microphyll.**

megaplex ('mɛgəˌplɛks) NOUN **a** a cinema complex containing a large number of separate screens, and usually a restaurant or bar. **b** (*as modifier*): *a megaplex cinema.*

megapode ('mɛgəˌpəʊd) NOUN any ground-living gallinaceous bird of the family *Megapodiidae,* of Australia, New Guinea, and adjacent islands. Their eggs incubate in mounds of sand, rotting vegetation, etc., by natural heat. Also called: **mound-builder.** See also **brush turkey, mallee fowl.**

Megara ('mɛgərə) NOUN a town in E central Greece: an ancient trading city, founding many colonies in the 7th and 8th centuries B.C. Pop.: 26 562 (1991 est.).

megaron ('mɛgəˌrɒn) NOUN, *plural* **-ra** (-rə). a tripartite rectangular room containing a central hearth surrounded by four pillars, found in Bronze Age Greece and Asia Minor.
▷HISTORY from Greek, literally: hall, from *megas* large

megascopic (ˌmɛgə'skɒpɪk) ADJECTIVE another word for **macroscopic.**

megasporangium (ˌmɛgəspɔː'rændʒɪəm) NOUN, *plural* **-gia** (-dʒɪə). the structure in certain spore-bearing plants in which the megaspores are formed: corresponds to the ovule in seed plants. Compare **microsporangium.**

megaspore ('mɛgəˌspɔː) NOUN [1] Also called: **macrospore.** the larger of the two types of spore produced by some spore-bearing plants, which develops into the female gametophyte. Compare **microspore** (sense 1). [2] the cell in flowering plants that gives rise to the embryo sac.
▸ˌ**mega'sporic** ADJECTIVE

megasporophyll (ˌmɛgə'spɔːrəfɪl) NOUN a leaf on which the megaspores are formed: corresponds to the carpel of a flowering plant. Compare **microsporophyll.**
▷HISTORY C20: from MEGA- + SPOROPHYLL

megass *or* **megasse** (mə'gæs) NOUN another name for **bagasse** (sense 2).
▷HISTORY C19: of obscure origin

megastar ('mɛgəˌstɑː) NOUN a very well-known personality in the entertainment business.

megathere ('mɛgəˌθɪə) NOUN any of various gigantic extinct American sloths of the genus *Megatherium* and related genera, common in late Cenozoic times.
▷HISTORY C19: from New Latin *megathērium,* from MEGA- + *-there,* from Greek *thērion* wild beast
▸ˌ**mega'therian** ADJECTIVE

megaton ('mɛgəˌtʌn) NOUN [1] one million tons. [2] an explosive power, esp of a nuclear weapon, equal to the power of one million tons of TNT. Abbreviation: **mt.**
▸**megatonic** (ˌmɛgə'tɒnɪk) ADJECTIVE

megavolt ('mɛgəˌvɒlt) NOUN one million volts. Symbol: MV.

megawatt ('mɛgəˌwɒt) NOUN one million watts. Symbol: MW.

Me generation NOUN the generation, originally in the 1970s, characterized by self-absorption; in the 1980s, characterized by material greed.

Megger ('mɛgə) NOUN *Trademark* an instrument that generates a high voltage in order to test the resistance of insulation, etc.

Meghalaya (ˌmeɪgə'leɪə) NOUN a state of NE India, created in 1969 from part of Assam. Capital: Shillong. Pop.: 2 306 069 (2001). Area: 22 429 sq. km (7800 sq. miles).

Megiddo (mə'gɪdəʊ) NOUN an ancient town in N Palestine, strategically located on a route linking Egypt to Mesopotamia: site of many battles, including an important Egyptian victory over rebel chieftains in 1469 or 1468 B.C. See also **Armageddon.**

megillah (mə'gɪlə; *Hebrew* migi'la) NOUN, *plural* **-lahs** *or* **-loth** (*Hebrew* -'lɔt). *Judaism* [1] a scroll of the Book of Esther, read on the festival of Purim. [2] a scroll of the Book of Ruth, Song of Songs, Lamentations, or Ecclesiastes. [3] *Slang* anything, such as a story or letter, that is too long or unduly drawn out.
▷HISTORY Hebrew: scroll, from *galal* to roll

megilp *or* **magilp** (mə'gɪlp) NOUN an oil-painting medium of linseed oil mixed with mastic varnish or turpentine.
▷HISTORY C18: of unknown origin

megohm ('mɛgˌəʊm) NOUN one million ohms. Symbol: MΩ.

megrim[1] ('miːgrɪm) NOUN *Archaic* [1] (*often plural*) a caprice. [2] a migraine.
▷HISTORY C14: see MIGRAINE

megrim[2] ('miːgrɪm) NOUN a flatfish, *Lepidorhombus whiffiagonis,* of the turbot family, having a yellowish translucent body up to 50 cm (20 in.) in length, found in European waters, and caught for food.
▷HISTORY C19: of uncertain origin

megrims ('miːgrɪmz) NOUN (*functioning as singular*) [1] *Archaic* a fit of depression. [2] *Archaic* a disease of horses and cattle; staggers.

mehndi ('mendiː) NOUN (esp in India) the practice of painting designs on the hands, feet, etc. using henna.
▷HISTORY C20: from Hindi

meibomian cyst (maɪ'bəʊmɪən) NOUN another name for **chalazion.**
▷HISTORY C19: named after H. *Meibom* (1638–1700), German anatomist

meibomian gland NOUN any of the small sebaceous glands in the eyelid, beneath the conjunctiva.

meiny *or* **meinie** ('meɪnɪ) NOUN, *plural* **meinies.** *Obsolete* [1] a retinue or household. [2] *Scot* a crowd.
▷HISTORY C13: from Old French *mesnie,* from Vulgar Latin *mansiōnāta* (unattested), from Latin *mansiō* a lodging; see MANSION

meiocyte ('maɪəʊˌsaɪt) NOUN *Botany* a cell that divides by meiosis to produce four haploid spores (**meiospores**).

meiofauna ('maɪəʊˌfɔːnə) NOUN the component of the fauna of a sea or lake bed comprising small (but not microscopic) animals, such as tiny worms and crustaceans.
▷HISTORY C20: from Greek *meiōn* less + FAUNA
▸ˌ**meio'faunal** ADJECTIVE

meiosis (maɪ'əʊsɪs) NOUN, *plural* **-ses** (-ˌsiːz). [1] a type of cell division in which a nucleus divides into four daughter nuclei, each containing half the chromosome number of the parent nucleus: occurs in all sexually reproducing organisms in which haploid gametes or spores are produced. Compare **mitosis.** See also **prophase** (sense 2). [2] *Rhetoric* another word for **litotes.**
▷HISTORY C16: via New Latin from Greek: a lessening, from *meioun* to diminish, from *meiōn* less
▸**meiotic** (maɪ'ɒtɪk) ADJECTIVE ▸**mei'otically** ADVERB

Meissen (*German* 'maisən) NOUN a town in E Germany, in Saxony, in Dresden district on the River Elbe: famous for its porcelain (Dresden china), first made here in 1710. Pop.: 38 100 (latest est.).

Meissner effect ('maɪsnə) NOUN *Physics* the phenomenon in which magnetic flux is excluded from a substance when it is in a superconducting state, except for a thin layer at the surface.
▷HISTORY C20: named after Fritz Walther *Meissner* (1882–1974), German physicist

-meister ('maɪstə) NOUN COMBINING FORM a person who excels at a particular activity: *spinmeister; horror-meister.*
▷HISTORY C20: from German *Meister* master

Meistersinger ('maɪstəˌsɪŋə) NOUN, *plural* **-singer** *or* **-singers.** a member of one of the various German guilds of workers or craftsmen organized to compose and perform poetry and music. These flourished in the 15th and 16th centuries.
▷HISTORY C19: German: master singer

meitnerium ('maɪtnɪərɪəm) NOUN a synthetic element produced in small quantities by high-energy ion bombardment. Symbol: Mt; atomic no.: 109.
▷HISTORY C20: named after Lise *Meitner* (1878–1968), Austrian nuclear physicist

Méjico ('mɛxiko) NOUN the Spanish name for **Mexico.**

Mekka ('mɛkə) NOUN a variant spelling of **Mecca.**

Meknès (mɛk'nɛs) NOUN a city in N central Morocco, in the Middle Atlas Mountains: noted for the making of carpets. Pop.: 188 224 (1994).

Mekong (ˌmiː'kɒŋ) NOUN a river in SE Asia, rising in SW China in Qinghai province: flows southeast forming the border between Laos and Myanmar, and part of the border between Laos and Thailand, then continues south across Cambodia and Vietnam to the South China Sea by an extensive delta, one of the greatest rice-growing areas in Asia. Length: about 4025 km (2500 miles).

mel (mɛl) NOUN *Pharmacol* a pure form of honey formerly used in pharmaceutical products.
▷HISTORY from Latin

mela ('miːlə, 'mɛlə) NOUN an Asian cultural or religious fair or festival.
▷HISTORY C19: Hindi, from Sanskrit *mēlā* an assembly, from *mil* to meet

melaleuca (ˌmɛlə'luːkə) NOUN any shrub or tree of the mostly Australian myrtaceous genus *Melaleuca,* found in sandy or swampy regions.
▷HISTORY C19: New Latin, from Greek *melas* black + *leukos* white, from its black trunk and white branches

melamine ('mɛləˌmiːn) NOUN [1] a colourless crystalline compound used in making synthetic resins; 2,4,6-triamino-1,3,5-triazine. Formula: $C_3H_6N_6$. [2] melamine resin or a material made from this resin.
▷HISTORY C19: from German *Melamin,* from *Melam* distillate of ammonium thiocyanate, with *-am* representing *ammonia*

melamine resin NOUN a thermosetting amino resin, stable to heat and light, produced from melamine and used for moulded products, adhesives, and surface coatings.

melancholia (ˌmɛlən'kəʊlɪə) NOUN a former name for **depression.**
▸ˌ**melan'choliˌac** ADJECTIVE, NOUN

melancholic (ˌmɛlən'kɒlɪk) ADJECTIVE [1] relating to or suffering from melancholy or melancholia. ◆ NOUN [2] a person who suffers from melancholia.
▸ˌ**melan'cholically** ADVERB

melancholy ('mɛlənkəlɪ) NOUN, *plural* **-cholies.** [1] a constitutional tendency to gloominess or depression. [2] a sad thoughtful state of mind; pensiveness. [3] *Archaic* **a** a gloomy character, thought to be caused by too much black bile. **b** one of the four bodily humours; black bile. See **humour** (sense 8). ◆ ADJECTIVE [4] characterized by, causing, or expressing sadness, dejection, etc.
▷HISTORY C14: via Old French from Late Latin *melancholia,* from Greek *melankholia,* from *melas* black + *kholē* bile
▸**melancholily** ('mɛlənˌkɒlɪlɪ) ADVERB ▸'**melanˌcholiness** NOUN

Melanesia (ˌmɛlə'niːzɪə) NOUN one of the three divisions of islands in the Pacific (the others being Micronesia and Polynesia); the SW division of Oceania: includes Fiji, New Caledonia, Vanuatu, the Bismarck Archipelago, and the Louisiade, Solomon, Santa Cruz, and Loyalty Islands, which all lie northeast of Australia.
▷HISTORY C19: from Greek *melas* black + *nēsos* island; with reference to the dark skins of the inhabitants; on the model of *Polynesia*

Melanesian (ˌmɛlə'niːzɪən) ADJECTIVE [1] of or relating to Melanesia, its people, or their languages. ◆ NOUN [2] a native or inhabitant of Melanesia: generally Negroid with frizzy hair and small stature. [3] a group or branch of languages spoken in Melanesia, belonging to the Malayo-Polynesian family. [4] See also **Neo-Melanesian.**

melange *or* **mélange** (meɪ'lɑːnʒ) NOUN [1] a mixture; confusion. [2] *Geology* a totally disordered mixture of rocks of different shapes, sizes, ages, and origins.
▷HISTORY C17: from French *mêler* to mix. See MEDLEY

melanic (mə'lænɪk) ADJECTIVE relating to melanism or melanosis.

melanin ('mɛlənɪn) NOUN any of a group of black or dark brown pigments present in the hair, skin, and eyes of man and animals: produced in excess in certain skin diseases and in melanomas.

melanism ('mɛləˌnɪzəm) NOUN [1] the condition in man and animals of having dark-coloured or black skin, feathers, etc. **Industrial melanism** is the occurrence of dark varieties of animals, esp moths, in smoke-blackened industrial regions, in which they are well camouflaged. [2] another name for **melanosis.**
▸ˌ**mela'nistic** ADJECTIVE

melanite ('mɛləˌnaɪt) NOUN a black variety of andradite garnet.

melano- *or before a vowel* **melan-** COMBINING FORM

black or dark: *melanin; melanism; melanocyte; melanoma.*
▷**HISTORY** from Greek *melas* black

Melanochroi (ˌmɛləˈnɒkrəʊˌaɪ) PLURAL NOUN a postulated subdivision of the Caucasoid race, characterized by dark hair and pale complexion.
▷**HISTORY** C19: New Latin (coined by T. H. Huxley), from Greek, from *melas* dark + *ōchros* pale
▸**Melanochroid** (ˌmɛləˈnɒkrɔɪd) ADJECTIVE

melanocyte (ˈmɛlənəʊˌsaɪt) NOUN *Anatomy, zoology* a cell, usually in the epidermis, that contains melanin.

melanoid (ˈmɛləˌnɔɪd) ADJECTIVE 1 resembling melanin; dark coloured. 2 characterized by or resembling melanosis.

melanoma (ˌmɛləˈnəʊmə) NOUN, *plural* **-mas** *or* **-mata** (-mətə). *Pathol* a malignant tumour composed of melanocytes, occurring esp in the skin, often as a result of excessive exposure to sunlight.

melanosis (ˌmɛləˈnəʊsɪs) *or* **melanism** (ˈmɛləˌnɪzəm) NOUN *Pathol* a skin condition characterized by excessive deposits of melanin.
▸**melanotic** (ˌmɛləˈnɒtɪk) ADJECTIVE

melanous (ˈmɛlənəs) ADJECTIVE having a dark complexion and black hair.
▸**melanosity** (ˌmɛləˈnɒsɪtɪ) NOUN

melaphyre (ˈmɛləˌfaɪə) NOUN *Geology, obsolete* a type of weathered amygdaloidal basalt or andesite.
▷**HISTORY** C19: via French from Greek *melas* black + *(por)phura* purple

melatonin (ˌmɛləˈtəʊnɪn) NOUN the hormone-like secretion of the pineal gland, causing skin colour changes in some animals and thought to be involved in reproductive function.
▷**HISTORY** C20: probably from MELA(NOCYTE) + (SERO)TONIN

Melba (ˈmɛlbə) NOUN **do a Melba.** *Austral, slang* to make repeated farewell appearances.
▷**HISTORY** from Dame Nellie *Melba*, stage name of Helen Porter Mitchell (1861–1931), Australian operatic soprano

Melba sauce NOUN a sweet sauce made from fresh raspberries and served with peach melba, fruit sundaes, etc.
▷**HISTORY** C20: named after Dame Nellie *Melba*, stage name of Helen Porter Mitchell (1861–1931), Australian operatic soprano

Melba toast NOUN very thin crisp toast.
▷**HISTORY** C20: named after Dame Nellie *Melba*, stage name of Helen Porter Mitchell (1861–1931), Australian operatic soprano

Melbourne (ˈmɛlbən) NOUN a port in SE Australia, capital of Victoria, on Port Phillip Bay: the second largest city in the country; settled in 1835 and developed rapidly with the discovery of rich goldfields in 1851; three universities. Pop.: 2 865 329 (1998 est.).

Melburnian (mɛlˈbɜːnɪən) NOUN 1 a native or inhabitant of Melbourne. ◆ ADJECTIVE 2 of or relating to Melbourne or its inhabitants.

Melchite (ˈmɛlkaɪt) *Eastern Churches* ◆ ADJECTIVE 1 of or relating to the Uniat Greek Catholic Church in Syria, Egypt, and Israel. ◆ NOUN 2 a member of this Church.
▷**HISTORY** C17: from Church Latin *Melchīta*, from Medieval Greek *Melkhītēs*, literally: royalist, from Syriac *malkā* king

Melchizedek (mɛlˈkɪzəˌdɛk) NOUN *Old Testament* the priest-king of Salem who blessed Abraham (Genesis 14:18-19) and was taken as a prototype of Christ's priesthood (Hebrews 7). Douay spelling: **Melchisedech.**

meld[1] (mɛld) VERB 1 (in some card games) to declare or lay down (cards), which then score points. ◆ NOUN 2 the act of melding. 3 a set of cards for melding.
▷**HISTORY** C19: from German *melden* to announce; related to Old English *meldian*

meld[2] (mɛld) VERB to blend or become blended; combine.
▷**HISTORY** C20: blend of MELT + WELD[1]

Meldrew (ˈmɛldruː) NOUN *Informal* a person, esp a middle-aged or elderly man, who is habitually peevish, pessimistic, and cynical; curmudgeon.
▷**HISTORY** C20: named after Victor *Meldrew*, curmudgeonly hero of the 1990s BBC television situation comedy *One Foot in the Grave*, written by David Renwick
▸ˈ**Meldrewish** ADJECTIVE

Meleager (ˌmɛlɪˈeɪgə) NOUN *Greek myth* one of the Argonauts, slayer of the Calydonian boar.

melee *or* **mêlée** (ˈmɛleɪ) NOUN a noisy riotous fight or brawl.
▷**HISTORY** C17: from French *mêlée*. See MEDLEY

meliaceous (ˌmiːlɪˈeɪʃəs) ADJECTIVE of, relating to, or belonging to the *Meliaceae*, a family of tropical and subtropical trees, including mahogany, some of which yield valuable timber.
▷**HISTORY** C19: from New Latin *Melia* type genus, from Greek: ash

melic (ˈmɛlɪk) ADJECTIVE (of poetry, esp ancient Greek lyric poems) intended to be sung.
▷**HISTORY** C17: via Latin from Greek *melikos*, from *melos* song

melick (ˈmɛlɪk) NOUN either of two pale green perennial grasses of the genus *Melica*, related to fescue, esp **wood melick** (*M. uniflora*) having branching flower heads, that are common in woodlands.
▷**HISTORY** New Latin *melica*, of unknown origin

Melilla (*French* melija) NOUN the chief town of a Spanish enclave in Morocco, on the Mediterranean coast: founded by the Phoenicians; exports iron ore. Pop.: 59 576 (1996 est.).

melilot (ˈmɛlɪˌlɒt) NOUN any leguminous plant of the Old World genus *Melilotus*, having narrow clusters of small white or yellow fragrant flowers. Also called: **sweet clover.**
▷**HISTORY** C15: via Old French from Latin *melilōtos*, from Greek: sweet clover, from *meli* honey + *lōtos* LOTUS

melinite (ˈmɛlɪˌnaɪt) NOUN a high explosive made from picric acid.
▷**HISTORY** C19: via French from Greek *mēlinos* (colour) of a quince, from *mēlon* fruit, quince

meliorate (ˈmiːlɪəˌreɪt) VERB a variant of **ameliorate.**
▸ˈ**meliorable** ADJECTIVE ▸**meliorative** (ˈmiːlɪərətɪv) ADJECTIVE, NOUN ▸ˈ**melioˌrator** NOUN

melioration (ˌmiːlɪəˈreɪʃən) NOUN the act or an instance of improving or the state of being improved.

meliorism (ˈmiːlɪəˌrɪzəm) NOUN the notion that the world can be improved by human effort.
▷**HISTORY** C19: from Latin *melior* better
▸ˈ**meliorist** ADJECTIVE, NOUN ▸ˌ**melioˈristic** ADJECTIVE

melisma (mɪˈlɪzmə) NOUN, *plural* **-mata** (-mətə) *or* **-mas.** *Music* an expressive vocal phrase or passage consisting of several notes sung to one syllable.
▷**HISTORY** C19: from Greek: melody
▸**melismatic** (ˌmɛlɪzˈmætɪk) ADJECTIVE

Melitopol (*Russian* mɪliˈtɔpəlj) NOUN a city in the SE Ukraine. Pop.: 171 000 (1998 est.).

Melk (mɛlk) NOUN a town in N Austria, on the River Danube: noted for its baroque Benedictine abbey. Pop.: 5163 (1991).

melliferous (mɪˈlɪfərəs) *or* **mellific** (mɪˈlɪfɪk) ADJECTIVE forming or producing honey.
▷**HISTORY** C17: from Latin *mellifer*, from *mel* honey + *ferre* to bear

mellifluous (mɪˈlɪfluəs) *or* **mellifluent** ADJECTIVE (of sounds or utterances) smooth or honeyed; sweet.
▷**HISTORY** C15: from Late Latin *mellifluus* flowing with honey, from Latin *mel* honey + *fluere* to flow
▸**melˈlifluously** *or* **melˈlifluently** ADVERB ▸**melˈlifluousness** *or* **melˈlifluence** NOUN

melliphagous (mɪˈlɪfəgəs) *or* **mellivorous** (mɪˈlɪvərəs) ADJECTIVE *Zoology* (of an animal) feeding on honey.
▷**HISTORY** C19: from Latin *mel* honey + Greek *-phagos*, from *phagein* to consume

mellophone (ˈmɛləˌfəʊn) NOUN *Music* a brass band instrument similar in tone to a French horn.
▷**HISTORY** C20: from MELLOW + -PHONE

mellow (ˈmɛləʊ) ADJECTIVE 1 (esp of fruits) full-flavoured; sweet; ripe. 2 (esp of wines) well-matured. 3 (esp of colours or sounds) soft or rich. 4 kind-hearted, esp through maturity or old age. 5 genial, as through the effects of alcohol. 6 (of soil) soft and loamy. ◆ VERB 7 to make or become mellow; soften; mature. 8 (foll by *out*) to become calm and relaxed or (esp of a drug) to have a calming or relaxing effect on (someone).
▷**HISTORY** C15: perhaps from Old English *meru* soft (as through ripeness)
▸ˈ**mellowly** ADVERB ▸ˈ**mellowness** NOUN

melodeon *or* **melodion** (mɪˈləʊdɪən) NOUN *Music* 1 a type of small accordion. 2 a type of keyboard instrument similar to the harmonium.
▷**HISTORY** C19: from German, from *Melodie* melody

melodic (mɪˈlɒdɪk) ADJECTIVE 1 of or relating to melody. 2 of or relating to a part in a piece of music. 3 tuneful or melodious.
▸**meˈlodically** ADVERB

melodic minor scale NOUN *Music* a minor scale modified from the natural by the sharpening of the sixth and seventh when taken in ascending order and the restoration of their original pitches when taken in descending order. See **minor** (sense 4a). Compare **harmonic minor scale.**

melodious (mɪˈləʊdɪəs) ADJECTIVE 1 having a tune that is pleasant to the ear. 2 of or relating to melody; melodic.
▸**meˈlodiously** ADVERB ▸**meˈlodiousness** NOUN

melodist (ˈmɛlədɪst) NOUN 1 a composer of melodies. 2 a singer.

melodize *or* **melodise** (ˈmɛləˌdaɪz) VERB 1 (*tr*) to provide with a melody. 2 (*tr*) to make melodious. 3 (*intr*) to sing or play melodies.
▸ˈ**meloˌdizer** *or* ˈ**meloˌdiser** NOUN

melodrama (ˈmɛləˌdrɑːmə) NOUN 1 a play, film, etc., characterized by extravagant action and emotion. 2 (formerly) a romantic drama characterized by sensational incident, music, and song. 3 overdramatic emotion or behaviour. 4 a poem or part of a play or opera spoken to a musical accompaniment.
▷**HISTORY** C19: from French *mélodrame*, from Greek *melos* song + *drame* DRAMA
▸**melodramatist** (ˌmɛləˈdræmətɪst) NOUN ▸**melodramatic** (ˌmɛlədrəˈmætɪk) ADJECTIVE ▸ˌ**melodraˈmatically** ADVERB

melodramatize *or* **melodramatise** (ˌmɛləʊˈdræməˌtaɪz) VERB (*tr*) to make melodramatic.

melody (ˈmɛlədɪ) NOUN, *plural* **-dies.** 1 *Music* **a** a succession of notes forming a distinctive sequence; tune. **b** the horizontally represented aspect of the structure of a piece of music. Compare **harmony** (sense 4b). 2 sounds that are pleasant because of tone or arrangement, esp words of poetry.
▷**HISTORY** C13: from Old French, from Late Latin *melōdia*, from Greek *melōidia* singing, from *melos* song + *-ōidia*, from *aoidein* to sing

meloid (ˈmɛlɔɪd) NOUN 1 any long-legged beetle of the family *Meloidae*, which includes the blister beetles and oil beetles. ◆ ADJECTIVE 2 of, relating to, or belonging to the *Meloidae*.
▷**HISTORY** C19: from New Latin *Meloē* name of genus

melon (ˈmɛlən) NOUN 1 any of several varieties of two cucurbitaceous vines (see **muskmelon, watermelon**), cultivated for their edible fruit. 2 the fruit of any of these plants, which has a hard rind and juicy flesh. 3 **cut a melon.** *US and Canadian, slang* to declare an abnormally high dividend to shareholders.
▷**HISTORY** C14: via Old French from Late Latin *mēlo*, shortened form of *mēlopepō*, from Greek *mēlopepōn*, from *mēlon* apple + *pepōn* gourd

Melos (ˈmiːlɒs) NOUN an island in the SW Aegean Sea, in the Cyclades: of volcanic origin, with hot springs; centre of early Aegean civilization, where the Venus de Milo was found. Pop.: 5000 (latest est.). Area: 132 sq. km (51 sq. miles). Modern Greek name: **Mílos.**

Melpomene (mɛlˈpɒmɪnɪ) NOUN *Greek myth* the Muse of tragedy.

Melrose Abbey (ˈmɛlrəʊz) NOUN a ruined Cistercian abbey in Melrose in Scottish Borders: founded in 1136 and sacked by the English in 1385 and 1547: repaired in 1822 by Sir Walter Scott.

melt (mɛlt) VERB **melts, melting, melted; melted** *or* **molten** (ˈməʊltən). 1 to liquefy (a solid) or (of a solid) to become liquefied, as a result of the action of heat. 2 to become or make liquid; dissolve: *cakes that melt in the mouth.* 3 (often foll by *away*) to disappear; fade. 4 (foll by *down*) to melt (metal scrap) for reuse. 5 (often foll by *into*) to blend or cause to blend gradually. 6 to make or become emotional or sentimental; soften. ◆ NOUN 7 the act or process of melting. 8 something melted or an amount melted.

▷HISTORY Old English *meltan* to digest; related to Old Norse *melta* to malt (beer), digest, Greek *meldein* to melt
▸ **'meltable** ADJECTIVE ▸ **ˌmelta'bility** NOUN ▸ **'melter** NOUN ▸ **'meltingly** ADVERB ▸ **'meltingness** NOUN

meltage ('mɛltɪdʒ) NOUN the process or result of melting or the amount melted: *rapid meltage of ice.*

meltdown ('mɛltˌdaʊn) NOUN 1 (in a nuclear reactor) the melting of the fuel rods as a result of a defect in the cooling system, with the possible escape of radiation into the environment. 2 *Informal* a sudden disastrous failure with potential for widespread harm, as a stock-exchange crash. 3 *Informal* the process or state of irreversible breakdown or decline: *the community is slowly going into meltdown.*

meltemi (mɛl'tɛmɪ) NOUN a northerly wind in the northeast Mediterranean; etesian wind.
▷HISTORY C20: from Modern Greek, from Turkish *meltem*

melting point NOUN the temperature at which a solid turns into a liquid. It is equal to the freezing point.

melting pot NOUN 1 a pot in which metals or other substances are melted, esp in order to mix them. 2 an area in which many races, ideas, etc., are mixed.

melton ('mɛltən) NOUN a heavy smooth woollen fabric with a short nap, used esp for overcoats. Also called: **melton cloth.**
▷HISTORY C19: from MELTON MOWBRAY, Leicestershire, a former centre for making this cloth

Melton Mowbray ('mɛltən 'məʊbrɪ) NOUN a town in central England, in Leicestershire: pork pies and Stilton cheese. Pop.: 24 348 (1991).

meltwater ('mɛltˌwɔːtə) NOUN melted snow or ice.

melungeon (mə'lʌndʒən) NOUN any of a dark-skinned group of people of the Appalachians in E Tennessee, of mixed Indian, White, and Black ancestry.
▷HISTORY C20: of unknown origin

Melville Island ('mɛlvɪl) NOUN 1 a Canadian island in the Arctic Ocean, north of Victoria Island: in the Northwest Territories and Nunavut. Area: 41 865 sq. km (16 164 sq. miles). 2 an island in the Arafura Sea, off the N central coast of Australia, separated from the mainland by Clarence Strait. Area: 6216 sq. km (2400 sq. miles).

Melville Peninsula NOUN a peninsula of N Canada, in Nunavut, between the Gulf of Boothia and Foxe Basin.

mem (mɛm) NOUN the 13th letter in the Hebrew alphabet (מ or, at the end of a word, ם), transliterated as *m.*
▷HISTORY Hebrew, literally: water

member ('mɛmbə) NOUN 1 a person who belongs to a club, political party, etc. 2 any individual plant or animal in a taxonomic group: *a member of the species.* 3 any part of an animal body, such as a limb. 4 another word for **penis.** 5 any part of a plant, such as a petal, root, etc. 6 *Maths* any individual object belonging to a set or logical class. 7 a distinct part of a whole, such as a proposition in a syllogism. 8 a component part of a building or construction.
▷HISTORY C13: from Latin *membrum* limb, part
▸ **'memberless** ADJECTIVE

Member ('mɛmbə) NOUN (*sometimes not capital*) 1 short for **Member of Parliament.** 2 short for **Member of Congress.** 3 a member of some other legislative body.

Member of Congress NOUN a member of the US Congress, esp of the House of Representatives.

Member of Parliament NOUN a member of the House of Commons or similar legislative body, as in many Commonwealth countries. Abbreviation: **MP.**

membership ('mɛmbəˌʃɪp) NOUN 1 the members of an organization collectively. 2 the state of being a member.

membrane ('mɛmbreɪn) NOUN 1 any thin pliable sheet of material. 2 a pliable sheetlike usually fibrous tissue that covers, lines, or connects plant and animal organs or cells. 3 *Biology* a double layer of lipid, containing some proteins, that surrounds biological cells and some of their internal structures. 4 *Physics* a two-dimensional entity postulated as a fundamental constituent of matter in superstring theories of particle physics. 5 a skin of parchment forming part of a roll.
▷HISTORY C16: from Latin *membrāna* skin covering a part of the body, from *membrum* MEMBER

membrane bone NOUN any bone that develops within membranous tissue, such as the clavicle and bones of the skull, without cartilage formation. Compare **cartilage bone.**

membrane transport NOUN the process by which physiologically important substances, such as calcium ions, sugars, etc., are conveyed across a biological membrane.

membranous ('mɛmbrənəs, mɛm'breɪnəs), **membraneous** (mɛm'breɪnɪəs), *or* **membranaceous** (ˌmɛmbrə'neɪʃəs) ADJECTIVE of or relating to a membrane.
▸ **'membranously** ADVERB

meme (miːm) NOUN an idea or element of social behaviour passed on through generations in a culture, esp by imitation.
▷HISTORY C20: possibly from MIMIC, on the model of GENE

Memel ('meːməl) NOUN 1 the German name for **Klaipeda.** 2 the lower course of the Neman River.

memento (mɪ'mɛntəʊ) NOUN, *plural* **-tos** *or* **-toes.** 1 something that reminds one of past events; souvenir. 2 *RC Church* either of two prayers occurring during the Mass.
▷HISTORY C15: from Latin, imperative of *meminisse* to remember

memento mori ('mɔːriː) NOUN an object, such as a skull, intended to remind people of the inevitability of death.
▷HISTORY C16: Latin: remember you must die

Memnon ('mɛmnɒn) NOUN 1 *Greek myth* a king of Ethiopia, son of Eos: slain by Achilles in the Trojan War. 2 a colossal statue of Amenhotep III at Thebes in ancient Egypt, which emitted a sound thought by the Greeks to be the voice of Memnon.
▸ **Memnonian** (mɛm'nəʊnɪən) ADJECTIVE

memo ('mɛməʊ, 'miːməʊ) NOUN, *plural* **memos.** short for **memorandum.**

memoir ('mɛmwɑː) NOUN 1 a biography or historical account, esp one based on personal knowledge. 2 an essay or monograph, as on a specialized topic. 3 *Obsolete* a memorandum.
▷HISTORY C16: from French, from Latin *memoria* MEMORY
▸ **'memoirist** NOUN

memoirs ('mɛmwɑːz) PLURAL NOUN 1 a collection of reminiscences about a period, series of events, etc., written from personal experience or special sources. 2 an autobiographical record. 3 a collection or record, as of transactions of a society, etc.

memorabilia (ˌmɛmərə'bɪlɪə) PLURAL NOUN, *singular* **-rabile** (-'ræbɪlɪ). 1 memorable events or things. 2 objects connected with famous people or events.
▷HISTORY C17: from Latin, from *memorābilis* MEMORABLE

memorable ('mɛmərəbᵊl, 'mɛmrə-) ADJECTIVE worth remembering or easily remembered; noteworthy.
▷HISTORY C15: from Latin *memorābilis,* from *memorāre* to recall, from *memor* mindful
▸ **ˌmemora'bility** *or* **'memorableness** NOUN ▸ **'memorably** ADVERB

memorandum (ˌmɛmə'rændəm) NOUN, *plural* **-dums** *or* **-da** (-də). 1 a written statement, record, or communication such as within an office. 2 a note of things to be remembered. 3 an informal diplomatic communication, often unsigned: often summarizing the point of view of a government. 4 *Law* a short written summary of the terms of a transaction. ♦ Often (esp for senses 1, 2) shortened to: **memo.**
▷HISTORY C15: from Latin: (something) to be remembered

memorial (mɪ'mɔːrɪəl) ADJECTIVE 1 serving to preserve the memory of the dead or a past event. 2 of or involving memory. ♦ NOUN 3 something serving as a remembrance. 4 a written statement of facts submitted to a government, authority, etc., in conjunction with a petition. 5 an informal diplomatic paper.
▷HISTORY C14: from Late Latin *memoriāle* a reminder, neuter of *memoriālis* belonging to remembrance
▸ **me'morially** ADVERB

Memorial Day NOUN a holiday in the United States, May 30th in most states, commemorating the servicemen killed in all American wars.

memorialist (mɪ'mɔːrɪəlɪst) NOUN 1 a person who writes or presents a memorial. 2 a writer of a memoir or memoirs.

memorialize *or* **memorialise** (mɪ'mɔːrɪəˌlaɪz) VERB (*tr*) 1 to honour or commemorate. 2 to present or address a memorial to.
▸ **meˌmoriali'zation** *or* **meˌmoriali'sation** NOUN
▸ **me'morialˌizer** *or* **me'morialˌiser** NOUN

memoria technica (mɪ'mɔːrɪə 'tɛknɪkə) NOUN a method or device for assisting the memory.
▷HISTORY C18: New Latin: artificial memory

memorize *or* **memorise** ('mɛməˌraɪz) VERB (*tr*) to commit to memory; learn so as to remember.
▸ **'memoˌrizable** *or* **'memoˌrisable** ADJECTIVE
▸ **ˌmemori'zation** *or* **ˌmemori'sation** NOUN ▸ **'memoˌrizer** *or* **'memoˌriser** NOUN

memory ('mɛmərɪ) NOUN, *plural* **-ries.** 1 **a** the ability of the mind to store and recall past sensations, thoughts, knowledge, etc.: *he can do it from memory.* **b** the part of the brain that appears to have this function. 2 the sum of everything retained by the mind. 3 a particular recollection of an event, person, etc. 4 the time over which recollection extends: *within his memory.* 5 commemoration or remembrance: *in memory of our leader.* 6 the state of being remembered, as after death. 7 Also called: **RAM, main store, store.** a part of a computer in which information is stored for immediate use by the central processing unit. See also **backing store, virtual storage.** 8 the tendency for a material, system, etc., to show effects that depend on its past treatment or history. 9 the ability of a material, etc., to return to a former state after a constraint has been removed.
▷HISTORY C14: from Old French *memorie,* from Latin *memoria,* from *memor* mindful

memory mapping NOUN a technique whereby computer peripherals may be addressed as though they formed part of the main memory of the computer.

memory span NOUN *Psychol* the capacity of short-term memory, usually between 5 and 10 items.

memory trace NOUN *Psychol* the hypothetical structural alteration in brain cells following learning. See also **engram.**

Memphian ('mɛmfɪən) ADJECTIVE 1 of or relating to ancient Memphis or its inhabitants. ♦ NOUN 2 an inhabitant or native of ancient Memphis.

Memphis ('mɛmfɪs) NOUN 1 a port in SW Tennessee, on the Mississippi River: the largest city in the state; a major cotton and timber market; Memphis State University (1909). Pop.: 650 100 (2000 est.). 2 a ruined city in N Egypt, the ancient centre of Lower Egypt, on the Nile: administrative and artistic centre, sacred to the worship of Ptah.

Memphremagog (ˌmɛmfriː'meɪgɒg) NOUN **Lake.** a lake on the border between the US and Canada, in N Vermont and S Quebec. Length: about 43 km (27 miles). Width: up to 6 km (4 miles).

memsahib ('mɛmˌsɑːɪb, -hɪb) NOUN (formerly in India) a term of respect used of a European married woman.
▷HISTORY C19: from MA'AM + SAHIB

men (mɛn) NOUN the plural of **man.**

menace ('mɛnɪs) VERB 1 to threaten with violence, danger, etc. ♦ NOUN 2 *Literary* a threat or the act of threatening. 3 something menacing; a source of danger. 4 *Informal* a nuisance.
▷HISTORY C13: ultimately related to Latin *minax* threatening, from *minārī* to threaten
▸ **'menacer** NOUN ▸ **'menacing** ADJECTIVE ▸ **'menacingly** ADVERB

menad ('miːnæd) NOUN a variant spelling of **maenad.**

menadione (ˌmɛnə'daɪəʊn) NOUN a yellow crystalline compound used in fungicides and as an additive to animal feeds. Formula: $C_{11}H_8O_2$. Also called: **vitamin K_3.**
▷HISTORY C20: from ME(THYL) + NA(PHTHA) + DI-[1] + -ONE

Menado (mɛˈnɑːdəʊ) *or* **Manado** NOUN a port in NE Indonesia, on NE Sulawesi: founded by the Dutch in 1657. Pop.: 398 900 (1995 est.).

ménage (meɪˈnɑːʒ; *French* menaʒ) NOUN the persons of a household.
▷HISTORY C17: from French, from Vulgar Latin *mansiōnāticum* (unattested) household; see MANSION

ménage à trois *French* (menaʒ a trwɑ) NOUN, *plural* ***ménages à trois*** (menaʒ a trwɑ). a sexual arrangement involving a married couple and the lover of one of them.
▷HISTORY literally: household of three

menagerie (mɪˈnædʒərɪ) NOUN 1 a collection of wild animals kept for exhibition. 2 the place where such animals are housed.
▷HISTORY C18: from French: household management, which formerly included care of domestic animals. See MÉNAGE

Menai Strait (ˈmɛnaɪ) NOUN a channel of the Irish Sea between the island of Anglesey and the mainland of NW Wales: famous suspension bridge (1819–26) designed by Thomas Telford and tubular bridge (1846–50) by Robert Stephenson. Length: 24 km (15 miles). Width: up to 3 km (2 miles).

Menam (miːˈnæm) NOUN another name for the **Chao Phraya**.

menaquinone (ˌmɛnəkwɪˈnəʊn) NOUN a form of vitamin K synthesized by bacteria in the intestine or in putrefying organic matter. Also called: **vitamin K_2**.
▷HISTORY C20: from *me(thyl)-na(phtho)quinone*

menarche (mɛˈnɑːkɪ) NOUN the first occurrence of menstruation in a woman's life.
▷HISTORY C20: New Latin, from Greek *mēn* month + *arkhē* beginning
▸**menˈarcheal** *or* **menˈarchial** ADJECTIVE

mend (mɛnd) VERB 1 (*tr*) to repair (something broken or unserviceable). 2 to improve or undergo improvement; reform (often in the phrase **mend one's ways**). 3 (*intr*) to heal or recover. 4 (*intr*) (of conditions) to improve; become better. 5 (*tr*) *Northern English* to feed or stir (a fire). ◆ NOUN 6 the act of repairing. 7 a mended area, esp on a garment. 8 **on the mend.** becoming better, esp in health.
▷HISTORY C12: shortened from AMEND
▸**ˈmendable** ADJECTIVE ▸**ˈmender** NOUN

mendacity (mɛnˈdæsɪtɪ) NOUN, *plural* **-ties.** 1 the tendency to be untruthful. 2 a falsehood.
▷HISTORY C17: from Late Latin *mendācitās,* from Latin *mendāx* untruthful
▸**mendacious** (mɛnˈdeɪʃəs) ADJECTIVE ▸**menˈdaciously** ADVERB ▸**menˈdaciousness** NOUN

mendelevium (ˌmɛndɪˈliːvɪəm) NOUN a transuranic element artificially produced by bombardment of einsteinium. Symbol: Md; atomic no.: 101; half-life of most stable isotope, ^{258}Md: 60 days (approx.); valency: 2 or 3.
▷HISTORY C20: named after Dmitri Ivanovich *Mendeleyev* (1834–1907), Russian chemist

Mendelian (mɛnˈdiːlɪən) ADJECTIVE of or relating to Mendel's laws.

Mendelism (ˈmɛndəˌlɪzəm) *or* **Mendelianism** (mɛnˈdiːlɪəˌnɪzəm) NOUN the science of heredity based on Mendel's laws with some modifications in the light of more recent knowledge.

Mendel's laws (ˈmɛndᵊlz) PLURAL NOUN the principles of heredity proposed by Gregor Mendel (1822–84), the Austrian monk and botanist. The **Law of Segregation** states that each hereditary character is determined by a pair of units in the reproductive cells: the pairs separate during meiosis so that each gamete carries only one unit of each pair. The **Law of Independent Assortment** states that the separation of the units of each pair is not influenced by that of any other pair.

Menderes (ˌmɛndɛˈrɛs) NOUN 1 a river in SW Turkey flowing southwest, then west to the Aegean. Length: about 386 km (240 miles). Ancient name: **Maeander.** 2 a river in NW Turkey flowing west and northwest to the Dardanelles. Length: 104 km (65 miles). Ancient name: **Scamander.**

mendicant (ˈmɛndɪkənt) ADJECTIVE 1 begging. 2 (of a member of a religious order) dependent on alms for sustenance: *mendicant friars.* 3 characteristic of a beggar. ◆ NOUN 4 a mendicant friar. 5 a less common word for **beggar.**
▷HISTORY C16: from Latin *mendīcāre* to beg, from *mendīcus* beggar, from *mendus* flaw
▸**ˈmendicancy** *or* **mendicity** (mɛnˈdɪsɪtɪ) NOUN

mending (ˈmɛndɪŋ) NOUN something to be mended, esp clothes.

Mendips (ˈmɛndɪps) PLURAL NOUN a range of limestone hills in SW England, in N Somerset: includes the Cheddar Gorge and numerous caves. Highest point: 325 m (1068 ft.). Also called: **Mendip Hills.**

Mendoza (mɛnˈdəʊzə; *Spanish* menˈdoθa) NOUN a city in W central Argentina, in the foothills of the Sierra de los Paramillos: largely destroyed by an earthquake in 1861; commercial centre of an intensively cultivated irrigated region; University of Cuyo (1939). Pop.: 119 681 (1999 est.).

meneer (məˈnɪə) NOUN a South African title of address equivalent to *sir* when used alone or *Mr* when placed before a name.
▷HISTORY Afrikaans

Menelaus (ˌmɛnɪˈleɪəs) NOUN *Greek myth* a king of Sparta and the brother of Agamemnon. He was the husband of Helen, whose abduction led to the Trojan War.

mene, mene, tekel, upharsin (ˈmiːniː ˈmiːniː ˈtɛkəl juːˈfɑːsɪn) NOUN *Old Testament* the words that appeared on the wall during Belshazzar's Feast (Daniel 5:25), interpreted by Daniel to mean that God had doomed the kingdom of Belshazzar.
▷HISTORY Aramaic: numbered, numbered, weighed, divided

menfolk (ˈmɛnˌfəʊk) *or US sometimes* **menfolks** PLURAL NOUN men collectively, esp the men of a particular family.

menhaden (mɛnˈheɪdᵊn) NOUN, *plural* **-den.** a marine North American fish, *Brevoortia tyrannus:* source of fishmeal, fertilizer, and oil: family *Clupeidae* (herrings, etc.).
▷HISTORY C18: from Algonquian; probably related to Narragansett *munnawhatteaúg* fertilizer, menhaden

menhir (ˈmɛnhɪə) NOUN a single standing stone, often carved, dating from the middle Bronze Age in the British Isles and from the late Neolithic Age in W Europe.
▷HISTORY C19: from Breton *men* stone + *hir* long

menial (ˈmiːnɪəl) ADJECTIVE 1 consisting of or occupied with work requiring little skill, esp domestic duties such as cleaning. 2 of, involving, or befitting servants. 3 servile. ◆ NOUN 4 a domestic servant. 5 a servile person.
▷HISTORY C14: from Anglo-Norman *meignial,* from Old French *meinie* household. See MEINY
▸**ˈmenially** ADVERB

Ménière's syndrome *or* **disease** (meɪnˈjɛəz) NOUN a disorder of the inner ear characterized by a ringing or buzzing in the ear, dizziness, and impaired hearing.
▷HISTORY C19: named after Prosper *Ménière* (1799–1862), French physician

menilite (ˈmɛnɪˌlaɪt) NOUN another name for **liver opal**, esp a brown or grey variety

meninges (mɪˈnɪndʒiːz) PLURAL NOUN, *singular* **meninx** (ˈmiːnɪŋks). the three membranes (**dura mater, arachnoid, pia mater**) that envelop the brain and spinal cord.
▷HISTORY C17: from Greek, pl of *meninx* membrane
▸**meningeal** (mɪˈnɪndʒɪəl) ADJECTIVE

meningitis (ˌmɛnɪnˈdʒaɪtɪs) NOUN inflammation of the membranes that surround the brain or spinal cord, caused by infection.
▸**meningitic** (ˌmɛnɪnˈdʒɪtɪk) ADJECTIVE

meningocele (mɛˈnɪŋgəʊˌsiːl) NOUN *Pathol* protrusion of the meninges through the skull or backbone.
▷HISTORY C19: from *meningo-* (see MENINGES) + -CELE

meningococcal (mɛˌnɪŋgəʊˈkɒkəl) ADJECTIVE of or relating to the meningococcus bacterium.

meningococcus (mɛˌnɪŋgəʊˈkɒkəs) NOUN, *plural* **-cocci** (-ˈkɒkaɪ). the bacterium that causes cerebrospinal meningitis.

meniscus (mɪˈnɪskəs) NOUN, *plural* **-nisci** (-ˈnɪsaɪ) *or* **-niscuses.** 1 the curved upper surface of a liquid standing in a tube, produced by the surface tension. 2 a crescent or half-moon-shaped body or design. 3 a crescent-shaped fibrous cartilage between the bones at certain joints, esp at the knee. 4 a crescent-shaped lens; a concavo-convex or convexo-concave lens.
▷HISTORY C17: from New Latin, from Greek *mēniskos* crescent, diminutive of *mēnē* moon
▸**meˈniscoid** ADJECTIVE

menispermaceous (ˌmɛnɪspɜːˈmeɪʃəs) ADJECTIVE of, relating to, or belonging to the *Menispermaceae,* a family of mainly tropical and subtropical plants, most of which are woody climbers with small flowers.
▷HISTORY C19: from New Latin *Mēnispermum* name of genus, from Greek *mēnē* moon + *sperma* seed

Mennonite (ˈmɛnəˌnaɪt) NOUN a member of a Protestant sect that rejects infant baptism, Church organization, and the doctrine of transubstantiation and in most cases refuses military service, public office, and the taking of oaths.
▷HISTORY C16: from German *Mennonit,* after *Menno* Simons (1496–1561), Frisian religious leader
▸**ˈMennoˌnitism** NOUN

meno (ˈmɛnəʊ) ADVERB *Music* 1 (esp preceding a dynamic or tempo marking) to be played less quickly, less softly, etc. 2 short for **meno mosso.**
▷HISTORY from Italian, from Latin *minus* less

meno- COMBINING FORM menstruation: *menorrhagia.*
▷HISTORY from Greek *mēn* month

menology (mɪˈnɒlədʒɪ) NOUN, *plural* **-gies.** 1 an ecclesiastical calendar of the months. 2 *Eastern Churches* a liturgical book containing the lives of the saints arranged by months.
▷HISTORY C17: from New Latin *mēnologium,* from Late Greek *mēnologion,* from Greek *mēn* month + *logos* word, account

Menomini *or* **Menominee** (məˈnɒmənɪ) NOUN 1 (*plural* **-ni, -nis** *or* **-nee, -nees**) a member of a North American Indian people formerly living between Lake Michigan and Lake Superior. 2 the language of this people, belonging to the Algonquian family.

meno mosso (ˈmɛnəʊ ˈmɒsəʊ) ADVERB *Music* to be played at reduced speed. Often shortened to: **meno.**
▷HISTORY Italian: less rapid

menopause (ˈmɛnəʊˌpɔːz) NOUN the period during which a woman's menstrual cycle ceases, normally occurring at an age of 45 to 50. Nontechnical name: **change of life.**
▷HISTORY C19: from French, from Greek *mēn* month + *pausis* halt
▸**ˌmenoˈpausal** *or* (*rarely*) **ˌmenoˈpausic** ADJECTIVE

menorah (mɪˈnɔːrə; *Hebrew* məˈnaurɑ) NOUN *Judaism* 1 a seven-branched candelabrum used in the Temple and now an emblem of Judaism and the badge of the state of Israel. 2 a candelabrum having eight branches and a shammes that is lit during the festival of Hanukkah.
▷HISTORY from Hebrew: candlestick

Menorca (meˈnɔrka) NOUN the Spanish name for **Minorca** (sense 1).

menorrhagia (ˌmɛnɔːˈreɪdʒɪə) NOUN excessive bleeding during menstruation.
▸**menorrhagic** (ˌmɛnəˈrædʒɪk) ADJECTIVE

menorrhoea (ˌmɛnəˈrɪə) NOUN normal bleeding in menstruation.

Mensa[1] (ˈmɛnsə) NOUN, *Latin genitive* **Mensae** (ˈmɛnsiː). a faint constellation in the S hemisphere lying between Hydrus and Volans and containing part of the Large Magellanic Cloud.
▷HISTORY Latin, literally: the table

Mensa[2] (ˈmɛnsə) NOUN an international society, membership of which is restricted to people whose intelligence test scores exceed those expected of 98 per cent of the population.

mensal[1] (ˈmɛnsᵊl) ADJECTIVE *Rare* monthly.
▷HISTORY C15: from Latin *mensis* month

mensal[2] (ˈmɛnsᵊl) ADJECTIVE *Rare* relating to or used at the table.
▷HISTORY C15: from Latin *mensālis,* from *mensa* table

menses (ˈmɛnsiːz) NOUN, *plural* **menses.** 1 another name for **menstruation.** 2 the period of time, usually from three to five days, during which menstruation occurs. 3 the matter discharged during menstruation.
▷HISTORY C16: from Latin, pl of *mensis* month

Menshevik (ˈmɛnʃɪvɪk) *or* **Menshevist** NOUN a member of the moderate wing of the Russian Social

Democratic Party, advocating gradual reform to achieve socialism. Compare **Bolshevik.**
▷HISTORY C20: from Russian, literally: minority, from *menshe* less, from *malo* few
▸'**Menshevism** NOUN

mens rea ('mɛnz 'reɪə) NOUN *Law* a criminal intention or knowledge that an act is wrong. It is assumed to be an ingredient of all criminal offences although some minor statutory offences are punishable irrespective of it.
▷HISTORY Latin, literally: guilty mind

men's room NOUN *Chiefly US and Canadian* a public lavatory for men.

menstrual ('mɛnstruəl) ADJECTIVE of or relating to menstruation or the menses.

menstruate ('mɛnstruˌeɪt) VERB (*intr*) to undergo menstruation.
▷HISTORY C17: from Latin *menstruāre,* from *mensis* month

menstruation (ˌmɛnstru'eɪʃən) NOUN the approximately monthly discharge of blood and cellular debris from the uterus by nonpregnant women from puberty to the menopause. Also called: **menses.** Nontechnical name: **period.**
▸**menstruous** ('mɛnstruəs) ADJECTIVE

menstruum ('mɛnstruəm) NOUN, *plural* **-struums** *or* **-strua** (-struə). *Obsolete* 1 a solvent, esp one used in the preparation of a drug. 2 a solid formulation of a drug.
▷HISTORY C17 (meaning: solvent), C14 (menstrual discharge): from Medieval Latin, from Latin *mēnstruus* monthly, from *mēnsis* month; from an alchemical comparison between a base metal being transmuted into gold and the supposed action of the menses

mensurable ('mɛnsjurəbᵊl, -ʃə-) ADJECTIVE a less common word for **measurable.**
▷HISTORY C17: from Late Latin *mēnsūrābilis,* from *mēnsūra* MEASURE
▸ˌ**mensura'bility** NOUN

mensural ('mɛnʃərəl) ADJECTIVE 1 of or involving measure. 2 *Music* of or relating to music in which notes have fixed values in relation to each other.
▷HISTORY C17: from Late Latin *mēnsūrālis,* from *mēnsūra* MEASURE

mensuration (ˌmɛnʃə'reɪʃən) NOUN 1 the study of the measurement of geometric magnitudes such as length. 2 the act or process of measuring; measurement.
▸ˌ**mensu'rational** ADJECTIVE ▸**mensurative** ('mɛnʃərətɪv) ADJECTIVE

menswear ('mɛnzˌwɛə) NOUN clothing for men.

-ment SUFFIX FORMING NOUNS, esp FROM VERBS 1 indicating state, condition, or quality: *enjoyment.* 2 indicating the result or product of an action: *embankment.* 3 indicating process or action: *management.*
▷HISTORY from French, from Latin *-mentum*

mental¹ ('mɛntᵊl) ADJECTIVE 1 of or involving the mind or an intellectual process. 2 occurring only in the mind: *mental calculations.* 3 affected by mental illness: *a mental patient.* 4 concerned with care for persons with mental illness: *a mental hospital.* 5 *Slang* insane.
▷HISTORY C15: from Late Latin *mentālis,* from Latin *mēns* mind
▸'**mentally** ADVERB

mental² ('mɛntᵊl) ADJECTIVE *Anatomy* of or relating to the chin. Also: **genial.**
▷HISTORY C18: from Latin *mentum* chin

mental age NOUN *Psychol* the mental ability of a child, expressed in years and based on a comparison of his test performance with the performance of children with a range of chronological ages. See also **intelligence quotient.**

mental block NOUN See **block** (sense 21).

mental cruelty NOUN behaviour that causes distress to another person but that does not involve physical assault.

mental deficiency NOUN *Psychiatry* a less common term for **mental retardation.**

mental disorder NOUN *Law* (in England, according to the Mental Health Act 1983) mental illness, arrested or incomplete development of mind, psychopathic disorder, or any other disorder or disability of the mind.
▸**mentally disordered** ADJECTIVE

mental handicap NOUN a general or specific intellectual disability, resulting directly or indirectly from injury to the brain or from abnormal neurological development.
▸**mentally handicapped** ADJECTIVE

mental healing NOUN the healing of a disorder by mental concentration or suggestion.
▸**mental healer** NOUN

mental home, hospital, *or* **institution** NOUN a home, hospital, or institution for people who are mentally ill.

mental illness NOUN any of various disorders in which a person's thoughts, emotions, or behaviour are so abnormal as to cause suffering to himself, herself, or other people.

mental impairment NOUN *Law* (in England, according to the Mental Health Act 1983) a state of arrested or incomplete development of mind, which includes significant impairment of intelligence and social functioning and is associated with abnormally aggressive or seriously irresponsible conduct.
▸**mentally impaired** ADJECTIVE

mentalism ('mɛntᵊˌlɪzəm) NOUN *Philosophy* the doctrine that mind is the fundamental reality and that objects of knowledge exist only as aspects of the subject's consciousness. Compare **physicalism, idealism** (sense 3). See also **monism** (sense 1), **materialism** (sense 2).
▸'**mentalist** NOUN ▸ˌ**mental'istic** ADJECTIVE
▸ˌ**mental'istically** ADVERB

mentality (mɛn'tælɪtɪ) NOUN, *plural* **-ties.** 1 the state or quality of mental or intellectual ability. 2 a way of thinking; mental inclination or character: *his weird mentality.*

mental lexicon NOUN the store of words in a person's mind.

mental reservation NOUN a tacit withholding of full assent or an unexpressed qualification made when one is taking an oath, making a statement, etc.

mental retardation NOUN *Psychiatry* the condition of having a low intelligence quotient (below 70).

mentation (mɛn'teɪʃən) NOUN the process or result of mental activity.

menthaceous (mɛn'θeɪʃəs) ADJECTIVE of, relating to, or belonging to the labiate plant genus *Mentha* (mints, etc.) the members of which have scented leaves.
▷HISTORY from New Latin, from Latin *mentha* MINT¹

menthol ('mɛnθɒl) NOUN an optically active organic compound found in peppermint oil and used as an antiseptic, in inhalants, and as an analgesic. Formula: $C_{10}H_{20}O$.
▷HISTORY C19: from German, from Latin *mentha* MINT¹

mentholated ('mɛnθəˌleɪtɪd) ADJECTIVE containing, treated, or impregnated with menthol.

mention ('mɛnʃən) VERB (*tr*) 1 to refer to or speak about briefly or incidentally. 2 to acknowledge or honour. 3 **not to mention (something).** to say nothing of (something too obvious to mention). ◆ NOUN 4 a recognition or acknowledgment. 5 a slight reference or allusion: *he only got a mention in the article; the author makes no mention of that.* 6 the act of mentioning. 7 *Philosophy, logic, linguistics* the occurrence (of an expression) in such a context that it is itself referred to rather than performing its own linguistic function. In *"Fido" names Fido,* the word *Fido* is first mentioned and then used to refer to the dog. Compare **use** (sense 18). See also **formal mode.**
▷HISTORY C14: via Old French from Latin *mentiō* a calling to mind, naming, from *mēns* mind
▸'**mentionable** ADJECTIVE ▸'**mentioner** NOUN

Mentmore ('mɛntˌmɔː) NOUN a mansion in Mentmore in Buckinghamshire: built by Sir Joseph Paxton in the 19th century for the Rothschild family; now owned by the Maharishi University of Natural Law.

Menton (mɛn'təʊn; *French* mɑ̃tɔ̃) NOUN a town and resort in SE France, on the Mediterranean: belonged to Monaco from the 14th century until 1848, then an independent republic until purchased by France in 1860. Pop.: 25 500 (latest est.).

mentor ('mɛntɔː) NOUN a wise or trusted adviser or guide.
▷HISTORY C18: from MENTOR
▸**men'torial** ADJECTIVE

Mentor ('mɛntɔː) NOUN the friend whom Odysseus put in charge of his household when he left for Troy. He was the adviser of the young Telemachus.

mentoring ('mɛntərɪŋ) NOUN (in business) the practice of assigning a junior member of staff to the care of a more experienced person who assists him in his career.

menu ('mɛnjuː) NOUN 1 a list of dishes served at a meal or that can be ordered in a restaurant. 2 a list of options displayed on a visual display unit from which the operator selects an action to be carried out by positioning the cursor or by depressing the appropriate key.
▷HISTORY C19: from French *menu* small, detailed (list), from Latin *minūtus* MINUTE²

menu-driven ADJECTIVE (of a computer system) operated through menus.

meow, miaou, miaow (mɪ'aʊ, mjaʊ), *or* **miaul** (mɪ'aʊl, mjaʊl) VERB 1 (*intr*) (of a cat) to make a characteristic crying sound. ◆ INTERJECTION 2 an imitation of this sound.

MEP (in Britain) ABBREVIATION FOR Member of the European Parliament.

mepacrine ('mɛpəkrɪn) NOUN *Brit* a drug, mepacrine dihydrochloride, one of the first synthetic substitutes for quinine, formerly widely used to treat malaria but now largely replaced by chloroquine. Formula: $C_{23}H_{30}ClN_3O.2HCl.2H_2O$. US name: **quinacrine.**
▷HISTORY C20: from ME(THYL) + PA(LUDISM + A)CR(ID)INE

Mephistopheles (ˌmɛfɪ'stɒfɪˌliːz) *or* **Mephisto** (mə'fɪstəʊ) NOUN a devil in medieval mythology and the one to whom Faust sold his soul in the Faust legend.
▸**Mephistophelean** *or* **Mephistophelian** (ˌmɛfɪstə'fiːlɪən) ADJECTIVE

mephitic (mɪ'fɪtɪk) *or* **mephitical** ADJECTIVE 1 poisonous; foul. 2 foul-smelling; putrid.
▷HISTORY C17: from Late Latin *mephīticus* pestilential
▸**me'phitically** ADVERB

meprobamate (mə'prəʊbəˌmeɪt, ˌmɛprəʊ'bæmeɪt) NOUN a white bitter powder used as a hypnotic. Formula: $C_9H_{18}N_2O_4$.
▷HISTORY ME(THYL) + PRO(PYL + CAR)BAMATE

mer. ABBREVIATION FOR meridian.

-mer SUFFIX FORMING NOUNS *Chem* denoting a substance of a particular class: *monomer; polymer.*
▷HISTORY from Greek *meros* part

Merano (mə'rɑːnəʊ; *Italian* me'raːno) NOUN a town and resort in NE Italy, in the foothills of the central Alps: capital of the Tyrol (12th–15th century); under Austrian rule until 1919. Pop.: 33 638 (1993 est.). German name: **Meran** (me'raːn).

meranti (mɪ'ræntɪ) NOUN wood from any of several Malaysian trees of the dipterocarpaceous genus *Shorea.*
▷HISTORY C18: from Malay

merbromin (mə'brəʊmɪn) NOUN a green iridescent crystalline compound that forms a red solution in water: used in medicine as an antiseptic. Formula: $C_{20}H_8Br_2HgNa_2O_6$. See also **Mercurochrome.**
▷HISTORY C20: blend of MERCURIC + *dibromofluorescein*

Merca ('mɛəkə) NOUN a port in S Somalia on the Indian Ocean. Pop.: 100 000 (latest est.).

Mercalli scale (mɜː'kælɪ) NOUN a 12-point scale for expressing the intensity of an earthquake, ranging from 1 (not felt, except by few under favourable circumstances) to 12 (total destruction). Compare **Richter scale.** See also **intensity** (sense 4).
▷HISTORY C20: named after Giuseppe *Mercalli* (1850–1914), Italian volcanologist and seismologist

mercantile ('mɜːkənˌtaɪl) ADJECTIVE 1 of, relating to, or characteristic of trade or traders; commercial. 2 of or relating to mercantilism.
▷HISTORY C17: from French, from Italian, from *mercante* MERCHANT

mercantile agency NOUN an enterprise that collects and supplies information about the financial credit standing of individuals and enterprises.

mercantile paper NOUN another name for **commercial paper.**

mercantilism (ˈmɜːkəntɪˌlɪzəm) NOUN [1] Also called: **mercantile system.** *Economics* a theory prevalent in Europe during the 17th and 18th centuries asserting that the wealth of a nation depends on its possession of precious metals and therefore that the government of a nation must maximize the foreign trade surplus, and foster national commercial interests, a merchant marine, the establishment of colonies, etc. [2] a rare word for **commercialism** (sense 1).
▸ **ˈmercanˌtilist** NOUN, ADJECTIVE

mercaptan (mɜːˈkæptæn) NOUN another name (not in technical usage) for **thiol.**
▷HISTORY C19: from German, from Medieval Latin *mercurium captans*, literally: seizing quicksilver

mercaptide (məˈkæptaɪd, mɜː-) NOUN a salt of a mercaptan, containing the ion RS^-, where R is an alkyl or aryl group.

mercapto- (mɜːˈkæptəʊ) COMBINING FORM (in chemical compounds) indicating the presence of an HS- group.

mercaptopurine (məˌkæptəʊˈpjʊəriːn) NOUN a drug used in the treatment of leukaemia. Formula: $C_5H_4N_4S$.

mercat (ˈmɛrkət) NOUN a Scot word for **market.**

Mercator projection (mɜːˈkeɪtə) NOUN an orthomorphic map projection on which parallels and meridians form a rectangular grid, scale being exaggerated with increasing distance from the equator. Also called: **Mercator's projection.**
▷HISTORY C17: named after Gerardus *Mercator*, Latinized name of Gerhard Kremer (1512–94), Flemish cartographer and mathematician

mercenary (ˈmɜːsɪnərɪ, -sɪnrɪ) ADJECTIVE [1] influenced by greed or desire for gain. [2] of or relating to a mercenary or mercenaries. ◆ NOUN, *plural* **-naries.** [3] a man hired to fight for a foreign army, etc. [4] *Rare* any person who works solely for pay.
▷HISTORY C16: from Latin *mercēnārius*, from *mercēs* wages
▸ **ˈmercenarily** ADVERB ▸ **ˈmercenariness** NOUN

mercer (ˈmɜːsə) NOUN *Brit* a dealer in textile fabrics and fine cloth.
▷HISTORY C13: from Old French *mercier* dealer, from Vulgar Latin *merciārius* (unattested), from Latin *merx* goods, wares
▸ **ˈmercery** NOUN

mercerize *or* **mercerise** (ˈmɜːsəˌraɪz) VERB (*tr*) to treat (cotton yarn) with an alkali to increase its strength and reception to dye and impart a lustrous silky appearance.
▷HISTORY C19: named after John *Mercer* (1791–1866), English maker of textiles
▸ **ˌmerceriˈzation** *or* **ˌmerceriˈsation** NOUN

merchandise NOUN (ˈmɜːtʃənˌdaɪs, -ˌdaɪz) [1] commercial goods; commodities. ◆ VERB (ˈmɜːtʃənˌdaɪz) [2] to engage in the commercial purchase and sale of (goods or services); trade.
▷HISTORY C13: from Old French. See MERCHANT
▸ **ˈmerchanˌdiser** NOUN

merchandising (ˈmɜːtʃənˌdaɪzɪŋ) NOUN [1] the selection and display of goods in a retail outlet. [2] commercial goods, esp ones issued to exploit the popularity of a pop group, sporting event, etc.

merchant (ˈmɜːtʃənt) NOUN [1] a person engaged in the purchase and sale of commodities for profit, esp on international markets; trader. [2] *Chiefly US and Canadian* a person engaged in retail trade. [3] (esp in historical contexts) any trader. [4] *Derogatory* a person dealing or involved in something undesirable: *a gossip merchant.* [5] (*modifier*) **a** of the merchant navy: *a merchant sailor.* **b** of or concerned with trade: *a merchant ship.* ◆ VERB [6] (*tr*) to conduct trade in; deal in.
▷HISTORY C13: from Old French, probably from Vulgar Latin *mercātāre* (unattested), from Latin *mercārī* to trade, from *merx* goods, wares
▸ **ˈmerchant-ˌlike** ADJECTIVE

merchantable (ˈmɜːtʃəntəbᵊl) ADJECTIVE suitable for trading.

merchant bank NOUN (in Britain) a financial institution engaged primarily in accepting foreign bills, advising companies on flotations and takeovers, underwriting new issues, hire-purchase finance, making long-term loans to companies, and managing investment portfolios, funds, and trusts.
▸ **merchant banker** NOUN

merchantman (ˈmɜːtʃəntmən) NOUN, *plural* **-men.** a merchant ship.

merchant navy *or* **marine** NOUN the ships or crew engaged in a nation's commercial shipping.

merchant prince NOUN a very wealthy merchant.

merchet (ˈmɜːtʃɪt) NOUN (in feudal England) a fine paid by a tenant, esp a villein, to his lord for allowing the marriage of his daughter.
▷HISTORY C13: from Anglo-French, literally: MARKET

Mercia (ˈmɜːʃɪə) NOUN a kingdom and earldom of central and S England during the Anglo-Saxon period that reached its height under King Offa (757–96).

Mercian (ˈmɜːʃɪən) ADJECTIVE [1] of or relating to Mercia or the dialect spoken there. ◆ NOUN [2] the dialect of Old and Middle English spoken in the Midlands of England south of the River Humber. See also **Anglian, Northumbrian.**

merciful (ˈmɜːsɪfʊl) ADJECTIVE showing or giving mercy; compassionate.
▸ **ˈmercifulness** NOUN

mercifully (ˈmɜːsɪfʊlɪ) ADVERB [1] in a way that shows mercy; compassionately: *mercifully put down.* [2] (*sentence modifier*) fortunately; one is relieved to say that: *mercifully, all went well.*

merciless (ˈmɜːsɪlɪs) ADJECTIVE without mercy; pitiless, cruel, or heartless.
▸ **ˈmercilessly** ADVERB ▸ **ˈmercilessness** NOUN

Mercosur (ˈmɜːkəˌsə) NOUN a trading block composed of Argentina, Bolivia, Brazil, Chile, Paraguay, and Uruguay.
▷HISTORY C20: from Spanish *Mercado Común del Cono Sur* common market of the southern cone

mercurate (ˈmɜːkjʊˌreɪt) VERB [1] (*tr*) to treat or mix with mercury. [2] to undergo or cause to undergo a chemical reaction in which a mercury atom is added to a compound.
▸ **ˌmercuˈration** NOUN

mercurial (mɜːˈkjʊərɪəl) ADJECTIVE [1] of, like, containing, or relating to mercury. [2] volatile; lively: *a mercurial temperament.* [3] (*sometimes capital*) of, like, or relating to the god or the planet Mercury. ◆ NOUN [4] *Med* any salt of mercury for use as a medicine.
▷HISTORY C14: from Latin *mercuriālis*
▸ **merˈcurially** ADVERB ▸ **merˈcurialness** *or* **merˌcuriˈality** NOUN

mercurialism (mɜːˈkjʊərɪəˌlɪzᵊm) NOUN poisoning caused by chronic ingestion of mercury.

mercurialize *or* **mercurialise** (mɜːˈkjʊərɪəˌlaɪz) VERB (*tr*) [1] to make mercurial. [2] to treat with mercury or a mercury compound.
▸ **merˌcurialiˈzation** *or* **merˌcurialiˈsation** NOUN

mercuric (mɜːˈkjʊərɪk) ADJECTIVE of or containing mercury in the divalent state; denoting a mercury(II) compound.

mercuric chloride NOUN a white poisonous soluble crystalline substance used as a pesticide, antiseptic, and preservative for wood. Formula: $HgCl_2$. Systematic name: **mercury(II) chloride.** Also called: **bichloride of mercury, corrosive sublimate.**

mercuric oxide NOUN a soluble poisonous substance existing in red and yellow powdered forms: used as pigments. Formula: HgO. Systematic name: **mercury(II) oxide.**

mercuric sulphide NOUN a compound of mercury, usually existing as a black solid (**metacinnabarite**) or a red solid (**cinnabar** or **vermilion**), which is used as a pigment. Formula: HgS. Systematic name: **mercury(II) sulphide.**

Mercurochrome (məˈkjʊərəˌkrəʊm) NOUN *Trademark* a solution of merbromin, used as topical antibacterial agent.

mercurous (ˈmɜːkjʊrəs) ADJECTIVE of or containing mercury in the monovalent state; denoting a mercury(I) compound. Mercurous salts contain the divalent ion Hg_2^{2+}.

mercurous chloride NOUN a white tasteless insoluble powder used as a fungicide and formerly as a medical antiseptic, cathartic, and diuretic. Formula: Hg_2Cl_2. Systematic name: **mercury(I) chloride.** Also called: **calomel.**

mercury (ˈmɜːkjʊrɪ) NOUN, *plural* **-ries.** [1] Also called: **quicksilver, hydrargyrum.** a heavy silvery-white toxic liquid metallic element occurring principally in cinnabar: used in thermometers, barometers, mercury-vapour lamps, and dental amalgams. Symbol: Hg; atomic no.: 80; atomic wt.: 200.59; valency: 1 or 2; relative density: 13.546; melting pt.: –38.842°C; boiling pt.: 357°C. [2] any plant of the euphorbiaceous genus *Mercurialis.* See **dog's mercury.** [3] *Archaic* a messenger or courier.
▷HISTORY C14: from Latin *Mercurius* messenger of Jupiter, god of commerce; related to *merx* merchandise

Mercury[1] (ˈmɜːkjʊrɪ) NOUN *Roman myth* the messenger of the gods. Greek counterpart: **Hermes.**

Mercury[2] (ˈmɜːkjʊrɪ) NOUN the second smallest planet and the nearest to the sun. Mean distance from sun: 57.9 million km; period of revolution around sun: 88 days; period of axial rotation: 59 days; diameter and mass: 38 and 5.4 per cent that of earth respectively.

mercury arc NOUN **a** an electric discharge through ionized mercury vapour, producing a brilliant bluish-green light containing ultraviolet radiation. **b** (*as modifier*): *a mercury-arc rectifier.* See also **ignitron.**

mercury chloride NOUN See **mercurous chloride, mercuric chloride.**

mercury switch NOUN *Electrical engineering* a switch in which a circuit is completed between two terminals by liquid mercury when the switch is tilted.

mercury-vapour lamp NOUN a lamp in which an electric discharge through a low pressure of mercury vapour is used to produce a greenish-blue light. It is used for street lighting and is also a source of ultraviolet radiation.

mercy (ˈmɜːsɪ) NOUN, *plural* **-cies.** [1] compassionate treatment of or attitude towards an offender, adversary, etc., who is in one's power or care; clemency; pity. [2] the power to show mercy: *to throw oneself on someone's mercy.* [3] a relieving or welcome occurrence or state of affairs: *his death was a mercy after weeks of pain.* [4] **at the mercy of.** in the power of.
▷HISTORY C12: from Old French, from Latin *mercēs* wages, recompense, price, from *merx* goods

mercy flight NOUN an aircraft flight to bring a seriously ill or injured person to hospital from an isolated community.

mercy killing NOUN another term for **euthanasia.**

mercy seat NOUN [1] *Old Testament* the gold platform covering the Ark of the Covenant and regarded as the throne of God where he accepted sacrifices and gave commandments (Exodus 25:17, 22). [2] *Christianity* the throne of God.

mere[1] (mɪə) ADJECTIVE, *superlative* **merest.** being nothing more than something specified: *she is a mere child.*
▷HISTORY C15: from Latin *merus* pure, unmixed

mere[2] (mɪə) NOUN [1] *Dialect or archaic* a lake or marsh. [2] *Obsolete* the sea or an inlet of it.
▷HISTORY Old English *mere* sea, lake; related to Old Saxon *meri* sea, Old Norse *marr*, Old High German *mari;* compare Latin *mare*

mere[3] (mɪə) NOUN *Archaic* a boundary or boundary marker.
▷HISTORY Old English *gemǣre*

mere[4] (ˈmɛrɪ) NOUN *NZ* a short flat striking weapon.
▷HISTORY Maori

-mere NOUN COMBINING FORM indicating a part or division: *blastomere.*
▷HISTORY from Greek *meros* part, portion
▸ **-meric** ADJECTIVE COMBINING FORM

merely (ˈmɪəlɪ) ADVERB only; nothing more than.

merengue (məˈrɛŋgeɪ) NOUN [1] a type of lively dance music originating in the Dominican Republic, which combines African and Spanish elements. [2] a Caribbean dance in duple time with syncopated rhythm performed to such music.
▷HISTORY from American Spanish and Haitian Creole

mereology (ˌmiːrɪˈɒlədʒɪ) NOUN the formal study of the logical properties of the relation of part and whole.
▷HISTORY C20: via French from Greek *meros* part + -LOGY
▸ **ˌmereoˈlogical** ADJECTIVE

meretricious (ˌmɛrɪˈtrɪʃəs) ADJECTIVE [1]

superficially or garishly attractive. [2] insincere: *meretricious praise.* [3] *Archaic* of, like, or relating to a prostitute.
▷**HISTORY** C17: from Latin *merētrīcius,* from *merētrix* prostitute, from *merēre* to earn money
▸**ˌmereˈtriciously** ADVERB ▸**ˌmereˈtriciousness** NOUN

merganser (mɜːˈgænsə) NOUN, *plural* **-sers** *or* **-ser.** any of several typically crested large marine diving ducks of the genus *Mergus,* having a long slender hooked bill with serrated edges. Also called: **sawbill.** See also **goosander.**
▷**HISTORY** C18: from New Latin, from Latin *mergus* waterfowl, from *mergere* to plunge + *anser* goose

merge (mɜːdʒ) VERB [1] to meet and join or cause to meet and join. [2] to blend or cause to blend; fuse.
▷**HISTORY** C17: from Latin *mergere* to plunge
▸**ˈmergence** NOUN

merger (ˈmɜːdʒə) NOUN [1] *Commerce* the combination of two or more companies, either by the creation of a new organization or by absorption by one of the others. Often called (Brit): **amalgamation.** [2] *Law* the extinguishment of an estate, interest, contract, right, offence, etc., by its absorption into a greater one. [3] the act of merging or the state of being merged.

Mergui Archipelago (mɜːˈgwiː) NOUN a group of over 200 islands in the Andaman Sea, off the Tenasserim coast of S Myanmar: mountainous and forested.

Meriç (məˈriːtʃ) NOUN the Turkish name for the **Maritsa.**

Mérida (*Spanish* ˈmeriða) NOUN [1] a city in SE Mexico, capital of Yucatán state: founded in 1542 on the site of the ancient Mayan city of T'ho; centre of the henequen industry; university. Pop.: 660 848 (2000). [2] a city in W Venezuela: founded in 1558 by Spanish conquistadores; University of Los Andes (1785). Pop.: 230 101 (2000 est.). [3] a market town in W Spain, in Estremadura, on the Guadiana River: founded in 25 B.C.; became the capital of Lusitania and one of the chief cities of Iberia. Pop.: 49 830 (1991). Latin name: **Augusta Emerita.**

meridian (məˈrɪdɪən) NOUN [1] **a** one of the imaginary lines joining the north and south poles at right angles to the equator, designated by degrees of longitude from 0° at Greenwich to 180°. **b** the great circle running through both poles. See **prime meridian.** [2] *Astronomy* **a** the great circle on the celestial sphere passing through the north and south celestial poles and the zenith and nadir of the observer. **b** (*as modifier*): *a meridian instrument.* [3] Also called: **meridian section.** *Maths* a section of a surface of revolution, such as a paraboloid, that contains the axis of revolution. [4] the peak; zenith: *the meridian of his achievements.* [5] (in acupuncture, etc.) any of the channels through which vital energy is believed to circulate round the body. [6] *Obsolete* noon. ◆ ADJECTIVE [7] along or relating to a meridian. [8] of or happening at noon. [9] relating to the peak of something.
▷**HISTORY** C14: from Latin *merīdiānus* of midday, from *merīdiēs* midday, from *medius* MID[1] + *diēs* day

meridian circle NOUN an instrument used in astronomy for determining the declination and right ascension of stars. It consists of a telescope attached to a graduated circle.

meridional (məˈrɪdɪənᵊl) ADJECTIVE [1] along, relating to, or resembling a meridian. [2] characteristic of or located in the south, esp of Europe. ◆ NOUN [3] an inhabitant of the south, esp of France.
▷**HISTORY** C14: from Late Latin *merīdiōnālis* southern; see MERIDIAN; for form, compare *septentriōnālis* SEPTENTRIONAL
▸**meˈridionally** ADVERB

mering (ˈmɪərɪŋ) NOUN *Chiefly Irish* **a** another word for **mere**[3]. **b** (*as modifier*): *the mering wall.*
▷**HISTORY** C16: from MERE[3]

meringue (məˈræŋ) NOUN [1] stiffly beaten egg whites mixed with sugar and baked, often as a topping for pies, cakes, etc. [2] a small cake or shell of this mixture, often filled with cream.
▷**HISTORY** C18: from French, origin obscure

merino (məˈriːnəʊ) NOUN, *plural* **-nos.** [1] a breed of sheep, originating in Spain, bred for their fleece. [2] the long fine wool of this sheep. [3] the yarn made from this wool, often mixed with cotton. [4] **pure merino.** *Austral informal* **a** *History* a free settler rather than a convict. **b** an affluent and socially prominent person. **c** (*as modifier*): *a pure merino cricketer.* ◆ ADJECTIVE [5] made from merino wool.
▷**HISTORY** C18: from Spanish, origin uncertain

Merionethshire (ˌmɛrɪˈɒnɪθˌʃɪə, -ʃə) NOUN (until 1974) a county of N Wales, now part of Gwynedd.

meristem (ˈmɛrɪˌstɛm) NOUN a plant tissue responsible for growth, whose cells divide and differentiate to form the tissues and organs of the plant. Meristems occur within the stem (see **cambium**) and leaves and at the tips of stems and roots.
▷**HISTORY** C19: from Greek *meristos* divided, from *merizein* to divide, from *meris* portion
▸**meristematic** (ˌmɛrɪstɪˈmætɪk) ADJECTIVE

meristic (məˈrɪstɪk) ADJECTIVE *Biology* [1] of or relating to the number of organs or parts in an animal or plant body: *meristic variation.* [2] segmented: *meristic worms.*

merit (ˈmɛrɪt) NOUN [1] worth or superior quality; excellence: *work of great merit.* [2] (*often plural*) a deserving or commendable quality or act: *judge him on his merits.* [3] *Christianity* spiritual credit granted or received for good works. [4] the fact or state of deserving; desert. [5] an obsolete word for **reward.** ◆ VERB **-its, -iting, -ited.** [6] (*tr*) to be worthy of; deserve: *he merits promotion.* ◆ See also **merits.**
▷**HISTORY** C13: via Old French from Latin *meritum* reward, desert, from *merēre* to deserve
▸**ˈmerited** ADJECTIVE ▸**ˈmeritless** ADJECTIVE

meritocracy (ˌmɛrɪˈtɒkrəsɪ) NOUN, *plural* **-cies.** [1] rule by persons chosen not because of birth or wealth, but for their superior talents or intellect. [2] the persons constituting such a group. [3] a social system formed on such a basis.
▸**ˈmeritoˌcrat** NOUN ▸**meritocratic** (ˌmɛrɪtəˈkrætɪk) ADJECTIVE

meritorious (ˌmɛrɪˈtɔːrɪəs) ADJECTIVE praiseworthy; showing merit.
▷**HISTORY** C15: from Latin *meritōrius* earning money
▸**ˌmeriˈtoriously** ADVERB ▸**ˌmeriˈtoriousness** NOUN

merits (ˈmɛrɪts) PLURAL NOUN [1] the actual and intrinsic rights and wrongs of an issue, esp in a law case, as distinct from extraneous matters and technicalities. [2] **on its** (**his, her,** etc.) **merits.** on the intrinsic qualities or virtues.

merit system NOUN *US* the system of employing and promoting civil servants solely on the basis of ability rather than patronage. Compare **spoils system.**

merkin (ˈmɜːkɪn) NOUN [1] an artificial hairpiece for the pudendum; a pubic wig. [2] *Obsolete* the pudendum itself.
▷**HISTORY** C16: of unknown origin

merle[1] *or* **merl** (mɜːl; *Scot* mɛrl) NOUN *Scot* another name for the (European) **blackbird.**
▷**HISTORY** C15: via Old French from Latin *merula*

merle[2] (mɜːl) ADJECTIVE (of a dog, esp a collie) having a bluish-grey coat with speckles or streaks of black. Often called: **blue merle.**
▷**HISTORY** C20: from dialect *mirlet, mirly* speckled

merlin (ˈmɜːlɪn) NOUN a small falcon, *Falco columbarius,* that has a dark plumage with a black-barred tail: used in falconry. See also **pigeon hawk.**
▷**HISTORY** C14: from Old French *esmerillon,* from *esmeril,* of Germanic origin

Merlin (ˈmɜːlɪn) NOUN (in Arthurian legend) a wizard and counsellor to King Arthur eternally imprisoned in a tree by a woman to whom he revealed his secret craft.

merlon (ˈmɜːlən) NOUN *Fortifications* the solid upright section in a crenellated battlement.
▷**HISTORY** C18: from French, from Italian *merlone,* from *merlo* battlement

Merlot (ˈmɜːləʊ) NOUN (*sometimes not capital*) [1] a black grape grown in France and now throughout the wine-producing world, used, often in a blend, for making wine. [2] any of various wines made from this grape.
▷**HISTORY** from French *merlot,* literally: young blackbird, diminutive of *merle* MERLE[1], probably alluding to the colour of the grape

mermaid (ˈmɜːˌmeɪd) NOUN an imaginary sea creature fabled to have a woman's head and upper body and a fish's tail.
▷**HISTORY** C14: from *mere* lake, inlet + MAID

mermaid's purse NOUN another name for **sea purse.**

merman (ˈmɜːˌmæn) NOUN, *plural* **-men.** a male counterpart of the mermaid.
▷**HISTORY** C17: see MERMAID

mero- COMBINING FORM part or partial: *merocrine.*
▷**HISTORY** from Greek *meros* part, share

meroblastic (ˌmɛrəʊˈblæstɪk) ADJECTIVE *Embryol* of or showing cleavage of only the non-yolky part of the zygote, as in birds' eggs. Compare **holoblastic.**
▸**ˌmeroˈblastically** ADVERB

merocrine (ˈmɛrəˌkraɪn, -krɪn) ADJECTIVE (of the secretion of glands) characterized by formation of the product without undergoing disintegration. Compare **holocrine, apocrine.**
▷**HISTORY** C20: from MERO- + Greek *krinein* to separate

Meroë (ˈmɛrəʊˌiː) NOUN an ancient city in N Sudan, on the Nile; capital of a kingdom that flourished from about 700 B.C. to about 350 A.D.

meronym (ˈmɛrəʊˌnɪm) NOUN a part of something used to refer to the whole, such as *faces* meaning *people,* as in *they've seen a lot of faces come and go.*
▷**HISTORY** from Greek *meros* part + *onuma* name

meroplankton (ˌmɛrəʊˈplæŋktən) NOUN plankton consisting of organisms at a certain stage of their life cycles, esp larvae, the other stages not being spent as part of the plankton community. Compare **holoplankton.**

-merous ADJECTIVE COMBINING FORM (in biology) having a certain number or kind of parts: *dimerous.*
▷**HISTORY** from Greek *meros* part, division

Merovingian (ˌmɛrəʊˈvɪndʒɪən) ADJECTIVE [1] of or relating to a Frankish dynasty founded by Clovis I, which ruled Gaul and W Germany from about 500 to 751 A.D. ◆ NOUN [2] a member or supporter of this dynasty.
▷**HISTORY** C17: from French, from Medieval Latin *Merovingi* offspring of *Merovaeus,* Latin form of *Merowig,* traditional founder of the line

merozoite (ˌmɛrəʊˈzəʊaɪt) NOUN any of the cells formed by fission of a schizont during the life cycle of sporozoan protozoans, such as the malaria parasite. Compare **trophozoite.**
▷**HISTORY** C20: from MERO- + ZO(O) + -ITE[1]

merriment (ˈmɛrɪmənt) NOUN gaiety, fun, or mirth.

merry (ˈmɛrɪ) ADJECTIVE **-rier, -riest.** [1] cheerful; jolly. [2] very funny; hilarious. [3] *Brit informal* slightly drunk. [4] *Archaic* delightful. [5] **make merry.** to revel; be festive. [6] **play merry hell with.** *Informal* to disturb greatly; disrupt.
▷**HISTORY** Old English *merige* agreeable
▸**ˈmerrily** ADVERB ▸**ˈmerriness** NOUN

merry-andrew NOUN a joker, clown, or buffoon.
▷**HISTORY** C17: original reference of *Andrew* unexplained

merry dancers PLURAL NOUN *Scot* the aurora borealis.

merry-go-round NOUN [1] another name for **roundabout** (sense 1). [2] a whirl of activity or events: *the merry-go-round of the fashion world.*

merrymaking (ˈmɛrɪˌmeɪkɪŋ) NOUN fun, revelry, or festivity.
▸**ˈmerryˌmaker** NOUN

merry men PLURAL NOUN *Facetious* a person's assistants or followers.
▷**HISTORY** C19: originally, the companions of a knight, outlaw, etc.

merrythought (ˈmɛrɪˌθɔːt) NOUN *Brit* a less common word for **wishbone.**

merse (mɜːs; *Scot* mɛrs) NOUN *Scot* [1] low level ground by a river or shore, often alluvial and fertile. [2] a marsh.
▷**HISTORY** Old English *merse* marsh

Merse (mɜːs; *Scot* mɛrs) NOUN **the.** a fertile lowland area of SE Scotland, in Scottish Borders, north of the Tweed.

Merseburg (*German* ˈmɛrzəbʊrk) NOUN a city in E Germany, on the Saale River, in Saxony-Anhalt: residence of the dukes of Saxe-Merseburg (1656–1738); chemical industry. Pop.: 46 250 (latest est.).

Mersey (ˈmɜːzɪ) NOUN a river in W England, rising

in N Derbyshire and flowing northwest and west to the Irish Sea through a large estuary on which is situated the port of Liverpool. Length: about 112 km (70 miles).

Mersey beat NOUN **a** the characteristic pop music of the Beatles and other groups from Liverpool in the 1960s. **b** (*as modifier*): *the Merseybeat years.*

Merseyside ('mɜːzɪˌsaɪd) NOUN a metropolitan county of NW England, administered since 1986 by the unitary authorities of Sefton, Liverpool, St Helens, Knowsley, and Wirral. Area: 652 sq. km (252 sq. miles).

Mersin (mɛə'siːn) NOUN a port in S Turkey, on the Mediterranean: oil refinery. Pop.: 501 398 (1997). Also called: **Içel.**

Merthyr Tydfil ('mɜːθə 'tɪdvɪl) NOUN 1 a town in SE Wales, in Merthyr Tydfil county borough: formerly an important centre for the mining industry. Pop.: 39 482 (1991). 2 a county borough in SE Wales, created from part of N Mid Glamorgan in 1996. Pop.: 55 983 (2001). Area: 111 sq. km (43 sq. miles).

Merton ('mɜːtᵊn) NOUN a borough in SW Greater London. Pop.: 187 908 (2001). Area: 38 sq. km (15 sq. miles).

mes- COMBINING FORM a variant of **meso-** before a vowel: *mesarch; mesencephalon; mesenteron.*

mesa ('meɪsə) NOUN a flat tableland with steep edges, common in the southwestern US.
▷HISTORY from Spanish: table

mésalliance (mɛ'zælɪəns; *French* mezaljɑ̃s) NOUN marriage with a person of lower social status.
▷HISTORY C18: from French: MISALLIANCE

mesarch ('mɛsɑːk) ADJECTIVE *Botany* (of a xylem strand) having the first-formed xylem surrounded by that formed later, as in fern stems. Compare **exarch², endarch.**
▷HISTORY C19: from MES(O)- + Greek *arkhē* beginning

Mesa Verde ('meɪsə 'vɜːd) NOUN a high plateau in SW Colorado: remains of numerous prehistoric cliff dwellings, inhabited by the Pueblo Indians.

mescal (mɛ'skæl) NOUN 1 Also called: **peyote.** a spineless globe-shaped cactus, *Lophophora williamsii*, of Mexico and the southwestern US. Its button-like tubercles (**mescal buttons**) contain mescaline and are chewed by certain Indian tribes for their hallucinogenic effects. 2 a colourless alcoholic spirit distilled from the fermented juice of certain agave plants.
▷HISTORY C19: from American Spanish, from Nahuatl *mexcalli* the liquor, from *metl* MAGUEY + *ixcalli* stew

mescaline *or* **mescalin** ('mɛskəˌliːn, -lɪn) NOUN a hallucinogenic drug derived from mescal buttons. Formula: $C_{11}H_{17}NO_3$.

mesdames ('meɪˌdæm; *French* medam) NOUN the plural of **madame** and **madam** (sense 1).

mesdemoiselles (ˌmeɪdmwə'zɛl; *French* medmwazɛl) NOUN the plural of **mademoiselle.**

meseems (mɪ'siːmz) VERB, *past* **meseemed.** (*tr; takes a clause as object*) *Archaic* it seems to me.

mesembryanthemum (mɪzˌɛmbrɪ'ænθɪməm) NOUN any plant of a South African genus (*Mesembryanthemum*) of succulent-leaved prostrate or erect plants widely grown in gardens and greenhouses: family *Aizoaceae.* See **fig marigold, ice plant, Livingstone daisy.**
▷HISTORY C18: New Latin, from Greek *mesēmbria* noon + *anthemon* flower

mesencephalon (ˌmɛsɛn'sɛfəˌlɒn) NOUN the part of the brain that develops from the middle portion of the embryonic neural tube. Compare **prosencephalon, rhombencephalon.** Nontechnical name: **midbrain.**
▸**mesencephalic** (ˌmɛsɛnsɪ'fælɪk) ADJECTIVE

mesenchyme ('mɛsɛŋˌkaɪm) NOUN *Embryol* the part of the mesoderm that develops into connective tissue, cartilage, lymph, blood, etc.
▷HISTORY C19: New Latin, from MESO- + -ENCHYMA
▸**mesenchymal** (mɛs'ɛŋkɪməl) *or* **mesenchymatous** (ˌmɛsɛŋ'kɪmətəs) ADJECTIVE

mesenteritis (mɛsˌɛntə'raɪtɪs) NOUN inflammation of the mesentery.

mesenteron (mɛs'ɛntəˌrɒn) NOUN, *plural* **-tera** (-tərə). a former name for **midgut** (sense 1).
▸**mesˌenter'onic** ADJECTIVE

mesentery ('mɛsəntərɪ, 'mɛz-) NOUN, *plural* **-teries.** the double layer of peritoneum that is attached to the back wall of the abdominal cavity and supports most of the small intestine.
▷HISTORY C16: from New Latin *mesenterium;* see MESO- + ENTERON
▸ˌ**mesen'teric** ADJECTIVE

mesh (mɛʃ) NOUN 1 a network; net. 2 an open space between the strands of a network. 3 (*often plural*) the strands surrounding these spaces. 4 anything that ensnares, or holds like a net: *the mesh of the secret police.* 5 the engagement of teeth on interacting gearwheels: *the gears are in mesh.* 6 a measure of spacing of the strands of a mesh or grid, expressed as the distance between strands for coarse meshes or a number of strands per unit length for fine meshes. ◆ VERB 7 to entangle or become entangled. 8 (of gear teeth) to engage or cause to engage. 9 (*intr; often foll by with*) to coordinate (with): *to mesh with a policy.* 10 to work or cause to work in harmony.
▷HISTORY C16: probably from Dutch *maesche;* related to Old English *masc,* Old High German *masca*
▸'**meshy** ADJECTIVE

Meshach ('miːʃæk) NOUN *Old Testament* one of Daniel's three companions who, together with Shadrach and Abednego, was miraculously saved from destruction in Nebuchadnezzar's fiery furnace (Daniel 3:12-30).

mesh connection NOUN *Electrical engineering* (in a polyphase system) an arrangement in which the end of each phase is connected to the beginning of the next, forming a ring, each junction being connected to a terminal. See also **delta connection, star connection.**

Meshed (mɛ'ʃɛd) NOUN a variant of **Mashhad.**

meshuga *Yiddish* (mɪ'ʃʊgə) ADJECTIVE crazy.
▷HISTORY from Hebrew

mesiad ('miːzɪæd) ADJECTIVE *Anatomy, zoology* relating to or situated at the middle or centre.

mesial ('miːzɪəl) ADJECTIVE *Anatomy* another word for **medial** (sense 1).
▷HISTORY C19: from MESO- + -IAL
▸'**mesially** ADVERB

mesic ('miːzɪk) ADJECTIVE 1 of, relating to, or growing in conditions of medium water supply: *mesic plants.* 2 of or relating to a meson.
▸'**mesically** ADVERB

mesitylene (mɪ'sɪtɪˌliːn, 'mɛsɪtɪˌliːn) NOUN a colourless liquid that occurs in crude petroleum; 1,3,5-trimethylbenzene. Formula: $C_6H_3(CH_3)_3$.
▷HISTORY C19: from *mesityl,* from *mesite,* from New Latin *mesita,* from Greek *mesitēs* mediator + -ENE

mesmeric (mɛz'mɛrɪk) ADJECTIVE 1 holding (someone) as if spellbound. 2 of or relating to mesmerism.
▸**mes'merically** ADVERB

mesmerism ('mɛzməˌrɪzəm) NOUN *Psychol* 1 a hypnotic state induced by the operator's imposition of his will on that of the patient. 2 an early doctrine concerning this.
▷HISTORY C19: named after F. A. *Mesmer* (1734–1815), Austrian physician
▸'**mesmerist** NOUN

mesmerize *or* **mesmerise** ('mɛzməˌraɪz) VERB (*tr*) 1 a former word for **hypnotize.** 2 to hold (someone) as if spellbound.
▸ˌ**mesmeri'zation** *or* ˌ**mesmeri'sation** NOUN ▸'**mesmerˌizer** *or* '**mesmerˌiser** NOUN

mesnalty ('miːnəltɪ) NOUN, *plural* **-ties.** *History* the lands of a mesne lord.
▷HISTORY C16: from legal French, from MESNE

mesne (miːn) ADJECTIVE *Law* 1 intermediate or intervening: used esp of any assignment of property before the last: *a mesne assignment.* 2 **mesne profits.** rents or profits accruing during the rightful owner's exclusion from his land.
▷HISTORY C15: from legal French *meien* in the middle, MEAN³

mesne lord NOUN (in feudal society) a lord who held land from a superior lord and kept his own tenants on it.

meso- *or before a vowel* **mes-** COMBINING FORM middle or intermediate: *mesomorph.*
▷HISTORY from Greek *misos* middle

Mesoamerica *or* **Meso-America** (ˌmɛsəʊə'mɛrɪkə) NOUN another name for **Central America.**
▸ˌ**Mesoa'merican** *or* ˌ**Meso-A'merican** ADJECTIVE, NOUN

mesobenthos (ˌmɛzə'bɛnθəs, ˌmɛsə-) NOUN flora and fauna living at the bottom of seas 182 to 914 metres deep.
▷HISTORY from MESO- + Greek *benthos* depth of the sea

mesoblast ('mɛsəʊˌblæst) NOUN another name for **mesoderm.**
▸ˌ**meso'blastic** ADJECTIVE

mesocarp ('mɛsəʊˌkɑːp) NOUN the middle layer of the pericarp of a fruit, such as the flesh of a peach.

mesocephalic (ˌmɛsəʊsɪ'fælɪk) *Anatomy* ◆ ADJECTIVE 1 having a medium-sized head, esp one with a cephalic index between 75 and 80. ◆ NOUN 2 an individual with such a head. ◆ Compare **brachycephalic, dolichocephalic.**
▸**mesocephaly** (ˌmɛsəʊ'sɛfəlɪ) NOUN

mesocratic (ˌmɛsə'krætɪk) ADJECTIVE (of igneous rocks) containing 30–60 per cent of ferromagnesian minerals.
▷HISTORY C20: from MESO- + -CRAT, with allusion to the moderately dark colour of the rock. Compare LEUCOCRATIC

mesoderm ('mɛsəʊˌdɜːm) NOUN the middle germ layer of an animal embryo, giving rise to muscle, blood, bone, connective tissue, etc. See also **ectoderm, endoderm.**
▸ˌ**meso'dermal** *or* ˌ**meso'dermic** ADJECTIVE

mesogastrium (ˌmɛsəʊ'gæstrɪəm) NOUN the mesentery supporting the embryonic stomach.
▸ˌ**meso'gastric** ADJECTIVE

mesoglea *or* **mesogloea** (ˌmɛsəʊ'gliːə) NOUN the gelatinous material between the outer and inner cellular layers of jellyfish and other coelenterates.
▷HISTORY C19: New Latin, from MESO- + Greek *gloia* glue

mesognathous (mɪ'sɒgnəθəs) ADJECTIVE *Anthropol* having slightly projecting jaws.
▸**me'sognathism** *or* **me'sognathy** NOUN

mesokurtic (ˌmɛsəʊ'kɜːtɪk) ADJECTIVE *Statistics* (of a distribution) having kurtosis $B_2 = 3$, concentrated around its mean like a normal distribution. Compare **leptokurtic, platykurtic.**
▷HISTORY C20: from MESO- + Greek *kurtos* arched, bulging + -IC

Mesolithic (ˌmɛsəʊ'lɪθɪk) NOUN 1 the period between the Palaeolithic and the Neolithic, in Europe from about 12 000 to 3000 B.C., characterized by the appearance of microliths. ◆ ADJECTIVE 2 of or relating to the Mesolithic.

Mesolonghi (ˌmɛsə'lɔːŋgɪ) NOUN a variant of **Missolonghi.**

Mesolóngion (ˌmɛsə'lɒŋgɪˌɒn) NOUN transliteration of the Modern Greek name for **Missolonghi.**

mesomorph ('mɛsəʊˌmɔːf) NOUN a person with a muscular body build: said to be correlated with somatotonia. Compare **ectomorph, endomorph** (sense 1).

mesomorphic (ˌmɛsəʊ'mɔːfɪk) ADJECTIVE *also* **mesomorphous.** 1 *Chem* existing in or concerned with an intermediate state of matter between a true liquid and a true solid. See also **liquid crystal, smectic, nematic.** 2 relating to or being a mesomorph.
▸ˌ**meso'morphism** NOUN ▸'**mesoˌmorphy** NOUN

meson ('miːzɒn) NOUN any of a group of elementary particles, such as a pion or kaon, that usually has a rest mass between those of an electron and a proton, and an integral spin. They are responsible for the force between nucleons in the atomic nucleus. Former name: **mesotron.** See also **muon.**
▷HISTORY C20: from MESO- + -ON
▸**me'sonic** *or* '**mesic** ADJECTIVE

mesonephros (ˌmɛsəʊ'nɛfrɒs) NOUN the middle part of the embryonic kidney in vertebrates, becoming the adult kidney in fishes and amphibians and the epididymis in reptiles, birds, and mammals. See also **pronephros, metanephros.**
▷HISTORY C19: New Latin, from MESO- + Greek *nephros* kidney
▸ˌ**meso'nephric** ADJECTIVE

mesopause ('mɛsəʊˌpɔːz) NOUN *Meteorol* the zone

of minimum temperature between the mesosphere and the thermosphere.

mesopelagic (ˌmɛsəʊpəˈlædʒɪk) ADJECTIVE of, relating to, or inhabiting the intermediate depths of the ocean between approximately 100 and 1000 metres.

mesophilic (ˌmɛsəʊˈfɪlɪk) ADJECTIVE *Biology* (esp of bacteria) having an ideal growth temperature of 20–45°C.
▸**mesophile** (ˈmɛsəʊˌfaɪl) NOUN

mesophyll (ˈmɛsəʊˌfɪl) NOUN the soft chlorophyll-containing tissue of a leaf between the upper and lower layers of epidermis: involved in photosynthesis.
▸**ˌmesoˈphyllic** *or* **ˌmesoˈphyllous** ADJECTIVE

mesophyte (ˈmɛsəʊˌfaɪt) NOUN any plant that grows in surroundings receiving an average supply of water.
▸**mesophytic** (ˌmɛsəʊˈfɪtɪk) ADJECTIVE

Mesopotamia (ˌmɛsəpəˈteɪmɪə) NOUN a region of SW Asia between the lower and middle reaches of the Tigris and Euphrates rivers: site of several ancient civilizations.
▷HISTORY Latin from Greek *mesopotamia* (*khora*) (the land) between rivers

Mesopotamian (ˌmɛsəpəˈteɪmɪən) ADJECTIVE 1 of or relating to Mesopotamia, a region of SW Asia, or its inhabitants. ◆ NOUN 2 a native or inhabitant of Mesopotamia.

mesosphere (ˈmɛsəʊˌsfɪə) NOUN 1 the atmospheric layer lying between the stratosphere and the thermosphere, characterized by a rapid decrease in temperature with height. 2 the solid part of the earth's mantle lying between the asthenosphere and the core.
▸**mesospheric** (ˌmɛsəʊˈsfɛrɪk) ADJECTIVE

mesothelioma (ˌmɛzəʊˌθiːlɪˈəʊmə) NOUN, *plural* **-mata** (-mətə) *or* **-mas**. a tumour of the epithelium lining the lungs, abdomen, or heart: often associated with exposure to asbestos dust.
▷HISTORY C20: from MESOTHELI(UM) + -OMA

mesothelium (ˌmɛsəʊˈθiːlɪəm) NOUN, *plural* **-liums** *or* **-lia** (-lɪə). epithelium, derived from embryonic mesoderm lining body cavities.
▷HISTORY from New Latin, from MESO- + (EPI)THELIUM
▸**ˌmesoˈthelial** ADJECTIVE

mesothorax (ˌmɛsəʊˈθɔːræks) NOUN, *plural* **-raxes** *or* **-races** (-rəˌsiːz). the middle segment of the thorax of an insect, bearing the second pair of walking legs and the first pair of wings. See also **prothorax, metathorax.**
▸**mesothoracic** (ˌmɛsəʊθɔːˈræsɪk) ADJECTIVE

mesothorium (ˌmɛsəʊˈθɔːrɪəm) NOUN *Physics, obsolete* either of the two radioactive elements which are decay products of thorium. **Mesothorium I** is now called radium-228. **Mesothorium II** is now called actinium-228.

mesotron (ˈmɛsəˌtrɒn) NOUN a former name for **meson.**

Mesozoic (ˌmɛsəʊˈzəʊɪk) ADJECTIVE 1 of, denoting, or relating to an era of geological time that began 250 000 000 years ago with the Triassic period and lasted about 185 000 000 years until the end of the Cretaceous period. ◆ NOUN 2 **the.** the Mesozoic era.

mesquite *or* **mesquit** (mɛˈskiːt, ˈmɛskiːt) NOUN any small leguminous tree of the genus *Prosopis*, esp the tropical American *P. juliflora*, whose sugary pods (**mesquite beans**) are used as animal fodder. Also called: **algarroba, honey locust, honey mesquite.**
▷HISTORY C19: from Mexican Spanish, from Nahuatl *mizquitl*

mess (mɛs) NOUN 1 a state of confusion or untidiness, esp if dirty or unpleasant: *the house was in a mess.* 2 a chaotic or troublesome state of affairs; muddle: *his life was a mess.* 3 *Informal* a dirty or untidy person or thing. 4 *Archaic* a portion of food, esp soft or semiliquid food. 5 a place where service personnel eat or take recreation: *an officers' mess.* 6 a group of people, usually servicemen, who eat together. 7 the meal so taken. 8 **mess of pottage.** a material gain involving the sacrifice of a higher value. ◆ VERB 9 (*tr; often foll by up*) to muddle or dirty. 10 (*intr*) to make a mess. 11 (*intr; often foll by with*) to interfere; meddle. 12 (*intr; often foll by with or together*) *Military* to group together, esp for eating.
▷HISTORY C13: from Old French *mes* dish of food, from Late Latin *missus* course (at table), from Latin *mittere* to send forth, set out

mess about *or* **around** VERB (*adverb*) 1 (*intr*) to occupy oneself trivially; potter. 2 (when *intr*, often foll by *with*) to interfere or meddle (with). 3 (*intr; sometimes foll by with*) *Chiefly US* to engage in adultery.

message (ˈmɛsɪdʒ) NOUN 1 a communication, usually brief, from one person or group to another. 2 an implicit meaning or moral, as in a work of art. 3 a formal communiqué. 4 an inspired communication of a prophet or religious leader. 5 a mission; errand. 6 (*plural*) *Scot* shopping: *going for the messages.* 7 **get the message.** *Informal* to understand what is meant. ◆ VERB 8 (*tr*) to send as a message, esp to signal (a plan, etc.).
▷HISTORY C13: from Old French, from Vulgar Latin *missāticum* (unattested) something sent, from Latin *missus*, past participle of *mittere* to send

message stick NOUN a stick bearing carved symbols, carried by a native Australian as identification.

message switching NOUN *Computing* the maintenance of a telecommunication link between two devices for the duration of a message.

messaging (ˈmɛsɪdʒɪŋ) NOUN the practice of sending and receiving written communications by computer or mobile phone.

messaline (ˌmɛsəˈliːn, ˈmɛsəˌliːn) NOUN a light lustrous twilled-silk fabric.
▷HISTORY C20: from French, origin obscure

Messapian (məˈseɪpɪən) *or* **Messapic** (məˈseɪpɪk, -ˈsæpɪk) NOUN a scantily recorded language of an ancient people of Calabria (the **Messapii**), thought by some to be related to ancient Illyrian.

Messeigneurs *French* (mesɛɲœr) NOUN the plural of **Monseigneur.**

Messene (mɛˈsiːnɪ) NOUN an ancient Greek city in the SW Peloponnese: founded in 369 B.C. as the capital of Messenia.

messenger (ˈmɛsɪndʒə) NOUN 1 a person who takes messages from one person or group to another or others. 2 a person who runs errands or is employed to run errands. 3 a carrier of official dispatches; courier. 4 *Nautical* **a** a light line used to haul in a heavy rope. **b** an endless belt of chain, rope, or cable, used on a powered winch to take off power. 5 *Archaic* a herald.
▷HISTORY C13: from Old French *messagier*, from MESSAGE

messenger RNA NOUN *Biochem* a form of RNA, transcribed from a single strand of DNA, that carries genetic information required for protein synthesis from DNA to the ribosomes. Sometimes shortened to: **mRNA.** See also **transfer RNA, genetic code.**

Messenia (məˈsiːnɪə) NOUN the southwestern area of the Peloponnese in S Greece.

mess hall NOUN a military dining room, usually large.

Messiah (mɪˈsaɪə) NOUN 1 *Judaism* the awaited redeemer of the Jews, to be sent by God to free them. 2 Jesus Christ, when regarded in this role. 3 an exceptional or hoped for liberator of a country or people.
▷HISTORY C14: from Old French *Messie*, ultimately from Hebrew *māshīach* anointed
▸**Mesˈsiahˌship** NOUN

messianic (ˌmɛsɪˈænɪk) ADJECTIVE 1 (*sometimes capital*) *Bible* **a** of or relating to the Messiah, his awaited deliverance of the Jews, or the new age of peace expected to follow this. **b** of or relating to Jesus Christ or the salvation believed to have been brought by him. 2 **a** of or relating to any popular leader promising deliverance or an ideal era of peace and prosperity. **b** of or relating to promises of this kind or to an ideal era of this kind.
▸**ˌmessiˈanically** ADVERB ▸**messianism** (mɛˈsaɪənɪzəm) NOUN

Messidor *French* (mesidɔr) NOUN the month of harvest: the tenth month of the French revolutionary calendar, extending from June 20 to July 19.
▷HISTORY C19: from French, from Latin *messis* harvest + Greek *dōron* gift

Messier catalogue (ˈmɛsɪeɪ) NOUN *Astronomy* a catalogue of 103 nonstellar objects, such as nebulae and galaxies, prepared in 1781–86. An object is referred to by its number in this catalogue, for example the Andromeda Galaxy is referred to as *M31*.
▷HISTORY C18: named after Charles *Messier* (1730–1817), French astronomer

messieurs (ˈmɛsəz; *French* mesjø) NOUN the plural of **monsieur.**

Messina (mɛˈsiːnə) NOUN a port in NE Sicily, on the **Strait of Messina**: colonized by Greeks around 730 B.C.; under Spanish rule (1282–1676 and 1678–1713); university (1549). Pop.: 259 156 (2000 est.).

mess jacket NOUN a waist-length jacket tapering to a point at the back, worn by officers in the mess for formal dinners.

mess kit NOUN *Military* 1 *Brit* formal evening wear for officers. 2 Also called: **mess gear.** eating utensils used esp in the field.

messmate (ˈmɛsˌmeɪt) NOUN 1 a person with whom one shares meals in a mess, esp in the army. 2 *Austral* any of various eucalyptus trees that grow amongst other species.

Messrs (ˈmɛsəz) NOUN the plural of **Mr.**
▷HISTORY C18: abbreviation from French *messieurs*

messuage (ˈmɛswɪdʒ) NOUN *Property law* a dwelling house together with its outbuildings, curtilage, and the adjacent land appropriated to its use.
▷HISTORY C14: from Norman French: household, perhaps through misspelling of Old French *mesnage* MÉNAGE

messy (ˈmɛsɪ) ADJECTIVE **messier, messiest.** dirty, confused, or untidy.
▸**ˈmessily** ADVERB ▸**ˈmessiness** NOUN

mestee (mɛˈstiː) NOUN a variant of **mustee.**

mester (ˈmɛstə) NOUN *South Yorkshire dialect* 1 master: used as a term of address for a man who is the head of a house. 2 **bad mester.** a term for the devil, used when speaking to children.

mestizo (mɛˈstiːzəʊ, mɪ-) NOUN, *plural* **-zos** *or* **-zoes.** a person of mixed parentage, esp the offspring of a Spanish American and an American Indian.
▷HISTORY C16: from Spanish, ultimately from Latin *miscēre* to mix
▸**mestiza** (mɛˈstiːzə) FEMININE NOUN

mestome (ˈmɛstəʊm) *or* **mestom** NOUN *Botany* **a** conducting tissue associated with parenchyma. **b** (*as modifier*): *a mestome sheath.*
▷HISTORY C19: from Greek *mestōma* filling up

mestranol (ˈmɛstrəˌnɒl, -ˌnəʊl) NOUN a synthetic oestrogen used in combination with progestogens as an oral contraceptive. Formula: $C_{21}H_{26}O_2$.
▷HISTORY C20: from M(ETHYL) + (O)ESTR(OGEN) + (*pregn*)*an*(*e*) ($C_{21}H_{36}$) + -OL

met (mɛt) VERB the past tense and past participle of **meet.**

met. ABBREVIATION FOR: 1 meteorological: *the met. office weather report.* 2 meteorology.

Meta (ˈmeɪtə; *Spanish* ˈmeta) NOUN a river in Colombia, rising in the Andes and flowing northeast and east, forming part of the border between Colombia and Venezuela, to join the Orinoco River. Length: about 1000 km (620 miles).

meta- *or sometimes before a vowel* **met-** PREFIX 1 indicating change, alteration, or alternation: *metabolism; metamorphosis.* 2 (of an academic discipline, esp philosophy) concerned with the concepts and results of the named discipline: *metamathematics; meta-ethics.* See also **metatheory.** 3 occurring or situated behind or after: *metaphase.* 4 (*often in italics*) denoting that an organic compound contains a benzene ring with substituents in the 1,3-positions: *metadinitrobenzene; meta-cresol.* Abbreviation: ***m-***. Compare **ortho-** (sense 4), **para-**[1] (sense 6). 5 denoting an isomer, polymer, or compound related to a specified compound (often differing from similar compounds that are prefixed by *para-*): *metaldehyde.* 6 denoting an oxyacid that is a lower hydrated form of the anhydride or a salt of such an acid: *metaphosphoric acid.* Compare **ortho-** (sense 5).
▷HISTORY Greek, from *meta* with, after, between, among. Compare Old English *mid, mith* with, Old Norse *meth* with, between

metabolic pathway NOUN any of the sequences of biochemical reactions, catalysed by enzymes, that occur in all living cells: concerned mainly with the exchange of energy and chemicals. See also **Krebs cycle.**

metabolism (mɪˈtæbəˌlɪzəm) NOUN [1] the sum total of the chemical processes that occur in living organisms, resulting in growth, production of energy, elimination of waste material, etc. See **anabolism, basal metabolism, catabolism.** [2] the sum total of the chemical processes affecting a particular substance in the body: *carbohydrate metabolism; iodine metabolism.*
▷HISTORY C19: from Greek *metabolē* change, from *metaballein* to change, from META- + *ballein* to throw
▸**metabolic** (ˌmɛtəˈbɒlɪk) ADJECTIVE ▸ˌ**metaˈbolically** ADVERB

metabolite (mɪˈtæbəˌlaɪt) NOUN a substance produced during or taking part in metabolism.
▷HISTORY C19: METABOL(ISM) + -ITE[1]

metabolize *or* **metabolise** (mɪˈtæbəˌlaɪz) VERB to bring about or subject to metabolism.
▸**meˈtaboˌlizable** *or* **meˈtaboˌlisable** ADJECTIVE

metabolome (mɪˈtæbəˌləʊm) NOUN the full complement of metabolites present in a cell, tissue, or organism in a particular physiological or developmental state.
▷HISTORY C20: from METABOL(ITE) + -OME

metabolomics (mɪˈtæˌbəˈlɒmɪks) NOUN (*functioning as singular*) the study of all the metabolites present in cells, tissues, and organs.

metaboly (mɪˈtæbəlɪ) NOUN *Biology* the ability of some cells, esp protozoans, to alter their shape.

metacarpal (ˌmɛtəˈkɑːpᵊl) *Anatomy* ◆ ADJECTIVE [1] of or relating to the metacarpus. ◆ NOUN [2] a metacarpal bone.

metacarpus (ˌmɛtəˈkɑːpəs) NOUN, *plural* **-pi** (-paɪ). [1] the skeleton of the hand between the wrist and the fingers, consisting of five long bones. [2] the corresponding bones in other vertebrates.

metacentre *or US* **metacenter** (ˈmɛtəˌsɛntə) NOUN the intersection of a vertical line through the centre of buoyancy of a floating body at equilibrium with the formerly vertical line through the centre of gravity of the body when the body is tilted.
▸ˌ**metaˈcentric** ADJECTIVE

metachromatic (ˌmɛtəkrəʊˈmætɪk) ADJECTIVE [1] (of tissues and cells stained for microscopical examination) taking a colour different from that of the dye solution. [2] (of dyes) capable of staining tissues or cells a colour different from that of the dye solution. [3] of or relating to metachromatism.

metachromatism (ˌmɛtəˈkrəʊməˌtɪzəm) NOUN a change in colour, esp when caused by a change in temperature.
▷HISTORY C19: from META- + CHROMATO- + -ISM

metachrosis (ˌmɛtəˈkrəʊsɪs) NOUN *Zoology* the ability of some animals, such as chameleons, to change their colour.
▷HISTORY C19: from META- + Greek *khrōs* colour

metacinnabarite (ˌmɛtəsɪˈnæbəˌraɪt) NOUN the black solid form of mercuric sulphide.

metacognition (ˌmɛtəkɒɡˈnɪʃən) NOUN *Psychol* thinking about one's own mental processes.

metacomputer (ˌmɛtəkəmˈpjuːtə) NOUN an interconnected and balanced set of computers that operate as a single unit.
▸ˌ**metacomˈputing** NOUN

meta-ethics NOUN (*functioning as singular*) the philosophical study of questions about the nature of ethical judgment as distinct from questions of normative ethics, for example, whether ethical judgments state facts or express attitudes, whether there are objective standards of morality, and how moral judgments can be justified.
▸ˌ**meta-ˈethical** ADJECTIVE

metafemale (ˌmɛtəˈfiːmeɪl) NOUN *Genetics* a sterile female organism, esp a fruit fly (*Drosophila*) that has three X chromosomes. Former name: **superfemale.**

metagalaxy (ˌmɛtəˈɡæləksɪ) NOUN, *plural* **-axies.** the total system of galaxies and intergalactic space making up the universe.
▸**metagalactic** (ˌmɛtəɡəˈlæktɪk) ADJECTIVE

metage (ˈmiːtɪdʒ) NOUN [1] the official measuring of weight or contents. [2] a charge for this.
▷HISTORY C16: from METE[1]

metagenesis (ˌmɛtəˈdʒɛnɪsɪs) NOUN another name for **alternation of generations.**
▸**metagenetic** (ˌmɛtədʒɪˈnɛtɪk) *or* ˌ**metaˈgenic** ADJECTIVE
▸ˌ**metageˈnetically** ADVERB

metagnathous (mɪˈtæɡnəθəs) ADJECTIVE (of the beaks of birds such as the crossbill) having crossed tips.
▷HISTORY C19: from META- + -GNATHOUS
▸**meˈtagnaˌthism** NOUN

metal (ˈmɛtᵊl) NOUN [1] **a** any of a number of chemical elements, such as iron or copper, that are often lustrous ductile solids, have basic oxides, form positive ions, and are good conductors of heat and electricity. **b** an alloy, such as brass or steel, containing one or more of these elements. [2] *Printing* type made of metal. [3] the substance of glass in a molten state or as the finished product. [4] short for **road metal.** [5] *Informal* short for **heavy metal** (sense 1). [6] *Navy* **a** the total weight of projectiles that can be shot by a ship's guns at any one time. **b** the total weight or number of a ship's guns. [7] *Astronomy* any element heavier than helium. Also called: **heavy element.** [8] *Heraldry* gold or silver. [9] (*plural*) the rails of a railway. ◆ ADJECTIVE [10] made of metal. ◆ VERB **-als, -alling, -alled** *or US* **-als, -aling, -aled.** (*tr*) [11] to fit or cover with metal. [12] to make or mend (a road) with **road metal.**
▷HISTORY C13: from Latin *metallum* mine, product of a mine, from Greek *metallon*
▸ˈ**metalled** ADJECTIVE ▸ˈ**metal-ˌlike** ADJECTIVE

metal. *or* **metall.** ABBREVIATION FOR: [1] metallurgical. [2] metallurgy.

metalanguage (ˈmɛtəˌlæŋɡwɪdʒ) NOUN a language or system of symbols used to discuss another language or system. See also **formal language, natural language.** Compare **object language.**

metal detector NOUN a device that gives an audible or visual signal when its search head comes close to a metallic object embedded in food, buried in the ground, etc.

metalled (ˈmɛtᵊld) ADJECTIVE [1] made or mended with **road metal.** [2] fitted or covered with metal.

metallic (mɪˈtælɪk) ADJECTIVE [1] of, concerned with, or consisting of metal or a metal. [2] suggestive of a metal: *a metallic click; metallic lustre.* [3] *Chem* (of a metal element) existing in the free state rather than in combination: *metallic copper.*
▸**meˈtallically** ADVERB

metallic bond NOUN *Chem* the covalent bonding between atoms in metals, in which the valence electrons are free to move through the crystal.

metallic lens NOUN an arrangement of louvres used to direct and focus electromagnetic or sound waves.

metallic soap NOUN any one of a number of colloidal stearates, palmitates, or oleates of various metals, including aluminium, calcium, magnesium, iron, and zinc. They are used as bases for ointments, fungicides, fireproofing and waterproofing agents, and dryers for paints and varnishes.

metalliferous (ˌmɛtᵊˈlɪfərəs) ADJECTIVE containing a high concentration of metallic elements: *a metalliferous ore.*
▷HISTORY C17: from Latin *metallifer* yielding metal, from *metallum* metal + *ferre* to bear

metalline (ˈmɛtəˌlaɪn) ADJECTIVE [1] of, resembling, or relating to metals. [2] containing metals or metal ions.

metallist *or US* **metalist** (ˈmɛtᵊlɪst) NOUN [1] a person who works with metals. [2] a person who advocates a system of currency based on a metal, such as gold or silver.

metallize, metallise, *or US* **metalize** (ˈmɛtəˌlaɪz) VERB (*tr*) to make metallic or to coat or treat with metal.
▸ˌ**metalliˈzation** *or* ˌ**metalliˈsation** *or* (*US*) ˌ**metaliˈzation** NOUN

metallo- COMBINING FORM denoting metal: *metallography; metalloid; metallurgy.*
▷HISTORY from Greek *metallon*

metallocene (mɪˈtæləʊˌsiːn) NOUN *Chem* any one of a class of organometallic sandwich compounds of the general formula $M(C_5H_5)_2$, where M is a metal atom. See **ferrocene.**
▷HISTORY C20: from METALLO- + *-cene,* as in FERROCENE

metallography (ˌmɛtəˈlɒɡrəfɪ) NOUN [1] the branch of metallurgy concerned with the composition and structure of metals and alloys. [2] a lithographic process using metal plates instead of stone; metal lithography.
▸ˌ**metalˈlographer** *or* ˌ**metalˈlographist** NOUN
▸**metallographic** (mɪˌtæləˈɡræfɪk) ADJECTIVE
▸**meˌtalloˈgraphically** ADVERB

metalloid (ˈmɛtəˌlɔɪd) NOUN [1] a nonmetallic element, such as arsenic or silicon, that has some of the properties of a metal. ◆ ADJECTIVE *also* **metalloidal** (ˌmɛtəˈlɔɪdᵊl). [2] of or being a metalloid. [3] resembling a metal.

metallophone (mɛˈtæləˌfəʊn) NOUN any of various musical instruments consisting of tuned metal bars struck with a hammer, such as the glockenspiel.

metallurgy (mɛˈtælədʒɪ; *US* ˈmɛtᵊˌlɜːdʒɪ) NOUN the scientific study of the extraction, refining, alloying, and fabrication of metals and of their structure and properties.
▸ˌ**metalˈlurgic** *or* ˌ**metalˈlurgical** ADJECTIVE
▸ˌ**metalˈlurgically** ADVERB ▸**metallurgist** (mɛˈtælədʒɪst, ˈmɛtəˌlɜːdʒɪst) NOUN

metal spraying NOUN a process in which a layer of one metal is sprayed onto another in the molten state.

metal tape NOUN a magnetic recording tape coated with pure iron rather than iron oxide or chromedioxide: it gives enhanced recording quality.

metalwork (ˈmɛtᵊlˌwɜːk) NOUN [1] the craft of working in metal. [2] work in metal or articles made from metal.

metalworking (ˈmɛtᵊlˌwɜːkɪŋ) NOUN the processing of metal to change its shape, size, etc., as by rolling, forging, etc., or by making metal articles.
▸ˈ**metalˌworker** NOUN

metamale (ˈmɛtəˌmeɪl) NOUN *Genetics* a sterile male organism, esp a fruit fly (*Drosophila*) that has one X chromosome and three sets of autosomes. Former name: **supermale.**

metamathematics (ˌmɛtəˌmæθɪˈmætɪks) NOUN (*functioning as singular*) the logical analysis of the reasoning, principles, and rules that control the use and combination of mathematical symbols, numbers, etc.
▸ˌ**metaˌmatheˈmatical** ADJECTIVE ▸ˌ**metaˌmathemaˈtician** NOUN

metamer (ˈmɛtəmə) NOUN any of two or more isomeric compounds exhibiting metamerism.

metamere (ˈmɛtəˌmɪə) NOUN one of the similar body segments into which earthworms, crayfish, and similar animals are divided longitudinally. Also called: **somite.**
▷HISTORY C19: from META- + -MERE
▸**metameral** (mɪˈtæmərəl) ADJECTIVE

metameric (ˌmɛtəˈmɛrɪk) ADJECTIVE [1] divided into or consisting of metameres. See also **metamerism** (sense 1). [2] of or concerned with metamerism.
▸ˌ**metaˈmerically** ADVERB

metamerism (mɪˈtæməˌrɪzəm) NOUN [1] Also called: **(metameric) segmentation.** the division of an animal into similar segments (metameres). In many vertebrates it is confined to the embryonic nervous and muscular systems. [2] *Chem* a type of isomerism in which molecular structures differ by the attachment of different groups to the same atom, as in $CH_3OC_3H_7$ and $C_2H_5OC_2H_5$.

metamict (ˈmɛtəˌmɪkt) ADJECTIVE of or denoting the amorphous state of a substance that has lost its crystalline structure as a result of the radioactivity of uranium or thorium within it: *metamict minerals.*
▷HISTORY C19: from Danish *metamikt,* from META- + Greek *miktos* mixed
▸ˌ**metamictiˈzation** *or* ˌ**metamictiˈsation** NOUN

metamorphic (ˌmɛtəˈmɔːfɪk) *or* **metamorphous** ADJECTIVE [1] relating to or resulting from metamorphosis or metamorphism. [2] (of rocks) altered considerably from their original structure and mineralogy by pressure and heat. Compare **igneous, sedimentary.**

metamorphism (ˌmɛtəˈmɔːfɪzəm) NOUN [1] the process by which metamorphic rocks are formed. [2] a variant of **metamorphosis.**

metamorphose (ˌmɛtəˈmɔːfəʊz) VERB to undergo or cause to undergo metamorphosis or metamorphism.

metamorphosis (ˌmɛtəˈmɔːfəsɪs) NOUN, *plural* **-ses** (-ˌsiːz). [1] a complete change of physical form

or substance. [2] a complete change of character, appearance, etc. [3] a person or thing that has undergone metamorphosis. [4] *Zoology* the rapid transformation of a larva into an adult that occurs in certain animals, for example the stage between tadpole and frog or between chrysalis and butterfly.
▷HISTORY C16: via Latin from Greek: transformation, from META- + *morphē* form

metanephros (ˌmɛtəˈnɛfrɒs) NOUN, *plural* **-roi** (-rɔɪ). the last-formed posterior part of the embryonic kidney in reptiles, birds, and mammals, which remains functional in the adult. See also **pronephros, mesonephros.**
▷HISTORY C19: New Latin, from META- + Greek *nephros* kidney

metaphase (ˈmɛtəˌfeɪz) NOUN [1] *Biology* the second stage of mitosis during which the condensed chromosomes attach to the centre of the spindle. See also **prophase** (sense 1), **anaphase** (sense 1), **telophase** (sense 1). [2] the corresponding stage of the first division of meiosis.

metaphor (ˈmɛtəfə, -ˌfɔː) NOUN a figure of speech in which a word or phrase is applied to an object or action that it does not literally denote in order to imply a resemblance, for example *he is a lion in battle*. Compare **simile.**
▷HISTORY C16: from Latin, from Greek *metaphora*, from *metapherein* to transfer, from META- + *pherein* to bear
▸**metaphoric** (ˌmɛtəˈfɒrɪk) *or* **ˌmetaˈphorical** ADJECTIVE ▸**ˌmetaˈphorically** ADVERB ▸**ˌmetaˈphoricalness** NOUN

metaphosphate (ˌmɛtəˈfɒsfeɪt) NOUN any salt of metaphosphoric acid.

metaphosphoric acid (ˌmɛtəfɒsˈfɒrɪk) NOUN a glassy deliquescent highly polymeric solid, used as a dehydrating agent. Formula: $(HPO_3)_n$. See also **polyphosphoric acid.**

metaphrase (ˈmɛtəˌfreɪz) NOUN [1] a literal translation. Compare **paraphrase.** ◆ VERB *(tr)* [2] to alter or manipulate the wording of. [3] to translate literally.
▷HISTORY C17: from Greek *metaphrazein* to translate

metaphrast (ˈmɛtəˌfræst) NOUN a person who metaphrases, esp one who changes the form of a text, as by rendering verse into prose.
▷HISTORY C17: from Medieval Greek *metaphrastēs* translator
▸**ˌmetaˈphrastic** *or* **ˌmetaˈphrastical** ADJECTIVE
▸**ˌmetaˈphrastically** ADVERB

metaphysic (ˌmɛtəˈfɪzɪk) NOUN [1] the system of first principles and assumptions underlying an enquiry or philosophical theory. [2] an obsolete word for **metaphysician.** ◆ ADJECTIVE [3] *Rare* another word for **metaphysical.**

metaphysical (ˌmɛtəˈfɪzɪkᵊl) ADJECTIVE [1] relating to or concerned with metaphysics. [2] (of a statement or theory) having the form of an empirical hypothesis, but in fact immune from empirical testing and therefore (in the view of the logical positivists) literally meaningless. [3] (popularly) abstract, abstruse, or unduly theoretical. [4] incorporeal; supernatural.
▸**ˌmetaˈphysically** ADVERB

Metaphysical (ˌmɛtəˈfɪzɪkᵊl) ADJECTIVE [1] denoting or relating to certain 17th-century poets who combined intense feeling with ingenious thought and often used elaborate imagery and conceits. Notable among them were Donne, Herbert, and Marvell. ◆ NOUN [2] a poet of this group.

metaphysicize *or* **metaphysicise** (ˌmɛtəˈfɪzɪˌsaɪz) VERB [1] *(intr)* to think, write, etc., metaphysically. [2] *(tr)* to treat (a subject) metaphysically.

metaphysics (ˌmɛtəˈfɪzɪks) NOUN *(functioning as singular)* [1] the branch of philosophy that deals with first principles, esp of being and knowing. [2] the philosophical study of the nature of reality, concerned with such questions as the existence of God, the external world, etc. [3] See **descriptive metaphysics.** [4] (popularly) abstract or subtle discussion or reasoning.
▷HISTORY C16: from Medieval Latin, from Greek *ta meta ta phusika* the things after the physics, from the arrangement of the subjects treated in the works of Aristotle
▸**metaphysician** (ˌmɛtəfɪˈzɪʃən) *or* **metaphysicist** (ˌmɛtəˈfɪzɪsɪst) NOUN

metaplasia (ˌmɛtəˈpleɪzɪə) NOUN the transformation of one kind of tissue into a different kind.

metaplasm (ˈmɛtəˌplæzəm) NOUN the nonliving constituents, such as starch and pigment granules, of the cytoplasm of a cell.
▸**ˌmetaˈplasmic** ADJECTIVE

metapolitics (ˌmɛtəˈpɒlɪtɪks) NOUN *(functioning as singular)* political theory (often used derogatorily).
▸**metapolitical** (ˌmɛtəpəˈlɪtɪkᵊl) ADJECTIVE

metapsychology (ˌmɛtəsaɪˈkɒlədʒɪ) NOUN *Psychol* [1] the study of philosophical questions, such as the relation between mind and body, that go beyond the laws of experimental psychology. [2] any attempt to state the general laws of psychology. [3] another word for **parapsychology.**
▸**metapsychological** (ˌmɛtəˌsaɪkəˈlɒdʒɪkᵊl) ADJECTIVE

metarchon (mɪˈtɑːkɒn) NOUN a nontoxic substance, such as a chemical to mask pheromones, that reduces the persistence of a pest.

metasoma (ˌmɛtəˈsəʊmə) NOUN *Zoology* the posterior part of an arachnid's abdomen (opisthosoma) that never carries appendages.

metasomatism (ˌmɛtəˈsəʊməˌtɪzəm) *or* **metasomatosis** (ˌmɛtəˌsəʊməˈtəʊsɪs) NOUN change in the composition of a rock or mineral by the addition or replacement of chemicals.
▷HISTORY C19: from New Latin; see META-, SOMATO-

metastable (ˌmɛtəˈsteɪbᵊl) *Physics* ◆ ADJECTIVE [1] (of a body or system) having a state of apparent equilibrium although capable of changing to a more stable state. [2] (of an atom, molecule, ion, or atomic nucleus) existing in an excited state with a relatively long lifetime. ◆ NOUN [3] a metastable atom, ion, molecule, or nucleus.
▸**ˌmetastaˈbility** NOUN

metastasis (mɪˈtæstəsɪs) NOUN, *plural* **-ses** (-ˌsiːz). [1] *Pathol* the spreading of a disease, esp cancer cells, from one part of the body to another. [2] a transformation or change, as in rhetoric, from one point to another. [3] a rare word for **metabolism.**
▷HISTORY C16: via Latin from Greek: transition
▸**metastatic** (ˌmɛtəˈstætɪk) ADJECTIVE ▸**ˌmetaˈstatically** ADVERB

metastasize *or* **metastasise** (mɪˈtæstəˌsaɪz) VERB *(intr) Pathol* (esp of cancer cells) to spread to a new site in the body via blood or lymph vessels.

metatarsal (ˌmɛtəˈtɑːsᵊl) *Anatomy* ◆ ADJECTIVE [1] of or relating to the metatarsus. ◆ NOUN [2] any bone of the metatarsus.

metatarsus (ˌmɛtəˈtɑːsəs) NOUN, *plural* **-si** (-saɪ). [1] the skeleton of the human foot between the toes and the tarsus, consisting of five long bones. [2] the corresponding skeletal part in other vertebrates.

metatheory (ˈmɛtəˌθɪərɪ) NOUN [1] philosophical discussion of the foundations, structure, or results of some theory, such as metamathematics. [2] a formal system that describes the structure of some other system. See also **metalanguage.**
▸**metatheoretical** (ˌmɛtəθɪəˈrɛtɪkᵊl) ADJECTIVE

metatherian (ˌmɛtəˈθɪərɪən) ADJECTIVE [1] of, relating to, or belonging to the *Metatheria*, a subclass of mammals comprising the marsupials. ◆ NOUN [2] any metatherian mammal; a marsupial. ◆ Compare **eutherian, prototherian.**
▷HISTORY C19: from New Latin, from META- + Greek *thērion* animal

metathesis (mɪˈtæθəsɪs) NOUN, *plural* **-ses** (-ˌsiːz). [1] the transposition of two sounds or letters in a word. [2] *Chem* another name for **double decomposition.**
▷HISTORY C16: from Late Latin, from Greek, from *metatithenai* to transpose
▸**metathetic** (ˌmɛtəˈθɛtɪk) *or* **ˌmetaˈthetical** ADJECTIVE

metathesize *or* **metathesise** (mɪˈtæθɪˌsaɪz) VERB to change or cause to change by metathesis.

metathorax (ˌmɛtəˈθɔːræks) NOUN, *plural* **-raxes** *or* **-races** (-rəˌsiːz). the third and last segment of an insect's thorax, which bears the third pair of walking legs and the second pair of wings. See also **prothorax, mesothorax.**
▸**metathoracic** (ˌmɛtəθɔːˈræsɪk) ADJECTIVE

metaxylem (ˌmɛtəˈzaɪlɛm) NOUN xylem tissue that consists of rigid thick-walled cells and occurs in parts of the plant that have finished growing. Compare **protoxylem.**

metazoan (ˌmɛtəˈzəʊən) NOUN [1] any multicellular animal of the group *Metazoa*: includes all animals except sponges. ◆ ADJECTIVE *also* **metazoic.** [2] of, relating to, or belonging to the *Metazoa*.
▷HISTORY C19: from New Latin *Metazoa*; see META-, -ZOA

mete[1] (miːt) VERB *(tr)* [1] (usually foll by *out*) *Formal* to distribute or allot (something, often unpleasant). ◆ VERB, NOUN [2] *Poetic, dialect* (to) measure.
▷HISTORY Old English *metan*; compare Old Saxon *metan*, Old Norse *meta*, German *messen* to measure

mete[2] (miːt) NOUN *Rare* a mark, limit, or boundary (esp in the phrase **metes and bounds**).
▷HISTORY C15: from Old French, from Latin *mēta* goal, turning post (in race)

metecdysis (ˌmɛtɛkˈdaɪsɪs) NOUN, *plural* **-ses** (-ˌsiːz). the period following the moult (ecdysis) of an arthropod, when the new cuticle is forming.

metempirical (ˌmɛtɛmˈpɪrɪkᵊl) *or* **metempiric** ADJECTIVE [1] beyond the realm of experience. [2] of or relating to metempirics.
▸**ˌmetemˈpirically** ADVERB

metempirics (ˌmɛtɛmˈpɪrɪks) NOUN *(functioning as singular)* the branch of philosophy that deals with things existing beyond the realm of experience.
▸**ˌmetemˈpiricist** NOUN

metempsychosis (ˌmɛtəmsaɪˈkəʊsɪs) NOUN, *plural* **-ses** (-siːz). [1] the migration of a soul from one body to another. [2] the entering of a soul after death upon a new cycle of existence in a new body either of human or animal form.
▷HISTORY C16: via Late Latin from Greek, from *metempsukhousthai*, from META- + *-em-* in + *psukhē* soul
▸**ˌmetempsyˈchosist** NOUN

metencephalon (ˌmɛtɛnˈsɛfəˌlɒn) NOUN, *plural* **-lons** *or* **-la** (-lə). the part of the embryonic hindbrain that develops into the cerebellum and pons Varolii.
▸**metencephalic** (ˌmɛtɛnsɪˈfælɪk) ADJECTIVE

meteor (ˈmiːtɪə) NOUN [1] a very small meteoroid that has entered the earth's atmosphere. Such objects have speeds approaching 70 kilometres per second. [2] Also called: **shooting star, falling star.** the bright streak of light appearing in the sky due to the incandescence of such a body heated by friction at its surface.
▷HISTORY C15: from Medieval Latin *meteōrum*, from Greek *meteōron* something aloft, from *meteōros* lofty, from *meta-* (intensifier) + *aeirein* to raise

meteoric (ˌmiːtɪˈɒrɪk) ADJECTIVE [1] of, formed by, or relating to meteors. [2] like a meteor in brilliance, speed, or transience. [3] *Rare* of or relating to the weather; meteorological.
▸**ˌmeteˈorically** ADVERB

meteoric water NOUN *Geology* ground water that has recently originated from the atmosphere.

meteorism (ˈmiːtɪəˌrɪzəm) NOUN *Med* another name for **tympanites.**

meteorite (ˈmiːtɪəˌraɪt) NOUN a rocklike object consisting of the remains of a meteoroid that has fallen on earth. It may be stony (see **chondrite**), iron, or stony iron (see **pallasite**).
▸**meteoritic** (ˌmiːtɪəˈrɪtɪk) ADJECTIVE

meteoritics (ˌmiːtɪəˈrɪtɪks) NOUN *(functioning as singular)* the branch of science concerned with meteors and meteorites.
▸**ˌmeteorˈiticist** NOUN

meteorograph (ˈmiːtɪərəˌɡrɑːf, -ˌɡræf) NOUN *Obsolete* an instrument that records various meteorological conditions.
▸**ˌmeteoroˈgraphic** *or* **ˌmeteoroˈgraphical** ADJECTIVE

meteoroid (ˈmiːtɪəˌrɔɪd) NOUN any of the small celestial bodies that are thought to orbit the sun, possibly as the remains of comets. When they enter the earth's atmosphere, they become visible as meteors.
▸**ˌmeteorˈoidal** ADJECTIVE

meteorol. *or* **meteor.** ABBREVIATION FOR: [1] meteorological. [2] meteorology.

meteorology (ˌmiːtɪəˈrɒlədʒɪ) NOUN the study of the earth's atmosphere, esp of weather-forming processes and weather forecasting.
▷HISTORY C17: from Greek *meteōrologia*, from *meteōron* something aloft + *-logia* -LOGY. See METEOR
▸**meteorological** (ˌmiːtɪərəˈlɒdʒɪkᵊl) *or* **ˌmeteoroˈlogic** ADJECTIVE ▸**ˌmeteoroˈlogically** ADVERB ▸**ˌmeteorˈologist** NOUN

meteor shower NOUN a transient rain of

meteors, such as the Perseids, occurring at regular intervals and coming from a particular region in the sky. It is caused by the earth passing through a large number of meteoroids (a **meteor swarm**).

meter[1] ('mi:tə) NOUN the US spelling of **metre**[1].

meter[2] ('mi:tə) NOUN the US spelling of **metre**[2].

meter[3] ('mi:tə) NOUN 1 any device that measures and records the quantity of a substance, such as gas, that has passed through it during a specified period. 2 any device that measures and sometimes records an electrical or magnetic quantity, such as current, voltage, etc. 3 See **parking meter.** ♦ VERB *(tr)* 4 to measure (a rate of flow) with a meter. 5 to print with stamps by means of a postage meter.
▷HISTORY C19: see METE[1]

-meter NOUN COMBINING FORM 1 indicating an instrument for measuring: *barometer.* 2 *Prosody* indicating a verse having a specified number of feet: *pentameter.*
▷HISTORY from Greek *metron* measure

metered mail NOUN mail franked privately, under licence, with a machine bearing special markings (**meter marks**).

meter maid NOUN *Informal* a female traffic warden.

metestrus (mεt'εstrəs, -'i:strəs) NOUN the US spelling of **metoestrus.**
▸**met'estrous** ADJECTIVE

Meth. ABBREVIATION FOR Methodist.

meth- COMBINING FORM indicating a chemical compound derived from methane or containing methyl groups: *methacrylate resin.*

methacrylate (mεθ'ækrɪˌleɪt) NOUN 1 any ester of methacrylic acid. 2 See **methacrylate resin.**

methacrylate resin NOUN any acrylic resin derived from methacrylic acid.

methacrylic acid (ˌmεθə'krɪlɪk) NOUN a colourless crystalline water-soluble substance used in the manufacture of acrylic resins; 2-methylpropenoic acid. Formula: CH_2:C(CH_3)COOH.

methadone ('mεθəˌdəʊn) *or* **methadon** ('mεθəˌdɒn) NOUN a narcotic analgesic drug similar to morphine, used to treat opiate addiction. Formula: $C_{21}H_{27}NO$.
▷HISTORY C20: from *(di)meth(yl)* + A(MINO) + D(IPHENYL) + -ONE

methaemoglobin (mεtˌhi:mə'gləʊbɪn, mεˌθi:mə-) NOUN a brown compound of oxygen and haemoglobin formed in the blood by the action of certain drugs.

methamphetamine (ˌmεθæm'fεtəmɪn) NOUN a variety of amphetamine used for its stimulant action.
▷HISTORY C20: from METH- + AMPHETAMINE

methanal ('mεθəˌnæl) NOUN the systematic name for **formaldehyde.**

methane ('mi:θeɪn) NOUN a colourless odourless flammable gas, the simplest alkane and the main constituent of natural gas: used as a fuel. Formula: CH_4. See also **marsh gas, firedamp.**
▷HISTORY C19: from METH(YL) + -ANE

methane series NOUN another name for the **alkane series.** See **alkane.**

methanoic acid ('mεθəˌnəʊɪk) NOUN the systematic name for **formic acid.**

methanol ('mεθəˌnɒl) NOUN a colourless volatile poisonous liquid compound used as a solvent and fuel. Formula: CH_3OH. Also called: **methyl alcohol, wood alcohol.**
▷HISTORY C20: from METHANE + -OL[1]

metheglin (mə'θεglɪn) NOUN (esp formerly) spiced or medicated mead.
▷HISTORY C16: from Welsh *meddyglyn,* from *meddyg* healer (from Latin *medicus* MEDICAL) + *llyn* liquor

methenamine (mε'θi:nəˌmi:n, -ˌmaɪn) NOUN another name for **hexamethylenetetramine.**
▷HISTORY C20: METH- + -ENE + AMINE

methinks (mɪ'θɪŋks) VERB, *past* **methought.** *(tr; takes a clause as object) Archaic* it seems to me.

methionine (mε'θaɪəˌni:n, -ˌnaɪn) NOUN an essential amino acid containing sulphur, which occurs in many proteins: important in methylating reactions.
▷HISTORY C20: METH- + THIONINE

metho ('mεθəʊ) NOUN *Austral* an informal name for **methylated spirits.**

method ('mεθəd) NOUN 1 a way of proceeding or doing something, esp a systematic or regular one. 2 orderliness of thought, action, etc. 3 *(often plural)* the techniques or arrangement of work for a particular field or subject. 4 *Bell-ringing* any of several traditional sets of changes. See **major** (sense 19), **minor** (sense 8).
▷HISTORY C16: via French from Latin *methodus,* from Greek *methodos,* literally: a going after, from *meta-* after + *hodos* way

Method ('mεθəd) NOUN *(sometimes not capital)* **a** a technique of acting based on the theories of Stanislavsky, in which the actor bases his role on the inner motivation of the character he plays. **b** *(as modifier): a Method actor.*

methodical (mɪ'θɒdɪkᵊl) *or less commonly* **methodic** ADJECTIVE characterized by method or orderliness; systematic.
▸**me'thodically** ADVERB ▸**me'thodicalness** NOUN

Methodism ('mεθəˌdɪzəm) NOUN the system and practices of the Methodist Church, developed by the English preacher John Wesley (1703–91) and his followers.

Methodist ('mεθədɪst) NOUN 1 a member of any of the Nonconformist denominations that derive from the system of faith and practice initiated by the English preacher John Wesley (1703–91) and his followers. ♦ ADJECTIVE *also* **Methodistic, Methodistical.** 2 of or relating to Methodism or the Church embodying it (the **Methodist Church**).
▸**ˌMethod'istically** ADVERB

methodize *or* **methodise** ('mεθəˌdaɪz) VERB *(tr)* to organize according to a method; systematize.
▸**ˌmethodi'zation** *or* **ˌmethodi'sation** NOUN ▸**'methodˌizer** *or* **'methodˌiser** NOUN

methodology (ˌmεθə'dɒlədʒɪ) NOUN, *plural* **-gies.** 1 the system of methods and principles used in a particular discipline. 2 the branch of philosophy concerned with the science of method and procedure.
▸**methodological** (ˌmεθədə'lɒdʒɪkᵊl) ADJECTIVE ▸**ˌmethodo'logically** ADVERB ▸**ˌmethod'ologist** NOUN

methotrexate (ˌmεθəʊ'trεkseɪt, ˌmi:θəʊ-) NOUN an antimetabolite drug used in the treatment of certain cancers. Formula: $C_{20}H_{22}N_8O_5$.

methought (mɪ'θɔ:t) VERB *Archaic* the past tense of **methinks.**

methoxide (mεθ'ɒksaɪd) NOUN a saltlike compound in which the hydrogen atom in the hydroxyl group of methanol has been replaced by a metal atom, usually an alkali metal atom as in sodium methoxide, $NaOCH_3$. Also called: **methylate.**

meths (mεθs) NOUN *Chiefly Brit, Austral, and NZ* an informal name for **methylated spirits.**

Methuselah[1] (mə'θju:zələ) NOUN a wine bottle holding the equivalent of eight normal bottles.

Methuselah[2] (mɪ'θju:zələ) NOUN *Old Testament* a patriarch supposed to have lived 969 years (Genesis 5:21–27) who has come to be regarded as epitomizing longevity. Douay spelling: **Mathusala.**

methyl ('mi:θaɪl, 'mεθɪl) NOUN 1 *(modifier)* of, consisting of, or containing the monovalent group of atoms CH_3. 2 an organometallic compound in which methyl groups are bound directly to a metal atom.
▷HISTORY C19: from French *méthyle,* back formation from METHYLENE
▸**methylic** (mə'θɪlɪk) ADJECTIVE

methyl acetate NOUN a colourless volatile flammable liquid ester with a fragrant odour, used as a solvent, esp in paint removers. Formula: CH_3COOCH_3.

methylal ('mεθɪˌlæl) NOUN a colourless volatile flammable liquid with an odour resembling that of chloroform, used as a solvent and in the manufacture of perfumes and adhesives. Formula: $(CH_3O)_2CH_2$. Also called: **formal.**

methyl alcohol NOUN another name for **methanol.**

methylamine (mi:'θaɪləˌmi:n) NOUN a colourless flammable water-soluble gas, used in the manufacture of herbicides, dyes, and drugs. Formula: CH_3NH_2.

methylate ('mεθɪˌleɪt) VERB 1 *(tr)* to mix with methanol. 2 to undergo or cause to undergo a chemical reaction in which a methyl group is introduced into a molecule. ♦ NOUN 3 another name for **methoxide.**
▸**ˌmethyl'ation** NOUN ▸**'methylˌator** NOUN

methylated spirits *or* **spirit** NOUN *(functioning as singular or plural)* alcohol that has been denatured by the addition of methanol and pyridine and a violet dye. Also called: **metho, meths.**

methyl bromide NOUN a colourless poisonous gas or volatile liquid with an odour resembling that of chloroform, used as a solvent, and extinguishant. Formula: CH_3Br.

methyl chloride NOUN a colourless gas with an ether-like odour, used as a refrigerant and anaesthetic. Formula: CH_3Cl. Systematic name: **chloromethane.**

methyl chloroform NOUN the traditional name for **trichloroethane.**

methyldopa (ˌmi:θaɪl'dəʊpə) NOUN a drug used to treat hypertension. Formula: $C_{10}H_{13}NO_4$.
▷HISTORY C20: from *methyl* + *d(ihydr)o(xy)p(henyl)a(lanine)*

methylene ('mεθɪˌli:n) NOUN *(modifier)* of, consisting of, or containing the divalent group of atoms $=CH_2$: *a methylene group or radical.*
▷HISTORY C19: from French *méthylène,* from Greek *methu* wine + *hulē* wood + -ENE: originally referring to a substance distilled from wood

methylene blue NOUN a dark-green crystalline compound forming a blue aqueous solution, used as a mild antiseptic and biological stain. Formula: $C_{16}H_{18}N_3SCl.3H_2O$. Also called: **methylthionine chloride.**

methylene chloride NOUN another name for **dichloromethane.**

methyl ethyl ketone NOUN another name for **butanone.**

methyl isobutyl ketone (ˌaɪsəʊ'bju:taɪl, -tɪl) NOUN a colourless insoluble liquid ketone used as a solvent for organic compounds, esp nitrocellulose; 4-methylpentan-2-one. Formula: $(CH_3)_2CHCH_2COCH_3$. Also called: **hexone.**

methyl methacrylate NOUN a colourless liquid compound, used in the manufacture of certain methacrylate resins. Formula: $CH_2C(CH_3)COOCH_3$.

methylnaphthalene (ˌmi:θaɪl'næpθəˌli:n) NOUN either of two isomeric derivatives of naphthalene: a liquid (1-methylnaphthalene), used in standardizing diesel fuels, or a solid (2-methylnaphthalene), an insecticide.

methylthionine chloride (ˌmi:θaɪl'θaɪəˌni:n) NOUN another name for **methylene blue.**

metic ('mεtɪk) NOUN (in ancient Greece) an alien having some rights of citizenship in the city in which he lives.
▷HISTORY C19: from Greek *metoikos,* from META- (indicating change) + *-oikos* dwelling

meticulous (mɪ'tɪkjʊləs) ADJECTIVE very precise about details, even trivial ones; painstaking.
▷HISTORY C16 (meaning: timid): from Latin *meticulōsus* fearful, from *metus* fear
▸**me'ticulously** ADVERB ▸**me'ticulousness** NOUN

métier ('mεtɪeɪ) NOUN 1 a profession or trade, esp that to which one is well suited. 2 a person's strong point or speciality.
▷HISTORY C18: from French, ultimately from Latin *ministerium* service

me-time NOUN the time a person has to himself or herself, in which to do something for his or her own enjoyment.

Métis (mε'ti:s) NOUN, *plural* **-tis** (-'ti:s, -'ti:z). 1 a person of mixed parentage. 2 *Canadian* **a** the offspring or a descendant of a French Canadian and a North American Indian. **b** a member or descendant of a group of such people, who established themselves in Manitoba and Saskatchewan as a distinct political and cultural force during the nineteenth century. 3 *US* a person having one eighth Black ancestry; octoroon.
▷HISTORY C19: from French, from Vulgar Latin *mixtīcius* (unattested) of mixed race; compare MESTIZO
▸**Métisse** (mε'ti:s) FEMININE NOUN

metoestrus (mεt'i:strəs, -'εstrəs) *or US* **metestrus** NOUN *Zoology* the period in the oestrous cycle following oestrus, characterized by lack of sexual activity.
▸**met'oestrous** *or (US)* **met'estrous** ADJECTIVE

metol ('mi:tɒl) NOUN a colourless soluble organic substance used, in the form of its sulphate, as a photographic developer; *p*-methylaminophenol. See also **aminophenol.**
▷HISTORY C20: from German, an arbitrary coinage

Metonic cycle (mɪ'tɒnɪk) NOUN a cycle of nearly 235 synodic months after which the phases of the moon recur on the same days of the year. See also **golden number.**
▷HISTORY C17: named after *Meton,* 5th-century B.C. Athenian astronomer

metonym ('mɛtənɪm) NOUN a word used in a metonymy. For example *the bottle* is a metonym for *alcoholic drink.*

metonymy (mɪ'tɒnɪmɪ) NOUN, *plural* **-mies.** the substitution of a word referring to an attribute for the thing that is meant, as for example the use of *the crown* to refer to a monarch. Compare **synecdoche.**
▷HISTORY C16: from Late Latin from Greek: a changing of name, from *meta-* (indicating change) + *onoma* name
▸**metonymical** (ˌmɛtə'nɪmɪkᵊl) *or* ˌ**meto'nymic** ADJECTIVE
▸ˌ**meto'nymically** ADVERB

me-too NOUN *Slang* a person who does something merely because someone else has done it.

me-tooism (ˌmi:'tu:izəm) NOUN the practice of imitating other people's work or ideas.

metope ('mɛtəʊp, 'mɛtəpɪ) NOUN *Architect* a square space between two triglyphs in a Doric frieze.
▷HISTORY C16: via Latin from Greek *metopē,* from *meta* between + *opē* one of the holes for the beam-ends

metopic (mɪ'tɒpɪk) ADJECTIVE of or relating to the forehead.

metralgia (mɪ'trældʒɪə) NOUN pain in the uterus.
▷HISTORY C20: from METRO-[1] + -ALGIA

metre[1] *or US* **meter** ('mi:tə) NOUN [1] a metric unit of length equal to approximately 1.094 yards. [2] the basic SI unit of length; the length of the path travelled by light in free space during a time interval of 1/299 792 458 of a second. In 1983 this definition replaced the previous one based on krypton-86, which in turn had replaced the definition based on the platinum-iridium metre bar kept in Paris. Symbol: m.
▷HISTORY C18: from French; see METRE[2]

metre[2] *or US* **meter** ('mi:tə) NOUN [1] *Prosody* the rhythmic arrangement of syllables in verse, usually according to the number and kind of feet in a line. [2] *Music* another word (esp US) for **time** (sense 22).
▷HISTORY C14: from Latin *metrum,* from Greek *metron* measure

metre-kilogram-second NOUN See **mks units.**

metric ('mɛtrɪk) ADJECTIVE [1] of or relating to the metre or metric system. [2] *Maths* denoting or relating to a set containing pairs of points for each of which a non-negative real number $\rho(x, y)$ (the distance) can be defined, satisfying specific conditions. ◆ NOUN [3] *Maths* the function $\rho(x, y)$ satisfying the conditions of membership of such a set (a **metric space**).

metrical ('mɛtrɪkᵊl) *or* **metric** ('mɛtrɪk) ADJECTIVE [1] of or relating to measurement. [2] of or in poetic metre.
▸'**metrically** ADVERB

metrical psalm NOUN a translation of one of the psalms into rhyming strict-metre verse usually sung as a hymn.

metricate ('mɛtrɪˌkeɪt) VERB to convert (a measuring system, instrument, etc.) from nonmetric to metric units.
▸ˌ**metri'cation** NOUN

metric hundredweight NOUN See **hundredweight** (sense 3).

metric madness NOUN *Informal* excessive devotion to metrication.

metric martyr NOUN *Brit* a shopkeeper or trader willing to be prosecuted for continuing to use only imperial measures as a protest against the perceived imposition of metric measures by the European Union.

metrics ('mɛtrɪks) NOUN (*functioning as singular*) *Prosody* the art of using poetic metre.

metric system NOUN any decimal system of units based on the metre. For scientific purposes the Système International d'Unités (SI units) is used.

metric ton NOUN another name (not in technical use) for **tonne.**

metrify ('mɛtrɪˌfaɪ) VERB **-fies, -fying, -fied.** (*tr*) *Prosody* to render into poetic metre.
▸'**metriˌfier** NOUN

metrist ('mɛtrɪst) NOUN *Prosody* a person skilled in the use of poetic metre.

metritis (mɪ'traɪtɪs) NOUN inflammation of the uterus.

metro ('mɛtrəʊ) *or* **métro** (*French* metro) NOUN, *plural* **-ros.** an underground, or largely underground, railway system in certain cities, esp in Europe, such as that in Paris.
▷HISTORY C20: from French, short for *chemin de fer métropolitain* metropolitan railway

metro-[1] *or before a vowel* **metr-** COMBINING FORM indicating the uterus: *metrorrhagia.*
▷HISTORY from Greek *mētra* womb

metro-[2] COMBINING FORM indicating a measure: *metronome.*
▷HISTORY from Greek *metron* measure

metrology (mɪ'trɒlədʒɪ) NOUN, *plural* **-gies.** [1] the science of weights and measures; the study of units of measurement. [2] a particular system of units.
▷HISTORY C19: from Greek *metron* measure
▸**metrological** (ˌmɛtrə'lɒdʒɪkᵊl) ADJECTIVE
▸ˌ**metro'logically** ADVERB ▸**me'trologist** NOUN

metronidazole (ˌmɛtrə'naɪdəˌzəʊl) NOUN a pale yellow crystalline compound used to treat vaginal trichomoniasis. Formula: $C_6H_9N_3O_3$.
▷HISTORY C20: from ME(THYL) + (NI)TRO- + *-n-* + (IM)ID(E) + AZOLE

metronome ('mɛtrəˌnəʊm) NOUN a mechanical device which indicates the exact tempo of a piece of music by producing a clicking sound from a pendulum with an adjustable period of swing.
▷HISTORY C19: from Greek *metron* measure + *nomos* rule, law
▸**metronomic** (ˌmɛtrə'nɒmɪk) ADJECTIVE

metronymic (ˌmɛtrə'nɪmɪk) *or less commonly* **matronymic** ADJECTIVE [1] (of a name) derived from the name of its bearer's mother or another female ancestor. ◆ NOUN [2] a metronymic name.
▷HISTORY C19: from Greek *mētronumikos,* from *mētēr* mother + *onoma* name

metropolis (mɪ'trɒpəlɪs) NOUN, *plural* **-lises.** [1] the main city, esp of a country or region; capital. [2] a centre of activity. [3] the chief see in an ecclesiastical province.
▷HISTORY C16: from Late Latin from Greek: mother city or state, from *mētēr* mother + *polis* city

metropolitan (ˌmɛtrə'pɒlɪtən) ADJECTIVE [1] of or characteristic of a metropolis. [2] constituting a city and its suburbs: *the metropolitan area.* [3] of, relating to, or designating an ecclesiastical metropolis. [4] of or belonging to the home territories of a country, as opposed to overseas territories: *metropolitan France.* ◆ NOUN [5] **a** *Eastern Churches* the head of an ecclesiastical province, ranking between archbishop and patriarch. **b** *Church of England* an archbishop. **c** *RC Church* an archbishop or bishop having authority in certain matters over the dioceses in his province.
▸ˌ**metro'politanism** NOUN

metropolitan county NOUN (in England) any of the six conurbations established as administrative units in the new local government system in 1974; the metropolitan county councils were abolished in 1986.

metropolitan district NOUN any of the districts making up the metropolitan counties of England: since 1986 they have functioned as unitary authorities, forming the sole principal tier of local government. Each metropolitan district has an elected council responsible for education, social services, etc. See also **district** (sense 4).

Metropolitan Museum of Art NOUN the principal museum in New York City: founded in 1870 and housed in its present premises in Central Park since 1880.

metrorrhagia (ˌmi:trɔ:'reɪdʒɪə, ˌmɛt-) NOUN abnormal bleeding from the uterus.

-metry NOUN COMBINING FORM indicating the process or science of measuring: *anthropometry; geometry.*
▷HISTORY from Old French *-metrie,* from Latin *-metria,* from Greek, from *metron* measure
▸**-metric** ADJECTIVE COMBINING FORM

mettle ('mɛtᵊl) NOUN [1] courage; spirit. [2] inherent character. [3] **on one's mettle.** roused to putting forth one's best efforts.
▷HISTORY C16: originally variant spelling of METAL

mettled ('mɛtᵊld) *or* **mettlesome** ('mɛtᵊlsəm) ADJECTIVE spirited, courageous, or valiant.

Metz (mɛts; *French* mɛs) NOUN a city in NE France on the River Moselle: a free imperial city in the 13th century; annexed by France in 1552; part of Germany (1871–1918); centre of the Lorraine iron-mining region. Pop.: 123 776 (1999).

meu (mju:) NOUN another name for **spignel.**
▷HISTORY C16: from Latin *mēum,* from Greek *mēon*

meum et tuum *Latin* ('meɪʊm ɛt 'tu:ʊm) mine and thine: used to express rights to property.
▷HISTORY C16: neuter of *mēus* mine and *tuus* yours

meunière (mən'jɛə; *French* mønjɛr) ADJECTIVE (of fish) dredged with flour, fried in butter, and served with butter, lemon juice, and parsley.
▷HISTORY French, literally: miller's wife

Meurthe-et-Moselle (*French* mœrtemozɛl) NOUN a department of NE France, in Lorraine region. Capital: Nancy. Pop.: 713 779 (1999). Area: 5280 sq. km (2059 sq. miles).

Meuse (mɜ:z; *French* møz) NOUN [1] a department of N France, in Lorraine region: heavy fighting occurred here in World War I. Capital: Bar-le-Duc. Pop.: 192 198 (1999). Area: 6241 sq. km (2434 sq. miles). [2] a river in W Europe, rising in NE France and flowing north across E Belgium and the S Netherlands to join the Waal River before entering the North Sea. Length: 926 km (575 miles). Dutch name: **Maas.**

MeV SYMBOL FOR million electronvolts (10^6 electronvolts).

mevrou (mə'frəʊ) NOUN a South African title of address equivalent to *Mrs* when placed before a surname or *madam* when used alone.
▷HISTORY Afrikaans

mew[1] (mju:) VERB [1] (*intr*) (esp of a cat) to make a characteristic high-pitched cry. ◆ NOUN [2] such a sound.
▷HISTORY C14: imitative

mew[2] (mju:) NOUN any seagull, esp the common gull, *Larus canus.* Also called: **mew gull, sea mew.**
▷HISTORY Old English *mǣw;* compare Old Saxon *mēu,* Middle Dutch *mēwe*

mew[3] (mju:) NOUN [1] a room or cage for hawks, esp while moulting. ◆ VERB [2] (*tr; often foll by up*) to confine (hawks or falcons) in a shelter, cage, etc., usually by tethering them to a perch. [3] to confine, conceal.
▷HISTORY C14: from Old French *mue,* from *muer* to moult, from Latin *mūtāre* to change

mew[4] (mju:) VERB [1] (*intr*) (of hawks or falcons) to moult. [2] (*tr*) *Obsolete* to shed (one's covering, clothes, etc.).
▷HISTORY C14: from Old French *muer* to moult, from Latin *mūtāre* to change

Mewar (me'wɑ:) NOUN another name for **Udaipur** (sense 1).

mewl (mju:l) VERB [1] (*intr*) (esp of a baby) to cry weakly; whimper (often in the phrase **mewl and puke**). ◆ NOUN [2] such a cry.
▷HISTORY C17: imitative
▸'**mewler** NOUN

mews (mju:z) NOUN (*functioning as singular or plural*) *Chiefly Brit* [1] a yard or street lined by buildings originally used as stables but now often converted into dwellings. [2] the buildings around a mews. [3] *Informal* an individual residence in a mews.
▷HISTORY C14: pl of MEW[3], originally referring to royal stables built on the site of hawks' mews at Charing Cross in London

MEX INTERNATIONAL CAR REGISTRATION FOR Mexico.

Mex. ABBREVIATION FOR: [1] Mexican. [2] Mexico.

Mexicali (ˌmɛksɪ'kɑ:lɪ; *Spanish* mɛxi'kali) NOUN a city in NW Mexico, capital of Baja California Norte state, on the border with the US adjoining Calexico, California: centre of a rich irrigated agricultural region. Pop.: 550 000 (2000 est.).

Mexican ('mɛksɪkən) ADJECTIVE [1] of or relating to

Mexico or its inhabitants. ◆ NOUN [2] a native or inhabitant of Mexico.

Mexican hairless NOUN a breed of small hairless dog with mottled skin, originating from Mexico.

Mexican War NOUN the war fought between the US and Mexico (1846–48), through which the US acquired the present-day Southwest.

Mexican wave NOUN the rippling effect produced when the spectators in successive sections of a sports stadium stand up while raising their arms and then sit down.
▷**HISTORY** C20: so called because it was first demonstrated at the World Cup in Mexico in 1986

Mexico (ˈmɛksɪˌkəʊ) NOUN [1] a republic in North America, on the Gulf of Mexico and the Pacific: early Mexican history includes the Maya, Toltec, and Aztec civilizations; conquered by the Spanish between 1519 and 1525 and achieved independence in 1821; lost Texas to the US in 1836 and California and New Mexico in 1848. It is generally mountainous with three ranges of the Sierra Madre (east, west, and south) and a large central plateau. Official language: Spanish. Religion: Roman Catholic majority. Currency: peso. Capital: Mexico City. Pop.: 99 969 000 (2001 est.). Area: 1 967 183 sq. km (761 530 sq. miles). Official name: **United Mexican States.** Spanish name: **Méjico.** [2] a state of Mexico, on the central plateau surrounding Mexico City, which is not administratively part of the state. Capital: Toluca. Pop.: 11 704 934 (1995 est.). Area: 21 460 sq. km (8287 sq. miles). [3] **Gulf of.** an arm of the Atlantic, bordered by the US, Cuba, and Mexico: linked with the Atlantic by the Straits of Florida and with the Caribbean by the Yucatán Channel. Area: about 1 600 000 sq. km (618 000 sq. miles).

Mexico City NOUN the capital of Mexico, on the central plateau at an altitude of 2240 m (7350 ft.): founded as the Aztec capital (Tenochtitlán) in about 1300; conquered and rebuilt by the Spanish in 1521; forms, with its suburbs, the federal district of Mexico; the largest industrial complex in the country. Pop.: 8 591 309 (2000 est.).

MEZ ABBREVIATION FOR Central European Time.
▷**HISTORY** from German *Mitteleuropäische Zeit*

mezcal (mɛˈskæl) NOUN a variant spelling of **mescal.**

mezcaline (ˈmɛskəˌliːn) NOUN a variant spelling of **mescaline.**

meze (ˈmɛzɛ) NOUN a type of hors d'oeuvre eaten esp with an apéritif or other drink in Greece and the Near East.
▷**HISTORY** C20: from Turkish *meze* snack, appetizer

mezereon (mɛˈzɪərɪən) NOUN [1] a Eurasian thymelaeaceous shrub, *Daphne mezereum,* with fragrant early-blooming purplish-pink flowers and small scarlet fruits. [2] another name for **mezereum.**
▷**HISTORY** C15: via Medieval Latin from Arabic *māzaryūn*

mezereum (mɪˈzɪərɪəm) *or* **mezereon** NOUN the dried bark of certain shrubs of the genus *Daphne,* esp mezereon, formerly used as a vesicant and to treat arthritis.

Mézières (*French* mezjɛr) NOUN a town in NE France, on the River Meuse opposite Charleville. See **Charleville-Mézières.**

mezuzah (məˈzuzə, -ˈzuː-; *Hebrew* məzuˈzɑ; *Yiddish* məˈzuzə) NOUN, *plural* **-zuzahs** *or* **-zuzoth** (*Hebrew* -zuˈzɔt). *Judaism* [1] a piece of parchment inscribed with biblical passages and fixed to the doorpost of the rooms of a Jewish house. [2] a metal case for such a parchment, sometimes worn as an ornament.
▷**HISTORY** from Hebrew, literally: doorpost

mezzanine (ˈmɛzəˌniːn, ˈmɛtsəˌniːn) NOUN [1] Also called: **mezzanine floor, entresol.** an intermediate storey, esp a low one between the ground and first floor of a building. [2] *Theatre, US and Canadian* the first balcony. [3] *Theatre, Brit* a room or floor beneath the stage. ◆ ADJECTIVE [4] Often shortened to: **mezz.** of or relating to an intermediate stage in a financial process: *mezzanine funding.*
▷**HISTORY** C18: from French, from Italian, diminutive of *mezzano* middle, from Latin *mediānus* MEDIAN

mezza voce (ˈmɛtsə ˈvəʊtʃɪ; *Italian* ˈmɛddza ˈvotʃe) ADVERB *Music* (in singing) softly; quietly.
▷**HISTORY** Italian, literally: half voice

mezzo (ˈmɛtsəʊ) *Music* ◆ ADVERB [1] moderately; quite: *mezzo forte; mezzo piano.* ◆ NOUN, *plural* **-zos.** [2] See **mezzo-soprano** (sense 1).
▷**HISTORY** C19: from Italian, literally: half, from Latin *medius* middle

mezzo-relievo *or* **mezzo-rilievo** (ˌmɛtsəʊrɪˈliːvəʊ) NOUN carving in which the depth of the relief is halfway between that of high relief and low relief.
▷**HISTORY** from Italian: half relief

mezzo-soprano NOUN, *plural* **-nos.** [1] a female voice intermediate between a soprano and contralto and having a range from the A below middle C to the F an eleventh above it. Sometimes shortened to: **mezzo.** [2] a singer with such a voice.

mezzotint (ˈmɛtsəʊˌtɪnt) NOUN [1] a method of engraving a copper plate by scraping and burnishing the roughened surface. [2] a print made from a plate so treated. ◆ VERB [3] (*tr*) to engrave (a copper plate) in this fashion.
▷**HISTORY** C18: from Italian *mezzotinto* half tint
▸**ˈmezzoˌtinter** NOUN

mf *Music* ABBREVIATION FOR mezzo forte.
▷**HISTORY** Italian: moderately loud

MF ABBREVIATION FOR: [1] *Radio* **medium frequency.** [2] Middle French.

M.F.A. (in the US and Canada) ABBREVIATION FOR Master of Fine Arts.

MFAT (ˈɛmfæt) NOUN (in New Zealand) ACRONYM FOR Ministry of Foreign Affairs and Trade.

mfd ABBREVIATION FOR manufactured.

mfg ABBREVIATION FOR manufacturing.

MFH *Hunting* ABBREVIATION FOR Master of Foxhounds.

mfr ABBREVIATION FOR: [1] manufacture. [2] manufacturer.

mg[1] SYMBOL FOR milligram.

mg[2] THE INTERNET DOMAIN NAME FOR Madagascar.

Mg THE CHEMICAL SYMBOL FOR magnesium.

MG ABBREVIATION FOR machine gun.

MGB ABBREVIATION FOR Ministry of State Security; the Soviet secret police from 1946 to 1954.
▷**HISTORY** from Russian *Ministerstvo gosudarstvennoi bezopasnosti*

MGL INTERNATIONAL CAR REGISTRATION FOR Mongolia.

Mgr ABBREVIATION FOR: [1] manager. [2] Monseigneur. [3] Monsignor.

mh THE INTERNET DOMAIN NAME FOR Marshall Islands.

MHA (in Australia and Newfoundland, Canada) ABBREVIATION FOR Member of the House of Assembly.

MHC ABBREVIATION FOR major histocompatibility complex; a series of genes located on chromosome 6 that code for antigens. They are important in determining histocompatibility.

MHD ABBREVIATION FOR magnetohydrodynamics.

MHG ABBREVIATION FOR Middle High German.

mho (məʊ) NOUN, *plural* **mhos.** the former name for **siemens.**
▷**HISTORY** C19: formed by reversing the letters of OHM (first used by Lord Kelvin)

MHR (in the US and Australia) ABBREVIATION FOR Member of the House of Representatives.

MHz SYMBOL FOR megahertz.

mi *or* **me** (miː) NOUN *Music* (in tonic sol-fa) the third degree of any major scale; mediant.
▷**HISTORY** C16: see GAMUT

MI ABBREVIATION FOR: [1] Michigan. [2] Military Intelligence.

mi. ABBREVIATION FOR mile.

MI5 ABBREVIATION FOR Military Intelligence, section five; a former official and present-day popular name for the counterintelligence agency of the British Government.

MI6 ABBREVIATION FOR Military Intelligence, section six; a former official and present-day popular name for the intelligence and espionage agency of the British Government.

MIA ABBREVIATION FOR: [1] *Military, chiefly US* missing in action: officially unaccounted for following combat. [2] (in Australia) Murrumbidgee Irrigation Area.

Miami (maɪˈæmɪ) NOUN a city and resort in SE Florida, on Biscayne Bay: developed chiefly after 1896, esp with the Florida land boom of the 1920s; centre of an extensive tourist area. Pop.: 362 470 (2000).

mia mia (ˈmiːə ˈmiːə) NOUN a native Australian's hut.
▷**HISTORY** from a native Australian language

Miami Beach NOUN a resort in SE Florida, on an island separated from Miami by Biscayne Bay. Pop.: 87 933 (2000).

miaou *or* **miaow** (mɪˈaʊ, mjaʊ) VERB, INTERJECTION variant spellings of **meow.**

miasma (mɪˈæzmə) NOUN, *plural* **-mata** (-mətə) *or* **-mas.** [1] an unwholesome or foreboding atmosphere. [2] pollution in the atmosphere, esp noxious vapours from decomposing organic matter.
▷**HISTORY** C17: New Latin, from Greek: defilement, from *miainein* to defile
▸**miˈasmal** *or* **miasmatic** (ˌmiːəzˈmætɪk) *or* **ˌmiasˈmatical** *or* **miˈasmic** ADJECTIVE

miaul (mɪˈaʊl) VERB (*intr*) another word for **meow.**

mic (maɪk) NOUN *Informal* short for **microphone.**

Mic. *Bible* ABBREVIATION FOR Micah.

mica (ˈmaɪkə) NOUN any of a group of lustrous rock-forming minerals consisting of hydrous silicates of aluminium, potassium, etc., in monoclinic crystalline form, occurring in igneous and metamorphic rock. Because of their resistance to electricity and heat they are used as dielectrics, in heating elements, etc.
▷**HISTORY** C18: from Latin: grain, morsel
▸**micaceous** (maɪˈkeɪʃəs) ADJECTIVE

Micah (ˈmaɪkə) NOUN *Old Testament* [1] a Hebrew prophet of the late 8th century B.C. [2] the book containing his prophecies. Douay spelling: **Micheas** (maɪˈkiːəs).

Micawber (mɪˈkɔːbə) NOUN a person who idles and trusts to fortune.
▷**HISTORY** C19: after a character in *David Copperfield,* a novel (1850) by English novelist Charles Dickens (1812–70)
▸**Miˈcawberish** ADJECTIVE ▸**Miˈcawberism** NOUN

mice (maɪs) NOUN the plural of **mouse.**

micelle, micell (mɪˈsɛl), *or* **micella** (mɪˈsɛlə) NOUN *Chem* **a** a charged aggregate of molecules of colloidal size in a solution. **b** any molecular aggregate of colloidal size, such as a particle found in coal.
▷**HISTORY** C19: from New Latin *micella,* diminutive of Latin *mīca* crumb
▸**miˈcellar** ADJECTIVE

mich (mɪtʃ) VERB (*intr*) a variant spelling of **mitch.**

Mich. ABBREVIATION FOR Michigan.

Michaelmas (ˈmɪkᵊlməs) NOUN Sept. 29, the feast of St Michael the archangel; in England, Ireland, and Wales, one of the four quarter days.

Michaelmas daisy NOUN *Brit* any of various plants of the genus *Aster* that have small autumn-blooming purple, pink, or white flowers: family *Asteraceae* (composites).

Michaelmas term NOUN the autumn term at Oxford and Cambridge Universities, the Inns of Court, and some other educational establishments.

Michelson-Morley experiment (ˌmaɪkᵊlsᵊnˈmɔːlɪ) NOUN an experiment first performed in 1887 by A. A. Michelson and E. W. Morley, in which an interferometer was used to attempt to detect a difference in the velocities of light in directions parallel and perpendicular to the earth's motion. The negative result was explained by the special theory of relativity.

michigan (ˈmɪʃɪgən) NOUN the US name for **newmarket** (sense 2).

Michigan (ˈmɪʃɪgən) NOUN [1] a state of the N central US, occupying two peninsulas between Lakes Superior, Huron, Michigan, and Erie: generally low-lying. Capital: Lansing. Pop.: 9 938 444 (2000). Area: 147 156 sq. km (56 817 sq. miles). Abbreviations: **Mich,** (with zip code) **MI.** [2] **Lake.** a lake in the N central US between Wisconsin and Michigan: the third largest of the five Great Lakes and the only one wholly in the US; linked with Lake Huron by the Straits of Mackinac. Area: 58 000 sq. km (22 400 sq. miles).

Michigander (ˌmɪʃɪˈgændə) NOUN a native or inhabitant of Michigan.

Michiganite (ˈmɪʃɪgənˌaɪt) NOUN [1] a native or

inhabitant of Michigan. ◆ ADJECTIVE 2 of or relating to Michigan or its inhabitants.

Michoacán (*Spanish* mitʃoa'kan) NOUN a state of SW Mexico, on the Pacific: rich mineral resources. Capital: Morelia. Pop.: 3 979 177 (2000). Area: 59 864 sq. km (23 114 sq. miles).

micht (mɪxt) VERB, NOUN a Scot word for **might**[1] and **might**[2].

Mick (mɪk) *or* **Mickey** ('mɪkɪ) NOUN (*sometimes not capital*) *Derogatory* a slang name for an Irishman or a Roman Catholic.
▷ HISTORY C19: from the nickname for *Michael*

mickey[1] *or* **micky** ('mɪkɪ) NOUN **take the mickey (out of).** *Informal* to tease.
▷ HISTORY C20: of unknown origin

mickey[2] *or* **micky** ('mɪkɪ) NOUN *Austral informal* a young bull, esp one that is wild and unbranded.

mickey[3] ('mɪkɪ) NOUN *Canadian* a liquor bottle of 0.375 litre capacity, flat on one side and curved on the other to fit into a pocket.
▷ HISTORY C20: of unknown origin

Mickey Finn NOUN *Slang* **a** a drink containing a drug to make the drinker unconscious, usually formed by the combination of chloral hydrate and alcohol. It can be poisonous. **b** the drug itself. ◆ Often shortened to: **Mickey.**
▷ HISTORY C20: of unknown origin

Mickey Mouse ADJECTIVE (*sometimes not capitals*) *Slang* 1 ineffective; trivial; insignificant: *he settled for a Mickey Mouse job instead of something challenging.* 2 *Chiefly US and Canadian* (of music, esp that of dance bands) mechanical or spiritless.
▷ HISTORY C20: from the name of a cartoon character known for his simple-minded attitudes, created by Walt Disney (1901–66), the US film producer

mickle ('mɪkᵊl) *or* **muckle** ('mʌkᵊl) *Scot and Northern English dialect* ◆ ADJECTIVE 1 great or abundant. ◆ ADVERB 2 much; greatly. ◆ NOUN 3 a great amount, esp in the proverb, *mony a little makes a mickle.* 4 *Scot* a small amount, esp in the proverb, *many a mickle maks a muckle.*
▷ HISTORY C13 *mikel,* from Old Norse *mikell,* replacing Old English *micel* MUCH

Micmac ('mɪkmæk) NOUN 1 (*plural* **-macs** *or* **-mac**) a member of a North American Indian people formerly living in the Maritime Provinces of Canada. 2 the language of this people, belonging to the Algonquian family.

MICR ABBREVIATION FOR **magnetic ink character recognition.**

micra ('maɪkrə) NOUN a plural of **micron.**

micro ('maɪkrəʊ) ADJECTIVE 1 very small. ◆ NOUN, *plural* **-cros.** 2 short for **microcomputer, microlepidoptera, microprocessor, microwave oven.**

micro- *or* **micr-** COMBINING FORM 1 small or minute: *microspore.* 2 involving the use of a microscope: *micrography.* 3 indicating a method or instrument for dealing with small quantities: *micrometer.* 4 (in pathology) indicating abnormal smallness or underdevelopment: *microcephaly; microcyte.* Compare **macro-** (sense 2). 5 denoting 10^{-6}: *microsecond.* Symbol: µ.
▷ HISTORY from Greek *mikros* small

microaerophile (ˌmaɪkrəʊ'ɛərəʊˌfaɪl) NOUN an organism, esp a bacterium, that thrives in an environment low in oxygen.
▸ **microaerophilic** (ˌmaɪkrəʊˌɛərəʊ'fɪlɪk) ADJECTIVE

microanalysis (ˌmaɪkrəʊə'nælɪsɪs) NOUN, *plural* **-ses** (-ˌsiːz). the qualitative or quantitative chemical analysis of very small amounts of substances.
▸ **microanalyst** (ˌmaɪkrəʊ'ænəlɪst) NOUN ▸ **microanalytic** (ˌmaɪkrəʊˌænə'lɪtɪk) *or* **ˌmicroˌana'lytical** ADJECTIVE

microbalance ('maɪkrəʊˌbæləns) NOUN a precision balance designed to weigh quantities between 10^{-6} and 10^{-9} kilogram.

microbarograph (ˌmaɪkrəʊ'bærəˌgrɑːf, -ˌgræf) NOUN a barograph that records minute changes in atmospheric pressure.

microbe ('maɪkrəʊb) NOUN any microscopic organism, esp a disease-causing bacterium.
▷ HISTORY C19: from French, from MICRO- + Greek *bios* life
▸ **mi'crobial** *or* **mi'crobic** *or* (*less commonly*) **mi'crobian** ADJECTIVE

microbiology (ˌmaɪkrəʊbaɪ'ɒlədʒɪ) NOUN the branch of biology involving the study of microorganisms.
▸ **microbiological** (ˌmaɪkrəʊˌbaɪə'lɒdʒɪkᵊl) *or* **ˌmicroˌbio'logic** ADJECTIVE ▸ **ˌmicroˌbio'logically** ADVERB ▸ **ˌmicrobi'ologist** NOUN

microbrewery ('maɪkrəʊˌbrʊərɪ) NOUN, *plural* **-ries.** a small, usually independent brewery that produces limited quantities of specialized beers, often sold for consumption on the premises.

microbubbles ('maɪkrəʊˌbʌbᵊlz) PLURAL NOUN *Medicine* a contrast medium used with ultrasound, consisting of tiny bubbles of gas introduced into the vascular system or Fallopian tubes to enhance the images obtained.

microburst ('maɪkrəʊˌbɜːst) NOUN another name for **downburst.**

microcelebrity (ˌmaɪkrəʊsɪ'lɛbrɪtɪ) NOUN, *plural* **-ties.** a celebrity whose fame is relatively narrow in scope and likely to be transient.

microcephaly (ˌmaɪkrəʊ'sɛfəlɪ) NOUN the condition of having an abnormally small head or cranial capacity. Compare **megacephaly.**
▸ **microcephalic** (ˌmaɪkrəʊsɪ'fælɪk) ADJECTIVE, NOUN ▸ **ˌmicro'cephalous** ADJECTIVE

microchemistry (ˌmaɪkrəʊ'kɛmɪstrɪ) NOUN chemical experimentation with minute quantities of material.
▸ **ˌmicro'chemical** ADJECTIVE

microchip ('maɪkrəʊˌtʃɪp) NOUN 1 a small piece of semiconductor material carrying many integrated circuits. ◆ VERB **-chips, -chipping, -chipped.** 2 (*tr*) to implant (an animal) with a microchip tag linked to a national computer network for purposes of identification.

microcircuit ('maɪkrəʊˌsɜːkɪt) NOUN a miniature electronic circuit, esp one in which a number of permanently connected components are contained in one small chip of semiconducting material. See **integrated circuit.**
▸ **ˌmicro'circuitry** NOUN

microclimate ('maɪkrəʊˌklaɪmɪt) NOUN *Ecology* 1 the atmospheric conditions affecting an individual or a small group of organisms, esp when they differ from the climate of the rest of the community. 2 the entire environment of an individual or small group of organisms.
▸ **microclimatic** (ˌmaɪkrəʊklaɪ'mætɪk) ADJECTIVE ▸ **ˌmicrocli'matically** ADVERB

microclimatology (ˌmaɪkrəʊˌklaɪmə'tɒlədʒɪ) NOUN the study of climate on a small scale, as of a city.
▸ **microclimatologic** (ˌmaɪkrəʊˌklaɪmətə'lɒdʒɪk) *or* **ˌmicroˌclimato'logical** ADJECTIVE ▸ **ˌmicroˌclima'tologist** NOUN

microcline ('maɪkrəʊˌklaɪn) NOUN a white, creamy yellow, red, or green mineral of the feldspar group, found in igneous, sedimentary, and metamorphic rocks: used in the manufacture of glass and ceramics. Composition: potassium aluminium silicate. Formula: $KAlSi_3O_8$. Crystal structure: triclinic.
▷ HISTORY C19: from German *Mikroklin,* from *mikro-* MICRO- + Greek *klinein* to lean; so called because its cleavage plane is slightly different from 90°

micrococcus (ˌmaɪkrəʊ'kɒkəs) NOUN, *plural* **-cocci** (-'kɒksaɪ). any spherical Gram-positive bacterium of the genus *Micrococcus*: family *Micrococcaceae.*

microcomputer ('maɪkrəʊkəmˌpjuːtə) NOUN a small computer in which the central processing unit is contained in one or more silicon chips. Sometimes shortened to: **micro.**

microcopy ('maɪkrəʊˌkɒpɪ) NOUN, *plural* **-copies.** a greatly reduced photographic copy of a printed page, drawing, etc., on microfilm or microfiche. Sometimes called: **microphotograph.**

microcosm ('maɪkrəʊˌkɒzəm) *or* **microcosmos** (ˌmaɪkrəʊ'kɒzmɒs) NOUN 1 a miniature representation of something, esp a unit, group, or place regarded as a copy of a larger one. 2 man regarded as epitomizing the universe. ◆ Compare **macrocosm.**
▷ HISTORY C15: via Medieval Latin from Greek *mikros kosmos* little world
▸ **ˌmicro'cosmic** *or* **ˌmicro'cosmical** ADJECTIVE

microcosmic salt NOUN a white soluble solid obtained from human urine; ammonium sodium hydrogen phosphate. It is used as a flux in bead tests on metal oxides.

micro-credit ('maɪkrəʊˌkrɛdɪt) NOUN the practice of lending small amounts of money on minimal security, esp to help small businesses and communities in the developing world.

microcrystalline (ˌmaɪkrəʊ'krɪstᵊˌlaɪn) ADJECTIVE (of a solid) composed of microscopic crystals.

microcyte ('maɪkrəʊˌsaɪt) NOUN an unusually small red blood cell.
▸ **microcytic** (ˌmaɪkrəʊ'sɪtɪk) ADJECTIVE

microdetector (ˌmaɪkrəʊdɪ'tɛktə) NOUN any instrument for measuring small quantities or detecting small effects, esp a sensitive galvanometer.

microdont ('maɪkrəʊˌdɒnt) *or* **microdontous** (ˌmaɪkrəʊ'dɒntəs) ADJECTIVE having unusually small teeth.

microdot ('maɪkrəʊˌdɒt) NOUN 1 a microcopy about the size of a pinhead, used esp in espionage. 2 a tiny tablet containing LSD.

microeconomics (ˌmaɪkrəʊˌiːkə'nɒmɪks, -ˌɛkə-) NOUN (*functioning as singular*) the branch of economics concerned with particular commodities, firms, or individuals and the economic relationships between them. Compare **macroeconomics.**
▸ **ˌmicroˌeco'nomic** ADJECTIVE

microelectronics (ˌmaɪkrəʊɪlɛk'trɒnɪks) NOUN (*functioning as singular*) the branch of electronics concerned with microcircuits.
▸ **ˌmicroelec'tronic** ADJECTIVE

microenvironment ('maɪkrəʊɪnˌvaɪrənmənt) NOUN *Ecology* the environment of a small area, such as that around a leaf or plant.

microfarad ('maɪkrəʊˌfærəd) NOUN one millionth of a farad; 10^{-6} farad. Symbol: µF.

microfibre *or US* **microfiber** ('maɪkrəʊˌfaɪbə) NOUN a very fine synthetic fibre used for textiles.

microfiche ('maɪkrəʊˌfiːʃ) NOUN a sheet of film, usually the size of a filing card, on which books, newspapers, documents, etc., can be recorded in miniaturized form. Sometimes shortened to: **fiche.** See also **ultrafiche.**
▷ HISTORY C20: from French, from MICRO- + *fiche* small card, from Old French *fichier* to fix

microfilament (ˌmaɪkrəʊ'fɪləmənt) NOUN thin filament, composed of the protein actin and associated proteins, that occurs abundantly in muscle and in the cytoplasm of other cells.

microfilaria (ˌmaɪkrəʊfɪ'lɛərɪə) NOUN, *plural* **-iae** (-ɪˌiː). *Zoology* the early larval stage of certain parasitic nematodes (filariae), found in the blood of infected individuals.

microfilm ('maɪkrəʊˌfɪlm) NOUN 1 a strip of film of standard width on which books, newspapers, documents, etc., can be recorded in miniaturized form. ◆ VERB 2 to photograph (a page, document, etc.) on microfilm. ◆ See also **microfiche.**

microfilm plotter NOUN *Computing* a type of incremental plotter that has a film rather than a paper output.

microform ('maɪkrəʊˌfɔːm) NOUN *Computing* a method of storing symbolic information by using photographic reduction techniques, such as microfilm, microfiche, etc.

microfossil ('maɪkrəʊˌfɒsᵊl) NOUN a fossil generally less than 0.5 millimetre in size, such as a protozoan, bacterium, or pollen grain.

microgamete (ˌmaɪkrəʊ'gæmiːt) NOUN the smaller and apparently male of two gametes in conjugating protozoans. Compare **macrogamete.**

microglia (ˌmaɪkrəʊ'glɪə) NOUN one of the two types of non-nervous tissue (glia) found in the central nervous system, having macrophage activity. Compare **macroglia.**

micrograph ('maɪkrəʊˌgrɑːf, -ˌgræf) NOUN 1 a photograph or drawing of an object as viewed through a microscope. 2 an instrument or machine for producing very small writing or engraving.

micrography (maɪ'krɒgrəfɪ) NOUN 1 the description, study, drawing, or photography of microscopic objects. 2 the technique of using a microscope. 3 the art or practice of writing in minute characters.

▸mi'crographer NOUN ▸micrographic (ˌmaɪkrəʊ'græfɪk) ADJECTIVE ▸ˌmicro'graphically ADVERB

microgravity ('maɪkrəʊˌgrævɪtɪ) NOUN the very low apparent gravity experienced in a spacecraft in earth orbit.

microgroove ('maɪkrəʊˌgru:v) NOUN **a** the narrow groove in a long-playing gramophone record. **b** (*as modifier*): *a microgroove record.*

microhabitat (ˌmaɪkrəʊ'hæbɪtæt) NOUN *Ecology* the smallest part of the environment that supports a distinct flora and fauna, such as a fallen log in a forest.

microinstruction ('maɪkrəʊɪnˌstrʌkʃən) NOUN *Computing* an instruction produced within an arithmetic and logic unit in accordance with a microprogram, that activates a particular circuit to perform part of the operation specified by a machine instruction.

microlepidoptera (ˌmaɪkrəʊˌlepɪ'dɒptərə) PLURAL NOUN a collector's name for the smaller moths: a term without taxonomic significance. Compare **macrolepidoptera.**

microlight *or* **microlite** ('maɪkrəʊˌlaɪt) NOUN a small private aircraft carrying no more than two people, with an empty weight of not more than 150 kg and a wing area not less than 10 square metres: used in pleasure flying and racing.

microlith ('maɪkrəʊˌlɪθ) NOUN *Archaeol* a small Mesolithic flint tool which was made from a blade and formed part of hafted tools.
▸ˌmicro'lithic ADJECTIVE

micromanage ('maɪkrəʊˌmænɪdʒ) VERB (*tr*) to control (a business or project) with excessive attention to minor details.

micromarketing (ˌmaɪkrəʊ'mɑ:kɪtɪŋ) NOUN the marketing of products or services designed to meet the needs of a very small section of the market.

micromere ('maɪkrəʊˌmɪə) NOUN *Embryol* any of the small cells formed by unequal cleavage of a fertilized ovum.

micrometeorite (ˌmaɪkrəʊ'mi:tɪəˌraɪt) NOUN a tiny meteorite having a diameter of 10–40 micrometres, found esp in rainwater and seawater, having entered the atmosphere as a **micrometeoroid** (extremely small meteoroid).

micrometeorology (ˌmaɪkrəʊˌmi:tɪə'rɒlədʒɪ) NOUN the study of the layer of air immediately above the earth and of small-scale meteorological processes.

micrometer (maɪ'krɒmɪtə) NOUN **1** any of various instruments or devices for the accurate measurement of distances or angles. **2** Also called: **micrometer gauge, micrometer calliper.** a type of gauge for the accurate measurement of small distances, thicknesses, diameters, etc. The gap between its measuring faces is adjusted by a fine screw, the rotation of the screw giving a sensitive measure of the distance moved by the face.
▸mi'crometry NOUN ▸micrometric (ˌmaɪkrəʊ'mɛtrɪk) *or* ˌmicro'metrical ADJECTIVE

micrometer screw NOUN a screw with a fine thread of definite pitch, such as that of a micrometer gauge.

micrometre ('maɪkrəʊˌmi:tə) NOUN a unit of length equal to 10^{-6} metre. Symbol: µm. Former name: **micron.**

microminiaturization *or* **microminiaturisation** (ˌmaɪkrəʊˌmɪnɪtʃəraɪ'zeɪʃən) NOUN the production and application of very small semiconductor components and the circuits and equipment in which they are used.

micron ('maɪkrɒn) NOUN, *plural* **-crons** *or* **-cra** (-krə). a unit of length equal to 10^{-6} metre. It is being replaced by the micrometre, the equivalent SI unit.
▷HISTORY C19: New Latin, from Greek *mikros* small

Micronesia (ˌmaɪkrəʊ'ni:zɪə) NOUN **1** one of the three divisions of islands in the Pacific (the others being Melanesia and Polynesia); the NW division of Oceania: includes the Mariana, Caroline, Marshall, and Kiribati island groups, and Nauru Island. **2** **Federated States of.** an island group in the W Pacific, formerly within the United States Trust Territory of the Pacific Islands: comprises the islands of Truk, Yap, Ponape, and Kosrae: formed in 1979 when the islands became self-governing: status of free association with the US from 1982. Languages: English and Micronesian languages. Religion: Christian majority. Currency: US dollar. Capital: Palikir. Pop.: 118 000 (2001 est.).
▷HISTORY C19: from MICRO- + Greek *nēsos* island; so called from the small size of many of the islands; on the model of *Polynesia*

Micronesian (ˌmaɪkrəʊ'ni:zɪən) ADJECTIVE **1** of or relating to Micronesia, its inhabitants, or their languages. ◆ NOUN **2** a native or inhabitant of Micronesia, more akin to the Polynesians than the Melanesians, but having Mongoloid traces. **3** a group of languages spoken in Micronesia, belonging to the Malayo-Polynesian family.

micronucleus (ˌmaɪkrəʊ'nju:klɪəs) NOUN, *plural* **-clei** (-klɪˌaɪ) *or* **-cleuses.** the smaller of two nuclei in ciliated protozoans, involved in reproduction. Compare **macronucleus.**

micronutrient (ˌmaɪkrəʊ'nju:trɪənt) NOUN any substance, such as a vitamin or trace element, essential for healthy growth and development but required only in minute amounts.

microorganism (ˌmaɪkrəʊ'ɔ:gəˌnɪzəm) NOUN any organism, such as a bacterium, protozoan, or virus, of microscopic size.

micropalaeontology (ˌmaɪkrəʊˌpælɪɒn'tɒlədʒɪ) NOUN the branch of palaeontology concerned with the study of microscopic fossils.
▸micropalaeontological (ˌmaɪkrəʊˌpælɪɒntə'lɒdʒɪkᵊl) *or* ˌmicroˌpalaeonto'logic ADJECTIVE ▸ˌmicroˌpalaeon'tologist NOUN

microparasite (ˌmaɪkrəʊ'pærəˌsaɪt) NOUN any parasitic microorganism.
▸microparasitic (ˌmaɪkrəʊˌpærə'sɪtɪk) ADJECTIVE

micropayment ('maɪkrəʊˌpeɪmənt) NOUN a system whereby a user pays a small fee to access a specific area of a website.

microphagous (maɪ'krɒfəgəs) ADJECTIVE *Zoology* (of an animal) feeding on small particles of food.

microphanerophyte (ˌmaɪkrəʊ'fænərəʊˌfaɪt) NOUN *Botany* any shrub or tree having a height of 2 to 8 metres.

microphone ('maɪkrəˌfəʊn) NOUN a device used in sound-reproduction systems for converting sound into electrical energy, usually by means of a ribbon or diaphragm set into motion by the sound waves. The vibrations are converted into the equivalent audio-frequency electric currents. Informal name: **mike.** See also **carbon microphone.** Compare **loudspeaker.**

microphonic (ˌmaɪkrə'fɒnɪk) ADJECTIVE **1** of or relating to microphones. **2** (of valves or other electronic components) unusually sensitive to incident sound or mechanical shock.

microphotograph (ˌmaɪkrəʊ'fəʊtəˌgrɑ:f, -ˌgræf) NOUN **1** a photograph in which the image is greatly reduced and therefore requires optical enlargement for viewing purposes. **2** a less common name for **microcopy** or **photomicrograph** (sense 1).
▸ˌmicroˌphoto'graphic ADJECTIVE ▸microphotography (ˌmaɪkrəʊfə'tɒgrəfɪ) NOUN

microphyll ('maɪkrəʊfɪl) NOUN *Botany* the relatively small type of leaf produced by club mosses and horsetails. Compare **megaphyll.**

microphysics (ˌmaɪkrəʊ'fɪzɪks) NOUN (*functioning as singular*) the branch of physics concerned with small objects and systems, such as atoms, molecules, nuclei, and elementary particles.
▸ˌmicro'physical ADJECTIVE

microphyte ('maɪkrəʊˌfaɪt) NOUN an obsolete name for a **bacterium.**
▸microphytic (ˌmaɪkrəʊ'fɪtɪk) ADJECTIVE

micropower ('maɪkrəʊˌpaʊə) NOUN power distributed on a small scale using local generators.

microprint ('maɪkrəʊˌprɪnt) NOUN a microphotograph reproduced on paper and read by a magnifying device. It is used in order to reduce the size of large books, etc.

microprism ('maɪkrəʊˌprɪzəm) NOUN *Photog* a small prism incorporated in the focusing screen of many single-lens reflex cameras. The prism stops shimmering when the subject is in focus.

microprocessor (ˌmaɪkrəʊ'prəʊsɛsə) NOUN *Computing* a single integrated circuit performing the basic functions of the central processing unit in a small computer.

microprogram ('maɪkrəʊˌprəʊgræm) NOUN *Computing* a sequence of microinstructions that controls the operation of an arithmetic and logic unit so that machine code instructions are executed.

micropropagation (ˌmaɪkrəʊˌprɒpə'geɪʃən) NOUN *Botany* the production of a large number of individual plants from a small piece of plant tissue cultured in a nutrient medium.

micropsia (maɪ'krɒpsɪə) NOUN a defect of vision in which objects appear to be smaller than they appear to a person with normal vision.

micropterous (maɪ'krɒptərəs) ADJECTIVE (of certain animals, esp some types of ant) having small reduced wings.

micropyle ('maɪkrəʊˌpaɪl) NOUN **1** a small opening in the integuments of a plant ovule through which the male gametes pass. **2** a small pore in the shell of an insect's eggs through which the sperm passes.
▷HISTORY C19: from MICRO- + Greek *pulē* gate
▸ˌmicro'pylar ADJECTIVE

micropyrometer (ˌmaɪkrəʊpaɪ'rɒmɪtə) NOUN a pyrometer for measuring the temperature of very small objects.

microreader ('maɪkrəʊˌri:də) NOUN an apparatus that produces an enlarged image of a microphotograph.

microsatellite (ˌmaɪkrəʊ'sætᵊˌlaɪt) NOUN *Genetics* a section of DNA consisting of very short nucleotide sequences repeated many times, the number of repeats varying between members of the species: used as a marker in determining genetic diversity, identifying important genetic traits, and in forensics, population studies, and paternity studies.

micro-scooter NOUN a foldable lightweight aluminium foot-propelled scooter, used by both adults and children.

microscope ('maɪkrəˌskəʊp) NOUN **1** an optical instrument that uses a lens or combination of lenses to produce a magnified image of a small, close object. Modern optical microscopes have magnifications of about 1500 to 2000. See also **simple microscope, compound microscope, ultramicroscope.** **2** any instrument, such as the electron microscope, for producing a magnified visual image of a small object.

microscopic (ˌmaɪkrə'skɒpɪk) *or less commonly* **microscopical** ADJECTIVE **1** not large enough to be seen with the naked eye but visible under a microscope. Compare **macroscopic.** **2** very small; minute. **3** of, concerned with, or using a microscope. **4** characterized by or done with great attention to detail.
▸ˌmicro'scopically ADVERB

Microscopium (ˌmaɪkrə'skəʊpɪəm) NOUN, *Latin genitive* **Microscopii** (ˌmaɪkrə'skəʊpɪˌaɪ). a faint constellation in the S hemisphere lying near Sagittarius and Capricornus.

microscopy (maɪ'krɒskəpɪ) NOUN **1** the study, design, and manufacture of microscopes. **2** investigation by use of a microscope.
▸microscopist (maɪ'krɒskəpɪst) NOUN

microsecond ('maɪkrəʊˌsɛkənd) NOUN one millionth of a second. Symbol: µs.

microseism ('maɪkrəʊˌsaɪzəm) NOUN a very slight tremor of the earth's surface, thought not to be caused by an earthquake.
▸microseismic (ˌmaɪkrəʊ'saɪzmɪk) *or* ˌmicro'seismical ADJECTIVE

microsite ('maɪkrəʊˌsaɪt) NOUN a website that is intended for a specific limited purpose and is often temporary.

microsleep ('maɪkrəʊˌsli:p) NOUN a period of sleep which is so momentary as to be imperceptible.

microsmatic (ˌmaɪkrɒz'mætɪk) ADJECTIVE (of humans and certain animals) having a poor sense of smell.
▷HISTORY from MICRO- + Greek *osmē* smell

microsome ('maɪkrəʊˌsəʊm) NOUN any of the small particles consisting of ribosomes and fragments of attached endoplasmic reticulum that can be isolated from cells by centrifugal action.
▸ˌmicro'somal ADJECTIVE

microspecies ('maɪkrəʊˌspi:ʃi:z) NOUN, *plural* **-cies.** another name for **biotype.**

microsporangium (ˌmaɪkrəʊspɔ:'rændʒɪəm)

NOUN, *plural* **-gia** (-dʒɪə). the structure in certain spore-bearing plants in which the microspores are formed: corresponds to the pollen sac in seed plants. Compare **megasporangium.**

microspore (ˈmaɪkrəʊˌspɔː) NOUN 1 the smaller of two types of spore produced by some spore-bearing plants, which develops into the male gametophyte. Compare **megaspore** (sense 1). 2 the pollen grain of seed plants.
▸ ˌ**microˈsporic** *or* ˌ**microˈsporous** ADJECTIVE

microsporophyll (ˌmaɪkrəʊˈspɔːrəfɪl) NOUN a leaf on which the microspores are formed: corresponds to the stamen of a flowering plant. Compare **megasporophyll.**
▷HISTORY C19: from MICRO- + SPOROPHYLL

microstomatous (ˌmaɪkrəʊˈstɒmətəs) *or* **microstomous** (maɪˈkrɒstəməs) ADJECTIVE *Anatomy* having an unusually small mouth.

microstructure (ˈmaɪkrəʊˌstrʌktʃə) NOUN structure on a microscopic scale, esp the structure of an alloy as observed by etching, polishing, and observation under a microscope.

microsurgery (ˌmaɪkrəʊˈsɜːdʒərɪ) NOUN intricate surgery performed on cells, tissues, etc., using a specially designed operating microscope and miniature precision instruments.
▸ ˌ**microˈsurgical** ADJECTIVE

microswitch (ˈmaɪkrəʊˌswɪtʃ) NOUN *Electrical engineering* a switch that operates by small movements of a lever.

microtechnology (ˌmaɪkrəʊtɛkˈnɒlədʒɪ) NOUN technology that uses microelectronics.

microtome (ˈmaɪkrəʊˌtəʊm) NOUN an instrument used for cutting thin sections, esp of biological material, for microscopical examination.

microtomy (maɪˈkrɒtəmɪ) NOUN, *plural* **-mies.** the cutting of sections with a microtome.
▸ **microtomic** (ˌmaɪkrəʊˈtɒmɪk) *or* ˌ**microˈtomical** ADJECTIVE ▸ **miˈcrotomist** NOUN

microtone (ˈmaɪkrəʊˌtəʊn) NOUN any musical interval smaller than a semitone.
▸ ˌ**microˈtonal** ADJECTIVE ▸ ˌ**microtoˈnality** NOUN
▸ ˌ**microˈtonally** ADVERB

microtubule (ˌmaɪkrəʊˈtjuːbjuːl) NOUN *Biology* a tubular aggregate of protein subunits that forms structures, such as the mitotic spindle or the cilia of animal cells or of protozoans, in which the protein interacts with other proteins to generate various cellular movements.

microvillus (ˌmaɪkrəʊˈvɪləs) NOUN, *plural* **-li** (-laɪ). *Physiol* a thin protuberance present in great abundance at the surface of some epithelial cells, notably in the gut, thus increasing the surface area available for absorption.

microwave (ˈmaɪkrəʊˌweɪv) NOUN 1 **a** electromagnetic radiation in the wavelength range 0.3 to 0.001 metres: used in radar, cooking, etc. **b** (*as modifier*): *microwave generator.* 2 short for **microwave oven.** ◆ VERB (*tr*) 3 to cook in a microwave oven.

microwave background NOUN a background of microwave electromagnetic radiation with a black-body spectrum discovered in 1965, understood to be the thermal remnant of the big bang with which the universe began.

microwave detector NOUN a device for recording the speed of a motorist.

microwave oven NOUN an oven in which food is cooked by microwaves. Often shortened to: **micro, microwave.**

microwave spectroscopy NOUN a type of spectroscopy in which information is obtained on the structure and chemical bonding of molecules and crystals by measurements of the wavelengths of microwaves emitted or absorbed by the sample.
▸ **microwave spectroscope** NOUN

microwriter (ˈmaɪkrəʊˌraɪtə) NOUN a small device with six keys for creating text that can be printed or displayed on a visual display unit.

micrurgy (ˈmaɪkrɜːdʒɪ) NOUN 1 *Biology* the manipulation and examination of single cells under a microscope. 2 dissection under a microscope.
▷HISTORY C20: from MICRO- + Greek *-ourgia* work

micturate (ˈmɪktjʊˌreɪt) VERB (*intr*) a less common word for **urinate.**
▷HISTORY C19: from Latin *micturīre* to desire to urinate, from *mingere* to urinate

▸ **micturition** (ˌmɪktjʊˈrɪʃən) NOUN

mid[1] (mɪd) ADJECTIVE 1 *Phonetics* of, relating to, or denoting a vowel whose articulation lies approximately halfway between high and low, such as *e* in English *bet.* ◆ NOUN 2 an archaic word for **middle.**
▷HISTORY C12 *midre* (inflected form of *midd,* unattested); related to Old Norse *mithr,* Gothic *midjis*

mid[2] *or* **'mid** (mɪd) PREPOSITION a poetic word for **amid.**

mid. ABBREVIATION FOR middle.

Mid. ABBREVIATION FOR Midshipman.

mid- COMBINING FORM indicating a middle part, point, time, or position: *midday; mid-April; mid-Victorian.*
▷HISTORY Old English; see MIDDLE, MID[1]

midair (ˌmɪdˈɛə) NOUN **a** some point above ground level, in the air. **b** (*as modifier*): *a midair collision of aircraft.*

Midas (ˈmaɪdəs) NOUN 1 *Greek legend* a king of Phrygia given the power by Dionysus of turning everything he touched to gold. 2 **the Midas touch.** ability to make money.

MIDAS (ˈmaɪdəs) NOUN ACRONYM FOR Missile Defence Alarm System.

mid-Atlantic ADJECTIVE characterized by a blend of British and American styles, elements, etc.: *a disc jockey's mid-Atlantic accent.*

midbrain (ˈmɪdˌbreɪn) NOUN the nontechnical name for **mesencephalon.**

midday (ˈmɪdˈdeɪ) NOUN **a** the middle of the day; noon. **b** (*as modifier*): *a midday meal.*

Middelburg (ˈmɪdəlˌbɜːg; *Dutch* ˈmɪdəlbyrx) NOUN a city in the SW Netherlands, capital of Zeeland province, on Walcheren Island: an important trading centre in the Middle Ages and member of the Hanseatic League; 12th-century abbey; market town. Pop.: 40 118 (1994).

middelmannetjie (ˌmɪdəlˈmænɪkɪ) NOUN a continuous hump between wheel ruts on a dirt road.
▷HISTORY from Afrikaans, literally: little man in the middle

midden (ˈmɪdən) NOUN 1 **a** *Archaic or dialect* a dunghill or pile of refuse. **b** *Dialect* a dustbin. **c** *Northern English dialect* an earth closet. 2 See **kitchen midden.**
▷HISTORY C14: from Scandinavian; compare Danish *mødding* from *møg* MUCK + *dynge* pile

middle (ˈmɪdəl) ADJECTIVE 1 equally distant from the ends or periphery of something; central. 2 intermediate in status, situation, etc. 3 located between the early and late parts of a series, time sequence, etc. 4 not extreme, esp in size; medium. 5 (esp in Greek and Sanskrit grammar) denoting a voice of verbs expressing reciprocal or reflexive action. Compare **active** (sense 5), **passive** (sense 5). 6 (*usually capital*) (of a language) intermediate between the earliest and the modern forms: *Middle English.* ◆ NOUN 7 an area or point equal in distance from the ends or periphery or in time between the early and late parts. 8 an intermediate part or section, such as the waist. 9 *Grammar* the middle voice. 10 *Logic* See **middle term.** 11 the ground between rows of growing plants. 12 a discursive article in a journal, placed between the leading articles and the book reviews. ◆ VERB (*tr*) 13 to place in the middle. 14 *Nautical* to fold in two. 15 *Football* to return (the ball) from the wing to midfield. 16 *Cricket* to hit (the ball) with the middle of the bat.
▷HISTORY Old English *middel;* compare Old Frisian *middel,* Dutch *middel,* German *mittel*

middle age NOUN the period of life between youth and old age, usually (in man) considered to occur approximately between the ages of 40 and 60.

middle-aged ADJECTIVE of, relating to, or being in the time in a person's life between youth and old age.

Middle Ages NOUN **the.** *European history* 1 (broadly) the period from the end of classical antiquity (or the deposition of the last W Roman emperor in 476 A.D.) to the Italian Renaissance (or the fall of Constantinople in 1453). 2 (narrowly) the period from about 1000 A.D. to the 15th century. Compare **Dark Ages.**

middle-age spread *or* **middle-aged spread** NOUN the fat that appears round many people's waist during middle age.

Middle America NOUN 1 the territories between the US and South America: Mexico, Central America, Panama, and the Greater and Lesser Antilles. 2 the US middle class, esp those groups that are politically conservative.

Middle American ADJECTIVE 1 of or relating to the territories between the US and South America or their inhabitants. 2 of or relating to the US middle class, esp those groups that are politically conservative. ◆ NOUN 1 a native or inhabitant of Middle America. 2 a member of the US middle class.

Middle Atlantic States *or* **Middle States** PLURAL NOUN the states of New York, Pennsylvania, and New Jersey.

middlebreaker (ˈmɪdəlˌbreɪkə) *or* **middlebuster** NOUN a type of plough that cuts a furrow with the soil heaped on each side, often used for sowing. Also called: **lister.**

middlebrow (ˈmɪdəlˌbraʊ) *Disparaging* ◆ NOUN 1 a person with conventional tastes and limited cultural appreciation. ◆ ADJECTIVE *also* **middlebrowed.** 2 of or appealing to middlebrows: *middlebrow culture.*
▸ ˈ**middleˌbrowism** NOUN

middle C NOUN *Music* the note graphically represented on the first ledger line below the treble staff or the first ledger line above the bass staff and corresponding in pitch to an internationally standardized fundamental frequency of 261.63 hertz.

middle class NOUN 1 Also called: **bourgeoisie.** a social stratum that is not clearly defined but is positioned between the lower and upper classes. It consists of businessmen, professional people, etc., along with their families, and is marked by bourgeois values. Compare **lower class, upper class, working class.** ◆ ADJECTIVE **middle-class.** 2 of, relating to, or characteristic of the middle class.

middle common room NOUN (in certain universities and colleges) a common room for the use of postgraduate students. Compare **junior common room, senior common room.**

Middle Congo NOUN one of the four territories of former French Equatorial Africa, in W central Africa: became an autonomous member of the French Community, as the Republic of the Congo, in 1958.

middle-distance ADJECTIVE 1 *Athletics* relating to or denoting races of a length between the sprints and the distance events, esp the 800 metres and the 1500 metres. ◆ NOUN **middle distance.** 2 part of a painting, esp a landscape between the foreground and far distance.

Middle Dutch NOUN the Dutch language from about 1100 to about 1500. Abbreviation: **MD.**

middle ear NOUN the sound-conducting part of the ear, containing the malleus, incus, and stapes.

Middle East NOUN 1 (loosely) the area around the E Mediterranean, esp Israel and the Arab countries from Turkey to North Africa and eastwards to Iran. 2 (formerly) the area extending from the Tigris and Euphrates to Myanmar.

Middle Eastern ADJECTIVE of or relating to the Middle East or its inhabitants.

middle eight NOUN the third contrasting eight-bar section of a 32-bar pop song.

Middle England NOUN a characterization of a predominantly middle-class, middle-income section of British society living mainly in suburban and rural England.

Middle English NOUN the English language from about 1100 to about 1450: main dialects are Kentish, Southwestern (West Saxon), East Midland (which replaced West Saxon as the chief literary form and developed into Modern English), West Midland, and Northern (from which the Scots of Lowland Scotland and other modern dialects developed). Compare **Old English, Modern English.** Abbreviation: **ME.**

middle game NOUN *Chess* the central phase between the opening and the endgame.

Middle Greek NOUN another name for **Medieval Greek.**

middle ground NOUN 1 another term for **middle distance.** 2 a position of compromise between two opposing views, parties, etc.

Middle High German NOUN High German from about 1200 to about 1500. Abbreviation: **MHG.**

Middle Irish NOUN Irish Gaelic from about 1100 to about 1500.

Middle Kingdom NOUN 1 a period of Egyptian history extending from the late 11th to the 13th dynasty (?2040–?1670 B.C.). 2 **a** the former Chinese empire (from the belief that it lay at the centre of the earth). **b** the original 18 provinces of China; China proper.

Middle Low German NOUN Low German from about 1200 to about 1500. Abbreviation: **MLG.**

middleman (ˈmɪdᵊlˌmæn) NOUN, *plural* **-men.** 1 an independent trader engaged in the distribution of goods from producer to consumer. 2 an intermediary. 3 *Theatre* the interlocutor in minstrel shows.

middle management NOUN a level of management in an organization or business consisting of executives or senior supervisory staff in charge of the detailed running of an organization or business and reporting to top management. Compare **top management.**
▸**middle manager** NOUN

middlemost (ˈmɪdᵊlˌməʊst) ADJECTIVE another word for **midmost.**

middle name NOUN 1 a name between a person's first name and surname. 2 a characteristic quality for which a person is known: *caution is my middle name.*

middle-of-the-road ADJECTIVE 1 not extreme, esp in political views; moderate. 2 of, denoting, or relating to popular music having a wide general appeal.
▸ˈ**middle-of-the-ˈroader** NOUN

Middle Palaeolithic NOUN 1 the period between the Lower and the Upper Palaeolithic, usually taken as equivalent to the Mousterian. ◆ ADJECTIVE 2 of or relating to this period.

middle passage NOUN **the.** *History* the journey across the Atlantic Ocean from the W coast of Africa to the Caribbean: the longest part of the journey of the slave ships sailing to the Caribbean or the Americas.

Middle Persian NOUN the classical form of modern Persian, spoken from about 300 A.D. to about 900. See also **Pahlavi**².

Middlesbrough (ˈmɪdᵊlzbrə) NOUN 1 an industrial town in NE England, in Middlesbrough unitary authority, North Yorkshire: on the Tees estuary; university (1992). Pop.: 145 800 (1994 est.). 2 a unitary authority in NE England, in North Yorkshire: formerly (1974–96) part of Cleveland county. Pop.: 134 847 (2001). Area: 54 sq. km (21 sq. miles).

middle school NOUN (in England and Wales) a school for children aged between 8 or 9 and 12 or 13. Compare **first school.**

Middlesex (ˈmɪdᵊlˌseks) NOUN a former county of SE England: became mostly part of N and W Greater London in 1965. Abbreviation: **Middx.**

Middle States PLURAL NOUN another name for the **Middle Atlantic States.**

Middle Temple NOUN (in England) one of the four legal societies in London which together form the Inns of Court.

middle term NOUN *Logic* the term that appears in both the major and minor premises of a syllogism, but not in the conclusion. Also called: **mean, middle.**

Middleton (ˈmɪdᵊltən) NOUN a town in NW England, in Oldham unitary authority, Greater Manchester. Pop.: 45 621 (1991).

middle watch NOUN *Nautical* the watch between midnight and 4 a.m.

middleweight (ˈmɪdᵊlˌweɪt) NOUN 1 **a** a professional boxer weighing 154–160 pounds (70–72.5 kg). **b** an amateur boxer weighing 71–75 kg (157–165 pounds). **c** (*as modifier*): *a middleweight contest.* 2 a wrestler in a similar weight category (usually 172–192 pounds (78–87 kg)).

Middle West NOUN another name for the **Midwest.**

Middle Western ADJECTIVE another name for **Midwestern.**

Middle Westerner NOUN another name for **Midwesterner.**

middle white NOUN (*often capitals*) a breed of medium-sized white pig commonly kept for pork and bacon, and for fattening.

middle youth NOUN the period of life between about 30 and 50.

middling (ˈmɪdlɪŋ) ADJECTIVE 1 mediocre in quality, size, etc.; neither good nor bad, esp in health (often in the phrase **fair to middling**). ◆ ADVERB 2 *Informal* moderately: *middling well.*
▷**HISTORY** C15 (northern English and Scottish): from MID¹ + -LING²
▸ˈ**middlingly** ADVERB

middlings (ˈmɪdlɪŋz) PLURAL NOUN 1 the poorer or coarser part of flour or other products. 2 commodities of intermediate grade, quality, size, or price. 3 *Chiefly US* the part of a pig between the ham and shoulder.

Middx ABBREVIATION FOR Middlesex.

middy (ˈmɪdɪ) NOUN, *plural* **-dies.** 1 *Informal* See **midshipman** (sense 1). 2 See **middy blouse.** 3 *Austral* a middle-sized glass of beer.

middy blouse NOUN a blouse with a sailor collar, worn by women and children, esp formerly.

Mideast (ˌmɪdˈiːst) NOUN *Chiefly US* another name for **Middle East.**

midfield (ˌmɪdˈfiːld) NOUN *Soccer* **a** the general area between the two opposing defences. **b** (*as modifier*): *a midfield player.*

mid-flight ADJECTIVE, ADVERB 1 during a flight; whilst airborne: *a mid-flight celebration; doors opening mid-flight.* ◆ NOUN 2 **in mid-flight.** during a flight; whilst airborne.

Midgard (ˈmɪdɡɑːd), **Midgarth** (ˈmɪdɡɑːð), *or* **Mithgarthr** (ˈmɪðɡɑːðə) NOUN *Norse myth* the dwelling place of mankind, formed from the body of the giant Ymir and linked by the bridge Bifrost to Asgard, home of the gods.
▷**HISTORY** C19: from Old Norse *mithgarthr;* see MID¹, YARD²

midge (mɪdʒ) NOUN 1 any fragile mosquito-like dipterous insect of the family *Chironomidae,* occurring in dancing swarms, esp near water. 2 any similar or related insect, such as the biting midge and gall midge. 3 a small or diminutive person or animal.
▷**HISTORY** Old English *mycge;* compare Old High German *mucca,* Danish *myg*
▸ˈ**midgy** ADJECTIVE

midget (ˈmɪdʒɪt) NOUN 1 a dwarf whose skeleton and features are of normal proportions. 2 **a** something small of its kind. **b** (*as modifier*): *a midget car.*
▷**HISTORY** C19: from MIDGE + -ET

Mid Glamorgan NOUN a former county of S Wales, formed in 1974 from parts of Breconshire, Glamorgan, and Monmouthshire: replaced in 1996 by the county boroughs of Bridgend, Rhondda Cynon Taff, Merthyr Tydfil, and part of Caerphilly.

midgut (ˈmɪdˌɡʌt) NOUN 1 the middle part of the digestive tract of vertebrates, including the small intestine. 2 the middle part of the digestive tract of arthropods. ◆ See also **foregut, hindgut.**

Midheaven (ˈmɪdˈhevᵊn) NOUN *Astrology* 1 the point on the ecliptic, measured in degrees, that crosses the meridian of a particular place at a particular time. On a person's birth chart it relates to the time of birth. Abbreviation: **MC.** 2 the sign of the zodiac containing this point.
▷**HISTORY** C16: initials *MC* represent Latin *medium caeli* middle of the sky

midi (ˈmɪdɪ) ADJECTIVE **a** (of a skirt, coat, etc.) reaching to below the knee or midcalf. **b** (*as noun*): *she wore her new midi.*
▷**HISTORY** C20: from MID-; on the model of MAXI and MINI

Midi (*French* midi) NOUN 1 the south of France. 2 **Canal du.** a canal in S France, extending from the River Garonne at Toulouse to the Mediterranean at Sète and providing a link between the Mediterranean and Atlantic coasts: built between 1666 and 1681. Length: 181 km (150 miles).

MIDI (ˈmɪdɪ) NOUN (*modifier*) a generally accepted specification for the external control of electronic musical instruments: *a MIDI synthesizer; a MIDI system.*
▷**HISTORY** C20: from *m(usical) i(nstrument) d(igital) i(nterface)*

Midian (ˈmɪdɪən) NOUN *Old Testament* 1 a son of Abraham (Genesis 25:1–2). 2 a nomadic nation claiming descent from him.
▸ˈ**Midianˌite** NOUN, ADJECTIVE ▸ˈ**Midianˌitish** ADJECTIVE

midinette (ˌmɪdɪˈnet; *French* midinɛt) NOUN, *plural* **-nettes** (-ˈnets; *French* -nɛt). a Parisian seamstress or salesgirl in a clothes shop.
▷**HISTORY** C20: from French, from *midi* noon + *dinette* light meal, since the girls had time for no more than a snack at midday

Midi-Pyrénées (*French* midipirene) NOUN a region of SW France: consists of N slopes of the Pyrenees in the south, a fertile lowland area in the west crossed by the River Garonne, and the edge of the Massif Central in the north and east.

midiron (ˈmɪdˌaɪən) NOUN *Golf* a club, usually a No. 5, 6, or 7 iron, used for medium-length approach shots.

midi system NOUN a complete set of hi-fi sound equipment designed as a single unit that is more compact than the standard equipment.

midland (ˈmɪdlənd) NOUN **a** the central or inland part of a country. **b** (*as modifier*): *a midland region.*

Midlander (ˈmɪdləndə) NOUN a native or inhabitant of the Midlands of England.

Midlands (ˈmɪdləndz) NOUN (*functioning as plural or singular*) **the.** the central counties of England, including Warwickshire, Northamptonshire, Leicestershire, Nottinghamshire, Derbyshire, Staffordshire, the former West Midlands metropolitan county, and Worcestershire: characterized by manufacturing industries.

midlife crisis (ˈmɪdˌlaɪf) NOUN a crisis that may be experienced in middle age involving frustration, panic, and feelings of pointlessness, sometimes resulting in radical and often ill-advised changes of lifestyle.

mid-list NOUN **a** a section of a publisher's list containing those books that are not bestsellers. **b** (*as modifier*): *a mid-list writer.* ◆ See also **backlist, front list.**

Midlothian (mɪdˈləʊðɪən) NOUN a council area of SE central Scotland: the historical county of Midlothian (including Edinburgh) became part of Lothian region in 1975; separate unitary authorities were created for Midlothian and City of Edinburgh in 1996; mainly agricultural. Administrative centre: Dalkeith. Pop.: 80 941 (2001). Area: 356 sq. km (137 sq. miles).

midmost (ˈmɪdˌməʊst) ADJECTIVE, ADVERB in the middle or midst.

midnight (ˈmɪdˌnaɪt) NOUN 1 **a** the middle of the night; 12 o'clock at night. **b** (*as modifier*): *the midnight hour.* 2 **burn the midnight oil.** to work or study late into the night.
▸ˈ**midˌnightly** ADJECTIVE, ADVERB

midnight blue NOUN **a** a very dark blue colour; bluish black. **b** (*as adjective*): *a midnight-blue suit.*

midnight sun NOUN the sun visible at midnight during local summer inside the Arctic and Antarctic circles.

mid-off NOUN *Cricket* 1 the fielding position on the off side closest to the bowler. 2 a fielder in this position.

mid-on NOUN *Cricket* 1 the fielding position on the on side closest to the bowler. 2 a fielder in this position.

midpoint (ˈmɪdˌpɔɪnt) NOUN 1 the point on a line that is at an equal distance from either end. 2 a point in time halfway between the beginning and end of an event.

midrash (ˈmɪdræʃ; *Hebrew* miˈdraʃ) NOUN, *plural* **midrashim** (mɪˈdrɔʃɪm; *Hebrew* midraˈʃim). *Judaism* 1 a homily on a scriptural passage derived by traditional Jewish exegetical methods and consisting usually of embellishment of the scriptural narrative. 2 one of a number of collections of such homilies composed between 400 and 1200 A.D.
▷**HISTORY** C17: from Hebrew: commentary, from *darash* to search
▸**midrashic** (mɪdˈræʃɪk) ADJECTIVE

midrib ('mɪdˌrɪb) NOUN the main vein of a leaf, running down the centre of the blade.

midriff ('mɪdrɪf) NOUN 1 **a** the middle part of the human body, esp between waist and bust. **b** (*as modifier*): *midriff bulge*. 2 *Anatomy* another name for the **diaphragm** (sense 1). 3 the part of a woman's garment covering the midriff. 4 *US* a woman's garment which exposes the midriff.
▷HISTORY Old English *midhrif*, from MID[1] + *hrif* belly

midsection ('mɪdˌsɛkʃən) NOUN 1 the middle of something. 2 the middle region of the human body; midriff.

midship ('mɪdˌʃɪp) *Nautical* ◆ ADJECTIVE 1 in, of, or relating to the middle of a vessel. ◆ NOUN 2 the middle of a vessel.

midshipman ('mɪdˌʃɪpmən) NOUN, *plural* **-men**. 1 a probationary rank held by young naval officers under training, or an officer holding such a rank. 2 any of several American toadfishes of the genus *Porichthys*, having small light-producing organs on the undersurface of their bodies.

midships ('mɪdˌʃɪps) ADVERB, ADJECTIVE *Nautical* See **amidships**.

midsole (ˌmɪd'səʊl) NOUN a layer between the inner and the outer sole of a shoe, contoured for absorbing shock.

midst[1] (mɪdst) NOUN 1 **in the midst of.** surrounded or enveloped by; at a point during, esp a climactic one. 2 **in our midst.** among us. 3 *Archaic* the centre.
▷HISTORY C14: back formation from *amiddes* AMID

midst[2] (mɪdst) PREPOSITION *Poetic* See **amid**.

midstream ('mɪdˌstriːm) NOUN 1 the middle of a stream or river. 2 the middle of a process or action: *they tried to change the rules in midstream*. ◆ ADVERB, ADJECTIVE 3 in or towards the middle of a stream or river: *moored midstream*.

midsummer ('mɪd'sʌmə) NOUN 1 **a** the middle or height of the summer. **b** (*as modifier*): *a midsummer carnival*. 2 another name for **summer solstice**.

midsummer madness NOUN foolish or extravagant behaviour, supposed to occur during the summer.

midsummer-men NOUN (*functioning as singular or plural*) another name for **rose-root**.

Midsummer's Day *or* **Midsummer Day** NOUN June 24, the feast of St John the Baptist; in England, Ireland, and Wales, one of the four quarter days. See also **summer solstice**.

midterm ('mɪd'tɜːm) NOUN 1 **a** the middle of a term in a school, university, etc. **b** (*as modifier*): *midterm exam*. 2 *US politics* **a** the middle of a term of office, esp of a presidential term, when congressional and local elections are held. **b** (*as modifier*): *midterm elections*. 3 **a** the middle of the gestation period. **b** (*as modifier*): *midterm checkup*. See **term** (sense 6).

midtown ('mɪdˌtaʊn) NOUN *US and Eastern Canadian* the centre of a town. See also **downtown**, **uptown**.

mid-Victorian ADJECTIVE 1 *Brit History* of or relating to the middle period of the reign of Queen Victoria (1837–1901). ◆ NOUN 2 a person of the mid-Victorian era.

midway ('mɪdˌweɪ) ADJECTIVE, ADVERB 1 in or at the middle of the distance; halfway. ◆ NOUN 2 *US and Canadian* a place in a fair, carnival, etc., where sideshows are located. 3 *Obsolete* a middle place, way, etc.

Midway Islands PLURAL NOUN an atoll in the central Pacific, about 2100 km (1300 miles) northwest of Honolulu: annexed by the US in 1867: scene of a decisive battle (June, 1942), in which the US combined fleets destroyed Japan's carrier fleet. Pop.: 450 (1995 est.). Area: 5 sq. km (2 sq. miles).

midweek ('mɪd'wiːk) NOUN **a** the middle of the week. **b** (*as modifier*): *a midweek holiday*.
▸ **ˌmid'weekly** ADJECTIVE

Midwest ('mɪd'wɛst) *or* **Middle West** NOUN the N central part of the US; the region consisting of the states from Ohio westwards that border on the Great Lakes, often extended to include the upper Mississippi and Missouri valleys.

Midwestern ('mɪd'wɛstən) *or* **Middle Western** ADJECTIVE of or relating to the Midwest of the US or its inhabitants.

Midwesterner ('mɪd'wɛstənə) *or* **Middle Westerner** NOUN a native or inhabitant of the Midwest of the US.

mid-wicket NOUN *Cricket* 1 the fielding position on the on side, approximately midway between square leg and mid-on. 2 a fielder in this position.

midwife ('mɪdˌwaɪf) NOUN, *plural* **-wives** (-ˌwaɪvz). a person qualified to deliver babies and to care for women before, during, and after childbirth.
▷HISTORY C14: from Old English *mid* with + *wif* woman

midwifery ('mɪdˌwɪfərɪ) NOUN the art or practice of a midwife; obstetrics.

midwife toad NOUN a European toad, *Alytes obstetricans*, the male of which carries the fertilized eggs on its hind legs until they hatch: family *Discoglossidae*.

midwinter ('mɪd'wɪntə) NOUN 1 **a** the middle or depth of the winter. **b** (*as modifier*): *a midwinter festival*. 2 another name for **winter solstice**.

midyear ('mɪd'jɪə) NOUN **a** the middle of the year. **b** (*as modifier*): *a midyear examination*.

mielie ('miːlɪ) NOUN a variant of **mealie**.

mien (miːn) NOUN *Literary* a person's manner, bearing, or appearance, expressing personality or mood: *a noble mien*.
▷HISTORY C16: probably variant of obsolete *demean* appearance; related to French *mine* aspect

Mieres (*Spanish* 'mjeres) NOUN a city in N Spain, south of Oviedo: steel and chemical industries; iron and coal mines. Pop.: 26 500 (latest est.).

mifepristone (mɪ'fɛprɪˌstəʊn) NOUN an antiprogestogenic steroid, used in the medical termination of pregnancy. Formula: $C_{29}H_{35}NO_2$.
▷HISTORY C20: from *ami*no*phe*nol + *pr*opyne + *oest*radiol + -ONE

miff (mɪf) *Informal* ◆ VERB 1 to take offence or offend. ◆ NOUN 2 a petulant mood. 3 a petty quarrel.
▷HISTORY C17: perhaps an imitative expression of bad temper

miffy ('mɪfɪ) ADJECTIVE **-fier, -fiest.** *Informal* easily upset; oversensitive.
▸ **'miffily** ADVERB ▸ **'miffiness** NOUN

MiG (mɪg) NOUN any of various types of Soviet fighter aircraft.
▷HISTORY from *Mi*(*koyan*) and *G*(*urevich*), names of designers

might[1] (maɪt) VERB (takes an implied infinitive or an infinitive without *to*) used as an auxiliary. 1 making the past tense or subjunctive mood of **may**[1]: *he might have come last night*. 2 (often foll by *well*) expressing theoretical possibility: *he might well come*. In this sense *might* looks to the future and functions as a weak form of *may*. See **may**[1] (sense 2).

> **Language note** See at **may**[1].

might[2] (maɪt) NOUN 1 power, force, or vigour, esp of a great or supreme kind. 2 physical strength. 3 **(with) might and main.** See **main**[1] (sense 8).
▷HISTORY Old English *miht*; compare Old High German *maht*, Dutch *macht*

mightily ('maɪtɪlɪ) ADVERB 1 to a great extent, amount, or degree. 2 with might; powerfully or vigorously.

mighty ('maɪtɪ) ADJECTIVE **mightier, mightiest.** 1 **a** having or indicating might; powerful or strong. **b** (*as collective noun; preceded by* the): *the mighty*. 2 very large; vast. 3 very great in extent, importance, etc. ◆ ADVERB 4 *Informal, chiefly US and Canadian* (intensifier): *he was mighty tired*.
▸ **'mightiness** NOUN

migmatite ('mɪgməˌtaɪt) NOUN a composite rock body containing two types of rock (esp igneous and metamorphic rock) that have interacted with each other but are nevertheless still distinguishable.
▷HISTORY C20: alteration of Swedish *migmatit*, from Greek *migma* mixture + -ITE[1]

mignon ('mɪnjɒn; *French* miɲɔ̃) ADJECTIVE small and pretty; dainty.
▷HISTORY C16: from French, from Old French *mignot* dainty
▸ **mignonne** ('mɪnjɒn; *French* miɲɔn) FEMININE NOUN

mignonette (ˌmɪnjə'nɛt) NOUN 1 any of various mainly Mediterranean plants of the resedaceous genus *Reseda*, such as *R. odorata* (**garden mignonette**), that have spikes of small greenish-white flowers with prominent anthers. 2 a type of fine pillow lace. ◆ ADJECTIVE 3 of a greyish-green colour; reseda.
▷HISTORY C18: from French, diminutive of MIGNON

migraine ('miːgreɪn, 'maɪ-) NOUN a throbbing headache usually affecting only one side of the head and commonly accompanied by nausea and visual disturbances.
▷HISTORY C18: (earlier form, C14 *mygrame* MEGRIM[1]): from French, from Late Latin *hēmicrānia* pain in half of the head, from Greek *hēmikrania*, from HEMI- + *kranion* CRANIUM
▸ **'migrainous** ADJECTIVE

migrant ('maɪgrənt) NOUN 1 a person or animal that moves from one region, place, or country to another. 2 an itinerant agricultural worker who travels from one district to another. 3 *Chiefly Austral* **a** an immigrant, esp a recent one. **b** (*as modifier*): *a migrant hostel*. ◆ ADJECTIVE 4 moving from one region, place, or country to another; migratory.
▷HISTORY C17: from Latin *migrāre* to change one's abode

migrate (maɪ'greɪt) VERB (*intr*) 1 to go from one region, country, or place of abode to settle in another, esp in a foreign country. 2 (of birds, fishes, etc.) to journey between different areas at specific times of the year.
▷HISTORY C17: from Latin *migrāre* to change one's abode
▸ **mi'grator** NOUN

migration (maɪ'greɪʃən) NOUN 1 the act or an instance of migrating. 2 a group of people, birds, etc., migrating in a body. 3 *Chem* a movement of atoms, ions, or molecules, such as the motion of ions in solution under the influence of electric fields.
▸ **mi'grational** ADJECTIVE

migratory ('maɪgrətərɪ, -trɪ) ADJECTIVE 1 of, relating to, or characterized by migration. 2 nomadic; itinerant.

MIG welding (mɪg) NOUN metal inert gas welding: a method of welding in which the filler metal wire supplies the electric current to maintain the arc, which is shielded from the access of air by an inert gas, usually argon. Compare **TIG welding**.

mihi ('miːhɪ) NOUN *NZ* a Maori ceremonial greeting.
▷HISTORY Maori

MIHL ABBREVIATION FOR music-induced hearing loss; a condition that can afflict both rock and classical musicians in which loss of sensitivity to high notes can be followed by headaches and tinnitus.

mihrab ('miːræb, -rəb) NOUN *Islam* the niche in a mosque showing the direction of Mecca.
▷HISTORY from Arabic

mikado (mɪ'kɑːdəʊ) NOUN, *plural* **-dos.** (*often capital*) *Archaic* the Japanese emperor. Compare **tenno**.
▷HISTORY C18: from Japanese, from *mi-* honourable + *kado* gate

mike (maɪk) NOUN *Informal* short for **microphone**. ◆ See also **mike up**.

Mike (maɪk) NOUN *Communications* a code word for the letter *m*.

mike up VERB (*tr*), ADVERB to supply with a microphone.

Míkonos (*Greek* 'mikonos) NOUN transliteration of the modern Greek name for **Mykonos**.

mikvah *or* **mikveh** (mik'vɑ, 'mikvə) NOUN *Judaism* a pool used esp by women for ritual purification after their monthly period.
▷HISTORY from Hebrew

mil (mɪl) NOUN 1 a unit of length equal to one thousandth of an inch. 2 an obsolete pharmaceutical unit of volume equal to one millilitre. 3 a unit of angular measure, used in gunnery, equal to one sixty-four-hundredth of a circumference.
▷HISTORY C18: short for Latin *millēsimus* thousandth

mil AN INTERNET DOMAIN NAME FOR a US military department.

mil. ABBREVIATION FOR: 1 military. 2 militia.

milady *or* **miladi** (mɪ'leɪdɪ) NOUN, *plural* **-dies.** (formerly) a continental title used for an English gentlewoman.

milage ('maɪlɪdʒ) NOUN a variant spelling of **mileage.**

Milan (mɪ'læn) NOUN a city in N Italy, in central Lombardy: Italy's second largest city and chief financial and industrial centre; a centre of the Renaissance under the Visconti and Sforza families. Pop.: 1 300 977 (2000 est.). Italian name: **Milano** (mi'la:no).

Milanese (ˌmɪlə'ni:z) ADJECTIVE [1] of or relating to Milan, its people, culture, etc. [2] of a fine lightweight knitted fabric of silk, rayon, etc. ◆ NOUN [3] the Italian dialect spoken in Milan. [4] (*plural* **-ese**) a native or inhabitant of Milan.

milatainment (ˌmɪlə'taɪnmənt) NOUN entertainment programmes about the military, often with a documentary or factual element.
▷HISTORY C21: from MIL(ITARY) + (ENTER)TAINMENT

Milazzo (*Italian* mi'lattso) NOUN a port in NE Sicily: founded in the 8th century B.C.; scene of a battle (1860), in which Garibaldi defeated the Bourbon forces. Pop.: 32 000 (latest est.). Ancient name: **Mylae** ('maɪˌli:).

milch (mɪltʃ) NOUN [1] (*modifier*) (esp of cattle) yielding milk. [2] **milch cow.** *Informal* a source of easy income, esp a person.
▷HISTORY C13: from Old English *-milce* (in compounds); related to Old English *melcan* to milk

milchik *or* **milchig** ('mɪlxɪk) ADJECTIVE *Judaism* containing or used in the preparation of milk products and so not to be used with meat products. Also called: **milky.** Compare **fleishik.** See also **kashruth.**
▷HISTORY Yiddish, from *milch* milk, ultimately from Old High German; compare MILCH; see also MILK

mild (maɪld) ADJECTIVE [1] (of a taste, sensation, etc.) not powerful or strong; bland: *a mild curry.* [2] gentle or temperate in character, climate, behaviour, etc. [3] not extreme; moderate: *a mild rebuke.* [4] feeble; unassertive. ◆ NOUN [5] *Brit* draught beer, of darker colour than bitter and flavoured with fewer hops.
▷HISTORY Old English *milde;* compare Old Saxon *mildi,* Old Norse *mildr*
▸'**mildly** ADVERB ▸'**mildness** NOUN

milden ('maɪldən) VERB to make or become mild or milder.

mildew ('mɪlˌdju:) NOUN [1] any of various diseases of plants that affect mainly the leaves and are caused by parasitic fungi. See also **downy mildew, powdery mildew.** [2] any fungus causing this kind of disease. [3] another name for **mould**[2]. ◆ VERB [4] to affect or become affected with mildew.
▷HISTORY Old English *mildēaw,* from *mil-* honey (compare Latin *mel,* Greek *mēli*) + *dēaw* DEW
▸'**milˌdewy** ADJECTIVE

mild steel NOUN any of a class of strong tough steels that contain a low quantity of carbon (0.1–0.25 per cent).

mile (maɪl) NOUN [1] Also called: **statute mile.** a unit of length used in the UK, the US, and certain other countries, equal to 1760 yards. 1 mile is equivalent to 1.609 34 kilometres. [2] See **nautical mile.** [3] See **Swedish mile.** [4] any of various units of length used at different times and places, esp the Roman mile, equivalent to 1620 yards. [5] (*often plural*) *Informal* a great distance; great deal: *he missed by a mile.* [6] a race extending over a mile. ◆ ADVERB [7] **miles.** (intensifier): *he likes his new job miles better.*
▷HISTORY Old English *mīl,* from Latin *mīlia* (*passuum*) a thousand (paces)

mileage *or* **milage** ('maɪlɪdʒ) NOUN [1] a distance expressed in miles. [2] the total number of miles that a motor vehicle has travelled. [3] allowance for travelling expenses, esp as a fixed rate per mile. [4] the number of miles a motor vehicle will travel on one gallon of fuel. [5] *Informal* use, benefit, or service provided by something: *this scheme has a lot of mileage left.* [6] *Informal* grounds, substance, or weight: *some mileage in the objectors' arguments.*

mileometer *or* **milometer** (maɪ'lɒmɪtə) NOUN a device that records the number of miles that a bicycle or motor vehicle has travelled. Usual US and Canadian name: **odometer.**

milepost ('maɪlˌpəʊst) NOUN [1] *Horse racing* a marking post on a racecourse a mile before the finishing line. [2] Also called (esp Brit): **milestone.** *Chiefly US and Canadian* a signpost that shows the distance in miles to or from a place.

miler ('maɪlə) NOUN an athlete, horse, etc., that runs or specializes in races of one mile.

miles gloriosus *Latin* ('mi:leɪs ˌglɔ:rɪ'əʊsʊs) NOUN, *plural* ***milites gloriosi*** ('mi:lɪˌteɪs ˌglɔ:rɪ'əʊsaɪ). a braggart soldier, esp as a stock figure in comedy.
▷HISTORY from the title of a comedy by Plautus

Milesian[1] (maɪ'li:zɪən) ADJECTIVE [1] of or relating to Miletus. ◆ NOUN [2] an inhabitant of Miletus.
▷HISTORY via Latin from Greek *Milēsios*

Milesian[2] (maɪ'li:zɪən) *Facetious* ◆ ADJECTIVE [1] Irish. ◆ NOUN [2] an Irishman.
▷HISTORY C16: from *Milesius,* a fictitious king of Spain whose sons were supposed to have conquered Ireland

milestone ('maɪlˌstəʊn) NOUN [1] a stone pillar that shows the distance in miles to or from a place. [2] a significant event in life, history, etc.

Miletus (mɪ'li:təs) NOUN an ancient city on the W coast of Asia Minor: a major Ionian centre of trade and learning in the ancient world.

milfoil ('mɪlˌfɔɪl) NOUN [1] another name for **yarrow.** [2] See **water milfoil.**
▷HISTORY C13: from Old French, from Latin *milifolium,* from *mille* thousand + *folium* leaf

Milford Haven ('mɪlfəd) NOUN a port in SW Wales, in Pembrokeshire on **Milford Haven** (a large inlet of St George's Channel): major oil port. Pop.: 13 194 (1991).

miliaria (ˌmɪlɪ'eərɪə) NOUN an acute itching eruption of the skin, caused by blockage of the sweat glands. Nontechnical names: **heat rash, prickly heat.**
▷HISTORY C19: from New Latin, from Latin *miliārius* MILIARY

miliary ('mɪljərɪ) ADJECTIVE [1] resembling or relating to millet seeds. [2] (of a disease or skin eruption) characterized by small lesions resembling millet seeds: *miliary tuberculosis.*
▷HISTORY C17: from Latin *miliārius,* from *milium* MILLET

miliary fever NOUN an acute infectious fever characterized by profuse sweating and the formation on the skin of minute fluid-filled vesicles. Nontechnical name: **sweating sickness.**

milieu ('mi:ljɜ:; *French* miljø) NOUN, *plural* **-lieux** (-ljɜ:, -ljɜ:z; *French* -ljø) *or* **-lieus.** surroundings, location, or setting.
▷HISTORY C19: from French, from *mi-* MID[1] + *lieu* place

militant ('mɪlɪtənt) ADJECTIVE [1] aggressive or vigorous, esp in the support of a cause: *a militant protest.* [2] warring; engaged in warfare. ◆ NOUN [3] a militant person.
▷HISTORY C15: from Latin *mīlitāre* to be a soldier, from *mīles* soldier
▸'**militancy** *or* (*less commonly*) '**militantness** NOUN
▸'**militantly** ADVERB

Militant ('mɪlɪtənt) NOUN [1] short for **Militant Tendency.** [2] a member of Militant Tendency.

Militant Tendency NOUN a Trotskyist group formerly operating within the Labour Party.

militaria (ˌmɪlɪ'teərɪə) PLURAL NOUN items of military interest, such as weapons, uniforms, medals, etc., esp from the past.

militarism ('mɪlɪtəˌrɪzəm) NOUN [1] military spirit; pursuit of military ideals. [2] domination by the military in the formulation of policies, ideals, etc., esp on a political level. [3] a policy of maintaining a strong military organization in aggressive preparedness for war.

militarist ('mɪlɪtərɪst) NOUN [1] a supporter of or believer in militarism. [2] a devotee of military history, strategy, etc.
▸ˌ**militaˈristic** ADJECTIVE ▸ˌ**militaˈristically** ADVERB

militarize *or* **militarise** ('mɪlɪtəˌraɪz) VERB (*tr*) [1] to convert to military use. [2] to imbue with militarism.
▸ˌ**militariˈzation** *or* ˌ**militariˈsation** NOUN

military ('mɪlɪtərɪ, -trɪ) ADJECTIVE [1] of or relating to the armed forces (esp the army), warlike matters, etc. [2] of, characteristic of, or about soldiers. ◆ NOUN, *plural* **-taries** *or* **-tary.** [3] (preceded by *the*) the armed services (esp the army).
▷HISTORY C16: via French from Latin *mīlitāris,* from *mīles* soldier
▸'**militarily** ADVERB

military academy NOUN a training establishment for young officer cadets entering the army.

military engineering NOUN the design, construction, etc., of military fortifications and communications.

military honours PLURAL NOUN ceremonies performed by troops in honour of royalty, at the burial of an officer, etc.

military-industrial complex NOUN (in the US) the combined interests of the military establishment and industries involved in producing military material considered as exerting influence on US foreign and economic policy.

military law NOUN articles or regulations that apply to those belonging to the armed services. Compare **martial law.**

military orchid NOUN another name for **soldier orchid.**

military pace NOUN the pace of a single step in marching, taken to be 30 inches for quick time (120 paces to the minute) in both the British and US armies.

military police NOUN a corps within an army that performs police and disciplinary duties.
▸**military policeman** NOUN

militate ('mɪlɪˌteɪt) VERB (*intr;* usually foll by *against* or *for*) (of facts, actions, etc.) to have influence or effect: *the evidence militated against his release.*
▷HISTORY C17: from Latin *mīlitātus,* from *mīlitāre* to be a soldier
▸ˌ**miliˈtation** NOUN

Language note See at **mitigate.**

militia (mɪ'lɪʃə) NOUN [1] a body of citizen (as opposed to professional) soldiers. [2] an organization containing men enlisted for service in emergency only.
▷HISTORY C16: from Latin: soldiery, from *mīles* soldier

militiaman (mɪ'lɪʃəmən) NOUN, *plural* **-men.** a man serving with the militia.

milium ('mɪlɪəm) NOUN, *plural* **-ia** (-ɪə). *Pathol* a small whitish nodule on the skin, usually resulting from a clogged sebaceous gland.
▷HISTORY C19: from Latin: millet

milk (mɪlk) NOUN [1] **a** a whitish nutritious fluid produced and secreted by the mammary glands of mature female mammals and used for feeding their young until weaned. **b** the milk of cows, goats, or other animals used by man as a food or in the production of butter, cheese, etc. Related adjectives: **lacteal, lactic.** [2] any similar fluid in plants, such as the juice of a coconut. [3] any of various milklike pharmaceutical preparations, such as milk of magnesia. [4] **cry over spilt milk.** to lament something that cannot be altered. ◆ VERB [5] to draw milk from the udder of (a cow, goat, or other animal). [6] (*intr*) (of cows, goats, or other animals) to yield milk. [7] (*tr*) to draw off or tap in small quantities: *to milk the petty cash.* [8] (*tr*) to extract as much money, help, etc., as possible from: *to milk a situation of its news value.* [9] (*tr*) to extract venom, sap, etc., from.
▷HISTORY Old English *milc;* compare Old Saxon *miluk,* Old High German *miluh,* Old Norse *mjolk*

milk-and-water ADJECTIVE (**milk and water** *when postpositive*) weak, feeble, or insipid.

milk bar NOUN [1] a snack bar at which milk drinks and light refreshments are served. [2] (in Australia) a shop selling, in addition to milk, basic provisions and other items.

milk cap NOUN any of a large genus (*Lactarius*) of basidiomycetous fungi that are brittle to touch and exude a milky liquid when crushed. Some are funnel-shaped and some parasol-shaped, and most, except for *L. deliciosus,* are inedible.

milk chocolate NOUN chocolate that has been made with milk, having a creamy taste. Compare **plain chocolate.**

milker ('mɪlkə) NOUN [1] a cow, goat, etc., that yields milk, esp of a specified quality or amount: *a poor milker.* [2] a person who milks. [3] another name for **milking machine.**

milk fever NOUN [1] a fever that sometimes occurs shortly after childbirth, once thought to result from engorgement of the breasts with milk but now thought to be caused by infection. [2] Also called: **parturient fever, eclampsia.** *Vet science* a disease of cows, goats, etc., occurring shortly after parturition, characterized by low blood calcium levels, paralysis, and loss of consciousness.

milkfish ('mɪlkˌfɪʃ) NOUN, *plural* **-fish** *or* **-fishes.** a large silvery tropical clupeoid food and game fish, *Chanos chanos:* family *Chanidae.*

milk float NOUN *Brit* a small motor vehicle used to deliver milk to houses.

milk glass NOUN opaque white glass, originally produced in imitation of Chinese porcelain.

milking machine NOUN an apparatus for milking cows.

milking shed NOUN a building in which a herd of cows is milked. Compare **milking parlour** (see **parlour** (sense 6)).

milking stool NOUN a low three-legged stool.

milk lameness NOUN *Vet science* a disease of cattle that produce a high milk yield, characterized by hip lameness associated with a low concentration of phosphorus in the blood.

milk leg NOUN inflammation and thrombosis of the femoral vein following childbirth, characterized by painful swelling of the leg. Also called: **white leg.** Technical name: **phlegmasia alba dolens.**

milkmaid ('mɪlkˌmeɪd) NOUN a girl or woman who milks cows.

milkman ('mɪlkmən) NOUN, *plural* **-men.** [1] a man who delivers or sells milk. [2] a man who milks cows; dairyman.

milko ('mɪlkəʊ) NOUN, *plural* **milkos.** *Austral* an informal name for **milkman** (sense 1).

milk of magnesia NOUN a suspension of magnesium hydroxide in water, used as an antacid and laxative.

milk pudding NOUN *Chiefly Brit* a hot or cold pudding made by boiling or baking milk with a grain, esp rice.

milk punch NOUN a spiced drink made of milk and spirits.

milk round NOUN *Brit* [1] a route along which a milkman regularly delivers milk. [2] **a** a regular series of visits, esp as made by recruitment officers from industry to universities. **b** (*as modifier*): *milk-round recruitment.*

milk run NOUN *Aeronautics informal* a routine and uneventful flight, esp on a dangerous mission.
▷HISTORY C20: referring to the regular and safe routine of a milkman's round

milk shake NOUN a cold frothy drink made of milk, flavouring, and sometimes ice cream, whisked or beaten together.

milk sickness NOUN [1] an acute disease characterized by weakness, vomiting, and constipation, caused by ingestion of the flesh or dairy products of cattle affected with trembles. [2] *Vet science* another name for **trembles** (sense 1).

milk snake NOUN a nonvenomous brown-and-grey North American colubrid snake *Lampropeltis doliata,* related to the king snakes.

milksop ('mɪlkˌsɒp) NOUN [1] a feeble or ineffectual man or youth. [2] *Brit* a dish of bread soaked in warm milk, given esp to infants and invalids.
▸'**milkˌsoppy** *or* '**milkˌsopping** ADJECTIVE ▸'**milkˌsopism** NOUN

milk stout NOUN *Brit* a rich mellow stout lacking a bitter aftertaste.
▷HISTORY C20: so called because its ingredients include LACTOSE

milk sugar NOUN another name for **lactose.**

milk thistle NOUN another name for **sow thistle.**

milktoast ('mɪlkˌtəʊst) NOUN a variant spelling of **milquetoast.**

milk tooth NOUN any of the first teeth to erupt; a deciduous tooth. Also called: **baby tooth.** See also **dentition.**

milk vetch NOUN any of various leguminous plants of the genus *Astragalus,* esp *A. glycyphyllos,* with clusters of purple, white, or yellowish flowers: formerly reputed to increase milk production in goats.

milkweed ('mɪlkˌwiːd) NOUN [1] Also called: **silkweed.** any plant of the mostly North American genus *Asclepias,* having milky sap and pointed pods that split open to release tufted seeds: family *Asclepiadaceae.* See also **asclepias.** [2] any of various other plants having milky sap. [3] **orange milkweed.** another name for **butterfly weed.** [4] another name for **monarch** (the butterfly).

milkwort ('mɪlkˌwɜːt) NOUN any of several plants of the genus *Polygala,* having small blue, pink, or white flowers with two petal-like sepals: family *Polygalaceae.* They were formerly believed to increase milk production in cows. See also **senega.**

milky ('mɪlkɪ) ADJECTIVE **milkier, milkiest.** [1] resembling milk, esp in colour or cloudiness. [2] of or containing milk. [3] spiritless or spineless. [4] *Judaism* another word for **milchik.**
▸'**milkily** ADVERB ▸'**milkiness** NOUN

Milky Way NOUN **the.** [1] the diffuse band of light stretching across the night sky that consists of millions of faint stars, nebulae, etc., within our Galaxy. [2] another name for the **Galaxy.**
▷HISTORY C14: translation of Latin *via lactea*

mill[1] (mɪl) NOUN [1] a building in which grain is crushed and ground to make flour. [2] a factory, esp one which processes raw materials: *a steel mill.* [3] any of various processing or manufacturing machines, esp one that grinds, presses, or rolls. [4] any of various small hand mills used for grinding pepper, salt, or coffee for domestic purposes. See also **coffee mill, pepper mill.** [5] a hard roller for impressing a design, esp in a textile-printing machine or in a machine for printing banknotes. [6] a system, institution, etc., that influences people or things in the manner of a factory: *going through the educational mill.* [7] an unpleasant experience; ordeal (esp in the phrases **go** *or* **be put through the mill**). [8] a fist fight. [9] **run of the mill.** ordinary or routine. ◆ VERB [10] (*tr*) to grind, press, or pulverize in or as if in a mill. [11] (*tr*) to process or produce in or with a mill. [12] to cut or roll (metal) with or as if with a milling machine. [13] (*tr*) to groove or flute the edge of (a coin). [14] (*intr;* often foll by *about* or *around*) to move about in a confused manner. [15] (*usually tr*) *Now rare* to beat (chocolate, etc.). [16] *Archaic slang* to fight, esp with the fists.
▷HISTORY Old English *mylen* from Late Latin *molīna* a mill, from Latin *mola* mill, millstone, from *molere* to grind
▸'**millable** ADJECTIVE

mill[2] (mɪl) NOUN a US and Canadian monetary unit used in calculations, esp for property taxes, equal to one thousandth of a dollar.
▷HISTORY C18: short for Latin *mīllēsimum* a thousandth (part)

millboard ('mɪlˌbɔːd) NOUN strong pasteboard, used esp in book covers.
▷HISTORY C18: changed from *milled board*

milldam ('mɪlˌdæm) NOUN a dam built in a stream to raise the water level sufficiently for it to turn a millwheel.

milled (mɪld) ADJECTIVE [1] (of coins, etc.) having a grooved or fluted edge. [2] made or treated in a mill.

millefeuille *French* (milfœj) NOUN *Brit* a small iced cake made of puff pastry filled with jam and cream. US name: **napoleon.**
▷HISTORY literally: thousand leaves

millefiori (ˌmɪlɪ'fjɔːrɪ) NOUN **a** decorative glassware in which coloured glass rods are fused and cut to create flower patterns: an ancient technique revived in Venice in the sixteenth century and in France and England in the nineteenth century. **b** (*as modifier*): *a millefiori paperweight.*
▷HISTORY C19: from Italian: thousand flowers

millefleurs ('miːlˌflɜː) NOUN a design of stylized floral patterns, used in textiles, tapestries, etc.
▷HISTORY French: thousand flowers

millenarian (ˌmɪlɪ'nɛərɪən) *or* **millenary** ADJECTIVE [1] of or relating to a thousand or to a thousand years. [2] of or relating to the millennium or millenarianism. ◆ NOUN [3] an adherent of millenarianism.

millenarianism (ˌmɪlɪ'nɛərɪəˌnɪzəm) NOUN [1] *Christianity* the belief in a future millennium following the Second Coming of Christ during which he will reign on earth in peace: based on Revelation 20:1–5. [2] any belief in a future period of ideal peace and happiness.

millenary (mɪ'lɛnərɪ) NOUN, *plural* **-naries.** [1] a sum or aggregate of one thousand, esp one thousand years. [2] another word for a **millennium.** ◆ ADJECTIVE, NOUN [3] another word for **millenarian.**
▷HISTORY C16: from Late Latin *millēnārius* containing a thousand, from Latin *mille* thousand

millennium (mɪ'lɛnɪəm) NOUN, *plural* **-nia** (-nɪə) *or* **-niums.** [1] **the.** *Christianity* the period of a thousand years of Christ's awaited reign upon earth. [2] a period or cycle of one thousand years. [3] a time of peace and happiness, esp in the distant future. [4] a thousandth anniversary.
▷HISTORY C17: from New Latin, from Latin *mille* thousand + *annus* year; for form, compare QUADRENNIUM
▸**mil'lennial** ADJECTIVE ▸**mil'lennialist** NOUN ▸**mil'lennially** ADVERB

millennium bug NOUN *Computing* any software problem arising from the change in date at the start of the 21st century.

millepede ('mɪlɪˌpiːd) *or* **milleped** ('mɪlɪˌpɛd) NOUN variants of **millipede.**

millepore ('mɪlɪˌpɔː) NOUN any tropical colonial coral-like medusoid hydrozoan of the order *Milleporina,* esp of the genus *Millepora,* having a calcareous skeleton.
▷HISTORY C18: from New Latin, from Latin *mille* thousand + *porus* hole

miller ('mɪlə) NOUN [1] a person who keeps, operates, or works in a mill, esp a corn mill. [2] another name for **milling machine.** [3] a person who operates a milling machine. [4] any of various pale coloured or white moths, especially the medium-sized noctuid *Apatele leporina.* [5] an edible basidiomycetous fungus, *Clitopilus prunulus,* with a white funnel-shaped cap and pinkish spores, often forming rings in grass.

millerite ('mɪləˌraɪt) NOUN a yellow mineral consisting of nickel sulphide in hexagonal crystalline form: a minor ore of nickel. Formula: NiS.
▷HISTORY C19: named after W. H. *Miller* (1801–80), English mineralogist

miller's disease NOUN *Vet science* osteofibrosis of horses due to low concentration of phosphorus in the blood caused by eating bran exclusively.

miller's thumb NOUN any of several small freshwater European fishes of the genus *Cottus,* esp *C. gobio,* having a flattened body: family *Cottidae* (bullheads, etc.).
▷HISTORY C15: from the alleged likeness of the fish's head to a thumb

millesimal (mɪ'lɛsɪməl) ADJECTIVE [1] **a** denoting a thousandth. **b** (*as noun*): *a millesimal.* [2] of, consisting of, or relating to a thousandth.
▷HISTORY C18: from Latin *mīllēsimus*

millet ('mɪlɪt) NOUN [1] a cereal grass, *Setaria italica,* cultivated for grain and animal fodder. [2] **a** an East Indian annual grass, *Panicum miliaceum,* cultivated for grain and forage, having pale round shiny seeds. **b** the seed of this plant. [3] any of various similar or related grasses, such as pearl millet and Indian millet. Related adjective: **miliary.**
▷HISTORY C14: via Old French from Latin *milium;* related to Greek *melinē* millet

milli- PREFIX denoting 10^{-3}: *millimetre.* Symbol: m.
▷HISTORY from French, from Latin *mille* thousand, this meaning being maintained in words borrowed from Latin (*millipede*)

milliard ('mɪlɪˌɑːd, 'mɪljɑːd) NOUN *Brit* (no longer in technical use) a thousand million. US and Canadian equivalent: **billion.**
▷HISTORY C19: from French

milliary ('mɪljərɪ) ADJECTIVE relating to or marking a distance equal to an ancient Roman mile of a thousand paces.
▷HISTORY C17: from Latin *milliārius* containing a thousand, from *mille* thousand

millibar ('mɪlɪˌbɑː) NOUN a cgs unit of atmospheric pressure equal to 10^{-3} bar, 100 newtons per square metre or 0.7500617 millimetre of mercury.

millieme (miːl'jɛm) NOUN a Tunisian monetary unit worth one thousandth of a dinar. Also called: **millime.**
▷HISTORY from French *millième* thousandth

millième (miːl'jɛm) NOUN an Egyptian monetary unit worth one thousandth of a lira.

milligram *or* **milligramme** (ˈmɪlɪˌɡræm) NOUN one thousandth of a gram. Symbol: mg.
▷HISTORY C19: from French

millilitre *or US* **milliliter** (ˈmɪlɪˌliːtə) NOUN one thousandth of a litre. Symbol: ml.

millimetre *or US* **millimeter** (ˈmɪlɪˌmiːtə) NOUN one thousandth of a metre. Symbol: mm.

millimicron (ˈmɪlɪˌmaɪkrɒn) NOUN an obsolete name for a nanometre; one millionth of a millimetre.

milliner (ˈmɪlɪnə) NOUN a person who makes or sells women's hats.
▷HISTORY C16: originally *Milaner,* a native of *Milan,* at that time famous for its fancy goods

millinery (ˈmɪlɪnərɪ, -nrɪ) NOUN [1] hats, trimmings, etc., sold by a milliner. [2] the business or shop of a milliner.

milling (ˈmɪlɪŋ) NOUN [1] the act or process of grinding, cutting, pressing, or crushing in a mill. [2] the vertical grooves or fluting on the edge of a coin, etc. [3] (in W North America) a method of halting a stampede of cattle by turning the leaders in a wide arc until the herd turns in upon itself in a tightening spiral.

milling machine NOUN a machine tool in which a horizontal arbor or vertical spindle rotates a cutting tool above a horizontal table, which is used to move a workpiece.

million (ˈmɪljən) NOUN, *plural* **-lions** *or* **-lion.** [1] the cardinal number that is the product of 1000 multiplied by 1000. See also **number** (sense 1). [2] a numeral, 1 000 000, 10^6, M, etc., representing this number. [3] *(often plural) Informal* an extremely large but unspecified number, quantity, or amount: *I have millions of things to do.* ♦ DETERMINER [4] (preceded by *a* or by a numeral) **a** amounting to a million: *a million light years away.* **b** *(as pronoun)*: *I can see a million under the microscope.* [5] **gone a million.** *Austral informal* done for; sunk. ♦ Related prefix: **mega-.**
▷HISTORY C17: via Old French from early Italian *millione,* from *mille* thousand, from Latin

millionaire *or* **millionnaire** (ˌmɪljəˈnɛə) NOUN a person whose assets are worth at least a million of the standard monetary units of his country.
▸ˌ**millionˈairess** *or* ˌ**millionˈnairess** FEMININE NOUN

millionth (ˈmɪljənθ) NOUN [1] **a** one of 1 000 000 approximately equal parts of something. **b** *(as modifier)*: *a millionth part.* [2] one of 1 000 000 equal divisions of a particular scientific quantity. Related prefix: **micro-.** [3] the fraction equal to one divided by 1 000 000. ♦ ADJECTIVE [4] *(usually prenominal)* **a** being the ordinal number of 1 000 000 in numbering or counting order, etc. **b** *(as noun)*: *the millionth to be manufactured.*

millipede, millepede (ˈmɪlɪˌpiːd), *or* **milleped** NOUN any terrestrial herbivorous arthropod of the class *Diplopoda,* having a cylindrical body made up of many segments, each of which bears two pairs of walking legs. See also **myriapod.**
▷HISTORY C17: from Latin, from *mille* thousand + *pēs* foot

millisecond (ˈmɪlɪˌsɛkənd) NOUN one thousandth of a second. Symbol: ms.

millpond (ˈmɪlˌpɒnd) NOUN [1] a pool formed by damming a stream to provide water to turn a millwheel. [2] any expanse of calm water: *the sea was a millpond.*

millrace (ˈmɪlˌreɪs) *or* **millrun** NOUN [1] the current of water that turns a millwheel. [2] the channel for this water.

mill-rind NOUN an iron support fitted across an upper millstone.

millrun (ˈmɪlˌrʌn) NOUN [1] another name for **millrace.** [2] *Mining* **a** the process of milling an ore or rock in order to determine the content or quality of the mineral. **b** the mineral so examined. ♦ ADJECTIVE **mill-run.** [3] *Chiefly US* (of commodities) taken straight from the production line; unsorted as to quality.

Mills bomb (mɪlz) NOUN a type of high-explosive hand grenade.
▷HISTORY C20: named after Sir William *Mills* (1856–1932), English inventor

millstone (ˈmɪlˌstəʊn) NOUN [1] one of a pair of heavy flat disc-shaped stones that are rotated one against the other to grind grain. [2] a heavy burden, such as a responsibility or obligation: *his debts were a millstone round his neck.*

millstream (ˈmɪlˌstriːm) NOUN a stream of water used to turn a millwheel.

millwheel (ˈmɪlˌwiːl) NOUN a wheel, esp a waterwheel, that drives a mill.

millwork (ˈmɪlˌwɜːk) NOUN work done in a mill.

millwright (ˈmɪlˌraɪt) NOUN a person who designs, builds, or repairs grain mills or mill machinery.

milo (ˈmaɪləʊ) NOUN, *plural* **-los.** any of various early-growing cultivated varieties of sorghum with heads of yellow or pinkish seeds resembling millet.
▷HISTORY C19: from Sotho *maili*

milometer (maɪˈlɒmɪtə) NOUN a variant spelling of **mileometer.**

milord (mɪˈlɔːd) NOUN (formerly) a continental title used for an English gentleman.
▷HISTORY C19: via French from English *my lord*

Mílos (ˈmilɔs) NOUN transliteration of the Modern Greek name for **Melos.**

milquetoast (ˈmɪlkˌtəʊst) NOUN *US and Canadian* a meek, submissive, or timid person.
▷HISTORY C20: from Caspar *Milquetoast,* a cartoon character invented by H. T. Webster (1885–1952)

milreis (ˈmɪlˌreɪs; *Portuguese* milˈrɛiʃ) NOUN, *plural* **-reis.** a former monetary unit of Portugal and Brazil, divided into 1000 reis.
▷HISTORY C16: from Portuguese, from *mil* thousand + *réis,* plural of *real* royal

milt (mɪlt) NOUN [1] the testis of a fish. [2] the spermatozoa and seminal fluid produced by a fish. [3] *Rare* the spleen of certain animals, esp fowls and pigs. ♦ VERB [4] to fertilize (the roe of a female fish) with milt, esp artificially.
▷HISTORY Old English *milte* spleen; in the sense: fish sperm, probably from Middle Dutch *milte*

milter (ˈmɪltə) NOUN a male fish that is mature and ready to breed.

Miltonic (mɪlˈtɒnɪk) *or* **Miltonian** (mɪlˈtəʊnɪən) ADJECTIVE characteristic of or resembling the literary style of the English poet John Milton (1608–74), esp in being sublime and majestic.

Milton Keynes (ˈmɪltən ˈkiːnz) NOUN [1] a new town in central England, in Milton Keynes unitary authority, N Buckinghamshire: founded in 1967: electronics, clothing, machinery; seat of the Open University. Pop.: 207 063 (2001). [2] a unitary authority in central England, in Buckinghamshire. Pop.: 188 400 (1994 est.). Area: 310 sq. km (119 sq. miles).

Milton Work count NOUN *Bridge* a system of hand valuation in which aces count 4, kings 3, queens 2, and jacks 1.
▷HISTORY C20: named after *Milton Work,* authority on auction bridge

Milwaukee (mɪlˈwɔːkiː) NOUN a port in SE Wisconsin, on Lake Michigan: the largest city in the state; established as a trading post in the 18th century; an important industrial centre. Pop.: 596 974 (2000).

Milwaukeean (mɪlˈwɔːkɪən) ADJECTIVE [1] of or relating to Milwaukee or its inhabitants. ♦ NOUN [2] a native or inhabitant of Milwaukee.

mim (mɪm) ADJECTIVE *Dialect* prim, modest, or demure.
▷HISTORY C17: perhaps imitative of lip-pursing

Mimas (ˈmaɪməs, -mæs) NOUN a satellite of the planet Saturn.

mime (maɪm) NOUN [1] the theatrical technique of expressing an idea or mood or portraying a character entirely by gesture and bodily movement without the use of words. [2] Also called: **mime artist.** a performer specializing in such a technique, esp a comic actor. [3] a dramatic presentation using such a technique. [4] (in the classical theatre) **a** a comic performance depending for effect largely on exaggerated gesture and physical action. **b** an actor in such a performance. ♦ VERB [5] to express (an idea) in actions or gestures without speech. [6] (of singers or musicians) to perform as if singing (a song) or playing (a piece of music) that is actually prerecorded.
▷HISTORY Old English *mīma,* from Latin *mīmus* mimic actor, from Greek *mimos* imitator
▸ˈ**mimer** NOUN

Mimeograph (ˈmɪmɪəˌɡrɑːf, -ˌɡræf) NOUN [1] *Trademark* an office machine for printing multiple copies of text or line drawings from an inked drum to which a cut stencil is fixed. [2] a copy produced by this machine. ♦ VERB [3] to print copies from (a prepared stencil) using this machine.

mimesis (mɪˈmiːsɪs) NOUN [1] *Art, literature* the imitative representation of nature or human behaviour. [2] **a** any disease that shows symptoms of another disease. **b** a condition in a hysterical patient that mimics an organic disease. [3] *Biology* another name for **mimicry** (sense 2). [4] *Rhetoric* representation of another person's alleged words in a speech.
▷HISTORY C16: from Greek, from *mimeisthai* to imitate

mimetic (mɪˈmɛtɪk) ADJECTIVE [1] of, resembling, or relating to mimesis or imitation, as in art, etc. [2] *Biology* of or exhibiting mimicry.
▸**miˈmetically** ADVERB

mimetite (ˈmɪmɪˌtaɪt, ˈmaɪmɪ-) NOUN a rare secondary mineral consisting of a chloride and arsenate of lead in the form of white or yellowish needle-like hexagonal crystals. Formula: $Pb_5Cl(AsO_4)_3$.
▷HISTORY C19: from German, from Greek *mimētēs* imitator (of pyromorphite)

mimic (ˈmɪmɪk) VERB **-ics, -icking, -icked.** *(tr)* [1] to imitate (a person, a manner, etc.), esp for satirical effect; ape. [2] to take on the appearance of; resemble closely: *certain flies mimic wasps.* [3] to copy closely or in a servile manner. ♦ NOUN [4] a person or an animal, such as a parrot, that is clever at mimicking. [5] an animal that displays mimicry. ♦ ADJECTIVE [6] of, relating to, or using mimicry; imitative. [7] simulated, make-believe, or mock.
▷HISTORY C16: from Latin *mīmicus,* from Greek *mimikos,* from *mimos* MIME
▸ˈ**mimicker** NOUN

mimic panel NOUN a panel simulating the geographical layout of a television studio, railway points system, traffic interchange, etc., in which small indicator lamps display the selected state of the lighting circuits, signalling, traffic lights, etc.

mimicry (ˈmɪmɪkrɪ) NOUN, *plural* **-ries.** [1] the act or art of copying or imitating closely; mimicking. [2] the resemblance shown by one animal species, esp an insect, to another, which protects it from predators.

MIMinE ABBREVIATION FOR Member of the Institute of Mining Engineers.

miminy-piminy (ˌmɪmɪnɪˈpɪmɪnɪ) ADJECTIVE a variant of **niminy-piminy.**

Mimir (ˈmiːmɪə) NOUN *Norse myth* a giant who guarded the well of wisdom near the roots of Yggdrasil.

mimosa (mɪˈməʊsə, -zə) NOUN [1] any tropical shrub or tree of the leguminous genus *Mimosa,* having ball-like clusters of yellow or pink flowers and compound leaves that are often sensitive to touch or light. See also **sensitive plant.** [2] any similar or related tree.
▷HISTORY C18: from New Latin, probably from Latin *mīmus* MIME, because the plant's sensitivity to touch imitates the similar reaction of animals

mimsy (ˈmɪmzɪ) ADJECTIVE **-sier, -siest.** prim, underwhelming, and ineffectual.
▷HISTORY C19: a blend of MISERABLE and FLIMSY, coined by the English writer Lewis Carroll (1832–98), real name *Charles Lutwidge Dodgson*

mimulus (ˈmɪmjʊləs) NOUN See **monkey flower.**
▷HISTORY New Latin, from Greek *mimō* ape (from the shape of the corolla)

MIMunE ABBREVIATION FOR Member of the Institution of Municipal Engineers.

min SYMBOL FOR minim (liquid measure).

Min (mɪn) NOUN any of the dialects or forms of Chinese spoken in Fukien province. Also called: **Fukien.**

min. ABBREVIATION FOR: [1] minimum. [2] minute(s).

Min. ABBREVIATION FOR: [1] Minister. [2] Ministry.

mina (ˈmaɪnə) NOUN, *plural* **-nae** (-niː) *or* **-nas.** an ancient unit of weight and money, used in Asia Minor, equal to one sixtieth of a talent.
▷HISTORY C16: via Latin from Greek *mna,* of Semitic origin; related to Hebrew *māneh* mina

minacious (mɪˈneɪʃəs) ADJECTIVE threatening.

▷HISTORY C17: from Latin *minax,* from *minārī* to threaten
▸**miˈnaciously** ADVERB ▸**minacity** (mɪˈnæsɪtɪ) NOUN

Mina Hassan Tani (ˈmiːnə hɑːˈsɑːn ˈtɑːnɪ) NOUN a port in NW Morocco, on the Sebou River 16 km (10 miles) from the Atlantic. Pop.: 234 000 (1993 est.). Also called: **Kénitra.** Former name (1932–56): **Port Lyautey.**

minaret (ˌmɪnəˈrɛt, ˈmɪnəˌrɛt) NOUN [1] a slender tower of a mosque having one or more balconies from which the muezzin calls the faithful to prayer. [2] any structure resembling this.
▷HISTORY C17: from French, from Turkish, from Arabic *manārat* lamp, from *nār* fire
▸**ˌminaˈreted** ADJECTIVE

Minas Basin (ˈmaɪnəs) NOUN a bay in E Canada, in central Nova Scotia: the NE arm of the Bay of Fundy, with which it is linked by **Minas Channel.**

Minas Gerais (*Portuguese* ˈminaʒ ʒəˈraiʒ) NOUN an inland state of E Brazil: situated on the high plateau of the Brazilian Highlands; large reserves of iron ore and manganese. Capital: Belo Horizonte. Pop.: 17 835 488 (2000). Area: 587 172 sq. km (226 707 sq. miles).

minatory (ˈmɪnətərɪ, -trɪ) *or* **minatorial** ADJECTIVE threatening or menacing.
▷HISTORY C16: from Late Latin *minātōrius,* from Latin *minārī* to threaten
▸**ˈminatorily** *or* **ˌminaˈtorially** ADVERB

mince (mɪns) VERB [1] (*tr*) to chop, grind, or cut into very small pieces. [2] (*tr*) to soften or moderate, esp for the sake of convention or politeness: *I didn't mince my words.* [3] (*intr*) to walk or speak in an affected dainty manner. ◆ NOUN [4] *Chiefly Brit* minced meat. [5] *Informal* nonsensical rubbish.
▷HISTORY C14: from Old French *mincier,* from Vulgar Latin *minūtiāre* (unattested), from Late Latin *minūtia* smallness; see MINUTIAE

mincemeat (ˈmɪnsˌmiːt) NOUN [1] a mixture of dried fruit, spices, etc., used esp for filling pies. [2] minced meat. [3] **make mincemeat of.** *Informal* to defeat completely.

mince pie NOUN [1] a small round pastry tart filled with mincemeat. [2] (*usually plural*) *Cockney rhyming slang* an eye.

mincer (mɪnsə) NOUN an appliance used to mince meat.

Minch (mɪntʃ) NOUN **the.** a channel of the Atlantic divided into the **North Minch** between the mainland of Scotland and the Isle of Lewis, and the **Little Minch** between the Isle of Skye and Harris and North Uist.

Mincha *Hebrew* (minˈxɑː; *Yiddish* ˈminxa) NOUN *Judaism* the afternoon service.

mincing (ˈmɪnsɪŋ) ADJECTIVE (of a person) affectedly elegant in gait, manner, or speech.
▸**ˈmincingly** ADVERB

mind (maɪnd) NOUN [1] the human faculty to which are ascribed thought, feeling, etc.; often regarded as an immaterial part of a person. [2] intelligence or the intellect, esp as opposed to feelings or wishes. [3] recollection or remembrance; memory: *it comes to mind.* [4] the faculty of original or creative thought; imagination: *it's all in the mind.* [5] a person considered as an intellectual being: *the great minds of the past.* [6] opinion or sentiment: *we are of the same mind; to change one's mind; to have a mind of one's own; to know one's mind; to speak one's mind.* [7] condition, state, or manner of feeling or thought: *no peace of mind; his state of mind.* [8] an inclination, desire, or purpose: *I have a mind to go.* [9] attention or thoughts: *keep your mind on your work.* [10] a sound mental state; sanity (esp in the phrase **out of one's mind**). [11] intelligence, as opposed to material things: *the mind of the universe.* [12] (in Cartesian philosophy) one of two basic modes of existence, the other being matter. [13] **blow someone's mind.** *Slang* **a** to cause someone to have a psychedelic experience. **b** to astound or surprise someone. [14] **give (someone) a piece of one's mind.** to criticize or censure (someone) frankly or vehemently. [15] **in** *or* **of two minds.** undecided; wavering: *he was in two minds about marriage.* [16] **make up one's mind.** to decide (something or to do something): *he made up his mind to go.* [17] **on one's mind.** in one's thoughts. [18] **put (one) in mind of.** to remind (one) of. ◆ VERB [19] (when *tr, may take a clause as object*) to take offence at: *do you mind if I smoke? I don't mind.* [20] to pay attention to (something); heed; notice: *to mind one's own business.* [21] (*tr; takes a clause as object*) to make certain; ensure: *mind you tell her.* [22] (*tr*) to take care of; have charge of: *to mind the shop.* [23] (when *tr, may take a clause as object*) to be cautious or careful about (something): *mind how you go; mind your step.* [24] (*tr*) to obey (someone or something); heed: *mind your father!* [25] to be concerned (about); be troubled (about): *never mind your hat; never mind about your hat; never mind.* [26] (*tr; passive; takes an infinitive*) to be intending or inclined (to do something): *clearly he was not minded to finish the story.* [27] (*tr*) *Scot and English dialect* to remember: *do ye mind his name?* [28] (*tr*) *Scot* to remind: *that minds me of another story.* [29] **mind you.** an expression qualifying a previous statement: *Dogs are nice. Mind you, I don't like all dogs.* ◆ Related adjectives: **mental, noetic, phrenic.** ◆ See also **mind out.**
▷HISTORY Old English *gemynd* mind; related to Old High German *gimunt* memory

Mindanao (ˌmɪndəˈnaʊ) NOUN the second largest island of the Philippines, in the S part of the archipelago: mountainous and volcanic. Chief towns: Davao, Zamboanga. Pop.: 14 298 000 (1990 est.). Area: (including offshore islands) 94 631 sq. km (36 537 sq. miles).

mind-bending ADJECTIVE *Informal* [1] very difficult to understand; complex. [2] altering one's state of consciousness: *mind-bending drugs.* [3] reaching the limit of credibility: *they offered a mind-bending salary.* ◆ NOUN [4] the process of brainwashing.

mind-blowing ADJECTIVE *Informal* producing euphoria; psychedelic.

mind-body problem NOUN the traditional philosophical problem concerning the nature of mind, body, and the relationship between them. See **dualism** (sense 2), **interactionism, parallelism** (sense 3), **monism** (sense 1), **idealism** (sense 3), **materialism** (sense 2), **identity theory, behaviourism** (sense 2).

mind-boggling ADJECTIVE *Informal* astonishing; bewildering.

minded (ˈmaɪndɪd) ADJECTIVE [1] having a mind, inclination, intention, etc., as specified: *politically minded.* [2] (*in combination*): *money-minded.*

Mindel (ˈmɪndᵊl) NOUN the second major Pleistocene glaciation of Alpine Europe. See also **Günz, Riss, Würm.**
▷HISTORY C20: named after the River *Mindel,* in Bavaria, Germany

minder (ˈmaɪndə) NOUN [1] someone who looks after someone or something. [2] short for **child minder.** [3] *Slang* an aide to someone in public life, esp a politician or political candidate, who keeps control of press and public relations. [4] *Slang* someone acting as a bodyguard, guard, or assistant, esp in the criminal underworld.

mind-expanding ADJECTIVE (of a drug such as LSD) causing a sensation of heightened consciousness; psychedelic.

mindfuck (ˈmaɪndˌfʌk) NOUN *Taboo slang* the deliberate infliction of psychological damage.

mindful (ˈmaɪndfʊl) ADJECTIVE (usually *postpositive* and foll by *of*) keeping aware; heedful: *mindful of your duties.*
▸**ˈmindfully** ADVERB ▸**ˈmindfulness** NOUN

mindless (ˈmaɪndlɪs) ADJECTIVE [1] stupid or careless. [2] requiring little or no intellectual effort: *a mindless task.*
▸**ˈmindlessly** ADVERB ▸**ˈmindlessness** NOUN

mind-numbing ADJECTIVE extremely boring and uninspiring.
▸**ˈmind-ˌnumbingly** ADVERB

Mindoro (mɪnˈdɔːrəʊ) NOUN a mountainous island in the central Philippines, south of Luzon. Pop.: 912 000 (1995 est.). Area: 9736 sq. km (3759 sq. miles).

mind out VERB (*intr, adverb*) *Brit* to be careful or pay attention.

mind-reader NOUN a person seemingly able to discern the thoughts of another.
▸**ˈmind-ˌreading** NOUN

mind-set NOUN the ideas and attitudes with which a person approaches a situation, esp when these are seen as being difficult to alter.

mind's eye NOUN the visual memory or the imagination.

mindshare (ˈmaɪndˌʃɛə) NOUN the level of awareness in the minds of consumers that a particular product commands.

mind-your-own-business NOUN a Mediterranean urticaceous plant, *Helxine soleirolii,* with small dense leaves: used for cover.

mine¹ (maɪn) PRONOUN [1] something or someone belonging to or associated with me: *mine is best.* [2] **of mine.** belonging to or associated with me. ◆ DETERMINER [3] (*preceding a vowel*) an archaic word for **my**: *mine eyes; mine host.*
▷HISTORY Old English *mīn;* compare Old High German, Old Norse *mīn,* Dutch *mijn*

mine² (maɪn) NOUN [1] a system of excavations made for the extraction of minerals, esp coal, ores, or precious stones. [2] any deposit of ore or minerals. [3] a lucrative source or abundant supply: *she was a mine of information.* [4] a device containing an explosive designed to destroy ships, vehicles, or personnel, usually laid beneath the ground or in water. [5] a tunnel or sap dug to undermine a fortification. [6] a groove or tunnel made by certain insects, esp in a leaf. ◆ VERB [7] to dig into (the earth) for (minerals). [8] to make (a hole, tunnel, etc.) by digging or boring. [9] to place explosive mines in position below the surface of (the sea or land). [10] to undermine (a fortification) by digging mines or saps. [11] another word for **undermine.**
▷HISTORY C13: from Old French, probably of Celtic origin; compare Irish *mein,* Welsh *mwyn* ore, mine
▸**ˈminable** *or* **ˈmineable** ADJECTIVE

mine detector NOUN an instrument designed to detect explosive mines.
▸**mine detection** NOUN

mine dump NOUN *South African* a large mound of residue, esp from gold-mining operations.

minefield (ˈmaɪnˌfiːld) NOUN [1] an area of ground or water containing explosive mines. [2] a subject, situation, etc., beset with hidden problems.

minehunter (ˈmaɪnˌhʌntə) NOUN a naval vessel that searches for mines by electronic means.

minelayer (ˈmaɪnˌleɪə) NOUN a warship or aircraft designed for the carrying and laying of mines.

miner (ˈmaɪnə) NOUN [1] a person who works in a mine. [2] Also called: **continuous miner.** a large machine for the automatic extraction of minerals, esp coal, from a mine. [3] any of various insects or insect larvae that bore into and feed on plant tissues. See also **leaf miner.** [4] *Austral* any of several honey-eaters of the genus *Manorina,* esp *M. melanocephala* (**noisy miner**), of scrub regions.

mineral (ˈmɪnərəl, ˈmɪnrəl) NOUN [1] any of a class of naturally occurring solid inorganic substances with a characteristic crystalline form and a homogeneous chemical composition. [2] any inorganic matter. [3] any substance obtained by mining, esp a metal ore. [4] (*often plural*) *Brit* short for **mineral water.** [5] *Brit* a soft drink containing carbonated water and flavourings. Usual US word: **soda.** ◆ ADJECTIVE [6] of, relating to, containing, or resembling minerals.
▷HISTORY C15: from Medieval Latin *minerāle* (n), from *minerālis* (adj); related to *minera* mine, ore, of uncertain origin

mineral. ABBREVIATION FOR mineralogy *or* mineralogical.

mineralize *or* **mineralise** (ˈmɪnərəˌlaɪz, ˈmɪnrə-) VERB (*tr*) [1] **a** to impregnate (organic matter, water, etc.) with a mineral substance. **b** to convert (such matter) into a mineral; petrify. [2] (of gases, vapours, etc., in magma) to transform (a metal) into an ore.
▸**ˌmineraliˈzation** *or* **ˌmineraliˈsation** NOUN

mineralizer *or* **mineraliser** (ˈmɪnərəˌlaɪzə) NOUN [1] any of various gases dissolved in magma that affect the crystallization of igneous rocks and the formation of minerals when the magma cools. [2] an element, such as oxygen, that combines with a metal to form an ore.

mineral jelly NOUN another name for **petrolatum.**

mineral kingdom NOUN all nonliving material, esp rocks and minerals. Compare **animal kingdom, plant kingdom.**

mineralocorticoid (ˌmɪnərələʊˈkɔːtɪˌkɔɪd) NOUN any corticosteroid that controls electrolyte and water balance, esp by promoting retention of sodium by the kidney tubules.

mineralogy (ˌmɪnəˈrælədʒɪ) NOUN the branch of geology concerned with the study of minerals. ▸**mineralogical** (ˌmɪnərəˈlɒdʒɪkəl) *or* ˌ**mineralˈogic** ADJECTIVE ▸ˌ**mineralˈogically** ADVERB ▸ˌ**minerˈalogist** NOUN

mineral oil NOUN 1 *Brit* any oil of mineral origin, esp petroleum. 2 a US and Canadian name for **liquid paraffin.**

mineral pitch NOUN another name for **asphalt.**

mineral spring NOUN a spring of water that contains a high proportion of dissolved mineral salts.

mineral tar NOUN a natural black viscous tar intermediate in properties between petroleum and asphalt. Also called: **maltha.**

mineral water NOUN water containing dissolved mineral salts or gases, usually having medicinal properties.

mineral wax NOUN another name for **ozocerite.**

mineral wool NOUN a fibrous material made by blowing steam or air through molten slag and used for packing and insulation. Also called: **rock wool.**

miner's right NOUN *Austral and NZ history* a licence to prospect for minerals, esp gold.
▷HISTORY C19

Minerva (mɪˈnɜːvə) NOUN the Roman goddess of wisdom. Greek counterpart: **Athena.**

minestrone (ˌmɪnɪˈstrəʊnɪ) NOUN a soup made from a variety of vegetables and pasta.
▷HISTORY from Italian, from *minestrare* to serve

minesweeper (ˈmaɪnˌswiːpə) NOUN a naval vessel equipped to detect and clear mines.
▸ˈ**mineˌsweeping** NOUN

Ming (mɪŋ) NOUN 1 the imperial dynasty of China from 1368 to 1644. ♦ ADJECTIVE 2 of or relating to Chinese porcelain produced during the Ming dynasty, characterized by the use of brilliant colours and a fine-quality body.

minge (mɪndʒ) NOUN *Brit, taboo slang* 1 the female genitals. 2 women collectively considered as sexual objects.
▷HISTORY C20: from Romany; of obscure origin

minger (ˈmɪŋə) NOUN *Brit informal* an unattractive or malodorous person.

minging (ˈmɪŋɪŋ) ADJECTIVE *Brit informal* 1 ugly, disgusting, or malodorous. 2 extremely poor in quality.
▷HISTORY C20: originally Scottish, of obscure origin

mingle (ˈmɪŋgəl) VERB 1 to mix or cause to mix. 2 (*intr; often foll by with*) to come into close association.
▷HISTORY C15: from Old English *mengan* to mix; related to Middle Dutch *mengen,* Old Frisian *mengja*
▸ˈ**mingler** NOUN

Mingrelian (mɪŋˈgriːlɪən) *or* **Mingrel** (ˈmɪŋgrəl) NOUN 1 a member of a people of Georgia living in the mountains northeast of the Black Sea. 2 the language of this people, belonging to the South Caucasian family and closely related to Georgian. ♦ ADJECTIVE 3 of or relating to the Mingrelians or their language.

ming tree NOUN an artificial plant resembling a bonsai plant.
▷HISTORY perhaps from MING

mingy (ˈmɪndʒɪ) ADJECTIVE **-gier, -giest.** *Brit informal* miserly, stingy, or niggardly.
▷HISTORY C20: probably a blend of MEAN[2] + STINGY[1]

Minho (ˈmiɲu) NOUN the Portuguese name for the **Miño.**

mini (ˈmɪnɪ) ADJECTIVE 1 (of a woman's dress, skirt, etc.) very short; thigh-length. 2 (*prenominal*) small; miniature. ♦ NOUN, *plural* **minis.** 3 something very small of its kind, esp a small car or a miniskirt.

mini- COMBINING FORM smaller or shorter than the standard size: *minibus; miniskirt.*
▷HISTORY C20: from MINIATURE and MINIMUM

miniature (ˈmɪnɪtʃə) NOUN 1 a model, copy, or similar representation on a very small scale. 2 anything that is very small of its kind. 3 a very small painting, esp a portrait, showing fine detail on ivory or vellum. 4 a very small bottle of whisky or other spirits, which can hold 50 millilitres. 5 an illuminated letter or other decoration in a manuscript. 6 **in miniature.** on a small scale: *games are real life in miniature.* ♦ ADJECTIVE 7 greatly reduced in size. 8 on a small scale; minute.
▷HISTORY C16: from Italian, from Medieval Latin *miniātūra,* from *miniāre* to paint red, (in illuminating manuscripts); from MINIUM

miniature camera NOUN a small camera using 35 millimetre film.

miniaturist (ˈmɪnɪtʃərɪst) NOUN a person who paints miniature portraits.

miniaturize *or* **miniaturise** (ˈmɪnɪtʃəˌraɪz) VERB (*tr*) to make or construct (something, esp electronic equipment) on a very small scale; reduce in size.
▸ˌ**miniaturiˈzation** *or* ˌ**miniaturiˈsation** NOUN

minibar (ˈmɪnɪˌbɑː) NOUN a selection of drinks and confectionery provided in a hotel bedroom and charged to the guest's bill if used.

minibus (ˈmɪnɪˌbʌs) NOUN a small bus able to carry approximately ten passengers.

minicab (ˈmɪnɪˌkæb) NOUN *Brit* a small saloon car used as a taxi.

minicom (ˈmɪnɪˌkɒm) NOUN a device used by deaf and hard-of-hearing people, allowing typed telephone messages to be sent and received.

minicomputer (ˌmɪnɪkəmˈpjuːtə) NOUN a small comparatively cheap digital computer.

minidisc (ˈmɪnɪˌdɪsk) NOUN a small recordable compact disc.

minidish (ˈmɪnɪˌdɪʃ) NOUN a small parabolic aerial for reception or transmission to a communications satellite.

minidress (ˈmɪnɪˌdrɛs) NOUN a very short dress, at least four inches above the knee. Often shortened to: **mini.**

Minié ball (ˈmɪnɪˌeɪ; *French* miɲe) NOUN a conical rifle bullet, used in the 19th century, manufactured with a hollow base designed to expand when fired to fit the rifling.
▷HISTORY C19: named after Capt. C. E. *Minié* (1814–1879), French army officer who invented it

minify (ˈmɪnɪˌfaɪ) VERB **-fies, -fying, -fied.** (*tr*) *Rare* to minimize or lessen the size or importance of (something).
▷HISTORY C17: from Latin *minus* less; for form, compare MAGNIFY
▸**minification** (ˌmɪnɪfɪˈkeɪʃən) NOUN

minikin (ˈmɪnɪkɪn) *Obsolete* ♦ NOUN 1 a small, dainty, or affected person or thing. ♦ ADJECTIVE 2 dainty, prim, or affected.
▷HISTORY C16: from Dutch *minneken,* diminutive of *minne* love

minim (ˈmɪnɪm) NOUN 1 a unit of fluid measure equal to one sixtieth of a drachm. It is approximately equal to one drop. Symbol: M, ɱ. 2 *Music* a note having the time value of half a semibreve. Usual US and Canadian name: **half-note.** 3 a small or insignificant person or thing. 4 a downward stroke in calligraphy. ♦ ADJECTIVE 5 *Rare* very small; tiny.
▷HISTORY C15 (in its musical meaning): from Latin *minimus* smallest

minima (ˈmɪnɪmə) NOUN a plural of **minimum.**

minimal (ˈmɪnɪməl) ADJECTIVE of the least possible; minimum or smallest.
▸ˈ**minimally** ADVERB

minimal art NOUN abstract painting or sculpture in which expressiveness and illusion are minimized by the use of simple geometric shapes, flat colour, and arrangements of ordinary objects.
▸**minimal artist** NOUN

minimalism (ˈmɪnɪməˌlɪzəm) NOUN 1 another name for **minimal art.** 2 a type of music based on simple elements and avoiding elaboration or embellishment. 3 design or style in which the simplest and fewest elements are used to create the maximum effect.

minimalist (ˈmɪnɪməlɪst) NOUN 1 a person advocating a minimal policy, style, technique, action, etc. 2 a minimal artist. ♦ ADJECTIVE 3 of or relating to minimal art or artists.

Minimalist (ˈmɪnɪməlɪst) NOUN (in early 20th-century Russia) 1 a member of the faction of the Social Revolutionaries that advocated immediate postrevolutionary democracy. 2 a less common name for a **Menshevik.** ♦ Compare **Maximalist.**

minimally *or* **minimal invasive** ADJECTIVE (of surgery) involving as little incision into the body as possible, through the use of techniques such as keyhole surgery and laser treatment.

minimal pair NOUN *Linguistics* a pair of speech elements in a given language differing in only one respect and thus serving to identify minimum units such as phonemes, morphemes, etc. For example, *tin* and *din* constitute a minimal pair in English.

minimax (ˈmɪnɪˌmæks) NOUN 1 *Maths* the lowest of a set of maximum values. 2 (in game theory, etc.) the procedure of choosing the strategy that least benefits the most advantaged member of a group. Compare **maximin.**
▷HISTORY C20: from MINI(MUM) + MAX(IMUM)

Mini-Me (ˈmɪnɪˌmiː) NOUN *Informal* 1 a person who resembles a smaller or younger version of another person. 2 a person who adopts the opinions or mannerisms of a more powerful or senior person in order to win favour, achieve promotion, etc.
▷HISTORY C20: after a cloned character in the 1999 film *Austin Powers: The Spy who Shagged Me*

minimize *or* **minimise** (ˈmɪnɪˌmaɪz) VERB (*tr*) 1 to reduce to or estimate at the least possible degree or amount: *to minimize a risk.* 2 to rank or treat at less than the true worth; belittle: *to minimize someone's achievements.*
▸ˌ**minimiˈzation** *or* ˌ**minimiˈsation** NOUN ▸ˈ**miniˌmizer** *or* ˈ**miniˌmiser** NOUN

minimum (ˈmɪnɪməm) NOUN, *plural* **-mums** *or* **-ma** (-mə). 1 the least possible amount, degree, or quantity. 2 the least amount recorded, allowed, or reached: *the minimum in our temperature record this month was 50°.* 3 (*modifier*) being the least possible, recorded, allowed, etc.: *minimum age.* 4 *Maths* a value of a function that is less than any neighbouring value. ♦ ADJECTIVE 5 of or relating to a minimum or minimums.
▷HISTORY C17: from Latin: smallest thing, from *minimus* least

minimum lending rate NOUN (in Britain) the minimum rate at which the Bank of England would lend to discount houses between 1971 and 1981, after which it was replaced by the less formal base rate. Abbreviation: **MLR.**

minimum wage NOUN the lowest wage that an employer is permitted to pay by law or union contract.

minimus (ˈmɪnɪməs) ADJECTIVE (*immediately postpositive*) *Brit* the youngest: sometimes used after the surname of a schoolboy having elder brothers at the same school: *Hunt minimus.*

mining (ˈmaɪnɪŋ) NOUN 1 the act, process, or industry of extracting coal, ores, etc., from the earth. 2 *Military* the process of laying mines.

mining bee NOUN a solitary bee of the genera *Andrena* and *Halictus,* which sometimes resemble honey bees.
▷HISTORY named from their burrowing habits

minion (ˈmɪnjən) NOUN 1 a favourite or dependant, esp a servile or fawning one. 2 a servile agent: *the minister's minions.* 3 a size of printer's type, approximately equal to 7 point. ♦ ADJECTIVE 4 dainty, pretty, or elegant.
▷HISTORY C16: from French *mignon,* from Old French *mignot,* of Gaulish origin

minipill (ˈmɪnɪˌpɪl) NOUN a low-dose oral contraceptive containing a progestogen only.

miniseries (ˈmɪnɪˌsɪəriːz) NOUN a television programme in several parts that is shown on consecutive days or weeks for a short period.

miniskirt (ˈmɪnɪˌskɜːt) NOUN a very short skirt, originally in the 1960s one at least four inches above the knee. Often shortened to: **mini.**
▸ˈ**miniˌskirted** ADJECTIVE

minister (ˈmɪnɪstə) NOUN 1 (esp in Presbyterian and some Nonconformist Churches) a member of the clergy. 2 a person appointed to head a government department. 3 any diplomatic agent accredited to a foreign government or head of state. 4 short for **minister plenipotentiary** or **envoy extraordinary and minister plenipotentiary.** See **envoy**[1] (sense 1). 5 Also called (in full): **minister resident.** a diplomat ranking after an envoy extraordinary and minister plenipotentiary. 6 a person who attends to the needs of others, esp in religious matters. 7 a person who acts as the agent or servant of a person or thing. ♦ VERB 8 (*intr; often foll by to*) to attend to

the needs (of); take care (of). 9 (*tr*) *Archaic* to provide; supply.
▷HISTORY C13: via Old French from Latin: servant; related to *minus* less
▸'**minister,ship** NOUN

ministerial (ˌmɪnɪ'stɪərɪəl) ADJECTIVE 1 of or relating to a minister of religion or his office. 2 of or relating to a government minister or ministry: *a ministerial act.* 3 (*often capital*) of or supporting the ministry or government against the opposition. 4 *Law* relating to or possessing delegated executive authority. 5 *Law* (of an office, duty, etc.) requiring the following of instructions, without power to exercise any personal discretion in doing so. 6 acting as an agent or cause; instrumental.
▸ˌ**minis'terially** ADVERB

ministerialist (ˌmɪnɪ'stɪərɪəlɪst) NOUN *Brit* a supporter of the governing ministry.

ministerium (ˌmɪnɪ'stɪərɪəm) NOUN, *plural* **-ria** (-rɪə). the body of the Lutheran ministers in a district.
▷HISTORY C19: Latin: MINISTRY

minister of state NOUN 1 (in the British Parliament) a minister, usually below cabinet rank, appointed to assist a senior minister with heavy responsibilities. 2 any government minister.

Minister of the Crown NOUN *Brit* any Government minister of cabinet rank.

minister plenipotentiary NOUN, *plural* **ministers plenipotentiary**. See **envoy**[1] (sense 1).

ministrant ('mɪnɪstrənt) ADJECTIVE 1 ministering or serving as a minister. ◆ NOUN 2 a person who ministers.
▷HISTORY C17: from Latin *ministrans,* from *ministrāre* to wait upon

ministration (ˌmɪnɪ'streɪʃən) NOUN 1 the act or an instance of serving or giving aid. 2 the act or an instance of ministering religiously.
▷HISTORY C14: from Latin *ministrātiō,* from *ministrāre* to wait upon
▸**ministrative** ('mɪnɪstrətɪv) ADJECTIVE

ministroke (ˌmɪnɪ'strəʊk) NOUN an informal name for **TIA**.

ministry ('mɪnɪstrɪ) NOUN, *plural* **-tries**. 1 **a** the profession or duties of a minister of religion. **b** the performance of these duties. 2 ministers of religion or government ministers considered collectively. 3 the tenure of a minister. 4 **a** a government department headed by a minister. **b** the buildings of such a department.
▷HISTORY C14: from Latin *ministerium* service, from *minister* servant; see MINISTER

Minitrack ('mɪnɪˌtræk) NOUN *Trademark, obsolete* a system for tracking the course of rockets or satellites by radio signals received at ground stations.

minium ('mɪnɪəm) NOUN another name for **red lead**.
▷HISTORY C14 (meaning: vermilion): from Latin

minivan ('mɪnɪˌvæn) NOUN a small van, esp one with seats in the back for carrying passengers.

miniver ('mɪnɪvə) NOUN white fur, used in ceremonial costumes.
▷HISTORY C13: from Old French *menu vair,* from *menu* small + *vair* variegated fur, VAIR

minivet ('mɪnɪvɛt) NOUN any brightly coloured tropical Asian cuckoo shrike of the genus *Pericrocotus*.
▷HISTORY C19: of unknown origin

mink (mɪŋk) NOUN, *plural* **mink** *or* **minks**. 1 any of several semiaquatic musteline mammals of the genus *Mustela,* of Europe, Asia, and North America, having slightly webbed feet. 2 the highly valued fur of these animals, esp that of the American mink (*M. vison*). 3 a garment made of this, esp a woman's coat or stole.
▷HISTORY C15: from Scandinavian; compare Danish *mink,* Swedish *mänk*

minke whale ('mɪŋkə) NOUN a type of small whalebone whale or rorqual, *Balaenoptera acutorostrata,* up to 10 metres long. Also called: **minke**.
▷HISTORY C20: probably from Norwegian *minkehval,* from *minke* lesser + *hval* whale

Minkowski space-time (mɪŋ'kɒfskɪ) NOUN a four-dimensional space in which three coordinates specify the position of a point in space and the fourth represents the time at which an event occurred at that point.
▷HISTORY C20: named after Hermann *Minkowski* (1864–1909), Russian-born German mathematician

min min (mɪn mɪn) NOUN *Austral* will-o'-the-wisp.
▷HISTORY from a native Australian language

Minn. ABBREVIATION FOR Minnesota.

Minna ('mɪnə) NOUN a city in W central Nigeria, capital of Niger state. Pop.: 136 900 (1996 est.).

Minneapolis (ˌmɪnɪ'æpəlɪs) NOUN a city in SE Minnesota, on the Mississippi River adjacent to St Paul: the largest city in the state; important centre for the grain trade. Pop.: 382 618 (2000 est.).

minneola (ˌmɪnɪ'əʊlə) NOUN a juicy citrus fruit that is a cross between a tangerine and a grapefruit.
▷HISTORY C20: perhaps from *Mineola,* Texas

minnesinger ('mɪnɪˌsɪŋə) NOUN one of the German lyric poets and musicians of the 12th to 14th centuries.
▷HISTORY C19: from German: love-singer

Minnesota (ˌmɪnɪ'səʊtə) NOUN 1 a state of the N central US: chief US producer of iron ore. Capital: St Paul. Pop.: 4 919 479 (2000). Area: 218 600 sq. km (84 402 sq. miles). Abbreviations: **Minn,** (with zip code) **MN.** 2 a river in S Minnesota, flowing southeast and northeast to the Mississippi River near St Paul. Length: 534 km (332 miles).

Minnesotan (ˌmɪnɪ'səʊtən) NOUN 1 a native or inhabitant of Minnesota. ◆ ADJECTIVE 2 of or relating to Minnesota or its inhabitants.

minnow ('mɪnəʊ) NOUN, *plural* **-nows** *or* **-now**. 1 a small slender European freshwater cyprinid fish, *Phoxinus phoxinus*. 2 any other small cyprinid. 3 *Angling* a spinning lure imitating a minnow. 4 a small or insignificant person.
▷HISTORY C15: related to Old English *myne* minnow; compare Old High German *muniwa* fish

Miño (*Spanish* 'miɲo) NOUN a river in SW Europe, rising in NW Spain and flowing southwest (as part of the border between Spain and Portugal) to the Atlantic. Length: 338 km (210 miles). Portuguese name: **Minho**.

Minoan (mɪ'nəʊən) ADJECTIVE 1 denoting the Bronze Age culture of Crete from about 3000 B.C. to about 1100 B.C. Compare **Mycenaean.** 2 of or relating to the linear writing systems used in Crete and later in mainland Greece. See **Linear A, Linear B.** ◆ NOUN 3 a Cretan belonging to the Minoan culture.
▷HISTORY C19: named after MINOS, from the excavations at his supposed palace at Knossos

minor ('maɪnə) ADJECTIVE 1 lesser or secondary in amount, extent, importance, or degree: *a minor poet; minor burns.* 2 of or relating to the minority. 3 below the age of legal majority. 4 *Music* **a** (of a scale) having a semitone between the second and third and fifth and sixth degrees (**natural minor**). See also **harmonic minor scale, melodic minor scale. b** (of a key) based on the minor scale. **c** (*postpositive*) denoting a specified key based on the minor scale: *C minor.* **d** (of an interval) reduced by a semitone from the major. **e** (of a chord, esp a triad) having a minor third above the root. **f** (esp in jazz) of or relating to a chord built upon a minor triad and containing a minor seventh: *a minor ninth.* See also **minor key, minor mode.** 5 *Logic* (of a term or premise) having less generality or scope than another term or proposition. 6 *US education* of or relating to an additional secondary subject taken by a student. 7 (*immediately postpositive*) *Brit* the younger or junior: sometimes used after the surname of a schoolboy if he has an older brother in the same school: *Hunt minor.* 8 (*postpositive*) *Bell-ringing* of, relating to, or denoting a set of changes rung on six bells: *grandsire minor.* ◆ NOUN 9 a person or thing that is lesser or secondary. 10 a person below the age of legal majority. 11 *US and Canadian education* a subsidiary subject in which a college or university student needs fewer credits than in his or her major. 12 *Music* a minor key, chord, mode, or scale. 13 *Logic* a minor term or premise. 14 *Maths* **a** a determinant associated with a particular element of a given determinant and formed by removing the row and column containing that element. **b** Also called: **cofactor, signed minor.** the number equal to this reduced determinant. 15 (*capital*) another name for **Minorite.** ◆ VERB 16 (*intr;* usually foll by *in*) *US education* to take a minor. ◆ Compare **major.**
▷HISTORY C13: from Latin: less, smaller; related to Old High German *minniro* smaller, Gothic *minniza* least, Latin *minuere* to diminish, Greek *meiōn* less

minor axis NOUN the shorter or shortest axis of an ellipse or ellipsoid.

Minorca (mɪ'nɔːkə) NOUN 1 an island in the W Mediterranean, northeast of Majorca: the second largest of the Balearic Islands. Chief town: Mahón. Pop.: 55 500 (latest est.). Area: 702 sq. km (271 sq. miles). Spanish name: **Menorca.** 2 a breed of light domestic fowl with glossy white, black, or blue plumage.

Minorcan (mɪ'nɔːkən) ADJECTIVE 1 of or relating to Minorca or its inhabitants. ◆ NOUN 2 a native or inhabitant of Minorca.

minor canon NOUN *Church of England* a clergyman who is attached to a cathedral to assist at daily services but who is not a member of the chapter.

Minorite ('maɪnəˌraɪt) NOUN a member of the Franciscan Friars Minor. Also called: **Minor.**
▷HISTORY C16: from Medieval Latin *frātrēs minōrēs* lesser brethren, name adopted by St Francis as a token of humility

minority (maɪ'nɒrɪtɪ, mɪ-) NOUN, *plural* **-ties**. 1 the smaller in number of two parts, factions, or groups. 2 a group that is different racially, politically, etc., from a larger group of which it is a part. 3 **a** the state of being a minor. **b** the period during which a person is below legal age. ◆ Compare **majority.** 4 (*modifier*) relating to or being a minority: *a minority interest; a minority opinion.*
▷HISTORY C16: from Medieval Latin *minōritās,* from Latin MINOR

minority carrier NOUN the entity responsible for carrying the lesser part of the current in a semiconductor. Compare **majority carrier.**

minor key NOUN *Music* a key based on notes taken from a corresponding minor scale.

minor league NOUN 1 *US and Canadian* any professional league in baseball other than a major league. Compare **major league.** 2 (*modifier*) of relatively little importance: *that firm is very minor league.*

minor mode NOUN *Music* any arrangement of notes present in or characteristic of a minor scale or key.

minor orders PLURAL NOUN *RC Church* the four lower degrees of holy orders, namely porter, exorcist, lector, and acolyte. Compare **major orders.**

minor planet NOUN another name for **asteroid** (sense 1).

minor premise NOUN *Logic* the premise of a syllogism containing the subject of its conclusion.

minor seventh chord NOUN a chord consisting of a minor triad with an added minor seventh above the root. Compare **major seventh chord.** Often shortened to: **minor seventh.**

minor suit NOUN *Bridge* diamonds or clubs. Compare **major suit.**

minor term NOUN *Logic* the subject of the conclusion of a syllogism, also occurring as the subject or predicate in the minor premise.

Minos ('maɪnɒs) NOUN *Greek myth* a king of Crete for whom Daedalus built the Labyrinth to contain the Minotaur.

Minotaur ('maɪnətɔː) NOUN *Greek myth* a monster with the head of a bull and the body of a man. It was kept in the Labyrinth in Crete, feeding on human flesh, until destroyed by Theseus.
▷HISTORY C14: via Latin from Greek *Minōtauros,* from MINOS + *tauros* bull

Minsk (mɪnsk) NOUN the capital of Belarus: an industrial city and educational and cultural centre, with a university (1921). Pop.: 1 717 000 (1998 est.).

minster ('mɪnstə) NOUN *Brit* any of certain cathedrals and large churches, usually originally connected to a monastery.
▷HISTORY Old English *mynster,* probably from Vulgar Latin *monisterium* (unattested), variant of Church Latin *monastērium* MONASTERY

minstrel ('mɪnstrəl) NOUN 1 a medieval wandering musician who performed songs or recited poetry with instrumental accompaniment.

[2] a performer in a minstrel show. [3] *Archaic or poetic* any poet, musician, or singer.
▷**HISTORY** C13: from Old French *menestral,* from Late Latin *ministeriālis* an official, from Latin MINISTER

minstrel show NOUN a theatrical entertainment consisting of songs, dances, comic turns, etc., performed by a troupe of actors wearing black face make-up.

minstrelsy ('mɪnstrəlsɪ) NOUN, *plural* **-sies.** [1] the art of a minstrel. [2] the poems, music, or songs of a minstrel. [3] a troupe of minstrels.

mint[1] (mɪnt) NOUN [1] any N temperate plant of the genus *Mentha*, having aromatic leaves and spikes of small typically mauve flowers: family *Lamiaceae* (labiates). The leaves of some species are used for seasoning and flavouring. See also **peppermint, spearmint, horsemint, water mint.** [2] **stone mint.** another name for **dittany** (sense 2). [3] a sweet flavoured with mint.
▷**HISTORY** Old English *minte,* from Latin *mentha,* from Greek *minthē;* compare Old High German *minza*
▸**'minty** ADJECTIVE

mint[2] (mɪnt) NOUN [1] a place where money is coined by governmental authority. [2] a very large amount of money: *he made a mint in business.* ◆ ADJECTIVE [3] (of coins, postage stamps, etc.) in perfect condition as issued. [4] *Brit informal* excellent; impressive. [5] **in mint condition.** in perfect condition; as if new. ◆ VERB [6] to make (coins) by stamping metal. [7] *(tr)* to invent (esp phrases or words).
▷**HISTORY** Old English *mynet* coin, from Latin *monēta* money, mint, from the temple of Juno *Monēta,* used as a mint in ancient Rome
▸**'minter** NOUN

mintage ('mɪntɪdʒ) NOUN [1] the process of minting. [2] money minted. [3] a fee paid for minting a coin. [4] an official impression stamped on a coin.

mint bush NOUN an aromatic shrub of the genus *Prostanthera* with a mintlike odour: family *Lamiaceae* (labiates): native to Australia.

minted ('mɪntɪd) ADJECTIVE *Brit, slang* wealthy.

mint julep NOUN *Chiefly US* a long drink consisting of bourbon whiskey, crushed ice, sugar, and sprigs of mint.

Minton ('mɪntən) NOUN **a** fine-quality porcelain ware produced in Stoke-on-Trent since 1798. **b** *(as modifier): Minton plate.*
▷**HISTORY** C19: named after Thomas *Minton* (1765–1836), English potter

mint sauce NOUN a sauce made from mint leaves, sugar, and vinegar, usually served with lamb.

minuend ('mɪnjʊˌɛnd) NOUN the number from which another number, the **subtrahend** is to be subtracted.
▷**HISTORY** C18: from Latin *minuendus (numerus)* (the number) to be diminished

minuet (ˌmɪnjʊ'ɛt) NOUN [1] a stately court dance of the 17th and 18th centuries in triple time. [2] a piece of music composed for or in the rhythm of this dance, sometimes as a movement in a suite, sonata, or symphony. See also **scherzo.**
▷**HISTORY** C17: from French *menuet* dainty (referring to the dance steps), from *menu* small

minus ('maɪnəs) PREPOSITION [1] reduced by the subtraction of: *four minus two* (written 4 – 2). [2] *Informal* deprived of; lacking: *minus the trimmings, that hat would be ordinary.* ◆ ADJECTIVE [3] **a** indicating or involving subtraction: *a minus sign.* **b** Also: **negative.** having a value or designating a quantity less than zero: *a minus number.* [4] on the negative part of a scale or coordinate axis: *a value of minus 40°C.* [5] involving a disadvantage, harm, etc.: *a minus factor.* [6] *(postpositive) Education* slightly below the standard of a particular grade: *he received a B minus for his essay.* [7] *Botany* designating the strain of a fungus that can only undergo sexual reproduction with a plus strain. [8] denoting a negative electric charge. ◆ NOUN [9] short for **minus sign.** [10] a negative quantity. [11] a disadvantage, loss, or deficit. [12] *Informal* something detrimental or negative. ◆ Mathematical symbol: –.
▷**HISTORY** C15: from Latin, neuter of MINOR

minuscule ('mɪnəˌskjuːl) NOUN [1] a lower-case letter. [2] writing using such letters. [3] a small cursive 7th-century style of lettering derived from the uncial. ◆ ADJECTIVE [4] relating to, printed in, or written in small letters. Compare **majuscule.** [5] very small. [6] (of letters) lower-case.
▷**HISTORY** C18: from French, from Latin *(littera) minuscula* very small (letter), diminutive of MINOR
▸**minuscular** (mɪ'nʌskjʊlə) ADJECTIVE

minus sign NOUN the symbol –, indicating subtraction or a negative quantity.

minute[1] ('mɪnɪt) NOUN [1] a period of time equal to 60 seconds; one sixtieth of an hour. [2] a unit of angular measure equal to one sixtieth of a degree. Symbol: ′. Also called: **minute of arc.** [3] any very short period of time; moment. [4] a short note or memorandum. [5] the distance that can be travelled in a minute: *it's only two minutes away.* [6] **up to the minute.** **(up-to-the-minute** *when prenominal)* very latest or newest. ◆ VERB *(tr)* [7] to record in minutes: *to minute a meeting.* [8] to time in terms of minutes. ◆ See also **minutes.**
▷**HISTORY** C14: from Old French from Medieval Latin *minūta,* n. use of Latin *minūtus* MINUTE[2]

minute[2] (maɪ'njuːt) ADJECTIVE [1] very small; diminutive; tiny. [2] unimportant; petty. [3] precise or detailed: *a minute examination.*
▷**HISTORY** C15: from Latin *minūtus,* past participle of *minuere* to diminish
▸**mi'nuteness** NOUN

minute gun ('mɪnɪt) NOUN a gun fired at one-minute intervals as a sign of distress or mourning.

minute hand ('mɪnɪt) NOUN the pointer on a timepiece that indicates minutes, typically the longer hand of two. Compare **hour hand, second hand.**

minutely[1] (maɪ'njuːtlɪ) ADVERB in great detail.

minutely[2] ('mɪnɪtlɪ) ADJECTIVE [1] occurring every minute. ◆ ADVERB [2] every minute.

Minuteman ('mɪnɪtˌmæn) NOUN, *plural* **-men.** [1] *(sometimes not capital)* (in the War of American Independence) a colonial militiaman who promised to be ready to fight at one minute's notice. [2] a US three-stage intercontinental ballistic missile.

minute mark ('mɪnɪt) NOUN the symbol ′ used for minutes of arc and linear feet.

minutes ('mɪnɪts) PLURAL NOUN an official record of the proceedings of a meeting, conference, convention, etc.

minute steak ('mɪnɪt) NOUN a small thinly-cut piece of steak that can be cooked quickly.

minutiae (mɪ'njuːʃɪˌiː) PLURAL NOUN, *singular* **-tia** (-ʃɪə). small, precise, or trifling details.
▷**HISTORY** C18: pl of Late Latin *minūtia* smallness, from Latin *minūtus* MINUTE[2]

minx (mɪŋks) NOUN a bold, flirtatious, or scheming woman.
▷**HISTORY** C16: of unknown origin
▸**'minxish** ADJECTIVE

Minya ('mɪnjə) NOUN See **El Minya.**

minyan *Hebrew* (min'jan; *English* 'mɪnjən) NOUN, *plural* ***minyanim*** (minja'nim) *or* ***minyans.*** the number of persons required by Jewish law to be present for a religious service, namely, at least ten males over thirteen years of age.
▷**HISTORY** literally: number

Miocene ('maɪəˌsiːn) ADJECTIVE [1] of, denoting, or formed in the fourth epoch of the Tertiary period, between the Oligocene and Pliocene epochs, which lasted for 19 million years. ◆ NOUN [2] **the.** this epoch or rock series.
▷**HISTORY** C19: from Greek *meiōn* less + -CENE

miombo (mɪ'ɒmbɒ) NOUN (in E Africa) a dry wooded area with sparse deciduous growth.
▷**HISTORY** C19: probably from a Niger-Congo language

miosis *or* **myosis** (maɪ'əʊsɪs) NOUN, *plural* **-ses** (-siːz). [1] excessive contraction of the pupil of the eye, as in response to drugs. [2] a variant spelling of **meiosis** (sense 1).
▷**HISTORY** C20: from Greek *muein* to shut the eyes + -OSIS
▸**miotic** *or* **myotic** (maɪ'ɒtɪk) ADJECTIVE, NOUN

MIP ABBREVIATION FOR: [1] monthly investment plan. [2] maximum investment plan: an endowment assurance policy designed to produce maximum profits.

MIPS (mɪps) NOUN *Computing* ACRONYM FOR million instructions per second.

Miquelon ('miːkəˌlɒn; *French* miklɔ̃) NOUN a group of islands in the French territory of **Saint Pierre and Miquelon.**

mir *Russian* (mir) NOUN, *plural* ***miri*** ('miri). a peasant commune in prerevolutionary Russia.
▷**HISTORY** literally: world

Mir (mɪə) NOUN the Russian (formerly Soviet) manned space station launched in February 1986 and scuttled in 2001.
▷**HISTORY** C20: Russian: peace

mirabelle ('mɪrəˌbɛl) NOUN [1] a small sweet yellow-orange fruit that is a variety of greengage. [2] a liqueur distilled from this.
▷**HISTORY** C18: from French

mirabile dictu *Latin* (mɪ'ræbɪleɪ 'dɪktuː) wonderful to relate; amazing to say.

Mira Ceti ('maɪrə 'siːtaɪ) NOUN a binary star one component of which, a red supergiant, is a long-period variable with an average period of 332 days.

miracidium (ˌmaɪrə'sɪdɪəm) NOUN, *plural* **-ia** (-ɪə). the flat ciliated larva of flukes that hatches from the egg and gives rise asexually to other larval forms.
▷**HISTORY** C20: New Latin, via Late Latin *miracidion,* from Greek *meirax* boy, girl
▸**ˌmira'cidial** ADJECTIVE

miracle ('mɪrək^əl) NOUN [1] an event that is contrary to the established laws of nature and attributed to a supernatural cause. [2] any amazing or wonderful event. [3] a person or thing that is a marvellous example of something: *the bridge was a miracle of engineering.* [4] short for **miracle play.** [5] *(modifier)* being or seeming a miracle: *a miracle cure.*
▷**HISTORY** C12: from Latin *mīrāculum,* from *mīrārī* to wonder at

miracle play NOUN a medieval play based on a biblical story or the life of a saint. Compare **mystery play.**

miraculous (mɪ'rækjʊləs) ADJECTIVE [1] of, like, or caused by a miracle; marvellous. [2] surprising. [3] having the power to work miracles.
▸**mi'raculously** ADVERB ▸**mi'raculousness** NOUN

mirador (ˌmɪrə'dɔː) NOUN a window, balcony, or turret.
▷**HISTORY** C17: from Spanish, from *mirar* to look

Miraflores (ˌmɪrə'flɔːrəs; *Spanish* mira'flores) NOUN **Lake.** an artificial lake in Panama, in the S Canal Zone of the Panama Canal.

mirage (mɪ'rɑːʒ) NOUN [1] an image of a distant object or sheet of water, often inverted or distorted, caused by atmospheric refraction by hot air. [2] something illusory.
▷**HISTORY** C19: from French, from *(se) mirer* to be reflected

Miranda (mɪ'rændə) NOUN one of the larger satellites of the planet Uranus.

MIRAS ('maɪˌræs) NOUN (formerly in Britain) ACRONYM FOR mortgage interest relief at source.

mire (maɪə) NOUN [1] a boggy or marshy area. [2] mud, muck, or dirt. ◆ VERB [3] to sink or cause to sink in a mire. [4] *(tr)* to make dirty or muddy. [5] *(tr)* to involve, esp in difficulties.
▷**HISTORY** C14: from Old Norse *mýrr;* related to MOSS
▸**'miriness** NOUN ▸**'miry** ADJECTIVE

Mirena (maɪ'riːnə) NOUN *Trademark* a type of intrauterine system. See **IUS.**

mirepoix (mɪə'pwɑː) NOUN a mixture of sautéed root vegetables used as a base for braising meat or for various sauces.
▷**HISTORY** French, probably named in honour of C. P. G. F. de Lévis, Duke of *Mirepoix,* 18th-century French general

Miriam ('mɪrɪəm) NOUN *Old Testament* the sister of Moses and Aaron. (Numbers 12:1–15). Douay name: **Mary.**

mirk (mɜːk) NOUN a variant spelling of **murk.**
▸**'mirky** ADJECTIVE ▸**'mirkily** ADVERB ▸**'mirkiness** NOUN

mirliton ('mɜːlɪtɒn) NOUN another name (chiefly US) for **chayote.**
▷**HISTORY** C19: French, literally: reed pipe, of imitative origin

mirror ('mɪrə) NOUN [1] a surface, such as polished metal or glass coated with a metal film, that reflects light without diffusion and produces an image of an object placed in front of it. [2] such a reflecting

surface mounted in a frame. 3 any reflecting surface. 4 a thing that reflects or depicts something else: *the press is a mirror of public opinion.* ◆ VERB 5 (*tr*) to reflect, represent, or depict faithfully: *he mirrors his teacher's ideals.*
▷HISTORY C13: from Old French from *mirer* to look at, from Latin *mīrārī* to wonder at
▸ˈ**mirror-ˌlike** ADJECTIVE

mirror ball NOUN a large revolving ball covered with small pieces of mirror glass so that it reflects light in changing patterns: used in discos and ballrooms.

mirror canon NOUN *Music* 1 a canon in which the parts are written as though seen in a mirror placed between them: one part or set of parts is the upside-down image of the other. 2 sometimes, less accurately, a piece that can be played backwards.

mirror carp NOUN a variety of the common carp (*Cyprinus carpio*) with reduced scales, giving a smooth shiny body surface.

mirror finish NOUN a smooth highly polished surface produced on metal by mechanical or electrolytic polishing or lapping.

mirror image NOUN 1 an image as observed in a mirror. 2 an object that corresponds to another object in the same way as it would correspond to its image in a mirror.

mirror lens NOUN *Photog* a lens of long focal length in which some of the lens elements are replaced by mirrors in order to shorten its overall length and reduce its weight.

mirror symmetry NOUN symmetry about a plane (**mirror plane**) that divides the object or system into two mutual mirror images.

mirror writing NOUN backward writing that forms a mirror image of normal writing.

mirth (mɜːθ) NOUN laughter, gaiety, or merriment.
▷HISTORY Old English *myrgth;* compare MERRY
▸ˈ**mirthful** ADJECTIVE ▸ˈ**mirthfully** ADVERB ▸ˈ**mirthfulness** NOUN ▸ˈ**mirthless** ADJECTIVE ▸ˈ**mirthlessly** ADVERB ▸ˈ**mirthlessness** NOUN

MIRV (mɜːv) NOUN ACRONYM FOR multiple independently targeted re-entry vehicle: **a** a missile that has several warheads, each one being directed to different enemy targets. **b** any of the warheads.

mirza (ˈmɜːzə, mɪəˈzɑː) NOUN (in Iran) 1 a title of respect placed before the surname of an official, scholar, or other distinguished man. 2 a royal prince: used as a title after a name.
▷HISTORY C17: from Persian: son of a lord

mis-[1] PREFIX 1 wrong, bad, or erroneous; wrongly, badly, or erroneously: *misunderstanding; misfortune; misspelling; mistreat; mislead.* 2 lack of; not: *mistrust.*
▷HISTORY Old English *mis(se)-;* related to Middle English *mes-,* from Old French *mes-;* compare Old High German *missa-,* Old Norse *mis-*

mis-[2] PREFIX a variant of **miso-** before a vowel.

misadventure (ˌmɪsədˈvɛntʃə) NOUN 1 an unlucky event; misfortune. 2 *Law* accidental death not due to crime or negligence.

misaligned (ˌmɪsəˈlaɪnd) ADJECTIVE placed or positioned wrongly or badly.
▸ˌ**misaˈlignment** NOUN

misalliance (ˌmɪsəˈlaɪəns) NOUN an unsuitable alliance or marriage.

misandry (ˈmɪsændrɪ) NOUN hatred of men.
▷HISTORY C20: from Greek, from MISO- + *-andria,* from *anēr* man
▸**misˈandrist** NOUN, ADJECTIVE ▸**misˈandrous** ADJECTIVE

misanthrope (ˈmɪzənˌθrəʊp) *or* **misanthropist** (mɪˈzænθrəpɪst) NOUN a person who dislikes or distrusts other people or mankind in general.
▷HISTORY C17: from Greek *mīsanthrōpos,* from *misos* hatred + *anthrōpos* man
▸**misanthropic** (ˌmɪzənˈθrɒpɪk) *or* ˌ**misanˈthropical** ADJECTIVE ▸ˌ**misanˈthropically** ADVERB ▸**misanthropy** (mɪˈzænθrəpɪ) NOUN

misapply (ˌmɪsəˈplaɪ) VERB **-plies, -plying, -plied.** (*tr*) 1 to apply wrongly or badly. 2 another word for **misappropriate.**
▸**misapplication** (ˌmɪsæplɪˈkeɪʃən) NOUN

misapprehend (ˌmɪsæprɪˈhɛnd) VERB (*tr*) to misunderstand.
▸**misapprehension** (ˌmɪsæprɪˈhɛnʃən) NOUN ▸ˌ**misappreˈhensive** ADJECTIVE ▸ˌ**misappreˈhensively** ADVERB ▸ˌ**misappreˈhensiveness** NOUN

misappropriate (ˌmɪsəˈprəʊprɪˌeɪt) VERB (*tr*) to appropriate for a wrong or dishonest use; embezzle or steal.
▸ˌ**misapˌpropriˈation** NOUN

misbecome (ˌmɪsbɪˈkʌm) VERB **-comes, -coming, -came.** (*tr*) to be unbecoming to or unsuitable for.

misbegotten (ˌmɪsbɪˈgɒtᵊn) ADJECTIVE 1 unlawfully obtained: *misbegotten gains.* 2 badly conceived, planned, or designed: *a misbegotten scheme.* 3 Also: **misbegot** (ˌmɪsbɪˈgɒt). *Literary and dialect* illegitimate; bastard.

misbehave (ˌmɪsbɪˈheɪv) VERB to behave (oneself) badly.
▸ˌ**misbeˈhaver** NOUN ▸**misbehaviour** (ˌmɪsbɪˈheɪvjə) NOUN

misbelief (ˌmɪsbɪˈliːf) NOUN a false or unorthodox belief.

misc. ABBREVIATION FOR miscellaneous.

miscalculate (ˌmɪsˈkælkjʊˌleɪt) VERB (*tr*) to calculate wrongly.
▸ˌ**miscalcuˈlation** NOUN ▸ˌ**misˈcalcuˌlator** NOUN

miscall (ˌmɪsˈkɔːl) VERB (*tr*) 1 to call by the wrong name. 2 *Dialect* to abuse or malign.
▸ˌ**misˈcaller** NOUN

miscanthus (mɪsˈkænθəs) NOUN any tall perennial bamboo-like grass of the genus *Miscanthus,* native from southern Africa to SE Asia and cultivated for ornament in temperate regions.

miscarriage (mɪsˈkærɪdʒ) NOUN 1 (*also* ˈmɪskær-) spontaneous expulsion of a fetus from the womb, esp prior to the 20th week of pregnancy. 2 an act of mismanagement or failure: *a miscarriage of justice.* 3 *Brit* the failure of freight to reach its destination.

miscarry (mɪsˈkærɪ) VERB **-ries, -rying, -ried.** (*intr*) 1 to expel a fetus prematurely from the womb; abort. 2 to fail: *all her plans miscarried.* 3 *Brit* (of freight, mail, etc.) to fail to reach a destination.

miscast (ˌmɪsˈkɑːst) VERB **-casts, -casting, -cast.** (*tr*) 1 to cast badly. 2 (*often passive*) **a** to cast (a role or the roles) in (a play, film, etc.) inappropriately: *Falstaff was certainly miscast.* **b** to assign an inappropriate role to: *he was miscast as Othello.*

miscegenation (ˌmɪsɪdʒɪˈneɪʃən) NOUN interbreeding of races, esp where differences of pigmentation are involved.
▷HISTORY C19: from Latin *miscēre* to mingle + *genus* race
▸**miscegenetic** (ˌmɪsɪdʒɪˈnɛtɪk) ADJECTIVE

miscellanea (ˌmɪsəˈleɪnɪə) PLURAL NOUN a collection of miscellaneous items, esp literary works.
▷HISTORY C16: from Latin: neuter pl of *miscellāneus* MISCELLANEOUS

miscellaneous (ˌmɪsəˈleɪnɪəs) ADJECTIVE 1 composed of or containing a variety of things; mixed; varied. 2 having varied capabilities, sides, etc.
▷HISTORY C17: from Latin *miscellāneus,* from *miscellus* mixed, from *miscēre* to mix
▸ˌ**miscelˈlaneously** ADVERB ▸ˌ**miscelˈlaneousness** NOUN

miscellanist (mɪˈsɛlənɪst) NOUN a writer of miscellanies.

miscellany (mɪˈsɛlənɪ; *US* ˈmɪsəˌleɪnɪ) NOUN, *plural* **-nies.** 1 a mixed assortment of items. 2 (*sometimes plural*) a miscellaneous collection of essays, poems, etc., by different authors in one volume.
▷HISTORY C16: from French *miscellanées* (pl) MISCELLANEA

mischance (mɪsˈtʃɑːns) NOUN 1 bad luck. 2 a stroke of bad luck.

mischief (ˈmɪstʃɪf) NOUN 1 wayward but not malicious behaviour, usually of children, that causes trouble, irritation, etc. 2 a playful inclination to behave in this way or to tease or disturb. 3 injury or harm caused by a person or thing. 4 a person, esp a child, who is mischievous. 5 a source of trouble, difficulty, etc.: *floods are a great mischief to the farmer.*
▷HISTORY C13: from Old French *meschief* disaster, from *meschever* to meet with calamity; from *mes-* MIS-[1] + *chever* to reach an end, from *chef* end, CHIEF

mischievous (ˈmɪstʃɪvəs) ADJECTIVE 1 inclined to acts of mischief. 2 teasing; slightly malicious: *a mischievous grin.* 3 causing or intended to cause harm: *a mischievous plot.*
▸ˈ**mischievously** ADVERB ▸ˈ**mischievousness** NOUN

misch metal (mɪʃ) NOUN an alloy of cerium and other rare earth metals, used esp as a flint in cigarette lighters.
▷HISTORY C20: from German *Mischmetall,* from *mischen* to mix

miscible (ˈmɪsɪbᵊl) ADJECTIVE capable of mixing: *alcohol is miscible with water.*
▷HISTORY C16: from Medieval Latin *miscibilis,* from Latin *miscēre* to mix
▸ˌ**misciˈbility** NOUN

misconceive (ˌmɪskənˈsiːv) VERB to have the wrong idea; fail to understand.
▸ˌ**misconˈceiver** NOUN

misconceived (ˌmɪskənˈsiːvd) ADJECTIVE faultily or wrongly planned or based.

misconception (ˌmɪskənˈsɛpʃən) NOUN a false or mistaken view, opinion, or attitude.

misconduct NOUN (mɪsˈkɒndʌkt) 1 behaviour, such as adultery or professional negligence, that is regarded as immoral or unethical. ◆ VERB (ˌmɪskənˈdʌkt) (*tr*) 2 to conduct (oneself) in such a way. 3 to manage (something) badly.

misconstruction (ˌmɪskənˈstrʌkʃən) NOUN 1 a false interpretation of evidence, facts, etc. 2 a faulty construction, esp in grammar.

misconstrue (ˌmɪskənˈstruː) VERB **-strues, -struing, -strued.** (*tr*) to interpret mistakenly.

miscount (ˌmɪsˈkaʊnt) VERB 1 to count or calculate incorrectly. ◆ NOUN 2 a false count or calculation.

miscreance (ˈmɪskrɪəns) *or* **miscreancy** NOUN *Archaic* lack of religious belief or faith.

miscreant (ˈmɪskrɪənt) NOUN 1 a wrongdoer or villain. 2 *Archaic* an unbeliever or heretic. ◆ ADJECTIVE 3 evil or villainous. 4 *Archaic* unbelieving or heretical.
▷HISTORY C14: from Old French *mescreant* unbelieving, from *mes-* MIS-[1] + *creant,* ultimately from Latin *credere* to believe

miscreate VERB (ˌmɪskrɪˈeɪt) 1 to create (something) badly or incorrectly. ◆ ADJECTIVE (ˈmɪskrɪɪt, -ˌeɪt) 2 *Archaic* badly or unnaturally formed or made.
▸ˌ**miscreˈation** NOUN

miscue (ˌmɪsˈkjuː) NOUN 1 *Billiards* a faulty stroke in which the cue tip slips off the cue ball or misses it altogether. 2 *Informal* a blunder or mistake. ◆ VERB **-cues, -cuing, -cued.** 3 (*intr*) *Billiards* to make a miscue. 4 (*intr*) *Theatre* to fail to answer one's own cue or answer the cue of another. 5 *Radio* to start (a record or tape) at the wrong point. 6 (*intr*) *Informal* to blunder.

miscue analysis NOUN *Brit education* analysis of the errors a pupil makes while reading.

misdate (mɪsˈdeɪt) VERB (*tr*) to date (a letter, event, etc.) wrongly.

misdeal (ˌmɪsˈdiːl) VERB **-deals, -dealing, -dealt.** 1 (*intr*) to deal out cards incorrectly. ◆ NOUN 2 a faulty deal.
▸ˌ**misˈdealer** NOUN

misdeed (ˌmɪsˈdiːd) NOUN an evil or illegal action.

misdemean (ˌmɪsdɪˈmiːn) VERB a rare word for **misbehave.**

misdemeanant (ˌmɪsdɪˈmiːnənt) NOUN *Criminal law* (formerly) a person who has committed or been convicted of a misdemeanour. Compare **felon**[1].

misdemeanour *or US* **misdemeanor** (ˌmɪsdɪˈmiːnə) NOUN 1 *Criminal law* (formerly) an offence generally less heinous than a felony and which until 1967 involved a different form of trial. Compare **felony.** 2 any minor offence or transgression.

misdiagnose (ˌmɪsˈdaɪəgˌnəʊz) VERB (*tr*) to diagnose (an illness or problem) wrongly or mistakenly.

misdiagnosis (ˌmɪsdaɪəgˈnəʊsɪs) NOUN, *plural* **-ses** (-siːz). the act or an instance of misdiagnosing or being misdiagnosed.

misdirect (ˌmɪsdɪˈrɛkt) VERB (*tr*) 1 to give (a person) wrong directions or instructions. 2 to address (a letter, parcel, etc.) wrongly.
▸ˌ**misdiˈrection** NOUN

misdoubt (mɪsˈdaʊt) VERB an archaic word for **doubt** or **suspect.**

mise (miːz, maɪz) NOUN *Law* 1 the issue in the obsolete writ of right. 2 an agreed settlement.

▷HISTORY C15: from Old French: action of putting, from *mettre* to put

mise en place *French* (miz ɑ̃ plas) NOUN (in a restaurant kitchen) the preparation of equipment and food before service begins.

mise en scène *French* (miz ɑ̃ sɛn) NOUN 1 **a** the arrangement of properties, scenery, etc., in a play. **b** the objects so arranged; stage setting. 2 the environment of an event.

Miseno (*Italian* mi'zɛ:no) NOUN a cape in SW Italy, on the N shore of the Bay of Naples: remains of the town of **Misenum**, a naval base constructed by Agrippa in 31 B.C.

miser^{1} ('maɪzə) NOUN 1 a person who hoards money or possessions, often living miserably. 2 selfish person.
▷HISTORY C16: from Latin: wretched

miser^{2} ('maɪzə) NOUN *Civil engineering* a large hand-operated auger used for loose soils.
▷HISTORY C19: origin unknown

miserabilism ('mɪzərəbɪˌlɪzəm, 'mɪzrə-) *or* **miserablism** ('mɪzərəˌblɪzəm, 'mɪzrə-) NOUN the quality of seeming to enjoy being depressed, or the type of gloomy music, art, etc., that evokes this.

miserabilist ('mɪzərəbɪlɪst, 'mɪzrə-) *or* **miserabilist** ('mɪzərəblɪst, 'mɪzrə-) NOUN 1 a person who appears to enjoy being depressed, esp a performer of or listener to gloomy music. ◆ ADJECTIVE 2 of, resembling, or likely to be enjoyed by a miserabilist or miserabilists.

miserable ('mɪzərəbᵊl, 'mɪzrə-) ADJECTIVE 1 unhappy or depressed; wretched. 2 causing misery, discomfort, etc.: *a miserable life.* 3 contemptible: *a miserable villain.* 4 sordid or squalid: *miserable living conditions.* 5 *Scot, Austral, and NZ* mean; stingy. 6 (pejorative intensifier): *you miserable wretch.*
▷HISTORY C16: from Old French, from Latin *miserābilis* worthy of pity, from *miserārī* to pity, from *miser* wretched
▸**'miserableness** NOUN ▸**'miserably** ADVERB

misère (mɪ'zɛə) NOUN 1 a call in solo whist and other card games declaring a hand that will win no tricks. 2 a hand that will win no tricks.
▷HISTORY C19: from French: misery

miserere (ˌmɪzə'rɛərɪ, -'rɪərɪ) NOUN another word for **misericord** (sense 1).

Miserere (ˌmɪzə'rɛərɪ, -'rɪərɪ) NOUN the 51st psalm, the Latin version of which begins "Miserere mei, Deus" ("Have mercy on me, O God").

misericord *or* **misericorde** (mɪ'zɛrɪˌkɔ:d) NOUN 1 a ledge projecting from the underside of the hinged seat of a choir stall in a church, on which the occupant can support himself while standing. 2 *Christianity* **a** a relaxation of certain monastic rules for infirm or aged monks or nuns. **b** a monastery where such relaxations can be enjoyed. 3 a small medieval dagger used to give the death stroke to a wounded foe.
▷HISTORY C14: from Old French, from Latin *misericordia* compassion, from *miserēre* to pity + *cor* heart

miserly ('maɪzəlɪ) ADJECTIVE of or resembling a miser; avaricious.
▸**'miserliness** NOUN

misery ('mɪzərɪ) NOUN, *plural* **-eries.** 1 intense unhappiness, discomfort, or suffering; wretchedness. 2 a cause of such unhappiness, discomfort, etc. 3 squalid or poverty-stricken conditions. 4 *Brit informal* a person who is habitually depressed: *he is such a misery.* 5 *Dialect* a pain or ailment.
▷HISTORY C14: via Anglo-Norman from Latin *miseria,* from *miser* wretched

misfeasance (mɪs'fi:zəns) NOUN *Law* the improper performance of an act that is lawful in itself. Compare **malfeasance, nonfeasance.**
▷HISTORY C16: from Old French *mesfaisance,* from *mesfaire* to perform misdeeds
▸**mis'feasor** NOUN

misfile (ˌmɪs'faɪl) VERB to file (papers, records, etc.) wrongly.

misfire (ˌmɪs'faɪə) VERB (*intr*) 1 (of a firearm or its projectile) to fail to fire, explode, or ignite as or when expected. 2 (of a motor engine or vehicle, etc.) to fail to fire at the appropriate time, often causing a backfire. 3 to fail to operate or occur as intended. ◆ NOUN 4 the act or an instance of misfiring.

misfit NOUN ('mɪsˌfɪt) 1 a person not suited in behaviour or attitude to a particular social environment. 2 something that does not fit or fits badly. ◆ VERB (ˌmɪs'fɪt) **-fits, -fitting, -fitted.** (*intr*) 3 to fail to fit or be fitted.

misfortune (mɪs'fɔ:tʃən) NOUN 1 evil fortune; bad luck. 2 an unfortunate or disastrous event; calamity.

misgive (mɪs'gɪv) VERB **-gives, -giving, -gave, -given.** to make or be apprehensive or suspicious.

misgiving (mɪs'gɪvɪŋ) NOUN (*often plural*) a feeling of uncertainty, apprehension, or doubt.

misgovern (ˌmɪs'gʌvən) VERB to govern badly.
▸**ˌmis'government** NOUN ▸**ˌmis'governor** NOUN

misguide (ˌmɪs'gaɪd) VERB (*tr*) to guide or direct wrongly or badly.
▸**ˌmis'guidance** NOUN ▸**ˌmis'guider** NOUN

misguided (ˌmɪs'gaɪdɪd) ADJECTIVE foolish or unreasonable, esp in action or behaviour.
▸**ˌmis'guidedly** ADVERB

mishandle (ˌmɪs'hændᵊl) VERB (*tr*) to handle or treat badly or inefficiently.

mishap ('mɪshæp) NOUN 1 an unfortunate accident. 2 bad luck.

mishear (ˌmɪs'hɪə) VERB **-hears, -hearing, -heard.** to fail to hear correctly.

mishit *Sport* ◆ NOUN ('mɪsˌhɪt) 1 a faulty shot or stroke. ◆ VERB (ˌmɪs'hɪt) **-hits, -hitting, -hit.** 2 to hit (a ball) with a faulty stroke.

mishmash ('mɪʃˌmæʃ) NOUN a confused collection or mixture; hotchpotch.
▷HISTORY C15: reduplication of MASH

Mishmi ('mɪʃmɪ) NOUN 1 (*plural* **-mi** *or* **-mis**) a member of a Mongoloid hill people of the Brahmaputra area of NE India. 2 the language of this people, belonging to the Tibeto-Burman branch of the Sino-Tibetan family. ◆ ADJECTIVE 3 of or relating to this people or their language.

Mishna ('mɪʃnə; *Hebrew* miʃ'na) NOUN, *plural* **Mishnayoth** (mɪʃ'nɑ:jəʊt; *Hebrew* miʃna'jɔt). *Judaism* a compilation of precepts passed down as an oral tradition and collected by Judah ha-Nasi in the late second century A.D. It forms the earlier part of the Talmud. See also **Gemara.**
▷HISTORY C17: from Hebrew: instruction by repetition, from *shānāh* to repeat
▸**Mishnaic** (mɪʃ'neɪɪk) ▸**'Mishnic** *or* **'Mishnical** ADJECTIVE

misinform (ˌmɪsɪn'fɔ:m) VERB (*tr*) to give incorrect information to.
▸**ˌmisin'formant** *or* **ˌmisin'former** NOUN ▸**misinformation** (ˌmɪsɪnfə'meɪʃən) NOUN

misinterpret (ˌmɪsɪn'tɜ:prɪt) VERB (*tr*) to interpret badly, misleadingly, or incorrectly.
▸**ˌmisinˌterpre'tation** NOUN ▸**ˌmisin'terpreter** NOUN

misjoinder (mɪs'dʒɔɪndə) NOUN *Law* the improper joining of parties as coplaintiffs or codefendants or of different causes of action in one suit. Compare **nonjoinder.**

misjudge (ˌmɪs'dʒʌdʒ) VERB to judge (a person or persons) wrongly or unfairly.
▸**ˌmis'judger** NOUN ▸**ˌmis'judgment** *or* **ˌmis'judgement** NOUN

Miskolc (*Hungarian* 'miʃkolts) NOUN a city in NE Hungary: the second most important industrial centre in Hungary; iron and steel industries. Pop.: 172 357 (2000 est.).

mislay (mɪs'leɪ) VERB **-lays, -laying, -laid.** (*tr*) 1 to lose (something) temporarily, esp by forgetting where it is. 2 to lay (something) badly.
▸**mis'layer** NOUN

mislead (mɪs'li:d) VERB **-leads, -leading, -led.** (*tr*) 1 to give false or misleading information to. 2 to lead or guide in the wrong direction.
▸**mis'leader** NOUN

misleading (mɪs'li:dɪŋ) ADJECTIVE tending to confuse or mislead; deceptive.
▸**mis'leadingly** ADVERB

mislike (mɪs'laɪk) *Archaic* ◆ VERB (*tr*) 1 to dislike. ◆ NOUN *also* **misliking.** 2 dislike or aversion.
▸**mis'liker** NOUN

mismanage (ˌmɪs'mænɪdʒ) VERB (*tr*) to manage badly or wrongly.
▸**ˌmis'management** NOUN ▸**ˌmis'manager** NOUN

mismatch (ˌmɪs'mætʃ) VERB 1 to match badly, esp in marriage. ◆ NOUN 2 a bad or inappropriate match.

misnomer (ˌmɪs'nəʊmə) NOUN 1 an incorrect or unsuitable name or term for a person or thing. 2 the act of referring to a person by the wrong name.
▷HISTORY C15: via Anglo-Norman from Old French *mesnommer* to misname, from Latin *nōmināre* to call by name

miso ('mi:səʊ) NOUN a thick brown salty paste made from soya beans, used to flavour savoury dishes, esp soups.
▷HISTORY from Japanese

miso- *or before a vowel* **mis-** COMBINING FORM indicating hatred: *misogyny.*
▷HISTORY from Greek *misos* hatred

misogamy (mɪ'sɒgəmɪ, maɪ-) NOUN hatred of marriage.
▸**mi'sogamist** NOUN

misogyny (mɪ'sɒdʒɪnɪ, maɪ-) NOUN hatred of women.
▷HISTORY C17: from Greek, from MISO- + *gunē* woman
▸**mi'sogynist** NOUN, ADJECTIVE ▸**miˌsogy'nistic** *or* **mi'sogynous** ADJECTIVE

misology (mɪ'sɒlədʒɪ, maɪ-) NOUN hatred of reasoning or reasoned argument.
▷HISTORY C19: from Greek *misologia,* from *misos* hatred + *logos* word, reasoning. See LOGOS
▸**mi'sologist** NOUN

misoneism (ˌmɪsəʊ'ni:ˌɪzəm, ˌmaɪ-) NOUN hatred of anything new.
▷HISTORY C19: from Italian *misoneismo;* see MISO-, NEO-, -ISM
▸**ˌmiso'neist** NOUN ▸**ˌmisone'istic** ADJECTIVE

mispickel ('mɪsˌpɪkᵊl) NOUN another name for **arsenopyrite.**
▷HISTORY C17: from German

misplace (ˌmɪs'pleɪs) VERB (*tr*) 1 to put (something) in the wrong place, esp to lose (something) temporarily by forgetting where it was placed; mislay. 2 (*often passive*) to bestow (trust, confidence, affection, etc.) unadvisedly.
▸**ˌmis'placement** NOUN

misplaced modifier NOUN *Grammar* a participle intended to modify a noun but having the wrong grammatical relationship to it as for example *having left* in the sentence *Having left Europe for good, Peter's future seemed bleak indeed.* Usual US and Canadian name: **dangling participle.**

misplay (ˌmɪs'pleɪ) VERB 1 (*tr*) to play badly or wrongly in games or sports: *the batsman misplayed the ball.* ◆ NOUN 2 a wrong or unskilful play.

misplead (mɪs'pli:d) VERB **-pleads, -pleading, -pleaded, -plead** (-'plɛd) *or* **-pled.** (*tr*) to plead incorrectly.

mispleading (mɪs'pli:dɪŋ) NOUN *Law* an error or omission in pleading.

misprint NOUN ('mɪsˌprɪnt) 1 an error in printing, made through damaged type, careless reading, etc. ◆ VERB (ˌmɪs'prɪnt) 2 (*tr*) to print (a letter) incorrectly.

misprision^{1} (mɪs'prɪʒən) NOUN **a** a failure to inform the proper authorities of the commission of an act of treason. **b** the deliberate concealment of the commission of a felony.
▷HISTORY C15: via Anglo-French from Old French *mesprision* error, from *mesprendre* to mistake, from *mes-* MIS-^{1} + *prendre* to take

misprision^{2} (mɪs'prɪʒən) NOUN *Archaic* 1 contempt. 2 failure to appreciate the value of something.
▷HISTORY C16: from MISPRIZE

misprize *or* **misprise** (mɪs'praɪz) VERB to fail to appreciate the value of; undervalue or disparage.
▷HISTORY C15: from Old French *mesprisier,* from *mes-* MIS-^{1} + *prisier* to PRIZE^{2}

mispronounce (ˌmɪsprə'naʊns) VERB to pronounce (a word) wrongly.
▸**mispronunciation** (ˌmɪsprəˌnʌnsɪ'eɪʃən) NOUN

misquote (ˌmɪs'kwəʊt) VERB to quote (a text, speech, etc.) inaccurately.
▸**ˌmisquo'tation** NOUN

misread (ˌmɪs'ri:d) VERB **-reads, -reading, -read** (-'rɛd). (*tr*) 1 to read incorrectly. 2 to misinterpret.

misreport (ˌmɪsrɪ'pɔ:t) VERB 1 (*tr*) to report

falsely or inaccurately. ◆ NOUN [2] an inaccurate or false report.
▸ ˌmisreˈporter NOUN

misrepresent (ˌmɪsrɛprɪˈzɛnt) VERB (*tr*) to represent wrongly or inaccurately.
▸ ˌmisrepresenˈtation NOUN ▸ ˌmisrepreˈsentative ADJECTIVE ▸ ˌmisrepreˈsenter NOUN

misrule (ˌmɪsˈruːl) VERB [1] (*tr*) to govern inefficiently or without humanity or justice. ◆ NOUN [2] inefficient or inhumane government. [3] disorder.

miss[1] (mɪs) VERB [1] to fail to reach, hit, meet, find, or attain (some specified or implied aim, goal, target, etc.). [2] (*tr*) to fail to attend or be present for: *to miss a train; to miss an appointment.* [3] (*tr*) to fail to see, hear, understand, or perceive: *to miss a point.* [4] (*tr*) to lose, overlook, or fail to take advantage of: *to miss an opportunity.* [5] (*tr*) to leave out; omit: *to miss an entry in a list.* [6] (*tr*) to discover or regret the loss or absence of: *he missed his watch; she missed him.* [7] (*tr*) to escape or avoid (something, esp a danger), usually narrowly: *he missed death by inches.* [8] **miss the boat** *or* **bus.** to lose an opportunity. ◆ NOUN [9] a failure to reach, hit, meet, find, etc. [10] **give (something) a miss.** *Informal* to avoid (something): *give the lecture a miss; give the pudding a miss.* ◆ See also **miss out**.
▷HISTORY Old English *missan* (meaning: to fail to hit); related to Old High German *missan,* Old Norse *missa*
▸ ˈmissable ADJECTIVE

miss[2] (mɪs) NOUN *Informal* an unmarried woman or girl, esp a schoolgirl.
▷HISTORY C17: shortened form of MISTRESS

Miss (mɪs) NOUN a title of an unmarried woman or girl, usually used before the surname or sometimes alone in direct address.
▷HISTORY C17: shortened from MISTRESS

Miss. ABBREVIATION FOR Mississippi.

missal (ˈmɪsᵊl) NOUN *RC Church* a book containing the prayers, rites, etc., of the Masses for a complete year.
▷HISTORY C14: from Church Latin *missale* (n), from *missālis* concerning the MASS

mis-sell VERB, *plural* **-sells, -selling, -sold.** to sell a financial product that is inappropriate for the needs of the customer.

missel thrush (ˈmɪsᵊl) NOUN a variant spelling of **mistle thrush.**

misshape VERB (ˌmɪsˈʃeɪp) **-shapes, -shaping, -shaped, -shaped** *or* **-shapen.** (*tr*) [1] to shape badly; deform. ◆ NOUN (ˈmɪsˌʃeɪp) [2] something that is badly shaped.

misshapen (ˌmɪsˈʃeɪpᵊn) ADJECTIVE badly shaped; deformed.
▸ ˌmisˈshapenly ADVERB ▸ ˌmisˈshapenness NOUN

missile (ˈmɪsaɪl) NOUN [1] any object or weapon that is thrown at a target or shot from an engine, gun, etc. [2] **a** a rocket-propelled weapon that flies either in a fixed trajectory (**ballistic missile**) or in a trajectory that can be controlled during flight (**guided missile**). **b** (*as modifier*): *a missile carrier.*
▷HISTORY C17: from Latin: *missilis,* from *mittere* to send

missileer (ˌmɪsaɪˈlɪə) NOUN a serviceman or servicewoman who is responsible for firing missiles.

missilery *or* **missilry** (ˈmɪsaɪlrɪ) NOUN [1] missiles collectively. [2] the design, operation, or study of missiles.

missing (ˈmɪsɪŋ) ADJECTIVE [1] not present; absent or lost. [2] not able to be traced and not known to be dead: *nine men were missing after the attack.* [3] **go missing.** to become lost or disappear.

missing fundamental NOUN a tone, not present in the sound received by the ear, whose pitch is that of the difference between the two tones that are sounded.

missing link NOUN [1] (*sometimes capitals;* usually preceded by *the*) a hypothetical extinct animal or animal group, formerly thought to be intermediate between the anthropoid apes and man. [2] any missing section or part in an otherwise complete series.

missiology (ˌmɪsɪˈɒlədʒɪ) NOUN *Christian theol* the study of the missionary function of the Christian Church.

mission (ˈmɪʃən) NOUN [1] a specific task or duty assigned to a person or group of people: *their mission was to irrigate the desert.* [2] a person's vocation (often in the phrase **mission in life**). [3] a group of persons representing or working for a particular country, business, etc., in a foreign country. [4] **a** a special embassy sent to a foreign country for a specific purpose. **b** *US* a permanent legation. [5] **a** a group of people sent by a religious body, esp a Christian church, to a foreign country to do religious and social work. **b** the campaign undertaken by such a group. [6] **a** the work or calling of a missionary. **b** a building or group of buildings in which missionary work is performed. **c** the area assigned to a particular missionary. [7] the dispatch of aircraft or spacecraft to achieve a particular task. [8] a church or chapel that has no incumbent of its own. [9] a charitable centre that offers shelter, aid, or advice to the destitute or underprivileged. [10] (*modifier*) of or relating to an ecclesiastical mission: *a mission station.* [11] *South African* a long and difficult process. [12] (*modifier*) *US* (of furniture) in the style of the early Spanish missions of the southwestern US. ◆ VERB [13] (*tr*) to direct a mission to or establish a mission in (a given region).
▷HISTORY C16: from Latin *missiō,* from *mittere* to send

missionary (ˈmɪʃənərɪ) NOUN, *plural* **-aries.** [1] a member of a religious mission. ◆ ADJECTIVE [2] of or relating to missionaries: *missionary work.* [3] resulting from a desire to convert people to one's own beliefs: *missionary zeal.*

missionary position NOUN *Informal* a position for sexual intercourse in which the man lies on top of the woman and they are face to face.
▷HISTORY C20: from the belief that missionaries advocated this as the proper position to primitive peoples among whom it was unknown

Missionary Ridge NOUN a ridge in NW Georgia and SE Tennessee: site of a battle (1863) during the Civil War: Northern victory leading to the campaign in Georgia.

mission creep NOUN the tendency for a task, esp a military operation, to become unintentionally wider in scope than its initial objectives.

missioner (ˈmɪʃənə) NOUN [1] a less common name for **missionary.** [2] a person heading a parochial mission in a Christian country.

mission statement NOUN an official statement of the aims and objectives of a business or other organization.

missis (ˈmɪsɪz, -ɪs) NOUN a variant spelling of **missus.**

Mississauga (ˌmɪsəˈsɔːgə) NOUN a town in SE Ontario: a SW suburb of Toronto. Pop.: 463 388 (1991).

Mississippi (ˌmɪsɪˈsɪpɪ) NOUN [1] a state of the southeastern US, on the Gulf of Mexico: consists of a largely forested undulating plain, with swampy regions in the northwest and on the coast, the Mississippi River forming the W border; cotton, rice, and oil. Capital: Jackson. Pop.: 2 844 658 (2000). Area: 122 496 sq. km (47 296 sq. miles). Abbreviations: **Miss,** (with zip code) **MS.** [2] a river in the central US, rising in NW Minnesota and flowing generally south to the Gulf of Mexico through several mouths, known as the Passes: the second longest river in North America (after its tributary, the Missouri), with the third largest drainage basin in the world (after the Amazon and the Congo). Length: 3780 km (2348 miles).

Mississippian (ˌmɪsɪˈsɪpɪən) ADJECTIVE [1] of or relating to the state of Mississippi or the Mississippi River. [2] (in North America) of, denoting, or formed in the lower of two subdivisions of the Carboniferous period (see also **Pennsylvanian** (sense 2)), which lasted for 30 million years. ◆ NOUN [3] an inhabitant or native of the state of Mississippi. [4] **the.** the Mississippian period or rock system equivalent to the lower Carboniferous of Europe.

missive (ˈmɪsɪv) NOUN [1] a formal or official letter. [2] a formal word for **letter.** ◆ ADJECTIVE [3] *Rare* sent or intended to be sent.
▷HISTORY C15: from Medieval Latin *missivus,* from *mittere* to send

Missolonghi (ˌmɪsəˈlɒŋgɪ) *or* **Mesolonghi** NOUN a town in W Greece, near the Gulf of Patras: famous for its defence against the Turks in 1822–23 and 1825–26 and for its association with Lord Byron, who died here in 1824. Pop.: 11 275 (latest est.). Modern Greek name: **Mesolóngion.**

Missouri (mɪˈzʊərɪ) NOUN [1] a state of the central US: consists of rolling prairies in the north, the Ozark Mountains in the south, and part of the Mississippi flood plain in the southeast, with the Mississippi forming the E border; chief US producer of lead and barytes. Capital: Jefferson City. Pop.: 5 595 211 (2000). Area: 178 699 sq. km (68 995 sq. miles). Abbreviations: **Mo,** (with zip code) **MO.** [2] a river in the W and central US, rising in SW Montana: flows north, east, and southeast to join the Mississippi above St Louis; the longest river in North America; chief tributary of the Mississippi. Length: 3970 km (2466 miles).

Missourian (mɪˈzʊərɪən) NOUN [1] a native or inhabitant of Missouri. ◆ ADJECTIVE [2] of or relating to Missouri or its inhabitants.

miss out VERB [1] (*tr, adverb*) to leave out; overlook. [2] (*intr, adverb;* often foll by *on*) to fail to experience: *by leaving early you missed out on the celebrations.*

misspell (ˌmɪsˈspɛl) VERB **-spells, -spelling, -spelt** *or* **-spelled.** to spell (a word or words) wrongly.

misspelling (ˌmɪsˈspɛlɪŋ) NOUN a wrong spelling.

misspend (ˌmɪsˈspɛnd) VERB **-spends, -spending, -spent.** to spend thoughtlessly or wastefully.
▸ ˌmisˈspender NOUN

misstate (ˌmɪsˈsteɪt) VERB (*tr*) to state incorrectly.
▸ ˌmisˈstatement NOUN

misstep (ˌmɪsˈstɛp) NOUN [1] a false step. [2] an error.

missus *or* **missis** (ˈmɪsɪz, -ɪs) NOUN [1] (usually preceded by *the*) *Informal* one's wife or the wife of the person addressed or referred to. [2] an informal term of address for a woman.
▷HISTORY C19: spoken version of MISTRESS

missy (ˈmɪsɪ) NOUN, *plural* **missies.** *Informal* an affectionate or sometimes disparaging form of address to a young girl.

mist (mɪst) NOUN [1] a thin fog resulting from condensation in the air near the earth's surface. [2] *Meteorol* such an atmospheric condition with a horizontal visibility of 1–2 kilometres. [3] a fine spray of any liquid, such as that produced by an aerosol container. [4] *Chem* a colloidal suspension of a liquid in a gas. [5] condensed water vapour on a surface that blurs the surface. [6] something that causes haziness or lack of clarity, such as a film of tears. ◆ VERB [7] to cover or be covered with or as if with mist.
▷HISTORY Old English; related to Middle Dutch, Swedish *mist,* Greek *omikhlē* fog

mistakable *or* **mistakeable** (mɪˈsteɪkəbᵊl) ADJECTIVE liable to be mistaken.
▸ misˈtakably *or* misˈtakeably ADVERB

mistake (mɪˈsteɪk) NOUN [1] an error or blunder in action, opinion, or judgment. [2] a misconception or misunderstanding. ◆ VERB **-takes, -taking, -took, -taken.** [3] (*tr*) to misunderstand; misinterpret: *she mistook his meaning.* [4] (*tr;* foll by *for*) to take (for), interpret (as), or confuse (with): *she mistook his direct manner for honesty.* [5] (*tr*) to choose badly or incorrectly: *he mistook his path.* [6] (*intr*) to make a mistake in action, opinion, judgment, etc.
▷HISTORY C13 (meaning: to do wrong, err): from Old Norse *mistaka* to take erroneously
▸ misˈtaker NOUN

mistaken (mɪˈsteɪkən) ADJECTIVE [1] (*usually predicative*) wrong in opinion, judgment, etc.: *she is mistaken.* [2] arising from error in judgment, opinion, etc.: *a mistaken viewpoint.*
▸ misˈtakenly ADVERB ▸ misˈtakenness NOUN

mistal (ˈmɪstəl) NOUN *Dialect* a cow shed; byre.
▷HISTORY C17: of uncertain origin

Mistassini (ˌmɪstəˈsiːnɪ) NOUN **Lake.** a lake in E Canada, in N Quebec: the largest lake in the province; drains through the Rupert River into James Bay. Area: 2175 sq. km (840 sq. miles). Length: about 160 km (100 miles).

mister (ˈmɪstə) (*sometimes capital*) NOUN [1] an informal form of address for a man. [2] *Naval* **a** the official form of address for subordinate or senior warrant officers. **b** the official form of address for all officers in a merchant ship, other than the captain. **c** *US Navy* the official form of address used by the commanding officer to his officers, esp to

the more junior. 3 *Brit* the form of address for a surgeon. 4 the form of address for officials holding certain positions: *mister chairman.* ◆ VERB 5 (*tr*) *Informal* to call (someone) mister.
▷HISTORY C16: variant of MASTER

Mister (ˈmɪstə) NOUN the full form of **Mr.**

Misti (*Spanish* ˈmisti) NOUN See **El Misti.**

mistigris (ˈmɪstɪgriː) NOUN 1 the joker or a blank card used as a wild card in a variety of draw poker. 2 the variety of draw poker using this card.
▷HISTORY C19: from French *mistigris* jack of clubs, game in which this card was wild

mistime (ˌmɪsˈtaɪm) VERB (*tr*) to time (an action, utterance, etc.) wrongly.

misting (ˈmɪstɪŋ) NOUN the act or an instance of having an artificial suntan applied to the skin by a fine spray of liquid.

mistle thrush *or* **missel thrush** (ˈmɪsᵊl) NOUN a large European thrush, *Turdus viscivorus,* with a brown back and spotted breast, noted for feeding on mistletoe berries.
▷HISTORY C18: from Old English *mistel* MISTLETOE

mistletoe (ˈmɪsᵊlˌtəʊ) NOUN 1 a Eurasian evergreen shrub, *Viscum album,* with leathery leaves, yellowish flowers, and waxy white berries: grows as a partial parasite on various trees: used as a Christmas decoration: family *Viscaceae.* 2 any of several similar and related American plants in the families *Loranthaceae* or *Viscaceae*, esp *Phoradendron flavescens.* 3 **mistletoe cactus.** an epiphytic cactus, *Rhipsalis cassytha,* that grows in tropical America.
▷HISTORY Old English *misteltān,* from *mistel* mistletoe + *tān* twig; related to Old Norse *mistilteinn*

mistletoe bird NOUN a small Australian flower-pecker, *Dicaeum hirundinaceum,* that feeds on mistletoe berries.

mistook (mɪˈstʊk) VERB the past tense of **mistake.**

mistral (ˈmɪstrəl, mɪˈstrɑːl) NOUN a strong cold dry wind that blows through the Rhône valley and S France to the Mediterranean coast, mainly in the winter.
▷HISTORY C17: via French from Provençal, from Latin *magistrālis* MAGISTRAL, as in *magistrālis ventus* master wind

mistreat (ˌmɪsˈtriːt) VERB (*tr*) to treat badly.
▸ˌ**misˈtreatment** NOUN

mistress (ˈmɪstrɪs) NOUN 1 a woman who has a continuing extramarital sexual relationship with a man. 2 a woman in a position of authority, ownership, or control, such as the head of a household. 3 a woman or female personification having control over something specified: *she was mistress of her own destiny.* 4 *Chiefly Brit* short for **schoolmistress.** 5 an archaic or dialect word for **sweetheart.**
▷HISTORY C14: from Old French; see MASTER, -ESS

Mistress (ˈmɪstrɪs) NOUN an archaic or dialect title equivalent to **Mrs.**

Mistress of the Robes NOUN (in Britain) a lady of high rank in charge of the Queen's wardrobe.

mistrial (mɪsˈtraɪəl) NOUN 1 a trial made void because of some error, such as a defect in procedure. 2 (in the US) an inconclusive trial, as when a jury cannot agree on a verdict.

mistrust (ˌmɪsˈtrʌst) VERB 1 to have doubts or suspicions about (someone or something). ◆ NOUN 2 distrust.
▸ˌ**misˈtruster** NOUN ▸ˌ**misˈtrustful** ADJECTIVE ▸ˌ**misˈtrustfully** ADVERB ▸ˌ**misˈtrustfulness** NOUN

misty (ˈmɪstɪ) ADJECTIVE **mistier, mistiest.** 1 consisting of or resembling mist. 2 obscured by or as if by mist. 3 indistinct; blurred: *the misty past.*
▸ˈ**mistily** ADVERB ▸ˈ**mistiness** NOUN

misunderstand (ˌmɪsʌndəˈstænd) VERB **-stands, -standing, -stood.** to fail to understand properly.

misunderstanding (ˌmɪsʌndəˈstændɪŋ) NOUN 1 a failure to understand properly. 2 a disagreement.

misunderstood (ˌmɪsʌndəˈstʊd) ADJECTIVE not properly or sympathetically understood: *a misunderstood work of art; a misunderstood adolescent.*

misuse NOUN (ˌmɪsˈjuːs) *also* **misusage.** 1 erroneous, improper, or unorthodox use: *misuse of words.* 2 cruel or inhumane treatment. ◆ VERB (ˌmɪsˈjuːz) (*tr*) 3 to use wrongly. 4 to treat badly or harshly.

misuser (ˌmɪsˈjuːzə) NOUN *Law* an abuse of some right, privilege, office, etc., such as one that may lead to its forfeiture.
▷HISTORY C17: from Old French *mesuser* (infinitive used as noun)

MIT ABBREVIATION FOR Massachusetts Institute of Technology.

mitch *or* **mich** (mɪtʃ) VERB (*intr*) *Dialect* to play truant from school.
▷HISTORY C13: probably from Old French *muchier, mucier* to hide, lurk

mite[1] (maɪt) NOUN any of numerous small free-living or parasitic arachnids of the order *Acarina* (or *Acari*) that can occur in terrestrial or aquatic habitats. See also **gall mite, harvest mite, itch mite, spider mite.** Related adjective: **acaroid.** Compare **tick**[2].
▷HISTORY Old English *mīte;* compare Old High German *mīza* gnat, Dutch *mijt*

mite[2] (maɪt) NOUN 1 a very small particle, creature, or object. 2 a very small contribution or sum of money. See also **widow's mite.** 3 a former Flemish coin of small value. 4 **a mite.** *Informal* somewhat: *he's a mite foolish.*
▷HISTORY C14: from Middle Low German, Middle Dutch *mīte;* compare MITE[1]

miter (ˈmaɪtə) NOUN, VERB the usual US spelling of **mitre.**

miterwort (ˈmaɪtəˌwɜːt) NOUN the US spelling of **mitrewort.**

mither[1] (ˈmɪðər) NOUN a Scot word for **mother**[1].

mither[2] (ˈmaɪðə) VERB (*intr*) *Northern English dialect* to fuss over or moan about something.
▷HISTORY C17: of unknown origin

Mithgarthr (ˈmɪðˌgɑːðə) NOUN a variant of **Midgard.**

Mithraism (ˈmɪθreɪˌɪzəm) *or* **Mithraicism** (mɪθˈreɪɪˌsɪzəm) NOUN the ancient Persian religion of Mithras. It spread to the Roman Empire during the first three centuries A.D.
▸**Mithraic** (mɪθˈreɪɪk) *or* ˌ**Mithraˈistic** ADJECTIVE
▸ˈ**Mithraist** NOUN, ADJECTIVE

Mithras (ˈmɪθræs) *or* **Mithra** (ˈmɪθrə) NOUN *Persian myth* the god of light, identified with the sun, who slew a primordial bull and fertilized the world with its blood.

mithridate (ˈmɪθrɪˌdeɪt) NOUN *Obsolete* a substance believed to be an antidote to every poison and a cure for every disease.
▷HISTORY C16: from Late Latin *mithradatium,* after *Mithridates* VI (?132–63 B.C.), king of Pontus, alluding to his legendary immunity to poisons

mithridatism (ˈmɪθrɪdeɪˌtɪzəm) NOUN immunity to large doses of poison by prior ingestion of gradually increased doses.
▸**mithridatic** (ˌmɪθrɪˈdætɪk, -ˈdeɪ-) ADJECTIVE

miticide (ˈmɪtɪˌsaɪd) NOUN any drug or agent that destroys mites.
▸ˌ**mitiˈcidal** ADJECTIVE

mitigate (ˈmɪtɪˌgeɪt) VERB to make or become less severe or harsh; moderate.
▷HISTORY C15: from Latin *mītigāre,* from *mītis* mild + *agere* to make
▸**mitigable** (ˈmɪtɪgəbᵊl) ADJECTIVE ▸ˌ**mitiˈgation** NOUN
▸ˈ**mitiˌgative** *or* ˈ**mitiˌgatory** ADJECTIVE ▸ˈ**mitiˌgator** NOUN

> **Language note** *Mitigate* is sometimes wrongly used where *militate* is meant: *his behaviour militates* (not *mitigates*) *against his chances of promotion.*

mitigating circumstances PLURAL NOUN circumstances that may be considered to lessen the culpability of an offender.

Mitilíni (mitiˈlini) NOUN transliteration of the Modern Greek name for **Mytilene** (sense 1).

mitis (ˈmaɪtɪs, ˈmiː-) *or* **mitis metal** NOUN a malleable iron, fluid enough for casting, made by adding a small amount of aluminium to wrought iron.
▷HISTORY C19: from Latin: soft

Mitnaged (ˌmitnɑˈged) *or* **Misnaged** (misˈnɑged) NOUN, *plural* **Mitnagdim** (ˌmitnɑgˈdim) *or* **Misnagdim** (misˈnɑgdim). *Judaism* an orthodox opponent of Chassidism. See **Chassid.**
▷HISTORY from Hebrew, literally: opponent

mitochondrial DNA NOUN DNA found in mitochondria, which contains some structural genes and is generally inherited only through the female line.

mitochondrion (ˌmaɪtəʊˈkɒndrɪən) NOUN, *plural* **-dria** (-drɪə). a small spherical or rodlike body, bounded by a double membrane, in the cytoplasm of most cells: contains enzymes responsible for energy production. Also called: **chondriosome.**
▷HISTORY C19: New Latin, from Greek *mitos* thread + *khondrion* small grain
▸ˌ**mitoˈchondrial** ADJECTIVE

mitogen (ˈmaɪtədʒən) NOUN any agent that induces mitosis.
▸**mitogenic** (ˌmaɪtəʊˈdʒenɪk) ADJECTIVE

mitosis (maɪˈtəʊsɪs, mɪ-) NOUN a method of cell division, in which the nucleus divides into daughter nuclei, each containing the same number of chromosomes as the parent nucleus. See **prophase, metaphase, anaphase, telophase.** Compare **meiosis** (sense 1).
▷HISTORY C19: from New Latin, from Greek *mitos* thread
▸**mitotic** (maɪˈtɒtɪk, mɪ-) ADJECTIVE ▸**miˈtotically** ADVERB

mitrailleuse (ˌmɪtraɪˈɜːz) NOUN 1 an early form of breech-loading machine gun having several parallel barrels. 2 any French machine gun.
▷HISTORY C19: from French, from *mitraille* small shot, from Old French *mistraille* pieces of money, from MITE[2]

mitral (ˈmaɪtrəl) ADJECTIVE 1 of or like a mitre. 2 *Anatomy* of or relating to the mitral valve.

mitral valve NOUN the valve between the left atrium and the left ventricle of the heart, consisting of two membranous flaps, that prevents regurgitation of blood into the atrium. Also called: **bicuspid valve.**

mitre *or US* **miter** (ˈmaɪtə) NOUN 1 *Christianity* the liturgical headdress of a bishop or abbot, in most western churches consisting of a tall pointed cleft cap with two bands hanging down at the back. 2 short for **mitre joint.** 3 a bevelled surface of a mitre joint. 4 (in sewing) a diagonal join where the hems along two sides meet at a corner of the fabric. ◆ VERB (*tr*) 5 to make a mitre joint between (two pieces of material, esp wood). 6 to make a mitre in (a fabric). 7 to confer a mitre upon: *a mitred abbot.*
▷HISTORY C14: from Old French, from Latin *mitra,* from Greek *mitra* turban

mitre block NOUN a block of wood with slots for cutting mitre joints with a saw.

mitre box NOUN an open-ended box with sides having narrow slots to guide a saw in cutting mitre joints.

mitre gear NOUN one of a pair of similar bevel gears or shafts at right angles to each other having a pitch cone angle of 45°.

mitre joint NOUN a corner joint formed between two pieces of material, esp wood, by cutting bevels of equal angles at the ends of each piece. Sometimes shortened to: **mitre.**

mitre square NOUN a tool with two blades that are at a fixed angle to one another, used to bevel a mitre joint.

mitrewort *or US* **miterwort** (ˈmaɪtəˌwɜːt) NOUN any of several Asian and North American saxifragaceous plants of the genus *Mitella,* having clusters of small white flowers and capsules resembling a bishop's mitre. Also called: **bishop's-cap.**

mitt (mɪt) NOUN 1 any of various glovelike hand coverings, such as one that does not cover the fingers. 2 short for **mitten** (sense 1). 3 *Baseball* a large round thickly padded leather mitten worn by the catcher. See also **glove** (sense 2). 4 (*often plural*) a slang word for **hand.** 5 *Slang* a boxing glove.
▷HISTORY C18: shortened from MITTEN

Mittelland Canal (*German* ˈmɪtəllant) NOUN a canal in Germany, linking the Rivers Rhine and Elbe. Length: 325 km (202 miles).

mitten (ˈmɪtᵊn) NOUN 1 a glove having one section for the thumb and a single section for the other fingers. Sometimes shortened to **mitt.** 2 *Slang* a boxing glove.
▷HISTORY C14: from Old French *mitaine,* of uncertain origin

mittimus (ˈmɪtɪməs) NOUN, *plural* **-muses.** *Law* a

warrant of commitment to prison or a command to a jailer directing him to hold someone in prison.
▷**HISTORY** C15: from Latin: we send, the first word of such a command

Mitty ('mɪtɪ) NOUN **Walter. a** a fictional character given to grand and elaborate fantasies; daydreamer. **b** (*as modifier*): *a Walter Mitty character; a Mitty act.*
▷**HISTORY** C20: from a short story *The Secret Life of Walter Mitty* (1939), by James Thurber (1894–1961), the US humorist and illustrator
▸ **ˌMitty'esque** *or* **'Mitty-ˌlike** ADJECTIVE

mitzvah ('mɪtsvə; *Hebrew* mits'vɑ) NOUN, *plural* **-vahs** *or* **-voth** (*Hebrew* -'vɔt). *Judaism* 1 a commandment or precept, esp one found in the Bible. 2 a good deed.
▷**HISTORY** from Hebrew: commandment

mix (mɪks) VERB 1 (*tr*) to combine or blend (ingredients, liquids, objects, etc.) together into one mass. 2 (*intr*) to become or have the capacity to become combined, joined, etc.: *some chemicals do not mix.* 3 (*tr*) to form (something) by combining two or more constituents: *to mix cement.* 4 (*tr; often foll by in or into*) to add as an additional part or element (to a mass or compound): *to mix flour into a batter.* 5 (*tr*) to do at the same time; combine: *to mix study and pleasure.* 6 (*tr*) to consume (drinks or foods) in close succession. 7 to come or cause to come into association socially: *Pauline has never mixed well.* 8 (*intr; often foll by with*) to go together; complement. 9 (*tr*) to crossbreed (differing strains of plants or breeds of livestock), esp more or less at random. 10 (*tr*) *Electronics* to combine (two or more signals). 11 *Music* **a** (in sound recording) to balance and adjust (the recorded tracks) on a multitrack tape machine. **b** (in live performance) to balance and adjust (the output levels from microphones and pick-ups). 12 (*tr*) to merge (two lengths of film) so that the effect is imperceptible. 13 **mix it.** *Informal* **a** to cause mischief or trouble, often for a person named: *she tried to mix it for John.* **b** to fight. ◆ NOUN 14 the act or an instance of mixing. 15 the result of mixing; mixture. 16 a mixture of ingredients, esp one commercially prepared for making a cake, bread, etc. 17 *Music* the sound obtained by mixing. 18 *Building trades, civil engineering* the proportions of cement, sand, and aggregate in mortar, plaster, or concrete. 19 *Informal* a state of confusion, bewilderment. ◆ See also **mix-up**.
▷**HISTORY** C15: back formation from *mixt* mixed, via Old French from Latin *mixtus*, from *miscēre* to mix
▸ **'mixable** ADJECTIVE ▸ **ˌmixa'bility** NOUN

mixdown ('mɪksˌdaʊn) NOUN (in sound recording) the transfer of a multitrack master mix to two-track stereo tape.

mixed (mɪkst) ADJECTIVE 1 formed or blended together by mixing. 2 composed of different elements, races, sexes, etc.: *a mixed school.* 3 consisting of conflicting elements, thoughts, attitudes, etc.: *mixed feelings; mixed motives.* 4 (of a legal action) **a** having the nature of both a real and a personal action, such as a demand for the return of wrongfully withheld property as well as for damages to compensate for the loss. **b** having aspects or issues determinable by different persons or bodies: *a mixed question of law and fact.* 5 (of an inflorescence) containing cymose and racemose branches. 6 (of a nerve) containing both motor and sensory nerve fibres. 7 *Maths* **a** (of a number) consisting of the sum of an integer and a fraction, as 5½. **b** (of a decimal) consisting of the sum of an integer and a decimal fraction, as 17.43. **c** (of an algebraic expression) consisting of the sum of a polynomial and a rational fraction, such as $2x + 4x^2 + 2/3x$.
▸ **mixedly** ('mɪksɪdlɪ) ADVERB ▸ **mixedness** ('mɪksɪdnɪs) NOUN

mixed bag NOUN *Informal* something composed of diverse elements, characteristics, people, etc.

mixed blessing NOUN an event, situation, etc., having both advantages and disadvantages.

mixed bud NOUN a bud containing both rudimentary flowers and foliage leaves.

mixed crystal NOUN *Chem* a crystal consisting of a solid solution of two or more distinct compounds.

mixed doubles PLURAL NOUN *Tennis* a doubles game with a man and a woman as partners on each side.

mixed economy NOUN an economy in which some industries are privately owned and others are publicly owned or nationalized.

mixed farming NOUN combined arable and livestock farming (on **mixed farms**).

mixed-flow turbine NOUN a water turbine in which water flows radially and axially through the rotating vanes.

mixed grill NOUN a dish made of several kinds of grilled meats, often served with grilled tomatoes and mushrooms.

mixed language NOUN any language containing items of vocabulary or other linguistic characteristics borrowed from two or more existing languages. See also **pidgin, creole** (sense 1), **lingua franca**.

mixed marriage NOUN a marriage between persons of different races or religions.

mixed media NOUN **a** the integrated use of different forms of media, esp within the arts. **b** (*as modifier*): *mixed-media musical presentations.*

mixed metaphor NOUN a combination of incongruous metaphors, as *when the Nazi jackboots sing their swan song.*

mixed-up ADJECTIVE in a state of mental confusion; perplexed.

mixer ('mɪksə) NOUN 1 a person or thing that mixes. 2 *Informal* **a** a person considered in relation to his ability to mix socially. **b** a person who creates trouble for others. 3 a kitchen appliance, usually electrical, used for mixing foods, etc. 4 a drink such as ginger ale, fruit juice, etc., used in preparing cocktails. 5 *Electronics* a device in which two or more input signals are combined to give a single output signal. 6 short for **sound mixer, vision mixer**.

mixer tap NOUN a tap in which hot and cold water supplies have a joint outlet but are controlled separately.

Mixe-Zoque ('mɪks'zɒk) NOUN 1 a member of an American Indian people of Mexico. 2 any of the languages of this people.

mixmaster ('mɪksˌmɑːstə) NOUN *Informal* a disc jockey.

mixologist (ˌmɪk'sɒlədʒɪst) NOUN *Humorous* a person who serves drinks, esp cocktails, at a bar.

mixolydian (ˌmɪksəʊ'lɪdɪən) ADJECTIVE *Music* of, relating to, or denoting an authentic mode represented by the ascending natural diatonic scale from G to G. See **Hypo-**.
▷**HISTORY** C16: from Greek *mixoludios* half-Lydian

mixte ('mɪkstɪ) ADJECTIVE of or denoting a type of bicycle frame, usually for women, in which angled twin lateral tubes run back to the rear axle.
▷**HISTORY** C20: from French

Mixtec ('miːstɛk) NOUN 1 (*plural* **-tecs** *or* **-tec**) a member of an American Indian people of Mexico. 2 the language of this people.
▸ **Mix'tecan** ADJECTIVE, NOUN

mixter-maxter ('mɪkstər'mækstər) *Scot* ◆ ADJECTIVE 1 chaotic or confused. ◆ NOUN 2 a chaotic or confused mixture; jumble.
▷**HISTORY** C19: reduplicated form based on MIX

mixture ('mɪkstʃə) NOUN 1 the act of mixing or state of being mixed. 2 something mixed; a result of mixing. 3 *Chem* a substance consisting of two or more substances mixed together without any chemical bonding between them. 4 *Pharmacol* a liquid medicine in which an insoluble compound is suspended in the liquid. 5 *Music* an organ stop that controls several ranks of pipes sounding the upper notes in a harmonic series. 6 the mixture of petrol vapour and air in an internal-combustion engine.
▷**HISTORY** C16: from Latin *mixtūra*, from *mixtus*, past participle of *miscēre* to mix

mix-up NOUN 1 a confused condition or situation. 2 *Informal* a fight. ◆ VERB **mix up**. (*tr, adverb*) 3 to make into a mixture: *to mix up ingredients.* 4 to confuse or confound: *Tom mixes John up with Bill.* 5 (*often passive*) to put (someone) into a state of confusion: *I'm all mixed up.* 6 (foll by *in* or *with*; usually passive) to involve (in an activity or group, esp one that is illegal): *why did you get mixed up in that drugs racket?* 7 **mix it up**. *US and Canadian informal* to fight.

Mizar ('maɪzɑː) NOUN a multiple star having four components that lies in the Plough in the constellation Ursa Major and forms a visible binary with the star Alcor. Visual magnitude: 2.1; spectral type: A2V.
▷**HISTORY** from Arabic *mi'zar* cloak

Mizoram (mɪ'zɔːrəm) NOUN a state (since 1986) in NE India, created in 1972 from the former Mizo Hills District of Assam. Capital: Aijal. Pop.: 891 058 (2001). Area: about 21 081 sq. km (8140 sq. miles).

mizuna (mɪ'zuːnə) NOUN a Japanese variety of lettuce having crisp green leaves.
▷**HISTORY** Japanese

mizzen *or* **mizen** ('mɪzᵊn) *Nautical* ◆ NOUN 1 a sail set on a mizzenmast. 2 short for **mizzenmast**. ◆ ADJECTIVE 3 of or relating to any kind of gear used with a mizzenmast: *a mizzen staysail.*
▷**HISTORY** C15: from French *misaine*, from Italian *mezzana, mezzano* middle

mizzenmast *or* **mizenmast** ('mɪzᵊnˌmɑːst; *Nautical* 'mɪzᵊnməst) NOUN *Nautical* 1 (on a yawl, ketch, or dandy) the after mast. 2 (on a vessel with three or more masts) the third mast from the bow.

mizzle[1] ('mɪzᵊl) VERB, NOUN a dialect word for **drizzle**.
▷**HISTORY** C15: perhaps from Low German *miseln* to drizzle; compare Dutch dialect *miezelen* to drizzle
▸ **'mizzly** ADJECTIVE

mizzle[2] ('mɪzᵊl) VERB (*intr*) *Brit, slang* to decamp.
▷**HISTORY** C18: of unknown origin

mizzy maze ('mɪzɪ) NOUN *Southwestern English dialect* a state of confusion.

mk[1] *Currency* SYMBOL FOR: 1 mark. 2 markka.

mk[2] THE INTERNET DOMAIN NAME FOR Macedonia.

Mk ABBREVIATION FOR mark (type of car).

MK INTERNATIONAL CAR REGISTRATION FOR (Federal Republic of) Macedonia.
▷**HISTORY** from Macedonian *Makedonija*

MKSA system NOUN another name for **Giorgi system**.

mks units PLURAL NOUN a metric system of units based on the metre, kilogram, and second as the units of length, mass, and time; it forms the basis of the SI units.

mkt ABBREVIATION FOR market.

ml[1] SYMBOL FOR: 1 millilitre. 2 mile.

ml[2] THE INTERNET DOMAIN NAME FOR Mali.

ML ABBREVIATION FOR Medieval Latin.

MLA ABBREVIATION FOR: 1 Member of the Legislative Assembly (of Northern Ireland). 2 Modern Language Association (of America).

MLC (in India and Australia) ABBREVIATION FOR Member of the Legislative Council.

MLD ABBREVIATION FOR minimum lethal dose (the smallest amount of a drug or toxic agent that will kill a laboratory animal).

MLF ABBREVIATION FOR multilateral (nuclear) force.

MLG ABBREVIATION FOR Middle Low German.

MLitt ABBREVIATION FOR Master of Letters.
▷**HISTORY** Latin *Magister Litterarum*

Mlle *plural* **Mlles** the French equivalent of **Miss**.
▷**HISTORY** from French *Mademoiselle*

MLR ABBREVIATION FOR **minimum lending rate**.

mm[1] 1 SYMBOL FOR millimetre. ◆ 2 ABBREVIATION FOR mutatis mutandis.

mm[2] THE INTERNET DOMAIN NAME FOR Myanmar.

MM 1 ABBREVIATION FOR Military Medal. 2 the French equivalent of **Messrs.**
▷**HISTORY** from French *Messieurs*

MMC (formerly, in Britain) ABBREVIATION FOR Monopolies and Mergers Commission.

MMDS ABBREVIATION FOR multipoint microwave distribution system: a radio alternative to cable television. Sometimes shortened to: **MDS**.

Mme *plural* **Mmes** the French equivalent of **Mrs.**
▷**HISTORY** from French *Madame, Mesdames*

mmf ABBREVIATION FOR magnetomotive force.

mmHg ABBREVIATION FOR millimetre(s) of mercury (a unit of pressure equal to the pressure that can support a column of mercury 1 millimetre high).

MMM (in Canada) ABBREVIATION FOR Member of the Order of Military Merit.

MMP ABBREVIATION FOR mixed member

proportional: a system of proportional representation, used in Germany and New Zealand.

MMR NOUN a combined vaccine against measles, mumps, and rubella, given to young children.

MMus. ABBREVIATION FOR Master of Music.

MMV (in Canada) ABBREVIATION FOR Medal of Military Valour.

mn THE INTERNET DOMAIN NAME FOR Mongolia.

Mn THE CHEMICAL SYMBOL FOR manganese.

MN ABBREVIATION FOR: 1 (in Britain) Merchant Navy. 2 Minnesota.

MNA (in Canada) ABBREVIATION FOR Member of the National Assembly (of Quebec).

mnemonic (nɪˈmɒnɪk) ADJECTIVE 1 aiding or meant to aid one's memory. 2 of or relating to memory or mnemonics. ◆ NOUN 3 something, such as a verse, to assist memory.
▷HISTORY C18: from Greek *mnēmonikos,* from *mnēmōn* mindful, from *mnasthai* to remember
▸**mneˈmonically** ADVERB

mnemonics (nɪˈmɒnɪks) NOUN *(usually functioning as singular)* 1 the art or practice of improving or of aiding the memory. 2 a system of rules to aid the memory.

Mnemosyne (niːˈmɒzɪˌniː, -ˈmɒs-) NOUN *Greek myth* the goddess of memory and mother by Zeus of the Muses.

mo¹ (məʊ) NOUN *Informal* 1 *Chiefly Brit* short for **moment** (sense 1) (esp in the phrase **half a mo**). 2 *Chiefly Austral* short for **moustache** (sense 1).

mo² THE INTERNET DOMAIN NAME FOR Macau.

Mo THE CHEMICAL SYMBOL FOR molybdenum.

MO ABBREVIATION FOR: 1 Missouri. 2 Medical Officer. 3 modus operandi.

Mo. ABBREVIATION FOR Missouri.

m.o. *or* **MO** ABBREVIATION FOR: 1 mail order. 2 money order.

-mo SUFFIX FORMING NOUNS (in bookbinding) indicating book size by specifying the number of leaves formed by folding one sheet of paper: *12mo, twelvemo,* or *duodecimo; 16mo* or *sixteenmo.*
▷HISTORY abstracted from DUODECIMO

moa (ˈməʊə) NOUN any large flightless bird of the recently extinct order *Dinornithiformes* of New Zealand (see **ratite**).
▷HISTORY C19: from Maori

Moab (ˈməʊæb) NOUN *Old Testament* an ancient kingdom east of the Dead Sea, in what is now the SW part of Jordan: flourished mainly from the 9th to the 6th centuries B.C.
▸**Moabite** (ˈməʊəˌbaɪt) ADJECTIVE, NOUN

Moabite (ˈməʊəˌbaɪt) *Old Testament* ◆ ADJECTIVE 1 of or relating to Moab, an ancient kingdom east of the Dead Sea, or its inhabitants. ◆ NOUN 2 a native or inhabitant of Moab.

moa hunter NOUN the name given by anthropologists to the early Maori inhabitants of New Zealand.

moai (ˈməʊaɪ) NOUN, *plural* **moai**. any of the gigantic carved stone figures found on Easter Island (Rapa Nui).
▷HISTORY from Rapanui (the Polynesian language of Easter Island), literally: statue, figurine

moan (məʊn) NOUN 1 a low prolonged mournful sound expressive of suffering or pleading. 2 any similar mournful sound, esp that made by the wind. 3 a grumble or complaint. ◆ VERB 4 to utter (words) in a low mournful manner. 5 *(intr)* to make a sound like a moan. 6 *(usually intr)* to grumble or complain (esp in the phrase **moan and groan**).
▷HISTORY C13: related to Old English *mǣnan* to grieve over
▸**ˈmoaner** NOUN ▸**ˈmoanful** ADJECTIVE ▸**ˈmoaning** NOUN, ADJECTIVE ▸**ˈmoaningly** ADVERB

moat (məʊt) NOUN 1 a wide water-filled ditch surrounding a fortified place, such as a castle. ◆ VERB 2 *(tr)* to surround with or as if with a moat: *a moated grange.*
▷HISTORY C14: from Old French *motte* mound

mob (mɒb) NOUN 1 **a** a riotous or disorderly crowd of people; rabble. **b** *(as modifier)*: *mob law; mob violence.* 2 *Often derogatory* a group or class of people, animals, or things. 3 *Austral and NZ* a flock (of sheep) or a herd (of cattle, esp when droving). 4 *Often derogatory* the masses. 5 *Slang* a gang of criminals. ◆ VERB **mobs, mobbing, mobbed.** *(tr)* 6 to attack in a group resembling a mob. 7 to surround, esp in order to acclaim: *they mobbed the film star.* 8 to crowd into (a building, plaza, etc.). 9 (of a group of animals of a prey species) to harass (a predator). ◆ See also **mobs.**
▷HISTORY C17: shortened from Latin *mōbile vulgus* the fickle populace; see MOBILE
▸**ˈmobber** NOUN ▸**ˈmobbish** ADJECTIVE

MOB ABBREVIATION FOR mobile phone.

mobcap (ˈmɒbˌkæp) NOUN a woman's large cotton cap with a pouched crown and usually a frill, worn esp during the 18th century. Often shortened to: **mob.**
▷HISTORY C18: from obsolete *mob* woman, esp a loose-living woman, + CAP

mobe (məʊb) NOUN *Informal* a mobile phone.

mob-handed ADJECTIVE, ADVERB *Informal* in or with a large group of people: *the police turned up mob-handed.*

mobie (ˈməʊbɪ) NOUN *Informal* a mobile phone.

mobile (ˈməʊbaɪl) ADJECTIVE 1 having freedom of movement; movable. 2 changing quickly in expression: *a mobile face.* 3 *Sociol* (of individuals or social groups) moving within and between classes, occupations, and localities: *upwardly mobile.* 4 (of military forces) able to move freely and quickly to any given area. 5 *(postpositive) Informal* having transport available: *are you mobile tonight?* ◆ NOUN 6 **a** a sculpture suspended in midair with delicately balanced parts that are set in motion by air currents. **b** *(as modifier)*: *mobile sculpture.* 7 short for **mobile phone.**
▷HISTORY C15: via Old French from Latin *mōbilis,* from *movēre* to move

Mobile (ˈməʊbiːl, məʊˈbiːl) NOUN a port in SW Alabama, on **Mobile Bay** (an inlet of the Gulf of Mexico): the state's only port and its first permanent settlement, made by French colonists in 1711. Pop.: 198 915 (2000).

-mobile (məʊˌbiːl) SUFFIX FORMING NOUNS indicating a vehicle designed for a particular person or purpose: *Popemobile.*

Mobile Command NOUN *Canadian* the Canadian army and other land forces.

mobile home NOUN living quarters mounted on wheels and capable of being towed by a motor vehicle.

mobile library NOUN a vehicle providing lending library facilities. US and Canadian equivalent: **bookmobile.**

mobile phone NOUN a portable telephone that works by means of a cellular radio system.

mobility (məʊˈbɪlɪtɪ) NOUN 1 the ability to move physically: *a handicapped person's mobility may be limited; mobility is part of physical education.* 2 *Sociol* (of individuals or social groups) movement within or between classes and occupations. See also **vertical mobility, horizontal mobility.** 3 time that a resident of a secure unit is allowed to spend outside the unit, as preparation for an eventual return to society.

mobility housing NOUN *Social welfare* houses designed or adapted for people who have difficulty in walking but are not necessarily chairbound. See also **wheelchair housing.**

mobilize *or* **mobilise** (ˈməʊbɪˌlaɪz) VERB 1 to prepare for war or other emergency by organizing (national resources, the armed services, etc.). 2 *(tr)* to organize for a purpose; marshal. 3 *(tr)* to put into motion, circulation, or use.
▸**ˈmobiˌlizable** *or* **ˈmobiˌlisable** ADJECTIVE ▸**ˌmobiliˈzation** *or* **ˌmobiliˈsation** NOUN

Möbius strip (ˈmɜːbɪəs; *German* ˈmøːbius) NOUN *Maths* a one-sided continuous surface, formed by twisting a long narrow rectangular strip of material through 180° and joining the ends.
▷HISTORY C19: named after August *Möbius* (1790–1868), German mathematician who invented it

moblog (ˈmɒblɒg) NOUN a chronicle, which may be shared with others, of someone's thoughts and experiences recorded in the form of mobile phone calls, text messages, and photographs.
▷HISTORY C21: MOB(ILE) + LOG¹

mobocracy (mɒˈbɒkrəsɪ) NOUN, *plural* **-cies.** 1 rule or domination by a mob. 2 the mob that rules.
▸**mobocrat** (ˈmɒbəˌkræt) NOUN ▸**ˌmoboˈcratic** *or* **ˌmoboˈcratical** ADJECTIVE

mobs (mɒbz) *Informal* ◆ PLURAL NOUN 1 (usually foll by *of*) great numbers or quantities; lots: *mobs of people.* ◆ ADVERB 2 *Austral and NZ* a great deal: *mobs better.*

mobster (ˈmɒbstə) NOUN a US slang word for **gangster.**

Mobutu (məˈbuːtuː) NOUN the former name (until 1997) of **Lake Albert.**

moby (ˈməʊbɪ) NOUN, *plural* **-bies.** *Informal* a mobile phone.

MoC ABBREVIATION FOR mother of the chapel.

MOC INTERNATIONAL CAR REGISTRATION FOR Mozambique.
▷HISTORY from Portuguese *Moçambique*

Moçambique (musəmˈbikə) NOUN the Portuguese name for **Mozambique.**

moccasin (ˈmɒkəsɪn) NOUN 1 a shoe of soft leather, esp deerskin, worn by North American Indians. 2 any soft shoe resembling this. 3 *NZ* a sheepshearer's footgear, usually made of sacking. 4 short for **water moccasin.**
▷HISTORY C17: from Algonquian; compare Narraganset *mocussin* shoe

moccasin flower NOUN any of several North American orchids of the genus *Cypripedium* with a pink solitary flower. See also **lady's-slipper, cypripedium** (sense 1).

moccasin telegraph NOUN *Canadian informal* the transmission of rumour or secret information; the grapevine.

mocha (ˈmɒkə) NOUN 1 a strongly flavoured dark brown coffee originally imported from Arabia. 2 a flavouring made from coffee and chocolate. 3 a soft glove leather with a suede finish, made from goatskin or sheepskin. 4 **a** a dark brown colour. **b** *(as adjective)*: *mocha shoes.*

Mocha *or* **Mokha** (ˈmɒkə) NOUN a port in Yemen, on the Red Sea; in North Yemen until 1990: formerly important for the export of Arabian coffee. Pop.: about 2000 (1990 est.).

mocha stone NOUN another name for **moss agate.**

mock (mɒk) VERB 1 (when *intr,* often foll by *at*) to behave with scorn or contempt (towards); show ridicule (for). 2 *(tr)* to imitate, esp in fun; mimic. 3 *(tr)* to deceive, disappoint, or delude. 4 *(tr)* to defy or frustrate: *the team mocked the visitors' attempt to score.* ◆ NOUN 5 the act of mocking. 6 a person or thing mocked. 7 a counterfeit; imitation. 8 *(often plural) Informal* (in England and Wales) the school examinations taken as practice before public examinations. ◆ ADJECTIVE *(prenominal)* 9 sham or counterfeit. 10 serving as an imitation or substitute, esp for practice purposes: *a mock battle; mock finals.* ◆ See also **mock-up.**
▷HISTORY C15: from Old French *mocquer*
▸**ˈmockable** ADJECTIVE ▸**ˈmocker** NOUN ▸**ˈmocking** NOUN, ADJECTIVE ▸**ˈmockingly** ADVERB

mocker (ˈmɒkə) *Austral, slang, old-fashioned* ◆ NOUN 1 clothing. ◆ VERB *(tr)* 2 **all mockered up.** dressed up.
▷HISTORY of unknown origin

mockernut (ˈmɒkəˌnʌt) NOUN 1 Also called: **black hickory.** a species of smooth-barked hickory, *Carya tomentosa,* with fragrant foliage that turns bright yellow in autumn. 2 the nut of this tree.
▷HISTORY so called because the nut is difficult to extract

mockers (ˈmɒkəz) PLURAL NOUN **put the mockers on.** *Informal* to ruin the chances of success of. Also (Austral): **put the mock** (*or* **mocks**) **on.**
▷HISTORY C20: perhaps from MOCK

mockery (ˈmɒkərɪ) NOUN, *plural* **-eries.** 1 ridicule, contempt, or derision. 2 a derisive action or comment. 3 an imitation or pretence, esp a derisive one. 4 a person or thing that is mocked. 5 a person, thing, or action that is inadequate or disappointing.

mock-heroic ADJECTIVE 1 (of a literary work, esp a poem) imitating the style of heroic poetry in order to satirize an unheroic subject, as in Pope's *The Rape of the Lock.* ◆ NOUN 2 burlesque imitation of the heroic style or of a single work in this style.

mockingbird (ˈmɒkɪŋˌbɜːd) NOUN 1 any American songbird of the family *Mimidae,* having a long tail and grey plumage: noted for their ability to mimic the song of other birds. [2] *Austral* a small scrub bird, *Atrichornis rufescens,* noted for its mimicry.

mock moon NOUN another name for **paraselene.**

mockney (ˈmɒknɪ) NOUN [1] (*often capital*) a person who affects a cockney accent. [2] an affected cockney accent. ◆ ADJECTIVE [3] denoting an affected cockney accent or a person who has one.
▷HISTORY C20: MOCK + COCKNEY

mock orange NOUN [1] Also called: **syringa.** any shrub of the genus *Philadelphus,* esp *P. coronarius,* with white fragrant flowers that resemble those of the orange: family *Philadelphaceae.* [2] any other shrub or tree that resembles the orange tree.

mock sun NOUN another name for **parhelion.**

mock turtle soup NOUN an imitation turtle soup made from a calf's head.

mockumentary (ˌmɒkjʊˈmɛntərɪ, -trɪ) NOUN, *plural* **-ries.** a satirical television or radio programme in the form of a parody of a documentary.
▷HISTORY C20: from MOCK + (DOC)UMENTARY

mock-up NOUN [1] a working full-scale model of a machine, apparatus, etc., for testing, research, etc. [2] a layout of printed matter. ◆ VERB **mock up.** [3] (*tr, adverb*) to build or make a mock-up of.

mod[1] (mɒd) NOUN *Brit* **a** a member of a group of teenagers in the mid-1960s, noted for their clothes-consciousness and opposition to the rockers. **b** a member of a revived group of this type in the late 1970s and early 1980s, noted for their clothes-consciousness and opposition to the skinheads. **c** (*as modifier*): *a mod haircut.*
▷HISTORY C20: from MODERNIST

mod[2] (mɒd) NOUN an annual Highland Gaelic meeting with musical and literary competitions.
▷HISTORY C19: from Gaelic *mòd* assembly, from Old Norse; related to MOOT

mod[3] (mɒd) *Maths* ABBREVIATION FOR modulus.

MOD (in Britain) ABBREVIATION FOR Ministry of Defence.

mod. ABBREVIATION FOR: [1] moderate. [2] moderato. [3] modern.

modal (ˈməʊdəl) ADJECTIVE [1] of, relating to, or characteristic of mode or manner. [2] *Grammar* (of a verb form or auxiliary verb) expressing a distinction of mood, such as that between possibility and actuality. The modal auxiliaries in English include *can, could, may, must, need, ought, shall, should, will,* and *would.* [3] *Philosophy, logic* **a** qualifying or expressing a qualification of the truth of some statement, for example, as necessary or contingent. **b** relating to analogous qualifications such as that of rules as obligatory or permissive. [4] *Metaphysics* of or relating to the form of a thing as opposed to its attributes, substance, etc. [5] *Music* of or relating to a mode. [6] of or relating to a statistical mode.
▸ˈ**modally** ADVERB

modality (məʊˈdælɪtɪ) NOUN, *plural* **-ties.** [1] the condition of being modal. [2] a quality, attribute, or circumstance that denotes mode, mood, or manner. [3] *Logic* the property of a statement of being classified under one of the concepts studied by modal logic, esp necessity or possibility. [4] any physical or electrical therapeutic method or agency. [5] any of the five senses.

modal logic NOUN [1] the logical study of such philosophical concepts as necessity, possibility, contingency, etc. [2] the logical study of concepts whose formal properties resemble certain moral, epistemological, and psychological concepts. See also **alethic, deontic, epistemic, doxastic.** [3] any formal system capable of being interpreted as a model for the behaviour of such concepts.

mod cons PLURAL NOUN *Informal* modern conveniences; the usual installations of a modern house, such as hot water, heating, etc.

mode (məʊd) NOUN [1] a manner or way of doing, acting, or existing. [2] the current fashion or style. [3] *Music* **a** any of the various scales of notes within one octave, esp any of the twelve natural diatonic scales taken in ascending order used in plainsong, folk song, and art music until 1600. **b** (in the music of classical Greece) any of the descending diatonic scales from which the liturgical modes evolved. **c** either of the two main scale systems in music since 1600: *major mode; minor mode.* [4] *Logic, linguistics* another name for **modality** (sense 3), **mood**[2] (sense 2). [5] *Philosophy* a complex combination of ideas the realization of which is not determined by the component ideas. [6] that one of a range of values that has the highest frequency as determined statistically. Compare **mean**[3] (sense 4), **median** (sense 6). [7] the quantitative mineral composition of an igneous rock. [8] *Physics* one of the possible configurations of a travelling or stationary wave. [9] *Physics* one of the fundamental vibrations.
▷HISTORY C14: from Latin *modus* measure, manner

model (ˈmɒdəl) NOUN [1] **a** a representation, usually on a smaller scale, of a device, structure, etc. **b** (*as modifier*): *a model train.* [2] **a** a standard to be imitated: *she was my model for good scholarship.* **b** (*as modifier*): *a model wife.* [3] a representative form, style, or pattern. [4] a person who poses for a sculptor, painter, or photographer. [5] a person who wears clothes to display them to prospective buyers; mannequin. [6] a preparatory sculpture in clay, wax, etc., from which the finished work is copied. [7] a design or style, esp one of a series of designs of a particular product: *last year's model.* [8] *Brit* **a** an original unique article of clothing. **b** (*as modifier*): *a model coat.* [9] a simplified representation or description of a system or complex entity, esp one designed to facilitate calculations and predictions. [10] *Logic* **a** an interpretation of a formal system under which the theorems derivable in that system are mapped onto truths. **b** a theory in which a given sentence is true. ◆ VERB **-els, -elling, -elled** *or US* **-els, -eling, -eled.** [11] to make a model of (something or someone). [12] to form in clay, wax, etc.; mould. [13] to display (clothing and accessories) as a mannequin. [14] to plan or create according to a model or models. [15] to arrange studio lighting so that highlights and shadows emphasize the desired features of a human form or an inanimate object.
▷HISTORY C16: from Old French *modelle,* from Italian *modello,* from Latin *modulus,* diminutive of *modus* MODE
▸ˈ**modeller** *or* (*US*) ˈ**modeler** NOUN

modelling *or US* **modeling** (ˈmɒdəlɪŋ) NOUN [1] the act or an instance of making a model. [2] the practice or occupation of a person who models clothes. [3] a technique in psychotherapy in which the therapist encourages the patient to model his behaviour on his own.

model theory NOUN the branch of logic that deals with the properties of models; the semantic study of formal systems.
▸ˈ**model-**ˌ**theo**ˈ**retic** ADJECTIVE

modem (ˈməʊdɛm) NOUN *Computing* a device for connecting two computers by a telephone line, consisting of a modulator that converts computer signals into audio signals and a corresponding demodulator.
▷HISTORY C20: from *mo(dulator) dem(odulator)*

Modena (*Italian* ˈmɔːdena) NOUN [1] a city in N Italy, in Emilia-Romagna: ruled by the Este family (18th–19th century); university (1678). Pop.: 176 022 (2000 est.). Ancient name: **Mutina.** [2] (*sometimes not capital*) a popular variety of domestic fancy pigeon originating in Modena.

moderate ADJECTIVE (ˈmɒdərɪt, ˈmɒdrɪt) [1] not extreme or excessive; within due or reasonable limits: *moderate demands.* [2] not violent; mild or temperate. [3] of average quality or extent: *moderate success.* ◆ NOUN (ˈmɒdərɪt, ˈmɒdrɪt) [4] a person who holds moderate views, esp in politics. ◆ VERB (ˈmɒdəˌreɪt) [5] to become or cause to become less extreme or violent. [6] (when *intr,* often foll by *over*) to preside over a meeting, discussion, etc. [7] *Brit and NZ* to act as an external moderator of the overall standards and marks for (some types of educational assessment). [8] *Physics* to slow down (neutrons), esp by using a moderator. [9] (*tr*) to monitor (the conversations in an on-line chatroom) for bad language, inappropriate content, etc.
▷HISTORY C14: from Latin *moderātus* observing moderation, from *moderārī* to restrain
▸ˈ**moderately** ADVERB ▸ˈ**moderateness** NOUN
▸ˈ**moderatism** NOUN

moderate breeze NOUN a wind of force four on the Beaufort scale.

moderate gale NOUN a gale of force seven on the Beaufort scale, capable of swaying trees.

moderation (ˌmɒdəˈreɪʃən) NOUN [1] the state or an instance of being moderate; mildness; balance. [2] the act of moderating. [3] **in moderation.** within moderate or reasonable limits.

Moderations (ˌmɒdəˈreɪʃənz) PLURAL NOUN short for **Honour Moderations.**

moderato (ˌmɒdəˈrɑːtəʊ) ADVERB *Music* [1] at a moderate tempo. [2] (preceded by a tempo marking) a direction indicating that the tempo specified is to be used with restraint: *allegro moderato.*
▷HISTORY C18: from Italian, from Latin *moderātus;* see MODERATE

moderator (ˈmɒdəˌreɪtə) NOUN [1] a person or thing that moderates. [2] *Presbyterian Church* a minister appointed to preside over a Church court, synod, or general assembly. [3] a presiding officer at a public or legislative assembly. [4] a material, such as heavy water or graphite, used for slowing down neutrons in the cores of nuclear reactors so that they have more chance of inducing nuclear fission. [5] an examiner at Oxford or Cambridge Universities in first public examinations. [6] (in Britain and New Zealand) one who is responsible for consistency of standards in the grading of some educational assessments. [7] a person who moniters the conversations in an on-line chatroom for bad language, inappropriate content, etc.
▸ˈ**mode**ˌ**ratorship** NOUN

modern (ˈmɒdən) ADJECTIVE [1] of, involving, or befitting the present or a recent time; contemporary. [2] of, relating to, or characteristic of contemporary styles or schools of art, literature, music, etc., esp those of an experimental kind. [3] belonging or relating to the period in history from the end of the Middle Ages to the present. ◆ NOUN [4] a contemporary person. [5] *Printing* a type style that originated around the beginning of the 19th century, characterized chiefly by marked contrast between thick and thin strokes. Compare **old face.**
▷HISTORY C16: from Old French, from Late Latin *modernus,* from *modō* (adv) just recently, from *modus* MODE
▸ˈ**modernly** ADVERB ▸ˈ**modernness** NOUN

modern apprenticeship NOUN an arrangement that allows a school leaver to gain vocational qualifications while being trained in a job.

modern dance NOUN a style of free and expressive theatrical dancing not bound by the classical rules of ballet.

moderne (məˈdɛən) ADJECTIVE *Chiefly US* of or relating to the style of architecture and design, prevalent in Europe and the US in the late 1920s and 1930s, typified by the use of straight lines, tubular chromed steel frames, contrasting inlaid woods, etc. Compare **Art Deco.**

Modern English NOUN the English language since about 1450, esp any of the standard forms developed from the S East Midland dialect of Middle English. See also **English, Middle English, Old English.**

modern greats PLURAL NOUN (at Oxford University) the Honour School of Philosophy, Politics, and Economics.

Modern Greek NOUN the Greek language since about 1453 A.D. (the fall of Byzantium). Compare **Demotic, Katharevusa.**

Modern Hebrew NOUN the official language of the state of Israel; a revived form of ancient Hebrew.

modernism (ˈmɒdəˌnɪzəm) NOUN [1] modern tendencies, characteristics, thoughts, etc., or the support of these. [2] something typical of contemporary life or thought. [3] a 20th-century divergence in the arts from previous traditions, esp in architecture. See **International Style.** [4] (*capital*) *RC Church* the movement at the end of the 19th and beginning of the 20th centuries that sought to adapt doctrine to the supposed requirements of modern thought.
▸ˈ**modernist** NOUN, ADJECTIVE ▸ˌ**modern**ˈ**istic** ADJECTIVE
▸ˌ**modern**ˈ**istically** ADVERB

modernity (mɒˈdɜːnɪtɪ) NOUN, *plural* **-ties.** [1] the quality or state of being modern. [2] something modern.

modernize *or* **modernise** (ˈmɒdəˌnaɪz) VERB [1] (*tr*) to make modern in appearance or style: *to modernize a room.* [2] (*intr*) to adopt modern ways, ideas, etc.

▸ˌ**moderniˈzation** *or* **moderniˈsation** NOUN ▸ˈ**modernˌizer** *or* ˈ**modernˌiser** NOUN

modern jazz NOUN any of the styles of jazz that evolved between the early 1940s and the later emergence of avant-garde jazz, characterized by a greater harmonic and rhythmic complexity than hitherto.

modern language NOUN any of the languages spoken in present-day Europe, with the exception of English.

modern pentathlon NOUN an athletic contest consisting of five different events: horse riding with jumps, fencing with electric épée, freestyle swimming, pistol shooting, and cross-country running.

modern sequence dancing NOUN a form of dancing in which ballroom dance steps are used as the basis of a wide variety of different dances typically performed in a sequence.

modest (ˈmɒdɪst) ADJECTIVE 1 having or expressing a humble opinion of oneself or one's accomplishments or abilities. 2 reserved or shy: *modest behaviour.* 3 not ostentatious or pretentious. 4 not extreme or excessive; moderate. 5 decorous or decent.
▹HISTORY C16: via Old French from Latin *modestus* moderate, from *modus* MODE
▸ˈ**modestly** ADVERB

modesty (ˈmɒdɪstɪ) NOUN, *plural* **-ties.** 1 the quality or condition of being modest. 2 (*modifier*) designed to prevent inadvertent exposure of part of the body: *a modesty flap.*

modge (mɒdʒ) VERB (*tr*) *Midland English dialect* to do shoddily; make a mess of.
▹HISTORY C20: perhaps a variant of *mudge* to crush (hops)

modicum (ˈmɒdɪkəm) NOUN a small amount or portion.
▹HISTORY C15: from Latin: a little way, from *modicus* moderate

modification (ˌmɒdɪfɪˈkeɪʃən) NOUN 1 the act of modifying or the condition of being modified. 2 something modified; the result of a modification. 3 a small change or adjustment. 4 *Grammar* the relation between a modifier and the word or phrase that it modifies.
▸ˈ**modifiˌcatory** *or* ˈ**modifiˌcative** ADJECTIVE

modified-release ADJECTIVE denoting a formulation of a medicinal drug taken orally that releases the active ingredients over several hours, in order to maintain a relatively constant plasma concentration of the drug. Also called: **sustained-release, continuous-release.**

modifier (ˈmɒdɪˌfaɪə) NOUN 1 Also called: **qualifier.** *Grammar* a word or phrase that qualifies the sense of another word; for example, the noun *alarm* is a modifier of *clock* in *alarm clock* and the phrase *every day* is an adverbial modifier of *walks* in *he walks every day.* 2 a person or thing that modifies.

modify (ˈmɒdɪˌfaɪ) VERB **-fies, -fying, -fied.** (*mainly tr*) 1 to change the structure, character, intent, etc., of. 2 to make less extreme or uncompromising: *to modify a demand.* 3 *Grammar* (of a word or group of words) to bear the relation of modifier to (another word or group of words). 4 *Linguistics* to change (a vowel) by umlaut. 5 (*intr*) to be or become modified.
▹HISTORY C14: from Old French *modifier,* from Latin *modificāre* to limit, control, from *modus* measure + *facere* to make
▸ˈ**modiˌfiable** ADJECTIVE ▸ˌ**modiˌfiaˈbility** *or* ˈ**modiˌfiableness** NOUN

modillion (məˈdɪljən) NOUN *Architect* one of a set of ornamental brackets under a cornice, esp as used in the Corinthian order. Compare **mutule.**
▹HISTORY C16: via French from Italian *modiglione,* probably from Vulgar Latin *mutiliō* (unattested), from Latin *mūtulus* MUTULE

modiolus (məʊˈdaɪələs, mə-) NOUN, *plural* **-li** (-ˌlaɪ). the central bony pillar of the cochlea.
▹HISTORY C19: New Latin, from Latin: hub of a wheel, from *modus* a measure

modish (ˈməʊdɪʃ) ADJECTIVE in the current fashion or style; contemporary.
▸ˈ**modishly** ADVERB ▸ˈ**modishness** NOUN

modiste (məʊˈdiːst) NOUN a fashionable dressmaker or milliner.
▹HISTORY C19: from French, from *mode* fashion

Modred (ˈməʊdrɪd) *or* **Mordred** (ˈmɔːdrɛd) NOUN (in Arthurian legend) a knight of the Round Table who rebelled against and killed his uncle King Arthur.

Mods (mɒdz), PLURAL NOUN (at Oxford University) short for **Honour Moderations.**

modular (ˈmɒdjʊlə) ADJECTIVE of, consisting of, or resembling a module or modulus.
▸**modularity** (ˌmɒdjʊˈlærɪtɪ) NOUN

modulate (ˈmɒdjʊˌleɪt) VERB 1 (*tr*) to change the tone, pitch, or volume of. 2 (*tr*) to adjust or regulate the degree of. 3 *Music* **a** to subject to or undergo modulation in music. **b** (often foll by *to*) to make or become in tune (with a pitch, key, etc.). 4 (*tr*) *Physics, electronics* to cause to vary by a process of modulation.
▹HISTORY C16: from Latin *modulātus* in due measure, melodious, from *modulārī* to regulate, from *modus* measure
▸**modulability** (ˌmɒdjʊləˈbɪlɪtɪ) NOUN ▸ˈ**modulative** *or* ˈ**modulatory** ADJECTIVE ▸ˈ**moduˌlator** NOUN

modulation (ˌmɒdjʊˈleɪʃən) NOUN 1 the act of modulating or the condition of being modulated. 2 *Music* the transition from one key to another. 3 *Grammar* **a** another word for **intonation** (sense 1). **b** the grammatical expression of modality. 4 *Electrical engineering* **a** the act or process of superimposing the amplitude, frequency, phase, etc., of a wave or signal onto another wave (the carrier wave) or signal or onto an electron beam. See also **amplitude modulation, frequency modulation, phase modulation, velocity modulation. b** the variation of the modulated signal.

module (ˈmɒdjuːl) NOUN 1 a self-contained unit or item, such as an assembly of electronic components and associated wiring or a segment of computer software, which itself performs a defined task and can be linked with other such units to form a larger system. 2 a standard unit of measure, esp one used to coordinate the dimensions of buildings and components; in classical architecture, half the diameter of a column at the base of the shaft. 3 a standardized unit designed to be added to or used as part of an arrangement of similar units, as in furniture. 4 *Astronautics* any of several self-contained separable units making up a spacecraft or launch vehicle, each of which has one or more specified tasks: *command module; service module.* 5 *Education* a short course of study, esp of a vocational or technical subject, that together with other such completed courses can count towards a particular qualification.
▹HISTORY C16: from Latin *modulus,* diminutive of *modus* MODE

modulus (ˈmɒdjʊləs) NOUN, *plural* **-li** (-ˌlaɪ). 1 *Physics* a coefficient expressing a specified property of a specified substance. See **bulk modulus, modulus of rigidity, Young's modulus.** 2 *Maths* another name for the **absolute value** (sense 2) of a complex number. 3 *Maths* the number by which a logarithm to one base is multiplied to give the corresponding logarithm to another base. 4 *Maths* an integer that can be divided exactly into the difference between two other integers: *7 is a modulus of 25 and 11.* See also **congruence** (sense 2).
▹HISTORY C16: from Latin, diminutive of *modus* measure

modulus of elasticity NOUN the ratio of the stress applied to a body or substance to the resulting strain within the elastic limit. Also called: **elastic modulus.** See also **Young's modulus, bulk modulus, modulus of rigidity.**

modulus of rigidity NOUN a modulus of elasticity equal to the ratio of the tangential force per unit area to the resulting angular deformation. Symbol: G.

modus operandi (ˈməʊdəs ˌɒpəˈrændiː, -ˈrændaɪ) NOUN, *plural* **modi operandi** (ˈməʊdiː ˌɒpəˈrændiː, ˈməʊdaɪ ˌɒpəˈrændaɪ). procedure; method of operating.
▹HISTORY C17: from Latin

modus ponens *Latin* (ˈməʊdəs ˈpəʊˌnɛnz) NOUN *Logic* the principle that whenever a conditional statement and its antecedent are given to be true its consequent may be validly inferred, as in *if it's Tuesday this must be Belgium* and *it's Tuesday so this must be Belgium.*
▹HISTORY literally: mood that affirms

modus tollens *Latin* (ˈməʊdəs ˈtɒlˌɛnz) NOUN *Logic* the principle that whenever a conditional statement and the negation of its consequent are given to be true, the negation of its antecedent may be validly inferred, as in *if it's Tuesday this must be Belgium* and *this isn't Belgium so it's not Tuesday.*
▹HISTORY literally: mood that denies

modus vivendi (ˈməʊdəs vɪˈvɛndiː, -ˈvɛndaɪ) NOUN, *plural* **modi vivendi** (ˈməʊdiː vɪˈvɛndiː, ˈməʊdaɪ vɪˈvɛndaɪ). a working arrangement between conflicting interests; practical compromise.
▹HISTORY C19: from Latin: way of living

moer (muːr) NOUN *South African, taboo slang* a despicable person.
▹HISTORY from Afrikaans

Moers (*German* møːrs) NOUN a city in W Germany, in North Rhine-Westphalia: coalmining centre. Pop. 106 704 (1999 est.).

mofette (məʊˈfɛt) NOUN an opening in a region of nearly extinct volcanic activity, through which carbon dioxide, nitrogen, and other gases pass.
▹HISTORY C19: from French, from Neapolitan Italian *mofeta;* compare dialect German *muffezen* to smell fetid

moffie (ˈmɒfɪ) *South African, slang* ◆ NOUN 1 a homosexual. ◆ ADJECTIVE 2 homosexual.
▹HISTORY C18: from *mophrodite,* a variant of HERMAPHRODITE

mofo (ˈməʊfəʊ) NOUN, *plural* **mofos.** *Slang, chiefly US short for* **motherfucker.**

Mogadishu (ˌmɒgəˈdɪʃuː) *or* **Mogadiscio** (ˌmɒgəˈdɪʃɪˌəʊ, -ˈdɪʃəʊ) NOUN the capital and chief port of Somalia, on the Indian Ocean: founded by Arabs around the 10th century; taken by the Sultan of Zanzibar in 1871 and sold to Italy in 1905. Pop.: 1 162 000 (1999 est.).

Mogadon (ˈmɒgəˌdɒn) NOUN *Trademark* a drug of the benzodiazepine group, a brand of nitrazepam, used to treat insomnia.

Mogador (ˌmɒgəˈdɔː; *French* mɔgadɔr) NOUN the former name (until 1956) of **Essaouira.**

Mogen David (ˈməʊgən ˈdeɪvɪd) NOUN another name for the **Star of David.**

moggy (ˈmɒgɪ) NOUN, *plural* **moggies.** *Brit* a slang name for **cat**[1] (sense 1). Sometimes shortened to: **mog.**
▹HISTORY C20: of dialect origin, originally a pet name for a cow

Mogilev (*Russian* məgiˈljɔf) *or* **Mohilev** NOUN an industrial city in E Belarus on the Dnieper River: passed to Russia in 1772 after Polish rule. Pop.: 369 000 (1998 est.).

mogul[1] (ˈməʊgʌl, məʊˈgʌl) NOUN 1 an important or powerful person. 2 a type of steam locomotive with a wheel arrangement of two leading wheels, six driving wheels, and no trailing wheels.
▹HISTORY C18: from MOGUL

mogul[2] (ˈməʊgəl) NOUN a mound of hard snow on a ski slope.
▹HISTORY C20: perhaps from South German dialect *Mugl*

Mogul (ˈməʊgʌl, məʊˈgʌl) NOUN 1 a member of the Muslim dynasty of Indian emperors established by Baber in 1526. See **Great Mogul.** 2 a Muslim Indian, Mongol, or Mongolian. ◆ ADJECTIVE 3 of or relating to the Moguls or their empire.
▹HISTORY C16: from Persian *mughul* Mongol

mogul skiing NOUN a skiing event in which skiers descend a slope which is covered in mounds of snow, making two jumps during the descent.

MOH (formerly in Britain) ABBREVIATION FOR Medical Officer of Health.

mohair (ˈməʊˌhɛə) NOUN 1 Also called: **angora.** the long soft silky hair that makes up the outer coat of the Angora goat. 2 **a** a fabric made from the yarn of this hair and cotton or wool. **b** (*as modifier*): *a mohair suit.*
▹HISTORY C16: variant (influenced by *hair*) of earlier *mocayare,* ultimately from Arabic *mukhayyar,* literally: choice, from *khayyara* to choose

Moham. ABBREVIATION FOR Mohammedan.

Mohammedan (məʊˈhæmɪdᵊn) NOUN, ADJECTIVE

another word, formerly common in Western usage but never used among Muslims, for **Muslim.**

Mohammedanism (məʊ'hæmɪdᵊ,nɪzəm) NOUN a name, formerly common in Western usage but never used among Muslims, for the Muslim religion; Islam. See **Islam.**

Mohammedanize *or* **Mohammedanise** (məʊ'hæmɪdᵊ,naɪz) VERB (*tr*) another word, formerly common in Western usage but never used among Muslims, for **Islamize.**

Moharram (məʊ'hærəm) NOUN a variant of **Muharram.**

Mohave *or* **Mojave** (məʊ'hɑːvɪ) NOUN [1] (*plural* **-ves** *or* **-ve**) a member of a North American Indian people formerly living along the Colorado River. [2] the language of this people, belonging to the Yuman family.

Mohave Desert NOUN another name for **Mojave Desert.**

mohawk ('məʊhɔːk) NOUN [1] *Skating* a half turn from either edge of either skate to the corresponding edge of the other skate. [2] the US and Canadian name for **mohican.**
▷HISTORY C19: after MOHAWK¹

Mohawk¹ ('məʊhɔːk) NOUN [1] (*plural* **-hawks** *or* **-hawk**) a member of a North American Indian people formerly living along the Mohawk River; one of the Iroquois peoples. [2] the language of this people, belonging to the Iroquoian family.

Mohawk² ('məʊhɔːk) NOUN a river in E central New York State, flowing south and east to the Hudson River at Cohoes: the largest tributary of the Hudson. Length: 238 km (148 miles).

mohel ('mɔɛl, mɔɪl) NOUN *Judaism* a man qualified to conduct circumcisions.
▷HISTORY from Hebrew

Mohenjo-Daro (mə'hɛndʒəʊ'dɑːrəʊ) NOUN an excavated city in SE Pakistan, southwest of Sukkur near the River Indus: flourished during the third millennium B.C.

mohican (məʊ'hiːkən) NOUN [1] a punk hairstyle in which the head is shaved at the sides and the remaining strip of hair is worn stiffly erect and sometimes brightly coloured. [2] a person wearing such a hairstyle.

Mohican ('məʊɪkən, məʊ'hiːkən) *or* **Mahican** (mə'hiːkən) NOUN [1] (*plural* **-cans** *or* **-can**) a member of a North American Indian people formerly living along the Hudson river and east of it. [2] the language of this people, belonging to the Algonquian family.

Moho ('məʊhəʊ) NOUN short for **Mohorovičić discontinuity.**

Mohock ('məʊhɒk) NOUN (in 18th-century London) one of a group of aristocratic ruffians, who attacked people in the streets at night.
▷HISTORY C18: variant of MOHAWK¹

Mohole ('məʊ,həʊl) NOUN an abandoned research project to drill through the earth's crust down to the Mohorovičić discontinuity to obtain samples of mantle rocks.
▷HISTORY C20: from *Moho(rovičić)* + HOLE. See MOHOROVIČIĆ DISCONTINUITY

Mohorovičić discontinuity (,məʊhə'rəʊvɪtʃɪtʃ) NOUN the boundary between the earth's crust and mantle, across which there is a sudden change in the velocity of seismic waves. Often shortened to: **Moho.**
▷HISTORY C20: named after Andrija *Mohorovičić* (1857–1936), Croatian geologist

Mohr's circle (mɔːz) NOUN a graphical construction enabling the stresses in the cross-section of a body to be determined if the principal stresses are known.
▷HISTORY C20: named after Otto *Mohr* (1773–1839), German scientist

Mohs scale (məʊz) NOUN a scale for expressing the hardness of solids by comparing them with ten standards ranging from talc, with a value of 1, to diamond, with a value of 10.
▷HISTORY C19: named after Friedrich *Mohs* (1773–1839), German mineralogist

mohur ('məʊhə) NOUN a former Indian gold coin worth 15 rupees.
▷HISTORY C17: from Hindi

MOI ABBREVIATION FOR Ministry of Information (now superseded by **COI**).

moidore ('mɔɪdɔː) NOUN a former Portuguese gold coin.
▷HISTORY C18: from Portuguese *moeda de ouro* money of gold

moiety ('mɔɪɪtɪ) NOUN, *plural* **-ties.** *Archaic* [1] a half. [2] one of two parts or divisions of something.
▷HISTORY C15: from Old French *moitié,* from Latin *mediētās* middle, from *medius*

moil (mɔɪl) *Archaic or dialect* ◆ VERB [1] to moisten or soil or become moist, soiled, etc. [2] (*intr*) to toil or drudge (esp in the phrase **toil and moil**). ◆ NOUN [3] toil; drudgery. [4] confusion; turmoil.
▷HISTORY C14 (to moisten; later: to work hard in unpleasantly wet conditions) from Old French *moillier,* ultimately from Latin *mollis* soft
▸'**moiler** NOUN

Moirai ('mɔɪriː) PLURAL NOUN, *singular* **Moira** ('mɔɪrə). **the.** the Greek goddesses of fate. Roman counterparts: **the Parcae.** See **Fates.**

moire (mwɑː) NOUN a fabric, usually silk, having a watered effect.
▷HISTORY C17: from French, earlier *mouaire,* from MOHAIR

moiré ('mwɑːreɪ) ADJECTIVE [1] having a watered or wavelike pattern. ◆ NOUN [2] such a pattern, impressed on fabrics by means of engraved rollers. [3] any fabric having such a pattern; moire. [4] Also: **moiré pattern.** a pattern seen when two geometrical patterns, such as grids, are visually superimposed.
▷HISTORY C17: from French, from *moire* MOHAIR

Moism ('məʊɪzəm) NOUN the religious and ethical teaching of Mo-Zi, the Chinese religious philosopher (?470–?391 B.C.), and his followers, emphasizing universal love, ascetic self-discipline, and obedience to the will of Heaven.

moist (mɔɪst) ADJECTIVE [1] slightly damp or wet. [2] saturated with or suggestive of moisture.
▷HISTORY C14: from Old French, ultimately related to Latin *mūcidus* musty, from *mūcus* MUCUS
▸'**moistly** ADVERB ▸'**moistness** NOUN

moisten ('mɔɪsᵊn) VERB to make or become moist.
▸'**moistener** NOUN

moisture ('mɔɪstʃə) NOUN water or other liquid diffused as vapour or condensed on or in objects.
▸'**moistureless** ADJECTIVE

moisturize *or* **moisturise** ('mɔɪstʃə,raɪz) VERB (*tr*) to add or restore moisture to (the air, the skin, etc.).

moisturizer *or* **moisturiser** ('mɔɪstʃə,raɪzə) NOUN a cosmetic cream, lotion, etc. applied to the skin to add or restore moisture to it.

moither ('mɔɪðə) *or* **moider** ('mɔɪdə) VERB *Dialect* [1] (*tr; usually passive*) to bother or bewilder. [2] (*intr*) to talk in a rambling or confused manner.
▷HISTORY C17: of obscure origin

Mojave (məʊ'hɑːvɪ) NOUN a variant spelling of **Mohave.**

Mojave Desert *or* **Mohave Desert** NOUN a desert in S California, south of the Sierra Nevada: part of the Great Basin. Area: 38 850 sq. km (15 000 sq. miles).

mojo ('məʊdʒəʊ) NOUN, *plural* **mojos** *or* **mojoes.** *US, slang* [1] **a** an amulet, charm, or magic spell. **b** (*as modifier*): *ancient mojo spells.* [2] the art of casting magic spells.
▷HISTORY C20: of W African origin

moke (məʊk) NOUN [1] *Brit* a slang name for **donkey** (sense 1). [2] *Austral, slang* an inferior type of horse.
▷HISTORY C19: origin obscure

Mokha ('məʊkə, 'mɒk-) NOUN a variant of **Mocha.**

moki ('məʊkɪ) NOUN, *plural* **mokis** *or* **moki.** either of two edible sea fish of New Zealand, the blue cod (*Percis colias*) or the bastard trumpeter (*Latridopsis ciliaris*).
▷HISTORY Maori

moko ('məʊkəʊ) NOUN, *plural* **mokos.** *NZ* a Maori tattoo or tattoo pattern.
▷HISTORY Maori

mokopuna (,məʊkəʊ'puːnə) NOUN *NZ* a grandchild or young person.
▷HISTORY Maori

mokoro (mo'koro) NOUN, *plural* **-ro** or **-ros.** (in Botswana) the traditional dugout canoe of the people of the Okavango Delta.
▷HISTORY from a Bantu language of Botswana

Mokpo (,məʊk'pəʊ) NOUN a port in SW South Korea, on the Yellow Sea. Pop.: 247 524 (1995).

moksha ('mɒkʃə) NOUN *Hinduism* freedom from the endless cycle of transmigration into a state of bliss.
▷HISTORY from Sanskrit *mokṣa* liberation

mol THE CHEMICAL SYMBOL FOR mole³.

mol. ABBREVIATION FOR: [1] molecular. [2] molecule.

mola ('məʊlə) NOUN, *plural* **-la** *or* **-las.** another name for **sunfish** (sense 1).
▷HISTORY C17: from Latin, literally: millstone

molal ('məʊləl) ADJECTIVE *Chem* of or consisting of a solution containing one mole of solute per thousand grams of solvent.
▷HISTORY C20: from MOLE³ + -AL¹

molality (mɒ'lælɪtɪ) NOUN, *plural* **-ties.** (not in technical usage) a measure of concentration equal to the number of moles of solute in a thousand grams of solvent.

molar¹ ('məʊlə) NOUN [1] any of the 12 broad-faced grinding teeth in man. [2] a corresponding tooth in other mammals. ◆ ADJECTIVE [3] of, relating to, or designating any of these teeth. [4] used for or capable of grinding.
▷HISTORY C16: from Latin *molāris* for grinding, from *mola* millstone

molar² ('məʊlə) ADJECTIVE [1] (of a physical quantity) per unit amount of substance: *molar volume.* [2] (not recommended in technical usage) (of a solution) containing one mole of solute per litre of solution.
▷HISTORY C19: from Latin *mōlēs* a mass

molarity (mɒ'lærɪtɪ) NOUN another name (not in technical usage) for **concentration** (sense 4).

molasse (mə'læs) NOUN a soft sediment produced by the erosion of mountain ranges after the final phase of mountain building.
▷HISTORY C18: from French, perhaps alteration of *mollasse,* from Latin *mollis* soft

molasses (mə'læsɪz) NOUN (*functioning as singular*) [1] the thick brown uncrystallized bitter syrup obtained from sugar during refining. [2] the US and Canadian name for **treacle** (sense 1).
▷HISTORY C16: from Portuguese *melaço,* from Late Latin *mellāceum* must, from Latin *mel* honey

mold (məʊld) NOUN, VERB the US spelling of **mould.**

Moldau ('mɔldau) NOUN [1] the German name for **Moldavia.** [2] the German name for the **Vltava.**

Moldavia (mɒl'deɪvɪə) NOUN [1] another name for **Moldova.** [2] a former principality of E Europe, consisting of the basins of the Rivers Prut and Dniester: the E part (Bessarabia) became Moldova; the W part remains a province of Romania. Romanian name: **Moldova** (mol'dova). German name: **Moldau.**

Moldavian (mɒl'deɪvɪən) ADJECTIVE, NOUN [1] another name for **Moldovan.** ◆ ADJECTIVE [2] of or relating to the former E European principality of Moldavia or its inhabitants. ◆ NOUN [3] a native or inhabitant of Moldavia.

moldavite ('mɒldə,vaɪt) NOUN a green tektite found in the Czech Republic, thought to be the product of an ancient meteorite impact in Germany.
▷HISTORY C19: named after MOLDAVIA

moldboard ('məʊld,bɔːd) NOUN the US spelling of **mouldboard.**

molder ('məʊldə) VERB, NOUN the US spelling of **moulder.**

molding ('məʊldɪŋ) NOUN the US spelling of **moulding.**

Moldova (mɒl'dəʊvə) NOUN a republic in SE Europe: comprising the E part of the former principality of Moldavia, the E part of which (Bessarabia) was ceded to the Soviet Union in 1940 and formed the Moldavian Soviet Socialist Republic until it gained independence in 1991; an agricultural region with many vineyards. Official language: Romanian. Religion: nonreligious and Christian. Currency: leu. Capital: Kishinev. Pop.: 4 431 000 (2001 est.). Area: 33 670 sq. km (13 000 sq. miles). Also called: **Moldavia** (mɒl'deɪvɪə).

Moldovan (mɒl'dəʊvən) *or* **Moldavian** ADJECTIVE [1] of or relating to Moldova or its inhabitants. ◆ NOUN [2] a native or inhabitant of Moldova.

moldy (ˈməʊldɪ) ADJECTIVE **moldier, moldiest.** the US spelling of **mouldy.**
▸ **ˈmoldiness** NOUN

mole[1] (məʊl) NOUN *Pathol* a nontechnical name for **naevus.**
▹HISTORY Old English *māl;* related to Old High German *meil* spot

mole[2] (məʊl) NOUN [1] any small burrowing mammal, of the family *Talpidae,* of Europe, Asia, and North and Central America: order *Insectivora* (insectivores). They have velvety, typically dark fur and forearms specialized for digging. [2] **golden mole.** any small African burrowing molelike mammal of the family *Chrysochloridae,* having copper-coloured fur: order *Insectivora* (insectivores). [3] *Informal* a spy who has infiltrated an organization and, often over a long period, become a trusted member of it.
▹HISTORY C14: from Middle Dutch *mol,* of Germanic origin; compare Middle Low German *mol*

mole[3] (məʊl) NOUN the basic SI unit of amount of substance; the amount that contains as many elementary entities as there are atoms in 0.012 kilogram of carbon-12. The entity must be specified and may be an atom, a molecule, an ion, a radical, an electron, a photon, etc. Symbol: mol.
▹HISTORY C20: from German *Mol,* short for *Molekül* MOLECULE

mole[4] (məʊl) NOUN [1] a breakwater. [2] a harbour protected by a breakwater. [3] a large tunnel excavator for use in soft rock.
▹HISTORY C16: from French *môle,* from Latin *mōlēs* mass

mole[5] (məʊl) NOUN *Pathol* a fleshy growth in the uterus formed by the degeneration of fetal tissues.
▹HISTORY C17: medical use of Latin *mola* millstone

mole[6] (ˈməʊleɪ) NOUN a spicy Mexican sauce made from chili and chocolate.
▹HISTORY C20: from Mexican Spanish from Nahuatl *molli* sauce

Molech (ˈməʊlɛk) NOUN *Old Testament* a variant of **Moloch.**

mole cricket NOUN any subterranean orthopterous insect of the family *Gryllotalpidae,* of Europe and North America, similar and related to crickets but having the first pair of legs specialized for digging.

molecular (məʊˈlɛkjʊlə, mə-) ADJECTIVE [1] of or relating to molecules: *molecular hydrogen.* [2] *Logic* (of a sentence, formula, etc.) capable of analysis into atomic formulae of the appropriate kind.
▸ **molecularity** (məʊˌlɛkjʊˈlærɪtɪ) NOUN ▸ **moˈlecularly** ADVERB

molecular beam *or* **ray** NOUN *Physics* a parallel beam of molecules that are at low pressure and suffer no interatomic or intermolecular collisions.

molecular biology NOUN the study of biological phenomena at the molecular level.

molecular cloud NOUN a cool dense interstellar region composed of a wide variety of molecules, mainly hydrogen, plus some dust, in which stars are forming.

molecular distillation NOUN distillation in which a substance is heated under vacuum, the pressure being so low that no intermolecular collisions can occur before condensation.

molecular film NOUN another name for **monolayer.**

molecular formula NOUN a chemical formula indicating the numbers and types of atoms in a molecule: *H_2SO_4 is the molecular formula of sulphuric acid.* Compare **empirical formula, structural formula.**

molecular genetics NOUN (*functioning as singular*) the study of the molecular constitution of genes and chromosomes.

molecular sieve NOUN *Chem* a material that can absorb large amounts of certain compounds while not absorbing others and is thus suitable for use in separating mixtures.

molecular volume NOUN the volume occupied by one mole of a substance. Also called: **molar volume.**

molecular weight NOUN the former name for **relative molecular mass.**

molecule (ˈmɒlɪˌkjuːl) NOUN [1] the simplest unit of a chemical compound that can exist, consisting of two or more atoms held together by chemical bonds. [2] a very small particle.
▹HISTORY C18: via French from New Latin *mōlēcula,* diminutive of Latin *mōlēs* mass, MOLE[4]

mole drain NOUN an underground cylindrical drainage channel cut by a special plough to drain heavy agricultural soil.

molehill (ˈməʊlˌhɪl) NOUN [1] the small mound of earth thrown up by a burrowing mole. [2] **make a mountain out of a molehill.** to exaggerate an unimportant matter out of all proportion.

mole rat NOUN [1] any burrowing molelike African rodent of the family *Bathyergidae.* [2] any similar rodent, esp any member of the genus *Spalax,* of Asia and North Africa: family *Spalacidae.* [3] another name for **bandicoot rat** (see **bandicoot** (sense 2)).

mole run NOUN (*usually plural*) *Informal* any part of a system of underground tunnels, rooms, etc., prepared for use in the event of nuclear war.

moleskin (ˈməʊlˌskɪn) NOUN [1] the dark grey dense velvety pelt of a mole, used as a fur. [2] a hard-wearing cotton fabric of twill weave used for work clothes, etc. [3] (*modifier*) made from moleskin: *a moleskin waistcoat.*

moleskins (ˈməʊlˌskɪnz) PLURAL NOUN clothing of moleskin.

molest (məˈlɛst) VERB (*tr*) [1] to disturb or annoy by malevolent interference. [2] to accost or attack, esp with the intention of assaulting sexually.
▹HISTORY C14: from Latin *molestāre* to annoy, from *molestus* troublesome, from *mōlēs* mass
▸ **molestation** (ˌməʊlɛˈsteɪʃən) NOUN ▸ **moˈlester** NOUN

moline (məˈlaɪn) ADJECTIVE *Heraldry* (of a cross) having arms of equal length, forked and curved back at the ends.
▹HISTORY C16: probably from Anglo-French *moliné,* from *molin* MILL[1], referring to the arms curved back like the ends of a mill-rind

Molinism (ˈmɒlɪnɪzəm) NOUN *RC Church* a doctrine of grace that attempts to reconcile the efficacy of divine grace with human free will in responding to it.
▹HISTORY C17: named after *Luis de Molina* (1535–1600), Spanish Jesuit who taught such a doctrine

Molise (*Italian* moˈliːze) NOUN a region of S central Italy, the second smallest of the regions: separated from **Abruzzi e Molise** in 1965. Capital: Campobasso. Pop.: 327 987 (2000 est.). Area: 4438 sq. km (1731 sq. miles).

moll (mɒl) NOUN *Slang* [1] the female accomplice of a gangster. [2] a prostitute.
▹HISTORY C17: from *Moll,* familiar form of *Mary*

mollah (ˈmɔːlə) NOUN an older spelling of **mullah.**

mollify (ˈmɒlɪˌfaɪ) VERB **-fies, -fying, -fied.** (*tr*) [1] to pacify; soothe. [2] to lessen the harshness or severity of.
▹HISTORY C15: from Old French *mollifier,* via Late Latin, from Latin *mollis* soft + *facere* to make
▸ **ˈmolliˌfiable** ADJECTIVE ▸ **ˌmollifiˈcation** NOUN ▸ **ˈmolliˌfier** NOUN

mollusc *or US* **mollusk** (ˈmɒləsk) NOUN any invertebrate of the phylum *Mollusca,* having a soft unsegmented body and often a shell, secreted by a fold of skin (the mantle). The group includes the gastropods (snails, slugs, etc.), bivalves (clams, mussels, etc.), and cephalopods (cuttlefish, octopuses, etc.).
▹HISTORY C18: via New Latin from Latin *molluscus,* from *mollis* soft
▸ **molluscan** *or* (*US*) **molluskan** (mɒˈlʌskən) ADJECTIVE, NOUN ▸ **ˈmollusc-ˌlike** *or* (*US*) **ˈmollusk-ˌlike** ADJECTIVE

molluscoid (mɒˈlʌskɔɪd) *or* **molluscoidal** (ˌmɒlʌsˈkɔɪdᵊl) ADJECTIVE of, relating to, or belonging to the *Molluscoidea,* a former phylum including the brachiopods and bryozoans now classified separately.
▹HISTORY C19: via New Latin from Latin *molluscus* soft

Mollweide projection (ˈmɒlˌvaɪdə) NOUN an equal-area map projection with the parallels and the central meridian being straight lines and the other meridians curved. It is often used to show world distributions of various phenomena.
▹HISTORY C19: named after Karl B. *Mollweide* (1774–1825), German mathematician and astronomer

molly[1] (ˈmɒlɪ) NOUN, *plural* **-lies.** any brightly coloured tropical or subtropical American freshwater cyprinodont fish of the genus *Mollienisia.*
▹HISTORY C19: from New Latin *Mollienisia,* from Comte F. N. *Mollien* (1758–1850), French statesman

molly[2] (ˈmɒlɪ) NOUN, *plural* **-lies.** *Irish informal* an effeminate, weak, or cowardly boy or man.
▹HISTORY C18: perhaps from *Molly,* pet name for *Mary*

mollycoddle (ˈmɒlɪˌkɒdᵊl) VERB [1] (*tr*) to treat with indulgent care; pamper. ◆ NOUN [2] a pampered person.
▹HISTORY C19: from MOLLY[2] + CODDLE
▸ **ˈmollyˌcoddler** NOUN

mollyhawk (ˈmɒlɪˌhɔːk) NOUN *NZ* the juvenile of the southern black-backed gull (*Larus dominicanus*).

Molly Maguire (ˈmɒlɪ məˈgwaɪə) NOUN [1] *Irish history* a member of a secret society that terrorized law officers during the 1840s to prevent evictions. [2] (in Pennsylvania from about 1865 to 1877) a member of a society of miners that terrorized mine owners and their agents in an effort to obtain better pay.
▹HISTORY C19: the name refers to the female disguise adopted by members of these societies

mollymawk (ˈmɒlɪˌmɔːk) NOUN *NZ* an informal name for **mallemuck.**

moloch (ˈməʊlɒk) NOUN a spiny Australian desert-living lizard, *Moloch horridus,* that feeds on ants: family *Agamidae* (agamas). Also called: **mountain devil, spiny lizard.**

Moloch (ˈməʊlɒk) *or* **Molech** (ˈməʊlɛk) NOUN *Old Testament* a Semitic deity to whom parents sacrificed their children.

Molokai (ˌməʊləʊˈkɑːɪ) NOUN an island in central Hawaii. Pop.: 6717 (1990). Area: 676 sq. km (261 sq. miles).

Molopo (məˈləʊpəʊ) NOUN a seasonal river rising in N South Africa and flowing west and southwest to the Orange river. Length: about 1000 km (600 miles).

Molossian (məˈlɒsɪən), **Molossian dog,** *or* **Molossian hound** NOUN a breed of dog native to Epirus in NW Greece, used in classical antiquity as a hunting dog and guard dog.
▹HISTORY from *Molossia,* a district of Epirus

Molotov (ˈmɒləˌtɒf; *Russian* ˈmɔlətəf) NOUN the former name (1940–62) for **Perm.**

Molotov cocktail (ˈmɒləˌtɒf) NOUN an elementary incendiary weapon, usually a bottle of petrol with a short-delay fuse or wick; petrol bomb.
▹HISTORY C20: named after Vyacheslav Mikhailovich *Molotov* (1890–1986), Soviet statesman

molt (məʊlt) VERB, NOUN the usual US spelling of **moult.**

molten (ˈməʊltən) ADJECTIVE [1] liquefied; melted: *molten lead.* [2] made by having been melted: *molten casts.* ◆ VERB [3] the past participle of **melt.**

molto (ˈmɒltəʊ) ADVERB *Music* (preceded or followed by a musical direction, esp a tempo marking) very: *allegro molto; molto adagio.*
▹HISTORY from Italian, from Latin *multum* (adv) much

Moluccas (məʊˈlʌkəz, mə-) *or* **Molucca Islands** PLURAL NOUN a group of islands in the Malay Archipelago, between Sulawesi (Celebes) and New Guinea. Capital: Amboina. Pop.: 2 223 000 (1999 est.). Area: about 74 505 sq. km (28 766 sq. miles). Indonesian name: **Maluku.** Former name: **Spice Islands.**

mol. wt. ABBREVIATION FOR molecular weight.

moly (ˈməʊlɪ) NOUN, *plural* **-lies.** [1] *Greek myth* a magic herb given by Hermes to Odysseus to nullify the spells of Circe. [2] a liliaceous plant, *Allium moly,* that is native to S Europe and has yellow flowers in a dense cluster.
▹HISTORY C16: from Latin *mōly,* from Greek *mōlu*

molybdate (mɒˈlɪbdeɪt) NOUN a salt or ester of a molybdic acid.

molybdenite (mɒˈlɪbdɪˌnaɪt) NOUN a soft grey mineral consisting of molybdenum sulphide in hexagonal crystalline form with rhenium as an impurity: the main source of molybdenum and rhenium. Formula: MoS_2.

molybdenous (mɒˈlɪbdɪnəs) ADJECTIVE of or containing molybdenum in the divalent state.

molybdenum (mɒˈlɪbdɪnəm) NOUN a very hard ductile silvery-white metallic element occurring

principally in molybdenite: used mainly in alloys, esp to harden and strengthen steels. Symbol: Mo; atomic no.: 42; atomic wt.: 95.94; valency: 2–6; relative density: 10.22; melting pt.: 2623°C; boiling pt.: 4639°C.
▷HISTORY C19: from New Latin, from Latin *molybdaena* galena, from Greek *molubdaina,* from *molubdos* lead

molybdic (mɒˈlɪbdɪk) ADJECTIVE of or containing molybdenum in the trivalent or hexavalent state.

molybdous (mɒˈlɪbdəs) ADJECTIVE of or containing molybdenum, esp in a low valence state.

mom (mɒm) NOUN *Chiefly US and Canadian* an informal word for **mother**[1].

Mombasa (mɒmˈbæsə) NOUN a port in S Kenya, on a coral island in a bay of the Indian Ocean: the chief port for Kenya, Uganda, and NE Tanzania; became British in 1887, capital of the East African Protectorate until 1907. Pop.: 461 753 (1999).

moment (ˈməʊmənt) NOUN 1 a short indefinite period of time: *he'll be here in a moment.* 2 a specific instant or point in time: *at that moment the doorbell rang.* 3 **the moment.** the present point of time: *at the moment it's fine.* 4 import, significance, or value: *a man of moment.* 5 *Physics* **a** a tendency to produce motion, esp rotation about a point or axis. **b** the product of a physical quantity, such as force or mass, and its distance from a fixed reference point. See also **moment of inertia.** 6 *Statistics* the mean of a specified power of the deviations of all the values of a variable in its frequency distribution. The power of the deviations indicates the order of the moment and the deviations may be from the origin (giving a **moment about the origin**) or from the mean (giving a **moment about the mean**).
▷HISTORY C14: from Old French, from Latin *mōmentum,* from *movēre* to move

momentarily (ˈməʊməntərəlɪ, -trɪlɪ) ADVERB 1 for an instant; temporarily. 2 from moment to moment; every instant. 3 *US and Canadian* very soon. ◆ Also (for senses 1, 2): **momently** (ˈməʊməntlɪ).

momentary (ˈməʊməntərɪ, -trɪ) ADJECTIVE lasting for only a moment; temporary.
▸ˈ**momentariness** NOUN

moment of inertia NOUN the tendency of a body to resist angular acceleration, expressed as the sum of the products of the mass of each particle in the body and the square of its perpendicular distance from the axis of rotation. Symbol: *I.*

moment of truth NOUN 1 a moment when a person or thing is put to the test. 2 the point in a bullfight when the matador is about to kill the bull.

momentous (məʊˈmɛntəs) ADJECTIVE of great significance.
▸**moˈmentously** ADVERB ▸**moˈmentousness** NOUN

momentum (məʊˈmɛntəm) NOUN, *plural* **-ta** (-tə) *or* **-tums.** 1 *Physics* the product of a body's mass and its velocity. Symbol: *p.* See also **angular momentum.** 2 the impetus of a body resulting from its motion. 3 driving power or strength.
▷HISTORY C17: from Latin: movement; see MOMENT

momism (ˈmɒmɪzəm) NOUN *US informal* the excessive domination of a child by his or her mother.

momma (ˈmɒmə) NOUN a variant (esp US and Canadian) of **mamma**[1].

mommy track (ˈmɒmɪ) NOUN *US* a path in life in which a woman devotes most of her time to her children and home rather than to her career.

Momus (ˈməʊməs) NOUN, *plural* **-muses** *or* **-mi** (-maɪ). 1 *Greek myth* the god of blame and mockery. 2 a cavilling critic.

Mon (məʊn) NOUN 1 (*plural* **Mon** *or* **Mons**) a member of a people of Myanmar and Thailand related to the Khmer of Cambodia. 2 the language of this people, belonging to the Mon-Khmer family. ◆ Also called: **Talaing.**

Mon. ABBREVIATION FOR Monday.

mon- COMBINING FORM a variant of **mono-** before a vowel.

mona (ˈməʊnə) NOUN a W African guenon monkey, *Cercopithecus mona,* with dark fur on the back and white or yellow underparts.
▷HISTORY C18: from Spanish or Portuguese: monkey

Monacan (ˈmɒnəkən, məˈnɑː-) ADJECTIVE 1 of or relating to Monaco or its inhabitants. ◆ NOUN 2 a native or inhabitant of Monaco.

monachal (ˈmɒnəkᵊl) ADJECTIVE a less common word for **monastic.**
▷HISTORY C16: from Old French, from Church Latin *monachālis,* from *monachus* MONK
▸ˈ**monachism** NOUN ▸ˈ**monachist** ADJECTIVE, NOUN

monacid (mɒnˈæsɪd) *or* **monacidic** (ˌmɒnəˈsɪdɪk) ADJECTIVE variants of **monoacid.**

Monaco (ˈmɒnəˌkəʊ, məˈnɑːkəʊ; *French* mɔnako) NOUN a principality in SW Europe, on the Mediterranean and forming an enclave in SE France: the second smallest sovereign state in the world (after the Vatican); consists of **Monaco-Ville** (the capital) on a rocky headland, **La Condamine** (a business area and port), **Monte Carlo** (the resort centre), and **Fontvieille** a light industrial area. Language: French. Religion: Roman Catholic. Currency: euro. Pop.: 31 800 (2001 est.). Area: 189 hectares (476 acres). Related adjective: **Monegasque.**

monad (ˈmɒnæd, ˈməʊ-) NOUN 1 (*plural* **-ads** *or* **-ades** (-əˌdiːz)) *Philosophy* **a** any fundamental singular metaphysical entity, esp if autonomous. **b** (in the metaphysics of Leibnitz) a simple indestructible nonspatial element regarded as the unit of which reality consists. **c** (in the pantheistic philosophy of Giordano Bruno) a fundamental metaphysical unit that is spatially extended and psychically aware. 2 a single-celled organism, esp a flagellate protozoan. 3 an atom, ion, or radical with a valency of one. ◆ Also called (for senses 1, 2): **monas.**
▷HISTORY C17: from Late Latin *monas,* from Greek: unit, from *monos* alone
▸**moˈnadical** ADJECTIVE ▸**moˈnadically** ADVERB

monadelphous (ˌmɒnəˈdɛlfəs) ADJECTIVE 1 (of stamens) having united filaments forming a tube around the style. 2 (of flowers) having monadelphous stamens.
▷HISTORY C19: from MONO- + Greek *adelphos* brother, twin + -OUS

monadic (mɒˈnædɪk) ADJECTIVE 1 being or relating to a monad. 2 *Logic, maths* (of an operator, predicate, etc.) having only a single argument place.

monadism (ˈmɒnəˌdɪzəm, ˈməʊ-) *or* **monadology** (ˌmɒnəˈdɒlədʒɪ, ˌməʊ-) NOUN (esp in the writings of Gottfried Leibnitz, the German rationalist philosopher and mathematician (1646–1716)) the philosophical doctrine that monads are the ultimate units of reality.
▸ˌ**monadˈistic** ADJECTIVE

monadnock (məˈnædnɒk) NOUN a residual hill that consists of hard rock in an otherwise eroded area.
▷HISTORY C19: named after Mount *Monadnock,* in New Hampshire

Monaghan (ˈmɒnəhən) NOUN 1 a county of NE Republic of Ireland, in Ulster province: many small lakes. County town: Monaghan. Pop.: 51 313 (1996). Area: 1292 sq. km (499 sq. miles). 2 a town in NE Republic of Ireland, county town of Co. Monaghan. Pop. 6200 (1995 est.).

monal *or* **monaul** (ˈmɒnɔːl) NOUN any of several S Asian pheasants of the genus *Lophophorus,* the males of which have a brilliantly coloured plumage.
▷HISTORY C18: from Hindi

Mona Lisa (ˈməʊnə ˈliːzə) NOUN a portrait of a young woman painted by Leonardo da Vinci, admired for her enigmatic smile. Also called: **La Gioconda.**

monandrous (mɒˈnændrəs) ADJECTIVE 1 having or preferring only one male sexual partner over a period of time. 2 (of plants) having flowers with only one stamen. 3 (of flowers) having only one stamen.
▷HISTORY C19: from MONO- + -ANDROUS
▸**moˈnandry** NOUN

monanthous (mɒˈnænθəs) ADJECTIVE (of certain plants) having or producing only one flower.
▷HISTORY C19: from MONO- + Greek *anthos* flower

Mona Passage (ˈməʊnə) NOUN a strait between Puerto Rico and the Dominican Republic, linking the Atlantic with the Caribbean.

monarch (ˈmɒnək) NOUN 1 a sovereign head of state, esp a king, queen, or emperor, who rules usually by hereditary right. 2 a supremely powerful or pre-eminent person or thing. 3 Also called: **milkweed.** a large migratory butterfly, *Danaus plexippus,* that has orange-and-black wings and feeds on the milkweed plant: family *Danaidae.*
▷HISTORY C15: from Late Latin *monarcha,* from Greek; see MONO-, -ARCH
▸**monarchal** (mɒˈnɑːkᵊl) *or* **monarchial** (mɒˈnɑːkɪəl) ADJECTIVE ▸**moˈnarchally** ADVERB ▸**moˈnarchical** *or* **moˈnarchic** ADJECTIVE ▸**moˈnarchically** ADVERB
▸ˈ**monarchism** NOUN ▸ˈ**monarchist** NOUN, ADJECTIVE
▸ˌ**monarˈchistic** ADJECTIVE

monarchy (ˈmɒnəkɪ) NOUN, *plural* **-chies.** 1 a form of government in which supreme authority is vested in a single and usually hereditary figure, such as a king, and whose powers can vary from those of an absolute despot to those of a figurehead. 2 a country reigned over by a king, prince, or other monarch.

monarda (mɒˈnɑːdə) NOUN any mintlike North American plant of the genus *Monarda:* family *Lamiaceae* (labiates). See also **horsemint** (sense 2), **bergamot** (sense 4).
▷HISTORY C19: from New Latin, named after N. *Monardés* (1493–1588), Spanish botanist

monas (ˈmɒnæs, ˈməʊ-) NOUN, *plural* **monades** (ˈmɒnəˌdiːz). another word for **monad** (senses 1, 2).

monastery (ˈmɒnəstərɪ, -strɪ) NOUN, *plural* **-teries.** the residence of a religious community, esp of monks, living in seclusion from secular society and bound by religious vows.
▷HISTORY C15: from Church Latin *monastērium,* from Late Greek *monastērion,* from Greek *monázein* to live alone, from *monos* alone
▸**monasterial** (ˌmɒnəˈstɪərɪəl) ADJECTIVE

monastic (məˈnæstɪk) ADJECTIVE *also less commonly* **monastical.** 1 of or relating to monasteries or monks, nuns, etc. 2 resembling this sort of life; reclusive. ◆ NOUN 3 a person who is committed to this way of life, esp a monk.
▸**moˈnastically** ADVERB

monasticism (məˈnæstɪˌsɪzəm) NOUN the monastic system, movement, or way of life.

Monastral (məˈnæstrəl) ADJECTIVE *Trademark* denoting certain fast pigments used in paints and inks, derived from phthalocyanine.

monatomic (ˌmɒnəˈtɒmɪk) *or* **monoatomic** (ˌmɒnəʊəˈtɒmɪk) ADJECTIVE *Chem* 1 (of an element) having or consisting of single atoms: *argon is a monatomic gas.* 2 (of a compound or molecule) having only one atom or group that can be replaced in a chemical reaction. 3 a less common word for **monovalent.**

monaul (ˈmɒnɔːl) NOUN a variant spelling of **monal.**

monaural (mɒˈnɔːrəl) ADJECTIVE 1 relating to, having, or hearing with only one ear. 2 another word for **monophonic.**
▸**monˈaurally** ADVERB

monaxial (mɒˈnæksɪəl) ADJECTIVE another word for **uniaxial.**

monazite (ˈmɒnəˌzaɪt) NOUN a yellow to reddish-brown mineral consisting of a phosphate of thorium, cerium, and lanthanum in monoclinic crystalline form.
▷HISTORY C19: from German, from Greek *monazein* to live alone, so called because of its rarity

Mönchengladbach (*German* mœnçənˈglatbax) NOUN a city in W Germany, in W North Rhine-Westphalia: headquarters of NATO forces in N central Europe; textile industry. Pop.: 264 100 (1999 est.). Former name: **München-Gladbach.**

Moncton (ˈmɒŋktən) NOUN a city in E Canada, in SE New Brunswick. Pop.: 80 744 (1991).

mondain (*French* mɔ̃dɛ̃) NOUN 1 a man who moves in fashionable society. ◆ ADJECTIVE 2 characteristic of fashionable society; worldly.
▷HISTORY C19: from French; see MUNDANE

mondaine (*French* mɔ̃dɛn) NOUN 1 a woman who moves in fashionable society. ◆ ADJECTIVE 2 characteristic of fashionable society; worldly.
▷HISTORY C19: from French; see MUNDANE

Monday (ˈmʌndɪ) NOUN the second day of the week; first day of the working week.
▷HISTORY Old English *mōnandæg* moon's day, translation of Late Latin *lūnae diēs*

Monday Club NOUN (in Britain) a club made up of right-wing Conservatives who originally met together for lunch on Monday: founded in 1961.

Mondayize *or* **Mondayise** (ˈmʌndɪˌaɪz) VERB (*tr*) *NZ* to move (a statutory holiday, such as the

Queen's birthday) to the nearest Monday in order to secure a long weekend.
▸ ˌ**Mondayi'zation** *or* ˌ**Mondayi'sation** NOUN

Monday morning quarterback NOUN *Chiefly US and Canadian informal* a person who criticizes or suggests alternative courses of action from a position of hindsight after the event in question.

mondegreen ('mɒndɪˌgriːn) NOUN a word or phrase that is misinterpreted as another word or phrase, usually with an amusing result.
▹ HISTORY C20: from the Scottish ballad 'The Bonny Earl of Murray', in which the line *laid him on the green* can be misheard as *Lady Mondegreen*

Mondeo Man (mɒn'deɪəʊ) NOUN *Brit informal* a middle-class man, seen as typically driving a Ford Mondeo and preferring to do this rather than use public transport.

mondial ('mɒndɪəl) ADJECTIVE of or involving the whole world.
▹ HISTORY C20: from French, ultimately from Latin *mundus*

Mond process (mɒnd; *German* mɔnt) NOUN a process for obtaining nickel by heating the ore in carbon monoxide to produce nickel carbonyl vapour, which is then decomposed at a higher temperature to yield the metal.
▹ HISTORY C19: named after Ludwig *Mond* (1839–1909), German chemist and industrialist

monecious (mɒ'niːʃəs) ADJECTIVE a variant spelling of **monoecious**.
▸ **mo'neciously** ADVERB

Monegasque (ˌmɒnə'gæsk) NOUN [1] a native or inhabitant of Monaco. ◆ ADJECTIVE [2] of or relating to Monaco or its inhabitants.
▹ HISTORY from French, from Provençal *mounegasc*, from *Mounegue* Monaco

Monel metal *or* **Monell metal** (mɒ'nel) NOUN *Trademark* any of various silvery corrosion-resistant alloys containing copper (28 per cent), nickel (67 per cent), and smaller quantities of such metals as iron, manganese, and aluminium.
▹ HISTORY C20: named after A. *Monell* (died 1921), president of the International Nickel Co., New York, which introduced the alloys

moneme ('məʊniːm) NOUN *Linguistics* a less common word for **morpheme**.
▹ HISTORY C20: from MONO- + -EME

monetarism ('mʌnɪtəˌrɪzəm) NOUN [1] the theory that inflation is caused by an excess quantity of money in an economy. [2] an economic policy based on this theory and on a belief in the efficiency of free market forces, that gives priority to achieving price stability by monetary control, balanced budgets, etc., and maintains that unemployment results from excessive real wage rates and cannot be controlled by Keynesian demand management.
▸ **'monetarist** NOUN, ADJECTIVE

monetary ('mʌnɪtərɪ, -trɪ) ADJECTIVE [1] of or relating to money or currency. [2] of or relating to monetarism: *a monetary policy*.
▹ HISTORY C19: from Late Latin *monētārius*, from Latin *monēta* MONEY
▸ **'monetarily** ADVERB

monetary unit NOUN a unit of value and money of a country, esp the major or standard unit.

monetize *or* **monetise** ('mʌnɪˌtaɪz) VERB (*tr*) [1] to establish as the legal tender of a country. [2] to give a legal value to (a coin).
▸ ˌ**moneti'zation** *or* ˌ**moneti'sation** NOUN

money ('mʌnɪ) NOUN [1] a medium of exchange that functions as legal tender. [2] the official currency, in the form of banknotes, coins, etc., issued by a government or other authority. [3] a particular denomination or form of currency: *silver money*. [4] property or assets with reference to their realizable value. [5] *formal plural* **moneys** *or* **monies** a pecuniary sum or income. [6] an unspecified amount of paper currency or coins: *money to lend*. [7] **for one's money.** in one's opinion. [8] **in the money.** *Informal* well-off; rich. [9] **money for old rope.** *Informal* profit obtained by little or no effort. [10] **money to burn.** more money than one needs. [11] **one's money's worth.** full value for the money one has paid for something. [12] **put money into.** to invest money in. [13] **put money on.** to place a bet on. [14] **put one's money where one's mouth is.** See **mouth** (sense 19). Related adjective: **pecuniary.**
▹ HISTORY C13: from Old French *moneie*, from Latin *monēta* coinage; see MINT[2]

moneybags ('mʌnɪˌbægz) NOUN (*functioning as singular*) *Informal* a very rich person.

moneychanger ('mʌnɪˌtʃeɪndʒə) NOUN [1] a person engaged in the business of exchanging currencies or money. [2] *Chiefly US* a machine for dispensing coins.

money cowry NOUN [1] a tropical marine gastropod, *Cypraea moneta*. [2] the shell of this mollusc, used as money in some parts of Africa and S Asia.

moneyed *or* **monied** ('mʌnɪd) ADJECTIVE [1] having a great deal of money; rich. [2] arising from or characterized by money.

moneyer ('mʌnɪə) NOUN [1] *Archaic* a person who coins money. [2] an obsolete word for **banker**[1].

money-grubbing ADJECTIVE *Informal* seeking greedily to obtain money at every opportunity.
▸ **'money-ˌgrubber** NOUN

moneylender ('mʌnɪˌlendə) NOUN a person who lends money at interest as a living.
▸ **'moneyˌlending** ADJECTIVE, NOUN

moneymaker ('mʌnɪˌmeɪkə) NOUN [1] a person who is intent on accumulating money. [2] a person or thing that is or might be profitable.
▸ **'moneyˌmaking** ADJECTIVE, NOUN

money market NOUN *Finance* the financial institutions dealing with short-term loans and capital and with foreign exchange. Compare **capital market.**

money of account NOUN another name (esp US and Canadian) for **unit of account.**

money order NOUN another name (esp US and Canadian) for **postal order.**

money-purchase ADJECTIVE another name for **defined-contribution.**

money shot NOUN *Slang* a shot in a pornographic film in which a male performer is seen to ejaculate.
▹ HISTORY C20: from the idea that the performer is only paid if he does this

money spider NOUN any of certain small shiny brownish spiders of the family *Linyphiidae*.

money-spinner NOUN *Informal* an enterprise, idea, person, or thing that is a source of wealth.

moneyspinning ('mʌnɪˌspɪnɪŋ) ADJECTIVE *Informal* earning money or making a profit.

money supply NOUN the total amount of money in a country's economy at a given time. See also **M0, M1, M2, M3, M3c, M4, M5.**

money wages PLURAL NOUN *Economics* wages evaluated with reference to the money paid rather than the equivalent purchasing power. Also called: **nominal wages.** Compare **real wages.**

moneywort ('mʌnɪˌwɜːt) NOUN a European and North American creeping primulaceous plant, *Lysimachia nummularia*, with round leaves and yellow flowers. Also called: **creeping Jennie.**

mong (mʌŋ) NOUN *Austral informal* short for **mongrel.**

monged (mɒŋd) ADJECTIVE *Slang* under the influence of drugs.
▹ HISTORY C20: from a shortening of MONGOL

monger ('mʌŋgə) NOUN [1] (*in combination except in archaic use*) a trader or dealer: *ironmonger*. [2] (*in combination*) a promoter of something unpleasant: *warmonger*.
▹ HISTORY Old English *mangere*, ultimately from Latin *mangō* dealer; compare Old High German *mangari*
▸ **'mongering** NOUN, ADJECTIVE

mongo *or* **mongoe** ('mɒŋgəʊ) NOUN a variant of **mungo.**

möngö *or* **mongoe** ('mɒŋgəʊ) NOUN, *plural* **-gos** *or* **-goes.** a Mongolian monetary unit worth one hundredth of a tugrik.

mongol ('mɒŋgᵊl) NOUN *Offensive* a person affected by Down's syndrome.

Mongol ('mɒŋgɒl, -gᵊl) NOUN [1] a native or inhabitant of Mongolia, esp a nomad. [2] the Mongolian language.

Mongolia (mɒŋ'gəʊlɪə) NOUN [1] a republic in E central Asia: made a Chinese province in 1691; became autonomous in 1911 and a republic in 1924; multiparty democracy introduced in 1990. It consists chiefly of a high plateau, with the Gobi Desert in the south, a large lake district in the northwest, and the Altai and Khangai Mountains in the west. Official language: Khalkha. Religion: nonreligious majority. Currency: tugrik. Capital: Ulan Bator. Pop.: 2 435 000 (2001 est.). Area: 1 565 000 sq. km (604 095 sq. miles). Former names: **Outer Mongolia** (until 1924), **Mongolian People's Republic** (1924–92). [2] a vast region of central Asia, inhabited chiefly by Mongols: now divided into the republic of Mongolia, the Inner Mongolian Autonomous Region of China, and the Tuva Republic of S Russia; at its height during the 13th century under Genghis Khan.

mongolian (mɒŋ'gəʊlɪən) ADJECTIVE (not in technical use) of, relating to, or affected by Down's syndrome.

Mongolian (mɒŋ'gəʊlɪən) ADJECTIVE [1] of or relating to Mongolia, its people, or their language. ◆ NOUN [2] a native of Mongolia. [3] the language of Mongolia: see **Khalkha.**

Mongolian People's Republic NOUN the former name of **Mongolia** (sense 1).

Mongolic (mɒŋ'gɒlɪk) NOUN [1] a branch or subfamily of the Altaic family of languages, including Mongolian, Kalmuck, and Buryat. [2] another word for **Mongoloid.**

mongolism ('mɒŋgəˌlɪzəm) NOUN *Pathol* a former name (not in technical use) for **Down's syndrome.**
▹ HISTORY C20: so named because Down's syndrome produces facial features similar to those of the Mongoloid peoples

mongoloid ('mɒŋgəˌlɔɪd) (not in technical use) ADJECTIVE [1] relating to or characterized by Down's syndrome. ◆ NOUN [2] a person affected by Down's syndrome.

Mongoloid ('mɒŋgəˌlɔɪd) ADJECTIVE [1] denoting, relating to, or belonging to one of the major racial groups of mankind, characterized by yellowish complexion, straight black hair, slanting eyes, short nose, and scanty facial hair, including most of the peoples of Asia, the Eskimos, and the North American Indians. ◆ NOUN [2] a member of this group.

mongoose ('mɒŋˌguːs) NOUN, *plural* **-gooses.** any small predatory viverrine mammal of the genus *Herpestes* and related genera, occurring in Africa and from S Europe to SE Asia, typically having a long tail and brindled coat.
▹ HISTORY C17: from Marathi *mangūs*, of Dravidian origin

mongrel ('mʌŋgrəl) NOUN [1] a plant or animal, esp a dog, of mixed or unknown breeding; a crossbreed or hybrid. [2] *Derogatory* a person of mixed race. ◆ ADJECTIVE [3] of mixed origin, breeding, character, etc.
▹ HISTORY C15: from obsolete *mong* mixture; compare Old English *gemong* a mingling
▸ **'mongrelism** NOUN ▸ **'mongrelly** ADJECTIVE

mongrelize *or* **mongrelise** ('mʌŋgrəˌlaɪz) VERB (*tr*) to make mixed or mongrel in breed, race, character, kind, etc.
▸ ˌ**mongreli'zation** *or* ˌ**mongreli'sation** NOUN ▸ **'mongrelˌizer** *or* **'mongrelˌiser** NOUN

'mongst (mʌŋst) PREPOSITION *Poetic* short for **amongst.**

monied ('mʌnɪd) ADJECTIVE a less common spelling of **moneyed.**

monies ('mʌnɪz) NOUN *Formal* a plural of **money.**

moniker *or* **monicker** ('mɒnɪkə) NOUN *Slang* a person's name or nickname.
▹ HISTORY C19: from Shelta *munnik*, altered from Irish *ainm* name

monilial (mə'nɪlɪəl) ADJECTIVE *Pathol* denoting a thrush infection, caused by the fungus *Candida* (formerly *Monilia*) *albicans*.
▹ HISTORY C20: from New Latin *monilia*, from Latin *monīle* necklace (referring to the beadlike form of the fungus)

moniliform (mɒ'nɪlɪˌfɔːm) ADJECTIVE *Biology* shaped like a string of beads: *moniliform fungi*.
▹ HISTORY C19: from New Latin *monīliformis*, from Latin *monīle* necklace + *forma* shape

monism ('mɒnɪzəm) NOUN [1] *Philosophy* the doctrine that the person consists of only a single substance, or that there is no crucial difference between mental and physical events or properties.

Compare **dualism** (sense 2). See also **materialism** (sense 2), **idealism** (sense 3). 2 *Philosophy* the doctrine that reality consists of an unchanging whole in which change is mere illusion. Compare **pluralism** (sense 5). 3 the epistemological theory that the object and datum of consciousness are identical. 4 the attempt to explain anything in terms of one principle only.
▷HISTORY C19: from Greek *monos* single + -ISM
▸'**monist** NOUN, ADJECTIVE ▸**mo'nistic** ADJECTIVE ▸**mo'nistically** ADVERB

monition (məʊ'nɪʃən) NOUN 1 a warning or caution; admonition. 2 *Christianity* a formal notice from a bishop or ecclesiastical court requiring a person to refrain from committing a specific offence.
▷HISTORY C14: via Old French from Latin *monitiō*, from *monēre* to warn

monitor ('mɒnɪtə) NOUN 1 a person or piece of equipment that warns, checks, controls, or keeps a continuous record of something. 2 *Education* **a** a senior pupil with various supervisory duties. **b** a pupil assisting a teacher in classroom organization, etc. 3 a television screen used to display certain kinds of information in a television studio, airport, etc. 4 the unit in a desk computer that contains the screen. 5 **a** a loudspeaker used in a recording studio control room to determine quality or balance. **b** a loudspeaker used on stage to enable musicians to hear themselves. 6 a device for controlling the direction of a water jet in fire fighting. 7 any large predatory lizard of the genus *Varanus* and family *Varanidae*, inhabiting warm regions of Africa, Asia, and Australia. See also **Komodo dragon.** 8 Also called: **giant.** *Mining* a nozzle for directing a high-pressure jet of water at the material to be excavated. 9 (formerly) a small heavily armoured shallow-draught warship used for coastal assault. ◆ VERB *(tr)* 10 to act as a monitor of. 11 to observe or record (the activity or performance) of (an engine or other device). 12 to check (the technical quality of) (a radio or television broadcast).
▷HISTORY C16: from Latin, from *monēre* to advise
▸**monitorial** (ˌmɒnɪ'tɔːrɪəl) ADJECTIVE ▸ˌ**moni'torially** ADVERB ▸'**monitorˌship** NOUN ▸'**monitress** FEMININE NOUN

monitory ('mɒnɪtərɪ, -trɪ) ADJECTIVE *also* **monitorial.** 1 warning or admonishing: *a monitory look.* ◆ NOUN, *plural* **-ries.** 2 *Rare* a letter containing a monition.

monk (mʌŋk) NOUN 1 a male member of a religious community bound by vows of poverty, chastity, and obedience. Related adjective: **monastic.** 2 *(sometimes capital)* a fancy pigeon having a bald pate and often large feathered feet.
▷HISTORY Old English *munuc*, from Late Latin *monachus*, from Late Greek: solitary (man), from Greek *monos* alone

monkery ('mʌŋkərɪ) NOUN, *plural* **-eries.** *Derogatory* 1 monastic life or practices. 2 a monastery or monks collectively.

monkey ('mʌŋkɪ) NOUN 1 any of numerous long-tailed primates excluding the prosimians (lemurs, tarsiers, etc.): comprise the families *Cercopithecidae* (see **Old World monkey**), *Cebidae* (see **New World monkey**), and *Callithricidae* (marmosets). Related adjective: **simian.** 2 any primate except man. 3 a naughty or mischievous person, esp a child. 4 the head of a pile-driver (**monkey engine**) or of some similar mechanical device. 5 *(modifier) Nautical* denoting a small light structure or piece of equipment contrived to suit an immediate purpose: *a monkey foresail; a monkey bridge.* 6 *US and Canadian, slang* an addict's dependence on a drug (esp in the phrase **have a monkey on one's back**). 7 *Slang* a butt of derision; someone made to look a fool (esp in the phrase **make a monkey of**). 8 *Slang* (esp in bookmaking) £500. 9 *US and Canadian, slang* $500. 10 *Austral slang, archaic* a sheep. 11 **give a monkey's.** *Brit, slang* to care about or regard as important: *who gives a monkey's what he thinks?* ◆ VERB 12 *(intr; usually foll by around, with, etc.)* to meddle, fool, or tinker. 13 *(tr) Rare* to imitate; ape.
▷HISTORY C16: perhaps from Low German; compare Middle Low German *Moneke* name of the ape's son in the tale of Reynard the Fox

monkey bread NOUN 1 the gourdlike fruit of the baobab tree. 2 **monkey bread tree.** another name for **baobab.**

monkey business NOUN *Informal* mischievous, suspect, dishonest, or meddlesome behaviour or acts.

monkey climb NOUN a wrestling throw in which a contestant seizes his opponent's arms or neck, places his feet on his opponent's stomach, and falls backwards, straightening his legs and throwing the opponent over his head.

monkey flower NOUN any of various scrophulariaceous plants of the genus *Mimulus*, cultivated for their yellow or red flowers. See also **musk** (sense 3).

monkey jacket NOUN a short close-fitting jacket, esp a waist-length jacket similar to a mess jacket.

monkey nut NOUN *Brit* another name for a **peanut.**

monkey orchid NOUN a European orchid, *Orchis simia*, rare in Britain, having a short dense flower spike that opens from the top downwards. The flowers are white streaked with pink or violet and have five spurs thought to resemble a monkey's arms, legs, and tail.

monkeypot ('mʌŋkɪˌpɒt) NOUN 1 any of various tropical trees of the genus *Lecythis:* family *Lecythidaceae.* 2 the large urn-shaped pod of any of these trees, formerly used to catch monkeys by baiting it with sugar. 3 a melting pot used in making flint glass.

monkey puzzle NOUN a South American coniferous tree, *Araucaria araucana*, having branches shaped like a candelabrum and stiff sharp leaves: family *Araucariaceae.* Also called: **Chile pine.**
▷HISTORY so called because monkeys allegedly have difficulty climbing them

monkey suit NOUN *US, slang* a man's evening dress.

monkey's wedding NOUN *South African informal* a combination of sunshine and light rain.

monkey tricks *or US* **monkey shines** PLURAL NOUN *Informal* mischievous behaviour or acts, such as practical jokes.

monkey wrench NOUN a wrench with adjustable jaws.

monkfish ('mʌŋkˌfɪʃ) NOUN, *plural* **-fish** *or* **-fishes.** 1 Also called (US): **goosefish.** any of various anglers of the genus *Lophius.* 2 another name for the **angel shark.**

Mon-Khmer NOUN 1 a family of languages spoken chiefly in Cambodia, Myanmar, and Assam; probably a member of the Austro-Asiatic phylum. ◆ ADJECTIVE 2 of or belonging to this family of languages.

monkhood ('mʌŋkhʊd) NOUN 1 the condition of being a monk. 2 monks collectively.

monkish ('mʌŋkɪʃ) ADJECTIVE of, relating to, or resembling a monk or monks.
▸'**monkishly** ADVERB ▸'**monkishness** NOUN

monk's cloth NOUN a heavy cotton fabric of basket weave, used mainly for bedspreads.
▷HISTORY C19: so called because a similar material was used for making monks' habits

monkshood ('mʌŋksˌhʊd) NOUN any of several poisonous N temperate plants of the ranunculaceous genus *Aconitum*, esp *A. napellus*, that have hooded blue-purple flowers.

Monmouth ('mɒnməθ) NOUN a market town in E Wales, in Monmouthshire: Norman castle, where Henry V was born in 1387. Pop.: 7246 (1991).

Monmouthshire ('mɒnməθˌʃɪə, -ʃə) NOUN a county of E Wales: administratively part of England for three centuries (until 1830); mainly absorbed into the county of Gwent in 1974; reinstated with reduced boundaries in 1996: chiefly agricultural, with the Black Mountains in the N. Administrative centre: Cwmbran. Pop.: 84 879 (2001). Area: 851 sq. km (329 sq. miles).

mono ('mɒnəʊ) ADJECTIVE 1 short for **monophonic.** ◆ NOUN 2 monophonic sound; monophony.

mono- *or before a vowel* **mon-** COMBINING FORM 1 one; single: *monochrome; monorail.* 2 indicating that a chemical compound contains a single specified atom or group: *monoxide.*
▷HISTORY from Greek *monos*

monoacid (ˌmɒnəʊ'æsɪd), **monacid, monoacidic** (ˌmɒnəʊə'sɪdɪk), *or* **monacidic** ADJECTIVE *Chem* (of a base) capable of reacting with only one molecule of a monobasic acid; having only one hydroxide ion per molecule.

monoamine (ˌmɒnəʊ'eɪmiːn) NOUN a substance, such as adrenaline, noradrenaline, or serotonin, that contains a single amine group.

monoamine oxidase NOUN *Biochem* an enzyme present in nerve tissue that is responsible for the inactivation of neurotransmitters.

monoamine oxidase inhibitor NOUN *Biochem* an agent that inhibits the action of monoamine oxidase. Such inhibitors are used in the treatment of depression. Abbreviation: **MAOI.**

monoatomic (ˌmɒnəʊə'tɒmɪk) ADJECTIVE a variant of **monatomic.**

monobasic (ˌmɒnəʊ'beɪsɪk) ADJECTIVE *Chem* (of an acid, such as hydrogen chloride) having only one replaceable hydrogen atom per molecule.

monobrow ('mɒnəʊˌbraʊ) NOUN *Informal* the appearance of a single eyebrow as a result of the eyebrows joining above a person's nose.

monocarp ('mɒnəʊˌkɑːp) NOUN a plant that is monocarpic.

monocarpellary (ˌmɒnəʊ'kɑːpɪlərɪ) *or* **monocarpous** (ˌmɒnəʊ'kɑːpəs) ADJECTIVE 1 (of flowers) having only one carpel. 2 (of a plant gynoecium) consisting of one carpel.

monocarpic (ˌmɒnəʊ'kɑːpɪk) *or* **monocarpous** ADJECTIVE *Botany* another name for **semelparous.** Also: **hapaxanthic.**

Monoceros (mə'nɒsərəs) NOUN, *Latin genitive* **Monocerotis** (məˌnɒsə'rəʊtɪs). a faint constellation on the celestial equator crossed by the Milky Way and lying close to Orion and Canis Major.
▷HISTORY C14: via Old French from Latin: unicorn, from Greek *monokeros* with a single horn, from MONO- + *keras* horn

monochasium (ˌmɒnəʊ'keɪzɪəm) NOUN, *plural* **-sia** (-zɪə). *Botany* a cymose inflorescence in which each branch gives rise to one other branch only, as in the forget-me-not and buttercup. Compare **dichasium.**
▷HISTORY C19: MONO- + *-chasium* as in DICHASIUM
▸ˌ**mono'chasial** ADJECTIVE

monochlamydeous (ˌmɒnəʊklə'mɪdɪəs) ADJECTIVE (of a flower) having a perianth of one whorl of members; not having a separate calyx and corolla.
▷HISTORY C19: from Greek, from MONO- + *khlamus* a cloak + -EOUS

monochloride (ˌmɒnə'klɔːraɪd) NOUN a chloride containing one atom of chlorine per molecule.

monochord ('mɒnəʊˌkɔːd) NOUN an instrument employed in acoustic analysis or investigation, consisting usually of one string stretched over a resonator of wood. Also called: **sonometer** (sə'nɒmɪtə).
▷HISTORY C15: from Old French, from Late Latin, from Greek *monokhordon*, from MONO- + *khordē* string

monochromat (ˌmɒnəʊ'krəʊmæt) *or* **monochromate** (ˌmɒnəʊ'krəʊmeɪt) NOUN a person who perceives all colours as a single hue.

monochromatic (ˌmɒnəʊkrəʊ'mætɪk) *or* **monochroic** (ˌmɒnəʊ'krəʊɪk) ADJECTIVE 1 Also: **homochromatic.** (of light or other electromagnetic radiation) having only one wavelength. 2 *Physics* (of moving particles) having only one kinetic energy. 3 of or relating to monochromatism. ◆ NOUN 4 a person who is totally colour-blind.
▸ˌ**monochro'matically** ADVERB

monochromatism (ˌmɒnəʊ'krəʊməˌtɪzəm) NOUN a visual defect in which all colours appear as variations of a single hue.

monochromator (ˌmɒnəʊ'krəʊmeɪtə) NOUN *Physics* a device that isolates a single wavelength of radiation.

monochrome ('mɒnəˌkrəʊm) NOUN 1 a black-and-white photograph or transparency. 2 *Photog* black and white. 3 **a** a painting, drawing, etc., done in a range of tones of a single colour. **b** the technique or art of this. 4 *(modifier)* executed in or resembling monochrome: *a monochrome print.* ◆ ADJECTIVE 5 devoid of any distinctive or stimulating characteristics. ◆ Also called (for senses 3, 4): **monotint.**
▷HISTORY C17: via Medieval Latin from Greek *monokhrōmos* of one colour

▸ˌmono'chromic *or* ˌmono'chromical ADJECTIVE
▸'monoˌchromist NOUN

monocle ('mɒnəkᵊl) NOUN a lens for correcting defective vision of one eye, held in position by the facial muscles.
▷HISTORY C19: from French, from Late Latin *monoculus* one-eyed, from MONO- + *oculus* eye
▸'monocled ADJECTIVE

monocline ('mɒnəʊˌklaɪn) NOUN a local steepening in stratified rocks with an otherwise gentle dip.
▷HISTORY C19: from MONO- + Greek *klīnein* to lean
▸ˌmono'clinal ADJECTIVE, NOUN ▸ˌmono'clinally ADVERB

monoclinic (ˌmɒnəʊ'klɪnɪk) ADJECTIVE *Crystallog* relating to or belonging to the crystal system characterized by three unequal axes, one pair of which are not at right angles to each other.
▷HISTORY C19: from MONO- + Greek *klīnein* to lean + -IC

monoclinous (ˌmɒnəʊ'klaɪnəs, 'mɒnəʊˌklaɪnəs) ADJECTIVE (of flowering plants) having the male and female reproductive organs on the same flower. Compare **diclinous.**
▷HISTORY C19: from MONO- + Greek *klīnē* bed + -OUS
▸'monoˌclinism NOUN

monoclonal antibody (ˌmɒnəʊ'kləʊnᵊl) NOUN an antibody, produced by a single clone of cells grown in culture, that is both pure and specific and is capable of proliferating indefinitely to produce unlimited quantities of identical antibodies: used in diagnosis, therapy, and biotechnology.

monocoque ('mɒnəˌkɒk) NOUN 1 a type of aircraft fuselage, car body, etc., in which all or most of the loads are taken by the skin. 2 a type of racing-car, racing-cycle, or powerboat design with no separate chassis and body. ◆ ADJECTIVE 3 of or relating to the design characteristic of a monocoque.
▷HISTORY C20: from French, from MONO- + *coque* shell

monocotyledon (ˌmɒnəʊˌkɒtɪ'liːdᵊn) NOUN any flowering plant of the class *Monocotyledonae,* having a single embryonic seed leaf, leaves with parallel veins, and flowers with parts in threes: includes grasses, lilies, palms, and orchids. Often shortened to: **monocot.** Compare **dicotyledon.**
▸ˌmonoˌcoty'ledonous ADJECTIVE

monocracy (mɒ'nɒkrəsɪ) NOUN, *plural* **-cies.** government by one person.
▸**monocrat** ('mɒnəˌkræt) NOUN ▸ˌmono'cratic ADJECTIVE

monocular (mɒ'nɒkjʊlə) ADJECTIVE 1 having to do with or using only one eye. ◆ NOUN 2 a device for use with one eye, such as a field glass.
▷HISTORY C17: from Late Latin *monoculus* one-eyed
▸mo'nocularly ADVERB

monoculture ('mɒnəʊˌkʌltʃə) NOUN the continuous growing of one type of crop.

monocycle ('mɒnəˌsaɪkᵊl) NOUN another name for **unicycle.**

monocyclic (ˌmɒnəʊ'saɪklɪk) ADJECTIVE 1 Also: **mononuclear.** (of a chemical compound) containing only one ring of atoms. 2 (of sepals, petals, or stamens) arranged in a single whorl. 3 (of a plant) having a life cycle that is completed in one year.

monocyte ('mɒnəʊˌsaɪt) NOUN a large phagocytic leucocyte with a spherical nucleus and clear cytoplasm.
▸**monocytic** (ˌmɒnə'sɪtɪk) ADJECTIVE ▸ˌmono'cytoid ADJECTIVE

monodactylous (ˌmɒnəʊ'dæktɪləs) ADJECTIVE (of certain animals) having a single functional digit.

monodisperse (ˌmɒnəʊdɪs'pɜːs) ADJECTIVE *Chem* (of a colloidal system) having particles of similar size.

monodont ('mɒnəʊˌdɒnt) ADJECTIVE (of certain animals, esp the male narwhal) having a single tooth throughout life.

monodrama ('mɒnəʊˌdrɑːmə) NOUN a play or other dramatic piece for a single performer.
▸ˌmonodra'matic ADJECTIVE

monody ('mɒnədɪ) NOUN, *plural* **-dies.** 1 (in Greek tragedy) an ode sung by a single actor. 2 any poem of lament for someone's death. 3 *Music* a style of composition consisting of a single vocal part, usually with accompaniment.
▷HISTORY C17: via Late Latin from Greek *monōidia,* from MONO- + *aeidein* to sing
▸**monodic** (mɒ'nɒdɪk) *or* mo'nodical ADJECTIVE
▸mo'nodically ADVERB ▸'monodist NOUN

monoecious, monecious (mɒ'niːʃəs), *or* **monoicous** (mɒ'nɔɪkəs) ADJECTIVE 1 (of some flowering plants) having the male and female reproductive organs in separate flowers on the same plant. 2 (of some animals and lower plants) hermaphrodite. ◆ Compare **dioecious.**
▷HISTORY C18: from New Latin *monoecia,* from MONO- + Greek *oikos* house
▸mo'noeciously *or* mo'neciously ADVERB

monofilament (ˌmɒnə'fɪləmənt) *or* **monofil** ('mɒnəfɪl) NOUN 1 synthetic thread or yarn composed of a single strand rather than twisted fibres. 2 a fishing line made of monofilaments.

monogamist (mɒ'nɒgəmɪst) NOUN a person who advocates or practises monogamy.
▸moˌnoga'mistic ADJECTIVE

monogamy (mɒ'nɒgəmɪ) NOUN 1 the state or practice of having only one husband or wife over a period of time. Compare **bigamy, polygamy** (sense 1), **digamy.** 2 *Zoology* the practice of having only one mate.
▷HISTORY C17: via French from Late Latin *monogamia,* from Greek; see MONO- + -GAMY
▸mo'nogamous ADJECTIVE ▸mo'nogamously ADVERB
▸mo'nogamousness NOUN

monogenesis (ˌmɒnəʊ'dʒɛnɪsɪs) *or* **monogeny** (mɒ'nɒdʒɪnɪ) NOUN 1 the hypothetical descent of all organisms from a single cell or organism. 2 asexual reproduction in animals. 3 the direct development of an ovum into an organism resembling the adult. 4 the hypothetical descent of all human beings from a single pair of ancestors. ◆ Compare **polygenesis.**

monogenetic (ˌmɒnəʊdʒɪ'nɛtɪk) *or* **monogenous** (mɒ'nɒdʒənəs) ADJECTIVE 1 of, relating to, or showing monogenesis. 2 of or relating to parasitic animals, such as some flukes, that complete their life cycle on only one host. 3 (of rocks and rock formations) formed from one source or by one process.

monogenic (ˌmɒnəʊ'dʒɛnɪk) ADJECTIVE 1 *Genetics* of or relating to an inherited character difference that is controlled by a single gene. 2 (of animals) producing offspring of one sex.

monogram ('mɒnəˌgræm) NOUN 1 a design of one or more letters, esp initials, embroidered on clothing, printed on stationery, etc. ◆ VERB **monograms, monogramming, monogrammed.** 2 (*tr; usually passive*) to decorate (clothing, stationery, etc.) with a monogram.
▷HISTORY C17: from Late Latin *monogramma,* from Greek; see MONO-, -GRAM
▸**monogrammatic** (ˌmɒnəgrə'mætɪk) ADJECTIVE

monograph ('mɒnəˌgrɑːf, -ˌgræf) NOUN 1 a paper, book, or other work concerned with a single subject or aspect of a subject. ◆ VERB 2 (*tr*) to write a monograph on.
▸**monographer** (mɒ'nɒgrəfə) *or* mo'nographist NOUN
▸ˌmono'graphic ADJECTIVE ▸ˌmono'graphically ADVERB

monogyny (mɒ'nɒdʒɪnɪ) NOUN the custom of having only one female sexual partner over a period of time.
▸mo'nogynist NOUN ▸mo'nogynous ADJECTIVE

monohull ('mɒnəʊˌhʌl) NOUN a sailing vessel with a single hull. Compare **multihull.**

monohybrid (ˌmɒnəʊ'haɪbrɪd) NOUN *Genetics* the offspring of two individuals that differ in respect of a single gene.

monohydrate (ˌmɒnəʊ'haɪdreɪt) NOUN a hydrate, such as ferrous sulphate monohydrate, $FeSO_4.H_2O$, containing one molecule of water per molecule of the compound.
▸ˌmono'hydrated ADJECTIVE

monohydric (ˌmɒnəʊ'haɪdrɪk) ADJECTIVE another word for **monohydroxy,** esp when applied to alcohols

monohydroxy (ˌmɒnəʊhaɪ'drɒksɪ) ADJECTIVE (of a chemical compound) containing one hydroxyl group per molecule. Also: **monohydric.**

monoicous (mɒ'nɔɪkəs) ADJECTIVE a variant of **monoecious.**
▸mo'noicously ADVERB

monolatry (mɒ'nɒlətrɪ) NOUN the exclusive worship of one god without excluding the existence of others.
▸**monolater** (mɒ'nɒlətə) *or* mo'nolatrist NOUN
▸mo'nolatrous ADJECTIVE

monolayer ('mɒnəʊˌleɪə) NOUN a single layer of atoms or molecules adsorbed on a surface. Also called: **molecular film.**

monolingual (ˌmɒnəʊ'lɪŋgwəl) ADJECTIVE 1 knowing or expressed in only one language. ◆ NOUN 2 a monolingual person. ◆ Compare **bilingual, multilingual.**

monolith ('mɒnəlɪθ) NOUN 1 a large block of stone or anything that resembles one in appearance, intractability, etc. 2 a statue, obelisk, column, etc., cut from one block of stone. 3 a large hollow foundation piece sunk as a caisson and having a number of compartments that are filled with concrete when it has reached its correct position.
▷HISTORY C19: via French from Greek *monolithos* made from a single stone

monolithic (ˌmɒnə'lɪθɪk) ADJECTIVE 1 of, relating to, or like a monolith. 2 characterized by hugeness, impenetrability, or intractability: *a monolithic government.* 3 *Electronics* (of an integrated circuit) having all components manufactured into or on top of a single chip of silicon. Compare **hybrid** (sense 6).
▸ˌmono'lithically ADVERB

monologue ('mɒnəˌlɒg) NOUN 1 a long speech made by one actor in a play, film, etc., esp when alone. 2 a dramatic piece for a single performer. 3 any long speech by one person, esp when interfering with conversation.
▷HISTORY C17: via French from Greek *monologos* speaking alone
▸**monologic** (ˌmɒnə'lɒdʒɪk) *or* ˌmono'logical ADJECTIVE
▸**monologist** ('mɒnəˌlɒgɪst, mə'nɒləgɪst) NOUN
▸**monology** (mɒ'nɒlədʒɪ) NOUN

Language note See at **soliloquy.**

monomania (ˌmɒnəʊ'meɪnɪə) NOUN an excessive mental preoccupation with one thing, idea, etc.
▸ˌmono'maniˌac NOUN, ADJECTIVE ▸**monomaniacal** (ˌmɒnəʊmə'naɪəkᵊl) ADJECTIVE

monomark ('mɒnəmɑːk) NOUN *Brit* a series of letters or figures to identify goods, personal articles, etc.

monomer ('mɒnəmə) NOUN *Chem* a compound whose molecules can join together to form a polymer.
▸**monomeric** (ˌmɒnə'mɛrɪk) ADJECTIVE

monomerous (mɒ'nɒmərəs) ADJECTIVE (of flowers) having whorls consisting of only one member.
▷HISTORY C19: from Greek *monomerēs* of one part; see MONO-, -MERE

monometallic (ˌmɒnəʊmɪ'tælɪk) ADJECTIVE 1 (esp of coins) consisting of one metal only. 2 relating to monometallism.

monometallism (ˌmɒnəʊ'mɛtᵊˌlɪzəm) NOUN 1 the use of one metal, esp gold or silver, as the sole standard of value and currency. 2 the economic policies supporting a monometallic standard.
▸ˌmono'metallist NOUN

monometer (mɒ'nɒmɪtə) NOUN *Prosody* a line of verse consisting of one metrical foot.
▸**monometrical** (ˌmɒnəʊ'mɛtrɪkᵊl) *or* ˌmono'metric ADJECTIVE

monomial (mɒ'nəʊmɪəl) NOUN 1 *Maths* an expression consisting of a single term, such as 5*ax.* ◆ ADJECTIVE 2 consisting of a single algebraic term. 3 *Biology* of, relating to, or denoting a taxonomic name that consists of a single term.
▷HISTORY C18: MONO- + (BIN)OMIAL

monomode ('mɒnəʊˌməʊd) ADJECTIVE denoting or relating to a type of optical fibre with a core less than 10 micrometres in diameter.

monomolecular (ˌmɒnəʊmə'lɛkjʊlə) ADJECTIVE of, concerned with, or involving single molecules: *a monomolecular layer.*

monomorphic (ˌmɒnəʊ'mɔːfɪk) *or* **monomorphous** ADJECTIVE 1 (of an individual organism) showing little or no change in structure during the entire life history. 2 (of a species) existing or having parts that exist in only one form.

3 (of a chemical compound) having only one crystalline form.
▸**,mono'morphism** NOUN

Monongahela (mə,nɒŋgə'hi:lə) NOUN a river in the northeastern US, flowing generally north to the Allegheny River at Pittsburgh, Pennsylvania, forming the Ohio River. Length: 206 km (128 miles).

mononuclear (,mɒnəʊ'nju:klɪə) ADJECTIVE 1 (of a cell) having only one nucleus. 2 another word for **monocyclic** (sense 1).

mononucleosis (,mɒnəʊ,nju:klɪ'əʊsɪs) NOUN 1 *Pathol* the presence of a large number of monocytes in the blood. 2 See **infectious mononucleosis.**

mononym ('mɒnəʊ,nɪm) NOUN a person who is famous enough to be known only by one name, usually the first name.
▷HISTORY C20: from MONO- + (EPO)NYM

monopetalous (,mɒnəʊ'pɛtələs) ADJECTIVE (of flowers) having only one petal.

monophagous (mə'nɒfəgəs) ADJECTIVE feeding on only one type of food: *monophagous insects.*
▸**mo'nophagy** NOUN

monophobia (,mɒnəʊ'fəʊbɪə) NOUN a strong fear of being alone.
▸**,mono'phobic** ADJECTIVE

monophonic (,mɒnəʊ'fɒnɪk) ADJECTIVE 1 Also: **monaural.** (of a system of broadcasting, recording, or reproducing sound) using only one channel between source and loudspeaker. Sometimes shortened to: **mono.** Compare **stereophonic.** 2 *Music* of or relating to a style of musical composition consisting of a single melodic line. See also **monody** (sense 3).
▸**monophony** (mɒ'nɒfənɪ) NOUN

monophthong ('mɒnəf,θɒŋ) NOUN a simple or pure vowel.
▷HISTORY C17: from Greek *monophthongos,* from MONO- + *thongos* sound
▸**monophthongal** (,mɒnəf'θɒŋgəl) ADJECTIVE

monophyletic (,mɒnəʊfaɪ'lɛtɪk) ADJECTIVE 1 relating to or characterized by descent from a single ancestral group of animals or plants. 2 (of animals or plants) of or belonging to a single stock.

monophyllous (,mɒnəʊ'fɪləs) ADJECTIVE *Botany* having or consisting of only one leaf or leaflike part.

Monophysite (mɒ'nɒfɪ,saɪt) *Christianity* ◆ NOUN 1 a person who holds that there is only one nature in the person of Christ, which is primarily divine with human attributes. ◆ ADJECTIVE 2 of or relating to this belief.
▷HISTORY C17: via Church Latin from Late Greek, from MONO- + *phusis* nature
▸**Monophysitic** (,mɒnəʊfɪ'sɪtɪk) ADJECTIVE
▸**Mo'nophy,sitism** NOUN

monoplane ('mɒnəʊ,pleɪn) NOUN an aeroplane with only one pair of wings. Compare **biplane.**

monoplegia (,mɒnəʊ'pli:dʒɪə) NOUN *Pathol* paralysis limited to one limb or a single group of muscles.
▸**monoplegic** (,mɒnəʊ'pli:dʒɪk) ADJECTIVE

monoploid ('mɒnə,plɔɪd) ADJECTIVE, NOUN a less common word for **haploid.**

monopode ('mɒnə,pəʊd) NOUN 1 a member of a legendary one-legged race of Africa. 2 another word for **monopodium.**
▷HISTORY C19: from Late Latin *monopodius*

monopodium (,mɒnə'pəʊdɪəm) NOUN, *plural* **-dia** (-dɪə). the main axis of growth in the pine tree and similar plants: the main stem, which elongates from the tip and gives rise to lateral branches. Compare **sympodium.**
▷HISTORY C19: New Latin, from Greek *monopous,* from MONO- + *pous* foot
▸**,mono'podial** ADJECTIVE ▸**,mono'podially** ADVERB

monopole ('mɒnə,pəʊl) NOUN *Physics* 1 a magnetic pole considered in isolation. 2 Also called: **magnetic monopole.** a hypothetical elementary particle postulated in certain theories of particle physics to exist as an isolated north or south magnetic pole.

monopolistic competition NOUN *Economics* the form of imperfect competition that exists when there are many producers or sellers of similar but differentiated goods or services.

monopolize *or* **monopolise** (mə'nɒpə,laɪz) VERB (*tr*) 1 to have, control, or make use of fully, excluding others. 2 to obtain, maintain, or exploit a monopoly of (a market, commodity, etc.).
▸**mo,nopoli'zation** *or* **mo,nopoli'sation** NOUN
▸**mo'nopo,lizer** *or* **mo'nopo,liser** NOUN

monopoly (mə'nɒpəlɪ) NOUN, *plural* **-lies.** 1 exclusive control of the market supply of a product or service. 2 **a** an enterprise exercising this control. **b** the product or service so controlled. 3 *Law* the exclusive right or privilege granted to a person, company, etc., by the state to purchase, manufacture, use, or sell some commodity or to carry on trade in a specified country or area. 4 exclusive control, possession, or use of something.
▷HISTORY C16: from Late Latin, from Greek *monopōlion,* from MONO- + *pōlein* to sell
▸**mo'nopolism** NOUN ▸**mo'nopolist** NOUN ▸**mo,nopo'listic** ADJECTIVE ▸**mo,nopo'listically** ADVERB

Monopoly (mə'nɒpəlɪ) NOUN *Trademark* a board game for two to six players who throw dice to advance their tokens around a board, the object being to acquire the property on which their tokens land.

monopropellant (,mɒnəʊprə'pɛlənt) NOUN a solid or liquid rocket propellant containing both the fuel and the oxidizer.

monopsony (mə'nɒpsənɪ) NOUN, *plural* **-nies.** a situation in which the entire market demand for a product or service consists of only one buyer.
▷HISTORY C20: MONO- + Greek *opsōnia* purchase, from *opsōnein* to buy
▸**mo,nopso'nistic** ADJECTIVE

monopteros (mɒn'ɒptə,rɒs) *or* **monopteron** NOUN, *plural* **-teroi** (-tə,rɔɪ) *or* **-tera** (-tərə). a circular classical building, esp a temple, that has a single ring of columns surrounding it.
▷HISTORY C18: Late Latin from Greek, from MONO- + *pteron* a wing
▸**mon'opteral** ADJECTIVE

monorail ('mɒnəʊ,reɪl) NOUN a single-rail railway, often elevated and with suspended cars.

monorchid ('mɒnɔ:kɪd) ADJECTIVE 1 having only one testicle. ◆ NOUN 2 an animal or person with only one testicle.

monosaccharide (,mɒnəʊ'sækə,raɪd, -rɪd) NOUN a simple sugar, such as glucose or fructose, that does not hydrolyse to yield other sugars.

monosemy ('mɒnəʊ,si:mɪ) NOUN the fact of having only a single meaning; absence of ambiguity in a word. Compare **polysemy.**
▷HISTORY C20: from MONO- + (POLY)SEMY

monosepalous (,mɒnəʊ'sɛpələs) ADJECTIVE (of flowers) having only one sepal.

monoski ('mɒnəʊ,ski:) NOUN a wide ski on which the skier stands with both feet.
▸**'mono,skier** NOUN ▸**'mono,skiing** NOUN

monosodium glutamate (,mɒnəʊ'səʊdɪəm) NOUN a white crystalline substance, the sodium salt of glutamic acid, that has little flavour itself but enhances the flavour of proteins either by increasing the amount of saliva produced in the mouth or by stimulating the taste buds: used as a food additive, esp in Chinese foods. Formula: $NaC_5H_8O_4$. Also called: **sodium glutamate.** Abbreviation: **MSG.**

monosome ('mɒnə,səʊm) NOUN an unpaired chromosome, esp an X-chromosome in an otherwise diploid cell.
▸**monosomic** (,mɒnə'səʊmɪk) ADJECTIVE

monospermous (,mɒnəʊ'spɜ:məs) *or* **monospermal** ADJECTIVE (of certain plants) producing only one seed.

monostable (,mɒnəʊ'steɪbəl) ADJECTIVE *Physics* (of an electronic circuit) having only one stable state but able to pass into a second state in response to an input pulse.

monostich ('mɒnə,stɪk) NOUN a poem of a single line.
▷HISTORY C16: via Late Latin from Greek; see MONO-, STICH
▸**,mono'stichic** ADJECTIVE

monostichous (,mɒnəʊ'staɪkəs) ADJECTIVE *Botany* (of parts) forming one row.

monostome ('mɒnə,stəʊm) *or* **monostomous** (mɒ'nɒstəməs) ADJECTIVE *Zoology, botany* having only one mouth, pore, or similar opening.

monostrophe (mɒ'nɒstrəfɪ, 'mɒnə,strəʊf) NOUN a poem in which all the stanzas or strophes are written in the same metre.
▸**monostrophic** (,mɒnə'strɒfɪk) ADJECTIVE

monostylous (,mɒnəʊ'staɪləs) ADJECTIVE *Botany* having only one style.

monosyllabic (,mɒnəsɪ'læbɪk) ADJECTIVE 1 (of a word) containing only one syllable. 2 characterized by monosyllables; curt: *a monosyllabic answer.*
▸**,monosyl'labically** ADVERB

monosyllable ('mɒnə,sɪləbəl) NOUN a word of one syllable, esp one used as a sentence.
▸**,mono'sylla,bism** NOUN

monosymmetric (,mɒnəsɪ'metrɪk) *or* **monosymmetrical** ADJECTIVE 1 *Crystallog* variants of **monoclinic.** 2 *Botany* variants of **zygomorphic.**
▸**,monosym'metrically** ADVERB ▸**monosymmetry** (,mɒnə'sɪmɪtrɪ) NOUN

monoterpene ('mɒnə,tɜ:pi:n) NOUN *Chem* an isoprene unit, C_5H_8, forming a terpene.

monotheism ('mɒnəʊθɪ,ɪzəm) NOUN the belief or doctrine that there is only one God.
▸**'mono,theist** NOUN, ADJECTIVE ▸**,monothe'istic** ADJECTIVE
▸**,monothe'istically** ADVERB

monotint ('mɒnə,tɪnt) NOUN another word for **monochrome** (senses 3, 4).

monotocous (mə'nɒtəkəs) ADJECTIVE (of certain animals) producing a single offspring at a birth.
▷HISTORY from MONO- + Greek *tokos* birth

monotone ('mɒnə,təʊn) NOUN 1 a single unvaried pitch level in speech, sound, etc. 2 utterance, etc., without change of pitch. 3 lack of variety in style, expression. etc. ◆ ADJECTIVE 4 unvarying or monotonous. 5 Also: **monotonic** (,mɒnə'tɒnɪk). *Maths* (of a sequence or function) consistently increasing or decreasing in value.

monotonize *or* **monotonise** (mə'nɒtə,naɪz) VERB (*tr*) to make monotonous.

monotonous (mə'nɒtənəs) ADJECTIVE 1 dull and tedious, esp because of repetition. 2 unvarying in pitch or cadence.
▸**mo'notonously** ADVERB ▸**mo'notonousness** NOUN

monotony (mə'nɒtənɪ) NOUN, *plural* **-nies.** 1 wearisome routine; dullness. 2 lack of variety in pitch or cadence.

monotreme ('mɒnəʊ,tri:m) NOUN any mammal of the primitive order *Monotremata,* of Australia and New Guinea: egg-laying toothless animals with a single opening (cloaca) for the passage of eggs or sperm, faeces, and urine. The group contains only the echidnas and the platypus.
▷HISTORY C19: via New Latin from MONO- + Greek *trēma* hole
▸**monotrematous** (,mɒnəʊ'tri:mətəs) ADJECTIVE

monotrichous (mɒ'nɒtrɪkəs) *or* **monotrichic** (,mɒnəʊ'trɪkɪk) ADJECTIVE (of bacteria) having a single flagellum.

monotype ('mɒnə,taɪp) NOUN 1 a single print made from a metal or glass plate on which a picture has been painted. 2 *Biology* a monotypic genus or species.

Monotype ('mɒnə,taɪp) NOUN 1 *Trademark* any of various typesetting systems, esp originally one in which each character was cast individually from hot metal. 2 type produced by such a system.

monotypic (,mɒnəʊ'tɪpɪk) ADJECTIVE 1 (of a genus or species) consisting of only one type of animal or plant. 2 of or relating to a monotype.

monounsaturated (,mɒnəʊʌn'sætʃə,reɪtɪd) ADJECTIVE of or relating to a class of vegetable oils, such as olive oil, the molecules of which have long chains of carbon atoms containing only one double bond. See also **polyunsaturated.**

monovalent (,mɒnəʊ'veɪlənt) ADJECTIVE *Chem* **a** having a valency of one. **b** having only one valency. ◆ Also: **univalent.**
▸**,mono'valence** *or* **,mono'valency** NOUN

monoxide (mɒ'nɒksaɪd) NOUN an oxide that contains one oxygen atom per molecule: *carbon monoxide, CO.*

Monroe doctrine NOUN a principle of US foreign policy that opposes the influence or interference of outside powers in the Americas.

Monrovia (mɒn'rəʊvɪə) NOUN the capital and chief port of Liberia, on the Atlantic: founded in

1822 as a home for freed American slaves; University of Liberia (1862). Pop.: 479 000 (1999 est.).

Mons (*French* mɔ̃s) NOUN a town in SW Belgium, capital of Hainaut province: scene of the first battle (1914) of the British Expeditionary Force during World War I. Pop.: 92 666 (1995 est.). Flemish name: **Bergen.**

Monseigneur *French* (mɔ̃sɛɲœr) NOUN, *plural* ***Messeigneurs*** (mesɛɲœr). a title given to French bishops, prelates, and princes. Abbreviation: **Mgr.**
▷HISTORY literally: my lord

monsieur (*French* məsjø; *English* məsˈjɜː) NOUN, *plural* **messieurs** (*French* mesjø; *English* ˈmɛsəz). a French title of address equivalent to *sir* when used alone or *Mr* when placed before a name.
▷HISTORY literally: my lord

Monsignor (mɒnˈsiːnjə; *Italian* monsiɲˈɲor) NOUN, *plural* **Monsignors** *or* **Monsignori** (*Italian* monsiɲˈɲoːri). *RC Church* an ecclesiastical title attached to certain offices or distinctions usually bestowed by the Pope. Abbreviations: **Mgr, Msgr.**
▷HISTORY C17: from Italian, from French MONSEIGNEUR

monsoon (mɒnˈsuːn) NOUN 1 a seasonal wind of S Asia that blows from the southwest in summer, bringing heavy rains, and from the northeast in winter. 2 the rainy season when the SW monsoon blows, from about April to October. 3 any wind that changes direction with the seasons.
▷HISTORY C16: from obsolete Dutch *monssoen,* from Portuguese *monção,* from Arabic *mawsim* season
▸**monˈsoonal** ADJECTIVE

mons pubis (ˈmɒnz ˈpjuːbɪs) NOUN, *plural* **montes pubis** (ˈmɒntiːz). the fatty cushion of flesh in human males situated over the junction of the pubic bones. Compare **mons veneris.**
▷HISTORY C17: New Latin: hill of the pubes

monster (ˈmɒnstə) NOUN 1 an imaginary beast, such as a centaur, usually made up of various animal or human parts. 2 a person, animal, or plant with a marked structural deformity. 3 a cruel, wicked, or inhuman person. 4 **a** a very large person, animal, or thing. **b** (*as modifier*): *a monster cake.*
▷HISTORY C13: from Old French *monstre,* from Latin *monstrum* portent, from *monēre* to warn

monstera (mɒnˈstɪərə) NOUN any plant of the tropical climbing genus *Monstera,* some species of which are grown as greenhouse or pot plants for their unusual leathery perforated leaves: family *Araceae. M. deliciosa* is the Swiss cheese plant.
▷HISTORY New Latin, perhaps because the leaves were regarded as an aberration

monstering (ˈmɒnstərɪŋ) NOUN *Informal* a severe reprimand or scolding; highly critical verbal attack.

monstrance (ˈmɒnstrəns) NOUN *RC Church* a receptacle, usually of gold or silver, with a transparent container in which the consecrated Host is exposed for adoration.
▷HISTORY C16: from Medieval Latin *mōnstrantia,* from Latin *mōnstrāre* to show

monstrosity (mɒnˈstrɒsɪtɪ) NOUN, *plural* **-ties.** 1 an outrageous or ugly person or thing; monster. 2 the state or quality of being monstrous.

monstrous (ˈmɒnstrəs) ADJECTIVE 1 abnormal, hideous, or unnatural in size, character, etc. 2 (of plants and animals) abnormal in structure. 3 outrageous, atrocious, or shocking: *it is monstrous how badly he is treated.* 4 huge: *a monstrous fire.* 5 of, relating to, or resembling a monster.
▸**ˈmonstrously** ADVERB ▸**ˈmonstrousness** NOUN

mons veneris (ˈmɒnz ˈvɛnərɪs) NOUN, *plural* **montes veneris** (ˈmɒntiːz). the fatty cushion of flesh in human females situated over the junction of the pubic bones. Compare **mons pubis.**
▷HISTORY C17: New Latin: hill of Venus

Mont. ABBREVIATION FOR Montana.

montage (mɒnˈtɑːʒ; *French* mɔ̃taʒ) NOUN 1 the art or process of composing pictures by the superimposition or juxtaposition of miscellaneous elements, such as other pictures or photographs. 2 such a composition. 3 a method of film editing involving the juxtaposition or partial superimposition of several shots to form a single image. 4 a rapidly cut film sequence of this kind.
▷HISTORY C20: from French, from *monter* to MOUNT[1]

Montagnais (ˌmɒntənˈjeɪ) NOUN, *plural* **-gnais** (jeɪ, jeɪz), **-gnaises** (jeɪz). 1 a member of an Innu people living in Labrador and eastern Quebec. 2 the Algonquian language of this people.
▷HISTORY C18: from French: of the mountain, from *montagne* MOUNTAIN

Montagnard (ˌmɒntənˈjɑːd, -ˈjɑː) NOUN, *plural* **-gnards** *or* **-gnard.** 1 a member of a hill people living on the border between Vietnam, Laos, and NE Cambodia. 2 a member of a North American Indian people living in the N Rocky Mountains.
▷HISTORY C19: from French: mountaineer, from *montagne* MOUNTAIN

Montague grammar (ˈmɒntəˌgjuː) NOUN *Logic, linguistics* a model-theoretic semantic theory for natural language that seeks to encompass indexical expressions and opaque contexts within an extensional theory by constructing set-theoretic representations of the intension of an expression in terms of functions of possible worlds.
▷HISTORY named after Richard Merett *Montague* (1930–71), US logician

Montagu's harrier (ˈmɒntəˌgjuːz) NOUN a brownish European bird of prey, *Circus pygargus,* with long narrow wings and a long tail: family *Accipitridae* (hawks, harriers, etc.).
▷HISTORY C19: named after Col. George *Montagu* (1751–1815), British naturalist

Montana (mɒnˈtænə) NOUN a state of the western US: consists of the Great Plains in the east and the Rocky Mountains in the west. Capital: Helena. Pop.: 902 195 (2000 est.). Area: 377 070 sq. km (145 587 sq. miles). Abbreviations: **Mont,** (with zip code) **MT.**

Montanan (mɒnˈtænən) NOUN 1 a native or inhabitant of Montana. ◆ ADJECTIVE 2 of or relating to Montana or its inhabitants.

montane (ˈmɒnteɪn) ADJECTIVE of or inhabiting mountainous regions: *a montane flora.*
▷HISTORY C19: from Latin *montānus,* from *mons* MOUNTAIN

montan wax (ˈmɒntæn) NOUN a hard wax obtained from lignite and peat, varying in colour from white to dark brown. It is used in polishes and candles.
▷HISTORY C20: from Latin *montānus* of a mountain

Montauban (*French* mɔ̃tobɑ̃) NOUN a city in SW France: a stronghold in the 16th and 17th centuries, taken by Richelieu in 1629. Pop.: 53 280 (1990).

Montbéliard (*French* mɔ̃beljar) NOUN an industrial town in E France: former capital of the duchy of Burgundy Pop.: 30 639 (1990).

Mont Blanc (*French* mɔ̃ blɑ̃) NOUN a massif in SW Europe, mainly between France and Italy: the highest mountain in the Alps; beneath it is **Mont Blanc Tunnel,** 12 km (7.5 miles) long. Highest peak (in France): 4807 m (15 771 ft.). Italian name: **Monte Bianco** (ˈmonte ˈbjaŋko).

montbretia (mɒnˈbriːʃə) NOUN a widely cultivated plant of the African iridaceous genus *Crocosmia,* a cross between *C. aurea* and *C. pottsii,* with ornamental orange or yellow flowers, grown mostly as pot plants.
▷HISTORY C19: New Latin, named after A. F. E. Coquebert de *Montbret* (1780–1801), French botanist

Mont Cenis (*French* mɔ̃səni) NOUN See (Mont) **Cenis.**

Mont Cervin (mɔ̃ sɛrvɛ̃) NOUN the French name for the **Matterhorn.**

mont-de-piété *French* (mɔ̃dpjete) NOUN, *plural* ***monts-de-piété*** (mɔ̃dpjete). (formerly) a public pawnshop.
▷HISTORY from Italian *monte di pietà* bank of pity

monte (ˈmɒntɪ) NOUN 1 a gambling card game of Spanish origin. 2 *Austral informal* a certainty.
▷HISTORY C19: from Spanish: mountain, hence pile of cards

Monte Carlo (ˈmɒntɪ ˈkɑːləʊ; *French* mɔ̃te karlo) NOUN a town and resort forming part of the principality of Monaco, on the Riviera: famous casino and the destination of an annual car rally (the **Monte Carlo Rally**). Pop.: 12 000 (latest est.).

Monte Carlo method NOUN a heuristic mathematical technique for evaluation or estimation of intractable problems by probabilistic simulation and sampling.
▷HISTORY C20: named after the casino at Monte Carlo, where systems for winning at roulette, etc., are often tried

Monte Cassino (ˈmɒntɪ kəˈsiːnəʊ; *Italian* ˈmonte kasˈsiːno) NOUN a hill above Cassino in central Italy: site of Benedictine monastery (530 A.D.); in 1944 mistaken for German observation post and destroyed by the Allies.

Monte Corno (*Italian* ˈmonte ˈkorno) NOUN See (Monte) **Corno.**

Montego Bay (mɒnˈtiːgəʊ) NOUN a port and resort in NW Jamaica: the second largest town on the island Pop.: 83 446 (1991).

monteith (mɒnˈtiːθ) NOUN a large ornamental bowl, usually of silver, for cooling wineglasses, which are suspended from the notched rim.
▷HISTORY C17: said to be from the name of a Scot who wore a cloak with a scalloped edge

Montenegrin (ˌmɒntɪˈniːgrɪn) ADJECTIVE 1 of or relating to Montenegro or its inhabitants. ◆ NOUN 2 a native or inhabitant of Montenegro.

Montenegro (ˌmɒntɪˈniːgrəʊ) NOUN a constituent republic of the Union of Serbia and Montenegro, bordering on the Adriatic: declared a kingdom in 1910 and united with Serbia, Croatia, and other territories in 1918 to form Yugoslavia; remained united with Serbia as the Federal Republic of Yugoslavia when the other Yugoslav constituent republics became independent in 1991–92; Union of Serbia and Montenegro formed in 2002. Capital: Podgorica. Pop.: 631 164 (1997 est.). Area: 13 812 sq. km (5387 sq. miles).

Monterey (ˌmɒntəˈreɪ) NOUN a city in W California: capital of Spain's Pacific empire from 1774 to 1825; taken by the US (1846). Pop.: 31 954 (1990).

Monterey cypress NOUN another name for **macrocarpa.**

montero (mɒnˈtɛərəʊ; *Spanish* monˈtero) NOUN, *plural* **-ros** (-rəʊz; *Spanish* -ros). a round cap with a flap at the back worn by hunters, esp in Spain in the 17th and 18th centuries.
▷HISTORY C17: from Spanish, literally: mountaineer

Monterrey (ˌmɒntəˈreɪ; *Spanish* monteˈrrei) NOUN a city in NE Mexico, capital of Nuevo Léon state: the third largest city in Mexico; a major industrial centre, esp for metals. Pop.: 1 108 400 (2000 est.).

Montessori method NOUN a method of nursery education in which children are provided with generous facilities for practical play and allowed to develop at their own pace.

Montevideo (ˌmɒntɪvɪˈdeɪəʊ; *Spanish* monteβiˈðeo) NOUN the capital and chief port of Uruguay, in the south on the Río de la Plata estuary: the largest city in the country: University of the Republic (1849); resort. Pop.: 1 378 707 (1996).

Montezuma's revenge (mɒntɪˈzuːməz) NOUN *Informal* an acute attack of infectious diarrhoea, esp when experienced in Mexico by tourists.
▷HISTORY C20: after *Montezuma* II (1466–1520), the Aztec emperor of Mexico overthrown and killed by the Spanish conquistador Hernando Cortés (1485–1527)

montgolfier (mɒntˈgɒlfɪə; *French* mɔ̃gɔlfje) NOUN *Obsolete* a hot-air balloon.
▷HISTORY C18: after Jacques Etienne *Montgolfier* (1745–99) and his brother Joseph Michel Montgolfier (1740–1810), the French inventors who built (1782) and ascended in (1783) the first practical hot-air balloon

Montgomery (məntˈgʌmərɪ) NOUN a city in central Alabama, on the Alabama River: state capital; capital of the Confederacy (1861). Pop.: 201 568 (2000).

Montgomeryshire (məntˈgʌmərɪˌʃɪə, -ʃə) NOUN (until 1974) a county of central Wales, now part of Powys.

month (mʌnθ) NOUN 1 one of the twelve divisions (**calendar months**) of the calendar year. 2 a period of time extending from one date to a corresponding date in the next calendar month. 3 a period of four weeks or of 30 days. 4 the period of time (**tropical month**) taken by the moon to return to the same longitude after one complete

revolution around the earth; 27.321 58 days (approximately 27 days, 7 hours, 43 minutes, 4.5 seconds). 5 the period of time (**sidereal month**) taken by the moon to make one complete revolution around the earth, measured between two successive conjunctions with a distant star; 27.321 66 days (approximately 27 days, 7 hours, 43 minutes, 11 seconds). 6 Also called: **lunation.** the period of time (**lunar** or **synodic month**) taken by the moon to make one complete revolution around the earth, measured between two successive new moons; 29.530 59 days (approximately 29 days, 12 hours, 44 minutes, 3 seconds). 7 **a month of Sundays.** *Informal* a long unspecified period. ◆ Related adjective: **mensal.**
▷HISTORY Old English *mōnath;* related to Old High German *mānōd,* Old Norse *mānathr;* compare Gothic *mena* moon

monthly ('mʌnθlɪ) ADJECTIVE 1 occurring, done, appearing, payable, etc., once every month. 2 lasting or valid for a month: *a monthly subscription.* ◆ ADVERB 3 once a month. ◆ NOUN, *plural* **-lies.** 4 a book, periodical, magazine, etc., published once a month. 5 *Informal* a menstrual period.

month's mind NOUN *RC Church* a Mass celebrated in remembrance of a person one month after his death.

monticule ('mɒntɪˌkjuːl) NOUN a small hill or mound, such as a secondary volcanic cone.
▷HISTORY C18: via French from Late Latin *monticulus,* diminutive of Latin *mons* mountain

Montluçon (*French* mɔ̃lysɔ̃) NOUN an industrial city in central France, on the Cher River. Pop.: 56 435 (latest est.).

Montmartre (*French* mɔ̃martrə) NOUN a district of N Paris, on a hill above the Seine: the highest point in the city; famous for its associations with many artists.

montmorillonite (ˌmɒntməˈrɪləˌnaɪt) NOUN a clay mineral consisting of hydrated aluminium silicate: an important component of bentonite.
▷HISTORY C19: named after *Montmorillon,* French town where it was first found, + -ITE[1]

Montparnasse (*French* mɔ̃parnas) NOUN a district of S Paris, on the left bank of the Seine: noted for its cafés, frequented by artists, writers, and students.

Montpelier (mɒntˈpiːljə) NOUN a city in N central Vermont, on the Winooski River: the state capital Pop.: 8254 (1990).

Montpellier (*French* mɔ̃pɛlje) NOUN a city in S France, the chief town of Languedoc: its university was founded by Pope Nicholas IV in 1289; wine trade. Pop.: 225 392 (1999).

Montreal (ˌmɒntrɪˈɔːl) NOUN a city and major port in central Canada, in S Quebec on **Montreal Island** at the junction of the Ottawa and St Lawrence Rivers. Pop.: 1 016 376 (1996), with a conurbation of 3 127 242 (1991). French name: **Montréal** (mɔ̃real).

Montreuil (*French* mɔ̃trœj) NOUN an E suburb of Paris: formerly famous for peaches, but now increasingly industrialized. Pop.: 94 754 (1990).

Montreux (*French* mɔ̃trø) NOUN a town and resort in W Switzerland, in Vaud canton on Lake Geneva annual television festival. Pop.: 19 850 (1990).

Mont-Saint-Michel (*French* mɔ̃sɛ̃miʃɛl) NOUN a rocky islet off the coast of NW France, accessible at low tide by a causeway, in the **Bay of St Michel** (an inlet of the Gulf of St Malo): Benedictine abbey (966), used as a prison from the Revolution until 1863; reoccupied by Benedictine monks since 1966. Area: 1 hectare (3 acres).

Montserrat NOUN 1 (ˌmɒntsəˈræt) a volcanic island in the Caribbean, in the Leeward Islands: a UK Overseas Territory: much of the island rendered uninhabitable by volcanic eruptions in 1997. Capital: Plymouth. Pop.: 4 500 (1998 est.). Area: 103 sq. km (40 sq. miles). 2 (*Spanish* mɔnsɛˈrrat) a mountain in NE Spain, northwest of Barcelona: famous Benedictine monastery. Height: 1235 m (4054 ft.). Ancient name: **Mons Serratus** (mɒnz səˈrætəs).

monument ('mɒnjʊmənt) NOUN 1 an obelisk, statue, building, etc., erected in commemoration of a person or event or in celebration of something. 2 a notable building or site, esp one preserved as public property. 3 a tomb or tombstone. 4 a literary or artistic work regarded as commemorative of its creator or a particular period. 5 *US* a boundary marker. 6 an exceptional example: *his lecture was a monument of tedium.* 7 an obsolete word for **statue.**
▷HISTORY C13: from Latin *monumentum,* from *monēre* to remind, advise

Monument ('mɒnjʊmənt) NOUN **the.** a tall columnar building designed (1671) by Sir Christopher Wren to commemorate the Fire of London (1666), which destroyed a large part of the medieval city.

monumental (ˌmɒnjʊˈmentᵊl) ADJECTIVE 1 like a monument, esp in large size, endurance, or importance: *a monumental work of art.* 2 of, relating to, or being a monument. 3 *Informal* (intensifier): *monumental stupidity.*
▸ **ˌmonumenˈtality** NOUN ▸ **ˌmonuˈmentally** ADVERB

mony ('mɒnɪ) DETERMINER a Scot word for **many.**

Monza (*Italian* ˈmontsa) NOUN a city in N Italy, northeast of Milan: the ancient capital of Lombardy; scene of the assassination of King Umberto I in 1900; motor-racing circuit. Pop.: 119 516 (2000 est.).

monzonite ('mɒnzəˌnaɪt) NOUN a coarse-grained plutonic igneous rock consisting of equal amounts of plagioclase and orthoclase feldspar, with ferromagnesian minerals.
▷HISTORY C19: from German, named after *Monzoni,* Tyrolean mountain where it was found
▸ **monzonitic** (ˌmɒnzəˈnɪtɪk) ADJECTIVE

moo (muː) VERB 1 (*intr*) (of a cow, bull, etc.) to make a characteristic deep long sound; low. ◆ INTERJECTION 2 an instance or imitation of this sound.

mooch (muːtʃ) VERB *Slang* 1 (*intr;* often foll by *around*) to loiter or walk aimlessly. 2 (*intr*) to behave in an apathetic way. 3 (*intr*) to sneak or lurk; skulk. 4 (*tr*) to cadge. 5 (*tr*) *Chiefly US and Canadian* to steal.
▷HISTORY C17: perhaps from Old French *muchier* to skulk
▸ **ˈmoocher** NOUN

mood[1] (muːd) NOUN 1 a temporary state of mind or temper: *a cheerful mood.* 2 a sullen or gloomy state of mind, esp when temporary: *she's in a mood.* 3 a prevailing atmosphere or feeling. 4 **in the mood.** in a favourable state of mind (for something or to do something).
▷HISTORY Old English *mōd* mind, feeling; compare Old Norse *mōthr* grief, wrath

mood[2] (muːd) NOUN 1 *Grammar* a category of the verb or verbal inflections that expresses semantic and grammatical differences, including such forms as the indicative, subjunctive, and imperative. 2 *Logic* one of the possible arrangements of the syllogism, classified solely by whether the component propositions are universal or particular and affirmative or negative. Compare **figure** (sense 18). ◆ Also called: **mode.**
▷HISTORY C16: from MOOD[1], influenced in meaning by MODE

moody ('muːdɪ) ADJECTIVE **moodier, moodiest.** 1 sullen, sulky, or gloomy. 2 temperamental or changeable.
▸ **ˈmoodily** ADVERB ▸ **ˈmoodiness** NOUN

Moog (muːg, məʊg) NOUN *Trademark, Music* a type of synthesizer.
▷HISTORY C20: named after Robert *Moog* (born 1934), US engineer

mooi (mɔɪ) ADJECTIVE *South African, slang* pleasing; nice.
▷HISTORY Afrikaans

mook (muːk) NOUN *US, slang* a person regarded with contempt, esp a stupid person.
▷HISTORY of uncertain origin

moolah ('muːlɑː) NOUN a slang word for **money.**

mooli ('muːlɪ) NOUN a type of large white radish.
▷HISTORY E African native name

mooloo ('muːluː) NOUN *NZ* a person from the Waikato.
▷HISTORY originally the name of the cow mascot of the Waikato rugby team

moolvie *or* **moolvi** ('muːlviː) NOUN (esp in India) a Muslim doctor of the law, teacher, or learned man also used as a title of respect.
▷HISTORY C17: from Urdu, from Arabic *mawlawīy;* compare MULLAH

Moomba ('muːmbə) NOUN *Austral* 1 a festival held annually in Melbourne since 1954, named in the belief that *moomba* was an Aboriginal word meaning "Let's get together and have fun". 2 a natural gas field in South Australia.
▷HISTORY from a native Australian language *moom* buttocks, anus

moon (muːn) NOUN 1 (*sometimes capital*) the natural satellite of the earth. Diameter: 3476 km; mass: 7.35×10^{22} kg; mean distance from earth: 384 400 km; periods of rotation and revolution: 27.32 days. Related adjective: **lunar.** 2 the face of the moon as it is seen during its revolution around the earth, esp at one of its phases: *new moon; full moon.* 3 any natural satellite of a planet. 4 moonlight; moonshine. 5 something resembling a moon. 6 a month, esp a lunar one. 7 **once in a blue moon.** very seldom. 8 **over the moon.** *Informal* extremely happy; ecstatic. 9 **reach for the moon.** to desire or attempt something unattainable or difficult to obtain. ◆ VERB 10 (when *tr,* often foll by *away;* when *intr,* often foll by *around*) to be idle in a listless way, as if in love, or to idle (time) away. 11 (*intr*) *Slang* to expose one's buttocks to passers-by.
▷HISTORY Old English *mōna;* compare Old Frisian *mōna,* Old High German *māno*
▸ **ˈmoonless** ADJECTIVE

Moon (muːn) NOUN a system of embossed alphabetical signs for blind readers, the fourteen basic characters of which can, by rotation, mimic most of the letters of the Roman alphabet, thereby making learning easier for those who learned to read before going blind. Compare **Braille[1].**
▷HISTORY C19: from William *Moon* (1919–94), British inventor of the system

moonbeam ('muːnˌbiːm) NOUN a ray of moonlight.

moon blindness NOUN 1 *Ophthalmol* a nontechnical name for **nyctalopia.** 2 Also called: **mooneye.** *Vet science* a disorder affecting horses, which causes inflammation of the eyes and sometimes blindness.
▸ **ˈmoon-ˌblind** ADJECTIVE

mooncalf ('muːnˌkɑːf) NOUN, *plural* **-calves** (-ˌkɑːvz). 1 a born fool; dolt. 2 a person who idles time away. 3 *Obsolete* a freak or monster.

Moon Child NOUN a euphemistic name for **Cancer** (sense 2b).

mooned (muːnd) ADJECTIVE decorated with a moon.

mooneye ('muːnˌaɪ) NOUN 1 any of several North American large-eyed freshwater clupeoid fishes of the family *Hiodontidae,* esp *Hiodon tergisus.* See also **goldeye.** 2 *Vet science* another name for **moon blindness** (sense 2).

moon-eyed ADJECTIVE 1 having the eyes open wide, as in awe. 2 *Vet science* affected with moon blindness.

moon-faced ADJECTIVE having a round face; full-faced.

moonfish ('muːnˌfɪʃ) NOUN, *plural* **-fishes** *or* **-fish.** 1 any of several deep-bodied silvery carangid fishes, occurring in warm and tropical American coastal waters. 2 any of various other round silvery fishes, such as the Indo-Pacific *Monodactylus argenteus.* 3 another name for **opah.**

moonflower ('muːnˌflaʊə) NOUN 1 any of several night-blooming convolvulaceous plants, esp the white-flowered *Calonyction* (or *Ipomoea*) *aculeatum.* 2 Also called: **angels' tears.** a Mexican solanaceous plant, *Datura suaveolens,* planted in the tropics for its white night-blooming flowers.

Moonie ('muːnɪ) NOUN *Informal* 1 a member of the Unification Church. 2 (*plural;* preceded by *the*) the Unification Church.
▷HISTORY C20: named after the founder Sun Myung *Moon* (born 1920), S Korean industrialist

moonlight ('muːnˌlaɪt) NOUN 1 Also called: **moonshine.** light from the sun received on earth after reflection by the moon. 2 (*modifier*) illuminated by the moon: *a moonlight walk.* 3 short for **moonlight flit.** ◆ VERB **-lights, -lighting, -lighted.** 4 (*intr*) *Informal* to work at a secondary job, esp at night, and often illegitimately.
▸ **ˈmoonˌlighter** NOUN

moonlight flit NOUN *Brit informal* a hurried departure at night, esp from rented accommodation to avoid payment of rent owed. Often shortened to: **moonlight**.

moonlighting (ˈmuːnˌlaɪtɪŋ) NOUN [1] working at a secondary job. [2] (in 19th-century Ireland) the carrying out of cattle-maiming, murders, etc., during the night in protest against the land-tenure system.

moonlit (ˈmuːnlɪt) ADJECTIVE illuminated by the moon.

moon pool NOUN (in the oil industry) an open shaft in the centre of the hull of a ship engaged in deep-sea drilling through which drilling takes place.

moonquake (ˈmuːnˌkweɪk) NOUN a light tremor of the moon, detected on the moon's surface.

moonraker (ˈmuːnˌreɪkə) NOUN *Nautical* a small square sail set above a skysail.

moon rat NOUN a ratlike SE Asian nocturnal mammal, *Echinosorex gymnurus*, with greyish fur and an elongated snout: family *Erinaceidae* (hedgehogs): the largest living insectivore.

moonrise (ˈmuːnˌraɪz) NOUN the moment when the moon appears above the horizon.

moonscape (ˈmuːnˌskeɪp) NOUN the general surface of the moon or a representation of it.

moonseed (ˈmuːnˌsiːd) NOUN any menispermaceous climbing plant of the genus *Menispermum* and related genera, having red or black fruits with crescent-shaped or ring-shaped seeds.

moonset (ˈmuːnˌsɛt) NOUN the moment when the moon disappears below the horizon.

moonshine (ˈmuːnˌʃaɪn) NOUN [1] another word for **moonlight** (sense 1). [2] *US and Canadian* illegally distilled or smuggled whisky or other spirit. [3] foolish talk or thought.

moonshiner (ˈmuːnˌʃaɪnə) NOUN *US and Canadian* a person who illegally makes or smuggles distilled spirits.

moonshot (ˈmuːnˌʃɒt) NOUN the launching of a spacecraft, rocket, etc., to the moon.

moonstone (ˈmuːnˌstəʊn) NOUN a gem variety of orthoclase or albite that is white and translucent with bluish reflections.

moonstruck (ˈmuːnˌstrʌk) *or* **moonstricken** (ˈmuːnˌstrɪkən) ADJECTIVE deranged or mad.

moonwort (ˈmuːnˌwɜːt) NOUN [1] Also called (US): **grape fern**. any of various ferns of the genus *Botrychium*, esp *B. lunaria*, which has crescent-shaped leaflets. [2] another name for **honesty** (sense 4).

moony (ˈmuːnɪ) ADJECTIVE **moonier, mooniest**. [1] *Informal* dreamy or listless. [2] of or like the moon. [3] *Brit, slang* crazy or foolish.
▸ **ˈmoonily** ADVERB ▸ **ˈmooniness** NOUN

moor[1] (mʊə, mɔː) NOUN a tract of unenclosed ground, usually having peaty soil covered with heather, coarse grass, bracken, and moss.
▷HISTORY Old English *mōr*; related to Old Saxon *mōr*, Old High German *muor* swamp
▸ **ˈmoory** ADJECTIVE

moor[2] (mʊə, mɔː) VERB [1] to secure (a ship, boat, etc.) with cables or ropes. [2] (of a ship, boat, etc.) to be secured in this way. [3] (not in technical usage) a less common word for **anchor** (sense 11).
▷HISTORY C15: of Germanic origin; related to Old English *mǣrelsrāp* rope for mooring

Moor (mʊə, mɔː) NOUN a member of a Muslim people of North Africa, of mixed Arab and Berber descent. In the 8th century they were converted to Islam and established power in North Africa and Spain, where they established a civilization (756–1492).
▷HISTORY C14: via Old French from Latin *Maurus*, from Greek *Mauros*, possibly from Berber

moorage (ˈmʊərɪdʒ, ˈmɔːrɪdʒ) NOUN [1] a place for mooring a vessel. [2] a charge for mooring. [3] the act of mooring.

moorburn *or* **muirburn** (ˈmuːrˌbʌrn, ˈmʊəˌbɜːn) NOUN *Scot* the practice of burning off old growth on a heather moor to encourage new growth for grazing.

moorcock (ˈmʊəˌkɒk, ˈmɔː-) NOUN the male of the red grouse.

Moore (ˈmʊʊre) NOUN another name for **Mossi**.

moorfowl (ˈmʊəˌfaʊl, ˈmɔː-) NOUN (in British game laws) an archaic name for **red grouse**. Compare **heathfowl**.

moor grass NOUN a grass characteristic of moors, especially **purple moor grass** (*Molinia caerulea*) of heath and fenland and **blue moor grass** (*Sesleria caerulea*) of limestone uplands.

moorhen (ˈmʊəˌhɛn, ˈmɔː-) NOUN [1] a bird, *Gallinula chloropus*, inhabiting ponds, lakes, etc., having a black plumage, red bill, and a red shield above the bill: family *Rallidae* (rails). [2] the female of the red grouse.

mooring (ˈmʊərɪŋ, ˈmɔː-) NOUN [1] a place for mooring a vessel. [2] a permanent anchor, dropped in the water and equipped with a floating buoy, to which vessels can moor. ◆ See also **moorings**.

mooring mast NOUN a mast or tower to which a balloon or airship may be moored. Also called: **mooring tower**.

moorings (ˈmʊərɪŋz, ˈmɔː-) PLURAL NOUN [1] *Nautical* the ropes, anchors, etc., used in mooring a vessel. [2] (*sometimes singular*) something that provides security or stability.

Moorish (ˈmʊərɪʃ, ˈmɔː-) ADJECTIVE [1] of or relating to the Moors. [2] denoting the style of architecture used in Spain from the 13th to 16th century, characterized by the horseshoe arch. Also: **Morisco** *or* **Moresco**.

Moorish idol NOUN a tropical marine spiny-finned fish, *Zanclus canescens*, that is common around coral reefs: family *Zanclidae*. It has a deeply compressed body with yellow and black stripes, a beaklike snout, and an elongated dorsal fin.

moorland (ˈmʊələnd, ˈmɔː-) NOUN *Brit* an area of moor.

moorwort (ˈmʊəˌwɜːt, ˈmɔː-) NOUN another name for **marsh andromeda**.

moose (muːs) NOUN, *plural* **moose**. a large North American deer, *Alces alces*, having large flattened palmate antlers: also occurs in Europe and Asia where it is called an elk.
▷HISTORY C17: from Algonquian; related to Narraganset *moos*, from *moosu* he strips, alluding to the moose's habit of stripping trees

Moose Jaw NOUN a city in W Canada, in S Saskatchewan. Pop.: 33 593 (1991).

moose milk NOUN *Canadian* a mixed alcoholic drink made with ingredients such as milk and eggs and usually rum.

moose pasture NOUN *Canadian informal* land considered to be worthless, esp when lacking in extractable mineral deposits.

moot (muːt) ADJECTIVE [1] subject or open to debate: *a moot point*. ◆ VERB [2] (*tr*) to suggest or bring up for debate. [3] (*intr*) to plead or argue theoretical or hypothetical cases, as an academic exercise or as vocational training for law students. ◆ NOUN [4] a discussion or debate of a hypothetical case or point, held as an academic activity. [5] (in Anglo-Saxon England) an assembly, mainly in a shire or hundred, dealing with local legal and administrative affairs.
▷HISTORY Old English *gemōt*; compare Old Saxon *mōt*, Middle High German *muoze* meeting
▸ **ˈmooter** NOUN

moot court NOUN a mock court trying hypothetical legal cases.

mop[1] (mɒp) NOUN [1] an implement with a wooden handle and a head made of twists of cotton or a piece of synthetic sponge, used for polishing or washing floors, or washing dishes. [2] something resembling this, such as a tangle of hair. ◆ VERB **mops, mopping, mopped**. [3] (*tr*; often foll by *up*) to clean or soak up with or as if with a mop. ◆ See also **mop up**.
▷HISTORY C15 *mappe*, from earlier *mappel*, from Medieval Latin *mappula* cloth, from Latin *mappa* napkin

mop[2] (mɒp) *Rare* ◆ VERB **mops, mopping, mopped**. [1] (*intr*) to make a grimace or sad expression (esp in the phrase **mop and mow**). ◆ NOUN [2] such a face or expression.
▷HISTORY C16: perhaps from Dutch *moppen* to pour; compare Dutch *mop* pug dog

mop[3] (mɒp) NOUN (in various parts of England) an annual fair at which formerly servants were hired.
▷HISTORY C17: from the practice of servants carrying a mop, broom, or flail, etc., to signify the job sought

mopani *or* **mopane** (mɒˈpɑːnɪ) NOUN a leguminous tree, *Colophospermum* (or *Copaifera*) *mopane*, native to southern Africa, that is highly resistant to drought and produces very hard wood. Also called: **ironwood**.
▷HISTORY C19: from Setswana (a Bantu language) *mo-pane*

mopani worm NOUN an edible caterpillar that feeds on mopani leaves.

mopboard (ˈmɒpˌbɔːd) NOUN a US word for **skirting board**.

mope (məʊp) VERB (*intr*) [1] to be gloomy or apathetic. [2] to move or act in an aimless way. ◆ NOUN [3] a gloomy person. ◆ See also **mopes**.
▷HISTORY C16: perhaps from obsolete *mope* fool and related to MOP[2]
▸ **ˈmoper** NOUN ▸ **ˈmopy** ADJECTIVE

moped (ˈməʊpɛd) NOUN *Brit* a light motorcycle, not over 50cc.
▷HISTORY C20: from MOTOR + PEDAL[1], originally equipped with auxiliary pedals

mopes (məʊps) PLURAL NOUN **the.** low spirits.

mopoke (ˈməʊˌpəʊk) NOUN [1] Also called (NZ): **ruru**. a small spotted owl, *Ninox novaeseelandiae*, of Australia and New Zealand. In Australia the tawny frogmouth, *Podargus strigoides*, is very often wrongly identified as the mopoke. [2] *Austral and NZ, slang* a slow or lugubrious person. ◆ Also called: **morepork**.
▷HISTORY C19: imitative of the bird's cry

moppet (ˈmɒpɪt) NOUN a less common word for **poppet** (sense 1).
▷HISTORY C17: from obsolete *mop* rag doll; of obscure origin

mop up VERB (*tr, adverb*) [1] to clean with a mop. [2] *Informal* to complete (a task, etc.). [3] *Military* to clear (remaining enemy forces) after a battle, as by killing, taking prisoner, etc. ◆ NOUN **mop-up**. [4] the act or an instance of mopping up.

moquette (mɒˈkɛt) NOUN a thick velvety fabric used for carpets, upholstery, etc.
▷HISTORY C18: from French; of uncertain origin

mor (mɔː) NOUN a layer of acidic humus formed in cool moist areas where decomposition is slow. Compare **mull**[4].
▷HISTORY Danish

MOR ABBREVIATION FOR middle-of-the-road: used esp in radio programming.

Mor. ABBREVIATION FOR Morocco.

mora (ˈmɔːrə) NOUN, *plural* **-rae** (-riː) *or* **-ras**. *Prosody* the quantity of a short syllable in verse represented by the breve (˘).
▷HISTORY C16: from Latin: pause

moraceous (mɔːˈreɪʃəs) ADJECTIVE of, relating to, or belonging to the *Moraceae*, a mostly tropical and subtropical family of trees and shrubs, including fig, mulberry, breadfruit, and hop, many of which have latex in the stems and heads enclosed in a fleshy receptacle.
▷HISTORY C20: via New Latin from Latin *morus* mulberry tree

Moradabad (ˌmɔːrədəˈbæd) NOUN a city in N India, in N Uttar Pradesh. Pop.: 429 214 (1991).

moraine (mɒˈreɪn) NOUN a mass of debris, carried by glaciers and forming ridges and mounds when deposited.
▷HISTORY C18: from French, from Savoy dialect *morena*, of obscure origin
▸ **moˈrainal** *or* **moˈrainic** ADJECTIVE

moral (ˈmɒrəl) ADJECTIVE [1] concerned with or relating to human behaviour, esp the distinction between good and bad or right and wrong behaviour: *moral sense*. [2] adhering to conventionally accepted standards of conduct. [3] based on a sense of right and wrong according to conscience: *moral courage*; *moral law*. [4] having psychological rather than tangible effects: *moral support*. [5] having the effects but not the appearance of (victory or defeat): *a moral victory*; *a moral defeat*. [6] having a strong probability: *a moral certainty*. [7] *Law* (of evidence, etc.) based on a knowledge of the tendencies of human nature. ◆ NOUN [8] the lesson to be obtained from a fable or event: *point the moral*. [9] a concise truth; maxim. [10] (*plural*) principles of behaviour in accordance with standards of right and wrong.

▷HISTORY C14: from Latin *mōrālis* relating to morals or customs, from *mōs* custom
▸ **'morally** ADVERB

morale (mɒ'rɑːl) NOUN the degree of mental or moral confidence of a person or group; spirit of optimism.
▷HISTORY C18: morals, from French, n. use of MORAL (adj)

moral hazard NOUN *Insurance* a risk incurred by an insurance company with respect to the possible lack of honesty or prudence among policyholders.

moralism ('mɒrəˌlɪzəm) NOUN [1] the habit or practice of moralizing. [2] a moral saying. [3] the practice of moral principles without reference to religion.

moralist ('mɒrəlɪst) NOUN [1] a person who seeks to regulate the morals of others or to imbue others with a sense of morality. [2] a person who lives in accordance with moral principles. [3] a philosopher who is concerned with casuistic discussions of right action, or who seeks a general characterization of right action, often contrasted with a moral philosopher whose concern is with general philosophical questions about ethics.
▸ **ˌmoral'istic** ADJECTIVE ▸ **ˌmoral'istically** ADVERB

morality (mə'rælɪtɪ) NOUN, *plural* **-ties.** [1] the quality of being moral. [2] conformity, or degree of conformity, to conventional standards of moral conduct. [3] a system of moral principles. [4] an instruction or lesson in morals. [5] short for **morality play.**

morality play NOUN a type of drama written between the 14th and 16th centuries concerned with the conflict between personified virtues and vices.

moralize *or* **moralise** ('mɒrəˌlaɪz) VERB [1] *(intr)* to make moral pronouncements. [2] *(tr)* to interpret or explain in a moral sense. [3] *(tr)* to improve the morals of.
▸ **ˌmorali'zation** *or* **ˌmorali'sation** NOUN ▸ **'moralˌizer** *or* **'moralˌiser** NOUN

moral majority NOUN a presumed majority of people believed to be in favour of a stricter code of public morals.
▷HISTORY C20: after *Moral Majority,* a right-wing US religious organization, based on SILENT MAJORITY

moral philosophy NOUN the branch of philosophy dealing with both argument about the content of morality and meta-ethical discussion of the nature of moral judgment, language, argument, and value.

Moral Rearmament NOUN a worldwide movement for moral and spiritual renewal founded by Frank Buchman in 1938. Also called: **Buchmanism.** Former name: **Oxford Group.**

moral theology NOUN the branch of theology dealing with ethics.

Morar ('mɔːrə) NOUN **Loch.** a lake in W Scotland, in the SW Highlands: the deepest in Scotland. Length: 18 km (11 miles). Depth: 296 m (987 ft.).

morass (mə'ræs) NOUN [1] a tract of swampy low-lying land. [2] a disordered or muddled situation or circumstance, esp one that impedes progress.
▷HISTORY C17: from Dutch *moeras,* ultimately from Old French *marais* MARSH

moratorium (ˌmɒrə'tɔːrɪəm) NOUN, *plural* **-ria** (-rɪə) *or* **-riums.** [1] a legally authorized postponement of the fulfilment of an obligation. [2] an agreed suspension of activity.
▷HISTORY C19: New Latin, from Late Latin *morātōrius* dilatory, from *mora* delay
▸ **moratory** ('mɒrətərɪ, -trɪ) ADJECTIVE

Morava (mə'rɑːvə) NOUN [1] a river in central Europe, rising in the Sudeten Mountains, in the Czech Republic, and flowing south through Slovakia to the Danube: forms part of the border between the Czech Republic, Slovakia, and Austria. Length: 370 km (230 miles). German name: **March.** [2] a river in E Serbia and Montenegro, formed by the confluence of the Southern Morava and the Western Morava near Stalac: flows north to the Danube. Length: 209 km (130 miles). [3] ('mɔrava) the Czech name for **Moravia.**

Moravia (mə'reɪvɪə, mɒ-) NOUN a region of the Czech Republic around the Morava River, bounded by the Bohemian-Moravian Highlands, the Sudeten Mountains, and the W Carpathians: became a separate Austrian crownland in 1848; part of Czechoslovakia 1918–92; valuable mineral resources. Czech name: **Morava.** German name: **Mähren.**

Moravian (mə'reɪvɪən, mɒ-) ADJECTIVE [1] of or relating to Moravia, its people, or their dialect of Czech. [2] of or relating to the Moravian Church. ◆ NOUN [3] the Moravian dialect. [4] a native or inhabitant of Moravia. [5] a member of the Moravian Church.
▸ **Mo'ravianism** NOUN

Moravian Church NOUN a Protestant Church originating in Moravia in 1722 as a revival of the sect of Bohemian Brethren. It has close links with the Lutheran Church.

Moravian Gate NOUN a low mountain pass linking S Poland and Moravia (the Czech Republic), between the SE Sudeten Mountains and the W Carpathian Mountains.

moray (mɒ'reɪ) NOUN, *plural* **-rays.** any voracious marine coastal eel of the family *Muraenidae,* esp *Muraena helena,* marked with brilliant patterns and colours.
▷HISTORY C17: from Portuguese *moréia,* from Latin *mūrēna,* from Greek *muraina*

Moray ('mʌrɪ) NOUN a council area and historical county of NE Scotland: part of Grampian region from 1975 to 1996: mainly hilly, with the Cairngorm mountains in the S. Administrative centre: Elgin. Pop.: 86 940 (2001). Area: 2238 sq. km (874 sq. miles). Former name: **Elgin.**

Moray Firth NOUN an inlet of the North Sea on the NE coast of Scotland. Length: about 56 km (35 miles).

morbid ('mɔːbɪd) ADJECTIVE [1] having an unusual interest in death or unpleasant events. [2] gruesome. [3] relating to or characterized by disease; pathologic: *a morbid growth.*
▷HISTORY C17: from Latin *morbidus* sickly, from *morbus* illness
▸ **'morbidly** ADVERB ▸ **'morbidness** NOUN

morbid anatomy NOUN the branch of medical science concerned with the study of the structure of diseased organs and tissues.

morbidity (mɔː'bɪdɪtɪ) NOUN [1] the state of being morbid. [2] Also called: **morbidity rate.** the relative incidence of a particular disease in a specific locality.

morbific (mɔː'bɪfɪk) ADJECTIVE causing disease; pathogenic.
▸ **mor'bifically** ADVERB

Morbihan (*French* mɔrbiɑ̃) NOUN a department of NW France, in S Brittany. Capital: Vannes. Pop.: 643 873 (1999). Area: 7092 sq. km (2766 sq. miles).

morbilli (mɔː'bɪlaɪ) NOUN a technical name for **measles.**
▷HISTORY C17: from Medieval Latin *morbillus* pustule, diminutive of Latin *morbus* illness

morceau *French* (mɔrso) NOUN, *plural* ***-ceaux*** (-so). [1] a fragment or morsel. [2] a short composition, esp a musical one.
▷HISTORY C18: from Old French: MORSEL

morcha ('mɔːtʃɑː) NOUN (in India) a hostile demonstration against the government.
▷HISTORY Hindi: entrenchment

mordacious (mɔː'deɪʃəs) ADJECTIVE sarcastic, caustic, or biting.
▷HISTORY C17: from Latin *mordax,* from *mordēre* to bite
▸ **mor'daciously** ADVERB ▸ **mordacity** (mɔː'dæsɪtɪ) *or* **mor'daciousness** NOUN

mordant ('mɔːdᵊnt) ADJECTIVE [1] sarcastic or caustic. [2] having the properties of a mordant. [3] pungent. ◆ NOUN [4] a substance used before the application of a dye, possessing the ability to fix colours in textiles, leather, etc. See also **lake**[2] (sense 1). [5] an acid or other corrosive fluid used to etch lines on a printing plate. ◆ VERB [6] *(tr)* to treat (a fabric, yarn, etc.) with a mordant.
▷HISTORY C15: from Old French: biting, from *mordre* to bite, from Latin *mordēre*
▸ **'mordancy** NOUN ▸ **'mordantly** ADVERB

mordent ('mɔːdᵊnt) NOUN *Music* a melodic ornament consisting of the rapid alternation of a note with a note one degree lower than it. Also called: **lower mordent.**
▷HISTORY C19: from German, from Italian *mordente,* from *mordere* to bite

Mordred ('mɔːdrɛd) NOUN a variant of **Modred.**

Mordvin ('mɔːdvɪn) NOUN [1] *(plural* **-vin** *or* **-vins)** a member of a Finnish people of the middle Volga region, living chiefly in the Mordvinian Republic. [2] the language of this people, belonging to the Finno-Ugric family.

Mordvinian Republic (mɔː'dvɪnɪən) NOUN a constituent republic of W central Russia, in the middle Volga basin. Capital: Saransk. Pop.: 929 000 (2000 est.). Area: 26 200 sq. km (10 110 sq. miles). Also called: **Mordovian Republic** (mɔː'dəʊvɪən), **Mordovia.**

more (mɔː) DETERMINER [1] **a** the comparative of **much** or **many:** *more joy than you know; more pork sausages.* **b** *(as pronoun; functioning as singular or plural): he has more than she has; even more are dying every day.* [2] **a** additional; further: *no more bananas.* **b** *(as pronoun; functioning as singular or plural): I can't take any more; more than expected.* [3] **more of.** to a greater extent or degree: *we see more of Sue these days; more of a nuisance than it should be.* ◆ ADVERB [4] used to form the comparative of some adjectives and adverbs: *a more believable story; more quickly.* [5] the comparative of **much:** *people listen to the radio more now.* [6] additionally; again: *I'll look at it once more.* [7] **more or less. a** as an estimate; approximately. **b** to an unspecified extent or degree: *the party was ruined, more or less.* [8] **more so.** to a greater extent or degree. [9] **neither more nor less than.** simply. [10] **think more of.** to have a higher opinion of. [11] **what is more.** moreover.
▷HISTORY Old English *māra;* compare Old Saxon, Old High German *mēro,* Gothic *maiza.* See also MOST

Language note See at **most.**

Morea (mɔː'rɪə) NOUN the medieval name for the **Peloponnese.**

Morecambe ('mɔːkəm) NOUN a port and resort in NW England, in NW Lancashire on **Morecambe Bay** (an inlet of the Irish Sea). Pop. (with Heysham): 46 657 (1991).

moreen (mɒ'riːn) NOUN a heavy, usually watered, fabric of wool or wool and cotton, used esp in furnishing.
▷HISTORY C17: perhaps from MOIRE, influenced by VELVETEEN

moreish *or* **morish** ('mɔːrɪʃ) ADJECTIVE *Informal* (of food) causing a desire for more: *these cakes are very moreish.*

morel (mɒ'rɛl) NOUN any edible saprotrophic ascomycetous fungus of the genus *Morchella,* in which the mushroom has a pitted cap: order *Pezizales.*
▷HISTORY C17: from French *morille,* probably of Germanic origin; compare Old High German *morhila,* diminutive of *morha* carrot

Morelia (*Spanish* mo'relja) NOUN a city in central Mexico, capital of Michoacán state: a cultural centre during colonial times; two universities. Pop.: 549 404 (2000 est.). Former name (until 1828): **Valladolid.**

morello (mə'rɛləʊ) NOUN, *plural* **-los.** a variety of small very dark sour cherry, *Prunus cerasus austera.*
▷HISTORY C17: perhaps from Medieval Latin *amārellum* diminutive of Latin *amārus* bitter, but also influenced by Italian *morello* blackish

Morelos (*Spanish* mo'relɔs) NOUN an inland state of S central Mexico, on the S slope of the great plateau. Capital: Cuernavaca. Pop.: 1 552 878 (2000 est.). Area: 4988 sq. km (1926 sq. miles).

moreover (mɔː'rəʊvə) SENTENCE CONNECTOR in addition to what has already been said; furthermore.

morepork ('mɔːˌpɔːk) NOUN another name (esp NZ) for **mopoke.**

mores ('mɔːreɪz) PLURAL NOUN *Sociol* the customs and conventions embodying the fundamental values of a group or society.
▷HISTORY C20: from Latin, plural of *mōs* custom

Moresco (mə'rɛskəʊ) NOUN, ADJECTIVE a variant of **Morisco.**

Moresque (mɔː'rɛsk) ADJECTIVE [1] (esp of decoration and architecture) of Moorish style. ◆

NOUN [2] **a** Moorish design or decoration. **b** a specimen of this.
▷HISTORY C17: from French, from Italian *moresco,* from *Moro* MOOR

Moreton Bay bug (ˈmɔːtᵊn) NOUN a flattish edible shellfish, *Thenus orientalis,* of Northern Australian waters.
▷HISTORY named after *Moreton Bay,* Queensland, Australia

Moreton Bay fig NOUN a large Australian fig tree, *Ficus macrophylla,* having glossy leaves and smooth bark.
▷HISTORY named after *Moreton Bay,* Queensland, Australia

Morgan (ˈmɔːɡən) NOUN an American breed of small compact saddle horse.
▷HISTORY C19: named after Justin *Morgan* (1747–98), American owner of the original sire

morganatic (ˌmɔːɡəˈnætɪk) ADJECTIVE of or designating a marriage between a person of high rank and a person of low rank, by which the latter is not elevated to the higher rank and any issue have no rights to the succession of the higher party's titles, property, etc.
▷HISTORY C18: from the Medieval Latin phrase *mātrimōnium ad morganāticum* marriage based on the morning-gift (a token present after consummation representing the husband's only liability); *morganātica,* ultimately from Old High German *morgan* morning; compare Old English *morgengiefu* morning-gift
▸**ˌmorgaˈnatically** ADVERB

morganite (ˈmɔːɡəˌnaɪt) NOUN a pink variety of beryl, used as a gemstone.
▷HISTORY C20: named after John Pierpoint *Morgan* (1837–1913), US financier, philanthropist, and art collector

Morgan le Fay (ˈmɔːɡən lə ˈfeɪ) *or* **Morgain le Fay** (ˈmɔːɡaɪn, -ɡən) NOUN a wicked sorceress of Arthurian legend, the half-sister of King Arthur.

morgen (ˈmɔːɡən) NOUN [1] a South African unit of area, equal to about two acres or 0.8 hectare. [2] a unit of area, formerly used in Prussia and Scandinavia, equal to about two thirds of an acre.
▷HISTORY C17: from Dutch: morning, a morning's ploughing

morgue[1] (mɔːɡ) NOUN [1] another word for **mortuary** (sense 1). [2] *Informal* a room or file containing clippings, files, etc., used for reference in a newspaper.
▷HISTORY C19: from French *la Morgue,* a Paris mortuary

morgue[2] *French* (mɔrɡ) NOUN superiority; haughtiness.

MORI (ˈmɔːrɪ) NOUN ACRONYM FOR Market and Opinion Research Institute: *a MORI poll.*

moribund (ˈmɒrɪˌbʌnd) ADJECTIVE [1] near death. [2] stagnant; without force or vitality.
▷HISTORY C18: from Latin, from *morī* to die
▸**ˌmoriˈbundity** NOUN ▸**ˈmoriˌbundly** ADVERB

morion[1] (ˈmɔːrɪən) NOUN a 16th-century helmet with a brim and wide comb.
▷HISTORY C16: via Old French from Spanish *morrión,* perhaps from *morra* crown of the head

morion[2] (ˈmɔːrɪən) NOUN a smoky brown, grey, or blackish variety of quartz, used as a gemstone.
▷HISTORY C18: via French from Latin *mōrion,* a misreading of *mormorion*

Moriori (ˌmɒrɪˈɔːrɪ) NOUN [1] a Polynesian people of New Zealand, esp of the Chatham Islands, closely related to the mainland Maori: now racially intermixed. [2] (*plural* **-ri** *or* **-ris**) a member of this people. [3] the language of the Moriori, belonging to the Malayo-Polynesian family. ♦ ADJECTIVE [4] of or relating to the Moriori or their language.

Morisco (məˈrɪskəʊ) *or* **Moresco** (məˈrɛskəʊ) NOUN, *plural* **-cos** *or* **-coes.** [1] a Spanish Moor. [2] a morris dance. ♦ ADJECTIVE [3] another word for **Moorish.**
▷HISTORY C16: from Spanish, from *Moro* MOOR

morish (ˈmɔːrɪʃ) ADJECTIVE a variant spelling of **moreish.**

Morley (ˈmɔːlɪ) NOUN an industrial town in N England, in Leeds unitary authority, West Yorkshire. Pop.: 47 579 (1991).

Mormon (ˈmɔːmən) NOUN [1] a member of the Church of Jesus Christ of Latter-day Saints, founded in 1830 at La Fayette, New York, by Joseph Smith (1805–44). [2] a prophet whose supposed revelations were recorded by Joseph Smith in the Book of Mormon. ♦ ADJECTIVE [3] of or relating to the Mormons, their Church, or their beliefs.
▸**ˈMormonism** NOUN

morn (mɔːn) NOUN [1] a poetic word for **morning.** [2] **the morn.** *Scot* tomorrow. [3] **the morn's nicht.** *Scot* tomorrow night.
▷HISTORY Old English *morgen;* compare Old High German *morgan,* Old Norse *morginn*

mornay (ˈmɔːneɪ) ADJECTIVE (*often immediately postpositive*) denoting a cheese sauce used in several dishes: *eggs mornay.*
▷HISTORY perhaps named after Philippe de *Mornay,* Seigneur du Plessis-Marly (1549–1623), French Huguenot leader

morning (ˈmɔːnɪŋ) NOUN [1] the first part of the day, ending at or around noon. [2] sunrise; daybreak; dawn. [3] the beginning or early period: *the morning of the world.* [4] **the morning after.** *Informal* the aftereffects of excess, esp a hangover. [5] (*modifier*) of, used, or occurring in the morning: *morning coffee.* ♦ See also **mornings.**
▷HISTORY C13 *morwening,* from MORN, formed on the model of EVENING

morning-after pill NOUN an oral contraceptive that is effective if taken some hours after intercourse.

morning coat NOUN a cutaway frock coat, part of morning dress. Also called: **tail coat, swallow-tailed coat.**

morning dress NOUN formal day dress for men, comprising a morning coat, usually with grey trousers and top hat.

morning-glory NOUN, *plural* **-ries.** any of various mainly tropical convolvulaceous plants of the genus *Ipomoea* and related genera, with trumpet-shaped blue, pink, or white flowers, which close in late afternoon.

mornings (ˈmɔːnɪŋz) ADVERB *Informal* in the morning, esp regularly, or during every morning.

morning sickness NOUN nausea occurring shortly after rising: an early symptom of pregnancy.

morning star NOUN a planet, usually Venus, seen just before sunrise during the time that the planet is west of the sun. Also called: **daystar.** Compare **evening star.**

morning tea NOUN *Austral and NZ* a mid-morning snack with a cup of tea. Brit equivalent: **elevenses.**

morning watch NOUN *Nautical* the watch between 4 and 8 a.m.

Moro (ˈmɔːrəʊ) NOUN [1] (*plural* **-ros** *or* **-ro**) a member of a group of predominantly Muslim peoples of the S Philippines: noted for their manufacture of weapons. [2] the language of these peoples, belonging to the Malayo-Polynesian family.
▷HISTORY C19: via Spanish from Latin *Maurus* MOOR

Moroccan (məˈrɒkən) ADJECTIVE [1] of or relating to Morocco or its inhabitants. ♦ NOUN [2] a native or inhabitant of Morocco.

morocco (məˈrɒkəʊ) NOUN **a** a fine soft leather made from goatskins, used for bookbinding, shoes, etc. **b** (*as modifier*): *morocco leather.*
▷HISTORY C17: after MOROCCO, where it was originally made

Morocco (məˈrɒkəʊ) NOUN a kingdom in NW Africa, on the Mediterranean and the Atlantic: conquered by the Arabs in about 683, who introduced Islam; at its height under Berber dynasties (11th–13th centuries); became a French protectorate in 1912 and gained independence in 1956. It is mostly mountainous, with the Atlas Mountains in the centre and the Rif range along the Mediterranean coast, with the Sahara in the south and southeast; an important exporter of phosphates. Official language: Arabic; Berber and French are also widely spoken. Official religion: (Sunni) Muslim. Currency: dirham. Capital: Rabat. Pop.: 29 237 000 (2001 est.). Area: 458 730 sq. km (177 117 sq. miles). French name: **Maroc.**

moron (ˈmɔːrɒn) NOUN [1] a foolish or stupid person. [2] a person having an intelligence quotient of between 50 and 70, able to work under supervision.
▷HISTORY C20: from Greek *mōros* foolish
▸**moronic** (mɒˈrɒnɪk) ADJECTIVE ▸**moˈronically** ADVERB
▸**ˈmoronism** *or* **moˈronity** NOUN

Moroni (məˈrəʊnɪ; *French* mɔrɔni) NOUN the capital of Comoros, on the island of Njazídja (Grande Comore). Pop. 30 000 (1991).

morose (məˈrəʊs) ADJECTIVE ill-tempered or gloomy.
▷HISTORY C16: from Latin *mōrōsus* peevish, capricious, from *mōs* custom, will, caprice
▸**moˈrosely** ADVERB ▸**moˈroseness** NOUN

Morpeth (ˈmɔːpəθ) NOUN a town in NE England, the administrative centre of Northumberland. Pop. 14 393 (1991).

morph[1] (mɔːf) NOUN *Linguistics* the phonological representation of a morpheme.
▷HISTORY C20: shortened form of MORPHEME

morph[2] (mɔːf) NOUN *Biology* any of the different forms of individual found in a polymorphic species.
▷HISTORY C20: from Greek *morphē* shape

morph[3] (mɔːf) VERB [1] to undergo or cause to undergo morphing. [2] to transform or be transformed completely in appearance or character: *he morphed from nerd into pop icon.* ♦ NOUN [3] a morphed image.

morph. *or* **morphol.** ABBREVIATION FOR: [1] morphological. [2] morphology.

-morph NOUN COMBINING FORM indicating shape, form, or structure of a specified kind: *ectomorph.*
▷HISTORY from Greek *-morphos,* from *morphē* shape
▸**-morphic** *or* **-morphous** ADJECTIVE COMBINING FORM
▸**-morphy** NOUN COMBINING FORM

morphallaxis (ˌmɔːfəˈlæksɪs) NOUN, *plural* **-laxes** (-ˈlæksiːz). *Zoology* the transformation of one part into another that sometimes occurs during regeneration of organs in certain animals.
▷HISTORY C20: New Latin, from MORPHO- + Greek *allaxis* exchange, from *allassein* to exchange, from *allos* other

morpheme (ˈmɔːfiːm) NOUN *Linguistics* a speech element having a meaning or grammatical function that cannot be subdivided into further such elements.
▷HISTORY C20: from French, from Greek *morphē* form, coined on the model of PHONEME; see -EME
▸**morˈphemic** ADJECTIVE ▸**morˈphemically** ADVERB

Morpheus (ˈmɔːfɪəs, -fjuːs) NOUN *Greek myth* the god of sleep and dreams.
▸**ˈMorphean** ADJECTIVE

morphic resonance (ˈmɔːfɪk) NOUN the idea that, through a telepathic effect or sympathetic vibration, an event or act can lead to similar events or acts in the future or an idea conceived in one mind can then arise in another.

morphine (ˈmɔːfiːn) *or* **morphia** (ˈmɔːfɪə) NOUN an alkaloid extracted from opium: used in medicine as an analgesic and sedative, although repeated use causes addiction. Formula: $C_{17}H_{19}NO_3$.
▷HISTORY C19: from French, from MORPHEUS

morphing (ˈmɔːfɪŋ) NOUN a computer technique used for graphics and in films, in which one image is gradually transformed into another image without individual changes being noticeable in the process.
▷HISTORY C20: from METAMORPHOSIS

morphinism (ˈmɔːfɪˌnɪzəm) NOUN morphine addiction.

morpho- *or before a vowel* **morph-** COMBINING FORM [1] indicating form or structure: *morphology.* [2] morpheme: *morphophonemics.*
▷HISTORY from Greek *morphē* form, shape

morphogenesis (ˌmɔːfəʊˈdʒɛnɪsɪs) NOUN [1] the development of form and structure in an organism during its growth from embryo to adult. [2] the evolutionary development of form in an organism or part of an organism.
▸**morphogenetic** (ˌmɔːfəʊdʒɪˈnɛtɪk) *or* **ˌmorphoˈgenic** ADJECTIVE

morphology (mɔːˈfɒlədʒɪ) NOUN [1] the branch of biology concerned with the form and structure of organisms. [2] the form and structure of words in a language, esp the consistent patterns of inflection, combination, derivation and change, etc., that may be observed and classified. [3] the form and structure of anything.
▸**morphologic** (ˌmɔːfəˈlɒdʒɪk) *or* **ˌmorphoˈlogical**

ADJECTIVE ▸ˌmorphoˈlogically ADVERB ▸morˈphologist NOUN

morphometrics (ˌmɔːfəʊˈmɛtrɪks) NOUN (*functioning as singular*) *Zoology* a technique of taxonomic analysis using measurements of the form of organisms.
▸ˌmorphoˈmetric ADJECTIVE

morphophoneme (ˌmɔːfəʊˈfəʊniːm) NOUN *Linguistics* the set of phonemes or sequences of phonemes that constitute the various allomorphs of a morpheme.
▷HISTORY C20: from MORPHEME + PHONEME

morphophonemics (ˌmɔːfəʊfəʊˈniːmɪks) NOUN (*functioning as singular*) *Linguistics* the study of the phonemic realization of the allomorphs of the morphemes of a language.
▸ˌmorphophoˈnemic ADJECTIVE

morphosis (mɔːˈfəʊsɪs) NOUN, *plural* **-ses** (-siːz). *Biology* development in an organism or its parts characterized by structural change.
▷HISTORY C17: via New Latin from Greek, from *morphoun* to form, from *morphē* form
▸morphotic (mɔːˈfɒtɪk) ADJECTIVE

morrell (məˈrɛl) NOUN a tall eucalyptus, *Eucalyptus longicornis,* of SW Australia, having pointed buds.
▷HISTORY from a native Australian language

Morris chair (ˈmɒrɪs) NOUN an armchair with an adjustable back and large cushions.
▷HISTORY C19: named after William *Morris* (1834–96), English poet, designer, craftsman, and socialist writer

morris dance (ˈmɒrɪs) NOUN any of various old English folk dances usually performed by men (**morris men**) to the accompaniment of violin, concertina, etc. The dancers are adorned with bells and often represent characters from folk tales. Often shortened to: **morris.**
▷HISTORY C15 *moreys daunce* Moorish dance. See MOOR
▸morris dancing NOUN

morro (ˈmɒrəʊ; *Spanish* ˈmorro) NOUN, *plural* **-ros** (-rəʊz; *Spanish* -ros). a rounded hill or promontory.
▷HISTORY from Spanish

morrow (ˈmɒrəʊ) NOUN (usually preceded by *the*) *Archaic or poetic* [1] the next day. [2] the period following a specified event. [3] the morning.
▷HISTORY C13 *morwe,* from Old English *morgen* morning; see MORN

Mors (mɔːz) NOUN the Roman god of death. Greek counterpart: **Thanatos.**

morse (mɔːs) NOUN a clasp or fastening on a cope.
▷HISTORY C15: from Old French *mors,* from Latin *morsus* clasp, bite, from *mordēre* to bite

Morse code (mɔːs) NOUN a telegraph code formerly used internationally for transmitting messages; it was superseded by satellite technology (the Global Marine Distress and Safety System) in 1999. Letters, numbers, etc., are represented by groups of shorter dots and longer dashes, or by groups of the corresponding sounds, *dits* and *dahs,* the groups being separated by spaces. Also called: **international Morse code.**
▷HISTORY C19: named after Samuel Finley Breese *Morse* (1791–1872), US inventor of the first electric telegraph

morsel (ˈmɔːsᵊl) NOUN [1] a small slice or mouthful of food. [2] a small piece; bit. [3] *Irish informal* a term of endearment for a child.
▷HISTORY C13: from Old French, from *mors* a bite, from Latin *morsus,* from *mordēre* to bite

Morse taper NOUN *Trademark, Engineering* a taper that is one of a standard series used in the shank of tools to fit a matching taper in the mandrel of a machine tool.
▷HISTORY probably named after the *Morse* Twist Drill Co., Massachusetts, US

mort[1] (mɔːt) NOUN a call blown on a hunting horn to signify the death of the animal hunted.
▷HISTORY C16: via Old French from Latin *mors* death

mort[2] (mɔːt) NOUN a great deal; a great many.
▷HISTORY possibly a shortened form of MORTAL used as an intensifier

mortal (ˈmɔːtᵊl) ADJECTIVE [1] (of living beings, esp human beings) subject to death. [2] of or involving life or the world. [3] ending in or causing death; fatal: *a mortal blow.* [4] deadly or unrelenting: *a mortal enemy.* [5] of or like the fear of death; dire: *mortal terror.* [6] great or very intense: *mortal pain.* [7] possible: *there was no mortal reason to go.* [8] *Slang* long and tedious: *for three mortal hours.* ◆ NOUN [9] a mortal being. [10] *Informal* a person: *a mean mortal.*
▷HISTORY C14: from Latin *mortālis,* from *mors* death
▸ˈmortally ADVERB

mortality (mɔːˈtælɪtɪ) NOUN, *plural* **-ties.** [1] the condition of being mortal. [2] great loss of life, as in war or disaster. [3] the number of deaths in a given period. [4] mankind; humanity. [5] an obsolete word for **death.**

mortality rate NOUN another term for **death rate.**

mortality table NOUN *Insurance* an actuarial table indicating life expectancy and death frequency for a given age, occupation, etc.

mortal sin NOUN *Christianity* a sin regarded as involving total loss of grace. Compare **venial sin.**

mortar (ˈmɔːtə) NOUN [1] a mixture of cement or lime or both with sand and water, used as a bond between bricks or stones or as a covering on a wall. [2] a muzzle-loading cannon having a short barrel and relatively wide bore that fires low-velocity shells in high trajectories over a short range. [3] a similar device for firing lifelines, fireworks, etc. [4] a vessel, usually bowl-shaped, in which substances are pulverized with a pestle. [5] *Mining* a cast-iron receptacle in which ore is crushed. ◆ VERB (*tr*) [6] to join (bricks or stones) or cover (a wall) with mortar. [7] to fire on with mortars. [8] *Midland English dialect* to trample (on).
▷HISTORY C13: from Latin *mortārium* basin in which mortar is mixed; in some senses, via Old French *mortier* substance mixed inside such a vessel

mortarboard (ˈmɔːtəˌbɔːd) NOUN [1] a black tasselled academic cap with a flat square top covered with cloth. [2] Also called: **hawk.** a small square board with a handle on the underside for carrying mortar.

mortgage (ˈmɔːgɪdʒ) NOUN [1] an agreement under which a person borrows money to buy property, esp a house, and the lender may take possession of the property if the borrower fails to repay the money. [2] the deed effecting such an agreement. [3] the loan obtained under such an agreement: *a mortgage of £48 000.* [4] a regular payment of money borrowed under such an agreement: *a mortgage of £247 per month.* ◆ VERB (*tr*) [5] to pledge (a house or other property) as security for the repayment of a loan. ◆ ADJECTIVE [6] of or relating to a mortgage: *a mortgage payment.*
▷HISTORY C14: from Old French, literally: dead pledge, from *mort* dead + *gage* security, GAGE[1]
▸ˈmortgageable ADJECTIVE

mortgagee (ˌmɔːgɪˈdʒiː) NOUN *Law* [1] the party to a mortgage who makes the loan. [2] a person who holds mortgaged property as security for repayment of a loan.

mortgage rate NOUN the level of interest charged by building societies and banks on house-purchase loans.

mortgagor (ˈmɔːgɪdʒə, ˌmɔːgɪˈdʒɔː) *or* **mortgager** NOUN *Property law* a person who borrows money by mortgaging his property to the lender as security.

mortician (mɔːˈtɪʃən) NOUN *Chiefly US* another word for **undertaker.**
▷HISTORY C19: from MORTUARY + *-ician,* as in *physician*

mortification (ˌmɔːtɪfɪˈkeɪʃən) NOUN [1] a feeling of loss of prestige or self-respect; humiliation. [2] something causing this. [3] *Christianity* the practice of mortifying the senses. [4] another word for **gangrene.**

mortify (ˈmɔːtɪˌfaɪ) VERB **-fies, -fying, -fied.** [1] (*tr*) to humiliate or cause to feel shame. [2] (*tr*) *Christianity* to subdue and bring under control by self-denial, disciplinary exercises, etc. [3] (*intr*) to undergo tissue death or become gangrenous.
▷HISTORY C14: via Old French from Church Latin *mortificāre* to put to death, from Latin *mors* death + *facere* to do
▸ˈmortiˌfier NOUN ▸ˈmortiˌfying ADJECTIVE ▸ˈmortiˌfyingly ADVERB

mortise *or* **mortice** (ˈmɔːtɪs) NOUN [1] a slot or recess, usually rectangular, cut into a piece of wood, stone, etc., to receive a matching projection (tenon) of another piece, or a mortise lock. [2] *Printing* a cavity cut into a letterpress printing plate into which type or another plate is inserted. ◆ VERB (*tr*) [3] to cut a slot or recess in (a piece of wood, stone, etc.). [4] to join (two pieces of wood, stone, etc.) by means of a mortise and tenon. [5] to cut a cavity in (a letterpress printing plate) for the insertion of type, etc.
▷HISTORY C14: from Old French *mortoise,* perhaps from Arabic *murtazza* fastened in position
▸ˈmortiser NOUN

mortise lock NOUN a lock set into a mortise in a door so that the mechanism of the lock is enclosed by the door.

mortmain (ˈmɔːtˌmeɪn) NOUN *Law* the state or condition of lands, buildings, etc., held inalienably, as by an ecclesiastical or other corporation.
▷HISTORY C15: from Old French *mortemain,* from Medieval Latin *mortua manus* dead hand, inalienable ownership

mortsafe (ˈmɔːtˌseɪf) NOUN a heavy iron cage or grille placed over the grave of a newly deceased person during the 19th century in order to deter body snatchers.
▷HISTORY C19: from *mort* dead body (via Old French from Latin *mors* death) + SAFE

mortuary (ˈmɔːtʃʊərɪ) NOUN, *plural* **-aries.** [1] Also called: **morgue.** a building where dead bodies are kept before cremation or burial. ◆ ADJECTIVE [2] of or relating to death or burial.
▷HISTORY C14 (as n, a funeral gift to a parish priest): via Medieval Latin *mortuārium* (n) from Latin *mortuārius* of the dead

morula (ˈmɒrjʊlə) NOUN, *plural* **-las** *or* **-lae** (-ˌliː). *Embryol* a solid ball of cells resulting from cleavage of a fertilized ovum.
▷HISTORY C19: via New Latin, diminutive of Latin *morum* mulberry, from Greek *moron*
▸ˈmorular ADJECTIVE

morwong (ˈmɔːˌwɒŋ) NOUN a food fish of Australasian coastal waters belonging to the *Cheilodactylidae* family.
▷HISTORY from a native Australian language

moryah (mɒrˈjæ) INTERJECTION *Irish* an exclamation of annoyance, disbelief, etc.
▷HISTORY from Irish Gaelic *Mar dhea* forsooth

MOS *Electronics* ABBREVIATION FOR metal oxide silicon.

mosaic (məˈzeɪɪk) NOUN [1] a design or decoration made up of small pieces of coloured glass, stone, etc. [2] the process of making a mosaic. [3] **a** a mottled yellowing that occurs in the leaves of plants affected with any of various virus diseases. **b** Also called: **mosaic disease.** any of the diseases, such as **tobacco mosaic**, that produce this discoloration. [4] *Genetics* another name for **chimera** (sense 4). [5] an assembly of aerial photographs forming a composite picture of a large area on the ground. [6] a light-sensitive surface on a television camera tube, consisting of a large number of granules of photoemissive material deposited on an insulating medium.
▷HISTORY C16: via French and Italian from Medieval Latin *mōsaicus,* from Late Greek *mouseion* mosaic work, from Greek *mouseios* of the Muses, from *mousa* MUSE
▸mosaicist (məˈzeɪɪsɪst) NOUN

Mosaic (məʊˈzeɪɪk) *or* **Mosaical** ADJECTIVE of or relating to Moses or the laws and traditions ascribed to him.

mosaic disease (məˈzeɪɪk) NOUN a serious viral disease of plants, esp tobacco, maize, and sugar cane, in which the leaves become mottled by discoloration.

mosaic gold (məˈzeɪɪk) NOUN stannic sulphide, esp when suspended in lacquer for use in gilding surfaces.

Mosaic law (məʊˈzeɪɪk) NOUN *Old Testament* the laws of the Hebrews ascribed to Moses and contained in the Pentateuch.

mosasaur (ˈməʊsəˌsɔː) *or* **mosasaurus** (ˌməʊsəˈsɔːrəs) NOUN, *plural* **-saurs** *or* **-sauri** (-ˈsɔːraɪ). any of various extinct Cretaceous giant marine lizards of the genus *Mosasaurus* and related genera, typically having paddle-like limbs.
▷HISTORY C18: from Latin *Mosa* the river MEUSE (near which remains were first found) + -SAUR

moschatel (ˌmɒskəˈtɛl) NOUN a small N temperate plant, *Adoxa moschatellina,* with greenish-white

musk-scented flowers on top of the stem, arranged as four pointing sideways at right angles to each other and one facing upwards: family *Adoxaceae.* Also called: **townhall clock, five-faced bishop.**
▷HISTORY C18: via French from Italian *moscatella,* diminutive of *moscato* MUSK

Moscow (ˈmɒskəʊ) NOUN the capital of Russia and of the Moscow Autonomous Region, on the Moskva River: dates from the 11th century; capital of the grand duchy of Russia from 1547 to 1712; capital of the Soviet Union 1918–91; centres on the medieval Kremlin; chief political, cultural, and industrial centre of Russia, with two universities. Pop.: 8 389 700 (1999 est.). Russian name: **Moskva.** Related noun: **Muscovite.**

Moselle (məʊˈzɛl) NOUN 1 a department of NE France, in Lorraine region. Capital: Metz. Pop. 1 023 447 (1999). Area: 6253 sq. km (2439 sq. miles). 2 a river in W Europe, rising in NE France and flowing northwest, forming part of the border between Luxembourg and Germany, then northeast to the Rhine: many vineyards along its lower course. Length: 547 km (340 miles). German name: **Mosel** (ˈmoːzᵊl). 3 (*sometimes not capital*) a German white wine from the Moselle valley.

Moses basket (ˈməʊzɪz) NOUN a portable cradle for a baby, often made of straw or wicker.
▷HISTORY C20: from Moses being left in a cradle of bulrushes (Exodus 2:3)

mosey (ˈməʊzɪ) VERB (*intr*) *Informal* (often foll by *along* or *on*) to walk in a leisurely manner; amble.
▷HISTORY C19: origin unknown

MOSFET (ˈmɒsfɛt) NOUN *Electronics* metal-oxide-silicon field-effect transistor; a type of IGFET.

mosh (mɒʃ) NOUN 1 a type of dance, performed to loud rock music, in which people throw themselves about in a frantic and violent manner. ◆ VERB 2 (*intr*) to dance in this manner.
▷HISTORY C20: of uncertain origin

moshav (*Hebrew* məˈʃav) NOUN, *plural* **-shavim** (-ʃaˈvim). a cooperative settlement in Israel, consisting of a number of small farms.
▷HISTORY C20: from Hebrew *mōshābh* a dwelling

mosh pit NOUN *Informal* an area at a rock-music concert, usually in front of the stage, where members of the audience dance in a frantic and violent manner.

Moskva (*Russian* masˈkva) NOUN 1 transliteration of the Russian name for **Moscow.** 2 a river in W central Russia, rising in the Smolensk-Moscow upland, and flowing southeast through Moscow to the Oka River: linked with the River Volga by the Moscow Canal. Length: about 500 km (310 miles).

Moslem (ˈmɒzləm) NOUN, *plural* **-lems** *or* **-lem,** ADJECTIVE a variant of **Muslim.**
▸**Moslemic** (mɒzˈlɛmɪk) ADJECTIVE ▸ˈ**Moslemism** NOUN

Mosotho (mʊˈsuːtuː) NOUN, *plural* **-tho** *or* **-thos.** a member of the Basotho people. Former name: **Basuto.**

mosque (mɒsk) NOUN a Muslim place of worship, usually having one or more minarets and often decorated with elaborate tracery and texts from the Koran. Also called: **masjid, musjid.**
▷HISTORY C14: earlier *mosquee,* from Old French via Italian *moschea,* ultimately from Arabic *masjid* temple, place of prostration

mosquito (məˈskiːtəʊ) NOUN, *plural* **-toes** *or* **-tos.** any dipterous insect of the family *Culicidae:* the females have a long proboscis adapted for piercing the skin of man and animals to suck their blood. See also **aedes, anopheles, culex.**
▷HISTORY C16: from Spanish, diminutive of *mosca* fly, from Latin *musca*

mosquito boat NOUN another name for **MTB.**

mosquito hawk NOUN another name for **nighthawk** (sense 1).

mosquito net *or* **netting** NOUN a fine curtain or net put in windows, around beds, etc., to keep mosquitoes out.

moss (mɒs) NOUN 1 any bryophyte of the phylum *Bryophyta,* typically growing in dense mats on trees, rocks, moist ground, etc. See also **peat moss.** 2 a clump or growth of any of these plants. 3 any of various similar but unrelated plants, such as club moss, Spanish moss, Ceylon moss, rose moss, and reindeer moss. 4 *Scot and Northern English* a peat bog or marsh.
▷HISTORY Old English *mos* swamp; compare Middle Dutch, Old High German *mos* bog, Old Norse *mosi;* compare also Old Norse *mýrr* MIRE
▸ˈ**moss,like** ADJECTIVE ▸ˈ**mossy** ADJECTIVE ▸ˈ**mossiness** NOUN

Mossad (ˈmɒsæd) NOUN the secret intelligence service of Israel.
▷HISTORY C20: Hebrew *Mosad LeModi'in U-LeTafkidim Miyuhadim* establishment for information and special tasks

moss agate NOUN a variety of chalcedony with dark greenish mossy markings, used as a gemstone.

mossback (ˈmɒs,bæk) NOUN *US and Canadian* 1 an old turtle, shellfish, etc., that has a growth of algae on its back. 2 *Informal* a provincial or conservative person.
▸ˈ**moss,backed** ADJECTIVE

Mössbauer effect (ˈmɒs,baʊə; *German* ˈmœsbauər) NOUN *Physics* the phenomenon in which an atomic nucleus in a crystal of certain substances emits a gamma ray without any recoil to the atom. The study of the emitted gamma rays (**Mössbauer spectroscopy**) is used to determine the energy levels in a nucleus, the structure of molecules, etc.
▷HISTORY C20: named after Rudolf Ludwig *Mössbauer* (born 1929), German physicist

mossbunker (ˈmɒs,bʌŋkə) NOUN *US* another name for **menhaden.**
▷HISTORY C18: from Dutch *marsbanker* scad, horse-mackerel

moss-grown ADJECTIVE covered with moss.

Mossi (ˈmɒsɪ) NOUN 1 (*plural* **-sis** *or* **-si**) a member of a Negroid people of W Africa, living chiefly in Burkina-Faso: noted for their use of cowry shells as currency and for their trading skill. 2 the language of this people, belonging to the Gur branch of the Niger-Congo family. ◆ Also called: **Moore.**

mossie[1] *or* **mozzie** (ˈmɒzɪ) NOUN *Austral and NZ* an informal name for **mosquito.**

mossie[2] (ˈmɒsɪ) NOUN another name for the **Cape sparrow.**
▷HISTORY Afrikaans

moss layer NOUN See **layer** (sense 2).

mosso (ˈmɒsəʊ) ADVERB *Music* to be performed with rapidity. See also **meno mosso.**
▷HISTORY Italian, past participle of *muovere* to MOVE

moss pink NOUN a North American plant, *Phlox subulata,* forming dense mosslike mats: cultivated for its pink, white, or lavender flowers: family *Polemoniaceae.* Also called: **ground pink.**

moss rose NOUN a variety of rose, *Rosa centifolia muscosa,* that has a mossy stem and calyx and fragrant pink flowers.

moss stitch NOUN a knitting stitch made up of alternate plain and purl stitches.

mosstrooper (ˈmɒs,truːpə) NOUN a raider in the border country of England and Scotland in the mid-17th century.
▷HISTORY C17 *moss,* in northern English dialect sense: bog

most (məʊst) DETERMINER 1 **a** a great majority of; nearly all: *most people like eggs.* **b** (*as pronoun; functioning as singular or plural*): *most of them don't know; most of it is finished.* 2 **the most. a** the superlative of **many** and **much**: *you have the most money; the most apples.* **b** (*as pronoun*): *the most he can afford is two pounds.* 3 **at (the) most.** at the maximum: *that girl is four at the most.* 4 **for the most part.** generally. 5 **make the most of.** to use to the best advantage: *she makes the most of her accent.* 6 **than most.** than most others: *the leaves are greener than most.* 7 **the most.** *Slang, chiefly US* wonderful: *that chick's the most.* ◆ ADVERB 8 **the most.** used to form the superlative of some adjectives and adverbs: *the most beautiful daughter of all.* 9 the superlative of **much**: *people welcome a drink most after work.* 10 (intensifier): *a most absurd story.* 11 *US and Canadian informal or dialect* almost: *most every town in this state.*
▷HISTORY Old English *māst* or *mǣst,* whence Middle English *moste, mēst;* compare Old Frisian *maest,* Old High German *meist,* Old Norse *mestr*

Language note *More* and *most* should be distinguished when used in comparisons. *More* applies to cases involving two persons, objects, etc., *most* to cases involving three or more: *John is the more intelligent of the two; he is the most intelligent of the students.*

-most SUFFIX *forming the superlative degree of some adjectives and adverbs*: *hindmost; uppermost.*
▷HISTORY Old English *-mǣst, -mest,* originally a superlative suffix, later mistakenly taken as derived from *mǣst* (adv) most

Mostaganem (mə,stægəˈnɛm) NOUN a port in NW Algeria, on the Mediterranean Sea: exports wine, fruit, and vegetables. Pop.: 124 399 (1998).

Most Honourable NOUN a courtesy title applied to marquesses and members of the Privy Council and the Order of the Bath.

mostly (ˈməʊstlɪ) ADVERB 1 almost entirely; chiefly. 2 on many or most occasions; usually.

Most Reverend NOUN (in Britain) a courtesy title applied to Anglican and Roman Catholic archbishops.

Mosul (ˈməʊsᵊl) NOUN a city in N Iraq, on the River Tigris opposite the ruins of Nineveh: an important commercial centre with nearby Ayn Zalah oilfield; university. Pop.: 664 220 (latest est.).

mot[1] (məʊ) NOUN short for **bon mot.**
▷HISTORY C16: via French from Vulgar Latin *mottum* (unattested) utterance, from Latin *muttum* a mutter, from *muttīre* to mutter

mot[2] (mɒt) NOUN *Dublin, slang* a girl or young woman, esp one's girlfriend.
▷HISTORY perhaps a variant of *mort,* obsolete slang for girl or woman, of unknown origin

MOT ABBREVIATION FOR: 1 (in New Zealand and formerly in Britain) Ministry of Transport (in Britain now part of the **DTLR**). 2 (in Britain) MOT test: a compulsory annual test for all road vehicles over a certain age, which require a valid **MOT certificate.**

mote[1] (məʊt) NOUN a tiny speck.
▷HISTORY Old English *mot;* compare Middle Dutch *mot* grit, Norwegian *mutt* speck

mote[2] (məʊt) VERB, *past* **moste** (məʊst). (takes an infinitive without *to*) *Archaic* may or might.
▷HISTORY Old English *mōt,* first person singular present tense of *mōtan* to be allowed

motel (məʊˈtɛl) NOUN a roadside hotel for motorists, usually having direct access from each room or chalet to a parking space or garage.
▷HISTORY C20: from *motor* + *hotel*

motet (məʊˈtɛt) NOUN a polyphonic choral composition used as an anthem in the Roman Catholic service.
▷HISTORY C14: from Old French, diminutive of *mot* word; see MOT[1]

moth (mɒθ) NOUN any of numerous insects of the order *Lepidoptera* that typically have stout bodies with antennae of various shapes (but not clubbed), including large brightly coloured species, such as hawk moths, and small inconspicuous types, such as the clothes moths. Compare **butterfly** (sense 1).
▷HISTORY Old English *moththe;* compare Middle Dutch *motte,* Old Norse *motti*

mothball (ˈmɒθ,bɔːl) NOUN 1 Also called: **camphor ball.** a small ball of camphor or naphthalene used to repel clothes moths in stored clothing, blankets, etc. 2 **put in mothballs.** to postpone work on (a project, activity, etc.). ◆ VERB (*tr*) 3 to prepare (a ship, aircraft, etc.) for a long period of storage by sealing all openings with plastic to prevent corrosion. 4 to take (a factory, plant, etc.) out of operation but maintain it so that it can be used in the future. 5 to postpone work on (a project, activity, etc.).

moth-eaten ADJECTIVE 1 decayed, decrepit, or outdated. 2 eaten away by or as if by moths.

mother[1] (ˈmʌðə) NOUN 1 **a** a female who has given birth to offspring. **b** (*as modifier*): *a mother bird.* 2 (*often capital, esp as a term of address*) a person's own mother. 3 a female substituting in the function of a mother. 4 (*often capital*) *Chiefly archaic* a term of address for an old woman. 5 **a** motherly qualities, such as maternal affection: *it appealed to the mother in her.* **b** (*as modifier*): *mother*

love. **c** (*in combination*): *mothercraft.* [6] **a** a female or thing that creates, nurtures, protects, etc., something. **b** (*as modifier*): *mother church; mother earth.* [7] a title given to certain members of female religious orders: *mother superior.* [8] *Christian Science* God as the eternal Principle. [9] (*modifier*) native or innate: *mother wit.* [10] *Offensive taboo slang chiefly US* short for **motherfucker.** [11] **be mother.** to pour the tea: *I'll be mother.* [12] **the mother of all ….** *Informal* the greatest example of its kind: *the mother of all parties.* ◆ VERB (*tr*) [13] to give birth to or produce. [14] to nurture, protect, etc. as a mother. ◆ Related adjective: **maternal.**
▷HISTORY Old English *mōdor;* compare Old Saxon *mōdar,* Old High German *muotar,* Latin *māter,* Greek *mētēr*
▸ **'mothering** NOUN

mother² ('mʌðə) NOUN a stringy slime containing various bacteria that forms on the surface of liquids undergoing acetous fermentation. It can be added to wine, cider, etc. to promote vinegar formation. Also called: **mother of vinegar.**
▷HISTORY C16: perhaps from MOTHER¹, but compare Spanish *madre* scum, Dutch *modder* dregs, Middle Low German *modder* decaying object, *mudde* sludge
▸ **'mothery** ADJECTIVE

motherboard ('mʌðə,bɔːd) NOUN (in an electronic system) a printed circuit board through which signals between all other boards are routed.

Mother Carey's chicken ('kɛərɪz) NOUN another name for **storm petrel.**
▷HISTORY origin unknown

mother country NOUN [1] the original country of colonists or settlers. [2] another term for **fatherland.**

motherese (,mʌðə'riːz) NOUN the simplified and repetitive type of speech, with exaggerated intonation and rhythm, often used by adults when speaking to babies.

motherfucker ('mʌðə,fʌkə) NOUN *Offensive taboo slang, chiefly US* a person or thing, esp an exasperating or unpleasant one. Often shortened to: **mother.**

Mother Goose NOUN the imaginary author of the collection of nursery rhymes published in 1781 in London as *Mother Goose's Melody.*
▷HISTORY C18: translated from French *Contes de ma mère l'Oye* (1697), title of a collection of tales by Charles *Perrault* (1628–1703), French author

motherhood ('mʌðə,hʊd) NOUN [1] the state of being a mother. [2] the qualities characteristic of a mother.

Mother Hubbard ('hʌbəd) NOUN (*sometimes not capitals*) a woman's full-length unbelted dress.
▷HISTORY C19: after *Mother Hubbard,* a character in a nursery rhyme

Mothering Sunday ('mʌðərɪŋ) NOUN See **Mother's Day.**

mother-in-law NOUN, *plural* **mothers-in-law.** the mother of one's wife or husband.

mother-in-law's tongue NOUN See **sansevieria.**

motherland ('mʌðə,lænd) NOUN another word for **fatherland.**

motherless ('mʌðələs) ADJECTIVE [1] not having a mother. ◆ ADVERB [2] (intensifier): *Austral informal motherless broke.*

mother lode NOUN *Mining* the principal lode in a system.

motherly ('mʌðəlɪ) ADJECTIVE of or resembling a mother, esp in warmth, or protectiveness.
▸ **'motherliness** NOUN

Mother of God NOUN a title given to the Virgin Mary: used in Orthodox and Roman Catholic churches to emphasize the belief that Jesus was God.

Mother of Parliaments NOUN **the.** the British Parliament: the model and creator of many other Parliaments.
▷HISTORY C19: first used of England in 1865 by John Bright (1811–89), British Liberal statesman

mother-of-pearl NOUN a hard iridescent substance, mostly calcium carbonate, that forms the inner layer of the shells of certain molluscs, such as the oyster. It is used to make buttons, inlay furniture, etc. Also called: **nacre.** Related adjective: **nacreous.**

mother-of-pearl moth NOUN a pyralid moth, *Pleuroptya ruralis,* having a pale sheen, that is often seen around nettles, on which its green larvae feed.

mother of the chapel NOUN (in British trade unions in the publishing and printing industries) a woman shop steward. Abbreviation: **MoC.**

mother-of-thousands NOUN [1] a S European perennial creeping plant, *Linaria cymbalaria,* having small pale blue or lilac flowers. [2] a saxifragaceous plant, *Saxifraga sarmentosa* or *S. stolonifera,* having white flowers and creeping red runners.

Mother's Day NOUN [1] *US, Canadian, Austral, and NZ* the second Sunday in May, observed as a day in honour of mothers. [2] *Brit and S African* the fourth Sunday in Lent, when mothers traditionally receive presents from their children. Also called: **Mothering Sunday.**

mother ship NOUN a ship providing facilities and supplies for a number of small vessels.

Mother Shipton ('ʃɪptᵊn) NOUN a day-flying noctuid moth, *Callistege mi,* mottled brown in colour and named from a fancied resemblance between its darker marking and a haggish profile.
▷HISTORY named after *Mother Shipton,* a legendary prophetess in 15th-century Yorkshire

mother superior NOUN, *plural* **mother superiors** *or* **mothers superior.** the head of a community of nuns.

mother tongue NOUN [1] the language first learned by a child. [2] a language from which another has evolved.

Motherwell ('mʌðəwəl) NOUN a town in S central Scotland, the administrative centre of North Lanarkshire on the River Clyde: industrial centre. Pop.: 30 717 (1991).

mother wit NOUN native practical intelligence; common sense.

motherwort ('mʌðə,wɜːt) NOUN any of several plants of the Eurasian genus *Leonurus,* esp *L cardiaca,* having divided leaves and clusters of small purple or pink flowers: family *Lamiaceae* (labiates).
▷HISTORY C14: so named because it was thought to be beneficial in uterine disorders

mothproof ('mɒθ,pruːf) ADJECTIVE [1] (esp of clothes) chemically treated so as to repel clothes moths. ◆ VERB [2] (*tr*) to make (clothes, etc.) mothproof.

mothy ('mɒθɪ) ADJECTIVE **mothier, mothiest.** [1] ragged; moth-eaten. [2] containing moths; full of moths.

motif (məʊ'tiːf) NOUN [1] a distinctive idea, esp a theme elaborated on in a piece of music, literature, etc. [2] Also: **motive.** a recurring form or shape in a design or pattern. [3] a single added piece of decoration, such as a symbol or name on a jumper, sweatshirt, etc.
▷HISTORY C19: from French. See MOTIVE

motile ('məʊtaɪl) ADJECTIVE [1] capable of moving spontaneously and independently. ◆ NOUN [2] *Psychol* a person whose mental imagery strongly reflects movement, esp his own.
▷HISTORY C19: from Latin *mōtus* moved, from *movēre* to move
▸ **motility** (məʊ'tɪlɪtɪ) NOUN

motion ('məʊʃən) NOUN [1] the process of continual change in the physical position of an object; movement: *linear motion.* ◆ Related adjective: **kinetic.** [2] a movement or action, esp of part of the human body; a gesture. [3] **a** the capacity for movement. **b** a manner of movement, esp walking; gait. [4] a mental impulse. [5] a formal proposal to be discussed and voted on in a debate, meeting, etc. [6] *Law* an application made to a judge or court for an order or ruling necessary to the conduct of legal proceedings. [7] *Brit* **a** the evacuation of the bowels. **b** excrement. [8] **a** part of a moving mechanism. **b** the action of such a part. [9] *Music* the upward or downward course followed by a part or melody. Parts whose progressions are in the same direction exhibit **similar motion,** while two parts whose progressions are in opposite directions exhibit **contrary motion.** See also **parallel** (sense 3). [10] **go through the motions. a** to act or perform the task (of doing something) mechanically or without sincerity. **b** to mimic the action (of something) by gesture. [11] **in motion.** operational or functioning (often in the phrases **set in motion, set the wheels in motion**). ◆ VERB [12] (when *tr, may take a clause as object or an infinitive*) to signal or direct (a person) by a movement or gesture.
▷HISTORY C15: from Latin *mōtiō* a moving, from *movēre* to move
▸ **'motional** ADJECTIVE

motion capture NOUN a process by which a device can be used to capture patterns of live movement; the data is then transmitted to a computer, where simulation software displays it applied to a virtual actor.

motionless ('məʊʃənlɪs) ADJECTIVE not moving; absolutely still.
▸ **'motionlessly** ADVERB ▸ **'motionlessness** NOUN

motion picture NOUN a US and Canadian term for **film** (sense 1).

motion sickness NOUN the state or condition of being dizzy or nauseous from riding in a moving vehicle.

motion study NOUN short for **time and motion study.**

motivate ('məʊtɪ,veɪt) VERB (*tr*) to give incentive to.

motivation (,məʊtɪ'veɪʃən) NOUN [1] the act or an instance of motivating. [2] desire to do; interest or drive. [3] incentive or inducement. [4] *Psychol* the process that arouses, sustains and regulates human and animal behaviour.
▸ **,moti'vational** ADJECTIVE ▸ **'moti,vative** ADJECTIVE

motivational research NOUN the application of psychology to the study of consumer behaviour, esp the planning of advertising and sales campaigns. Also called: **motivation research.**

motive ('məʊtɪv) NOUN [1] the reason for a certain course of action, whether conscious or unconscious. [2] a variant of **motif** (sense 2). ◆ ADJECTIVE [3] of or causing motion or action: *a motive force.* [4] of or acting as a motive; motivating. ◆ VERB (*tr*) [5] to motivate.
▷HISTORY C14: from Old French *motif,* from Late Latin *mōtīvus* (adjective) moving, from Latin *mōtus,* past participle of *movēre* to move
▸ **'motiveless** ADJECTIVE ▸ **'motivelessly** ADVERB
▸ **'motivelessness** NOUN

motive power NOUN [1] any source of energy used to produce motion. [2] the means of supplying power to an engine, vehicle, etc. [3] any driving force.

motivity (məʊ'tɪvɪtɪ) NOUN the power of moving or of initiating motion.

mot juste *French* (mo ʒyst) NOUN, *plural* ***mots justes*** (mo ʒyst). the appropriate word or expression.

motley ('mɒtlɪ) ADJECTIVE [1] made up of elements of varying type, quality, etc. [2] multicoloured. ◆ NOUN [3] a motley collection or mixture. [4] the particoloured attire of a jester. [5] *Obsolete* a jester.
▷HISTORY C14: perhaps from *mot* speck, MOTE¹

motmot ('mɒtmɒt) NOUN any tropical American bird of the family *Momotidae,* having a long tail and blue and brownish-green plumage: order *Coraciiformes* (kingfishers, etc.).
▷HISTORY C19: from American Spanish, imitative of the bird's call

motocross ('məʊtə,krɒs) NOUN [1] a motorcycle race across very rough ground. [2] another name for **rallycross.** See also **autocross.**
▷HISTORY C20: from MOTO(R) + CROSS(-COUNTRY)

motoneuron (,məʊtəʊ'njʊərɒn) NOUN *Anatomy* an efferent nerve cell; motor neuron.

moto perpetuo ('məʊtəʊ pə'pɛtjʊəʊ) NOUN *Music* a fast instrumental passage made up of notes of equal length.
▷HISTORY Italian, literally: perpetual motion

motor ('məʊtə) NOUN [1] **a** the engine, esp an internal-combustion engine, of a vehicle. **b** (*as modifier*): *a motor scooter.* [2] Also called: **electric motor.** a machine that converts electrical energy into mechanical energy by means of the forces exerted on a current-carrying coil placed in a magnetic field. [3] any device that converts another form of energy into mechanical energy to produce motion. [4] an indispensable part or player that moves a process or system along. [5] **a** *Chiefly Brit* a car or other motor vehicle. **b** *as modifier: motor spares.* ◆ ADJECTIVE [6] producing or causing motion. [7] *Physiol* **a** of or relating to nerves or neurons that carry impulses that cause muscles to contract. **b** of or relating to movement or to muscles that induce movement. ◆ VERB [8] (*intr*) to travel by car. [9] (*tr*)

Brit to transport by car. [10] (*intr*) *Informal* to move fast; make good progress. [11] (*tr*) to motivate.
▷HISTORY C16: from Latin *mōtor* a mover, from *movēre* to move

motorable (ˈməʊtərəbᵊl) ADJECTIVE (of a road) suitable for use by motor vehicles.

motorbicycle (ˈməʊtəˌbaɪsɪkᵊl) NOUN [1] a motorcycle. [2] a moped.

motorbike (ˈməʊtəˌbaɪk) NOUN a less formal name for **motorcycle.**

motorboat (ˈməʊtəˌbəʊt) NOUN any boat powered by a motor.

motorbus (ˈməʊtəˌbʌs) NOUN a bus driven by an internal-combustion engine.

motorcade (ˈməʊtəˌkeɪd) NOUN a parade of cars or other motor vehicles.
▷HISTORY C20: from MOTOR + CAVALCADE

motor camp NOUN *NZ* a camp for motorists, tents, and caravans.

motorcar (ˈməʊtəˌkɑː) NOUN [1] a more formal word for **car** (sense 1). [2] a self-propelled electric railway car.

motor caravan NOUN *Brit* a motor vehicle fitted with equipment for cooking, sleeping, etc., like that of a caravan.

motorcoach (ˈməʊtəˌkəʊtʃ) NOUN a coach driven by an internal-combustion engine.

motorcycle (ˈməʊtəˌsaɪkᵊl) NOUN [1] Also called: **motorbike.** a two-wheeled vehicle, having a stronger frame than a bicycle, that is driven by a petrol engine, usually with a capacity of between 125 cc and 1000 cc. ◆ VERB (*intr*) [2] to ride on a motorcycle.
▸ **ˈmotorˌcyclist** NOUN

motor drive NOUN *Photog* a battery-operated motorized system to give fast film advance between exposures. Compare **autowinder.**

-motored ADJECTIVE (*in combination*) having a specified type of motor or number of motors.

motor generator NOUN a generator driven by an electric motor, by means of which the voltage, frequency, or phases of an electrical power supply can be changed.

motorist (ˈməʊtərɪst) NOUN a driver of a car, esp when considered as a car-owner.

motorize *or* **motorise** (ˈməʊtəˌraɪz) VERB (*tr*) [1] to equip with a motor. [2] to provide (military units) with motor vehicles.
▸ **ˌmotoriˈzation** *or* **ˌmotoriˈsation** NOUN

motorman (ˈməʊtəmən) NOUN, *plural* **-men.** [1] the driver of an electric train. [2] the operator of a motor.

motor neurone disease NOUN a progressively degenerative disease of the motor system causing muscle weakness and wasting.

motor park NOUN a W African name for **car park.**

motor scooter NOUN a light motorcycle with small wheels and an enclosed engine. Often shortened to: **scooter.**

motor vehicle NOUN a road vehicle driven by a motor or engine, esp an internal-combustion engine.

motor vessel *or* **ship** NOUN a ship whose main propulsion system is a diesel or other internal-combustion engine.

motorway (ˈməʊtəˌweɪ) NOUN *Brit* a main road for fast-moving traffic, having limited access, separate carriageways for vehicles travelling in opposite directions, and usually a total of four or six lanes. US names: **superhighway,** (also Canadian) **expressway.**

Motown (ˈməʊˌtaʊn) NOUN *Trademark* music combining rhythm and blues and pop, or gospel rhythms and modern ballad harmony.
▷HISTORY C20: from *Motown Records* of Detroit; from *Mo(tor)Town,* a nickname for Detroit, Michigan, centre of the US car industry

motser *or* **motza** (ˈmɒtsə) NOUN *Austral informal* a large sum of money, esp a gambling win.
▷HISTORY of uncertain origin; possibly Yiddish

motte (mɒt) NOUN *History* a natural or man-made mound on which a castle was erected.
▷HISTORY C14: see MOAT

MOT test NOUN (in Britain) See **MOT** (sense 2).

mottle (ˈmɒtᵊl) VERB [1] (*tr*) to colour with streaks or blotches of different shades. ◆ NOUN [2] a mottled appearance, as of the surface of marble. [3] one streak or blotch of colour in a mottled surface.
▷HISTORY C17: back formation from MOTLEY

motto (ˈmɒtəʊ) NOUN, *plural* **-toes** *or* **-tos.** [1] a short saying expressing the guiding maxim or ideal of a family, organization, etc., esp when part of a coat of arms. [2] a short explanatory phrase inscribed on or attached to something. [3] a verse or maxim contained in a paper cracker. [4] a quotation prefacing a book or chapter of a book. [5] a recurring musical phrase.
▷HISTORY C16: via Italian from Latin *muttum* utterance

motty (ˈmɒtɪ) NOUN *Irish* the target at which coins are aimed in pitch-and-toss.

Motu (ˈməʊtuː) NOUN [1] (*plural* **-tu** *or* **-tus**) a member of an aboriginal people of S Papua. [2] the language of this people, belonging to the Malayo-Polynesian family. [3] Also called: **Hiri Motu,** (esp formerly) **Police Motu.** a pidgin version of this language, widely used in Papua-New Guinea. Compare **Neo-Melanesian.**

motu proprio (ˈməʊtuː ˈprəʊprɪˌəʊ) NOUN an administrative papal bull.
▷HISTORY Latin: of his own accord

moue *French* (mu) NOUN a disdainful or pouting look.

mouflon *or* **moufflon** (ˈmuːflɒn) NOUN a wild short-fleeced mountain sheep, *Ovis musimon,* of Corsica and Sardinia.
▷HISTORY C18: via French from Corsican *mufrone,* from Late Latin *mufrō*

mouillé (ˈmwiːeɪ) ADJECTIVE *Phonetics* palatalized, as in the sounds represented by Spanish *ll* or *ñ,* Italian *gl* or *gn* (pronounced as (ʎ) and (ɲ) respectively), or French *ll* (representing a (j) sound).
▷HISTORY C19: from French, past participle of *mouiller* to moisten, from Latin *mollis* soft

moujik (ˈmuːʒɪk) NOUN a variant spelling of **muzhik.**

mould^{1} *or US* **mold** (məʊld) NOUN [1] a shaped cavity used to give a definite form to fluid or plastic material. [2] a frame on which something may be constructed. [3] something shaped in or made on a mould. [4] shape, form, design, or pattern. [5] specific nature, character, or type: *heroic mould.* ◆ VERB (*tr*) [6] to make in a mould. [7] to shape or form, as by using a mould. [8] to influence or direct: *to mould opinion.* [9] to cling to: *the skirt moulds her figure.* [10] *Metallurgy* to make (a material such as sand) into a mould that is used in casting.
▷HISTORY C13 (n): changed from Old French *modle,* from Latin *modulus* a small measure, MODULE
▸ **ˈmouldable** *or* (*US*) **ˈmoldable** ADJECTIVE ▸ **ˌmouldaˈbility** *or* (*US*) **ˌmoldaˈbility** NOUN

mould^{2} *or US* **mold** (məʊld) NOUN [1] a coating or discoloration caused by various saprotrophic fungi that develop in a damp atmosphere on the surface of stored food, fabrics, wallpaper, etc. [2] any of the fungi that causes this growth. ◆ VERB [3] to become or cause to become covered with this growth. Also called: **mildew.**
▷HISTORY C15: dialect (Northern English) *mowlde* mouldy, from the past participle of *moulen* to become mouldy, probably of Scandinavian origin; compare Old Norse *mugla* mould

mould^{3} *or US* **mold** (məʊld) NOUN [1] loose soil, esp when rich in organic matter. [2] *Poetic* the earth.
▷HISTORY Old English *molde;* related to Old High German *molta* soil, Gothic *mulde*

mouldboard *or US* **moldboard** (ˈməʊldˌbɔːd) NOUN the curved blade of a plough, which turns over the furrow.

moulder^{1} *or US* **molder** (ˈməʊldə) VERB (often foll by *away*) to crumble or cause to crumble, as through decay.
▷HISTORY C16: verbal use of MOULD^{3}

moulder^{2} *or US* **molder** (ˈməʊldə) NOUN [1] a person who moulds or makes moulds. [2] *Printing* one of the set of electrotypes used for making duplicates.

moulding *or US* **molding** (ˈməʊldɪŋ) NOUN [1] *Architect* **a** a shaped outline, esp one used on cornices, etc. **b** a shaped strip made of wood, stone, etc. [2] something moulded.

moulding board NOUN a board on which dough is kneaded.

mouldwarp (ˈməʊldˌwɔːp) *or* **mouldywarp** (ˈməʊldɪˌwɔːp) NOUN an archaic or dialect name for a **mole**^{1} (sense 1).
▷HISTORY C14 *moldewarpe;* ultimately from Germanic *moldeworpon* (unattested) earth-thrower, from *moldā* MOULD^{3} + *wurp, werp* to throw (both unattested)

mouldy *or US* **moldy** (ˈməʊldɪ) ADJECTIVE **mouldier, mouldiest** *or US* **moldier, moldiest.** [1] covered with mould. [2] stale or musty, esp from age or lack of use. [3] *Slang* boring; dull.
▸ **ˈmouldiness** *or* (*US*) **ˈmoldiness** NOUN

mouldy fig NOUN *Dated slang* a rigid adherent to older jazz forms.

moulin (ˈmuːlɪn) NOUN a vertical shaft in a glacier, maintained by a constant descending stream of water and debris.
▷HISTORY C19: from French: a mill

Moulins (*French* mulɛ̃) NOUN a market town in central France, on the Allier River. Pop.: 23 350 (1990).

Moulmein *or* **Maulmain** (maʊlˈmeɪn) NOUN a port in S Myanmar, near the mouth of the Salween River: exports teak and rice. Pop.: 307 600 (1993 est.).

moult *or US* **molt** (məʊlt) VERB [1] (of birds, mammals, reptiles, and arthropods) to shed (feathers, hair, skin, or cuticle). ◆ NOUN [2] the periodic process of moulting. See also **ecdysis.**
▷HISTORY C14 *mouten,* from Old English *mūtian,* as in *bimūtian* to exchange for, from Latin *mūtāre* to change
▸ **ˈmoulter** *or* (*US*) **ˈmolter** NOUN

mound^{1} (maʊnd) NOUN [1] a raised mass of earth, debris, etc. [2] any heap or pile: *a mound of washing.* [3] a small natural hill. [4] *Archaeol* another word for **barrow**^{2}. [5] an artificial ridge of earth, stone, etc., as used for defence. ◆ VERB [6] (often foll by *up*) to gather into a mound; heap. [7] (*tr*) to cover or surround with a mound: *to mound a grave.* ◆ Related adjective: **tumular.**
▷HISTORY C16: earthwork, perhaps from Old English *mund* hand, hence defence: compare Middle Dutch *mond* protection

mound^{2} (maʊnd) NOUN *Heraldry* a rare word for **orb** (sense 1).
▷HISTORY C13 (meaning: world, C16: orb): from French *monde,* from Latin *mundus* world

Mound Builder NOUN a member of a group of prehistoric inhabitants of the Mississippi region who built altar-mounds, tumuli, etc.

mound-builder NOUN another name for **megapode.**

mount^{1} (maʊnt) VERB [1] to go up (a hill, stairs, etc.); climb. [2] to get up on (a horse, a platform, etc.). [3] (*intr;* often foll by *up*) io increase; accumulate: *excitement mounted.* [4] (*tr*) to fix onto a backing, setting, or support: *to mount a photograph; to mount a slide.* [5] (*tr*) to provide with a horse for riding, or to place on a horse. [6] (of male animals) to climb onto (a female animal) for copulation. [7] (*tr*) to prepare (a play, musical comedy, etc.) for production. [8] (*tr*) to plan and organize (a compaign, an exhibition, etc.). [9] (*tr*) *Military* to prepare or launch (an operation): *the Allies mounted an offensive.* [10] (*tr*) to prepare (a skeleton, dead animal, etc.) for exhibition as a specimen. [11] (*tr*) to place or carry (weapons) in such a position that they can be fired. [12] **mount guard.** See **guard** (sense 26). ◆ NOUN [13] a backing, setting, or support onto which something is fixed. [14] the act or manner of mounting. [15] a horse for riding. [16] a slide used in microscopy. [17] *Philately* **a** a small transparent pocket in an album for a postage stamp. **b** another word for **hinge** (sense 5).
▷HISTORY C16: from Old French *munter,* from Vulgar Latin *montāre* (unattested) from Latin *mons* MOUNT^{2}
▸ **ˈmountable** ADJECTIVE ▸ **ˈmounter** NOUN

mount^{2} (maʊnt) NOUN [1] a mountain or hill: used in literature and (when cap.) in proper names: *Mount Everest.* [2] (in palmistry) any of the seven cushions of flesh on the palm of the hand.
▷HISTORY Old English *munt,* from Latin *mons* mountain, but influenced in Middle English by Old French *mont*

mountain (ˈmaʊntɪn) NOUN [1] **a** a natural upward projection of the earth's surface, higher and steeper than a hill and often having a rocky summit. **b** (*as*

modifier): *mountain people; mountain scenery*. **c** (*in combination*): *a mountaintop*. [2] a huge heap or mass: *a mountain of papers*. [3] anything of great quantity or size. [4] a surplus of a commodity, esp in the European Union: *the butter mountain*. [5] **a mountain to climb.** *Brit informal* a serious or considerable difficulty or obstruction to overcome. [6] **make a mountain out of a molehill.** See **molehill** (sense 2).
▷HISTORY C13: from Old French *montaigne*, from Vulgar Latin *montānea* (unattested) mountainous, from Latin *montānus*, from *mons* mountain

Mountain ('maʊntɪn) NOUN **the.** an extremist faction during the French Revolution led by Danton and Robespierre.
▷HISTORY C18: so called because its members sat in the highest row of seats at the National Convention Hall in 1793

mountain ash NOUN [1] any of various trees of the rosaceous genus *Sorbus*, such as *S. aucuparia* (**European mountain ash** or **rowan**), having clusters of small white flowers and bright red berries. [2] any of several Australian eucalyptus trees, such as *Eucalyptus regnans*.

mountain avens NOUN See **avens** (sense 2).

mountain bike NOUN a type of sturdy bicycle with at least 16 and up to 21 gears, straight handlebars, and heavy-duty tyres.

mountain cat NOUN any of various wild feline mammals, such as the bobcat, lynx, or puma.

mountain chain NOUN a series of ranges of mountains.

mountain devil NOUN another name for **moloch.**

mountaineer (ˌmaʊntɪ'nɪə) NOUN [1] a person who climbs mountains. [2] a person living in a mountainous area. ◆ VERB [3] (*intr*) to climb mountains.
▸ˌ**mountain'eering** NOUN

mountain everlasting NOUN another name for **cat's-foot.**

mountain goat NOUN [1] short for **Rocky Mountain goat.** [2] any wild goat inhabiting mountainous regions.

mountain laurel NOUN any of various ericaceous shrubs or trees of the genus *Kalmia*, esp *K. latifolia* of E North America, which has leathery poisonous leaves and clusters of pink or white flowers. Also called: **calico bush.**

mountain lion NOUN another name for **puma.**

mountainous ('maʊntɪnəs) ADJECTIVE [1] of or relating to mountains: *a mountainous region*. [2] like a mountain, esp in size or impressiveness.
▸'**mountainously** ADVERB ▸'**mountainousness** NOUN

mountain range NOUN a series of adjoining mountains or of lines of mountains of similar origin.

mountain sheep NOUN [1] another name for **bighorn.** [2] any wild sheep inhabiting mountainous regions.

mountain sickness NOUN [1] Also called: **altitude sickness.** nausea, headache, and shortness of breath caused by climbing to high altitudes (usually above 12 000 ft.). [2] *Vet science* a disease of cattle kept at high altitude in S and N America, characterized by congestive heart failure.

Mountain Standard Time NOUN one of the standard times used in North America, seven hours behind Greenwich Mean Time. Abbreviation: **MST.**

Mount Cook lily NOUN a large white buttercup, *Ranunculus lyallii*, of the South Island alpine country of New Zealand. Also called: **great mountain buttercup.**

Mount Desert Island NOUN an island off the coast of Maine: lakes and granite peaks. Area: 279 sq km (108 sq. miles).

mountebank ('maʊntɪˌbæŋk) NOUN [1] (formerly) a person who sold quack medicines in public places. [2] a charlatan; fake. ◆ VERB [3] (*intr*) to play the mountebank.
▷HISTORY C16: from Italian *montambanco* a climber on a bench, from *montare* to MOUNT[2] + *banco* BENCH (see also BANK[1])
▸ˌ**mounte'bankery** NOUN

mounted ('maʊntɪd) ADJECTIVE [1] equipped with or riding horses: *mounted police*. [2] provided with a support, backing, etc.

Mountie *or* **Mounty** ('maʊntɪ) NOUN, *plural* **Mounties.** *Informal* a member of the Royal Canadian Mounted Police.
▷HISTORY nickname evolved from MOUNTED

mounting ('maʊntɪŋ) NOUN another word for **mount**[1] (sense 13).

mounting-block NOUN a block of stone formerly used to aid a person when mounting a horse.

Mount Isa ('aɪzə) NOUN a city in NE Australia in NW Queensland: mining of copper and other minerals. Pop.: 24 104 (1988 est.).

Mount McKinley National Park (mə'kɪnlɪ) NOUN a national park in S central Alaska: contains part of the Alaska Range Area: 7847 sq. km (3030 sq. miles).

Mount Rainier National Park ('raɪnɪə, reɪ'nɪə, rə-) NOUN a national park in W Washington, in the Cascade Range. Area: 976 sq. km (377 sq. miles).

mourn (mɔːn) VERB [1] to feel or express sadness for the death or loss of (someone or something). [2] (*intr*) to observe the customs of mourning, as by wearing black. [3] (*tr*) to grieve over (loss or misfortune).
▷HISTORY Old English *murnan;* compare Old High German *mornēn* to be troubled, Gothic *maurnan* to grieve, Greek *mermeros* worried

Mourne Mountains (mɔːn) PLURAL NOUN a mountain range in SE Northern Ireland. Highest peak: Slieve Donard, 853 m (2798 ft).

mourner ('mɔːnə) NOUN [1] a person who mourns, esp at a funeral. [2] (at US revivalist meetings) a person who repents publicly.

mournful ('mɔːnful) ADJECTIVE [1] evoking grief; sorrowful. [2] gloomy; sad.
▸'**mournfully** ADVERB ▸'**mournfulness** NOUN

mourning ('mɔːnɪŋ) NOUN [1] the act or feelings of one who mourns; grief. [2] the conventional symbols of grief, such as the wearing of black. [3] the period of time during which a death is officially mourned. [4] **in mourning.** observing the conventions of mourning. ◆ ADJECTIVE [5] of or relating to mourning.
▸'**mourningly** ADVERB

mourning band NOUN a piece of black material, esp an armband, worn to indicate that the wearer is in mourning.

mourning cloak NOUN the US name for **Camberwell beauty.**

mourning dove NOUN a brown North American dove, *Zenaidura macroura*, with a plaintive song.

mouse (maʊs) NOUN, *plural* **mice** (maɪs). [1] any of numerous small long-tailed rodents of the families *Muridae* and *Cricetidae* that are similar to but smaller than rats. See also **fieldmouse, harvest mouse, house mouse.** Related adjective: **murine.** [2] any of various related rodents, such as the jumping mouse. [3] a quiet, timid, or cowardly person. [4] *Computing* a hand-held device used to control the cursor movement and select computing functions without keying. [5] *Slang* a black eye. [6] *Nautical* another word for **mousing.** ◆ VERB (maʊz) [7] to stalk and catch (mice). [8] (*intr*) to go about stealthily. [9] (*tr*) *Nautical* to secure (a hook) with mousing.
▷HISTORY Old English *mūs;* compare Old Saxon *mūs*, German *Maus*, Old Norse *mūs*, Latin *mūs*, Greek *mūs*
▸'**mouseˌlike** ADJECTIVE

mousebird ('maʊsˌbɜːd) NOUN another name for **coly.**

mouse deer NOUN another name for **chevrotain.**

mouse-ear NOUN short for **mouse-ear chickweed** (see **chickweed** (sense 2)).

mouser ('maʊzə, 'maʊsə) NOUN a cat or other animal that is used to catch mice: usually qualified: *a good mouser*.

mousetail ('maʊsˌteɪl) NOUN any of various N temperate ranunculaceous plants of the genus *Myosurus*, esp *M. minimus*, with tail-like flower spikes.

mousetrap ('maʊsˌtræp) NOUN [1] any trap for catching mice, esp one with a spring-loaded metal bar that is released by the taking of the bait. [2] *Brit informal* cheese of indifferent quality.

mousey ('maʊsɪ) ADJECTIVE **mousier, mousiest.** a variant spelling of **mousy.**
▸'**mousily** ADVERB ▸'**mousiness** NOUN

mousing ('maʊzɪŋ) NOUN *Nautical* a lashing, shackle, etc., for closing off a hook to prevent a load from slipping off.

moussaka *or* **mousaka** (mʊ'sɑːkə) NOUN a dish originating in the Balkan States, consisting of meat, aubergines, and tomatoes, topped with cheese sauce.
▷HISTORY C20: from Modern Greek

mousse (muːs) NOUN [1] a light creamy dessert made with eggs, cream, fruit, etc., set with gelatine. [2] a similar dish made from fish or meat. [3] the layer of small bubbles on the top of a glass of champagne or other sparkling wine. [4] short for **styling mousse.**
▷HISTORY C19: from French: froth

mousseline (*French* muslin) NOUN [1] a fine fabric made of rayon or silk. [2] a type of fine glass. [3] short for **mousseline sauce.**
▷HISTORY C17: French: MUSLIN

mousseline de laine *French* (muslin də lɛn) NOUN a light woollen fabric.
▷HISTORY literally: muslin of wool

mousseline de soie *French* (muslin də swa) NOUN a thin gauzelike fabric of silk or rayon.
▷HISTORY literally: muslin of silk

mousseline sauce NOUN a light sauce, made by adding whipped cream or egg whites to hollandaise sauce.
▷HISTORY from French *mousseline*, literally: muslin

moustache *or US* **mustache** (mə'stɑːʃ) NOUN [1] the unshaved growth of hair on the upper lip, and sometimes down the sides of the mouth. [2] a similar growth of hair or bristles (in animals) or feathers (in birds). [3] a mark like a moustache.
▷HISTORY C16: via French from Italian *mostaccio*, ultimately from Doric Greek *mustax* upper lip
▸**mous'tached** *or* (*US*) **mus'tached** ADJECTIVE

moustache cup NOUN a cup with a partial cover to protect a drinker's moustache.

Mousterian (muː'stɪərɪən) NOUN [1] a culture characterized by flint flake tools and associated with Neanderthal man, found throughout Europe, North Africa, and the Near East, dating from before 70 000–32 000 B.C. ◆ ADJECTIVE [2] of or relating to this culture.
▷HISTORY C20: from French *Moustérien* from archaeological finds of the same period in the cave of *Le Moustier*, Dordogne, France

mousy *or* **mousey** ('maʊsɪ) ADJECTIVE **mousier, mousiest.** [1] resembling a mouse, esp in having a light brown or greyish hair colour. [2] shy or ineffectual: *a mousy little woman*. [3] infested with mice.
▸'**mousily** ADVERB ▸'**mousiness** NOUN

mouth NOUN (maʊθ), *plural* **mouths** (maʊðz). [1] the opening through which many animals take in food and issue vocal sounds. [2] the system of organs surrounding this opening, including the lips, tongue, teeth, etc. [3] the visible part of the lips on the face. Related adjectives: **oral, oscular.** [4] a person regarded as a consumer of food: *four mouths to feed*. [5] verbal expression (esp in the phrase **give mouth to**). [6] a particular manner of speaking: *a foul mouth*. [7] *Informal* boastful, rude, or excessive talk: *he is all mouth*. [8] the point where a river issues into a sea or lake. [9] the opening of a container, such as a jar. [10] the opening of or place leading into a cave, tunnel, volcano, etc. [11] that part of the inner lip of a horse on which the bit acts, esp when specified as to sensitivity: *a hard mouth*. [12] *Music* the narrow slit in an organ pipe. [13] the opening between the jaws of a vice or other gripping device. [14] a pout; grimace. [15] **by word of mouth.** orally rather than by written means. [16] **down in** *or* **at the mouth.** in low spirits. [17] **have a big mouth** *or* **open one's big mouth.** *Informal* to speak indiscreetly, loudly, or excessively. [18] **keep one's mouth shut.** to keep a secret. [19] **put one's money where one's mouth is.** to take appropriate action to support what one has said. [20] **put words into someone's mouth. a** to represent, often inaccurately, what someone has said. **b** to tell someone what to say. [21] **run off at the mouth.** *Informal* to talk incessantly, esp about unimportant matters. ◆ VERB (maʊð) [22] to speak or say (something) insincerely, esp in public. [23] (*tr*) to form (words) with movements of the lips but without speaking. [24] (*tr*) to accustom (a horse) to wearing a bit. [25] (*tr*) to take (something) into the mouth or to move

(something) around inside the mouth. 26 (*intr; usually foll by at*) to make a grimace.
▷**HISTORY** Old English *mūth;* compare Old Norse *muthr,* Gothic *munths,* Dutch *mond*
▸**mouther** ('maʊðə) NOUN

mouthbrooder ('maʊθˌbru:də) *or* **mouthbreeder** ('maʊθˌbri:də) NOUN any of various African cichlid fishes of the genera *Tilapia Haplochromis* that carry their eggs and young around in the mouth.

mouthfeel ('maʊθˌfi:l) NOUN the texture of a substance as it is perceived in the mouth: *the wine has a good mouthfeel.*

mouthful ('maʊθˌfʊl) NOUN, *plural* **-fuls.** 1 as much as is held in the mouth at one time. 2 a small quantity, as of food. 3 a long word or phrase that is difficult to say. 4 *Brit informal* an abusive response. 5 *Informal, chiefly US and Canadian* an impressive remark (esp in the phrase **say a mouthful**).

mouth organ NOUN another name for **harmonica** (sense 1).

mouthpart ('maʊθˌpɑ:t) NOUN any of the paired appendages in arthropods that surround the mouth and are specialized for feeding.

mouthpiece ('maʊθˌpi:s) NOUN 1 the part of a wind instrument into which the player blows. 2 the part of a telephone receiver into which a person speaks. 3 the part of a container forming its mouth. 4 a person who acts as a spokesman, as for an organization. 5 a publication, esp a periodical, expressing the official views of an organization. 6 *Boxing* another name for **gumshield.**

mouth-to-mouth ADJECTIVE designating a method of artificial respiration involving blowing air rhythmically into the mouth of a person who has stopped breathing, to stimulate return of spontaneous breathing.

mouthwash ('maʊθˌwɒʃ) NOUN a medicated aqueous solution, used for gargling and for cleansing the mouth.

mouthwatering ('maʊθˌwɔ:tərɪŋ) ADJECTIVE whetting the appetite, as from smell, appearance, or description.

mouthy ('maʊðɪ) ADJECTIVE **mouthier, mouthiest.** bombastic; excessively talkative.

mouton ('mu:tɒn) NOUN sheepskin processed to resemble the fur of another animal, esp beaver or seal.
▷**HISTORY** from French: sheep. See MUTTON

movable *or* **moveable** ('mu:vəb^{ə}l) ADJECTIVE 1 able to be moved or rearranged; not fixed. 2 (esp of religious festivals such as Easter) varying in date from year to year. 3 (usually spelt **moveable**) *Law* denoting or relating to personal property as opposed to realty. 4 *Printing* (of type) cast singly so that each character is on a separate piece of type suitable for composition by hand, as founder's type. ♦ NOUN 5 (*often plural*) a movable article, esp a piece of furniture.
▸ˌ**mova'bility** *or* '**movableness** NOUN ▸'**movably** ADVERB

move (mu:v) VERB 1 to go or take from one place to another; change in location or position. 2 (*usually intr*) to change (one's dwelling, place of business, etc.). 3 to be or cause to be in motion; stir. 4 (*intr*) (of machines, etc.) to work or operate. 5 (*tr*) to cause (to do something); prompt. 6 (*intr*) to begin to act: *move soon or we'll lose the order.* 7 (*intr*) to associate oneself with a specified social circle: *to move in exalted spheres.* 8 (*intr*) to make progress. 9 (*tr*) to arouse affection, pity, or compassion in; touch. 10 (in board games) to change the position of (a piece) or (of a piece) to change position. 11 (*intr*) (of merchandise) to be disposed of by being bought. 12 (when *tr, often takes a clause as object;* when *intr,* often foll by *for*) to suggest (a proposal) formally, as in debating or parliamentary procedure. 13 (*intr; usually foll by on or along*) to go away or to another place; leave. 14 to cause (the bowels) to evacuate or (of the bowels) to be evacuated. 15 (*intr*) *Informal* to be exciting or active: *the party started moving at twelve.* 16 **move heaven and earth.** to take every step possible (to achieve something). ♦ NOUN 17 the act of moving; movement. 18 one of a sequence of actions, usually part of a plan; manoeuvre. 19 the act of moving one's residence, place of business, etc. 20 (in board games) **a** a player's turn to move his piece or take other permitted action. **b** a permitted manoeuvre of a piece. 21 **get a move on.** *Informal* **a** to get started. **b** to hurry up. 22 **make a move.** (*usually used with a negative*) *Informal* to take even the slightest action: *don't make a move without phoning me.* 23 **make one's move.** to commit oneself to a position or course of action. 24 **on the move. a** travelling from place to place. **b** advancing; succeeding. **c** very active; busy.
▷**HISTORY** C13: from Anglo-French *mover,* from Latin *movēre*

move in VERB (*mainly adverb*) 1 (*also preposition*) Also: (when *preposition*) **move into.** to occupy or take possession of (a new residence, place of business, etc.) or help (someone) to do this. 2 (*intr; often foll by on*) *Informal* to creep close (to), as in preparing to capture. 3 (*intr; often foll by on*) *Informal* to try to gain power or influence (over) or interfere (with).

movement ('mu:vmənt) NOUN 1 **a** the act, process, or result of moving. **b** an instance of moving. 2 the manner of moving. 3 **a** a group of people with a common ideology, esp a political or religious one. **b** the organized action of such a group. 4 a trend or tendency in a particular sphere. 5 the driving and regulating mechanism of a watch or clock. 6 (*often plural*) a person's location and activities during a specific time. 7 **a** the evacuation of the bowels. **b** the matter evacuated. 8 *Music* a principal self-contained section of a symphony, sonata, etc., usually having its own structure. 9 tempo or pace, as in music or literature. 10 *Fine arts* the appearance of motion in painting, sculpture, etc. 11 *Prosody* the rhythmic structure of verse. 12 a positional change by one or a number of military units. 13 a change in the market price of a security or commodity.

move out VERB (*adverb*) to vacate a residence, place of business, etc., or help (someone) to do this.

mover ('mu:və) NOUN 1 *Informal* a person, business, idea, etc., that is advancing or progressing. 2 a person who moves a proposal, as in a debate. 3 *US and Canadian* a removal firm or a person who works for one.

movers and shakers PLURAL NOUN *Informal* the people with power and influence in a particular field of activity.
▷**HISTORY** C20: perhaps from the line "We are the movers and shakers of the world for ever" in 'Ode' by Arthur O'Shaughnessy (1844–81), British poet

movie ('mu:vɪ) NOUN **a** an informal word for **film** (sense 1). **b** (*as modifier*): *movie ticket.*
▷**HISTORY** C20: from MOV(ING PICTURE) + -IE

movie camera NOUN the US and Canadian term for **cine camera.**

movie film NOUN the US and Canadian term for **cine film.**

Movietone ('mu:vɪˌtəʊn) NOUN *Trademark, US* the earliest technique of including a soundtrack on film.

moving ('mu:vɪŋ) ADJECTIVE 1 arousing or touching the emotions. 2 changing or capable of changing position. 3 causing motion.
▸'**movingly** ADVERB

moving average NOUN *Statistics* (of a sequence of values) a derived sequence of the averages of successive subsequences of a given number of members, often used in time series to even out short-term fluctuations and make a trend clearer: *the 3-term moving average of 4, 6, 8, 7, 9, 8 is 6, 7, 8.*

moving coil ADJECTIVE denoting an electromechanical device in which a suspended coil is free to move in a magnetic field. A current passing through the coil causes it to move, as in loudspeakers and electrical measuring instruments, or movement of the coil gives rise to induced currents, as in microphones and some record-player pick-ups.

moving picture NOUN a US and Canadian name for **film** (sense 1).

moving staircase *or* **stairway** NOUN less common terms for **escalator** (sense 1).

Moviola (ˌmu:vɪ'əʊlə) NOUN *Trademark* a viewing machine used in cutting and editing film.

mow^1 (məʊ) VERB **mows, mowing, mowed, mowed** *or* **mown.** 1 to cut down (grass, crops, etc.) with a hand implement or machine. 2 (*tr*) to cut the growing vegetation of (a field, lawn, etc.).
▷**HISTORY** Old English *māwan;* related to Old High German *māen,* Middle Dutch *maeyen* to mow, Latin *metere* to reap, Welsh *medi*
▸'**mower** NOUN

mow^2 (maʊ) NOUN 1 the part of a barn where hay, straw, etc., is stored. 2 the hay, straw, etc., stored.
▷**HISTORY** Old English *mūwa;* compare Old Norse *mūgr* heap, Greek *mukōn*

mow^3 (maʊ) NOUN, VERB an archaic word for **grimace.**
▷**HISTORY** C14: from Old French *moe* a pout, or Middle Dutch *mouwe*

mowburnt ('məʊˌbɜ:nt) ADJECTIVE (of hay, straw, etc.) damaged by overheating in a mow.

mowdie ('maʊdɪ) *or* **mowdiewart** ('maʊdɪˌwært) NOUN Scot words for **mole^2.**
▷**HISTORY** C18: a Scot variant of MOULDWARP

mow down VERB (*tr, adverb*) to kill in large numbers, esp by gunfire.

mown (məʊn) VERB a past participle of **mow^1.**

MOX (mɒks) NOUN a blend of plutonium and uranium oxides, used as a nuclear fuel in breeder reactors.
▷**HISTORY** C20: from *m(ixed) ox(ides)*

moxa ('mɒksə) NOUN 1 a downy material obtained from various plants and used in Oriental medicine by being burned on the skin as a cauterizing agent or counterirritant for the skin. 2 any of various plants yielding this material, such as the wormwood *Artemisia chinensis.*
▷**HISTORY** C17: anglicized version of Japanese *mogusa,* contraction of *moe gusa* burning herb

moxibustion (ˌmɒksɪ'bʌstʃən) NOUN a method of treatment, originally in Chinese medicine, in which a moxa is burned on the skin.
▷**HISTORY** C20: from MOXA + (COM)BUSTION

moxie ('mɒksɪ) NOUN *US and Canadian, slang* courage, nerve, or vigour.
▷**HISTORY** from the trademark *Moxie,* a soft drink

Moyle (mɔɪl) NOUN a district of NE Northern Ireland, in Co. Antrim. Pop.: 15 933 (2001) Area: 494 sq. km (191 sq. miles).

moz *or* **mozz** (mɒz) NOUN *Austral, slang, obsolete* 1 a hoodoo; hex. 2 **put the moz on.** to jinx.
▷**HISTORY** short for *mozzle,* from Hebrew *mazzal* luck

Mozambican *or* **Mozambiquan** (ˌməʊzəm'bi:kən) ADJECTIVE 1 of or relating to Mozambique or its inhabitants. ♦ NOUN 2 a native or inhabitant of Mozambique.

Mozambique (ˌməʊzəm'bi:k) NOUN a republic in SE Africa: colonized by the Portuguese from 1505 onwards and a slave-trade centre until 1878; made an overseas province of Portugal in 1951; became an independent republic in 1975; became a member of the Commonwealth in 1995. Official language: Portuguese. Religion: animist majority. Currency: metical. Capital: Maputo. Pop.: 19 371 000 (2001 est.). Area: 812 379 sq. km (313 661 sq. miles). Portuguese name: **Moçambique.** Also called (until 1975): **Portuguese East Africa.**

Mozambique Channel NOUN a strait between Mozambique and Madagascar. Length: about 1600 km (1000 miles). Width: 400 km (250 miles).

Mozarab (məʊ'zærəb) NOUN (formerly) a Christian of Moorish Spain.
▷**HISTORY** C18: via Spanish from Arabic *musta'rib* a would-be Arab
▸**Moz'arabic** ADJECTIVE

mozzarella (ˌmɒtsə'rɛlə) NOUN a moist white Italian curd cheese made originally from buffalo milk.
▷**HISTORY** from Italian, diminutive of *mozza* a type of cheese, from *mozzare* to cut off

mozzetta (məʊ'zɛtə; *Italian* mot'tsetta) *or* **mozetta** NOUN *RC Church* a short hooded cape worn by the pope, cardinals, etc.
▷**HISTORY** C18: from Italian, shortened from *almozzetta,* from Medieval Latin *almutia* ALMUCE

mozzie ('mɒzɪ) NOUN a variant spelling of **mossie^1.**

mp^1 ABBREVIATION FOR: 1 melting point. 2 *Music* mezzo piano.
▷**HISTORY** Italian: moderately soft

mp^2 THE INTERNET DOMAIN NAME FOR Northern Mariana Islands.

MP ABBREVIATION FOR: [1] (in Britain and Canada) Member of Parliament. [2] (in Britain) Metropolitan Police. [3] Military Police. [4] Mounted Police.

MP3 ABBREVIATION FOR: [1] MPEG-1 Audio Layer-3: tradename for software created by the Motion Picture Experts Group that enables files to be compressed quickly to 10% or less of their original size for storage on disk or hard drive or esp for transfer across the Internet. [2] an audio or video file created in this way.

MPC (in Britain) ABBREVIATION FOR: [1] Medical Practices Committee. [2] Monetary Policy Committee (of the Bank of England).

MPEG (ˈɛmˌpeg) NOUN *Computing* a standard file format for compressing video images and audio sounds.
▷HISTORY C20: technique devised by the *M(otion) P(icture) E(xperts) G(roup)*

mpg ABBREVIATION FOR miles per gallon.

MPG (in Britain) ABBREVIATION FOR main professional grade: the basic salary scale for classroom teachers.

mph ABBREVIATION FOR miles per hour.

MPhil *or* **MPh** ABBREVIATION FOR Master of Philosophy.

MPLA ABBREVIATION FOR Movimento Popular de Libertacão de Angola.
▷HISTORY Portuguese: Popular Movement for the Liberation of Angola

MP/M NOUN *Computing* a multiuser operating system that resembles a CP/M.

MPP (in Canada) ABBREVIATION FOR Member of the Provincial Parliament (of Ontario).

MPS ABBREVIATION FOR: [1] Member of the Pharmaceutical Society. [2] Member of the Philological Society.

Mpumalanga (mˈpʌmɑːˌlɑːŋgə) NOUN a province of E South Africa; formed in 1994 from part of the former province of Transvaal: agriculture and service industries. Capital: Nelspruit. Pop.: 3 003 327 (1999 est.). Area: 78 370 sq. km (30 259 sq. miles).

MPV ABBREVIATION FOR **multipurpose vehicle**.

mq THE INTERNET DOMAIN NAME FOR Martinique.

Mr (ˈmɪstə) NOUN, *plural* **Messrs** (ˈmɛsəz). [1] a title used before a man's name or names or before some office that he holds: *Mr Jones; Mr President.* [2] (in military contexts) a title used in addressing a warrant officer, officer cadet, or junior naval officer. [3] a title placed before the surname of a surgeon.
▷HISTORY C17: abbreviation of MISTER

MR ABBREVIATION FOR: [1] (in Britain) **Master of the Rolls.** [2] motivation(al) research.

MRA ABBREVIATION FOR: [1] magnetic resonance. [2] **Moral Rearmament.**

Mr Big NOUN *Slang, chiefly US* the head of an organization, esp of a criminal organization.

MRBM ABBREVIATION FOR **medium-range ballistic missile.**

MRC (in Britain) ABBREVIATION FOR Medical Research Council.

MRCA ABBREVIATION FOR multirole combat aircraft.

MRE ABBREVIATION FOR meal ready to eat, a US military precooked ration pack.

MRI ABBREVIATION FOR magnetic resonance imaging.

MRIA ABBREVIATION FOR Member of the Royal Irish Academy.

mridang (mrɪˈdʌŋ) NOUN a drum used in Indian music.
▷HISTORY Hindi

MRM ABBREVIATION FOR mechanically recovered meat: a reconstituted meat product created from offal and other meat waste, often used in hamburgers, sausages, pies, etc.

mRNA ABBREVIATION FOR messenger RNA.

MRP ABBREVIATION FOR manufacturers' recommended price.

Mr Right NOUN *Informal* the man considered by a woman to be her perfect marriage partner.

Mrs (ˈmɪsɪz) NOUN, *plural* **Mrs** *or* **Mesdames.** a title used before the name or names of a married woman.
▷HISTORY C17: originally an abbreviation of MISTRESS

MRSA ABBREVIATION FOR methicillin-resistant *Staphylococcus aureus*: a bacterium that enters the skin through open wounds to cause septicaemia and is extremely resistant to most antibiotics. It has been responsible for outbreaks of untreatable infections among patients in hospitals.

MRSC ABBREVIATION FOR Member of the Royal Society of Chemistry.

Mrs Mop NOUN *Informal* a cleaning lady.

ms THE INTERNET DOMAIN NAME FOR Montserrat.

Ms (mɪz, məs) NOUN a title substituted for **Mrs** or **Miss** before a woman's name to avoid making a distinction between married and unmarried women.

MS ABBREVIATION FOR: [1] Master of Surgery. [2] (on gravestones) memoriae sacrum. [Latin: sacred to the memory of] [3] Mississippi. [4] motor ship. [5] **multiple sclerosis.** ◆ [6] INTERNATIONAL CAR REGISTRATION FOR Mauritius.

MS. *or* **ms.** *plural* **MSS.** *or* **mss.** ABBREVIATION FOR manuscript.

msb *Computing* ABBREVIATION FOR most significant bit; the bit of binary number with the greatest numerical value or the bit in some other binary pattern which occupies this position.

MSc ABBREVIATION FOR Master of Science.

MSC (in Canada) ABBREVIATION FOR Meritorious Service Cross.

MSD (in New Zealand) ABBREVIATION FOR Ministry of Social Development.

MS-DOS (ɛmˈɛsˈdɒs) NOUN *Trademark, computing* a type of disk operating system.
▷HISTORY C20: from *M(icro)s(oft)*, the company that developed it, + DOS

MSF (formerly, in Britain) ABBREVIATION FOR Manufacturing, Science, Finance (a trade union).

MSG ABBREVIATION FOR **monosodium glutamate.**

Msgr ABBREVIATION FOR Monsignor.

MSI *Electronics* ABBREVIATION FOR medium-scale integration.

msl *or* **MSL** ABBREVIATION FOR mean sea level.

MSM (in Canada) ABBREVIATION FOR Meritorious Service Medal.

MSP ABBREVIATION FOR Member of the Scottish Parliament.

MSS *or* **mss** ABBREVIATION FOR manuscripts.

MST ABBREVIATION FOR **Mountain Standard Time.**

Ms-Th *Physics* SYMBOL FOR mesothorium.

mt THE INTERNET DOMAIN NAME FOR Malta.

Mt *or* **mt** ABBREVIATION FOR: [1] mount: *Mt Everest.* [2] Also: **mtn.** mountain.

MT ABBREVIATION FOR Montana.

MTB NOUN *Brit* a motor torpedo boat.

MTBE ABBREVIATION FOR methyl tertiary-butyl ether: a lead-free antiknock petrol additive.

MTBF ABBREVIATION FOR mean time between failures.

MTech ABBREVIATION FOR Master of Technology.

mtg ABBREVIATION FOR meeting.

MTNG *Text messaging* ABBREVIATION FOR meeting.

Mt Rev. ABBREVIATION FOR Most Reverend.

MTV ABBREVIATION FOR music television: a US music channel that operates 24 hours a day.

mu[1] (mjuː) NOUN the 12th letter in the Greek alphabet (Μ, μ), a consonant, transliterated as *m*.

mu[2] THE INTERNET DOMAIN NAME FOR Mauritius.

MU ABBREVIATION FOR Musicians' Union.

Muay Thai (ˈmuːeɪ ˈtaɪ) NOUN a martial art developed in Thailand in which blows may be struck with the fists, elbows, knees, and shins.

muc- COMBINING FORM a variant of **muco-** before a vowel.

much (mʌtʃ) DETERMINER [1] **a** (*usually used with a negative*) a great quantity or degree of: *there isn't much honey left.* **b** (*as pronoun*): *much has been learned from this.* [2] **a bit much.** *Informal* rather excessive. [3] **as much.** exactly that: *I suspected as much when I heard.* [4] **make much of.** See **make of** (sense 4). [5] **not much of.** not to any appreciable degree or extent: *he's not much of an actor really.* [6] **not up to much.** *Informal* of a low standard: *this beer is not up to much.* [7] **think much of.** (*used with a negative*) to have a high opinion of: *I don't think much of his behaviour.* ◆ ADVERB [8] considerably: *they're much better now.* [9] practically; nearly (esp in the phrase **much the same**). [10] (*usually used with a negative*) often; a great deal: *it doesn't happen much in this country.* [11] **(as) much as.** even though; although: *much as I'd like to, I can't come.* ◆ ADJECTIVE [12] (*predicative; usually used with a negative*) impressive or important: *this car isn't much.* ◆ See also **more, most.**
▷HISTORY Old English *mycel;* related to Old English *micel* great, Old Saxon *mikil,* Gothic *mikils;* compare also Latin *magnus,* Greek *megas*

muchness (ˈmʌtʃnɪs) NOUN [1] *Archaic or informal* magnitude. [2] **much of a muchness.** *Brit* very similar.

mucic acid (ˈmjuːsɪk) NOUN a colourless crystalline solid carboxylic acid found in milk sugar and used in the manufacture of pyrrole. Formula: $C_4H_4(OH)_4(COOH)_2$.
▷HISTORY C19: *mucic,* from French *mucique;* see MUCUS, -IC

mucid (ˈmjuːsɪd) ADJECTIVE *Rare* mouldy, musty, or slimy.
▷HISTORY C17: from Latin *mūcidus,* from *mucēre* to be mouldy
▸**muˈcidity** *or* **ˈmucidness** NOUN

mucigen (ˈmjuːsɪdʒən) NOUN a substance present in mucous cells that is converted into mucin.

mucilage (ˈmjuːsɪlɪdʒ) NOUN [1] a sticky preparation, such as gum or glue, used as an adhesive. [2] a complex glutinous carbohydrate secreted by certain plants.
▷HISTORY C14: via Old French from Late Latin *mūcilāgo* mouldy juice; see MUCID
▸**mucilaginous** (ˌmjuːsɪˈlædʒɪnəs) ADJECTIVE ▸**ˌmuciˈlaginously** ADVERB ▸**ˌmuciˈlaginousness** NOUN

mucin (ˈmjuːsɪn) NOUN *Biochem* any of a group of nitrogenous mucoproteins occurring in saliva, skin, tendon, etc., that produce a very viscous solution in water.
▷HISTORY C19: via French from Latin MUCUS
▸**ˈmucinous** ADJECTIVE

muck (mʌk) NOUN [1] farmyard dung or decaying vegetable matter. [2] Also called: **muck soil.** an organic soil rich in humus and used as a fertilizer. [3] dirt or filth. [4] earth, rock material, etc., removed during mining excavations. [5] *Slang, chiefly Brit* rubbish. [6] See **Lord Muck, Lady Muck.** [7] **make a muck of.** *Slang, chiefly Brit* to ruin or spoil. ◆ VERB (*tr*) [8] to spread manure upon (fields, gardens, etc.). [9] to soil or pollute. [10] (often foll by *out*) to clear muck from. ◆ See also **muck about, muck in, muck up.**
▷HISTORY C13: probably of Scandinavian origin; compare Old Norse *myki* dung, Norwegian *myk*

muck about VERB *Brit, slang* [1] (*intr*) to waste time; misbehave. [2] (when *intr,* foll by *with*) to interfere with, annoy, or waste the time of.

muckamuck (ˈmʌkəˌmʌk) *Canadian W coast* ◆ NOUN [1] food. ◆ VERB [2] (*intr*) to consume food; eat.
▷HISTORY Chinook Jargon

mucker (ˈmʌkə) NOUN [1] *Mining* a person who shifts broken rock or waste. [2] *Brit, slang* **a** a friend; mate. **b** a coarse person.
▸**ˈmuckerish** ADJECTIVE

muck in VERB (*intr, adverb*) *Brit, slang* to share something, such as duties, work, etc. (with other people).

muckle (ˈmʌkᵊl) *Scot* ◆ ADJECTIVE [1] large; much. ◆ ADVERB [2] much; greatly.
▷HISTORY dialect variant of MICKLE

muckrake (ˈmʌkˌreɪk) NOUN [1] an agricultural rake for spreading manure. ◆ VERB [2] (*intr*) to seek out and expose scandal, esp concerning public figures.
▸**ˈmuckˌraker** NOUN ▸**ˈmuckˌraking** NOUN

mucksweat (ˈmʌkˌswet) NOUN *Brit informal* profuse sweat or a state of profuse sweating.

muck up VERB (*adverb*) *Informal* [1] (*tr*) *Brit and Austral* to ruin or spoil; make a mess of. [2] (*intr*) *Austral* to misbehave.

muck-up day NOUN *Austral, slang* the last day of school before the annual examinations, marked by practical jokes and other student pranks.

muckworm (ˈmʌkˌwɜːm) NOUN [1] any larva or worm that lives in mud. [2] *Informal* a miser.

mucky (ˈmʌkɪ) ADJECTIVE **muckier, muckiest.** [1] dirty. [2] of or like muck.
▸**ˈmuckily** ADVERB ▸**ˈmuckiness** NOUN

muco- *or before a vowel* **muc-** COMBINING FORM mucus or mucous: *mucoprotein; mucin.*

mucoid ('mju:kɔɪd) *or* **mucoidal** ADJECTIVE of the nature of or resembling mucin.

mucopolysaccharide (ˌmju:kəʊˌpɒlɪ'sækəraɪd) NOUN *Biochem* any of a group of complex polysaccharides composed of repeating units of two sugars, one of which contains an amino group.

mucoprotein (ˌmju:kəʊ'prəʊti:n) NOUN any of a group of conjugated proteins containing small quantities of mucopolysaccharides; glycoprotein.

mucopurulent (ˌmju:kəʊ'pjʊərələnt) ADJECTIVE *Pathol* composed of or containing both mucus and pus.

mucor ('mju:kɔ:) NOUN any fungus belonging to the genus *Mucor,* which comprises many common moulds.
▷HISTORY C20: New Latin, from Latin: mould

mucosa (mju:'kəʊsə) NOUN, *plural* **-sae** (-si:). another word for **mucous membrane.**
▷HISTORY C19: New Latin, from Latin *mūcōsus* slimy
▸**mu'cosal** ADJECTIVE

mucous ('mju:kəs) *or* **mucose** ('mju:kəʊs, -kəʊz) ADJECTIVE of, resembling, or secreting mucus.
▷HISTORY C17: from Latin *mūcōsus* slimy, from MUCUS
▸**mucosity** (mju:'kɒsɪtɪ) NOUN

> **Language note** The noun *mucus* is often misspelled *mucous. Mucous* can only be correctly used as an adjective.

mucous membrane NOUN a mucus-secreting membrane that lines body cavities or passages that are open to the external environment. Also called: **mucosa.**
▸**mucomembranous** (ˌmju:kəʊ'mɛmbrənəs) ADJECTIVE

mucro ('mju:krəʊ) NOUN, *plural* **mucrones** (mju:'krəʊni:z). *Biology* a short pointed projection from certain parts or organs, as from the tip of a leaf.
▷HISTORY C17: from Latin *mūcrō* point

mucronate ('mju:krəʊnɪt, -ˌneɪt) *or* **mucronated** ADJECTIVE terminating in a sharp point.
▷HISTORY C18: from Latin *mūcrōnātus* pointed, from MUCRO
▸ˌ**mucro'nation** NOUN

mucus ('mju:kəs) NOUN the slimy protective secretion of the mucous membranes, consisting mainly of mucin.
▷HISTORY C17: from Latin: nasal secretions; compare *mungere* to blow the nose; related to Greek *muxa* mucus, *muktēr* nose

> **Language note** See at **mucous.**

mud (mʌd) NOUN [1] a fine-grained soft wet deposit that occurs on the ground after rain, at the bottom of ponds, lakes, etc. [2] *Informal* slander or defamation. [3] **clear as mud.** *Informal* not at all clear. [4] **drag (someone's) name in the mud.** to disgrace or defame (someone). [5] **here's mud in your eye.** *Informal* a humorous drinking toast. [6] **(someone's) name is mud.** *Informal* (someone) is disgraced. [7] **throw** (*or* **sling**) **mud at.** *Informal* to slander; vilify. ◆ VERB **muds, mudding, mudded.** [8] (*tr*) to soil or cover with mud.
▷HISTORY C14: probably from Middle Low German *mudde;* compare Middle High German *mot* swamp, mud, Swedish *modd* slush

mud bath NOUN [1] a medicinal bath in heated mud. [2] a dirty or muddy occasion, state, etc.

mudcat ('mʌdˌkæt) NOUN any of several large North American catfish living in muddy rivers, esp in the Mississippi valley.

mud crab NOUN a large edible crab, *Scylla serrata,* of Australian mangrove regions.

mud dauber NOUN any of various wasps of the family *Sphecidae,* that construct cells of mud or clay in which they lay their eggs and store live insects as food for the developing larvae. See also **digger wasp.**

muddle ('mʌdᵊl) VERB (*tr*) [1] (often foll by *up*) to mix up (objects, items, etc.); jumble. [2] to confuse. [3] to make (water) muddy or turbulent. [4] *US* to mix or stir (alcoholic drinks, etc.). ◆ NOUN [5] a state of physical or mental confusion.
▷HISTORY C16: perhaps from Middle Dutch *moddelen* to make muddy
▸'**muddled** ADJECTIVE ▸'**muddledness** *or* '**muddlement** NOUN ▸'**muddling** ADJECTIVE, NOUN ▸'**muddlingly** ADVERB ▸'**muddly** ADJECTIVE

muddle along *or* **on** VERB (*intr, adverb*) to proceed in a disorganized way.

muddleheaded (ˌmʌdᵊl'hɛdɪd) ADJECTIVE mentally confused or vague.
▸ˌ**muddle'headedness** NOUN

muddler ('mʌdlə) NOUN [1] a person who muddles or muddles through. [2] *US* an instrument for mixing drinks thoroughly.

muddle through VERB (*intr, adverb*) *Chiefly Brit* to succeed in some undertaking in spite of lack of organization.

muddy ('mʌdɪ) ADJECTIVE **-dier, -diest.** [1] covered or filled with mud. [2] not clear or bright: *muddy colours.* [3] cloudy: *a muddy liquid.* [4] (esp of thoughts) confused or vague. ◆ VERB **-dies, -dying, -died.** [5] to become or cause to become muddy.
▸'**muddily** ADVERB ▸'**muddiness** NOUN

Mudéjar *Spanish* (mu'ðexar) NOUN, *plural* ***-jares*** (-xares). [1] *Medieval history* a Spanish Moor, esp one permitted to stay in Spain after the Christian reconquest. ◆ ADJECTIVE [2] of or relating to a style of architecture orginated by Mudéjares.
▷HISTORY from Arabic *mudajjan* one permitted to remain

mud fever NOUN another name for **scratches.**

mudfish ('mʌdˌfɪʃ) NOUN, *plural* **-fish** *or* **-fishes**. any of various fishes, such as the bowfin and cichlids, that live at or frequent the muddy bottoms of rivers, lakes, etc.

mud flat NOUN a tract of low muddy land, esp near an estuary, that is covered at high tide and exposed at low tide.

mudflow ('mʌdˌfləʊ) NOUN *Geology* a flow of soil or fine-grained sediment mixed with water down a steep unstable slope.

mud gecko NOUN *Austral* another name for **crocodile.**

mudguard ('mʌdˌgɑ:d) NOUN a curved part of a motorcycle, bicycle, etc., attached above the wheels to reduce the amount of water or mud thrown up by them. US and Canadian name: **fender.**

mud hen NOUN any of various birds that frequent marshes or similar places, esp the coots, rails, etc.

mudir (mu:'dɪə) NOUN a local governor.
▷HISTORY C19: via Turkish, from Arabic, from *adāra* to administrate

mudlark ('mʌdˌlɑ:k) NOUN [1] *Slang, now rare* a street urchin. [2] (formerly) one who made a living by picking up odds and ends in the mud of tidal rivers. [3] *Austral, slang* a racehorse that runs well on a wet or muddy course.

mud map NOUN *Austral informal* a map drawn on the ground with a stick, or any other roughly drawn map.

mudpack ('mʌdˌpæk) NOUN a cosmetic astringent paste containing fuller's earth, used to improve the complexion.

mud pie NOUN a mass of mud moulded into a pie-like shape by a child.

mud puppy NOUN any aquatic North American salamander of the genus *Necturus,* esp *N. maculosus,* having red feathery external gills and other persistent larval features: family *Proteidae.* See also **neoteny.**

mudra (mə'drɑ:) NOUN any of various ritual hand movements in Hindu religious dancing.
▷HISTORY Sanskrit, literally: sign, token

mudskipper ('mʌdˌskɪpə) NOUN any of various gobies of the genus *Periophthalmus* and related genera that occur in tropical coastal regions of Africa and Asia and can move on land by means of their strong pectoral fins.

mudslinging ('mʌdˌslɪŋɪŋ) NOUN casting malicious slurs on an opponent, esp in politics.
▸'**mud,slinger** NOUN

mudstone ('mʌdˌstəʊn) NOUN a dark grey clay rock similar to shale but with the lamination less well developed.

mud turtle NOUN any of various small turtles of the genus *Kinosternon* and related genera that inhabit muddy rivers in North and Central America: family *Kinosternidae.*

mud volcano NOUN a cone-shaped mound formed from fine mud ejected, with gases and water, from hot springs, geysers, etc., in volcanic regions.

muenster ('mʊnstə) NOUN a whitish-yellow semihard whole milk cheese, often flavoured with caraway or aniseed.
▷HISTORY after *Muenster,* Haut-Rhin, France

muesli ('mju:zlɪ) NOUN a mixture of rolled oats, nuts, fruit, etc., eaten with milk.
▷HISTORY Swiss German, from German *Mus* mush, purée + *-li,* diminutive suffix

muesli bar NOUN a snack made of compressed muesli ingredients.

muezzin (mu:'ɛzɪn) NOUN *Islam* the official of a mosque who calls the faithful to prayer five times a day from the minaret.
▷HISTORY C16: changed from Arabic *mu'adhdhin*

muff¹ (mʌf) NOUN [1] an open-ended cylinder of fur or cloth into which the hands are placed for warmth. [2] the tuft on either side of the head of certain fowls.
▷HISTORY C16: probably from Dutch *mof,* ultimately from French *mouffle* MUFFLE¹

muff² (mʌf) VERB [1] to perform (an action) awkwardly. [2] (*tr*) to bungle (a shot, catch, etc.) in a game. ◆ NOUN [3] any unskilful play in a game, esp a dropped catch. [4] any clumsy or bungled action. [5] a bungler.
▷HISTORY C19: of uncertain origin

muffin ('mʌfɪn) NOUN [1] *Brit* a thick round baked yeast roll, usually toasted and served with butter. [2] *US and Canadian* a small cup-shaped sweet bread roll, usually eaten hot with butter.
▷HISTORY C18: perhaps from Low German *muffen,* cakes

muffin man NOUN *Brit* (formerly) an itinerant seller of muffins.

muffle¹ ('mʌfᵊl) VERB (*tr*) [1] (often foll by *up*) to wrap up (the head) in a scarf, cloak, etc., esp for warmth. [2] to deaden (a sound or noise), esp by wrapping. [3] to prevent (the expression of something) by (someone). ◆ NOUN [4] something that muffles. [5] a kiln with an inner chamber for firing porcelain, enamel, etc., at a low temperature.
▷HISTORY C15: probably from Old French; compare Old French *moufle* mitten, *emmouflé* wrapped up

muffle² ('mʌfᵊl) NOUN the fleshy hairless part of the upper lip and nose in ruminants and some rodents.
▷HISTORY C17: from French *mufle,* of unknown origin

muffler ('mʌflə) NOUN [1] a thick scarf, collar, etc. [2] the US and Canadian name for **silencer** (sense 1). [3] something that muffles.

mufti¹ ('mʌftɪ) NOUN, *plural* **-tis.** [1] a Muslim legal expert and adviser on the law of the Koran. [2] (in the former Ottoman empire) the leader of the religious community.
▷HISTORY C16: from Arabic *muftī,* from *aftā* to give a (legal) decision

mufti² ('mʌftɪ) NOUN, *plural* **-tis.** civilian dress, esp as worn by a person who normally wears a military uniform.
▷HISTORY C19: perhaps from MUFTI¹

Mufulira (ˌmu:fu:'lɪərə) NOUN a mining town in the Copper Belt of Zambia. Pop.: 152 944 (1990).

mug¹ (mʌg) NOUN [1] a drinking vessel with a handle, usually cylindrical and made of earthenware. [2] Also called: **mugful.** the quantity held by a mug or its contents.
▷HISTORY C16: probably from Scandinavian; compare Swedish *mugg*

mug² (mʌg) NOUN [1] *Slang* a person's face or mouth: *get your ugly mug out of here!* [2] *Slang* a grimace. [3] *Brit, slang* a gullible person, esp one who is swindled easily. [4] **a mug's game.** a worthless activity. ◆ VERB **mugs, mugging, mugged.** [5] (*tr*) *Informal* to attack or rob (someone) violently. [6] (*intr*) *Brit, slang* to pull faces or overact, esp in front of a camera. ◆ See also **mug up.**
▷HISTORY C18: perhaps from MUG¹, since drinking vessels were sometimes modelled into the likeness of a face

mugga ('mʌɡə) NOUN an Australian eucalyptus tree with dark bark and pink flowers, *Eucalyptus sideroxylon*.
▷**HISTORY** from a native Australian language

mugger[1] ('mʌɡə) NOUN [1] *Informal* a person who commits robbery with violence, esp in the street. [2] *Chiefly US and Canadian* a person who overacts.

mugger[2], **muggar,** *or* **muggur** ('mʌɡə) NOUN a large freshwater crocodile, *Crocodylus niloticus*, inhabiting marshes and pools of India and Ceylon. Also called: **marsh crocodile.**
▷**HISTORY** C19: from Hindi *magar*

muggins ('mʌɡɪnz) NOUN [1] *Brit, slang* **a** a simpleton; silly person. **b** a title used humorously to refer to oneself. [2] a variation on the game of dominoes. [3] a card game.
▷**HISTORY** C19: probably from the surname *Muggins*

muggy ('mʌɡɪ) ADJECTIVE **-gier, -giest.** (of weather, air, etc.) unpleasantly warm and humid.
▷**HISTORY** C18: dialect *mug* drizzle, probably from Scandinavian; compare Old Norse *mugga* mist
▸**'muggily** ADVERB ▸**'mugginess** NOUN

mug punter NOUN *Brit, slang* a customer or client who is gullible and easily swindled.

mug up VERB (*adverb*) *Brit, slang* to study (a subject) hard, esp for an exam.
▷**HISTORY** C19: of unknown origin

mugwort ('mʌɡˌwɜːt) NOUN [1] a N temperate perennial herbaceous plant, *Artemisia vulgaris*, with aromatic leaves and clusters of small greenish-white flowers: family *Asteraceae* (composites). [2] another name for **crosswort.**
▷**HISTORY** Old English *mucgwyrt*, perhaps from Old English *mycg* MIDGE

mugwump ('mʌɡˌwʌmp) NOUN *US* a neutral or independent person, esp in politics.
▷**HISTORY** C19: from Algonquian: great chief, from *mogki* great + *-omp* man
▸**'mugˌwumpery** *or* **'mugˌwumpism** NOUN ▸**'mugˌwumpish** ADJECTIVE

Muhammadan *or* **Muhammedan** (mʊ'hæmədᵊn) NOUN, ADJECTIVE another word (not in Muslim use) for **Muslim.**

Muharram (muː'hærəm) *or* **Moharram** NOUN the first month of the Islamic year.
▷**HISTORY** from Arabic: sacred

Mühlhausen (myːl'hauzən) NOUN the German name for **Mulhouse.**

muir (muːr, mjuːr, myr) NOUN **a** a Scot word for **moor**[1]. **b** (*in place names*): *Sheriffmuir*.

muirburn ('muːrˌbʌrn, 'mjuːr-, 'myr-) NOUN *Scot* a variant of **moorburn.**

Muir Glacier (mjʊə) NOUN a glacier in SE Alaska, in the St Elias Mountains, flowing southeast from Mount Fairweather. Area: about 900 sq. km (350 sq. miles).

mujaheddin, mujahedeen, *or* **mujahideen** (ˈmuːdʒəhəˈdiːn) PLURAL NOUN (preceded by *the; sometimes capital*) (in Afghanistan and Iran) fundamentalist Muslim guerrillas; in Afghanistan in 1992 the mujaheddin overthrew the government but were unable to agree on a constitution due to factional conflict and in 1996 Taliban forces seized power.
▷**HISTORY** C20: from Arabic *mujāhidīn* fighters, ultimately from JIHAD

mujik ('muːʒɪk) NOUN a variant spelling of **muzhik.**

Mukden ('mʊkdən) NOUN a former name of **Shenyang.**

mukluk ('mʌklʌk) NOUN a soft boot, usually of sealskin, worn by Eskimos.
▷**HISTORY** from Eskimo *muklok* large seal

muktuk ('mʌktʌk) NOUN *Canadian* the thin outer skin of the beluga, used as food.
▷**HISTORY** from Inuktitut

mulatto (mjuː'lætəʊ) NOUN, *plural* **-tos** *or* **-toes.** [1] a person having one Black and one White parent. ◆ ADJECTIVE [2] of a light brown colour.
▷**HISTORY** C16: from Spanish *mulato* young mule, variant of *mulo* MULE[1]

mulberry ('mʌlbərɪ, -brɪ) NOUN, *plural* **-ries.** [1] any moraceous tree of the temperate genus *Morus*, having edible blackberry-like fruit, such as *M. alba* (**white mulberry**), the leaves of which are used to feed silkworms. [2] the fruit of any of these trees. [3] any of several similar or related trees, such as the paper mulberry and Indian mulberry. [4] **a** a dark purple colour. **b** (*as adjective*): *a mulberry dress*.
▷**HISTORY** C14: from Latin *mōrum*, from Greek *moron;* related to Old English *mōrberie;* compare Dutch *moerbezie*, Old High German *mūrberi*

Mulberry Harbour NOUN either of two prefabricated floating harbours towed across the English Channel to the French coast for the Allied invasion of Normandy in 1944.
▷**HISTORY** from the code name Operation *Mulberry*

mulch (mʌltʃ) NOUN [1] half-rotten vegetable matter, peat, etc., used to prevent soil erosion or enrich the soil. ◆ VERB [2] (*tr*) to cover (the surface of land) with mulch.
▷**HISTORY** C17: from obsolete *mulch* soft; related to Old English *mylisc* mellow; compare dialect German *molsch* soft, Latin *mollis* soft

Mulciber ('mʌlsɪbə) NOUN another name for **Vulcan**[1].

mulct (mʌlkt) VERB (*tr*) [1] to cheat or defraud. [2] to fine (a person). ◆ NOUN [3] a fine or penalty.
▷**HISTORY** C15: via French from Latin *multa* a fine

mule[1] (mjuːl) NOUN [1] the sterile offspring of a male donkey and a female horse, used as a beast of burden. Compare **hinny**[1]. [2] any hybrid animal: *a mule canary*. [3] Also called: **spinning mule.** a machine invented by Samuel Crompton that spins cotton into yarn and winds the yarn on spindles. [4] *Informal* an obstinate or stubborn person. [5] *Slang* a person who is paid to transport illegal drugs for a dealer.
▷**HISTORY** C13: from Old French *mul*, from Latin *mūlus* ass, mule

mule[2] (mjuːl) NOUN a backless shoe or slipper.
▷**HISTORY** C16: from Old French from Latin *mulleus* a magistrate's shoe

mule deer NOUN a W North American deer, *Odocoileus hemionus*, with long ears and a black-tipped tail.

mules (mjuːlz) VERB (*tr*) *Austral* to perform the Mules operation on (a sheep).

mule skinner NOUN *US and Canadian* an informal term for **muleteer.**

Mules operation (mjuːlz) NOUN *Austral* the surgical removal of folds of skin in the breech of a sheep to reduce blowfly strike.
▷**HISTORY** named after J. H. W. *Mules* (died 1946), Australian grazier who first suggested it

muleta (mjuː'lɛtə) NOUN the small cape attached to a stick used by the matador during the final stages of a bullfight.
▷**HISTORY** Spanish: small mule, crutch, from *mula* MULE[1]

muleteer (ˌmjuːlɪ'tɪə) NOUN a person who drives mules.

muley ('mjuːlɪ) *or* **mulley** ('mʌlɪ) ADJECTIVE [1] (of cattle) having no horns. ◆ NOUN [2] any hornless cow.
▷**HISTORY** C16: variant of dialect *moiley*, from Gaelic *maol*, Welsh *moel* bald

mulga ('mʌlɡə) NOUN *Austral* [1] any of various Australian acacia shrubs, esp *Acacia aneura*, which grows in the central desert regions and has leaflike leafstalks. [2] scrub comprised of a dense growth of acacia. [3] the outback; bush.
▷**HISTORY** from a native Australian language

Mulhacén (*Spanish* mula'θen) NOUN a mountain in S Spain, in the Sierra Nevada: the highest peak in Spain Height: 3478 m (11 410 ft.).

Mülheim an der Ruhr (*German* 'myːlhaim an der 'ruːr) *or* **Mülheim** NOUN an industrial city in W Germany, in North Rhine-Westphalia on the River Ruhr: river port. Pop.: 174 300 (1999 est.).

Mulhouse (*French* myluz) NOUN a city in E France, on the Rhône-Rhine canal: under German rule (1871–1918); textiles. Pop.: 110 359 (1999). German name: **Mühlhausen.**

muliebrity (ˌmjuːlɪ'ɛbrɪtɪ) NOUN [1] the condition of being a woman. [2] femininity.
▷**HISTORY** C16: via Late Latin from Latin *muliēbris* womanly, from *mulier* woman

mulish ('mjuːlɪʃ) ADJECTIVE stubborn; obstinate; headstrong.
▸**'mulishly** ADVERB ▸**'mulishness** NOUN

Mulki ('mʊlkɪ) NOUN a native or inhabitant of the former Hyderabad State in India.
▷**HISTORY** Urdu, from *mulk* country

mull[1] (mʌl) VERB (*tr; often foll by over*) to study or ponder.
▷**HISTORY** C19: probably from MUDDLE

mull[2] (mʌl) VERB (*tr*) to heat (wine, ale, etc.) with sugar and spices to make a hot drink.
▷**HISTORY** C17: of unknown origin

mull[3] (mʌl) NOUN a light muslin fabric of soft texture.
▷**HISTORY** C18: earlier *mulmull*, from Hindi *malmal*

mull[4] (mʌl) NOUN a layer of nonacidic humus formed in well drained and aerated soils. Compare **mor.**
▷**HISTORY** C20: from Danish *muld;* see MOULD[3]

mull[5] (mʌl) NOUN *Scot* a promontory.
▷**HISTORY** C14: related to Gaelic *maol*, Icelandic *múli*

Mull (mʌl) NOUN a mountainous island off the west coast of Scotland, in the Inner Hebrides, separated from the mainland by the **Sound of Mull.** Chief town: Tobermory. Pop.: 2605 (latest est.). Area: 909 sq. km (351 sq. miles).

mullah, mulla ('mʌlə, 'mʊlə), *or* **mollah** ('mɒlə) NOUN (formerly) a Muslim scholar, teacher, or religious leader: also used as a title of respect.
▷**HISTORY** C17: from Turkish *molla*, Persian and Hindi *mulla*, from Arabic *mawlā* master

mullein *or* **mullen** ('mʌlɪn) NOUN any of various European herbaceous plants of the scrophulariaceous genus *Verbascum*, such as *V. thapsus* (**common mullein** or **Aaron's rod**), typically having tall spikes of yellow flowers and broad hairy leaves.
▷**HISTORY** C15: from Old French *moleine*, probably from Old French *mol* soft, from Latin *mollis*

muller ('mʌlə) NOUN a flat heavy implement of stone or iron used to grind material against a slab of stone.
▷**HISTORY** C15: probably from *mullen* to grind to powder; compare Old English *myl* dust

mullered ('mʌləd) ADJECTIVE *Slang* [1] drunk. [2] heavily defeated; trounced.
▷**HISTORY** C20: of unknown origin

Müllerian mimicry (muː'lɪərɪən) NOUN *Zoology* mimicry in which two or more harmful or inedible species resemble each other, so that predators tend to avoid them.
▷**HISTORY** C19: named after J.F.T. *Müller* (1821–97), German zoologist who first described it

Müller-Lyer illusion ('muːlə'laɪə) NOUN an optical illusion in which a line with inward pointing arrowheads is seen as longer than an equal line with outward pointing arrowheads.
▷**HISTORY** C19: named after Franz *Müller-Lyer* (1857–1916), German sociologist and psychiatrist

mullet[1] ('mʌlɪt) NOUN [1] any of various teleost food fishes belonging to the families *Mugilidae* (see **grey mullet**) or *Mullidae* (see **red mullet**). [2] the US name for **grey mullet.**
▷**HISTORY** C15: via Old French from Latin *mullus*, from Greek *mullos*

mullet[2] ('mʌlɪt) NOUN a hairstyle in which the hair is short at the top and long at the back.
▷**HISTORY** C20: origin unknown

mulley ('mʌlɪ) ADJECTIVE, NOUN a variant of **muley.**

mulligan ('mʌlɪɡən) NOUN *US and Canadian* a stew made from odds and ends of food.
▷**HISTORY** C20: perhaps from the surname

mulligatawny (ˌmʌlɪɡə'tɔːnɪ) NOUN a curry-flavoured soup of Anglo-Indian origin, made with meat stock.
▷**HISTORY** C18: from Tamil *milakutanni*, from *milaku* pepper + *tanni* water

Mullingar (ˌmʌlɪn'ɡɑː) NOUN a town in N central Republic of Ireland, the county town of Co. Westmeath; site of cathedral; cattle raised. Pop.: 11 800 (1995 est.).

mullion ('mʌlɪən) NOUN [1] a vertical member between the casements or panes of a window or the panels of a screen. [2] one of the ribs on a rock face. ◆ VERB [3] (*tr*) to furnish (a window, screen, etc.) with mullions.
▷**HISTORY** C16: variant of Middle English *munial*, from Old French *moinel*, of unknown origin

mullite ('mʌlaɪt) NOUN a colourless mineral consisting of aluminium silicate in orthorhombic crystalline form: used as a refractory. Formula: $Al_6Si_2O_{13}$.

▷HISTORY from island of MULL

mullock ('mʌlək) NOUN [1] *Austral* waste material from a mine. [2] *Dialect* a mess or muddle. [3] **poke mullock at.** *Austral informal* to ridicule.
▷HISTORY C14: related to Old English *myl* dust, Old Norse *mylja* to crush; see MULLER
▸ **'mullocky** ADJECTIVE

mulloway ('mʌlə,weɪ) NOUN a large Australian marine sciaenid fish, *Sciaena antarctica,* valued for sport and food.
▷HISTORY C19: of unknown origin

Multan (,mʊl'tɑ:n) NOUN a city in central Pakistan, near the Chenab River. Pop.: 1 182 441 (1998 est.).

multangular (mʌl'tæŋgjʊlə) *or* **multiangular** ADJECTIVE having many angles.

multeity (mʌl'ti:ɪtɪ) NOUN manifoldness.
▷HISTORY C19: from Latin *multus* many, perhaps formed by analogy with HAECCEITY

multi- COMBINING FORM [1] many or much: *multiflorous; multimillion.* [2] more than one: *multiparous; multistorey.*
▷HISTORY from Latin *multus* much, many

multiaccess (,mʌltɪ'ækses) NOUN *Computing* a system in which several users are permitted to have apparently simultaneous access to a computer.

multichannel analyser (,mʌltɪ'tʃænᵊl) NOUN an electronic instrument, such as a pulse height analyser, that splits an input waveform into a large number of channels in accordance with a particular parameter of the input.

multicide ('mʌltɪ,saɪd) NOUN mass murder.

multicollinearity (,mʌltɪkəʊ,lɪnɪ'ærɪtɪ) NOUN *Statistics* the condition occurring when two or more of the independent variables in a regression equation are correlated.

multicoloured ('mʌltɪ,kʌləd) ADJECTIVE having many colours.

multicultural (,mʌltɪ'kʌltʃərəl) ADJECTIVE consisting of, relating to, or designed for the cultures of several different races.

multiculturalism (,mʌltɪ'kʌltʃərə,lɪzəm) NOUN [1] the state or condition of being multicultural. [2] the policy of maintaining a diversity of ethnic cultures within a community.

multidisciplinary (,mʌltɪ'dɪsɪ,plɪnərɪ) ADJECTIVE of or relating to the study of one topic, involving several subject disciplines.

multiethnic (,mʌltɪ'ɛθnɪk) ADJECTIVE consisting of, relating to, or designed for various different races.

multifaceted (,mʌltɪ'fæsɪtɪd) ADJECTIVE [1] (of a gem) having many facets. [2] having many aspects, abilities, etc.

multifactorial (,mʌltɪfæk'tɔ:rɪəl) ADJECTIVE [1] *Genetics* of or designating inheritance that depends on more than one gene. [2] involving or including a number of elements or factors.

multifarious (,mʌltɪ'fɛərɪəs) ADJECTIVE having many parts of great variety.
▷HISTORY C16: from Late Latin *multifārius* manifold, from Latin *multifāriam* on many sides
▸ **,multi'fariously** ADVERB ▸ **,multi'fariousness** NOUN

multifid ('mʌltɪfɪd) *or* **multifidous** (mʌl'tɪfɪdəs) ADJECTIVE having or divided into many lobes or similar segments: *a multifid leaf.*
▷HISTORY C18: from Latin *multifidus,* from *multus* many + *findere* to split
▸ **'multifidly** ADVERB

multiflora rose (,mʌltɪ'flɔ:rə) NOUN an Asian climbing shrubby rose, *Rosa multiflora,* having clusters of small fragrant flowers: the source of many cultivated roses.

multifoil ('mʌltɪ,fɔɪl) NOUN an ornamental design having a large number of foils. See also **trefoil** (sense 4), **quatrefoil** (sense 2), **cinquefoil** (sense 2).

multifold ('mʌltɪ,fəʊld) ADJECTIVE many times doubled; manifold.

multifoliate (,mʌltɪ'fəʊlɪɪt, -,eɪt) ADJECTIVE *Botany* having many leaves or leaflets: *a multifoliate compound leaf.*

multiform ('mʌltɪ,fɔ:m) ADJECTIVE having many forms or kinds.
▸ **multiformity** (,mʌltɪ'fɔ:mɪtɪ) NOUN

multifunctional (,mʌltɪ'fʌŋkʃənᵊl) *or* **multifunction** ('mʌltɪ,fʌŋkʃən) ADJECTIVE having or able to perform many functions.

multigravida (,mʌltɪ'grævɪdə) NOUN a woman who is pregnant for at least the third time. Compare **multipara.**
▷HISTORY C20: New Latin; see MULTI-, GRAVID

multigym ('mʌltɪ,dʒɪm) NOUN an exercise apparatus incorporating a variety of weights, used for toning the muscles.

multihull ('mʌltɪ,hʌl) NOUN a sailing vessel with two or more hulls. Compare **monohull.**

multilateral (,mʌltɪ'lætərəl, -'lætrəl) ADJECTIVE [1] of or involving more than two nations or parties: *a multilateral pact.* [2] having many sides.
▸ **,multi'laterally** ADVERB

multilingual (,mʌltɪ'lɪŋgwəl) ADJECTIVE [1] able to speak more than two languages. [2] written or expressed in more than two languages. Compare **bilingual, monolingual.**

multimedia (,mʌltɪ'mi:dɪə) PLURAL NOUN [1] the combined use of media such as television, slides, etc., esp in education. ◆ ADJECTIVE [2] of or relating to the use of a combination of media: *multimedia teaching aids.* [3] *Computing* of or relating to any of various systems which can manipulate data in a variety of forms, such as sound, graphics, or text.

multimeter ('mʌltɪ,mi:tə) NOUN an electrical test instrument offering measurement of several values, usually voltage, current, and resistance.

multimillionaire (,mʌltɪ,mɪljə'nɛə) NOUN a person with a fortune of several million pounds, dollars, etc.

multinational (,mʌltɪ'næʃənᵊl) ADJECTIVE [1] (of a large business company) operating in several countries. ◆ NOUN [2] such a company.

multinomial (,mʌltɪ'nəʊmɪəl) NOUN another name for **polynomial** (sense 2b).
▷HISTORY C17: from MULTI- + *-nomial* as in BINOMIAL

multinuclear (,mʌltɪ'nju:klɪə) *or* **multinucleate** (,mʌltɪ'nju:klɪɪt, -,eɪt) ADJECTIVE (of a cell, microorganism, etc.) having two or more nuclei.

multipack ('mʌltɪ,pæk) NOUN a form of packaging of foodstuffs, etc., that contains several units and is offered at a price below that of the equivalent number of units.

multipara (mʌl'tɪpərə) NOUN, *plural* **-rae** (-,ri:). a woman who has given birth to more than one viable fetus or living child. Compare **multigravida.**
▷HISTORY C19: New Latin, feminine of *multiparus* MULTIPAROUS

multiparous (mʌl'tɪpərəs) ADJECTIVE [1] (of certain species of mammal) producing many offspring at one birth. [2] of, relating to, or designating a multipara.
▷HISTORY C17: from New Latin *multiparus*
▸ **multiparity** (,mʌltɪ'pærɪtɪ) NOUN

multipartite (,mʌltɪ'pɑ:taɪt) ADJECTIVE [1] divided into many parts or sections. [2] *Government* a less common word for **multilateral.**

multi-part stationery NOUN *Computing* continuous stationery comprising two or more sheets, either carbonless or with carbon paper between the sheets.

multiparty (,mʌltɪ'pɑ:tɪ) ADJECTIVE of or relating to a state, political system, etc., in which more than one political party is permitted: *multiparty democracy.*

multipath ('mʌltɪ,pɑ:θ) ADJECTIVE relating to television or radio signals that travel by more than one route from a transmitter and arrive at slightly different times, causing ghost images or audio distortion.

multiped ('mʌltɪ,pɛd) *or* **multipede** ('mʌltɪ,pi:d) *Rare* ◆ ADJECTIVE [1] having many feet. ◆ NOUN [2] an insect or animal having many feet.
▷HISTORY C17: from Latin *multipēs*

multiphase ('mʌltɪ,feɪz) ADJECTIVE another word for **polyphase** (sense 1).

multiplane ('mʌltɪ,pleɪn) NOUN an aircraft that has more than one pair of wings. Compare **monoplane.**

multiple ('mʌltɪpᵊl) ADJECTIVE [1] having or involving more than one part, individual, etc. [2] *Electronics, US and Canadian* (of a circuit) having a number of conductors in parallel. ◆ NOUN [3] the product of a given number or polynomial and any other one: *6 is a multiple of 2.* [4] *Telephony* an electrical circuit accessible at a number of points to any one of which a connection can be made. [5] short for **multiple store.**
▷HISTORY C17: via French from Late Latin *multiplus,* from Latin MULTIPLEX
▸ **'multiply** ADVERB

multiple alleles PLURAL NOUN three or more alternative forms of a particular gene existing in a population.
▸ **multiple allelism** NOUN

multiple-choice ADJECTIVE having a number of possible given answers out of which the correct one must be chosen.

multiple factors PLURAL NOUN *Genetics* two or more genes that act as a unit, producing cumulative effects in the phenotype.

multiple fission NOUN *Zoology* asexual reproduction in unicellular organisms, esp sporozoans, in which the nucleus divides a number of times, followed by division of the cytoplasm, to form daughter cells.

multiple fruit NOUN a fruit, such as a pineapple, formed from the ovaries of individual flowers in an inflorescence.

multiple personality NOUN *Psychiatry* a mental disorder in which an individual's personality appears to have become separated into two or more distinct personalities, each with its own complex organization. Nontechnical name: **split personality.**

multiplepoinding (,mʌltɪpᵊl'pɪndɪŋ) NOUN *Scots law* an action to determine the division of a property or fund between several claimants, brought by or on behalf of the present holder.

multiple sclerosis NOUN a chronic progressive disease of the central nervous system characterized by loss of some of the myelin sheath surrounding certain nerve fibres and resulting in speech and visual disorders, tremor, muscular incoordination, partial paralysis, etc. Also called: **disseminated sclerosis.**

multiple star NOUN a system of three or more stars associated by gravitation. See also **binary star.**

multiple store NOUN one of several retail enterprises under the same ownership and management. Also called: **multiple shop.**

multiplet ('mʌltɪ,plɛt, -plɪt) NOUN *Physics* [1] a set of closely spaced lines in a spectrum, resulting from small differences between the energy levels of atoms or molecules. [2] a group of related elementary particles that differ only in electric charge.
▷HISTORY from MULTIPLE; on the model of DOUBLET

multiple voting NOUN the practice of voting in more than one constituency in the same election.

multiplex ('mʌltɪ,plɛks) NOUN [1] *Telecomm* **a** the use of a common communications channel for sending two or more messages or signals. In **frequency-division multiplex** the frequency band transmitted by the common channel is split into narrower bands each of which constitutes a distinct channel. In **time-division multiplex** different channels are established by intermittent connections to the common channel. **b** (*as modifier*): *a multiplex transmitter.* [2] **a** a purpose-built complex containing a number of cinemas and usually a restaurant or bar. **b** (*as modifier*): *a multiplex cinema.* ◆ ADJECTIVE [3] designating a method of map-making using three cameras to produce a stereoscopic effect. [4] a less common word for **multiple.** ◆ VERB [5] to send (messages or signals) or (of messages or signals) be sent by multiplex.
▷HISTORY C16: from Latin: having many folds, from MULTI- + *plicāre* to fold
▸ **'multi,plexer** NOUN

multiplicand (,mʌltɪplɪ'kænd) NOUN a number to be multiplied by another number, the **multiplier.**
▷HISTORY C16: from Latin *multiplicandus,* gerund of *multiplicāre* to MULTIPLY

multiplicate ('mʌltɪplɪ,keɪt) ADJECTIVE *Rare* manifold.

multiplication (,mʌltɪplɪ'keɪʃən) NOUN [1] an arithmetical operation, defined initially in terms of repeated addition, usually written $a \times b$, $a.b$, or ab, by which the product of two quantities is calculated: to multiply a by positive integral b is to add a to itself b times. Multiplication by fractions can then be defined in the light of the associative

and commutative properties; multiplication by $1/n$ is equivalent to multiplication by 1 followed by division by n: for example $0.3 \times 0.7 = 0.3 \times 7/10 = (0.3 \times 7)/10 = 2.1/10 = 0.21$. [2] the act of multiplying or state of being multiplied. [3] the act or process in animals, plants, or people of reproducing or breeding.
▸ **ˌmultipliˈcational** ADJECTIVE

multiplication sign NOUN the symbol ×, placed between numbers to be multiplied, as in $3 \times 4 \times 5 = 60$.

multiplication table NOUN one of a group of tables giving the results of multiplying two numbers together.

multiplicative (ˈmʌltɪplɪˌkeɪtɪv, ˌmʌltɪˈplɪkətɪv) ADJECTIVE [1] tending or able to multiply. [2] *Maths* involving multiplication.
▸ **ˈmultipliˌcatively** ADVERB

multiplicity (ˌmʌltɪˈplɪsɪtɪ) NOUN, *plural* **-ties**. [1] a large number or great variety. [2] the state of being multiple. [3] *Physics* **a** the number of levels into which the energy of an atom, molecule, or nucleus splits as a result of coupling between orbital angular momentum and spin angular momentum. **b** the number of elementary particles in a multiplet.

multiplier (ˈmʌltɪˌplaɪə) NOUN [1] a person or thing that multiplies. [2] the number by which another number, the **multiplicand** is multiplied. [3] *Physics* any device or instrument, such as a photomultiplier, for increasing an effect. [4] *Economics* **a** the ratio of the total change in income resulting from successive rounds of spending) to an initial autonomous change in expenditure. **b** (*as modifier*): *multiplier effects.*

multiply (ˈmʌltɪˌplaɪ) VERB **-plies, -plying, -plied.** [1] to increase or cause to increase in number, quantity, or degree. [2] (*tr*) to combine (two numbers or quantities) by multiplication. [3] (*intr*) to increase in number by reproduction.
▹ **HISTORY** C13: from Old French *multiplier,* from Latin *multiplicāre* to multiply, from *multus* much, many + *plicāre* to fold
▸ **ˈmultiˌpliable** *or* **ˈmultiˌplicable** ADJECTIVE

multiprocessor (ˌmʌltɪˈprəʊsesə) NOUN *Computing* a number of central processing units linked together to enable parallel processing to take place.

multiprogramming (ˌmʌltɪˈprəʊgræmɪŋ) NOUN a time-sharing technique by which several computer programs are each run for a short period in rotation.

multipurpose (ˌmʌltɪˈpɜːpəs) ADJECTIVE able to be used for many purposes: *a multipurpose gadget.*

multipurpose vehicle NOUN a large car, similar to a van, designed to carry up to eight passengers. Abbreviation: **MPV.**

multiracial (ˌmʌltɪˈreɪʃəl) ADJECTIVE comprising people of many races.
▸ **ˌmultiˈracialism** NOUN

multirole (ˈmʌltɪˌrəʊl) ADJECTIVE having a number of roles, functions, etc.

multiseriate (ˌmʌltɪˈsɪərɪeɪt) ADJECTIVE *Botany* arranged in rows or composed of more than one cell layer.

multiskilling (ˈmʌltɪˌskɪlɪŋ) NOUN the practice of training employees to do a number of different tasks.

multistage (ˈmʌltɪˌsteɪdʒ) ADJECTIVE [1] (of a rocket or missile) having several stages, each of which can be jettisoned after it has burnt out. [2] (of a turbine, compressor, or supercharger) having more than one rotor. [3] (of any process or device) having more than one stage.

multistorey (ˌmʌltɪˈstɔːrɪ) ADJECTIVE [1] (of a building) having many storeys. ◆ NOUN [2] a multistorey car park.

multitask (ˈmʌltɪˌtɑːsk) VERB (*intr*) to work at several different tasks simultaneously.

multitasking (ˈmʌltɪˌtɑːskɪŋ) NOUN [1] *Computing* the execution of various diverse tasks simultaneously. [2] the carrying out of two or more tasks at the same time by one person.

multitrack (ˈmʌltɪˌtræk) ADJECTIVE (in sound recording) using tape containing two or more tracks, usually four to twenty-four.

multitude (ˈmʌltɪˌtjuːd) NOUN [1] a large gathering of people. [2] **the.** the common people. [3] a large number. [4] the state or quality of being numerous.
▹ **HISTORY** C14: via Old French from Latin *multitūdō*

multitudinous (ˌmʌltɪˈtjuːdɪnəs) ADJECTIVE [1] very numerous. [2] *Rare* great in extent, variety, etc. [3] *Poetic* crowded.
▸ **ˌmultiˈtudinously** ADVERB ▸ **ˌmultiˈtudinousness** NOUN

multi-user ADJECTIVE (of a computer) capable of being used by several people at once.

multi-utility NOUN, *plural* **-ties.** a public utility that provides more than one essential service, such as supplying both gas and electricity.

multivalent (ˌmʌltɪˈveɪlənt) ADJECTIVE another word for **polyvalent.**
▸ **ˌmultiˈvalency** NOUN

multivariate (ˌmʌltɪˈvɛərɪɪt) ADJECTIVE *Statistics* (of a distribution) involving a number of distinct, though not usually independent, random variables.

multiversity (ˌmʌltɪˈvɜːsɪtɪ) NOUN *Chiefly US and Canadian* a university with many constituent and affiliated institutions.
▹ **HISTORY** C20: MULTI- + UNIVERSITY

multivibrator (ˌmʌltɪvaɪˈbreɪtə) NOUN an electronic oscillator consisting of two transistors or other electronic devices, coupled so that the input of each is derived from the output of the other.

multivocal (ˌmʌltɪˈvəʊkəl) ADJECTIVE having many meanings.
▹ **HISTORY** C19: from Latin *multus* many + *vocare* to call; on the model of EQUIVOCAL

multiwindow (ˌmʌltɪˈwɪndəʊ) NOUN a visual display unit screen that can be divided to show a number of different documents simultaneously.

multum in parvo (ˈmʊltʊm ɪn ˈpɑːvəʊ) much in a small space.
▹ **HISTORY** Latin

multure (ˈmʌltʃə) NOUN *Scot* [1] a fee formerly paid to a miller for grinding grain. [2] the right to receive such a fee.
▹ **HISTORY** C13: from Old French *moulture,* from Medieval Latin *molitūra* a grinding, from Latin *molere*

mum[1] (mʌm) NOUN *Chiefly Brit* an informal word for **mother**[1].
▹ **HISTORY** C19: a child's word

mum[2] (mʌm) ADJECTIVE [1] keeping information to oneself; silent. ◆ NOUN [2] **mum's the word.** silence or secrecy is to be observed.
▹ **HISTORY** C14: suggestive of closed lips

mum[3] *or* **mumm** (mʌm) VERB **mums, mumming, mummed.** (*intr*) to act in a mummer's play.
▹ **HISTORY** C16: verbal use of MUM[2]

mum[4] (mʌm) NOUN *Brit, obsolete* a type of beer made from cereals, beans, etc.
▹ **HISTORY** C17: from German *Mumme,* perhaps from the name of its original brewer

Mumbai (mʊmˈbaɪ) NOUN the Hindi name for **Bombay.**

mumble (ˈmʌmbəl) VERB [1] to utter indistinctly, as with the mouth partly closed; mutter. [2] *Rare* to chew (food) ineffectually or with difficulty. ◆ NOUN [3] an indistinct or low utterance or sound.
▹ **HISTORY** C14 *momelen,* from MUM[2]
▸ **ˈmumbler** NOUN ▸ **ˈmumbling** ADJECTIVE ▸ **ˈmumblingly** ADVERB

mumbletypeg (ˈmʌmbəltɪˌpɛg) NOUN *US* a game in which players throw a knife in various prescribed ways, the aim being to make the blade stick in the ground.
▹ **HISTORY** C17: from *mumble the peg,* a loser in the game being required to pull the knife out of the ground using the teeth

mumbo jumbo (ˈmʌmbəʊ) NOUN, *plural* **mumbo jumbos.** [1] foolish religious reverence, ritual, or incantation. [2] meaningless or unnecessarily complicated language. [3] an object of superstitious awe or reverence.
▹ **HISTORY** C18: probably from Mandingo *mama dyumbo,* name of a tribal god

mumchance (ˈmʌmˌtʃɑːns) ADJECTIVE silent; struck dumb.
▹ **HISTORY** C16 (masquerade, dumb show): from Middle Low German *mummenschanze* masked serenade; from *mummen* (see MUMMER) + *schanze* CHANCE

mu meson (mjuː) NOUN a former name for **muon.**

mummer (ˈmʌmə) NOUN [1] one of a group of masked performers in folk play or mime. [2] a mime artist. [3] *Humorous or derogatory* an actor.
▹ **HISTORY** C15: from Old French *momeur,* from *momer* to mime; related to *momon* mask

Mummerset (ˈmʌməsɪt, -ˌsɛt) NOUN an imitation West Country accent used in drama.
▹ **HISTORY** C20: from MUMMER + (SOMER)SET

mummery (ˈmʌmərɪ) NOUN, *plural* **-meries.** [1] a performance by mummers. [2] hypocritical or ostentatious ceremony.

mummify (ˈmʌmɪˌfaɪ) VERB **-fies, -fying, -fied.** [1] (*tr*) to preserve the body of (a human or animal) as a mummy. [2] (*intr*) to dry up; shrivel. [3] (*tr*) to preserve (an outdated idea, institution, etc.) while making lifeless.
▸ **ˌmummifiˈcation** NOUN

mummy[1] (ˈmʌmɪ) NOUN, *plural* **-mies.** [1] an embalmed or preserved body, esp as prepared for burial in ancient Egypt. [2] *Obsolete* the substance of such a body used medicinally. [3] a mass of pulp. [4] a dark brown pigment.
▹ **HISTORY** C14: from Old French *momie,* from Medieval Latin *mumia,* from Arabic *mūmiyah* asphalt, from Persian *mūm* wax

mummy[2] (ˈmʌmɪ) NOUN, *plural* **-mies.** *Chiefly Brit* a child's word for **mother.**
▹ **HISTORY** C19: variant of MUM[1]

mump[1] (mʌmp) VERB (*intr*) *Archaic* to be silent.
▹ **HISTORY** C16 (to grimace, sulk, be silent): of imitative origin, alluding to the shape of the mouth when mumbling or chewing

mump[2] (mʌmp) VERB (*intr*) *Archaic* to beg.
▹ **HISTORY** C17: perhaps from Dutch *mompen* to cheat

mumps (mʌmps) NOUN (*functioning as singular or plural*) an acute contagious viral disease of the parotid salivary glands, characterized by swelling of the affected parts, fever, and pain beneath the ear: usually affects children. Also called: **epidemic parotitis.**
▹ **HISTORY** C16: from MUMP[1] (to grimace)
▸ **ˈmumpish** ADJECTIVE

mumsy (ˈmʌmzɪ) ADJECTIVE **-sier, -siest.** out of fashion; homely or drab.

munch (mʌntʃ) VERB to chew (food) steadily, esp with a crunching noise.
▹ **HISTORY** C14 *monche,* of imitative origin; compare CRUNCH
▸ **ˈmuncher** NOUN

Munchausen (*German* ˈmynçhauzən) NOUN [1] an exaggerated story. [2] a person who tells such a story.
▹ **HISTORY** C19: after Baron *Münchhausen,* subject of a series of exaggerated adventure tales written in English by R. E. Raspe (1737–94)

Munchausen's syndrome NOUN a mental disorder in which a patient feigns illness to obtain hospital treatment.

Munchausen's syndrome by proxy *or* **Munchausen by proxy** NOUN a mental disorder in which an individual derives emotional satisfaction from inflicting injury on others and then subjecting them to medical treatment.

München (ˈmynçən) NOUN the German name for **Munich.**

München-Gladbach (mynçənˈglatbax) NOUN the former name of **Mönchengladbach.**

munchies (ˈmʌntʃɪz) PLURAL NOUN *Slang* [1] **the.** a craving for food, induced by alcohol or drugs. [2] snacks or food collectively.

munchkin (ˈmʌntʃkɪn) NOUN [1] *Informal, chiefly US* an undersized person or a child, esp an appealing one. [2] a breed of medium-sized cat with short legs.
▹ **HISTORY** C20: from the *Munchkins,* a dwarfish race of people in L. Frank Baum's *The Wonderful Wizard of Oz* (1900)

Munda (ˈmʊndə) NOUN [1] a family of languages spoken by scattered peoples throughout central India. [2] (*plural* **-das**) a member of any of these peoples.

mundane (ˈmʌndeɪn, mʌnˈdeɪn) ADJECTIVE [1] everyday, ordinary, or banal. [2] relating to the world or worldly matters.
▹ **HISTORY** C15: from French *mondain,* via Late Latin, from Latin *mundus* world

▶'**mundanely** ADVERB ▶**mun'danity** *or* '**mundaneness** NOUN

munga ('mʌŋgə) NOUN *NZ informal* an army canteen.
▷**HISTORY** C20: perhaps from French *manger* to eat or from Maori *manga* food remains

mung bean (mʌŋ) NOUN [1] an E Asian bean plant, *Phaseolus aureus,* grown for forage and as the source of bean sprouts used in oriental cookery. [2] the seed of this plant.
▷**HISTORY** C20 *mung,* changed from *mungo,* from Tamil *mūngu,* ultimately from Sanskrit *mudga*

mungo ('mʌŋgəʊ), **mongo,** *or* **mongoe** NOUN, *plural* **-gos** *or* **-goes.** a cheap felted fabric made from waste wool.
▷**HISTORY** C19: of unknown origin

Munich ('mju:nɪk) NOUN a city in SW Germany, capital of the state of Bavaria, on the Isar River: became capital of Bavaria in 1508; headquarters of the Nazi movement in the 1920s; a major financial, commercial, and manufacturing centre. Pop.: 1 193 600 (1999 est.). German name: **München.**

Munich Pact *or* **Agreement** NOUN the pact signed by Germany, the United Kingdom, France, and Italy on Sept. 29, 1938, to settle the crisis over Czechoslovakia, by which the Sudetenland was ceded to Germany.

municipal (mju:'nɪsɪpᵊl) ADJECTIVE of or relating to a town, city, or borough or its local government.
▷**HISTORY** C16: from Latin *mūnicipium* a free town, from *mūniceps* citizen from *mūnia* responsibilities + *capere* to take
▶**mu'nicipalism** NOUN ▶**mu'nicipalist** NOUN ▶**mu'nicipally** ADVERB

municipality (mju:ˌnɪsɪ'pælɪtɪ) NOUN, *plural* **-ties.** [1] a city, town, or district enjoying some degree of local self-government. [2] the governing body of such a unit.

municipalize *or* **municipalise** (mju:'nɪsɪpəˌlaɪz) VERB *(tr)* [1] to bring under municipal ownership or control. [2] to make a municipality of.
▶**muˌnicipali'zation** *or* **muˌnicipali'sation** NOUN

munificent (mju:'nɪfɪsənt) ADJECTIVE [1] (of a person) very generous; bountiful. [2] (of a gift) generous; liberal.
▷**HISTORY** C16: back formation from Latin *mūnificentia* liberality, from *mūnificus,* from *mūnus* gift + *facere* to make
▶**mu'nificence** *or* **mu'nificentness** NOUN ▶**mu'nificently** ADVERB

muniment ('mju:nɪmənt) NOUN *Rare* a means of defence.
▷**HISTORY** C15: via Old French, from Latin *mūnīre* to defend

muniments ('mju:nɪmənts) PLURAL NOUN [1] *Law* the title deeds and other documentary evidence relating to the title to land. [2] *Archaic* furnishings or supplies.

munition (mju:'nɪʃən) VERB *(tr)* to supply with munitions.
▷**HISTORY** C16: via French from Latin *mūnītiō* fortification, from *mūnīre* to fortify. See AMMUNITION
▶**mu'nitioner** NOUN

munitions (mju:'nɪʃənz) PLURAL NOUN *(sometimes singular)* military equipment and stores, esp ammunition.

munnion ('mʌnjən) NOUN an archaic word for **mullion.**
▷**HISTORY** C16: from *monial* mullion

Munro (mʌn'rəʊ) NOUN, *plural* **Munros.** *Mountaineering* any separate mountain peak over 3000 feet high: originally used of Scotland only but now sometimes extended to other parts of the British Isles.
▷**HISTORY** C20: named after Hugh Thomas *Munro* (1856–1919), who published a list of these in 1891

Munsell scale ('mʌnsᵊl) NOUN a standard chromaticity scale used in specifying colour. It gives approximately equal changes in visual hue.
▷**HISTORY** C20: named after A. H. *Munsell* (1858–1918), US inventor

münster ('mynstə) NOUN a variant of **muenster.**

Munster ('mʌnstə) NOUN a province of SW Republic of Ireland: the largest of the four provinces and historically a kingdom; consists of the counties of Clare, Cork, Kerry, Limerick, Tipperary, and Waterford. Capital: Cork. Pop.: 1 033 903 (1996). Area: 24 125 sq. km (9315 sq. miles).

Münster (*German* 'mynstər) NOUN a city in NW Germany, in North Rhine-Westphalia on the Dortmund-Ems Canal: one of the treaties comprising the Peace of Westphalia (1648) was signed here; became capital of Prussian Westphalia in 1815. Pop.: 264 700 (1999 est.).

munt (munt) NOUN *South African and Zimbabwean, slang, derogatory* a Black African.
▷**HISTORY** from Zulu *umuntu* person

munter ('mʌntə) NOUN *Slang* an unattractive person.
▷**HISTORY** C20: of unknown origin

muntin ('mʌntɪn) NOUN another name (esp US) for **glazing-bar.**
▷**HISTORY** C17: variant of C15 *mountant,* from Old French *montant,* present participle of *monter* to MOUNT[1]

muntjac *or* **muntjak** ('mʌntˌdʒæk) NOUN any small Asian deer of the genus *Muntiacus,* typically having a chestnut-brown coat, small antlers, and a barklike cry. Also called: **barking deer.**
▷**HISTORY** C18: probably changed from Javanese *mindjangan* deer

Muntz metal (mʌnts) NOUN a type of brass consisting of three parts copper and two parts zinc, used in casting and extrusion.
▷**HISTORY** C19: named after G. F. *Muntz* (1794–1857), English metallurgist

muon ('mju:ɒn) NOUN a positive or negative elementary particle with a mass 207 times that of an electron and spin ½. It was originally called the **mu meson** but is now classified as a lepton.
▷**HISTORY** C20: short for MU MESON
▶**muonic** (mju:'ɒnɪk) ADJECTIVE

muon-catalysed fusion NOUN *Physics* an experimental form of nuclear fusion in which hydrogen and deuterium muonic atoms are formed. Because the mass of the muon is much larger than that of the electron, the atoms are smaller, and the nuclei are close enough for fusion to occur.

muonic atom NOUN *Physics* an atom in which an orbiting electron has been replaced by a muon.

muppet ('mʌpɪt) NOUN *Slang* a stupid person.
▷**HISTORY** C20: from the name for the puppets used in the television programme *The Muppet Show*

murage ('mjʊərɪdʒ) NOUN *Brit, archaic* a tax levied for the construction or maintenance of town walls.
▷**HISTORY** C13: from Old French, ultimately from Latin *mūrus* wall

mural ('mjʊərəl) NOUN [1] a large painting or picture on a wall. ◆ ADJECTIVE [2] of or relating to a wall.
▷**HISTORY** C15: from Latin *mūrālis,* from *mūrus* wall
▶'**muralist** NOUN

Murcia (*Spanish* 'murθja) NOUN [1] a region and ancient kingdom of SE Spain, on the Mediterranean: taken by the Moors in the 8th century; an independent Muslim kingdom in the 11th and 12th centuries. [2] a city in SE Spain, capital of Murcia province: trading centre for a rich agricultural region; silk industry; university (1915). Pop.: 34 904 (1995 est.).

murdabad ('mʊədɑ:ˌbɑ:d) VERB *(tr) Indian* down with; death to: used as part of a slogan in India, Pakistan, etc. Compare **zindabad.**
▷**HISTORY** from Urdu, from Persian *murda* dead

murder ('mɜ:də) NOUN [1] the unlawful premeditated killing of one human being by another. Compare **manslaughter, homicide.** [2] *Informal* something dangerous, difficult, or unpleasant: *driving around London is murder.* [3] **cry blue murder.** *Informal* to make an outcry. [4] **get away with murder.** *Informal* to escape censure; do as one pleases. ◆ VERB *(mainly tr)* [5] *(also intr)* to kill (someone) unlawfully with premeditation or during the commission of a crime. [6] to kill brutally. [7] *Informal* to destroy; ruin: *he murdered her chances of happiness.* [8] *Informal* to defeat completely; beat decisively: *the home team murdered their opponents.* ◆ Also (archaic or dialect): **murther.**
▷**HISTORY** Old English *morthor;* related to Old English *morth,* Old Norse *morth,* Latin *mors* death; compare French *meurtre*
▶'**murderer** NOUN ▶'**murderess** FEMININE NOUN

murderous ('mɜ:dərəs) ADJECTIVE [1] intending, capable of, or guilty of murder. [2] *Informal* very dangerous, difficult, or unpleasant: *a murderous road.*
▶'**murderously** ADVERB ▶'**murderousness** NOUN

mure (mjʊə) VERB *(tr)* an archaic or literary word for **immure.**
▷**HISTORY** C14: from Old French *murer,* from Latin *mūrus* wall

Mureş ('mʊərɛʃ) NOUN a river in SE central Europe, rising in central Romania in the Carpathian Mountains and flowing west to the Tisza River at Szeged, Hungary. Length: 885 km (550 miles). Hungarian name: **Maros.**

murex ('mjʊərɛks) NOUN, *plural* **murices** ('mjʊərɪˌsi:z). any of various spiny-shelled marine gastropods of the genus *Murex* and related genera: formerly used as a source of the dye Tyrian purple.
▷**HISTORY** C16: from Latin *mūrex* purple fish; related to Greek *muax* sea mussel

muriate ('mjʊərɪɪt, -ˌeɪt) NOUN an obsolete name for a **chloride.**
▷**HISTORY** C18: back formation from *muriatic;* see MURIATIC ACID

muriatic acid (ˌmjʊərɪ'ætɪk) NOUN a former name for **hydrochloric acid.**
▷**HISTORY** C17: from Latin *muriāticus* pickled, from *muria* brine

muricate ('mjʊərɪˌkeɪt) *or* **muricated** ADJECTIVE *Biology* having a surface roughened by numerous short points: *muricate stems.*
▷**HISTORY** C17: from Latin *mūricātus* pointed like a MUREX

murine ('mjʊəraɪn, -rɪn) ADJECTIVE [1] of, relating to, or belonging to the *Muridae,* an Old World family of rodents, typically having long hairless tails: includes rats and mice. [2] resembling a mouse or rat. ◆ NOUN [3] any animal belonging to the *Muridae.*
▷**HISTORY** C17: from Latin *mūrīnus* of mice, from *mūs* MOUSE

murk *or* **mirk** (mɜ:k) NOUN [1] gloomy darkness. ◆ ADJECTIVE [2] an archaic variant of **murky.**
▷**HISTORY** C13: probably from Old Norse *myrkr* darkness; compare Old English *mirce* dark

murky *or* **mirky** ('mɜ:kɪ) ADJECTIVE **murkier, murkiest** *or* **mirkier, mirkiest.** [1] gloomy or dark. [2] cloudy or impenetrable as with smoke or fog.
▶'**murkily** *or* '**mirkily** ADVERB ▶'**murkiness** *or* '**mirkiness** NOUN

Murman Coast ('mʊəmən) *or* **Murmansk Coast** NOUN a coastal region of NW Russia, in the north of the Kola Peninsula within the Arctic Circle, but ice-free.

Murmansk (*Russian* 'murmənsk) NOUN a port in NW Russia, on the Kola Inlet of the Barents Sea: founded in 1915; the world's largest town north of the Arctic Circle, with a large fishing fleet. Pop.: 382 700 (1999 est.).

murmur ('mɜ:mə) NOUN [1] a continuous low indistinct sound, as of distant voices. [2] an indistinct utterance: *a murmur of satisfaction.* [3] a complaint; grumble: *he made no murmur at my suggestion.* [4] *Med* any abnormal soft blowing sound heard within the body, usually over the chest. See also **heart murmur.** ◆ VERB **-murs, -muring, -mured.** [5] to utter (something) in a murmur. [6] *(intr)* to complain in a murmur.
▷**HISTORY** C14: as n, from Latin *murmur;* vb via Old French *murmurer* from Latin *murmurāre* to rumble
▶'**murmurer** NOUN ▶'**murmuring** NOUN, ADJECTIVE ▶'**murmuringly** ADVERB ▶'**murmurous** ADJECTIVE

murphy ('mɜ:fɪ) NOUN, *plural* **-phies.** a dialect or informal word for **potato.**
▷**HISTORY** C19: from the common Irish surname *Murphy*

Murphy bed NOUN *US and Canadian* a bed designed to be folded or swung into a cabinet when not in use.
▷**HISTORY** C20: named after William *Murphy,* US inventor

Murphy's Law NOUN *Informal* another term for **Sod's law.**
▷**HISTORY** C20: of uncertain origin

murra ('mʌrə) NOUN See **murrhine** (sense 2).

murragh ('mʌrə) NOUN an angler's name for the

great red sedge, a large caddis fly, *Phryganea grandis,* of still and running water, esteemed by trout.
▷HISTORY perhaps from MURREY

murrain ('mʌrɪn) NOUN *Archaic* [1] any plaguelike disease in cattle. [2] a plague.
▷HISTORY C14: from Old French *morine,* from *morir* to die, from Latin *morī*

Murray ('mʌrɪ) NOUN a river in SE Australia, rising in New South Wales and flowing northwest into SE South Australia, then south into the sea at Encounter Bay: the main river of Australia, important for irrigation and power. Length: 2590 km (1609 miles).

Murray cod NOUN a large Australian freshwater fish, *Maccullochella peeli,* chiefly of the Murray and Darling rivers.

murre (mɜː) NOUN *US and Canadian* any guillemot of the genus *Uria.*
▷HISTORY C17: origin unknown

murree *or* **murri** ('mʌrɪ) NOUN, *plural* **-rees** *or* **-ris**. a native Australian.
▷HISTORY C19: from a native Australian language

murrelet ('mɜːlɪt) NOUN any of several small diving birds of the genus *Brachyramphus* and related genera, similar and related to the auks: family *Alcidae,* order *Charadriiformes.*
▷HISTORY C19: from MURRE + -LET

murrey ('mʌrɪ) ADJECTIVE *Brit, archaic* mulberry-coloured.
▷HISTORY C14: from Old French *moré,* ultimately from Latin *mōrum* mulberry

murrhine *or* **murrine** ('mʌraɪn, -ɪn) ADJECTIVE [1] of or relating to an unknown substance used in ancient Rome to make vases, cups, etc. ◆ NOUN [2] Also called: **murra**. the substance so used.
▷HISTORY C16: from Latin *murr(h)inus* belonging to *murra*

murrhine glass NOUN a type of Eastern glassware made from fluorspar and decorated with pieces of coloured metal.

Murrumbidgee (ˌmʌrəm'bɪdʒɪ) NOUN a river in SE Australia, rising in S New South Wales and flowing north and west to the Murray River: important for irrigation. Length: 1690 km (1050 miles).

murther ('mɜːðə) NOUN, VERB an archaic word for **murder**.
▸ **'murtherer** NOUN

murti ('muːrtɪ) NOUN *Hinduism* an image of a deity, which itself is considered divine once consecrated.
▷HISTORY from Sanskrit, literally: embodiment

mus. ABBREVIATION FOR: [1] museum. [2] music.

musaceous (mjuː'zeɪʃəs) ADJECTIVE of, relating to, or belonging to the *Musaceae,* a family of tropical flowering plants having large leaves and clusters of elongated berry fruits: includes the banana, edible plantain, and Manila hemp.
▷HISTORY C19: from New Latin *Mūsāceae,* from *Mūsa* genus name, from Arabic *mawzah* banana

Musaf *Hebrew* (mʊ'sɑf; *Yiddish* 'mʊsəf) NOUN *Judaism* the additional prayers added to the morning service on Sabbaths, festivals, and Rosh Chodesh.
▷HISTORY literally: addition

musar *Hebrew* (mʊ'sɑː; *Yiddish* 'mʊsə) NOUN *Judaism* [1] rabbinic literature concerned with ethics, right conduct, etc. [2] any moralizing speech, esp one which is critical.
▷HISTORY literally: instruction

MusB *or* **MusBac** ABBREVIATION FOR Bachelor of Music.

Musca ('mʌskə) NOUN, *Latin genitive* **Muscae** ('mʌskiː). a small constellation in the S hemisphere lying between the Southern Cross and Chamaeleon.
▷HISTORY Latin: a fly

muscadel *or* **muscadelle** (ˌmʌskə'dɛl) NOUN another name for **muscatel**.

Muscadet ('mʌskəˌdeɪ; *French* myskadɛ) NOUN (*sometimes not capital*) [1] a white grape, grown esp in the Loire valley, used for making wine. [2] any of various dry white wines made from this grape.
▷HISTORY C20: from the region of Brittany where the grape was first grown

muscadine ('mʌskədɪn, -ˌdaɪn) NOUN [1] a woody climbing vitaceous plant, *Vitis rotundifolia,* of the southeastern US. [2] Also called: **scuppernong, bullace grape**. the thick-skinned musk-scented purple grape produced by this plant: used to make wine.
▷HISTORY C16: from MUSCADEL

muscae volitantes ('mʌsiː vɒlɪ'tæntiːz) PLURAL NOUN *Pathol* moving black specks or threads seen before the eyes, caused by opaque fragments floating in the vitreous humour or a defect in the lens.
▷HISTORY C18: New Latin: flying flies

muscarine ('mʌskərɪn, -ˌriːn) NOUN a poisonous alkaloid occurring in certain mushrooms. Formula: $C_9H_{21}NO_3$.
▷HISTORY C19: from Latin *muscārius* of flies, from *musca* fly

muscat ('mʌskət, -kæt) NOUN [1] any of various grapevines that produce sweet white grapes used for making wine or raisins. [2] another name for **muscatel** (sense 1).
▷HISTORY C16: via Old French from Provençal *muscat,* from *musc* MUSK

Muscat ('mʌskət, -kæt) NOUN the capital of the Sultanate of Oman, a port on the Gulf of Oman: a Portuguese port from the early 16th century; controlled by Persia (1650–1741). Pop.: 51 969 (1993). Arabic name: **Masqat**.

Muscat and Oman NOUN the former name (until 1970) of (the Sultanate of) **Oman**.

muscatel (ˌmʌskə'tɛl), **muscadel,** *or* **muscadelle** NOUN [1] Also called: **muscat**. a rich sweet wine made from muscat grapes. [2] the grape or raisin from a muscat vine.
▷HISTORY C14: from Old French *muscadel,* from Old Provençal, from *moscadel,* from *muscat* musky. See MUSK

muscid ('mʌsɪd) NOUN [1] any fly of the dipterous family *Muscidae,* including the housefly and tsetse fly. ◆ ADJECTIVE [2] of, relating to, or belonging to the *Muscidae.*
▷HISTORY C19: via New Latin from Latin *musca* fly

muscle ('mʌsᵊl) NOUN [1] a tissue composed of bundles of elongated cells capable of contraction and relaxation to produce movement in an organ or part. [2] an organ composed of muscle tissue. [3] strength or force. ◆ VERB [4] (*intr;* often foll by *in, on,* etc.) *Informal* to force one's way (in).
▷HISTORY C16: from medical Latin *musculus* little mouse, from the imagined resemblance of some muscles to mice, from Latin *mūs* mouse
▸ **'muscly** ADJECTIVE

muscle-bound ADJECTIVE [1] having overdeveloped and inelastic muscles. [2] lacking flexibility.

muscle fibre NOUN any of the numerous elongated contractile cells that make up striated muscle.

muscleman ('mʌsᵊlˌmæn) NOUN, *plural* **-men**. [1] a man with highly developed muscles. [2] a henchman employed by a gangster to intimidate or use violence upon victims.

muscle mary NOUN, *plural* **maries**. *Informal* a homosexual man who practises bodybuilding.

muscle sense NOUN another name for **kinaesthesia**.

muscovado *or* **muscavado** (ˌmʌskə'vɑːdəʊ) NOUN raw sugar obtained from the juice of sugar cane by evaporating the molasses.
▷HISTORY C17: from Portuguese *açúcar mascavado* separated sugar; *mascavado* from *mascavar* to separate, probably from Latin

muscovite ('mʌskəˌvaɪt) NOUN a pale brown, or green, or colourless mineral of the mica group, found in plutonic rocks such as granite and in sedimentary rocks. It is used in the manufacture of lubricants, insulators, paints, and Christmas "snow". Composition: potassium aluminium silicate. Formula: $KAl_2(AlSi_3)O_{10}(OH)_2$. Crystal structure: monoclinic. See also **mica**.
▷HISTORY C19: from the phrase *Muscovy glass,* an early name for mica

Muscovite ('mʌskəˌvaɪt) NOUN [1] a native or inhabitant of Moscow. ◆ ADJECTIVE [2] an archaic word for **Russian**.

Muscovy ('mʌskəvɪ) NOUN [1] a Russian principality (13th to 16th centuries), of which Moscow was the capital. [2] an archaic name for **Russia** and **Moscow**.

Muscovy duck *or* **musk duck** NOUN a large crested widely domesticated South American duck, *Cairina moschata,* having a greenish-black plumage with white markings and a large red caruncle on the bill.
▷HISTORY C17: originally *musk duck,* a name later mistakenly associated with MUSCOVY

muscular ('mʌskjʊlə) ADJECTIVE [1] having well-developed muscles; brawny. [2] of, relating to, or consisting of muscle.
▷HISTORY C17: from New Latin *muscularis,* from *musculus* MUSCLE
▸ **muscularity** (ˌmʌskjʊ'lærɪtɪ) NOUN ▸ **'muscularly** ADVERB

muscular dystrophy NOUN a genetic disease characterized by progressive deterioration and wasting of muscle fibres, causing difficulty in walking.

musculature ('mʌskjʊlətʃə) NOUN [1] the arrangement of muscles in an organ or part. [2] the total muscular system of an organism.

musculocutaneous (ˌmʌskjʊləʊkjuː'teɪnɪəs) ADJECTIVE of, relating to, or supplying the muscles and skin: *musculocutaneous nerve.*

MusD *or* **MusDoc** ABBREVIATION FOR Doctor of Music.

muse¹ (mjuːz) VERB [1] (when *intr,* often foll by *on* or *about*) to reflect (about) or ponder (on), usually in silence. [2] (*intr*) to gaze thoughtfully. ◆ NOUN [3] *Archaic* a state of abstraction.
▷HISTORY C14: from Old French *muser,* perhaps from *mus* snout, from Medieval Latin *mūsus*
▸ **'muser** NOUN ▸ **'museful** ADJECTIVE ▸ **'musefully** ADVERB

muse² (mjuːz) NOUN a goddess that inspires a creative artist, esp a poet.
▷HISTORY C14: from Old French, from Latin *Mūsa,* from Greek *Mousa* a Muse

Muse (mjuːz) NOUN *Greek myth* any of nine sister goddesses, each of whom was regarded as the protectress of a different art or science. Daughters of Zeus and Mnemosyne, the nine are Calliope, Clio, Erato, Euterpe, Melpomene, Polyhymnia, Terpsichore, Thalia, and Urania.

museology (ˌmjuːzɪ'ɒlədʒɪ) NOUN the science of museum organization.
▸ **ˌmuseo'logical** ADJECTIVE ▸ **ˌmuse'ologist** NOUN

musette (mjuː'zɛt; *French* myzɛt) NOUN [1] a type of bagpipe with a bellows popular in France during the 17th and 18th centuries. [2] a dance, with a drone bass originally played by a musette.
▷HISTORY C14: from Old French, diminutive of *muse* bagpipe

musette bag NOUN *US* an army officer's haversack.

museum (mjuː'zɪəm) NOUN a place or building where objects of historical, artistic, or scientific interest are exhibited, preserved, or studied.
▷HISTORY C17: via Latin from Greek *Mouseion* home of the Muses, from *Mousa* MUSE

museum beetle NOUN See **dermestid**.

museum piece NOUN [1] an object of sufficient age or interest to be kept in a museum. [2] *Informal* a person or thing regarded as antiquated or decrepit.

mush¹ (mʌʃ) NOUN [1] a soft pulpy mass or consistency. [2] *US* a thick porridge made from corn meal. [3] *Informal* cloying sentimentality. [4] *Radio* interference in reception, esp a hissing noise. ◆ VERB [5] (*tr*) to reduce (a substance) to a soft pulpy mass.
▷HISTORY C17: from obsolete *moose* porridge; probably related to MASH; compare Old English *mōs* food

mush² (mʌʃ) *Canadian* ◆ INTERJECTION [1] an order to dogs in a sled team to start up or go faster. ◆ VERB [2] to travel by or drive a dog sled. [3] (*intr*) to travel on foot, esp with snowshoes. ◆ NOUN [4] a journey with a dogsled.
▷HISTORY C19: perhaps from French *marchez* or *marchons,* imperatives of *marcher* to advance
▸ **'musher** NOUN

mush³ (mʊʃ) NOUN *Brit* a slang word for **face** (sense 1).
▷HISTORY C19: from MUSH¹, alluding to the softness of the face

mush⁴ (mʊʃ) NOUN *Brit, slang* a familiar or contemptuous term of address.
▷HISTORY C19: probably from Gypsy *moosh* a man

mush area NOUN a region where signals from two or more radio transmitters overlap, causing fading and distortion.

mushroom ('mʌʃruːm, -rʊm) NOUN [1] **a** the fleshy spore-producing body of any of various basidiomycetous fungi, typically consisting of a cap (see **pileus**) at the end of a stem arising from an underground mycelium. Some species, such as the field mushroom, are edible. Compare **toadstool. b** (*as modifier*): *mushroom soup.* [2] the fungus producing any of these structures. [3] **a** something resembling a mushroom in shape or rapid growth. **b** (*as modifier*): *mushroom expansion.* ◆ VERB (*intr*) [4] to grow rapidly: *demand mushroomed overnight.* [5] to assume a mushroom-like shape. [6] to gather mushrooms.
▷HISTORY C15: from Old French *mousseron,* from Late Latin *mussiriō,* of obscure origin

mushroom cloud NOUN the large mushroom-shaped cloud of dust, debris, etc. produced by a nuclear explosion.

mushy ('mʌʃɪ) ADJECTIVE **mushier, mushiest.** [1] soft and pulpy. [2] *Informal* excessively sentimental or emotional.
▸'**mushily** ADVERB ▸'**mushiness** NOUN

music ('mjuːzɪk) NOUN [1] an art form consisting of sequences of sounds in time, esp tones of definite pitch organized melodically, harmonically, rhythmically and according to tone colour. [2] such an art form characteristic of a particular people, culture, or tradition: *Indian music; rock music; baroque music.* [3] the sounds so produced, esp by singing or musical instruments. [4] written or printed music, such as a score or set of parts. [5] any sequence of sounds perceived as pleasing or harmonious. [6] *Rare* a group of musicians: *the Queen's music.* [7] **face the music.** *Informal* to confront the consequences of one's actions. [8] **music to one's ears.** something that is very pleasant to hear: *his news is music to my ears.*
▷HISTORY C13: via Old French from Latin *mūsica,* from Greek *mousikē* (*tekhnē*) (art) belonging to the Muses, from *Mousa* MUSE

musical ('mjuːzɪk^{ə}l) ADJECTIVE [1] of, relating to, or used in music: *a musical instrument.* [2] harmonious; melodious: *musical laughter.* [3] talented in or fond of music. [4] involving or set to music: *a musical evening.* ◆ NOUN [5] short for **musical comedy.**
▸'**musically** ADVERB ▸'**musicalness** *or* ˌ**musi'cality** NOUN

musical chairs NOUN (*functioning as singular*) [1] a party game in which players walk around chairs while music is played, there being one fewer chair than players. Whenever the music stops, the player who fails to find a chair is eliminated. [2] any situation involving a number of people in a series of interrelated changes.

musical comedy NOUN [1] a play or film, usually having a light romantic story, that consists of dialogue interspersed with singing and dancing. [2] such plays and films collectively.

musicale (ˌmjuːzɪ'kɑːl) NOUN *US and Canadian* a party or social evening with a musical programme.
▷HISTORY C19: shortened from French *soirée musicale* musical evening

musical glasses PLURAL NOUN another term for **glass harmonica.**

music box *or* **musical box** NOUN a mechanical instrument that plays tunes by means of pins on a revolving cylinder striking the tuned teeth of a comblike metal plate, contained in a box.

music centre NOUN a single hi-fi unit containing e.g. a turntable, amplifier, radio, cassette player, and compact disc player.

music drama NOUN [1] an opera in which the musical and dramatic elements are of equal importance and strongly interfused. [2] the genre of such operas.
▷HISTORY C19: translation of German *Musikdrama,* coined by Wagner to describe his later operas

music hall NOUN *Chiefly Brit* [1] **a** a variety entertainment consisting of songs, comic turns, etc. US and Canadian name: **vaudeville. b** (*as modifier*): *a music-hall song.* [2] a theatre at which such entertainments are staged.

musician (mjuː'zɪʃən) NOUN a person who plays or composes music, esp as a profession.
▸**mu'sicianly** ADJECTIVE

musicianship (mjuː'zɪʃənʃɪp) NOUN skill or artistry in performing music.

music of the spheres NOUN the celestial music supposed by Pythagoras to be produced by the regular movements of the stars and planets.

musicology (ˌmjuːzɪ'kɒlədʒɪ) NOUN the scholarly study of music.
▸**musicological** (ˌmjuːzɪkə'lɒdʒɪk^{ə}l) ADJECTIVE ▸ˌ**musico'logically** ADVERB ▸ˌ**musi'cologist** NOUN

music paper NOUN paper ruled or printed with a stave for writing music.

music roll NOUN a roll of perforated paper for use in a mechanical instrument such as a player piano.

music stand NOUN a frame, usually of wood or metal, upon which a musical score or orchestral part is supported.

music theatre NOUN a modern musical-dramatic work that is performed on a smaller scale than, and without the conventions of, traditional opera.

musique concrète *French* (myzik kɔ̃krɛt) NOUN another term for **concrete music.**

musjid ('mʌsdʒɪd) NOUN a variant spelling of **masjid.**

musk (mʌsk) NOUN [1] a strong-smelling glandular secretion of the male musk deer, used in perfumery. [2] a similar substance produced by certain other animals, such as the civet and otter, or manufactured synthetically. [3] any of several scrophulariaceous plants of the genus *Mimulus,* esp the North American *M. moschatus,* which has yellow flowers and was formerly cultivated for its musky scent. See also **monkey flower.** [4] the smell of musk or a similar heady smell. [5] (*modifier*) containing or resembling musk: *musk oil; a musk flavour.*
▷HISTORY C14: from Late Latin *muscus,* from Greek *moskhos,* from Persian *mushk,* probably from Sanskrit *mushká* scrotum (from the appearance of the musk deer's musk bag), diminutive of *mūsh* MOUSE

musk deer NOUN a small central Asian mountain deer, *Moschus moschiferus.* The male has long tusklike canine teeth and secretes musk.

musk duck NOUN [1] another name for **Muscovy duck.** [2] a duck, *Biziura lobata,* inhabiting swamps, lakes, and streams in Australia. The male has a leathery pouch beneath the bill and emits a musky odour.

muskeg ('mʌsˌkɛg) NOUN *Chiefly Canadian* [1] undrained boggy land characterized by sphagnum moss vegetation: *vast areas of muskeg.* [2] a bog or swamp of this nature.
▷HISTORY C19: from Algonquian: grassy swamp

muskellunge ('mʌskəˌlʌndʒ), **maskalonge** ('mæskəˌlɒndʒ), *or* **maskanonge** ('mæskəˌnɒndʒ) NOUN, *plural* **-lunges, -longes, -nonges** *or* **-lunge, -longe, -nonge.** a large North American freshwater game fish, *Esox masquinongy:* family *Esocidae* (pikes, etc.). Often (informal) shortened to: **musky** *or* **muskie.**
▷HISTORY C18 *maskinunga,* of Algonquian origin; compare Ojibwa *mashkinonge* big pike

musket ('mʌskɪt) NOUN a long-barrelled muzzle-loading shoulder gun used between the 16th and 18th centuries by infantry soldiers.
▷HISTORY C16: from French *mousquet,* from Italian *moschetto* arrow, earlier: sparrow hawk, from *moscha* a fly, from Latin *musca*

musketeer (ˌmʌskɪ'tɪə) NOUN (formerly) a soldier armed with a musket.

musketry ('mʌskɪtrɪ) NOUN [1] muskets or musketeers collectively. [2] the technique of using small arms.

muskie ('mʌskɪ) NOUN *Canadian* an informal name for the **muskellunge.**

musk mallow NOUN [1] a malvaceous plant, *Malva moschata,* of Europe and N Africa, with purple-spotted stems, pink flowers, and a faint scent of musk. [2] another name for **abelmosk.**

muskmelon ('mʌskˌmɛlən) NOUN [1] any of several varieties of the melon *Cucumis melo,* such as the cantaloupe and honeydew. [2] the fruit of any of these melons, having ribbed or warty rind and sweet yellow, white, or green flesh with a musky aroma.

Muskogean *or* **Muskhogean** (mʌs'kəʊgɪən) NOUN a family of North American Indian languages, probably distantly related to the Algonquian family.

musk orchid NOUN a small Eurasian orchid, *Herminium monorchis,* with dense spikes of musk-scented greenish-yellow flowers.

musk ox NOUN a large bovid mammal, *Ovibos moschatus,* which has a dark shaggy coat, short legs, and widely spaced downward-curving horns and emits a musky smell: now confined to the tundras of Canada and Greenland.

muskrat ('mʌskˌræt) NOUN, *plural* **-rats** *or* **-rat.** [1] a North American beaver-like amphibious rodent, *Ondatra zibethica,* closely related to but larger than the voles: family *Cricetidae.* [2] the brown fur of this animal. [3] either of two closely related rodents, *Ondatra obscurus* or *Neofiber alleni* (**round-tailed muskrat**). ◆ Also called: **musquash.**
▷HISTORY C17: by folk etymology, from the same source as MUSQUASH

musk rose NOUN a prickly shrubby Mediterranean rose, *Rosa moschata,* cultivated for its white musk-scented flowers.

musk turtle NOUN any of several small turtles of the genus *Sternotherus,* esp *S. odoratus* (**common musk turtle** or **stinkpot**), that emit a strong unpleasant odour: family *Kinosternidae.*

musky[1] ('mʌskɪ) ADJECTIVE **muskier, muskiest.** resembling the smell of musk; having a heady or pungent sweet aroma.
▸'**muskiness** NOUN

musky[2] ('mʌskɪ) NOUN, *plural* **muskies.** an informal name for the **muskellunge.**

Muslim ('mʊzlɪm, 'mʌz-) *or* **Moslem** NOUN, *plural* **-lims** *or* **-lim.** [1] a follower of the religion of Islam. ◆ ADJECTIVE [2] of or relating to Islam, its doctrines, culture, etc. ◆ Also (but not in Muslim use): **Muhammadan, Muhammedan, Mohammedan.**
▷HISTORY C17: from Arabic, literally: one who surrenders
▸'**Muslimism** *or* '**Moslemism** NOUN

muslin ('mʌzlɪn) NOUN a fine plain-weave cotton fabric.
▷HISTORY C17: from French *mousseline,* from Italian *mussolina,* from Arabic *mawṣilīy* of Mosul, from *Mawṣil* Mosul, Iraq, where it was first produced

MusM ABBREVIATION FOR Master of Music.

muso ('mjuːzəʊ) NOUN, *plural* **musos.** *Slang* [1] *Brit, derogatory* a musician, esp a pop musician, regarded as being overconcerned with technique rather than musical content or expression. [2] *Austral* any musician, esp a professional one.

musquash ('mʌskwɒʃ) NOUN another name for **muskrat,** esp the fur
▷HISTORY C17: from Algonquian: compare Natick *musquash,* Abnaki *muskwessu*

muss (mʌs) *US and Canadian informal* ◆ VERB [1] (*tr;* often foll by *up*) to make untidy; rumple. ◆ NOUN [2] a state of disorder; muddle.
▷HISTORY C19: probably a blend of MESS + FUSS

mussel ('mʌs^{ə}l) NOUN [1] any of various marine bivalves of the genus *Mytilus* and related genera, esp *M. edulis* (**edible mussel**), having a dark slightly elongated shell and living attached to rocks, etc. [2] any of various freshwater bivalves of the genera *Anodonta, Unio,* etc., attached to rocks, sand, etc. having a flattened oval shell (a source of mother-of-pearl). The **zebra mussel,** *Dreissena polymorpha,* can be a serious nuisance in water mains.
▷HISTORY Old English *muscle,* from Vulgar Latin *muscula* (unattested), from Latin *musculus,* diminutive of *mūs* mouse

musselcracker ('mʌs^{ə}lˌkrækə) NOUN *South African* a large variety of sea bream, *Sparodon durbanensis,* that feeds on shellfish and is a popular food and game fish.

Mussulman *or* **Mussalman** ('mʌs^{ə}lmən) NOUN, *plural* **-mans.** an archaic word for **Muslim.**
▷HISTORY C16: from Persian *Musulmān* (pl) from Arabic *Muslimūn,* pl of MUSLIM

mussy ('mʌsɪ) ADJECTIVE **mussier, mussiest.** untidy or disordered.
▸'**mussily** ADVERB ▸'**mussiness** NOUN

must[1] (mʌst; *unstressed* məst, məs) VERB (takes an infinitive without *to* or an implied infinitive) used as an auxiliary: [1] to express obligation or compulsion: *you must pay your dues.* In this sense, *must* does not form a negative. If used with a negative infinitive it indicates obligatory prohibition. [2] to indicate necessity: *I must go to the*

bank tomorrow. [3] to indicate the probable correctness of a statement: *he must be there by now.* [4] to indicate inevitability: *all good things must come to an end.* [5] to express resolution: **a** on the part of the speaker when used with *I* or *we*: *I must finish this.* **b** on the part of another or others as imputed to them by the speaker, when used with *you, he, she, they,* etc.: *let him get drunk if he must.* [6] (used emphatically) to express conviction or certainty on the part of the speaker: *he must have reached the town by now, surely; you must be joking.* [7] (foll by *away*) used with an implied verb of motion to express compelling haste: *I must away.* ◆ NOUN [8] an essential or necessary thing: *strong shoes are a must for hill walking.*
▷HISTORY Old English *mōste* past tense of *mōtan* to be allowed, be obliged to; related to Old Saxon *mōtan,* Old High German *muozan,* German *müssen*

must² (mʌst) NOUN the newly pressed juice of grapes or other fruit ready for fermentation.
▷HISTORY Old English, from Latin *mustum* new wine, must, from *mustus* (adj) newborn

must³ (mʌst) NOUN mustiness or mould.
▷HISTORY C17: back formation from MUSTY

must⁴ (mʌst) NOUN a variant spelling of **musth.**

must- COMBINING FORM indicating that something is highly recommended or desirable: *a must-see film; this season's must-haves.*

mustache (mə'stɑːʃ) NOUN the US spelling of **moustache.**
▸**mus'tached** ADJECTIVE

mustachio (mə'stɑːʃɪˌəʊ) NOUN, *plural* **-chios.** (*often plural when considered as two halves*) *Often humorous* a moustache, esp when bushy or elaborately shaped.
▷HISTORY C16: from Spanish *mostacho* and Italian *mostaccio*

mustachioed (mə'stɑːʃɪˌəʊd) ADJECTIVE *Often humorous* having a moustache, esp when bushy or elaborately shaped.

mustang ('mʌstæŋ) NOUN a small breed of horse, often wild or half wild, found in the southwestern US.
▷HISTORY C19: from Mexican Spanish *mestengo,* from *mesta* a group of stray animals

mustard ('mʌstəd) NOUN [1] any of several Eurasian plants of the genus *Brassica,* esp black mustard and white mustard, having yellow or white flowers and slender pods and cultivated for their pungent seeds: family *Brassicaceae* (crucifers). See also **charlock.** [2] a paste made from the powdered seeds of any of these plants and used as a condiment. [3] **a** a brownish-yellow colour. **b** (*as adjective*): *a mustard carpet.* [4] *Slang, chiefly US* zest or enthusiasm. [5] **cut the mustard.** *Slang* to come up to expectations.
▷HISTORY C13: from Old French *moustarde,* from Latin *mustum* MUST², since the original condiment was made by adding must

mustard and cress NOUN seedlings of white mustard and garden cress, used in salads.

mustard gas NOUN an oily liquid vesicant compound used in chemical warfare. Its vapour causes blindness and burns. Formula: $(ClCH_2CH_2)_2S$.

mustard oil NOUN an oil that is obtained from mustard seeds and used in making soap.

mustard plaster NOUN *Med* a mixture of powdered black mustard seeds and an adhesive agent applied to the skin for its relaxing, stimulating, or counterirritant effects.

mustee (mʌ'stiː, 'mʌstiː) *or* **mestee** (mɛ'stiː) NOUN [1] the offspring of a White and a quadroon. [2] any person of mixed ancestry.
▷HISTORY C17: shortened from MESTIZO

musteline ('mʌstɪˌlaɪn, -lɪn) ADJECTIVE [1] of, relating to, or belonging to the *Mustelidae,* a family of typically predatory mammals including weasels, ferrets, minks, polecats, badgers, skunks, and otters: order *Carnivora* (carnivores). ◆ NOUN [2] any musteline animal.
▷HISTORY C17: from Latin *mustēlīnus,* from *mustēla* weasel, from *mūs* mouse + *-tēla,* of unknown origin

muster ('mʌstə) VERB [1] to call together (numbers of men) for duty, inspection, etc., or (of men) to assemble in this way. [2] **muster in** *or* **out.** *US* to enlist into or discharge from military service. [3] (*tr*) *Austral and NZ* to round up (livestock). [4] (*tr;* sometimes foll by *up*) to summon or gather: *to muster one's arguments; to muster up courage.* ◆ NOUN [5] an assembly of military personnel for duty, inspection, etc. [6] a collection, assembly, or gathering. [7] *Austral and NZ* the rounding up of livestock. [8] a flock of peacocks. [9] **pass muster.** to be acceptable.
▷HISTORY C14: from old French *moustrer,* from Latin *monstrāre* to show, from *monstrum* portent, omen

muster roll NOUN a list of the officers and men in a regiment, ship's company, etc.

musth *or* **must** (mʌst) NOUN (often preceded by *in*) a state of frenzied sexual excitement in the males of certain large mammals, esp elephants, associated with discharge from a gland between the ear and eye.
▷HISTORY C19: from Urdu *mast,* from Persian: drunk

musty ('mʌstɪ) ADJECTIVE **-tier, -tiest.** [1] smelling or tasting old, stale, or mouldy. [2] old-fashioned, dull, or hackneyed: *musty ideas.*
▷HISTORY C16: perhaps a variant of obsolete *moisty,* influenced by MUST³
▸**'mustily** ADVERB ▸**'mustiness** NOUN

mut (mʌt) NOUN *Printing* another word for **em** (sense 1).
▷HISTORY C20: shortened from MUTTON

mutable ('mjuːtəbᵊl) ADJECTIVE [1] able to or tending to change. [2] *Astrology* of or relating to four of the signs of the zodiac, Gemini, Virgo, Sagittarius, and Pisces, which are associated with the quality of adaptability. Compare **cardinal** (sense 9), **fixed** (sense 10).
▷HISTORY C14: from Latin *mūtābilis* fickle, from *mūtāre* to change
▸ˌ**muta'bility** *or* (*less commonly*) **'mutableness** NOUN
▸**'mutably** ADVERB

mutagen ('mjuːtədʒən) NOUN a substance or agent that can induce genetic mutation.
▷HISTORY C20: from MUTATION + -GEN
▸**mutagenic** (ˌmjuːtə'dʒɛnɪk) ADJECTIVE ▸ˌ**mutagen'icity** NOUN

mutagenesis (ˌmjuːtə'dʒɛnɪsɪs) NOUN *Genetics* the generation, usually intentional, of mutations.
▷HISTORY C20: from MUTATION + -GENESIS

mutagenize *or* **mutagenise** ('mjuːtədʒəˌnaɪz) VERB (*tr*) to subject (cells, DNA, etc.) to mutagens to induce mutations.

mutant ('mjuːtᵊnt) NOUN [1] Also called: **mutation.** an animal, organism, or gene that has undergone mutation. ◆ ADJECTIVE [2] of, relating to, undergoing, or resulting from change or mutation.
▷HISTORY C20: from Latin *mutāre* to change

Mutare (muː'tɑːrɪ) NOUN a city in E Zimbabwe, near the Mozambique border: rail and trade centre in a mining and tobacco-growing region. Pop.: 165 000 (1998 est.). Former name (until 1982): **Umtali.**

mutate (mjuː'teɪt) VERB to undergo or cause to undergo mutation.
▷HISTORY C19: from Latin *mūtātus* changed, from *mūtāre* to change
▸**mutative** ('mjuːtətɪv, mjuː'teɪtɪv) ADJECTIVE

mutation (mjuː'teɪʃən) NOUN [1] the act or process of mutating; change; alteration. [2] a change or alteration. [3] a change in the chromosomes or genes of a cell. When this change occurs in the gametes the structure and development of the resultant offspring may be affected. See also **inversion** (sense 11). [4] another word for **mutant** (sense 1). [5] a physical characteristic of an individual resulting from this type of chromosomal change. [6] *Phonetics* **a** (in Germanic languages) another name for **umlaut. b** (in Celtic languages) a phonetic change in certain initial consonants caused by a preceding word.
▸**mu'tational** ADJECTIVE ▸**mu'tationally** ADVERB

mutation stop NOUN an organ pipe sounding the harmonic of the note normally produced.

mutatis mutandis *Latin* (muː'tɑːtɪs muː'tændɪs) the necessary changes having been made.

Mutazilite (muː'tɑːzɪˌlaɪt) NOUN a member of an 8th-century liberal Muslim sect, later merged into the Shiahs.
▷HISTORY from Arabic *mu'tazilah* body of seceders + -ITE¹

mutch¹ (mʌtʃ) NOUN a close-fitting linen cap formerly worn by women and children in Scotland.
▷HISTORY C15: from Middle Dutch *mutse* cap, from Medieval Latin *almucia* ALMUCE

mutch² (mʌtʃ) VERB *Dialect* [1] (*tr*) to cadge; beg. [2] (*intr*) another word for **mitch.**

mutchkin ('mʌtʃkɪn) NOUN a Scottish unit of liquid measure equal to slightly less than one pint.
▷HISTORY C15: from Middle Dutch *mudseken,* from Latin *modius* measure for grain

mute¹ (mjuːt) ADJECTIVE [1] not giving out sound or speech; silent. [2] unable to speak; dumb. [3] unspoken or unexpressed: *mute dislike.* [4] *Law* (of a person arraigned on indictment) refusing to answer a charge. [5] *Phonetics* another word for **plosive.** [6] (of a letter in a word) silent. ◆ NOUN [7] a person who is unable to speak. [8] *Law* a person who refuses to plead when arraigned on indictment for an offence. [9] any of various devices used to soften the tone of stringed or brass instruments. [10] *Phonetics* a plosive consonant; stop. [11] a silent letter. [12] an actor in a dumb show. [13] a hired mourner at a funeral. ◆ VERB (*tr*) [14] to reduce the volume of (a musical instrument) by means of a mute, soft pedal, etc. [15] to subdue the strength of (a colour, tone, lighting, etc.).
▷HISTORY C14 *muwet* from Old French *mu,* from Latin *mūtus* silent
▸**'mutely** ADVERB ▸**'muteness** NOUN

mute² (mjuːt) *Archaic* ◆ VERB [1] (of birds) to discharge (faeces). ◆ NOUN [2] birds' faeces.
▷HISTORY C15: from Old French *meutir,* variant of *esmeltir,* of Germanic origin; probably related to SMELT¹ and MELT

muted ('mjuːtɪd) ADJECTIVE [1] (of a sound or colour) softened: *a muted pink shirt.* [2] (of an emotion or action) subdued or restrained: *his response was muted.* [3] (of a musical instrument) being played while fitted with a mute: *muted trumpet.*

mute swan NOUN a Eurasian swan, *Cygnus olor,* with a pure white plumage, an orange-red bill with a black base, and a curved neck. Compare **whistling swan.**

muti ('mʊtɪ) NOUN *South African informal* medicine, esp herbal medicine.
▷HISTORY from Zulu *umuthi* tree, medicine

muticous ('mjuːtɪkəs) ADJECTIVE *Botany* lacking an awn, spine, or point. Also: **muticate.**
▷HISTORY C19: from Latin *muticus* awnless, curtailed

mutilate ('mjuːtɪˌleɪt) VERB (*tr*) [1] to deprive of a limb, essential part, etc.; maim; dismember. [2] to mar, expurgate, or damage (a text, book, etc).
▷HISTORY C16: from Latin *mutilāre* to cut off; related to *mutilus* maimed
▸ˌ**muti'lation** NOUN ▸**'mutiˌlative** ADJECTIVE ▸**'mutiˌlator** NOUN

mutineer (ˌmjuːtɪ'nɪə) NOUN a person who mutinies.

mutinous ('mjuːtɪnəs) ADJECTIVE [1] openly rebellious or disobedient: *a mutinous child.* [2] characteristic or indicative of mutiny.
▸**'mutinously** ADVERB ▸**'mutinousness** NOUN

mutiny ('mjuːtɪnɪ) NOUN, *plural* **-nies.** [1] open rebellion against constituted authority, esp by seamen or soldiers against their officers. ◆ VERB **-nies, -nying, -nied.** [2] (*intr*) to engage in mutiny.
▷HISTORY C16: from obsolete *mutine,* from Old French *mutin* rebellious, from *meute* mutiny, ultimately from Latin *movēre* to move

mutism ('mjuːtɪzəm) NOUN [1] the state of being mute. [2] *Psychiatry* **a** a refusal to speak although the mechanism of speech is not damaged. **b** the lack of development of speech, due usually to early deafness.

mutt (mʌt) NOUN *Slang* [1] an inept, ignorant, or stupid person. [2] a mongrel dog; cur.
▷HISTORY C20: shortened from MUTTONHEAD

mutter ('mʌtə) VERB [1] to utter (something) in a low and indistinct tone. [2] (*intr*) to grumble or complain. [3] (*intr*) to make a low continuous murmuring sound. ◆ NOUN [4] a muttered sound or complaint.
▷HISTORY C14 *moteren;* related to Norwegian (dialect) *mutra,* Old High German *mutilōn;* compare Old English *mōtian* to speak

▸'**mutterer** NOUN ▸'**muttering** NOUN, ADJECTIVE
▸'**mutteringly** ADVERB

mutton ('mʌtᵊn) NOUN 1 the flesh of sheep, esp of mature sheep, used as food. 2 **mutton dressed as lamb.** an older woman dressed up to look young. 3 *Printing* another word for **em** (sense 1). Compare **nut** (sense 12).
▷HISTORY C13 *moton* sheep, from Old French, from Medieval Latin *multō*, of Celtic origin; the term was adopted in printing to distinguish the pronunciation of *em quad* from *en quad*
▸'**muttony** ADJECTIVE

mutton bird NOUN 1 any of several shearwaters, having a dark plumage with greyish underparts, esp the sooty shearwater (*Puffinus griseus*) of New Zealand, which is collected for food by Maoris. It inhabits the Pacific Ocean and in summer nests in Australia and New Zealand. 2 *Austral* any of various petrels, esp the sort-tailed shearwater, *Puffinus tenuirostris*, which inhabits the Pacific Ocean and in summer rests in S Australia.
▷HISTORY C19: so named because their cooked flesh is claimed to taste like mutton

mutton-birder NOUN *NZ* a person who hunts mutton birds.

mutton chop NOUN a piece of mutton from the loin.

muttonchops ('mʌtᵊn,tʃɒps) PLURAL NOUN side whiskers trimmed in the shape of chops, widening out from the temples.

muttonhead ('mʌtᵊn,hɛd) NOUN *Slang* a stupid or ignorant person; fool.
▸'**mutton,headed** ADJECTIVE

Muttra ('mʌtrə) NOUN the former name of **Mathura.**

mutual ('mjuːtʃʊəl) ADJECTIVE 1 experienced or expressed by each of two or more people or groups about the other; reciprocal: *mutual distrust.* 2 common to or shared by both or all of two or more parties: *a mutual friend; mutual interests.* 3 denoting an insurance company, etc., in which the policyholders share the profits and expenses and there are no shareholders.
▷HISTORY C15: from Old French *mutuel*, from Latin *mūtuus* reciprocal (originally: borrowed); related to *mūtāre* to change
▸**mutuality** (,mjuːtʃʊ'ælɪtɪ) *or* '**mutualness** NOUN
▸'**mutually** ADVERB

> **Language note** The use of *mutual* to mean *common to or shared by two or more parties* was formerly considered incorrect, but is now acceptable. Tautologous use of *mutual* should be avoided: *cooperation* (not *mutual cooperation*) *between the two countries.*

mutual fund NOUN the US and Canadian name for **unit trust.**

mutual inductance NOUN a measure of the mutual induction between two magnetically linked circuits, given as the ratio of the induced electromotive force to the rate of change of current producing it. It is usually measured in henries. Symbol: M or L_{12}. Also called: **coefficient of mutual induction.**

mutual induction NOUN the production of an electromotive force in a circuit by a current change in a second circuit magnetically linked to the first. See also **mutual inductance.** Compare **self-induction.**

mutual insurance NOUN a system of insurance by which all policyholders become company members under contract to pay premiums into a common fund out of which claims are paid. See also **mutual** (sense 3).

mutualism ('mjuːtʃʊə,lɪzəm) NOUN another name for **symbiosis.**
▸'**mutualist** NOUN, ADJECTIVE ▸,**mutual'istic** ADJECTIVE

mutualize *or* **mutualise** ('mjuːtʃʊə,laɪz) VERB 1 to make or become mutual. 2 (*tr*) *US* to organize or convert (a business enterprise) so that customers or employees own a majority of shares.
▸,**mutuali'zation** *or* ,**mutuali'sation** NOUN

mutual savings bank NOUN *Chiefly US* a savings bank having no subscribed capital stock and distributing all available net profit to depositors who, however, remain creditors without voting power.

mutuel ('mjuːtjʊəl) NOUN short for **pari-mutuel.**

mutule ('mjuːtjuːl) NOUN *Architect* one of a set of flat blocks below the corona of a Doric cornice. Compare **modillion.**
▷HISTORY C16: via French from Latin *mūtulus* modillion

muu-muu ('muː,muː) NOUN a loose brightly-coloured dress worn by women in Hawaii.
▷HISTORY from Hawaiian

Muzak ('mjuːzæk) NOUN *Trademark* recorded light music played in shops, restaurants, factories, etc., to entertain, increase sales or production, etc.

muzhik, moujik, *or* **mujik** ('muːʒɪk) NOUN a Russian peasant, esp under the tsars.
▷HISTORY C16: from Russian: peasant

muzz (mʌz) VERB (*tr*) *Brit informal* to make (something) muzzy.

muzzle ('mʌzᵊl) NOUN 1 the projecting part of the face, usually the jaws and nose, of animals such as the dog and horse. 2 a guard or strap fitted over an animal's nose and jaws to prevent it biting or eating. 3 the front end of a gun barrel. ◆ VERB (*tr*) 4 to prevent from being heard or noticed: *to muzzle the press.* 5 to put a muzzle on (an animal). 6 to take in (a sail).
▷HISTORY C15 *mosel*, from Old French *musel*, diminutive of *muse* snout, from Medieval Latin *mūsus*, of unknown origin
▸'**muzzler** NOUN

muzzle-loader NOUN a firearm receiving its ammunition through the muzzle.
▸'**muzzle-,loading** ADJECTIVE

muzzle velocity NOUN the velocity of a projectile as it leaves a firearm's muzzle.

muzzy ('mʌzɪ) ADJECTIVE **-zier, -ziest.** 1 blurred, indistinct, or hazy. 2 confused, muddled, or befuddled.
▷HISTORY C18: origin obscure
▸'**muzzily** ADVERB ▸'**muzziness** NOUN

mv[1] *Music* ABBREVIATION FOR mezzo voce.

mv[2] THE INTERNET DOMAIN NAME FOR Maldives.

MV ABBREVIATION FOR: 1 motor vessel. 2 **muzzle velocity.** ◆ 3 SYMBOL FOR megavolt.

MVD ABBREVIATION FOR Ministry of Internal Affairs; the police organization in the former Soviet Union, formed in 1946.
▷HISTORY from Russian *Ministerstvo vnutrennikh del*

MVDI (in New Zealand) ABBREVIATION FOR Motor Vehicle Dealers Institute.

MVO (in Britain) ABBREVIATION FOR Member of the Royal Victorian Order.

MVP (in the US and Australia) ABBREVIATION FOR most valuable player: the man or woman judged to be the outstanding player in a sport during a particular season or championship.

MVS ABBREVIATION FOR Master of Veterinary Surgery.

MVSc ABBREVIATION FOR Master of Veterinary Science.

mw THE INTERNET DOMAIN NAME FOR Malawi.

MW 1 SYMBOL FOR megawatt. ◆ ABBREVIATION FOR: 2 *Radio* **medium wave.** 3 Master of Wine. ◆ 4 INTERNATIONAL CAR REGISTRATION FOR Malawi.

mwalimu (mwɑː'liːmuː) NOUN *E African* a teacher.
▷HISTORY Swahili

Mweru ('mweəruː) NOUN a lake in central Africa, on the border between Zambia and the Democratic Republic of Congo (formerly Zaïre). Area: 4196 sq. km (1620 sq. miles).

mx THE INTERNET DOMAIN NAME FOR Mexico.

Mx *Physics* SYMBOL FOR maxwell.

MX *US* ABBREVIATION FOR missile-experimental: an intercontinental ballistic missile with up to ten nuclear warheads.

my (maɪ) DETERMINER 1 of, belonging to, or associated with the speaker or writer (me): *my own ideas; do you mind my smoking?* 2 used in various forms of address: *my lord; my dear boy.* 3 used in various exclamations: *my goodness!* ◆ INTERJECTION 4 an exclamation of surprise, awe, etc.: *my, how you've grown!*
▷HISTORY C12 *mī*, variant of Old English *mīn* when preceding a word beginning with a consonant

> **Language note** See at **me.**

my THE INTERNET DOMAIN NAME FOR Malaysia.

MY ABBREVIATION FOR motor yacht.

my- COMBINING FORM a variant of **myo-** before a vowel.

myalgia (maɪ'ældʒɪə) NOUN pain in a muscle or a group of muscles.
▷HISTORY C19: from MYO- + -ALGIA
▸**my'algic** ADJECTIVE

myalgic encephalopathy (maɪ'ældʒɪk ɛn,sɛfələ'pɒpəθɪ) NOUN a condition characterized by painful muscles, extreme fatigue, and general debility, sometimes occuring as a sequel to viral illness. Also called: **chronic fatigue syndrome.** Formerly called : **myalgic encephalomyelitis.** Abbreviation: **ME.**

myalism ('maɪə,lɪzəm) NOUN a kind of witchcraft, similar to obi, practised esp in the Caribbean.
▷HISTORY C19: from *myal*, probably of West African origin
▸'**myalist** NOUN

myall ('maɪəl) NOUN 1 any of several Australian acacias, esp *Acacia pendula*, having hard scented wood used for fences. 2 a native Australian living independently of society.
▷HISTORY C19: from a native Australian name

Myanmar *or* **Myanma** ('maɪænmɑː, 'mjænmɑː) NOUN a republic in SE Asia, on the Bay of Bengal and the Andaman Sea: unified from small states in 1752; annexed by Britain (1823–85) and made a province of India in 1886; became independent in 1948. It is generally mountainous, with the basins of the Chindwin and Irrawaddy Rivers in the central part and the Irrawaddy delta in the south. Official language: Burmese. Religion: Buddhist majority. Currency: kyat. Capital: Yangon. Pop.: 41 995 000 (2001 est.). Area: 676 577 sq. km (261 228 sq. miles). Official name: **the Union of Myanmar.** Former name (until 1989): **Burma.**

myasthenia (,maɪəs'θiːnɪə) NOUN 1 any muscular weakness. 2 short for **myasthenia gravis.**
▷HISTORY C19: from MYO- + ASTHENIA
▸**myasthenic** (,maɪəs'θɛnɪk) ADJECTIVE

myasthenia gravis ('grɑːvɪs) NOUN a chronic progressive disease in which the muscles, esp those of the head and face, become weak and easily fatigued.

myc- COMBINING FORM a variant of **myco-** before a vowel.

mycelium (maɪ'siːlɪəm) NOUN, *plural* **-lia** (-lɪə). the vegetative body of fungi: a mass of branching filaments (hyphae) that spread throughout the nutrient substratum.
▷HISTORY C19 (literally: nail of fungus): from MYCO- + Greek *hēlos* nail
▸**my'celial** ADJECTIVE ▸**myceloid** ('maɪsɪ,lɔɪd) ADJECTIVE

mycella (maɪ'sɛlə) NOUN a blue-veined Danish cream cheese, less strongly flavoured than Danish blue.
▷HISTORY C20: New Latin, from Greek *mukēs* fungus

Mycenae (maɪ'siːniː) NOUN an ancient Greek city in the NE Peloponnesus on the plain of Argos.

Mycenaean (,maɪsɪ'niːən) ADJECTIVE 1 of or relating to ancient Mycenae or its inhabitants. 2 of or relating to the Aegean civilization of Mycenae (1400 to 1100 B.C.).

-mycete NOUN COMBINING FORM indicating a fungus: *ascomycete.*
▷HISTORY from New Latin *-mycetes*, from Greek *mukētes*, plural of *mukēs* fungus

myceto- *or before a vowel* **mycet-** COMBINING FORM fungus: *mycetophagous.*
▷HISTORY from Greek *mukēs* fungus

mycetoma (,maɪsɪ'təʊmə) NOUN, *plural* **-mas** *or* **-mata** (-mətə). a chronic fungal infection, esp of the foot, characterized by swelling, usually resulting from a wound.

mycetophagous (,maɪsɪ'tɒfəgəs) ADJECTIVE *Zoology* feeding on fungi.

mycetozoan (maɪ,siːtəʊ'zəʊən) NOUN a former name for a **slime mould.**

-mycin NOUN COMBINING FORM indicating an antibiotic compound derived from a fungus: *streptomycin.*
▷HISTORY from Greek *mukēs* fungus + -IN

myco- *or before a vowel* **myc-** COMBINING FORM indicating fungus: *mycology.*

▷HISTORY from Greek *mukēs* fungus

mycobacterium (ˌmaɪkəʊbækˈtɪərɪəm) NOUN, *plural* **-ria** (-rɪə). any of the rod-shaped Gram-positive bacteria of the genus *Mycobacterium*, some of which cause human diseases, such as tuberculosis and leprosy.

mycobiont (ˌmaɪkəʊˈbaɪɒnt) NOUN *Botany* the fungal constituent of a lichen. Compare **phycobiont.**

mycol. ABBREVIATION FOR: [1] mycological. [2] mycology.

mycology (maɪˈkɒlədʒɪ) NOUN [1] the branch of biology concerned with the study of fungi. [2] the fungi of a particular region.
▸**mycological** (ˌmaɪkəˈlɒdʒɪkᵊl) *or* ˌ**mycoˈlogic** ADJECTIVE ▸**myˈcologist** NOUN

mycoplasma (ˌmaɪkəʊˈplæzmə) NOUN any prokaryotic microorganism of the genus *Mycoplasma,* some species of which cause disease (**mycoplasmosis**) in animals and humans.

mycorrhiza *or* **mycorhiza** (ˌmaɪkəˈraɪzə) NOUN, *plural* **-zae** (-ziː) *or* **-zas.** an association of a fungus and a plant in which the fungus lives within or on the outside of the plant's roots forming a symbiotic or parasitic relationship. See **ectotrophic mycorrhiza, endotrophic mycorrhiza.**
▷HISTORY C19: from MYCO- + Greek *rhiza* root
▸ˌ**mycorˈrhizal** *or* ˌ**mycoˈrhizal** ADJECTIVE

mycosis (maɪˈkəʊsɪs) NOUN any infection or disease caused by fungus.
▸**mycotic** (maɪˈkɒtɪk) ADJECTIVE

Mycostatin (ˌmaɪkəʊˈstætɪn) NOUN *Trademark* (in the US and Australia) a brand of **nystatin.**

mycotoxin (ˌmaɪkəˈtɒksɪn) NOUN any of various toxic substances produced by fungi some of which may affect food and others of which are alleged to have been used in warfare. See also **aflatoxin, yellow rain.**
▸ˌ**mycotoxˈology** NOUN

mycotrophic (ˌmaɪkəʊˈtrɒfɪk) ADJECTIVE *Botany* (of a plant) symbiotic with a fungus, esp a mycorrhizal fungus.

mydriasis (mɪˈdraɪəsɪs, maɪ-) NOUN abnormal dilation of the pupil of the eye, produced by drugs, coma, etc.
▷HISTORY C17: via Late Latin from Greek; origin obscure

mydriatic (ˌmɪdrɪˈætɪk) ADJECTIVE [1] relating to or causing mydriasis. ◆ NOUN [2] a mydriatic drug.

myel- *or before a consonant* **myelo-** COMBINING FORM the spinal cord or bone marrow: *myeloid.*
▷HISTORY from Greek *muelos* marrow, spinal cord, from *mus* muscle

myelencephalon (ˌmaɪɪlɛnˈsɛfəˌlɒn) NOUN, *plural* **-lons** *or* **-la** (-lə). the part of the embryonic hindbrain that develops into the medulla oblongata. Nontechnical name: **afterbrain.**
▸**myelencephalic** (ˌmaɪɪlɛnsəˈfælɪk) ADJECTIVE

myelin (ˈmaɪɪlɪn) *or* **myeline** (ˈmaɪɪˌliːn) NOUN a white tissue forming an insulating sheath (**myelin sheath**) around certain nerve fibres. Damage to the myelin sheath causes neurological disease, as in multiple sclerosis.
▸ˌ**myeˈlinic** ADJECTIVE

myelinated (ˈmaɪɪlɪˌneɪtɪd) ADJECTIVE (of a nerve fibre) having a myelin sheath.

myelitis (ˌmaɪɪˈlaɪtɪs) NOUN inflammation of the spinal cord or of the bone marrow.

myeloblast (ˈmaɪələʊˌblɑːst) NOUN a cell that gives rise to a granulocyte, normally occurring in the bone marrow but detected in the blood in certain diseases, esp leukaemia.
▸**myeloblastic** (ˌmaɪələʊˈblæstɪk) ADJECTIVE

myelocyte (ˈmaɪələʊˌsaɪt) NOUN an immature granulocyte, normally occurring in the bone marrow but detected in the blood in certain diseases.
▸**myelocytic** (ˌmaɪələʊˈsɪtɪk) ADJECTIVE

myelogram (maɪˈɛləˌgræm) NOUN an X-ray of the spinal cord, after injection with a radio-opaque medium.
▸ˌ**myeˈlography** NOUN

myeloid (ˈmaɪɪˌlɔɪd) ADJECTIVE of or relating to the spinal cord or the bone marrow.

myeloma (ˌmaɪɪˈləʊmə) NOUN, *plural* **-mas** *or* **-mata** (-mətə). a usually malignant tumour of the bone marrow or composed of cells normally found in bone marrow.
▸ˌ**myeˈlomaˌtoid** ADJECTIVE

myiasis (ˈmaɪəsɪs) NOUN, *plural* **-ses** (-ˌsiːz). [1] infestation of the body by the larvae of flies. [2] any disease resulting from such infestation.
▷HISTORY C19: New Latin, from Greek *muia* a fly

Mykonos (ˈmɪkənɒs, -əʊs, ˈmiːkə-) NOUN a Greek island in the S Aegean Sea, one of the Cyclades: a popular tourist resort with many churches. Pop.: 5500 (latest est.). Greek name: **Míkonos.**

My Lai (ˈmaɪ ˈlaɪ, ˈmiː) NOUN a village in S Vietnam where in 1968 US troops massacred over 400 civilians.

mylonite (ˈmaɪləˌnaɪt, ˈmɪlə-) NOUN a fine-grained metamorphic rock, often showing banding and micaceous fracture, formed by the crushing, grinding, or rolling of the original structure.
▷HISTORY C19: from Greek *mulōn* mill

mynah *or* **myna** (ˈmaɪnə) NOUN any of various tropical Asian starlings of the genera *Acridotheres, Gracula,* etc., esp *G. religiosa* (see **hill mynah**), some of which can mimic human speech.
▷HISTORY C18: from Hindi *mainā,* from Sanskrit *madana*

Mynheer (məˈnɪə) NOUN a Dutch title of address equivalent to *Sir* when used alone or to *Mr* when placed before a name.
▷HISTORY C17: from Dutch *mijnheer* my lord

myo- *or before a vowel* **my-** COMBINING FORM muscle: *myocardium.*
▷HISTORY from Greek *mus* MUSCLE

myocardial (ˌmaɪəʊˈkɑːdɪəl) ADJECTIVE of or relating to the muscular tissue of the heart.

myocardial infarction NOUN destruction of an area of heart muscle as the result of occlusion of a coronary artery. Compare **coronary thrombosis.**

myocardiograph (ˌmaɪəʊˈkɑːdɪəˌgrɑːf, -ˌgræf) NOUN an instrument for recording the movements of heart muscle.

myocarditis (ˌmaɪəʊkɑːˈdaɪtɪs) NOUN inflammation of the heart muscle.

myocardium (ˌmaɪəʊˈkɑːdɪəm) NOUN, *plural* **-dia** (-dɪə). the muscular tissue of the heart.
▷HISTORY C19: *myo-* + *cardium,* from Greek *kardia* heart

myoelectric (ˌmaɪəʊɪˈlɛktrɪk) ADJECTIVE denoting a type of powered artificial hand or limb that detects electrical changes in the muscles of the stump and converts these into movements.

myogenic (ˌmaɪəˈdʒɛnɪk) ADJECTIVE originating in or forming muscle tissue.

myoglobin (ˌmaɪəʊˈgləʊbɪn) NOUN a protein that is the main oxygen-carrier of muscle.

myograph (ˈmaɪəˌgrɑːf, -ˌgræf) NOUN an instrument for recording tracings (**myograms**) of muscular contractions.
▸ˌ**myoˈgraphic** ADJECTIVE ▸ˌ**myoˈgraphically** ADVERB
▸**myography** (maɪˈɒgrəfɪ) NOUN

myology (maɪˈɒlədʒɪ) NOUN the branch of medical science concerned with the structure and diseases of muscles.
▸**myologic** (ˌmaɪəˈlɒdʒɪk) *or* ˌ**myoˈlogical** ADJECTIVE
▸**myˈologist** NOUN

myoma (maɪˈəʊmə) NOUN, *plural* **-mas** *or* **-mata** (-mətə). a benign tumour composed of muscle tissue.
▸**myˈomatous** ADJECTIVE

myomectomy (ˌmaɪəˈmɛktəmɪ) NOUN, *plural* **-mies.** surgical removal of a myoma, especially in the uterus.

myopathy (maɪˈɒpəθɪ) NOUN, *plural* **-thies.** any disease affecting muscles or muscle tissue.

myope (ˈmaɪəʊp) NOUN any person afflicted with myopia.
▷HISTORY C18: via French from Greek *muōps;* see MYOPIA

myophily *or* **myiophily** (maɪˈɒfɪlɪ) NOUN pollination of plants by flies.
▷HISTORY from Greek *muia* fly + *philos* loving
▸**myˈophilous** *or* **myiˈophilous** ADJECTIVE

myopia (maɪˈəʊpɪə) NOUN inability to see distant objects clearly because the images are focused in front of the retina; short-sightedness.
▷HISTORY C18: via New Latin from Greek *muōps* short-sighted, from *muein* to close (the eyes), blink + *ōps* eye
▸**myopic** (maɪˈɒpɪk) ADJECTIVE ▸**myˈopically** ADVERB

myosin (ˈmaɪəsɪn) NOUN the chief protein of muscle that interacts with actin to form actomyosin during muscle contraction; it is also present in many other cell types.
▷HISTORY C19: from MYO- + -OSE² + -IN

myosis (maɪˈəʊsɪs) NOUN, *plural* **-ses** (-siːz). a variant spelling of **miosis.**

myosotis (ˌmaɪəˈsəʊtɪs) *or* **myosote** (ˈmaɪəˌsəʊt) NOUN any plant of the boraginaceous genus *Myosotis.* See **forget-me-not.**
▷HISTORY C18: New Latin from Greek *muosōtis* mouse-ear (referring to its furry leaves), from *muos,* genitive of *mus* mouse + *-ōt-,* stem of *ous* ear

myotome (ˈmaɪəˌtəʊm) NOUN [1] any segment of embryonic mesoderm that develops into skeletal muscle in the adult. [2] any of the segmentally arranged blocks of muscle in lower vertebrates such as fishes.

myotonia (ˌmaɪəˈtəʊnɪə) NOUN lack of muscle tone, frequently including muscle spasm or rigidity. Also called: **amyotonia.**
▸**myotonic** (ˌmaɪəˈtɒnɪk) ADJECTIVE

myria- COMBINING FORM indicating a very great number: *myriapod.*
▷HISTORY from Greek *murios* countless

myriad (ˈmɪrɪəd) ADJECTIVE [1] innumerable. ◆ NOUN [2] (*also used in plural*) a large indefinite number. [3] *Archaic* ten thousand.
▷HISTORY C16: via Late Latin from Greek *murias* ten thousand

myriapod (ˈmɪrɪəˌpɒd) NOUN [1] any terrestrial arthropod of the group *Myriapoda,* having a long segmented body and many walking limbs: includes the centipedes and millipedes. ◆ ADJECTIVE [2] of, relating to, or belonging to the *Myriapoda.*
▷HISTORY C19: from New Latin *Myriapoda.* See MYRIAD, -POD
▸**myriapodan** (ˌmɪrɪˈæpədᵊn) ADJECTIVE ▸ˌ**myriˈapodous** ADJECTIVE

myrica (mɪˈraɪkə) NOUN the dried root bark of the wax myrtle, used as a tonic and to treat diarrhoea.
▷HISTORY C18: via Latin from Greek *murikē* the tamarisk

myrmeco- COMBINING FORM ant: *myrmecology; myrmecophile.*
▷HISTORY from Greek *murmēx*

myrmecochory (ˌmɜːmɪkəʊˈkɔːrɪ) NOUN the dispersal of fruits and seeds by ants.

myrmecology (ˌmɜːmɪˈkɒlədʒɪ) NOUN the branch of zoology concerned with the study of ants.
▸**myrmecological** (ˌmɜːmɪkəˈlɒdʒɪkᵊl) ADJECTIVE
▸ˌ**myrmeˈcologist** NOUN

myrmecophagous (ˌmɜːmɪˈkɒfəgəs) ADJECTIVE [1] (of jaws) specialized for feeding on ants. [2] feeding on ants.

myrmecophile (ˈmɜːmɪkəʊˌfaɪl) NOUN an animal that lives in a colony of ants.
▸**myrmecophilous** (ˌmɜːmɪˈkɒfɪləs) ADJECTIVE

myrmecophily (ˌmɜːmɪˈkɒfɪlɪ) NOUN *Biology* [1] symbiosis with ants. [2] pollination of plants by ants.

Myrmidon (ˈmɜːmɪˌdɒn, -dᵊn) NOUN, *plural* **Myrmidons** *or* **Myrmidones** (mɜːˈmɪdᵊˌniːz). [1] *Greek myth* one of a race of people whom Zeus made from a nest of ants. They settled in Thessaly and were led against Troy by Achilles. [2] (*often not capital*) a follower or henchman.

myrobalan (maɪˈrɒbələn, mɪ-) NOUN [1] the dried plumlike fruit of various tropical trees of the genus *Terminalia,* used in dyeing, tanning, ink, and medicine. [2] a dye extracted from this fruit. [3] another name for **cherry plum.**
▷HISTORY C16: via Latin from Greek *murobalanos,* from *muron* ointment + *balanos* acorn

myrrh (mɜː) NOUN [1] any of several burseraceous trees and shrubs of the African and S Asian genus *Commiphora,* esp *C. myrrha,* that exude an aromatic resin. Compare **balm of Gilead** (sense 1). [2] the resin obtained from such a plant, used in perfume, incense, and medicine. [3] another name for **sweet cicely** (sense 1).
▷HISTORY Old English *myrre,* via Latin from Greek *murrha,* ultimately from Akkadian *murrū;* compare Hebrew *mōr,* Arabic *murr*

myrtaceous (mɜːˈteɪʃəs) ADJECTIVE of, relating to, or belonging to the *Myrtaceae,* a family of mostly tropical and subtropical trees and shrubs having oil glands in the leaves: includes eucalyptus, clove, myrtle, and guava.
▷HISTORY C19: via New Latin from Latin *myrtus* myrtle, from Greek *murtos*

myrtle (ˈmɜːtᵊl) NOUN 1 any evergreen shrub or tree of the myrtaceous genus *Myrtus,* esp *M. communis,* a S European shrub with pink or white flowers and aromatic blue-black berries. 2 short for **crape myrtle.** 3 **bog myrtle**. another name for **sweet gale.** 4 **creeping** *or* **trailing myrtle.** *US and Canadian* another name for **periwinkle** (the plant).
▷HISTORY C16: from Medieval Latin *myrtilla,* from Latin *myrtus,* from Greek *murtos*

myself (maɪˈsɛlf) PRONOUN 1 **a** the reflexive form of *I* or *me*. **b** (intensifier): *I myself know of no answer.* 2 *(preceded by a copula)* my usual self: *I'm not myself today.* 3 *Not standard* used instead of *I* or *me* in compound noun phrases: *John and myself are voting together.*

Mysia (ˈmɪsɪə) NOUN an ancient region in the NW corner of Asia Minor.

Mysian (ˈmɪsɪən) ADJECTIVE 1 of or relating to Mysia, an ancient region in Asia Minor, or its inhabitants. ◆ NOUN 2 a native or inhabitant of Mysia.

Mysore (maɪˈsɔː) NOUN 1 a city in S India, in S Karnataka state: former capital of the state of Mysore; manufacturing and trading centre; university (1916). Pop.: 480 692 (1991). 2 the former name (until 1973) of **Karnataka.**

mystagogue (ˈmɪstəˌɡɒɡ) NOUN (in Mediterranean mystery religions) a person who instructs those who are preparing for initiation into the mysteries.
▷HISTORY C16: via Latin from Greek *mustagōgos,* from *mustēs* candidate for initiation + *agein* to lead. See MYSTIC
▸**mystagogic** (ˌmɪstəˈɡɒdʒɪk) *or* **ˌmystaˈgogical** ADJECTIVE ▸**ˌmystaˈgogically** ADVERB ▸**mystagogy** (ˈmɪstəˌɡɒdʒɪ) NOUN

mysterious (mɪˈstɪərɪəs) ADJECTIVE 1 characterized by or indicative of mystery. 2 puzzling, curious, or enigmatic.
▸**mysˈteriously** ADVERB ▸**mysˈteriousness** NOUN

mystery¹ (ˈmɪstərɪ, -trɪ) NOUN, *plural* **-teries.** 1 an unexplained or inexplicable event, phenomenon, etc. 2 a person or thing that arouses curiosity or suspense because of an unknown, obscure, or enigmatic quality. 3 the state or quality of being obscure, inexplicable, or enigmatic. 4 a story, film, etc., which arouses suspense and curiosity because of facts concealed. 5 *Christianity* any truth that is divinely revealed but otherwise unknowable. 6 *Christianity* a sacramental rite, such as the Eucharist, or *(when plural)* the consecrated elements of the Eucharist. 7 *(often plural)* any of various rites of certain ancient Mediterranean religions. 8 short for **mystery play.**
▷HISTORY C14: via Latin from Greek *mustērion* secret rites. See MYSTIC

mystery² (ˈmɪstərɪ) NOUN, *plural* **-teries.** *Archaic* 1 a trade, occupation, or craft. 2 a guild of craftsmen.
▷HISTORY C14: from Medieval Latin *mistērium,* from Latin *ministerium* occupation, from *minister* official

mystery bag NOUN *Austral, slang* 1 a sausage. 2 a meat pie.

mystery play NOUN (in the Middle Ages) a type of drama based on the life of Christ. Compare **miracle play.**

mystery tour NOUN an excursion to an unspecified destination.

mystic (ˈmɪstɪk) NOUN 1 a person who achieves mystical experience or an apprehension of divine mysteries. ◆ ADJECTIVE 2 another word for **mystical.**
▷HISTORY C14: via Latin from Greek *mustikos,* from *mustēs* mystery initiate; related to *muein* to initiate into sacred rites

mystical (ˈmɪstɪkᵊl) ADJECTIVE 1 relating to or characteristic of mysticism. 2 *Christianity* having a divine or sacred significance that surpasses natural human apprehension. 3 having occult or metaphysical significance, nature, or force. 4 a less common word for **mysterious.**
▸**ˈmystically** ADVERB ▸**ˈmysticalness** NOUN

mysticism (ˈmɪstɪˌsɪzəm) NOUN 1 belief in or experience of a reality surpassing normal human understanding or experience, esp a reality perceived as essential to the nature of life. 2 a system of contemplative prayer and spirituality aimed at achieving direct intuitive experience of the divine. 3 obscure or confused belief or thought.

mystify (ˈmɪstɪˌfaɪ) VERB **-fies, -fying, -fied.** *(tr)* 1 to confuse, bewilder, or puzzle. 2 to make mysterious or obscure.
▷HISTORY C19: from French *mystifier,* from *mystère* MYSTERY¹ or *mystique* MYSTIC
▸**ˌmystifiˈcation** NOUN ▸**ˈmystiˌfier** NOUN ▸**ˈmystiˌfying** ADJECTIVE ▸**ˈmystiˌfyingly** ADVERB

mystique (mɪˈstiːk) NOUN an aura of mystery, power, and awe that surrounds a person or thing: *the mystique of the theatre; the mystique of computer programming.*
▷HISTORY C20: from French (adj): MYSTIC

myth (mɪθ) NOUN 1 **a** a story about superhuman beings of an earlier age taken by preliterate society to be a true account, usually of how natural phenomena, social customs, etc., came into existence. **b** another word for **mythology** (senses 1, 3). 2 a person or thing whose existence is fictional or unproven. 3 (in modern literature) a theme or character type embodying an idea: *Hemingway's myth of the male hero.* 4 *Philosophy* (esp in the writings of Plato) an allegory or parable.
▷HISTORY C19: via Late Latin from Greek *muthos* fable, word

myth. ABBREVIATION FOR: 1 mythological. 2 mythology.

mythical (ˈmɪθɪkᵊl) *or* **mythic** (ˈmɪθɪk) ADJECTIVE 1 of or relating to myth. 2 imaginary or fictitious.
▸**ˈmythically** ADVERB

mythicize *or* **mythicise** (ˈmɪθɪˌsaɪz) VERB *(tr)* to make into or treat as a myth.
▸**ˌmythiciˈzation** *or* **ˌmythiciˈsation** NOUN ▸**ˈmythicist** *or* **ˈmythiˌcizer** *or* **ˈmythiˌciser** NOUN

mytho- COMBINING FORM myth: *mythogenesis; mythography.*

mythological (ˌmɪθəˈlɒdʒɪkᵊl) ADJECTIVE 1 of or relating to mythology. 2 mythical.
▸**ˌmythoˈlogically** ADVERB

mythologist (mɪˈθɒlədʒɪst) NOUN 1 an expert in or student of mythology. 2 a writer or editor of myths.

mythologize *or* **mythologise** (mɪˈθɒləˌdʒaɪz) VERB 1 to tell, study, or explain (myths). 2 *(intr)* to create or make up myths. 3 *(tr)* to convert into a myth.
▸**myˌthologiˈzation** *or* **myˌthologiˈsation** NOUN ▸**myˈthologer** *or* **myˈtholoˌgizer** *or* **myˈtholoˌgiser** NOUN

mythology (mɪˈθɒlədʒɪ) NOUN, *plural* **-gies.** 1 a body of myths, esp one associated with a particular culture, institution, person, etc. 2 a body of stories about a person, institution, etc.: *the mythology of Hollywood.* 3 myths collectively. 4 the study or collecting of myths.

mythomania (ˌmɪθəʊˈmeɪnɪə) NOUN *Psychiatry* the tendency to lie, exaggerate, or relate incredible imaginary adventures as if they had really happened, occurring in some mental disorders.
▸**mythomaniac** (ˌmɪθəʊˈmeɪnɪˌæk) NOUN, ADJECTIVE

mythopoeia (ˌmɪθəʊˈpiːə) *or* **mythopoesis** (ˌmɪθəpəʊˈiːsɪs) NOUN the composition or making of myths.
▷HISTORY C19: from Greek, from *muthopoiein,* from *muthos* myth + *poiein* to make

mythopoeic (ˌmɪθəʊˈpiːɪk) ADJECTIVE of or relating to the composition of myths; productive of myths.
▸**ˌmythoˈpoeism** NOUN ▸**ˌmythoˈpoeist** NOUN

mythos (ˈmaɪθɒs, ˈmɪθɒs) NOUN, *plural* **-thoi** (-θɔɪ). 1 the complex of beliefs, values, attitudes, etc., characteristic of a specific group or society. 2 another word for **myth** or **mythology.**

Mytilene (ˌmɪtɪˈliːnɪ) NOUN 1 a port on the Greek island of Lesbos: Roman remains; Byzantine fortress Pop.: 25 000 (latest est.). Modern Greek name: **Mitilíni.** 2 a former name for **Lesbos.**

myxo (ˈmɪksəʊ) NOUN *Austral, slang* short for **myxomatosis.**

myxo- *or before a vowel* **myx-** COMBINING FORM mucus or slime: *myxomycete.*
▷HISTORY from Greek *muxa* slime, mucus

myxoedema *or US* **myxedema** (ˌmɪksɪˈdiːmə) NOUN a disease resulting from underactivity of the thyroid gland characterized by puffy eyes, face, and hands and mental sluggishness. See also **cretinism.**
▸**myxoedemic** (ˌmɪksɪˈdɛmɪk) *or* **myxoedematous** (ˌmɪksɪˈdɛmətəs, -ˈdiː-) *or (US)* **ˌmyxeˈdemic** *or* **ˌmyxeˈdematous** ADJECTIVE

myxoma (mɪkˈsəʊmə) NOUN, *plural* **-mas** *or* **-mata** (-mətə). a tumour composed of mucous connective tissue, usually situated in subcutaneous tissue.
▸**myxomatous** (mɪkˈsɒmətəs) ADJECTIVE

myxomatosis (ˌmɪksəməˈtəʊsɪs) NOUN an infectious and usually fatal viral disease of rabbits characterized by swelling of the mucous membranes and formation of skin tumours; transmitted by flea bites.

myxomycete (ˌmɪksəʊmaɪˈsiːt) NOUN a slime mould, esp a slime mould of the phylum *Myxomycota* (division *Myxomycetes* in traditional classifications).
▸**ˌmyxomyˈcetous** ADJECTIVE

myxovirus (ˈmɪksəʊˌvaɪərəs) NOUN any of a group of viruses that cause influenza, mumps, and certain other diseases.

mz THE INTERNET DOMAIN NAME FOR Mozambique.

mzee (ᵊmˈzeɪ) *E African* ◆ NOUN 1 an old person. ◆ ADJECTIVE 2 advanced in years.
▷HISTORY C19: from Swahili

mzungu (ᵊmˈzʊŋɡuː) NOUN *E African* a White person.
▷HISTORY C20: from Swahili

Nn

n *or* **N** (ɛn) NOUN, *plural* **n's, N's** *or* **Ns.** [1] the 14th letter and 11th consonant of the modern English alphabet. [2] a speech sound represented by this letter, usually an alveolar nasal, as in *nail.*

n[1] SYMBOL FOR: [1] neutron. [2] *Optics* index of refraction. [3] nano-.

n[2] (ɛn) DETERMINER an indefinite number (of): *there are n objects in a box.*

N SYMBOL FOR: [1] Also: **kt.** *Chess* knight. [2] neper. [3] neutral. [4] newton(s). [5] *Chem* nitrogen. [6] North. [7] Avogadro's number. [8] noun. ◆ [9] INTERNATIONAL CAR REGISTRATION FOR Norway.

n. ABBREVIATION FOR: [1] natus. [2] neuter. [3] new. [4] nominative. [5] noun.
▷**HISTORY** (for sense 1) Latin: born

***n*-** PREFIX *Chem* short for **normal** (sense 6).

na[1] (nɑː) a variant of **nae.**

na[2] THE INTERNET DOMAIN NAME FOR Namibia.

Na THE CHEMICAL SYMBOL FOR sodium.
▷**HISTORY** Latin *natrium*

NA [1] ABBREVIATION FOR North America. ◆ [2] INTERNATIONAL CAR REGISTRATION FOR Netherlands Antilles.

n/a ABBREVIATION FOR not applicable.

NAACP (in the US) ABBREVIATION FOR National Association for the Advancement of Colored People.

NAAFI *or* **Naafi** (ˈnæfɪ) NOUN [1] ACRONYM FOR Navy, Army, and Air Force Institutes: an organization providing canteens, shops, etc., for British military personnel at home or overseas. [2] a canteen, shop, etc., run by this organization.

naan (nɑːn) NOUN another name for **nan bread.**

naartjie (ˈnɑːtʃɪ) NOUN *South African* a tangerine.
▷**HISTORY** Afrikaans

nab (næb) VERB **nabs, nabbing, nabbed.** (*tr*) *Informal* [1] to arrest. [2] to catch (someone) in wrongdoing. [3] to seize suddenly; snatch.
▷**HISTORY** C17: perhaps of Scandinavian origin; compare Danish *nappe,* Swedish *nappa* to snatch. See KIDNAP

Nabataean *or* **Nabatean** (ˌnæbəˈtiːən) NOUN [1] a member of an Arab trading people who flourished southeast of Palestine, around Petra, in the Hellenistic and Roman periods. [2] the extinct form of Aramaic spoken by this people.

Nabis (*French* nabi) PLURAL NOUN, *singular* **-bi** (-bi). a group of French artists much influenced by Gauguin, including Bonnard and Vuillard, who reacted against the naturalism of the impressionists. See also **synthetism.**
▷**HISTORY** C19: French, from Hebrew *nābhi* prophet

nabla (ˈnæblə) NOUN *Maths* another name for **del.**
▷**HISTORY** C19: from Greek *nabla* stringed instrument, because it is shaped like a harp

Nablus (ˈnɑːbləs) NOUN a town in the West Bank: near the site of ancient Shechem. Pop.: 100 231 (1997).

nabob (ˈneɪbɒb) NOUN [1] *Informal* a rich, powerful, or important man. [2] (formerly) a European who made a fortune in the Orient, esp in India. [3] another name for a **nawab.**
▷**HISTORY** C17: from Portuguese *nababo,* from Hindi *nawwāb;* see NAWAB
▸**nabobery** (ˈneɪbɒbərɪ, neɪˈbɒbərɪ) *or* ˈ**nabobism** NOUN
▸ˈ**nabobish** ADJECTIVE

Nabonidus (ˌnæbəˈnaɪdəs) NOUN *Old Testament* the father of Belshazzar; last king of Babylon before it was captured by Cyrus in 539 B.C.

Naboth (ˈneɪbɒθ) NOUN *Old Testament* an inhabitant of Jezreel, murdered by King Ahab at the instigation of his wife Jezebel for refusing to sell his vineyard (I Kings 21).

nacelle (nəˈsɛl) NOUN a streamlined enclosure on an aircraft, not part of the fuselage, to accommodate an engine, passengers, crew, etc.
▷**HISTORY** C20: from French: small boat, from Late Latin *nāvicella,* a diminutive of Latin *nāvis* ship

nacho (ˈnɑːtʃəʊ) NOUN, *plural* **nachos.** *Mexican cookery* a snack consisting of a piece of tortilla topped with cheese, hot peppers, etc., and grilled.

NACODS (ˈneɪkɒdz) NOUN ACRONYM FOR National Association of Colliery Overmen, Deputies, and Shotfirers.

nacre (ˈneɪkə) NOUN the technical name for **mother-of-pearl.**
▷**HISTORY** C16: via French from Old Italian *naccara,* from Arabic *naqqārah* shell, drum
▸ˈ**nacred** ADJECTIVE

nacreous (ˈneɪkrɪəs) ADJECTIVE [1] relating to or consisting of mother-of-pearl. [2] having the lustre of mother-of-pearl: *nacreous minerals.*

NACRO *or* **Nacro** (ˈnækrəʊ) NOUN ACRONYM FOR National Association for the Care and Resettlement of Offenders.

NAD NOUN *Biochem* nicotinamide adenine dinucleotide; a coenzyme that is a hydrogen carrier in metabolic reactions, esp in tissue respiration. Former name: **DPN.**

nada (ˈnɑːdə) NOUN *Chiefly US informal* nothing.
▷**HISTORY** C20: Spanish

Na-Dene *or* **Na-Déné** (nɑːˈdeɪnɪ, nəˈdiːn) NOUN a phylum of North American Indian languages including Athapascan, Tlingit, and Haida.
▷**HISTORY** from Haida *na* to dwell + Athapascan *dene* people; coined by Edward Sapir (1884–1939), American anthropologist

NADH NOUN *Biochem* the chemically reduced form of NAD.

nadir (ˈneɪdɪə, ˈnæ-) NOUN [1] the point on the celestial sphere directly below an observer and diametrically opposite the zenith. [2] the lowest or deepest point; depths: *the nadir of despair.*
▷**HISTORY** C14: from Old French, from Arabic *nazīr as-samt,* literally: opposite the zenith

nadors (ˈnɑːˌdɔːz) NOUN *South African* a thirst brought on by excessive consumption of alcohol.
▷**HISTORY** from Afrikaans *na* after + *dors* thirst

NADP NOUN *Biochem* nicotinamide adenine dinucleotide phosphate; a coenzyme with functions similar to those of NAD. Former name: **TPN.**

NADPH NOUN *Biochem* the chemically reduced form of NADP.

nads (nædz) PLURAL NOUN *Slang* another word for **testicles.**
▷**HISTORY** C20: (GO)NAD

nae (neɪ) *or* **na** (nɑː) a Scot word for **no** or **not.**

naevus *or US* **nevus** (ˈniːvəs) NOUN, *plural* **-vi** (-vaɪ). any congenital growth or pigmented blemish on the skin; birthmark or mole.
▷**HISTORY** C19: from Latin; related to (*g*)*natus* born, produced by nature
▸ˈ**naevoid** *or US* ˈ**nevoid** ADJECTIVE

naff (næf) ADJECTIVE *Brit, slang* inferior; in poor taste.
▷**HISTORY** C19: perhaps back slang for *fan,* short for FANNY
▸ˈ**naffness** NOUN

naff off SENTENCE SUBSTITUTE *Brit, slang* a forceful expression of dismissal or contempt.

NAFTA (ˈnæftə) NOUN ACRONYM FOR North American Free Trade Agreement.

nag[1] (næg) VERB **nags, nagging, nagged.** [1] to scold or annoy constantly. [2] (when *intr,* often foll by *at*) to be a constant source of discomfort or worry (to): *toothache nagged him all day.* ◆ NOUN [3] a person, esp a woman, who nags.
▷**HISTORY** C19: of Scandinavian origin; compare Swedish *nagga* to GNAW, irritate, German *nagen*
▸ˈ**nagger** NOUN ▸ˈ**naggingly** ADVERB

nag[2] (næg) NOUN [1] *Often derogatory* a horse. [2] a small riding horse.
▷**HISTORY** C14: of Germanic origin; related to NEIGH

Naga (ˈnɑːgə) NOUN [1] (*plural* **Nagas** *or* **Naga**) a member of a people of NE India and W Myanmar: until the early 20th century they practised head-hunting. [2] the language of this people, belonging to the Sino-Tibetan family of languages and having many dialects.

Nagaland (ˈnɑːgəˌlænd) NOUN a state of NE India: formed in 1962 from parts of Assam and the North-East Frontier Agency; inhabited chiefly by Naga tribes; consists of almost inaccessible forested hills and mountains (the **Naga Hills**); shifting cultivation predominates. Capital: Kohima. Pop.: 1 988 636 (2001). Area: 16 579 sq. km (6401 sq. miles).

nagana (nəˈgɑːnə) NOUN a disease of all domesticated animals of central and southern Africa, caused by parasitic protozoa of the genus *Trypanosoma* transmitted by tsetse flies.
▷**HISTORY** from Zulu *u-nakane*

Nagano (nəˈgɑːnəʊ) NOUN a city in central Japan, on central Honshu: Buddhist shrine; two universities. Pop.: 358 512 (1995).

Nagari (ˈnɑːgərɪ) NOUN [1] a set of scripts, including Devanagari, used as the writing systems for several languages of India. [2] another word for **Devanagari.**

Nagasaki (ˌnɑːgəˈsɑːkɪ) NOUN a port in SW Japan, on W Kyushu: almost completely destroyed in 1945 by the second atomic bomb dropped on Japan by the US; shipbuilding industry. Pop.: 438 724 (1995).

nagor (ˈneɪgɔː) NOUN another name for **reedbuck.**
▷**HISTORY** C18: from French, arbitrarily named by Buffon, from earlier *nanguer*

Nagorno-Karabakh Autonomous Region (nəˈgɔːnəʊkərʌˈbɑːk) NOUN an administrative division in S Azerbaijan. In 1990–94 Armenian claims to the region led to violent unrest and fighting between national forces. Capital: Stepanakert. Pop.: 193 300 (1991 est.). Area: 4400 sq. km (1700 sq. miles).

Nagoya (ˈnɑːgɔɪjə) NOUN a city in central Japan, on S Honshu on Ise Bay: a major industrial centre. Pop.: 2 152 258 (1995).

Nagpur (nægˈpʊə) NOUN a city in central India, in NE Maharashtra state: became capital of the kingdom of Nagpur (1743); capital of the Central Provinces (later Madhya Pradesh) from 1861 to 1956. Pop.: 1 624 752 (1991).

Nagyszeben (ˈnɒdjseːˌbɛn) NOUN the Hungarian name for **Sibiu.**

Nagyvárad (ˈnɒdjvaːrɒd) NOUN the Hungarian name for **Oradea.**

Nah. *Bible* ABBREVIATION FOR Nahum.

Naha (ˈnɑːhə) NOUN a port in S Japan, on the SW coast of Okinawa Island: chief city of the Ryukyu Islands. Pop.: 301 928 (1995).

Nahal (nəˈhɑːl) NOUN [1] (in Israel) a military youth organization. [2] (*not capital*) an agricultural settlement, esp in a border area, set up or manned by Nahal members.
▷**HISTORY** C20: from Hebrew acronym for *No'ar Halutzi Lohem* Pioneer and Military Youth

NAHT (in Britain) ABBREVIATION FOR National Association of Head Teachers.

Nahuatl (ˈnɑːwɑːtᵊl, nɑːˈwɑːtᵊl) NOUN [1] (*plural* **-tl** *or* **-tls**) a member of one of a group of Central American and Mexican Indian peoples including the Aztecs. [2] the language of these peoples, belonging to the Uto-Aztecan family. ◆ Also **Nahuatlan.**

Nahum (ˈneɪhəm) NOUN *Old Testament* [1] a Hebrew prophet of the 7th century B.C. [2] the book containing his oracles.

NAI (in Britain) ABBREVIATION FOR **nonaccidental injury.**

naiad (ˈnaɪæd) NOUN, *plural* **-ads** *or* **-ades** (-əˌdiːz). [1] *Greek myth* a nymph dwelling in a lake, river, spring, or fountain. [2] the aquatic larva of the

dragonfly, mayfly, and related insects. 3 Also called: **water nymph.** any monocotyledonous submerged aquatic plant of the genus *Naias* (or *Najas*), having narrow leaves and small flowers: family *Naiadaceae* (or *Najadaceae*). 4 any of certain freshwater mussels of the genus *Unio.* See **mussel** (sense 2).
▷HISTORY C17: via Latin from Greek *nāias* water nymph; related to *náein* to flow

NAIC ABBREVIATION FOR National Astronomy and Ionosphere Center (headquarters Cornell University, New York State).

naïf (nɑːˈiːf) ADJECTIVE, NOUN a less common word for **naive.**

nail (neɪl) NOUN 1 a fastening device usually made from round or oval wire, having a point at one end and a head at the other. 2 anything resembling such a fastening device, esp in function or shape. 3 the horny plate covering part of the dorsal surface of the fingers or toes. See **fingernail, toenail.** Related adjectives: **ungual, ungular.** 4 the claw of a mammal, bird, or reptile. 5 *Slang* a hypodermic needle, used for injecting drugs. 6 a unit of length, formerly used for measuring cloth, equal to two and a quarter inches. 7 **a nail in one's coffin.** an experience or event that tends to shorten life or hasten the end of something. 8 **bite one's nails. a** to chew off the ends of one's fingernails. **b** to be worried or apprehensive. 9 **hard as nails. a** in tough physical condition. **b** without sentiment or feelings. 10 **hit the nail on the head.** to do or say something correct or telling. 11 **on the nail.** (of payments) at once (esp in the phrase **pay on the nail**). ◆ VERB *(tr)* 12 to attach with or as if with nails. 13 *Informal* to arrest or seize. 14 *Informal* to hit or bring down, as with a shot: *I nailed the sniper.* 15 *Informal* to expose or detect (a lie or liar). 16 to fix or focus (one's eyes, attention, etc.) on an object. 17 to stud with nails. ◆ See also **nail down, nail up.**
▷HISTORY Old English *nægl;* related to Old High German *nagal* nail, Latin *unguis* fingernail, claw, Greek *onux*
▸**ˈnailer** NOUN ▸**ˈnail-less** ADJECTIVE

nail bar NOUN a type of beauty salon specializing in manicure and the decoration of, esp women's, fingernails.

nailbiter (ˈneɪlˌbaɪtə) NOUN 1 a person who bites his or her nails. 2 a person who is anxious or tense. 3 something that causes anxiety or tension.

nail-biting NOUN 1 the act or habit of biting one's fingernails. 2 **a** anxiety or tension. **b** *(as modifier): nail-biting suspense.*

nail bomb NOUN an explosive device containing nails, used by terrorists to cause serious injuries in crowded situations.

nailbrush (ˈneɪlˌbrʌʃ) NOUN a small stiff-bristled brush for cleaning the fingernails.

nail down VERB *(tr, adverb)* 1 to fasten down with or as if with nails. 2 *Informal* to extort a definite promise or consent from: *I nailed him down on the deadline.* 3 *Informal* to settle in a definite way: *they nailed down the agreement.*

nailed-on ADJECTIVE *Slang* certain, definite; guaranteed to be successful.

nailfile (ˈneɪlˌfaɪl) NOUN a small file, chiefly either of metal or of board coated with emery, used to trim the nails.

nailhead (ˈneɪlˌhɛd) NOUN a decorative device, as on tooled leather, resembling the round head of a nail.

nail polish, varnish, *or US* **enamel** NOUN a quick-drying lacquer applied to colour the nails or make them shiny or esp both.

nail set *or* **punch** NOUN a punch for driving the head of a nail below or flush with the surrounding surface.

nail technician NOUN a person whose job is to take care of and decorate people's fingernails.

nail up VERB *(tr, adverb)* to shut in or fasten tightly with or as if with nails.

nainsook (ˈneɪnsʊk, ˈnæn-) NOUN a light soft plain-weave cotton fabric, used esp for babies' wear.
▷HISTORY C19: from Hindi *nainsukh,* literally: delight to the eye, from *nain* eye + *sukh* delight, from Sanskrit *sukha*

naira (ˈnaɪrə) NOUN the standard monetary unit of Nigeria, divided into 100 kobo.
▷HISTORY C20: altered from NIGERIA

NAI register NOUN *Social welfare* (in Britain) a list of children deemed to be at risk of abuse or injury from their parents or guardians, compiled and held by a local authority, area health authority, or NSPCC Special Unit. Also called: **child abuse register.**

Nairnshire (ˈnɛənˌʃɪə, -ʃə) NOUN (until 1975) a county of NE Scotland, now part of Highland.

Nairobi (naɪˈrəʊbɪ) NOUN the capital of Kenya, in the southwest at an altitude of 1650 m (5500 ft.): founded in 1899; became capital in 1905; commercial and industrial centre; the **Nairobi National Park** (a game reserve) is nearby. Pop.: 2 143 254 (1999).

NAIRU (ˈnaɪruː) NOUN *Economics* ACRONYM FOR non-accelerating inflation rate of unemployment: the rate of unemployment at which inflation is neither accelerating nor decelerating. Also called: **natural rate of unemployment.**

Naismith's rule (ˈneɪsmɪθs) NOUN *Mountaineering* a rule of thumb for calculating the time needed for a climbing expedition, allowing 1 hour for every 3 miles of distance plus 1 hour for every 2000 feet of height.
▷HISTORY C19: named after W. W. *Naismith* (1856–1935), Scottish climber, who formulated it

naissant (ˈneɪsᵊnt) ADJECTIVE *Heraldry* (of a beast) having only the forepart shown above a horizontal division of a shield.
▷HISTORY C16: from Old French, literally: being born. See NASCENT

naive, naïve (nɑːˈiːv, naɪˈiːv), *or* **naïf** ADJECTIVE 1 **a** having or expressing innocence and credulity; ingenuous. **b** *(as collective noun;* preceded by *the): only the naive believed him.* 2 artless or unsophisticated. 3 lacking developed powers of analysis, reasoning, or criticism: *a naive argument.* 4 another word for **primitive** (sense 5). ◆ NOUN 5 *Rare* a person who is naive, esp in artistic style. See **primitive** (sense 10).
▷HISTORY C17: from French, feminine of *naïf,* from Old French *naif* native, spontaneous, from Latin *nātīvus* NATIVE, from *nasci* to be born
▸**naˈively, naˈïvely,** *or* **naˈïfly** ADVERB ▸**naˈiveness, naˈïveness,** *or* **naˈïfness** NOUN

naive realism NOUN *Philosophy* the doctrine that in perception of physical objects what is before the mind is the object itself and not a representation of it. Compare **representationalism** (sense 1).

naivety (naɪˈiːvtɪ), **naiveté,** *or* **naïveté** (ˌnɑːiːvˈteɪ) NOUN, *plural* **-ties** *or* **-tés.** 1 the state or quality of being naive; ingenuousness; simplicity. 2 a naive act or statement.

naked (ˈneɪkɪd) ADJECTIVE 1 having the body completely unclothed; undressed. Compare **bare**[1]. 2 having no covering; bare; exposed: *a naked flame.* 3 with no qualification or concealment; stark; plain: *the naked facts.* 4 unaided by any optical instrument, such as a telescope or microscope (esp in the phrase **the naked eye**). 5 with no defence, protection, or shield. 6 (usually foll by *of*) stripped or destitute: *naked of weapons.* 7 (of the seeds of gymnosperms) not enclosed in a pericarp. 8 (of flowers) lacking a perianth. 9 (of stems) lacking leaves and other appendages. 10 (of animals) lacking hair, feathers, scales, etc. 11 *Law* **a** unsupported by authority or financial or other consideration: *a naked contract.* **b** lacking some essential condition to render valid; incomplete.
▷HISTORY Old English *nacod;* related to Old High German *nackot* (German *nackt*), Old Norse *noktr,* Latin *nudus*
▸**ˈnakedly** ADVERB ▸**ˈnakedness** NOUN

naked ladies NOUN *(functioning as singular)* another name for **autumn crocus.**

naked lady NOUN a leafless pink orchid found in Australia and New Zealand.

naked singularity NOUN *Astronomy* an infinitely dense point mass without a surrounding black hole. See also **black hole.**

naker (ˈneɪkə, ˈnæk-) NOUN one of a pair of small kettledrums used in medieval music.
▷HISTORY C14: from Old French *nacre,* via Medieval Greek *anakara,* from Arabic *naqāra*

nakfa (ˈnækfə) NOUN the standard currency unit of Eritrea.

Nakhichevan (nəˌkɪtʃɛˈvɑːn) NOUN a city in W Azerbaijan, capital of the Nakhichevan Autonomous Republic: an ancient trading town; ceded to Russia in 1828. Pop.: 66 800 (1994). Ancient name: **Naxuana** (ˌnækˈswɑːnə).

Nakhichevan Autonomous Republic (nəˌkɪtʃɛˈvɑːn) NOUN a region belonging to Azerbaijan, from which it is separated by part of Armenia; annexed by Russia in 1828; unilaterally declared secession from the Soviet Union in 1990. Capital: Nakhichevan. Pop.: 315 000 (1994). Area: 5500 sq. km (2120 sq. miles).

Nakuru (nəˈkuːruː) NOUN a town in W Kenya, on Lake Nakuru: commercial centre of an agricultural region. Pop.: 231 262 (1999).

nalbuphine hydrochloride (ˈnælbuːˌfiːn) NOUN an opiate drug used as a painkiller. See also **Nubain.**

Nalchik (*Russian* ˈnaljtʃik) NOUN a city in SW Russia, capital of the Kabardino-Balkar Republic, in a valley of the Greater Caucasus: health resort. Pop.: 234 700 (1999 est.).

NALGO (ˈnælgəʊ) NOUN (formerly, in Britain) ACRONYM FOR National and Local Government Officers' Association.

naloxone (nəˈlɒksəʊn) NOUN a chemical substance that counteracts the effects of opiates by binding to opiate receptors on cells.
▷HISTORY C20: from *N-al(lylnor)ox(ymorph)one,* the chemical name

Nam *or* **'Nam** (næm) NOUN *Chiefly US informal* Vietnam.

NAM INTERNATIONAL CAR REGISTRATION FOR Namibia.

Nama (ˈnɑːmə) *or* **Namaqua** (nəˈmɑːkwə) NOUN 1 *(plural* **-ma, -mas** *or* **-qua, -quas)** a member of a Khoikhoi people living chiefly in Namaqualand. 2 the Khoikhoi language spoken by this people, belonging to the Khoisan family. See also **Damara.**
▸**ˈNaman** *or* **Naˈmaquan** NOUN, ADJECTIVE

Namangan (*Russian* nəmanˈgan) NOUN a city in E Uzbekistan. Pop.: 291 000 (1998 est.).

Namaqualand (nəˈmɑːkwəˌlænd) NOUN a semiarid coastal region of SW Africa, extending from near Windhoek, Namibia, into W South Africa: divided by the Orange River into **Little Namaqualand** in South Africa, and **Great Namaqualand** in Namibia; rich mineral resources. Area: 47 961 sq. km (18 518 sq. miles). Also called: **Namaland** (ˈnɑːməˌlænd).

namas kar (nəˈmʌs kɑː) NOUN a salutation used in India.
▷HISTORY Sanskrit, from *namas* salutation, bow + *kara* doing

namby-pamby (ˌnæmbɪˈpæmbɪ) ADJECTIVE 1 sentimental or prim in a weak insipid way: *namby-pamby manners.* 2 clinging, feeble, or spineless: *a namby-pamby child.* ◆ NOUN, *plural* **-bies.** 3 a person who is namby-pamby.
▷HISTORY C18: a nickname of Ambrose Phillips (died 1749), whose pastoral verse was ridiculed for being insipid

Nam Co (ˈnɑːm ˈkɔː) *or* **Nam Tso** NOUN a salt lake in SW China, in SE Tibet at an altitude of 4629 m (15 186 ft.). Area: about 1800 sq. km (700 sq. miles). Also called: **Tengri Nor.**

name (neɪm) NOUN 1 a word or term by which a person or thing is commonly and distinctively known. Related adjective: **nominal.** 2 mere outward appearance or form as opposed to fact (esp in the phrase **in name**): *he was a ruler in name only.* 3 a word, title, or phrase descriptive of character, usually abusive or derogatory: *to call a person names.* 4 reputation, esp, if unspecified, good reputation: *he's made quite a name for himself.* 5 **a** a famous person or thing: *a name in the advertising world.* **b** *Chiefly US and Canadian (as modifier): a name product.* 6 a member of Lloyd's who provides part of the capital of a syndicate and shares in its profits or losses but does not arrange its business. 7 **in** *or* **under the name of.** using as a name. 8 **in the name of. a** for the sake of. **b** by the sanction or authority of. 9 **know by name.** to have heard of without having met. 10 **name of the game. a** anything that is essential, significant, or important. **b** expected or normal conditions, circumstances, etc.: *in gambling, losing money's the name of the game.* 11 **to one's name.** belonging to one: *I haven't a penny to my name.* ◆ VERB *(tr)* 12 to give a name to; call by a name: *she named the child Edward.* 13 to refer to by name; cite:

he named three French poets. 14 to determine, fix, or specify: *they have named a date for the meeting.* 15 to appoint to or cite for a particular title, honour, or duty; nominate: *he was named Journalist of the Year.* 16 to ban (an MP) from the House of Commons by mentioning him formally by name as being guilty of disorderly conduct. 17 **name and shame.** to reveal the identity of a person or organization guilty of illegal or unacceptable behaviour in order to embarrass them into not repeating the offence. 18 **name names.** to cite people, esp in order to blame or accuse them. 19 **name the day.** to choose the day for one's wedding. 20 **you name it.** whatever you need, mention, etc.
▷HISTORY Old English *nama,* related to Latin *nomen,* Greek *noma,* Old High German *namo,* German *Namen*
▶ **'namable** *or* **'nameable** ADJECTIVE

name-calling NOUN verbal abuse, esp as a crude form of argument.

namecheck ('neɪm,tʃɛk) VERB *(tr)* 1 to mention (someone) specifically by name. ◆ NOUN 2 a specific mention of someone's name, for example on a radio programme.

name day NOUN 1 *RC Church* the feast day of a saint whose name one bears. 2 another name for **ticket day.**

name-dropping NOUN *Informal* the practice of referring frequently to famous or fashionable people, esp as though they were intimate friends, in order to impress others.
▶ **'name-,dropper** NOUN

nameless ('neɪmlɪs) ADJECTIVE 1 without a name; anonymous. 2 incapable of being named; indescribable: *a nameless horror seized him.* 3 too unpleasant or disturbing to be mentioned: *nameless atrocities.* 4 having no legal name; illegitimate: *a nameless child.*
▶ **'namelessly** ADVERB ▶ **'namelessness** NOUN

namely ('neɪmlɪ) ADVERB that is to say: *it was another colour, namely green.*

Namen ('naːmə) NOUN the Flemish name for **Namur.**

name part NOUN another name for **title role.**

nameplate ('neɪm,pleɪt) NOUN a small panel on or next to the door of a room or building, bearing the occupant's name and profession.

namesake ('neɪm,seɪk) NOUN 1 a person or thing named after another. 2 a person or thing with the same name as another.
▷HISTORY C17: probably a shortening of the phrase describing people connected *for the name's sake*

nametape ('neɪm,teɪp) NOUN a narrow cloth tape bearing the owner's name and attached to an article.

Namhoi ('nɑːm'hɔɪ) NOUN another name for **Foshan.**

Namibe (næ'miːb) NOUN a port in SW Angola: fishing industry. Pop.: 77 000 (latest est.).

Namibia (nɑː'mɪbɪə, nə-) NOUN a country in southern Africa bordering on South Africa: annexed by Germany in 1884 and mandated by the League of Nations to South Africa in 1920. The mandate was terminated by the UN in 1966 but this was ignored by South Africa, as was the 1971 ruling by the International Court of Justice that the territory be surrendered. Independence was achieved in 1990 and Namibia became a member of the Commonwealth; Walvis Bay remained a South African enclave until 1994 when it was returned to Namibia. Official language: English; Afrikaans and German also spoken. Religion: mostly animist, with some Christians. Currency: dollar. Capital: Windhoek. Pop.: 1 798 000 (2001 est.). Area: 823 328 sq. km (317 887 sq. miles). Also called: **South West Africa.** Former name (1885–1919): **German Southwest Africa.**

Namibian (nɑː'mɪbɪən, nə-) ADJECTIVE 1 of or relating to Namibia or its inhabitants. ◆ NOUN 2 a native or inhabitant of Namibia.

namma hole ('næmə) NOUN *Austral* a natural well in a rock.
▷HISTORY C19: from a native Australian language

nam pla (,næm 'plɑː) NOUN a fermented fish sauce with a strong aroma and a salty taste, often used in Thai cookery.
▷HISTORY Thai

Nam Tso ('nɑːm 'tsɔː) NOUN a variant transliteration of the Chinese name for **Nam Co.**

Namur (næ'mʊə; *French* namyr) NOUN 1 a province of S Belgium. Capital: Namur. Pop.: 443 903 (2000 est.). Area: 3660 sq. km (1413 sq. miles). 2 a town in S Belgium, capital of Namur province: strategically situated on a promontory between the Sambre and Meuse Rivers, besieged and captured many times. Pop.: 105 419 (2000 est.). Flemish name: **Namen.**

nan (næn), **nana,** *or* **nanna** ('nænə) NOUN a child's words for **grandmother.**
▷HISTORY see NANNY; compare Greek *nanna* aunt, Medieval Latin *nonna* old woman

nana ('nɑːnə) NOUN 1 *Slang* a fool. 2 *Austral, slang* the head. 3 **do one's nana.** *Austral, slang* to become very angry. 4 **off one's nana.** *Austral, slang* mad; insane.
▷HISTORY C19: probably from BANANA

Nanaimo bar (nə'naɪməʊ) NOUN *Canadian* a chocolate-coated sweet with a filling made from butter and icing sugar.
▷HISTORY C20: named after *Nanaimo,* a city on Vancouver Island

nan bread *or* **naan** (nɑːn) NOUN (in Indian cookery) a slightly leavened bread in a large flat leaf shape.
▷HISTORY from Hindi

Nanchang *or* **Nan-ch'ang** ('næn'tʃæŋ) NOUN a walled city in SE China, capital of Jiangxi province, on the Kan River: largest city in the Poyang basin. Pop.: 1 264 739 (1999 est.).

Nan-ching ('næn'tʃɪŋ) NOUN a variant spelling of **Nanjing.**

nancy ('nænsɪ) NOUN, *plural* **-cies. a** an effeminate or homosexual boy or man. **b** *(as modifier)*: *his nancy ways.* ◆ Also called **nancy boy.**
▷HISTORY C20: from the girl's name *Nancy*

Nancy ('nænsɪ; *French* nɑ̃si) NOUN a city in NE France: became the capital of the dukes of Lorraine in the 12th century, becoming French in 1766; administrative and financial centre. Pop.: 103 605 (1999).

Nanda Devi ('nʌndə 'diːvɪ) NOUN a mountain in N India, in Uttaranchal in the Himalayas. Height: 7817 m (25 645 ft.).

NAND circuit *or* **gate** (nænd) NOUN *Electronics* a computer logic circuit having two or more input wires and one output wire that has an output signal if one or more of the input signals are at a low voltage. Compare **OR circuit.**
▷HISTORY C20: from *not* + AND; see NOT CIRCUIT, AND CIRCUIT

nandrolone ('nændrə,ləʊn) NOUN an anabolic steroid present in the body in small amounts but also produced by metabolism of other steroids, sometimes taken as performance-enhancing drugs by athletes and bodybuilders.

nane (nen) PRONOUN a Scot word for **none**[1].

Nanga Parbat ('nʌŋgə 'pɑːbʌt) NOUN a mountain in N India, in NW Kashmir in the W Himalayas. Height: 8126 m (26 660 ft.).

Nanhai ('nɑːn'haɪ) NOUN the Chinese name for the **South China Sea.**

Nanjing ('næn'dʒɪŋ), **Nanking** ('næn'kɪŋ), *or* **Nan-ching** NOUN a port in E central China, capital of Jiangsu province, on the Yangtze River: capital of the Chinese empire and a literary centre from the 14th to 17th centuries; capital of Nationalist China (1928–37); site of a massacre of about 300 000 civilians by the invading Japanese army in 1937; university (1928). Pop.: 2 388 915 (1999 est.).

nankeen (næŋ'kiːn) *or* **nankin** ('nænkɪn) NOUN 1 a hard-wearing buff-coloured cotton fabric. 2 **a** a pale greyish-yellow colour. **b** *(as adjective)*: *a nankeen carpet.*
▷HISTORY C18: named after *Nanking,* China, where it originated

Nanning *or* **Nan-ning** ('næn'nɪŋ) NOUN a port in S China, capital of Guanxi Zhuang AR, on the Xiang River: rail links with North Vietnam. Pop.: 984 061 (1999 est.).

nanny ('nænɪ) NOUN, *plural* **-nies.** 1 a nurse or nursemaid for children. 2 **a** any person or thing regarded as treating people like children, esp by being patronizing or overprotective. **b** *(as modifier)*: *the nanny state.* 3 a child's word for **grandmother.** ◆ VERB **nannies, nannying, nannied.** 4 *(intr)* to nurse or look after someone else's children. 5 *(tr)* to be overprotective towards.
▷HISTORY C19: child's name for a nurse

nannygai ('nænɪ,gaɪ) NOUN, *plural* **-gais.** an edible sea fish, *Centroberyx affinis,* of Australia which is red in colour and has large prominent eyes. Also called: **red fish.**
▷HISTORY C19: from a native Australian language

nanny goat NOUN a female goat. Compare **billy goat.**

nanny state NOUN a government that makes decisions for people that they might otherwise make for themselves, esp those relating to private and personal behaviour.

nano- COMBINING FORM 1 denoting 10^{-9}: *nanosecond.* Symbol: n. 2 indicating extreme smallness: *nanoplankton.*
▷HISTORY from Latin *nānus* dwarf, from Greek *nanos*

nanometre ('nænəʊ,miːtə) NOUN one thousand-millionth of a metre. Symbol: nm.

nanook ('nænuːk) NOUN *N Canadian* the polar bear.
▷HISTORY from Eskimo *nanug*

nanophysics ('nænəʊ,fɪzɪks) NOUN the physics of structures and artefacts with dimensions in the namometre range or of phenomena occurring in nanoseconds.

nanoplankton *or* **nannoplankton** ('nænəʊ,plæŋktən) NOUN microscopic organisms in plankton.

nanosecond ('nænəʊ,sɛkənd) NOUN one thousand-millionth of a second. Symbol: ns.

nanotechnology (,nænəʊtɛk'nɒlədʒɪ) NOUN a branch of technology dealing with the manufacture of objects with dimensions of less than 100 nanometres and the manipulation of individual molecules and atoms.

nanoworld ('nænəʊ,wɜːld) NOUN the world at a microscopic level, as dealt with by nanotechnology.

Nansen bottle ('nænsən) NOUN an instrument used by oceanographers for obtaining samples of sea water from a desired depth.
▷HISTORY C19: named after Fridtjof *Nansen* (1861–1930), Norwegian arctic explorer, statesman, and scientist

Nansen passport ('nænsən) NOUN a passport issued to stateless persons by the League of Nations after World War I.
▷HISTORY C20: named after Fridtjof *Nansen* (1861–1930), Norwegian arctic explorer, statesman, and scientist

Nan Shan ('næn 'ʃæn) PLURAL NOUN a mountain range in N central China, mainly in Qinghai province, with peaks over 6000 m (20 000 ft.).

Nanterre (*French* nɑ̃tɛr) NOUN a town in N France, on the Seine: an industrial suburb of Paris. Pop.: 84 565 (1990).

Nantes (*French* nɑ̃t) NOUN 1 a port in W France, at the head of the Loire estuary: scene of the signing of the Edict of Nantes and of the Noyades (drownings) during the French Revolution; extensive shipyards, and large metallurgical and food processing industries. Pop.: 268 695 (1999). 2 *History* See **Edict of Nantes.**

Nantong *or* **Nantung** ('næn'tʌŋ) NOUN a city in E China, in Jiangsu province on the Yangtze estuary. Pop.: 468 215 (1999 est.).

Nantucket (næn'tʌkɪt) NOUN an island off SE Massachusetts: formerly a centre of the whaling industry; now a resort. Length: nearly 24 km (15 miles). Width: 5 km (3 miles). Pop.: 6012 (1990).

Naoise ('niːʃə) NOUN *Irish myth* the husband of Deirdre, killed by his uncle Conchobar. See also **Deirdre.**

Naomi ('neɪəmɪ) NOUN *Old Testament* the mother-in-law of Ruth (Ruth 1:2). Douay spelling: **Noemi.**

naos ('neɪɒs) NOUN, *plural* **naoi** ('neɪɔɪ). 1 *Rare* an ancient classical temple. 2 *Architect* another name for **cella.**
▷HISTORY C18: from Greek: inner part of temple

nap[1] (næp) VERB **naps, napping, napped.** *(intr)* 1 to sleep for a short while; doze. 2 to be unaware or inattentive; be off guard (esp in the phrase **catch**

someone napping). ◆ NOUN [3] a short light sleep; doze.
▷HISTORY Old English *hnappian;* related to Middle High German *napfen*

nap² (næp) NOUN [1] **a** the raised fibres of velvet or similar cloth. **b** the direction in which these fibres lie when smoothed down. [2] any similar downy coating. [3] *Austral informal* blankets, bedding. ◆ VERB **naps, napping, napped.** [4] *(tr)* to raise the nap of (cloth, esp velvet) by brushing or similar treatment.
▷HISTORY C15: probably from Middle Dutch *noppe;* related to Old English *hnoppian* to pluck

nap³ (næp) NOUN [1] Also called: **napoleon.** a card game similar to whist, usually played for stakes. [2] a call in this card game, undertaking to win all five tricks. [3] *Horse racing* a tipster's choice for an almost certain winner. [4] **go nap. a** to undertake to win all five tricks at nap. **b** to risk everything on one chance. [5] **not go nap on.** *Austral, slang* to hold in disfavour. [6] **nap hand.** a position in which there is a very good chance of success if a risk is taken. ◆ VERB **naps, napping, napped.** [7] *(tr) Horse racing* to name (a horse) as likely to win a race.
▷HISTORY C19: short for NAPOLEON, the original name of the card game

napalm ('neɪpɑːm, 'næ-) NOUN [1] a thick and highly incendiary liquid, usually consisting of petrol gelled with aluminium soaps, used in firebombs, flame-throwers, etc. ◆ VERB [2] *(tr)* to attack with napalm.
▷HISTORY C20: from NA(PHTHENE) + PALM(ITATE)

nape¹ (neɪp) NOUN the back of the neck. Related adjective: **nuchal.**
▷HISTORY C13: of unknown origin

nape² (neɪp) VERB *(tr) US, military slang* to attack with napalm.

napery ('neɪpərɪ) NOUN *Rare* household linen, esp table linen.
▷HISTORY C14: from Old French *naperie,* from *nape* tablecloth, from Latin *mappa.* See NAPKIN

Naphtali ('næftəˌlaɪ) NOUN *Old Testament* [1] Jacob's sixth son, whose mother was Rachel's handmaid (Genesis 30:7–8). [2] the tribe descended from him. [3] the territory of this tribe, between the Sea of Galilee and the mountains of central Galilee. Douay spelling: **Nephtali.**

naphtha ('næfθə, 'næp-) NOUN [1] a distillation product from coal tar boiling in the approximate range 80–170°C and containing aromatic hydrocarbons. [2] a distillation product from petroleum boiling in the approximate range 100–200°C and containing aliphatic hydrocarbons: used as a solvent and in petrol. [3] an obsolete name for **petroleum.**
▷HISTORY C16: via Latin from Greek, of Iranian origin; related to Persian *neft* naphtha

naphthalene, naphthaline ('næfθəˌliːn, 'næp-), *or* **naphthalin** ('næfθəlɪn, 'næp-) NOUN a white crystalline volatile solid with a characteristic penetrating odour: an aromatic hydrocarbon used in mothballs and in the manufacture of dyes, explosives, etc. Formula: $C_{10}H_8$.
▷HISTORY C19: from NAPHTHA + ALCOHOL + -ENE
▸**naphthalic** (næf'θælɪk, næp-) ADJECTIVE

naphthene ('næfθiːn, 'næp-) NOUN any of a class of cycloalkanes, mainly derivatives of cyclopentane, found in petroleum.
▷HISTORY C20: from NAPHTHA + -ENE

naphthol ('næfθɒl, 'næp-) NOUN a white crystalline solid having two isomeric forms, **alpha-naphthol,** used in dyes, and **beta-naphthol,** used in dyes and as an antioxidant. Formula: $C_{10}H_7OH$.
▷HISTORY C19: from NAPHTHA + -OL[1]

naphthyl ('næfθaɪl, -θɪl, 'næp-) NOUN *(modifier)* of, consisting of, or containing either of two forms of the monovalent group $C_{10}H_7$–.
▷HISTORY C19: from NAPHTHA + -YL

Napier ('neɪpɪə) NOUN a port in New Zealand, on E North Island on Hawke Bay: wool trade centre. Pop.: 53 500 (1995 est.).

Napierian logarithm (nə'pɪərɪən, neɪ-) NOUN another name for **natural logarithm.**

Napier's bones ('neɪpɪəz) PLURAL NOUN a set of graduated rods formerly used for multiplication and division.
▷HISTORY C17: based on a method invented by John *Napier* (1550–1617), Scottish mathematician

napiform ('neɪpɪˌfɔːm) ADJECTIVE *Botany* shaped like a turnip.
▷HISTORY C19: from Latin *nāpus* turnip

napkin ('næpkɪn) NOUN [1] Also called: **table napkin.** a usually square piece of cloth or paper used while eating to protect the clothes, wipe the mouth, etc.; serviette. [2] *Rare* a similar piece of cloth used for example as a handkerchief or headscarf. [3] a more formal name for **nappy¹**. [4] a less common term for **sanitary towel.**
▷HISTORY C15: from Old French, from *nape* tablecloth, from Latin *mappa* small cloth, towel; see MAP

Naples ('neɪpᵊlz) NOUN [1] a port in SW Italy, capital of Campania region, on the Bay of Naples: the third largest city in the country; founded by Greeks in the 6th century B.C.; incorporated into the Kingdom of the Two Sicilies in 1140 and its capital (1282–1503); university (1224). Pop.: 1 002 619 (2000 est.). Ancient name: **Neapolis.** Italian name: **Napoli.** Related adjective: **Neapolitan.** [2] **Bay of.** an inlet of the Tyrrhenian Sea in the SW coast of Italy.

Naples yellow NOUN [1] a yellow pigment, used by artists; lead antimonate. [2] a similar pigment consisting of a mixture of zinc oxide with yellow colouring matter. [3] the colour of either of these pigments.

napoleon (nə'pəʊlɪən) NOUN [1] a former French gold coin worth 20 francs bearing a portrait of either Napoleon I (1769–1821), Emperor of the French (1804–15), or Napoleon III (1808–73), Emperor of the French (1852–70). [2] *Cards* the full name for **nap³** (sense 1). [3] the US name for ***millefeuille.***
▷HISTORY C19: from French *napoléon,* after *Napoleon* I

Napoleonic (nəˌpəʊlɪ'ɒnɪk) ADJECTIVE relating to or characteristic of Napoleon I (1769–1821), Emperor of the French (1804–15), or his era.

Napoleonic Code NOUN the English name for the ***Code Napoléon.***

Napoleonic Wars PLURAL NOUN the series of wars fought between France, under Napoleon Bonaparte, and (principally) Great Britain, Prussia, Russia, and Austria either alone or in alliances (1799–1815).

Napoli ('naːpoli) NOUN the Italian name for **Naples.**

nappa ('næpə) NOUN a soft leather, used in gloves and clothes, made from sheepskin, lambskin, or kid.
▷HISTORY C19: named after *Napa,* California, where it was originally made

nappe (næp) NOUN [1] a large sheet or mass of rock, commonly a recumbent fold, that has been thrust from its original position by earth movements. [2] the sheet of water that flows over a dam or weir. [3] *Geometry* either of the two parts into which a cone (sense 2) is divided by the vertex.
▷HISTORY C20: from French: tablecloth

napper¹ ('næpə) NOUN a person or thing that raises the nap on cloth.

napper² ('næpə) NOUN *Brit* a slang or dialect word for **head** (sense 1).
▷HISTORY C18: from NAP[1]

nappy¹ ('næpɪ) NOUN, *plural* **-pies.** *Brit* a piece of soft material, esp towelling or a disposable material, wrapped around a baby in order to absorb its excrement. Also called: **napkin.** US and Canadian name: **diaper.**
▷HISTORY C20: changed from NAPKIN

nappy² ('næpɪ) ADJECTIVE **-pier, -piest.** [1] having a nap; downy; fuzzy. [2] (of alcoholic drink, esp beer) **a** having a head; frothy. **b** strong or heady. [3] *Dialect, chiefly Brit* slightly intoxicated; tipsy. [4] (of a horse) jumpy or irritable; nervy. ◆ NOUN [5] any strong alcoholic drink, esp heady beer.
▸**'nappiness** NOUN

nappy rash NOUN *Brit* (in babies) any irritation to the skin around the genitals, anus, or buttocks, usually caused by contact with urine or excrement. Formal name: **napkin rash.** US and Canadian name: **diaper rash.**

Nara ('nɑːrə) NOUN a city in central Japan, on S Honshu: the first permanent capital of Japan (710–784). Pop.: 359 234 (1995).

Narayanganj (nə'rɑːjənˌgʌndʒ) NOUN a city in central Bangladesh, on the Ganges delta just southeast of Dhaka. Pop.: 276 549 (1991).

Narbada (nə'bʌdə) NOUN another name for the **Narmada.**

Narbonne (*French* narbɔn) NOUN a city in S France: capital of the Roman province of **Gallia Narbonensis;** harbour silted up in the 14th century. Pop.: 47 090 (1990).

narc (nɑːk) NOUN *US, slang* a narcotics agent.

narceine *or* **narceen** ('nɑːsiːn) NOUN a narcotic alkaloid that occurs in opium. Formula: $C_{23}H_{27}O_8N$.
▷HISTORY C19: via French from Greek *narkē* numbness

narcissism ('nɑːsɪˌsɪzəm) *or* **narcism** ('nɑːˌsɪzəm) NOUN [1] an exceptional interest in or admiration for oneself, esp one's physical appearance. [2] sexual satisfaction derived from contemplation of one's own physical or mental endowments.
▷HISTORY C19: from NARCISSUS
▸**'narcissist** NOUN ▸**ˌnarcis'sistic** ADJECTIVE

narcissus (nɑː'sɪsəs) NOUN, *plural* **-cissuses** *or* **-cissi** (-'sɪsaɪ, -'sɪsiː). any amaryllidaceous plant of the Eurasian genus *Narcissus,* esp *N. poeticus,* whose yellow, orange, or white flowers have a crown surrounded by spreading segments.
▷HISTORY C16: via Latin from Greek *nárkissos,* perhaps from *narkē* numbness, because of narcotic properties attributed to species of the plant

Narcissus (nɑː'sɪsəs) NOUN *Greek myth* a beautiful youth who fell in love with his reflection in a pool and pined away, becoming the flower that bears his name.

narco- *or sometimes before a vowel* **narc-** COMBINING FORM [1] indicating numbness or torpor: *narcolepsy.* [2] connected with or derived from illicit drug production: *narcoeconomies.*
▷HISTORY from Greek *narkē* numbness

narcoanalysis (ˌnɑːkəʊə'nælɪsɪs) NOUN psychoanalysis of a patient in a trance induced by a narcotic drug.

narcolepsy ('nɑːkəˌlɛpsɪ) NOUN *Pathol* a rare condition characterized by sudden and uncontrollable episodes of deep sleep.
▸**ˌnarco'leptic** ADJECTIVE

narcosis (nɑː'kəʊsɪs) NOUN unconsciousness induced by narcotics or general anaesthetics.

narcotic (nɑː'kɒtɪk) NOUN [1] any of a group of drugs, such as heroin, morphine, and pethidine, that produce numbness and stupor. They are used medicinally to relieve pain but are sometimes also taken for their pleasant effects; prolonged use may cause addiction. [2] anything that relieves pain or induces sleep, mental numbness, etc. [3] any illegal drug. ◆ ADJECTIVE [4] of, relating to, or designating narcotics. [5] of or relating to narcotics addicts or users. [6] of or relating to narcosis.
▷HISTORY C14: via Medieval Latin from Greek *narkōtikós,* from *narkoūn* to render numb, from *narkē* numbness
▸**nar'cotically** ADVERB

narcotism ('nɑːkəˌtɪzəm) NOUN stupor or addiction induced by narcotic drugs.

narcotize *or* **narcotise** ('nɑːkəˌtaɪz) VERB *(tr)* to place under the influence of a narcotic drug.
▸**ˌnarcoti'zation** *or* **ˌnarcoti'sation** NOUN

nard (nɑːd) NOUN [1] another name for **spikenard** (senses 1, 2). [2] any of several plants, such as certain valerians, whose aromatic roots were formerly used in medicine.
▷HISTORY C14: via Latin from Greek *nárdos,* perhaps ultimately from Sanskrit *nalada* Indian spikenard, perhaps via Semitic (Hebrew *nērd,* Arabic *nārdīn*)

nardoo ('nɑːduː) NOUN [1] any of certain cloverlike ferns of the genus *Marsilea,* which grow in swampy areas. [2] the spores of such a plant, used as food in Australia.
▷HISTORY C19: from a native Australian language

nares ('nɛəriːz) PLURAL NOUN, *singular* **naris** ('nɛərɪs). *Anatomy* the nostrils.
▷HISTORY C17: from Latin; related to Old English *nasu,* Latin *nāsus* nose

narghile, nargile, *or* **nargileh** ('nɑːgɪlɪ, -ˌleɪ) NOUN another name for **hookah.**
▷HISTORY C19: from French *narguilé,* from Persian *nārgīleh* a pipe having a bowl made of coconut shell, from *nārgīl* coconut

narial ('nɛərɪəl) *or* **narine** ('nɛərɪn, -raɪn) ADJECTIVE *Anatomy* of or relating to the nares.
▷HISTORY C19: from Latin *nāris* nostril

nark (nɑːk) *Slang* ◆ NOUN 1 *Brit, Austral, and NZ* an informer or spy, esp. one working for the police (**copper's nark**). 2 *Brit* a person who complains irritatingly: *an old nark.* 3 *Austral and NZ* a spoilsport. ◆ VERB 4 *Brit, Austral, and NZ* to annoy, upset, or irritate: *he was narked by her indifference.* 5 *(intr) Brit, Austral, and NZ* to inform or spy, esp. for the police. 6 *(intr) Brit* to complain irritatingly. 7 **nark at (someone).** *NZ* to nag (someone). 8 **nark it.** *Brit* stop it!
▷HISTORY C19: probably from Romany *nāk* nose

narky ('nɑːkɪ) ADJECTIVE **narkier, narkiest.** *Slang* irritable, complaining, or sarcastic.

Narmada (nə'mʌdə) *or* **Narbada** NOUN a river in central India, rising in Madhya Pradesh and flowing generally west to the Gulf of Cambay in a wide estuary: the second most sacred river in India. Length: 1290 km (801 miles).

Narraganset *or* **Narragansett** (ˌnærə'gænsɪt) NOUN 1 *(plural* **-set, -sets** *or* **-sett, -setts**) a member of a North American Indian people formerly living in Rhode Island. 2 the language of this people, belonging to the Algonquian family.

Narragansett Bay NOUN an inlet of the Atlantic in SE Rhode Island: contains several islands, including Rhode Island, Prudence Island, and Conanicut Island.

narrate (nə'reɪt) VERB 1 to tell (a story); relate. 2 to speak in accompaniment of (a film, television programme, etc.).
▷HISTORY C17: from Latin *narrāre* to recount, from *gnārus* knowing
▸**nar'ratable** ADJECTIVE

narration (nə'reɪʃən) NOUN 1 the act or process of narrating. 2 a narrated account or story; narrative. 3 (in traditional rhetoric) the third step in making a speech, the putting forward of the question.

narrative ('nærətɪv) NOUN 1 an account, report, or story, as of events, experiences, etc. 2 (sometimes preceded by *the*) the part of a literary work that relates events. 3 the process or technique of narrating. ◆ ADJECTIVE 4 telling a story: *a narrative poem.* 5 of or relating to narration: *narrative art.*
▸**'narratively** ADVERB

narrator (nə'reɪtə) NOUN 1 a person who tells a story or gives an account of something. 2 a person who speaks in accompaniment of a film, television programme, etc.

narrow ('nærəʊ) ADJECTIVE 1 small in breadth, esp in comparison to length. 2 limited in range or extent. 3 limited in outlook; lacking breadth of vision. 4 limited in means or resources; meagre: *narrow resources.* 5 barely adequate or successful (esp in the phrase **a narrow escape**). 6 painstakingly thorough; minute: *a narrow scrutiny.* 7 *Finance* denoting an assessment of liquidity as including notes and coin in circulation with the public, banks' till money, and banks' balances: *narrow money.* Compare **broad** (sense 14). 8 *Dialect* overcareful with money; parsimonious. 9 *Phonetics* **a** another word for **tense**[1] (sense 4). **b** relating to or denoting a transcription used to represent phonetic rather than phonemic distinctions. **c** another word for **close**[1] (sense 21). 10 (of agricultural feeds) especially rich in protein. 11 **narrow squeak.** *Informal* an escape only just managed. ◆ VERB 12 to make or become narrow; limit; restrict. ◆ NOUN 13 a narrow place, esp a pass or strait. ◆ See also **narrows.**
▷HISTORY Old English *nearu;* related to Old Saxon *naru*
▸**'narrowly** ADVERB ▸**'narrowness** NOUN

narrow boat NOUN a long narrow bargelike boat with a beam of 2.1 metres (7 feet) or less, used on canals.

narrowcast ('nærəʊˌkɑːst) VERB **-casts, -casting, -cast** *or* **-casted.** 1 *(tr)* to supply (television programmes) to a small area by cable television. 2 *(intr)* (of programmers or advertisers) to target a specialized audience on radio or television. ◆ Compare **broadcast.**
▸**'narrowˌcasting** NOUN

narrow gauge NOUN 1 a railway track with a smaller distance between the lines than the standard gauge of 56½ inches. ◆ ADJECTIVE **narrow-gauge, narrow-gauged.** 2 of, relating to, or denoting a railway with a narrow gauge.

narrow-minded ADJECTIVE having a biased or illiberal viewpoint; bigoted, intolerant, or prejudiced.
▸**ˌnarrow-'mindedly** ADVERB ▸**ˌnarrow-'mindedness** NOUN

narrows ('nærəʊz) PLURAL NOUN a narrow part of a strait, river, current, etc.

narrow seas PLURAL NOUN *Archaic* the channels between Great Britain and the Continent and Great Britain and Ireland.

narthex ('nɑːθɛks) NOUN 1 a portico at the west end of a basilica or church, esp one that is at right angles to the nave. 2 a rectangular entrance hall between the porch and nave of a church.
▷HISTORY C17: via Latin from Medieval Greek: enclosed porch, enclosure (earlier: box), from Greek *narthēx* giant fennel, the stems of which were used to make boxes

Narva (*Russian* 'narvə) NOUN a port in Estonia on the Narva River near the Gulf of Finland: developed around a Danish fortress in the 13th century; textile centre. Pop.: 77 770 (1995).

Narvik ('nɑːvɪk; *Norwegian* 'narvik) NOUN a port in N Norway: scene of two naval battles in 1940; exports iron ore from Kiruna and Gällivare (Sweden). Pop.: 18 500 (1990).

narwhal, narwal ('nɑːwəl), *or* **narwhale** ('nɑːˌweɪl) NOUN an arctic toothed whale, *Monodon monoceros,* having a black-spotted whitish skin and, in the male, a long spiral tusk: family *Monodontidae.*
▷HISTORY C17: of Scandinavian origin; compare Danish, Norwegian *narhval,* from Old Norse *nāhvalr,* from *nār* corpse + *hvalr* whale, from its white colour, supposed to resemble a human corpse

nary ('nɛərɪ) ADVERB *Dialect* not; never: *nary a man was left.*
▷HISTORY C19: variant of *ne'er a* never a

NASA ('næsə) NOUN (in the US) ACRONYM FOR National Aeronautics and Space Administration.

nasal ('neɪzᵊl) ADJECTIVE 1 of or relating to the nose. 2 *Phonetics* pronounced with the soft palate lowered allowing air to escape via the nasal cavity instead of or as well as through the mouth. ◆ NOUN 3 a nasal speech sound, such as English *m, n,* or *ng.* 4 another word for **nosepiece** (sense 1).
▷HISTORY C17: from French from Late Latin *nāsālis,* from Latin *nāsus* nose
▸**nasality** (neɪ'zælɪtɪ) NOUN ▸**'nasally** ADVERB

nasal index NOUN the ratio of the widest part of the nose to its length multiplied by 100.

nasalize *or* **nasalise** ('neɪzᵊˌlaɪz) VERB *(tr)* to pronounce nasally.
▸**ˌnasali'zation** *or* **ˌnasali'sation** NOUN

nascent ('næsᵊnt, 'neɪ-) ADJECTIVE 1 starting to grow or develop; being born. 2 *Chem* (of an element or simple compound, esp hydrogen) created within the reaction medium in the atomic form and having a high activity.
▷HISTORY C17: from Latin *nascēns* present participle of *nāscī* to be born
▸**'nascence** *or* **'nascency** NOUN

NASDAQ ('næzdæk) NOUN (in the US) ACRONYM FOR National Association of Securities Dealers Automated Quotations System.

naseberry ('neɪzˌbɛrɪ) NOUN, *plural* **-berries.** another name for **sapodilla.**
▷HISTORY C17: from Spanish *néspera* medlar + BERRY

Naseby ('neɪzbɪ) NOUN a village in Northamptonshire: site of a major Parliamentarian victory (1645) in the Civil War, when Cromwell routed Prince Rupert's force.

nashi ('næʃɪ) NOUN, *plural* **nashi** *or* **nashis.** another name for **Asian pear.**
▷HISTORY Japanese: pear

Nasho ('næʃəʊ) NOUN *Obsolete Austral, slang* 1 compulsory military training; conscription. 2 *(plural* **Nashos**) a conscript.
▷HISTORY C20: shortening and alteration of *national service*

Nashville ('næʃvɪl) NOUN a city in central Tennessee, the state capital, on the Cumberland River: an industrial and commercial centre, noted for its recording industry. Pop.: 545 524 (2000).

nasi goreng ('nɑːsɪ gə'rɛŋ) NOUN a dish, originating in Malaysia, consisting of rice fried with a selection of other ingredients.
▷HISTORY C20: from Malay *nasi* (cooked) rice + *goreng* fry

Nasik ('nɑːsɪk) NOUN a city in W India, in Maharashtra: a centre for Hindu pilgrims. Pop.: 656 925 (1991).

nasion ('neɪzɪən) NOUN a craniometric point where the top of the nose meets the ridge of the forehead.
▷HISTORY C20: New Latin, from Latin *nāsus* nose
▸**'nasial** ADJECTIVE

Naskapi (nə'skæpɪ) NOUN a member of an Innu people living in Quebec.
▷HISTORY from Cree

naso- COMBINING FORM nose: *nasopharynx.*
▷HISTORY from Latin *nāsus* nose

nasofrontal (ˌneɪzəʊ'frʌntᵊl) ADJECTIVE *Anatomy* of or relating to the nasal and frontal bones.

nasogastric (ˌneɪzəʊ'gæstrɪk) ADJECTIVE *Anatomy* of or relating to the nose and stomach: *a nasogastric tube.*

nasopharynx (ˌneɪzəʊ'færɪŋks) NOUN, *plural* **-pharynges** (-fə'rɪndʒiːz) *or* **-pharynxes.** the part of the pharynx situated above and behind the soft palate.
▸**nasopharyngeal** (ˌneɪzəʊfə'rɪndʒɪəl, -ˌfærɪn'dʒɪəl) ADJECTIVE

Nassau NOUN 1 (*German* 'nasau) a region of W central Germany: formerly a duchy (1816–66), from which a branch of the House of Orange arose (represented by the present rulers of the Netherlands and Luxembourg); annexed to the Prussian province of Hesse-Nassau in 1866; corresponds to present-day W Hesse and NE Rhineland-Palatinate states; formerly (1949–90) part of West Germany. 2 ('næsɔː) the capital and chief port of the Bahamas, on the NE coast of New Providence Island: resort. Pop.: 214 000 (1999 est.).

nassella tussock (nə'sɛlə) NOUN a type of tussock grass, originally of South America, now regarded as a noxious weed in New Zealand.

Nassella Tussock Board NOUN *NZ* one of many local statutory organizations set up in different regions of New Zealand to eradicate the invasive nassella tussock weed.

nastic movement ('næstɪk) NOUN a response of plant parts that is independent of the direction of the external stimulus, such as the opening of buds caused by an alteration in light intensity.
▷HISTORY C19 *nastic,* from Greek *nastos* close-packed, from *nassein* to press down

nasturtium (nə'stɜːʃəm) NOUN any of various plants of the genus *Tropaeolum,* esp *T. major,* having round leaves and yellow, red, or orange trumpet-shaped spurred flowers: family *Tropaeolaceae.*
▷HISTORY C17: from Latin: kind of cress, from *nāsus* nose + *tortus* twisted, from *torquēre* to twist, distort; so called because the pungent smell causes one to wrinkle one's nose

nasty ('nɑːstɪ) ADJECTIVE **-tier, -tiest.** 1 unpleasant, offensive, or repugnant. 2 (of an experience, condition, etc.) unpleasant, dangerous, or painful: *a nasty wound.* 3 spiteful, abusive, or ill-natured. 4 obscene or indecent. 5 **nasty piece of work.** *Brit informal* a cruel or mean person. ◆ NOUN, *plural* **-ties.** 6 an offensive or unpleasant person or thing: *a video nasty.*
▷HISTORY C14: origin obscure; probably related to Swedish dialect *nasket* and Dutch *nestig* dirty
▸**'nastily** ADVERB ▸**'nastiness** NOUN

-nasty NOUN COMBINING FORM indicating a nastic movement to a certain stimulus: *nyctinasty.*
▷HISTORY from Greek *nastos* pressed down, close-pressed
▸**-nastic** ADJECTIVE COMBINING FORM

NAS/UWT (in Britain) ABBREVIATION FOR National Association of Schoolmasters/Union of Women Teachers.

Nat (næt) NOUN *Informal* 1 a member or supporter of the Scottish National Party. 2 *NZ* a member of the National Party. 3 *NZ* a Member of Parliament for the National Party.

nat. ABBREVIATION FOR: 1 national. 2 natural.

natal[1] ('neɪtᵊl) ADJECTIVE 1 of or relating to birth. 2 a rare word for **native**: *natal instincts.*
▷HISTORY C14: from Latin *nātālis* of one's birth, from *nātus,* from *nascī* to be born

natal[2] ('neɪtᵊl) ADJECTIVE *Anatomy* of or relating to the buttocks.

▷**HISTORY** from New Latin *nates* buttocks

Natal NOUN [1] (nə'tæl) a former province of E South Africa, between the Drakensberg and the Indian Ocean: set up as a republic by the Boers in 1838; became a British colony in 1843; joined South Africa in 1910; replaced by KwaZulu/Natal in 1994. Capital: Pietermaritzburg. [2] (*Portuguese* na'tal) a port in NE Brazil, capital of Rio Grande do Norte state, near the mouth of the Potengi River. Pop. (urban area): 709 422 (2000).

natality (neɪ'tælɪtɪ) NOUN, *plural* **-ties.** another name (esp US) for **birth rate.**

natant ('neɪtᵊnt) ADJECTIVE [1] (of aquatic plants) floating on the water. [2] *Rare* floating or swimming.
▷**HISTORY** C18: from Latin *natāns,* present participle of *natāre* to swim

natation (nə'teɪʃən) NOUN a formal or literary word for **swimming.**
▷**HISTORY** C16: from Latin *natātiō* a swimming, from *natāre* to swim
▸**na'tational** ADJECTIVE

natatorium (ˌneɪtə'tɔːrɪəm) NOUN, *plural* **-riums** *or* **-ria** (-rɪə). *Rare* a swimming pool, esp an indoor pool.
▷**HISTORY** C20: from Late Latin: swimming place, pool

natatory (nə'teɪtərɪ) *or* **natatorial** (ˌnætə'tɔːrɪəl, ˌneɪtə'tɔːrɪəl) ADJECTIVE of or relating to swimming.
▷**HISTORY** C18: from Late Latin *natātōrius,* from *natāre* to swim

natch (nætʃ) SENTENCE SUBSTITUTE *Informal* short for **naturally** (sense 3).

nates ('neɪtiːz) PLURAL NOUN, *singular* **-tis** (-tɪs). a technical word for the **buttocks.**
▷**HISTORY** C17: from Latin; compare Greek *nōton* back, *nosthi* buttocks

NATFHE ABBREVIATION FOR National Association of Teachers in Further and Higher Education.

Nathan ('neɪθən) NOUN *Old Testament* a prophet at David's court (II Samuel 7:1–17; 12:1–15).

Nathanael (nə'θænjəl) NOUN *New Testament* a Galilean who is perhaps to be identified with Bartholomew among the apostles (John 1:45–51; 21:1).

natheless ('neɪθlɪs) *or* **nathless** ('næθlɪs) *Archaic* ◆ SENTENCE CONNECTOR [1] another word for **nonetheless.** ◆ PREPOSITION [2] notwithstanding; despite.
▷**HISTORY** Old English *nāthylǣs,* from *nā* never + *thȳ* for that + *lǣs* less

nation ('neɪʃən) NOUN [1] an aggregation of people or peoples of one or more cultures, races, etc., organized into a single state: *the Australian nation.* [2] a community of persons not constituting a state but bound by common descent, language, history, etc.: *the French-Canadian nation.* [3] **a** a federation of tribes, esp American Indians. **b** the territory occupied by such a federation.
▷**HISTORY** C13: via Old French from Latin *nātiō* birth, tribe, from *nascī* to be born
▸**'nation,hood** NOUN ▸**'nationless** ADJECTIVE

national ('næʃənᵊl) ADJECTIVE [1] of, involving, or relating to a nation as a whole. [2] of, relating to, or characteristic of a particular nation: *the national dress of Poland.* [3] *Rare* nationalistic or patriotic. ◆ NOUN [4] a citizen or subject. [5] a national newspaper.
▸**'nationally** ADVERB

National ('næʃənᵊl) NOUN **the.** short for the **Grand National.**

national accounting NOUN another name for **social accounting.**

national agreement NOUN written formal agreements covering rates of pay and other terms and conditions of employment that are the result of collective bargaining at national level between one or more trade unions and employers in a sector of the economy.

national anthem NOUN a patriotic hymn or other song adopted by a nation for use on public or state occasions.

National Assembly NOUN *French history* the body constituted by the French third estate in June 1789 after the calling of the Estates General. It was dissolved in Sept. 1791 to be replaced by the new Legislative Assembly.

national assistance NOUN (in Britain) formerly a weekly allowance paid to certain people by the state to bring their incomes up to minimum levels established by law. Now replaced by **income support.**

national bank NOUN [1] (in the US) a commercial bank incorporated under a Federal charter and legally required to be a member of the Federal Reserve System. Compare **state bank.** [2] a bank owned and operated by a government.

National Bureau of Standards NOUN (in the US) an organization, founded in 1901, whose function is to establish and maintain standards for units of measurements. Compare **British Standards Institution, International Standards Organization.**

national code NOUN another term for **Australian Rules.**

National Convention NOUN [1] a convention held every four years by each major US political party to choose its presidential candidate. [2] *French history* the longest lasting of the revolutionary assemblies, lasting from Sept. 1792 to Oct. 1795, when it was replaced by the Directory.

National Country Party NOUN (in Australia) a former name for **National Party.** Abbreviation: **NCP.**

National Covenant NOUN See **Covenant.**

National Curriculum NOUN (in England and Wales) the curriculum of subjects taught in state schools progressively from 1989. There are ten foundation subjects: English, maths, and science (the core subjects); art, design and technology, geography, history, music, physical education, and a foreign language. Pupils are assessed according to specified attainment targets throughout each of four key stages. Schools must also provide religious education and from 1999 lessons in citizenship.

national debt NOUN the total outstanding borrowings of a nation's central government. Also called (esp US): **public debt.**

National Economic Development Council NOUN an advisory body on general economic policy in Britain, composed of representatives of government, management, and trade unions: established in 1962; abolished in 1992. Abbreviations: **NEDC,** (informal) **Neddy.**

National Enterprise Board NOUN a public corporation established in 1975 to help the economy of the UK. In 1981 it merged with the National Research and Development Council to form the British Technology Group. Abbreviation: **NEB.**

National Front NOUN (in Britain) a small political party of the right with racist and other extremist policies. Abbreviation: **NF.**

National Gallery NOUN a major art gallery in London, in Trafalgar Square. Founded in 1824, it contains the largest collection of paintings in Britain.

national grid NOUN [1] *Brit* a network of high-voltage power lines connecting major power stations. [2] a grid of metric coordinates used by the Ordnance Survey in Britain and Ireland and in New Zealand by the New Zealand Lands and Survey Department and printed on their maps.

National Guard NOUN [1] (*sometimes not capitals*) the armed force, first commanded by Lafayette, that was established in France in 1789 and existed intermittently until 1871. [2] (in the US) a state military force that can be called into federal service by the president.

National Health Service NOUN (in Britain) the system of national medical services since 1948, financed mainly by taxation.

national hunt NOUN *Brit* (*often capital*) **a** the racing of horses on racecourses with jumps. **b** (*as modifier*): *a National Hunt jockey.*

national income NOUN *Economics* the total of all incomes accruing over a specified period to residents of a country and consisting of wages, salaries, profits, rent, and interest.

national insurance NOUN (in Britain) state insurance based on weekly contributions from employees and employers and providing payments to the unemployed, the sick, the retired, etc., as well as medical services. See also **social security.**

nationalism ('næʃənəˌlɪzəm, 'næʃnə-) NOUN [1] a sentiment based on common cultural characteristics that binds a population and often produces a policy of national independence or separatism. [2] loyalty or devotion to one's country; patriotism. [3] exaggerated, passionate, or fanatical devotion to a national community. See also **chauvinism.**
▸**'nationalist** NOUN, ADJECTIVE ▸**ˌnational'istic** ADJECTIVE

Nationalist China NOUN an unofficial name for (the Republic of) **China.**

nationality (ˌnæʃə'nælɪtɪ) NOUN, *plural* **-ties.** [1] the state or fact of being a citizen of a particular nation. [2] a body of people sharing common descent, history, language, etc.; a nation. [3] a national group: *30 different nationalities are found in this city.* [4] national character or quality. [5] the state or fact of being a nation; national status.

nationalize *or* **nationalise** ('næʃənəˌlaɪz, 'næʃnə-) VERB (*tr*) [1] to put (an industry, resources, etc.) under state control or ownership. [2] to make national in scope, character, or status. [3] a less common word for **naturalize.**
▸**ˌnationali'zation** *or* **ˌnationali'sation** NOUN

National Liberation Front NOUN [1] (*sometimes not capitals*) a revolutionary movement that seeks the national independence of a country, usually by guerrilla warfare. [2] Also called: **National Liberation Front of South Vietnam.** a political organization formed in South Vietnam in 1960 by the Vietcong.

national park NOUN an area of countryside for public use designated by a national government as being of notable scenic, environmental, or historical importance.

National Park NOUN a mountainous volcanic region in New Zealand, in the central North Island: ski resort.

National Party NOUN [1] (in New Zealand) the more conservative of the two main political parties. [2] (in Australia) a political party drawing its main support from rural areas. Former name: **National Country Party.** [3] (in South Africa) a political party composed mainly of centre-to-right-wing Afrikaners, which ruled from 1948 until the country's first multiracial elections in 1994: renamed the **New National Party** (NNP) in 1999. See also **Progressive Federal Party, United Party.**

National Physical Laboratory NOUN a UK establishment founded in 1900 at Teddington to carry out research in physics and monitor standards of measurement. Abbreviation: **NPL.**

National Portrait Gallery NOUN an art gallery in London, established in 1856, displaying portraits and photographs of eminent figures in British history.

National Savings Bank NOUN (in Britain) a government savings bank, run through the post office, esp for small savers.

National School NOUN [1] (in Ireland) a state primary school. [2] (in England in the 19th century) a school run by the Church of England for the children of the poor.

national service NOUN compulsory military service.

National Socialism NOUN *German history* the doctrines and practices of the Nazis, involving the supremacy of the Austrian-born German dictator Adolf Hitler (1889–1945) as Führer (1934–45), anti-Semitism, state control of the economy, and national expansion. Also called: **Nazism, Naziism.**
▸**National Socialist** NOUN, ADJECTIVE

national superannuation NOUN *NZ* a means-related pension paid to elderly people.

National Tests PLURAL NOUN (*sometimes not capitals*) *Brit education* externally devised assessments in the core subjects of English, mathematics and science which school students in England and Wales sit at the end of Key Stages 1 to 3. Often referred to as: **SATs.**

National Theatre NOUN the former name of the **Royal National Theatre.**

National Trust NOUN [1] (in Britain) an organization concerned with the preservation of historic buildings and monuments and areas of the countryside of great beauty in England, Wales, and Northern Ireland. It was founded in 1895 and incorporated by act of parliament in 1907. The **National Trust for Scotland** was founded in 1931. [2] (in Australia) a similar organization in each of the states.

nation-building NOUN *South African* the advocacy of national solidarity in South Africa in the post-apartheid era.

Nation of Islam NOUN the official name for the **Black Muslims.** Abbreviation: **NOI.**

nation-state NOUN an independent state inhabited by all the people of one nation and one nation only.

nationwide ('neɪʃənˌwaɪd) ADJECTIVE covering or available to the whole of a nation; national: *a nationwide survey*.

native ('neɪtɪv) ADJECTIVE [1] relating or belonging to a person or thing by virtue of conditions existing at the time of birth: *my native city*. [2] inherent, natural, or innate: *a native strength*. [3] born in a specified place: *a native Indian*. [4] (when *postpositive*, foll by *to*) originating in a specific place or area: *kangaroos are native to Australia*. [5] characteristic of or relating to the indigenous inhabitants of a country or area: *the native art of the New Guinea Highlands*. [6] (of chemical elements, esp metals) found naturally in the elemental form. [7] unadulterated by civilization, artifice, or adornment; natural. [8] *Archaic* related by birth or race. [9] **go native.** (of a settler) to adopt the lifestyle of the local population, esp when it appears less civilized. ◆ NOUN [10] (usually foll by *of*) a person born in a particular place: *a native of Geneva*. [11] (usually foll by *of*) a species originating in a particular place or area: *the kangaroo is a native of Australia*. [12] a member of an indigenous people of a country or area, esp a non-White people, as opposed to colonial settlers and immigrants. [13] *Derogatory, rare* any non-White.
▷HISTORY C14: from Latin *nātīvus* innate, natural, from *nascī* to be born
▸'**natively** ADVERB ▸'**nativeness** NOUN

Native American NOUN another name for an **American Indian.**

native bear NOUN an Austral name for **koala.**

native-born ADJECTIVE born in the country or area indicated.

native bush NOUN *NZ* indigenous forest.

native cat NOUN *Austral* any of various Australian catlike carnivorous marsupials of the genus *Dasyurus*.

native companion NOUN *Austral* another name for the **brolga.**
▷HISTORY C19: so called because the birds were observed in pairs

native dog NOUN *Austral* a dingo.

native oak NOUN *Austral* another name for **casuarina.**

native speaker NOUN a person having a specified native language: *a native speaker of Cree*.

Native States PLURAL NOUN the former 562 semi-independent states of India, ruled by Indians but subject to varying degrees of British authority: merged with provinces by 1948; largest states were Hyderabad, Gwalior, Baroda, Mysore, Cochin, Jammu and Kashmir, Travancore, Sikkim, and Indore. Also called: **Indian States and Agencies.**

nativism ('neɪtɪˌvɪzəm) NOUN [1] *Chiefly US* the policy of favouring the natives of a country over the immigrants. [2] *Anthropol* the policy of protecting and reaffirming native tribal cultures in reaction to acculturation. [3] the doctrine that the mind and its capacities are innately structured and that much knowledge is innate.
▸'**nativist** NOUN, ADJECTIVE ▸ˌ**nativ'istic** ADJECTIVE

nativity (nə'tɪvɪtɪ) NOUN, *plural* **-ties.** birth or origin, esp in relation to the circumstances surrounding it.
▷HISTORY C14: via Old French from Late Latin *nātīvitas* birth: see NATIVE

Nativity (nə'tɪvɪtɪ) NOUN [1] the birth of Jesus Christ. [2] the feast of Christmas as a commemoration of this. [3] **a** an artistic representation of the circumstances of the birth of Christ. **b** (*as modifier*): *a Nativity play*.

natl ABBREVIATION FOR national.

NATO *or* **Nato** ('neɪtəʊ) NOUN ACRONYM FOR North Atlantic Treaty Organization, an international organization composed of the US, Canada, Britain, and a number of European countries: established by the **North Atlantic Treaty** (1949) for purposes of collective security. In 1994 it launched the partnerships for peace initiative, in order to forge alliances with former Warsaw Pact countries; in 1997 a treaty of cooperation with Russia was signed and in 1999 Hungary, Poland, and the Czech Republic became full NATO members.

natrium ('neɪtrɪəm) NOUN an obsolete name for **sodium.**
▷HISTORY C19: New Latin; see NATRON

natrolite ('nætrəˌlaɪt, 'neɪ-) NOUN a colourless, white, or yellow zeolite mineral consisting of sodium aluminium silicate in the form of needle-like orthorhombic crystals. Formula: $Na_2Al_2Si_3O_{10}.2H_2O$.
▷HISTORY C19: from NATRON + -LITE

natron ('neɪtrən) NOUN a whitish or yellow mineral that consists of hydrated sodium carbonate and occurs in saline deposits and salt lakes. Formula: $Na_2CO_3.10H_2O$.
▷HISTORY C17: via French and Spanish from Arabic *natrūn*, from Greek *nitron*

NATSOPA (næt'səʊpə) NOUN (formerly, in Britain) ACRONYM FOR National Society of Operative Printers, Graphical and Media Personnel.

natter ('nætə) *Chiefly Brit* ◆ VERB [1] (*intr*) to talk idly and at length; chatter or gossip. ◆ NOUN [2] prolonged idle chatter or gossip.
▷HISTORY C19: changed from *gnatter* to grumble, of imitative origin; compare Low German *gnatteren*
▸'**natterer** NOUN

natterjack ('nætəˌdʒæk) NOUN a European toad, *Bufo calamita*, of sandy regions, having a greyish-brown body marked with reddish warty processes: family *Bufonidae*.
▷HISTORY C18: of unknown origin

natty ('nætɪ) ADJECTIVE **-tier, -tiest.** *Informal* smart in appearance or dress; spruce; dapper: *a natty outfit*.
▷HISTORY C18: perhaps from obsolete *netty*, from *net* NEAT[1]; compare Old French *net* trim
▸'**nattily** ADVERB ▸'**nattiness** NOUN

natural ('nætʃrəl, -tʃərəl) ADJECTIVE [1] of, existing in, or produced by nature: *natural science; natural cliffs*. [2] in accordance with human nature: *it is only natural to want to be liked*. [3] as is normal or to be expected; ordinary or logical: *the natural course of events*. [4] not acquired; innate: *a natural gift for sport*. [5] being so through innate qualities: *a natural leader*. [6] not supernatural or strange: *natural phenomena*. [7] not constrained or affected; genuine or spontaneous. [8] not artificially dyed or coloured: *a natural blonde*. [9] following or resembling nature or life; lifelike: *she looked more natural without her make-up*. [10] not affected by man or civilization; uncultivated; wild: *in the natural state this animal is not ferocious*. [11] illegitimate; born out of wedlock. [12] not adopted but rather related by blood: *her natural parents*. [13] *Music* **a** not sharp or flat. **b** (*postpositive*) denoting a note that is neither sharp nor flat: *B natural*. **c** (of a key or scale) containing no sharps or flats. Compare **flat**[1] (sense 23), **sharp** (sense 12). [14] *Music* of or relating to a trumpet, horn, etc., without valves or keys, on which only notes of the harmonic series of the keynote can be obtained. [15] determined by inborn conviction: *natural justice; natural rights*. [16] *Cards* **a** (of a card) not a joker or wild card. **b** (of a canasta or sequence) containing no wild cards. **c** (of a bid in bridge) describing genuine values; not conventional. [17] based on the principles and findings of human reason and what is to be learned of God from nature rather than on revelation: *natural religion*. ◆ NOUN [18] *Informal* a person or thing regarded as certain to qualify for success, selection, etc.: *the horse was a natural for first place*. [19] *Music* **a** Also called (US): **cancel.** an accidental cancelling a previous sharp or flat. Usual symbol: ♮. **b** a note affected by this accidental. Compare **flat**[1] (sense 35), **sharp** (sense 19). [20] *Pontoon* the combination of an ace with a ten or court card when dealt to a player as his or her first two cards. [21] *Obsolete* an imbecile; idiot.
▸'**naturally** ADVERB ▸'**naturalness** NOUN

natural-born ADJECTIVE being as specified through one's birth: *a natural-born Irishman*.

natural childbirth NOUN a method of childbirth characterized by the absence of anaesthetics, in which the expectant mother is given special breathing and relaxing exercises.

natural classification NOUN *Biology* classification of organisms according to relationships based on descent from a common ancestor.

natural deduction NOUN a system of formal logic that has no axioms but permits the assumption of premises of an argument. Such a system uses sequents to record which assumptions are operative at any stage. Compare **axiomatic** (sense 3).

natural frequency NOUN *Physics* the frequency at which a system vibrates when set in free vibration. Compare **forcing frequency.**

natural gas NOUN a gaseous mixture consisting mainly of methane trapped below ground; used extensively as a fuel.

natural gender NOUN grammatical gender that reflects, as in English, the sex or animacy of the referent of a noun rather than the form or any other feature of the word.

natural history NOUN [1] the study of animals and plants in the wild state. [2] the study of all natural phenomena. [3] the sum of these phenomena in a given place or at a given time: *the natural history of Iran*.
▸**natural historian** NOUN

natural immunity NOUN immunity with which an individual is born, which has a genetic basis.

naturalism ('nætʃrəˌlɪzəm, -tʃərə-) NOUN [1] **a** a movement, esp in art and literature, advocating detailed realistic and factual description, esp that in 19th-century France in the writings of the novelists Emile Zola (1840–1902), Gustave Flaubert (1821–80), etc. **b** the characteristics or effects of this movement. [2] a school of painting or sculpture characterized by the faithful imitation of appearances for their own sake. [3] the belief that all religious truth is based not on revelation but rather on the study of natural causes and processes. [4] *Philosophy* **a** a scientific account of the world in terms of causes and natural forces that rejects all spiritual, supernatural, or teleological explanations. **b** the meta-ethical thesis that moral properties are reducible to natural ones, or that ethical judgments are derivable from nonethical ones. See **naturalistic fallacy.** Compare **descriptivism.** [5] action or thought caused by natural desires and instincts. [6] devotion to that which is natural.

naturalist ('nætʃrəlɪst, -tʃərəl-) NOUN [1] a person who is expert or interested in botany or zoology, esp in the field. [2] a person who advocates or practises naturalism, esp in art or literature.

naturalistic (ˌnætʃrə'lɪstɪk, -tʃərə-) ADJECTIVE [1] of, imitating, or reproducing nature in effect or characteristics. [2] of or characteristic of naturalism, esp in art or literature. [3] of or relating to naturalists. [4] (of an ethical theory) permitting the inference of ethical judgments from statements of nonethical fact. See **Hume's law.**
▸ˌ**natural'istically** ADVERB

naturalistic fallacy NOUN the supposed fallacy of inferring evaluative conclusions from purely factual premises. See **Hume's law.** Compare **non-naturalism.**

naturalize *or* **naturalise** ('nætʃrəˌlaɪz, -tʃərə-) VERB [1] (*tr*) to give citizenship to (a person of foreign birth). [2] to be or cause to be adopted in another place, as a word, custom, etc. [3] (*tr*) to introduce (a plant or animal from another region) and cause it to adapt to local conditions. [4] (*intr*) (of a plant or animal) to adapt successfully to a foreign environment and spread there. [5] (*tr*) to explain (something unusual) with reference to nature, excluding the supernatural. [6] (*tr*) to make natural or more lifelike.
▸ˌ**naturali'zation** *or* ˌ**naturali'sation** NOUN

natural justice NOUN the principles and procedures that govern the adjudication of disputes between persons or organizations, chief among which are that the adjudication should be unbiased and given in good faith, and that each party should have equal access to the tribunal and should be aware of arguments and documents adduced by the other.

natural language NOUN [1] a language that has evolved naturally as a means of communication among people. Compare **artificial language, formal language.** [2] languages of this kind considered collectively.

natural law NOUN 1 an ethical belief or system of beliefs supposed to be inherent in human nature and discoverable by reason rather than revelation. 2 a nonlogically necessary truth; law of nature. See also **nomological** (sense 2). 3 the philosophical doctrine that the authority of the legal system or of certain laws derives from their justifiability by reason, and indeed that a legal system which cannot be so justified has no authority.

natural logarithm NOUN a logarithm to the base e (see **e** (sense 1)). Usually written $\log_e$ or ln. Also called: **Napierian logarithm.** Compare **common logarithm.**

naturally ('nætʃrəlɪ, -tʃərə-) ADVERB 1 in a natural or normal way. 2 through nature; inherently; instinctively. ◆ ADVERB, SENTENCE SUBSTITUTE 3 of course; surely.

natural number NOUN any of the numbers 0,1,2,3,4,... that can be used to count the members of a set; the nonnegative integers.

natural philosophy NOUN (now only used in Scottish universities) physical science, esp physics. ▸**natural philosopher** NOUN

natural rate of unemployment NOUN another name for **NAIRU.**

natural resources PLURAL NOUN naturally occurring materials such as coal, fertile land, etc., that can be used by man.

natural science NOUN 1 the sciences collectively that are involved in the study of the physical world and its phenomena, including biology, physics, chemistry, and geology, but excluding social sciences, abstract or theoretical sciences, such as mathematics, and applied sciences. 2 any one of these sciences. ▸**natural scientist** NOUN

natural selection NOUN a process resulting in the survival of those individuals from a population of animals or plants that are best adapted to the prevailing environmental conditions. The survivors tend to produce more offspring than those less well adapted, so that the characteristics of the population change over time, thus accounting for the process of evolution.

natural slope NOUN *Civil engineering* the maximum angle at which soil will lie in a bank without slipping.

natural theology NOUN the attempt to derive theological truth, and esp the existence of God, from empirical facts by reasoned argument. Compare **revealed religion, fideism, revelation** (sense 3). ▸**natural theologian** NOUN

natural virtues PLURAL NOUN (esp among the scholastics) those virtues of which man is capable without direct help from God, specifically justice, temperance, prudence, and fortitude. Compare **theological virtues.**

natural wastage NOUN another term for **attrition** (sense 3).

nature ('neɪtʃə) NOUN 1 the fundamental qualities of a person or thing; identity or essential character. 2 (*often capital, esp when personified*) the whole system of the existence, arrangement, forces, and events of all physical life that are not controlled by man. 3 all natural phenomena and plant and animal life, as distinct from man and his creations. 4 a wild primitive state untouched by man or civilization. 5 natural unspoilt scenery or countryside. 6 disposition or temperament. 7 tendencies, desires, or instincts governing behaviour. 8 the normal biological needs or urges of the body. 9 sort; kind; character. 10 the real appearance of a person or thing: *a painting very true to nature.* 11 accepted standards of basic morality or behaviour. 12 *Biology* the complement of genetic material that partly determines the structure of an organism; genotype. Compare **nurture** (sense 3). 13 *Irish* sympathy and fondness for one's own people or native place: *she is full of nature.* 14 **against nature.** unnatural or immoral. 15 **by nature.** essentially or innately. 16 **call of nature.** *Informal, euphemistic or humorous* the need to urinate or defecate. 17 **from nature.** using natural models in drawing, painting, etc. 18 **in** (*or* **of**) **the nature of.** essentially the same as; by way of.
▷HISTORY C13: via Old French from Latin *nātūra,* from *nātus,* past participle of *nascī* to be born

Nature Conservancy Council NOUN (in Britain) a body set up by act of parliament in 1973 to establish and manage nature reserves, identify SSSIs, and provide information and advice about nature conservation. In 1991–92 it was replaced by English Nature, Scottish Natural Heritage, and the Countryside Council for Wales. Abbreviation: **NCC.**

nature reserve NOUN an area of land that is protected and managed in order to preserve a particular type of habitat and its flora and fauna which are often rare or endangered.

nature strip NOUN *Austral informal* a grass strip in front of a house between a fence or footpath and a roadway.

nature study NOUN the study of the natural world, esp animals and plants, by direct observation at an elementary level.

nature trail NOUN a path through countryside designed and usually signposted to draw attention to natural features of interest.

naturism ('neɪtʃəˌrɪzəm) NOUN another name for **nudism.**
▸'**naturist** NOUN, ADJECTIVE

naturopathy (ˌneɪtʃə'rɒpəθɪ) NOUN a method of treating disorders, involving the use of herbs and other naturally grown foods, sunlight, fresh air, etc. Also called: **nature cure.**
▸**naturopath** ('neɪtʃərəˌpæθ) NOUN ▸**naturopathic** (ˌneɪtʃərə'pæθɪk) ADJECTIVE

NAU INTERNATIONAL CAR REGISTRATION FOR Nauru.

nauch (nɔːtʃ) NOUN a variant spelling of **nautch.**

Naucratis ('nɔːkrətɪs) NOUN an ancient Greek city in N Egypt, in the Nile delta: founded in the 7th century B.C.

naught (nɔːt) NOUN 1 *Archaic or literary* nothing or nothingness; ruin or failure. 2 a variant spelling (esp US) of **nought.** 3 **set at naught.** to have disregard or scorn for; disdain. ◆ ADVERB 4 *Archaic or literary* not at all: *it matters naught.* ◆ ADJECTIVE 5 *Obsolete* worthless, ruined, or wicked.
▷HISTORY Old English *nāwiht,* from *nā* NO[1] + *wiht* thing, person; see WIGHT[1], WHIT

naughty ('nɔːtɪ) ADJECTIVE **-tier, -tiest.** 1 (esp of children or their behaviour) mischievous or disobedient; bad. 2 mildly indecent; titillating. ◆ NOUN, *plural* **-ties.** 3 *Austral and NZ, slang* an act of sexual intercourse.
▷HISTORY C14 (originally: needy, of poor quality): from NAUGHT
▸'**naughtily** ADVERB ▸'**naughtiness** NOUN

naughty nineties NOUN **the.** (in Britain) the 1890s, considered to be a period of fun loving and laxity, esp in sexual morals.

naumachia (nɔː'meɪkɪə) *or* **naumachy** ('nɔːməkɪ) NOUN, *plural* **-chiae** (-kɪˌiː), **-chias,** *or* **-chies.** (in ancient Rome) 1 a mock sea fight performed as an entertainment. 2 an artificial lake used in such a spectacle.
▷HISTORY C16: via Latin from Greek *naumakhia,* from *naus* ship + *makhē* battle

nauplius ('nɔːplɪəs) NOUN, *plural* **-plii** (-plɪˌaɪ). the larva of many crustaceans, having a rounded unsegmented body with three pairs of limbs.
▷HISTORY C19: from Latin: type of shellfish, from Greek *Nauplios,* one of the sons of Poseidon

Nauru (nɑː'uːruː) NOUN an island republic in the SW Pacific, west of Kiribati: administered jointly by Australia, New Zealand, and Britain as a UN trust territory before becoming independent in 1968 as a special member of the Commonwealth (not represented at meetings of Commonwealth heads of state). The economy is based on export of phosphates. Languages: Nauruan (a Malayo-Polynesian language) and English. Religion: Christian. Currency: Australian dollar. Pop.: 12 100 (2001 est.). Area: 2130 hectares (5263 acres). Former name: **Pleasant Island.**

Nauruan (nɑː'uːruːən) ADJECTIVE 1 of or relating to Nauru, its inhabitants, or their language. ◆ NOUN 2 a native or inhabitant of Nauru. 3 the Malayo-Polynesian language of Nauru.

nausea ('nɔːzɪə, -sɪə) NOUN 1 the sensation that precedes vomiting. 2 a feeling of disgust or revulsion.
▷HISTORY C16: via Latin from Greek: seasickness, from *naus* ship

nauseate ('nɔːzɪˌeɪt, -sɪ-) VERB 1 (*tr*) to arouse feelings of disgust or revulsion in. 2 to feel or cause to feel sick.
▸'**nauseˌating** ADJECTIVE ▸ˌ**nause'ation** NOUN

nauseous ('nɔːzɪəs, -sɪəs) ADJECTIVE 1 feeling sick. 2 causing nausea. 3 distasteful to the mind or senses; repulsive.
▸'**nauseously** ADVERB ▸'**nauseousness** NOUN

Nausicaä (nɔː'sɪkɪə) NOUN *Greek myth* a daughter of Alcinous, king of the Phaeacians, who assisted the shipwrecked Odysseus after discovering him on a beach.

-naut NOUN COMBINING FORM indicating a person engaged in the navigation of a vehicle, esp one used for scientific investigation: *astronaut.*

nautch *or* **nauch** (nɔːtʃ) NOUN **a** an intricate traditional Indian dance performed by professional dancing girls. **b** (*as modifier*): *a nautch girl.*
▷HISTORY C18: from Hindi *nāc,* from Sanskrit *nrtya,* from *nrtyati* he acts or dances

nautical ('nɔːtɪk[ə]l) ADJECTIVE of, relating to, or involving ships, navigation, or sailors.
▷HISTORY C16: from Latin *nauticus,* from Greek *nautikos,* from *naus* ship
▸'**nautically** ADVERB

nautical mile NOUN 1 Also called: **international nautical mile, air mile.** a unit of length, used esp in navigation, equivalent to the average length of a minute of latitude, and corresponding to a latitude of 45°, i.e. 1852 m (6076.12 ft.). 2 a former British unit of length equal to 1853.18 m (6080 ft.), which was replaced by the international nautical mile in 1970. Former name: **geographical mile.** Compare **sea mile.**

nautiloid ('nɔːtɪˌlɔɪd) NOUN 1 any mollusc of the *Nautiloidea,* a group of cephalopods that includes the pearly nautilus and many extinct forms. ◆ ADJECTIVE 2 of, relating to, or belonging to the *Nautiloidea.*

nautilus ('nɔːtɪləs) NOUN, *plural* **-luses** *or* **-li** (-ˌlaɪ). 1 any cephalopod mollusc of the genus *Nautilus,* esp the pearly nautilus. 2 short for **paper nautilus.**
▷HISTORY C17: via Latin from Greek *nautilos* sailor, from *naus* ship

NAV ABBREVIATION FOR **net asset value.**

Navaho *or* **Navajo** ('nævəˌhəʊ, 'nɑː-) NOUN 1 (*plural* **-ho, -hos, -hoes** *or* **-jo, -jos, -joes**) a member of a North American Indian people of Arizona, New Mexico, and Utah. 2 the language of this people, belonging to the Athapascan group of the Na-Dene phylum.
▷HISTORY C18: from Spanish *Navajó* pueblo, from Tena *Navahu* large planted field

naval ('neɪv[ə]l) ADJECTIVE 1 of, relating to, characteristic of, or having a navy. 2 of or relating to ships; nautical.
▷HISTORY C16: from Latin *nāvālis,* from *nāvis* ship; related to Greek *naus,* Old Norse *nōr* ship, Sanskrit *nau*

naval architecture NOUN the designing of ships.
▸**naval architect** NOUN

navar ('nævɑː) NOUN a system of air navigation in which a ground radar station relays signals to each aircraft indicating the relative positions of neighbouring aircraft.
▷HISTORY C20: from *nav(igational and traffic control rad)ar*

Navaratri (nævə'rɑːtrɪ) NOUN an annual Hindu festival celebrated over nine days in September–October. Observed throughout India, it commemorates the slaying of demons by Rama and the goddess Durga; in some places it is dedicated to all female deities. Also called: **Durga Puja.**
▷HISTORY from Sanskrit *navaratri* nine nights

navarin ('nævərɪn; *French* navarɛ̃) NOUN a stew of mutton or lamb with root vegetables.
▷HISTORY from French

Navarino (nava'riːno) NOUN 1 the Italian name for **Pylos.** 2 a sea battle (Oct. 20, 1827) in which the defeat of the Turkish-Egyptian fleet by a combined British, French, and Russian fleet decided Greek independence.

Navarre (nə'vɑː) NOUN a former kingdom of SW Europe: established in the 9th century by the Basques; the parts south of the Pyrenees joined Spain in 1515 and the N parts passed to France in 1589. Capital: Pamplona. Spanish name: **Navarra** (na'βarra).

nave[1] (neɪv) NOUN the central space in a church,

extending from the narthex to the chancel and often flanked by aisles.
▷**HISTORY** C17: via Medieval Latin from Latin *nāvis* ship, from the similarity of shape

nave[2] (neɪv) NOUN the central block or hub of a wheel.
▷**HISTORY** Old English *nafu, nafa;* related to Old High German *naba*

navel (ˈneɪvəl) NOUN [1] the scar in the centre of the abdomen, usually forming a slight depression, where the umbilical cord was attached. Technical name: **umbilicus.** Related adjective: **umbilical.** [2] a central part, location, or point; middle. [3] short for **navel orange.**
▷**HISTORY** Old English *nafela;* related to Old Frisian *navla,* Old High German *nabulo* (German *Nabel*), Latin *umbilīcus*

navel-gazing NOUN *Informal* self-absorbed behaviour.

navel orange NOUN a sweet orange that is usually seedless and has at its apex a navel-like depression enclosing an underdeveloped secondary fruit.

navelwort (ˈneɪvəlˌwɜːt) NOUN another name for **pennywort** (sense 1).

navew (ˈneɪvjuː) NOUN another name for **turnip** (senses 1, 2).
▷**HISTORY** C16: from Old French *navel,* from Latin *nāpus*

navicert (ˈnævɪˌsɜːt) NOUN a certificate specifying the contents of a neutral ship's cargo, issued esp in time of war by a blockading power.
▷**HISTORY** C20: from Latin *nāvi(s)* ship + CERT(IFICATE)

navicular (nəˈvɪkjʊlə) *Anatomy* ◆ ADJECTIVE [1] shaped like a boat. ◆ NOUN *also* **naviculare** (nəˌvɪkjʊˈlɑːrɪ). [2] a small boat-shaped bone of the wrist or foot.
▷**HISTORY** C16: from Late Latin *nāviculāris,* from Latin *nāvicula,* diminutive of *nāvis* ship

navig. ABBREVIATION FOR navigation.

navigable (ˈnævɪgəbəl) ADJECTIVE [1] wide, deep, or safe enough to be sailed on or through: *a navigable channel.* [2] capable of being steered or controlled: *a navigable raft.*
▸ **ˌnavigaˈbility** *or* **ˈnavigableness** NOUN ▸ **ˈnavigably** ADVERB

navigate (ˈnævɪˌgeɪt) VERB [1] to plan, direct, or plot the path or position of (a ship, an aircraft, etc.). [2] (*tr*) to travel over, through, or on (water, air, or land) in a boat, aircraft, etc. [3] *Informal* to direct (oneself, one's way, etc.) carefully or safely: *he navigated his way to the bar.* [4] (*intr*) (of a passenger in a motor vehicle) to give directions to the driver; point out the route. [5] (*intr*) *Rare* to voyage in a ship; sail.
▷**HISTORY** C16: from Latin *nāvigāre* to sail, from *nāvis* ship + *agere* to drive

navigation (ˌnævɪˈgeɪʃən) NOUN [1] the skill or process of plotting a route and directing a ship, aircraft, etc., along it. [2] the act or practice of navigating: *dredging made navigation of the river possible.* [3] *US, rare* ship traffic; shipping. [4] *Midland English, dialect* an inland waterway; canal.
▸ **ˌnaviˈgational** ADJECTIVE

Navigation Acts PLURAL NOUN a series of acts of Parliament, the first of which was passed in 1381, that attempted to restrict to English ships the right to carry goods to and from England and its colonies. The attempt to enforce the acts helped cause the War of American Independence.

navigator (ˈnævɪˌgeɪtə) NOUN [1] a person who is skilled in or performs navigation, esp on a ship or aircraft. [2] (esp formerly) a person who explores by ship. [3] an instrument or device for assisting a pilot to navigate an aircraft.

Návpaktos (*Greek* ˈnafpaktos) NOUN the Greek name for **Lepanto.**

navvy (ˈnævɪ) NOUN, *plural* **-vies.** *Brit informal* a labourer on a building site, excavations, etc.
▷**HISTORY** C19: shortened from *navigator,* builder of a navigation (sense 4)

navy (ˈneɪvɪ) NOUN, *plural* **-vies.** [1] the warships and auxiliary vessels of a nation or ruler. [2] (*often capital; usually preceded by the*) the branch of a country's armed services comprising such ships, their crews, and all their supporting services and equipment. [3] short for **navy blue.** [4] *Archaic or literary* a fleet of ships. [5] (*as modifier*): *a navy custom.*
▷**HISTORY** C14: via Old French from Vulgar Latin *nāvia* (unattested) ship, from Latin *nāvis* ship

navy blue NOUN **a** a dark greyish-blue colour. **b** (*as adjective*): *a navy-blue suit.* ◆ Sometimes shortened to **navy.**
▷**HISTORY** C19: from the colour of the British naval uniform

navy cut NOUN tobacco finely cut from a block.

Navy List NOUN (in Britain) an official list of all serving commissioned officers of the Royal Navy and reserve officers liable for recall.

navy yard NOUN a naval shipyard, esp in the US.

nawab (nəˈwɑːb) NOUN (formerly) a Muslim ruling prince or powerful landowner in India. Also called: **nabob.**
▷**HISTORY** C18: from Hindi *nawwāb,* from Arabic *nuwwāb,* plural of *na'ib* viceroy, governor

Naxalite (ˈnʌksəˌlaɪt) NOUN a member of an extreme Maoist group in India that originated in 1967 in West Bengal and which employs tactics of agrarian terrorism and direct action.
▷**HISTORY** C20: named after *Naxalbari,* a town in West Bengal where the movement started

Naxos (ˈnæksɒs) NOUN a Greek island in the S Aegean, the largest of the Cyclades: ancient centre of the worship of Dionysius. Pop.: 14 000 (latest est.). Area: 438 sq. km (169 sq. miles).

nay (neɪ) SENTENCE SUBSTITUTE [1] a word for **no**[1]: archaic or dialectal except in voting by voice. ◆ NOUN [2] **a** a person who votes in the negative. **b** a negative vote. ◆ ADVERB [3] (*sentence modifier*) *Archaic* an emphatic form of **no**[1]. ◆ Compare **aye**[1].
▷**HISTORY** C12: from Old Norse *nei,* from *ne* not + *ei* ever, AY[1]

Nayarit (*Spanish* najaˈrit) NOUN a state of W Mexico, on the Pacific: includes the offshore Tres Marías Islands. Capital: Tepic. Pop.: 919 739 (2000). Area: 27 621 sq. km (10 772 sq. miles).

Nazarene (ˌnæzəˈriːn, ˈnæz-) NOUN *also* **Nazarite.** [1] an early name for a **Christian** (Acts 24:5) or (when preceded by *the*) for Jesus Christ (?4 B.C.–?29 A.D.), the founder of Christianity. [2] a member of one of several groups of Jewish-Christians found principally in Syria. [3] a member of an association of German artists called the Nazarenes or Brotherhood of St Luke, including Friedrich Overbeck (1789–1869) and Peter von Cornelius (1783–1867), founded (1809) in Vienna to revive German religious art after the examples of the Middle Ages and early Renaissance. ◆ ADJECTIVE [4] of or relating to Nazareth or the Nazarenes.

Nazareth (ˈnæzərɪθ) NOUN a town in N Israel, in Lower Galilee: the home of Jesus in his youth. Pop.: 51 000 (latest est.).

Nazarite[1] (ˈnæzəˌraɪt) NOUN another word for **Nazarene** (senses 1, 2).

Nazarite[2] *or* **Nazirite** (ˈnæzəˌraɪt) NOUN a religious ascetic of ancient Israel.
▷**HISTORY** C16: from Latin *Nazaraeus,* from Hebrew *nāzīr,* from *nāzar* to consecrate + -ITE[1]

Naze (neɪz) NOUN **the.** [1] a flat marshy headland in SE England, in Essex on the North Sea coast. [2] another name for **Lindesnes.**

Nazi (ˈnɑːtsɪ) NOUN, *plural* **Nazis.** [1] a member of the fascist National Socialist German Workers' Party, which was founded in 1919 and seized political control in Germany in 1933 under the Austrian-born German dictator Adolf Hitler (1889–1945). [2] *Derogatory* anyone who thinks or acts like a Nazi, esp showing racism, brutality, etc. ◆ ADJECTIVE [3] of, characteristic of, or relating to the Nazis.
▷**HISTORY** C20: from German, phonetic spelling of the first two syllables of *Nationalsozialist* National Socialist
▸ **Nazism** (ˈnɑːtˌsɪzəm) *or* **Naziism** (ˈnɑːtsɪˌɪzəm) NOUN

Nazify (ˈnɑːtsɪˌfaɪ) VERB **-fies, -fying, -fied.** (*tr*) to make Nazi in character.
▸ **ˌNazifiˈcation** NOUN

nb *Cricket* ABBREVIATION FOR no ball.

Nb THE CHEMICAL SYMBOL FOR niobium.

NB[1] ABBREVIATION FOR New Brunswick.

NB[2], **N.B., nb,** *or* **n.b.** ABBREVIATION FOR nota bene.
▷**HISTORY** Latin: note well

NBA ABBREVIATION FOR: [1] (in the US) National Basketball Association. [2] (the former) **Net Book Agreement.**

NBC ABBREVIATION FOR: [1] (in the US) National Broadcasting Company. [2] (of weapons or warfare) nuclear, biological, and chemical.

NBG *Informal* ABBREVIATION FOR no bloody good. Also: **nbg.**

nc THE INTERNET DOMAIN NAME FOR New Caledonia.

NC *or* **N.C.** ABBREVIATION FOR: [1] North Carolina. [2] *Brit education* **National Curriculum.**

NCC (in Britain) ABBREVIATION FOR (the former) **Nature Conservancy Council.**

NCCL ABBREVIATION FOR National Council for Civil Liberties.

NCEA (in New Zealand) ABBREVIATION FOR National Certificate of Educational Attainment.

NCIS (in Britain) ABBREVIATION FOR National Criminal Intelligence Service.

NCM (in the Canadian armed forces) ABBREVIATION FOR noncommissioned member.

NCO ABBREVIATION FOR noncommissioned officer.

NCP (in Australia) ABBREVIATION FOR **National Country Party.**

NCVO (in Britain) ABBREVIATION FOR National Council for Voluntary Organizations.

nd ABBREVIATION FOR no date.

Nd THE CHEMICAL SYMBOL FOR neodymium.

ND, N.D., *or* **N. Dak.** ABBREVIATION FOR North Dakota.

NDE ABBREVIATION FOR **near-death experience.**

Ndebele (ənˈdɛbɛlɛ) NOUN [1] (*plural* **Ndebele**) a member of a Negroid people of Zimbabwe. See also **Matabele.** [2] the language of this people, belonging to the Bantu grouping of the Niger-Congo family.

Ndjamena *or* **N'djamena** (əndʒɑːˈmeɪnə) NOUN the capital of Chad, in the southwest, at the confluence of the Shari and Logone Rivers: trading centre for livestock. Pop.: 530 965 (1993). Former name (until 1973): **Fort Lamy.**

Ndola (ənˈdəʊlə) NOUN a city in N Zambia: copper, cobalt, and sugar refineries. Pop.: 376 311 (1990).

NDP ABBREVIATION FOR: [1] **net domestic product.** [2] (in Canada) **New Democratic Party.**

NDT ABBREVIATION FOR **nondestructive testing.**

ne THE INTERNET DOMAIN NAME FOR Niger.

Ne THE CHEMICAL SYMBOL FOR neon.

NE[1] [1] SYMBOL FOR northeast(ern). ◆ [2] ABBREVIATION FOR Nebraska.

NE[2] *or* **N.E.** ABBREVIATION FOR New England.

NE1 *Text messaging* ABBREVIATION FOR anyone.

ne- COMBINING FORM a variant of **neo-,** esp before a vowel *Nearctic.*

Neagh (neɪ) NOUN **Lough.** a lake in Northern Ireland, in SW Co. Antrim: the largest lake in the British Isles. Area: 388 sq. km (150 sq. miles).

Neanderthal (nɪˈændəˌtɑːl) (*sometimes not capital*) ADJECTIVE [1] relating to or characteristic of Neanderthal man. [2] primitive; uncivilized. [3] *Informal* ultraconservative; reactionary. ◆ NOUN [4] a person showing any such characteristics.

Neanderthal man (nɪˈændəˌtɑːl) NOUN a type of primitive man, *Homo neanderthalensis,* or *H. sapiens neanderthalensis,* occurring throughout much of Europe in late Palaeolithic times: it is thought that they did not interbreed with other early humans and are not the ancestors of modern humans.
▷**HISTORY** C19: from the anthropological findings (1857) in the Neandertal, a valley near Düsseldorf, Germany

neanic (nɪˈænɪk) ADJECTIVE *Zoology* of or relating to the early stages in the life cycle of an organism, esp the pupal stage of an insect.
▷**HISTORY** C19: from Greek *neanikus* youthful

neap (niːp) ADJECTIVE [1] of, relating to, or constituting a neap tide. ◆ NOUN [2] short for **neap tide.**
▷**HISTORY** Old English, as in *nēpflōd* neap tide, of uncertain origin

Neapolitan (ˌnɪəˈpɒlɪtən) NOUN [1] a native or inhabitant of Naples. ◆ ADJECTIVE [2] of or relating to Naples.

▷HISTORY C15: from Latin *Neāpolītānus,* ultimately from Greek *Neapolis* new town

Neapolitan ice cream NOUN ice cream, usually in brick form, with several layers of different colours and flavours.

Neapolitan sixth NOUN (in musical harmony) a chord composed of the subdominant of the key, plus a minor third and a minor sixth. Harmonically it is equivalent to the first inversion of a major chord built upon the flattened supertonic.

neap tide NOUN either of the two tides that occur at the first or last quarter of the moon when the tide-generating forces of the sun and moon oppose each other and produce the smallest rise and fall in tidal level. Compare **spring tide** (sense 1).

near (nɪə) PREPOSITION [1] at or to a place or time not far away from; close to. ◆ ADVERB [2] at or to a place or time not far away; close by. [3] **near to.** not far from; near. [4] short for **nearly** (esp in phrases such as **damn near**): *I was damn near killed.* ◆ ADJECTIVE [5] at or in a place not far away. [6] (*prenominal*) only just successful or only just failing: *a near escape.* [7] (*postpositive*) *Informal* miserly, mean. [8] (*prenominal*) closely connected or intimate: *a near relation.* ◆ VERB [9] to come or draw close (to). ◆ NOUN [10] Also called: **nearside. a** the left side of a horse, team of animals, vehicle, etc. **b** (*as modifier*): *the near foreleg.*
▷HISTORY Old English *nēar* (adv), comparative of *nēah* close, NIGH; related to Old Frisian *niār,* Old Norse *nǣr,* Old High German *nāhōr*
▸**'nearness** NOUN

near- COMBINING FORM nearly; almost: *a near-perfect landing.*

nearby ADJECTIVE ('nɪəˌbaɪ), ADVERB (ˌnɪə'baɪ) not far away; close at hand.

Nearctic (nɪ'ɑːktɪk) ADJECTIVE of or denoting a zoogeographical region consisting of North America, north of the tropic of Cancer, and Greenland.

near-death experience NOUN an experience, instances of which have been widely reported, in which a person near death is apparently outside his body and aware of it and the attendant circumstances as separate from him. Abbreviation: **NDE.**

Near East NOUN [1] another term for the **Middle East.** [2] (formerly) the Balkan States and the area of the Ottoman Empire.

near gale NOUN *Meteorol* a wind of force seven on the Beaufort scale or from 32–38 mph.

nearly ('nɪəlɪ) ADVERB [1] not quite; almost; practically. [2] **not nearly.** nowhere near; not at all: *not nearly enough money.* [3] closely: *the person most nearly concerned.*

near-market research NOUN scientific research that, while not linked to the development of a specific product, is likely to be commercially exploitable.

near miss NOUN [1] a bomb, shell, etc., that does not exactly hit the target. [2] any attempt or shot that just fails to be successful. [3] an incident in which two vehicles narrowly avoid collision.

near money NOUN liquid assets that can be converted to cash very quickly, such as a bank deposit or bill of exchange.

near point NOUN *Optics* the nearest point to the eye at which an object remains in focus.

near rhyme NOUN *Prosody* another term for **half-rhyme.**

nearside ('nɪəˌsaɪd) NOUN [1] (usually preceded by *the*) *Chiefly Brit* **a** the side of a vehicle normally nearer the kerb (in Britain, the left side). **b** (*as modifier*): *the nearside door.* ◆ Compare **offside.** [2] **a** the left side of an animal, team of horses, etc. **b** (*as modifier*): *the nearside flank.*

near-sighted (ˌnɪə'saɪtɪd) ADJECTIVE relating to or suffering from myopia.
▸**ˌnear-'sightedly** ADVERB ▸**ˌnear-'sightedness** NOUN

near thing NOUN *Informal* an event or action whose outcome is nearly a failure, success, disaster, etc.

nearthrosis (ˌniːɑː'θrəʊsɪs) NOUN, *plural* **-ses** (-siːz). another name for **pseudoarthrosis.**

neat¹ (niːt) ADJECTIVE [1] clean, tidy, and orderly. [2] liking or insisting on order and cleanliness; fastidious. [3] smoothly or competently done; efficient: *a neat job.* [4] pat or slick: *his excuse was suspiciously neat.* [5] (of alcoholic drinks) without added water, lemonade, etc.; undiluted. [6] a less common word for **net²**: *neat profits.* [7] *Slang, chiefly US and Canadian* good; pleasing; admirable.
▷HISTORY C16: from Old French *net,* from Latin *nitidus* clean, shining, from *nitēre* to shine; related to Middle Irish *niam* beauty, brightness, Old Persian *naiba-* beautiful
▸**'neatly** ADVERB ▸**'neatness** NOUN

neat² (niːt) NOUN, *plural* **neat.** *Archaic or dialect* a domestic bovine animal.
▷HISTORY Old English *neat*

neaten ('niːtᵊn) VERB (*tr*) to make neat; tidy.

neath *or* **'neath** (niːθ) PREPOSITION *Archaic* short for **beneath.**

Neath Port Talbot ('niːθ 'pɔːt 'tɔːlbət, 'tæl-) NOUN a county borough in S Wales, created from part of West Glamorgan in 1996. Administrative centre: Port Talbot. Pop.: 134 471 (2001). Area: 439 sq. km (169 sq. miles).

neat's-foot oil NOUN a yellow fixed oil obtained by boiling the feet and shinbones of cattle and used esp to dress leather.

neb (nɛb) NOUN *Archaic or dialect* [1] *Chiefly Scot and northern English* the peak of a cap. [2] the beak of a bird or the nose or snout of an animal. [3] a person's mouth or nose. [4] the projecting part or end of anything. [5] **a** a peak, esp in N England. **b** a prominent gritstone overhang.
▷HISTORY Old English *nebb;* related to Old Norse *nef,* Old High German *snabul* (German *Schnabel*)

NEB ABBREVIATION FOR: [1] New English Bible. [2] (the former) National Enterprise Board.

Nebelung ('neɪbəˌlʊŋ) NOUN a breed of cat with a long body, long silky bluish hair, and a plumelike tail.

Nebo ('niːbəʊ) NOUN **Mount.** a mountain in Jordan, northeast of the Dead Sea: the highest point of a ridge known as Pisgah, from which Moses viewed the Promised Land just before his death (Deuteronomy 34:1). Height: 802 m (2631 ft.).

Nebr. ABBREVIATION FOR Nebraska.

Nebraska (nɪ'bræskə) NOUN a state of the western US: consists of an undulating plain. Capital: Lincoln. Pop.: 1 711 263 (2000 est.). Area: 197 974 sq. km (76 483 sq. miles). Abbreviations: **Nebr.,** (with zip code) **NE.**

Nebraskan (nɪ'bræskən) ADJECTIVE [1] of or relating to Nebraska or its inhabitants. ◆ NOUN [2] a native or inhabitant of Nebraska.

Nebuchadnezzar¹ (ˌnɛbjʊkəd'nɛzə) NOUN a wine bottle, used esp for display, holding the equivalent of twenty normal bottles (approximately 520 ounces).
▷HISTORY C20: named after NEBUCHADNEZZAR², from the custom of naming large wine bottles after Old Testament figures; compare JEROBOAM

Nebuchadnezzar² (ˌnɛbjʊkəd'nɛzə) *or* **Nebuchadrezzar** NOUN *Old Testament* a king of Babylon, 605–562 B.C., who conquered and destroyed Jerusalem and exiled the Jews to Babylon (II Kings 24–25).

nebula ('nɛbjʊlə) NOUN, *plural* **-lae** (-ˌliː) *or* **-las.** [1] *Astronomy* a diffuse cloud of particles and gases (mainly hydrogen) that is visible either as a hazy patch of light (either an **emission** or a **reflection nebula**) or an irregular dark region against a brighter background (**dark nebula**). Compare **planetary nebula.** [2] *Pathol* **a** opacity of the cornea. **b** cloudiness of the urine. [3] any substance for use in an atomizer spray.
▷HISTORY C17: from Latin: mist, cloud; related to Greek *nephélē* cloud, Old High German *nebul* cloud, Old Norse *njól* night
▸**'nebular** ADJECTIVE

nebular hypothesis NOUN the theory that the solar system evolved from the gravitational collapse of nebular matter.

nebulize *or* **nebulise** ('nɛbjʊˌlaɪz) VERB (*tr*) to convert (a liquid) into a mist or fine spray; atomize.
▸**ˌnebuli'zation** *or* **ˌnebuli'sation** NOUN

nebulizer *or* **nebuliser** ('nɛbjʊˌlaɪzə) NOUN a device for converting a drug in liquid form into a mist or fine spray which is inhaled through a mask to provide medication for the respiratory system. Also called: **inhalator.**

nebulosity (ˌnɛbjʊ'lɒsɪtɪ) NOUN, *plural* **-ties.** [1] the state or quality of being nebulous. [2] *Astronomy* a nebula.

nebulous ('nɛbjʊləs) ADJECTIVE [1] lacking definite form, shape, or content; vague or amorphous: *nebulous reasons.* [2] of, characteristic of, or resembling a nebula. [3] *Rare* misty or hazy.
▸**'nebulously** ADVERB ▸**'nebulousness** NOUN

NEC ABBREVIATION FOR National Executive Committee.

necessaries ('nɛsɪsərɪz) PLURAL NOUN [1] (*sometimes singular*) what is needed; essential items: *the necessaries of life.* [2] *Law* food, clothing, etc., essential for the maintenance of a dependant in the condition of life to which he or she is accustomed.

necessarily ('nɛsɪsərɪlɪ, ˌnɛsɪ'sɛrɪlɪ) ADVERB [1] as an inevitable or natural consequence: *girls do not necessarily like dolls.* [2] as a certainty: *he won't necessarily come.*

necessary ('nɛsɪsərɪ) ADJECTIVE [1] needed to achieve a certain desired effect or result; required. [2] resulting from necessity; inevitable: *the necessary consequences of your action.* [3] *Logic* **a** (of a statement, formula, etc.) true under all interpretations or in all possible circumstances. **b** (of a proposition) determined to be true by its meaning, so that its denial would be self-contradictory. **c** (of a property) essential, so that without it its subject would not be the entity it is. **d** (of an inference) always yielding a true conclusion when its premises are true; valid. **e** (of a condition) entailed by the truth of some statement or the obtaining of some state of affairs. ◆ Compare **sufficient** (sense 2). [4] *Philosophy* (in a nonlogical sense) expressing a law of nature, so that if it is in this sense necessary that all As are B, even although it is not contradictory to conceive of an A which is not B, we are licensed to infer that if something were an A it would have to be B. [5] *Rare* compelled, as by necessity or law; not free. ◆ NOUN [6] *Informal* (preceded by *the*) the money required for a particular purpose. [7] **do the necessary.** *Informal* to do something that is necessary in a particular situation. ◆ See also **necessaries.**
▷HISTORY C14: from Latin *necessārius* indispensable, from *necesse* unavoidable

necessitarianism (nɪˌsɛsɪ'tɛərɪəˌnɪzəm) *or* **necessarianism** (ˌnɛsɪ'sɛərɪəˌnɪzəm) NOUN *Philosophy* another word for **determinism.** Compare **libertarian.**
▸**neˌcessi'tarian** *or* **ˌneces'sarian** NOUN, ADJECTIVE

necessitate (nɪ'sɛsɪˌteɪt) VERB (*tr*) [1] to cause as an unavoidable and necessary result. [2] (*usually passive*) to compel or require (someone to do something).
▸**neˌcessi'tation** NOUN ▸**ne'cessitative** ADJECTIVE

necessitous (nɪ'sɛsɪtəs) ADJECTIVE very needy; destitute; poverty-stricken.
▸**ne'cessitously** ADVERB

necessity (nɪ'sɛsɪtɪ) NOUN, *plural* **-ties.** [1] (*sometimes plural*) something needed for a desired result; prerequisite: *necessities of life.* [2] a condition or set of circumstances, such as physical laws or social rules, that inevitably requires a certain result: *it is a matter of necessity to wear formal clothes when meeting the Queen.* [3] the state or quality of being obligatory or unavoidable. [4] urgent requirement, as in an emergency or misfortune: *in time of necessity we must all work together.* [5] poverty or want. [6] *Rare* compulsion through laws of nature; fate. [7] *Philosophy* **a** a condition, principle, or conclusion that cannot be otherwise. **b** the constraining force of physical determinants on all aspects of life. Compare **freedom** (sense 8). [8] *Logic* **a** the property of being necessary. **b** a statement asserting that some property is essential or statement is necessarily true. **c** the operator that indicates that the expression it modifies is true in all possible worlds. Usual symbol: □ or L. [9] **of necessity.** inevitably; necessarily.

neck (nɛk) NOUN [1] the part of an organism connecting the head with the rest of the body. Related adjectives: **cervical, jugular.** [2] the part of a garment around or nearest the neck. [3] something resembling a neck in shape or position: *the neck of a bottle.* [4] *Anatomy* a constricted portion of an organ or part, such as the cervix of the uterus. [5] a

narrow or elongated projecting strip of land; a peninsula or isthmus. [6] a strait or channel. [7] the part of a violin, cello, etc., that extends from the body to the tuning pegs and supports the fingerboard. [8] a solid block of lava from the opening of an extinct volcano, exposed after erosion of the surrounding rock. [9] *Botany* the upper, usually tubular, part of the archegonium of mosses, ferns, etc. [10] the length of a horse's head and neck taken as an approximate distance by which one horse beats another in a race: *to win by a neck.* [11] *Informal* a short distance, amount, or margin: *he is always a neck ahead in new techniques.* [12] *Informal* impudence; audacity: *he had the neck to ask for a rise.* [13] *Architect* the narrow band at the top of the shaft of a column between the necking and the capital, esp as used in the Tuscan order. [14] another name for **beard** (sense 7) (on printer's type). [15] **break one's neck.** *Informal* to exert oneself greatly, esp by hurrying, in order to do something. [16] **by the neck.** *Irish and Scot, slang* (of a bottle of beer) served unpoured: *give me two bottles of stout by the neck.* [17] **get it in the neck.** *Informal* to be reprimanded or punished severely. [18] **neck and neck.** absolutely level or even in a race or competition. [19] **neck of the woods.** *Informal* an area or locality: *a quiet neck of the woods.* [20] **risk one's neck.** to take a great risk. [21] **save one's** *or* **someone's neck.** *Informal* to escape from or help someone else to escape from a difficult or dangerous situation. [22] **stick one's neck out.** *Informal* to risk criticism, ridicule, failure, etc., by speaking one's mind. [23] **up to one's neck (in).** deeply involved (in). ◆ VERB [24] *(intr) Informal* to kiss, embrace, or fondle someone or one another passionately. [25] *(tr) Brit informal* to swallow (something, esp a drink): *he's been necking pints all night.*
▷HISTORY Old English *hnecca;* related to Old High German *hnack,* Old Irish *cnocc* hill
▸ **'necker** NOUN

Neckar ('nɛkɑː) NOUN a river in SW Germany, rising in the Black Forest and flowing generally north into the Rhine at Mannheim. Length: 394 km (245 miles).

neckband ('nɛkˌbænd) NOUN a band around the neck of a garment as finishing, decoration, or a base for a collar.

neckcloth ('nɛkˌklɒθ) NOUN a large ornamental usually white cravat worn formerly by men.

neckerchief ('nɛkətʃɪf, -ˌtʃiːf) NOUN a piece of ornamental cloth, often square, worn around the neck.
▷HISTORY C14: from NECK + KERCHIEF

Necker cube ('nɛkə) NOUN a line drawing showing the 12 edges of a transparent cube, so that it can be seen alternately facing in two different directions: an example of an ambiguous figure.
▷HISTORY C19: named after Louis Albert *Necker* (1786–1861), Swiss mineralogist

necking ('nɛkɪŋ) NOUN [1] *Informal* the activity of kissing and embracing passionately. [2] Also called: **gorgerin.** *Architect* one or more mouldings at the top of a column between the shaft and the capital.

necklace ('nɛklɪs) NOUN [1] a chain, band, or cord, often bearing beads, pearls, jewels, etc., worn around the neck as an ornament, esp by women. [2] (in South Africa) a tyre soaked in petrol, placed round a person's neck, and set on fire in order to burn the person to death. ◆ VERB [3] *(tr) South African* to kill (someone) by placing a burning tyre round his or her neck.

necklace bomb NOUN a bomb consisting of linked charges hung around a victim's neck, used by terrorists or in hostage situations.

necklet ('nɛklɪt) NOUN an ornament worn round the neck.

neckline ('nɛkˌlaɪn) NOUN the shape or position of the upper edge of a dress, blouse, etc.: *a plunging neckline.*

neckpiece ('nɛkˌpiːs) NOUN a piece of fur, cloth, etc., worn around the neck or neckline.

necktie ('nɛkˌtaɪ) NOUN the US name for **tie** (sense 11).

neckwear ('nɛkˌwɛə) NOUN articles of clothing, such as ties, scarves, etc., worn around the neck.

necro- *or before a vowel* **necr-** COMBINING FORM indicating death, a dead body, or dead tissue: *necrology; necrophagous; necrosis.*
▷HISTORY from Greek *nekros* corpse

necrobiosis (ˌnɛkrəʊbaɪ'əʊsɪs) NOUN *Physiol* the normal degeneration and death of cells. Compare **necrosis.**
▸ **necrobiotic** (ˌnɛkrəʊbaɪ'ɒtɪk) ADJECTIVE

necrolatry (nɛ'krɒlətrɪ) NOUN the worship of the dead.

necrology (nɛ'krɒlədʒɪ) NOUN, *plural* **-gies.** [1] a list of people recently dead. [2] a less common word for **obituary.**
▸ **necrological** (ˌnɛkrə'lɒdʒɪkᵊl) ADJECTIVE ▸ **ne'crologist** NOUN

necromancy ('nɛkrəʊˌmænsɪ) NOUN [1] the art or practice of supposedly conjuring up the dead, esp in order to obtain from them knowledge of the future. [2] black magic; sorcery.
▷HISTORY C13: (as in sense 1) ultimately from Greek *nekromanteia,* from *nekros* corpse; (as in sense 2) from Medieval Latin *nigromantia,* from Latin *niger* black, which replaced *necro-* through folk etymology
▸ **'necroˌmancer** NOUN ▸ **ˌnecro'mantic** ADJECTIVE

necromania (ˌnɛkrəʊ'meɪnɪə) NOUN another word for **necrophilia.**
▸ **ˌnecro'maniˌac** NOUN

necrophagous (nə'krɒfəgəs) ADJECTIVE (of an animal, bird, etc.) feeding on carrion.

necrophilia (ˌnɛkrəʊ'fɪlɪə) NOUN sexual attraction for or sexual intercourse with dead bodies. Also called: **necromania, necrophilism.**
▸ **ˌnecro'philiˌac** *or* **necrophile** ('nɛkrəʊˌfaɪl) NOUN
▸ **ˌnecro'philic** ADJECTIVE

necrophilism (nɛ'krɒfɪˌlɪzəm) NOUN [1] another word for **necrophilia.** [2] a strong desire to be dead.

necrophobia (ˌnɛkrəʊ'fəʊbɪə) NOUN an abnormal fear of death or dead bodies.
▸ **'necroˌphobe** NOUN ▸ **ˌnecro'phobic** ADJECTIVE

necrophorous (nɪ'krɒfərəs) ADJECTIVE denoting animals, such as certain beetles, that carry away the bodies of dead animals.

necropolis (nɛ'krɒpəlɪs) NOUN, *plural* **-lises** *or* **-leis** (-ˌleɪs). a burial site or cemetery.
▷HISTORY C19: Greek, from *nekros* dead + *polis* city

necropsy ('nɛkrɒpsɪ) *or* **necroscopy** (nɛ'krɒskəpɪ) NOUN, *plural* **-sies** *or* **-pies.** another name for **autopsy.**
▷HISTORY C19: from Greek *nekros* dead body + *opsis* sight

necrose (nɛ'krəʊs, 'nɛkrəʊs) VERB *(intr)* to cause or undergo necrosis.
▷HISTORY C19: back formation from NECROSIS

necrosis (nɛ'krəʊsɪs) NOUN [1] the death of one or more cells in the body, usually within a localized area, as from an interruption of the blood supply to that part. [2] death of plant tissue due to disease, frost, etc.
▷HISTORY C17: New Latin from Greek *nekrōsis,* from *nekroun* to kill, from *nekros* corpse
▸ **necrotic** (nɛ'krɒtɪk) ADJECTIVE

necrotic enteritis NOUN *Vet science* an infectious disease of calves, lambs, foals, and piglets, characterized by acute diarrhoea and death, caused by the toxin of the organism *Clostridium perfringens type C.*

necrotomy (nɛ'krɒtəmɪ) NOUN, *plural* **-mies.** [1] dissection of a dead body. [2] surgical excision of dead tissue from a living organism.

necrotroph ('nɛkrəʊˌtrəʊf) NOUN a parasitic organism that kills the living cells of its host and then feeds on the dead matter.
▸ **necrotrophic** (ˌnɛkrəʊ'trɒfɪk) ADJECTIVE

nectar ('nɛktə) NOUN [1] a sugary fluid produced in the nectaries of plants and collected by bees and other animals. [2] *Classical myth* the drink of the gods. Compare **ambrosia** (sense 1). [3] any delicious drink, esp a sweet one. [4] something very pleasant or welcome: *your words are nectar to me.* [5] *Chiefly US* **a** the undiluted juice of a fruit. **b** a mixture of fruit juices.
▷HISTORY C16: via Latin from Greek *néktar,* perhaps *nek-* death (related to *nekros* corpse) + *-tar,* related to Sanskrit *tarati* he overcomes; compare Latin *nex* death and *trans* across
▸ **nectareous** (nɛk'tɛərɪəs) *or* **'nectarous** ADJECTIVE

nectarine ('nɛktərɪn) NOUN [1] a variety of peach tree, *Prunus persica nectarina.* [2] the fruit of this tree, which has a smooth skin.
▷HISTORY C17: apparently from NECTAR

nectarivorous (ˌnɛktə'rɪvərəs) ADJECTIVE *Zoology* feeding on nectar.

nectary ('nɛktərɪ) NOUN, *plural* **-ries.** [1] any of various glandular structures secreting nectar that occur in the flowers, leaves, stipules, etc., of a plant. [2] any of the abdominal tubes in aphids through which honeydew is secreted.
▷HISTORY C18: from New Latin *nectarium,* from NECTAR
▸ **nectarial** (nɛk'tɛərɪəl) ADJECTIVE

NEDC ABBREVIATION FOR (the former) National Economic Development Council. Also (informal): **Neddy** ('nɛdɪ).

neddy ('nɛdɪ) NOUN, *plural* **-dies.** [1] a child's word for a **donkey.** [2] *Informal* a silly person; fool. [3] *Austral informal* a horse, esp a racehorse: *he lost his money on the neddies.*
▷HISTORY C18: from *Ned,* pet form of *Edward*

Nederland ('neːdərlɑnt) NOUN the Dutch name for the **Netherlands.**

née *or* **nee** (neɪ) ADJECTIVE indicating the maiden name of a married woman: *Mrs Bloggs née Blandish.*
▷HISTORY C19: from French: past participle (fem) of *naître* to be born, from Latin *nascī*

need (niːd) VERB [1] *(tr)* to be in want of: *to need money.* [2] *(tr)* to require or be required of necessity (to be or do something); be obliged: *to need to do more work.* [3] (takes an infinitive without *to*) used as an auxiliary in negative and interrogative sentences to express necessity or obligation and does not add *-s* when used with *he, she, it,* and singular nouns: *need he go?* [4] *(intr) Archaic* to be essential or necessary to: *there needs no reason for this.* ◆ NOUN [5] the fact or an instance of feeling the lack of something: *he has need of a new coat.* [6] a requirement: *the need for vengeance.* [7] necessity or obligation resulting from some situation: *no need to be frightened.* [8] distress or extremity: *a friend in need.* [9] extreme poverty or destitution; penury. ◆ See also **needs.**
▷HISTORY Old English *nēad, nied;* related to Old Frisian *nēd,* Old Saxon *nōd,* Old High German *nōt*

needful ('niːdfʊl) ADJECTIVE [1] necessary; needed; required. [2] *Archaic* needy; poverty-stricken. ◆ NOUN [3] *Informal* money or funds: *do you have the needful?* [4] **do the needful.** to perform a necessary task.
▸ **'needfully** ADVERB ▸ **'needfulness** NOUN

neediness ('niːdɪnɪs) NOUN the state of being needy; poverty.

needle ('niːdᵊl) NOUN [1] a pointed slender piece of metal, usually steel, with a hole or eye in it through which thread is passed for sewing. [2] a somewhat larger rod with a point at one or each end, used in knitting. [3] a similar instrument with a hook at one end for crocheting. [4] **a** another name for **stylus** (sense 3). **b** a small thin pointed device, esp one made of stainless steel, used to transmit the vibrations from a gramophone record to the pick-up. [5] *Med* **a** the long hollow pointed part of a hypodermic syringe, which is inserted into the body. **b** an informal name for **hypodermic syringe.** [6] *Surgery* a pointed steel instrument, often curved, for suturing, puncturing, or ligating. [7] a long narrow stiff leaf, esp of a conifer, in which water loss is greatly reduced: *pine needles.* [8] any slender sharp spine, such as the spine of a sea urchin. [9] any slender pointer for indicating the reading on the scale of a measuring instrument. [10] short for **magnetic needle.** [11] a crystal resembling a needle in shape. [12] a sharp pointed metal instrument used in engraving and etching. [13] anything long and pointed, such as an obelisk: *a needle of light.* [14] a short horizontal beam passed through a wall and supported on vertical posts to take the load of the upper part of the wall. [15] *Informal* **a** anger or intense rivalry, esp in a sporting encounter. **b** *(as modifier): a needle match.* [16] **have** *or* **get the needle (to).** *Brit informal* to feel dislike, distaste, nervousness, or annoyance (for): *she got the needle after he had refused her invitation.* ◆ VERB [17] *(tr) Informal* to goad or provoke, as by constant criticism. [18] *(tr)* to sew, embroider, or prick (fabric) with a needle. [19] *(tr) US* to increase the alcoholic strength of (beer or other beverages). [20] *(intr)* (of a substance) to form needle-shaped crystals.
▷HISTORY Old English *nǣdl;* related to Gothic *nēthla,* German *Nadel*

needle bearing NOUN *Engineering* an antifriction roller bearing in which long rollers of very small diameter fill the race without a cage to provide spacers between them.

needlecord ('niːdəlˌkɔːd) NOUN a corduroy fabric with narrow ribs.

needlecraft ('niːdəlˌkrɑːft) NOUN the art or practice of needlework.

needle exchange NOUN a centre where drug users can exchange used hypodermic syringes for new ones.

needlefish ('niːdəlˌfɪʃ) NOUN, *plural* **-fish** *or* **-fishes.** [1] any ferocious teleost fish of the family *Belonidae* of warm and tropical regions, having an elongated body and long toothed jaws. [2] another name for **pipefish.**

needle fly NOUN a small stonefly of the genus *Leuctra,* whose rolled-up wings at rest give it a slender pointed appearance.

needleful ('niːdəlfʊl) NOUN a length of thread cut for use in a needle.

needlepoint ('niːdəlˌpɔɪnt) NOUN [1] embroidery done on canvas with the same stitch throughout so as to resemble tapestry. [2] another name for **point lace.**

needless ('niːdlɪs) ADJECTIVE not required or desired; unnecessary.
▸**'needlessly** ADVERB ▸**'needlessness** NOUN

needlestick ('niːdəlˌstɪk) ADJECTIVE (of an injury) caused by accidentally pricking the skin with a hypodermic needle.

needle time NOUN the limited time allocated by a radio channel to the broadcasting of music from records.

needle valve NOUN a valve containing a tapered rod that can be moved in or out to control the flow of a fluid.

needlewoman ('niːdəlˌwʊmən) NOUN, *plural* **-women.** a woman who does needlework; seamstress.

needlework ('niːdəlˌwɜːk) NOUN [1] work done with a needle, esp sewing and embroidery. [2] the result of such work.

needs (niːdz) ADVERB [1] (preceded or foll by *must*) of necessity: *we must needs go; we will go, if needs must.* ◆ PLURAL NOUN [2] what is required; necessities: *the needs of the third world; his needs are modest.*

needs test NOUN *Social welfare* an examination of a person's physical or social, rather than financial, circumstances, to determine whether he is eligible for a particular welfare benefit or service. Compare **means test.**

needy ('niːdɪ) ADJECTIVE **needier, neediest. a** in need of practical or emotional support; distressed. **b** (*as collective noun; preceded by the*): *the needy.*

Néel point *or* **temperature** (neɪ'ɛl) NOUN the temperature above which an antiferromagnetic substance loses its antiferromagnetism and becomes paramagnetic.

neem (niːm) NOUN a large tree of India, *Azadirachta indica,* all parts of which are useful to man: the leaves act as a natural pesticide, the fruit and seeds yield a medicinal oil, the bark is used to make a tonic, and the trunk exudes a gum.
▷**HISTORY** C19: from Hindi *nīm,* from Sanskrit *nimba*

neep (niːp) NOUN *Brit* a dialect name for a **turnip.**
▷**HISTORY** Old English *nǣp,* from Latin *nāpus* turnip

ne'er (nɛə) ADVERB a poetic contraction of **never.**

Ne'erday ('nerde) NOUN *Scot* New Year's Day.

ne'er-do-well NOUN [1] an improvident, irresponsible, or lazy person. ◆ ADJECTIVE [2] useless; worthless: *your ne'er-do-well schemes.*

nefarious (nɪ'fɛərɪəs) ADJECTIVE evil; wicked; sinful.
▷**HISTORY** C17: from Latin *nefārius,* from *nefās* unlawful deed, from *nē* not + *fās* divine law
▸**ne'fariously** ADVERB ▸**ne'fariousness** NOUN

NEG (in transformational grammar) ABBREVIATION FOR negative.

neg. ABBREVIATION FOR negative(ly).

negate (nɪ'geɪt) VERB (*tr*) [1] to make ineffective or void; nullify; invalidate. [2] to deny or contradict.
▷**HISTORY** C17: from Latin *negāre,* from *neg-,* variant of *nec* not + *aio* I say
▸**ne'gator** *or* **ne'gater** NOUN

negation (nɪ'geɪʃən) NOUN [1] the opposite or absence of something. [2] a negative thing or condition. [3] the act or an instance of negating. [4] *Logic* **a** the operator that forms one sentence from another and corresponds to the English *not.* **b** a sentence so formed. It is usually written $-p$, $\sim p$, $\bar{p}$, or $\neg p$, where *p* is the given sentence, and is false when the given sentence is true, and true when it is false.

negative ('nɛgətɪv) ADJECTIVE [1] expressing or meaning a refusal or denial: *a negative answer.* [2] lacking positive or affirmative qualities, such as enthusiasm, interest, or optimism. [3] showing or tending towards opposition or resistance. [4] **a** measured in a direction opposite to that regarded as positive. **b** having the same magnitude but opposite sense to an equivalent positive quantity. [5] *Biology* indicating movement or growth away from a particular stimulus: *negative geotropism.* [6] *Med* (of the results of a diagnostic test) indicating absence of the disease or condition for which the test was made. [7] another word for **minus** (senses 3b, 5). [8] *Physics* **a** (of an electric charge) having the same polarity as the charge of an electron. **b** (of a body, system, ion, etc.) having a negative electric charge; having an excess of electrons. **c** (of a point in an electric circuit) having a lower electrical potential than some other point with an assigned zero potential. [9] short for **electronegative.** [10] of or relating to a photographic negative. [11] *Logic* (of a categorial proposition) denying the satisfaction by the subject of the predicate, as in *some men are irrational; no pigs have wings.* [12] *Astrology* of, relating to, or governed by the signs of the zodiac of the earth and water classifications, which are thought to be associated with a receptive passive nature. [13] short for **Rh negative.** ◆ NOUN [14] a statement or act of denial, refusal, or negation. [15] a negative person or thing. [16] *Photog* a piece of photographic film or a plate, previously exposed and developed, showing an image that, in black-and-white photography, has a reversal of tones. In colour photography the image is in complementary colours to the subject so that blue sky appears yellow, green grass appears purple, etc. [17] *Physics* a negative object, such as a terminal or a plate in a voltaic cell. [18] a sentence or other linguistic element with a negative meaning, as the English word *not.* [19] a quantity less than zero or a quantity to be subtracted. [20] *Logic* a negative proposition. [21] *Archaic* the right of veto. [22] **in the negative.** indicating denial or refusal. ◆ SENTENCE SUBSTITUTE [23] (esp in military communications) a signal code word for **no**[1]. ◆ VERB (*tr*) [24] to deny or nullify; negate. [25] to show to be false; disprove. [26] to refuse consent to or approval of: *the proposal was negatived.* ◆ Compare **positive, affirmative.**
▸**'negatively** ADVERB ▸**'negativeness** *or* **ˌnega'tivity** NOUN

negative equity NOUN the state of holding a property the value of which is less than the amount of mortgage still unpaid.

negative feedback NOUN See **feedback.**

negative hallucination NOUN *Psychol* an apparent abnormal inability to perceive an object.

negative polarity NOUN *Grammar* the grammatical character of a word or phrase, such as *ever* or *any,* that may normally only be used in a semantically or syntactically negative or interrogative context.

negative-raising NOUN *Transformational grammar* a rule that moves a negative element out of the complement clause of certain verbs, such as *think,* into the main clause, as in the derivation of *He doesn't think that he'll finish.*

negative reinforcement NOUN *Psychol* the reinforcing of a response by giving an aversive stimulus when the response is not made and omitting the aversive stimulus when the response is made.

negative resistance NOUN a characteristic of certain electronic components in which an increase in the applied voltage increases the resistance, producing a proportional decrease in current.

negative sign NOUN the symbol (–) used to indicate a negative quantity or a subtraction; minus sign.

negative tax NOUN a payment by the State to a person with a low income, the magnitude of the payment increasing as the income decreases. It is regarded as a form of social welfare. Also called: **negative income tax.**

negativism ('nɛgətɪvˌɪzəm) NOUN [1] a tendency to be or a state of being unconstructively critical. [2] any sceptical or derisive system of thought. [3] *Psychiatry* refusal to do what is expected or suggested or the tendency to do the opposite.
▸**'negativist** NOUN, ADJECTIVE ▸**ˌnegativ'istic** ADJECTIVE

negator (nɪ'geɪtə) NOUN *Electronics* another name for **NOT circuit.**

negatron ('nɛgəˌtrɒn) NOUN an obsolete word for **electron.**
▷**HISTORY** C20: from NEGA(TIVE + ELEC)TRON

Negev ('nɛgɛv) *or* **Negeb** ('nɛgɛb) NOUN the S part of Israel, on the Gulf of Aqaba: a triangular-shaped semidesert region, with large areas under irrigation; scene of fighting between Israeli and Egyptian forces in 1948. Chief town: Beersheba. Area: 12 820 sq. km (4950 sq. miles).

neglect (nɪ'glɛkt) VERB (*tr*) [1] to fail to give due care, attention, or time to: *to neglect a child.* [2] to fail (to do something) through thoughtlessness or carelessness: *he neglected to tell her.* [3] to ignore or disregard: *she neglected his frantic signals.* ◆ NOUN [4] lack of due care or attention; negligence: *the child starved through neglect.* [5] the act or an instance of neglecting or the state of being neglected.
▷**HISTORY** C16: from Latin *neglegere* to neglect, from *nec* not + *legere* to select
▸**ne'glecter** *or* **ne'glector** NOUN

neglectful (nɪ'glɛktfʊl) ADJECTIVE (when *postpositive,* foll by *of*) not giving due care and attention (to); careless; heedless.
▸**ne'glectfully** ADVERB ▸**ne'glectfulness** NOUN

negligee *or* **negligée** ('nɛglɪˌʒeɪ) NOUN [1] a woman's light dressing gown, esp one that is lace-trimmed. [2] any informal attire.
▷**HISTORY** C18: from French *négligée,* past participle (fem) of *négliger* to NEGLECT

negligence ('nɛglɪdʒəns) NOUN [1] the state or quality of being negligent. [2] a negligent act. [3] *Law* a civil wrong whereby a person or party is in breach of a legal duty of care to another which results in loss or injury to the claimant.

negligent ('nɛglɪdʒənt) ADJECTIVE [1] habitually neglecting duties, responsibilities, etc.; lacking attention, care, or concern; neglectful. [2] careless or nonchalant.
▸**'negligently** ADVERB

negligible ('nɛglɪdʒəbəl) ADJECTIVE so small, unimportant, etc., as to be not worth considering; insignificant.
▸**ˌnegligi'bility** *or* **'negligibleness** NOUN ▸**'negligibly** ADVERB

negotiable (nɪ'gəʊʃəbəl) ADJECTIVE [1] able to be negotiated. [2] (of a bill of exchange, promissory note, etc.) legally transferable in title from one party to another.
▸**neˌgotia'bility** NOUN

negotiable instrument NOUN a legal document, such as a cheque or bill of exchange, that is freely negotiable.

negotiant (nɪ'gəʊʃɪənt) NOUN a person, nation, organization, etc., involved in a negotiation.

negotiate (nɪ'gəʊʃɪˌeɪt) VERB [1] to work or talk (with others) to achieve (a transaction, an agreement, etc.). [2] (*tr*) to succeed in passing through, around, or over: *to negotiate a mountain pass.* [3] (*tr*) *Finance* **a** to transfer (a negotiable commercial paper) by endorsement to another in return for value received. **b** to sell (financial assets). **c** to arrange for (a loan).
▷**HISTORY** C16: from Latin *negōtiārī* to do business, from *negōtium* business, from *nec* not + *ōtium* leisure
▸**ne'gotiˌator** NOUN

negotiation (nɪˌgəʊʃɪ'eɪʃən) NOUN [1] a discussion set up or intended to produce a settlement or agreement. [2] the act or process of negotiating.

Negress ('niːgrɪs) NOUN a female Black person.

Negrillo (nɪ'grɪləʊ) NOUN, *plural* **-los** *or* **-loes.** a member of a dwarfish Negroid race of central and southern Africa.
▷**HISTORY** C19: from Spanish, diminutive of *negro* black

Negri Sembilan ('nɛgrɪ sɛm'biːlən) NOUN a state of S Peninsular Malaysia: mostly mountainous, with large areas under paddy and rubber. Capital:

Seremban. Pop.: 830 080 (2000). Area: 6643 sq. km (2565 sq. miles).

Negritic (nɪ'grɪtɪk) ADJECTIVE relating to the Negroes or the Negritos.

Negrito (nɪ'gri:təʊ) NOUN, *plural* **-tos** *or* **-toes**. a member of any of various dwarfish Negroid peoples of SE Asia and Melanesia.
▷HISTORY C19: from Spanish, diminutive of *negro* black

negritude ('ni:grɪˌtju:d, 'nɛg-) NOUN [1] the fact of being a Negro. [2] awareness and cultivation of the Negro heritage, values, and culture.
▷HISTORY C20: from French, from *nègre* NEGRO[1]

Negro[1] ('ni:grəʊ) *Old-fashioned or offensive* ◆ NOUN, *plural* **-groes**. [1] a member of any of the dark-skinned indigenous peoples of Africa and their descendants elsewhere. ◆ ADJECTIVE [2] relating to or characteristic of Negroes.
▷HISTORY C16: from Spanish or Portuguese: black, from Latin *niger* black
▸**'Negro,ism** NOUN

Negro[2] ('neɪgrəʊ, 'nɛg-) NOUN **Río.** [1] a river in NW South America, rising in E Colombia (as the Guainía) and flowing east, then south as part of the border between Colombia and Venezuela, entering Brazil and continuing southeast to join the Amazon at Manáus. Length: about 2250 km (1400 miles). [2] a river in S central Argentina, formed by the confluence of the Neuquén and Limay Rivers and flowing east and southeast to the Atlantic. Length: about 1014 km (630 miles). [3] a river in central Uruguay, rising in S Brazil and flowing southwest into the Uruguay River. Length: about 467 km (290 miles).

Negroid ('ni:grɔɪd) ADJECTIVE [1] denoting, relating to, or belonging to one of the major racial groups of mankind, characterized by brown-black skin, tightly-curled hair, a short nose, and full lips. This group includes the indigenous peoples of Africa south of the Sahara, their descendants elsewhere, and some Melanesian peoples. ◆ NOUN [2] a member of this racial group.

Negrophil ('ni:grəʊfɪl) *or* **Negrophile** ('ni:grəʊˌfaɪl) NOUN a person who admires Negroes and their culture.
▸**Negrophilism** (ni:'grɒfɪˌlɪzəm) NOUN

Negrophobe ('ni:grəʊˌfəʊb) NOUN a person who dislikes or fears Negroes.
▸**ˌNegro'phobia** NOUN ▸**ˌNegro'phobic** ADJECTIVE

Negropont ('nɛgrəʊˌpɒnt) NOUN [1] the former English name for **Euboea.** [2] the medieval English name for **Chalcis.**

Negros ('neɪgrəʊs; *Spanish* 'neγrɔs) NOUN an island of the central Philippines, one of the Visayan Islands. Capital: Bacolod. Pop.: 3 168 000 (1990 est.). Area: 12 704 sq. km (4904 sq. miles).

Negro spiritual ('ni:grəʊ) NOUN a type of religious song originating among Black slaves in the American South.

negus ('ni:gəs) NOUN, *plural* **-guses**. a hot drink of port and lemon juice, usually spiced and sweetened.
▷HISTORY C18: named after Col. Francis *Negus* (died 1732), its English inventor

Negus ('ni:gəs) NOUN, *plural* **-guses**. a title of the emperor of Ethiopia.
▷HISTORY from Amharic: king

Neh. *Bible* ABBREVIATION FOR Nehemiah.

Nehemiah (ˌni:ɪ'maɪə) NOUN *Old Testament* [1] a Jewish official at the court of Artaxerxes, king of Persia, who in 444 B.C. became a leader in the rebuilding of Jerusalem after the Babylonian captivity. [2] the book recounting the acts of Nehemiah.

neigh (neɪ) NOUN [1] the high-pitched cry of a horse; whinny. ◆ VERB [2] (*intr*) to make a neigh or a similar noise. [3] (*tr*) to utter with a sound like a neigh.
▷HISTORY Old English *hnǣgan;* related to Old Saxon *hnēgian*

neighbour *or US* **neighbor** ('neɪbə) NOUN [1] a person who lives near or next to another. [2] **a** a person or thing near or next to another. **b** (*as modifier*): *neighbour states.* ◆ VERB [3] (when *intr,* often foll by *on*) to be or live close (to a person or thing).
▷HISTORY Old English *nēahbūr,* from *nēah* NIGH + *būr, gebūr* dweller; see BOOR

▸**'neighbouring** *or US* **'neighboring** ADJECTIVE
▸**'neighbourless** *or US* **'neighborless** ADJECTIVE

neighbourhood *or US* **neighborhood** ('neɪbəˌhʊd) NOUN [1] the immediate environment; surroundings; vicinity. Related adjective: **vicinal.** [2] a district where people live. [3] the people in a particular area; neighbours. [4] neighbourly feeling. [5] *Maths* the set of all points whose distance from a given point is less than a specified value. [6] (*modifier*) of or for a neighbourhood: *a neighbourhood community worker.* [7] **in the neighbourhood of.** approximately (a given number).

neighbourhood watch NOUN a scheme under which members of a community agree together to take responsibility for keeping an eye on each other's property, as a way of preventing crime.

neighbourly *or US* **neighborly** ('neɪbəlɪ) ADJECTIVE kind, friendly, or sociable, as befits a neighbour.
▸**'neighbourliness** *or US* **'neighborliness** NOUN

Neisse ('naɪsə) NOUN [1] Also called: **Glatzer Neisse** ('glɑ:tsə). Polish name: **Nysa.** a river in SW Poland, rising on the northern Czech border, and flowing northeast to join the Oder near Brzeg. Length: about 193 km (120 miles). [2] Also called: **Lusatian Neisse.** a river in E Europe, rising near Liberec in the Czech Republic and flowing north to join the Oder: forms part of the German-Polish border. Length: 225 km (140 miles).

neither ('naɪðə, 'ni:ðə) DETERMINER [1] **a** not one nor the other (of two); not either: *neither foot is swollen.* **b** (*as pronoun*): *neither can win.* ◆ CONJUNCTION [2] (*coordinating*) **a** (used preceding alternatives joined by *nor*) not: *neither John nor Mary nor Joe went.* **b** another word for **nor** (sense 2). ◆ ADVERB [3] (*sentence modifier*) *Not standard* another word for **either** (sense 4).
▷HISTORY C13 (literally, *ne either* not either): changed from Old English *nāwther,* from *nāhwæther,* from *nā* not + *hwæther* which of two; see WHETHER

> **Language note** A verb following a compound subject that uses *neither...nor* should be in the singular if both subjects are in the singular: *neither Jack nor John has done the work.*

Nejd (nɛʒd, neɪd) NOUN a region of central Saudi Arabia: formerly an independent sultanate of Arabia; united with Hejaz to form the kingdom of Saudi Arabia (1932).

nek (nɛk) NOUN (*capital when part of name*) *South African* a mountain pass: *Lundeans Nek.*

nekton ('nɛktɒn) NOUN the population of free-swimming animals that inhabits the middle depths of a sea or lake. Compare **plankton.**
▷HISTORY C19: via German from Greek *nēkton* a swimming thing, from *nēkhein* to swim
▸**nek'tonic** ADJECTIVE

nelly ('nɛlɪ) NOUN **not on your nelly.** (*sentence substitute*) *Brit, slang* not under any circumstances; certainly not.

nelson ('nɛlsən) NOUN any wrestling hold in which a wrestler places his arm or arms under his opponent's arm or arms from behind and exerts pressure with his palms on the back of his opponent's neck. See **full nelson, half-nelson.**
▷HISTORY C19: from a proper name

Nelson ('nɛlsən) NOUN [1] a town in NW England, in E Lancashire: textile industry. Pop.: 29 120 (1991). [2] a port in New Zealand, on N South Island on Tasman Bay. Pop.: 51 200 (1995 est.). [3] **River.** a river in central Canada, in N central Manitoba, flowing from Lake Winnipeg northeast to Hudson Bay. Length: about 650 km (400 miles).

nelumbo (nɪ'lʌmbəʊ) NOUN, *plural* **-bos**. either of the two aquatic plants of the genus *Nelumbo:* family *Nelumbonaceae.* See **lotus** (sense 4), **water chinquapin.**
▷HISTORY C19: New Latin, from Sinhalese *nelumbu* lotus

Neman *or* **Nyeman** (*Russian* 'njɛmən) NOUN a river in NE Europe, rising in Belarus and flowing northwest through Lithuania to the Baltic. Length: 937 km (582 miles). Polish name: **Niemen.**

nemathelminth (ˌnɛmə'θɛlmɪnθ) NOUN any unsegmented worm of the group *Nemathelminthes,* including the nematodes, nematomorphs, and acanthocephalans.

nematic (nɪ'mætɪk) ADJECTIVE *Chem* (of a substance) existing in or having a mesomorphic state in which a linear orientation of the molecules causes anisotropic properties. Compare **smectic.** See also **liquid crystal.**
▷HISTORY C20: NEMAT(O)- (referring to the threadlike chains of molecules in liquid) + -IC

nemato- *or before a vowel* **nemat-** COMBINING FORM indicating a threadlike form: *nematocyst.*
▷HISTORY from Greek *nēma* thread

nematocyst ('nɛmətəˌsɪst, nɪ'mætə-) NOUN a structure in coelenterates, such as jellyfish, consisting of a capsule containing a hollow coiled thread that can be everted to sting or paralyse prey and enemies.
▸**ˌnemato'cystic** ADJECTIVE

nematode ('nɛməˌtəʊd) NOUN any unsegmented worm of the phylum (or class) *Nematoda,* having a tough outer cuticle. The group includes free-living forms and disease-causing parasites, such as the hookworm and filaria. Also called: **nematode worm, roundworm.**

Nembutal ('nɛmbjʊˌtɑ:l) NOUN a trademark for **pentobarbital sodium.**

nem. con. ABBREVIATION FOR nemine contradicente.
▷HISTORY Latin: no-one contradicting; unanimously

Nemea (nɪ'mi:ə) NOUN (in ancient Greece) a valley in N Argolis in the NE Peloponnese; site of the **Nemean Games,** a Panhellenic festival and athletic competition held every other year.

Nemean (nɪ'mi:ən) ADJECTIVE of or relating to the valley of Nemea in ancient Greece or its inhabitants.

Nemean lion NOUN *Greek myth* an enormous lion that was strangled by Hercules as his first labour.

nemertean (nɪ'mɜ:tɪən) *or* **nemertine** ('nɛməˌtaɪn) NOUN [1] Also called: **ribbon worm.** any soft flattened ribbon-like marine worm of the phylum (or class) *Nemertea* (or *Nemertina*), having an eversible threadlike proboscis. ◆ ADJECTIVE [2] of, relating to, or belonging to the *Nemertea.*
▷HISTORY C19: via New Latin from Greek *Nēmertēs* a NEREID[1]

nemesia (nɪ'mi:ʒə) NOUN any plant of the southern African scrophulariaceous genus *Nemesia:* cultivated for their brightly coloured (often reddish) flowers.
▷HISTORY C19: New Latin, from Greek *nemesion,* name of a plant resembling this

Nemesis ('nɛmɪsɪs) NOUN, *plural* **-ses** (-ˌsi:z). [1] *Greek myth* the goddess of retribution and vengeance. [2] (*sometimes not capital*) any agency of retribution and vengeance.
▷HISTORY C16: via Latin from Greek: righteous wrath, from *némein* to distribute what is due

nemophila (nə'mɒfɪlə) NOUN any of a genus, *Nemophila,* of low-growing hairy annual plants, esp *N. menziesii,* grown for its blue or white flowers: family *Hydrophyllaceae.*
▷HISTORY New Latin, from Greek *nemos* a grove + *philein* to love

nene ('neɪˌneɪ) NOUN a rare black-and-grey short-winged Hawaiian goose, *Branta sandvicensis,* having partly webbed feet.
▷HISTORY from Hawaiian

neo- *or sometimes before a vowel* **ne-** COMBINING FORM [1] (*sometimes capital*) new, recent, or a new or modern form or development: *neoclassicism; neocolonialism.* [2] (*usually capital*) the most recent subdivision of a geological period: *Neogene.*
▷HISTORY from Greek *neos* new

neoanthropic (ˌni:əʊæn'θrɒpɪk) ADJECTIVE *Anthropol* of, relating to, or resembling modern man.

neoarsphenamine (ˌni:əʊɑ:s'fɛnəˌmi:n, -fɪ'næmɪn) NOUN a derivative of arsenic formerly used in treating syphilis.

Neocene ('ni:əˌsi:n) ADJECTIVE, NOUN a former word for **Neogene.**

neoclassicism (ˌni:əʊ'klæsɪˌsɪzəm) NOUN [1] a late 18th- and early 19th-century style in architecture, decorative art, and fine art, based on the imitation of surviving classical models and types. [2] *Mu* movement of the 1920s, involving Hindemith Stravinsky, etc., that sought to avoid the emotionalism of late romantic music by reviv

the use of counterpoint, forms such as the classical suite, and small instrumental ensembles.
▸ ˌneoˈclassicist NOUN

neocolonialism (ˌniːəʊkəˈləʊnɪəˌlɪzəm) NOUN (in the modern world) political control by an outside power of a country that is in theory sovereign and independent, esp through the domination of its economy.
▸ ˌneocoˈlonial ADJECTIVE ▸ ˌneocoˈlonialist NOUN

Neo-Darwinism (ˌniːəʊˈdɑːwɪnˌɪzəm) NOUN the modern version of the Darwinian theory of evolution, which incorporates the principles of genetics to explain how inheritable variations can arise by mutation.
▸ ˌNeo-Darˈwinian ADJECTIVE, NOUN

neodymium (ˌniːəʊˈdɪmɪəm) NOUN a toxic silvery-white metallic element of the lanthanide series, occurring principally in monazite: used in colouring glass. Symbol: Nd; atomic no.: 60; atomic wt.: 144.24; valency: 3; relative density: 6.80 and 7.00 (depending on allotrope); melting pt.: 1024°C; boiling pt.: 3127°C.
▷HISTORY C19: New Latin; see NEO- + DIDYMIUM

Neogaea (ˌniːəʊˈdʒiːə) NOUN a zoogeographical area comprising the Neotropical region. Compare **Arctogaea, Notogaea.**
▷HISTORY C19: New Latin, from NEO- + GAEA, from Greek *gaia* earth

Neogaean (ˌniːəʊˈdʒiːən) ADJECTIVE of or relating to Neogaea, a zoogeographical area comprising the Neotropical region.

Neogene (ˈniːəˌdʒiːn) ADJECTIVE [1] of, denoting, or formed during the Miocene and Pliocene epochs. ◆ NOUN [2] **the.** the Neogene period or system.

neogothic (ˌnɪəʊˈgɒθɪk) NOUN another name for **Gothic Revival.**

neoimpressionism (ˌniːəʊɪmˈprɛʃəˌnɪzəm) NOUN a movement in French painting initiated mainly by Georges Seurat (1859–91) in the 1880s and combining his vivid colour technique with strictly formal composition. See also **pointillism.**
▸ ˌneoimˈpressionist NOUN, ADJECTIVE

Neo-Lamarckism (ˌniːəʊləˈmɑːkɪzəm) NOUN a theory of evolution based on Lamarckism, proposing that environmental factors could lead to adaptive genetic changes.
▸ ˌNeo-LaˈmarckianADJECTIVE, NOUN

Neo-Latin (ˌniːəʊˈlætɪn) NOUN [1] another term for **New Latin.** ◆ ADJECTIVE [2] denoting or relating to New Latin. [3] denoting or relating to language that developed from Latin; Romance.

neoliberalism (ˌniːəʊˈlɪbərəˌlɪzəm, -ˈlɪbrəˌlɪzəm) NOUN a modern politico-economic theory favouring free trade, privatization, minimal government intervention in business, reduced public expenditure on social services, etc.
▸ ˌneoˈliberal ADJECTIVE, NOUN

neolith (ˈniːəʊlɪθ) NOUN a Neolithic stone implement.

Neolithic (ˌniːəʊˈlɪθɪk) NOUN [1] the cultural period that lasted in SW Asia from about 9000 to 6000 B.C. and in Europe from about 4000 to 2400 B.C. and was characterized by primitive crop growing and stock rearing and the use of polished stone and flint tools and weapons. ◆ ADJECTIVE [2] relating to this period. ◆ See also **Mesolithic, Palaeolithic.**

neologism (nɪˈɒləˌdʒɪzəm) *or* **neology** NOUN, *plural* **-gisms** *or* **-gies.** [1] a newly coined word, or a phrase or familiar word used in a new sense. [2] the practice of using or introducing neologisms. [3] *Rare* a tendency towards adopting new views, esp rationalist views, in matters of religion.
▷HISTORY C18: via French from NEO- + *-logism,* from Greek *logos* word, saying
▸ neˈologist NOUN ▸ neˌoloˈgistic *or* neˌoloˈgistical *or* neological (ˌnɪəˈlɒdʒɪkəl) ADJECTIVE ▸ neˌoloˈgistically *or* ˌneoˈlogically ADVERB

neologize *or* **neologise** (nɪˈɒləˌdʒaɪz) VERB (*intr*) to invent or use neologisms.

Neo-Melanesian NOUN an English-based creole language widely spoken in the SW Pacific, with borrowings from other languages, esp Motu. Also called: **Beach-la-Mar.**

neomycin (ˌniːəʊˈmaɪsɪn) NOUN an antibiotic obtained from the bacterium *Streptomyces fradiae,* administered locally in the treatment of skin and eye infections or orally for bowel infections. Formula: $C_{12}H_{26}N_4O_6$.
▷HISTORY C20: from NEO- + Greek *mukēs* fungus + -IN

neon (ˈniːɒn) NOUN [1] a colourless odourless rare gaseous element, an inert gas occurring in trace amounts in the atmosphere: used in illuminated signs and lights. Symbol: Ne; atomic no.: 10; atomic wt.: 20.1797; valency: 0; density: 0.899 90 kg/m^3; melting pt.: –248.59°C; boiling pt.: –246.08°C. [2] (*modifier*) of or illuminated by neon or neon lamps: *neon sign.*
▷HISTORY C19: via New Latin from Greek *neon* new

neonatal (ˌniːəʊˈneɪtəl) ADJECTIVE of or relating to newborn children, esp in the first week of life and up to four weeks old.
▸ ˌneoˈnatally ADVERB

neonate (ˈniːəʊˌneɪt) NOUN a newborn child, esp in the first week of life and up to four weeks old.

neonaticide (ˌniːəʊˈneɪtɪˌsaɪd) NOUN the act of killing a baby in the first 24 hours of its life.

neonatology (ˌniːəʊnəˈtɒlədʒɪ) NOUN the branch of medicine concerned with the development and disorders of newborn babies.
▸ ˌneonaˈtologist NOUN

neon lamp NOUN a glass bulb or tube containing neon at low pressure that gives a pink or red glow when a voltage is applied.

neo-noir (ˌniːəʊˈnwɑː) ADJECTIVE (of a film) set in contemporary modern times, but showing characteristics of a film noir, in plot or style.

neo-orthodoxy (ˌniːəʊˈɔːθəˌdɒksɪ) NOUN a movement in 20th-century Protestantism, reasserting certain older traditional Christian doctrines.
▸ ˌneo-ˈorthodox ADJECTIVE

neophilia (ˌniːəʊˈfɪlɪə) NOUN a tendency to like anything new; love of novelty.
▸ ˈneoˌphiliac NOUN

neophobia (ˌniːəʊˈfəʊbɪə) NOUN a tendency to dislike anything new; fear of novelty.
▸ ˈneoˌphobe NOUN ▸ ˌneoˈphobic ADJECTIVE

neophyte (ˈniːəʊˌfaɪt) NOUN [1] a person newly converted to a religious faith. [2] *RC Church* a novice in a religious order. [3] a novice or beginner.
▷HISTORY C16: via Church Latin from New Testament Greek *neophutos* recently planted, from *neos* new + *phuton* a plant
▸ neophytic (ˌniːəʊˈfɪtɪk) ADJECTIVE

neoplasm (ˈniːəʊˌplæzəm) NOUN *Pathol* any abnormal new growth of tissue; tumour.
▸ neoplastic (ˌniːəʊˈplæstɪk) ADJECTIVE

neoplasticism (ˌniːəʊˈplæstɪˌsɪzəm) NOUN the style of abstract painting evolved by the Dutch painter Piet Mondrian (1872–1944) and the Dutch de Stijl movement, characterized by the use of horizontal and vertical lines and planes and by black, white, grey, and primary colours.

neoplasty (ˈniːəʊˌplæstɪ) NOUN the surgical formation of new tissue structures or repair of damaged structures.

Neo-Platonism *or* **Neoplatonism** (ˌniːəʊˈpleɪtəˌnɪzəm) NOUN a philosophical system which was first developed in the 3rd century A.D. as a synthesis of Platonic, Pythagorean, and Aristotelian elements, and which, although originally opposed to Christianity, later incorporated it. It dominated European thought until the 13th century and re-emerged during the Renaissance.
▸ Neo-Platonic (ˌniːəʊpləˈtɒnɪk) ADJECTIVE
▸ ˌNeo-ˈPlatonist NOUN, ADJECTIVE

neoprene (ˈniːəʊˌpriːn) NOUN a synthetic rubber obtained by the polymerization of chloroprene. It is resistant to oil and ageing and is used in waterproof products, such as diving suits, paints, and adhesives.
▷HISTORY C20: from NEO- + PR(OPYL) + -ENE

Neoptolemus (ˌniːɒpˈtɒləməs) NOUN *Greek myth* a son of Achilles and slayer of King Priam of Troy. Also called: **Pyrrhus.**

neorealism (ˌniːəʊˈriːəlɪzəm) NOUN *Films* a movement to depict directly the poor in society: originating in postwar Italy.
▸ ˌneoˈrealist NOUN, ADJECTIVE

neoteny (nɪˈɒtənɪ) NOUN the persistence of larval or fetal features in the adult form of an animal. For example, the adult axolotl, a salamander, retains larval external gills. See also **paedogenesis.**
▷HISTORY C19: from New Latin *neotenia,* from Greek NEO- + *teinein* to stretch
▸ neotenic (ˌniːəʊˈtɛnɪk) *or* neˈotenous ADJECTIVE

neoteric (ˌniːəʊˈtɛrɪk) *Rare* ◆ ADJECTIVE [1] belonging to a new fashion or trend; modern: *a neoteric genre.* ◆ NOUN [2] a new writer or philosopher.
▷HISTORY C16: via Late Latin from Greek *neōterikos* young, fresh, from *neoteros* younger, more recent, from *neos* new, recent
▸ ˌneoˈterically ADVERB

Neotropical (ˌniːəʊˈtrɒpɪkəl) ADJECTIVE of or denoting a zoogeographical region consisting of South America and North America south of the tropic of Cancer.

neotype (ˈniːəʊˌtaɪp) NOUN *Biology* a specimen selected to replace a type specimen that has been lost or destroyed.

Neozoic (ˌniːəʊˈzəʊɪk) ADJECTIVE *Obsolete* of or formed at any time after the end of the Mesozoic era.

NEP [1] ABBREVIATION FOR **New Economic Policy.** ◆ [2] INTERNATIONAL CAR REGISTRATION FOR Nepal.

NEPAD (ˈniːpæd) NOUN ACRONYM FOR New Partnership for African Development.

Nepal (nɪˈpɔːl) NOUN a kingdom in S Asia: the world's only Hindu kingdom; united in 1768 by the Gurkhas; consists of swampy jungle in the south and great massifs, valleys, and gorges of the Himalayas over the rest of the country, with many peaks over 8000 m (26 000 ft.) (notably Everest and Kangchenjunga). A multiparty democracy was instituted in 1990. Official language: Nepali. Official religion: Hinduism; Mahayana Buddhist minority. Currency: rupee. Capital: Katmandu. Pop.: 25 284 000 (2001 est.). Area: 147 181 sq. km (56 815 sq. miles).

Nepalese (ˌnɛpəˈliːz) ADJECTIVE [1] of or relating to Nepal or its inhabitants. ◆ NOUN [2] a native or inhabitant of Nepal.

Nepali (nɪˈpɔːlɪ) NOUN [1] the official language of Nepal, also spoken in Sikkim and parts of India. It forms the E group of Pahari and belongs to the Indic branch of Indo-European. [2] (*plural* **-pali** *or* **-palis**) a native or inhabitant of Nepal; a Nepalese. ◆ ADJECTIVE [3] of or relating to Nepal, its inhabitants, or their language; Nepalese.

nepenthe (nɪˈpɛnθɪ) NOUN [1] a drug, or the plant providing it, that ancient writers referred to as a means of forgetting grief or trouble. [2] anything that produces sleep, forgetfulness, or pleasurable dreaminess.
▷HISTORY C16: via Latin from Greek *nēpenthes* sedative made from a herb, from *nē-* not + *penthos* grief
▸ neˈpenthean ADJECTIVE

neper (ˈneɪpə, ˈniː-) NOUN a unit expressing the ratio of two quantities, esp amplitudes in telecommunications, equal to the natural logarithm of the ratio of the two quantities. Symbol: Np, N.
▷HISTORY C20: named after John *Napier* (1550–1617), Scottish mathematician; the name was approved in 1928

nepeta (ˈnɛpətə) NOUN See **catmint.**
▷HISTORY Latin: catmint

nepheline (ˈnɛfɪlɪn, -ˌliːn) *or* **nephelite** (ˈnɛfɪˌlaɪt) NOUN a whitish mineral consisting of sodium potassium aluminium silicate in hexagonal crystalline form: used in the manufacture of glass and ceramics. Formula: $(Na,K)(AlSi)_2O_4$.
▷HISTORY C19: from French *néphéline,* from Greek *nephelē* cloud, so called because pieces of it become cloudy if dipped in nitric acid

nephelinite (ˈnɛfɪlɪˌnaɪt) NOUN a fine-grained basic laval rock consisting of pyroxene and nepheline.

nephelometer (ˌnɛfɪˈlɒmɪtə) NOUN *Chem* an instrument for measuring the size or density of particles suspended in a fluid.
▷HISTORY C19 (in the sense: an instrument for measuring the cloudiness of the sky): from Greek *nephelē* cloud + -O- + -METER
▸ nephelometric (ˌnɛfɪləʊˈmɛtrɪk) ADJECTIVE
▸ ˌnepheˈlometry NOUN

nephew ('nɛvjuː, 'nɛf-) NOUN a son of one's sister or brother.
▷**HISTORY** C13: from Old French *neveu,* from Latin *nepōs;* related to Old English *nefa,* Old High German *nevo* relative

nepho- COMBINING FORM concerning cloud or clouds.
▷**HISTORY** from Greek *nephos* cloud

nephogram ('nɛfəˌɡræm) NOUN *Meteorol* a photograph of a cloud.

nephograph ('nɛfəˌɡrɑːf, -ˌɡræf) NOUN an instrument for photographing clouds.

nephology (nɪ'fɒlədʒɪ) NOUN the study of clouds.
▸**nephological** (ˌnɛfə'lɒdʒɪkᵊl) ADJECTIVE ▸**ne'phologist** NOUN

nephoscope ('nɛfəˌskəʊp) NOUN an instrument for measuring the altitude, velocity, and direction of movement of clouds.

nephralgia (nɪ'frældʒɪə) NOUN pain in a kidney.
▸**ne'phralgic** ADJECTIVE

nephrectomy (nɪ'frɛktəmɪ) NOUN, *plural* **-mies.** surgical removal of a kidney.

nephridium (nɪ'frɪdɪəm) NOUN, *plural* **-ia** (-ɪə). a simple excretory organ of many invertebrates, consisting of a tube through which waste products pass to the exterior.
▷**HISTORY** C19: New Latin: little kidney
▸**ne'phridial** ADJECTIVE

nephrite ('nɛfraɪt) NOUN a tough fibrous amphibole mineral: a variety of jade consisting of calcium magnesium silicate in monoclinic crystalline form. Formula: $Ca_2Mg_5Si_8O_{22}(OH)_2$. Also called: **kidney stone.**
▷**HISTORY** C18: via German *Nephrit* from Greek *nephrós* kidney, so called because it was thought to be beneficial in kidney disorders

nephritic (nɪ'frɪtɪk) ADJECTIVE [1] of or relating to the kidneys. [2] relating to or affected with nephritis.

nephritis (nɪ'fraɪtɪs) NOUN inflammation of a kidney.

nephro- *or before a vowel* **nephr-** COMBINING FORM kidney or kidneys: *nephrotomy.*
▷**HISTORY** from Greek *nephros*

nephroblastoma (ˌnɛfrəʊblæs'təʊmə) NOUN, *plural* **-mata** *or* **-mas.** a malignant tumour arising from the embryonic kidney that occurs in young children, esp in the age range 3–8 years.

nephrolepis (ˌnɛfrə'liːpɪs) NOUN any fern of the tropical genus *Nephrolepis,* some species of which are grown as ornamental greenhouse or house plants for their handsome deeply-cut drooping fronds: family *Polypodiaceae.* Also called: **ladder fern, Boston fern.**
▷**HISTORY** New Latin, from Greek *nephros* kidney + *lepis* scale (from the shape of the indusium)

nephrology (nɪ'frɒlədʒɪ) NOUN the branch of medicine concerned with diseases of the kidney.
▸**ne'phrologist** NOUN

nephron ('nɛfrɒn) NOUN any of the minute urine-secreting tubules that form the functional unit of the kidneys.

nephroscope ('nɛfrəˌskəʊp) NOUN a tubular medical instrument inserted through an incision in the skin to enable examination of a kidney.
▸**nephroscopy** (nɪ'frɒskəpɪ) NOUN

nephrosis (nɪ'frəʊsɪs) NOUN any noninflammatory degenerative kidney disease.
▸**nephrotic** (nɪ'frɒtɪk) ADJECTIVE

nephrotomy (nɪ'frɒtəmɪ) NOUN, *plural* **-mies.** surgical incision into a kidney.

nepionic (ˌnɛpɪ'ɒnɪk) ADJECTIVE *Zoology* of or relating to the juvenile period in the life cycle of an organism.

nepit ('niːpɪt) NOUN another word for **nit**[4].

ne plus ultra *Latin* ('neɪ 'plʊs 'ʊltrɑː) NOUN the extreme or perfect point or state.
▷**HISTORY** literally: not more beyond (that is, go no further), allegedly a warning to sailors inscribed on the Pillars of Hercules at Gibraltar

nepotism ('nɛpəˌtɪzəm) NOUN favouritism shown to relatives or close friends by those with power or influence.
▷**HISTORY** C17: from Italian *nepotismo,* from *nepote* NEPHEW, from the former papal practice of granting special favours to nephews or other relatives
▸**nepotic** (nɪ'pɒtɪk) *or* ˌ**nepo'tistic** ADJECTIVE ▸**'nepotist** NOUN

Neptune[1] ('nɛptjuːn) NOUN the Roman god of the sea. Greek counterpart: **Poseidon.**

Neptune[2] ('nɛptjuːn) NOUN the eighth planet from the sun, having eight satellites, the largest being Triton and Nereid, and a faint planar system of rings or ring fragments. Mean distance from sun: 4497 million km; period of revolution around sun: 164.8 years; period of rotation: 14 to 16 hours; diameter and mass: 4.0 and 17.2 times that of earth respectively.

Neptunian (nɛp'tjuːnɪən) ADJECTIVE [1] of or relating to the Roman god Neptune or the sea. [2] of, occurring on, or relating to the planet Neptune. [3] *Geology* (of sedimentary rock formations such as dykes) formed under water.

neptunium (nɛp'tjuːnɪəm) NOUN a silvery metallic transuranic element synthesized in the production of plutonium and occurring in trace amounts in uranium ores. Symbol: Np; atomic no.: 93; half-life of most stable isotope, ^{237}Np: 2.14×10^6 years; valency: 3, 4, 5, or 6; relative density: 20.25; melting pt.: 639±1°C; boiling pt.: 3902°C (est.).
▷**HISTORY** C20: from NEPTUNE[2], the planet beyond Uranus, because neptunium is the element beyond uranium in the periodic table

neptunium series NOUN a radioactive series that starts with plutonium-241 and ends with bismuth-209. Neptunium-237 is the longest-lived member of the series. The series does not occur in nature.

neral ('nɪəræl) NOUN *Chem* the *trans-* isomer of citral.
▷**HISTORY** C20: from *nerol* (an alcohol from NEROLI OIL) + -AL[3]

NERC ABBREVIATION FOR Natural Environment Research Council.

nerd *or* **nurd** (nɜːd) NOUN *Slang* [1] a boring or unpopular person, esp one obsessed with something specified: *a computer nerd.* [2] a stupid and feeble person.
▸**'nerdish** *or* **'nurdish** ADJECTIVE ▸**'nerdy** *or* **'nurdy** ADJECTIVE

Nereid[1] ('nɪərɪɪd) NOUN, *plural* **Nereides** (nə'riːəˌdiːz). *Greek myth* any of the 50 sea nymphs who were the daughters of the sea god Nereus.
▷**HISTORY** C17: via Latin from Greek *Nērēid,* from NEREUS; compare Latin *nāre* to swim

Nereid[2] ('nɪərɪɪd) NOUN a satellite of the planet Neptune, in a large and highly eccentric orbit.

nereis ('nɪərɪɪs) NOUN any polychaete worm of the genus *Nereis.* See **ragworm.**
▷**HISTORY** C18: from Latin; see NEREID[1]

Nereus ('nɪərɪˌuːs) NOUN *Greek myth* a sea god who lived in the depths of the sea with his wife Doris and their daughters the Nereides.

nerine (nə'riːnɪ) NOUN any plant of the bulbous S. African genus *Nerine,* related to the amaryllis; several species are grown as garden or pot plants for their beautiful pink, orange, red, or white flowers. *N. sarniensis* is the pink-flowered Guernsey lily: family *Amaryllidaceae.*
▷**HISTORY** Latin, from Greek *nērēis* a sea nymph

neritic (nɛ'rɪtɪk) ADJECTIVE of or formed in the region of shallow seas near a coastline.
▷**HISTORY** C20: perhaps from Latin *nērīta* sea mussel, from Greek *nēritēs,* from NEREUS

Nernst heat theorem (nɛənst) NOUN the principle that reactions in crystalline solids involve changes in entropy that tend to zero as the temperature approaches absolute zero. See **law of thermodynamics** (sense 1).

neroli oil *or* **neroli** ('nɪərəlɪ) NOUN a brown oil distilled from the flowers of various orange trees, esp the Seville orange: used in perfumery.
▷**HISTORY** C17: named after Anne Marie de la Tremoïlle of *Neroli,* French-born Italian princess believed to have discovered it

nervate ('nɜːveɪt) ADJECTIVE (of leaves) having veins.

nervation (nɜː'veɪʃən) *or* **nervature** ('nɜːvətʃə) NOUN a less common word for **venation.**

nerve (nɜːv) NOUN [1] any of the cordlike bundles of fibres that conduct sensory or motor impulses between the brain or spinal cord and another part of the body. Related adjective: **neural.** [2] courage, bravery, or steadfastness. [3] **lose one's nerve.** to become timid, esp failing to perform some audacious act. [4] *Informal* boldness or effrontery; impudence: *he had the nerve to swear at me.* [5] muscle or sinew (often in the phrase **strain every nerve**). [6] a large vein in a leaf. [7] any of the veins of an insect's wing. [8] **touch, hit,** *or* **strike a (raw) nerve.** to mention or bring to mind a sensitive issue or subject. ◆ VERB *(tr)* [9] to give courage to (oneself); steel (oneself). [10] to provide with nerve or nerves. ◆ See also **nerves.**
▷**HISTORY** C16: from Latin *nervus;* related to Greek *neuron;* compare Sanskrit *snāvan* sinew

nerve block NOUN induction of anaesthesia in a specific part of the body by injecting a local anaesthetic close to the sensory nerves that supply it.

nerve cell NOUN another name for **neurone.**

nerve centre NOUN [1] a group of nerve cells associated with a specific function. [2] a principal source of control over any complex activity: *Wall Street is the financial nerve centre of America.*

nerve fibre NOUN a threadlike extension of a nerve cell; axon.

nerve gas NOUN (esp in chemical warfare) any of various poisonous gases that have a paralysing effect on the central nervous system that can be fatal.

nerve growth factor NOUN [1] a polypeptide produced by neurones and their supporting tissues as well as some other tissues that stimulates the growth of neurones. [2] any of various related polypeptides that promote the growth of neurones. Abbreviation: **NGF.**

nerve impulse NOUN the electrical wave transmitted along a nerve fibre, usually following stimulation of the nerve-cell body. See also **action potential.**

nerveless ('nɜːvlɪs) ADJECTIVE [1] calm and collected. [2] listless or feeble.
▸**'nervelessly** ADVERB ▸**'nervelessness** NOUN

nerve-racking *or* **nerve-wracking** ADJECTIVE very distressing, exhausting, or harrowing.

nerves (nɜːvz) PLURAL NOUN *Informal* [1] the imagined source of emotional control: *my nerves won't stand it.* [2] anxiety, tension, or imbalance: *she's all nerves.* [3] **bundle of nerves.** a very nervous person. [4] **get on one's nerves.** to irritate, annoy, or upset one.

nervine ('nɜːviːn) ADJECTIVE [1] having a soothing or calming effect upon the nerves. ◆ NOUN [2] *Obsolete* a nervine drug or agent.
▷**HISTORY** C17: from New Latin *nervīnus,* from Latin *nervus* NERVE

nerving ('nɜːvɪŋ) NOUN *Vet science* surgical removal of part of a nerve trunk, or the use of chemicals to block the nerve supply, to relieve pain; usually because of chronic and disabling inflammation.

nervous ('nɜːvəs) ADJECTIVE [1] very excitable or sensitive; highly strung. [2] (often foll by *of*) apprehensive or worried: *I'm nervous of traffic.* [3] of, relating to, or containing nerves; neural: *nervous tissue.* [4] affecting the nerves or nervous tissue: *a nervous disease.* [5] *Archaic* active, vigorous, or forceful.
▸**'nervously** ADVERB ▸**'nervousness** NOUN

nervous breakdown NOUN any mental illness not primarily of organic origin, in which the patient ceases to function properly, often accompanied by severely impaired concentration, anxiety, insomnia, and lack of self-esteem; used esp of episodes of depression.

nervous system NOUN the sensory and control apparatus of all multicellular animals above the level of sponges, consisting of a network of nerve cells (see **neurone**). See also **central nervous system.**

nervure ('nɜːvjʊə) NOUN [1] *Entomol* any of the stiff chitinous rods that form the supporting framework of an insect's wing; vein. [2] *Botany* any of the veins or ribs of a leaf.
▷**HISTORY** C19: from French; see NERVE, -URE

nervy ('nɜːvɪ) ADJECTIVE **nervier, nerviest.** [1] *Brit informal* tense or apprehensive. [2] having or needing bravery or endurance. [3] *US and Canadian informal* brash or cheeky. [4] *Archaic* muscular; sinewy.
▸**'nervily** ADVERB ▸**'nerviness** NOUN

nescience ('nɛsɪəns) NOUN a formal or literary word for **ignorance.**
▷HISTORY C17: from Late Latin *nescientia,* from Latin *nescīre* to be ignorant of, from *ne* not + *scīre* to know; compare SCIENCE
▸'**nescient** ADJECTIVE

nesh (nɛʃ) ADJECTIVE *Dialect* [1] sensitive to the cold. [2] timid or cowardly.
▷HISTORY from Old English *hnesce;* related to Gothic *hnasqus* tender, soft; of obscure origin

ness (nɛs) NOUN **a** *Archaic* a promontory or headland. **b** (*capital as part of a name*): *Orford Ness.*
▷HISTORY Old English *næs* headland; related to Old Norse *nes,* Old English *nasu* NOSE

Ness (nɛs) NOUN **Loch.** a lake in NW Scotland, in the Great Glen: said to be inhabited by a legendary aquatic monster. Length: 36 km (22.5 miles). Depth: 229 m (754 ft.).

-ness SUFFIX FORMING NOUNS CHIEFLY FROM ADJECTIVES AND PARTICIPLES indicating state, condition, or quality, or an instance of one of these: *greatness; selfishness; meaninglessness; a kindness.*
▷HISTORY Old English *-nes,* of Germanic origin; related to Gothic *-nassus*

nesselrode ('nɛsᵊl,rəʊd) NOUN a rich frozen pudding, made of chestnuts, eggs, cream, etc.
▷HISTORY C19: named after Count Karl Robert *Nesselrode* (1780–1862), Russian diplomat, whose chef invented the dish

Nessus ('nɛsəs) NOUN *Greek myth* a centaur that killed Hercules. A garment dipped in its blood fatally poisoned Hercules, who had been given it by Deianira who thought it was a love charm.

nest (nɛst) NOUN [1] a place or structure in which birds, fishes, insects, reptiles, mice, etc., lay eggs or give birth to young. [2] a number of animals of the same species and their young occupying a common habitat: *an ants' nest.* [3] a place fostering something undesirable: *a nest of thievery.* [4] the people in such a place: *a nest of thieves.* [5] a cosy or secluded place. [6] a set of things, usually of graduated sizes, designed to fit together: *a nest of tables.* [7] *Military* a weapon emplacement: *a machine-gun nest.* ◆ VERB [8] (*intr*) to make or inhabit a nest. [9] (*intr*) to hunt for birds' nests. [10] (*tr*) to place in a nest.
▷HISTORY Old English; related to Latin *nīdus* (nest) and to BENEATH, SIT
▸'**nester** NOUN ▸'**nest,like** ADJECTIVE

NESTA ('nɛstə) NOUN (in Britain) ACRONYM FOR National Endowment for Science, Technology and the Arts.

nest box *or* **nesting box** NOUN [1] a box in a henhouse in which domestic chickens lay eggs. [2] a box designed as a nesting place for wild birds and positioned in a garden, park, or reserve to encourage them to breed there.

nest egg NOUN [1] a fund of money kept in reserve; savings. [2] a natural or artificial egg left in a nest to induce hens to lay their eggs in it.

nesting ('nɛstɪŋ) NOUN the tendency to arrange one's immediate surroundings, such as a work station, to create a place where one feels secure, comfortable, or in control.

nestle ('nɛsᵊl) VERB [1] (*intr; often foll by up or down*) to snuggle, settle, or cuddle closely. [2] (*intr*) to be in a sheltered or protected position; lie snugly. [3] (*tr*) to shelter or place snugly or partly concealed, as in a nest.
▷HISTORY Old English *nestlian.* See NEST
▸'**nestler** NOUN

nestling ('nɛstlɪŋ, 'nɛslɪŋ) NOUN [1] **a** a young bird not yet fledged. **b** (*as modifier*): *a nestling thrush.* [2] any young person or animal.
▷HISTORY C14: from NEST + -LING[1]

Nestor ('nɛstɔː) NOUN [1] *Greek myth* the oldest and wisest of the Greeks in the Trojan War. [2] (*sometimes not capital*) a wise old man; sage.

Nestorianism (nɛ'stɔːrɪə,nɪzəm) NOUN the doctrine that Christ was two distinct persons, divine and human, implying a denial that the Virgin Mary was the mother of God. It is attributed to Nestorius (died ?451 A.D.), the Syrian patriarch of Constantinople, and survives in the Iraqi Church.
▸**Nes'torian** NOUN, ADJECTIVE

net[1] (nɛt) NOUN [1] an openwork fabric of string, rope, wire, etc.; mesh. Related adjective: **retiary.** [2] a device made of net, used to protect or enclose things or to trap animals. [3] **a** a thin light mesh fabric of cotton, nylon, or other fibre, used for curtains, dresses, etc. **b** (*as modifier*): *net curtains.* [4] a plan, strategy, etc., intended to trap or ensnare: *the murderer slipped through the police net.* [5] *Sport* **a** a strip of net that divides the playing area into two equal parts. **b** a shot that hits the net, whether or not it goes over. [6] the goal in soccer, hockey, etc. [7] (*often plural*) *Cricket* **a** a pitch surrounded by netting, used for practice. **b** a practice session in a net. [8] *Informal* short for **Internet.** [9] another word for **network** (sense 2). ◆ VERB **nets, netting, netted.** [10] (*tr*) to catch with or as if with a net; ensnare. [11] (*tr*) to shelter or surround with a net. [12] (*intr*) *Sport* to hit a shot into the net. [13] to make a net out of (rope, string, etc.).
▷HISTORY Old English *net;* related to Gothic *nati,* Dutch *net*

net[2] *or* **nett** (nɛt) ADJECTIVE [1] remaining after all deductions, as for taxes, expenses, losses, etc.: *net profit.* Compare **gross** (sense 2). [2] (of weight) after deducting tare. [3] ultimate; final; conclusive (esp in the phrase **net result**). ◆ NOUN [4] net income, profits, weight, etc. ◆ VERB **nets, netting, netted.** [5] (*tr*) to yield or earn as clear profit.
▷HISTORY C14: clean, neat, from French *net* NEAT[1]; related to Dutch *net,* German *nett*

net[3] AN INTERNET DOMAIN NAME FOR a company or organization.

net asset value NOUN the total value of the assets of an organization less its liabilities and capital charges. Abbreviation: **NAV.**

netball ('nɛt,bɔːl) NOUN a team game similar to basketball, played mainly by women.
▸'**net,baller** NOUN

Net Book Agreement NOUN a former agreement between UK publishers and booksellers that until 1995 prohibited booksellers from undercutting the price of books sold in bookshops. Abbreviation: **NBA.**

net domestic product NOUN *Economics* the gross domestic product minus an allowance for the depreciation of capital goods. Abbreviation: **NDP.**

Neth. ABBREVIATION FOR Netherlands.

nethead ('nɛt,hɛd) NOUN *Informal* a person who is enthusiastic about or an expert on the Internet.
▷HISTORY C20: from (INTER)NET + HEAD, meaning enthusiast, expert

nether ('nɛðə) ADJECTIVE placed or situated below, beneath, or underground: *nether regions; a nether lip.*
▷HISTORY Old English *niothera, nithera,* literally: further down, from *nither* down. Related to Old Irish *nitaram,* German *nieder*

Netherlander ('nɛðə,lændə) NOUN a native or inhabitant of the Netherlands.

Netherlands ('nɛðələndz) NOUN (*functioning as singular or plural*) **the.** [1] Also called: **Holland.** a kingdom in NW Europe, on the North Sea: declared independence from Spain in 1581 as the United Provinces; became a major maritime and commercial power in the 17th century, gaining many overseas possessions; a member of the European Union. It is mostly flat and low-lying, with about 40 per cent of the land being below sea level, much of it on polders protected by dykes. Official language: Dutch. Religion: Christian majority, Protestant and Roman Catholic, large nonreligious minority. Currency: euro. Capital: Amsterdam, with the seat of government at The Hague. Pop.: 15 968 000 (2001 est.). Area: 41 526 sq. km (16 033 sq. miles). Dutch name: **Nederland.** [2] the kingdom of the Netherlands together with the Flemish-speaking part of Belgium, esp as ruled by Spain and Austria before 1581; the Low Countries.

Netherlands Antilles PLURAL NOUN **the.** two groups of islands in the Caribbean, in the Lesser Antilles: overseas division of the Netherlands, consisting of the S group of Curaçao, Aruba, and Bonaire, and the N group of Saint Eustatius, Saba, and the S part of Saint Martin; economy based on refining oil from Venezuela. Capital: Willemstad (on Curaçao). Pop.: 205 000 (2001 est.). Area: 996 sq. km (390 sq. miles). Former names: **Curaçao** (until 1949), **Dutch West Indies, Netherlands West Indies.**

Netherlands East Indies PLURAL NOUN **the.** a former name (1798–1945) for **Indonesia.**

Netherlands Guiana NOUN a former name for **Surinam.**

Netherlands West Indies PLURAL NOUN **the.** a former name for the **Netherlands Antilles.**

nethermost ('nɛðə,məʊst) ADJECTIVE farthest down; lowest.

nether world NOUN [1] the world after death; the underworld. [2] hell. [3] a criminal underworld. ◆ Also called (for senses 1, 2) **nether regions.**

netiquette ('nɛtɪ,kɛt) NOUN the informal code of behaviour on the Internet.
▷HISTORY C20: from NET(WORK) + (ET)IQUETTE

netizen ('nɛtɪzᵊn) NOUN *Informal* a person who regularly uses the Internet.
▷HISTORY C20: from (INTER)NET + (CIT)IZEN

net national product NOUN gross national product minus an allowance for the depreciation of capital goods. Abbreviation: **NNP.**

net present value NOUN *Accounting* an assessment of the long-term profitability of a project made by adding together all the revenue it can be expected to achieve over its whole life and deducting all the costs involved, discounting both future costs and revenue at an appropriate rate. Abbreviation: **NPV.**

net profit NOUN gross profit minus all operating costs not included in the calculation of gross profit, esp wages, overheads, and depreciation.

net realizable value NOUN the net value of an asset if it were to be sold, taking into account the cost of making the sale and of bringing the asset into a saleable state. Abbreviation: **NRV.**

netsuke ('nɛtsʊkɪ) NOUN (in Japan) a carved toggle, esp of wood or ivory, originally used to tether a medicine box, purse, etc., worn dangling from the waist.
▷HISTORY C19: from Japanese

nett (nɛt) ADJECTIVE, NOUN, VERB a variant spelling of **net**[2].

nettie ('nɛtɪ) NOUN *Informal* a habitual and enthusiastic user of the Internet.
▷HISTORY C20: from (INTER)NET

netting ('nɛtɪŋ) NOUN any netted fabric or structure.

nettle ('nɛtᵊl) NOUN [1] any weedy plant of the temperate urticaceous genus *Urtica,* such as *U. dioica* (**stinging nettle**), having serrated leaves with stinging hairs and greenish flowers. [2] any of various other urticaceous plants with stinging hairs or spines. [3] any of various plants that resemble urticaceous nettles, such as the dead-nettle, hemp nettle, and horse nettle. [4] **grasp the nettle.** to attempt or approach something with boldness and courage. ◆ VERB (*tr*) [5] to bother; irritate. [6] to sting as a nettle does.
▷HISTORY Old English *netele;* related to Old High German *nazza* (German *Nessel*)
▸'**nettle-,like** ADJECTIVE ▸'**nettly** ADJECTIVE

nettle rash NOUN a nontechnical name for **urticaria.**

nettlesome ('nɛtᵊlsəm) ADJECTIVE causing or susceptible to irritation.

net ton NOUN the full name for **ton**[1] (sense 2).

netty ('nɛtɪ) NOUN, *plural* **-ties.** *Northeast English, dialect* a lavatory, originally an earth closet.
▷HISTORY of obscure origin

Neturei Karta (nə'tʊrɛɪ 'kɑrtɑ) NOUN a small ultra-orthodox Jewish group living mainly in Jerusalem and New York who oppose the establishment of a Jewish state by temporal means.
▷HISTORY Aramaic: guardians of the walls

network ('nɛt,wɜːk) NOUN [1] an interconnected group or system: *a network of shops.* [2] Also: **net.** a system of intersecting lines, roads, veins, etc. [3] another name for **net**[1] (sense 1) or **netting.** [4] *Radio, television* a group of broadcasting stations that all transmit the same programme simultaneously. [5] *Electronics* a system of interconnected components or circuits. [6] *Computing* a system of interconnected computer systems, terminals, and other equipment allowing information to be exchanged. ◆ VERB [7] (*tr*) *Radio, television* to broadcast on stations throughout the country: *the Scotland-England match was networked.* [8] *Computing* (of computers, terminals, etc.) to connect or be connected. [9] (*intr*) to form business contacts through informal social meetings.

networker ('nɛt,wɜːkə) NOUN a person who forms business contacts through informal social meetings

networking ('nɛtˌwɜːkɪŋ) NOUN [1] *Computing* the interconnection of two or more networks in different places, as in working at home with a link to a central computer in an office. [2] forming business connections and contacts through informal social meetings. ◆ ADJECTIVE [3] of or for networking: *networking systems.*

Neubrandenburg (*German* nɔyˈbrandənbʊrk) NOUN a city in NE Germany, in Mecklenburg-West Pomerania: 14th-century city walls. Pop.: 87 880 (1991).

Neuchâtel (*French* nøʃɑtɛl) NOUN [1] a canton in the Jura Mountains of W Switzerland. Capital: Neuchâtel. Pop.: 165 600 (2000 est.). Area: 798 sq. km (308 sq. miles). [2] a town in W Switzerland, capital of Neuchâtel canton, on Lake Neuchâtel: until 1848 the seat of the last hereditary rulers in Switzerland. Pop.: 32 509 (1990). [3] **Lake.** a lake in W Switzerland: the largest lake wholly in Switzerland. Area: 216 sq. km (83 sq. miles). ◆ German name (for senses 1, 2) **Neuenburg** (ˈnɔyənbʊrk).

Neufchâtel (*French* nøʃɑtɛl) NOUN a soft creamy whole milk cheese, similar to cream cheese.
▷HISTORY named after *Neufchâtel*, town in N France where it is made

Neuilly-sur-Seine (*French* nœjisyrsɛn) NOUN a town in N France, on the Seine: a suburb of NW Paris. Pop.: 61 768 (1990).

neuk (njuːk) NOUN a Scot word for **nook.**

neume *or* **neum** (njuːm) NOUN *Music* one of a series of notational symbols used before the 14th century.
▷HISTORY C15: from Medieval Latin *neuma* group of notes sung on one breath, from Greek *pneuma* breath
▸**ˈneumic** ADJECTIVE

Neumünster (*German* nɔyˈmynstər) NOUN a town in N Germany, in Schleswig-Holstein: manufacturing of textiles and machinery. Pop.: 81 175 (1991).

neural (ˈnjʊərəl) ADJECTIVE of or relating to a nerve or the nervous system.
▸**ˈneurally** ADVERB

neural chip NOUN another name for **neurochip.**

neural computer NOUN another name for **neurocomputer.**

neuralgia (njʊˈrældʒə) NOUN severe spasmodic pain caused by damage to or malfunctioning of a nerve and often following the course of the nerve.
▸**neuˈralgic** ADJECTIVE

neural network NOUN [1] an interconnected system of neurons, as in the brain or other parts of the nervous system. [2] Also called: **neural net.** an analogous network of electronic components, esp one in a computer designed to mimic the operation of the human brain.

neural tube NOUN the structure in mammalian embryos that develops into the brain and spinal cord. Incomplete development results in **neural-tube defects,** such as spina bifida, in a newborn baby.

neuraminidase (ˌnjʊərəˈmɪnɪdeɪz) NOUN any of various enzymes, found esp in viruses, that catalyse the breakdown of glucosides containing neuraminic acid, an amino sugar.
▷HISTORY C20: from *neuramin(ic acid)* (from NEURO- + AMINE + -IC) + -IDE + -ASE

neurasthenia (ˌnjʊərəsˈθiːnɪə) NOUN an obsolete technical term for a neurosis characterized by extreme lassitude and inability to cope with any but the most trivial tasks.
▸**neurasthenic** (ˌnjʊərəsˈθɛnɪk) ADJECTIVE
▸**ˌneurasˈthenically** ADVERB

neurectomy (njʊˈrɛktəmɪ) NOUN, *plural* **-mies.** the surgical removal of a nerve segment.

neurilemma (ˌnjʊərɪˈlɛmə) NOUN a variant of **neurolemma.**
▷HISTORY C19: from French *névrilème*, from Greek *neuron* nerve + *eilēma* covering, but influenced also by Greek *lemma* husk

neuritis (njʊˈraɪtɪs) NOUN inflammation of a nerve or nerves, often accompanied by pain and loss of function in the affected part.
▸**neuritic** (njʊˈrɪtɪk) ADJECTIVE

neuro- *or before a vowel* **neur-** COMBINING FORM indicating a nerve or the nervous system: *neuroblast; neurology.*
▷HISTORY from Greek *neuron* nerve; related to Latin *nervus*

neuroanatomy (ˌnjʊərəʊəˈnætəmɪ) NOUN the study of the structure of the nervous system.
▸**ˌneuroaˈnatomist** NOUN

neurobiology (ˌnjʊərəʊbaɪˈɒlədʒɪ) NOUN the study of the anatomy, physiology, and biochemistry of the nervous system.
▸**ˌneurobiˈologist** NOUN

neuroblast (ˈnjʊərəʊˌblæst) NOUN an embryonic nerve cell.

neurochip (ˈnjʊərəʊˌtʃɪp) NOUN *Computing* a semiconductor chip designed for use in an electronic neural network. Also called: **neural chip.**

neurocoele (ˈnjʊərəˌsiːl) NOUN *Embryol* a cavity in the embryonic brain and spinal cord that develops into the ventricles and central canal respectively.
▷HISTORY C19: from NEURO- + Greek *koilos* hollow

neurocomputer (ˈnjʊərəʊkəmˌpjuːtə) NOUN a type of computer designed to mimic the action of the human brain by use of an electronic neural network. Also called: **neural computer.**

neuroendocrine (ˌnjʊərəʊˈɛndəʊˌkraɪn) ADJECTIVE of, relating to, or denoting the dual control of certain body functions by both nervous and hormonal stimulation: *neuroendocrine system.*

neuroendocrinology (ˌnjʊərəʊˌɛndəʊkrɪˈnɒlədʒɪ) NOUN the study of neuroendocrine systems and neurohormones.

neurofibril (ˌnjʊərəʊˈfaɪbrɪl) NOUN any of the delicate threads within the body of a nerve cell that extend into the axon and dendrites.
▸**ˌneuroˈfibrilar, ˌneurofiˈbrillar,** *or* **ˌneurofiˈbrillary** ADJECTIVE

neurofibromatosis (ˌnjʊərəʊˌfaɪbrəməˈtəʊsɪs) NOUN a condition characterized by the formation of benign tumours on the fibrous coverings of the peripheral nerves and the development of areas of *café-au-lait* spots.

neurogenic (ˌnjʊərəʊˈdʒɛnɪk) ADJECTIVE originating in or stimulated by the nervous system or nerve impulses.

neuroglia (njʊˈrɒglɪə) NOUN another name for **glia.**

neurohormone (ˈnjʊərəʊˌhɔːməʊn) NOUN a hormone, such as noradrenaline, oxytocin, or vasopressin, that is produced by specialized nervous tissue rather than by endocrine glands.

neurohypophysis (ˌnjʊərəʊhaɪˈpɒfɪsɪs) NOUN, *plural* **-ses** (-ˌsiːz). the posterior lobe of the pituitary gland. Compare **adenohypophysis.**

neurol. ABBREVIATION FOR neurology.

neurolemma (ˌnjʊərəʊˈlɛmə) NOUN the thin membrane that forms a sheath around nerve fibres. Also: **neurilemma.**
▷HISTORY C19: New Latin, from NEURO- + Greek *eilēma* covering

neuroleptic (ˌnjʊərəʊˈlɛptɪk) ADJECTIVE [1] capable of affecting the brain, esp by reducing the intensity of nerve function; tranquillizing. ◆ NOUN [2] a neuroleptic drug; major tranquillizer: used in the treatment of psychoses.

neurolinguistics (ˌnjʊərəʊlɪŋˈgwɪstɪks) NOUN (*functioning as singular*) the branch of linguistics that deals with the encoding of the language faculty in the brain.

neurological (ˌnjʊərəˈlɒdʒɪkᵊl) ADJECTIVE of or relating to the nervous system or neurology.

neurology (njʊˈrɒlədʒɪ) NOUN the study of the anatomy, physiology, and diseases of the nervous system.
▸**neuˈrologist** NOUN

neuroma (njʊˈrəʊmə) NOUN, *plural* **-mata** (-mətə) *or* **-mas.** any tumour composed of nerve tissue.
▸**neuromatous** (njʊˈrɒmətəs) ADJECTIVE

neuromuscular (ˌnjʊərəʊˈmʌskjʊlə) ADJECTIVE of, relating to, or affecting nerves and muscles.

neurone (ˈnjʊərəʊn) *or* **neuron** (ˈnjʊərɒn) NOUN a cell specialized to conduct nerve impulses: consists of a cell body, axon, and dendrites. Also called: **nerve cell.**
▸**neuˈronal** ADJECTIVE ▸**neuronic** (njʊˈrɒnɪk) ADJECTIVE

neuropath (ˈnjʊərəʊˌpæθ) NOUN a person suffering from or predisposed to a disorder of the nervous system.

neuropathology (ˌnjʊərəʊpəˈθɒlədʒɪ) NOUN the study of diseases of the nervous system.
▸**neuropathological** (ˌnjʊərəʊˌpæθəˈlɒdʒɪkᵊl) ADJECTIVE
▸**ˌneuropaˈthologist** NOUN

neuropathy (njʊˈrɒpəθɪ) NOUN disease of the nervous system.
▸**neuropathic** (ˌnjʊərəʊˈpæθɪk) ADJECTIVE
▸**ˌneuroˈpathically** ADVERB

neuropeptide (ˌnjʊərəʊˈpɛptaɪd) NOUN a peptide produced by neural tissue, esp one with hormonal activity.

neurophysiology (ˌnjʊərəʊˌfɪzɪˈɒlədʒɪ) NOUN the study of the functions of the nervous system.
▸**neurophysiological** (ˌnjʊərəʊˌfɪzɪəˈlɒdʒɪkᵊl) ADJECTIVE
▸**ˌneuroˌphysioˈlogically** ADVERB ▸**ˌneuroˌphysiˈologist** NOUN

neuropil (ˈnjʊərəʊpɪl) NOUN a dense network of neurons and glia in the central nervous system.
▷HISTORY from NEURO- + Greek *pilos* hair

neuropsychiatry (ˌnjʊərəʊsaɪˈkaɪətrɪ) NOUN the branch of psychiatry that investigates the links between mental illness and organic disease of the brain.
▸**neuropsychiatric** (ˌnjʊərəʊˌsaɪkɪˈætrɪk) ADJECTIVE
▸**ˌneuropsyˈchiatrist** NOUN

neuropsychology (ˌnjʊərəʊsaɪˈkɒlədʒɪ) NOUN the study of the effects of brain damage on behaviour and the mind.
▸**ˌneuropsyˈchologist** NOUN

neuropteran *or* **neuropteron** (njʊˈrɒptərən) NOUN, *plural* **-terans** *or* **-tera** (-tərə). any neuropterous insect.

neuropterous (njʊˈrɒptərəs) *or* **neuropteran** ADJECTIVE of, relating to, or belonging to the *Neuroptera,* an order of insects having two pairs of large much-veined wings and biting mouthparts: includes the lacewings and antlions.
▷HISTORY C18: from New Latin *Neuroptera;* see NEURO-, -PTEROUS

neuroscience (ˈnjʊərəʊˌsaɪəns) NOUN the study of the anatomy, physiology, biochemistry, and pharmacology of the nervous system.

neurosis (njʊˈrəʊsɪs) NOUN, *plural* **-ses** (-siːz). a relatively mild mental disorder, characterized by symptoms such as hysteria, anxiety, depression, or obsessive behaviour. Also called: **psychoneurosis.**

neurosurgery (ˌnjʊərəʊˈsɜːdʒərɪ) NOUN the branch of surgery concerned with the nervous system.
▸**ˌneuroˈsurgeon** NOUN ▸**ˌneuroˈsurgical** ADJECTIVE
▸**ˌneuroˈsurgically** ADVERB

neurotic (njʊˈrɒtɪk) ADJECTIVE [1] of, relating to, or afflicted by neurosis. ◆ NOUN [2] a person who is afflicted with a neurosis or who tends to be emotionally unstable or unusually anxious.
▸**neuˈrotically** ADVERB

neuroticism (njʊˈrɒtɪˌsɪzəm) NOUN a personality trait characterized by instability, anxiety, aggression, etc.

neurotomy (njʊˈrɒtəmɪ) NOUN, *plural* **-mies.** the surgical cutting of a nerve, esp to relieve intractable pain.
▸**neuˈrotomist** NOUN

neurotoxin (ˌnjʊərəʊˈtɒksɪn) NOUN any of several natural substances that interfere with the electrical activities of nerves, thus preventing them from functioning.
▸**ˌneuroˈtoxic** ADJECTIVE

neurotransmitter (ˌnjʊərəʊtrænzˈmɪtə) NOUN a chemical by which a nerve cell communicates with another nerve cell or with a muscle.

neurovascular (ˌnʊərəʊˈvæskjʊlə) ADJECTIVE of, relating to, or affecting both the nerves and the blood vessels.

Neusatz (ˈnɔyzats) NOUN the German name for **Novi Sad.**

Neuss (*German* nɔys) NOUN an industrial city in W Germany, in North Rhine-Westphalia west of Düsseldorf: founded as a Roman fortress in the 1st century A.D. Pop.: 149 206 (1999 est.). Latin name: **Novaesium.**

neuston (ˈnjuːstᵊn) NOUN [1] organisms, similar to plankton, that float on the surface film of open water. [2] the ecosystem of the surface film of open water in which such organisms as copepods graze on tiny flagellates, bacteria, etc.
▷HISTORY C20: via German from Greek *neustos* swimming, from *nein* to swim
▸**neusˈtonic** ADJECTIVE

Neustria ('nju:strɪə) NOUN the western part of the kingdom of the Merovingian Franks formed in 561 A.D. in what is now N France.

Neustrian ('nju:strɪən) ADJECTIVE of or relating to Neustria, the western part of the kingdom of the Merovingian Franks, or its inhabitants.

neut. ABBREVIATION FOR neuter.

neuter ('nju:tə) ADJECTIVE 1 *Grammar* **a** denoting or belonging to a gender of nouns which for the most part have inanimate referents or do not specify the sex of their referents. **b** (*as noun*): *German "Mädchen" (meaning "girl") is a neuter.* 2 (of animals and plants) having nonfunctional, underdeveloped, or absent reproductive organs. 3 sexless or giving no indication of sex: *a neuter sort of name.* ◆ NOUN 4 a sexually underdeveloped female insect, such as a worker bee. 5 a castrated animal, esp a domestic animal. 6 a flower in which the stamens and pistil are absent or nonfunctional. ◆ VERB 7 (*tr*) to castrate or spay (an animal).
▷HISTORY C14: from Latin, from *ne* not + *uter* either (of two)

neutral ('nju:trəl) ADJECTIVE 1 not siding with any party to a war or dispute. 2 of, belonging to, or appropriate to a neutral party, country, etc.: *neutral land.* 3 of no distinctive quality, characteristics, or type; indifferent. 4 (of a colour such as white or black) having no hue; achromatic. 5 (of a colour) dull, but harmonizing with most other colours. 6 a less common term for **neuter** (sense 2). 7 *Chem* neither acidic nor alkaline. 8 *Physics* having zero charge or potential. 9 *Rare* having no magnetism. 10 *Phonetics* (of a vowel) articulated with the tongue relaxed in mid-central position and the lips midway between spread and rounded: *the word "about" begins with a neutral vowel.* ◆ NOUN 11 a neutral person, nation, etc. 12 a citizen of a neutral state. 13 the position of the controls of a gearbox that leaves the transmission disengaged.
▷HISTORY C16: from Latin *neutrālis;* see NEUTER
▸'**neutrally** ADVERB

neutral axis NOUN *Engineering* the line or plane through the section of a beam or plate which does not suffer extension or compression when the beam or plate bends.

neutral density NOUN **a** black, white, or a shade of grey; a colourless tone. **b** (*as modifier*): *a neutral-density filter.*

neutralism ('nju:trəˌlɪzəm) NOUN (in international affairs) the policy, practice, or attitude of neutrality, noninvolvement, or nonalignment with power blocs.
▸'**neutralist** NOUN, ADJECTIVE

neutrality (nju:'trælɪtɪ) NOUN 1 the state or character of being neutral, esp in a dispute, contest, etc. 2 the condition of being chemically or electrically neutral.

neutralize *or* **neutralise** ('nju:trəˌlaɪz) VERB (*mainly tr*) 1 (*also intr*) to render or become ineffective or neutral by counteracting, mixing, etc.; nullify. 2 (*also intr*) to make or become electrically or chemically neutral. 3 to exclude (a country) from the sphere of warfare or alliances by international agreement: *the great powers neutralized Belgium in the 19th century.* 4 to render (an army) incapable of further military action.
▸ˌ**neutrali'zation** *or* ˌ**neutrali'sation** NOUN ▸'**neutralˌizer** *or* '**neutralˌiser** NOUN

neutral monism NOUN the philosophical doctrine that mind and body are both constructs of the same elements which cannot themselves be classified either as mental or physical. See also **monism** (sense 1).

neutral spirits NOUN (*functioning as singular or plural*) *US* ethanol of more than 190° proof.

neutretto (nju:'trɛtəʊ) NOUN, *plural* **-tos.** *Physics* 1 the neutrino associated with the muon. 2 (formerly) any of various hypothetical neutral particles.
▷HISTORY C20: from NEUTR(INO) + diminutive suffix *-etto*

neutrino (nju:'tri:nəʊ) NOUN, *plural* **-nos.** *Physics* a stable leptonic neutral elementary particle with very small or possibly zero rest mass and spin ½ that travels at the speed of light. Three types exist, associated with the electron, the muon, and the tau particle.
▷HISTORY C20: from Italian, diminutive of *neutrone* NEUTRON

neutrino astronomy NOUN the detection of neutrinos emitted by the sun or by supernovae from which information about the solar interior can be obtained.

neutron ('nju:trɒn) NOUN *Physics* a neutral elementary particle with a rest mass of $1.674\,92716 \times 10^{-27}$ kilogram and spin ½; classified as a baryon. In the nucleus of an atom it is stable but when free it decays.
▷HISTORY C20: from NEUTRAL, on the model of ELECTRON

neutron bomb NOUN a type of nuclear weapon designed to provide a high yield of neutrons but to cause little blast or long-lived radioactive contamination. The neutrons destroy all life in the target area, which theoretically can be entered relatively soon after the attack. Technical name: **enhanced radiation weapon.**

neutron gun NOUN *Physics* a device used for producing a beam of fast neutrons.

neutron number NOUN the number of neutrons in the nucleus of an atom. Symbol: *N.*

neutron poison NOUN *Physics* a nonfissionable material used to absorb neutrons and thus to control nuclear reactions.

neutron star NOUN a star that has collapsed under its own gravity to a diameter of about 10 to 15 kilometres. It is composed mostly of neutrons, has a mass of between 1.4 and about 3 times that of the sun, and a density in excess of 10^{17} kilograms per cubic metre.

neutropenia (ˌnju:trə'pi:nɪə) NOUN an abnormal reduction in the number of neutrophils in the blood, as seen in certain anaemias and leukaemias.

neutrophil ('nju:trəˌfɪl) *or* **neutrophile** ('nju:trəˌfaɪl) NOUN 1 a leucocyte having a lobed nucleus and a fine granular cytoplasm, which stains with neutral dyes. ◆ ADJECTIVE 2 (of cells and tissues) readily stainable by neutral dyes.

Nev. ABBREVIATION FOR Nevada.

Neva ('ni:və; *Russian* nɪ'va) NOUN a river in NW Russia, flowing west to the Gulf of Finland by the delta on which Saint Petersburg stands. Length: 74 km (46 miles).

Nevada (nɪ'vɑ:də) NOUN a state of the western US: lies almost wholly within the Great Basin, a vast desert plateau; noted for production of gold and copper. Capital: Carson City. Pop.: 1 998 257 (2000). Area: 284 612 sq. km (109 889 sq. miles). Abbreviations: **Nev.,** (with zip code) **NV.**

névé ('neveɪ) NOUN 1 Also called: **firn.** a mass of porous ice, formed from snow, that has not yet become frozen into glacier ice. 2 a snowfield at the head of a glacier that becomes transformed to ice.
▷HISTORY C19: from Swiss French *névé* glacier, from Late Latin *nivātus* snow-cooled, from *nix* snow

never ('nɛvə) ADVERB, SENTENCE SUBSTITUTE 1 at no time; not ever. 2 certainly not; by no means; in no case. ◆ INTERJECTION 3 Also: **well I never!** surely not!
▷HISTORY Old English *nǣfre,* from *ne* not + *ǣfre* EVER

Language note In informal speech and writing, *never* can be used instead of *not* with the simple past tenses of certain verbs for emphasis (*I never said that; I never realized how clever he was*), but this usage should be avoided in serious writing.

never-ending ADJECTIVE having or seeming to have no end; interminable.

nevermore (ˌnɛvə'mɔ:) ADVERB *Literary* never again.

never-never *Informal* ◆ NOUN 1 the hire-purchase system of buying. 2 *Austral* remote desert country, as that of W Queensland and central Australia. ◆ ADJECTIVE 3 imaginary; idyllic (esp in the phrase **never-never land**).

Nevers (*French* nəvɛr) NOUN a city in central France: capital of the former duchy of Nivernais; engineering industry. Pop.: 43 890 (1990).

nevertheless (ˌnɛvəðə'lɛs) SENTENCE CONNECTOR in spite of that; however; yet.

Nevis NOUN 1 ('ni:vɪs, 'nɛvɪs) an island in the Caribbean, part of St Kitts-Nevis; the volcanic cone of **Nevis Peak,** which rises to 1002 m (3287 ft.), lies in the centre of the island. Capital: Charlestown. Pop.: 8010 (1995 est.). Area: 129 sq. km (50 sq. miles). 2 ('nɛvɪs) See **Ben Nevis.**

nevus ('ni:vəs) NOUN, *plural* **-vi** (-vaɪ). the usual US spelling of **naevus.**

new (nju:) ADJECTIVE 1 **a** recently made or brought into being: *a new dress; our new baby.* **b** (*as collective noun;* preceded by *the*): *the new.* 2 of a kind never before existing; novel: *a new concept in marketing.* 3 having existed before but only recently discovered: *a new comet.* 4 markedly different from what was before: *the new liberalism.* 5 fresh and unused; not second-hand: *a new car.* 6 (*prenominal*) having just or recently become: *a new bride.* 7 (often foll by *to* or *at*) recently introduced (to); inexperienced (in) or unaccustomed (to): *new to this neighbourhood.* 8 (*capital in names or titles*) more or most recent of two or more things with the same name: *the New Testament.* 9 (*prenominal*) fresh; additional: *I'll send some new troops.* 10 (often foll by *to*) unknown; novel: *this is new to me.* 11 (of a cycle) beginning or occurring again: *a new year.* 12 (*prenominal*) (of crops) harvested early: *new carrots.* 13 changed, esp for the better: *she returned a new woman from her holiday.* 14 up-to-date; fashionable. 15 (*capital when part of a name; prenominal*) being the most recent, usually living, form of a language: *New High German.* 16 (**be**) **the new.** (to be) set to become the new vogue: *comedy is the new rock'n'roll.* 17 **turn over a new leaf.** to reform; make a fresh start. ◆ ADVERB (*usually in combination*) 18 recently, freshly: *new-laid eggs.* 19 anew; again. ◆ See also **news.** ◆ Related prefix: **neo-.**
▷HISTORY Old English *nīowe;* related to Gothic *niujis,* Old Norse *naujas,* Latin *novus*
▸'**newness** NOUN

New Age NOUN 1 **a** a philosophy, originating in the late 1980s, characterized by a belief in alternative medicine, astrology, spiritualism, etc. **b** (*as modifier*): *New Age therapies.* 2 short for **New Age music.**

New Age music *or* **New Age** NOUN a type of gentle melodic popular music originating in the US in the late 1980s, which takes in elements of jazz, folk, and classical music and is played largely on synthesizers and acoustic instruments.

New Amsterdam NOUN the Dutch settlement established on Manhattan (1624–26); capital of New Netherlands; captured by the English and renamed New York in 1664.

Newark ('nju:ək) NOUN 1 a town in N central England, in Nottinghamshire. Pop.: 35 129 (1991). Official name: **Newark-on-Trent.** 2 a port in NE New Jersey, just west of New York City, on Newark Bay and the Passaic River: the largest city in the state; founded in 1666 by Puritans from Connecticut; industrial and commercial centre. Pop.: 273 546 (2000).

New Australia NOUN the colony on socialist principles founded by William Lane in Paraguay in 1893.

New Australian NOUN an immigrant to Australia, esp one whose native tongue is not English.

New Bedford NOUN a port and resort in SE Massachusetts, near Buzzards Bay: settled by Plymouth colonists in 1652; a leading whaling port (18th–19th centuries). Pop.: 93 768 (2000).

newbie ('nju:bɪ) NOUN *Slang* a newcomer, esp in computing or on the Internet.
▷HISTORY C20: origin unknown; possibly from *new boy*

newborn ('nju:ˌbɔ:n) ADJECTIVE 1 **a** recently or just born. **b** (*as collective noun;* preceded by *the*): *the newborn.* 2 (of hope, faith, etc.) reborn.

New Britain NOUN an island in the S Pacific, northeast of New Guinea: the largest island of the Bismarck Archipelago; part of Papua New Guinea; mountainous, with several active volcanoes. Capital: Rabaul. Pop.: 435 307 (1999 est.). Area: 36 519 sq. km (14 100 sq. miles).

new broom NOUN a newly appointed person eager to make changes.

New Brunswick NOUN a province of SE Canada on the Gulf of St Lawrence and the Bay of Fundy: extensively forested. Capital: Fredericton. Pop.:

757 100 (2001 est.). Area: 72 092 sq. km (27 835 sq. miles). Abbreviation: **NB.**

New Brunswicker ('brʌnzwɪkə) NOUN a native or inhabitant of New Brunswick.

new brutalism NOUN another name for **brutalism.**

Newburg ('nju:bɜ:g) ADJECTIVE (*immediately postpositive*) (of shellfish, esp lobster) cooked in a rich sauce of butter, cream, sherry, and egg yolks.
▷HISTORY of unknown origin

Newbury ('nju:bərɪ) NOUN a market town in West Berkshire unitary authority, S England: scene of a Parliamentarian victory (1643) and a Royalist victory (1644) during the Civil War; telecommunications, racecourse. Pop.: 33 273 (1991).

Newby Hall ('nju:bɪ) NOUN a mansion near Ripon in Yorkshire: built in 1705 and altered (1770–76) by Robert Adam.

New Caledonia NOUN an island in the SW Pacific, east of Australia: forms, with its dependencies, an overseas territory of France; discovered by Captain Cook in 1774; rich mineral resources. Capital: Nouméa. Pop.: 216 000 (2001 est.). Area: 19 103 sq. km (7374 miles). French name: **Nouvelle-Calédonie.**

New Castile NOUN a region and former province of central Spain. Chief town: Toledo.

Newcastle ('nju:ˌkɑ:səl) NOUN a port in SE Australia, in E New South Wales near the mouth of the Hunter River: important industrial centre, with extensive steel, metalworking, engineering, shipbuilding, and chemical industries. It suffered Australia's first fatal earthquake in 1989. Pop.: 139 171 (1998 est.).

Newcastle disease NOUN an acute viral disease of birds, esp poultry, characterized by pneumonia and inflammation of the central nervous system.
▷HISTORY C20: named after NEWCASTLE UPON TYNE, where it was recorded in 1926

Newcastle-under-Lyme NOUN a town in W central England, in Staffordshire. Pop.: 73 731 (1991). Often shortened to: **Newcastle.**

Newcastle upon Tyne NOUN [1] a port in NE England in Newcastle upon Tyne unitary authority, Tyne and Wear, near the mouth of the River Tyne opposite Gateshead: Roman remains; engineering industries, including ship repairs; two universities (1937, 1992). Pop.: 189 150 (1991). Often shortened to: **Newcastle.** [2] a unitary authority in NE England, in Tyne and Wear. Pop.: 259 573 (2001). Area: 112 sq. km (43 sq. miles).

new chum NOUN [1] *Austral and NZ, archaic informal* a recent British immigrant. [2] *Austral* a novice in any activity. [3] *Austral* (in the 19th century) a new arrival in a hulk.

New Church NOUN another name for the **New Jerusalem Church.**

newcomer ('nju:ˌkʌmə) NOUN a person who has recently arrived or started to participate in something.

New Country NOUN a style of country music that emerged in the late 1980s characterized by a more contemporary sound and down-to-earth rather than sentimental lyrics.

new criticism NOUN an approach to literary criticism through close analysis of the text.
▸**new critic** NOUN ▸**new critical** ADJECTIVE

New Deal NOUN [1] the domestic policies of Franklin D. Roosevelt for economic and social reform. [2] the period of the implementation of these policies (1933–40).
▸**New Dealer** NOUN

New Delhi NOUN See **Delhi.**

New Democratic Party NOUN the Canadian social democratic party formed in 1961. Abbreviation: **NDP.**

New Economic Policy NOUN an economic programme in the former Soviet Union from 1921 to 1928, that permitted private ownership of industries, etc. Abbreviation: **NEP.**

new economy NOUN the postindustrial world economy based on Internet trading and advanced technology.

newel ('nju:əl) NOUN [1] the central pillar of a winding staircase, esp one that is made of stone. [2] see **newel post.**
▷HISTORY C14: from Old French *nouel* knob, from Medieval Latin *nōdellus,* diminutive of *nōdus* NODE

newel post NOUN the post at the top or bottom of a flight of stairs that supports the handrail. Sometimes shortened to: **newel.**

New England NOUN [1] the NE part of the US, consisting of the states of Maine, New Hampshire, Vermont, Massachusetts, Rhode Island, and Connecticut: settled originally chiefly by Puritans in the mid-17th century. [2] a region in SE Australia, in the northern tablelands of New South Wales.

New Englander ('ɪŋgləndə) NOUN a native or inhabitant of New England.

New England Range NOUN a mountain range in SE Australia, in NE New South Wales: part of the Great Dividing Range. Highest peak: Ben Lomond, 1520 m (4986 ft.).

New English Bible NOUN a new Modern English version of the Bible and Apocrypha, published in full in 1970.

newfangled ('nju:'fæŋgəld) ADJECTIVE [1] newly come into existence or fashion, esp excessively modern. [2] *Rare* excessively fond of new ideas, fashions, etc.
▷HISTORY C14 *newefangel* liking new things, from *new* + *-fangel,* from Old English *fōn* to take
▸'**new'fangledness** NOUN

new-fashioned ADJECTIVE of or following a recent design, trend, etc.

Newfie ('nju:fɪ) NOUN *Informal* [1] a native or inhabitant of Newfoundland. [2] the province or island of Newfoundland.

New Forest NOUN a region of woodland and heath in S England, in SW Hampshire: a hunting ground of the West Saxon kings; tourist area, noted for its ponies. Area: 336 sq. km (130 sq. miles).

New Forest disease NOUN *Vet science* an infectious eye disease causing acute eye pain in cattle.

New Forest fly NOUN *Vet science* a blood-sucking fly, *Hippobosca equinus,* that attacks horses and cattle.

new-found ADJECTIVE newly or recently discovered: *new-found confidence.*

Newfoundland ('nju:fəndlənd, -fənlənd, -ˌlænd, nju:'faʊndlənd) NOUN [1] an island of E Canada, separated from the mainland by the Strait of Belle Isle: with the Coast of Labrador forms the province of Newfoundland; consists of a rugged plateau with the Long Range Mountains in the west. Area: 110 681 sq. km (42 734 sq. miles). [2] a province of E Canada, consisting of the island of Newfoundland and the Coast of Labrador. Capital: St John's. Pop.: 533 800 (2001 est.). Area: 404 519 sq. km (156 185 sq. miles). Abbreviations: **Nfld** *or* **NF.** [3] a very large heavy breed of dog similar to a Saint Bernard with a flat coarse usually black coat.

Newfoundlander (nju:'faʊndləndə) NOUN a native or inhabitant of Newfoundland.

Newfoundland Standard Time NOUN one of the standard times used in Canada, three and a half hours behind Greenwich Mean Time.

New France NOUN the former French colonies and possessions in North America, most of which were lost to England and Spain by 1763: often restricted to the French possessions in Canada.

Newgate ('nju:gɪt, -ˌgeɪt) NOUN a famous London prison, in use from the Middle Ages: demolished in 1902.

New Georgia NOUN [1] a group of islands in the SW Pacific, in the Solomon Islands. [2] the largest island in this group. Area: about 1300 sq. km (500 sq. miles).

New Granada NOUN [1] a former Spanish presidency and later viceroyalty in South America. At its greatest extent it consisted of present-day Panama, Colombia, Venezuela, and Ecuador. [2] the name of Colombia when it formed, with Panama, part of Great Colombia (1819–30).

New Guinea NOUN [1] an island in the W Pacific, north of Australia: divided politically into Irian Jaya (a province of Indonesia) in the west and Papua New Guinea in the east. There is a central chain of mountains and a lowland area of swamps in the south and along the Sepik River in the north. Area: 775 213 sq. km (299 310 sq. miles). [2] **Trust Territory of.** (until 1975) an administrative division of the former Territory of Papua and New Guinea, consisting of the NE part of the island of New Guinea together with the Bismarck Archipelago; now part of Papua New Guinea.

New Guinea macrophylum (ˌmækrəʊ'faɪləm) NOUN the older term for **Trans-New Guinea phylum.**

New Guinea Pidgin NOUN the variety of Neo-Melanesian spoken in Papua New Guinea and neighbouring islands.

Newham ('nju:əm) NOUN a borough of E Greater London, on the River Thames: established in 1965. Pop.: 243 737 (2001). Area: 36 sq. km (14 sq. miles).

New Hampshire NOUN a state of the northeastern US: generally hilly. Capital: Concord. Pop.: 1 235 786 (2000 est.). Area: 23 379 sq. km (9027 sq. miles). Abbreviations: **N.H.,** (with zip code) **NH.**

New Harmony NOUN a village in SW Indiana, on the Wabash River: scene of two experimental cooperative communities, the first founded in 1815 by George Rapp, a German religious leader, and the second by Robert Owen in 1825.

Newhaven ('nju:ˌheɪvən) NOUN a ferry port and resort on the S coast of England, in East Sussex. Pop.: 11 208 (1991).

New Haven NOUN an industrial city and port in S Connecticut, on Long Island Sound: settled in 1638 by English Puritans, who established it as a colony in 1643; seat of Yale University (1701). Pop.: 123 626 (2000 est.).

New Hebrides PLURAL NOUN the former name (until 1980) of **Vanuatu.**

New Ireland NOUN an island in the S Pacific, in the Bismarck Archipelago, separated from New Britain by St George's Channel: part of Papua New Guinea. Chief town and port: Kavieng. Pop.: 87 194 (1990.). Area (including adjacent islands): 9850 sq. km (3800 sq. miles).

newish ('nju:ɪʃ) ADJECTIVE fairly new.
▸'**newishly** ADVERB ▸'**newishness** NOUN

new issue NOUN *Stock Exchange* an issue of shares being offered to the public for the first time.

New Jersey NOUN a state of the eastern US, on the Atlantic and Delaware Bay: mostly low-lying, with a heavy industrial area in the northeast and many coastal resorts. Capital: Trenton. Pop.: 8 414 350 (2000). Area: 19 479 sq. km (7521 sq. miles). Abbreviations: **N.J.,** (with zip code) **NJ.**

New Jerusalem NOUN *Christianity* heaven regarded as the prototype of the earthly Jerusalem; the heavenly city.

New Jerusalem Church NOUN a sect founded in 1787, based on Swedenborgianism. Often shortened to: **New Church.**

New Journalism NOUN a style of journalism originating in the US in the 1960s, which uses techniques borrowed from fiction to portray a situation or event as vividly as possible.

New Kingdom NOUN a period of Egyptian history, extending from the 18th to the 20th dynasty (?1570–?1080 B.C.).

New Latin NOUN the form of Latin used since the Renaissance, esp for scientific nomenclature. Also called: **Neo-Latin.**

New Learning NOUN the classical and Biblical studies of Renaissance Europe in the 15th and 16th centuries.

New Left NOUN a loose grouping of left-wing radicals, esp among students, that arose in many countries after 1960.

New Look NOUN **the.** a fashion in women's clothes introduced in 1947, characterized by long full skirts.

newly ('nju:lɪ) ADVERB [1] recently; lately or just: *a newly built shelf.* [2] again; afresh; anew: *newly raised hopes.* [3] in a new manner; differently: *a newly arranged hairdo.*

Newlyn datum ('nju:lɪn) NOUN another name for **ordnance datum.**
▷HISTORY named after *Newlyn,* Cornwall, where the observations were taken

newlywed ('nju:lɪˌwed) NOUN (*often plural*) a recently married person.

New Man NOUN **the.** a type of modern man who allows the caring side of his nature to show by being supportive and by sharing child care and housework.

newmarket ('nju:ˌmɑ:kɪt) NOUN [1] a double-breasted waisted coat with a full skirt worn, esp for riding, in the 19th century. [2] a simple gambling card game.

Newmarket ('nju:ˌmɑ:kɪt) NOUN a town in SE England, in W Suffolk: a famous horse-racing centre since the reign of James I. Pop.: 18 430 (1991).

new maths NOUN *(functioning as singular) Brit* an approach to mathematics in which the basic principles of set theory are introduced at an elementary level.

new media NOUN **a** the Internet and other postindustrial forms of telecommunication. **b** *(as modifier)*: *the new-media industry.* Compare **old media**.

New Mexican ADJECTIVE [1] of or relating to New Mexico or its inhabitants. ◆ NOUN [2] a native or inhabitant of New Mexico.

New Mexico NOUN a state of the southwestern US: has high semiarid plateaus and mountains, crossed by the Rio Grande and the Pecos River; large Spanish-American and Indian populations; contains over two-thirds of US uranium reserves. Capital: Santa Fé. Pop.: 1 819 046 (2000). Area: 314 451 sq. km (121 412 sq. miles). Abbreviations: **N. Mex, N.M.,** (with zip code) **NM**.

New Model Army NOUN the army established (1645) during the Civil War by the English parliamentarians, which exercised considerable political power under Cromwell.

new moon NOUN [1] the moon when it appears as a narrow waxing crescent. [2] the time at which this occurs. [3] *Astronomy* one of the four principal phases of the moon, occurring when it lies between the earth and the sun.

New National Party NOUN see **National Party** (sense 3).

New Netherland ('nɛðələnd) NOUN a Dutch North American colony of the early 17th century, centred on the Hudson valley. Captured by the English in 1664, it was divided into New York and New Jersey.

New Orleans ('ɔ:li:ənz, -lənz, ɔ:'li:nz) NOUN a port in SE Louisiana, on the Mississippi River about 172 km (107 miles) from the sea: the largest city in the state and the second most important port in the US; founded by the French in 1718; belonged to Spain (1763–1803). It is largely below sea level, built around the Vieux Carré (French quarter); famous for its annual Mardi Gras festival and for its part in the history of jazz; a major commercial, industrial, and transportation centre. Pop.: 484 674 (2000).

New Orleans jazz NOUN the jazz originating in New Orleans from about 1914; traditional jazz.

new penny NOUN another name for **penny** (sense 1).

new planets PLURAL NOUN the outer planets Uranus, Neptune, and Pluto, only discovered comparatively recently.

New Plymouth NOUN a port in New Zealand, on W North Island: founded in 1841. Pop.: 49 800 (1995 est.).

Newport ('nju:ˌpɔ:t) NOUN [1] a city and port in SE Wales, in Newport county borough on the River Usk: electronics. Pop.: 129 900 (1991). [2] a county borough in SE Wales, created from part of Gwent in 1996. Pop.: 137 017 (2001). Area: 190 sq. km (73 sq. miles). [3] a port in SE Rhode Island: founded in 1639, it became one of the richest towns of colonial America; centre of a large number of US naval establishments. Pop.: 28 227 (1990). [4] a town in S England, administrative centre of the Isle of Wight. Pop.: 20 574 (1991).

Newport News NOUN *(functioning as singular)* a port in SE Virginia, at the mouth of the James River: an industrial centre, with one of the world's largest shipyards. Pop.: 180 150 (1996 est.).

New Providence NOUN an island in the Atlantic, in the Bahamas. Chief town: Nassau. Pop.: 172 196 (1990). Area: 150 sq. km (58 sq. miles).

New Quebec NOUN a region of E Canada, formerly the Ungava district of Northwest Territories (1895–1912), extending from the line of the Eastmain and Hamilton Rivers north between Hudson Bay and Labrador: absorbed by Quebec in 1912: contains extensive iron deposits. Area: about 777 000 sq. km (300 000 sq. miles).

New Right NOUN a range of radical right-wing groups and ideologies which advocate laissez-faire economic policies, anti-welfarism, and the belief in the rights of the individual over the common good.

New Romney NOUN a market town in SE England, in Kent on Romney Marsh: of early importance as one of the Cinque Ports, but is now over 1.6 km (1 mile) inland. Pop.: 4565 (latest est.). Former name (until 1563): **Romney**.

Newry ('njʊərɪ) NOUN a city and port in Northern Ireland, in Newry and Mourne district, Co. Down: close to the border with the Republic of Ireland, it has been the scene of sectarian violence in recent years. Pop.: 22 975 (1991).

Newry and Mourne ('mɔ:n) NOUN a district of SE Northern Ireland, in Co. Down. Pop.: 87 058 (2001). Area: 909 sq. km (351 sq. miles).

news (nju:z) NOUN *(functioning as singular)* [1] current events; important or interesting recent happenings. [2] information about such events, as in the mass media. [3] **a the.** a presentation, such as a radio broadcast, of information of this type: *the news is at six.* **b** *(in combination)*: *a newscaster.* [4] interesting or important information not previously known or realized: *it's news to me.* [5] a person, fashion, etc., widely reported in the mass media: *she is no longer news in the film world.*
▷HISTORY C15: from Middle English *newes,* plural of *newe* new *(adj)* on model of Old French *noveles* or Medieval Latin *nova* new things
▸ **'newsless** ADJECTIVE

newsagency ('nju:zˌeɪdʒənsɪ) NOUN *Austral* a newsagent's shop.

news agency NOUN an organization that collects news reports for newspapers, periodicals, etc. Also called: **press agency**.

newsagent ('nju:zˌeɪdʒənt) *or US* **newsdealer** ('nju:zˌdi:lə) NOUN a shopkeeper who sells newspapers, stationery, etc.

newsboy ('nju:zˌbɔɪ) NOUN a boy who sells or delivers newspapers.

newscast ('nju:zˌkɑ:st) NOUN a radio or television broadcast of the news.
▷HISTORY C20: from NEWS + (BROAD)CAST
▸ **'newsˌcaster** NOUN

news conference NOUN another name for **press conference**.

newsflash ('nju:zˌflæʃ) NOUN a brief item of important news, often interrupting a radio or television programme.

newsgirl ('nju:zˌgɜ:l) NOUN [1] *Informal* a female newsreader or reporter. [2] a girl who sells or delivers newspapers.

newsgroup ('nju:zˌgru:p) NOUN *Computing* a forum where subscribers exchange information about a specific subject by electronic mail.

newshawk ('nju:zˌhɔ:k) NOUN *US and Canadian informal* a newspaper reporter. Also called: **newshound** ('nju:zˌhaʊnd).

New Siberian Islands PLURAL NOUN an archipelago in the Arctic Ocean, off the N mainland of Russia, in the Sakha Republic. Area: about 37 555 sq. km (14 500 sq. miles).

newsletter ('nju:zˌlɛtə) NOUN [1] Also called: **news-sheet**. a printed periodical bulletin circulated to members of a group. [2] *History* a written or printed account of the news.

newsman ('nju:zˌmæn) NOUN, *plural* **-men**. *Informal* a male newsreader or reporter.

newsmonger ('nju:zˌmʌŋgə) NOUN *Old-fashioned* a gossip.

new sol (sɒl) NOUN the standard monetary unit of Peru, divided into 100 céntimos. Spanish name: **nuevo sol**.

New South NOUN *Austral informal* See **New South Wales**.

New South Wales NOUN a state of SE Australia: originally contained over half the continent, but was reduced by the formation of other states (1825–1911); consists of a narrow coastal plain, separated from extensive inland plains by the Great Dividing Range; the most populous state; mineral resources. Capital: Sydney. Pop.: 6 441 680 (1999 est.). Area: 801 428 sq. km (309 433 sq. miles).

New Spain NOUN a Spanish viceroyalty of the 16th to 19th centuries, composed of Mexico, Central America north of Panama, the Spanish West Indies, the southwestern US, and the Philippines.

newspaper ('nju:zˌpeɪpə) NOUN [1] **a** a weekly or daily publication consisting of folded sheets and containing articles on the news, features, reviews, and advertisements. Often shortened to: **paper**. **b** *(as modifier)*: *a newspaper article.* [2] a less common name for **newsprint**.

newspaperman ('nju:zˌpeɪpəˌmæn) NOUN, *plural* **-men**. [1] a man who works for a newspaper as a reporter or editor. [2] the male owner or proprietor of a newspaper.

newspaperwoman ('nju:zˌpeɪpəˌwʊmən) NOUN, *plural* **-women**. [1] a woman who works for a newspaper as a reporter or editor. [2] the female owner or proprietor of a newspaper.

newspeak ('nju:ˌspi:k) NOUN the language of bureaucrats and politicians, regarded as deliberately ambiguous and misleading.
▷HISTORY C20: from *1984*, a novel by George Orwell

newsprint ('nju:zˌprɪnt) NOUN an inexpensive wood-pulp paper used for newspapers.

newsreader ('nju:zˌri:də) NOUN a news announcer on radio or television.

newsreel ('nju:zˌri:l) NOUN a short film with a commentary presenting current events.

newsroom ('nju:zˌru:m, -ˌrʊm) NOUN a room in a newspaper office or television or radio station, where news is received and prepared for publication or broadcasting.

newsstand ('nju:zˌstænd) NOUN a portable stand or stall in the street, from which newspapers are sold.

New Stone Age NOUN (not now in technical use) another term for **Neolithic**.

New Style NOUN the present method of reckoning dates using the Gregorian calendar.

news vendor NOUN a person who sells newspapers.

newswoman ('nju:zˌwʊmən) NOUN, *plural* **-women**. *Informal* a female newsreader or reporter.

newsworthy ('nju:zˌwɜ:ðɪ) ADJECTIVE sufficiently interesting to be reported in a news bulletin.
▸ **'newsˌworthiness** NOUN

newsy ('nju:zɪ) ADJECTIVE **newsier, newsiest**. full of news, esp gossipy or personal news: *a newsy letter.*
▸ **'newsiness** NOUN

newt (nju:t) NOUN [1] any of various small semiaquatic urodele amphibians, such as *Triturus vulgaris* (**common newt**) of Europe, having a long slender body and tail and short feeble legs. [2] *Chiefly Brit* any other urodele amphibian, including the salamanders.
▷HISTORY C15: from *a newt,* a mistaken division of *an ewt; ewt,* from Old English *eveta* EFT[1]

New Test. ABBREVIATION FOR New Testament.

New Testament NOUN the collection of writings consisting of the Gospels, Acts of the Apostles, Pauline and other Epistles, and the book of Revelation, composed soon after Christ's death and added to the Jewish writings of the Old Testament to make up the Christian Bible.

New Thought NOUN a movement interested in spiritual healing and the power of constructive thinking.

newton ('nju:tᵊn) NOUN the derived SI unit of force that imparts an acceleration of 1 metre per second per second to a mass of 1 kilogram; equivalent to 10^5 dynes or 7.233 poundals. Symbol: N.
▷HISTORY C20: named after Sir Isaac *Newton* (1642–1727), English mathematician, physicist, astronomer, and philosopher

Newton ('nju:tᵊn) NOUN one of the deepest craters on the moon, over 7300 metres deep and about 113 kilometres in diameter, situated in the SE quadrant

Newtonian (nju:'təʊnɪən) ADJECTIVE of, relating to, or based on the theories of Sir Isaac Newton, the English mathematician, physicist, astronomer, and philosopher (1642–1727).

Newtonian mechanics NOUN (*functioning as singular*) a system of mechanics based on Newton's laws of motion.

Newtonian telescope NOUN a type of astronomical reflecting telescope in which light is reflected from a large concave mirror, onto a plane mirror, and through a hole in the side of the body of the telescope to form an image.

Newton's cradle NOUN an ornamental puzzle consisting of a frame in which five metal balls are suspended in such a way that when one is moved it sets all the others in motion in turn.

Newton's law of gravitation NOUN the principle that two particles attract each other with forces directly proportional to the product of their masses divided by the square of the distance between them.

Newton's laws of motion PLURAL NOUN three laws of mechanics describing the motion of a body. **The first law** states that a body remains at rest or in uniform motion in a straight line unless acted upon by a force. **The second law** states that a body's rate of change of momentum is proportional to the force causing it. **The third law** states that when a force acts on a body due to another body then an equal and opposite force acts simultaneously on that body.

Newtown ('nju:taʊn) NOUN a new town in central Wales, in Powys. Pop.: 10 548 (1991).

new town NOUN (in Britain) a town that has been planned as a complete unit and built with government sponsorship, esp to accommodate overspill population.

Newtownabbey (ˌnju:tᵊn'æbɪ) NOUN [1] a town in Northern Ireland, in Newtownabbey district, Co. Antrim on Belfast Lough: the third largest town in Northern Ireland, formed in 1958 by the amalgamation of seven villages; light industrial centre, esp for textiles. Pop.: 57 103 (1991). [2] a district of E Northern Ireland, in Co. Antrim. Pop.: 79 995 (2001). Area: 151 sq. km (58 sq. miles).

Newtown St Boswells ('nju:taʊn sənt 'bɒzwəlz) NOUN a village in SE Scotland, administrative centre of Scottish Borders: agricultural centre. Pop.: 1108 (1991).

new-variant Creutzfeldt-Jakob disease *or* **variant Creutzfeldt-Jakob disease** NOUN a form of Creutzfeldt-Jakob disease thought to be transmitted by eating beef or beef products infected with BSE. Often shortened to: **new-variant CJD, variant CJD.** Abbrevs: **nvCJD, vCJD.**

new wave NOUN a movement in art, film-making, politics, etc., that consciously breaks with traditional ideas.

New Wave[1] NOUN **the.** a movement in the French cinema of the 1960s, led by such directors as Godard, Truffaut, and Resnais, and characterized by a fluid use of the camera and an abandonment of traditional editing techniques. Also called: **Nouvelle Vague.**

New Wave[2] NOUN rock music of the late 1970s, related to punk but more complex: sometimes used to include punk.

New Windsor NOUN the official name of **Windsor**[1] (sense 1).

new wool NOUN wool that is being processed or woven for the first time. Usual US term: **virgin wool.**

New World NOUN **the.** the Americas; the western hemisphere.

New World monkey NOUN any monkey of the family *Cebidae,* of Central and South America, having widely separated nostrils: many are arboreal and have a prehensile tail. Compare **Old World monkey.**

New Year NOUN the first day or days of the year in various calendars, usually celebrated as a holiday.

New Year's Day NOUN January 1, celebrated as a holiday in many countries. Often (US and Canadian informal) shortened to: **New Year's.**

New Year's Eve NOUN the evening of Dec. 31, often celebrated with parties. See also **Hogmanay.**

New York NOUN [1] Also called: **New York City.** a city in SE New York State, at the mouth of the Hudson River: the largest city and chief port of the US; settled by the Dutch as New Amsterdam in 1624 and captured by the British in 1664, when it was named New York; consists of five boroughs (Manhattan, the Bronx, Queens, Brooklyn, and Richmond) and many islands, with its commercial and financial centre in Manhattan; the country's leading commercial and industrial city. Pop.: 8 008 278 (2000). Abbreviations: **N.Y.C., NYC.** [2] a state of the northeastern US: consists chiefly of a plateau with the Finger Lakes in the centre, the Adirondack Mountains in the northeast, the Catskill Mountains in the southeast, and Niagara Falls in the west. Capital: Albany. Pop.: 18 976 457 (2000). Area: 123 882 sq. km (47 831 sq. miles). Abbreviations: **N.Y.,** (with zip code) **NY.**

New York Bay NOUN an inlet of the Atlantic at the mouth of the Hudson River: forms the harbour of the port of New York.

New Yorker NOUN a native or inhabitant of New York.

New York State Barge Canal NOUN a system of inland waterways in New York State, connecting the Hudson River with Lakes Erie and Ontario and, via Lake Champlain, with the St Lawrence. Length: 845 km (525 miles).

New Zealand ('zi:lənd) NOUN an independent dominion within the Commonwealth, occupying two main islands (the North Island and the South Island), Stewart Island, the Chatham Islands, and a number of minor islands in the SE Pacific: original Maori inhabitants ceded sovereignty to the British government in 1840; became a dominion in 1907; a major world exporter of dairy products, wool, and meat. Official languages: English and Maori. Religion: Christian majority, nonreligious and Maori minorities. Currency: New Zealand dollar. Capital: Wellington. Pop.: 3 861 000 (2001 est.). Area: 270 534 sq. km (104 454 sq. miles).

New Zealander ('zi:ləndə) NOUN a native or inhabitant of New Zealand.

New Zealand greenstone NOUN a variety of nephrite from New Zealand, used as a gemstone.

New Zealand on Air NOUN the operational name for the New Zealand Broadcasting Commission.

next (nɛkst) ADJECTIVE [1] immediately following: *the next patient to be examined; do it next week.* [2] immediately adjoining: *the next room.* [3] closest to in degree: *the tallest boy next to James; the next-best thing.* [4] **the next (Sunday) but one.** the (Sunday) after the next. ◆ ADVERB [5] at a time or on an occasion immediately to follow: *the patient to be examined next; next, he started to unscrew the telephone receiver.* [6] **next to. a** adjacent to; at or on one side of: *the house next to ours.* **b** following in degree: *next to your mother, who do you love most?* **c** almost: *next to impossible.* ◆ PREPOSITION [7] *Archaic* next to.
▷**HISTORY** Old English *nēhst,* superlative of *nēah* NIGH; compare NEAR, NEIGHBOUR

next door ADJECTIVE (**next-door** *when prenominal*), ADVERB at, in, or to the adjacent house, flat, building, etc.: *we live next door to the dentist; the next-door house.*

next friend NOUN *Law* (formerly) a person acting on behalf of an infant or other person under legal disability. Official name: **litigation friend.**

next of kin NOUN a person's closest relative or relatives.

nexus ('nɛksəs) NOUN, *plural* **nexus.** [1] a means of connection between members of a group or things in a series; link; bond. [2] a connected group or series.
▷**HISTORY** C17: from Latin: a binding together, from *nectere* to bind

Nez Percé ('nɛz 'pɜ:s; *French* ne pɛrse) NOUN [1] (*plural* **Nez Percés** ('pɜ:sɪz; *French* pɛrse) *or* **Nez Percé**) a member of a North American Indian people of the Pacific coast, a tribe of the Sahaptin. [2] the Sahaptin language of this people.
▷**HISTORY** French, literally: pierced nose

nf THE INTERNET DOMAIN NAME FOR Norfolk Island.

NF ABBREVIATION FOR: [1] Norman French (language). [2] (in Britain) **National Front.** [3] (esp in postal addresses) Newfoundland.

N/F *or* **NF** *Banking* ABBREVIATION FOR no funds.

NFA ABBREVIATION FOR: [1] (in the US) National Futures Association. [2] (in Britain) no fixed abode.

NFB (in Canada) ABBREVIATION FOR National Film Board.

NFL (in the US) ABBREVIATION FOR National Football League.

NFS (in Britain) ABBREVIATION FOR National Fire Service.

NFT ABBREVIATION FOR National Film Theatre.

NFU (in Britain) ABBREVIATION FOR National Farmers' Union.

NFWI (in Britain) ABBREVIATION FOR National Federation of Women's Institutes.

ng THE INTERNET DOMAIN NAME FOR Nigeria.

NG ABBREVIATION FOR: [1] (in the US) National Guard. [2] New Guinea. [3] Also: **ng.** no good.

NGA (formerly, in Britain) ABBREVIATION FOR National Graphical Association.

ngaio ('naɪəʊ) NOUN, *plural* **ngaios.** a small New Zealand tree, *Myoporum laetum,* yielding useful timber: family *Myoporaceae.*
▷**HISTORY** from Maori

Ngaliema Mountain (ᵊŋɡɑ:'ljeɪmə) NOUN the Congolese name for (Mount) **Stanley.**

ngati ('nɑ:ti:) NOUN *NZ* (occurring as part of the name of a tribe) tribe or clan.
▷**HISTORY** Maori

NGC ABBREVIATION FOR New General Catalogue of Nebulae and Clusters of Stars; a catalogue in which over 8000 nebulae, galaxies, and clusters are listed numerically.

NGF ABBREVIATION FOR **nerve growth factor.**

NGk ABBREVIATION FOR New Greek.

NGL ABBREVIATION FOR natural gas liquids: liquid hydrocarbons derived from natural gas.

NGO ABBREVIATION FOR: [1] Non-Governmental Organization. [2] (in India) nongazetted officer.

ngoma (ᵊŋ'ɡəʊmə, ᵊŋ'ɡɒm-) NOUN *E African* a type of drum.
▷**HISTORY** Swahili

ngultrum (ᵊŋ'ɡu:ltrəm) NOUN the standard monetary unit of Bhutan, divided into 100 chetrum.

Nguni (ᵊŋ'ɡu:nɪ) NOUN a group of Bantu languages of southern Africa, consisting chiefly of Zulu, Xhosa, and Swazi.

ngwee (ᵊŋ'ɡweɪ) NOUN a Zambian monetary unit worth one hundredth of a kwacha.

NH *or* **N.H.** ABBREVIATION FOR New Hampshire.

Nha Trang ('njɑ: 'træŋ) NOUN a port in SE Vietnam, on the South China Sea: nearby temples of the Cham civilization; fishing industry. Pop.: 221 331 (1992 est.).

NHI (in Britain) ABBREVIATION FOR National Health Insurance.

NHL (in Canada) ABBREVIATION FOR National Hockey League.

NHS (in Britain) ABBREVIATION FOR **National Health Service.**

ni THE INTERNET DOMAIN NAME FOR Nicaragua.

Ni THE CHEMICAL SYMBOL FOR nickel.

NI ABBREVIATION FOR: [1] (in Britain) **national insurance.** [2] Northern Ireland. [3] *NZ* North Island.

niacin ('naɪəsɪn) NOUN another name for **nicotinic acid.**
▷**HISTORY** C20: from NI(COTINIC) AC(ID) + -IN

Niagara (naɪ'æɡrə, -'æɡərə) NOUN [1] a river in NE North America, on the border between W New York State and Ontario, Canada, flowing from Lake Erie to Lake Ontario. Length: 45 km (28 miles). [2] a torrent.

Niagara Falls NOUN [1] (*functioning as plural*) the falls of the Niagara River, on the border between the US and Canada: divided by Goat Island into the American Falls, 50 m (167 ft.) high, and the Horseshoe or Canadian Falls, 47 m (158 ft.) high. [2] (*functioning as singular*) a city in W New York State, situated at the falls of the Niagara River. Pop.: 61 840 (1990). [3] (*functioning as singular*) a city in S Canada, in SE Ontario on the Niagara River just below the falls: linked to the city of Niagara Falls in the US by three bridges. Pop.: 76 917 (1996).

Niamey (njɑ:'meɪ) NOUN the capital of Niger, in the southwest on the River Niger: became capital in 1926; airport and land route centre. Pop.: 495 000 (1995 est.).

nib (nɪb) NOUN [1] the writing point of a pen, esp an insertable tapered metal part with a split tip. [2]

a point, tip, or beak. 3 (*plural*) crushed cocoa beans. ◆ VERB **nibs, nibbing, nibbed.** (*tr*) 4 to provide with a nib. 5 to prepare or sharpen the nib of.
▷HISTORY C16 (in the sense: beak): origin obscure; compare Northern German *nibbe* tip. See NEB, NIBBLE
▸ '**nib,like** ADJECTIVE

nibble ('nɪbᵊl) VERB (when *intr*, often foll by *at*) 1 (esp of animals, such as mice) to take small repeated bites (of). 2 to take dainty or tentative bites: *to nibble at a cake.* 3 to bite (at) gently or caressingly. 4 (*intr*) to make petty criticisms. 5 (*intr*) to consider tentatively or cautiously: *to nibble at an idea.* ◆ NOUN 6 a small mouthful. 7 an instance or the act of nibbling. 8 (*plural*) *Informal* small items of food, esp savouries, usually served with drinks.
▷HISTORY C15: related to Low German *nibbelen.* Compare NIB, NEB

nibbler ('nɪblə) NOUN 1 a person, animal, or thing that nibbles. 2 *Engineering* a tool that cuts sheet material by a series of small rapidly reciprocating cuts.

Nibelung ('ni:bə,lʊŋ) NOUN, *plural* **-lungs** *or* **-lungen** (-,lʊŋən). *German myth* 1 any of the race of dwarfs who possessed a treasure hoard stolen by Siegfried. 2 one of Siegfried's companions or followers. 3 (in the *Nibelungenlied*) a member of the family of Gunther, king of Burgundy.

Nibelungenlied *German* ('ni:bəlʊŋənli:t) NOUN a medieval High German heroic epic of unknown authorship based on German history and legend and written about 1200.
▷HISTORY literally: song of the Nibelungs

niblick ('nɪblɪk) NOUN *Golf* (formerly) a club, a No. 9 iron, giving a great deal of lift.
▷HISTORY C19: of unknown origin

nibs (nɪbz) PLURAL NOUN **his nibs.** *Slang* a mock title used of someone in authority.
▷HISTORY C19: of unknown origin

NIC 1 ABBREVIATION FOR newly industrialized country. ◆ 2 INTERNATIONAL CAR REGISTRATION FOR Nicaragua.

nicad ('naɪ,kæd) NOUN a rechargeable dry-cell battery with a nickel anode and a cadmium cathode.
▷HISTORY C20: NI(CKEL) + CAD(MIUM)

Nicaea (naɪ'si:ə) NOUN an ancient city in NW Asia Minor, in Bithynia: site of the **first council of Nicaea** (325 A.D.), which composed the Nicene Creed.

Nicaean (naɪ'si:ən) ADJECTIVE a variant of **Nicene.**

NICAM ('naɪkæm) NOUN ACRONYM FOR near-instantaneous companding system: a technique for coding audio signals into digital form.

Nicaragua (,nɪkə'rægjʊə, -gwə; *Spanish* nika'raɣwa) NOUN 1 a republic in Central America, on the Caribbean and the Pacific: colonized by the Spanish from the 1520s; gained independence in 1821 and was annexed by Mexico, becoming a republic in 1838. Official language: Spanish. Religion: Roman Catholic majority. Currency: córdoba. Capital: Managua. Pop.: 4 918 000 (2001 est.). Area: 131 812 sq. km (50 893 sq. miles). 2 **Lake.** a lake in SW Nicaragua, separated from the Pacific by an isthmus 19 km (12 miles) wide: the largest lake in Central America. Area: 8264 sq. km (3191 sq. miles).

Nicaraguan (,nɪkə'rægjʊən, -gwən) ADJECTIVE 1 of or relating to Nicaragua or its inhabitants. ◆ NOUN 2 a native or inhabitant of Nicaragua.

niccolite ('nɪkə,laɪt) NOUN a copper-coloured mineral consisting of nickel arsenide in hexagonal crystalline form, occurring associated with copper and silver ores: a source of nickel. Formula: NiAs. Also called **nickeline.**
▷HISTORY C19: from New Latin *niccolum* NICKEL + -ITE[1]

nice (naɪs) ADJECTIVE 1 pleasant or commendable: *a nice day.* 2 kind or friendly: *a nice gesture of help.* 3 good or satisfactory: *they made a nice job of it.* 4 subtle, delicate, or discriminating: *a nice point in the argument.* 5 precise; skilful: *a nice fit.* 6 *Now rare* fastidious; respectable: *he was not too nice about his methods.* 7 *Obsolete* **a** foolish or ignorant. **b** delicate. **c** shy; modest. **d** wanton. 8 **nice and.** pleasingly: *it's nice and cool.*
▷HISTORY C13 (originally: foolish): from Old French *nice* simple, silly, from Latin *nescius* ignorant, from *nescīre* to be ignorant; see NESCIENCE
▸ '**nicely** ADVERB ▸ '**niceness** NOUN ▸ '**nicish** ADJECTIVE

Nice (*French* nis) NOUN a city in SE France, on the Mediterranean: a leading resort of the French Riviera; founded by Phocaeans from Marseille in about the 3rd century B.C. Pop.: 342 738 (1999).

NICE (naɪs) NOUN (in Britain) ACRONYM FOR National Institute for Clinical Excellence: a body established in 1999 to provide authoritative guidance on current best practice in medicine and to promote high-quality cost-effective medical treatment in the NHS.

nice-looking ADJECTIVE *Informal* attractive in appearance; pretty or handsome.

Nicene ('naɪsi:n) *or* **Nicaean** (naɪ'si:ən) ADJECTIVE of or relating to Nicaea, an ancient city in NW Asia Minor, or its inhabitants.

Nicene Council NOUN 1 the first council of Nicaea, the first general council of the Church, held in 325 A.D. to settle the Arian controversy. 2 the second council of Nicaea, the seventh general council of the Church, held in 787 A.D. to settle the question of images.

Nicene Creed NOUN 1 the formal summary of Christian beliefs promulgated at the first council of Nicaea in 325 A.D. 2 a longer formulation of Christian beliefs authorized at the council of Constantinople in 381, and now used in most Christian liturgies.

nicety ('naɪsɪtɪ) NOUN, *plural* **-ties.** 1 a subtle point of delicacy or distinction: *a nicety of etiquette.* 2 (*usually plural*) a refinement or delicacy: *the niceties of first-class travel.* 3 subtlety, delicacy, or precision. 4 excessive refinement; fastidiousness. 5 **to a nicety.** with precision.

nicey-nicey (,naɪsɪ'naɪsɪ) ADJECTIVE, ADVERB *Informal* trying to be pleasant, but in a way that suggests artifice or exaggeration; ingratiating(ly).

niche (nɪtʃ, ni:ʃ) NOUN 1 a recess in a wall, esp one that contains a statue. 2 any similar recess, such as one in a rock face. 3 a position particularly suitable for the person occupying it: *he found his niche in politics.* 4 (*modifier*) relating to or aimed at a small specialized group or market. 5 *Ecology* the role of a plant or animal within its community and habitat, which determines its activities, relationships with other organisms, etc. ◆ VERB 6 (*tr*) to place (a statue) in a niche; ensconce (oneself).
▷HISTORY C17: from French, from Old French *nichier* to nest, from Vulgar Latin *nīdicāre* (unattested) to build a nest, from Latin *nīdus* NEST

Nichiren ('ni:tʃi:,rɛn) NOUN a Buddhist sect of Japan based on the teachings of the Buddhist priest Nichiren (1222–82), who claimed that the Lotus Sutra contained the only way to salvation.

Nichrome ('naɪkrəʊm) NOUN *Trademark* any of various alloys containing nickel, iron, and chromium, with smaller amounts of other components. It is used in electrical heating elements, furnaces, etc.

nicht (nɪxt) NOUN a Scot word for **night.**

nick[1] (nɪk) NOUN 1 a small notch or indentation on an edge or surface. 2 a groove on the shank of a printing type, used to orientate type and often to distinguish the fount. 3 *Brit* a slang word for **prison** or **police station.** 4 **in good nick.** *Informal* in good condition. 5 **in the nick of time.** at the last possible moment; at the critical moment. ◆ VERB 6 (*tr*) to chip or cut. 7 (*tr*) *Slang, chiefly Brit* **a** to steal. **b** to take into legal custody; arrest. 8 (*intr; often foll by off*) *Informal* to move or depart rapidly. 9 to divide and reset (certain of the tail muscles of a horse) to give the tail a high carriage. 10 (*tr*) to guess, catch, etc., exactly. 11 (*intr*) (of breeding stock) to mate satisfactorily. 12 **nick (someone) for.** *US and Canadian, slang* to defraud (someone) to the extent of.
▷HISTORY C15: perhaps changed from C14 *nocke* NOCK

nick[2] (nɪk) NOUN *Computing* an alias adopted by a member of a chatroom or forum; nickname.
▷HISTORY short for NICKNAME

nickel ('nɪkᵊl) NOUN 1 a malleable ductile silvery-white metallic element that is strong and corrosion-resistant, occurring principally in pentlandite and niccolite: used in alloys, esp in toughening steel, in electroplating, and as a catalyst in organic synthesis. Symbol: Ni; atomic no.: 28; atomic wt.: 58.6934; valency: 0, 1, 2, or 3; relative density: 8.902; melting pt.: 1455°C; boiling pt.: 2914°C. 2 a US and Canadian coin and monetary unit worth five cents. ◆ VERB **-els, -elling, -elled** *or US* **-els, -eling, -eled.** 3 (*tr*) to plate with nickel.
▷HISTORY C18: shortened form of German *Kupfernickel* NICCOLITE, literally: copper demon, so called by miners because it was mistakenly thought to contain copper

nickel bloom NOUN another name for **annabergite.**

nickelic (nɪ'kɛlɪk) ADJECTIVE 1 of or containing metallic nickel. 2 of or containing nickel in the trivalent state.

nickeliferous (,nɪkə'lɪfərəs) ADJECTIVE containing nickel.

nickeline ('nɪkə,li:n) NOUN another name for **niccolite.**

nickelodeon (,nɪkə'ləʊdɪən) NOUN *US* 1 an early form of jukebox. 2 (formerly) a cinema charging five cents for admission. 3 (formerly) a Pianola, esp one operated by inserting a five-cent piece.
▷HISTORY C20: from NICKEL + (MEL)ODEON

nickelous ('nɪkələs) ADJECTIVE of or containing nickel, esp in the divalent state.

nickel plate NOUN a thin layer of nickel deposited on a surface, usually by electrolysis.

nickel silver NOUN any of various white alloys containing copper (46–63 per cent), zinc (18–36 per cent), and nickel (6–30 per cent): used in making tableware, etc. Also called: **German silver, pakthong.**

nickel steel NOUN *Engineering* steel containing between 0.5 and 6.0 per cent nickel to increase its strength.

nicker[1] ('nɪkə) VERB (*intr*) 1 (of a horse) to neigh softly. 2 to laugh quietly; snigger.
▷HISTORY C18: perhaps from NEIGH

nicker[2] ('nɪkə) NOUN, *plural* **-er.** *Brit, slang* a pound sterling.
▷HISTORY C20: of unknown origin

nick-nack ('nɪk,næk) NOUN a variant spelling of **knick-knack.**

nickname ('nɪk,neɪm) NOUN 1 a familiar, pet, or derisory name given to a person, animal, or place: *his nickname was Lefty because he was left-handed.* 2 a shortened or familiar form of a person's name: *Joe is a nickname for Joseph.* ◆ VERB 3 (*tr*) to call by a nickname; give a nickname to.
▷HISTORY C15 *a nekename,* mistaken division of *an ekename* an additional name, from *eke* addition + NAME

nickpoint ('nɪk,pɔɪnt) NOUN a variant spelling (esp US) of **knickpoint.**

nicky-tam ('nɪkɪ'tæm) NOUN *Scot* a strap or string secured round a trouser leg below the knee, formerly worn esp by farm workers to keep the trouser bottoms clear of dirt.
▷HISTORY C20: from *knicker* + *tam, taum* a fishing line or string

Nicobar Islands ('nɪkə,bɑ:) PLURAL NOUN a group of 19 islands in the Indian Ocean, south of the Andaman Islands, with which they form a territory of India. Area: 1645 sq. km (635 sq. miles).

Nicodemus (,nɪkə'di:məs) NOUN *New Testament* a Pharisee and a member of the Sanhedrin, who supported Jesus against the other Pharisees (John 8:50–52).

Nicol prism ('nɪkᵊl) NOUN a device composed of two prisms of Iceland spar or calcite cut at specified angles and cemented together with Canada balsam. It is used for producing plane-polarized light.
▷HISTORY C19: named after William *Nicol* (?1768–1851), Scottish physicist, its inventor

Nicosia (,nɪkə'si:ə, -'sɪə) NOUN the capital of Cyprus, in the central part on the Pedieos River: capital since the 10th century. Pop. (Greek and Turkish): 230 935 (1998 est.). Greek name: **Levkosia** *or* **Leukosia.** Turkish name: **Lefkoşa.**

nicotiana (nɪ,kəʊʃɪ'ɑ:nə, -'eɪnə) NOUN any solanaceous plant of the American and Australian genus *Nicotiana,* such as tobacco, having white, yellow, or purple fragrant flowers.
▷HISTORY C16: see NICOTINE

nicotinamide (,nɪkə'tɪnə,maɪd, -'ti:n-) NOUN the amide of nicotinic acid: a component of the vitamin B complex and essential in the diet for the prevention of pellagra. Formula: $C_6H_6ON_2$.

nicotine (ˈnɪkəˌtiːn) NOUN a colourless oily acrid toxic liquid that turns yellowish-brown in air and light: the principal alkaloid in tobacco, used as an agricultural insecticide. Formula: $C_{10}H_{14}N_2$.
▷HISTORY C19: from French, from New Latin *herba nicotiana* Nicot's plant, named after J. *Nicot* (1530–1600), French diplomat who introduced tobacco into France
▸ˈ**nicoˌtined** ADJECTIVE ▸**nicotinic** (ˌnɪkəˈtɪnɪk) ADJECTIVE

nicotinic acid NOUN a vitamin of the B complex that occurs in milk, liver, yeast, etc. Lack of it in the diet leads to the disease pellagra. Formula: $(C_5H_4N)COOH$. Also called: **niacin.**

nicotinism (ˈnɪkətiːˌnɪzəm) NOUN *Pathol* a toxic condition of the body or a bodily organ or part caused by nicotine.

Nictheroy (*Portuguese* niteˈrɔi) NOUN another name for **Niterói.**

nictitate (ˈnɪktɪˌteɪt) *or* **nictate** (ˈnɪkteɪt) VERB technical words for **blink** (sense 1).
▷HISTORY C19: from Medieval Latin *nictitāre* to wink repeatedly, from Latin *nictāre* to wink, from *nicere* to beckon
▸ˌ**nictiˈtation** *or* **nicˈtation** NOUN

nictitating membrane NOUN (in reptiles, birds, and some mammals) a thin fold of skin beneath the eyelid that can be drawn across the eye. Also called: **third eyelid, haw.**

Nidaros (*Norwegian* ˈniːdaroːs) NOUN the former name (1930–31) of **Trondheim.**

nidation (naɪˈdeɪʃən) NOUN *Physiol* another name for **implantation** (sense 2).
▷HISTORY from Latin *nīdus* nest

niddering *or* **nidering** (ˈnɪdərɪŋ) *Archaic* ◆ NOUN [1] a coward. ◆ ADJECTIVE [2] cowardly.
▷HISTORY C16: a mistaken reading of Old English *nithing* coward; related to *nīth* malice

niddick (ˈnɪdɪk) NOUN *Southwest English, dialect* the nape of the neck.

niddle-noddle (ˈnɪdəlˌnɒdəl) ADJECTIVE [1] nodding. ◆ VERB [2] to nod rapidly or unsteadily.
▷HISTORY C18: reduplication of NOD

NIDDM ABBREVIATION FOR noninsulin-dependent diabetes mellitus; a form of diabetes in which insulin production is inadequate or the body becomes resistant to insulin.

nide (naɪd) NOUN another word for **nye.**
▷HISTORY C17: from Latin *nīdus* nest

nidicolous (nɪˈdɪkələs) ADJECTIVE (of young birds) remaining in the nest for some time after hatching.
▷HISTORY C19: from Latin *nīdus* nest + *colere* to inhabit

nidifugous (nɪˈdɪfjʊgəs) ADJECTIVE (of young birds) leaving the nest very soon after hatching.
▷HISTORY C19: from Latin *nīdus* nest + *fugere* to flee

nidify (ˈnɪdɪˌfaɪ) *or* **nidificate** (ˈnɪdɪfɪˌkeɪt) VERB **-fies, -fying, -fied.** (*intr*) (of a bird) to make or build a nest.
▷HISTORY C17: from Latin *nīdificāre*, from *nīdus* a nest + *facere* to make
▸ˌ**nidifiˈcation** NOUN

nid-nod (ˈnɪdˌnɒd) VERB **-nods, -nodding, -nodded.** to nod repeatedly.
▷HISTORY C18: reduplication of NOD

nidus (ˈnaɪdəs) NOUN, *plural* **-di** (-daɪ). [1] the nest in which insects or spiders deposit their eggs. [2] *Pathol* a focus of infection. [3] a cavity in which plant spores develop.
▷HISTORY C18: from Latin: NEST
▸ˈ**nidal** ADJECTIVE

niece (niːs) NOUN a daughter of one's sister or brother.
▷HISTORY C13: from Old French: niece, granddaughter, ultimately from Latin *neptis* granddaughter

Niederösterreich (ˈniːdərøːstəraɪç) NOUN the German name for **Lower Austria.**

Niedersachsen (ˈniːdərzaksən) NOUN the German name for **Lower Saxony.**

niello (nɪˈɛləʊ) NOUN, *plural* **-li** (-lɪ) *or* **-los.** [1] a black compound of sulphur and silver, lead, or copper used to incise a design on a metal surface. [2] the process of decorating surfaces with niello. [3] a surface or object decorated with niello. ◆ VERB **-los, -loing, -loed.** [4] (*tr*) to decorate or treat with niello.
▷HISTORY C19: from Italian from Latin *nigellus* blackish, from *niger* black
▸**niˈellist** NOUN

Niemen (ˈnjɛmɛn) NOUN the Polish name for the **Neman.**

Niersteiner (*German* ˈniːrʃtaɪnər) NOUN a white wine from the region around Nierstein, Germany.

nieve (niːv) NOUN *Scot and northern English, dialect* the closed hand; fist.
▷HISTORY C14: from Old Norse *hnefi*

Nièvre (*French* njɛvrə) NOUN a department of central France, in Burgundy region. Capital: Nevers. Pop.: 225 198 (1999). Area: 6888 sq. km (2686 sq. miles).

nife (naɪf, ˈnaɪfɪ) NOUN the earth's core, thought to be composed of nickel and iron.
▷HISTORY C20: from the chemical symbols *Ni* (nickel) and *Fe* (iron)

nifedipine (naɪˈfɛdɪpiːn) NOUN *Med* a calcium-channel blocker used in the treatment of hypertension, angina pectoris, and heart failure.

niff (nɪf) *Brit, slang* ◆ NOUN [1] a bad smell. ◆ VERB (*intr*) [2] to smell badly; stink.
▷HISTORY C20: perhaps from SNIFF
▸ˈ**niffy** ADJECTIVE

Niflheim (ˈnɪvəlˌheɪm) NOUN *Norse myth* the abode of the dead.
▷HISTORY Old Norse, literally: mist home

nifty (ˈnɪftɪ) ADJECTIVE **-tier, -tiest.** *Informal* [1] pleasing, apt, or stylish. [2] quick, agile: *he's nifty on his feet.*
▷HISTORY C19: of uncertain origin
▸ˈ**niftily** ADVERB ▸ˈ**niftiness** NOUN

nigella (naɪˈdʒɛlə) NOUN any plant of the ranunculaceous genus *Nigella*, from the Mediterranean and W Asia, esp *N. damascena:* see **love-in-a-mist.**
▷HISTORY New Latin, diminutive of Latin *niger* black, from the colour of the seeds

Niger NOUN [1] (niːˈʒɛə, ˈnaɪdʒə) a landlocked republic in West Africa: important since earliest times for its trans-Saharan trade routes; made a French colony in 1922 and became fully independent in 1960; exports peanuts and livestock. Official language: French. Religion: Muslim majority. Currency: franc. Capital: Niamey. Pop.: 10 355 000 (2001 est.). Area: 1 267 000 sq. km (489 000 sq. miles). [2] (ˈnaɪdʒə) a river in West Africa, rising in S Guinea and flowing in a great northward curve through Mali, then southwest through Niger and Nigeria to the Gulf of Guinea: the third longest river in Africa, with the largest delta, covering an area of 36 260 sq. km (14 000 sq. miles). Length: 4184 km (2600 miles). [3] (ˈnaɪdʒə) a state of W central Nigeria, formed in 1976 from part of North-Western State. Capital: Minna. Pop.: 2 775 526 (1995 est.). Area: 76 363 sq. km (29 476 sq. miles).

Niger-Congo NOUN [1] a family of languages of Africa consisting of the Bantu languages together with most of the languages of the coastal regions of West Africa. The chief branches are Benue-Congo (including Bantu), Kwa, Mande, and West Atlantic. ◆ ADJECTIVE [2] relating to or belonging to this family of languages.

Nigeria (naɪˈdʒɪərɪə) NOUN a republic in West Africa, on the Gulf of Guinea: Lagos annexed by the British in 1861; protectorates of Northern and Southern Nigeria formed in 1900 and united as a colony in 1914; gained independence as a member of the Commonwealth in 1960 (membership suspended from 1995 to 1999 following human rights violations); Eastern Region seceded as the Republic of Biafra for the duration of the severe civil war (1967–70); ruled by military governments from 1966. It consists of a belt of tropical rain forest in the south, with semidesert in the extreme north and highlands in the east; the main export is petroleum. Official language: English; Hausa, Ibo, and Yoruba are the chief regional languages. Religion: animist, Muslim, and Christian. Currency: naira. Capital: Abuja. Pop.: 126 636 000 (2001 est.). Area: 923 773 sq. km (356 669 sq. miles).

Nigerian (naɪˈdʒɪərɪən) ADJECTIVE [1] of or relating to Nigeria or its inhabitants. ◆ NOUN [2] a native or inhabitant of Nigeria.

Nigerien (niːˈʒɛərɪən) ADJECTIVE [1] of or relating to Niger or its inhabitants. ◆ NOUN [2] a native or inhabitant of Niger.

Niger seed NOUN another name for **ramtil** (sense 2).

niggard (ˈnɪgəd) NOUN [1] a stingy person. ◆ ADJECTIVE [2] *Archaic* miserly.
▷HISTORY C14: perhaps of Scandinavian origin; related to Swedish dialect *nygg* and Old English *hnēaw* stingy

niggardly (ˈnɪgədlɪ) ADJECTIVE [1] stingy or ungenerous. [2] meagre: *a niggardly salary.* ◆ ADVERB [3] stingily; grudgingly.
▸ˈ**niggardliness** NOUN

nigger (ˈnɪgə) NOUN [1] *Offensive* **a** another name for a Negro. **b** (*as modifier*): *nigger minstrels.* [2] *Offensive* a member of any dark-skinned race. [3] **nigger in the woodpile.** a hidden snag or hindrance.
▷HISTORY C18: from C16 dialect *neeger*, from French *nègre*, from Spanish NEGRO[1]

niggle (ˈnɪgəl) VERB [1] (*intr*) to find fault continually. [2] (*intr*) to be preoccupied with details; fuss. [3] (*tr*) to irritate; worry. ◆ NOUN [4] a slight or trivial objection or complaint. [5] a slight feeling as of misgiving, uncertainty, etc.
▷HISTORY C16: from Scandinavian; related to Norwegian *nigla.* Compare NIGGARD
▸ˈ**niggler** NOUN ▸ˈ**niggly** ADJECTIVE

niggling (ˈnɪglɪŋ) ADJECTIVE [1] petty. [2] fussy. [3] irritating. [4] requiring painstaking work. ◆ NOUN [5] an act or instance of niggling.
▸ˈ**nigglingly** ADVERB

nigh (naɪ) ADJECTIVE, ADVERB, PREPOSITION an archaic, poetic, or dialect word for **near.**
▷HISTORY Old English *nēah, nēh;* related to German *nah*, Old Frisian *nei.* Compare NEAR, NEXT

night (naɪt) NOUN [1] the period of darkness each 24 hours between sunset and sunrise, as distinct from day. [2] (*modifier*) of, occurring, working, etc., at night: *a night nurse.* [3] the occurrence of this period considered as a unit: *four nights later they left.* [4] the period between sunset and retiring to bed; evening. [5] the time between bedtime and morning: *she spent the night alone.* [6] the weather conditions of the night: *a clear night.* [7] the activity or experience of a person during a night. [8] (*sometimes capital*) any evening designated for a special observance or function. [9] nightfall or dusk. [10] a state or period of gloom, ignorance, etc. [11] **make a night of it.** to go out and celebrate for most of the night. [12] **night and day.** continually: *that baby cries night and day.* ◆ Related adjective: **nocturnal.**
▷HISTORY Old English *niht;* compare Dutch *nacht*, Latin *nox*, Greek *nux*
▸ˈ**nightless** ADJECTIVE ▸ˈ**nightˌlike** ADJECTIVE

night blindness NOUN *Pathol* a nontechnical term for **nyctalopia.**
▸ˈ**nightˌblind** ADJECTIVE

night-blooming cereus NOUN any of several cacti of the genera *Hylocereus, Selenicereus*, etc., having large fragrant flowers that open at night.

nightcap (ˈnaɪtˌkæp) NOUN [1] a bedtime drink, esp an alcoholic or hot one. [2] a soft cap formerly worn in bed.

nightclothes (ˈnaɪtˌkləʊðz) PLURAL NOUN clothes worn in bed.

nightclub (ˈnaɪtˌklʌb) NOUN a place of entertainment open until late at night, usually offering food, drink, a floor show, dancing, etc.
▸ˈ**nightˌclubber** NOUN

night dancer NOUN (in Uganda) a person believed to employ the help of the dead in destroying other people.

nightdress (ˈnaɪtˌdrɛs) NOUN *Brit* a loose dress worn in bed by women. Also called: **nightgown, nightie.**

nightfall (ˈnaɪtˌfɔːl) NOUN the approach of darkness; dusk.

night fighter NOUN an interceptor aircraft used for operations at night.

nightgown (ˈnaɪtˌgaʊn) NOUN [1] another name for **nightdress.** [2] a man's nightshirt.

nighthawk (ˈnaɪtˌhɔːk) NOUN [1] Also called: **bullbat, mosquito hawk.** any American nightjar of the genus *Chordeiles* and related genera, having a dark plumage and, in the male, white patches on the wings and tail. [2] *Informal* another name for **night owl.**

night heron NOUN any nocturnal heron of the genus *Nycticorax* and related genera, having short legs and neck, a heavy body, and a short heavy bill.

nightie *or* **nighty** ('naɪtɪ) NOUN, *plural* **nighties**. *Informal* short for **nightdress**.

nightingale ('naɪtɪŋˌgeɪl) NOUN [1] a brownish European songbird, *Luscinia megarhynchos,* with a broad reddish-brown tail: well known for its musical song, usually heard at night. [2] any of various similar or related birds, such as *Luscinia luscinia* (**thrush nightingale**).
▷HISTORY Old English *nihtegale,* literally: night-singer, from NIGHT + *galan* to sing

Nightingale ward NOUN a long hospital ward with beds on either side and the nurses' station in the middle.

nightjar ('naɪtˌdʒɑː) NOUN any nocturnal bird of the family *Caprimulgidae,* esp *Caprimulgus europaeus* (**European nightjar**): order *Caprimulgiformes*. They have a cryptic plumage and large eyes and feed on insects.
▷HISTORY C17: NIGHT + JAR², so called from its discordant cry

night latch NOUN a door lock that is operated by means of a knob on the inside and a key on the outside.

night letter NOUN (formerly, in the US and Canada) a telegram sent for delivery the next day at a cheaper rate than a regular telegram.

nightlife ('naɪtˌlaɪf) NOUN social life or entertainment taking place in the late evening or night, as in nightclubs.

night-light NOUN a dim light burning at night, esp for children.

nightlong ('naɪtˌlɒŋ) ADJECTIVE, ADVERB throughout the night.

nightly ('naɪtlɪ) ADJECTIVE [1] happening or relating to each night. [2] happening at night. ◆ ADVERB [3] at night or each night.

nightmare ('naɪtˌmɛə) NOUN [1] a terrifying or deeply distressing dream. [2] **a** an event or condition resembling a terrifying dream: *the nightmare of shipwreck.* **b** (*as modifier*): *a nightmare drive.* [3] a thing that is feared. [4] (formerly) an evil spirit supposed to harass or suffocate sleeping people.
▷HISTORY C13 (meaning: incubus; C16: bad dream): from NIGHT + Old English *mare, mære* evil spirit, from Germanic; compare Old Norse *mara* incubus, Polish *zmora,* French *cauchemar* nightmare
▸'**nightˌmarish** ADJECTIVE ▸'**nightˌmarishly** ADVERB
▸'**nightˌmarishness** NOUN

night-night SENTENCE SUBSTITUTE an informal word for **good night**.

night nurse NOUN a nurse whose duty is to look after a patient or patients during the night.

night owl *or* **hawk** NOUN *Informal* a person who is or prefers to be up and about late at night.

night raven NOUN *Poetic* any bird, esp the night heron, that is most active at night.

nightrider ('naɪtˌraɪdə) NOUN a member of a band of mounted and usually masked Whites in the southern US who carried out acts of revenge and intimidation at night after the Civil War.
▸'**nightˌriding** NOUN

night robe NOUN a US and Canadian name for **nightdress**.

nights (naɪts) ADVERB *Informal* at night, esp regularly: *he works nights.*

night safe NOUN a safe built into the outside wall of a bank, in which customers can deposit money at times when the bank is closed.

night school NOUN an educational institution that holds classes in the evening for those who are not free during the day.

nightshade ('naɪtˌʃeɪd) NOUN [1] any of various solanaceous plants, such as deadly nightshade, woody nightshade, and black nightshade. [2] See **enchanter's nightshade**.
▷HISTORY Old English *nihtscada,* apparently NIGHT + SHADE, referring to the poisonous or soporific qualities of these plants

night shift NOUN [1] a group of workers who work a shift during the night in an industry or occupation where a day shift or a back shift are also worked. [2] the period worked. ◆ See also **back shift**.

nightshirt ('naɪtˌʃɜːt) NOUN a loose knee-length or longer shirtlike garment worn in bed by men.

night soil NOUN human excrement collected at night from cesspools, privies, etc., and sometimes used as a fertilizer.

nightspot ('naɪtˌspɒt) NOUN an informal word for **nightclub**.

night stick NOUN a US and Canadian name for **truncheon**.

night terrors PLURAL NOUN a condition in which a person, usually a child, suddenly starts from sleep in a state of extreme fear but cannot later remember the incident.

night-time NOUN **a** the time from sunset to sunrise; night as distinct from day. **b** (*as modifier*): *a night-time prowler.*

night watch NOUN [1] a watch or guard kept at night, esp for security. [2] the period of time the watch is kept. [3] a person who keeps such a watch; night watchman.

night watchman NOUN [1] Also called: **night watch**. a person who keeps guard at night on a factory, public building, etc. [2] *Cricket* a batsman sent in to bat to play out time when a wicket has fallen near the end of a day's play.

nightwear ('naɪtˌwɛə) NOUN apparel worn in bed or before retiring to bed; pyjamas, nightdress, dressing gown, etc.

nigrescent (naɪ'grɛsᵊnt) ADJECTIVE blackish; dark.
▷HISTORY C18: from Latin *nigrescere* to grow black, from *niger* black; see NEGRO¹
▸**ni'grescence** NOUN

nigritude ('nɪgrɪˌtjuːd) NOUN *Rare* blackness; darkness.
▷HISTORY C17: from Latin *nigritūdō,* from *niger* black

nigrosine ('nɪgrəˌsiːn, -sɪn) *or* **nigrosin** ('nɪgrəsɪn) NOUN any of a class of black pigments and dyes obtained from aniline: used in inks and shoe polishes and for dyeing textiles.
▷HISTORY C19: from Latin *niger* black + -OSE¹ + -INE¹

NIHE (in Ireland) ABBREVIATION FOR National Institute for Higher Education.

nihil *Latin* ('naɪhɪl, 'niːhɪl) NOUN nil; nothing.

nihilism ('naɪɪˌlɪzəm) NOUN [1] a complete denial of all established authority and institutions. [2] *Philosophy* an extreme form of scepticism that systematically rejects all values, belief in existence, the possibility of communication, etc. [3] a revolutionary doctrine of destruction for its own sake. [4] the practice or promulgation of terrorism.
▷HISTORY C19: from Latin *nihil* nothing + -ISM, on the model of German *Nihilismus*
▸'**nihilist** NOUN, ADJECTIVE ▸ˌ**nihil'istic** ADJECTIVE

Nihilism ('naɪɪˌlɪzəm) NOUN (in tsarist Russia) any of several revolutionary doctrines that upheld terrorism.

nihility (naɪ'hɪlɪtɪ) NOUN the state or condition of being nothing; nothingness; nullity.

nihil obstat ('ɒbstæt) the phrase used by a Roman Catholic censor to declare publication inoffensive to faith or morals.
▷HISTORY Latin, literally: nothing hinders

Nihon ('niː'hɒn) NOUN transliteration of a Japanese name for **Japan**.

NII (in Britain) ABBREVIATION FOR nuclear installations inspectorate.

Niigata ('niːɪˌgɑːtə) NOUN a port in central Japan, on NW Honshu at the mouth of the Shinano River: the chief port on the Sea of Japan. Pop.: 494 785 (1995).

Nijmegen ('naɪˌmeɪgən; *Dutch* 'nɛimeːxə) NOUN an industrial town in the E Netherlands, in Gelderland province on the Waal River: the oldest town in the country; scene of the signing (1678) of the peace treaty between Louis XIV, the Netherlands, Spain, and the Holy Roman Empire. Pop.: 151 864 (1999 est.). Latin name: **Noviomagus**. German name: **Nimwegen**.

-nik SUFFIX FORMING NOUNS denoting a person associated with a specified state, belief, or quality: *beatnik; refusenik.*
▷HISTORY C20: from Russian *-nik,* as in SPUTNIK, and influenced by Yiddish *-nik* (agent suffix)

Nikaria (nɪ'kɛərɪə, naɪ-) NOUN another name for **Icaria**.

nikau *or* **nikau palm** ('niːkaʊ) NOUN a palm tree of the genus *Rhopalostylis,* esp *R. sapida,* native to New Zealand. The leaves were used by the Maoris to build their whares and the top of the stem is sometimes eaten.
▷HISTORY Maori

Nike ('naɪkiː) NOUN *Greek myth* the winged goddess of victory. Roman counterpart: **Victoria**.
▷HISTORY from Greek: victory

Nikkei Stock Average ('nɪkeɪ) NOUN an index of prices on the Tokyo Stock Exchange.
▷HISTORY C20: from *Nik(on) Kei(zai Shimbun),* a Japanese newspaper group

Nikko ('niːkəʊ) NOUN a town in central Japan, on NE Honshu: a major pilgrimage centre, with a 4th-century Shinto shrine, a Buddhist temple (767), and the shrines and mausoleums of the Tokugawa shoguns. Pop.: 20 128 (1990).

Nikolainkaupunki (*Finnish* ˌnikəlaɪn'kaupuŋki) NOUN the former name of **Vaasa**.

Nikolayev (*Russian* nika'lajɪf) NOUN a city in the S Ukraine on the Southern Bug about 64 km (40 miles) from the Black Sea: founded as a naval base in 1788; one of the leading Black Sea ports. Pop.: 517 900 (1998 est.). Former name: **Vernoleninsk**.

nil (nɪl) NOUN another word for nothing: used esp in the scoring of certain games.
▷HISTORY C19: from Latin

nil desperandum ('nɪl ˌdɛspə'rændəm) SENTENCE SUBSTITUTE never despair.
▷HISTORY from Latin, literally: nothing to be despaired of

Nile (naɪl) NOUN a river in Africa, rising in S central Burundi in its remotest headstream, the **Luvironza**: flows into Lake Victoria and leaves the lake as the **Victoria Nile**, flowing to Lake Albert, which is drained by the **Albert Nile**, becoming the White Nile on the border between Uganda and the Sudan; joined by its chief tributary, the **Blue Nile** (which rises near Lake Tana, Ethiopia) at Khartoum, and flows north to its delta on the Mediterranean; the longest river in the world. Length: (from the source of the Luvironza to the Mediterranean) 6741 km (4187 miles).

Nile blue NOUN **a** a pale greenish-blue colour. **b** (*as adjective*): *a Nile-blue carpet.*

Nile green NOUN **a** a pale bluish-green colour. **b** (*as adjective*): *a Nile-green dress.*

nilgai ('nɪlgaɪ), **nilghau,** *or* **nylghau** ('nɪlgɔː) NOUN, *plural* **-gai, -gais** *or* **-ghau, -ghaus**. a large Indian antelope, *Boselaphus tragocamelus.* The male is blue-grey with white markings and has small horns; the female is brownish and has no horns.
▷HISTORY C19: from Hindi *nīlgāw* blue bull, from Sanskrit *nīla* dark blue + *go* bull

Nilgiri Hills ('nɪlgɪrɪ) *or* **Nilgiris** PLURAL NOUN a plateau in S India, in Tamil Nadu. Average height: 2000 m (6500 ft.), reaching 2635 m (8647 ft.) in Doda Betta.

Nilometer (naɪ'lɒmɪtə) NOUN *Archaic* a graduated pillar by which the rise and fall of the Nile can be measured.

Nilo-Saharan (ˌnaɪləʊsə'hɑːrən) NOUN [1] a family of languages of Africa, spoken chiefly by Nilotic peoples in a region extending from the Sahara to Kenya and Tanzania, including the Chari-Nile, Saharan, Songhai, and other branches. Classification is complicated by the fact that many languages spoken in this region belong to the unrelated Afro-Asiatic, Kordofanian, and Niger-Congo families. ◆ ADJECTIVE [2] relating to or belonging to this family of languages.

Nilotic (naɪ'lɒtɪk) ADJECTIVE [1] of or relating to the Nile. [2] of, relating to, or belonging to a tall Negroid pastoral people inhabiting the S Sudan, parts of Kenya and Uganda, and neighbouring countries. [3] relating to or belonging to the group of languages spoken by the Nilotic peoples. ◆ NOUN [4] a group of languages of E Africa, including Luo, Dinka, and Masai, now generally regarded as belonging to the Chari-Nile branch of the Nilo-Saharan family.
▷HISTORY C17: via Latin from Greek *Neilotikós,* from *Neilos* the NILE

nil return NOUN a reply of zero to a request for a quantified reply.

nim (nɪm) NOUN a game in which two players alternately remove one or more small items, such as

matchsticks, from one of several rows or piles, the object being to take (or avoid taking) the last item remaining on the table.
▷**HISTORY** C20: perhaps from archaic *nim* to take, from Old English *niman*

nimble (ˈnɪmbᵊl) ADJECTIVE 1 agile, quick, and neat in movement: *nimble fingers*. 2 alert; acute: *a nimble intellect*.
▷**HISTORY** Old English *nǣmel* quick to grasp, and *numol* quick at seizing, both from *niman* to take
▸**ˈnimbleness** NOUN ▸**ˈnimbly** ADVERB

nimblewit (ˈnɪmbəlˌwɪt) NOUN *Chiefly US and Canadian* an alert, bright, and clever person.
▸**ˈnimbleˌwitted** ADJECTIVE

nimbostratus (ˌnɪmbəʊˈstreɪtəs, -ˈstrɑːtəs) NOUN, *plural* **-ti** (-taɪ). a dark-coloured rain-bearing stratus cloud.

nimbus (ˈnɪmbəs) NOUN, *plural* **-bi** (-baɪ) *or* **-buses**. 1 **a** a dark grey rain-bearing cloud. **b** (*in combination*): *cumulonimbus clouds*. 2 **a** an emanation of light surrounding a saint or deity. **b** a representation of this emanation. 3 a surrounding aura or atmosphere.
▷**HISTORY** C17: from Latin: cloud, radiance
▸**ˈnimbused** ADJECTIVE

NIMBY (ˈnɪmbɪ) NOUN ACRONYM FOR not in my back yard: a person who objects to the occurrence of something if it will affect them or take place in their locality.

nimbyism (ˈnɪmbɪˌɪzəm) NOUN the practice of objecting to something that will affect one or take place in one's locality.

Nîmes (*French* nim) NOUN a city in S France: Roman remains including an amphitheatre and the Pont du Gard aqueduct. Pop.: 133 424 (1999).

nimiety (nɪˈmaɪɪtɪ) NOUN, *plural* **-ties**. a rare word for **excess**.
▷**HISTORY** C16: from Late Latin *nimietās*, from Latin *nimis* too much

niminy-piminy (ˈnɪmɪnɪˈpɪmɪnɪ) ADJECTIVE excessively refined; prim.
▷**HISTORY** C19: imitative of a prim affected enunciation

nimonic alloy (nɪˈmɒnɪk) NOUN any of various nickel-based alloys used at high temperatures, as in gas turbine blades.
▷**HISTORY** C20: from NI(CKEL) + MO(LYBDENUM) + -IC

n'importe *French* (nɛ̃pɔrt) no matter.

nimps (nɪmps) ADJECTIVE *Northern English, dialect* easy.

Nimrod (ˈnɪmrɒd) NOUN 1 *Old Testament* a hunter, who was famous for his prowess (Genesis 10:8–9). 2 a person who is dedicated to or skilled in hunting. Douay spelling: **Nemrod**.
▸**Nimˈrodian** *or* **Nimˈrodic** ADJECTIVE

Nimrud (nɪmˈruːd) NOUN an ancient city in Assyria, near the present-day city of Mosul (Iraq): founded in about 1250 B.C. and destroyed by the Medes in 612 B.C.; excavated by Sir Austen Henry Layard.

Nimwegen (ˈnɪmveːgən) NOUN the German name for **Nijmegen**.

Niña (ˈniːnə; *Spanish* ˈniɲa) NOUN **the**. one of the three ships commanded by Columbus in 1492.

nincompoop (ˈnɪnkəmˌpuːp, ˈnɪŋ-) NOUN a stupid person; fool; idiot.
▷**HISTORY** C17: of unknown origin

nine (naɪn) NOUN 1 the cardinal number that is the sum of one and eight. See also **number** (sense 1). 2 a numeral, 9, IX, etc., representing this number. 3 something representing, represented by, or consisting of nine units, such as a playing card with nine symbols on it. 4 Also: **nine o'clock**. nine hours after noon or midnight: *the play starts at nine*. 5 **dressed (up) to the nines**. *Informal* elaborately dressed. 6 **999**. (in Britain) the telephone number of the emergency services. 7 **nine to five**. normal office hours: *he works nine to five; a nine-to-five job*. ◆ DETERMINER 8 **a** amounting to nine: *nine days*. **b** (*as pronoun*): *nine of the ten are ready*. ◆ Related prefix: **nona-**.
▷**HISTORY** Old English *nigon*; related to Gothic *niun*, Latin *novem*

nine-days wonder NOUN something that arouses great interest, but only for a short period.

nine-eleven, 9-11, *or* **9/11** NOUN the 11th of September 2001, the day on which the twin towers of the World Trade Center in New York were flown into and destroyed by aeroplanes hijacked by Islamic fundamentalists. Also called: **September eleven**.
▷**HISTORY** C21: from the US custom of expressing dates in figures, the day of the month following the number of the month

ninefold (ˈnaɪnˌfəʊld) ADJECTIVE 1 equal to or having nine times as many or as much. 2 composed of nine parts. ◆ ADVERB 3 by or up to nine times as many or as much.

ninepins (ˈnaɪnˌpɪnz) NOUN 1 (*functioning as singular*) another name for **skittles**. 2 (*singular*) one of the pins used in this game.

nineteen (ˌnaɪnˈtiːn) NOUN 1 the cardinal number that is the sum of ten and nine and is a prime number. See also **number** (sense 1). 2 a numeral, 19, XIX, etc., representing this number. 3 something represented by, representing, or consisting of 19 units. 4 **talk nineteen to the dozen**. to talk incessantly. ◆ DETERMINER 5 **a** amounting to nineteen: *nineteen pictures*. **b** (*as pronoun*): *only nineteen voted*.
▷**HISTORY** Old English *nigontīne*

nineteenth (ˌnaɪnˈtiːnθ) ADJECTIVE 1 (*usually prenominal*) **a** coming after the eighteenth in numbering or counting order, position, time, etc., being the ordinal number of *nineteen*. Often written: 19th. **b** (*as noun*): *the nineteenth was rainy*. ◆ NOUN 2 **a** one of 19 approximately equal parts of something. **b** (*as modifier*): *a nineteenth part*. 3 the fraction that is equal to one divided by 19 (1/19).

nineteenth hole NOUN *Golf, slang* the bar in a golf clubhouse.
▷**HISTORY** C20: from its being the next objective after a standard 18-hole round

nineteenth man NOUN 1 *Australian Rules football* the first reserve in a team. 2 any person acting as a reserve or substitute.

ninetieth (ˈnaɪntɪɪθ) ADJECTIVE 1 (*usually prenominal*) **a** being the ordinal number of *ninety* in numbering or counting order, position, time, etc. Often written: 90th. **b** (*as noun*): *the ninetieth in succession*. ◆ NOUN 2 **a** one of 90 approximately equal parts of something. **b** (*as modifier*): *a ninetieth part*. 3 the fraction equal to one divided by 90 (1/90).

ninety (ˈnaɪntɪ) NOUN, *plural* **-ties**. 1 the cardinal number that is the product of ten and nine. See also **number** (sense 1). 2 a numeral, 90, XC, etc., representing this number. 3 something represented by, representing, or consisting of 90 units. ◆ DETERMINER 4 **a** amounting to ninety: *ninety times out of a hundred*. **b** (*as pronoun*): *at least ninety are thought to be missing*.
▷**HISTORY** Old English *nigontig*

Nineveh (ˈnɪnɪvə) NOUN the ancient capital of Assyria, on the River Tigris opposite the present-day city of Mosul (N Iraq): at its height in the 8th and 7th centuries B.C.; destroyed in 612 B.C. by the Medes and Babylonians.

Ninevite (ˈnɪnˌɪvaɪt) NOUN a native or inhabitant of Nineveh, the ancient capital of Assyria.

Ningbo *or* **Ningpo** (ˈnɪŋˈpəʊ) NOUN a port in E China, in NE Zhejiang, on the Yung River, about 20 km (12 miles) from its mouth at Hangzhou Bay: one of the first sites of European settlement in China. Pop.: 1 704 819 (1999 est.).

Ningsia *or* **Ninghsia** (ˈnɪŋˈʃjɑː) NOUN 1 a former province of NW China: mostly included in the Inner Mongolian AR in 1956, with the smaller part constituted as the Ningxia Hui AR in 1958. 2 the former name of **Yinchuan**.

Ningxia Hui Autonomous Region (ˈnɪŋˈʃjɑː ˈhuːɪ) NOUN an administrative division of NW China, south of the Inner Mongolian AR. Capital: Yinchuan. Pop.: 5 620 000 (2000 est.). Area: 66 400 sq. km (25 896 sq. miles).

ninhydrin (nɪnˈhaɪdrɪn) NOUN a chemical reagent used for the detection and analysis of primary amines, esp amino acids, with which it forms a derivative with an intense purple colour.
▷**HISTORY** C20: from the chemical name *triketo hydrindene*

ninja (ˈnɪndʒə) NOUN, *plural* **-ja** *or* **-jas**. (*sometimes capital*) a person skilled in **ninjutsu**, a Japanese martial art characterized by stealthy movement and camouflage.
▷**HISTORY** Japanese

ninny (ˈnɪnɪ) NOUN, *plural* **-nies**. a dull-witted person.
▷**HISTORY** C16: perhaps from *an innocent* simpleton
▸**ˈninnyish** ADJECTIVE

ninon (ˈniːnɒn, ˈnaɪnɒn; *French* ninɔ̃) NOUN a fine strong silky fabric.
▷**HISTORY** C20: from French

ninth (naɪnθ) ADJECTIVE 1 (*usually prenominal*) **a** coming after the eighth in counting order, position, time, etc.; being the ordinal number of *nine*. Often written: 9th. **b** (*as noun*): *he came on the ninth; ninth in line*. ◆ NOUN 2 **a** one of nine equal or nearly equal parts of an object, quantity, measurement, etc. **b** (*as modifier*): *a ninth part*. 3 the fraction equal to one divided by nine (1/9). 4 *Music* **a** an interval of one octave plus a second. **b** one of two notes constituting such an interval. **c** See **ninth chord**. ◆ ADVERB 5 Also: **ninthly**. after the eighth person, position, event, etc. ◆ SENTENCE CONNECTOR 6 Also: **ninthly**. as the ninth point: linking what follows to the previous statement.
▷**HISTORY** Old English *nigotha*; related to Old High German *niunto*, Old Norse *nīundi*

ninth chord NOUN a chord much used in jazz and pop, consisting of a major or minor triad with the seventh and ninth added above the root. Often shortened to: **ninth**.

Niobe (ˈnaɪəbɪ) NOUN *Greek myth* a daughter of Tantalus, whose children were slain after she boasted of them: although turned into stone, she continued to weep.
▸**Niobean** (naɪˈəʊbɪən) ADJECTIVE

niobic (naɪˈəʊbɪk, -ˈɒbɪk) ADJECTIVE of or containing niobium in the pentavalent state. Also: **columbic**.

niobite (ˈnaɪəˌbaɪt) NOUN another name for **columbite**.
▷**HISTORY** C19: NIOBIUM + -ITE[1]

niobium (naɪˈəʊbɪəm) NOUN a ductile white superconductive metallic element that occurs principally in columbite and tantalite: used in steel alloys. Symbol: Nb; atomic no.: 41; atomic wt.: 92.90638; valency: 2, 3, or 5; relative density: 8.57; melting pt.: 2469±10°C; boiling pt.: 4744°C. Former name: **columbium**.
▷**HISTORY** C19: from New Latin, from NIOBE (daughter of Tantalus), so named because it occurred in TANTALITE

niobous (naɪˈəʊbəs) ADJECTIVE of or containing niobium in the trivalent state. Also: **columbous**.

Niort (*French* njɔr) NOUN a market town in W France. Pop.: 58 660 (1990).

nip[1] (nɪp) VERB **nips, nipping, nipped**. (*mainly tr*) 1 to catch or tightly compress, as between a finger and the thumb; pinch. 2 (often foll by *off*) to remove by clipping, biting, etc. 3 (when *intr*, often foll by *at*) to give a small sharp bite (to): *the dog nipped at his heels*. 4 (esp of the cold) to affect with a stinging sensation. 5 to harm through cold: *the frost nipped the young plants*. 6 to check or destroy the growth of (esp in the phrase **nip in the bud**). 7 *Slang* to steal. 8 (*intr*; foll by *along, up, out*, etc.) *Brit informal* to hurry; dart. 9 *Slang, chiefly US and Canadian* to snatch. ◆ NOUN 10 the act of nipping; a pinch, snip, etc. 11 **a** a frosty or chilly quality. **b** severe frost or cold: *the first nip of winter*. 12 a small piece or quantity: *he went out for a nip of fresh air*. 13 a sharp flavour or tang. 14 *Archaic* a taunting remark. 15 **nip and tuck**. **a** *Chiefly US and Canadian* neck and neck. **b** *Informal* plastic surgery performed for cosmetic reasons. 16 **put the nips in**. *Austral and NZ, slang* to exert pressure on someone, esp in order to extort money.
▷**HISTORY** C14: of Scandinavian origin; compare Old Norse *hnippa* to prod

nip[2] (nɪp) NOUN 1 a small drink of spirits; dram. 2 *Chiefly Brit* a measure of spirits usually equal to one sixth of a gill. ◆ VERB **nips, nipping, nipped**. 3 to drink (spirits), esp habitually in small amounts.
▷**HISTORY** C18: shortened from *nipperkin* a vessel holding a half-pint or less, of uncertain origin; compare Dutch *nippen* to sip

Nip (nɪp) NOUN *Slang* a derogatory word for a **Japanese**.
▷**HISTORY** C20: short for *Nipponese*

nipa (ˈniːpə, ˈnaɪ-) NOUN 1 a palm tree, *Nipa fruticans*, of S and SE Asia, having feathery leaves,

used for thatching, and edible fruit. 2 the fruit or thatch obtained from this tree. 3 the sap of this tree, used to make a liquor.
▷HISTORY C16: from Malay *nīpah*

nip curn (kɜːn) NOUN *Northern English, dialect* a tightfisted woman.
▷HISTORY from NIP (to bite) and *curn* currant; the allusion being that the currant is divided in two to make it go further

Nipigon (ˈnɪpəɡɒn) NOUN **Lake.** a lake in central Canada, in NW Ontario, draining into Lake Superior via the **Nipigon River.** Area: 4843 sq. km (1870 sq. miles).

Nipissing (ˈnɪpɪsɪŋ) NOUN **Lake.** a lake in central Canada, in E Ontario between the Ottawa River and Georgian Bay. Area: 855 sq. km (330 sq. miles).

nipper (ˈnɪpə) NOUN 1 a person or thing that nips. 2 the large pincer-like claw of a lobster, crab, or similar crustacean. 3 *Informal* a small child. 4 *Austral* a type of small prawn used as bait.

nippers (ˈnɪpəz) PLURAL NOUN an instrument or tool, such as a pair of pliers, for snipping, pinching, or squeezing.

nipping (ˈnɪpɪŋ) ADJECTIVE 1 sharp and biting: *a nipping wind.* 2 sarcastic; bitter.
▸**ˈnippingly** ADVERB

nipple (ˈnɪpᵊl) NOUN 1 Also called: **mamilla, papilla, teat.** the small conical projection in the centre of the areola of each breast, which in women contains the outlet of the milk ducts. Related adjective: **mamillary.** 2 something resembling a nipple in shape or function. 3 Also called: **grease nipple.** a small drilled bush, usually screwed into a bearing, through which grease is introduced. 4 *US and Canadian* an informal word for **dummy** (sense 11).
▷HISTORY C16: from earlier *neble, nible,* perhaps from NEB, NIB

nipplewort (ˈnɪpᵊlˌwɜːt) NOUN an annual Eurasian plant, *Lapsana communis,* with pointed oval leaves and small yellow flower heads: family *Asteraceae* (composites).

Nippon (ˈnɪpɒn) NOUN transliteration of a Japanese name for **Japan.**

Nipponese (ˌnɪpəˈniːz) ADJECTIVE, NOUN another word for **Japanese.**

Nippur (nɪˈpʊə) NOUN an ancient Sumerian and Babylonian city, the excavated site of which is in SE Iraq: an important religious centre, abandoned in the 12th or 13th century.

nippy (ˈnɪpɪ) ADJECTIVE **-pier, -piest.** 1 (of weather) chilly, keen, or frosty. 2 *Brit informal* **a** quick; nimble; active. **b** (of a motor vehicle) small and relatively powerful. 3 (of the taste of food) biting, sharp, or pungent. 4 (of a dog) inclined to bite.
▸**ˈnippily** ADVERB ▸**ˈnippiness** NOUN

NIREX (ˈnaɪreks) NOUN ACRONYM FOR Nuclear Industry Radioactive Waste Executive.

nirvana (nɪəˈvɑːnə, nɜː-) NOUN *Buddhism, Hinduism* final release from the cycle of reincarnation attained by extinction of all desires and individual existence, culminating (in Buddhism) in absolute blessedness, or (in Hinduism) in absorption into Brahman.
▷HISTORY C19: from Sanskrit: extinction, literally: a blowing out, from *nir-* out + *vāti* it blows
▸**nirˈvanic** ADJECTIVE

Niš *or* **Nish** (niːʃ) NOUN an industrial town in E Serbia and Montenegro, in SE Serbia: situated on routes between central Europe and the Aegean. Pop.: 182 583 (1991).

Nisan (niːˈsan) NOUN (in the Jewish calendar) the first month of the year according to biblical reckoning and the seventh month of the civil year, usually falling within March and April.
▷HISTORY from Hebrew

Nisei (ˈniːseɪ) NOUN a native-born citizen of the United States or Canada whose parents were Japanese immigrants.
▷HISTORY Japanese, literally: second generation

nisgul (ˈnɪsɡʌl) NOUN *Midland English, dialect* the smallest and weakest bird in a brood of chickens.

nish (nɪʃ) NOUN *Northern English, dialect* nothing.

Nishapur (ˌniːʃɑːˈpʊə) NOUN a town in NE Iran, at an altitude of 1195 m (3920 ft.): birthplace and burial place of Omar Khayyám. Pop.: 135 681 (1991).

Nishinomiya (ˌniːʃɪˈnɒmɪjə) NOUN an industrial city in central Japan, on S Honshu, northwest of Osaka. Pop.: 390 388 (1995).

nisi (ˈnaɪsaɪ) ADJECTIVE (*postpositive*) *Law* (of a court order) coming into effect on a specified date unless cause is shown within a certain period why it should not: *a decree nisi.*
▷HISTORY C19: from Latin: unless, if not

nisi prius (ˈpraɪəs) NOUN 1 *English legal history* **a** a direction that a case be brought up to Westminster for trial before a single judge and a jury. **b** the writ giving this direction. **c** trial before the justices taking the assizes. 2 (in the US) a court where civil actions are tried by a single judge sitting with a jury as distinguished from an appellate court.
▷HISTORY C15: from Latin: unless previously

Nissen hut (ˈnɪsᵊn) NOUN a military shelter of semicircular cross section, made of corrugated steel sheet. US and Canadian equivalent: **Quonset hut.**
▷HISTORY C20: named after Lt Col. Peter *Nissen* (1871–1930), British mining engineer, its inventor

nisus (ˈnaɪsəs) NOUN, *plural* **-sus.** an impulse towards or striving after a goal.
▷HISTORY C17: from Latin: effort, from *nītī* to strive

nit¹ (nɪt) NOUN 1 the egg of a louse, usually adhering to human hair. 2 the larva of a louse or similar insect.
▷HISTORY Old English *hnitu;* related to Dutch *neet,* Old High German *hniz*

nit² (nɪt) NOUN a unit of luminance equal to 1 candela per square metre.
▷HISTORY C20: from Latin *nitor* brightness

nit³ (nɪt) NOUN *Informal, chiefly Brit* short for **nitwit.**

nit⁴ (nɪt) NOUN a unit of information equal to 1.44 bits. Also called: **nepit.**
▷HISTORY C20: from *N(apierian dig)it*

nit⁵ (nɪt) NOUN **keep nit.** *Austral informal* to keep watch, esp during illegal activity.
▷HISTORY C19: from NIX¹

niter (ˈnaɪtə) NOUN the usual US spelling of **nitre.**

niterie (ˈnaɪtərɪ, -trɪ) NOUN *Slang* a nightclub.

Niterói (*Portuguese* niteˈrɔi) NOUN a port in SE Brazil, on Guanabara Bay opposite Rio de Janeiro: contains Brazil's chief shipyards. Pop.: 458 465 (2000). Also called: **Nictheroy.**

nither (ˈnaɪðə) VERB (*intr*) *Northern English, dialect* to shiver.

nitid (ˈnɪtɪd) ADJECTIVE *Poetic* bright; glistening.
▷HISTORY C17: from Latin *nitidus,* from *nitēre* to shine

niton (ˈnaɪtɒn) NOUN a less common name for **radon.**
▷HISTORY C20: from Latin *nitēre* to shine

nit-picking *Informal* ◆ NOUN 1 a concern with insignificant details, esp with the intention of finding fault. ◆ ADJECTIVE 2 showing such a concern; fussy.
▷HISTORY C20: from NIT¹ + PICK¹
▸**ˈnit-ˌpicker** NOUN

nitramine (ˈnaɪtrəˌmiːn) NOUN another name for **tetryl.**

nitrate (ˈnaɪtreɪt) NOUN 1 any salt or ester of nitric acid, such as sodium nitrate, $NaNO_3$. 2 a fertilizer consisting of or containing nitrate salts. ◆ VERB 3 (*tr*) to treat with nitric acid or a nitrate. 4 to convert or be converted into a nitrate. 5 to undergo or cause to undergo the chemical process in which a nitro group is introduced into a molecule.
▸**niˈtration** NOUN

nitrazepam (naɪˈtreɪzɪˌpæm, naɪˈtræz-) NOUN a synthetic chemical compound belonging to the benzodiazepine group of drugs; a minor tranquillizer used mainly in sleeping tablets, such as Mogadon. Formula: $C_{15}H_{11}N_3O_3$.
▷HISTORY C20: from NITRO- + *-azepam;* see DIAZEPAM

nitre *or US* **niter** (ˈnaɪtə) NOUN another name for **potassium nitrate** or **sodium nitrate.**
▷HISTORY C14: via Old French from Latin *nitrum,* from Greek *nitron* NATRON

nitric (ˈnaɪtrɪk) ADJECTIVE of or containing nitrogen, esp in the pentavalent state.

nitric acid NOUN a colourless or yellowish fuming corrosive liquid usually used in aqueous solution. It is an oxidizing agent and a strong monobasic acid: important in the manufacture of fertilizers, explosives, and many other chemicals. Formula: HNO_3. Former name: **aqua fortis.**

nitric bacteria PLURAL NOUN bacteria that convert nitrites to nitrates in the soil. See also **nitrobacteria.**

nitric oxide NOUN a colourless slightly soluble gas forming red fumes of nitrogen dioxide in air. Formula: NO. Systematic name: **nitrogen monoxide.**

nitride (ˈnaɪtraɪd) NOUN a compound of nitrogen with a more electropositive element, for example magnesium nitride, Mg_3N_2.

nitriding (ˈnaɪtraɪdɪŋ) NOUN a type of case-hardening in which steel is heated for long periods in ammonia vapour so that nitrogen produced by dissociation on the surface enters the steel.

nitrification (ˌnaɪtrɪfɪˈkeɪʃən) NOUN 1 the oxidation of the ammonium compounds in dead organic material into nitrites and nitrates by soil nitrobacteria, making nitrogen available to plants. See also **nitrogen cycle.** 2 **a** the addition of a nitro group to an organic compound. **b** the substitution of a nitro group for another group in an organic compound.

nitrify (ˈnaɪtrɪˌfaɪ) VERB **-fies, -fying, -fied.** (*tr*) 1 to treat or cause to react with nitrogen or a nitrogen compound. 2 to treat (soil) with nitrates. 3 (of nitrobacteria) to convert (ammonium compounds) into nitrates by oxidation.
▸**ˈnitriˌfiable** ADJECTIVE

nitrile (ˈnaɪtrɪl, -traɪl) NOUN any one of a class of organic compounds containing the monovalent group, -CN. Also called (not in technical usage): **cyanide.**

nitrite (ˈnaɪtraɪt) NOUN any salt or ester of nitrous acid.

nitro (ˈnaɪtrəʊ) NOUN *Slang* short for **nitroglycerine.**

nitro- *or before a vowel* **nitr-** COMBINING FORM 1 indicating that a chemical compound contains a nitro group, $-NO_2$: *nitrobenzene.* 2 indicating that a chemical compound is a nitrate ester: *nitrocellulose.*
▷HISTORY from Greek *nitron* NATRON

nitrobacteria (ˌnaɪtrəʊbækˈtɪərɪə) PLURAL NOUN, *singular* **-terium** (-ˈtɪərɪəm). soil bacteria of the order *Pseudomonadales* that are involved in nitrification, including species of *Nitrosomonas* and *Nitrobacter.*

nitrobenzene (ˌnaɪtrəʊˈbenziːn) NOUN a yellow oily toxic water-insoluble liquid compound, used as a solvent and in the manufacture of aniline. Formula: $C_6H_5NO_2$.

nitrocellulose (ˌnaɪtrəʊˈseljʊˌləʊs) NOUN another name (not in chemical usage) for **cellulose nitrate.**

Nitro-chalk NOUN *Trademark* a chemical fertilizer containing calcium carbonate and ammonium nitrate.

nitrochloroform (ˌnaɪtrəʊˈklɔːrəˌfɔːm) NOUN another name for **chloropicrin.**

nitro compound (ˈnaɪtrəʊ) NOUN any one of a class of usually organic compounds that contain the monovalent group, $-NO_2$ (**nitro group** or **radical**), linked to a carbon atom. The commonest example is nitrobenzene, $C_6H_5NO_2$.

nitrogen (ˈnaɪtrədʒən) NOUN **a** a colourless odourless relatively unreactive gaseous element that forms 78 per cent (by volume) of the air, occurs in many compounds, and is an essential constituent of proteins and nucleic acids: used in the manufacture of ammonia and other chemicals and as a refrigerant. Symbol: N; atomic no.: 7; atomic wt.: 14.00674; valency: 3 or 5; density: 1/2506 kg/m^3; melting pt.: –210.00°C; boiling pt.: –195.8°C. **b** (*as modifier*): *nitrogen cycle.*

nitrogen cycle NOUN the natural circulation of nitrogen by living organisms. Nitrates in the soil, derived from dead organic matter by bacterial action (see **nitrification, nitrogen fixation**), are absorbed and synthesized into complex organic compounds by plants and reduced to nitrates again when the plants and the animals feeding on them die and decay.

nitrogen dioxide NOUN a red-brown poisonous irritating gas that, at ordinary temperatures, exists in equilibrium with dinitrogen tetroxide. It is an intermediate in the manufacture of nitric acid, a nitrating agent, and an oxidizer for rocket fuels. Formula: NO_2.

nitrogen fixation NOUN 1 the conversion of atmospheric nitrogen into nitrogen compounds by

certain bacteria, such as *Rhizobium* in the root nodules of legumes. [2] a process, such as the Haber process, in which atmospheric nitrogen is converted into a nitrogen compound, used esp for the manufacture of fertilizer.
▸ **'nitrogen-ˌfixing** ADJECTIVE

nitrogenize *or* **nitrogenise** (naɪˈtrɒdʒɪˌnaɪz) VERB to combine or treat with nitrogen or a nitrogen compound.
▸ **niˌtrogeniˈzation** *or* **niˌtrogeniˈsation** NOUN

nitrogen monoxide NOUN the systematic name for **nitric oxide.**

nitrogen mustard NOUN any of a class of organic compounds resembling mustard gas in their molecular structure. General formula: $RN(CH_2CH_2Cl)_2$, where R is an organic group: important in the treatment of cancer.

nitrogenous (naɪˈtrɒdʒɪnəs) ADJECTIVE containing nitrogen or a nitrogen compound: *a nitrogenous fertilizer.*

nitrogen peroxide NOUN [1] an obsolete name for **nitrogen dioxide.** [2] the equilibrium mixture of nitrogen dioxide and dinitrogen tetroxide.

nitrogen tetroxide NOUN [1] another name for **dinitrogen tetroxide.** [2] a brown liquefied mixture of nitrogen dioxide and dinitrogen tetroxide, used as a nitrating, bleaching, and oxidizing agent.

nitroglycerine (ˌnaɪtrəʊˈglɪsəˌriːn) *or* **nitroglycerin** (ˌnaɪtrəʊˈglɪsərɪn) NOUN a pale yellow viscous explosive liquid substance made from glycerol and nitric and sulphuric acids and used in explosives and in medicine as a vasodilator. Formula: $CH_2NO_3CHNO_3CH_2NO_3$. Also called: **trinitroglycerine.**

nitrohydrochloric acid (ˌnaɪtrəʊˌhaɪdrəʊˈklɒrɪk) NOUN another name for **aqua regia.**

nitrometer (naɪˈtrɒmɪtə) NOUN an instrument for measuring the amount of nitrogen in a substance.
▸ **nitrometric** (ˌnaɪtrəʊˈmɛtrɪk) ADJECTIVE

nitromethane (ˌnaɪtrəʊˈmiːθeɪn) NOUN an oily colourless liquid obtained from methane and used as a solvent and rocket fuel and in the manufacture of synthetic resins. Formula: CH_3NO_2.

nitroparaffin (ˌnaɪtrəʊˈpærəfɪn) NOUN any of a class of colourless toxic compounds with the general formula $C_nH_{2n+1}NO_2$.

nitrophilous (naɪˈtrɒfɪləs) ADJECTIVE (of plants) growing in soil well supplied with nitrogen.

nitrosamine (ˌnaɪtrəʊsəˈmiːn, ˌnaɪtrəʊsˈæmiːn) NOUN any one of a class of neutral, usually yellow oily compounds containing the divalent group =NNO.

nitroso (naɪˈtrəʊsəʊ) NOUN (*modifier*) of, consisting of, or containing the monovalent group O:N-: *a nitroso compound.*
▷ **HISTORY** C19: from Latin *nitrōsus* full of natron; see NITRE

nitrosyl (ˈnaɪtrəsɪl, -ˌsaɪl) NOUN (*modifier*) another word for **nitroso**, esp when applied to inorganic compounds: *nitrosyl chloride.*
▷ **HISTORY** C19: see NITROSO

nitrous (ˈnaɪtrəs) ADJECTIVE of, derived from, or containing nitrogen, esp in a low valency state.
▷ **HISTORY** C17: from Latin *nitrōsus* full of natron

nitrous acid NOUN a weak monobasic acid known only in solution and in the form of nitrite salts. Formula: HNO_2. Systematic name: **dioxonitric(III) acid.**

nitrous bacteria PLURAL NOUN bacteria that convert ammonia to nitrites in the soil. See also **nitrobacteria.**

nitrous oxide NOUN a colourless nonflammable slightly soluble gas with a sweet smell: used as an anaesthetic in dentistry and surgery. Formula: N_2O. Systematic name: **dinitrogen oxide.** Also called: **laughing gas.**

nitty¹ (ˈnɪtɪ) ADJECTIVE **-tier, -tiest.** infested with nits.

nitty² (ˈnɪtɪ) ADJECTIVE **-tier, -tiest.** *Informal* foolish; stupid.
▷ **HISTORY** C20: from NITWIT

nitty-gritty (ˈnɪtɪˈgrɪtɪ) NOUN **the.** *Informal* the basic facts of a matter, situation, etc.; the core.
▷ **HISTORY** C20: perhaps rhyming compound formed from GRIT

nitwit (ˈnɪtˌwɪt) NOUN *Informal* a foolish person.
▷ **HISTORY** C20: perhaps from NIT¹ + WIT¹

Niue (ˈnjuːeɪ) NOUN an island in the S Pacific, between Tonga and the Cook Islands: annexed by New Zealand (1901); achieved full internal self-government in 1974. Chief town and port: Alofi. Pop.: 1977 (1993 est.). Area: 260 sq. km (100 sq. miles). Also called: **Savage Island.**

Niuean (njuːˈɪən) ADJECTIVE [1] of or relating to the S Pacific island of Niue or its inhabitants. ◆ NOUN [2] a native or inhabitant of Niue.

nival (ˈnaɪvᵊl) ADJECTIVE of or growing in or under snow.
▷ **HISTORY** C17: from Latin *nivālis*, from *nix* snow

nivation (naɪˈveɪʃən) NOUN the weathering of rock around a patch of snow by alternate freezing and thawing.
▷ **HISTORY** C19: from Latin *nix*, stem *niv-* snow

niveous (ˈnɪvɪəs) ADJECTIVE resembling snow, esp in colour.
▷ **HISTORY** C17: from Latin *niveus*, from *nix* snow

Nivernais (*French* nivɛrnɛ) NOUN a former province of central France, around Nevers.

Nivôse *French* (nivoz) NOUN the fourth month of the French revolutionary calendar, extending from Dec. 22 to Jan. 20.
▷ **HISTORY** C18: via French from Latin *nivōsus* snowy, from *nix* snow

nix¹ (nɪks) *US and Canadian informal* ◆ SENTENCE SUBSTITUTE [1] another word for **no¹** (sense 1). [2] be careful! watch out! ◆ NOUN [3] a rejection or refusal. [4] nothing at all. ◆ VERB [5] (*tr*) to veto, deny, reject, or forbid (plans, suggestions, etc.).
▷ **HISTORY** C18: from German, colloquial form of *nichts* nothing

nix² (nɪks) NOUN *German myth* a male water sprite, usually unfriendly to humans.
▷ **HISTORY** C19: from German *Nixe* nymph or water spirit, from Old High German *nihhus;* related to Old English *nicor* sea monster

nixer (ˈnɪksə) NOUN *Dublin, dialect* a spare-time job.
▷ **HISTORY** from NIX¹, (in the sense), no (tax or insurance) + -ER¹

nixie (ˈnɪksɪ) NOUN *German myth* a female water sprite, usually unfriendly to humans.
▷ **HISTORY** C19: see NIX

Nixie tube (ˈnɪksɪ) NOUN *Electronics* another name for **digitron.**

nizam (naɪˈzæm) NOUN (formerly) a Turkish regular soldier.
▷ **HISTORY** C18: ultimately from Arabic *nizām* order, arrangement

Nizam (nɪˈzɑːm) NOUN the title of the ruler of Hyderabad, India, from 1724 to 1948.

Nizhni Novgorod (*Russian* ˈniʒnij ˈnɔvgərət) NOUN a city and port in central Russia, at the confluence of the Volga and Oka Rivers: situated on the Volga route from the Baltic to central Asia; birthplace of Maxim Gorki. Pop.: 1 364 900 (1999 est.). Former name (1932–91): **Gorki.**

Nizhni Tagil (*Russian* ˈniʒnij taˈgil) NOUN a city in central Russia, on the E slopes of the Ural Mountains: a major metallurgical centre. Pop.: 395 800 (1999 est.).

NJ *or* **N.J.** ABBREVIATION FOR New Jersey.

Njord (njɔːd) *or* **Njorth** (njɔːθ) NOUN *Norse myth* the god of the sea, fishing, and prosperity.

NKGB ABBREVIATION FOR (formerly) People's Commissariat of State Security: the Soviet secret police from 1943 to 46.
▷ **HISTORY** from Russian *Narodny komissariat gosudarstvennoi bezopasnosti*

nkosi (ᵊŋˈkɔːsɪ) NOUN *South African* a term of address to a superior; master; chief.
▷ **HISTORY** Nguni *inkosi* chief, lord

Nkosi Sikele' iAfrica (ŋˈkosɪ ˌsɪkeˈlɛlɪ ˌɑfrɪˈkɑ) NOUN the unofficial anthem of the Black people of South Africa, officially recognized as a national anthem (along with 'Die Stem') in 1991.
▷ **HISTORY** from Xhosa, Lord Bless Africa

NKVD ABBREVIATION FOR (formerly) People's Commissariat of Internal Affairs: the Soviet police and secret police from 1934 to 1943: the police from 1943–46.
▷ **HISTORY** from Russian *Narodny komissariat vnutrennikh del* People's Commissariat of Internal Affairs

nl¹ ABBREVIATION FOR: [1] non licet. [2] non liquet.
▷ **HISTORY** Latin: (for sense 1) it is not permitted: (for sense 2) it is not clear

nl² THE INTERNET DOMAIN NAME FOR the Netherlands.

NL ABBREVIATION FOR: [1] New Latin. ◆ [2] INTERNATIONAL CAR REGISTRATION FOR the Netherlands.

NLC ABBREVIATION FOR National Liberal Club.

NLF ABBREVIATION FOR National Liberation Front.

NLLST ABBREVIATION FOR National Lending Library for Science and Technology.

NLS ABBREVIATION FOR National Library of Scotland.

NLW ABBREVIATION FOR National Library of Wales.

nm ABBREVIATION FOR: [1] nautical mile. [2] nanometre.

NM *or* **N. Mex.** ABBREVIATION FOR New Mexico.

NMR ABBREVIATION FOR nuclear magnetic resonance.

NNE SYMBOL FOR north-northeast.

NNP ABBREVIATION FOR: [1] **net national product.** [2] (in South Africa) New National Party.

NNW SYMBOL FOR north-northwest.

no¹ (nəʊ) SENTENCE SUBSTITUTE [1] used to express denial, disagreement, refusal, disapproval, disbelief, or acknowledgment of negative statements. [2] used with question intonation to query a previous negative statement, as in disbelief: *Alfred isn't dead yet. No?* ◆ NOUN, *plural* **noes** *or* **nos.** [3] an answer or vote of *no.* [4] (*often plural*) a person who votes in the negative. [5] **the noes have it.** there is a majority of votes in the negative. [6] **not take no for an answer.** to continue in a course of action despite refusals. ◆ Compare **yes,** (for senses 3–5) **aye¹.**
▷ **HISTORY** Old English *nā*, from *ne* not, no + *ā* ever; see AY¹

no² (nəʊ) DETERMINER [1] not any, not a, or not one: *there's no money left; no card in the file.* [2] not by a long way; not at all: *she's no youngster.* [3] (foll by comparative adjectives and adverbs) not: *no less than forty men; no more quickly than before.* [4] **no go.** See **go** (sense 74).
▷ **HISTORY** Old English *nā*, changed from *nān* NONE¹

no³ THE INTERNET DOMAIN NAME FOR Norway.

No¹ *or* **Noh** (nəʊ) NOUN, *plural* **No** *or* **Noh.** the stylized classic drama of Japan, developed in the 15th century or earlier, using music, dancing, chanting, elaborate costumes, and themes from religious stories or myths.
▷ **HISTORY** from Japanese *nō* talent, from Chinese *neng*

No² THE CHEMICAL SYMBOL FOR nobelium.

No³ (nəʊ) NOUN **Lake.** a lake in the S central Sudan, where the Bahr el Jebel (White Nile) is joined by the Bahr el Ghazal. Area: about 103 sq. km (40 sq. miles).

No1 *Text messaging* ABBREVIATION FOR no-one.

No. ABBREVIATION FOR: [1] north(ern). [2] (*plural* **Nos** *or* **nos**) Also: **no.** number.
▷ **HISTORY** from French *numéro*

n.o. *Cricket* ABBREVIATION FOR not out.

no' (no, nəʊ) ADVERB *Scot* not.

no-account ADJECTIVE [1] worthless; good-for-nothing. ◆ NOUN [2] a worthless person.

Noachian (nəʊˈeɪkɪən) *or* **Noachic** (nəʊˈækɪk, -ˈeɪkɪk) ADJECTIVE *Old Testament* of or relating to the patriarch Noah.

noah (ˈnəʊə) NOUN *Austral* a shark.
▷ **HISTORY** from Australian rhyming slang *Noah's Ark*

Noah (ˈnəʊə) NOUN *Old Testament* a Hebrew patriarch, who saved himself, his family, and specimens of each species of animal and bird from the Flood by building a ship (**Noah's Ark**) in which they all survived (Genesis 6–8).

Noahide Laws (ˈnəʊəˌhaɪd) PLURAL NOUN *Judaism* the seven laws given to Noah after the Flood, which decree the establishment of a fair system of justice in society, and prohibit idolatry, blasphemy, murder, adultery and incest, robbery, and the eating of flesh taken from a living animal.

nob¹ (nɒb) NOUN *Cribbage* [1] the jack of the suit turned up. [2] **one for his nob.** the call made with this jack, scoring one point.
▷ **HISTORY** C19: of uncertain origin

nob² (nɒb) NOUN *Slang, chiefly Brit* a person of social distinction.

▷HISTORY C19: of uncertain origin
▸ 'nobby ADJECTIVE ▸ 'nobbily ADVERB

nob[3] (nɒb) NOUN *Slang* the head.
▷HISTORY C17: perhaps a variant of KNOB

nob[4] (nɒb) NOUN a variant spelling of **knob** (sense 4).

no-ball NOUN [1] *Cricket* an illegal ball, as for overstepping the crease, throwing, etc., for which the batting side scores a run, and from which the batsman can be out only by being run out. [2] *Rounders* an illegal ball, esp one bowled too high or too low. ◆ SENTENCE SUBSTITUTE [3] *Cricket, rounders* a call by the umpire indicating a no-ball. ◆ VERB [4] (*tr*) *Cricket* (of an umpire) **a** to declare (a bowler) to have bowled a no-ball. **b** to declare (a delivery) to be a no-ball.

nobble ('nɒbᵊl) VERB (*tr*) *Brit, slang* [1] to disable (a racehorse), esp with drugs. [2] to win over or outwit (a person) by underhand means. [3] to suborn (a person, esp a juror) by threats, bribery, etc. [4] to steal; filch. [5] to get hold of; grab. [6] to kidnap.
▷HISTORY C19: back formation from *nobbler,* from false division of *an hobbler* (one who hobbles horses) as *a nobbler*
▸ 'nobbler NOUN

nobbut ('nɒbət) ADVERB *Dialect* nothing but; only.
▷HISTORY C14: from NO[2] + BUT[1]

nobelium (nəʊ'bi:lɪəm) NOUN a transuranic element produced artificially from curium. Symbol: No; atomic no.: 102; half-life of most stable isotope, ^{255}No: 180 seconds (approx.); valency: 2 or 3.
▷HISTORY C20: New Latin, named after *Nobel* Institute, Stockholm, where it was discovered

Nobel prize (nuə'bɛl) NOUN a prize for outstanding contributions to chemistry, physics, physiology or medicine, literature, economics, and peace that may be awarded annually. It was established in 1901; the prize for economics being added in 1969. The recipients are chosen by an international committee centred in Sweden, except for the peace prize which is awarded in Oslo by a committee of the Norwegian parliament.

nobiliary (nə'bɪlɪərɪ) ADJECTIVE of or relating to the nobility.
▷HISTORY C18: from French *nobiliaire;* see NOBLE, -ARY

nobiliary particle NOUN a preposition, such as French *de* or German *von,* occurring as part of a title or surname: *Marquis de Sade.*

nobility (nəʊ'bɪlɪtɪ) NOUN, *plural* **-ties.** [1] a socially or politically privileged class whose titles are conferred by descent or by royal decree. [2] the state or quality of being morally or spiritually good; dignity: *the nobility of his mind.* [3] (in the British Isles) the class of people holding the title of dukes, marquesses, earls, viscounts, or barons and their feminine equivalents collectively; peerage.

noble ('nəʊbᵊl) ADJECTIVE [1] of or relating to a hereditary class with special social or political status, often derived from a feudal period. [2] of or characterized by high moral qualities; magnanimous: *a noble deed.* [3] having dignity or eminence; illustrious. [4] grand or imposing; magnificent: *a noble avenue of trees.* [5] of superior quality or kind; excellent: *a noble strain of horses.* [6] *Chem* **a** (of certain elements) chemically unreactive. **b** (of certain metals, esp copper, silver, and gold) resisting oxidation. [7] *Falconry* **a** designating long-winged falcons that capture their quarry by stooping on it from above. Compare **ignoble. b** designating the type of quarry appropriate to a particular species of falcon. ◆ NOUN [8] a person belonging to a privileged social or political class whose status is usually indicated by a title conferred by sovereign authority or descent. [9] (in the British Isles) a person holding the title of duke, marquess, earl, viscount, or baron, or a feminine equivalent. [10] a former Brit. gold coin having the value of one third of a pound.
▷HISTORY C13: via Old French from Latin *nōbilis,* originally, capable of being known, hence well-known, noble, from *noscere* to know
▸ 'nobleness NOUN ▸ 'nobly ADVERB

noble art *or* **science** NOUN **the.** boxing.

noble gas NOUN another name for **inert gas** (sense 1).

nobleman ('nəʊbᵊlmən) NOUN, *plural* **-men.** a man of noble rank, title, or status; peer; aristocrat.

noble rot NOUN *Winemaking* a condition in which grapes are deliberately affected by *Botrytis cinerea,* resulting in the shrivelling of the ripened grapes, which in turn leads to an increased sugar content.
▷HISTORY C20: translation of French *pourriture noble*

noble savage NOUN (in romanticism) an idealized view of primitive man.

noblesse (nəʊ'blɛs) NOUN *Literary* [1] noble birth or condition. [2] the noble class.
▷HISTORY C13: from Old French; see NOBLE

noblesse oblige (nəʊ'blɛs əʊ'bli:ʒ; *French* nɔblɛs ɔbliʒ) NOUN *Often ironic* the supposed obligation of nobility to be honourable and generous.
▷HISTORY French, literally: nobility obliges

noblewoman ('nəʊbᵊlwʊmən) NOUN, *plural* **-women.** a woman of noble rank, title, or status; peer; aristocrat.

nobody ('nəʊbədɪ) PRONOUN [1] no person; no-one. ◆ NOUN, *plural* **-bodies.** [2] an insignificant person.

> **Language note** See at **everyone.**

no-brainer ('nəʊˌbreɪnə) NOUN *Slang* something which requires little or no mental effort.

nociceptive (ˌnəʊsɪ'sɛptɪv) ADJECTIVE causing or reacting to pain.
▷HISTORY C20: from Latin *nocēre* to injure + RECEPTIVE

nocireceptor ('nəʊsɪrɪˌsɛptə) *or* **nociceptor** ('nəʊsɪˌsɛptə) NOUN *Physiol* a receptor sensitive to pain.

nock (nɒk) NOUN [1] a notch on an arrow that fits on the bowstring. [2] either of the grooves at each end of a bow that hold the bowstring. ◆ VERB (*tr*) [3] to fit (an arrow) on a bowstring. [4] to put a groove or notch in (a bow or arrow).
▷HISTORY C14: related to Swedish *nock* tip

nocking point NOUN a marked part of the bowstring where the arrow is placed.

no-claims bonus NOUN a reduction on an insurance premium, esp one covering a motor vehicle, if no claims have been made within a specified period. Also called: **no-claim bonus.**

noctambulism (nɒk'tæmbjʊˌlɪzəm) *or* **noctambulation** NOUN another word for **somnambulism.**
▷HISTORY C19: from Latin *nox* night + *ambulāre* to walk
▸ noc'tambulist NOUN

nocti- *or before a vowel* **noct-** COMBINING FORM night: *noctilucent.*
▷HISTORY from Latin *nox, noct-*

noctiluca (ˌnɒktɪ'lu:kə) NOUN, *plural* **-cae** (-si:). any bioluminescent marine dinoflagellate of the genus *Noctiluca.*
▷HISTORY C17: from Latin, from *nox* night + *lūcēre* to shine

noctilucent (ˌnɒktɪ'lu:sᵊnt) ADJECTIVE shining at night, usu. of very thin high altitude clouds observable in the summer twilight sky.
▸ ˌnocti'lucence NOUN

noctuid ('nɒktjʊɪd) NOUN [1] any nocturnal moth of the family *Noctuidae:* includes the underwings and antler moth. See also **cutworm, army worm.** ◆ ADJECTIVE [2] of, relating to, or belonging to the *Noctuidae.*
▷HISTORY C19: via New Latin from Latin *noctua* night owl, from *nox* night

noctule ('nɒktju:l) NOUN any of several large Old World insectivorous bats of the genus *Nyctalus,* esp *N. noctula:* family *Vespertilionidae.*
▷HISTORY C18: probably from Late Latin *noctula* small owl, from Latin *noctua* night owl

nocturn ('nɒktɜ:n) NOUN *RC Church* any of the main sections of the office of matins.
▷HISTORY C13: from Medieval Latin *nocturna* (n), from Latin *nocturnus* nocturnal, from *nox* night

nocturnal (nɒk'tɜ:nᵊl) ADJECTIVE [1] of, used during, occurring in, or relating to the night. [2] (of animals) active at night. [3] (of plants) having flowers that open at night and close by day. ◆ Compare **diurnal.**
▷HISTORY C15: from Late Latin *nocturnālis,* from Latin *nox* night
▸ ˌnoctur'nality NOUN ▸ noc'turnally ADVERB

nocturne ('nɒktɜ:n) NOUN [1] a short, lyrical piece of music, esp one for the piano. [2] a painting or tone poem of a night scene.

nocuous ('nɒkjʊəs) ADJECTIVE *Rare* harmful; noxious.
▷HISTORY C17: from Latin *nocuus,* from *nocēre* to hurt
▸ 'nocuously ADVERB ▸ 'nocuousness NOUN

nod (nɒd) VERB **nods, nodding, nodded.** [1] to lower and raise (the head) briefly, as to indicate agreement, invitation, etc. [2] (*tr*) to express or indicate by nodding: *she nodded approval.* [3] (*tr*) to bring or direct by nodding: *she nodded me towards the manager's office.* [4] (*intr*) (of flowers, trees, etc.) to sway or bend forwards and back. [5] (*intr*) to let the head fall forward through drowsiness; be almost asleep: *the old lady sat nodding by the fire.* [6] (*intr*) to be momentarily inattentive or careless: *even Homer sometimes nods.* [7] **nodding acquaintance.** a slight, casual, or superficial knowledge (of a subject or a person). ◆ NOUN [8] a quick down-and-up movement of the head, as in assent, command, etc.: *she greeted him with a nod.* [9] a short sleep; nap. See also **land of Nod.** [10] a swaying motion, as of flowers, etc., in the wind. [11] **on the nod.** *Informal* **a** agreed, as in a committee meeting, without any formal procedure. **b** (formerly) on credit. [12] **the nod.** *Boxing informal* the award of a contest to a competitor on the basis of points scored. ◆ See also **nod off, nod out.**
▷HISTORY C14 *nodde,* of obscure origin
▸ 'nodding ADJECTIVE, NOUN

nodal ('nəʊdᵊl) ADJECTIVE of or like a node.
▸ no'dality NOUN ▸ 'nodally ADVERB

nodding dog NOUN a small model of a dog carried as a mascot in a motor vehicle, with a head so mounted that it moves up and down with the motion of the vehicle.

nodding donkey NOUN *Informal* (in the oil industry) a type of reciprocating pump used to extract oil from an inland well.
▷HISTORY C20: so called from its shape and movement

noddle[1] ('nɒdᵊl) NOUN *Informal, chiefly Brit* the head or brains: *use your noddle!*
▷HISTORY C15: origin obscure

noddle[2] ('nɒdᵊl) VERB *Informal, chiefly Brit* to nod (the head), as through drowsiness.
▷HISTORY C18: from NOD

noddy[1] ('nɒdɪ) NOUN, *plural* **-dies.** [1] any of several tropical terns of the genus *Anous,* esp *A. stolidus* (**common noddy**), typically having a dark plumage. [2] a fool or dunce.
▷HISTORY C16: perhaps noun use of obsolete *noddy* foolish, drowsy, perhaps from NOD (vb); the bird is so called because it allows itself to be caught by hand

noddy[2] ('nɒdɪ) NOUN, *plural* **-dies.** (*usually plural*) *Television* film footage of an interviewer's reactions to comments made by an interviewee, used in editing the interview after it has been recorded.
▷HISTORY C20: from NOD

noddy[3] ('nɒdɪ) ADJECTIVE *Informal* very easy to use or understand; simplistic.
▷HISTORY C20: origin unknown

node (nəʊd) NOUN [1] a knot, swelling, or knob. [2] the point on a plant stem from which the leaves or lateral branches grow. [3] *Physics* a point at which the amplitude of one of the two kinds of displacement in a standing wave has zero or minimum value. Generally the other kind of displacement has its maximum value at this point. See also **standing wave.** Compare **antinode.** [4] Also called: **crunode.** *Maths* a point at which two branches of a curve intersect, each branch having a distinct tangent. [5] *Maths, linguistics* one of the objects of which a graph or a tree consists; vertex. [6] *Astronomy* either of the two points at which the orbit of a body intersects the plane of the ecliptic. When the body moves from the south to the north side of the ecliptic it passes the **ascending node** and from the north to the south side it passes the **descending node.** [7] *Anatomy* **a** any natural bulge or swelling of a structure or part, such as those that occur along the course of a lymphatic vessel (**lymph node**). **b** a finger joint or knuckle. [8] *Computing* an interconnection point on a computer network.
▷HISTORY C16: from Latin *nōdus* knot

node house NOUN a prefabricated shelter used by welders during the construction of an oil rig.

node of Ranvier ('rɑ:nvɪ,eɪ) NOUN any of the gaps that occur at regular intervals along the length of the sheath of a myelinated nerve fibre, at which the axon is exposed.
▷HISTORY C19: named after Louis-Antoine *Ranvier* (1835–1922), French histologist

nodical ('nəʊdɪkᵊl, 'nɒdɪ-) ADJECTIVE of or relating to the nodes of a celestial body, esp of the moon.

nodical month NOUN another name for **draconic month.**

nod off VERB (*intr, adverb*) *Informal* to fall asleep.

nodose ('nəʊdəʊs, nəʊ'dəʊs) *or* **nodous** ('nəʊdəs) ADJECTIVE having nodes or knotlike swellings: *nodose stems.*
▷HISTORY C18: from Latin *nōdōsus* knotty
▸**nodosity** (nəʊ'dɒsɪtɪ) NOUN

nod out VERB (*intr, adverb*) *Slang* to lapse into stupor, esp on heroin.

nodule ('nɒdju:l) NOUN [1] a small knot, lump, or node. [2] Also called: **root nodule.** any of the knoblike outgrowths on the roots of clover and many other legumes: contain bacteria involved in nitrogen fixation. [3] *Anatomy* any small node or knoblike protuberance. [4] a small rounded lump of rock or mineral substance, esp in a matrix of different rock material.
▷HISTORY C17: from Latin *nōdulus,* from *nōdus* knot
▸'**nodular,** '**nodulose,** *or* '**nodulous** ADJECTIVE

nodus ('nəʊdəs) NOUN, *plural* **-di** (-daɪ). [1] a problematic idea, situation, etc. [2] another word for **node.**
▷HISTORY C14: from Latin: knot

Noel *or* **Noël** (nəʊ'ɛl) NOUN [1] (esp in carols) another word for **Christmas.** [2] (*often not capital*) *Rare* a Christmas carol.
▷HISTORY C19: from French, from Latin *nātālis* a birthday; see NATAL[1]

noesis (nəʊ'i:sɪs) NOUN [1] *Philosophy* the exercise of reason, esp in the apprehension of universal forms. Compare **dianoia.** [2] *Psychol* the mental process used in thinking and perceiving; the functioning of the intellect. See also **cognition.**
▷HISTORY C19: from Greek *noēsis* thought, from *noein* to think

noetic (nəʊ'ɛtɪk) ADJECTIVE of or relating to the mind, esp to its rational and intellectual faculties.
▷HISTORY C17: from Greek *noētikos,* from *noein* to think, from *nous* the mind

no-fly zone NOUN [1] an area in which aeroplanes may not fly, esp during wartime. [2] a taboo subject.

nog[1] *or* **nogg** (nɒg) NOUN [1] Also called: **flip.** a drink, esp an alcoholic one, containing beaten egg. [2] *East Anglian, dialect* strong local beer.
▷HISTORY C17 (originally: a strong beer): of obscure origin

nog[2] (nɒg) NOUN [1] a wooden peg or block built into a masonry or brick wall to provide a fixing for nails. [2] short for **nogging** (sense 1).
▷HISTORY C17: origin unknown

noggin ('nɒgɪn) NOUN [1] a small quantity of spirits, usually 1 gill. [2] a small mug or cup. [3] an informal word for **head** (sense 1).
▷HISTORY C17: of obscure origin

nogging ('nɒgɪŋ) NOUN [1] Also called: **nog,** (Scot and NZ) **dwang.** a short horizontal timber member used between the studs of a framed partition. [2] masonry or brickwork between the timber members of a framed construction. [3] a number of wooden pieces fitted between the timbers of a half-timbered wall.

no-go area NOUN [1] a district in a town that is barricaded off, usually by a paramilitary organization, within which the police, army, etc., can only enter by force. [2] an area that is barred to certain individuals, groups, etc.

Noh (nəʊ) NOUN a variant spelling of **No**[1].

no-hoper NOUN *Informal* a useless person; failure.

nohow ('nəʊ,haʊ) ADVERB *Not standard* (*in negative constructions*) **a** under any conditions. **b** in any manner.

NOI ABBREVIATION FOR **Nation of Islam.**

noil (nɔɪl) NOUN *Textiles* the short or knotted fibres that are separated from the long fibres, or staple, by combing.
▷HISTORY C17: of unknown origin

nointer ('nɔɪntə) NOUN *Austral, slang* a mischievous child; rascal.

noir (nwɑ:) ADJECTIVE (of a film) showing characteristics of a *film noir*, in plot or style.

noise (nɔɪz) NOUN [1] a sound, esp one that is loud or disturbing. [2] loud shouting; clamour; din. [3] any undesired electrical disturbance in a circuit, degrading the useful information in a signal. See also **signal-to-noise ratio.** [4] undesired or irrelevant elements in a visual image: *removing noise from pictures.* [5] talk or interest: *noise about strikes.* [6] (*plural*) conventional comments or sounds conveying a reaction, attitude, feeling, etc.: *she made sympathetic noises.* [7] **make a noise.** to talk a great deal or complain. [8] **make noises about.** *Informal* to give indications of one's intentions: *the government is making noises about new social security arrangements.* [9] **noises off.** *Theatre* sounds made offstage intended for the ears of the audience: used as a stage direction. ◆ VERB [10] (*tr; usually foll by abroad* or *about*) to spread (news, gossip, etc.). [11] (*intr*) *Rare* to talk loudly or at length. [12] (*intr*) *Rare* to make a din or outcry; be noisy.
▷HISTORY C13: from Old French, from Latin: NAUSEA

noise generator NOUN [1] a device used in synthesizers to produce high-frequency sound effects. [2] a generator of electronic noise used to test equipment.

noiseless ('nɔɪzlɪs) ADJECTIVE making little or no sound; silent.
▸'**noiselessly** ADVERB ▸'**noiselessness** NOUN

noisemaker ('nɔɪz,meɪkə) NOUN *US and Canadian* something, such as a clapper or bell, used to make a loud noise at football matches, celebrations, etc.
▸'**noise,making** NOUN, ADJECTIVE

noisenik ('nɔɪz,nɪk) NOUN a rock musician who performs loud harsh music.

noise pollution NOUN annoying or harmful noise in an environment.

noisette (nwɑ:'zɛt) ADJECTIVE [1] flavoured or made with hazelnuts. ◆ NOUN [2] a small round boneless slice of lamb from the fillet or leg. [3] a chocolate made with hazelnuts.
▷HISTORY from French: hazelnut

noisome ('nɔɪsəm) ADJECTIVE [1] (esp of smells) offensive. [2] harmful or noxious.
▷HISTORY C14: from obsolete *noy,* variant of ANNOY + -SOME[1]
▸'**noisomely** ADVERB ▸'**noisomeness** NOUN

noisy ('nɔɪzɪ) ADJECTIVE **noisier, noisiest.** [1] making a loud or constant noise. [2] full of or characterized by noise.
▸'**noisily** ADVERB ▸'**noisiness** NOUN

noisy miner NOUN a honey-eater, *Manorina melanocephala*, of eastern Australia, having a grey-white plumage and brown wings and noted for its raucous cries.

nolens volens *Latin* ('nəʊlɛnz 'vəʊlɛnz) ADVERB whether willing or unwilling.

noli-me-tangere ('nəʊlɪ,meɪ'tæŋgərɪ) NOUN [1] a warning against interfering or against touching a person or thing. [2] a work of art depicting Christ appearing to Mary Magdalene after His Resurrection. [3] another name for **touch-me-not.** [4] a cancerous ulcer affecting soft tissue and bone.
▷HISTORY from Latin: do not touch me, the words spoken by Christ to Mary Magdalene (Vulgate, John 20:17)

nolle prosequi ('nɒlɪ 'prɒsɪ,kwaɪ) NOUN *Law* an entry made on the court record when the plaintiff in a civil suit or prosecutor in a criminal prosecution undertakes not to continue the action or prosecution. Compare **non prosequitur.**
▷HISTORY Latin: do not pursue (prosecute)

nolo contendere ('nəʊləʊ kɒn'tɛndərɪ) NOUN *Law, chiefly US* a plea made by a defendant to a criminal charge having the same effect in those proceedings as a plea of guilty but not precluding him from denying the charge in a subsequent action.
▷HISTORY Latin: I do not wish to contend

nol. pros. *or* **nolle pros.** ABBREVIATION FOR nolle prosequi.

nom. ABBREVIATION FOR: [1] nominal. [2] nominative.

noma ('nəʊmə) NOUN a gangrenous inflammation of the mouth, esp one affecting malnourished children.
▷HISTORY C19: New Latin, from Latin *nomē* ulcer, from Greek *nomē* feeding; related to Greek *nemein* to feed

nomad ('nəʊmæd) NOUN [1] a member of a people or tribe who move from place to place to find pasture and food. [2] a person who continually moves from place to place; wanderer.
▷HISTORY C16: via French from Latin *nomas* wandering shepherd, from Greek; related to *nemein* to feed, pasture
▸'**nomadism** NOUN

nomadic (nəʊ'mædɪk) ADJECTIVE relating to or characteristic of nomads or their way of life.
▸**no'madically** ADVERB

nomadize *or* **nomadise** ('nəʊmæd,aɪz) VERB [1] (*intr*) to live as nomads. [2] (*tr*) to make into nomads. [3] (*tr*) to people (a place) with nomads.

no-man's-land NOUN [1] land between boundaries, esp an unoccupied zone between opposing forces. [2] an unowned or unclaimed piece of land. [3] an ambiguous area of activity or thought.

nomarch ('nɒmɑ:k) NOUN [1] the head of an ancient Egyptian nome. [2] the senior administrator in a Greek nomarchy.
▷HISTORY C17: from Greek *nomarkhēs*

nomarchy ('nɒmɑ:kɪ, -əkɪ) NOUN, *plural* **-chies.** any of the provinces of modern Greece; nome.
▷HISTORY C19: from Greek; see NOME, -ARCHY

no-mates ADJECTIVE *Slang* (*used postpositively after a name*) designating a person with no friends: *Norman No-Mates.*

nombles ('nʌmbᵊlz) PLURAL NOUN a variant spelling of **numbles.**

nombril ('nɒmbrɪl) NOUN *Heraldry* a point on a shield between the fesse point and the lowest point.
▷HISTORY C16: from French, literally: navel

nom de guerre ('nɒm də 'gɛə) NOUN, *plural* **noms de guerre** ('nɒm də 'gɛə). an assumed name; pseudonym.
▷HISTORY French, literally: war name

nom de plume ('nɒm də 'plu:m) NOUN, *plural* **noms de plume** ('nɒm də 'plu:m). another term for **pen name.**

nome (nəʊm) NOUN [1] any of the former provinces of modern Greece; nomarchy. [2] an administrative division of ancient Egypt.
▷HISTORY C18: from Greek *nomos* pasture, region

nomen ('nəʊmɛn) NOUN, *plural* **nomina** ('nɒmɪnə). an ancient Roman's second name, designating his gens or clan. See also **agnomen, cognomen, praenomen.**
▷HISTORY Latin: a name

nomenclator ('nəʊmɛn,kleɪtə) NOUN a person who invents or assigns names, as in scientific classification.
▷HISTORY C16: from Latin, from *nōmen* name + *calāre* to call

nomenclature (nəʊ'mɛnklətʃə; US 'nəʊmən,kleɪtʃər) NOUN the terminology used in a particular science, art, activity, etc.
▷HISTORY C17: from Latin *nōmenclātūra* list of names; see NOMENCLATOR

nomenklatura (,nəʊmɛnklə'tjʊ:rə) NOUN (formerly, in the USSR and E Europe) a list of individuals drawn up by the Communist Party from which were selected candidates for vacant senior positions in the state, party, and other important organizations.
▷HISTORY C20: Russian, from Latin *nōmenclātūra* list of names

nominal ('nɒmɪnᵊl) ADJECTIVE [1] in name only; theoretical: *the nominal leader.* [2] minimal in comparison with real worth or what is expected; token: *a nominal fee.* [3] of, relating to, constituting, bearing, or giving a name. [4] *Grammar* of or relating to a noun or noun phrase. ◆ NOUN [5] *Grammar* a nominal element; a noun, noun phrase, or syntactically similar structure. [6] *Bell-ringing* the harmonic an octave above the strike tone of a bell.
▷HISTORY C15: from Latin *nōminālis* of a name, from *nōmen* name
▸'**nominally** ADVERB

nominal aphasia NOUN aphasia in which the

primary symptom is an inability to recognize words and to speak the right word.

nominalism ('nɒmɪnᵊˌlɪzəm) NOUN the philosophical theory that the variety of objects to which a single general word, such as *dog,* applies have nothing in common but the name. Compare **conceptualism, realism.**
▸ **'nominalist** NOUN, ADJECTIVE ▸ **ˌnominal'istic** ADJECTIVE

nominal scale NOUN *Statistics* a discrete classification of data, in which data are neither measured nor ordered but subjects are merely allocated to distinct categories: for example, a record of students' course choices constitutes nominal data which could be correlated with school results. Compare **ordinal scale, interval scale, ratio scale.**

nominal value NOUN another name for **par value.**

nominal wages PLURAL NOUN another name for **money wages.**

nominate VERB ('nɒmɪˌneɪt) *(mainly tr)* 1 to propose as a candidate, esp for an elective office. 2 to appoint to an office or position. 3 to name (someone) to act on one's behalf, esp to conceal one's identity. 4 *(intr) Austral* to stand as a candidate in an election. 5 *Archaic* to name, entitle, or designate. ◆ ADJECTIVE ('nɒmɪnɪt) 6 *Rare* having a particular name.
▷HISTORY C16: from Latin *nōmināre* to call by name, from *nōmen* name
▸ **'nomiˌnator** NOUN

nomination (ˌnɒmɪ'neɪʃən) NOUN the act of nominating or state of being nominated, esp as an election candidate.

nominative ('nɒmɪnətɪv, 'nɒmnə-) ADJECTIVE 1 *Grammar* denoting a case of nouns and pronouns in inflected languages that is used esp to identify the subject of a finite verb. See also **subjective** (sense 6). 2 appointed rather than elected to a position, office, etc. 3 bearing the name of a person. ◆ NOUN 4 *Grammar* **a** the nominative case. **b** a word or speech element in the nominative case.
▷HISTORY C14: from Latin *nōminātīvus* belonging to naming, from *nōmen* name
▸ **nominatival** (ˌnɒmɪnə'taɪvᵊl, ˌnɒmnə-) ADJECTIVE
▸ **'nominatively** ADVERB

nominee (ˌnɒmɪ'niː) NOUN 1 a person who is nominated to an office or as a candidate. 2 **a** a person or organization named to act on behalf of someone else, esp to conceal the identity of the nominator. **b** *(as modifier): nominee shareholder.*
▷HISTORY C17: from NOMINATE + -EE

nomism ('nəʊmɪzəm) NOUN adherence to a law or laws as a primary exercise of religion.
▷HISTORY C20: from Greek *nomos* law, custom
▸ **no'mistic** ADJECTIVE

nomo- COMBINING FORM indicating law or custom: *nomology.*
▷HISTORY from Greek *nomos* law, custom

nomocracy (nɒ'mɒkrəsɪ, nəʊ-) NOUN, *plural* **-cies.** government based on the rule of law rather than arbitrary will, terror, etc.
▷HISTORY C19: from Greek, from *nomos* law + -CRACY

nomogram ('nɒməˌgræm, 'nəʊmə-) *or* **nomograph** NOUN 1 an arrangement of two linear or logarithmic scales such that an intersecting straight line enables intermediate values or values on a third scale to be read off. 2 any graphic representation of numerical relationships.
▷HISTORY C20: from Greek *nomos* law + -GRAM, on the model of French *nomogramme*

nomography (nɒ'mɒgrəfɪ) NOUN, *plural* **-phies.** the science of constructing nomographs. See **nomogram.**
▸ **no'mographer** NOUN ▸ **nomographic** (ˌnɒmə'græfɪk) *or* **ˌnomo'graphical** ADJECTIVE ▸ **ˌnomo'graphically** ADVERB

nomological (ˌnɒmə'lɒdʒɪkᵊl) ADJECTIVE 1 of or relating to nomology. 2 stating or relating to a nonlogical necessity or law of nature. The difference between a nomological and a merely universal statement is that from the universal *all As are Bs* one cannot, but from the nomological *all As must be Bs* one can, infer the counterfactual *if this were an A it would (have to) be a B.*
▸ **ˌnomo'logically** ADVERB

nomology (nɒm'ɒlədʒɪ) NOUN 1 the science of law and law-making. 2 the branch of science concerned with the formulation of laws explaining natural phenomena.
▸ **no'mologist** NOUN

nomothetic (ˌnɒmə'θɛtɪk) *or* **nomothetical** ADJECTIVE 1 giving or enacting laws; legislative. 2 *Psychol* of or relating to the search for general laws or traits, esp in personality theory. Compare **idiographic.**
▷HISTORY C17: from Greek *nomothetikos,* from *nomothetēs* lawgiver

-nomy NOUN COMBINING FORM indicating a science or the laws governing a certain field of knowledge: *agronomy; economy.*
▷HISTORY from Greek *-nomia* law; related to *nemein* to distribute, control
▸ **-nomic** ADJECTIVE COMBINING FORM

non- PREFIX 1 indicating negation: *nonexistent.* 2 indicating refusal or failure: *noncooperation.* 3 indicating exclusion from a specified class of persons or things: *nonfiction.* 4 indicating lack or absence, esp of a quality associated with what is specified: *nonobjective; nonevent.*
▷HISTORY from Latin *nōn* not

nona- *or before a vowel* **non-** COMBINING FORM nine: *nonagon.*
▷HISTORY from Latin *nōnus*

nonacademic (ˌnɒnækə'dɛmɪk) ADJECTIVE not related to, involved in, or trained in academic disciplines.

nonacceptance (ˌnɒnək'sɛptəns) NOUN the act or an instance of not accepting or being accepted.

nonaccidental injury (ˌnɒnæksɪ'dɛntᵊl) NOUN *Social welfare* damage, such as a bruise, burn, or fracture, deliberately inflicted on a child or an old person. Abbreviation: **NAI.** See also **child abuse.**

nonaddictive (ˌnɒnə'dɪktɪv) ADJECTIVE not of, relating to, or causing addiction.

nonage ('nəʊnɪdʒ) NOUN 1 *Law* the state of being under any of various ages at which a person may legally enter into certain transactions, such as the making of binding contracts, marrying, etc. 2 any period of immaturity.

nonagenarian (ˌnəʊnədʒɪ'nɛərɪən) NOUN 1 a person who is from 90 to 99 years old. ◆ ADJECTIVE 2 of, relating to, or denoting a nonagenarian.
▷HISTORY C19: from Latin *nōnāgēnārius,* from *nōnāginta* ninety

nonaggression (ˌnɒnə'grɛʃən) NOUN **a** restraint of aggression, esp between states. **b** *(as modifier): a nonaggression pact.*

nonagon ('nɒnəˌgɒn) NOUN a polygon having nine sides. Also called: **enneagon.**
▸ **nonagonal** (nɒn'ægənᵊl) ADJECTIVE

nonagricultural (ˌnɒnægrɪ'kʌltʃərəl) ADJECTIVE not of or relating to agriculture.

nonalcoholic (ˌnɒnælkə'hɒlɪk) ADJECTIVE not containing alcohol: *nonalcoholic drinks.*

nonaligned (ˌnɒnə'laɪnd) ADJECTIVE (of states) not part of a major alliance or power bloc, esp not allied to the US, China, or formerly the Soviet Union.
▸ **ˌnona'lignment** NOUN

nonanoic acid (ˌnɒnə'nəʊɪk) NOUN a colourless oily fatty acid with a rancid odour: used in making pharmaceuticals, lacquers, and plastics. Formula: $CH_3(CH_2)_7COOH$. Also called: **pelargonic acid.**
▷HISTORY C19: from *nonane* a paraffin, ninth in the methane series, from Latin *nōnus* ninth + -ANE

non-A, non-B hepatitis NOUN a form of viral hepatitis, not caused by the agents responsible for hepatitis A and hepatitis B, that is commonly transmitted by infected blood transfusions. The causative virus has been isolated. Also called: **hepatitis C.**

nonappearance (ˌnɒnə'pɪərəns) NOUN failure to appear or attend, esp as a defendant or witness in court.

nonattendance (ˌnɒnə'tɛndəns) NOUN the act or an instance of not attending an event, meeting, etc.

nonbeing (nɒn'biːɪŋ) NOUN the philosophical problem arising from the fact that the ability to refer appears to presuppose the existence of whatever is referred to, and yet we can talk intelligibly about nonexistent objects. See also **subsistence** (sense 5).

nonbeliever (ˌnɒnbɪ'liːvə) NOUN a person who does not believe, esp in God and religion.

nonbiological (ˌnɒnbaɪə'lɒdʒɪkᵊl) ADJECTIVE 1 not related by birth: *nonbiological mother.* 2 (of a detergent) not containing enzymes said to be capable of removing stains of organic origin from items to be washed. 3 not of or relating to biology.

non-Catholic ADJECTIVE 1 not of or relating to the Roman Catholic Church. ◆ NOUN 2 a person who does not practise Roman Catholicism.

nonce[1] (nɒns) NOUN the present time or occasion (now only in the phrase **for the nonce**).
▷HISTORY C12: from the phrase *for the nonce,* a mistaken division of *for then anes,* literally: for the once, from *then* dative singular of *the* + *anes* ONCE

nonce[2] (nɒns) NOUN *Prison slang* a rapist or child molester; a sexual offender.
▷HISTORY C20: of unknown origin

nonce word NOUN a word coined for a single occasion.

nonchalant ('nɒnʃələnt) ADJECTIVE casually unconcerned or indifferent; uninvolved.
▷HISTORY C18: from French, from *nonchaloir* to lack warmth, from NON- + *chaloir,* from Latin *calēre* to be warm
▸ **'nonchalance** NOUN ▸ **'nonchalantly** ADVERB

non-Christian ADJECTIVE 1 (of a person, country, etc.) not adhering to the Christian faith. ◆ NOUN 2 a person who does not adhere to the Christian faith.

noncognitivism (nɒn'kɒgnɪtɪˌvɪzəm) NOUN *Philosophy* the semantic meta-ethical thesis that moral judgments do not express facts and so do not have a truth value thus excluding both naturalism and non-naturalism. See **emotivism, prescriptivism.**

non-com ('nɒnˌkɒm) NOUN *US* short for **noncommissioned officer.**

noncombatant (nɒn'kɒmbətənt) NOUN 1 a civilian in time of war. 2 a member of the armed forces whose duties do not include fighting, such as a chaplain or surgeon.

noncommercial (ˌnɒnkə'mɜːʃəl) ADJECTIVE not of, connected with, or involved in commerce: *noncommercial organizations.*

noncommissioned officer (ˌnɒnkə'mɪʃənd) NOUN (in the armed forces) a person, such as a sergeant or corporal, who is appointed from the ranks as a subordinate officer.

noncommittal (ˌnɒnkə'mɪtᵊl) ADJECTIVE 1 not involving or revealing commitment to any particular opinion or course of action: *a noncommittal reply.* 2 *Rare* having no outstanding quality, meaning, etc.

noncommunist (nɒn'kɒmjʊnɪst) ADJECTIVE 1 relating to a government or state that does not practise communism. ◆ NOUN 2 a person who does not practise communism: *re-enter politics as a noncommunist.*

noncompetitive (ˌnɒnkəm'pɛtɪtɪv) ADJECTIVE not involving or determined by rivalry or competition.

noncompliance (ˌnɒnkəm'plaɪəns) NOUN the act or state of not complying.

non compos mentis *Latin* ('nɒn 'kɒmpəs 'mɛntɪs) ADJECTIVE mentally incapable of managing one's own affairs; of unsound mind.
▷HISTORY Latin: not in control of one's mind

nonconductor (ˌnɒnkən'dʌktə) NOUN a substance that is a poor conductor of heat, electricity, or sound.

nonconformist (ˌnɒnkən'fɔːmɪst) NOUN 1 a person who does not conform to generally accepted patterns of behaviour or thought. ◆ ADJECTIVE 2 of or characterized by behaviour that does not conform to generally accepted patterns.
▸ **ˌnoncon'formism** NOUN

Nonconformist (ˌnɒnkən'fɔːmɪst) NOUN 1 a member of a Protestant denomination that dissents from an Established Church, esp the Church of England. ◆ ADJECTIVE 2 of, relating to, or denoting Nonconformists.
▸ **ˌNoncon'formity** *or* **ˌNoncon'formism** NOUN

nonconformity (ˌnɒnkən'fɔːmɪtɪ) NOUN 1 failure or refusal to conform. 2 absence of agreement or harmony.

noncontributory (ˌnɒnkən'trɪbjʊtərɪ, -trɪ) ADJECTIVE 1 **a** denoting an insurance or pension scheme for employees, the premiums of which are paid entirely by the employer. **b** (of a state benefit) not dependent on national insurance contributions. [2] not providing contribution; noncontributing.

noncontroversial (ˌnɒnkɒntrəˈvɜːʃəl) ADJECTIVE not causing dispute, argument, debate, etc.

nonconventional (ˌnɒnkənˈvɛnʃənᵊl) ADJECTIVE [1] not established by accepted usage or general agreement; non-traditional: *a nonconventional lifestyle.* [2] (of weapons, warfare, etc.) nuclear or chemical.

noncooperation (ˌnɒnkəʊˌɒpəˈreɪʃən) NOUN [1] failure or refusal to cooperate. [2] refusal to pay taxes, obey government decrees, etc., as a protest.
▸**noncooperative** (ˌnɒnkəʊˈɒpərətɪv) ADJECTIVE
▸**ˌnoncoˈoperˌator** NOUN

noncritical (nɒnˈkrɪtɪkᵊl) ADJECTIVE not containing or making severe or negative judgments.

nondemocratic (ˌnɒndɛməˈkrætɪk) ADJECTIVE not adhering to the principles or practice of democracy.

nondenominational (ˌnɒndɪˌnɒmɪˈneɪʃənᵊl) ADJECTIVE not of or related to any religious denomination.

nondescript (ˈnɒndɪˌskrɪpt) ADJECTIVE [1] lacking distinct or individual characteristics; having no outstanding features. ◆ NOUN [2] a nondescript person or thing.
▷HISTORY C17: from NON- + Latin *dēscriptus*, past participle of *dēscribere* to copy, DESCRIBE

nondestructive testing (ˌnɒndɪˈstrʌktɪv) NOUN any of several methods of detecting flaws in metals without causing damage. The most common techniques involve the use of X-rays, gamma rays, and ultrasonic vibrations. Abbreviation: **NDT.**

nondirective therapy (ˌnɒndɪˈrɛktɪv, ˌnɒndaɪ-) NOUN *Psychiatry* another name for **client-centred therapy.**

nondisjunction (ˌnɒndɪsˈdʒʌŋkʃən) NOUN the failure of paired homologous chromosomes to move to opposite poles of the cell during meiosis.

nondomiciled (nɒnˈdɒmɪsaɪld) ADJECTIVE of, relating to, or denoting a person who is not domiciled in his country of origin.

nondrinker (nɒnˈdrɪŋkə) NOUN someone who does not drink alcohol.

nondrip (nɒnˈdrɪp) ADJECTIVE (of paint) specially formulated to minimize dripping during application.

none¹ (nʌn) PRONOUN [1] not any of a particular class: *none of my letters has arrived.* [2] no-one; nobody: *there was none to tell the tale.* [3] no part (of a whole); not any (of): *none of it looks edible.* [4] **none other.** no other person: *none other than the Queen herself.* [5] **none the.** (foll by a comparative adjective) in no degree: *she was none the worse for her ordeal.* [6] **none too.** not very: *he was none too pleased with his car.*
▷HISTORY Old English *nān*, literally: not one

> **Language note** *None* is a singular pronoun and should be used with a singular form of a verb: *none of the students has* (not *have*) *a car.*

none² (nəʊn) NOUN another word for **nones.**

noneconomic (ˌnɒniːkəˈnɒmɪk, -ɛkəˈnɒmɪk) ADJECTIVE not of or relating to economic factors: *noneconomic benefits.*

noneffective (ˌnɒnɪˈfɛktɪv) *Chiefly US* ◆ ADJECTIVE [1] not effective. [2] unfit for or incapable of active military service. ◆ NOUN [3] *Military* a noneffective person.

nonego (nɒnˈiːgəʊ, -ˈɛgəʊ) NOUN *Philosophy* everything that is outside one's conscious self, such as one's environment.

nonentity (nɒnˈɛntɪtɪ) NOUN, *plural* **-ties.** [1] an insignificant person or thing. [2] a nonexistent thing. [3] the state of not existing; nonexistence.

nonequivalence (ˌnɒnɪˈkwɪvələns) NOUN [1] the relationship of being unequal or incomparable. [2] *Logic* **a** the relation between two statements only one of which can be true in any circumstances. **b** a function of two statements that takes the value true only when one but not both of its arguments is true. **c** a compound statement asserting that just one of its components is true. ◆ Also called **exclusive or.**

nones (nəʊnz) NOUN (*functioning as singular or plural*) [1] (in the Roman calendar) the ninth day before the ides of each month: the seventh day of March, May, July, and October, and the fifth of each other month. See also **calends.** [2] *Chiefly RC Church* the fifth of the seven canonical hours of the divine office, originally fixed at the ninth hour of the day, about 3 p.m.
▷HISTORY Old English *nōn*, from Latin *nōna hora* ninth hour, from *nōnus* ninth

nonessential (ˌnɒnɪˈsɛnʃəl) ADJECTIVE [1] not essential; not necessary. [2] *Biochem* (of an amino acid in a particular organism) able to be synthesized from other substances. ◆ NOUN [3] a nonessential person or thing.

nonesuch *or* **nonsuch** (ˈnʌnˌsʌtʃ) NOUN [1] *Archaic* a matchless person or thing; nonpareil. [2] another name for **black medick.**

nonet (nɒˈnɛt) NOUN [1] a piece of music composed for a group of nine instruments. [2] an instrumental group of nine players.
▷HISTORY C19: from Italian *nonetto*, from *nono* ninth, from Latin *nōnus*

nonetheless (ˌnʌnðəˈlɛs) SENTENCE CONNECTOR despite that; however; nevertheless.

non-Euclidean geometry NOUN the branch of modern geometry in which certain axioms of Euclidean geometry are restated. It introduces fundamental changes into the concept of space.

nonevent (ˌnɒnɪˈvɛnt) NOUN a disappointing or insignificant occurrence, esp one predicted to be important.

nonexclusive (ˌnɒnɪksˈkluːsɪv) ADJECTIVE not belonging to a particular individual or group: *a nonexclusive deal.*

nonexecutive (ˌnɒnɪgˈzɛkjʊtɪv) ADJECTIVE not having the function or purpose of carrying plans, orders, laws, etc., into practical effect: *a nonexecutive role on the board.*

nonexecutive director NOUN a director of a commercial company who is not a full-time member of the company but is brought in to advise the other directors.

nonexistent (ˌnɒnɪgˈzɪstənt) ADJECTIVE [1] not having being or existence. [2] not present under specified conditions or in a specified place.
▸**ˌnonexˈistence** NOUN

nonfatal (nɒnˈfeɪtᵊl) ADJECTIVE not resulting in or capable of causing death.

nonfattening (nɒnˈfætᵊnɪŋ) ADJECTIVE not causing weight gain: *a nonfattening alternative.*

nonfeasance (nɒnˈfiːzᵊns) NOUN *Law* a failure to act when under an obligation to do so. Compare **malfeasance, misfeasance.**
▷HISTORY C16: from NON- + *feasance* (obsolete) performing or doing, from French *faisance*, from *faire* to do, from Latin *facere*

nonferrous (nɒnˈfɛrəs) ADJECTIVE [1] denoting any metal other than iron. [2] not containing iron: *a nonferrous alloy.*

nonfiction (nɒnˈfɪkʃən) NOUN [1] writing dealing with facts and events rather than imaginative narration. [2] (*modifier*) relating to or denoting nonfiction.
▸**nonˈfictional** ADJECTIVE ▸**nonˈfictionally** ADVERB

nonflammable (nɒnˈflæməbᵊl) ADJECTIVE incapable of burning or not easily set on fire; not flammable.

nong (nɒŋ) NOUN *Austral, slang* a stupid or incompetent person.
▷HISTORY C19: perhaps alteration of obsolete English dialect *nigmenog* silly fellow, of unknown origin

nongovernmental (ˌnɒngʌvəˈmɛntᵊl) ADJECTIVE not related to government affairs or procedures.

nonharmonic (ˌnɒnhɑːˈmɒnɪk) ADJECTIVE *Music* not relating to the harmony formed by a chord or chords.

non-Hodgkin's lymphoma (-ˈhɒdʒkɪnz) NOUN any form of lymphoma other than Hodgkin's disease.

nonillion (nəʊˈnɪljən) NOUN [1] (in Britain, France, and Germany) the number represented as one followed by 54 zeros (10^{54}). [2] (in the US and Canada) the number represented as one followed by 30 zeros (10^{30}). Brit word: **quintillion.**
▷HISTORY C17: from French, from Latin *nōnus* ninth, on the model of MILLION
▸**noˈnillionth** ADJECTIVE, NOUN

non-impact printer NOUN *Computing* any printing device in which the images are created without being struck onto the paper, such as a laser printer or ink-jet printer.

nonindustrial (ˌnɒnɪnˈdʌstrɪəl) ADJECTIVE not of or relating to an industrial society, place, or age.

nonintellectual (ˌnɒnɪntɪˈlɛktʃʊəl) ADJECTIVE not appealing to or characteristic of people with a developed intellect.

nonintervention (ˌnɒnɪntəˈvɛnʃən) NOUN refusal to intervene, esp the abstention by a state from intervening in the affairs of other states or in its own internal disputes.
▸**ˌnoninterˈventional** ADJECTIVE ▸**ˌnoninterˈventionist** NOUN, ADJECTIVE

noninvasive (ˌnɒnɪnˈveɪsɪv) ADJECTIVE (of medical treatment) not involving the making of a relatively large incision in the body or the insertion of instruments, etc., into the patient.

noniron (nɒnˈaɪən) ADJECTIVE (of a fabric) composed of any of various man-made fibres that are crease-resistant and do not require ironing.

nonjoinder (nɒnˈdʒɔɪndə) NOUN *Law* the failure to join as party to a suit a person who should have been included either as a plaintiff or as a defendant. Compare **misjoinder.**

nonjudgmental *or* **nonjudgemental** (ˌnɒndʒʌdʒˈmɛntᵊl) ADJECTIVE of, relating to, or denoting an attitude, approach, etc., that is open and not incorporating a judgment one way or the other.

nonjuror (nɒnˈdʒʊərə) NOUN a person who refuses to take an oath, as of allegiance.

Nonjuror (nɒnˈdʒʊərə) NOUN any of a group of clergy in England and Scotland who declined to take the oath of allegiance to William and Mary in 1689.

nonlethal (nɒnˈliːθəl) ADJECTIVE not resulting in or capable of causing death.

non licet (ˈnɒn ˈlaɪsɪt) ADJECTIVE not permitted; unlawful.
▷HISTORY C17: Latin, literally: it is not allowed

nonlinear (nɒnˈlɪnɪə) ADJECTIVE [1] not of, in, along, or relating to a line. [2] denoting digital editing in which edits are saved on computer, rather than videotape, thus enabling further edits to be made.

non liquet (ˈnɒn ˈlaɪkwɪt) ADJECTIVE *Roman law* (of a cause, evidence, etc.) not clear.
▷HISTORY C17: Latin, literally: it is not clear

nonliterary (nɒnˈlɪtərərɪ, -ˈlɪtrərɪ) ADJECTIVE not of, relating to, concerned with, or characteristic of literature or scholarly writing.

nonlocal (nɒnˈləʊkᵊl) ADJECTIVE not of, affecting, or confined to a limited area or part: *the nonlocal aspect of the psyche.*

non-malignant (ˌnɒnməˈlɪgnənt) ADJECTIVE (of a tumour) not uncontrollable or resistant to therapy.

nonmedical (nɒnˈmɛdɪkᵊl) ADJECTIVE not of, relating to, or using medical theory or practice.

nonmember (nɒnˈmɛmbə) NOUN a person who is not a member of a club, etc.

nonmetal (nɒnˈmɛtᵊl) NOUN any of a number of chemical elements that form negative ions, have acidic oxides, and are generally poor conductors of heat and electricity.

nonmetallic (ˌnɒnmɪˈtælɪk) ADJECTIVE [1] not of metal. [2] of, concerned with, or being a nonmetal.

nonmonetary advantages (nɒnˈmʌnɪtərɪ) PLURAL NOUN the beneficial aspects of an employment, such as the stimulation of the work, attractiveness of the workplace, or its nearness to one's home, that do not reflect its financial remuneration.

nonmoral (nɒnˈmɒrəl) ADJECTIVE not involving or related to morality or ethics; neither moral nor immoral.

non-native NOUN a person who is not a native of a particular place or country.

non-naturalism NOUN the meta-ethical doctrine that moral properties exist but are not reducible to "natural", empirical, or supernatural ones, and that moral judgments therefore state a special kind of fact. Compare **naturalistic fallacy.** See also **descriptivism.**

non-negotiable ADJECTIVE not open to negotiation or discussion: *the policy is non-negotiable.*

Nonne's syndrome (nɒnz) NOUN another name for **cerebellar syndrome.**

non-nuclear ADJECTIVE [1] not of, concerned with, or operated by energy from fission or fusion of atomic nuclei: *non-nuclear weapons.* [2] not involving, concerned with, or possessing nuclear weapons: *non-nuclear states.*

nonobjective (ˌnɒnəb'dʒɛktɪv) ADJECTIVE of or designating an art movement in which things are depicted in an abstract or purely formalized way, not as they appear in reality.

nonofficial (ˌnɒnə'fɪʃəl) ADJECTIVE not official or formal.

no-nonsense (ˌnəʊ'nɒnsəns) ADJECTIVE sensible, practical, straightforward; without nonsense of any kind: *a businesslike no-nonsense approach; a severe no-nonsense look.*

nonoperational (ˌnɒnɒpər'eɪʃənᵊl) ADJECTIVE not in working order or ready to use.

nonorthodox (nɒn'ɔːθəˌdɒks) ADJECTIVE not conforming with established or accepted standards, as in religion, behaviour, or attitudes.

nonparametric statistics (ˌnɒnpærə'mɛtrɪk) NOUN *(functioning as singular)* the branch of statistics that studies data measurable on an ordinal or nominal scale, to which arithmetic operations cannot be applied.

nonpareil ('nɒnpərəl, ˌnɒnpə'reɪl) NOUN [1] a person or thing that is unsurpassed or unmatched; peerless example. [2] (formerly) a size of printers' type equal to 6 point. [3] *US* a small bead of coloured sugar used to decorate cakes, biscuits, etc. [4] *Chiefly US* a flat round piece of chocolate covered with this sugar. ◆ ADJECTIVE [5] having no match or equal; peerless.
▷HISTORY C15: from French, from NON- + *pareil* similar

nonparous (nɒn'pærəs) ADJECTIVE never having given birth.

nonparticipating (ˌnɒnpɑː'tɪsɪˌpeɪtɪŋ) ADJECTIVE [1] not participating. [2] (of an assurance policy, share, etc.) not carrying the right to share in a company's profit.

nonpartisan *or* **nonpartizan** (ˌnɒnpɑːtɪ'zæn) ADJECTIVE not partisan or aligned, esp not affiliated to, influenced by, or supporting any one political party.
▸ **ˌnonpartiˈsanˌship** *or* **ˌnonpartiˈzanˌship** NOUN

nonparty (nɒn'pɑːtɪ) ADJECTIVE not connected with any one political party.

nonpaying (nɒn'peɪɪŋ) ADJECTIVE (of guests, customers, etc.) not expected or requested to pay.

nonpayment (nɒn'peɪmənt) NOUN the act or state of not paying.

nonpermanent (nɒn'pɜːmənənt) ADJECTIVE not existing or intended to exist for an indefinite time.

nonpersistent (ˌnɒnpə'sɪstənt) ADJECTIVE (of pesticides) breaking down rapidly after application; not persisting in the environment.

non-person NOUN a person regarded as nonexistent or unimportant; a nonentity.

nonphysical (nɒn'fɪzɪkᵊl) ADJECTIVE [1] not of or relating to the body or nature. [2] not sexual; platonic: *intimate nonphysical friendships.*

nonplaying (nɒn'pleɪɪŋ) ADJECTIVE belonging to a team, group, etc., but not participating in their pursuit: *appointed nonplaying captain.*

nonplus (nɒn'plʌs) VERB **-plusses, -plussing, -plussed** *or US* **-pluses, -plusing, -plused.** [1] *(tr)* to put at a loss; confound: *he was nonplussed by the sudden announcement.* ◆ NOUN, *plural* **-pluses.** [2] a state of utter perplexity prohibiting action or speech.
▷HISTORY C16: from Latin *nōn plūs* no further (that is, nothing further can be said or done)

nonpoisonous (nɒn'pɔɪzənəs) ADJECTIVE not having the effects or qualities of a poison.

nonpolitical (ˌnɒnpə'lɪtɪkᵊl) ADJECTIVE not of, dealing with, or relating to politics: *a nonpolitical organization.*

nonpolluting (ˌnɒnpə'luːtɪŋ) ADJECTIVE (of a fuel, vehicle, technology, etc.) not resulting in or causing pollution.

nonporous (nɒn'pɔːrəs) ADJECTIVE not permeable to water, air, or other fluids.

nonpractising (nɒn'præktɪsɪŋ) ADJECTIVE of or relating to a person who no longer observes or pursues their religious faith.

nonproductive (ˌnɒnprə'dʌktɪv) ADJECTIVE [1] (of workers) not directly responsible for producing goods. [2] having disappointing results; unproductive.
▸ **ˌnonproˈductiveness** NOUN ▸ **nonproductivity** (ˌnɒnprɒdʌk'tɪvɪtɪ) NOUN

nonprofessional (ˌnɒnprə'fɛʃənᵊl) ADJECTIVE [1] not of, relating to, suitable for, or engaged in a profession. [2] not undertaken or performed for gain or by people who are paid.

nonprofit (nɒn'prɒfɪt) *US* ◆ ADJECTIVE [1] another word for **non-profit-making.** ◆ NOUN [2] an organization that is not intended to make a profit.

non-profit-making ADJECTIVE not yielding a profit, esp because organized or established for some other reason: *a non-profit-making organization.*

nonproliferation (ˌnɒnprəˌlɪfər'eɪʃən) NOUN [1] **a** limitation of the production or spread of something, esp nuclear or chemical weapons. **b** *(as modifier)*: *a nonproliferation treaty.* [2] failure or refusal to proliferate.

non pros. *Law* ABBREVIATION FOR non prosequitur.

non-pros (ˌnɒn'prɒs) NOUN [1] short for **non prosequitur.** ◆ VERB **-prosses, -prossing, -prossed.** [2] *(tr)* to enter a judgment of non prosequitur against (a plaintiff).

non prosequitur ('nɒn prəʊ'sɛkwɪtə) NOUN *Law* (formerly) a judgment in favour of a defendant when the plaintiff failed to take the necessary steps in an action within the time allowed. Compare **nolle prosequi.**
▷HISTORY Latin, literally: he does not prosecute

nonracial (nɒn'reɪʃəl) ADJECTIVE not related to racial factors or discrimination.

nonrational (nɒn'ræʃənᵊl) ADJECTIVE not in accordance with the principles of logic or reason.

nonrecognition (ˌnɒnrɛkəg'nɪʃən) NOUN the act or an instance of refusing to acknowledge formally a government or the independence of a country.

nonreflexive (ˌnɒnrɪ'flɛksɪv) ADJECTIVE *Logic* (of a relation) neither reflexive nor irreflexive; holding between some members of its domain and themselves, and failing to hold between others.

nonreligious (ˌnɒnrɪ'lɪdʒəs) ADJECTIVE not of or relating to religious beliefs and practices.

nonrenewable (ˌnɒnrɪ'njuːəbᵊl) ADJECTIVE not able to be restored, replaced, recommenced, etc.: *nonrenewable resources.*

nonrepresentational (ˌnɒnrɛprɪzɛn'teɪʃənᵊl) ADJECTIVE *Art* another word for **abstract** (sense 4).

nonresident (nɒn'rɛzɪdənt) NOUN [1] a person who is not residing in the place implied or specified: *the hotel restaurant is open to nonresidents.* [2] a British person employed abroad on a contract for a minimum of one year, who is exempt from UK income tax provided that he does not spend more than 90 days in the UK during that tax year. ◆ ADJECTIVE [3] not residing in the place specified.
▸ **nonˈresidence** *or* **nonˈresidency** NOUN

nonresidential (ˌnɒnrɛzɪ'dɛnʃəl) ADJECTIVE [1] not suitable or allocated for residence: *nonresidential areas.* [2] not having residence: *nonresidential customers.*

nonresistant (ˌnɒnrɪ'zɪstənt) ADJECTIVE [1] incapable of resisting something, such as a disease; susceptible. [2] *History* (esp in 17th-century England) practising passive obedience to royal authority even when its commands were unjust.
▸ **ˌnonreˈsistance** NOUN

nonrestrictive (ˌnɒnrɪ'strɪktɪv) ADJECTIVE [1] not restrictive or limiting. [2] *Grammar* denoting a relative clause that is not restrictive. Compare **restrictive** (sense 2).

nonreturn (ˌnɒnrɪ'tɜːn) ADJECTIVE denoting a mechanism that permits flow in a pipe, tunnel, etc., in one direction only: *a nonreturn valve.*

nonreturnable (ˌnɒnrɪ'tɜːnəbᵊl) ADJECTIVE denoting a container, esp a bottle, on which no returnable deposit is paid on purchase of the contents.

nonreturn valve NOUN another name for **check valve.**

nonrhotic (nɒn'rəʊtɪk) ADJECTIVE *Phonetics* denoting or speaking a dialect of English in which preconsonantal *r*s are not pronounced.
▸ **ˌnonrhoˈticity** NOUN

nonrigid (nɒn'rɪdʒɪd) ADJECTIVE [1] not rigid; flexible. [2] (of the gas envelope of an airship) flexible and held in shape only by the internal gas pressure.

nonscheduled (nɒn'ʃɛdjuːld; *also, esp US* nɒn'skɛdʒʊəld) ADJECTIVE [1] not according to a schedule or plan; unscheduled. [2] (of an airline) operating without published flight schedules.

nonscientific (ˌnɒnsaɪən'tɪfɪk) ADJECTIVE not of, relating to, derived from, or used in science.

nonsectarian (ˌnɒnsɛk'tɛərɪən) ADJECTIVE not narrow-minded, esp as a result of rigid adherence to a particular sect; broad-minded.

nonselective (ˌnɒnsɪ'lɛktɪv) ADJECTIVE (of a school, education system, etc.) admitting all pupils regardless of ability; inclusive.

nonsense ('nɒnsəns) NOUN [1] something that has or makes no sense; unintelligible language; drivel. [2] conduct or action that is absurd. [3] foolish or evasive behaviour or manners: *she'll stand no nonsense.* [4] See **no-nonsense.** [5] things of little or no value or importance; trash. ◆ INTERJECTION [6] an exclamation of disagreement.
▸ **nonsensical** (nɒn'sɛnsɪkᵊl) ADJECTIVE ▸ **nonˈsensically** ADVERB ▸ **nonˈsensicalness** *or* **nonˌsensiˈcality** NOUN

nonsense correlation NOUN *Statistics* a correlation supported by data but having no basis in reality, as between incidence of the common cold and ownership of televisions.

nonsense syllable NOUN *Psychol* a syllable, like *bik,* having no meaning. Lists of such syllables have been used to investigate memory and learning.

nonsense verse NOUN verse in which the sense is nonexistent or absurd, such as that of Edward Lear.

non seq. ABBREVIATION FOR non sequitur.

non sequitur ('nɒn 'sɛkwɪtə) NOUN [1] a statement having little or no relevance to what preceded it. [2] *Logic* a conclusion that does not follow from the premises. Abbreviation: **non seq.**
▷HISTORY Latin, literally: it does not follow

nonsexist (nɒn'sɛksɪst) ADJECTIVE not discriminating on the basis of sex, esp not against women.

nonsexual (nɒn'sɛksjʊəl) ADJECTIVE not of, relating to, or characterized by sex or sexuality.

nonslip (nɒn'slɪp) ADJECTIVE designed to reduce or prevent slipping.

nonsmoker (nɒn'sməʊkə) NOUN [1] a person who does not smoke. [2] a train compartment in which smoking is forbidden.
▸ **nonˈsmoking** ADJECTIVE

nonspeaking (nɒn'spiːkɪŋ) ADJECTIVE (of a part in a play) not having any lines to speak.

nonspecialist (nɒn'spɛʃəlɪst) NOUN [1] someone who does not specialize in a particular area, activity, field of research, etc. ◆ ADJECTIVE [2] not specializing in a particular area, activity, field of research, etc.

nonspecific (ˌnɒnspɪ'sɪfɪk) ADJECTIVE not explicit, particular, or definite.

nonspecific urethritis NOUN inflammation of the urethra as a result of a venereal infection that cannot be traced to a specific cause. Abbreviation: **NSU.**

nonspecular reflection (nɒn'spɛkjʊlə) NOUN *Physics* the diffuse reflection of sound or light waves.

nonsporting (nɒn'spɔːtɪŋ) ADJECTIVE [1] not of or related to sport. [2] having no aptitude for sport.

nonstandard (nɒn'stændəd) ADJECTIVE [1] denoting or characterized by idiom, vocabulary, etc., that is not regarded as correct and acceptable by educated native speakers of a language; not standard. [2] deviating from a given standard.

nonstarter (nɒn'stɑːtə) NOUN [1] a horse that fails to run in a race for which it has been entered. [2] a person or thing that is useless, has little chance of success, etc.

nonstative (nɒnˈsteɪtɪv) *Grammar* ◆ ADJECTIVE 1 denoting a verb describing an action rather than a state, as for example *throw* or *thank* as opposed to *know* or *hate*. Compare **stative.** ◆ NOUN 2 a nonstative verb. ◆ Also **active.**

nonstick (ˈnɒnˈstɪk) ADJECTIVE (of saucepans, frying pans, etc.) coated with a substance such as polytetrafluoroethylene (PTFE) that prevents food sticking to them.

nonstoichiometric (nɒnˌstɔɪkɪəˈmɛtrɪk) ADJECTIVE *Chem* (of a solid compound) having a composition in which the ratio of the atoms present is not a simple integer.

nonstop (ˈnɒnˈstɒp) ADJECTIVE, ADVERB done without pause or interruption: *a nonstop flight.*

nonstrategic (ˌnɒnstrəˈtiːdʒɪk) ADJECTIVE not of, relating to, or characteristic of strategy.

nonstriated (nɒnˈstraɪeɪtɪd) ADJECTIVE (esp of certain muscle fibres) having no striations.

non-striker NOUN *Cricket* the batsman who is not facing the bowling.

nonsuch (ˈnʌnˌsʌtʃ) NOUN a variant spelling of **nonesuch.**

Nonsuch Palace (ˈnʌnˌsʌtʃ) NOUN a former royal palace in Cuddington in London: built in 1538 for Henry VIII; later visited by Elizabeth I, James I, Charles I, and Charles II; demolished (1682–1702).

nonsuit (nɒnˈsuːt, -ˈsjuːt) *Law* ◆ NOUN 1 an order of a judge dismissing a suit when the plaintiff fails to show he has a good cause of action or fails to produce any evidence. ◆ VERB 2 (*tr*) to order the dismissal of the suit of (a person).

nonsurgical (nɒnˈsɜːdʒɪkᵊl) ADJECTIVE not of, relating to, involving, or used in surgery.

nonswimmer (nɒnˈswɪmə) NOUN a person who cannot swim.

nonsymmetric (ˌnɒnsɪˈmetrɪk) ADJECTIVE *Logic, maths* (of a relation) not symmetric, asymmetric, or antisymmetric; holding between some pairs of arguments *x* and *y* and failing to hold for some other pairs when it holds between *y* and *x*.

nontaxable (nɒnˈtæksəbᵊl) ADJECTIVE not subject to tax.

nonteaching (nɒnˈtiːtʃɪŋ) ADJECTIVE of or relating to a post within an academic or vocational environment which does not entail teaching.

nontechnical (nɒnˈtɛknɪkᵊl) ADJECTIVE not relating to, characteristic of, or skilled in a particular field of activity and its terminology.

nontoxic (nɒnˈtɒksɪk) ADJECTIVE not of, relating to, or caused by a toxin or poison: *safe, nontoxic paint.*

nontraditional (ˌnɒntrəˈdɪʃənᵊl) ADJECTIVE not traditional; unconventional: *nontraditional lifestyles.*

nontransitive (nɒnˈtrænsɪtɪv) ADJECTIVE *Logic* (of a relation) neither transitive nor intransitive.

non troppo (ˈnɒn ˈtrɒpəʊ) ADVERB *Music* (preceded by a musical direction, esp a tempo marking) not to be observed too strictly (esp in the phrases **allegro ma non troppo, adagio ma non troppo**).

non-U (nɒnˈjuː) ADJECTIVE *Brit informal* (esp of language) not characteristic of or used by the upper class. Compare **U**[1].

nonunion (nɒnˈjuːnjən) ADJECTIVE 1 not belonging or related to a trade union: *nonunion workers.* 2 not favouring or employing union labour: *a nonunion shop.* 3 not produced by union labour: *nonunion shirts.* ◆ NOUN 4 *Pathol* failure of broken bones or bone fragments to heal.

nonunionism (nɒnˈjuːnjəˌnɪzəm) NOUN *Chiefly US* opposition to trade unionism.
▸ **nonˈunionist** NOUN, ADJECTIVE

nonvenomous (nɒnˈvɛnəməs) ADJECTIVE (of a snake, spider, etc.) not venomous.

nonverbal (nɒnˈvɜːbᵊl) ADJECTIVE not spoken: *the nonverbal signals of body movement.*

nonverbal communication NOUN *Psychol* those aspects of communication, such as gestures and facial expressions, that do not involve verbal communication but which may include nonverbal aspects of speech itself (accent, tone of voice, speed of speaking, etc.).

nonvintage (nɒnˈvɪntɪdʒ) ADJECTIVE 1 (of wine) not of an outstandingly good year. 2 not representative of the best: *two nonvintage teams.*

nonviolence (nɒnˈvaɪələns) NOUN abstention from the use of physical force to achieve goals.
▸ **nonˈviolent** ADJECTIVE

nonvoter (nɒnˈvəʊtə) NOUN 1 a person who does not vote. 2 a person not eligible to vote.

nonvoting (nɒnˈvəʊtɪŋ) ADJECTIVE 1 of or relating to a nonvoter. 2 *Finance* (of shares) not entitling the holder to vote at company meetings.

non-White NOUN a person not of the Caucasoid or White race.

nonworking (nɒnˈwɜːkɪŋ) ADJECTIVE 1 not engaged in payed employment: *nonworking mothers.* 2 (of machinery, technology, etc.) not operating properly or effectively: *nonworking telephones.*

noodle[1] (ˈnuːdᵊl) NOUN (*often plural*) a ribbon-like strip of pasta: noodles are often served in soup or with a sauce.
▷ **HISTORY** C18: from German *Nudel,* origin obscure

noodle[2] (ˈnuːdᵊl) NOUN 1 *US and Canadian* a slang word for **head** (sense 1). 2 a simpleton.
▷ **HISTORY** C18: perhaps a blend of NOODLE[1] and NOODLE[1]

noodle[3] (ˈnuːdᵊl) VERB (*intr*) *Slang* to improvise aimlessly on a musical instrument.

Noogoora burr (nəˈguːrə) NOUN *Austral* a European cocklebur, *Xanthium pungens,* that is poisonous to stock.
▷ **HISTORY** from *Noogoora* a sheep station in Queensland

nook (nʊk) NOUN 1 a corner or narrow recess, as in a room. 2 a secluded or sheltered place; retreat.
▷ **HISTORY** C13: origin obscure; perhaps related to Norwegian dialect *nok* hook

nooky *or* **nookie** (ˈnʊkɪ) NOUN *Slang* sexual intercourse.
▷ **HISTORY** C20: of uncertain origin; perhaps from NOOK

noon (nuːn) NOUN 1 **a** the middle of the day; 12 o'clock in the daytime or the time or point at which the sun crosses the local meridian. **b** (*as modifier*): *the noon sun.* 2 *Poetic* the highest, brightest, or most important part; culmination.
▷ **HISTORY** Old English *nōn,* from Latin *nōna* (*hōra*) ninth hour (originally 3 p.m., the ninth hour from sunrise)

noonday (ˈnuːnˌdeɪ) NOUN **a** the middle of the day; noon. **b** (*as modifier*): *the noonday sun.*

no-one *or* **no one** PRONOUN no person; nobody.

> **Language note** See at **everyone.**

nooning (ˈnuːnɪŋ) NOUN *Dialect, chiefly US* 1 a midday break for rest or food. 2 midday; noon.

noontime (ˈnuːnˌtaɪm) *or* **noontide** NOUN **a** the middle of the day; noon. **b** (*as modifier*): *a noontime drink.*

Noordbrabant (noːrdˈbraːbɑnt) NOUN the Dutch name for **North Brabant.**

Noordholland (noːrtˈhɔlɑnt) NOUN the Dutch name for **North Holland.**

noose (nuːs) NOUN 1 a loop in the end of a rope or cord, such as a lasso, snare, or hangman's halter, usually tied with a slipknot. 2 something that restrains, binds, or traps. 3 **put one's head in a noose.** to bring about one's own downfall. ◆ VERB (*tr*) 4 to secure or catch in or as if in a noose. 5 to make a noose of or in.
▷ **HISTORY** C15: perhaps from Provençal *nous,* from Latin *nōdus* NODE

Nootka (ˈnʊtkə, ˈnuːt-) NOUN 1 (*plural* **-ka** *or* **-kas**) a member of a North American Indian people living in British Columbia and Vancouver Island. 2 the language of this people, belonging to the Wakashan family.

nopal (ˈnəʊpᵊl) NOUN 1 any of various cactuses of the genus *Nopalea,* esp the red-flowered *N. cochinellifera,* which is a host plant of the cochineal insect. 2 a cactus, *Opuntia lindheimeri,* having yellow flowers and purple fruits. See also **prickly pear.**
▷ **HISTORY** C18: from Spanish, from Nahuatl *nopálli* cactus

no-par ADJECTIVE (of securities) without a par value.

nope (nəʊp) SENTENCE SUBSTITUTE an informal word for **no**[1].
▷ **HISTORY** C19: originally US, a variant of NO[1]

Nopo (ˈnəʊˌpəʊ) ACRONYM FOR no person operation; denoting driverless trains suggested as a means of increasing the efficiency of some railway systems.

nor (nɔː; *unstressed* nə) CONJUNCTION (*coordinating*), PREPOSITION 1 (used to join alternatives, the first of which is preceded by *neither*) and not: *neither measles nor mumps.* 2 (foll by an auxiliary verb or *have, do,* or *be* used as main verbs) (and) not...either: *they weren't talented — nor were they particularly funny.* 3 *Dialect* than: *better nor me.* 4 *Poetic* neither: *nor wind nor rain.*
▷ **HISTORY** C13: contraction of Old English *nōther,* from *nāhwæther* NEITHER

nor- COMBINING FORM 1 indicating that a chemical compound is derived from a specified compound by removal of a group or groups: *noradrenaline.* 2 indicating that a chemical compound is a normal isomer of a specified compound.
▷ **HISTORY** by shortening from NORMAL

noradrenaline (ˌnɔːrəˈdrɛnəlɪn, -liːn) *or* **noradrenalin** NOUN a hormone secreted by the adrenal medulla, increasing blood pressure and heart rate, and by the endings of sympathetic nerves, when it acts as a neurotransmitter both centrally and peripherally. Formula: $C_8H_{11}NO_3$. US name: **norepinephrine.**

Noraid (ˈnɔːrˌeɪd) NOUN an American organization that supports the Republicans in Northern Ireland.

NOR circuit *or* **gate** (nɔː) NOUN *Computing* a logic circuit having two or more input wires and one output wire that has a high-voltage output signal only if all input signals are at a low voltage. Compare **AND circuit.**
▷ **HISTORY** C20: from NOR, so named because the action performed is similar to the operation of the conjunction *nor* in logic

Nord (*French* nɔr) NOUN a department of N France, in Nord-Pas-de-Calais region. Capital: Lille. Pop.: 2 555 020 (1999). Area: 5774 sq. km (2252 sq. miles).

Nordenskjöld Sea (*Swedish* ˈnuːrdənʃœld) NOUN the former name of the **Laptev Sea.**
▷ **HISTORY** named after Nils Adolf Erik *Nordenskjöld* (1832–1901), Swedish Arctic explorer and geologist

nordic (ˈnɔːdɪk) ADJECTIVE *Skiing* of or relating to competitions in cross-country racing and ski-jumping. Compare **alpine** (sense 4).

Nordic (ˈnɔːdɪk) ADJECTIVE of, relating to, or belonging to a subdivision of the Caucasoid race typified by the tall blond blue-eyed long-headed inhabitants of N Britain, Scandinavia, N Germany, and the Netherlands.
▷ **HISTORY** C19: from French *nordique,* from *nord* NORTH

Nordkyn Cape (*Norwegian* ˈnuːrçyːn) NOUN a cape in N Norway: the northernmost point of the European mainland.

Nord-Pas-de-Calais (*French* nɔrpɑdəkalɛ) NOUN a region of N France, on the Straits of Dover (the **Pas de Calais**): coal-mining, textile, and metallurgical industries.

Nordrhein-Westfalen (ˈnɔrtrainvɛstˈfaːlən) NOUN the German name for **North Rhine-Westphalia.**

norepinephrine (ˌnɔːrɛpɪˈnɛfrɪn, -riːn) NOUN the US name for **noradrenaline.**

Norfolk (ˈnɔːfək) NOUN 1 a county of E England, on the North Sea and the Wash: low-lying, with large areas of fens in the west and the Broads in the east; rich agriculturally. Administrative centre: Norwich. Pop.: 796 733 (2001). Area: 5368 sq. km (2072 sq. miles). 2 a port in SE Virginia, on the Elizabeth River and Hampton Roads: headquarters of the US Atlantic fleet; shipbuilding. Pop.: 234 403 (2000).

Norfolk Island NOUN an island in the S Pacific, between New Caledonia and N New Zealand: an Australian external territory; discovered by Captain Cook in 1774; a penal settlement in early years. Pop.: 2665 (1993). Area: 36 sq. km (14 sq. miles).

Norfolk Island pine NOUN a tall coniferous tree, *Araucaria heterophylla,* native to Norfolk Island and widely cultivated.

Norfolk jacket NOUN a man's single-breasted

belted jacket with one or two chest pockets and a box pleat down the back.
▷HISTORY C19: worn in NORFOLK for duck shooting

Norfolk terrier NOUN a small wiry-coated breed of terrier having a short tail and pendent ears.

Norge (ˈnɔrgə) NOUN the Norwegian name for **Norway**.

nori (ˈnɔːrɪ) NOUN an edible seaweed often used in Japanese cookery, esp for wrapping sushi or rice balls.
▷HISTORY Japanese

noria (ˈnɔːrɪə) NOUN a water wheel with buckets attached to its rim for raising water from a stream into irrigation canals: common in Spain and the Orient.
▷HISTORY C18: via Spanish from Arabic *nāʿūra*, from *naʿara* to creak

Noricum (ˈnɒrɪkəm) NOUN an Alpine kingdom of the Celts, south of the Danube: comprises present-day central Austria and parts of Bavaria; a Roman province from about 16 B.C.

norite (ˈnɔːraɪt) NOUN a variety of gabbro composed mainly of hypersthene and labradorite feldspar.
▷HISTORY C19: from Norwegian *norit*, from NORGE Norway + *-it* -ITE[1]

nork (nɔːk) NOUN (*usually plural*) *Austral, slang* a female breast.
▷HISTORY C20: of unknown origin

norland (ˈnɔːlənd) NOUN *Archaic* the north part of a country or the earth.
▷HISTORY C17: contraction of NORTH + LAND

norm (nɔːm) NOUN [1] an average level of achievement or performance, as of a group or person. [2] a standard of achievement or behaviour that is required, desired, or designated as normal. [3] *Sociol* an established standard of behaviour shared by members of a social group to which each member is expected to conform. [4] *Maths* **a** the length of a vector expressed as the square root of the sum of the square of its components. **b** another name for **mode** (sense 6). [5] *Geology* the theoretical standard mineral composition of an igneous rock.
▷HISTORY C19: from Latin *norma* carpenter's rule, square

Norm (nɔːm) NOUN a stereotype of the unathletic Australian male.
▷HISTORY from a cartoon figure in the government-sponsored *Life, Be In It* campaign

norm. ABBREVIATION FOR normal.

Norm. ABBREVIATION FOR Norman.

Norma (ˈnɔːmə) NOUN, *Latin genitive* **Normae** (ˈnɔːmiː). a constellation in the S hemisphere crossed by the Milky Way lying near Scorpius and Ara.

normal (ˈnɔːməl) ADJECTIVE [1] usual; regular; common; typical: *the normal way of doing it; the normal level.* [2] constituting a standard: *if we take this as normal.* [3] *Psychol* **a** being within certain limits of intelligence, educational success or ability, etc. **b** conforming to the conventions of one's group. [4] *Biology, med* (of laboratory animals) maintained in a natural state for purposes of comparison with animals treated with drugs, etc. [5] *Chem* (of a solution) containing a number of grams equal to the equivalent weight of the solute in each litre of solvent. Symbol: *N.* [6] *Chem* denoting a straight-chain hydrocarbon: *a normal alkane.* Prefix: ***n*-**, e.g. *n*-octane. [7] *Geometry* another word for **perpendicular** (sense 1). ◆ NOUN [8] the usual, average, or typical state, degree, form, etc. [9] anything that is normal. [10] *Geometry* a line or plane perpendicular to another line or plane or to the tangent of a curved line or plane at the point of contact.
▷HISTORY C16: from Latin *normālis* conforming to the carpenter's square, from *norma* NORM
▸**normality** (nɔːˈmælɪtɪ) *or (esp US)* ˈ**normalcy** NOUN

normal curve NOUN *Statistics* a symmetrical bell-shaped curve representing the probability density function of a normal distribution. The area of a vertical section of the curve represents the probability that the random variable lies between the values which delimit the section.

normal distribution NOUN *Statistics* a continuous distribution of a random variable with its mean, median, and mode equal, the probability density function of which is given by ($\underline{exp}[(x-\mu)^2/2\sigma^2]/\sigma\sqrt{(2\pi)}$) where μ is the mean and σ^2 the variance. Also called: **Gaussian distribution.**

normalization *or* **normalisation** (ˌnɔːməlaɪˈzeɪʃən) NOUN [1] the act or process of normalizing. [2] *Social welfare* the policy of offering mentally or physically handicapped people patterns, conditions, and experiences of everyday life as close as possible to those of nonhandicapped people, by not segregating them physically, socially, and administratively from the rest of society.

normalize *or* **normalise** (ˈnɔːməˌlaɪz) VERB (*tr*) [1] to bring or make into the normal state. [2] to bring into conformity with a standard. [3] to heat (steel) above a critical temperature and allow it to cool in air to relieve internal stresses; anneal.

normally (ˈnɔːməlɪ) ADVERB [1] as a rule; usually; ordinarily. [2] in a normal manner.

normal matrix NOUN a square matrix *A* for which *AA** = *A***A*, where *A** is the Hermitian conjugate of *A*.

normal school NOUN (in France, and formerly England, the US, and Canada) a school or institution for training teachers.
▷HISTORY C19: from French *école normale:* the first French school so named was intended as a model for similar institutions

Norman (ˈnɔːmən) NOUN [1] (in the Middle Ages) a member of the people of Normandy descended from the 10th-century Scandinavian conquerors of the country and the native French. [2] a native or inhabitant of Normandy. [3] another name for **Norman French.** ◆ ADJECTIVE [4] of, relating to, or characteristic of the Normans, esp the Norman kings of England, the Norman people living in England, or their dialect of French. [5] of, relating to, or characteristic of Normandy or its inhabitants. [6] denoting, relating to, or having the style of Romanesque architecture used in Britain from the Norman Conquest until the 12th century. It is characterized by the rounded arch, the groin vault, massive masonry walls, etc.

Norman arch NOUN *Chiefly Brit* a semicircular arch, esp one in the Romanesque style of architecture developed by the Normans in England. Also called: **Roman arch.**

Norman Conquest NOUN the invasion and settlement of England by the Normans, following the Battle of Hastings (1066).

Normandy (ˈnɔːməndɪ) NOUN a former province of N France, on the English Channel: settled by Vikings under Rollo in the 10th century; scene of the Allied landings in 1944. Chief town: Rouen. French name: **Normandie** (nɔrmɑ̃di).

Norman English NOUN the dialect of English used by the Norman conquerors of England.

Norman French NOUN the medieval Norman and English dialect of Old French. See also **Anglo-French** (sense 3).

Normanize *or* **Normanise** (ˈnɔːməˌnaɪz) VERB to make or become Norman in character, style, customs, etc.
▸ˌ**Normaniˈzation** *or* ˌ**Normaniˈsation** NOUN

normative (ˈnɔːmətɪv) ADJECTIVE [1] implying, creating, or prescribing a norm or standard, as in language: *normative grammar.* [2] expressing value judgments or prescriptions as contrasted with stating facts: *normative economics.* [3] of, relating to, or based on norms.
▸ˈ**normatively** ADVERB ▸ˈ**normativeness** NOUN

normotensive (ˌnɔːməʊˈtɛnsɪv) ADJECTIVE having or denoting normal blood pressure.

Norn[1] (nɔːn) NOUN *Norse myth* any of the three virgin goddesses of fate, who predestine the lives of the gods and men.
▷HISTORY C18: Old Norse

Norn[2] (nɔːn) NOUN the medieval Norse language of the Orkneys, Shetlands, and parts of N Scotland. It was extinct by 1750.
▷HISTORY C17: from Old Norse *norrǿna* Norwegian, from *northr* north

Norrköping (*Swedish* ˈnɔrtçøːpiŋ) NOUN a port in SE Sweden, near the Baltic. Pop.: 122 212 (2000 est.).

Norroy (ˈnɒrɔɪ) NOUN the third King-of-Arms in England: since 1943, called **Norroy and Ulster.**
▷HISTORY C15: Old French *nor* north + *roy* king

Norse (nɔːs) ADJECTIVE [1] of, relating to, or characteristic of ancient and medieval Scandinavia or its inhabitants. [2] of, relating to, or characteristic of Norway. ◆ NOUN [3] **a** the N group of Germanic languages, spoken in Scandinavia; Scandinavian. **b** any one of these languages, esp in their ancient or medieval forms. See also **Proto-Norse, Old Norse.** [4] **the Norse.** (*functioning as plural*) **a** the Norwegians. **b** the Vikings.

Norseman (ˈnɔːsmən) NOUN, *plural* **-men.** another name for a **Viking.**

north (nɔːθ) NOUN [1] one of the four cardinal points of the compass, at 0° or 360°, that is 90° from east and west and 180° from south. [2] the direction along a meridian towards the North Pole. [3] the direction in which a compass needle points; magnetic north. [4] **the North.** (*often capital*) any area lying in or towards the north. Related adjectives: **arctic, boreal.** [5] *Cards* (*usually capital*) the player or position at the table corresponding to north on the compass. ◆ ADJECTIVE [6] situated in, moving towards, or facing the north. [7] (esp of the wind) from the north. ◆ ADVERB [8] in, to, or towards the north. [9] *Archaic* (of the wind) from the north. ◆ Symbol **N.**
▷HISTORY Old English; related to Old Norse *northr*, Dutch *noord*, Old High German *nord*

North (nɔːθ) NOUN **the.** [1] the northern area of England, generally regarded as reaching approximately the southern boundaries of Yorkshire and Lancashire. [2] (in the US) the area approximately north of Maryland and the Ohio River, esp those states north of the Mason-Dixon Line that were known as the Free States during the Civil War. [3] the northern part of North America, esp the area consisting of Alaska, the Yukon, the Northwest Territories, and Nunavut; the North Country. [4] the countries of the world that are economically and technically advanced. [5] *Poetic* the north wind. ◆ ADJECTIVE [6] **a** of or denoting the northern part of a specified country, area, etc. **b** (*as part of a name*): *North Africa.*

North Africa NOUN the part of Africa between the Mediterranean and the Sahara: consists chiefly of Morocco, Algeria, Tunisia, Libya, and N Egypt.

North African ADJECTIVE [1] of or relating to North Africa or its inhabitants. ◆ NOUN [2] a native or inhabitant of North Africa.

Northallerton (nɔːˈθælətən) NOUN a market town in N England, administrative centre of North Yorkshire. Pop.: 13 774 (1991).

North America NOUN the third largest continent, linked with South America by the Isthmus of Panama and bordering on the Arctic Ocean, the N Pacific, the N Atlantic, the Gulf of Mexico, and the Caribbean. It consists generally of a great mountain system (the Western Cordillera) extending along the entire W coast, actively volcanic in the extreme north and south, with the Great Plains to the east and the Appalachians still further east, separated from the Canadian Shield by an arc of large lakes (Great Bear, Great Slave, Winnipeg, Superior, Michigan, Huron, Erie, Ontario); reaches its greatest height of 6194 m (20 320 ft.) in Mount McKinley, Alaska, and its lowest point of 85 m (280 ft.) below sea level in Death Valley, California, and ranges from snowfields, tundra, and taiga in the north to deserts in the southwest and tropical forests in the extreme south. Pop.: 421 006 000 (1996 est.). Area: over 24 000 000 sq. km (9 500 000 sq. miles).

North American ADJECTIVE [1] of or relating to North America or its inhabitants. ◆ NOUN [2] a native or inhabitant of North America.

North American Free Trade Agreement NOUN an international trade agreement between the United States, Canada, and Mexico. Abbreviation: **NAFTA.**

Northampton (nɔːˈθæmptən, nɔːθˈhæmp-) NOUN [1] a town in central England, administrative centre of Northamptonshire, on the River Nene: footwear and engineering industries. Pop.: 179 596 (1991). [2] short for **Northamptonshire.**

Northamptonshire (nɔːˈθæmptənˌʃɪə, -ʃə, nɔːθˈhæmp-) NOUN a county of central England: agriculture, food processing, engineering, and footwear industries. Administrative centre:

Northampton. Pop.: 629 676 (1994 est.). Area: 2367 sq. km (914 sq. miles). Abbreviation: **Northants.**

Northants (nɔːˈθænts) ABBREVIATION FOR Northamptonshire.

North Atlantic Drift *or* **Current** NOUN the warm ocean current flowing northeast, under the influence of prevailing winds, from the Gulf of Mexico towards NW Europe and warming its climate. Also called: **Gulf Stream.**

North Atlantic Treaty Organization NOUN the full name of **NATO.**

North Ayrshire (ˈɛəʃɪə, -ʃə) NOUN a council area of W central Scotland, on the Firth of Clyde: comprises the N part of the historical county of Ayrshire, including the Isle of Arran; formerly part of Strathclyde Region (1975–96): chiefly agricultural, with fishing and tourism. Administrative centre: Irvine. Pop.: 135 817 (2001). Area: 884 sq. km (341 sq. miles).

North Borneo NOUN the former name (until 1963) of **Sabah.**

northbound (ˈnɔːθˌbaʊnd) ADJECTIVE going or leading towards the north.

North Brabant NOUN a province of the S Netherlands: formed part of the medieval duchy of Brabant. Capital: ’s Hertogenbosch. Pop.: 2 356 000 (2000 est.). Area: 4965 sq. km (1917 sq. miles). Dutch name: **Noordbrabant.**

north by east NOUN [1] one point on the compass east of north, 11° 15′ clockwise from north. ◆ ADJECTIVE, ADVERB [2] in, from, or towards this direction.

north by west NOUN [1] one point on the compass west of north, 348° 45′ clockwise from north. ◆ ADJECTIVE, ADVERB [2] in, from, or towards this direction.

North Cape NOUN [1] a cape on N Magerøy Island, in the Arctic Ocean off the N coast of Norway. [2] a cape on N North Island, New Zealand.

North Carolina NOUN a state of the southeastern US, on the Atlantic: consists of a coastal plain rising to the Piedmont Plateau and the Appalachian Mountains in the west. Capital: Raleigh. Pop.: 8 049 313 (2000). Area: 126 387 sq. km (48 798 sq. miles). Abbreviations: **N.C.,** (with zip code) **NC.**

North Carolinian (ˌkærəˈlɪnɪən) ADJECTIVE [1] of or relating to North Carolina or its inhabitants. ◆ NOUN [2] a native or inhabitant of North Carolina.

North Channel NOUN a strait between NE Ireland and SW Scotland, linking the North Atlantic with the Irish Sea.

North Country NOUN (usually preceded by *the*) [1] another name for **North**[1] (sense 1). [2] the geographic region formed by Alaska, the Yukon, the Northwest Territories, and Nunavut.

northcountryman (ˌnɔːθˈkʌntrɪmən) NOUN, *plural* **-men.** a native or inhabitant of the North of England.

Northd ABBREVIATION FOR Northumberland.

North Dakota NOUN a state of the western US: mostly undulating prairies and plains, rising from the Red River valley in the east to the Missouri plateau in the west, with the infertile Bad Lands in the extreme west. Capital: Bismarck. Pop.: 642 200 (2000). Area: 183 019 sq. km (70 664 sq. miles). Abbreviations: **N.Dak, N.D.,** (with zip code) **ND.**

North Dakotan ADJECTIVE [1] of or relating to North Dakota or its inhabitants. ◆ NOUN [2] a native or inhabitant of North Dakota.

North Down NOUN a district of E Northern Ireland, in Co. Down. Pop.: 76 323 (1991). Area: 82 sq. km (32 sq. miles).

northeast (ˌnɔːθˈiːst; *Nautical* ˌnɔːrˈiːst) NOUN [1] the point of the compass or direction midway between north and east, 45° clockwise from north. [2] (*often capital;* usually preceded by *the*) any area lying in or towards this direction. ◆ ADJECTIVE *also* **northeastern.** [3] (*sometimes capital*) of or denoting the northeastern part of a specified country, area, etc.: *northeast Lincolnshire.* [4] situated in, proceeding towards, or facing the northeast. [5] (esp of the wind) from the northeast. ◆ ADVERB [6] in, to, towards, or (esp of the wind) from the northeast. ◆ Symbol **NE.**

▸**ˌnorthˈeasternmost** ADJECTIVE

Northeast (ˌnɔːθˈiːst) NOUN (usually preceded by *the*) the northeastern part of England, esp Northumberland, Durham, and the Tyneside area.

northeast by east NOUN [1] one point on the compass east of northeast, 56° 15′ clockwise from north. ◆ ADJECTIVE, ADVERB [2] in, from, or towards this direction.

northeast by north NOUN [1] one point on the compass north of northeast, 33° 45′ clockwise from north. ◆ ADJECTIVE, ADVERB [2] in, from, or towards this direction.

northeaster (ˌnɔːθˈiːstə; *Nautical* ˌnɔːrˈiːstə) NOUN a strong wind or storm from the northeast.

northeasterly (ˌnɔːθˈiːstəlɪ; *Nautical* ˌnɔːrˈiːstəlɪ) ADJECTIVE, ADVERB [1] in, towards, or (esp of a wind) from the northeast. ◆ NOUN, *plural* **-lies.** [2] a wind or storm from the northeast.

North East Frontier Agency NOUN the former name (until 1972) of **Arunachal Pradesh.**

North East Lincolnshire (ˈlɪŋkənˌʃɪə, -ʃə) NOUN a unitary authority in NE England, in Lincolnshire: formerly (1974–96) part of the county of Humberside. Pop.: 157 983 (2001). Area: 192 sq. km (74 sq. miles).

Northeast Passage NOUN a shipping route along the Arctic coasts of Europe and Asia, between the Atlantic and Pacific: first navigated by Nordenskjöld (1878–79).

northeastward (ˌnɔːθˈiːstwəd; *Nautical* ˌnɔːrˈiːstwəd) ADJECTIVE [1] towards or (esp of a wind) from the northeast. ◆ NOUN [2] a direction towards or area in the northeast.

▸**ˌnorthˈeastwardly** ADJECTIVE, ADVERB

northeastwards (ˌnɔːθˈiːstwədz; *Nautical* ˌnɔːrˈiːstwədz) *or* **northeastward** ADVERB to the northeast.

norther (ˈnɔːðə) NOUN *Chiefly southern US* a wind or storm from the north.

northerly (ˈnɔːðəlɪ) ADJECTIVE [1] of, relating to, or situated in the north. ◆ ADVERB, ADJECTIVE [2] towards or in the direction of the north. [3] from the north: *a northerly wind.* ◆ NOUN, *plural* **-lies.** [4] a wind from the north.

▸**ˈnortherliness** NOUN

northern (ˈnɔːðən) ADJECTIVE [1] situated in or towards the north: *northern towns.* [2] directed or proceeding towards the north: *a northern flow of traffic.* [3] (esp of winds) proceeding from the north. [4] (*sometimes capital*) of, relating to, or characteristic of the north or North. [5] (*sometimes capital*) *Astronomy* north of the celestial equator.

Northern Cape NOUN the largest but least populated province in South Africa, in the NW part of the country; created in 1994 from part of Cape Province: agriculture, mining (esp diamonds). Capital: Kimberley. Pop.: 875 222 (1999 est.). Area: 139 703 sq. km (361 830 sq. miles).

Northern Cross NOUN a group of the five brightest stars that form a large cross in the constellation Cygnus.

Northern Dvina NOUN See **Dvina** (sense 1).

Northerner (ˈnɔːðənə) NOUN (*sometimes not capital*) a native or inhabitant of the north of any specified region, esp England or the US.

northern hemisphere NOUN (*often capitals*) [1] that half of the globe lying north of the equator. [2] *Astronomy* that half of the celestial sphere north of the celestial equator. ◆ Abbreviation: **N hemisphere.**

Northern Ireland NOUN that part of the United Kingdom occupying the NE part of Ireland: separated from the rest of Ireland, which became independent in law in 1920; it remained part of the United Kingdom, with a separate Parliament (Stormont), inaugurated in 1921, and limited self-government: scene of severe conflict between Catholics and Protestants, including terrorist bombing from 1969: direct administration from Westminster from 1972: assembly and powersharing executive established in 1998–99 following the Good Friday Agreement of 1998. Capital: Belfast. Pop.: 1 685 267 (2001). Area: 14 121 sq. km (5452 sq. miles).

Northern Isles PLURAL NOUN the Orkneys and Shetland.

northern lights PLURAL NOUN another name for **aurora borealis.**

northernmost (ˈnɔːðənˌməʊst) ADJECTIVE situated or occurring farthest north.

Northern Province NOUN the former name for **Limpopo** (sense 1).

Northern Rhodesia NOUN the former name (until 1964) of **Zambia.**

Northern Sotho NOUN another name for **Pedi** (the language).

Northern Territories PLURAL NOUN a former British protectorate in W Africa, established in 1897; attached to the Gold Coast in 1901; now constitutes the Northern Region of Ghana (since 1957).

Northern Territory NOUN an administrative division of N central Australia, on the Timor and Arafura Seas: includes Ashmore and Cartier Islands; the Arunta Desert lies in the east, the Macdonnell Ranges in the south, and Arnhem Land in the north (containing Australia’s largest Aboriginal reservation). Capital: Darwin. Pop.: 192 880 (1999 est.). Area: 1 347 525 sq. km (520 280 sq. miles).

North Germanic NOUN a subbranch of the Germanic languages that consists of Danish, Norwegian, Swedish, Icelandic, and their associated dialects. See also **Old Norse.**

North Holland NOUN a province of the NW Netherlands, on the peninsula between the North Sea and IJsselmeer: includes the West Frisian Island of Texel. Capital: Haarlem. Pop.: 2 518 400 (2000 est.). Area: 2663 sq. km (1029 sq. miles). Dutch name: **Noordholland.**

northing (ˈnɔːθɪŋ, -ðɪŋ) NOUN [1] *Navigation* movement or distance covered in a northerly direction, esp as expressed in the resulting difference in latitude. [2] *Astronomy* a north or positive declination. [3] *Cartography* **a** the distance northwards of a point from a given parallel indicated by the second half of a map grid reference. **b** a latitudinal grid line. Compare **easting** (sense 2).

North Island NOUN the northernmost of the two main islands of New Zealand. Pop.: 2 849 724 (2001). Area: 114 729 sq. km (44 297 sq. miles).

North Korea NOUN a republic in NE Asia, on the Sea of Japan and the Yellow Sea: established in 1948 as a people’s republic; mostly rugged and mountainous, with fertile lowlands in the west. Language: Korean. Currency: won. Capital: Pyongyang. Pop.: 21 968 000 (2001 est.). Area: 122 313 sq. km (47 225 sq. miles). Official name: **Democratic People’s Republic of Korea.** Korean name: **Chosŏn.**

North Korean ADJECTIVE [1] of or relating to North Korea or its inhabitants. ◆ NOUN [2] a native or inhabitant of North Korea.

North Lanarkshire (ˈlænəkˌʃɪə, -ʃə) NOUN a council area of central Scotland: consists mainly of the NE part of the historical county of Lanarkshire; formerly (1974–96) part of Strathclyde Region: engineering and metalworking industries. Administrative centre: Motherwell. Pop.: 321 067 (2001). Area: 1771 sq. km (684 sq. miles).

Northland (ˈnɔːθlənd) NOUN [1] the peninsula containing Norway and Sweden. [2] (in Canada) the far north.

Northlander (ˈnɔːθləndə) NOUN [1] a native or inhabitant of the peninsula containing Norway and Sweden. [2] (in Canada) a native or inhabitant of the far north.

North Lincolnshire (ˈlɪŋkənˌʃɪə, -ʃə) NOUN a unitary authority of NE England, in Lincolnshire: formerly (1975–96) part of the county of Humberside. Pop.: 152 839 (2001). Area: 1497 sq. km (578 sq. miles).

Northman (ˈnɔːθmən) NOUN, *plural* **-men.** another name for a **Viking.**

north-northeast NOUN [1] the point on the compass or the direction midway between north and northeast, 22° 30′ clockwise from north. ◆ ADJECTIVE, ADVERB [2] in, from, or towards this direction. ◆ Symbol **NNE.**

north-northwest NOUN [1] the point on the compass or the direction midway between northwest and north, 337° 30′ clockwise from north. ◆ ADJECTIVE, ADVERB [2] in, from, or towards this direction. ◆ Symbol **NNW.**

North Ossetian Republic (əˈsiːʃən) NOUN a

constituent republic of S Russia, on the N slopes of the central Caucasus Mountains. Capital: Vladikavkaz. Pop.: 674 000 (2000 est.). Area: about 8000 sq. km (3088 sq. miles). Also called: **North Ossetia, Alania.**

North Pole NOUN [1] the northernmost point on the earth's axis, at a latitude of 90°N. [2] Also called: **north celestial pole.** *Astronomy* the point of intersection of the earth's extended axis and the northern half of the celestial sphere, lying about 1° from Polaris. [3] (*usually not capitals*) the pole of a freely suspended magnet, which is attracted to the earth's magnetic North Pole.

North Rhine-Westphalia NOUN a state of W Germany: formed in 1946 by the amalgamation of the Prussian province of Westphalia with the N part of the Prussian Rhine province and later with the state of Lippe; part of West Germany until 1990: highly industrialized. Capital: Düsseldorf. Pop.: 17 999 000 (2000 est.). Area: 34 039 sq. km (13 142 sq. miles). German name: **Nordrhein-Westfalen.**

North Riding NOUN (until 1974) an administrative division of Yorkshire, now constituting most of North Yorkshire.

North Saskatchewan NOUN a river in W Canada, rising in W Alberta and flowing northeast, east, and southeast to join the South Saskatchewan River and form the Saskatchewan River. Length: 1223 km (760 miles).

North Sea NOUN an arm of the Atlantic between Great Britain and the N European mainland. Area: about 569 800 sq. km (220 000 sq. miles). Former name: **German Ocean.**

North-Sea gas NOUN (in Britain) natural gas obtained from deposits below the North Sea.

North Somerset (ˈsʌməsɛt) NOUN a unitary authority of SW England, in Somerset: formerly (1974–96) part of the county of Avon. Pop.: 188 556 (2001). Area: 375 sq. km (145 sq. miles).

North Star NOUN **the.** another name for **Polaris** (sense 1).

North Tyneside (ˈtaɪnsaɪd) NOUN a unitary authority of NE England, in Tyne and Wear. Pop.: 191 663 (2001). Area: 84 sq. km (32 sq. miles).

Northumberland (nɔːˈθʌmbələnd) NOUN the northernmost county of England, on the North Sea: hilly in the north (the Cheviots) and west (the Pennines), with many Roman remains, notably Hadrian's Wall; shipbuilding, coal mining. Administrative centre: Morpeth. Pop.: 307 186 (2001). Area: 5032 sq. km (1943 sq. miles). Abbreviation: **Northd.**

Northumbria (nɔːˈθʌmbrɪə) NOUN [1] (in Anglo-Saxon Britain) a region that stretched from the Humber to the Firth of Forth: formed in the 7th century A.D., it became an important intellectual centre; a separate kingdom until 876 A.D. [2] an area of NE England roughly corresponding to the Anglo-Saxon region of Northumbria.

Northumbrian (nɔːˈθʌmbrɪən) ADJECTIVE [1] of or relating to the English county of Northumberland, its inhabitants, or their dialect of English. [2] of or relating to ancient Northumbria, its inhabitants, or their dialect. ◆ NOUN [3] **a** the dialect of Old and Middle English spoken north of the River Humber. See also **Anglian, Mercian. b** the dialect of Modern English spoken in Northumberland.

North Vietnam NOUN a region of N Vietnam, on the Gulf of Tonkin: an independent Communist state from 1954 until 1976. Area: 164 061 sq. km (63 344 sq. miles).

northward (ˈnɔːθwəd; *Nautical* ˈnɔːðəd) ADJECTIVE [1] moving, facing, or situated towards the north. ◆ NOUN [2] the northward part, direction, etc.; the north. ◆ ADVERB [3] a variant of **northwards.**
▸ **ˈnorthwardly** ADJECTIVE, ADVERB

northwards (ˈnɔːθwədz) *or* **northward** ADVERB towards the north.

northwest (ˌnɔːθˈwɛst; *Nautical* ˌnɔːˈwɛst) NOUN [1] the point of the compass or direction midway between north and west, clockwise 315° from north. [2] (*often capital;* usually preceded by *the*) any area lying in or towards this direction. ◆ ADJECTIVE *also* **northwestern.** [3] (*sometimes capital*) of or denoting the northwestern part of a specified country, area, etc.: *northwest Greenland.* ◆ ADJECTIVE, ADVERB [4] in, to, towards, or (esp of the wind) from the northwest. ◆ Symbol **NW.**
▸ **ˌnorthˈwesternmost** ADJECTIVE

Northwest (ˌnɔːθˈwɛst) NOUN (usually preceded by *the*) [1] the northwestern part of England, esp Lancashire and the Lake District. [2] the northwestern part of the US, consisting of the states of Washington, Oregon, and sometimes Idaho. [3] (in Canada) the region north and west of the Great Lakes.

North West NOUN a province in N South Africa, created in 1994 from the NE part of Cape Province and part of Transvaal: agriculture and service industries. Capital: Mafikeng Mmabatho. Pop.: 3 562 280 (1990 est.). Area: 116 320 sq. km (44 911 sq. miles).

northwest by north NOUN [1] one point on the compass north of northwest, 326° 15′ clockwise from north. ◆ ADJECTIVE, ADVERB [2] in, from, or towards this direction.

northwest by west NOUN [1] one point on the compass south of northwest, 303° 45′ clockwise from north. ◆ ADJECTIVE, ADVERB [2] in, from, or towards this direction.

northwester (ˌnɔːθˈwɛstə; *Nautical* ˌnɔːˈwɛstə) NOUN a strong wind or storm from the northwest.

northwesterly (ˌnɔːθˈwɛstəlɪ; *Nautical* ˌnɔːˈwɛstəlɪ) ADJECTIVE, ADVERB [1] in, towards, or (esp of a wind) from the northwest. ◆ NOUN, *plural* **-lies.** [2] a wind or storm from the northwest.

North-West Frontier Province NOUN a province in N Pakistan between Afghanistan and Jammu and Kashmir: part of British India from 1901 until 1947; of strategic importance, esp for the Khyber Pass. Capital: Peshawar. Pop.: 17 555 000 (1998 est.). Area: 74 522 sq. km (28 773 sq. miles).

Northwest Passage NOUN the passage by sea from the Atlantic to the Pacific along the N coast of America: attempted for over 300 years by Europeans seeking a short route to the Far East, before being successfully navigated by Amundsen (1903–06).

Northwest Territories PLURAL NOUN a territory of NW Canada including part of Victoria Island and several other islands of the Arctic; comprised over a third of Canada's total area until Nunavut became a separate territory in 1999: rich mineral resources. Pop.: 41 800 (1999 est.). Area: 2 082 910 sq. km (804 003 sq. miles). Abbreviation: **NWT.**

Northwest Territory NOUN See **Old Northwest.**

northwestward (ˌnɔːθˈwɛstwəd; *Nautical* ˌnɔːˈwɛstwəd) ADJECTIVE [1] towards or (esp of a wind) from the northwest. ◆ NOUN [2] a direction towards or area in the northwest.
▸ **ˌnorthˈwestwardly** ADJECTIVE, ADVERB

northwestwards (ˌnɔːθˈwɛstwədz; *Nautical* ˌnɔːˈwɛstwədz) *or* **northwestward** ADVERB towards or (esp of a wind) from the northwest.

Northwich (ˈnɔːθwɪtʃ) NOUN a town in NW England, in Cheshire: salt and chemical industries. Pop.: 34 520 (1991).

North Yemen NOUN a former republic in SW Arabia, on the Red Sea; now part of Yemen: declared a republic in 1962: united with South Yemen in 1990. Official name: **Yemen Arab Republic.** See also **Yemen, South Yemen.**

North Yorkshire NOUN a county in N England, formed in 1974 from most of the North Riding of Yorkshire and parts of the East and West Ridings: the geographical and ceremonial county includes the unitary authorities of Middlesbrough, Redcar and Cleveland, and part of Stockton on Tees (all within Cleveland until 1996), and York (created in 1997). Administrative centre: Northallerton. Pop. (excluding unitary authorities): 569 660 (2001). Area (excluding unitary authorities): 8037 sq. km (3102 sq. miles).

Norw. ABBREVIATION FOR: [1] Norway. [2] Norwegian.

Norway (ˈnɔːˌweɪ) NOUN a kingdom in NW Europe, occupying the W part of the Scandinavian peninsula: first united in the Viking age (800–1050); under the rule of Denmark (1523–1814) and Sweden (1814–1905); became an independent monarchy in 1905. Its coastline is deeply indented by fjords and fringed with islands, rising inland to plateaus and mountains. Norway has a large fishing fleet and its merchant navy is among the world's largest. Official language: Norwegian. Official religion: Evangelical Lutheran. Currency: krone. Capital: Oslo. Pop.: 4 516 000 (2001 est.). Area: 323 878 sq. km (125 050 sq. miles). Norwegian name: **Norge.**

Norway lobster NOUN a European lobster, *Nephrops norvegicus,* fished for food.

Norway maple NOUN a large Eurasian maple tree, *Acer platanoides,* with broad five-lobed pale green leaves.

Norway rat NOUN another name for **brown rat.**

Norway spruce NOUN a European spruce tree, *Picea abies,* planted for timber and ornament, having drooping branches and dark green needle-like leaves.

Norwegian (nɔːˈwiːdʒən) ADJECTIVE [1] of, relating to, or characteristic of Norway, its language, or its people. ◆ NOUN [2] any of the various North Germanic languages of Norway. See also **Nynorsk, Bokmål.** Compare **Norse.** [3] a native, citizen, or inhabitant of Norway.

Norwegian buhund (ˈbuːˌhʊnd) NOUN a slightly-built medium-sized dog of a breed with erect pointed ears and a short thick tail carried curled over its back.
▷ **HISTORY** from Norwegian *bu* homestead, livestock + *hund* dog

Norwegian forest cat NOUN a breed of long-haired cat with a long bushy tail and a long mane.

Norwegian Sea NOUN part of the Arctic Ocean between Greenland and Norway.

nor'wester (ˌnɔːˈwɛstə) NOUN [1] a less common name for **sou'wester.** [2] a drink of strong liquor. [3] a strong northwest wind. [4] *NZ* a hot dry wind from the Southern Alps.
▷ **HISTORY** C18 (in the sense: storm from the northwest): a contraction of NORTHWESTER

Norwich (ˈnɒrɪdʒ) NOUN a city in E England, administrative centre of Norfolk: cathedral (founded 1096); University of East Anglia (1963); traditionally a centre of the footwear industry, now has engineering, financial services. Pop.: 171 304 (1991).

Norwich terrier NOUN a small wiry-coated breed of terrier having either erect or pendent ears.

Nos. *or* **nos.** ABBREVIATION FOR numbers.

nose (nəʊz) NOUN [1] the organ of smell and entrance to the respiratory tract, consisting of a prominent structure divided into two hair-lined air passages by a median septum. Related adjectives: **nasal, rhinal.** [2] the sense of smell itself: in hounds and other animals, the ability to follow trails by scent (esp in the phrases **a good nose, a bad nose**). [3] another word for **bouquet** (sense 2). [4] instinctive skill or facility, esp in discovering things (sometimes in the phrase **follow one's nose**): *he had a nose for good news stories.* [5] any part regarded as resembling a nose in form or function, such as a nozzle or spout. [6] the forward part of a vehicle, aircraft, etc., esp the front end of an aircraft. [7] narrow margin of victory (in the phrase **(win) by a nose**). [8] **cut off one's nose to spite one's face.** to carry out a vengeful action that hurts oneself more than another. [9] **get up (someone's) nose.** *Informal* to annoy or irritate (someone). [10] **keep one's nose clean.** to stay out of trouble; behave properly. [11] **keep one's nose to the grindstone.** to work hard and continuously. [12] **lead (someone) by the nose.** to make (someone) do unquestioningly all one wishes; dominate (someone). [13] **look down one's nose at.** *Informal* to be contemptuous or disdainful of. [14] **nose to tail.** (of vehicles) moving or standing very close behind one another. [15] **on the nose.** *Slang* **a** (in horse-race betting) to win only: *I bet twenty pounds on the nose on that horse.* **b** *Chiefly US and Canadian* precisely; exactly. **c** *Austral* bad or bad-smelling. [16] **pay through the nose.** *Informal* to pay an exorbitant price. [17] **poke, stick, etc., one's nose into.** *Informal* to pry into or interfere in. [18] **put someone's nose out of joint.** *Informal* to thwart or offend someone, esp by supplanting him or gaining something he regards as his. [19] **rub someone's nose in it.** *Informal* to remind someone unkindly of his failing or error. [20] **see no further than (the end of) one's nose.** *Informal* **a** to be short-sighted; suffer from myopia. **b** to lack insight or foresight. [21] **turn up one's nose (at).** *Informal* to behave disdainfully (towards). [22] **under one's nose.** **a**

directly in front of one. **b** without one noticing. 23 **with one's nose in the air.** haughtily. ◆ VERB 24 (*tr*) (esp of horses, dogs, etc.) to rub, touch, or sniff with the nose; nuzzle. 25 to smell or sniff (wine, etc.). 26 (*intr;* usually foll by *after* or *for*) to search (for) by or as if by scent. 27 to move or cause to move forwards slowly and carefully: *the car nosed along the cliff top; we nosed the car into the garage.* 28 (*intr;* foll by *into, around, about,* etc.) to pry or snoop (into) or meddle (in). ◆ See also **nose out.**
▷HISTORY Old English *nosu;* related to Old Frisian *nose,* Norwegian *nosa* to smell and *nus* smell
▸'**noseless** ADJECTIVE ▸'**nose,like** ADJECTIVE

nosebag ('nəʊzˌbæg) NOUN a bag, fastened around the head of a horse and covering the nose, in which feed is placed.

noseband ('nəʊzˌbænd) NOUN the detachable part of a horse's bridle that goes around the nose. Also called: **nosepiece.**
▸'**nose,banded** ADJECTIVE

nosebleed ('nəʊzˌbliːd) NOUN bleeding from the nose, as the result of injury, etc. Technical name: **epistaxis.**

nose cone NOUN the conical forward section of a missile, spacecraft, etc., designed to withstand high temperatures, esp during re-entry into the earth's atmosphere.

nose dive NOUN 1 a sudden plunge with the nose or front pointing downwards, esp of an aircraft. 2 *Informal* a sudden drop or sharp decline: *prices took a nose dive.* ◆ VERB **nose-dive.** 3 to perform or cause to perform a nose dive. 4 (*intr*) *Informal* to drop suddenly.

nose flute NOUN (esp in the South Sea Islands) a type of flute blown through the nose.

nosegay ('nəʊzˌgeɪ) NOUN a small bunch of flowers; posy.
▷HISTORY C15: from NOSE + archaic *gay* a toy

nose job NOUN *Slang* a surgical remodelling of the nose for cosmetic reasons.

nose out VERB (*tr, adverb*) 1 to discover by smelling. 2 to discover by cunning or persistence: *the reporter managed to nose out a few facts.* 3 *Informal* to beat by a narrow margin: *he was nosed out of first place by the champion.*

nosepiece ('nəʊzˌpiːs) NOUN 1 Also called: **nasal.** a piece of armour, esp part of a helmet, that serves to protect the nose. 2 the connecting part of a pair of spectacles that rests on the nose; bridge. 3 the part of a microscope to which one or more objective lenses are attached. 4 a less common word for **noseband.**

nose rag NOUN *Slang* a handkerchief.

nose ring NOUN a ring fixed through the nose, as for leading a bull.

nose wheel NOUN a wheel fitted to the forward end of a vehicle, esp the landing wheel under the nose of an aircraft.

nosey ('nəʊzɪ) ADJECTIVE a variant spelling of **nosy.**

nosh (nɒʃ) *Slang* ◆ NOUN 1 food or a meal. ◆ VERB 2 to eat.
▷HISTORY C20: from Yiddish; compare German *naschen* to nibble
▸'**nosher** NOUN

noshery *or* **nosherie** ('nɒʃərɪ) NOUN, *plural* **-eries.** *Informal* a restaurant or other place where food is served.

no-show NOUN a person who fails to take up a reserved seat, place, etc., without having cancelled it.

nosh-up NOUN *Brit, slang* a large and satisfying meal.

no-side NOUN *Rugby* the end of a match, signalled by the referee's whistle.

nosing ('nəʊzɪŋ) NOUN 1 the edge of a step or stair tread that projects beyond the riser. 2 a projecting edge of a moulding, esp one that is half-round.
▷HISTORY C18: from NOSE + -ING[1]

noso- *or before a vowel* **nos-** COMBINING FORM disease: *nosology.*
▷HISTORY from Greek *nosos*

nosocomial (ˌnɒsə'kəʊmɪəl) ADJECTIVE *Med* originating in hospital: *nosocomial disease.*
▷HISTORY C19: New Latin *nosocomialis,* via Late Latin from Greek, from *nosokomos* one that tends the sick, from *nosos* (see NOSO-) + *komein* to tend

nosography (nɒ'sɒgrəfɪ) NOUN a written classification and description of various diseases.
▸**no'sographer** NOUN ▸**nosographic** (ˌnɒsə'græfɪk) ADJECTIVE

nosology (nɒ'sɒlədʒɪ) NOUN the branch of medicine concerned with the classification of diseases.
▸**nosological** (ˌnɒsə'lɒdʒɪkəl) ADJECTIVE ▸ˌ**noso'logically** ADVERB ▸**no'sologist** NOUN

nosophobia (ˌnɒsə'fəʊbɪə) NOUN the morbid dread of contracting disease.

nostalgia (nɒ'stældʒə, -dʒɪə) NOUN 1 a yearning for the return of past circumstances, events, etc. 2 the evocation of this emotion, as in a book, film, etc. 3 longing for home or family; homesickness.
▷HISTORY C18: New Latin (translation of German *Heimweh* homesickness), from Greek *nostos* a return home + -ALGIA

nostalgic (nɒ'stældʒɪk) ADJECTIVE 1 of or characterized by nostalgia. ◆ NOUN 2 a person who indulges in nostalgia.

nostalgist (nɒ'stældʒɪst) NOUN a person who indulges in nostalgia.

nostoc ('nɒstɒk) NOUN any cyanobacterium of the genus *Nostoc,* occurring in moist places as rounded colonies consisting of coiled filaments in a gelatinous substance.
▷HISTORY C17: New Latin, coined by Paracelsus

nostology (nɒ'stɒlədʒɪ) NOUN *Med* another word for **gerontology.**
▷HISTORY C20: from Greek *nostos* a return home (with reference to ageing or second childhood) + -LOGY
▸**nostologic** (ˌnɒstə'lɒdʒɪk) ADJECTIVE

nostril ('nɒstrɪl) NOUN either of the two external openings of the nose. Related adjectives: **narial, narine.**
▷HISTORY Old English *nosthyrl,* from *nosu* NOSE + *thyrel* hole

nostro account ('nɒstrəʊ) NOUN a bank account conducted by a British bank with a foreign bank, usually in the foreign currency. Compare **vostro account.**

nostrum ('nɒstrəm) NOUN 1 a patent or quack medicine. 2 a favourite remedy, as for political or social problems.
▷HISTORY C17: from Latin: our own (make), from *noster* our

nosy *or* **nosey** ('nəʊzɪ) ADJECTIVE **nosier, nosiest.** *Informal* prying or inquisitive.
▸'**nosily** ADVERB ▸'**nosiness** NOUN

nosy parker NOUN *Informal* a prying person.
▷HISTORY C20: apparently arbitrary use of surname *Parker*

not (nɒt) ADVERB 1 **a** used to negate the sentence, phrase, or word that it modifies: *I will not stand for it.* **b** (*in combination*): *they cannot go.* 2 **not that.** (*conjunction*) Also (archaic): **not but what.** which is not to say or suppose that: *I expect to lose the game — not that I mind.* ◆ SENTENCE SUBSTITUTE 3 used to indicate denial, negation, or refusal: *certainly not.*
▷HISTORY C14 *not,* variant of *nought* nothing, from Old English *nāwiht,* from *nā* no + *wiht* creature, thing. See NAUGHT, NOUGHT

not- COMBINING FORM a variant of **noto-** before a vowel.

nota ('nəʊtə) NOUN the plural of **notum.**

nota bene *Latin* ('nəʊtə 'biːnɪ) note well; take note. Abbreviations: **NB, N.B., nb, n.b.**

notability (ˌnəʊtə'bɪlɪtɪ) NOUN, *plural* **-ties.** 1 the state or quality of being notable. 2 a distinguished person; notable.

notable ('nəʊtəbəl) ADJECTIVE 1 worthy of being noted or remembered; remarkable; distinguished. ◆ NOUN 2 a notable person.
▷HISTORY C14: via Old French from Latin *notābilis,* from *notāre* to NOTE
▸'**notableness** NOUN

notably ('nəʊtəblɪ) ADVERB particularly or especially; in a way worthy of being noted.

notarize *or* **notarise** ('nəʊtəˌraɪz) VERB (*tr*) to attest to or authenticate (a document, contract, etc.), as a notary.

notary ('nəʊtərɪ) NOUN, *plural* **-ries.** 1 a notary public. 2 (formerly) a clerk licensed to prepare legal documents. 3 *Archaic* a clerk or secretary.
▷HISTORY C14: from Latin *notārius* clerk, from *nota* a mark, note
▸**notarial** (nəʊ'tɛərɪəl) ADJECTIVE ▸**no'tarially** ADVERB ▸'**notaryship** NOUN

notary public NOUN, *plural* **notaries public.** a public official, usually a solicitor, who is legally authorized to administer oaths, attest and certify certain documents, etc.

notate (nəʊ'teɪt) VERB to write (esp music) in notation.
▷HISTORY C20: back formation from NOTATION

notation (nəʊ'teɪʃən) NOUN 1 any series of signs or symbols used to represent quantities or elements in a specialized system, such as music or mathematics. 2 the act or process of notating. 3 **a** the act of noting down. **b** a note or record.
▷HISTORY C16: from Latin *notātiō* a marking, from *notāre* to NOTE
▸**no'tational** ADJECTIVE

notch (nɒtʃ) NOUN 1 a V-shaped cut or indentation; nick. 2 a cut or nick made in a tally stick or similar object. 3 *US and Canadian* a narrow pass or gorge. 4 *Informal* a step or level (esp in the phrase **a notch above**). ◆ VERB (*tr*) 5 to cut or make a notch in. 6 to record with or as if with a notch. 7 (usually foll by *up*) *Informal* to score or achieve: *the team notched up its fourth win.*
▷HISTORY C16: from incorrect division of *an otch* (as *a notch*), from Old French *oche* notch, from Latin *obsecāre* to cut off, from *secāre* to cut

notch effect NOUN *Metallurgy, building trades* the increase in stress in an area of a component near a crack, depression, etc., or a change in section, such as a sharp angle: can be enough to cause failure of the component although the calculated average stress may be quite safe.

notchy ('nɒtʃɪ) ADJECTIVE (of a motor-vehicle gear mechanism) requiring careful gear-changing, as if having to fit the lever into narrow notches.

NOT circuit *or* **gate** (nɒt) NOUN *Computing* a logic circuit that has a high-voltage output signal if the input signal is low, and vice versa: used extensively in computers. Also called: **inverter, negator.**
▷HISTORY C20: so named because the action performed on electrical signals is similar to the operation of *not* in logical constructions

note (nəʊt) NOUN 1 a brief summary or record in writing, esp a jotting for future reference. 2 a brief letter, usually of an informal nature. 3 a formal written communication, esp from one government to another. 4 a short written statement giving any kind of information. 5 a critical comment, explanatory statement, or reference in the text of a book, often preceded by a number. 6 short for **banknote.** 7 a characteristic element or atmosphere: *a note of sarcasm.* 8 a distinctive vocal sound, as of a species of bird or animal: *the note of the nightingale.* 9 any of a series of graphic signs representing a musical sound whose pitch is indicated by position on the stave and whose duration is indicated by the sign's shape. 10 Also called (esp US and Canadian): **tone.** a musical sound of definite fundamental frequency or pitch. 11 a key on a piano, organ, etc. 12 a sound, as from a musical instrument, used as a signal or warning: *the note to retreat was sounded.* 13 short for **promissory note.** 14 *Archaic or poetic* a tune or melody. 15 **of note. a** distinguished or famous: *an athlete of note.* **b** worth noticing or paying attention to; important: *nothing of note.* 16 **strike the right** (*or* **a false**) **note.** to behave appropriately (or inappropriately). 17 **take note.** (often foll by *of*) to observe carefully; pay close attention (to). ◆ VERB (*tr; may take a clause as object*) 18 to notice; perceive: *he noted that there was a man in the shadows.* 19 to pay close attention to; observe: *they noted every movement.* 20 to make a written note or memorandum of: *she noted the date in her diary.* 21 to make particular mention of; remark upon: *I note that you do not wear shoes.* 22 to write down (music, a melody, etc.) in notes. 23 to take (an unpaid or dishonoured bill of exchange) to a notary public to re-present the bill and if it is still unaccepted or unpaid to note the circumstances in a register. See **protest** (sense 12). 24 a less common word for **annotate.** ◆ See also **notes.**
▷HISTORY C13: via Old French from Latin *nota* sign, indication
▸'**noteless** ADJECTIVE

notebook ('nəʊtˌbʊk) NOUN 1 a book for recording notes or memoranda. 2 a book for registering promissory notes.

notebook computer NOUN a portable computer smaller than a laptop model, often approximately the size of a sheet of A4 paper.

notecase ('nəʊtˌkeɪs) NOUN a less common word for **wallet** (sense 1).

noted ('nəʊtɪd) ADJECTIVE 1 distinguished; celebrated; famous. 2 of special note or significance; noticeable: *a noted increase in the crime rate.*
▸ **'notedly** ADVERB

notelet ('nəʊtlɪt) NOUN a folded card with a printed design on the front, for writing a short informal letter.

note of hand NOUN another name for **promissory note.**

notepaper ('nəʊtˌpeɪpə) NOUN paper for writing letters; writing paper.

note-perfect ADJECTIVE 1 (of a singer or musician) able to sing or play without making any errors. 2(of a piece of music) sung or performed without any errors.

note row (rəʊ) NOUN *Music* another name for **tone row.**

notes (nəʊts) PLURAL NOUN 1 short descriptive or summarized jottings taken down for future reference. 2 a record of impressions, reflections, etc., esp as a literary form.

notes inégales *French* (nɔts inegal) PLURAL NOUN 1 (esp in French baroque music) notes written down evenly but executed as if they were divided into pairs of long and short notes. 2 the style of playing in this manner.
▷ HISTORY literally: unequal notes

note value NOUN another term for **time value.**

noteworthy ('nəʊtˌwɜːðɪ) ADJECTIVE worthy of notice; notable.
▸ **'noteˌworthily** ADVERB ▸ **'noteˌworthiness** NOUN

not-for-profit organization *or esp US* **nonprofit organization** NOUN an organization that is not intended to make a profit, esp one set up to provide a public service.

nothing ('nʌθɪŋ) PRONOUN 1 (*indefinite*) no thing; not anything, as of an implied or specified class of things: *I can give you nothing.* 2 no part or share: *to have nothing to do with this crime.* 3 a matter of no importance or significance: *it doesn't matter, it's nothing.* 4 indicating the absence of anything perceptible; nothingness. 5 indicating the absence of meaning, value, worth, etc.: *to amount to nothing.* 6 zero quantity; nought. 7 **be nothing to. a** not to concern or be significant to (someone). **b** to be not nearly as good as. 8 **have** *or* **be nothing to do with.** to have no connection with. 9 **have (got) nothing on. a** to have no engagements to keep. **b** to be undressed or naked. **c** *Informal* to compare unfavourably with. 10 **in nothing flat.** *Informal* in almost no time; very quickly or soon. 11 **nothing but.** not something other than; only. 12 **nothing doing.** *Informal* an expression of dismissal, disapproval, lack of compliance with a request, etc. 13 **nothing if not.** at the very least; certainly. 14 **nothing less than** *or* **nothing short of.** downright; truly. 15 **(there's) nothing for it.** (there's) no choice; no other course. 16 **there's nothing like.** a general expression of praise: *there's nothing like a good cup of tea.* 17 **there's nothing to it.** it is very simple, easy, etc. 18 **think nothing of. a** to regard as routine, easy, or natural. **b** to have no compunction or hesitation about. **c** to have a very low opinion of. 19 **to say nothing of.** as well as; even disregarding: *he was warmly dressed in a shirt and heavy jumper, to say nothing of his thick overcoat.* 20 **stop at nothing.** to be prepared to do anything; be unscrupulous or ruthless. ◆ ADVERB 21 in no way; not at all: *he looked nothing like his brother.* ◆ NOUN 22 *Informal* a person or thing of no importance or significance. 23 **sweet nothings.** words of endearment or affection.

> **Language note** *Nothing* normally takes a singular verb, but when *nothing but* is followed by a plural form of a noun, a plural verb is usually used: *it was a large room where nothing but souvenirs were sold.*

▷ HISTORY Old English *nāthing, nān thing,* from *nān* NONE[1] + THING[1]

nothingness ('nʌθɪŋnɪs) NOUN 1 the state or condition of being nothing; nonexistence. 2 absence of consciousness or life. 3 complete insignificance or worthlessness. 4 something that is worthless or insignificant.

notice ('nəʊtɪs) NOUN 1 the act of perceiving; observation; attention: *to escape notice.* 2 **take notice.** to pay attention; attend. 3 **take no notice of.** to ignore or disregard. 4 information about a future event; warning; announcement. 5 a displayed placard or announcement giving information. 6 advance notification of intention to end an arrangement, contract, etc., as of renting or employment (esp in the phrase **give notice**). 7 **at short, two hours', etc., notice.** with notification only a little, two hours, etc., in advance. 8 *Chiefly Brit* dismissal from employment. 9 favourable, interested, or polite attention: *she was beneath his notice.* 10 a theatrical or literary review: *the play received very good notices.* ◆ VERB (*tr*) 11 to become conscious or aware of; perceive; note. 12 to point out or remark upon. 13 to pay polite or interested attention to. 14 to recognize or acknowledge (an acquaintance).
▷ HISTORY C15: via Old French from Latin *notitia* fame, from *nōtus* known, celebrated

noticeable ('nəʊtɪsəbᵊl) ADJECTIVE easily seen or detected; perceptible: *the stain wasn't noticeable.*
▸ **ˌnoticea'bility** NOUN ▸ **'noticeably** ADVERB

notice board NOUN *Brit* a board on which notices, advertisements, bulletins, etc., are displayed. US and Canadian name: **bulletin board.**

notifiable ('nəʊtɪˌfaɪəbᵊl) ADJECTIVE 1 denoting certain infectious diseases of humans, such as smallpox and tuberculosis, outbreaks of which must be reported to the public health authorities. 2 denoting certain infectious diseases of animals, such as BSE, foot-and-mouth disease, and rabies, outbreaks of which must be reported to the appropriate veterinary authority.

notification (ˌnəʊtɪfɪ'keɪʃən) NOUN 1 the act of notifying. 2 a formal announcement. 3 something that notifies; a notice.

notify ('nəʊtɪˌfaɪ) VERB **-fies, -fying, -fied.** (*tr*) 1 to inform; tell. 2 *Chiefly Brit* to draw attention to; make known; announce.
▷ HISTORY C14: from Old French *notifier,* from Latin *notificāre* to make known, from *nōtus* known + *facere* to make
▸ **'notiˌfier** NOUN

no-tillage NOUN a system of farming in which planting is done in a narrow trench, without tillage, and weeds are controlled with herbicide.

notion ('nəʊʃən) NOUN 1 a vague idea; impression. 2 an idea, concept, or opinion. 3 an inclination or whim. ◆ See also **notions.**
▷ HISTORY C16: from Latin *nōtiō* a becoming acquainted (with), examination (of), from *noscere* to know

notional ('nəʊʃənᵊl) ADJECTIVE 1 relating to, expressing, or consisting of notions or ideas. 2 not evident in reality; hypothetical or imaginary: *a notional tax credit.* 3 characteristic of a notion or concept, esp in being speculative or imaginary; abstract. 4 *Grammar* **a** (of a word) having lexical meaning. **b** another word for **semantic.**
▸ **'notionally** ADVERB

notions ('nəʊʃənz) PLURAL NOUN *Chiefly US and Canadian* pins, cotton, ribbon, and similar wares used for sewing; haberdashery.

notitia (nəʊ'tɪʃɪə) NOUN a register or list, esp of ecclesiastical districts.
▷ HISTORY C18: Latin, literally: knowledge, from *notus* known

noto- *or before a vowel* **not-** COMBINING FORM the back: *notochord.*
▷ HISTORY from Greek *nōton* the back

notochord ('nəʊtəˌkɔːd) NOUN a fibrous longitudinal rod in all embryo and some adult chordate animals, immediately above the gut, that supports the body. It is replaced in adult vertebrates by the vertebral column.
▸ **ˌnoto'chordal** ADJECTIVE

Notogaea (ˌnəʊtə'dʒiːə) NOUN a zoogeographical area comprising the Australasian region. Compare **Arctogaea, Neogaea.**
▷ HISTORY C19: from Greek *notos* south wind + *gaia* land

Notogaean (ˌnəʊtə'dʒiːən) NOUN 1 a native or inhabitant of Notogaea, a zoogeographical area comprising the Australasian region. ◆ ADJECTIVE 2 of or relating to Notogaea or its inhabitants.

notorious (nəʊ'tɔːrɪəs) ADJECTIVE 1 well-known for some bad or unfavourable quality, deed, etc.; infamous. 2 *Rare* generally known or widely acknowledged.
▷ HISTORY C16: from Medieval Latin *notōrius* well-known, from *nōtus* known, from *noscere* to know
▸ **notoriety** (ˌnəʊtə'raɪɪtɪ) *or* **no'toriousness** NOUN
▸ **no'toriously** ADVERB

notornis (nəʊ'tɔːnɪs) NOUN a rare flightless rail of the genus *Notornis,* of New Zealand. See **takahe.**
▷ HISTORY C19: New Latin, from Greek *notos* south + *ornis* bird

nototherium (ˌnəʊtəʊ'θɪərɪəm) NOUN an extinct Pleistocene rhinoceros-sized marsupial of the genus *Nototherium,* related to the wombats.
▷ HISTORY C19: New Latin, from Greek *notos* south (referring to their discovery in the S hemisphere) + *thērion* beast

notour ('nəʊtə) ADJECTIVE (in Scots Law) short for **notorious.** A **notour bankrupt** is one who has failed to discharge his debts within the days of grace allowed by the court.

not proven ('prəʊvᵊn) ADJECTIVE (*postpositive*) a third verdict available to Scottish courts, returned when there is evidence against the defendant but insufficient to convict.

Notre Dame ('nəʊtrə 'dɑːm, 'nɒtrə; *French* nɔtrə dam) NOUN the early Gothic cathedral of Paris, on the Île de la Cité: built between 1163 and 1257.

no-trump *Bridge* ◆ NOUN *also* **no-trumps.** 1 a bid or contract to play without trumps. ◆ ADJECTIVE *also* **no-trumper.** 2 (of a hand) of balanced distribution suitable for playing without trumps.

Nottingham ('nɒtɪŋəm) NOUN 1 a city in N central England, unitary administrative centre of Nottinghamshire, on the River Trent: scene of the outbreak of the Civil War (1642); famous for its associations with the Robin Hood legend; two universities. Pop.: 283 800 (1995 est.). 2 a unitary authority in N central England, in Nottinghamshire. Pop.: 266 995 (2001). Area: 78 sq. km (30 sq. miles).

Nottinghamshire ('nɒtɪŋəmˌʃɪə, -ʃə) NOUN an inland county of central England: generally low-lying, with part of the S Pennines and the remnant of Sherwood Forest in the east. Nottingham became an independent unitary authority in 1998. Administrative centre: Nottingham. Pop. (excluding Nottingham): 748 503 (2001). Area (excluding Nottingham): 2086 sq. km (805 sq. miles). Abbreviation: **Notts.**

Nottm ABBREVIATION FOR Nottingham.

Notts (nɒts) ABBREVIATION FOR Nottinghamshire.

notum ('nəʊtəm) NOUN, *plural* **-ta** (-tə). a cuticular plate covering the dorsal surface of a thoracic segment of an insect.
▷ HISTORY C19: New Latin, from Greek *nōton* back
▸ **'notal** ADJECTIVE

Notus ('nəʊtəs) NOUN *Classical myth* a personification of the south or southwest wind.

notwithstanding (ˌnɒtwɪθ'stændɪŋ, -wɪð-) PREPOSITION 1 (*often immediately postpositive*) in spite of; despite. ◆ CONJUNCTION 2 (*subordinating*) despite the fact that; although. ◆ SENTENCE CONNECTOR 3 in spite of that; nevertheless.
▷ HISTORY C14: NOT + *withstanding,* from Old English *withstandan,* on the model of Medieval Latin *non obstante,* Old French *non obstant*

Nouakchott (*French* nwakʃɔt) NOUN the capital of Mauritania, near the Atlantic coast: replaced St Louis as capital in 1957; situated on important caravan routes. Pop. (urban area): 881 000 (1999 est.).

nougat ('nuːgɑː, 'nʌgət) NOUN a hard chewy pink or white sweet containing chopped nuts, cherries, etc.
▷ HISTORY C19: via French from Provençal *nogat,* from *noga* nut, from Latin *nux* nut

nought (nɔːt) NOUN *also* **naught, ought, aught.** 1 another name for **zero:** used esp in counting or

numbering. ◆ NOUN, ADJECTIVE, ADVERB 2 a variant spelling of **naught**.
▷HISTORY Old English *nōwiht*, from *ne* not, no + *ōwiht* something; see WHIT

noughties ('nɔːtɪz) PLURAL NOUN *Informal* the years from 2000 to 2009.

noughts and crosses NOUN (*functioning as singular*) a game in which two players, one using a nought, "O", the other a cross, "X", alternately mark one square out of nine formed by two pairs of crossed lines, the winner being the first to get three of his symbols in a row. US and Canadian term: **tick-tack-toe,** (US) **crisscross.**

Nouméa (ˌnuː'meɪə; *French* numea) NOUN the capital and chief port of the French Overseas Territory of New Caledonia. Pop.: 76 293 (1996).

noumenon ('nuːmɪnən, 'naʊ-) NOUN, *plural* **-na** (-nə). 1 (in the philosophy of Kant) a thing as it is in itself, not perceived or interpreted, incapable of being known, but only inferred from the nature of experience. Compare **phenomenon** (sense 3). See also **thing-in-itself.** 2 the object of a purely intellectual intuition.
▷HISTORY C18: via German from Greek: thing being thought of, from *noein* to think, perceive; related to *nous* mind
▸'**noumenal** ADJECTIVE ▸'**noumenalism** NOUN ▸'**noumenalist** NOUN, ADJECTIVE ▸ˌ**noume'nality** NOUN ▸'**noumenally** ADVERB

noun (naʊn) NOUN **a** a word or group of words that refers to a person, place, or thing or any syntactically similar word. **b** (*as modifier*): *a noun phrase*. Abbreviations: **N, n.** Related adjective: **nominal.**
▷HISTORY C14: via Anglo-French from Latin *nōmen* NAME
▸'**nounal** ADJECTIVE ▸'**nounally** ADVERB ▸'**nounless** ADJECTIVE

noun phrase NOUN *Grammar* a constituent of a sentence that consists of a noun and any modifiers it may have, a noun clause, or a word, such as a pronoun, that takes the place of a noun. Abbreviation: **NP.**

nourish ('nʌrɪʃ) VERB (*tr*) 1 to provide with the materials necessary for life and growth. 2 to support or encourage (an idea, feeling, etc.); foster: *to nourish resentment*.
▷HISTORY C14: from Old French *norir*, from Latin *nūtrīre* to feed, care for
▸'**nourisher** NOUN ▸'**nourishing** ADJECTIVE ▸'**nourishingly** ADVERB

nourishment ('nʌrɪʃmənt) NOUN 1 the act or state of nourishing. 2 a substance that nourishes; food; nutriment.

nous (naʊs) NOUN 1 *Metaphysics* mind or reason, esp when regarded as the principle governing all things. 2 *Brit, slang* common sense; intelligence.
▷HISTORY C17: from Greek, literally: mind

nouveau *or before a plural noun* **nouveaux** ('nuːvəʊ) ADJECTIVE (*prenominal*) *Facetious or derogatory* having recently become the thing specified: *a nouveau hippy*.
▷HISTORY C20: French, literally: new; on the model of NOUVEAU RICHE

nouveau riche (ˌnuːvəʊ 'riːʃ; *French* nuvo riʃ) NOUN, *plural* **nouveaux riches** (ˌnuːvəʊ 'riːʃ; *French* nuvo riʃ). 1 (often *plural* and preceded by *the*) a person who has acquired wealth recently and is regarded as vulgarly ostentatious or lacking in social graces. ◆ ADJECTIVE 2 of or characteristic of the nouveaux riches.
▷HISTORY French, literally: new rich

nouveau roman *French* (nuvo rɔmɑ̃) NOUN, *plural* ***nouveaux romans*** (nuvo rɔmɑ̃). another term for **anti-roman.** See **antinovel.**
▷HISTORY literally: new novel

Nouvelle-Calédonie (nuvɛlkaledɔni) NOUN the French name for **New Caledonia.**

nouvelle cuisine ('nuːvel kwiː'ziːn) NOUN a style of preparing and presenting food, often raw or only lightly cooked, with light sauces, and unusual combinations of flavours and garnishes.
▷HISTORY C20: French, literally: new cookery

Nouvelle Vague *French* (nuvɛl vag) NOUN *Films* another term for **New Wave[1].**

Nov. ABBREVIATION FOR November.

nova ('nəʊvə) NOUN, *plural* **-vae** (-viː) *or* **-vas.** a variable star that undergoes a cataclysmic eruption, observed as a sudden large increase in brightness with a subsequent decline over months or years; it is a close binary system with one component a white dwarf. Compare **supernova.**
▷HISTORY C19: New Latin *nova* (*stella*) new (star), from Latin *novus* new

novaculite (nəʊ'vækjʊˌlaɪt) NOUN a fine-grained dense hard rock containing quartz and feldspar: used as a whetstone.
▷HISTORY C18: from Latin *novācula* sharp knife, razor, from *novāre* to renew

Nova Lisboa (*Portuguese* 'nɔvə liʒ'βoə) NOUN the former name (1928–73) of **Huambo.**

Novara (*Italian* no'vaːra) NOUN a city in NW Italy, in NE Piedmont: scene of the Austrian defeat of the Piedmontese in 1849. Pop.: 102 037 (2000 est.).

Nova Scotia ('nəʊvə 'skəʊʃə) NOUN 1 a peninsula in E Canada, between the Gulf of St Lawrence and the Bay of Fundy. 2 a province of E Canada, consisting of the Nova Scotia peninsula and Cape Breton Island: first settled by the French as Acadia. Capital: Halifax. Pop.: 942 700 (2001 est.). Area: 52 841 sq. km (20 402 sq. miles). Abbreviation: **NS.**

Nova Scotia duck tolling retriever NOUN a Canadian variety of retriever.

Nova Scotian ('nəʊvə 'skəʊʃən) NOUN 1 a native or inhabitant of Nova Scotia. ◆ ADJECTIVE 2 of or relating to Nova Scotia or its inhabitants.

novation (nəʊ'veɪʃən) NOUN 1 *Law* the substitution of a new obligation for an old one by mutual agreement between the parties, esp of one debtor or creditor for another. 2 an obsolete word for **innovation.**
▷HISTORY C16: from Late Latin *novātio* a renewing, from Latin *novāre* to renew

Novaya Zemlya (*Russian* 'nɔvəjə zɪm'lja) NOUN an archipelago in the Arctic Ocean, off the NE coast of Russia: consists of two large islands and many islets. Area: about 81 279 sq. km (31 382 sq. miles).

novel[1] ('nɒvᵊl) NOUN 1 an extended work in prose, either fictitious or partly so, dealing with character, action, thought, etc., esp in the form of a story. 2 **the.** the literary genre represented by novels. 3 (*usually plural*) *Obsolete* a short story or novella, as one of those in the *Decameron* of Boccaccio.
▷HISTORY C15: from Old French *novelle*, from Latin *novella* (*narrātiō*) new (story); see NOVEL[2]

novel[2] ('nɒvᵊl) ADJECTIVE of a kind not seen before; fresh; new; original: *a novel suggestion*.
▷HISTORY C15: from Latin *novellus* new, diminutive of *novus* new

novel[3] ('nɒvᵊl) NOUN *Roman law* a new decree or an amendment to an existing statute. See also **Novels.**

novelese (ˌnɒvə'liːz) NOUN *Derogatory* a style of writing characteristic of poor novels.

novelette (ˌnɒvə'lɛt) NOUN 1 an extended prose narrative story or short novel. 2 a novel that is regarded as being slight, trivial, or sentimental. 3 a short piece of lyrical music, esp one for the piano.

novelettish (ˌnɒvə'lɛtɪʃ) ADJECTIVE characteristic of a novelette; trite or sentimental.

novelist ('nɒvəlɪst) NOUN a writer of novels.

novelistic (ˌnɒvə'lɪstɪk) ADJECTIVE of or characteristic of novels, esp in style or method of treatment: *his novelistic account annoyed other historians*.

novelize *or* **novelise** ('nɒvəˌlaɪz) VERB to convert (a true story, film, etc.) into a novel.
▸ˌ**noveli'zation** *or* ˌ**noveli'sation** NOUN

novella (nəʊ'vɛlə) NOUN, *plural* **-las** *or* **-le** (-leɪ). 1 (formerly) a short narrative tale, esp a popular story having a moral or satirical point, such as those in Boccaccio's *Decameron*. 2 a short novel; novelette.
▷HISTORY C20: from Italian; see NOVEL[1]

Novels ('nɒvᵊlz) PLURAL NOUN *Roman law* the new statutes of Justinian and succeeding emperors supplementing the Institutes, Digest, and Code: now forming part of the Corpus Juris Civilis.
▷HISTORY Latin *Novellae* (*constitūtiōnēs*) new (laws)

novelty ('nɒvᵊltɪ) NOUN, *plural* **-ties.** 1 **a** the quality of being new and fresh and interesting. **b** (*as modifier*): *novelty value*. 2 a new or unusual experience or occurrence. 3 (*often plural*) a small usually cheap new toy, ornament, or trinket.
▷HISTORY C14: from Old French *novelté*; see NOVEL[2]

November (nəʊ'vɛmbə) NOUN 1 the eleventh month of the year, consisting of 30 days. 2 *Communications* a code word for the letter *n*.
▷HISTORY C13: via Old French from Latin: ninth month, from *novem* nine

novena (nəʊ'viːnə) NOUN, *plural* **-nas** *or* **-nae** (-niː). *RC Church* a devotion consisting of prayers or services on nine consecutive days.
▷HISTORY C19: from Medieval Latin, from Latin *novem* nine

novercal (nəʊ'vɜːkᵊl) ADJECTIVE *Rare* stepmotherly.
▷HISTORY C17: from Latin *novercālis*, from *noverca* stepmother

Novgorod (*Russian* 'nɔvgərət) NOUN a city in NW Russia, on the Volkhov River; became a principality in 862 under Rurik, an event regarded as the founding of the Russian state; a major trading centre in the Middle Ages; destroyed by Ivan the Terrible in 1570. Pop.: 231 700 (1999 est.).

novice ('nɒvɪs) NOUN 1 **a** a person who is new to or inexperienced in a certain task, situation, etc.; beginner; tyro. **b** (*as modifier*): *novice driver*. 2 a probationer in a religious order. 3 a sportsman, esp an oarsman, who has not won a recognized prize, performed to an established level, etc. 4 a racehorse, esp a steeplechaser or hurdler, that has not won a specified number of races.
▷HISTORY C14: via Old French from Latin *novīcius*, from *novus* new

Novi Sad (*Serbo-Croat* 'nɔviː 'saːd) NOUN a port in NE Serbia and Montenegro, in Serbia, on the River Danube: founded in 1690 as the seat of the Serbian patriarch; university (1960). Pop.: 179 626 (1991). German name: **Neusatz.**

novitiate *or* **noviciate** (nəʊ'vɪʃɪɪt, -ˌeɪt) NOUN 1 the state of being a novice, esp in a religious order, or the period for which this lasts. 2 the part of a religious house where the novices live. 3 a less common word for **novice.**
▷HISTORY C17: from French *noviciat*, from Latin *novīcius* NOVICE

Novocaine ('nəʊvəˌkeɪn) NOUN a trademark for **procaine hydrochloride.** See **procaine.**

Novokuznetsk (*Russian* nɔvəkuz'njetsk) NOUN a city in S central Russia: iron and steel works. Pop.: 562 800 (1999 est.). Former name (1932–61): **Stalinsk.**

Novosibirsk (*Russian* nəvəsi'birsk) NOUN a city in W central Russia, on the River Ob: the largest town in Siberia; developed with the coming of the Trans-Siberian railway in 1893; important industrial centre. Pop.: 1 402 400 (1999 est.).

now (naʊ) ADVERB 1 at or for the present time or moment. 2 at this exact moment; immediately. 3 in these times; nowadays. 4 given the present circumstances: *now we'll have to stay to the end*. 5 (preceded by *just*) very recently: *he left just now*. 6 (often preceded by *just*) very soon: *he is leaving just now*. 7 (**every**) **now and again** *or* **then.** occasionally; on and off. 8 **for now.** for the time being. 9 **now now!** (*interjection*) an exclamation used to rebuke or pacify someone. 10 **now then. a** (*sentence connector*) used to preface an important remark, the next step in an argument, etc. **b** (*interjection*) an expression of mild reproof: *now then, don't tease!* ◆ CONJUNCTION 11 (*subordinating*; often foll by *that*) seeing that; since it has become the case that: *now you're in charge, things will be better*. ◆ SENTENCE CONNECTOR 12 **a** used as a transitional particle or hesitation word: *now, I can't really say*. **b** used for emphasis: *now listen to this*. **c** used at the end of a command, esp in dismissal: *run along, now*. ◆ NOUN 13 the present moment or time: *now is the time to go*. ◆ ADJECTIVE 14 *Informal* of the moment; fashionable: *the now look is street fashion*.
▷HISTORY Old English *nū*; compare Old Saxon *nū*, German *nun*, Latin *nunc*, Greek *nu*

nowadays ('naʊəˌdeɪz) ADVERB in these times.
▷HISTORY C14: from NOW + *adays* from Old English *a* on + *dæges* genitive of DAY

noway ('nəʊˌweɪ) ADVERB 1 Also in the US (not standard): **noways.** in no manner; not at all; nowise. ◆ SENTENCE SUBSTITUTE **no way.** 2 used to make an emphatic refusal, denial etc.

Nowel *or* **Nowell** (nəʊ'ɛl) NOUN archaic spellings of **Noel.**

nowhence ('nəʊˌwɛns) ADVERB *Archaic* from no place; from nowhere.

nowhere ('nəʊˌwɛə) ADVERB 1 in, at, or to no

place; not anywhere. 2 **get nowhere (fast).** *Informal* to fail completely to make any progress. 3 **nowhere near.** far from; not nearly. ◆ NOUN 4 a nonexistent or insignificant place. 5 **middle of nowhere.** a completely isolated, featureless, or insignificant place.

nowhither ('nəʊˌwɪðə) ADVERB *Archaic* to no place; to nowhere.
▷**HISTORY** Old English *nāhwider.* See NEITHER

no-win ADJECTIVE offering no possibility of a favourable outcome (esp in the phrase **a no-win situation**).

nowise ('nəʊˌwaɪz) ADVERB another word for **noway.**

nowt[1] (naʊt) NOUN *Northern English* a dialect word for **nothing.**
▷**HISTORY** from NAUGHT

nowt[2] (naʊt) NOUN *Scot and northern English* a dialect word for **bullock** and **cattle.**
▷**HISTORY** C13: from Old Norse *naut;* see NEAT[2]

nowty ('naʊtɪ) ADJECTIVE **nowtier, nowtiest.** *Northern English, dialect* bad-tempered.

Nox (nɒks) NOUN the Roman goddess of the night. Greek counterpart: **Nyx.**

noxious ('nɒkʃəs) ADJECTIVE 1 poisonous or harmful. 2 harmful to the mind or morals; corrupting.
▷**HISTORY** C17: from Latin *noxius* harmful, from *noxa* injury
▸**'noxiously** ADVERB ▸**'noxiousness** NOUN

noyade (nwɑː'jɑːd; *French* nwajad) NOUN *French history* execution by drowning, esp as practised during the Reign of Terror at Nantes from 1793 to 1794.
▷**HISTORY** C19: from French, from *noyer* to drown, from Late Latin *necāre* to drown, from Latin: to put to death

noyau ('nwaɪəʊ) NOUN a liqueur made from brandy flavoured with nut kernels.
▷**HISTORY** C18: from French: kernel, from Latin *nux* nut

Noyon (*French* nwajɔ̃) NOUN a town in N France: scene of the coronations of Charlemagne (768) and Hugh Capet (987); birthplace of John Calvin. Pop.: 14 426 (1990).

nozzle ('nɒzᵊl) NOUN 1 a projecting pipe or spout from which fluid is discharged. 2 Also called: **propelling nozzle.** a pipe or duct, esp in a jet engine or rocket, that directs the effluent and accelerates or diffuses the flow to generate thrust. 3 a socket, such as the part of a candlestick that holds the candle.
▷**HISTORY** C17 *nosle, nosel,* diminutive of NOSE

np[1] ABBREVIATION FOR: 1 *Printing* new paragraph. 2 *Law* nisi prius. 3 no place of publication.

np[2] THE INTERNET DOMAIN NAME FOR Nepal.

Np 1 SYMBOL FOR neper. ◆ 2 THE CHEMICAL SYMBOL FOR neptunium.

NP ABBREVIATION FOR: 1 neuropsychiatric. 2 neuropsychiatry. 3 Also: **np. Notary Public.** 4 noun phrase.

NPA ABBREVIATION FOR Newspaper Publishers' Association.

NPC (in New Zealand) ABBREVIATION FOR National Provincial Championship, an interprovincial rugby competition.

NPD *Commerce* ABBREVIATION FOR new product development.

NPL ABBREVIATION FOR National Physical Laboratory.

NPV ABBREVIATION FOR: 1 **net present value.** 2 no par value.

NQA (in New Zealand) ABBREVIATION FOR National Qualifications Authority.

nr[1] ABBREVIATION FOR near.

nr[2] THE INTERNET DOMAIN NAME FOR Nauru.

NRA (in Britain) ABBREVIATION FOR: 1 National Rifle Association. 2 National Rivers Authority.

NRC (in Canada) ABBREVIATION FOR National Research Council.

NRL (in Australia) ABBREVIATION FOR National Rugby League.

NRMA (in Australia) ABBREVIATION FOR National Roads and Motorists Association.

NRN *Text messaging* ABBREVIATION FOR no reply necessary.

NRT ABBREVIATION FOR nicotine replacement therapy: a type of treatment designed to help people give up smoking in which gradually decreasing doses of nicotine are administered through patches on the skin etc. to avoid the effects of sudden withdrawal from the drug.

NRV ABBREVIATION FOR **net realizable value.**

ns ABBREVIATION FOR: 1 new series. 2 not specified.

NS ABBREVIATION FOR: 1 New Style (method of reckoning dates). 2 not sufficient *or* not satisfactory. 3 (esp in postal addresses) Nova Scotia. 4 nuclear ship.

NSAID ABBREVIATION FOR nonsteroidal anti-inflammatory drug: any of a class of drugs, including aspirin and ibuprofen, used for reducing inflammation and pain in rheumatic diseases. Possible adverse effects include gastric ulceration.

NSB ABBREVIATION FOR **National Savings Bank.**

NSF *or* **N/S/F** *Banking* ABBREVIATION FOR not sufficient funds.

NSG *Brit education* ABBREVIATION FOR nonstatutory guidelines: practical nonmandatory advice and information on the implementation of the National Curriculum.

NSPCC ABBREVIATION FOR National Society for the Prevention of Cruelty to Children.

NSU ABBREVIATION FOR **nonspecific urethritis.**

NSW ABBREVIATION FOR New South Wales.

NT ABBREVIATION FOR: 1 National Trust. 2 New Testament. 3 Northern Territory (of Australia). 4 (esp in postal addresses) Northwest Territories (of Australia). 5 (esp in postal addresses) Nunavut. 6 no-trump. 7 (in Ireland) National Teacher (teacher in a National School).

-n't CONTRACTION OF not: used as an enclitic after *be* and *have* when they function as main verbs and after auxiliary verbs or verbs operating syntactically as auxiliaries: *can't; don't; shouldn't; needn't; daren't; isn't.*

nth (ɛnθ) ADJECTIVE 1 *Maths* of or representing an unspecified ordinal number, usually the greatest in a series of values: *the nth power.* 2 *Informal* being the last, most recent, or most extreme of a long series: *for the nth time, eat your lunch!* 3 **to the nth degree.** *Informal* to the utmost extreme; as much as possible.

Nth ABBREVIATION FOR North.

NTO (in Britain) ABBREVIATION FOR National Training Organization.

NTP ABBREVIATION FOR normal temperature and pressure: standard conditions of 0°C temperature and 101.325 kPa (760 mmHg) pressure. Also: **STP.**

NTS ABBREVIATION FOR National Trust for Scotland.

n-tuple NOUN *Logic, maths* an ordered set of *n* elements.

nt. wt. *or* **nt wt** ABBREVIATION FOR net weight.

n-type ADJECTIVE 1 (of a semiconductor) having more conduction electrons than mobile holes. 2 associated with or resulting from the movement of electrons in a semiconductor: *n-type conductivity.* ◆ Compare **p-type.**

nu[1] (njuː) NOUN the 13th letter in the Greek alphabet (Ν, ν), a consonant, transliterated as *n.*
▷**HISTORY** from Greek, of Semitic origin; compare NUN[2]

nu[2] THE INTERNET DOMAIN NAME FOR Niue.

nu- PREFIX *Informal* indicating an updated or modern version of something: *nu-metal music.*
▷**HISTORY** C20: from NEW

nuance (njuː'ɑːns, 'njuːɑːns) NOUN 1 a subtle difference in colour, meaning, tone, etc.; a shade or graduation. ◆ VERB (*tr; passive*) 2 to give subtle differences to: *carefully nuanced words.*
▷**HISTORY** C18: from French, from *nuer* to show light and shade, ultimately from Latin *nūbēs* a cloud

nub (nʌb) NOUN 1 a small lump or protuberance. 2 a small piece or chunk. 3 the point or gist: *the nub of a story.* 4 a small fibrous knot in yarn.
▷**HISTORY** C16: variant of *knub,* from Middle Low German *knubbe* KNOB

Nuba ('njuːbə) NOUN 1 (*plural* **-bas** *or* **-ba**) a member of a formerly warlike Nilotic people living chiefly in the hills of S central Sudan. 2 the language or group of related dialects spoken by this people, belonging to the Chari-Nile branch of the Nilo-Saharan family.

Nubain ('njuːˌbeɪn) NOUN *Trademark* an opiate drug, nalbuphine hydrochloride, used as a painkiller and, illegally, by bodybuilders and others to increase their pain threshold and as a recreational drug, being a cheap alternative to heroin.

nubbin ('nʌbɪn) NOUN *Chiefly US and Canadian* something small or undeveloped, esp a fruit or ear of corn.
▷**HISTORY** C19: diminutive of NUB

nubble ('nʌbᵊl) NOUN a small lump.
▷**HISTORY** C19: diminutive of NUB
▸**'nubbly** ADJECTIVE

nubby ('nʌbɪ) ADJECTIVE having small lumps or protuberances; knobbly.

nubecula (njuː'bɛkjʊlə) NOUN, *plural* **-lae** (-liː). See **Magellanic Cloud.**
▷**HISTORY** C19: from Latin, diminutive of *nubes* cloud

Nubia ('njuːbɪə) NOUN an ancient region of NE Africa, on the Nile, extending from Aswan to Khartoum.

Nubian ('njuːbɪən) NOUN 1 a native or inhabitant of Nubia, an ancient region of NE Africa. 2 the language spoken by the people of Nubia. ◆ ADJECTIVE 3 of or relating to Nubia or its inhabitants. 4 *Informal* of or relating to Black culture.

Nubian Desert NOUN a desert in the NE Sudan, between the Nile valley and the Red Sea: mainly a sandstone plateau.

nubile ('njuːbaɪl) ADJECTIVE (of a girl or woman) 1 ready or suitable for marriage by virtue of age or maturity. 2 sexually attractive.
▷**HISTORY** C17: from Latin *nūbilis,* from *nūbere* to marry
▸**nubility** (njuː'bɪlɪtɪ) NOUN

Nubuck ('njuːˌbʌk) NOUN (*sometimes not capital*) leather that has been rubbed on the flesh side of the skin to give it a fine velvet-like finish.

nucellus (njuː'sɛləs) NOUN, *plural* **-li** (-laɪ). the central part of a plant ovule containing the embryo sac.
▷**HISTORY** C19: New Latin, from Latin *nucella,* from *nux* nut
▸**nu'cellar** ADJECTIVE

nucha ('njuːkə) NOUN, *plural* **-chae** (-kiː). *Zoology, anatomy* the back or nape of the neck.
▷**HISTORY** C14: from Medieval Latin, from Arabic *nukhā'* spinal marrow
▸**'nuchal** ADJECTIVE

nucivorous (njuː'sɪvərəs) ADJECTIVE (of animals) feeding on nuts.
▷**HISTORY** from Latin *nux* nut + -VOROUS

nuclear ('njuːklɪə) ADJECTIVE 1 of, concerned with, or involving the nucleus of an atom: *nuclear fission.* 2 *Biology* of, relating to, or contained within the nucleus of a cell: *a nuclear membrane.* 3 of, relating to, forming, or resembling any other kind of nucleus. 4 of, concerned with, or operated by energy from fission or fusion of atomic nuclei: *a nuclear weapon.* 5 involving, concerned with, or possessing nuclear weapons: *nuclear war; a nuclear strike.*

nuclear bomb NOUN a bomb whose force is due to uncontrolled nuclear fusion or nuclear fission.

nuclear chemistry NOUN the branch of chemistry concerned with nuclear reactions.

nuclear energy NOUN energy released during a nuclear reaction as a result of fission or fusion. Also called: **atomic energy.**

nuclear family NOUN *Sociol, anthropol* a primary social unit consisting of parents and their offspring. Compare **extended family.**

nuclear fission NOUN the splitting of an atomic nucleus into approximately equal parts, either spontaneously or as a result of the impact of a particle usually with an associated release of energy. Sometimes shortened to **fission.** Compare **nuclear fusion.**

nuclear-free zone NOUN an area barred, esp by local authorities, to the storage or deployment of nuclear weapons.

nuclear fuel NOUN a fuel that provides nuclear

energy, used in nuclear power stations, nuclear submarines, etc.

nuclear fusion NOUN a reaction in which two nuclei combine to form a nucleus with the release of energy. Sometimes shortened to **fusion.** Compare **nuclear fission.** See also **thermonuclear reaction.**

nuclear isomer NOUN the more formal name for **isomer** (sense 2).
▸**nuclear isomerism** NOUN

nuclear magnetic resonance NOUN a technique for determining the magnetic moments of nuclei by subjecting a substance to high-frequency radiation and a large magnetic field. The technique is used as a method of determining structure. Abbreviation: **NMR.** See also **electron spin resonance.**

nuclear magnetic resonance scanner NOUN a machine for the medical technique in which changes in the constituent atoms of the body under the influence of a powerful electromagnet are used to generate computed images of the internal organs.

nuclear medicine NOUN the branch of medicine concerned with the use of radionuclides in the diagnosis and treatment of disease.

nuclear option NOUN 1 the use of or power to use nuclear weapons. 2 the use of or power to use a measure considered to be particularly drastic: *the nuclear option of a confidence vote.*

nuclear physics NOUN (*functioning as singular*) the branch of physics concerned with the structure and behaviour of the nucleus and the particles of which it consists.
▸**nuclear physicist** NOUN

nuclear power NOUN power, esp electrical or motive, produced by a nuclear reactor. Also called: **atomic power.**

nuclear reaction NOUN a process in which the structure and energy content of an atomic nucleus is changed by interaction with another nucleus or particle.

nuclear reactor NOUN a device in which a nuclear reaction is maintained and controlled for the production of nuclear energy. Sometimes shortened to **reactor.** Former name: **atomic pile.** See also **fission reactor, fusion reactor.**

nuclear threshold NOUN the point in war at which a combatant brings nuclear weapons into use.

nuclear transfer NOUN the procedure used to produce the first cloned mammals, in which the nucleus of a somatic cell is transferred into an egg cell whose own nucleus has been removed: this cell is then stimulated by an electric shock to divide and form an embryo.

nuclear waste NOUN another name for **radioactive waste.**

nuclear winter NOUN a period of extremely low temperatures and little light that has been suggested would occur as a result of a nuclear war.

nuclease ('nju:klɪˌeɪz) NOUN any of a group of enzymes that hydrolyse nucleic acids to simple nucleotides.

nucleate ADJECTIVE ('nju:klɪɪt, 'nju:klɪˌeɪt) 1 having a nucleus. ◆ VERB (-ˌeɪt) (*intr*) 2 to form a nucleus.
▸ˌ**nucle'ation** NOUN ▸'**nucleˌator** NOUN

nucleating agent NOUN *Meteorol* a substance used to seed clouds to control rainfall and fog formation.

nuclei ('nju:klɪˌaɪ) NOUN a plural of **nucleus.**

nucleic acid (nju:'kli:ɪk, -'kleɪ-) NOUN *Biochem* any of a group of complex compounds with a high molecular weight that are vital constituents of all living cells. See also **RNA, DNA.**

nuclein ('nju:klɪɪn) NOUN any of a group of proteins, containing phosphorus, that occur in the nuclei of living cells.

nucleo- *or before a vowel* **nucle-** COMBINING FORM 1 nucleus or nuclear: *nucleoplasm.* 2 nucleic acid: *nucleoprotein.*

nucleolus (ˌnju:klɪ'əʊləs) NOUN, *plural* **-li** (-laɪ). a small rounded body within a resting nucleus that contains RNA and proteins and is involved in the production of ribosomes. Also called: '**nucleˌole.**
▷HISTORY C19: from Latin, diminutive of NUCLEUS
▸ˌ**nucle'olar** *or* '**nucleoˌlate** *or* '**nucleoˌlated** ADJECTIVE

nucleon ('nju:klɪˌɒn) NOUN a proton or neutron, esp one present in an atomic nucleus.
▷HISTORY C20: from NUCLE(US) + -ON

nucleonics (ˌnju:klɪ'ɒnɪks) NOUN (*functioning as singular*) the branch of physics concerned with the applications of nuclear energy.
▸ˌ**nucle'onic** ADJECTIVE ▸ˌ**nucle'onically** ADVERB

nucleon number NOUN another name for **mass number.**

nucleophilic (ˌnju:klɪəʊ'fɪlɪk) ADJECTIVE *Chem* having or involving an affinity for positive charge. Nucleophilic reagents (**nucleophiles**) are molecules, atoms, and ions that behave as electron donors. Compare **electrophilic.**

nucleoplasm ('nju:klɪəˌplæzəm) NOUN the protoplasm in the nucleus of a plant or animal cell that surrounds the chromosomes and nucleolus. Also called: **karyoplasm.**
▸ˌ**nucleo'plasmic** *or* ˌ**nucleoplas'matic** ADJECTIVE

nucleoprotein (ˌnju:klɪəʊ'prəʊti:n) NOUN a compound within a cell nucleus that consists of a protein bound to a nucleic acid.

nucleoside ('nju:klɪəˌsaɪd) NOUN *Biochem* a compound containing a purine or pyrimidine base linked to a sugar (usually ribose or deoxyribose).
▷HISTORY C20: from NUCLEO- + -OSE[2] + -IDE

nucleosome ('nju:klɪəˌsəʊm) NOUN a repeating structural unit of chromatin that contains DNA and histones.

nucleosynthesis (ˌnju:klɪəʊ'sɪnθɪsɪs) NOUN *Astronomy* the formation of heavier elements from lighter elements by nuclear fusion in stars.

nucleotide ('nju:klɪəˌtaɪd) NOUN *Biochem* a compound consisting of a nucleoside linked to phosphoric acid. Nucleic acids are made up of long chains (polynucleotides) of such compounds.
▷HISTORY C20: from NUCLEO- + *t* (added for ease of pronunciation) + -IDE

nucleus ('nju:klɪəs) NOUN, *plural* **-clei** (-klɪˌaɪ) *or* **-cleuses.** 1 a central or fundamental part or thing around which others are grouped; core. 2 a centre of growth or development; basis; kernel: *the nucleus of an idea.* 3 *Biology* (in the cells of eukaryotes) a large compartment, bounded by a double membrane, that contains the chromosomes and associated molecules and controls the characteristics and growth of the cell. 4 *Anatomy* any of various groups of nerve cells in the central nervous system. 5 *Astronomy* the central portion in the head of a comet, consisting of small solid particles of ice and frozen gases, which vaporize on approaching the sun to form the coma and tail. 6 *Physics* the positively charged dense region at the centre of an atom, composed of protons and neutrons, about which electrons orbit. 7 *Chem* a fundamental group of atoms in a molecule serving as the base structure for related compounds and remaining unchanged during most chemical reactions: *the benzene nucleus.* 8 *Botany* **a** the central point of a starch granule. **b** a rare name for **nucellus.** 9 *Phonetics* the most sonorous part of a syllable, usually consisting of a vowel or frictionless continuant. 10 *Logic* the largest individual that is a mereological part of every member of a given class.
▷HISTORY C18: from Latin: kernel, from *nux* nut

nuclide ('nju:klaɪd) NOUN a species of atom characterized by its atomic number and its mass number. See also **isotope.**
▷HISTORY C20: from NUCLEO- + *-ide,* from Greek *eidos* shape

nuddy ('nʌdɪ) NOUN **in the nuddy.** *Informal, chiefly Brit and Austral* in the nude; naked.
▷HISTORY C20: originally Australian, a variant of NUDE

nude (nju:d) ADJECTIVE 1 completely unclothed; undressed. 2 having no covering; bare; exposed. 3 *Law* **a** lacking some essential legal requirement, esp supporting evidence. **b** (of a contract, agreement, etc.) made without consideration and void unless under seal. ◆ NOUN 4 the state of being naked (esp in the phrase **in the nude**). 5 a naked figure, esp in painting, sculpture, etc.
▷HISTORY C16: from Latin *nūdus*
▸'**nudely** ADVERB ▸'**nudeness** NOUN

nudge (nʌdʒ) VERB (*tr*) 1 to push or poke (someone) gently, esp with the elbow, to get attention; jog. 2 to push slowly or lightly: *as I drove out, I just nudged the gatepost.* 3 to give (someone) a gentle reminder or encouragement. ◆ NOUN 4 a gentle poke or push.
▷HISTORY C17: perhaps from Scandinavian; compare Icelandic *nugga* to push
▸'**nudger** NOUN

nudi- COMBINING FORM naked or bare: *nudibranch.*
▷HISTORY from Latin *nūdus*

nudibranch ('nju:dɪˌbræŋk) NOUN any marine gastropod of the order *Nudibranchia,* characterized by a shell-less, often beautifully coloured, body bearing external gills and other appendages. Also called: **sea slug.**
▷HISTORY C19: from NUDI- + *branche,* from Latin *branchia* gills

nudicaudate (ˌnju:dɪ'kɔ:deɪt) ADJECTIVE (of such animals as rats) having a hairless tail.

nudicaul ('nju:dɪˌkɔ:l) *or* **nudicaulous** (ˌnju:dɪ'kɔ:ləs) ADJECTIVE (of plants) having stems without leaves.
▷HISTORY C20: from NUDI- + *caul,* from Latin *caulis* stem

nudism ('nju:dɪzəm) NOUN the practice of nudity, esp for reasons of health, religion, etc.
▸'**nudist** NOUN, ADJECTIVE

nudity ('nju:dɪtɪ) NOUN, *plural* **-ties.** 1 the state or fact of being nude; nakedness. 2 *Rare* a nude figure, esp in art.

nudum pactum ('nju:dʊm 'pæktʊm) NOUN *Law* an agreement made without consideration and void unless made under seal.
▷HISTORY Latin: nude (sense 3b) agreement

nuée ardente ('nʊeɪ ɑ:'dɑ̃t) NOUN a rapidly moving turbulent incandescent cloud of gas, ash, and rock fragments flowing close to the ground after violent ejection from a volcano. See also **ignimbrite.**
▷HISTORY C20: from French, literally: burning cloud

Nuevo Laredo (*Spanish* 'nweβo la'reðo) NOUN a city and port of entry in NE Mexico, in Tamaulipas state on the Rio Grande opposite Laredo, Texas: oil industries. Pop.: 309 000 (2000 est.).

Nuevo León ('nweɪvəʊ leɪ'əʊn, nu:'eɪ-; *Spanish* 'nweβo le'ɔn) NOUN a state of NE Mexico: the first centre of heavy industry in Latin America. Capital: Monterrey. Pop.: 3 826 240 (2000). Area: 64 555 sq. km (24 925 sq. miles).

nuevo sol ('nweɪvəʊ 'sɒl) NOUN the Spanish name for **new sol.**

Nuffield teaching project ('nʌfi:ld) NOUN (in Britain) a complete school programme in mathematics, science, languages, etc., with suggested complementary theory and practical work.

nugatory ('nju:gətərɪ, -trɪ) ADJECTIVE 1 of little value; trifling. 2 not valid: *a nugatory law.*
▷HISTORY C17: from Latin *nūgātōrius,* from *nūgārī* to jest, from *nūgae* trifles

nuggar ('nʌgə) NOUN a sailing boat used to carry cargo on the Nile.
▷HISTORY from Arabic

nugget ('nʌgɪt) NOUN 1 a small piece or lump, esp of gold in its natural state. 2 something small but valuable or excellent.
▷HISTORY C19: origin unknown

Nugget ('nʌgɪt) *NZ* ◆ NOUN 1 *Trademark* shoe polish. ◆ VERB 2 (*tr; sometimes not capital*) *informal* to shine (shoes).

nuggety ('nʌgɪtɪ) ADJECTIVE 1 of or resembling a nugget. 2 *Austral and NZ informal* (of a person) thickset; stocky.

nuisance ('nju:səns) NOUN 1 **a** a person or thing that causes annoyance or bother. **b** (*as modifier*): *nuisance calls.* 2 *Law* something unauthorized that is obnoxious or injurious to the community at large (**public nuisance**) or to an individual, esp in relation to his ownership or occupation of property (**private nuisance**). 3 **nuisance value.** the usefulness of a person's or thing's capacity to cause difficulties or irritation.
▷HISTORY C15: via Old French from *nuire* to injure, from Latin *nocēre*

Nuits-Saint-Georges (*French* nɥisɛ̃ʒɔrʒ) NOUN a fine red wine produced near the town of Nuits-Saint-Georges in Burgundy.

NUJ (in Britain) ABBREVIATION FOR National Union of Journalists.

Nu Jiang ('nu: 'dʒjæŋ) NOUN the Chinese name for the **Salween.**

nuke (nju:k) *Slang* ◆ VERB 1 *(tr)* to attack or destroy with nuclear weapons. ◆ NOUN 2 a nuclear bomb. 3 a military strike with nuclear weapons. 4 nuclear power. 5 *Chiefly US* a nuclear power plant.

Nuku'alofa (ˌnu:ku:ə'lɔ:fə) NOUN the capital of Tonga, a port on the N coast of Tongatapu Island. Pop.: 37 000 (1999 est.).

Nukus (*Russian* nu'kus) NOUN a city in Uzbekistan, capital of the Kara-Kalpak Autonomous Republic, on the Amu Darya River. Pop.: 185 000 (1998 est.).

null (nʌl) ADJECTIVE 1 without legal force; invalid; (esp in the phrase **null and void**). 2 without value or consequence; useless. 3 lacking distinction; characterless: *a null expression.* 4 nonexistent; amounting to nothing. 5 *Maths* **a** quantitatively zero. **b** relating to zero. **c** (of a set) having no members. **d** (of a sequence) having zero as a limit. 6 *Physics* involving measurement in which an instrument has a zero reading, as with a Wheatstone bridge.
▷HISTORY C16: from Latin *nullus* none, from *ne* not + *ullus* any

nullah ('nʌlɑ:) NOUN a stream or drain.
▷HISTORY C18: from Hindi *nālā*

nulla-nulla (ˌnʌlə'nʌlə) NOUN *Austral* a wooden club used by native Australians.
▷HISTORY from a native Australian language

Nullarbor Plain ('nʌləˌbɔ:) NOUN a vast low plateau of S Australia: extends north from the Great Australian Bight to the Great Victoria Desert; has no surface water or trees. Area: 260 000 sq. km (100 000 sq. miles).

null hypothesis NOUN *Statistics* the residual hypothesis if the alternative hypothesis tested against it fails to achieve a predetermined significance level. See **hypothesis testing.** Compare **alternative hypothesis.**

nullifidian (ˌnʌlɪ'fɪdɪən) NOUN 1 a person who has no faith or belief; sceptic; disbeliever. ◆ ADJECTIVE 2 having no faith or belief.
▷HISTORY C16: from Latin, from *nullus* no + *fidēs* faith

nullify ('nʌlɪˌfaɪ) VERB **-fies, -fying, -fied.** *(tr)* 1 to render legally void or of no effect. 2 to render ineffective or useless; cancel out.
▷HISTORY C16: from Late Latin *nullificāre* to despise, from Latin *nullus* of no account + *facere* to make
▸**ˌnullifi'cation** NOUN ▸**'nulliˌfier** NOUN

nullipara (nʌ'lɪpərə) NOUN, *plural* **-rae** (-ˌri:). a woman who has never borne a child.
▷HISTORY C19: New Latin, from *nullus* no, not any + *-para,* from *parere* to bring forth; see -PAROUS
▸**nul'liparous** ADJECTIVE

nullipore ('nʌlɪˌpɔ:) NOUN any of several red seaweeds that secrete and become encrusted with calcium carbonate: family *Rhodophyceae.*
▷HISTORY C19: from Latin, from *nullus* no + PORE²

nulli secundus *Latin* ('nuli: sə'kundus) ADJECTIVE second to none.

nullity ('nʌlɪtɪ) NOUN, *plural* **-ties.** 1 the state of being null. 2 a null or legally invalid act or instrument. 3 something null, ineffective, characterless, etc.
▷HISTORY C16: from Medieval Latin *nullitās,* from Latin *nullus* no, not any

NUM (in Britain and South Africa) ABBREVIATION FOR National Union of Mineworkers.

Num. *Bible* ABBREVIATION FOR Numbers.

Numantia (nju:'mæntɪə) NOUN an ancient city in N Spain: a centre of Celtic resistance to Rome in N Spain: captured by Scipio the Younger in 133 B.C.

Numantian (nju:'mæntɪən) ADJECTIVE 1 of or relating to Numantia or its inhabitants. ◆ NOUN 2 a native or inhabitant of Numantia.

numb (nʌm) ADJECTIVE 1 deprived of feeling through cold, shock, etc. 2 unable to move; paralysed. 3 characteristic of or resembling numbness: *a numb sensation.* ◆ VERB 4 *(tr)* to make numb; deaden, shock, or paralyse.
▷HISTORY C15 *nomen,* literally: taken (with paralysis), from Old English *niman* to take; related to Old Norse *nema,* Old High German *niman*
▸**'numbly** ADVERB ▸**'numbness** NOUN

numbat ('nʌmˌbæt) NOUN a small Australian marsupial, *Myrmecobius fasciatus,* having a long snout and tongue and strong claws for hunting and feeding on termites: family *Dasyuridae.* Also called: **banded anteater.**
▷HISTORY C20: from a native Australian language

number ('nʌmbə) NOUN 1 a concept of quantity that is or can be derived from a single unit, the sum of a collection of units, or zero. Every number occupies a unique position in a sequence, enabling it to be used in counting. It can be assigned to one or more sets that can be arranged in a hierarchical classification: every number is a **complex number**; a complex number is either an **imaginary number** or a **real number**, and the latter can be a **rational number** or an **irrational number**; a rational number is either an **integer** or a **fraction**, while an irrational number can be a **transcendental number** or an **algebraic number**. See also **cardinal number, ordinal number.** 2 the symbol used to represent a number; numeral. 3 a numeral or string of numerals used to identify a person or thing, esp in numerical order: *a telephone number.* 4 the person or thing so identified or designated: *she was number seven in the race.* 5 the sum or quantity of equal or similar units or things: *a large number of people.* 6 one of a series, as of a magazine or periodical; issue. 7 **a** a self-contained piece of pop or jazz music. **b** a self-contained part of an opera or other musical score, esp one for the stage. 8 a group or band of people, esp an exclusive group: *he was not one of our number.* 9 *Slang* a person, esp a woman: *who's that nice little number?* 10 *Informal* an admired article, esp an item of clothing for a woman: *that little number is by Dior.* 11 *Slang* a cannabis cigarette: *roll another number.* 12 a grammatical category for the variation in form of nouns, pronouns, and any words agreeing with them, depending on how many persons or things are referred to, esp as singular or plural in number and in some languages dual or trial. 13 **any number of.** several or many. 14 **by numbers.** *Military* (of a drill procedure, etc.) performed step by step, each move being made on the call of a number. 15 **do a number on (someone).** *US, slang* to manipulate or trick (someone). 16 **get** *or* **have someone's number.** *Informal* to discover someone's true character or intentions. 17 **in numbers.** in large numbers; numerously. 18 **one's number is up.** *Brit informal* one is finished; one is ruined or about to die. 19 **without** *or* **beyond number.** of too great a quantity to be counted; innumerable. ◆ VERB *(mainly tr)* 20 to assign a number to. 21 to add up to; total. 22 *(also intr)* to list (items) one by one; enumerate. 23 *(also intr)* to put or be put into a group, category, etc.: *they were numbered among the worst hit.* 24 to limit the number of: *his days were numbered.*
▷HISTORY C13: from Old French *nombre,* from Latin *numerus*

number crunching NOUN *Computing* the large-scale processing of numerical data.
▸**number cruncher** NOUN

numbered account NOUN *Banking* an account identified only by a number, esp one in a Swiss bank that could contain funds illegally obtained.

number eight wire NOUN *NZ* 1 a standard gauge of fencing wire. 2 this wire or something similar used for emergency repairs.

numberless ('nʌmbəlɪs) ADJECTIVE 1 too many to be counted; countless. 2 not containing or consisting of numbers.
▸**'numberlessly** ADVERB ▸**'numberlessness** NOUN

number line NOUN an infinite line on which points represent the real numbers.

number off VERB *(adverb)* to call out or cause to call out one's number or place in a sequence, esp in a rank of soldiers: *the sergeant numbered his men off from the right.*

number one NOUN 1 the first in a series or sequence. 2 an informal phrase for **oneself, myself,** etc.: *to look after number one.* 3 *Informal* the most important person; leader, chief: *he's number one in the organization.* 4 *Informal* the bestselling pop record in any one week. 5 *Euphemistic* the act or an instance of urination. 6 a haircut in which the hair is cut very close to the head with an electric shaver. ◆ ADJECTIVE 7 first in importance, urgency, quality, etc.: *number one priority.* 8 *Informal* (of a pop record) having reached the top of the charts.

numberplate ('nʌmbəˌpleɪt) NOUN a plate mounted on the front and back of a motor vehicle bearing the registration number. Usual US term: **license plate,** (Canadian) **licence plate.**

Numbers ('nʌmbəz) NOUN *(functioning as singular)* the fourth book of the Old Testament, recording the numbers of the Israelites who followed Moses out of Egypt.

numbers game *or* **racket** NOUN *US* an illegal lottery in which money is wagered on a certain combination of digits appearing at the beginning of a series of numbers published in a newspaper, as in share prices or sports results. Often shortened to: **numbers.**

Number Ten NOUN 10 Downing Street, the British prime minister's official London residence.

number theory NOUN the study of integers, their properties, and the relationship between integers.

number two NOUN 1 *Euphemistic* the act or an instance of defecation. 2 a haircut in which the hair is cut close to the head with an electric shaver.

number work NOUN simple arithmetic and similar mathematical procedures as used and studied at primary level. Also called (esp formerly): **sums.**

numbfish ('nʌmˌfɪʃ) NOUN, *plural* **-fish** *or* **-fishes.** any of several electric rays, such as *Narcine tasmaniensis* (**Australian numbfish**).
▷HISTORY C18: so called because it numbs its victims

numbles ('nʌmbᵊlz) PLURAL NOUN *Archaic* the heart, lungs, liver, etc., of a deer or other animal, cooked for food.
▷HISTORY C14: from Old French *nombles,* plural of *nomble* thigh muscle of a deer, changed from Latin *lumbulus* a little loin, from *lumbus* loin; see HUMBLE PIE

numbskull *or* **numskull** ('nʌmˌskʌl) NOUN a stupid person; dolt; blockhead.
▷HISTORY C18: from NUMB + SKULL

numdah ('nʌmdɑ:) NOUN 1 a coarse felt made esp in India. 2 a saddle pad made from this. 3 an embroidered rug made from this. ◆ Also called (for senses 1, 2): **numnah.**
▷HISTORY C19: from Urdu *namdā*

numen ('nju:mɛn) NOUN, *plural* **-mina** (-mɪnə). 1 (esp in ancient Roman religion) a deity or spirit presiding over a thing or place. 2 a guiding principle, force, or spirit.
▷HISTORY C17: from Latin: a nod (indicating a command), divine power; compare *nuere* to nod

numerable ('nju:mərəbᵊl) ADJECTIVE able to be numbered or counted.
▸**'numerably** ADVERB

numeracy ('nju:mərəsɪ) NOUN the ability to use numbers, esp in arithmetical operations.

numeral ('nju:mərəl) NOUN 1 a symbol or group of symbols used to express a number: for example, *6* (*Arabic*), *VI* (*Roman*), *110* (*binary*). ◆ ADJECTIVE 2 of, consisting of, or denoting a number.
▷HISTORY C16: from Late Latin *numerālis* belonging to number, from Latin *numerus* number

numerary ('nju:mərərɪ) ADJECTIVE of or relating to numbers.

numerate ADJECTIVE ('nju:mərɪt) 1 able to use numbers, esp in arithmetical operations. Compare **literate.** ◆ VERB ('nju:məˌreɪt) *(tr)* 2 to read (a numerical expression). 3 a less common word for **enumerate.**
▷HISTORY C18 (vb): from Latin *numerus* number + -ATE¹, by analogy with *literate*

numeration (ˌnju:mə'reɪʃən) NOUN 1 the act or process of writing, reading, or naming numbers. 2 a system of numbering or counting.
▸**'numerative** ADJECTIVE

numerator ('nju:məˌreɪtə) NOUN 1 *Maths* the dividend of a fraction: *the numerator of* ⅞ *is 7.* Compare **denominator.** 2 a person or thing that numbers; enumerator.

numerical (nju:'mɛrɪkᵊl) *or* **numeric** ADJECTIVE 1 of, relating to, or denoting a number or numbers. 2 measured or expressed in numbers: *numerical value.* 3 *Maths* **a** containing or using constants, coefficients, terms, or elements represented by numbers: $3x^2 + 4y = 2$ is a numerical equation. Compare **literal** (sense 6). **b** another word for **absolute** (sense 11a).
▸**nu'merically** ADVERB

numerical analysis NOUN a branch of mathematics concerned with methods, usually iterative, for obtaining solutions to problems by means of a computer.

numerical control NOUN *Engineering* a form of computer control applied to machine tools, by which an operation is directed from numerical data stored on tape or punched on cards.

numerical identity NOUN *Logic* the relation that holds between two relata when they are the selfsame entity, that is, when the terms designating them have the same reference. Compare **qualitative identity.** See also **Leibnitz's law.**

numerology (ˌnjuːməˈrɒlədʒɪ) NOUN the study of numbers, such as the figures in a birth date, and of their supposed influence on human affairs.
▸**numerological** (ˌnjuːmərəˈlɒdʒɪkᵊl) ADJECTIVE
▸ˌ**numerˈologist** NOUN

numerous (ˈnjuːmərəs) ADJECTIVE [1] being many. [2] consisting of many units or parts: *a numerous collection.*
▸ˈ**numerously** ADVERB ▸ˈ**numerousness** NOUN

nu-metal (ˌnjuːˈmɛtᵊl) NOUN **a** a type of rock music popular from the late 1990s, featuring much of the sound typical of heavy metal but also influenced by rap and hip-hop. **b** (*as modifier*): *a nu-metal band.*
▷**HISTORY** C20: from NU-, a form of NEW + (HEAVY) METAL

Numidia (njuːˈmɪdɪə) NOUN an ancient country of N Africa, corresponding roughly to present-day Algeria: flourished until its invasion by Vandals in 429; chief towns were Cirta and Hippo Regius.

Numidian (njuːˈmɪdɪən) ADJECTIVE [1] of or relating to Numidia or its inhabitants. ◆ NOUN [2] a native or inhabitant of Numidia.

Numidian crane NOUN another name for **demoiselle crane** (see **demoiselle** (sense 1)).

numina (ˈnjuːmɪnə) NOUN the plural of **numen.**

numinous (ˈnjuːmɪnəs) ADJECTIVE [1] denoting, being, or relating to a numen; divine. [2] arousing spiritual or religious emotions. [3] mysterious or awe-inspiring.
▷**HISTORY** C17: from Latin *numin-*, NUMEN + -OUS

numismatics (ˌnjuːmɪzˈmætɪks) NOUN (*functioning as singular*) the study or collection of coins, medals, etc. Also called: **numismatology.**
▷**HISTORY** C18: from French *numismatique*, from Latin *nomisma*, from Greek: piece of currency, from *nomizein* to have in use, from *nōmos* use
▸ˌ**numisˈmatic** ADJECTIVE ▸ˌ**numisˈmatically** ADVERB

numismatist (njuːˈmɪzmətɪst) *or* **numismatologist** (njuːˌmɪzməˈtɒlədʒɪst) NOUN a person who studies or collects coins, medals, etc.

nummary (ˈnʌmərɪ) ADJECTIVE of or relating to coins.
▷**HISTORY** C17: from Latin *nummārius*, from *nummus* coin

nummular (ˈnʌmjʊlə) ADJECTIVE shaped like a coin; disc-shaped; circular.
▷**HISTORY** C19: from Latin *nummulus* a small coin

nummulite (ˈnʌmjʊˌlaɪt) NOUN any of various large fossil protozoans of the family *Nummulitidae*, common in Tertiary times: phylum *Foraminifera* (foraminifers).
▷**HISTORY** C19: from New Latin *Nummulites* genus name, from Latin *nummulus*, from *nummus* coin
▸**nummulitic** (ˌnʌmjʊˈlɪtɪk) ADJECTIVE

numnah (ˈnʌmnɑː) NOUN another word for **numdah** (senses 1, 2).

numpty (ˈnʌmptɪ) NOUN, *plural* **-ties.** *Scot informal* a stupid person.
▷**HISTORY** C20: of unknown origin

numskull (ˈnʌmˌskʌl) NOUN a variant spelling of **numbskull.**

nun¹ (nʌn) NOUN [1] a female member of a religious order. [2] (*sometimes capital*) a variety of domestic fancy pigeon usually having a black-and-white plumage with a ridged peak or cowl of short white feathers.
▷**HISTORY** Old English *nunne*, from Church Latin *nonna*, from Late Latin: form of address used for an elderly woman
▸ˈ**nunlike** ADJECTIVE

nun² (nʊn) NOUN the 14th letter in the Hebrew alphabet (נ or, at the end of a word, ן), transliterated as *n.*

nunatak (ˈnʌnəˌtæk) NOUN an isolated mountain peak projecting through the surface of surrounding glacial ice and supporting a distinct fauna and flora after recession of the ice.
▷**HISTORY** C19: via Danish from Eskimo

Nunavut (ˈnuːnəvuːt) NOUN a territory of NW Canada, formed in 1999 from part of the Northwest Territories as a semiautonomous region for the Inuit; includes Baffin Island and Ellesmere Island. Capital: Iqaluit. Pop.: 26 745 (2001). Area: 2 093 190 sq. km (808 185 sq. miles).

nun buoy (nʌn) NOUN *Nautical* a buoy, conical at the top, marking the right side of a channel leading into a harbour: green in British waters but red in US waters. Compare **can buoy.**
▷**HISTORY** C18: from obsolete *nun* a child's spinning top + BUOY

Nunc Dimittis (ˈnʌŋk dɪˈmɪtɪs, ˈnʊŋk) NOUN [1] the Latin name for the Canticle of Simeon (Luke 2:29–32). [2] a musical setting of this.
▷**HISTORY** from the opening words (Vulgate): now let depart

nunciature (ˈnʌnsɪətʃə) NOUN the office or term of office of a nuncio.
▷**HISTORY** C17: from Italian *nunziatura;* see NUNCIO

nuncio (ˈnʌnʃɪˌəʊ, -sɪ-) NOUN, *plural* **-cios.** *RC Church* a diplomatic representative of the Holy See, ranking above an internuncio and esp having ambassadorial status.
▷**HISTORY** C16: via Italian from Latin *nuntius* messenger

nuncle (ˈnʌŋkᵊl) NOUN an archaic or dialect word for **uncle.**
▷**HISTORY** C16: from division of *mine uncle* as *my nuncle*

nuncupative (ˈnʌŋkjʊˌpeɪtɪv, nʌŋˈkjuːpətɪv) ADJECTIVE (of a will) declared orally by the testator and later written down.
▷**HISTORY** C16: from Late Latin *nuncupātīvus* nominal, from Latin *nuncupāre* to name

Nuneaton (nʌnˈiːtᵊn) NOUN a town in central England, in Warwickshire. Pop.: 66 715 (1991).

nunhood (ˈnʌnhʊd) NOUN [1] the condition, practice, or character of a nun. [2] nuns collectively.

nunnery (ˈnʌnərɪ) NOUN, *plural* **-neries.** the convent or religious house of a community of nuns.

nunny bag (ˈnʌnɪ) NOUN *Canadian* a small sealskin haversack, used chiefly in Newfoundland.
▷**HISTORY** C19 *nunny*, probably from Scottish dialect *noony* luncheon, from NOON

nun's cloth *or* **veiling** (nʌnz) NOUN a thin soft plain-weave silk or worsted fabric used for veils, dresses, etc.

Nupe (ˈnuːpeɪ) NOUN [1] (*plural* **-pe** *or* **-pes**) a member of a Negroid people of Nigeria, noted as fishermen, who live near the confluence of the Niger and Benue Rivers. [2] the language of this people, belonging to the Kwa branch of the Niger-Congo family.

NUPE (ˈnjuːpɪ) NOUN (formerly, in Britain) ACRONYM FOR National Union of Public Employees.

nuptial (ˈnʌpʃəl, -tʃəl) ADJECTIVE [1] relating to marriage; conjugal: *nuptial vows.* [2] *Zoology* of or relating to mating: *the nuptial flight of a queen bee.*
▷**HISTORY** C15: from Latin *nuptiālis*, from *nuptiae* marriage, from *nubere* to marry
▸ˈ**nuptially** ADVERB

nuptials (ˈnʌpʃəlz, -tʃəlz) PLURAL NOUN (*sometimes singular*) a marriage ceremony; wedding.

NUR (in Britain, formerly) ABBREVIATION FOR National Union of Railwaymen.

nurd (nɜːd) NOUN a variant spelling of **nerd.**

Nuremberg (ˈnjʊərəmˌbɜːg) NOUN a city in S Germany, in N Bavaria: scene of annual Nazi rallies (1933–38), the anti-Semitic Nuremberg decrees (1935), and the trials of Nazi leaders for their war crimes (1945–46); important metalworking and electrical industries. Pop.: 486 400 (1999 est.). German name: **Nürnberg.**

Nuri (ˈnʊərɪ) NOUN [1] (*plural* **-ris** *or* **-ri**) Also called: **Kafir.** a member of an Indo-European people of Nuristan and neighbouring parts of Pakistan. [2] Also called: **Kafiri.** the Indo-Iranian language of this people.

Nuristan (ˌnʊərɪˈstɑːn) NOUN a region of E Afghanistan: consists mainly of high mountains (including part of the Hindu Kush), steep narrow valleys, and forests. Area: about 13 000 sq. km (5000 sq. miles). Former name: **Kafiristan.**

Nürnberg (ˈnyrnbɛrk) NOUN the German name for **Nuremberg.**

nurse (nɜːs) NOUN [1] a person, usually a woman, who tends the sick, injured, or infirm. [2] short for **nursemaid.** [3] a woman employed to breast-feed another woman's child; wet nurse. [4] a worker in a colony of social insects that takes care of the larvae. ◆ VERB (*mainly tr*) [5] (*also intr*) to tend (the sick). [6] (*also intr*) to feed (a baby) at the breast; suckle. [7] to try to cure (an ailment). [8] to clasp carefully or fondly: *she nursed the crying child in her arms.* [9] (*also intr*) (of a baby) to suckle at the breast (of). [10] to look after (a child) as one's employment. [11] to attend to carefully; foster, cherish: *he nursed the magazine through its first year; having a very small majority he nursed the constituency diligently.* [12] to harbour; preserve: *to nurse a grudge.* [13] *Billiards* to keep (the balls) together for a series of cannons.
▷**HISTORY** C16: from earlier *norice*, Old French *nourice*, from Late Latin *nūtrīcia* nurse, from Latin *nūtrīcius* nourishing, from *nūtrīre* to nourish

nursehound (ˈnɜːsˌhaʊnd) NOUN a species of European dogfish, *Scyliorrhinus caniculus.*
▷**HISTORY** C20: NURSE (SHARK) + HOUND[1]

nursemaid (ˈnɜːsˌmeɪd) *or* **nurserymaid** (ˈnɜːsrɪˌmeɪd) NOUN a woman or girl employed to look after someone else's children. Often shortened to **nurse.**

nurse practitioner NOUN a nurse who has specialized advanced skills in diagnosis, psychosocial assessment, and patient management and is permitted to prescribe certain drugs.

nursery (ˈnɜːsrɪ) NOUN, *plural* **-ries.** [1] **a** a room in a house set apart for use by children. **b** (*as modifier*): *nursery wallpaper.* [2] a place where plants, young trees, etc., are grown commercially. [3] an establishment providing residential or day care for babies and very young children; crèche. [4] short for **nursery school.** [5] anywhere serving to foster or nourish new ideas, etc. [6] Also called: **nursery cannon.** *Billiards* **a** a series of cannons with the three balls adjacent to a cushion, esp near a corner pocket. **b** a cannon in such a series.

nurseryman (ˈnɜːsrɪmən) NOUN, *plural* **-men.** a person who owns or works in a nursery in which plants are grown.

nursery rhyme NOUN a short traditional verse or song for children, such as *Little Jack Horner.*

nursery school NOUN a school for young children, usually from three to five years old.

nursery slopes PLURAL NOUN gentle slopes used by beginners in skiing.

nursery stakes PLURAL NOUN a race for two-year-old horses.

nurse shark NOUN any of various sharks of the family *Orectolobidae*, such as *Ginglymostoma cirratum* of the Atlantic Ocean, having an external groove on each side of the head between the mouth and nostril.
▷**HISTORY** C15 *nusse fisshe* (later influenced in spelling by NURSE), perhaps from division of obsolete *an huss* shark, dogfish (of uncertain origin) as *a nuss*

nursing (ˈnɜːsɪŋ) NOUN **a** the practice or profession of caring for the sick and injured. **b** (*as modifier*): *a nursing home.*

nursing bottle NOUN another term (esp US) for **feeding bottle.**

nursing father NOUN a biblical name for **foster father.**

nursing home NOUN [1] a private hospital or residence staffed and equipped to care for aged or infirm persons. [2] *Brit* a private maternity home.

nursing mother NOUN [1] a mother who is breast-feeding her baby. [2] a biblical name for **foster mother.**

nursing officer NOUN (in Britain) the official name for **matron** (sense 4).

nursling *or* **nurseling** (ˈnɜːslɪŋ) NOUN a child or young animal that is being suckled, nursed, or fostered.

nurture (ˈnɜːtʃə) NOUN [1] the act or process of

promoting the development, etc., of a child. 2 something that nourishes. 3 *Biology* the environmental factors that partly determine the structure of an organism. See also **nature** (sense 12). ◆ VERB (*tr*) 4 to feed or support. 5 to educate or train.
▷HISTORY C14: from Old French *norriture,* from Latin *nutrīre* to nourish
▸'**nurturable** ADJECTIVE ▸'**nurturer** NOUN

NUS (in Britain) ABBREVIATION FOR National Union of Students.

Nusa Tenggara ('nu:sə tɛŋ'gɑ:rə) NOUN an island chain east of Java, mostly in Indonesia: the main islands are Bali, Lombok, Sumbawa, Sumba, Flores, Alor, and Timor. Pop.: 7 237 600 (1995 est.). Area: 73 144 sq. km (28 241 sq. miles). Former name: **Lesser Sunda Islands.**

nut (nʌt) NOUN 1 a dry one-seeded indehiscent fruit that usually possesses a woody wall. 2 (*not in technical use*) any similar fruit, such as the walnut, having a hard shell and an edible kernel. 3 the edible kernel of such a fruit. 4 *Slang* **a** an eccentric person. **b** a person who is mentally disturbed. 5 a slang word for **head** (sense 1). 6 **do one's nut.** *Brit, slang* to be extremely angry; go into a rage. 7 **off one's nut.** *Slang* mad, crazy, or foolish. 8 a person or thing that presents difficulties (esp in the phrase **a tough** *or* **hard nut to crack**). 9 a small square or hexagonal block, usu. metal, with a threaded hole through the middle for screwing on the end of a bolt. 10 *Mountaineering* a variously shaped small metal block, usually a wedge or hexagonal prism (originally an ordinary engineer's nut) with a wire or rope loop attached, for jamming into a crack to provide security. Also called: **chock.** 11 Also called (US and Canadian): **frog.** *Music* **a** the ledge or ridge at the upper end of the fingerboard of a violin, cello, etc., over which the strings pass to the tuning pegs. **b** the end of a violin bow that is held by the player. 12 *Printing* another word for **en.** 13 a small usually gingery biscuit. 14 *Brit* a small piece of coal. ◆ VERB **nuts, nutting, nutted.** 15 (*intr*) to gather nuts. 16 (*tr*) *Slang* to butt (someone) with the head. ◆ See also **nuts.**
▷HISTORY Old English *hnutu;* related to Old Norse *hnot,* Old High German *hnuz* (German *Nuss*)
▸'**nut,like** ADJECTIVE

NUT (in Britain) ABBREVIATION FOR National Union of Teachers.

nutant ('nju:tənt) ADJECTIVE *Botany* having the apex hanging down: *nutant flowers.*
▷HISTORY C18: from Latin *nūtāre* to nod

nutation (nju:'teɪʃən) NOUN 1 *Astronomy* a periodic variation in the precession of the earth's axis causing the earth's poles to oscillate about their mean position. 2 *Physics* a periodic variation in the uniform precession of the axis of any spinning body, such as a gyroscope, about the horizontal. 3 Also called: **circumnutation.** the spiral growth of a shoot, tendril, or similar plant organ, caused by variation in the growth rate in different parts. 4 the act or an instance of nodding the head.
▷HISTORY C17: from Latin *nutātiō,* from *nūtāre* to nod
▸**nu'tational** ADJECTIVE

nutbrown ('nʌt'braʊn) ADJECTIVE of a brownish colour, esp a reddish-brown: *nutbrown hair.*

nutcase ('nʌt,keɪs) NOUN *Slang* an insane or very foolish person.

nutcracker ('nʌt,krækə) NOUN 1 (*often plural*) a device for cracking the shells of nuts. 2 either of two birds, *Nucifraga caryocatactes* of the Old World or *N. columbianus* (**Clark's nutcracker**) of North America, having speckled plumage and feeding on nuts, seeds, etc.: family *Corvidae* (crows).

nutgall ('nʌt,gɔ:l) NOUN a nut-shaped gall caused by gall wasps on the oak and other trees.

nuthatch ('nʌt,hætʃ) NOUN any songbird of the family *Sittidae,* esp *Sitta europaea,* having strong feet and bill, and feeding on insects, seeds, and nuts.
▷HISTORY C14 *notehache,* from *note* nut + *hache* hatchet, from the bird's habit of splitting nuts; see NUT, HACK[1]

nuthouse ('nʌt,haʊs) NOUN *Slang* a mental hospital or asylum.

nut key NOUN *Mountaineering* a tool for extracting a nut, chock, etc., from a crack after use.

nutlet ('nʌtlɪt) NOUN 1 any of the one-seeded portions of a fruit, such as a labiate fruit, that fragments when mature. 2 the stone of a drupe, such as a plum. 3 a small nut.

nutmeg ('nʌtmɛg) NOUN 1 an East Indian evergreen tree, *Myristica fragrans,* cultivated in the tropics for its hard aromatic seed: family *Myristicaceae.* See also **mace**[2]. 2 the seed of this tree, used as a spice. 3 any of several similar trees or their fruit. 4 a greyish-brown colour. ◆ VERB **-megs, -megging, -megged.** (*tr*) 5 *Brit sport, informal* to kick or hit the ball between the legs of (an opposing player).
▷HISTORY C13: from Old French *nois muguede,* from Old Provençal *noz muscada* musk-scented nut, from Latin *nux* NUT + *muscus* MUSK

nut oil NOUN oil obtained from walnuts, hazelnuts, etc., used in paints and varnishes and in cooking.

nut pine NOUN either of two varieties of the pine tree *Pinus cembroides,* of Mexico, Arizona, and California, having edible nuts.

nutraceutical (,nju:trə'sju:tɪkəl) NOUN another name for **functional food.**

nutria ('nju:trɪə) NOUN 1 another name for **coypu,** esp the fur 2 a brown colour with a grey tinge.
▷HISTORY C19: from Spanish: otter, variant of *lutria,* ultimately from Latin *lūtra* otter

nutrient ('nju:trɪənt) NOUN 1 any of the mineral substances that are absorbed by the roots of plants for nourishment. 2 any substance that nourishes an organism. ◆ ADJECTIVE 3 providing or contributing to nourishment: *a nutrient solution.*
▷HISTORY C17: from Latin *nūtrīre* to nourish

nutriment ('nju:trɪmənt) NOUN any material providing nourishment.
▷HISTORY C16: from Latin *nūtrīmentum,* from *nūtrīre* to nourish
▸**nutrimental** (,nju:trɪ'mɛntəl) ADJECTIVE

nutrition (nju:'trɪʃən) NOUN 1 a process in animals and plants involving the intake of nutrient materials and their subsequent assimilation into the tissues. Related adjectives: **alimentary, trophic.** 2 the act or process of nourishing. 3 the study of nutrition, esp in humans.
▷HISTORY C16: from Late Latin *nūtrītiō,* from *nūtrīre* to nourish
▸**nu'tritional** *or* (*less commonly*) **nu'tritionary** ADJECTIVE
▸**nu'tritionally** ADVERB

nutritionist (nju:'trɪʃənɪst) NOUN a person who specializes in nutrition and the nutritive value of various foods.

nutritious (nju:'trɪʃəs) ADJECTIVE nourishing, sometimes to a high degree.
▷HISTORY C17: from Latin *nūtrīcius* nourishing, from *nūtrix* a NURSE
▸**nu'tritiously** ADVERB ▸**nu'tritiousness** NOUN

nutritive ('nju:trɪtɪv) ADJECTIVE 1 providing nourishment. 2 of, concerning, or promoting nutrition. ◆ NOUN 3 a nutritious food.
▸'**nutritively** ADVERB

nuts (nʌts) ADJECTIVE 1 a slang word for **insane.** 2 (foll by *about* or *on*) *Slang* extremely fond (of) or enthusiastic (about). ◆ INTERJECTION 3 *Slang* an expression of disappointment, contempt, refusal, or defiance. ◆ PLURAL NOUN 4 a slang word for **testicles.**

nuts and bolts PLURAL NOUN *Informal* the essential or practical details.

nutshell ('nʌt,ʃɛl) NOUN 1 the shell around the kernel of a nut. 2 **in a nutshell.** in essence; briefly.

nutso ('nʌtsəʊ) ADJECTIVE *Informal chiefly US* insane.

nutter ('nʌtə) NOUN *Brit, slang* a mad or eccentric person.

nutting ('nʌtɪŋ) NOUN the act or pastime of gathering nuts.

nutty ('nʌtɪ) ADJECTIVE **-tier, -tiest.** 1 containing or abounding in nuts. 2 resembling nuts, esp in taste. 3 a slang word for **insane.** 4 (foll by *over* or *about*) *Informal* extremely fond (of) or enthusiastic (about).
▸'**nuttily** ADVERB ▸'**nuttiness** NOUN

nutwood ('nʌt,wʊd) NOUN 1 any of various nut-bearing trees, such as walnut. 2 the wood of any of these trees.

Nuuk (nu:k) NOUN the capital of Greenland, in the southwest: the oldest Danish settlement in Greenland, founded in 1721. Pop.: 13 838 (2000 est.). Former name (until 1979): **Godthaab.**

Nuxalk (nu:'xɒlk) NOUN a member of a Salishan Native Canadian people of British Columbia. Formerly called: **Bella Coola.**
▷HISTORY from Salish

nux vomica ('nʌks 'vɒmɪkə) NOUN 1 an Indian spiny loganiaceous tree, *Strychnos nux-vomica,* with orange-red berries containing poisonous seeds. 2 any of the seeds of this tree, which contain strychnine and other poisonous alkaloids. 3 a medicine manufactured from the seeds of this tree, formerly used as a heart stimulant.
▷HISTORY C16: from Medieval Latin: vomiting nut

nuzzle ('nʌzəl) VERB 1 to push or rub gently against the nose or snout. 2 (*intr*) to nestle; lie close. 3 (*tr*) to dig out with the snout.
▷HISTORY C15 *nosele,* from NOSE (n)

NV ABBREVIATION FOR Nevada.

NVQ (in Britain) ABBREVIATION FOR national vocational qualification: a qualification which rewards competence in a specified type of employment.

NW SYMBOL FOR northwest(ern).

n-word NOUN (*sometimes capital; preceded by the*) a euphemistic way of referring to the word **nigger.**

NWT ABBREVIATION FOR Northwest Territories (of Canada).

NY *or* **N.Y.** ABBREVIATION FOR New York (city or state).

nyaff (njæf) NOUN *Scot* a small or contemptible person.
▷HISTORY C19: perhaps imitative of the bark of a small dog

nyala ('njɑ:lə) NOUN, *plural* **-la** *or* **-las.** 1 a spiral-horned southern African antelope, *Tragelaphus angasi,* with a fringe of white hairs along the length of the back and neck. 2 **mountain nyala.** a similar and related Ethiopian animal, *T. buxtoni,* lacking the white crest.
▷HISTORY from Zulu

Nyanja ('njændʒə) NOUN 1 (*plural* **-ja** *or* **-jas**) a member of a Negroid people of central Africa, living chiefly in Malawi. 2 the language of this people, belonging to the Bantu group of the Niger-Congo family. Nyanja forms the basis of a pidgin used as a lingua franca in central Africa.

nyanza ('njænzə, nɪ'ænzə) NOUN (*capital when part of a name*) (in E Africa) a lake.
▷HISTORY from Bantu

Nyasa *or* **Nyassa** (nɪ'æsə, naɪ'æsə) NOUN **Lake.** a lake in central Africa at the S end of the Great Rift Valley: the third largest lake in Africa, drained by the Shiré River into the Zambezi. Area: about 28 500 sq. km (11 000 sq. miles). Malawi name: **Lake Malawi.**

Nyasaland (nɪ'æsə,lænd, naɪ'æsə-) NOUN the former name (until 1964) of **Malawi.**

NYC ABBREVIATION FOR New York City.

nyctaginaceous (,nɪktədʒɪ'neɪʃəs) ADJECTIVE of, relating to, or belonging to the *Nyctaginaceae,* a family of mostly tropical plants, including bougainvillea, having large coloured bracts surrounding each flower.
▷HISTORY from New Latin, from *Nyctago* type genus, from Greek *nukt-, nux* night

nyctalopia (,nɪktə'ləʊpɪə) NOUN inability to see normally in dim light. Nontechnical name: **night blindness.** Compare **hemeralopia.**
▷HISTORY C17: via Late Latin from Greek *nuktálōps,* from *nux* night + *alaos* blind + *ōps* eye

nyctanthous (nɪk'tænθəs) ADJECTIVE (of plants) flowering at night.

nyctinasty ('nɪktɪ,næstɪ) NOUN *Botany* a nastic movement, such as the closing of petals, that occurs in response to the alternation of day and night.
▷HISTORY C20: from Greek *nukt-, nux* night + -NASTY
▸,**nycti'nastic** ADJECTIVE

nyctitropism (nɪk'tɪtrə,pɪzəm) NOUN a tendency of some plant parts to assume positions at night that are different from their daytime positions.
▷HISTORY C19: *nyct-,* from Greek *nukt-, nux* night + -TROPISM
▸**nyctitropic** (,nɪktɪ'trɒpɪk) ADJECTIVE

nyctophobia (,nɪktəʊ'fəʊbɪə) NOUN *Psychiatry* an abnormal dread of night or darkness.

▷HISTORY *nyct-,* from Greek *nukt-, nux* night + -PHOBIA
▸ˌnyctoˈphobic ADJECTIVE

nye (naɪ) NOUN a flock of pheasants. Also called: **nide, eye.**
▷HISTORY C15: from Old French *ni,* from Latin *nīdus* nest

Nyeman (*Russian* ˈnjɛmən) NOUN a variant spelling of **Neman.**

Nyíregyháza (*Hungarian* ˈnjiːrɛtjhaːzɔ) NOUN a market town in NE Hungary. Pop.: 112 419 (2000 est.).

Nykøbing (*Danish* ˈnykøːbeŋ) NOUN a port in Denmark, on the W coast of Falster Island. Pop.: 64 428 (latest est.).

nylghau (ˈnɪlgɔː) NOUN, *plural* **-ghau** *or* **-ghaus.** another name for **nilgai.**

nylon (ˈnaɪlɒn) NOUN 1 a class of synthetic polyamide materials made by copolymerizing dicarboxylic acids with diamines. They can be moulded into a variety of articles, such as combs and machine parts. Nylon monofilaments are used for bristles, etc., and nylon fibres can be spun into yarn. 2 **a** yarn or cloth made of nylon, used for clothing, stockings, etc. **b** (*as modifier*): *a nylon dress.* ◆ See also **nylons.**
▷HISTORY C20: originally a trademark

NYLON (ˈnaɪlɒn) NOUN *Informal* a high-earning business executive who enjoys a transatlantic lifestyle, living part of the year in New York City and part in London.
▷HISTORY C20: from *N(ew) Y(ork)* + *Lon(don)*

nylons (ˈnaɪlɒnz) PLURAL NOUN stockings made of nylon or other man-made material.

nymph (nɪmf) NOUN 1 *Myth* a spirit of nature envisaged as a beautiful maiden. 2 *Chiefly poetic* a beautiful young woman. 3 the larva of insects such as the dragonfly and mayfly. It resembles the adult, apart from having underdeveloped wings and reproductive organs, and develops into the adult without a pupal stage.
▷HISTORY C14: via Old French from Latin, from Greek *numphē* nymph; related to Latin *nūbere* to marry
▸ˈ**nymphal** *or* **nymphean** (ˈnɪmfɪən) ADJECTIVE
▸ˈ**nymphlike** ADJECTIVE

nympha (ˈnɪmfə) NOUN, *plural* **-phae** (-fiː). *Anatomy* either one of the labia minora. Also called: **labium minus pudendi.**
▷HISTORY C17: from Latin: bride, NYMPH

nymphaeaceous (ˌnɪmfɪˈeɪʃəs) ADJECTIVE of, relating to, or belonging to the *Nymphaeaceae,* a family of plants, including the water lilies, that grow in water or marshes and have typically floating leaves and showy flowers.
▷HISTORY from New Latin, from Latin *nymphaea* water lily, ultimately from Greek *numphaios* sacred to nymphs

nymphalid (ˈnɪmfəlɪd) NOUN 1 any butterfly of the family *Nymphalidae,* typically having brightly coloured wings: includes the fritillaries, tortoiseshells, red admirals, and peacock. ◆ ADJECTIVE 2 of, relating to, or belonging to the *Nymphalidae.*
▷HISTORY C19: from New Latin, from *Nymphālis* genus name, from Latin; see NYMPH

nymphet (ˈnɪmfɪt) NOUN a young girl who is sexually precocious and desirable.
▷HISTORY C17 (meaning: a young nymph): diminutive of NYMPH

nympho (ˈnɪmfəʊ) NOUN, *plural* **-phos.** *Informal* a nymphomaniac.

nympholepsy (ˈnɪmfəˌlɛpsɪ) NOUN, *plural* **-sies.** a state of violent emotion, esp when associated with a desire for something one cannot have.
▷HISTORY C18: from NYMPHOLEPT, on the model of *epilepsy*
▸ˌ**nymphoˈleptic** ADJECTIVE

nympholept (ˈnɪmfəˌlɛpt) NOUN a person afflicted by nympholepsy.
▷HISTORY C19: from Greek *numpholēptos* caught by nymphs, from *numphē* nymph + *lambanein* to seize

nymphomania (ˌnɪmfəˈmeɪnɪə) NOUN a neurotic condition in women in which the symptoms are a compulsion to have sexual intercourse with as many men as possible and an inability to have lasting relationships with them. Compare **satyriasis.**
▷HISTORY C18: New Latin, from Greek *numphē* nymph + -MANIA
▸ˌ**nymphoˈmaniac** NOUN, ADJECTIVE ▸**nymphomaniacal** (ˌnɪmfəʊməˈnaɪək^{ə}l) ADJECTIVE

Nynorsk (*Norwegian* ˈnyːnɔːsk; *English* ˈniːnɔːsk) NOUN one of the two mutually intelligible official forms of written Norwegian: it also exists in spoken form and is derived from the dialect of W and N Norway. Also called: **Landsmål.** Compare **Bokmål.**
▷HISTORY Norwegian: new Norse

Nyoro (ˈnjɔːrəʊ) NOUN 1 (*plural* **-ro** *or* **-ros**) a member of a Negroid people of W Uganda. 2 the language of this people, belonging to the Bantu group of the Niger-Congo family.

Nysa (ˈnɪsə) NOUN the Polish name for the **Neisse** (sense 1).

NYSE ABBREVIATION FOR New York Stock Exchange.

nystagmus (nɪˈstægməs) NOUN involuntary movement of the eye comprising a smooth drift followed by a flick back, occurring in several situations, for example after the body has been rotated or in disorders of the cerebellum.

nystatin (ˈnɪstətɪn) NOUN an antibiotic obtained from the bacterium *Streptomyces noursei:* used in the treatment of infections caused by certain fungi, esp *Candida albicans.*
▷HISTORY C20: from *New York State,* where it was originated + -IN

Nyx (nɪks) NOUN *Greek myth* the goddess of the night, daughter of Chaos. Roman counterpart: **Nox.**

nz THE INTERNET DOMAIN NAME FOR New Zealand.

NZ[1] INTERNATIONAL CAR REGISTRATION FOR New Zealand.

NZ[2] *or* **N. Zeal.** ABBREVIATION FOR New Zealand.

NZC ABBREVIATION FOR New Zealand Cricket.

NZCER ABBREVIATION FOR New Zealand Council for Educational Research.

NZE ABBREVIATION FOR New Zealand English.

NZEF ABBREVIATION FOR New Zealand Expeditionary Force, the New Zealand army that served in 1914–18. **2NZEF** is used to refer to the Second New Zealand Expeditionary Force, in World War II.

NZEFIP ABBREVIATION FOR New Zealand Expeditionary Force in the Pacific, the 3rd division of the New Zealand Expeditionary Force serving in the Pacific campaign in World War II.

NZEI ABBREVIATION FOR New Zealand Educational Institute.

NZLR ABBREVIATION FOR New Zealand Law Reports.

NZMA ABBREVIATION FOR New Zealand Medical Association.

NZOM ABBREVIATION FOR New Zealand Order of Merit.

NZPA ABBREVIATION FOR New Zealand Press Association.

NZR ABBREVIATION FOR (the former) New Zealand Railways.

NZRFU ABBREVIATION FOR New Zealand Rugby Football Union.

NZRN ABBREVIATION FOR New Zealand Registered Nurse.

NZSE ABBREVIATION FOR New Zealand Stock Exchange.

NZSO ABBREVIATION FOR New Zealand Symphony Orchestra.

Oo

o *or* **O** (əʊ) NOUN, *plural* **o's, O's,** *or* **Os.** [1] the 15th letter and fourth vowel of the modern English alphabet. [2] any of several speech sounds represented by this letter, in English as in *code, pot, cow, move,* or *form.* [3] another name for **nought.**

O^{1} SYMBOL FOR: [1] *Chem* oxygen. [2] a human blood type of the ABO group. See **universal donor.** [3] *Logic* a particular negative categorial proposition, such as *some men are not married:* often symbolized as **SoP**. Compare **A, E, I**^{2}. ◆ ABBREVIATION FOR: [4] *Austral, slang* offence.
▷**HISTORY** (for sense 3) From Latin (*neg*)*o* I deny

O^{2} (əʊ) INTERJECTION [1] a variant spelling of **oh.** [2] an exclamation introducing an invocation, entreaty, wish, etc.: *O God!; O for the wings of a dove!*

o- PREFIX short for **ortho-** (sense 4).

o' (ə) PREPOSITION *Informal or archaic* shortened form of **of**: *a cup o' tea.*

O'- PREFIX (in surnames of Irish Gaelic origin) descendant of: *O'Corrigan.*
▷**HISTORY** from Irish Gaelic *ó, ua* descendant

-o SUFFIX forming informal and slang variants and abbreviations, esp. of nouns: *wino; lie doggo; Jacko.*
▷**HISTORY** probably special use of OH

-o- CONNECTIVE VOWEL used to connect elements in a compound word: *chromosome; filmography.* Compare -i-.
▷**HISTORY** from Greek, stem vowel of many nouns and adjectives in combination

oaf (əʊf) NOUN a stupid or loutish person.
▷**HISTORY** C17: variant of Old English *ælf* ELF
▸**'oafish** ADJECTIVE ▸**'oafishly** ADVERB ▸**'oafishness** NOUN

Oahu (əʊ'ɑːhuː) NOUN an island in central Hawaii: the third largest of the Hawaiian Islands. Chief town: Honolulu. Pop.: 836 231 (1990). Area: 1574 sq. km (608 sq. miles).

oak (əʊk) NOUN [1] any deciduous or evergreen tree or shrub of the fagaceous genus *Quercus,* having acorns as fruits and lobed leaves. See also **holm oak, cork oak, red oak, Turkey oak, durmast.** Related adjective: **quercine.** [2] **a** the wood of any of these trees, used esp. as building timber and for making furniture. **b** (*as modifier*): *an oak table.* [3] any of various trees that resemble the oak, such as the poison oak, silky oak, and Jerusalem oak. [4] **a** anything made of oak, esp. a heavy outer door to a set of rooms in an Oxford or Cambridge college. **b sport one's oak.** to shut this door as a sign one does not want visitors. [5] the leaves of an oak tree, worn as a garland. [6] the dark brownish colour of oak wood. [7] *Austral* any of various species of casuarina, such as desert oak, swamp oak, or she-oak.
▷**HISTORY** Old English *āc;* related to Old Norse *eik,* Old High German *eih,* Latin *aesculus*

oak apple *or* **gall** NOUN any of various brownish round galls on oak trees, containing the larva of certain wasps.

Oak-apple Day NOUN (in Britain) May 29, the anniversary of the Restoration (1660), formerly commemorated by the wearing of oak apples or oak leaves, recalling the **Boscobel oak** in which Charles II hid after the battle of Worcester.

oaken ('əʊkən) ADJECTIVE made of the wood of the oak.

oak fern NOUN a graceful light green polypody fern, *Thelypteris dryopteris,* having a creeping rhizome, found in acid woodlands and on rocks in the northern hemisphere.

Oakham ('əʊkəm) NOUN a market town in E central England, the administrative centre of Rutland. Pop.: 8691 (1991).

Oakland ('əʊklənd) NOUN a port and industrial centre in W California, on San Francisco Bay; damaged by earthquake in 1989. Pop.: 399 484 (2000).

oak-leaf cluster NOUN *US* an insignia consisting of oak leaves and acorns awarded to holders of certain military decorations to indicate a further award of the same decoration.

Oaks (əʊks) NOUN (*functioning as singular*) **the.** [1] a horse race for fillies held annually at Epsom since 1779: one of the classics of English flat racing. [2] any of various similar races.
▷**HISTORY** named after an estate near Epsom

oakum ('əʊkəm) NOUN loose fibre obtained by unravelling old rope, used esp. for caulking seams in wooden ships.
▷**HISTORY** Old English *ācuma,* variant of *ācumba,* literally: off-combings, from *ā-* off + *-cumba,* from *cemban* to COMB

Oakville ('əʊkvɪl) NOUN a city in SE Canada, in SE Ontario on Lake Ontario southwest of Toronto: motor-vehicle industry. Pop.: 128 405 (1996).

oaky^{1} ('əʊkɪ) ADJECTIVE **oakier, oakiest.** [1] hard like the wood of an oak. [2] (of a wine) having a pleasant flavour imparted by the oak barrel in which it was stored.

oaky^{2} ('əʊkɪ) NOUN, *plural* **oakies.** *Midland English, dialect* an ice cream.

Oamaru stone ('ɒmaruː) NOUN a kind of limestone, of building quality, found at Oamaru on South Island, New Zealand.

O & M ABBREVIATION FOR organization and method (in studies of working methods).

oanshagh ('oːnʃəx) NOUN *Irish* a foolish girl or woman.
▷**HISTORY** from Irish Gaelic *óinseach*

OAP (in Britain) ABBREVIATION FOR **old age pension** *or* **pensioner.**

OAPEC (əʊ'eɪpɛk) NOUN ACRONYM FOR Organization of Arab Petroleum Exporting Countries.

oar (ɔː) NOUN [1] a long shaft of wood for propelling a boat by rowing, having a broad blade that is dipped into and pulled against the water. Oars were also used for steering certain kinds of ancient sailing boats. [2] short for **oarsman.** [3] **put one's oar in.** to interfere or interrupt. ◆ VERB [4] to row or propel with or as if with oars: *the two men were oaring their way across the lake.*
▷**HISTORY** Old English *ār,* of Germanic origin; related to Old Norse *ār*
▸**'oarless** ADJECTIVE ▸**'oar,like** ADJECTIVE

oared (ɔːd) ADJECTIVE [1] equipped with oars. [2] (*in combination*) having oars as specified: *two-oared.*

oarfish ('ɔːˌfɪʃ) NOUN, *plural* **-fish** *or* **-fishes.** a very long ribbonfish, *Regalecus glesne,* with long slender ventral fins. Also called: **king of the herrings.**
▷**HISTORY** C19: referring to the flattened oarlike body

oarlock ('ɔːˌlɒk) NOUN the usual US and Canadian word for **rowlock.**

oarsman ('ɔːzmən) NOUN, *plural* **-men.** a man who rows, esp. one who rows in a racing boat.
▸**'oarsman,ship** NOUN

oarweed ('ɔːˌwiːd) NOUN any of various brown seaweeds, especially a kelp of the genus *Laminaria,* with long broad fronds, common below the low-water mark.
▷**HISTORY** from earlier *oreweed,* from *wore,* from Old English *wār* seaweed + WEED^{1}

OAS ABBREVIATION FOR: [1] **Organization of American States.** [2] *Organisation de l'armée secrète*; an organization of European settlers in Algeria who opposed Algerian independence by acts of terrorism (1961–63).

oasis (əʊ'eɪsɪs) NOUN, *plural* **-ses** (-siːz). [1] a fertile patch in a desert occurring where the water table approaches or reaches the ground surface. [2] a place of peace, safety, or happiness in the midst of trouble or difficulty.
▷**HISTORY** C17: via Latin from Greek, probably of Egyptian origin

Oasis (əʊ'eɪsɪs) NOUN *Trademark* a block of light porous material, used as a base for flower arrangements.

oast (əʊst) NOUN *Chiefly Brit* [1] a kiln for drying hops. [2] Also called: **oast house.** a building containing such kilns, usually having a conical or pyramidal roof.
▷**HISTORY** Old English *āst;* related to Old Norse *eisa* fire

oat (əʊt) NOUN [1] an erect annual grass, *Avena sativa,* grown in temperate regions for its edible seed. [2] (*usually plural*) the seeds or fruits of this grass. [3] any of various other grasses of the genus *Avena,* such as the wild oat. [4] *Poetic* a flute made from an oat straw. [5] **feel one's oats.** *US and Canadian informal* **a** to feel exuberant. **b** to feel self-important. [6] **get one's oats.** *Slang* to have sexual intercourse. [7] **sow one's (wild) oats.** to indulge in adventure or promiscuity during youth.
▷**HISTORY** Old English *āte,* of obscure origin

oatcake ('əʊtˌkeɪk) NOUN a brittle unleavened oatmeal biscuit.

oaten ('əʊtᵊn) ADJECTIVE made of oats or oat straw.

oat grass NOUN any of various oatlike grasses, esp. of the genera *Arrhenatherum* and *Danthonia,* of Eurasia and N. Africa.

oath (əʊθ) NOUN, *plural* **oaths** (əʊðz). [1] a solemn pronouncement to affirm the truth of a statement or to pledge a person to some course of action, often involving a sacred being or object as witness. Related adjective: **juratory.** [2] the form of such a pronouncement. [3] an irreverent or blasphemous expression, esp. one involving the name of a deity; curse. [4] **on, upon,** *or* **under oath. a** under the obligation of an oath. **b** *Law* having sworn to tell the truth, usually with one's hand on the Bible. [5] **take an oath.** to declare formally with an oath or pledge, esp. before giving evidence.
▷**HISTORY** Old English *āth;* related to Old Saxon, Old Frisian *ēth,* Old High German *eid*

oatmeal ('əʊtˌmiːl) NOUN [1] meal ground from oats, used for making porridge, oatcakes, etc. [2] **a** a greyish-yellow colour. **b** (*as adjective*): *an oatmeal coat.*

OAU ABBREVIATION FOR the former Organization of African Unity, now the **African Union.**

Oaxaca (wə'hɑːkə; *Spanish* oa'xaka) NOUN [1] a state of S Mexico, on the Pacific: includes most of the Isthmus of Tehuantepec; inhabited chiefly by Indians. Capital: Oaxaca de Juárez. Pop.: 3 432 180 (2000). Area: 95 363 sq. km (36 820 sq. miles). [2] a city in S Mexico, capital of Oaxaca state: founded in 1486 by the Aztecs and conquered by Spain in 1521. Pop.: 252 586 (2000 est.). Official name: **Oaxaca de Juárez** (de 'xwareθ).

Ob (*Russian* ɔpj) NOUN a river in N central Russia, formed at Bisk by the confluence of the Biya and Katun Rivers and flowing generally north to the **Gulf of Ob** (an inlet of the Arctic Ocean): one of the largest rivers in the world, with a drainage basin of about 2 930 000 sq. km (1 131 000 sq. miles). Length: 3682 km (2287 miles).

OB *Brit* ABBREVIATION FOR: [1] Old Boy. [2] outside broadcast.

ob. ABBREVIATION FOR: [1] (on tombstones) obiit. [2] obiter. [3] oboe.
▷**HISTORY** (for sense 1) Latin: he (or she) died; (for sense 2) Latin: incidentally; in passing

ob- PREFIX inverse or inversely: *obovate.*
▷**HISTORY** from Old French, from Latin *ob.* In compound words of Latin origin, *ob-* (and *oc-, of-, op-*) indicates: to, towards (*object*); against (*oppose*); away from (*obsolete*); before (*obstetric*); down, over (*obtect*); for the sake of (*obsecrate*); and is used as an intensifier (*oblong*)

oba ('ɔːbɑː, -bə) NOUN (in W Africa) a Yoruba chief or ruler.

Obad. *Bible* ABBREVIATION FOR Obadiah.

Obadiah (ˌəʊbə'daɪə) NOUN *Old Testament* [1] a Hebrew prophet. [2] the book containing his oracles, chiefly directed against Edom. Douay spelling: **Abdias** (æb'daɪəs).

Oban ('əubən) NOUN a small port and resort in W Scotland, in Argyll and Bute on the Firth of Lorne. Pop.: 8203 (1991).

obb. ABBREVIATION FOR obbligato.

obbligato *or* **obligato** (ˌɒblɪ'gɑːtəʊ) *Music* ◆ ADJECTIVE [1] not to be omitted in performance. ◆ NOUN, *plural* **-tos** *or* **-ti** (-tiː). [2] an essential part in a score: *with oboe obbligato.* ◆ See also **ad-lib.**
▷HISTORY C18: from Italian, from *obbligare* to OBLIGE

obconic (ɒb'kɒnɪk) *or* **obconical** ADJECTIVE *Botany* (of a fruit or similar part) shaped like a cone and attached at the pointed end.

obcordate (ɒb'kɔːdeɪt) ADJECTIVE *Botany* heart-shaped and attached at the pointed end: *obcordate leaves.*

obdt ABBREVIATION FOR obedient.

obdurate ('ɒbdjurɪt) ADJECTIVE [1] not easily moved by feelings or supplication; hardhearted. [2] impervious to persuasion, esp. to moral persuasion.
▷HISTORY C15: from Latin *obdūrāre* to make hard, from *ob-* (intensive) + *dūrus* hard; compare ENDURE
▸ **'obduracy** *or* **'obdurateness** NOUN ▸ **'obdurately** ADVERB

OBE ABBREVIATION FOR: [1] Officer of the Order of the British Empire (a Brit title). [2] **out-of-body experience.**

obeah ('əubɪə) NOUN another word for **obi**[2].

obedience (ə'biːdɪəns) NOUN [1] the condition or quality of being obedient. [2] the act or an instance of obeying; dutiful or submissive behaviour. [3] the authority vested in a Church or similar body. [4] the collective group of persons submitting to this authority. See also **passive obedience.**

obedient (ə'biːdɪənt) ADJECTIVE obeying or willing to obey.
▷HISTORY C13: from Old French, from Latin *oboediens,* present participle of *oboedīre* to OBEY
▸ **o'bediently** ADVERB

obedientiary (əʊˌbiːdɪ'ɛnʃərɪ) NOUN, *plural* **-ries.** *Christianity* the holder of any monastic office under the superior.
▷HISTORY C18: from Medieval Latin *obedientiarius;* see OBEDIENT, -ARY

obeisance (əʊ'beɪsəns, əʊ'biː-) NOUN [1] an attitude of deference or homage. [2] a gesture expressing obeisance.
▷HISTORY C14: from Old French *obéissant,* present participle of *obéir* to OBEY
▸ **o'beisant** ADJECTIVE ▸ **o'beisantly** ADVERB

obelisk ('ɒbɪlɪsk) NOUN [1] a stone pillar having a square or rectangular cross section and sides that taper towards a pyramidal top, often used as a monument in ancient Egypt. [2] *Printing* another name for **dagger** (sense 2).
▷HISTORY C16: via Latin from Greek *obeliskos* a little spit, from *obelos* spit
▸ **ˌobe'liscal** ADJECTIVE ▸ **ˌobe'liskoid** ADJECTIVE

obelize *or* **obelise** ('ɒbɪˌlaɪz) VERB (*tr*) to mark (a word or passage) with an obelus.
▷HISTORY C17: from Greek *obelizein*

obelus ('ɒbɪləs) NOUN, *plural* **-li** (-ˌlaɪ). [1] a mark (— or ÷) used in editions of ancient documents to indicate spurious words or passages. [2] another name for **dagger** (sense 2).
▷HISTORY C14: via Late Latin from Greek *obelos* spit

Oberammergau (*German* oːbər'amərgau) NOUN a village in S Germany, in Bavaria in the foothills of the Alps: famous for its Passion Play, performed by the villagers every ten years (except during the World Wars) since 1634, in thanksgiving for the end of the Black Death. Pop.: 4740 (latest est.).

Oberhausen (*German* 'oːbərhauzən) NOUN an industrial city in W Germany, in North Rhine-Westphalia on the Rhine-Herne Canal: site of the first ironworks in the Ruhr. Pop.: 222 300 (1999 est.).

Oberland ('əubəˌlænd) NOUN the lower parts of the Bernese Alps in central Switzerland, mostly in S Bern canton.

Oberon[1] ('əubəˌrɒn) NOUN (in medieval folklore) the king of the fairies, husband of Titania.

Oberon[2] ('əubəˌrɒn) NOUN the outermost of the satellites of Uranus.

Oberösterreich ('oːbərˌøːstəraiç) NOUN the German name for **Upper Austria.**

obese (əʊ'biːs) ADJECTIVE excessively fat or fleshy; corpulent.
▷HISTORY C17: from Latin *obēsus,* from *ob-* (intensive) + *edere* to eat
▸ **o'besity** *or* **o'beseness** NOUN

obey (ə'beɪ) VERB [1] to carry out (instructions or orders); comply with (demands). [2] to behave or act in accordance with (one's feelings, whims, etc.).
▷HISTORY C13: from Old French *obéir,* from Latin *oboedīre,* from *ob-* to, towards + *audīre* to hear
▸ **o'beyer** NOUN

obfuscate ('ɒbfʌsˌkeɪt) VERB (*tr*) [1] to obscure or darken. [2] to perplex or bewilder.
▷HISTORY C16: from Latin *ob-* (intensive) + *fuscāre* to blacken, from *fuscus* dark
▸ **ˌobfus'catory** ADJECTIVE

obfuscation (ˌɒbfʌs'keɪʃən) NOUN the act or an instance of making something obscure, dark, or difficult to understand.

obi[1] ('əubɪ) NOUN, *plural* **obis** *or* **obi.** [1] a broad sash tied in a large flat bow at the back, worn by Japanese women and children as part of the national costume. [2] a narrow sash worn by Japanese men.
▷HISTORY C19: from Japanese

obi[2] ('əubɪ) *or* **obeah** NOUN, *plural* **obis** *or* **obeahs.** [1] a kind of witchcraft originating in Africa and practised by some West Indians. [2] a charm or amulet used in this.
▷HISTORY of West African origin; compare Edo *obi* poison
▸ **'obiism** NOUN

obit ('ɒbɪt, 'əubɪt) NOUN *Informal* [1] short for **obituary.** [2] a memorial service.

obiter dictum ('ɒbɪtə 'dɪktəm, 'əu-) NOUN, *plural* **obiter dicta** ('dɪktə). [1] *Law* an observation by a judge on some point of law not directly in issue in the case before him and thus neither requiring his decision nor serving as a precedent, but nevertheless of persuasive authority. [2] any comment, remark, or observation made in passing.
▷HISTORY Latin: something said in passing

obituary (ə'bɪtjuərɪ) NOUN, *plural* **-aries.** a published announcement of a death, often accompanied by a short biography of the dead person.
▷HISTORY C18: from Medieval Latin *obituārius,* from Latin *obīre* to fall, from *ob-* down + *īre* to go
▸ **o'bituarist** NOUN

obj. ABBREVIATION FOR: [1] *Grammar* object(ive). [2] objection.

object[1] ('ɒbdʒɪkt) NOUN [1] a tangible and visible thing. [2] a person or thing seen as a focus or target for feelings, thought, etc.: *an object of affection.* [3] an aim, purpose, or objective. [4] *Informal* a ridiculous or pitiable person, spectacle, etc. [5] *Philosophy* that towards which cognition is directed, as contrasted with the thinking subject; anything regarded as external to the mind, esp. in the external world. [6] *Grammar* a noun, pronoun, or noun phrase whose referent is the recipient of the action of a verb. See also **direct object, indirect object.** [7] *Grammar* a noun, pronoun, or noun phrase that is governed by a preposition. [8] **no object.** not a hindrance or obstacle: *money is no object.* [9] *Computing* a self-contained identifiable component of a software system or design: *object-oriented programming.*
▷HISTORY C14: from Late Latin *objectus* something thrown before (the mind), from Latin *obicere;* see OBJECT[2]

object[2] (əb'dʒɛkt) VERB [1] (*tr; takes a clause as object*) to state as an objection: *he objected that his motives had been good.* [2] (*intr;* often foll by *to*) to raise or state an objection (to); present an argument (against).
▷HISTORY C15: from Latin *obicere,* from *ob-* against + *jacere* to throw

object ball NOUN *Billiards, snooker* any ball except the cue ball, esp. one which the striker aims to hit with the cue ball.

object glass NOUN *Optics* another name for **objective** (sense 11).

objectify (əb'dʒɛktɪˌfaɪ) VERB **-fies, -fying, -fied.** (*tr*) to represent concretely; present as an object.
▸ **obˌjectifi'cation** NOUN

objection (əb'dʒɛkʃən) NOUN [1] an expression, statement, or feeling of opposition or dislike. [2] a cause for such an expression, statement, or feeling. [3] the act of objecting.

objectionable (əb'dʒɛkʃənəbəl) ADJECTIVE unpleasant, offensive, or repugnant.
▸ **obˌjectiona'bility** *or* **ob'jectionableness** NOUN
▸ **ob'jectionably** ADVERB

objective (əb'dʒɛktɪv) ADJECTIVE [1] existing independently of perception or an individual's conceptions: *are there objective moral values?* [2] undistorted by emotion or personal bias. [3] of or relating to actual and external phenomena as opposed to thoughts, feelings, etc. [4] *Med* (of disease symptoms) perceptible to persons other than the individual affected. [5] *Grammar* denoting a case of nouns and pronouns, esp. in languages having only two cases, that is used to identify the direct object of a finite verb or preposition and for various other purposes. In English the objective case of pronouns is also used in many elliptical constructions (as in *Poor me! Who, him?*), as the subject of a gerund (as in *It was me helping him*), informally as a predicate complement (as in *It's me*), and in nonstandard use as part of a compound subject (as in *John, Larry, and me went fishing*). See also **accusative.** [6] of, or relating to a goal or aim. ◆ NOUN [7] the object of one's endeavours; goal; aim. [8] Also called: **objective point.** *Military* a place or position towards which forces are directed. [9] an actual phenomenon; reality. [10] *Grammar* **a** the objective case. **b** a word or speech element in the objective case. [11] Also called: **object glass.** *Optics* **a** the lens or combination of lenses nearest to the object in an optical instrument. **b** the lens or combination of lenses forming the image in a camera or projector. ◆ Abbreviation: **obj.** Compare **subjective.**
▸ **objectival** (ˌɒbdʒɛk'taɪvəl) ADJECTIVE ▸ **ob'jectively** ADVERB ▸ **ˌobjec'tivity** *or* (*less commonly*) **ob'jectiveness** NOUN

objective danger NOUN *Mountaineering* a danger, such as a stone fall or avalanche, to which climbing skill is irrelevant.

objective genitive NOUN *Grammar* a use of the genitive case to express an objective relationship, as in Latin *timor mortis* (fear of death).

objective point NOUN *Military* another term for **objective** (sense 8).

objective test NOUN a test, such as one using multiple-choice questions, in which the feelings or opinions of the person marking it cannot affect the marks given.

objectivism (əb'dʒɛktɪˌvɪzəm) NOUN [1] the tendency to stress what is objective. [2] *Philosophy* **a** the meta-ethical doctrine that there are certain moral truths that are independent of the attitudes of any individuals. **b** the philosophical doctrine that reality is objective, and that sense data correspond with it.
▸ **ob'jectivist** NOUN, ADJECTIVE ▸ **obˌjectiv'istic** ADJECTIVE
▸ **obˌjectiv'istically** ADVERB

object language NOUN a language described by or being investigated by another language. Compare **metalanguage.**

object lesson NOUN [1] a convincing demonstration of some principle or ideal. [2] (esp. formerly) a lesson in which a material object forms the basis of the teaching and is available to be inspected.

object program NOUN a computer program translated from the equivalent source program into machine language by the compiler or assembler.

object relations theory NOUN a form of psychoanalytic theory postulating that people relate to others in order to develop themselves.

objet d'art *French* (ɔbʒɛ dar) NOUN, *plural* ***objets d'art*** (ɔbʒɛ dar). a small object considered to be of artistic worth.
▷HISTORY literally: object of art

objet de vertu (ɒb'ʒeɪ də vɜː'tuː) NOUN, *plural* **objets de vertu** (ɒb'ʒeɪ də vɜː'tuː). another name for **object of virtu:** see **virtu.**
▷HISTORY French, coined by the British as a translation of *object of virtu* but literally meaning only "object of virtue"

objet trouvé *French* (ɔbʒɛ truve) NOUN, *plural* ***objets trouvés*** (ɔbʒɛ truve). any ordinary object considered from an aesthetic viewpoint.
▷HISTORY C20: literally: found object

objure (ɒb'dʒuə) VERB *Rare* [1] (*tr*) to put on oath. [2] (*intr*) to swear.

▷HISTORY C17: from Latin *objūrāre* to bind by oath
▸ˌobjuˈration NOUN

objurgate (ˈɒbdʒəˌɡeɪt) VERB (*tr*) to scold or reprimand.
▷HISTORY C17: from Latin *objurgāre*, from *ob-* against + *jurgāre* to scold
▸ˌobjurˈgation NOUN ▸ˈobjurˌgator NOUN ▸**objurgatory** (ɒbˈdʒɜːɡətərɪ, -trɪ) *or* obˈjurgative ADJECTIVE

oblanceolate (ɒbˈlɑːnsɪəlɪt, -ˌleɪt) ADJECTIVE *Botany* (esp. of leaves) having a rounded apex and a tapering base.

oblast (ˈɒblɑːst) NOUN [1] an administrative division of the constituent republics of Russia. [2] an administrative and territorial division in some republics of the former Soviet Union.
▷HISTORY from Russian, from Old Slavonic, *vlast* government

oblate¹ (ˈɒbleɪt) ADJECTIVE having an equatorial diameter of greater length than the polar diameter: *the earth is an oblate sphere*. Compare **prolate.**
▷HISTORY C18: from New Latin *oblātus* lengthened, from Latin *ob-* towards + *lātus*, past participle of *ferre* to bring
▸ˈoblately ADVERB

oblate² (ˈɒbleɪt) NOUN a person dedicated to a monastic or religious life.
▷HISTORY C19: from French *oblat*, from Medieval Latin *oblātus*, from Latin *offerre* to OFFER

oblation (ɒˈbleɪʃən) NOUN *Christianity* [1] the offering of the bread and wine of the Eucharist to God. [2] any offering made for religious or charitable purposes.
▷HISTORY C15: from Church Latin *oblātiō*; see OBLATE²
▸**oblatory** (ˈɒblətərɪ, -trɪ) *or* obˈlational ADJECTIVE

obligate (ˈɒblɪˌɡeɪt) VERB [1] to compel, constrain, or oblige morally or legally. [2] (in the US) to bind (property, funds, etc.) as security. ◆ ADJECTIVE [3] compelled, bound, or restricted. [4] *Biology* able to exist under only one set of environmental conditions: *an obligate parasite cannot live independently of its host*. Compare **facultative** (sense 4).
▷HISTORY C16: from Latin *obligāre* to OBLIGE
▸ˈobligable ADJECTIVE ▸obˈligative ADJECTIVE ▸ˈobliˌgator NOUN

obligation (ˌɒblɪˈɡeɪʃən) NOUN [1] a moral or legal requirement; duty. [2] the act of obligating or the state of being obligated. [3] *Law* a legally enforceable agreement to perform some act, esp. to pay money, for the benefit of another party. [4] *Law* **a** a written contract containing a penalty. **b** an instrument acknowledging indebtedness to secure the repayment of money borrowed. [5] a person or thing to which one is bound morally or legally. [6] something owed in return for a service or favour. [7] a service or favour for which one is indebted.
▸ˌobliˈgational ADJECTIVE

obligato (ˌɒblɪˈɡɑːtəʊ) ADJECTIVE, NOUN *Music* a variant spelling of **obbligato.**

obligatory (ɒˈblɪɡətərɪ, -trɪ) ADJECTIVE [1] required to be done, obtained, possessed, etc. [2] of the nature of or constituting an obligation.
▸obˈligatorily ADVERB

oblige (əˈblaɪdʒ) VERB [1] (*tr; often passive*) to bind or constrain (someone to do something) by legal, moral, or physical means. [2] (*tr; usually passive*) to make indebted or grateful (to someone) by doing a favour or service: *we are obliged to you for dinner*. [3] to do a service or favour to (someone): *she obliged the guest with a song*.
▷HISTORY C13: from Old French *obliger*, from Latin *obligāre*, from *ob-* to, towards + *ligāre* to bind
▸oˈbliger NOUN

obligee (ˌɒblɪˈdʒiː) NOUN [1] a person in whose favour an obligation, contract, or bond is created; creditor. [2] a person who receives a bond.

obligement (əˈblaɪdʒmənt) NOUN *Now chiefly Scot* a kind helpful action; favour.

obliging (əˈblaɪdʒɪŋ) ADJECTIVE ready to do favours; agreeable; kindly.
▸oˈbligingly ADVERB ▸oˈbligingness NOUN

obligor (ˌɒblɪˈɡɔː) NOUN [1] a person who binds himself by contract to perform some obligation; debtor. [2] a person who gives a bond.

oblique (əˈbliːk) ADJECTIVE [1] at an angle; slanting; sloping. [2] *Geometry* **a** (of lines, planes, etc.) neither perpendicular nor parallel to one another or to another line, plane, etc. **b** not related to or containing a right angle. [3] indirect or evasive. [4] *Grammar* denoting any case of nouns, pronouns, etc., other than the nominative and vocative. [5] *Biology* having asymmetrical sides or planes: *an oblique leaf*. [6] (of a map projection) constituting a type of zenithal projection in which the plane of projection is tangential to the earth's surface at some point between the equator and the poles. ◆ NOUN [7] something oblique, esp. a line. [8] another name for **solidus** (sense 1). [9] *Navigation* the act of changing course by less than 90°. [10] an aerial photograph taken at an oblique angle. ◆ VERB (*intr*) [11] to take or have an oblique direction. [12] (of a military formation) to move forward at an angle.
▷HISTORY C15: from Old French, from Latin *oblīquus*, of obscure origin
▸oˈbliquely ADVERB ▸oˈbliqueness NOUN

oblique angle NOUN an angle that is not a right angle or any multiple of a right angle.

oblique fault NOUN a fault that runs obliquely to, rather than parallel to or perpendicular to, the strike of the affected rocks.

oblique sailing NOUN a ship's movement on a course that is not due north, south, east, or west.

oblique-slip fault NOUN a fault on which the movement is along both the strike and the dip of the fault.

obliquity (əˈblɪkwɪtɪ) NOUN, *plural* **-ties.** [1] the state or condition of being oblique. [2] a deviation from the perpendicular or horizontal. [3] a moral or mental deviation. [4] Also called: **obliquity of the ecliptic.** *Astronomy* the angle between the plane of the earth's orbit and that of the celestial equator, equal to approximately 23° 27′ at present.
▸oˈbliquitous ADJECTIVE

obliterate (əˈblɪtəˌreɪt) VERB (*tr*) to destroy every trace of; wipe out completely.
▷HISTORY C16: from Latin *oblitterāre* to erase, from *ob-* out + *littera* letter
▸oˌbliteˈration NOUN ▸oˈbliterative ADJECTIVE ▸oˈbliterˌator NOUN

oblivion (əˈblɪvɪən) NOUN [1] the condition of being forgotten or disregarded. [2] the state of being mentally withdrawn or blank. [3] *Law* an intentional overlooking, esp. of political offences; amnesty; pardon.
▷HISTORY C14: via Old French from Latin *oblīviō* forgetfulness, from *oblīviscī* to forget

oblivious (əˈblɪvɪəs) ADJECTIVE (foll by *to* or *of*) unaware or forgetful.
▸obˈliviously ADVERB ▸obˈliviousness NOUN

> **Language note** It was formerly considered incorrect to use *oblivious* to mean *unaware*, but this use is now acceptable.

oblong (ˈɒbˌlɒŋ) ADJECTIVE [1] having an elongated, esp. rectangular, shape. ◆ NOUN [2] a figure or object having this shape.
▷HISTORY C15: from Latin *oblongus*, from *ob-* (intensive) + *longus* LONG¹

obloquy (ˈɒbləkwɪ) NOUN, *plural* **-quies.** [1] defamatory or censorious statements, esp. when directed against one person. [2] disgrace brought about by public abuse.
▷HISTORY C15: from Latin *obloquium* contradiction, from *ob-* against + *loquī* to speak

obmutescence (ˌɒbmjuːˈtɛsəns) NOUN *Archaic* persistent silence.
▷HISTORY C17: from Latin *obmūtescere* to become mute
▸ˌobmuˈtescent ADJECTIVE

obnoxious (əbˈnɒkʃəs) ADJECTIVE [1] extremely unpleasant. [2] *Obsolete* exposed to harm, injury, etc.
▷HISTORY C16: from Latin *obnoxius*, from *ob-* to + *noxa* injury, from *nocēre* to harm
▸obˈnoxiously ADVERB ▸obˈnoxiousness NOUN

obnubilate (ɒbˈnjuːbɪˌleɪt) VERB (*tr*) *Literary* to darken or obscure.
▷HISTORY C16: ultimately from Latin *obnūbilāre* to cover with clouds, from *nubes* cloud

oboe (ˈəʊbəʊ) NOUN [1] a woodwind instrument of the family that includes the bassoon and cor anglais, consisting of a conical tube fitted with a mouthpiece having a double reed. It has a penetrating nasal tone. Range: about two octaves plus a sixth upwards from B flat below middle C. [2] a person who plays this instrument in an orchestra: *second oboe*. ◆ Archaic form: **hautboy.**
▷HISTORY C18: via Italian *oboe*, phonetic approximation to French *haut bois*, literally: high wood (referring to its pitch)
▸ˈoboist NOUN

oboe da caccia (də ˈkætʃə) NOUN a member of the oboe family; the predecessor of the cor anglais.
▷HISTORY Italian: hunting oboe

oboe d'amore (dɑːˈmɔːreɪ) NOUN a type of oboe pitched a minor third lower than the oboe itself. It is used chiefly in the performance of baroque music.
▷HISTORY Italian: oboe of love

obolus (ˈɒbələs) *or* **obol** (ˈɒbɒl) NOUN, *plural* **-li** (-ˌlaɪ) *or* **-ols.** [1] a modern Greek unit of weight equal to one tenth of a gram. [2] a silver coin of ancient Greece worth one sixth of a drachma.
▷HISTORY C16: via Latin from Greek *obolos* small coin, nail; related to *obelos* spit, variant of OBELUS

obovate (ɒbˈəʊveɪt) ADJECTIVE (of a leaf or similar flat part) shaped like the longitudinal section of an egg with the narrower end at the base; inversely ovate.

obovoid (ɒbˈəʊvɔɪd) ADJECTIVE (of a fruit or similar solid part) egg-shaped with the narrower end at the base. Compare **ovoid** (sense 2).

obreption (ɒˈbrɛpʃən) NOUN *Now rare* the obtaining of something, such as a gift, in Scots Law esp. a grant from the Crown, by giving false information. Compare **subreption** (sense 1).
▷HISTORY C17: from Latin *obreptio*, from *obrepere* to creep up to

obs. ABBREVIATION FOR obsolete.

obscene (əbˈsiːn) ADJECTIVE [1] offensive or outrageous to accepted standards of decency or modesty. [2] *Law* (of publications) having a tendency to deprave or corrupt. [3] disgusting; repellent: *an obscene massacre*.
▷HISTORY C16: from Latin *obscēnus* inauspicious, perhaps related to *caenum* filth
▸obˈscenely ADVERB

obscenity (əbˈsɛnɪtɪ) NOUN, *plural* **-ties.** [1] the state or quality of being obscene. [2] an obscene act, statement, word, etc.

obscurant (əbˈskjʊərənt) NOUN [1] an opposer of reform and enlightenment. ◆ ADJECTIVE [2] of or relating to an obscurant. [3] causing obscurity.
▸ˌobscuˈrantism NOUN ▸ˌobscuˈrantist NOUN, ADJECTIVE

obscure (əbˈskjʊə) ADJECTIVE [1] unclear or abstruse. [2] indistinct, vague, or indefinite. [3] inconspicuous or unimportant. [4] hidden, secret, or remote. [5] (of a vowel) reduced to or transformed into a neutral vowel (ə). [6] gloomy, dark, clouded, or dim. ◆ VERB (*tr*) [7] to make unclear, vague, or hidden. [8] to cover or cloud over. [9] *Phonetics* to pronounce (a vowel) with articulation that causes it to become a neutral sound represented by (ə). ◆ NOUN [10] a rare word for **obscurity.**
▷HISTORY C14: via Old French from Latin *obscūrus* dark
▸**obscuration** (ˌɒbskjʊˈreɪʃən) NOUN ▸obˈscurely ADVERB ▸obˈscureness NOUN

obscurity (əbˈskjʊərɪtɪ) NOUN, *plural* **-ties.** [1] the state or quality of being obscure. [2] an obscure person or thing.

obscurum per obscurius (əbˈskjʊərəm pɜːr əbˈskjʊərɪəs) NOUN another term for **ignotum per ignotius.**
▷HISTORY Latin: the obscure by the more obscure

obsecrate (ˈɒbsɪˌkreɪt) VERB (*tr*) a rare word for **beseech.**
▷HISTORY C16: from Latin *obsecrāre* to entreat (in the name of the gods), from *ob-* for the sake of + *sacrāre* to hold in reverence; see SACRED
▸ˌobseˈcration NOUN

obsequent (ˈɒbsɪkwənt) ADJECTIVE (of a river) flowing into a subsequent stream in the opposite direction to the original slope of the land.
▷HISTORY C16 (in the obsolete sense: yielding): from Latin *obsequī*, from *sequī* to follow

obsequies (ˈɒbsɪkwɪz) PLURAL NOUN, *singular* **-quy.** funeral rites.
▷HISTORY C14: via Anglo-Norman from Medieval

Latin *obsequiae* (influenced by Latin *exsequiae*), from *obsequium* compliance
▸**obsequial** (ɒbˈsiːkwɪəl) ADJECTIVE

obsequious (əbˈsiːkwɪəs) ADJECTIVE [1] obedient or attentive in an ingratiating or servile manner. [2] *Now rare* submissive or compliant.
▷HISTORY C15: from Latin *obsequiōsus* compliant, from *obsequium* compliance, from *obsequi* to follow, from *ob-* to + *sequi* to follow
▸**obˈsequiously** ADVERB ▸**obˈsequiousness** NOUN

observance (əbˈzɜːvəns) NOUN [1] recognition of or compliance with a law, custom, practice, etc. [2] the act of such recognition. [3] a ritual, ceremony, or practice, esp. of a religion. [4] observation or attention. [5] the degree of strictness of a religious order or community in following its rule. [6] *Archaic* respectful or deferential attention.

observant (əbˈzɜːvənt) ADJECTIVE [1] paying close attention to detail; watchful or heedful. [2] adhering strictly to rituals, ceremonies, laws, etc.
▸**obˈservantly** ADVERB

observation (ˌɒbzəˈveɪʃən) NOUN [1] the act of observing or the state of being observed. [2] a comment or remark. [3] detailed examination of phenomena prior to analysis, diagnosis, or interpretation: *the patient was under observation.* [4] the facts learned from observing. [5] an obsolete word for **observance.** [6] *Navigation* **a** a sight taken with an instrument to determine the position of an observer relative to that of a given heavenly body. **b** the data so taken.
▸**ˌobserˈvational** ADJECTIVE ▸**ˌobserˈvationally** ADVERB

observation car NOUN a railway carriage fitted with large expanses of glass to provide a good view of the scenery.

observation post NOUN *Military* a position from which observations can be made or from which fire can be directed. Abbreviation: **OP.**

observatory (əbˈzɜːvətərɪ, -trɪ) NOUN, *plural* **-ries.** [1] an institution or building specially designed and equipped for observing meteorological and astronomical phenomena. [2] any building or structure providing an extensive view of its surroundings.

observe (əbˈzɜːv) VERB [1] (*tr; may take a clause as object*) to see; perceive; notice: *we have observed that you steal.* [2] (when *tr, may take a clause as object*) to watch (something) carefully; pay attention to (something). [3] to make observations of (something), esp. scientific ones. [4] (when *intr,* usually foll by *on* or *upon;* when *tr, may take a clause as object*) to make a comment or remark: *the speaker observed that times had changed.* [5] (*tr*) to abide by, keep, or follow (a custom, tradition, law, holiday, etc.).
▷HISTORY C14: via Old French from Latin *observāre,* from *ob-* to + *servāre* to watch
▸**obˈservable** ADJECTIVE ▸**obˈservableness** *or* **obˌservaˈbility** NOUN ▸**obˈservably** ADVERB

observer (əbˈzɜːvə) NOUN [1] a person or thing that observes. [2] a person who attends a conference solely to note the proceedings. [3] a person trained to identify aircraft, esp., formerly, a member of an aircrew.

obsess (əbˈsɛs) VERB [1] (*tr;* when *passive,* foll by *with* or *by*) to preoccupy completely; haunt. [2] (*intr;* usually foll by *on* or *over*) to worry neurotically; brood.
▷HISTORY C16: from Latin *obsessus* besieged, past participle of *obsidēre,* from *ob-* in front of + *sedēre* to sit

obsession (əbˈsɛʃən) NOUN [1] *Psychiatry* a persistent idea or impulse that continually forces its way into consciousness, often associated with anxiety and mental illness. [2] a persistent preoccupation, idea, or feeling. [3] the act of obsessing or the state of being obsessed.
▸**obˈsessional** ADJECTIVE ▸**obˈsessionally** ADVERB

obsessive (əbˈsɛsɪv) ADJECTIVE [1] *Psychiatry* motivated by a persistent overriding idea or impulse, often associated with anxiety and mental illness. [2] continually preoccupied with a particular activity, person, or thing. ◆ NOUN [3] *Psychiatry* a person subject to obsession. [4] a person who is continually preoccupied with a particular activity, person, or thing.
▸**obˈsessively** ADVERB ▸**obˈsessiveness** NOUN

obsessive-compulsive disorder NOUN *Psychiatry* an anxiety disorder in which patients are driven to repeat the same act, such as washing their hands, over and over again, usually for many hours. Abbreviation: **OCD.**

obsidian (ɒbˈsɪdɪən) NOUN a dark volcanic glass formed by very rapid solidification of lava. Also called: **Iceland agate.**
▷HISTORY C17: from Latin *obsidiānus,* erroneous transcription of *obsiānus* (*lapis*) (stone of) *Obsius,* the name (in Pliny) of the discoverer of a stone resembling obsidian

obsolesce (ˌɒbsəˈlɛs) VERB (*intr*) to become obsolete.

obsolescent (ˌɒbsəˈlɛsᵊnt) ADJECTIVE becoming obsolete or out of date.
▷HISTORY C18: from Latin *obsolescere;* see OBSOLETE
▸**ˌobsoˈlescence** NOUN ▸**ˌobsoˈlescently** ADVERB

obsolete (ˈɒbsəˌliːt, ˌɒbsəˈliːt) ADJECTIVE [1] out of use or practice; not current. [2] out of date; unfashionable or outmoded. [3] *Biology* (of parts, organs, etc.) vestigial; rudimentary.
▷HISTORY C16: from Latin *obsolētus* worn out, past participle of *obsolēre* (unattested), from *ob-* opposite to + *solēre* to be used
▸**ˈobsoˌletely** ADVERB ▸**ˈobsoˌleteness** NOUN

> **Language note** The word *obsoleteness* is hardly ever used, *obsolescence* standing as the noun form for both *obsolete* and *obsolescent.*

obstacle (ˈɒbstəkᵊl) NOUN [1] a person or thing that opposes or hinders something. [2] *Brit* a fence or hedge used in showjumping.
▷HISTORY C14: via Old French from Latin *obstāculum,* from *obstāre,* from *ob-* against + *stāre* to stand

obstacle race NOUN a race in which competitors have to negotiate various obstacles.

obstet. ABBREVIATION FOR obstetric(s).

obstetric (ɒbˈstɛtrɪk) *or* **obstetrical** ADJECTIVE of or relating to childbirth or obstetrics.
▷HISTORY C18: via New Latin from Latin *obstetrīcius,* from *obstetrix* a midwife, literally: woman who stands opposite, from *obstāre* to stand in front of; see OBSTACLE
▸**obˈstetrically** ADVERB

obstetrician (ˌɒbstɪˈtrɪʃən) NOUN a physician who specializes in obstetrics.

obstetrics (ɒbˈstɛtrɪks) NOUN (*functioning as singular*) the branch of medicine concerned with childbirth and the treatment of women before and after childbirth.

obstinacy (ˈɒbstɪnəsɪ) NOUN, *plural* **-cies.** [1] the state or quality of being obstinate. [2] an obstinate act, attitude, etc.

obstinate (ˈɒbstɪnɪt) ADJECTIVE [1] adhering fixedly to a particular opinion, attitude, course of action, etc. [2] self-willed or headstrong. [3] difficult to subdue or alleviate; persistent: *an obstinate fever.*
▷HISTORY C14: from Latin *obstinātus,* past participle of *obstināre* to persist in, from *ob-* (intensive) + *stin-,* variant of *stare* to stand
▸**ˈobstinately** ADVERB

obstipation (ˌɒbstɪˈpeɪʃən) NOUN *Pathol* a severe form of constipation, usually resulting from obstruction of the intestinal tract.
▷HISTORY C16: from Latin *obstīpātiō,* from *ob-* (intensive) + *stīpāre* to press together

obstreperous (əbˈstrɛpərəs) ADJECTIVE noisy or rough, esp. in resisting restraint or control.
▷HISTORY C16: from Latin, from *obstrepere,* from *ob-* against + *strepere* to roar
▸**obˈstreperously** ADVERB ▸**obˈstreperousness** NOUN

obstruct (əbˈstrʌkt) VERB (*tr*) [1] to block (a road, passageway, etc.) with an obstacle. [2] to make (progress or activity) difficult. [3] to impede or block a clear view of.
▷HISTORY C17: Latin *obstructus* built against, past participle of *obstruere,* from *ob-* against + *struere* to build
▸**obˈstructor** NOUN ▸**obˈstructive** ADJECTIVE, NOUN ▸**obˈstructively** ADVERB ▸**obˈstructiveness** NOUN

obstruction (əbˈstrʌkʃən) NOUN [1] a person or thing that obstructs. [2] the act or an instance of obstructing. [3] delay of business, esp. in a legislature by means of procedural devices. [4] *Sport* the act of unfairly impeding an opposing player. [5] the state or condition of being obstructed.
▸**obˈstructional** ADJECTIVE ▸**obˈstructionally** ADVERB

obstructionist (əbˈstrʌkʃənɪst) NOUN **a** a person who deliberately obstructs business, esp. in a legislature. **b** (*as modifier*): *obstructionist tactics.*
▸**obˈstructionism** NOUN

obstruent (ˈɒbstrʊənt) *Med* ◆ ADJECTIVE [1] causing obstruction, esp. of the intestinal tract. ◆ NOUN [2] anything that causes obstruction.
▷HISTORY C17: from Latin *obstruere* to OBSTRUCT

obtain (əbˈteɪn) VERB [1] (*tr*) to gain possession of; acquire; get. [2] (*intr*) to be customary, valid, or accepted: *a new law obtains in this case.* [3] (*tr*) *Archaic* to arrive at. [4] (*intr*) *Archaic* to win a victory; succeed.
▷HISTORY C15: via Old French from Latin *obtinēre* to take hold of, from *ob-* (intensive) + *tenēre* to hold
▸**obˈtainable** ADJECTIVE ▸**obˌtainaˈbility** NOUN ▸**obˈtainer** NOUN ▸**obˈtainment** NOUN

obtaining by deception NOUN *Law* the offence of dishonestly obtaining the property of another by some deception or misrepresentation of facts.

obtect (ɒbˈtɛkt) ADJECTIVE (of a pupa) encased in a hardened secretion so that the wings, legs, etc., are held immovably to the body, as in butterflies. Also: **obtected.**
▷HISTORY C19: from Latin *obtectus* covered, past participle of *obtegere,* from *ob-* (intensive) + *tegere* to cover

obtemper (ɒbˈtɛmpə) VERB *Scots law* to comply (with).
▷HISTORY C15: from Latin *obtemperāre* to obey, from *ob-* towards + *temperāre* to temper

obtest (ɒbˈtɛst) VERB *Rare* [1] (*tr; may take a clause as object or an infinitive*) to beg (someone) earnestly. [2] (when *tr, takes a clause as object;* when *intr,* may be foll by *with* or *against*) to object; protest. [3] (*tr*) to call (a supernatural power) to witness.
▷HISTORY C16: from Latin *obtestārī* to protest, from *ob-* to + *testārī* to bear or call as witness
▸**ˌobtesˈtation** NOUN

obtrude (əbˈtruːd) VERB [1] to push (oneself, one's opinions, etc.) on others in an unwelcome way. [2] (*tr*) to push out or forward.
▷HISTORY C16: from Latin *obtrūdere,* from *ob-* against + *trūdere* to push forward
▸**obˈtruder** NOUN ▸**obtrusion** (əbˈtruːʒən) NOUN

obtrusive (əbˈtruːsɪv) ADJECTIVE [1] obtruding or tending to obtrude. [2] sticking out; protruding; noticeable.
▸**obˈtrusively** ADVERB ▸**obˈtrusiveness** NOUN

obtund (ɒbˈtʌnd) VERB (*tr*) *Rare* to deaden or dull.
▷HISTORY C14: from Latin *obtundere* to beat against, from *ob-* against + *tundere* to belabour
▸**obˈtundent** ADJECTIVE, NOUN

obturate (ˈɒbtjʊəˌreɪt) VERB (*tr*) to stop up (an opening, esp. the breech of a gun).
▷HISTORY C17: from Latin *obtūrāre* to block up, of obscure origin
▸**ˌobtuˈration** NOUN ▸**ˈobtuˌrator** NOUN

obtuse (əbˈtjuːs) ADJECTIVE [1] mentally slow or emotionally insensitive. [2] *Maths* **a** (of an angle) lying between 90° and 180°. **b** (of a triangle) having one interior angle greater than 90°. [3] not sharp or pointed. [4] indistinctly felt, heard, etc.; dull: *obtuse pain.* [5] (of a leaf or similar flat part) having a rounded or blunt tip.
▷HISTORY C16: from Latin *obtūsus* dulled, past participle of *obtundere* to beat down; see OBTUND
▸**obˈtusely** ADVERB ▸**obˈtuseness** NOUN

obverse (ˈɒbvɜːs) ADJECTIVE [1] facing or turned towards the observer. [2] forming or serving as a counterpart. [3] (of certain plant leaves) narrower at the base than at the top. ◆ NOUN [4] a counterpart or complement. [5] the side of a coin that bears the main design or device. Compare **reverse** (sense 15). [6] *Logic* a categorial proposition derived from another by replacing the original predicate by its negation and changing the proposition from affirmative to negative or vice versa, as *no sum is correct* from *every sum is incorrect.*
▷HISTORY C17: from Latin *obversus* turned towards, past participle of *obvertere,* from *ob-* to + *vertere* to turn
▸**obˈversely** ADVERB

obvert (ɒbˈvɜːt) VERB (*tr*) [1] *Logic* to deduce the

obverse of (a proposition). 2 *Rare* to turn so as to show the main or other side.
▷HISTORY C17: from Latin *obvertere* to turn towards; see OBVERSE
▸**ob'version** NOUN

obviate ('ɒbvɪˌeɪt) VERB (*tr*) to do away with or counter.
▷HISTORY C16: from Late Latin *obviātus* prevented, past participle of *obviāre;* see OBVIOUS
▸**ˌobvi'ation** NOUN

> **Language note** Only things which have not yet occurred can be *obviated*. For example, one can *obviate* a possible future difficulty, but not one which already exists.

obvious ('ɒbvɪəs) ADJECTIVE 1 easy to see or understand; evident. 2 exhibiting motives, feelings, intentions, etc., clearly or without subtlety. 3 naive or unsubtle: *the play was rather obvious.* 4 *Obsolete* being or standing in the way.
▷HISTORY C16: from Latin *obvius,* from *obviam* in the way, from *ob-* against + *via* way
▸**'obviousness** NOUN

obviously ('ɒbvɪəslɪ) ADVERB 1 in a way that is easy to see or understand; evidently. 2 without subtlety. 3 (*sentence modifier*) it is obvious that; clearly: *obviously not everyone wants a bank account.*

obvolute ('ɒbvəˌluːt) ADJECTIVE 1 (of leaves or petals in the bud) folded so that the margins overlap each other. 2 turned in or rolled.
▷HISTORY C18: from Latin *obvolūtus* past participle of *obvolvere,* from *ob-* to, over + *volvere* to roll
▸**ˌobvo'lution** NOUN ▸**'obvoˌlutive** ADJECTIVE

OC ABBREVIATION FOR: 1 Officer Commanding. 2 Officer of the Order of Canada.

o/c ABBREVIATION FOR overcharge.

oca ('əʊkə) NOUN any of various South American herbaceous plants of the genus *Oxalis,* cultivated for their edible tubers: family *Oxalidaceae.*
▷HISTORY C20: via Spanish from Quechua *okka*

OCAM ABBREVIATION FOR *Organisation commune africaine et malgache*: an association of the 14 principal Francophone states of Africa, established in 1965 to further political cooperation and economic and social development.

O Canada NOUN the Canadian national anthem.

ocarina (ˌɒkə'riːnə) NOUN an egg-shaped wind instrument with a protruding mouthpiece and six to eight finger holes, producing an almost pure tone. Also called (US informal): **sweet potato.**
▷HISTORY C19: from Italian: little goose, from *oca* goose, ultimately from Latin *avis* bird

Occam's razor NOUN a variant spelling of **Ockham's razor.**

occasion (ə'keɪʒən) NOUN 1 (sometimes foll by *of*) the time of a particular happening or event. 2 (sometimes foll by *for*) a reason or cause (to do or be something); grounds: *there was no occasion to complain.* 3 an opportunity (to do something); chance. 4 a special event, time, or celebration: *the party was quite an occasion.* 5 **on occasion.** every so often. 6 **rise to the occasion.** to have the courage, wit, etc., to meet the special demands of a situation. 7 **take occasion.** to avail oneself of an opportunity (to do something). ◆ VERB 8 (*tr*) to bring about, esp. incidentally or by chance. ◆ See also **occasions.**
▷HISTORY C14: from Latin *occāsiō* a falling down, from *occidere,* from *ob-* down + *cadere* to fall

occasional (ə'keɪʒənᵊl) ADJECTIVE 1 taking place from time to time; not frequent or regular. 2 of, for, or happening on special occasions. 3 serving as an occasion (for something).

occasionalism (ə'keɪʒənəˌlɪzəm) NOUN the post-Cartesian theory that the seeming interconnection of mind and matter is effected by God.

occasional licence NOUN *Brit* a licence granted to sell alcohol only at specified times.

occasionally (ə'keɪʒənəlɪ) ADVERB from time to time.

occasional table NOUN a small table with no regular use.

occasions (ə'keɪʒənz) PLURAL NOUN *Archaic* 1 (*sometimes singular*) needs; necessities. 2 personal or business affairs.

occident ('ɒksɪdənt) NOUN a literary or formal word for **west.** Compare **orient.**
▷HISTORY C14: via Old French from Latin *occidere* to fall, go down (with reference to the setting sun); see OCCASION

Occident ('ɒksɪdənt) NOUN (usually preceded by *the*) 1 the countries of Europe and America. 2 the western hemisphere.

occidental (ˌɒksɪ'dɛntᵊl) ADJECTIVE a literary or formal word for **western.** Compare **oriental.**

Occidental (ˌɒksɪ'dɛntᵊl) (*sometimes not capital*) ADJECTIVE 1 of or relating to the Occident. ◆ NOUN 2 an inhabitant, esp. a native, of the Occident.
▸**ˌOcci'dentalism** NOUN ▸**ˌOcci'dentalist** NOUN, ADJECTIVE
▸**ˌOcci'dentally** ADVERB

Occidentalize *or* **Occidentalise** (ˌɒksɪ'dɛntəˌlaɪz) VERB to make or become Occidental.
▸**ˌOcciˌdentali'zation** *or* **ˌOcciˌdentali'sation** NOUN

occipital (ɒk'sɪpɪtᵊl) ADJECTIVE 1 of or relating to the back of the head or skull. ◆ NOUN 2 short for **occipital bone.**

occipital bone NOUN the saucer-shaped bone that forms the back part of the skull and part of its base.

occipital lobe NOUN the posterior portion of each cerebral hemisphere, concerned with the interpretation of visual sensory impulses.

occiput ('ɒksɪˌpʌt, -pət) NOUN, *plural* **occiputs** *or* **occipita** (ɒk'sɪpɪtə). the back part of the head or skull.
▷HISTORY C14: from Latin, from *ob-* at the back of + *caput* head

occlude (ə'kluːd) VERB 1 (*tr*) to block or stop up (a passage or opening); obstruct. 2 (*tr*) to prevent the passage of. 3 (*tr*) *Chem* (of a solid) to incorporate (a substance) by absorption or adsorption. 4 *Meteorol* to form or cause to form an occluded front. 5 *Dentistry* to produce or cause to produce occlusion, as in chewing.
▷HISTORY C16: from Latin *occlūdere,* from *ob-* (intensive) + *claudere* to close
▸**oc'cludent** ADJECTIVE

occluded front NOUN *Meteorol* the line or plane occurring where the cold front of a depression has overtaken the warm front, raising the warm sector from ground level. Also called: **occlusion.**

occlusion (ə'kluːʒən) NOUN 1 the act or process of occluding or the state of being occluded. 2 *Meteorol* another term for **occluded front.** 3 *Dentistry* the normal position of the teeth when the jaws are closed. 4 *Phonetics* the complete closure of the vocal tract at some point, as in the closure prior to the articulation of a plosive.
▸**occlusal** (ə'kluːsəl) ADJECTIVE

occlusive (ə'kluːsɪv) ADJECTIVE 1 of or relating to the act of occlusion. ◆ NOUN 2 *Phonetics* an occlusive speech sound.
▸**oc'clusiveness** NOUN

occult ADJECTIVE (ɒ'kʌlt, 'ɒkʌlt) 1 **a** of or characteristic of magical, mystical, or supernatural arts, phenomena, or influences. **b** (*as noun*): *the occult.* 2 beyond ordinary human understanding. 3 secret or esoteric. ◆ VERB (ɒ'kʌlt) 4 *Astronomy* (of a celestial body) to hide (another celestial body) from view by occultation or (of a celestial body) to become hidden by occultation. 5 to hide or become hidden or shut off from view. 6 (*intr*) (of lights, esp. in lighthouses) to shut off at regular intervals.
▷HISTORY C16: from Latin *occultus,* past participle of *occulere,* from *ob-* over, up + *-culere,* related to *celāre* to conceal
▸**oc'cultly** ADVERB ▸**oc'cultness** NOUN

occultation (ˌɒkʌl'teɪʃən) NOUN 1 the temporary disappearance of one celestial body as it moves out of sight behind another body. 2 the act of occulting or the state of being occulted.

occultism ('ɒkʌlˌtɪzəm) NOUN belief in and the study and practice of magic, astrology, etc.
▸**'occultist** NOUN, ADJECTIVE

occupancy ('ɒkjʊpənsɪ) NOUN, *plural* **-cies.** 1 the act of occupying; possession of a property. 2 *Law* the possession and use of property by or without agreement and without any claim to ownership. 3 *Law* the act of taking possession of unowned property, esp. land, with the intent of thus acquiring ownership. 4 the condition or fact of being an occupant, esp. a tenant. 5 the period of time during which one is an occupant, esp. of property.

occupant ('ɒkjʊpənt) NOUN 1 a person, thing, etc., holding a position or place. 2 *Law* a person who has possession of something, esp. an estate, house, etc.; tenant. 3 *Law* a person who acquires by occupancy the title to something previously without an owner.

occupation (ˌɒkjʊ'peɪʃən) NOUN 1 a person's regular work or profession; job or principal activity. 2 any activity on which time is spent by a person. 3 the act of occupying or the state of being occupied. 4 the control of a country by a foreign military power. 5 the period of time that a nation, place, or position is occupied. 6 (*modifier*) for the use of the occupier of a particular property: *occupation road; occupation bridge.*

occupational (ˌɒkjʊ'peɪʃənᵊl) ADJECTIVE of, relating to, or caused by an occupation: *an occupational pension scheme; an occupational disease.*
▸**ˌoccu'pationally** ADVERB

occupational pension NOUN 1 a pension scheme provided for the members of a particular occupation or by a specific employer or group of employers. 2 a pension derived from such a scheme.

occupational psychology NOUN *Psychol* the study of human behaviour at work, including ergonomics, selection procedures, and the effects of stress.

occupational therapy NOUN *Med* treatment of people with physical, emotional, or social problems, using purposeful activity to help them overcome or learn to deal with their problems.
▸**occupational therapist** NOUN

occupation franchise NOUN *Brit* the right of a tenant to vote in national and local elections.

occupation groupings PLURAL NOUN a system of classifying people according to occupation, based originally on information obtained by government census and subsequently developed by market research. The classifications are used by the advertising industry to identify potential markets. The groups are **A, B, C1, C2, D,** and **E.**

occupier ('ɒkjʊˌpaɪə) NOUN 1 *Brit* a person who is in possession or occupation of a house or land. 2 a person or thing that occupies.

occupy ('ɒkjʊˌpaɪ) VERB **-pies, -pying, -pied.** (*tr*) 1 to live or be established in (a house, flat, office, etc.). 2 (*often passive*) to keep (a person) busy or engrossed; engage the attention of. 3 (*often passive*) to take up (a certain amount of time or space). 4 to take and hold possession of, esp. as a demonstration: *students occupied the college buildings.* 5 to fill or hold (a position or rank).
▷HISTORY C14: from Old French *occuper,* from Latin *occupāre* to seize hold of, from *ob-* (intensive) + *capere* to take

occur (ə'kɜː) VERB **-curs, -curring, -curred.** (*intr*) 1 to happen; take place; come about. 2 to be found or be present; exist. 3 (foll by *to*) to be realized or thought of (by); suggest itself (to).
▷HISTORY C16: from Latin *occurrere* to run up to, from *ob-* to + *currere* to run

> **Language note** It is usually regarded as incorrect to talk of pre-arranged events *occurring* or *happening*: *the wedding took place* (not *occurred* or *happened*) *in the afternoon.*

occurrence (ə'kʌrəns) NOUN 1 something that occurs; a happening; event. 2 the act or an instance of occurring: *a crime of frequent occurrence.*

occurrent (ə'kʌrənt) ADJECTIVE *Philosophy* (of a property) relating to some observable feature of its bearer. Compare **disposition** (sense 4).

occy ('ɒkɪ) ADJECTIVE *Midland English, dialect* **all over the occy.** in every direction.

OCD ABBREVIATION FOR **obsessive-compulsive disorder.**

ocean ('əʊʃən) NOUN 1 a very large stretch of sea, esp. one of the five oceans of the world, the Atlantic, Pacific, Indian, Arctic, and Antarctic. 2 the body of salt water covering approximately 70

per cent of the earth's surface. [3] a huge quantity or expanse: *an ocean of replies*. [4] *Literary* the sea.
▷HISTORY C13: via Old French from Latin *ōceanus,* from Greek *ōkeanos* OCEANUS

oceanarium (ˌəʊʃəˈnɛərɪəm) NOUN, *plural* **-iums** *or* **-ia** (-ɪə). a large saltwater aquarium for marine life.

ocean floor spreading NOUN another term for **seafloor spreading.**

ocean-going ADJECTIVE (of a ship, boat, etc.) suited for travel on the open ocean.

ocean greyhound NOUN a fast ship, esp. a liner.

Oceania (ˌəʊʃɪˈɑːnɪə) NOUN the islands of the central and S Pacific, including Melanesia, Micronesia, and Polynesia: sometimes also including Australasia and the Malay Archipelago.

Oceanian (ˌəʊʃɪˈɑːnɪən) ADJECTIVE [1] of or relating to Oceania or its inhabitants. ◆ NOUN [2] a native or inhabitant of Oceania.

oceanic (ˌəʊʃɪˈænɪk) ADJECTIVE [1] of or relating to the ocean. [2] living in the depths of the ocean beyond the continental shelf at a depth exceeding 200 metres: *oceanic fauna*. [3] huge or overwhelming. [4] (of geological formations) of volcanic origin, arising from the ocean: *oceanic islands*.

Oceanic (ˌəʊʃɪˈænɪk) NOUN [1] a branch, group, or subfamily of the Malayo-Polynesian family of languages, comprising Polynesian and Melanesian. ◆ ADJECTIVE [2] of, relating to, or belonging to this group of languages. [3] of or relating to Oceania.

oceanic ridge NOUN any section of the narrow, largely continuous range of submarine mountains that extends into all the major oceans and at which new oceanic lithosphere is created by the rise of magma from the earth's interior. See also **seafloor spreading.**

oceanic trench NOUN a long narrow steep-sided depression in the earth's oceanic crust, usually lying above a subduction zone.

Oceanid (əʊˈsɪənɪd) NOUN, *plural* **Oceanids** *or* **Oceanides** (ˌəʊsɪˈænɪˌdiːz). *Greek myth* any of the ocean nymphs born of Oceanus and Tethys.

Ocean of Storms NOUN the largest of the dark plains (maria) on the surface of the moon, situated in the second and third quadrant. Also called: **Oceanus Procellarum** (ˌəʊʃɪˈænəs ˌprəʊseˈlærəm).

oceanog. ABBREVIATION FOR oceanography.

oceanography (ˌəʊʃəˈnɒɡrəfɪ, ˌəʊʃɪə-) NOUN the branch of science dealing with the physical, chemical, geological, and biological features of the oceans and ocean basins.
▸ˌ**oceanˈographer** NOUN ▸**oceanographic** (ˌəʊʃənəˈɡræfɪk, ˌəʊʃɪə-) *or* ˌ**oceanoˈgraphical** ADJECTIVE ▸ˌ**oceanoˈgraphically** ADVERB

oceanology (ˌəʊʃəˈnɒlədʒɪ, ˌəʊʃɪə-) NOUN the study of the sea, esp. of its economic geography.

Oceanus (əʊˈsɪənəs) NOUN *Greek myth* a Titan, divinity of the stream believed to flow around the earth.

ocellus (ɒˈsɛləs) NOUN, *plural* **-li** (-laɪ). [1] the simple eye of insects and some other invertebrates, consisting basically of light-sensitive cells. [2] any eyelike marking in animals, such as the eyespot on the tail feather of a peacock. [3] *Botany* **a** an enlarged discoloured cell in a leaf. **b** a swelling on the sporangium of certain fungi.
▷HISTORY C19: via New Latin from Latin: small eye, from *oculus* eye
▸**oˈcellar** ADJECTIVE ▸**ocellate** (ˈɒsɪˌleɪt) *or* **ocellated** (ˈɒsɪˌleɪtɪd) ADJECTIVE ▸ˌ**ocelˈlation** NOUN

ocelot (ˈɒsɪˌlɒt, ˈəʊ-) NOUN a feline mammal, *Felis pardalis,* inhabiting the forests of Central and South America and having a dark-spotted buff-brown coat.
▷HISTORY C18: via French from Nahuatl *ocelotl* jaguar

och (ɒx) *Scot and Irish* ◆ INTERJECTION [1] an expression of surprise, contempt, annoyance, impatience, or disagreement. ◆ SENTENCE CONNECTOR [2] an expression used to preface a remark, gain time, etc.: *och, I suppose so*. ◆ Also: **ach.**

oche (ˈɒkɪ) NOUN *Darts* the mark or ridge on the floor behind which a player must stand to throw.
▷HISTORY of unknown origin; perhaps connected with obsolete *oche* to chop off, from Old French *ocher* to cut a notch in

ocher (ˈəʊkə) NOUN, ADJECTIVE, VERB the US spelling of **ochre.**
▸ˈ**ocherous** *or* ˈ**ochery** ADJECTIVE ▸**ochroid** (ˈəʊkrɔɪd) ADJECTIVE

ochlocracy (ɒkˈlɒkrəsɪ) NOUN, *plural* **-cies**. rule by the mob; mobocracy.
▷HISTORY C16: via French, from Greek *okhlokratia,* from *okhlos* mob + *kratos* power
▸**ochlocrat** (ˈɒkləˌkræt) NOUN ▸**ochlocratic** (ˌɒklɒˈkrætɪk) ADJECTIVE

ochlophobia (ˌɒkləˈfəʊbɪə) NOUN *Psychol* the fear of crowds.
▷HISTORY C19: from New Latin, from Greek *okhlos* mob + -PHOBIA

ochone (ɒˈxəʊn) INTERJECTION *Scot and Irish* an expression of sorrow or regret.
▷HISTORY from Gaelic *ochóin*

ochre *or US* **ocher** (ˈəʊkə) NOUN [1] any of various natural earths containing ferric oxide, silica, and alumina: used as yellow or red pigments. [2] **a** a moderate yellow-orange to orange colour. **b** (*as adjective*): *an ochre dress*. ◆ VERB [3] (*tr*) to colour with ochre.
▷HISTORY C15: from Old French *ocre,* from Latin *ōchra,* from Greek *ōkhra,* from *ōkhros* pale yellow
▸**ochreous** (ˈəʊkrɪəs, ˈəʊkərəs), **ochrous** (ˈəʊkrəs), **ochry** (ˈəʊkərɪ, ˈəʊkrɪ), *or US* ˈ**ocherous,** ˈ**ochery** ADJECTIVE
▸**ochroid** (ˈəʊkrɔɪd) ADJECTIVE

ochrea *or* **ocrea** (ˈɒkrɪə) NOUN, *plural* **-reae** (-rɪˌiː). a cup-shaped structure that sheathes the stems of certain plants, formed from united stipules or leaf bases.
▷HISTORY C19: from Latin *ocrea* greave, legging, of obscure origin

ocicat (ˈɒsɪˌkæt) NOUN a breed of large short-haired cat with a spotted coat.
▷HISTORY C20: from OC(ELOT) + *-i-* + CAT

-ock SUFFIX FORMING NOUNS indicating smallness: *hillock*.
▷HISTORY Old English *-oc, -uc*

ocker (ˈɒkə) *Austral, slang* ◆ NOUN [1] (*often capital*) an uncultivated or boorish Australian. ◆ ADJECTIVE, ADVERB [2] typical of such a person.
▷HISTORY C20: of uncertain origin

Ockham's razor *or* **Occam's razor** (ˈɒkəmz) NOUN a maxim, attributed to the English nominalist philosopher William of Ockham (died ?1349), stating that in explaining something assumptions must not be needlessly multiplied. Also called: **the principle of economy.**

ockodols (ˈɒkədɒlz) PLURAL NOUN *Northern English, dialect* one's feet when wearing boots.

o'clock (əˈklɒk) ADVERB [1] used after a number from one to twelve to indicate the hour of the day or night. [2] used after a number to indicate direction or position relative to the observer, twelve o'clock being directly ahead or overhead and other positions being obtained by comparisons with a clock face.
▷HISTORY C18: abbreviation for *of the clock*

ocotillo (ˌəʊkəˈtiːljəʊ) NOUN, *plural* **-los**. a cactus-like tree, *Fouquieria splendens,* of Mexico and the southwestern US, with scarlet tubular flowers: used for hedges and candlewood: family *Fouquieriaceae*.
▷HISTORY Mexican Spanish: diminutive of *ocote* pine, from Nahuatl *ocotl* torch

OCR ABBREVIATION FOR optical character reader *or* recognition.

ocrea (ˈɒkrɪə) NOUN, *plural* **-reae** (-rɪˌiː). a variant spelling of **ochrea.**

ocreate (ˈɒkrɪɪt, -ˌeɪt) ADJECTIVE [1] *Botany* possessing an ocrea; sheathed. [2] *Ornithol* another word for **booted** (sense 2).

OCS ABBREVIATION FOR Officer Candidate School.

Oct. ABBREVIATION FOR October.

oct- COMBINING FORM a variant of **octo-** before a vowel.

octa (ˈɒktə) NOUN a variant spelling of **okta.**

octa- COMBINING FORM a variant of **octo-.**

octachord (ˈɒktəˌkɔːd) NOUN [1] an eight-stringed musical instrument. [2] a series of eight notes, esp. a scale.

octad (ˈɒktæd) NOUN [1] a group or series of eight. [2] *Chem* an element or group with a valency of eight.
▷HISTORY C19: from Greek *oktás,* from *oktō* eight
▸**ocˈtadic** ADJECTIVE

octagon (ˈɒktəɡən) *or less commonly* **octangle** NOUN a polygon having eight sides.
▷HISTORY C17: via Latin from Greek *oktagōnos,* having eight angles

octagonal (ɒkˈtæɡənᵊl) ADJECTIVE [1] having eight sides and eight angles. [2] of or relating to an octagon.
▸**ocˈtagonally** ADVERB

octahedral (ˌɒktəˈhiːdrəl) ADJECTIVE [1] having eight plane surfaces. [2] shaped like an octahedron.

octahedrite (ˌɒktəˈhiːdraɪt) NOUN another name for **anatase.**

octahedron (ˌɒktəˈhiːdrən) NOUN, *plural* **-drons** *or* **-dra** (-drə). a solid figure having eight plane faces.

octal notation *or* **octal** (ˈɒktəl) NOUN a number system having a base 8: often used in computing, one octal digit being equivalent to a group of three bits.

octamerous (ɒkˈtæmərəs) ADJECTIVE consisting of eight parts, esp. (of flowers) having the parts arranged in groups of eight.

octameter (ɒkˈtæmɪtə) NOUN *Prosody* a verse line consisting of eight metrical feet.

octane (ˈɒkteɪn) NOUN a liquid alkane hydrocarbon found in petroleum and existing in 18 isomeric forms, esp. the isomer *n*-octane. Formula: C_8H_{18}. See also **isooctane.**

octanedioic acid (ˌɒkteɪndaɪˈəʊɪk) NOUN a colourless crystalline dicarboxylic acid found in suberin and castor oil and used in the manufacture of synthetic resins. Formula: $HOOC(CH_2)_6COOH$. Also called: **suberic acid.**
▷HISTORY C20: from OCTANE + DIOL

octane number *or* **rating** NOUN a measure of the quality of a petrol expressed as the percentage of isooctane in a mixture of isooctane and *n*-heptane that gives a fuel with the same antiknock qualities as the given petrol.

octangle (ˈɒktæŋɡᵊl) NOUN a less common name for **octagon.**

octangular (ɒkˈtæŋɡjʊlə) ADJECTIVE having eight angles.

Octans (ˈɒktænz) NOUN, *Latin genitive* **Octantis** (ɒkˈtæntɪs). a faint constellation in the S hemisphere in which the S celestial pole is situated.

octant (ˈɒktənt) NOUN [1] *Maths* **a** any of the eight parts into which the three planes containing the Cartesian coordinate axes divide space. **b** an eighth part of a circle. [2] *Astronomy* the position of a celestial body when it is at an angular distance of 45° from another body. [3] an instrument used for measuring angles, similar to a sextant but having a graduated arc of 45°.
▷HISTORY C17: from Latin *octans* half quadrant, from *octo* eight

octarchy (ˈɒktɑːkɪ) NOUN, *plural* **-chies**. [1] government by eight rulers. [2] a confederacy of eight kingdoms, tribes, etc.

octaroon (ˌɒktəˈruːn) NOUN a variant spelling of **octoroon.**

octavalent (ˌɒktəˈveɪlənt) ADJECTIVE *Chem* having a valency of eight.

octave (ˈɒktɪv) NOUN [1] **a** the interval between two musical notes one of which has twice the pitch of the other and lies eight notes away from it counting inclusively along the diatonic scale. **b** one of these two notes, esp. the one of higher pitch. **c** (*as modifier*): *an octave leap*. ◆ See also **perfect** (sense 9), **diminished** (sense 2), **interval** (sense 5). [2] *Prosody* a rhythmic group of eight lines of verse. [3] (ˈɒkteɪv) **a** a feast day and the seven days following. **b** the final day of this period. [4] the eighth of eight basic positions in fencing. [5] any set or series of eight. ◆ ADJECTIVE [6] consisting of eight parts.
▷HISTORY C14: (originally: eighth day) via Old French from Medieval Latin *octāva diēs* eighth day (after a festival), from Latin *octo* eight

octave coupler NOUN a mechanism on an organ and on some harpsichords that enables keys or pedals an octave apart to be played simultaneously.

octavo (ɒkˈteɪvəʊ) NOUN, *plural* **-vos**. [1] Also called: **eightvo.** a book size resulting from folding a sheet of paper of a specified size to form eight leaves: *demi-octavo*. Often written: **8vo, 8°.** [2] a book of this

size. [3] (formerly) a size of cut paper 8 inches by 5 inches (20.3 cm by 12.7 cm).
▷**HISTORY** C16: from New Latin phrase *in octavo* in an eighth (of a whole sheet)

octennial (ɒk'tɛnɪəl) ADJECTIVE [1] occurring every eight years. [2] lasting for eight years.
▷**HISTORY** C17: from Latin *octennium* eight years, from *octo* eight + *annus* year
▸**oc'tennially** ADVERB

octet (ɒk'tɛt) NOUN [1] any group of eight, esp. eight singers or musicians. [2] a piece of music composed for such a group. [3] *Prosody* another word for **octave** (sense 2). [4] *Chem* a group of eight electrons forming a stable shell in an atom. ◆ Also (for senses 1, 2, 3): **octette.**
▷**HISTORY** C19: from Latin *octo* eight, on the model of DUET

octillion (ɒk'tɪljən) NOUN [1] (in Britain and Germany) the number represented as one followed by 48 zeros (10^{48}). [2] (in the US, Canada, and France) the number represented as one followed by 27 zeros (10^{27}).
▷**HISTORY** C17: from French, on the model of MILLION
▸**oc'tillionth** ADJECTIVE

octo-, octa-, *or before a vowel* **oct-** COMBINING FORM eight: *octosyllabic; octagon.*
▷**HISTORY** from Latin *octo*, Greek *okto*

October (ɒk'təʊbə) NOUN the tenth month of the year, consisting of 31 days.
▷**HISTORY** Old English, from Latin, from *octo* eight, since it was the eighth month in Roman reckoning

October Revolution NOUN another name for the **Russian Revolution** (sense 2).

Octobrist (ɒk'təʊbrɪst) NOUN a member of a Russian political party favouring the constitutional reforms granted in a manifesto issued by Nicholas II in Oct. 1905.

octocentenary (ˌɒktəʊsɛn'tiːnərɪ) NOUN, *plural* **-naries.** an eight-hundredth anniversary.

octodecimo (ˌɒktəʊ'dɛsɪməʊ) NOUN, *plural* **-mos.** *Bookbinding* another word for **eighteenmo.**
▷**HISTORY** C18: from New Latin phrase *in octodecimo* in an eighteenth (of a whole sheet)

octogenarian (ˌɒktəʊdʒɪ'nɛərɪən) *or less commonly* **octogenary** (ɒk'tɒdʒɪnərɪ) NOUN, *plural* **-narians** *or* **-naries.** [1] a person who is from 80 to 89 years old. ◆ ADJECTIVE [2] of or relating to an octogenarian.
▷**HISTORY** C19: from Latin *octōgēnārius* containing eighty, from *octōgēnī* eighty each

octonary ('ɒktənərɪ) *Rare* ◆ ADJECTIVE [1] relating to or based on the number eight. ◆ NOUN, *plural* **-naries.** [2] *Prosody* a stanza of eight lines. [3] a group of eight.
▷**HISTORY** C16: from Latin *octōnārius*, from *octōnī* eight at a time

octopod ('ɒktəˌpɒd) NOUN [1] any cephalopod mollusc of the order *Octopoda,* including octopuses and the paper nautilus, having eight tentacles, and lacking an internal shell. ◆ ADJECTIVE [2] of, relating to, or belonging to the *Octopoda*.

octopus ('ɒktəpəs) NOUN, *plural* **-puses.** [1] any cephalopod mollusc of the genera *Octopus, Eledone,* etc., having a soft oval body with eight long suckered tentacles and occurring at the sea bottom: order *Octopoda* (octopods). [2] a powerful influential organization with far-reaching effects, esp. harmful ones. [3] another name for **spider** (sense 8).
▷**HISTORY** C18: via New Latin from Greek *oktōpous* having eight feet

octoroon *or* **octaroon** (ˌɒktə'ruːn) NOUN a person having one quadroon and one White parent and therefore having one-eighth Black blood. Compare **quadroon.**
▷**HISTORY** C19: OCTO- + *-roon* as in QUADROON

octosyllable ('ɒktəˌsɪləb^{ə}l) NOUN [1] a line of verse composed of eight syllables. [2] a word of eight syllables.
▸**octosyllabic** (ˌɒktəsɪ'læbɪk) ADJECTIVE

octroi ('ɒktrwɑː) NOUN [1] (in some European countries, esp. France) a duty on various goods brought into certain towns or cities. [2] the place where such a duty is collected. [3] the officers responsible for its collection.
▷**HISTORY** C17: from French *octroyer* to concede, from Medieval Latin *auctorizāre* to AUTHORIZE

octuple ('ɒktjʊp^{ə}l) NOUN [1] a quantity or number eight times as great as another. ◆ ADJECTIVE [2] eight times as much or as many. [3] consisting of eight parts. ◆ VERB [4] (*tr*) to multiply by eight.
▷**HISTORY** C17: from Latin *octuplus,* from *octo* eight + *-plus* as in *duplus* double

ocular ('ɒkjʊlə) ADJECTIVE [1] of or relating to the eye. ◆ NOUN [2] another name for **eyepiece.**
▷**HISTORY** C16: from Latin *oculāris* from *oculus* eye
▸**'ocularly** ADVERB

ocularist ('ɒkjʊlərɪst) NOUN a person who makes artificial eyes.

oculate ('ɒkjʊˌleɪt) ADJECTIVE *Zoology* [1] possessing eyes. [2] relating to or resembling eyes: *oculate markings*.

oculist ('ɒkjʊlɪst) NOUN *Med* a former term for **ophthalmologist.**
▷**HISTORY** C17: via French from Latin *oculus* eye

oculo- *or sometimes before a vowel* **ocul-** COMBINING FORM indicating the eye: *oculomotor.*
▷**HISTORY** from Latin *oculus* eye

oculomotor (ˌɒkjʊləʊ'məʊtə) ADJECTIVE relating to or causing eye movements.
▷**HISTORY** C19: from OCULO- + MOTOR

oculomotor nerve NOUN the third cranial nerve, which supplies most of the eye muscles.

od (ɒd, əʊd), **odyl,** *or* **odyle** ('ɒdɪl) NOUN *Archaic* a hypothetical force formerly thought to be responsible for many natural phenomena, such as magnetism, light, and hypnotism.
▷**HISTORY** C19: coined arbitrarily by Baron Karl von Reichenbach (1788–1869), German scientist
▸**'odic** ADJECTIVE

Od, 'Od, *or* **Odd** (ɒd) NOUN *Euphemistic* (used in mild oaths) an archaic word for **God.**

OD^{1} (ˌəʊ'diː) *Informal* ◆ NOUN [1] an overdose of a drug. ◆ VERB **OD's, OD'ing, OD'd.** [2] (*intr*) to take an overdose of a drug.
▷**HISTORY** C20: from *o(ver)d(ose)*

OD^{2} ABBREVIATION FOR: [1] Officer of the Day. [2] Old Dutch. [3] **ordnance datum.** [4] outside diameter. [5] Also: **o.d.** *Military* olive drab. [6] Also: **O/D.** *Banking* **a** on demand. **b** overdraft. **c** overdrawn.

ODA (in Britain, formerly) ABBREVIATION FOR Overseas Development Administration, now superseded by the Department for International Development (DFID).

odalisque *or* **odalisk** ('əʊdəlɪsk) NOUN a female slave or concubine.
▷**HISTORY** C17: via French, changed from Turkish *ōdalik,* from *ōdah* room + *-lik* n suffix

odd (ɒd) ADJECTIVE [1] unusual or peculiar in appearance, character, etc. [2] occasional, incidental, or random: *odd jobs.* [3] leftover or additional: *odd bits of wool.* [4] **a** not divisible by two. **b** represented or indicated by a number that is not divisible by two: *graphs are on odd pages.* Compare **even**^{1} (sense 7). [5] being part of a matched pair or set when the other or others are missing: *an odd sock; odd volumes.* [6] (*in combination*) used to designate an indefinite quantity more than the quantity specified in round numbers: *fifty-odd pounds.* [7] out-of-the-way or secluded: *odd corners.* [8] *Maths* (of a function) changing sign but not absolute value when the sign of the independent variable is changed, as in $y=x^3$. Compare **even**^{1} (sense 13). [9] **odd man out.** a person or thing excluded from others forming a group, unit, etc. ◆ NOUN [10] *Golf* **a** one stroke more than the score of one's opponent. **b** an advantage or handicap of one stroke added to or taken away from a player's score. [11] a thing or person that is odd in sequence or number. ◆ See also **odds.**
▷**HISTORY** C14: *odde:* from Old Norse *oddi* point, angle, triangle, third or odd number. Compare Old Norse *oddr* point, spot, place; Old English *ord* point, beginning
▸**'oddly** ADVERB ▸**'oddness** NOUN

oddball ('ɒdˌbɔːl) *Informal* ◆ NOUN [1] Also called: **odd bod, odd fish.** a strange or eccentric person. ◆ ADJECTIVE [2] strange or peculiar.

Oddfellow ('ɒdˌfɛləʊ) NOUN a member of the **Independent Order of Oddfellows,** a secret benevolent and fraternal association founded in England in the 18th century.

oddity ('ɒdɪtɪ) NOUN, *plural* **-ties.** [1] an odd person or thing. [2] an odd quality or characteristic. [3] the condition of being odd.

odd-jobman *or* **odd-jobber** NOUN, *plural* **-men** *or* **-bers.** a person who does casual work, esp. domestic repairs.

odd lot NOUN [1] a batch of merchandise that contains less than or more than the usual number of units. [2] *Stock Exchange* a number of securities less than the standard trading unit of 100.

oddment ('ɒdmənt) NOUN [1] (*often plural*) an odd piece or thing; leftover. [2] (*plural*) *NZ* pieces of wool, such as belly wool or neck wool, removed from a fleece and sold separately.

odd-pinnate ADJECTIVE (of a plant leaf) pinnate with a single leaflet at the apex.

odds (ɒdz) PLURAL NOUN [1] (foll by *on* or *against*) the probability, expressed as a ratio, that a certain event will take place: *the odds against the outsider are a hundred to one.* [2] the amount, expressed as a ratio, by which the wager of one better is greater than that of another: *he was offering odds of five to one.* [3] the likelihood that a certain state of affairs will be found to be so: *the odds are that he is drunk.* [4] the chances or likelihood of success in a certain undertaking: *their odds were very poor after it rained.* [5] an equalizing allowance, esp. one given to a weaker side in a contest. [6] the advantage that one contender is judged to have over another: *the odds are on my team.* [7] *Brit* a significant difference (esp. in the phrase **it makes no odds**). [8] **at odds. a** on bad terms. **b** appearing not to correspond or match: *the silvery hair was at odds with her youthful shape.* [9] **give** *or* **lay odds.** to offer a bet with favourable odds. [10] **take odds.** to accept such a bet. [11] **over the odds. a** more than is expected, necessary, etc.: *he got two pounds over the odds for this job.* **b** unfair or excessive. [12] **what's the odds?** *Brit informal* what difference does it make?

odds and ends PLURAL NOUN miscellaneous items or articles.

odds and sods PLURAL NOUN *Brit informal* miscellaneous people or things.

odds-on ADJECTIVE [1] (of a chance, horse, etc.) rated at even money or less to win. [2] regarded as more or most likely to win, succeed, happen, etc.

ode (əʊd) NOUN [1] a lyric poem, typically addressed to a particular subject, with lines of varying lengths and complex rhythms. See also **Horatian ode, Pindaric ode.** [2] (formerly) a poem meant to be sung.
▷**HISTORY** C16: via French from Late Latin *ōda,* from Greek *ōidē,* from *aeidein* to sing

-ode^{1} NOUN COMBINING FORM denoting resemblance: *nematode.*
▷**HISTORY** from Greek *-ōdēs,* from *eidos* shape, form

-ode^{2} NOUN COMBINING FORM denoting a path or way: *electrode.*
▷**HISTORY** from Greek *-odos,* from *hodos* a way

odea ('əʊdɪə) NOUN the plural of **odeum.**

Odelsting *or* **Odelsthing** ('əʊd^{ə}lsˌtɪŋ) NOUN the lower chamber of the Norwegian parliament. See also **Lagting, Storting.**

Odense (*Danish* 'oːðənsə) NOUN a port in S Denmark, on Funen Island: cathedral founded by King Canute in the 11th century. Pop.: 189 912 (2000 est.).

Oder ('əʊdə) NOUN a river in central Europe, rising in the NE Czech Republic and flowing north and west, forming part of the border between Germany and Poland, to the Baltic. Length: 913 km (567 miles). Czech and Polish name: **Odra.**

Oder-Neisse Line ('əʊdə'naɪsə) NOUN the present-day boundary between Germany and Poland along the Rivers Oder and Neisse. Established in 1945, it originally separated the Soviet Zone of Germany from the regions under Polish administration.

Odessa (əʊ'dɛsə; *Russian* a'djɛsə) NOUN a port in the S Ukraine on the Black Sea: the chief Russian grain port in the 19th century; university (1865); industrial centre and important naval base. Pop.: 1 027 400 (1998 est.).

odeum ('əʊdɪəm) NOUN, *plural* **odea** ('əʊdɪə). (esp. in ancient Greece and Rome) a building for musical performances. Also called: **odeon.**
▷**HISTORY** C17: from Latin, from Greek *ōideion,* from *ōidē* ODE

ODI ABBREVIATION FOR *Cricket* one-day international.

Odin (ˈəʊdɪn) *or* **Othin** (ˈəʊðɪn) NOUN *Norse myth* the supreme creator god; the divinity of wisdom, culture, war, and the dead. Germanic counterpart: **Wotan, Woden.**

odious (ˈəʊdɪəs) ADJECTIVE offensive; repugnant.
▷HISTORY C17: from Latin; see ODIUM
▸ˈ**odiously** ADVERB ▸ˈ**odiousness** NOUN

odium (ˈəʊdɪəm) NOUN 1 the dislike accorded to a hated person or thing. 2 hatred; repugnance.
▷HISTORY C17: from Latin; related to *ōdī* I hate, Greek *odussasthai* to be angry

odometer (ɒˈdɒmɪtə, əʊ-) NOUN the usual US and Canadian name for **mileometer.**
▷HISTORY C18 *hodometer,* from Greek *hodos* way + -METER
▸**oˈdometry** NOUN

-odont ADJECTIVE AND NOUN COMBINING FORM having teeth of a certain type; -toothed: *acrodont.*
▷HISTORY from Greek *odōn* tooth

odontalgia (ˌɒdɒnˈtældʒɪə) NOUN a technical name for **toothache.**
▸ˌ**odonˈtalgic** ADJECTIVE

odonto- *or before a vowel* **odont-** COMBINING FORM indicating a tooth or teeth: *odontology.*
▷HISTORY from Greek *odōn* tooth

odontoblast (ɒˈdɒntəˌblæst) NOUN any of a layer of cells lining the pulp cavity of a tooth and giving rise to the dentine.
▸**oˌdontoˈblastic** ADJECTIVE

odontoglossum (ɒˌdɒntəˈglɒsəm) NOUN any epiphytic orchid of the tropical American genus *Odontoglossum,* having clusters of brightly coloured flowers.

odontoid (ɒˈdɒntɔɪd) ADJECTIVE 1 toothlike. 2 of or relating to the odontoid process.

odontoid process NOUN *Anatomy* the toothlike upward projection at the back of the second vertebra of the neck.

odontolite (ɒˈdɒntəˌlaɪt) NOUN another name for **bone turquoise.**

odontology (ˌɒdɒnˈtɒlədʒɪ) NOUN the branch of science concerned with the anatomy, development, and diseases of teeth and related structures.
▸**odontological** (ɒˌdɒntəˈlɒdʒɪkəl) ADJECTIVE
▸ˌ**odonˈtologist** NOUN

odontophore (ɒˈdɒntəˌfɔː) NOUN an oral muscular protrusible structure in molluscs that supports the radula.
▸**odontophoral** (ˌɒdɒnˈtɒfərəl) *or* ˌ**odonˈtophorous** ADJECTIVE

odontorhynchous (ɒˌdɒntəˈrɪŋkəs) ADJECTIVE (of birds) having toothlike ridges inside the beak.
▷HISTORY C19: from ODONTO- + Greek *rhunkhos* snout + -OUS

odor (ˈəʊdə) NOUN the US spelling of **odour.**
▸ˈ**odorless** ADJECTIVE

odoriferous (ˌəʊdəˈrɪfərəs) ADJECTIVE having or emitting an odour, esp. a fragrant one.
▸ˌ**odorˈiferously** ADVERB ▸ˌ**odorˈiferousness** NOUN

odorimetry (ˌəʊdəˈrɪmɪtrɪ) NOUN *Chem* the measurement of the strength and permanence of odours. Also called: **olfactometry.**

odoriphore (əʊˈdɒrɪˌfɔː) NOUN *Chem* the group of atoms in an odorous molecule responsible for its odour.

odorous (ˈəʊdərəs) ADJECTIVE having or emitting a characteristic smell or odour.
▸ˈ**odorously** ADVERB ▸ˈ**odorousness** NOUN

odour *or US* **odor** (ˈəʊdə) NOUN 1 the property of a substance that gives it a characteristic scent or smell. 2 a pervasive quality about something: *an odour of dishonesty.* 3 repute or regard (in the phrases **in good odour, in bad odour**).
▷HISTORY C13: from Old French *odur,* from Latin *odor;* related to Latin *olēre* to smell, Greek *ōzein*
▸ˈ**odourless** *or US* ˈ**odorless** ADJECTIVE

odour of sanctity NOUN *Derogatory* sanctimoniousness.
▷HISTORY C18: originally, the sweet smell said to be exhaled by the bodies of dead saints

Odra (ˈɔdra) NOUN the Czech and Polish name for the **Oder.**

odyl *or* **odyle** (ˈɒdɪl) NOUN other words for **od.**

Odysseus (əˈdiːsɪəs) NOUN *Greek myth* one of the foremost of the Greek heroes at the siege of Troy, noted for his courage and ingenuity. His return to his kingdom of Ithaca was fraught with adventures in which he lost all his companions and he was acknowledged by his wife Penelope only after killing her suitors. Roman name: **Ulysses.**

Odyssey (ˈɒdɪsɪ) NOUN 1 a Greek epic poem, attributed to Homer (c. 800 B.C.), describing the ten-year homeward wanderings of Odysseus after the fall of Troy. 2 (*often not capital*) any long eventful journey.
▸**Odyssean** (ˌɒdɪˈsiːən) ADJECTIVE

Oe SYMBOL FOR oersted.

OE ABBREVIATION FOR Old English (language).

o.e. *Commerce* ABBREVIATION FOR omissions excepted.

OECD ABBREVIATION FOR Organization for Economic Cooperation and Development; an association of 21 nations to promote growth and trade, set up in 1961 to supersede the OEEC.

oecology (iːˈkɒlədʒɪ) NOUN a less common spelling of **ecology.**
▸**oecological** (ˌɛkəˈlɒdʒɪkəl, ˌiː-) ADJECTIVE
▸ˌ**oecoˈlogically** ADVERB ▸**oeˈcologist** NOUN

oecumenical (ˌiːkjʊˈmɛnɪkəl) ADJECTIVE a less common spelling of **ecumenical.**

OED ABBREVIATION FOR Oxford English Dictionary.

oedema *or* **edema** (ɪˈdiːmə) NOUN, *plural* **-mata** (-mətə). 1 *Pathol* an excessive accumulation of serous fluid in the intercellular spaces of tissue. 2 *Plant pathol* an abnormal swelling in a plant caused by a large mass of parenchyma or an accumulation of water in the tissues.
▷HISTORY C16: via New Latin from Greek *oidēma,* from *oidein* to swell
▸**oedematous, edematous** (ɪˈdɛmətəs), **oeˈdemaˌtose,** *or* **eˈdemaˌtose** ADJECTIVE

Oedipus (ˈiːdɪpəs) NOUN *Greek myth* the son of Laius and Jocasta, the king and queen of Thebes, who killed his father, being unaware of his identity, and unwittingly married his mother, by whom he had four children. When the truth was revealed, he put out his eyes and Jocasta killed herself.

Oedipus complex NOUN *Psychoanal* a group of emotions, usually unconscious, involving the desire of a child, esp. a male child, to possess sexually the parent of the opposite sex while excluding the parent of the same sex. Compare **Electra complex.**
▸ˈ**oedipal** *or* ˌ**oediˈpean** ADJECTIVE

oedometer (iːˈdɒmɪtə) NOUN *Civil engineering* an instrument for measuring the rate and amount of consolidation of a soil specimen under pressure.
▷HISTORY C20: from Greek *oidēma* (see OEDEMA) + -METER

OEEC ABBREVIATION FOR Organization for European Economic Cooperation; an organization of European nations set up in 1948 to allocate postwar US aid and to stimulate trade and cooperation. It was superseded by the OECD in 1961.

oeil-de-boeuf *French* (œjdəbœf) NOUN, *plural* ***oeils-de-boeuf*** (œjdəbœf). a circular window, esp. in 17th- and 18th-century French architecture.
▷HISTORY literally: bull's eye

oeillade (ɜːˈjɑːd; *French* œjad) NOUN *Literary* an amorous or suggestive glance; ogle.
▷HISTORY C16: from French, from *oeil* eye, from Latin *oculus* + *-ade* as in FUSILLADE

OEM ABBREVIATION FOR original equipment manufacturer: a computer company whose products are made by customizing basic parts supplied by others.

oenology *or* **enology** (iːˈnɒlədʒɪ) NOUN the study of wine.
▷HISTORY C19: from Greek *oinos* wine + -LOGY
▸**oenological** *or* **enological** (ˌiːnəˈlɒdʒɪkəl) ADJECTIVE
▸**oeˈnologist** *or* **eˈnologist** NOUN

oenomel (ˈiːnəˌmɛl) NOUN 1 a drink made of wine and honey. 2 *Literary* a source of strength and sweetness.
▷HISTORY C16: via Latin from Greek *oinos* wine + *meli* honey

Oenone (iːˈnəʊnɪ) NOUN *Greek myth* a nymph of Mount Ida, whose lover Paris left her for Helen.

oenophile (ˈiːnəˌfaɪl) NOUN a lover or connoisseur of wines.
▷HISTORY C20: from Greek *oinos* wine + -PHILE

oenothera (ˌiːnəˈθɪərə) NOUN any plant of the large taxonomically complicated American genus *Oenothera,* typically having yellow flowers that open in the evening: family *Onagraceae.* See **evening primrose.**

o'er (ɔː, əʊə) PREPOSITION, ADVERB a poetic contraction of **over.**

oersted (ˈɜːstɛd) NOUN the cgs unit of magnetic field strength; the field strength that would cause a unit magnetic pole to experience a force of 1 dyne in a free space. It is equivalent to 79.58 amperes per metre. Symbol: Oe.
▷HISTORY C20: named after H. C. *Oersted* (1777–1851), Danish physicist, who discovered electromagnetism

oesophagoscope *or US* **esophagoscope** (iːˈsɒfəgəʊˌskəʊp) NOUN *Med* an instrument for examining the oesophagus.
▸**oesophagoscopy** (iːˌsɒfəˈgɒskəpɪ) NOUN

oesophagus *or US* **esophagus** (iːˈsɒfəgəs) NOUN, *plural* **-gi** (-ˌgaɪ). the part of the alimentary canal between the pharynx and the stomach; gullet.
▷HISTORY C16: via New Latin from Greek *oisophagos,* from *oisein,* future infinitive of *pherein* to carry + *-phagos,* from *phagein* to eat
▸**oesophageal** *or US* **esophageal** (iːˌsɒfəˈdʒiːəl) ADJECTIVE

oestradiol (ˌiːstrəˈdaɪɒl, ˌɛstrə-) *or US* **estradiol** NOUN the most potent oestrogenic hormone secreted by the mammalian ovary: synthesized and used to treat oestrogen deficiency and cancer of the breast. Formula: $C_{18}H_{24}O_2$.
▷HISTORY C20: from New Latin, from OESTRIN + DI-[1] + -OL[1]

oestrin (ˈiːstrɪn, ˈɛstrɪn) *or US* **estrin** NOUN an obsolete term for **oestrogen.**
▷HISTORY C20: from OESTR(US) + -IN

oestriol (ˈiːstrɪˌɒl, ˈɛstrɪ-) *or US* **estriol** NOUN a weak oestrogenic hormone secreted by the mammalian ovary: a synthetic form is used to treat oestrogen deficiency. Formula: $C_{18}H_{24}O_3$.
▷HISTORY C20: from OESTRIN + TRI- + -OL[1]

oestrogen (ˈiːstrədʒən, ˈɛstrə-) *or US* **estrogen** NOUN any of several steroid hormones, that are secreted chiefly by the ovaries and placenta, that induce oestrus, stimulate changes in the female reproductive organs during the oestrous cycle, and promote development of female secondary sexual characteristics.
▷HISTORY C20: from OESTRUS + -GEN
▸**oestrogenic** (ˌiːstrəˈdʒɛnɪk, ˌɛstrə-) *or US* **estrogenic** (ˌɛstrəˈdʒɛnɪk, ˌiːstrə-) ADJECTIVE ▸ˌ**oestroˈgenically** *or US* ˌ**estroˈgenically** ADVERB

oestrone (ˈiːstrəʊn, ˈɛstrəʊn) *or US* **estrone** NOUN a weak oestrogenic hormone secreted by the mammalian ovary and having the same medical uses as oestradiol. Formula: $C_{18}H_{22}O_2$.
▷HISTORY C20: from OESTR(US) + -ONE

oestrous cycle NOUN a hormonally controlled cycle of activity of the reproductive organs in many female mammals. The follicular stage (growth of the Graafian follicles, thickening of the lining of the uterus, secretion of oestrogen, and ovulation (see **oestrus**)), is succeeded by the luteal phase (formation of the corpus luteum and secretion of progesterone), followed by regression and a return to the first stage.

oestrus (ˈiːstrəs, ˈɛstrəs) *or US* **estrus, estrum** (ˈiːstrəm, ˈɛstrəm) NOUN a regularly occurring period of sexual receptivity in most female mammals, except humans, during which ovulation occurs and copulation can take place; heat.
▷HISTORY C17: from Latin *oestrus* gadfly, hence frenzy, from Greek *oistros*
▸ˈ**oestrous,** ˈ**oestral,** *or US* ˈ**estrous,** ˈ**estral** ADJECTIVE

oeuvre *French* (œvrə) NOUN 1 a work of art, literature, music, etc. 2 the total output of a writer, painter, etc.
▷HISTORY ultimately from Latin *opera,* plural of *opus* work

of (ɒv; *unstressed* əv) PREPOSITION 1 used with a verbal noun or gerund to link it with a following noun that is either the subject or the object of the verb embedded in the gerund: *the breathing of a fine swimmer* (subject); *the breathing of clean air* (object). 2 used to indicate possession, origin, or association: *the house of my sister; to die of hunger.* 3 used after words or phrases expressing quantities: *a pint of milk.* 4 constituted by, containing, or characterized by: *a family of idiots; a rod of iron; a*

man of some depth. [5] used to indicate separation, as in time or space: *within a mile of the town; within ten minutes of the beginning of the concert.* [6] used to mark apposition: *the city of Naples; a speech on the subject of archaeology.* [7] about; concerning: *speak to me of love.* [8] used in passive constructions to indicate the agent: *he was beloved of all.* [9] *Informal* used to indicate a day or part of a period of time when some activity habitually occurs: *I go to the pub of an evening.* [10] *US* before the hour of: *a quarter of nine.*
▷HISTORY Old English (as prep and adv); related to Old Norse *af,* Old High German *aba,* Latin *ab,* Greek *apo*

> **Language note** See at **off**.

OF ABBREVIATION FOR Old French (language).
ofay ('əʊfeɪ) NOUN *US, slang* a derogatory term for a White person.
▷HISTORY C20: origin unknown
Ofcom ('ɒfkɒm) NOUN (in Britain) ACRONYM FOR Office of Communications: a government body regulating the telecommunications industries; a super-regulator merging the Radio Authority, Independent Television Commission, and Oftel.
off (ɒf) PREPOSITION [1] used to indicate actions in which contact is absent or rendered absent, as between an object and a surface: *to lift a cup off the table.* [2] used to indicate the removal of something that is or has been appended to or in association with something else: *to take the tax off potatoes.* [3] out of alignment with: *we are off course.* [4] situated near to or leading away from: *just off the High Street.* [5] not inclined towards: *I'm off work; I've gone off you.* ◆ ADVERB [6] *(particle)* so as to be deactivated or disengaged: *turn off the radio.* [7] *(particle)* **a** so as to get rid of: *sleep off a hangover.* **b** so as to be removed from, esp. as a reduction: *he took ten per cent off.* [8] spent away from work or other duties: *take the afternoon off.* [9] **a** on a trip, journey, or race: *I saw her off at the station.* **b** *(particle)* so as to be completely absent, used up, or exhausted: *this stuff kills off all vermin.* [10] out from the shore or land: *the ship stood off.* [11] **a** out of contact; at a distance: *the ship was 10 miles off.* **b** out of the present location: *the girl ran off.* [12] away in the future: *August is less than a week off.* [13] *(particle)* so as to be no longer taking place: *the match has been rained off.* [14] *(particle)* removed from contact with something, as clothing from the body: *the girl took all her clothes off.* [15] offstage: *noises off.* [16] *Commerce* (used with a preceding number) indicating the number of items required or produced: *please supply 100 off.* [17] **off and on** *or* **on and off.** occasionally; intermittently: *he comes here off and on.* [18] **off with.** *(interjection)* a command, often peremptory, or an exhortation to remove or cut off (something specified): *off with his head; off with that coat, my dear.* ◆ ADJECTIVE [19] not on; no longer operative: *the off position on the dial.* [20] *(postpositive)* not or no longer taking place; cancelled or postponed: *the meeting is off.* [21] in a specified condition regarding money, provisions, etc.: *well off; how are you off for bread?* [22] unsatisfactory or disappointing: *his performance was rather off; an off year for good tennis.* [23] *(postpositive)* in a condition as specified: *I'd be better off without this job.* [24] *(postpositive)* no longer on the menu; not being served at the moment: *sorry, love, haddock is off.* [25] *(postpositive)* (of food or drink) having gone bad, sour, etc.: *this milk is off.* ◆ NOUN [26] *Cricket* **a** the part of the field on that side of the pitch to which the batsman presents his bat when taking strike: thus for a right-hander, off is on the right-hand side. Compare **leg** (sense 13). **b** *(in combination)* a fielding position in this part of the field: *mid-off.* **c** *(as modifier)*: *the off stump.* ◆ VERB [27] *(tr)* to kill (someone).
▷HISTORY originally variant of OF; fully distinguished from it in the 17th century

> **Language note** In standard English, *off* is not followed by *of*: *he stepped off (not off of) the platform.*

off-air ADJECTIVE, ADVERB [1] obtained by reception of a radiated broadcasting signal rather than by line feed: *an off-air recording.* [2] connected with a radio or television programme but not broadcast: *an off-air phone-in.*
offal ('ɒfᵊl) NOUN [1] the edible internal parts of an animal, such as the heart, liver, and tongue. [2] dead or decomposing organic matter. [3] refuse; rubbish.
▷HISTORY C14: from OFF + FALL, referring to parts fallen or cut off; compare German *Abfall* rubbish
Offaly ('ɒfəlɪ) NOUN an inland county of E central Republic of Ireland, in Leinster province: formerly an ancient kingdom, which also included parts of Tipperary, Leix, and Kildare. County town: Tullamore. Pop.: 59 117 (1996). Area: 2000 sq. km (770 sq. miles).
off-balance sheet reserve NOUN *Accounting* a sum of money or an asset that should appear on a company's balance but does not; hidden reserve.
offbeat ('ɒf,biːt) NOUN [1] *Music* any of the normally unaccented beats in a bar, such as the second and fourth beats in a bar of four-four time. They are stressed in most rock and some jazz and dance music, such as the bossa nova. ◆ ADJECTIVE [2] **a** unusual, unconventional, or eccentric. **b** *(as noun)*: *he liked the offbeat in fashion.*
off break NOUN *Cricket* a bowled ball that spins from off to leg on pitching.
off-Broadway ADJECTIVE [1] designating the kind of experimental, low-budget, or noncommercial productions associated with theatre outside the Broadway area in New York. [2] (of theatres) not located in Broadway. ◆ Compare **off-off-Broadway.**
off-centre ADJECTIVE [1] displaced from a centre point or axis. [2] slightly eccentric or unconventional; not completely sound or balanced.
off chance NOUN [1] a slight possibility. [2] **on the off chance.** with the hope: *on the off chance of getting the job.*
off colour ADJECTIVE (**off-colour** *when prenominal*) [1] *Chiefly Brit* slightly ill; unwell. [2] indecent or indelicate; risqué.
offcut ('ɒf,kʌt) NOUN a piece of paper, plywood, fabric, etc., remaining after the main pieces have been cut; remnant.
Offenbach (*German* 'ɔfənbax) NOUN a city in central Germany, on the River Main in Hesse opposite Frankfurt am Main: leather-goods industry. Pop.: 116 400 (1999 est.).
offence *or US* **offense** (ə'fɛns) NOUN [1] a violation or breach of a law, custom, rule, etc. [2] **a** any public wrong or crime. **b** a nonindictable crime punishable on summary conviction. [3] annoyance, displeasure, or resentment. [4] **give offence (to).** to cause annoyance or displeasure (to). [5] **take offence.** to feel injured, humiliated, or offended. [6] a source of annoyance, displeasure, or anger. [7] attack; assault. [8] *Archaic* injury or harm. [9] ('ɒfɛns) *American football* (usually preceded by *the*) **a** the team that has possession of the ball. **b** the members of a team that play in such circumstances.
▸ **of'fenceless** *or US* **of'fenseless** ADJECTIVE
offend (ə'fɛnd) VERB [1] to hurt the feelings, sense of dignity, etc., of (a person). [2] *(tr)* to be disagreeable to; disgust: *the smell offended him.* [3] *(intr except in archaic uses)* to break (a law or laws in general).
▷HISTORY C14: via Old French *offendre* to strike against, from Latin *offendere,* from *ob-* against + *fendere* to strike
▸ **of'fender** NOUN ▸ **of'fending** ADJECTIVE
offensive (ə'fɛnsɪv) ADJECTIVE [1] unpleasant or disgusting, as to the senses. [2] causing anger or annoyance; insulting. [3] for the purpose of attack rather than defence. ◆ NOUN [4] (usually preceded by *the*) an attitude or position of aggression. [5] an assault, attack, or military initiative, esp. a strategic one.
▸ **of'fensively** ADVERB ▸ **of'fensiveness** NOUN
offer ('ɒfə) VERB [1] to present or proffer (something, someone, oneself, etc.) for acceptance or rejection. [2] *(tr)* to present as part of a requirement: *she offered English as a second subject.* [3] *(tr)* to provide or make accessible: *this stream offers the best fishing.* [4] *(intr)* to present itself: *if an opportunity should offer.* [5] *(tr)* to show or express willingness or the intention (to do something). [6] *(tr)* to put forward (a proposal, opinion, etc.) for consideration. [7] *(tr)* to present for sale. [8] *(tr)* to propose as payment; bid or tender. [9] (when *tr,* often foll by *up*) to present (a prayer, sacrifice, etc.) as or during an act of worship. [10] *(tr)* to show readiness for: *to offer battle.* [11] *(intr) Archaic* to make a proposal of marriage. [12] *(tr;* sometimes foll by *up* or *to*) *Engineering* to bring (a mechanical piece) near to or in contact with another, and often to proceed to fit the pieces together. ◆ NOUN [13] something, such as a proposal or bid, that is offered. [14] the act of offering or the condition of being offered. [15] *Contract law* a proposal made by one person that will create a binding contract if accepted unconditionally by the person to whom it is made. See also **acceptance.** [16] a proposal of marriage. [17] short for **offer price.** [18] **on offer.** for sale at a reduced price.
▷HISTORY Old English, from Latin *offerre* to present, from *ob-* to + *ferre* to bring
▸ **'offerer** *or* **'offeror** NOUN
Offer ('ɒfə), NOUN (formerly, in Britain) ACRONYM FOR Office of Electricity Regulation: merged with Ofgas in 1999 to form Ofgem.
offer document NOUN a document sent by a person or firm making a takeover bid to the shareholders of the target company, giving details of the offer that has been made and, usually, reasons for accepting it.
offering ('ɒfərɪŋ) NOUN [1] something that is offered. [2] a contribution to the funds of a religious organization. [3] a sacrifice, as of an animal, to a deity.
offer price NOUN *Stock Exchange* the price at which a market maker is prepared to sell a specific security. Often shortened to **offer.** Compare **bid price.**
offertory ('ɒfətərɪ) NOUN, *plural* **-tories.** [1] the oblation of the bread and wine at the Eucharist. [2] the offerings of the worshippers at this service. [3] the prayers said or sung while the worshippers' offerings are being received.
▷HISTORY C14: from Church Latin *offertōrium* place appointed for offerings, from Latin *offerre* to OFFER
off-glide NOUN *Phonetics* a glide caused by the movement of the articulators away from their position in articulating the previous speech sound. Compare **on-glide.**
offhand (,ɒf'hænd) ADJECTIVE *also* **offhanded,** ADVERB [1] without care, thought, or consideration; sometimes, brusque or ungracious: *an offhand manner.* [2] without preparation or warning; impromptu.
▸ **,off'handedly** ADVERB ▸ **,off'handedness** NOUN
office ('ɒfɪs) NOUN [1] **a** a room or set of rooms in which business, professional duties, clerical work, etc., are carried out. **b** *(as modifier)*: *office furniture; an office boy.* [2] *(often plural)* the building or buildings in which the work of an organization, such as a business or government department, is carried out. [3] a commercial or professional business: *the architect's office approved the plans.* [4] the group of persons working in an office: *it was a happy office until she came.* [5] *(capital when part of a name)* (in Britain) a department of the national government: *the Home Office.* [6] *(capital when part of a name)* (in the US) **a** a governmental agency, esp. of the Federal government. **b** a subdivision of such an agency or of a department: *Office of Science and Technology.* [7] **a** a position of trust, responsibility, or duty, esp. in a government or organization: *the office of president; to seek office.* **b** *(in combination)*: *an office-holder.* [8] duty or function: *the office of an administrator.* [9] *(often plural)* a minor task or service: *domestic offices.* [10] *(often plural)* an action performed for another, usually a beneficial action: *through his good offices.* [11] a place where tickets, information, etc., can be obtained: *a ticket office.* [12] *Christianity* **a** *(often plural)* a ceremony or service, prescribed by ecclesiastical authorities, esp. one for the dead. **b** the order or form of these. **c** *RC Church* the official daily service. **d** short for **divine office.** [13] *(plural)* the parts of a house or estate where work is done, goods are stored, etc. [14] *(usually plural) Brit, euphemistic* a lavatory (esp. in the phrase **usual offices**). [15] **in** (*or* **out of**) **office.** (of a government) in (or out of) power. [16] **the office.** *Slang* a hint or signal.
▷HISTORY C13: via Old French from Latin *officium* service, duty, from *opus* work, service + *facere* to do
office bearer NOUN a person who holds an office, as in a society, company, club, etc.; official.

office block NOUN a large building designed to provide office accommodation.

office boy NOUN a former name for **office junior.**

office hours PLURAL NOUN [1] the hours during which an office is open for business. [2] the number of hours worked in an office.

office junior NOUN a young person, esp. a school-leaver, employed in an office for running errands and doing other minor jobs.

officer ('ɒfɪsə) NOUN [1] a person in the armed services who holds a position of responsibility, authority, and duty, esp. one who holds a commission. [2] See **police officer.** [3] (on a non-naval ship) any person including the captain and mate, who holds a position of authority and responsibility: *radio officer; engineer officer.* [4] a person appointed or elected to a position of responsibility or authority in a government, society, etc. [5] a government official: *a customs officer.* [6] (in the Order of the British Empire) a member of the grade below commander. ◆ VERB (*tr*) [7] to furnish with officers. [8] to act as an officer over (some section, group, organization, etc.).

officer of arms NOUN *Heraldry* a pursuivant or herald.

officer of the day NOUN a military officer whose duty is to take charge of the security of the unit or camp for a day. Also called: **orderly officer.**

officer of the guard NOUN a junior officer whose duty is to command a ceremonial guard. Abbreviation: **OG.**

official (ə'fɪʃəl) ADJECTIVE [1] of or relating to an office, its administration, or its duration. [2] sanctioned by, recognized by, or derived from authority: *an official statement.* [3] appointed by authority, esp. for some special duty. [4] having a formal ceremonial character: *an official dinner.* ◆ NOUN [5] a person who holds a position in an organization, government department, etc., esp. a subordinate position.

Official (ə'fɪʃəl) ADJECTIVE [1] of or relating to one of the two factions of the IRA and Sinn Féin created by a split in 1969. The Official movement subsequently renounced terrorism and entered constitutional politics in the Irish Republic as the Workers' Party (now the Democratic Left). ◆ NOUN [2] (formerly) a member of the Official IRA and Sinn Féin. Compare **Provisional.**

officialdom (ə'fɪʃəldəm) NOUN [1] the outlook or behaviour of officials, esp. those rigidly adhering to regulations; bureaucracy. [2] officials or bureaucrats collectively.

officialese (əˌfɪʃə'li:z) NOUN language characteristic of official documents, esp. when verbose or pedantic.

officially (ə'fɪʃəlɪ) ADVERB [1] in a formal or authoritative manner: *the Queen officially opened the dome.* [2] in a way that is formally acknowledged but is not necessarily the case: *officially on the dole but actually holding a job.*

Official Receiver NOUN an officer appointed by the Department of Trade and Industry to receive the income and manage the estate of a bankrupt pending the appointment of a trustee in bankruptcy. See also **receiver** (sense 2).

Official Referee NOUN *Law* (in England) a circuit judge attached to the High Court who is empowered to try certain cases, esp. where a detailed examination of accounts or other documents is involved.

Official Solicitor NOUN an officer of the Supreme Court of Judicature with special responsibilities for protecting the interests of persons under disability.

official strike NOUN a collective stoppage of work by part or all of the workforce of an organization with the approval of the trade union concerned. The stoppage may be accompanied by the payment of strike pay by the trade union concerned.

officiant (ə'fɪʃɪənt) NOUN a person who presides and officiates at a religious ceremony.

officiary (ə'fɪʃɪərɪ) NOUN, *plural* **-aries.** [1] a body of officials. ◆ ADJECTIVE [2] of, relating to, or derived from office.

officiate (ə'fɪʃɪˌeɪt) VERB (*intr*) [1] to hold the position, responsibility, or function of an official. [2] to conduct a religious or other ceremony.
▷**HISTORY** C17: from Medieval Latin *officiāre,* from Latin *officium;* see OFFICE
▸**ofˌfici'ation** NOUN ▸**of'ficiˌator** NOUN

officinal (ɒ'fɪsɪnəl, ˌɒfɪ'saɪnəl) *Pharmacol, obsolete* ◆ ADJECTIVE [1] (of pharmaceutical products) available without prescription. [2] (of a plant) having pharmacological properties. ◆ NOUN [3] an officinal preparation or plant.
▷**HISTORY** C17: from Medieval Latin *officīnālis,* from Latin *officīna* workshop; see OFFICE
▸**of'ficinally** ADVERB

officious (ə'fɪʃəs) ADJECTIVE [1] unnecessarily or obtrusively ready to offer advice or services. [2] marked by such readiness. [3] *Diplomacy* informal or unofficial. [4] *Obsolete* attentive or obliging.
▷**HISTORY** C16: from Latin *officiōsus* kindly, from *officium* service; see OFFICE
▸**of'ficiously** ADVERB ▸**of'ficiousness** NOUN

offing ('ɒfɪŋ) NOUN [1] the part of the sea that can be seen from the shore. [2] **in the offing.** likely to occur soon.

offish ('ɒfɪʃ) ADJECTIVE *Informal* aloof or distant in manner.
▸**'offishly** ADVERB ▸**'offishness** NOUN

off key ADJECTIVE (**off-key** *when prenominal*), ADVERB [1] *Music* **a** not in the correct key. **b** out of tune. [2] out of keeping; discordant.

off-licence NOUN *Brit* [1] a shop, or a counter in a pub or hotel, where alcoholic drinks are sold for consumption elsewhere. US equivalents: **package store, liquor store.** [2] a licence permitting such sales.

off limits ADJECTIVE (**off-limits** *when prenominal*) [1] not to be entered; out of bounds. ◆ ADVERB [2] in or into an area forbidden by regulations.

off line ADJECTIVE (**off-line** *when prenominal*) [1] of, relating to, or concerned with a part of a computer system not connected to the central processing unit but controlled by a computer storage device. Compare **on line.** [2] disconnected from a computer; switched off. [3] extra to or not involving a continuous sequence of operations, such as a production line. [4] *Radio, television* (of processes, such as editing) not carried out on the actual transmission medium.

off-load VERB (*tr*) to get rid of (something unpleasant or burdensome), as by delegation to another.

off message ADJECTIVE (**off-message** *when prenominal*) not adhering to or reflecting the official line of a political party, government, or other organization.

off-off-Broadway ADJECTIVE of or relating to highly experimental informal small-scale theatrical productions in New York, usually taking place in cafés, small halls, etc. Compare **off-Broadway.**

off-peak ADJECTIVE of or relating to services as used outside periods of intensive use or electricity supplied at cheaper rates during the night.

off-piste ADJECTIVE of or relating to skiing on virgin snow off the regular runs.

off plan ADJECTIVE (**off-plan** *when prenominal*) (of a new building) considered with reference to its plans, before it has been built.

offprint ('ɒfˌprɪnt) NOUN [1] Also called (US): **separate.** a separate reprint of an article that originally appeared in a larger publication. ◆ VERB [2] (*tr*) to reprint (an article taken from a larger publication) separately.

off-putting ADJECTIVE *Brit informal* disconcerting or disturbing.

off-road ADJECTIVE (of a motor vehicle) designed or built for use away from public roads, esp. on rough terrain.

off-roader NOUN a motor vehicle designed for use away from public roads, esp. on rough terrain.

off-sales PLURAL NOUN *Brit* sales of alcoholic drink for consumption off the premises by a pub or an off-licence attached to a pub.

offscourings ('ɒfˌskaʊərɪŋz) PLURAL NOUN scum; dregs.

off season ADJECTIVE (**off-season** *when prenominal*) [1] denoting or occurring during a period of little activity in a trade or business. ◆ NOUN [2] such a period. ◆ ADVERB [3] in an off-season period.

offset NOUN ('ɒfˌsɛt). [1] something that counterbalances or compensates for something else. [2] an allowance made to counteract some effect. [3] **a** a printing method in which the impression is made onto an intermediate surface, such as a rubber blanket, which transfers it to the paper. **b** (*modifier*) relating to, involving, or printed by offset: *offset letterpress; offset lithography.* [4] another name for **set-off.** [5] *Botany* **a** a short runner in certain plants, such as the houseleek, that produces roots and shoots at the tip. **b** a plant produced from such a runner. [6] a ridge projecting from a range of hills or mountains. [7] the horizontal component of displacement on a fault. [8] a narrow horizontal or sloping surface formed where a wall is reduced in thickness towards the top. [9] a person or group descended collaterally from a particular group or family; offshoot. [10] *Surveying* a measurement of distance to a point at right angles to a survey line. ◆ VERB (ˌɒf'sɛt), **-sets, -setting, -set.** [11] (*tr*) to counterbalance or compensate for. [12] (*tr*) to print (pictures, text, etc.) using the offset process. [13] (*tr*) to construct an offset in (a wall). [14] (*intr*) to project or develop as an offset.

offshoot ('ɒfˌʃu:t) NOUN [1] a shoot or branch growing from the main stem of a plant. [2] something that develops or derives from a principal source or origin.

offshore (ˌɒf'ʃɔ:) ADJECTIVE, ADVERB [1] from, away from, or at some distance from the shore. [2] *NZ* overseas; abroad. ◆ ADJECTIVE [3] sited or conducted at sea as opposed to on land: *offshore industries.* [4] based or operating abroad in places where the tax system is more advantageous than that of the home country: *offshore banking; offshore fund.*

offside ('ɒf'saɪd) ADJECTIVE, ADVERB [1] *Sport* (in football, hockey, etc.) in a position illegally ahead of the ball or puck when it is played, usually when within one's opponents' half or the attacking zone. ◆ NOUN [2] (usually preceded by *the*) *Chiefly Brit* **a** the side of a vehicle nearest the centre of the road (in Britain, the right side). **b** (*as modifier*): *the offside passenger door.* ◆ Compare **nearside.**

offsider (ˌɒf'saɪdə) NOUN *Austral and NZ* a partner or assistant.

off-site ADJECTIVE, ADVERB away from the principal area of activity.

offspring ('ɒfˌsprɪŋ) NOUN [1] the immediate descendant or descendants of a person, animal, etc.; progeny. [2] a product, outcome, or result.

offstage ('ɒf'steɪdʒ) ADJECTIVE, ADVERB out of the view of the audience; off the stage.

off-street ADJECTIVE located away from a street: *off-street parking.*

off the record ADJECTIVE (**off-the-record** *when prenominal*) [1] not intended for publication or disclosure; confidential. ◆ ADVERB [2] with such an intention; unofficially.

off the shelf ADVERB [1] from stock and readily available: *you can have this model off the shelf.* ◆ ADJECTIVE (**off-the-shelf** *when prenominal*) [2] of or relating to a product that is readily available: *an off-the-shelf model.* [3] of or denoting a company that has been registered with the Registrar of Companies for the sole purpose of being sold.

off-the-wall ADJECTIVE (**off the wall** *when postpositive*) *Slang* new or unexpected in an unconventional or eccentric way: *an off-the-wall approach to humour.*
▷**HISTORY** C20: possibly from the use of the phrase in handball and squash to describe a shot that is unexpected

off-white NOUN [1] a colour, such as cream or bone, consisting of white mixed with a tinge of grey or with a pale hue. ◆ ADJECTIVE [2] of such a colour: *an off-white coat.*

off-year election NOUN (in the US) an election held in a year when a presidential election does not take place.

Ofgas ('ɒfˌgæs) NOUN (formerly, in Britain) ACRONYM FOR Office of Gas Supply: merged with Offer in 1999 to form Ofgem.

Ofgem ('ɒfˌdʒɛm) NOUN (in Britain) ACRONYM FOR Office of Gas and Electricity Markets: a government body set up in 1999 to monitor the activities of the power suppliers and to protect the interests of their customers.

oflag ('ɒf,lɑːg) NOUN a German prisoner-of-war camp for officers in World War II.
▷HISTORY German, short for *Offizierslager* officers' camp

Oflot ('ɒf,lɒt) NOUN (in Britain, formerly) ACRONYM FOR Office of the National Lottery, now superseded by the National Lottery Commission.

OFM ABBREVIATION FOR Ordo Fratrum Minorum (the Franciscans).
▷HISTORY Latin: Order of Minor Friars

OFris ABBREVIATION FOR Old Frisian.

OFS ABBREVIATION FOR (Orange) Free State.

Ofsted ('ɒf,stɛd) NOUN (in Britain) ACRONYM FOR Office for Standards in Education: a government body set up in 1993 to inspect and assess the educational standards of schools and colleges in England and Wales.

oft (ɒft) ADVERB short for **often** (archaic or poetic except in combinations such as **oft-repeated** and **oft-recurring**).
▷HISTORY Old English *oft;* related to Old High German *ofto*

OFT (in Britain) ABBREVIATION FOR Office of Fair Trading.

Oftel ('ɒf,tɛl) NOUN (in Britain) ACRONYM FOR Office of Telecommunications: a government body set up in 1984 to supervise telecommunications activities in the UK, and to protect the interests of the consumers.

often ('ɒfᵊn, 'ɒftᵊn) ADVERB 1 frequently or repeatedly; much of the time. Archaic equivalents: **oftentimes, ofttimes.** 2 **as often as not.** quite frequently. 3 **every so often.** at intervals. 4 **more often than not.** in more than half the instances. ◆ ADJECTIVE 5 *Archaic* repeated; frequent.
▷HISTORY C14: variant of OFT before vowels and *h*

Ofwat ('ɒf,wɒt) NOUN (in Britain) ACRONYM FOR Office of Water Services: a government body set up in 1989 to regulate the activities of the water companies in England and Wales, and to protect the interests of their consumers.

OG ABBREVIATION FOR: 1 officer of the guard. 2 Also: **o.g.** *Philately* original gum.

o.g. ABBREVIATION FOR own goal.

Ogaden (,ɒgə'dɛn) NOUN **the.** a region of SE Ethiopia, bordering on Somalia: consists of a desert plateau, inhabited by Somali nomads; a secessionist movement, supported by Somalia, has existed within the region since the early 1960s and led to bitter fighting between Ethiopia and Somalia (1977–78).

Ogasawara Gunto (,ɒgəsə'wɑːrə 'gʌntəʊ) NOUN transliteration of the Japanese name for the **Bonin Islands.**

Ogbomosho (,ɒgbə'məʊʃəʊ) NOUN a city in SW Nigeria: the third largest town in Nigeria; trading centre for an agricultural region. Pop.: 730 000 (1996 est.).

ogdoad ('ɒgdəʊ,æd) NOUN a group of eight.
▷HISTORY C17: via Late Latin from Greek *ogdoos* eighth, from *oktō* eight

ogee ('əʊdʒiː) NOUN *Architect* 1 Also called: **talon.** a moulding having a cross section in the form of a letter S. 2 short for **ogee arch.**
▷HISTORY C15: probably variant of OGIVE

ogee arch NOUN *Architect* a pointed arch having an S-shaped curve on both sides. Sometimes shortened to **ogee.** Also called: **keel arch.**

Ogen melon ('əʊgɛn) NOUN a variety of small melon having a green skin and sweet pale green flesh.
▷HISTORY C20: named after a kibbutz in Israel where it was first developed

ogham *or* **ogam** ('ɒgəm, ɔːm) NOUN an ancient alphabetical writing system used by the Celts in Britain and Ireland, consisting of straight lines drawn or carved perpendicular to or at an angle to another long straight line.
▷HISTORY C17: from Old Irish *ogom,* of uncertain origin but associated with the name *Ogma,* legendary inventor of this alphabet

ogive ('əʊdʒaɪv, əʊ'dʒaɪv) NOUN 1 a diagonal rib or groin of a Gothic vault. 2 another name for **lancet arch.** 3 *Statistics* a graph the ordinates of which represent cumulative frequencies of the values indicated by the corresponding abscissas. 4 the conical head of a missile or rocket that protects the payload during its passage through the atmosphere.
▷HISTORY C17: from Old French, of uncertain origin
▸**o'gival** ADJECTIVE

ogle ('əʊgᵊl) VERB 1 to look at (someone) amorously or lustfully. 2 (*tr*) to stare or gape at. ◆ NOUN 3 a flirtatious or lewd look.
▷HISTORY C17: probably from Low German *oegeln,* from *oegen* to look at
▸**'ogler** NOUN

Ogooué *or* **Ogowe** (ɒ'gəʊweɪ) NOUN a river in W central Africa, rising in SW Congo-Brazzaville and flowing generally northwest and north through Gabon to the Atlantic. Length: about 970 km (683 miles).

Ogopogo (,əʊgəʊ'pəʊgəʊ) NOUN an aquatic monster said to live in Okanagan Lake in British Columbia, Canada.
▷HISTORY apparently an arbitrary coinage

Ogpu ('ɒgpuː) NOUN the Soviet police and secret police from 1923 to 1934.
▷HISTORY C20: from Russian *O(byedinyonnoye) g(osudarstvennoye) p(oliticheskoye) u(pravleniye)* United State Political Administration

O grade NOUN (formerly, in Scotland) 1 **a** the basic level of the Scottish Certificate of Education, now replaced by **Standard Grade. b** (*as modifier*): *O grade history.* 2 a pass in a particular subject at O grade: *she has ten O grades.* ◆ Formal name: **Ordinary grade.**

ogre ('əʊgə) NOUN 1 (in folklore) a giant, usually given to eating human flesh. 2 any monstrous or cruel person.
▷HISTORY C18: from French, perhaps from Latin *Orcus* god of the infernal regions
▸**'ogreish** ADJECTIVE ▸**'ogress** FEMININE NOUN

Ogun (əʊ'gʊn) NOUN a state of SW Nigeria, formed in 1976 from part of Western State. Capital: Abeokuta. Pop.: 2 614 747 (1995 est.). Area: 16 762 sq. km (6472 sq. miles).

Ogygian (əʊ'dʒɪdʒɪən) ADJECTIVE of very great age; prehistoric.
▷HISTORY C19: from Greek *ōgugios* relating to *Ogyges,* the most ancient king of Greece, mythical ruler of Boeotia or Attica

oh (əʊ) INTERJECTION 1 an exclamation expressive of surprise, pain, pleasure, etc. ◆ SENTENCE CONNECTOR 2 an expression used to preface a remark, gain time, etc.: *oh, I suppose so.*

OH ABBREVIATION FOR Ohio.

OHG ABBREVIATION FOR Old High German.

Ohio (əʊ'haɪəʊ) NOUN 1 a state of the central US, in the Midwest on Lake Erie: consists of prairies in the W and the Allegheny plateau in the E, the Ohio River forming the S and most of the E borders. Capital: Columbus. Pop.: 11 353 140 (2000). Area: 107 044 sq. km (41 330 sq. miles). Abbreviation and zip code: **OH.** 2 a river in the eastern US, formed by the confluence of the Allegheny and Monongahela Rivers at Pittsburgh: flows generally W and SW to join the Mississippi at Cairo, Illinois, as its chief E tributary. Length: 1570 km (975 miles).

ohm (əʊm) NOUN the derived SI unit of electrical resistance; the resistance between two points on a conductor when a constant potential difference of 1 volt between them produces a current of 1 ampere. Symbol: Ω.
▷HISTORY C19: named after Georg Simon *Ohm* (1787–1854), German physicist

ohmage ('əʊmɪdʒ) NOUN electrical resistance in ohms.

ohmic ('əʊmɪk) ADJECTIVE of or relating to a circuit element, the electrical resistance of which obeys Ohm's law.

ohmmeter ('əʊm,miːtə) NOUN an instrument for measuring electrical resistance.

OHMS (in Britain and the dominions of the Commonwealth) ABBREVIATION FOR On Her (*or* His) Majesty's Service.

Ohm's law NOUN the principle that the electric current passing through a conductor is directly proportional to the potential difference across it, provided that the temperature remains constant. The constant of proportionality is the resistance of the conductor.
▷HISTORY C19: named after Georg Simon *Ohm* (1787–1854), German physicist

oho (əʊ'həʊ) INTERJECTION an exclamation expressing surprise, exultation, or derision.

ohv ABBREVIATION FOR overhead valve.

OIC *Text messaging* ABBREVIATION FOR oh I see.

-oid SUFFIX FORMING ADJECTIVES AND ASSOCIATED NOUNS indicating likeness, resemblance, or similarity: *anthropoid.*
▷HISTORY from Greek *-oeidēs* resembling, form of, from *eidos* form

-oidea SUFFIX FORMING PLURAL PROPER NOUNS forming the names of zoological classes or superfamilies: *Crinoidea; Canoidea.*
▷HISTORY from New Latin, from Latin *-oīdēs* -OID

oidium (əʊ'ɪdɪəm) NOUN, *plural* **-ia** (-ɪə). *Botany* any of various fungal spores produced in the form of a chain by the development of septa in a hypha.
▷HISTORY New Latin: from OO- + *-idium* diminutive suffix

oik (ɔɪk) NOUN *Brit, derogatory, slang* a person regarded as inferior because ignorant, ill-educated, or lower-class.

oil (ɔɪl) NOUN 1 any of a number of viscous liquids with a smooth sticky feel. They are usually flammable, insoluble in water, soluble in organic solvents, and are obtained from plants and animals, from mineral deposits, and by synthesis. They are used as lubricants, fuels, perfumes, foodstuffs, and raw materials for chemicals. See also **essential oil, fixed oil.** 2 **a** another name for **petroleum. b** (*as modifier*): *an oil engine; an oil rig.* 3 **a** Also called: **lubricating oil.** any of a number of substances usually derived from petroleum and used for lubrication. **b** (*in combination*): *an oilcan; an oilstone.* **c** (*as modifier*): *an oil pump.* 4 Also called: **fuel oil.** a petroleum product used as a fuel in domestic heating, industrial furnaces, marine engines, etc. 5 *Brit* **a** paraffin, esp. when used as a domestic fuel. **b** (*as modifier*): *an oil lamp; an oil stove.* 6 any substance of a consistency resembling that of oil: *oil of vitriol.* 7 the solvent, usually linseed oil, with which pigments are mixed to make artists' paints. 8 **a** (*often plural*) oil colour or paint. **b** (*as modifier*): *an oil painting.* 9 an oil painting. 10 **the good (dinkum) oil.** *Austral and NZ, slang* facts or news. 11 **strike oil. a** to discover petroleum while drilling for it. **b** *Informal* to become very rich or successful. ◆ VERB (*tr*) 12 to lubricate, smear, polish, etc., with oil or an oily substance. 13 *Informal* to bribe (esp. in the phrase **oil someone's palm**). 14 **oil the wheels.** to make things run smoothly. 15 See **well-oiled.**
▷HISTORY C12: from Old French *oile,* from Latin *oleum* (olive) oil, from *olea* olive tree, from Greek *elaia* OLIVE
▸**'oil-,like** ADJECTIVE

oil beetle NOUN any of various beetles of the family *Meloidae* that exude an oily evil-smelling blood from their joints, which deters enemies.

oilbird ('ɔɪl,bɜːd) NOUN a nocturnal gregarious cave-dwelling bird, *Steatornis caripensis,* of N South America and Trinidad, having a hooked bill and dark plumage: family *Steatornithidae,* order *Caprimulgiformes.* Also called: **guacharo.**

oil cake NOUN stock feed consisting of compressed cubes made from the residue of the crushed seeds of oil-bearing crops such as linseed.

oilcan ('ɔɪl,kæn) NOUN a container with a long nozzle for applying lubricating oil to machinery.

oilcloth ('ɔɪl,klɒθ) NOUN 1 waterproof material made by treating one side of a cotton fabric with a drying oil, or a synthetic resin. 2 another name for **linoleum.**

oil-cooled ADJECTIVE *Engineering* (of an engine, apparatus, etc.) having its heat removed by the circulation of oil.
▸**oil cooler** NOUN

oilcup ('ɔɪl,kʌp) NOUN a cup-shaped oil reservoir in a machine providing continuous lubrication for a bearing.

oil drum NOUN a metal drum used to contain or transport oil.

oiled silk NOUN silk treated with oil to make it waterproof.

oiler ('ɔɪlə) NOUN 1 a person, device, etc., that

lubricates or supplies oil. 2 an oil tanker. 3 an oil well.

oilfield ('ɔɪl,fiːld) NOUN an area containing reserves of petroleum, esp. one that is already being exploited.

oilfired ('ɔɪl,faɪəd) ADJECTIVE (of central heating) using oil as fuel.

oilgas ('ɔɪl,gæs) NOUN a gaseous mixture of hydrocarbons used as a fuel, obtained by the destructive distillation of mineral oils.

oil hardening NOUN a process of hardening high-carbon or alloy steels by heating and cooling in oil. Compare **air hardening.**

oilman ('ɔɪlmən) NOUN, *plural* **-men.** 1 a person who owns or operates oil wells. 2 a person who makes or sells oil.

oil of turpentine NOUN another name for **turpentine** (sense 3).

oil of vitriol NOUN another name for **sulphuric acid.**

oil paint *or* **colour** NOUN paint made of pigment ground in oil, usually linseed oil, used for oil painting.

oil painting NOUN 1 a picture painted with oil paints. 2 the art or process of painting with oil paints. 3 **he's** *or* **she's no oil painting.** *Informal* he or she is not good-looking.

oil palm NOUN a tropical African palm tree, *Elaeis guineensis,* the fruits of which yield palm oil.

oil rig NOUN See **rig** (sense 6).

Oil Rivers PLURAL NOUN the delta of the Niger River in S Nigeria.

oil sand NOUN a sandstone impregnated with hydrocarbons, esp. such deposits in Alberta, Canada.

oil-seed rape NOUN another name for **rape**[2].

oil shale NOUN a fine-grained shale containing oil, which can be extracted by heating.

oilskin ('ɔɪl,skɪn) NOUN 1 **a** a cotton fabric treated with oil and pigment to make it waterproof. **b** (*as modifier*): *an oilskin hat.* 2 (*often plural*) a protective outer garment of this fabric.

oil slick NOUN a mass of floating oil covering an area of water, esp. oil that has leaked or been discharged from a ship.

oilstone ('ɔɪl,stəʊn) NOUN a stone with a fine grain lubricated with oil and used for sharpening cutting tools. See also **whetstone.**

oil varnish NOUN another name for **varnish** (sense 1).

oil well NOUN a boring into the earth or sea bed for the extraction of petroleum.

oily ('ɔɪlɪ) ADJECTIVE **oilier, oiliest.** 1 soaked in or smeared with oil or grease. 2 consisting of, containing, or resembling oil. 3 flatteringly servile or obsequious.
▸ **'oilily** ADVERB ▸ **'oiliness** NOUN

oink (ɔɪŋk) INTERJECTION an imitation or representation of the grunt of a pig.

ointment ('ɔɪntmənt) NOUN 1 a fatty or oily medicated formulation applied to the skin to heal or protect. 2 a similar substance used as a cosmetic.
▷ HISTORY C14: from Old French *oignement,* from Latin *unguentum* UNGUENT

Oireachtas ('ɛrəkθəs; *Gaelic* 'ɛrəxtəs) NOUN the parliament of the Republic of Ireland, consisting of the president, the Dáil Éireann, and the Seanad Éireann. See also **Dáil Éireann, Seanad Éireann.**
▷ HISTORY Irish: assembly, from Old Irish *airech* nobleman

Oise (*French* waz) NOUN 1 a department of N France, in Picardy region. Capital: Beauvais. Pop.: 766 441 (1999). Area: 5887 sq. km (2296 sq. miles). 2 a river in N France, rising in Belgium, in the Ardennes, and flowing southwest to join the Seine at Conflans. Length: 302 km (188 miles).

Oita ('ɔɪtə) NOUN an industrial city in SW Japan, on NE Kyushu: dominated most of Kyushu in the 16th century. Pop.: 426 981 (1995).

OJ ABBREVIATION FOR Order of Jamaica.

Ojibwa (əʊ'dʒɪbwə) NOUN 1 (*plural* **-was** *or* **-wa**) a member of a North American Indian people living in a region west of Lake Superior. 2 the language of this people, belonging to the Algonquian family. ◆ Also called: **Chippewa.**

OK ABBREVIATION FOR Oklahoma.

O.K. (,əʊ'keɪ) *Informal* ◆ SENTENCE SUBSTITUTE 1 an expression of approval, agreement, etc. ◆ ADJECTIVE (*usually postpositive*), ADVERB 2 in good or satisfactory condition. ◆ VERB **O.K.s, O.K.ing** (,əʊ'keɪɪŋ), **O.K.ed** (,əʊ'keɪd). 3 (*tr*) to approve or endorse. ◆ NOUN, *plural* **O.K.s.** 4 approval or agreement. ◆ Also: **OK, o.k., okay.**
▷ HISTORY C19: perhaps from *o(ll) k(orrect),* jocular alteration of *all correct*

oka ('əʊkə) *or* **oke** (əʊk) NOUN 1 a unit of weight used in Turkey, equal to about 2.75 pounds or 1.24 kilograms. 2 a unit of liquid measure used in Turkey, equal to about 1.3 pints or 0.75 litres.
▷ HISTORY C17: from Turkish *ōqah,* from Arabic *ūqiyah,* probably from Greek *ounkia;* perhaps related to Latin *uncia* one twelfth; see OUNCE[1]

Oka ('əʊkə) NOUN a brine-cured Canadian cheese.
▷ HISTORY named after *Oka,* Quebec, where it is made at a monastery

Okanagan (,əʊkə'nɑːgən) NOUN 1 Also (US): **Okanogan.** a river in North America that flows south from Okanagan Lake in Canada into the Columbia River in NE Washington, US. Length: about 483 km (300 miles). 2 Also: **Okanogan, Okinagan.** a member of a North American Indian people living in the Okanagan River valley in British Columbia and Washington. 3 Also: **Okanogan, Okinagan.** the language of this people, belonging to the Salish family.

Okanagan Lake NOUN a lake in SW Canada, in S British Columbia: drained by the Okanagan River into the Columbia River. Length: about 111 km (69 miles). Width: from 3.2–6.4 km (2–4 miles).

okapi (əʊ'kɑːpɪ) NOUN, *plural* **-pis** *or* **-pi.** a ruminant mammal, *Okapia johnstoni,* of the forests of central Africa, having a reddish-brown coat with horizontal white stripes on the legs and small horns: family *Giraffidae.*
▷ HISTORY C20: from a Central African word

Okavango *or* **Okovango** (,əʊkə'vɑːŋgəʊ) NOUN a river in SW central Africa, rising in central Angola and flowing southeast, then east as part of the border between Angola and Namibia, then southeast across the Caprivi Strip into Botswana to form a great marsh known as the **Okavango Basin.** Length: about 1600 km (1000 miles).

okay (,əʊ'keɪ) SENTENCE SUBSTITUTE, ADJECTIVE, VERB, NOUN a variant of **O.K.**

Okayama (,ɒkə'jɑːmə) NOUN a city in SW Japan, on W Honshu on the Inland Sea. Pop.: 616 056 (1995).

oke[1] (əʊk) NOUN another name for **oka.**

oke[2] (əʊk) ADJECTIVE, ADVERB *Informal* another term for **O.K.**

oke[3] (əʊk) NOUN *South African* an informal word for **man.**
▷ HISTORY from Afrikaans

Okeechobee (,əʊkɪ'tʃəʊbɪ) NOUN **Lake.** a lake in S Florida, in the Everglades: second largest freshwater lake wholly within the US. Area: 1813 sq. km (700 sq. miles).

Okefenokee Swamp (,əʊkɪfɪ'nəʊkɪ) NOUN a swamp in the US, in SE Georgia and N Florida: protected flora and fauna. Area: 1554 sq. km (600 sq. miles).

okey-doke ('əʊkɪ'dəʊk) *or* **okey-dokey** ('əʊkɪ'dəʊkɪ) SENTENCE SUBSTITUTE, ADJECTIVE, ADVERB *Informal* another term for **O.K.**

Okhotsk ('əʊkɒtsk; *Russian* a'xɔtsk) NOUN **Sea of.** part of the NW Pacific, surrounded by the Kamchatka Peninsula, the Kurile Islands, Sakhalin Island, and the E coast of Siberia. Area: 1 589 840 sq. km (613 838 sq. miles).

Okie ('əʊkɪ) NOUN *US, slang, sometimes considered offensive* 1 an inhabitant of Oklahoma. 2 an impoverished migrant farm worker, esp. one who left Oklahoma during the Depression of the 1930s to work elsewhere in the US.

Okinawa (,əʊkɪ'nɑːwə) NOUN a coral island of SW Japan, the largest of the Ryukyu Islands in the N Pacific: scene of heavy fighting in World War II; administered by the US (1945–72); agricultural. Chief town: Naha City. Pop.: 1 273 508 (1995). Area: 1176 sq. km (454 sq. miles).

Okla. ABBREVIATION FOR Oklahoma.

Oklahoma (,əʊklə'həʊmə) NOUN a state in the S central US: consists of plains in the west, rising to mountains in the southwest and east; important for oil. Capital: Oklahoma City. Pop.: 3 450 654 (2000). Area: 181 185 sq. km (69 956 sq. miles). Abbreviations: **Okla.,** (with zip code) **OK.**

Oklahoma City NOUN a city in central Oklahoma: the state capital and a major agricultural and industrial centre. Pop.: 506 132 (2000).

Oklahoman (,əʊklə'həʊmən) NOUN 1 a native or inhabitant of Oklahoma. ◆ ADJECTIVE 2 of or relating to Oklahoma or its inhabitants.

Okovango (,əʊkə'vɑːŋgəʊ) NOUN a variant spelling of **Okavango.**

okra ('əʊkrə) NOUN 1 Also called: **ladies' fingers.** an annual malvaceous plant, *Hibiscus esculentus,* of the Old World tropics, with yellow-and-red flowers and edible oblong sticky green pods. 2 the pod of this plant, eaten in soups, stews, etc. See also **gumbo** (sense 1).
▷ HISTORY C18: of W African origin

okta *or* **octa** ('ɒktə) NOUN a unit used in meteorology to measure cloud cover, equivalent to a cloud cover of one eighth of the sky.
▷ HISTORY C20: from Greek *okta-, oktō* eight

-ol[1] SUFFIX FORMING NOUNS denoting an organic chemical compound containing a hydroxyl group, esp. alcohols and phenols: *ethanol; quinol.*
▷ HISTORY from ALCOHOL

-ol[2] NOUN COMBINING FORM (*not used systematically*) a variant of **-ole**[1].

Öland (*Swedish* 'øːland) NOUN an island in the Baltic Sea, separated from the mainland of SE Sweden by Kalmar Sound: the second largest Swedish island. Chief town: Borgholm. Pop.: 24 100 (latest est.). Area: 1347 sq. km (520 sq. miles).

old (əʊld) ADJECTIVE 1 having lived or existed for a relatively long time: *an old man; an old tradition; old wine; an old house; an old country.* 2 **a** of or relating to advanced years or a long life: *old age.* **b** (*as collective noun;* preceded by *the*): *the old.* **c old and young.** people of all ages. 3 decrepit or senile. 4 worn with age or use: *old clothes; an old car.* 5 **a** (*postpositive*) having lived or existed for a specified period: *a child who is six years old.* **b** (*in combination*): *a six-year-old child.* **c** (*as noun in combination*): *a six-year-old.* 6 (*capital when part of a name or title*) earlier or earliest of two or more things with the same name: *the old edition; the Old Testament; old Norwich.* 7 (*capital when part of a name*) designating the form of a language in which the earliest known records are written: *Old English.* 8 (*prenominal*) familiar through long acquaintance or repetition: *an old friend; an old excuse.* 9 practised; hardened: *old in cunning.* 10 (*prenominal;* often preceded by *good*) cherished; dear: used as a term of affection or familiarity: *good old George.* 11 *Informal* (with any of several nouns) used as a familiar form of address to a person: *old thing; old bean; old stick; old fellow.* 12 skilled through long experience (esp. in the phrase **an old hand**). 13 out-of-date; unfashionable. 14 remote or distant in origin or time of origin: *an old culture.* 15 (*prenominal*) former; previous: *my old house was small.* 16 **a** (*prenominal*) established for a relatively long time: *an old member.* **b** (*in combination*): *old-established.* 17 sensible, wise, or mature: *old beyond one's years.* 18 (of a river, valley, or land surface) in the final stage of the cycle of erosion, characterized by flat extensive flood plains and minimum relief. See also **youthful** (sense 4), **mature** (sense 6). 19 (intensifier) (esp. in phrases such as **a good old time, any old thing, any old how,** etc.). 20 (of crops) harvested late. 21 **good old days.** an earlier period of time regarded as better than the present. 22 **little old.** *Informal* indicating affection, esp. humorous affection: *my little old wife.* 23 **the old one** (*or* **gentleman**). *Informal* a jocular name for **Satan.** ◆ NOUN 24 an earlier or past time (esp. in the phrase **of old**): *in days of old.*
▷ HISTORY Old English *eald;* related to Old Saxon *ald,* Old High German, German *alt,* Latin *altus* high
▸ **'oldish** ADJECTIVE ▸ **'oldness** NOUN

old age pension NOUN a former name for the state **retirement pension.**
▸ **old age pensioner** NOUN

Old Bailey NOUN the chief court exercising criminal jurisdiction in London; the Central Criminal Court of England.

Old Bill NOUN *Brit, slang* 1 a policeman. 2 (*functioning as plural;* preceded by *the*) policemen collectively or in general.
▷HISTORY C20: of uncertain origin: perhaps derived from the World War I cartoon of a soldier with a drooping moustache

old bird NOUN *Jocular* a wary and astute person.

old boy NOUN 1 (*sometimes capitals*) *Brit* a male ex-pupil of a school. 2 *Informal, chiefly Brit* **a** a familiar name used to refer to a man. **b** an old man.

old boy network NOUN *Brit informal* the appointment to power of former pupils of the same small group of public schools or universities.

Old Bulgarian NOUN another name for **Old Church Slavonic.**

Old Castile NOUN a region of N Spain, on the Bay of Biscay: formerly a province. Spanish name: **Castilla la Vieja.**

Old Catholic ADJECTIVE 1 of or relating to several small national Churches which have broken away from the Roman Catholic Church on matters of doctrine. ◆ NOUN 2 a member of one of these Churches.

old chum NOUN *Austral informal* (formerly) 1 a person who is experienced, esp. in life in colonial Australia. 2 an experienced convict.

Old Church Slavonic *or* **Slavic** NOUN the oldest recorded Slavonic language: the form of Old Slavonic into which the Bible was translated in the ninth century, preserved as a liturgical language of various Orthodox Churches: belonging to the South Slavonic subbranch of languages.

old clothes man NOUN a person who deals in second-hand clothes.

Old Contemptibles PLURAL NOUN the British expeditionary force to France in 1914.
▷HISTORY so named from the Kaiser's alleged reference to them as a "contemptible little army"

old country NOUN the country of origin of an immigrant or an immigrant's ancestors.

Old Dart NOUN **the.** *Austral, slang* England.
▷HISTORY C19: of unknown origin

Old Delhi NOUN See **Delhi.**

Old Dutch NOUN the Dutch language up to about 1100, derived from the Low Franconian dialect of Old Low German. See also **Franconian.** Abbreviation: **OD.**

olden ('əʊldᵊn) ADJECTIVE an archaic or poetic word for **old** (often in phrases such as **in olden days** and **in olden times**).

Oldenburg ('əʊldᵊn,bɜːg; *German* 'ɔldənburk) NOUN 1 a city in NW Germany, in Lower Saxony: former capital of Oldenburg state. Pop.: 154 100 (1999 est.). 2 a former state of NW Germany: became part of Lower Saxony in 1946.

Old English NOUN 1 Also called: **Anglo-Saxon.** the English language from the time of the earliest settlements in the fifth century A.D. to about 1100. The main dialects were West Saxon (the chief literary form), Kentish, and Anglian. Compare **Middle English, Modern English.** Abbreviation: **OE.** 2 *Printing* a Gothic typeface commonly used in England up until the 18th century.

Old English sheepdog NOUN a breed of large bobtailed sheepdog with a profuse shaggy coat.

older ('əʊldə) ADJECTIVE 1 the comparative of **old.** 2 Also (of people, esp members of the same family): **elder.** having lived or existed longer; of greater age.

old-established ADJECTIVE established for a long time.

olde-worlde ('əʊldɪ'wɜːldɪ) ADJECTIVE *Sometimes facetious* old-world or quaint.

old face NOUN *Printing* a type style that originated in the 18th century, characterized by little contrast between thick and thin strokes. Compare **modern** (sense 5).

oldfangled ('əʊld'fæŋgᵊld) ADJECTIVE *Derogatory* out-of-date; old-fashioned.
▷HISTORY C20: formed on analogy with NEWFANGLED

old-fashioned ADJECTIVE 1 belonging to, characteristic of, or favoured by former times; outdated: *old-fashioned ideas.* 2 favouring or adopting the dress, manners, fashions, etc., of a former time. 3 quizzically doubtful or disapproving: *she did not reply, but gave him an old-fashioned look.* 4 *Scot and northern English, dialect* old for one's age: *an old-fashioned child.* ◆ NOUN 5 a cocktail containing spirit, bitters, fruit, etc.
▸,**old-'fashionedly** ADVERB

Old French NOUN the French language in its earliest forms, from about the 9th century up to about 1400. Abbreviation: **OF.**

Old Frisian NOUN the Frisian language up to about 1400. Abbreviation: **OFris.**

old girl NOUN 1 (*sometimes capitals*) *Brit* a female ex-pupil of a school. 2 *Informal chiefly Brit* **a** a familiar name used to refer to a woman. **b** an old woman.

Old Glory NOUN a nickname for the flag of the United States of America.

old gold NOUN **a** a dark yellow colour, sometimes with a brownish tinge. **b** (*as adjective*): *an old-gold carpet.*

old guard NOUN 1 a group that works for a long-established or old-fashioned cause or principle. 2 the conservative element in a political party or other group.
▷HISTORY C19: from OLD GUARD

Old Guard NOUN the French imperial guard created by Napoleon in 1804.

Oldham ('əʊldəm) NOUN 1 a town in NW England, in Oldham unitary authority, Greater Manchester. Pop.: 103 931 (1991). 2 a unitary authority in NW England, in Greater Manchester. Pop.: 217 393 (2001). Area: 141 sq. km (54 sq. miles).

old hand NOUN 1 a person who is skilled at something through long experience. 2 *Austral informal* (in the nineteenth century) an ex-convict. 3 *Austral informal* a person who is long established in a place.

Old Harry NOUN *Informal* a jocular name for **Satan.**

old hat ADJECTIVE (*postpositive*) old-fashioned or trite.

Old High German NOUN a group of West Germanic dialects that eventually developed into modern German; High German up to about 1200: spoken in the Middle Ages on the upper Rhine, in Bavaria, Alsace, and elsewhere, including Alemannic, Bavarian, Langobardic, and Upper Franconian. Abbreviation: **OHG.**

Old Icelandic NOUN the dialect of Old Norse spoken and written in Iceland; the Icelandic language up to about 1600.

old identity NOUN *NZ* a person known for a long time in the one locality.

oldie ('əʊldɪ) NOUN *Informal* an old person or thing.

Old Irish NOUN the Celtic language of Ireland up to about 900 A.D., introduced to Scotland by Irish settlers about 500 A.D.

Old Kingdom NOUN a period of Egyptian history: usually considered to extend from the third to the sixth dynasty (?2700–?2150 B.C.).

old lady NOUN 1 an informal term for **mother**[1] or **wife** (sense 1). 2 a large noctuid moth, *Mormo maura,* that has drab patterned wings originally thought to resemble an elderly Victorian lady's shawl.

Old Latin NOUN the Latin language before the classical period, up to about 100 B.C.

old-line ADJECTIVE 1 *US and Canadian* conservative; old-fashioned. 2 well-established; traditional.
▸,**old-'liner** NOUN

Old Low German NOUN the Saxon and Low Franconian dialects of German up to about 1200; the old form of modern Low German and Dutch. Abbreviation: **OLG.**

old maid NOUN 1 a woman regarded as unlikely ever to marry; spinster. 2 *Informal* a prim, fastidious, or excessively cautious person. 3 a card game using a pack from which one card has been removed, in which players try to avoid holding the unpaired card at the end of the game.
▸,**old-'maidish** ADJECTIVE

old man NOUN 1 an informal term for **father** or **husband** (sense 1). 2 (*sometimes capitals*) *Informal* a man in command, such as an employer, foreman, or captain of a ship. 3 *Sometimes facetious* an affectionate term used in addressing a man. 4 another name for **southernwood.** 5 *Austral informal* **a** an adult male kangaroo. **b** (*as modifier*) very large. 6 *Christianity* the unregenerate aspect of human nature.

old man's beard NOUN any of various plants having a white feathery appearance, esp. traveller's joy and Spanish moss.

old master NOUN 1 one of the great European painters of the period 1500 to 1800. 2 a painting by one of these.

old media NOUN **a** the media in existence before the arrival of the Internet, such as newspapers, books, television, and cinema. **b** (*as modifier*): *Warner's vast old-media holdings.* Compare **new media.**

old moon NOUN 1 a phase of the moon lying between last quarter and new moon, when it appears as a waning crescent. 2 the moon when it appears as a waning crescent. 3 the time at which this occurs.

Old Nick NOUN *Informal* a jocular name for **Satan.**

Old Norse NOUN the language or group of dialects of medieval Scandinavia and Iceland from about 700 to about 1350, forming the North Germanic branch of the Indo-European family of languages. See also **Proto-Norse, Old Icelandic.** Abbreviation: **ON.**

Old North French NOUN any of the dialects of Old French spoken in N France, such as Norman French.

Old Northwest NOUN (in the early US) the land between the Great Lakes, the Mississippi, and the Ohio River. Awarded to the US in 1783, it was organized into the **Northwest Territory** in 1787 and now forms the states of Ohio, Indiana, Illinois, Wisconsin, Michigan, and part of Minnesota.

Old Persian NOUN an ancient language belonging to the West Iranian branch of the Indo-European family, recorded in cuneiform inscriptions of the 6th to the 4th centuries B.C. See also **Middle Persian.**

Old Prussian NOUN the former language of the non-German Prussians, belonging to the Baltic branch of the Indo-European family: extinct by 1700.

Old Red Sandstone NOUN 1 a thick sequence of sedimentary rock (generally, but not always, red) deposited in Britain and NW Europe during the Devonian period. 2 (in Britain) another term for **Devonian.** ◆ Abbreviation: **ORS.**

old rose NOUN **a** a greyish-pink colour. **b** (*as adjective*): *old-rose gloves.*

Old Saxon NOUN the Saxon dialect of Low German up to about 1200, from which modern Low German is derived. Abbreviation: **OS.**

old school NOUN 1 *Chiefly Brit* a school formerly attended by a person. 2 a group of people favouring traditional ideas or conservative practices.

old school tie NOUN 1 *Brit* a distinctive tie that indicates which school the wearer attended. 2 the attitudes, loyalties, values, etc., associated with British public schools.

old skool NOUN **a** the hip-hop music of the 1980s or modern music imitating this style. **b** (*as modifier*): *old-skool hip-hop.*
▷HISTORY C20: *skool* is a phonetic rendering of SCHOOL

Old Slavonic *or* **Slavic** NOUN the South Slavonic language up to about 1400: the language of the Macedonian Slavs that developed into Serbo-Croat and Bulgarian. See also **Old Church Slavonic.**

old sod NOUN *Informal* one's native country: *back to the old sod.*

old soldier NOUN 1 a former soldier or veteran. 2 an experienced or practised person.

Old South NOUN the American South before the Civil War.

old squaw NOUN *US and Canadian* a long-tailed northern sea duck, *Clangula hyemalis,* having dark wings and a white-and-brown head and body. Also called: **oldwife.**

old stager NOUN a person with experience; old hand.

oldster ('əʊldstə) NOUN 1 *Informal* an older

person. 2 *Brit Navy* a person who has been a midshipman for four years.

Old Stone Age NOUN (*not now in technical usage*) another term for **Palaeolithic.**

old style NOUN *Printing* a type style reviving the characteristics of old face.

Old Style NOUN the former method of reckoning dates using the Julian calendar. Compare **New Style.**

old sweat NOUN *Brit informal* 1 an old soldier; veteran. 2 a person who has a great deal of experience in some activity.

old talk *Caribbean* ◆ NOUN 1 superficial chatting. ◆ VERB **old-talk.** 2 (*intr*) to indulge in such chatting.

Old Test. ABBREVIATION FOR Old Testament.

Old Testament NOUN the collection of books comprising the sacred Scriptures of the Hebrews and essentially recording the history of the Hebrew people as the chosen people of God; the first part of the Christian Bible.

old-time ADJECTIVE (*prenominal*) of or relating to a former time; old-fashioned: *old-time dancing.*

old-time dance NOUN *Brit* a formal or formation dance, such as the lancers.
▸**old-time dancing** NOUN

old-timer NOUN 1 a person who has been in a certain place, occupation, etc., for a long time. 2 *US* an old man.

Olduvai Gorge ('ɒldʊˌvaɪ) NOUN a gorge in N Tanzania, north of the Ngorongoro Crater: fossil evidence of early man and other closely related species, together with artefacts.

oldwife ('əʊldˌwaɪf) NOUN, *plural* **-wives.** 1 another name for **old squaw.** 2 any of various fishes, esp. the menhaden or the alewife.

old wives' tale NOUN a belief, usually superstitious or erroneous, passed on by word of mouth as a piece of traditional wisdom.

old woman NOUN 1 an informal term for **mother**[1] or **wife** (sense 1). 2 a timid, fussy, or cautious person.
▸ˌ**old-'womanish** ADJECTIVE

Old World NOUN that part of the world that was known before the discovery of the Americas, comprising Europe, Asia, and Africa; the eastern hemisphere.

old-world ADJECTIVE of or characteristic of former times, esp., in Europe, quaint or traditional.
▸ˌ**old-'worldly** ADVERB

Old World monkey NOUN any monkey of the family *Cercopithecidae,* including macaques, baboons, and mandrills. They are more closely related to anthropoid apes than are the New World monkeys, having nostrils that are close together and nonprehensile tails. Compare **New World monkey.**

olé (əʊ'leɪ) INTERJECTION 1 an exclamation of approval or encouragement customary at bullfights, flamenco dancing, and other Spanish or Latin American events. ◆ NOUN 2 a cry of olé.
▷**HISTORY** Spanish, from Arabic *wa-llāh,* from *wa* and + *allāh* God

-ole[1] *or* **-ol** NOUN COMBINING FORM 1 denoting an organic unsaturated compound containing a 5-membered ring: *thiazole.* 2 denoting an aromatic organic ether: *anisole.*
▷**HISTORY** from Latin *oleum* oil, from Greek *elaion,* from *elaia* olive

-ole[2] SUFFIX OF NOUNS indicating something small: *arteriole.*
▷**HISTORY** from Latin *-olus,* diminutive suffix

olea ('əʊlɪə) NOUN a plural of **oleum.**

oleaceous (ˌəʊlɪ'eɪʃəs) ADJECTIVE of, relating to, or belonging to the *Oleaceae,* a family of trees and shrubs, including the ash, jasmine, privet, lilac, and olive.
▷**HISTORY** C19: via New Latin from Latin *olea* OLIVE; see also OIL

oleaginous (ˌəʊlɪ'ædʒɪnəs) ADJECTIVE 1 resembling or having the properties of oil. 2 containing or producing oil.
▷**HISTORY** C17: from Latin *oleāginus,* from *olea* OLIVE; see also OIL

oleander (ˌəʊlɪ'ændə) NOUN a poisonous evergreen Mediterranean apocynaceous shrub or tree, *Nerium oleander,* with fragrant white, pink, or purple flowers. Also called: **rosebay.**
▷**HISTORY** C16: from Medieval Latin, variant of *arodandrum,* perhaps from Latin RHODODENDRON

olearia (ˌɒlɪ'ɛərɪə) NOUN *Austral* another word for **daisy bush.**

oleaster (ˌəʊlɪ'æstə) NOUN 1 any of several shrubs of the genus *Elaeagnus,* esp. *E. angustifolia,* of S Europe, Asia, and North America, having silver-white twigs, yellow flowers, and an olive-like fruit: family *Elaeagnaceae.* 2 Also called: **wild olive.** a wild specimen of the cultivated olive.
▷**HISTORY** Latin: from *olea;* see OLIVE, OIL

oleate ('əʊlɪˌeɪt) NOUN any salt or ester of oleic acid, containing the ion $C_{17}H_{33}COO^-$ or the group $C_{17}H_{33}COO$-: common components of natural fats.

olecranon (əʊ'lɛkrəˌnɒn, ˌəʊlɪ'kreɪnən) NOUN *Anatomy* the bony projection of the ulna behind the elbow joint.
▷**HISTORY** C18: from Greek, shortened from *ōlenokrānon,* from *ōlenē* elbow + *krānion* head
▸**olecranal** (əʊ'lɛkrən^əl, ˌəʊlɪ'kreɪn^əl) ADJECTIVE

olefine *or* **olefin** ('əʊlɪˌfiːn, -fɪn, 'ɒl-) NOUN other names for **alkene.**
▷**HISTORY** C19: from French *oléfiant,* ultimately from Latin *oleum* oil + *facere* to make
▸ˌ**ole'finic** ADJECTIVE

oleic acid (əʊ'liːɪk) NOUN a colourless oily liquid unsaturated acid occurring, as the glyceride, in almost all natural fats used in making soaps, ointments, cosmetics, and lubricating oils. Formula: $CH_3(CH_2)_7CH{:}CH(CH_2)_7COOH$. Systematic name: ***cis*-9-octadecenoic acid.**
▷**HISTORY** C19 *oleic,* from Latin *oleum* oil + -IC

olein ('əʊlɪɪn) NOUN another name for **triolein.**
▷**HISTORY** C19: from French *oléine,* from Latin *oleum* oil + -IN

oleo- COMBINING FORM oil: *oleomargarine.*
▷**HISTORY** from Latin *oleum* OIL

oleograph ('əʊlɪəˌgrɑːf, -ˌgræf) NOUN 1 a chromolithograph printed in oil colours to imitate the appearance of an oil painting. 2 the pattern formed by a drop of oil spreading on water.
▸**oleographic** (ˌəʊlɪə'græfɪk) ADJECTIVE ▸**oleography** (ˌəʊlɪ'ɒgrəfɪ) NOUN

oleomargarine (ˌəʊlɪəʊˌmɑːdʒə'riːn) *or* **oleomargarin** (ˌəʊlɪəʊ'mɑːdʒərɪn) NOUN other names (esp US) for **margarine.**

oleo oil ('əʊlɪəʊ) NOUN an oil extracted from beef fat, consisting mainly of a mixture of olein and palmitin. It is used in the manufacture of margarine.

oleoresin (ˌəʊlɪəʊ'rɛzɪn) NOUN 1 a semisolid mixture of a resin and essential oil, obtained from certain plants. 2 *Pharmacol* a liquid preparation of resins and oils, obtained by extraction from plants.
▸ˌ**oleo'resinous** ADJECTIVE

oleum ('əʊlɪəm) NOUN, *plural* **olea** ('əʊlɪə) *or* **oleums.** another name for **fuming sulphuric acid.**
▷**HISTORY** from Latin: oil, referring to its oily consistency

O level NOUN (formerly, in Britain) 1 **a** the basic level of the General Certificate of Education, now replaced by **GCSE. b** (*as modifier*): *O level maths.* 2 a pass in a particular subject at O level: *he has eight O levels.* ◆ Formal name: **Ordinary level.**

olfaction (ɒl'fækʃən) NOUN 1 the sense of smell. 2 the act or function of smelling.

olfactometry (ˌɒlfæk'tɒmɪtrɪ) NOUN *Chem* another name for **odorimetry.**

olfactory (ɒl'fæktərɪ, -trɪ) ADJECTIVE 1 of or relating to the sense of smell. ◆ NOUN, *plural* **-ries.** 2 (*usually plural*) an organ or nerve concerned with the sense of smell.
▷**HISTORY** C17: from Latin *olfactus,* past participle of *olfacere,* from *olere* to smell + *facere* to make

olfactory bulb NOUN the anterior and slightly enlarged end of the olfactory tract, from which the cranial nerves concerned with the sense of smell originate.

olfactory nerve NOUN either one of the first pair of cranial nerves, supplying the mucous membrane of the nose.

olfactory tract NOUN a long narrow triangular band of white tissue originating in the olfactory bulb and extending back to the point at which its fibres enter the base of the cerebrum.

OLG ABBREVIATION FOR Old Low German.

olibanum (ɒ'lɪbənəm) NOUN another name for **frankincense.**
▷**HISTORY** C14: from Medieval Latin, from Greek *libanos*

olid ('ɒlɪd) ADJECTIVE foul-smelling.
▷**HISTORY** C17: from Latin *olidus,* from *olēre* to smell

oligaemia *or US* **oligemia** (ˌɒlɪ'giːmɪə) NOUN *Med* a reduction in the volume of the blood, as occurs after haemorrhage.
▸ˌ**oli'gaemic** *or US* ˌ**oli'gemic** ADJECTIVE

oligarch ('ɒlɪˌgɑːk) NOUN a member of an oligarchy.

oligarchy ('ɒlɪˌgɑːkɪ) NOUN, *plural* **-chies.** 1 government by a small group of people. 2 a state or organization so governed. 3 a small body of individuals ruling such a state. 4 *Chiefly US* a small clique of private citizens who exert a strong influence on government.
▷**HISTORY** C16: via Medieval Latin from Greek *oligarkhia,* from *olígos* few + -ARCHY
▸ˌ**oli'garchic** *or* ˌ**oli'garchical** ADJECTIVE ▸ˌ**oli'garchically** ADVERB

oligo- *or before a vowel* **olig-** COMBINING FORM indicating a few or little: *oligopoly.*
▷**HISTORY** from Greek *olígos* little, few

Oligocene ('ɒlɪgəʊˌsiːn, ɒ'lɪg-) ADJECTIVE 1 of, denoting, or formed in the third epoch of the Tertiary period, which lasted for 10 000 000 years. ◆ NOUN 2 **the.** the Oligocene epoch or rock series.
▷**HISTORY** C19: OLIGO- + -CENE

oligochaete ('ɒlɪgəʊˌkiːt) NOUN 1 any freshwater or terrestrial annelid worm of the class *Oligochaeta,* having bristles (chaetae) borne singly along the length of the body: includes the earthworms. ◆ ADJECTIVE 2 of, relating to, or belonging to the class *Oligochaeta.*
▷**HISTORY** C19: from New Latin; see OLIGO-, CHAETA

oligoclase ('ɒlɪgəʊˌkleɪs) NOUN a white, bluish, or reddish-yellow feldspar mineral of the plagioclase series, consisting of aluminium silicates of sodium and calcium. Formula: $NaAlSi_3O_8.CaAl_2Si_2O_8$.
▷**HISTORY** C19: from OLIGO- + -CLASE

oligomer (ɒ'lɪgəmə) NOUN a compound of relatively low molecular weight containing up to five monomer units. Compare **polymer, copolymer.**
▷**HISTORY** C20: from OLIGO- + *-mer,* as in *polymer*

oligomerous (ˌɒlɪ'gɒmərəs) ADJECTIVE *Biology* having a small number of component parts.

oligonucleotide (ˌɒlɪgəʊ'njuːklɪəˌtaɪd) NOUN a polymer consisting of a small number of nucleotides.

oligopeptide (ˌɒlɪgəʊ'pɛptaɪd) NOUN *Biochem* a peptide comprising a small number of amino acids.

oligopoly (ˌɒlɪ'gɒpəlɪ) NOUN, *plural* **-lies.** *Economics* a market situation in which control over the supply of a commodity is held by a small number of producers each of whom is able to influence prices and thus directly affect the position of competitors.
▷**HISTORY** C20: from OLIGO- + Greek *pōlein* to sell, on the model of MONOPOLY
▸ˌ**oliˌgopo'listic** ADJECTIVE

oligopsony (ˌɒlɪ'gɒpsənɪ) NOUN, *plural* **-nies.** a market situation in which the demand for a commodity is represented by a small number of purchasers.
▷**HISTORY** C20: from OLIGO- + *-opsony,* from Greek *opsōnia* purchase of food
▸ˌ**oliˌgopso'nistic** ADJECTIVE

oligosaccharide (ˌɒlɪgəʊ'sækəˌraɪd, -rɪd) NOUN any one of a class of carbohydrates consisting of a few monosaccharide units linked together. Compare **polysaccharide.**

oligospermia (ˌɒlɪgəʊ'spɜːmɪə) NOUN the condition of having less than the normal number of spermatozoa in the semen: a cause of infertility in men.

oligotrophic (ˌɒlɪgəʊ'trɒfɪk) ADJECTIVE (of lakes and similar habitats) poor in nutrients and plant life and rich in oxygen. Compare **eutrophic.**
▷**HISTORY** C20: from OLIGO- + Greek *trophein* to nourish + -IC
▸**oligotrophy** (ˌɒlɪ'gɒtrəfɪ) NOUN

oliguria (ˌɒlɪ'gjʊərɪə) *or* **oliguresis** (ˌɒlɪgjʊ'riːsɪs) NOUN excretion of an abnormally small volume of urine, often as the result of a kidney disorder. Compare **anuria.**
▷**HISTORY** C19: from OLIGO- + -URIA

▸**oliguretic** (ˌɒlɪgjuˈrɛtɪk) ADJECTIVE

Ólimbos (ˈɔlimbɔs) NOUN transliteration of the Modern Greek name for (Mount) **Olympus** (sense 1).

olio (ˈəʊlɪˌəʊ) NOUN, *plural* **olios.** 1 a dish of many different ingredients. 2 a miscellany or potpourri.
▹HISTORY C17: from Spanish *olla* stew, from Latin: jar

olivaceous (ˌɒlɪˈveɪʃəs) ADJECTIVE of an olive colour.

olivary (ˈɒlɪvərɪ) ADJECTIVE 1 shaped like an olive. 2 *Anatomy* of or relating to either of two masses of tissue (**olivary bodies**) on the forward portion of the medulla oblongata.
▹HISTORY C16: from Latin *olivārius*, from *oliva* OLIVE

olive (ˈɒlɪv) NOUN 1 an evergreen oleaceous tree, *Olea europaea*, of the Mediterranean region but cultivated elsewhere, having white fragrant flowers, and edible shiny black fruits. 2 the fruit of this plant, eaten as a relish and used as a source of olive oil. 3 the wood of the olive tree, used for ornamental work. 4 any of various trees or shrubs resembling the olive. 5 **a** a yellow-green colour. **b** (*as adjective*): *an olive coat.* 6 an angler's name for the dun of various mayflies or an artificial fly in imitation of this. ◆ ADJECTIVE 7 of, relating to, or made of the olive tree, its wood, or its fruit.
▹HISTORY C13: via Old French from Latin *oliva*, related to Greek *elaia* olive tree; compare Greek *elaion* oil

olive branch NOUN 1 a branch of an olive tree used to symbolize peace. 2 any offering of peace or conciliation.

olive brown NOUN **a** a dull yellowish-brown to yellowish-green colour. **b** (*as adjective*): *an olive-brown coat.*

olive crown NOUN (esp. in ancient Greece and Rome) a garland of olive leaves awarded as a token of victory.

olive drab NOUN *US* 1 **a** a dull but fairly strong greyish-olive colour. **b** (*as adjective*): *an olive-drab jacket.* 2 cloth or clothes in this colour, esp. the uniform of the US Army. Abbreviation: **OD.**

olive green NOUN **a** a colour that is greener, stronger, and brighter than olive; deep yellowish-green. **b** (*as adjective*): *an olive-green coat.*

olivenite (ɒˈlɪvɪˌnaɪt) NOUN a green to black rare secondary mineral consisting of hydrated basic copper arsenate in orthorhombic crystalline form. Formula: $Cu_2(AsO_4)(OH)$.
▹HISTORY C19: from German *Oliven(erz)* olive (ore) + -ITE[1]

olive oil NOUN a pale yellow oil pressed from ripe olive fruits and used in cooking, medicines, soaps, etc.

Olives (ˈɒlɪvz) NOUN **Mount of.** a hill to the east of Jerusalem: in New Testament times the village Bethany (Mark 11:11) was on its eastern slope and Gethsemane on its western one.

olivine (ˈɒlɪˌviːn, ˌɒlɪˈviːn) NOUN 1 an olive-green mineral of the olivine group, found in igneous and metamorphic rocks. The clear-green variety (peridot) is used as a gemstone. Composition: magnesium iron silicate. Formula: $(MgFe)_2SiO_4$. Crystal structure: orthorhombic. also called **chrysolite.** 2 any mineral in the group having the general formula $(Mg,Fe,Mn,Ca)_2SiO_4$.
▹HISTORY C18: from German, named after its colour

olla (ˈɒlə; *Spanish* ˈoʎa) NOUN 1 a cooking pot. 2 short for **olla podrida.**
▹HISTORY Spanish, from Latin *olla*, variant of *aulla* pot

olla podrida (pɒˈdriːdə; *Spanish* poˈðriða) NOUN 1 a Spanish dish, consisting of a stew with beans, sausages, etc. 2 an assortment; miscellany.
▹HISTORY literally: rotten pot

oller (ˈɒlə) NOUN *Northern English, dialect* waste ground.

ollie (ˈɒlɪ) NOUN, *plural* **-lies.** (in skateboarding and snowboarding) a jump into the air executed by stamping on the tail of the board.
▹HISTORY C20: of uncertain origin

olm (əʊlm, ɒlm) NOUN a pale blind eel-like salamander, *Proteus anguinus*, of underground streams in SE Europe, that retains its larval form throughout its life: family *Proteidae*. See also **mud puppy.**

▹HISTORY C20: from German

Olmec (ˈɒlmɛk) NOUN, *plural* **-mecs** *or* **-mec.** 1 a member of an ancient Central American Indian people who inhabited the southern Gulf Coast of Mexico and flourished between about 1200 and 400 B.C. ◆ ADJECTIVE 2 of or relating to these people or their civilization or culture.

Olmütz (ˈɔlmyts) NOUN the German name for **Olomouc.**

ologoan (ˌʌləˈgoːn) VERB (*intr*) *Irish* to complain loudly without reason: *she's always ologoaning about something.*
▹HISTORY from Irish Gaelic *olagón* lament

ology (ˈɒlədʒɪ) NOUN, *plural* **-gies.** *Informal* a science or other branch of knowledge.
▹HISTORY C19: abstracted from words with this ending, such as *theology, biology*, etc.; see -LOGY

Olomouc (*Czech* ˈɔlɔmɔuts) NOUN a city in the Czech Republic, in North Moravia on the Morava River: capital of Moravia until 1640; university (1576). Pop.: 103 015 (2000 est.). German name: **Olmütz.**

oloroso (ˌɒləˈrəʊsəʊ) NOUN a full-bodied golden-coloured sweet sherry.
▹HISTORY from Spanish: fragrant

Olsztyn (*Polish* ˈɔlʃtin) NOUN a town in NE Poland: founded in 1334 by the Teutonic Knights; communications centre. Pop.: 170 904 (1999 est.).

Olympia (əˈlɪmpɪə) NOUN 1 a plain in Greece, in the NW Peloponnese: in ancient times a major sanctuary of Zeus and site of the original Olympic Games. 2 a port in W Washington, the state capital, on Puget Sound. Pop.: 33 840 (1990).

Olympiad (əˈlɪmpɪˌæd) NOUN 1 a staging of the modern Olympic Games. 2 the four-year period between consecutive celebrations of the Olympic Games; a unit of ancient Greek chronology dating back to 776 B.C. 3 an international contest in chess, bridge, etc.

Olympian (əˈlɪmpɪən) ADJECTIVE 1 of or relating to Mount Olympus or to the classical Greek gods. 2 majestic or godlike in manner or bearing. 3 superior to mundane considerations, esp. when impractical. 4 of or relating to ancient Olympia or its inhabitants. ◆ NOUN 5 a god of Olympus. 6 an inhabitant or native of ancient Olympia. 7 *Chiefly US* a competitor in the Olympic Games.

Olympic (əˈlɪmpɪk) ADJECTIVE 1 of or relating to the Olympic Games. 2 of or relating to ancient Olympia.

Olympic Games NOUN (*functioning as singular or plural*) 1 the greatest Panhellenic festival, held every fourth year in honour of Zeus at ancient Olympia. From 472 B.C., it consisted of five days of games, sacrifices, and festivities. 2 Also called: **the Olympics.** the modern revival of these games, consisting of international athletic and sporting contests held every four years in a selected country since their inception in Athens in 1896. See also **Winter Olympic Games.**

Olympic Mountains PLURAL NOUN a mountain range in NW Washington: part of the Coast Range. Highest peak: Mount Olympus, 2427 m (7965 ft.).

Olympic Peninsula NOUN a large peninsula of W Washington.

Olympus (əʊˈlɪmpəs) NOUN 1 **Mount.** a mountain in NE Greece: the highest mountain in Greece, believed in Greek mythology to be the dwelling place of the greater gods. Height: 2911 m (9550 ft.). Modern Greek name: **Ólimbos.** 2 **Mount.** a mountain in NW Washington: highest peak of the Olympic Mountains. Height: 2427 m (7965 ft.). 3 a poetic word for **heaven.**

Olympus Mons NOUN the highest of the giant shield volcanoes on Mars, lying 18°N of the equator. Height: 26 km; base diameter: over 600 km.

Olynthus (əʊˈlɪnθəs) NOUN an ancient city in N Greece: the centre of Chalcidice.

om THE INTERNET DOMAIN NAME FOR Oman.

Om (əʊm) NOUN *Hinduism* a sacred syllable typifying the three gods Brahma, Vishnu, and Siva, who are concerned in the threefold operation of integration, maintenance, and disintegration.
▹HISTORY from Sanskrit

OM 1 ABBREVIATION FOR Order of Merit (a Brit title). ◆ 2 *Currency* SYMBOL FOR (the former) Ostmark.

-oma NOUN COMBINING FORM indicating a tumour: *carcinoma.*
▹HISTORY from Greek *-ōma*

omadhaun (ˈɒmədɑːn) NOUN *Irish* a foolish man or boy.
▹HISTORY C19: from Irish Gaelic *amadán*

Omagh (əʊˈmɑː, ˈəʊmə) NOUN 1 a market town in Northern Ireland. Pop.: 17 280 (1991). 2 a district of W Northern Ireland, in Co. Tyrone. Pop.: 47 952 (1991). Area: 1130 sq. km (436 sq. miles).

Omaha (ˈəʊməˌhɑː) NOUN a city in E Nebraska, on the Missouri River opposite Council Bluffs, Iowa: the largest city in the state; the country's largest livestock market and meat-packing centre. Pop.: 390 007 (2000).

Oman (əʊˈmɑːn) NOUN a sultanate in SE Arabia, on the **Gulf of Oman** and the Arabian Sea: the most powerful state in Arabia in the 19th century, ruling Zanzibar, much of the Persian coast, and part of Pakistan. Official language: Arabic. Official religion: Muslim. Currency: rial. Capital: Muscat. Pop.: 2 497 000 (2001 est.). Area: about 306 000 sq. km (118 150 sq. miles). Former name (until 1970): **Muscat and Oman.**

OMAN INTERNATIONAL CAR REGISTRATION FOR Oman.

Omani (əʊˈmɑːnɪ) NOUN 1 a native or inhabitant of Oman. ◆ ADJECTIVE 2 of or relating to Oman or its inhabitants.

omasum (əʊˈmeɪsəm) NOUN, *plural* **-sa** (-sə). another name for **psalterium.**
▹HISTORY C18: from Latin: bullock's tripe

ombre *or US* **omber** (ˈɒmbə) NOUN an 18th-century card game.
▹HISTORY C17: from Spanish *hombre* man, referring to the player who attempts to win the stakes

ombro- COMBINING FORM indicating rain: *ombrogenous; ombrophilous.*
▹HISTORY from Greek *ombros* shower of rain

ombrogenous (ɒmˈbrɒdʒɪnəs) ADJECTIVE (of plants) able to flourish in wet conditions.

ombrophilous (ɒmˈbrɒfɪləs) ADJECTIVE (of plants) tolerant of wet conditions.

ombrophobous (ɒmˈbrɒfəbəs) ADJECTIVE (of plants) not able to tolerate wet conditions.

ombudsman (ˈɒmbʊdzmən) NOUN, *plural* **-men.** 1 a commissioner who acts as independent referee between individual citizens and their government or its administration. 2 (in Britain) an official, without power of sanction or mechanism of appeal, who investigates complaints of maladministration by members of the public against national or local government or its servants. Formal names: **Commissioner for Local Administration, Health Service Commissioner, Parliamentary Commissioner.** See also **Financial Ombudsman.**
▹HISTORY C20: from Swedish: commissioner

Omdurman (ˌɒmdɜːˈmɑːn) NOUN a city in the central Sudan, on the White Nile, opposite Khartoum: the largest town in the Sudan; scene of the **Battle of Omdurman** (1898), in which the Mahdi's successor was defeated by Lord Kitchener's forces. Pop.: 1 267 077 (1993).

-ome NOUN COMBINING FORM denoting a mass or part of a specified kind: *rhizome.*
▹HISTORY variant of -OMA

omega (ˈəʊmɪgə) NOUN 1 the 24th and last letter of the Greek alphabet (Ω, ω), a long vowel, transliterated as *o* or *ō*. 2 the ending or last of a series.
▹HISTORY C16: from Greek *ō mega* big o; see MEGA-, OMICRON

omega minus NOUN an unstable negatively charged elementary particle, classified as a baryon, that has a mass 3273 times that of the electron.

omega-3 fatty acid NOUN an unsaturated fatty acid that occurs naturally in fish oil and is valuable in reducing blood-cholesterol levels.

omelette *or esp US* **omelet** (ˈɒmlɪt) NOUN a savoury or sweet dish of beaten eggs cooked in fat.
▹HISTORY C17: from French *omelette*, changed from *alumette*, from *alumelle* sword blade, changed by mistaken division from *la lemelle*, from Latin (see LAMELLA); apparently from the flat shape of the omelette

omen (ˈəʊmən) NOUN 1 a phenomenon or occurrence regarded as a sign of future happiness or

disaster. [2] prophetic significance. ◆ VERB [3] (*tr*) to portend.
▷**HISTORY** C16: from Latin

omentum (əʊˈmɛntəm) NOUN, *plural* **-ta** (-tə). *Anatomy* a double fold of peritoneum connecting the stomach with other abdominal organs.
▷**HISTORY** C16: from Latin: membrane, esp. a caul, of obscure origin

omer (ˈəʊmə) NOUN an ancient Hebrew unit of dry measure equal to one tenth of an ephah.
▷**HISTORY** C17: from Hebrew *ʿōmer* a measure

Omer (ˈəʊmə) NOUN *Judaism* a period of seven weeks extending from the second day of Passover to the first day of Shavuoth, and observed as a period of semimourning.
▷**HISTORY** named because sacrifices of an OMER of grain were made

omertà *Italian* (omerˈta) NOUN a conspiracy of silence.

omicron (əʊˈmaɪkrɒn, ˈɒmɪkrɒn) NOUN the 15th letter in the Greek alphabet (Ο, ο), a short vowel, transliterated as *o*.
▷**HISTORY** from Greek *ō mikron* small o; see MICRO-, OMEGA

omigod (ˌəʊmaɪˈgɒd) INTERJECTION an exclamation of surprise, pleasure, dismay, etc.
▷**HISTORY** C20: from *Oh, my God*

ominous (ˈɒmɪnəs) ADJECTIVE [1] foreboding evil. [2] serving as or having significance as an omen.
▷**HISTORY** C16: from Latin *ōminōsus,* from OMEN
▸**ˈominously** ADVERB ▸**ˈominousness** NOUN

omission (əʊˈmɪʃən) NOUN [1] something that has been omitted or neglected. [2] the act of omitting or the state of having been omitted.
▷**HISTORY** C14: from Latin *omissiō,* from *omittere* to OMIT
▸**oˈmissive** ADJECTIVE ▸**oˈmissiveness** NOUN

omit (əʊˈmɪt) VERB **omits, omitting, omitted.** (*tr*) [1] to neglect to do or include. [2] to fail (to do something).
▷**HISTORY** C15: from Latin *omittere,* from *ob-* away + *mittere* to send
▸**omissible** (əʊˈmɪsɪbᵊl) ADJECTIVE ▸**oˈmitter** NOUN

OMM (in Canada) ABBREVIATION FOR Officer of the Order of Military Merit.

ommatidium (ˌɒməˈtɪdɪəm) NOUN, *plural* **-tidia** (-ˈtɪdɪə). any of the numerous cone-shaped units that make up the compound eyes of some arthropods.
▷**HISTORY** C19: via New Latin from Greek *ommatidion,* from *omma* eye
▸**ˌommaˈtidial** ADJECTIVE

ommatophore (ɒˈmætəˌfɔː) NOUN *Zoology* a movable stalk or tentacle bearing an eye, occurring in lower animals such as crabs and snails.
▷**HISTORY** C19: from Greek *omma* eye + -PHORE
▸**ommatophorous** (ˌɒməˈtɒfərəs) ADJECTIVE

Ommiad (əʊˈmaɪæd) NOUN, *plural* **-ads** *or* **-ades** (-əˌdiːz). a variant spelling of **Omayyad.**

omni- COMBINING FORM all or everywhere: *omnipresent.*
▷**HISTORY** from Latin *omnis* all

omnia vincit amor *Latin* (ˈɒmnɪə ˈvɪnsɪt ˈæmɔː) love conquers all things.
▷**HISTORY** from Virgil's Eclogues 10:69

omnibus (ˈɒmnɪˌbʌs, -bəs) NOUN, *plural* **-buses.** [1] a less common word for **bus** (sense 1). [2] Also called: **omnibus volume.** a collection of works by one author or several works on a similar topic, reprinted in one volume. [3] Also called: **omnibus edition.** a television or radio programme consisting of two or more programmes broadcast earlier in the week. ◆ ADJECTIVE [4] (*prenominal*) of, dealing with, or providing for many different things or cases.
▷**HISTORY** C19: from Latin, literally: for all, from *omnis* all

omnicompetent (ˌɒmnɪˈkɒmpɪtənt) ADJECTIVE able to judge or deal with all matters.
▸**ˌomniˈcompetence** NOUN

omnidirectional (ˌɒmnɪdɪˈrɛkʃənᵊl, -daɪ-) ADJECTIVE [1] (of an antenna) capable of transmitting and receiving radio signals equally in any direction in the horizontal plane. [2] (of a microphone or antenna) equally sensitive in all directions.

omnifarious (ˌɒmnɪˈfɛərɪəs) ADJECTIVE of many or all varieties or forms.
▷**HISTORY** C17: from Late Latin *omnifārius,* from Latin *omnis* all + *-farius* doing, related to *facere* to do
▸**ˌomniˈfariously** ADVERB ▸**ˌomniˈfariousness** NOUN

omnific (ɒmˈnɪfɪk) *or* **omnificent** (ɒmˈnɪfɪsᵊnt) ADJECTIVE *Rare* creating all things.
▷**HISTORY** C17: via Medieval Latin from Latin *omni-* + *-ficus,* from *facere* to do
▸**omˈnificence** NOUN

omnipotent (ɒmˈnɪpətənt) ADJECTIVE [1] having very great or unlimited power. ◆ NOUN [2] **the Omnipotent.** an epithet for God.
▷**HISTORY** C14: via Old French from Latin *omnipotens* all-powerful, from OMNI- + *potens,* from *posse* to be able
▸**omˈnipotence** NOUN ▸**omˈnipotently** ADVERB

omnipresent (ˌɒmnɪˈprɛzᵊnt) ADJECTIVE (esp. of a deity) present in all places at the same time.
▸**ˌomniˈpresence** NOUN

omnirange (ˈɒmnɪˌreɪndʒ) NOUN a very-high-frequency ground radio navigational system to assist a pilot in plotting his exact position.

omniscient (ɒmˈnɪsɪənt) ADJECTIVE [1] having infinite knowledge or understanding. [2] having very great or seemingly unlimited knowledge.
▷**HISTORY** C17: from Medieval Latin *omnisciens,* from Latin OMNI- + *scīre* to know
▸**omˈniscience** NOUN ▸**omˈnisciently** ADVERB

omnium-gatherum (ˈɒmnɪəmˈgæðərəm) NOUN *Often facetious* a miscellaneous collection; assortment.
▷**HISTORY** C16: from Latin *omnium* of all, from *omnis* all + Latinized form of English *gather*

omnivore (ˈɒmnɪˌvɔː) NOUN an omnivorous person or animal.

omnivorous (ɒmˈnɪvərəs) ADJECTIVE [1] eating food of both animal and vegetable origin, or any type of food indiscriminately. [2] taking in or assimilating everything, esp. with the mind.
▷**HISTORY** C17: from Latin *omnivorus* all-devouring, from OMNI- + *vorāre* to eat greedily
▸**omˈnivorously** ADVERB ▸**omˈnivorousness** NOUN

omophagia (ˌəʊməˈfeɪdʒɪə) *or* **omophagy** (əʊˈmɒfədʒɪ) NOUN the eating of raw food, esp. meat.
▷**HISTORY** C18: via New Latin from Greek *ōmophagia,* from *ōmos* raw + *-phagia;* see -PHAGY
▸**omophagic** (ˌəʊməˈfædʒɪk) *or* **omophagous** (əʊˈmɒfəgəs) ADJECTIVE

omov (ˈəʊmɒv) NOUN ACRONYM FOR one member one vote.

Omphale (ˈɒmfəˌliː) NOUN *Greek myth* a queen of Lydia, whom Hercules was required to serve as a slave to atone for the murder of Iphitus.

omphalos (ˈɒmfəˌlɒs) NOUN [1] (in the ancient world) a sacred conical object, esp. a stone. The most famous omphalos at Delphi was assumed to mark the centre of the earth. [2] the central point. [3] *Literary* another word for **navel.**
▷**HISTORY** Greek: navel

OMS ABBREVIATION FOR Organisation Mondiale de la Santé.
▷**HISTORY** French: World Health Organization

Omsk (ɒmsk) NOUN a city in W central Russia, at the confluence of the Irtysh and Om Rivers: a major industrial centre, with pipelines from the second Baku oilfield. Pop.: 1 157 600 (1999 est.).

Omuta (ˈəʊmuːˌtɑː) NOUN a city in SW Japan, on W Kyushu on Ariake Bay: former coal-mining centre; chemical industries and manufacturing. Pop.: 146 691 (1996).

on (ɒn) PREPOSITION [1] in contact or connection with the surface of; at the upper surface of: *an apple on the ground; a mark on the table cloth.* [2] attached to: *a puppet on a string.* [3] carried with: *I've no money on me.* [4] in the immediate vicinity of; close to or along the side of: *a house on the sea; this verges on the ridiculous!* [5] within the time limits of a day or date: *he arrived on Thursday.* [6] being performed upon or relayed through the medium of: *what's on the television?* [7] at the occasion of: *on his retirement.* [8] used to indicate support, subsistence, contingency, etc.: *he lives on bread; it depends on what you want.* [9] **a** regularly taking (a drug): *she's on the pill.* **b** addicted to: *he's on heroin.* [10] by means of (something considered as a mode of transport) (esp. in such phrases as **on foot, on wheels, on horseback,** etc.). [11] in the process or course of: *on a journey; on strike.* [12] concerned with or relating to: *a tax on potatoes; a programme on archaeology.* [13] used to indicate the basis, grounds, or cause, as of a statement or action: *I have it on good authority.* [14] against: used to indicate opposition: *they marched on the city at dawn.* [15] used to indicate a meeting or encounter: *he crept up on her.* [16] (used with an adjective preceded by *the*) indicating the manner or way in which an action is carried out: *on the sly; on the cheap.* [17] *Informal or dialect* to the loss or disadvantage of: *the old car gave out on us.* ◆ ADVERB (*often used as a particle*) [18] in the position or state required for the commencement or sustained continuation, as of a mechanical operation: *the radio's been on all night.* [19] **a** attached to, surrounding, or placed in contact with something: *the girl had nothing on.* **b** taking place: *what's on tonight?* [20] in a manner indicating continuity, persistence, concentration, etc.: *don't keep on about it; the play went on all afternoon.* [21] in a direction towards something, esp. forwards; so as to make progress: *we drove on towards London; march on!* [22] **on and off** *or* **off and on.** intermittently; from time to time. [23] **on and on.** without ceasing; continually. ◆ ADJECTIVE [24] functioning; operating: *turn the switch to the on position.* [25] (*postpositive*) *Informal* **a** staked or wagered as a bet: *ten pounds on that horse.* **b** performing, as on stage: *I'm on in five minutes.* **c** definitely taking place: *the match is on for Friday; their marriage is still on.* **d** charged to: *the drinks are on me.* **e** tolerable, practicable, acceptable, etc.: *your plan just isn't on.* **f** (of a person) willing to do something. [26] **on at.** *Informal* nagging: *she was always on at her husband.* [27] **on it.** *Austral informal* drinking alcoholic liquor. [28] *Cricket* (of a bowler) bowling. ◆ NOUN [29] *Cricket* **a** (*modifier*) relating to or denoting the leg side of a cricket field or pitch: *the on side; an on drive.* **b** (*in combination*) used to designate certain fielding positions on the leg side: *long-on; mid-on.*
▷**HISTORY** Old English *an, on;* related to Old Saxon *an,* Old High German, Gothic *ana*

On (ɒn) NOUN the ancient Egyptian and biblical name for **Heliopolis.**

ON ABBREVIATION FOR: [1] Old Norse. [2] (esp. in postal addresses) Ontario.

-on SUFFIX FORMING NOUNS [1] indicating a chemical substance: *interferon; parathion.* [2] (in physics) indicating an elementary particle or quantum: *electron; photon.* [3] (in chemistry) indicating an inert gas: *neon; radon.* [4] (in biochemistry) a molecular unit: *codon; operon.*
▷**HISTORY** from ION

onager (ˈɒnədʒə) NOUN, *plural* **-gri** (-ˌgraɪ) *or* **-gers.** [1] a Persian variety of the wild ass, *Equus hemionus.* Compare **kiang.** [2] an ancient war engine for hurling stones.
▷**HISTORY** C14: from Late Latin: military engine for stone throwing, from Latin: wild ass, from Greek *onagros,* from *onos* ass + *agros* field

onagraceous (ˌɒnəˈgreɪʃəs) ADJECTIVE of, relating to, or belonging to the *Onagraceae,* a family of flowering plants including fuchsia and willowherb.
▷**HISTORY** C19: via New Latin *Onagrăceae,* from Latin *onager;* see ONAGER

onanism (ˈəʊnəˌnɪzəm) NOUN another name for **masturbation** or **coitus interruptus.**
▷**HISTORY** C18: after *Onan,* son of Judah; see Genesis 38:9
▸**ˈonanist** NOUN, ADJECTIVE ▸**ˌonanˈistic** ADJECTIVE

onbeat (ˈɒnˌbiːt) NOUN *Music* the first and third beats in a bar of four-four time.

ONC (in Britain, formerly) ABBREVIATION FOR Ordinary National Certificate.

once (wʌns) ADVERB [1] one time; on one occasion or in one case. [2] at some past time; formerly: *I could speak French once.* [3] by one step or degree (of relationship): *a cousin once removed.* [4] (*in conditional clauses, negatives, etc.*) ever; at all: *if you once forget it.* [5] multiplied by one. [6] **once and away. a** conclusively. **b** occasionally. [7] **once and for all.** conclusively; for the last time. [8] **once in a while.** occasionally; now and then. [9] **once or twice** *or* **once and again.** a few times. [10] **once upon a time.** used to begin fairy tales and children's stories. ◆ CONJUNCTION [11] (*subordinating*) as soon as; if ever or whenever: *once you begin, you'll enjoy it.* ◆ NOUN [12] one occasion or case: *you may do it, this once.* [13] **all at once. a** suddenly or without warning. **b**

simultaneously. [14] **at once. a** immediately. **b** simultaneously. [15] **for once.** this time, if (or but) at no other time.
▷HISTORY C12 *ones, ānes,* adverbial genitive of *on, ān* ONE

once-over NOUN *Informal* [1] a quick examination or appraisal. [2] a quick but comprehensive piece of work. [3] a violent beating or thrashing (esp. in the phrase **give (a person** or **thing) the** (or **a**) **once-over**).

oncer ('wʌnsə) NOUN [1] *Brit, slang* (formerly) a one-pound note. [2] *Austral, slang* a person elected to Parliament who can only expect to serve one term. [3] *NZ* something that happens on only one occasion.
▷HISTORY C20: from ONCE

onchocerciasis (ˌɒŋkəʊsə'kaɪəsɪs) NOUN, *plural* **-ses** (-siːz). a disease found in parts of Africa and tropical America that is caused by a parasitic worm, *Onchocerca volvulus,* and transmitted to humans by various species of black fly. It results in inflammation of the skin and in some cases blindness. Also called: **river blindness.**
▷HISTORY C20: from *Onchocerca,* the genus of worms + -IASIS

onco- COMBINING FORM denoting a tumour: *oncology.*
▷HISTORY from Greek *onkos*

oncogene ('ɒŋkəʊˌdʒiːn) NOUN any of several genes, first identified in viruses but present in all cells, that when abnormally activated can cause cancer.

oncogenic (ˌɒŋkəʊ'dʒɛnɪk) *or* **oncogenous** (ɒŋ'kɒdʒənəs) ADJECTIVE causing the formation of a tumour: *an oncogenic virus.*
▸**ˌonco'genesis** NOUN

oncology (ɒŋ'kɒlədʒɪ) NOUN the branch of medicine concerned with the study, classification, and treatment of tumours.
▸**oncological** (ˌɒŋkə'lɒdʒɪkᵊl) ADJECTIVE ▸**on'cologist** NOUN

oncoming ('ɒnˌkʌmɪŋ) ADJECTIVE [1] coming nearer in space or time; approaching. ◆ NOUN [2] the approach or onset: *the oncoming of winter.*

oncost ('ɒnˌkɒst) NOUN *Brit* [1] another word for **overhead** (sense 7). [2] (*sometimes plural*) another word for **overheads.**

OND (in Britain, formerly) ABBREVIATION FOR Ordinary National Diploma.

ondes Martenot (ɔ̃d mɑːtə'nəʊ) NOUN *Music* an electronic keyboard instrument in which the frequency of an oscillator is varied to produce separate musical notes.
▷HISTORY C20: French, literally: Martenot waves, invented by Maurice *Martenot* (1898–1980)

on dit *French* (ɔ̃ di) NOUN, *plural* ***on dits*** (ɔ̃ di). a rumour; piece of gossip.
▷HISTORY literally: it is said, they say

Ondo ('ɒndəʊ) NOUN a state of SW Nigeria, on the Bight of Benin: formed in 1976 from part of Western State. Capital: Akure. Pop.: 4 343 230 (1995 est.). Area: 20 959 sq. km (8092 sq. miles).

ondograph ('ɒndəʊˌgrɑːf, -ˌgræf) NOUN an instrument for producing a graphical recording of an alternating current by measuring the charge imparted to a capacitor at different points in the cycle.
▷HISTORY C20: from French, from *onde* wave + -GRAPH

one (wʌn) DETERMINER [1] **a** single; lone; not two or more: *one car.* **b** (*as pronoun*): *one is enough for now; one at a time.* **c** (*in combination*): *one-eyed; one-legged.* [2] **a** distinct from all others; only; unique: *one girl in a million.* **b** (*as pronoun*): *one of a kind.* [3] **a** a specified (person, item, etc.) as distinct from another or others of its kind: *raise one hand and then the other.* **b** (*as pronoun*): *which one is correct?* [4] a certain, indefinite, or unspecified (time); some: *one day you'll be sorry.* [5] *Informal* an emphatic word for **a**[1] or **an**[1]. *it was one hell of a fight.* [6] a certain (person): *one Miss Jones was named.* [7] **(all) in one.** combined; united. [8] **all one. a** all the same. **b** of no consequence: *it's all one to me.* [9] **at one.** (often foll by *with*) in a state of agreement or harmony. [10] **be made one.** (of a man and a woman) to become married. [11] **many a one.** many people. [12] **neither one thing nor the other.** indefinite, undecided, or mixed. [13] **never a one.** none. [14] **one and all.** everyone, without exception. [15] **one by one.** one at a time; individually. [16] **one or two.** a few. [17] **one way and another.** on balance. [18] **off on one.** *Informal* exhibiting bad temper; ranting. [19] **one with another.** on average. ◆ PRONOUN [20] an indefinite person regarded as typical of every person: *one can't say any more than that.* [21] any indefinite person: used as the subject of a sentence to form an alternative grammatical construction to that of the passive voice: *one can catch fine trout in this stream.* [22] *Archaic* an unspecified person: *one came to him.* ◆ NOUN [23] the smallest whole number and the first cardinal number; unity. See also **number** (sense 1). [24] a numeral (1, I, i, etc.) representing this number. [25] *Music* the numeral 1 used as the lower figure in a time signature to indicate that the beat is measured in semibreves. [26] something representing, represented by, or consisting of one unit. [27] Also called: **one o'clock.** one hour after noon or midnight. [28] a blow or setback (esp. in the phrase **one in the eye for**). [29] **the one.** (in Neo-Platonic philosophy) the ultimate being. [30] **the Holy One** *or* **the One above.** God. [31] **the Evil One.** Satan; the devil. ◆ Related prefixes: **mono-, uni-.** Related adjective: **single.**
▷HISTORY Old English *ān,* related to Old French *ān, ēn,* Old High German *ein,* Old Norse *einn,* Latin *unus,* Greek *oinē* ace

-one SUFFIX FORMING NOUNS indicating that a chemical compound is a ketone: *acetone.*
▷HISTORY arbitrarily from Greek *-ōnē,* feminine patronymic suffix, but perhaps influenced by *-one* in OZONE

one another PRONOUN the reflexive form of plural pronouns when the action, attribution, etc., is reciprocal: *they kissed one another; knowing one another.* Also: **each other.**

one-armed bandit NOUN a fruit machine operated by pulling down a lever at one side.

one-down ADJECTIVE *Informal* having conceded an advantage or lead to someone or something.

Onega (*Russian* a'njɛgə) NOUN a lake in NW Russia, mostly in the Karelian Republic: the second largest lake in Europe. Area: 9891 sq. km (3819 sq. miles).

one-horse ADJECTIVE [1] drawn by or using one horse. [2] (*prenominal*) *Informal* small or obscure: *a one-horse town.*

Oneida (əʊ'naɪdə) NOUN, *plural* **-das** *or* **-da.** [1] **Lake.** a lake in central New York State: part of the New York State Barge Canal system. Length: about 35 km (22 miles). Greatest width: 9 km (6 miles). [2] (preceded by *the; functioning as plural*) a North American Indian people formerly living east of Lake Ontario; one of the Iroquois peoples. [3] a member of this people. [4] the language of this people, belonging to the Iroquoian family.
▷HISTORY from Iroquois *onēyóte',* literally: standing stone

oneiric (əʊ'naɪərɪk) ADJECTIVE of or relating to dreams.

oneiro- COMBINING FORM indicating a dream: *oneirocritic.*
▷HISTORY from Greek *oneiros* dream

oneirocritic (əʊˌnaɪərəʊ'krɪtɪk) NOUN a person who interprets dreams.
▷HISTORY C17: from Greek *oneirokritikos*
▸**oˌneiro'critical** ADJECTIVE ▸**oˌneiro'critically** ADVERB

oneiromancy (əʊ'naɪərəʊˌmænsɪ) NOUN *Rare* divination by the interpretation of dreams.
▷HISTORY C17: from Greek *oneiros* dream + -MANCY
▸**o'neiroˌmancer** NOUN

one-liner NOUN *Informal* a short joke or witty remark or riposte.

one-man ADJECTIVE consisting of or done by or for one man: *a one-man band; a one-man show.*

one-many ADJECTIVE *Maths, logic* (of a relation) holding between more than one ordered pair of elements with the same first member.

oneness ('wʌnnɪs) NOUN [1] the state or quality of being one; singleness. [2] the state of being united; agreement. [3] uniqueness. [4] sameness.

one-night stand NOUN [1] a performance given only once at any one place. [2] *Informal* **a** a sexual encounter lasting only one evening or night. **b** a person regarded as being only suitable for such an encounter.

one-off NOUN *Brit* **a** something that is carried out or made only once. **b** (*as modifier*): *a one-off job.* Also: **one-shot.**
▷HISTORY See OFF (sense 15)

one-on-one ADJECTIVE denoting a relationship or encounter in which someone is involved with only one other person: *a one-on-one meeting.*

one-parent family NOUN a household consisting of at least one dependent child and the mother or father, the other parent being dead or permanently absent.

one-piece ADJECTIVE [1] (of a garment, esp. a bathing costume) made in one piece. ◆ NOUN [2] a garment, esp. a bathing costume, made in one piece.

oner ('wʌnə) NOUN *Brit informal* [1] a single continuous action (esp. in the phrase **down it in a oner**). [2] an outstanding person or thing. [3] a heavy blow.
▷HISTORY C20: from ONE

onerous ('ɒnərəs, 'əʊ-) ADJECTIVE [1] laborious or oppressive. [2] *Law* (of a contract, lease, etc.) having or involving burdens or obligations that counterbalance or outweigh the advantages.
▷HISTORY C14: from Latin *onerōsus* burdensome, from *onus* load
▸**'onerously** ADVERB ▸**'onerousness** NOUN

oneself (wʌn'sɛlf) PRONOUN [1] **a** the reflexive form of **one** (senses 20, 21). **b** (intensifier): *one doesn't do that oneself.* [2] (*preceded by a copula*) one's normal or usual self: *one doesn't feel oneself after such an experience.*

one-sided ADJECTIVE [1] considering or favouring only one side of a matter, problem, etc. [2] having all the advantage on one side. [3] larger or more developed on one side. [4] having, existing on, or occurring on one side only. [5] another term for **unilateral.** [6] denoting a surface on which any two points can be joined without crossing an edge. See **Möbius strip.**
▸**ˌone-'sidedly** ADVERB ▸**ˌone-'sidedness** NOUN

one-step NOUN [1] an early 20th-century ballroom dance with long quick steps, the precursor of the foxtrot. [2] a piece of music composed for or in the rhythm of this dance.

one-stop ADJECTIVE having or providing a range of related services or goods in one place: *a one-stop shop.*

one-tailed ADJECTIVE *Statistics* (of a significance test) concerned with the hypothesis that an observed value of a sampling statistic either significantly exceeds or falls significantly below a given value, where the error is relevant only in one direction: for instance, in testing whether scales are fair a customer does not regard overweight goods as a relevant error. Compare **two-tailed.**

One Thousand Guineas NOUN See **Thousand Guineas.**

one-time ADJECTIVE [1] (*prenominal*) at some time in the past; former. ◆ ADVERB [2] *Caribbean informal* at once.

one-to-one ADJECTIVE [1] (of two or more things) corresponding exactly. [2] denoting a relationship or encounter in which someone is involved with only one other person: *one-to-one tuition.* [3] *Maths* characterized by or involving the pairing of each member of one set with only one member of another set, without remainder. ◆ NOUN [4] a conversation, encounter, or relationship between two people.

one-track ADJECTIVE [1] *Informal* obsessed with one idea, subject, etc. [2] having or consisting of a single track.

one-trick pony NOUN *Informal, chiefly US* a person or thing considered as being limited to only one single talent, capability, quality, etc.

one-two NOUN [1] *Boxing* a jab with the leading hand followed by a cross with the other hand. [2] *Soccer* another term for **wall pass.**

one-up ADJECTIVE *Informal* having or having scored an advantage or lead over someone or something.

one-upmanship (wʌn'ʌpmənʃɪp) NOUN *Informal* the art or practice of achieving or maintaining an advantage over others, often by slightly unscrupulous means.

one-way ADJECTIVE [1] moving or allowing travel in one direction only: *one-way traffic; a one-way* *ticket.* 2 entailing no reciprocal obligation, action, etc.: *a one-way agreement.*

one-way ticket NOUN the US and Canadian name for **single ticket.**

on-glide NOUN *Phonetics* a glide immediately preceding a speech sound, for which the articulators are taking position. Compare **off-glide.**

ongoing ('ɒn,gəʊɪŋ) ADJECTIVE 1 actually in progress: *ongoing projects.* 2 continually moving forward; developing. 3 remaining in existence; continuing.

ongoings ('ɒngəʊɪŋz) PLURAL NOUN a Scot word for **goings-on.**

onie ('əʊnɪ) DETERMINER *Scot* a variant spelling of **ony.**

onion ('ʌnjən) NOUN 1 an alliaceous plant, *Allium cepa,* having greenish-white flowers: cultivated for its rounded edible bulb. 2 the bulb of this plant, consisting of concentric layers of white succulent leaf bases with a pungent odour and taste. 3 any of several related plants similar to *A. cepa,* such as *A. fistulosum* (Welsh onion). 4 **know one's onions.** *Brit, slang* to be fully acquainted with a subject.
▷HISTORY C14: via Anglo-Norman from Old French *oignon,* from Latin *unio* onion, related to UNION
▸'**oniony** ADJECTIVE

onion dome NOUN a bulb-shaped dome characteristic of Byzantine and Russian church architecture.

onion fly NOUN a small grey dipterous insect, *Delia antiqua,* that is a serious pest of onions. The larvae destroy the bulbs.

onionskin ('ʌnjən,skɪn) NOUN a glazed translucent paper.

onion weed NOUN a plant of Australia and New Zealand, *Nuthoscordum inodorum,* having a strong onion-like smell and reproducing from bulbs and seeds.

Onitsha (ə'nɪtʃə) NOUN a port in S Nigeria, in Anambra State on the Niger River: industrial centre. Pop.: 371 900 (1996 est.).

onium compound *or* **salt** ('əʊnɪəm) NOUN *Chem* any salt in which the positive ion (**onium ion**) is formed by the attachment of a proton to a neutral compound, as in ammonium, oxonium, and sulphonium compounds.
▷HISTORY C20: from (AMM)ONIUM

on key ADJECTIVE (**on-key** *when prenominal*), ADVERB 1 in the right key. 2 in tune.

on line *or* **online** ('ɒn,laɪn) ADJECTIVE (**on-line** *or* **online** *when prenominal*) 1 of, relating to, or concerned with a peripheral device that is directly connected to and controlled by the central processing unit of a computer. 2 of or relating to the Internet: *online shopping.* 3 occurring as part of, or involving, a continuous sequence of operations, such as a production line. ◆ Compare **off line.**

onliner (ɒn'laɪnə) NOUN a person who uses the Internet regularly.

onlooker ('ɒn,lʊkə) NOUN a person who observes without taking part.
▸'**on,looking** ADJECTIVE

only ('əʊnlɪ) ADJECTIVE (*prenominal*) 1 **the.** being single or very few in number: *the only men left in town were too old to bear arms.* 2 (of a child) having no siblings. 3 unique by virtue of being superior to anything else; peerless. 4 **one and only. a** (*adjective*) incomparable; unique. **b** (*as noun*) the object of all one's love: *you are my one and only.* ◆ ADVERB 5 without anyone or anything else being included; alone: *you have one choice only; only a genius can do that.* 6 merely or just: *it's only Henry.* 7 no more or no greater than: *we met only an hour ago.* 8 *Irish* (intensifier): *she was only marvellous; it was only dreadful.* 9 used in conditional clauses introduced by *if* to emphasize the impossibility of the condition ever being fulfilled: *if I had only known, this would never have happened.* 10 not earlier than; not...until: *I only found out yesterday.* 11 **if only** *or* **if...only.** an expression used to introduce a wish, esp. one felt to be unrealizable. 12 **only if.** never...except when. 13 **only too. a** (intensifier): *he was only too pleased to help.* **b** most regrettably (esp. in the phrase **only too true**). ◆ SENTENCE CONNECTOR 14 but; however: used to introduce an exception or condition: *play outside: only don't go into the street.*
▷HISTORY Old English *ānlīc,* from *ān* ONE + *-līc* -LY[2]

> **Language note** In informal English, *only* is often used as a sentence connector: *I would have phoned you, only I didn't know your number.* This use should be avoided in formal writing: *I would have phoned you if I'd known your number.* In formal speech and writing, *only* is placed directly before the word or words that it modifies: *she could interview only three applicants in the morning.* In all but the most formal contexts, however, it is generally regarded as acceptable to put *only* before the verb: *she could only interview three applicants in the morning.* Care must be taken not to create ambiguity, esp. in written English, in which intonation will not, as it does in speech, help to show to which item in the sentence *only* applies. A sentence such as *she only drinks tea in the afternoon* is capable of two interpretations and is therefore better rephrased either as *she drinks only tea in the afternoon* (i.e. no other drink) or *she drinks tea only in the afternoon* (i.e. at no other time).

only-begotten ADJECTIVE *Archaic* (of a child) being the only offspring of its father.

on message ADJECTIVE (**on-message** *when prenominal*) adhering to or reflecting the official line of a political party, government, or other organization.

o.n.o. (in advertisements in Britain, Australia, and New Zealand) ABBREVIATION FOR or near(est) offer: *£50 o.n.o.*

on-off ADJECTIVE 1 (of an electrical switch, button, etc.) having an 'on' position and an 'off' position. 2 existing at times and not at others; discontinuous: *an on-off relationship.*

onomasiology (,ɒnəʊ,meɪsɪ'ɒlədʒɪ) NOUN 1 another name for **onomastics** (sense 1). 2 the branch of semantics concerned with the meanings of and meaning relations between individual words.

onomastic (,ɒnə'mæstɪk) ADJECTIVE 1 of or relating to proper names. 2 *Law* denoting a signature in a different handwriting from that of the document to which it is attached.
▷HISTORY C17: from Greek *onomastikos,* from *onomazein* to name, from *onoma* NAME

onomastics (,ɒnə'mæstɪks) NOUN 1 (*functioning as singular*) the study of proper names, esp. of their origins. 2 (*functioning as singular or plural*) a systematization of the facts about how proper names are formed in a given language.

onomatopoeia (,ɒnə,mætə'piːə) NOUN 1 the formation of words whose sound is imitative of the sound of the noise or action designated, such as *hiss, buzz,* and *bang.* 2 the use of such words for poetic or rhetorical effect.
▷HISTORY C16: via Late Latin from Greek *onoma* name + *poiein* to make
▸,**ono,mato'poeic** *or* **onomatopoetic** (,ɒnə,mætəpəʊ'ɛtɪk) ADJECTIVE ▸,**ono,mato'poeically** *or* ,**ono,matopo'etically** ADVERB

Onondaga (,ɒnən'dɑːgə) NOUN 1 **Lake.** a salt lake in central New York State. Area: about 13 sq. km (5 sq. miles). 2 (*plural* **-gas** *or* **-ga**) a member of a North American Indian Iroquois people formerly living between Lake Champlain and the St Lawrence River. 3 the language of this people, belonging to the Iroquoian family.
▷HISTORY from Iroquois *onōtáge',* literally: on the top of the hill (the name of their principal village)

Onondagan (,ɒnən'dɑːgən) ADJECTIVE of or relating to the Onondaga people or their language.

onrush ('ɒn,rʌʃ) NOUN a forceful forward rush or flow.

ONS (in Britain) ABBREVIATION FOR Office for National Statistics.

onset ('ɒn,sɛt) NOUN 1 an attack; assault. 2 a start; beginning.

onshore ('ɒn'ʃɔː) ADJECTIVE, ADVERB 1 towards the land: *an onshore gale.* 2 on land; not at sea.

onside (,ɒn'saɪd) ADJECTIVE, ADVERB 1 *Sport* (of a player) in a legal position, as when behind the ball or with a required number of opponents between oneself and the opposing team's goal line. ◆ ADJECTIVE 2 taking one's part or side; working towards the same goal (esp. in the phrase **get someone onside**). Compare **offside.**

onslaught ('ɒn,slɔːt) NOUN a violent attack.
▷HISTORY C17: from Middle Dutch *aenslag,* from *aan* ON + *slag* a blow, related to SLAY

Ont. ABBREVIATION FOR Ontario.

Ontarian (ɒn'tɛərɪən) *or* **Ontarioan** (ɒn'tɛərɪ,əʊən) NOUN 1 a native or inhabitant of Ontario. ◆ ADJECTIVE 2 of or relating to Ontario or its inhabitants.

Ontario (ɒn'tɛərɪəʊ) NOUN 1 a province of central Canada: lies mostly on the Canadian Shield and contains the fertile plain of the lower Great Lakes and the St Lawrence River, one of the world's leading industrial areas; the second largest and the most populous province. Capital: Toronto. Pop.: 11 874 400 (2001 est.). Area: 891 198 sq. km (344 092 sq. miles). Abbreviations: **Ont.** *or* **ON.** 2 **Lake.** a lake between the US and Canada, bordering on New York State and Ontario province: the smallest of the Great Lakes; linked with Lake Erie by the Niagara River and Welland Canal; drained by the St Lawrence. Area: 19 684 sq. km (7600 sq. miles).

onto *or* **on to** ('ɒntu; *unstressed* 'ɒntə) PREPOSITION 1 to a position that is on: *step onto the train as it passes.* 2 having become aware of (something illicit or secret): *the police are onto us.* 3 into contact with: *get onto the factory.*

> **Language note** *Onto* is now generally accepted as a word in its own right. *On to* is still used, however, where *on* is considered to be part of the verb: *he moved on to a different town* as contrasted with *he jumped onto the stage.*

onto- COMBINING FORM existence or being: *ontogeny; ontology.*
▷HISTORY from Late Greek, from *ōn* (stem *ont-*) being, present participle of *einai* to be

ontogeny (ɒn'tɒdʒənɪ) *or* **ontogenesis** (,ɒntə'dʒɛnɪsɪs) NOUN the entire sequence of events involved in the development of an individual organism. Compare **phylogeny.**
▸**ontogenic** (,ɒntə'dʒɛnɪk) *or* **ontogenetic** (,ɒntədʒɪ'nɛtɪk) ADJECTIVE ▸,**onto'genically** *or* ,**ontoge'netically** ADVERB

ontological argument NOUN *Philosophy* 1 the traditional a priori argument for the existence of God on the grounds that the concept itself necessitates existence. Compare **cosmological argument, teleological argument.** 2 any analogous argument from the nature of some concept to the existence of whatever instantiates it.

ontology (ɒn'tɒlədʒɪ) NOUN 1 *Philosophy* the branch of metaphysics that deals with the nature of being. 2 *Logic* the set of entities presupposed by a theory.
▸,**onto'logical** ADJECTIVE ▸,**onto'logically** ADVERB

onus ('əʊnəs) NOUN, *plural* **onuses.** a responsibility, task, or burden.
▷HISTORY C17: from Latin: burden

onus probandi ('əʊnəs prəʊ'bændɪ) NOUN *Law* the Latin phrase for **burden of proof.**

onward ('ɒnwəd) ADJECTIVE 1 directed or moving forwards, onwards, etc. ◆ ADVERB 2 a variant of **onwards.**

onwards ('ɒnwədz) *or* **onward** ADVERB at or towards a point or position ahead, in advance, etc.

ony ('əʊnɪ) DETERMINER a Scot word for **any.**

onychia (,ɒnɪ'kɪə) NOUN *Vet science* inflammation of the nails or claws of animals.

onychophoran (,ɒnɪ'kɒfərən) NOUN any wormlike invertebrate of the phylum *Onychophora,* having a segmented body, short unjointed limbs, and breathing by means of tracheae: intermediate in structure and evolutionary development between annelids and arthropods.
▷HISTORY from New Latin *Onychophora,* from Greek *onukh-* nail, claw + -PHORE

-onym NOUN COMBINING FORM indicating a name or word: *acronym; pseudonym.*
▷HISTORY from Greek *-onumon,* from *onuma,* Doric variant of *onoma* name

onymous ('ɒnɪməs) ADJECTIVE (of a book) bearing its author's name.
▷HISTORY C18: back formation from ANONYMOUS

onyx ('ɒnɪks) NOUN 1 a variety of chalcedony

with alternating black and white parallel bands, used as a gemstone. Formula: SiO_2. [2] a compact variety of calcite used as an ornamental stone; onyx marble. Formula: $CaCO_3$.
▷HISTORY C13: from Latin from Greek: fingernail (so called from its veined appearance)

ONZ ABBREVIATION FOR Order of New Zealand (a NZ title).

oo- *or* **oö-** COMBINING FORM egg or ovum: *oosperm*.
▷HISTORY from Greek *ōion* EGG[1]

oocyst (ˈəʊəˌsɪst) NOUN an encysted zygote of sporozoan protozoans that undergoes sporogony to produce infective sporozoites.

oocyte (ˈəʊəˌsaɪt) NOUN an immature female germ cell that gives rise to an ovum after two meiotic divisions.

oodles (ˈuːdᵊlz) PLURAL NOUN *Informal* great quantities: *oodles of money*.
▷HISTORY C20: of uncertain origin

oof (uːf) NOUN *Slang* money.
▷HISTORY C19: from Yiddish *ooftisch,* from German *auf dem Tische* on the table (referring to gambling stakes)
▸ **ˈoofy** ADJECTIVE

oogamy (əʊˈɒɡəmɪ) NOUN sexual reproduction involving a small motile male gamete and a large much less motile female gamete: occurs in all higher animals and some plants.
▸ **oˈogamous** ADJECTIVE

oogenesis (ˌəʊəˈdʒɛnɪsɪs) NOUN the formation and maturation of ova from undifferentiated cells in the ovary. See also **oocyte.**
▸ **oogenetic** (ˌəʊədʒɪˈnɛtɪk) ADJECTIVE

oogonium (ˌəʊəˈɡəʊnɪəm) NOUN, *plural* **-nia** (-nɪə) *or* **-niums.** [1] an immature female germ cell forming oocytes by repeated divisions. [2] a female sex organ of some algae and fungi producing female gametes (oospheres).
▸ **ooˈgonial** ADJECTIVE

ooh (uː) INTERJECTION an exclamation of surprise, pleasure, pain, etc.

Ookpik (ˈuːkpɪk) NOUN *Trademark, Canadian* a sealskin doll resembling an owl, first made in 1963 by an Inuit and used abroad as a symbol of Canadian handicrafts.
▷HISTORY from Eskimo *ukpik* a snowy owl

oolite (ˈəʊəˌlaɪt) NOUN any sedimentary rock, esp. limestone, consisting of tiny spherical concentric grains within a fine matrix.
▷HISTORY C18: from French from New Latin *oolitēs,* literally: egg stone; probably a translation of German *Rogenstein* roe stone
▸ **oolitic** (ˌəʊəˈlɪtɪk) ADJECTIVE

oolith (ˈəʊəˌlɪθ) NOUN any of the tiny spherical grains of sedimentary rock of which oolite is composed.

oology (əʊˈɒlədʒɪ) NOUN the branch of ornithology concerned with the study of birds' eggs.
▸ **oological** (ˌəʊəˈlɒdʒɪkᵊl) ADJECTIVE ▸ **oˈologist** NOUN

oolong (ˈuːˌlɒŋ) NOUN a kind of dark tea, grown in China, that is partly fermented before being dried.
▷HISTORY C19: from Chinese *wu lung,* from *wu* black + *lung* dragon

oom (ˈuːəm) NOUN *South African* a title of respect used to address an elderly man.
▷HISTORY Afrikaans: literally, uncle

oomiak *or* **oomiac** (ˈuːmɪˌæk) NOUN other words for **umiak.**

oompah (ˈuːmˌpɑː) NOUN a representation of the sound made by a deep brass instrument, esp. in military band music.

oomph (ʊmf) NOUN *Informal* [1] enthusiasm, vigour, or energy. [2] sex appeal.
▷HISTORY C20: perhaps imitative of the bellow of a mating bull

oomycete (ˌəʊəˈmaɪsiːt) NOUN any organism of the phylum *Oomycota* (or *Oomycetes*), formerly classified as fungi but now usually included in the kingdom *Protoctista* or *Protista*: includes the water moulds and downy mildews.

oont (ʊnt) NOUN *Anglo-Indian, dialect* a camel.
▷HISTORY C19: from Hindi *unt*

oophorectomy (ˌəʊəfəˈrɛktəmɪ) NOUN, *plural* **-mies.** surgical removal of an ovary or ovarian tumour. Also called: **ovariectomy.** Compare **ovariotomy.**
▷HISTORY C19: from New Latin *ōophoron* ovary, from Greek *ōion* egg + *phoros* bearing, + -ECTOMY

oophoritis (ˌəʊəfəˈraɪtɪs) NOUN inflammation of an ovary; ovaritis.
▸ **oophoritic** (ˌəʊəfəˈrɪtɪk) ADJECTIVE

oophyte (ˈəʊəˌfaɪt) NOUN the gametophyte in mosses, liverworts, and ferns.
▸ **oophytic** (ˌəʊəˈfɪtɪk) ADJECTIVE

oops (ʊps, uːps) INTERJECTION an exclamation of surprise or of apology as when someone drops something or makes a mistake.

Oort cloud (ɔːt) NOUN a mass of comets orbiting the sun far beyond the orbit of Pluto, whose existence was first proposed by Jan Hendrick Oort (1900–92) in 1950.

oose (uːs) NOUN *Scot, dialect* dust; fluff.
▷HISTORY of unknown origin
▸ **ˈoosy** ADJECTIVE

oosperm (ˈəʊəˌspɜːm) NOUN a fertilized ovum; zygote.

oosphere (ˈəʊəˌsfɪə) NOUN a large female gamete produced in the oogonia of algae and fungi.

oospore (ˈəʊəˌspɔː) NOUN a thick-walled sexual spore that develops from a fertilized oosphere in some algae and fungi.
▸ **ˌooˈsporic** *or* **ˌooˈsporous** ADJECTIVE

Oostende (oːstˈɛndə) NOUN the Flemish name for **Ostend.**

ootheca (ˌəʊəˈθiːkə) NOUN, *plural* **-cae** (-siː). a capsule containing eggs that is produced by some insects and molluscs.
▷HISTORY C19: New Latin, from OO- + *thēkē* case
▸ **ˌooˈthecal** ADJECTIVE

ootid (ˈəʊətɪd) NOUN *Zoology* an immature female gamete that develops into an ovum.
▷HISTORY C20: from OO- + (SPERMA)TID

ooze¹ (uːz) VERB [1] (*intr*) to flow or leak out slowly, as through pores or very small holes. [2] to exude or emit (moisture, gas, etc.). [3] (*tr*) to overflow with: *to ooze charm.* [4] (*intr;* often foll by *away*) to disappear or escape gradually. ◆ NOUN [5] a slow flowing or leaking. [6] an infusion of vegetable matter, such as sumach or oak bark, used in tanning.
▷HISTORY Old English *wōs* juice

ooze² (uːz) NOUN [1] a soft thin mud found at the bottom of lakes and rivers. [2] a fine-grained calcareous or siliceous marine deposit consisting of the hard parts of planktonic organisms. [3] muddy ground, esp. of bogs.
▷HISTORY Old English *wāse* mud; related to Old French *wāse,* Old Norse *veisa*

ooze leather NOUN a very soft leather with a suedelike finish.
▷HISTORY C19: from OOZE¹ (sense 6)

oozy¹ (ˈuːzɪ) ADJECTIVE **oozier, ooziest.** moist or dripping.

oozy² (ˈuːzɪ) ADJECTIVE **oozier, ooziest.** of, resembling, or containing mud; slimy.
▸ **ˈoozily** ADVERB ▸ **ˈooziness** NOUN

OP ABBREVIATION FOR: [1] *Military* observation post. [2] Ordo Praedicatorum (the Dominicans). [3] organophosphate.
▷HISTORY (for sense 2) Latin: Order of Preachers

op. ABBREVIATION FOR: [1] operation. [2] opus. [3] operator. [4] operational.

o.p. *or* **O.P.** ABBREVIATION FOR out of print.

opacity (əʊˈpæsɪtɪ) NOUN, *plural* **-ties.** [1] the state or quality of being opaque. [2] the degree to which something is opaque. [3] an opaque object or substance. [4] obscurity of meaning; unintelligibility. [5] *Physics, photog* the ratio of the intensity of light incident on a medium, such as a photographic film, to that transmitted through the medium. [6] *Logic, philosophy* the property of being an opaque context.

opah (ˈəʊpə) NOUN a large soft-finned deep-sea teleost fish, *Lampris regius* (or *luna*), of the Atlantic and Pacific Oceans and the Mediterranean Sea, having a deep, brilliantly coloured body: family *Lampridae.* Also called: **moonfish, kingfish.**
▷HISTORY C18: of West African origin

opal (ˈəʊpᵊl) NOUN an amorphous, usually iridescent, mineral that can be of almost any colour, found in igneous rocks and around hot springs. It is used as a gemstone. Composition: hydrated silica. Formula: $SiO_2.nH_2O$.
▷HISTORY C16: from Latin *opalus,* from Greek *opallios,* from Sanskrit *upala* precious stone
▸ **ˈopal-ˌlike** ADJECTIVE

opalesce (ˌəʊpəˈlɛs) VERB (*intr*) to exhibit a milky iridescence.

opalescent (ˌəʊpəˈlɛsᵊnt) ADJECTIVE having or emitting an iridescence like that of an opal.
▸ **ˌopalˈescence** NOUN

opal glass NOUN glass that is opalescent or white, made by the addition of fluorides.

opaline (ˈəʊpəˌlaɪn) ADJECTIVE [1] opalescent. ◆ NOUN [2] an opaque or semiopaque whitish glass.

opaque (əʊˈpeɪk) ADJECTIVE [1] not transmitting light; not transparent or translucent. [2] not reflecting light; lacking lustre or shine; dull. [3] not transmitting radiant energy, such as electromagnetic or corpuscular radiation, or sound. [4] hard to understand; unintelligible. [5] unintelligent; dense. ◆ NOUN [6] *Photog* an opaque pigment used to block out particular areas on a negative. ◆ VERB **opaques, opaquing, opaqued.** (*tr*) [7] to make opaque. [8] *Photog* to block out particular areas, such as blemishes, on (a negative), using an opaque.
▷HISTORY C15: from Latin *opācus* shady
▸ **oˈpaquely** ADVERB ▸ **oˈpaqueness** NOUN

opaque context NOUN *Philosophy, logic* an expression in which the replacement of a term by another with the same reference may change the truth-value of the whole. *John believes that Cicero was a Roman* is opaque, since even though Cicero and Tully are the same person John may know that the given statement is true but not that Tully was a Roman. Compare **transparent context.** See also **intensional, Electra paradox.**

opaque projector NOUN the US and Canadian name for **episcope.**

op art (ɒp) NOUN a style of abstract art chiefly concerned with the exploitation of optical effects such as the illusion of movement.
▷HISTORY C20 *op,* short for *optical*

OPC *or* **opc** ABBREVIATION FOR ordinary Portland cement.

op. cit. (in textual annotations) ABBREVIATION FOR opere citato.
▷HISTORY Latin: in the work cited

ope (əʊp) VERB, ADJECTIVE an archaic or poetic word for **open.**

OPEC (ˈəʊˌpɛk) NOUN ACRONYM FOR Organization of Petroleum-Exporting Countries: an organization formed in 1961 to administer a common policy for the sale of petroleum. Its members are Algeria, Indonesia, Iran, Iraq, Kuwait, Libya, Nigeria, Qatar, Saudi Arabia, the United Arab Emirates, and Venezuela. Ecuador and Gabon were members but withdrew in 1992 and 1995 respectively.

op-ed (ˈɒpˌɛd) NOUN **a** a page of a newspaper where varying opinions are expressed by columnists, commentators, etc. **b** (*as modifier*): *an op-ed column in the New York Times.*
▷HISTORY C20: from *op(posite) ed(itorial page)*

open (ˈəʊpᵊn) ADJECTIVE [1] not closed or barred: *the door is open.* [2] affording free passage, access, view, etc.; not blocked or obstructed: *the road is open for traffic.* [3] not sealed, fastened, or wrapped: *an open package.* [4] having the interior part accessible: *an open drawer.* [5] extended, expanded, or unfolded: *an open newspaper; an open flower.* [6] ready for business: *the shops are open.* [7] able to be obtained; available: *the position advertised last week is no longer open.* [8] unobstructed by buildings, trees, etc.: *open countryside.* [9] free to all to join, enter, use, visit, etc.: *an open competition.* [10] unengaged or unoccupied: *the doctor has an hour open for you to call.* [11] See **open season.** [12] not decided or finalized: *an open question.* [13] ready to entertain new ideas; not biased or prejudiced: *an open mind.* [14] unreserved or candid: *she was very open in her description.* [15] liberal or generous: *an open hand.* [16] extended or eager to receive (esp. in the phrase **with open arms**). [17] exposed to view; blatant: *open disregard of the law.* [18] liable or susceptible: *you will leave yourself open to attack if you speak.* [19] (of climate or seasons) free from frost; mild. [20] free from navigational hazards, such as ice, sunken ships, etc.: *open water.* [21] *US* without legal restrictions or enforceable regulations, esp. in relation to gambling, vice, etc.: *an open town.* 22 without barriers to prevent absconding: *an open prison.* 23 having large or numerous spacing or apertures: *open ranks.* 24 full of small openings or gaps; porous: *an open texture.* 25 *Printing* (of type matter) generously leaded or widely spaced. 26 *Music* **a** (of a violin or guitar string) not stopped with the finger. **b** (of a pipe, such as an organ pipe) not closed at either end. **c** (of a note) played on such a string or pipe. 27 *Commerce* **a** in operation; active: *an open account.* **b** unrestricted; unlimited: *open credit; open insurance cover.* 28 See **open cheque.** 29 (of a return ticket) not specifying a date for travel. 30 *Sport* **a** (of a goal, court, etc.) unguarded or relatively unprotected: *the forward missed an open goal.* **b** (of a stance, esp. in golf) characterized by the front of the body being turned forward. 31 (of a wound) exposed to the air. 32 (esp. of the large intestine) free from obstruction. 33 undefended and of no military significance: *an open city.* 34 *Phonetics* **a** denoting a vowel pronounced with the lips relatively wide apart. **b** denoting a syllable that does not end in a consonant, as in *pa.* 35 *Chess* (of a file) having no pawns on it. 36 *Maths* (of a set) containing points whose neighbourhood consists of other points of the same set: *points inside a circle are an open set.* 37 *Computing* (of software or a computer system) designed to an internationally agreed standard in order to allow communication between computers, irrespective of size, maufacturer, etc. ◆ VERB 38 to move or cause to move from a closed or fastened position: *to open a window.* 39 (when *intr*, foll by *on* or *onto*) to render, be, or become accessible or unobstructed: *to open a road; to open a parcel; the door opens into the hall.* 40 (*intr*) to come into or appear in view: *the lake opened before us.* 41 (*tr*) to puncture (a boil) so as to permit drainage. 42 to extend or unfold or cause to extend or unfold: *to open a newspaper.* 43 to disclose or uncover or be disclosed or uncovered: *to open one's heart.* 44 to cause (the mind) to become receptive or (of the mind) to become receptive. 45 to operate or cause to operate: *to open a shop.* 46 (when *intr,* sometimes foll by *out*) to make or become less compact or dense in structure: *to open ranks.* 47 to set or be set in action; start: *to open a discussion; to open the batting.* 48 (*tr*) to arrange for (a bank account, savings account, etc.) usually by making an initial deposit. 49 to turn to a specified point in (a book, magazine, etc.): *open at page one.* 50 *Law* to make the opening statement in (a case before a court of law). 51 (*intr*) *Cards* to bet, bid, or lead first on a hand. ◆ NOUN 52 (often preceded by *the*) any wide or unobstructed space or expanse, esp. of land or water. 53 See **open air.** 54 *Sport* a competition which anyone may enter. 55 **bring** (*or* **come**) **into the open.** to make (or become) evident or public. ◆ See also **open up.**

▷**HISTORY** Old English; related to Old French *open, epen,* Old Saxon *opan,* Old High German *offan*

▸ **'openable** ADJECTIVE ▸ **'openly** ADVERB ▸ **'openness** NOUN

open air NOUN **a** the place or space where the air is unenclosed; the outdoors. **b** (*as modifier*): *an open-air concert.*

open-and-shut ADJECTIVE easily decided or solved; obvious: *an open-and-shut case.*

open book NOUN a person or thing without secrecy or concealment that can be easily known or interpreted.

Open Brethren NOUN one of the two main divisions of the Plymouth Brethren that, in contrast to the Exclusive Brethren, permits contacts with members outside the sect.

opencast mining ('əupᵊn,kɑːst) NOUN *Brit* mining by excavating from the surface. Also called: (esp US) **strip mining,** (Austral and NZ) **open-cut mining.**

▷**HISTORY** C18: from OPEN + archaic *cast* ditch or cutting

open chain NOUN a chain of atoms in a molecule that is not joined at its ends into the form of a ring.

open cheque NOUN an uncrossed cheque that can be cashed at the drawee bank.

open circuit NOUN an incomplete electrical circuit in which no current flows. Compare **closed circuit.**

Open College NOUN **the.** (in Britain) a college of art founded in 1987 for mature students studying foundation courses in arts and crafts by television programmes, written materials, and tutorials.

open court NOUN a court or trial to which members of the public are freely admitted.

open cut NOUN *Civil engineering* an excavation made in the open rather than in a tunnel. See **cut-and-cover.**

open-cut mining NOUN the Austral and NZ name for **opencast mining.**

open day NOUN an occasion on which an institution, such as a school, is open for inspection by the public. Also called: **at-home.** US and Canadian name: **open house.**

open door NOUN 1 a policy or practice by which a nation grants opportunities for trade to all other nations equally. 2 free and unrestricted admission. ◆ ADJECTIVE **open-door.** 3 open to all; accessible. 4 (in industrial relations) designating a policy of management being prepared to talk to workers in the office at any time.

open-ended ADJECTIVE 1 without definite limits, as of duration or amount: *an open-ended contract.* 2 denoting a question, esp. one on a questionnaire, that cannot be answered "yes", "no", or "don't know".

opener ('əupənə) NOUN 1 an instrument used to open sealed containers such as tins or bottles: *a bottle opener.* 2 a person who opens, esp. the player who makes the first bid or play. 3 the first or opening section or episode in a series. 4 *US* the first song, act, etc., in a variety show. 5 (*plural*) a start; beginning (esp. in the phrase **for openers**).

open-eyed ADJECTIVE 1 with the eyes wide open, as in amazement. 2 watchful; alert.

open-faced ADJECTIVE 1 having an ingenuous expression. 2 (of a watch) having no lid or cover other than the glass.

open-field ADJECTIVE (*prenominal*) *Medieval history* of or denoting the system in which an arable area was divided into unenclosed strips, esp. cultivated by different tenants.

open game NOUN *Chess* a relatively simple game involving open ranks and files, permitting tactical play, and usually following symmetrical development. Compare **closed game.**

open-handed ADJECTIVE generous; liberal.
▸ **,open-'handedly** ADVERB ▸ **,open-'handedness** NOUN

open-hearted ADJECTIVE 1 kindly and warm. 2 disclosing intentions and thoughts clearly; candid.
▸ **,open-'heartedly** ADVERB ▸ **,open-'heartedness** NOUN

open-hearth furnace NOUN (esp. formerly) a steel-making reverbatory furnace in which pig iron and scrap are contained in a shallow hearth and heated by producer gas.

open-hearth process NOUN a process for making steel using an open-hearth furnace.

open-heart surgery NOUN surgical repair of the heart during which the blood circulation is often maintained mechanically.

open house NOUN 1 a US and Canadian name for **at-home** or **open day.** 2 **keep open house.** to be always ready to provide hospitality. 3 *US and NZ* a house available for inspection by prospective buyers.

opening ('əupənɪŋ) NOUN 1 the act of making or becoming open. 2 a vacant or unobstructed space, esp. one that will serve as a passageway; gap. 3 *Chiefly US* a tract in a forest in which trees are scattered or absent. 4 the first part or stage of something. 5 **a** the first performance of something, esp. a theatrical production. **b** (*as modifier*): *the opening night.* 6 a specific or formal sequence of moves at the start of any of certain games, esp. chess or draughts. 7 an opportunity or chance, esp. for employment or promotion in a business concern. 8 *Law* the preliminary statement made by counsel to the court or jury before adducing evidence in support of his case.

opening time NOUN *Brit* the time at which public houses can legally start selling alcoholic drinks.

open learning NOUN a system of further education on a flexible part-time basis.

open letter NOUN a letter, esp. one of protest, addressed to a person but also made public, as through the press.

open market NOUN **a** a market in which prices are determined by supply and demand, there are no barriers to entry, and trading is not restricted to a specific area. **b** (*as modifier*): *open-market value.*

open-market operations PLURAL NOUN *Finance* the purchase and sale on the open market of government securities by the Bank of England for the purpose of regulating the supply of money and credit to the economy.

open marriage NOUN a marriage in which the partners are free to pursue their own social and sexual lives.

open mike NOUN **a** a session in a pub or club where members of the public are invited to perform comedy or to sing. **b** (*as modifier*): *an open-mike slot for young hopefuls.*

open-minded ADJECTIVE having a mind receptive to new ideas, arguments, etc.; unprejudiced.
▸ **,open-'mindedly** ADVERB ▸ **,open-'mindedness** NOUN

open-mouthed ADJECTIVE 1 having an open mouth, esp. in surprise. 2 greedy or ravenous. 3 clamorous or vociferous.

open order NOUN *Military* a formation that allows additional space between the ranks of a guard or inspected unit to allow the inspecting officer to pass.

open-plan ADJECTIVE having no or few dividing walls between areas: *an open-plan office floor.*

open policy NOUN an insurance policy in which the amount payable in the event of a claim is settled after the loss or damage has occurred. Compare **valued policy.**

open position NOUN *Commerce* a situation in which a dealer in commodities, securities, or currencies has either unsold stock or uncovered sales.

open primary NOUN *US Government* a primary in which any registered voter may participate. Compare **closed primary.**

open prison NOUN a penal establishment in which the prisoners are trusted to serve their sentences and so do not need to be locked up, thus extending the range of work and occupation they can safely undertake.

open punctuation NOUN punctuation characterized by sparing use of stops, esp. of the comma. Compare **close punctuation.**

open question NOUN 1 a matter which is undecided. 2 a question that cannot be answered with a yes or no but requires a developed answer.

open-reel ADJECTIVE another term for **reel-to-reel.**

open sandwich NOUN a slice of bread covered with a spread or filling but without a top.

open season NOUN 1 a specified period of time in the year when it is legal to hunt or kill game or fish protected at other times by law. 2 (often foll by *on*) a time when criticism or mistreatment is common: *open season on women employees.*

open secret NOUN something that is supposed to be secret but is widely known.

open sentence NOUN *Logic* an expression containing a free variable that can be replaced by a name to yield a sentence, as *x is wise.* Also called: **propositional function, sentential function.**

open sesame NOUN a very successful means of achieving a result.

▷**HISTORY** from the magical words used by Ali Baba in *The Arabian Nights' Entertainments* to open the door of the robbers' den

open set NOUN *Maths* 1 a set which is not a closed set. 2 an interval on the real line excluding its end points, as [0, 1], the set of reals between, but excluding, 0 and 1.

open shop NOUN an establishment in which persons are hired and employed irrespective of their membership or nonmembership of a trade union. Compare **closed shop, union shop.**

open slather NOUN See **slather** (sense 2).

open texture NOUN *Philosophy* the failure of natural languages to determine future usage, particularly the ability of predicates to permit the construction of borderline cases.

Open University NOUN **the.** (in Britain) a university founded in 1969 for mature students studying by television and radio lectures, correspondence courses, local counselling, and summer schools.

open up VERB (*adverb*) [1] (*intr*) to start firing a gun or guns. [2] (*intr*) to speak freely or without restraint. [3] (*intr*) *Informal* (of a motor vehicle) to accelerate. [4] (*tr*) to render accessible: *the motorway opened up the remoter areas.* [5] to make or become more exciting or lively: *the game opened up after half-time.*

open verdict NOUN a finding by a coroner's jury of death without stating the cause.

openwork ('əupᵊnˌwɜːk) NOUN ornamental work, as of metal or embroidery, having a pattern of openings or holes.

opera¹ ('ɒpərə, 'ɒprə) NOUN [1] an extended dramatic work in which music constitutes a dominating feature, either consisting of separate recitatives, arias, and choruses, or having a continuous musical structure. [2] the branch of music or drama represented by such works. [3] the score, libretto, etc., of an opera. [4] a theatre where opera is performed.
▷HISTORY C17: via Italian from Latin: work, a work, plural of *opus* work

opera² ('ɒpərə) NOUN a plural of **opus**.

operable ('ɒpərəbᵊl, 'ɒprə-) ADJECTIVE [1] capable of being treated by a surgical operation. [2] capable of being operated. [3] capable of being put into practice.
▸ˌ**opera'bility** NOUN ▸'**operably** ADVERB

opéra bouffe ('ɒpərə 'buːf; *French* ɔpera buf) NOUN, *plural* **opéras bouffes** (*French* ɔpera buf). a type of light or satirical opera common in France during the 19th century.
▷HISTORY from French: comic opera

opera buffa ('buːfə; *Italian* 'opera 'buffa) NOUN, *plural* **opera buffas** *or* **opere buffe** (*Italian* 'opere 'buffe). comic opera, esp. that originating in Italy during the 18th century.
▷HISTORY from Italian: comic opera

opera cloak NOUN a large cloak worn over evening clothes. Also called: **opera hood.**

opéra comique (kɒ'miːk; *French* ɔpera kɔmik) NOUN, *plural* **opéras comiques** (*French* ɔpera kɔmik). a type of opera, not necessarily comic, current in France during the 19th century and characterized by spoken dialogue. It originated in satirical parodies of grand opera.

opera glasses PLURAL NOUN small low-powered binoculars used by audiences in theatres and opera houses.

opera hat NOUN a collapsible top hat operated by a spring. Also called: **gibus.**

opera house NOUN a theatre designed for opera.

operand ('ɒpəˌrænd) NOUN a quantity or function upon which a mathematical or logical operation is performed.
▷HISTORY C19: from Latin *operandum* (something) to be worked upon, from *operārī* to work

operant ('ɒpərənt) ADJECTIVE [1] producing effects; operating. ◆ NOUN [2] a person or thing that operates. [3] *Psychol* any response by an organism that is not directly caused by a stimulus.

operant learning NOUN *Psychol* another name for **instrumental learning.**

opera seria ('sɪərɪə; *Italian* 'opera 'sɛːrja) NOUN, *plural* **opere serie** (*Italian* 'opere 'sɛːrje). a type of opera current in 18th-century Italy based on a serious plot, esp. a mythological tale.
▷HISTORY from Italian: serious opera

operate ('ɒpəˌreɪt) VERB [1] to function or cause to function. [2] (*tr*) to control the functioning of: *operate a machine.* [3] to manage, direct, run, or pursue (a business, system, etc.). [4] (*intr*) to perform a surgical operation (upon a person or animal). [5] (*intr*) to produce a desired or intended effect. [6] (*tr*; usually foll by *on*) to treat or process in a particular or specific way. [7] (*intr*) to conduct military or naval operations. [8] (*intr*) to deal in securities on a stock exchange.
▷HISTORY C17: from Latin *operārī* to work

operatic (ˌɒpə'rætɪk) ADJECTIVE [1] of or relating to opera. [2] histrionic or exaggerated.
▸ˌ**oper'atically** ADVERB

operating budget NOUN *Accounting* a forecast of the sales revenue, production costs, overheads, cash flow, etc., of an organization, used to monitor its trading activities, usually for one year.

operating system NOUN the set of software that controls the overall operation of a computer system, typically by performing such tasks as memory allocation, job scheduling, and input/output control.

operating table NOUN the table on which the patient lies during a surgical operation.

operating theatre NOUN a room in which surgical operations are performed.

operation (ˌɒpə'reɪʃən) NOUN [1] the act, process, or manner of operating. [2] the state of being in effect, in action, or operative (esp. in the phrases **in** *or* **into operation**). [3] a process, method, or series of acts, esp. of a practical or mechanical nature. [4] *Surgery* any manipulation of the body or one of its organs or parts to repair damage, arrest the progress of a disease, remove foreign matter, etc. [5] **a** a military or naval action, such as a campaign, manoeuvre, etc. **b** (*capital and prenominal when part of a name*): *Operation Crossbow.* [6] *Maths* **a** any procedure, such as addition, multiplication, involution, or differentiation, in which one or more numbers or quantities are operated upon according to specific rules. **b** a function from a set onto itself. [7] a commercial or financial transaction.

operational (ˌɒpə'reɪʃənᵊl) ADJECTIVE [1] of or relating to an operation or operations. [2] in working order and ready for use. [3] *Military* capable of, needed in, or actually involved in operations.
▸ˌ**oper'ationally** ADVERB

operational amplifier NOUN a high-gain direct-coupled amplifier, the response of which may be controlled by negative-feedback circuits externally connected.

operationalism (ˌɒpə'reɪʃənəˌlɪzəm) *or* **operationism** (ˌɒpə'reɪʃəˌnɪzəm) NOUN *Philosophy* the theory that scientific terms are defined by the experimental operations which determine their applicability.
▸ˌ**operˌational'istic** ADJECTIVE

Operation Barbarossa NOUN the codename for Hitler's invasion (1941) of Russia.

Operation Desert Storm NOUN the codename for the US-led UN operation to liberate Kuwait from Iraq (1991).

Operation Overlord NOUN the codename for the Allied invasion (June 1944) of northern France.

Operation Sealion NOUN the codename for Hitler's proposed invasion (1940) of Great Britain.

operations research NOUN the analysis of problems in business and industry involving the construction of models and the application of linear programming, critical path analysis, and other quantitative techniques. Also: **operational research.**

operations room NOUN a room from which all the operations of a military, police, or other disciplined activity are controlled.

operative ('ɒpərətɪv) ADJECTIVE [1] in force, effect, or operation. [2] exerting force or influence. [3] producing a desired effect; significant: *the operative word.* [4] of or relating to a surgical procedure. ◆ NOUN [5] a worker, esp. one with a special skill. [6] *US* a private detective.
▸'**operatively** ADVERB ▸'**operativeness** *or* ˌ**opera'tivity** NOUN

operatize *or* **operatise** ('ɒpərəˌtaɪz) VERB (*tr*) to turn (a play, novel, etc.) into an opera.

operator ('ɒpəˌreɪtə) NOUN [1] a person who operates a machine, instrument, etc., esp., a person who makes connections on a telephone switchboard or at an exchange. [2] a person who owns or operates an industrial or commercial establishment. [3] a speculator, esp one who operates on currency or stock markets. [4] *Informal* a person who manipulates affairs and other people. [5] *Maths* any symbol, term, letter, etc., used to indicate or express a specific operation or process, such as Δ (the differential operator).

operculum (əʊ'pɜːkjʊləm) NOUN, *plural* **-la** (-lə) *or* **-lums.** [1] *Zoology* **a** the hard bony flap covering the gill slits in fishes. **b** the bony plate in certain gastropods covering the opening of the shell when the body is withdrawn. [2] *Botany* the covering of the spore-bearing capsule of a moss. [3] *Biology* any other covering or lid in various organisms.
▷HISTORY C18: via New Latin from Latin: lid, from *operīre* to cover
▸**o'percular** *or* **operculate** (əʊ'pɜːkjʊlɪt, -ˌleɪt) ADJECTIVE

operetta (ˌɒpə'retə) NOUN a type of comic or light-hearted opera.
▷HISTORY C18: from Italian: a small OPERA¹
▸ˌ**oper'ettist** NOUN

operon ('ɒpəˌrɒn) NOUN *Genetics* a group of adjacent genes in bacteria functioning as a unit, consisting of structural genes and an **operator.**
▷HISTORY C20: from OPERATE

operose ('ɒpəˌrəʊs) ADJECTIVE *Rare* [1] laborious. [2] industrious; busy.
▷HISTORY C17: from Latin *operōsus* painstaking, from *opus* work
▸'**operˌosely** ADVERB ▸'**operˌoseness** NOUN

ophicleide ('ɒfɪˌklaɪd) NOUN *Music* an obsolete keyed wind instrument of bass pitch.
▷HISTORY C19: from French *ophicléide,* from Greek *ophis* snake + *kleis* key

ophidian (əʊ'fɪdɪən) ADJECTIVE [1] snakelike. [2] of, relating to, or belonging to the *Ophidia,* a suborder of reptiles that comprises the snakes. ◆ NOUN [3] any reptile of the suborder *Ophidia;* a snake.
▷HISTORY C19: from New Latin *Ophidia* name of suborder, from Greek *ophidion,* from *ophis* snake

ophiology (ˌɒfɪ'ɒlədʒɪ) NOUN the branch of zoology that is concerned with the study of snakes.
▷HISTORY C19: from Greek *ophis* snake + -LOGY
▸**ophiological** (ˌɒfɪə'lɒdʒɪkᵊl) ADJECTIVE ▸ˌ**ophi'ologist** NOUN

Ophir ('əʊfə) NOUN *Bible* a region, probably situated on the SW coast of Arabia on the Red Sea, renowned, esp. in King Solomon's reign, for its gold and precious stones (I Kings 9:28; 10:10).

ophite ('əʊfaɪt) NOUN any of several greenish mottled rocks with ophitic texture, such as dolerite and diabase.
▷HISTORY C17: from Latin *ophītēs,* from Greek, from *ophis* snake: because the mottled appearance resembles the markings of a snake

ophitic (əʊ'fɪtɪk) ADJECTIVE (of the texture of rocks such as dolerite) having small elongated unorientated feldspar crystals enclosed within pyroxene grains.

Ophiuchus (ɒ'fjuːkəs) NOUN, *Latin genitive* **Ophiuchi** (ɒ'fjuːkaɪ). a large constellation lying on the celestial equator between Hercules and Scorpius and containing the dark nebula, **Ophiuchus Nebula.**
▷HISTORY C17: via Latin from Greek *Ophioukhos,* from *ophis* snake + *ekhein* to hold

ophthalmia (ɒf'θælmɪə) NOUN inflammation of the eye, often including the conjunctiva.
▷HISTORY C16: via Late Latin from Greek, from *ophthalmos* eye; see OPTIC

ophthalmic (ɒf'θælmɪk) ADJECTIVE of or relating to the eye.

ophthalmic optician NOUN See **optician.**

ophthalmitis (ˌɒfθæl'maɪtɪs) NOUN inflammation of the eye.

ophthalmo- *or before a vowel* **ophthalm-** COMBINING FORM indicating the eye or the eyeball: *ophthalmoscope.*
▷HISTORY from Greek *ophthalmos* EYE¹

ophthalmol. *or* **ophthal.** ABBREVIATION FOR ophthalmology.

ophthalmologist (ˌɒfθæl'mɒlədʒɪst) NOUN a medical practitioner specializing in the diagnosis and treatment of eye diseases.

ophthalmology (ˌɒfθæl'mɒlədʒɪ) NOUN the branch of medicine concerned with the eye and its diseases.
▸**ophthalmological** (ɒfˌθælmə'lɒdʒɪkᵊl) ADJECTIVE

ophthalmoscope (ɒf'θælməˌskəʊp) NOUN an instrument for examining the interior of the eye.
▸**ophthalmoscopic** (ɒfˌθælmə'skɒpɪk) ADJECTIVE

ophthalmoscopy (ˌɒfθæl'mɒskəpɪ) NOUN examination of the interior of the eye with an ophthalmoscope.

-opia NOUN COMBINING FORM indicating a visual defect or condition: *myopia.*
▷HISTORY from Greek, from *ōps* eye
▸**-opic** ADJECTIVE COMBINING FORM

opiate NOUN ('əʊpɪɪt) [1] any of various narcotic drugs, such as morphine and heroin, that act on opioid receptors. [2] any other narcotic or sedative

drug. 3 something that soothes, deadens, or induces sleep. ◆ ADJECTIVE ('əʊpɪɪt) 4 containing or consisting of opium. 5 inducing relaxation; soporific. ◆ VERB ('əʊpɪˌeɪt) (*tr*) *Rare* 6 to treat with an opiate. 7 to dull or deaden.
▷HISTORY C16: from Medieval Latin *opiātus;* from Latin *opium* poppy juice, OPIUM

opine (əʊ'paɪn) VERB (when *tr, usually takes a clause as object*) to hold or express an opinion: *he opined that it was all a sad mistake.*
▷HISTORY C16: from Latin *opīnārī*

opinion (ə'pɪnjən) NOUN 1 judgment or belief not founded on certainty or proof. 2 the prevailing or popular feeling or view: *public opinion.* 3 evaluation, impression, or estimation of the value or worth of a person or thing. 4 an evaluation or judgment given by an expert: *a medical opinion.* 5 the advice given by a barrister or counsel on a case submitted to him or her for a view on the legal points involved. 6 **a matter of opinion.** a point open to question. 7 **be of the opinion (that).** to believe (that).
▷HISTORY C13: via Old French from Latin *opīniō* belief, from *opīnārī* to think; see OPINE

opinionated (ə'pɪnjəˌneɪtɪd) ADJECTIVE holding obstinately and unreasonably to one's own opinions; dogmatic.
▶**o'pinionˌatedly** ADVERB ▶**o'pinionˌatedness** NOUN

opinionative (ə'pɪnjənətɪv) ADJECTIVE *Rare* 1 of or relating to opinion. 2 another word for **opinionated.**
▶**o'pinionatively** ADVERB ▶**o'pinionativeness** NOUN

opinion poll NOUN another term for a **poll** (sense 3).

opioid ('əʊpɪˌɔɪd) NOUN **a** any of a group of substances that resemble morphine in their physiological or pharmacological effects, esp. in their pain-relieving properties. **b** (*modifier*) of or relating to such substances: *opioid receptor; opioid analgesic.*

opisthobranch (ə'pɪsθəˌbræŋk) NOUN any marine gastropod of the class *Opisthobranchia* (or *Opisthobranchiata*), in which the shell is reduced or absent: includes the pteropods, sea hares, and nudibranchs.
▷HISTORY via New Latin from Greek *opisthen* behind + -BRANCH

opisthognathous (ˌɒpɪs'θɒgnəθəs) ADJECTIVE (of a person or animal) having receding jaws.
▷HISTORY C19: from Greek *opisthen* behind + -GNATHOUS
▶**ˌopis'thognathism** NOUN

opisthosoma (ɒˌpɪsθə'səʊmə) NOUN *Zoology* the abdomen of a spider or other arachnid.
▷HISTORY C19: from Greek *opisthen* behind + SOMA[1]

opium ('əʊpɪəm) NOUN 1 the dried juice extracted from the unripe seed capsules of the opium poppy that contains alkaloids such as morphine and codeine: used in medicine as an analgesic. 2 something having a tranquillizing or stupefying effect.
▷HISTORY C14: from Latin: poppy juice, from Greek *opion,* diminutive of *opos* juice of a plant

opium den NOUN a place where opium is sold and used.

opiumism ('əʊpɪəˌmɪzəm) NOUN *Pathol* addiction to opium or a condition resulting from prolonged use of opium.

opium poppy NOUN a poppy, *Papaver somniferum,* of SW Asia, with greyish-green leaves and typically white or reddish flowers: widely cultivated as a source of opium.

Opium Wars PLURAL NOUN two wars (1839–42; 1856–60) between China and Britain resulting from the Chinese refusal to allow the importation of opium from India. China ceded Hong Kong after the British victory in 1842. The British and French victory in the second war established free trade in Chinese ports and the legalization of the opium trade.

Oporto (ə'pɔːtəʊ) NOUN a port in NW Portugal, near the mouth of the Douro River: the second largest city in Portugal, famous for port wine (begun in 1678). Pop.: 262 928 (2001). Portuguese name: **Pôrto.**

opossum (ə'pɒsəm) NOUN, *plural* **-sums** *or* **-sum.** 1 any thick-furred marsupial, esp. *Didelphis marsupialis* (**common opossum**), of the family *Didelphidae* of S North, Central, and South America, having an elongated snout and a hairless prehensile tail. Sometimes (informal) shortened to **possum.** 2 Also called (Austral and NZ): **possum.** any of various similar animals, esp. the phalanger, *Trichosurus vulpecula,* of the New Zealand bush.
▷HISTORY C17: from Algonquian *aposoum;* related to Delaware *apässum,* literally: white beast

opossum block NOUN (in New Zealand) a block of bush allocated to a licensed opossum trapper.

opossum shrimp NOUN any of various shrimplike crustaceans of the genera *Mysis, Praunus,* etc., of the order *Mysidacea,* in which the females carry the eggs and young around in a ventral brood pouch.

oppidan ('ɒpɪdən) *Rare* ◆ ADJECTIVE 1 of a town; urban. ◆ NOUN 2 a person living in a town.
▷HISTORY C16: from Latin *oppidānus,* from *oppidum* town

oppilate ('ɒpɪˌleɪt) VERB (*tr*) *Pathol, obsolete* to block (the pores, bowels, etc.).
▷HISTORY C16: from Latin *oppīlāre,* from *ob-* against + *pīlāre* to pack closely
▶**ˌoppi'lation** NOUN

opponent (ə'pəʊnənt) NOUN 1 a person who opposes another in a contest, battle, etc. 2 *Anatomy* an opponent muscle. ◆ ADJECTIVE 3 opposite, as in position. 4 *Anatomy* (of a muscle) bringing two parts into opposition. 5 opposing; contrary.
▷HISTORY C16: from Latin *oppōnere* to oppose, from *ob-* against + *pōnere* to place
▶**op'ponency** NOUN

opportune ('ɒpəˌtjuːn) ADJECTIVE 1 occurring at a time that is suitable or advantageous. 2 fit or suitable for a particular purpose or occurrence.
▷HISTORY C15: via Old French from Latin *opportūnus,* from *ob-* to + *portus* harbour (originally: coming to the harbour, obtaining timely protection)
▶**'opporˌtunely** ADVERB ▶**'opporˌtuneness** NOUN

opportunist (ˌɒpə'tjuːnɪst) NOUN 1 a person who adapts his actions, responses, etc., to take advantage of opportunities, circumstances, etc. ◆ ADJECTIVE 2 taking advantage of opportunities and circumstances in this way.
▶**ˌoppor'tunism** NOUN

opportunistic (ˌɒpətju'nɪstɪk) ADJECTIVE 1 of or characterized by opportunism. 2 *Med* (of an infection) caused by any microorganism that is harmless to a healthy person but debilitates a person whose immune system has been weakened by disease or drug treatment.
▶**ˌopportu'nistically** ADVERB

opportunity (ˌɒpə'tjuːnɪtɪ) NOUN, *plural* **-ties.** 1 a favourable, appropriate, or advantageous combination of circumstances. 2 a chance or prospect.

opportunity cost NOUN *Economics* the benefit that could have been gained from an alternative use of the same resource.

opportunity shop NOUN *Austral and NZ* a shop selling second-hand goods for charitable funds. Also called: **op-shop.**

opposable (ə'pəʊzəbᵊl) ADJECTIVE 1 capable of being opposed. 2 Also: **apposable.** (of the thumb of primates, esp. man) capable of being moved into a position facing the other digits so as to be able to touch the ends of each. 3 capable of being placed opposite something else.
▶**op'posably** ADVERB ▶**opˌposa'bility** NOUN

oppose (ə'pəʊz) VERB 1 (*tr*) to fight against, counter, or resist strongly. 2 (*tr*) to be hostile or antagonistic to; be against. 3 (*tr*) to place or set in opposition; contrast or counterbalance. 4 (*tr*) to place opposite or facing. 5 (*intr*) to be or act in opposition.
▷HISTORY C14: via Old French from Latin *oppōnere,* from *ob-* against + *pōnere* to place
▶**op'poser** NOUN ▶**op'posing** ADJECTIVE ▶**op'posingly** ADVERB ▶**oppositive** (ə'pɒzɪtɪv) ADJECTIVE

opposed-cylinder ADJECTIVE (of an internal-combustion engine) having cylinders on opposite sides of the crankcase in the same plane.

opposite ('ɒpəzɪt, -sɪt) ADJECTIVE 1 situated or being on the other side or at each side of something between: *their houses were at opposite ends of the street.* 2 facing or going in contrary directions: *opposite ways.* 3 diametrically different in character, tendency, belief, etc.: *opposite views.* 4 *Botany* **a** (of leaves, flowers, etc.) arranged in pairs on either side of the stem. **b** (of parts of a flower) arranged opposite the middle of another part. 5 *Maths* **a** (of two vertices or sides in an even-sided polygon) separated by the same number of vertices or sides in both a clockwise and anticlockwise direction. **b** (of a side in a triangle) facing a specified angle. Abbreviation: **opp.** ◆ NOUN 6 a person or thing that is opposite; antithesis. 7 *Maths* the side facing a specified angle in a right-angled triangle. 8 a rare word for **opponent.** ◆ PREPOSITION 9 Also: **opposite to.** facing; corresponding to (something on the other side of a division): *the house opposite ours.* 10 as a co-star with: *she played opposite Olivier in "Hamlet".* ◆ ADVERB 11 on opposite sides: *she lives opposite.*
▶**'oppositely** ADVERB ▶**'oppositeness** NOUN

opposite number NOUN a person holding an equivalent and corresponding position on another side or situation.

opposite prompt NOUN *Theatre* another name for **stage right.** See **prompt.**

opposite sex NOUN **the.** women in relation to men or men in relation to women.

opposition (ˌɒpə'zɪʃən) NOUN 1 the act of opposing or the state of being opposed. 2 hostility, unfriendliness, or antagonism. 3 a person or group antagonistic or opposite in aims to another. 4 **a** (usually preceded by *the*) a political party or group opposed to the ruling party or government. **b** (*capital as part of a name, esp. in Britain and other Commonwealth countries*): *Her Majesty's Loyal Opposition.* **c in opposition.** (of a political party) opposing the government. 5 a position facing or opposite another. 6 the act of placing something facing or opposite something else. 7 something that acts as an obstacle to some course or progress. 8 *Astronomy* **a** the position of an outer planet or the moon when it is in line or nearly in line with the earth as seen from the sun and is approximately at its nearest to the earth. **b** the position of two celestial bodies when they appear to be diametrically opposite each other on the celestial sphere. 9 *Astrology* an exact aspect of 180° between two planets, etc., an orb of 8° being allowed. Compare **conjunction** (sense 5), **square** (sense 10), **trine** (sense 1). 10 *Logic* **a** the relation between propositions having the same subject and predicate but differing in quality, quantity, or both, as with *all men are wicked; no men are wicked; some men are not wicked.* **b square of opposition.** a diagram representing these relations with the contradictory propositions at diagonally opposite corners. 11 **the opposition.** *Chess* a relative position of the kings in the endgame such that the player who has the move is at a disadvantage: *his opponent has the opposition.*
▶**ˌoppo'sitional** ADJECTIVE ▶**ˌoppo'sitionist** NOUN ▶**ˌoppo'sitionless** ADJECTIVE

oppress (ə'prɛs) VERB (*tr*) 1 to subjugate by cruelty, force, etc. 2 to afflict or torment. 3 to lie heavy on (the mind, imagination, etc.). 4 an obsolete word for **overwhelm.**
▷HISTORY C14: via Old French from Medieval Latin *oppressāre,* from Latin *opprimere,* from *ob-* against + *premere* to press
▶**op'pressingly** ADVERB ▶**op'pressor** NOUN

oppression (ə'prɛʃən) NOUN 1 the act of subjugating by cruelty, force, etc. or the state of being subjugated in this way. 2 the condition of being afflicted or tormented. 3 the condition of having something lying heavily on one's mind, imagination, etc.

oppressive (ə'prɛsɪv) ADJECTIVE 1 cruel, harsh, or tyrannical. 2 heavy, constricting, or depressing.
▶**op'pressively** ADVERB ▶**op'pressiveness** NOUN

opprobrious (ə'prəʊbrɪəs) ADJECTIVE 1 expressing scorn, disgrace, or contempt. 2 shameful or infamous.
▶**op'probriously** ADVERB ▶**op'probriousness** NOUN

opprobrium (ə'prəʊbrɪəm) NOUN 1 the state of being abused or scornfully criticized. 2 reproach or censure. 3 a cause of disgrace or ignominy.
▷HISTORY C17: from Latin *ob-* against + *probrum* a shameful act

oppugn (ə'pjuːn) VERB (*tr*) to call into question; dispute.

▷HISTORY C15: from Latin *oppugnāre,* from *ob-* against + *pugnāre* to fight, from *pugnus* clenched fist; see PUGNACIOUS
▶**op'pugner** NOUN

oppugnant (ə'pʌgnənt) ADJECTIVE *Rare* combative, antagonistic, or contrary.
▶**op'pugnancy** NOUN ▶**op'pugnantly** ADVERB

OPRA ('ɒprə) NOUN (in Britain) ACRONYM FOR Occupational Pensions Regulatory Authority.

Ops (ɒps) NOUN the Roman goddess of abundance and fertility, wife of Saturn. Greek counterpart: **Rhea.**

ops. ABBREVIATION FOR operations.

op-shop NOUN *Austral and NZ informal* short for **opportunity shop.**

opsimath ('ɒpsɪˌmæθ) NOUN a person who learns late in life.
▷HISTORY C19: from Greek *opsimathēs,* from *opse* late + *math-* learn
▶**opsimathy** (ɒp'sɪməθɪ) NOUN

opsin ('ɒpsɪn) NOUN the protein that together with retinene makes up the purple visual pigment rhodopsin.
▷HISTORY C20: back formation from RHODOPSIN

-opsis NOUN COMBINING FORM indicating a specified appearance or resemblance: *coreopsis.*
▷HISTORY from Greek *opsis* sight

opsonic index NOUN the ratio of the number of bacteria destroyed by phagocytes in the blood of a test patient to the number destroyed in the blood of a normal individual.

opsonin ('ɒpsənɪn) NOUN a constituent of blood serum that renders invading bacteria more susceptible to ingestion by phagocytes in the serum.
▷HISTORY C20: from Greek *opsōnion* victuals
▶**opsonic** (ɒp'sɒnɪk) ADJECTIVE

opsonize, opsonise ('ɒpsəˌnaɪz), *or* **opsonify** (ɒp'sɒnɪˌfaɪ) VERB (*tr*) to subject (bacteria) to the action of opsonins.
▶**ˌopsoni'zation, ˌopsoni'sation,** *or* **opˌsonifi'cation** NOUN

opt (ɒpt) VERB (when *intr,* foll by *for*) to show preference (for) or choose (to do something). See also **opt out.**
▷HISTORY C19: from French *opter,* from Latin *optāre* to choose

optative ('ɒptətɪv) ADJECTIVE [1] indicating or expressing choice, preference, or wish. [2] *Grammar* denoting a mood of verbs in Greek, Sanskrit, etc., expressing a wish. ◆ NOUN [3] *Grammar* **a** the optative mood. **b** a verb in this mood.
▷HISTORY C16: via French *optatif,* from Late Latin *optātīvus,* from Latin *optāre* to desire

optic ('ɒptɪk) ADJECTIVE [1] of or relating to the eye or vision. [2] a less common word for **optical.** ◆ NOUN [3] an informal word for **eye**[1].
▷HISTORY C16: from Medieval Latin *opticus,* from Greek *optikos,* from *optos* visible, seen; related to *ōps* eye

Optic ('ɒptɪk) NOUN *Trademark, Brit* a device attached to an inverted bottle for dispensing measured quantities of liquid, such as whisky, gin, etc.

optical ('ɒptɪkᵊl) ADJECTIVE [1] of, relating to, producing, or involving light. [2] of or relating to the eye or to the sense of sight; optic. [3] (esp. of a lens) aiding vision or correcting a visual disorder.
▶**'optically** ADVERB

optical activity NOUN the ability of substances that are optical isomers to rotate the plane of polarization of a transmitted beam of plane-polarized light.

optical bench NOUN an apparatus fitted for experimentation in optics, typically consisting of a table and an adjustable arrangement of light source, lenses, prisms, etc.

optical character reader NOUN a computer peripheral device enabling letters, numbers, or other characters usually printed on paper to be optically scanned and input to a storage device, such as magnetic tape. The device uses the process of **optical character recognition.** Abbreviation (for both *reader* and *recognition*): **OCR.**

optical crown NOUN an optical glass of low dispersion and relatively low refractive index. It is used in the construction of lenses.

optical density NOUN *Physics* the former name for **reflection density** or **transmission density.**

optical disc NOUN *Computing* an inflexible disc on which information is stored in digital form by laser technology. Also called: **video disc.**

optical double star NOUN two stars that appear close together when viewed through a telescope but are not physically associated and are often separated by a great distance. Compare **binary star.**

optical fibre NOUN a communications cable consisting of a thin glass fibre in a protective sheath. Light transmitted along the fibre may be modulated with vision, sound, or data signals. See also **fibre optics.**

optical flint NOUN an optical glass of high dispersion and high refractive index containing lead oxide. They are used in the manufacture of lenses, artificial gems, and cut glass. Also called: **flint glass.**

optical glass NOUN any of several types of clear homogeneous glass of known refractive index used in the construction of lenses, etc. See **optical flint, optical crown.**

optical illusion NOUN [1] an object causing a false visual impression. [2] an instance of deception by such an object.

optical isomerism NOUN isomerism of chemical compounds in which the two isomers differ only in that their molecules are mirror images of each other. See also **dextrorotation, laevorotatory, racemize.**
▶**optical isomer** NOUN

optical mark reading NOUN the reading of marks by an optical device whereby the information can be stored in machine-readable form.

optical pyrometer NOUN See **pyrometer.**

optical rotation NOUN the angle through which plane-polarized light is rotated in its passage through a substance exhibiting optical activity.

optical scanner NOUN a computer peripheral device enabling printed material, including characters and diagrams, to be scanned and converted into a form that can be stored in a computer. See also **optical character reader.**

optical sound NOUN sound recorded in the form of a photographic image on cinematograph films.

optic axis NOUN the direction in a uniaxial crystal or one of the two directions in a biaxial crystal along which a ray of unpolarized light may pass without undergoing double refraction.

optic disc NOUN a small oval-shaped area on the retina marking the site of entrance into the eyeball of the optic nerve. See **blind spot** (sense 1).

optician (ɒp'tɪʃən) NOUN a general name used to refer to: **a ophthalmic optician.** Also called: **optometrist.** a person qualified to examine the eyes and prescribe and supply spectacles and contact lenses. **b dispensing optician.** a person who supplies and fits spectacle frames but is not qualified to prescribe lenses. ◆ See also **optometrist.** Compare **ophthalmologist.**

optic nerve NOUN the second cranial nerve, which provides a sensory pathway from the retina to the brain.

optics ('ɒptɪks) NOUN (*functioning as singular*) the branch of science concerned with vision and the generation, nature, propagation, and behaviour of electromagnetic light.

optic thalamus NOUN *Anatomy* an older term for **thalamus** (senses 1, 2).

optimal ('ɒptɪməl) ADJECTIVE another word for **optimum** (sense 2).
▶**ˌopti'mality** NOUN ▶**'optimally** ADVERB

optimism ('ɒptɪˌmɪzəm) NOUN [1] the tendency to expect the best and see the best in all things. [2] hopefulness; confidence. [3] the doctrine of the ultimate triumph of good over evil. [4] the philosophical doctrine that this is the best of all possible worlds. ◆ Compare **pessimism.**
▷HISTORY C18: from French *optimisme,* from Latin *optimus* best, superlative of *bonus* good
▶**'optimist** NOUN ▶**ˌopti'mistic** *or* **ˌopti'mistical** ADJECTIVE
▶**ˌopti'mistically** ADVERB

optimize *or* **optimise** ('ɒptɪˌmaɪz) VERB [1] (*tr*) to take the full advantage of. [2] (*tr*) to plan or carry out (an economic activity) with maximum efficiency. [3] (*intr*) to be optimistic. [4] (*tr*) to write or modify (a computer program) to achieve maximum efficiency in storage capacity, time, cost, etc. [5] (*tr*) to find the best compromise among several often conflicting requirements, as in engineering design.
▶**ˌoptimi'zation** *or* **ˌoptimi'sation** NOUN

optimum ('ɒptɪməm) NOUN, *plural* **-ma** (-mə) *or* **-mums.** [1] a condition, degree, amount or compromise that produces the best possible result. ◆ ADJECTIVE [2] most favourable or advantageous; best: *optimum conditions.*
▷HISTORY C19: from Latin: the best (thing), from *optimus* best; see OPTIMISM

optimum population NOUN *Economics* a population that is sufficiently large to provide an adequate workforce with minimal unemployment.

option ('ɒpʃən) NOUN [1] the act or an instance of choosing or deciding. [2] the power or liberty to choose. [3] an exclusive opportunity, usually for a limited period, to buy something at a future date: *he has a six month option on the Canadian rights to this book.* [4] *Commerce* the right to buy (**call option**) or sell (**put option**) a fixed quantity of a commodity, security, foreign exchange, etc., at a fixed price at a specified date in the future. See also **traded option.** [5] something chosen; choice. [6] *NZ* short for **local option.** [7] **keep** (*or* **leave**) **one's options open.** not to commit oneself. [8] See **soft option.** ◆ VERB [9] (*tr*) to obtain or grant an option on.
▷HISTORY C17: from Latin *optiō* free choice, from *optāre* to choose

optional ('ɒpʃənᵊl) ADJECTIVE possible but not compulsory; left to personal choice.
▶**'optionally** ADVERB

option money NOUN *Commerce* the price paid for buying an option.

optoelectronics (ˌɒptəʊɪlɛk'trɒnɪks) NOUN (*functioning as singular*) the study or use of devices in which an optical input produces an electrical output, or in which electrical stimulation produces visible or infrared output.
▶**ˌoptoelec'tronic** ADJECTIVE

optometer (ɒp'tɒmɪtə) NOUN any of various instruments for measuring the refractive power of the eye.

optometrist (ɒp'tɒmɪtrɪst) NOUN a person who is qualified to examine the eyes and prescribe and supply spectacles and contact lenses. Also called (esp Brit): **ophthalmic optician.** Compare **optician, ophthalmologist.**

optometry (ɒp'tɒmɪtrɪ) NOUN the science or practice of testing visual acuity and prescribing corrective lenses.
▶**optometric** (ˌɒptə'mɛtrɪk) ADJECTIVE

optophone ('ɒptəˌfəʊn) NOUN a device for blind people that converts printed words into sounds.

opt out VERB [1] (*intr, adverb;* often foll by *of*) to choose not to be involved (in) or part (of). ◆ NOUN **opt-out.** [2] the act of opting out, esp. of local-authority administration: *opt-outs by hospitals and schools.*

opulent ('ɒpjʊlənt) ADJECTIVE [1] having or indicating wealth. [2] abundant or plentiful.
▷HISTORY C17: from Latin *opulens,* from *opēs* (pl) wealth
▶**'opulence** *or* (*less commonly*) **'opulency** NOUN
▶**'opulently** ADVERB

opuntia (ɒ'pʌnʃɪə) NOUN any cactus of the genus *Opuntia,* esp. prickly pear, having fleshy branched stems and green, red, or yellow flowers.
▷HISTORY C17: New Latin, from Latin *Opuntia* (*herba*) the Opuntian (plant), from *Opus,* ancient town of Locris, Greece

opus ('əʊpəs, 'ɒp-) NOUN, *plural* **opuses** *or* **opera** ('ɒpərə). [1] an artistic composition, esp. a musical work. [2] (*often capital*) (usually followed by a number) a musical composition by a particular composer, generally catalogued in order of publication: *Beethoven's opus 61 is his violin concerto.* Abbreviation: **op.**
▷HISTORY C18: from Latin: a work; compare Sanskrit *apas* work

opus anglicanum ('əʊpəs æŋglɪ'kɑːnəm) NOUN fine embroidery, esp. of church vestments, produced in England *c.*1200–*c.*1350; characterized by the rich materials used, esp. silver gilt thread.
▷HISTORY Latin: English work

opuscule (ɒˈpʌskjuːl) NOUN *Rare* a small or insignificant artistic work.
▷HISTORY C17: via French from Latin *opusculum,* from *opus* work
▸**oˈpuscular** ADJECTIVE

Opus Dei (ˈəʊpəs ˈdeɪɪ) NOUN 1 another name for **divine office.** 2 an international Roman Catholic organization of lay people and priests founded in Spain in 1928 by Josemaria Escrivá de Balaguer (1902–75), with the aim of spreading Christian principles.

or[1] (ɔː; *unstressed* ə) CONJUNCTION (*coordinating*) 1 used to join alternatives: *apples or pears; apples or pears or cheese; apples, pears, or cheese.* 2 used to join rephrasings of the same thing: *to serve in the army, or rather to fight in the army; twelve, or a dozen.* 3 used to join two alternatives when the first is preceded by *either* or *whether*: *whether it rains or not we'll be there; either yes or no.* 4 **one or two, four or five,** etc. a few. 5 **or else.** See **else** (sense 3). 6 a poetic word for **either** or **whether**, as the first element in correlatives, with *or* also preceding the second alternative ◆ See also **exclusive or, inclusive or.**
▷HISTORY C13: contraction of *other,* used to introduce an alternative, changed (through influence of EITHER) from Old English *oththe;* compare Old High German *odar* (German *oder*)

or[2] (ɔː) *Archaic* ◆ CONJUNCTION 1 (*subordinating;* foll by *ever* or *ere*) before; when. ◆ PREPOSITION 2 before.
▷HISTORY Old English *ār* soon; related to Old Norse *ār* early, Old High German *ēr*

or[3] (ɔː) ADJECTIVE (*usually postpositive*) *Heraldry* of the metal gold.
▷HISTORY C16: via French from Latin *aurum* gold

OR ABBREVIATION FOR: 1 **operations research.** 2 Oregon. 3 *Military* **other ranks.**

-or[1] SUFFIX FORMING NOUNS FROM VERBS a person or thing that does what is expressed by the verb: *actor; conductor; generator; sailor.*
▷HISTORY via Old French *-eur, -eor,* from Latin *-or* or *-ātor*

-or[2] SUFFIX FORMING NOUNS 1 indicating state, condition, or activity: *terror; error.* 2 the US spelling of **-our.**

ora (ˈɔːrə) NOUN the plural of **os**[2].

orache *or esp US* **orach** (ˈɒrɪtʃ) NOUN any of several herbaceous plants or small shrubs of the chenopodiaceous genus *Atriplex,* esp. *A. hortensis* (**garden orache**), which is cultivated as a vegetable. They have typically greyish-green lobed leaves and inconspicuous flowers.
▷HISTORY C15: from Old French *arache,* from Latin *atriplex,* from Greek *atraphaxus,* of obscure origin

oracle (ˈɒrəkᵊl) NOUN 1 a prophecy, often obscure or allegorical, revealed through the medium of a priest or priestess at the shrine of a god. 2 a shrine at which an oracular god is consulted. 3 an agency through which a prophecy is transmitted. 4 any person or thing believed to indicate future action with infallible authority. 5 a statement believed to be infallible and authoritative. 6 *Bible* **a** a message from God. **b** the holy of holies in the Israelite temple. ◆ See also **oracles.**
▷HISTORY C14: via Old French from Latin *ōrāculum,* from *ōrāre* to request

oracles (ˈɒrəkᵊlz) PLURAL NOUN another term for **Scripture** (sense 1).

oracular (ɒˈrækjʊlə) ADJECTIVE 1 of or relating to an oracle: *Apollo had an oracular shrine at Delphi.* 2 wise and prophetic: *an oracular political thriller.* 3 mysterious or ambiguous.
▸**oˈracularly** ADVERB

oracy (ˈɔːrəsɪ) NOUN the capacity to express oneself in and understand speech.
▷HISTORY C20: from Latin *or-, os* mouth, by analogy with *literacy*

Oradea (*Romanian* oˈradea) NOUN an industrial city in NW Romania, in Transylvania: ceded by Hungary (1919). Pop.: 223 288 (1997 est.). German name: **Grosswardein.** Hungarian name: **Nagyvárad.**

ora et labora *Latin* (ˈɔːrɑː ɛt ˈlæbɔːˌrɑː) pray and work.

oral (ˈɔːrəl, ˈɒrəl) ADJECTIVE 1 spoken or verbal: *an oral agreement.* 2 relating to, affecting, or for use in the mouth: *an oral thermometer.* 3 of or relating to the surface of an animal, such as a jellyfish, on which the mouth is situated. 4 denoting a drug to be taken by mouth: *an oral contraceptive.* Compare **parenteral.** 5 of, relating to, or using spoken words. 6 *Phonetics* pronounced with the soft palate in a raised position completely closing the nasal cavity and allowing air to pass out only through the mouth. 7 *Psychoanal* **a** relating to a stage of psychosexual development during which the child's interest is concentrated on the mouth. **b** denoting personality traits, such as dependence, selfishness, and aggression, resulting from fixation at the oral stage. Compare **anal** (sense 2), **genital** (sense 2), **phallic** (sense 2). ◆ NOUN 8 an examination in which the questions and answers are spoken rather than written.
▷HISTORY C17: from Late Latin *ōrālis,* from Latin *ōs* face
▸**ˈorally** ADVERB

oral eroticism NOUN *Psychoanal* libidinal pleasure derived from the lips and mouth, for example by kissing.

oral history NOUN the memories of living people about events or social conditions which they experienced in their earlier lives taped and preserved as historical evidence.

oral hygiene NOUN another name for **dental hygiene.**

oral hygienist NOUN another name for **dental hygienist.**

Oral Law NOUN *Judaism* the traditional body of religious law believed to have been revealed to Moses as an interpretation of the Torah and passed on orally until it was codified and recorded, principally in the Mishna and Gemara.

oral society NOUN a society that has not developed literacy.

Oran (əˈræn, əˈrɑːn; *French* ɔrɑ̃) NOUN a port in NW Algeria: the second largest city in the country; scene of the destruction by the British of most of the French fleet in the harbour in 1940 to prevent its capture by the Germans. Pop.: 692 516 (1998).

orang (ɔːˈræŋ, ˈɔːræŋ) NOUN short for **orang-utan.**

orange (ˈɒrɪndʒ) NOUN 1 any of several citrus trees, esp. *Citrus sinensis* (**sweet orange**) and the Seville orange, cultivated in warm regions for their round edible fruit. See also **tangerine** (sense 1). 2 **a** the fruit of any of these trees, having a yellowish-red bitter rind and segmented juicy flesh. See also **navel orange. b** (*as modifier*): *orange peel.* 3 the hard wood of any of these trees. 4 any of a group of colours, such as that of the skin of an orange, that lie between red and yellow in the visible spectrum in the approximate wavelength range 620–585 nanometres. 5 a dye or pigment producing these colours. 6 orange cloth or clothing: *dressed in orange.* 7 any of several trees or herbaceous plants that resemble the orange, such as mock orange. ◆ ADJECTIVE 8 of the colour orange.
▷HISTORY C14: via Old French from Old Provençal *auranja,* from Arabic *nāranj,* from Persian *nārang,* from Sanskrit *nāranga,* probably of Dravidian origin

Orange NOUN 1 (ˈɒrɪndʒ) a river in S Africa, rising in NE Lesotho and flowing generally west across the South African plateau to the Atlantic: the longest river in South Africa. Length: 2093 km (1300 miles). 2 (*French* ɔrɑ̃ʒ) a town in SE France: a small principality in the Middle Ages, the descendants of which formed the House of Orange. Pop.: 28 136 (1990). Ancient name: **Arausio** (əˈraʊsɪəʊ).

orangeade (ˌɒrɪndʒˈeɪd) NOUN an effervescent or still orange-flavoured drink.

orange blossom NOUN the flowers of the orange tree, traditionally worn by brides.

orange chromide (ˈkrəʊmaɪd) NOUN an Asian cichlid fish, *Etropus maculatus,* with a brownish-orange spotted body.

orange flower water NOUN a distilled infusion of orange blossom, used in cakes, confectionery, etc.

Orange Free State NOUN a former province of central South Africa, between the Orange and Vaal rivers: settled by Boers in 1836 after the Great Trek; annexed by Britain in 1848; became a province of South Africa in 1910; replaced in 1994 by the new province of Free State; economy based on agriculture and mineral resources (esp. gold and uranium). Capital: Bloemfontein.

Orangeism (ˈɒrɪndʒˌɪzəm) NOUN the practices or principles of Orangemen, esp. Protestant supremacy in the Republic of Ireland, Northern Ireland, or Canada.

Orangeman (ˈɒrɪndʒmən) NOUN, *plural* **-men.** a member of a society founded in Ireland (1795) to uphold the Protestant religion, the Protestant dynasty, and the Protestant constitution. **Orange Lodges** have since spread to many parts of the former British Empire.
▷HISTORY C18: after William, prince of *Orange* (king of England as William III)

Orangeman's Day NOUN the 12th of July, celebrated by Protestants in Northern Ireland to commemorate the anniversary of the Battle of the Boyne (1690).

orange peel NOUN 1 the thick pitted rind of an orange. 2 anything resembling this in surface texture, such as skin or porcelain.

orange-peel fungus NOUN See **elf-cup.**

orange pekoe NOUN a superior grade of black tea made from the small leaves at the tips of the plant stems and growing in India and Sri Lanka.

orange roughy (ˈrʌfɪ) NOUN a marine food fish, *Hoplosthenus atlanticus,* of S Pacific waters.

orangery (ˈɒrɪndʒərɪ, -dʒrɪ) NOUN, *plural* **-eries.** a building, such as a greenhouse, in which orange trees are grown.

orange stick NOUN a small stick used to clean the fingernails and cuticles, having one pointed and one rounded end.

orange-tip NOUN a European butterfly, *Anthocharis cardamines,* having whitish wings with orange-tipped forewings: family *Pieridae.*

orangewood (ˈɒrɪndʒˌwʊd) NOUN **a** the hard fine-grained yellowish wood of the orange tree. **b** (*as modifier*): *an orangewood table.*

orang-utan (ɔːˌræŋuːˈtæn, ˌɔːræŋˈuːtæn) *or* **orang-utang** (ɔːˌræŋuːˈtæŋ, ˌɔːræŋˈuːtæŋ) NOUN a large anthropoid ape, *Pongo pygmaeus,* of the forests of Sumatra and Borneo, with shaggy reddish-brown hair and strong arms. Sometimes shortened to **orang.**
▷HISTORY C17: from Malay *orang hutan,* from *ōrang* man + *hūtan* forest

ora pro nobis *Latin* (ˈɔːrɑː prəʊ ˈnəʊbɪs) a Latin invocation meaning *pray for us.*

orate (ɔːˈreɪt) VERB (*intr*) 1 to make or give an oration. 2 to speak pompously and lengthily.

oration (ɔːˈreɪʃən) NOUN 1 a formal public declaration or speech. 2 any rhetorical, lengthy, or pompous speech. 3 an academic exercise or contest in public speaking.
▷HISTORY C14: from Latin *ōrātiō* speech, harangue, from *ōrāre* to plead, pray

orator (ˈɒrətə) NOUN 1 a public speaker, esp. one versed in rhetoric. 2 a person given to lengthy or pompous speeches. 3 *Obsolete* the claimant in a cause of action in chancery.

Oratorian (ˌɒrəˈtɔːrɪən) NOUN a member of the religious congregation of the Oratory.

oratorio (ˌɒrəˈtɔːrɪəʊ) NOUN, *plural* **-rios.** a dramatic but unstaged musical composition for soloists, chorus, and orchestra, based on a religious theme.
▷HISTORY C18: from Italian, literally: ORATORY[2], referring to the Church of the Oratory at Rome where musical services were held

oratory[1] (ˈɒrətərɪ, -trɪ) NOUN 1 the art of public speaking. 2 rhetorical skill or style.
▷HISTORY C16: from Latin (*ars*) *ōrātōria* (the art of) public speaking
▸**ˌoraˈtorical** ADJECTIVE ▸**ˌoraˈtorically** ADVERB

oratory[2] (ˈɒrətərɪ, -trɪ) NOUN, *plural* **-ries.** a small room or secluded place, set apart for private prayer.
▷HISTORY C14: from Anglo-Norman, from Church Latin *ōrātōrium* place of prayer, from *ōrāre* to plead, pray

Oratory (ˈɒrətərɪ, -trɪ) NOUN *RC Church* 1 Also called: **Congregation of the Oratory.** the religious society of secular priests (**Oratorians**) living in a community founded by St Philip Neri. 2 any church belonging to this society: *the Brompton Oratory.*

orb (ɔːb) NOUN 1 (in royal regalia) an ornamental sphere surmounted by a cross, representing the power of a sovereign. 2 a sphere; globe. 3 *Poetic* another word for **eye**[1]. 4 *Obsolete or poetic* **a** a

celestial body, esp. the earth or sun. **b** the orbit of a celestial body. 5 an archaic word for **circle.** ◆ VERB 6 to make or become circular or spherical. 7 (*tr*) an archaic word for **encircle.**
▷HISTORY C16: from Latin *orbis* circle, disc

orbicular (ɔːˈbɪkjʊlə), **orbiculate,** *or* **orbiculated** ADJECTIVE 1 circular or spherical. 2 (of a leaf or similar flat part) circular or nearly circular. 3 *Rare* rounded or total.
▸**orbicularity** (ɔːˌbɪkjʊˈlærɪtɪ) NOUN ▸**orˈbicularly** ADVERB

orbit (ˈɔːbɪt) NOUN 1 *Astronomy* the curved path, usually elliptical, followed by a planet, satellite, comet, etc., in its motion around another celestial body under the influence of gravitation. 2 a range or field of action or influence; sphere: *he is out of my orbit.* 3 *Anatomy* the bony cavity containing the eyeball. Nontechnical name: **eye socket.** 4 *Zoology* **a** the skin surrounding the eye of a bird. **b** the hollow in which lies the eye or eyestalk of an insect or other arthropod. 5 *Physics* the path of an electron in its motion around the nucleus of an atom. ◆ VERB 6 to move around (a body) in a curved path, usually circular or elliptical. 7 (*tr*) to send (a satellite, spacecraft, etc.) into orbit. 8 (*intr*) to move in or as if in an orbit.
▷HISTORY C16: from Latin *orbita* course, from *orbis* circle, ORB

orbital (ˈɔːbɪtᵊl) ADJECTIVE 1 of or denoting an orbit. ◆ NOUN 2 a region surrounding an atomic nucleus in which the probability distribution of the electrons is given by a wave function.
▸**ˈorbitally** ADVERB

orbital velocity NOUN the velocity required by a spacecraft, satellite, etc., to enter and maintain a given orbit.

orbiter (ˈɔːbɪtə) NOUN a spacecraft or satellite designed to orbit a planet or other body without landing on it. Compare **lander.**

orc (ɔːk) NOUN 1 any of various whales, such as the killer and grampus. 2 a mythical monster.
▷HISTORY C16: via Latin *orca,* perhaps from Greek *orux* whale

Orcadian (ɔːˈkeɪdɪən) NOUN 1 a native or inhabitant of the Orkneys. ◆ ADJECTIVE 2 of or relating to the Orkneys.
▷HISTORY from Latin *Orcades* the Orkney Islands

orcein (ˈɔːsiːɪn) NOUN a brown crystalline material formed by the action of ammonia on orcinol and present in orchil: used as a dye, biological stain, and antiseptic. Formula: $C_{28}H_{24}O_7N_2$.
▷HISTORY C19: see ORCINOL

orchard (ˈɔːtʃəd) NOUN 1 an area of land devoted to the cultivation of fruit trees. 2 a collection of fruit trees especially cultivated.
▷HISTORY Old English *orceard, ortigeard,* from *ort-,* from Latin *hortus* garden + *geard* YARD[2]

orchard bush NOUN *W African* open savanna country with occasional trees and scrub, as found north of the W African forest belt.

orchardman (ˈɔːtʃədmən) NOUN, *plural* **-men.** a person who grows and sells orchard fruits.

orchestra (ˈɔːkɪstrə) NOUN 1 a large group of musicians, esp. one whose members play a variety of different instruments. See also **symphony orchestra, string orchestra, chamber orchestra.** 2 a group of musicians, each playing the same type of instrument: *a balalaika orchestra.* 3 Also called: **orchestra pit.** the space reserved for musicians in a theatre, immediately in front of or under the stage. 4 *Chiefly US and Canadian* the stalls in a theatre. 5 (in the ancient Greek theatre) the semicircular space in front of the stage.
▷HISTORY C17: via Latin from Greek: the space in the theatre reserved for the chorus, from *orkheisthai* to dance
▸**orchestral** (ɔːˈkɛstrəl) ADJECTIVE ▸**orˈchestrally** ADVERB

orchestrate (ˈɔːkɪˌstreɪt) VERB (*tr*) 1 to score or arrange (a piece of music) for orchestra. 2 to arrange, organize, or build up for special or maximum effect.
▸**ˌorchesˈtration** NOUN ▸**ˈorchesˌtrator** NOUN

orchestrina (ˌɔːkɪsˈtriːnə) *or* **orchestrion** (ɔːˈkɛstrɪən) NOUN any of various types of mechanical musical instrument designed to imitate the sound of an orchestra.

orchid (ˈɔːkɪd) NOUN any terrestrial or epiphytic plant of the family *Orchidaceae,* often having flowers of unusual shapes and beautiful colours, specialized for pollination by certain insects. See **bee orchid, burnt-tip orchid, fly orchid, frog orchid, lady orchid, lizard orchid, man orchid, monkey orchid, purple-fringed orchid, pyramidal orchid, scented orchid, spider orchid, spotted orchid.**
▷HISTORY C19: from New Latin *Orchideae;* see ORCHIS

orchidaceous (ˌɔːkɪˈdeɪʃəs) ADJECTIVE of, relating to, or belonging to the *Orchidaceae,* a family of flowering plants including the orchids.

orchidectomy (ˌɔːkɪˈdɛktəmɪ) NOUN, *plural* **-mies.** the surgical removal of one or both testes.
▷HISTORY C19: from Greek *orkhis* testicle + -ECTOMY

orchil (ˈɔːkɪl, -tʃɪl) *or* **archil** NOUN 1 any of various lichens, esp. any of the genera *Roccella, Dendrographa,* and *Lecanora.* 2 Also called: **cudbear.** a purplish dye obtained by treating these lichens with aqueous ammonia: contains orcinol, orcein, and litmus.
▷HISTORY C15: from Old French *orcheil,* of uncertain origin

orchis (ˈɔːkɪs) NOUN 1 any terrestrial orchid of the N temperate genus *Orchis,* having fleshy tubers and spikes of typically pink flowers. 2 any of various temperate or tropical orchids of the genus *Habenaria,* such as the fringed orchis.
▷HISTORY C16: via Latin from Greek *orkhis* testicle; so called from the shape of its roots

orchitis (ɔːˈkaɪtɪs) NOUN inflammation of one or both testicles.
▷HISTORY C18: from New Latin, from Greek *orkhis* testicle + -ITIS
▸**orchitic** (ɔːˈkɪtɪk) ADJECTIVE

orcinol (ˈɔːsɪˌnɒl) *or* **orcin** (ˈɔːsɪn) NOUN a colourless crystalline water-soluble solid that occurs in many lichens and from which the dyes found in litmus are derived. Formula: $CH_3C_6H_3(OH)_2$.
▷HISTORY C20: from New Latin *orcina,* from Italian *orcello* ORCHIL

OR circuit *or* **gate** (ɔː) NOUN *Computing* a logic circuit having two or more input wires and one output wire that gives a high-voltage output signal if one or more input signals are at a high voltage: used extensively as a basic circuit in computers. Compare **AND circuit, NAND circuit.**
▷HISTORY C20: so named from its similarity to the function of *or* in logical constructions

Orcus (ˈɔːkəs) NOUN another name for **Dis** (sense 1).

Ord (ɔːd) NOUN a river in NE Western Australia, rising on the Kimberley Plateau and flowing generally north to the Timor Sea: subject of a major irrigation scheme. Length: about 500 km (300 miles).

ordain (ɔːˈdeɪn) VERB (*tr*) 1 to consecrate (someone) as a priest; confer holy orders upon. 2 (*may take a clause as object*) to decree, appoint, or predestine irrevocably. 3 (*may take a clause as object*) to order, establish, or enact with authority. 4 *Obsolete* to select for an office.
▷HISTORY C13: from Anglo-Norman *ordeiner,* from Late Latin *ordināre,* from Latin *ordo* ORDER
▸**orˈdainer** NOUN ▸**orˈdainment** NOUN

ordeal (ɔːˈdiːl) NOUN 1 a severe or trying experience. 2 *History* a method of trial in which the guilt or innocence of an accused person was determined by subjecting him to physical danger, esp. by fire or water. The outcome was regarded as an indication of divine judgment.
▷HISTORY Old English *ordāl, ordēl;* related to Old Frisian *ordēl,* Old High German *urteili* (German *Urteil*) verdict. See DEAL[1], DOLE[1]

order (ˈɔːdə) NOUN 1 a state in which all components or elements are arranged logically, comprehensibly, or naturally. 2 an arrangement or disposition of things in succession; sequence: *alphabetical order.* 3 an established or customary method or state, esp. of society. 4 a peaceful or harmonious condition of society: *order reigned in the streets.* 5 (*often plural*) a class, rank, or hierarchy: *the lower orders.* 6 *Biology* any of the taxonomic groups into which a class is divided and which contains one or more families. *Carnivora, Primates,* and *Rodentia* are three orders of the class *Mammalia.* 7 an instruction that must be obeyed; command. 8 a decision or direction of a court or judge entered on the court record but not included in the final judgment. 9 **a** a commission or instruction to produce or supply something in return for payment. **b** the commodity produced or supplied. **c** (*as modifier*): *order form.* 10 a procedure followed by an assembly, meeting, etc. 11 (*capital when part of a name*) a body of people united in a particular aim or purpose. 12 Also called: **religious order.** (*usually capital*) a group of persons who bind themselves by vows in order to devote themselves to the pursuit of religious aims. 13 *History* a society of knights constituted as a fraternity, such as the Knights Templars. 14 **a** a group of people holding a specific honour for service or merit, conferred on them by a sovereign or state. **b** the insignia of such a group. 15 **a** any of the five major classical styles of architecture classified by the style of columns and entablatures used. See also **Doric, Ionic, Corinthian, Tuscan, Composite. b** any style of architecture. 16 *Christianity* **a** the sacrament by which bishops, priests, etc., have their offices conferred upon them. **b** any of the degrees into which the ministry is divided. **c** the office of an ordained Christian minister. 17 a form of Christian Church service prescribed to be used on specific occasions. 18 *Judaism* one of the six sections of the Mishna or the corresponding tractates of the Talmud. 19 *Maths* **a** the number of times a function must be differentiated to obtain a given derivative. **b** the order of the highest derivative in a differential equation. **c** the number of rows or columns in a determinant or square matrix. **d** the number of members of a finite group. 20 short for **order of magnitude.** 21 *Military* (often preceded by *the*) the dress, equipment, or formation directed for a particular purpose or undertaking: *drill order; battle order.* 22 **a tall order.** something difficult, demanding, or exacting. 23 **in order. a** in sequence. **b** properly arranged. **c** appropriate or fitting. 24 **in order to.** (*preposition;* foll by an infinitive) so that it is possible to: *to eat in order to live.* 25 **in order that.** (*conjunction*) with the purpose that; so that. 26 **keep order.** to maintain or enforce order. 27 **of** *or* **in the order of.** having an approximately specified size or quantity. 28 **on order.** having been ordered or commissioned but not having been delivered. 29 **out of order. a** not in sequence. **b** not working. **c** not following the rules or customary procedure. 30 **to order. a** according to a buyer's specifications. **b** on request or demand. ◆ VERB 31 (*tr*) to give a command to (a person or animal to do or be something). 32 to request (something) to be supplied or made, esp. in return for payment: *he ordered a hamburger.* 33 (*tr*) to instruct or command to move, go, etc. (to a specified place): *they ordered her into the house.* 34 (*tr; may take a clause as object*) to authorize; prescribe: *the doctor ordered a strict diet.* 35 (*tr*) to arrange, regulate, or dispose (articles) in their proper places. 36 (of fate or the gods) to will; ordain. 37 (*tr*) *Rare* to ordain. ◆ INTERJECTION 38 an exclamation of protest against an infringement of established procedure. 39 an exclamation demanding that orderly behaviour be restored. ◆ See also **orders.**
▷HISTORY C13: from Old French *ordre,* from Latin *ordō*
▸**ˈorderer** NOUN ▸**ˈorderless** ADJECTIVE

order about *or* **around** VERB (*tr*) to bully or domineer.

order arms INTERJECTION, NOUN *Military* the order in drill to hold the rifle close to the right side with the butt resting on the ground.

order-driven ADJECTIVE denoting an electronic market system, esp. for stock exchanges, in which prices are determined by the publication of orders to buy or sell. Compare **quote-driven.**

ordered set NOUN *Logic, maths* a sequence of elements that is distinguished from the other sequences of the same element by the order of the elements. Thus <a, b> is not identical with <b, a>.

order in council NOUN (in Britain and various other Commonwealth countries) a decree of the Cabinet, usually made under the authority of a statute: in theory a decree of the sovereign and Privy Council.

ordering (ˈɔːdərɪŋ) NOUN *Logic* any of a number of categories of relations that permit at least some members of their domain to be placed in order. A **linear** or **simple ordering** is reflexive, antisymmetric, transitive, and connected, as *less than or equal to* on the integers. A **partial ordering** is reflexive, antisymmetric, and transitive, as set inclusion. Either of these orderings is called *strict* if it is asymmetric instead of reflexive and antisymmetric. It is a *well-ordering* if every nonempty subset has a least member under the relation.

orderly ('ɔːdəlɪ) ADJECTIVE 1 in order, properly arranged, or tidy. 2 obeying or appreciating method, system, and arrangement. 3 harmonious or peaceful. 4 *Military* of or relating to orders: *an orderly book*. ◆ ADVERB 5 *Now rare* according to custom or rule. ◆ NOUN, *plural* **-lies**. 6 *Med* a male hospital attendant. 7 *Military* a junior rank detailed to carry orders or perform minor tasks for a more senior officer.
▸ **'orderliness** NOUN

orderly officer NOUN another name for **officer of the day**.

orderly room NOUN *Military* a room in the barracks of a battalion or company used for general administrative purposes.

Order of Australia NOUN an order awarded to Australians for outstanding achievement or for service to Australia or to humanity at large; established in 1975.

Order of Canada NOUN an order awarded to Canadians for outstanding achievement; established in 1967.

order of magnitude NOUN the approximate size of something, esp. measured in powers of 10: *the order of magnitude of the deficit was as expected; their estimates differ by an order of magnitude*. Also called: **order**.

Order of Merit NOUN *Brit* an order conferred on civilians and servicemen for eminence in any field.

Order of Military Merit NOUN an order awarded to members of the Canadian Forces for conspicuous merit; established in 1972.

order of the day NOUN 1 the general directive of a commander in chief or the specific instructions of a commanding officer. 2 *Informal* the prescribed or only thing offered or available: *prunes were the order of the day*. 3 (in Parliament and similar legislatures) any item of public business ordered to be considered on a specific day. 4 an agenda or programme.

Order of the Garter NOUN the highest order of British knighthood (but see also **Order of the Thistle**) open to women since 1987. It consists of the sovereign, 24 knight companions, and extra members created by statute. Also called: **the Garter**.

Order of the Thistle NOUN an ancient Scottish order of knighthood revived by James VII of Scotland in 1687. It consists of the sovereign, 16 knights brethren, and extra members created by statute. It is the equivalent of the Order of the Garter, and is usually conferred on Scots. Also called: **the Thistle**.

order paper NOUN a list indicating the order in which business is to be conducted, esp. in Parliament.

orders ('ɔːdəz) PLURAL NOUN 1 short for **holy orders**. 2 **in (holy) orders**. ordained. 3 **take (holy) orders**. to become ordained. 4 short for **major orders** or **minor orders**.

ordinal ('ɔːdɪnᵊl) ADJECTIVE 1 denoting a certain position in a sequence of numbers. 2 of, relating to, or characteristic of an order in biological classification. ◆ NOUN 3 short for **ordinal number**. 4 a book containing the forms of services for the ordination of ministers. 5 *RC Church* a service book.
▷ HISTORY C14 (in the sense: orderly): from Late Latin *ordinalis* denoting order or place in a series, from Latin *ordō* ORDER

ordinal number NOUN 1 a number denoting relative position in a sequence, such as *first, second, third*. Sometimes shortened to **ordinal**. 2 *Logic, maths* a measure of not only the size of a set but also the order of its elements. ◆ Compare **cardinal number**.

ordinal scale NOUN *Statistics* a scale on which data is shown simply in order of magnitude since there is no standard of measurement of differences: for instance, a squash ladder is an ordinal scale since one can say only that one person is better than another, but not by how much. Compare **interval scale, ratio scale, nominal scale**.

ordinance ('ɔːdɪnəns) NOUN an authoritative regulation, decree, law, or practice.
▷ HISTORY C14: from Old French *ordenance*, from Latin *ordināre* to set in order

ordinand ('ɔːdɪˌnænd) NOUN *Christianity* a candidate for ordination.

ordinarily ('ɔːdᵊnrɪlɪ, 'ɔːdᵊˌnerɪlɪ) ADVERB in ordinary, normal, or usual practice; usually; normally.

ordinary ('ɔːdᵊnrɪ) ADJECTIVE 1 of common or established type or occurrence. 2 familiar, everyday, or unexceptional. 3 uninteresting or commonplace. 4 having regular or ex officio jurisdiction: *an ordinary judge*. 5 *Maths* (of a differential equation) containing two variables only and derivatives of one of the variables with respect to the other. ◆ NOUN, *plural* **-naries**. 6 a common or average situation, amount, or degree (esp. in the phrase **out of the ordinary**). 7 a normal or commonplace person or thing. 8 *Civil law* a judge who exercises jurisdiction in his own right. 9 (*usually capital*) an ecclesiastic, esp. a bishop, holding an office to which certain jurisdictional powers are attached. 10 *RC Church* **a** the parts of the Mass that do not vary from day to day. Compare **proper** (sense 13). **b** a prescribed form of divine service, esp. the Mass. 11 the US name for **penny-farthing**. 12 *Heraldry* any of several conventional figures, such as the bend, the fesse, and the cross, commonly charged upon shields. 13 *History* a clergyman who visited condemned prisoners before their death. 14 *Brit, obsolete* **a** a meal provided regularly at a fixed price. **b** the inn providing such meals. 15 **in ordinary**. *Brit* (used esp. in titles) in regular service or attendance: *physician in ordinary to the sovereign*.
▷ HISTORY C16 (adj) and C13 (some n senses): ultimately from Latin *ordinārius* orderly, from *ordō* order

Ordinary grade NOUN (in Scotland) the formal name for **O grade**.

ordinary lay NOUN the form of lay found in a cable-laid rope.

Ordinary level NOUN (in Britain) the formal name for **O level**.

ordinary rating NOUN a rank in the Royal Navy comparable to that of a private in the army.

ordinary ray NOUN the plane-polarized ray of light that obeys the laws of refraction in a doubly-refracting crystal. See **double refraction**. Compare **extraordinary ray**.

ordinary seaman NOUN a seaman of the lowest rank, being insufficiently experienced to be an able-bodied seaman.

ordinary shares PLURAL NOUN *Brit* shares representing part of the capital issued by a company and entitling their holders to a dividend that varies according to the prosperity of the company, to vote at all meetings of members, and to a claim on the net assets of the company, after the holders of preference shares have been paid. US equivalent: **common stock**. Compare **preference shares**. See also **A shares**.

ordinate ('ɔːdɪnɪt) NOUN the vertical or *y*-coordinate of a point in a two-dimensional system of Cartesian coordinates. Compare **abscissa**.
▷ HISTORY C16: from New Latin phrase (*linea*) *ordināte* (*applicāta*) (line applied) in an orderly manner, from *ordināre* to arrange in order

ordination (ˌɔːdɪ'neɪʃən) NOUN 1 **a** the act of conferring holy orders. **b** the reception of holy orders. 2 the condition of being ordained or regulated. 3 an arrangement or order.

ordnance ('ɔːdnəns) NOUN 1 cannon or artillery. 2 military supplies; munitions. 3 **the**. a department of an army or government dealing with military supplies.
▷ HISTORY C14: variant of ORDINANCE

ordnance datum NOUN mean sea level calculated from observation taken at Newlyn, Cornwall, and used as the official basis for height calculation on British maps. Abbreviation: **OD**.

Ordnance Survey NOUN the official map-making body of the British or Irish government.

ordonnance ('ɔːdənəns; *French* ɔrdɔnɑ̃s) NOUN 1 the proper disposition of the elements of a building or an artistic or literary composition. 2 an ordinance, law, or decree, esp. in French law.
▷ HISTORY C17: from Old French *ordenance* arrangement, influenced by *ordonner* to order

Ordovician (ˌɔːdəʊ'vɪʃɪən) ADJECTIVE 1 of, denoting, or formed in the second period of the Palaeozoic era, between the Cambrian and Silurian periods, which lasted for 45 000 000 years during which marine invertebrates flourished. ◆ NOUN 2 **the**. the Ordovician period or rock system.
▷ HISTORY C19: from Latin *Ordovices* ancient Celtic tribe in N Wales

ordure ('ɔːdjʊə) NOUN 1 excrement; dung. 2 something regarded as being morally offensive.
▷ HISTORY C14: via Old French, from *ord* dirty, from Latin *horridus* shaggy

Ordzhonikidze *or* **Orjonikidze** (*Russian* ardʒəni'kidzɪ) NOUN the former name (until 1991) of **Vladikavkaz**.

ore (ɔː) NOUN any naturally occurring mineral or aggregate of minerals from which economically important constituents, esp. metals, can be extracted.
▷ HISTORY Old English *ār, ōra;* related to Gothic *aiz,* Latin *aes,* Dutch *oer*

öre ('ørə) NOUN, *plural* **öre**. a Scandinavian monetary unit worth one hundredth of a Swedish krona and (**øre**) one hundredth of a Danish and Norwegian krone.

oread ('ɔːrɪˌæd) NOUN *Greek myth* a mountain nymph.
▷ HISTORY C16: via Latin from Greek *Oreias,* from *oros* mountain

Örebro (*Swedish* œːrə'bruː) NOUN a town in S Sweden: one of Sweden's oldest towns; scene of the election of Jean Bernadotte as heir to the throne in 1810. Pop.: 123 503 (2000 est.).

orectic (ɒ'rɛktɪk) ADJECTIVE of or relating to the desires.
▷ HISTORY C18: from Greek *orektikos* causing desire, from *oregein* to desire

ore dressing NOUN the first stage in the extraction of a metal from an ore in which as much gangue as possible is removed and the ore is prepared for smelting, refining, etc. Also called: **mineral dressing, mineral processing**.

Oreg. ABBREVIATION FOR Oregon.

oregano (ˌɒrɪ'gɑːnəʊ) NOUN 1 a Mediterranean variety of wild marjoram (*Origanum vulgare*), with pungent leaves. 2 the dried powdered leaves of this plant, used to season food. ◆ See also **origanum**.
▷ HISTORY C18: American Spanish, from Spanish, from Latin *orīganum,* from Greek *origanon* an aromatic herb, perhaps marjoram

Oregon ('ɒrɪgən) NOUN a state of the northwestern US, on the Pacific: consists of the Coast and Cascade Ranges in the west and a plateau in the east; important timber production. Capital: Salem. Pop.: 3 421 399 (2000). Area: 251 418 sq. km (97 073 sq. miles). Abbreviations: **Oreg.**, (with zip code) **OR**.

Oregon fir *or* **pine** NOUN other names for **Douglas fir**.

Oregon grape NOUN 1 an evergreen berberidaceous shrub, *Mahonia aquifolium,* of NW North America, having yellow fragrant flowers and small blue edible berries. 2 the berry of this shrub.

Oregon trail NOUN an early pioneering route across the central US, from Independence, W Missouri, to the Columbia River country of N Oregon: used chiefly between 1804 and 1860. Length: about 3220 km (2000 miles).

Orel *or* **Oryol** (*Russian* a'rjɔl) NOUN a city in W Russia; founded in 1564 but damaged during World War II. Pop.: 346 500 (1999 est.).

Ore Mountains (ɔː) PLURAL NOUN another name for the **Erzgebirge**.

Orenburg ('ɒrənˌbɜːg; *Russian* arɪn'burk) NOUN a city in W Russia, on the Ural River. Pop.: 526 800 (1999 est.). Former name (1938–57): **Chkalov**.

Orense (*Spanish* o'rense) NOUN a city in NW Spain, in Galicia on the Miño River: warm springs. Pop.: 107 965 (1998 est.).

Orestes (ɒ'rɛstiːz) NOUN *Greek myth* the son of Agamemnon and Clytemnestra, who killed his mother and her lover Aegisthus in revenge for their murder of his father.

Øresund (œːrəˈsʊnd) NOUN the Danish name for the **Sound**. Swedish name: **Öresund**.

orf NOUN *Vet science* an infectious disease of sheep and sometimes goats and cattle, characterized by scabby pustular lesions on the muzzle and lips; caused by a paramyxovirus. technical name: **contagious pustular dermatitis**.

orfe (ɔːf) NOUN a small slender European cyprinoid fish, *Idus idus,* occurring in two colour varieties, namely the **silver orfe** and the **golden orfe,** popular aquarium fishes. Compare **goldfish**.
▷HISTORY C17: from German; related to Latin *orphus,* Greek *orphos* the sea perch

orfray (ˈɔːfrɪ) NOUN a less common spelling of **orphrey**.

org AN INTERNET DOMAIN NAME FOR an organization, usually a nonprofit-making organization.

org. ABBREVIATION FOR: 1 organic. 2 organization.

organ (ˈɔːgən) NOUN 1 **a** Also called: **pipe organ**. a large complex musical keyboard instrument in which sound is produced by means of a number of pipes arranged in sets or stops, supplied with air from a bellows. The largest instruments possess three or more manuals and one pedal keyboard and have the greatest range of any instrument. **b** (*as modifier*): *organ pipe; organ stop; organ loft.* 2 any instrument, such as a harmonium, in which sound is produced in this way. See also **reed organ, harmonica**. 3 short for **electric organ** (sense 1a), **electronic organ**. 4 a fully differentiated structural and functional unit, such as a kidney or a root, in an animal or plant. 5 an agency or medium of communication, esp. a periodical issued by a specialist group or party. 6 an instrument with which something is done or accomplished. 7 a euphemistic word for **penis**.
▷HISTORY C13: from Old French *organe,* from Latin *organum* implement, from Greek *organon* tool; compare Greek *ergein* to work

organa (ˈɔːgənə) NOUN a plural of **organon** and **organum**.

organdie *or esp US* **organdy** (ˈɔːgəndɪ, ɔːˈgæn-) NOUN, *plural* **-dies**. a fine and slightly stiff cotton fabric used esp. for dresses.
▷HISTORY C19: from French *organdi,* of unknown origin

organelle (ˌɔːgəˈnɛl) NOUN a structural and functional unit, such as a mitochondrion, in a cell or unicellular organism.
▷HISTORY C20: from New Latin *organella,* from Latin *organum:* see ORGAN

organ-grinder NOUN a street musician playing a hand organ for money.

organic (ɔːˈgænɪk) ADJECTIVE 1 of, relating to, derived from, or characteristic of living plants and animals. 2 of or relating to animal or plant constituents or products having a carbon basis. 3 of or relating to one or more organs of an animal or plant. 4 of, relating to, or belonging to the class of chemical compounds that are formed from carbon: *an organic compound.* Compare **inorganic** (sense 2). 5 constitutional in the structure of something; fundamental; integral. 6 of or characterized by the coordination of integral parts; organized. 7 developing naturally: *organic change through positive education.* 8 of or relating to the essential constitutional laws regulating the government of a state: *organic law.* 9 of, relating to, or grown with the use of fertilizers or pesticides deriving from animal or vegetable matter, rather than from chemicals. ◆ NOUN 10 any substance, such as a fertilizer or pesticide, that is derived from animal or vegetable matter.
▸**orˈganically** ADVERB

organic chemistry NOUN the branch of chemistry concerned with the compounds of carbon: originally confined to compounds produced by living organisms but now extended to include man-made substances based on carbon, such as plastics. Compare **inorganic chemistry**.

organic disease NOUN any disease in which there is a physical change in the structure of an organ or part. Compare **functional disease**.

organicism (ɔːˈgænɪˌsɪzəm) NOUN 1 the theory that the functioning of living organisms is determined by the working together of all organs as an integrated system. 2 the theory that all symptoms are caused by organic disease. 3 the theory that each organ of the body has its own peculiar constitution.
▸**orˈganicist** NOUN, ADJECTIVE ▸**orˌganiˈcistic** ADJECTIVE

organic psychosis NOUN a severe mental illness produced by damage to the brain, as a result of poisoning, alcoholism, disease, etc. Compare **functional** (sense 4b).

organism (ˈɔːgəˌnɪzəm) NOUN 1 any living biological entity, such as an animal, plant, fungus, or bacterium. 2 anything resembling a living creature in structure, behaviour, etc.
▸**ˌorganˈismal** *or* **ˌorganˈismic** ADJECTIVE ▸**ˌorganˈismally** ADVERB

organist (ˈɔːgənɪst) NOUN a person who plays the organ.

organization *or* **organisation** (ˌɔːgənaɪˈzeɪʃən) NOUN 1 the act of organizing or the state of being organized. 2 an organized structure or whole. 3 a business or administrative concern united and constructed for a particular end. 4 a body of administrative officials, as of a political party, a government department, etc. 5 order or system; method.
▸**ˌorganiˈzational** *or* **ˌorganiˈsational** ADJECTIVE
▸**ˌorganiˈzationally** *or* **ˌorganiˈsationally** ADVERB

organizational culture NOUN the customs, rituals, and values shared by the members of an organization that have to be accepted by new members.

organizational psychology NOUN the study of the structure of an organization and of the ways in which the people in it interact, usually undertaken in order to improve the organization.

organization chart NOUN a diagram representing the management structure of a company, showing the responsibilities of each department, the relationships of the departments to each other, and the hierarchy of management.

organization man NOUN 1 a person who subordinates his personal life to the demands of the organization he works for. 2 a person who specializes in or is good at organization.

Organization of African Unity NOUN the former name for the **African Union**. Abbreviation: **OAU**.

Organization of American States NOUN an association consisting of the US and other republics in the W hemisphere, founded at Bogotá in 1948 to promote military, economic, social, and cultural cooperation among the member states. Abbreviation: **OAS**. See also **Pan American Union**.

organize *or* **organise** (ˈɔːgəˌnaɪz) VERB 1 to form (parts or elements of something) into a structured whole; coordinate. 2 (*tr*) to arrange methodically or in order. 3 (*tr*) to provide with an organic structure. 4 (*tr*) to enlist (the workers) of (a factory, concern, or industry) in a trade union. 5 (*intr*) to join or form an organization or trade union. 6 (*tr*) *Informal* to put (oneself) in an alert and responsible frame of mind.
▷HISTORY C15: from Medieval Latin *organizare,* from Latin *organum* ORGAN

organized *or* **organised** (ˈɔːgəˌnaɪzd) ADJECTIVE 1 planned and controlled on a large scale and involving many people: *organized crime.* 2 orderly and efficient: *a highly organized campaign.* 3 (of the workers in a factory or office) belonging to a trade union: *organized labour.*

organizer *or* **organiser** (ˈɔːgəˌnaɪzə) NOUN 1 a person who organizes or is capable of organizing. 2 a container with a number of compartments for storage: *hanging organizers to keep your clothes smart.* 3 *Embryol* any part of an embryo or any substance produced by it that induces specialization of undifferentiated cells.

organo- COMBINING FORM 1 (in biology or medicine) indicating an organ or organs: *organogenesis.* 2 (in chemistry) indicating a compound containing an organic group: *organometallic; organosulphur; organophosphate.*

organ of Corti (ˈkɔːtɪ) NOUN the sense organ of the cochlea by which sounds are converted into nerve impulses.
▷HISTORY named after Alfonso *Corti* (died 1876), Italian anatomist

organogenesis (ˌɔːgənəʊˈdʒɛnɪsɪs) NOUN 1 the formation and development of organs in an animal or plant. 2 Also called: **organogeny** (ˌɔːgənˈɒdʒənɪ). the study of this process.
▸**organogenetic** (ˌɔːgənəʊdʒɪˈnɛtɪk) ADJECTIVE
▸**ˌorganogeˈnetically** ADVERB

organography (ˌɔːgəˈnɒgrəfɪ) NOUN the description of the organs and major structures of animals and plants.
▸**organographic** (ˌɔːgənəʊˈgræfɪk) *or* **ˌorganoˈgraphical** ADJECTIVE ▸**ˌorganˈographist** NOUN

organoleptic (ˌɔːgənəʊˈlɛptɪk) ADJECTIVE *Physiol* 1 able to stimulate an organ, esp. a special sense organ. 2 able to perceive a sensory stimulus.

organology (ˌɔːgəˈnɒlədʒɪ) NOUN the study of the structure and function of the organs of animals and plants.
▸**organological** (ˌɔːgənəʊˈlɒdʒɪkᵊl) ADJECTIVE
▸**ˌorganˈologist** NOUN

organometallic (ɔːˌgænəʊmɪˈtælɪk) ADJECTIVE of, concerned with, or being an organic compound with one or more metal atoms in its molecules: *an organometallic compound.*

organon (ˈɔːgəˌnɒn) *or* **organum** NOUN, *plural* **organa** (ˈɔːgənə), **-nons** *or* **-na, -nums.** *Epistemology* 1 a system of logical or scientific rules, esp. that of Aristotle. 2 *Archaic* a sense organ, regarded as an instrument for acquiring knowledge.
▷HISTORY C16: from Greek: implement; see ORGAN

organophosphate (ɔːˌgænəʊˈfɒsfeɪt) NOUN any of a group of organic compounds containing phosphate groups and used as a pesticide.

organotherapy (ˌɔːgənəʊˈθɛrəpɪ) NOUN the treatment of disease with extracts of animal endocrine glands.
▸**organotherapeutic** (ˌɔːgənəʊˌθɛrəˈpjuːtɪk) ADJECTIVE

organotin (ˌɔːgænəʊˈtɪn) ADJECTIVE of, concerned with, or being an organic compound with one or more tin atoms in its molecules: used as a pesticide, hitherto considered to decompose safely, now found to be toxic in the food chain.

organ screen NOUN a wooden or stone screen that supports the organ in a cathedral or church and divides the choir from the nave.

organum (ˈɔːgənəm) NOUN, *plural* **-na** (-nə) *or* **-nums.** 1 a form of polyphonic music originating in the ninth century, consisting of a plainsong melody with parts added at the fourth and fifth. 2 a variant of **organon**.
▷HISTORY C17: via Latin from Greek; see ORGAN

organza (ɔːˈgænzə) NOUN a thin stiff fabric of silk, cotton, nylon, rayon, etc.
▷HISTORY C20: perhaps related to ORGANZINE

organzine (ˈɔːgənˌziːn, ɔːˈgænziːn) NOUN 1 a strong thread made of twisted strands of raw silk. 2 fabric made of such threads.
▷HISTORY C17: from French *organsin,* from Italian *organzino,* probably from *Urgench,* a town in Uzbekistan where the fabric was originally produced

orgasm (ˈɔːgæzəm) NOUN 1 the most intense point during sexual excitement, characterized by extremely pleasurable sensations and in the male accompanied by ejaculation of semen. 2 *Rare* intense or violent excitement.
▷HISTORY C17: from New Latin *orgasmus,* from Greek *orgasmos,* from *organ* to mature, swell
▸**orˈgasmic** *or* **orˈgastic** ADJECTIVE

orgeat (ˈɔːʒɑː; *French* ɔrʒa) NOUN a drink made from barley or almonds, and orange flower water.
▷HISTORY C18: via French, from *orge* barley, from Latin *hordeum*

orgone (ˈɔːgəʊn) NOUN a substance postulated by Wilhelm Reich, who thought it was present everywhere and needed to be incorporated in people for sexual activity and mental health.
▷HISTORY C20: from ORG(ASM) + (HORM)ONE

orgulous (ˈɔːgjʊləs) ADJECTIVE *Archaic* proud.
▷HISTORY C13: from Old French, from *orgueil* pride, from Frankish *urgōli* (unattested)

orgy (ˈɔːdʒɪ) NOUN, *plural* **-gies.** 1 a wild gathering marked by promiscuous sexual activity, excessive drinking, etc. 2 an act of immoderate or frenzied indulgence. 3 (*often plural*) secret religious rites of Dionysus, Bacchus, etc., marked by drinking, dancing, and songs.
▷HISTORY C16: from French *orgies,* from Latin *orgia,* from Greek: nocturnal festival
▸**ˌorgiˈastic** ADJECTIVE

oribi ('ɒrɪbɪ) NOUN, *plural* **-bi** *or* **-bis.** a small African antelope, *Ourebia ourebi,* of grasslands and bush south of the Sahara, with fawn-coloured coat and, in the male, ridged spikelike horns.
▷HISTORY C18: from Afrikaans, probably from Khoikhoi *arab*

oriel window ('ɔːrɪəl) NOUN a bay window, esp. one that is supported by one or more brackets or corbels. Sometimes shortened to **oriel.**
▷HISTORY C14: from Old French *oriol* gallery, perhaps from Medieval Latin *auleolum* niche

orient NOUN ('ɔːrɪənt) 1 *Poetic* another word for **east.** Compare **occident.** 2 *Archaic* the eastern sky or the dawn. 3 **a** the iridescent lustre of a pearl. **b** (*as modifier*): *orient pearls.* 4 a pearl of high quality. ◆ ADJECTIVE ('ɔːrɪənt) 5 *Now chiefly poetic* eastern. 6 *Archaic* (of the sun, stars, etc.) rising. ◆ VERB ('ɔːrɪˌɛnt) 7 to adjust or align (oneself or something else) according to surroundings or circumstances. 8 (*tr*) to position, align, or set (a map, surveying instrument, etc.) with reference to the points of the compass or other specific directions. 9 (*tr*) to set or build (a church) in an easterly direction.
▷HISTORY C18: via French from Latin *oriēns* rising (sun), from *orīrī* to rise

Orient ('ɔːrɪənt) NOUN (usually preceded by *the*) 1 the countries east of the Mediterranean. 2 the eastern hemisphere.

oriental (ˌɔːrɪ'ɛntᵊl) ADJECTIVE another word for **eastern.** Compare **occidental.**

Oriental (ˌɔːrɪ'ɛntᵊl) ADJECTIVE 1 (*sometimes not capital*) of or relating to the Orient. 2 of or denoting a zoogeographical region consisting of southeastern Asia from India to Borneo, Java, and the Philippines. ◆ NOUN 3 a breed of slender muscular cat with large ears, long legs, and a long tail. 4 (*sometimes not capital*) an inhabitant, esp. a native, of the Orient.

Oriental almandine NOUN a variety of corundum resembling almandine in colour and used as a gemstone.

Oriental emerald NOUN a green variety of corundum used as a gemstone.

Orientalism (ˌɔːrɪ'ɛntəˌlɪzəm) NOUN 1 knowledge of or devotion to the Orient. 2 an Oriental quality, style, or trait.
▸ **ˌOri'entalist** NOUN ▸ **ˌOriˌental'istic** ADJECTIVE

Orientalize *or* **Orientalise** (ˌɔːrɪ'ɛntəˌlaɪz) VERB to make, become, or treat as Oriental.
▸ **ˌOriˌentali'zation** *or* **ˌOriˌentali'sation** NOUN

Oriental topaz NOUN a variety of corundum resembling topaz in colour and used as a gemstone.

orientate ('ɔːrɪɛnˌteɪt) VERB a variant of **orient.**

orientation (ˌɔːrɪɛn'teɪʃən) NOUN 1 the act or process of orienting or the state of being oriented. 2 position or positioning with relation to the points of the compass or other specific directions. 3 the adjustment or alignment of oneself or one's ideas to surroundings or circumstances. 4 Also called: **orientation course.** *Chiefly US and Canadian* **a** a course, programme, lecture, etc., introducing a new situation or environment. **b** (*as modifier*): *an orientation talk.* 5 *Psychol* the knowledge of one's own temporal, social, and practical circumstances in life. 6 basic beliefs or preferences: *sexual orientation.* 7 *Biology* the change in position of the whole or part of an organism in response to a stimulus, such as light. 8 *Chem* the relative dispositions of atoms, ions, or groups in molecules or crystals. 9 the siting of a church on an east-west axis, usually with the altar at the E end.
▸ **ˌorien'tational** ADJECTIVE

-oriented SUFFIX FORMING ADJECTIVES designed for, directed towards, motivated by, or concerned with: *computer-oriented courses; managers who are profit-oriented.*

orienteer (ˌɔːrɪən'tɪə) VERB (*intr*) 1 to take part in orienteering. ◆ NOUN 2 a person who takes part in orienteering.

orienteering (ˌɔːrɪɛn'tɪərɪŋ) NOUN a sport in which contestants race on foot over a course consisting of checkpoints found with the aid of a map and a compass.
▷HISTORY C20: from Swedish *orientering;* compare ORIENT

orifice ('ɒrɪfɪs) NOUN *Chiefly technical* an opening or mouth into a cavity; vent; aperture.
▷HISTORY C16: via French from Late Latin *ōrificium,* from Latin *ōs* mouth + *facere* to make

orifice meter NOUN *Engineering* a plate having a central hole that is placed across the flow of a liquid, usually between flanges in a pipeline. The pressure difference generated by the flow velocity through the hole enables the flow quantity to be measured.

oriflamme ('ɒrɪˌflæm) NOUN a scarlet flag, originally of the abbey of St. Denis in N France, adopted as the national banner of France in the Middle Ages.
▷HISTORY C15: via Old French, from Latin *aurum* gold + *flamma* flame

orig. ABBREVIATION FOR: 1 origin. 2 original(ly).

origami (ˌɒrɪ'gɑːmɪ) NOUN the art or process, originally Japanese, of paper folding.
▷HISTORY from Japanese, from *ori* a folding + *kami* paper

origan ('ɒrɪgən) NOUN another name for **marjoram** (sense 2).
▷HISTORY C16: from Latin *orīganum,* from Greek *origanon* an aromatic herb, perhaps marjoram; compare OREGANO

origanum (ə'rɪgənəm) NOUN any plant of the herbaceous aromatic Mediterranean genus *Origanum:* family *Lamiaceae.* See **oregano, marjoram, dittany** (sense 1).
▷HISTORY New Latin, from Greek *origanon* wild marjoram

origin ('ɒrɪdʒɪn) NOUN 1 a primary source; derivation. 2 the beginning of something; first stage or part. 3 (*often plural*) ancestry or parentage; birth; extraction. 4 *Anatomy* **a** the end of a muscle, opposite its point of insertion. **b** the beginning of a nerve or blood vessel or the site where it first starts to branch out. 5 *Maths* **a** the point of intersection of coordinate axes or planes. **b** the point whose coordinates are all zero. See also **pole²** (sense 8). 6 *Commerce* the country from which a commodity or product originates: *shipment from origin.*
▷HISTORY C16: from French *origine,* from Latin *orīgō* beginning, birth, from *orīrī* to rise, spring from

original (ə'rɪdʒɪnᵊl) ADJECTIVE 1 of or relating to an origin or beginning. 2 fresh and unusual; novel. 3 able to think of or carry out new ideas or concepts. 4 being that from which a copy, translation, etc., is made. ◆ NOUN 5 the first and genuine form of something, from which others are derived. 6 a person or thing used as a model in art or literature. 7 a person whose way of thinking is unusual or creative. 8 an unconventional or strange person. 9 the first form or occurrence of something. 10 an archaic word for **originator,** see **originate.**

originality (əˌrɪdʒɪ'nælɪtɪ) NOUN, *plural* **-ties.** 1 the quality or condition of being original. 2 the ability to create or innovate. 3 something original.

originally (ə'rɪdʒɪnəlɪ) ADVERB 1 in the first place. 2 in an original way. 3 with reference to the origin or beginning.

original sin NOUN a state of sin held to be innate in mankind as the descendants of Adam.

originate (ə'rɪdʒɪˌneɪt) VERB 1 to come or bring into being. 2 (*intr*) *US and Canadian* (of a bus, train, etc.) to begin its journey at a specified point.
▸ **oˌrigi'nation** NOUN ▸ **o'rigiˌnator** NOUN

orinasal (ˌɔːrɪ'neɪzᵊl) *Phonetics* ◆ ADJECTIVE 1 pronounced with simultaneous oral and nasal articulation, such as the French nasalized vowels æ̃ (as in *un*), ɔ̃ (as in *bon*), and ɑ̃ (as in *blanc*). ◆ NOUN 2 an orinasal speech sound.
▷HISTORY C19: from Latin *ōr-* (from *ōs* mouth) + NASAL
▸ **ˌori'nasally** ADVERB

O-ring NOUN a rubber ring used in machinery as a seal against oil, air, etc.

Orinoco (ˌɒrɪ'nəʊkəʊ) NOUN a river in N South America, rising in S Venezuela and flowing west, then north as part of the border between Colombia and Venezuela, then east to the Atlantic by a great delta: the third largest river system in South America, draining an area of 945 000 sq. km (365 000 sq. miles); reaches a width of 22 km (14 miles) during the rainy season. Length: about 2575 km (1600 miles).

oriole ('ɔːrɪˌəʊl) NOUN 1 any songbird of the mainly tropical Old World family *Oriolidae,* such as *Oriolus oriolus* (**golden oriole**), having a long pointed bill and a mostly yellow-and-black plumage. 2 any American songbird of the family *Icteridae,* esp. those of the genus *Icterus,* such as the Baltimore oriole, with a typical male plumage of black with either orange or yellow.
▷HISTORY C18: from Medieval Latin *oryolus,* from Latin *aureolus,* diminutive of *aureus,* from *aurum* gold

Orion¹ (ə'raɪən) NOUN *Greek myth* a Boeotian giant famed as a great hunter, who figures in several tales.

Orion² (ə'raɪən) NOUN, *Latin genitive* **Orionis** (ˌɔːrɪ'əʊnɪs). a conspicuous constellation near Canis Major containing two first magnitude stars (Betelgeuse and Rigel) and a distant bright emission nebula (the **Orion Nebula**) associated with a system of giant molecular clouds and star formation.

orisha *or* **orixa** (ə'rɪʃə) NOUN any of the minor gods or spirits of traditional Yoruba religion and its S American and Caribbean offshoots such as Santeria and Candomblé.
▷HISTORY from Yoruba *orisha* and the Portuguese spelling *orixá*

orison ('ɒrɪzᵊn) NOUN *Literary* another word for **prayer¹.**
▷HISTORY C12: from Old French *oreison,* from Late Latin *ōrātiō,* from Latin: speech, from *ōrāre* to speak

Orissa (ɒ'rɪsə) NOUN a state of E India, on the Bay of Bengal: part of the province of Bihar and Orissa (1912–36); enlarged by the addition of 25 native states in 1949. Capital: Bhubaneswar. Pop.: 36 706 920 (2001). Area: 155 707 sq. km (60 119 sq. miles).

orixa (ə'rɪʃə) NOUN another name for **orisha.**

Oriya (ɒ'riːə) NOUN 1 (*plural* **-ya**) a member of a people of India living chiefly in Orissa and neighbouring states. 2 the state language of Orissa, belonging to the Indic branch of the Indo-European family.

Orizaba (ˌɔːrɪ'zɑːbə; *Spanish* ori'θaβa) NOUN 1 a city and resort in SE Mexico, in Veracruz state. Pop.: 118 400 (2000 est.). 2 **Pico de.** the Spanish name for **Citlaltépetl.**

Orjonikidze (*Russian* ardʒəni'kidzɪ) NOUN a variant spelling of **Ordzhonikidze.**

Orkneyman ('ɔːknɪmən) NOUN, *plural* **-men.** a native or inhabitant of the Orkneys.
▸ **'Orkneyˌwoman** NOUN

Orkneys ('ɔːknɪz), **Orkney** ('ɔːknɪ), *or* **Orkney Islands** PLURAL NOUN a group of over 70 islands off the N coast of Scotland, separated from the mainland by the Pentland Firth: constitutes an island authority of Scotland; low-lying and treeless; prehistoric remains. Administrative centre: Kirkwall. Pop.: 19 245 (2001). Area: 974 sq. km (376 sq. miles). Related word: **Orcadian.**

Orlando (ɔː'lændəʊ) NOUN a city in the US, in Florida: site of Walt Disney World. Pop.: 185 951 (2000).

orle (ɔːl) NOUN *Heraldry* a border around a shield.
▷HISTORY C16: from French, from *ourler* to hem

Orléanais (*French* ɔrleanɛ) NOUN a former province of N central France, centred on Orléans.

Orleanist (ɔː'lɪənɪst) NOUN an adherent of the Orléans branch of the French Bourbons.

Orléans (ɔː'lɪənz; *French* ɔrleɑ̃) NOUN a city in N central France, on the River Loire: famous for its deliverance by Joan of Arc from the long English siege in 1429; university (1305); an important rail and road junction. Pop.: 112 833 (1999).

Orlon ('ɔːlɒn) NOUN *Trademark* a crease-resistant acrylic fibre or fabric used for clothing, furnishings, etc.

orlop *or* **orlop deck** ('ɔːlɒp) NOUN *Nautical* (in a vessel with four or more decks) the lowest deck.
▷HISTORY C15: from Dutch *overloopen* to run over, spill. See OVER, LEAP

Orly ('ɔːliː; *French* ɔrli) NOUN a suburb of SE Paris, France, with an international airport.

Ormazd *or* **Ormuzd** ('ɔːməzd) NOUN *Zoroastrianism* the creative deity, embodiment of good and opponent of Ahriman. Also called: **Ahura Mazda.**

▷HISTORY from Persian, from Avestan *Ahura-Mazda,* from *ahura* spirit + *mazdā* wise

ormer ('ɔːmə) NOUN [1] Also called: **sea-ear.** an edible marine gastropod mollusc, *Haliotis tuberculata,* that has an ear-shaped shell perforated with holes and occurs near the Channel Islands. [2] any other abalone.
▷HISTORY C17: from French (Guernsey dialect), apparently from Latin *auris* ear + *mare* sea

ormolu ('ɔːməˌluː) NOUN [1] **a** a gold-coloured alloy of copper, tin, or zinc used to decorate furniture, mouldings, etc. **b** (*as modifier*): *an ormolu clock.* [2] gold prepared to be used for gilding.
▷HISTORY C18: from French *or moulu* ground gold

Ormuz ('ɔːmʌz) NOUN a variant spelling of **Hormuz**.

ornament NOUN ('ɔːnəmənt) [1] anything that enhances the appearance of a person or thing. [2] decorations collectively: *she was totally without ornament.* [3] a small decorative object. [4] something regarded as a source of pride or beauty. [5] *Music* any of several decorations, such as the trill, mordent, etc., occurring chiefly as improvised embellishments in baroque music. ◆ VERB ('ɔːnəˌmɛnt) (*tr*) [6] to decorate with or as if with ornaments. [7] to serve as an ornament to.
▷HISTORY C14: from Latin *ornāmentum,* from *ornāre* to adorn
▸**ˌornamen'tation** NOUN

ornamental (ˌɔːnə'mɛntᵊl) ADJECTIVE [1] of value as an ornament; decorative. [2] (of a plant) used to decorate houses, gardens, etc. ◆ NOUN [3] a plant cultivated for show or decoration.
▸**ˌorna'mentally** ADVERB

ornate (ɔː'neɪt) ADJECTIVE [1] heavily or elaborately decorated. [2] (of style in writing) overembellished; flowery.
▷HISTORY C15: from Latin *ornāre* to decorate
▸**or'nately** ADVERB ▸**or'nateness** NOUN

Orne (*French* ɔrn) NOUN a department of NW France, in Basse-Normandie. Capital: Alençon. Pop.: 292 337 (1999). Area: 6144 sq. km (2396 sq. miles).

ornery ('ɔːnərɪ) ADJECTIVE *US and Canadian, dialect or informal* [1] stubborn or vile-tempered. [2] low; treacherous: *an ornery trick.* [3] ordinary.
▷HISTORY C19: alteration of ORDINARY
▸**'orneriness** NOUN

ornis ('ɔːnɪs) NOUN a less common word for **avifauna.**
▷HISTORY C19: from Greek: bird

ornithic (ɔː'nɪθɪk) ADJECTIVE of or relating to birds or a bird fauna.
▷HISTORY C19: from Greek *ornithikos,* from *ornis* bird

ornithine ('ɔːnɪˌθiːn) NOUN an amino acid produced from arginine by hydrolysis: involved in the formation of urea in the liver; diaminopentanoic acid. Formula: $NH_2(CH_2)_3CHNH_2COOH$.
▷HISTORY C19: from *ornithuric* (*acid*) secreted in the urine of birds, from ORNITHO- + URIC

ornithischian (ˌɔːnɪ'θɪskɪən) ADJECTIVE [1] of, relating to, or belonging to the *Ornithischia,* an order of dinosaurs that included the ornithopods, stegosaurs, ankylosaurs, and triceratops. ◆ NOUN [2] any dinosaur of the order *Ornithischia*; a bird-hipped dinosaur.
▷HISTORY C20: from ORNITHO- + Greek *ischion* hip joint

ornitho- *or before a vowel* **ornith-** COMBINING FORM bird or birds: *ornithology; ornithomancy; ornithopter; ornithoscopy; ornithosis.*
▷HISTORY from Greek *ornis, ornith-* bird

ornithol. *or* **ornith.** ABBREVIATION FOR: [1] ornithological. [2] ornithology.

ornithology (ˌɔːnɪ'θɒlədʒɪ) NOUN the study of birds, including their physiology, classification, ecology, and behaviour.
▸**ornithological** (ˌɔːnɪθə'lɒdʒɪkᵊl) ADJECTIVE ▸**ˌornitho'logically** ADVERB ▸**ˌorni'thologist** NOUN

ornithomancy ('ɔːnɪθəʊˌmænsɪ) NOUN divination from the flight and cries of birds.

ornithophily (ˌɔːnɪ'θɒfɪlɪ) NOUN pollination of flowers by birds.
▸**ˌorni'thophilous** ADJECTIVE

ornithopod ('ɔːnɪθəˌpɒd) NOUN any herbivorous typically bipedal ornithischian dinosaur of the suborder *Ornithopoda,* including the iguanodon.

ornithopter ('ɔːnɪˌθɒptə) NOUN a heavier-than-air craft sustained in and propelled through the air by flapping wings. Also called: **orthopter.**

ornithorhynchus (ˌɔːnɪθəʊ'rɪŋkəs) NOUN the technical name for **duck-billed platypus.**
▷HISTORY C19: New Latin, from ORNITHO- + Greek *rhunkhos* bill

ornithoscopy (ˌɔːnɪ'θɒskəpɪ) NOUN divination from the observation of birds.

ornithosis (ˌɔːnɪ'θəʊsɪs) NOUN a disease identical to psittacosis that occurs in birds other than parrots and can be transmitted to man.

oro-¹ COMBINING FORM mountain: *orogeny; orography.*
▷HISTORY from Greek *oros*

oro-² COMBINING FORM oral; mouth: *oromaxillary.*
▷HISTORY from Latin, from *ōs*

orobanchaceous (ˌɔːrəʊbæŋ'keɪʃəs) ADJECTIVE of, relating to, or belonging to the *Orobanchaceae,* a family of flowering plants all of which are root parasites, including broomrapes.
▷HISTORY via Latin from Greek *orobankhē* broomrape

orogeny (ɒ'rɒdʒɪnɪ) *or* **orogenesis** (ˌɒrəʊ'dʒɛnɪsɪs) NOUN the formation of mountain ranges by intense upward displacement of the earth's crust, usually associated with folding, thrust faulting, and other compressional processes.
▸**orogenic** (ˌɒrəʊ'dʒɛnɪk) *or* **orogenetic** (ˌɒrəʊdʒɪ'nɛtɪk) ADJECTIVE ▸**ˌoro'genically** *or* **ˌoroge'netically** ADVERB

orography (ɒ'rɒgrəfɪ) *or* **orology** (ɒ'rɒlədʒɪ) NOUN the study or mapping of relief, esp. of mountains.
▸**o'rographer** *or* **o'rologist** NOUN ▸**orographic** (ˌɒrəʊ'græfɪk) *or* **orological** (ˌɒrəʊ'lɒdʒɪkᵊl) ADJECTIVE ▸**ˌoro'graphically** *or* **ˌoro'logically** ADVERB

oroide ('ɔːrəʊˌaɪd) NOUN an alloy containing copper, tin, and other metals, used as imitation gold.
▷HISTORY C19: from French *or* gold + -OID

orometer (ɒ'rɒmɪtə) NOUN an aneroid barometer with an altitude scale.
▷HISTORY C19: from ORO-¹ (mountain, altitude) + -METER

oronasal (ˌɔːrəʊ'neɪzᵊl) ADJECTIVE *Anatomy* of or relating to the mouth and nose.

Orontes (ɒ'rɒntiːz) NOUN a river in SW Asia, rising in Lebanon and flowing north through Syria into Turkey, where it turns west to the Mediterranean. Length: 571 km (355 miles). Arabic name: **'Asi.**

orotund ('ɒrəʊˌtʌnd) ADJECTIVE [1] (of the voice) resonant; booming. [2] (of speech or writing) bombastic; pompous.
▷HISTORY C18: from Latin phrase *ore rotundo* with rounded mouth

orphan ('ɔːfən) NOUN [1] **a** a child, one or (more commonly) both of whose parents are dead. **b** (*as modifier*): *an orphan child.* [2] *Printing* the first line of a paragraph separated from the rest of the paragraph by occurring at the foot of a page. ◆ VERB [3] (*tr*) to deprive of one or both parents.
▷HISTORY C15: from Late Latin *orphanus,* from Greek *orphanos;* compare Latin *orbus* bereaved

orphanage ('ɔːfənɪdʒ) NOUN [1] an institution for orphans and abandoned children. [2] the state of being an orphan.

orpharion (ɔː'færɪən) NOUN a large lute in use during the 16th and 17th centuries.
▷HISTORY C16: from ORPHEUS + *Arion,* musicians of Greek mythology

Orphean ('ɔːfɪən) ADJECTIVE [1] of or relating to Orpheus. [2] melodious or enchanting.

Orpheus ('ɔːfɪəs, -fjuːs) NOUN *Greek myth* a poet and lyre-player credited with the authorship of the poems forming the basis of Orphism. He married Eurydice and sought her in Hades after her death. He failed to win her back and was killed by a band of bacchantes.

Orphic ('ɔːfɪk) ADJECTIVE [1] of or relating to Orpheus or Orphism. [2] (*sometimes not capital*) mystical or occult.
▸**'Orphically** ADVERB

Orphism ('ɔːfɪzəm) NOUN a mystery religion of ancient Greece, widespread from the 6th century B.C. onwards, combining pre-Hellenic beliefs, the Thracian cult of (Dionysius) Zagreus, etc.
▸**Or'phistic** ADJECTIVE

orphrey *or less commonly* **orfray** ('ɔːfrɪ) NOUN a richly embroidered band or border, esp. on an ecclesiastical vestment.
▷HISTORY C13 *orfreis,* from Old French, from Late Latin *aurifrisium, auriphrygium,* from Latin *aurum* gold + *Phrygius* Phrygian

orpiment ('ɔːpɪmənt) NOUN a yellow mineral consisting of arsenic trisulphide in monoclinic crystalline form occurring in association with realgar: it is an ore of arsenic. Formula: As_2S_3.
▷HISTORY C14: via Old French from Latin *auripigmentum* gold pigment

orpine ('ɔːpaɪn) *or* **orpin** ('ɔːpɪn) NOUN a succulent perennial N temperate crassulaceous plant, *Sedum telephium,* with toothed leaves and heads of small purplish-white flowers. Also called: (Brit) **livelong,** (US) **live-forever.**
▷HISTORY C14: from Old French, apparently from ORPIMENT (perhaps referring to the yellow flowers of a related species)

Orpington¹ ('ɔːpɪŋtən) NOUN [1] a heavy breed of domestic fowl of various single colours, laying brown eggs. [2] a breed of brown duck with an orange bill.

Orpington² ('ɔːpɪŋtən) NOUN a district of SE London, part of the Greater London borough of Bromley from 1965.

orra ('ɒrə) ADJECTIVE *Scot* [1] odd or unmatched; supernumerary. [2] occasional or miscellaneous. [3] **orra man** *or* **orraman.** an odd-jobman.
▷HISTORY C18: of unknown origin

orrery ('ɒrərɪ) NOUN, *plural* **-ries.** a mechanical model of the solar system in which the planets can be moved at the correct relative velocities around the sun.
▷HISTORY C18: originally made for Charles Boyle, Earl of *Orrery*

orris¹ *or* **orrice** ('ɒrɪs) NOUN [1] any of various irises, esp. *Iris florentina,* that have fragrant rhizomes. [2] Also called: **orrisroot.** the rhizome of such a plant, prepared and used as perfume.
▷HISTORY C16: variant of IRIS

orris² ('ɒrɪs) NOUN a kind of lace made of gold or silver, used esp. in the 18th century.
▷HISTORY from Old French *orfreis,* from Latin *auriphrygium* Phrygian gold

Orsk (*Russian* ɔrsk) NOUN a city in W Russia, on the Ural River: a major railway and industrial centre, with an oil refinery linked by pipeline with the Emba field (on the Caspian). Pop.: 274 400 (1995 est.).

ortanique (ˌɔːtə'niːk) NOUN a hybrid between an orange and a tangerine.
▷HISTORY C20: from OR(ANGE) + TAN(GERINE) + (UN)IQUE

Ortegal (*Spanish* ɔrte'ɣal) NOUN **Cape.** a cape in NW Spain, projecting into the Bay of Biscay.

Orth. ABBREVIATION FOR Orthodox (religion).

orthicon ('ɔːθɪˌkɒn) NOUN a television camera tube in which an optical image produces a corresponding electrical charge pattern on a mosaic surface that is scanned from behind by an electron beam. The resulting discharge of the mosaic provides the output signal current. See also **image orthicon.**
▷HISTORY C20: from ORTHO- + ICON(OSCOPE)

ortho- *or before a vowel* **orth-** COMBINING FORM [1] straight or upright: *orthotropous.* [2] perpendicular or at right angles: *orthoclastic.* [3] correct or right: *orthodontics; orthodox; orthography; orthoptics.* [4] (*often in italics*) denoting an organic compound containing a benzene ring with substituents attached to adjacent carbon atoms (the 1,2-positions): *orthodinitrobenzene.* Abbreviation: ***o-***. Compare **para-¹** (sense 6), **meta-** (sense 4). [5] denoting an oxyacid regarded as the highest hydrated form of the anhydride or a salt of such an acid: *orthophosphoric acid.* Compare **meta-** (sense 6). [6] denoting a diatomic substance in which the spins of the two atoms are parallel: *orthohydrogen.* Compare **para-¹** (sense 8).
▷HISTORY from Greek *orthos* straight, right, upright

orthoboric acid (ˌɔːθəʊ'bɔːrɪk) NOUN the more formal name for **boric acid** (sense 1).

orthocentre *or US* **orthocenter** ('ɔːθəʊˌsɛntə) NOUN the point of intersection of any two altitudes of a triangle.

orthocephalic (ˌɔːθəʊsɪˈfælɪk) *or* **orthocephalous** (ˌɔːθəʊˈsɛfələs) ADJECTIVE having a skull whose breadth is between 70 and 75 per cent of its length.
▸ **ˌorthoˈcephaly** NOUN

orthochromatic (ˌɔːθəʊkrəʊˈmætɪk) ADJECTIVE *Photog* of or relating to an emulsion giving a rendering of relative light intensities of different colours that corresponds approximately to the colour sensitivity of the eye, esp. one that is insensitive to red light. Sometimes shortened to **ortho.** Compare **panchromatic.**
▸ **orthochromatism** (ˌɔːθəʊˈkrəʊməˌtɪzəm) NOUN

orthoclase (ˈɔːθəʊˌkleɪs, -ˌkleɪz) NOUN a white to pale yellow, red, or green mineral of the feldspar group, found in igneous, sedimentary, and metamorphic rocks. It is used in the manufacture of glass and ceramics. Composition: potassium aluminium silicate. Formula: $KAlSi_3O_8$. Crystal structure: monoclinic.

orthodontics (ˌɔːθəʊˈdɒntɪks) *or* **orthodontia** (ˌɔːθəʊˈdɒntɪə) NOUN (*functioning as singular*) the branch of dentistry concerned with preventing or correcting irregularities of the teeth. Also called: **dental orthopaedics.**
▸ **ˌorthoˈdontic** ADJECTIVE ▸ **ˌorthoˈdontist** NOUN

orthodox (ˈɔːθəˌdɒks) ADJECTIVE 1 conforming with established or accepted standards, as in religion, behaviour, or attitudes. 2 conforming to the Christian faith as established by the early Church.
▷ HISTORY C16: via Church Latin from Greek *orthodoxos,* from *orthos* correct + *doxa* belief
▸ **ˈorthoˌdoxly** ADVERB

Orthodox (ˈɔːθəˌdɒks) ADJECTIVE 1 of or relating to the Orthodox Church of the East. 2 (*sometimes not capital*) **a** of or relating to Orthodox Judaism. **b** (of an individual Jew) strict in the observance of Talmudic law and in personal devotions.

Orthodox Church NOUN 1 Also called: **Byzantine Church, Eastern Orthodox Church, Greek Orthodox Church.** the collective body of those Eastern Churches that were separated from the western Church in the 11th century and are in communion with the Greek patriarch of Constantinople. 2 any of these Churches.

Orthodox Judaism NOUN the form of Judaism characterized by allegiance to the traditional interpretation and to strict observance of the Mosaic Law as interpreted in the Talmud, etc., and regarded as divinely revealed. Compare **Conservative Judaism, Reform Judaism.**

orthodoxy (ˈɔːθəˌdɒksɪ) NOUN, *plural* **-doxies.** 1 orthodox belief or practice. 2 the quality of being orthodox.

orthoepy (ˈɔːθəʊˌɛpɪ) NOUN the study of correct or standard pronunciation.
▷ HISTORY C17: from Greek *orthoepeia,* from ORTHO- straight + *epos* word
▸ **orthoepic** (ˌɔːθəʊˈɛpɪk) ADJECTIVE ▸ **ˌorthoˈepically** ADVERB

orthogenesis (ˌɔːθəʊˈdʒɛnɪsɪs) NOUN 1 *Biology* **a** evolution of a group of organisms predetermined to occur in a particular direction. **b** the theory that proposes such a development. 2 the theory that there is a series of stages through which all cultures pass in the same order.
▸ **orthogenetic** (ˌɔːθəʊdʒɪˈnɛtɪk) ADJECTIVE
▸ **ˌorthogeˈnetically** ADVERB

orthogenic (ˌɔːθəʊˈdʒɛnɪk) ADJECTIVE 1 *Med* relating to corrective procedures designed to promote healthy development. 2 of or relating to orthogenesis.
▸ **ˌorthoˈgenically** ADVERB

orthognathous (ɔːˈθɒgnəθəs) ADJECTIVE *Anatomy* having normally aligned jaws.
▸ **orˈthognaˌthism** *or* **orˈthognathy** NOUN

orthogonal (ɔːˈθɒgənᵊl) ADJECTIVE 1 relating to, consisting of, or involving right angles; perpendicular. 2 *Maths* **a** (of a pair of vectors) having a defined scalar product equal to zero. **b** (of a pair of functions) having a defined product equal to zero.
▸ **orˈthogonally** ADVERB

orthogonal matrix NOUN *Maths* a matrix that is the inverse of its transpose so that any two rows or any two columns are orthogonal vectors. Compare **symmetric matrix.**

orthogonal projection NOUN *Engineering* the method used in engineering drawing of projecting views of the object being described, such as plan, elevation, side view, etc., at right angles to each other.

orthographic (ˌɔːθəʊˈgræfɪk) *or* **orthographical** ADJECTIVE of or relating to spelling.
▸ **ˌorthoˈgraphically** ADVERB

orthographic projection NOUN 1 a style of engineering drawing in which true dimensions are represented as if projected from infinity on three planes perpendicular to each other, avoiding the effects of perspective. 2 a type of zenithal map projection in which the area is mapped as if projected from infinity, with resulting distortion of scale away from the centre.

orthography (ɔːˈθɒgrəfɪ) NOUN, *plural* **-phies.** 1 a writing system. 2 **a** a spelling considered to be correct. **b** the principles underlying spelling. 3 the study of spelling. 4 orthographic projection.
▸ **orˈthographer** *or* **orˈthographist** NOUN

orthohydrogen (ˌɔːθəʊˈhaɪdrədʒən) NOUN *Chem* the form of molecular hydrogen, constituting about 75 per cent of the total at normal temperatures, in which the nuclei of the atoms spin in the same direction. Compare **parahydrogen.**

orthomorphic (ˌɔːθəʊˈmɔːfɪk) ADJECTIVE *Geography* another word for **conformal** (sense 2).

orthopaedic *or US* **orthopedic** (ˌɔːθəʊˈpiːdɪk) ADJECTIVE 1 of or relating to orthopaedics. 2 designed to help correct or ameliorate the discomfort of disorders of the spine and joints: *orthopaedic mattresses.*

orthopaedics *or US* **orthopedics** (ˌɔːθəʊˈpiːdɪks) NOUN (*functioning as singular*) 1 the branch of surgery concerned with disorders of the spine and joints and the repair of deformities of these parts. 2 **dental orthopaedics.** another name for **orthodontics.**
▸ **ˌorthoˈpaedist** *or US* **ˌorthoˈpedist** NOUN

orthophosphate (ˌɔːθəʊˈfɒsfeɪt) NOUN any salt or ester of orthophosphoric acid.

orthophosphoric acid (ˌɔːθəʊfɒsˈfɒrɪk) NOUN a colourless soluble solid tribasic acid used in the manufacture of fertilizers and soaps. Formula: H_3PO_4. Also called: **phosphoric acid.**

orthophosphorous acid (ˌɔːθəʊˈfɒsfərəs) NOUN a white or yellowish hygroscopic crystalline dibasic acid. Formula: H_3PO_3. Also called: **phosphorous acid.**

orthopraxy (ˈɔːθəˌpræksɪ) NOUN *Theol* the belief that right action is as important as religious faith.
▷ HISTORY from Greek *orthos* correct + *praxis* deed, action

orthopsychiatry (ˌɔːθəʊsaɪˈkaɪətrɪ) NOUN the study and treatment of mental disorders with emphasis on prevention during childhood.
▸ **orthopsychiatric** (ˌɔːθəʊˌsaɪkɪˈætrɪk) ADJECTIVE
▸ **ˌorthopsyˈchiatrist** NOUN

orthopter (ˈɔːθɒptə) NOUN another name for **ornithopter.**

orthopteran (ɔːˈθɒptərən) NOUN, *plural* **-terans.** 1 Also: **orthopteron** (*plural* **-tera** (-tərə)). any orthopterous insect. ◆ ADJECTIVE 2 another word for **orthopterous.**

orthopterous (ɔːˈθɒptərəs) *or* **orthopteran** ADJECTIVE of, relating to, or belonging to the *Orthoptera,* a large order of insects, including crickets, locusts, and grasshoppers, having leathery forewings and membranous hind wings, hind legs adapted for leaping, and organs of stridulation.

orthoptic (ɔːˈθɒptɪk) ADJECTIVE relating to normal binocular vision.

orthoptics (ɔːˈθɒptɪks) NOUN (*functioning as singular*) the science or practice of correcting defective vision, as by exercises to strengthen weak eye muscles.

orthoptist (ɔːˈθɒptɪst) NOUN a person who is qualified to practise orthoptics.

orthopyroxene (ˌɔːθəʊpaɪˈrɒksiːn) NOUN a member of the pyroxene group of minerals having an orthorhombic crystal structure, such as enstatite and hypersthene.

orthorhombic (ˌɔːθəʊˈrɒmbɪk) ADJECTIVE *Crystallog* relating to the crystal system characterized by three mutually perpendicular unequal axes. Also: **rhombic, trimetric.**

orthoscope (ˈɔːθəʊˌskəʊp) NOUN *Med, obsolete* a 19th-century instrument for viewing the fundus of the eye through a layer of water, which eliminates distortion caused by the cornea.

orthoscopic (ˌɔːθəʊˈskɒpɪk) ADJECTIVE 1 of, relating to, or produced by normal vision. 2 yielding an undistorted image.

orthosis (ɔːˈθəʊsɪs) NOUN, *plural* **-ses** (-siːz). an artificial or mechanical aid, such as a brace, to support or assist movement of a weak or injured part of the body.

orthostichy (ɔːˈθɒstɪkɪ) NOUN, *plural* **-chies.** 1 an imaginary vertical line that connects a row of leaves on a stem. 2 an arrangement of leaves so connected. ◆ Compare **parastichy.**
▷ HISTORY C19: from ORTHO- + Greek *stikhos* line
▸ **orˈthostichous** ADJECTIVE

orthotics (ɔːˈθɒtɪks) NOUN (*functioning as singular*) the provision and use of artificial or mechanical aids, such as braces, to prevent or assist movement of weak or injured joints or muscles.

orthotist (ɔːˈθɒtɪst) NOUN a person who is qualified to practise orthotics.

orthotone (ˈɔːθəʊˌtəʊn) ADJECTIVE 1 (of a word) having an independent accent. ◆ NOUN 2 an independently accented word.

orthotropic (ˌɔːθəʊˈtrɒpɪk) ADJECTIVE 1 *Botany* relating to or showing growth that is in direct line with the stimulus. 2 (of a material) having different elastic properties in different planes.
▸ **orthotropism** (ɔːˈθɒtrəˌpɪzəm) NOUN

orthotropous (ɔːˈθɒtrəpəs) ADJECTIVE (of a plant ovule) growing straight during development so that the micropyle is at the apex. Compare **anatropous.**

Ortles (*Italian* ˈɔrtles) PLURAL NOUN a range of the Alps in N Italy. Highest peak: 3899 m (12 792 ft.). Also called: **Ortler** (ˈɔːtlə).

ortolan (ˈɔːtələn) NOUN 1 Also called: **ortolan bunting.** a brownish Old World bunting, *Emberiza hortulana,* regarded as a delicacy. 2 any of various other small birds eaten as delicacies, esp. the bobolink.
▷ HISTORY C17: via French from Latin *hortulānus,* from *hortulus,* diminutive of *hortus* garden

orts (ɔːts) PLURAL NOUN (*sometimes singular*) *Archaic or dialect* scraps or leavings.
▷ HISTORY C15: of Germanic origin; related to Dutch *oorete,* from *oor-* remaining + *ete* food

Oruro (*Spanish* oˈruro) NOUN a city in W Bolivia: a former silver-mining centre; university (1892); tin, copper, and tungsten. Pop.: 232 311 (2000 est.).

Orvieto (*Italian* orˈvjɛːto) NOUN 1 a market town in central Italy, in Umbria: Etruscan remains. Pop.: 21 575 (1990). Latin name: **Urbs Vetus** (ˈʊəbz ˈviːtəs). 2 a light white wine from this region.

Orwellian (ɔːˈwɛlɪən) ADJECTIVE of, relating to, or reminiscent of George Orwell (real name *Eric Arthur Blair*), the English novelist (1903–50), particularly his portrayal of an authoritarian state.

-ory[1] SUFFIX FORMING NOUNS 1 indicating a place for: *observatory.* 2 something having a specified use: *directory.*
▷ HISTORY via Old French *-orie,* from Latin *-ōrium, -ōria*

-ory[2] SUFFIX FORMING ADJECTIVES of or relating to; characterized by; having the effect of: *contributory; promissory.*
▷ HISTORY via Old French *-orie,* from Latin *-ōrius*

Oryol (*Russian* aˈrjɔl) NOUN a variant spelling of **Orel.**

oryx (ˈɒrɪks) NOUN, *plural* **-yxes** *or* **-yx.** any large African antelope of the genus *Oryx,* typically having long straight nearly upright horns.
▷ HISTORY C14: via Latin from Greek *orux* stonemason's axe, used also of the pointed horns of an antelope

os[1] (ɒs) NOUN, *plural* **ossa** (ˈɒsə). *Anatomy* the technical name for **bone.**
▷ HISTORY C16: from Latin: bone; compare Greek *osteon*

os[2] (ɒs) NOUN, *plural* **ora** (ˈɔːrə). *Anatomy, zoology* a mouth or mouthlike part or opening.
▷ HISTORY C18: from Latin

os[3] (əʊs) NOUN, *plural* **osar** (ˈəʊsɑː). another name for **esker.**

▷**HISTORY** C19 *osar* (plural), from Swedish *ås* (singular) ridge

Os THE CHEMICAL SYMBOL FOR osmium.

OS ABBREVIATION FOR: 1 Old School. 2 Old Style (method of reckoning dates). 3 Ordinary Seaman. 4 (in Britain) **Ordnance Survey**. 5 outsize. 6 Old Saxon (language).

o.s., OS, *or* **O/S** ABBREVIATION FOR: 1 out of stock. 2 *Banking* outstanding.

OSA ABBREVIATION FOR Order of Saint Augustine.

Osage (əʊ'seɪdʒ, 'əʊseɪdʒ) NOUN 1 (*plural* **Osages** *or* **Osage**) a member of a North American Indian people formerly living in an area between the Missouri and Arkansas Rivers. 2 the language of this people, belonging to the Siouan family.

Osage orange NOUN 1 a North American moraceous tree, *Maclura pomifera*, grown for hedges and ornament. 2 the warty orange-like fruit of this plant.

Osaka (əʊ'sɑːkə) NOUN a port in S Japan, on S Honshu on **Osaka Bay** (an inlet of the Pacific): the third largest city in Japan (the chief commercial city during feudal times); university (1931); an industrial and commercial centre. Pop.: 2 602 352 (1995).

OSB ABBREVIATION FOR Order of Saint Benedict.

Osborne House ('ɒzˌbɔːn) NOUN a house near Cowes on the Isle of Wight: the favourite residence of Queen Victoria, who died there; now a convalescent home.

Oscan ('ɒskən) NOUN 1 an extinct language of ancient S Italy belonging to the Italic branch of the Indo-European family. See also **Osco-Umbrian.** 2 a speaker of this language; Samnite. ◆ ADJECTIVE 3 of or relating to this language.

oscar ('ɒskə) NOUN *Austral, slang, rare* cash; money.
▷**HISTORY** C20: rhyming slang, from *Oscar* Asche (1871–1936), Australian actor

Oscar ('ɒskə) NOUN 1 **a** any of several small gold statuettes awarded annually in the United States by the Academy of Motion Picture Arts and Sciences for outstanding achievements in films. Official name: **Academy Award. b** (*sometimes not capital*) an award made in recognition of outstanding endeavour in any of various other fields: *the TV Oscars*. 2 (*without capital*) any annual award for excellence. 3 *Communications* a code word for the letter *o*.
▷**HISTORY** C20: sense 1 said to have been named after a remark made by an official on first seeing the statuette, that it reminded her of her uncle Oscar

OSCE ABBREVIATION FOR Organization for Security and Cooperation in Europe.

oscillate ('ɒsɪˌleɪt) VERB 1 (*intr*) to move or swing from side to side regularly. 2 (*intr*) to waver between opinions, courses of action, etc. 3 *Physics* to undergo or produce or cause to undergo or produce oscillation.
▷**HISTORY** C18: from Latin *oscillāre* to swing, from *oscillum* a swing

oscillating universe theory NOUN the theory that the universe is oscillating between periods of expansion and collapse.

oscillation (ˌɒsɪ'leɪʃən) NOUN 1 *Physics, statistics* **a** regular fluctuation in value, position, or state about a mean value, such as the variation in an alternating current or the regular swinging of a pendulum. **b** a single cycle of such a fluctuation. 2 the act or process of oscillating.
▸**oscillatory** ('ɒsɪlətərɪ, -trɪ) ADJECTIVE

oscillator ('ɒsɪˌleɪtə) NOUN 1 a circuit or instrument for producing an alternating current or voltage of a required frequency. 2 any instrument for producing oscillations. 3 a person or thing that oscillates.

oscillogram (ɒ'sɪləˌgræm) NOUN the recording obtained from an oscillograph or the trace on an oscilloscope screen.

oscillograph (ɒ'sɪləˌgrɑːf, -ˌgræf) NOUN a device for producing a graphical record of the variation of an oscillating quantity, such as an electric current.
▸**oscillographic** (ɒˌsɪlə'græfɪk) ADJECTIVE ▸**oscillography** (ˌɒsɪ'lɒgrəfɪ) NOUN

oscilloscope (ɒ'sɪləˌskəʊp) NOUN an instrument for producing a representation of a quantity that rapidly changes with time on the screen of a cathode-ray tube. The changes are converted into electric signals, which are applied to plates in the cathode-ray tube. Changes in the magnitude of the potential across the plates deflect the electron beam and thus produce a trace on the screen.

oscine ('ɒsaɪn, 'ɒsɪn) ADJECTIVE of, relating to, or belonging to the *Oscines*, a suborder of passerine birds that includes most of the songbirds.
▷**HISTORY** C17: via New Latin from Latin *oscen* singing bird

oscitancy ('ɒsɪtənsɪ) *or* **oscitance** NOUN, *plural* **-tancies** *or* **-tances.** 1 the state of being drowsy, lazy, or inattentive. 2 the act of yawning. ◆ Also called: **oscitation.**
▷**HISTORY** C17: from Latin *oscitāre* to gape, yawn
▸**'oscitant** ADJECTIVE

Osco-Umbrian (ˌɒskəʊ'ʌmbrɪən) NOUN 1 a group of extinct languages of ancient Italy, including Oscan, Umbrian, and Sabellian, which were displaced by Latin. ◆ ADJECTIVE 2 relating to or belonging to this group of languages.

osculant ('ɒskjʊlənt) ADJECTIVE 1 *Biology* (of an organism or group of organisms) possessing some of the characteristics of two different taxonomic groups. 2 *Zoology* closely joined or adhering.
▷**HISTORY** C19: from Latin *ōsculārī* to kiss; see OSCULUM

oscular ('ɒskjʊlə) ADJECTIVE 1 *Zoology* of or relating to an osculum. 2 of or relating to the mouth or to kissing.

osculate ('ɒskjʊˌleɪt) VERB 1 *Usually humorous* to kiss. 2 (*intr*) (of an organism or group of organisms) to be intermediate between two taxonomic groups. 3 *Geometry* to touch in osculation.
▷**HISTORY** C17: from Latin *ōsculārī* to kiss; see OSCULUM

osculation (ˌɒskjʊ'leɪʃən) NOUN 1 Also called: **tacnode.** *Maths* a point at which two branches of a curve have a common tangent, each branch extending in both directions of the tangent. 2 *Rare* the act or an instance of kissing.
▸**osculatory** ('ɒskjʊlətərɪ, -trɪ) ADJECTIVE

osculum ('ɒskjʊləm) NOUN, *plural* **-la** (-lə). *Zoology* a mouthlike aperture, esp. the opening in a sponge out of which water passes.
▷**HISTORY** C17: from Latin: a kiss, little mouth, diminutive of *ōs* mouth

OSD ABBREVIATION FOR Order of Saint Dominic.

-ose[1] SUFFIX FORMING ADJECTIVES possessing; resembling: *verbose; grandiose.*
▷**HISTORY** from Latin *-ōsus;* see -OUS

-ose[2] SUFFIX FORMING NOUNS 1 indicating a carbohydrate, esp. a sugar: *lactose*. 2 indicating a decomposition product of protein: *albumose*.
▷**HISTORY** from GLUCOSE

OSF ABBREVIATION FOR Order of Saint Francis.

Oshawa ('ɒʃəwə) NOUN a city in central Canada, in SE Ontario on Lake Ontario: motor-vehicle industry. Pop.: 134 364 (1996).

Oshogbo (ə'ʃɒgbəʊ) NOUN a city in SW Nigeria: trade centre. Pop.: 476 800 (1996 est.).

OSI ABBREVIATION FOR open systems interconnection; an international standardization model to facilitate communications among computers with different protocols.

osier ('əʊzɪə) NOUN 1 any of various willow trees, esp. *Salix viminalis,* whose flexible branches or twigs are used for making baskets, etc. 2 a twig or branch from such a tree. 3 any of several North American dogwoods, esp. the red osier.
▷**HISTORY** C14: from Old French, probably from Medieval Latin *ausēria,* perhaps of Gaulish origin; compare Breton *aoz*

Osijek (*Serbo-Croat* 'ɔsijɛk) NOUN a town in NE Croatia on the Drava River: under Turkish rule from 1526 to 1687. Pop.: 129 792 (1991). Ancient name: **Mursa** ('mʊəsə).

Osiris (əʊ'saɪrɪs) NOUN an ancient Egyptian god, ruler of the underworld and judge of the dead.
▸**O'sirian** ADJECTIVE

-osis SUFFIX FORMING NOUNS 1 indicating a process or state: *metamorphosis*. 2 indicating a diseased condition: *tuberculosis*. Compare **-iasis.** 3 indicating the formation or development of something: *fibrosis*.
▷**HISTORY** from Greek, suffix used to form nouns from verbs with infinitives in *-oein* or *-oun*

Oslo ('ɒzləʊ; *Norwegian* 'uslu) NOUN the capital and chief port of Norway, in the southeast at the head of **Oslo Fjord** (an inlet of the Skagerrak): founded in about 1050; university (1811); a major commercial and industrial centre, producing about a quarter of Norway's total output. Pop.: 507 467 (2000 est.). Former names: **Christiania** (1624–1877), **Kristiania** (1877–1924).

Osmanli (ɒz'mænlɪ) ADJECTIVE 1 of or relating to the Ottoman Empire. ◆ NOUN 2 (*plural* **-lis**) (formerly) a subject of the Ottoman Empire. 3 the Turkish language, esp. as written in Arabic letters under the Ottoman Empire.
▷**HISTORY** C19: from Turkish, from Osman I (1259–1326), Turkish sultan

osmic ('ɒzmɪk) ADJECTIVE of or containing osmium in a high valence state, esp. the tetravalent state.

osmious ('ɒzmɪəs) ADJECTIVE another word for **osmous.**

osmiridium (ˌɒzmɪ'rɪdɪəm) NOUN a very hard corrosion-resistant white or grey natural alloy of osmium and iridium in variable proportions, often containing smaller amounts of platinum, ruthenium, and rhodium: used esp. in pen nibs. Also: **iridosmine.**
▷**HISTORY** C19: from OSM(IUM) + IRIDIUM

osmium ('ɒzmɪəm) NOUN a very hard brittle bluish-white metal occurring with platinum and alloyed with iridium in osmiridium: used to produce platinum alloys, mainly for pen tips and instrument pivots, as a catalyst, and in electric-light filaments. Symbol: Os; atomic no.: 76; atomic wt.: 190.2; valency: 0 to 8; relative density: 22.57; melting pt.: 3033±30°C; boiling pt.: 5012±100°C.
▷**HISTORY** C19: from Greek *osmē* smell, so called from its penetrating odour

osmium tetroxide NOUN a yellowish poisonous water-soluble crystalline substance with a penetrating odour, used as a reagent and catalyst in organic synthesis. Formula: OsO_4.

osmometer (ɒz'mɒmɪtə) NOUN an instrument for measuring osmotic pressure.
▷**HISTORY** C20: from OSMO(SIS) + -METER
▸**osmometric** (ˌɒzmə'mɛtrɪk) ADJECTIVE
▸**ˌosmo'metrically** ADVERB ▸**os'mometry** NOUN

osmoregulation (ˌɒzməʊˌrɛgjʊ'leɪʃən) NOUN *Zoology* the adjustment of the osmotic pressure of a cell or organism in relation to the surrounding fluid.

osmose ('ɒzməʊs, -məʊz, 'ɒs-) VERB 1 to undergo or cause to undergo osmosis. ◆ NOUN 2 a former name for **osmosis.**
▷**HISTORY** C19 (n): abstracted from the earlier terms *endosmose* and *exosmose;* related to Greek *ōsmos* push

osmosis (ɒz'məʊsɪs, ɒs-) NOUN 1 the passage of a solvent through a semipermeable membrane from a less concentrated to a more concentrated solution until both solutions are of the same concentration. 2 diffusion through any membrane or porous barrier, as in dialysis. 3 gradual or unconscious assimilation or adoption, as of ideas.
▷**HISTORY** C19: Latinized form from OSMOSE (n), from Greek *ōsmos* push, thrust
▸**osmotic** (ɒz'mɒtɪk, ɒs-) ADJECTIVE ▸**os'motically** ADVERB

osmotic pressure NOUN the pressure necessary to prevent osmosis into a given solution when the solution is separated from the pure solvent by a semipermeable membrane.

osmous ('ɒzməs) ADJECTIVE of or containing osmium in a low valence state, esp. the divalent state. Also: **osmious.**

osmunda (ɒz'mʌndə) *or* **osmund** ('ɒzmənd) NOUN any fern of the genus *Osmunda,* such as the royal fern, having large spreading fronds: family *Osmundaceae*.
▷**HISTORY** C13: from Old French *osmonde,* of unknown origin

Osnabrück (*German* ɔsna'bryk) NOUN an industrial city in NW Germany, in Lower Saxony: a member of the Hanseatic League in the Middle Ages; one of the treaties comprising the Peace of Westphalia (1648) was signed here. Pop.: 164 900 (1999 est.).

osnaburg ('ɒznəˌbɜːg) NOUN a coarse plain-woven cotton used for sacks, furnishings, etc.
▷HISTORY C16: corruption of OSNABRÜCK, where it was originally made

osprey ('ɒsprɪ, -preɪ) NOUN 1 a large broad-winged fish-eating diurnal bird of prey, *Pandion haliaetus,* with a dark back and whitish head and underparts: family *Pandioridae.* Often called (US and Canadian): **fish hawk.** 2 any of the feathers of various other birds, used esp. as trimming for hats.
▷HISTORY C15: from Old French *ospres,* apparently from Latin *ossifraga,* literally: bone-breaker, from *os* bone + *frangere* to break

ossa ('ɒsə) NOUN the plural of **os**[1].

Ossa ('ɒsə) NOUN a mountain in NE Greece, in E Thessaly: famous in mythology for the attempt of the twin giants, Otus and Ephialtes, to reach heaven by piling Ossa on Olympus and Pelion on Ossa. Height: 1978 m (6489 ft.).

ossein ('ɒsɪɪn) NOUN a protein that forms the organic matrix of bone, constituting about 40 per cent of its matter.
▷HISTORY C19: from Latin *osseus* bony, from *os* bone

osseous ('ɒsɪəs) ADJECTIVE consisting of or containing bone, bony.
▷HISTORY C17: from Latin *osseus,* from *os* bone
▸**'osseously** ADVERB

Osset ('ɒsɪt) NOUN a member of an Iranian people living in S Russia and N Georgia, chiefly in Ossetia in the Caucasus.

Ossetia (ɒ'siːʃə) NOUN a region of central Asia, in the Caucasus: consists administratively of the North Ossetian Republic in Russia and the South Ossetian Autonomous Region in Georgia.

Ossetic (ɒ'sɛtɪk) *or* **Ossetian** (ɒ'siːʃən) ADJECTIVE 1 of or relating to Ossetia, its people, or their language. ◆ NOUN 2 the language of the Ossets, belonging to the East Iranian branch of the Indo-European family.

Ossi ('ɒsɪ; *German* 'ɔsi) NOUN *Informal* a native, inhabitant, or citizen of that part of Germany that was formerly East Germany.
▷HISTORY C20: from German *ostdeutsch* East German

ossicle ('ɒsɪkᵊl) NOUN a small bone, esp. one of those in the middle ear.
▷HISTORY C16: from Latin *ossiculum,* from *os* bone
▸**ossicular** (ɒ'sɪkjʊlə) ADJECTIVE

Ossie ('ɒzɪ) ADJECTIVE, NOUN a variant spelling of **Aussie.**

ossiferous (ɒ'sɪfərəs) ADJECTIVE *Geology* containing or yielding bones: *ossiferous caves.*

ossification (ˌɒsɪfɪ'keɪʃən) NOUN 1 the formation of or conversion into bone. 2 the process of ossifying or the state of being ossified.

ossifrage ('ɒsɪfrɪdʒ, -ˌfreɪdʒ) NOUN an archaic name for the **lammergeier** and **osprey** (sense 1).
▷HISTORY C17: from Latin *ossifraga* sea eagle; see OSPREY

ossify ('ɒsɪˌfaɪ) VERB **-fies, -fying, -fied.** 1 to convert or be converted into bone. 2 (*intr*) (of habits, attitudes, etc.) to become inflexible.
▷HISTORY C18: from French *ossifier,* from Latin *os* bone + *facere* to make
▸**'ossiˌfier** NOUN

osso bucco ('ɒsəʊ 'bʊkəʊ) NOUN a stew, originally from Italy, made with knuckle of veal, cooked in tomato sauce.
▷HISTORY C20: from Italian: marrowbone

ossuary ('ɒsjʊərɪ) NOUN, *plural* **-aries.** any container for the burial of human bones, such as an urn or vault.
▷HISTORY C17: from Late Latin *ossuārium,* from Latin *os* bone

OST (in the US) ABBREVIATION FOR Office of Science and Technology.

osteal ('ɒstɪəl) ADJECTIVE 1 of or relating to bone or to the skeleton. 2 composed of bone; osseous.
▷HISTORY C19: from Greek *osteon* bone

osteichthyan (ˌɒstɪ'ɪkθɪən) NOUN *Zoology* a technical name for **bony fish.**
▷HISTORY New Latin, from Greek *osteon* bone + *ikhthus* fish

osteitis (ˌɒstɪ'aɪtɪs) NOUN inflammation of a bone.
▸**osteitic** (ˌɒstɪ'ɪtɪk) ADJECTIVE

osteitis deformans (dɪ'fɔːmənz) NOUN another name for **Paget's disease** (sense 1).

Ostend (ɒs'tɛnd) NOUN a port and resort in NW Belgium, in West Flanders on the North Sea. Pop.: 68 858 (1995 est.). French name: **Ostende** (ɔstɑ̃d). Flemish name: **Oostende.**

ostensible (ɒ'stɛnsɪbᵊl) ADJECTIVE 1 apparent; seeming. 2 pretended.
▷HISTORY C18: via French from Medieval Latin *ostensibilis,* from Latin *ostendere* to show, from *ob-* before + *tendere* to extend
▸**osˌtensi'bility** NOUN

ostensibly (ɒ'stɛnsɪblɪ) ADVERB (*sentence modifier*) apparently; seemingly.

ostensive (ɒ'stɛnsɪv) ADJECTIVE 1 obviously or manifestly demonstrative. 2 a less common word for **ostensible.** 3 *Philosophy* (of a definition) given by demonstrative means, esp. by pointing.
▷HISTORY C17: from Late Latin *ostentīvus,* from Latin *ostendere* to show; see OSTENSIBLE
▸**os'tensively** ADVERB

ostensory (ɒs'tɛnsərɪ) NOUN, *plural* **-sories.** *RC Church* another word for **monstrance.**
▷HISTORY C18: from Medieval Latin *ostensorium;* see OSTENSIBLE

ostentation (ˌɒstɛn'teɪʃən) NOUN pretentious, showy, or vulgar display.

ostentatious (ˌɒstɛn'teɪʃəs) ADJECTIVE characterized by pretentious, showy, or vulgar display.
▸**ˌosten'tatiously** ADVERB

osteo- *or before a vowel* **oste-** COMBINING FORM indicating bone or bones: *osteopathy.*
▷HISTORY from Greek *osteon*

osteoarthritis (ˌɒstɪəʊɑː'θraɪtɪs) NOUN chronic inflammation of the joints, esp. those that bear weight, with pain and stiffness. Also called: **degenerative joint disease.**
▸**osteoarthritic** (ˌɒstɪəʊɑː'θrɪtɪk) ADJECTIVE, NOUN

osteoblast ('ɒstɪəʊˌblæst) NOUN a bone-forming cell.
▸**ˌosteo'blastic** ADJECTIVE

osteoclasis (ˌɒstɪ'ɒkləsɪs) NOUN 1 surgical fracture of a bone to correct deformity. 2 absorption of bone tissue.

osteoclast ('ɒstɪəʊˌklæst) NOUN 1 a surgical instrument for fracturing bone. 2 a large multinuclear cell formed in bone marrow that is associated with the normal absorption of bone.
▸**ˌosteo'clastic** ADJECTIVE

osteofibrosis (ˌɒstɪəʊˌfaɪ'brəʊsɪs) NOUN loss of calcium from the bones, causing them to become fragile.

osteogenesis (ˌɒstɪəʊ'dʒɛnɪsɪs) NOUN the formation of bone.
▸**ˌosteo'genic** ADJECTIVE

osteogenesis imperfecta (ˌɪmpə'fɛktə) NOUN a hereditary disease caused by a collagen abnormality, causing fragility of the skeleton which results in fractures and deformities. Also called: **brittle bone syndrome.**

osteoid ('ɒstɪˌɔɪd) ADJECTIVE of or resembling bone; bony.

osteology (ˌɒstɪ'ɒlədʒɪ) NOUN the study of the structure and function of bones.
▸**osteological** (ˌɒstɪə'lɒdʒɪkᵊl) ADJECTIVE
▸**ˌosteo'logically** ADVERB ▸**ˌoste'ologist** NOUN

osteoma (ˌɒstɪ'əʊmə) NOUN, *plural* **-mata** (-mətə) *or* **-mas.** a benign tumour composed of bone or bonelike tissue.

osteomalacia (ˌɒstɪəʊmə'leɪʃɪə) NOUN a disease in adults characterized by softening of the bones, resulting from a deficiency of vitamin D and of calcium and phosphorus.
▷HISTORY C19: from New Latin, from OSTEO- + Greek *malakia* softness
▸**ˌosteoma'lacial** *or* **osteomalacic** (ˌɒstɪəʊmə'læsɪk) ADJECTIVE

osteomyelitis (ˌɒstɪəʊˌmaɪɪ'laɪtɪs) NOUN inflammation of bone marrow, caused by infection.

osteopath ('ɒstɪəˌpæθ) *or* (*less commonly*) **osteopathist** (ˌɒstɪ'ɒpəθɪst) NOUN a person who practises osteopathy.

osteopathy (ˌɒstɪ'ɒpəθɪ) NOUN a system of healing based on the manipulation of bones or other parts of the body.
▸**osteopathic** (ˌɒstɪə'pæθɪk) ADJECTIVE ▸**ˌosteo'pathically** ADVERB

osteophyte ('ɒstɪəˌfaɪt) NOUN a small abnormal bony outgrowth.
▸**osteophytic** (ˌɒstɪə'fɪtɪk) ADJECTIVE

osteoplastic (ˌɒstɪə'plæstɪk) ADJECTIVE 1 of or relating to osteoplasty. 2 of or relating to the formation of bone.

osteoplasty ('ɒstɪəˌplæstɪ) NOUN, *plural* **-ties.** the branch of surgery concerned with bone repair or bone grafting.

osteoporosis (ˌɒstɪəʊpɔː'rəʊsɪs) NOUN porosity and brittleness of the bones due to loss of calcium from the bone matrix.
▷HISTORY C19: from OSTEO- + PORE[2] + -OSIS
▸**ˌosteopo'rotic** ADJECTIVE

osteotome ('ɒstɪəˌtəʊm) NOUN a surgical instrument for cutting bone, usually a special chisel.

osteotomy (ˌɒstɪ'ɒtəmɪ) NOUN, *plural* **-mies.** the surgical cutting or dividing of bone, usually to correct a deformity.

Österreich ('øːstəraiç) NOUN the German name for **Austria.**

Ostia ('ɒstɪə) NOUN an ancient town in W central Italy, originally at the mouth of the Tiber but now about 6 km (4 miles) inland: served as the port of ancient Rome; harbours built by Claudius and Trajan; ruins excavated since 1854.

ostiary ('ɒstɪərɪ) NOUN, *plural* **-aries.** *RC Church* another word for **porter**[2] (sense 4).
▷HISTORY C15: from Latin *ostiārius* doorkeeper, from *ostium* door

ostinato (ˌɒstɪ'nɑːtəʊ) NOUN **a** a continuously reiterated musical phrase. **b** (*as modifier*): *an ostinato passage.*
▷HISTORY Italian: from Latin *obstinātus* OBSTINATE

ostiole ('ɒstɪˌəʊl) NOUN *Biology* 1 the pore in the reproductive bodies of certain algae and fungi through which spores pass. 2 any small pore.
▷HISTORY C19: from Latin *ostiolum,* diminutive of *ostium* door
▸**ostiolar** ('ɒstɪələ) *or* **'ostioˌlate** ADJECTIVE

ostium ('ɒstɪəm) NOUN, *plural* **-tia** (-tɪə). *Biology* 1 any of the pores in sponges through which water enters the body. 2 any of the openings in the heart of an arthropod through which blood enters. 3 any similar opening.
▷HISTORY C17: from Latin: door, entrance

ostler *or* **hostler** ('ɒslə) NOUN *Archaic* a stableman, esp. one at an inn.
▷HISTORY C15: variant of *hostler,* from HOSTEL

Ostmark ('ɒstˌmɑːk; *German* 'ɔstmark) NOUN (formerly) the standard monetary unit of East Germany, divided into 100 pfennigs.
▷HISTORY German, literally: east mark

ostosis (ɒs'təʊsɪs) NOUN the formation of bone; ossification.

Ostpreussen ('ɔstprɔysən) NOUN the German name for **East Prussia.**

ostracize *or* **ostracise** ('ɒstrəˌsaɪz) VERB (*tr*) 1 to exclude or banish (a person) from a particular group, society, etc. 2 (in ancient Greece) to punish by temporary exile.
▷HISTORY C17: from Greek *ostrakizein* to select someone for banishment by voting on potsherds; see OSTRACON
▸**'ostracism** NOUN ▸**'ostraˌcizable** *or* **'ostraˌcisable** ADJECTIVE ▸**'ostraˌcizer** *or* **'ostraˌciser** NOUN

ostracod ('ɒstrəˌkɒd) NOUN any minute crustacean of the mainly freshwater subclass *Ostracoda,* in which the body is enclosed in a transparent two-valved carapace.
▷HISTORY C19: via New Latin from Greek *ostrakōdēs* having a shell, from *ostrakon* shell
▸**ostracodan** (ˌɒstrə'kəʊdən) *or* **ˌostra'codous** ADJECTIVE

ostracoderm ('ɒstrəkəˌdɜːm, ɒs'trækə-) NOUN any extinct Palaeozoic fishlike jawless vertebrate of the group *Ostracodermi,* characterized by a heavily armoured body.
▷HISTORY C19: via New Latin from Greek *ostrakon* shell + -DERM

ostracon ('ɒstrəˌkɒn) NOUN (in ancient Greece) a potsherd used for ostracizing.
▷HISTORY from Greek

Ostrava (*Czech* 'ɔstrava) NOUN an industrial city in

the E Czech Republic, on the River Oder: the chief coal-mining area in the Czech Republic, in Upper Silesia. Pop.: 321 263 (2000 est.).

ostrich (ˈɒstrɪtʃ) NOUN, *plural* **-triches** *or* **-trich.** 1 a fast-running flightless African bird, *Struthio camelus,* that is the largest living bird, with stout two-toed feet and dark feathers, except on the naked head, neck, and legs: order *Struthioniformes* (see **ratite**). Related adjective: **struthious.** 2 **American ostrich.** another name for **rhea.** 3 a person who refuses to recognize the truth, reality, etc.: a reference to the ostrich's supposed habit of burying its head in the sand.
▷HISTORY C13: from Old French *ostrice,* from Latin *avis* bird + Late Latin *struthio* ostrich, from Greek *strouthion*

Ostrogoth (ˈɒstrəˌɡɒθ) NOUN a member of the eastern group of the Goths, who formed a kingdom in Italy from 493 to 552.
▷HISTORY C17: from Late Latin *Ostrogothī,* from *ostro-* east, eastward + GOTH
▸ˌ**Ostroˈgothic** ADJECTIVE

Ostyak (ˈɒstɪˌæk) NOUN 1 (*plural* **-aks** *or* **-ak**) a member of an Ugrian people living in NW Siberia E of the Urals. 2 the language of this people, belonging to the Finno-Ugric family: related to Hungarian.

Osun (əʊˈsʌn) NOUN a state of SW Nigeria. Capital: Oshogbo. Pop.: 2 463 185 (1995 est.). Area 9251 sq. km (3570 sq. miles).

Oświęcim (*Polish* ɔʃˈfjɛntʃim) NOUN the Polish name for **Auschwitz.**

OT ABBREVIATION FOR: 1 occupational therapy. 2 occupational therapist. 3 Old Testament. 4 overtime.

ot- COMBINING FORM a variant of **oto-** before a vowel: *otalgia.*

Otago (ɒˈtɑːɡəʊ) NOUN a council region of New Zealand, formerly a province, founded by Scottish settlers in the south of South Island. The University of Otago (1869) in Dunedin is the oldest university in New Zealand. Chief town: Dunedin. Pop.: 192 936 (2001).

otalgia (əʊˈtældʒɪə, -dʒə) NOUN the technical name for **earache.**

OTC ABBREVIATION FOR: 1 (in Britain) Officers' Training Corps. 2 **over-the-counter.** 3 oxytetracycline.

OTE ABBREVIATION FOR on-target earnings: referring to the salary a salesperson should be able to achieve.

O tempora! O mores! *Latin* (əʊ ˈtɛmpɔːrɑː əʊ ˈmɔːreɪz) SENTENCE SUBSTITUTE oh the times! oh the customs!: an exclamation at the evil of them.
▷HISTORY from Cicero's oration *In Catilinam*

other (ˈʌðə) DETERMINER 1 **a** (when used before a singular noun, usually preceded by *the*) the remaining (one or ones in a group of which one or some have been specified): *I'll read the other sections of the paper later.* **b the other.** (*as pronoun; functioning as singular*): *one walks while the other rides.* 2 (a) different (one or ones from that or those already specified or understood): *he found some other house; no other man but you; other days were happier.* 3 additional; further: *there are no other possibilities.* 4 (preceded by *every*) alternate; two: *it buzzes every other minute.* 5 **other than. a** apart from; besides: *a lady other than his wife.* **b** different from: *he couldn't be other than what he is.* Archaic form: **other from.** 6 **no other.** *Archaic* nothing else: *I can do no other.* 7 **or other.** (preceded by a phrase or word with *some*) used to add vagueness to the preceding pronoun, noun, noun phrase, or adverb: *some dog or other bit him; he's somewhere or other.* 8 **other things being equal.** conditions being the same or unchanged. 9 **the other day, night,** etc. a few days, nights, etc., ago. 10 **the other thing.** an unexpressed alternative. ◆ PRONOUN 11 another: *show me one other.* 12 (*plural*) additional or further ones: *the police have found two and are looking for others.* 13 (*plural*) other people or things. 14 **the others.** the remaining ones (of a group): *take these and leave the others.* 15 (*plural*) different ones (from those specified or understood): *they'd rather have others, not these.* See also **each other, one another.** ◆ ADVERB 16 (usually used with a negative and foll by *than*) otherwise; differently: *they couldn't behave other than they do.*
▷HISTORY Old English *ōther;* related to Old Saxon *āthar, ōthar,* Old High German *andar*

> **Language note** See at **otherwise.**

other-directed ADJECTIVE guided by values derived from external influences. Compare **inner-directed.**

otherness (ˈʌðənɪs) NOUN the quality of being different or distinct in appearance, character, etc.

other ranks PLURAL NOUN (*rarely used in singular*) *Chiefly Brit* (in the armed forces) all those who do not hold a commissioned rank.

otherwhere (ˈʌðəˌwɛə) ADVERB *Archaic, poetic* elsewhere.

otherwise (ˈʌðəˌwaɪz) SENTENCE CONNECTOR 1 or else; if not, then: *go home — otherwise your mother will worry.* ◆ ADVERB 2 differently: *I wouldn't have thought otherwise.* 3 in other respects: *an otherwise hopeless situation.* ◆ ADJECTIVE 4 (*predicative*) of an unexpected nature; different: *the facts are otherwise.* ◆ PRONOUN 5 something different in outcome: *success or otherwise.*
▷HISTORY C14: from Old English *on ōthre wīsan* in other manner

> **Language note** The expression *otherwise than* means *in any other way than* and should not be followed by an adjective: *no-one taught by this method can be other than* (not *otherwise than*) *successful; you are not allowed to use the building otherwise than as a private dwelling.*

other world NOUN the spirit world or afterlife.

otherworldly (ˌʌðəˈwɜːldlɪ) ADJECTIVE 1 of or relating to the spiritual or imaginative world. 2 impractical or unworldly.
▸ˌ**otherˈworldliness** NOUN

Othin (ˈəʊðɪn) NOUN a variant of **Odin.**

Othman (ˈɒθmən, ɒθˈmɑːn) ADJECTIVE, NOUN a variant of **Ottoman.**

otic (ˈəʊtɪk, ˈɒtɪk) ADJECTIVE of or relating to the ear.
▷HISTORY C17: from Greek *ōtikos,* from *ous* ear

-otic SUFFIX FORMING ADJECTIVES 1 relating to or affected by: *sclerotic.* 2 causing: *narcotic.*
▷HISTORY from Greek *-ōtikos*

otiose (ˈəʊtɪˌəʊs, -ˌəʊz) ADJECTIVE 1 serving no useful purpose: *otiose language.* 2 *Rare* indolent; lazy.
▷HISTORY C18: from Latin *ōtiōsus* leisured, from *ōtium* leisure
▸**otiosity** (ˌəʊtɪˈɒsɪtɪ) *or* ˈ**otioseness** NOUN

otitis (əʊˈtaɪtɪs) NOUN inflammation of the ear, esp. the middle ear (**otitis media**), with pain, impaired hearing, etc., or the outer ear (**otitis externa**), with inflammation between the ear drum and the external opening. See also **labyrinthitis.**

oto- *or before a vowel* **ot-** COMBINING FORM indicating the ear: *otitis; otolith.*
▷HISTORY from Greek *ous, ōt-* ear

otocyst (ˈəʊtəʊˌsɪst) NOUN 1 another name for **statocyst.** 2 the embryonic structure in vertebrates that develops into the inner ear in the adult.
▸ˌ**otoˈcystic** ADJECTIVE

otolaryngology (ˌəʊtəʊˌlærɪŋˈɡɒlədʒɪ) NOUN the branch of medicine concerned with the ear, nose, and throat and their diseases. Sometimes called: **otorhinolaryngology.**
▸**otolaryngological** (ˌəʊtəʊləˌrɪŋɡəˈlɒdʒɪkᵊl) ADJECTIVE
▸ˌ**otoˌlarynˈgologist** NOUN

otolith (ˈəʊtəʊˌlɪθ) NOUN 1 any of the granules of calcium carbonate in the inner ear of vertebrates. Movement of otoliths, caused by a change in position of the animal, stimulates sensory hair cells, which convey the information to the brain. 2 another name for **statolith** (sense 1).
▸ˌ**otoˈlithic** ADJECTIVE

otology (əʊˈtɒlədʒɪ) NOUN the branch of medicine concerned with the ear.
▸**otological** (ˌəʊtəˈlɒdʒɪkᵊl) ADJECTIVE ▸**oˈtologist** NOUN

otorrhoea (ˌəʊtəˈrɪə) NOUN *Pathol* a discharge from the ears.

otoscope (ˈəʊtəˌskəʊp) NOUN another name for **auriscope.**
▸**otoscopic** (ˌəʊtəˈskɒpɪk) ADJECTIVE

OTPOTSS *or* **otpotss** ABBREVIATION FOR orientation towards people of the same sex (i.e. homosexuality).

Otranto (*Italian* ˈɔːtranto) NOUN a small port in SE Italy, in Apulia on the **Strait of Otranto**: the most easterly town in Italy; dates back to Greek times and was an important Roman port; its ruined castle was the setting of Horace Walpole's *Castle of Otranto.* Pop.: 5075 (latest est.).

OTT *Slang* ABBREVIATION FOR over the top: see **top**[1] (sense 19b).

ottar (ˈɒtə) NOUN a variant of **attar.**

ottava (əʊˈtɑːvə) NOUN an interval of an octave. See **all'ottava.**
▷HISTORY Italian: OCTAVE

ottava rima (ˈriːmə) NOUN *Prosody* a stanza form consisting of eight iambic pentameter lines, rhyming a b a b a b c c.
▷HISTORY Italian: eighth rhyme

Ottawa (ˈɒtəwə) NOUN 1 the capital of Canada, in E Ontario on the Ottawa River: name changed from Bytown to Ottawa in 1854. Pop.: 323 340 (1996). 2 a river in central Canada, rising in W Quebec and flowing west, then southeast to join the St Lawrence River as its chief tributary at Montreal; forms the border between Quebec and Ontario for most of its length. Length: 1120 km (696 miles).

otter (ˈɒtə) NOUN, *plural* **-ters** *or* **-ter.** 1 any freshwater carnivorous musteline mammal of the subfamily *Lutrinae,* esp. *Lutra lutra* (**Eurasian otter**), typically having smooth fur, a streamlined body, and webbed feet. 2 the fur of any of these animals. 3 Also called: **otter board.** a type of fishing tackle consisting of a weighted board to which hooked and baited lines are attached. ◆ VERB 4 to fish using an otter.
▷HISTORY Old English *otor;* related to Old Norse *otr,* Old High German *ottar*

Otterburn (ˈɒtəˌbɜːn) NOUN a village in NE England, in central Northumberland: scene of a battle (1388) in which the Scots, led by the earl of Douglas, defeated the English, led by Hotspur.

otter hound NOUN a dog used for otter hunting, esp. one of a breed, now rare, that stands about 60 cm (24 in.) high and has a harsh thick coat, often greyish with tan markings.

otter shell NOUN See **gaper** (sense 2).

otter shrew NOUN any small otter-like amphibious mammal, esp. *Potamogale velox,* of the family *Potamogalidae* of W and central Africa: order *Insectivora* (insectivores).

otto (ˈɒtəʊ) NOUN another name for **attar.**

Otto cycle NOUN an engine cycle used on four-stroke petrol engines (**Otto engines**) in which, ideally, combustion and rejection of heat both take place at constant volume. Compare **diesel cycle.**
▷HISTORY C19: named after Nikolaus August *Otto* (1832–91), German engineer

ottoman (ˈɒtəmən) NOUN, *plural* **-mans.** 1 **a** a low padded seat, usually armless, sometimes in the form of a chest. **b** a cushioned footstool. 2 a corded fabric.
▷HISTORY C17: from French *ottomane,* feminine of OTTOMAN

Ottoman (ˈɒtəmən) *or* **Othman** ADJECTIVE 1 *History* of or relating to the Ottomans or the Ottoman Empire. 2 denoting or relating to the Turkish language. ◆ NOUN, *plural* **-mans.** 3 a member of a Turkish people who invaded the Near East in the late 13th century.
▷HISTORY C17: from French, via Medieval Latin, from Arabic *Othmānī* Turkish, from Turkish *Othman Osman* I (1259–1326), founder of the Ottoman Empire

Ottoman Empire NOUN the former Turkish empire in Europe, Asia, and Africa, which lasted from the late 13th century until the end of World War I. Also called: **Turkish Empire.**

ou (əʊ) NOUN *South African, slang* a man, bloke, or chap.
▷HISTORY Afrikaans

OU ABBREVIATION FOR: 1 the Open University. 2 Oxford University.

ouabain (ˈwɑːbɑːɪn) NOUN a poisonous white crystalline glycoside extracted from certain trees and used as a heart stimulant and, by some African tribes, on poison darts. Formula: $C_{29}H_{44}O_{12}.8H_2O$.

▷**HISTORY** C19: from French *ouabaïo,* from Somali *waba yo* native name of tree

Ouachita *or* **Washita** ('wɒʃɪ,tɔː) NOUN a river in the S central US, rising in the **Ouachita Mountains** and flowing east, south, and southeast into the Red River in E Louisiana. Length: 974 km (605 miles).

Ouagadougou (,wɑːgə'duːguː) NOUN the capital of Burkina-Faso, on the central plateau: terminus of the railway from Abidjan (Côte d'Ivoire). Pop.: 690 000 (1993 est.).

ouananiche (,wɑːnə'niːʃ) NOUN a landlocked variety of the Atlantic salmon, *Salmo salar,* found in lakes in SE Canada.

▷**HISTORY** from Canadian French, from Montagnais *wananish,* diminutive of *wanans* salmon

oubaas ('əʊ,bɑːs) NOUN *South African* a person who is senior in years or rank.

▷**HISTORY** Afrikaans

Oubangui (uː'bɑːŋgiː, juː'bæŋgɪ) NOUN the French name for **Ubangi.**

oubliette (,uːblɪ'ɛt) NOUN a dungeon the only entrance to which is through the top.

▷**HISTORY** C19: from French, from *oublier* to forget

ouch[1] (aʊtʃ) INTERJECTION an exclamation of sharp sudden pain.

ouch[2] (aʊtʃ) NOUN *Archaic* 1 a brooch or clasp set with gems. 2 the setting of a gem.

▷**HISTORY** C15 *an ouch,* mistaken division of C14 *a nouche,* from Old French *nouche,* of Germanic origin; compare Old High German *nusca* buckle

oud (uːd) NOUN an Arabic stringed musical instrument resembling a lute or mandolin.

▷**HISTORY** from Arabic *al 'ūd,* literally: the wood. Compare LUTE[1]

Oudh (aʊd) NOUN 1 a region of N India, in central Uttar Pradesh: annexed by Britain in 1856 and a centre of the Indian Mutiny (1857–58); joined with Agra in 1877, becoming the United Provinces of Agra and Oudh in 1902, which were renamed Uttar Pradesh in 1950. 2 another name for **Ayodha.**

Ouessant (wesɑ̃) NOUN the French name for **Ushant.**

ought[1] (ɔːt) VERB (foll by *to; takes an infinitive or implied infinitive*) used as an auxiliary: 1 to indicate duty or obligation: *you ought to pay your dues.* 2 to express prudent expediency: *you ought to be more careful with your money.* 3 (usually with reference to future time) to express probability or expectation: *you ought to finish this work by Friday.* 4 to express a desire or wish on the part of the speaker: *you ought to come next week.*

▷**HISTORY** Old English *āhte,* past tense of *āgan* to OWE; related to Gothic *aihta*

> **Language note** In correct English, *ought* is not used with *did* or *had. I ought not to do it,* not *I didn't ought to do it; I ought not to have done it,* not *I hadn't ought to have done it.*

ought[2] (ɔːt) PRONOUN, ADVERB a variant spelling of **aught**[1].

ought[3] (ɔːt) NOUN a less common word for **nought** (zero).

▷**HISTORY** C19: mistaken division of *a nought* as *an ought;* see NOUGHT

ouguiya (uː'giːjə) NOUN the standard monetary unit of Mauritania, divided into 5 khoums.

Ouija board ('wiːdʒə) NOUN *Trademark* a board on which are marked the letters of the alphabet. Answers to questions are spelt out by a pointer or glass held by the fingertips of the participants, and are supposedly formed by spiritual forces.

▷**HISTORY** C19: from French *oui* yes + German *ja* yes

Oujda (uːdʒ'dɑː) NOUN a city in NE Morocco, near the border with Algeria: frontier post. Pop.: 146 142 (1994).

Oulu ('ɔulu) NOUN an industrial city and port in W Finland, on the Gulf of Bothnia: university (1959). Pop.: 117 670 (2000 est.). Swedish name: **Uleåborg.**

ouma ('əʊmɑː) NOUN *South African* 1 grandmother, esp. in titular use with surname. 2 *Slang* any elderly woman.

▷**HISTORY** Afrikaans

ounce[1] (aʊns) NOUN 1 a unit of weight equal to one sixteenth of a pound (avoirdupois); 1 ounce is equal to 437.5 grains or 28.349 grams. Abbreviation: **oz.** 2 a unit of weight equal to one twelfth of a Troy or Apothecaries' pound; 1 ounce is equal to 480 grains or 31.103 grams. 3 short for **fluid ounce.** 4 a small portion or amount.

▷**HISTORY** C14: from Old French *unce,* from Latin *uncia* a twelfth; from *ūnus* one

ounce[2] (aʊns) NOUN another name for **snow leopard.**

▷**HISTORY** C18: from Old French *once,* by mistaken division of *lonce* as if *l'once,* from Latin LYNX

oupa ('əʊpɑː) NOUN *South African* 1 grandfather, esp. in titular use with surname. 2 *Slang* any elderly man.

▷**HISTORY** Afrikaans

our (aʊə) DETERMINER 1 of, belonging to, or associated in some way with us: *our best vodka; our parents are good to us.* 2 belonging to or associated with all people or people in general: *our nearest planet is Venus.* 3 a formal word for *my* used by editors or other writers, and monarchs. 4 *Informal* (often sarcastic) used instead of *your: are our feet hurting?* 5 *Dialect* belonging to the family of the speaker: *it's our Sandra's birthday tomorrow.*

▷**HISTORY** Old English *ūre* (genitive plural), from US; related to Old French, Old Saxon *ūser,* Old High German *unsēr,* Gothic *unsara*

-our SUFFIX FORMING NOUNS indicating state, condition, or activity: *behaviour; labour.*

▷**HISTORY** in Old French *-eur,* from Latin *-or,* noun suffix

Our Father NOUN another name for the **Lord's Prayer,** taken from its opening words

Our Lady NOUN a title given to the **Virgin Mary.**

ours (aʊəz) PRONOUN 1 something or someone belonging to or associated with us: *ours have blue tags.* 2 **of ours.** belonging to or associated with us.

ourself (aʊə'self) PRONOUN *Archaic* a variant of **myself,** formerly used by monarchs or editors in formal contexts

ourselves (aʊə'sɛlvz) PRONOUN 1 **a** the reflexive form of *we* or *us.* **b** (intensifier): *we ourselves will finish it.* 2 (*preceded by a copula*) our usual selves: *we are ourselves when we're together.* 3 *Not standard* used instead of *we* or *us* in compound noun phrases: *other people and ourselves.*

-ous SUFFIX FORMING ADJECTIVES 1 having, full of, or characterized by: *dangerous; spacious; languorous.* 2 (in chemistry) indicating that an element is chemically combined in the lower of two possible valency states: *ferrous; stannous.* Compare **-ic** (sense 2).

▷**HISTORY** from Old French, from Latin *-ōsus* or *-us,* Greek *-os,* adj suffixes

Ouse (uːz) NOUN 1 Also called: **Great Ouse.** a river in E England, rising in Northamptonshire and flowing northeast to the Wash near King's Lynn; for the last 56 km (35 miles) follows mainly artificial channels. Length: 257 km (160 miles). 2 a river in NE England, in Yorkshire, formed by the confluence of the Swale and Ure Rivers: flows southeast to the Humber. Length: 92 km (57 miles). 3 a river in S England, rising in Sussex and flowing south to the English Channel. Length: 48 km (30 miles).

ousel ('uːzᵊl) NOUN a variant spelling of **ouzel.**

oust (aʊst) VERB (*tr*) 1 to force out of a position or place; supplant or expel. 2 *Property law* to deprive (a person) of the possession of land.

▷**HISTORY** C16: from Anglo-Norman *ouster,* from Latin *obstāre* to withstand, from *ob-* against + *stāre* to stand

ouster ('aʊstə) NOUN *Property law* the act of dispossessing of freehold property; eviction; ejection.

out (aʊt) ADVERB 1 (*often used as a particle*) at or to a point beyond the limits of some location; outside: *get out at once.* 2 (*particle*) out of consciousness: *she passed out at the sight of blood.* 3 (*particle*) used to indicate a burst of activity as indicated by the verb: *fever broke out.* 4 (*particle*) used to indicate obliteration of an object: *the graffiti were painted out.* 5 (*particle*) used to indicate an approximate drawing or description: *sketch out; chalk out.* 6 (*often used as a particle*) away from one's custody or ownership, esp. on hire: *to let out a cottage.* 7 on sale or on view to the public: *the book is being brought out next May.* 8 (of a young woman) in or into polite society: *Lucinda had a fabulous party when she came out.* 9 (of a jury) withdrawn to consider a verdict in private. 10 (*particle*) used to indicate exhaustion or extinction: *the sugar's run out; put the light out.* 11 (*particle*) used to indicate a goal or object achieved at the end of the action specified by the verb: *he worked it out; let's fight it out, then!* 12 (*preceded by a superlative*) existing: *the friendliest dog out.* 13 an expression in signalling, radio, etc., to indicate the end of a transmission. 14 *Austral and NZ, archaic* in or to Australia or New Zealand: *he came out last year.* 15 **out of. a** at or to a point outside: *out of his reach.* **b** away from; not in: *stepping out of line; out of focus.* **c** because of, motivated by: *doing it out of jealousy.* **d** from (a material or source): *made out of plastic.* **e** not or no longer having any of (a substance, material, etc.): *we're out of sugar.* ◆ ADJECTIVE (*postpositive*) 16 not or not any longer worth considering: *that plan is out because of the weather.* 17 not allowed: *smoking on duty is out.* 18 (*also prenominal*) not in vogue; unfashionable: *that sort of dress is out these days.* 19 (of a fire or light) no longer burning or providing illumination: *the fire is out.* 20 not working: *the radio's out.* 21 unconscious: *he was out for two minutes.* 22 **out to it.** *Austral and NZ informal* asleep or unconscious, esp. because drunk. 23 not in; not at home: *call back later, they're out now.* 24 desirous of or intent on (something or doing something): *I'm out for as much money as I can get.* 25 Also: **out on strike.** on strike: *the machine shop is out.* 26 (in several games and sports) denoting the state in which a player is caused to discontinue active participation, esp. in some specified role. 27 used up; exhausted: *our supplies are completely out.* 28 worn into holes: *this sweater is out at the elbows.* 29 inaccurate, deficient, or discrepant: *out by six pence.* 30 not in office or authority: *his party will be out at the election.* 31 completed or concluded, as of time: *before the year is out.* 32 in flower: *the roses are out now.* 33 in arms, esp., in rebellion: *one of his ancestors was out in the Forty-Five.* 34 (*also prenominal*) being out: *the out position on the dial.* 35 *Informal* not concealing one's homosexuality. ◆ PREPOSITION 36 out of; out through: *he ran out the door.* 37 *Archaic or dialect* outside; beyond: *he comes from out our domain.* ◆ INTERJECTION 38 **a** an exclamation, usually peremptory, of dismissal, reproach, etc. **b** (in wireless telegraphy) an expression used to signal that the speaker is signing off. 39 **out with it.** a command to make something known immediately, without missing any details. ◆ NOUN 40 *Chiefly US* a method of escape from a place, difficult situation, punishment, etc. 41 *Baseball* an instance of the putting out of a batter; putout. 42 *Printing* **a** the omission of words from a printed text; lacuna. **b** the words so omitted. 43 **ins and outs.** See **in** (sense 29). ◆ VERB 44 (*tr*) to put or throw out. 45 (*intr*) to be made known or effective despite efforts to the contrary (esp. in the phrase **will out**): *the truth will out.* 46 (*tr*) *Informal* (of homosexuals) to expose (a public figure) as being a fellow homosexual. 47 (*tr*) *Informal* to expose something secret, embarrassing, or unknown about (a person): *he was eventually outed as a talented goal scorer.*

▷**HISTORY** Old English *ūt;* related to Old Saxon, Old Norse *ūt,* Old High German *ūz,* German *aus*

> **Language note** The use of *out* as a preposition, though common in American English, is regarded as incorrect in British English: *he climbed out of* (not *out*) *a window; he went out through the door.*

out- PREFIX 1 excelling or surpassing in a particular action: *outlast; outlive.* 2 indicating an external location or situation away from the centre: *outpost; outpatient.* 3 indicating emergence, an issuing forth, etc.: *outcrop; outgrowth.* 4 indicating the result of an action: *outcome.*

outage ('aʊtɪdʒ) NOUN 1 a quantity of goods missing or lost after storage or shipment. 2 a period of power failure, machine stoppage, etc.

out and about ADJECTIVE regularly going out of the house to work, take part in social activity, etc., esp. after an illness.

out and away ADVERB by far.

out-and-out ADJECTIVE (*prenominal*) thoroughgoing; complete.

out-and-outer NOUN *Slang* 1 a thorough or

thoroughgoing person or thing. 2 a person or thing that is excellent of its kind. 3 an extremist.

outasight (ˌautə'saɪt) *or* **out-of-sight** ADJECTIVE, INTERJECTION *Slang* another term for **far-out**.

outback ('autˌbæk) NOUN **a** the remote bush country of Australia. **b** (*as modifier*): *outback life*.

outbalance (ˌaut'bæləns) VERB another word for **outweigh**.

outbid (ˌaut'bɪd) VERB **-bids, -bidding, -bid, -bidden** *or* **-bid**. (*tr*) to bid higher than; outdo in bidding.

outboard ('autˌbɔːd) ADJECTIVE 1 (of a boat's engine) portable, with its own propeller, and designed to be attached externally to the stern. Compare **inboard** (sense 1). 2 in a position away from, or further away from, the centre line of a vessel or aircraft, esp. outside the hull or fuselage. ◆ ADVERB 3 away from the centre line of a vessel or aircraft, esp. outside the hull or fuselage. ◆ NOUN 4 an outboard motor. 5 a boat fitted with an outboard motor.

outbound ('autˌbaund) ADJECTIVE going out; outward bound.

outbrave (ˌaut'breɪv) VERB (*tr*) 1 to surpass in bravery. 2 to confront defiantly.

outbreak ('autˌbreɪk) NOUN a sudden, violent, or spontaneous occurrence, esp. of disease or strife.

outbreed (ˌaut'briːd) VERB **-breeds, -breeding, -bred**. 1 (*intr*) *Anthropol* to produce offspring through sexual relations outside a particular family or tribe. 2 to breed (animals that are not closely related) or (of such animals) to be bred.
▸ **ˌout'breeding** NOUN

outbuilding ('autˌbɪldɪŋ) NOUN a building subordinate to but separate from a main building; outhouse.

outburst ('autˌbɜːst) NOUN 1 a sudden and violent expression of emotion. 2 an explosion or eruption.

outcast ('autˌkɑːst) NOUN 1 a person who is rejected or excluded from a social group. 2 a vagabond or wanderer. 3 anything thrown out or rejected. ◆ ADJECTIVE 4 rejected, abandoned, or discarded; cast out.

outcaste ('autˌkɑːst) NOUN 1 a person who has been expelled from a caste. 2 a person having no caste. ◆ VERB 3 (*tr*) to cause (someone) to lose his caste.

outclass (ˌaut'klɑːs) VERB (*tr*) 1 to surpass in class, quality, etc. 2 to defeat easily.

outcome ('autˌkʌm) NOUN something that follows from an action, dispute, situation, etc.; result; consequence.

outcrop NOUN ('autˌkrɒp) 1 part of a rock formation or mineral vein that appears at the surface of the earth. 2 an emergence; appearance. ◆ VERB (ˌaut'krɒp) **-crops, -cropping, -cropped**. (*intr*) 3 (of rock strata, mineral veins, etc.) to protrude through the surface of the earth. 4 another word for **crop out**.

outcross VERB (ˌaut'krɒs) 1 to breed (animals or plants of the same breed but different strains). ◆ NOUN ('autˌkrɒs) 2 an animal or plant produced as a result of outcrossing. 3 an act of outcrossing.

outcry NOUN ('autˌkraɪ), PLURAL **-cries**. 1 a widespread or vehement protest. 2 clamour; uproar. 3 *Commerce* a method of trading in which dealers shout out bids and offers at a prearranged meeting: *sale by open outcry*. ◆ VERB (ˌaut'kraɪ) **-cries, -crying, -cried**. 4 (*tr*) to cry louder or make more noise than (someone or something).

outdate (ˌaut'deɪt) VERB (*tr*) (of something new) to cause (something else) to become old-fashioned or obsolete.

outdated (ˌaut'deɪtɪd) ADJECTIVE old-fashioned or obsolete.

outdistance (ˌaut'dɪstəns) VERB (*tr*) to leave far behind.

outdo (ˌaut'duː) VERB **-does, -doing, -did, -done**. (*tr*) to surpass or exceed in performance or execution.

outdoor ('aut'dɔː) ADJECTIVE (*prenominal*) taking place, existing, or intended for use in the open air: *outdoor games; outdoor clothes*. Also: **out-of-door**.

outdoor relief NOUN another name for **out-relief**.

outdoors (ˌaut'dɔːz) ADVERB 1 Also: **out-of-doors**. in the open air; outside. ◆ NOUN 2 the world outside or far away from human habitation: *the great outdoors*.

outdoorsy (ˌaut'dɔːzɪ) ADJECTIVE *Informal* characteristic of, or taking part in activities relating to, the outdoors.

outer ('autə) ADJECTIVE (*prenominal*) 1 being or located on the outside; external. 2 further from the middle or central part. ◆ NOUN 3 *Archery* **a** the white outermost ring on a target. **b** a shot that hits this ring. 4 *Austral* the unsheltered part of the spectator area at a sports ground. 5 **on the outer**. *Austral and NZ informal* excluded or neglected.

outer bar NOUN (in England) a collective name for junior barristers who plead from outside the bar of the court. Compare **Queen's Counsel**.

outercourse ('autəˌkɔːs) NOUN sexual activity between partners that does not include actual penetration.

outer garments PLURAL NOUN the garments that are worn over a person's other clothes.

Outer Hebrides PLURAL NOUN See **Hebrides**.

Outer Mongolia NOUN the former name (until 1924) of the republic of **Mongolia**.

outermost ('autəˌməust) ADJECTIVE furthest from the centre or middle; outmost.

outer planet NOUN any of the planets Jupiter, Saturn, Uranus, Neptune, and Pluto, whose orbit lies outside the asteroid belt.

outer space NOUN (*not in technical usage*) any region of space beyond the atmosphere of the earth.

outface (ˌaut'feɪs) VERB (*tr*) 1 to face or stare down. 2 to confront boldly or defiantly.

outfall ('autˌfɔːl) NOUN the end of a river, sewer, drain, etc., from which it discharges.

outfield ('autˌfiːld) NOUN 1 *Cricket* the area of the field relatively far from the pitch; the deep. Compare **infield** (sense 1). 2 *Baseball* **a** the area of the playing field beyond the lines connecting first, second, and third bases. **b** the positions of the left fielder, centre fielder, and right fielder taken collectively. Compare **infield** (sense 2). 3 *Agriculture* farmland most distant from the farmstead.
▸ **'outˌfielder** NOUN

outfighting ('autˌfaɪtɪŋ) NOUN fighting at a distance and not at close range.

outfit ('autˌfɪt) NOUN 1 a set of articles or equipment for a particular task, occupation, etc. 2 a set of clothes, esp. a carefully selected one. 3 *Informal* any group or association regarded as a cohesive unit, such as a military company, business house, etc. 4 the act of fitting out. 5 *Canadian* (formerly) the annual shipment of trading goods and supplies sent by a fur company to its trading posts. ◆ VERB **-fits, -fitting, -fitted**. 6 to furnish or be furnished with an outfit, equipment, etc.

outfitter ('autˌfɪtə) NOUN *Chiefly Brit* 1 a shop that sells men's clothes. 2 a person who provides outfits.

outflank (ˌaut'flæŋk) VERB (*tr*) 1 to go around the flank of (an opposing army). 2 to get the better of.

outflow ('autˌfləu) NOUN 1 anything that flows out, such as liquid, money, ideas, etc. 2 the amount that flows out. 3 the act or process of flowing out.

outfoot (ˌaut'fut) VERB (*tr*) 1 (of a boat) to go faster than (another boat). 2 to surpass in running, dancing, etc.

outfox (ˌaut'fɒks) VERB (*tr*) to surpass in guile or cunning.

outgas (ˌaut'gæs) VERB **-gases** *or* **-gasses, -gassing, -gassed**. to undergo or cause to undergo the removal of adsorbed or absorbed gas from solids, often by heating in free space.

outgeneral (ˌaut'dʒenərəl) VERB **-als, -alling, -alled** *or* *US* **-als, -aling, -aled**. (*tr*) to surpass in generalship.

outgo VERB (ˌaut'gəu) **-goes, -going, -went, -gone**. 1 (*tr*) to exceed or outstrip. ◆ NOUN ('autˌgəu) 2 cost; outgoings; outlay. 3 something that goes out; outflow.

outgoing ('autˌgəuɪŋ) ADJECTIVE 1 departing; leaving. 2 leaving or retiring from office: *the outgoing chairman*. 3 friendly and sociable. ◆ NOUN 4 the act of going out.

outgoings ('autˌgəuɪŋz) PLURAL NOUN expenditure.

out-group NOUN *Sociol* persons excluded from an in-group.

outgrow (ˌaut'grəu) VERB **-grows, -growing, -grew, -grown**. (*tr*) 1 to grow too large for (clothes, shoes, etc.). 2 to lose (a habit, idea, reputation, etc.) in the course of development or time. 3 to grow larger or faster than.

outgrowth ('autˌgrəuθ) NOUN 1 a thing growing out of a main body. 2 a development, result, or consequence. 3 the act of growing out.

outgun (ˌaut'gʌn) VERB (*tr*) **-guns, -gunning, -gunned** 1 to surpass in fire power. 2 to surpass in shooting. 3 *Informal* to surpass or excel.

outhaul ('autˌhɔːl) NOUN *Nautical* a line or cable for tightening the foot of a sail by hauling the clew out along the boom or yard. Also: **outhauler**.

out-Herod VERB (*tr*) to surpass in evil, excesses, or cruelty.
▷HISTORY C17: originally *out-Herod Herod*, from Shakespeare's *Hamlet* (act 3, scene 2); see also HEROD: portrayed in medieval mystery plays as a ranting tyrant

outhit (ˌaut'hɪt) VERB **-hits, -hitting, -hit**. (*tr*) to hit something further than (someone else).

outhouse ('autˌhaus) NOUN 1 a building near to, but separate from, a main building; outbuilding. 2 *US* an outside lavatory.

outing ('autɪŋ) NOUN 1 a short outward and return journey; trip; excursion. 2 *Informal* the naming by homosexuals of other prominent homosexuals, often against their will.

outjockey (ˌaut'dʒɒkɪ) VERB (*tr*) to outwit by deception.

outland ADJECTIVE ('autˌlænd, -lənd) 1 outlying or distant. 2 *Archaic* foreign; alien. ◆ NOUN ('autˌlænd) 3 (*usually plural*) the outlying areas of a country or region.

outlander ('autˌlændə) NOUN a foreigner or stranger.

outlandish (aut'lændɪʃ) ADJECTIVE 1 grotesquely unconventional in appearance, habits, etc. 2 *Archaic* foreign.
▸ **out'landishly** ADVERB ▸ **out'landishness** NOUN

outlaw ('autˌlɔː) NOUN 1 (formerly) a person excluded from the law and deprived of its protection. 2 any fugitive from the law, esp. a habitual transgressor. 3 a wild or untamed beast. ◆ VERB (*tr*) 4 to put (a person) outside the law and deprive of its protection. 5 (in the US) to deprive (a contract) of legal force. 6 to ban.

outlawry ('autˌlɔːrɪ) NOUN, *plural* **-ries**. 1 the act of outlawing or the state of being outlawed. 2 disregard for the law.

outlay NOUN ('autˌleɪ) 1 an expenditure of money, effort, etc. ◆ VERB (ˌaut'leɪ), **-lays, -laying, -laid**. 2 (*tr*) to spend (money).

outlet ('autlɛt, -lɪt) NOUN 1 an opening or vent permitting escape or release. 2 a means for release or expression of emotion, creative energy, etc. 3 **a** a market for a product or service. **b** a commercial establishment retailing the goods of a particular producer or wholesaler. 4 **a** a channel that drains a body of water. **b** the mouth of a river. 5 a point in a wiring system from which current can be taken to supply electrical devices. 6 *Anatomy* the beginning or end of a passage, esp. the lower opening of the pelvis (**pelvic outlet**).

outlier ('autˌlaɪə) NOUN 1 an outcrop of rocks that is entirely surrounded by older rocks. 2 a person, thing, or part situated away from a main or related body. 3 a person who lives away from his place of work, duty, etc. 4 *Statistics* a point in a sample widely separated from the main cluster of points in the sample. See **scatter diagram**.

outline ('autˌlaɪn) NOUN 1 a preliminary or schematic plan, draft, account, etc. 2 (*usually plural*) the important features of an argument, theory, work, etc. 3 the line by which an object or figure is or appears to be bounded. 4 **a** a drawing or manner of drawing consisting only of external lines. **b** (*as modifier*): *an outline map*. ◆ VERB (*tr*) 5 to draw or display the outline of. 6 to give the main features or general idea of.

outlive (ˌaut'lɪv) VERB (*tr*) 1 to live longer than (someone). 2 to live beyond (a date or period): *he outlived the century*. 3 to live through (an experience).

outlook (ˈaʊtˌlʊk) NOUN [1] a mental attitude or point of view. [2] the probable or expected condition or outcome of something: *the weather outlook*. [3] the view from a place. [4] view or prospect. [5] the act or state of looking out.

outlying (ˈaʊtˌlaɪɪŋ) ADJECTIVE distant or remote from the main body or centre, as of a town or region.

outman (ˌaʊtˈmæn) VERB **-mans, -manning, -manned.** (*tr*) [1] to surpass in manpower. [2] to surpass in manliness.

outmanoeuvre *or US* **outmaneuver** (ˌaʊtməˈnuːvə) VERB (*tr*) to secure a strategic advantage over by skilful manoeuvre.

outmoded (ˌaʊtˈməʊdɪd) ADJECTIVE [1] no longer fashionable or widely accepted. [2] no longer practical or usable.
► **ˌoutˈmodedly** ADVERB ► **ˌoutˈmodedness** NOUN

outmost (ˈaʊtˌməʊst) ADJECTIVE another word for **outermost.**

outness (ˈaʊtnɪs) NOUN [1] the state or quality of being external. [2] outward expression.

outnumber (ˌaʊtˈnʌmbə) VERB (*tr*) to exceed in number.

out-of-body experience NOUN a vivid feeling of being detached from one's body, usually involving observing it and its environment from nearby. Abbreviations: **OBE, OOBE.** Compare **near-death experience.**

out of bounds ADJECTIVE (*postpositive,*), ADVERB [1] (often foll by *to*) not to be entered (by); barred (to): *out of bounds to civilians*. [2] outside specified or prescribed limits.

out of date ADJECTIVE (**out-of-date** *when prenominal*), ADVERB no longer valid, current, or fashionable; outmoded.

out-of-door ADJECTIVE (*prenominal*) another term for **outdoor.**

out-of-doors ADVERB, ADJECTIVE (*postpositive*) in the open air; outside. Also: **outdoors.**

out of pocket ADJECTIVE (**out-of-pocket** *when prenominal*) [1] (*postpositive*) having lost money, as in a commercial enterprise. [2] without money to spend. [3] (*prenominal*) (of expenses) unbudgeted and paid for in cash.

out-of-the-way ADJECTIVE (*prenominal*) [1] distant from more populous areas. [2] uncommon or unusual.

outpace (aʊtˈpeɪs) VERB (*tr*) to run or move faster than (someone or something else).

outpatient (ˈaʊtˌpeɪʃənt) NOUN a nonresident hospital patient. Compare **inpatient.**

outperform (ˌɒʊtpəˈfɔːm) VERB (*tr*) to perform better than (someone or something).

outplacement (ˈaʊtˌpleɪsmənt) NOUN a service that offers counselling and careers advice, esp. to redundant executives, which is paid for by their previous employer.

outplay (aʊtˈpleɪ) VERB (*tr*) to perform better than one's opponent in a sport or game.

outpoint (ˌaʊtˈpɔɪnt) VERB (*tr*) [1] to score more points than. [2] *Nautical* to sail closer to the wind (point higher) than (another sailing vessel).

outport (ˈaʊtˌpɔːt) NOUN [1] *Chiefly Brit* a subsidiary port built in deeper water than the original port. [2] *Canadian* one of the many isolated fishing villages located in the bays and other indentations of the Newfoundland coast.

outporter (ˈaʊtˌpɔːtə) NOUN *Canadian* an inhabitant or native of a Newfoundland outport.

outpost (ˈaʊtˌpəʊst) NOUN [1] *Military* **a** a position stationed at a distance from the area occupied by a major formation. **b** the troops assigned to such a position. [2] an outlying settlement or position. [3] a limit or frontier.

outpour NOUN (ˈaʊtˌpɔː) [1] the act of flowing or pouring out. [2] something that pours out. ◆ VERB (ˌaʊtˈpɔː) [3] to pour or cause to pour out freely or rapidly.

outpouring (ˈaʊtˌpɔːrɪŋ) NOUN [1] a passionate or exaggerated outburst; effusion. [2] another word for **outpour** (senses 1, 2).

output (ˈaʊtˌpʊt) NOUN [1] the act of production or manufacture. [2] Also called: **outturn.** the amount produced, as in a given period: *a high weekly output*. [3] the material produced, manufactured, yielded, etc. [4] *Electronics* **a** the power, voltage, or current delivered by a circuit or component. **b** the point at which the signal is delivered. [5] the power, energy, or work produced by an engine or a system. [6] *Computing* **a** the information produced by a computer. **b** the operations and devices involved in producing this information. See also **input/output.** [7] (*modifier*) of or relating to electronic, computer, or other output: *output signal; output device; output tax*. ◆ VERB **-puts, -putting, -putted** *or* **-put.** (*tr*) [8] *Computing* to cause (data) to be emitted as output.

outrage (ˈaʊtˌreɪdʒ) NOUN [1] a wantonly vicious or cruel act. [2] a gross violation of decency, morality, honour, etc. [3] profound indignation, anger, or hurt, caused by such an act. ◆ VERB (*tr*) [4] to cause profound indignation, anger, or resentment in. [5] to offend grossly (feelings, decency, human dignity, etc.). [6] to commit an act of wanton viciousness, cruelty, or indecency on. [7] a euphemistic word for **rape**[1].
▷**HISTORY** C13 (meaning: excess): via French from *outré* beyond, from Latin *ultrā*

outrageous (aʊtˈreɪdʒəs) ADJECTIVE [1] being or having the nature of an outrage. [2] grossly offensive to decency, authority, etc. [3] violent or unrestrained in behaviour or temperament. [4] extravagant or immoderate.
► **outˈrageously** ADVERB ► **outˈrageousness** NOUN

outrank (ˌaʊtˈræŋk) VERB (*tr*) [1] to be of higher rank than. [2] to take priority over.

outré (ˈuːtreɪ) ADJECTIVE deviating from what is usual or proper.
▷**HISTORY** C18: from French past participle of *outrer* to pass beyond

outreach VERB (ˌaʊtˈriːtʃ) [1] (*tr*) to surpass in reach. [2] (*tr*) to go beyond. [3] to reach or cause to reach out. ◆ NOUN (ˈaʊtˌriːtʃ) [4] the act or process of reaching out. [5] the length or extent of reach. [6] *Social welfare* any systematic effort to provide unsolicited and predefined help to groups or individuals deemed to need it. [7] (*modifier*) (of welfare work or workers) propagating take-up of a service by seeking out appropriate people and persuading them to accept what is judged good for them. Compare **detached** (sense 3).

out-relief NOUN *English history* money given to poor people not living in a workhouse. Also called: **outdoor relief.**

outride VERB (ˌaʊtˈraɪd), **-rides, -riding, -rode, -ridden.** (*tr*) [1] to outdo by riding faster, farther, or better than. [2] (of a vessel) to ride out (a storm). ◆ NOUN (ˈaʊtˌraɪd) [3] *Prosody, rare* an extra unstressed syllable within a metrical foot.

outrider (ˈaʊtˌraɪdə) NOUN [1] a person who goes ahead of a car, group of people, etc., to ensure a clear passage. [2] a person who goes in advance to investigate, discover a way, etc.; scout. [3] a person who rides in front of or beside a carriage, esp. as an attendant or guard. [4] *US* a mounted herdsman.

outrigger (ˈaʊtˌrɪgə) NOUN [1] a framework for supporting a pontoon outside and parallel to the hull of a boat to provide stability. [2] a boat equipped with such a framework, esp. one of the canoes of the South Pacific. [3] any projecting framework attached to a boat, aircraft, building, etc., to act as a support. [4] *Rowing* another name for **rigger** (sense 2).
▷**HISTORY** C18: from OUT- + RIG[1] + -ER[1]; perhaps influenced by archaic *outligger* outlier

outright ADJECTIVE (ˈaʊtˌraɪt) (*prenominal*) [1] without qualifications or limitations: *outright ownership*. [2] complete; total: *an outright lie*. [3] straightforward; direct: *an outright manner*. ◆ ADVERB (ˌaʊtˈraɪt) [4] without restrictions: *buy outright*. [5] without reservation or concealment: *ask outright*. [6] instantly: *he was killed outright*. [7] *Obsolete* straight ahead or out.

outro (ˈaʊtrəʊ) NOUN, *plural* **-tros.** *Music informal* an instrumental passage that concludes a piece of music.
▷**HISTORY** C20: modelled on INTRO

outrun (ˌaʊtˈrʌn) VERB **-runs, -running, -ran, -run.** (*tr*) [1] to run faster, farther, or better than. [2] to escape from by or as if by running. [3] to go beyond; exceed.

outrunner (ˈaʊtˌrʌnə) NOUN [1] an attendant who runs in front of a carriage, etc. [2] the leading dog in a sled team.

outrush (ˈaʊtˌrʌʃ) NOUN a flowing or rushing out.

outsell (ˌaʊtˈsɛl) VERB **-sells, -selling, -sold.** (*tr*) to sell or be sold in greater quantities than.

outsert (ˈaʊtˌsɜːt) NOUN another word for **wrapround** (sense 5).
▷**HISTORY** C20: based on INSERT

outset (ˈaʊtˌsɛt) NOUN a start; beginning (esp. in the phrase **from** (*or* **at**) **the outset**).

outshine (ˌaʊtˈʃaɪn) VERB **-shines, -shining, -shone.** [1] (*tr*) to shine more brightly than. [2] (*tr*) to surpass in excellence, beauty, wit, etc. [3] (*intr*) *Rare* to emit light.

outshoot VERB (ˌaʊtˈʃuːt), **-shoots, -shooting, -shot.** [1] (*tr*) to surpass or excel in shooting. [2] to go or extend beyond (something). ◆ NOUN (ˈaʊtˌʃuːt) [3] a thing that projects or shoots out. [4] the act or state of shooting out or protruding.

outside PREPOSITION (ˌaʊtˈsaɪd) [1] (sometimes foll by *of*) on or to the exterior of: *outside the house*. [2] beyond the limits of: *outside human comprehension*. [3] apart from; other than: *no-one knows outside you and me*. ◆ ADJECTIVE (ˈaʊtˌsaɪd) [4] (*prenominal*) situated on the exterior: *an outside lavatory*. [5] remote; unlikely: *an outside chance*. [6] not a member of. [7] the greatest possible or probable (prices, odds, etc.). ◆ ADVERB (ˌaʊtˈsaɪd) [8] outside a specified thing or place; out of doors. [9] *Slang* not in prison. ◆ NOUN (ˈaʊtˈsaɪd) [10] the external side or surface: *the outside of the garage*. [11] the external appearance or aspect. [12] the exterior or outer part of something. [13] (of a path, pavement, etc.) the side nearest the road or away from a wall or building. [14] *Sport* an outside player, as in football. [15] (*plural*) the outer sheets of a ream of paper. [16] *Canadian* (in the north) the settled parts of Canada. [17] **at the outside.** *Informal* at the most or at the greatest extent: *two days at the outside*. [18] **outside in.** another term for **inside out.** See **inside** (sense 5).

> **Language note** The use of *outside of* and *inside of*, although fairly common, is generally thought to be incorrect or non-standard: *she waits outside* (not *outside of*) *the school*.

outside broadcast NOUN *Radio, television* a broadcast not made from a studio.

outside director NOUN a director of a company who is not employed by that company but is often employed by a holding or associated company.

outsider (ˌaʊtˈsaɪdə) NOUN [1] a person or thing excluded from or not a member of a set, group, etc. [2] a contestant, esp. a horse, thought unlikely to win in a race. [3] *Canadian* (in the north) a person who does not live in the Arctic regions.

outsider art NOUN art produced by untutored artists working by themselves and for themselves.
► **outsider artist** NOUN

outside work NOUN work done off the premises of a business.

out sister NOUN a member of a community of nuns who performs tasks in the outside world on behalf of the community.

outsize (ˈaʊtˌsaɪz) ADJECTIVE [1] Also: **outsized.** very large or larger than normal: *outsize tomatoes*. ◆ NOUN [2] something outsize, such as a garment or person. [3] (*modifier*) relating to or dealing in outsize clothes: *an outsize shop*.

outskirts (ˈaʊtˌskɜːts) PLURAL NOUN (*sometimes singular*) outlying or bordering areas, districts, etc., as of a city.

outsmart (ˌaʊtˈsmɑːt) VERB (*tr*) *Informal* to get the better of; outwit.

outsole (ˈaʊtˌsəʊl) NOUN the outermost sole of a shoe.

outsource (ˌaʊtˈsɔːs) VERB (*tr*) (of a manufacturer) [1] to subcontract (work) to another company. [2] to buy in (components for a product) rather than manufacture them.

outspan *South African* ◆ NOUN (ˈaʊtˌspæn) [1] an area on a farm kept available for travellers to rest and refresh animals. [2] the act of unharnessing or unyoking. ◆ VERB (ˌaʊtˈspæn) **-spans, -spanning, -spanned.** [3] to unharness or unyoke (animals).

▷HISTORY C19: partial translation of Afrikaans *uitspan,* from *uit* out + *spannen* to stretch

outspoken (ˌaʊtˈspəʊkən) ADJECTIVE 1 candid or bold in speech. 2 said or expressed with candour or boldness.
▸**outˈspokenness** NOUN

outspread VERB (ˌaʊtˈsprɛd), **-spreads, -spreading, -spread.** 1 to spread out or cause to spread out. ◆ ADJECTIVE (ˈaʊtˈsprɛd) 2 spread or stretched out. 3 scattered or diffused widely. ◆ NOUN (ˈaʊtˌsprɛd) 4 a spreading out.

outsprint (ˌaʊtˈsprɪnt) VERB (*tr*) to run faster than (someone).

outstand (ˌaʊtˈstænd) VERB **-stands, -standing, -stood.** 1 (*intr*) to be outstanding or excel. 2 (*intr*) *Nautical* to stand out to sea. 3 (*tr*) *Archaic* to last beyond.

outstanding (ˌaʊtˈstændɪŋ) ADJECTIVE 1 superior; excellent; distinguished. 2 prominent, remarkable, or striking. 3 still in existence; unsettled, unpaid, or unresolved. 4 (of shares, bonds, etc.) issued and sold. 5 projecting or jutting upwards or outwards.
▸**ˌoutˈstandingly** ADVERB

outstation (ˈaʊtˌsteɪʃən) NOUN 1 a station or post in a remote region. 2 in a radio network, any station other than the base station. 3 *Austral* a station set up independently of the head station of a large sheep or cattle farm. 4 **outstation movement.** *Austral* the programme to resettle native Australians on their tribal lands. ◆ ADVERB 5 (in Malaysia) away from (the speaker's) town or area.

outstay (ˌaʊtˈsteɪ) VERB (*tr*) 1 to stay longer than. 2 to stay beyond (a limit). 3 **outstay one's welcome.** See **overstay** (sense 4).

outstretch (ˌaʊtˈstrɛtʃ) VERB (*tr*) 1 to extend or expand; stretch out. 2 to stretch or extend beyond.

outstrip (ˌaʊtˈstrɪp) VERB **-strips, -stripping, -stripped.** (*tr*) 1 to surpass in a sphere of activity, competition, etc. 2 to be or grow greater than. 3 to go faster than and leave behind.

outswing (ˈaʊtˌswɪŋ) NOUN *Cricket* the movement of a ball from leg to off through the air. Compare **inswing.**

outswinger (ˈaʊtˌswɪŋə) NOUN 1 *Cricket* a ball bowled so as to move from leg to off through the air. 2 *Soccer* a ball kicked, esp. from a corner, so as to move through the air in a curve away from the goal or the centre.

outtake (ˈaʊtˌteɪk) NOUN an unreleased take from a recording session, film, or television programme.

outtalk (ˌaʊtˈtɔːk) VERB (*tr*) to talk more, longer, or louder than (someone).

out there ADJECTIVE *Slang* (**out-there** *when prenominal*) unconventional or eccentric: *he blends sublime pop moments with some real out-there stuff.*

outthink (ˌaʊtˈθɪŋk) VERB **-thinks, -thinking, -thought.** (*tr*) 1 to outdo in thinking. 2 to outwit.

out-tray NOUN (in an office) a tray for outgoing correspondence, documents, etc.

outturn (ˈaʊtˌtɜːn) NOUN 1 another word for **output** (sense 2). 2 outcome; result.

outvote (ˌaʊtˈvəʊt) VERB (*tr*) to defeat by a majority of votes.

outward (ˈaʊtwəd) ADJECTIVE 1 of or relating to what is apparent or superficial. 2 of or relating to the outside of the body. 3 belonging or relating to the external, as opposed to the mental, spiritual, or inherent. 4 of, relating to, or directed towards the outside or exterior. 5 (of a ship, part of a voyage, etc.) leaving for a particular destination. 6 **the outward man. a** the body as opposed to the soul. **b** *Facetious* clothing. ◆ ADVERB 7 (of a ship) away from port. 8 a variant of **outwards.** ◆ NOUN 9 the outward part; exterior.
▸**ˈoutwardness** NOUN

Outward Bound NOUN *Trademark* (in Britain) a scheme to provide adventure training for young people.

outwardly (ˈaʊtwədlɪ) ADVERB 1 in outward appearance. 2 with reference to the outside or outer surface; externally.

outwards (ˈaʊtwədz) *or* **outward** ADVERB towards the outside; out.

outwash (ˈaʊtˌwɒʃ) NOUN a mass of gravel, sand, etc., carried and deposited by the water derived from melting glaciers.

outwear (ˌaʊtˈwɛə) VERB **-wears, -wearing, -wore, -worn.** (*tr*) 1 to use up or destroy by wearing. 2 to last or wear longer than. 3 to outlive, outgrow, or develop beyond. 4 to deplete or exhaust in strength, determination, etc.

outweigh (ˌaʊtˈweɪ) VERB (*tr*) 1 to prevail over; overcome: *his desire outweighed his discretion.* 2 to be more important or significant than. 3 to be heavier than.

outwit (ˌaʊtˈwɪt) VERB **-wits, -witting, -witted.** (*tr*) 1 to get the better of by cunning or ingenuity. 2 *Archaic* to be of greater intelligence than.

outwith (ˌaʊtˈwɪθ) PREPOSITION *Scot* outside; beyond.

outwork NOUN (ˈaʊtˌwɜːk) 1 (*often plural*) defences which lie outside main defensive works. 2 work performed away from the factory, office, etc., by which it has been commissioned. ◆ VERB (ˌaʊtˈwɜːk), **-works, -working, -worked** *or* **-wrought.** (*tr*) 3 to work better, harder, etc., than. 4 to work out to completion.
▸**ˈoutˌworker** NOUN

outworn (ˈaʊtwɔːn, ˌaʊtˈwɔːn) ADJECTIVE no longer accepted, used, believed, etc.; obsolete or outmoded.

ouzel *or* **ousel** (ˈuːzᵊl) NOUN 1 short for **ring ouzel** or **water ouzel** (see **dipper**). 2 an archaic name for the (European) **blackbird.**
▷HISTORY Old English *ōsle,* related to Old High German *amsala* (German *Amsel*), Latin *merula* MERLE[1]

ouzo (ˈuːzəʊ) NOUN a strong aniseed-flavoured spirit from Greece.
▷HISTORY Modern Greek *ouzon,* of obscure origin

ova (ˈəʊvə) NOUN the plural of **ovum.**

oval (ˈəʊvᵊl) ADJECTIVE 1 having the shape of an ellipse or ellipsoid. ◆ NOUN 2 anything that is oval in shape, such as a sports ground.
▷HISTORY C16: from Medieval Latin *ōvālis,* from Latin *ōvum* egg
▸**ˈovally** ADVERB ▸**ˈovalness** *or* **ovality** (əʊˈvælɪtɪ) NOUN

Oval (ˈəʊvᵊl) NOUN **the.** a cricket ground in south London, in the borough of Lambeth.

Oval Office NOUN **the.** 1 the private office of the president of the US, a large oval room in the White House. 2 the US presidency.

ovals of Cassini (kəˈsiːnɪ) PLURAL NOUN *Maths* the locus of a point *x,* whose distance from two fixed points, *a* and *b,* is such that |*x*–*a*| |*x*–*b*| is a constant.
▷HISTORY C18: named after J. D. Cassini (1625–1712), Italian-French astronomer and mathematician

Ovambo (əʊˈvæmbəʊ, ɔːˈvambɔː) NOUN 1 (*plural* **-bo** *or* **-bos**) a member of a mixed Khoikhoi and Negroid people of southern Africa, living chiefly in N Namibia: noted for their skill in metal work. 2 the language of this people, belonging to the Bantu group of the Niger-Congo family.

ovariectomy (əʊˌvɛərɪˈɛktəmɪ) NOUN, *plural* **-mies.** *Surgery* another name for **oophorectomy.**

ovariotomy (əʊˌvɛərɪˈɒtəmɪ) NOUN, *plural* **-mies.** surgical incision into an ovary. Compare **oophorectomy.**

ovaritis (ˌəʊvəˈraɪtɪs) NOUN inflammation of an ovary; oophoritis.

ovary (ˈəʊvərɪ) NOUN, *plural* **-ries.** 1 either of the two female reproductive organs, which produce ova and secrete oestrogen hormones. 2 the corresponding organ in vertebrate and invertebrate animals. 3 *Botany* the hollow basal region of a carpel containing one or more ovules. In some plants the carpels are united to form a single compound ovary.
▷HISTORY C17: from New Latin *ōvārium,* from Latin *ōvum* egg
▸**ovarian** (əʊˈvɛərɪən) ADJECTIVE

ovate (ˈəʊveɪt) ADJECTIVE 1 shaped like an egg. 2 (esp. of a leaf) shaped like the longitudinal section of an egg, with the broader end at the base. Compare **obovate.**
▷HISTORY C18: from Latin *ōvātus* egg-shaped; see OVUM
▸**ˈovately** ADVERB

ovation (əʊˈveɪʃən) NOUN 1 an enthusiastic reception, esp. one of prolonged applause: *a standing ovation.* 2 a victory procession less glorious than a triumph awarded to a Roman general.
▷HISTORY C16: from Latin *ovātiō* rejoicing, from *ovāre* to exult
▸**oˈvational** ADJECTIVE

ovel (ˈɒvəl) NOUN *Judaism* a mourner, esp. during the first seven days after a death. See also **shivah.**
▷HISTORY from Hebrew

oven (ˈʌvᵊn) NOUN 1 an enclosed heated compartment or receptacle for baking or roasting food. 2 a similar device, usually lined with a refractory material, used for drying substances, firing ceramics, heat-treating, etc. ◆ VERB 3 (*tr*) to cook in an oven.
▷HISTORY Old English *ofen;* related to Old High German *ofan,* Old Norse *ofn*
▸**ˈoven-ˌlike** ADJECTIVE

ovenable (ˈʌvᵊnəbᵊl) ADJECTIVE 1 (of food) suitable for cooking in an oven. 2 (of a container) suitable for use in an oven.

ovenbird (ˈʌvᵊnˌbɜːd) NOUN 1 any of numerous small brownish South American passerine birds of the family *Furnariidae* that build oven-shaped clay nests. 2 a common North American warbler, *Seiurus aurocapillus,* that has an olive-brown striped plumage with an orange crown and builds a cup-shaped nest on the ground.

oven-ready ADJECTIVE (of various foods) bought already prepared so that they are ready to be cooked in the oven.

ovenware (ˈʌvᵊnˌwɛə) NOUN heat-resistant dishes in which food can be both cooked and served.

over (ˈəʊvə) PREPOSITION 1 directly above; on the top of; via the top or upper surface of: *over one's head.* 2 on or to the other side of: *over the river.* 3 during; through, or throughout (a period of time). 4 in or throughout all parts of: *to travel over England.* 5 throughout the whole extent of: *over the racecourse.* 6 above; in preference to: *I like that over everything else.* 7 by the agency of (an instrument of telecommunication): *we heard it over the radio.* 8 more than: *over a century ago.* 9 on the subject of; about: *an argument over nothing.* 10 while occupied in: *discussing business over golf.* 11 having recovered from the effects of: *she's not over that last love affair yet.* 12 **over and above.** added to; in addition to: *he earns a large amount over and above his salary.* ◆ ADVERB 13 in a state, condition, situation, or position that is or has been placed or put over something: *to climb over.* 14 (*particle*) so as to cause to fall: *knocking over a policeman.* 15 at or to a point across intervening space, water, etc.: *come over and see us; over in America.* 16 throughout a whole area: *the world over.* 17 (*particle*) from beginning to end, usually cursorily: *to read a document over.* 18 throughout a period of time: *stay over for this week.* 19 (esp. in signalling and radio) it is now your turn to speak, act, etc. 20 more than is expected or usual: *not over well.* 21 **over again.** once more. 22 **over against. a** opposite to. **b** contrasting with. 23 **over and over.** (often foll by *again*) repeatedly. 24 **over the odds. a** in addition, esp. when not expected. **b** unfair or excessive. ◆ ADJECTIVE 25 (*postpositive*) finished; no longer in progress: *is the concert over yet?* ◆ ADVERB, ADJECTIVE 26 remaining; surplus (often in the phrase **left over**). ◆ NOUN 27 *Cricket* **a** a series of six balls bowled by a bowler from the same end of the pitch. **b** the play during this.
▷HISTORY Old English *ofer;* related to Old High German *ubir, obar,* Old Norse *yfir,* Latin *super,* Greek *huper*

over- PREFIX 1 excessive or excessively; beyond an agreed or desirable limit: *overcharge; overdue; oversimplify.* 2 indicating superior rank: *overseer.* 3 indicating location or movement above: *overhang.* 4 indicating movement downwards: *overthrow.*

overabundance (ˌəʊvərəˈbʌndəns) NOUN a supply or amount that is greater than required: *an overabundance of milk.*

overachieve (ˌəʊvərəˈtʃiːv) VERB (*intr*) to perform (for example, in examinations) better than would be expected on the basis of one's age or talents.
▸**ˌoveraˈchiever** NOUN

overact (ˌəʊvərˈækt) VERB to act or behave in an exaggerated manner, as in a theatrical production. Also: **overplay.**

overactive (ˌəʊvərˈæktɪv) ADJECTIVE 1 inordinately active. 2 (of the thyroid or adrenal gland, nervous system, etc.) functioning at too high a capacity.

overage (ˌəʊvərˈeɪdʒ) ADJECTIVE beyond a specified age.

overaggressive (ˌəʊvərəˈɡrɛsɪv) ADJECTIVE excessively quarrelsome or belligerent.

overall ADJECTIVE (ˈəʊvərˌɔːl) (*prenominal*) [1] from one end to the other. [2] including or covering everything: *the overall cost*. ◆ ADVERB (ˌəʊvərˈɔːl) [3] in general; on the whole. ◆ NOUN (ˈəʊvərˌɔːl) [4] *Brit* a protective work garment usually worn over ordinary clothes. [5] (*plural*) hard-wearing work trousers with a bib and shoulder straps or jacket attached.

overambitious (ˌəʊvəræmˈbɪʃəs) ADJECTIVE excessively ambitious: *The aims were overambitious, therefore few were achieved*.

overanxious (ˌəʊvərˈæŋkʃəs, -ˈæŋʃəs) ADJECTIVE excessively worried, tense, or uneasy.

overarch (ˌəʊvərˈɑːtʃ) VERB (*tr*) to form an arch over.

overarching (ˌəʊvərˈɑːtʃɪŋ) ADJECTIVE overall; all-encompassing: *an overarching concept*.

overarm (ˈəʊvərˌɑːm) ADJECTIVE [1] *Sport* bowled, thrown, or performed with the arm raised above the shoulder. ◆ ADVERB [2] with the arm raised above the shoulder.

overattentive (ˌəʊvərəˈtɛntɪv) ADJECTIVE excessively careful to fulfil the needs and wants (of).

overawe (ˌəʊvərˈɔː) VERB (*tr*) to subdue, restrain, or overcome by affecting with a feeling of awe.

overbalance VERB (ˌəʊvəˈbæləns) [1] to lose or cause to lose balance. [2] (*tr*) another word for **outweigh**. ◆ NOUN (ˈəʊvəˌbæləns) [3] excess of weight, value, etc.

overbear (ˌəʊvəˈbɛə) VERB **-bears, -bearing, -bore, -borne**. [1] (*tr*) to dominate or overcome: *to overbear objections*. [2] (*tr*) to press or bear down with weight or physical force. [3] to produce or bear (fruit, progeny, etc.) excessively.

overbearing (ˌəʊvəˈbɛərɪŋ) ADJECTIVE [1] domineering or dictatorial in manner or action. [2] of particular or overriding importance or significance.
▸ **ˌoverˈbearingly** ADVERB

overbid VERB (ˌəʊvəˈbɪd), **-bids, -bidding, -bid, -bidden** *or* **-bid**. [1] (*intr*) *Bridge* to bid for more tricks than one can expect to win. [2] to bid more than the value of (something). ◆ NOUN (ˈəʊvəˌbɪd) [3] a bid higher than someone else's bid.

overbite (ˈəʊvəˌbaɪt) NOUN *Dentistry* an extension of the upper front teeth over the lower front teeth when the mouth is closed. Also called: **vertical overlap**.

overblouse (ˈəʊvəˌblaʊz) NOUN a blouse designed to be worn not tucked into trousers or a skirt but to fit loosely over the waist or hips.

overblow (ˌəʊvəˈbləʊ) VERB **-blows, -blowing, -blew, -blown**. [1] *Music* to blow into (a wind instrument) with greater force than normal in order to obtain a harmonic or overtone instead of the fundamental tone. [2] to blow (a wind instrument) or (of a wind instrument) to be blown too hard. [3] to blow over, away, or across.

overblown (ˌəʊvəˈbləʊn) ADJECTIVE [1] overdone or excessive. [2] bombastic; turgid: *overblown prose*. [3] (of flowers, such as the rose) past the stage of full bloom.

overboard (ˈəʊvəˌbɔːd) ADVERB [1] from on board a vessel into the water. [2] **go overboard**. *Informal* **a** to be extremely enthusiastic. **b** to go to extremes. [3] **throw overboard**. to reject or abandon.

overboot (ˈəʊvəˌbuːt) NOUN a protective boot worn over an ordinary boot or shoe.

overbuild (ˌəʊvəˈbɪld) VERB **-builds, -building, -built**. (*tr*) [1] to build over or on top of. [2] to erect too many buildings in (an area). [3] to build too large or elaborately.

overburden VERB (ˌəʊvəˈbɜːdᵊn) [1] (*tr*) to load with excessive weight, work, etc. ◆ NOUN (ˈəʊvəˌbɜːdᵊn) [2] an excessive burden or load. [3] *Geology* the sedimentary rock material that covers coal seams, mineral veins, etc.
▸ **ˌoverˈburdensome** ADJECTIVE

overcall *Bridge* ◆ NOUN (ˈəʊvəˌkɔːl) [1] a bid higher than the preceding one. ◆ VERB (ˌəʊvəˈkɔːl) [2] to bid higher than (an opponent).

overcapacity (ˌəʊvəkəˈpæsɪtɪ) NOUN the situation in which an industry or business cannot sell as much as it produces.

overcapitalize *or* **overcapitalise** (ˌəʊvəˈkæpɪtəˌlaɪz) VERB (*tr*) [1] to provide or issue capital for (an enterprise) in excess of profitable investment opportunities. [2] to estimate the capital value of (a company) at an unreasonably or unlawfully high level. [3] to overestimate the market value of (property).
▸ **ˌoverˌcapitaliˈzation** *or* **ˌoverˌcapitaliˈsation** NOUN

overcast ADJECTIVE (ˈəʊvəˌkɑːst) [1] covered over or obscured, esp. by clouds. [2] *Meteorol* (of the sky) more than 95 per cent cloud-covered. [3] gloomy or melancholy. [4] sewn over by overcasting. ◆ VERB (ˌəʊvəˈkɑːst) [5] to make or become overclouded or gloomy. [6] to sew (an edge, as of a hem) with long stitches passing successively over the edge. ◆ NOUN (ˈəʊvəˌkɑːst) [7] a covering, as of clouds or mist. [8] *Meteorol* the state of the sky when more than 95 per cent of it is cloud-covered. [9] *Mining* a crossing of two passages without an intersection.

overcharge VERB (ˌəʊvəˈtʃɑːdʒ) [1] to charge too much. [2] (*tr*) to fill or load beyond capacity. [3] *Literary* another word for **exaggerate**. ◆ NOUN (ˈəʊvəˌtʃɑːdʒ) [4] an excessive price or charge. [5] an excessive load.

overcheck (ˈəʊvəˌtʃɛk) NOUN [1] a thin leather strap attached to a horse's bit to keep its head up. [2] (in textiles) **a** a checked pattern laid over another checked pattern. **b** a fabric patterned in such a way.

overcloud (ˌəʊvəˈklaʊd) VERB [1] to make or become covered with clouds. [2] to make or become dark or dim.

overcoat (ˈəʊvəˌkəʊt) NOUN a warm heavy coat worn over the outer clothes in cold weather.

overcome (ˌəʊvəˈkʌm) VERB **-comes, -coming, -came, -come**. [1] (*tr*) to get the better of in a conflict. [2] (*tr; often passive*) to render incapable or powerless by laughter, sorrow, exhaustion, etc.: *he was overcome by fumes*. [3] (*tr*) to surmount (obstacles, objections, etc.). [4] (*intr*) to be victorious.

overcommit (ˌəʊvəkəˈmɪt) VERB **-mits, -mitting, -mitted**. (*tr*) to promise, undertake, or allocate more than the available resources justify.

overcompensate (ˌəʊvəˈkɒmpɛnˌseɪt) VERB [1] to compensate (a person or thing) excessively. [2] (*intr*) *Psychol* to engage in overcompensation.
▸ **ˌoverˈcompenˌsatory** ADJECTIVE

overcompensation (ˌəʊvəˌkɒmpɛnˈseɪʃən) NOUN *Psychol* an attempt to make up for a character trait by overexaggerating its opposite.

overcomplex (ˌəʊvəˈkɒmplɛks) ADJECTIVE excessively complicated, intricate, or involved: *an overcomplex pattern*.

overconfident (ˌəʊvəˈkɒnfɪdənt) ADJECTIVE excessively confident.
▸ **ˌoverˈconfidence** NOUN

overconsumption (ˌəʊvəkənˈsʌmpʃən) NOUN the state or an instance of consuming too much food, drink, fuel, etc.

overcook (ˌəʊvəˈkʊk) VERB (*tr*) to cook (something) until dry, burnt, or inedible.

overcrop (ˌəʊvəˈkrɒp) VERB **-crops, -cropping, -cropped**. (*tr*) to exhaust (land) by excessive cultivation.

overcrowd (ˌəʊvəˈkraʊd) VERB (*tr*) to fill (a room, vehicle, city, etc.) with more people or things than is desirable.

overcrowding (ˌəʊvəˈkraʊdɪŋ) NOUN a state of being filled with more people or things than is desirable; congestion.

overdependence (ˌəʊvədɪˈpɛndəns) NOUN the state or fact of being too dependent, esp. for help or support.

overdependent (ˌəʊvədɪˈpɛndənt) ADJECTIVE excessively dependent on a person or thing for aid, support, etc.

overdevelop (ˌəʊvədɪˈvɛləp) VERB (*tr*) [1] to develop too much or too far. [2] *Photog* to process (a film, plate, or print) in developer for more than the required time, at too great a concentration, etc.
▸ **ˌoverdeˈvelopment** NOUN

overdeviate (ˌəʊvəˈdiːvɪˌeɪt) VERB to cause (a frequency-modulated radio transmitter) to exceed its specified frequency excursion from the rest frequency.

overdo (ˌəʊvəˈduː) VERB **-does, -doing, -did, -done**. (*tr*) [1] to take or carry too far; do to excess. [2] to exaggerate, overelaborate, or overplay. [3] to cook or bake too long. [4] **overdo it** *or* **things**. to overtax one's strength, capacity, etc.

overdose NOUN (ˈəʊvəˌdəʊs) [1] (esp. of drugs) an excessive dose. ◆ VERB (ˌəʊvəˈdəʊs) [2] to take an excessive dose or give an excessive dose to.
▸ **ˌoverˈdosage** NOUN

overdraft (ˈəʊvəˌdrɑːft) NOUN [1] a draft or withdrawal of money in excess of the credit balance on a bank or building-society cheque account. [2] the amount of money drawn or withdrawn thus.

overdraught (ˈəʊvəˌdrɑːft) NOUN a current of air passed above a fire, as in a furnace.

overdraw (ˌəʊvəˈdrɔː) VERB **-draws, -drawing, -drew, -drawn**. [1] to draw on (a bank account) in excess of the credit balance. [2] (*tr*) to strain or pull (a bow) too far. [3] (*tr*) to exaggerate in describing or telling.

overdress VERB (ˌəʊvəˈdrɛs) [1] to dress (oneself or another) too elaborately or finely. ◆ NOUN (ˈəʊvəˌdrɛs) [2] a dress that may be worn over a jumper, blouse, etc.

overdrive NOUN (ˈəʊvəˌdraɪv) [1] a very high gear in a motor vehicle used at high speeds to reduce wear and save fuel. [2] **in** *or* **into overdrive**. in *or* into a state of intense activity. ◆ VERB (ˌəʊvəˈdraɪv), **-drives, -driving, -drove, -driven**. [3] (*tr*) to drive too hard or too far; overwork or overuse.

overdub (in multitrack recording) ◆ VERB (ˌəʊvəˈdʌb), **-dubs, -dubbing, -dubbed**. [1] to add (new sound) on a spare track or tracks. ◆ NOUN (ˈəʊvəˌdʌb) [2] the addition of new sound to a recording; the blending of various layers of sound in one recording.

overdue (ˌəʊvəˈdjuː) ADJECTIVE past the time specified, required, or preferred for arrival, occurrence, payment, etc.

overdye (ˌəʊvəˈdaɪ) VERB (*tr*) [1] to dye (a fabric, yarn, etc.) excessively. [2] to dye for a second or third time with a different colour.

overeager (ˌəʊvərˈiːɡə) ADJECTIVE excessively eager or keen: *overeager supporters*.

overeat (ˌəʊvərˈiːt) VERB **-eats, -eating, -ate, -eaten** (*intr*) to consume too much food.

overelaborate (ˌəʊvərɪˈlæbərɪt) ADJECTIVE [1] excessively ornate, detailed, or complex (ˌəʊvərɪˈlæbəˌreɪt). ◆ VERB (*tr*) [2] to detail or develop (an idea, plan, etc.) excessively.
▸ **ˌovereˌlaboˈration** NOUN

overemphasize *or* **overemphasise** (ˌəʊvərˈɛmfəˌsaɪz) VERB (*tr*) to give excessive emphasis or prominence to (something).
▸ **ˌoverˈemphasis** NOUN

overenthusiastic (ˌəʊvərɪnˈθjuːzɪˌæstɪk) ADJECTIVE excessively enthusiastic.

overestimate VERB (ˌəʊvərˈɛstɪˌmeɪt) [1] (*tr*) to value or estimate too highly. ◆ NOUN (ˌəʊvərˈɛstɪmɪt) [2] an estimate that is too high.
▸ **ˌoverˌestiˈmation** NOUN

overexcited (ˌəʊvərɪkˈsaɪtɪd) ADJECTIVE excessively excited.

overexpansion (ˌəʊvərɪksˈpænʃən) NOUN an excessive increase, enlargement, or development, esp. in the activities of a company.

overexpose (ˌəʊvərɪksˈpəʊz) VERB (*tr*) [1] to expose too much or for too long. [2] *Photog* to expose (a film, plate, or paper) for too long a period or with too bright a light.
▸ **ˌoverexˈposure** NOUN

overfall (ˈəʊvəˌfɔːl) NOUN [1] a turbulent stretch of water caused by marine currents over an underwater ridge. [2] a mechanism that allows excess water to escape from a dam or lock. [3] the point at which a sewer or land drainage discharges into the sea or a river.

overfamiliar (ˌəʊvəfəˈmɪlɪə) ADJECTIVE [1] excessively friendly, informal, or intimate. [2] too well-known or easily recognized: *an overfamiliar action movie*.
▸ **ˌoverfaˌmiliˈarity** NOUN

overflight (ˈəʊvəˌflaɪt) NOUN the flight of an aircraft over a specific area or territory.

overflow VERB (ˌəʊvəˈfləʊ), **-flows, -flowing, -flowed**

or (formerly) **-flown.** 1 to flow or run over (a limit, brim, bank, etc.). 2 to fill or be filled beyond capacity so as to spill or run over. 3 *(intr; usually foll by with)* to be filled with happiness, tears, etc. 4 *(tr)* to spread or cover over; flood or inundate. ◆ NOUN ('əʊvəˌfləʊ) 5 overflowing matter, esp. liquid. 6 any outlet that enables surplus liquid to be discharged or drained off, esp. one just below the top of a tank or cistern. 7 the amount by which a limit, capacity, etc., is exceeded. 8 *Computing* a condition that occurs when numeric operations produce results too large to store in the register available.

overfly (ˌəʊvə'flaɪ) VERB **-flies, -flying, -flew, -flown.** *(tr)* to fly over (a territory) or past (a point).

overfold ('əʊvəˌfəʊld) NOUN *Geology* a fold in which one or both limbs have been inclined more than 90° from their original orientation.

overfond (ˌəʊvə'fɒnd) ADJECTIVE *(postpositive; followed by of)* excessively keen (on).

overfull (ˌəʊvə'fʊl) ADJECTIVE excessively full; overflowing.

overfunding ('əʊvəˌfʌndɪŋ) NOUN (in Britain) a government policy in which it sells more of its securities than would be required to finance public spending, with the object of absorbing surplus funds to curb inflation.

overgarment ('əʊvəˌgɑːmənt) NOUN any garment worn over other clothes, esp. to protect them from wear or dirt.

overgear (ˌəʊvə'gɪə) VERB *(tr; usually passive)* to cause (a company) to have too high a proportion of loan stock and preference shares in comparison to its ordinary share capital.

overgenerous (ˌəʊvə'dʒɛnərəs, -'dʒɛnrəs) ADJECTIVE excessively willing and liberal in giving away one's time, money, etc.

overglaze ('əʊvəˌgleɪz) ADJECTIVE (of decoration or colours) applied to porcelain or pottery above the glaze.

overgraze (ˌəʊvə'greɪz) VERB *(tr)* to graze (land) beyond its capacity to sustain stock.

overground ('əʊvəˌgraʊnd) ADJECTIVE on or above the surface of the ground: *an overground railway.*

overgrow (ˌəʊvə'grəʊ) VERB **-grows, -growing, -grew, -grown.** 1 *(tr)* to grow over or across (an area, path, lawn, etc.). 2 *(tr)* to choke or supplant by a stronger growth. 3 *(tr)* to grow too large for. 4 *(intr)* to grow beyond normal size.
▸ **'overˌgrowth** NOUN

overhand ('əʊvəˌhænd) ADJECTIVE 1 thrown or performed with the hand raised above the shoulder. 2 sewn with thread passing over two edges in one direction. ◆ ADVERB 3 with the hand above the shoulder; overarm. 4 with shallow stitches passing over two edges. ◆ VERB 5 to sew (two edges) overhand.

overhand knot NOUN a knot formed by making a loop in a piece of cord and drawing one end through it. Also called: **thumb knot.**

overhang VERB (ˌəʊvə'hæŋ), **-hangs, -hanging, -hung.** 1 to project or extend beyond (a surface, building, etc.). 2 *(tr)* to hang or be suspended over. 3 *(tr)* to menace, threaten, or dominate. ◆ NOUN ('əʊvəˌhæŋ) 4 a formation, object, part of a structure, etc., that extends beyond or hangs over something, such as an outcrop of rock overhanging a mountain face. 5 the amount or extent of projection. 6 *Aeronautics* **a** half the difference in span of the main supporting surfaces of a biplane or other multiplane. **b** the distance from the outer supporting strut of a wing to the wing tip. 7 *Finance* the shares, collectively, that the underwriters have to buy when a new issue has not been fully taken up by the market.

overhaul VERB (ˌəʊvə'hɔːl) *(tr)* 1 to examine carefully for faults, necessary repairs, etc. 2 to make repairs or adjustments to (a car, machine, etc.). 3 to overtake. ◆ NOUN ('əʊvəˌhɔːl) 4 a thorough examination and repair.

overhead ADJECTIVE ('əʊvəˌhɛd) 1 situated or operating above head height or some other reference level. 2 *(prenominal)* inclusive: *the overhead price included meals.* ◆ ADVERB (ˌəʊvə'hɛd) 3 over or above head height, esp. in the sky. ◆ NOUN ('əʊvəˌhɛd) 4 **a** a stroke in racket games played from above head height. **b** *(as modifier)*: *an overhead smash.* 5 *Nautical* the interior lining above one's head below decks in a vessel. 6 short for **overhead door.** 7 *(modifier)* of, concerned with, or resulting from overheads: *overhead costs.* ◆ See also **overheads.**

overhead camshaft NOUN a type of camshaft situated above the cylinder head in an internal-combustion engine. It is usually driven by a chain or a toothed belt from the crankshaft and the cams bear directly onto the valve stems or rocker arms.

overhead door NOUN a door that rotates on a horizontal axis and is supported horizontally when open. Sometimes shortened to **overhead.**

overhead projector NOUN a projector that throws an enlarged image of a transparency onto a surface above and behind the person using it. Alterations and additions can be made to the material on the transparency while the projector is in use.

overheads ('əʊvəˌhɛdz) PLURAL NOUN business expenses, such as rent, that are not directly attributable to any department or product and can therefore be assigned only arbitrarily. Also called: **burden, fixed costs, indirect costs, oncost.** Compare **prime cost.**

overhead-valve engine NOUN a type of internal-combustion engine in which the inlet and exhaust valves are in the cylinder head above the pistons. US name: **valve-in-head engine.** Compare **side-valve engine.**

overhear (ˌəʊvə'hɪə) VERB **-hears, -hearing, -heard.** *(tr)* to hear (a person, remark, etc.) without the knowledge of the speaker.

overheat (ˌəʊvə'hiːt) VERB 1 to make or become excessively hot. 2 *(tr; often passive)* to make very agitated, irritated, etc. 3 *(intr)* (of an economy) to tend towards inflation, often as a result of excessive growth in demand. 4 *(tr)* to cause (an economy) to tend towards inflation. ◆ NOUN 5 the condition of being overheated.

Overijssel *(Dutch* oːvər'ɛisəl) NOUN a province of the E Netherlands: generally low-lying. Capital: Zwolle. Pop.: 1 077 600 (2000 est.). Area: 3929 sq. km (1517 sq. miles).

overindulge (ˌəʊvərɪn'dʌldʒ) VERB 1 to indulge (in something, esp. food or drink) immoderately; binge. 2 *(tr)* to yield excessively to the wishes of; spoil.
▸ **ˌoverin'dulgence** NOUN ▸ **ˌoverin'dulgent** ADJECTIVE

overissue ('əʊvərˌɪsjuː, -ˌɪʃuː) VERB **-sues, -suing, -sued.** *(tr)* 1 to issue (shares, banknotes, etc.) in excess of demand or ability to pay. ◆ NOUN 2 shares, banknotes, etc., thus issued.

overjoy (ˌəʊvə'dʒɔɪ) VERB *(tr)* to give great delight to.
▸ **ˌover'joyed** ADJECTIVE

overkill ('əʊvəˌkɪl) NOUN 1 the capability to deploy more weapons, esp. nuclear weapons, than is necessary to ensure military advantage. 2 any capacity or treatment that is greater than that required or appropriate.

overland ('əʊvəˌlænd) ADJECTIVE *(prenominal)*, ADVERB 1 over or across land. ◆ VERB 2 *Austral history* to drive (cattle or sheep) overland.
▸ **'overˌlander** NOUN

overlap VERB (ˌəʊvə'læp), **-laps, -lapping, -lapped.** 1 (of two things) to extend or lie partly over (each other). 2 to cover and extend beyond (something). 3 *(intr)* to coincide partly in time, subject, etc. ◆ NOUN ('əʊvəˌlæp) 4 a part that overlaps or is overlapped. 5 the amount, length, etc., overlapping. 6 the act or fact of overlapping. 7 a place of overlapping. 8 *Geology* the horizontal extension of the upper beds in a series of rock strata beyond the lower beds, usually caused by submergence of the land.

overlarge (ˌəʊvə'lɑːdʒ) ADJECTIVE excessively large.

overlay VERB (ˌəʊvə'leɪ), **-lays, -laying, -laid.** *(tr)* 1 to lay or place something over or upon (something else). 2 (often foll by *with*) to cover, overspread, or conceal (with). 3 (foll by *with*) to cover (a surface) with an applied decoration: *ebony overlaid with silver.* 4 to achieve the correct printing pressure all over (a forme or plate) by adding to the appropriate areas of the packing. ◆ NOUN ('əʊvəˌleɪ) 5 something that is laid over something else; covering. 6 an applied decoration or layer, as of gold leaf. 7 a transparent sheet giving extra details to a map or diagram over which it is designed to be placed. 8 *Printing* material, such as paper, used to overlay a forme or plate.

overleaf (ˌəʊvə'liːf) ADVERB on the other side of the page. Also: **overpage.**

overlie (ˌəʊvə'laɪ) VERB **-lies, -lying, -lay, -lain.** *(tr)* 1 to lie or rest upon. Compare **overlay.** 2 to kill (a baby or newborn animal) by lying upon it.

overlive (ˌəʊvə'lɪv) VERB 1 to live longer than (another person). 2 to survive or outlive (an event).

overload VERB (ˌəʊvə'ləʊd) 1 *(tr)* to put too large a load on or in. ◆ NOUN ('əʊvəˌləʊd) 2 an excessive load.

overlong (ˌəʊvə'lɒŋ) ADJECTIVE, ADVERB too or excessively long.

overlook VERB (ˌəʊvə'lʊk) *(tr)* 1 to fail to notice or take into account. 2 to disregard deliberately or indulgently. 3 to look at or over from above: *the garden is overlooked by the prison.* 4 to afford a view of from above: *the house overlooks the bay.* 5 to rise above. 6 to look after. 7 to look at carefully. 8 to bewitch or cast the evil eye upon (someone). ◆ NOUN ('əʊvəˌlʊk) *US* 9 a high place affording a view. 10 an act of overlooking.

overlooker ('əʊvəˌlʊkə) NOUN another word (less common) for **overseer** (sense 1).

overlord ('əʊvəˌlɔːd) NOUN a supreme lord or master.
▸ **'overˌlordship** NOUN

overly ('əʊvəlɪ) ADVERB too; excessively.

overman VERB (ˌəʊvə'mæn) **-mans, -manning, -manned.** 1 *(tr)* to supply with an excessive number of men. ◆ NOUN ('əʊvəˌmæn), *plural* **-men.** 2 a man who oversees others. 3 the Nietzschean superman.

overmantel ('əʊvəˌmæntᵊl) NOUN an ornamental shelf over a mantelpiece, often with a mirror.

overmaster (ˌəʊvə'mɑːstə) VERB *(tr)* to overpower.

overmatch *Chiefly US* ◆ VERB (ˌəʊvə'mætʃ) *(tr)* 1 to be more than a match for. 2 to match with a superior opponent. ◆ NOUN ('əʊvəˌmætʃ) 3 a person superior in ability. 4 a match in which one contestant is superior.

overmatter ('əʊvəˌmætə) NOUN *Printing* type that has been set but cannot be used for printing owing to lack of space. Also called: **overset.**

overmuch (ˌəʊvə'mʌtʃ) ADVERB, ADJECTIVE 1 too much; very much. ◆ NOUN 2 an excessive amount.

overnice (ˌəʊvə'naɪs) ADJECTIVE too fastidious, precise, etc.

overnight ADVERB (ˌəʊvə'naɪt) 1 for the duration of the night: *we stopped overnight.* 2 in or as if in the course of one night; suddenly: *the situation changed overnight.* ◆ ADJECTIVE ('əʊvəˌnaɪt) *(usually prenominal)* 3 done in, occurring in, or lasting the night: *an overnight stop.* 4 staying for one night: *overnight guests.* 5 lasting one night: *an overnight trip; an overnight bank loan.* 6 for use during a single night: *overnight clothes.* 7 occurring in or as if in the course of one night; sudden: *an overnight victory.* ◆ VERB *(intr)* 8 to stay the night.

overoptimism (ˌəʊvər'ɒptɪˌmɪzəm) NOUN excessive hopefulness or confidence.

overoptimistic (ˌəʊvərˌɒptɪ'mɪstɪk) ADJECTIVE excessively optimistic.

overpage (ˌəʊvə'peɪdʒ) ADVERB another word for **overleaf.**

overparted (ˌəʊvə'pɑːtɪd) ADJECTIVE (of a performer) having been cast in a role that is beyond his or her abilities.

overpass NOUN ('əʊvəˌpɑːs) 1 another name for **flyover** (sense 1). ◆ VERB (ˌəʊvə'pɑːs) **-passes, -passing, -passed, -past.** *(tr) Now rare* 2 to pass over, through, or across. 3 to exceed. 4 to get over. 5 to ignore.

overpay (ˌəʊvə'peɪ) VERB **-pays, -paying, -paid.** 1 to pay (someone) at too high a rate. 2 to pay (someone) more than is due, as by an error.

overpersuade (ˌəʊvəpə'sweɪd) VERB *(tr)* to persuade (someone) against his inclination or judgment.

overpitch (ˌəʊvə'pɪtʃ) VERB *Cricket* to bowl (a ball) so that it pitches too close to the stumps.

overplay (ˌəʊvə'pleɪ) VERB 1 *(tr)* to exaggerate the importance of. 2 another word for **overact.** 3

overplay one's hand. to overestimate the worth or strength of one's position.

overplus ('əʊvəˌplʌs) NOUN surplus or excess quantity.

overpopulated (ˌəʊvəˈpɒpjʊˌleɪtɪd) ADJECTIVE having too many inhabitants for the available space or resources.

overpopulation (ˌəʊvəˌpɒpjʊˈleɪʃən) NOUN the population of an area in too large numbers.

overpower (ˌəʊvəˈpaʊə) VERB (*tr*) 1 to conquer or subdue by superior force. 2 to have such a strong effect on as to make helpless or ineffective. 3 to supply with more power than necessary.

overpowering (ˌəʊvəˈpaʊərɪŋ) ADJECTIVE 1 so strong or intense as to be unbearable. 2 so powerful as to crush or conquer.
▸ **ˌoverˈpoweringly** ADVERB

overpressure ('əʊvəˌprɛʃə) NOUN the blast effect of a nuclear weapon expressed as an amount of pressure greater than normal barometric pressure.

overpriced (ˌəʊvəˈpraɪst) ADJECTIVE charging or charged at too high a price.

overprint VERB (ˌəʊvəˈprɪnt) 1 (*tr*) to print (additional matter or another colour) on a sheet of paper. ◆ NOUN ('əʊvəˌprɪnt) 2 additional matter or another colour printed onto a previously printed sheet. 3 additional matter, other than a change in face value, applied to a finished postage stamp by printing, stamping, etc. See also **surcharge** (sense 5), **provisional** (sense 2).

overproduction (ˌəʊvəprəˈdʌkʃən) NOUN the production of more of a product or commodity than is required.

overprotect (ˌəʊvəprəˈtɛkt) VERB (*tr*) to protect more than necessary, esp. to shield a child excessively so as to inhibit its development.
▸ **ˌoverproˈtective** ADJECTIVE

overqualified (ˌəʊvəˈkwɒlɪˌfaɪd) ADJECTIVE having more managerial experience or academic qualifications than required for a particular job.

overrate (ˌəʊvəˈreɪt) VERB (*tr*) to assess too highly.

overreach (ˌəʊvəˈriːtʃ) VERB 1 (*tr*) to defeat or thwart (oneself) by attempting to do or gain too much. 2 (*tr*) to aim for but miss by going too far or attempting too much. 3 to get the better of (a person) by trickery. 4 (*tr*) to reach or extend beyond or over. 5 (*intr*) to reach or go too far. 6 (*intr*) (of a horse) to strike the back of a forefoot with the edge of the opposite hind foot.

overreact (ˌəʊvərɪˈækt) VERB (*intr*) to react excessively to something.
▸ **ˌoverreˈaction** NOUN

overrefine (ˌəʊvərɪˈfaɪn) VERB 1 to refine (something) to excess. 2 (*intr*) to make excessively fine distinctions.
▸ **ˌoverreˈfinement** NOUN

overreliance (ˌəʊvərɪˈlaɪəns) NOUN the state or fact of being too reliant on someone or something.

overrich (ˌəʊvəˈrɪtʃ) ADJECTIVE 1 (of food) excessively flavoursome or fatty. 2 being excessively abundant, strong, etc.: *overrich heroin.*

override (ˌəʊvəˈraɪd) VERB **-rides, -riding, -rode, -ridden.** (*tr*) 1 to set aside or disregard with superior authority or power. 2 to supersede or annul. 3 to dominate or vanquish by or as if by trampling down. 4 to take manual control of (a system that is usually under automatic control). 5 to extend or pass over, esp. to overlap. 6 to ride (a horse) too hard. 7 to ride over or across. ◆ NOUN 8 a device or system that can override an automatic control.

overrider ('əʊvəˌraɪdə) NOUN either of two metal or rubber attachments fitted to the bumper of a motor vehicle to prevent the bumpers interlocking with those of another vehicle.

overriding (ˌəʊvəˈraɪdɪŋ) ADJECTIVE taking precedence.

overripe (ˌəʊvəˈraɪp) ADJECTIVE 1 (of food, cheese, etc.) past the usual stage of being ready to eat or use. 2 overused or overly sentimental and emotional: *his love songs are overripe ballads.*

overrule (ˌəʊvəˈruːl) VERB (*tr*) 1 to disallow the arguments of (a person) by the use of authority. 2 to rule or decide against (an argument, decision, etc.). 3 to prevail over, dominate, or influence. 4 to exercise rule over.

overrun VERB (ˌəʊvəˈrʌn) **-runs, -running, -ran, -run.** 1 (*tr*) to attack or invade and defeat conclusively. 2 (*tr*) to swarm or spread over rapidly. 3 to run over (something); overflow. 4 to extend or run beyond a limit. 5 (*intr*) (of an engine) to run with a closed throttle at a speed dictated by that of the vehicle it drives, as on a decline. 6 (*tr*) **a** to print (a book, journal, etc.) in a greater quantity than ordered. **b** to print additional copies of (a publication). 7 (*tr*) *Printing* to transfer (set type and other matter) from one column, line, or page, to another. 8 (*tr*) *Archaic* to run faster than. ◆ NOUN ('əʊvəˌrʌn) 9 the act or an instance of overrunning. 10 the amount or extent of overrunning. 11 the number of copies of a publication in excess of the quantity ordered. 12 the cleared level area at the end of an airport runway.

overrun brake NOUN a brake fitted to a trailer or other towed vehicle that prevents the towed vehicle travelling faster than the towing vehicle when slowing down or descending an incline.

oversaturated (ˌəʊvəˈsætʃəˌreɪtɪd) ADJECTIVE (of igneous rocks) containing excess silica.

overscore (ˌəʊvəˈskɔː) VERB (*tr*) to cancel or cross out by drawing a line or lines over or through.

overseas ADVERB (ˌəʊvəˈsiːz) 1 beyond the sea; abroad. ◆ ADJECTIVE ('əʊvəˈsiːz) 2 of, to, in, from, or situated in countries beyond the sea. 3 Also: **oversea** (ˌəʊvəˈsiː). of or relating to passage over the sea. ◆ NOUN (ˌəʊvəˈsiːz) 4 (*functioning as singular*) *Informal* a foreign country or foreign countries collectively.

overseas *or* **international telegram** NOUN *Brit* another name for **cable** (sense 5).

oversee (ˌəʊvəˈsiː) VERB **-sees, -seeing, -saw, -seen.** (*tr*) 1 to watch over and direct; supervise. 2 to watch secretly or accidentally.

overseer ('əʊvəˌsiːə) NOUN 1 Also called (less commonly): **overlooker.** a person who oversees others, esp. workmen. 2 *Brit history* short for **overseer of the poor;** a minor official of a parish attached to the workhouse or poorhouse.

oversell (ˌəʊvəˈsɛl) VERB **-sells, -selling, -sold.** 1 (*tr*) to sell more of (a commodity) than can be supplied. 2 to use excessively aggressive methods in selling (commodities). 3 (*tr*) to exaggerate the merits of.

oversensitive (ˌəʊvəˈsɛnsɪtɪv) ADJECTIVE excessively responsive to or aware of feelings, reactions, etc.

overset VERB (ˌəʊvəˈsɛt) **-sets, -setting, -set.** (*tr*) 1 to disturb or upset. 2 *Printing* to set (type or copy) in excess of the space available. ◆ NOUN ('əʊvəˌsɛt) 3 another name for **overmatter.**

oversew ('əʊvəˌsəʊ, ˌəʊvəˈsəʊ) VERB **-sews, -sewing, -sewed, -sewn.** to sew (two edges) with close stitches that pass over them both.

oversexed (ˌəʊvəˈsɛkst) ADJECTIVE having an excessive preoccupation with or need for sexual activity.

overshadow (ˌəʊvəˈʃædəʊ) VERB (*tr*) 1 to render insignificant or less important in comparison. 2 to cast a shadow or gloom over.

overshoe ('əʊvəˌʃuː) NOUN a protective shoe worn over an ordinary shoe.

overshoot (ˌəʊvəˈʃuːt) VERB **-shoots, -shooting, -shot.** 1 to shoot or go beyond (a mark or target). 2 to cause (an aircraft) to fly or taxi too far along (a runway) during landing or taking off, or (of an aircraft) to fly or taxi too far along a runway. 3 (*tr*) to pass swiftly over or down over, as water over a wheel. ◆ NOUN 4 an act or instance of overshooting. 5 the extent of such overshooting. 6 a momentary excessive response of an electrical or mechanical system.

overshot ('əʊvəˌʃɒt) ADJECTIVE 1 having or designating an upper jaw that projects beyond the lower jaw, esp. when considered as an abnormality. 2 (of a water wheel) driven by a flow of water that passes over the wheel rather than under it. Compare **undershot.**

overside ('əʊvəˌsaɪd) ADVERB over the side (of a ship).

oversight ('əʊvəˌsaɪt) NOUN 1 an omission or mistake, esp. one made through failure to notice something. 2 supervision.

oversimplify (ˌəʊvəˈsɪmplɪˌfaɪ) VERB **-fies, -fying, -fied.** to simplify (something) to the point of distortion or error.
▸ **ˌoverˌsimplifiˈcation** NOUN

oversize ADJECTIVE (ˌəʊvəˈsaɪz) 1 Also: **oversized.** larger than the usual size. ◆ NOUN ('əʊvəˌsaɪz) 2 a size larger than the usual or proper size. 3 something that is oversize.

overskirt ('əʊvəˌskɜːt) NOUN an outer skirt, esp. one that reveals a decorative underskirt.

overslaugh ('əʊvəˌslɔː) NOUN 1 *Military* the passing over of one duty for another that takes precedence. ◆ VERB 2 (*tr*) *US* to pass over; ignore.
▷ **HISTORY** C18: from Dutch *overslaan* to pass over

oversleep (ˌəʊvəˈsliːp) VERB **-sleeps, -sleeping, -slept.** (*intr*) to sleep beyond the intended time for getting up.

oversleeve ('əʊvəˌsliːv) NOUN a protective sleeve covering an ordinary sleeve.

overspend VERB (ˌəʊvəˈspɛnd) **-spends, -spending, -spent.** 1 to spend in excess of (one's desires or what one can afford or is allocated). 2 (*tr; usually passive*) to wear out; exhaust. ◆ NOUN ('əʊvəˌspɛnd) 3 the amount by which someone or something is overspent.

overspill NOUN ('əʊvəˌspɪl) 1 **a** something that spills over or is in excess. **b** (*as modifier*): *overspill population.* ◆ VERB (ˌəʊvəˈspɪl) **-spills, -spilling, -spilt** *or* **-spilled.** 2 (*intr*) to overflow.

overstaff (ˌəʊvəˈstɑːf) VERB (*tr*) to provide an excessive number of staff for (a factory, hotel, etc.).

overstate (ˌəʊvəˈsteɪt) VERB (*tr*) to state too strongly; exaggerate or overemphasize.
▸ **ˌoverˈstatement** NOUN

overstay (ˌəʊvəˈsteɪ) VERB (*tr*) 1 to stay beyond the time, limit, or duration of. 2 *Finance* to delay a transaction in (a market) until after the point at which the maximum profit would have been made. 3 *NZ* to stay in New Zealand beyond (the period sanctioned by the immigration authorities or the period of a visitor's permit). 4 **overstay** *or* **outstay one's welcome.** to stay (at a party, on a visit, etc.), longer than pleases the host or hostess.

overstayer ('əʊvəˌsteɪə) NOUN a person who illegally remains in a country after the period of the permitted visit has expired.

oversteer (ˌəʊvəˈstɪə) VERB (*intr*) (of a vehicle) to turn more sharply, for a particular turn of the steering wheel, than is desirable or anticipated.

overstep (ˌəʊvəˈstɛp) VERB **-steps, -stepping, -stepped.** (*tr*) to go beyond (a certain or proper limit).

overstock (ˌəʊvəˈstɒk) VERB (*tr*) 1 to hold or supply (a commodity) in excess of requirements. 2 to run more farm animals on (a piece of land) than it is capable of maintaining.

overstretch (ˌəʊvəˈstrɛtʃ) VERB (*tr*) 1 to make excessive demands or put excessive pressure on (oneself, finances, etc.). 2 to stretch (muscles or limbs) too much or too hard.

overstrung (ˌəʊvəˈstrʌŋ) ADJECTIVE 1 too highly strung; tense. 2 (of a piano) having two sets of strings crossing each other at an oblique angle.

overstuff (ˌəʊvəˈstʌf) VERB (*tr*) 1 to force too much into. 2 to cover (furniture) entirely with upholstery.

oversubscribe (ˌəʊvəsəbˈskraɪb) VERB (*tr; often passive*) to subscribe or apply for in excess of available supply.
▸ **ˌoversubˈscription** NOUN

oversupply ('əʊvəˌsəplaɪ) NOUN 1 the supply of too much or too many. ◆ VERB (ˌəʊvəˈsəplaɪ) **-plies, -plying, -plied.** 2 (*tr*) to supply too much (material, etc.) or too many (goods, people, etc.).

overt ('əʊvɜːt, əʊˈvɜːt) ADJECTIVE 1 open to view; observable. 2 *Law* open; deliberate. Criminal intent may be inferred from an overt act.
▷ **HISTORY** C14: via Old French, from *ovrir* to open, from Latin *aperīre*
▸ **oˈvertly** ADVERB ▸ **oˈvertness** NOUN

overtake (ˌəʊvəˈteɪk) VERB **-takes, -taking, -took, -taken.** 1 *Chiefly Brit* to move past (another vehicle or person) travelling in the same direction. 2 (*tr*) to pass or do better than, after catching up with. 3 (*tr*) to come upon suddenly or unexpectedly: *night overtook him.* 4 (*tr*) to catch up with; draw level with.

overtask (ˌəʊvəˈtɑːsk) VERB (*tr*) to impose too heavy a task upon.

overtax (ˌəʊvəˈtæks) VERB (*tr*) 1 to tax too heavily. 2 to impose too great a strain on.

over-the-counter ADJECTIVE 1 **a** (of securities) not listed or quoted on a stock exchange. **b** (of a security market) dealing in such securities. **c** (of security transactions) conducted through a broker's office directly between purchaser and seller and not on a stock exchange. 2 (of medicinal drugs) able to be sold without a prescription. Abbreviation: **OTC.** Compare **POM.**

overthrow VERB (ˌəʊvəˈθrəʊ), **-throws, -throwing, -threw, -thrown.** 1 (*tr*) to effect the downfall or destruction of (a ruler, institution, etc.), esp. by force. 2 (*tr*) to throw or turn over. 3 (*tr*) to throw (something, esp. a ball) too far. ◆ NOUN (ˈəʊvəˌθrəʊ) 4 an act of overthrowing. 5 downfall; destruction. 6 *Cricket* **a** a ball thrown back too far by a fielder. **b** a run scored because of this.

overthrust (ˈəʊvəˌθrʌst) NOUN *Geology* a reverse fault in which the rocks on the upper surface of a fault plane have moved over the rocks on the lower surface. Compare **underthrust.**

overtime NOUN (ˈəʊvəˌtaɪm) 1 **a** work at a regular job done in addition to regular working hours. **b** (*as modifier*): *overtime pay.* 2 the rate of pay established for such work. 3 time in excess of a set period. 4 *Sport, US and Canadian* extra time. ◆ ADVERB (ˈəʊvəˌtaɪm) 5 beyond the regular or stipulated time. ◆ VERB (ˌəʊvəˈtaɪm) 6 (*tr*) to exceed the required time for (a photographic exposure).

overtired (ˌəʊvəˈtaɪəd) ADJECTIVE extremely tired; exhausted: *overtired and overworked.*

overtone (ˈəʊvəˌtəʊn) NOUN 1 (*often plural*) additional meaning or nuance: *overtones of despair.* 2 *Music, acoustics* any of the tones, with the exception of the fundamental, that constitute a musical sound and contribute to its quality, each having a frequency that is a multiple of the fundamental frequency. See also **harmonic** (sense 7), **partial** (sense 6).

overtop (ˌəʊvəˈtɒp) VERB **-tops, -topping, -topped.** (*tr*) 1 to exceed in height. 2 to surpass; excel. 3 to rise over the top of.

overtopping (ˌəʊvəˈtɒpɪŋ) NOUN the rising of water over the top of a barrier.

overtrade (ˌəʊvəˈtreɪd) VERB (*intr*) (of an enterprise) to trade in excess of capacity or working capital.

overtrick (ˈəʊvəˌtrɪk) NOUN *Bridge* a trick by which a player exceeds his contract.

overtrump (ˌəʊvəˈtrʌmp) VERB *Cards* to play a trump higher than (one previously played to the trick).

overture (ˈəʊvəˌtjʊə) NOUN 1 *Music* **a** a piece of orchestral music containing contrasting sections that is played at the beginning of an opera or oratorio, often containing the main musical themes of the work. **b** a similar piece preceding the performance of a play. **c** Also called: **concert overture.** a one-movement orchestral piece, usually having a descriptive or evocative title. **d** a short piece in three movements (**French overture** or **Italian overture**) common in the 17th and 18th centuries. 2 (*often plural*) a proposal, act, or gesture initiating a relationship, negotiation, etc. 3 something that introduces what follows. ◆ VERB (*tr*) 4 to make or present an overture to. 5 to introduce with an overture.
▷ **HISTORY** C14: via Old French, from Late Latin *apertūra* opening, from Latin *aperīre* to open; see OVERT

overturn VERB (ˌəʊvəˈtɜːn) 1 to turn or cause to turn from an upright or normal position. 2 (*tr*) to overthrow or destroy. 3 (*tr*) to invalidate; reverse: *the bill was passed in the Commons but overturned in the Lords.* ◆ NOUN (ˈəʊvəˌtɜːn) 4 the act of overturning or the state of being overturned.

over-under *US* ◆ ADJECTIVE 1 (of a two-barrelled firearm) having one barrel on top of the other. ◆ NOUN 2 an over-under firearm.

over-use VERB (ˌəʊvəˈjuːz) (*tr*) 1 to use excessively. ◆ NOUN (ˌəʊvəˈjuːs) 2 excessive use.

overview (ˈəʊvəˌvjuː) NOUN a general survey.

overvoltage (ˈəʊvəˌvəʊltɪdʒ) NOUN a voltage above the normal level.

overwatch (ˌəʊvəˈwɒtʃ) VERB (*tr*) 1 to watch over. 2 *Archaic* to fatigue with long watching or lack of sleep.

overweening (ˌəʊvəˈwiːnɪŋ) ADJECTIVE 1 (of a person) excessively arrogant or presumptuous. 2 (of opinions, appetites, etc.) excessive; immoderate.
▷ **HISTORY** C14: OVER- + *weening,* from Old English *wēnan:* see WEEN
▸ ˌ**over'weeningly** ADVERB ▸ ˌ**over'weeningness** NOUN

overweigh (ˌəʊvəˈweɪ) VERB (*tr*) 1 to exceed in weight; overbalance. 2 to weigh down; oppress.

overweight ADJECTIVE (ˌəʊvəˈweɪt) 1 weighing more than is usual, allowed, or healthy. ◆ NOUN (ˈəʊvəˌweɪt) 2 *Finance* **a** having a higher proportion of one's investments in a particular sector of the market than the size of that sector relative to the total market would suggest: *portfolio managers are currently overweight in bonds.* **b** (of a fund etc.) invested disproportionately in this way. 3 extra or excess weight. 4 *Archaic* greater importance or effect. ◆ VERB (ˌəʊvəˈweɪt) (*tr*) 5 to give too much emphasis or consideration to. 6 to add too much weight to. 7 to weigh down.

overwhelm (ˌəʊvəˈwɛlm) VERB (*tr*) 1 to overpower the thoughts, emotions, or senses of. 2 to overcome with irresistible force. 3 to overcome, as with a profusion or concentration of something. 4 to cover over or bury completely. 5 to weigh or rest upon overpoweringly. 6 *Archaic* to overturn.

overwhelming (ˌəʊvəˈwɛlmɪŋ) ADJECTIVE overpowering in effect or force.
▸ ˌ**over'whelmingly** ADVERB

overwind (ˌəʊvəˈwaɪnd) VERB **-winds, -winding, -wound.** (*tr*) to wind (a watch) beyond the proper limit.

overwinter (ˌəʊvəˈwɪntə) VERB 1 (*intr*) to spend winter (in or at a particular place). 2 (*tr*) to keep (animals or plants) alive through the winter. 3 (*intr*) (of an animal or plant) to remain alive throughout the winter.

overword (ˈəʊvəˌwɜːd) NOUN a repeated word or phrase.

overwork VERB (ˌəʊvəˈwɜːk) (*mainly tr*) 1 (*also intr*) to work or cause to work too hard or too long. 2 to use too much: *to overwork an excuse.* 3 to decorate the surface of. 4 to work up. ◆ NOUN (ˈəʊvəˌwɜːk) 5 excessive or excessively tiring work.
▸ ˌ**over'worked** ADJECTIVE

overwrite (ˌəʊvəˈraɪt) VERB **-writes, -writing, -wrote, -written.** 1 to write (something) in an excessively ornate or prolix style. 2 to write too much about (someone or something). 3 to write on top of (other writing). 4 to record on a storage medium, such as a magnetic disk, thus destroying what was originally recorded there.

overwrought (ˌəʊvəˈrɔːt) ADJECTIVE 1 full of nervous tension; agitated. 2 too elaborate; fussy: *an overwrought style.* 3 (*often postpositive* and foll by *with*) with the surface decorated or adorned.

overzealous (ˌəʊvəˈzɛləs) ADJECTIVE excessively zealous.

ovi- *or* **ovo-** COMBINING FORM egg or ovum: *oviform; ovotestis.*
▷ **HISTORY** from Latin *ōvum*

oviduct (ˈɒvɪˌdʌkt, ˈəʊ-) NOUN the tube through which ova are conveyed from an ovary. Also called (in mammals): **Fallopian tube.**
▸ **oviducal** (ˌɒvɪˈdjuːkᵊl, ˌəʊ-) *or* ˌ**ovi'ductal** ADJECTIVE

Oviedo (*Spanish* oˈβjeðo) NOUN a city in NW Spain: capital of Asturias from 810 until 1002; centre of a coal- and iron-mining area. Pop.: 199 549 (1998 est.).

oviferous (əʊˈvɪfərəs) *or* **ovigerous** (əʊˈvɪdʒərəs) ADJECTIVE *Zoology* carrying or producing eggs or ova: *the oviferous legs of certain spiders.*

oviform (ˈəʊvɪˌfɔːm) ADJECTIVE *Biology* shaped like an egg.

ovine (ˈəʊvaɪn) ADJECTIVE of, relating to, or resembling a sheep.
▷ **HISTORY** C19: from Late Latin *ovīnus,* from Latin *ovis* sheep

oviparous (əʊˈvɪpərəs) ADJECTIVE (of fishes, reptiles, birds, etc.) producing eggs that hatch outside the body of the mother. Compare **ovoviviparous, viviparous** (sense 1).
▸ **oviparity** (ˌəʊvɪˈpærɪtɪ) NOUN ▸ **o'viparously** ADVERB

oviposit (ˌəʊvɪˈpɒzɪt) VERB (*intr*) (of insects and fishes) to deposit eggs through an ovipositor.
▷ **HISTORY** C19: OVI- + *positus,* past participle of Latin *pōnere* to place
▸ **oviposition** (ˌəʊvɪpəˈzɪʃən) NOUN

ovipositor (ˌəʊvɪˈpɒzɪtə) NOUN 1 the egg-laying organ of most female insects, consisting of a pair of specialized appendages at the end of the abdomen. 2 a similar organ in certain female fishes, formed by an extension of the edges of the genital opening.

ovisac (ˈəʊvɪˌsæk) NOUN a capsule or sac, such as an ootheca, in which egg cells are produced.

ovo- COMBINING FORM a variant of **ovi-.**

ovoid (ˈəʊvɔɪd) ADJECTIVE 1 egg-shaped. 2 *Botany* (of a fruit or similar part) egg-shaped with the broader end at the base. Compare **obovoid.** ◆ NOUN 3 something that is ovoid.

ovolo (ˈəʊvəˌləʊ) NOUN, *plural* **-li** (-ˌlaɪ). *Architect* a convex moulding having a cross section in the form of a quarter of a circle or ellipse. Also called: **quarter round, thumb.** Compare **congé** (sense 3), **echinus** (sense 1).
▷ **HISTORY** C17: from Italian: a little egg, from *ovo* egg, from Latin *ōvum*

ovotestis (ˌəʊvəʊˈtɛstɪs) NOUN, *plural* **-tes** (-tiːz). the reproductive organ of snails, which produces both ova and spermatozoa.

ovoviviparous (ˌəʊvəʊvaɪˈvɪpərəs) ADJECTIVE (of certain reptiles, fishes, etc.) producing eggs that hatch within the body of the mother. Compare **oviparous, viviparous** (sense 1).
▸ **ovoviviparity** (ˌəʊvəʊˌvaɪvɪˈpærɪtɪ) NOUN

ovulate (ˈɒvjʊˌleɪt) VERB (*intr*) to produce or discharge eggs from an ovary.
▷ **HISTORY** C19: from OVULE
▸ ˌ**ovu'lation** NOUN

ovulation method NOUN another name for **Billings method.**

ovule (ˈɒvjuːl) NOUN 1 a small body in seed-bearing plants that consists of the integument(s), nucellus, and embryosac (containing the egg cell) and develops into the seed after fertilization. 2 *Zoology* an immature ovum.
▷ **HISTORY** C19: via French from Medieval Latin *ōvulum* a little egg, from Latin *ōvum* egg
▸ ˈ**ovular** ADJECTIVE

ovum (ˈəʊvəm) NOUN, *plural* **ova** (ˈəʊvə). an unfertilized female gamete; egg cell.
▷ **HISTORY** from Latin: egg

ow (aʊ) INTERJECTION an exclamation of pain.

owe (əʊ) VERB (*mainly tr*) 1 to be under an obligation to pay (someone) to the amount of. 2 (*intr*) to be in debt: *he still owes for his house.* 3 (often foll by *to*) to have as a result (of): *he owes his success to chance.* 4 to feel the need or obligation to do, give, etc.: *to owe somebody thanks; to owe it to oneself to rest.* 5 to hold or maintain in the mind or heart (esp. in the phrase **owe a grudge**).
▷ **HISTORY** Old English *āgan* to have (C12: to have to); related to Old Saxon *ēgan,* Old High German *eigan*

owelty (ˈəʊəltɪ) NOUN, *plural* **-ties.** *Law* equality, esp. in financial transactions.
▷ **HISTORY** C16: from Anglo-French *owelté,* ultimately from Latin *aequalitas,* from *aequalis* EQUAL

Owen gun (ˈəʊən) NOUN a type of simple recoil-operated 9 mm sub-machine-gun first used by Australian forces in World War II.
▷ **HISTORY** named after E. E. *Owen* (1915–49), its Australian inventor

Owen Stanley Range (ˈəʊən) NOUN a mountain range in SE New Guinea. Highest peak: Mount Victoria, 4073 m (13 363 ft.).

ower *or* **owre** (ˈaʊər) PREPOSITION, ADVERB, ADJECTIVE a Scot word for **over.**

Owerri (əˈwɛrɪ) NOUN a market town in S Nigeria, capital of Imo state. Pop.: 35 010 (latest est.).

owing (ˈəʊɪŋ) ADJECTIVE 1 (*postpositive*) owed; due. 2 **owing to.** (*preposition*) because of or on account of.

owl (aʊl) NOUN 1 any nocturnal bird of prey of the order *Strigiformes,* having large front-facing eyes, a small hooked bill, soft feathers, and a short neck. 2 any of various breeds of owl-like fancy domestic pigeon (esp. the **African owl, Chinese owl,** and **English owl**). 3 a person who looks or behaves like an owl, esp. in having a solemn manner.
▷ **HISTORY** Old English *ūle;* related to Dutch *uil,* Old High German *ūwila,* Old Norse *ugla*
▸ ˈ**owl-**ˌ**like** ADJECTIVE

owlet (ˈaʊlɪt) NOUN a young or nestling owl.

owlish (ˈaʊlɪʃ) ADJECTIVE 1 like an owl. 2 solemn and wise in appearance.
▸ **ˈowlishly** ADVERB ▸ **ˈowlishness** NOUN

own (əʊn) DETERMINER (*preceded by a possessive*) 1 **a** (intensifier): *John's own idea; your own mother.* **b** (*as pronoun*): *I'll use my own.* 2 on behalf of oneself or in relation to oneself: *he is his own worst enemy.* 3 **come into one's own. a** to become fulfilled: *she really came into her own when she got divorced.* **b** to receive what is due to one. 4 **get one's own back.** *Informal* to have revenge. 5 **hold one's own.** to maintain one's situation or position, esp. in spite of opposition or difficulty. 6 **on one's own. a** without help. **b** by oneself; alone. ◆ VERB 7 (*tr*) to have as one's possession. 8 (when *intr,* often foll by *up, to,* or *up to*) to confess or admit; acknowledge. 9 (*tr; takes a clause as object*) *Now rare* to concede: *I own that you are right.*
▹HISTORY Old English *āgen,* originally past participle of *āgan* to have; related to Old Saxon *ēgan,* Old Norse *eiginn.* See OWE

own brand NOUN **a** an item packaged and marketed under the brand name of a particular retailer, usually a large supermarket chain, rather than that of the manufacturer. **b** (*as modifier*): *own-brand products.* ◆ Also: **own label.**

owner (ˈəʊnə) NOUN a person who owns; legal possessor.

owner-occupier NOUN *Brit* a person who owns or is in the process of buying the house or flat he lives in.
▸ **ˌowner-ˈoccuˌpied** ADJECTIVE ▸ **ˈowner-ˌoccuˈpation** NOUN

ownership (ˈəʊnəʃɪp) NOUN 1 the state or fact of being an owner. 2 legal right of possession; proprietorship.

ownership flat NOUN *NZ* a flat owned by the occupier.

own goal NOUN 1 *Soccer* a goal scored by a player accidentally playing the ball into his own team's net. Abbreviation: **o.g.** 2 *Informal* any action that results in disadvantage to the person who took it or to a party, group, etc. with which that person is associated.

owt (aʊt) PRONOUN *Northern English* a dialect word for **anything.**
▹HISTORY a variant of AUGHT[1]

ox (ɒks) NOUN, *plural* **oxen** (ˈɒksən). 1 an adult castrated male of any domesticated species of cattle, esp. *Bos taurus,* used for draught work and meat. 2 any bovine mammal, esp. any of the domestic cattle.
▹HISTORY Old English *oxa;* related to Old Saxon, Old High German *ohso,* Old Norse *oxi*

oxa- *or before a vowel* **ox-** COMBINING FORM indicating that a chemical compound contains oxygen, used esp. to denote that a heterocyclic compound is derived from a specified compound by replacement of a carbon atom with an oxygen atom: *oxazine.*

oxalate (ˈɒksəˌleɪt) NOUN a salt or ester of oxalic acid.

oxalic acid (ɒkˈsælɪk) NOUN a colourless poisonous crystalline dicarboxylic acid found in many plants: used as a bleach and a cleansing agent for metals. Formula: $(COOH)_2$. Systematic name: **ethanedioic acid.**
▹HISTORY C18: from French *oxalique,* from Latin *oxalis* garden sorrel; see OXALIS

oxalis (ˈɒksəlɪs, ɒkˈsælɪs) NOUN any plant of the genus *Oxalis,* having clover-like leaves which contain oxalic acid and white, pink, red, or yellow flowers: family *Oxalidaceae.* See also **wood sorrel.**
▹HISTORY C18: via Latin from Greek: sorrel, sour wine, from *oxus* acid, sharp

oxazine (ˈɒksəˌziːn) NOUN any of 13 heterocyclic compounds with the formula C_4H_5NO.
▹HISTORY from OXY-[2] + AZINE

oxblood (ˈɒksˌblʌd) *or* **oxblood red** ADJECTIVE of a dark reddish-brown colour.

oxbow (ˈɒksˌbəʊ) NOUN 1 a U-shaped piece of wood fitted under and around the neck of a harnessed ox and attached to the yoke. 2 Also called: **oxbow lake, cutoff.** a small curved lake lying on the flood plain of a river and constituting the remnant of a former meander.

Oxbridge (ˈɒksˌbrɪdʒ) NOUN **a** the British universities of Oxford and Cambridge, esp. considered as ancient and prestigious academic institutions, bastions of privilege and superiority, etc. **b** (*as modifier*): *Oxbridge graduates.*

oxen (ˈɒksən) NOUN the plural of **ox.**

oxeye (ˈɒksˌaɪ) NOUN 1 any Eurasian plant of the genus *Buphthalmum,* having daisy-like flower heads with yellow rays and dark centres: family *Asteraceae* (composites). 2 any of various North American plants of the related genus *Heliopsis,* having daisy-like flowers. 3 **oxeye daisy.** another name for **daisy** (sense 2).

ox-eyed ADJECTIVE having large round eyes, like those of an ox.

ox-eye herring NOUN a herring-like sea fish, *Megalops cyprinoides,* of northern Australian waters, related to the tarpon.

OXFAM *or* **Oxfam** (ˈɒksfæm) NOUN ACRONYM FOR Oxford Committee for Famine Relief.

Oxford (ˈɒksfəd) NOUN 1 a city in S England, administrative centre of Oxfordshire, at the confluence of the Rivers Thames and Cherwell: Royalist headquarters during the Civil War; seat of Oxford University, consisting of 40 separate colleges, the oldest being University College (1249), and Oxford Brookes University (1993); motor-vehicle industry. Pop.: 118 795 (1991). Related word: **Oxonian.** 2 Also called: **Oxford Down.** a breed of sheep with middle-length wool and a dark brown face and legs. 3 a type of stout laced shoe with a low heel. 4 a lightweight fabric of plain or twill weave used esp. for men's shirts.

Oxford accent NOUN the accent associated with Oxford English.

Oxford bags PLURAL NOUN trousers with very wide baggy legs, originally popular in the 1920s. Often shortened to **bags.**

Oxford blue NOUN 1 **a** a dark blue colour. **b** (*as adjective*): *an Oxford-blue scarf.* 2 a person who has been awarded a blue from Oxford University.

Oxford English NOUN that form of the received pronunciation of English supposed to be typical of Oxford University and regarded by many as affected or pretentious.

Oxford frame NOUN a type of picture frame in which the sides of the frame cross each other and project outwards.

Oxford Group NOUN an early name for **Moral Rearmament.**

Oxford Movement NOUN a movement within the Church of England that began at Oxford in 1833 and was led by Pusey, Newman, and Keble. It affirmed the continuity of the Church with early Christianity and strove to restore the High-Church ideals of the 17th century. Its views were publicized in a series of tracts (**Tracts for the Times**) 1833–41. The teaching and practices of the Movement are maintained in the High-Church tradition within the Church of England. Also called: **Tractarianism.**

Oxfordshire (ˈɒksfədˌʃɪə, -ʃə) NOUN an inland county of S central England: situated mostly in the basin of the Upper Thames, with the Cotswolds in the west and the Chilterns in the southeast. Administrative centre: Oxford. Pop.: 605 492 (2001). Area: 2608 sq. km (1007 sq. miles). Abbreviation: **Oxon.**

oxhide (ˈɒksˌhaɪd) NOUN leather made from the hide of an ox.

oxidant (ˈɒksɪdənt) NOUN a substance that acts or is used as an oxidizing agent. Also called (esp in rocketry): **oxidizer.**

oxidase (ˈɒksɪˌdeɪs, -ˌdeɪz) NOUN any of a group of enzymes that bring about biological oxidation.

oxidate (ˈɒksɪˌdeɪt) VERB another word for **oxidize.**

oxidation (ˌɒksɪˈdeɪʃən) NOUN **a** the act or process of oxidizing. **b** (*as modifier*): *an oxidation state; an oxidation potential.*
▸ **ˌoxiˈdational** ADJECTIVE ▸ **ˈoxiˌdative** ADJECTIVE

oxidation-reduction NOUN **a** a reversible chemical process usually involving the transfer of electrons, in which one reaction is an oxidation and the reverse reaction is a reduction. **b** Also: **redox.** (*as modifier*): *an oxidation-reduction reaction.*

oxidative phosphorylation NOUN the process by which the energy liberated by oxidation of metabolites is used to synthesize the energy-rich molecule ATP.

oxide (ˈɒksaɪd) NOUN 1 any compound of oxygen with another element. 2 any organic compound in which an oxygen atom is bound to two alkyl or aryl groups; an ether or epoxide.
▹HISTORY C18: from French, from *ox*(*ygène*) + (*ac*)*ide;* see OXYGEN, ACID

oxidimetry (ˌɒksɪˈdɪmɪtrɪ) NOUN *Chem* a branch of volumetric analysis in which oxidizing agents are used in titrations.
▹HISTORY C20: from OXID(ATION) + -METRY
▸ **oxidimetric** (ˌɒksɪdɪˈmɛtrɪk) ADJECTIVE

oxidize *or* **oxidise** (ˈɒksɪˌdaɪz) VERB 1 to undergo or cause to undergo a chemical reaction with oxygen, as in formation of an oxide. 2 to form or cause to form a layer of metal oxide, as in rusting. 3 to lose or cause to lose hydrogen atoms. 4 to undergo or cause to undergo a decrease in the number of electrons. Compare **reduce** (sense 12c).
▸ **ˌoxidiˈzation** *or* **ˌoxidiˈsation** NOUN

oxidizer *or* **oxidiser** (ˈɒksɪˌdaɪzə) NOUN an oxidant, esp. a substance that combines with the fuel in a rocket engine.

oxidizing agent NOUN *Chem* a substance that oxidizes another substance, being itself reduced in the process. Common oxidizing agents are oxygen, hydrogen peroxide, and ferric salts. Compare **reducing agent.**

oxime (ˈɒksiːm) NOUN any of a class of compounds with the general formula RR′NOH, where R is an organic group and R′ is either an organic group (**ketoxime**) or hydrogen atom (**aldoxime**): used in the chemical analysis of carbonyl compounds.
▹HISTORY C19: from OX(YGEN) + IM(ID)E

oxlip (ˈɒksˌlɪp) NOUN 1 Also called: **paigle.** a primulaceous Eurasian woodland plant, *Primula elatior,* with small drooping pale yellow flowers. 2 Also called: **false oxlip.** a similar and related plant that is a natural hybrid between the cowslip and primrose.
▹HISTORY Old English *oxanslyppe,* literally: ox's slippery dropping; see SLIP[3], compare COWSLIP

Oxo (ˈɒksəʊ) NOUN *Trademark* extract of beef in the shape of small cubes which are mixed with boiling water and used for flavouring, as stock, a drink, etc.
▹HISTORY C20: from OX + -O

oxo- *or before a vowel* **ox-** COMBINING FORM indicating that a chemical compound contains oxygen linked to another atom by a double bond, used esp. to denote that a compound is derived from a specified compound by replacement of a methylene group with a carbonyl group: *oxobutanoic acid.*

oxo acid (ˈɒksəʊ) NOUN another name for **oxyacid.**

Oxon ABBREVIATION FOR Oxfordshire.
▹HISTORY from Latin *Oxonia*

Oxon. (ˈɒksən) ABBREVIATION FOR (in degree titles) of Oxford.
▹HISTORY from Latin *Oxoniensis*

Oxonian (ɒkˈsəʊnɪən) ADJECTIVE 1 of or relating to Oxford or Oxford University. ◆ NOUN 2 a member of Oxford University. 3 an inhabitant or native of Oxford.

oxonium compound *or* **salt** (ɒkˈsəʊnɪəm) NOUN *Chem* any of a class of salts derived from certain organic ethers or alcohols by adding a proton to the oxygen atom and thus producing a positive ion (**oxonium ion**).

oxpecker (ˈɒksˌpɛkə) NOUN either of two African starlings, *Buphagus africanus* or *B. erythrorhynchus,* having flattened bills with which they obtain food from the hides of cattle. Also called: **tick-bird.**

oxtail (ˈɒksˌteɪl) NOUN the skinned tail of an ox, used esp. in soups and stews.

oxter (ˈɒkstə) NOUN *Scot, Irish, and northern English, dialect* the armpit.
▹HISTORY C16: from Old English *oxta;* related to Old High German *Ahsala,* Latin *axilla*

oxtongue (ˈɒksˌtʌŋ) NOUN 1 any of various Eurasian plants of the genus *Picris,* having oblong bristly leaves and clusters of dandelion-like flowers: family *Asteraceae* (composites). 2 any of various other plants having bristly tongue-shaped leaves, such as alkanet. 3 the tongue of an ox, braised or boiled as food.

Oxus ('ɒksəs) NOUN the ancient name for the **Amu Darya**.

oxy-[1] COMBINING FORM denoting something sharp; acute: *oxytone*.
▷HISTORY from Greek, from *oxus*

oxy-[2] COMBINING FORM [1] containing or using oxygen: *oxyacetylene*. [2] a former equivalent of **hydroxy-**.

oxyacetylene (ˌɒksɪə'sɛtɪˌliːn) NOUN **a** a mixture of oxygen and acetylene; used in a blowpipe for cutting or welding metals at high temperatures. **b** (*as modifier*): *an oxyacetylene burner*.

oxyacid (ˌɒksɪ'æsɪd) NOUN any acid that contains oxygen. Also called: **oxo acid**.

oxycephaly (ˌɒksɪ'sɛfəlɪ) NOUN *Pathol* the condition of having a conical skull.
▷HISTORY C20: from Greek *oxus* sharp + -CEPHALY
▸**oxycephalic** (ˌɒksɪsɪ'fælɪk) *or* ˌ**oxy'cephalous** ADJECTIVE

oxycodone hydrochloride (ˌɒksɪ'kəudəun) NOUN an opiate drug used as a painkiller. See also **OxyContin**.

OxyContin (ˌɒksɪ'kɒntɪn) NOUN *Trademark* an opiate drug, oxycodone hydrochloride, used as a painkiller and, illegally, as an alternative to heroin.

oxygen ('ɒksɪdʒən) NOUN **a** a colourless odourless highly reactive gaseous element: the most abundant element in the earth's crust (49.2 per cent). It is essential for aerobic respiration and almost all combustion and is widely used in industry. Symbol: O; atomic no.: 8; atomic wt.: 15.9994; valency: 2; density: 1.429 kg/m^3; melting pt.: –218.79°C; boiling pt.: –182.97°C. **b** (*as modifier*): *an oxygen mask*.
▸**oxygenic** (ˌɒksɪ'dʒɛnɪk) *or* **oxygenous** (ɒk'sɪdʒɪnəs) ADJECTIVE

oxygen acid NOUN another name for **oxyacid**.

oxygenate ('ɒksɪdʒɪˌneɪt), **oxygenize,** *or* **oxygenise** VERB to enrich or be enriched with oxygen: *to oxygenate blood*.
▸ˌ**oxygen'ation** NOUN ▸**'oxygeˌnizer** *or* **'oxygeˌniser** NOUN

oxygenator ('ɒksɪdʒɪˌneɪtə) NOUN an apparatus that oxygenates the blood, esp. while a patient is undergoing an operation.

oxygen bar NOUN an establishment where customers pay to inhale pure oxygen in order to combat the effects of air pollution.

oxygen effect NOUN *Biology* the increased sensitivity to radiation of living organisms, tissues, etc., when they are exposed in the presence of oxygen.

oxygen mask NOUN a device, worn over the nose and mouth, to which oxygen is supplied from a cylinder or other source: used to aid breathing.

oxygen tent NOUN *Med* a transparent enclosure covering a bedridden patient, into which oxygen is released to help maintain respiration.

oxygen weed NOUN *NZ* another name for **water hyacinth**.

oxyhaemoglobin *or US* **oxyhemoglobin** (ˌɒksɪˌhiːməu'gləubɪn, -ˌhɛm-) NOUN *Biochem* the bright red product formed when oxygen from the lungs combines with haemoglobin in the blood.

oxyhydrogen (ˌɒksɪ'haɪdrədʒən) NOUN **a** a mixture of hydrogen and oxygen used to provide an intense flame for welding. **b** (*as modifier*): *an oxyhydrogen blowpipe*.

oxymoron (ˌɒksɪ'mɔːrɒn) NOUN, *plural* **-mora** (-'mɔːrə). *Rhetoric* an epigrammatic effect, by which contradictory terms are used in conjunction: *living death*; *fiend angelical*.
▷HISTORY C17: via New Latin from Greek *oxumōron*, from *oxus* sharp + *mōros* stupid

oxyntic (ɒk'sɪntɪk) ADJECTIVE *Physiol* of or denoting stomach cells that secrete acid: *oxyntic cells*.
▷HISTORY C19: from Greek *oxus* acid, sharp

oxysalt (ˌɒksɪ'sɔːlt) NOUN any salt of an oxyacid.

oxysulphide (ˌɒksɪ'sʌlfaɪd) NOUN *Chem* a compound containing an element combined with oxygen and sulphur.

oxytetracycline (ˌɒksɪˌtɛtrə'saɪklɪn) NOUN a broad-spectrum antibiotic, obtained from the bacterium *Streptomyces rimosus*, used in treating various infections. Formula: $C_{22}H_{24}N_2O_9$. Abbreviation: **OTC**.

oxytocic (ˌɒksɪ'təusɪk) ADJECTIVE [1] accelerating childbirth by stimulating uterine contractions. ◆ NOUN [2] an oxytocic drug or agent.
▷HISTORY C19: from Greek, from OXY-[1] + *tokos* childbirth

oxytocin (ˌɒksɪ'təusɪn) NOUN a polypeptide hormone, secreted by the pituitary gland, that stimulates contractions of the uterus or oviduct and ejection of milk in mammals; alphahypophame: used therapeutically for aiding childbirth. Formula: $C_{43}H_{68}N_{12}O_{12}S_2$. Compare **vasopressin**.

oxytone ('ɒksɪˌtəun) (in the classical Greek language) ◆ ADJECTIVE [1] (of a word) having an accent on the final syllable. ◆ NOUN [2] an oxytone word. ◆ Compare **paroxytone, proparoxytone**.
▷HISTORY C18: from Greek *oxytonos*, from *oxus* sharp + *tonos* tone

oyer (ɔɪə) NOUN [1] *English legal history* (in the 13th century) an assize. [2] (formerly) the reading out loud of a document in court. [3] See **oyer and terminer**.

oyer and terminer ('tɜːmɪnə) NOUN [1] *English law* (formerly) a commission issued to judges to try cases on assize. It became obsolete with the abolition of assizes and the setting up of crown courts in 1972. [2] the court in which such a hearing was held. [3] (in the US) a court exercising higher criminal jurisdiction.
▷HISTORY C15: from Anglo-Norman, from *oyer* to hear + *terminer* to judge

oyez *or* **oyes** (əu'jɛs, -'jɛz) INTERJECTION [1] a cry, usually uttered three times, by a public crier or court official for silence and attention before making a proclamation. ◆ NOUN [2] such a cry.
▷HISTORY C15: via Anglo-Norman from Old French *oiez!* hear!

-oyl SUFFIX OF NOUNS (in chemistry) indicating an acyl group or radical: *ethanoyl*; *methanoyl*.
▷HISTORY C20: from O(XYGEN) + -YL

Oyo ('əujəu) NOUN a state of SW Nigeria, formed in 1976 from part of Western State. Capital: Ibadan. Pop.: 3 900 803 (1995 est.). Area: 28 454 sq. km (10 986 sq. miles).

oyster ('ɔɪstə) NOUN [1] **a** any edible marine bivalve mollusc of the genus *Ostrea*, having a rough irregularly shaped shell and occurring on the sea bed, mostly in coastal waters. **b** (*as modifier*): *oyster farm*; *oyster knife*. [2] any of various similar and related molluscs, such as the pearl oyster and the **saddle oyster** (*Anomia ephippium*). [3] the oyster-shaped piece of dark meat in the hollow of the pelvic bone of a fowl. [4] something from which advantage, delight, profit, etc., may be derived: *the world is his oyster*. [5] *Informal* a very uncommunicative person. ◆ VERB [6] (*intr*) to dredge for, gather, or raise oysters.
▷HISTORY C14 *oistre*, from Old French *uistre*, from Latin *ostrea*, from Greek *ostreon*; related to Greek *osteon* bone, *ostrakon* shell

oyster bed NOUN a place, esp. on the sea bed, where oysters breed and grow naturally or are cultivated for food or pearls. Also called: **oyster bank, oyster park**.

oystercatcher ('ɔɪstəˌkætʃə) NOUN any shore bird of the genus *Haematopus* and family *Haematopodidae*, having a black or black-and-white plumage and a long stout laterally compressed red bill.

oyster crab NOUN any of several small soft-bodied crabs of the genus *Pinnotheres*, esp. *P. ostreum*, that live as commensals in the mantles of oysters.

oysterman ('ɔɪstəmən) NOUN, *plural* **-men**. *Chiefly US* [1] a person who gathers, cultivates, or sells oysters. [2] a boat used in gathering oysters.

oyster mushroom NOUN an edible fungus, *Pleurotus ostreatus*, having an oyster-shaped cap, commonly found growing in clusters on the trunks of broad-leaved trees.

oyster pink NOUN **a** a delicate pinkish-white colour, sometimes with a greyish tinge. **b** (*as adjective*): *oyster-pink shoes*.

oyster plant NOUN another name for **salsify** (sense 1) and **sea lungwort** (see **lungwort** (sense 2)).

oyster white NOUN **a** a greyish-white colour. **b** (*as adjective*): *oyster-white walls*.

oz *or* **oz.** ABBREVIATION FOR ounce.
▷HISTORY from Italian *onza*

Oz (ɒz) NOUN *Austral, slang* Australia.

Ozalid ('ɒzəlɪd) NOUN [1] *Trademark* a method of duplicating typematter, illustrations, etc., when printed on translucent paper. It is used for proofing. [2] a reproduction produced by this method.
▷HISTORY C20: formed by reversing DIAZO and inserting *l*

Ozark Plateau ('əuzɑːk) NOUN *or* **Ozark Mountains** *or* **Ozarks** PLURAL NOUN an eroded plateau in S Missouri, N Arkansas, and NE Oklahoma. Area: about 130 000 sq. km (50 000 sq. miles).

ozocerite *or* **ozokerite** (əu'zəukəˌraɪt) NOUN a brown or greyish wax that occurs associated with petroleum and is used for making candles and wax paper. Also called: **earth wax, mineral wax**.
▷HISTORY C19: from German *Ozokerit*, from Greek *ozein* to smell + *kēros* beeswax

ozone ('əuzəun, əu'zəun) NOUN [1] a colourless gas with a chlorine-like odour, formed by an electric discharge in oxygen: a strong oxidizing agent, used in bleaching, sterilizing water, purifying air, etc. Formula: O_3; density: 2.14 kg/m^3; melting pt.: –192°C; boiling pt.: –110.51°C. Technical name: **trioxygen**. [2] *Informal* clean bracing air, as found at the seaside.
▷HISTORY C19: from German *Ozon*, from Greek: smell
▸**ozonic** (əu'zɒnɪk) *or* **'ozonous** ADJECTIVE

ozone-friendly ADJECTIVE not harmful to the ozone layer; using substances that do not produce gases harmful to the ozone layer: *an ozone-friendly refrigerator*.

ozone layer NOUN the region of the stratosphere with the highest concentration of ozone molecules, which by absorbing high-energy solar ultraviolet radiation protects organisms on earth. Also called: **ozonosphere**.

ozonide (əu'zəunaɪd) NOUN any of a class of unstable explosive compounds produced by the addition of ozone to a double bond in an organic compound.

ozoniferous (ˌəuzəu'nɪfərəs) ADJECTIVE containing ozone.

ozonize *or* **ozonise** ('əuzəuˌnaɪz) VERB (*tr*) [1] to convert (oxygen) into ozone. [2] to treat (a substance) with ozone.
▸ˌ**ozoni'zation** *or* ˌ**ozoni'sation** NOUN ▸**'ozoˌnizer** *or* **'ozoˌniser** NOUN

ozonolysis (ˌəuzəu'nɒlɪsɪs) NOUN *Chem* the process of treating an organic compound with ozone to form an ozonide: used to locate double bonds in molecules.

ozonosphere (əu'zəunəˌsfɪə, -'zɒnə-) NOUN another name for **ozone layer**.

ozs *or* **ozs.** ABBREVIATION FOR ounces.

ozzie ('ɒzɪ) NOUN *Northern English informal* a hospital.

Pp

p *or* **P** (piː) NOUN, *plural* **p's, P's** *or* **Ps.** [1] the 16th letter and 12th consonant of the modern English alphabet. [2] a speech sound represented by this letter, usually a voiceless bilabial stop, as in *pig.* [3] **mind one's p's and q's.** to be careful to behave correctly and use polite or suitable language.

p SYMBOL FOR: [1] (in Britain) penny *or* pence. [2] *Music* piano: an instruction to play quietly. [3] pico-. [4] *Physics* **a** momentum. **b** proton. **c** pressure.

P SYMBOL FOR: [1] *Chem* phosphorus. [2] *Physics* **a** pressure. **b** power. **c** parity. **d** poise. [3] (on road signs) parking. [4] *Chess* pawn. [5] *Currency* **a** (the former) peseta. **b** peso. **c** pataca. **d** pula. ◆ ABBREVIATION FOR: [6] pharmacy only: used to label medicines that can be obtained without a prescription, but only at a shop at which there is a pharmacist. ◆ [7] INTERNATIONAL CAR REGISTRATION FOR Portugal.

p. ABBREVIATION FOR: [1] (*plural* **pp**) page. [2] part. [3] participle. [4] past. [5] per. [6] post. [Latin: after] [7] pro.
▷HISTORY Latin: in favour of; for

p- PREFIX short for **para-**[1] (sense 6).

P45 NOUN (in Britain) [1] a severance form issued by the Inland Revenue via an employer to a person leaving employment. [2] **get one's P45.** *Informal* to be dismissed from one's employment.

pa[1] (pɑː) NOUN an informal word for **father.**

pa[2] *or* **pah** (pɑː) NOUN *NZ* [1] a Maori village or settlement. [2] *History* a Maori defensive position and settlement on a hilltop. [3] **go back to the pa.** to abandon city life in favour of rural life.
▷HISTORY Maori

pa[3] THE INTERNET DOMAIN NAME FOR Panama.

Pa [1] THE CHEMICAL SYMBOL FOR protactinium. ◆ [2] SYMBOL FOR pascal.

PA ABBREVIATION FOR: [1] Pennsylvania. [2] personal appearance. [3] personal assistant. [4] *Military* Post Adjutant. [5] **power of attorney.** [6] press agent. [7] Press Association. [8] *Banking* private account. [9] public-address system. [10] publicity agent. [11] Publishers Association. [12] purchasing agent. [13] *Insurance* **particular average.** [14] (in New Zealand) **probationary assistant.** ◆ [15] INTERNATIONAL CAR REGISTRATION FOR Panama.

Pa. ABBREVIATION FOR Pennsylvania.

p.a. ABBREVIATION FOR per annum.
▷HISTORY Latin: yearly

paal (pɑːl) NOUN *Caribbean* a stake driven into the ground.
▷HISTORY from Dutch: a pile, stake

pa'anga (pɑːˈɑːŋgə) NOUN the standard monetary unit of Tonga, divided into 100 seniti.

PABA (ˈpɑːbə) NOUN ACRONYM FOR para-aminobenzoic acid.

Pablum (ˈpɑːbləm) NOUN *Trademark* a cereal food for infants, developed in Canada.

pabulum (ˈpæbjʊləm) NOUN *Rare* [1] food. [2] food for thought, esp when bland or dull.
▷HISTORY C17: from Latin, from *pascere* to feed

PABX (in Britain) ABBREVIATION FOR **private automatic branch exchange.** See also **PBX.**

PAC ABBREVIATION FOR Pan-Africanist Congress.

Pac. ABBREVIATION FOR Pacific.

paca (ˈpɑːkə, ˈpækə) NOUN a large burrowing hystricomorph rodent, *Cuniculus paca,* of Central and South America, having white-spotted brown fur and a large head: family *Dasyproctidae.*
▷HISTORY C17: from Spanish, from Tupi

pace[1] (peɪs) NOUN [1] **a** a single step in walking. **b** the distance covered by a step. [2] a measure of length equal to the average length of a stride, approximately 3 feet. See also **Roman pace, geometric pace, military pace.** [3] speed of movement, esp of walking or running. [4] rate or style of proceeding at some activity: *to live at a fast pace.* [5] manner or action of stepping, walking, etc.; gait. [6] any of the manners in which a horse or other quadruped walks or runs, the three principal paces being the walk, trot, and canter (or gallop). [7] a manner of moving, natural to the camel and sometimes developed in the horse, in which the two legs on the same side of the body are moved and put down at the same time. [8] *Architect* a step or small raised platform. [9] **keep pace with.** to proceed at the same speed as. [10] **put (someone) through his paces.** to test the ability of (someone). [11] **set the pace.** to determine the rate at which a group runs or walks or proceeds at some other activity. [12] **stand** *or* **stay the pace.** to keep up with the speed or rate of others. ◆ VERB [13] (*tr*) to set or determine the pace for, as in a race. [14] (often foll by *about, up and down,* etc.) to walk with regular slow or fast paces, as in boredom, agitation, etc.: *to pace the room.* [15] (*tr; often foll by out*) to measure by paces: *to pace out the distance.* [16] (*intr*) to walk with slow regular strides: *to pace along the street.* [17] (*intr*) (of a horse) to move at the pace (the specially developed gait).
▷HISTORY C13: via Old French from Latin *passūs* step, from *pandere* to spread, unfold, extend (the legs as in walking)

pace[2] *Latin* (ˈpeɪsɪ; *English* ˈpɑːkɛ) PREPOSITION with due deference to: used to acknowledge politely someone who disagrees with the speaker or writer.
▷HISTORY C19: from Latin, from *pāx* peace

PACE (peɪs) NOUN (in England and Wales) ACRONYM FOR Police and Criminal Evidence Act.

pace bowler NOUN *Cricket* a bowler who characteristically delivers the ball rapidly.

pacemaker (ˈpeɪsˌmeɪkə) NOUN [1] a person, horse, vehicle, etc., used in a race or speed trial to set the pace. [2] a person, an organization, etc., regarded as being the leader in a particular field of activity. [3] Also called: **cardiac pacemaker.** a small area of specialized tissue within the wall of the right atrium of the heart whose spontaneous electrical activity initiates and controls the beat of the heart. [4] Also called: **artificial pacemaker.** an electronic device for use in certain cases of heart disease to assume the functions of the natural cardiac pacemaker.

pacer (ˈpeɪsə) NOUN [1] a horse trained to move at a special gait, esp for racing. [2] another word for **pacemaker** (sense 1).

pacesetter (ˈpeɪsˌsetə) NOUN another word for **pacemaker** (senses 1, 2).

paceway (ˈpeɪsˌweɪ) NOUN *Austral* a racecourse for trotting and pacing.

pacey *or* **pacy** (ˈpeɪsɪ) ADJECTIVE **pacier, paciest.** fast-moving, quick, lively: *a pacey story.*

pacha (ˈpɑːʃə, ˈpæʃə) NOUN a variant spelling of **pasha.**

pachalic (ˈpɑːʃəlɪk) NOUN a variant spelling of **pashalik.**

pachinko (pəˈtʃɪŋkəʊ) NOUN a Japanese game similar to pinball.
▷HISTORY C20: possibly from Japanese *pachin,* imitative of the sound of a ball being fired by a trigger

pachisi (pəˈtʃiːzɪ, pɑː-) NOUN an Indian game somewhat resembling backgammon, played on a cruciform board using six cowries as dice.
▷HISTORY C18: from Hindi *pacīsī,* from *pacīs* twenty-five (the highest score possible in one throw)

pachouli (ˈpætʃʊlɪ, pəˈtʃuːlɪ) NOUN a variant spelling of **patchouli.**

Pachuca (*Spanish* paˈtʃuka) NOUN a city in central Mexico, capital of Hidalgo state, in the Sierra Madre Oriental: silver mines; university (1961). Pop.: 231 089 (2000 est.).

Pachuco (pəˈtʃuːkəʊ) NOUN, *plural* **-cos.** *US* a young Mexican living in the US, esp one of low social status who belongs to a street gang.
▷HISTORY C20: from Mexican Spanish

pachyderm (ˈpækɪˌdɜːm) NOUN any very large thick-skinned mammal, such as an elephant, rhinoceros, or hippopotamus.
▷HISTORY C19: from French *pachyderme,* from Greek *pakhudermos* thick-skinned, from *pakhus* thick + *derma* skin
▸ˌ**pachy'dermatous** ADJECTIVE

pachymeningitis (ˌpækɪˌmɛnɪnˈdʒaɪtɪs) NOUN *Pathol* inflammation of the dura mater of the brain and spinal cord.

pachytene (ˈpækɪˌtiːn) NOUN the third stage of the prophase of meiosis during which the chromosomes become shorter and thicker and divide into chromatids.
▷HISTORY from Greek *pakhus* thick + *tainia* band

pacific (pəˈsɪfɪk) ADJECTIVE [1] tending or conducive to peace; conciliatory. [2] not aggressive; opposed to the use of force. [3] free from conflict; peaceful.
▷HISTORY C16: from Old French *pacifique,* from Latin *pācificus,* from *pāx* peace + *facere* to make
▸**pa'cifically** ADVERB

Pacific (pəˈsɪfɪk) NOUN [1] **the.** short for **Pacific Ocean.** ◆ ADJECTIVE [2] of or relating to the Pacific Ocean or its islands.

pacification (ˌpæsɪfɪˈkeɪʃən) NOUN the act, process, or policy of pacifying.
▸ˈ**pacifiˌcatory** ADJECTIVE

Pacific Islands PLURAL NOUN a former Trust Territory; an island group in the W Pacific Ocean, mandated to Japan after World War I and assigned to the US by the United Nations in 1947: comprised 2141 islands (96 inhabited) of the Caroline, Marshall, and Mariana groups (excluding Guam). In 1978 the Northern Marianas became a commonwealth in union with the US. The three remaining entities consisting of the Marshall Islands, the Republic of Belau (formerly Palau), and the Federated States of Micronesia became self-governing during the period 1979–80. In 1982 they signed agreements of free association with the US. Administrative centre: Saipan (Mariana Islands). Land area: about 1800 sq. km (700 sq. miles), scattered over about 7 500 000 sq. km (3 000 000 sq. miles) of ocean.

Pacific Northwest NOUN the region of North America lying north of the Columbia River and west of the Rockies.

Pacific Ocean NOUN the world's largest and deepest ocean, lying between Asia and Australia and North and South America: almost landlocked in the north, linked with the Arctic Ocean only by the Bering Strait, and extending to Antarctica in the south; has exceptionally deep trenches, and a large number of volcanic and coral islands. Area: about 165 760 000 sq. km (64 000 000 sq. miles). Average depth: 4215 m (14 050 ft.). Greatest depth: Challenger Deep (in the Marianas Trench), 11 033 m (37 073 ft.). Greatest width: (between Panama and Mindanao, Philippines) 17 066 km (10 600 miles).

Pacific rim NOUN the regions, countries, etc., that lie on the western shores of the Pacific Ocean, esp in the context of their developing manufacturing capacity and consumer markets.

Pacific Rose NOUN a large variety of eating apple from New Zealand, with sweet flesh.

Pacific Standard Time NOUN one of the standard times used in North America, based on the local time of the 120° meridian, eight hours behind Greenwich Mean Time. Abbreviation: **PST.**

pacifier (ˈpæsɪˌfaɪə) NOUN [1] a person or thing that pacifies. [2] *US and Canadian* a baby's dummy or teething ring.

pacifism (ˈpæsɪˌfɪzəm) NOUN [1] the belief that violence of any kind is unjustifiable and that one should not participate in war. [2] the belief that international disputes can be settled by arbitration rather than war.

pacifist ('pæsɪfɪst) NOUN 1 a person who supports pacifism. 2 a person who refuses military service. ◆ ADJECTIVE 3 advocating, relating to, or characterized by pacifism.

pacify ('pæsɪˌfaɪ) VERB **-fies, -fying, -fied.** (*tr*) 1 to calm the anger or agitation of; mollify. 2 to restore to peace or order, esp by the threat or use of force.
▷HISTORY C15: from Old French *pacifier;* see PACIFIC
▸ **'paciˌfiable** ADJECTIVE

pack[1] (pæk) NOUN 1 **a** a bundle or load, esp one carried on the back. **b** (*as modifier*): *a pack animal.* 2 a collected amount of anything. 3 a complete set of similar things, esp a set of 52 playing cards. 4 a group of animals of the same kind, esp hunting animals: *a pack of hounds.* 5 any group or band that associates together, esp for criminal purposes. 6 *Rugby* the forwards of a team or both teams collectively, as in a scrum or in rucking. 7 the basic organizational unit of Cub Scouts and Brownie Guides. 8 **a** a small package, carton, or container, used to retail commodities, esp foodstuffs, cigarettes, etc. **b** (*in combination*): *pack-sealed.* 9 a US and Canadian word for **packet** (sense 1). 10 short for **pack ice.** 11 the quantity of something, such as food, packaged for preservation. 12 *Med* **a** a sheet or blanket, either damp or dry, for wrapping about the body, esp for its soothing effect. **b** a material such as cotton or gauze for temporarily filling a bodily cavity, esp to control bleeding. 13 short for **backpack** or **rucksack.** 14 *Mining* a roof support, esp one made of rubble. 15 short for **face pack.** 16 a parachute folded and ready for use. 17 *Computing* another name for **deck** (sense 5). 18 **go to the pack.** *Austral and NZ, informal* to fall into a lower state or condition. ◆ VERB 19 to place or arrange (articles) in (a container), such as clothes in a suitcase. 20 (*tr*) to roll up into a bundle. 21 (when *passive,* often foll by *out*) to press tightly together; cram: *the audience packed into the foyer; the hall was packed out.* 22 (*tr;* foll by *in* or *into*) to fit (many things, experiences, etc.) into a limited space or time: *she packed a lot of theatre visits into her holiday.* 23 to form (snow, ice, etc.) into a hard compact mass or (of snow, ice, etc.) to become compacted. 24 (*tr*) to press in or cover tightly: *to pack a hole with cement.* 25 (*tr*) to load (a horse, donkey, etc.) with a burden. 26 (often foll by *off* or *away*) to send away or go away, esp hastily. 27 (*tr*) to seal (a joint) by inserting a layer of compressible material between the faces. 28 (*tr*) to fill (a bearing or gland) with grease to lubricate it. 29 (*tr*) to separate (two adjoining components) so that they have a predetermined gap between them, by introducing shims, washers, plates, etc. 30 (*tr*) *Med* to treat with a pack. 31 (*tr*) *Slang* to be capable of inflicting (a blow): *he packs a mean punch.* 32 (*tr*) *US, informal* to carry or wear habitually: *he packs a gun.* 33 (*intr;* often foll by *down*) *Rugby* to form a scrum. 34 (*tr;* often foll by *into, to,* etc.) *US, Canadian, and NZ* to carry (goods), esp on the back: *will you pack your camping equipment into the mountains?* 35 **pack one's bags.** *Informal* to get ready to leave. 36 **send packing.** *Informal* to dismiss peremptorily. ◆ See also **pack in, pack up.**
▷HISTORY C13: related to Middle Low German *pak,* of obscure origin
▸ **'packable** ADJECTIVE

pack[2] (pæk) VERB (*tr*) to fill (a legislative body, committee, etc.) with one's own supporters: *to pack a jury.*
▷HISTORY C16: perhaps changed from PACT

package ('pækɪdʒ) NOUN 1 any wrapped or boxed object or group of objects. 2 **a** a proposition, offer, or thing for sale in which separate items are offered together as a single or inclusive unit. **b** (*as modifier*): *a package holiday; a package deal.* 3 a complete unit consisting of a number of component parts sold separately. 4 the act or process of packing or packaging. 5 *Computing* a set of programs designed for a specific type of problem in statistics, production control, etc., making it unnecessary for a separate program to be written for each problem. 6 a US and Canadian word for **packet**[1]. ◆ VERB (*tr*) 7 to wrap in or put into a package. 8 to design and produce a package for (retail goods). 9 to group (separate items) together as a single unit. 10 to compile (complete books) for a publisher to market.

packager ('pækɪdʒə) NOUN an independent firm specializing in design and production, as of illustrated books or television programmes which are sold to publishers or television companies as finished products.

package store NOUN *US* a store where alcoholic drinks are sold for consumption elsewhere. Canadian name (also sometimes used in the US): **liquor store.** Brit equivalent: **off-licence.**

packaging ('pækɪdʒɪŋ) NOUN 1 **a** the box or wrapping in which a product is offered for sale. **b** the design of such a box or wrapping, esp with reference to its ability to attract customers. 2 the presentation of a person, product, television programme, etc., to the public in a way designed to build up a favourable image. 3 the work of a packager.

pack animal NOUN an animal, such as a donkey, used to transport goods, equipment, etc.

pack drill NOUN a military punishment by which the offender is made to march about carrying a full pack of equipment.

packed (pækt) ADJECTIVE 1 completely filled; full: *a packed theatre.* 2 (of a picnic type of meal) prepared and put in a container or containers beforehand; prepacked: *a packed lunch.*

packer ('pækə) NOUN 1 a person or company whose business is to pack goods, esp food: *a meat packer.* 2 a person or machine that packs.

packet ('pækɪt) NOUN 1 a small or medium-sized container of cardboard, paper, etc., often together with its contents: *a packet of biscuits.* Usual US and Canadian word: **package, pack.** 2 a small package; parcel. 3 Also called: **packet boat.** a boat that transports mail, passengers, goods, etc., on a fixed short route. 4 *Slang* a large sum of money: *to cost a packet.* 5 *Computing* a unit into which a larger piece of data is broken down for more efficient transmission. See also **packet switching.** ◆ VERB 6 (*tr*) to wrap up in a packet or as a packet.
▷HISTORY C16: from Old French *pacquet,* from *pacquer* to pack, from Old Dutch *pak* a pack

packet switching NOUN *Computing* the concentration of data into units that are allocated an address prior to transmission.

packframe ('pækˌfreɪm) NOUN *Mountaineering* a light metal frame with shoulder straps, used for carrying heavy or awkward loads.

packhorse ('pækˌhɔːs) NOUN a horse used to transport goods, equipment, etc.

pack ice NOUN a large area of floating ice, usually occurring in polar seas, consisting of separate pieces that have become massed together. Also called: **ice pack.**

pack in VERB (*tr, adverb*) 1 *Brit and NZ, informal* to stop doing (something) (esp in the phrase **pack it in**). 2 to carry (something) to base camp, etc. by pack.

packing ('pækɪŋ) NOUN 1 **a** material used to cushion packed goods. **b** (*as modifier*): *a packing needle.* 2 the packaging of foodstuffs. 3 *Med* **a** the application of a medical pack. **b** gauze or other absorbent material for packing a wound. 4 *Printing* sheets of material, esp paper, used to cover the platen or impression cylinder of a letterpress machine. 5 any substance or material used to make watertight or gastight joints, esp in a stuffing box. 6 *Engineering* pieces of material of various thicknesses used to adjust the position of a component or machine before it is secured in its correct position or alignment.

packing box NOUN another name for **stuffing box.**

packing density NOUN *Computing* a measure of the amount of data that can be held by unit length of a storage medium, such as magnetic tape.

packing fraction NOUN a measure of the stability of a nucleus, equal to the difference between its mass in amu and its mass number, divided by the mass number.

pack of lies NOUN a completely false story, account, etc.

pack rat NOUN any rat of the genus *Neotoma,* of W North America, having a long tail that is furry in some species: family *Cricetidae.* Also called: **wood rat.**

packsack ('pækˌsæk) NOUN a US and Canadian word for **knapsack.**

packsaddle ('pækˌsædᵊl) NOUN a saddle hung with packs, equipment, etc., used on a pack animal.

pack shot NOUN (in television advertising) a close-up of the product being advertised, usually so that the viewer can register its logo and packaging.

packthread ('pækˌθrɛd) NOUN a strong twine for sewing or tying up packages.

pack up VERB (*adverb*) 1 to put (things) away in a proper or suitable place. 2 *Informal* to give up (an attempt) or stop doing (something): *if you don't do your work better, you might as well pack up.* 3 (*intr*) (of an engine, machine, etc.) to fail to operate; break down. 4 *Engineering* to use packing to adjust the height of a component or machine before it is secured in its correct position or alignment.

pact (pækt) NOUN an agreement or compact between two or more parties, nations, etc., for mutual advantage.
▷HISTORY C15: from Old French *pacte,* from Latin *pactum,* from *pacīscī* to agree

pacy ('peɪsɪ) ADJECTIVE a variant spelling of **pacey.**

pad[1] (pæd) NOUN 1 a thick piece of soft material used to make something comfortable, give it shape, or protect it. 2 a guard made of flexible resilient material worn in various sports to protect parts of the body. 3 Also called: **stamp pad, ink pad.** a block of firm absorbent material soaked with ink for transferring to a rubber stamp. 4 Also called: **notepad, writing pad.** a number of sheets of paper fastened together along one edge. 5 a flat piece of stiff material used to back a piece of blotting paper. 6 **a** the fleshy cushion-like underpart of the foot of a cat, dog, etc. **b** any of the parts constituting such a structure. 7 any of various level surfaces or flat-topped structures, such as a launch pad. 8 *Entomol* a nontechnical name for **pulvillus.** 9 the large flat floating leaf of the water lily. 10 *Electronics* a resistive attenuator network inserted in the path of a signal to reduce amplitude or to match one circuit to another. 11 *Slang* a person's residence. 12 *Slang* a bed or bedroom. ◆ VERB **pads, padding, padded.** (*tr*) 13 to line, stuff, or fill out with soft material, esp in order to protect or give shape to. 14 (often foll by *out*) to inflate with irrelevant or false information: *to pad out a story.*
▷HISTORY C16: origin uncertain; compare Low German *pad* sole of the foot

pad[2] (pæd) VERB **pads, padding, padded.** 1 (*intr;* often foll by *along, up,* etc.) to walk with a soft or muffled tread. 2 (when *intr,* often foll by *around*) to travel (a route) on foot, esp at a slow pace; tramp: *to pad around the country.* ◆ NOUN 3 a dull soft sound, esp of footsteps. 4 *Archaic* short for **footpad.** 5 *Archaic or dialect* a slow-paced horse; nag. 6 *Austral* a path or track: *a cattle pad.*
▷HISTORY C16: perhaps from Middle Dutch *paden,* from *pad* PATH

padang ('pædæŋ) NOUN (in Malaysia) a playing field.
▷HISTORY from Malay: plain

Padang ('pɑːdɑːŋ) NOUN a port in W Indonesia, in W Sumatra at the foot of the **Padang Highlands** on the Indian Ocean. Pop.: 721 500 (1995 est.).

padauk *or* **padouk** (pə'daʊk, -'dɔːk) NOUN 1 any of various tropical African or Asian leguminous trees of the genus *Pterocarpus* that have reddish wood. 2 the wood of any of these trees, used in decorative cabinetwork. ◆ See also **amboyna.**
▷HISTORY from a native Burmese word

padded cell NOUN a room, esp one in a mental hospital, with padded surfaces in which violent inmates are placed.

padding ('pædɪŋ) NOUN 1 any soft material used to pad clothes, furniture, etc. 2 superfluous material put into a speech or written work to pad it out; waffle. 3 inflated or false entries in a financial account, esp an expense account.

paddle[1] ('pædᵊl) NOUN 1 a short light oar with a flat blade at one or both ends, used without a rowlock to propel a canoe or small boat. 2 Also called: **float.** a blade of a water wheel or paddle wheel. 3 a period of paddling: *to go for a paddle upstream.* 4 **a** a paddle wheel used to propel a boat. **b** (*as modifier*): *a paddle steamer.* 5 the sliding panel in a lock or sluicegate that regulates the level or flow of water. 6 any of various instruments shaped like a paddle and used for beating, mixing, etc. 7 a table-tennis bat. 8 the flattened limb of a seal, turtle, or similar aquatic animal, specialized for swimming. ◆ VERB 9 to propel (a canoe, small boat, etc.) with a paddle. 10 **paddle one's own canoe. a** to

be self-sufficient. **b** to mind one's own business. 11 (*tr*) to convey by paddling: *we paddled him to the shore.* 12 (*tr*) to stir or mix with or as if with a paddle. 13 to row (a boat) steadily, esp (of a racing crew) to row firmly but not at full pressure. 14 (*intr*) (of steamships) to be propelled by paddle wheels. 15 (*intr*) to swim with short rapid strokes, like a dog. 16 (*tr*) *US and Canadian, informal* to spank.
▷HISTORY C15: of unknown origin
▶'**paddler** NOUN

paddle[2] ('pædᵊl) VERB (*mainly intr*) 1 to walk or play barefoot in shallow water, mud, etc. 2 to dabble the fingers, hands, or feet in water. 3 to walk unsteadily, like a baby. 4 (*tr*) *Archaic* to fondle with the fingers. ◆ NOUN 5 the act of paddling in water.
▷HISTORY C16: of uncertain origin
▶'**paddler** NOUN

paddlefish ('pædᵊl,fɪʃ) NOUN, *plural* **-fish** *or* **-fishes.** 1 a primitive bony fish, *Polyodon spathula,* of the Mississippi River, having a long paddle-like projection to the snout: family *Polyodontidae.* 2 a similar and related Chinese fish, *Psephurus gladius,* of the Yangtze River.

paddle wheel NOUN a large wheel fitted with paddles, turned by an engine to propel a vessel on the water.

paddle worm NOUN any of a family of green-blue faintly iridescent active marine polychaete worms of the genus *Phyllodoce,* having paddle-shaped swimming lobes, found under stones on the shore.

paddock[1] ('pædək) NOUN 1 a small enclosed field, often for grazing or training horses, usually near a house or stable. 2 (in horse racing) the enclosure in which horses are paraded and mounted before a race, together with the accompanying rooms. 3 (in motor racing) an area near the pits where cars are worked on before races. 4 *Austral and NZ* any area of fenced land. 5 *Austral and NZ* a playing field. 6 **the long paddock.** *Austral, informal* a stockroute or roadside area offering feed to sheep and cattle in dry times. ◆ VERB 7 (*tr*) to confine (horses, etc.) in a paddock.
▷HISTORY C17: variant of dialect *parrock,* from Old English *pearruc* enclosure, of Germanic origin. See PARK

paddock[2] ('pædək) NOUN *Archaic or dialect* a frog or toad. Also called (Scot): **puddock.**
▷HISTORY C12: from *pad* toad, probably from Old Norse *padda;* see -OCK

paddock-basher NOUN *Austral, slang* a vehicle suited to driving on rough terrain.

paddy[1] ('pædɪ) NOUN, *plural* **-dies.** 1 Also called: **paddy field.** a field planted with rice. 2 rice as a growing crop or when harvested but not yet milled.
▷HISTORY from Malay *pādī*

paddy[2] ('pædɪ) NOUN, *plural* **-dies.** *Brit, informal* a fit of temper.
▷HISTORY C19: from PADDY

Paddy ('pædɪ) NOUN, *plural* **-dies.** (*sometimes not capital*) an informal, often derogatory, name for an Irishman.
▷HISTORY from *Patrick*

paddy-last NOUN *Irish* the last person in a race or competition: *she was paddy-last.*

paddymelon ('pædɪ,mɛlən) NOUN 1 *Austral* a South African cucurbitaceous vine, *Cucumis myriocarpus,* widely naturalized in Australia. 2 *Austral* the melon-like fruit of this plant. 3 *Austral* a variant spelling of **pademelon.**
▷HISTORY C19: of uncertain origin

paddy wagon NOUN *US, Austral, and NZ* an informal word for **patrol wagon.**

paddywhack *or* **paddywack** ('pædɪ,wæk) NOUN *Informal* 1 *Brit* another word for **paddy**[2]. 2 a spanking or smack.

pademelon *or* **paddymelon** ('pædɪ,mɛlən) NOUN a small wallaby of the genus *Thylogale,* of coastal scrubby regions of Australia.
▷HISTORY C19: from a native Australian name

Paderborn (*German* pa:dər'bɔrn) NOUN a market town in NW Germany, in North Rhine-Westphalia: scene of the meeting between Charlemagne and Pope Leo III (799 A.D.) that led to the foundation of the Holy Roman Empire. Pop.: 131 851 (1999 est.).

Padishah ('pɑ:dɪ,ʃɑ:) NOUN a title of the shah of Iran.
▷HISTORY from Persian *pādi* lord + SHAH

padkos ('pad,kɒs) PLURAL NOUN *South African* snacks and provisions for a journey.
▷HISTORY Afrikaans, literally: road food

padlock ('pæd,lɒk) NOUN 1 a detachable lock having a hinged or sliding shackle, which can be used to secure a door, lid, etc., by passing the shackle through rings or staples. ◆ VERB 2 (*tr*) to fasten with or as if with a padlock.
▷HISTORY C15 *pad,* of obscure origin

Padma Shri ('pʌdmə 'ʃri:) NOUN (in India) an award for distinguished service in any field.
▷HISTORY Hindi: lotus decoration

padouk (pə'daʊk, -'dɔ:k) NOUN a variant spelling of **padauk.**

Padova ('pa:dova) NOUN the Italian name for **Padua.**

padre ('pɑ:drɪ) NOUN *Informal* (*sometimes capital*) 1 father: used to address or refer to a clergyman, esp a priest. 2 a chaplain to the armed forces.
▷HISTORY via Spanish or Italian from Latin *pater* father

padrone (pə'drəʊnɪ) NOUN, *plural* **-nes** *or* **-ni** (-ni:). 1 the owner or proprietor of an inn, esp in Italy. 2 *US* an employer who completely controls his workers, esp a man who exploits Italian immigrants in the US.
▷HISTORY C17: from Italian; see PATRON[1]

padsaw ('pæd,sɔ:) NOUN a small narrow saw used for cutting curves.
▷HISTORY C19: from PAD[1] (in the sense: a handle that can be fitted to various tools) + SAW[1]

Padua ('pædʒʊə, 'pædjʊə) NOUN a city in NE Italy, in Veneto: important in Roman and Renaissance times; university (1222); botanical garden (1545). Pop.: 211 391 (2000 est.). Latin name: **Patavium** (pə'teɪvɪəm). Italian name: **Padova.**

paduasoy ('pædjʊə,sɔɪ) NOUN 1 a rich strong silk fabric used for hangings, vestments, etc. 2 a garment made of this.
▷HISTORY C17: changed (through influence of PADUA) from earlier *poudesoy,* from French *pou-de-soie,* of obscure origin

Padus ('peɪdəs) NOUN the Latin name for the **Po**[2].

paean *or sometimes US* **pean** ('pi:ən) NOUN 1 a hymn sung in ancient Greece in invocation of or thanksgiving to a deity. 2 any song of praise. 3 enthusiastic praise: *the film received a paean from the critics.*
▷HISTORY C16: via Latin from Greek *paiān* hymn to Apollo, from his title *Paiān,* denoting the physician of the gods

paederast ('pɛdə,ræst) NOUN a less common spelling of **pederast.**
▶,**paeder'astic** ADJECTIVE ▶'**paeder,asty** NOUN

paediatrician *or chiefly US* **pediatrician** (,pi:dɪə'trɪʃən) NOUN a medical practitioner who specializes in paediatrics.

paediatrics *or chiefly US* **pediatrics** (,pi:dɪ'ætrɪks) NOUN (*functioning as singular*) the branch of medical science concerned with children and their diseases.
▶,**paedi'atric** *or* (*chiefly US*) ,**pedi'atric** ADJECTIVE

paedo-, *or before a vowel* **paed-,** *esp US* **pedo-, ped-** COMBINING FORM indicating a child or children: *paedology.*
▷HISTORY from Greek *pais, paid-* child

paedogenesis (,pi:dəʊ'dʒɛnɪsɪs) NOUN sexual reproduction in an animal that retains its larval features. See also **neoteny.**
▶**paedogenetic** (,pi:dəʊdʒə'nɛtɪk) *or* ,**paedo'genic** ADJECTIVE

paedology *or US* **pedology** (pi:'dɒlədʒɪ) NOUN the study of the character, growth, and development of children.
▶**paedological** *or US* **pedological** (,pi:dᵊ'lɒdʒɪkᵊl) ADJECTIVE ▶**pae'dologist** *or US* **pe'dologist** NOUN

paedomorphosis (,pi:də'mɔ:fəsɪs) NOUN the resemblance of adult animals to the young of their ancestors: seen in the evolution of modern man, who shows resemblances to the young stages of australopithecines.

paedophile *or esp US* **pedophile** ('pi:dəʊ,faɪl) NOUN a person who is sexually attracted to children.

paedophilia *or esp US* **pedophilia** (,pi:dəʊ'fɪlɪə) NOUN the condition of being sexually attracted to children.
▶**paedo'phili,ac** *or* ,**paedo'phili,ac** *or* (*esp US*) ,**pedo'phili,ac** NOUN, ADJECTIVE

paella (paɪ'ɛlə; *Spanish* pa'eʎa) NOUN, *plural* **-las** (-ləz; *Spanish* -ʎas). 1 a Spanish dish made from rice, shellfish, chicken, and vegetables. 2 the large flat frying pan in which a paella is cooked.
▷HISTORY from Catalan, from Old French *paelle,* from Latin *patella* small pan

paeon ('pi:ən) NOUN *Prosody* a metrical foot of four syllables, with one long one and three short ones in any order.
▷HISTORY C17: via Latin *paeon* from Greek *paiōn;* variant of PAEAN
▶**pae'onic** ADJECTIVE

paeony ('pi:ənɪ) NOUN, *plural* **-nies.** a variant spelling of **peony.**

Paestum ('pɛstəm) NOUN an ancient Greek colony on the coast of Lucania in S Italy.

PAGAD ABBREVIATION FOR *South African* People Against Gangsterism and Drugs, a popular organization formed in the Western Cape around 1995.

pagan ('peɪgən) NOUN 1 a member of a group professing a polytheistic religion or any religion other than Christianity, Judaism, or Islam. 2 a person without any religion; heathen. ◆ ADJECTIVE 3 of or relating to pagans or their faith or worship. 4 heathen; irreligious.
▷HISTORY C14: from Church Latin *pāgānus* civilian (hence, not a soldier of Christ), from Latin: countryman, villager, from *pāgus* village
▶'**pagandom** NOUN ▶'**paganish** ADJECTIVE ▶'**paganism** NOUN ▶'**paganist** ADJECTIVE, NOUN ▶,**pagan'istic** ADJECTIVE ▶,**pagan'istically** ADVERB

paganize *or* **paganise** ('peɪgə,naɪz) VERB to become pagan, render pagan, or convert to paganism.
▶,**pagani'zation** *or* ,**pagani'sation** NOUN ▶'**pagan,izer** *or* '**pagan,iser** NOUN

page[1] (peɪdʒ) NOUN 1 one side of one of the leaves of a book, newspaper, letter, etc. or the written or printed matter it bears. Abbreviation: **p** (*plural* **pp**). 2 such a leaf considered as a unit: *insert a new page.* 3 a screenful of information from a website, teletext service, etc., displayed on a television monitor or visual display unit. 4 an episode, phase, or period: *a glorious page in the revolution.* 5 *Printing* the type as set up for printing a page. ◆ VERB 6 another word for **paginate.** 7 (*intr; foll by* through) to look through (a book, report, etc.); leaf through.
▷HISTORY C15: via Old French from Latin *pāgina*

page[2] (peɪdʒ) NOUN 1 a boy employed to run errands, carry messages, etc., for the guests in a hotel, club, etc. 2 a youth in attendance at official functions or ceremonies, esp weddings. 3 *Medieval history* **a** a boy in training for knighthood in personal attendance on a knight. **b** a youth in the personal service of a person of rank, esp in a royal household: *page of the chamber.* 4 (in the US) an attendant at Congress or other legislative body. 5 *Canadian* a person employed in the debating chamber of the House of Commons, the Senate, or a legislative assembly to carry messages for members. ◆ VERB (*tr*) 6 to call out the name of (a person), esp by a loudspeaker system, so as to give him a message. 7 to call (a person) by an electronic device, such as a pager. 8 to act as a page to or attend as a page.
▷HISTORY C13: via Old French from Italian *paggio,* probably from Greek *paidion* boy, from *pais* child

pageant ('pædʒənt) NOUN 1 an elaborate colourful parade or display portraying scenes from history, esp one involving rich costume. 2 any magnificent or showy display, procession, etc.
▷HISTORY C14: from Medieval Latin *pāgina* scene of a play, from Latin: PAGE[1]

pageantry ('pædʒəntrɪ) NOUN, *plural* **-ries.** 1 spectacular display or ceremony. 2 *Archaic* pageants collectively.

pageboy ('peɪdʒ,bɔɪ) NOUN 1 a smooth medium-length hairstyle with the ends of the hair curled under and a long fringe falling onto the forehead from the crown. 2 a less common word for **page²** (sense 1). 3 another word for **page²** (sense 2).

pager (ˈpeɪdʒə) NOUN a small electronic device, capable of receiving short messages; usually carried by people who need to be contacted urgently (e.g. doctors).

Paget's disease (ˈpædʒɪts) NOUN 1 Also called: **osteitis deformans.** a chronic disease of the bones characterized by inflammation and deformation. 2 Also called: **Paget's cancer.** cancer of the nipple and surrounding tissue.
▷HISTORY C19: named after Sir James *Paget* (1814–99), British surgeon and pathologist, who described these diseases

page-turner NOUN an exciting novel, such as a thriller, with a fast-moving story.

paginal (ˈpædʒɪnᵊl) ADJECTIVE 1 page-for-page: *paginal facsimile.* 2 of, like, or consisting of pages.
▷HISTORY C17: from Late Latin *pāginālis,* from Latin *pāgina* page

paginate (ˈpædʒɪˌneɪt) VERB (tr) to number the pages of (a book, manuscript, etc.) in sequence. Compare **foliate.**
▸ **ˌpagiˈnation** NOUN

pagoda (pəˈgəʊdə) NOUN an Indian or Far Eastern temple, esp a tower, usually pyramidal and having many storeys.
▷HISTORY C17: from Portuguese *pagode,* ultimately from Sanskrit *bhagavatī* divine

pagoda tree NOUN a Chinese leguminous tree, *Sophora japonica,* with ornamental white flowers and dark green foliage.

Pago Pago (ˈpɑːŋgəʊ ˈpɑːŋgəʊ) NOUN a port in American Samoa, on SE Tutuila Island. Pop.: 4000 (1990). Former name: **Pango Pango.**

pagurian (pəˈgjʊərɪən) *or* **pagurid** (pəˈgjʊərɪd, ˈpægjʊrɪd) NOUN 1 any decapod crustacean of the family *Paguridae,* which includes the hermit crabs. ◆ ADJECTIVE 2 of, relating to, or belonging to the *Paguridae.*
▷HISTORY C19: from Latin *pagurus,* from Greek *pagouros* kind of crab

pah (pɑː) INTERJECTION an exclamation of disgust, disbelief, etc.

Pahang (pəˈhʌŋ) NOUN a state of Peninsular Malaysia, on the South China Sea: the largest Malayan state; mountainous and heavily forested. Capital: Kuantan. Pop.: 1 231 176 (2000). Area: 35 964 sq. km (13 886 sq. miles).

Pahari (pəˈhɑːrɪ) NOUN a group of Indo-European languages spoken in the Himalayas, divided into **Eastern Pahari** (Nepali) and **Western Pahari** (consisting of many dialects).

Pahlavi (ˈpɑːləvɪ) *or* **Pehlevi** NOUN the Middle Persian language, esp as used in classical Zoroastrian and Manichean literature.
▷HISTORY C18: from Persian *pahlavī,* from Old Persian *Parthava* PARTHIA

Pahsien (ˈpɑːˈʃjɛn) NOUN another name for **Chongqing.**

paid (peɪd) VERB 1 the past tense and past participle of **pay¹**. 2 **put paid to.** *Chiefly Brit and NZ* to end or destroy: *breaking his leg put paid to his hopes of running in the Olympics.*

paid-up ADJECTIVE 1 having paid the due, full, or required fee to be a member of an organization, club, political party, etc. 2 denoting a security in which all the instalments have been paid; fully paid: *a paid-up share.* 3 denoting all the money that a company has received from its shareholders: *the paid-up capital.* 4 denoting an endowment assurance policy on which the payment of premiums has stopped and the surrender value has been used to purchase a new single-premium policy.

paigle (ˈpeɪgᵊl) NOUN another name for the **cowslip** and **oxlip.**
▷HISTORY C16: of uncertain origin

Paignton (ˈpeɪntən) NOUN a town and resort in SW England, in Torbay unitary authority, Devon.

pail (peɪl) NOUN 1 a bucket, esp one made of wood or metal. 2 Also called: **pailful.** the quantity that fills a pail.
▷HISTORY Old English *pægel;* compare Catalan *paella* frying pan, PAELLA

paillasse (ˈpælɪˌæs, ˌpælɪˈæs) NOUN a variant spelling (esp US) of **palliasse.**

paillette (pælˈjɛt; *French* pajɛt) NOUN 1 a sequin or spangle sewn onto a costume. 2 a small piece of metal or foil, used in enamelling for decoration.
▷HISTORY C19: from French, diminutive of *paille* straw, from Latin *palea*

pain (peɪn) NOUN 1 the sensation of acute physical hurt or discomfort caused by injury, illness, etc. 2 emotional suffering or mental distress. 3 **on pain of.** subject to the penalty of. 4 Also called: **pain in the neck** *or* **arse.** *Informal* a person or thing that is a nuisance. ◆ VERB (tr) 5 to cause (a person) distress, hurt, grief, anxiety, etc. 6 *Informal* to annoy; irritate. ◆ See also **pains.**
▷HISTORY C13: from Old French *peine,* from Latin *poena* punishment, grief, from Greek *poinē* penalty

pained (peɪnd) ADJECTIVE having or expressing pain or distress, esp mental or emotional distress: *a pained expression.*

painful (ˈpeɪnfʊl) ADJECTIVE 1 causing pain; distressing: *a painful duty.* 2 affected with pain: *a painful leg.* 3 tedious or difficult. 4 *Informal* extremely bad: *a painful performance.*
▸ **ˈpainfully** ADVERB ▸ **ˈpainfulness** NOUN

painkiller (ˈpeɪnˌkɪlə) NOUN 1 an analgesic drug or agent. 2 anything that relieves pain.

painless (ˈpeɪnlɪs) ADJECTIVE 1 not causing pain or distress. 2 not affected by pain.
▸ **ˈpainlessly** ADVERB ▸ **ˈpainlessness** NOUN

pains (peɪnz) PLURAL NOUN 1 care, trouble, or effort (esp in the phrases **take pains, be at pains to**). 2 painful sensations experienced during contractions in childbirth; labour pains.

painstaking (ˈpeɪnzˌteɪkɪŋ) ADJECTIVE extremely careful, esp as to fine detail: *painstaking research.*
▸ **ˈpainsˌtakingly** ADVERB ▸ **ˈpainsˌtakingness** NOUN

paint (peɪnt) NOUN 1 a substance used for decorating or protecting a surface, esp a mixture consisting of a solid pigment suspended in a liquid, that when applied to a surface dries to form a hard coating. 2 a dry film of paint on a surface. 3 the solid pigment of a paint before it is suspended in liquid. 4 *Informal* face make-up, such as rouge. 5 short for **greasepaint.** ◆ VERB 6 to make (a picture) of (a figure, landscape, etc.) with paint applied to a surface such as canvas. 7 to coat (a surface) with paint, as in decorating. 8 (tr) to apply (liquid) onto (a surface): *her mother painted the cut with antiseptic.* 9 (tr) to apply make-up onto (the face, lips, etc.). 10 (tr) to describe vividly in words. 11 **paint the town red.** *Informal* to celebrate uninhibitedly; go on a spree.
▷HISTORY C13: from Old French *peint* painted, from *peindre* to paint, from Latin *pingere* to paint, adorn
▸ **ˈpainty** ADJECTIVE

paintball game (ˈpeɪntˌbɔːl) NOUN a game in which teams of players simulate a military skirmish, shooting each other with paint pellets that explode on impact, marking the players who have been shot.

paintbox (ˈpeɪntˌbɒks) NOUN a box containing a tray of dry watercolour paints.

paintbrush (ˈpeɪntˌbrʌʃ) NOUN a brush used to apply paint.

Painted Desert NOUN a section of the high plateau country of N central Arizona, along the N side of the Little Colorado River Valley: brilliant-coloured rocks; occupied largely by Navaho and Hopi Indians. Area: about 20 000 sq. km (7500 sq. miles).

painted lady NOUN a migratory nymphalid butterfly, *Vanessa cardui,* with pale brownish-red mottled wings.

painted woman NOUN *Old-fashioned, derogatory* a woman whose appearance suggests she is promiscuous.

painter¹ (ˈpeɪntə) NOUN 1 a person who paints surfaces as a trade. 2 an artist who paints pictures.

painter² (ˈpeɪntə) NOUN a line attached to the bow of a boat for tying it up.
▷HISTORY C15: probably from Old French *penteur* strong rope

painterly (ˈpeɪntəlɪ) ADJECTIVE 1 having qualities peculiar to painting, esp the depiction of shapes by means of solid masses of colour, rather than by lines. Compare **linear** (sense 5). 2 of or characteristic of a painter; artistic.

painter's colic NOUN *Pathol* another name for **lead colic.**
▷HISTORY C19: so called because it frequently affected people who worked with lead-based paints or similar substances

painting (ˈpeɪntɪŋ) NOUN 1 the art or process of applying paints to a surface such as canvas, to make a picture or other artistic composition. 2 a composition or picture made in this way. 3 the act of applying paint to a surface with a brush.

paint stripper *or* **remover** NOUN a liquid, often caustic, used to remove paint from a surface.

paintwork (ˈpeɪntˌwɜːk) NOUN a surface, such as wood or a car body, that is painted.

pair¹ (pɛə) NOUN, *plural* **pairs** *or functioning as singular or plural* **pair.** 1 two identical or similar things matched for use together: *a pair of socks.* 2 two persons, animals, things, etc., used or grouped together: *a pair of horses; a pair of scoundrels.* 3 an object considered to be two identical or similar things joined together: *a pair of trousers.* 4 two people joined in love or marriage. 5 a male and a female animal of the same species, esp such animals kept for breeding purposes. 6 *Parliamentary procedure* **a** two opposed members who both agree not to vote on a specified motion or for a specific period of time. **b** the agreement so made. 7 two playing cards of the same rank or denomination: *a pair of threes.* 8 one member of a matching pair: *I can't find the pair to this glove.* 9 *Cricket* short for a **pair of spectacles** (see **spectacles** (sense 2)). 10 *Rowing* See **pair-oar.** 11 *Brit and US, dialect* a group or set of more than two. 12 *Logic, maths* **a** a set with two members. **b** an ordered set with two members. ◆ VERB 13 (often foll by *off*) to arrange or fall into groups of twos. 14 to group or be grouped in matching pairs: *to pair socks.* 15 to join or be joined in marriage; mate or couple. 16 (when *tr, usually passive*) *Parliamentary procedure* to form or cause to form a pair: *18 members were paired for the last vote.* ◆ See also **pairs.**
▷HISTORY C13: from Old French *paire,* from Latin *paria* equal (things), from *pār* equal

> **Language note** Like other collective nouns, *pair* takes a singular or a plural verb according to whether it is seen as a unit or as a collection of two things: *the pair are said to dislike each other; a pair of good shoes is essential.*

pair² (per) ADJECTIVE a Scot word for **poor.**

pair bond NOUN the exclusive relationship formed between a male and a female, esp in some species of animals and birds during courtship and breeding.
▸ **pair bonding** NOUN

pair-oar NOUN *Rowing* a racing shell in which two oarsmen sit one behind the other and pull one oar each. Also called: **pair.** Compare **double scull.**

pair production NOUN the production of an electron and a positron from a gamma-ray photon in a strong field as that passes close to an atomic nucleus.

pair royal NOUN (in some card games) a set of three cards of the same denomination.

pairs (pɛəz) PLURAL NOUN another name for **Pelmanism** (sense 2).

pair trawling NOUN the act or practice of using two boats to trawl for fish.

paisa (ˈpaɪsɑː) NOUN, *plural* **-se** (-seɪ). a monetary unit of Bangladesh, Bhutan, India, Nepal, and Pakistan worth one hundredth of a rupee.
▷HISTORY from Hindi

paisano (paɪˈsɑːnəʊ; *Spanish* paiˈsano) NOUN, *plural* **-nos** (-nəʊz; *Spanish* -nos). *Southwestern US* (often a term of address) 1 *Informal* a friend; pal. 2 a fellow countryman.
▷HISTORY C20: via Spanish from French *paysan* PEASANT

paisley (ˈpeɪzlɪ) NOUN 1 a pattern of small curving shapes with intricate detailing, usually printed in bright colours. 2 a soft fine wool fabric traditionally printed with this pattern. 3 a garment made of this fabric, esp a shawl popular in

the late 19th century. 4 (*modifier*) of or decorated with this pattern: *a paisley scarf*.
▷**HISTORY** C19: named after PAISLEY

Paisley ('peɪzlɪ) NOUN an industrial town in SW Scotland, the administrative centre of Renfrewshire: one of the world's chief centres for the manufacture of thread, linen, and gauze in the 19th century. Pop.: 75 526 (1991).

paitrick ('petrɪk) NOUN a Scot word for **partridge.**

Paiute *or* **Piute** ('paɪˌuːt, paɪ'juːt) NOUN 1 (*plural* **-utes** *or* **-ute**) a member of either of two North American Indian peoples (**Northern Paiute** and **Southern Paiute**) of the Southwestern US, related to the Aztecs. 2 the language of either of these peoples, belonging to the Shoshonean subfamily of the Uto-Aztecan family.

pajamas (pə'dʒɑːməz) PLURAL NOUN the US spelling of **pyjamas.**

pakahi ('pɑːkəhiː) NOUN *NZ* **a** acid land that is unsuitable for cultivation. **b** (*as modifier*): *pakahi soil*.
▷**HISTORY** C19: from Maori

pakapoo ('pækəpuː) NOUN, *plural* **-poos.** *Austral and NZ* 1 a Chinese lottery with betting slips marked with Chinese characters. 2 **like a pakapoo ticket.** untidy, incomprehensible.
▷**HISTORY** C19: from Chinese

pak-choi cabbage ('pɑːk'tʃɔɪ) NOUN another name for **bok choy.**

Pakeha ('pɑːkɪˌhɑː) NOUN (in New Zealand) a person who is not of Maori ancestry, esp a White person.
▷**HISTORY** from Maori

Pakeha Maori NOUN (in the 19th century) a European who adopted the Maori way of life.

Paki ('pækɪ) *Brit, slang, offensive* ◆ NOUN, *plural* **Pakis.** 1 a Pakistani or person of Pakistani descent. 2 (loosely) a person from any part of the Indian subcontinent. ◆ ADJECTIVE 3 Pakistani or of Pakistani descent. 4 (loosely) denoting a person from the Indian subcontinent.

Paki-bashing NOUN *Brit, slang* the activity of making vicious and unprovoked physical assaults upon Pakistani immigrants or people of Pakistani descent.
▸**'Paki-ˌbasher** NOUN

pakirikiri ('pɑːkɪriːˌkɪriː) NOUN *NZ* another name for **blue cod.**

Pakistan (ˌpɑːkɪ'stɑːn) NOUN 1 a republic in S Asia, on the Arabian Sea: the Union of Pakistan, formed in 1947, comprised West and East Pakistan; East Pakistan gained independence as Bangladesh in 1971 and West Pakistan became Pakistan; a member of the Commonwealth from 1947, it withdrew from 1972 until 1989; contains the fertile plains of the Indus valley rising to mountains in the north and west. Official language: Urdu. Official religion: Muslim. Currency: rupee. Capital: Islamabad. Pop.: 144 617 000 (2001 est.). Area: 801 508 sq. km (309 463 sq. miles). 2 a former republic in S Asia consisting of the provinces of West Pakistan and East Pakistan (now Bangladesh), 1500 km (900 miles) apart: formed in 1947 from the predominantly Muslim parts of India.

Pakistani (ˌpɑːkɪ'stɑːnɪ) NOUN 1 a native or inhabitant of Pakistan. ◆ ADJECTIVE 2 of or relating to Pakistan or its inhabitants.

pakoko ('pɑːkəʊkəʊ) NOUN *NZ* another name for **bully**[2].

pakora (pə'kɔːrə) NOUN an Indian dish consisting of pieces of vegetable, chicken, etc., dipped in a spiced batter and deep-fried: served with a piquant sauce.
▷**HISTORY** C20: from Hindi

pakthong (pæk'θɒŋ) NOUN another name for **nickel silver.**

pal (pæl) *Informal* ◆ NOUN 1 a close friend; comrade. 2 an accomplice. ◆ VERB **pals, palling, palled.** 3 (*intr*; usually foll by *with* or *about*) to associate as friends. ◆ See also **pal up.**
▷**HISTORY** C17: from English Gypsy: brother, ultimately from Sanskrit *bhrātar* BROTHER

PAL (pæl) NOUN ACRONYM FOR phase alternation line: a colour-television broadcasting system used generally in Europe.

Pal. ABBREVIATION FOR Palestine.

palace ('pælɪs) NOUN (*capital when part of a name*) 1 the official residence of a reigning monarch or member of a royal family: *Buckingham Palace*. 2 the official residence of various high-ranking church dignitaries or members of the nobility, as of an archbishop. 3 a large and richly furnished building resembling a royal palace. ◆ Related adjectives: **palatial, palatine.**
▷**HISTORY** C13: from Old French *palais*, from Latin *Palātium* PALATINE[2], the site of the palace of the emperors

palace revolution NOUN a coup d'état made by those already in positions of power, usually with little violence.

paladin ('pælədɪn) NOUN 1 one of the legendary twelve peers of Charlemagne's court. 2 a knightly champion.
▷**HISTORY** C16: via French from Italian *paladino*, from Latin *palātīnus* imperial official, from *Palātium* PALATINE[2]

palaeanthropic (ˌpælɪæn'θrɒpɪk) ADJECTIVE relating to or denoting the earliest variety of man.

Palaearctic (ˌpælɪ'ɑːktɪk) ADJECTIVE of or denoting a zoogeographical region consisting of Europe, Africa north of the Sahara, and most of Asia north of the Himalayas.

palaeethnology (ˌpælɪɛθ'nɒlədʒɪ) NOUN the study of prehistoric man.
▸**palaeethnological** (ˌpælɪˌɛθnə'lɒdʒɪkəl) ADJECTIVE
▸**ˌpalaeeth'nologist** NOUN

palaeo-, *or before a vowel* **palae-,** *esp US* **paleo-, pale-** COMBINING FORM old, ancient, or prehistoric: *palaeography*.
▷**HISTORY** from Greek *palaios* old

palaeoanthropology (ˌpælɪəʊˌænθrə'pɒlədʒɪ) NOUN the branch of anthropology concerned with primitive man.

palaeobotany (ˌpælɪəʊ'bɒtənɪ) NOUN the study of fossil plants.
▸**palaeobotanical** (ˌpælɪəʊbə'tænɪkəl) *or* **ˌpalaeobo'tanic** ADJECTIVE ▸**ˌpalaeo'botanist** NOUN

Palaeocene ('pælɪəʊˌsiːn) ADJECTIVE 1 of, denoting, or formed in the first epoch of the Tertiary period, which lasted for 10 million years. ◆ NOUN 2 **the.** the Palaeocene epoch or rock series.
▷**HISTORY** C19: from French from *paléo-* PALAEO- + Greek *kainos* new, recent

palaeoclimatology (ˌpælɪəʊˌklaɪmə'tɒlədʒɪ) NOUN the study of climates of the geological past.
▸**ˌpalaeoˌclima'tologist** NOUN

palaeocurrent ('pælɪəʊˌkʌrənt) NOUN *Geology* an ancient current, esp of water, evidence of which has been preserved in sedimentary rocks as fossilized ripple marks, etc.

palaeoecology (ˌpælɪəʊɪ'kɒlədʒɪ) NOUN the study of fossil animals and plants in order to deduce their ecology and the environmental conditions in which they lived.
▸**ˌpalaeoˌeco'logical** ADJECTIVE ▸**ˌpalaeoe'cologist** NOUN

palaeoethnobotany (ˌpælɪəʊˌɛθnəʊ'bɒtənɪ) NOUN the study of fossil seeds and grains to further archaeological knowledge, esp of the domestication of cereals.

Palaeogene ('pælɪəˌdʒiːn) ADJECTIVE 1 of or formed in the Palaeocene, Eocene, and Oligocene epochs. ◆ NOUN 2 **the.** the Palaeogene period or system.

palaeogeography (ˌpælɪəʊdʒɪ'ɒgrəfɪ) NOUN the study of geographical features of the geological past.
▸**ˌpalaeoge'ographer** NOUN ▸**palaeogeographical** (ˌpælɪəʊˌdʒiːəʊ'græfɪkəl) *or* **ˌpalaeoˌgeo'graphic** ADJECTIVE ▸**ˌpalaeoˌgeo'graphically** ADVERB

palaeography (ˌpælɪ'ɒgrəfɪ) NOUN 1 the study of the handwritings of the past, and often the manuscripts as well, so that they may be dated, read, etc., and may serve as historical and literary sources. 2 a handwriting of the past.
▸**palae'ographer** NOUN ▸**palaeographic** (ˌpælɪəʊ'græfɪk) *or* **ˌpalaeo'graphical** ADJECTIVE

palaeolith ('pælɪəʊˌlɪθ) NOUN a stone tool dating to the Palaeolithic.

Palaeolithic (ˌpælɪəʊ'lɪθɪk) NOUN 1 the period of the emergence of primitive man and the manufacture of unpolished chipped stone tools, about 2.5 million to 3 million years ago until about 12 000 B.C. See also **Lower Palaeolithic, Middle Palaeolithic, Upper Palaeolithic.** ◆ ADJECTIVE 2 (*sometimes not capital*) of or relating to this period.

Palaeolithic man NOUN any of various primitive types of man, such as Neanderthal man and Java man, who lived in the Palaeolithic.

palaeomagnetism (ˌpælɪəʊ'mægnɪˌtɪzəm) NOUN the study of the fossil magnetism in rocks, used to determine the past configurations of the continents and to investigate the past shape and magnitude of the earth's magnetic field.
▸**ˌpalaeomag'netic** ADJECTIVE

palaeontography (ˌpælɪɒn'tɒgrəfɪ) NOUN the branch of palaeontology concerned with the description of fossils.
▷**HISTORY** C19: from PALAEO- + ONTO- + -GRAPHY
▸**palaeontographic** (ˌpælɪˌɒntə'græfɪk) *or* **ˌpalaeˌonto'graphical** ADJECTIVE

palaeontol. ABBREVIATION FOR palaeontology.

palaeontology (ˌpælɪɒn'tɒlədʒɪ) NOUN 1 the study of fossils to determine the structure and evolution of extinct animals and plants and the age and conditions of deposition of the rock strata in which they are found. See also **palaeobotany, palaeozoology.** 2 another name for **palaeozoology.**
▷**HISTORY** C19: from PALAEO- + ONTO- + -LOGY
▸**palaeontological** (ˌpælɪˌɒntə'lɒdʒɪkəl) ADJECTIVE
▸**ˌpalaeˌonto'logically** ADVERB ▸**ˌpalaeon'tologist** NOUN

palaeopathology (ˌpælɪəʊpə'θɒlədʒɪ) NOUN the study of diseases of ancient man and fossil animals.
▸**'palaeoˌpatho'logical** ADJECTIVE ▸**ˌpalaeopa'thologist** NOUN

Palaeozoic (ˌpælɪəʊ'zəʊɪk) ADJECTIVE 1 of, denoting, or relating to an era of geological time that began 600 million years ago with the Cambrian period and lasted about 375 million years until the end of the Permian period. ◆ NOUN 2 **the.** the Palaeozoic era.
▷**HISTORY** C19: from PALAEO- + Greek *zōē* life + -IC

palaeozoology (ˌpælɪəʊzuː'ɒlədʒɪ) NOUN the study of fossil animals. Also called: **palaeontology.**
▸**palaeozoological** (ˌpælɪəʊˌzuə'lɒdʒɪkəl) ADJECTIVE
▸**ˌpalaeozo'ologist** NOUN

palaestra *or esp US* **palestra** (pə'lɛstrə, -'liː-) NOUN, *plural* **-tras** *or* **-trae** (-triː). (in ancient Greece or Rome) a public place devoted to the training of athletes.
▷**HISTORY** C16: via Latin from Greek *palaistra*, from *palaiein* to wrestle

Palagi (pɑː'lʌŋiː) NOUN, *plural* **-gi.** *NZ* a Samoan name for a **European.**
▷**HISTORY** from Samoan *papālagi*

palais de danse *French* (palɛ də dɑ̃s) NOUN a dance hall.

palais glide ('pæleɪ) NOUN a dance with high kicks and gliding steps in which performers link arms in a row.
▷**HISTORY** C20: from PALAIS DE DANSE

palanquin *or* **palankeen** (ˌpælən'kiːn) NOUN a covered litter, formerly used in the Orient, carried on the shoulders of four men.
▷**HISTORY** C16: from Portuguese *palanquim*, from Prakrit *pallanka*, from Sanskrit *paryanka* couch

palatable ('pælətəbəl) ADJECTIVE 1 pleasant to taste. 2 acceptable or satisfactory: *a palatable suggestion*.
▸**ˌpalata'bility** *or* **'palatableness** NOUN ▸**'palatably** ADVERB

palatal ('pælətəl) ADJECTIVE 1 Also: **palatine.** of or relating to the palate. 2 *Phonetics* of, relating to, or denoting a speech sound articulated with the blade of the tongue touching the hard palate. ◆ NOUN 3 Also called: **palatine.** the bony plate that forms the palate. 4 *Phonetics* a palatal speech sound, such as the semivowel (j).
▸**'palatally** ADVERB

palatalize *or* **palatalise** ('pælətəˌlaɪz) VERB (*tr*) to pronounce (a speech sound) with the blade of the tongue touching the palate.
▸**ˌpalatali'zation** *or* **ˌpalatali'sation** NOUN

palate ('pælɪt) NOUN 1 the roof of the mouth, separating the oral and nasal cavities. See **hard palate, soft palate.** Related adjective: **palatine.** 2 the sense of taste: *she had no palate for the wine*. 3 relish or enjoyment. 4 *Botany* (in some two-lipped corollas) the projecting part of the lower lip that closes the opening of the corolla.
▷**HISTORY** C14: from Latin *palātum*, perhaps of Etruscan origin

Language note Avoid confusion with **palette** or **pallet.**

palatial (pəˈleɪʃəl) ADJECTIVE of, resembling, or suitable for a palace; sumptuous.
▸**paˈlatially** ADVERB ▸**paˈlatialness** NOUN

palatinate (pəˈlætɪnɪt) NOUN a territory ruled by a palatine prince or noble or count palatine.

Palatinate (pəˈlætɪnɪt) NOUN 1 **the.** either of two territories in SW Germany, once ruled by the counts palatine. **Upper Palatinate** is now in Bavaria; **Lower** or **Rhine Palatinate** is now in Rhineland-Palatinate, Baden-Württemberg, and Hesse. German name: **Pfalz.** 2 a native or inhabitant of the Palatinate.

palatine[1] (ˈpæləˌtaɪn) ADJECTIVE 1 (of an individual) possessing royal prerogatives in a territory. 2 of, belonging to, characteristic of, or relating to a count palatine, county palatine, palatinate, or palatine. 3 of or relating to a palace. ◆ NOUN 4 *Feudal history* the lord of a palatinate. 5 any of various important officials at the late Roman, Merovingian, or Carolingian courts. 6 (in Colonial America) any of the proprietors of a palatine colony, such as Carolina.
▷HISTORY C15: via French from Latin *palātīnus* belonging to the palace, from *palātium*; see PALACE

palatine[2] (ˈpæləˌtaɪn) ADJECTIVE 1 of or relating to the palate. ◆ NOUN 2 either of two bones forming the hard palate.
▷HISTORY C17: from French *palatin,* from Latin *palātum* palate

Palatine[1] (ˈpæləˌtaɪn) ADJECTIVE 1 of or relating to the Palatinate. ◆ NOUN 2 a Palatinate.

Palatine[2] (ˈpæləˌtaɪn) NOUN 1 one of the Seven Hills of Rome: traditionally the site of the first settlement of Rome. ◆ ADJECTIVE 2 of, relating to, or designating this hill.

Palau Islands (pɑːˈlaʊ) PLURAL NOUN a former name (until 1981) of the (Republic of) **Belau.**

palaver (pəˈlɑːvə) NOUN 1 tedious or time-consuming business, esp when of a formal nature: *all the palaver of filling in forms.* 2 loud and confused talk and activity; hubbub. 3 (often used humorously) a conference. 4 *Now rare* talk intended to flatter or persuade. 5 *W African* **a** an argument. **b** trouble arising from an argument. ◆ VERB 6 *(intr)* (often used humorously) to have a conference. 7 *(intr)* to talk loudly and confusedly. 8 *(tr)* to flatter or cajole.
▷HISTORY C18: from Portuguese *palavra* talk, from Latin *parabola* PARABLE

Palawan (*Spanish* paˈlavan) NOUN an island of the SW Philippines between the South China Sea and the Sulu Sea: the westernmost island in the country; mountainous and forested. Capital: Puerto Princesa. Pop.: 311 550 (latest est.). Area: 11 785 sq. km (4550 sq. miles).

palazzo pants (pəˈlætsəʊ) PLURAL NOUN women's trousers with very wide legs.
▷HISTORY C20: *palazzo* from Italian, literally: PALACE

pale[1] (peɪl) ADJECTIVE 1 lacking brightness of colour; whitish: *pale morning light.* 2 (of a colour) whitish; produced by a relatively small quantity of colouring agent. 3 dim or wan: *the pale stars.* 4 feeble: *a pale effort.* 5 *South African* a euphemism for **White**[1]. ◆ VERB 6 to make or become pale or paler; blanch. 7 *(intr; often foll by before)* to lose superiority or importance (in comparison to): *her beauty paled before that of her hostess.*
▷HISTORY C13: from Old French *palle,* from Latin *pallidus* pale, from *pallēre* to look wan
▸**ˈpalely** ADVERB ▸**ˈpaleness** NOUN

pale[2] (peɪl) NOUN 1 a wooden post or strip used as an upright member in a fence. 2 an enclosing barrier, esp a fence made of pales. 3 an area enclosed by a pale. 4 a sphere of activity within which certain restrictions are applied. 5 *Heraldry* an ordinary consisting of a vertical stripe, usually in the centre of a shield. 6 **beyond the pale.** outside the limits of social convention. ◆ VERB 7 *(tr)* to enclose with pales.
▷HISTORY C14: from Old French *pal,* from Latin *pālus* stake; compare POLE[1]

palea (ˈpeɪlɪə) *or* **pale** NOUN, *plural* **paleae** (ˈpeɪlɪˌiː) *or* **pales.** *Botany* 1 the inner of two bracts surrounding each floret in a grass spikelet. ◆ Compare **lemma.** 2 any small membranous bract or scale.
▷HISTORY C18: from Latin: straw, chaff; see PALLET[1]
▸**paleaceous** (ˌpeɪlɪˈeɪʃəs) ADJECTIVE

paleface (ˈpeɪlˌfeɪs) NOUN a derogatory term for a White person, said to have been used by North American Indians.

Palembang (pɑːˈlɛmbɑːŋ) NOUN a port in W Indonesia, in S Sumatra; oil refineries; university (1955). Pop.: 1 352 300 (1995 est.).

Palencia (*Spanish* paˈlenθia) NOUN a city in N central Spain: earliest university in Spain (1208); seat of Castilian kings (12th–13th centuries); communications centre. Pop.: 77 752 (1991).

Palenque (*Spanish* paˈleŋke) NOUN the site of an ancient Mayan city in S Mexico famous for its architectural ruins.

paleo- *or before a vowel* **pale-** COMBINING FORM variants (esp US) of **palaeo-.**

Palermo (pəˈlɛəməʊ, -ˈlɜː-; *Italian* paˈlɛrmo) NOUN the capital of Sicily, on the NW coast: founded by the Phoenicians in the 8th century B.C. Pop.: 683 794 (2000 est.).

Palestine (ˈpælɪˌstaɪn) NOUN 1 Also called: **the Holy Land, Canaan.** the area between the Jordan River and the Mediterranean Sea in which most of the biblical narrative is located. 2 the province of the Roman Empire in this region. 3 the former British mandatory territory created by the League of Nations in 1922 (but effective from 1920), and including all of the present territories of Israel and Jordan between whom it was partitioned by the UN in 1948.

Palestine Liberation Organization NOUN an organization founded in 1964 with the aim of creating a state for Palestinians; it recognized the state of Israel in 1993 and Israel granted Palestinians autonomy in the Gaza Strip and West Bank. Abbreviation: **PLO.**

Palestinian (ˌpælɪˈstɪnɪən) ADJECTIVE 1 of or relating to Palestine. ◆ NOUN 2 a native or inhabitant of the former British mandate, or their descendants, esp such Arabs now living in the Palestinian Administered Territories, Jordan, Lebanon, or Israel, or as refugees from Israeli-occupied territory.

Palestinian Administered Territories NOUN the Gaza Strip and the West Bank in Israel: these areas were granted autonomous status under the control of the Palestinian National Authority following the 1993 peace agreement between Israel and the Palestine Liberation Organization. Also called: **Palestinian Autonomous Areas.**

Palestinian National Authority NOUN the authority formed in 1994 to govern the Palestinian Administered Territories: it controls policy on health, education, social welfare, direct taxation, tourism, and culture and manages elections to the Palestinian Council. Abbreviation: **PNA.**

palestra (pəˈlɛstrə, -ˈliː-) NOUN, *plural* **-tras** *or* **-trae** (-triː). the usual US spelling of **palaestra.**

paletot (ˈpæltəʊ) NOUN 1 a loose outer garment. 2 a woman's fitted coat often worn over a crinoline or bustle.
▷HISTORY C19: from French

palette (ˈpælɪt) NOUN 1 Also: **pallet.** a flat piece of wood, plastic, etc., used by artists as a surface on which to mix their paints. 2 the range of colours characteristic of a particular artist, painting, or school of painting: *a restricted palette.* 3 the available range of colours or patterns that can be displayed by a computer on a visual display unit. 4 either of the plates of metal attached by a strap to the cuirass in a suit of armour to protect the armpits.
▷HISTORY C17: from French, diminutive of *pale* shovel, from Latin *pala* spade

> **Language note** Avoid confusion with **palate** or **pallet.**

palette *or* **pallet knife** NOUN 1 a round-ended spatula with a thin flexible blade used esp by artists for mixing, applying, and scraping off paint, esp oil paint. 2 a knife with a round-ended flexible blade used in cookery for scraping out a mixture from a bowl, spreading icing, etc.

palfrey (ˈpɔːlfrɪ) NOUN *Archaic* a light saddle horse, esp ridden by women.
▷HISTORY C12: from Old French *palefrei,* from Medieval Latin *palafredus,* from Late Latin *paraverēdus,* from Greek *para* beside + Latin *verēdus* light fleet horse, of Celtic origin

Pali (ˈpɑːlɪ) NOUN an ancient language of India derived from Sanskrit; the language of the Buddhist scriptures.
▷HISTORY C19: from Sanskrit *pāli-bhāsa,* from *pāli* canon + *bhāsa* language, of Dravidian origin

palikar (ˈpælɪˌkɑː) NOUN a Greek soldier in the war of independence against Turkey (1821–28).
▷HISTORY C19: from Modern Greek *palikari* youth

palilalia (ˌpælɪˈleɪlɪə) NOUN a speech disorder in which a word or phrase is rapidly repeated.
▷HISTORY C20: from Greek *palin* again + *lalein* to babble

palimony (ˈpælɪmənɪ) NOUN *US* alimony awarded to a nonmarried partner after the break-up of a long-term relationship.
▷HISTORY C20: from a blend of *pal* + *alimony*

palimpsest (ˈpælɪmpˌsɛst) NOUN 1 a manuscript on which two or more successive texts have been written, each one being erased to make room for the next. ◆ ADJECTIVE 2 (of a text) written on a palimpsest. 3 (of a document) used as a palimpsest.
▷HISTORY C17: from Latin *palimpsestus* parchment cleaned for reuse, from Greek *palimpsēstos,* from *palin* again + *psēstos* rubbed smooth, from *psēn* to scrape

palindrome (ˈpælɪnˌdrəʊm) NOUN a word or phrase the letters of which, when taken in reverse order, give the same word or phrase, such as *able was I ere I saw Elba.*
▷HISTORY C17: from Greek *palindromos* running back again, from *palin* again + -DROME
▸**palindromic** (ˌpælɪnˈdrɒmɪk) ADJECTIVE

paling (ˈpeɪlɪŋ) NOUN 1 a fence made of pales. 2 pales collectively. 3 a single pale. 4 the act of erecting pales.

palingenesis (ˌpælɪnˈdʒɛnɪsɪs) NOUN, *plural* **-ses** (-ˌsiːz). 1 *Christianity* spiritual rebirth through metempsychosis of Christian baptism. 2 *Biology* another name for **recapitulation** (sense 2).
▷HISTORY C19: from Greek *palin* again + *genesis* birth, GENESIS
▸**palingenetic** (ˌpælɪndʒəˈnɛtɪk) ADJECTIVE
▸**ˌpalingeˈnetically** ADVERB

palinka (pəˈlɪŋkə) NOUN a type of apricot brandy, originating in Central and Eastern Europe.

palinode (ˈpælɪˌnəʊd) NOUN 1 a poem in which the poet recants something he has said in a former poem. 2 *Rare* a recantation.
▷HISTORY C16: from Latin *palinōdia* repetition of a song, from Greek, from *palin* again + *ōidē* song, ODE

palinopsia (ˌpælɪˈnɒpsɪə) *or* **palinopia** (ˌpælɪˈnəʊpɪə) NOUN a visual disorder in which the patient perceives a prolonged afterimage.
▷HISTORY from Greek *palin* again + *ōps* eye

palisade (ˌpælɪˈseɪd) NOUN 1 a strong fence made of stakes driven into the ground, esp for defence. 2 one of the stakes used in such a fence. 3 *Botany* a layer of elongated mesophyll cells containing many chloroplasts, situated below the outer epidermis of a leaf blade. ◆ VERB 4 *(tr)* to enclose with a palisade.
▷HISTORY C17: via French, from Old Provençal *palissada,* ultimately from Latin *pālus* stake; see PALE[2], POLE[1]

palisades (ˌpælɪˈseɪdz, ˈpælɪˌseɪdz) PLURAL NOUN *US and Canadian* high cliffs in a line, often along a river, resembling a palisade.

palish (ˈpeɪlɪʃ) ADJECTIVE rather pale.

Palk Strait (pɔːk, pɔːlk) NOUN a channel between SE India and N Ceylon. Width: about 64 km (40 miles).

pall[1] (pɔːl) NOUN 1 a cloth covering, usually black, spread over a coffin or tomb. 2 a coffin, esp during the funeral ceremony. 3 a dark heavy covering; shroud: *the clouds formed a pall over the sky.* 4 a depressing or oppressive atmosphere: *her bereavement cast a pall on the party.* 5 *Heraldry* an ordinary consisting of a Y-shaped bearing. 6 *Christianity* **a** a small square linen cloth with which the chalice is covered at the Eucharist. **b** an archaic word for **pallium** (sense 2). 7 an obsolete word for **cloak.** ◆ VERB 8 *(tr)* to cover or depress with a pall.
▷HISTORY Old English *pæll,* from Latin: PALLIUM

pall[2] (pɔːl) VERB 1 *(intr; often foll by on)* to become or appear boring, insipid, or tiresome (to): *history*

classes palled on me. 2 to cloy or satiate, or become cloyed or satiated.
▷HISTORY C14: variant of APPAL

Palladian[1] (pəˈleɪdɪən) ADJECTIVE denoting, relating to, or having the neoclassical style of architecture created by Palladio.
▷HISTORY C18: after Andrea Palladio (1508–80), Italian architect
▸**Palˈladian,ism** NOUN

Palladian[2] (pəˈleɪdɪən) ADJECTIVE 1 of or relating to the goddess Pallas Athena. 2 *Literary* wise or learned.
▷HISTORY C16: from Latin *Palladius,* from Greek *Pallas,* an epithet applied to Athena, meaning perhaps "(spear) brandisher" or perhaps "virgin"

palladic (pəˈlædɪk, -ˈleɪ-) ADJECTIVE of or containing palladium in the trivalent or tetravalent state.

palladium[1] (pəˈleɪdɪəm) NOUN a ductile malleable silvery-white element of the platinum metal group occurring principally in nickel-bearing ores: used as a hydrogenation catalyst and, alloyed with gold, in jewellery. Symbol: Pd; atomic no.: 46; atomic wt.: 106.42; valency: 2, 3, or 4; relative density: 1202; melting pt.: 1555°C; boiling pt.: 2964°C.
▷HISTORY C19: named after the asteroid PALLAS, at the time (1803) a recent discovery

palladium[2] (pəˈleɪdɪəm) NOUN something believed to ensure protection; safeguard.
▷HISTORY C17: after the PALLADIUM

Palladium (pəˈleɪdɪəm) NOUN a statue of Pallas Athena, esp the one upon which the safety of Troy depended.

palladous (pəˈleɪdəs, ˈpælədəs) ADJECTIVE of or containing palladium in the divalent state.

Pallas (ˈpæləs) NOUN *Astronomy* the second largest asteroid (diameter 520 km), revolving around the sun in a period of 4.62 years.

Pallas Athena *or* **Pallas** NOUN another name for **Athena.**

pallbearer (ˈpɔːlˌbɛərə) NOUN a person who carries or escorts the coffin at a funeral.

pallescent (pæˈlɛsənt) ADJECTIVE *Botany* becoming paler in colour with increasing age.

pallet[1] (ˈpælɪt) NOUN 1 a straw-filled mattress or bed. 2 any hard or makeshift bed.
▷HISTORY C14: from Anglo-Norman *paillet,* from Old French *paille* straw, from Latin *palea* straw

> **Language note** Avoid confusion with **palate** or **palette.**

pallet[2] (ˈpælɪt) NOUN 1 an instrument with a handle and a flat, sometimes flexible, blade used by potters for shaping. 2 a standard-sized platform of box section open at two ends on which goods may be stacked. The open ends allow the entry of the forks of a lifting truck so that the palletized load can be raised and moved about easily. 3 *Horology* the locking lever that engages and disengages alternate end pawls with the escape wheel to give impulses to the balance. 4 a variant spelling of **palette** (sense 1). 5 *Music* a flap valve of wood faced with leather that opens to allow air from the wind chest to enter an organ pipe, causing it to sound.
▷HISTORY C16: from Old French *palette* a little shovel, from *pale* spade, from Latin *pala* spade

> **Language note** Avoid confusion with **palate** or **palette.**

palletize *or* **palletise** (ˈpælɪˌtaɪz) VERB (*tr*) to stack or transport on a pallet or pallets.
▸**ˌpalletiˈzation** *or* **ˌpalletiˈsation** NOUN

pallet knife NOUN a variant spelling of **palette knife.**

pallet truck NOUN a powered truck with a mast, sometimes telescopic, on which slides a carriage which can be raised and lowered hydraulically. The carriage has extended forks which can be passed under a palletized load for stacking or moving to a new position. Also called: **stacking truck.**

palliasse *or esp US* **paillasse** (ˈpælɪˌæs, ˌpælɪˈæs) NOUN a straw-filled mattress; pallet.
▷HISTORY C18: from French *paillasse,* from Italian *pagliaccio,* ultimately from Latin *palea* PALLET[1]

palliate (ˈpælɪˌeɪt) VERB (*tr*) 1 to lessen the severity of (pain, disease, etc.) without curing or removing; alleviate; mitigate. 2 to cause (an offence) to seem less serious by concealing evidence; extenuate.
▷HISTORY C16: from Late Latin *palliāre* to cover up, from Latin *pallium* a cloak, PALLIUM
▸**ˌpalliˈation** NOUN ▸**ˈpalliˌator** NOUN

palliative (ˈpælɪətɪv) ADJECTIVE 1 serving to palliate; relieving without curing. ◆ NOUN 2 something that palliates, such as a sedative drug or agent.
▸**ˈpalliatively** ADVERB

pallid (ˈpælɪd) ADJECTIVE 1 lacking colour or brightness; wan: *a pallid complexion.* 2 lacking vigour; vapid: *a pallid performance.*
▷HISTORY C17: from Latin *pallidus,* from *pallēre* to be PALE[1]
▸**ˈpallidly** ADVERB ▸**ˈpallidness** *or* **palˈlidity** NOUN

pallium (ˈpælɪəm) NOUN, *plural* **-lia** (-lɪə) *or* **-liums.** 1 a garment worn by men in ancient Greece or Rome, made by draping a large rectangular cloth about the body. 2 *Chiefly RC Church* a woollen vestment consisting of a band encircling the shoulders with two lappets hanging from it front and back: worn by the pope, all archbishops, and (as a mark of special honour) some bishops. 3 Also called: **mantle.** *Anatomy* the cerebral cortex and contiguous white matter. 4 *Zoology* another name for **mantle** (sense 5).
▷HISTORY C16: from Latin: cloak; related to Latin *palla* mantle

pall-mall (ˈpælˈmæl) NOUN *Obsolete* 1 a game in which a ball is driven by a mallet along an alley and through an iron ring. 2 the alley itself.
▷HISTORY C17: from obsolete French, from Italian *pallamaglio,* from *palla* ball + *maglio* mallet

Pall Mall (ˈpæl ˈmæl) NOUN a street in London, noted for its many clubs.

pallor (ˈpælə) NOUN a pale condition, esp when unnatural: *fear gave his face a deathly pallor.*
▷HISTORY C17: from Latin: whiteness (of the skin), from *pallēre* to be PALE[1]

pally (ˈpælɪ) ADJECTIVE **-lier, -liest.** *Informal* on friendly or familiar terms.

pally up VERB (*intr, adverb;* often foll by *with*) *Informal* to become friends (with).

palm[1] (pɑːm) NOUN 1 the inner part of the hand from the wrist to the base of the fingers. Related adjectives: **thenar, volar.** 2 a corresponding part in animals, esp apes and monkeys. 3 a linear measure based on the breadth or length of a hand, equal to three to four inches or seven to ten inches respectively. 4 the part of a glove that covers the palm. 5 a hard leather shield worn by sailmakers to protect the palm of the hand. 6 **a** the side of the blade of an oar that faces away from the direction of a boat's movement during a stroke. **b** the face of the fluke of an anchor. 7 a flattened or expanded part of the antlers of certain deer. 8 **in the palm of one's hand.** at one's mercy or command. ◆ VERB (*tr*) 9 to conceal in or about the hand, as in sleight-of-hand tricks. 10 to touch or soothe with the palm of the hand. ◆ See also **palm off.**
▷HISTORY C14 *paume,* via Old French from Latin *palma;* compare Old English *folm* palm of the hand, Greek *palamē*

palm[2] (pɑːm) NOUN 1 any treelike plant of the tropical and subtropical monocotyledonous family *Arecaceae* (formerly *Palmae* or *Palmaceae*), usually having a straight unbranched trunk crowned with large pinnate or palmate leaves. 2 a leaf or branch of any of these trees, a symbol of victory, success, etc. 3 merit or victory. 4 an emblem or insignia representing a leaf or branch worn on certain military decorations.
▷HISTORY Old English, from Latin *palma,* from the likeness of its spreading fronds to a hand; see PALM[1]

Palma (*Spanish* ˈpalma) NOUN the capital of the Balearic Islands, on the SW coast of Majorca: a tourist centre. Pop.: 296 754 (1991). Official name: **Palma de Mallorca.**

palmaceous (pælˈmeɪʃəs) ADJECTIVE of, relating to, or belonging to the palm family, *Arecaceae* (formerly *Palmae* or *Palmaceae*).

palmar (ˈpælmə) ADJECTIVE of or relating to the palm of the hand.

palmary (ˈpælmərɪ) ADJECTIVE *Rare* worthy of praise.
▷HISTORY C17: from Latin *palmārius* relating to the palm of victory; see PALM[2]

Palmas (ˈpælməs) NOUN a city in N Brazil, capital of Tocantins state. Pop.: 5750 (1990).

palmate (ˈpælmeɪt, -mɪt) *or* **palmated** ADJECTIVE 1 shaped like an open hand: *palmate antlers.* 2 *Botany* having more than three lobes or segments that spread out from a common point: *palmate leaves.* 3 (of the feet of most water birds) having three toes connected by a web.
▷HISTORY C18: from Latin *palmatus,* from *palma* palm; see PALM[2]

palmation (pælˈmeɪʃən) NOUN 1 the state of being palmate. 2 a projection or division of a palmate structure.

Palm Beach NOUN a town in SE Florida, on an island between Lake Worth (a lagoon) and the Atlantic: major resort and tourist centre. Pop.: 9814 (1990).

palm civet NOUN any of various small civet-like arboreal viverrine mammals of the genera *Paradoxurus, Hemigalus,* etc., of Africa and S and SE Asia.

palmcorder (ˈpɑːmˌkɔːdə) NOUN a small camcorder which can be held in the palm of the hand.

palmer (ˈpɑːmə) NOUN 1 (in Medieval Europe) a pilgrim bearing a palm branch as a sign of his visit to the Holy Land. 2 (in Medieval Europe) an itinerant monk. 3 (in Medieval Europe) any pilgrim. 4 any of various artificial angling flies characterized by hackles around the length of the body.
▷HISTORY C13: from Old French *palmier,* from Medieval Latin *palmārius,* from Latin *palma* palm

Palmer Archipelago NOUN a group of islands between South America and Antarctica: part of the British colony of Falkland Islands and Dependencies. Former name: **Antarctic Archipelago.**

Palmer Land NOUN the S part of the Antarctic Peninsula.

Palmer Peninsula NOUN the former name (until 1964) for the **Antarctic Peninsula.**

Palmerston (ˈpɑːməstən) NOUN the former name (1869–1911) of **Darwin.**

Palmerston North NOUN a city in New Zealand, in the S North Island on the Manawatu River. Pop. (urban area): 76 300 (1995 est.).

palmer worm NOUN the hairy black and white caterpillar of the goldtail moth.
▷HISTORY C16: originally applied to various destructive caterpillars of migratory habits

palmette (pælˈmɛt) NOUN *Archaeol* an ornament or design resembling the palm leaf.
▷HISTORY C19: from French: a little PALM[2]

palmetto (pælˈmɛtəʊ) NOUN, *plural* **-tos** *or* **-toes.** 1 any of several small chiefly tropical fan palms, esp any of the genus *Sabal,* of the southeastern US. See also **cabbage palmetto, saw palmetto.** 2 any of various other fan palms such as palms of the genera *Serenoa, Thrinax,* and *Chamaerops.*
▷HISTORY C16: from Spanish *palmito* a little PALM[2]

Palmira (*Spanish* palˈmira) NOUN a city in W Colombia: agricultural trading centre. Pop.: 226 500 (1999 est.).

palmistry (ˈpɑːmɪstrɪ) NOUN the process or art of interpreting character, telling fortunes, etc., by the configuration of lines, marks, and bumps on a person's hand. Also called: **chiromancy.**
▷HISTORY C15 *pawmestry,* from *paume* PALM[1]; the second element is unexplained
▸**ˈpalmist** NOUN

palmitate (ˈpælmɪˌteɪt) NOUN any salt or ester of palmitic acid.

palmitic acid (pælˈmɪtɪk) NOUN a white crystalline solid that is a saturated fatty acid: used in the manufacture of soap and candles. Formula: $(C_{15}H_{31})COOH$. Systematic name: **hexadecanoic acid.**
▷HISTORY C19: from French *palmitique;* see PALM[2], -ITE[2], -IC

palmitin (ˈpælmɪtɪn) NOUN the colourless glyceride of palmitic acid, occurring in many natural oils and fats. Formula: $(C_{15}H_{31}COO)_3C_3H_5$. Also called: **tripalmitin.**

▷HISTORY C19: from French *palmitine,* probably from *palmite* pith of the palm tree; see PALM[2]

palm off VERB (*tr, adverb;* often foll by *on*) 1 to offer, sell, or spend fraudulently: *to palm off a counterfeit coin.* 2 to divert in order to be rid of: *I palmed the unwelcome visitor off on John.*

palm oil NOUN a yellow butter-like oil obtained from the fruit of the oil palm, used as an edible fat and in soap.

palm-oil chop NOUN a W African dish made with meat and palm oil.

Palm Springs NOUN a city in the US, in California: a popular tourist resort. Pop.: 40 181 (1990).

palm sugar NOUN sugar obtained from the sap of certain species of palm trees.

Palm Sunday NOUN the Sunday before Easter commemorating Christ's triumphal entry into Jerusalem.

palmtop computer (ˈpɑːmˌtɒp) NOUN a computer that has a small screen and compressed keyboard and is small enough to be held in the hand, often used as a personal organizer. Often shortened to: **palmtop.** Compare **laptop computer.**

palm vaulting NOUN a less common name for **fan vaulting.**

palm wine NOUN (esp in W Africa) the sap drawn from the palm tree, esp when allowed to ferment.

palmy (ˈpɑːmɪ) ADJECTIVE **palmier, palmiest.** 1 prosperous, flourishing, or luxurious: *a palmy life.* 2 covered with, relating to, or resembling palms: *a palmy beach.*

palmyra (pælˈmaɪrə) NOUN a tall tropical Asian palm, *Borassus flabellifer,* with large fan-shaped leaves used for thatching and weaving; grown also for its edible seedlings.
▷HISTORY C17: from Portuguese *palmeira* palm tree (see PALM[2]); perhaps influenced by PALMYRA, city in Syria

Palmyra (pælˈmaɪrə) NOUN 1 an ancient city in central Syria: said to have been built by Solomon. Biblical name: **Tadmor.** 2 an island in the central Pacific, in the Line Islands: under US administration.

Palo Alto NOUN 1 (ˈpæləʊ ˈæltəʊ) a city in W California, southeast of San Francisco: founded in 1891 as the seat of Stanford University. Pop.: 55 900 (1990). 2 (*Spanish* ˈpalo ˈalto) a battlefield in E Mexico, northwest of Monterrey, where the first battle (1846) of the Mexican War took place, in which the Mexicans under General Mariano Arista were defeated by the Americans under General Zachary Taylor.

palo cortado (ˈpæləʊ kɔrˈtɑdəʊ) NOUN a rich, dry sherry.
▷HISTORY Spanish, literally: crossed stick (referring to the classification system in which butts of palo cortado are marked with a vertical line and one or more horizontal lines)

palolo worm (pəˈləʊləʊ) NOUN any of several polychaete worms of the family *Eunicidae, esp Eunice viridis,* of the S Pacific Ocean: reproductive segments are shed from the posterior end of the body when breeding.
▷HISTORY C20 *palolo,* from Samoan or Tongan

Palomar (ˈpæləˌmɑː) NOUN **Mount.** a mountain in S California, northeast of San Diego: site of **Mount Palomar Observatory,** which has a large (200-inch) reflecting telescope. Height: 1871 m (6140 ft.).

palomino (ˌpæləˈmiːnəʊ) NOUN, *plural* **-nos.** a golden horse with a cream or white mane and tail.
▷HISTORY American Spanish, from Spanish: dovelike, from Latin *palumbīnus,* from *palumbēs* ring dove

palooka (pəˈluːkə) NOUN *US, slang* a stupid or clumsy boxer or other person.
▷HISTORY C20: origin uncertain

Palos (*Spanish* ˈpalɔs) NOUN a village and former port in SW Spain: starting point of Columbus' voyage of discovery to America (1492).

palp (pælp) *or* **palpus** (ˈpælpəs) NOUN, *plural* **palps** *or* **palpi** (ˈpælpaɪ). 1 either of a pair of sensory appendages that arise from the mouthparts of crustaceans and insects. 2 either of a pair of tactile organs arising from the head or anterior end of certain annelids and molluscs.
▷HISTORY C19: from French, from Latin *palpus* a touching
▶ˈ**palpal** ADJECTIVE

palpable (ˈpælpəbᵊl) ADJECTIVE 1 (*usually prenominal*) easily perceived by the senses or the mind; obvious: *the excuse was a palpable lie.* 2 capable of being touched; tangible. 3 *Med* capable of being discerned by the sense of touch: *a palpable tumour.*
▷HISTORY C14: from Late Latin *palpābilis* that may be touched, from Latin *palpāre* to stroke, touch
▶ˌ**palpaˈbility** *or* ˈ**palpableness** NOUN ▶ˈ**palpably** ADVERB

palpate[1] (ˈpælpeɪt) VERB (*tr*) *Med* to examine (an area of the body) by the sense of touch and pressure.
▷HISTORY C19: from Latin *palpāre* to stroke
▶**palˈpation** NOUN

palpate[2] (ˈpælpeɪt) ADJECTIVE *Zoology* of, relating to, or possessing a palp or palps.

palpebral (ˈpælpɪbrəl) ADJECTIVE of or relating to the eyelid.
▷HISTORY C19: from Late Latin *palpebrālis,* from Latin *palpebra* eyelid; probably related to *palpāre* to stroke

palpebrate ADJECTIVE (ˈpælpɪbrɪt, -ˌbreɪt) 1 having eyelids. ◆ VERB (ˈpælpɪˌbreɪt) 2 (*intr*) to wink or blink, esp repeatedly.

palpitate (ˈpælpɪˌteɪt) VERB (*intr*) 1 (of the heart) to beat with abnormal rapidity. 2 to flutter or tremble.
▷HISTORY C17: from Latin *palpitāre* to throb, from *palpāre* to stroke
▶ˈ**palpitant** ADJECTIVE ▶ˌ**palpiˈtation** NOUN

palsgrave (ˈpɔːlzgreɪv) NOUN *Archaic* a German count palatine.
▷HISTORY C16: from Dutch, from Middle Dutch *paltsgrave,* from *palts* estate of a palatine + *grave* count
▶**palsgravine** (ˈpɔːlzgrəˌviːn) FEMININE NOUN

palstave (ˈpɔːlˌsteɪv) NOUN *Archaeol* a kind of celt, usually of bronze, made to fit into a split wooden handle rather than having a socket for the handle.
▷HISTORY C19: from Danish *paalstav,* from Old Norse, from *páll* spade + *stafr* STAFF[1]

palsy (ˈpɔːlzɪ) *Pathol* ◆ NOUN, *plural* **-sies.** 1 paralysis, esp of a specified type: *cerebral palsy.* ◆ VERB **-sies, -sying, -sied.** (*tr*) 2 to paralyse.
▷HISTORY C13 *palesi,* from Old French *paralisie,* from Latin PARALYSIS
▶ˈ**palsied** ADJECTIVE

palsy-walsy (ˈpælzɪˌwælzɪ) ADJECTIVE *Informal* excessively friendly.

palter (ˈpɔːltə) VERB (*intr*) 1 to act or talk insincerely. 2 to haggle.
▷HISTORY C16: of unknown origin
▶ˈ**palterer** NOUN

paltry (ˈpɔːltrɪ) ADJECTIVE **-trier, -triest.** 1 insignificant; meagre. 2 worthless or petty.
▷HISTORY C16: from Low Germanic *palter, paltrig* ragged
▶ˈ**paltrily** ADVERB ▶ˈ**paltriness** NOUN

paludal (pəˈljuːdᵊl, ˈpæljʊdᵊl) ADJECTIVE *Rare* 1 of, relating to, or produced by marshes. 2 malarial.
▷HISTORY C19: from Latin *palus* marsh; related to Sanskrit *palvala* pond

paludism (ˈpæljʊˌdɪzəm) NOUN *Pathol* a rare word for **malaria.**
▷HISTORY C19: from Latin *palus* marsh

Paludrine (ˈpæljʊdrɪn) NOUN *Trademark* proguanil hydrochloride, a synthetic antimalarial drug first produced in 1944.

pal up VERB (*intr, adverb;* often foll by *with*) *Informal* to become friends (with): *he palled up with the other boys.*

paly (ˈpeɪlɪ) ADJECTIVE (*usually postpositive*) *Heraldry* vertically striped.
▷HISTORY C15: from Old French *palé,* from Latin *pālus* stake; see PALE[2]

palynology (ˌpælɪˈnɒlədʒɪ) NOUN the study of living and fossil pollen grains and plant spores.
▷HISTORY C20: from Greek *palunein* to scatter + -LOGY
▶**palynological** (ˌpælɪnəˈlɒdʒɪkᵊl) ADJECTIVE
▶ˌ**palyˈnologist** NOUN

Pama-Nyungan (ˈpɑːməˈnjuŋgən) ADJECTIVE 1 of or relating to the largest superfamily of languages within the phylum of languages spoken by the native Australians. ◆ NOUN 2 this phylum.

Pamirs (pəˈmɪəz) PLURAL NOUN **the.** a mountainous area of central Asia, mainly in Tajikistan and partly in Kyrgyzstan, extending into China and Afghanistan: consists of a complex of high ranges, from which the Tian Shan projects to the north, the Kunlun and Karakoram to the east, and the Hindu Kush to the west; Kommunizma Peak is situated in the Tajik Pamirs. Highest peak: Kongur Shan, 7719 m (25 326 ft.). Also called: **Pamir.**

Pamlico Sound (ˈpæmlɪkəʊ) NOUN an inlet of the Atlantic between the E coast of North Carolina and its chain of offshore islands. Length: 130 km (80 miles).

pampas (ˈpæmpəz) NOUN (*functioning as singular or more often plural*) **a** the extensive grassy plains of temperate South America, esp in Argentina. **b** (*as modifier*): *pampas dwellers.*
▷HISTORY C18: from American Spanish *pampa* (sing), from Quechua *bamba* plain
▶**pampean** (ˈpæmpɪən, pæmˈpiːən) ADJECTIVE

pampas grass (ˈpæmpəs, -pəz) NOUN any of various large grasses of the South American genus *Cortaderia* and related genera, widely cultivated for their large feathery silver-coloured flower branches.

Pampeluna (ˌpæmpəˈluːnə) NOUN the former name of **Pamplona.**

pamper (ˈpæmpə) VERB (*tr*) 1 to treat with affectionate and usually excessive indulgence; coddle; spoil. 2 *Archaic* to feed to excess.
▷HISTORY C14: of Germanic origin; compare German dialect *pampfen* to gorge oneself
▶ˈ**pamperer** NOUN

pampero (pæmˈpɛərəʊ; *Spanish* pamˈpero) NOUN, *plural* **-ros** (-rəʊz; *Spanish* -ros). a dry cold wind in South America blowing across the pampas from the south or southwest.
▷HISTORY C19: from American Spanish: (wind) of the PAMPAS

pamphlet (ˈpæmflɪt) NOUN 1 a brief publication generally having a paper cover; booklet. 2 a brief treatise, often on a subject of current interest, published in pamphlet form.
▷HISTORY C14 *pamflet,* from Anglo-Latin *panfletus,* from Medieval Latin *Pamphilus* title of a popular 12th-century amatory poem from Greek *Pamphilos* masculine proper name

pamphleteer (ˌpæmflɪˈtɪə) NOUN 1 a person who writes or issues pamphlets, esp of a controversial nature. ◆ VERB 2 (*intr*) to write or issue pamphlets.

pamphrey (ˈpæmfrɪ) NOUN *Ulster, dialect* a cabbage.
▷HISTORY of unknown origin

Pamphylia (pæmˈfɪlɪə) NOUN an area on the S coast of ancient Asia Minor.

Pamplona (pæmˈpləʊnə; *Spanish* pamˈplona) NOUN a city in N Spain in the foothills of the Pyrenees: capital of the kingdom of Navarre from the 11th century until 1841. Pop.: 171 150 (1998 est.). Former name: **Pampeluna.**

pampoen (ˌpamˈpʊn) NOUN *South African* 1 a pumpkin. 2 *Informal* a fool.

pampootie (ˌpæmˈpuːtiː) NOUN a rawhide slipper worn by men in the Aran Islands.
▷HISTORY C19: of uncertain origin

pan[1] (pæn) NOUN 1 **a** a wide metal vessel used in cooking. **b** (*in combination*): *saucepan.* 2 Also called: **panful.** the amount such a vessel will hold. 3 any of various similar vessels used esp in industry, as for boiling liquids. 4 a dish used by prospectors, esp gold prospectors, for separating a valuable mineral from the gravel or earth containing it by washing and agitating. 5 either of the two dishlike receptacles on a balance. 6 Also called: **lavatory pan.** *Brit* the bowl of a lavatory. 7 **a** a natural or artificial depression in the ground where salt can be obtained by the evaporation of brine. **b** a natural depression containing water or mud. 8 *Caribbean* the indented top from an oil drum used as the treble drum in a steel band. 9 See **hardpan, brainpan.** 10 a small ice floe. 11 a slang word for **face** (sense 1a). 12 a small cavity containing priming powder in the locks of old guns. 13 a hard substratum of soil. 14 short for **pan loaf.** ◆ VERB **pans, panning, panned.** 15 (when *tr,* often foll by *off* or *out*) to wash (gravel) in a pan to separate particles of (valuable minerals) from it. 16 (*intr;* often foll by *out*) (of

gravel) to yield valuable minerals by this process. [17] *(tr) Informal* to criticize harshly: *the critics panned his new play.* ◆ See also **pan out.**
▷HISTORY Old English *panne;* related to Old Saxon, Old Norse *panna,* Old High German *pfanna*

pan[2] (pæn) NOUN [1] the leaf of the betel tree. [2] a preparation of this leaf which is chewed, together with betel nuts and lime, in India and the East Indies.
▷HISTORY C17: from Hindi, from Sanskrit *parna* feather, wing, leaf

pan[3] (pæn) VERB **pans, panning, panned.** [1] to move (a film camera) or (of a film camera) to be moved so as to follow a moving object or obtain a panoramic effect. ◆ NOUN [2] **a** the act of panning. **b** *(as modifier): a pan shot.*
▷HISTORY C20: shortened from *panoramic*

Pan (pæn) NOUN *Greek myth* the god of fields, woods, shepherds, and flocks, represented as a man with a goat's legs, horns, and ears. Related adjectives: **Pandean, Panic.**

Pan. ABBREVIATION FOR Panama.

pan- COMBINING FORM [1] all or every: *panchromatic.* [2] including or relating to all parts or members: *Pan-African; pantheistic.*
▷HISTORY from Greek *pan,* neuter of *pas* all

panacea (ˌpænəˈsɪə) NOUN a remedy for all diseases or ills.
▷HISTORY C16: via Latin from Greek *panakeia* healing everything, from *pan* all + *akēs* remedy
▸**ˌpanaˈcean** ADJECTIVE

panache (pəˈnæʃ, -ˈnɑːʃ) NOUN [1] a dashing manner; style; swagger: *he rides with panache.* [2] a feathered plume on a helmet.
▷HISTORY C16: via French from Old Italian *pennacchio,* from Late Latin *pinnāculum* feather, from Latin *pinna* feather; compare Latin *pinnāculum* PINNACLE

panada (pəˈnɑːdə) NOUN a mixture of flour, water, etc., or of breadcrumbs soaked in milk, used as a thickening.
▷HISTORY C16: from Spanish, from *pan* bread, from Latin *pānis*

Pan-African ADJECTIVE [1] of or relating to all African countries or the advocacy of political unity among African countries. ◆ NOUN [2] a supporter of the Pan-African movement.
▸**ˈPan-ˈAfricanˌism** NOUN

Pan-Africanist Congress NOUN a South African political party, founded as a liberation movement in 1959. Abbreviation: **PAC.**

Panaji (pɑːˈnɑːdʒiː) NOUN a variant of **Panjim.**

Panama (ˌpænəˈmɑː, ˈpænəˌmɑː) NOUN [1] a republic in Central America, occupying the Isthmus of Panama: gained independence from Spain in 1821 and joined Greater Colombia; became independent in 1903, with the immediate area around the canal forming the Canal Zone under US jurisdiction; Panama assumed sovereignty over the Canal Zone in 1979 and full control in 1999. Official language: Spanish; English is also widely spoken. Religion: Roman Catholic majority. Currency: balboa. Capital: Panama City. Pop.: 2 903 000 (2001 est.). Area: 75 650 sq. km (29 201 sq. miles). [2] **Isthmus of.** an isthmus linking North and South America, between the Pacific and the Caribbean. Length: 676 km (420 miles). Width (at its narrowest point): 50 km (31 miles). Former name: (Isthmus of) **Darien.** [3] **Gulf of.** a wide inlet of the Pacific in Panama.

Panama Canal NOUN a canal across the Isthmus of Panama, linking the Atlantic and Pacific Oceans: extends from Colón on the Caribbean Sea southeast to Balboa on the Gulf of Panama; built by the US (1904–14), after an unsuccessful previous attempt (1880–89) by the French under de Lesseps. Length: 64 km (40 miles).

Panama Canal Zone NOUN See **Canal Zone.**

Panama City NOUN the capital of Panama, near the Pacific entrance of the Panama Canal: developed rapidly with the building of the Panama Canal; seat of the University of Panama (1935). Pop.: 415 964 (2000).

Panama hat NOUN *(sometimes not capital)* a hat made of the plaited leaves of the jipijapa plant of Central and South America. Often shortened to: **panama** *or* **Panama.**

Panamanian (ˌpænəˈmeɪnɪən) ADJECTIVE [1] of or relating to Panama or its inhabitants. ◆ NOUN [2] a native or inhabitant of Panama.

Pan-American ADJECTIVE of, relating to, or concerning North, South, and Central America collectively or the advocacy of political or economic unity among American countries.
▸**ˈPan-Aˈmericanˌism** NOUN

Pan American Union NOUN the secretariat and major official agency of the Organization of American States.

pan and tilt head NOUN *Films, television* a mounting device on which a camera may be rotated in a horizontal plane (pan) or in a vertical plane (tilt).

Pan-Arabism (ˈærəˌbɪzəm) NOUN the principle of, support for, or the movement towards Arab political union or cooperation.
▸**ˈPan-ˈArab** ADJECTIVE, NOUN ▸**ˈPan-ˈArabic** ADJECTIVE

panatella (ˌpænəˈtɛlə) NOUN a long slender cigar.
▷HISTORY American Spanish *panetela* long slim biscuit, from Italian *panatella* small loaf, from *pane* bread, from Latin *pānis*

Panathenaea (pæˌnæθɪˈniːə) NOUN (in ancient Athens) a summer festival on the traditional birthday of Athena.

Panay (pɑːˈnaɪ) NOUN an island in the central Philippines, the westernmost of the Visayan Islands. Pop.: 2 595 315 (latest est.). Area: 12 300 sq. km (4750 sq. miles).

pancake (ˈpænˌkeɪk) NOUN [1] **a** a thin flat cake made from batter and fried on both sides, often served rolled and filled with a sweet or savoury mixture. **b** *(as modifier): pancake mix.* [2] a Scot name for **drop scone.** [3] a stick or flat cake of compressed make-up. [4] Also called: **pancake landing.** an aircraft landing made by levelling out a few feet from the ground and then dropping onto it. ◆ VERB [5] to cause (an aircraft) to make a pancake landing or (of an aircraft) to make a pancake landing.

Pancake Day NOUN another name for **Shrove Tuesday.**

pancake ice NOUN thin slabs of newly formed ice in polar seas.

pancetta (pænˈtʃɛtə; *Italian* panˈtʃetta) NOUN a lightly spiced cured bacon from Italy.
▷HISTORY Italian, literally: little belly

panchax (ˈpænˌtʃæks) NOUN any of several brightly coloured tropical Asian cyprinodont fishes of the genus *Aplocheilus,* such as *A. panchax* (**blue panchax**).
▷HISTORY C19: from New Latin (former generic name), of obscure origin

Panchayat (pənˈtʃɑːjət) NOUN a village council in India.
▷HISTORY Hindi, from Sanskrit *panch* five, because such councils originally consisted of five members

Panchen Lama (ˈpɑːntʃən) NOUN one of the two Grand Lamas of Tibet, ranking below the Dalai Lama. Also called: **Tashi Lama.**
▷HISTORY from Tibetan *panchen,* literally: great jewel, from the title of the lama (in full: great jewel among scholars)

panchromatic (ˌpænkrəʊˈmætɪk) ADJECTIVE *Photog* (of an emulsion or film) made sensitive to all colours by the addition of suitable dyes to the emulsion. Compare **orthochromatic.**
▸**panchromatism** (pænˈkrəʊməˌtɪzəm) NOUN

pancosmism (pænˈkɒzˌmɪzəm) NOUN the philosophical doctrine that the material universe is all that exists.
▷HISTORY C19: see PAN-, COSMOS, -ISM

pancratium (pænˈkreɪʃɪəm) NOUN, *plural* **-tia** (-ʃɪə). (in ancient Greece) a wrestling and boxing contest.
▷HISTORY C17: via Latin from Greek *pankration,* from PAN- + *kratos* strength
▸**pancratic** (pænˈkrætɪk) ADJECTIVE

pancreas (ˈpæŋkrɪəs) NOUN a large elongated glandular organ, situated behind the stomach, that secretes insulin and pancreatic juice.
▷HISTORY C16: via New Latin from Greek *pankreas,* from PAN- + *kreas* flesh
▸**pancreatic** (ˌpæŋkrɪˈætɪk) ADJECTIVE

pancreatic juice NOUN the clear alkaline secretion of the pancreas that is released into the duodenum and contains several digestive enzymes.

pancreatin (ˈpæŋkrɪətɪn) NOUN the powdered extract of the pancreas of certain animals, such as the pig, used in medicine as an aid to digestion by virtue of the enzymes it contains.

pancreatitis (ˌpæŋkrɪəˈtaɪtɪs) NOUN inflammation of the pancreas.

pancreozymin (ˌpæŋkrɪəʊˈzaɪmɪn) NOUN another name for **cholecystokinin.**

panda (ˈpændə) NOUN [1] Also called: **giant panda.** a large black-and-white herbivorous bearlike mammal, *Ailuropoda melanoleuca,* related to the raccoons and inhabiting the high mountain bamboo forests of China: family *Procyonidae.* [2] **lesser** *or* **red panda.** a closely related smaller animal resembling a raccoon, *Ailurus fulgens,* of the mountain forests of S Asia, having a reddish-brown coat and ringed tail.
▷HISTORY C19: via French from a native Nepalese word

panda car NOUN *Brit* a police patrol car, esp a blue and white one.
▷HISTORY C20: so called because it was originally white with black or blue markings, supposedly resembling the markings of the giant panda

pandanaceous (ˌpændəˈneɪʃəs) ADJECTIVE of, relating to, or belonging to the *Pandanaceae,* an Old World tropical family of monocotyledonous plants including the screw pines.

pandanus (pænˈdeɪnəs) NOUN, *plural* **-nuses.** any of various Old World tropical palmlike plants of the genus *Pandanus,* having large aerial prop roots and leaves that yield a fibre used for making mats, etc.: family *Pandanaceae.* See also **screw pine.**
▷HISTORY C19: via New Latin from Malay *pandan*

Pandarus (ˈpændərəs) NOUN [1] *Greek myth* the leader of the Lycians, allies of the Trojans in their war with the Greeks. He broke the truce by shooting Menelaus with an arrow and was killed in the ensuing battle by Diomedes. [2] (in medieval legend) the procurer of Cressida on behalf of Troilus.

Pandean (pænˈdiːən) ADJECTIVE of or relating to the god Pan.

pandect (ˈpændɛkt) NOUN [1] a treatise covering all aspects of a particular subject. [2] *(often plural)* the complete body of laws of a country; legal code.
▷HISTORY C16: via Late Latin from Greek *pandektēs* containing everything, from PAN- + *dektēs* receiver, from *dekhesthai* to receive

Pandects of Justinian PLURAL NOUN another name for **Digest.**

pandemic (pænˈdɛmɪk) ADJECTIVE [1] (of a disease) affecting persons over a wide geographical area; extensively epidemic. ◆ NOUN [2] a pandemic disease.
▷HISTORY C17: from Late Latin *pandēmus,* from Greek *pandēmos* general, from PAN- + *demos* the people

pandemonium (ˌpændɪˈməʊnɪəm) NOUN [1] wild confusion; uproar. [2] a place of uproar and chaos.
▷HISTORY C17: coined by Milton to designate the capital of hell in *Paradise Lost,* from PAN- + Greek *daimōn* DEMON
▸**ˌpandeˈmoniˌac** *or* **pandemonic** (ˌpændɪˈmɒnɪk) ADJECTIVE

pander (ˈpændə) VERB [1] *(intr; foll by to)* to give gratification (to weaknesses or desires). [2] (archaic when *tr*) to act as a go-between in a sexual intrigue (for). ◆ NOUN *also* **ˈpanderer.** [3] a person who caters for vulgar desires, esp in order to make money. [4] a person who procures a sexual partner for another; pimp.
▷HISTORY C16 (n): from *Pandare* PANDARUS

pandiculation (pænˌdɪkjʊˈleɪʃən) NOUN [1] the act of stretching and yawning, esp on waking. [2] a yawn.
▷HISTORY C17: from Latin *pandiculari,* from *pendere* to stretch

pandit (ˈpʌndɪt; *spelling pron* ˈpændɪt) NOUN *Hinduism* a variant of **pundit** (sense 3).

P & L ABBREVIATION FOR profit and loss.

P & O ABBREVIATION FOR the Peninsular and Oriental Steam Navigation Company.

pandora (pænˈdɔːrə) NOUN [1] a handsome red sea bream, *Pagellus erythrinus,* of European coastal waters, caught for food in the Mediterranean. [2] a marine bivalve mollusc of the genus *Pandora* that

lives on the surface of sandy shores and has thin equal valves. 3 *Music* another word for **bandore.**
▷HISTORY after PANDORA

Pandora (pænˈdɔːrə) *or* **Pandore** (pænˈdɔː, ˈpændɔː) NOUN *Greek myth* the first woman, made out of earth as the gods' revenge on man for obtaining fire from Prometheus. Given a box (**Pandora's box**) that she was forbidden to open, she disobeyed out of curiosity and released from it all the ills that beset man, leaving only hope within.
▷HISTORY from Greek, literally: all-gifted

pandore (ˈpændɔː) NOUN *Music* another word for **bandore.**

pandour (ˈpænduə) NOUN one of an 18th-century force of Croatian soldiers in the Austrian service, notorious for their brutality.
▷HISTORY C18: via French from Hungarian *pandur,* from Croat: guard, probably from Medieval Latin *banderius* summoner, from *bannum* BAN[1]

pandowdy (pænˈdaudɪ) NOUN, *plural* **-dies.** *US* a deep-dish pie made from fruit, esp apples, with a cake topping: *apple pandowdy.*
▷HISTORY C19: of unknown origin

p & p *Brit* ABBREVIATION FOR postage and packing.

pandurate (ˈpændjuˌreɪt) *or* **panduriform** (pænˈdjuərɪˌfɔːm) ADJECTIVE (of plant leaves) shaped like the body of a fiddle.
▷HISTORY C19: from Late Latin *pandūra* BANDORE

pandy (ˈpændɪ) *Chiefly Scot and Irish* ◆ NOUN, *plural* **-dies.** 1 (in schools) a stroke on the hand with a strap as a punishment. ◆ VERB **-dies, -dying, -died.** 2 (*tr*) to punish with such strokes.
▷HISTORY C19: from Latin *pande* (*manum*) stretch out (the hand), from *pandere* to spread or extend

pane[1] (peɪn) NOUN 1 a sheet of glass in a window or door. 2 a panel of a window, door, wall, etc. 3 a flat section or face, as of a cut diamond. 4 *Philately* **a** any of the rectangular marked divisions of a sheet of stamps made for convenience in selling. **b** a single page in a stamp booklet. See also **tête-bêche, se tenant.**
▷HISTORY C13: from Old French *pan* portion, from Latin *pannus* rag

pane[2] (peɪn) NOUN, VERB a variant of **peen.**

pané *French* (pane) ADJECTIVE (of fish, meat, etc.) dipped or rolled in breadcrumbs before cooking.

paneer (pəˈnɪə) NOUN a soft white cheese, used in Indian cookery.
▷HISTORY C20: from Hindi *panīr* cheese

panegyric (ˌpænɪˈdʒɪrɪk) NOUN a formal public commendation; eulogy.
▷HISTORY C17: via French and Latin from Greek, from *panēguris* public gathering, from PAN- + *aguris* assembly
▸ˌ**paneˈgyrical** ADJECTIVE ▸ˌ**paneˈgyrically** ADVERB
▸ˌ**paneˈgyrist** NOUN

panegyrize *or* **panegyrise** (ˈpænɪdʒɪˌraɪz) VERB to make a eulogy or eulogies (about).

panel (ˈpænᵊl) NOUN 1 a flat section of a wall, door, etc. 2 any distinct section or component of something formed from a sheet of material, esp of a car body, the spine of a book, etc. 3 a piece of material inserted in a skirt, dress, etc. 4 **a** a group of persons selected to act as a team in a quiz, to judge a contest, to discuss a topic before an audience, etc. **b** (*as modifier*): *a panel game.* 5 a public discussion by such a group: *a panel on public health.* 6 *Law* **a** a list of persons summoned for jury service. **b** the persons on a specific jury. 7 *Scots law* a person indicted or accused of crime after appearing in court. 8 **a** a thin board used as a surface or backing for an oil painting. **b** a painting done on such a surface. 9 any picture with a length much greater than its breadth. 10 See **instrument panel.** 11 (formerly, in Britain) **a** a list of patients insured under the National Health Insurance Scheme. **b** a list of medical practitioners within a given area available for consultation by these patients. 12 **on the panel.** *Brit, informal* receiving sickness benefit, esp from the government. ◆ VERB **-els, -elling, -elled** *or US* **-els, -eling, -eled.** (*tr*) 13 to furnish or decorate with panels. 14 to divide into panels. 15 *Law* **a** to empanel (a jury). **b** (in Scotland) to bring (a person) to trial; indict.
▷HISTORY C13: from Old French: portion, from *pan* piece of cloth, from Latin *pannus;* see PANE[1]

panel beater NOUN a person who beats out the bodywork of motor vehicles.

panel heating NOUN a system of space heating with panels that contain heating pipes or electrical conductors.

panelling *or US* **paneling** (ˈpænᵊlɪŋ) NOUN 1 panels collectively, as on a wall or ceiling. 2 material used for making panels.

panellist *or US* **panelist** (ˈpænᵊlɪst) NOUN a member of a panel, esp on a radio or television programme.

panel pin NOUN a light slender nail with a narrow head.

panel saw NOUN a saw with a long narrow blade for cutting thin wood.

panel truck NOUN the US and Canadian name for **delivery van.**

panel van NOUN 1 *Austral* a small van with two rear doors, esp one having windows and seats in the rear. 2 *NZ* a small enclosed delivery van.

panettone (pænəˈtəunɪ; *Italian* panetˈtoːne) NOUN, *plural* **-nes** *or* **-ni** (-nɪ). a kind of Italian spiced brioche containing sultanas: traditionally eaten at Christmas in Italy.
▷HISTORY Italian, from *panetto* small loaf, from *pane* bread, from Latin *pānis*

Pan-European ADJECTIVE of or relating to all European countries or the advocacy of political or economic unity among European countries.

pang (pæŋ) NOUN a sudden brief sharp feeling, as of loneliness, physical pain, or hunger.
▷HISTORY C16: variant of earlier *prange,* of Germanic origin

panga (ˈpæŋgə) NOUN a broad heavy knife of E Africa, used as a tool or weapon.
▷HISTORY from a native E African word

Pangaea *or* **Pangea** (pænˈdʒiːə) NOUN the ancient supercontinent, comprising all the present continents joined together, which began to break up about 200 million years ago. See also **Laurasia, Gondwanaland.**
▷HISTORY C20: from Greek, literally: all-earth

pangenesis (pænˈdʒɛnɪsɪs) NOUN a former theory of heredity, that each body cell produces hereditary particles that circulate in the blood before collecting in the reproductive cells. See also **blastogenesis** (sense 1).
▸**pangenetic** (ˌpændʒəˈnɛtɪk) ADJECTIVE
▸ˌ**pangeˈnetically** ADVERB

Pan-Germanism NOUN (esp in the 19th century) the movement for the unification of Germany.

Pang-fou (ˈpæŋˈfuː) NOUN a variant transliteration of the Chinese name for **Bengbu.**

Pangloss (ˈpænglɒs) NOUN a person who views a situation with unwarranted optimism.
▸**Panˈglossian** ADJECTIVE
▷HISTORY C19: after Dr *Pangloss,* a character in Voltaire's *Candide* (1759)

pangolin (pæŋˈgəulɪn) NOUN any mammal of the order *Pholidota* found in tropical Africa, S Asia, and Indonesia, having a body covered with overlapping horny scales and a long snout specialized for feeding on ants and termites. Also called: **scaly anteater.**
▷HISTORY C18: from Malay *peng-gōling,* from *gōling* to roll over; from its ability to roll into a ball

Pango Pango (ˈpɑːŋgəu ˈpɑːŋgəu) NOUN the former name of **Pago Pago.**

pangram (ˈpæŋˌgræm) NOUN a sentence incorporating all the letters of the alphabet, such as *the quick brown fox jumps over the lazy dog.*

panhandle[1] (ˈpænˌhændᵊl) NOUN 1 (*sometimes capital*) (in the US) a narrow strip of land that projects from one state into another. 2 (in a South African city) a plot of land without street frontage.

panhandle[2] (ˈpænˌhændᵊl) VERB *US and Canadian, informal* to accost and beg from (passers-by), esp on the street.
▷HISTORY C19: probably a back formation from *panhandler* a person who begs with a pan
▸ˈ**panˌhandler** NOUN

Panhellenic (ˌpænhɛˈlɛnɪk) ADJECTIVE of or relating to all the Greeks, all Greece, or Panhellenism.

Panhellenism (ˌpænˈhɛlɪˌnɪzəm) NOUN the principle of or support for the union of all Greeks or all Greece.
▸ˌ**Panˈhellenist** NOUN ▸ˌ**Panˌhellenˈistic** ADJECTIVE

panic (ˈpænɪk) NOUN 1 a sudden overwhelming feeling of terror or anxiety, esp one affecting a whole group of people. 2 (*modifier*) of or resulting from such terror: *panic measures.* ◆ VERB **-ics, -icking, -icked.** 3 to feel or cause to feel panic.
▷HISTORY C17: from French *panique,* from New Latin *pānicus,* from Greek *panikos* emanating from PAN, considered as the source of irrational fear
▸ˈ**panicky** ADJECTIVE

Panic (ˈpænɪk) ADJECTIVE of or relating to the god Pan.

panic attack NOUN an episode of acute and disabling anxiety associated with such physical symptoms as hyperventilation and sweating. See also **panic disorder.**

panic bolt NOUN a bolt on the inside esp of double doors that is released by pressure on a waist-high bar: used for emergency exits in theatres, shops, etc.

panic button NOUN 1 a button or switch that operates any of various safety devices, for use in an emergency. 2 **hit** *or* **press the panic button.** *Informal* to react to a situation by demanding emergency action; become excited; panic.

panic buying NOUN the buying up of large quantities of a commodity which, it is feared, is likely to be in short supply.

panic disorder NOUN *Psychiatry* a condition in which a person experiences recurrent panic attacks.

panic grass NOUN any of various grasses of the genus *Panicum,* such as millet, grown in warm and tropical regions for fodder and grain.
▷HISTORY C15 *panic,* from Latin *pānicum,* probably a back formation from *pānicula* PANICLE

panicle (ˈpænɪkᵊl) NOUN 1 a compound raceme, occurring esp in grasses. 2 any branched inflorescence.
▷HISTORY C16: from Latin *pānicula* tuft, diminutive of *panus* thread, ultimately from Greek *penos* web; related to *penion* bobbin
▸ˈ**panicled** ADJECTIVE

panicmonger (ˈpænɪkˌmʌŋgə) NOUN a person who spreads panic.

panic room NOUN a secure room with a separate telephone line within a house, to which a person can flee if someone breaks in.

panic stations PLURAL NOUN *Informal* a state of alarm; panicky reaction: *when he realized he'd lost the keys it was panic stations.*

panic-stricken *or* **panic-struck** ADJECTIVE affected by panic.

paniculate (pəˈnɪkjuˌleɪt, -lɪt) *or* **paniculated** ADJECTIVE *Botany* growing or arranged in panicles: *a paniculate inflorescence.*
▸**paˈnicuˌlately** ADVERB

panidiomorphic (pæˌnɪdɪəuˈmɔːfɪk) ADJECTIVE (of igneous rocks) having well-developed crystals.
▷HISTORY C19: from PAN- + IDIOMORPHIC

Panjabi (pʌnˈdʒɑːbɪ) NOUN, ADJECTIVE a variant spelling of **Punjabi.**

panjandrum (pænˈdʒændrəm) NOUN a pompous self-important official or person of rank.
▷HISTORY C18: after a character, the *Grand Panjandrum,* in a nonsense work (1755) by Samuel Foote, English playwright and actor

Panjim (ˈpɑːnˌʒɪm) *or* **Panaji** NOUN the capital of the Indian union territory of Goa, Daman, and Diu: a port on the Arabian Sea on the coast of Goa. Pop.: 85 515 (1991).

pan loaf NOUN *Irish and Scot, dialect* a loaf of bread with a light crust all the way round. Often shortened to: **pan.** Compare **batch**[1] (sense 4).

panmixia (pænˈmɪksɪə) *or* **panmixis** (pænˈmɪksɪs) NOUN (in population genetics) random mating within an interbreeding population.
▷HISTORY C20: from New Latin, from Greek PAN- + *mixis* act of mating
▸**panmictic** (pænˈmiktik) ADJECTIVE

Panmunjom (ˈpɑːnˈmunˈdʒɒm) NOUN a village in the demilitarized zone of Korea: site of truce talks leading to the end of the Korean War (1950–53).

pannage (ˈpænɪdʒ) NOUN *Archaic* 1 pasturage for pigs, esp in a forest. 2 the right to pasture pigs in a forest. 3 payment for this. 4 acorns, beech mast, etc., on which pigs feed.
▷HISTORY C13: from Old French *pasnage,* ultimately

from Latin *pastion-, pastiō* feeding, from *pascere* to feed

panne (pæn) NOUN a lightweight velvet fabric.
▷HISTORY C19: via Old French, from Latin *pinna* wing, feather

pannier (ˈpænɪə) NOUN 1 a large basket, esp one of a pair slung over a beast of burden. 2 one of a pair of bags slung either side of the back wheel of a motorcycle, bicycle, etc. 3 (esp in the 18th century) **a** a hooped framework to distend a woman's skirt. **b** one of two puffed-out loops of material worn drawn back onto the hips to reveal the underskirt.
▷HISTORY C13: from Old French *panier,* from Latin *pānārium* basket for bread, from *pānis* bread

pannikin (ˈpænɪkɪn) NOUN *Chiefly Brit* a small metal cup or pan.
▷HISTORY C19: from PAN[1] + -KIN

pannikin boss NOUN *Austral, informal* a person in charge of a few fellow workers.

Pannonia (pəˈnəʊnɪə) NOUN a region of the ancient world south and west of the Danube: made a Roman province in 6 A.D.

pannus (ˈpænəs) NOUN an inflammatory fleshy lesion on the surface of the eye.
▷HISTORY C15: from Latin, literally cloth

panocha (pəˈnəʊtʃə) *or* **penuche** NOUN 1 a coarse grade of sugar made in Mexico. 2 (in the US) a sweet made from brown sugar and milk, often with chopped nuts.
▷HISTORY Mexican Spanish, diminutive of Spanish *pan* bread, from Latin *pānis*

panoply (ˈpænəplɪ) NOUN, *plural* **-plies.** 1 a complete or magnificent array. 2 the entire equipment of a warrior.
▷HISTORY C17: via French from Greek *panoplia* complete armour, from PAN- + *hopla* armour, pl of *hoplon* tool
▸ˈ**panoplied** ADJECTIVE

panoptic (pænˈɒptɪk) *or* **panoptical** ADJECTIVE taking in all parts, aspects, etc., in a single view; all-embracing: *a panoptic survey.*
▷HISTORY C19: from Greek *panoptēs* seeing everything, from PAN- + *optos* visible
▸**panˈoptically** ADVERB

panorama (ˌpænəˈrɑːmə) NOUN 1 an extensive unbroken view, as of a landscape, in all directions. 2 a wide or comprehensive survey: *a panorama of the week's events.* 3 a large extended picture or series of pictures of a scene, unrolled before spectators a part at a time so as to appear continuous. 4 another name for **cyclorama.**
▷HISTORY C18: from PAN- + Greek *horāma* view
▸**panoramic** (ˌpænəˈræmɪk) ADJECTIVE ▸ˌ**panoˈramically** ADVERB

panoramic sight NOUN a type of artillery sight with a large field of view.

pan out VERB (*intr, adverb*) *Informal* to work out; turn out; result.

panpipes (ˈpænˌpaɪps) PLURAL NOUN (*often singular; often capital*) a number of reeds or whistles of graduated lengths bound together to form a musical wind instrument. Also called: **pipes of Pan, syrinx.**

pan potentiometer NOUN a control on a stereo sound mixing desk by means of which the relative levels in right- and left-hand channels can be adjusted and hence the apparent position of the recorded or broadcast sound source within the stereo panorama can be controlled. Often shortened to: **pan pot.**
▷HISTORY C20: from PAN(ORAMIC) + POTENTIOMETER

panradiometer (ˌpænreɪdɪˈɒmɪtə) NOUN *Physics* an instrument used for measuring radiant heat independently of wavelength.

Pan-Slavism NOUN (esp in the 19th century) the movement for the union of the Slavic peoples, esp under the hegemony of tsarist Russia.
▸ˈ**Pan-ˈSlavic** ADJECTIVE

pansophy (ˈpænsəfɪ) NOUN universal knowledge.
▷HISTORY C17: from New Latin *pansophia;* see PAN-, -SOPHY
▸**pansophic** (pænˈsɒfɪk) *or* **panˈsophical** ADJECTIVE
▸**panˈsophically** ADVERB

pansy (ˈpænzɪ) NOUN, *plural* **-sies.** 1 any violaceous garden plant that is a variety of *Viola tricolor,* having flowers with rounded velvety petals, white, yellow, or purple in colour. See also **wild pansy.** 2 *Slang, offensive* an effeminate or homosexual man or boy. 3 **a** a strong violet colour. **b** (*as adjective*): *a pansy carpet.*
▷HISTORY C15: from Old French *pensée* thought, from *penser* to think, from Latin *pensāre*

pant (pænt) VERB 1 to breathe with noisy deep gasps, as when out of breath from exertion or excitement. 2 to say (something) while breathing thus. 3 (*intr; often foll by for*) to have a frantic desire (for); yearn. 4 (*intr*) to pulsate; throb rapidly. ◆ NOUN 5 the act or an instance of panting. 6 a short deep gasping noise; puff.
▷HISTORY C15: from Old French *pantaisier,* from Greek *phantasioun* to have visions, from *phantasia* FANTASY

Pantagruel (pænˈtægruːɛl) NOUN a gigantic prince, noted for his ironical buffoonery, in the satire *Gargantua and Pantagruel* (1534) by the French writer François Rabelais (?1494–1553).
▸ˌ**Pantagruˈelian** *or* ˌ**Pantagruˈelic** ADJECTIVE
▸ˌ**Pantaˈgruelˌism** NOUN ▸ˌ**Pantaˈgruelist** NOUN

pantalets *or* **pantalettes** (ˌpæntəˈlɛts) PLURAL NOUN 1 long drawers, usually trimmed with ruffles, extending below the skirts: worn during the early and mid 19th century. 2 a pair of ruffles for the ends of such drawers.
▷HISTORY C19: diminutive of PANTALOONS

pantaloon (ˌpæntəˈluːn) NOUN *Theatre* 1 (in pantomime) an absurd old man, the butt of the clown's tricks. 2 (*usually capital*) (in commedia dell'arte) a lecherous old merchant dressed in pantaloons.
▷HISTORY C16: from French *Pantalon,* from Italian *Pantalone,* local nickname for a Venetian, probably from *San Pantaleone,* a fourth-century Venetian saint

pantaloons (ˌpæntəˈluːnz) PLURAL NOUN 1 **a** *History* men's tight-fitting trousers, esp those fastening under the instep worn in the late 18th and early 19th centuries. **b** children's trousers resembling these. 2 *Informal or facetious* any trousers, esp baggy ones.

pantechnicon (pænˈtɛknɪkən) NOUN *Brit* 1 a large van, esp one used for furniture removals. 2 a warehouse where furniture is stored.
▷HISTORY C19: from PAN- + Greek *tekhnikon* relating to the arts, from *tekhnē* art; originally the name of a London bazaar, the building later being used as a furniture warehouse

Pantelleria (*Italian* pantelleˈriːa) NOUN an Italian island in the Mediterranean, between Sicily and Tunisia: of volcanic origin; used by the Romans as a place of banishment. Pop.: 7316 (1991 est.). Area: 83 sq. km (32 sq. miles). Ancient name: **Cossyra** (kəˈsaɪrə).

Pan-Teutonism NOUN another name for **Pan-Germanism.**

Panth (pʌnθ) NOUN the Sikh community.
▷HISTORY from Punjabi: path

pantheism (ˈpænθɪˌɪzəm) NOUN 1 the doctrine that God is the transcendent reality of which man, nature, and the material universe are manifestations. 2 any doctrine that regards God as identical with the material universe or the forces of nature. 3 readiness to worship all or a large number of gods.
▸ˈ**pantheist** NOUN ▸ˌ**pantheˈistic** *or* ˌ**pantheˈistical** ADJECTIVE ▸ˌ**pantheˈistically** ADVERB

pantheon (pænˈθiːən, ˈpænθɪən) NOUN 1 (esp in ancient Greece or Rome) a temple to all the gods. 2 all the gods collectively of a religion. 3 a monument or building commemorating a nation's dead heroes.
▷HISTORY C14: via Latin from Greek *Pantheion,* from PAN- + *-theios* divine, from *theos* god

Pantheon (pænˈθiːən, ˈpænθɪən) NOUN a circular temple in Rome dedicated to all the gods, built by Agrippa in 27 B.C., rebuilt by Hadrian 120–24 A.D., and used since 609 A.D. as a Christian church.

panther (ˈpænθə) NOUN, *plural* **-thers** *or* **-ther.** 1 another name for **leopard** (sense 1), esp the black variety (**black panther**) 2 *US and Canadian* any of various related animals, esp the puma.
▷HISTORY C14: from Old French *pantère,* from Latin *panthēra,* from Greek *panthēr;* perhaps related to Sanskrit *pundarīka* tiger

panties (ˈpæntɪz) PLURAL NOUN a pair of women's or children's underpants.

pantihose (ˈpæntɪˌhəʊz) PLURAL NOUN another name (esp US and Austral) for **tights** (sense 1).
▷HISTORY C20: from PANTIES + HOSE[2]

pantile (ˈpænˌtaɪl) NOUN 1 a roofing tile, with an S-shaped cross section, laid so that the downward curve of one tile overlaps the upward curve of the adjoining tile. 2 a tapering roofing tile with a semicircular cross section, laid alternately so that the convex side of one tile overlaps the concave side of adjoining tiles.
▷HISTORY C17: from PAN[1] + TILE

pantisocracy (ˌpæntɪˈsɒkrəsɪ) NOUN a community, social group, etc., in which all have rule and everyone is equal.
▷HISTORY C18 (coined by Robert Southey (1774–1843), English poet): from Greek, from PANTO- + *isos* equal + -CRACY

panto (ˈpæntəʊ) NOUN, *plural* **-tos.** *Brit, informal* short for **pantomime** (sense 1).

panto- *or before a vowel* **pant-** COMBINING FORM all: *pantisocracy; pantofle; pantograph; pantomime.*
▷HISTORY from Greek *pant-, pas*

pantofle, pantoffle (pænˈtɒfᵊl), *or* **pantoufle** (pænˈtuːfᵊl) NOUN *Archaic* a kind of slipper.
▷HISTORY C15: from French *pantoufle,* from Old Italian *pantofola,* perhaps from Medieval Greek *pantophellos* shoe made of cork, from PANTO- + *phellos* cork

pantograph (ˈpæntəˌgrɑːf) NOUN 1 an instrument consisting of pivoted levers for copying drawings, maps, etc., to any desired scale. 2 a sliding type of current collector, esp a diamond-shaped frame mounted on a train roof in contact with an overhead wire. 3 a device consisting of a parallelogram of jointed rods used to suspend a studio lamp so that its height can be adjusted.
▸**pantographer** (pænˈtɒgrəfə) NOUN ▸**pantographic** (ˌpæntəˈgræfɪk) ADJECTIVE ▸ˌ**pantoˈgraphically** ADVERB
▸**panˈtography** NOUN

pantomime (ˈpæntəˌmaɪm) NOUN 1 (in Britain) **a** a kind of play performed at Christmas time characterized by farce, music, lavish sets, stock roles, and topical jokes. Sometimes shortened to: **panto. b** (*as modifier*): *a pantomime horse.* 2 a theatrical entertainment in which words are replaced by gestures and bodily actions. 3 action without words as a means of expression. 4 (in ancient Rome) an actor in a dumb show. 5 *Informal, chiefly Brit* a confused or farcical situation. ◆ VERB 6 another word for **mime** (sense 5).
▷HISTORY C17: via Latin from Greek *pantomīmos;* see PANTO-, MIME
▸**pantomimic** (ˌpæntəˈmɪmɪk) ADJECTIVE ▸**pantomimist** (ˈpæntəˌmaɪmɪst) NOUN

pantothenic acid (ˌpæntəˈθɛnɪk) NOUN an oily acid that is a vitamin of the B complex: occurs widely in animal and vegetable foods and is essential for cell growth. Formula: $C_9H_{17}NO_5$.
▷HISTORY C20: from Greek *pantothen* from every side

pantoum (pænˈtuːm) NOUN *Prosody* a verse form consisting of a series of quatrains in which the second and fourth lines of each verse are repeated as the first and third lines of the next.
▷HISTORY C19: via French from Malay *pantun*

pantry (ˈpæntrɪ) NOUN, *plural* **-tries.** a small room or cupboard in which provisions, cooking utensils, etc., are kept; larder.
▷HISTORY C13: via Anglo-Norman, from Old French *paneterie* store for bread, ultimately from Latin *pānis* bread

pants (pænts) PLURAL NOUN 1 *Brit* an undergarment reaching from the waist to the thighs or knees. 2 the usual US and Canadian name for **trousers.** 3 **bore, scare,** etc., **the pants off.** *Informal* to bore, scare, etc., extremely. ◆ ADJECTIVE 4 *Brit, slang* inferior.
▷HISTORY C19: shortened from *pantaloons;* see PANTALOON

pantsuit (ˈpæntˌsjuːt, -ˌsuːt) NOUN the US and Canadian term for **trouser suit.**

panty girdle (ˈpæntɪ) NOUN a foundation garment with a crotch, often of lighter material than a girdle.

pantyhose ('pæntɪˌhəʊz) NOUN the NZ spelling of **pantihose.**

pantywaist ('pæntɪˌweɪst) NOUN *US, informal* a man or boy considered as childish, lacking in courage, etc.
▷HISTORY C20: originally a child's garment of trousers buttoned to a jacket at the waist

panzer ('pænzə; *German* 'pantsər) NOUN [1] (*modifier*) of, relating to, or characteristic of the fast mechanized armoured units employed by the German army in World War II: *a panzer attack.* [2] a vehicle belonging to a panzer unit, esp a tank. [3] (*plural*) armoured troops.
▷HISTORY C20: from German, from Middle High German, from Old French *panciere* coat of mail, from Latin *pantex* PAUNCH

panzootic (ˌpænzəʊ'ɒtɪk) NOUN *Vet science* a disease that affects all the animals in a geographical area.

Pão de Açúcar (pə̃un di a'sukar) NOUN the Portuguese name for the **Sugar Loaf Mountain.**

Paoting *or* **Pao-ting** ('paʊ'tɪŋ) NOUN a variant transliteration of the Chinese name for **Baoding.**

Paotow ('paʊ'taʊ) NOUN a variant transliteration of the Chinese name for **Baotou.**

pap[1] (pæp) NOUN [1] any soft or semiliquid food, such as bread softened with milk, esp for babies or invalids; mash. [2] *South African* porridge made from maize. [3] worthless or oversimplified ideas; drivel: *intellectual pap.*
▷HISTORY C15: from Middle Low German *pappe,* via Medieval Latin from Latin *pappāre* to eat; compare Dutch *pap,* Italian *pappa*

pap[2] (pæp) NOUN [1] *Scot and northern English, dialect* a nipple or teat. [2] **a** something resembling a breast or nipple, such as (formerly) one of a pair of rounded hilltops. **b** (*capital as part of a name*): *the Pap of Glencoe.*
▷HISTORY C12: of Scandinavian origin, imitative of a sucking sound; compare Latin *papilla* nipple, Sanskrit *pippalaka*

papa[1] (pə'pɑː) NOUN *Old-fashioned* an informal word for **father** (sense 1).
▷HISTORY C17: from French, a children's word for father; compare Late Latin *pāpa,* Greek *pappa*

papa[2] ('pɑːpɑː) NOUN *RC Church* another name for the **pope**[1] (sense 1).
▷HISTORY C16: from Italian

papa[3] ('pɑːpa) NOUN *NZ rare.* a soft blue-grey clay of marine siltstone or sandstone.
▷HISTORY Maori

Papa ('pɑːpɑː) NOUN *Communications* a code word for the letter *p.*

papacy ('peɪpəsɪ) NOUN, *plural* **-cies.** [1] the office or term of office of a pope. [2] the system of government in the Roman Catholic Church that has the pope as its head.
▷HISTORY C14: from Medieval Latin *pāpātia,* from *pāpa* POPE[1]

papain (pə'peɪɪn, -'paɪɪn) NOUN a proteolytic enzyme occurring in the unripe fruit of the papaya tree, *Carica papaya:* used as a meat tenderizer and in medicine as an aid to protein digestion.
▷HISTORY C19: from PAPAYA

papal ('peɪpᵊl) ADJECTIVE of or relating to the pope or the papacy.
▸ **'papally** ADVERB

papal cross NOUN a cross with three crosspieces.

Papal States PLURAL NOUN the temporal domain of the popes in central Italy from 756 A.D. until the unification of Italy in 1870. Also called: **States of the Church.**

Papanicolaou test *or* **smear** (ˌpæpə'nɪkəluː) NOUN the full name for **Pap test.**

paparazzo (ˌpæpə'rætsəʊ) NOUN, *plural* **-razzi** (-'rætsiː). a freelance photographer who specializes in candid camera shots of famous people and often invades their privacy to obtain such photographs.
▷HISTORY C20: from Italian

papaveraceous (pəˌpeɪvə'reɪʃəs) ADJECTIVE of, relating to, or belonging to the *Papaveraceae,* a family of plants having large showy flowers and a cylindrical seed capsule with pores beneath the lid: includes the poppies and greater celandine.
▷HISTORY C19: from New Latin, from Latin *papāver* POPPY

papaverine (pə'peɪvəˌriːn, -rɪn) NOUN a white crystalline almost insoluble alkaloid found in opium and used as an antispasmodic to treat coronary spasms and certain types of colic. Formula: $C_{20}H_{21}NO_4$.
▷HISTORY C19: from Latin *papāver* POPPY

papaw (pə'pɔː) *or* **pawpaw** NOUN [1] another name for **papaya.** [2] Also called: **custard apple. a** a bush or small tree, *Asimina triloba,* of central North America, having small fleshy edible fruit: family *Annonaceae.* **b** the fruit of this tree.
▷HISTORY C16: from Spanish PAPAYA

papaya (pə'paɪə) NOUN [1] a Caribbean evergreen tree, *Carica papaya,* with a crown of large dissected leaves and large green hanging fruit: family *Caricaceae.* [2] the fruit of this tree, having a yellow sweet edible pulp and small black seeds. ◆ Also called **papaw, pawpaw.**
▷HISTORY C15 *papaye,* from Spanish *papaya,* from an American Indian language; compare Carib *ababai*
▸ **pa'payan** ADJECTIVE

Papeete (ˌpɑːpɪ'iːtɪ) NOUN the capital of French Polynesia, on the NW coast of Tahiti: one of the largest towns in the S Pacific. Pop.: 25 353 (1996), with a conurbation of 121 000 (1996 est.).

paper ('peɪpə) NOUN [1] a substance made from cellulose fibres derived from rags, wood, etc., often with other additives, and formed into flat thin sheets suitable for writing on, decorating walls, wrapping, etc. Related adjective: **papyraceous.** [2] a single piece of such material, esp if written or printed on. [3] (*usually plural*) documents for establishing the identity of the bearer; credentials. [4] (*plural*) Also called: **ship's papers.** official documents relating to the ownership, cargo, etc., of a ship. [5] (*plural*) collected diaries, letters, etc. [6] See **newspaper** or **wallpaper.** [7] *Government* See **white paper, green paper, command paper.** [8] a lecture or short published treatise on a specific subject. [9] a short essay, as by a student. [10] **a** a set of written examination questions. **b** the student's answers. [11] *Commerce* See **commercial paper.** [12] *Theatre, slang* a free ticket. [13] **on paper.** in theory, as opposed to fact: *it was a good idea on paper, but failed in practice.* ◆ ADJECTIVE [14] made of paper: *paper cups do not last long.* [15] thin like paper: *paper walls.* [16] (*prenominal*) existing only as recorded on paper but not yet in practice: *paper profits; paper expenditure.* [17] taking place in writing: *paper battles.* ◆ VERB [18] to cover (walls) with wallpaper. [19] (*tr*) to cover or furnish with paper. [20] (*tr*) *Theatre, slang* to fill (a performance) by giving away free tickets (esp in the phrase **paper the house**). ◆ See also **paper over.**
▷HISTORY C14: from Latin PAPYRUS
▸ **'paperer** NOUN

paperback ('peɪpəˌbæk) NOUN [1] a book or edition with covers made of flexible card, sold relatively cheaply. Compare **hardback.** ◆ ADJECTIVE *also* **'paperˌbound, soft-cover.** [2] of or denoting a paperback or publication of paperbacks. ◆ VERB (*tr*) [3] to publish in paperback.
▸ **'paperˌbacker** NOUN

paperbark ('peɪpəˌbɑːk) NOUN [1] any of several Australian myrtaceous trees of the genus *Melaleuca,* esp *M. quinquenervia,* of swampy regions, having spear-shaped leaves and papery bark that can be peeled off in thin layers. [2] the papery bark of any of these trees.

paperboard ('peɪpəˌbɔːd) NOUN **a** a thick cardboard made of compressed layers of paper pulp; pasteboard. **b** (*as modifier*): *a paperboard box.*

paperboy ('peɪpəˌbɔɪ) NOUN a boy employed to deliver newspapers, magazines, etc.
▸ **'paperˌgirl** FEMININE NOUN

paper chase NOUN a former type of cross-country run in which a runner laid a trail of paper for others to follow.

paperclip ('peɪpəˌklɪp) NOUN a clip for holding sheets of paper together, esp one made of bent wire.

paper-cutter NOUN a machine for cutting paper, usually a blade mounted over a table on which paper can be aligned.

paper filigree NOUN another name for **rolled paperwork.**

paperhanger ('peɪpəˌhæŋə) NOUN [1] a person who hangs wallpaper as an occupation. [2] *US, slang* a counterfeiter.
▸ **'paperˌhanging** NOUN

paperknife ('peɪpəˌnaɪf) NOUN, *plural* **-knives.** a knife with a comparatively blunt blade, esp one of wood, bone, etc., for opening sealed envelopes.

paperless ('peɪpəlɪs) ADJECTIVE of, relating to, or denoting a means of communication, record keeping, etc., esp electronic, that does not use paper: *the paperless office.*

paper money NOUN paper currency issued by the government or the central bank as legal tender and which circulates as a substitute for specie.

paper mulberry NOUN a small moraceous E Asian tree, *Broussonetia papyrifera,* the inner bark of which was formerly used for making paper in Japan. See also **tapa.**

paper nautilus NOUN any cephalopod mollusc of the genus *Argonauta, esp A. argo,* of warm and tropical seas, having a papery external spiral shell: order *Octopoda* (octopods). Also called: **argonaut.** Compare **pearly nautilus.**

paper over VERB (*tr, adverb*) to conceal (something controversial or unpleasant).

paper tape NOUN a strip of paper for recording information in the form of rows of either six or eight holes, some or all of which are punched to produce a combination used as a discrete code symbol, formerly used in computers, telex machines, etc. US equivalent: **perforated tape.**

paper tiger NOUN a nation, institution, etc., that appears powerful but is in fact weak or insignificant.
▷HISTORY C20: translation of a Chinese phrase first applied to the US

paperweight ('peɪpəˌweɪt) NOUN a small heavy object placed on loose papers to prevent them from scattering.

paperwork ('peɪpəˌwɜːk) NOUN clerical work, such as the completion of forms or the writing of reports or letters.

papery ('peɪpərɪ) ADJECTIVE like paper, esp in thinness, flimsiness, or dryness.
▸ **'paperiness** NOUN

papeterie ('pæpətrɪ; *French* papetri) NOUN a box or case for papers and other writing materials.
▷HISTORY C19: from French, from *papetier* maker of paper, from *papier* PAPER

Paphian ('peɪfɪən) ADJECTIVE [1] of or relating to Paphos. [2] of or relating to Aphrodite. [3] *Literary* of sexual love.

Paphlagonia (ˌpæflə'gəʊnɪə) NOUN an ancient country and Roman province in N Asia Minor, on the Black Sea.

Paphos[1] ('peɪfɒs) NOUN a village in SW Cyprus, near the sites of two ancient cities: famous as the centre of Aphrodite worship and traditionally the place at which she landed after her birth among the waves. Pop.: 32 575 (1992 est.).

Paphos[2] ('peɪfɒs) *or* **Paphus** ('peɪfəs) NOUN *Greek myth* the son of Pygmalion and Galatea, who succeeded his father on the throne of Cyprus.

Papiamento (*Spanish* papja'mento) NOUN a creolized Spanish spoken in the Netherlands Antilles.
▷HISTORY Spanish, from *papia* talk

papier collé (*French* papje kɔle) NOUN a type of collage, usually of an abstract design.
▷HISTORY French, literally: glued paper

papier-mâché (ˌpæpjeɪ'mæʃeɪ; *French* papjemɑʃe) NOUN [1] a hard strong substance suitable for painting on, made of paper pulp or layers of paper mixed with paste, size, etc., and moulded when moist. ◆ ADJECTIVE [2] made of papier-mâché.
▷HISTORY C18: from French, literally: chewed paper

papilla (pə'pɪlə) NOUN, *plural* **-lae** (-liː). [1] the small projection of tissue at the base of a hair, tooth, or feather. [2] any other similar protuberance. [3] any minute blunt hair or process occurring in plants.
▷HISTORY C18: from Latin: nipple; related to Latin *papula* pimple
▸ **pa'pillary** *or* **'papillate** *or* **'papillose** ADJECTIVE

papilloma (ˌpæpɪ'ləʊmə) NOUN, *plural* **-mata** (-mətə) *or* **-mas.** *Pathol* a benign tumour derived from epithelial tissue and forming a rounded or lobulated mass.

▷HISTORY C19: from PAPILLA + -OMA
▸ˌpapil'lomatous ADJECTIVE ▸ˌpapilˌloma'tosis NOUN

papillon ('pæpɪˌlɒn) NOUN a breed of toy spaniel with large ears.
▷HISTORY French: butterfly, from Latin *pāpiliō*

papillote ('pæpɪˌləʊt) NOUN [1] a paper frill around cutlets, etc. [2] **en papillote** (*French* ɑ̃ papijɔt). (of food) cooked in oiled greaseproof paper or foil.
▷HISTORY C18: from French PAPILLON

papist ('peɪpɪst) NOUN, ADJECTIVE (*often capital*) *Usually disparaging* another term for **Roman Catholic.**
▷HISTORY C16: from French *papiste,* from Church Latin *pāpa* POPE[1]
▸pa'pistical *or* pa'pistic ADJECTIVE ▸'papistry NOUN

papoose *or* **pappoose** (pə'puːs) NOUN [1] an American Indian baby or child. [2] a pouchlike bag used for carrying a baby, worn on the back.
▷HISTORY C17: from Algonquian *papoos*

pappus ('pæpəs) NOUN, *plural* **pappi** ('pæpaɪ). a ring of fine feathery hairs surrounding the fruit in composite plants, such as the thistle; aids dispersal of the fruits by the wind.
▷HISTORY C18: via New Latin, from Greek *pappos* grandfather, old man, old man's beard, hence: pappus, down
▸'pappose *or* 'pappous ADJECTIVE

pappy[1] ('pæpɪ) ADJECTIVE **-pier, -piest.** resembling pap; mushy.

pappy[2] ('pæpɪ) NOUN, *plural* **-pies.** *US* an informal word for **father.**

paprika ('pæprɪkə, pæ'priː-) NOUN [1] a mild powdered seasoning made from a sweet variety of red pepper. [2] the fruit or plant from which this seasoning is obtained.
▷HISTORY C19: via Hungarian from Serbian, from *papar* PEPPER

Pap test *or* **smear** (pæp) NOUN *Med* [1] another name for **cervical smear.** [2] a similar test for precancerous cells in other organs. ◆ Also called **Papanicolaou smear.**
▷HISTORY C20: named after George *Papanicolaou* (1883–1962), US anatomist, who devised it

Papua ('pæpjʊə) NOUN [1] **Territory of.** a former territory of Australia, consisting of SE New Guinea and adjacent islands: now part of Papua New Guinea. Former name (1888–1906): **British New Guinea.** [2] **Gulf of.** an inlet of the Coral Sea in the SE coast of New Guinea.

Papuan ('pæpjʊən) ADJECTIVE [1] of or relating to Papua or any of the languages spoken there. ◆ NOUN [2] a native or inhabitant of Papua New Guinea. [3] any of several languages of Papua New Guinea that apparently do not belong to the Malayo-Polynesian family.

Papua New Guinea NOUN a country in the SW Pacific; consists of the E half of New Guinea, the Bismarck Archipelago, the W Solomon Islands, Trobriand Islands, D'Entrecasteaux Islands, Woodlark Island, and the Louisiade Archipelago; administered by Australia from 1949 until 1975, when it became an independent member of the Commonwealth. Official language: English; Tok Pisin (English Creole) and Motu are widely spoken. Religion: Christian majority. Currency: kina. Capital: Port Moresby. Pop.: 5 287 000 (2001 est.). Area: 461 693 sq. km (178 260 sq. miles).

papule ('pæpjuːl) *or* **papula** ('pæpjʊlə) NOUN, *plural* **-ules** *or* **-ulae** (-jʊˌliː). *Pathol* a small solid usually round elevation of the skin.
▷HISTORY C19: from Latin *papula* pustule, pimple
▸'papular ADJECTIVE ▸ˌpapu'liferous ADJECTIVE

papyraceous (ˌpæpɪ'reɪʃəs) ADJECTIVE of, relating to, made of, or resembling paper.
▷HISTORY C18: from PAPYRUS + -ACEOUS. See PAPER

papyrology (ˌpæpɪ'rɒlədʒɪ) NOUN the study of ancient papyri.
▸papyrological (ˌpæpɪrə'lɒdʒɪkᵊl) ADJECTIVE
▸ˌpapy'rologist NOUN

papyrus (pə'paɪrəs) NOUN, *plural* **-ri** (-raɪ) *or* **-ruses.** [1] a tall aquatic cyperaceous plant, *Cyperus papyrus,* of S Europe and N and central Africa with small green-stalked flowers arranged like umbrella spokes around the stem top. [2] a kind of paper made from the stem pith of this plant, used by the ancient Egyptians, Greeks, and Romans. [3] an ancient document written on this paper.
▷HISTORY C14: via Latin from Greek *papūros* reed used in making paper

par (pɑː) NOUN [1] an accepted level or standard, such as an average (esp in the phrase **up to par**). [2] a state of equality (esp in the phrase **on a par with**). [3] *Finance* the established value of the unit of one national currency in terms of the unit of another where both are based on the same metal standard. [4] *Commerce* **a** See **par value. b** the condition of equality between the current market value of a share, bond, etc., and its face value (the **nominal par**). This equality is indicated by **at par,** while **above** (*or* **below**) **par** indicates that the market value is above (or below) face value. [5] *Golf* an estimated standard score for a hole or course that a good player should make: *par for the course was 72.* [6] **below** *or* **under par.** not feeling or performing as well as normal. [7] **par for the course.** an expected or normal occurrence or situation. ◆ ADJECTIVE [8] average or normal. [9] (*usually prenominal*) *Commerce* of or relating to par: *par value.*
▷HISTORY C17: from Latin *pār* equal, on a level; see PEER[1]

par. ABBREVIATION FOR: [1] paragraph. [2] parenthesis. [3] parish.

Par. ABBREVIATION FOR Paraguay.

par- PREFIX a variant of **para-**[1] before a vowel.

para[1] ('pɑːrə) NOUN, *plural* **-ras** *or* **-ra.** a monetary unit of Serbia worth one hundredth of a dinar; formerly a monetary unit of Yugoslavia.
▷HISTORY C17: Serbo-Croat, via Turkish from Persian *pārah* piece, portion

para[2] ('pærə) NOUN *Informal* [1] **a** a soldier in an airborne unit. **b** an airborne unit. [2] a paragraph.

Pará (*Portuguese* pa'ra) NOUN [1] a state of N Brazil, on the Atlantic: mostly dense tropical rainforest. Capital: Belém. Pop.: 6 188 685 (2000). Area: 1 248 042 sq. km (474 896 sq. miles). [2] another name for **Belém.** [3] an estuary in N Brazil into which flow the Tocantins River and a branch of the Amazon. Length: about 320 km (200 miles).

para-[1] *or before a vowel* **par-** PREFIX [1] beside; near: *parameter; parathyroid.* [2] beyond: *parapsychology.* [3] resembling: *paramnesia.* [4] defective; abnormal: *paraesthesia.* [5] subsidiary to: *paraphysis.* [6] (*usually in italics*) denoting that an organic compound contains a benzene ring with substituents attached to atoms that are directly opposite across the ring (the 1,4- positions): *paradinitrobenzene; para*-cresol. Abbreviation: *p*-. Compare **ortho-** (sense 4), **meta-** (sense 4). [7] denoting an isomer, polymer, or compound related to a specified compound: *paraldehyde; paracasein.* [8] denoting the form of a diatomic substance in which the spins of the two constituent atoms are antiparallel: *parahydrogen.* Compare **ortho-** (sense 6).
▷HISTORY from Greek *para* (prep) alongside, beyond

para-[2] COMBINING FORM indicating an object that acts as a protection against something: *parachute; parasol.*
▷HISTORY via French from Italian *para-,* from *parare* to defend, shield against, ultimately from Latin *parāre* to prepare

para-aminobenzoic acid NOUN *Biochem* an acid present in yeast and liver: used in the manufacture of dyes and pharmaceuticals. Formula: $C_6H_4(NH_2)COOH$.

parabasis (pə'ræbəsɪs) NOUN, *plural* **-ses** (-ˌsiːz). (in classical Greek comedy) an address from the chorus to the audience.
▷HISTORY C19: from Greek, from *parabanein* to step forward

parabiosis (ˌpærəbaɪ'əʊsɪs) NOUN [1] the natural union of two individuals, such as Siamese twins, so that they share a common circulation of the blood. [2] a similar union induced for experimental or therapeutic purposes.
▷HISTORY C20: from PARA-[1] + Greek *biōsis* manner of life, from *bios* life
▸parabiotic (ˌpærəbaɪ'ɒtɪk) ADJECTIVE

parablast ('pærəˌblæst) NOUN the yolk of an egg, such as a hen's egg, that undergoes meroblastic cleavage.
▷HISTORY C19: from PARA-[1] + -BLAST
▸ˌpara'blastic ADJECTIVE

parable ('pærəbᵊl) NOUN [1] a short story that uses familiar events to illustrate a religious or ethical point. Related adjectives: **parabolic, parabolical.** [2] any of the stories of this kind told by Jesus Christ.
▷HISTORY C14: from Old French *parabole,* from Latin *parabola* comparison, from Greek *parabolē* analogy, from *paraballein* to throw alongside, from PARA-[1] + *ballein* to throw
▸parabolist (pə'ræbəlɪst) NOUN

parabola (pə'ræbələ) NOUN a conic section formed by the intersection of a cone by a plane parallel to its side. Standard equation: $y^2 = 4ax$, where $2a$ is the distance between focus and directrix.
▷HISTORY C16: via New Latin from Greek *parabolē* a setting alongside; see PARABLE

parabolic[1] (ˌpærə'bɒlɪk) ADJECTIVE [1] of, relating to, or shaped like a parabola. [2] shaped like a paraboloid: *a parabolic mirror.*

parabolic[2] (ˌpærə'bɒlɪk) *or* **parabolical** ADJECTIVE of or resembling a parable.
▸ˌpara'bolically ADVERB

parabolic aerial NOUN a formal name for **dish aerial.**

parabolize[1] *or* **parabolise** (pə'ræbəˌlaɪz) VERB (*tr*) to explain by a parable.

parabolize[2] *or* **parabolise** (pə'ræbəˌlaɪz) VERB (*tr*) to shape like a parabola or paraboloid.
▸paˌraboli'zation *or* paˌraboli'sation NOUN

paraboloid (pə'ræbəˌlɔɪd) NOUN a geometric surface whose sections parallel to two coordinate planes are parabolic and whose sections parallel to the third plane are either elliptical or hyperbolic. Equations $x^2/a^2 \pm y^2/b^2 = 2cz$.
▸paˌrabo'loidal ADJECTIVE

parabrake ('pærəˌbreɪk) NOUN another name for **brake parachute.**

paracasein (ˌpærə'keɪsɪɪn, -siːn) NOUN *US* another name for **casein.**

paracentesis (ˌpærəsɛn'tiːsɪs) NOUN *Med* the surgical puncture of a body cavity in order to draw off excess fluid.

paracetamol (ˌpærə'siːtəˌmɒl, -'sɛtə-) NOUN a mild analgesic and antipyretic drug used as an alternative to aspirin. US name: **acetaminophen.**
▷HISTORY C20: from *para-acetamidophenol*

parachronism (pə'rækrəˌnɪzəm) NOUN an error in dating, esp by giving too late a date. Compare **prochronism.**
▷HISTORY C17: from PARA-[1] + *-chronism,* as in ANACHRONISM

parachute ('pærəˌʃuːt) NOUN [1] **a** a device used to retard the fall of a man or package from an aircraft, consisting of a large fabric canopy connected to a harness. **b** (*as modifier*): *parachute troops.* Sometimes shortened to: **chute.** See also **brake parachute.** ◆ VERB [2] (of troops, supplies, etc.) to land or cause to land by parachute from an aircraft. [3] (in an election) to bring in (a candidate, esp someone well known) from outside the constituency.
▷HISTORY C18: from French, from PARA-[2] + *chute* fall
▸'paraˌchutist NOUN

paraclete ('pærəˌkliːt) NOUN *Rare* a mediator or advocate.

Paraclete ('pærəˌkliːt) NOUN *Christianity* the Holy Ghost as comforter or advocate.
▷HISTORY C15: via Old French from Church Latin *Paraclētus,* from Late Greek *Paraklētos* advocate, from Greek *parakalein* to summon as a helper, from PARA-[1] + *kalein* to call

parade (pə'reɪd) NOUN [1] an ordered, esp ceremonial, march, assembly, or procession, as of troops being reviewed: *on parade.* [2] Also called: **parade ground.** a place where military formations regularly assemble. [3] a visible show or display: *to make a parade of one's grief.* [4] a public promenade or street of shops. [5] a successive display of things or people. [6] the interior area of a fortification. [7] a parry in fencing. [8] **rain on someone's parade.** to hinder someone's enjoyment; upset someone's plans. [9] **on parade. a** on display. **b** showing oneself off. ◆ VERB [10] (when *intr,* often foll by *through* or *along*) to walk or march, esp in a procession (through): *to parade the streets.* [11] (*tr*) to exhibit or flaunt: *he was parading his medals.* [12] (*tr*) to cause to assemble in formation, as for a military parade. [13] (*intr*) to walk about in a public place.
▷HISTORY C17: from French: a making ready, a setting out, a boasting display; compare Italian

parata, Spanish *parada,* all ultimately from Latin *parāre* to prepare
▸**pa'rader** NOUN

paradiddle ('pærəˌdɪd(ə)l) NOUN a group of four drum beats produced by using alternate sticks in the pattern right-left-right-right or left-right-left-left.
▹HISTORY C20: of imitative origin

paradigm ('pærəˌdaɪm) NOUN [1] *Grammar* the set of all the inflected forms of a word or a systematic arrangement displaying these forms. [2] a pattern or model. [3] a typical or stereotypical example (esp in the phrase **paradigm case**). [4] (in the philosophy of science) a very general conception of the nature of scientific endeavour within which a given enquiry is undertaken.
▹HISTORY C15: via French and Latin from Greek *paradeigma* pattern, from *paradeiknunai* to compare, from PARA-[1] + *deiknunai* to show
▸**paradigmatic** (ˌpærədɪg'mætɪk) ADJECTIVE

paradigm shift NOUN a radical change in underlying beliefs or theory.
▹HISTORY C20: coined by T.S. Kuhn (1922–96), US philosopher of science

paradisal (ˌpærə'daɪs(ə)l), **paradisiacal** (ˌpærədɪ'saɪək(ə)l), *or* **paradisiac** (ˌpærə'dɪsɪˌæk) ADJECTIVE of, relating to, or resembling paradise.

paradise ('pærəˌdaɪs) NOUN [1] heaven as the ultimate abode or state of the righteous. [2] *Islam* the sensual garden of delights that the Koran promises the faithful after death. [3] Also called: **limbo.** (according to some theologians) the intermediate abode or state of the just prior to the Resurrection of Jesus, as in Luke 23:43. [4] the place or state of happiness enjoyed by Adam before the first sin; the Garden of Eden. [5] any place or condition that fulfils all one's desires or aspirations. [6] a park in which foreign animals are kept.
▹HISTORY Old English, from Church Latin *paradīsus,* from Greek *paradeisos* garden, of Persian origin; compare Avestan *pairidaēza* enclosed area, from *pairi-* around + *daēza* wall

paradise duck NOUN a large duck, *Casarca variegata,* of New Zealand, having a brightly coloured plumage.

paradise fish NOUN any of several beautifully coloured labyrinth fishes of the genus *Macropodus, esp M. opercularis,* of S and SE Asia.

parador ('pærədɔː; *Spanish* 'paraðor) NOUN, *plural* **-dors** *or* **-dores**. a state-run hotel in Spain.
▹HISTORY Spanish

parados ('pærəˌdɒs) NOUN a bank behind a trench or other fortification, giving protection from being fired on from the rear.
▹HISTORY C19: from French, from PARA-[2] + *dos* back, from Latin *dorsum;* compare PARASOL, PARAPET

paradox ('pærəˌdɒks) NOUN [1] a seemingly absurd or self-contradictory statement that is or may be true: *religious truths are often expressed in paradox.* [2] a self-contradictory proposition, such as *I always tell lies.* [3] a person or thing exhibiting apparently contradictory characteristics. [4] an opinion that conflicts with common belief.
▹HISTORY C16: from Late Latin *paradoxum,* from Greek *paradoxos* opposed to existing notions, from PARA-[1] + *doxa* opinion
▸**ˌpara'doxical** ADJECTIVE ▸**ˌpara'doxically** ADVERB

paradoxical intention NOUN (in psychotherapy) the deliberate practice of a neurotic habit or thought, undertaken in order to remove it.

paradoxical sleep NOUN *Physiol* sleep that appears to be deep but that is characterized by a brain wave pattern similar to that of wakefulness, rapid eye movements, and heavier breathing.

paradrop ('pærəˌdrɒp) NOUN the delivery of personnel or equipment from an aircraft by parachute.

paraesthesia *or US* **paresthesia** (ˌpæres'θiːzɪə) NOUN *Pathol* an abnormal or inappropriate sensation in an organ, part, or area of the skin, as of burning, prickling, tingling, etc.
▸**paraesthetic** *or US* **paresthetic** (ˌpæres'θetɪk) ADJECTIVE

paraffin ('pærəfɪn) *or less commonly* **paraffine** ('pærəˌfiːn) NOUN [1] Also called: **paraffin oil,** (esp US and Canadian) **kerosene.** a liquid mixture consisting mainly of alkane hydrocarbons with boiling points in the range 150°–300°C, used as an aircraft fuel, in domestic heaters, and as a solvent. [2] another name for **alkane.** [3] See **paraffin wax.** [4] See **liquid paraffin.** ◆ VERB (*tr*) [5] to treat with paraffin or paraffin wax.
▹HISTORY C19: from German, from Latin *parum* too little + *affinis* adjacent; so called from its chemical inertia

paraffin wax NOUN a white insoluble odourless waxlike solid consisting mainly of alkane hydrocarbons with melting points in the range 50°–60°C, used in candles, waterproof paper, and as a sealing agent. Also called: **paraffin.**

paraformaldehyde (ˌpærəfɔː'mældɪˌhaɪd) *or* **paraform** NOUN a white amorphous solid polymeric form of formaldehyde: used as a convenient source of formaldehyde and as a fumigant. Formula: $(CH_2O)n$, where *n* lies between 6 and 50.

paragenesis (ˌpærə'dʒenɪsɪs) *or* **paragenesia** (ˌpærədʒɪ'niːzɪə) NOUN a characteristic association of minerals in a particular type of rock or ore deposit.
▸**paragenetic** (ˌpærədʒɪ'netɪk) ADJECTIVE
▸**ˌparage'netically** ADVERB

paragliding ('pærəˌglaɪdɪŋ) NOUN the sport of cross-country gliding using a specially designed parachute shaped like flexible wings. The parachutist glides from an aeroplane to a predetermined landing area.
▸**'paraˌglider** NOUN

paragnathous (ˌpærəg'neɪθəs) ADJECTIVE (of certain vertebrates) having the upper and lower jaws of equal length.

paragoge (ˌpærə'gəudʒɪ) *or* **paragogue** ('pærəˌgɒg) NOUN the addition of a sound or a syllable to the end of a word, such as *st* in *amongst.*
▹HISTORY C17: via Late Latin from Greek *paragōgē* an alteration, ultimately from *paragein* to lead past, change
▸**paragogic** (ˌpærə'gɒdʒɪk) *or* **ˌpara'gogical** ADJECTIVE
▸**ˌpara'gogically** ADVERB

paragon ('pærəgən) NOUN [1] a model of excellence; pattern: *a paragon of virtue.* [2] a size of printer's type, approximately equal to 20 point. ◆ VERB (*tr*) [3] *Archaic* **a** to equal or surpass. **b** to compare. **c** to regard as a paragon.
▹HISTORY C16: via French from Old Italian *paragone* comparison, from Medieval Greek *parakonē* whetstone, from Greek *parakonan* to sharpen against, from PARA-[1] + *akonan* to sharpen, from *akonē* whetstone

paragraph ('pærəˌgrɑːf, -ˌgræf) NOUN [1] (in a piece of writing) one of a series of subsections each usually devoted to one idea and each usually marked by the beginning of a new line, indentation, increased interlinear space, etc. [2] *Printing* the character ¶, used as a reference mark or to indicate the beginning of a new paragraph. [3] a short article in a newspaper. ◆ VERB (*tr*) [4] to form into paragraphs. [5] to express or report in a paragraph.
▹HISTORY C16: from Medieval Latin *paragraphus,* from Greek *paragraphos* line drawing attention to part of a text, from *paragraphein* to write beside, from PARA-[1] + *graphein* to write
▸**paragraphic** (ˌpærə'græfɪk) *or* **ˌpara'graphical** ADJECTIVE
▸**ˌpara'graphically** ADVERB

paragraphia (ˌpærə'grɑːfɪə) NOUN *Psychiatry* the habitual writing of a different word or letter from the one intended, often the result of a mental disorder or brain injury.
▹HISTORY C20: from New Latin; see PARA-[1], -GRAPH

Paraguay ('pærəˌgwaɪ) NOUN [1] an inland republic in South America: colonized by the Spanish from 1537, gaining independence in 1811; lost 142 500 sq. km (55 000 sq. miles) of territory and over half its population after its defeat in the war against Argentina, Brazil, and Uruguay (1865–70). It is divided by the Paraguay River into a sparsely inhabited semiarid region (Chaco) in the west, and a central region of wooded hills, tropical forests, and rich grasslands, rising to the Paraná plateau in the east. Official languages: Spanish and Guarani. Religion: Roman Catholic majority. Currency: guarani. Capital: Asunción. Pop.: 5 636 000 (2001 est.). Area: 406 750 sq. km (157 047 sq. miles). [2] a river in South America flowing south through Brazil and Paraguay to the Paraná River. Length: about 2400 km (1500 miles).

Paraguayan (ˌpærə'gwaɪən) ADJECTIVE [1] of or relating to Paraguay or its inhabitants. ◆ NOUN [2] a native or inhabitant of Paraguay.

Paraguay tea NOUN another name for **maté.**

parahydrogen (ˌpærə'haɪdrədʒən) NOUN *Chem* the form of molecular hydrogen (constituting about 25 per cent of the total at normal temperatures) in which the nuclei of the two atoms in each molecule spin in opposite directions. Compare **orthohydrogen.**

Paraíba (*Portuguese* para'iba) NOUN [1] a state of NE Brazil, on the Atlantic: consists of a coastal strip, with hills and plains inland; irrigated agriculture. Capital: João Pessoa. Pop.: 3 436 718 (2000). Area: 56 371 sq. km (21 765 sq. miles). [2] Also called: **Paraíba do Sul** ('du: sul). a river in SE Brazil, flowing southwest and then northeast to the Atlantic near Campos. Length: 1060 km (660 miles). [3] Also called: **Paraíba do Norte** ('du: 'nɔrtə). a river in NE Brazil, in Paraíba state, flowing northeast and east to the Atlantic. Length: 386 km (240 miles). [4] the former name (until 1930) of **João Pessoa.**

para-influenza virus NOUN any of a group of viruses that cause respiratory infections with influenza-like symptoms, esp in children.

parakeet *or* **parrakeet** ('pærəˌkiːt) NOUN any of numerous small usually brightly coloured long-tailed parrots, such as *Psittacula krameri* (**ring-necked parakeet**), of Africa.
▹HISTORY C16: from Spanish *periquito* and Old French *paroquet* parrot, of uncertain origin

parakelia *or* **parakeelya** (ˌpærə'kiːljə) NOUN a succulent herb of the genus *Calandrinia,* with purple flowers, that thrives in inland Australia.
▹HISTORY from a native Australian language

paralalia (ˌpærə'leɪlɪə) NOUN any of various speech disorders, esp the production of a sound different from that intended.

paralanguage ('pærəˌlæŋgwɪdʒ) NOUN *Linguistics* nonverbal elements in speech, such as intonation, that may affect the meaning of an utterance.

paraldehyde (pə'rældɪˌhaɪd) NOUN a colourless liquid substance that is a cyclic trimer of acetaldehyde: used in making dyestuffs and as a hypnotic and anticonvulsant drug. Formula: $(C_2H_4O)_3$.

paralegal (ˌpærə'liːg(ə)l) NOUN [1] a person trained to undertake legal work but not qualified as a professional solicitor or barrister. ◆ ADJECTIVE [2] of or designating such a person.

paralexia (ˌpærə'lɛksɪə) NOUN a disorder of the ability to read in which words and syllables are meaninglessly transposed.
▸**ˌpara'lexic** ADJECTIVE

paralimnion (ˌpærə'lɪmnɪɒn) NOUN *Ecology* the region of a lake floor between the shoreline or water's edge and the zone of rooted vegetation.
▹HISTORY from PARA-[1] + Greek *limnē* lake

paralinguistics (ˌpærəlɪŋ'gwɪstɪks) NOUN (*functioning as singular*) the study of paralanguage.
▸**ˌparalin'guistic** ADJECTIVE

paralipomena (ˌpærəlaɪ'pɒmənə) PLURAL NOUN [1] things added in a supplement to a work. [2] *Old Testament* another name for the Books of **Chronicles.**
▹HISTORY C14: via late Latin from Greek *paraleipomena,* from PARA-[1] (on one side) + *leipein* to leave

paralipsis (ˌpærə'lɪpsɪs) *or* **paraleipsis** (ˌpærə'laɪpsɪs) NOUN, *plural* **-ses** (-siːz). a rhetorical device in which an idea is emphasized by the pretence that it is too obvious to discuss, as in *there are many drawbacks to your plan, not to mention the cost.*
▹HISTORY C16: via Late Latin from Greek: neglect, from *paraleipein* to leave aside, from PARA-[1] + *leipein* to leave

parallax ('pærəˌlæks) NOUN [1] an apparent change in the position of an object resulting from a change in position of the observer. [2] *Astronomy* the angle subtended at a celestial body, esp a star, by the radius of the earth's orbit. **Annual** or **heliocentric parallax** is the apparent displacement of a nearby star resulting from its observation from the earth. **Diurnal** or **geocentric parallax** results from the observation of a planet, the sun, or the moon from the surface of the earth.
▹HISTORY C17: via French from New Latin

parallaxis, from Greek: change, from *parallassein* to change, from PARA-[1] + *allassein* to alter
▸**parallactic** (ˌpærəˈlæktɪk) ADJECTIVE ▸ˌ**paralˈlactically** ADVERB

parallel (ˈpærəˌlɛl) ADJECTIVE (when *postpositive,* usually foll by *to*) 1 separated by an equal distance at every point; never touching or intersecting: *parallel walls.* 2 corresponding; similar: *parallel situations.* 3 *Music* **a** Also: **consecutive.** (of two or more parts or melodies) moving in similar motion but keeping the same interval apart throughout: *parallel fifths.* **b** denoting successive chords in which the individual notes move in parallel motion. 4 *Grammar* denoting syntactic constructions in which the constituents of one construction correspond to those of the other. 5 *Computing* operating on several items of information, instructions, etc., simultaneously. Compare **serial** (sense 6). ◆ NOUN 6 *Maths* one of a set of parallel lines, planes, etc. 7 an exact likeness. 8 a comparison. 9 Also called: **parallel of latitude.** any of the imaginary lines around the earth parallel to the equator, designated by degrees of latitude ranging from 0° at the equator to 90° at the poles. 10 **a** a configuration of two or more electrical components connected between two points in a circuit so that the same voltage is applied to each (esp in the phrase **in parallel**). **b** (*as modifier*): *a parallel circuit.* ◆ Compare **series** (sense 6). 11 *Printing* the character (‖) used as a reference mark. 12 a trench or line lying in advance of and parallel to other defensive positions. ◆ VERB **-lels, -leling, -leled.** (*tr*) 13 to make parallel. 14 to supply a parallel to. 15 to be a parallel to or correspond with: *your experience parallels mine.*
▹**HISTORY** C16: via French and Latin from Greek *parallēlos* alongside one another, from PARA-[1] + *allēlos* one another

parallel bars PLURAL NOUN *Gymnastics* **a** (*functioning as plural*) a pair of wooden bars on uprights, sometimes at different heights, for various exercises. **b** (*functioning as singular*) an event in a gymnastic competition in which competitors exercise on such bars.

parallelepiped, parallelopiped (ˌpærəˌlɛləˈpaɪpɛd), *or* **parallelepipedon** (ˌpærəˌlɛləˈpaɪpɪdən) NOUN a geometric solid whose six faces are parallelograms.
▹**HISTORY** C16: from Greek *parallēlepipedon;* from *parallēlos* PARALLEL + *epipedon* plane surface, from EPI- + *pedon* ground

parallel importing NOUN the importing of certain goods, esp pharmaceutical drugs, by dealers who undersell local manufacturers.

paralleling (ˈpærəˌlɛlɪŋ) NOUN a form of trading in which companies buy highly priced goods in a market in which the prices are low in order to be able to sell them in a market in which the prices are higher.

parallelism (ˈpærəlɛˌlɪzəm) NOUN 1 the state of being parallel. 2 *Grammar* the repetition of a syntactic construction in successive sentences for rhetorical effect. 3 *Philosophy* the dualistic doctrine that mental and physical processes are regularly correlated but are not causally connected, so that, for example, pain always accompanies, but is not caused by, a pin-prick. Compare **interactionism, occasionalism.**
▸ˈ**paralˌlelist** NOUN, ADJECTIVE

parallelogram (ˌpærəˈlɛləˌgræm) NOUN a quadrilateral whose opposite sides are parallel and equal in length. See also **rhombus, rectangle, trapezium, trapezoid.**
▹**HISTORY** C16: via French from Late Latin, from Greek *parallēlogrammon,* from *parallēlos* PARALLEL + *grammē* line, related to *graphein* to write

parallelogram rule NOUN *Maths, physics* a rule for finding the resultant of two vectors by constructing a parallelogram with two adjacent sides representing the magnitudes and directions of the vectors, the diagonal through the point of intersection of the vectors representing their resultant.

parallel processing NOUN the performance by a computer system of two or more simultaneous operations.

parallel resonance NOUN the resonance that results when circuit elements are connected with their inductance and capacitance in parallel, so that the impedance of the combination rises to a maximum at the resonant frequency. Compare **series resonance.**

parallel ruler NOUN *Engineering* a drawing instrument in which two parallel edges are connected so that they remain parallel, although the distance between them can be varied.

parallel turn NOUN *Skiing* a turn, executed by shifting one's weight, in which the skis stay parallel.

paralogism (pəˈræləˌdʒɪzəm) NOUN 1 *Logic, psychol* an argument that is unintentionally invalid. Compare **sophism.** 2 any invalid argument or conclusion.
▹**HISTORY** C16: via Late Latin from Greek *paralogismos,* from *paralogizesthai* to argue fallaciously, from PARA-[1] + *-logizesthai,* ultimately from *logos* word
▸**paˈralogist** NOUN ▸**paˌraloˈgistic** ADJECTIVE

Paralympian (ˌpærəˈlɪmpɪən) NOUN a competitor in the Paralympics.

Paralympic (ˌpærəˈlɪmpɪk) ADJECTIVE of or relating to the Paralympics.

Paralympics (ˌpærəˈlɪmpɪks) PLURAL NOUN **the.** a sporting event, modelled on the Olympic Games, held solely for disabled competitors. Also called: **the Parallel Olympics.**
▹**HISTORY** C20: PARALLEL + OLYMPICS

paralyse *or US* **paralyze** (ˈpærəˌlaɪz) VERB (*tr*) 1 *Pathol* to affect with paralysis. 2 *Med* to render (a part of the body) insensitive to pain, touch, etc., esp by injection of an anaesthetic. 3 to make immobile; transfix.
▹**HISTORY** C19: from French *paralyser,* from *paralysie* PARALYSIS
▸ˌ**paralyˈsation** *or US* ˌ**paralyˈzation** NOUN ▸ˈ**paraˌlyser** *or US* ˈ**paraˌlyzer** NOUN

paralysis (pəˈrælɪsɪs) NOUN, *plural* **-ses** (-ˌsiːz). 1 *Pathol* **a** impairment or loss of voluntary muscle function or of sensation (**sensory paralysis**) in a part or area of the body, usually caused by a lesion or disorder of the muscles or the nerves supplying them. **b** a disease characterized by such impairment or loss; palsy. 2 cessation or impairment of activity: *paralysis of industry by strikes.*
▹**HISTORY** C16: via Latin from Greek *paralusis;* see PARA-[1], -LYSIS

paralysis agitans (ˈædʒɪˌtænz) NOUN another name for **Parkinson's disease.**

paralytic (ˌpærəˈlɪtɪk) ADJECTIVE 1 of, relating to, or of the nature of paralysis. 2 afflicted with or subject to paralysis. 3 *Brit, informal* very drunk. ◆ NOUN 4 a person afflicted with paralysis.
▸ˌ**paraˈlytically** ADVERB

paramagnetism (ˌpærəˈmægnɪˌtɪzəm) NOUN *Physics* the phenomenon exhibited by substances that have a relative permeability slightly greater than unity and a positive susceptibility. The effect is due to the alignment of unpaired spins of electrons in atoms of the material. Compare **diamagnetism, ferromagnetism.**
▸**paramagnetic** (ˌpærəmægˈnɛtɪk) ADJECTIVE

Paramaribo (ˌpærəˈmærɪˌbəʊ; *Dutch* paːraːˈmaːriːboː) NOUN the capital and chief port of Surinam, 27 km (17 miles) from the Atlantic on the Surinam River: the only large town in the country. Pop.: 233 000 (1999 est.).

paramatta *or* **parramatta** (ˌpærəˈmætə) NOUN a lightweight twill-weave fabric of wool formerly with silk or cotton, used for dresses, etc., now used esp for rubber-proofed garments.
▹**HISTORY** C19: named after *Parramatta,* New South Wales, Australia, where it was originally produced

paramecium (ˌpærəˈmiːsɪəm) NOUN, *plural* **-cia** (-sɪə). any freshwater protozoan of the genus *Paramecium,* having an oval body covered with cilia and a ventral ciliated groove for feeding: phylum *Ciliophora* (ciliates).
▹**HISTORY** C18: New Latin, from Greek *paramēkēs* elongated, from PARA-[1] + *mēkos* length

paramedic (ˌpærəˈmɛdɪk) *or* **paramedical** NOUN 1 a person, such as a laboratory technician, who supplements the work of the medical profession. 2 a member of an ambulance crew trained in a number of life-saving skills, including infusion and cardiac care. ◆ ADJECTIVE 3 of or designating such a person.

parament (ˈpærəmənt) NOUN, *plural* **paraments** *or* **paramenta** (ˌpærəˈmɛntə). (*often plural*) an ecclesiastical vestment or decorative hanging.
▹**HISTORY** C14: from Old French *parament,* from Medieval Latin *paramentum,* from Latin *parāre* to prepare

parameter (pəˈræmɪtə) NOUN 1 one of a number of auxiliary variables in terms of which all the variables in an implicit functional relationship can be explicitly expressed. See **parametric equations.** 2 a variable whose behaviour is not being considered and which may for present purposes be regarded as a constant, as *y* in the partial derivative $\partial f(x,y)/\partial x$. 3 *Statistics* a characteristic of the distribution of a population, such as its mean, as distinct from that of a sample. Compare **statistic.** 4 *Informal* any constant or limiting factor: *a designer must work within the parameters of budget and practicality.*
▹**HISTORY** C17: from New Latin; see PARA-[1], -METER
▸**parametric** (ˌpærəˈmɛtrɪk) *or* ˌ**paraˈmetrical** ADJECTIVE

parametric amplifier NOUN a type of high-frequency amplifier in which energy from a pumping oscillator is transferred to the input signal through a circuit with a varying parameter, usually a varying reactance.

parametric equalizer NOUN an electronic device for cutting or boosting selected frequencies by continuous narrowing or widening of the frequencies to be filtered. Compare **graphic equalizer.**

parametric equations PLURAL NOUN a set of equations expressing a number of quantities as explicit functions of the same set of independent variables and equivalent to some direct functional relationship of these quantities: *a circle* $x^2 + y^2 = r^2$ *has parametric equations* $x = r \cos \theta$ *and* $y = r \sin \theta$ *in terms of the parameters r and* θ.

parametric statistics NOUN (*functioning as singular*) the branch of statistics concerned with data measurable on interval or ratio scales, so that arithmetic operations are applicable to them, enabling parameters such as the mean of the distribution to be defined.

paramilitary (ˌpærəˈmɪlɪtərɪ, -trɪ) ADJECTIVE 1 denoting or relating to a group of personnel with military structure functioning either as a civil force or in support of military forces. 2 denoting or relating to a force with military structure conducting armed operations against a ruling or occupying power. ◆ NOUN 3 **a** a paramilitary force. **b** a member of such a force.

paramnesia (ˌpæræmˈniːzɪə) NOUN *Psychiatry* a disorder of the memory or the faculty of recognition in which dreams may be confused with reality.

paramo (ˈpærəˌməʊ) NOUN, *plural* **-mos.** a high plateau in the Andes between the tree line and the permanent snow line.
▹**HISTORY** C18: American Spanish, from Spanish: treeless plain

paramorph (ˈpærəˌmɔːf) NOUN 1 a mineral that has undergone paramorphism. 2 a plant or animal that is classified on the basis of inadequate data and differs taxonomically from other members of the species in which it has been placed.
▸ˌ**paraˈmorphic** *or* ˌ**paraˈmorphous** ADJECTIVE

paramorphine (ˌpærəˈmɔːfiːn) NOUN another name for **thebaine.**

paramorphism (ˌpærəˈmɔːˌfɪzəm) NOUN a process by which the crystalline structure of a mineral alters without any change in its chemical composition.

paramount (ˈpærəˌmaʊnt) ADJECTIVE 1 of the greatest importance or significance; pre-eminent. ◆ NOUN 2 *Rare* a supreme ruler.
▹**HISTORY** C16: via Anglo-Norman from Old French *paramont,* from *par* by + *-amont* above, from Latin *ad montem* to the mountain
▸ˈ**paraˌmountcy** NOUN ▸ˈ**paraˌmountly** ADVERB

paramour (ˈpærəˌmʊə) NOUN 1 *Now usually derogatory* a lover, esp an adulterous woman. 2 an archaic word for **beloved** (sense 2).
▹**HISTORY** C13: from Old French, literally: through love

Paraná NOUN 1 (parəˈna) a state of S Brazil, on the Atlantic: consists of a coastal plain and a large rolling plateau with extensive forests. Capital: Curitiba. Pop.: 9 558 126 (2000). Area: 199 555 sq. km (77 048 sq. miles). 2 (paraˈna) a city in E Argentina, on the Paraná River opposite Santa Fe:

capital of Argentina (1853–1862). Pop.: 256 602 (1999 est.). 3 (*Portuguese* parə'na; *Spanish* para'na) a river in central South America, formed in S Brazil by the confluence of the Rio Grande and the Paranaíba River and flowing generally south to the Atlantic through the Río de la Plata estuary. Length: 2900 km (1800 miles).

Paraná pine (pə'rɑːnə) NOUN 1 a large pine tree, *Araucaria angustifolia,* of South America yielding softwood timber: family *Araucariaceae.* 2 the wood of this tree.

parang ('pɑːræŋ) NOUN a short stout straight-edged knife used by the Dyaks of Borneo.
▷HISTORY C19: from Malay

paranoia (ˌpærə'nɔɪə) NOUN 1 a form of schizophrenia characterized by a slowly progressive deterioration of the personality, involving delusions and often hallucinations. 2 a mental disorder characterized by any of several types of delusions, in which the personality otherwise remains relatively intact. 3 *Informal* intense fear or suspicion, esp when unfounded.
▷HISTORY C19: via New Latin from Greek: frenzy, from *paranoos* distraught, from PARA-[1] + *noos* mind
▸**paranoiac** (ˌpærə'nɔɪɪk) *or* **paranoic** (ˌpærə'nəʊɪk) ADJECTIVE, NOUN

paranoid ('pærəˌnɔɪd) ADJECTIVE 1 of, characterized by, or resembling paranoia. 2 *Informal* exhibiting undue suspicion, fear of persecution, etc. ♦ NOUN 3 a person who shows the behaviour patterns associated with paranoia.

paranormal (ˌpærə'nɔːməl) ADJECTIVE 1 beyond normal explanation. ♦ NOUN 2 **the.** paranormal happenings generally.

paranymph ('pærəˌnɪmf) NOUN *Archaic* a bridesmaid or best man.
▷HISTORY C16: via Late Latin from Greek *paranumphos,* from PARA-[1] + *numphē* bride (literally: person beside the bride)

paraparesis (ˌpærəpə'riːsɪs) NOUN muscle weakness, esp of the legs, allowing limited movement; partial paralysis.
▸**paraparetic** (ˌpærəpə'rɛtɪk) ADJECTIVE

parapente ('pærəˌpentɪ) NOUN 1 another name for **paraskiing.** 2 the form of parachute used in this sport.

parapet ('pærəpɪt, -ˌpɛt) NOUN 1 a low wall or railing along the edge of a balcony, roof, etc. 2 Also called: **breastwork.** a rampart, mound of sandbags, bank, etc., in front of a trench, giving protection from fire from the front.
▷HISTORY C16: from Italian *parapetto,* literally: chest-high wall, from PARA-[2] + *petto,* from Latin *pectus* breast

paraph ('pærəf) NOUN a flourish after a signature, originally to prevent forgery.
▷HISTORY C14: via French from Medieval Latin *paraphus,* variant of *paragraphus* PARAGRAPH

paraphasia (ˌpærə'feɪzɪə) NOUN a defect of speech in which the normal flow of words is interrupted by inappropriate words and phrases.
▷HISTORY C20: from Greek PARA-[1] + *-phasia,* from *phanai* to speak

paraphernalia (ˌpærəfə'neɪlɪə) PLURAL NOUN (*sometimes functioning as singular*) 1 miscellaneous articles or equipment. 2 *Law* (formerly) articles of personal property given to a married woman by her husband before or during marriage and regarded in law as her possessions over which she has some measure of control.
▷HISTORY C17: via Medieval Latin from Latin *parapherna* personal property of a married woman, apart from her dowry, from Greek, from PARA-[1] + *phernē* dowry, from *pherein* to carry

paraphilia (ˌpærə'fɪlɪə) NOUN any abnormal sexual behaviour; sexual anomaly or deviation.
▷HISTORY C20: from PARA-[1] + *-philia,* from Greek *philos* loving

paraphimosis (ˌpærəˌfɪ'məʊsɪs) NOUN inability to retract the penis into the prepuce as a result of narrowing of the prepuce.

paraphrase ('pærəˌfreɪz) NOUN 1 an expression of a statement or text in other words, esp in order to clarify. 2 the practice of making paraphrases. ♦ VERB 3 to put (something) into other words; restate (something).
▷HISTORY C16: via French from Latin *paraphrasis,* from Greek, from *paraphrazein* to recount

▸**paraphrastic** (ˌpærə'fræstɪk) ADJECTIVE

paraphysis (pə'ræfɪsɪs) NOUN, *plural* **-ses** (-ˌsiːz). any of numerous sterile cells occurring between the sex organs of mosses and algae and between the spore-producing bodies of basidiomycetous and ascomycetous fungi.
▷HISTORY C19: New Latin from Greek: subsidiary growth, from PARA-[1] + *phusis* growth
▸**pa'raphysate** ADJECTIVE

paraplegia (ˌpærə'pliːdʒə) NOUN *Pathol* paralysis of the lower half of the body, usually as the result of disease or injury of the spine. Compare **hemiplegia, quadriplegia.**
▷HISTORY C17: via New Latin from Greek: a blow on one side, from PARA-[1] + *plēssein* to strike

paraplegic (ˌpærə'pliːdʒɪk) ADJECTIVE 1 *Pathol* of, relating to, or afflicted with paraplegia. ♦ NOUN 2 *Pathol* a person afflicted with paraplegia.

parapodium (ˌpærə'pəʊdɪəm) NOUN, *plural* **-dia** (-dɪə). 1 any of the paired unjointed lateral appendages of polychaete worms, used in locomotion, respiration, etc. 2 any of various similar appendages of other invertebrates, esp certain molluscs.
▷HISTORY New Latin: from PARA-[1] + -PODIUM

parapraxis (ˌpærə'præksɪs) NOUN *Psychoanal* a minor error in action, such as slips of the tongue, supposedly the result of repressed impulses. See also **Freudian slip.**
▷HISTORY C20: from PARA-[1] + Greek *praxis* a doing, deed

parapsychology (ˌpærəsaɪ'kɒlədʒɪ) NOUN the study of mental phenomena, such as telepathy, which are beyond the scope of normal physical explanation.
▸**parapsychological** (ˌpærəsaɪkə'lɒdʒɪkəl) ADJECTIVE
▸**ˌparapsy'chologist** NOUN

Paraquat ('pærəˌkwɒt) NOUN *Trademark* a yellow extremely poisonous soluble solid used in solution as a weedkiller.

Pará rubber (pə'rɑː, 'pɑːrə) NOUN a South American rubber obtained from any of various euphorbiaceous trees of the genus *Hevea, esp H. brasiliensis.* See also **rubber tree.**
▷HISTORY C19: from PARÁ

parasailing ('pærəˌseɪlɪŋ) NOUN a sport in which a water-skier wearing a parachute is towed by a speedboat, becomes airborne, and sails along in the air.

parasang ('pærəˌsæŋ) NOUN a Persian unit of distance equal to about 5.5 km or 3.4 miles.
▷HISTORY C16: via Latin and Greek from a Persian word related to modern Persian *farsang*

parascending ('pærəˌsendɪŋ) NOUN a sport in which a participant wears a parachute and becomes airborne by being towed by a vehicle into the wind and then descends by parachute.

parascience ('pærəˌsaɪəns) NOUN the study of subjects that are outside the scope of traditional science because they cannot be explained by accepted scientific theory or tested by conventional scientific methods.

paraselene (ˌpærəsɪ'liːnɪ) NOUN, *plural* **-nae** (-niː). *Meteorol* a bright image of the moon on a lunar halo. Also called: **mock moon.** Compare **parhelion.**
▷HISTORY C17: New Latin, from PARA-[1] + Greek *selēnē* moon
▸**ˌparase'lenic** ADJECTIVE

Parashah ('pærəˌʃɑː; *Hebrew* para'ʃa) NOUN, *plural* **-shoth** (-ˌʃəʊt; *Hebrew* -'ʃɔt). *Judaism* 1 any of the sections of the Torah read in the synagogue. 2 any of the subsections of the weekly lessons read on Sabbaths in the synagogue. ♦ Also called (Yiddish) **Parsha.**
▷HISTORY from Hebrew, from *pārāsh* to divide, separate

parasite ('pærəˌsaɪt) NOUN 1 an animal or plant that lives in or on another (the host) from which it obtains nourishment. The host does not benefit from the association and is often harmed by it. 2 a person who habitually lives at the expense of others; sponger. 3 (formerly) a sycophant.
▷HISTORY C16: via Latin from Greek *parasitos* one who lives at another's expense, from PARA-[1] + *sitos* grain
▸**parasitic** (ˌpærə'sɪtɪk) *or* **ˌpara'sitical** ADJECTIVE
▸**ˌpara'sitically** ADVERB

parasite drag NOUN the part of the drag on an aircraft that is contributed by nonlifting surfaces, such as fuselage, nacelles, etc. Also called: **parasite resistance.**

parasiticide (ˌpærə'sɪtɪˌsaɪd) NOUN 1 any substance capable of destroying parasites. ♦ ADJECTIVE 2 destructive to parasites.
▸**ˌparaˌsiti'cidal** ADJECTIVE

parasitic male NOUN *Zoology* a male animal that is much smaller than the female and is totally dependent on the female for its nutrition, such as the male of some species of deep-sea angler fish.

parasitic oscillation NOUN (in an electronic circuit) oscillation at any undesired frequency. Sometimes shortened to: **parasitic.**

parasitism ('pærəsaɪˌtɪzəm) NOUN 1 the relationship between a parasite and its host. 2 the state of being infested with parasites. 3 the state of being a parasite.

parasitize *or* **parasitise** ('pærəsɪˌtaɪz, -saɪ-) VERB (*tr*) 1 to infest or infect with parasites. 2 to live on (another organism) as a parasite.

parasitoid ('pærəsɪˌtɔːd) NOUN *Zoology* an animal, esp an insect, that is parasitic during the larval stage of its life cycle but becomes free-living when adult.

parasitology (ˌpærəsaɪ'tɒlədʒɪ) NOUN the branch of biology that is concerned with the study of parasites.
▸**parasitological** (ˌpærəˌsaɪtəl'lɒdʒɪkəl) ADJECTIVE
▸**ˌparasit'ologist** NOUN

paraskiing ('pærəˌskiːɪŋ) NOUN the sport of jumping off high mountains wearing skis and a light parachute composed of inflatable fabric tubes that form a semirigid wing. Also called: **parapente.**

parasol ('pærəˌsɒl) NOUN an umbrella used for protection against the sun; sunshade.
▷HISTORY C17: via French from Italian *parasole,* from PARA-[2] + *sole* sun, from Latin *sōl*

parasol mushroom NOUN any of several fungi of the basidiomycetous genus *Lepiota,* having an umbrella-shaped cap, white gills, and a slender brownish stem with a prominent white ring.

parastatal (ˌpærə'steɪtəl) NOUN 1 a state-owned organization, esp in Africa. ♦ ADJECTIVE 2 of or relating to such an organization.

parastichy (pə'ræstɪkɪ) NOUN, *plural* **-chies.** 1 a hypothetical spiral line connecting the bases of a series of leaves on a stem. 2 an arrangement of leaves so connected. ♦ Compare **orthostichy.**
▷HISTORY C19: from PARA-[1] + Greek *stikhia,* from *stikhos* row, rank
▸**pa'rastichous** ADJECTIVE

parasuicide (ˌpærə'suːɪˌsaɪd) NOUN 1 the deliberate infliction of injury on oneself or the taking of a drug overdose as an attempt at suicide which may not be intended to be successful. 2 a person who commits such an act.

parasymbiosis (ˌpærəˌsɪmbɪ'əʊsɪs) NOUN the symbiotic relationship that occurs between certain species of fungi and lichens (which are themselves symbiotic associations between a fungus and an alga).
▸**ˌpara'symbiont** NOUN ▸**ˌparaˌsymbi'otic** ADJECTIVE

parasympathetic (ˌpærəˌsɪmpə'θɛtɪk) ADJECTIVE *Anatomy, physiol* of or relating to the division of the autonomic nervous system that acts in opposition to the sympathetic system by slowing the heartbeat, constricting the bronchi of the lungs, stimulating the smooth muscles of the digestive tract, etc. Compare **sympathetic** (sense 4).

parasynapsis (ˌpærəsɪ'næpsɪs) NOUN another name for **synapsis** (sense 1).
▸**ˌparasyn'aptic** ADJECTIVE

parasynthesis (ˌpærə'sɪnθɪsɪs) NOUN formation of words by means of compounding a phrase and adding an affix, as for example *light-headed,* which is *light* + *head* with the affix *-ed.*
▸**parasynthetic** (ˌpærəsɪn'θɛtɪk) ADJECTIVE

parasyntheton (ˌpærə'sɪnθətɒn) NOUN, *plural* **-ta** (-tə). a word formed by parasynthesis; for example, *kind-hearted.*
▷HISTORY from Greek

parataxis (ˌpærə'tæksɪs) NOUN the juxtaposition of clauses in a sentence without the use of a conjunction, as for example *None of my friends stayed — they all left early.*

▷HISTORY C19: New Latin from Greek, from *paratassein,* literally: to arrange side by side, from PARA-[1] + *tassein* to arrange
▸**paratactic** (ˌpærəˈtæktɪk) ADJECTIVE ▸**ˌparaˈtactically** ADVERB

paratha (pəˈrɑːtə) NOUN (in Indian cookery) a flat unleavened bread, resembling a small nan bread, that is fried on a griddle.
▷HISTORY from Hindi *parāṭhā*

parathion (ˌpærəˈθaɪɒn) NOUN a slightly water-soluble toxic oil, odourless and colourless when pure, used as an insecticide. Formula: $C_{10}H_{14}NO_5PS$.
▷HISTORY C20: from PARA-[1] + THIO- + -ON

parathyroid (ˌpærəˈθaɪrɔɪd) ADJECTIVE [1] situated near the thyroid gland. [2] of or relating to the parathyroid glands. ◆ NOUN [3] See **parathyroid gland.**

parathyroid gland NOUN any one of the small egg-shaped endocrine glands situated near or embedded within the thyroid gland: they secrete parathyroid hormone.

parathyroid hormone NOUN the hormone secreted by the parathyroid glands that controls the level of calcium in the blood: a deficiency of the hormone often results in tetany. Also called: **parathormone** (ˌpærəˈθɔːməʊn).

paratonic (ˌpærəˈtɒnɪk) ADJECTIVE *Botany* (of a plant movement) occurring in response to an external stimulus.

paratroops (ˈpærəˌtruːps) PLURAL NOUN troops trained and equipped to be dropped by parachute into a battle area. Also called: **paratroopers, parachute troops.**

paratyphoid (ˌpærəˈtaɪfɔɪd) *Pathol* ◆ ADJECTIVE [1] resembling typhoid fever or its causative agent. [2] of or relating to paratyphoid fever. ◆ NOUN [3] See **paratyphoid fever.**

paratyphoid fever NOUN *Pathol* a disease resembling but less severe than typhoid fever, characterized by chills, headache, nausea, vomiting, and diarrhoea, caused by bacteria of the genus *Salmonella.*

paravane (ˈpærəˌveɪn) NOUN a torpedo-shaped device towed from the bow of a vessel so that the cables will cut the anchors of any moored mines.
▷HISTORY C20: from PARA-[2] + VANE

par avion *French* (par avjɔ̃) ADVERB by aeroplane: used in labelling mail sent by air.

paraxial (pæˈræksɪəl) ADJECTIVE *Physics* (of a light ray) parallel to the axis of an optical system.

parazoan (ˌpærəˈzəʊən) NOUN, *plural* **-zoa** (-ˈzəʊə). any multicellular invertebrate of the group *Parazoa,* which consists of the sponges (phylum *Porifera*). Compare **metazoan.**
▷HISTORY C19: from *parazoa,* formed on the model of *protozoa* and *metazoa,* from PARA-[1] + Greek *zōon* animal

parboil (ˈpɑːˌbɔɪl) VERB (*tr*) [1] to boil until partially cooked, often before further cooking. [2] to subject to uncomfortable heat.
▷HISTORY C15: from Old French *parboillir,* from Late Latin *perbullīre* to boil thoroughly (see PER-, BOIL[1]); modern meaning due to confusion of *par-* with *part*

parbuckle (ˈpɑːˌbʌkəl) NOUN [1] a rope sling for lifting or lowering a heavy cylindrical object, such as a cask or tree trunk. ◆ VERB [2] (*tr*) to raise or lower (an object) with such a sling.
▷HISTORY C17 *parbunkel:* of uncertain origin

Parcae (ˈpɑːsiː) PLURAL NOUN, *singular* **Parca** (ˈpɑːkə). **the.** the Roman goddesses of fate. Greek counterparts: **the Moirai.**

parcel (ˈpɑːsəl) NOUN [1] something wrapped up; package. [2] a group of people or things having some common characteristic. [3] a quantity of some commodity offered for sale; lot. [4] a distinct portion of land. [5] an essential part of something (esp in the phrase **part and parcel**). ◆ VERB **-cels, -celling, -celled** *or US* **-cels, -celing, -celed.** (*tr*) [6] (often foll by *up*) to make a parcel of; wrap up. [7] (often foll by *out*) to divide (up) into portions. [8] *Nautical* to bind strips of canvas around (a rope). ◆ ADVERB [9] an archaic word for **partly.**
▷HISTORY C14: from Old French *parcelle,* from Latin *particula* PARTICLE

parcel-gilt ADJECTIVE partly gilded, esp (of an item of silverware) having the inner surface gilded.
▷HISTORY C15: from *parcel* (in the obsolete adv sense: partly) + GILT[1]

parcenary (ˈpɑːsɪnərɪ) NOUN joint heirship. Also called: **coparcenary.**
▷HISTORY C16: from Old French *parçonerie,* from *parçon* distribution; see PARCENER

parcener (ˈpɑːsɪnə) NOUN a person who takes an equal share with another or others; coheir. Also called: **coparcener.**
▷HISTORY C13: from Old French *parçonier,* from *parçon* distribution, from Latin *partītiō* a sharing, from *partīre* to divide

parch (pɑːtʃ) VERB [1] to deprive or be deprived of water; dry up: *the sun parches the fields.* [2] (*tr; usually passive*) to make very thirsty: *I was parched after the run.* [3] (*tr*) to roast (corn, etc.) lightly.
▷HISTORY C14: of obscure origin

Parcheesi (pɑːˈtʃiːzɪ) NOUN *Trademark* a modern board game derived from the ancient game of pachisi.

parchment (ˈpɑːtʃmənt) NOUN [1] the skin of certain animals, such as sheep, treated to form a durable material, as for bookbinding, or (esp formerly) manuscripts. [2] a manuscript, bookbinding, etc., made of or resembling this material. [3] a type of stiff yellowish paper resembling parchment.
▷HISTORY C13: from Old French *parchemin,* via Latin from Greek *pergamēnē,* from *Pergamēnos* of Pergamum (where parchment was made); the form of Old French *parchemin* was influenced by *parche* leather, from Latin *Parthica* (*pellis*) Parthian (leather)
▸**ˈparchmenty** ADJECTIVE

parclose (ˈpɑːˌkləʊz) NOUN a screen or railing in a church separating off an altar, chapel, etc.
▷HISTORY C14: from Old French, noun use of past participle of *parclore* to close off; see PER-, CLOSE[1]

pard[1] (pɑːd) NOUN *US* short for **pardner.**

pard[2] (pɑːd) NOUN *Archaic* a leopard or panther.
▷HISTORY C13: via Old French from Latin *pardus,* from Greek *pardos*

pardalote (ˈpɑːdəˌləʊt) NOUN any of various small Australian songbirds of the genus *Pardalotus*, esp the diamond bird.
▷HISTORY C19: from New Latin, from Greek *pardalōtos* spotted like a leopard; see PARD[2]

pardner (ˈpɑːdnə) NOUN *US, dialect* friend or partner: used as a term of address.

pardon (ˈpɑːdən) VERB (*tr*) [1] to excuse or forgive (a person) for (an offence, mistake, etc.): *to pardon someone; to pardon a fault.* ◆ NOUN [2] forgiveness; allowance. [3] **a** a release from punishment for an offence. **b** the warrant granting such release. [4] a Roman Catholic indulgence. ◆ SENTENCE SUBSTITUTE [5] Also: **pardon me, I beg your pardon. a** sorry; excuse me. **b** what did you say?
▷HISTORY C13: from Old French, from Medieval Latin *perdōnum,* from *perdōnāre* to forgive freely, from Latin *per* (intensive) + *dōnāre* to grant
▸**ˈpardonable** ADJECTIVE ▸**ˈpardonably** ADVERB
▸**ˈpardonless** ADJECTIVE

pardoner (ˈpɑːdənə) NOUN (before the Reformation) a person licensed to sell ecclesiastical indulgences.

Pardubice (*Czech* ˈpardubitsɛ) NOUN a city in the central Czech Republic, on the Elbe River: 13th-century cathedral; oil refinery. Pop.: 163 000 (1993).

pare (pɛə) VERB (*tr*) [1] to peel or cut (the outer layer) from (something). [2] to cut the edges from (the nails); trim. [3] to decrease bit by bit.
▷HISTORY C13: from Old French *parer* to adorn, from Latin *parāre* to make ready
▸**ˈparer** NOUN

paregoric (ˌpærəˈɡɒrɪk) NOUN a medicine containing opium, benzoic acid, camphor (English paregoric) or ammonia (Scottish paregoric), and anise oil, formerly widely used to relieve diarrhoea and coughing in children.
▷HISTORY C17 (meaning: relieving pain): via Late Latin from Greek *parēgorikos* soothing, from *parēgoros* relating to soothing speech, from PARA-[1] (beside, alongside of) + *-ēgor-,* from *agoreuein* to speak in assembly, from *agora* assembly

pareira (pəˈrɛərə) NOUN the root of a South American menispermaceous climbing plant, *Chondrodendron tomentosum,* used as a diuretic, tonic, and as a source of curare.
▷HISTORY C18: from Portuguese *pareira brava,* literally: wild vine

paren. ABBREVIATION FOR parenthesis.

parenchyma (pəˈrɛŋkɪmə) NOUN [1] unspecialized plant tissue consisting of simple thin-walled cells with intervening air spaces: constitutes the greater part of fruits, stems, roots, etc. [2] animal tissue that constitutes the essential or specialized part of an organ as distinct from the blood vessels, connective tissue, etc., associated with it. [3] loosely-packed tissue filling the spaces between the organs in lower animals such as flatworms.
▷HISTORY C17: via New Latin from Greek *parenkhuma* something poured in beside, from PARA-[1] + *enkhuma* infusion
▸**parenchymatous** (ˌpærɛŋˈkɪmətəs) ADJECTIVE

parent (ˈpɛərənt) NOUN [1] a father or mother. [2] a person acting as a father or mother; guardian. [3] *Rare* an ancestor. [4] a source or cause. [5] **a** an organism or organization that has produced one or more organisms or organizations similar to itself. **b** (*as modifier*): *a parent organism.* [6] *Physics, chem* **a** a precursor, such as a nucleus or compound, of a derived entity. **b** (*as modifier*): *a parent nucleus; a parent ion.*
▷HISTORY C15: via Old French from Latin *parens* parent, from *parere* to bring forth
▸**ˈparenthood** NOUN

parentage (ˈpɛərəntɪdʒ) NOUN [1] ancestry. [2] derivation from a particular origin. [3] a less common word for **parenthood.**

parental (pəˈrɛntəl) ADJECTIVE [1] of or relating to a parent or parenthood. [2] *Genetics* designating the first generation in a line, which gives rise to all succeeding (filial) generations.
▸**paˈrentally** ADVERB

parent company NOUN a company that owns more than half the shares of another company.

parenteral (pæˈrɛntərəl) ADJECTIVE *Med* [1] (esp of the route by which a drug is administered) by means other than through the digestive tract, esp by injection. [2] designating a drug to be injected.
▷HISTORY C20: from PARA-[1] + ENTERO- + -AL[1]
▸**parˈenterally** ADVERB

parenthesis (pəˈrɛnθɪsɪs) NOUN, *plural* **-ses** (-ˌsiːz). [1] a phrase, often explanatory or qualifying, inserted into a passage with which it is not grammatically connected, and marked off by brackets, dashes, etc. [2] Also called: **bracket.** either of a pair of characters, (), used to enclose such a phrase or as a sign of aggregation in mathematical or logical expressions. [3] an intervening occurrence; interlude; interval. [4] **in parenthesis.** inserted as a parenthesis.
▷HISTORY C16: via Late Latin from Greek: something placed in besides, from *parentithenai,* from PARA-[1] + EN-[2] + *tithenai* to put
▸**parenthetic** (ˌpærənˈθɛtɪk) *or* **ˌparenˈthetical** ADJECTIVE
▸**ˌparenˈthetically** ADVERB

parenthesize *or* **parenthesise** (pəˈrɛnθɪˌsaɪz) VERB (*tr*) [1] to place in parentheses. [2] to insert as a parenthesis. [3] to intersperse (a speech, writing, etc.) with parentheses.

parenting (ˈpɛərəntɪŋ) NOUN the care and upbringing of a child.

parentless (ˈpɛərəntˌlɪs) ADJECTIVE having no living parents; orphaned.

parent metal NOUN *Engineering, metallurgy* the metal of components that are being welded by a molten filler metal.

Parents Anonymous NOUN (in Britain) an association of local voluntary self-help groups offering help through an anonymous telephone service to parents who fear they will injure their children, or who have other problems in managing their children.

parent teacher association NOUN a social group of the parents of children at a school and their teachers formed in order to foster better understanding between them and to organize activities on behalf of the school. Abbreviation: **PTA.**

parergon (pəˈrɛəɡɒn) NOUN, *plural* **-ga** (-ɡə). work that is not one's main employment.
▷HISTORY C17: from Latin, from Greek, from PARA-[1] + *ergon* work

paresis (pə'ri:sɪs, 'pærɪsɪs) NOUN, *plural* **-ses** (-,si:z). *Pathol* [1] incomplete or slight paralysis of motor functions. [2] short for **general paresis**. See **general paralysis of the insane.**
▷HISTORY C17: via New Latin from Greek: a relaxation, from *parienai* to let go, from PARA-[1] + *hienai* to release
▸**paretic** (pə'rɛtɪk) ADJECTIVE

paresthesia (,pærɛs'θi:zɪə) NOUN *Pathol* the usual US spelling of **paraesthesia.**
▸**paresthetic** (,pærɛs'θɛtɪk) ADJECTIVE

Pareto (*Italian* pa'rɛ:to) ADJECTIVE denoting a law, mathematical formula, etc., originally used by Vilfredo Pareto (1848–1923), Italian sociologist and economist, to express the frequency distribution of incomes in a society.

pareu ('pɑ:reɪ,u:) NOUN a rectangle of fabric worn by Polynesians as a skirt or loincloth.
▷HISTORY from Tahitian

parev, pareve, *or* **parve** ('pɑrvə, 'pɑrəv) ADJECTIVE *Judaism* containing neither meat nor milk products and so fit for use with either meat or milk dishes. Compare **milchik, fleishik.** See also **kashruth.**

par excellence *French* (par ɛkselɑ̃s; *English* pɑ:r 'ɛksələns) ADVERB to a degree of excellence; beyond comparison: *she is the charitable lady par excellence.*
▷HISTORY literally: by (way of) excellence

parfait (pɑ:'feɪ) NOUN a rich frozen dessert made from eggs and cream with ice cream, fruit, etc.
▷HISTORY from French: PERFECT

parfleche ('pɑ:flɛʃ) NOUN *US and Canadian* [1] a sheet of rawhide that has been dried after soaking in lye and water to remove the hair. [2] an object, such as a case, made of this.
▷HISTORY C19: from Canadian French, from French *parer* to ward off, protect + *flèche* arrow

parget ('pɑ:dʒɪt) NOUN [1] Also called: **pargeting. a** plaster, mortar, etc., used to line chimney flues or cover walls. **b** plasterwork that has incised ornamental patterns. [2] another name for **gypsum** (esp when used in building). ◆ VERB (*tr*) [3] to cover or decorate with parget.
▷HISTORY C14: from Old French *pargeter* to throw over, from *par* PER- + *geter,* from Medieval Latin *jactāre* to throw

parhelic circle NOUN *Meteorol* a luminous band at the same altitude as the sun, parallel to the horizon, caused by reflection of the sun's rays by ice crystals in the atmosphere.

parhelion (pɑ:'hi:lɪən) NOUN, *plural* **-lia** (-lɪə). one of several bright spots on the parhelic circle or solar halo, caused by the diffraction of light by ice crystals in the atmosphere, esp around sunset. Also called: **mock sun, sundog.** Compare **anthelion.**
▷HISTORY C17: via Latin from Greek *parēlion,* from PARA-[1] (beside) + *hēlios* sun
▸**parhelic** (pɑ:'hi:lɪk, -'hɛlɪk) *or* **parheliacal** (,pɑ:hɪ'laɪək(ə)l) ADJECTIVE

pari- COMBINING FORM equal or equally; even (in number): *parisyllabic; paripinnate.*
▷HISTORY from Latin *par*

pariah (pə'raɪə, 'pærɪə) NOUN [1] a social outcast. [2] (formerly) a member of a low caste in South India.
▷HISTORY C17: from Tamil *paraiyan* drummer, from *parai* drum; so called because members of the caste were the drummers at festivals

pariah dog NOUN another term for **pye-dog.**

Parian ('pɛərɪən) ADJECTIVE [1] denoting or relating to a fine white marble mined in classical times in Paros. [2] denoting or relating to a fine biscuit porcelain used mainly for statuary. [3] of or relating to Paros. ◆ NOUN [4] a native or inhabitant of Paros. [5] Parian marble. [6] Parian porcelain.

Paricutín (*Spanish* pariku'tin) NOUN a volcano in W central Mexico, in Michoacán state, formed in 1943 after a week of earth tremors; grew to a height of 2500 m (8200 ft.) in a year and buried the village of Paricutín.

paries ('pɛərɪ,i:z) NOUN, *plural* **parietes** (pə'raɪɪ,ti:z). the wall of an organ or bodily cavity.
▷HISTORY C18: from Latin: wall

parietal (pə'raɪɪt(ə)l) ADJECTIVE [1] *Anatomy, biology* of, relating to, or forming the walls or part of the walls of a bodily cavity or similar structure: *the parietal bones of the skull.* [2] of or relating to the side of the skull. [3] (of plant ovaries) having ovules attached to the walls. [4] *US* living or having authority within a college. ◆ NOUN [5] a parietal bone.
▷HISTORY C16: from Late Latin *parietālis,* from Latin *pariēs* wall

parietal bone NOUN either of the two bones forming part of the roof and sides of the skull.

parietal cell NOUN any one of the cells in the lining of the stomach that produce hydrochloric acid.

parietal lobe NOUN the portion of each cerebral hemisphere concerned with the perception and interpretation of sensations of touch, temperature, and taste and with muscular movements.

pari-mutuel (,pærɪ'mju:tjʊəl) NOUN, *plural* **pari-mutuels** *or* **paris-mutuels** (,pærɪ'mju:tjʊəlz). **a** a system of betting in which those who have bet on the winners of a race share in the total amount wagered less a percentage for the management. **b** (*as modifier*): *the pari-mutuel machine.*
▷HISTORY C19: from French, literally: mutual wager

paring ('pɛərɪŋ) NOUN (*often plural*) something pared or cut off.

pari passu *Latin* (,pærɪ 'pæsu:, 'pɑ:rɪ) ADVERB *Usually legal* with equal speed or progress; equably: often used to refer to the right of creditors to receive assets from the same source without one taking precedence.

paripinnate (,pærɪ'pɪneɪt) ADJECTIVE (of pinnate leaves) having an even number of leaflets and no terminal leaflet. Compare **imparipinnate.**

Paris ('pærɪs; *French* pari) NOUN [1] the capital of France, in the north on the River Seine: constitutes a department; dates from the 3rd century B.C., becoming capital of France in 987; centre of the French Revolution; centres around its original site on an island in the Seine, the **Île de la Cité,** containing Notre Dame; university (1150). Pop.: 2 123 261 (1999). Ancient name: **Lutetia.** [2] **Treaty of Paris. a** a treaty of 1783 between the US, Britain, France, and Spain, ending the War of American Independence. **b** a treaty of 1763 signed by Britain, France, and Spain that ended their involvement in the Seven Years' War. **c** a treaty of 1898 between Spain and the US bringing to an end the Spanish-American War.
▷HISTORY via French and Old French, from Late Latin (*Lūtētia*) *Parisiōrum* (marshes) of the *Parisii,* a tribe of Celtic Gaul

Paris Club NOUN another name for **Group of Ten.**

Paris Commune NOUN *French history* the council established in Paris in the spring of 1871 in opposition to the National Assembly and esp to the peace negotiated with Prussia following the Franco-Prussian War. Troops of the Assembly crushed the Commune with great bloodshed.

Paris green NOUN an emerald-green poisonous insoluble substance used as a pigment and insecticide. It is a double salt of copper arsenite and copper acetate. Formula: $3Cu(AsO_2)_2.Cu(C_2H_3O_2)_2$.

parish ('pærɪʃ) NOUN [1] a subdivision of a diocese, having its own church and a clergyman. Related adjective: **parochial.** [2] the churchgoers of such a subdivision. [3] (in England and, formerly, Wales) the smallest unit of local government in rural areas. [4] (in Louisiana) a unit of local government corresponding to a county in other states of the US. [5] the people living in a parish. [6] **on the parish.** *History* receiving parochial relief.
▷HISTORY C13: from Old French *paroisse,* from Church Latin *parochia,* from Late Greek *paroikia,* from *paroikos* Christian, sojourner, from Greek: neighbour, from PARA-[1] (beside) + *oikos* house

Parishad ('pʌrɪʃəd) NOUN (in India) an assembly.
▷HISTORY Hindi

parish clerk NOUN a person designated to assist in various church duties.

parish council NOUN (in England and, formerly, Wales) the administrative body of a parish. See **parish** (sense 3).

parishioner (pə'rɪʃənə) NOUN a member of a particular parish.

parish pump ADJECTIVE of only local interest; parochial.

parish register NOUN a book in which the births, baptisms, marriages, and deaths in a parish are recorded.

Parisian (pə'rɪzɪən) ADJECTIVE [1] of or relating to Paris or its inhabitants. ◆ NOUN [2] a native or inhabitant of Paris.

parison ('pærɪs(ə)n) NOUN an unshaped mass of glass before it is moulded into its final form.
▷HISTORY C19: from French *paraison,* from *parer* to prepare

parisyllabic (,pærɪsɪ'læbɪk) ADJECTIVE (of a noun or verb, in inflected languages) containing the same number of syllables in all or almost all inflected forms. Compare **imparisyllabic.**

parity[1] ('pærɪtɪ) NOUN, *plural* **-ties.** [1] equality of rank, pay, etc. [2] close or exact analogy or equivalence. [3] *Finance* **a** the amount of a foreign currency equivalent at the established exchange rate to a specific sum of domestic currency. **b** a similar equivalence between different forms of the same national currency, esp the gold equivalent of a unit of gold-standard currency. [4] equality between prices of commodities or securities in two separate markets. [5] *Physics* **a** a property of a physical system characterized by the behaviour of the sign of its wave function when all spatial coordinates are reversed in direction. The wave function either remains unchanged (**even parity**) or changes in sign (**odd parity**). **b** a quantum number describing this property, equal to +1 for even parity systems and –1 for odd parity systems. Symbol: *P.* See also **conservation of parity.** [6] *Maths* a relationship between two integers. If both are odd or both even they have the same parity; if one is odd and one even they have different parity. [7] (in the US) a system of government support for farm products.
▷HISTORY C16: from Late Latin *pāritās;* see PAR

parity[2] ('pærɪtɪ) NOUN [1] the condition or fact of having given birth. [2] the number of children to which a woman has given birth.
▷HISTORY C19: from Latin *parere* to bear

parity check NOUN a check made of computer data to ensure that the total number of bits of value 1 (or 0) in each unit of information remains odd or even after transfer between a peripheral device and the memory or vice versa.

park (pɑ:k) NOUN [1] a large area of land preserved in a natural state for recreational use by the public. See also **national park.** [2] a piece of open land in a town with public amenities. [3] *NZ* an area, esp of mountain country, reserved for recreational purposes. [4] a large area of land forming a private estate. [5] *English law* an enclosed tract of land where wild beasts are protected, acquired by a subject by royal grant or prescription. Compare **forest** (sense 5). [6] an area designed and landscaped to accommodate a group of related enterprises, businesses, research establishments, etc.: *science park.* [7] *US and Canadian* See **amusement park.** [8] *US, Canadian, and NZ* See **car park.** [9] *US and Canadian* a playing field or sports stadium. [10] **the park.** *Brit, informal* a soccer pitch. [11] a gear selector position on the automatic transmission of a motor vehicle that acts as a parking brake. [12] the area in which the equipment and supplies of a military formation are assembled. [13] a high valley surrounded by mountains in the western US. ◆ VERB [14] to stop and leave (a vehicle) temporarily. [15] to manoeuvre (a motor vehicle) into a space for it to be left: *try to park without hitting the kerb.* [16] *Stock Exchange* to register (securities) in the name of another or of nominees in order to conceal their real ownership. [17] (*tr*) *Informal* to leave or put somewhere: *park yourself in front of the fire.* [18] (*intr*) *Military* to arrange equipment in a park. [19] (*tr*) to enclose in or as a park.
▷HISTORY C13: from Old French *parc,* from Medieval Latin *parricus* enclosure, from Germanic; compare Old High German *pfarrih* pen, Old English *pearruc* PADDOCK[1]
▸**'park,like** ADJECTIVE

parka ('pɑ:kə) NOUN a warm hip-length weatherproof coat with a hood, originally worn by Eskimos.
▷HISTORY C19: from Aleutian: skin

parkade ('pɑ:keɪd) NOUN *Canadian* a building used as a car park.
▷HISTORY C20: from PARK + (ARC)ADE

Parker Morris standard NOUN (*often plural*) (in Britain) a set of minimum criteria for good housing construction, design, and facilities, recommended by the 1961 report of the Central Housing Advisory Committee chaired by Sir Parker Morris.

Subsequent governments have urged private and local authority house-builders to achieve these standards.

parkette (ˌpɑːk'ɛt) NOUN *Canadian* a small public park.

parkie ('pɑːkɪ) NOUN *Informal* a park keeper.

parkin ('pɑːkɪn) *or* **perkin** NOUN (in Britain and New Zealand) a moist spicy ginger cake usually containing oatmeal.
▷HISTORY C19: of unknown origin

parking disc NOUN See **disc** (sense 7a).

parking lot NOUN the US and Canadian term for **car park.**

parking meter NOUN a timing device, usually coin-operated, that indicates how long a vehicle may be left parked.

parking orbit NOUN an orbit around the earth or moon in which a spacecraft can be placed temporarily in order to prepare for the next step in its programme.

parking ticket NOUN a summons served for a parking offence.

Parkinson's disease ('pɑːkɪnsənz) NOUN a progressive chronic disorder of the central nervous system characterized by impaired muscular coordination and tremor. Often shortened to: **Parkinson's.** Also called: **Parkinsonism, Parkinson's syndrome, paralysis agitans, shaking palsy.**
▷HISTORY C19: named after James *Parkinson* (1755–1824), British surgeon, who first described it

Parkinson's law NOUN the notion, expressed facetiously as a law of economics, that work expands to fill the time available for its completion.
▷HISTORY C20: named after C. N. *Parkinson* (1909–93), British historian and writer, who formulated it

park keeper NOUN (in Britain) an official employed by a local authority to patrol and supervise a public park.

parkland ('pɑːkˌlænd) NOUN grassland with scattered trees.

park savanna NOUN savanna grassland scattered with trees.

parkway ('pɑːkˌweɪ) NOUN (in the US and Canada) a wide road planted with trees, turf, etc.

parky ('pɑːkɪ) ADJECTIVE **parkier, parkiest.** (*usually postpositive*) *Brit, informal* (of the weather) chilly; cold.
▷HISTORY C19: perhaps from PERKY

parlance ('pɑːləns) NOUN [1] a particular manner of speaking, esp when specialized; idiom: *political parlance.* [2] *Archaic* any discussion, such as a debate.
▷HISTORY C16: from Old French, from *parler* to talk, via Medieval Latin from Late Latin *parabola* speech, PARABLE; compare PARLEY

parlando (pɑː'lændəʊ) ADJECTIVE, ADVERB *Music* to be performed as though speaking.
▷HISTORY Italian: speaking, from *parlare* to speak

parlay ('pɑːlɪ) *US and Canadian* ◆ VERB (*tr*) [1] to stake (winnings from one bet) on a subsequent wager. Brit equivalent: **double up.** [2] to exploit (one's talent) to achieve worldly success. ◆ NOUN [3] a bet in which winnings from one wager are staked on another, or a series of such bets.
▷HISTORY C19: variant of *paroli,* via French from Neapolitan Italian *parolo,* from *paro* a pair, from Latin *pār* equal, PAR

parley ('pɑːlɪ) NOUN [1] a discussion, esp between enemies under a truce to decide terms of surrender, etc. ◆ VERB [2] (*intr*) to discuss, esp with an enemy under a truce. [3] (*tr*) to speak (a foreign language).
▷HISTORY C16: from French, from *parler* to talk, from Medieval Latin *parabolāre,* from Late Latin *parabola* speech, PARABLE
▸**'parleyer** NOUN

parleyvoo (ˌpɑːlɪ'vuː) *Informal* ◆ VERB (*intr*) [1] to speak French. ◆ NOUN [2] the French language. [3] a Frenchman.
▷HISTORY C20: jocular respelling of *parlez-vous (français)?* do you speak (French)?

parliament ('pɑːləmənt) NOUN [1] an assembly of the representatives of a political nation or people, often the supreme legislative authority. [2] any legislative or deliberative assembly, conference, etc. [3] Also: **parlement.** (in France before the Revolution) any of several high courts of justice in which royal decrees were registered.
▷HISTORY C13: from Anglo-Latin *parliamentum,* from Old French *parlement,* from *parler* to speak; see PARLEY

Parliament ('pɑːləmənt) NOUN [1] the highest legislative authority in Britain, consisting of the House of Commons, which exercises effective power, the House of Lords, and the sovereign. [2] a similar legislature in another country. [3] the two chambers of a Parliament. [4] the lower chamber of a Parliament. [5] any of the assemblies of such a body created by a general election and royal summons and dissolved before the next election.

parliamentarian (ˌpɑːləmɛn'tɛərɪən) NOUN [1] an expert in parliamentary procedures, etc. [2] (*sometimes capital*) *Brit* a Member of Parliament. ◆ ADJECTIVE [3] of or relating to a parliament or parliaments.

Parliamentarian (ˌpɑːləmɛn'tɛərɪən) NOUN [1] a supporter of Parliament during the English Civil War. ◆ ADJECTIVE [2] of or relating to Parliament or its supporters during the English Civil War.

parliamentarianism (ˌpɑːləmɛn'tɛərɪəˌnɪzəm) *or* **parliamentarism** (ˌpɑːlə'mɛntəˌrɪzəm) NOUN the system of parliamentary government.

parliamentary (ˌpɑːlə'mɛntərɪ, -trɪ) ADJECTIVE (*sometimes capital*) [1] of or characteristic of a parliament or Parliament. [2] proceeding from a parliament or Parliament: *a parliamentary decree.* [3] conforming to or derived from the procedures of a parliament or Parliament: *parliamentary conduct.* [4] having a parliament or Parliament. [5] of or relating to Parliament or its supporters during the English Civil War.

parliamentary agent NOUN (in Britain) a person who is employed to manage the parliamentary business of a private group.

Parliamentary Commissioner *or in full* **Parliamentary Commissioner for Administration** NOUN (in Britain) the official name for **ombudsman** (sense 2).

parliamentary private secretary NOUN (in Britain) a backbencher in Parliament who assists a minister, esp in liaison with backbenchers. Abbreviation: **PPS.**

parliamentary secretary NOUN (in Britain) a Member of Parliament appointed, usually as a junior minister, to assist a Minister of the Crown with departmental responsibilities.

parlor car NOUN (in the US and Canada) a comfortable railway coach with individual reserved seats.

parlour *or US* **parlor** ('pɑːlə) NOUN [1] *Old-fashioned* a living room, esp one kept tidy for the reception of visitors. [2] a reception room in a priest's house, convent, etc. [3] a small room for guests away from the public rooms in an inn, club, etc. [4] *Chiefly US, Canadian, and NZ* a room or shop equipped as a place of business: *a billiard parlor.* [5] *Caribbean* a small shop, esp one selling cakes and nonalcoholic drinks. [6] Also called: **milking parlour.** a building equipped for the milking of cows.
▷HISTORY C13: from Anglo-Norman *parlur,* from Old French *parleur* room in convent for receiving guests, from *parler* to speak; see PARLEY

parlour game NOUN an informal indoor game.

parlous ('pɑːləs) *Archaic or humorous* ◆ ADJECTIVE [1] dangerous or difficult. [2] cunning. ◆ ADVERB [3] extremely.
▷HISTORY C14 *perlous,* variant of PERILOUS
▸**'parlously** ADVERB ▸**'parlousness** NOUN

Parma NOUN [1] (*Italian* 'parma) a city in N Italy, in Emilia-Romagna: capital of the duchy of Parma and Piacenza from 1545 until it became part of Italy in 1860; important food industry (esp Parmesan cheese). Pop.: 168 717 (2000 est.). [2] ('pɑːmə) a city in NE Ohio, south of Cleveland. Pop.: 85 006 (1996 est.).

Parmentier ('pɑːmənˌtjeɪ; *French* parmɑ̃tje) ADJECTIVE (of soups, etc.) containing or garnished with potatoes.
▷HISTORY C19: named after A. *Parmentier* (1737–1813), French horticulturist

Parmesan (ˌpɑːmɪ'zæn, 'pɑːmɪˌzæn) ADJECTIVE [1] of or relating to Parma or its inhabitants. ◆ NOUN [2] a native or inhabitant of Parma.

Parmesan cheese NOUN a hard dry cheese made from skimmed milk, used grated, esp on pasta dishes and soups.

Parmigiano Reggiano (ˌpɑːmɪˌdʒɑːnəʊ rɛ'dʒɑːnəʊ) NOUN, *plural* **-nos.** another name for **Parmesan cheese.**

Parnaíba *or* **Parnahiba** (*Portuguese* parna'iba) NOUN a river in NE Brazil, rising in the Serra das Mangabeiras and flowing generally northeast, to the Atlantic. Length: about 1450 km (900 miles).

Parnassian[1] (pɑː'næsɪən) ADJECTIVE of or relating to Mount Parnassus or poetry.

Parnassian[2] (pɑː'næsɪən) NOUN [1] one of a school of French poets of the late 19th century who wrote verse that emphasized metrical form and restricted emotion. ◆ ADJECTIVE [2] of or relating to the Parnassians or their poetry.
▷HISTORY C19: from French *parnassien,* from *Parnasse* PARNASSUS; from *Le Parnasse contemporain,* title of an anthology produced by these poets
▸**Par'nassianˌism** *or* **Par'nasˌsism** NOUN

Parnassus (pɑː'næsəs) NOUN [1] **Mount.** a mountain in central Greece, in NW Boeotia: in ancient times sacred to Dionysus, Apollo, and the Muses, with the Castalian Spring and Delphi on its slopes. Height: 2457 m (8061 ft.). Modern Greek names: **Parnassós** (ˌparna'sɔs), **Liákoura.** [2] **a** the world of poetry. **b** a centre of poetic or other creative activity. [3] a collection of verse or belles-lettres.

Parnell shout NOUN *NZ, informal* a social occasion where each person in a group pays for his or her own entertainment or meal.
▷HISTORY from *Parnell,* suburb of Auckland, where very independent people on low incomes were supposed to live

parochial (pə'rəʊkɪəl) ADJECTIVE [1] narrow in outlook or scope; provincial. [2] of or relating to a parish or parishes.
▷HISTORY C14: via Old French from Church Latin *parochiālis;* see PARISH
▸**pa'rochialˌism** NOUN ▸**paˌrochi'ality** NOUN ▸**pa'rochially** ADVERB

parochial church council NOUN *Church of England* an elected body of lay representatives of the members of a parish that administers the affairs of the parish.

parody ('pærədɪ) NOUN, *plural* **-dies.** [1] a musical, literary, or other composition that mimics the style of another composer, author, etc., in a humorous or satirical way. [2] mimicry of someone's individual manner in a humorous or satirical way. [3] something so badly done as to seem an intentional mockery; travesty. ◆ VERB **-dies, -dying, -died.** [4] (*tr*) to make a parody of.
▷HISTORY C16: via Latin from Greek *paroidiā* satirical poem, from PARA-[1] + *ōidē* song
▸**parodic** (pə'rɒdɪk) *or* **pa'rodical** ADJECTIVE ▸**'parodist** NOUN

paroecious (pə'riːʃəs) *or* **paroicous** (pə'rɔɪkəs) ADJECTIVE (of mosses and related plants) having the male and female reproductive organs at different levels on the same stem.
▷HISTORY C19: from Greek *paroikos* living nearby, from PARA-[1] (beside) + *oikos* house; compare PARISH

parol ('pærəl, pə'rəʊl) *Law* ◆ NOUN [1] (formerly) the pleadings in an action when presented by word of mouth. [2] an oral statement; word of mouth (now only in the phrase **by parol**). ◆ ADJECTIVE [3] **a** (of a contract, lease, etc.) made orally or in writing but not under seal. **b** expressed or given by word of mouth: *parol evidence.*
▷HISTORY C15: from Old French *parole* speech; see PAROLE

parole (pə'rəʊl) NOUN [1] **a** the freeing of a prisoner before his sentence has expired, on the condition that he is of good behaviour. **b** the duration of such conditional release. [2] a promise given by a prisoner, as to be of good behaviour if granted liberty or partial liberty. [3] a variant spelling of **parol.** [4] *US Military* a password. [5] *Linguistics* language as manifested in the individual speech acts of particular speakers. Compare **langue, performance** (sense 7), **competence** (sense 5). [6] **on parole. a** conditionally released from detention. **b** *Informal* (of a person) under scrutiny, esp for a recurrence of an earlier shortcoming. ◆ VERB (*tr*) [7] to place (a person) on parole.
▷HISTORY C17: from Old French, from the phrase

parole d'honneur word of honour; *parole* from Late Latin *parabola* speech
▸**pa'rolable** ADJECTIVE ▸**parolee** (pə,rəʊ'li:) NOUN

paronomasia (ˌpærənəʊ'meɪzɪə) NOUN *Rhetoric* a play on words, esp a pun.
▷HISTORY C16: via Latin from Greek: a play on words, from *paronomazein* to make a change in naming, from PARA-[1] (beside) + *onomazein* to name, from *onoma* a name
▸**paronomastic** (ˌpærənəʊ'mæstɪk) ADJECTIVE ▸**ˌparono'mastically** ADVERB

paronym ('pærənɪm) NOUN *Linguistics* a cognate word.
▷HISTORY C19: via Late Latin from Greek *paronumon,* from PARA-[1] (beside) + *onoma* a name
▸**ˌparo'nymic** *or* **paronymous** (pə'rɒnɪməs) ADJECTIVE ▸**pa'ronymously** ADVERB

Páros ('pærɒs) NOUN a Greek island in the S Aegean Sea, in the Cyclades: site of the discovery (1627) of the Parian Chronicle, a marble tablet outlining Greek history from before 1000 B.C. to about 354 B.C. (now at Oxford University). Pop.: 8000 (latest est.). Area: 166 sq. km (64 sq. miles).

parosmia (pæ'rɒzmɪə) NOUN any disorder of the sense of smell.
▷HISTORY C19: from PARA-[1] + Greek *osmē* smell

parotic (pə'rɒtɪk) ADJECTIVE situated near the ear.
▷HISTORY C19: from New Latin *paroticus,* from Greek PARA-[1] (near) + *-oticus,* from *ous* ear

parotid (pə'rɒtɪd) ADJECTIVE 1 relating to or situated near the parotid gland. ◆ NOUN 2 See **parotid gland.**
▷HISTORY C17: via French, via Latin from Greek *parōtis,* from PARA-[1] (near) + *-ōtis,* from *ous* ear

parotid gland NOUN a large salivary gland, in man situated in front of and below each ear.

parotitis (ˌpærə'taɪtɪs) *or* **parotiditis** (pə,rɒtɪ'daɪtɪs) NOUN inflammation of the parotid gland. See also **mumps.**
▸**parotitic** (ˌpærə'tɪtɪk) *or* **parotiditic** (pə,rɒtɪ'dɪtɪk) ADJECTIVE

parotoid (pə'rɒtɔɪd) NOUN 1 Also called: **parotoid gland.** any of various warty poison glands on the head and back of certain toads and salamanders. ◆ ADJECTIVE 2 resembling a parotid gland.
▷HISTORY C19: from Greek *parot(is)* (see PAROTID) + -OID

-parous ADJECTIVE COMBINING FORM giving birth to: *oviparous.*
▷HISTORY from Latin *-parus,* from *parere* to bring forth

parousia (pə'ru:sɪə) NOUN *Christianity* another term for the **Second Coming.**
▷HISTORY C19: from Greek: presence

paroxetine (pæ'rɒksəti:n) NOUN an antidepressant drug that acts by preventing the re-uptake after release of serotonin in the brain, thereby prolonging its action: used for treating depression, obsessive-compulsive disorders, and panic disorder. Formula: $C_{19}H_{20}FNO_3$.

paroxysm ('pærək,sɪzəm) NOUN 1 an uncontrollable outburst: *a paroxysm of giggling.* 2 *Pathol* **a** a sudden attack or recurrence of a disease. **b** any fit or convulsion.
▷HISTORY C17: via French from Medieval Latin *paroxysmus* annoyance, from Greek *paroxusmos,* from *paroxunein* to goad, from PARA-[1] (intensifier) + *oxunein* to sharpen, from *oxus* sharp
▸**ˌparox'ysmal** *or* **ˌparox'ysmic** ADJECTIVE ▸**ˌparox'ysmally** ADVERB

paroxytone (pə'rɒksɪ,təʊn) ADJECTIVE 1 (in the classical Greek language) of, relating to, or denoting words having an acute accent on the next to last syllable. ◆ NOUN 2 a paroxytone word. ◆ Compare **oxytone.**
▷HISTORY C18: via New Latin from Greek *paroxutonos,* from PARA-[1] (beside) + *-oxutonos* OXYTONE
▸**paroxytonic** (ˌpærɒksɪ'tɒnɪk) ADJECTIVE

parpend ('pɑ:pənd) *or US* **parpen** ('pɑ:pən) NOUN other names for **perpend**[1].

parquet ('pɑ:keɪ, -kɪ) NOUN 1 a floor covering of pieces of hardwood fitted in a decorative pattern; parquetry. 2 Also called: **parquet floor.** a floor so covered. 3 *US* the stalls of a theatre. 4 the main part of the Paris Bourse, where officially listed securities are traded. Compare **coulisse** (sense 3). 5 (in France) the department of government responsible for the prosecution of crimes. ◆ VERB (*tr*) 6 to cover (a floor) with parquet.
▷HISTORY C19: from Old French: small enclosure, from *parc* enclosure; see PARK

parquet circle NOUN *US* the seating area of the main floor of a theatre that lies to the rear of the auditorium and underneath the balcony. Also called: **parterre.**

parquetry ('pɑ:kɪtrɪ) NOUN a geometric pattern of inlaid pieces of wood, often of different kinds, esp as used to cover a floor or to ornament furniture. Compare **marquetry.**

parr (pɑ:) NOUN, *plural* **parrs** *or* **parr.** a salmon up to two years of age, with dark spots and transverse bands.
▷HISTORY C18: of unknown origin

parra ('pærə) NOUN *Austral, informal* a tourist or non-resident on a beach.
▷HISTORY C20: possibly from *Parramatta,* a district of Sydney

parrakeet ('pærə,ki:t) NOUN a variant spelling of **parakeet.**

parramatta (ˌpærə'mætə) NOUN a variant spelling of **paramatta.**

parrel *or* **parral** ('pærəl) NOUN *Nautical* a ring that holds the jaws of a boom to the mast but lets it slide up and down.
▷HISTORY C15: probably from obsolete *aparail* equipment, a variant of APPAREL

parricide ('pærɪ,saɪd) NOUN 1 the act of killing either of one's parents. 2 a person who kills his parent.
▷HISTORY C16: from Latin *parricīdium* murder of a parent or relative, and from *parricīda* one who murders a relative, from *parri-* (element related to Greek *pēos* kinsman) + *-cīdium, -cīda* -CIDE
▸**ˌparri'cidal** ADJECTIVE

parritch ('pærɪtʃ, 'pɑ:r-) NOUN a Scot word for **porridge.**

parrot ('pærət) NOUN 1 any bird of the tropical and subtropical order *Psittaciformes,* having a short hooked bill, compact body, bright plumage, and an ability to mimic sounds. Related adjective: **psittacine.** 2 a person who repeats or imitates the words or actions of another unintelligently. 3 **sick as a parrot.** *Usually facetious* extremely disappointed. ◆ VERB **-rots, -roting, -roted.** 4 (*tr*) to repeat or imitate mechanically without understanding.
▷HISTORY C16: probably from French *paroquet;* see PARAKEET
▸**'parrotry** NOUN

parrot-fashion ADVERB *Informal* without regard for meaning; by rote: *she learned it parrot-fashion.*

parrot fever *or* **disease** NOUN another name for **psittacosis.**

parrotfish ('pærət,fɪʃ) NOUN, *plural* **-fish** *or* **-fishes.** 1 any brightly coloured tropical marine percoid fish of the family *Scaridae,* having parrot-like jaws. 2 *Austral* any of various brightly coloured marine fish of the family *Labridae.* 3 any of various similar fishes.

parrot toadstool NOUN See **wax cap.**

parry ('pærɪ) VERB **-ries, -rying, -ried.** 1 to ward off (an attack) by blocking or deflecting, as in fencing. 2 (*tr*) to evade (questions), esp adroitly. ◆ NOUN, *plural* **-ries.** 3 an act of parrying, esp (in fencing) using a stroke or circular motion of the blade. 4 a skilful evasion, as of a question.
▷HISTORY C17: from French *parer* to ward off, from Latin *parāre* to prepare

parse (pɑ:z) VERB *Grammar* 1 to assign constituent structure to (a sentence or the words in a sentence). 2 (*intr*) (of a word or linguistic element) to play a specified role in the structure of a sentence.
▷HISTORY C16: from Latin *pars* (*ōrātionis*) part (of speech)
▸**'parsable** ADJECTIVE

parsec ('pɑ:,sɛk) NOUN a unit of astronomical distance equal to the distance from earth at which stellar parallax would be 1 second of arc; equivalent to 3.0857×10^{16} m or 3.262 light years.
▷HISTORY C20: from PARALLAX + SECOND[2]

Parsee *or* **Parsi** ('pɑ:si:) NOUN 1 an adherent of a monotheistic religion of Zoroastrian origin, the practitioners of which were driven out of Persia by the Muslims in the eighth century A.D. It is now found chiefly in western India. ◆ ADJECTIVE 2 of or relating to the Parsees or their religion.
▷HISTORY C17: from Persian *Pārsī* a Persian, from Old Persian *Pārsa* PERSIA
▸**'Parsee,ism** NOUN

parser ('pɑ:zə) NOUN *Computing* a program or part of a program that interprets input to a computer by recognizing key words or analysing sentence structure.

Parsha ('pɑ:ʃə; *Yiddish* 'parʃə) NOUN the Yiddish word for **Parashah.**

Parsifal ('pɑ:sɪf^{ə}l, -,fɑ:l) *or* **Parzival** NOUN *German myth* the hero of a medieval cycle of legends about the Holy Grail. English eqivalent: **Percival.**

parsimony ('pɑ:sɪmənɪ) NOUN extreme care or reluctance in spending; frugality; niggardliness.
▷HISTORY C15: from Latin *parcimōnia,* from *parcere* to spare
▸**parsimonious** (ˌpɑ:sɪ'məʊnɪəs) ADJECTIVE ▸**ˌparsi'moniously** ADVERB

parsley ('pɑ:slɪ) NOUN 1 a S European umbelliferous plant, *Petroselinum crispum,* widely cultivated for its curled aromatic leaves, which are used in cooking. 2 any of various similar and related plants, such as fool's-parsley, stone parsley, and cow parsley.
▷HISTORY C14 *persely,* from Old English *petersilie* + Old French *persil, peresil,* both ultimately from Latin *petroselīnum* rock parsley, from Greek *petroselinon,* from *petra* rock + *selinon* parsley

parsley fern NOUN 1 a small bright green tufted European fern, *Cryptogramma crispa,* that grows on acid scree and rock in uplands. 2 any of several other plants with crisped foliage, resembling that of parsley.

parsley piert (pɪət) NOUN a small N temperate rosaceous plant, *Aphanes arvensis,* having fan-shaped leaves and small greenish flowers.
▷HISTORY C17: from French *perce pierre,* literally: break stone

parsnip ('pɑ:snɪp) NOUN 1 a strong-scented umbelliferous plant, *Pastinaca sativa,* cultivated for its long whitish root. 2 the root of this plant, eaten as a vegetable. 3 any of several similar plants, esp the cow parsnip.
▷HISTORY C14: from Old French *pasnaie,* from Latin *pastināca,* from *pastināre* to dig, from *pastinum* two-pronged tool for digging; also influenced by Middle English *nepe* TURNIP

parson ('pɑ:s^{ə}n) NOUN 1 a parish priest in the Church of England, formerly applied only to those who held ecclesiastical benefices. 2 any clergyman. 3 *NZ* a nonconformist minister.
▷HISTORY C13: from Medieval Latin *persōna* parish priest, representative of the parish, from Latin: personage; see PERSON
▸**parsonic** (pɑ:'sɒnɪk) *or* **par'sonical** ADJECTIVE

parsonage ('pɑ:s^{ə}nɪdʒ) NOUN the residence of a parson who is not a rector or vicar, as provided by the parish.

parson bird NOUN another name for **tui.**
▷HISTORY C19: so called because of its dark plumage with white neck feathers

parson's nose NOUN the fatty extreme end portion of the tail of a fowl when cooked. Also called: **pope's nose.**

part (pɑ:t) NOUN 1 a piece or portion of a whole. 2 an integral constituent of something: *dancing is part of what we teach.* 3 **a** an amount less than the whole; bit: *they only recovered part of the money.* **b** (*as modifier*): *an old car in part exchange for a new one.* 4 one of several equal or nearly equal divisions: *mix two parts flour to one part water.* 5 **a** an actor's role in a play. **b** the speech and actions which make up such a role. **c** a written copy of these. 6 a person's proper role or duty: *everyone must do his part.* 7 (*often plural*) region; area: *you're well known in these parts.* 8 *Anatomy* any portion of a larger structure. 9 a component that can be replaced in a machine, engine, etc.: *spare parts.* 10 the US, Canadian, and Austral word for **parting** (sense 1). 11 *Music* **a** one of a number of separate melodic lines making up the texture of music. **b** one of such melodic lines, which is assigned to one or more instrumentalists or singers: *the viola part; the soprano solo part.* **c** such a line performed from a separately written or printed copy. See **part song.** 12 **for the most part.** generally. 13 **for one's part.** as far as one is concerned. 14 **in part.** to

some degree; partly. 15 **of many parts.** having many different abilities. 16 **on the part of.** on behalf of. 17 **part and parcel.** an essential ingredient. 18 **play a part.** **a** to pretend to be what one is not. **b** (foll by *in*) to have something to do (with); be instrumental (in): *to play a part in the king's downfall.* 19 **take in good part.** to respond to (teasing) with good humour. 20 **take part in.** to participate in. 21 **take someone's part.** to support someone in an argument. ◆ VERB 22 to divide or separate from one another; take or come apart: *to part the curtains; the seams parted when I washed the dress.* 23 to go away or cause to go away from one another; stop or cause to stop seeing each other: *the couple parted amicably.* 24 (*intr;* foll by *from*) to leave; say goodbye (to). 25 (*intr;* foll by *with*) to relinquish, esp reluctantly: *I couldn't part with my teddy bear.* 26 (*tr;* foll by *from*) to cause to relinquish, esp reluctantly: *he's not easily parted from his cash.* 27 (*intr*) to split; separate: *the path parts here.* 28 (*tr*) to arrange (the hair) in such a way that a line of scalp is left showing. 29 (*intr*) a euphemism for **die**[1] (sense 1). 30 (*intr*) *Archaic* to depart. 31 **part company. a** to end a friendship or association, esp as a result of a quarrel; separate: *they were in partnership, but parted company last year.* **b** (foll by *with*) to leave; go away from; be separated from. ◆ ADVERB 32 to some extent; partly. ◆ See also **parts.**
▷HISTORY C13: via Old French from Latin *partīre* to divide, from *pars* a part

part. ABBREVIATION FOR: 1 participle. 2 particular.

partake (pɑːˈteɪk) VERB **-takes, -taking, -took, -taken.** (*mainly intr*) 1 (foll by *in*) to have a share; participate: *to partake in the excitement.* 2 (foll by *of*) to take or receive a portion, esp of food or drink: *each partook of the food offered to him.* 3 (foll by *of*) to suggest or have some of the quality (of): *music partaking of sadness.* 4 (*tr*) *Archaic* to share in.
▷HISTORY C16: back formation from *partaker,* earlier *part taker,* based on Latin *particeps* participant; see PART, TAKE
▸**parˈtaker** NOUN

> **Language note** *Partake of* is sometimes wrongly used as if it were a synonym of *eat* or *drink.* Correctly, one can only *partake of* food or drink which is available for several people to share.

partan (ˈpɑːtᵊn; *Scot* ˈpartᵊn) NOUN a Scot word for **crab**[1] (senses 1, 2).
▷HISTORY C15: of Celtic origin

parted (ˈpɑːtɪd) ADJECTIVE 1 *Botany* divided almost to the base: *parted leaves.* 2 *Heraldry* showing two coats of arms divided by a vertical central line.

parterre (pɑːˈtɛə) NOUN 1 a formally patterned flower garden. 2 *Brit Irish* the pit in a theatre. 3 *US* another name for **parquet circle.**
▷HISTORY C17: from French, from *par* along + *terre* ground

part exchange NOUN a transaction in which used goods are taken as partial payment for more expensive ones of the same type.

parthenocarpy (pɑːˈθiːnəʊˌkɑːpɪ) NOUN the development of fruit without fertilization or formation of seeds.
▷HISTORY C20: from Greek *parthenos* virgin + *karpos* fruit
▸**parˌthenoˈcarpic** *or* **parˌthenoˈcarpous** ADJECTIVE

parthenogenesis (ˌpɑːθɪnəʊˈdʒɛnɪsɪs) NOUN 1 a type of reproduction, occurring in some insects and flowers, in which the unfertilized ovum develops directly into a new individual. 2 human conception without fertilization by a male; virgin birth.
▷HISTORY C19: from Greek *parthenos* virgin + *genesis* birth
▸**parthenogenetic** (ˌpɑːθɪˌnəʊdʒɪˈnɛtɪk) ADJECTIVE
▸**ˌpartheˌnogeˈnetically** ADVERB

Parthenon (ˈpɑːθəˌnɒn, -nən) NOUN the temple on the Acropolis in Athens built in the 5th century B.C. and regarded as the finest example of the Greek Doric order.

Parthenopaeus (ˌpɑːθənəʊˈpiːəs) NOUN *Greek myth* one of the Seven against Thebes, son of Atalanta.

Parthenope (pɑːˈθɛnəpɪ) NOUN *Greek myth* a siren, who drowned herself when Odysseus evaded the lure of the sirens' singing. Her body was said to have been cast ashore at what became Naples.

Parthenos (ˈpɑːθɪˌnɒs) NOUN an epithet meaning "Virgin", applied by the Greeks to several goddesses, esp Athena.

parthenospore (pɑːˈθiːnəʊˌspɔː) NOUN another name for **azygospore.**

Parthia (ˈpɑːθɪə) NOUN a country in ancient Asia, southeast of the Caspian Sea, that expanded into a great empire dominating SW Asia in the 2nd century B.C. It was destroyed by the Sassanids in the 3rd century A.D.

Parthian (ˈpɑːθɪən) ADJECTIVE 1 of or relating to Parthia, a country in ancient Asia, or its inhabitants. ◆ NOUN 2 a native or inhabitant of Parthia.

Parthian shot NOUN a hostile remark or gesture delivered while departing.
▷HISTORY alluding to the custom of Parthian archers who shot their arrows backwards while retreating

partial (ˈpɑːʃəl) ADJECTIVE 1 relating to only a part; not general or complete: *a partial eclipse.* 2 biased: *a partial judge.* 3 (*postpositive;* foll by *to*) having a particular liking (for). 4 *Botany* **a** constituting part of a larger structure: *a partial umbel.* **b** used for only part of the life cycle of a plant: *a partial habitat.* **c** (of a parasite) not exclusively parasitic. 5 *Maths* designating or relating to an operation in which only one of a set of independent variables is considered at a time. ◆ NOUN 6 Also called: **partial tone.** *Music, acoustics* any of the component tones of a single musical sound, including both those that belong to the harmonic series of the sound and those that do not. 7 *Maths* a partial derivative.
▷HISTORY C15: from Old French *parcial,* from Late Latin *partiālis* incomplete, from Latin *pars* PART
▸**ˈpartially** ADVERB ▸**ˈpartialness** NOUN

> **Language note** See at **partly.**

partial derivative NOUN the derivative of a function of two or more variables with respect to one of the variables, the other or others being considered constant. Written $\partial f/\partial x$.

partial eclipse NOUN an eclipse, esp of the sun, in which the body is only partially hidden. Compare **total eclipse, annular eclipse.**

partial fraction NOUN *Maths* one of a set of fractions into which a more complicated fraction can be resolved.

partiality (ˌpɑːʃɪˈælɪtɪ) NOUN, *plural* **-ties.** 1 favourable prejudice or bias. 2 (usually foll by *for*) liking or fondness. 3 the state or condition of being partial.

partially sighted ADJECTIVE **a** unable to see properly so that even with corrective aids normal activities are prevented or seriously hindered. **b** (*as collective noun;* preceded by *the*): *the partially sighted.*
▸**partial sight** NOUN

partial pressure NOUN the pressure that a gas, in a mixture of gases, would exert if it alone occupied the whole volume occupied by the mixture.

partial product NOUN the result obtained when a number is multiplied by one digit of a multiplier.

partial reinforcement NOUN *Psychol* the process of randomly rewarding an organism for making a response on only some of the occasions it makes it.

partible (ˈpɑːtəbᵊl) ADJECTIVE (esp of property or an inheritance) divisible; separable.
▷HISTORY C16: from Late Latin *partibilis,* from *part-, pars* PART

Participaction (pɑːˌtɪsɪˈpækʃən) NOUN (in Canada) a non-profit-making organization set up to promote physical fitness.
▷HISTORY from PARTICIP(ATION) + ACTION

participate (pɑːˈtɪsɪˌpeɪt) VERB (*intr;* often foll by *in*) to take part, be or become actively involved, or share (in).
▷HISTORY C16: from Latin *participāre,* from *pars* PART + *capere* to take
▸**parˈticipant** ADJECTIVE, NOUN ▸**parˌticiˈpation** NOUN
▸**parˈticiˌpator** NOUN ▸**parˈticipatory** ADJECTIVE

participating insurance NOUN a system of insurance by which policyholders receive dividends from the company's profit or surplus.

participle (ˈpɑːtɪsɪpᵊl, pɑːˈtɪsɪpᵊl) NOUN a nonfinite form of verbs, in English and other languages, used adjectivally and in the formation of certain compound tenses. See also **present participle, past participle.**
▷HISTORY C14: via Old French from Latin *participium,* from *particeps* partaker, from *pars* PART + *capere* to take
▸**participial** (ˌpɑːtɪˈsɪpɪəl) ADJECTIVE, NOUN
▸**ˌpartiˈcipially** ADVERB

particle (ˈpɑːtɪkᵊl) NOUN 1 an extremely small piece of matter; speck. 2 a very tiny amount; iota: *it doesn't make a particle of difference.* 3 a function word, esp (in certain languages) a word belonging to an uninflected class having suprasegmental or grammatical function: *the Greek particles "mēn" and "de" are used to express contrast; questions in Japanese are indicated by the particle "ka"; English "up" is sometimes regarded as an adverbial particle.* 4 a common affix, such as *re-, un-,* or *-ness.* 5 *Physics* a body with finite mass that can be treated as having negligible size, and internal structure. 6 See **elementary particle.** 7 *RC Church* a small piece broken off from the Host at Mass. 8 *Archaic* a section or clause of a document.
▷HISTORY C14: from Latin *particula* a small part, from *pars* PART

particle accelerator NOUN a machine for accelerating charged elementary particles to very high energies, used for research in nuclear physics. See also **linear accelerator, cyclotron, betatron, synchrotron, synchrocyclotron.**

particle beam NOUN 1 a stream of energized particles produced by a particle accelerator. 2 such a stream emitted by a particle beam weapon.

particle beam weapon NOUN a weapon that fires particle beams into the atmosphere or space.

particle board NOUN another name for **chipboard.**

particle physics NOUN the study of fundamental particles and their properties. Also called: **high-energy physics.**

particle separation NOUN *Transformational grammar* a rule that moves the particle of a phrasal verb, thus deriving a sentence like *He looked the answer up* from a structure that also underlies *He looked up the answer.*

parti-coloured *or* **party-coloured** (ˈpɑːtɪˌkʌləd) ADJECTIVE having different colours in different parts; variegated.
▷HISTORY C16 *parti,* from (obsolete) *party* of more than one colour, from Old French: striped, from Latin *partīre* to divide

particular (pəˈtɪkjʊlə) ADJECTIVE 1 (*prenominal*) of or belonging to a single or specific person, thing, category, etc.; specific; special: *the particular demands of the job; no particular reason.* 2 (*prenominal*) exceptional or marked: *a matter of particular importance.* 3 (*prenominal*) relating to or providing specific details or circumstances: *a particular account.* 4 exacting or difficult to please, esp in details; fussy. 5 (of the solution of a differential equation) obtained by giving specific values to the arbitrary constants in a general equation. 6 *Logic* (of a proposition) affirming or denying something about only some members of a class of objects, as in *some men are not wicked.* Compare **universal** (sense 10). 7 *Property law* denoting an estate that precedes the passing of the property into ultimate ownership. See also **remainder** (sense 3), **reversion** (sense 4). ◆ NOUN 8 a separate distinct item that helps to form a generalization: opposed to *general.* 9 (*often plural*) an item of information; detail: *complete in every particular.* 10 *Logic* another name for **individual** (sense 7a). 11 *Philosophy* an individual object, as contrasted with a universal. See **universal** (sense 12b). 12 **in particular.** especially, particularly, or exactly.
▷HISTORY C14: from Old French *particuler,* from Late Latin *particulāris* concerning a part, from Latin *particula* PARTICLE V

particular average NOUN *Insurance* partial damage to or loss of a ship or its cargo affecting only the shipowner or one cargo owner. Abbreviation: **PA.** Compare **general average.**

particularism (pəˈtɪkjʊləˌrɪzəm) NOUN 1 exclusive attachment to the interests of one group,

class, sect, etc., esp at the expense of the community as a whole. [2] the principle of permitting each state or minority in a federation the right to further its own interests or retain its own laws, traditions, etc. [3] *Theol* the doctrine that divine grace is restricted to the elect.
▸ **par'ticularist** NOUN, ADJECTIVE ▸ **par,ticular'istic** ADJECTIVE

particularity (pə,tɪkjʊ'lærɪtɪ) NOUN, *plural* **-ties.** [1] (*often plural*) a specific circumstance: *the particularities of the affair.* [2] great attentiveness to detail; fastidiousness. [3] the quality of being precise: *a description of great particularity.* [4] the state or quality of being particular as opposed to general; individuality: *the particularity of human situations.*

particularize *or* **particularise** (pə'tɪkjʊlə,raɪz) VERB [1] to treat in detail; give details (about). [2] (*intr*) to go into detail.
▸ **par,ticulari'zation** *or* **par,ticulari'sation** NOUN
▸ **par'ticular,izer** *or* **par'ticular,iser** NOUN

particularly (pə'tɪkjʊləlɪ) ADVERB [1] very much; exceptionally: *I wasn't particularly successful.* [2] in particular; specifically: *pensioners, particularly the less well-off.*

Particulars of Claim PLURAL NOUN *Law* (in England) the first reading made by the claimant in a county court action, showing the facts upon which he or she relies in support of a claim and the relief asked for.

particulate (pɑː'tɪkjʊlɪt, -,leɪt) NOUN [1] a substance consisting of separate particles. ◆ ADJECTIVE [2] of or made up of separate particles. [3] *Genetics* of, relating to, or designating inheritance of characteristics, esp with emphasis on the role of genes.

parting ('pɑːtɪŋ) NOUN [1] *Brit* the line of scalp showing when sections of hair are combed in opposite directions. US, Canadian, and Austral equivalent: **part.** [2] the act of separating or the state of being separated. [3] **a** a departure or leave-taking, esp one causing a final separation. **b** (*as modifier*): *a parting embrace.* [4] a place or line of separation or division. [5] *Chem* a division of a crystal along a plane that is not a cleavage plane. [6] a euphemism for **death.** ◆ ADJECTIVE (*prenominal*) [7] *Literary* departing: *the parting day.* [8] serving to divide or separate.

parting strip NOUN a thin strip of wood, metal, etc., used to separate two adjoining materials.

parti pris *French* (parti pri) NOUN a preconceived opinion.
▹HISTORY C19: literally: side taken

Parti Québecois (*French* parti) NOUN (in Canada) a political party in Quebec, formed in 1968 and originally advocating the separation of Quebec from the rest of the country. Abbreviation: **PQ.**

partisan[1] *or* **partizan** (,pɑːtɪ'zæn, 'pɑːtɪ,zæn) NOUN [1] an adherent or devotee of a cause, party, etc. [2] **a** a member of an armed resistance group within occupied territory, esp in Italy or the Balkans in World War II. **b** (*as modifier*): *partisan forces.* ◆ ADJECTIVE [3] of, relating to, or characteristic of a partisan. [4] relating to or excessively devoted to one party, faction, etc.; one-sided: *partisan control.*
▹HISTORY C16: via French, from Old Italian *partigiano,* from *parte* faction, from Latin *pars* PART
▸ **,parti'sanship** *or* **,parti'zanship** NOUN

partisan[2] *or* **partizan** ('pɑːtɪzᵊn) NOUN a spear or pike with two opposing axe blades or spikes.
▹HISTORY C16: from French *partizane,* from Old Italian *partigiana,* from *partigiano* PARTISAN[1]

partita (pɑː'tiːtə) NOUN, *plural* **-te** (-teɪ) *or* **-tas.** *Music* a type of suite.
▹HISTORY Italian: divided (piece), from Latin *partīre* to divide

partite ('pɑːtaɪt) ADJECTIVE [1] (*in combination*) composed of or divided into a specified number of parts: *bipartite.* [2] (esp of plant leaves) divided almost to the base to form two or more parts.
▹HISTORY C16: from Latin *partīre* to divide

partition (pɑː'tɪʃən) NOUN [1] a division into parts; separation. [2] something that separates, such as a large screen dividing a room in two. [3] a part or share. [4] a division of a country into two or more separate nations. [5] *Property law* a division of property, esp realty, among joint owners. [6] *Maths* any of the ways by which an integer can be expressed as a sum of integers. [7] *Logic, maths* **a** the division of a class into a number of disjoint and exhaustive subclasses. **b** such a set of subclasses. [8] *Biology* a structure that divides or separates. [9] *Rhetoric* the second part of a speech where the chief lines of thought are announced. ◆ VERB (*tr*) [10] (often foll by *off*) to separate or apportion into sections: *to partition a room off with a large screen.* [11] to divide (a country) into two or more separate nations. [12] *Property law* to divide (property, esp realty) among joint owners, by dividing either the property itself or the proceeds of sale.
▹HISTORY C15: via Old French from Latin *partītiō,* from *partīre* to divide
▸ **par'titioner** *or* **par'titionist** NOUN

partition coefficient NOUN *Chem* the ratio of the concentrations of a substance in two heterogenous phases in equilibrium with each other.

partitive ('pɑːtɪtɪv) ADJECTIVE [1] *Grammar* indicating that a noun involved in a construction refers only to a part or fraction of what it otherwise refers to. The phrase *some of the butter* is a partitive construction; in some inflected languages it would be translated by the genitive case of the noun. [2] serving to separate or divide into parts. ◆ NOUN [3] *Grammar* a partitive linguistic element or feature.
▹HISTORY C16: from Medieval Latin *partītīvus* serving to divide, from Latin *partīre* to divide
▸ **'partitively** ADVERB

partlet ('pɑːtlɪt) NOUN a woman's garment covering the neck and shoulders, worn esp during the 16th century.
▹HISTORY C16: a variant of Middle English *patelet* strip of cloth, from Middle French *patelette*

partly ('pɑːtlɪ) ADVERB to some extent; not completely.

> **Language note** *Partly* and *partially* are to some extent interchangeable, but *partly* should be used when referring to a part or parts of something: *the building is partly* (not *partially*) *of stone,* while *partially* is preferred for the meaning *to some extent: his mother is partially* (not *partly*) *sighted.*

partner ('pɑːtnə) NOUN [1] an ally or companion: *a partner in crime.* [2] a member of a partnership. [3] one of a pair of dancers or players on the same side in a game: *my bridge partner.* [4] either member of a couple in a relationship. ◆ VERB [5] to be or cause to be a partner (of).
▹HISTORY C14: variant (influenced by PART) of PARCENER
▸ **'partnerless** ADJECTIVE

partners ('pɑːtnəz) PLURAL NOUN *Nautical* a wooden construction around an opening in a deck, as to support a mast.

partnership ('pɑːtnəʃɪp) NOUN [1] **a** a contractual relationship between two or more persons carrying on a joint business venture with a view to profit, each incurring liability for losses and the right to share in the profits. **b** the deed creating such a relationship. **c** the persons associated in such a relationship. [2] the state or condition of being a partner.

part-off NOUN *Caribbean* a screen used to divide off part of a room, such as the eating place of a parlour.

part of speech NOUN a class of words sharing important syntactic or semantic features; a group of words in a language that may occur in similar positions or fulfil similar functions in a sentence. The chief parts of speech in English are noun, pronoun, adjective, determiner, adverb, verb, preposition, conjunction, and interjection. Abbreviation: **POS.**

parton ('pɑː,tɒn) NOUN *Physics* a hypothetical elementary particle postulated as a constituent of neutrons and protons.
▹HISTORY from PART + -ON

partook (pɑː'tʊk) VERB the past tense of **partake.**

partridge ('pɑːtrɪdʒ) NOUN, *plural* **-tridges** *or* **-tridge.** [1] any of various small Old World gallinaceous game birds of the genera *Perdix, Alectoris,* etc., esp *P. perdix* (**common** or **European partridge**): family *Phasianidae* (pheasants). [2] *US and Canadian* any of various other gallinaceous birds, esp the bobwhite and ruffed grouse.
▹HISTORY C13: from Old French *perdriz,* from Latin *perdix,* from Greek

partridgeberry ('pɑːtrɪdʒ,berɪ) NOUN, *plural* **-ries.** [1] Also called: **boxberry, twinberry.** a creeping woody rubiaceous plant, *Mitchella repens,* of E North America with small white fragrant flowers and scarlet berries. [2] the berry of the wintergreen. [3] another name for **wintergreen** (sense 1).

partridge-wood NOUN the dark striped wood of the tropical American leguminous tree, *Andira inermis,* used for cabinetwork.

parts (pɑːts) PLURAL NOUN [1] personal abilities or talents: *a man of many parts.* [2] short for **private parts.**

Parts of Holland NOUN See **Holland**[1] (sense 3).

Parts of Kesteven NOUN See (Parts of) **Kesteven.**

Parts of Lindsey NOUN See (Parts of) **Lindsey.**

part song NOUN [1] a song composed in harmonized parts. [2] (*in more technical usage*) a piece of homophonic choral music in which the topmost part carries the melody.

part-time ADJECTIVE [1] for less than the entire time appropriate to an activity: *a part-time job; a part-time waitress.* ◆ ADVERB **part time.** [2] on a part-time basis: *he works part time.* ◆ Compare **full-time.**
▸ **,part-'timer** NOUN

parturient (pɑː'tjʊərɪənt) ADJECTIVE [1] of or relating to childbirth. [2] giving birth. [3] producing or about to produce a new idea, etc.
▹HISTORY C16: via Latin *parturīre,* from *parere* to bring forth
▸ **par'turiency** NOUN

parturient fever NOUN another name for **milk fever.**

parturifacient (pɑː,tjʊərɪ'feɪʃənt) ADJECTIVE, NOUN a medical word for **oxytocic.**
▹HISTORY C19: from Latin *parturīre* to be in travail + *facere* to make

parturition (,pɑːtjʊ'rɪʃən) NOUN the act or process of giving birth.
▹HISTORY C17: from Late Latin *parturītiō,* from *parturīre* to be in labour

partway ('pɑːt,weɪ) ADVERB some of the way; partly: *I stopped reading partway through the chapter.*

part work NOUN *Brit* a series of magazines issued as at weekly or monthly intervals, which are designed to be bound together to form a complete course or book.

part-writing NOUN *Music* the aspect of composition concerned with the writing of parts, esp counterpoint.

party ('pɑːtɪ) NOUN, *plural* **-ties.** [1] **a** a social gathering for pleasure, often held as a celebration. **b** (*as modifier*): *party spirit.* **c** (*in combination*): *partygoer.* [2] a group of people associated in some activity: *a rescue party.* [3] **a** (*often capital*) a group of people organized together to further a common political aim, such as the election of its candidates to public office. **b** (*as modifier*): *party politics.* [4] the practice of taking sides on public issues. [5] a person, esp one who participates in some activity such as entering into a contract. [6] the person or persons taking part in legal proceedings, such as plaintiff or prosecutor: *a party to the action.* [7] *Informal, humorous* a person: *he's an odd old party.* ◆ VERB **-ties, -tying, -tied.** (*intr*) [8] *Informal* to celebrate; revel. ◆ ADJECTIVE [9] *Heraldry* (of a shield) divided vertically into two colours, metals, or furs.
▹HISTORY C13: from Old French *partie* part, faction, from Latin *partīre* to divide; see PART

party line NOUN [1] a telephone line serving two or more subscribers. [2] the policies or dogma of a political party, to which all members are expected to subscribe. [3] *Chiefly US* the boundary between adjoining property.

party list NOUN (*modifier*) of or relating to a system of voting in which people vote for a party rather than for a candidate. Parties are assigned the number of seats which reflects their share of the vote. See **proportional representation.**

party man NOUN a loyal member of a political party, esp one who is extremely loyal or devoted.

party politics PLURAL NOUN politics conducted through, by, or for parties, as opposed to other interests or the public good.

party pooper ('pu:pə) NOUN *Informal* a person whose behaviour or personality spoils other people's enjoyment.
▷HISTORY C20: originally US

party popper NOUN a small plastic cylinder which, when a string is pulled, makes a small bang and fires thin paper streamers into the air.

party wall NOUN *Property law* a wall separating two properties or pieces of land and over which each of the adjoining owners has certain rights.

parulis (pə'ru:lɪs) NOUN, *plural* **-lides** (-lɪ,di:z). *Pathol* another name for **gumboil.**
▷HISTORY C19: from PARA-[1] + Greek *oulon* gum

parure (pə'rʊə) NOUN a set of jewels or other ornaments.
▷HISTORY C15: from Old French *pareure* adornment, from *parer* to embellish, from Latin *parāre* to arrange

par value NOUN the value imprinted on the face of a share certificate or bond and used to assess dividend, capital ownership, or interest. Also called: **face value.** Compare **market value, book value** (sense 2).

Parvati ('pʌrvətɪ) NOUN *Hinduism* goddess consort of the god Siva, associated with mountains.
▷HISTORY from Sanskrit: the mountain-dwelling one

parve ('pɑrvə) ADJECTIVE a variant of **parev.**

parvenu ('pɑ:və,nju:) NOUN [1] a person, esp a man, who, having risen socially or economically, is considered to be an upstart or to lack the appropriate refinement for his or her new position. ◆ ADJECTIVE [2] of or characteristic of a parvenu.
▷HISTORY C19: from French, from *parvenir* to attain, from Latin *pervenīre,* from *per* through + *venīre* to come

parvenue ('pɑ:və,nju:) NOUN [1] a woman who, having risen socially or economically, is considered to be an upstart or to lack the appropriate refinement for her new position. ◆ ADJECTIVE [2] of or characteristic of a parvenue.
▷HISTORY C19: see PARVENU

parvifoliate (,pɑ:vɪ'fəʊlɪ,eɪt) ADJECTIVE (of plants) having small leaves in comparison with the size of the stem.

parvis *or* **parvise** ('pɑ:vɪs) NOUN a court or portico in front of a building, esp a church.
▷HISTORY C14: via Old French from Late Latin *paradīsus* PARADISE

parvovirus ('pɑ:vəʊ,vaɪrəs) NOUN any of a group of viruses characterized by their very small size, each of which is specific to a particular species, as for example canine parvovirus.
▷HISTORY C20: New Latin from Latin *parvus* little + VIRUS

Parzival (*German* 'partsifal) NOUN a variant of **Parsifal.**

pas (pɑ:; *French* pɑ) NOUN, *plural* **pas** (pɑ:z; *French* pɑ). [1] a dance step or movement, esp in ballet. [2] *Rare* the right to precede; precedence.
▷HISTORY C18: French, literally: step

PA's PLURAL NOUN *Mountaineering* a type of rock boot.
▷HISTORY C20: named after *P*ierre *A*llain, French climber

Pasadena (,pæsə'di:nə) NOUN a city in SW California, east of Los Angeles. Pop.: 133 936 (2000).

Pasargadae (pæ'sɑ:gə,di:) NOUN an ancient city in Persia, northeast of Persepolis in present-day Iran: built by Cyrus the Great.

Pasay ('pɑ:saɪ) NOUN a city in the Philippines, on central Luzon just south of Manila, on Manila Bay. Pop.: 354 908 (2000). Also called: **Rizal.**

pascal ('pæskᵊl) NOUN the derived SI unit of pressure; the pressure exerted on an area of 1 square metre by a force of 1 newton; equivalent to 10 dynes per square centimetre or 1.45×10^{-4} pound per square inch. Symbol: Pa.
▷HISTORY C20: named after Blaise *Pascal* (1623–62), French philosopher, mathematician, and physicist

Pascal ('pæs,kæl, -kᵊl) NOUN a high-level computer programming language developed as a teaching language: used for general-purpose programming.

Pascal's triangle NOUN a triangle consisting of rows of numbers; the apex is 1 and each row starts and ends with 1, other numbers being obtained by adding together the two numbers on either side in the row above: used to calculate probabilities.
▷HISTORY C17: named after Blaise *Pascal* (1623–62), French philosopher, mathematician, and physicist

Pascal's wager NOUN *Philosophy* the argument that it is in one's rational self-interest to act as if God exists, since the infinite punishments of hell, provided they have a positive probability, however small, outweigh any countervailing advantage.
▷HISTORY C17: named after Blaise *Pascal* (1623–62), French philosopher, mathematician, and physicist

Pasch (pɑ:sk, pæsk) NOUN an archaic name for **Passover** (sense 1) or **Easter.**
▷HISTORY C12: from Old French *pasche,* via Church Latin and Greek from Hebrew *pesakh* PESACH

paschal ('pæskᵊl) ADJECTIVE [1] of or relating to Passover. [2] of or relating to Easter.

paschal flower NOUN another name for **pasqueflower.**

Paschal Lamb NOUN [1] (*sometimes not capitals*) *Old Testament* the lamb killed and eaten on the first day of the Passover. [2] Christ regarded as this sacrifice.

pas de basque (,pɑ: də 'bɑ:sk; *French* pɑ də bask) NOUN, *plural* **pas de basque.** a dance step performed usually on the spot, consisting of one long and two short movements during which the weight is transferred from one foot to the other: used esp in reels and jigs.
▷HISTORY from French, literally: Basque step

Pas-de-Calais (*French* pɑdkalɛ) NOUN a department of N France, in Nord-Pas-de-Calais region, on the Straits of Dover (the **Pas de Calais**): the part of France closest to the British Isles. Capital: Arras. Pop.: 1 441 568 (1999). Area: 6752 sq. km (2633 sq. miles).

pas de chat (*French* pɑdʃa) NOUN, *plural* **pas de chat.** *Ballet* a catlike leap.
▷HISTORY French: cat's step

pas de deux (*French* pɑddø) NOUN, *plural* **pas de deux.** *Ballet* a sequence for two dancers.
▷HISTORY French: step for two

pase ('pɑ:seɪ) NOUN *Bullfighting* a movement of the cape or muleta by a matador to attract the bull's attention and guide its attack.
▷HISTORY from Spanish, literally: pass

pash[1] (pæʃ) NOUN *Slang* infatuation.
▷HISTORY C20: from PASSION

pash[2] (pæʃ) *Obsolete or dialect* ◆ VERB [1] to throw or be thrown and break or be broken to bits; smash. ◆ NOUN [2] a crushing blow.
▷HISTORY C17 (n): from earlier *passhen* to throw with violence, probably of imitative origin

pasha *or* **pacha** ('pɑ:ʃə, 'pæʃə) NOUN (formerly) a provincial governor or other high official of the Ottoman Empire or the modern Egyptian kingdom: placed after a name when used as a title.
▷HISTORY C17: from Turkish *paşa*

pashalik *or* **pashalic** ('pɑ:ʃəlɪk) NOUN the province or jurisdiction of a pasha.
▷HISTORY C18: from Turkish

pashka ('pæʃkə) NOUN a rich Russian dessert made of cottage cheese, cream, almonds, currants, etc., set in a special wooden mould and traditionally eaten at Easter.

pashm ('pæʃəm) NOUN the underfur of various Tibetan animals, esp goats, used for cashmere shawls.
▷HISTORY from Persian, literally: wool

pashmina (pæʃ'mi:nə) NOUN a scarf or shawl made of pashm.
▷HISTORY from Persian *pashmina*; see PASHM

Pashto, Pushto ('pʌʃtəʊ), *or* **Pushtu** NOUN [1] a language of Afghanistan and NW Pakistan, belonging to the East Iranian branch of the Indo-European family: since 1936 the official language of Afghanistan. [2] (*plural* **-to** *or* **-tos, -tu** *or* **-tus**) a speaker of the Pashto language; a Pathan. ◆ ADJECTIVE [3] denoting or relating to this language or a speaker of it.

Pasiphaë[1] (pə'sɪfɪ:) NOUN *Greek myth* the wife of Minos and mother (by a bull) of the Minotaur.

Pasiphaë[2] (pə'sɪfɪ:) NOUN *Astronomy* a small outer satellite of the planet Jupiter.

paso doble ('pæsəʊ 'dəʊbleɪ; *Spanish* 'paso 'doβle) NOUN, *plural* **paso dobles** *or* **pasos dobles** (*Spanish* 'pasos 'doβles). [1] a modern ballroom dance in fast duple time. [2] a piece of music composed for or in the rhythm of this dance.
▷HISTORY Spanish: double step

PASOK ('pæsɒk) NOUN ACRONYM FOR Panhellenic Socialist Movement.
▷HISTORY C20: Modern Greek *Pa(nhellenion) So(sialistiko) K(enema)*

pas op ('pɑ:s ,ɒp) INTERJECTION *South African* beware.
▷HISTORY Afrikaans

paspalum (pæs'peɪləm) NOUN any of various grasses of the genus *Paspalum* of Australia and New Zealand having wide leaves.
▷HISTORY from New Latin, from Greek *paspalos,* a variety of millet

pasqueflower ('pɑ:sk,flaʊə, 'pæsk-) NOUN [1] a purple-flowered herbaceous ranunculaceous plant, *Anemone pulsatilla* (or *Pulsatilla vulgaris*), of N and Central Europe and W Asia. [2] any of several related North American plants, such as *A. patens.* ◆ Also called **paschal flower, pulsatilla.**
▷HISTORY C16: from French *passefleur,* from *passer* to excel + *fleur* flower; changed to *pasqueflower* Easter flower, because it blooms at Easter

pasquinade (,pæskwɪ'neɪd) *or* **pasquil** ('pæskwɪl) NOUN [1] an abusive lampoon or satire, esp one posted in a public place. ◆ VERB **-ades, -ading, -aded** *or* **-quils, -quilling, -quilled.** [2] (*tr*) to ridicule with pasquinade.
▷HISTORY C17: from Italian *Pasquino* name given to an ancient Roman statue disinterred in 1501, which was annually posted with satirical verses
▸ **,pasquin'ader** NOUN

pass (pɑ:s) VERB [1] to go onwards or move by or past (a person, thing, etc.). [2] to run, extend, or lead through, over, or across (a place): *the route passes through the city.* [3] to go through or cause to go through (an obstacle or barrier): *to pass a needle through cloth.* [4] to move or cause to move onwards or over: *he passed his hand over her face.* [5] (*tr*) to go beyond or exceed: *this victory passes all expectation.* [6] to gain or cause to gain an adequate or required mark, grade, or rating in (an examination, course, etc.): *the examiner passed them all.* [7] (often foll by *away* or *by*) to elapse or allow to elapse: *we passed the time talking.* [8] **pass the time of day (with).** to spend time amicably (with), esp in chatting, with no particular purpose. [9] (*intr*) to take place or happen: *what passed at the meeting?* [10] to speak or exchange or be spoken or exchanged: *angry words passed between them.* [11] to spread or cause to spread: *we passed the news round the class.* [12] to transfer or exchange or be transferred or exchanged: *the bomb passed from hand to hand.* [13] (*intr*) to undergo change or transition: *to pass from joy to despair.* [14] (when *tr,* often foll by *down*) to transfer or be transferred by inheritance: *the house passed to the younger son.* [15] to agree to or sanction or to be agreed to or receive the sanction of a legislative body, person of authority, etc.: *the assembly passed 10 resolutions.* [16] (*tr*) (of a legislative measure) to undergo (a procedural stage) and be agreed: *the bill passed the committee stage.* [17] (when *tr,* often foll by *on* or *upon*) to pronounce or deliver (judgment, findings, etc.): *the court passed sentence.* [18] to go or allow to go without comment or censure: *the intended insult passed unnoticed.* [19] (*intr*) to opt not to exercise a right, as by not answering a question or not making a bid or a play in card games. [20] *Physiol* to discharge (urine, faeces, etc.) from the body. [21] **pass water.** to urinate. [22] (*intr*) to come to an end or disappear: *his anger soon passed.* [23] (*intr;* usually foll by *for* or *as*) to be likely to be mistaken for or accepted as (someone or something else): *you could easily pass for your sister.* [24] (*intr;* foll by *away, on,* or *over*) a euphemism for **die**[1] (sense 1). [25] (*tr*) *Chiefly US* to fail to declare (a dividend). [26] (*intr;* usually foll by *on* or *upon*) *Chiefly US* (of a court, jury, etc.) to sit in judgment; adjudicate. [27] *Sport* to hit, kick, or throw (the ball) to another player. [28] **bring to pass.** *Archaic* to cause to happen. [29] **come to pass.** to happen. ◆ NOUN [30] the act of passing. [31] **a** a route through a range of mountains where the summit is lower or where there is a gap between peaks. **b** (*capital as part of a name*): *the Simplon Pass.* [32] a way through any difficult region. [33] a permit, licence, or authorization to do something without restriction: *she has a pass to visit*

the museum on Sundays. 34 **a** a document allowing entry to and exit from a military installation. **b** a document authorizing leave of absence. 35 *Brit* **a** the passing of a college or university examination to a satisfactory standard but not as high as honours. **b** (*as modifier*): *a pass degree.* ◆ Compare **honours** (sense 2). 36 a dive, sweep, or bombing or landing run by an aircraft. 37 a motion of the hand or of a wand as a prelude to or part of a conjuring trick. 38 *Informal* an attempt, in words or action, to invite sexual intimacy (esp in the phrase **make a pass at**). 39 a state of affairs or condition, esp a bad or difficult one (esp in the phrase **a pretty pass**). 40 *Sport* the transfer of a ball from one player to another. 41 *Fencing* a thrust or lunge with a sword. 42 *Bridge* the act of passing (making no bid). 43 *Bullfighting* a variant of **pase.** 44 *Archaic* a witty sally or remark. ◆ INTERJECTION 45 *Bridge* a call indicating that a player has no bid to make. ◆ See also **pass by, pass off, pass out, pass over, pass up.**
▷HISTORY C13: from Old French *passer* to pass, surpass, from Latin *passūs* step, PACE[1]

pass. ABBREVIATION FOR passive.

passable ('pɑːsəbᵊl) ADJECTIVE 1 adequate, fair, or acceptable: *a passable but not outstanding speech.* 2 (of an obstacle) capable of being passed or crossed. 3 (of currency) valid for general circulation. 4 (of a proposed law) able to be ratified or enacted.
▸ **'passableness** NOUN

passably ('pɑːsəblɪ) ADVERB 1 fairly; somewhat. 2 acceptably; well enough: *she sings passably.*

passacaglia (ˌpæsə'kɑːljə) NOUN 1 an old Spanish dance in slow triple time. 2 a slow instrumental piece characterized by a series of variations on a particular theme played over a repeated bass part. See also **chaconne** (sense 1).
▷HISTORY C17: earlier *passacalle,* from Spanish *pasacalle* street dance, from *paso* step + *calle* street; the ending *-alle* was changed to *-aglia* to suggest an Italian origin

passade (pæ'seɪd) NOUN *Dressage* the act of moving back and forth in the same place.
▷HISTORY C17: via French from Italian *passata,* from *passare* to PASS

passage[1] ('pæsɪdʒ) NOUN 1 a channel, opening, etc., through or by which a person or thing may pass. 2 *Music* a section or division of a piece, movement, etc. 3 a way, as in a hall or lobby. 4 a section of a written work, speech, etc., esp one of moderate length. 5 a journey, esp by ship: *the outward passage took a week.* 6 the act or process of passing from one place, condition, etc., to another: *passage of a gas through a liquid.* 7 the permission, right, or freedom to pass: *to be denied passage through a country.* 8 the enactment of a law or resolution by a legislative or deliberative body. 9 an evacuation of the bowels. 10 *Rare* an exchange or interchange, as of blows, words, etc. (esp in the phrase **passage of arms**).
▷HISTORY C13: from Old French from *passer* to PASS

passage[2] ('pæsɪdʒ, 'pæsɑːʒ) *Dressage* ◆ NOUN 1 a sideways walk in which diagonal pairs of feet are lifted alternately. 2 a cadenced lofty trot, the moment of suspension being clearly defined. ◆ VERB 3 to move or cause to move at a passage.
▷HISTORY C18: from French *passager,* variant of *passéger,* from Italian *passeggiare* to take steps, ultimately from Latin *passūs* step, PACE[1]

passage hawk *or* **passager hawk** ('pæsɪdʒə) NOUN a young hawk or falcon caught while on migration. Compare **eyas, haggard**[1] (sense 4).

passageway ('pæsɪdʒˌweɪ) NOUN a way, esp one in or between buildings; passage.

passage work NOUN *Music* scales, runs, etc., in a piece of music which have no structural significance but provide an opportunity for virtuoso display.

Passamaquoddy Bay (ˌpæsəmə'kwɒdɪ) NOUN an inlet of the Bay of Fundy between New Brunswick (Canada) and Maine (US) at the mouth of the St Croix River.

passant ('pæsᵊnt) ADJECTIVE (*usually postpositive*) *Heraldry* (of a beast) walking, with the right foreleg raised.
▷HISTORY C14: from Old French, present participle of *passer* to PASS

passata (pə'sɑːtə) NOUN a sauce made from sieved tomatoes, often used in Italian cookery.
▷HISTORY Italian

pass band NOUN the band of frequencies that is transmitted with maximum efficiency through a circuit, filter, etc.

passbook ('pɑːsˌbʊk) NOUN 1 a book for keeping a record of withdrawals from and payments into a building society. 2 another name for **bankbook.** 3 a customer's book in which is recorded by a trader a list of credit sales to that customer. 4 (formerly in South Africa) an official document serving to identify the bearer, his race, his residence, and his employment.

pass by VERB 1 (*intr*) to go or move past. 2 (*tr, adverb*) to overlook or disregard: *to pass by difficult problems.*

Passchendaele ('pæʃənˌdeɪl) NOUN a village in NW Belgium, in West Flanders province: the scene of heavy fighting during the third battle of Ypres in World War I during which 245 000 British troops were lost.

passé ('pɑːseɪ, 'pɑseɪ; *French* pɑse) ADJECTIVE 1 out-of-date: *passé ideas.* 2 past the prime; faded: *a passé society beauty.*
▷HISTORY C18: from French, past participle of *passer* to PASS

passel ('pæsᵊl) NOUN *Informal or dialect, chiefly US* a group or quantity of no fixed number.
▷HISTORY variant of PARCEL

passementerie (pæs'mɛntrɪ; *French* pɑsmɑ̃tri) NOUN a decorative trimming of gimp, cord, beads, braid, etc.
▷HISTORY C16: from Old French *passement,* from *passer* to trim, PASS

passenger ('pæsɪndʒə) NOUN 1 **a** a person travelling in a car, train, boat, etc., not driven by him. **b** (*as modifier*): *a passenger seat.* 2 *Chiefly Brit* a member of a group or team who is a burden on the others through not participating fully in the work.
▷HISTORY C14: from Old French *passager* passing, from PASSAGE[1]

passenger pigeon NOUN a gregarious North American pigeon, *Ectopistes migratorius:* became extinct at the beginning of the 20th century.

passe-partout (ˌpæspɑː'tuː; *French* pɑspartu) NOUN 1 a mounting for a picture in which strips of strong gummed paper are used to bind together the glass, picture, and backing. 2 the gummed paper used for this. 3 a mat, often decorated, on which a picture is mounted. 4 something that secures entry everywhere, esp a master key.
▷HISTORY C17: from French, literally: pass everywhere

passepied (pɑːs'pjeɪ) NOUN, *plural* **-pieds** (-'pjeɪ). 1 a lively minuet of Breton origin, in triple time, popular in the 17th century. 2 a piece of music composed for or in the rhythm of this dance.
▷HISTORY C17: from French: pass the foot

passer-by NOUN, *plural* **passers-by.** a person that is passing or going by, esp on foot.

passerine ('pæsəˌraɪn, -ˌriːn) ADJECTIVE 1 of, relating to, or belonging to the *Passeriformes,* an order of birds characterized by the perching habit: includes the larks, finches, crows, thrushes, starlings, etc. ◆ NOUN 2 any bird belonging to the order *Passeriformes.*
▷HISTORY C18: from Latin *passer* sparrow

pas seul (*French* pɑ sœl) NOUN, *plural* **pas seuls** (*French* pɑ sœl). a dance sequence for one person.
▷HISTORY French, literally: step on one's own

passible ('pæsɪbᵊl) ADJECTIVE susceptible to emotion or suffering; able to feel.
▷HISTORY C14: from Medieval Latin *passibilis,* from Latin *patī* to suffer; see PASSION
▸ **ˌpassi'bility** NOUN

passifloraceous (ˌpæsɪflɔː'reɪʃəs) ADJECTIVE of, relating to, or belonging to the *Passifloraceae,* a tropical and subtropical family of climbing plants including the passionflowers: the flowers have five petals and threadlike parts forming a dense mass (corona) around the central disc.
▷HISTORY C19: from New Latin *Passiflora,* the type genus (passionflower)

passim *Latin* ('pæsɪm) ADVERB here and there; throughout: used to indicate that what is referred to occurs frequently in the work cited.

passing ('pɑːsɪŋ) ADJECTIVE 1 transitory or momentary: *a passing fancy.* 2 cursory or casual in action or manner: *a passing reference.* ◆ ADVERB, ADJECTIVE 3 *Archaic* to an extreme degree: *the events were passing strange.* ◆ NOUN 4 a place where or means by which one may pass, cross, ford, etc. 5 a euphemism for **death.** 6 **in passing.** by the way; incidentally: *he mentioned your visit in passing.*

passing bell NOUN a bell rung to announce a death or a funeral. Also called: **death bell, death knell.**

passing note *or US* **passing tone** NOUN *Music* a nonharmonic note through which a melody passes from one harmonic note to the next. Compare **auxiliary note.**

passing shot NOUN *Tennis* a winning shot hit outside an opponent's reach.

passion ('pæʃən) NOUN 1 ardent love or affection. 2 intense sexual love. 3 a strong affection or enthusiasm for an object, concept, etc.: *a passion for poetry.* 4 any strongly felt emotion, such as love, hate, envy, etc. 5 a state or outburst of extreme anger: *he flew into a passion.* 6 the object of an intense desire, ardent affection, or enthusiasm. 7 an outburst expressing intense emotion: *he burst into a passion of sobs.* 8 *Philosophy* **a** any state of the mind in which it is affected by something external, such as perception, desire, etc., as contrasted with action. **b** feelings, desires or emotions, as contrasted with reason. 9 the sufferings and death of a Christian martyr.
▷HISTORY C12: via French from Church Latin *passiō* suffering, from Latin *patī* to suffer

Passion ('pæʃən) NOUN 1 the sufferings of Christ from the Last Supper to his death on the cross. 2 any of the four Gospel accounts of this. 3 a musical setting of this: *the St Matthew Passion.*

passional ('pæʃənᵊl) ADJECTIVE 1 of, relating to, or due to passion or the passions. ◆ NOUN 2 a book recounting the sufferings of Christian martyrs or saints.

passionate ('pæʃənɪt) ADJECTIVE 1 manifesting or exhibiting intense sexual feeling or desire: *a passionate lover.* 2 capable of, revealing, or characterized by intense emotion: *a passionate plea.* 3 easily roused to anger; quick-tempered.
▸ **'passionately** ADVERB ▸ **'passionateness** NOUN

passionflower ('pæʃənˌflaʊə) NOUN any passifloraceous plant of the tropical American genus *Passiflora,* cultivated for their red, yellow, greenish, or purple showy flowers: some species have edible fruit. See also **granadilla.**
▷HISTORY C17: so called from the alleged resemblance between parts of the flower and the instruments of Christ's crucifixion

passion fruit NOUN the edible fruit of any of various passionflowers, esp granadilla.

passionless ('pæʃənlɪs) ADJECTIVE 1 empty of emotion or feeling: *a passionless marriage.* 2 calm and detached; dispassionate.
▸ **'passionlessly** ADVERB ▸ **'passionlessness** NOUN

Passion play NOUN a play depicting the Passion of Christ.

Passion Sunday NOUN the fifth Sunday in Lent (the second Sunday before Easter), when Passiontide begins.

Passiontide ('pæʃənˌtaɪd) NOUN the last two weeks of Lent, extending from Passion Sunday to Holy Saturday.

Passion Week NOUN 1 the week between Passion Sunday and Palm Sunday. 2 (formerly) Holy Week; the week before Easter.

passivate ('pæsɪˌveɪt) VERB (*tr*) to render (a metal) less susceptible to corrosion by coating the surface with a substance, such as an oxide.

passive ('pæsɪv) ADJECTIVE 1 not active or not participating perceptibly in an activity, organization, etc. 2 unresisting and receptive to external forces; submissive. 3 not working or operating. 4 affected or acted upon by an external object or force. 5 *Grammar* denoting a voice of verbs in sentences in which the grammatical subject is not the logical subject but rather the recipient of the action described by the verb, as *was broken* in the sentence *The glass was broken by a boy.* Compare **active** (sense 5a). 6 *Chem* (of a substance, esp a metal) apparently chemically unreactive, usually as a result of the formation of a thin

protective layer that prevents further reaction. [7] *Electronics, telecomm* **a** containing no source of power and therefore capable only of attenuating a signal: *a passive network.* **b** not capable of amplifying a signal or controlling a function: *a passive communications satellite.* [8] *Finance* (of a bond, share, debt, etc.) yielding no interest. ◆ NOUN [9] *Grammar* **a** the passive voice. **b** a passive verb.
▷HISTORY C14: from Latin *passīvus* susceptible of suffering, from *patī* to undergo
▸ **'passively** ADVERB ▸ **pas'sivity** *or* **'passiveness** NOUN

passive euthanasia NOUN a form of euthanasia in which medical treatment that will keep a dying patient alive for a time is withdrawn.

passive obedience NOUN [1] unquestioning obedience to authority. [2] the surrender of a person's will to another person.

passive resistance NOUN resistance to a government, law, etc., made without violence, as by fasting, demonstrating peacefully, or refusing to cooperate.

passive safety NOUN the practice of taking measures to reduce the consequences of accidents, as opposed to attempting to avoid them altogether. Compare **active safety.**

passive smoking NOUN the inhalation of smoke from other people's cigarettes by a nonsmoker.
▸ **passive smoker** NOUN

passive vocabulary NOUN all the words, collectively, that a person can understand. Compare **active vocabulary.**

passivism ('pæsɪˌvɪzəm) NOUN [1] the theory, belief, or practice of passive resistance. [2] the quality, characteristics, or fact of being passive.
▸ **'passivist** NOUN, ADJECTIVE

passkey ('pɑːsˌkiː) NOUN [1] any of various keys, esp a latchkey. [2] another term for **master key** or **skeleton key.**

pass law NOUN (formerly, in South Africa) a law restricting the movement of Black Africans, esp from rural to urban areas.

pass off VERB (*adverb*) [1] to be or cause to be accepted or circulated in a false character or identity: *he passed the fake diamonds off as real.* [2] (*intr*) to come to a gradual end; disappear: *eventually the pain passed off.* [3] to emit (a substance) as a gas or vapour, or (of a substance) to be emitted in this way. [4] (*intr*) to take place: *the meeting passed off without disturbance.* [5] (*tr*) to set aside or disregard: *I managed to pass off his insult.*

pass out VERB (*adverb*) [1] (*intr*) *Informal* to become unconscious; faint. [2] (*intr*) *Brit* (esp of an officer cadet) to qualify for a military commission; complete a course of training satisfactorily: *General Smith passed out from Sandhurst in 1933.* [3] (*tr*) to distribute.

pass over VERB [1] (*tr, adverb*) to take no notice of; disregard: *they passed me over in the last round of promotions.* [2] (*intr, preposition*) to disregard (something bad or embarrassing): *we shall pass over your former faults.*

Passover ('pɑːsˌəʊvə) NOUN [1] Also called: **Pesach, Pesah, Feast of the Unleavened Bread.** an eight-day Jewish festival beginning on Nisan 15 and celebrated in commemoration of the passing over or sparing of the Israelites in Egypt, when God smote the firstborn of the Egyptians (Exodus 12). Related adjective: **Paschal.** [2] another term for the **Paschal Lamb.**
▷HISTORY C16: from *pass over,* translation of Hebrew *pesah,* from *pāsah* to pass over

passport ('pɑːspɔːt) NOUN [1] an official document issued by a government, identifying an individual, granting him permission to travel abroad, and requesting the protection of other governments for him. [2] a licence granted by a state to a foreigner, allowing the passage of his person or goods through the country. [3] another word for **sea letter** (sense 1). [4] a quality, asset, etc., that gains a person admission or acceptance.
▷HISTORY C15: from French *passeport,* from *passer* to PASS + PORT[1]

pass up VERB (*tr, adverb*) [1] *Informal* to let go by; ignore: *I won't pass up this opportunity.* [2] to take no notice of (someone).

passus ('pæsəs) NOUN, *plural* **-sus** *or* **-suses.** (esp in medieval literature) a division or section of a poem, story, etc.
▷HISTORY C16: from Latin: step, PACE[1]

password ('pɑːsˌwɜːd) NOUN [1] a secret word, phrase, etc., that ensures admission or acceptance by proving identity, membership, etc. [2] an action, quality, etc., that gains admission or acceptance. [3] a sequence of characters used to gain access to a computer system.

past (pɑːst) ADJECTIVE [1] completed, finished, and no longer in existence: *past happiness.* [2] denoting or belonging to all or a segment of the time that has elapsed at the present moment: *the past history of the world.* [3] denoting a specific unit of time that immediately precedes the present one: *the past month.* [4] (*prenominal*) denoting a person who has held and relinquished an office or position; former: *a past president.* [5] *Grammar* denoting any of various tenses of verbs that are used in describing actions, events, or states that have been begun or completed at the time of utterance. Compare **aorist, imperfect** (sense 4), **perfect** (sense 8). ◆ NOUN [6] **the past.** the period of time or a segment of it that has elapsed: *forget the past.* [7] the history, experience, or background of a nation, person, etc.: *a soldier with a distinguished past.* [8] an earlier period of someone's life, esp one that contains events kept secret or regarded as disreputable. [9] *Grammar* **a** a past tense. **b** a verb in a past tense. ◆ ADVERB [10] at a specified or unspecified time before the present; ago: *three years past.* [11] on or onwards: *I greeted him but he just walked past.* ◆ PREPOSITION [12] beyond in time: *it's past midnight.* [13] beyond in place or position: *the library is past the church.* [14] moving beyond; in a direction that passes: *he walked past me.* [15] beyond or above the reach, limit, or scope of: *his foolishness is past comprehension.* [16] beyond or above in number or amount: *to count past ten.* [17] **past it.** *Informal* unable to perform the tasks one could do when one was younger. [18] **not put it past someone.** to consider someone capable of (the action specified).
▷HISTORY C14: from *passed,* past participle of PASS

> **Language note** The past participle of *pass* is sometimes wrongly spelt *past: the time for recriminations has passed* (not *past*).

pasta ('pæstə) NOUN any of several variously shaped edible preparations made from a flour and water dough, such as spaghetti.
▷HISTORY Italian, from Late Latin: PASTE[1]

paste[1] (peɪst) NOUN [1] a mixture or material of a soft or malleable consistency, such as toothpaste. [2] an adhesive made from water and flour or starch, used esp for joining pieces of paper. [3] a preparation of food, such as meat, that has been powdered to a creamy mass, for spreading on bread, crackers, etc. [4] any of various sweet doughy confections: *almond paste.* [5] dough, esp when prepared with shortening, as for making pastry. [6] **a** Also called: **strass.** a hard shiny glass used for making imitation gems. **b** an imitation gem made of this glass. [7] the combined ingredients of porcelain. See also **hard paste, soft paste.** ◆ VERB (*tr*) [8] (often foll by *on* or *onto*) to attach by or as if by using paste: *he pasted posters onto the wall.* [9] (usually foll by *with*) to cover (a surface) with paper, usually attached with an adhesive: *he pasted the wall with posters.*
▷HISTORY C14: via Old French from Late Latin *pasta* dough, from Greek *pastē* barley porridge, from *pastos,* from *passein* to sprinkle

paste[2] (peɪst) VERB (*tr*) *Slang* to hit, esp with the fists; punch or beat soundly.
▷HISTORY C19: variant of BASTE[3]

pasteboard ('peɪstˌbɔːd) NOUN [1] **a** a stiff board formed from layers of paper or pulp pasted together, esp as used in bookbinding. **b** (*as modifier*): *a pasteboard book cover.* [2] *Slang* a card or ticket. ◆ ADJECTIVE [3] flimsy; insubstantial. [4] sham; fake.

pastel ('pæstᵊl, pæ'stɛl) NOUN [1] **a** a substance made of ground pigment bound with gum, used for making sticks for drawing. **b** a crayon of this. **c** a drawing done in such crayons. [2] the medium or technique of pastel drawing. [3] a pale delicate colour. [4] a light prose work, esp a poetic one. [5] another name for **woad.** ◆ ADJECTIVE [6] (of a colour) pale; delicate: *pastel blue.*
▷HISTORY C17: via French from Italian *pastello,* from Late Latin *pastellus* woad compounded into a paste, diminutive of *pasta* PASTE[1]
▸ **'pastelist** *or* **'pastellist** NOUN

pastern ('pæstən) NOUN [1] the part of a horse's foot between the fetlock and the hoof. [2] Also called: **fetter bone.** either of the two bones that constitute this part.
▷HISTORY C14: from Old French *pasturon,* from *pasture* a hobble, from Latin *pāstōrius* of a shepherd, from PASTOR

paste-up NOUN *Printing* [1] an assembly of typeset matter, illustrations, etc., pasted on a sheet of paper or board and used as a guide or layout in the production of a publication. [2] a sheet of paper or board on which are pasted artwork, typeset matter, etc., for photographing prior to making a printing plate; another name for **camera-ready copy.** [3] another name for **collage** (senses 1, 2).

pasteurism ('pæstəˌrɪzəm, -stjə-, 'pɑː-) NOUN *Med* [1] a method of securing immunity from rabies in a person who has been bitten by a rabid animal, by daily injections of progressively more virulent suspensions of the infected spinal cord of a rabbit that died of rabies. [2] a similar method of treating patients with other viral infections by the serial injection of progressively more virulent suspensions of the causative virus. ◆ Also called **Pasteur treatment.**

pasteurization *or* **pasteurisation** (ˌpæstəraɪ'zeɪʃən, -stjə-, ˌpɑː-) NOUN the process of heating beverages, such as milk, beer, wine, or cider, or solid foods, such as cheese or crab meat, to destroy harmful or undesirable microorganisms or to limit the rate of fermentation by the application of controlled heat.

pasteurize *or* **pasteurise** ('pæstəˌraɪz, -stjə-, 'pɑː-) VERB (*tr*) [1] to subject (milk, beer, etc.) to pasteurization. [2] *Rare* to subject (a patient) to pasteurism.

pasteurizer *or* **pasteuriser** ('pæstəˌraɪzə, -stjə-, 'pɑː-) NOUN [1] an apparatus for pasteurizing substances (esp milk). [2] a person who carries out pasteurization.

pastiche (pæ'stiːʃ) *or* **pasticcio** (pæ'stɪtʃəʊ) NOUN [1] a work of art that mixes styles, materials, etc. [2] a work of art that imitates the style of another artist or period.
▷HISTORY C19: French *pastiche,* Italian *pasticcio,* literally: piecrust (hence, something blended), from Late Latin *pasta* PASTE[1]

pasticheur (ˌpæstiː'ʃɜː) NOUN a person who creates or performs pastiches.

pastille *or* **pastil** ('pæstɪl) NOUN [1] a small flavoured or medicated lozenge for chewing. [2] an aromatic substance burnt to fumigate the air. [3] *Med* a small coated paper disc formerly used to estimate the dose or intensity of radiation (esp of X-rays): it changes colour when exposed. [4] a variant of **pastel** (sense 1).
▷HISTORY C17: via French from Latin *pastillus* small loaf, from *pānis* bread

pastime ('pɑːsˌtaɪm) NOUN an activity or entertainment which makes time pass pleasantly: *golf is my favourite pastime.*
▷HISTORY C15: from PASS + TIME, on the model of French *passe-temps*

pasting ('peɪstɪŋ) NOUN *Slang* a thrashing; heavy defeat.

pastis (pæ'stɪs, -'stiːs) NOUN an anise-flavoured alcoholic drink.
▷HISTORY from French, of uncertain origin

pastitsio (pæs'tɪtsɪəʊ) NOUN a Greek dish consisting of minced meat and macaroni topped with béchamel sauce.
▷HISTORY C20: from Modern Greek

past life therapy NOUN a form of hypnosis or meditation based on the belief that an individual's present problems are rooted in events that occurred before birth in this life.

past master NOUN [1] a person with talent for, or experience in, a particular activity: *a past master of tact.* [2] a person who has held the office of master in a Freemasons' lodge, guild, etc.

Pasto (*Spanish* 'pasto) NOUN a city in SE Colombia, at an altitude of 2590 m (8500 ft.). Pop.: 332 396 (1999 est.).

pastor (ˈpɑːstə) NOUN [1] a clergyman or priest in charge of a congregation. [2] a person who exercises spiritual guidance over a number of people. [3] an archaic word for **shepherd** (sense 1). [4] Also called: **rosy pastor.** a S Asian starling, *Sturnus roseus,* having glossy black head and wings and a pale pink body.
▷HISTORY C14: from Latin: shepherd, from *pascere* to feed
▸ˈ**pastor**ˌ**ship** NOUN

pastoral (ˈpɑːstərəl) ADJECTIVE [1] of, characterized by, or depicting rural life, scenery, etc. [2] (of a literary work) dealing with an idealized form of rural existence in a conventional way. [3] (of land) used for pasture. [4] denoting or relating to the branch of theology dealing with the duties of a clergyman or priest to his congregation. [5] of or relating to a clergyman or priest in charge of a congregation or his duties as such. [6] of or relating to a teacher's responsibility for the personal, as the distinct from the educational, development of pupils. [7] of or relating to shepherds, their work, etc. ◆ NOUN [8] a literary work or picture portraying rural life, esp the lives of shepherds in an idealizing way. See also **eclogue.** [9] *Music* a variant of **pastorale.** [10] *Christianity* **a** a letter from a clergyman to the people under his charge. **b** the letter of a bishop to the clergy or people of his diocese. **c** Also called: **pastoral staff.** the crosier or staff carried by a bishop as a symbol of his pastoral responsibilities.
▷HISTORY C15: from Latin, from PASTOR
▸ˈ**pastoral**ˌ**ism** NOUN ▸ˈ**pastorally** ADVERB

pastorale (ˌpæstəˈrɑːl) NOUN, *plural* **-rales.** *Music* [1] a composition evocative of rural life, characterized by moderate compound duple or quadruple time and sometimes a droning accompaniment. [2] a musical play based on a rustic story, popular during the 16th century.
▷HISTORY C18: Italian, from Latin: PASTORAL

pastoralist (ˈpɑːstərəlɪst) NOUN *Austral* a grazier or land-holder raising sheep, cattle, etc., on a large scale.

pastorate (ˈpɑːstərɪt) NOUN [1] the office or term of office of a pastor. [2] a body of pastors; pastors collectively.

past participle NOUN a participial form of verbs used to modify a noun that is logically the object of a verb, also used in certain compound tenses and passive forms of the verb in English and other languages.

past perfect *Grammar* ◆ ADJECTIVE [1] denoting a tense of verbs used in relating past events where the action had already occurred at the time of the action of a main verb that is itself in a past tense. In English this is a compound tense formed with *had* plus the past participle. ◆ NOUN [2] **a** the past perfect tense. **b** a verb in this tense.

pastrami (pəˈstrɑːmɪ) NOUN highly seasoned smoked beef, esp prepared from a shoulder cut.
▷HISTORY from Yiddish, from Romanian *pastramă,* from *păstra* to preserve

pastry (ˈpeɪstrɪ) NOUN, *plural* **-tries.** [1] a dough of flour, water, shortening, and sometimes other ingredients. [2] baked foods, such as tarts, made with this dough. [3] an individual cake or pastry pie.
▷HISTORY C16: from PASTE[1]

pastry cream NOUN a creamy custard, often flavoured, used as a filling for éclairs, flans, etc. Also called: **pastry custard.**

pasturage (ˈpɑːstʃərɪdʒ) NOUN [1] the right to graze or the business of grazing cattle. [2] another word for **pasture.**

pasture (ˈpɑːstʃə) NOUN [1] land covered with grass or herbage and grazed by or suitable for grazing by livestock. [2] a specific tract of such land. [3] the grass or herbage growing on it. ◆ VERB [4] (*tr*) to cause (livestock) to graze or (of livestock) to graze (a pasture).
▷HISTORY C13: via Old French from Late Latin *pāstūra,* from *pascere* to feed

pasty[1] (ˈpeɪstɪ) ADJECTIVE **pastier, pastiest.** [1] of or like the colour, texture, etc., of paste. [2] (esp of the complexion) pale or unhealthy-looking. ◆ NOUN, *plural* **pasties.** [3] either one of a pair of small round coverings for the nipples used by striptease dancers.
▸ˈ**pastily** ADVERB ▸ˈ**pastiness** NOUN

pasty[2] (ˈpæstɪ) NOUN, *plural* **pasties.** a round of pastry folded over a filling of meat, vegetables, etc.: *Cornish pasty.*
▷HISTORY C13: from Old French *pastée,* from Late Latin *pasta* dough

PA system NOUN See **public-address system.**

pat[1] (pæt) VERB **pats, patting, patted.** [1] to hit (something) lightly with the palm of the hand or some other flat surface: *to pat a ball.* [2] to slap (a person or animal) gently, esp on the back, as an expression of affection, congratulation, etc. [3] (*tr*) to shape, smooth, etc., with a flat instrument or the palm. [4] (*intr*) to walk or run with light footsteps. [5] **pat (someone) on the back.** *Informal* to congratulate or encourage (someone). ◆ NOUN [6] a light blow with something flat. [7] a gentle slap. [8] a small mass of something: *a pat of butter.* [9] the sound made by a light stroke or light footsteps. [10] **pat on the back.** *Informal* a gesture or word indicating approval or encouragement.
▷HISTORY C14: perhaps imitative

pat[2] (pæt) ADVERB [1] Also: **off pat.** exactly or fluently memorized or mastered: *he recited it pat.* [2] opportunely or aptly. [3] **stand pat. a** *Chiefly US and Canadian* to refuse to abandon a belief, decision, etc. **b** (in poker, etc.) to play without adding new cards to the hand dealt. ◆ ADJECTIVE [4] exactly right for the occasion; apt: *a pat reply.* [5] too exactly fitting; glib: *a pat answer to a difficult problem.* [6] exactly right: *a pat hand in poker.*
▷HISTORY C17: perhaps adverbial use ("with a light stroke") of PAT[1]

pat[3] (pæt) NOUN **on one's pat.** *Austral, informal* alone; on one's own.
▷HISTORY C20: rhyming slang, from *Pat* Malone

Pat (pæt) NOUN an informal name for an Irishman.
▷HISTORY from *Patrick*

patagium (pəˈteɪdʒɪəm) NOUN, *plural* **-gia** (-dʒɪə). [1] a web of skin between the neck, limbs, and tail in bats and gliding mammals that functions as a wing. [2] a membranous fold of skin connecting margins of a bird's wing to the shoulder.
▷HISTORY C19: New Latin from Latin, from Greek *patageion* gold border on a tunic

Patagonia (ˌpætəˈɡəʊnɪə) NOUN [1] the southernmost region of South America, in Argentina and Chile extending from the Andes to the Atlantic. Area: about 777 000 sq. km (300 000 sq. miles). [2] an arid tableland in the southernmost part of Argentina, rising towards the Andes in the west.

Patagonian (ˌpætəˈɡəʊnɪən) ADJECTIVE [1] of or relating to Patagonia or its inhabitants. ◆ NOUN [2] a native or inhabitant of Patagonia.

patch (pætʃ) NOUN [1] **a** a piece of material used to mend a garment or to make patchwork, a sewn-on pocket, etc. **b** (*as modifier*): *a patch pocket.* [2] a small piece, area, expanse, etc. [3] **a** a small plot of land. **b** its produce: *a patch of cabbages.* [4] a district for which particular officials, such as social workers or policemen, have responsibility: *he's a problem that's on your patch, John.* [5] *Pathol* any discoloured area on the skin, mucous membranes, etc., usually being one sign of a specific disorder. [6] *Med* **a** a protective covering for an injured eye. **b** any protective dressing. [7] an imitation beauty spot, esp one made of black or coloured silk, worn by both sexes, esp in the 18th century. [8] Also called: **flash.** *US* an identifying piece of fabric worn on the shoulder of a uniform, on a vehicle, etc. [9] a small contrasting section or stretch: *a patch of cloud in the blue sky.* [10] a scrap; remnant. [11] *Computing* a small set of instructions to correct or improve a computer program. [12] *Austral, informal* the insignia of a motorcycle club or gang. [13] **a bad patch.** a difficult or troubled time. [14] **not a patch on.** *Informal* not nearly as good as. ◆ VERB (*tr*) [15] to mend or supply (a garment, etc.) with a patch or patches. [16] to put together or produce with patches. [17] (of material) to serve as a patch to. [18] (often foll by *up*) to mend hurriedly or in a makeshift way. [19] (often foll by *up*) to make (up) or settle (a quarrel). [20] to connect (electric circuits) together temporarily by means of a patch board. [21] (usually foll by *through*) to connect (a telephone call) by means of a patch board. [22] *Computing* to correct or improve (a program) by adding a small set of instructions.
▷HISTORY C16 *pacche,* perhaps from French *pieche* PIECE
▸ˈ**patchable** ADJECTIVE ▸ˈ**patcher** NOUN

patch board *or* **panel** NOUN a device with a large number of sockets into which electrical plugs can be inserted to form many different temporary circuits: used in telephone exchanges, computer systems, etc. Also called: **plugboard.**

patchouli, pachouli, *or* **patchouly** (ˈpætʃʊlɪ, pəˈtʃuːlɪ) NOUN [1] any of several Asiatic trees of the genus *Pogostemon,* the leaves of which yield a heavy fragrant oil: family *Lamiaceae* (labiates). [2] the perfume made from this oil.
▷HISTORY C19: from Tamil *paccilai,* from *paccu* green + *ilai* leaf

patch pocket NOUN a pocket on the outside of a garment.

patch quilt NOUN *Irish* a patchwork quilt.

patch test NOUN *Med* a test to detect an allergic reaction by applying small amounts of a suspected substance to the skin and then examining the area for signs of irritation.

patchwork (ˈpætʃˌwɜːk) NOUN [1] needlework done by sewing pieces of different materials together. [2] something, such as a theory, made up of various parts: *a patchwork of cribbed ideas.*

patchy (ˈpætʃɪ) ADJECTIVE **patchier, patchiest.** [1] irregular in quality, occurrence, intensity, etc.: *a patchy essay.* [2] having or forming patches.
▸ˈ**patchily** ADVERB ▸ˈ**patchiness** NOUN

patd ABBREVIATION FOR patented.

pate (peɪt) NOUN the head, esp with reference to baldness or (in facetious use) intelligence.
▷HISTORY C14: of unknown origin

pâté (ˈpæteɪ; *French* pɑte) NOUN [1] a spread of very finely minced liver, poultry, etc., served usually as an hors d'oeuvre. [2] a savoury pie of meat or fish.
▷HISTORY from French: PASTE[1]

pâté de foie gras (pɑte də fwa ɡrɑ) NOUN, *plural* **pâtés de foie gras** (pɑte də fwa ɡrɑ). a smooth rich paste made from the liver of a specially fattened goose, considered a great delicacy.
▷HISTORY French: pâté of fat liver

patella (pəˈtɛlə) NOUN, *plural* **-lae** (-liː). [1] *Anatomy* a small flat triangular bone in front of and protecting the knee joint. Nontechnical name: **kneecap.** [2] *Biology* a cuplike structure, such as the spore-producing body of certain ascomycetous fungi. [3] *Archaeol* a small pan.
▷HISTORY C17: from Latin, from *patina* shallow pan
▸**pa**ˈ**tellar** ADJECTIVE

patellate (pəˈtɛlɪt, -ˌleɪt) ADJECTIVE having the shape of a patella. Also: **patelliform** (pəˈtɛlɪˌfɔːm).

paten (ˈpætᵊn)**, patin,** *or* **patine** (ˈpætɪn) NOUN a plate, usually made of silver or gold, esp the plate on which the bread is placed in the Eucharist.
▷HISTORY C13: from Old French *patene,* from Medieval Latin, from Latin *patina* pan

patency (ˈpeɪtᵊnsɪ) NOUN [1] the condition of being obvious. [2] the state of a bodily passage, duct, etc., of being open or unobstructed. [3] *Phonetics* the degree to which the vocal tract remains unobstructed in the articulation of a speech sound. See also **closure** (sense 7).

patent (ˈpeɪtᵊnt, ˈpætᵊnt) NOUN [1] **a** a government grant to an inventor assuring him the sole right to make, use, and sell his invention for a limited period. **b** a document conveying such a grant. [2] an invention, privilege, etc., protected by a patent. [3] **a** an official document granting a right. **b** any right granted by such a document. [4] (in the US) **a** a grant by the government of title to public lands. **b** the instrument by which such title is granted. **c** the land so granted. [5] a sign that one possesses a certain quality. ◆ ADJECTIVE [6] open or available for inspection (esp in the phrases **letters patent, patent writ**). [7] (ˈpeɪtᵊnt) obvious: *their scorn was patent to everyone.* [8] concerning protection, appointment, etc., of or by a patent or patents. [9] proprietary. [10] (esp of a bodily passage or duct) being open or unobstructed. [11] *Biology* spreading out widely: *patent branches.* [12] (of plate glass) ground and polished on both sides. ◆ VERB (*tr*) [13] to obtain a patent for. [14] (in the US) to grant (public land or mineral rights) by a patent. [15] *Metallurgy* to heat (a metal) above a transformation temperature and cool it at a rate that allows cold working.
▷HISTORY C14: via Old French from Latin *patēre* to lie open; n use, short for *letters patent,* from Medieval Latin *litterae patentes* letters lying open (to public inspection)

▸ 'patentable ADJECTIVE ▸ ˌpatenta'bility NOUN

Language note The pronunciation "'pætᵊnt" is heard in *letters patent* and *Patent Office* and is the usual US pronunciation for all senses. In Britain "'pætᵊnt" is sometimes heard for senses 1, 2 and 3, but "'peɪtᵊnt" is commoner and is regularly used in collocations like *patent leather*.

patentee (ˌpeɪtᵊn'tiː, ˌpæ-) NOUN a person, group, company, etc., that has been granted a patent.

patent fastener NOUN (in Ireland) another name for **press stud**.

patent leather NOUN leather or imitation leather processed with lacquer to give a hard glossy surface.

patent log NOUN *Nautical* any of several mechanical devices for measuring the speed of a vessel and the distance travelled, consisting typically of a trailing rotor that registers its rotations on a meter. Compare **chip log**.

patently ('peɪtᵊntlɪ) ADVERB obviously: *he was patently bored*.

patent medicine NOUN a medicine protected by a patent and available without a doctor's prescription.

Patent Office ('pætᵊnt) NOUN a government department that issues patents. Abbreviation: **Pat. Off.**

patentor (ˌpeɪtᵊn'tɔː, ˌpæ-) NOUN a person who or official body that grants a patent or patents.

patent right NOUN the exclusive right granted by a patent.

Patent Rolls PLURAL NOUN (in Britain) the register of patents issued.

patent still NOUN a type of still in which the distillation is continuous.
▷HISTORY so called because a still of this type was patented in 1830

pater ('peɪtə) NOUN *Brit* a public school slang word for **father**: now chiefly used facetiously.
▷HISTORY from Latin

paterfamilias (ˌpeɪtəfə'mɪlɪˌæs) NOUN, *plural* **patresfamilias** (ˌpɑːtreɪzfə'mɪlɪˌæs). [1] the male head of a household. [2] *Roman law* **a** the head of a household having authority over its members. **b** the parental or other authority of another person.
▷HISTORY Latin: father of the family

paternal (pə'tɜːnᵊl) ADJECTIVE [1] relating to or characteristic of a father, esp in showing affection, encouragement, etc.; fatherly. [2] (*prenominal*) related through the father: *his paternal grandfather*. [3] inherited or derived from the male parent.
▷HISTORY C17: from Late Latin *paternālis*, from Latin *pater* father
▸ pa'ternally ADVERB

paternalism (pə'tɜːnəˌlɪzəm) NOUN the attitude or policy of a government or other authority that manages the affairs of a country, company, community, etc., in the manner of a father, esp in usurping individual responsibility and the liberty of choice.
▸ pa'ternalist NOUN, ADJECTIVE ▸ paˌternal'istic ADJECTIVE ▸ paˌternal'istically ADVERB

paternity (pə'tɜːnɪtɪ) NOUN [1] **a** the fact or state of being a father. **b** (*as modifier*): *a paternity suit was filed against the man*. [2] descent or derivation from a father. [3] authorship or origin: *the paternity of the theory is disputed*.
▷HISTORY C15: from Late Latin *paternitās*, from Latin *pater* father

paternity leave NOUN [1] a period of paid absence from work, in the UK currently two weeks, to which a man is legally entitled immediately after the birth of his child. [2] a period of paid or unpaid absence from work granted to a man by his employer immediately after the birth of his child.

paternity suit NOUN *Law* the US (and in Britain a nontechnical) term for **affiliation proceedings**.

paternoster (ˌpætə'nɒstə) NOUN [1] *RC Church* the beads at the ends of each decade of the rosary marking the points at which the Paternoster is recited. [2] any fixed form of words used as a prayer or charm. [3] Also called: **paternoster line**. a type of fishing tackle in which short lines and hooks are attached at intervals to the main line. [4] a type of lift in which platforms are attached to continuous chains. The lift does not stop at each floor but passengers enter while it is moving.
▷HISTORY Latin, literally: our father (from the opening of the Lord's Prayer)

Paternoster (ˌpætə'nɒstə) NOUN (*sometimes not capital*) *RC Church* [1] the Lord's Prayer, esp in Latin. [2] the recital of this as an act of devotion.
▷HISTORY see PATERNOSTER

Paterson ('pætəsᵊn) NOUN a city in NE New Jersey: settled by the Dutch in the late 17th century. Pop.: 149 222 (1999).

Paterson's curse NOUN an Austral name for **viper's bugloss** (sense 2).

path (pɑːθ) NOUN, *plural* **paths** (pɑːðz). [1] a road or way, esp a narrow trodden track. [2] a surfaced walk, as through a garden. [3] the course or direction in which something moves: *the path of a whirlwind*. [4] a course of conduct: *the path of virtue*.
▷HISTORY Old English *pæth*; related to Old High German, German *Pfad*
▸ 'pathless ADJECTIVE

path. (pæθ) ABBREVIATION FOR: [1] pathological. [2] pathology.

-path NOUN COMBINING FORM [1] denoting a person suffering from a specified disease or disorder: *neuropath*. [2] denoting a practitioner of a particular method of treatment: *osteopath*.
▷HISTORY back formation from -PATHY

Pathan (pə'tɑːn) NOUN a member of the Pashto-speaking people of Afghanistan, NW Pakistan, and elsewhere, most of whom are Muslim in religion.
▷HISTORY C17: from Hindi

pathetic (pə'θɛtɪk) ADJECTIVE [1] evoking or expressing pity, sympathy, etc. [2] distressingly inadequate: *the old man sat huddled in front of a pathetic fire*. [3] *Brit, informal* ludicrously or contemptibly uninteresting or worthless: *the standard of goalkeeping in amateur football today is pathetic*. [4] *Obsolete* of or affecting the feelings. ◆ PLURAL NOUN [5] pathetic sentiments.
▷HISTORY C16: from French *pathétique*, via Late Latin from Greek *pathetikos* sensitive, from *pathos* suffering; see PATHOS
▸ pa'thetically ADVERB

pathetic fallacy NOUN (in literature) the presentation of inanimate objects in nature as possessing human feelings.

pathfinder ('pɑːθˌfaɪndə) NOUN [1] a person who makes or finds a way, esp through unexplored areas or fields of knowledge. [2] an aircraft or parachutist who indicates a target area by dropping flares, etc. [3] a radar device used for navigation or homing onto a target.
▸ 'pathˌfinding NOUN

pathfinder prospectus NOUN a prospectus regarding the flotation of a new company that contains only sufficient details to test the market reaction.

pathic ('pæθɪk) NOUN [1] a catamite. [2] a person who suffers; victim. ◆ ADJECTIVE [3] of or relating to a catamite. [4] of or relating to suffering.
▷HISTORY C17: via Latin from Greek *pathikos* passive; see PATHOS

patho- *or before a vowel* **path-** COMBINING FORM disease: *pathology*.
▷HISTORY from Greek *pathos* suffering; see PATHOS

pathogen ('pæθəˌdʒɛn) *or* **pathogene** ('pæθəˌdʒiːn) NOUN any agent that can cause disease.

pathogenesis (ˌpæθə'dʒɛnɪsɪs) *or* **pathogeny** (pə'θɒdʒɪnɪ) NOUN the origin, development, and resultant effects of a disease.
▸ pathogenetic (ˌpæθəʊdʒɪ'nɛtɪk) ADJECTIVE

pathogenic (ˌpæθə'dʒɛnɪk) ADJECTIVE able to cause or produce disease: *pathogenic bacteria*.

pathognomonic (ˌpæθəgnə'mɒnɪk) ADJECTIVE *Pathol* characteristic or indicative of a particular disease.
▷HISTORY C17: from Greek *pathognōmonikos* expert in judging illness, from PATHO- + *gnōmōn* judge
▸ ˌpathogno'monically ADVERB

pathognomy (pə'θɒgnəmɪ) NOUN study or knowledge of the passions or emotions or their manifestations.
▷HISTORY C18: from PATHO- + *-gnomy*, as in PHYSIOGNOMY

pathol. ABBREVIATION FOR: [1] pathological. [2] pathology.

pathological (ˌpæθə'lɒdʒɪkᵊl) *or less commonly* **pathologic** ADJECTIVE [1] of or relating to pathology. [2] relating to, involving, or caused by disease. [3] *Informal* compulsively motivated: *a pathological liar*.
▸ ˌpatho'logically ADVERB

pathologize *or* **pathologise** (pə'θɒlə[dg]aɪz) VERB (*tr*) to represent (something) as a disease: *this pathologizing of parenthood*.

pathology (pə'θɒlədʒɪ) NOUN, *plural* **-gies**. [1] the branch of medicine concerned with the cause, origin, and nature of disease, including the changes occurring as a result of disease. [2] the manifestations of disease, esp changes occurring in tissues or organs. [3] any variant or deviant condition from normal.
▸ pa'thologist NOUN

pathos ('peɪθɒs) NOUN [1] the quality or power, esp in literature or speech, of arousing feelings of pity, sorrow, etc. [2] a feeling of sympathy or pity: *a stab of pathos*.
▷HISTORY C17: from Greek: suffering; related to *penthos* sorrow

pathway ('pɑːθˌweɪ) NOUN [1] another word for **path** (senses 1, 2). [2] a route to or way of access to; way of reaching or achieving something. [3] courses taken by a student to gain entry to a higher course or towards a final qualification. [4] *Biochem* a chain of reactions associated with a particular metabolic process.

-pathy NOUN COMBINING FORM [1] indicating feeling, sensitivity, or perception: *telepathy*. [2] indicating disease or a morbid condition: *psychopathy*. [3] indicating a method of treating disease: *osteopathy*.
▷HISTORY from Greek *patheia* suffering; see PATHOS
▸ -pathic ADJECTIVE COMBINING FORM

Patiala (ˌpʌtɪ'ɑːlə) NOUN a city in N India, in E Punjab: seat of the Punjabi University (1962). Pop.: 238 368 (1991).

patience ('peɪʃəns) NOUN [1] tolerant and even-tempered perseverance. [2] the capacity for calmly enduring pain, trying situations, etc. [3] *Chiefly Brit* any of various card games for one player only, in which the cards may be laid out in various combinations as the player tries to use up the whole pack. US equivalent: **solitaire**. [4] *Obsolete* permission; sufferance.
▷HISTORY C13: via Old French from Latin *patientia* endurance, from *patī* to suffer

patient ('peɪʃənt) ADJECTIVE [1] enduring trying circumstances with even temper. [2] tolerant; understanding. [3] capable of accepting delay with equanimity. [4] persevering or diligent: *a patient worker*. [5] *Archaic* admitting of a certain interpretation. ◆ NOUN [6] a person who is receiving medical care. [7] *Rare* a person or thing that is the recipient of some action.
▷HISTORY C14: see PATIENCE
▸ 'patiently ADVERB

patin *or* **patine** ('pætɪn) NOUN variants of **paten**.

patina¹ ('pætɪnə) NOUN, *plural* **-nas**. [1] a film of oxide formed on the surface of a metal, esp the green oxidation of bronze or copper. See also **verdigris** (sense 1). [2] any fine layer on a surface: *a patina of frost*. [3] the sheen on a surface that is caused by much handling.
▷HISTORY C18: from Italian: coating, from Latin: PATINA²

patina² ('pætɪnə) NOUN, *plural* **-nae** (-ˌniː). a broad shallow dish used in ancient Rome.
▷HISTORY from Latin, from Greek *patanē* platter

patio ('pætɪˌəʊ) NOUN, *plural* **-os**. [1] an open inner courtyard, esp one in a Spanish or Spanish-American house. [2] an area adjoining a house, esp one that is paved and used for outdoor activities.
▷HISTORY C19: from Spanish: courtyard

patisserie (pə'tiːsərɪ) NOUN [1] a shop where fancy pastries are sold. [2] such pastries.
▷HISTORY C18: French, from *pâtissier* pastry cook, ultimately from Late Latin *pasta* PASTE¹

Patmos ('pætmɒs) NOUN a Greek island in the Aegean, in the NW Dodecanese: St John's place of exile (about 95 A.D.), where he wrote the Apocalypse. Pop.: 2650 (1995 est.). Area: 34 sq. km (13 sq. miles).

Patna ('pætnə) NOUN a city in NE India, capital of Bihar state, on the River Ganges: founded in the 5th century B.C.; university (1917); centre of a rice-growing region. Pop.: 917 243 (1991).

Patna rice NOUN a variety of long-grain rice, used for savoury dishes.

Pat. Off. ABBREVIATION FOR Patent Office.

patois ('pætwɑ:; *French* patwa) NOUN, *plural* **patois** ('pætwɑ:z; *French* patwa). 1 an unwritten regional dialect of a language, esp of French, usually considered substandard. 2 the jargon of particular group.
▷HISTORY C17: from Old French: rustic speech, perhaps from *patoier* to handle awkwardly, from *patte* paw

pat. pend. ABBREVIATION FOR patent pending.

Patras (pə'træs, 'pætrəs) NOUN a port in W Greece, in the NW Peloponnese on the **Gulf of Patras** (an inlet of the Ionian Sea): one of the richest cities in Greece until the 3rd century B.C.; under Turkish rule from 1458 to 1687 and from 1715 until the War of Greek Independence, which began here in 1821. Pop.: 155 180 (1991). Modern Greek name: **Pátrai** ('patrɛ).

patri- COMBINING FORM father: *patricide; patrilocal.*
▷HISTORY from Latin *pater,* Greek *patēr* FATHER

patrial ('peɪtrɪəl) NOUN (in Britain formerly) a person having by statute the right of abode in the United Kingdom, and so not subject to immigration control.
▷HISTORY C20: from Latin *patria* native land

patriarch ('peɪtrɪˌɑ:k) NOUN 1 the male head of a tribe or family. Compare **matriarch** (sense 2). 2 a very old or venerable man. 3 *Old Testament* any of a number of persons regarded as the fathers of the human race, divided into the antediluvian patriarchs, from Adam to Noah, and the postdiluvian, from Noah to Abraham. 4 *Old Testament* any of the three ancestors of the Hebrew people: Abraham, Isaac, or Jacob. 5 *Old Testament* any of Jacob's twelve sons, regarded as the ancestors of the twelve tribes of Israel. 6 *Early Christian Church* the bishop of one of several principal sees, esp those of Rome, Antioch, and Alexandria. 7 *Eastern Orthodox Church* the bishops of the four ancient principal sees of Constantinople, Antioch, Alexandria, and Jerusalem, and also of Russia, Romania, and Serbia, the bishop of Constantinople (the **ecumenical Patriarch**) being highest in dignity among these. 8 *RC Church* **a** a title given to the pope. **b** a title given to a number of bishops, esp of the Uniat Churches, indicating their rank as immediately below that of the pope. 9 *Mormon Church* another word for **Evangelist** (sense 2). 10 *Eastern Christianity* the head of the Coptic, Armenian, Syrian Jacobite, or Nestorian Churches, and of certain other non-Orthodox Churches in the East. 11 the oldest or most venerable member of a group, community, etc.: *the patriarch of steam engines.* 12 a person regarded as the founder of a community, tradition, etc.
▷HISTORY C12: via Old French from Church Latin *patriarcha*
▸ˌ**patri'archal** ADJECTIVE ▸ˌ**patri'archally** ADVERB

patriarchal cross NOUN a cross with two high horizontal bars, the upper one shorter than the lower.

patriarchate ('peɪtrɪˌɑ:kɪt) NOUN 1 the office, jurisdiction, province, or residence of a patriarch. 2 a family or people under male domination or government.

patriarchy ('peɪtrɪˌɑ:kɪ) NOUN, *plural* **-chies.** 1 a form of social organization in which a male is the head of the family and descent, kinship, and title are traced through the male line. 2 any society governed by such a system.

patriate ('pætrɪˌeɪt, 'peɪtrɪˌeɪt) VERB (*tr*) to bring under the authority of an autonomous country, for example as in the transfer of the Canadian constitution from UK to Canadian responsibility.
▸ˌ**patri'ation** NOUN

patrician (pə'trɪʃən) NOUN 1 a member of the hereditary aristocracy of ancient Rome. In the early republic the patricians held almost all the higher offices. Compare **plebs** (sense 2). 2 a high nonhereditary title awarded by Constantine and his eastern Roman successors for services to the empire. 3 (in medieval Europe) **a** a title borne by numerous princes including several emperors from the 8th to the 12th centuries. **b** a member of the upper class in numerous Italian republics and German free cities. 4 an aristocrat. 5 a person of refined conduct, tastes, etc. ◆ ADJECTIVE 6 (esp in ancient Rome) of, relating to, or composed of patricians. 7 aristocratic. 8 oligarchic and often antidemocratic or nonpopular: *patrician political views.*
▷HISTORY C15: from Old French *patricien,* from Latin *patricius* noble, from *pater* father

patriciate (pə'trɪʃɪɪt, -ˌeɪt) NOUN 1 the dignity, position, or rank of a patrician. 2 the class or order of patricians.

patricide ('pætrɪˌsaɪd) NOUN 1 the act of killing one's father. 2 a person who kills his father.
▸ˌ**patri'cidal** ADJECTIVE

patriclinous (ˌpætrɪ'klaɪnəs), **patroclinous,** *or* **patroclinal** (ˌpætrə'klaɪnᵊl) ADJECTIVE (of animals and plants) showing the characters of the male parent. Compare **matriclinous.**
▷HISTORY C20: from Latin *pater* father + *clīnāre* to incline

patrilineal (ˌpætrɪ'lɪnɪəl) *or* **patrilinear** ADJECTIVE tracing descent, kinship, or title through the male line.
▸ˌ**patri'lineally** *or* ˌ**patri'linearly** ADVERB

patrilocal (ˌpætrɪ'ləʊkᵊl) ADJECTIVE having or relating to a marriage pattern in which the couple lives with the husband's family.
▸ˌ**patri'locally** ADVERB

patrimony ('pætrɪmənɪ) NOUN, *plural* **-nies.** 1 an inheritance from one's father or other ancestor. 2 the endowment of a church.
▷HISTORY C14 *patrimoyne,* from Old French, from Latin *patrimonium* paternal inheritance
▸**patrimonial** (ˌpætrɪ'məʊnɪəl) ADJECTIVE ▸ˌ**patri'monially** ADVERB

patriot ('peɪtrɪət, 'pæt-) NOUN a person who vigorously supports his country and its way of life.
▷HISTORY C16: via French from Late Latin *patriōta,* from Greek *patriotēs,* from *patris* native land; related to Greek *patēr* father; compare Latin *pater* father, *patria* fatherland
▸**patriotic** (ˌpætrɪ'ɒtɪk) ADJECTIVE ▸ˌ**patri'otically** ADVERB

Patriot ('peɪtrɪət) NOUN a US surface-to-air missile system with multiple launch stations and the capability to track multiple targets by radar.

patriotism ('pætrɪəˌtɪzəm) NOUN devotion to one's own country and concern for its defence. Compare **nationalism.**

patristic (pə'trɪstɪk) *or* **patristical** ADJECTIVE of or relating to the Fathers of the Church, their writings, or the study of these.
▸**pa'tristically** ADVERB ▸**pa'tristics** NOUN (*functioning as singular*)

Patroclus (pə'trɒkləs) NOUN *Greek myth* a friend of Achilles, killed in the Trojan War by Hector. His death made Achilles return to the fight after his quarrel with Agamemnon.

patrol (pə'trəʊl) NOUN 1 the action of going through or around a town, neighbourhood, etc., at regular intervals for purposes of security or observation. 2 a person or group that carries out such an action. 3 a military detachment with the mission of security, gathering information, or combat with enemy forces. 4 a division of a troop of Scouts or Guides. ◆ VERB **-trols, -trolling, -trolled.** 5 to engage in a patrol of (a place).
▷HISTORY C17: from French *patrouiller,* from *patouiller* to flounder in mud, from *patte* paw
▸**pa'troller** NOUN

patrol car NOUN a police car with a radio telephone used for patrolling streets and motorways. See also **panda car.**

patrolman (pə'trəʊlmən) NOUN, *plural* **-men.** 1 *Chiefly US* a man, esp a policeman, who patrols a certain area. 2 *Brit* a man employed to patrol an area to help motorists in difficulty.

patrology (pə'trɒlədʒɪ) NOUN 1 the study of the writings of the Fathers of the Church. 2 a collection of such writings.
▷HISTORY C17: from Greek *patr-, patēr* father + -LOGY
▸**patrological** (ˌpætrə'lɒdʒɪkᵊl) ADJECTIVE ▸**pa'trologist** NOUN

patrol wagon NOUN the usual US, Austral, and NZ term for **Black Maria.** Also called (US): **police wagon.**

patron[1] ('peɪtrən) NOUN 1 a person, esp a man, who sponsors or aids artists, charities, etc.; protector or benefactor. 2 a customer of a shop, hotel, etc., esp a regular one. 3 See **patron saint.** 4 (in ancient Rome) the protector of a dependant or client, often the former master of a freedman still retaining certain rights over him. 5 *Christianity* a person or body having the right to present a clergyman to a benefice.
▷HISTORY C14: via Old French from Latin *patrōnus* protector, from *pater* father
▸**patronal** (pə'trəʊnᵊl) ADJECTIVE ▸**'patronly** ADJECTIVE

patron[2] *French* (patrɔ̃) NOUN a man, who owns or manages a hotel, restaurant, or bar.

patron[3] ('pætərn) NOUN *Irish* a variant spelling of **pattern**[2].

patronage ('pætrənɪdʒ) NOUN 1 **a** the support given or custom brought by a patron or patroness. **b** the position of a patron. 2 (in politics) **a** the practice of making appointments to office, granting contracts, etc. **b** the favours so distributed. 3 **a** a condescending manner. **b** any kindness done in a condescending way. 4 *Christianity* the right to present a clergyman to a benefice.

patroness ('peɪtrənˌɛs) NOUN 1 a woman who sponsors or aids artists, charities, etc.; protector or benefactor. 2 See **patron saint.**
▷HISTORY see PATRON
▸**patronal** (pə'trəʊnᵊl) ADJECTIVE ▸**'patronly** ADJECTIVE

patronize *or* **patronise** ('pætrəˌnaɪz) VERB 1 to behave or treat in a condescending way. 2 (*tr*) to act as a patron or patroness by sponsoring or bringing trade to.
▸**'patronˌizer** *or* **'patronˌiser** NOUN

patronizing *or* **patronising** ('pætrəˌnaɪzɪŋ) ADJECTIVE having a superior manner; condescending.
▸**'patronˌizingly** *or* **'patronˌisingly** ADVERB

patronne *French* (patrɔn) NOUN a woman who owns or manages a hotel, restaurant, or bar.

patron saint NOUN a saint regarded as the particular guardian of a country, church, trade, person, etc.

patronymic (ˌpætrə'nɪmɪk) ADJECTIVE 1 (of a name) derived from the name of its bearer's father or ancestor. In Western cultures, many surnames are patronymic in origin, as for example Irish names beginning with *O'* and English names ending with *-son;* in other cultures, such as Russian, a special patronymic name is used in addition to the surname. ◆ NOUN 2 a patronymic name.
▷HISTORY C17: via Late Latin from Greek *patronumikos,* from *patēr* father + *onoma* NAME

patroon (pə'tru:n) NOUN (in the US) a Dutch land-holder in New Netherland and New York with manorial rights in the colonial era.
▷HISTORY C18: from Dutch: PATRON[1]
▸**pa'troonˌship** NOUN

patsy ('pætsɪ) NOUN, *plural* **-sies.** *Slang, chiefly US and Canadian* 1 a person who is easily cheated, victimized, etc. 2 a scapegoat.
▷HISTORY C20: of unknown origin

pattée ('pæteɪ, 'pætɪ) ADJECTIVE (*often postpositive*) (of a cross) having triangular arms widening outwards.
▷HISTORY from French *patte* paw

patten ('pætᵊn) NOUN a wooden clog or sandal on a raised wooden platform or metal ring.
▷HISTORY C14: from Old French *patin,* probably from *patte* paw

patter[1] ('pætə) VERB 1 (*intr*) to walk or move with quick soft steps. 2 to strike with or make a quick succession of light tapping sounds. 3 (*tr*) *Rare* to cause to patter. ◆ NOUN 4 a quick succession of light tapping sounds, as of feet: *the patter of mice.*
▷HISTORY C17: from PAT[1]

patter[2] ('pætə) NOUN 1 the glib rapid speech of comedians, salesmen, etc. 2 quick idle talk; chatter. 3 the jargon of a particular group; lingo. ◆ VERB 4 (*intr*) to speak glibly and rapidly. 5 to repeat (prayers) in a mechanical or perfunctory manner.
▷HISTORY C14: from Latin *pater* in *Pater Noster* Our Father

pattern[1] ('pætᵊn) NOUN 1 an arrangement of repeated or corresponding parts, decorative motifs,

etc.: *although the notes seemed random, a careful listener could detect a pattern.* 2 a decorative design: *a paisley pattern.* 3 a style: *various patterns of cutlery.* 4 a plan or diagram used as a guide in making something: *a paper pattern for a dress.* 5 a standard way of moving, acting, etc.: *traffic patterns.* 6 a model worthy of imitation: *a pattern of kindness.* 7 a representative sample. 8 a wooden or metal shape or model used in a foundry to make a mould. 9 **a** the arrangement of marks made in a target by bullets. **b** a diagram displaying such an arrangement. ◆ VERB *(tr)* 10 (often foll by *after* or *on*) to model. 11 to arrange as or decorate with a pattern.
▷**HISTORY** C14 *patron,* from Medieval Latin *patrōnus* example, from Latin: PATRON[1]

pattern[2] *or* **patron** ('pætərn) NOUN *Irish* an outdoor assembly with religious practices, traders' stalls, etc. on the feast day of a patron saint.
▷**HISTORY** C18: variant of PATRON[1]; see PATTERN[1]

patter song NOUN *Music* a humorous song or aria, the text of which consists of rapid strings of words.

patty ('pætɪ) NOUN, *plural* **-ties.** 1 a small flattened cake of minced food. 2 a small pie.
▷**HISTORY** C18: from French PÂTÉ

pattypan squash *or* **pattypan** ('pætɪˌpæn) NOUN *Chiefly US* a small round flattish squash with a scalloped rim and thin, pale green skin.
▷**HISTORY** C17: PATTY + PAN[1]

patu ('pɑːtuː) NOUN, *plural* **patus.** a short Maori club, now used ceremonially.
▷**HISTORY** Maori

patulous ('pætjʊləs) ADJECTIVE 1 *Botany* spreading widely or expanded: *patulous branches.* 2 *Rare* gaping.
▷**HISTORY** C17: from Latin *patulus* open, from *patēre* to lie open
▸ **'patulously** ADVERB ▸ **'patulousness** NOUN

patutuki ('pɑːtuːˌtuːkɪ) NOUN *NZ* another name for **blue cod.**

Pau (*French* po) NOUN a city in SW France: residence of the French kings of Navarre; tourist centre for the Pyrenees. Pop.: 82 157 (1990).

PAU ABBREVIATION FOR **Pan American Union.**

paua ('pɑːʊɑ) NOUN an edible abalone, *Haliotis iris,* of New Zealand, having an iridescent shell used esp for jewellery.
▷**HISTORY** from Maori

paucal ('pɔːkᵊl) *Grammar* ◆ NOUN 1 a grammatical number occurring in some languages for words in contexts where a few of their referents are described or referred to. ◆ ADJECTIVE 2 relating to or inflected for this number.
▷**HISTORY** from Latin *paucus* few

paucity ('pɔːsɪtɪ) NOUN 1 smallness of quantity; insufficiency; dearth. 2 smallness of number; fewness.
▷**HISTORY** C15: from Latin *paucitās* scarcity, from *paucus* few

pauldron ('pɔːldrən) NOUN either of two metal plates worn with armour to protect the shoulders.
▷**HISTORY** C15: from French *espauleron,* from *espaule* shoulder; see EPAULETTE

Pauli exclusion principle NOUN *Physics* the principle that two identical fermions cannot occupy the same quantum state in a body such as an atom; sometimes shortened to **exclusion principle.**
▷**HISTORY** C20: from Wolfgang *Pauli* (1900–58), US physicist born in Austria

Pauline ('pɔːlaɪn) ADJECTIVE relating to Saint Paul (died ?67 A.D.), the Christian missionary, martyr, and writer of many of the epistles in the New Testament, or to his doctrines.

Paul Jones NOUN an old-time dance in which partners are exchanged.
▷**HISTORY** C19: named after John *Paul Jones* (1747–92), Scots-born US naval commander

paulownia (pɔː'ləʊnɪə) NOUN any scrophulariaceous tree of the Japanese genus *Paulownia, esp P. tomentosa,* having large heart-shaped leaves and clusters of purplish or white flowers.
▷**HISTORY** C19: New Latin, named after Anna *Paulovna,* daughter of Paul I of Russia

Paul Pry NOUN a nosy person.
▷**HISTORY** C19: from a character in the play *Paul Pry* by John Poole (1825)

Paumotu Archipelago (paʊ'məʊtuː) NOUN another name for the **Tuamotu Archipelago.**

paunch (pɔːntʃ) NOUN 1 the belly or abdomen, esp when protruding. 2 another name for **rumen.** 3 *Nautical* a thick mat that prevents chafing. ◆ VERB *(tr)* 4 to stab in the stomach; disembowel.
▷**HISTORY** C14: from Anglo-Norman *paunche,* from Old French *pance,* from Latin *panticēs* (pl) bowels

paunchy ('pɔːntʃɪ) ADJECTIVE **-ier, -iest.** having a protruding belly or abdomen.
▸ **'paunchiness** NOUN

pauper ('pɔːpə) NOUN 1 a person who is extremely poor. 2 (formerly) a destitute person supported by public charity.
▷**HISTORY** C16: from Latin: poor
▸ **'pauperˌism** NOUN

pauperize *or* **pauperise** ('pɔːpəˌraɪz) VERB *(tr)* to make a pauper of; impoverish.

pauropod ('pɔːrəˌpɒd) NOUN a member of the *Pauropoda,* a class of minute myriapods less than 2 mm (1/20 in.) in size, having 8 to 10 pairs of legs and branched antennae.

pause (pɔːz) VERB *(intr)* 1 to cease an action temporarily; stop. 2 to hesitate; delay: *she replied without pausing.* ◆ NOUN 3 a temporary stop or rest, esp in speech or action; short break. 4 *Prosody* another word for **caesura.** 5 Also called: **fermata.** *Music* a continuation of a note or rest beyond its normal length. Usual symbol: 𝄐. 6 **give pause to.** to cause to hesitate.
▷**HISTORY** C15: from Latin *pausa* pause, from Greek *pausis,* from *pauein* to halt
▸ **'pausal** ADJECTIVE ▸ **'pauser** NOUN ▸ **'pausing** NOUN, ADJECTIVE

pav (pæv) NOUN *Austral and NZ, informal* short for **pavlova.**

pavage ('peɪvɪdʒ) NOUN 1 *History* a tax towards paving streets, or the right to levy such a tax. 2 the act of paving.

pavane *or* **pavan** (pə'vɑːn, -'væn, 'pævᵊn) NOUN 1 a slow and stately dance of the 16th and 17th centuries. 2 a piece of music composed for or in the rhythm of this dance, usually characterized by a slow stately triple time.
▷**HISTORY** C16 *pavan,* via French from Spanish *pavana,* from Old Italian *padovana* Paduan (dance), from *Padova* Padua

pave (peɪv) VERB *(tr)* 1 to cover (a road, path, etc.) with a firm surface suitable for travel, as with paving stones or concrete. 2 to serve as the material for a pavement or other hard layer: *bricks paved the causeway.* 3 (often foll by *with*) to cover with a hard layer (of): *shelves paved with marble.* 4 to prepare or make easier (esp in the phrase **pave the way**): *to pave the way for future development.*
▷**HISTORY** C14: from Old French *paver,* from Latin *pavīre* to ram down
▸ **'paver** NOUN

pavé ('pæveɪ) NOUN 1 a paved surface, esp an uneven one. 2 a style of setting gems so closely that no metal shows.

pavement ('peɪvmənt) NOUN 1 a hard-surfaced path for pedestrians alongside and a little higher than a road. US and Canadian word: **sidewalk.** 2 a paved surface, esp one that is a thoroughfare. 3 the material used in paving. 4 *Civil engineering* the hard layered structure that forms a road carriageway, airfield runway, vehicle park, or other paved areas. 5 *Geology* a level area of exposed rock resembling a paved road. See **limestone pavement.**
▷**HISTORY** C13: from Latin *pavīmentum* a hard floor, from *pavīre* to beat hard

Pavia ('pɑːvɪə) NOUN a town in N Italy, in Lombardy: noted for its Roman and medieval remains, including the tomb of St Augustine. Pop.: 80 650 (1990). Latin name: **Ticinum.**

pavid ('pævɪd) ADJECTIVE *Rare* fearful; timid.
▷**HISTORY** C17: from Latin *pavidus* fearful, from *pavēre* to tremble with fear

pavilion (pə'vɪljən) NOUN 1 *Brit* a building at a sports ground, esp a cricket pitch, in which players change. 2 a summerhouse or other decorative shelter. 3 a building or temporary structure, esp one that is open and ornamental, for housing exhibitions. 4 a large ornate tent, esp one with a peaked top, as used by medieval armies. 5 one of a set of buildings that together form a hospital or other large institution. 6 one of four main facets on a brilliant-cut stone between the girdle and the culet. ◆ VERB *(tr) Literary* 7 to place or set in or as if in a pavilion: *pavilioned in splendour.* 8 to provide with a pavilion or pavilions.
▷**HISTORY** C13: from Old French *pavillon* canopied structure, from Latin *pāpiliō* butterfly, tent

paving ('peɪvɪŋ) NOUN 1 a paved surface; pavement. 2 material used for a pavement, such as paving stones, bricks, or asphalt. ◆ ADJECTIVE 3 of or for a paved surface or pavement. 4 preparatory, facilitating, enabling: *paving legislation.*

paving stone NOUN a concrete or stone slab for paving.

paviour *or US* **pavior** ('peɪvjə) NOUN 1 a person who lays paving. 2 a machine for ramming down paving. 3 material used for paving.
▷**HISTORY** C15: from *paver,* from PAVE

pavis *or* **pavise** ('pævɪs) NOUN a large square shield, developed in the 15th century, at first portable but later heavy and set up in a permanent position.
▷**HISTORY** C14: from Old French *pavais,* from Italian *pavese* of *Pavia,* Italian city where these shields were originally made

Pavlodar (*Russian* pəvla'dar) NOUN a port in NE Kazakhstan on the Irtysh River: major industrial centre with an oil refinery. Pop.: 300 500 (1999).

pavlova (pæv'ləʊvə) NOUN a meringue cake topped with whipped cream and fruit.
▷**HISTORY** C20: named after Anna *Pavlova* (1885–1931), Russian ballerina

Pavlovian (pæv'ləʊvɪən) ADJECTIVE 1 of or relating to the work of Ivan Pavlov (1849–1936), the Russian physiologist. 2 (of a reaction or response) automatic; involuntary.

Pavo ('pɑːvəʊ) NOUN, *Latin genitive* **Pavonis** (pə'vəʊnɪs). a small constellation near the South Pole lying between Tucana and Ara.
▷**HISTORY** Latin: peacock

pavonine ('pævəˌnaɪn) ADJECTIVE of or resembling a peacock or the colours, design, or iridescence of a peacock's tail.
▷**HISTORY** C17: from Latin *pāvōnīnus,* from *pāvō* peacock

paw (pɔː) NOUN 1 any of the feet of a four-legged mammal, bearing claws or nails. 2 *Informal* a hand, esp one that is large, clumsy, etc. ◆ VERB 3 to scrape or contaminate with the paws or feet. 4 *(tr) Informal* to touch or caress in a clumsy, rough, or overfamiliar manner; maul.
▷**HISTORY** C13: via Old French from Germanic; related to Middle Dutch *pōte,* German *Pfote*

pawky ('pɔːkɪ) ADJECTIVE **pawkier, pawkiest.** *Scot* having or characterized by a dry wit.
▷**HISTORY** C17: from Scottish *pawk* trick, of unknown origin
▸ **'pawkily** ADVERB ▸ **'pawkiness** NOUN

pawl (pɔːl) NOUN a pivoted lever shaped to engage with a ratchet wheel to prevent motion in a particular direction.
▷**HISTORY** C17: perhaps from Dutch *pal* pawl

pawn[1] (pɔːn) VERB *(tr)* 1 to deposit (an article) as security for the repayment of a loan, esp from a pawnbroker. 2 to stake: *to pawn one's honour.* ◆ NOUN 3 an article deposited as security. 4 the condition of being so deposited (esp in the phrase **in pawn**). 5 a person or thing that is held as a security, esp a hostage. 6 the act of pawning.
▷**HISTORY** C15: from Old French *pan* security, from Latin *pannus* cloth, apparently because clothing was often left as a surety; compare Middle Flemish *paen* pawn, German *Pfand* pledge
▸ **'pawnage** NOUN

pawn[2] (pɔːn) NOUN 1 a chessman of the lowest theoretical value, limited to forward moves of one square at a time with the option of two squares on its initial move: it captures with a diagonal move only. Abbreviation: **P.** Compare **piece** (sense 12). 2 a person, group, etc., manipulated by another.
▷**HISTORY** C14: from Anglo-Norman *poun,* from Old French *pehon,* from Medieval Latin *pedō* infantryman, from Latin *pēs* foot

pawnbroker ('pɔːnˌbrəʊkə) NOUN a dealer licensed to lend money at a specified rate of interest on the security of movable personal property, which can be sold if the loan is not repaid within a specified period.
▸ **'pawnˌbroking** NOUN

Pawnee (pɔːˈniː) NOUN 1 (*plural* **-nees** *or* **-nee**) a member of a confederacy of related North American Indian peoples, formerly living in Nebraska and Kansas, now chiefly in Oklahoma. 2 the language of these peoples, belonging to the Caddoan family.

pawnshop (ˈpɔːnˌʃɒp) NOUN the premises of a pawnbroker.

pawn ticket NOUN a receipt for goods pawned.

pawpaw (ˈpɔːˌpɔː) NOUN a variant of **papaw** or **papaya.**

pax (pæks) NOUN 1 *Chiefly RC Church* **a** a greeting signifying Christian love transmitted from one to another of those assisting at the Eucharist; kiss of peace. **b** a small metal or ivory plate, often with a representation of the Crucifixion, formerly used to convey the kiss of peace from the celebrant at Mass to those attending it, who kissed the plate in turn. ◆ INTERJECTION 2 *Brit, school slang* a call signalling an end to hostilities or claiming immunity from the rules of a game: usually accompanied by a crossing of the fingers.
▷HISTORY Latin: peace

Pax (pæks) NOUN 1 the Roman goddess of peace. Greek counterpart: **Irene.** 2 a period of general peace, esp one in which there is one dominant nation.
▷HISTORY Latin: peace

PAX ABBREVIATION FOR private automatic exchange.

Pax Romana (ˈpæks rəʊˈmɑːnə) NOUN the Roman peace; the long period of stability under the Roman Empire.

pax vobiscum *Latin* (pæks vəʊˈbɪskʊm) peace be with you.

paxwax (ˈpæksˌwæks) NOUN *Dialect* a strong ligament in the neck of many mammals, which supports the head.
▷HISTORY C15: changed from C14 *fax wax,* probably from Old English *feax* hair of the head, *wax* growth

pay[1] (peɪ) VERB **pays, paying, paid.** 1 to discharge (a debt, obligation, etc.) by giving or doing something: *he paid his creditors.* 2 (when *intr,* often foll by *for*) to give (money) to (a person) in return for goods or services: *they pay their workers well; they pay by the hour.* 3 to give or afford (a person) a profit or benefit: *it pays one to be honest.* 4 (*tr*) to give or bestow (a compliment, regards, attention, etc.). 5 (*tr*) to make (a visit or call). 6 (*intr;* often foll by *for*) to give compensation or make amends. 7 (*tr*) to yield a return of: *the shares pay 15 per cent.* 8 to give or do (something equivalent) in return; pay back: *he paid for the insult with a blow.* 9 (*tr; past tense and past participle* **paid** or **payed**) *Nautical* to allow (a vessel) to make leeway. 10 *Austral, informal* to acknowledge or accept (something) as true, just, etc. 11 **pay one's way. a** to contribute one's share of expenses. **b** to remain solvent without outside help. ◆ NOUN 12 **a** money given in return for work or services; a salary or wage. **b** (*as modifier*): *a pay slip; pay claim.* 13 paid employment (esp in the phrase **in the pay of**). 14 (*modifier*) requiring the insertion of money or discs before or during use: *a pay phone; a pay toilet.* 15 (*modifier*) rich enough in minerals to be profitably mined or worked: *pay gravel.* ◆ See also **pay back, pay down, pay for, pay in, pay off, pay out, pay up.**
▷HISTORY C12: from Old French *payer,* from Latin *pācāre* to appease (a creditor), from *pāx* PEACE

pay[2] (peɪ) VERB **pays, paying, payed.** (*tr*) *Nautical* to caulk (the seams of a wooden vessel) with pitch or tar.
▷HISTORY C17: from Old French *peier,* from Latin *picāre,* from *pix* pitch

payable (ˈpeɪəbᵊl) ADJECTIVE 1 (often foll by *on*) to be paid: *payable on the third of each month.* 2 that is capable of being paid. 3 capable of being profitable. 4 (of a debt) imposing an obligation on the debtor to pay, esp at once.

pay-and-display ADJECTIVE denoting a car-parking system in which a motorist buys a permit to park for a specified period from a coin-operated machine and displays the permit on or near the windscreen of his or her car so that it can be seen by a parking attendant.

pay back VERB (*tr, adverb*) 1 to retaliate against: *to pay someone back for an insult.* 2 to give or do (something equivalent) in return for a favour, insult, etc. 3 to repay (a loan). ◆ NOUN **payback.** 4 **a** the return on an investment. **b** Also called: **payback period.** the time taken for a project to cover its outlay. 5 **a** something done in order to gain revenge. **b** (*as modifier*): *payback killings.*

pay bed NOUN an informal name for **amenity bed** or **private pay bed.**

payday (ˈpeɪˌdeɪ) NOUN the day on which wages or salaries are paid.

pay dirt NOUN 1 a deposit rich enough in minerals to be worth mining. 2 **strike** *or* **hit pay dirt.** *Informal* to achieve one's objective.

pay down VERB (*adverb*) to pay (a sum of money) at the time of purchase as the first of a series of instalments.

PAYE (in Britain and New Zealand) ABBREVIATION FOR pay as you earn; a system by which income tax levied on wage and salary earners is paid by employers directly to the government.

payee (peɪˈiː) NOUN 1 the person to whom a cheque, money order, etc., is made out. 2 a person to whom money is paid or due.

payer (ˈpeɪə) NOUN 1 a person who pays. 2 the person named in a commercial paper as responsible for its payment on redemption.

pay for VERB (*preposition*) 1 to make payment (of) for. 2 (*intr*) to suffer or be punished, as for a mistake, wrong decision, etc.: *in his old age he paid for the laxity of his youth.*

pay in VERB (*tr, adverb*) to hand (money, a cheque, etc.) to a cashier for depositing in a bank, etc.

paying guest NOUN a euphemism for **lodger.** Abbreviation: **PG.**

payload (ˈpeɪˌləʊd) NOUN 1 that part of a cargo earning revenue. 2 **a** the passengers, cargo, or bombs carried by an aircraft. **b** the equipment carried by a rocket, satellite, or spacecraft. 3 the explosive power of a warhead, bomb, etc., carried by a missile or aircraft: *a missile carrying a 50-megaton payload.*

paymaster (ˈpeɪˌmɑːstə) NOUN an official of a government, business, etc., responsible for the payment of wages and salaries.

payment (ˈpeɪmənt) NOUN 1 the act of paying. 2 a sum of money paid. 3 something given in return; punishment or reward.

payment by results NOUN a system of wage payment whereby all or part of the wage varies systematically according to the level of work performance of an employee.

paynim (ˈpeɪnɪm) NOUN *Archaic* 1 a heathen or pagan. 2 a Muslim.
▷HISTORY C13: from Old French *paienime,* from Late Latin *pāgānismus* paganism, from *pāgānus* PAGAN

pay off VERB 1 (*tr, adverb*) to pay all that is due in wages, etc., and discharge from employment. 2 (*tr, adverb*) to pay the complete amount of (a debt, bill, etc.). 3 (*intr, adverb*) to turn out to be profitable, effective, etc.: *the gamble paid off.* 4 (*tr, adverb* or *intr, preposition*) to take revenge on (a person) or for (a wrong done): *to pay someone off for an insult.* 5 (*tr, adverb*) *Informal* to give a bribe to. 6 (*intr, adverb*) *Nautical* (of a vessel) to make leeway. ◆ NOUN **payoff.** 7 the final settlement, esp in retribution: *the payoff came when the gang besieged the squealer's house.* 8 *Informal* the climax, consequence, or outcome of events, a story, etc., esp when unexpected or improbable. 9 the final payment of a debt, salary, etc. 10 the time of such a payment. 11 *Informal* a bribe.

payola (peɪˈəʊlə) NOUN *Informal chiefly US* 1 a bribe given to secure special treatment, esp to a disc jockey to promote a commercial product. 2 the practice of paying or receiving such bribes.
▷HISTORY C20: from PAY[1] + *-ola,* as in *Pianola*

pay out VERB (*adverb*) 1 to distribute (money); disburse. 2 (*tr*) to release (a rope) gradually, hand over hand. 3 (*tr*) to retaliate against. ◆ NOUN **payout.** 4 a sum of money paid out.

pay-per-click NOUN a system of payment used on the Internet in which an advertiser on a website pays the website owner according to the number of people who visit the advertiser's website via the hyperlinked advert on the owner's website.

pay-per-view NOUN **a** a system of television broadcasting by which subscribers pay for each programme they wish to receive. **b** (*as modifier*): *a pay-per-view channel.* ◆ Compare **free-to-air, pay television.**

payphone (ˈpeɪˌfəʊn) NOUN a public telephone operated by coins or a phonecard.

payroll (ˈpeɪˌrəʊl) NOUN 1 a list of employees, specifying the salary or wage of each. 2 **a** the total of these amounts or the actual money equivalent. **b** (*as modifier*): *a payroll tax.*

Paysandú (*Spanish* paisanˈdu) NOUN a port in W Uruguay, on the Uruguay River: the third largest city in the country. Pop.: 75 200 (latest est.).

Pays de la Loire (*French* pei də la lwar) NOUN a region of W France, on the Bay of Biscay: generally low-lying, drained by the River Loire and its tributaries; agricultural.

payt ABBREVIATION FOR payment.

pay television NOUN a system by which television programmes are transmitted in scrambled form, unintelligible except to those who have paid for descrambling equipment. Also called: **subscription television.** Compare **free-to-air, pay-per-view.**

pay up VERB (*adverb*) to pay (money) promptly, in full, or on demand.

pazzazz *or* **pazazz** (pəˈzæz) NOUN *Informal* variants of **pizzazz.**

Pb THE CHEMICAL SYMBOL FOR lead.
▷HISTORY from New Latin *plumbum*

PB ABBREVIATION FOR: 1 Pharmacopoeia Britannica. 2 Prayer Book. 3 *Athletics* personal best.

PBX (in Britain) ABBREVIATION FOR private branch exchange; a telephone system that handles the internal and external calls of a building, firm, etc.

pc ABBREVIATION FOR: 1 per cent. 2 postcard. 3 *Obsolete* (in prescriptions) post cibum. [Latin: after meals] 4 parsec.

PC ABBREVIATION FOR: 1 personal computer. 2 Parish Council(lor). 3 Past Commander. 4 (in Britain and Canada) Police Constable. 5 politically correct. 6 Prince Consort. 7 (in Britain and Canada) **Privy Council(lor).** 8 (in Canada) Progressive Conservative.

P/C, p/c, *or* **p.c.** ABBREVIATION FOR: 1 petty cash. 2 price current.

PCB ABBREVIATION FOR **polychlorinated biphenyl.**

PCC (in Britain) ABBREVIATION FOR Press Complaints Commission.

pcm ABBREVIATION FOR pulse code modulation.

PCOS ABBREVIATION FOR **polycystic ovary syndrome.**

PCP NOUN 1 *p*henyl*c*yclohexyl*p*iperidine (phencyclidine); a depressant drug used illegally as a hallucinogen. Informal name: **angel dust.** ◆ ABBREVIATION FOR: 2 *Pneumocystis carinii* pneumonia. See **pneumocystis.**

PCR ABBREVIATION FOR polymerase chain reaction: a technique for rapidly producing many copies of a fragment of DNA for diagnostic or research purposes.

pct *US* ◆ ABBREVIATION FOR per cent.

PCV (in Britain) ABBREVIATION FOR passenger carrying vehicle.

pd ABBREVIATION FOR: 1 paid. 2 Also: **PD.** per diem. 3 potential difference.

Pd THE CHEMICAL SYMBOL FOR palladium.

PD (in the US) ABBREVIATION FOR Police Department.

PDA ABBREVIATION FOR **personal digital assistant.**

pdl ABBREVIATION FOR **poundal.**

pdq *Slang* ◆ ABBREVIATION FOR pretty damn quick.

PDR ABBREVIATION FOR **price-dividend ratio.**

P-D ratio NOUN short for **price-dividend ratio.**

PDSA (in Britain) ABBREVIATION FOR People's Dispensary for Sick Animals.

pe[1] (peɪ; *Hebrew* pe) NOUN the 17th letter in the Hebrew alphabet (פ or, at the end of a word, ף) transliterated as *p* or, when final, *ph.*
▷HISTORY from Hebrew *peh* mouth

pe[2] THE INTERNET DOMAIN NAME FOR Peru.

PE ABBREVIATION FOR: 1 physical education. 2 **potential energy.** 3 Presiding Elder. 4 (esp in postal addresses) Prince Edward Island (Canadian Province). 5 Also: **p.e.** printer's error. 6 *Statistics* probable error. 7 Protestant Episcopal. 8 (in South Africa) Port Elizabeth. ◆ 9 INTERNATIONAL CAR REGISTRATION FOR Peru.

pea (piː) NOUN [1] an annual climbing leguminous plant, *Pisum sativum,* with small white flowers and long green pods containing edible green seeds: cultivated in temperate regions. [2] **a** the seed of this plant, eaten as a vegetable. **b** (*as modifier*): *pea soup.* [3] any of several other leguminous plants, such as the sweet pea, chickpea, and cowpea.
▷HISTORY C17: from PEASE (incorrectly assumed to be a plural)
▸ **'pea,like** ADJECTIVE

pea-brain NOUN *Informal* a foolish or unintelligent person.

peace (piːs) NOUN [1] **a** the state existing during the absence of war. **b** (*as modifier*): *peace negotiations.* [2] (*modifier*) denoting a person or thing symbolizing support for international peace: *peace women.* [3] (*often capital*) a treaty marking the end of a war. [4] a state of harmony between people or groups; freedom from strife. [5] law and order within a state; absence of violence or other disturbance: *a breach of the peace.* [6] absence of mental anxiety (often in the phrase **peace of mind**). [7] a state of stillness, silence, or serenity. [8] **at peace. a** in a state of harmony or friendship. **b** in a state of serenity. **c** dead: *the old lady is at peace now.* [9] **hold** *or* **keep one's peace.** to keep silent. [10] **keep the peace.** to maintain or refrain from disturbing law and order. [11] **make one's peace with.** to become reconciled with. [12] **make peace.** to bring hostilities to an end. ◆ VERB [13] (*intr*) *Obsolete except as an imperative* to be or become silent or still.
▷HISTORY C12: from Old French *pais,* from Latin *pāx*

peaceable ('piːsəbᵊl) ADJECTIVE [1] inclined towards peace. [2] tranquil; calm.
▸ **'peaceableness** NOUN ▸ **'peaceably** ADVERB

Peace Corps NOUN an agency of the US government that sends American volunteers to developing countries, where they work on educational and other projects: established in 1961.

peace dividend NOUN additional money available to a government from cuts in defence expenditure because of the end of a period of hostilities.

peaceful ('piːsfʊl) ADJECTIVE [1] not in a state of war or disagreement. [2] tranquil; calm. [3] not involving violence: *peaceful picketing.* [4] of, relating to, or in accord with a time of peace: *peaceful uses of atomic energy.* [5] inclined towards peace.
▸ **'peacefully** ADVERB ▸ **'peacefulness** NOUN

peacekeeping ('piːsˌkiːpɪŋ) NOUN **a** the maintenance of peace, esp the prevention of further fighting between hostile forces in an area. **b** (*as modifier*): *a UN peacekeeping force.*
▸ **'peace,keeper** NOUN

peacemaker ('piːsˌmeɪkə) NOUN a person who establishes peace, esp between others.
▸ **'peace,making** NOUN

peace offering NOUN [1] something given to an adversary in the hope of procuring or maintaining peace. [2] *Judaism* a sacrificial meal shared between the offerer and Jehovah to intensify the union between them.

peace pipe NOUN a long decorated pipe smoked by North American Indians on ceremonial occasions, esp as a token of peace. Also called: **calumet, pipe of peace.**

Peace River NOUN a river in W Canada, rising in British Columbia as the Finlay River and flowing northeast into the Slave River. Length: 1715 km (1065 miles).

peace sign NOUN a gesture made with the palm of the hand outwards and the index and middle fingers raised in a V. See also **V-sign** (sense 2).

peacetime ('piːsˌtaɪm) NOUN **a** a period without war; time of peace. **b** (*as modifier*): *a peacetime agreement.*

peach[1] (piːtʃ) NOUN [1] a small rosaceous tree, *Prunus persica,* with pink flowers and rounded edible fruit: cultivated in temperate regions. See also **nectarine** (sense 1). [2] the soft juicy fruit of this tree, which has a downy reddish-yellow skin, yellowish-orange sweet flesh, and a single stone. See also **nectarine** (sense 2). [3] **a** a pinkish-yellow to orange colour. **b** (*as adjective*): *a peach dress.* [4] *Informal* a person or thing that is especially pleasing.
▷HISTORY C14 *peche,* from Old French, from Medieval Latin *persica,* from Latin *Persicum mālum* Persian apple

peach[2] (piːtʃ) VERB (*intr except in obsolete uses*) *Slang* to inform against an accomplice.
▷HISTORY C15: variant of earlier *apeche,* from French, from Late Latin *impedicāre* to entangle; see IMPEACH
▸ **'peacher** NOUN

peach-blow NOUN [1] **a** a delicate purplish-pink colour. **b** (*as adjective*): *a peach-blow vase.* [2] a glaze of this colour on Oriental porcelain.
▷HISTORY C19: from PEACH[1] + BLOW[3]

peach brandy NOUN (esp in S. Africa) a brandy made from fermented peaches.

peach Melba NOUN a dessert made of halved peaches, vanilla ice cream, and Melba sauce.
▷HISTORY C20: named after Dame Nellie *Melba,* stage name of *Helen Porter Mitchell* (1861–1931), Australian operatic soprano

peachy ('piːtʃɪ) ADJECTIVE **peachier, peachiest.** [1] of or like a peach, esp in colour or texture. [2] *Informal* excellent; fine.
▸ **'peachily** ADVERB ▸ **'peachiness** NOUN

peacock ('piːˌkɒk) NOUN, *plural* **-cocks** *or* **-cock.** [1] a male peafowl, having a crested head and a very large fanlike tail marked with blue and green eyelike spots. Related adjective: **pavonine.** [2] another name for **peafowl.** [3] a vain strutting person. ◆ VERB [4] to display (oneself) proudly. [5] *Obsolete slang Austral* to acquire (the best pieces of land) in such a way that the surrounding land is useless to others.
▷HISTORY C14 *pecok, pe-* from Old English *pāwa* (from Latin *pāvō* peacock) + COCK[1]
▸ **'pea,cockish** ADJECTIVE ▸ **'pea,hen** FEMININE NOUN

peacock blue NOUN **a** a greenish-blue colour. **b** (*as adjective*): *a peacock-blue car.*

peacock butterfly NOUN a European nymphalid butterfly, *Inachis io,* having reddish-brown wings each marked with a purple eyespot.

peacock ore NOUN another name for **bornite.**

peacock's tail NOUN a handsome brown seaweed, *Padina pavonia* (though coloured yellow-olive, red, and green) whose fan-shaped fronds have concentric bands of iridescent hairs.

pea crab NOUN any of various globular soft-bodied crabs of the genus *Pinnotheres* and related genera that live commensally in the mantles of certain bivalves.

peafowl ('piːˌfaʊl) NOUN, *plural* **-fowls** *or* **-fowl.** [1] either of two large pheasants, *Pavo cristatus* (**blue peafowl**) of India and Ceylon and *P. muticus* (**green peafowl**) of SE Asia. The males (see **peacock** (sense 1)) have a characteristic bright plumage. [2] a rare closely related African species, *Afropavo congensis* (**Congo peafowl**), both sexes of which are brightly coloured.

peag *or* **peage** (piːg) NOUN less common words for **wampum.**
▷HISTORY shortened from Narraganset *wampompeag* WAMPUM

pea green NOUN **a** a yellowish-green colour. **b** (*as adjective*): *a pea-green teapot.*

pea jacket *or* **peacoat** ('piːˌkəʊt) NOUN a sailor's short heavy double-breasted overcoat of navy wool.
▷HISTORY C18: from Dutch *pijjekker,* from *pij* coat of coarse cloth + *jekker* jacket

peak (piːk) NOUN [1] a pointed end, edge, or projection: *the peak of a roof.* [2] the pointed summit of a mountain. [3] a mountain with a pointed summit. [4] the point of greatest development, strength, etc.: *the peak of his career.* [5] **a** a sharp increase in a physical quantity followed by a sharp decrease: *a voltage peak.* **b** the maximum value of this quantity. **c** (*as modifier*): *peak voltage.* [6] Also called: **visor.** a projecting piece on the front of some caps. [7] **a** See **widow's peak. b** the pointed end of a beard. [8] *Nautical* **a** the extreme forward (**forepeak**) or aft (**afterpeak**) part of the hull. **b** (of a fore-and-aft quadrilateral sail) the after uppermost corner. **c** the after end of a gaff. ◆ VERB [9] (*tr*) *Nautical* to set (a gaff) or tilt (oars) vertically. [10] to form or reach or cause to form or reach a peak or maximum. ◆ ADJECTIVE [11] of or relating to a period of highest use or demand, as for watching television, commuting, etc.: *peak viewing hours; peak time.*
▷HISTORY C16: perhaps from PIKE[2], influenced by BEAK[1]; compare Spanish *pico,* French *pic,* Middle Low German *pēk*
▸ **'peaky** ADJECTIVE

Peak District NOUN a region of N central England, mainly in N Derbyshire at the S end of the Pennines: consists of moors in the north and a central limestone plateau; many caves. Highest point: 727 m (2088 ft.).

peaked (piːkt) ADJECTIVE having a peak; pointed.

peak load NOUN the maximum load on an electrical power-supply system. Compare **base load.**

peak programme meter NOUN an instrument for assessing the maximum levels of an electrical sound signal. Abbreviations: **PPM, ppm.**

peaky ('piːkɪ) ADJECTIVE **-kier, -kiest.** wan, emaciated, or sickly.
▷HISTORY C16: of uncertain origin

peal[1] (piːl) NOUN [1] a loud prolonged usually reverberating sound, as of bells, thunder, or laughter. [2] *Bell-ringing* a series of changes rung in accordance with specific rules, consisting of not fewer than 5000 permutations in a ring of eight bells. [3] (*not in technical usage*) the set of bells in a belfry. ◆ VERB [4] (*intr*) to sound with a peal or peals. [5] (*tr*) to give forth loudly and sonorously. [6] (*tr*) to ring (bells) in peals.
▷HISTORY C14 *pele,* variant of *apele* APPEAL

peal[2] (piːl) NOUN a dialect name for a grilse or a young sea trout.

pean[1] ('piːən) NOUN a less common US spelling of **paean.**

pean[2] (piːn) NOUN *Heraldry* a fur of sable spotted with or.
▷HISTORY C16: of uncertain origin

Peano's axioms (pɪ'ɑːnəʊz) PLURAL NOUN a set of axioms that yield the arithmetic of the natural numbers.
▷HISTORY named after Giuseppe *Peano* (1858–1932), Italian mathematician

peanut ('piːˌnʌt) NOUN **a** a leguminous plant, *Arachis hypogaea,* of tropical America: widely cultivated for its edible seeds. The seed pods are forced underground where they ripen. See also **hog peanut. b** the edible nutlike seed of this plant, used for food and as a source of oil. Also called: **goober, goober pea,** (Brit) **groundnut,** (Brit) **monkey nut.** ◆ See also **peanuts.**

peanut butter NOUN a brownish oily paste made from peanuts.

peanut oil NOUN oil that is made from peanut seeds and used for cooking, in soaps, and in pharmaceutical products.

peanuts ('piːˌnʌts) NOUN *Slang* a trifling amount of money.

pear (pɛə) NOUN [1] a widely cultivated rosaceous tree, *Pyrus communis,* having white flowers and edible fruits. [2] the sweet gritty-textured juicy fruit of this tree, which has a globular base and tapers towards the apex. [3] the wood of this tree, used for making furniture. [4] **go pear-shaped.** *Informal* to go wrong: *the plan started to go pear-shaped.*
▷HISTORY Old English *pere,* ultimately from Latin *pirum*

pea rifle NOUN a small rifle.

pearl[1] (pɜːl) NOUN [1] a hard smooth lustrous typically rounded structure occurring on the inner surface of the shell of a clam or oyster: consists of calcium carbonate secreted in layers around an invading particle such as a sand grain; much valued as a gem. Related adjectives: **margaric, margaritic.** [2] any artificial gem resembling this. [3] See **mother-of-pearl.** [4] a person or thing that is like a pearl, esp in beauty or value. [5] a pale greyish-white colour, often with a bluish tinge. [6] a size of printer's type, approximately equal to 5 point. ◆ ADJECTIVE [7] of, made of, or set with pearl or mother-of-pearl. [8] having the shape or colour of a pearl. ◆ VERB [9] (*tr*) to set with or as if with pearls. [10] to shape into or assume a pearl-like form or colour. [11] (*intr*) to dive or search for pearls.
▷HISTORY C14: from Old French, from Vulgar Latin *pernula* (unattested), from Latin *perna* sea mussel

pearl[2] (pɜːl) NOUN, VERB a variant spelling of **purl**[1] (senses 2, 3, 5).

pearl ash NOUN the granular crystalline form of potassium carbonate.

pearl barley NOUN barley ground into small

round grains, used in cooking, esp in soups and stews.

pearler ('pɜːlə) NOUN [1] a person who dives for or trades in pearls. [2] a boat used while searching for pearls. [3] *Austral, informal* something impressive: *that shot was a real pearler.* ◆ ADJECTIVE [4] *Austral, informal* excellent; pleasing.

pearl grey NOUN **a** a light bluish-grey colour. **b** (*as adjective*): *pearl-grey shoes.*

Pearl Harbor NOUN an almost landlocked inlet of the Pacific on the S coast of the island of Oahu, Hawaii: site of a US naval base attacked by the Japanese in 1941, resulting in the US entry into World War II.

pearlite ('pɜːlaɪt) NOUN [1] the lamellar structure in carbon steels and some cast irons that consists of alternate plates of pure iron and iron carbide. [2] a variant spelling of **perlite.**
▸**pearlitic** (pɜː'lɪtɪk) ADJECTIVE

pearlized *or* **pearlised** ('pɜːlaɪzd) ADJECTIVE having or given a pearly lustre: *a pearlized lipstick.*

pearl millet NOUN a tall grass, *Pennisetum glaucum,* cultivated in Africa, E Asia, and the southern US as animal fodder and for its pearly white seeds, which are used as grain.

pearl oyster NOUN any of various tropical marine bivalves of the genus *Pinctada* and related genera: a major source of pearls.

Pearl River NOUN [1] a river in central Mississippi, flowing southwest and south to the Gulf of Mexico. Length: 789 km (490 miles). [2] the English name for the **Zhu Jiang.**

pearlwort ('pɜːlˌwɜːt) NOUN any caryophyllaceous plant of the genus *Sagina,* having small white flowers that are spherical in bud.

pearly ('pɜːlɪ) ADJECTIVE **pearlier, pearliest.** [1] resembling a pearl, esp in lustre. [2] of the colour pearl; pale bluish-grey. [3] decorated with pearls or mother-of-pearl. ◆ NOUN, *plural* **pearlies.** (in Britain) [4] a London costermonger who wears on ceremonial occasions a traditional dress of dark clothes covered with pearl buttons. [5] (*plural*) the clothes or the buttons themselves.
▸'**pearliness** NOUN

Pearly Gates PLURAL NOUN [1] *Informal* the entrance to heaven. [2] (*not capitals*) *Brit, slang* teeth.

pearly king NOUN the male London costermonger whose ceremonial clothes display the most lavish collection of pearl buttons. See also **pearly** (sense 4).

pearly nautilus NOUN any of several cephalopod molluscs of the genus *Nautilus, esp N. pompilius,* of warm and tropical seas, having a partitioned pale pearly external shell with brown stripes. Also called: **chambered nautilus.** Compare **paper nautilus.**

pearly queen NOUN the female London costermonger whose ceremonial clothes display the most lavish collection of pearl buttons. See also **pearly** (sense 4).

pearmain ('pɛəˌmeɪn) NOUN any of several varieties of apple having a red skin.
▷HISTORY C15: from Old French *permain* a type of pear, perhaps from Latin *Parmēnsis* of Parma

Pearson's correlation coefficient NOUN a statistic measuring the linear relationship between two variables in a sample and used as an estimate of the correlation in the whole population, given by $r = Cov\ (X, Y)/\sqrt{[(Var(X).Var(Y)]}$. In full: **Pearson's product moment correlation coefficient.**
▷HISTORY named after Karl *Pearson* (1857–1936), British mathematician

peart (pɪət) ADJECTIVE *Dialect* lively; spirited; brisk.
▷HISTORY C15: variant of PERT
▸'**peartly** ADVERB ▸'**peartness** NOUN

peasant ('pɛz^{ə}nt) NOUN [1] **a** a member of a class of low social status that depends on either cottage industry or agricultural labour as a means of subsistence. **b** (*as modifier*): *peasant dress.* [2] *Informal* a person who lives in the country; rustic. [3] *Informal* an uncouth or uncultured person.
▷HISTORY C15: from Anglo-French, from Old French *païsant,* from *païs* country, from Latin *pāgus* rural area; see PAGAN

peasantry ('pɛz^{ə}ntrɪ) NOUN [1] peasants as a class. [2] conduct characteristic of peasants. [3] the status of a peasant.

peasanty ('pɛzəntɪ) ADJECTIVE [1] having qualities ascribed to traditional country life or people; simple or unsophisticated. [2] crude, awkward, or uncouth.

pease (piːz) NOUN, *plural* **pease.** an archaic or dialect word for **pea.**
▷HISTORY Old English *peose,* via Late Latin from Latin *pisa* peas, pl of *pisum,* from Greek *pison*

pease-brose ('piːz'broz, -'brəʊz) NOUN *Scot* brose made from a meal of dried peas.

peasecod *or* **peascod** ('piːzˌkɒd) NOUN *Archaic* the pod of a pea plant.
▷HISTORY C14: from PEASE + COD^{2}

pease pudding NOUN (esp in Britain) a dish of split peas that have been soaked and boiled served with ham or pork.

peashooter ('piːˌʃuːtə) NOUN a tube through which pellets such as dried peas are blown, used as a toy weapon.

peasouper (ˌpiː'suːpə) NOUN [1] *Informal, chiefly Brit* dense dirty yellowish fog. [2] *Canadian* a disparaging name for a **French Canadian.**

peat^{1} (piːt) NOUN [1] **a** a compact brownish deposit of partially decomposed vegetable matter saturated with water: found in uplands and bogs in temperate and cold regions and used as a fuel (when dried) and as a fertilizer. **b** (*as modifier*): *peat bog.* [2] a piece of dried peat for use as fuel.
▷HISTORY C14: from Anglo-Latin *peta,* perhaps from Celtic; compare Welsh *peth* thing
▸'**peaty** ADJECTIVE

peat^{2} (piːt) NOUN [1] *Archaic, derogatory* a person, esp a woman. [2] *Obsolete* a term of endearment for a girl or woman.
▷HISTORY C16: of uncertain origin

peatland ('piːtˌlænd) NOUN an area of land consisting of peat bogs, usually containing many species of flora and fauna.

peat moss NOUN any of various mosses, esp sphagnum, that grow in wet places in dense masses and decay to form peat. Also called: **bog moss.** See also **sphagnum.**

peat reek NOUN [1] the smoke of a peat fire. [2] whisky distilled over a peat fire.

peau de soie ('pəʊ də swɑː; *French* po də swa) NOUN a rich reversible silk or rayon fabric.
▷HISTORY literally: skin of silk

peavey *or* **peavy** ('piːvɪ) NOUN, *plural* **-veys** *or* **-vies.** *US and Canadian* a wooden lever with a metal pointed end and a hinged hook, used for handling logs. Compare **cant hook.**
▷HISTORY C19: named after Joseph *Peavey,* American who invented it

pebble ('pɛb^{ə}l) NOUN [1] **a** a small smooth rounded stone, esp one worn by the action of water. **b** *Geology* a rock fragment, often rounded, with a diameter of 4–64 mm and thus smaller than a cobble but larger than a granule. [2] **a** a transparent colourless variety of rock crystal, used for making certain lenses. **b** such a lens. [3] (*modifier*) *Informal* (of a lens or of spectacles) thick, with a high degree of magnification or distortion. [4] **a** a grainy irregular surface, esp on leather. **b** leather having such a surface. [5] *Informal, chiefly Austral* a troublesome or obstinate person or animal. ◆ VERB (*tr*) [6] to pave, cover, or pelt with pebbles. [7] to impart a grainy surface to (leather).
▷HISTORY Old English *papolstān,* from *papol-* (perhaps of imitative origin) + *stān* stone
▸'**pebbly** ADJECTIVE

pebble dash NOUN *Brit* a finish for external walls consisting of small stones embedded in plaster.

pebble garden NOUN *NZ* a small ornamental garden mainly composed of an arrangement of pebbles.

pebbling ('pɛblɪŋ) NOUN *Curling* the act of spraying the rink with drops of hot water to slow down the stone.

pebi- ('pɛbɪ) PREFIX *Computing* denoting 2^{50}: *pebibyte.*
▷HISTORY C20: from PE(TA-) + BI(NARY)

pec (pɛk) NOUN (*usually plural*) *Informal* short for **pectoral muscle.**

pecan (pɪ'kæn, 'piːkən) NOUN [1] a hickory tree, *Carya pecan* (or *C. illinoensis*), of the southern US, having deeply furrowed bark and edible nuts. [2] the smooth oval nut of this tree, which has a sweet oily kernel.
▷HISTORY C18: from Algonquian *paccan;* related to Ojibwa *pagân* nut with a hard shell, Cree *pakan*

peccable ('pɛkəb^{ə}l) ADJECTIVE liable to sin; susceptible to temptation.
▷HISTORY C17: via French from Medieval Latin *peccābilis,* from Latin *peccāre* to sin
▸ˌ**pecca'bility** NOUN

peccadillo (ˌpɛkə'dɪləʊ) NOUN, *plural* **-loes** *or* **-los.** a petty sin or trifling fault.
▷HISTORY C16: from Spanish *pecadillo,* from *pecado* sin, from Latin *peccātum,* from *peccāre* to transgress

peccant ('pɛkənt) ADJECTIVE *Rare* [1] guilty of an offence; corrupt. [2] violating or disregarding a rule; faulty. [3] producing disease; morbid.
▷HISTORY C17: from Latin *peccans,* from *peccāre* to sin
▸'**peccancy** NOUN ▸'**peccantly** ADVERB

peccary ('pɛkərɪ) NOUN, *plural* **-ries** *or* **-ry.** either of two piglike artiodactyl mammals, *Tayassu tajacu* (**collared peccary**) or *T. albirostris* (**white-lipped peccary**) of forests of southern North America, Central and South America: family *Tayassuidae.*
▷HISTORY C17: from Carib

peccavi (pɛ'kɑːviː) NOUN, *plural* **-vis.** a confession of guilt.
▷HISTORY C16: from Latin, literally: I have sinned, from *peccāre*

pech (pɛx) VERB, NOUN a Scot word for **pant.**
▷HISTORY C15: of imitative origin

Pechora (*Russian* pɪ'tʃɔrə) NOUN a river in N Russia, rising in the Ural Mountains and flowing north in a great arc to the **Pechora Sea** (the SE part of the Barents Sea). Length: 1814 km (1127 miles).

peck^{1} (pɛk) NOUN [1] a unit of dry measure equal to 8 quarts or one quarter of a bushel. [2] a container used for measuring this quantity. [3] a large quantity or number.
▷HISTORY C13: from Anglo-Norman, of uncertain origin

peck^{2} (pɛk) VERB [1] (when *intr,* sometimes foll by *at*) to strike with the beak or with a pointed instrument. [2] (*tr;* sometimes foll by *out*) to dig (a hole) by pecking. [3] (*tr*) (of birds) to pick up (corn, worms, etc.) by pecking. [4] (*intr;* often foll by *at*) to nibble or pick (at one's food). [5] *Informal* to kiss (a person) quickly and lightly. [6] (*intr;* foll by *at*) to nag. ◆ NOUN [7] a quick light blow, esp from a bird's beak. [8] a mark made by such a blow. [9] *Informal* a quick light kiss.
▷HISTORY C14: of uncertain origin; compare PICK^{1}, Middle Low German *pekken* to jab with the beak

pecker ('pɛkə) NOUN [1] *Brit, slang* spirits (esp in the phrase **keep one's pecker up**). [2] *Informal* short for **woodpecker.** [3] *US and Canadian* a slang word for **penis.**

pecking order NOUN [1] Also called: **peck order.** a natural hierarchy in a group of gregarious birds, such as domestic fowl. [2] any hierarchical order, as among people in a particular group.

peckish ('pɛkɪʃ) ADJECTIVE *Informal, chiefly Brit* feeling slightly hungry; having an appetite.
▷HISTORY C18: from PECK^{2}

Pecksniffian (pɛk'snɪfɪən) ADJECTIVE affecting benevolence or high moral principles.
▷HISTORY C19: after Seth *Pecksniff,* character in *Martin Chuzzlewit* (1843), a novel by the English novelist Charles Dickens (1812–70)

pecorino (ˌpɛkə'riːnəʊ) NOUN an Italian cheese made from ewes' milk.
▷HISTORY C20: from Italian, literally: of ewes, from *pecora* sheep, from Latin *pecus*

Pecos ('peɪkəs; *Spanish* 'pekɔs) NOUN a river in the southwestern US, rising in N central New Mexico and flowing southeast to the Rio Grande. Length: about 1180 km (735 miles).

Pécs (*Hungarian* peːtʃ) NOUN an industrial city in SW Hungary: university (1367). Pop.: 157 332 (2000 est.).

pectase ('pɛkteɪs) NOUN an enzyme occurring in certain ripening fruits: involved in transforming pectin into a soluble form.
▷HISTORY C19: from PECTIN + -ASE

pectate ('pɛkteɪt) NOUN a salt or ester of pectic acid.
▷HISTORY C19: from PECTIC ACID + -ATE^{1}

pecten ('pɛktɪn) NOUN, *plural* **-tens** *or* **-tines** (-tɪˌniːz). [1] a comblike structure in the eye of birds and

reptiles, consisting of a network of blood vessels projecting inwards from the retina, which it is thought to supply with oxygen. 2 any other comblike part or organ. 3 any scallop of the genus *Pecten*, which swim by expelling water from their shell valves in a series of snapping motions.
▷HISTORY C18: from Latin: a comb, from *pectere*, related to Greek *pekein* to comb

pectic acid NOUN a complex acid containing arabinose and galactose that occurs in ripe fruit, beets, and other vegetables. Formula: $C_{35}H_{50}O_{33}$.

pectin (ˈpɛktɪn) NOUN *Biochem* any of the acidic hemicelluloses that occur in ripe fruit and vegetables: used in the manufacture of jams because of their ability to solidify to a gel when heated in a sugar solution (may be referred to on food labels as **E440(a)**).
▷HISTORY C19: from Greek *pēktos* congealed, from *pegnuein* to set
▸**ˈpectic** *or* **ˈpectinous** ADJECTIVE

pectinate (ˈpɛktɪˌneɪt) *or* **pectinated** ADJECTIVE shaped like a comb: *pectinate antennae*.
▷HISTORY C18: from Latin *pectinātus* combed; see PECTEN
▸**ˌpectiˈnation** NOUN

pectize *or* **pectise** (ˈpɛktaɪz) VERB to change into a jelly; gel.
▷HISTORY C19: from Greek *pēktos* solidified; see PECTIN
▸**ˈpectizable** *or* **ˈpectisable** ADJECTIVE ▸**ˌpectiˈzation** *or* **ˌpectiˈsation** NOUN

pectoral (ˈpɛktərəl) ADJECTIVE 1 of or relating to the chest, breast, or thorax: *pectoral fins*. 2 worn on the breast or chest: *a pectoral medallion*. 3 *Rare* heartfelt or sincere. ◆ NOUN 4 a pectoral organ or part, esp a muscle or fin. 5 a medicine or remedy for disorders of the chest or lungs. 6 anything worn on the chest or breast for decoration or protection.
▷HISTORY C15: from Latin *pectorālis*, from *pectus* breast
▸**ˈpectorally** ADVERB

pectoral fin NOUN either of a pair of fins, situated just behind the head in fishes, that help to control the direction of movement during locomotion.

pectoral girdle *or* **arch** NOUN a skeletal support to which the front or upper limbs of a vertebrate are attached.

pectoral muscle NOUN either of two large chest muscles (**pectoralis major** and **pectoralis minor**), that assist in movements of the shoulder and upper arm.

pectose (ˈpɛkˌtəʊz) NOUN an insoluble carbohydrate found in the cell walls of unripe fruit that is converted to pectin by enzymic processes.

peculate (ˈpɛkjʊˌleɪt) VERB to appropriate or embezzle (public money).
▷HISTORY C18: from Latin *pecūlārī*, from *pecūlium* private property (originally, cattle); see PECULIAR
▸**ˌpecuˈlation** NOUN ▸**ˈpecuˌlator** NOUN

peculiar (pɪˈkjuːlɪə) ADJECTIVE 1 strange or unusual; odd: *a peculiar individual; a peculiar idea*. 2 distinct from others; special. 3 (*postpositive*; foll by *to*) belonging characteristically or exclusively (to): *peculiar to North America*. ◆ NOUN 4 Also called: **arbitrary**. *Printing* a special sort, esp an accented letter. 5 *Church of England* a church or parish that is exempt from the jurisdiction of the ordinary in whose diocese it lies.
▷HISTORY C15: from Latin *pecūliāris* concerning private property, from *pecūlium*, literally: property in cattle, from *pecus* cattle
▸**peˈculiarly** ADVERB

peculiarity (pɪˌkjuːlɪˈærɪtɪ) NOUN, *plural* **-ties**. 1 a strange or unusual habit or characteristic. 2 a distinguishing trait, etc. that is characteristic of a particular person; idiosyncrasy. 3 the state or quality of being peculiar.

peculiar people PLURAL NOUN 1 (*sometimes capitals*) a small sect of faith healers founded in London in 1838, having no ministers or external organization. 2 the Jews considered as God's elect.

peculium (pɪˈkjuːlɪəm) NOUN *Roman law* property that a father or master allowed his child or slave to hold as his own.
▷HISTORY C17: from Latin; see PECULIAR

pecuniary (pɪˈkjuːnɪərɪ) ADJECTIVE 1 consisting of or relating to money. 2 *Law* (of an offence) involving a monetary penalty.
▷HISTORY C16: from Latin *pecūniāris*, from *pecūnia* money
▸**peˈcuniarily** ADVERB

pecuniary advantage NOUN *Law* financial advantage that is dishonestly obtained by deception and that constitutes a criminal offence.

ped- COMBINING FORM a variant (esp US) of **paedo-**.

-ped *or* **-pede** NOUN COMBINING FORM foot or feet: *quadruped; centipede*.
▷HISTORY from Latin *pēs, ped-* foot

pedagogics (ˌpɛdəˈgɒdʒɪks, -ˈgəʊ-) NOUN (*functioning as singular*) another word for **pedagogy**.

pedagogue *or sometimes US* **pedagog** (ˈpɛdəˌgɒg) NOUN 1 a teacher or educator. 2 a pedantic or dogmatic teacher.
▷HISTORY C14: from Latin *paedagōgus*, from Greek *paidagōgos* slave who looked after his master's son, from *pais* boy + *agōgos* leader
▸**ˌpedaˈgogic** *or* **ˌpedaˈgogical** ADJECTIVE ▸**ˌpedaˈgogically** ADVERB ▸**ˈpedaˌgogism** *or* **ˈpedaˌgoguism** NOUN

pedagogy (ˈpɛdəˌgɒgɪ, -ˌgɒdʒɪ, -ˌgəʊdʒɪ) NOUN the principles, practice, or profession of teaching.

pedal¹ (ˈpɛdᵊl) NOUN 1 **a** any foot-operated lever or other device, esp one of the two levers that drive the chain wheel of a bicycle, the foot brake, clutch control, or accelerator of a car, one of the levers on an organ controlling deep bass notes, or one of the levers on a piano used to create a muted effect or sustain tone. **b** (*as modifier*): *a pedal cycle; a pianist's pedal technique*. ◆ VERB **-als, -alling, -alled** *or US* **-als, -aling, -aled**. 2 to propel (a bicycle, boat, etc.) by operating the pedals. 3 (*intr*) to operate the pedals of an organ, piano, etc., esp in a certain way. 4 to work (pedals of any kind).
▷HISTORY C17: from Latin *pedālis*; see PEDAL²

pedal² (ˈpiːdᵊl) ADJECTIVE of or relating to the foot or feet.
▷HISTORY C17: from Latin *pedālis*, from *pēs* foot

pedalfer (pɪˈdælfə) NOUN a type of zonal soil deficient in lime but containing deposits of aluminium and iron, found in wet areas, esp those with high temperatures. Compare **pedocal**.
▷HISTORY C20: PEDO-² + ALUM + *-fer*, from Latin *ferrum* iron

pedalo (ˈpɛdᵊləʊ) NOUN, *plural* **-los** *or* **-loes**. a pleasure craft driven by pedal-operated paddle wheels.
▷HISTORY C20: from PEDAL¹

pedal point (ˈpɛdᵊl) NOUN *Music* a sustained bass note, over which the other parts move bringing about changing harmonies. Often shortened to: **pedal**.

pedal pushers PLURAL NOUN calf-length trousers or jeans worn by women.

pedal steel guitar NOUN a floor-mounted, multineck, lap steel guitar with each set of strings tuned to a different open chord and foot pedals to raise or lower the pitch.

pedant (ˈpɛdᵊnt) NOUN 1 a person who relies too much on academic learning or who is concerned chiefly with insignificant detail. 2 *Archaic* a schoolmaster or teacher.
▷HISTORY C16: via Old French from Italian *pedante* teacher; perhaps related to Latin *paedagōgus* PEDAGOGUE

pedantic (pɪˈdæntɪk) ADJECTIVE of, relating to, or characterized by pedantry.
▸**peˈdantically** ADVERB

pedantry (ˈpɛdᵊntrɪ) NOUN, *plural* **-ries**. the habit or an instance of being a pedant, esp in the display of useless knowledge or minute observance of petty rules or details.

pedate (ˈpɛdeɪt) ADJECTIVE 1 (of a plant leaf) divided into several lobes arising at a common point, the lobes often being stalked and the lateral lobes sometimes divided into smaller lobes. 2 *Zoology* having or resembling a foot: *a pedate appendage*.
▷HISTORY C18: from Latin *pedātus* equipped with feet, from *pēs* foot
▸**ˈpedately** ADVERB

pedatifid (pɪˈdætɪfɪd, -ˈdeɪ-) ADJECTIVE (of a plant leaf) pedately divided, with the divisions less deep than in a pedate leaf.

peddle (ˈpɛdᵊl) VERB 1 to go from place to place selling (goods, esp small articles). 2 (*tr*) to sell (illegal drugs, esp narcotics). 3 (*tr*) to advocate (ideas) persistently or importunately: *to peddle a new philosophy*. 4 (*intr*) *Archaic* to trifle.
▷HISTORY C16: back formation from PEDLAR

peddler (ˈpɛdlə) NOUN 1 a person who sells illegal drugs, esp narcotics. 2 the usual US spelling of **pedlar**.

-pede NOUN COMBINING FORM a variant of **-ped**.

pederast *or sometimes* **paederast** (ˈpɛdəˌræst) NOUN a man who practises pederasty.

pederasty *or sometimes* **paederasty** (ˈpɛdəˌræstɪ) NOUN homosexual relations between men and boys.
▷HISTORY C17: from New Latin *paederastia*, from Greek, from *pais* boy + *erastēs* lover, from *eran* to love
▸**ˌpederˈastic** *or* (*sometimes*) **ˌpaederˈastic** ADJECTIVE

pedes (ˈpɛdiːz) NOUN the plural of **pes**.

pedestal (ˈpɛdɪstᵊl) NOUN 1 a base that supports a column, statue, etc., as used in classical architecture. 2 a position of eminence or supposed superiority (esp in the phrases **place, put,** *or* **set on a pedestal**). 3 **a** either of a pair of sets of drawers used as supports for a writing surface. **b** (*as modifier*): *a pedestal desk*.
▷HISTORY C16: from French *piédestal*, from Old Italian *piedestallo*, from *pie* foot + *di* of + *stallo* a stall

pedestrian (pɪˈdɛstrɪən) NOUN 1 **a** a person travelling on foot; walker. **b** (*as modifier*): *a pedestrian precinct*. ◆ ADJECTIVE 2 dull; commonplace: *a pedestrian style of writing*.
▷HISTORY C18: from Latin *pedester*, from *pēs* foot

pedestrian crossing NOUN *Brit* a path across a road marked as a crossing for pedestrians. See also **zebra crossing, pelican crossing.** US and Canadian name: **crosswalk.**

pedestrianize *or* **pedestrianise** (pɪˈdɛstrɪəˌnaɪz) VERB (*tr*) to convert (a street) into an area for the use of pedestrians only, by excluding all motor vehicles.
▸**peˌdestrianiˈzation** *or* **peˌdestrianiˈsation** NOUN

Pedi (ˈpɛdɪ) NOUN 1 Also called: **Northern Sotho.** a member of a subgroup of the Sotho people resident in the Transvaal. 2 the dialect of Sotho spoken by this people.

pedi- COMBINING FORM indicating the foot: *pedicure*.
▷HISTORY from Latin *pēs, ped-* foot

pediatrician (ˌpiːdɪəˈtrɪʃən) NOUN the US spelling of **paediatrician.**

pediatrics (ˌpiːdɪˈætrɪks) NOUN the US spelling of **paediatrics.**

pedicab (ˈpɛdɪˌkæb) NOUN a pedal-operated tricycle, available for hire, with an attached seat for one or two passengers.

pedicel (ˈpɛdɪˌsɛl) NOUN 1 the stalk bearing a single flower of an inflorescence. 2 Also called: **peduncle.** *Biology* any short stalk bearing an organ or organism. 3 the second segment of an insect's antenna.
▷HISTORY C17: from New Latin *pedicellus*, from Latin *pedīculus*, from *pēs* foot
▸**pedicellate** (pɪˈdɪsɪˌleɪt) ADJECTIVE

pedicle (ˈpɛdɪkᵊl) NOUN *Biology* any small stalk; pedicel; peduncle.
▷HISTORY C17: from Latin *pedīculus* small foot; see PEDICEL

pedicular (pɪˈdɪkjʊlə) ADJECTIVE 1 relating to, infested with, or caused by lice. 2 *Biology* of or relating to a stem, stalk, or pedicle.
▷HISTORY C17: from Latin *pedīculāris*, from *pedīculus*, diminutive of *pedis* louse

pediculate (pɪˈdɪkjʊlɪt, -ˌleɪt) ADJECTIVE 1 of, relating to, or belonging to the *Pediculati*, a large order of teleost fishes containing the anglers. ◆ NOUN 2 any fish belonging to the order *Pediculati*.
▷HISTORY C19: from Latin *pedīculus* little foot; see PEDICEL

pediculosis (pɪˌdɪkjʊˈləʊsɪs) NOUN *Pathol* the state of being infested with lice.
▷HISTORY C19: via New Latin from Latin *pedīculus* louse; see PEDICULAR
▸**pediculous** (pɪˈdɪkjʊləs) ADJECTIVE

pedicure (ˈpɛdɪˌkjʊə) NOUN professional treatment of the feet, either by a medical expert or a cosmetician.

▷HISTORY C19: via French from Latin *pēs* foot + *curāre* to care for

pediform (ˈpɛdɪˌfɔːm) ADJECTIVE shaped like a foot.

pedigree (ˈpɛdɪˌɡriː) NOUN [1] **a** the line of descent of a purebred animal. **b** (*as modifier*): *a pedigree bull.* [2] a document recording this. [3] a genealogical table, esp one indicating pure ancestry. [4] derivation or background: *the pedigree of an idea.*
▷HISTORY C15: from Old French *pie de grue* crane's foot, alluding to the spreading lines used in a genealogical chart
▸**ˈpediˌgreed** ADJECTIVE

pediment (ˈpɛdɪmənt) NOUN [1] a low-pitched gable, esp one that is triangular, as used in classical architecture. [2] a gently sloping rock surface, formed through denudation under arid conditions.
▷HISTORY C16: from obsolete *periment,* perhaps workman's corruption of PYRAMID
▸**ˌpediˈmental** ADJECTIVE

pedipalp (ˈpɛdɪˌpælp) NOUN either member of the second pair of head appendages of arachnids: specialized for feeding, locomotion, etc.
▷HISTORY C19: from New Latin *pedipalpi,* from Latin *pēs* foot + *palpus* palp

pedlar, *or esp US* **peddler, pedler** (ˈpɛdlə) NOUN a person who peddles; hawker.
▷HISTORY C14: changed from *peder,* from *ped, pedde* basket, of obscure origin

pedo-^{1} *or before a vowel* **ped-** COMBINING FORM variants (esp US) of **paedo-**.

pedo-^{2} COMBINING FORM indicating soil: *pedocal.*
▷HISTORY from Greek *pedon*

pedocal (ˈpɛdəˌkæl) NOUN a type of zonal soil that is rich in lime and characteristic of relatively dry areas. Compare **pedalfer.**
▷HISTORY from PEDO-^{2} + CAL(CIUM)

pedology^{1} (pɪˈdɒlədʒɪ) NOUN a US spelling of **paedology.**

pedology^{2} (pɪˈdɒlədʒɪ) NOUN the study of the formation, characteristics, and distribution of soils.
▸**pedological** (ˌpiːdəˈlɒdʒɪkəl) ADJECTIVE ▸**peˈdologist** NOUN

pedometer (pɪˈdɒmɪtə) NOUN a device containing a pivoted weight that records the number of steps taken in walking and hence the distance travelled.

pedophilia (ˌpiːdəʊˈfɪlɪə) NOUN a variant spelling (esp US) of **paedophilia.**

peduncle (pɪˈdʌŋkəl) NOUN [1] the stalk of a plant bearing an inflorescence or solitary flower. [2] *Anatomy* a stalklike structure, esp a large bundle of nerve fibres within the brain. [3] *Pathol* a slender process of tissue by which a polyp or tumour is attached to the body. [4] *Biology* another name for **pedicel** (sense 2).
▷HISTORY C18: from New Latin *pedunculus,* from Latin *pedīculus* little foot; see PEDICLE
▸**peˈduncled** *or* **peduncular** (pɪˈdʌŋkjʊlə) ADJECTIVE

pedunculate (pɪˈdʌŋkjʊlɪt, -ˌleɪt) *or* **pedunculated** ADJECTIVE having, supported on, or growing from a peduncle.
▸**peˌduncuˈlation** NOUN

pedunculate oak NOUN a large deciduous oak tree, *Quercus robur,* of Eurasia, having lobed leaves and stalked acorns. Also called: **common oak.**

pee (piː) *Informal* ◆ VERB **pees, peeing, peed.** [1] (*intr*) to urinate. ◆ NOUN [2] urine. [3] the act of urinating.
▷HISTORY C18: a euphemism for PISS, based on the initial letter

Peebles (ˈpiːbəlz) NOUN a town in SE Scotland, in Scottish Borders. Pop.: 7065 (1991).

Peeblesshire (ˈpiːbəlzˌʃɪə, -ʃə) NOUN (until 1975) a county of SE Scotland, now part of Scottish Borders. Also called: **Tweeddale.**

peek (piːk) VERB [1] (*intr*) to glance quickly or furtively; peep. ◆ NOUN [2] a quick or furtive glance.
▷HISTORY C14 *pike,* related to Middle Dutch *kiken* to peek

peekaboo (ˈpiːkəˌbuː) NOUN [1] a game for young children, in which one person hides his face and suddenly reveals it and cries "peekaboo." ◆ ADJECTIVE [2] (of a garment) made of fabric that is almost transparent or patterned with small holes.
▷HISTORY C16: from PEEK + BOO

peel^{1} (piːl) VERB [1] (*tr*) to remove (the skin, rind, outer covering, etc.) of (a fruit, egg, etc.). [2] (*intr*) (of paint, etc.) to be removed from a surface, esp through weathering. [3] (*intr*) (of a surface) to lose its outer covering of paint, etc. esp through weathering. [4] (*intr*) (of a person or part of the body) to shed skin in flakes or (of skin) to be shed in flakes, esp as a result of sunburn. [5] *Croquet* to put (another player's ball) through a hoop or hoops. [6] **keep one's eyes peeled** (*or* **skinned**). to watch vigilantly. ◆ NOUN [7] the skin or rind of a fruit, etc. ◆ See also **peel off.**
▷HISTORY Old English *pilian* to strip off the outer layer, from Latin *pilāre* to make bald, from *pilus* a hair

peel^{2} (piːl) NOUN a long-handled shovel used by bakers for moving bread, in an oven.
▷HISTORY C14 *pele,* from Old French, from Latin *pāla* spade, from *pangere* to drive in; see PALETTE

peel^{3} (piːl) NOUN (in Britain) a fortified tower of the 16th century on the borders between England and Scotland, built to withstand raids.
▷HISTORY C14 (fence made of stakes): from Old French *piel* stake, from Latin *pālus;* see PALE^{2}, PALING

peeler^{1} (ˈpiːlə) NOUN [1] a special knife or mechanical device for peeling vegetables, fruit, etc.: *a potato peeler.* [2] *US, slang* a striptease dancer.

peeler^{2} (ˈpiːlə) NOUN *Brit, dated slang* another word for **policeman.**
▷HISTORY C19: from the founder of the police force, Sir Robert *Peel* (1788–1850), British Conservative statesman

peeling (ˈpiːlɪŋ) NOUN a strip of skin, rind, bark, etc., that has been peeled off: *a potato peeling.*

peel off VERB (*adverb*) [1] to remove or be removed by peeling. [2] (*intr*) *Slang* to undress. [3] (*intr*) (of an aircraft) to turn away as by banking, and leave a formation. [4] *Slang* to go away or cause to go away.

peely-wally *or* **peelie-wallie** (ˈpiːlɪˈwælɪ) ADJECTIVE *Scot, urban dialect* off colour; pale and ill-looking: *he's a wee bit peely-wally this morning.*
▷HISTORY apparently a reduplicated form of WALLY^{2} in the sense: faded

peen (piːn) NOUN [1] the end of a hammer head opposite the striking face, often rounded or wedge-shaped. ◆ VERB [2] (*tr*) to strike with the peen of a hammer or with a stream of metal shot in order to bend or shape (a sheet of metal).
▷HISTORY C17: variant of *pane,* perhaps from French *panne,* ultimately from Latin *pinna* point

Peenemünde (ˌpiːnəˈmʊndə) NOUN a village in N Germany, in Mecklenburg-West Pomerania on the Baltic coast: site of a German rocket-development centre in World War II.

peep^{1} (piːp) VERB (*intr*) [1] to look furtively or secretly, as through a small aperture or from a hidden place. [2] to appear partially or briefly: *the sun peeped through the clouds.* ◆ NOUN [3] a quick or furtive look. [4] the first appearance: *the peep of dawn.*
▷HISTORY C15: variant of PEEK

peep^{2} (piːp) VERB (*intr*) [1] (esp of young birds) to utter shrill small noises. [2] to speak in a thin shrill voice. ◆ NOUN [3] a peeping sound. [4] *US* any of various small sandpipers of the genus *Calidris* (or *Erolia*) and related genera, such as the pectoral sandpiper.
▷HISTORY C15: of imitative origin

peeper (ˈpiːpə) NOUN [1] a person who peeps. [2] (*often plural*) a slang word for **eye**^{1} (sense 1).

peephole (ˈpiːpˌhəʊl) NOUN a small aperture, such as one in the door of a flat for observing callers before opening.

Peeping Tom NOUN a man who furtively observes women undressing; voyeur.
▷HISTORY C19: after the tailor who, according to legend, peeped at Lady Godiva when she rode naked through Coventry

peepshow (ˈpiːpˌʃəʊ) NOUN [1] Also called: **raree show.** a small box with a peephole through which a series of pictures, esp of erotic poses, can be seen. [2] a booth from which a viewer can see a live nude model for a fee.

peep sight NOUN an adjustable rear gun sight with a narrow aperture through which the target and the front sight are aligned when aiming.

peepul (ˈpiːpəl) *or* **pipal** NOUN an Indian moraceous tree, *Ficus religiosa,* resembling the banyan: regarded as sacred by Buddhists. Also called: **bo tree.**
▷HISTORY C18: from Hindi *pīpal,* from Sanskrit *pippala*

peer^{1} (pɪə) NOUN [1] a member of a nobility; nobleman. [2] a person who holds any of the five grades of the British nobility: duke, marquess, earl, viscount, and baron. See also **life peer.** [3] **a** a person who is an equal in social standing, rank, age, etc. **b** (*as modifier*): *peer pressure.* [4] *Archaic* a companion; mate.
▷HISTORY C14 (in sense 3): from Old French *per,* from Latin *pār* equal

peer^{2} (pɪə) VERB (*intr*) [1] to look intently with or as if with difficulty: *to peer into the distance.* [2] to appear partially or dimly: *the sun peered through the fog.*
▷HISTORY C16: from Flemish *pieren* to look with narrowed eyes

peerage (ˈpɪərɪdʒ) NOUN [1] the whole body of peers; aristocracy. [2] the position, rank, or title of a peer. [3] (esp in the British Isles) a book listing the peers and giving genealogical and other information about them.

peeress (ˈpɪərɪs) NOUN [1] the wife or widow of a peer. [2] a woman holding the rank of a peer in her own right.

peer group NOUN a social group composed of individuals of approximately the same age.

peerie^{1} (ˈpiːrɪ) NOUN *Scot* a spinning top.
▷HISTORY C19: perhaps from *peir* a Scot variant of *pear,* alluding to the top's shape

peerie^{2} (ˈpiːrɪ) ADJECTIVE *Orkney and Shetland, dialect* small.
▷HISTORY C19: of uncertain origin; perhaps from Norwegian dialect *piren* niggardly, thin

peerless (ˈpɪəlɪs) ADJECTIVE having no equals; matchless.

peer of the realm NOUN, *plural* **peers of the realm.** (in Great Britain and Northern Ireland) any member of the nobility entitled to sit in the House of Lords.

peer-to-peer ADJECTIVE (of a computer network) designed so that computers can send information directly to one another without passing through a centralized server. Abbreviation: **P2P.**

peetweet (ˈpiːtˌwiːt) NOUN *US* another name for the **spotted sandpiper.**
▷HISTORY C19: imitative of its cry

peeve (piːv) *Informal* ◆ VERB [1] (*tr*) to irritate; vex; annoy. ◆ NOUN [2] something that irritates; vexation: *it was a pet peeve of his.*
▷HISTORY C20: back formation from PEEVISH
▸**peeved** ADJECTIVE

peevers (ˈpiːvərz) *or* **peever** NOUN (*functioning as singular*) *Scot, dialect* hopscotch.
▷HISTORY from *peever* (the stone used in the game), of obscure origin

peevish (ˈpiːvɪʃ) ADJECTIVE [1] fretful or irritable: *a peevish child.* [2] *Obsolete* perverse.
▷HISTORY C14: of unknown origin
▸**ˈpeevishly** ADVERB ▸**ˈpeevishness** NOUN

peewee (ˈpiːwiː) NOUN [1] a variant spelling of **pewee.** [2] a variant (esp Scot) of **peewit.** [3] *Austral* another name for **magpie lark.** [4] *Canadian* **a** an age level of 12 to 13 in amateur sport, esp ice hockey. **b** (*as modifier*): *peewee hockey.*

peewit (ˈpiːwɪt) NOUN another name for **lapwing.**
▷HISTORY C16: imitative of its call

peg (pɛɡ) NOUN [1] a small cylindrical pin or dowel, sometimes slightly tapered, used to join two parts together. [2] a pin pushed or driven into a surface: used to mark scores, define limits, support coats, etc. [3] *Music* any of several pins passing through the head (**peg box**) of a stringed instrument, which can be turned so as to tune strings wound around them. See also **pin** (sense 11). [4] Also called: **clothes peg.** *Brit* a split or hinged pin for fastening wet clothes to a line to dry. US and Canadian equivalent: **clothespin.** [5] *Informal* a person's leg. [6] *Northern English, dialect* a tooth. [7] *Brit* a small drink of wine or spirits, esp of brandy or whisky and soda. [8] an opportunity or pretext for doing something: *a peg on which to hang a theory.* [9] a mountaineering piton. [10] *Croquet* a post that a player's ball must strike to win the game. [11] *Angling* a fishing station allotted to an angler in a competition, marked by a peg in the ground. [12] *Informal* a level of self-esteem, importance, etc. (esp

in the phrases **bring** *or* **take down a peg**). 13 *Informal* See **peg leg.** 14 **off the peg.** *Chiefly Brit* (of clothes) ready to wear, as opposed to tailor-made. ◆ VERB **pegs, pegging, pegged.** 15 *(tr)* to knock or insert a peg into or pierce with a peg. 16 *(tr; sometimes foll by down)* to secure with pegs: *to peg a tent.* 17 *Mountaineering* to insert or use pitons. 18 *(tr)* to mark (a score) with pegs, as in some card games. 19 *(tr) Informal* to aim and throw (missiles) at a target. 20 *(intr; foll by away, along,* etc.) *Chiefly Brit* to work steadily: *he pegged away at his job for years.* 21 *(tr)* to stabilize (the price of a commodity, an exchange rate, etc.) by legislation or market operations. ◆ See also **peg down, peg out.**
▷HISTORY C15: from Low Germanic *pegge*

Pegasus[1] (ˈpɛɡəsəs) NOUN *Greek myth* an immortal winged horse, which sprang from the blood of the slain Medusa and enabled Bellerophon to achieve many great deeds as his rider.

Pegasus[2] (ˈpɛɡəsəs) NOUN, *Latin genitive* **Pegasi** (ˈpɛɡəˌsaɪ). a constellation in the N hemisphere lying close to Andromeda and Pisces.

pegboard (ˈpɛɡˌbɔːd) NOUN 1 a board having a pattern of holes into which small pegs can be fitted, used for playing certain games or keeping a score. 2 another name for **solitaire** (sense 1). 3 hardboard perforated by a pattern of holes in which articles may be pegged or hung, as for display.

peg climbing NOUN another name for **aid climbing.**

peg down VERB *(tr, adverb)* to make (a person) committed to a course of action or bound to follow rules: *you won't peg him down to any decision.*

pegging (ˈpɛɡɪŋ) NOUN another name for **aid climbing.**

peg leg NOUN *Informal* 1 an artificial leg, esp one made of wood. 2 a person with an artificial leg.

pegmatite (ˈpɛɡməˌtaɪt) NOUN any of a class of exceptionally coarse-grained intrusive igneous rocks consisting chiefly of quartz and feldspar: often occurring as dykes among igneous rocks of finer grain.
▷HISTORY C19: from Greek *pegma* something joined together
▸**pegmatitic** (ˌpɛɡməˈtɪtɪk) ADJECTIVE

peg out VERB *(adverb)* 1 *(intr) Informal* to collapse or die. 2 *Croquet* **a** *(intr)* to win a game by hitting the peg. **b** *(tr)* to cause (an opponent's ball) to hit the peg, rendering it out of the game. 3 *(intr) Cribbage* to score the point that wins the game. 4 *(tr)* to mark or secure with pegs: *to peg out one's claims to a piece of land.*

peg top NOUN a child's spinning top, usually made of wood with a metal centre pin.

peg-top ADJECTIVE (of skirts, trousers, etc.) wide at the hips then tapering off towards the ankle.

Pegu (pɛˈɡuː) NOUN a city in S Myanmar: capital of a united Burma (16th century). Pop.: 190 900 (1993 est.).

Pehlevi (ˈpeɪləvɪ) NOUN a variant of **Pahlavi**[2].

PEI ABBREVIATION FOR Prince Edward Island.

peignoir (ˈpeɪnwɑː) NOUN a woman's dressing gown or negligee.
▷HISTORY C19: from French, from *peigner* to comb, since the garment was worn while the hair was combed

Peipus (ˈpaɪpəs) NOUN a lake in W Russia, on the boundary with Estonia: drains into the Gulf of Finland. Area: 3512 sq. km (1356 sq. miles). Russian name: **Chudskoye Ozero.**

Peiraeus (paɪˈriːəs, pɪˈreɪ-) NOUN a variant spelling of **Piraeus.**

pejoration (ˌpiːdʒəˈreɪʃən) NOUN 1 *Linguistics* semantic change whereby a word acquires unfavourable connotations: *the English word "silly" changed its meaning from "holy" or "happy" by pejoration.* Compare **amelioration** (sense 3). 2 the process of worsening; deterioration.

pejorative (pɪˈdʒɒrətɪv, ˈpiːdʒər-) ADJECTIVE 1 (of words, expressions, etc.) having an unpleasant or disparaging connotation. ◆ NOUN 2 a pejorative word, expression, etc.
▷HISTORY C19: from French *péjoratif,* from Late Latin *pējōrātus,* past participle of *pējōrāre* to make worse, from Latin *pēior* worse
▸**peˈjoratively** ADVERB

pekan (ˈpɛkən) NOUN another name for **fisher** (sense 2).
▷HISTORY C18: from Canadian French *pékan,* of Algonquian origin; compare Abnaki *pékané*

peke (piːk) NOUN *Informal* a Pekingese dog.

Pekin (piːˈkɪn) NOUN a breed of white or cream duck with a bright orange bill.
▷HISTORY C18: via French from PEKING

Peking (ˈpiːˈkɪŋ) NOUN the former English name of **Beijing.**

Pekingese (ˌpiːkɪŋˈiːz) *or* **Pekinese** (ˌpiːkəˈniːz) NOUN 1 *(plural* **-ese***)* a small breed of pet dog with a profuse straight coat, curled plumed tail, and short wrinkled muzzle. 2 the dialect of Mandarin Chinese spoken in Beijing (formerly Peking), the pronunciation of which serves as a standard for the language. 3 *(plural* **-ese***)* a native or inhabitant of Beijing (formerly Peking). ◆ ADJECTIVE 4 of or relating to Beijing (formerly Peking) or its inhabitants.

Peking man NOUN an early type of man, *Homo erectus,* remains of which, of the Lower Palaeolithic age, were found in a cave near Peking (now Beijing), China, in 1927.

pekoe (ˈpiːkəʊ) NOUN a high-quality tea made from the downy tips of the young buds of the tea plant.
▷HISTORY C18: from Chinese (Amoy) *peh ho,* from *peh* white + *ho* down

pelage (ˈpɛlɪdʒ) NOUN the coat of a mammal, consisting of hair, wool, fur, etc.
▷HISTORY C19: via French from Old French *pel* animal's coat, from Latin *pilus* hair

pelagian (pɛˈleɪdʒɪən) ADJECTIVE of or inhabiting the open sea.
▷HISTORY C18: from Latin *pelagius,* from Greek *pelagios* of the sea, from *pelagos* sea

Pelagian (pɛˈleɪdʒɪən) ADJECTIVE 1 of or relating to the British monk Pelagius (?360–?420 A.D.), or his doctrines. ◆ NOUN 2 an adherent of the doctrines of Pelagius. ◆ See also **Pelagianism.**

Pelagian Islands (pɛˈleɪdʒɪən) PLURAL NOUN a group of Italian islands (Lampedusa, Linosa, and Lampione) in the Mediterranean, between Tunisia and Malta. Pop.: 4500 (latest est.). Area: about 27 sq. km (11 sq. miles). Italian name: **Isole Pelagie** (ˈiːzole peˈladʒe).

Pelagianism (pɛˈleɪdʒɪəˌnɪzəm) NOUN *Christianity* a heretical doctrine, first formulated by the British monk Pelagius (?360–?420 A.D.), that rejected the concept of original sin and maintained that the individual takes the initial steps towards salvation by his own efforts and not by the help of divine grace.

pelagic (pɛˈlædʒɪk) ADJECTIVE 1 of or relating to the open sea: *pelagic whaling.* 2 (of marine life) living or occurring in the upper waters of open sea. 3 (of geological formations) derived from material that has fallen to the bottom from the upper waters of the sea.
▷HISTORY C17: from Latin *pelagicus,* from *pelagus,* from Greek *pelagos* sea

pelargonic acid (ˌpɛləˈɡɒnɪk) NOUN another name for **nonanoic acid.**
▷HISTORY C19: so named because it was originally derived from PELARGONIUM leaves

pelargonium (ˌpɛləˈɡəʊnɪəm) NOUN any plant of the chiefly southern African geraniaceous genus *Pelargonium,* having circular or lobed leaves and red, pink, or white aromatic flowers: includes many cultivated geraniums.
▷HISTORY C19: via New Latin from Greek *pelargos* stork, on the model of GERANIUM; from the likeness of the seed vessels to a stork's bill

Pelasgian (pɛˈlæzdʒɪən) NOUN 1 a member of any of the pre-Hellenic peoples (the **Pelasgi**) who inhabited Greece and the islands and coasts of the Aegean Sea before the arrival of the Bronze Age Greeks. ◆ ADJECTIVE *also* **Pelasgic.** 2 of or relating to these peoples.

pelecypod (pɪˈlɛsɪˌpɒd) NOUN, ADJECTIVE another word for **bivalve** (senses 1, 2).
▷HISTORY C19: from Greek *pelekus* hatchet + -POD

Pelée (pəˈleɪ) NOUN **Mount.** a volcano in the Caribbean, in N Martinique: erupted in 1902, killing every person but one in the town of Saint Pierre. Height: 1463 m (4800 ft.).

pelerine (ˈpɛləˌriːn) NOUN a woman's narrow cape with long pointed ends in front.
▷HISTORY C18: from French *pèlerine,* feminine of *pèlerin* PILGRIM, that is, a pilgrim's cape

Pele's hair (ˈpeɪleɪz, ˈpiːliːz) NOUN fine threads of volcanic glass formed from molten lava by the action of wind, explosion, etc.
▷HISTORY C20: translation of Hawaiian *lauoho-o Pele,* from Pele, name of the goddess of volcanoes

Peleus (ˈpɛlɪəs, ˈpiːlɪəs) NOUN *Greek myth* a king of the Myrmidons; father of Achilles.

Pelew Islands (piːˈluː) PLURAL NOUN a former name of (the Republic of) **Belau.**

pelf (pɛlf) NOUN *Contemptuous* money or wealth, esp if dishonestly acquired; lucre.
▷HISTORY C14: from Old French *pelfre* booty; related to Latin *pilāre* to despoil

pelham (ˈpɛləm) NOUN a horse's bit for a double bridle, less severe than a curb but more severe than a snaffle.
▷HISTORY probably from the proper name *Pelham*

Pelias (ˈpiːlɪˌæs) NOUN *Greek myth* a son of Poseidon and Tyro. He feared his nephew Jason and sent him to recover the Golden Fleece, hoping he would not return.

pelican (ˈpɛlɪkən) NOUN any aquatic bird of the tropical and warm water family *Pelecanidae,* such as *P. onocrotalus* (**white pelican**): order *Pelecaniformes.* They have a long straight flattened bill, with a distensible pouch for engulfing fish.
▷HISTORY Old English *pellican,* from Late Latin *pelicānus,* from Greek *pelekān;* perhaps related to Greek *pelekus* axe, perhaps from the shape of the bird's bill; compare Greek *pelekas* woodpecker

pelican crossing NOUN a type of road crossing marked by black-and-white stripes or by two rows of metal studs and consisting of a pedestrian-operated traffic-light system.
▷HISTORY C20: from *pe(destrian) li(ght) con(trolled) crossing,* with *-con* adapted to *-can* of *pelican*

Pelion (ˈpiːlɪən) NOUN a mountain in NE Greece, in E Thessaly. In Greek mythology it was the home of the centaurs. Height: 1548 m (5079 ft.). Modern Greek name: **Pílion.**

pelisse (pɛˈliːs) NOUN 1 a fur-trimmed cloak. 2 a high-waisted loose coat, usually fur-trimmed, worn esp by women in the early 19th century.
▷HISTORY C18: via Old French from Medieval Latin *pellicia* cloak, from Latin *pellis* skin

pelite (ˈpiːlaɪt) NOUN any argillaceous rock such as shale.
▷HISTORY C19: from Greek *pēlos* mud
▸**pelitic** (pɪˈlɪtɪk) ADJECTIVE

Pella (ˈpɛlə) NOUN an ancient city in N Greece: the capital of Macedonia under Philip II.

pellagra (pəˈleɪɡrə, -ˈlæ-) NOUN *Pathol* a disease caused by a dietary deficiency of nicotinic acid, characterized by burning or itching often followed by scaling of the skin, inflammation of the mouth, diarrhoea, mental impairment, etc.
▷HISTORY C19: via Italian from *pelle* skin + *-agra,* from Greek *agra* paroxysm
▸**pelˈlagrous** ADJECTIVE

Pelles (ˈpɛliːz) NOUN (in Arthurian legend) the father of Elaine and one of the searchers for the Holy Grail.

pellet (ˈpɛlɪt) NOUN 1 a small round ball, esp of compressed matter: *a wax pellet.* 2 **a** an imitation bullet used in toy guns. **b** a piece of small shot. 3 a stone ball formerly used as a catapult or cannon missile. 4 Also called: **cast, casting.** *Ornithol* a mass of undigested food, including bones, fur, feathers, etc., that is regurgitated by certain birds, esp birds of prey. 5 a small pill. 6 a raised area on coins and carved or moulded ornaments. ◆ VERB *(tr)* 7 to strike with pellets. 8 to make or form into pellets.
▷HISTORY C14: from Old French *pelote,* from Vulgar Latin *pilota* (unattested), from Latin *pila* ball

pellicle (ˈpɛlɪkᵊl) NOUN 1 a thin skin or film. 2 the hard protective outer layer of certain protozoans, such as those of the genus *Paramecium.* 3 *Botany* **a** the thin outer layer of a mushroom cap. **b** a growth on the surface of a liquid culture. 4 *Photog* the thin layer of emulsion covering a plate, film, or paper.
▷HISTORY C16: via French from Latin *pellicula,* from *pellis* skin

▸**pellicular** (pɛˈlɪkjʊlə) ADJECTIVE

pellitory (ˈpɛlɪtərɪ, -trɪ) NOUN, *plural* **-ries.** [1] any of various urticaceous plants of the S and W European genus *Parietaria, esp P. diffusa* (**pellitory-of-the-wall** or **wall pellitory**), that grow in crevices and have long narrow leaves and small pink flowers. [2] **pellitory of Spain.** a small Mediterranean plant, *Anacyclus pyrethrum,* the root of which contains an oil formerly used to relieve toothache: family *Asteraceae* (composites).
▹HISTORY C16 *peletre,* from Old French *piretre,* from Latin *pyrethrum,* from Greek *purethron,* from *pur* fire, from the hot pungent taste of the root

pell-mell (ˈpɛlˈmɛl) ADVERB [1] in a confused headlong rush: *the hounds ran pell-mell into the yard.* [2] in a disorderly manner: *the things were piled pell-mell in the room.* ◆ ADJECTIVE [3] disordered; tumultuous: *a pell-mell rush for the exit.* ◆ NOUN [4] disorder; confusion.
▹HISTORY C16: from Old French *pesle-mesle,* jingle based on *mesler* to MEDDLE

pellucid (pɛˈluːsɪd) ADJECTIVE [1] transparent or translucent. [2] extremely clear in style and meaning; limpid.
▹HISTORY C17: from Latin *pellūcidus,* variant of *perlūcidus,* from *perlūcēre* to shine through, from *per* through + *lūcēre* to shine
▸**pelˈlucidly** ADVERB ▸**ˌpelluˈcidity** *or* **pelˈlucidness** NOUN

pellum (ˈpɛləm) NOUN *Southwest English, dialect* dust.

Pelmanism (ˈpɛlməˌnɪzəm) NOUN [1] a system of training to improve the memory. [2] *(often not capital)* Also called: **pairs,** (esp US) **concentration.** a memory card game in which a pack of cards is spread out face down and players try to turn up pairs with the same number.
▹HISTORY named after the *Pelman* Institute, founded in London in 1898

pelmet (ˈpɛlmɪt) NOUN an ornamental drapery or board fixed above a window to conceal the curtain rail.
▹HISTORY C19: probably from French *palmette* palm-leaf decoration on cornice moulding; see PALMETTE

Peloponnese (ˌpɛləpəˈniːs) NOUN **the.** the S peninsula of Greece, joined to central Greece by the Isthmus of Corinth: chief cities in ancient times were Sparta and Corinth, now Patras. Pop.: 632 955 (2001). Area: 21 439 sq. km (8361 sq. miles). Medieval name: **Morea.** Modern Greek name: **Peloponnesos.** Also called: **Peloponnesus.**

Peloponnesian (ˌpɛləpəˈniːʃən) ADJECTIVE of or relating to the Peloponnese or its inhabitants.

Peloponnesian War NOUN a war fought for supremacy in Greece from 431 to 404 B.C., in which Athens and her allies were defeated by the league centred on Sparta.

Pelops (ˈpiːlɒps) NOUN *Greek myth* the son of Tantalus, who as a child was killed by his father and served up as a meal for the gods.

peloria (pɛˈlɔːrɪə) NOUN the abnormal production of actinomorphic flowers in a plant of a species that usually produces zygomorphic flowers.
▹HISTORY C19: via New Latin from Greek *pelōros,* from *pelōr* monster
▸**peloric** (pɛˈlɔːrɪk, -ˈlɒ-) ADJECTIVE

pelorus (pɪˈlɔːrəs) NOUN, *plural* **-ruses.** a sighting device used in conjunction with a magnetic compass or a gyrocompass for measuring the relative bearings of observed points.
▹HISTORY of uncertain origin, perhaps from Latin *Pelōrus* a dangerous Sicilian promontory

pelota (pəˈlɒtə) NOUN any of various games played in Spain, Spanish America, SW France, etc., by two players who use a basket strapped to their wrists or a wooden racket to propel a ball against a specially marked wall.
▹HISTORY C19: from Spanish: ball, from Old French *pelote;* see PELLET

Pelotas (*Portuguese* peˈlɔtas) NOUN a port in S Brazil, in Rio Grande do Sul on the Canal de São Gonçalo. Pop.: 300 952 (2000 est.).

peloton (ˈpɛləˌtɒn) NOUN *Cycle racing* the main field of riders in a road race.
▹HISTORY C20: French, literally: pack

pelt^{1} (pɛlt) VERB [1] *(tr)* to throw (missiles) at (a person). [2] *(tr)* to hurl (insults) at (a person). [3] *(intr;* foll by *along, over,* etc.) to move rapidly; hurry. [4] *(intr;* often foll by *down)* to rain heavily. ◆ NOUN [5] a blow. [6] speed (esp in the phrase **at full pelt**).
▹HISTORY C15: of uncertain origin, perhaps from PELLET
▸**ˈpelter** NOUN

pelt^{2} (pɛlt) NOUN [1] the skin of a fur-bearing animal, such as a mink, esp when it has been removed from the carcass. [2] the hide of an animal, stripped of hair and ready for tanning.
▹HISTORY C15: perhaps back formation from PELTRY

peltast (ˈpɛltæst) NOUN (in ancient Greece) a lightly armed foot soldier.
▹HISTORY C17: from Latin *peltasta,* from Greek *peltastēs* soldier equipped with a *pelta,* a small leather shield

peltate (ˈpɛlteɪt) ADJECTIVE (of leaves) having the stalk attached to the centre of the lower surface.
▹HISTORY C18: from Latin *peltātus* equipped with a *pelta,* a small shield; see PELTAST
▸**ˈpeltately** ADVERB ▸**pelˈtation** NOUN

Peltier effect (ˈpɛltɪˌeɪ) NOUN *Physics* the production of heat at one junction and the absorption of heat at the other junction of a thermocouple when a current is passed around the thermocouple circuit. The heat produced is additional to the heat arising from the resistance of the wires. Compare **Seebeck effect.**
▹HISTORY C19: named after Jean *Peltier* (1785–1845), French physicist, who discovered it

Peltier element NOUN an electronic device consisting of metal strips between which alternate strips of n-type and p-type semiconductors are connected. Passage of a current causes heat to be absorbed from one set of metallic strips and emitted from the other by the Peltier effect.

Pelton wheel (ˈpɛltən) NOUN a type of impulse turbine in which specially shaped buckets mounted on the perimeter of a wheel are struck by a fast-flowing water jet.
▹HISTORY C19: named after L. A. *Pelton* (1829–1908), US engineer who invented it

peltry (ˈpɛltrɪ) NOUN, *plural* **-ries.** the pelts of animals collectively.
▹HISTORY C15: from Old French *peleterie* collection of pelts, from Latin *pilus* hair

pelvic (ˈpɛlvɪk) ADJECTIVE of, near, or relating to the pelvis.

pelvic fin NOUN either of a pair of fins attached to the pelvic girdle of fishes that help to control the direction of movement during locomotion.

pelvic floor NOUN the muscular area in the lower part of the abdomen, attached to the pelvis.

pelvic-floor exercises PLURAL, NOUN another name for **Kegel exercises.**

pelvic girdle *or* **arch** NOUN the skeletal structure to which the lower limbs in man, and the hind limbs or corresponding parts in other vertebrates, are attached.

pelvic inflammatory disease NOUN inflammation of a woman's womb, Fallopian tubes, or ovaries as a result of infection with one of a group of bacteria. Abbreviation: **PID.**

pelvimetry (pɛlˈvɪmɪtrɪ) NOUN *Obstetrics* measurement of the dimensions of the female pelvis.

pelvis (ˈpɛlvɪs) NOUN, *plural* **-vises** *or* **-ves** (-viːz). [1] the large funnel-shaped structure at the lower end of the trunk of most vertebrates: in man it is formed by the hipbones and sacrum. [2] the bones that form this structure. [3] any anatomical cavity or structure shaped like a funnel or cup. [4] short for **renal pelvis.**
▹HISTORY C17: from Latin: basin, laver

pelycosaur (ˈpɛlɪkəʊˌsɔː) NOUN any extinct mammal-like reptile of the order *Pelycosauria,* of Upper Carboniferous to Lower Permian times, from which the therapsids are thought to have evolved.
▹HISTORY C19: from New Latin *Pelycosauria,* from Greek *pelyx* bowl, PELVIS, + -SAUR

Pemba (ˈpɛmbə) NOUN an island in the Indian Ocean, off the E coast of Africa north of Zanzibar: part of Tanzania; produces most of the world's cloves. Chief town: Chake Chake. Pop.: 322 466 (1995 est.). Area: 984 sq. km (380 sq. miles).

Pembroke (ˈpɛmbrʊk) NOUN [1] a town in SW Wales, in Pembrokeshire on Milford Haven: 11th-century castle where Henry VII was born. Pop. (with Pembroke Dock): 15 424 (1991). [2] the smaller variety of corgi, usually having a short tail.

Pembrokeshire (ˈpɛmbrʊkˌʃɪə, -ʃə) NOUN a county of SW Wales, on the Irish Sea and the Bristol Channel: formerly (1974–96) part of Dyfed: a hilly peninsula with a deeply indented coast: tourism, agriculture, oil refining. Administrative centre: Haverfordwest. Pop.: 112 901 (2001). Area: 1589 sq. km (614 sq. miles).

Pembroke table NOUN a small table with drop leaves and often one or more drawers.
▹HISTORY perhaps named after Mary Herbert, Countess of *Pembroke* (1561–1621), who originally ordered its design

pemmican *or* **pemican** (ˈpɛmɪkən) NOUN a small pressed cake of shredded dried meat, pounded into paste with fat and berries or dried fruits, used originally by American Indians and now chiefly for emergency rations.
▹HISTORY C19: from Cree *pimikân,* from *pimii* fat, grease

pemphigus (ˈpɛmfɪgəs, pɛmˈfaɪ-) NOUN *Pathol* any of a group of blistering skin diseases, esp a potentially fatal form (**pemphigus vulgaris**) characterized by large blisters on the skin, mucous membranes of the mouth, genitals, intestines, etc., which eventually rupture and form painful denuded areas from which critical amounts of bodily protein, fluid, and blood may be lost.
▹HISTORY C18: via New Latin from Greek *pemphix* bubble

pen^{1} (pɛn) NOUN [1] an implement for writing or drawing using ink, formerly consisting of a sharpened and split quill, and now of a metal nib attached to a holder. See also **ballpoint, fountain pen.** [2] the writing end of such an implement; nib. [3] style of writing. [4] **the pen. a** writing as an occupation. **b** the written word: *the pen is mightier than the sword.* [5] the long horny internal shell of a squid. ◆ VERB **pens, penning, penned.** [6] *(tr)* to write or compose.
▹HISTORY Old English *pinne,* from Late Latin *penna* (quill) pen, from Latin: feather

pen^{2} (pɛn) NOUN [1] an enclosure in which domestic animals are kept: *sheep pen.* [2] any place of confinement. [3] a dock for servicing submarines, esp one having a bombproof roof. ◆ VERB **pens, penning, penned** *or* **pent.** [4] *(tr)* to enclose or keep in a pen.
▹HISTORY Old English *penn,* perhaps related to PIN

pen^{3} (pɛn) NOUN *US and Canadian, informal* short for **penitentiary** (sense 1).

pen^{4} (pɛn) NOUN a female swan.
▹HISTORY C16: of unknown origin

PEN (pɛn) NOUN ACRONYM FOR International Association of Poets, Playwrights, Editors, Essayists, and Novelists.

Pen. ABBREVIATION FOR Peninsula.

penal (ˈpiːnᵊl) ADJECTIVE [1] of, relating to, constituting, or prescribing punishment. [2] payable as a penalty: *a penal sum.* [3] used or designated as a place of punishment: *a penal institution.*
▹HISTORY C15: from Late Latin *poenālis* concerning punishment, from *poena* penalty
▸**ˈpenally** ADVERB

penal code NOUN the codified body of the laws in any legal system that relate to crime and its punishment.

penalize *or* **penalise** (ˈpiːnəˌlaɪz) VERB *(tr)* [1] to impose a penalty on (someone), as for breaking a law or rule. [2] to inflict a handicap or disadvantage on. [3] *Sport* to award a free stroke, point, or penalty against (a player or team). [4] to declare (an act) legally punishable; make subject to a penalty.
▸**ˌpenaliˈzation** *or* **ˌpenaliˈsation** NOUN

penal servitude NOUN *English criminal law* (formerly) the imprisonment of an offender and his subjection to hard labour. It was substituted for transportation in 1853 and abolished in 1948. Compare **hard labour.**

penalty (ˈpɛnᵊltɪ) NOUN, *plural* **-ties.** [1] a legal or official punishment, such as a term of imprisonment. [2] some other form of punishment, such as a fine or forfeit for not fulfilling a contract. [3] loss, suffering, or other unfortunate result of one's own action, error, etc. [4] *Sport, games* a handicap awarded against a player or team for

illegal play, such as a free shot at goal by the opposing team, loss of points, etc.
▷HISTORY C16: from Medieval Latin *poenālitās* penalty; see PENAL

penalty area NOUN *Soccer* a rectangular area in front of the goal, within which the goalkeeper may handle the ball and within which a penalty is awarded for a foul by the defending team.

penalty box NOUN [1] *Soccer* another name for **penalty area.** [2] *Ice hockey* a bench for players serving time penalties.

penalty corner NOUN *Hockey* a free hit from the goal line taken by the attacking side. Also called: **short corner.**

penalty kick NOUN [1] *Soccer* a free kick at the goal from a point (**penalty spot**) within the penalty area and 12 yards (about 11 m) from the goal, with only the goalkeeper allowed to defend it: awarded to the attacking team after a foul within the penalty area by a member of the defending team. [2] *Rugby Union* a kick awarded after a serious foul that can be aimed straight at the goal to score three points.

penalty killer NOUN *Ice hockey* a good player who, when his team is short-handed because of a penalty, is sent onto the ice to prevent the other side from scoring.

penalty point NOUN [1] *Brit* an endorsement on a driving licence due to a motoring offence: *he also got eight penalty points on his licence.* [2] a point awarded against a sports team or competitor for an infringement of the rules.

penalty rates PLURAL NOUN *Austral and NZ* rates of pay, such as double time, paid to employees working outside normal working hours.

penalty shoot-out NOUN [1] *Soccer* a method of deciding the winner of a drawn match, in which players from each team attempt to score with a penalty kick. [2] a similar method of resolving a tie in hockey, ice hockey, polo, etc.

penance ('pɛnəns) NOUN [1] voluntary self-punishment to atone for a sin, crime, etc. [2] a feeling of regret for one's wrongdoings. [3] *Christianity* **a** a punishment usually consisting of prayer, fasting, etc., undertaken voluntarily as an expression of penitence for sin. **b** a punishment of this kind imposed by church authority as a condition of absolution. ◆ VERB [4] (*tr*) (of ecclesiastical authorities) to impose a penance upon (a sinner).
▷HISTORY C13: via Old French from Latin *paenitentia* repentance; related to Latin *poena* penalty

Penang (pɪ'næŋ) NOUN [1] a state of Peninsular Malaysia: consists of the island of Penang and the province Wellesley on the mainland, which first united administratively in 1798 as a British colony. Capital: George Town. Pop.: 1 225 501 (2000). Area: 1031 sq. km (398 sq. miles). Also called: **Pulau Pinang.** [2] a forested island off the NW coast of Malaya, in the Strait of Malacca. Area: 293 sq. km (113 sq. miles). Former name (until about 1867): **Prince of Wales Island.** [3] another name for **George Town.**

penannular (pɛn'ænjʊlə) ADJECTIVE of or forming an almost complete ring.
▷HISTORY C19: from PENE- + ANNULAR

penates (pə'nɑːtiːz) PLURAL NOUN See **lares and penates.**
▷HISTORY Latin

pence (pɛns) NOUN a plural of **penny.**

> **Language note** Since the decimalization of British currency and the introduction of the abbreviation **p**, as in *10p*, *85p*, etc., the abbreviation has tended to replace *pence* in speech, as in *4p* (ˌfɔː'piː), *12p* (ˌtwɛlv'piː), etc.

pencel, pensel, or **pensil** ('pɛnsᵊl) NOUN a small pennon, originally one carried by a knight's squire.
▷HISTORY C13: via Anglo-French from Old French *penoncel* a little PENNON

penchant ('pɒŋʃɒŋ) NOUN a strong inclination or liking; bent or taste.
▷HISTORY C17: from French, from *pencher* to incline, from Latin *pendēre* to be suspended

Penchi ('pɛn'tʃiː) NOUN a variant transliteration of the Chinese name for **Benxi.**

pencil ('pɛnsᵊl) NOUN [1] **a** a thin cylindrical instrument used for writing, drawing, etc., consisting of a rod of graphite or other marking substance, usually either encased in wood and sharpened or held in a mechanical metal device. **b** (*as modifier*): *a pencil drawing.* [2] something similar in shape or function: *a styptic pencil; an eyebrow pencil.* [3] a narrow set of lines or rays, such as light rays, diverging from or converging to a point. [4] *Archaic* an artist's fine paintbrush. [5] *Rare* an artist's individual style or technique in drawing. ◆ VERB **-cils, -cilling, -cilled** or *US* **-cils, -ciling, -ciled.** (*tr*) [6] to draw, colour, or write with a pencil. [7] to mark with a pencil. [8] **pencil in.** to note, arrange, include, etc. provisionally or tentatively.
▷HISTORY C14: from Old French *pincel,* from Latin *pēnicillus* painter's brush, from *pēniculus* a little tail, from *pēnis* tail
▸ **'penciller** or *US* **'penciler** NOUN

pend (pɛnd) VERB (*intr*) [1] to await judgment or settlement. [2] *Dialect* to hang; depend. ◆ NOUN [3] *Scot* an archway or vaulted passage.
▷HISTORY C15: from Latin *pendēre* to hang; related to Latin *pendere* to suspend

pendant ('pɛndənt) NOUN [1] **a** an ornament that hangs from a piece of jewellery. **b** a necklace with such an ornament. [2] a hanging light, esp a chandelier. [3] a carved ornament that is suspended from a ceiling or roof. [4] something that matches or complements something else. [5] Also called: **pennant.** *Nautical* a length of wire or rope secured at one end to a mast or spar and having a block or other fitting at the lower end. ◆ ADJECTIVE [6] a variant spelling of **pendent.**
▷HISTORY C14: from Old French, from *pendre* to hang, from Latin *pendēre* to hang down; related to Latin *pendere* to hang, *pondus* weight, Greek *span* to pull

pendent ('pɛndənt) ADJECTIVE [1] dangling. [2] jutting. [3] (of a grammatical construction) incomplete: *a pendent nominative is a construction having no verb.* [4] a less common word for **pending** (senses 2, 3). ◆ NOUN [5] a variant spelling of **pendant.**
▷HISTORY C15: from Old French *pendant,* from *pendre* to hang; see PENDANT
▸ **'pendency** NOUN ▸ **'pendently** ADVERB

pendente lite (pɛn'dɛntɪ 'laɪtɪ) ADJECTIVE *Law* while a suit is pending.
▷HISTORY Latin, literally: with litigation pending

pendentive (pɛn'dɛntɪv) NOUN any of four triangular sections of vaulting with concave sides, positioned at a corner of a rectangular space to support a circular or polygonal dome.
▷HISTORY C18: from French *pendentif,* from Latin *pendens* hanging, from *pendere* to hang

pending ('pɛndɪŋ) PREPOSITION [1] while waiting for or anticipating. ◆ ADJECTIVE (*postpositive*) [2] not yet decided, confirmed, or finished: *what are the matters pending?* [3] imminent: *these developments have been pending for some time.*

Pendolino (ˌpɛndəʊ'liːnəʊ) NOUN an Italian high-speed tilting train, now used in several countries.

pendragon (pɛn'drægən) NOUN a supreme war chief or leader of the ancient Britons.
▷HISTORY Welsh, literally: head dragon
▸ **pen'dragon,ship** NOUN

pendule ('pɒndjuːl, 'pɛn-) NOUN *Mountaineering* a manoeuvre by which a climber on a rope from above swings in a pendulum-like series of movements to reach another line of ascent. Also called: **pendulum.**

pendulous ('pɛndjʊləs) ADJECTIVE hanging downwards, esp so as to swing from side to side.
▷HISTORY C17: from Latin *pendulus,* from *pendēre* to hang down
▸ **'pendulously** ADVERB ▸ **'pendulousness** NOUN

pendulum ('pɛndjʊləm) NOUN [1] a body mounted so that it can swing freely under the influence of gravity. It is either a bob hung on a light thread (**simple pendulum**) or a more complex structure (**compound pendulum**). [2] such a device used to regulate a clockwork mechanism. [3] something that changes its position, attitude, etc. fairly regularly: *the pendulum of public opinion.*
▷HISTORY C17: from Latin *pendulus* PENDULOUS

pene- or *before a vowel* **pen-** PREFIX almost: *peneplain.*
▷HISTORY from Latin *paene*

Penelope (pə'nɛləpɪ) NOUN *Greek myth* the wife of Odysseus, who remained true to him during his long absence despite the importunities of many suitors.

peneplain or **peneplane** ('piːnɪˌpleɪn, ˌpiːnɪ'pleɪn) NOUN a relatively flat land surface produced by a long period of erosion.
▷HISTORY C19: from PENE- + PLAIN[1]
▸ **ˌpenepla'nation** NOUN

penetralia (ˌpɛnɪ'treɪlɪə) PLURAL NOUN [1] the innermost parts. [2] secret matters.
▷HISTORY C17: from Latin, from *penetrālis* inner, from *penetrāre* to PENETRATE
▸ **ˌpene'tralian** ADJECTIVE

penetrance ('pɛnɪtrəns) NOUN *Genetics* the percentage frequency with which a gene exhibits its effect.
▷HISTORY C20: from PENETR(ANT) + -ANCE, on the model of German *penetranz*

penetrant ('pɛnɪtrənt) ADJECTIVE [1] sharp; penetrating. ◆ NOUN [2] *Chem* a substance that lowers the surface tension of a liquid and thus causes it to penetrate or be absorbed more easily. [3] a person or thing that penetrates.

penetrate ('pɛnɪˌtreɪt) VERB [1] to find or force a way into or through (something); pierce; enter. [2] to diffuse through (a substance); permeate. [3] (*tr*) to see through: *their eyes could not penetrate the fog.* [4] (*tr*) (of a man) to insert the penis into the vagina of (a woman). [5] (*tr*) to grasp the meaning of (a principle, etc.). [6] (*intr*) to be understood: *his face lit up as the new idea penetrated.*
▷HISTORY C16: from Latin *penetrāre;* related to *penitus* inner, and *penus* the interior of a house
▸ **'penetrable** ADJECTIVE ▸ **ˌpenetra'bility** NOUN
▸ **'penetrably** ADVERB ▸ **'penetrative** ADJECTIVE
▸ **'pene,trator** NOUN

penetrating ('pɛnɪˌtreɪtɪŋ) ADJECTIVE tending to or able to penetrate: *a penetrating mind; a penetrating voice.*
▸ **'pene,tratingly** ADVERB

penetration (ˌpɛnɪ'treɪʃən) NOUN [1] the act or an instance of penetrating. [2] the ability or power to penetrate. [3] keen insight or perception. [4] *Military* an offensive manoeuvre that breaks through an enemy's defensive position. [5] Also called: **market penetration.** the proportion of the total number of potential purchasers of a product or service who either are aware of its existence or actually buy it. [6] another name for **depth of field.**

penetrometer (ˌpɛnɪ'trɒmɪtə) NOUN *Physics* an instrument used to measure the penetrating power of radiation, such as X-rays.

Peneus (pɪ'niːəs) NOUN the ancient name for the **Salambria.**

pen friend NOUN another name for **pen pal.**

Penghu or **P'eng-hu** ('pɛŋ'huː) NOUN transliteration of the Chinese name for the **Pescadores.**

pengö ('pɛŋɡɜː) NOUN, *plural* **-gös.** (formerly) the standard monetary unit of Hungary, replaced by the forint in 1946.
▷HISTORY from Hungarian, from *pengeni* to sound

Pengpu ('pɛŋ'puː) NOUN a variant transliteration of the Chinese name for **Bengbu.**

penguin ('pɛŋɡwɪn) NOUN [1] any flightless marine bird, such as *Aptenodytes patagonica* (king penguin) and *Pygoscelis adeliae* (**Adélie penguin**), of the order *Sphenisciformes* of cool southern, esp Antarctic, regions: they have wings modified as flippers, webbed feet, and feathers lacking barbs. See also **emperor penguin, king penguin.** [2] an obsolete name for **great auk.**
▷HISTORY C16: perhaps from Welsh *pen gwyn,* from *pen* head + *gwyn* white

penicillate (ˌpɛnɪ'sɪlɪt, -eɪt) ADJECTIVE *Biology* having or resembling one or more tufts of fine hairs: *a penicillate caterpillar.*
▷HISTORY C19: from Latin *pēnicillus* brush, PENCIL
▸ **ˌpeni'cillately** ADVERB ▸ **ˌpenicil'lation** NOUN

penicillin (ˌpɛnɪ'sɪlɪn) NOUN any of a group of antibiotics with powerful bactericidal action, used to treat many types of infections, including pneumonia, gonorrhoea, and infections caused by streptococci and staphylococci: originally obtained from the fungus *Penicillium, esp P. notatum.* Formula:

$R\text{-}C_9H_{11}N_2O_4S$ where R is one of several side chains.
▷HISTORY C20: from PENICILLIUM

penicillium (ˌpenɪˈsɪlɪəm) NOUN, *plural* **-cilliums** *or* **-cillia** (-ˈsɪlɪə). any ascomycetous saprotrophic fungus of the genus *Penicillium,* which commonly grow as a green or blue mould on stale food: some species are used in cheese-making and others as a source of penicillin.
▷HISTORY C19: New Latin, from Latin *pēnicillus* tuft of hairs; named from the tufted appearance of the sporangia of this fungus

penile (ˈpiːnaɪl) ADJECTIVE of or relating to the penis.

penillion *or* **pennillion** (pɪˈnɪlɪən) PLURAL NOUN, *singular* **penill** (pɪˈnɪl). the Welsh art or practice of singing poetry in counterpoint to a traditional melody played on the harp.
▷HISTORY from Welsh: verses, plural of *penill* verse, stanza

peninsula (pɪˈnɪnsjʊlə) NOUN a narrow strip of land projecting into a sea or lake from the mainland.
▷HISTORY C16: from Latin, literally: almost an island, from *paene* PENE- + *insula* island
▸**penˈinsular** ADJECTIVE

Language note The noun *peninsula* is sometimes confused with the adjective *peninsular: the Iberian peninsula* (not *peninsular*).

Peninsula NOUN **the.** short for the **Iberian Peninsula.**

Peninsular War NOUN the war (1808–14) fought in the Iberian Peninsula by British, Portuguese, and Spanish forces against the French, resulting in the defeat of the French: part of the Napoleonic Wars.

peninsulate (pɪˈnɪnsjʊˌleɪt) VERB (*tr*) to cause (land) to become peninsular.

penis (ˈpiːnɪs) NOUN, *plural* **-nises** *or* **-nes** (-niːz). the male organ of copulation in higher vertebrates, also used for urine excretion in many mammals.
▷HISTORY C17: from Latin

penis envy NOUN *Psychoanal* a Freudian concept in which envy of the penis is postulated as the cause for some of the characteristics found in women.

penitent (ˈpenɪtənt) ADJECTIVE [1] feeling regret for one's sins; repentant. ◆ NOUN [2] a person who is penitent. [3] *Christianity* **a** a person who repents his sins and seeks forgiveness for them. **b** *RC Church* a person who confesses his sins to a priest and submits to a penance imposed by him.
▷HISTORY C14: from Church Latin *paenitēns* regretting, from *paenitēre* to repent, of obscure origin
▸**ˈpenitence** NOUN ▸**ˈpenitently** ADVERB

penitential (ˌpenɪˈtenʃəl) ADJECTIVE [1] of, showing, or constituting penance. ◆ NOUN [2] *Chiefly RC Church* a book or compilation of instructions for confessors. [3] a less common word for **penitent** (senses 2, 3).
▸**ˌpeniˈtentially** ADVERB

penitentiary (ˌpenɪˈtenʃərɪ) NOUN, *plural* **-ries.** [1] (in the US and Canada) a state or federal prison: in Canada, esp a federal prison for offenders convicted of serious crimes. Sometimes shortened to: **pen.** [2] *RC Church* **a** a cleric appointed to supervise the administration of the sacrament of penance in a particular area. **b** a priest who has special faculties to absolve particularly grave sins. **c** a cardinal who presides over a tribunal that decides all matters affecting the sacrament of penance. **d** this tribunal itself. ◆ ADJECTIVE [3] another word for **penitential** (sense 1). [4] *US and Canadian* (of an offence) punishable by imprisonment in a penitentiary.
▷HISTORY C15 (meaning also: an officer dealing with penances): from Medieval Latin *poenitentiārius,* from Latin *paenitēns* PENITENT

Penki (ˈpenˈtʃiː) NOUN a variant transliteration of the Chinese name for **Benxi.**

penknife (ˈpenˌnaɪf) NOUN, *plural* **-knives.** a small knife with one or more blades that fold into the handle; pocketknife.
▷HISTORY C15: so called because it was originally used for making and repairing quill pens

penman (ˈpenmən) NOUN, *plural* **-men.** [1] a person skilled in handwriting. [2] a person who writes by hand in a specified way: *a bad penman.* [3] an author.

penmanship (ˈpenmənʃɪp) NOUN style or technique of writing by hand. Also called: **calligraphy.**

Penn. *or* **Penna** ABBREVIATION FOR Pennsylvania.

penna (ˈpenə) NOUN, *plural* **-nae** (-niː). *Ornithol* any large feather that has a vane and forms part of the main plumage of a bird.
▷HISTORY Latin: feather
▸**pennaceous** (peˈneɪʃəs) ADJECTIVE

pen name NOUN an author's pseudonym. Also called: **nom de plume.**

pennant (ˈpenənt) NOUN [1] a type of pennon, esp one flown from vessels as identification or for signalling. [2] *Chiefly US, Canadian, and Austral* **a** a flag serving as an emblem of championship in certain sports. **b** (*as modifier*): *pennant cricket.* [3] *Nautical* another word for **pendant** (sense 5).
▷HISTORY C17: probably a blend of PENDANT and PENNON

pennate (ˈpeneɪt) *or* **pennated** ADJECTIVE *Biology* [1] having feathers, wings, or winglike structures. [2] another word for **pinnate.**
▷HISTORY C19: from Latin *pennātus,* from *penna* wing

penne (ˈpenɪ) NOUN pasta in the form of short tubes.
▷HISTORY C20: Italian, literally: quills

penni (ˈpenɪ) NOUN, *plural* **-niä** (-nɪə) *or* **-nis.** a former Finnish monetary unit worth one hundredth of a markka.
▷HISTORY Finnish, from Low German *pennig* PENNY

penniless (ˈpenɪlɪs) ADJECTIVE very poor; almost totally without money.
▸**ˈpennilessly** ADVERB ▸**ˈpennilessness** NOUN

pennillion (pɪˈnɪlɪən) NOUN a variant spelling of **penillion.**

Pennine Alps (ˈpenaɪn) PLURAL NOUN a range of the Alps between Switzerland and Italy. Highest peak: Monte Rosa, 4634 m (15 204 ft.).

Pennines (ˈpenaɪnz) PLURAL NOUN a system of hills in England, extending from the Cheviot Hills in the north to the River Trent in the south: forms the watershed for the main rivers of N England. Highest peak: Cross Fell, 893 m (2930 ft.). Also called: **the Pennine Chain.**

Pennine Way NOUN a long-distance footpath extending from Edale, Derbyshire, for 402 km (250 miles) to Kirk Yetholm, Scottish Borders.

penninite (ˈpenɪˌnaɪt) NOUN a bluish-green variety of chlorite occurring in the form of thick crystals.
▷HISTORY C20: from German *Pennin* Pennine (Alps) + -ITE[1]

pennon (ˈpenən) NOUN [1] a long flag, often tapering and rounded, divided, or pointed at the end, originally a knight's personal flag. [2] a small tapering or triangular flag borne on a ship or boat. [3] a poetic word for **wing.**
▷HISTORY C14: via Old French ultimately from Latin *penna* feather

Pennsylvania (ˌpensɪlˈveɪnɪə) NOUN a state of the northeastern US: almost wholly in the Appalachians, with the Allegheny Plateau to the west and a plain in the southeast; the second most important US state for manufacturing. Capital: Harrisburg. Pop.: 12 281 054 (2000). Area: 116 462 sq. km (44 956 sq. miles). Abbreviations: **Pa, Penn, Penna,** (with zip code) **PA.**

Pennsylvania Dutch NOUN [1] Also called: **Pennsylvania German.** a dialect of German spoken in E Pennsylvania. [2] **the Pennsylvania Dutch.** (*functioning as plural*) a group of German-speaking people in E Pennsylvania, descended from 18th-century settlers from SW Germany and Switzerland.

Pennsylvanian (ˌpensɪlˈveɪnɪən) ADJECTIVE [1] of the state of Pennsylvania. [2] (in North America) of, denoting, or formed in the upper of two divisions of the Carboniferous period (see also **Mississippian** (sense 2)), which lasted 30 million years, during which coal measures were formed. ◆ NOUN [3] an inhabitant or native of the state of Pennsylvania. [4] **the.** the Pennsylvanian period or rock system, equivalent to the Upper Carboniferous of Europe.

penny (ˈpenɪ) NOUN, *plural* **pennies** *or* **pence** (pens). [1] Also called (formerly): **new penny.** (in Britain) a bronze coin having a value equal to one hundredth of a pound. Symbol: p. [2] (in Britain before 1971) a bronze or copper coin having a value equal to one twelfth of a shilling or one two-hundred-and-fortieth of a pound. Abbreviation: **d.** [3] a former monetary unit of the Republic of Ireland worth one hundredth of a pound. [4] (*plural* **pennies**) (in the US and Canada) a cent. [5] a coin of similar value, as used in several other countries. [6] (*used with a negative*) *Informal, chiefly Brit* the least amount of money: *I don't have a penny.* [7] **a bad penny.** *Informal, chiefly Brit* an objectionable person or thing (esp in the phrase **turn up like a bad penny**). [8] **a pretty penny.** *Informal* a considerable sum of money. [9] **spend a penny.** *Brit, informal* to urinate. [10] **the penny dropped.** *Informal, chiefly Brit* the explanation of something was finally realized. [11] **two a penny.** plentiful but of little value.
▷HISTORY Old English *penig, pening;* related to Old Saxon *penni(n)g,* Old High German *pfeni(n)c,* German *Pfennig*

penny-a-liner NOUN *Now rare* a hack writer or journalist.

penny arcade NOUN *Chiefly US* a public place with various coin-operated machines for entertainment; amusement arcade.

Penny Black NOUN the first adhesive postage stamp, issued in Britain in 1840; an imperforate stamp bearing the profile of Queen Victoria on a dark background.

pennyboy (ˈpenɪˌbɔɪ) NOUN *Irish, slang* an employee whose duties include menial tasks, such as running errands.

pennycress (ˈpenɪˌkres) NOUN any of several plants of the genus *Thlaspi* of temperate Eurasia and North America, typically having small white or mauve flowers and rounded or heart-shaped leaves: family *Brassicaceae* (crucifers).

penny-dreadful NOUN, *plural* **-fuls.** *Brit, informal* a cheap, often lurid or sensational book or magazine.

penny-farthing NOUN *Brit* an early type of bicycle with a large front wheel and a small rear wheel, the pedals being attached to the front wheel. US name: **ordinary.**
▷HISTORY C20: so called because of the similarity between the relative sizes of the wheels and the relative sizes of the (old) penny and farthing coins

penny-pinching ADJECTIVE *Informal* excessively careful with money.
▸**ˈpenny-ˌpincher** NOUN

pennyroyal (ˌpenɪˈrɔɪəl) NOUN [1] a Eurasian plant, *Mentha pulegium,* with hairy leaves and small mauve flowers, that yields an aromatic oil used in medicine: family *Lamiaceae* (labiates). [2] Also called: **mock pennyroyal.** a similar and related plant, *Hedeoma pulegioides,* of E North America.
▷HISTORY C16: variant of Anglo-Norman *puliol real,* from Old French *pouliol* (from Latin *pūleium* pennyroyal) + *real* ROYAL

penny shares PLURAL NOUN *Stock Exchange* securities with a low market price, esp less than 20p, enabling small investors to purchase a large number for a relatively small outlay.

pennyweight (ˈpenɪˌweɪt) NOUN a unit of weight equal to 24 grains or one twentieth of an ounce (Troy).

penny whistle NOUN a type of flageolet with six finger holes, esp a cheap one made of metal. Also called: **tin whistle.**

penny-wise ADJECTIVE [1] greatly concerned with saving small sums of money. [2] **penny-wise and pound-foolish.** careful about trifles but wasteful in large ventures.

pennywort (ˈpenɪˌwɜːt) NOUN [1] Also called: **navelwort.** a crassulaceous Eurasian rock plant, *Umbilicus rupestris* (or *Cotyledon umbilicus*), with whitish-green tubular flowers and rounded leaves. [2] a marsh plant, *Hydrocotyle vulgaris,* of Europe and North Africa, having circular leaves and greenish-pink flowers: family *Hydrocotylaceae.* [3] a gentianaceous plant, *Obolaria virginica,* of E North America, with fleshy scalelike leaves and small white or purplish flowers. [4] any of various other plants with rounded penny-like leaves.

pennyworth (ˈpenɪˌwɜːθ) NOUN [1] the amount that can be bought for a penny. [2] a small amount: *he hasn't got a pennyworth of sense.*

penology (piːˈnɒlədʒɪ) NOUN 1 the branch of the social sciences concerned with the punishment of crime. 2 the science of prison management. ◆ Also **poenology.**
▷HISTORY C19: from Greek *poinē* punishment
▸**penological** (ˌpiːnəˈlɒdʒɪkᵊl) ADJECTIVE ▸**ˌpenoˈlogically** ADVERB ▸**peˈnologist** NOUN

pen pal NOUN a person with whom one regularly exchanges letters, often a person in another country whom one has not met. Also called: **pen friend.**

penpusher (ˈpɛnˌpʊʃə) NOUN a person who writes a lot, esp a clerk involved with boring paperwork.
▸**ˈpenˌpushing** ADJECTIVE, NOUN

Penrith (pɛnˈrɪθ) NOUN a market town in NW England, in Cumbria. Pop.: 12 049 (1991).

pensel *or* **pensil** (ˈpensᵊl) NOUN variants of **pencel.**

Penshurst Place (ˈpɛnzhɜːst) NOUN a 14th-century mansion near Tunbridge Wells in Kent: birthplace of Sir Philip Sidney; gardens laid out from 1560.

pensile (ˈpɛnsaɪl) ADJECTIVE *Ornithol* designating or building a hanging nest: *pensile birds.*
▷HISTORY C17: from Latin *pensilis* hanging down, from *pendēre* to hang
▸**pensility** (pɛnˈsɪlɪtɪ) *or* **ˈpensileness** NOUN

pension[1] (ˈpɛnʃən) NOUN 1 a regular payment made by the state to people over a certain age to enable them to subsist without having to work. 2 a regular payment made by an employer to former employees after they retire. 3 a regular payment made to a retired person as the result of his or her contributions to a personal pension scheme. 4 any regular payment made on charitable grounds, by way of patronage, or in recognition of merit, service, etc.: *a pension paid to a disabled soldier.* ◆ VERB 5 (*tr*) to grant a pension to.
▷HISTORY C14: via Old French from Latin *pēnsiō* a payment, from *pendere* to pay
▸**ˈpensionable** ADJECTIVE ▸**ˈpensionless** ADJECTIVE

pension[2] *French* (pɑ̃sjɔ̃) NOUN (in France and some other countries) 1 a relatively cheap boarding house. 2 another name for **full board.**
▷HISTORY C17: French; extended meaning of *pension* grant; see PENSION[1]

pensionary (ˈpɛnʃənərɪ) ADJECTIVE 1 constituting a pension. 2 maintained by or receiving a pension. ◆ NOUN, *plural* **-aries.** 3 a person whose service can be bought; hireling.

pensioneer trustee (ˌpɛnʃəˈnɪə) NOUN (in Britain) a person authorized by the Inland Revenue to oversee the management of a pension fund.

pensioner (ˈpɛnʃənə) NOUN 1 a person who is receiving a pension, esp an old-age pension from the state. 2 a person dependent on the pay or bounty of another. 3 *Obsolete Brit* another name for **gentleman-at-arms.**

pension mortgage NOUN an arrangement whereby a person takes out a mortgage and pays the capital repayment instalments into a pension fund and the interest to the mortgagee. The loan is repaid out of the tax-free lump sum proceeds of the pension plan on the borrower's retirement.

pension off VERB (*tr, adverb*) 1 to cause to retire from a post and pay a pension to. 2 to discard, because old and worn: *to pension off submarines.*

pensive (ˈpɛnsɪv) ADJECTIVE 1 deeply or seriously thoughtful, often with a tinge of sadness. 2 expressing or suggesting pensiveness.
▷HISTORY C14: from Old French *pensif,* from *penser* to think, from Latin *pensāre* to consider; compare PENSION[1]
▸**ˈpensively** ADVERB ▸**ˈpensiveness** NOUN

penstemon (pɛnˈstiːmən) NOUN a variant (esp US) of **pentstemon.**

penstock (ˈpɛnˌstɒk) NOUN 1 a conduit that supplies water to a hydroelectric power plant. 2 a channel bringing water from the head gates to a water wheel. 3 a sluice for controlling water flow.
▷HISTORY C17: from PEN[2] + STOCK

pent (pɛnt) VERB a past tense and past participle of **pen**[2].

penta- COMBINING FORM five: *pentagon; pentameter; pentaprism.*
▷HISTORY from Greek *pente* five

pentachlorophenol (ˌpɛntəˌklɔːrəˈfiːnɒl) NOUN a white crystalline water-insoluble compound used as a fungicide, herbicide, and preservative for wood. Formula: C_6Cl_5OH.

pentacle (ˈpɛntəkᵊl) NOUN another name for **pentagram.**
▷HISTORY C16: from Italian *pentacolo* something having five corners; see PENTA-

pentad (ˈpɛntæd) NOUN 1 a group or series of five. 2 the number or sum of five. 3 a period of five years. 4 *Chem* a pentavalent element, atom, or radical. 5 *Meteorol* a period of five days.
▷HISTORY C17: from Greek *pentas* group of five

pentadactyl (ˌpɛntəˈdæktɪl) ADJECTIVE (of the limbs of amphibians, reptiles, birds, and mammals) consisting of an upper arm or thigh, a forearm or shank, and a hand or foot bearing five digits.

pentagon (ˈpɛntəˌgɒn) NOUN a polygon having five sides.
▸**pentagonal** (pɛnˈtægənᵊl) ADJECTIVE

Pentagon (ˈpɛntəˌgɒn) NOUN 1 the five-sided building in Arlington, Virginia, that houses the headquarters of the US Department of Defense. 2 the military leadership of the US.

pentagram (ˈpɛntəˌgræm) NOUN 1 a star-shaped figure formed by extending the sides of a regular pentagon to meet at five points. 2 such a figure used as a magical or symbolic figure by the Pythagoreans, black magicians, etc. ◆ Also called **pentacle, pentangle.**

pentahedron (ˌpɛntəˈhiːdrən) NOUN, *plural* **-drons** *or* **-dra** (-drə). a solid figure having five plane faces. See also **polyhedron.**
▸**ˌpentaˈhedral** ADJECTIVE

pentamerous (pɛnˈtæmərəs) ADJECTIVE consisting of five parts, esp (of flowers) having the petals, sepals, and other parts arranged in groups of five.
▸**penˈtamerˌism** NOUN

pentameter (pɛnˈtæmɪtə) NOUN 1 a verse line consisting of five metrical feet. 2 (in classical prosody) a verse line consisting of two dactyls, one stressed syllable, two dactyls, and a final stressed syllable. ◆ ADJECTIVE 3 designating a verse line consisting of five metrical feet.

pentamidine (pɛnˈtæmɪˌdiːn, -dɪn) NOUN a drug used to treat protozoal infections, esp pneumonia caused by *Pneumocystis carinii* in patients with AIDS.

pentane (ˈpɛnteɪn) NOUN an alkane hydrocarbon having three isomers, esp the isomer with a straight chain of carbon atoms (*n*-pentane) which is a colourless flammable liquid used as a solvent. Formula: C_5H_{12}.

pentangle (ˈpɛnˌtæŋgᵊl) NOUN another name for **pentagram.**

pentangular (pɛnˈtæŋgjʊlə) ADJECTIVE having five angles.

pentanoic acid (ˌpɛntəˈnəʊɪk) NOUN a colourless liquid carboxylic acid with an unpleasant odour, used in making perfumes, flavourings, and pharmaceuticals. Formula: $CH_3(CH_2)_3COOH$. Also called: **valeric acid.**
▷HISTORY from PENTANE

pentaprism (ˈpɛntəˌprɪzəm) NOUN a five-sided prism that deviates light from any direction through an angle of 90°, typically used in single-lens reflex cameras between lens and viewfinder to present the image the right way round.

pentarchy (ˈpɛntɑːkɪ) NOUN, *plural* **-chies.** 1 government by five rulers. 2 a ruling body of five. 3 a union or association of five kingdoms, provinces, etc., each under its own ruler. 4 a country ruled by a body of five.
▸**penˈtarchical** ADJECTIVE

pentastich (ˈpɛntəˌstɪk) NOUN a poem, stanza, or strophe that consists of five lines.

Pentateuch (ˈpɛntəˌtjuːk) NOUN the first five books of the Old Testament regarded as a unity.
▷HISTORY C16: from Church Latin *pentateuchus,* from Greek PENTA- + *teukhos* tool (in Late Greek: scroll)
▸**ˌPentaˈteuchal** ADJECTIVE

pentathlon (pɛnˈtæθlən) NOUN an athletic contest consisting of five different events, based on a competition in the ancient Greek Olympics. Compare **decathlon.**
▷HISTORY C18: from Greek *pentathlon,* from PENTA- + *athlon* contest
▸**penˈtathlete** NOUN

pentatomic (ˌpɛntəˈtɒmɪk) ADJECTIVE *Chem* having five atoms in the molecule.

pentatonic scale (ˌpɛntəˈtɒnɪk) NOUN *Music* any of several scales consisting of five notes, the most commonly encountered one being composed of the first, second, third, fifth, and sixth degrees of the major diatonic scale.

pentavalent (ˌpɛntəˈveɪlənt) ADJECTIVE *Chem* having a valency of five. Also: **quinquevalent.**

pentazocine (pɛnˈtæzəʊˌsiːn) NOUN a powerful synthetic drug used in medical practice as a narcotic analgesic.

Pentecost (ˈpɛntɪˌkɒst) NOUN 1 a Christian festival occurring on Whit Sunday commemorating the descent of the Holy Ghost on the apostles. 2 Also called: **Feast of Weeks, Shavuot.** *Judaism* the harvest festival celebrated fifty days after the second day of Passover on the sixth and seventh days of Sivan, and commemorating the giving the Torah on Mount Sinai.
▷HISTORY Old English, from Church Latin *pentēcostē,* from Greek *pentēkostē* fiftieth

Pentecostal (ˌpɛntɪˈkɒstᵊl) ADJECTIVE 1 (*usually prenominal*) of or relating to any of various Christian groups that emphasize the charismatic aspects of Christianity and adopt a fundamental attitude to the Bible. 2 of or relating to Pentecost or the influence of the Holy Ghost. ◆ NOUN 3 a member of a Pentecostal Church.
▸**ˌPenteˈcostalˌism** NOUN ▸**ˌPenteˈcostalist** NOUN, ADJECTIVE

Pentelikon (pɛnˈtɛlɪkɒn) NOUN a mountain in SE Greece, near Athens: famous for its white marble, worked regularly from the 6th century B.C., from which the chief buildings and sculptures in Athens are made. Height: 1109 m (3638 ft.). Latin name: **Pentelicus.**

pentene (ˈpɛntiːn) NOUN a colourless flammable liquid alkene having several straight-chained isomeric forms, used in the manufacture of organic compounds. Formula: C_5H_{10}. Also called: **amylene.**

Penthesileia *or* **Penthesilea** (ˌpɛnθəsɪˈleɪə) NOUN *Greek myth* the daughter of Ares and queen of the Amazons, whom she led to the aid of Troy. She was slain by Achilles.

Pentheus (ˈpɛnθɪəs) NOUN *Greek myth* the grandson of Cadmus and his successor as king of Thebes, who resisted the introduction of the cult of Dionysus. In revenge the god drove him mad and he was torn to pieces by a group of bacchantes, one of whom was his mother.

penthouse (ˈpɛntˌhaʊs) NOUN 1 a flat or maisonette built onto the top floor or roof of a block of flats. 2 a construction on the roof of a building, esp one used to house machinery. 3 a shed built against a building, esp one that has a sloping roof. 4 *Real Tennis* the roofed corridor that runs along three sides of the court.
▷HISTORY C14 *pentis* (later *penthouse,* by folk etymology), from Old French *apentis,* from Late Latin *appendicium* appendage, from Latin *appendere* to hang from; see APPENDIX

pentimento (ˌpɛntɪˈmɛntəʊ) NOUN, *plural* **-ti** (-tiː). 1 the revealing of a painting or part of a painting that has been covered over by a later painting. 2 the part of a painting thus revealed.
▷HISTORY C20: Italian, literally: correction

pentito *Italian* (penˈtiːto) NOUN, *plural* **-ti** (-tiː). a person involved in organized crime who offers information to the police in return for immunity from prosecution.
▷HISTORY literally: penitent

Pentland Firth (ˈpɛntlənd) NOUN a channel between the mainland of N Scotland and the Orkney Islands: notorious for rough seas. Length: 32 km (20 miles). Width: up to 13 km (8 miles).

pentlandite (ˈpɛntlənˌdaɪt) NOUN a brownish-yellow mineral consisting of an iron and nickel sulphide in cubic crystalline form: the principal ore of nickel. Formula: (Fe,Ni)S.
▷HISTORY C19: from French; named after J. B. *Pentland* (1797–1873), Irish scientist who discovered it

pentobarbital sodium (ˌpɛntəˈbɑːbɪˌtəʊn) NOUN a barbiturate drug used in medicine as a sedative and hypnotic. Formula: $C_{11}H_{17}N_2O_3Na$. US equivalent: **sodium pentabarbital.**

pentode ('pɛntəʊd) NOUN 1 an electronic valve having five electrodes: a cathode, anode, and three grids. 2 (*modifier*) (of a transistor) having three terminals at the base or gate.
▷HISTORY C20: from PENTA- + Greek *hodos* way

pentomic (pɛn'tɒmɪk) ADJECTIVE denoting or relating to the subdivision of an army division into five battle groups, esp for nuclear warfare.
▷HISTORY C20: from PENTA- + ATOMIC

pentosan ('pɛntəˌsæn) NOUN *Biochem* any of a group of polysaccharides, having the general formula $(C_5H_8O_4)_n$: occur in plants, humus, etc.
▷HISTORY C20: from PENTOSE + -AN

pentose ('pɛntəʊs) NOUN any monosaccharide containing five atoms of carbon per molecule: occur mainly in plants and the nucleic acids.
▷HISTORY C20: from PENTA- + -OSE[2]

pentose phosphate pathway NOUN a sequence of metabolic reactions by which NADPH is synthesized, together with ribose phosphate, part of the synthesis of nucleic acids.

Pentothal sodium ('pɛntəˌθæl) NOUN a trademark for **thiopental sodium.**

pentoxide (pɛnt'ɒksaɪd) NOUN an oxide of an element with five atoms of oxygen per molecule.

pentstemon (pɛnt'stiːmən) *or esp US* **penstemon** NOUN any scrophulariaceous plant of the North American genus *Penstemon* (or *Pentstemon*), having white, pink, red, blue, or purple flowers with five stamens, one of which is bearded and sterile.
▷HISTORY C18: New Latin, from PENTA- + Greek *stēmōn* thread (here: stamen)

pent-up ADJECTIVE (**pent up** *when postpositive*) 1 not released; repressed: *pent-up emotions*. 2 kept unwillingly: *I've been pent up in this office for over a year*.

pentyl ('pɛntaɪl, -tɪl) NOUN (*modifier*) of, consisting of, or containing the monovalent group $CH_3CH_2CH_2CH_2CH_2$-: *a pentyl group or radical*.

pentyl acetate NOUN a colourless combustible liquid used as a solvent for paints, in the extraction of penicillin, in photographic film, and as a flavouring. Formula: $CH_3COOC_5H_{11}$. Also called: **amyl acetate.** Nontechnical name: **banana oil.**

pentylenetetrazol (ˌpɛntɪliːn'tɛtrəˌzɒl) NOUN a white crystalline water-soluble substance with a bitter taste, used in medicine to stimulate the central nervous system. Formula: $C_6H_{10}N_4$.
▷HISTORY C20: from *penta-methylene-tetrazole*

penuche (pə'nuːtʃɪ) NOUN a variant of **panocha.**

penuchle *or* **penuckle** ('piːnʌkᵊl) NOUN less common spellings of **pinochle.**

penult ('pɛnʌlt, pɪ'nʌlt) *or* **penultima** (pɪ'nʌltɪmə) NOUN the last syllable but one in a word.
▷HISTORY C16: Latin *paenultima syllaba*, from *paene ultima* almost the last

penultimate (pɪ'nʌltɪmɪt) ADJECTIVE 1 next to the last. ◆ NOUN 2 anything that is next to the last, esp a penult.
▷HISTORY C17: from Latin *paene* almost + ULTIMATE, on the model of Latin *paenultimus*

penumbra (pɪ'nʌmbrə) NOUN, *plural* **-brae** (-briː) *or* **-bras.** 1 a fringe region of half shadow resulting from the partial obstruction of light by an opaque object. 2 *Astronomy* the lighter and outer region of a sunspot. 3 *Painting* the point or area in which light and shade blend. ◆ Compare **umbra.**
▷HISTORY C17: via New Latin from Latin *paene* almost + *umbra* shadow
▸**pe'numbral** *or* **pe'numbrous** ADJECTIVE

penurious (pɪ'njʊərɪəs) ADJECTIVE 1 niggardly with money. 2 lacking money or means. 3 yielding little; scanty.
▸**pe'nuriously** ADVERB ▸**pe'nuriousness** NOUN

penury ('pɛnjʊrɪ) NOUN 1 extreme poverty. 2 extreme scarcity.
▷HISTORY C15: from Latin *pēnūria* dearth, of obscure origin

Penutian (pɪ'njuːtɪən, -ʃən) NOUN 1 a family of North American Indian languages of the Pacific coast. 2 a phylum of languages of North and South America, including Araucanian, Chinook, Mayan, and Sahaptin.

Penza (*Russian* 'pjɛnzə) NOUN a city in W Russia: manufacturing centre. Pop.: 533 300 (1999 est.).

Penzance (pɛn'zæns) NOUN a town in SW England, in SW Cornwall: the westernmost town in England; resort and fishing port. Pop.: 19 709 (1991).

peon[1] ('piːən, 'piːɒn) NOUN 1 a Spanish-American farm labourer or unskilled worker. 2 (formerly in Spanish America) a debtor compelled to work off his debts. 3 any very poor person.
▷HISTORY C19: from Spanish *peón* peasant, from Medieval Latin *pedō* man who goes on foot, from Latin *pēs* foot; compare Old French *paon* PAWN[2]

peon[2] (pjuːn, 'piːən, 'piːɒn) NOUN (in India, Sri Lanka, etc., esp formerly) 1 a messenger or attendant, esp in an office. 2 a native policeman. 3 a foot soldier.
▷HISTORY C17: from Portuguese *peão* orderly; see PEON[1]

peonage ('piːənɪdʒ) *or* **peonism** ('piːəˌnɪzəm) NOUN 1 the state of being a peon. 2 a system in which a debtor must work for his creditor until the debt is paid off.

peony *or* **paeony** ('piːənɪ) NOUN, *plural* **-nies.** 1 any of various ranunculaceous shrubs and plants of the genus *Paeonia*, of Eurasia and North America, having large pink, red, white, or yellow flowers. 2 the flower of any of these plants.
▷HISTORY Old English *peonie*, from Latin *paeōnia*, from Greek *paiōnia*; related to *paiōnios* healing, from *paiōn* physician

people ('piːpᵊl) NOUN (*usually functioning as plural*) 1 persons collectively or in general. 2 a group of persons considered together: *blind people*. 3 (*plural* **peoples**) the persons living in a country and sharing the same nationality: *the French people*. 4 one's family: *he took her home to meet his people*. 5 persons loyal to someone powerful: *the king's people accompanied him in exile*. 6 **the people. a** the mass of persons without special distinction, privileges, etc. **b** the body of persons in a country, esp those entitled to vote. ◆ VERB 7 (*tr*) to provide with or as if with people or inhabitants.
▷HISTORY C13: from Old French *pople*, from Latin *populus*; see POPULACE

> **Language note** See at **person.**

people carrier NOUN another name for **multipurpose vehicle.**

people mover NOUN 1 any of various automated forms of transport for large numbers of passengers over short distances, such as a moving pavement, driverless cars, etc. 2 another name for **multipurpose vehicle.**

people's democracy NOUN (in Communist ideology) a country or form of government in transition from bourgeois democracy to socialism. In this stage there is more than one class, the largest being the proletariat, led by the Communist Party, which is therefore the dominant power.

people's front NOUN a less common term for **popular front.**

people's panel NOUN a group of people composed of members of the public, brought together to discuss, investigate, or decide on a particular matter.

People's Party NOUN *US History* the political party of the Populists.

Peoria (piː'ɔːrɪə) NOUN a port in N central Illinois, on the Illinois River. Pop.: 112 936 (2000).

pep (pɛp) NOUN 1 high spirits, energy, or vitality. ◆ VERB **peps, pepping, pepped.** 2 (*tr*; usually foll by *up*) to liven by imbuing with new vigour.
▷HISTORY C20: short for PEPPER

PEP (pɛp) NOUN ACRONYM FOR: 1 personal equity plan: a method of saving in the UK with certain tax advantages, in which investments up to a fixed annual value can be purchased: replaced by the ISA in 1999 but arrangements for existing PEPs remain unchanged. ◆ ABBREVIATION FOR: 2 political and economic planning.

peperomia (pɛpə'rəʊmɪə) NOUN any plant of the large genus *Peperomia* from tropical and subtropical America with slightly fleshy ornamental leaves, some of which are grown as pot plants: family *Piperaceae*.
▷HISTORY New Latin, from Greek *peperi* pepper + *homoios* similar + -IA

peplos *or* **peplus** ('pɛpləs) NOUN, *plural* **-loses** *or* **-luses.** (in ancient Greece) the top part of a woman's attire, caught at the shoulders and hanging in folds to the waist. Also called: **peplum.**
▷HISTORY C18: from Greek, of obscure origin

peplum ('pɛpləm) NOUN, *plural* **-lums** *or* **-la** (-lə). 1 a flared ruffle attached to the waist of a jacket, bodice, etc. 2 a variant of **peplos.**
▷HISTORY C17: from Latin: full upper garment, from Greek *peplos* shawl

pepo ('piːpəʊ) NOUN, *plural* **-pos.** the fruit of any of various cucurbitaceous plants, such as the melon, squash, cucumber, and pumpkin, having a firm rind, fleshy watery pulp, and numerous seeds.
▷HISTORY C19: from Latin: pumpkin, from Greek *pepōn* edible gourd, from *peptein* to ripen

pepper ('pɛpə) NOUN 1 a woody climbing plant, *Piper nigrum*, of the East Indies, having small black berry-like fruits: family *Piperaceae*. 2 the dried fruit of this plant, which is ground to produce a sharp hot condiment. See also **black pepper, white pepper.** 3 any of various other plants of the genus *Piper*. See **cubeb, betel, kava.** 4 Also called: **capsicum.** any of various tropical plants of the solanaceous genus *Capsicum*, esp *C. frutescens*, the fruits of which are used as a vegetable and a condiment. See also **bird pepper, sweet pepper, red pepper, cayenne pepper.** 5 the fruit of any of these capsicums, which has a mild or pungent taste. 6 the condiment made from the fruits of any of these plants. 7 any of various similar but unrelated plants, such as water pepper. ◆ VERB (*tr*) 8 to season with pepper. 9 to sprinkle liberally; dot: *his prose was peppered with alliteration*. 10 to pelt with small missiles.
▷HISTORY Old English *piper*, from Latin *piper*, from Greek *peperi*; compare French *poivre*, Old Norse *piparr*

pepper-and-salt ADJECTIVE 1 (of cloth) marked with a fine mixture of black and white. 2 (of hair) streaked with grey.

peppercorn ('pɛpəˌkɔːn) NOUN 1 the small dried berry of the pepper plant (*Piper nigrum*). 2 something trifling.

peppercorn rent NOUN a rent that is very low or nominal.

peppered moth NOUN a European geometrid moth, *Biston betularia*, occurring in a pale grey speckled form in rural areas and a black form in industrial regions. See also **melanism** (sense 1).

peppergrass ('pɛpəˌgrɑːs) NOUN the usual US and Canadian name for **pepperwort** (sense 2).

pepper mill NOUN a small hand mill used to grind peppercorns.

peppermint ('pɛpəˌmɪnt) NOUN 1 a temperate mint plant, *Mentha piperita*, with purple or white flowers: cultivated for its downy leaves, which yield a pungent oil. 2 the oil from this plant, which is used as a flavouring. 3 a sweet flavoured with peppermint.

pepperoni (ˌpɛpə'rəʊnɪ) NOUN a highly seasoned dry sausage of pork and beef spiced with pepper, used esp on pizza.
▷HISTORY C20: from Italian *peperoni*, plural of *peperone* cayenne pepper

pepper pot NOUN 1 a small container with perforations in the top for sprinkling pepper. 2 a Caribbean stew of meat, rice, vegetables, etc., highly seasoned with cassareep.

pepper tree NOUN any of several evergreen anacardiaceous trees of the chiefly South American genus *Schinus*, esp *S. molle* (also called: **mastic tree**), having yellowish-white flowers and bright red ornamental fruits.

peppertree ('pɛpəˌtriː) NOUN *NZ* another name for **kawakawa.**

pepperwort ('pɛpəˌwɜːt) NOUN 1 any of various temperate and tropical aquatic or marsh ferns of the genus *Marsilea*, having floating leaves consisting of four leaflets: family *Marsileaceae*. 2 any of several plants of the genus *Lepidium*, esp *L. campestre*, of dry regions of Eurasia, having small white flowers and pungent seeds: family *Brassicaceae* (crucifers). Usual US and Canadian name: **peppergrass.**

peppery ('pɛpərɪ) ADJECTIVE 1 flavoured with or tasting of pepper. 2 quick-tempered; irritable. 3 full of bite and sharpness: *a peppery speech*.
▸'**pepperiness** NOUN

pep pill NOUN *Informal* a tablet containing a stimulant drug.

peppy ('pɛpɪ) ADJECTIVE **-pier, -piest.** *Informal* full of vitality; bouncy or energetic.
▸ **'peppily** ADVERB ▸ **'peppiness** NOUN

pepsin *or* **pepsine** ('pɛpsɪn) NOUN a proteolytic enzyme produced in the stomach in the inactive form pepsinogen, which, when activated by acid, splits proteins into peptones.
▹HISTORY C19: via German from Greek *pepsis*, from *peptein* to digest

pepsinate ('pɛpsɪˌneɪt) VERB (*tr*) [1] to treat (a patient) with pepsin. [2] to mix or infuse (something) with pepsin.

pepsinogen (pɛp'sɪnədʒən) NOUN the inactive precursor of pepsin produced by the stomach.

pep talk NOUN *Informal* an enthusiastic talk designed to increase confidence, production, cooperation, etc.

peptic ('pɛptɪk) ADJECTIVE [1] of, relating to, or promoting digestion. [2] of, relating to, or caused by pepsin or the action of the digestive juices.
▹HISTORY C17: from Greek *peptikos* capable of digesting, from *pepsis* digestion, from *peptein* to digest

peptic ulcer NOUN *Pathol* an ulcer of the mucous membrane lining those parts of the alimentary tract exposed to digestive juices. It can occur in the oesophagus, the stomach, the duodenum, the jejunum, or in parts of the ileum.

peptidase ('pɛptɪˌdeɪs, -ˌdeɪz) NOUN any of a group of proteolytic enzymes that hydrolyse peptides to amino acids.

peptide ('pɛptaɪd) NOUN any of a group of compounds consisting of two or more amino acids linked by chemical bonding between their respective carboxyl and amino groups. See also **peptide bond, polypeptide.**

peptide bond NOUN *Biochem* a chemical amide linkage, –NH–CO–, formed by the condensation of the amino group of one amino acid with the carboxyl group of another.

peptize *or* **peptise** ('pɛptaɪz) VERB (*tr*) *Chem* to disperse (a substance) into a colloidal state, usually to form a sol.
▸ **'peptizable** *or* **'peptisable** ADJECTIVE ▸ **ˌpepti'zation** *or* **ˌpepti'sation** NOUN ▸ **'peptizer** *or* **'peptiser** NOUN

peptone ('pɛptəʊn) NOUN *Biochem* any of a group of compounds that form an intermediary group in the digestion of proteins to amino acids. See also **proteose.**
▹HISTORY C19: from German *Pepton*, from Greek *pepton* something digested, from *peptein* to digest
▸ **peptonic** (pɛp'tɒnɪk) ADJECTIVE

peptonize *or* **peptonise** ('pɛptəˌnaɪz) VERB (*tr*) to hydrolyse (a protein) to peptones by enzymic action, esp by pepsin or pancreatic extract.
▸ **ˌpeptoni'zation** *or* **ˌpeptoni'sation** NOUN ▸ **'peptoˌnizer** *or* **'peptoˌniser** NOUN

Péquiste (peɪ'ki:st) NOUN (*sometimes not capital*) (in Canada) a member or supporter of the Parti Québecois.
▹HISTORY from the French pronunciation of PQ + *-iste*

Pequot ('pi:kwɒt) NOUN [1] (*plural* **-quot** *or* **-quots**) a member of a North American Indian people formerly living in S New England. [2] the language of this people, belonging to the Algonquian family.
▹HISTORY probably based on Narraganset *paquatanog* destroyers

per (pɜ:; *unstressed* pə) DETERMINER [1] for every: *three pence per pound.* ◆ PREPOSITION [2] (esp in some Latin phrases) by; through. [3] **as per.** according to: *as per specifications.* [4] **as per usual.** *Informal* as usual.
▹HISTORY C15: from Latin: by, for each

PER (in Britain) ABBREVIATION FOR Professional Employment Register.

per- PREFIX [1] through: *pervade.* [2] throughout: *perennial.* [3] away, beyond: *perfidy.* [4] completely, throughly: *perplex.* [5] (intensifier): *perfervid.* [6] indicating that a chemical compound contains a high proportion of a specified element: *peroxide; perchloride.* [7] indicating that a chemical element is in a higher than usual state of oxidation: *permanganate; perchlorate.* [8] (*not in technical usage*) a variant of **peroxy-**: *persulphuric acid.*
▹HISTORY from Latin *per* through

Pera ('pɪərə) NOUN the former name of **Beyoğlu.**

peracid (pɜ:r'æsɪd) NOUN [1] an acid, such as perchloric acid, in which the element forming the acid radical exhibits its highest valency. [2] (*not in technical usage*) an acid, such as persulphuric acid, that contains the -OOH group. Recommended names: **peroxo acid, peroxy acid.**
▸ **peracidity** (ˌpɛrə'sɪdɪtɪ) NOUN

peradventure (pərəd'vɛntʃə, ˌpɜ:r-) *Archaic* ◆ ADVERB [1] by chance; perhaps. ◆ NOUN [2] chance, uncertainty, or doubt.
▹HISTORY C13: from Old French *par aventure* by chance

Peraea *or* **Perea** (pə'ri:ə) NOUN a region of ancient Palestine, east of the River Jordan and the Dead Sea.

Perak ('peərə, 'pɪərə, pɪ'ræk) NOUN a state of NW Peninsular Malaysia, on the Strait of Malacca: tin mining. Capital: Ipoh. Pop.: 2 030 382 (2000). Area: 20 680 sq. km (8030 sq. miles).

perambulate (pə'ræmbjʊˌleɪt) VERB [1] to walk about (a place). [2] (*tr*) to walk round in order to inspect.
▹HISTORY C16: from Latin *perambulāre* to traverse, from *per* through + *ambulāre* to walk
▸ **perˌambu'lation** NOUN ▸ **perambulatory** (pə'ræmbjʊlətərɪ, -trɪ) ADJECTIVE

perambulator (pə'ræmbjʊˌleɪtə) NOUN [1] a formal word for **pram**[1]. [2] a wheel-like instrument used by surveyors to measure distances.

per annum (pər 'ænəm) ADVERB every year or by the year.

per ardua ad astra *Latin* (pɜ:r 'ɑ:djʊə æd 'æstrə) through difficulties to the stars: the motto of the RAF.

P/E ratio ABBREVIATION FOR price-earnings ratio.

perborate (pə'bɔ:reɪt) NOUN any of certain salts derived, or apparently derived, from perboric acid. Perborates are used as bleaches in washing powders. See **sodium perborate.**

percale (pə'keɪl, -'kɑ:l) NOUN a close-textured woven cotton fabric, plain or printed, used esp for sheets.
▹HISTORY C17: via French from Persian *pargālah* piece of cloth

percaline ('pɜ:kəˌli:n, -lɪn) NOUN a fine light cotton fabric, used esp for linings.
▹HISTORY C19: from French; see PERCALE

per capita (pə 'kæpɪtə) ADJECTIVE, ADVERB of or for each person.
▹HISTORY Latin, literally: according to heads

perceive (pə'si:v) VERB [1] to become aware of (something) through the senses, esp the sight; recognize or observe. [2] (*tr; may take a clause as object*) to come to comprehend; grasp.
▹HISTORY C13: from Old French *perçoivre*, from Latin *percipere* seize entirely, from PER- (thoroughly) + *capere* to grasp
▸ **per'ceivable** ADJECTIVE ▸ **perˌceiva'bility** NOUN ▸ **per'ceivably** ADVERB ▸ **per'ceiver** NOUN

perceived noise decibel NOUN a unit for measuring perceived levels of noise by comparison with the sound pressure level of a reference sound judged equally noisy by a normal listener. Abbreviation: **PNdB.**

per cent (pə 'sɛnt) ADVERB [1] Also: **per centum.** in or for every hundred. Symbol: %. ◆ NOUN *also* **per'cent.** [2] a percentage or proportion. [3] (*often plural*) securities yielding a rate of interest as specified: *he bought three percents.*
▹HISTORY C16: from Medieval Latin *per centum* out of every hundred

percentage (pə'sɛntɪdʒ) NOUN [1] proportion or rate per hundred parts. [2] *Commerce* the interest, tax, commission, or allowance on a hundred items. [3] any proportion in relation to the whole. [4] *Informal* profit or advantage.

percentile (pə'sɛntaɪl) NOUN one of 99 actual or notional values of a variable dividing its distribution into 100 groups with equal frequencies; the 90th percentile is the value of a variable such that 90% of the relevant population is below that value. Also called: **centile.**

percept ('pɜ:sɛpt) NOUN [1] a concept that depends on recognition by the senses, such as sight, of some external object or phenomenon. [2] an object or phenomenon that is perceived.
▹HISTORY C19: from Latin *perceptum*, from *percipere* to PERCEIVE

perceptible (pə'sɛptəbᵊl) ADJECTIVE able to be perceived; noticeable or recognizable.
▸ **perˌcepti'bility** NOUN ▸ **per'ceptibly** ADVERB

perception (pə'sɛpʃən) NOUN [1] the act or the effect of perceiving. [2] insight or intuition gained by perceiving. [3] the ability or capacity to perceive. [4] way of perceiving; awareness or consciousness; view: *advertising affects the customer's perception of a product.* [5] the process by which an organism detects and interprets information from the external world by means of the sensory receptors. [6] *Law* the collection, receipt, or taking into possession of rents, crops, etc.
▹HISTORY C15: from Latin *perceptiō* comprehension; see PERCEIVE
▸ **per'ceptional** ADJECTIVE

perceptive (pə'sɛptɪv) ADJECTIVE [1] quick at perceiving; observant. [2] perceptual. [3] able to perceive.
▸ **per'ceptively** ADVERB ▸ **per'ceptiveness** *or* **ˌpercep'tivity** NOUN

perceptual (pə'sɛptjʊəl) ADJECTIVE of or relating to perception.
▸ **per'ceptually** ADVERB

perceptual defence NOUN *Psychol* the process by which it is thought that certain stimuli are either not perceived or are distorted due to their offensive, unpleasant, or threatening nature.

perceptual mapping NOUN *Marketing* the use of a graph or map in the development of a new product, in which the proximity of consumers' images of the new product to those of an ideal product provide an indication of the new product's likely success.

perch[1] (pɜ:tʃ) NOUN [1] a pole, branch, or other resting place above ground on which a bird roosts or alights. [2] a similar resting place for a person or thing. [3] another name for **rod** (sense 7). [4] a solid measure for stone, usually taken as 198 inches by 18 inches by 12 inches. [5] a pole joining the front and rear axles of a carriage. [6] a frame on which cloth is placed for inspection. [7] *Obsolete or dialect* a pole. ◆ VERB [8] (usually foll by *on*) to alight, rest, or cause to rest on or as if on a perch: *the bird perched on the branch; the cap was perched on his head.* [9] (*tr*) to inspect (cloth) on a perch.
▹HISTORY C13 *perche* stake, from Old French, from Latin *pertica* long staff
▸ **'percher** NOUN

perch[2] (pɜ:tʃ) NOUN, *plural* **perch** *or* **perches.** [1] any freshwater spiny-finned teleost fish of the family *Percidae, esp those of the genus Perca,* such as *P. fluviatilis* of Europe and *P. flavescens* (**yellow perch**) of North America: valued as food and game fishes. [2] any of various similar or related fishes. Related adjective: **percoid.**
▹HISTORY C13: from Old French *perche*, from Latin *perca*, from Greek *perkē*; compare Greek *perkos* spotted

perchance (pə'tʃɑ:ns) ADVERB *Archaic or poetic* [1] perhaps; possibly. [2] by chance; accidentally.
▹HISTORY C14: from Anglo-French *par chance*; see PER, CHANCE

Percheron ('pɜ:ʃəˌrɒn) NOUN a compact heavy breed of carthorse, grey or black in colour.
▹HISTORY C19: from French, from *le Perche*, region of NW France where the breed originated

perchery ('pɜ:tʃərɪ) NOUN, *plural* **-eries.** **a** a barn in which hens are allowed to move without restriction. **b** (*as modifier*): *perchery eggs.*
▹HISTORY C20: from PERCH[1]

perchlorate (pə'klɔ:reɪt) NOUN any salt or ester of perchloric acid. Perchlorate salts contain the ion ClO_4^-.

perchloric acid (pə'klɔ:rɪk) NOUN a colourless syrupy oxyacid of chlorine containing a greater proportion of oxygen than chloric acid. It is a powerful oxidizing agent and is used as a laboratory reagent. Formula: $HClO_4$. Systematic name: **chloric(VII) acid.**

perchloride (pə'klɔ:raɪd) NOUN a chloride that contains more chlorine than other chlorides of the same element.

perchloroethylene (pəˌklɔ:rəʊ'ɛθɪli:n) *or* **perchloroethene** (pəˌklɔ:rəʊ'ɛθi:n) NOUN a colourless liquid used as a dry-cleaning solvent. Formula: CCl_2:CCl_2.

percipient (pəˈsɪpɪənt) ADJECTIVE [1] able to perceive. [2] perceptive. ♦ NOUN [3] a person or thing that perceives.
▷HISTORY C17: from Latin *percipiens* observing, from *percipere* to grasp; see PERCEIVE
▸**perˈcipience** NOUN ▸**perˈcipiently** ADVERB

Percival *or* **Perceval** (ˈpɜːsɪvᵊl) NOUN (in Arthurian legend) a knight in King Arthur's court. German equivalent: **Parzival.**

percoid (ˈpɜːkɔɪd) *or* **percoidean** (pəˈkɔɪdɪən) ADJECTIVE [1] of, relating to, or belonging to the *Percoidea,* a suborder of spiny-finned teleost fishes including the perches, sea bass, red mullet, cichlids, etc. [2] of, relating to, or resembling a perch. ♦ NOUN [3] any fish belonging to the suborder *Percoidea.*
▷HISTORY C19: from Latin *perca* PERCH² + -OID

percolate VERB (ˈpɜːkəˌleɪt) [1] to cause (a liquid) to pass through a fine mesh, porous substance, etc., or (of a liquid) to pass through a fine mesh, porous substance, etc.; trickle: *rain percolated through the roof.* [2] to permeate; penetrate gradually: *water percolated the road.* [3] (*intr*) *US, informal* to become active or lively: *she percolated with happiness.* [4] to make (coffee) or (of coffee) to be made in a percolator. ♦ NOUN (ˈpɜːkəlɪt, -ˌleɪt) [5] a product of percolation.
▷HISTORY C17: from Latin *percolāre,* from PER + *cōlāre* to strain, from *cōlum* a strainer; see COLANDER
▸**percolable** (ˈpɜːkələbᵊl) ADJECTIVE ▸**ˌpercoˈlation** NOUN ▸**ˈpercolative** ADJECTIVE

percolator (ˈpɜːkəˌleɪtə) NOUN a kind of coffeepot in which boiling water is forced up through a tube and filters down through the coffee grounds into a container.

per contra (ˈpɜː ˈkɒntrə) ADVERB on the contrary.
▷HISTORY from Latin

percuss (pəˈkʌs) VERB (*tr*) [1] to strike sharply, rapidly, or suddenly. [2] *Med* to tap on (a body surface) with the fingertips or a special hammer to aid diagnosis or for therapeutic purposes.
▷HISTORY C16: from Latin *percutere,* from *per-* through + *quatere* to shake
▸**perˈcussor** NOUN

percussion (pəˈkʌʃən) NOUN [1] the act, an instance, or an effect of percussing. [2] *Music* the family of instruments in which sound arises from the striking of materials with sticks, hammers, or the hands. [3] *Music* **a** instruments of this family constituting a section of an orchestra, band, etc. **b** (*as modifier*): *a percussion ensemble.* [4] *Med* the act of percussing a body surface. [5] the act of exploding a percussion cap.
▷HISTORY C16: from Latin *percussiō,* from *percutere* to hit; see PERCUSS

percussion cap NOUN a detonator consisting of a paper or thin metal cap containing material that explodes when struck and formerly used in certain firearms.

percussion instrument NOUN any of various musical instruments that produce a sound when their resonating surfaces are struck directly, as with a stick or mallet, or by leverage action. They may be of definite pitch (as a kettledrum or xylophone), indefinite pitch (as a gong or rattle), or a mixture of both (as various drums).

percussionist (pəˈkʌʃənɪst) NOUN *Music* a person who plays any of several percussion instruments, esp in an orchestra.

percussion lock NOUN a gunlock in which the hammer strikes a percussion cap.

percussion tool NOUN a power driven tool which operates by striking rapid blows: the power may be electricity or compressed air.

percussive (pəˈkʌsɪv) ADJECTIVE of, caused by, or relating to percussion.
▸**perˈcussively** ADVERB ▸**perˈcussiveness** NOUN

percutaneous (ˌpɜːkjuˈteɪnɪəs) ADJECTIVE *Med* effected through the skin, as in the absorption of an ointment.

Perdido (*Spanish* perˈðiðo) NOUN **Monte** (ˈmɔnte). a mountain in NE Spain, in the central Pyrenees. Height: 3352 m (10 997 ft.). French name: (Mont) **Perdu.**

per diem (ˈpɜː ˈdaɪɛm, ˈdiːɛm) ADVERB [1] every day or by the day. ♦ NOUN [2] **a** an allowance for daily expenses, usually those incurred while working. **b** (*as modifier*): *a per-diem allowance.*
▷HISTORY from Latin

perdition (pəˈdɪʃən) NOUN [1] *Christianity* **a** final and irrevocable spiritual ruin. **b** this state as one that the wicked are said to be destined to endure for ever. [2] another word for **hell.** [3] *Archaic* utter disaster, ruin, or destruction.
▷HISTORY C14: from Late Latin *perditiō* ruin, from Latin *perdere* to lose, from PER- (away) + *dāre* to give

perdu *or* **perdue** (ˈpɜːdjuː) ADJECTIVE [1] *Obsolete* (of a soldier) placed on hazardous sentry duty. [2] *Obsolete* (of a soldier) placed in a hazardous ambush. [3] (of a person or thing) hidden or concealed. ♦ NOUN [4] *Obsolete* a soldier placed on hazardous sentry duty. [5] *Obsolete* a soldier placed in a hazardous ambush.
▷HISTORY C16: via French: lost, from *perdre* to lose, from Latin *perdere* to destroy

Perdu (pɛrdy) NOUN **Mont.** the French name for (Monte) **Perdido.**

perdurable (pəˈdjuərəbᵊl) ADJECTIVE *Rare* extremely durable.
▷HISTORY C13: from Late Latin *perdūrābilis,* from Latin *per-* (intensive) + *dūrābilis* long-lasting, from *dūrus* hard
▸**ˌperduraˈbility** NOUN ▸**ˈperdurably** ADVERB

père *French* (pɛr; *English* pɛə) NOUN an addition to a French surname to specify the father rather than the son of the same name: *Dumas père.* Compare ***fils***¹.

Perea (pəˈriːə) NOUN a variant spelling of **Peraea.**

Père David's deer NOUN a large grey deer, *Elaphurus davidianus,* surviving only in captivity as descendants of a herd preserved in the Imperial hunting park near Beijing.
▷HISTORY C20: named after Father A. *David* (died 1900), French missionary

peregrinate (ˈpɛrɪgrɪˌneɪt) VERB [1] (*intr*) to travel or wander about from place to place; voyage. [2] (*tr*) to travel through (a place). ♦ ADJECTIVE [3] an obsolete word for **foreign.**
▷HISTORY C16: from Latin, from *peregrīnārī* to travel; see PEREGRINE
▸**ˈperegriˌnator** NOUN

peregrination (ˌpɛrɪgrɪˈneɪʃən) NOUN [1] a voyage, esp an extensive one. [2] the act or process of travelling.

peregrine (ˈpɛrɪgrɪn) ADJECTIVE *Archaic* [1] coming from abroad. [2] travelling or migratory; wandering.
▷HISTORY C14: from Latin *peregrīnus* foreign, from *pereger* being abroad, from *per* through + *ager* land (that is, beyond one's own land)

peregrine falcon NOUN a falcon, *Falco peregrinus,* occurring in most parts of the world, having a dark plumage on the back and wings and lighter underparts. See also **duck hawk.**

Pereira (*Spanish* peˈreira) NOUN a town in W central Colombia: cattle trading and coffee processing. Pop.: 381 275 (1999 est.).

pereira bark (pəˈrɛərə) NOUN the bark of a South American apocynaceous tree, *Geissospermum vellosii:* source of a substance formerly used for treating malaria.
▷HISTORY named after Jonathan *Pereira* (1804–53), English pharmacologist

peremptory (pəˈrɛmptərɪ) ADJECTIVE [1] urgent or commanding: *a peremptory ring on the bell.* [2] not able to be remitted or debated; decisive. [3] positive or assured in speech, manner, etc.; dogmatic. [4] *Law* **a** admitting of no denial or contradiction; precluding debate. **b** obligatory rather than permissive.
▷HISTORY C16: from Anglo-Norman *peremptorie,* from Latin *peremptōrius* decisive, from *perimere* to take away completely, from PER- (intensive) + *emere* to take
▸**perˈemptorily** ADVERB ▸**perˈemptoriness** NOUN

Perendale (ˈpɛrənˌdeɪl) NOUN *NZ* a Romney-Cheviot crossbreed of sheep.
▷HISTORY C20: named after Sir Geoffrey S. *Peren,* New Zealand agriculturist

perennate (ˈpɛrɪˌneɪt, pəˈrɛneɪt) VERB (*intr*) (of plants) to live from one growing season to another, usually with a period of reduced activity between seasons.
▷HISTORY C17: from Latin *perennātus,* from *perennāre,* from PER- (through) + *annus* year

perennial (pəˈrɛnɪəl) ADJECTIVE [1] lasting throughout the year or through many years. [2] everlasting; perpetual. ♦ NOUN [3] a woody or herbaceous plant that can continue its growth for at least two years. Compare **annual** (sense 3), **biennial** (sense 3).
▷HISTORY C17: from Latin *perennis* continual, from *per* through + *annus* year
▸**perˈennially** ADVERB

perentie *or* **perenty** (pəˈrɛntɪ) NOUN, *plural* **-ties.** a large dark-coloured monitor lizard, *Varanus giganteus,* of central and west Australia which grows to 7 ft.
▷HISTORY from a native Australian language

perestroika (ˌpɛrəˈstrɔɪkə) NOUN the policy of reconstructing the economy, etc., of the former Soviet Union under the leadership of Mikhail Gorbachov.
▷HISTORY C20: Russian, literally: reconstruction

perf. ABBREVIATION FOR: [1] perfect. [2] perforated. [3] perforation.

perfect ADJECTIVE (ˈpɜːfɪkt) [1] having all essential elements. [2] unblemished; faultless: *a perfect gemstone.* [3] correct or precise: *perfect timing.* [4] utter or absolute: *a perfect stranger.* [5] excellent in all respects: *a perfect day.* [6] *Maths* exactly divisible into equal integral or polynomial roots: *36 is a perfect square.* [7] *Botany* **a** (of flowers) having functional stamens and pistils. **b** (of plants) having all parts present. [8] *Grammar* denoting a tense of verbs used in describing an action that has been completed by the subject. In English this is a compound tense, formed with *have* or *has* plus the past participle. [9] *Music* **a** of or relating to the intervals of the unison, fourth, fifth, and octave. **b** (of a cadence) ending on the tonic chord, giving a feeling of conclusion. Also: **full, final.** Compare **imperfect** (sense 6). [10] *Archaic* positive certain, or assured. ♦ NOUN (ˈpɜːfɪkt) [11] *Grammar* **a** the perfect tense. **b** a verb in this tense. ♦ VERB (pəˈfɛkt) (*tr*) [12] to make perfect; improve to one's satisfaction: *he is in Paris to perfect his French.* [13] to make fully accomplished. [14] *Printing* to print the reverse side of (a printed sheet of paper).
▷HISTORY C13: from Latin *perfectus,* from *perficere* to perform, from *per* through + *facere* to do
▸**ˈperfectness** NOUN

> **Language note** For most of its meanings, the adjective *perfect* describes an absolute state, i.e. one that cannot be qualified; thus something is either *perfect* or *not perfect,* and cannot be *more perfect* or *less perfect.* However when *perfect* means excellent in all respects, a comparative can be used with it without absurdity: *the next day the weather was even more perfect.*

perfect binding NOUN See **adhesive binding.**

perfect competition NOUN *Economics* a market situation in which there exists a homogeneous product, freedom of entry, and a large number of buyers and sellers none of whom individually can affect price.

perfect game NOUN [1] *Baseball* a game in which no batter on the opposing team reaches first base. [2] *Tenpin bowling* a game in which a bowler scores twelve consecutive strikes.

perfect gas NOUN another name for **ideal gas.**

perfectible (pəˈfɛktəbᵊl) ADJECTIVE capable of becoming or being made perfect.
▸**perˌfectiˈbility** NOUN

perfection (pəˈfɛkʃən) NOUN [1] the act of perfecting or the state or quality of being perfect. [2] the highest degree of a quality, etc.: *the perfection of faithfulness.* [3] an embodiment of perfection.
▷HISTORY C13: from Latin *perfectiō* a completing, from *perficere* to finish

perfectionism (pəˈfɛkʃəˌnɪzəm) NOUN [1] *Philosophy* the doctrine that man can attain perfection in this life. [2] the demand for the highest standard of excellence.

perfectionist (pəˈfɛkʃənɪst) NOUN [1] a person who strives for or demands the highest standards of excellence in work, etc. [2] a person who believes the doctrine of perfectionism. ◆ ADJECTIVE 3 of or relating to perfectionism.

perfective (pəˈfɛktɪv) ADJECTIVE 1 tending to perfect. 2 *Grammar* denoting an aspect of verbs in some languages, including English, used to express that the action or event described by the verb is or was completed: *I lived in London for ten years* is perfective; *I have lived in London for ten years* is imperfective, since the implication is that I still live in London.

perfectly (ˈpɜːfɪktlɪ) ADVERB 1 completely, utterly, or absolutely. 2 in a perfect way; extremely well.

perfect number NOUN an integer, such as 28, that is equal to the sum of all its possible factors, excluding itself.

perfecto (pəˈfɛktəʊ) NOUN, *plural* **-tos**. a large cigar that is tapered from both ends.
▷HISTORY Spanish, literally: perfect

perfector *or* **perfecter** (ˈpɜːfɪktə) NOUN 1 a person who completes or makes something perfect. 2 *Printing* a machine or press capable of printing both sides of the paper in a single operation.

perfect participle NOUN another name for **past participle**.

perfect pitch NOUN another name (not in technical usage) for **absolute pitch** (sense 1).

perfect rhyme NOUN 1 Also called: **full rhyme**. rhyme between words in which the stressed vowels and any succeeding consonants are identical although the consonants preceding the stressed vowels may be different, as between *part/hart* or *believe/conceive*. 2 a rhyme between two words that are pronounced the same although differing in meaning, as in *bough/bow*.

perfervid (pɜːˈfɜːvɪd) ADJECTIVE *Literary* extremely ardent, enthusiastic, or zealous.
▷HISTORY C19: from New Latin *perfervidus,* from Latin *per-* (intensive) + *fervidus* FERVID
▸**perˈfervidly** ADVERB ▸**perˈfervidness** NOUN

perfidious (pəˈfɪdɪəs) ADJECTIVE guilty, treacherous, or faithless; deceitful.
▸**perˈfidiously** ADVERB ▸**perˈfidiousness** NOUN

perfidy (ˈpɜːfɪdɪ) NOUN, *plural* **-dies**. a perfidious act.
▷HISTORY C16: from Latin *perfidia,* from *perfidus* faithless, from *per* beyond + *fidēs* faith

perfin (ˈpɜːfɪn) NOUN *Philately* the former name for **spif**.
▷HISTORY from *perf(orated with) in(itials)*

perfing (ˈpɜːfɪŋ) NOUN *NZ* the practice of taking early retirement, with financial compensation, from the police force.
▷HISTORY from *P(olice) E(arly) R(etirement) F(und)*

perfoliate (pəˈfəʊlɪɪt, -ˌeɪt) ADJECTIVE (of a leaf) having a base that completely encloses the stem, so that the stem appears to pass through it.
▷HISTORY C17: from New Latin *perfoliātus,* from Latin *per-* through + *folium* leaf
▸**perˌfoliˈation** NOUN

perforate VERB (ˈpɜːfəˌreɪt) 1 to make a hole or holes in (something); penetrate. 2 (*tr*) to punch rows of holes between (stamps, coupons, etc.) for ease of separation. ◆ ADJECTIVE (ˈpɜːfərɪt) 3 *Biology* **a** pierced by small holes: *perforate shells*. **b** marked with small transparent spots. 4 *Philately* another word for **perforated** (sense 2).
▷HISTORY C16: from Latin *perforāre,* from *per-* through + *forāre* to pierce
▸**perforable** (ˈpɜːfərəbᵊl) ADJECTIVE ▸ˈ**perforative** *or* ˈ**perforatory** ADJECTIVE ▸ˈ**perfoˌrator** NOUN

perforated (ˈpɜːfəˌreɪtɪd) ADJECTIVE 1 pierced with one or more holes. 2 (esp of stamps) having perforations. Abbreviation: **perf**.

perforated tape NOUN a US name for **paper tape**.

perforation (ˌpɜːfəˈreɪʃən) NOUN 1 the act of perforating or the state of being perforated. 2 a hole or holes made in something. 3 **a** a method of making individual stamps, coupons, etc., easily separable by punching holes along their margins. **b** the holes punched in this way. Abbreviation: **perf**.

perforation gauge NOUN a graduated scale for measuring perforations and roulettes of postage stamps.

perforce (pəˈfɔːs) ADVERB by necessity; unavoidably.
▷HISTORY C14: from Old French *par force;* see PER, FORCE[1]

perform (pəˈfɔːm) VERB 1 to carry out or do (an action). 2 (*tr*) to fulfil or comply with: *to perform someone's request*. 3 to present or enact (a play, concert, etc.) before or otherwise entertain an audience: *the group performed Hamlet*. 4 (*intr*) *Informal* to accomplish sexual intercourse: *he performed well*.
▷HISTORY C14: from Anglo-Norman *perfourmer* (influenced by *forme* FORM), from Old French *parfournir,* from *par-* PER- + *fournir* to provide; see FURNISH
▸**perˈformable** ADJECTIVE ▸**perˈformer** NOUN

performance (pəˈfɔːməns) NOUN 1 the act, process, or art of performing. 2 an artistic or dramatic production: *last night's performance was terrible*. 3 manner or quality of functioning: *a machine's performance*. 4 *Informal* mode of conduct or behaviour, esp when distasteful or irregular: *what did you mean by that performance at the restaurant?* 5 *Informal* any tiresome procedure: *what a performance dressing the children to play in the snow!* 6 any accomplishment. 7 *Linguistics* (in transformational grammar) the form of the human language faculty, viewed as concretely embodied in speakers. Compare **competence** (sense 5), **langue, parole** (sense 5).

performance appraisal NOUN the assessment, at regular intervals, of an employee's performance at work.

performance art NOUN a theatrical presentation that incorporates various art forms, such as dance, sculpture, music, etc.

performance bond NOUN a bond given by a bank to a third party guaranteeing that if a specified customer fails to fulfil all the terms of a specified contract, the bank will be responsible for any loss sustained by the third party.

performance indicator NOUN a quantitative or qualitative measurement, or any other criterion, by which the performance, efficiency, achievement, etc. of a person or organization can be assessed, often by comparison with an agreed standard or target.

performance test NOUN *Psychol* a test designed to assess a person's manual ability.

performative (pəˈfɔːmətɪv) ADJECTIVE *Linguistics, philosophy* 1 **a** denoting an utterance that constitutes some act, esp the act described by the verb. For example, *I confess that I was there* is itself a confession, and so is performative in the narrower sense, while *I'd like you to meet …* (effecting an introduction) is performative only in the looser sense. See also **locutionary act, illocution, perlocution**. **b** (*as noun*): *that sentence is a performative*. 2 **a** denoting a verb that may be used as the main verb in such an utterance. **b** (*as noun*): *"promise" is a performative*.
▸**perˈformatively** ADVERB

performing (pəˈfɔːmɪŋ) ADJECTIVE (of an animal) trained to perform tricks before an audience, as in a circus.

performing arts PLURAL NOUN the arts that are primarily performed before an audience, such as dance and drama.

perfume NOUN (ˈpɜːfjuːm) 1 a mixture of alcohol and fragrant essential oils extracted from flowers, spices, etc., or made synthetically, used esp to impart a pleasant long-lasting scent to the body, stationery, etc. See also **cologne, toilet water**. 2 a scent or odour, esp a fragrant one. ◆ VERB (pəˈfjuːm) 3 (*tr*) to impart a perfume to.
▷HISTORY C16: from French *parfum,* probably from Old Provençal *perfum,* from *perfumar* to make scented, from *per* through (from Latin) + *fumar* to smoke, from Latin *fūmāre* to smoke

perfumer (pəˈfjuːmə) *or* **perfumier** (pəˈfjuːmjeɪ) NOUN a person who makes or sells perfume.

perfumery (pəˈfjuːmərɪ) NOUN, *plural* **-eries**. 1 a place where perfumes are sold. 2 a factory where perfumes are made. 3 the process of making perfumes. 4 perfumes in general.

perfunctory (pəˈfʌŋktərɪ) ADJECTIVE 1 done superficially, only as a matter of routine; careless or cursory. 2 dull or indifferent.
▷HISTORY C16: from Late Latin *perfunctōrius* negligent, from *perfunctus* dispatched, from *perfungī* to fulfil; see FUNCTION
▸**perˈfunctorily** ADVERB ▸**perˈfunctoriness** NOUN

perfuse (pəˈfjuːz) VERB (*tr*) 1 to suffuse or permeate (a liquid, colour, etc.) through or over (something). 2 *Surgery* to pass (a fluid) through organ tissue to ensure adequate exchange of oxygen and carbon monoxide.
▷HISTORY C16: from Latin *perfūsus* wetted, from *perfundere* to pour over, from PER- + *fundere* to pour
▸**perˈfusion** NOUN ▸**perˈfusionist** NOUN ▸**perˈfusive** ADJECTIVE ▸**perˈfused** ADJECTIVE

Pergamum (ˈpɜːgəməm) NOUN an ancient city in NW Asia Minor, in Mysia: capital of a major Hellenistic monarchy of the same name that later became a Roman province.

pergola (ˈpɜːgələ) NOUN a horizontal trellis or framework, supported on posts, that carries climbing plants and may form a covered walk.
▷HISTORY C17: via Italian from Latin *pergula* projection from a roof, from *pergere* to go forward

perhaps (pəˈhæps; *informal* præps) ADVERB 1 **a** possibly; maybe. **b** (*as sentence modifier*): *he'll arrive tomorrow, perhaps; perhaps you'll see him tomorrow*. ◆ SENTENCE SUBSTITUTE 2 it may happen, be so, etc.; maybe.
▷HISTORY C16 *perhappes,* from *per* by + *happes* chance, HAP[1]

peri (ˈpɪərɪ) NOUN, *plural* **-ris**. 1 (in Persian folklore) one of a race of beautiful supernatural beings. 2 any beautiful fairy-like creature.
▷HISTORY C18: from Persian: fairy, from Avestan *pairikā* witch

peri- PREFIX 1 enclosing, encircling, or around: *pericardium; pericarp; perigon*. 2 near or adjacent: *perihelion*.
▷HISTORY from Greek *peri* around, near, about

perianth (ˈpɛrɪˌænθ) NOUN the outer part of a flower, consisting of the calyx and corolla.
▷HISTORY C18: from French *périanthe,* from New Latin, from PERI- + Greek *anthos* flower

periapt (ˈpɛrɪˌæpt) NOUN *Rare* a charm or amulet.
▷HISTORY C16: via French from Greek *periapton,* from PERI- + *haptos* clasped, from *haptein* to fasten

periastron (ˌpɛrɪˈæstrɒn) NOUN *Astronomy* the point in the orbit of a body around a star when it is nearest to the star, esp applied to double-star systems.

periblem (ˈpɛrɪˌblɛm) NOUN *Botany* a layer of meristematic tissue in stems and roots that gives rise to the cortex.
▷HISTORY C19: via German from Greek *periblēma* protection, from *periballein* to throw around, from PERI- + *ballein* to throw

pericarditis (ˌpɛrɪkɑːˈdaɪtɪs) NOUN inflammation of the pericardium.
▸**pericarditic** (ˌpɛrɪkɑːˈdɪtɪk) ADJECTIVE

pericardium (ˌpɛrɪˈkɑːdɪəm) NOUN, *plural* **-dia** (-dɪə). the membranous sac enclosing the heart.
▷HISTORY C16: via New Latin from Greek *perikardion,* from PERI- + *kardia* heart
▸ˌ**periˈcardial** *or* ˌ**periˈcardiˌac** ADJECTIVE

pericarp (ˈpɛrɪˌkɑːp) NOUN 1 the part of a fruit enclosing the seeds that develops from the wall of the ovary. 2 a layer of tissue around the reproductive bodies of some algae and fungi.
▷HISTORY C18: via French from New Latin *pericarpium*
▸ˌ**periˈcarpial** *or* ˌ**periˈcarpic** ADJECTIVE

pericentre *or US* **pericenter** (ˈpɛrɪˌsɛntə) NOUN the point in an elliptical orbit that is nearest to the centre of mass of the system.

perichaetial (ˌpɛrɪˈkiːtɪəl) ADJECTIVE denoting the leaves in mosses that surround the archegonia and, later, the base of the sporophyte.

perichondrium (ˌpɛrɪˈkɒndrɪəm) NOUN, *plural* **-dria** (-drɪə). the white fibrous membrane that covers the surface of cartilage.
▷HISTORY C18: New Latin, from PERI- + Greek *chondros* cartilage
▸ˌ**periˈchondrial** ADJECTIVE

periclase (ˈpɛrɪˌkleɪs) NOUN a mineral consisting of magnesium oxide in the form of isometric crystals or grains: occurs in metamorphosed limestone.
▷HISTORY C19: from New Latin *periclasia,* from

Greek *peri* very + *klasis* a breaking, referring to its perfect cleavage
▸**periclastic** (ˌperɪˈklæstɪk) ADJECTIVE

Periclean (ˌperɪˈkliːən) ADJECTIVE of or relating to Pericles (?495–429 B.C.), the Athenian statesman, or to the period when Athens was the intellectual and artistic leader of the Greek city-states.

periclinal (ˌperɪˈklaɪnᵊl) ADJECTIVE 1 of or relating to a pericline. 2 *Botany* **a** denoting or relating to cell walls that are parallel to the surface of a plant part, such as a meristem. **b** (of chimeras) having one component completely enclosed by the other component.

pericline (ˈperɪˌklaɪn) NOUN 1 a white translucent variety of albite in the form of elongated crystals. 2 Also called: **dome.** a dome-shaped formation of stratified rock with its slopes following the direction of folding.
▹HISTORY C19: from Greek *periklinēs* sloping on all sides, from PERI- + *klinein* to lean

pericope (pəˈrɪkəpɪ) NOUN a selection from a book, esp a passage from the Bible read at religious services.
▹HISTORY C17: via Late Latin from Greek *perikopē* piece cut out, from PERI- + *kopē* a cutting
▸**pericopic** (ˌperɪˈkɒpɪk) ADJECTIVE

pericranium (ˌperɪˈkreɪnɪəm) NOUN, *plural* **-nia** (-nɪə). the fibrous membrane covering the external surface of the skull.
▹HISTORY C16: New Latin, from Greek *perikranion*
▸ˌ**periˈcranial** ADJECTIVE

pericycle (ˈperɪˌsaɪkᵊl) NOUN a layer of plant tissue beneath the endodermis: surrounds the conducting tissue in roots and certain stems.
▹HISTORY C19: from Greek *perikuklos*
▸**pericyclic** (ˌperɪˈsaɪklɪk, -ˈsɪk-) ADJECTIVE

pericynthion (ˌperɪˈsɪnθɪən) NOUN the point at which a spacecraft launched from earth into a lunar orbit is nearest the moon. Compare **perilune, apocynthion.**
▹HISTORY C20: from PERI- + *-cynthion,* from CYNTHIA

periderm (ˈperɪˌdɜːm) NOUN the outer corky protective layer of woody stems and roots, consisting of cork cambium, phelloderm and cork.
▹HISTORY C19: from New Latin *peridermis*
▸ˌ**periˈdermal** *or* ˌ**periˈdermic** ADJECTIVE

peridium (pəˈrɪdɪəm) NOUN, *plural* **-ridia** (-ˈrɪdɪə). the distinct outer layer of the spore-bearing organ in many fungi.
▹HISTORY C19: from Greek *pēridion* a little wallet, from *pēra* leather bag, of obscure origin

peridot (ˈperɪˌdɒt) NOUN a pale green transparent variety of the olivine chrysolite, used as a gemstone.
▹HISTORY C14: from Old French *peritot,* of unknown origin

peridotite (ˌperɪˈdəʊtaɪt) NOUN a dark coarse-grained ultrabasic plutonic igneous rock consisting principally of olivine.
▹HISTORY C19: from French, from PERIDOT
▸**peridotitic** (ˌperɪdəʊˈtɪtɪk) ADJECTIVE

perigee (ˈperɪˌdʒiː) NOUN the point in its orbit around the earth when the moon or an artificial satellite is nearest the earth. Compare **apogee** (sense 1).
▹HISTORY C16: via French from Greek *perigeion,* from PERI- + *gea* earth
▸ˌ**periˈgean** *or* ˌ**periˈgeal** ADJECTIVE

periglacial (ˌperɪˈgleɪʃəl) ADJECTIVE relating to a region bordering a glacier: *periglacial climate.*

perigon (ˈperɪgən) NOUN an angle of 360°. Also called: **round angle.**
▹HISTORY C19: from PERI- + Greek *gonia* angle

Perigordian (ˌperɪˈgɔːdɪən) ADJECTIVE 1 of, relating to, or characteristic of an Upper Palaeolithic culture in Europe, esp in France. ◆ NOUN 2 **the.** the Perigordian culture.
▹HISTORY C20: after *Périgord,* district in France

Périgueux (ˌperɪˈgɜː; *French* perigø) NOUN a town in SW France, capital of the Dordogne: noted for its Roman remains, medieval cathedral, and pâté de foie gras. Pop.: 32 850 (1990).

perigynous (pəˈrɪdʒɪnəs) ADJECTIVE 1 (of a flower) having a concave or flat receptacle with the gynoecium and other floral parts at the same level, as in the rose. 2 of or relating to the parts of a flower arranged in this way.
▹HISTORY C19: from New Latin *perigynus;* see PERI-, -GYNOUS
▸**peˈrigyny** NOUN

perihelion (ˌperɪˈhiːlɪən) NOUN, *plural* **-lia** (-lɪə). the point in its orbit when a planet or comet is nearest the sun. Compare **aphelion.**
▹HISTORY C17: from New Latin *perihēlium,* from PERI- + Greek *hēlios* sun

peril (ˈperɪl) NOUN exposure to risk or harm; danger or jeopardy.
▹HISTORY C13: via Old French from Latin *perīculum*

perilous (ˈperɪləs) ADJECTIVE very hazardous or dangerous: *a perilous journey.*
▸ˈ**perilously** ADVERB ▸ˈ**perilousness** NOUN

perilune (ˈperɪˌluːn) NOUN the point in a lunar orbit when a spacecraft launched from the moon is nearest the moon. Compare **apolune, pericynthion.**
▹HISTORY C20: from PERI- + *-lune,* from Latin *lūna* moon

perilymph (ˈperɪˌlɪmf) NOUN the fluid filling the space between the membranous and bony labyrinths of the internal ear.

perimeter (pəˈrɪmɪtə) NOUN 1 *Maths* **a** the curve or line enclosing a plane area. **b** the length of this curve or line. 2 **a** any boundary around something, such as a field. **b** (*as modifier*): *a perimeter fence; a perimeter patrol.* 3 a medical instrument for measuring the limits of the field of vision.
▹HISTORY C16: from French *périmètre,* from Latin *perimetros;* see PERI-, -METER
▸**perimetric** (ˌperɪˈmetrɪk) *or* ˌ**periˈmetrical** ADJECTIVE
▸ˌ**periˈmetrically** ADVERB ▸**peˈrimetry** NOUN

perimorph (ˈperɪˌmɔːf) NOUN a mineral that encloses another mineral of a different type.
▸ˌ**periˈmorphic** *or* ˌ**periˈmorphous** ADJECTIVE
▸ˌ**periˈmorˌphism** NOUN

perimysium (ˌperɪˈmɪzɪəm) NOUN, *plural* **-ia** (-ɪə). *Anatomy* the sheath of fibrous connective tissue surrounding the primary bundles of muscle fibres.
▹HISTORY C19: from PERI- + *-mysium,* from Greek *mus* muscle

perinatal (ˌperɪˈneɪtᵊl) ADJECTIVE of, relating to, or occurring in the period from about three months before to one month after birth.

perineal gland NOUN *Zoology* one of a pair of glands that are situated near the anus in some mammals and secrete an odorous substance.

perinephrium (ˌperɪˈnefrɪəm) NOUN, *plural* **-ria** (-rɪə). *Anatomy* the fatty and connective tissue surrounding the kidney.
▹HISTORY C19: from PERI- + *-nephrium,* from Greek *nephros* kidney
▸ˌ**periˈnephric** ADJECTIVE

perineum (ˌperɪˈniːəm) NOUN, *plural* **-nea** (-ˈniːə). 1 the region of the body between the anus and the genital organs, including some of the underlying structures. 2 the nearly diamond-shaped surface of the human trunk between the thighs.
▹HISTORY C17: from New Latin, from Greek *perinaion,* from PERI- + *inein* to empty out
▸ˌ**periˈneal** ADJECTIVE

perineuritis (ˌperɪnjʊˈraɪtɪs) NOUN inflammation of the perineurium.
▸**perineuritic** (ˌperɪnjʊˈrɪtɪk) ADJECTIVE

perineurium (ˌperɪˈnjʊərɪəm) NOUN the connective tissue forming a sheath around a single bundle of nerve fibres.
▹HISTORY C19: from New Latin, from PERI- + Greek *neuron* nerve
▸ˌ**periˈneurial** ADJECTIVE

period (ˈpɪərɪəd) NOUN 1 a portion of time of indefinable length: *he spent a period away from home.* 2 **a** a portion of time specified in some way: *the Arthurian period; Picasso's blue period.* **b** (*as modifier*): *period costume.* 3 a nontechnical name for an occurrence of menstruation. 4 *Geology* a unit of geological time during which a system of rocks is formed: *the Jurassic period.* 5 a division of time, esp of the academic day. 6 *Physics, maths* **a** the time taken to complete one cycle of a regularly recurring phenomenon; the reciprocal of frequency. Symbol: *T.* **b** an interval in which the values of a periodic function follow a certain pattern that is duplicated over successive intervals: $\sin x = \sin (x + 2\pi)$, *where* 2π *is the period.* 7 *Astronomy* **a** the time required by a body to make one complete rotation on its axis. **b** the time interval between two successive maxima or minima of light variation of a variable star. 8 *Chem* one of the horizontal rows of elements in the periodic table. Each period starts with an alkali metal and ends with a rare gas. Compare **group** (sense 11). 9 another term (esp US and Canadian) for **full stop.** 10 a complete sentence, esp a complex one with several clauses. 11 *Music* a passage or division of a piece of music, usually consisting of two or more contrasting or complementary musical phrases and ending on a cadence. Also called: **sentence.** 12 (in classical prosody) a unit consisting of two or more cola. 13 *Rare* a completion or end.
▹HISTORY C14 *peryod,* from Latin *periodus,* from Greek *periodos* circuit, from PERI- + *hodos* way

periodate (pɜːˈraɪəˌdeɪt) NOUN any salt or ester of a periodic acid.

periodic (ˌpɪərɪˈɒdɪk) ADJECTIVE 1 happening or recurring at intervals; intermittent. 2 of, relating to, or resembling a period. 3 having or occurring in repeated periods or cycles.
▸ˌ**periˈodically** ADVERB ▸**periodicity** (ˌpɪərɪəˈdɪsɪtɪ) NOUN

periodic acid (ˌpɜːraɪˈɒdɪk) NOUN any of various oxyacids of iodine containing a greater proportion of oxygen than iodic acid and differing from each other in water content, esp either of the crystalline compounds HIO_4 (**metaperiodic acid**) and H_5IO_6 (**paraperiodic acid**).
▹HISTORY C19: from PER- + IODIC

periodical (ˌpɪərɪˈɒdɪkᵊl) NOUN 1 a publication issued at regular intervals, usually monthly or weekly. ◆ ADJECTIVE 2 of or relating to such publications. 3 published at regular intervals. 4 periodic or occasional.

periodic function (ˌpɪərɪˈɒdɪk) NOUN *Maths* a function, such as sin *x,* whose value is repeated at constant intervals.

periodic law (ˌpɪərɪˈɒdɪk) NOUN the principle that the chemical properties of the elements are periodic functions of their atomic weights (also called: **Mendeleev's law**) or, more accurately, of their atomic numbers.

periodic sentence (ˌpɪərɪˈɒdɪk) NOUN *Rhetoric* a sentence in which the completion of the main clause is left to the end, thus creating an effect of suspense.

periodic system (ˌpɪərɪˈɒdɪk) NOUN the classification of the elements based on the periodic law.

periodic table (ˌpɪərɪˈɒdɪk) NOUN a table of the elements, arranged in order of increasing atomic number, based on the periodic law. Elements having similar chemical properties and electronic structures appear in vertical columns (groups).

periodic tenancy NOUN *Social welfare* the letting of a dwelling for a repeated short term, as by the week, month, or quarter, with no end date.

periodization *or* **periodisation** (ˌpɪərɪədaɪˈzeɪʃən) NOUN the act or process of dividing history into periods.

period of revolution NOUN *Astronomy* the mean time taken for one body, such as a planet, to complete a revolution about another, such as the sun.

periodontal (ˌperɪəˈdɒntᵊl) ADJECTIVE of, denoting, or affecting the gums and other tissues surrounding the teeth: *periodontal disease.*

periodontics (ˌperɪəˈdɒntɪks) NOUN (*functioning as singular*) the branch of dentistry concerned with diseases affecting the tissues and structures that surround teeth. Also called: **periodontology.**
▹HISTORY C19: from PERI- + *-odontics,* from Greek *odōn* tooth
▸ˌ**perioˈdontic** ADJECTIVE ▸ˌ**perioˈdontically** ADVERB

period piece NOUN an object, a piece of music, a play, etc., valued for its quality of evoking a particular historical period: often one regarded as of little except historical interest.

perionychium (ˌperɪəʊˈnɪkɪəm) NOUN, *plural* **-ia** (-ɪə). the skin that surrounds a fingernail or toenail.
▹HISTORY C19: New Latin, from PERI- + Greek *onux* a nail

periosteum (ˌperɪˈɒstɪəm) NOUN, *plural* **-tea** (-tɪə). a thick fibrous two-layered membrane covering the surface of bones.
▹HISTORY C16: New Latin, from Greek *periosteon,* from PERI- + *osteon* bone
▸ˌ**periˈosteal** ADJECTIVE

periostitis (ˌpɛrɪɒˈstaɪtɪs) NOUN inflammation of the periosteum.
▸**periostitic** (ˌpɛrɪɒˈstɪtɪk) ADJECTIVE

periotic (ˌpɛrɪˈəʊtɪk, -ˈɒtɪk) ADJECTIVE 1 of or relating to the structures situated around the internal ear. 2 situated around the ear.
▷HISTORY C19: from PERI- + *-otic,* from Greek *ous* ear

peripatetic (ˌpɛrɪpəˈtɛtɪk) ADJECTIVE 1 itinerant. 2 *Brit* employed in two or more educational establishments and travelling from one to another: *a peripatetic football coach.* ◆ NOUN 3 a peripatetic person.
▷HISTORY C16: from Latin *peripatēticus,* from Greek *peripatētikos,* from *peripatein* to pace to and fro
▸**ˌperipaˈtetically** ADVERB

Peripatetic (ˌpɛrɪpəˈtɛtɪk) ADJECTIVE 1 of or relating to the teachings of the Greek philosopher Aristotle (384–322 B.C.), who used to teach philosophy while walking about the Lyceum in ancient Athens. ◆ NOUN 2 a student of Aristotelianism.

peripatus (pəˈrɪpətəs) NOUN any of a genus of wormlike arthropods having a segmented body and short unjointed limbs: belonging to the phylum *Onychophora.*
▷HISTORY from New Latin, from Greek *peripatos* a pacing about; see PERIPATETIC

peripeteia, peripetia (ˌpɛrɪpɪˈtaɪə, -ˈtɪə), *or* **peripety** (pəˈrɪpətɪ) NOUN (esp in drama) an abrupt turn of events or reversal of circumstances.
▷HISTORY C16: from Greek, from PERI- + *piptein* to fall (to change suddenly, literally: to fall around)
▸**ˌperipeˈteian** *or* **ˌperipeˈtian** ADJECTIVE

peripheral (pəˈrɪfərəl) ADJECTIVE 1 not relating to the most important part of something; incidental, minor, or superficial. 2 of, relating to, or of the nature of a periphery. 3 *Anatomy* of, relating to, or situated near the surface of the body: *a peripheral nerve.*
▸**peˈripherally** ADVERB

peripheral device *or* **unit** NOUN *Computing* any device, such as a disk, printer, modem, or screen, concerned with input/output, storage, etc. Often shortened to: **peripheral.**

periphery (pəˈrɪfərɪ) NOUN, *plural* **-eries.** 1 the outermost boundary of an area. 2 the outside surface of something. 3 *Anatomy* the surface or outermost part of the body or one of its organs or parts.
▷HISTORY C16: from Late Latin *peripherīa,* from Greek, from PERI- + *pherein* to bear

periphrasis (pəˈrɪfrəsɪs) NOUN, *plural* **-rases** (-rəˌsiːz). 1 a roundabout way of expressing something; circumlocution. 2 an expression of this kind.
▷HISTORY C16: via Latin from Greek, from PERI- + *phrazein* to declare

periphrastic (ˌpɛrɪˈfræstɪk) ADJECTIVE 1 employing or involving periphrasis. 2 expressed in two or more words rather than by an inflected form of one: used esp of a tense of a verb where the alternative element is an auxiliary verb. For example, *He does go* and *He will go* involve periphrastic tenses.
▸**ˌperiˈphrastically** ADVERB

periphyton (pəˈrɪfɪˌtɒn) NOUN aquatic organisms, such as certain algae, that live attached to rocks or other surfaces.
▷HISTORY C20: from Greek, from PERI- + *phutos,* from *phuein* to grow

peripteral (pəˈrɪptərəl) ADJECTIVE having a row of columns on all sides.
▷HISTORY C19: from PERI- + *-pteral,* from Greek *pteron* wing

perique (pəˈriːk) NOUN a strong highly-flavoured tobacco cured in its own juices and grown in Louisiana.
▷HISTORY C19: apparently from *Périque,* nickname of Pierre Chenet, American tobacco planter who first grew it in Louisiana

perisarc (ˈpɛrɪˌsɑːk) NOUN the outer chitinous layer secreted by colonial hydrozoan coelenterates, such as species of *Obelia.*
▷HISTORY C19: from PERI- + *-sarc,* from Greek *sarx* flesh
▸**ˌperiˈsarcal** *or* **ˌperiˈsarcous** ADJECTIVE

periscope (ˈpɛrɪˌskəʊp) NOUN any of a number of optical instruments that enable the user to view objects that are not in the direct line of vision, such as one in a submarine for looking above the surface of the water. They have a system of mirrors or prisms to reflect the light and often contain focusing lenses.
▷HISTORY C19: from Greek *periskopein* to look around; see PERI-, -SCOPE

periscopic (ˌpɛrɪˈskɒpɪk) ADJECTIVE (of a lens) having a wide field of view.
▸**ˌperiˈscopically** ADVERB

perish (ˈpɛrɪʃ) VERB (*intr*) 1 to be destroyed or die, esp in an untimely way. 2 to rot: *leather perishes if exposed to bad weather.* 3 **perish the thought!** may it never be or happen thus. ◆ NOUN 4 **do a perish.** *Austral, informal* to die or come near to dying of thirst or starvation.
▷HISTORY C13: from Old French *périr,* from Latin *perīre* to pass away entirely, from PER- (away) + *īre* to go

perishable (ˈpɛrɪʃəbᵊl) ADJECTIVE 1 liable to rot or wither. ◆ NOUN 2 (*often plural*) a perishable article, esp food.
▸**ˌperishaˈbility** *or* **ˈperishableness** NOUN ▸**ˈperishably** ADVERB

perished (ˈpɛrɪʃt) ADJECTIVE *Informal* (of a person, part of the body, etc.) extremely cold.

perishing (ˈpɛrɪʃɪŋ) ADJECTIVE 1 *Informal* (of weather, etc.) extremely cold. 2 *Slang* (intensifier qualifying something undesirable): *it's a perishing nuisance!*
▸**ˈperishingly** ADVERB

perisperm (ˈpɛrɪˌspɜːm) NOUN the nutritive tissue surrounding the embryo in certain seeds, and developing from the nucellus of the ovule.
▸**ˌperiˈspermal** ADJECTIVE

perispomenon (ˌpɛrɪˈspəʊməˌnɒn) ADJECTIVE 1 (of a Greek word) bearing a circumflex accent on the last syllable. ◆ NOUN 2 a word having such an accent.
▷HISTORY from Greek, from PERI- (around) + *spaein* to pull, draw

perissodactyl (pəˌrɪsəʊˈdæktɪl) *or* **perissodactyle** (pəˌrɪsəʊˈdæktaɪl) NOUN 1 any placental mammal of the order *Perissodactyla,* having hooves with an odd number of toes: includes horses, tapirs, and rhinoceroses. ◆ ADJECTIVE 2 of, relating to, or belonging to the *Perissodactyla.*
▷HISTORY C19: from New Latin *perissodactylus,* from Greek *perissos* uneven + *daktulos* digit
▸**peˌrissoˈdactylous** ADJECTIVE

peristalsis (ˌpɛrɪˈstælsɪs) NOUN, *plural* **-ses** (-siːz). *Physiol* the succession of waves of involuntary muscular contraction of various bodily tubes, esp of the alimentary tract, where it effects transport of food and waste products.
▷HISTORY C19: from New Latin, from PERI- + Greek *stalsis* compression, from *stellein* to press together
▸**ˌperiˈstaltic** ADJECTIVE ▸**ˌperiˈstaltically** ADVERB

peristome (ˈpɛrɪˌstəʊm) NOUN 1 a fringe of pointed teeth surrounding the opening of a moss capsule. 2 any of various parts surrounding the mouth of invertebrates, such as echinoderms and earthworms, and of protozoans.
▷HISTORY C18: from New Latin *peristoma,* from PERI- + Greek *stoma* mouth
▸**ˌperiˈstomal** *or* **ˌperiˈstomial** ADJECTIVE

peristyle (ˈpɛrɪˌstaɪl) NOUN 1 a colonnade that surrounds a court or building. 2 an area that is surrounded by a colonnade.
▷HISTORY C17: via French from Latin *peristȳlum,* from Greek *peristulon,* from PERI- + *stulos* column
▸**ˌperiˈstylar** ADJECTIVE

perithecium (ˌpɛrɪˈθiːsɪəm) NOUN, *plural* **-cia** (-sɪə). *Botany* a flask-shaped structure containing asci that are discharged from an apical pore; a type of ascocarp.
▷HISTORY C19: from New Latin, from PERI- + Greek *thēkē* case

peritoneal dialysis a technique of dialysis used when haemodialysis is inappropriate; it makes use of the peritoneum as an autogenous semipermeable membrane.

peritoneum (ˌpɛrɪtəˈniːəm) NOUN, *plural* **-nea** (-ˈniːə) *or* **-neums.** a thin translucent serous sac that lines the walls of the abdominal cavity and covers most of the viscera.
▷HISTORY C16: via Late Latin from Greek *peritonaion,* from *peritonos* stretched around, from PERI- + *tenein* to stretch
▸**ˌperitoˈneal** ADJECTIVE

peritonitis (ˌpɛrɪtəˈnaɪtɪs) NOUN inflammation of the peritoneum.
▸**peritonitic** (ˌpɛrɪtəˈnɪtɪk) ADJECTIVE

peritrack (ˈpɛrɪˌtræk) NOUN another name for **taxiway.**

peritricha (pəˈrɪtrɪkə) PLURAL NOUN, *singular* **peritrich** (ˈpɛrɪˌtrɪk). 1 ciliate protozoans, of the order *Peritrichida,* in which the cilia are restricted to a spiral around the mouth. 2 bacteria having the entire cell surface covered with flagella.
▷HISTORY C19: from New Latin, from PERI- + Greek *thrix* hair
▸**peˈritrichous** ADJECTIVE

periwig (ˈpɛrɪˌwɪg) NOUN a wig, such as a peruke.
▷HISTORY C16 *perwyke,* changed from French *perruque* wig, PERUKE

periwinkle[1] (ˈpɛrɪˌwɪŋkᵊl) NOUN any of various edible marine gastropods of the genus *Littorina, esp L. littorea,* having a spirally coiled shell. Often shortened to: **winkle.**
▷HISTORY C16: of unknown origin

periwinkle[2] (ˈpɛrɪˌwɪŋkᵊl) NOUN 1 Also called (US): **creeping myrtle, trailing myrtle.** any of several Eurasian apocynaceous evergreen plants of the genus *Vinca,* such as *V. minor* (**lesser periwinkle**) and *V. major* (**greater periwinkle**), having trailing stems and blue flowers. 2 **a** a light purplish-blue colour. **b** (*as adjective*): *a periwinkle coat.*
▷HISTORY C14 *pervenke,* from Old English *perwince,* from Late Latin *pervinca*

perjink (pərˈdʒɪŋk) ADJECTIVE *Scot* prim or finicky.
▷HISTORY C19: of unknown origin

perjure (ˈpɜːdʒə) VERB (*tr*) *Criminal law* to render (oneself) guilty of perjury.
▷HISTORY C15: from Old French *parjurer,* from Latin *perjūrāre,* from PER- + *jūrāre* to make an oath, from *jūs* law
▸**ˈperjurer** NOUN

perjured (ˈpɜːdʒəd) ADJECTIVE *Criminal law* 1 **a** having sworn falsely. **b** having committed perjury. 2 involving or characterized by perjury: *perjured evidence.*

perjury (ˈpɜːdʒərɪ) NOUN, *plural* **-juries.** *Criminal law* the offence committed by a witness in judicial proceedings who, having been lawfully sworn or having affirmed, wilfully gives false evidence.
▷HISTORY C14: from Anglo-French *parjurie,* from Latin *perjūrium* a false oath; see PERJURE
▸**perjurious** (pɜːˈdʒʊərɪəs) ADJECTIVE ▸**perˈjuriously** ADVERB

perk[1] (pɜːk) ADJECTIVE 1 pert; brisk; lively. ◆ VERB 2 See **perk up.**
▷HISTORY C16: see PERK UP

perk[2] (pɜːk) VERB *Informal* 1 (*intr*) (of coffee) to percolate. 2 (*tr*) to percolate (coffee).

perk[3] (pɜːk) NOUN *Brit, informal* short for **perquisite.**

perkin (ˈpɜːkɪn) NOUN a variant of **parkin.**

Perkin's mauve (ˈpɜːkɪnz) NOUN another name for **mauve** (sense 2).
▷HISTORY C19: named after Sir William Henry *Perkin* (1838–1907), who first synthesized it

perk up VERB (*adverb*) 1 to make or become more cheerful, hopeful, or lively. 2 to rise or cause to rise briskly: *the dog's ears perked up.* 3 (*tr*) to make smarter in appearance: *she perked up her outfit with a bright scarf.* 4 (*intr*) *Austral, slang* to vomit.
▷HISTORY C14 *perk,* perhaps from Norman French *perquer;* see PERCH[1]

perky (ˈpɜːkɪ) ADJECTIVE **perkier, perkiest.** 1 jaunty; lively. 2 confident; spirited.
▸**ˈperkily** ADVERB ▸**ˈperkiness** NOUN

Perl (pɜːl) NOUN a computer language that is used for text manipulation, esp on the World Wide Web.
▷HISTORY C20: from *p(ractical) e(xtraction and) r(eport) l(anguage)*

perlemoen (ˈpɛələˌmʊn) NOUN *South African* another name for **abalone.**
▷HISTORY from Afrikaans, from Dutch *paarlemoer* mother of pearl

Perlis (ˈpɛəlɪs, ˈpɜː-) NOUN a state of NW Peninsular Malaysia, on the Andaman Sea: a dependency of Thailand until 1909. Capital: Kangar. Pop.: 198 335 (2000). Area: 803 sq. km (310 sq. miles).

perlite *or* **pearlite** ('pɜːlaɪt) NOUN a variety of obsidian consisting of masses of small pearly globules: used as a filler, insulator, and soil conditioner.
▷HISTORY C19: from French, from *perle* PEARL[1]
▸**perlitic** *or* **pearlitic** (pɜː'lɪtɪk) ADJECTIVE

perlocution (ˌpɜːlɒ'kjuːʃən) NOUN *Philosophy* the effect that someone has by uttering certain words, such as frightening a person. Also called: **perlocutionary act.** Compare **illocution.**
▷HISTORY C16 (in the obsolete sense: the action of speaking): from Medieval or New Latin *perlocūtiō;* see PER-, LOCUTION
▸ˌ**perlo'cutionary** ADJECTIVE

perm[1] (pɜːm) NOUN [1] a hairstyle produced by treatment with heat, chemicals, etc. which gives long-lasting waves, curls, or other shaping. Also called (esp formerly): **permanent wave.** [2] the act of giving or receiving such a hairstyle. ◆ VERB [3] (*tr*) to give a perm to (hair).

perm[2] (pɜːm) NOUN short for **permutation** (sense 4).

Perm (*Russian* pjermj) NOUN a port in W Russia, on the Kama River: oil refinery; university (1916). Pop.: 1 017 100 (1999 est.). Former name (1940–62): **Molotov.**

perma- PREFIX *Informal* indicating a fixed state: *a perma-tan; perma-grin.*

permaculture ('pɜːməˌkʌltʃə) NOUN the practice of producing food, energy, etc., using ways that do not deplete the earth's natural resources.
▷HISTORY C20: coined by Bill Mollison (born 1928), Australian ecologist, from *perma(nent agri)culture*

permafrost ('pɜːməˌfrɒst) NOUN ground that is permanently frozen, often to great depths, the surface sometimes thawing in the summer.
▷HISTORY C20: from PERMA(NENT) + FROST

permalloy (pɜːm'ælɔɪ) NOUN any of various alloys containing iron and nickel (45–80 per cent) and sometimes smaller amounts of chromium and molybdenum.
▷HISTORY C20: from PERM(EABILITY) + ALLOY

permanence ('pɜːmənəns) NOUN the state or quality of being permanent.

permanency ('pɜːmənənsɪ) NOUN, *plural* **-cies.** [1] a person or thing that is permanent. [2] another word for **permanence.**

permanent ('pɜːmənənt) ADJECTIVE [1] existing or intended to exist for an indefinite period: *a permanent structure.* [2] not expected to change for an indefinite time; not temporary: *a permanent condition.*
▷HISTORY C15: from Latin *permanens* continuing, from *permanēre* to stay to the end, from *per-* through + *manēre* to remain
▸'**permanently** ADVERB

Permanent Court of Arbitration NOUN the official name of the **Hague Tribunal.**

permanent hardness NOUN *Chem* hardness of water that cannot be removed by boiling as it results mainly from the presence of calcium and magnesium chlorides and sulphates.

permanent health insurance NOUN a form of insurance that provides up to 75 per cent of a person's salary, until retirement, in case of prolonged illness or disability.

permanent magnet NOUN a magnet, often of steel, that retains its magnetization after the magnetic field producing it has been removed.
▸**permanent magnetism** NOUN

permanent press NOUN **a** a chemical treatment for clothing that makes the fabric crease-resistant and sometimes provides a garment with a permanent crease or pleats. **b** (*as modifier*): *permanent-press skirts.*

permanent resident NOUN *Canadian* an immigrant who has been given official residential status, often prior to being granted citizenship.

permanent set NOUN *Engineering* the change in shape of a material that results when the load to which it is subjected causes the elastic limit to be exceeded and is then removed.

permanent wave NOUN another name (esp formerly) for **perm**[1] (sense 1).

permanent way NOUN *Chiefly Brit* the track of a railway, including the ballast, sleepers, rails, etc.

permanganate (pə'mæŋgəˌneɪt, -nɪt) NOUN a salt of permanganic acid.

permanganic acid (ˌpɜːmæn'gænɪk) NOUN a monobasic acid known only in solution and in the form of permanganate salts. Formula: $HMnO_4$. Systematic name: **manganic(VII) acid.**

perma-tan NOUN a permanent year-round suntan.

permeability (ˌpɜːmɪə'bɪlɪtɪ) NOUN [1] the state or quality of being permeable. [2] a measure of the response of a medium to a magnetic field, expressed as the ratio of the magnetic flux density in the medium to the field strength; measured in henries per metre. Symbol: μ. See also **relative permeability, magnetic constant.** [3] *Civil engineering* the rate of diffusion of a fluid under pressure through soil. [4] the rate at which gas diffuses through the surface of a balloon or airship, usually expressed in litres per square metre per day.

permeability coefficient NOUN the volume of an incompressible fluid that will flow in unit time through a unit cube of a porous substance across which a unit pressure difference is maintained.

permeable ('pɜːmɪəb[ə]l) ADJECTIVE capable of being permeated, esp by liquids.
▷HISTORY C15: from Late Latin *permeābilis,* from Latin *permeāre* to pervade; see PERMEATE
▸'**permeableness** NOUN ▸'**permeably** ADVERB

permeance ('pɜːmɪəns) NOUN [1] the act of permeating. [2] the reciprocal of the reluctance of a magnetic circuit. Symbol: Λ.
▸'**permeant** ADJECTIVE, NOUN

permeate ('pɜːmɪˌeɪt) VERB [1] to penetrate or pervade (a substance, area, etc.): *a lovely smell permeated the room.* [2] to pass through or cause to pass through by osmosis or diffusion: *to permeate a membrane.*
▷HISTORY C17: from Latin *permeāre,* from *per-* through + *meāre* to pass
▸ˌ**perme'ation** NOUN ▸'**permeative** ADJECTIVE

per mensem *Latin* ('pɜː 'mɛnsəm) ADVERB every month or by the month.

Permian ('pɜːmɪən) ADJECTIVE [1] of, denoting, or formed in the last period of the Palaeozoic era, between the Carboniferous and Triassic periods, which lasted for 60 000 000 years. ◆ NOUN [2] **the.** the Permian period or rock system.
▷HISTORY C19: after PERM, Russia

permie ('pɜːmɪ) NOUN a person, esp an office worker, employed by a firm on a permanent basis. Compare **temp.**
▷HISTORY C20: diminutive of PERMANENT

per mill *or* **mil** (pə 'mɪl) ADVERB by the thousand or in each thousand.
▷HISTORY C19: from PER + French or Latin *mille* thousand, on the model of PER CENT

permissible (pə'mɪsəb[ə]l) ADJECTIVE permitted; allowable.
▸**perˌmissi'bility** NOUN ▸**per'missibly** ADVERB

permission (pə'mɪʃən) NOUN authorization to do something.

permissive (pə'mɪsɪv) ADJECTIVE [1] tolerant; lenient: *permissive parents.* [2] indulgent in matters of sex: *a permissive society.* [3] granting permission. [4] *Archaic* not obligatory.
▸**per'missively** ADVERB ▸**per'missiveness** NOUN

permit VERB (pə'mɪt) **-mits, -mitting, -mitted.** [1] (*tr*) to grant permission to do something: *you are permitted to smoke.* [2] (*tr*) to consent to or tolerate: *she will not permit him to come.* [3] (when *intr,* often foll by *of;* when *tr,* often foll by an infinitive) to allow the possibility (of): *the passage permits of two interpretations; his work permits him to relax nowadays.* ◆ NOUN ('pɜːmɪt) [4] an official certificate or document granting authorization; licence. [5] permission, esp written permission.
▷HISTORY C15: from Latin *permittere,* from *per-* through + *mittere* to send
▸**per'mitter** NOUN

permittivity (ˌpɜːmɪ'tɪvɪtɪ) NOUN, *plural* **-ties.** a measure of the response of a substance to an electric field, expressed as the ratio of its electric displacement to the applied field strength; measured in farads per metre. Symbol: ε. See also **relative permittivity, electric constant.**

permutate ('pɜːmjʊˌteɪt) VERB to alter the sequence or arrangement (of); treat by permutation: *endlessly permutating three basic designs.*

permutation (ˌpɜːmjʊ'teɪʃən) NOUN [1] *Maths* **a** an ordered arrangement of the numbers, terms, etc., of a set into specified groups: *the permutations of a, b, and c, taken two at a time, are ab, ba, ac, ca, bc, cb.* **b** a group formed in this way. The number of permutations of *n* objects taken *r* at a time is $n!/(n-r)!$ Symbol: $_nP_r$. ◆ Compare **combination** (sense 6). [2] a combination of items made by reordering. [3] an alteration; transformation. [4] a fixed combination for selections of results on football pools. Usually shortened to: **perm.**
▷HISTORY C14: from Latin *permūtātiō,* from *permūtāre* to change thoroughly; see MUTATION
▸ˌ**permu'tational** ADJECTIVE

permute (pə'mjuːt) VERB (*tr*) [1] to change the sequence of. [2] *Maths* to subject to permutation.
▷HISTORY C14: from Latin *permūtāre,* from PER- + *mūtāre* to change, alter
▸**per'mutable** ADJECTIVE ▸**perˌmuta'bility** *or* **per'mutableness** NOUN ▸**per'mutably** ADVERB

Pernambuco (ˌpɜːnəm'bjuːkəʊ; *Portuguese* pernəm'buku) NOUN [1] a state of NE Brazil, on the Atlantic: consists of a humid coastal plain rising to a high inland plateau. Capital: Recife. Pop.: 7 910 992 (2001 est.). Area: 98 280 sq. km (37 946 sq. miles). [2] the former name of **Recife.**

pernicious (pə'nɪʃəs) ADJECTIVE [1] wicked or malicious: *pernicious lies.* [2] causing grave harm; deadly.
▷HISTORY C16: from Latin *perniciōsus,* from *perniciēs* ruin, from PER- (intensive) + *nex* death
▸**per'niciously** ADVERB ▸**per'niciousness** NOUN

pernicious anaemia NOUN a form of anaemia characterized by lesions of the spinal cord, weakness, sore tongue, numbness in the arms and legs, diarrhoea, etc.: associated with inadequate absorption of vitamin B_{12}.

pernickety (pə'nɪkɪtɪ) *or US* **persnickety** ADJECTIVE *Informal* [1] excessively precise and attentive to detail; fussy. [2] (of a task) requiring close attention; exacting.
▷HISTORY C19: originally Scottish, of unknown origin
▸**per'nicketiness** *or US* **per'snicketiness** NOUN

Pernik (*Bulgarian* 'pɛrnik) NOUN an industrial town in W Bulgaria, on the Struma River. Pop.: 99 643 (1990). Former name (1949–62): **Dimitrovo.**

Pernod ('pɛənəʊ; *French* pɛrno) NOUN *Trademark* an aniseed-flavoured apéritif from France.

peroneal (ˌpɛrə'niːəl) ADJECTIVE *Anatomy* of or relating to the fibula or the outer side of the leg.
▷HISTORY C19: from New Latin *peronē* fibula, from Greek: fibula

Peronist (pə'rɒnɪst) NOUN [1] a follower or admirer of Juan Domingo Peron, the Argentine soldier, statesman, and dictator (1895–1974). ◆ ADJECTIVE [2] of or relating to Peron, his policies, or his supporters.

perorate ('pɛrəˌreɪt) VERB (*intr*) [1] to speak at length, esp in a formal manner. [2] to conclude a speech or sum up, esp with a formal recapitulation.

peroration (ˌpɛrə'reɪʃən) NOUN *Rhetoric* the conclusion of a speech or discourse, in which points made previously are summed up or recapitulated, esp with greater emphasis.
▷HISTORY C15: from Latin *perōrātiō,* from *perōrāre,* from PER- (thoroughly) + *ōrāre* to speak

perovskite (pɛ'rɒvskaɪt) NOUN a yellow, brown, or greyish-black mineral form of calcium titanate with some rare-earth elements, which is used in certain high-temperature ceramic superconductors.
▷HISTORY C19: named after Count Lev Alekseevich *Perovski* (1792–1856), Russian statesman

peroxidase (pə'rɒksɪˌdeɪs, -ˌdeɪz) NOUN any of a group of enzymes that catalyse the oxidation of a compound by the decomposition of hydrogen peroxide or an organic peroxide. They generally consist of a protein combined with haem.

peroxidation (pəˌrɒksɪ'deɪʃən) NOUN a type of reaction in which oxygen atoms are formed leading to the production of peroxides. It is stimulated in the body by certain toxins and infections.

peroxide (pə'rɒksaɪd) NOUN [1] short for **hydrogen peroxide,** esp when used for bleaching hair [2] any of a class of metallic oxides, such as sodium peroxide, Na_2O_2, that contain the divalent ion $^-O\text{-}O^-$. [3] (*not in technical usage*) any of certain dioxides, such as manganese peroxide, MnO_2, that resemble peroxides in their formula but do not contain the $^-O\text{-}O^-$ ion. [4] any of a class of organic compounds whose molecules contain two oxygen atoms bound together. They tend to be explosive. [5] (*modifier*) of, relating to, bleached with, or resembling peroxide. ◆ VERB [6] (*tr*) to bleach (the hair) with peroxide.

peroxide blonde NOUN *Usually disparaging* a woman having hair that is bleached rather than naturally blonde and that looks harsh or unnatural.

peroxisome (pəˈrɒksɪˌsəʊm) NOUN a type of organelle present in most eukaryotic cells that carry out oxidative reactions, such as oxidation of alcohol in the liver.

peroxy- *or esp for inorganic compounds* **peroxo-** COMBINING FORM indicating the presence of the peroxide group, -O–O-: *peroxysulphuric acid*. Also (not in technical usage): **per-**.

peroxysulphuric acid (pəˌrɒksɪsʌlˈfjʊərɪk) NOUN a white hygroscopic crystalline unstable oxidizing acid. Formula: H_2SO_5. Also called (not in technical usage): **persulphuric acid, Caro's acid.**

perpend[1] (ˈpɜːpənd) *or* **perpent** NOUN a large stone that passes through a wall from one side to the other. Also called: **parpend, perpend stone.**
▷HISTORY C15: from Old French *parpain*, of uncertain origin

perpend[2] (pəˈpɛnd) VERB an archaic word for **ponder.**
▷HISTORY C16: from Latin *perpendere* to examine, from PER- (thoroughly) + *pendere* to weigh

perpendicular (ˌpɜːpənˈdɪkjʊlə) ADJECTIVE [1] Also: **normal.** at right angles to a horizontal plane. [2] denoting, relating to, or having the style of Gothic architecture used in England during the 14th and 15th centuries, characterized by tracery having vertical lines, a four-centred arch, and fan vaulting. [3] upright; vertical. ◆ NOUN [4] *Geometry* a line or plane perpendicular to another. [5] any instrument used for indicating the vertical line through a given point. [6] *Mountaineering* a nearly vertical face.
▷HISTORY C14: from Latin *perpendiculāris*, from *perpendiculum* a plumb line, from *per-* through + *pendēre* to hang
▸**perpendicularity** (ˌpɜːpənˌdɪkjʊˈlærɪtɪ) NOUN
▸**ˌperpenˈdicularly** ADVERB

perpetrate (ˈpɜːpɪˌtreɪt) VERB (*tr*) to perform or be responsible for (a deception, crime, etc.).
▷HISTORY C16: from Latin *perpetrāre*, from *per-* (thoroughly) + *patrāre* to perform, perhaps from *pater* father, leader in the performance of sacred rites
▸**ˌperpeˈtration** NOUN ▸**ˈperpeˌtrator** NOUN

> **Language note** *Perpetrate* and *perpetuate* are sometimes confused: *he must answer for the crimes he has perpetrated* (not *perpetuated*); *the book helped to perpetuate* (not *perpetrate*) *some of the myths surrounding his early life.*

perpetual (pəˈpɛtjʊəl) ADJECTIVE [1] (*usually prenominal*) eternal; permanent. [2] (*usually prenominal*) seemingly ceaseless because often repeated: *your perpetual complaints*. [3] *Horticulture* blooming throughout the growing season or year. ◆ NOUN [4] (of a crop plant) continually producing edible parts: *perpetual spinach*. [5] a plant that blooms throughout the growing season.
▷HISTORY C14: via Old French from Latin *perpetuālis* universal, from *perpes* continuous, from *per-* (thoroughly) + *petere* to go towards
▸**perˈpetually** ADVERB

perpetual check NOUN *Chess* a consecutive series of checks that the checked player cannot avoid, leading to a drawn game.

perpetual debenture NOUN a bond or debenture that can either never be redeemed or cannot be redeemed on demand.

perpetual inventory NOUN a form of stock control in which running records are kept of all acquisitions and disposals.

perpetual motion NOUN [1] Also called: **perpetual motion of the first kind.** motion of a hypothetical mechanism that continues indefinitely without any external source of energy. It is impossible in practice because of friction. [2] Also called: **perpetual motion of the second kind.** motion of a hypothetical mechanism that derives its energy from a source at a lower temperature. It is impossible in practice because of the second law of thermodynamics.

perpetuate (pəˈpɛtjʊˌeɪt) VERB (*tr*) to cause to continue or prevail: *to perpetuate misconceptions*.
▷HISTORY C16: from Latin *perpetuāre* to continue without interruption, from *perpetuus* PERPETUAL
▸**perˌpetuˈation** NOUN

> **Language note** See at **perpetrate.**

perpetuity (ˌpɜːpɪˈtjuːɪtɪ) NOUN, *plural* **-ties.** [1] eternity. [2] the state or quality of being perpetual. [3] *Property law* a limitation preventing the absolute disposal of an estate for longer than the period allowed by law. [4] an annuity with no maturity date and payable indefinitely. [5] **in perpetuity.** for ever.
▷HISTORY C15: from Old French *perpetuite*, from Latin *perpetuitās* continuity; see PERPETUAL

Perpignan (*French* pɛrpiɲɑ̃) NOUN a town in S France: historic capital of Roussillon. Pop.: 105 115 (1999).

perplex (pəˈplɛks) VERB (*tr*) [1] to puzzle; bewilder; confuse. [2] to complicate: *to perplex an issue*.
▷HISTORY C15: from obsolete *perplex* (adj) intricate, from Latin *perplexus* entangled, from *per-* (thoroughly) + *plectere* to entwine

perplexity (pəˈplɛksɪtɪ) NOUN, *plural* **-ties.** [1] the state of being perplexed. [2] the state of being intricate or complicated. [3] something that perplexes.

per pro (ˈpɜː ˈprəʊ) PREPOSITION by delegation to; through the agency of: used when signing documents on behalf of someone else.
▷HISTORY Latin: abbreviation of *per prōcūrātiōnem*

> **Language note** See at **pp.**

perquisite (ˈpɜːkwɪzɪt) NOUN [1] an incidental benefit gained from a certain type of employment, such as the use of a company car. [2] a customary benefit received in addition to a regular income. [3] a customary tip. [4] something expected or regarded as an exclusive right. ◆ Often (informal) shortened to **perk.**
▷HISTORY C15: from Medieval Latin *perquīsītum* an acquired possession, from Latin *perquīrere* to seek earnestly for something, from *per-* (thoroughly) + *quaerere* to ask for, seek

Perrier water *or* **Perrier** (ˈpɛrɪeɪ) NOUN *Trademark* a sparkling mineral water from the south of France.
▷HISTORY C20: named after a spring *Source Perrier*, at Vergèze, France

perron (ˈpɛrən) NOUN an external flight of steps, esp one at the front entrance of a building.
▷HISTORY C14: from Old French, from *pierre* stone, from Latin *petra*

perry (ˈpɛrɪ) NOUN, *plural* **-ries.** alcoholic drink made of pears, similar in taste to cider.
▷HISTORY C14 *pereye*, from Old French *peré*, ultimately from Latin *pirum* pear

persalt (ˈpɜːˌsɔːlt) NOUN any salt of a peracid.

perse (pɜːs) NOUN **a** a dark greyish-blue colour. **b** (*as adjective*): *perse cloth*.
▷HISTORY C14: from Old French, from Medieval Latin *persus*, perhaps changed from Latin *Persicus* Persian

per se (ˈpɜː ˈseɪ) ADVERB by or in itself; intrinsically.
▷HISTORY Latin

persecute (ˈpɜːsɪˌkjuːt) VERB (*tr*) [1] to oppress, harass, or maltreat, esp because of race, religion, etc. [2] to bother persistently.
▷HISTORY C15: from Old French *persecuter*, back formation from *persecuteur*, from Late Latin *persecūtor* pursuer, from *persequī* to take vengeance upon
▸**ˈperseˌcutive** ADJECTIVE ▸**ˈperseˌcutor** NOUN

persecution (ˌpɜːsɪˈkjuːʃən) NOUN the act of persecuting or the state of being persecuted.

persecution complex NOUN *Psychol* an acute irrational fear that other people are plotting one's downfall and that they are responsible for one's failures.

persecutory (ˈpɜːsɪˌkjuːtərɪ) ADJECTIVE involving or characteristic of persecution.

Perseid (ˈpɜːsɪɪd) NOUN any member of a meteor shower occurring annually around August 12th and appearing to radiate from a point in the constellation Perseus.
▷HISTORY C19: from Greek *Perseïdes* daughters of PERSEUS[1]

Persephone (pəˈsɛfənɪ) NOUN *Greek myth* a daughter of Zeus and Demeter, abducted by Hades and made his wife and queen of the underworld, but allowed part of each year to leave it. Roman counterpart: **Proserpina.**

Persepolis (pəˈsɛpəlɪs) NOUN the capital of ancient Persia in the Persian Empire and under the Seleucids: founded by Darius; sacked by Alexander the Great in 330 B.C.

Perseus[1] (ˈpɜːsɪəs) NOUN *Greek myth* a son of Zeus and Danaë, who with Athena's help slew the Gorgon Medusa and rescued Andromeda from a sea monster.

Perseus[2] (ˈpɜːsɪəs) NOUN, *Latin genitive* **Persei** (ˈpɜːsɪˌaɪ). a conspicuous constellation in the N hemisphere lying between Auriga and Cassiopeia and crossed by the Milky Way. It contains the eclipsing binary, Algol, and a rich cluster of galaxies.

perseverance (ˌpɜːsɪˈvɪərəns) NOUN [1] continued steady belief or efforts, withstanding discouragement or difficulty; persistence. [2] *Christianity* persistence in remaining in a state of grace until death.
▸**ˌperseˈverant** ADJECTIVE

perseveration (pɜːˌsɛvəˈreɪʃən) NOUN *Psychol* [1] the tendency for an impression, idea, or feeling to dissipate only slowly and to recur during subsequent experiences. [2] an inability to change one's method of working when transferred from one task to another.

persevere (ˌpɜːsɪˈvɪə) VERB (*intr; often foll by in*) to show perseverance.
▷HISTORY C14: from Old French *perseverer*, from Latin *persevērāre*, from *perseverus* very strict; see SEVERE
▸**ˌperseˈvering** ADJECTIVE ▸**ˌperseˈveringly** ADVERB

Pershing (ˈpɜːʃɪŋ) NOUN a US ballistic missile capable of carrying a nuclear or conventional warhead.
▷HISTORY C20: after John Joseph *Pershing* (1860–1948), US general

Persia (ˈpɜːʃə) NOUN [1] the former name (until 1935) of **Iran.** [2] another name for **Persian Empire.**

Persian (ˈpɜːʃən) ADJECTIVE [1] of or relating to ancient Persia or modern Iran, their inhabitants, or their languages. ◆ NOUN [2] a native, citizen, or inhabitant of modern Iran; an Iranian. [3] a member of an Indo-European people of West Iranian speech who established a great empire in SW Asia in the 6th century B.C. [4] (loosely) the language of Iran or Persia in any of its ancient or modern forms, belonging to the West Iranian branch of the Indo-European family. See also **Avestan, Old Persian, Pahlavi**[2]**, Farsi.**

Persian blinds PLURAL NOUN another term for **persiennes.**

Persian carpet *or* **rug** NOUN a carpet or rug made in Persia or other countries of the Near East by knotting silk or wool yarn by hand onto a woven backing, characterized by rich colours and flowing or geometric designs.

Persian cat NOUN a long-haired variety of domestic cat with a stocky body, round face, short nose, and short thick legs.

Persian Empire NOUN the S Asian empire established by Cyrus the Great in the 6th century B.C. and overthrown by Alexander the Great in the 4th century B.C. At its height it extended from India to Europe.

Persian greyhound NOUN another name for the **Saluki.**

Persian Gulf NOUN a shallow arm of the Arabian Sea between SW Iran and Arabia: linked with the Arabian Sea by the Strait of Hormuz and the Gulf of Oman; important for the oilfields on its shores. Area: 233 000 sq. km (90 000 sq. miles).

Persian lamb NOUN [1] a black loosely curled fur

obtained from the skin of the karakul lamb. [2] a karakul lamb.

Persian melon NOUN another name for **winter melon.**

persicaria (ˌpɜːsɪˈkɛərɪə) NOUN another name for **red shank.**

persiennes (ˌpɜːsɪˈɛnz) PLURAL NOUN outside window shutters having louvres to keep out the sun while maintaining ventilation. Also called: **Persian blinds.**

▷HISTORY C19: from French, from *persien* Persian

persiflage (ˈpɜːsɪˌflɑːʒ) NOUN light frivolous conversation, style, or treatment; friendly teasing.

▷HISTORY C18: via French, from *persifler* to tease, from *per-* (intensive) + *siffler* to whistle, from Latin *sībilāre* to whistle

persimmon (pɜːˈsɪmən) NOUN [1] any of several tropical trees of the genus *Diospyros,* typically having hard wood and large orange-red fruit: family *Ebenaceae*. [2] the sweet fruit of any of these trees, which is edible when completely ripe. ◆ See also **ebony** (sense 1).

▷HISTORY C17: of Algonquian origin; related to Delaware *pasĭmĕnan* dried fruit

Persis (ˈpɜːsɪs) NOUN an ancient region of SW Iran: homeland of the Achaemenid dynasty.

persist (pəˈsɪst) VERB (*intr*) [1] (often foll by *in*) to continue steadfastly or obstinately despite opposition or difficulty. [2] to continue to exist or occur without interruption: *the rain persisted throughout the night.*

▷HISTORY C16: from Latin *persistere,* from *per-* (intensive) + *sistere* to stand steadfast, from *stāre* to stand

▸**perˈsister** NOUN

persistence (pəˈsɪstəns) *or* **persistency** NOUN [1] the quality of persisting; tenacity. [2] the act of persisting; continued effort or existence. [3] the continuance of an effect after the cause of it has stopped: *persistence of vision.*

persistent (pəˈsɪstənt) ADJECTIVE [1] showing persistence. [2] incessantly repeated; unrelenting: *your persistent questioning.* [3] (of plant parts) remaining attached to the plant after the normal time of withering: *a fruit surrounded by a persistent perianth.* [4] *Zoology* **a** (of parts normally present only in young stages) present in the adult: *persistent gills in axolotls.* **b** continuing to grow or develop after the normal period of growth: *persistent teeth.* [5] (of a chemical, esp when used as an insecticide) slow to break down; not easily degradable.

▸**perˈsistently** ADVERB

persistent cruelty NOUN *Brit Law* conduct causing fear of danger to the life or health of a spouse (used in matrimonial proceedings before magistrates).

persistent organic pollutant NOUN a toxin resulting from a manufacturing process, which remains in the environment for many years. Abbreviation: **POP.**

persistent vegetative state NOUN *Med* an irreversible condition, resulting from brain damage, characterized by lack of consciousness, thought, and feeling, although reflex activities (such as breathing) continue. Abbreviation: **PVS.**

persnickety (pəˈsnɪkɪtɪ) ADJECTIVE the US word for **pernickety.**

person (ˈpɜːsᵊn) NOUN, *plural* **persons.** [1] an individual human being. [2] the body of a human being, sometimes including his or her clothing: *guns hidden on his person.* [3] a grammatical category into which pronouns and forms of verbs are subdivided depending on whether they refer to the speaker, the person addressed, or some other individual, thing, etc. [4] a human being or a corporation recognized in law as having certain rights and obligations. [5] *Philosophy* a being characterized by consciousness, rationality, and a moral sense, and traditionally thought of as consisting of both a body and a mind or soul. [6] *Archaic* a character or role; guise. [7] **in person. a** actually present: *the author will be there in person.* **b** without the help or intervention of others.

▷HISTORY C13: from Old French *persone,* from Latin *persōna* mask, perhaps from Etruscan *phersu* mask

> **Language note** *People* is the word usually used to refer to more than one individual: *there were a hundred people at the reception. Persons* is rarely used, except in official English: *several persons were interviewed.*

Person (ˈpɜːsᵊn) NOUN *Christianity* any of the three hypostases existing as distinct in the one God and constituting the Trinity. They are the **First Person,** the Father, the **Second Person,** the Son, and the **Third Person,** the Holy Ghost.

-person SUFFIX FORMING NOUNS sometimes used instead of *-man* and *-woman* or *-lady*: *chairperson; salesperson.*

> **Language note** See at **-man.**

persona (pɜːˈsəʊnə) NOUN, *plural* **-nae** (-niː). [1] (*often plural*) a character in a play, novel, etc. [2] an assumed identity or character. [3] (in Jungian psychology) the mechanism that conceals a person's true thoughts and feelings, esp in his adaptation to the outside world.

▷HISTORY Latin: mask

personable (ˈpɜːsənəbᵊl) ADJECTIVE pleasant in appearance and personality.

▸ˈ**personableness** NOUN ▸ˈ**personably** ADVERB

personage (ˈpɜːsənɪdʒ) NOUN [1] an important or distinguished person. [2] another word for **person** (sense 1): *a strange personage.* [3] *Rare* a figure in literature, history, etc.

persona grata *Latin* (pɜːˈsəʊnə ˈgrɑːtə) NOUN, *plural* ***personae gratae*** (pɜːˈsəʊniː ˈgrɑːtiː). an acceptable person, esp a diplomat acceptable to the government of the country to which he or she is sent.

personal (ˈpɜːsənᵊl) ADJECTIVE [1] of or relating to the private aspects of a person's life: *personal letters; a personal question.* [2] (*prenominal*) of or relating to a person's body, its care, or its appearance: *personal hygiene; great personal beauty.* [3] belonging to or intended for a particular person and no-one else: *as a personal favour; for your personal use.* [4] (*prenominal*) undertaken by an individual himself: *a personal appearance by a celebrity.* [5] referring to, concerning, or involving a person's individual personality, intimate affairs, etc., esp in an offensive way: *personal remarks; don't be so personal.* [6] having the attributes of an individual conscious being: *a personal God.* [7] of or arising from the personality: *personal magnetism.* [8] of, relating to, or denoting grammatical person. [9] *Law* of or relating to movable property, such as money. Compare **real**[1] (sense 8). ◆ NOUN [10] *Law* an item of movable property.

personal column NOUN a newspaper column containing personal messages, advertisements by charities, requests for friendship, holiday companions, etc.

personal computer NOUN a small inexpensive computer used in word processing, playing computer games, etc.

personal digital assistant NOUN a palmtop computer for storing information. Abbreviation: **PDA.**

personal equation NOUN [1] the variation or error in observation or judgment caused by individual characteristics. [2] the allowance made for such variation.

personal equity plan NOUN the full name for **PEP.**

personalism (ˈpɜːsənəˌlɪzəm) NOUN [1] a philosophical movement that stresses the value of persons. [2] an idiosyncratic mode of behaviour or expression.

▸ˌ**personalˈistic** ADJECTIVE ▸ˈ**personalist** NOUN, ADJECTIVE

personality (ˌpɜːsəˈnælɪtɪ) NOUN, *plural* **-ties.** [1] *Psychol* the sum total of all the behavioural and mental characteristics by means of which an individual is recognized as being unique. [2] the distinctive character of a person that makes him socially attractive: *a salesman needs a lot of personality.* [3] a well-known person in a certain field, such as sport or entertainment. [4] a remarkable person: *the old fellow is a real personality.* [5] the quality of being a unique person. [6] the distinctive atmosphere of a place or situation. [7] (*often plural*) a personal remark.

personality cult NOUN deliberately cultivated adulation of a person, esp a political leader.

personality disorder NOUN *Psychiatry* any of a group of mental disorders characterized by a permanent disposition to behave in ways causing suffering to oneself or others.

personality inventory NOUN *Psychol* a form of personality test in which the subject answers questions about himself. The results are used to determine dimensions of personality, such as extroversion.

personality type NOUN *Psychol* a cluster of personality traits commonly occurring together.

personalize *or* **personalise** (ˈpɜːsənəˌlaɪz) VERB (*tr*) [1] to endow with personal or individual qualities or characteristics. [2] to mark (stationery, clothing, etc.) with a person's initials, name, etc. [3] to take (a remark, etc.) personally. [4] another word for **personify.**

▸ˌ**personaliˈzation** *or* ˌ**personaliˈsation** NOUN

personally (ˈpɜːsənəlɪ) ADVERB [1] without the help or intervention of others: *I'll attend to it personally.* [2] (*sentence modifier*) in one's own opinion or as regards oneself: *personally, I hate onions.* [3] as if referring to oneself: *to take the insults personally.* [4] as a person: *we like him personally, but professionally he's incompetent.*

personal organizer NOUN [1] a diary that stores personal records, appointments, notes, etc. [2] a pocket-sized electronic device that performs the same functions.

personal pension NOUN [1] a private pension scheme in which an individual contributes part of his or her salary to a financial institution, which invests it so that a lump sum is available on retirement; this is then used to purchase an annuity. [2] a pension derived from such a scheme.

personal pronoun NOUN a pronoun having a definite person or thing as an antecedent and functioning grammatically in the same way as the noun that it replaces. In English, the personal pronouns include *I, you, he, she, it, we,* and *they,* and are inflected for case.

personal property NOUN *Law* movable property, such as furniture or money. Compare **real property.** Also called: **personalty.**

personal shopper NOUN a person employed, esp by a shop, to accompany and advise customers on shopping trips or to select items for them.

personal stereo NOUN a very small audio cassette player designed to be worn attached to a belt and used with lightweight headphones.

personal stylist NOUN a person employed by a rich or famous client to offer advice on clothes, hairstyles, and other aspects of personal appearance.

personalty (ˈpɜːsənəltɪ) NOUN, *plural* **-ties.** *Law* another word for **personal property.**

▷HISTORY C16: from Anglo-French, from Late Latin *persōnālitās* personality

persona non grata *Latin* (pɜːˈsəʊnə nɒn ˈgrɑːtə) NOUN, *plural* ***personae non gratae*** (pɜːˈsəʊniː nɒn ˈgrɑːtiː). [1] an unacceptable or unwelcome person. [2] a diplomatic or consular officer who is not acceptable to the government or sovereign to whom he or she is accredited.

personate[1] (ˈpɜːsəˌneɪt) VERB (*tr*) [1] to act the part of (a character in a play); portray. [2] a less common word for **personify.** [3] *Criminal law* to assume the identity of (another person) with intent to deceive.

▸ˌ**personˈation** NOUN ▸ˈ**personative** ADJECTIVE

▸ˈ**personˌator** NOUN

personate[2] (ˈpɜːsənɪt, -ˌneɪt) ADJECTIVE (of the corollas of certain flowers) having two lips in the form of a face.

▷HISTORY C18: from New Latin *persōnātus* masked, from Latin *persōna;* see PERSON

personification (pɜːˌsɒnɪfɪˈkeɪʃən) NOUN [1] the attribution of human characteristics to things, abstract ideas, etc., as for literary or artistic effect. [2] the representation of an abstract quality or idea in the form of a person, creature, etc., as in art and literature. [3] a person or thing that personifies. [4] a person or thing regarded as an embodiment of a quality: *he is the personification of optimism.*

personify (pɜːˈsɒnɪˌfaɪ) VERB **-fies, -fying, -fied.** (*tr*) [1] to attribute human characteristics to (a thing or abstraction). [2] to represent (an abstract quality) in human or animal form. [3] (of a person or thing) to represent (an abstract quality), as in art or literature. [4] to be the embodiment of.
▸**perˈsoniˌfiable** ADJECTIVE ▸**perˈsoniˌfier** NOUN

personned ADJECTIVE another word for **manned.**

personnel (ˌpɜːsəˈnɛl) NOUN [1] the people employed in an organization or for a service or undertaking. Compare **materiel.** [2] **a** the office or department that interviews, appoints, or keeps records of employees. Also called: **human resources. b** (*as modifier*): *a personnel officer.*
▷HISTORY C19: from French, ultimately from Late Latin *persōnālis* personal (adj); see PERSON

perspective (pəˈspɛktɪv) NOUN [1] a way of regarding situations, facts, etc., and judging their relative importance. [2] the proper or accurate point of view or the ability to see it; objectivity: *try to get some perspective on your troubles.* [3] the theory or art of suggesting three dimensions on a two-dimensional surface, in order to recreate the appearance and spatial relationships that objects or a scene in recession present to the eye. [4] the appearance of objects, buildings, etc., relative to each other, as determined by their distance from the viewer, or the effects of this distance on their appearance. [5] a view over some distance in space or time; vista; prospect. [6] a picture showing perspective.
▷HISTORY C14: from Medieval Latin *perspectīva ars* the science of optics, from Latin *perspicere* to inspect carefully, from *per-* (intensive) + *specere* to behold
▸**perˈspectively** ADVERB

Perspex (ˈpɜːspɛks) NOUN *Trademark* any of various clear acrylic resins, used chiefly as a substitute for glass.

perspicacious (ˌpɜːspɪˈkeɪʃəs) ADJECTIVE [1] acutely perceptive or discerning. [2] *Archaic* having keen eyesight.
▷HISTORY C17: from Latin *perspicax,* from *perspicere* to look at closely; see PERSPECTIVE
▸**ˌperspiˈcaciously** ADVERB ▸**perspicacity** (ˌpɜːspɪˈkæsɪtɪ) *or* **ˌperspiˈcaciousness** NOUN

perspicuity (ˌpɜːspɪˈkjuːɪtɪ) NOUN [1] the quality of being perspicuous. [2] another word for **perspicacity.**

perspicuous (pəˈspɪkjʊəs) ADJECTIVE (of speech or writing) easily understood; lucid.
▷HISTORY C15: from Latin *perspicuus* transparent, from *perspicere* to explore thoroughly; see PERSPECTIVE
▸**perˈspicuously** ADVERB ▸**perˈspicuousness** NOUN

perspiration (ˌpɜːspəˈreɪʃən) NOUN [1] the act or process of insensibly eliminating fluid through the pores of the skin, which evaporates immediately. [2] the sensible elimination of fluid through the pores of the skin, which is visible as droplets on the skin. [3] the salty fluid secreted through the pores of the skin; sweat.

perspiratory (pəˈspaɪərətərɪ, -trɪ) ADJECTIVE of, relating to, or stimulating perspiration.

perspire (pəˈspaɪə) VERB to secrete or exude (perspiration) through the pores of the skin.
▷HISTORY C17: from Latin *perspīrāre* to blow, from *per-* (through) + *spīrāre* to breathe; compare INSPIRE
▸**perˈspiringly** ADVERB

persuade (pəˈsweɪd) VERB (*tr; may take a clause as object or an infinitive*) [1] to induce, urge, or prevail upon successfully: *he finally persuaded them to buy it.* [2] to cause to believe; convince: *even with the evidence, the police were not persuaded.*
▷HISTORY C16: from Latin *persuādēre,* from *per-* (intensive) + *suādēre* to urge, advise
▸**perˈsuadable** *or* **perˈsuasible** ADJECTIVE ▸**perˌsuadaˈbility** *or* **perˌsuasiˈbility** NOUN ▸**perˈsuader** NOUN

persuasion (pəˈsweɪʒən) NOUN [1] the act of persuading or of trying to persuade. [2] the power to persuade. [3] the state of being persuaded; strong belief. [4] an established creed or belief, esp a religious one. [5] a sect, party, or faction.
▷HISTORY C14: from Latin *persuāsiō;* see PERSUADE

persuasive (pəˈsweɪsɪv) ADJECTIVE having the power or ability to persuade; tending to persuade: *a persuasive salesman.*
▸**perˈsuasively** ADVERB ▸**perˈsuasiveness** NOUN

persulphuric acid *or US* **persulfuric acid** (ˌpɜːsʌlˈfjʊərɪk) NOUN other names (not in technical usage) for **peroxysulphuric acid.**

pert (pɜːt) ADJECTIVE [1] saucy, impudent, or forward. [2] jaunty: *a pert little hat.* [3] *Obsolete* clever or brisk.
▷HISTORY C13: variant of earlier *apert,* from Latin *apertus* open, from *aperīre* to open; influenced by Old French *aspert,* from Latin *expertus* EXPERT
▸**ˈpertly** ADVERB ▸**ˈpertness** NOUN

PERT (pɜːt) NOUN ACRONYM FOR programme evaluation and review technique.

pertain (pəˈteɪn) VERB (*intr; often foll by to*) [1] to have reference, relation, or relevance: *issues pertaining to women.* [2] to be appropriate: *the product pertains to real user needs.* [3] to belong (to) or be a part (of); be an adjunct, attribute, or accessory (of).
▷HISTORY C14: from Latin *pertinēre,* from *per-* (intensive) + *tenēre* to hold

Perth (pɜːθ) NOUN [1] a city in central Scotland, in Perth and Kinross on the River Tay: capital of Scotland from the 12th century until the assassination of James I there in 1437. Pop.: 41 453 (1991). [2] a city in SW Australia, capital of Western Australia, on the Swan River: major industrial centre; University of Western Australia (1911). Pop.: 1 262 600 (1995 est.).

Perth and Kinross (kɪnˈrɒs) NOUN a council area of N central Scotland, corresponding mainly to the historical counties of Perthshire and Kinross-shire: part of Tayside Region from 1975 until 1996: chiefly mountainous, with agriculture, tourism, and forestry. Administrative centre: Perth. Pop.: 134 949 (2001). Area: 5321 sq. km (2019 sq. miles).

Perthshire (ˈpɜːθˌʃɪə, -ʃə) NOUN (until 1975) a county of central Scotland, now part of Perth and Kinross council area.

pertinacious (ˌpɜːtɪˈneɪʃəs) ADJECTIVE [1] doggedly resolute in purpose or belief; unyielding. [2] stubbornly persistent.
▷HISTORY C17: from Latin *pertināx,* from *per-* (intensive) + *tenāx* clinging, from *tenēre* to hold
▸**ˌpertiˈnaciously** ADVERB ▸**pertinacity** (ˌpɜːtɪˈnæsɪtɪ) *or* **ˌpertiˈnaciousness** NOUN

pertinent (ˈpɜːtɪnənt) ADJECTIVE relating to the matter at hand; relevant.
▷HISTORY C14: from Latin *pertinēns,* from *pertinēre* to PERTAIN
▸**ˈpertinence** NOUN ▸**ˈpertinently** ADVERB

perturb (pəˈtɜːb) VERB (*tr; often passive*) [1] to disturb the composure of; trouble. [2] to throw into disorder. [3] *Physics, astronomy* to cause (a planet, electron, etc.) to undergo a perturbation.
▷HISTORY C14: from Old French *pertourber,* from Latin *perturbāre* to confuse, from *per-* (intensive) + *turbāre* to agitate, from *turba* confusion
▸**perˈturbable** ADJECTIVE ▸**perˈturbably** ADVERB
▸**perˈturbing** ADJECTIVE ▸**perˈturbingly** ADVERB

perturbation (ˌpɜːtəˈbeɪʃən) NOUN [1] the act of perturbing or the state of being perturbed. [2] a cause of disturbance or upset. [3] *Physics* a secondary influence on a system that modifies simple behaviour, such as the effect of the other electrons on one electron in an atom. [4] *Astronomy* a small continuous deviation in the inclination and eccentricity of the orbit of a planet or comet, due to the attraction of neighbouring planets.

pertussis (pəˈtʌsɪs) NOUN the technical name for **whooping cough.**
▷HISTORY C18: New Latin, from Latin *per-* (intensive) + *tussis* cough
▸**perˈtussal** ADJECTIVE

Peru (pəˈruː) NOUN a republic in W South America, on the Pacific: the centre of the great Inca Empire when conquered by the Spanish in 1532; gained independence in 1824 by defeating Spanish forces with armies led by San Martín and Bolívar; consists of a coastal desert, rising to the Andes; an important exporter of minerals and a major fishing nation. Official languages: Spanish, Quechua, and Aymara. Official religion: Roman Catholic. Currency: nuevo sol. Capital: Lima. Pop.: 26 090 000 (2001 est.). Area: 1 285 215 sq. km (496 222 sq. miles).

Peru Current NOUN another name for the **Humboldt Current.**

Perugia (pəˈruːdʒə; *Italian* peˈruːdʒa) NOUN [1] a city in central Italy, in Umbria: centre of the Umbrian school of painting (15th century); university (1308); Etruscan and Roman remains. Pop.: 156 673 (2000 est.). Ancient name: **Perusia.** [2] **Lake.** another name for (Lake) **Trasimene.**

peruke (pəˈruːk) NOUN a type of wig for men, fashionable in the 17th and 18th centuries. Also called: **periwig.**
▷HISTORY C16: from French *perruque,* from Italian *perrucca* wig, of obscure origin

peruse (pəˈruːz) VERB (*tr*) [1] to read or examine with care; study. [2] to browse or read through in a leisurely way.
▷HISTORY C15 (meaning: to use up): from PER- (intensive) + USE
▸**peˈrusal** NOUN ▸**peˈruser** NOUN

Peruvian (pəˈruːvɪən) ADJECTIVE of or relating to Peru or its inhabitants. ◆ NOUN a native or inhabitant of Peru.

Peruvian bark NOUN another name for **cinchona** (sense 2).

perv (pɜːv) *Slang* ◆ NOUN [1] a pervert. [2] *Austral* an erotic glance or look. ◆ VERB *also* **perve.** (*intr*) [3] *Austral* to give a person an erotic look. ◆ See also **perv on.**

pervade (pɜːˈveɪd) VERB (*tr*) to spread through or throughout, esp subtly or gradually; permeate.
▷HISTORY C17: from Latin *pervādere,* from *per-* through + *vādere* to go
▸**perˈvader** NOUN ▸**pervasion** (pɜːˈveɪʒən) NOUN

pervasive (pɜːˈveɪsɪv) ADJECTIVE pervading or tending to pervade.
▷HISTORY C18: from Latin *pervāsus,* past participle of *pervādere* to PERVADE
▸**perˈvasively** ADVERB ▸**perˈvasiveness** NOUN

perverse (pəˈvɜːs) ADJECTIVE [1] deliberately deviating from what is regarded as normal, good, or proper. [2] persistently holding to what is wrong. [3] wayward or contrary; obstinate; cantankerous. [4] *Archaic* perverted.
▷HISTORY C14: from Old French *pervers,* from Latin *perversus* turned the wrong way
▸**perˈversely** ADVERB ▸**perˈverseness** NOUN

perversion (pəˈvɜːʃən) NOUN [1] any abnormal means of obtaining sexual satisfaction. [2] the act of perverting or the state of being perverted. [3] a perverted form or usage.

perversity (pəˈvɜːsɪtɪ) NOUN, *plural* **-ties.** [1] the quality or state of being perverse. [2] a perverse action, comment, etc.

perversive (pəˈvɜːsɪv) ADJECTIVE perverting or tending to pervert.

pervert VERB (*tr*) (pəˈvɜːt) [1] to use wrongly or badly. [2] to interpret wrongly or badly; distort. [3] to lead into deviant or perverted beliefs or behaviour; corrupt. [4] to debase. ◆ NOUN (ˈpɜːvɜːt) [5] a person who practises sexual perversion.
▷HISTORY C14: from Old French *pervertir,* from Latin *pervertere* to turn the wrong way, from *per-* (indicating deviation) + *vertere* to turn
▸**perˈverter** NOUN ▸**perˈvertible** ADJECTIVE

perverted (pəˈvɜːtɪd) ADJECTIVE [1] deviating greatly from what is regarded as normal or right; distorted. [2] of or practising sexual perversion. [3] incorrectly interpreted.
▸**perˈvertedly** ADVERB ▸**perˈvertedness** NOUN

pervious (ˈpɜːvɪəs) ADJECTIVE [1] able to be penetrated; permeable. [2] receptive to new ideas; open-minded.
▷HISTORY C17: from Latin *pervius,* from *per-* (through) + *via* a way
▸**ˈperviously** ADVERB ▸**ˈperviousness** NOUN

perv on VERB (*tr, preposition*) *Slang* to make unwanted sexual advances towards.

pes (peɪz, piːz) NOUN, *plural* **pedes** (ˈpediːz). [1] the technical name for the human **foot.** [2] the corresponding part in higher vertebrates. [3] any footlike part.
▷HISTORY C19: New Latin: foot

Pesach *or* **Pesah** (ˈpeɪsɑːk; *Hebrew* ˈpɛsax) NOUN other words for **Passover** (sense 1).
▷HISTORY from Hebrew *pesah;* see PASSOVER

pesade (peˈsɑːd) NOUN *Dressage* a position in which the horse stands on the hind legs with the forelegs in the air.
▷HISTORY C18: from French, from *posade,* from Italian *posata* a halt, from *posare* to stop, from Latin *pausa* end

Pesaro (*Italian* ˈpeːzaro) NOUN a port and resort in

E central Italy, in the Marches on the Adriatic. Pop.: 90 340 (1990). Ancient name: **Pisaurum** (pɪ'saʊrəm).

Pescadores (ˌpɛskə'dɔːrɪz) PLURAL NOUN a group of 64 islands in Formosa Strait, separated from Taiwan (to which it belongs) by the **Pescadores Channel.** Pop.: 90 719 (2001 est.). Area: 127 sq. km (49 sq. miles). Chinese names: **Penghu, P'eng-hu.**

Pescara (*Italian* pes'kaːra) NOUN a city and resort in E central Italy, on the Adriatic. Pop.: 115 698 (2000 est.).

peseta (pə'seɪtə; *Spanish* pe'seta) NOUN the former standard monetary unit of Spain and Andorra, divided into 100 céntimos; replaced by the euro in 2002.
▷**HISTORY** C19: from Spanish, diminutive of PESO

pesewa (pɪ'seɪwɑː) NOUN a Ghanaian monetary unit worth one hundredth of a cedi.

Peshawar (pə'ʃɔːə) NOUN a city in N Pakistan, at the E end of the Khyber Pass: one of the oldest cities in Pakistan and capital of the ancient kingdom of Gandhara; university (1950). Pop.: 988 055 (1998).

Peshitta (pə'ʃiːtə) *or* **Peshito** (pə'ʃiːtəʊ) NOUN the principal Syriac version of the Bible.
▷**HISTORY** C18 *Peshito,* from Syriac

pesky ('pɛskɪ) ADJECTIVE **peskier, peskiest.** *Informal, chiefly US and Canadian* troublesome: *pesky flies.*
▷**HISTORY** C19: probably changed from *pesty;* see PEST
▸**'peskily** ADVERB ▸**'peskiness** NOUN

peso ('peɪsəʊ; *Spanish* 'peso) NOUN, *plural* **-sos** (-səʊz; *Spanish* -sos). [1] the standard monetary unit, comprising 100 centavos, of Argentina, Chile, Colombia, Cuba, the Dominican Republic, Mexico, and the Philippines; formerly also of Guinea-Bissau, where it was replaced by the CFA franc. [2] the standard monetary unit of Uruguay, divided into 100 centesimos. [3] another name for **piece of eight.**
▷**HISTORY** C16: from Spanish: weight, from Latin *pēnsum* something weighed out, from *pendere* to weigh

pessary ('pɛsərɪ) NOUN, *plural* **-ries.** *Med* [1] a device for inserting into the vagina, either as a support for the uterus or (**diaphragm pessary**) to deliver a drug, such as a contraceptive. [2] a medicated vaginal suppository.
▷**HISTORY** C14: from Late Latin *pessārium,* from Latin *pessum,* from Greek *pessos* plug

pessimism ('pɛsɪˌmɪzəm) NOUN [1] the tendency to expect the worst and see the worst in all things. [2] the doctrine of the ultimate triumph of evil over good. [3] the doctrine that this world is corrupt and that man's sojourn in it is a preparation for some other existence.
▷**HISTORY** C18: from Latin *pessimus* worst, from *malus* bad
▸**'pessimist** NOUN ▸**ˌpessi'mistic** *or* (*less commonly*) **ˌpessi'mistical** ADJECTIVE ▸**ˌpessi'mistically** ADVERB

pest (pɛst) NOUN [1] a person or thing that annoys, esp by imposing itself when it is not wanted; nuisance. [2] **a** any organism that damages crops, injures or irritates livestock or man, or reduces the fertility of land. **b** (*as modifier*): *pest control.* [3] *Rare* an epidemic disease or pestilence.
▷**HISTORY** C16: from Latin *pestis* plague, of obscure origin

pester ('pɛstə) VERB (*tr*) to annoy or nag continually.
▷**HISTORY** C16: from Old French *empestrer* to hobble (a horse), from Vulgar Latin *impāstōriāre* (unattested) to use a hobble, from *pāstōria* (unattested) a hobble, from Latin *pāstōrius* relating to a herdsman, from *pastor* herdsman
▸**'pesterer** NOUN ▸**'pesteringly** ADVERB

pester power NOUN the ability possessed by a child to nag a parent relentlessly until the parent succumbs and agrees to the child's request.

pesthouse ('pɛstˌhaʊs) NOUN *Obsolete* a hospital for treating persons with infectious diseases. Also called: **lazaretto.**

pesticide ('pɛstɪˌsaɪd) NOUN a chemical used for killing pests, esp insects and rodents.
▸**ˌpesti'cidal** ADJECTIVE

pestiferous (pɛ'stɪfərəs) ADJECTIVE [1] *Informal* troublesome; irritating. [2] breeding, carrying, or spreading infectious disease. [3] corrupting; pernicious.
▷**HISTORY** C16: from Latin *pestifer,* from *pestis* contagious disease, PEST + *ferre* to bring
▸**pes'tiferously** ADVERB ▸**pes'tiferousness** NOUN

pestilence ('pɛstɪləns) NOUN [1] **a** any epidemic outbreak of a deadly and highly infectious disease, such as the plague. **b** such a disease. [2] an evil influence or idea.

pestilent ('pɛstɪlənt) ADJECTIVE [1] annoying; irritating. [2] highly destructive morally or physically; pernicious. [3] infected with or likely to cause epidemic or infectious disease.
▷**HISTORY** C15: from Latin *pestilens* unwholesome, from *pestis* plague
▸**'pestilently** ADVERB

pestilential (ˌpɛstɪ'lɛnʃəl) ADJECTIVE [1] dangerous or troublesome; harmful or annoying. [2] of, causing, or resembling pestilence.
▸**ˌpesti'lentially** ADVERB

pestle ('pɛsᵊl) NOUN [1] a club-shaped instrument for mixing or grinding substances in a mortar. [2] a tool for pounding or stamping. ◆ VERB [3] to pound (a substance or object) with or as if with a pestle.
▷**HISTORY** C14: from Old French *pestel,* from Latin *pistillum;* related to *pinsāre* to crush

pesto ('pɛstəʊ) NOUN a sauce for pasta, consisting of basil leaves, pine nuts, garlic, oil, and Parmesan cheese, all crushed together.
▷**HISTORY** Italian, shortened form of *pestato,* past participle of *pestare* to pound, crush

pet¹ (pɛt) NOUN [1] a tame animal kept in a household for companionship, amusement, etc. [2] a person who is fondly indulged; favourite: *teacher's pet.* ◆ ADJECTIVE [3] kept as a pet: *a pet dog.* [4] of or for pet animals: *pet food.* [5] particularly cherished; favourite: *a pet theory; a pet hatred.* [6] familiar or affectionate: *a pet name.* [7] **pet day.** *Scot and Irish* a single fine day during a period of bad weather. ◆ VERB **pets, petting, petted.** [8] (*tr*) to treat (a person, animal, etc.) as a pet; pamper. [9] (*tr*) to pat or fondle (an animal, child, etc.). [10] (*intr*) *Informal* (of two people) to caress each other in an erotic manner, as during lovemaking (often in the phrase **heavy petting**).
▷**HISTORY** C16: origin unknown
▸**'petter** NOUN

pet² (pɛt) NOUN [1] a fit of sulkiness, esp at what is felt to be a slight; pique. ◆ VERB **pets, petting, petted.** [2] (*intr*) to take offence; sulk.
▷**HISTORY** C16: of uncertain origin

PET ABBREVIATION FOR: [1] **positron emission tomography.** ◆ NOUN ACRONYM FOR: [2] potentially exempt transfer: a procedure in the UK whereby gifting property and cash is tax-free, provided that the donor lives for at least seven years after the gift is made.

Pet. *Bible* ◆ ABBREVIATION FOR Peter.

Peta ABBREVIATION FOR People for the Ethical Treatment of Animals.

peta- PREFIX denoting 10^{15}: *petametres.* Symbol: P.
▷**HISTORY** C20: so named because it is the SI prefix after TERA-; on the model of PENTA-, the prefix after TETRA-

petal ('pɛtᵊl) NOUN any of the separate parts of the corolla of a flower: often brightly coloured.
▷**HISTORY** C18: from New Latin *petalum,* from Greek *petalon* leaf; related to *petannunai* to lie open
▸**'petaline** ADJECTIVE ▸**'petal-ˌlike** ADJECTIVE ▸**'petalled** ADJECTIVE

-petal ADJECTIVE COMBINING FORM seeking: *centripetal.*
▷**HISTORY** from New Latin *-petus,* from Latin *petere* to seek

petaliferous (ˌpɛtə'lɪfərəs) *or* **petalous** ADJECTIVE bearing or having petals.

petalody ('pɛtəˌləʊdɪ) NOUN a condition in certain plants in which stamens or other parts of the flower assume the form and function of petals.
▷**HISTORY** C19: from Greek *petalōdēs* like a leaf, from *petalon* leaf
▸**petalodic** (ˌpɛtə'lɒdɪk) ADJECTIVE

petaloid ('pɛtəˌlɔɪd) ADJECTIVE *Biology* resembling a petal, esp in shape: *the petaloid pattern on a sea urchin.*

pétanque *French* (ˌpeɪ'tɑ̃k; *English* petɑ̃k) NOUN another name, esp in the South of France, for ***boules.***
▷**HISTORY** French, from Provençal *pèd tanco* foot fixed (to the ground)

petard (pɪ'tɑːd) NOUN [1] (formerly) a device containing explosives used to breach a wall, doors, etc. [2] **hoist with one's own petard.** being the victim of one's own schemes. [3] a type of explosive firework.
▷**HISTORY** C16: from French: firework, from *péter* to break wind, from Latin *pēdere*

petasus ('pɛtəsəs) *or* **petasos** ('pɛtəsəs, -ˌsɒs) NOUN a broad-brimmed hat worn by the ancient Greeks, such as one with wings on either side as traditionally worn by Mercury.
▷**HISTORY** C16: via Latin from Greek *petasos*

petaurist (pə'tɔːrɪst) NOUN another name for **flying phalanger.**
▷**HISTORY** C20: from Latin *petaurista* tightrope walker

petcock ('pɛtˌkɒk) NOUN a small valve for checking the water level in a steam boiler or draining condensed steam from the cylinder of a steam engine.
▷**HISTORY** C19: from PET¹ or perhaps French *pet,* from *péter* to break wind + COCK¹

petechia (pɪ'tiːkɪə) NOUN, *plural* **-chiae** (-kɪˌiː). a minute discoloured spot on the surface of the skin or mucous membrane, caused by an underlying ruptured blood vessel.
▷**HISTORY** C18: via New Latin from Italian *petecchia* freckle, of obscure origin
▸**pe'techial** ADJECTIVE

peter¹ ('piːtə) VERB (*intr; foll by out or away*) to fall (off) in volume, intensity, etc., and finally cease: *the cash petered out in three months.*
▷**HISTORY** C19: of unknown origin

peter² ('piːtə) *Bridge, whist* ◆ VERB (*intr*) [1] to play a high card before a low one in a suit, usually a conventional signal of a doubleton holding or of strength in that suit. ◆ NOUN [2] the act of petering.
▷**HISTORY** C20: perhaps a special use of PETER¹ (to fall off in power)

peter³ ('piːtə) NOUN *Slang* [1] a safe, till, or cash box. [2] a prison cell. [3] the witness box in a courtroom. [4] *Chiefly US* a slang word for **penis.**
▷**HISTORY** C17 (meaning a case): from the name *Peter*

Peter ('piːtə) NOUN *New Testament* either of the two epistles traditionally ascribed to the apostle Peter (in full **The First Epistle** and **The Second Epistle of Peter**).

Peterborough ('piːtəbərə, -brə) NOUN [1] a city in central England, in Peterborough unitary authority, N Cambridgeshire on the River Nene: industrial centre; under development as a new town since 1968. Pop.: 134 788 (1991 est.). [2] a unitary authority in central England, in Cambridgeshire. Pop.: 156 060 (2001). Area: 402 sq. km (155 sq. miles). [3] **Soke of.** a former administrative unit of E central England, generally considered part of Northamptonshire or Huntingdonshire: absorbed into Cambridgeshire in 1974. [4] a city in SE Canada, in SE Ontario: manufacturing centre. Pop.: 68 371 (1991). [5] a traditional type of wooden canoe formerly made in Peterborough, SE Ontario.

Peterlee ('piːtəˌliː) NOUN a new town in Co. Durham, founded in 1948. Pop.: 23 500 (1990).

Peterloo Massacre (ˌpiːtə'luː) NOUN an incident at St Peter's Fields, Manchester, in 1819 in which a radical meeting was broken up by a cavalry charge, resulting in about 500 injuries and 11 deaths.
▷**HISTORY** C19: from *St Peter's Fields* + WATERLOO

peterman ('piːtəmən) NOUN, *plural* **-men.** *Slang* a burglar skilled in safe-breaking.
▷**HISTORY** C19: from PETER³

Petermann Peak ('piːtəmən) NOUN a mountain in E Greenland. Height: 2932 m (9645 ft.).

Peter Pan NOUN a youthful, boyish, or immature man.
▷**HISTORY** C20: after the main character in *Peter Pan* (1904), a play by J. M. Barrie

Peter Pan collar NOUN a collar on a round neck, having two rounded ends at the front.

Peter Principle NOUN **the.** the theory, usually taken facetiously, that all members in a hierarchy rise to their own level of incompetence.
▷**HISTORY** C20: from the book *The Peter Principle* (1969) by Dr. Lawrence J. Peter and Raymond Hull, in which the theory was originally propounded

Petersburg ('piːtəzˌbɜːg) NOUN a city in SE Virginia, on the Appomattox River: scene of prolonged fighting (1864–65) during the final months of the American Civil War. Pop.: 38 386 (1990).

petersham ('pi:təʃəm) NOUN 1 a thick corded ribbon used to stiffen belts, button bands, etc. 2 a heavy woollen fabric used esp for coats. 3 a kind of overcoat made of such fabric.
▷HISTORY C19: named after Viscount *Petersham* (died 1851), English army officer

Peter's pence *or* **Peter pence** NOUN 1 an annual tax, originally of one penny, formerly levied for the maintenance of the Papal See: abolished by Henry VIII in 1534. 2 a voluntary contribution made by Roman Catholics in many countries for the same purpose.
▷HISTORY C13: referring to St PETER, considered as the first pope

Peters' projection NOUN a form of modified Mercator's map projection that gives prominence to Third World countries.
▷HISTORY C20: named after Arno *Peters,* German historian

pethidine ('pɛθɪˌdi:n) NOUN a white crystalline water-soluble drug used as an analgesic. Formula: $C_{15}H_{21}NO_2$.HCl. Also called: **pethidine hydrochloride.**
▷HISTORY C20: perhaps a blend of PIPERIDINE + ETHYL

pétillant *French* (petijɑ̃) ADJECTIVE (of wine) slightly effervescent.
▷HISTORY French, from *pétiller* to effervesce

petiolate ('pɛtɪəˌleɪt) *or* **petiolated** ADJECTIVE (of a plant or leaf) having a leafstalk. Compare **sessile** (sense 1).

petiole ('pɛtɪˌəʊl) NOUN 1 the stalk by which a leaf is attached to the rest of the plant. 2 *Zoology* a slender stalk or stem, such as the connection between the thorax and abdomen of ants.
▷HISTORY C18: via French from Latin *petiolus* little foot, from *pēs* foot

petiolule ('pi:tɪəʊlˌju:l) NOUN the stalk of any of the leaflets making up a compound leaf.
▷HISTORY C19: from New Latin *petiolūlus,* diminutive of Latin *petiolus;* see PETIOLE

petit ('pɛtɪ) ADJECTIVE *(prenominal) Chiefly law* of little or lesser importance; small: *petit jury.*
▷HISTORY C14: from Old French: little, of obscure origin

petit bourgeois ('pɛtɪ 'bʊəʒwɑ:; *French* pəti burʒwa) NOUN, *plural* **petits bourgeois** ('pɛtɪ 'bʊəʒwɑ:z; *French* pəti burʒwa). 1 Also called: **petite bourgeoisie, petty bourgeoisie.** the section of the middle class with the lowest social status, generally composed of shopkeepers, lower clerical staff, etc. 2 a member of this stratum. ◆ ADJECTIVE 3 of, relating to, or characteristic of the petit bourgeois, esp indicating a sense of self-righteousness and a high degree of conformity to established standards of behaviour.

petite (pə'ti:t) ADJECTIVE (of a woman) small, delicate, and dainty.
▷HISTORY C18: from French, feminine of *petit* small

petit four ('pɛtɪ 'fɔ:; *French* pəti fur) NOUN, *plural* **petits fours** ('pɛtɪ 'fɔ:z; *French* pəti fur). any of various very small rich sweet cakes and biscuits, usually decorated with fancy icing, marzipan, etc.
▷HISTORY French, literally: little oven

petition (pɪ'tɪʃən) NOUN 1 a written document signed by a large number of people demanding some form of action from a government or other authority. 2 any formal request to a higher authority or deity; entreaty. 3 *Law* a formal application in writing made to a court asking for some specific judicial action: *a petition for divorce.* 4 the action of petitioning. ◆ VERB 5 *(tr)* to address or present a petition to (a person in authority, government, etc.): *to petition Parliament.* 6 *(intr;* foll by *for)* to seek by petition: *to petition for a change in the law.*
▷HISTORY C14: from Latin *petītiō,* from *petere* to seek
▸**pe'titionary** ADJECTIVE

petitioner (pɪ'tɪʃənə) NOUN 1 a person who presents a petition. 2 *Chiefly Brit* the plaintiff in a divorce suit.

petitio principii (pɪ'tɪʃɪˌəʊ prɪn'kɪpɪˌaɪ) NOUN *Logic* a form of fallacious reasoning in which the conclusion has been assumed in the premises; begging the question. Sometimes shortened to: **petitio.**
▷HISTORY C16: Latin, translation of Greek *to en arkhei aiteisthai* an assumption at the beginning

petit jury NOUN a jury of 12 persons empanelled to determine the facts of a case and decide the issue pursuant to the direction of the court on points of law. Also called: **petty jury.** Compare **grand jury.**
▸**petit juror** NOUN

petit larceny NOUN 1 (formerly in England) the stealing of property valued at 12 pence or under. Abolished 1827. 2 (in some states of the US) the theft of property having a value below a certain figure. ◆ Also called **petty larceny.** Compare **grand larceny.**
▸**petit larcenist** NOUN

petit mal ('pɛtɪ 'mæl; *French* pəti mal) NOUN a mild form of epilepsy characterized by periods of impairment or loss of consciousness for up to 30 seconds. Compare **grand mal.**
▷HISTORY C19: French: little illness

petit point ('pɛtɪ 'pɔɪnt; *French* pəti pwɛ̃) NOUN 1 Also called: **tent stitch.** a small diagonal needlepoint stitch used for fine detail. 2 work done with such stitches, esp fine tapestry. ◆ Compare **gros point.**
▷HISTORY French: small point

petits pois *(French* pəti pwa) PLURAL NOUN small sweet fresh green peas.
▷HISTORY French: small peas

Petra ('pɛtrə, 'pi:trə) NOUN an ancient city in the south of present-day Jordan; capital of the Nabataean kingdom.

Petrarchan (pə'trɑ:kən) ADJECTIVE of or relating to Petrarch (Italian name *Francesco Petrarca*), the Italian lyric poet and scholar (1304–74).

Petrarchan sonnet NOUN a sonnet form associated with the poet Petrarch, having an octave rhyming a b b a a b b a and a sestet rhyming either c d e c d e or c d c d c d. Also called: **Italian sonnet.**

petrel ('pɛtrəl) NOUN any oceanic bird of the order *Procellariiformes,* having a hooked bill and tubular nostrils: includes albatrosses, storm petrels, and shearwaters. See also **storm petrel.**
▷HISTORY C17: variant of earlier *pitteral,* associated by folk etymology with St *Peter,* because the bird appears to walk on water

Petri dish ('pɛtrɪ) NOUN a shallow circular flat-bottomed dish, often with a fitting cover, used in laboratories, esp for producing cultures of microorganisms.
▷HISTORY C19: named after J. R. *Petri* (1852–1921), German bacteriologist

petrifaction (ˌpɛtrɪ'fækʃən) *or* **petrification** (ˌpɛtrɪfɪ'keɪʃən) NOUN 1 the act or process of forming petrified organic material. 2 the state of being petrified.

Petrified Forest NOUN a national park in E Arizona, containing petrified coniferous trees about 170 000 000 years old.

petrify ('pɛtrɪˌfaɪ) VERB **-fies, -fying, -fied.** 1 *(tr; often passive)* to convert (organic material, esp plant material) into a fossilized form by impregnation with dissolved minerals so that the original appearance is preserved. 2 to make or become dull, unresponsive, insensitive, etc.; deaden. 3 *(tr; often passive)* to stun or daze with horror, fear, etc.
▷HISTORY C16: from French *pétrifier,* ultimately from Greek *petra* stone, rock
▸**'petriˌfier** NOUN

Petrine ('pi:traɪn) ADJECTIVE 1 *New Testament* of or relating to St Peter (died ?67 A.D.), the Christian apostle regarded by Roman Catholics as the first pope, his position of leadership, or the epistles, etc., attributed to him. 2 *RC Church* of or relating to the supremacy in the Church that the pope is regarded as having inherited from St Peter: *the Petrine claims.*

petro- *or before a vowel* **petr-** COMBINING FORM 1 indicating stone or rock: *petrology.* 2 indicating petroleum, its products, etc.: *petrochemical.* 3 of or relating to a petroleum-producing country: *petrostate.*
▷HISTORY from Greek *petra* rock or *petros* stone

petrochemical (ˌpɛtrəʊ'kɛmɪkᵊl) NOUN 1 any substance, such as acetone or ethanol, obtained from petroleum or natural gas. ◆ ADJECTIVE 2 of, concerned with, or obtained from petrochemicals or related to petrochemistry.
▸**ˌpetro'chemically** ADVERB

petrochemistry (ˌpɛtrəʊ'kɛmɪstrɪ) NOUN 1 the chemistry of petroleum and its derivatives. 2 the branch of chemistry concerned with the chemical composition of rocks.

petrodollar ('pɛtrəʊˌdɒlə) NOUN money, paid in dollars, earned by a country for the exporting of petroleum.

petrog. ABBREVIATION FOR petrography.

petroglyph ('pɛtrəˌglɪf) NOUN a drawing or carving on rock, esp a prehistoric one.
▷HISTORY C19: via French from Greek *petra* stone + *gluphē* carving

Petrograd ('pɛtrəʊˌgræd; *Russian* pɪtra'grat) NOUN a former name (1914–24) of **Saint Petersburg.**

petrography (pɛ'trɒgrəfɪ) NOUN the branch of petrology concerned with the description and classification of rocks. Abbreviation: **petrog.**
▸**pe'trographer** NOUN ▸**petrographic** (ˌpɛtrə'græfɪk) *or* **ˌpetro'graphical** ADJECTIVE ▸**ˌpetro'graphically** ADVERB

petrol ('pɛtrəl) NOUN any one of various volatile flammable liquid mixtures of hydrocarbons, mainly hexane, heptane, and octane, obtained from petroleum and used as a solvent and a fuel for internal-combustion engines. Usually petrol also contains additives such as antiknock compounds and corrosion inhibitors. US and Canadian name: **gasoline.**
▷HISTORY C16: via French from Medieval Latin PETROLEUM

petrol. ABBREVIATION FOR petrology.

petrolatum (ˌpɛtrə'leɪtəm) NOUN a translucent gelatinous substance obtained from petroleum; used as a lubricant and in medicine as an ointment base and protective dressing. Also called: **mineral jelly, petroleum jelly.**
▷HISTORY C19: from PETROL + Latin *-atum* -ATE[1]

petrol bomb NOUN 1 a home-made incendiary device, consisting of a bottle filled with petrol and stoppered with a wick, that is thrown by hand; Molotov cocktail. ◆ VERB **petrol-bomb.** *(tr)* 2 to attack with petrol bombs.
▸**petrol bomber** NOUN

petrol engine NOUN an internal-combustion engine that uses petrol as fuel.

petroleum (pə'trəʊlɪəm) NOUN a dark-coloured thick flammable crude oil occurring in sedimentary rocks around the Persian Gulf, in parts of North and South America, and below the North Sea, consisting mainly of hydrocarbons. Fractional distillation separates the crude oil into petrol, paraffin, diesel oil, lubricating oil, etc. Fuel oil, paraffin wax, asphalt, and carbon black are extracted from the residue.
▷HISTORY C16: from Medieval Latin, from Latin *petra* stone + *oleum* oil

petroleum ether NOUN a volatile mixture of the higher alkane hydrocarbons, obtained as a fraction of petroleum and used as a solvent.

petroleum jelly NOUN another name for **petrolatum.**

petrolhead ('pɛtrəlˌhɛd) NOUN *Informal* a person who is excessively interested in or is devoted to travelling by car.

petrolic (pɛ'trɒlɪk) ADJECTIVE of, relating to, containing, or obtained from petroleum.

petrology (pɛ'trɒlədʒɪ) NOUN, *plural* **-gies.** the study of the composition, origin, structure, and formation of rocks. Abbreviation: **petrol.**
▸**petrological** (ˌpɛtrə'lɒdʒɪkᵊl) ADJECTIVE ▸**ˌpetro'logically** ADVERB ▸**pe'trologist** NOUN

petrol pump NOUN a device at a filling station that is used to deliver petrol to the tank of a car and which displays the quantity, quality, and usually the cost of the petrol delivered.

petrol station NOUN *Brit* another term for **filling station.**

petronel ('pɛtrəˌnɛl) NOUN a firearm of large calibre used in the 16th and early 17th centuries, esp by cavalry soldiers.
▷HISTORY C16: from French, literally: of the breast, from *poitrine* breast, from Latin *pectus*

Petropavlovsk *(Russian* pɪtra'pavləfsk) NOUN a city in N Kazakhstan on the Ishim River. Pop.: 203 500 (1999).

Petrópolis *(Portuguese* pe'trɔpulis) NOUN a city in SE Brazil, north of Rio de Janeiro: resort. Pop. (urban area): 270 489 (2000).

petrosal (pɛ'trəʊsᵊl) ADJECTIVE *Anatomy* of, relating

to, or situated near the dense part of the temporal bone that surrounds the inner ear.
▷HISTORY C18: from Latin *petrōsus* full of rocks, from *petra* a rock, from Greek

petrous ('pɛtrəs, 'pi:-) ADJECTIVE [1] *Anatomy* denoting the dense part of the temporal bone that surrounds the inner ear. [2] *Rare* like rock or stone.
▷HISTORY C16: from Latin *petrōsus* full of rocks

Petrovsk (*Russian* pɪ'trɔfsk) NOUN the former name (until 1921) of **Makhachkala.**

Petrozavodsk (*Russian* pɪtrəza'vɔtsk) NOUN a city in NW Russia, capital of the Karelian Autonomous Republic, on Lake Onega: developed around ironworks established by Peter the Great in 1703; university (1940). Pop.: 282 500 (1999 est.).

pe-tsai cabbage ('peɪ'tsaɪ) NOUN another name for **Chinese cabbage** (sense 1).
▷HISTORY from Chinese (Beijing) *pe ts'ai,* literally: white vegetable

Petsamo (*Finnish* 'pɛtsɑmɔ) NOUN a former territory of N Finland ceded by the Soviet Union to Finland in 1920 and taken back in 1940; now in NW Russia.

petticoat ('pɛtɪˌkəʊt) NOUN [1] a woman's light undergarment in the form of an underskirt or including a bodice supported by shoulder straps. [2] *Informal* **a** a humorous or mildly disparaging name for a woman. **b** (*as modifier*): *petticoat politics.*
▷HISTORY C15: see PETTY, COAT

pettifog ('pɛtɪˌfɒg) VERB **-fogs, -fogging, -fogged.** (*intr*) to be a pettifogger.

pettifogger ('pɛtɪˌfɒgə) NOUN [1] a lawyer of inferior status who conducts unimportant cases, esp one who is unscrupulous or resorts to trickery. [2] any person who quibbles or fusses over details.
▷HISTORY C16: from PETTY + *fogger,* of uncertain origin, perhaps from *Fugger,* name of a family (C15–16) of German financiers
▸**'pettiˌfoggery** NOUN

pettifogging ('pɛtɪˌfɒgɪŋ) ADJECTIVE [1] petty: *pettifogging details.* [2] mean; quibbling: *pettifogging lawyers.*

pettish ('pɛtɪʃ) ADJECTIVE peevish; petulant: *a pettish child.*
▷HISTORY C16: from PET^2
▸**'pettishly** ADVERB ▸**'pettishness** NOUN

pettitoes ('pɛtɪˌtəʊz) PLURAL NOUN pig's trotters, esp when used as food.
▷HISTORY C16: from Old French *petite oie,* literally: little goose (giblets of a goose)

petty ('pɛtɪ) ADJECTIVE **-tier, -tiest.** [1] trivial; trifling; inessential: *petty details.* [2] of a narrow-minded, mean, or small-natured disposition or character: *petty spite.* [3] minor or subordinate in rank: *petty officialdom.* [4] *Law* of lesser importance.
▷HISTORY C14: from Old French PETIT
▸**'pettily** ADVERB ▸**'pettiness** NOUN

petty cash NOUN a small cash fund kept on a firm's premises for the payment of minor incidental expenses.

petty jury NOUN a variant spelling of **petit jury.**
▸**petty juror** NOUN

petty larceny NOUN a variant spelling of **petit larceny.**

petty officer NOUN a noncommissioned officer in a naval service, comparable in rank to a sergeant in an army or marine corps.

petty sessions NOUN (*functioning as singular or plural*) another term for **magistrates' court.**

petulant ('pɛtjʊlənt) ADJECTIVE irritable, impatient, or sullen in a peevish or capricious way.
▷HISTORY C16: via Old French from Latin *petulāns* bold, from *petulāre* (unattested) to attack playfully, from *petere* to assail
▸**'petulance** *or* **'petulancy** NOUN ▸**'petulantly** ADVERB

petunia (pɪ'tju:nɪə) NOUN any solanaceous plant of the tropical American genus *Petunia:* cultivated for their white, pink, blue, or purple funnel-shaped flowers.
▷HISTORY C19: via New Latin from obsolete French *petun* variety of tobacco, from Tupi *petyn*

petuntse *or* **petuntze** (pɪ'tʌntsɪ, -'tʊn-) NOUN a fusible feldspathic mineral used in hard-paste porcelain; china stone.
▷HISTORY C18: from Chinese (Beijing) *pe tun tzu,* from *pe* white + *tun* heap + *tzu* offspring

Petworth House ('pɛtwɜ:θ) NOUN a mansion in Petworth in Sussex: rebuilt (1688–96) for Charles Seymour, 6th Duke of Somerset; gardens laid out by Capability Brown; subject of paintings by Turner.

pew (pju:) NOUN [1] (in a church) **a** one of several long benchlike seats with backs, used by the congregation. **b** an enclosed compartment reserved for the use of a family or other small group. [2] *Brit, informal* a seat (esp in the phrase **take a pew**).
▷HISTORY C14 *pywe,* from Old French *puye,* from Latin *podium* a balcony, from Greek *podion* supporting structure, from *pous* foot

pewee *or* **peewee** ('pi:wi:) NOUN any of several small North American flycatchers of the genus *Contopus,* having a greenish-brown plumage.
▷HISTORY C19: imitative of its cry

pewit ('pi:wɪt) NOUN another name for **lapwing.**
▷HISTORY C13: imitative of the bird's cry

pewter ('pju:tə) NOUN [1] **a** any of various alloys containing tin (80–90 per cent), lead (10–20 per cent), and sometimes small amounts of other metals, such as copper and antimony. **b** (*as modifier*): *pewter ware; a pewter tankard.* [2] **a** a bluish-grey colour. **b** (*as adjective*): *pewter tights.* [3] plate or kitchen utensils made from pewter.
▷HISTORY C14: from Old French *peaultre,* of obscure origin; related to Old Provençal *peltre* pewter
▸**'pewterer** NOUN

peyote (peɪ'əʊtɪ, pɪ-) NOUN another name for **mescal** (sense 1).
▷HISTORY Mexican Spanish, from Nahuatl *peyotl*

pf THE INTERNET DOMAIN NAME FOR French Polynesia.

pF SYMBOL FOR picofarad.

pf. ABBREVIATION FOR: [1] perfect. [2] Also: **pfg.** pfennig. [3] preferred.

pfa ABBREVIATION FOR please find attached.

Pfalz (pfalts) NOUN the German name for the **Palatinate.**

pfennig ('fɛnɪg; *German* 'pfɛnɪç) NOUN, *plural* **-nigs** *or* **-nige** (*German* -nɪgə). [1] a former German monetary unit worth one hundredth of a Deutschmark. [2] (formerly) a monetary unit worth one hundredth of an East German ostmark.
▷HISTORY German: PENNY

PFI (in Britain) ABBREVIATION FOR **Private Finance Initiative.**

Pforzheim (*German* 'pfɔrtshaim) NOUN a city in SW Germany, in W Baden-Württemberg: centre of the German watch and jewellery industry. Pop.: 117 500 (1999 est.).

pg THE INTERNET DOMAIN NAME FOR Papua New Guinea.

PG[1] SYMBOL FOR a film certified for viewing by anyone, but which contains scenes that may be unsuitable for children, for whom parental guidance is necessary.
▷HISTORY C20: from abbreviation of *parental guidance*

PG[2] ABBREVIATION FOR: [1] paying guest. [2] postgraduate.

pg. ABBREVIATION FOR page.

Pg. ABBREVIATION FOR: [1] Portugal. [2] Portuguese.

PGA ABBREVIATION FOR Professional Golfers' Association.

PGD ABBREVIATION FOR preimplantation genetic diagnosis; a technique using in vitro fertilization to ensure that a baby does not possess a known genetic defect of either parent. After genetic analysis of the embryos so formed, only those free of defect are implanted in the mother's womb.

PGR ABBREVIATION FOR **psychogalvanic response.**

ph THE INTERNET DOMAIN NAME FOR Philippines.

pH NOUN potential of hydrogen; a measure of the acidity or alkalinity of a solution equal to the common logarithm of the reciprocal of the concentration of hydrogen ions in moles per cubic decimetre of solution. Pure water has a pH of 7, acid solutions have a pH less than 7, and alkaline solutions a pH greater than 7.

Ph THE CHEMICAL SYMBOL FOR phenyl group or radical.

ph. ABBREVIATION FOR phase.

phacelia (fə'si:lɪə) NOUN any plant of the mostly annual American genus *Phacelia, esp P. campanularia,* grown for its large, deep blue bell flowers: family *Hydrophyllaceae.*
▷HISTORY New Latin, from Greek *phakelos* cluster (from the habit of the flowers) + -IA

Phaeacian (fi:'eɪʃən) NOUN *Greek myth* one of a race of people inhabiting the island of Scheria visited by Odysseus on his way home from the Trojan War.

Phaedra ('fi:drə) NOUN *Greek myth* the wife of Theseus, who falsely accused her stepson Hippolytus of raping her because he spurned her amorous advances.

phaeic ('fi:ɪk) ADJECTIVE (of animals) having dusky coloration; less dark than melanic.
▷HISTORY C19: from Greek *phaiós* dusky
▸**'phaeism** NOUN

Phaethon ('feɪəθən) NOUN an asteroid (6.9 km in diameter) that has an orbit approaching close to the sun and releases fragments of dust that enter the earth's atmosphere as meteors.

Phaëthon ('feɪəθən) NOUN *Greek myth* the son of Helios (the sun god) who borrowed his father's chariot and nearly set the earth on fire by approaching too close to it. Zeus averted the catastrophe by striking him down with a thunderbolt.

phaeton ('feɪtᵊn) NOUN a light four-wheeled horse-drawn carriage with or without a top, usually having two seats.
▷HISTORY C18: from PHAËTHON

phage (feɪdʒ) NOUN short for **bacteriophage.**

-phage NOUN COMBINING FORM indicating something that eats or consumes something specified: *bacteriophage.*
▷HISTORY from Greek *-phagos;* see PHAGO-
▸**-phagous** ADJECTIVE COMBINING FORM

phagedaena *or* **phagedena** (ˌfædʒɪ'di:nə) NOUN *Pathol* a rapidly spreading ulcer that destroys tissues as it increases in size.
▷HISTORY C17: via Latin from Greek, from *phagein* to eat

phago- *or before a vowel* **phag-** COMBINING FORM eating, consuming, or destroying: *phagocyte.*
▷HISTORY from Greek *phagein* to consume

phagocyte ('fægəˌsaɪt) NOUN an amoeboid cell or protozoan that engulfs particles, such as food substances or invading microorganisms.
▸**phagocytic** (ˌfægə'sɪtɪk) ADJECTIVE

phagocytosis (ˌfægəsaɪ'təʊsɪs) NOUN the process by which a cell, such as a white blood cell, ingests microorganisms, other cells, and foreign particles.

phagomania (ˌfægəʊ'meɪnɪə) NOUN a compulsive desire to eat.
▸**ˌphago'maniˌac** NOUN

-phagy *or* **-phagia** NOUN COMBINING FORM indicating an eating or devouring: *anthropophagy.*
▷HISTORY from Greek *-phagia;* see PHAGO-

phalange ('fælændʒ) NOUN, *plural* **phalanges** (fæ'lændʒi:z). *Anatomy* another name for **phalanx** (sense 5).
▷HISTORY C16: via French, ultimately from Greek PHALANX

phalangeal (fə'lændʒɪəl) ADJECTIVE *Anatomy* of or relating to a phalanx or phalanges.

phalanger (fə'lændʒə) NOUN any of various Australasian arboreal marsupials, such as *Trichosurus vulpecula* (**brush-tailed phalanger**), having dense fur and a long tail: family *Phalangeridae.* Also called (Austral and NZ): **possum.** See also **flying phalanger.**
▷HISTORY C18: via New Latin from Greek *phalaggion* spider's web, referring to its webbed hind toes

Phalangist (fə'lændʒɪst) NOUN **a** a member of a Lebanese Christian paramilitary organization founded in 1936 and originally based on similar ideas to the fascist Falange in Spain. **b** (*as modifier*): *Phalangist leaders.*

phalanstery ('fælənstərɪ, -strɪ) NOUN, *plural* **-steries.** [1] (in Fourierism) **a** buildings occupied by a phalanx. **b** a community represented by a phalanx. [2] any similar association or the buildings occupied by such an association.
▷HISTORY C19: from French *phalanstère,* from *phalange* PHALANX, on the model of *monastère* MONASTERY

phalanx ('fælæŋks) NOUN, *plural* **phalanxes** *or* **phalanges** (fæ'lændʒi:z). [1] an ancient Greek and Macedonian battle formation of hoplites presenting long spears from behind a wall of overlapping shields. [2] any closely ranked unit or mass of

people: *the police formed a phalanx to protect the embassy.* 3 a number of people united for a common purpose. 4 (in Fourierism) a group of approximately 1800 persons forming a commune in which all property is collectively owned. 5 *Anatomy* any of the bones of the fingers or toes. Related adjective: **phalangeal.** 6 *Botany* **a** a bundle of stamens, joined together by their stalks (filaments). **b** a form of vegetative spread in which the advance is on a broad front, as in the common reed. ◆ Compare **guerrilla.**
▷HISTORY C16: via Latin from Greek: infantry formation in close ranks, bone of finger or toe

phalarope ('fælə,rəʊp) NOUN any aquatic shore bird of the family *Phalaropidae,* such as *Phalaropus fulicarius* (**grey phalarope**), of northern oceans and lakes, having a long slender bill and lobed toes: order *Charadriiformes.*
▷HISTORY C18: via French from New Latin *Phalaropus,* from Greek *phalaris* coot + *pous* foot

phallic ('fælɪk) ADJECTIVE 1 of, relating to, or resembling a phallus: *a phallic symbol.* 2 *Psychoanal* **a** relating to a stage of psychosexual development during which a male child's interest is concentrated on the genital organs. **b** designating personality traits, such as conceit and self-assurance, due to fixation at the phallic stage of development. Compare **anal** (sense 2), **oral** (sense 7), **genital** (sense 2). **c** (in Freudian theory) denoting a phase of early childhood in which there is a belief that both sexes possess a phallus. 3 of or relating to phallicism.

phallicism ('fælɪ,sɪzəm) *or* **phallism** NOUN the worship or veneration of the phallus.
▸**'phallicist** *or* **'phallist** NOUN

phallocentric (,fæləʊ'sɛntrɪk) ADJECTIVE dominated by male attitudes.
▷HISTORY C20: from PHALLUS + -CENTRIC
▸**,phallocen'tricity** *or* **,phallo'centrism** NOUN

phalloidin (fə'lɔɪdɪn) NOUN a peptide toxin, responsible for the toxicity of the death cap mushroom, *Amanita phalloides.*
▷HISTORY C20: New Latin, from PHALLUS + -OID + -IN

phallus ('fæləs) NOUN, *plural* **-luses** *or* **-li** (-laɪ). 1 another word for **penis.** 2 an image of the penis, esp as a religious symbol of reproductive power.
▷HISTORY C17: via Late Latin from Greek *phallos*

-phane NOUN COMBINING FORM indicating something resembling a specified substance: *cellophane.*
▷HISTORY from Greek *phainein* to shine, (in passive) appear

phanerocrystalline (,fænərəʊ'krɪstəlɪn, -,laɪn) ADJECTIVE (of igneous and metamorphic rocks) having a crystalline structure in which the crystals are large enough to be seen with the naked eye.
▷HISTORY C19: from Greek *phaneros* visible + CRYSTALLINE

phanerogam ('fænərəʊ,gæm) NOUN any plant of the former major division *Phanerogamae,* which included all seed-bearing plants; a former name for **spermatophyte.** Compare **cryptogam.**
▷HISTORY C19: from New Latin *phanerogamus,* from Greek *phaneros* visible + *gamos* marriage
▸**,phanero'gamic** *or* **phanerogamous** (,fænə'rɒgəməs) ADJECTIVE

phanerophyte ('fænərə,faɪt, fə'nɛrə-) NOUN a tree or shrub that bears its perennating buds more than 25 cm above the level of the soil.
▷HISTORY C20: from Greek *phanero-* visible + -PHYTE

Phanerozoic (,fænərə'zəʊɪk) ADJECTIVE 1 of or relating to that part of geological time represented by rocks in which the evidence of life is abundant, comprising the Palaeozoic, Mesozoic, and Cenozoic eras. ◆ NOUN 2 **the.** the Phanerozoic era. ◆ Compare **Cryptozoic.**

phantasm ('fæntæzəm) NOUN 1 a phantom. 2 an illusory perception of an object, person, etc. 3 (in the philosophy of Plato) objective reality as distorted by perception.
▷HISTORY C13: from Old French *fantasme,* from Latin *phantasma,* from Greek; related to Greek *phantazein* to cause to be seen, from *phainein* to show
▸**phan'tasmal** *or* **phan'tasmic** ADJECTIVE ▸**phan'tasmally** *or* **phan'tasmically** ADVERB

phantasmagoria (,fæntæzmə'gɔːrɪə) *or* **phantasmagory** (fæn'tæzməgərɪ) NOUN 1 *Psychol* a shifting medley of real or imagined figures, as in a dream. 2 *Films* a sequence of pictures made to vary in size rapidly while remaining in focus. 3 *Rare* a shifting scene composed of different elements.
▷HISTORY C19: probably from French *fantasmagorie* production of phantasms, from PHANTASM + *-agorie,* perhaps from Greek *ageirein* to gather together
▸**phantasmagoric** (,fæntæzmə'gɒrɪk) *or* **,phantasma'gorical** ADJECTIVE ▸**,phantasma'gorically** ADVERB

phantasy ('fæntəsɪ) NOUN, *plural* **-sies.** an archaic spelling of **fantasy.**

phantom ('fæntəm) NOUN 1 **a** an apparition or spectre. **b** (*as modifier*): *a phantom army marching through the sky.* 2 the visible representation of something abstract, esp as appearing in a dream or hallucination: *phantoms of evil haunted his sleep.* 3 something apparently unpleasant or horrific that has no material form. 4 *Med* another name for **manikin** (sense 2b).
▷HISTORY C13: from Old French *fantosme,* from Latin *phantasma* PHANTASM

phantom limb NOUN the illusion that a limb still exists following its amputation, sometimes with pain (**phantom limb pain**).

phantom pregnancy NOUN the occurrence of signs of pregnancy, such as enlarged abdomen and absence of menstruation, when no embryo is present, due to hormonal imbalance. Also called: **false pregnancy, pseudopregnancy.** Technical name: **pseudocyesis.**

phantom withdrawal NOUN the unauthorized removal of funds from a bank account using an automated teller machine.

-phany NOUN COMBINING FORM indicating a manifestation: *theophany.*
▷HISTORY from Greek *-phania,* from *phainein* to show; see -PHANE
▸**-phanous** ADJECTIVE COMBINING FORM

phar., Phar., pharm., *or* **Pharm.** ABBREVIATION FOR: 1 pharmaceutical. 2 pharmacist. 3 pharmacopoeia. 4 pharmacy.

Pharaoh ('fɛərəʊ) NOUN the title of the ancient Egyptian kings.
▷HISTORY Old English *Pharaon,* via Latin, Greek, and Hebrew ultimately from Egyptian *pr-'o* great house
▸**Pharaonic** (fɛə'rɒnɪk) ADJECTIVE

Pharaoh ant *or* **Pharaoh's ant** NOUN a small yellowish-red ant, *Monomorium pharaonis,* of warm regions: accidentally introduced into many countries, infesting heated buildings.

Pharaoh hound NOUN a medium-sized powerful swift-moving short-haired breed of hound having a glossy tan coat, sometimes with white markings.

Pharisaic (,færɪ'seɪɪk) *or* **Pharisaical** ADJECTIVE 1 *Judaism* of, relating to, or characteristic of the Pharisees or Pharisaism. 2 (*often not capital*) righteously hypocritical.
▸**,Phari'saically** ADVERB ▸**,Phari'saicalness** NOUN

Pharisaism ('færɪseɪ,ɪzəm) *or* **Phariseeism** ('færɪsiː,ɪzəm) NOUN 1 *Judaism* the tenets and customs of the Pharisees. 2 (*often not capital*) observance of the external forms of religion without genuine belief; hypocrisy.

Pharisee ('færɪ,siː) NOUN 1 *Judaism* a member of an ancient Jewish sect that was opposed to the Sadducees, teaching strict observance of Jewish tradition as interpreted rabbinically and believing in life after death and in the coming of the Messiah. 2 (*often not capital*) a self-righteous or hypocritical person.
▷HISTORY Old English *Farīsēus,* ultimately from Aramaic *perīshāiyā,* pl of *perīsh* separated

pharmaceutical (,fɑːmə'sjuːtɪk^əl) *or less commonly* **pharmaceutic** ADJECTIVE of or relating to drugs or pharmacy.
▷HISTORY C17: from Late Latin *pharmaceuticus,* from Greek *pharmakeus* purveyor of drugs; see PHARMACY
▸**,pharma'ceutically** ADVERB

pharmaceutics (,fɑːmə'sjuːtɪks) NOUN 1 (*functioning as singular*) another term for **pharmacy** (sense 1). 2 (*functioning as plural*) pharmaceutical remedies.

pharmacist ('fɑːməsɪst) *or less commonly* **pharmaceutist** (,fɑːmə'sjuːtɪst) NOUN a person qualified to prepare and dispense drugs.

pharmaco- COMBINING FORM indicating drugs: *pharmacology; pharmacopoeia.*
▷HISTORY from Greek *pharmakon* drug, potion

pharmacodynamics (,fɑːməkəʊdaɪ'næmɪks) NOUN (*functioning as singular*) the branch of pharmacology concerned with the action of drugs on the physiology or pathology of the body.
▸**,pharmacody'namic** ADJECTIVE

pharmacognosy (,fɑːmə'kɒgnəsɪ) NOUN the branch of pharmacology concerned with crude drugs of plant and animal origin.
▷HISTORY C19: from PHARMACO- + *gnosy,* from Greek *gnosis* knowledge
▸**,pharma'cognosist** NOUN ▸**pharmacognostic** (,fɑːməkɒg'nɒstɪk) ADJECTIVE

pharmacokinetics (,fɑːməkəʊkɪ'nɛtɪks, -kaɪ-) NOUN the branch of pharmacology concerned with the way drugs are taken into, move around, and are eliminated from, the body.
▸**,pharmacoki'netic** ADJECTIVE ▸**,pharmacoki'netically** ADVERB ▸**pharmacokineticist** (,fɑːməkəʊkɪ'nɛtɪsɪst) NOUN

pharmacol. ABBREVIATION FOR pharmacology.

pharmacology (,fɑːmə'kɒlədʒɪ) NOUN the science of drugs, including their characteristics and uses.
▸**pharmacological** (,fɑːməkə'lɒdʒɪk^əl) ADJECTIVE ▸**,pharmaco'logically** ADVERB ▸**,pharma'cologist** NOUN

pharmacopoeia *or sometimes US* **pharmacopeia** (,fɑːməkə'piːə) NOUN an authoritative book containing a list of medicinal drugs with their uses, preparation, dosages, formulas, etc.
▷HISTORY C17: via New Latin from Greek *pharmakopoiia* art of preparing drugs, from PHARMACO- + *-poiia,* from *poiein* to make
▸**,pharmaco'poeial** *or* **,pharmaco'poeic** ADJECTIVE ▸**,pharmaco'poeist** NOUN

pharmacy ('fɑːməsɪ) NOUN, *plural* **-cies.** 1 Also called: **pharmaceutics.** the practice or art of preparing and dispensing drugs. 2 a dispensary.
▷HISTORY C14: from Medieval Latin *pharmacia,* from Greek *pharmakeia* making of drugs, from *pharmakon* drug

pharming ('fɑːmɪŋ) NOUN the practice of rearing or growing genetically-modified animals or plants in order to develop pharmaceutical products.
▷HISTORY C20: blend of PHARMACEUTICAL + FARMING

Pharos ('fɛərɒs) NOUN a large Hellenistic lighthouse built on an island off Alexandria in Egypt in about 280 B.C. and destroyed by an earthquake in the 14th century: usually included among the Seven Wonders of the World.

Pharsalus (fɑː'seɪləs) NOUN an ancient town in Thessaly in N Greece. Several major battles were fought nearby, including Caesar's victory over Pompey (48 B.C.).

pharyngeal (,færɪn'dʒiːəl) *or* **pharyngal** (fə'rɪŋg^əl) ADJECTIVE 1 of, relating to, or situated in or near the pharynx. 2 *Phonetics* pronounced or supplemented in pronunciation with an articulation in or constriction of the pharynx. ◆ NOUN 3 *Phonetics* a pharyngeal speech sound.
▷HISTORY C19: from New Latin *pharyngeus;* see PHARYNX

pharyngeal tonsil NOUN the technical name for **adenoids.**

pharyngitis (,færɪn'dʒaɪtɪs) NOUN inflammation of the pharynx.

pharyngo- *or before a vowel* **pharyng-** COMBINING FORM pharynx: *pharyngoscope.*

pharyngology (,færɪŋ'gɒlədʒɪ) NOUN the branch of medical science concerned with the pharynx and its diseases.
▸**pharyngological** (,færɪŋgə'lɒdʒɪk^əl) ADJECTIVE ▸**,pharyn'gologist** NOUN

pharyngoscope (fə'rɪŋgə,skəʊp) NOUN a medical instrument for examining the pharynx.
▸**pharyngoscopic** (fə,rɪŋgə'skɒpɪk) ADJECTIVE ▸**pharyngoscopy** (,færɪŋ'gɒskəpɪ) NOUN

pharyngotomy (,færɪŋ'gɒtəmɪ) NOUN, *plural* **-mies.** surgical incision into the pharynx.

pharynx ('færɪŋks) NOUN, *plural* **pharynges** (fæ'rɪndʒiːz) *or* **pharynxes.** the part of the alimentary canal between the mouth and the oesophagus. Compare **nasopharynx.** Related adjective: **pharyngeal.**
▷HISTORY C17: via New Latin from Greek *pharunx* throat; related to Greek *pharanx* chasm

phascogale (ˈfæskəgeɪl, ˌfæsˈkaːgəli) NOUN *Austral* another name for **tuan**[2].

phase (feɪz) NOUN 1 any distinct or characteristic period or stage in a sequence of events or chain of development: *there were two phases to the resolution; his immaturity was a passing phase.* 2 *Astronomy* one of the recurring shapes of the portion of the moon or an inferior planet illuminated by the sun: *the new moon, first quarter, full moon, and last quarter are the four principal phases of the moon.* 3 *Physics* **a** the fraction of a cycle of a periodic quantity that has been completed at a specific reference time, expressed as an angle. **b** (*as modifier*): *a phase shift.* 4 *Physics* a particular stage in a periodic process or phenomenon. 5 **in phase.** (of two waveforms) reaching corresponding phases at the same time. 6 **out of phase.** (of two waveforms) not in phase. 7 *Chem* a distinct state of matter characterized by homogeneous composition and properties and the possession of a clearly defined boundary. 8 *Zoology* a variation in the normal form of an animal, esp a colour variation, brought about by seasonal or geographical change. 9 *Biology* (*usually in combination*) a stage in mitosis or meiosis: *prophase; metaphase.* 10 *Electrical engineering* one of the circuits in a system in which there are two or more alternating voltages displaced by equal amounts in phase (sense 5). See also **polyphase** (sense 1). 11 (in systemic grammar) the type of correspondence that exists between the predicators in a clause that has two or more predicators; for example connection by *to,* as in *I managed to do it,* or *-ing,* as in *we heard him singing.* ◆ VERB (*tr*) 12 (*often passive*) to execute, arrange, or introduce gradually or in stages: *a phased withdrawal.* 13 (sometimes foll by *with*) to cause (a part, process, etc.) to function or coincide with (another part, process, etc.): *he tried to phase the intake and output of the machine; he phased the intake with the output.* 14 *Chiefly US* to arrange (processes, goods, etc.) to be supplied or executed when required.
▷HISTORY C19: from New Latin *phases,* pl of *phasis,* from Greek: aspect; related to Greek *phainein* to show
▸ˈ**phaseless** ADJECTIVE ▸ˈ**phasic** *or* ˈ**phaseal** ADJECTIVE

phase-contrast microscope NOUN a microscope that makes visible details of colourless transparent objects. It employs a method of illumination such that small differences of refractive index of the materials in the object cause differences of luminous intensity by interference.

phased array NOUN an array of radio antennae connected together to form a single antenna. The beam produced can be steered across the sky by adjusting the phases of the signals. The absence of moving parts enables the beams to be steered very rapidly, making it useful in radar.

phase in VERB (*tr, adverb*) to introduce in a gradual or cautious manner: *the legislation was phased in over two years.*

phase modulation NOUN a type of modulation, used in communication systems, in which the phase of a radio carrier wave is varied by an amount proportional to the instantaneous amplitude of the modulating signal.

phase out VERB 1 (*tr, adverb*) to discontinue or withdraw gradually. ◆ NOUN **phase-out.** 2 the action or an instance of phasing out: *a phase-out of conventional forces.*

phase rule NOUN the principle that in any system in equilibrium the number of degrees of freedom is equal to the number of components less the number of phases plus two. See also **degree of freedom, component** (sense 4).

phase shift keying NOUN See **PSK.**

phase speed *or* **velocity** NOUN *Physics* the speed at which the phase of a wave is propagated, the product of the frequency times the wavelength. This is the quantity that is determined by methods using interference. In a dispersive medium it differs from the group speed. Also called: **wave speed, wave velocity.**

phase-switching NOUN a technique used in radio interferometry in which the signal from one of the two antennae is periodically reversed in phase before being multiplied by the signal from the other antenna.

-phasia NOUN COMBINING FORM indicating speech disorder of a specified kind: *aphasia.*
▷HISTORY from Greek, from *phanai* to speak
▸**-phasic** ADJECTIVE AND NOUN COMBINING FORM

phasing (ˈfeɪzɪŋ) NOUN *Electrical engineering* a tonal sweep achieved by varying the phase relationship of two similar audio signals by mechanical or electronic means.

phasmid (ˈfæzmɪd) NOUN 1 any plant-eating insect of the mainly tropical order *Phasmida:* includes the leaf insects and stick insects. ◆ ADJECTIVE 2 of, relating to, or belonging to the order *Phasmida.*
▷HISTORY C19: from New Latin *Phasmida,* from Greek *phasma* spectre

phasor (ˈfeɪzɔː) NOUN *Electrical engineering* a rotating vector representing a quantity, such as an alternating current or voltage, that varies sinusoidally.

phat (fæt) ADJECTIVE *Slang* terrific; superb.
▷HISTORY C20: from Black slang, a corruption of FAT

phatic (ˈfætɪk) ADJECTIVE (of speech, esp of conversational phrases) used to establish social contact and to express sociability rather than specific meaning.
▷HISTORY C20: from Greek *phat(os)* spoken + -IC

PHC ABBREVIATION FOR Pharmaceutical Chemist.

PhD ABBREVIATION FOR Doctor of Philosophy. Also: **DPhil.**

pheasant (ˈfɛzᵊnt) NOUN 1 any of various long-tailed gallinaceous birds of the family *Phasianidae, esp Phasianus colchicus* (**ring-necked pheasant**), having a brightly-coloured plumage in the male: native to Asia but introduced elsewhere. 2 any of various other gallinaceous birds of the family *Phasianidae,* including the quails and partridges. 3 *US and Canadian* any of several other gallinaceous birds, esp the ruffed grouse.
▷HISTORY C13: from Old French *fesan,* from Latin *phāsiānus,* from Greek *phasianos ornis* Phasian bird, named after the River *Phasis,* in Colchis

pheasant's eye NOUN 1 an annual ranunculaceous plant, *Adonis annua* (or *autumnalis*), with scarlet flowers and finely divided leaves: native to S Europe but naturalized elsewhere. 2 a type of narcissus, *Narcissus poeticus,* that has white petals and a small red-ringed cup.

Phebe (ˈfiːbɪ) NOUN a variant spelling of **Phoebe**[1].

phellem (ˈfɛləm) NOUN *Botany* the technical name for **cork** (sense 4).
▷HISTORY C20: from Greek *phellos* cork + PHLOEM

phelloderm (ˈfɛləʊˌdɜːm) NOUN a layer of thin-walled cells produced by the inner surface of the cork cambium.
▷HISTORY C19: from Greek *phellos* cork + -DERM
▸ˌ**phelloˈdermal** ADJECTIVE

phellogen (ˈfɛlədʒən) NOUN *Botany* the technical name for **cork cambium.**
▷HISTORY C19: from Greek *phellos* cork + -GEN
▸**phellogenetic** (ˌfɛləʊdʒɪˈnɛtɪk) *or* **phellogenic** (ˌfɛləʊˈdʒɛnɪk) ADJECTIVE

phenacaine (ˈfiːnəˌkeɪn, ˈfɛn-) NOUN a crystalline basic compound that is the hydrochloride of holocaine: used as a local anaesthetic in ophthalmic medicine. Formula: $C_{18}H_{22}N_2O_2HCl$.
▷HISTORY C20: from PHENO- + ACETO- + COCAINE

phenacetin (fɪˈnæsɪtɪn) NOUN a white crystalline solid formerly used in medicine to relieve pain and fever. Because of its kidney toxicity it has been superseded by paracetamol. Formula: $CH_3CONHC_6H_4OC_2H_5$. Also called: **acetophenetidin.**
▷HISTORY C19: from PHENETIDINE + ACETYL + -IN

phenacite (ˈfɛnəˌsaɪt) *or* **phenakite** (ˈfɛnəˌkaɪt) NOUN a colourless or white glassy mineral consisting of beryllium silicate in hexagonal crystalline form: occurs in veins in granite. Formula: Be_2SiO_4.
▷HISTORY C19: from Greek *phenax* a cheat, because of its deceptive resemblance to quartz

phenanthrene (fɪˈnænθriːn) NOUN a colourless crystalline aromatic compound isomeric with anthracene: used in the manufacture of dyes, drugs, and explosives. Formula: $C_{14}H_{10}$.
▷HISTORY C19: from PHENO- + ANTHRACENE

phenazine (ˈfɛnəˌziːn) NOUN a yellow crystalline tricyclic compound that is the parent compound of many azine dyes and some antibiotics. Formula: $C_6H_4N_2C_6H_4$.
▷HISTORY C19: from PHENO- + AZINE

phencyclidine (fɛnˈsɪklɪˌdiːn) NOUN See **PCP.**

phenetics (fɪˈnɛtɪks) NOUN (*functioning as singular*) *Biology* a system of classification based on similarities between organisms without regard to their evolutionary relationships.
▷HISTORY C20: from PHEN(OTYPE) + (GEN)ETICS
▸**pheˈnetic** ADJECTIVE

phenetidine (fɪˈnɛtɪˌdiːn, -dɪn) NOUN a liquid amine that is a derivative of phenetole, existing in three isomeric forms: used in the manufacture of dyestuffs. Formula: $H_2NC_6H_4OC_2H_5$.
▷HISTORY C19: from PHENETOLE + -ID[3] + -INE[2]

phenetole (ˈfɛnɪˌtəʊl, -ˌtɒl) NOUN a colourless oily compound; phenyl ethyl ether. Formula: $C_6H_5OC_2H_5$.
▷HISTORY C19: from PHENO- + ETHYL + -OLE[1]

phenformin (fɛnˈfɔːmɪn) NOUN a biguanide administered orally in the treatment of diabetes to lower blood concentrations of glucose; it has been largely superseded by metformin. Formula: $C_{10}H_{15}N_5$.
▷HISTORY C20: from PHEN(YL) + FORM(ALDEHYDE) + -IN

phenix (ˈfiːnɪks) NOUN a US spelling of **phoenix.**

pheno- *or before a vowel* **phen-** COMBINING FORM 1 showing or manifesting: *phenotype.* 2 indicating that a molecule contains benzene rings: *phenobarbital.*
▷HISTORY from Greek *phaino-* shining, from *phainein* to show; its use in a chemical sense is exemplified in *phenol,* so called because originally prepared from illuminating gas

phenobarbital (ˌfiːnəʊˈbɑːbɪtᵊl) NOUN a white crystalline derivative of barbituric acid used as a sedative for treating insomnia and as an anticonvulsant in epilepsy. Formula: $C_{12}H_{12}N_2O_3$.

phenocopy (ˈfiːnəʊˌkɒpɪ) NOUN, *plural* **-copies.** a noninheritable change in an organism that is caused by environmental influence during development but resembles the effects of a genetic mutation.

phenocryst (ˈfiːnəˌkrɪst, ˈfɛn-) NOUN any of several large crystals that are embedded in a mass of smaller crystals in igneous rocks such as porphyry.
▷HISTORY C19: from PHENO- (shining) + CRYSTAL

phenol (ˈfiːnɒl) NOUN 1 Also called: **carbolic acid.** a white crystalline soluble poisonous acidic derivative of benzene, used as an antiseptic and disinfectant and in the manufacture of resins, nylon, dyes, explosives, and pharmaceuticals; hydroxybenzene. Formula: C_6H_5OH. 2 *Chem* any of a class of weakly acidic organic compounds whose molecules contain one or more hydroxyl groups bound directly to a carbon atom in an aromatic ring.

phenolate (ˈfiːnəˌleɪt) VERB 1 (*tr*) Also: **carbolize.** to treat or disinfect with phenol. ◆ NOUN 2 another name (not in technical usage) for **phenoxide.**

phenolic (fɪˈnɒlɪk) ADJECTIVE of, containing, or derived from phenol.

phenolic resin NOUN any one of a class of resins derived from phenol, used in paints, adhesives, and as thermosetting plastics. See also **Bakelite.**

phenology (fɪˈnɒlədʒɪ) NOUN the study of recurring phenomena, such as animal migration, esp as influenced by climatic conditions.
▷HISTORY C19: from PHENO(MENON) + -LOGY
▸**phenological** (ˌfiːnəˈlɒdʒɪkᵊl) ADJECTIVE ▸**pheˈnologist** NOUN

phenolphthalein (ˌfiːnɒlˈθeɪliːn, -lɪɪn, -ˈθæl-) NOUN a colourless crystalline compound used in medicine as a laxative and in chemistry as an indicator. Formula: $C_{20}H_{14}O_4$.

phenom (fɪˈnɒm) NOUN *Informal* a person or thing of outstanding abilities or qualities.
▷HISTORY C20: from PHENOM(ENON)

phenomena (fɪˈnɒmɪnə) NOUN a plural of **phenomenon.**

phenomenal (fɪˈnɒmɪnᵊl) ADJECTIVE 1 of or relating to a phenomenon. 2 extraordinary; outstanding; remarkable: *a phenomenal achievement.* 3 *Philosophy* known or perceived by the senses rather than the mind.
▸**pheˈnomenally** ADVERB

phenomenalism (fɪˈnɒmɪnəˌlɪzəm) NOUN *Philosophy* the doctrine that statements about physical objects and the external world can be analysed in terms of possible or actual experiences,

and that entities, such as physical objects, are only mental constructions out of phenomenal appearances. Compare **idealism** (sense 3), **realism** (sense 6).
▸**phe'nomenalist** NOUN, ADJECTIVE ▸**phe,nomenal'istically** ADVERB

phenomenology (fɪˌnɒmɪˈnɒlədʒɪ) NOUN *Philosophy* [1] the movement founded by Husserl that concentrates on the detailed description of conscious experience, without recourse to explanation, metaphysical assumptions, and traditional philosophical questions. [2] the science of phenomena as opposed to the science of being.
▸**phenomenological** (fɪˌnɒmɪnəˈlɒdʒɪkᵊl) ADJECTIVE ▸**phe,nomeno'logically** ADVERB ▸**phe,nome'nologist** NOUN

phenomenon (fɪˈnɒmɪnən) NOUN, *plural* **-ena** (-ɪnə) *or* **-enons.** [1] anything that can be perceived as an occurrence or fact by the senses. [2] any remarkable occurrence or person. [3] *Philosophy* **a** the object of perception, experience, etc. **b** (in the writings of Kant) a thing as it appears and is interpreted in perception and reflection, as distinguished from its real nature as a thing-in-itself. Compare **noumenon.**
▷HISTORY C16: via Late Latin from Greek *phainomenon,* from *phainesthai* to appear, from *phainein* to show

Language note Although *phenomena* is often treated as if it were singular, correct usage is to employ *phenomenon* with a singular construction and *phenomena* with a plural: *that is an interesting phenomenon* (not *phenomena*); *several new phenomena were recorded in his notes.*

phenothiazine (ˌfiːnəʊˈθaɪəziːn) NOUN [1] a colourless to light yellow insoluble crystalline compound used as an anthelmintic for livestock and in insecticides. Formula: $C_{12}H_9NS$. [2] any of several drugs derived from phenothiazine and used as strong tranquillizers and in the treatment of schizophrenia.

phenotype (ˈfiːnəʊˌtaɪp) NOUN the physical and biochemical characteristics of an organism as determined by the interaction of its genetic constitution and the environment. Compare **genotype.**
▸**phenotypic** (ˌfiːnəʊˈtɪpɪk) *or* **,pheno'typical** ADJECTIVE ▸**,pheno'typically** ADVERB

phenoxide (fɪˈnɒksaɪd) NOUN any of a class of salts of phenol. They contain the ion $C_6H_5O^-$. Also called: **phenolate.**

phenoxy resin (fɪˈnɒksɪ) NOUN *Chem* any of a class of resins derived from polyhydroxy ethers.

phenyl (ˈfiːnaɪl, ˈfɛnɪl) NOUN (*modifier*) of, containing, or consisting of the monovalent group C_6H_5, derived from benzene: *a phenyl group or radical.*

phenylalanine (ˌfiːnaɪlˈæləˌniːn, ˌfɛnɪl-) NOUN an aromatic essential amino acid; a component of proteins.

phenylamine (ˌfiːnaɪləˈmiːn, ˌfɛnɪl-) NOUN another name for **aniline.**

phenylbutazone (ˌfiːnaɪlˈbjuːtəˌzəʊn) NOUN an anti-inflammatory drug used in the treatment of rheumatic diseases; it has been largely superseded by other NSAIDs.
▷HISTORY C20: from *(dioxodi)phenylbut(ylpyr)azo(lidi)ne*

phenylketonuria (ˌfiːnaɪlˌkiːtəˈnjʊərɪə) NOUN a congenital metabolic disorder characterized by the abnormal accumulation of phenylalanine in the body fluids, resulting in various degrees of mental deficiency.
▷HISTORY C20: New Latin; see PHENYL, KETONE, -URIA

phenytoin (ˌfɛnɪˈtəʊɪn) NOUN an anticonvulsant drug used in the management of epilepsy and in the treatment of abnormal heart rhythms. Formula: $C_{15}H_{11}N_2O_2Na$. Also called: **diphenylhydantoin sodium.**
▷HISTORY C20: from *(di)pheny(lhydan)toin*

pheromone (ˈfɛrəˌməʊn) NOUN a chemical substance, secreted externally by certain animals, such as insects, affecting the behaviour or physiology of other animals of the same species.
▷HISTORY C20: *phero-,* from Greek *pherein* to bear + (HOR)MONE

phew (fjuː) INTERJECTION an exclamation of relief, surprise, disbelief, weariness, etc.

phi (faɪ) NOUN, *plural* **phis.** the 21st letter in the Greek alphabet, Φ, ϕ, a consonant, transliterated as *ph* or *f.*

phial (ˈfaɪəl) NOUN a small bottle for liquids; vial.
▷HISTORY C14: from Old French *fiole,* from Latin *phiola* saucer, from Greek *phialē* wide shallow vessel

Phi Beta Kappa (ˈfaɪ ˈbeɪtə ˈkæpə, ˈbiːtə) NOUN (in the US) [1] a national honorary society, founded in 1776, membership of which is based on high academic ability. [2] a member of this society.
▷HISTORY from the initials of the Greek motto *philosophia biou kubernētēs* philosophy the guide of life

phil. ABBREVIATION FOR: [1] philosophy. [2] philharmonic.

Phil. ABBREVIATION FOR: [1] Philippians. [2] Philippines. [3] Philadelphia. [4] Philharmonic.

Philadelphia (ˌfɪləˈdɛlfɪə) NOUN a city and port in SE Pennsylvania, at the confluence of the Delaware and Schuylkill Rivers: the fourth largest city in the US; founded by Quakers in 1682; cultural and financial centre of the American colonies and the federal capital (1790–1800); scene of the Continental Congresses (1774–83) and the signing of the Declaration of Independence (1776). Pop.: 1 517 550 (2000).

philadelphus (ˌfɪləˈdɛlfəs) NOUN any shrub of the N temperate genus *Philadelphus,* cultivated for their strongly scented showy flowers: family *Hydrangeaceae.* See also **mock orange** (sense 1).
▷HISTORY C19: New Latin, from Greek *philadelphon* mock orange, literally: loving one's brother

Philae (ˈfaɪliː) NOUN an island in Upper Egypt, in the Nile north of the Aswan Dam: of religious importance in ancient times; almost submerged since the raising of the level of the dam.

philander (fɪˈlændə) VERB (*intr;* often foll by *with*) (of a man) to flirt with women.
▷HISTORY C17: from Greek *philandros* fond of men, from *philos* loving + *anēr* man; used as a name for a lover in literary works
▸**phi'landerer** NOUN ▸**phi'landering** NOUN, ADJECTIVE

philanthropic (ˌfɪlənˈθrɒpɪk) *or* **philanthropical** ADJECTIVE showing concern for humanity, esp by performing charitable actions, donating money, etc.
▸**,philan'thropically** ADVERB

philanthropy (fɪˈlænθrəpɪ) NOUN, *plural* **-pies.** [1] the practice of performing charitable or benevolent actions. [2] love of mankind in general.
▷HISTORY C17: from Late Latin *philanthrōpia,* from Greek: love of mankind, from *philos* loving + *anthrōpos* man
▸**phi'lanthropist** *or* **philanthrope** (ˈfɪlənˌθrəʊp) NOUN

philately (fɪˈlætəlɪ) NOUN the collection and study of postage stamps and all related material concerned with postal history.
▷HISTORY C19: from French *philatélie,* from PHILO- + Greek *ateleia* exemption from charges (here referring to stamps), from A-[1] + *telos* tax, payment
▸**philatelic** (ˌfɪləˈtɛlɪk) ADJECTIVE ▸**,phila'telically** ADVERB ▸**phi'latelist** NOUN

-phile *or* **-phil** NOUN COMBINING FORM indicating a person or thing having a fondness or preference for something specified: *bibliophile; Francophile.*
▷HISTORY from Greek *philos* loving

Philem. *Bible* ◆ ABBREVIATION FOR Philemon.

Philemon[1] (faɪˈliːmɒn) NOUN *New Testament* [1] a Christian of Colossae whose escaped slave came to meet Paul. [2] the book (in full **The Epistle of Paul the Apostle to Philemon**), asking Philemon to forgive the slave for escaping.

Philemon[2] (faɪˈliːmɒn) NOUN *Greek myth* a poor Phrygian, who with his wife Baucis offered hospitality to the disguised Zeus and Hermes.

philharmonic (ˌfɪlhɑːˈmɒnɪk, ˌfɪlə-) ADJECTIVE [1] fond of music. [2] (*capital when part of a name*) denoting an orchestra, choir, society, etc., devoted to the performance, appreciation, and study of music. ◆ NOUN [3] (*capital when part of a name*) a specific philharmonic choir, orchestra, or society.
▷HISTORY C18: from French *philharmonique,* from Italian *filarmonico* music-loving; see PHILO-, HARMONY

philhellene (fɪlˈhɛliːn) *or* **philhellenist** (fɪlˈhɛlɪnɪst) NOUN [1] a lover of Greece and Greek culture. [2] *European history* a supporter of the cause of Greek national independence.
▸**philhellenic** (ˌfɪlhɛˈliːnɪk) ADJECTIVE ▸**philhellenism** (fɪlˈhɛlɪˌnɪzəm) NOUN

-philia NOUN COMBINING FORM [1] indicating a tendency towards: *haemophilia.* [2] indicating an abnormal liking for: *necrophilia.*
▷HISTORY from Greek *philos* loving
▸**-philiac** NOUN COMBINING FORM ▸**-philous** *or* **-philic** ADJECTIVE COMBINING FORM

philibeg (ˈfɪlɪˌbɛg) NOUN a variant spelling of **filibeg.**

Philippeville (ˈfɪlɪpˌvɪl) NOUN the former name of **Skikda.**

Philippi (fɪˈlɪpaɪ, ˈfɪlɪ-) NOUN an ancient city in NE Macedonia: scene of the victory of Antony and Octavian over Brutus and Cassius (42 B.C.).

Philippian (fɪˈlɪpɪən) ADJECTIVE [1] of or relating to the ancient Macedonian city of Philippi. ◆ NOUN [2] a native or inhabitant of Philippi.

Philippians (fɪˈlɪpɪənz) NOUN (*functioning as singular*) a book of the New Testament (in full **The Epistle of Paul the Apostle to the Philippians**).

philippic (fɪˈlɪpɪk) NOUN a bitter or impassioned speech of denunciation; invective.

Philippics (fɪˈlɪpɪks) PLURAL NOUN [1] Demosthenes' orations against Philip of Macedon. [2] Cicero's orations against Antony.

Philippine (ˈfɪlɪˌpiːn) ADJECTIVE another word for **Filipino** (sense 3).

Philippine mahogany (ˈfɪlɪˌpiːn) NOUN any of various Philippine hardwood trees of the genus *Shorea* and related genera: family *Dipterocarpaceae.*

Philippines (ˈfɪlɪˌpiːnz, ˌfɪlɪˈpiːnz) NOUN (*functioning as singular*) **Republic of the.** a republic in SE Asia, occupying an archipelago of about 7100 islands (including Luzon, Mindanao, Samar, and Negros): became a Spanish colony in 1571 but ceded to the US in 1898 after the Spanish-American War; gained independence in 1946. The islands are generally mountainous and volcanic. Official languages: Filipino, based on Tagalog, and English. Religion: Roman Catholic majority. Currency: peso. Capital: Manila. Pop.: 78 609 000 (2001 est.). Area: 300 076 sq. km (115 860 sq. miles). Related word: **Filipino.**

Philippine Sea NOUN part of the NW Pacific Ocean, east and north of the Philippines.

Philippopolis (ˌfɪlɪˈpɒpəlɪs) NOUN transliteration of the Greek name for **Plovdiv.**

Philistia (fɪˈlɪstɪə) NOUN an ancient country on the coast of SW Palestine.

Philistian (fɪˈlɪstɪən) ADJECTIVE of or relating to Philistia, an ancient country in Palestine, or its inhabitants.

Philistine (ˈfɪlɪˌstaɪn) NOUN [1] a person who is unreceptive to or hostile towards culture, the arts, etc.; a smug boorish person. [2] a member of the non-Semitic people who inhabited ancient Philistia. ◆ ADJECTIVE [3] (*sometimes not capital*) boorishly uncultured. [4] of or relating to the ancient Philistines.
▸**Philistinism** (ˈfɪlɪstɪˌnɪzəm) NOUN

Phillips curve NOUN *Economics* a curve that purports to plot the relationship between unemployment and inflation on the theory that as inflation falls unemployment rises and vice versa.
▷HISTORY C20: named after A. W. H. *Phillips* (1914–75), English economist who formulated the theory

Phillips screw NOUN *Trademark* a screw having a cruciform slot into which a screwdriver with a cruciform point (**Phillips screwdriver** (*Trademark*)) fits.

phillumenist (fɪˈljuːmənɪst, -ˈluː-) NOUN a person who collects matchbox labels.
▷HISTORY C20: from PHILO- + Latin *lumen* light + -IST
▸**phil'lumeny** NOUN

philo- *or before a vowel* **phil-** COMBINING FORM indicating a love of: *philology; philanthropic.*
▷HISTORY from Greek *philos* loving

Philoctetes (ˌfɪlɒkˈtiːtiːz, fɪˈlɒktɪˌtiːz) NOUN *Greek myth* a hero of the Trojan War, in which he killed Paris with the bow and poisoned arrows given to him by Hercules.

philodendron (ˌfɪləˈdɛndrən) NOUN, *plural* **-drons** *or* **-dra** (-drə). any aroid evergreen climbing plant of

the tropical American genus *Philodendron:* cultivated as house plants.
▷HISTORY C19: New Latin from Greek: lover of trees

philogyny (fɪˈlɒdʒɪnɪ) NOUN *Rare* fondness for women. Compare **misogyny**.
▷HISTORY C17: from Greek *philogunia,* from PHILO- + *gunē* woman
▶**phiˈlogynist** NOUN ▶**phiˈlogynous** ADJECTIVE

philol. ABBREVIATION FOR: [1] philological. [2] philology.

philology (fɪˈlɒlədʒɪ) NOUN [1] comparative and historical linguistics. [2] the scientific analysis of written records and literary texts. [3] (no longer in scholarly use) the study of literature in general.
▷HISTORY C17: from Latin *philologia,* from Greek: love of language
▶**philological** (ˌfɪləˈlɒdʒɪkᵊl) ADJECTIVE ▶**ˌphiloˈlogically** ADVERB ▶**phiˈlologist** *or (less commonly)* **phiˈlologer** NOUN

philomel (ˈfɪləˌmɛl) *or* **philomela** (ˌfɪləʊˈmiːlə) NOUN poetic names for a **nightingale**.
▷HISTORY C14 *philomene,* via Medieval Latin from Latin *philomēla,* from Greek

Philomela (ˌfɪləʊˈmiːlə) NOUN *Greek myth* an Athenian princess, who was raped and had her tongue cut out by her brother-in-law Tereus, and subsequently was transformed into a nightingale. See **Procne**.

philoprogenitive (ˌfɪləʊprəʊˈdʒɛnɪtɪv) ADJECTIVE *Rare* [1] fond of children. [2] producing many offspring.

philos. ABBREVIATION FOR: [1] philosopher. [2] philosophical.

philosopher (fɪˈlɒsəfə) NOUN [1] a student, teacher, or devotee of philosophy. [2] a person of philosophical temperament, esp one who is patient, wise, and stoical. [3] (formerly) an alchemist or devotee of occult science. [4] a person who establishes the ideology of a cult or movement: *the philosopher of the revolution.*

philosopher kings PLURAL NOUN [1] (in the political theory of Plato) the elite whose education has given them true knowledge of the Forms and esp of the Form of the Good, thus enabling them alone to rule justly. [2] *Informal* any ideologically motivated elite.

philosopher's stone NOUN a stone or substance thought by alchemists to be capable of transmuting base metals into gold.

philosophical (ˌfɪləˈsɒfɪkᵊl) *or* **philosophic** ADJECTIVE [1] of or relating to philosophy or philosophers. [2] reasonable, wise, or learned. [3] calm and stoical, esp in the face of difficulties or disappointments. [4] (formerly) of or relating to science or natural philosophy.
▶**ˌphiloˈsophically** ADVERB ▶**ˌphiloˈsophicalness** NOUN

philosophical logic NOUN the branch of philosophy that studies the relationship between formal logic and ordinary language, esp the extent to which the former can be held accurately to represent the latter.

philosophize *or* **philosophise** (fɪˈlɒsəˌfaɪz) VERB [1] (*intr*) to make philosophical pronouncements and speculations. [2] (*tr*) to explain philosophically.
▶**phiˌlosophiˈzation** *or* **phiˌlosophiˈsation** NOUN ▶**phiˈlosoˌphizer** *or* **phiˈlosoˌphiser** NOUN

philosophy (fɪˈlɒsəfɪ) NOUN, *plural* **-phies**. [1] the academic discipline concerned with making explicit the nature and significance of ordinary and scientific beliefs and investigating the intelligibility of concepts by means of rational argument concerning their presuppositions, implications, and interrelationships; in particular, the rational investigation of the nature and structure of reality (metaphysics), the resources and limits of knowledge (epistemology), the principles and import of moral judgment (ethics), and the relationship between language and reality (semantics). [2] the particular doctrines relating to these issues of some specific individual or school: *the philosophy of Descartes.* [3] the critical study of the basic principles and concepts of a discipline: *the philosophy of law.* [4] *Archaic or literary* the investigation of natural phenomena, esp alchemy, astrology, and astronomy. [5] any system of belief, values, or tenets. [6] a personal outlook or viewpoint. [7] serenity of temper.
▷HISTORY C13: from Old French *filosofie,* from Latin *philosophia,* from Greek, from *philosophos* lover of wisdom

-philous *or* **-philic** ADJECTIVE COMBINING FORM indicating love of or fondness for: *heliophilous.*
▷HISTORY from Latin *-philus,* from Greek *-philos;* see -PHILE

philtre *or US* **philter** (ˈfɪltə) NOUN a drink supposed to arouse love, desire, etc.
▷HISTORY C16: from Latin *philtrum,* from Greek *philtron* love potion, from *philos* loving

philtrum (ˈfɪltrəm) NOUN, *plural* **philtra**. the indentation above the upper lip.
▷HISTORY C17: from Latin, see PHILTRE

phimosis (faɪˈməʊsɪs) NOUN abnormal tightness of the foreskin, preventing its being retracted over the tip of the penis.
▷HISTORY C17: via New Latin from Greek: a muzzling, from *phimos* a muzzle

phi-phenomenon (ˈfaɪfɪˌnɒmɪnən) NOUN, *plural* **-na** (-nə). *Psychol* [1] the illusion that when two lights are rapidly turned on and off in succession something appears to move backwards and forwards between them while the lights stay stationary. [2] a similar illusion in which one light appears to move smoothly backwards and forwards.
▷HISTORY C20: arbitrary use of Greek *phi*

phiz (fɪz) NOUN *Slang, chiefly Brit* the face or a facial expression: *an ugly phiz.* Also called: **phizog** (ˈfɪzɒg, fɪˈzɒg).
▷HISTORY C17: colloquial shortening of PHYSIOGNOMY

phlebectomy (flɪˈbɛktəmɪ) NOUN the surgical excision of a vein or part of a vein.

phlebitis (flɪˈbaɪtɪs) NOUN inflammation of a vein.
▷HISTORY C19: via New Latin from Greek; see PHLEBO-, -ITIS
▶**phlebitic** (flɪˈbɪtɪk) ADJECTIVE

phlebo- *or before a vowel* **phleb-** COMBINING FORM indicating a vein: *phlebotomy.*
▷HISTORY from Greek *phleps, phleb-* vein

phlebography (flɪˈbɒgrəfɪ) NOUN another name for **venography**.

phlebosclerosis (ˌflɛbəʊsklɪˈrəʊsɪs) NOUN *Pathol* hardening and loss of elasticity of the veins. Also called: **venosclerosis**.

phlebotomize *or* **phlebotomise** (flɪˈbɒtəˌmaɪz) VERB (*tr*) *Surgery* to perform phlebotomy on (a patient).

phlebotomy (flɪˈbɒtəmɪ) NOUN, *plural* **-mies**. surgical incision into a vein. Also called: **venesection**.
▷HISTORY C14: from Old French *flebothomie,* from Late Latin *phlebotomia,* from Greek
▶**phlebotomic** (ˌflɛbəˈtɒmɪk) *or* **ˌphleboˈtomical** ADJECTIVE ▶**phleˈbotomist** NOUN

Phlegethon (ˈflɛgɪˌθɒn) NOUN *Greek myth* a river of fire in Hades.
▷HISTORY C14: from Greek, literally: blazing, from *phlegethein* to flame, blaze

phlegm (flɛm) NOUN [1] the viscid mucus secreted by the walls of the respiratory tract. [2] *Archaic* one of the four bodily humours. [3] apathy; stolidity; indifference. [4] self-possession; imperturbability; coolness.
▷HISTORY C14: from Old French *fleume,* from Late Latin *phlegma,* from Greek: inflammation, from *phlegein* to burn
▶**ˈphlegmy** ADJECTIVE

phlegmatic (flɛgˈmætɪk) *or* **phlegmatical** ADJECTIVE [1] having a stolid or unemotional disposition. [2] not easily excited.
▶**phlegˈmatically** ADVERB ▶**phlegˈmaticalness** *or* **phlegˈmaticness** NOUN

phloem (ˈfləʊɛm) NOUN tissue in higher plants that conducts synthesized food substances to all parts of the plant.
▷HISTORY C19: via German from Greek *phloos* bark

phlogistic (flɒˈdʒɪstɪk) ADJECTIVE [1] *Pathol* of inflammation; inflammatory. [2] *Chem* of, concerned with, or containing phlogiston.

phlogiston (flɒˈdʒɪstɒn, -tən) NOUN *Chem* a hypothetical substance formerly thought to be present in all combustible materials and to be released during burning.
▷HISTORY C18: via New Latin from Greek, from *phlogizein* to set alight; related to *phlegein* to burn

phlogopite (ˈflɒgəˌpaɪt) NOUN a brownish mica consisting of a hydrous silicate of potassium, magnesium, and aluminium, occurring principally in metamorphic limestones and ultrabasic rocks. Formula: $KMg_3AlSi_3O_{10}(OH)_2$. See also **mica**.
▷HISTORY C19: from Greek *phlogōpos* of fiery appearance, from *phlox* flame + *ōps* eye

phlox (flɒks) NOUN, *plural* **phlox** *or* **phloxes**. any polemoniaceous plant of the chiefly North American genus *Phlox:* cultivated for their clusters of white, red, or purple flowers.
▷HISTORY C18: via Latin from Greek: a plant of glowing colour, literally: flame

PHLS (in Britain) ABBREVIATION FOR Public Health Laboratory Service.

phlyctena *or* **phlyctaena** (flɪkˈtiːnə) NOUN, *plural* **-nae** (-niː). *Pathol* a small blister, vesicle, or pustule.
▷HISTORY C17: via New Latin from Greek *phluktaina,* from *phluzein* to swell

Phnom Penh *or* **Pnom Penh** (ˌnɒm ˈpɛn) NOUN the capital of Cambodia, a port in the south at the confluence of the Mekong and Tonle Sap Rivers: capital of the country since 1865; university (1960). Pop.: 938 000 (1999 est.).

-phobe NOUN COMBINING FORM indicating a person or thing that fears or hates: *Germanophobe; xenophobe.*
▷HISTORY from Greek *-phobos* fearing
▶**-phobic** ADJECTIVE COMBINING FORM

phobia (ˈfəʊbɪə) NOUN *Psychiatry* an abnormal intense and irrational fear of a given situation, organism, or object.
▷HISTORY C19: from Greek *phobos* fear

-phobia NOUN COMBINING FORM indicating an extreme abnormal fear of or aversion to: *acrophobia; claustrophobia.*
▷HISTORY via Latin from Greek, from *phobos* fear
▶**-phobic** ADJECTIVE COMBINING FORM

phobic (ˈfəʊbɪk) ADJECTIVE [1] of, relating to, or arising from a phobia. ◆ NOUN [2] a person suffering from a phobia.

Phobos (ˈfəʊbɒs) NOUN the larger of the two satellites of Mars and the closer to the planet. Approximate diameter (although it has an irregular shape): 23 km. Compare **Deimos**.

Phocaea (fəʊˈsiːə) NOUN an ancient port in Asia Minor, the northernmost of Ionian cities on the W coast of Asia Minor: an important maritime state (about 1000–600 B.C.).

phocine (ˈfəʊsaɪn) ADJECTIVE [1] of, relating to, or resembling a seal. [2] of, relating to, or belonging to the *Phocinae,* a subfamily that includes the harbour seal and grey seal.
▷HISTORY C19: ultimately from Greek *phōkē* a seal

Phocis (ˈfəʊsɪs) NOUN an ancient district of central Greece, on the Gulf of Corinth: site of the Delphic oracle.

phocomelia (ˌfəʊkəʊˈmiːlɪə) *or* **phocomely** (fəʊˈkɒməlɪ) NOUN a congenital deformity resulting from prenatal interference with the development of the fetal limbs, characterized esp by short stubby hands or feet attached close to the body.
▷HISTORY C19: via New Latin from Greek *phōkē* a seal + *melos* a limb
▶**ˌphocoˈmelic** ADJECTIVE

phoebe (ˈfiːbɪ) NOUN any of several greyish-brown North American flycatchers of the genus *Sayornis,* such as *S. phoebe* (**eastern phoebe**).
▷HISTORY C19: imitative of the bird's call

Phoebe[1] *or* **Phebe** (ˈfiːbɪ) NOUN [1] *Classical myth* a Titaness, who later became identified with Artemis (Diana) as goddess of the moon. [2] *Poetic* a personification of the moon.

Phoebe[2] (ˈfiːbɪ) NOUN the outermost satellite of the planet Saturn. It has retrograde motion and a dark surface.

Phoebus (ˈfiːbəs) NOUN [1] Also called: **Phoebus Apollo**. *Greek myth* Apollo as the sun god. [2] *Poetic* a personification of the sun.
▷HISTORY C14: via Latin from Greek *Phoibos* bright; related to *phaos* light

Phoenicia (fəˈnɪʃɪə, -ˈniː-) NOUN an ancient maritime country extending from the Mediterranean Sea to the Lebanon Mountains, now occupied by the coastal regions of Lebanon and parts of Syria and Israel: consisted of a group of city-states, at their height between about 1200 and

1000 B.C., that were leading traders of the ancient world.

Phoenician (fəˈniːʃən, -ˈnɪʃɪən) NOUN **1** a member of an ancient Semitic people of NW Syria who dominated the trade of the ancient world in the first millennium B.C. and founded colonies throughout the Mediterranean. **2** the extinct language of this people, belonging to the Canaanitic branch of the Semitic subfamily of the Afro-Asiatic family. ◆ ADJECTIVE **3** of or relating to Phoenicia, the Phoenicians, or their language.

phoenix *or US* **phenix** (ˈfiːnɪks) NOUN **1** a legendary Arabian bird said to set fire to itself and rise anew from the ashes every 500 years. **2** a person or thing of surpassing beauty or quality.
▷HISTORY Old English *fenix,* via Latin from Greek *phoinix;* identical in form with Greek *Phoinix* Phoenician, purple

Phoenix[1] (ˈfiːnɪks) NOUN, *Latin genitive* **Phoenices** (ˈfiːnɪˌsiːz). a constellation in the S hemisphere lying between Grus and Eridanus.

Phoenix[2] (ˈfiːnɪks) NOUN a city in central Arizona, capital city of the state, on the Salt River. Pop.: 1 321 045 (1996 est.).

Phoenix Islands PLURAL NOUN a group of eight coral islands in the central Pacific: administratively part of Kiribati. Area: 28 sq. km (11 sq. miles).

Pholus (ˈfəʊləs) NOUN a large astronomical object, some 2000 km in diameter, discovered in 1991. Its elliptical orbit around the earth, between the orbits of Neptune and Saturn, has a period of 93 years. It has been classified as an asteroid although it lies outside the main asteroid belt.

phon (fɒn) NOUN a unit of loudness that measures the intensity of a sound by the number of decibels it is above a reference tone having a frequency of 1000 hertz and a root-mean-square sound pressure of 20×10^{-6} pascal.
▷HISTORY C20: via German from Greek *phōnē* sound, voice

phon. ABBREVIATION FOR: **1** Also: **phonet.** phonetics. **2** phonology.

phonate (fəʊˈneɪt) VERB (*intr*) to articulate speech sounds, esp to cause the vocal cords to vibrate in the execution of a voiced speech sound.
▷HISTORY C19: from Greek *phōnē* voice
▸**phoˈnation** NOUN ▸**phonatory** (ˈfəʊnətərɪ, -trɪ) ADJECTIVE

phone[1] (fəʊn) NOUN, VERB short for **telephone.**

phone[2] (fəʊn) NOUN *Phonetics* a single uncomplicated speech sound.
▷HISTORY C19: from Greek *phōnē* sound, voice

-phone COMBINING FORM **1** (*forming nouns*) indicating voice, sound, or a device giving off sound: *microphone; telephone.* **2** (*forming nouns and adjectives*) (a person) speaking a particular language: *Francophone.*
▷HISTORY from Greek *phōnē* voice, sound
▸**-phonic** ADJECTIVE COMBINING FORM

phonecard (ˈfəʊnˌkɑːd) NOUN a card for use in a cardphone that operates for the number or duration of calls paid for in the purchase price of the card.

phone-in NOUN **a** a radio or television programme in which listeners' or viewers' questions, comments, etc., are telephoned to the studio and broadcast live. **b** (*as modifier*): *a phone-in discussion.*

phoneme (ˈfəʊniːm) NOUN *Linguistics* one of the set of speech sounds in any given language that serve to distinguish one word from another. A phoneme may consist of several phonetically distinct articulations, which are regarded as identical by native speakers, since one articulation may be substituted for another without any change of meaning. Thus /p/ and /b/ are separate phonemes in English because they distinguish such words as *pet* and *bet,* whereas the light and dark /l/ sounds in *little* are not separate phonemes since they may be transposed without changing meaning.
▷HISTORY C20: via French from Greek *phōnēma* sound, speech

phonemic (fəˈniːmɪk) ADJECTIVE *Linguistics* **1** of or relating to the phoneme. **2** relating to or denoting speech sounds that belong to different phonemes rather than being allophonic variants of the same phoneme. Compare **phonetic** (sense 2). **3** of or relating to phonemics.
▸**phoˈnemically** ADVERB

phonemics (fəˈniːmɪks) NOUN (*functioning as singular*) that aspect of linguistics concerned with the classification, analysis, interrelation, and environmental changes of the phonemes of a language.
▸**phoˈnemicist** NOUN

phonendoscope (fəˈnendəˌskəʊp) NOUN an instrument that amplifies small sounds, esp within the human body.
▷HISTORY C20: from PHONO- + ENDO- + -SCOPE

phoner (ˈfəʊnə) NOUN *Informal* a person making a telephone call.

phone sex NOUN sexual activity carried out verbally by telephone.

phonetic (fəˈnɛtɪk) ADJECTIVE **1** of or relating to phonetics. **2** denoting any perceptible distinction between one speech sound and another, irrespective of whether the sounds are phonemes or allophones. Compare **phonemic** (sense 2). **3** conforming to pronunciation: *phonetic spelling.*
▷HISTORY C19: from New Latin *phōnēticus,* from Greek *phōnētikos,* from *phōnein* to make sounds, speak
▸**phoˈnetically** ADVERB

phonetic alphabet NOUN a list of the words used in communications to represent the letters of the alphabet, as in E for Echo, T for Tango.

phonetician (ˌfəʊnɪˈtɪʃən) NOUN a person skilled in phonetics or one who employs phonetics in his work.

phonetics (fəˈnɛtɪks) NOUN (*functioning as singular*) the science concerned with the study of speech processes, including the production, perception, and analysis of speech sounds from both an acoustic and a physiological point of view. This science, though capable of being applied to language studies, technically excludes linguistic considerations. Compare **phonology.**

phonetist (ˈfəʊnɪtɪst) NOUN **1** another name for **phonetician. 2** a person who advocates or uses a system of phonetic spelling.

phoney *or esp US* **phony** (ˈfəʊnɪ) *Informal* ◆ ADJECTIVE **-nier, -niest. 1** not genuine; fake. **2** (of a person) insincere or pretentious. ◆ NOUN, *plural* **-neys** *or* **-nies. 3** an insincere or pretentious person. **4** something that is not genuine; a fake.
▷HISTORY C20: origin uncertain
▸**ˈphoneyness** *or* (*esp US*) **ˈphoniness** NOUN

phonics (ˈfɒnɪks) NOUN (*functioning as singular*) **1** an obsolete name for **acoustics** (sense 1). **2** a method of teaching people to read by training them to associate letters with their phonetic values.
▸**ˈphonic** ADJECTIVE ▸**ˈphonically** ADVERB

phono- *or before a vowel* **phon-** COMBINING FORM indicating a sound or voice: *phonograph; phonology.*
▷HISTORY from Greek *phōnē* sound, voice

phonochemistry (ˌfəʊnəʊˈkɛmɪstrɪ) NOUN the branch of chemistry concerned with the chemical effects of sound and ultrasonic waves.

phonogram (ˈfəʊnəˌgræm) NOUN **1** any written symbol standing for a sound, syllable, morpheme, or word. **2** a sequence of written symbols having the same sound in a variety of different words, for example, *ough* in *bought, ought,* and *brought.*
▸**ˌphonoˈgramic** *or* **ˌphonoˈgrammic** ADJECTIVE

phonograph (ˈfəʊnəˌgrɑːf, -ˌgræf) NOUN **1** an early form of gramophone capable of recording and reproducing sound on wax cylinders. **2** another US and Canadian word for **gramophone** or **record player.**

phonographic (ˌfəʊnəˈgræfɪk) ADJECTIVE **1** of or relating to phonography. **2** of or relating to the recording of music.

phonography (fəʊˈnɒgrəfɪ) NOUN **1** a writing system that represents sounds by individual symbols. Compare **logography. 2** the employment of such a writing system.
▸**phoˈnographer** *or* **phoˈnographist** NOUN

phonolite (ˈfəʊnəˌlaɪt) NOUN a fine-grained volcanic igneous rock consisting of alkaline feldspars and nepheline.
▷HISTORY C19: via French from German *Phonolith;* see PHONO-, -LITE
▸**phonolitic** (ˌfəʊnəˈlɪtɪk) ADJECTIVE

phonology (fəˈnɒlədʒɪ) NOUN, *plural* **-gies. 1** the study of the sound system of a language or of languages in general. Compare **syntax** (senses 1, 2), **semantics. 2** such a sound system.
▸**phonological** (ˌfəʊnəˈlɒdʒɪkəl, ˌfɒn-) ADJECTIVE
▸**ˌphonoˈlogically** ADVERB ▸**phoˈnologist** NOUN

phonometer (fəˈnɒmɪtə) NOUN an apparatus that measures the intensity of sound, esp one calibrated in phons.
▸**phonometric** (ˌfəʊnəˈmɛtrɪk) *or* **ˌphonoˈmetrical** ADJECTIVE

phonon (ˈfəʊnɒn) NOUN *Physics* a quantum of vibrational energy in the acoustic vibrations of a crystal lattice.
▷HISTORY C20: from PHONO- + -ON

phono plug (ˈfəʊnəʊ) NOUN *Electrical engineering* a type of coaxial connector, used esp in audio equipment.

phonoscope (ˈfəʊnəˌskəʊp) NOUN a device that renders visible the vibrations of sound waves.

phonotactics (ˈfəʊnəʊˌtæktɪks) NOUN (*functioning as singular*) *Linguistics* the study of the possible arrangement of the sounds of a language in the words of that language.
▷HISTORY C20: from PHONO- + *-tactics,* on the model of *syntactic;* see SYNTAX

phonotype (ˈfəʊnəˌtaɪp) NOUN *Printing* **1** a letter or symbol representing a sound. **2** text printed in phonetic symbols.
▸**phonotypic** (ˌfəʊnəˈtɪpɪk) *or* **ˌphonoˈtypical** ADJECTIVE

phonotypy (ˈfəʊnəˌtaɪpɪ) NOUN the transcription of speech into phonetic symbols.
▸**ˈphonoˌtypist** *or* **ˈphonoˌtyper** NOUN

phony (ˈfəʊnɪ) ADJECTIVE **-nier, -niest,** NOUN, *plural* **-nies.** a variant spelling (esp US) of **phoney.**
▸**ˈphoniness** NOUN

-phony NOUN COMBINING FORM indicating a specified type of sound: *cacophony; euphony.*
▷HISTORY from Greek *-phōnia,* from *phōnē* sound
▸**-phonic** ADJECTIVE COMBINING FORM

phony war NOUN **1** (in wartime) a period of apparent calm and inactivity, esp the period at the beginning of World War II. **2** (in peacetime) a contrived embattled atmosphere; mock war.

phooey (ˈfuːɪ) INTERJECTION *Informal* an exclamation of scorn, contempt, disbelief, etc.
▷HISTORY C20: probably variant of PHEW

-phore NOUN COMBINING FORM indicating a person or thing that bears or produces: *gonophore; semaphore.*
▷HISTORY from New Latin *-phorus,* from Greek *-phoros* bearing, from *pherein* to bear
▸**-phorous** ADJECTIVE COMBINING FORM

-phoresis NOUN COMBINING FORM indicating a transmission: *electrophoresis.*
▷HISTORY from Greek *phorēsis* being carried, from *pherein* to bear

phoresy (ˈfɒrəsɪ) NOUN an association in which one animal clings to another to ensure movement from place to place, as some mites use some insects.
▷HISTORY C20: from New Latin *phoresia,* from Greek *phorēsis,* from *pherein* to carry

phormium (ˈfɔːmɪəm) NOUN any plant of the New Zealand bulbous genus *Phormium,* with leathery evergreen leaves and red or yellow flowers in panicles.
▷HISTORY New Latin, from Greek *phormos* a basket (from a use for the fibres)

phosgene (ˈfɒzdʒiːn) NOUN a colourless easily liquefied poisonous gas, carbonyl chloride, with an odour resembling that of new-mown hay: used in chemical warfare as a lethal choking agent and in the manufacture of pesticides, dyes, and polyurethane resins. Formula: $COCl_2$.
▷HISTORY C19: from Greek *phōs* light + *-gene,* variant of -GEN

phosgenite (ˈfɒzdʒɪˌnaɪt) NOUN a rare fluorescent secondary mineral consisting of lead chloro-carbonate in the form of greyish tetragonal crystals. Formula: $Pb_2(Cl_2CO_3)$.

phosphatase (ˈfɒsfəˌteɪs, -ˌteɪz) NOUN any of a group of enzymes that catalyse the hydrolysis of organic phosphates.

phosphate (ˈfɒsfeɪt) NOUN **1** any salt or ester of any phosphoric acid, esp a salt of orthophosphoric acid. **2** (*often plural*) any of several chemical fertilizers containing phosphorous compounds.
▷HISTORY C18: from French *phosphat;* see PHOSPHORUS, -ATE[1]

▸**phosphatic** (fɒsˈfætɪk) ADJECTIVE

phosphatide (ˈfɒsfəˌtaɪd) NOUN another name for **phospholipid**.

phosphatidylcholine (ˌfɒsfətɪdaɪlˈkəʊliːn) NOUN the systematic name for **lecithin**.

phosphatidylethanolamine (ˌfɒsfətɪdaɪlˌɛθəˈnɒləmiːn) NOUN the systematic name for **cephalin**.

phosphatidylserine (ˌfɒsfətɪdaɪlˈsɪəriːn) NOUN any of a class of phospholipids occurring in biological membranes and fats.

phosphatize *or* **phosphatise** (ˈfɒsfəˌtaɪz) VERB [1] (*tr*) to treat with a phosphate or phosphates, as by applying a fertilizer. [2] to change or be changed into a phosphate.
▸ **ˌphosphatiˈzation** *or* **ˌphosphatiˈsation** NOUN

phosphaturia (ˌfɒsfəˈtjʊərɪə) NOUN *Pathol* an abnormally large amount of phosphates in the urine.
▹HISTORY C19: New Latin, from PHOSPHATE + -URIA
▸ **ˌphosphaˈturic** ADJECTIVE

phosphene (ˈfɒsfiːn) NOUN the sensation of light caused by pressure on the eyelid of a closed eye or by other mechanical or electrical interference with the visual system.
▹HISTORY C19: from Greek *phōs* light + *phainein* to show

phosphide (ˈfɒsfaɪd) NOUN any compound of phosphorus with another element, esp a more electropositive element.

phosphine (ˈfɒsfiːn) NOUN a colourless flammable gas that is slightly soluble in water and has a strong fishy odour: used as a pesticide. Formula: PH_3.

phosphite (ˈfɒsfaɪt) NOUN any salt or ester of phosphorous acid.

phospho- *or before a vowel* **phosph-** COMBINING FORM containing phosphorus: *phosphocreatine*.
▹HISTORY from French, from *phosphore* PHOSPHORUS

phosphocreatine (ˌfɒsfəˈkriːəˌtiːn) *or* **phosphocreatin** NOUN a compound of phosphoric acid and creatine found in vertebrate muscle.

phospholipid (ˌfɒsfəˈlɪpɪd) NOUN any of a group of compounds composed of fatty acids, phosphoric acid, and a nitrogenous base: important constituents of all membranes. Also called: **phosphatide**.

phosphonic acid (fɒsˈfɒnɪk) NOUN the systematic name for **phosphorous acid**.

phosphoprotein (ˌfɒsfəˈprəʊtiːn) NOUN any of a group of conjugated proteins, esp casein, in which the protein molecule is bound to phosphoric acid.

phosphor (ˈfɒsfə) NOUN a substance, such as the coating on a cathode-ray tube, capable of emitting light when irradiated with particles or electromagnetic radiation.
▹HISTORY C17: from French, ultimately from Greek *phōsphoros* PHOSPHORUS

phosphorate (ˈfɒsfəˌreɪt) VERB [1] to treat or combine with phosphorus. [2] (*tr*) *Rare* to cause (a substance) to exhibit phosphorescence.

phosphor bronze NOUN any of various hard corrosion-resistant alloys containing copper, tin (2–8 per cent), and phosphorus (0.1–0.4 per cent): used in gears, bearings, cylinder casings, etc.

phosphoresce (ˌfɒsfəˈrɛs) VERB (*intr*) to exhibit phosphorescence.

phosphorescence (ˌfɒsfəˈrɛsəns) NOUN [1] *Physics* **a** a fluorescence that persists after the bombarding radiation producing it has stopped. **b** a fluorescence for which the average lifetime of the excited atoms is greater than 10^{-8} seconds. [2] the light emitted in phosphorescence. [3] the emission of light during a chemical reaction, such as bioluminescence, in which insufficient heat is evolved to cause fluorescence. Compare **fluorescence**.

phosphorescent (ˌfɒsfəˈrɛsᵊnt) ADJECTIVE exhibiting or having the property of phosphorescence.
▸ **ˌphosphoˈrescently** ADVERB

phosphoric (fɒsˈfɒrɪk) ADJECTIVE of or containing phosphorus in the pentavalent state.

phosphoric acid NOUN [1] a colourless solid tribasic acid used in the manufacture of fertilizers and soap. Formula: H_3PO_4. Systematic name: **phosphoric(V) acid**. Also called: **orthophosphoric acid**. [2] any oxyacid of phosphorus produced by reaction between phosphorus pentoxide and water. See also **metaphosphoric acid, pyrophosphoric acid, hypophosphoric acid**.

phosphorism (ˈfɒsfəˌrɪzəm) NOUN poisoning caused by prolonged exposure to phosphorus.

phosphorite (ˈfɒsfəˌraɪt) NOUN [1] a fibrous variety of the mineral apatite. [2] any of various mineral deposits that consist mainly of calcium phosphate.
▸ **phosphoritic** (ˌfɒsfəˈrɪtɪk) ADJECTIVE

phosphoroscope (fɒsˈfɒrəˌskəʊp) NOUN an instrument for measuring the duration of phosphorescence after the source of radiation causing it has been removed.

phosphorous (ˈfɒsfərəs) ADJECTIVE of or containing phosphorus in the trivalent state.

phosphorous acid NOUN [1] a white or yellowish hygroscopic crystalline dibasic acid. Formula: H_3PO_3. Systematic name: **phosphonic acid**. Also called: **orthophosphorous acid**. [2] any oxyacid of phosphorus containing less oxygen than the corresponding phosphoric acid.

phosphorus (ˈfɒsfərəs) NOUN [1] an allotropic nonmetallic element occurring in phosphates and living matter. Ordinary phosphorus is a toxic flammable phosphorescent white solid; the red form is less reactive and nontoxic: used in matches, pesticides, and alloys. The radioisotope **phosphorus-32 (radiophosphorus)**, with a half-life of 14.3 days, is used in radiotherapy and as a tracer. Symbol: P; atomic no.: 15; atomic wt.: 30.973762; valency: 3 or 5; relative density: 1.82 (white), 2.20 (red); melting pt.: 44.1°C (white); boiling pt.: 280°C (white). [2] a less common name for a **phosphor**.
▹HISTORY C17: via Latin from Greek *phōsphoros* light-bringing, from *phōs* light + *pherein* to bring

Phosphorus (ˈfɒsfərəs) NOUN a morning star, esp Venus.

phosphorus pentoxide NOUN a white odourless solid produced when phosphorus burns: has a strong affinity for water with which it forms phosphoric acids. Formula: P_2O_5 (commonly existing as the dimer P_4O_{10}). Also called: **phosphoric anhydride**.

phosphorylase (fɒsˈfɒrɪˌleɪs, -ˌleɪz) NOUN any of a group of enzymes that catalyse the hydrolysis of glycogen to glucose-1-phosphate.
▹HISTORY C20: from PHOSPHORUS + -YL + -ASE

phosphorylation (ˌfɒsfərɪˈleɪʃən) NOUN the chemical or enzymic introduction into a compound of a phosphoryl group (a trivalent radical of phosphorus and oxygen).

phossy jaw (ˈfɒsɪ) NOUN a gangrenous condition of the lower jawbone caused by prolonged exposure to phosphorus fumes.
▹HISTORY C19: *phossy*, colloquial shortening of PHOSPHORUS

phot (fɒt, fəʊt) NOUN a unit of illumination equal to one lumen per square centimetre. 1 phot is equal to 10 000 lux.
▹HISTORY C20: from Greek *phōs* light

photic (ˈfəʊtɪk) ADJECTIVE [1] of or concerned with light. [2] *Biology* of or relating to the production of light by organisms. [3] Also: **photobathic**. designating the zone of the sea where photosynthesis takes place.
▹HISTORY C19: from PHOTO- + -IC

photo (ˈfəʊtəʊ) NOUN, *plural* **-tos**. short for **photograph** (sense 1).

photo- COMBINING FORM [1] of, relating to, or produced by light: *photosynthesis*. [2] indicating a photographic process: *photolithography*.
▹HISTORY from Greek *phōs*, *phōt-* light

photoactinic (ˌfəʊtəʊækˈtɪnɪk) ADJECTIVE emitting actinic radiation.

photoactive (ˌfəʊtəʊˈæktɪv) ADJECTIVE (of a substance) capable of responding to light or other electromagnetic radiation.

photo-ageing NOUN premature wrinkling of the skin caused by overexposure to sunlight.
▸ **ˌphoto-ˈaged** ADJECTIVE

photoautotrophic (ˌfəʊtəʊˌɔːtəʊˈtrɒfɪk) ADJECTIVE (of plants) capable of using light as the energy source in the synthesis of food from inorganic matter. See also **photosynthesis**.

photobathic (ˌfəʊtəʊˈbæθɪk) ADJECTIVE another word for **photic** (sense 3).
▹HISTORY from PHOTO- + Greek *bathus* deep + -IC

photobiology (ˌfəʊtəʊbaɪˈɒlədʒɪ) NOUN the branch of biology concerned with the effect of light on living organisms.
▸ **photobiological** (ˌfəʊtəʊˌbaɪəˈlɒdʒɪkᵊl) ADJECTIVE
▸ **ˌphotobiˈologist** NOUN

photo call NOUN a time arranged for photographers, esp press photographers, to take pictures of a celebrity, the cast of a play, etc., usually for publicity purposes.

photocatalysis (ˌfəʊtəʊkəˈtælɪsɪs) NOUN, *plural* **-ses** (-siːz). the alteration of the rate of a chemical reaction by light or other electromagnetic radiation.

photocathode (ˌfəʊtəʊˈkæθəʊd) NOUN a cathode that undergoes or is used for photoemission.

photocell (ˈfəʊtəʊˌsɛl) NOUN a device in which the photoelectric or photovoltaic effect or photoconductivity is used to produce a current or voltage when exposed to light or other electromagnetic radiation. They are used in exposure meters, burglar alarms, etc. Also called: **photoelectric cell, electric eye**.

photochemical (ˌfəʊtəʊˈkɛmɪkᵊl) ADJECTIVE of or relating to photochemistry; involving the chemical effects of light.
▸ **ˌphotoˈchemically** ADVERB

photochemistry (ˌfəʊtəʊˈkɛmɪstrɪ) NOUN the branch of chemistry concerned with the chemical effects of light and other electromagnetic radiations. Also called: **actinochemistry**.
▸ **ˌphotoˈchemist** NOUN

photochromic (ˌfəʊtəʊˈkrəʊmɪk) ADJECTIVE (of glass) changing colour with the intensity of incident light, used, for example, in sunglasses that darken as the sunlight becomes brighter.

photochronograph (ˌfəʊtəʊˈkrɒnəˌgrɑːf, -ˌgræf) NOUN *Physics* an instrument for measuring very small time intervals by the trace made by a beam of light on a moving photographic film.
▸ **photochronography** (ˌfəʊtəʊkrəˈnɒgrəfɪ) NOUN

photocompose (ˌfəʊtəʊkəmˈpəʊz) VERB (*tr*) to set (type matter) by photocomposition.
▸ **ˌphotocomˈposer** NOUN

photocomposition (ˌfəʊtəʊˌkɒmpəˈzɪʃən) NOUN *Printing* typesetting by exposing type characters onto photographic film or photosensitive paper in order to make printing plates. Also called: **photosetting, phototypesetting**.

photoconduction (ˌfəʊtəʊkənˈdʌkʃən) NOUN conduction of electricity resulting from the absorption of light. See **photoconductivity**.

photoconductivity (ˌfəʊtəʊˌkɒndʌkˈtɪvɪtɪ) NOUN the change in the electrical conductivity of certain substances, such as selenium, as a result of the absorption of electromagnetic radiation.
▸ **photoconductive** (ˌfəʊtəʊkənˈdʌktɪv) ADJECTIVE
▸ **ˌphotoconˈductor** NOUN

photocopier (ˈfəʊtəʊˌkɒpɪə) NOUN an instrument using light-sensitive photographic materials to reproduce written, printed, or graphic work.

photocopy (ˈfəʊtəʊˌkɒpɪ) NOUN, *plural* **-copies**. [1] a photographic reproduction of written, printed, or graphic work. See also **microcopy**. ◆ VERB **-copies, -copying, -copied**. [2] to reproduce (written, printed, or graphic work) on photographic material.

photocurrent (ˈfəʊtəʊˌkʌrənt) NOUN an electric current produced by electromagnetic radiation in the photoelectric effect, photovoltaic effect, or photoconductivity.

photodegradable (ˌfəʊtəʊdɪˈgreɪdəbᵊl) ADJECTIVE (of plastic) capable of being decomposed by prolonged exposure to light.

photodiode (ˌfəʊtəʊˈdaɪəʊd) NOUN a semiconductor diode, the conductivity of which is controlled by incident illumination.

photodisintegration (ˌfəʊtəʊdɪˌsɪntɪˈgreɪʃən) NOUN disintegration of an atomic nucleus as a result of its absorption of a photon, usually a gamma ray.

photodynamic (ˌfəʊtəʊdaɪˈnæmɪk) ADJECTIVE [1] of or concerned with photodynamics. [2] involving or producing an adverse or toxic reaction to light, esp ultraviolet light. [3] *Med* denoting a therapy for cancer in which a cytotoxic drug is activated by a laser beam.

photodynamics (ˌfəʊtəʊdaɪˈnæmɪks) NOUN (*functioning as singular*) the branch of biology concerned with the effects of light on the actions of plants and animals.

photoelasticity (ˌfəʊtəʊɪlæˈstɪsɪtɪ) NOUN the effects of stress, such as double refraction, on the optical properties of transparent materials.

photoelectric (ˌfəʊtəʊɪˈlɛktrɪk) *or* **photoelectrical** ADJECTIVE of or concerned with electric or electronic effects caused by light or other electromagnetic radiation.
▸ˌ**photoeˈlectrically** ADVERB ▸**photoelectricity** (ˌfəʊtəʊɪlɛkˈtrɪsɪtɪ) NOUN

photoelectric cell NOUN another name for **photocell.**

photoelectric effect NOUN [1] the ejection of electrons from a solid by an incident beam of sufficiently energetic electromagnetic radiation. [2] any phenomenon involving electricity and electromagnetic radiation, such as photoemission.

photoelectric magnitude NOUN *Astronomy* the magnitude of a star determined using a photometer plus a filter to select light or other radiation of the desired wavelength.

photoelectron (ˌfəʊtəʊɪˈlɛktrɒn) NOUN an electron ejected from an atom, molecule, or solid by an incident photon.

photoelectrotype (ˌfəʊtəʊɪˈlɛktrəʊˌtaɪp) NOUN an electrotype mode using photography.

photoemission (ˌfəʊtəʊɪˈmɪʃən) NOUN the emission of electrons due to the impact of electromagnetic radiation, esp as a result of the photoelectric effect.
▸ˌ**photoeˈmissive** ADJECTIVE

photoengrave (ˌfəʊtəʊɪnˈgreɪv) VERB (*tr*) to reproduce (an illustration) by photoengraving.
▸ˌ**photoenˈgraver** NOUN

photoengraving (ˌfəʊtəʊɪnˈgreɪvɪŋ) NOUN [1] a photomechanical process for producing letterpress printing plates. [2] a plate made by this process. [3] a print made from such a plate.

photo finish NOUN [1] a finish of a race in which contestants are so close that a photograph is needed to decide the result. [2] any race or competition in which the winners or placed contestants are separated by a very small margin.

Photofit (ˈfəʊtəʊˌfɪt) NOUN *Trademark* **a** a method of combining photographs of facial features, hair, etc., into a composite picture of a face: formerly used by the police to trace suspects from witnesses' descriptions. **b** (*as modifier*): *a Photofit picture.*

photoflash (ˈfəʊtəʊˌflæʃ) NOUN another name for **flashbulb.**

photoflood (ˈfəʊtəʊˌflʌd) NOUN a highly incandescent tungsten lamp used as an artificial light source for indoor photography, television, etc. The brightness is obtained by operating with higher than normal current.

photofluorography (ˌfəʊtəʊflʊəˈrɒgrəfɪ) NOUN *Med* the process of taking a photograph (**photofluorogram**) of a fluoroscopic image: used in diagnostic screening.

photog. ABBREVIATION FOR: [1] photograph. [2] photographer. [3] photographic. [4] photography.

photogelatine process (ˌfəʊtəʊˈdʒɛlətiːn) NOUN another name for **collotype** (sense 1).

photogene (ˈfəʊtəʊˌdʒiːn) NOUN another name for **afterimage.**
▹HISTORY C19: from Greek *phōtogenēs* light-produced. See PHOTO-, -GENE

photogenic (ˌfəʊtəˈdʒɛnɪk) ADJECTIVE [1] (esp of a person) having features, colouring, and a general facial appearance that look attractive in photographs. [2] *Biology* producing or emitting light: *photogenic bacteria.*
▸ˌ**photoˈgenically** ADVERB

photogeology (ˌfəʊtəʊdʒɪˈɒlədʒɪ) NOUN the study and identification of geological phenomena using aerial photographs.

photogram (ˈfəʊtəˌgræm) NOUN [1] a picture, usually abstract, produced on a photographic material without the use of a camera, as by placing an object on the material and exposing to light. [2] *Obsolete* a photograph, often of the more artistic kind rather than a mechanical record.

photogrammetry (ˌfəʊtəʊˈgræmɪtrɪ) NOUN the process of making measurements from photographs, used esp in the construction of maps from aerial photographs and also in military intelligence, medical and industrial research, etc.
▸**photogrammetric** (ˌfəʊtəʊgrəˈmɛtrɪk) ADJECTIVE
▸ˌ**photoˈgrammetrist** NOUN

photograph (ˈfəʊtəˌgrɑːf, -ˌgræf) NOUN [1] an image of an object, person, scene, etc., in the form of a print or slide recorded by a camera on photosensitive material. Often shortened to: **photo.** ◆ VERB [2] to take a photograph of (an object, person, scene, etc.).

photographer (fəˈtɒgrəfə) NOUN a person who takes photographs, either as a hobby or a profession.

photographic (ˌfəʊtəˈgræfɪk) ADJECTIVE [1] of or relating to photography: *a photographic society; photographic materials.* [2] like a photograph in accuracy or detail. [3] (of a person's memory) able to retain facts, appearances, etc., in precise detail, often after only a very short view of or exposure to them.
▸ˌ**photoˈgraphically** ADVERB

photography (fəˈtɒgrəfɪ) NOUN [1] the process of recording images on sensitized material by the action of light, X-rays, etc., and the chemical processing of this material to produce a print, slide, or cine film. [2] the art, practice, or occupation of taking and printing photographs, making cine films, etc.

photogravure (ˌfəʊtəʊgrəˈvjʊə) NOUN [1] any of various methods in which an intaglio plate for printing is produced by the use of photography. [2] matter printed from such a plate. ◆ Former name **heliogravure.**
▹HISTORY C19: from PHOTO- + French *gravure* engraving

photojournalism (ˌfəʊtəʊˈdʒɜːnəˌlɪzəm) NOUN journalism in which photographs are the predominant feature.
▸ˌ**photoˈjournalist** NOUN ▸ˌ**photoˌjournalˈistic** ADJECTIVE

photokinesis (ˌfəʊtəʊkɪˈniːsɪs, -kaɪ-) NOUN *Biology* the movement of an organism in response to the stimulus of light.
▸**photokinetic** (ˌfəʊtəʊkɪˈnɛtɪk, -kaɪ-) ADJECTIVE
▸ˌ**photokiˈnetically** ADVERB

photolithograph (ˌfəʊtəʊˈlɪθəˌgrɑːf, -ˌgræf) NOUN [1] a picture printed by photolithography. ◆ VERB [2] (*tr*) to reproduce (pictures, text, etc.) by photolithography.

photolithography (ˌfəʊtəʊlɪˈθɒgrəfɪ) NOUN [1] a lithographic printing process using photographically made plates. Often shortened to: **photolitho** (ˌfəʊtəʊˈlaɪθəʊ). [2] *Electronics* a process used in the manufacture of semiconductor devices, thin-film circuits, optical devices, and printed circuits in which a particular pattern is transferred from a photograph onto a substrate, producing a pattern that acts as a mask during an etching or diffusion process. See also **planar process.**
▸ˌ**photoliˈthographer** NOUN ▸**photolithographic** (ˌfəʊtəʊˌlɪθəˈgræfɪk) ADJECTIVE ▸ˌ**photoˌlithoˈgraphically** ADVERB

photoluminescence (ˌfəʊtəʊˌluːmɪˈnɛsəns) NOUN luminescence resulting from the absorption of light or infrared or ultraviolet radiation.
▸ˌ**photoˌlumiˈnescent** ADJECTIVE

photolysis (fəʊˈtɒlɪsɪs) NOUN chemical decomposition caused by light or other electromagnetic radiation. Compare **radiolysis.**
▸**photolytic** (ˌfəʊtəʊˈlɪtɪk) ADJECTIVE

photomap (ˈfəʊtəʊˌmæp) NOUN [1] a map constructed by adding grid lines, place names, etc., to one or more aerial photographs. ◆ VERB **-maps, -mapping, -mapped.** [2] (*tr*) to map (an area) using aerial photography.

photomechanical (ˌfəʊtəʊmɪˈkænɪkəl) ADJECTIVE [1] of or relating to any of various methods by which printing plates are made using photography. ◆ NOUN [2] a final paste-up of artwork or typeset matter or both for photographing and processing into a printing plate. Often shortened to: **mechanical.**
▸ˌ**photomeˈchanically** ADVERB

photomechanical transfer NOUN a method of producing photographic prints or offset printing plates from paper negatives by a chemical transfer process rather than by exposure to light.

photometer (fəʊˈtɒmɪtə) NOUN an instrument used in photometry, usually one that compares the illumination produced by a particular light source with that produced by a standard source. See also **spectrophotometer.**

photometry (fəʊˈtɒmɪtrɪ) NOUN [1] the measurement of the intensity of light. [2] the branch of physics concerned with such measurements.
▸**photometric** (ˌfəʊtəˈmɛtrɪk) ADJECTIVE
▸ˌ**photoˈmetrically** ADVERB ▸**phoˈtometrist** NOUN

photomicrograph (ˌfəʊtəʊˈmaɪkrəˌgrɑːf, -ˌgræf) NOUN [1] a photograph of a microscope image. [2] a less common name for **microphotograph** (sense 1). Sometimes called: **microphotograph.**
▸**photomicrographer** (ˌfəʊtəʊmaɪˈkrɒgrəfə) NOUN
▸**photomicrographic** (ˌfəʊtəʊˌmaɪkrəˈgræfɪk) ADJECTIVE
▸ˌ**photoˌmicroˈgraphically** ADVERB ▸ˌ**photomiˈcrography** NOUN

photomontage (ˌfəʊtəʊmɒnˈtɑːʒ) NOUN [1] the technique of producing a composite picture by combining several photographs: used esp in advertising. [2] the composite picture so produced.

photomosaic (ˌfəʊtəʊməˈzeɪɪk) NOUN a large-scale detailed picture made up of many photographs. See also **mosaic** (sense 5).

photomultiplier (ˌfəʊtəʊˈmʌltɪˌplaɪə) NOUN a device sensitive to electromagnetic radiation, consisting of a photocathode, from which electrons are released by incident photons, and an electron multiplier, which amplifies and produces a detectable pulse of current.

photomural (ˌfəʊtəʊˈmjʊərəl) NOUN a decoration covering all or part of a wall consisting of a single enlarged photograph or a montage.

photon (ˈfəʊtɒn) NOUN a quantum of electromagnetic radiation, regarded as a particle with zero rest mass and charge, unit spin, and energy equal to the product of the frequency of the radiation and the Planck constant.

photonasty (ˈfəʊtəʊˌnæstɪ) NOUN, *plural* **-ties.** a nastic movement in response to a change in light intensity.
▸ˌ**photoˈnastic** ADJECTIVE

photonegative (ˌfəʊtəʊˈnɛgətɪv) ADJECTIVE *Physics* (of a material) having an electrical conductivity that decreases with increasing illumination.

photoneutron (ˌfəʊtəʊˈnjuːtrɒn) NOUN a neutron emitted from a nucleus as a result of photodisintegration.

photonics (fəʊˈtɒnɪks) NOUN (*functioning as singular*) the study and design of devices and systems, such as optical fibres, that depend on the transmission, modulation, or amplification of streams of photons.

photonuclear (ˌfəʊtəʊˈnjuːklɪə) ADJECTIVE *Physics* of or concerned with a nuclear reaction caused by a photon.

photo-offset NOUN *Printing* an offset process in which the plates are produced photomechanically.

photo op NOUN short for **photo opportunity.**

photo opportunity NOUN an opportunity, either preplanned or accidental, for the press to photograph a politician, celebrity, or event.

photoperiod (ˌfəʊtəʊˈpɪərɪəd) NOUN the period of daylight in every 24 hours, esp in relation to its effects on plants and animals. See also **photoperiodism.**
▸ˌ**photoˌperiˈodic** ADJECTIVE ▸ˌ**photoˌperiˈodically** ADVERB

photoperiodism (ˌfəʊtəʊˈpɪərɪəˌdɪzəm) NOUN the response of plants and animals by behaviour, growth, etc., to photoperiods.

photophilous (fəʊˈtɒfələs) ADJECTIVE (esp of plants) growing best in strong light.
▸**phoˈtophily** NOUN

photophobia (ˌfəʊtəʊˈfəʊbɪə) NOUN [1] *Pathol* abnormal sensitivity of the eyes to light, esp as the result of inflammation. [2] *Psychiatry* abnormal fear of or aversion to sunlight or well-lit places.
▸ˌ**photoˈphobic** ADJECTIVE

photophore (ˈfəʊtəˌfɔː) NOUN *Zoology* any light-producing organ in animals, esp in certain fishes.

photopia (fəʊˈtəʊpɪə) NOUN the normal adaptation of the eye to light; day vision.
▹HISTORY C20: New Latin, from PHOTO- + -OPIA

▸**photopic** (fəʊˈtɒpɪk, -ˈtəʊ-) ADJECTIVE

photopolymer (ˌfəʊtəʊˈpɒlɪmə) NOUN a polymeric material that is sensitive to light: used in printing plates, microfilms, etc.

photopositive (ˌfəʊtəʊˈpɒzɪtɪv) ADJECTIVE *Physics* (of a material) having an electrical conductivity that increases with increasing illumination.

photorealism (ˌfəʊtəʊˈrɪəˌlɪzəm) NOUN a style of painting and sculpture that depicts esp commonplace urban images with meticulously accurate detail.
▸ˌ**photoˈrealist** NOUN, ADJECTIVE

photoreceptor (ˌfəʊtəʊrɪˈsɛptə) NOUN *Zoology, physiol* a light-sensitive cell or organ that conveys impulses through the sensory neuron connected to it.

photoreconnaissance (ˌfəʊtəʊrɪˈkɒnɪsəns) NOUN *Chiefly military* reconnaissance from the air by camera.

photo relief NOUN a method of showing the configuration of the relief of an area by photographing a model of it that is illuminated by a lamp in the northwest corner.

photorespiration (ˌfəʊtəʊˌrɛspəˈreɪʃən) NOUN (in plants) a reaction that occurs during photosynthesis in which oxygen is assimilated and used to oxidize carbohydrates, with the release of carbon dioxide: differs from normal respiration in that there is no production of energy in the form of ATP.

photosensitive (ˌfəʊtəʊˈsɛnsɪtɪv) ADJECTIVE sensitive to electromagnetic radiation, esp light: *a photosensitive photographic film.*
▸ˌ**photoˌsensiˈtivity** NOUN

photosensitize *or* **photosensitise** (ˌfəʊtəʊˈsɛnsɪˌtaɪz) VERB (*tr*) to make (an organism or substance) photosensitive.
▸ˌ**photoˌsensitiˈzation** *or* ˌ**photoˌsensitiˈsation** NOUN

photoset (ˈfəʊtəʊˌsɛt) VERB **-sets, -setting, -set.** (*tr*) to set (type matter) by photosetting.
▸ˈ**photoˌsetter** NOUN

photosetting (ˈfəʊtəʊˌsɛtɪŋ) NOUN *Printing* another word for **photocomposition.**

photosphere (ˈfəʊtəʊˌsfɪə) NOUN the visible surface of the sun, several hundred kilometres thick.
▸**photospheric** (ˌfəʊtəʊˈsfɛrɪk) ADJECTIVE

photostat (ˈfəʊtəʊˌstæt) NOUN 1 a machine or process used to make quick positive or negative photographic copies of written, printed, or graphic matter. 2 any copy made by such a machine. ◆ VERB **-stats, -statting** *or* **-stating, -statted** *or* **-stated.** 3 to make a photostat copy (of).
▸ˌ**photoˈstatic** ADJECTIVE

photosynthate (ˌfəʊtəʊˈsɪnˌθeɪt) NOUN any substance synthesized in photosynthesis, esp a sugar.

photosynthesis (ˌfəʊtəʊˈsɪnθɪsɪs) NOUN 1 (in plants) the synthesis of organic compounds from carbon dioxide and water (with the release of oxygen) using light energy absorbed by chlorophyll. 2 the corresponding process in certain bacteria.
▸**photosynthetic** (ˌfəʊtəʊsɪnˈθɛtɪk) ADJECTIVE
▸ˌ**photosynˈthetically** ADVERB

photosynthesize *or* **photosynthesise** (ˌfəʊtəʊˈsɪnθɪˌsaɪz) VERB (of plants and some bacteria) to carry out photosynthesis.

photosystem (ˈfəʊtəʊˌsɪstəm) NOUN *Botany* either of two pigment-containing systems, photosystem I or II, in which the light-dependent chemical reactions of photosynthesis occur in the chloroplasts of plants.

phototaxis (ˌfəʊtəʊˈtæksɪs) *or* **phototaxy** NOUN the movement of an entire organism in response to light.
▸**phototactic** (ˌfəʊtəʊˈtæktɪk) ADJECTIVE

phototherapy (ˌfəʊtəʊˈθɛrəpɪ) *or* **phototherapeutics** (ˌfəʊtəʊˌθɛrəˈpjuːtɪks) NOUN (*functioning as singular*) the use of light in the treatment of disease.
▸ˌ**photoˌtheraˈpeutic** ADJECTIVE ▸ˌ**photoˌtheraˈpeutically** ADVERB

photothermic (ˌfəʊtəʊˈθɜːmɪk) *or* **photothermal** ADJECTIVE of or concerned with light and heat, esp the production of heat by light.
▸ˌ**photoˈthermically** *or* ˌ**photoˈthermally** ADVERB

phototonus (fəʊˈtɒtənəs) NOUN the condition of plants that enables them to respond to the stimulus of light.
▷HISTORY C19: from PHOTO- + Greek *tonos* TONE
▸**phototonic** (ˌfəʊtəʊˈtɒnɪk) ADJECTIVE

phototopography (ˌfəʊtəʊtəˈpɒgrəfɪ) NOUN the preparation of topographic maps from photographs.

phototoxic (ˌfəʊtəʊˈtɒksɪk) ADJECTIVE (of cosmetics, skin creams, etc.) making the skin hazardously sensitive to sunlight.

phototransistor (ˌfəʊtəʊtrænˈzɪstə) NOUN a junction transistor, whose base signal is generated by illumination of the base. The emitter current, and hence collector current, increases with the intensity of the light.

phototroph (ˈfəʊtəʊˌtrɒf) NOUN an organism that obtains energy from sunlight for the synthesis of organic compounds.
▸**phototrophic** (ˌfəʊtəʊˈtrɒfɪk) ADJECTIVE

phototropism (ˌfəʊtəʊˈtrəʊpɪzəm) NOUN 1 the growth response of plant parts to the stimulus of light, producing a bending towards the light source. 2 the response of animals to light: sometimes used as another word for **phototaxis.**
▸ˌ**photoˈtropic** ADJECTIVE

phototropy (ˌfəʊtəʊˈtrəʊpɪ) NOUN *Chem* 1 an alteration in the colour of certain substances as a result of being exposed to light of different wavelengths. 2 the reversible loss of colour of certain dyestuffs when illuminated at a particular wavelength.

phototube (ˈfəʊtəʊˌtjuːb) NOUN a type of photocell in which radiation falling on a photocathode causes electrons to flow to an anode and thus produce an electric current.

phototype (ˈfəʊtəʊˌtaɪp) *Printing* ◆ NOUN 1 **a** a printing plate produced by photography. **b** a print produced from such a plate. ◆ VERB 2 (*tr*) to reproduce (an illustration) using a phototype.
▸**phototypic** (ˌfəʊtəʊˈtɪpɪk) ADJECTIVE ▸ˌ**photoˈtypically** ADVERB

phototypeset (ˌfəʊtəʊˈtaɪpˌsɛt) VERB **-sets, -setting, -set.** (*tr*) to set (type matter) by phototypesetting.

phototypesetting (ˌfəʊtəʊˈtaɪpˌsɛtɪŋ) NOUN *Printing* another word for **photocomposition.**

phototypography (ˌfəʊtəʊtaɪˈpɒgrəfɪ) NOUN any printing process involving the use of photography.
▸**phototypographical** (ˌfəʊtəʊˌtaɪpəˈgræfɪkᵊl) ADJECTIVE
▸ˌ**photoˌtypoˈgraphically** ADVERB

photovoltaic (ˌfəʊtəʊvɒlˈteɪɪk) ADJECTIVE of, concerned with, or producing electric current or voltage caused by electromagnetic radiation.

photovoltaic effect NOUN the effect observed when electromagnetic radiation falls on a thin film of one solid deposited on the surface of a dissimilar solid producing a difference in potential between the two materials.

photozincography (ˌfəʊtəʊzɪŋˈkɒgrəfɪ) NOUN a photoengraving process using a printing plate made of zinc.
▸**photozincograph** (ˌfəʊtəʊˈzɪŋkəˌgrɑːf, -ˌgræf) NOUN

phrasal (ˈfreɪzᵊl) ADJECTIVE of, relating to, or composed of phrases.
▸ˈ**phrasally** ADVERB

phrasal verb NOUN (in English grammar) a phrase that consists of a verb plus an adverbial or prepositional particle, esp one the meaning of which cannot be deduced by analysis of the meaning of the constituents: *"take in" meaning "deceive" is a phrasal verb.*

phrase (freɪz) NOUN 1 a group of words forming an immediate syntactic constituent of a clause. Compare **clause** (sense 1), **noun phrase, verb phrase.** 2 a particular expression, esp an original one. 3 *Music* a small group of notes forming a coherent unit of melody. 4 (in choreography) a short sequence of dance movements. ◆ VERB (*tr*) 5 *Music* to divide (a melodic line, part, etc.) into musical phrases, esp in performance. 6 to express orally or in a phrase.
▷HISTORY C16: from Latin *phrasis,* from Greek: speech, from *phrazein* to declare, tell

phrase book NOUN a book containing frequently used expressions and their equivalents in a foreign language, esp for the use of tourists.

phrase marker NOUN *Linguistics* a representation, esp one in the form of a tree diagram, of the constituent structure of a sentence.

phraseogram (ˈfreɪzɪəˌgræm) NOUN a symbol representing a phrase, as in shorthand.

phraseograph (ˈfreɪzɪəˌgrɑːf) NOUN a phrase for which there exists a phraseogram.
▸**phraseographic** (ˌfreɪzɪəˈgræfɪk) ADJECTIVE
▸**phraseography** (ˌfreɪzɪˈɒgrəfɪ) NOUN

phraseologist (ˌfreɪzɪˈɒlədʒɪst) NOUN a person who is interested in or collects phrases or who affects a particular phraseology.

phraseology (ˌfreɪzɪˈɒlədʒɪ) NOUN, *plural* **-gies.** 1 the manner in which words or phrases are used. 2 a set of phrases used by a particular group of people.
▸**phraseological** (ˌfreɪzɪəˈlɒdʒɪkᵊl) ADJECTIVE
▸ˌ**phraseoˈlogically** ADVERB

phrase-structure grammar NOUN a grammar in which relations among the words and morphemes of a sentence are described, but not deeper or semantic relations. Abbreviation: **PSG.** Compare **transformational grammar.**

phrase-structure rule NOUN *Generative grammar* a rule of the form A → X where A is a syntactic category label, such as *noun phrase* or *sentence,* and X is a sequence of such labels and/or morphemes, expressing the fact that A can be replaced by X in generating the constituent structure of a sentence. Also called: **rewrite rule.** Compare **transformational rule.**

phrasing (ˈfreɪzɪŋ) NOUN 1 the way in which something is expressed, esp in writing; wording. 2 *Music* the division of a melodic line, part, etc., into musical phrases.

phratry (ˈfreɪtrɪ) NOUN, *plural* **-tries.** *Anthropol* a group of people within a tribe who have a common ancestor.
▷HISTORY C19: from Greek *phratria* clan, from *phratēr* fellow clansman; compare Latin *frāter* brother
▸ˈ**phratric** ADJECTIVE

phreaking (ˈfriːkɪŋ) NOUN the act of gaining unauthorized access to telecommunication systems, esp to obtain free calls.
▷HISTORY C20: blend of FREAKING + PHONE

phreatic (frɪˈætɪk) ADJECTIVE *Geography* of or relating to ground water occurring below the water table. Compare **vadose.**
▷HISTORY C19: from Greek *phrear* a well

phreatophyte (frɪˈætəfaɪt) NOUN a plant having very long roots that reach down to the water table or the layer above it.
▷HISTORY C20: from Greek *phrear* a well + -PHYTE

phrenetic (frɪˈnɛtɪk) ADJECTIVE an obsolete spelling of **frenetic.**
▸**phreˈnetically** ADVERB ▸**phreˈneticness** NOUN

phrenic (ˈfrɛnɪk) ADJECTIVE 1 **a** of or relating to the diaphragm. **b** (*as noun*): *the phrenic.* 2 *Obsolete* of or relating to the mind.
▷HISTORY C18: from New Latin *phrenicus,* from Greek *phrēn* mind, diaphragm

phrenitis (frɪˈnaɪtɪs) NOUN *Rare* 1 another name for **encephalitis.** 2 a state of frenzy; delirium.
▷HISTORY C17: via Late Latin from Greek: delirium, from *phrēn* mind, diaphragm + -ITIS
▸**phrenitic** (frɪˈnɪtɪk) ADJECTIVE

phreno- *or before a vowel* **phren-** COMBINING FORM 1 mind or brain: *phrenology.* 2 of or relating to the diaphragm: *phrenic.*
▷HISTORY from Greek *phrēn* mind, diaphragm

phrenology (frɪˈnɒlədʒɪ) NOUN (formerly) the branch of science concerned with localization of function in the human brain, esp determination of the strength of the faculties by the shape and size of the skull overlying the parts of the brain thought to be responsible for them.
▸**phrenological** (ˌfrɛnəˈlɒdʒɪkᵊl) ADJECTIVE
▸**phreˈnologist** NOUN

phrensy (ˈfrɛnzɪ) NOUN, *plural* **-sies,** VERB an obsolete spelling of **frenzy.**

Phrixus (ˈfrɪksəs) NOUN *Greek myth* the son of Athamas and Nephele who escaped the wrath of his father's mistress, Ino, by flying to Colchis on a winged ram with a golden fleece. See also **Helle, Golden Fleece.**

phrygana (frɪˈgɑːnə) NOUN another name for **garigue,** used esp in Greece

Phrygia (ˈfrɪdʒɪə) NOUN an ancient country of W central Asia Minor.

Phrygian (ˈfrɪdʒɪən) ADJECTIVE 1 of or relating to ancient Phrygia, its inhabitants, or their extinct language. 2 *Music* of or relating to an authentic mode represented by the natural diatonic scale from E to E. See **Hypo-**. 3 *Music* (of a cadence) denoting a progression that leads a piece of music out of the major key and ends on the dominant chord of the relative minor key. ◆ NOUN 4 a native or inhabitant of ancient Phrygia. 5 an ancient language of Phrygia, belonging to the Thraco-Phrygian branch of the Indo-European family: recorded in a few inscriptions.

Phrygian cap NOUN a conical cap of soft material worn during ancient times that became a symbol of liberty during the French Revolution.

PHS (in the US) ABBREVIATION FOR Public Health Service.

PHSE ABBREVIATION FOR personal, social, and health education.

phthalate (ˈθælɪt, ˈfθæl-) NOUN a salt or ester of phthalic acid. Esters are commonly used as plasticizers in PVC; when ingested they can cause kidney and liver damage.

phthalein (ˈθeɪliːn, -lɪɪn, ˈθæl-, ˈfθæl-) NOUN any of a class of organic compounds obtained by the reaction of phthalic anhydride with a phenol and used in dyes.
▷HISTORY C19: from *phthal-*, shortened form of NAPHTHALENE + -IN

phthalic acid (ˈθælɪk, ˈfθæl-) NOUN a soluble colourless crystalline acid used in the synthesis of dyes and perfumes; 1,2-benzenedicarboxylic acid. Formula: $C_6H_4(COOH)_2$.
▷HISTORY C19 *phthalic*, from *phthal-* (see PHTHALEIN) + -IC

phthalic anhydride NOUN a white crystalline substance used mainly in producing dyestuffs. Formula: $C_6H_4(CO)_2O$.

phthalocyanine (ˌθæləʊˈsaɪəˌniːn, ˌθeɪ-, ˌfθæl-) NOUN 1 a cyclic blue-green organic pigment. Formula: $(C_6H_4C_2N)_4N_4H_4$. 2 any of a class of compounds derived by coordination of this compound with a metal atom. They are blue or green pigments used in printing inks, plastics, and enamels.
▷HISTORY C20: from *phthal-* (see PHTHALEIN) + CYANINE

phthiriasis (θɪˈraɪəsɪs) NOUN *Pathol* the state or condition of being infested with lice; pediculosis.
▷HISTORY C16: via Latin from Greek, from *phtheir* louse

phthisic (ˈθaɪsɪk, ˈfθaɪsɪk, ˈtaɪsɪk) *Obsolete* ◆ ADJECTIVE 1 relating to or affected with phthisis. ◆ NOUN 2 another name for **asthma**.
▷HISTORY C14: from Old French *tisike*, from Latin *phthisicus*, from Greek *phthisikos*; see PHTHISIS
▸ˈ**phthisical** ADJECTIVE

phthisis (ˈθaɪsɪs, ˈfθaɪ-, ˈtaɪ-) NOUN any disease that causes wasting of the body, esp pulmonary tuberculosis.
▷HISTORY C16: via Latin from Greek: a wasting away, from *phthinein* to waste away

Phuket (ˌpuːˈkɛt) NOUN 1 an island and province of S Thailand, in the Andaman Sea: mainly flat. Area: 534 sq. km (206 sq. miles). 2 the chief town of the island of Phuket; a popular tourist resort.

phut (fʌt) *Informal* ◆ NOUN 1 a representation of a muffled explosive sound. ◆ ADVERB 2 **go phut**. to break down or collapse.
▷HISTORY C19: of imitative origin

phyco- COMBINING FORM seaweed: *phycology*.
▷HISTORY from Greek *phukos*

phycobilin (ˌfaɪkəʊˈbaɪlɪn) NOUN *Biology* any of a class of red or blue-green pigments found in the red algae and cyanobacteria.

phycobiont (ˌfaɪkəʊˈbaɪɒnt) NOUN *Botany* the algal constituent of a lichen. Compare **mycobiont**.

phycology (faɪˈkɒlədʒɪ) NOUN the study of algae.
▸**phycological** (ˌfaɪkəˈlɒdʒɪkᵊl) ADJECTIVE ▸**phyˈcologist** NOUN

phycomycete (ˌfaɪkəʊˈmaɪsiːt) NOUN any of a primitive group of fungi, formerly included in the class *Phycomycetes* but now classified in different phyla: includes certain mildews and moulds.
▸ˌ**phycomyˈcetous** ADJECTIVE

phyla (ˈfaɪlə) NOUN the plural of **phylum**.

phylactery (fɪˈlæktərɪ) NOUN, *plural* **-teries**. 1 *Judaism* (*usually plural*) Also called: **Tefillah**. either of the pair of blackened square cases containing parchments inscribed with biblical passages, bound by leather thongs to the head and left arm, and worn by Jewish men during weekday morning prayers. 2 a reminder or aid to remembering. 3 *Archaic* an amulet or charm.
▷HISTORY C14: from Late Latin *phylactērium*, from Greek *phulaktērion* outpost, from *phulax* a guard

phyle (ˈfaɪlɪ) NOUN, *plural* **-lae** (-liː). a tribe or clan of an ancient Greek people such as the Ionians.
▷HISTORY C19: from Greek *phulē* tribe, clan
▸ˈ**phylic** ADJECTIVE

phyletic (faɪˈlɛtɪk) *or* **phylogenetic** (ˌfaɪləʊdʒɪˈnɛtɪk) ADJECTIVE of or relating to the evolution of a species or group of organisms.
▷HISTORY C19: from Greek *phuletikos* tribal
▸**phyˈletically** *or* ˌ**phylogeˈnetically** ADVERB

-phyll *or* **-phyl** NOUN COMBINING FORM leaf: *chlorophyll*.
▷HISTORY from Greek *phullon*

phyllid (ˈfɪlɪd) NOUN *Botany* the leaf of a liverwort or moss.

phyllite (ˈfɪlaɪt) NOUN a compact lustrous metamorphic rock, rich in mica, derived from a shale or other clay-rich rock.
▷HISTORY C19: from PHYLL(O)- + -ITE[1]
▸**phyllitic** (fɪˈlɪtɪk) ADJECTIVE

phyllo (ˈfɪləʊ) NOUN a variant of **filo**.
▷HISTORY C20: from Greek: leaf

phyllo- *or before a vowel* **phyll-** COMBINING FORM leaf: *phyllopod*.
▷HISTORY from Greek *phullon* leaf

phylloclade (ˈfɪləʊˌkleɪd) *or* **phylloclad** (ˈfɪləʊˌklæd) NOUN other names for **cladode**.
▷HISTORY C19: from New Latin *phyllocladium*, from PHYLLO- + Greek *klados* branch

phyllode (ˈfɪləʊd) NOUN a flattened leafstalk that resembles and functions as a leaf.
▷HISTORY C19: from New Latin *phyllodium*, from Greek *phullōdēs* leaflike
▸**phylˈlodial** ADJECTIVE

phylloid (ˈfɪlɔɪd) ADJECTIVE resembling a leaf.

phyllome (ˈfɪləʊm) NOUN a leaf or a leaflike organ.
▸**phyllomic** (fɪˈlɒmɪk, -ˈləʊ-) ADJECTIVE

phylloplane (ˈfɪləʊˌpleɪn) NOUN *Ecology* the surface of a leaf considered as a habitat, esp for microorganisms. Also called: **phyllosphere**.

phylloquinone (ˌfɪləʊkwɪˈnəʊn) NOUN a viscous fat-soluble liquid occurring in plants: essential for the production of prothrombin, required in blood clotting. Formula: $C_{31}H_{46}O_2$. Also called: **vitamin K_1**.

phyllosilicate (ˌfɪləʊˈsɪlɪkeɪt) NOUN any of a class of silicate minerals, including talc, consisting of thin sheets.

phyllosphere (ˈfɪləʊˌsfɪə) NOUN another name for **phylloplane**.

phyllotaxis (ˌfɪləˈtæksɪs) *or* **phyllotaxy** NOUN, *plural* **-taxes** (-ˈtæksiːz) *or* **-taxies**. 1 the arrangement of the leaves on a stem. 2 the study of this arrangement in different plants.
▸ˌ**phylloˈtactic** ADJECTIVE

-phyllous ADJECTIVE COMBINING FORM having leaves of a specified number or type: *monophyllous*.
▷HISTORY from Greek *-phullos* of a leaf

phylloxera (ˌfɪlɒkˈsɪərə, fɪˈlɒksərə) NOUN, *plural* **-rae** (-riː) *or* **-ras**. any homopterous insect of the genus *Phylloxera*, such as *P. vitifolia* (or *Viteus vitifolii*) (**vine phylloxera**), typically feeding on plant juices, esp of vines: family *Phylloxeridae*.
▷HISTORY C19: New Latin, from PHYLLO- + *xēros* dry

phylo- *or before a vowel* **phyl-** COMBINING FORM tribe; race; phylum: *phylogeny*.
▷HISTORY from Greek *phulon* race

phylogeny (faɪˈlɒdʒɪnɪ) *or* **phylogenesis** (ˌfaɪləʊˈdʒɛnɪsɪs) NOUN, *plural* **-nies** *or* **-geneses** (-ˈdʒɛnɪˌsiːz). *Biology* the sequence of events involved in the evolution of a species, genus, etc. Compare **ontogeny**.
▷HISTORY C19: from PHYLO- + -GENY
▸**phylogenic** (ˌfaɪləʊˈdʒɛnɪk) *or* **phylogenetic** (ˌfaɪləʊdʒɪˈnɛtɪk) ADJECTIVE

phylum (ˈfaɪləm) NOUN, *plural* **-la** (-lə). 1 a major taxonomic division of living organisms that contain one or more classes. An example is the phylum *Arthropoda* (insects, crustaceans, arachnids, etc., and myriapods). 2 any analogous group, such as a group of related language families or linguistic stocks.
▷HISTORY C19: New Latin, from Greek *phulon* race

phys. ABBREVIATION FOR: 1 physical. 2 physician. 3 physics. 4 physiological. 5 physiology.

physalis (faɪˈseɪlɪs) NOUN See **Chinese lantern, strawberry tomato**.
▷HISTORY New Latin, from Greek *physallis* a bladder (from the form of the calyx)

physiatrics (ˌfɪzɪˈætrɪks) NOUN (*functioning as singular*) *Med US* another name for **physiotherapy**.
▷HISTORY C19: from PHYSIO- + -IATRICS
▸ˌ**physiˈatric** *or* ˌ**physiˈatrical** ADJECTIVE

physic (ˈfɪzɪk) NOUN 1 *Rare* a medicine or drug, esp a cathartic or purge. 2 *Archaic* the art or skill of healing. 3 an archaic term for **physics** (sense 1). ◆ VERB **-ics, -icking, -icked**. 4 (*tr*) *Archaic* to treat (a patient) with medicine.
▷HISTORY C13: from Old French *fisique*, via Latin, from Greek *phusikē*, from *phusis* nature
▸ˈ**physicky** ADJECTIVE

physical (ˈfɪzɪkᵊl) ADJECTIVE 1 of or relating to the body, as distinguished from the mind or spirit. 2 of, relating to, or resembling material things or nature: *the physical universe*. 3 involving or requiring bodily contact: *rugby is a physical sport*. 4 of or concerned with matter and energy. 5 of or relating to physics. 6 perceptible to the senses; apparent: *a physical manifestation*. ◆ NOUN 7 short for **physical examination**. ◆ See also **physicals**.
▸ˈ**physically** ADVERB ▸ˈ**physicalness** NOUN

physical anthropology NOUN the branch of anthropology dealing with the genetic aspect of human development and its physical variations.

physical chemistry NOUN the branch of chemistry concerned with the way in which the physical properties of substances depend on and influence their chemical structure, properties, and reactions.

physical education NOUN training and practice in sports, gymnastics, etc., as in schools and colleges. Abbreviation: **PE**.

physical examination NOUN *Med* the process of examining the body by means of sight, touch, percussion, or auscultation to diagnose disease or verify fitness.

physical geography NOUN the branch of geography that deals with the natural features of the earth's surface.

physical handicap NOUN loss of or failure to develop a specific bodily function or functions, whether of movement, sensation, coordination, or speech, but excluding mental impairments or disabilities.
▸**physically handicapped** ADJECTIVE

physicalism (ˈfɪzɪkᵊˌlɪzəm) NOUN *Philosophy* the doctrine that all phenomena can be described in terms of space and time and that all meaningful statements are either analytic, as in logic and mathematics, or can be reduced to empirically verifiable assertions. See also **logical positivism, identity theory**.
▸ˈ**physicalist** NOUN, ADJECTIVE ▸ˌ**physicalˈistic** ADJECTIVE

physicality (ˌfɪzɪˈkælɪtɪ) NOUN 1 the state or quality of being physical. 2 the physical characteristics of a person, object, etc.

physical jerks PLURAL NOUN *Brit, informal* See **jerk**[1] (sense 6).

physical medicine NOUN the branch of medicine devoted to the management of physical disabilities, as resulting from rheumatic disease, asthma, poliomyelitis, etc. See also **rehabilitation** (sense 2).

physicals (ˈfɪzɪkᵊlz) PLURAL NOUN *Commerce* commodities that can be purchased and used, as opposed to those bought and sold in a futures market. Also called: **actuals**.

physical science NOUN any of the sciences concerned with nonliving matter, energy, and the physical properties of the universe, such as physics, chemistry, astronomy, and geology. Compare **life science**.

physical therapy NOUN another term for **physiotherapy**.

physician (fɪˈzɪʃən) NOUN 1 a person legally qualified to practise medicine, esp one specializing in areas of treatment other than surgery; doctor of medicine. 2 *Archaic* any person who treats diseases; healer.
▷HISTORY C13: from Old French *fisicien,* from *fisique* PHYSIC

physicist (ˈfɪzɪsɪst) NOUN a person versed in or studying physics.

physicochemical (ˌfɪzɪkəʊˈkɛmɪkᵊl) ADJECTIVE of, concerned with, or relating to physical chemistry or both physics and chemistry.
▸**ˌphysicoˈchemically** ADVERB

physics (ˈfɪzɪks) NOUN (*functioning as singular*) 1 the branch of science concerned with the properties of matter and energy and the relationships between them. It is based on mathematics and traditionally includes mechanics, optics, electricity and magnetism, acoustics, and heat. Modern physics, based on quantum theory, includes atomic, nuclear, particle, and solid-state studies. It can also embrace applied fields such as geophysics and meteorology. 2 physical properties of behaviour: *the physics of the electron.* 3 *Archaic* natural science or natural philosophy.
▷HISTORY C16: from Latin *physica,* translation of Greek *ta phusika* natural things, from *phusis* nature

physio (ˈfɪzɪəʊ) NOUN *Informal* short for **physiotherapy, physiotherapist.**

physio- *or before a vowel* **phys-** COMBINING FORM 1 of or relating to nature or natural functions: *physiology.* 2 physical: *physiotherapy.*
▷HISTORY from Greek *phusio,* from *phusis* nature, from *phuein* to make grow

physiocrat (ˈfɪzɪəʊˌkræt) NOUN a follower of Quesnay's doctrines of government, believing that the inherent natural order governing society was based on land and its natural products as the only true form of wealth.
▷HISTORY C18: from French *physiocrate;* see PHYSIO-, -CRAT
▸**physiocracy** (ˌfɪzɪˈɒkrəsɪ) NOUN ▸**ˌphysioˈcratic** ADJECTIVE

physiognomy (ˌfɪzɪˈɒnəmɪ) NOUN 1 a person's features or characteristic expression considered as an indication of personality. 2 the art or practice of judging character from facial features. 3 the outward appearance of something, esp the physical characteristics of a geographical region.
▷HISTORY C14: from Old French *phisonomie,* via Medieval Latin, from Late Greek *phusiognōmia,* erroneous for Greek *phusiognōmonia,* from *phusis* nature + *gnōmōn* judge
▸**physiognomic** (ˌfɪzɪəˈnɒmɪk) *or* **ˌphysiogˈnomical** ADJECTIVE ▸**ˌphysiogˈnomically** ADVERB ▸**ˌphysiˈognomist** NOUN

physiography (ˌfɪzɪˈɒgrəfɪ) NOUN another name for **geomorphology** or **physical geography.**
▸**ˌphysiˈographer** NOUN ▸**physiographic** (ˌfɪzɪəˈgræfɪk) *or* **ˌphysioˈgraphical** ADJECTIVE ▸**ˌphysioˈgraphically** ADVERB

physiol. ABBREVIATION FOR: 1 physiological. 2 physiology.

physiological (ˌfɪzɪəˈlɒdʒɪkᵊl) ADJECTIVE 1 of or relating to physiology. 2 of or relating to normal healthful functioning; not pathological.
▸**ˌphysioˈlogically** ADVERB

physiological psychology NOUN the branch of psychology concerned with the study and correlation of physiological and psychological events.

physiology (ˌfɪzɪˈɒlədʒɪ) NOUN 1 the branch of science concerned with the functioning of organisms. 2 the processes and functions of all or part of an organism.
▷HISTORY C16: from Latin *physiologia,* from Greek
▸**ˌphysiˈologist** NOUN

physiotherapy (ˌfɪzɪəʊˈθɛrəpɪ) NOUN the therapeutic use of physical agents or means, such as massage, exercises, etc. Also called: **physical therapy,** (informal) **physio,** (US) **physiatrics.**
▸**ˌphysioˈtherapist** NOUN

physique (fɪˈziːk) NOUN the general appearance of the body with regard to size, shape, muscular development, etc.
▷HISTORY C19: via French, from *physique* (adj) natural, from Latin *physicus* physical

physoclistous (ˌfaɪsəʊˈklɪstəs) ADJECTIVE (of fishes) having an air bladder that is not connected to the alimentary canal. Compare **physostomous.**
▷HISTORY C19: from Greek *phusa* bladder + *-clistous,* from *kleistos* closed

physostigmine (ˌfaɪsəʊˈstɪgmiːn) *or* **physostigmin** (ˌfaɪsəʊˈstɪgmɪn) NOUN an alkaloid found in the Calabar bean used esp in eye drops to reduce pressure inside the eyeball. Formula: $C_{15}H_{21}N_3O_2$. Also called: **eserine.**
▷HISTORY C19: from New Latin *Physostigma* genus name, from Greek *phusa* bladder + *stigma* mark

physostomous (faɪˈsɒstəməs) ADJECTIVE (of fishes) having a duct connecting the air bladder to part of the alimentary canal. Compare **physoclistous.**
▷HISTORY C19: from Greek *phusa* bladder + *-stomous,* from *stoma* mouth

-phyte NOUN COMBINING FORM indicating a plant of a specified type or habitat: *lithophyte; thallophyte.*
▷HISTORY from Greek *phuton* plant
▸**-phytic** ADJECTIVE COMBINING FORM

phyto- *or before a vowel* **phyt-** COMBINING FORM indicating a plant or vegetation: *phytogenesis.*
▷HISTORY from Greek *phuton* plant, from *phuein* to make grow

phytoalexin (ˌfaɪtəʊəˈlɛksɪn) NOUN *Botany* any of a group of substances produced by plants that inhibit the growth of pathogenic fungi that infect them.
▷HISTORY C20: from PHYTO- + Greek *alexein* to ward off

phytochemistry (ˌfaɪtəʊˈkɛmɪstrɪ) NOUN the branch of chemistry concerned with plants, their chemical composition and processes.
▸**ˌphytoˈchemist** NOUN

phytochrome (ˈfaɪtəʊˌkrəʊm) NOUN *Botany* a blue-green pigment existing in two interchangeable forms, present in most plants, that mediates many light-dependent processes, including photoperiodism and the greening of leaves.

phytogenesis (ˌfaɪtəʊˈdʒɛnɪsɪs) *or* **phytogeny** (faɪˈtɒdʒənɪ) NOUN the branch of botany concerned with the origin and evolution of plants.
▸**phytogenetic** (ˌfaɪtəʊdʒɪˈnɛtɪk) ADJECTIVE ▸**ˌphytogeˈnetically** ADVERB

phytogenic (ˌfaɪtəʊˈdʒɛnɪk) ADJECTIVE derived from plants: *coal is a phytogenic substance.*

phytogeography (ˌfaɪtəʊdʒɪˈɒgrəfɪ) NOUN the branch of botany that is concerned with the geographical distribution of plants.
▸**ˌphytogeˈographer** NOUN ▸**ˌphytoˌgeoˈgraphic** *or* **ˌphytoˌgeoˈgraphical** ADJECTIVE

phytography (faɪˈtɒgrəfɪ) NOUN the branch of botany that is concerned with the detailed description of plants.
▸**phytographic** (ˌfaɪtəˈgræfɪk) ADJECTIVE

phytohormone (ˌfaɪtəʊˈhɔːməʊn) NOUN a hormone-like substance produced by a plant.

phytology (faɪˈtɒlədʒɪ) NOUN a rare name for **botany** (sense 1).
▸**phytological** (ˌfaɪtəˈlɒdʒɪkᵊl) ADJECTIVE ▸**ˌphytoˈlogically** ADVERB ▸**phyˈtologist** NOUN

phyton (ˈfaɪtɒn) NOUN a unit of plant structure, usually considered as the smallest part of the plant that is capable of growth when detached from the parent plant.
▷HISTORY C20: from Greek. See -PHYTE

phytopathology (ˌfaɪtəʊpəˈθɒlədʒɪ) NOUN the branch of botany concerned with diseases of plants.
▸**phytopathological** (ˌfaɪtəʊˌpæθəˈlɒdʒɪkᵊl) ADJECTIVE ▸**ˌphytopaˈthologist** NOUN

phytophagous (faɪˈtɒfəgəs) ADJECTIVE (esp of insects) feeding on plants.
▸**phytophagy** (faɪˈtɒfədʒɪ) NOUN

phytoplankton (ˌfaɪtəˈplæŋktən) NOUN the photosynthesizing organisms in plankton, mainly unicellular algae and cyanobacteria. Compare **zooplankton.**
▸**phytoplanktonic** (ˌfaɪtəplæŋkˈtɒnɪk) ADJECTIVE

phytoremediation (ˌfaɪtəʊrɪˌmiːdɪˈeɪʃən) NOUN another name for **bioremediation.**

phytosociology (ˌfaɪtəʊˌsəʊsɪˈɒlədʒɪ, -ˌsəʊʃɪ-) NOUN the branch of ecology that is concerned with the origin, development, etc., of plant communities.
▸**phytosociological** (ˌfaɪtəʊˌsəʊsɪəˈlɒdʒɪkᵊl, -ˌsəʊʃɪə-) ADJECTIVE ▸**ˌphytoˌsocioˈlogically** ADVERB ▸**ˌphytoˌsociˈologist** NOUN

phytotoxin (ˌfaɪtəˈtɒksɪn) NOUN a toxin, such as strychnine, that is produced by a plant. Compare **zootoxin.**
▸**ˌphytoˈtoxic** ADJECTIVE

phytotron (ˈfaɪtəʊˌtrɒn) NOUN a building in which plants can be grown on a large scale, under controlled conditions.
▷HISTORY C20: from PHYTO- + -TRON, on the model of CYCLOTRON

pi¹ (paɪ) NOUN, *plural* **pis.** 1 the 16th letter in the Greek alphabet (Π, π), a consonant, transliterated as *p.* 2 *Maths* a transcendental number, fundamental to mathematics, that is the ratio of the circumference of a circle to its diameter. Approximate value: 3.141 592...; symbol: π.
▷HISTORY C18 (mathematical use): representing the first letter of Greek *periphereia* PERIPHERY

pi² *or* **pie** (paɪ) NOUN, *plural* **pies.** 1 a jumbled pile of printer's type. 2 a jumbled mixture. ◆ VERB **pies, piing, pied** *or* **pies, pieing, pied.** (*tr*) 3 to spill and mix (set type) indiscriminately. 4 to mix up.
▷HISTORY C17: of uncertain origin

pi³ (paɪ) ADJECTIVE *Brit slang* short for **pious** (senses 2, 3).

PI ABBREVIATION FOR: 1 Philippine Islands. 2 private investigator.

Piacenza (*Italian* pjaˈtʃentsa) NOUN a town in N Italy, in Emilia-Romagna on the River Po. Pop.: 101 692 (1994 est.). Latin name: **Placentia** (pləˈsɛntʃɪə).

piacular (paɪˈækjʊlə) ADJECTIVE 1 making expiation for a sacrilege. 2 requiring expiation.
▷HISTORY C17: from Latin *piāculum* propitiatory sacrifice, from *piāre* to appease

piaffe (pɪˈæf) NOUN *Dressage* a passage done on the spot.
▷HISTORY C18: from French, from *piaffer* to strut

pia mater (ˈpaɪə ˈmeɪtə) NOUN the innermost of the three membranes (see **meninges**) that cover the brain and spinal cord.
▷HISTORY C16: from Medieval Latin, literally: pious mother, intended to translate Arabic *umm raqīqah* tender mother

pianism (ˈpiːəˌnɪzəm) NOUN technique, skill, or artistry in playing the piano.
▸**ˌpiaˈnistic** ADJECTIVE

pianissimo (pɪəˈnɪsɪˌməʊ) ADJECTIVE, ADVERB *Music* (to be performed) very quietly. Symbol: *pp.*
▷HISTORY C18: from Italian, superlative of *piano* soft

pianist (ˈpɪənɪst) NOUN a person who plays the piano.

piano¹ (pɪˈænəʊ) NOUN, *plural* **-anos.** a musical stringed instrument resembling a harp set in a vertical or horizontal frame, played by depressing keys that cause hammers to strike the strings and produce audible vibrations. See also **grand piano, upright piano.**
▷HISTORY C19: short for PIANOFORTE

piano² (ˈpjɑːnəʊ) ADJECTIVE, ADVERB *Music* (to be performed) softly. Symbol: *p.*
▷HISTORY C17: from Italian, from Latin *plānus* flat; see PLAIN¹

piano accordion NOUN an accordion in which the right hand plays a piano-like keyboard. See **accordion.**
▸**piano accordionist** NOUN

pianoforte (pɪˈænəʊˈfɔːtɪ) NOUN the full name for **piano¹.**
▷HISTORY C18: from Italian, originally (*gravecembalo col*) *piano e forte* (harpsichord with) soft and loud; see PIANO², FORTE²

Pianola (pɪəˈnəʊlə) NOUN *Trademark* a type of mechanical piano in which the keys are depressed by air pressure from bellows, this air flow being regulated by perforations in a paper roll. Also called: **player piano.**

piano nobile (ˈpjɑːnəʊ ˈnəʊbɪlɪ) NOUN *Architect* the main floor of a large house, containing the reception rooms: usually of lofty proportions.
▷HISTORY Italian: great floor

piano player NOUN 1 another name for **pianist.** 2 any of various devices for playing a piano automatically.

piano roll NOUN a perforated roll of paper actuating the playing mechanism of a Pianola. Also called: **music roll.**

piano stool NOUN a stool on which a pianist sits when playing a piano, esp one whose height is adjustable.

piano trio NOUN [1] an instrumental ensemble consisting of a piano, a violin, and a cello. [2] a piece of music written for such an ensemble, usually having the form and commonest features of a sonata.

piassava (ˌpiːəˈsɑːvə) *or* **piassaba** (ˌpiːəˈsɑːbə) NOUN [1] either of two South American palm trees, *Attalea funifera* or *Leopoldinia piassaba*. [2] the coarse fibre obtained from either of these trees, used to make brushes and rope.
▷HISTORY C19: via Portuguese from Tupi *piaçaba*

piastre *or* **piaster** (pɪˈæstə) NOUN [1] (formerly) the standard monetary unit of South Vietnam, divided into 100 cents. [2] a fractional monetary unit of Egypt, Lebanon, and Syria worth one hundredth of a pound; formerly also used in the Sudan. [3] another name for **kuruş**. [4] a rare word for **piece of eight**.
▷HISTORY C17: from French *piastre*, from Italian *piastra d'argento* silver plate; related to Italian *piastro* PLASTER

Piauí (*Portuguese* pjaˈui) NOUN a state of NE Brazil, on the Atlantic: rises to a semiarid plateau, with the more humid Paranaíba valley in the west. Capital: Teresina. Pop.: 2 840 969 (2000). Area: 250 934 sq. km (96 886 sq. miles).

Piave (*Italian* ˈpjaːve) NOUN a river in NE Italy, rising near the border with Austria and flowing south and southeast to the Adriatic: the main line of Italian defence during World War I. Length: 220 km (137 miles).

piazza (pɪˈætsə, -ˈædzə; *Italian* ˈpjattsa) NOUN [1] a large open square in an Italian town. [2] *Chiefly Brit* a covered passageway or gallery.
▷HISTORY C16: from Italian: marketplace, from Latin *platēa* courtyard, from Greek *plateia*; see PLACE

pibroch (ˈpiːbrɒk; *Gaelic* ˈpiːbrɒx) NOUN [1] a form of music for Scottish bagpipes, consisting of a theme and variations. [2] a piece of such music.
▷HISTORY C18: from Gaelic *piobaireachd*, from *piobair* piper

pic (pɪk) NOUN, *plural* **pics** *or* **pix**. *Informal* a photograph, picture, or illustration.
▷HISTORY C20: shortened from PICTURE

pica[1] (ˈpaɪkə) NOUN [1] Also called: **em, pica em.** a printer's unit of measurement, equal to 12 points or 0.166 ins. [2] (formerly) a size of printer's type equal to 12 point. [3] a typewriter type size having 10 characters to the inch.
▷HISTORY C15: from Anglo-Latin *pīca* list of ecclesiastical regulations, apparently from Latin *pīca* magpie, with reference to its habit of making collections of miscellaneous items; the connection between the original sense (ecclesiastical list) and the typography meanings is obscure

pica[2] (ˈpaɪkə) NOUN *Pathol* an abnormal craving to ingest substances such as clay, dirt, or hair, sometimes occurring during pregnancy, in persons with chlorosis, etc.
▷HISTORY C16: from medical Latin, from Latin: magpie, being an allusion to its omnivorous feeding habits

picador (ˈpɪkəˌdɔː) NOUN *Bullfighting* a horseman who pricks the bull with a lance in the early stages of a fight to goad and weaken it.
▷HISTORY C18: from Spanish, literally: pricker, from *picar* to prick; see PIQUE[1]

Picardy (ˈpɪkədɪ) NOUN a region of N France: mostly low-lying; scene of heavy fighting in World War I. French name: **Picardie** (pikardi).

Picardy third NOUN *Music* a major chord used in the final chord of a piece of music in the minor mode. Also called: **tierce de Picardie.**
▷HISTORY translation of French *tierce de Picardie*, from its use in the church music of Picardy

picaresque (ˌpɪkəˈrɛsk) ADJECTIVE [1] of or relating to a type of fiction in which the hero, a rogue, goes through a series of episodic adventures. It originated in Spain in the 16th century. [2] of or involving rogues or picaroons.
▷HISTORY C19: via French from Spanish *picaresco*, from *pícaro* a rogue

picaroon *or* **pickaroon** (ˌpɪkəˈruːn) NOUN *Archaic* an adventurer or rogue.
▷HISTORY C17: from Spanish *picarón*, from *pícaro*

picayune (ˌpɪkəˈjuːn) ADJECTIVE *also* **picayunish**, *US and Canadian informal*. [1] of small value or importance. [2] mean; petty. ◆ NOUN [3] the half real, an old Spanish-American coin. [4] *US* any coin of little value, esp a five-cent piece.
▷HISTORY C19: from French *picaillon* coin from Piedmont, from Provençal *picaioun*, of unknown origin
▸ ˌ**picaˈyunishly** ADVERB ▸ ˌ**picaˈyunishness** NOUN

Piccadilly (ˌpɪkəˈdɪlɪ) NOUN one of the main streets of London, running from Piccadilly Circus to Hyde Park Corner.

piccalilli (ˈpɪkəˌlɪlɪ) NOUN a pickle of mixed vegetables, esp onions, cauliflower, and cucumber, in a mustard sauce.
▷HISTORY C18 *piccalillo*, perhaps a coinage based on PICKLE

piccanin (ˈpɪkəˌnɪn, ˌpɪkəˈnɪn) NOUN *South African offensive* a Black African child.
▷HISTORY variant of PICCANINNY

piccaninny *or esp US* **pickaninny** (ˌpɪkəˈnɪnɪ) NOUN, *plural* **-nies.** [1] *Offensive* a small Black or Aboriginal child. [2] (*modifier*) tiny: *a piccaninny fire won't last long.*
▷HISTORY C17: perhaps from Portuguese *pequenino* tiny one, from *pequeno* small

piccolo (ˈpɪkəˌləʊ) NOUN, *plural* **-los.** a woodwind instrument, the smallest member of the flute family, lying an octave above that of the flute. See **flute** (sense 1).
▷HISTORY C19: from Italian: small; compare English PETTY, French *petit*

pice (paɪs) NOUN, *plural* **pice.** a former Indian coin worth one sixty-fourth of a rupee.
▷HISTORY C17: from Mahratti *paisā*

piceous (ˈpɪsɪəs, ˈpaɪsɪəs) ADJECTIVE of, relating to, or resembling pitch.
▷HISTORY C17: from Latin *piceus*, from *pix* PITCH[2]

pi character NOUN *Printing* any special character, such as an accent or mathematical symbol, which is not normally obtained in a standard type fount.

pichiciego (ˌpɪtʃɪsɪˈeɪgəʊ) NOUN, *plural* **-gos.** [1] a very small Argentine armadillo, *Chlamyphorus truncatus*, with white silky hair and pale pink plates on the head and back. [2] **greater pichiciego.** a similar but larger armadillo, *Burmeisteria retusa*.
▷HISTORY C19: from Spanish, probably from Guarani *pichey* small armadillo + Spanish *ciego* blind

pick[1] (pɪk) VERB [1] to choose (something) deliberately or carefully, from or as if from a group or number; select. [2] to pluck or gather (fruit, berries, or crops) from (a tree, bush, field, etc.): *to pick hops; to pick a whole bush.* [3] (*tr*) to clean or prepare (fruit, poultry, etc.) by removing the indigestible parts. [4] (*tr*) to remove loose particles from (the teeth, the nose, etc.). [5] (esp of birds) to nibble or gather (corn, etc.). [6] (when *intr*, foll by *at*) to nibble (at) fussily or without appetite. [7] to separate (strands, fibres, etc.), as in weaving. [8] (*tr*) to provoke (an argument, fight, etc.) deliberately. [9] (*tr*) to steal (money or valuables) from (a person's pocket). [10] (*tr*) to open (a lock) with an instrument other than a key. [11] to pluck the strings of (a guitar, banjo, etc.). [12] (*tr*) to make (one's way) carefully on foot: *they picked their way through the rubble.* [13] **pick and choose.** to select fastidiously, fussily, etc. [14] **pick someone's brains.** to obtain information or ideas from someone. ◆ NOUN [15] freedom or right of selection (esp in the phrase **take one's pick**). [16] a person, thing, etc., that is chosen first or preferred: *the pick of the bunch.* [17] the act of picking. [18] the amount of a crop picked at one period or from one area. [19] *Printing* a speck of dirt or paper fibre or a blob of ink on the surface of set type or a printing plate. ◆ See also **pick at, pick off, pick on, pick out, pick-up.**
▷HISTORY C15: from earlier *piken* to pick, influenced by French *piquer* to pierce; compare Middle Low German *picken*, Dutch *pikken*
▸ ˈ**pickable** ADJECTIVE

pick[2] (pɪk) NOUN [1] a tool with a handle carrying a long steel head curved and tapering to a point at one or both ends, used for loosening soil, breaking rocks, etc. [2] any of various tools used for picking, such as an ice pick or toothpick. [3] a plectrum. ◆ VERB [4] (*tr*) to pierce, dig, or break up (a hard surface) with a pick. [5] (*tr*) to form (a hole) in this way.
▷HISTORY C14: perhaps variant of PIKE[2]

pick[3] (pɪk) (in weaving) VERB [1] (*tr*) to cast (a shuttle). ◆ NOUN [2] one casting of a shuttle. [3] a weft or filling thread.
▷HISTORY C14: variant of PITCH[1]

pickaback (ˈpɪkəˌbæk) NOUN, ADVERB, ADJECTIVE, VERB another word for **piggyback.**

pick and mix *or* **pick 'n' mix** NOUN [1] a selection of sweets from which the customer can choose, paid for by weight. ◆ ADJECTIVE **pick-and-mix.** [2] allowing the user to choose items or ideas and combine them as he or she wishes: *a pick-and-mix selection of fabric and wallpapers.*

pickaninny (ˌpɪkəˈnɪnɪ) NOUN, *plural* **-nies.** a variant spelling (esp US) of **piccaninny.**

pickaroon (ˌpɪkəˈruːn) NOUN a variant spelling of **picaroon.**

pick at VERB (*intr, preposition*) to make criticisms of in a niggling or petty manner.

pickaxe *or US* **pickax** (ˈpɪkˌæks) NOUN [1] a large pick or mattock. ◆ VERB [2] to use a pickaxe on (earth, rocks, etc.).
▷HISTORY C15: from earlier *pikois* (but influenced also by AXE), from Old French *picois*, from *pic* PICK[2]; compare also PIQUE[1]

picker (ˈpɪkə) NOUN [1] a person or thing that picks, esp that gathers fruit, crops, etc. [2] (in weaving) a person or the part of the loom that casts the shuttle.

pickerel (ˈpɪkərəl, ˈpɪkrəl) NOUN, *plural* **-el** *or* **-els.** any of several North American freshwater game fishes, such as *Esox americanus* and *E. niger*: family *Esocidae* (pikes, walleye, etc.).
▷HISTORY C14: a small pike; diminutive of PIKE[1]

pickerelweed (ˈpɪkərəlˌwiːd, ˈpɪkrəl-) NOUN any of several North American freshwater plants of the genus *Pontederia, esp P. cordata*, having arrow-shaped leaves and purple flowers: family *Pontederiaceae*.

picket (ˈpɪkɪt) NOUN [1] a pointed stake, post, or peg that is driven into the ground to support a fence, provide a marker for surveying, etc. [2] an individual or group that stands outside an establishment to make a protest, to dissuade or prevent employees or clients from entering, etc. [3] Also: **picquet.** a small detachment of troops or warships positioned towards the enemy to give early warning of attack. ◆ VERB [4] to post or serve as pickets at (a factory, embassy, etc.): *let's go and picket the shop.* [5] to guard (a main body or place) by using or acting as a picket. [6] (*tr*) to fasten (a horse or other animal) to a picket. [7] (*tr*) to fence (an area, boundary, etc.) with pickets.
▷HISTORY C18: from French *piquet*, from Old French *piquer* to prick; see PIKE[2]
▸ ˈ**picketer** NOUN

picket fence NOUN a fence consisting of pickets supported at close regular intervals by being driven into the ground, by interlacing with strong wire, or by nailing to horizontal timbers fixed to posts in the ground.

picket line NOUN a line of people acting as pickets.

pickin (ˈpɪkɪn) NOUN *W African* a small child.
▷HISTORY from Portuguese *pequeno*; see PICCANINNY

pickings (ˈpɪkɪŋz) PLURAL NOUN (*sometimes singular*) money, profits, etc., acquired easily or by more or less dishonest means; spoils.

pickle (ˈpɪkᵊl) NOUN [1] (*often plural*) vegetables, such as cauliflowers, onions, etc., preserved in vinegar, brine, etc. [2] any food preserved in this way. [3] a liquid or marinade, such as spiced vinegar, for preserving vegetables, meat, fish, etc. [4] *Chiefly US and Canadian* a cucumber that has been preserved and flavoured in a pickling solution, such as brine or vinegar. [5] *Informal* an awkward or difficult situation: *to be in a pickle.* [6] *Brit informal* a mischievous child. ◆ VERB (*tr*) [7] to preserve in a pickling liquid. [8] to immerse (a metallic object) in a liquid, such as an acid, to remove surface scale.
▷HISTORY C14: perhaps from Middle Dutch *pekel*; related to German *Pökel* brine
▸ ˈ**pickler** NOUN

pickled (ˈpɪkᵊld) ADJECTIVE [1] preserved in a pickling liquid. [2] *Informal* intoxicated; drunk.

picklock (ˈpɪkˌlɒk) NOUN [1] a person who picks locks, esp one who gains unlawful access to premises by this means. [2] an instrument for picking locks.

pick-me-up NOUN *Informal* a tonic or restorative, esp a special drink taken as a stimulant.

pick 'n' mix NOUN [1] a variant spelling of **pick and mix.**

pick off VERB (*tr, adverb*) to aim at and shoot one by one.

pick on VERB (*tr, preposition*) to select (someone) for something unpleasant, esp in order to bully, blame, or cause to perform a distasteful task.

pick out VERB (*tr, adverb*) [1] to select for use or special consideration, illustration, etc., as from a group. [2] to distinguish (an object from its surroundings), as in painting: *she picked out the woodwork in white.* [3] to perceive or recognize (a person or thing previously obscured): *we picked out his face among the crowd.* [4] to distinguish (sense or meaning) from or as if from a mass of detail or complication. [5] to play (a tune) tentatively, by or as if by ear.

pickpocket ('pɪkˌpɒkɪt) NOUN a person who steals from the pockets or handbags of others in public places.

pick-up NOUN [1] Also called: **pick-up arm, tone arm.** the light balanced arm of a record player that carries the wires from the cartridge to the preamplifier. [2] an electromagnetic transducer that converts the vibrations of the steel strings of an electric guitar or other amplified instrument into electric signals. [3] another name for **cartridge** (sense 3). [4] Also called: **pick-up truck.** a small truck with an open body and low sides, used for light deliveries. [5] *Informal, chiefly US* an ability to accelerate rapidly: *this car has good pick-up.* [6] *Informal* a casual acquaintance, usually one made with sexual intentions. [7] *Informal* **a** a stop to collect passengers, goods, etc. **b** the people or things collected. [8] *Slang* a free ride in a motor vehicle. [9] *Informal* an improvement. [10] *Slang* a pick-me-up. ◆ ADJECTIVE [11] *US and Canadian* organized, arranged, or assembled hastily and without planning: *a pick-up band; pick-up games.* ◆ VERB **pick up.** (*adverb*) [12] (*tr*) to gather up in the hand or hands. [13] (*tr*) to acquire, obtain, or purchase casually, incidentally, etc. [14] (*tr*) to catch (a disease): *she picked up a bad cold during the weekend.* [15] (*intr*) to improve in health, condition, activity, etc.: *the market began to pick up.* [16] (*reflexive*) to raise (oneself) after a fall or setback. [17] (*tr*) to notice or sense: *she picked up a change in his attitude.* [18] to resume where one left off; return to: *we'll pick up after lunch; they picked up the discussion.* [19] (*tr*) to learn gradually or as one goes along. [20] (*tr*) to take responsibility for paying (a bill): *he picked up the bill for dinner.* [21] (*tr*) *Informal* to reprimand: *he picked her up on her table manners.* [22] (*tr*) to collect or give a lift to (passengers, hitchhikers, goods, etc.). [23] (*tr*) *Informal* to become acquainted with, esp with a view to having sexual relations. [24] (*tr*) *Informal* to arrest. [25] to increase (speed): *the cars picked up down the straight.* [26] (*tr*) to receive (electrical signals, a radio signal, sounds, etc.), as for transmission or amplification. [27] **pick up the pieces.** to restore a situation to normality after a crisis or collapse.

Pickwickian (pɪk'wɪkɪən) ADJECTIVE [1] of, relating to, or resembling Mr Pickwick in *The Pickwick Papers,* a novel by English novelist Charles Dickens (1812–70), esp in being naive or benevolent. [2] (of the use or meaning of a word, etc.) odd or unusual.

picky ('pɪkɪ) ADJECTIVE **pickier, pickiest.** *Informal* fussy; finicky; choosy.
▸ **'pickily** ADVERB ▸ **'pickiness** NOUN

picnic ('pɪknɪk) NOUN [1] a trip or excursion to the country, seaside, etc., on which people bring food to be eaten in the open air. [2] **a** any informal meal eaten outside. **b** (*as modifier*): *a picnic lunch.* [3] *Informal, chiefly Austral* a troublesome situation or experience. [4] **no picnic.** *Informal* a hard or disagreeable task. ◆ VERB **-nics, -nicking, -nicked.** [5] (*intr*) to eat a picnic.
▷ HISTORY C18: from French *piquenique,* of unknown origin
▸ **'picnicker** NOUN

picnic races PLURAL NOUN *Austral* horse races for amateur riders held in rural areas.

pico- PREFIX denoting 10^{-12}: *picofarad.* Symbol: p.
▷ HISTORY from Spanish *pico* small quantity, odd number, peak

Pico de Aneto (*Spanish* 'piko de a'neto) NOUN See **Aneto.**

Pico de Teide (*Spanish* 'piko de 'teiðe) NOUN See **Teide.**

picofarad ('pi:kəʊˌfærəd, -æd) NOUN a million millionth of a farad; 10^{-12} farad. Symbol: pF.

picoline ('pɪkəˌli:n, -lɪn) NOUN a liquid derivative of pyridine found in bone oil and coal tar; methylpyridene. Formula: $C_5H_4N(CH_3)$.
▷ HISTORY C19: from Latin *pic-, pix* PITCH² + -OL² + -INE²
▸ **picolinic** (ˌpɪkə'lɪnɪk) ADJECTIVE

picong ('pɪkɒŋ) NOUN *Caribbean* any teasing or satirical banter, originally a verbal duel in song.
▷ HISTORY from Spanish *picón* mocking, from *picar* to pierce; compare PICADOR

picornavirus (pɪ'kɔ:nəˌvaɪrəs) NOUN any one of a group of small viruses that contain RNA; the group includes polioviruses, rhinoviruses, Coxsackie viruses, and the virus that causes foot-and-mouth disease.
▷ HISTORY C20: from PICO- + RNA + VIRUS

picosecond ('pi:kəʊˌsɛkənd, 'paɪkəʊ-) NOUN a million millionth of a second; 10^{-12} second.

picot ('pi:kəʊ) NOUN any of a pattern of small loops, as on lace.
▷ HISTORY C19: from French: small point, from *pic* point

picotee (ˌpɪkə'ti:) NOUN a type of carnation having pale petals edged with a darker colour, usually red.
▷ HISTORY C18: from French *picoté* marked with points, from PICOT

picquet ('pɪkɪt) NOUN a variant spelling of **picket** (sense 3).

picrate ('pɪkreɪt) NOUN [1] any salt or ester of picric acid, such as sodium picrate. [2] a charge-transfer complex formed by picric acid.

picric acid ('pɪkrɪk) NOUN a toxic sparingly soluble crystalline yellow acid used as a dye, antiseptic, and explosive. Formula: $C_6H_2OH(NO_2)_3$. Systematic name: **2,4,6-trinitrophenol.** See also **lyddite.**

picrite ('pɪkraɪt) NOUN a coarse-grained ultrabasic igneous rock consisting of olivine and augite with small amounts of plagioclase feldspar.

picro- *or before a vowel* **picr-** COMBINING FORM bitter: *picrotoxin.*
▷ HISTORY from Greek *pikros*

picrotoxin (ˌpɪkrə'tɒksɪn) NOUN a bitter poisonous crystalline compound formerly used as an antidote for barbiturate poisoning. Formula: $C_{30}H_{34}O_{13}$.

Pict (pɪkt) NOUN a member of any of the peoples who lived in Britain north of the Forth and Clyde in the first to the fourth centuries A.D.: later applied chiefly to the inhabitants of NE Scotland. Throughout Roman times the Picts carried out border raids.
▷ HISTORY Old English *Peohtas;* later forms from Late Latin *Pictī* painted men, from *pingere* to paint

Pictish ('pɪktɪʃ) NOUN [1] the language of the Picts, of which few records survive. Its origins are much disputed and it was extinct by about 900 A.D. ◆ ADJECTIVE [2] of or relating to the Picts.

pictogram ('pɪktəˌgræm) NOUN another word for **pictograph.**

pictograph ('pɪktəˌgrɑ:f, -ˌgræf) NOUN [1] a picture or symbol standing for a word or group of words, as in written Chinese. [2] a chart on which symbols are used to represent values, such as population levels or consumption.
▷ HISTORY C19: from Latin *pictus,* from *pingere* to paint
▸ **pictographic** (ˌpɪktə'græfɪk) ADJECTIVE ▸ **pictography** (pɪk'tɒgrəfɪ) NOUN

Pictor ('pɪktə) NOUN, *Latin genitive* **Pictoris** (pɪk'tɔ:rɪs). a faint constellation in the S hemisphere lying between Dorado and Carina.
▷ HISTORY Latin: painter

pictorial (pɪk'tɔ:rɪəl) ADJECTIVE [1] relating to, consisting of, or expressed by pictures. [2] (of books, newspapers, etc.) containing pictures. [3] of or relating to painting or drawing. [4] (of language, style, etc.) suggesting a picture; vivid; graphic. ◆ NOUN [5] **a** a magazine, newspaper, etc., containing many pictures. **b** (*capital when part of a name*): *the Sunday Pictorial.*
▷ HISTORY C17: from Late Latin *pictōrius,* from Latin *pictor* painter, from *pingere* to paint
▸ **pic'torially** ADVERB

picture ('pɪktʃə) NOUN [1] **a** a visual representation of something, such as a person or scene, produced on a surface, as in a photograph, painting, etc. **b** (*as modifier*): *picture gallery; picture postcard.* Related adjective: **pictorial.** [2] a mental image or impression: *a clear picture of events.* [3] a verbal description, esp one that is vivid. [4] a situation considered as an observable scene: *the political picture.* [5] a person or thing that bears a close resemblance to another: *he was the picture of his father.* [6] a person, scene, etc., considered as typifying a particular state or quality: *the picture of despair.* [7] a beautiful person or scene: *you'll look a picture.* [8] a complete image on a television screen, comprising two interlaced fields. [9] **a** a motion picture; film. **b** (*as modifier*): *picture theatre.* [10] **the pictures.** *Chiefly Brit and Austral* a cinema or film show. [11] another name for **tableau vivant.** [12] **get the picture.** *Informal* to understand a situation. [13] **in the picture.** informed about a given situation. ◆ VERB (*tr*) [14] to visualize or imagine. [15] to describe or depict, esp vividly. [16] (*often passive*) to put in a picture or make a picture of: *they were pictured sitting on the rocks.*
▷ HISTORY C15: from Latin *pictūra* painting, from *pingere* to paint

picture card NOUN another name for **court card.**

picturegoer ('pɪktʃəˌgəʊə) NOUN *Brit old-fashioned* a person who goes to the cinema, esp frequently.

picture hat NOUN a decorated hat with a very wide brim, esp as worn by women in paintings by Gainsborough and Reynolds.

picture house NOUN *Chiefly Brit* an old-fashioned name for **cinema** (sense 1a).

picture moulding NOUN [1] the edge around a framed picture. [2] Also called: **picture rail.** the moulding or rail near the top of a wall from which pictures can be hung.

picture palace NOUN *Brit* an old-fashioned name for **cinema** (sense 1a).

picturesque (ˌpɪktʃə'rɛsk) ADJECTIVE [1] visually pleasing, esp in being striking or vivid: *a picturesque view.* [2] having a striking or colourful character, nature, etc. [3] (of language) graphic; vivid.
▷ HISTORY C18: from French *pittoresque* (but also influenced by PICTURE), from Italian *pittoresco,* from *pittore* painter, from Latin *pictor*
▸ **ˌpictur'esquely** ADVERB ▸ **ˌpictur'esqueness** NOUN

picture tube NOUN another name for **television tube.**

picture window NOUN a large window having a single pane of glass, usually placed so that it overlooks a view.

picture writing NOUN [1] any writing system that uses pictographs. [2] a system of artistic expression and communication using pictures or symbolic figures.

picul ('pɪkᵊl) NOUN a unit of weight, used in China, Japan, and SE Asia, equal to approximately 60 kilograms or 133 pounds.
▷ HISTORY C16: from Malay *pīkul* a grown man's load

PID ABBREVIATION FOR **pelvic inflammatory disease.**

piddle ('pɪdᵊl) VERB [1] (*intr*) *Informal* to urinate. [2] (when *tr,* often foll by *away*) to spend (one's time) aimlessly; fritter.
▷ HISTORY C16: origin unknown
▸ **'piddler** NOUN

piddling ('pɪdlɪŋ) ADJECTIVE *Informal* petty; trifling; trivial.
▸ **'piddlingly** ADVERB

piddock ('pɪdək) NOUN any marine bivalve of the family *Pholadidae,* boring into rock, clay, or wood by means of sawlike shell valves. See also **shipworm.**
▷ HISTORY C19: origin uncertain

pidgin ('pɪdʒɪn) NOUN a language made up of elements of two or more other languages and used for contacts, esp trading contacts, between the speakers of other languages. Unlike creoles, pidgins do not constitute the mother tongue of any speech community.
▷ HISTORY C19: perhaps from Chinese pronunciation of English *business*

pidgin English NOUN a pidgin in which one of the languages involved is English.

pi-dog NOUN a variant spelling of **pye-dog**.

pie¹ (paɪ) NOUN [1] a baked food consisting of a sweet or savoury filling in a pastry-lined dish, often covered with a pastry crust. [2] **have a** (*or* **one's**) **finger in the pie. a** to have an interest in or take part in some activity. **b** to meddle or interfere. [3] **pie in the sky.** illusory hope or promise of some future good; false optimism.
▷HISTORY C14: of obscure origin

pie² (paɪ) NOUN an archaic or dialect name for **magpie.**
▷HISTORY C13: via Old French from Latin *pīca* magpie; related to Latin *pīcus* woodpecker

pie³ (paɪ) NOUN, VERB *Printing* a variant spelling of **pi²**.

pie⁴ (paɪ) NOUN a very small former Indian coin worth one third of a pice.
▷HISTORY C19: from Hindi *pā'ī*, from Sanskrit *pādikā* a fourth

pie⁵ *or* **pye** (paɪ) NOUN *History* a book for finding the Church service for any particular day.
▷HISTORY C15: from Medieval Latin *pica* almanac; see PICA¹

pie⁶ (paɪ) ADJECTIVE **be pie on.** *NZ informal* to be keen on.
▷HISTORY from Maori *pai ana*

piebald ('paɪˌbɔːld) ADJECTIVE [1] marked or spotted in two different colours, esp black and white: *a piebald horse*. ◆ NOUN [2] a black-and-white pied horse.
▷HISTORY C16: PIE² + BALD; see also PIED

pie cart NOUN *NZ* a mobile van selling warmed-up food and drinks.

piece (piːs) NOUN [1] an amount or portion forming a separate mass or structure; bit: *a piece of wood*. [2] a small part, item, or amount forming part of a whole, esp when broken off or separated: *a piece of bread*. [3] a length by which a commodity is sold, esp cloth, wallpaper, etc. [4] an instance or occurrence: *a piece of luck*. [5] *Slang* a girl or woman regarded as an object of sexual attraction: *a nice piece*. [6] an example or specimen of a style or type, such as an article of furniture: *a beautiful piece of Dresden china*. [7] *Informal* an opinion or point of view: *to state one's piece*. [8] a literary, musical, or artistic composition. [9] a coin having a value as specified: *fifty-pence piece*. [10] a small object, often individually shaped and designed, used in playing certain games, esp board games: *chess pieces*. [11] **a** a firearm or cannon. **b** (*in combination*): *fowling-piece*. [12] any chessman other than a pawn. [13] *US and Canadian* a short time or distance: *down the road a piece*. [14] *Scot and English dialect* **a** a slice of bread or a sandwich. **b** a packed lunch taken to work, school, etc. [15] (*usually plural*) *Austral and NZ* fragments of fleece wool. See also **oddment** (sense 2). [16] **give someone a piece of one's mind.** *Informal* to criticize or censure someone frankly or vehemently. [17] **go to pieces. a** (of a person) to lose control of oneself; have a breakdown. **b** (of a building, organization, etc.) to disintegrate. [18] **nasty piece of work.** *Brit informal* a cruel or mean person. [19] **of a piece.** of the same kind; alike. [20] **piece of cake.** *Informal* something easily obtained or achieved. ◆ VERB (*tr*) [21] (often foll by *together*) to fit or assemble piece by piece. [22] (often foll by *up*) to patch or make up (a garment) by adding pieces. [23] *Textiles* to join (broken threads) during spinning. ◆ See also **piece out**.
▷HISTORY C13 *pece*, from Old French, of Gaulish origin; compare Breton *pez* piece, Welsh *peth* portion

pièce de résistance *French* (pjɛs də rezistɑ̃s) NOUN [1] the principal or most outstanding item in a series or creative artist's work. [2] the main dish of a meal.
▷HISTORY lit: piece of resistance

piece-dyed ADJECTIVE (of fabric) dyed after weaving. Compare **yarn-dyed**.

piece goods PLURAL NOUN goods, esp fabrics, made in standard widths and lengths. Also called: **yard goods**.

piecemeal ('piːsˌmiːl) ADVERB [1] by degrees; bit by bit; gradually. [2] in or into pieces or piece from piece: *to tear something piecemeal*. ◆ ADJECTIVE [3] fragmentary or unsystematic: *a piecemeal approach*.
▷HISTORY C13 *pecemele*, from PIECE + *-mele*, from Old English *mælum* quantity taken at one time

piece of eight NOUN, *plural* **pieces of eight**. a former Spanish coin worth eight reals; peso.

piece out VERB (*tr, adverb*) [1] to extend by adding pieces. [2] to cause to last longer by using only a small amount at a time: *to piece out rations*.

piecer ('piːsə) NOUN *Textiles* a person who mends, repairs, or joins something, esp broken threads on a loom.

piece rate NOUN a fixed rate paid according to the quantity produced.

piecework ('piːsˌwɜːk) NOUN work paid for according to the quantity produced. Compare **timework**.

pie chart NOUN a circular graph divided into sectors proportional to the magnitudes of the quantities represented.

piecrust table ('paɪˌkrʌst) NOUN a round table, ornamented with carved moulding suggestive of a pie crust.

pied (paɪd) ADJECTIVE having markings of two or more colours.
▷HISTORY C14: from PIE²; an allusion to the magpie's black-and-white colouring

pied-à-terre (ˌpjeɪtɑːˈtɛə) NOUN, *plural* **pieds-à-terre** (ˌpjeɪtɑːˈtɛə). a flat, house, or other lodging for secondary or occasional use.
▷HISTORY French, literally: foot on (the) ground

piedmont ('piːdmɒnt) ADJECTIVE (*prenominal*) (of glaciers, plains, etc.) formed or situated at the foot of a mountain or mountain range.
▷HISTORY from Italian *piémonte* mountain foot

Piedmont ('piːdmɒnt) NOUN [1] a region of NW Italy: consists of the upper Po Valley; mainly agricultural. Chief town: Turin. Pop.: 4 287 465 (2000 est.). Area: 25 399 sq. km (9807 sq. miles). Italian name: **Piemonte.** [2] a low plateau of the eastern US, between the coastal plain and the Appalachian Mountains.

piedmontite *or* **piemontite** ('piːdmɒnˌtaɪt, -mən-) NOUN a dark red mineral occurring in metamorphic rocks: a complex hydrated silicate containing calcium, aluminium, iron, and manganese. Formula: $Ca_2(Al,Fe,Mn)_3(SiO_4)_3OH$.
▷HISTORY C19: from PIEDMONT in Italy

pie-dog NOUN a variant spelling of **pye-dog.**

Pied Piper NOUN [1] Also called: **the Pied Piper of Hamelin.** (in German legend) a piper who rid the town of Hamelin of rats by luring them away with his music and then, when he was not paid for his services, lured away its children. [2] (*sometimes not capitals*) a person who entices others to follow him.

pied-piping NOUN *Transformational grammar* the principle that a noun phrase may take with it the rest of a prepositional phrase or a larger noun phrase in which it is contained, when moved in a transformation. For example, when the interrogative pronoun is moved to initial position, other words are moved too, as in *to whom did you speak?*

pied wagtail NOUN a British songbird, *Motacilla alba yarrellii*, with a black throat and back, long black tail, and white underparts and face: family *Motacillidae* (wagtails and pipits).

pie-eyed ADJECTIVE a slang term for **drunk** (sense 1).

pieman ('paɪmən) NOUN, *plural* **-men**. *Brit obsolete* a seller of pies.

Piemonte (*Italian* pje'monte) NOUN the Italian name for **Piedmont** (sense 1).

pier (pɪə) NOUN [1] a structure with a deck that is built out over water, and used as a landing place, promenade, etc. [2] a pillar that bears heavy loads, esp one of rectangular cross section. [3] the part of a wall between two adjacent openings. [4] another name for **buttress** (sense 1).
▷HISTORY C12 *per*, from Anglo-Latin *pera* pier supporting a bridge

pierce (pɪəs) VERB (*mainly tr*) [1] to form or cut (a hole) in (something) with or as if with a sharp instrument. [2] to thrust into or penetrate sharply or violently: *the thorn pierced his heel*. [3] to force (a way, route, etc.) through (something). [4] (of light) to shine through or penetrate (darkness). [5] (*also intr*) to discover or realize (something) suddenly or (of an idea) to become suddenly apparent. [6] (of sounds or cries) to sound sharply through (the silence). [7] to move or affect (a person's emotions, bodily feelings, etc.) deeply or sharply: *the cold pierced their bones*. [8] (*intr*) to penetrate or be capable of penetrating: *piercing cold*.
▷HISTORY C13 *percen*, from Old French *percer*, ultimately from Latin *pertundere*, from *per* through + *tundere* to strike
▸ '**pierceable** ADJECTIVE ▸ '**piercer** NOUN

piercing ('pɪəsɪŋ) ADJECTIVE [1] (of a sound) sharp and shrill. [2] (of eyes or a look) intense and penetrating. [3] (of an emotion) strong and deeply affecting. [4] (of cold or wind) intense or biting. ◆ NOUN [5] the art or practice of piercing body parts for the insertion of jewellery. [6] an instance of the piercing of a body part.
▸ '**piercingly** ADVERB

pier glass NOUN a tall narrow mirror, usually one of a pair or set, designed to hang on the wall between windows, usually above a pier table.

Pieria (paɪ'ɪərɪə) NOUN a region of ancient Macedonia, west of the Gulf of Salonika: site of the Pierian Spring.

Pierian (paɪ'ɪərɪən) ADJECTIVE [1] of or relating to the Muses or artistic or poetic inspiration. [2] of or relating to Pieria.

Pierian Spring NOUN a sacred fountain in Pieria, in Greece, fabled to inspire those who drank from it.

Pierides (paɪ'ɪərɪˌdiːz) PLURAL NOUN *Greek myth* [1] another name for the Muses (see **Muse**). [2] nine maidens of Thessaly, who were defeated in a singing contest by the Muses and turned into magpies for their effrontery.

pieridine (paɪ'ɛərɪˌdaɪn) ADJECTIVE of, relating to, or belonging to the *Pieridae*, a family of butterflies including the whites and brimstones.

pieris ('paɪərɪs) NOUN any plant of a genus, *Pieris*, of American and Asiatic shrubs, esp *P. formosa forrestii*, grown for the bright red colour of its young foliage: family *Ericaceae*.
▷HISTORY New Latin, from Greek *Pierides*, a name for the Muses

Pierre (pɪə) NOUN a city in central South Dakota, capital of the state, on the Missouri River. Pop.: 12 906 (1990).

Pierrot ('pɪərəʊ; *French* pjɛro) NOUN [1] a male character from French pantomime with a whitened face, white costume, and pointed hat. [2] (*usually not capital*) a clown or masquerader so made up.

pier table NOUN a side table designed to stand against a wall between windows.

Piesporter ('piːzˌpɔːtə) NOUN any of various white wines from the area around the village of Piesport in the Moselle valley in Germany.

pietà (pɪɛ'tɑː) NOUN a sculpture, painting, or drawing of the dead Christ, supported by the Virgin Mary.
▷HISTORY Italian: pity, from Latin *pietās* PIETY

Pietermaritzburg (ˌpiːtə'mærɪtsˌbɜːg) NOUN a city in E South Africa, the capital of KwaZulu/Natal: founded in 1839 by the Boers: gateway to Natal's mountain resorts. Pop.: 378 126 (1996).

pietism ('paɪɪˌtɪzəm) NOUN [1] a less common word for **piety.** [2] excessive, exaggerated, or affected piety or saintliness.
▸ '**pietist** NOUN ▸ ˌ**pie'tistic** *or* ˌ**pie'tistical** ADJECTIVE

Pietism ('paɪɪˌtɪzəm) NOUN *History* a reform movement in the German Lutheran Churches during the 17th and 18th centuries that strove to renew the devotional ideal.
▸ '**Pietist** NOUN

piet-my-vrou ('piːtˌmeɪ'frəʊ) NOUN *South African* a cuckoo, *Notococcyx solitarius*, having a red breast.
▷HISTORY from Afrikaans *piet* Peter + *my* my + *vrou* wife: onomatopoeic, based on the bird's three clear notes

piety ('paɪɪtɪ) NOUN, *plural* **-ties.** [1] dutiful devotion to God and observance of religious principles. [2] the quality or characteristic of being pious. [3] a pious action, saying, etc. [4] *Now rare* devotion and obedience to parents or superiors.
▷HISTORY C13 *piete*, from Old French, from Latin *pietās* piety, dutifulness, from *pius* PIOUS

piezo- (paɪ'iːzəʊ-, piː'eɪzəʊ-, 'piːtsəʊ-) COMBINING FORM pressure: *piezometer*.
▷HISTORY from Greek *piezein* to press

piezochemistry (paɪˌiːzəʊˈkɛmɪstrɪ) NOUN the study of chemical reactions at high pressures.

piezoelectric crystal (paɪˌiːzəʊɪˈlɛktrɪk) NOUN a crystal, such as quartz, that produces a potential difference across its opposite faces when under mechanical stress. See also **piezoelectric effect.**

piezoelectric effect *or* **piezoelectricity** (paɪˌiːzəʊɪlɛkˈtrɪsɪtɪ) NOUN *Physics* **a** the production of electricity or electric polarity by applying a mechanical stress to certain crystals. **b** the converse effect in which stress is produced in a crystal as a result of an applied potential difference.
▸**piˌezoeˈlectrically** ADVERB

piezomagnetic effect (paɪˌiːzəʊmægˈnɛtɪk) *or* **piezomagnetism** (paɪˌiːzəʊˈmægnɪtɪzəm) NOUN *Physics* **a** the production of a magnetic field by applying a mechanical stress to certain crystals. **b** the converse effect in which stress is produced in a crystal as a result of an applied magnetic field.
▸**piˌezomagˈnetically** ADJECTIVE

piezometer (ˌpaɪɪˈzɒmɪtə) NOUN any instrument for the measurement of pressure (**piezometry**), esp very high pressure, or for measuring the compressibility of materials under pressure.
▸**piezometric** (paɪˌiːzəʊˈmɛtrɪk) ADJECTIVE
▸**piˌezoˈmetrically** ADVERB

piffle (ˈpɪfᵊl) *Informal* ◆ NOUN 1 nonsense: *to talk piffle.* ◆ VERB 2 (*intr*) to talk or behave feebly.
▷HISTORY C19: origin uncertain

piffling (ˈpɪflɪŋ) ADJECTIVE worthless, trivial.

pig (pɪg) NOUN 1 any artiodactyl mammal of the African and Eurasian family *Suidae, esp Sus scrofa* (**domestic pig**), typically having a long head with a movable snout, a thick bristle-covered skin, and, in wild species, long curved tusks. 2 a domesticated pig weighing more than 120 pounds (54 kg). 3 *Informal* a dirty, greedy, or bad-mannered person. 4 the meat of swine; pork. 5 *Derogatory* a slang word for **policeman.** 6 **a** a mass of metal, such as iron, copper, or lead, cast into a simple shape for ease of storing or transportation. **b** a mould in which such a mass of metal is formed. 7 *Brit informal* something that is difficult or unpleasant. 8 an automated device propelled through a duct or pipeline to clear impediments or check for faults, leaks, etc. 9 **a pig in a poke.** something bought or received without prior sight or knowledge. 10 **make a pig of oneself.** *Informal* to overindulge oneself. 11 **on the pig's back.** *Irish and NZ* successful; established: *he's on the pig's back now.* ◆ Related adjective (for senses 1, 2): **porcine.** ◆ VERB **pigs, pigging, pigged.** 12 (*intr*) (of a sow) to give birth. 13 (*intr*) Also: **pig it.** *Informal* to live in squalor. 14 (*tr*) *Informal* to devour (food) greedily. ◆ See also **pig out.**
▷HISTORY C13 *pigge,* of obscure origin

pig bed NOUN a bed of sand in which pig iron is cast.

pig dog NOUN *NZ* a dog bred for hunting wild pigs in the bush.

pigeon¹ (ˈpɪdʒɪn) NOUN 1 any of numerous birds of the family *Columbidae,* having a heavy body, small head, short legs, and long pointed wings: order *Columbiformes.* See **rock dove.** 2 *Slang* a victim or dupe.
▷HISTORY C14: from Old French *pijon* young dove, from Late Latin *pīpiō* young bird, from *pīpīre* to chirp

pigeon² (ˈpɪdʒɪn) NOUN *Brit informal* concern or responsibility (often in the phrase **it's his, her,** etc., **pigeon**).
▷HISTORY C19: altered from PIDGIN

pigeon breast NOUN a deformity of the chest characterized by an abnormal protrusion of the breastbone, caused by rickets or by obstructed breathing during infancy. Also called: **chicken breast.**

pigeon hawk NOUN the North American variety of the merlin.

pigeon-hearted *or* **pigeon-livered** ADJECTIVE of a timid or fearful disposition.

pigeonhole (ˈpɪdʒɪnˌhəʊl) NOUN 1 a small compartment for papers, letters, etc., as in a bureau. 2 a hole or recess in a dovecote for pigeons to nest in. 3 *Informal* a category or classification. ◆ VERB (*tr*) 4 to put aside or defer. 5 to classify or categorize, esp in a rigid manner.

pigeon pea NOUN another name for **dhal.**

pigeon-toed ADJECTIVE having the toes turned inwards.

pigeonwing (ˈpɪdʒɪnˌwɪŋ) NOUN *Chiefly US* a fancy step in dancing in which the feet are clapped together.

pigface (ˈpɪgˌfeɪs) NOUN *Austral* a creeping succulent plant of the genus *Carpobrotus,* having bright-coloured flowers and red fruits and often grown for ornament: family *Aizoaceae.*

pig fern NOUN *NZ* giant bracken.

pigfish (ˈpɪgˌfɪʃ) NOUN, *plural* **-fish** *or* **-fishes.** 1 Also called: **hogfish.** any of several grunts, esp *Orthopristis chrysopterus,* of the North American Atlantic coast. 2 any of several wrasses, such as *Achoerodus gouldii* (**giant pigfish**), that occur around the Great Barrier Reef.

piggery (ˈpɪgərɪ) NOUN, *plural* **-geries.** 1 a place where pigs are kept and reared. 2 great greediness; piggishness.

piggin (ˈpɪgɪn) NOUN a small wooden bucket or tub. Also called: **pipkin.**
▷HISTORY C16: origin unknown

piggish (ˈpɪgɪʃ) ADJECTIVE 1 like a pig, esp in appetite or manners. 2 *Informal, chiefly Brit* obstinate or mean.
▸**ˈpiggishly** ADVERB ▸**ˈpiggishness** NOUN

piggy (ˈpɪgɪ) NOUN, *plural* **-gies.** 1 a child's word for a pig, esp a piglet. 2 **piggy in the middle. a** a children's game in which one player attempts to retrieve a ball thrown over him or her by at least two other players. **b** a situation in which a person or group is caught up in a disagreement between other people or groups. 3 a child's word for toe or, sometimes, finger. ◆ ADJECTIVE **-gier, -giest.** 4 another word for **piggish.**

piggyback (ˈpɪgɪˌbæk) *or* **pickaback** NOUN 1 a ride on the back and shoulders of another person. 2 a system whereby a vehicle, aircraft, etc., is transported for part of its journey on another vehicle, such as a flat railway wagon, another aircraft, etc. ◆ ADVERB 3 on the back and shoulders of another person. 4 on or as an addition to something else. ◆ ADJECTIVE 5 of or for a piggyback: *a piggyback ride; piggyback lorry trains.* 6 of or relating to a type of heart transplant in which the transplanted heart functions in conjunction with the patient's own heart. ◆ VERB (*tr*) 7 to give (a person) a piggyback on one's back and shoulders. 8 to transport (one vehicle) on another.

piggy bank NOUN a child's coin bank shaped like a pig with a slot for coins.

pig-headed ADJECTIVE stupidly stubborn.
▸**ˌpig-ˈheadedly** ADVERB ▸**ˌpig-ˈheadedness** NOUN

pig iron NOUN crude iron produced in a blast furnace and poured into moulds in preparation for making wrought iron, steels, alloys, etc.

Pig Island NOUN *NZ informal* New Zealand.

Pig Islander NOUN *NZ informal* a New Zealander.

pig-jump VERB (*intr*) (of a horse) to jump from all four legs.

Pig Latin NOUN a secret language used by children in which any consonants at the beginning of a word are placed at the end, followed by *-ay;* for example *cathedral* becomes *athedralcay.*

piglet (ˈpɪglɪt) NOUN a young pig.

pigmeat (ˈpɪgˌmiːt) NOUN a less common name for **pork, ham¹** (sense 2) or **bacon** (sense 1).

pigment (ˈpɪgmənt) NOUN 1 a substance occurring in plant or animal tissue and producing a characteristic colour, such as chlorophyll in green plants and haemoglobin in red blood. 2 any substance used to impart colour. 3 a powder that is mixed with a liquid to give a paint, ink, etc.
▷HISTORY C14: from Latin *pigmentum,* from *pingere* to paint
▸**ˈpigmentary** ADJECTIVE

pigmentation (ˌpɪgmənˈteɪʃən) NOUN 1 coloration in plants, animals, or man caused by the presence of pigments. 2 the deposition of pigment in animals, plants, or man.

Pigmy (ˈpɪgmɪ) NOUN, *plural* **-mies.** a variant spelling of **Pygmy.**

pignut (ˈpɪgˌnʌt) NOUN 1 Also called: **hognut. a** the bitter nut of any of several North American hickory trees, esp *Carya glabra* (**brown hickory**). **b** any of the trees bearing such a nut. 2 another name for **earthnut.**

pig out VERB (*intr, adverb*) *Slang* to gorge oneself.

pigpen (ˈpɪgˌpɛn) NOUN a US and Canadian word for **pigsty.**

pig-root VERB (*intr*) *NZ* another term for **pig-jump.**

pigs (pɪgz) INTERJECTION *Austral slang* an expression of derision or disagreement. Also: **pig's arse, pig's bum.**

Pigs (pɪgz) NOUN **Bay of.** See **Bay of Pigs.**

pig's ear NOUN something that has been badly or clumsily done; a botched job (esp in the phrase **make a pig's ear of (something)**).

pig's fry NOUN the heart, liver, lights, and sweetbreads of a pig cooked, esp fried, together.

pigskin (ˈpɪgˌskɪn) NOUN 1 the skin of the domestic pig. 2 leather made of this skin. 3 *US and Canadian informal* a football. ◆ ADJECTIVE 4 made of pigskin.

pigstick (ˈpɪgˌstɪk) VERB (*intr*) (esp in India) to hunt and spear wild boar, esp from horseback.

pigsticker (ˈpɪgˌstɪkə) NOUN 1 a person who hunts wild boar. 2 *Slang* a large sharp hunting knife.

pigsticking (ˈpɪgˌstɪkɪŋ) NOUN the sport of hunting wild boar.

pigsty (ˈpɪgˌstaɪ) *or US and Canadian* **pigpen** NOUN, *plural* **-sties.** 1 a pen for pigs; sty. 2 *Brit* a dirty or untidy place.

pigswill (ˈpɪgˌswɪl) NOUN waste food or other edible matter fed to pigs. Also called: **pig's wash.**

pigtail (ˈpɪgˌteɪl) NOUN 1 a bunch of hair or one of two bunches on either side of the face, worn loose or plaited. 2 a twisted roll of tobacco.
▸**ˈpigˌtailed** ADJECTIVE

pigweed (ˈpɪgˌwiːd) NOUN 1 Also called: **redroot.** any of several coarse North American amaranthaceous weeds of the genus *Amaranthus, esp A. retroflexus,* having hairy leaves and green flowers. 2 a US name for **fat hen.**

pika (ˈpaɪkə) NOUN any burrowing lagomorph mammal of the family *Ochotonidae* of mountainous regions of North America and Asia, having short rounded ears, a rounded body, and rudimentary tail. Also called: **cony.**
▷HISTORY C19: from Tungusic *piika*

pikau (ˈpiːkaʊ) NOUN *NZ* a pack, knapsack, or rucksack.
▷HISTORY Maori

pike¹ (paɪk) NOUN, *plural* **pike** *or* **pikes.** 1 any of several large predatory freshwater teleost fishes of the genus *Esox, esp E. lucius* (**northern pike**), having a broad flat snout, strong teeth, and an elongated body covered with small scales: family *Esocidae.* 2 any of various similar fishes.
▷HISTORY C14: short for *pikefish,* from Old English *pīc* point, with reference to the shape of its jaw

pike² (paɪk) NOUN 1 a medieval weapon consisting of an iron or steel spearhead joined to a long pole, the pikestaff. 2 a point or spike. ◆ VERB 3 (*tr*) to stab or pierce using a pike.
▷HISTORY Old English *pīc* point, of obscure origin

pike³ (paɪk) NOUN short for **turnpike** (sense 1).

pike⁴ (paɪk) NOUN *Northern English dialect* a pointed or conical hill.
▷HISTORY Old English *pīc,* of obscure origin

pike⁵ (paɪk) *or* **piked** (paɪkt) ADJECTIVE (of the body position of a diver) bent at the hips but with the legs straight.
▷HISTORY C20: of obscure origin

pikelet (ˈpaɪklɪt) NOUN a dialect word for a **crumpet** (sense 1).
▷HISTORY C18: from Welsh *bara pyglyd* pitchy bread

pikeman (ˈpaɪkmən) NOUN, *plural* **-men.** (formerly) a soldier armed with a pike.

pikeperch (ˈpaɪkˌpɜːtʃ) NOUN, *plural* **-perch** *or* **-perches.** any of various pikelike freshwater teleost fishes of the genera *Stizostedion* (or *Lucioperca*), such as *S. lucioperca* of Europe: family *Percidae* (perches).

piker (ˈpaɪkə) NOUN *Slang* 1 *Austral* a wild bullock. 2 *Austral and NZ* a useless person; failure. 3 *US, Austral, and NZ* a lazy person; shirker. 4 a mean person.
▷HISTORY C19: perhaps related to PIKE³

Pikes Peak NOUN a mountain in central

Colorado, in the Rockies. Height: 4300 m (14 109 ft.).

pikestaff ('paɪkˌstɑːf) NOUN the wooden handle of a pike.

pilaster (pɪ'læstə) NOUN a shallow rectangular column attached to the face of a wall.
▷HISTORY C16: from French *pilastre,* from Latin *pīla* pillar
▸**pi'lastered** ADJECTIVE

Pilates (pɪ'lɑːtiːz) NOUN a system of gentle exercise performed lying down that stretches and lengthens the muscles, designed to improve posture, flexibility, etc.
▷HISTORY C20: named after Joseph *Pilates* (1880–1967), its German inventor

Pilatus (*German* pi'laːtʊs) NOUN a mountain in central Switzerland, in Unterwalden canton: derives its name from the legend that the body of Pontius Pilate lay in a former lake on the mountain. Height: 2122 m (6962 ft.).

pilau (pɪ'laʊ), **pilaf, pilaff** ('pɪlæf), **pilao** (pɪ'laʊ), *or* **pilaw** (pɪ'lɔː) NOUN a dish originating from the East, consisting of rice flavoured with spices and cooked in stock, to which meat, poultry, or fish may be added.
▷HISTORY C17: from Turkish *pilāw,* from Persian

pilch (pɪltʃ) NOUN *Brit archaic* 1 an outer garment, originally one made of skin. 2 an infant's outer wrapping, worn over the napkin.
▷HISTORY C17: from Old English *pylce* a garment made of skin and fur, from Late Latin *pellicia,* from Latin *pellis* fur

pilchard ('pɪltʃəd) NOUN 1 a European food fish, *Sardina* (or *Clupea*) *pilchardus,* with a rounded body covered with large scales: family *Clupeidae* (herrings). 2 a related fish, *Sardinops neopilchardus,* of S Australian waters.
▷HISTORY C16 *pylcher,* of obscure origin

Pilcomayo (*Spanish* pilko'majo) NOUN a river in S central South America, rising in W central Bolivia and flowing southeast, forming the border between Argentina and Paraguay, to the Paraguay River at Asunción. Length: about 1600 km (1000 miles).

pile[1] (paɪl) NOUN 1 a collection of objects laid on top of one another or of other material stacked vertically; heap; mound. 2 *Informal* a large amount of money (esp in the phrase **make a pile**). 3 (*often plural*) *Informal* a large amount: *a pile of work.* 4 a less common word for **pyre.** 5 a large building or group of buildings. 6 short for **voltaic pile.** 7 *Physics* a structure of uranium and a moderator used for producing atomic energy; nuclear reactor. 8 *Metallurgy* an arrangement of wrought-iron bars that are to be heated and worked into a single bar. 9 the point of an arrow. ◆ VERB 10 (often foll by *up*) to collect or be collected into or as if into a pile: *snow piled up in the drive.* 11 (*intr;* foll by *in, into, off, out,* etc.) to move in a group, esp in a hurried or disorganized manner: *to pile off the bus.* 12 **pile arms.** to prop a number of rifles together, muzzles together and upwards, butts forming the base. 13 **pile it on.** *Informal* to exaggerate. ◆ See also **pile up.**
▷HISTORY C15: via Old French from Latin *pīla* stone pier

pile[2] (paɪl) NOUN 1 a long column of timber, concrete, or steel that is driven into the ground to provide a foundation for a vertical load (a bearing pile) or a group of such columns to resist a horizontal load from earth or water pressure (a sheet pile). 2 *Heraldry* an ordinary shaped like a wedge, usually displayed point-downwards. ◆ VERB (*tr*) 3 to drive (piles) into the ground. 4 to provide or support (a structure) with piles.
▷HISTORY Old English *pīl,* from Latin *pīlum*

pile[3] (paɪl) NOUN 1 *Textiles* **a** the yarns in a fabric that stand up or out from the weave, as in carpeting, velvet, etc. **b** one of these yarns. 2 soft fine hair, fur, wool, etc.
▷HISTORY C15: from Anglo-Norman *pyle,* from Latin *pilus* hair

pilea ('pɪlɪə) NOUN any plant of the tropical annual or perennial genus *Pilea, esp P. muscosa,* the artillery or gunpowder plant, which releases a cloud of pollen when shaken; some others are grown for their ornamental foliage: family *Urticaceae.*
▷HISTORY New Latin, from Greek *pilos* cap (from the shape of the segments of the perianth)

pileate ('paɪlɪɪt, -ˌeɪt, 'pɪl-) *or* **pileated** ('paɪlɪˌeɪtɪd, 'pɪl-) ADJECTIVE 1 (of birds) having a crest. 2 *Botany* having a pileus.
▷HISTORY C18: from Latin *pīleātus* wearing a felt cap, from PILEUS

pile cap NOUN a reinforced or mass concrete connecting beam cast around the head of a group of piles enabling it to act as a single unit to support the imposed load.

pile-driver NOUN 1 a machine that drives piles into the ground either by repeatedly allowing a heavy weight to fall on the head of the pile or by using a steam hammer. 2 *Informal* a forceful punch or kick.

pileous ('paɪlɪəs, 'pɪl-) ADJECTIVE *Biology* 1 hairy. 2 of or relating to hair.
▷HISTORY C19: ultimately from Latin *pilus* a hair

piles (paɪlz) PLURAL NOUN a nontechnical name for **haemorrhoids.**
▷HISTORY C15: from Latin *pilae* balls (referring to the appearance of external piles)

pile shoe NOUN an iron casting shaped to a point and fitted to a lower end of a wooden or concrete pile. Also called: **shoe.**

pileum ('paɪlɪəm, 'pɪl-) NOUN, *plural* **-lea** (-lɪə). the top of a bird's head from the base of the bill to the occiput.
▷HISTORY C19: New Latin, from Latin PILEUS

pile up VERB (*adverb*) 1 to gather or be gathered in a pile; accumulate. 2 *Informal* to crash or cause to crash. ◆ NOUN **pile-up.** 3 *Informal* a multiple collision of vehicles.

pileus ('paɪlɪəs, 'pɪl-) NOUN, *plural* **-lei** (-lɪˌaɪ). the upper cap-shaped part of a mushroom or similar spore-producing body.
▷HISTORY C18 (botanical use): New Latin, from Latin: felt cap

pilewort ('paɪlˌwɜːt) NOUN any of several plants, such as lesser celandine, thought to be effective in treating piles.

pilfer ('pɪlfə) VERB to steal (minor items), esp in small quantities.
▷HISTORY C14 *pylfre* (n) from Old French *pelfre* booty; see PELF
▸**'pilferer** NOUN ▸**'pilfering** NOUN

pilferage ('pɪlfərɪdʒ) NOUN 1 the act or practice of stealing small quantities or articles. 2 the amount so stolen.

pilgarlic (pɪl'gɑːlɪk) NOUN 1 *Obsolete* a bald head or a man with a bald head. 2 *Dialect* a pitiable person.
▷HISTORY C16: literally: peeled garlic

pilgrim ('pɪlgrɪm) NOUN 1 a person who undertakes a journey to a sacred place as an act of religious devotion. 2 any wayfarer.
▷HISTORY C12: from Provençal *pelegrin,* from Latin *peregrīnus* foreign, from *per* through + *ager* field, land; see PEREGRINE

Pilgrim ('pɪlgrɪm) NOUN See **Canterbury Pilgrims** (sense 2).

pilgrimage ('pɪlgrɪmɪdʒ) NOUN 1 a journey to a shrine or other sacred place. 2 a journey or long search made for exalted or sentimental reasons. ◆ VERB 3 (*intr*) to make a pilgrimage.

Pilgrimage of Grace NOUN a rebellion in 1536 in N England against the Reformation and Henry VIII's government.

Pilgrim Fathers *or* **Pilgrims** PLURAL NOUN **the.** the English Puritans who sailed on the Mayflower to New England, where they founded Plymouth Colony in SE Massachusetts (1620).

pili[1] (pɪ'liː) NOUN, *plural* **-lis.** 1 a burseraceous Philippine tree, *Canarium ovatum,* with edible seeds resembling almonds. 2 Also called: **pili nut.** the seed of this tree.
▷HISTORY from Tagalog

pili[2] ('paɪlɪ) PLURAL NOUN, *singular* **pilus** ('paɪləs). *Bacteriol* short curled hairlike processes on the surface of certain bacteria that are involved in conjugation and the attachment of the bacteria to other cells.
▷HISTORY C20: from Latin: hairs

piliferous (paɪ'lɪfərəs) ADJECTIVE 1 (esp of plants or their parts) bearing or ending in a hair or hairs. 2 designating the outer layer of root epidermis, which bears the root hairs.
▷HISTORY C19: from Latin *pilus* hair + -FEROUS. Compare PILE[3]

piliform ('pɪlɪˌfɔːm) ADJECTIVE *Botany* resembling a long hair.

piling ('paɪlɪŋ) NOUN 1 the act of driving piles. 2 a number of piles. 3 a structure formed of piles.

Pílion ('piljɔn) NOUN transliteration of the Modern Greek name for **Pelion.**

pill[1] (pɪl) NOUN 1 a small spherical or ovoid mass of a medicinal substance, intended to be swallowed whole. 2 **the.** (*sometimes capital*) *Informal* an oral contraceptive. 3 something unpleasant that must be endured (esp in the phrase **bitter pill to swallow**). 4 *Slang* a ball or disc. 5 a small ball of matted fibres that forms on the surface of a fabric through rubbing. 6 *Slang* an unpleasant or boring person. ◆ VERB 7 (*tr*) to give pills to. 8 (*tr*) to make pills of. 9 (*intr*) **a** to form into small balls. **b** (of a fabric) to form small balls of fibre on its surface through rubbing. 10 (*tr*) *Slang* to blackball. ◆ See also **pills.**
▷HISTORY C15: from Middle Flemish *pille,* from Latin *pilula* a little ball, from *pila* ball

pill[2] (pɪl) VERB 1 *Archaic or dialect* to peel or skin (something). 2 *Archaic* to pillage or plunder (a place). 3 *Obsolete* to make or become bald.
▷HISTORY Old English *pilian,* from Latin *pilāre* to strip

pillage ('pɪlɪdʒ) VERB 1 to rob (a town, village, etc.) of (booty or spoils), esp during a war. ◆ NOUN 2 the act of pillaging. 3 something obtained by pillaging; booty.
▷HISTORY C14: via Old French from *piller* to despoil, probably from *peille* rag, from Latin *pīleus* felt cap
▸**'pillager** NOUN

pillar ('pɪlə) NOUN 1 an upright structure of stone, brick, metal, etc., that supports a superstructure or is used for ornamentation. 2 something resembling this in shape or function: *a pillar of stones; a pillar of smoke.* 3 a tall, slender, usually sheer rock column, forming a separate top. 4 a prominent supporter: *a pillar of the Church.* 5 **from pillar to post.** from one place to another. ◆ VERB 6 (*tr*) to support with or as if with pillars.
▷HISTORY C13: from Old French *pilier,* from Latin *pīla;* see PILE[1]

pillar box NOUN 1 (in Britain) a red pillar-shaped public letter box situated on a pavement. ◆ ADJECTIVE **pillar-box.** 2 characteristic of a pillar box (in the phrase **pillar-box red**).

Pillars of Hercules PLURAL NOUN the two promontories at the E end of the Strait of Gibraltar: the Rock of Gibraltar on the European side and the Jebel Musa on the African side; according to legend, formed by Hercules.

pill beetle NOUN a very common beetle, *Byrrhus pilula,* typical of the family *Byrrhidae,* that can feign death by withdrawing legs and antennae into grooves underneath the oval body.

pillbox ('pɪlˌbɒks) NOUN 1 a box for pills. 2 a small enclosed fortified emplacement, usually made of reinforced concrete. 3 a small round hat, now worn esp by women.

pill bug NOUN any of various woodlice of the genera *Armadillidium* and *Oniscus,* capable of rolling up into a ball when disturbed.

pillie ('pɪli) NOUN *Austral informal* a pilchard.

pillion ('pɪljən) NOUN 1 a seat or place behind the rider of a motorcycle, scooter, horse, etc. ◆ ADVERB 2 on a pillion: *to ride pillion.*
▷HISTORY C16: from Gaelic; compare Scottish *pillean,* Irish *pillīn* couch; related to Latin *pellis* skin

pilliwinks ('pɪlɪˌwɪŋks) PLURAL NOUN a medieval instrument of torture for the fingers and thumbs.
▷HISTORY C14: of uncertain origin

pillock ('pɪlək) NOUN *Brit slang* a stupid or annoying person.
▷HISTORY C14: from Scandinavian dialect *pillicock* penis

pillory ('pɪlərɪ) NOUN, *plural* **-ries.** 1 a wooden framework into which offenders were formerly locked by the neck and wrists and exposed to public abuse and ridicule. 2 exposure to public scorn or abuse. ◆ VERB **-ries, -rying, -ried.** (*tr*) 3 to expose to public scorn or ridicule. 4 to punish by putting in a pillory.
▷HISTORY C13: from Anglo-Latin *pillorium,* from Old French *pilori,* of uncertain origin; related to Provençal *espillori*

pillow (ˈpɪləʊ) NOUN 1 a cloth case stuffed with feathers, foam rubber, etc., used to support the head, esp during sleep. 2 Also called: **cushion.** a padded cushion or board on which pillow lace is made. 3 anything like a pillow in shape or function. ◆ VERB *(tr)* 4 to rest (one's head) on or as if on a pillow. 5 to serve as a pillow for.
▷**HISTORY** Old English *pylwe,* from Latin *pulvīnus* cushion; compare German *Pfühl*

pillow block NOUN *Machinery* a block that supports a journal bearing. Also called: **plummer block.**

pillowcase (ˈpɪləʊˌkeɪs) *or* **pillowslip** (ˈpɪləʊˌslɪp) NOUN a removable washable cover of cotton, linen, nylon, etc., for a pillow.

pillow fight NOUN a mock fight in which participants thump each other with pillows.

pillow lace NOUN lace made by winding thread around bobbins on a padded cushion or board. Compare **point lace.**

pillow lava NOUN lava that has solidified under water, having a characteristic structure comprising a series of close-fitting pillow-shaped masses.

pillow sham NOUN *Chiefly US* a decorative cover for a bed pillow.

pillow talk NOUN intimate conversation in bed.

pills (pɪlz) PLURAL NOUN a slang word for **testicles.**

pillwort (ˈpɪlˌwɜːt) NOUN a small Eurasian water fern, *Pilularia globulifera,* with globular spore-producing bodies and grasslike leaves.
▷**HISTORY** C19: from PILL[1] + WORT

pilocarpine (ˌpaɪləʊˈkɑːpaɪn, -pɪn) *or* **pilocarpin** (ˌpaɪləʊˈkɑːpɪn) NOUN an alkaloid extracted from the leaves of the jaborandi tree, formerly used to induce sweating. Formula: $C_{11}H_{16}N_2O_2$.
▷**HISTORY** C19: from New Latin *Pilocarpus* genus name, from Greek *pilos* hair + *karpos* fruit

pilomotor (ˌpaɪləʊˈməʊtə) ADJECTIVE *Physiol* causing movement of hairs: *pilomotor nerves.*

Pílos (ˈpilɔs) NOUN transliteration of the Modern Greek name for **Pylos.**

pilose (ˈpaɪləʊz) *or* **pilous** ADJECTIVE *Biology* covered with fine soft hairs: *pilose leaves.*
▷**HISTORY** C18: from Latin *pilōsus,* from *pilus* hair
▸**pilosity** (paɪˈlɒsɪtɪ) NOUN

pilot (ˈpaɪlət) NOUN 1 **a** a person who is qualified to operate an aircraft or spacecraft in flight. **b** *(as modifier): pilot error.* 2 **a** a person who is qualified to steer or guide a ship into or out of a port, river mouth, etc. **b** *(as modifier): a pilot ship.* 3 a person who steers a ship. 4 a person who acts as a leader or guide. 5 *Machinery* a guide, often consisting of a tongue or dowel, used to assist in joining two mating parts together. 6 *Machinery* a plug gauge for measuring an internal diameter. 7 *Films* a colour test strip accompanying black-and-white rushes from colour originals. 8 an experimental programme on radio or television. 9 See **pilot film.** 10 *(modifier)* used in or serving as a test or trial: *a pilot project.* 11 *(modifier)* serving as a guide: *a pilot beacon.* ◆ VERB *(tr)* 12 to act as pilot of. 13 to control the course of. 14 to guide or lead (a project, people, etc.).
▷**HISTORY** C16: from French *pilote,* from Medieval Latin *pilotus,* ultimately from Greek *pēdon* oar; related to Greek *pous* foot

pilotage (ˈpaɪlətɪdʒ) NOUN 1 the act of piloting an aircraft or ship. 2 a pilot's fee. 3 the navigation of an aircraft by the observation of ground features and use of charts.

pilot balloon NOUN a meteorological balloon used to observe air currents.

pilot bird NOUN a warbler of forest floors in SE Australia, *Pycnoptilus floccosus,* named from its alleged habit of accompanying the superb lyrebird.

pilot biscuit NOUN another term for **hardtack.**

pilot cloth NOUN a type of thick blue cloth used esp to make sailor's coats.

pilot engine NOUN a locomotive that leads one or more other locomotives at the head of a train of coaches or wagons.

pilot film NOUN a film of short duration serving as a guide to a projected series.

pilot fish NOUN 1 a small carangid fish, *Naucrates ductor,* of tropical and subtropical seas, marked with dark vertical bands: often accompanies sharks and other large fishes. 2 any of various similar or related fishes.

pilot house NOUN *Nautical* an enclosed structure on the bridge of a vessel from which it can be navigated; wheelhouse.

piloting (ˈpaɪlətɪŋ) NOUN 1 the navigational handling of a ship near land using buoys, soundings, landmarks, etc., or the finding of a ship's position by such means. 2 the occupation of a pilot.

pilot lamp NOUN a small light in an electric circuit or device that lights up when the circuit is closed or when certain conditions prevail.

pilot light NOUN 1 a small auxiliary flame that ignites the main burner of a gas appliance when the control valve opens. 2 a small electric light used as an indicator.

pilot officer NOUN the most junior commissioned rank in the British Royal Air Force and in certain other air forces.

pilot plant NOUN a small-scale industrial plant in which problems can be identified and solved before the full-scale plant is built.

pilot study NOUN a small-scale experiment or set of observations undertaken to decide how and whether to launch a full-scale project.

pilot whale NOUN any of several black toothed whales of the genus *Globicephala,* such as *G. melaena,* that occur in all seas except polar seas: family *Delphinidae.* Also called: **black whale, blackfish.**

pilous (ˈpaɪləs) ADJECTIVE a variant of **pilose.**

Pils (pɪlz, pɪls) NOUN a type of lager-like beer.
▷**HISTORY** C20: abbreviation of PILSNER

Pilsen (ˈpɪlzən) NOUN the German name for **Plzeň.**

Pilsner (ˈpɪlznə) *or* **Pilsener** NOUN a type of pale beer with a strong flavour of hops.
▷**HISTORY** named after PILSEN, where it was originally brewed

Piltdown man (ˈpɪltˌdaʊn) NOUN an advanced hominid postulated from fossil bones found in Sussex in 1912, but shown by modern dating methods in 1953 to be a hoax, which was perpetrated by a student museum assistant who was refused a wage.

pilule (ˈpɪljuːl) NOUN a small pill.
▷**HISTORY** C16: via French from Latin *pilula* little ball, from *pila* ball
▸ˈ**pilular** ADJECTIVE

pimento (pɪˈmentəʊ) NOUN, *plural* **-tos.** another name for **allspice** or **pimiento.**
▷**HISTORY** C17: from Spanish *pimiento* pepper plant, from Medieval Latin *pigmenta* spiced drink, from Latin *pigmentum* PIGMENT

pi meson NOUN another name for **pion.**

pimiento (pɪˈmjentəʊ, -ˈmen-) NOUN, *plural* **-tos.** a Spanish pepper, *Capsicum annuum,* with a red fruit used raw in salads, cooked as a vegetable, and as a stuffing for green olives. Also called: **pimento.**
▷**HISTORY** variant of PIMENTO

pimp[1] (pɪmp) NOUN 1 a man who solicits for a prostitute or brothel and lives off the earnings. 2 a man who procures sexual gratification for another; procurer; pander. ◆ VERB 3 *(intr)* to act as a pimp.
▷**HISTORY** C17: of unknown origin

pimp[2] (pɪmp) *Slang, chiefly Austral and NZ* ◆ NOUN 1 a spy or informer. ◆ VERB 2 *(intr; often foll by on)* to inform (on).
▷**HISTORY** of unknown origin

pimpernel (ˈpɪmpəˌnel, -nᵊl) NOUN 1 any of several plants of the primulaceous genus *Anagallis,* such as the scarlet pimpernel, typically having small star-shaped flowers. 2 any of several similar and related plants, such as *Lysimachia nemorum* (**yellow pimpernel**).
▷**HISTORY** C15: from Old French *pimpernelle,* ultimately from Latin *piper* PEPPER; compare Old English *pipeneale*

pimple (ˈpɪmpᵊl) NOUN 1 a small round usually inflamed swelling of the skin. 2 any of the bumps on the surface of a table tennis bat.
▷**HISTORY** C14: related to Old English *pipilian* to break out in spots; compare Latin *papula* pimple
▸ˈ**pimpled** ADJECTIVE ▸ˈ**pimply** ADJECTIVE ▸ˈ**pimpliness** NOUN

pin (pɪn) NOUN 1 **a** a short stiff straight piece of wire pointed at one end and either rounded or having a flattened head at the other: used mainly for fastening pieces of cloth, paper, etc., esp temporarily. **b** *(in combination): pinhole.* 2 short for **cotter pin, hairpin, panel pin, rolling pin** or **safety pin.** 3 an ornamental brooch, esp a narrow one. 4 a badge worn fastened to the clothing by a pin. 5 something of little or no importance (esp in the phrases **not care** *or* **give a pin (for)**). 6 a peg or dowel. 7 anything resembling a pin in shape, function, etc. 8 (in various bowling games) a usually club-shaped wooden object set up in groups as a target. 9 Also called: **cotter pin, safety pin.** a clip on a hand grenade that prevents its detonation until removed or released. 10 *Nautical* **a** See **belaying pin. b** the axle of a sheave. **c** the sliding closure for a shackle. 11 *Music* a metal tuning peg on a piano, the end of which is inserted into a detachable key by means of which it is turned. 12 *Surgery* a metal rod, esp of stainless steel, for holding together adjacent ends of fractured bones during healing. 13 *Chess* a position in which a piece is pinned against a more valuable piece or the king. 14 *Golf* the flagpole marking the hole on a green. 15 **a** the cylindrical part of a key that enters a lock. **b** the cylindrical part of a lock where this part of the key fits. 16 *Wrestling* a position in which a person is held tight or immobile, esp with both shoulders touching the ground. 17 a dovetail tenon used to make a dovetail joint. 18 (in Britain) a miniature beer cask containing 4½ gallons. 19 *(usually plural) Informal* a leg. 20 **be put to the pin on one's collar.** *Irish* to be forced to make an extreme effort. ◆ VERB **pins, pinning, pinned.** *(tr)* 21 to attach, hold, or fasten with or as if with a pin or pins. 22 to transfix with a pin, spear, etc. 23 (foll by *on*) *Informal* to place (the blame for something): *he pinned the charge on his accomplice.* 24 *Chess* to cause (an enemy piece) to be effectively immobilized by attacking it with a queen, rook, or bishop so that moving it would reveal a check or expose a more valuable piece to capture. 25 Also: **underpin.** to support (masonry), as by driving in wedges over a beam. ◆ See also **pin down.**
▷**HISTORY** Old English *pinn;* related to Old High German *pfinn,* Old Norse *pinni* nail

PIN (pɪn) NOUN ACRONYM FOR personal identification number: a number used by a holder of a cash card or credit card used in EFTPOS.

p-i-n ABBREVIATION FOR p-type, intrinsic, n-type: a form of construction of semiconductor devices.

pinaceous (paɪˈneɪʃəs) ADJECTIVE of, relating to, or belonging to the *Pinaceae,* a family of conifers with needle-like leaves: includes pine, spruce, fir, larch, and cedar.
▷**HISTORY** C19: via New Latin from Latin *pīnus* a pine

piña cloth (ˈpiːnjə) NOUN a fine fabric made from the fibres of the pineapple leaf.
▷**HISTORY** C19: from Spanish *piña* pineapple

piña colada (ˈpiːnjə kəˈlɑːdə) NOUN a drink consisting of pineapple juice, coconut, and rum.
▷**HISTORY** C20: from Spanish, literally: strained pineapple

pinafore (ˈpɪnəˌfɔː) NOUN 1 *Chiefly Brit* an apron, esp one with a bib. 2 *Chiefly Brit* short for **pinafore dress.** 3 *Chiefly US* an overdress buttoning at the back.
▷**HISTORY** C18: from PIN + AFORE

pinafore dress NOUN *Brit* a sleeveless dress worn over a blouse or sweater. Often shortened to: **pinafore.** US and Canadian name: **jumper.**

Pinar del Río (*Spanish* piˈnar ðel ˈrrio) NOUN a city in W Cuba: tobacco industry. Pop.: 128 570 (1994 est.).

pinaster (paɪˈnæstə, pɪ-) NOUN a Mediterranean pine tree, *Pinus pinaster,* with paired needles and prickly cones. Also called: **maritime** (*or* **cluster**) **pinaster.**
▷**HISTORY** C16: from Latin: wild pine, from *pīnus* pine

piñata (ˌpɪnˈjata) NOUN a papier-mâché party decoration filled with sweets, hung up during parties, and struck with a stick until it breaks open.
▷**HISTORY** Spanish, from Italian *pignatta,* probably from dialect *pigna,* from Latin *pinea* pine cone

pinball (ˈpɪnˌbɔːl) NOUN **a** a game in which the player shoots a small ball through several hazards on a table, electrically operated machine, etc. **b** (*as modifier*): *a pinball machine.*

pince-nez ('pæns,neɪ, 'pɪns-; *French* pɛ̃sne) NOUN, *plural* **pince-nez**. eyeglasses that are held in place only by means of a clip over the bridge of the nose.
▷**HISTORY** C19: French, literally: pinch-nose

pincer movement ('pɪnsə) NOUN a military tactical movement in which two columns of an army follow a curved route towards each other with the aim of isolating and surrounding an enemy. Also called: **envelopment**.

pincers ('pɪnsəz) PLURAL NOUN [1] Also called: **pair of pincers**. a gripping tool consisting of two hinged arms with handles at one end and, at the other, curved bevelled jaws that close on the workpiece: used esp for extracting nails. [2] the pair or pairs of jointed grasping appendages in lobsters and certain other arthropods.
▷**HISTORY** C14: from Old French *pinceour*, from Old French *pincier* to PINCH

pinch (pɪntʃ) VERB [1] to press (something, esp flesh) tightly between two surfaces, esp between a finger and the thumb (see **nip**[1]). [2] to confine, squeeze, or painfully press (toes, fingers, etc.) because of lack of space: *these shoes pinch.* [3] (*tr*) to cause stinging pain to: *the cold pinched his face.* [4] (*tr*) to make thin or drawn-looking, as from grief, lack of food, etc. [5] (usually foll by *on*) to provide (oneself or another person) with meagre allowances, amounts, etc. [6] **pinch pennies**. to live frugally because of meanness or to economize. [7] (*tr*) *Nautical* to sail (a sailing vessel) so close to the wind that her sails begin to luff and she loses way. [8] (*intr*; sometimes foll by *out*) (of a vein of ore) to narrow or peter out. [9] (usually foll by *off, out,* or *back*) to remove the tips of (buds, shoots, etc.) to correct or encourage growth. [10] (*tr*) *Informal* to steal or take without asking. [11] (*tr*) *Informal* to arrest. ◆ NOUN [12] a squeeze or sustained nip. [13] the quantity of a substance, such as salt, that can be taken between a thumb and finger. [14] a very small quantity. [15] a critical situation; predicament; emergency: *if it comes to the pinch we'll have to manage.* [16] (usually preceded by *the*) sharp, painful, or extreme stress, need, etc.: *feeling the pinch of poverty.* [17] See **pinch bar**. [18] *Slang* a robbery. [19] *Slang* a police raid or arrest. [20] **at a pinch**. if absolutely necessary. [21] **with a pinch** *or* **grain of salt**. without wholly believing; sceptically.
▷**HISTORY** C16: probably from Old Norman French *pinchier* (unattested); related to Old French *pincier* to pinch; compare Late Latin *punctiāre* to prick

pinch bar NOUN a crowbar with a lug formed on it to provide a fulcrum.

pinchbeck ('pɪntʃ,bɛk) NOUN [1] an alloy of copper and zinc, used as imitation gold. [2] a spurious or cheap imitation; sham. ◆ ADJECTIVE [3] made of pinchbeck. [4] sham, spurious, or cheap.
▷**HISTORY** C18 (the alloy), C19 (something spurious): after Christopher *Pinchbeck* (?1670–1732), English watchmaker who invented it

pinchcock ('pɪntʃ,kɒk) NOUN a clamp used to compress a flexible tube to control the flow of fluid through it.

pinch effect NOUN the constriction of a beam of charged particles, caused by a force on each particle due to its motion in the magnetic field generated by the movement of the other particles.

pinch-hit VERB **-hits, -hitting, -hit**. (*intr*) [1] *Baseball* to bat as a substitute for the scheduled batter. [2] *US and Canadian informal* to act as a substitute. [3] *Cricket* (of a batsman in a limited-overs match) to bat aggressively at the start of an innings in order to take advantage of fielding restrictions.
▸**pinch hitter** NOUN

pinchpenny ('pɪntʃ,pɛnɪ) ADJECTIVE [1] niggardly; miserly. ◆ NOUN, *plural* **-nies**. [2] a miserly person; niggard.

pinch point NOUN a traffic-calming measure in which the road narrows to one lane, with a sign indicating which oncoming driver should give way.

pin curl NOUN a small section of hair wound in a circle and secured with a hairpin to set it in a curl.

pincushion ('pɪn,kʊʃən) NOUN a small well-padded cushion in which pins are stuck ready for use.

pindan ('pɪn,dæn) NOUN [1] a desert region of Western Australia. [2] the vegetation growing in this region.
▷**HISTORY** from a native Australian language

Pindaric (pɪn'dærɪk) ADJECTIVE [1] of, relating to, or resembling the style of the Greek lyric poet Pindar (?518–?438 B.C.). [2] *Prosody* having a complex metrical structure, either regular or irregular. ◆ NOUN [3] See **Pindaric ode**.

Pindaric ode NOUN a form of ode associated with Pindar consisting of a triple unit or groups of triple units, with a strophe and an antistrophe of identical structure followed by an epode of a different structure. Often shortened to: **Pindaric**.

pindling ('pɪndlɪŋ) ADJECTIVE *Dialect* [1] *Western Brit* peevish or fractious. [2] *US* sickly or puny.
▷**HISTORY** C19: perhaps changed from *spindling*

pin down VERB (*tr, adverb*) [1] to force (someone) to make a decision or carry out a promise. [2] to define clearly: *he had a vague suspicion that he couldn't quite pin down.* [3] to confine to a place: *the fallen tree pinned him down.*

Pindus ('pɪndəs) NOUN a mountain range in central Greece between Epirus and Thessaly. Highest peak: Mount Smólikas, 2633 m (8639 ft.). Modern Greek name: **Píndhos** ('pinðɔs).

pine[1] (paɪn) NOUN [1] any evergreen resinous coniferous tree of the genus *Pinus*, of the N hemisphere, with long needle-shaped leaves and brown cones: family *Pinaceae*. See also **longleaf pine, nut pine, pitch pine, Scots pine**. [2] any other tree or shrub of the family *Pinaceae*. [3] the wood of any of these trees. [4] any of various similar but unrelated plants, such as ground pine and screw pine.
▷**HISTORY** Old English *pīn*, from Latin *pīnus* pine

pine[2] (paɪn) VERB [1] (*intr*; often foll by *for* or an infinitive) to feel great longing or desire; yearn. [2] (*intr*; often foll by *away*) to become ill, feeble, or thin through worry, longing, etc. [3] (*tr*) *Archaic* to mourn or grieve for.
▷**HISTORY** Old English *pīnian* to torture, from *pīn* pain, from Medieval Latin *pēna*, from Latin *poena* PAIN

pineal ('pɪnɪəl, paɪ'ni:əl) ADJECTIVE [1] resembling a pine cone. [2] of or relating to the pineal gland.
▷**HISTORY** C17: via French from Latin *pīnea* pine cone

pineal eye NOUN an outgrowth of the pineal gland that forms an eyelike structure on the top of the head in certain cold-blooded vertebrates.

pineal gland *or* **body** NOUN a pea-sized organ in the brain, situated beneath the posterior part of the corpus callosum, that secretes melatonin into the bloodstream. Technical names: **epiphysis, epiphysis cerebri**.

pineapple ('paɪn,æpᵊl) NOUN [1] a tropical American bromeliaceous plant, *Ananas comosus*, cultivated in the tropics for its large fleshy edible fruit. [2] the fruit of this plant, consisting of an inflorescence clustered around a fleshy axis and surmounted by a tuft of leaves. [3] *Military, slang* a hand grenade.
▷**HISTORY** C14 *pinappel* pine cone; C17: applied to the fruit because of its appearance

pineapple weed NOUN an Asian plant, *Matricaria matricarioides*, naturalized in Europe and North America, having greenish-yellow flower heads, and smelling of pineapple when crushed: family *Asteraceae* (composites).

pine cone NOUN the seed-producing structure of a pine tree. See **cone** (sense 3a).

pine end NOUN *Dialect* the gable or gable end of a building.

pine marten NOUN a marten, *Martes martes*, of N European and Asian coniferous woods, having dark brown fur with a creamy-yellow patch on the throat. See also **sweet marten**.

pinene ('paɪni:n) NOUN either of two isomeric terpenes, found in many essential oils and constituting the main part of oil of turpentine. The commonest structural isomer (α-**pinene**) is used in the manufacture of camphor, solvents, plastics, and insecticides. Formula: $C_{10}H_{16}$.
▷**HISTORY** C20: from PINE[1] + -ENE

pine needle NOUN any of the fine pointed leaves of a pine.

pine nut *or* **kernel** NOUN the edible seed of certain pine trees.

pinery ('paɪnərɪ) NOUN, *plural* **-neries**. [1] a place, esp a hothouse, where pineapples are grown. [2] a forest of pine trees, esp one cultivated for timber.

Pines (paɪnz) NOUN **Isle of**. the former name of the (Isle of) **Youth**.

pine tar NOUN a brown or black semisolid or viscous substance, produced by the destructive distillation of pine wood, used in roofing compositions, paints, medicines, etc.

pinetum (paɪ'ni:təm) NOUN, *plural* **-ta** (-tə). an area of land where pine trees and other conifers are grown.
▷**HISTORY** C19: from Latin, from *pīnus* PINE[1]

pin-eyed ADJECTIVE (of flowers, esp primulas) having the stigma in the mouth of the corolla, on the end of a long style with the stamens lower in the tube. Compare **thrum-eyed**.

pinfall ('pɪn,fɔ:l) NOUN *Wrestling* another name for **fall** (sense 48).

pinfeather ('pɪn,fɛðə) NOUN *Ornithol* a feather emerging from the skin and still enclosed in its horny sheath.

pinfish ('pɪn,fɪʃ) NOUN, *plural* **-fish** *or* **-fishes**. a small porgy, *Lagodon rhomboides*, occurring off the SE North American coast of the Atlantic. Also called: **sailor's choice**.
▷**HISTORY** so named because it has spines

pinfold ('pɪn,fəʊld) NOUN [1] **a** a pound for stray cattle. **b** a fold or pen for sheep or cattle. ◆ VERB [2] (*tr*) to gather or confine in or as if in a pinfold.
▷**HISTORY** Old English *pundfald*, from POUND[3] + FOLD[2]

ping (pɪŋ) NOUN [1] a short high-pitched resonant sound, as of a bullet striking metal or a sonar echo. ◆ VERB [2] (*intr*) to make such a noise.
▷**HISTORY** C19: of imitative origin
▸**'pinging** ADJECTIVE

pinger ('pɪŋə) NOUN a device that makes a pinging sound, esp one that can be preset to ring at a particular time.

pingo ('pɪŋgəʊ) NOUN, *plural* **-gos**. a mound of earth or gravel formed through pressure from a layer of water trapped between newly frozen ice and underlying permafrost in Arctic regions.
▷**HISTORY** C20: from Eskimo

Ping-Pong ('pɪŋ,pɒŋ) NOUN *Trademark* another name for **table tennis**. Also called: **ping pong**.

pinguid ('pɪŋgwɪd) ADJECTIVE fatty, oily, or greasy; soapy.
▷**HISTORY** C17: from Latin *pinguis* fat, rich
▸**pin'guidity** NOUN

pinhead ('pɪn,hɛd) NOUN [1] the head of a pin. [2] something very small. [3] *Informal* a stupid or contemptible person.

pinheaded ('pɪn,hɛdɪd) ADJECTIVE *Informal* stupid or silly.
▸**'pin,headedness** NOUN

pinhole ('pɪn,həʊl) NOUN [1] a small hole made with or as if with a pin. [2] *Archery* the exact centre of an archery target, in the middle of the gold zone.

pinhole camera NOUN a camera with a pinhole as an aperture instead of a lens.

pinion[1] ('pɪnjən) NOUN [1] *Chiefly poetic* a bird's wing. [2] the part of a bird's wing including the flight feathers. ◆ VERB (*tr*) [3] to hold or bind (the arms) of (a person) so as to restrain or immobilize him. [4] to confine or shackle. [5] to make (a bird) incapable of flight by removing that part of (the wing) from which the flight feathers grow.
▷**HISTORY** C15: from Old French *pignon* wing, from Latin *pinna* wing

pinion[2] ('pɪnjən) NOUN a cogwheel that engages with a larger wheel or rack, which it drives or by which it is driven.
▷**HISTORY** C17: from French *pignon* cogwheel, from Old French *peigne* comb, from Latin *pecten* comb; see PECTEN

Piniós (pi'njɔs) NOUN transliteration of the Modern Greek name for the **Salambria**.

pinite ('pɪnaɪt, 'paɪ-) NOUN a greyish-green or brown mineral containing amorphous aluminium and potassium sulphates.
▷**HISTORY** C19: from German *Pinit*, named after the *Pini* mine, Schneeberg, Saxony

pin joint NOUN a mechanical joint that will transmit axial load but will not transmit torque.

pink[1] (pɪŋk) NOUN [1] any of a group of colours

with a reddish hue that are of low to moderate saturation and can usually reflect or transmit a large amount of light; a pale reddish tint. 2 pink cloth or clothing: *dressed in pink.* 3 any of various Old World plants of the caryophyllaceous genus *Dianthus,* such as *D. plumarius* (**garden pink**), cultivated for their fragrant flowers. See also **carnation** (sense 1). 4 any of various plants of other genera, such as the moss pink. 5 the flower of any of these plants. 6 the highest or best degree, condition, etc. (esp in the phrases **in the pink of health, in the pink**). 7 **a** a huntsman's scarlet coat. **b** a huntsman who wears a scarlet coat. ◆ ADJECTIVE 8 of the colour pink. 9 *Brit informal* left-wing. 10 *US derogatory* **a** a sympathetic to or influenced by Communism. **b** leftist or radical, esp half-heartedly. 11 *Informal* of or relating to homosexuals or homosexuality: *the pink vote.* 12 (of a huntsman's coat) scarlet or red. ◆ VERB 13 (*intr*) another word for **knock** (sense 7).
▷HISTORY C16 (the flower), C18 (the colour): perhaps a shortening of PINKEYE
▸'**pinkish** ADJECTIVE ▸'**pinkness** NOUN ▸'**pinky** ADJECTIVE

pink² (pɪŋk) VERB (*tr*) 1 to prick lightly with a sword or rapier. 2 to decorate (leather, cloth, etc.) with a perforated or punched pattern. 3 to cut with pinking shears.
▷HISTORY C14: perhaps of Low German origin; compare Low German *pinken* to peck

pink³ (pɪŋk) NOUN a sailing vessel with a narrow overhanging transom.
▷HISTORY C15: from Middle Dutch *pinke,* of obscure origin

pink-collar ADJECTIVE of, relating to, or designating low-paid occupations traditionally associated with female workers. Compare **blue-collar, white-collar.**

pink elephants PLURAL NOUN a facetious name applied to hallucinations caused by drunkenness.

pinkeye ('pɪŋkˌaɪ) NOUN 1 Also called: **acute conjunctivitis.** an acute contagious inflammation of the conjunctiva of the eye, characterized by redness, discharge, etc.: usually caused by bacterial infection. 2 Also called: **infectious keratitis.** a similar condition affecting the cornea of horses and cattle.
▷HISTORY C16: partial translation of obsolete Dutch *pinck oogen* small eyes

pink-footed goose NOUN a Eurasian goose, *Anser brachyrhynchus,* having a reddish-brown head, pink legs, and a pink band on its black beak.

pink gin NOUN a mixture of gin and bitters.

pinkie *or* **pinky** ('pɪŋkɪ) NOUN, *plural* **-ies.** *Scot, US, and Canadian* the little finger.
▷HISTORY C19: from Dutch *pinkje,* diminutive of PINK¹; compare PINKEYE

pinking shears PLURAL NOUN scissors with a serrated edge on one or both blades, producing a wavy edge to material cut, thus preventing fraying.

pink noise NOUN noise containing a mixture of frequencies, but excluding higher frequencies.

pinko ('pɪŋkəʊ) NOUN, *plural* **-os** *or* **-oes.** *chiefly US derogatory* a person regarded as mildly left-wing.

pinkroot ('pɪŋkˌru:t) NOUN 1 any of several loganiaceous plants of the genus *Spigelia, esp S. marilandica,* of the southeastern US, having red-and-yellow flowers and pink roots. 2 the powdered root of this plant, used as a vermifuge. 3 a fungal disease of onions and related plants resulting in stunted growth and shrivelled pink roots.

pink salmon NOUN 1 any salmon having pale pink flesh, esp *Oncorhynchus gorbuscha,* of the Pacific Ocean. 2 the flesh of such a fish.

pink slip NOUN *US informal* a notice of redundancy issued to an employee.

Pinky bar NOUN *Trademark, NZ* a chocolate-covered marshmallow bar.

pin money NOUN 1 an allowance by a husband to his wife for personal expenditure. 2 money saved or earned to be used for incidental expenses.

pinna ('pɪnə) NOUN, *plural* **-nae** (-ni:) *or* **-nas.** 1 any leaflet of a pinnate compound leaf. 2 *Zoology* a feather, wing, fin, or similarly shaped part. 3 another name for **auricle** (sense 2).
▷HISTORY C18: via New Latin from Latin: wing, feather, fin

pinnace ('pɪnɪs) NOUN any of various kinds of ship's tender.
▷HISTORY C16: from French *pinace,* apparently from Old Spanish *pinaza,* literally: something made of pine, ultimately from Latin *pīnus* pine

pinnacle ('pɪnəkᵊl) NOUN 1 the highest point or level, esp of fame, success, etc. 2 a towering peak, as of a mountain. 3 a slender upright structure in the form of a cone, pyramid, or spire on the top of a buttress, gable, or tower. ◆ VERB (*tr*) 4 to set on or as if on a pinnacle. 5 to furnish with a pinnacle or pinnacles. 6 to crown with a pinnacle.
▷HISTORY C14: via Old French from Late Latin *pinnāculum* a peak, from Latin *pinna* wing

pinnate ('pɪneɪt, 'pɪnɪt) *or* **pinnated** ADJECTIVE 1 like a feather in appearance. 2 (of compound leaves) having the leaflets growing opposite each other in pairs on either side of the stem.
▷HISTORY C18: from Latin *pinnātus,* from *pinna* feather
▸'**pinnately** ADVERB ▸**pin'nation** NOUN

pinnati- COMBINING FORM pinnate or pinnately: *pinnatifid.*

pinnatifid (pɪ'nætɪfɪd) ADJECTIVE (of leaves) pinnately divided into lobes reaching more than halfway to the midrib.
▸**pin'natifidly** ADVERB

pinnatipartite (pɪˌnætɪ'pɑ:taɪt) ADJECTIVE (of leaves) pinnately divided into lobes reaching just over halfway to the midrib.

pinnatiped (pɪ'nætɪˌpɛd) ADJECTIVE (of birds) having lobate feet.

pinnatisect (pɪ'nætɪˌsɛkt) ADJECTIVE (of leaves) pinnately divided almost to the midrib but not into separate leaflets.

pinner ('pɪnə) NOUN 1 a person or thing that pins. 2 a small dainty apron. 3 a cap with two long flaps pinned on.

pinniped ('pɪnɪˌpɛd) *or* **pinnipedian** (ˌpɪnɪ'pi:dɪən) ADJECTIVE 1 of, relating to, or belonging to the *Pinnipedia,* an order of aquatic placental mammals having a streamlined body and limbs specialized as flippers: includes seals, sea lions, and the walrus. ◆ NOUN 2 any pinniped animal. ◆ Compare **fissiped.**
▷HISTORY C19: from New Latin *pinnipēs,* from Latin *pinna* feather, fin + *pēs* foot

pinnule ('pɪnju:l) *or* **pinnula** ('pɪnjʊlə) NOUN, *plural* **pinnules** *or* **pinnulae** ('pɪnjʊˌli:). 1 any of the lobes of a leaflet of a pinnate compound leaf, which is itself pinnately divided. 2 *Zoology* any feather-like part, such as any of the arms of a sea lily.
▷HISTORY C16: from Latin *pinnula,* diminutive of *pinna* feather
▸'**pinnular** ADJECTIVE

pinny ('pɪnɪ) NOUN, *plural* **-nies.** a child's or informal name for **pinafore** (sense 1).

pinochle, penuchle, penuckle, *or* **pinocle** ('pi:nʌkᵊl) NOUN 1 a card game for two to four players similar to bezique. 2 the combination of queen of spades and jack of diamonds in this game.
▷HISTORY C19: of unknown origin

pinole (pɪ'nəʊlɪ) NOUN (in the southwestern United States) flour made of parched ground corn, mesquite beans, sugar, etc.
▷HISTORY from American Spanish, from Nahuatl

pinotage ('pɪnətɑ:ʒ) NOUN 1 a red grape variety of South Africa, a cross between the Pinot Noir and the Hermitage. 2 any of the red wines made from this grape.

Pinot Grigio ('pi:nəʊ 'gri:dʒəʊ) NOUN 1 a variety of grape, grown in Italy for wine-making. 2 any of the white Italian wines made from this grape.
▷HISTORY Italian *grigio* grey

Pinot Noir ('pi:nəʊ nwɑ:) NOUN 1 a variety of black grape, grown esp for wine-making. 2 any of the red wines made from this grape.
▷HISTORY French

pinpoint ('pɪnˌpɔɪnt) VERB (*tr*) 1 to locate or identify exactly: *to pinpoint a problem; to pinpoint a place on a map.* ◆ NOUN 2 an insignificant or trifling thing. 3 the point of a pin. 4 (*modifier*) exact: *a pinpoint aim.*

pinprick ('pɪnˌprɪk) NOUN 1 a slight puncture made by or as if by a pin. 2 a small irritation. ◆ VERB 3 (*tr*) to puncture with or as if with a pin.

pin rail NOUN *Nautical* a strong wooden rail or bar containing holes for belaying pins to which lines are fastened on sailing vessels. Compare **fife rail.**

pins and needles NOUN (*functioning as singular*) *Informal* 1 a tingling sensation in the fingers, toes, legs, etc., caused by the return of normal blood circulation after its temporary impairment. 2 **on pins and needles.** in a state of anxious suspense or nervous anticipation.

Pinsk (*Russian* pinsk) NOUN a city in SW Belarus: capital of a principality (13th–14th centuries). Pop.: 132 000 (1998 est.).

pinstripe ('pɪnˌstraɪp) NOUN (in textiles) **a** a very narrow stripe in fabric or the fabric itself, used esp for men's suits. **b** (*as modifier*): *a pinstripe suit.*

pinswell ('pɪnˌswɛl) NOUN *Southwest English dialect* a small boil.

pint (paɪnt) NOUN 1 a unit of liquid measure of capacity equal to one eighth of a gallon. 1 Brit pint is equal to 0.568 litre, 1 US pint to 0.473 litre. 2 a unit of dry measure of capacity equal to one half of a quart. 1 US dry pint is equal to one sixty-fourth of a US bushel or 0.5506 litre. 3 a measure having such a capacity. 4 *Brit informal* **a** a pint of beer. **b** a drink of beer: *he's gone out for a pint.*
▷HISTORY C14: from Old French *pinte,* of uncertain origin; perhaps from Medieval Latin *pincta* marks used in measuring liquids, ultimately from Latin *pingere* to paint; compare Middle Low German, Middle Dutch *pinte*

pinta¹ ('pɪntə) NOUN a tropical infectious skin disease caused by the bacterium *Treponema carateum* and characterized by the formation of papules and loss of pigmentation in circumscribed areas. Also called: **mal de pinto.**
▷HISTORY C19: from American Spanish, from Spanish: spot, ultimately from Latin *pictus* painted, from *pingere* to paint

pinta² ('paɪntə) NOUN *Informal* a pint of milk.
▷HISTORY C20: phonetic rendering of *pint of*

Pinta ('pɪntə) NOUN **the.** one of the three ships commanded by Columbus on his first voyage to America (1492).

pintadera (ˌpɪntə'dɛərə) NOUN a decorative stamp, usually made of clay, found in the Neolithic of the E Mediterranean and in many American cultures.
▷HISTORY from Spanish, literally: an instrument for making decorations on bread, from *pintado* mottled, from *pintar* to PAINT

pintado petrel (pɪn'tɑ:dəʊ) NOUN another name for **Cape pigeon.**
▷HISTORY C19: Portuguese: past participle of *pintar* to paint, referring to the mottled coloration

pintail ('pɪnˌteɪl) NOUN, *plural* **-tails** *or* **-tail.** a greyish-brown duck, *Anas acuta,* with slender pointed wings and a pointed tail.

Pinteresque (ˌpɪntər'ɛsk) ADJECTIVE reminiscent of the plays of Harold Pinter, the English dramatist (born 1930), noted for their equivocal and halting dialogue.

pintle ('pɪntᵊl) NOUN 1 a pin or bolt forming the pivot of a hinge. 2 the link bolt, hook, or pin on a vehicle's towing bracket. 3 the needle or plunger of the injection valve of an oil engine.
▷HISTORY Old English *pintel* penis

pinto ('pɪntəʊ) *US and Canadian* ◆ ADJECTIVE 1 marked with patches of white; piebald. ◆ NOUN, *plural* **-tos.** 2 a pinto horse.
▷HISTORY C19: from American Spanish (originally: painted, spotted), ultimately from Latin *pingere* to paint

pinto bean NOUN a variety of kidney bean that has mottled seeds and is grown for food and fodder in the southwestern US.

pint-size *or* **pint-sized** ADJECTIVE *Informal* very small; tiny.

Pintubi ('pɪntəbɪ) NOUN 1 (*plural* **-bi** *or* **-bis**) an Aboriginal people of the southern border area of Western Australia and the Northern Territory. 2 the language of this people.

pin tuck NOUN a narrow ornamental fold used esp on shirt fronts and dress bodices.

pin-up NOUN 1 *Informal* **a** a picture of a sexually attractive person, esp when partially or totally undressed. **b** (*as modifier*): *a pin-up magazine.* 2 *Slang* a person who has appeared in such a picture. 3 a photograph of a famous personality. [4] (*modifier*) *US* designed to be hung from a wall: *a pin-up lamp.*

pinwheel ('pɪn,wiːl) NOUN [1] another name for **Catherine wheel** (sense 1). [2] a cogwheel whose teeth are formed by small pins projecting either axially or radially from the rim of the wheel. [3] the US and Canadian name for **windmill** (sense 3).

pinwork ('pɪn,wɜːk) NOUN (in needlepoint lace) the fine raised stitches.

pinworm ('pɪn,wɜːm) NOUN a parasitic nematode worm, *Enterobius vermicularis,* infecting the colon, rectum, and anus of humans: family *Oxyuridae.* Also called: **threadworm.**

pin wrench NOUN a wrench fitted with a cylindrical pin that registers in a hole in the part to be rotated, used to improve the application of the turning moment.

pinxit *Latin* ('pɪŋksɪt) he (or she) painted it: an inscription sometimes found on paintings following the artist's name.

piny ('paɪnɪ) ADJECTIVE **pinier, piniest.** of, resembling, or covered with pine trees.

Pinyin ('pɪn'jɪn) NOUN a system of romanized spelling developed in China in 1958: used to transliterate Chinese characters into the Roman alphabet.

piolet (pjəʊ'leɪ) NOUN a type of ice axe.
▷HISTORY C19: from French (Savoy) dialect *piola* axe

pion ('paɪɒn) *or* **pi meson** NOUN *Physics* a meson having a positive or negative charge and a rest mass 273.13 times that of the electron, or no charge and a rest mass 264.14 times that of the electron.
▷HISTORY C20: from Greek letter PI[1] + ON

pioneer (,paɪə'nɪə) NOUN [1] **a** a colonist, explorer, or settler of a new land, region, etc. **b** (*as modifier*): *a pioneer wagon.* [2] an innovator or developer of something new. [3] *Military* a member of an infantry group that digs entrenchments, makes roads, etc. [4] *Ecology* the first species of plant or animal to colonize an area of bare ground. ◆ VERB [5] to be a pioneer (in or of). [6] (*tr*) to initiate, prepare, or open up: *to pioneer a medical programme.*
▷HISTORY C16: from Old French *paonier* infantryman, from *paon* PAWN[2]; see also PEON[1]

Pioneer[1] (,paɪə'nɪə) NOUN a total abstainer from alcoholic drink, esp a member of the **Pioneer Total Abstinence Association,** a society devoted to abstention.

Pioneer[2] (,paɪə'nɪə) NOUN any of a series of US spacecraft that studied the solar system, esp **Pioneer 10,** which made the first flyby of Jupiter (1973), and **Pioneer 11,** which made the first flyby of Saturn (1979).

pious ('paɪəs) ADJECTIVE [1] having or expressing reverence for a god or gods; religious; devout. [2] marked by reverence. [3] marked by false reverence; sanctimonious. [4] sacred; not secular. [5] *Archaic* having or expressing devotion for one's parents or others.
▷HISTORY C17: from Latin *pius,* related to *piāre* to expiate
▸'**piously** ADVERB ▸'**piousness** NOUN

pip[1] (pɪp) NOUN [1] the seed of a fleshy fruit, such as an apple or pear. [2] any of the segments marking the surface of a pineapple. [3] a rootstock or flower of the lily of the valley or certain other plants.
▷HISTORY C18: short for PIPPIN

pip[2] (pɪp) NOUN [1] a short high-pitched sound, a sequence of which can act as a time signal, esp on radio. [2] a radar blip. [3] **a** a spot or single device, such as a spade, diamond, heart, or club on a playing card. **b** any of the spots on dice or dominoes. [4] *Informal* the emblem worn on the shoulder by junior officers in the British Army, indicating their rank. Also called: **star.** ◆ VERB **pips, pipping, pipped.** [5] (of a young bird) **a** (*intr*) to chirp; peep. **b** to pierce (the shell of its egg) while hatching. [6] (*intr*) to make a short high-pitched sound.
▷HISTORY C16 (in the sense: spot or speck); C17 (vb); C20 (in the sense: short high-pitched sound): of obscure, probably imitative origin; senses 1 and 5 are probably related to PEEP[2]

pip[3] (pɪp) NOUN [1] a contagious disease of poultry characterized by the secretion of thick mucus in the mouth and throat. [2] *Facetious slang* a minor human ailment. [3] *Brit, Austral, NZ & S African slang* a bad temper or depression (esp in the phrase **give (someone) the pip**). [4] **get** *or* **have the pip.** *NZ informal* to sulk. ◆ VERB **pips, pipping, pipped.** [5] *Brit slang* to cause to be annoyed or depressed.
▷HISTORY C15: from Middle Dutch *pippe,* ultimately from Latin *pituita* phlegm; see PITUITARY

pip[4] (pɪp) VERB **pips, pipping, pipped.** (*tr*) *Brit slang* [1] to wound or kill, esp with a gun. [2] to defeat (a person), esp when his success seems certain (often in the phrase **pip at the post**). [3] to blackball or ostracize.
▷HISTORY C19 (originally in the sense: to blackball): probably from PIP[2]

pipa ('piːpə) NOUN a tongueless South American toad, *Pipa pipa,* that carries its young in pits in the skin of its back.
▷HISTORY C18: from Surinam dialect, probably of African origin

pipage ('paɪpɪdʒ) NOUN [1] pipes collectively. [2] conveyance by pipes. [3] the money charged for such conveyance.

pipal ('paɪpᵊl) NOUN a variant of **peepul.**

pipe[1] (paɪp) NOUN [1] a long tube of metal, plastic, etc., used to convey water, oil, gas, etc. [2] a long tube or case. [3] **a** an object made in any of various shapes and sizes, consisting of a small bowl with an attached tubular stem, in which tobacco or other substances are smoked. **b** (*as modifier*): *a pipe bowl.* [4] Also called: **pipeful.** the amount of tobacco that fills the bowl of a pipe. [5] *Zoology, botany* any of various hollow organs, such as the respiratory passage of certain animals. [6] **a** any musical instrument whose sound production results from the vibration of an air column in a simple tube. **b** any of the tubular devices on an organ, in which air is made to vibrate either directly, as in a flue pipe, or by means of a reed. [7] an obsolete three-holed wind instrument, held in the left hand while played and accompanied by the tabor. See **tabor.** [8] **the pipes.** See **bagpipes.** [9] a shrill voice or sound, as of a bird. [10] **a** a boatswain's pipe. **b** the sound it makes. [11] (*plural*) *Informal* the respiratory tract or vocal cords. [12] *Metallurgy* a conical hole in the head of an ingot, made by escaping gas as the metal cools. [13] a cylindrical vein of rich ore, such as one of the vertical diamond-bearing veins at Kimberley, South Africa. [14] Also called: **volcanic pipe.** a vertical cylindrical passage in a volcano through which molten lava is forced during eruption. [15] *US slang* something easy to do, esp a simple course in college. [16] **put that in your pipe and smoke it.** *Informal* accept that fact if you can. ◆ VERB [17] to play (music) on a pipe. [18] (*tr*) to summon or lead by a pipe: *to pipe the dancers.* [19] to utter (something) shrilly. [20] **a** to signal orders to (the crew) by a boatswain's pipe. **b** (*tr*) to signal the arrival or departure of: *to pipe the admiral aboard.* [21] (*tr*) to convey (water, gas, etc.) by a pipe or pipes. [22] (*tr*) to provide with pipes. [23] (*tr*) to trim (an article, esp of clothing) with piping. [24] (*tr*) to force (cream, icing, etc.) through a shaped nozzle to decorate food. ◆ See also **pipe down, pipe up.**
▷HISTORY Old English *pīpe* (n), *pīpian* (vb), ultimately from Latin *pīpāre* to chirp
▸'**pipeless** ADJECTIVE ▸'**pipy** ADJECTIVE

pipe[2] (paɪp) NOUN [1] a large cask for wine, oil, etc. [2] a measure of capacity for wine equal to four barrels. 1 pipe is equal to 126 US gallons or 105 Brit gallons. [3] a cask holding this quantity with its contents.
▷HISTORY C14: via Old French (in the sense: tube, tubular vessel), ultimately from Latin *pīpāre* to chirp; compare PIPE[1]

pipe bomb NOUN a small explosive device hidden in a pipe or drain, detonated by means of a timer.

pipeclay ('paɪp,kleɪ) NOUN [1] a fine white pure clay, used in the manufacture of tobacco pipes and pottery and for whitening leather and similar materials. ◆ VERB [2] (*tr*) to whiten with pipeclay.

pipe cleaner NOUN a short length of thin wires twisted so as to hold tiny tufts of yarn: used to clean the stem of a tobacco pipe.

piped music NOUN light popular music prerecorded and played through amplifiers in a shop, restaurant, factory, etc., as background music. See also **Muzak.**

pipe down VERB (*intr, adverb*) *Informal* to stop talking, making noise, etc.

pipe dream NOUN a fanciful or impossible plan or hope.
▷HISTORY alluding to dreams produced by smoking an opium pipe

pipefish ('paɪp,fɪʃ) NOUN, *plural* **-fish** *or* **-fishes.** any of various teleost fishes of the genera *Nerophis, Syngnathus,* etc., having a long tubelike snout and an elongated body covered with bony plates: family *Syngnathidae.* Also called: **needlefish.**

pipefitting ('paɪp,fɪtɪŋ) NOUN [1] **a** the act or process of bending, cutting to length, and joining pipes. **b** the branch of plumbing involving this. [2] the threaded gland nuts, unions, adaptors, etc., used for joining pipes.
▸'**pipe,fitter** NOUN

pipe jacking NOUN a method of laying underground pipelines by assembling the pipes at the foot of an access shaft and pushing them through the ground.

pipeline ('paɪp,laɪn) NOUN [1] a long pipe, esp underground, used to transport oil, natural gas, etc., over long distances. [2] a medium of communication, esp a private one. [3] **in the pipeline.** in the process of being completed, delivered, or produced. ◆ VERB (*tr*) [4] to convey by pipeline. [5] to supply with a pipeline.

pipe major NOUN the noncommissioned officer, generally of warrant officer's rank, who is responsible for the training, duty, and discipline of a military or civilian pipe band.

pip-emma ('pɪp'ɛmə) ADVERB *Old-fashioned* in the afternoon; p.m. Compare **ack-emma.**
▷HISTORY World War I phonetic alphabet for P, M

pipe organ NOUN another name for **organ** (the musical instrument). Compare **reed organ.**

piper ('paɪpə) NOUN [1] a person who plays a pipe or bagpipes. [2] **pay the piper and call the tune.** to bear the cost of an undertaking and control it.

piperaceous (,pɪpə'reɪʃəs) ADJECTIVE of, relating to, or belonging to the *Piperaceae,* a family of pungent tropical shrubs and climbing flowering plants: includes pepper, betel, and cubeb.
▷HISTORY C17: via New Latin from Latin *piper* PEPPER

piperazine (pɪ'pɛrə,ziːn, -zɪn) NOUN a white crystalline deliquescent heterocyclic nitrogen compound used as an insecticide, corrosion inhibitor, and veterinary anthelmintic. Formula: $C_4H_{10}N_2$.

piperidine (pɪ'pɛrɪ,diːn, -dɪn) NOUN a colourless liquid heterocyclic compound with a peppery ammoniacal odour: used in making rubbers and curing epoxy resins. Formula: $C_5H_{11}N$.

piperine ('pɪpə,raɪn, -rɪn) NOUN a crystalline insoluble alkaloid that is the active ingredient of pepper, used as a flavouring and as an insecticide. Formula: $C_{17}H_{19}NO_3$.
▷HISTORY C19: from Latin *piper* PEPPER

pipe roll NOUN *History* an annual record of the accounts of a sheriff or other minister of the crown kept at the British Exchequer from the 12th to the 19th centuries. Also called: **the Great Roll of the Exchequer.**
▷HISTORY C17: from PIPE[1] and ROLL; perhaps from documents being rolled into a pipe shape

piperonal ('pɪpərəʊ,næl) NOUN a white fragrant aldehyde used in flavourings, perfumery, and suntan lotions. Formula: $C_8H_6O_3$. Also called: **heliotropin.**

pipes of Pan PLURAL NOUN another term for **panpipes.**

pipestone ('paɪp,stəʊn) NOUN a variety of consolidated red clay used by American Indians to make tobacco pipes.

pipette (pɪ'pɛt) NOUN [1] a calibrated glass tube drawn to a fine bore at one end, filled by sucking liquid into the bulb, and used to transfer or measure known volumes of liquid. ◆ VERB [2] (*tr*) to transfer or measure out (a liquid) using a pipette.
▷HISTORY C19: via French: little pipe, from *pipe* PIPE[1]

pipe up VERB (*intr, adverb*) [1] to commence singing or playing a musical instrument: *the band piped up.* [2] to speak up, esp in a shrill voice.

pipewort ('paɪp,wɜːt) NOUN a perennial plant, *Eriocaulon septangulare,* of wet places in W Republic of Ireland, the Scottish Hebrides, and the eastern

US, having a twisted flower stalk and a greenish-grey scaly flower head: family *Eriocaulaceae.*

pipi ('pɪpi:) NOUN, *plural* **pipi** *or* **pipis**. any of various shellfishes, esp *Plebidonax deltoides* of Australia or *Mesodesma novae-zelandiae* of New Zealand.
▷HISTORY Maori

piping ('paɪpɪŋ) NOUN [1] pipes collectively, esp pipes formed into a connected system, as in the plumbing of a house. [2] a cord of icing, whipped cream, etc., often used to decorate desserts and cakes. [3] a thin strip of covered cord or material, used to edge hems, etc. [4] the sound of a pipe or a set of bagpipes. [5] the art or technique of playing a pipe or bagpipes. [6] a shrill voice or sound, esp a whistling sound. ◆ ADJECTIVE [7] making a shrill sound. [8] *Archaic* relating to the pipe (associated with peace), as opposed to martial instruments, such as the fife or trumpet. ◆ ADVERB [9] **piping hot.** extremely hot.

pipistrelle (ˌpɪpɪ'strɛl) NOUN any of numerous small brownish insectivorous bats of the genus *Pipistrellus,* occurring in most parts of the world: family *Vespertilionidae.*
▷HISTORY C18: via French from Italian *pipistrello,* from Latin *vespertīliō* a bat, from *vesper* evening, because of its nocturnal habits

pipit ('pɪpɪt) NOUN any of various songbirds of the genus *Anthus* and related genera, having brownish speckled plumage and a long tail: family *Motacillidae.* Also called: **titlark.**
▷HISTORY C18: probably of imitative origin

pipiwharauroa ('pi:pi:ˌfæræu:ˌrɔ:ə) NOUN *NZ* a Pacific migratory bird with a metallic green-gold plumage.

pipkin ('pɪpkɪn) NOUN [1] a small metal or earthenware vessel. [2] another name for **piggin.**
▷HISTORY C16: perhaps a diminutive of PIPE²; see -KIN

pippin ('pɪpɪn) NOUN [1] any of several varieties of eating apple with a rounded oblate shape. [2] the seed of any of these fruits.
▷HISTORY C13: from Old French *pepin,* of uncertain origin

pipsissewa (pɪp'sɪsəwə) NOUN any of several ericaceous plants of the Asian and American genus *Chimaphila,* having jagged evergreen leaves and white or pinkish flowers. Also called: **wintergreen.**
▷HISTORY C19: from Cree *pipisisikweu,* literally: it breaks it into pieces, so called because it was believed to be efficacious in treating bladder stones

pipsqueak ('pɪpˌskwi:k) NOUN *Informal* a person or thing that is insignificant or contemptible.
▷HISTORY C20: from PIP² + SQUEAK

piquant ('pi:kənt, -kɑ:nt) ADJECTIVE [1] having an agreeably pungent or tart taste. [2] lively or stimulating to the mind.
▷HISTORY C16: from French (literally: prickling), from *piquer* to prick, goad; see PIQUE¹
▸'**piquancy** *or* (*less commonly*) '**piquantness** NOUN
▸'**piquantly** ADVERB

pique¹ (pi:k) NOUN [1] a feeling of resentment or irritation, as from having one's pride wounded. ◆ VERB **piques, piquing, piqued.** (*tr*) [2] to cause to feel resentment or irritation. [3] to excite or arouse. [4] (foll by *on* or *upon*) to pride or congratulate (oneself).
▷HISTORY C16: from French, from *piquer* to prick, sting; see PICK¹

pique² (pi:k) *Piquet* ◆ NOUN [1] a score of 30 points made by a player from a combination of cards held before play begins and from play while his opponent's score is nil. ◆ VERB [2] to score a pique (against).
▷HISTORY C17: from French *pic,* of uncertain origin

piqué ('pi:keɪ) NOUN a close-textured fabric of cotton, silk, or spun rayon woven with lengthwise ribs.
▷HISTORY C19: from French *piqué* pricked, from *piquer* to prick

piquet (pɪ'kɛt, -'keɪ) NOUN a card game for two people playing with a reduced pack and scoring points for card combinations and tricks won.
▷HISTORY C17: from French, of unknown origin; compare PIQUE²

Pir (pɪr) NOUN a title given to Sufi masters.
▷HISTORY Persian

piracy ('paɪrəsɪ) NOUN, *plural* **-cies.** [1] *Brit* robbery on the seas within admiralty jurisdiction. [2] a felony, such as robbery or hijacking, committed aboard a ship or aircraft. [3] the unauthorized use or appropriation of patented or copyrighted material, ideas, etc.
▷HISTORY C16: from Anglo-Latin *pirātia,* from Late Greek *peirāteia;* see PIRATE

Piraeus *or* **Peiraeus** (paɪ'ri:əs, pɪ'reɪ-) NOUN a port in SE Greece, adjoining Athens: the country's chief port; founded in the 5th century B.C. as the port of Athens. Pop.: 169 622 (1991). Modern Greek name: **Piraiévs** (ˌpirɛ'ɛfs).

piragua (pɪ'rɑ:gwə, -'ræg-) NOUN another word for **pirogue.**
▷HISTORY C17: via Spanish from Carib: dugout canoe

piranha *or* **piraña** (pɪ'rɑ:njə) NOUN any of various small freshwater voracious fishes of the genus *Serrasalmus* and related genera, of tropical America, having strong jaws and sharp teeth: family *Characidae* (characins).
▷HISTORY C19: via Portuguese from Tupi: fish with teeth, from *pirá* fish + *sainha* tooth

pirate ('paɪrɪt) NOUN [1] a person who commits piracy. [2] **a** a vessel used by pirates. **b** (*as modifier*): *a pirate ship.* [3] a person who illicitly uses or appropriates someone else's literary, artistic, or other work. [4] **a** a person or group of people who broadcast illegally. **b** (*as modifier*): *a pirate radio station.* ◆ VERB [5] (*tr*) to use, appropriate, or reproduce (artistic work, ideas, etc.) illicitly.
▷HISTORY C15: from Latin *pīrāta,* from Greek *peirātēs* one who attacks, from *peira* an attempt, attack
▸**piratical** (paɪ'rætɪkᵊl) *or* **pi'ratic** ADJECTIVE ▸**pi'ratically** ADVERB

piri-piri (ˌpɪrɪ'pɪrɪ) NOUN a hot sauce, of Portuguese colonial origin, made from red chilli peppers.
▷HISTORY from a Bantu language: literally, pepper

Pirithoüs (paɪ'rɪθəʊəs) NOUN *Greek myth* a prince of the Lapiths, who accomplished many great deeds with his friend Theseus.

pirn (pɜ:n; *Scot* pɪrn) NOUN *Scot* [1] a reel or bobbin. [2] (in weaving) the spool of a shuttle. [3] a fishing reel.
▷HISTORY C15: of uncertain origin

pirog (pɪ'rəʊg) NOUN, *plural* **-rogi** (-'rəʊgɪ). a large pie filled with meat, vegetables, etc.
▷HISTORY from Russian: pie

pirogue (pɪ'rəʊg) *or* **piragua** NOUN any of various kinds of dugout canoes.
▷HISTORY C17: via French from Spanish PIRAGUA

pirouette (ˌpɪrʊ'ɛt) NOUN [1] a body spin, esp in dancing, on the toes or the ball of the foot. ◆ VERB [2] (*intr*) to perform a pirouette.
▷HISTORY C18: from French, from Old French *pirouet* spinning top; related to Italian *pirolo* little peg

pirozhki *or* **piroshki** (pɪ'rɒʃkɪ) PLURAL NOUN, *singular* **pirozhok** ('pɪrəˌʒɒk). small triangular pastries filled with meat, vegetables, etc.
▷HISTORY C20: from Russian, from *pirozhók,* diminutive of PIROG

Pisa ('pi:zə; *Italian* 'pi:sa) NOUN a city in Tuscany, NW Italy, near the mouth of the River Arno: flourishing maritime republic (11th–12th centuries), contains a university (1343), a cathedral (1063), and the Leaning Tower (begun in 1174 and about 5 m (17 ft.) from perpendicular); tourism. Pop.: 102 150 (1990).

pis aller *French* (piz ale) NOUN a last resort; stopgap.
▷HISTORY literally: (at) the worst going

piscary ('pɪskərɪ) NOUN, *plural* **-ries.** [1] a place where fishing takes place. [2] the right to fish in certain waters.
▷HISTORY C15: from Latin *piscārius* fishing, from *piscis* a fish

piscatorial (ˌpɪskə'tɔ:rɪəl) *or* **piscatory** ('pɪskətərɪ, -trɪ) ADJECTIVE [1] of or relating to fish, fishing, or fishermen. [2] devoted to fishing.
▷HISTORY C19: from Latin *piscātōrius,* from *piscātor* fisherman
▸ˌ**pisca'torially** ADVERB

Pisces ('paɪsi:z, 'pɪ-) NOUN, *Latin genitive* **Piscium** ('paɪsɪəm). [1] *Astronomy* a faint extensive zodiacal constellation lying between Aquarius and Aries on the ecliptic. [2] *Astrology* **a** Also called: **the Fishes.** the twelfth sign of the zodiac, symbol ♓, having a mutable water classification and ruled by the planets Jupiter and Neptune. The sun is in this sign between about Feb. 19 and March 20. **b** a person born when the sun is in this sign. [3] **a** a taxonomic group that comprises all fishes. See **fish** (sense 1). **b** a taxonomic group that comprises the bony fishes only. See **teleost.** ◆ ADJECTIVE [4] *Astrology* born under or characteristic of Pisces. ◆ Also (for senses 2b, 4): **Piscean** ('paɪsɪən).
▷HISTORY C14: Latin: the fishes

pisci- COMBINING FORM fish: *pisciculture.*
▷HISTORY from Latin *piscis*

pisciculture ('pɪsɪˌkʌltʃə) NOUN the rearing and breeding of fish under controlled conditions.
▸ˌ**pisci'cultural** ADJECTIVE ▸ˌ**pisci'culturally** ADVERB
▸ˌ**pisci'culturist** NOUN, ADJECTIVE

piscina (pɪ'si:nə) NOUN, *plural* **-nae** (-ni:) *or* **-nas.** *RC Church* a stone basin, with a drain, in a church or sacristy where water used at Mass is poured away.
▷HISTORY C16: from Latin: fish pond, from *piscis* a fish
▸**piscinal** ('pɪsɪnᵊl) ADJECTIVE

piscine ('pɪsaɪn) ADJECTIVE of, relating to, or resembling a fish.

Piscis Austrinus ('pɪsɪs ɒ'straɪnəs, 'paɪ-) NOUN, *Latin genitive* **Piscis Austrini** (ɒ'straɪnaɪ). a small constellation in the S hemisphere lying between Aquarius and Grus and containing the first-magnitude star Fomalhaut.
▷HISTORY Latin: the Southern Fish

piscivorous (pɪ'sɪvərəs) ADJECTIVE feeding on fish: *piscivorous birds.*

pisé ('pi:zeɪ) NOUN rammed earth or clay used to make floors or walls. Also called: **pisé de terre.**
▷HISTORY C18: French, from past participle of *piser,* from Latin *pisare* to beat, pound

Pisgah ('pɪzgə) NOUN **Mount.** *Old Testament* the mountain slopes to the northeast of the Dead Sea, from one of which, Mount Nebo, Moses viewed Canaan.

pish (pʃ, pɪʃ) INTERJECTION [1] an exclamation of impatience or contempt. ◆ VERB [2] to make this exclamation at (someone or something).

pishogue (pɪ'ʃəʊg) NOUN *Irish* sorcery; witchcraft.
▷HISTORY from Irish *piseog, pisreog*

Pishpek (pɪʃ'pɛk) NOUN a variant transliteration of the Kyrgyz name for **Bishkek.**

pisiform ('pɪsɪˌfɔ:m) ADJECTIVE [1] *Zoology, botany* resembling a pea. ◆ NOUN [2] a small pealike bone on the ulnar side of the carpus.
▷HISTORY C18: via New Latin from Latin *pīsum* pea + *forma* shape

pismire ('pɪsˌmaɪə) NOUN an archaic or dialect word for an **ant.**
▷HISTORY C14 (literally: urinating ant, from the odour of formic acid characteristic of an ant hill): from PISS + obsolete *mire* ant, of Scandinavian origin; compare Old Norse *maurr,* Middle Low German *mīre* ant

pisolite ('paɪsəʊˌlaɪt) NOUN a sedimentary rock, commonly a limestone, consisting of pea-sized concentric formations (**pisoliths**) within a fine matrix.
▷HISTORY C18: from New Latin *pisolithus* pea stone, from Greek *pisos* pea + *lithos* -LITE
▸**pisolitic** (ˌpaɪsəʊ'lɪtɪk) ADJECTIVE

piss (pɪs) *Slang* ◆ VERB [1] (*intr*) to urinate. [2] (*tr*) to discharge as or in one's urine: *to piss blood.* ◆ NOUN [3] an act of urinating. [4] urine. [5] *Austral* beer. [6] **on the piss.** drinking alcohol, esp in large quantities. [7] **piece of piss.** something easily obtained of achieved. [8] **take the piss.** to tease or make fun of someone or something. [9] **piss all over.** to be far superior to: *a version that pisses all over the original.*
▷HISTORY C13: from Old French *pisser,* probably of imitative origin

piss about *or* **around** VERB (*adverb*) *Slang* [1] (*intr*) to behave in a casual or silly way. [2] (*tr*) to waste the time of.

piss artist NOUN *Slang* [1] a boastful or incompetent person. [2] a person who drinks heavily and gets drunk frequently.

pissed (pɪst) ADJECTIVE [1] *Brit, Austral, and NZ slang* intoxicated; drunk. 2 *US slang* annoyed, irritated, or disappointed.

pisser ('pɪsə) NOUN *Slang* 1 someone or something that pisses. 2 a disappointment or nuisance.

pisshead ('pɪsˌhɛd) NOUN *Slang* a drunkard.

piss off VERB (*adverb*) *Slang* 1 (*tr; often passive*) to annoy, irritate, or disappoint. 2 (*intr*) *Chiefly Brit* to go away; depart, often used to dismiss a person.

pissoir ('piːswɑː; *French* piswar) NOUN a public urinal, usu. enclosed by a wall or screen.
▷HISTORY French, from *pisser* to urinate

piss-poor ADJECTIVE *Slang* of a contemptibly low standard or quality; pathetic.

piss-up NOUN *Slang, chiefly Brit* a drinking session.

pistachio (pɪ'stɑːʃɪˌəʊ) NOUN, *plural* **-os.** 1 an anacardiaceous tree, *Pistacia vera,* of the Mediterranean region and W Asia, with small hard-shelled nuts. 2 Also called: **pistachio nut.** the nut of this tree, having an edible green kernel. 3 the sweet flavour of the pistachio nut, used esp in ice creams. ◆ ADJECTIVE 4 of a yellowish-green colour.
▷HISTORY C16: via Italian and Latin from Greek *pistakion* pistachio nut, from *pistakē* pistachio tree, from Persian *pistah*

pistareen (ˌpɪstə'riːn) NOUN a Spanish coin, used in the US and the West Indies until the 18th century.
▷HISTORY C18: perhaps changed from PESETA

piste (piːst) NOUN 1 a trail, slope, or course for skiing. 2 a rectangular area for fencing bouts.
▷HISTORY C18: via Old French from Old Italian *pista,* from *pistare* to tread down

pistil ('pɪstɪl) NOUN the female reproductive part of a flower, consisting of one or more separate or fused carpels; gynoecium.
▷HISTORY C18: from Latin *pistillum* PESTLE

pistillate ('pɪstɪlɪt, -ˌleɪt) ADJECTIVE (of plants) 1 having pistils but no anthers. 2 having or producing pistils.

Pistoia (*Italian* pis'toːja) NOUN a city in N Italy, in N Tuscany: scene of the defeat and death of Catiline in 62 B.C. Pop.: 89 972 (1990).

pistol ('pɪstᵊl) NOUN 1 a short-barrelled handgun. 2 **hold a pistol to a person's head.** to threaten a person in order to force him to do what one wants. ◆ VERB **-tols, -tolling, -tolled** *or US* **-tols, -toling, -toled.** 3 (*tr*) to shoot with a pistol.
▷HISTORY C16: from French *pistole,* from German, from Czech *píšťala* pistol, pipe; related to Russian *pischal* shepherd's pipes

pistole (pɪs'təʊl) NOUN any of various gold coins of varying value, formerly used in Europe.
▷HISTORY C16: from Old French, shortened from *pistolet,* literally: little PISTOL

pistoleer (ˌpɪstə'lɪə) NOUN *Obsolete* a person, esp a soldier, who is armed with or fires a pistol.

pistol grip NOUN **a** a handle shaped like the butt of a pistol. **b** (*as modifier*): *a pistol-grip camera.*

pistol-whip VERB **-whips, -whipping, -whipped.** (*tr*) to beat or strike with a pistol barrel.

piston ('pɪstən) NOUN a disc or cylindrical part that slides to and fro in a hollow cylinder. In an internal-combustion engine it is forced to move by the expanding gases in the cylinder head and is attached by a pivoted connecting rod to a crankshaft or flywheel, thus converting reciprocating motion into rotation.
▷HISTORY C18: via French from Old Italian *pistone,* from *pistare* to pound, grind, from Latin *pinsere* to crush, beat

piston ring NOUN a split ring, usually made of cast iron, that fits into a groove on the rim of a piston to provide a spring-loaded seal against the cylinder wall.

piston rod NOUN 1 the rod that connects the piston of a reciprocating steam engine to the crosshead. 2 a less common name for a **connecting rod.**

piston slap NOUN the characteristic sound of a seriously worn piston in a cylinder (usually of the engine of a motor car).

pit¹ (pɪt) NOUN 1 a large, usually deep opening in the ground. 2 **a** a mine or excavation with a shaft, esp for coal. **b** the shaft in a mine. **c** (*as modifier*): *pit pony; pit prop.* 3 a concealed danger or difficulty. 4 **the pit.** hell. 5 Also called: **orchestra pit.** the area that is occupied by the orchestra in a theatre, located in front of the stage. 6 an enclosure for fighting animals or birds, esp gamecocks. 7 *Anatomy* **a** a small natural depression on the surface of a body, organ, structure, or part; fossa. **b** the floor of any natural bodily cavity: *the pit of the stomach.* 8 *Pathol* a small indented scar at the site of a former pustule; pockmark. 9 any of various small areas in a plant cell wall that remain unthickened when the rest of the cell becomes lignified, esp the vascular tissue. 10 a working area at the side of a motor-racing track for servicing or refuelling vehicles. 11 a section on the floor of a commodity exchange devoted to a special line of trading. 12 a rowdy card game in which players bid for commodities. 13 an area of sand or other soft material at the end of a long-jump approach, behind the bar of a pole vault, etc., on which an athlete may land safely. 14 the ground floor of the auditorium of a theatre. 15 *Brit* a slang word for **bed** (sense 1) or **bedroom** (sense 1). 16 another word for **pitfall** (sense 2). ◆ VERB **pits, pitting, pitted.** 17 (*tr;* often foll by *against*) to match in opposition, esp as antagonists. 18 to mark or become marked with pits. 19 (*tr*) to place or bury in a pit. ◆ See also **pits.**
▷HISTORY Old English *pytt,* from Latin *puteus;* compare Old French *pet,* Old High German *pfuzzi*

pit² (pɪt) *Chiefly US and Canadian* ◆ NOUN 1 the stone of a cherry, plum, etc. ◆ VERB **pits, pitting, pitted.** 2 (*tr*) to extract the stone from (a fruit).
▷HISTORY C19: from Dutch: kernel; compare PITH

pit³ (pɪt) VERB a Scot word for **put.**

pita ('piːtə) NOUN 1 any of several agave plants yielding a strong fibre. See also **istle.** 2 a species of pineapple, *Ananas magdalenae,* the leaves of which yield a white fibre. 3 Also called: **pita fibre.** the fibre obtained from any of these plants, used in making cordage and paper.
▷HISTORY C17: via Spanish from Quechua

pitapat (ˌpɪtə'pæt) ADVERB 1 with quick light taps or beats. ◆ VERB **-pats, -patting, -patted.** 2 (*intr*) to make quick light taps or beats. ◆ NOUN 3 such taps or beats.

pit bull terrier NOUN a dog resembling the Staffordshire bull terrier but somewhat larger: developed for dog-fighting; it is not recognized by kennel clubs and is regarded as dangerous. It is not allowed in some countries, including the UK. Also called: **American pit bull terrier.**

Pitcairn Island (pɪt'kɛən, 'pɪtkɛən) NOUN an island in the S Pacific: forms with other islands a UK Overseas Territory; uninhabited until the landing in 1790 of the mutineers of H.M.S. *Bounty* and their Tahitian companions. Pop.: 54 (1999 est.). Area: 4.6 sq. km (1.75 sq. miles).

pitch¹ (pɪtʃ) VERB 1 to hurl or throw (something); cast; fling. 2 (*usually tr*) to set up (a camp, tent, etc.). 3 (*tr*) to place or thrust (a stake, spear, etc.) into the ground. 4 (*intr*) to move vigorously or irregularly to and fro or up and down. 5 (*tr*) to aim or fix (something) at a particular level, position, style, etc.: *if you advertise privately you may pitch the price too low.* 6 (*tr*) to aim to sell (a product) to a specified market or on a specified basis. 7 (*intr*) to slope downwards. 8 (*intr*) to fall forwards or downwards. 9 (*intr*) (of a vessel) to dip and raise its bow and stern alternately. 10 *Cricket* to bowl (a ball) so that it bounces on a certain part of the wicket, or (of a ball) to bounce on a certain part of the wicket. 11 (*intr*) (of a missile, aircraft, etc.) to deviate from a stable flight attitude by movement of the longitudinal axis about the lateral axis. Compare **yaw** (sense 1), **roll** (sense 14). 12 (*tr*) (in golf) to hit (a ball) steeply into the air, esp with backspin to minimize roll. 13 (*tr*) *Music* **a** to sing or play accurately (a note, interval, etc.). **b** (*usually passive*) (of a wind instrument) to specify or indicate its basic key or harmonic series by its size, manufacture, etc. 14 (*tr*) *Cards* to lead (a suit) and so determine trumps for that trick. 15 *Baseball* **a** (*tr*) to throw (a baseball) to a batter. **b** (*intr*) to act as pitcher in a baseball game. 16 *Southwest English dialect* (used with *it* as subject) to snow without the settled snow melting. 17 **in there pitching.** *US and Canadian informal* taking part with enthusiasm. 18 **pitch a tale** (*or* **yarn**). to tell a story, usually of a fantastic nature. ◆ NOUN 19 the degree of elevation or depression. 20 **a** the angle of descent of a downward slope. **b** such a slope. 21 the extreme height or depth. 22 *Mountaineering* a section of a route between two belay points, sometimes equal to the full length of the rope but often shorter. 23 the degree of slope of a roof, esp when expressed as a ratio of height to span. 24 the distance between corresponding points on adjacent members of a body of regular form, esp the distance between teeth on a gearwheel or between threads on a screw thread. 25 the distance between regularly spaced objects such as rivets, bolts, etc. 26 the pitching motion of a ship, missile, etc. 27 **a** the distance a propeller advances in one revolution, assuming no slip. **b** the blade angle of a propeller or rotor. 28 the distance between the back rest of a seat in a passenger aircraft and the back of the seat in front of it. 29 *Music* **a** the auditory property of a note that is conditioned by its frequency relative to other notes: *high pitch; low pitch.* **b** an absolute frequency assigned to a specific note, fixing the relative frequencies of all other notes. The fundamental frequencies of the notes A–G, in accordance with the frequency A = 440 hertz, were internationally standardized and accepted in 1939. See also **concert pitch** (sense 1), **international pitch.** 30 *Cricket* the rectangular area between the stumps, 22 yards long and 10 feet wide; the wicket. 31 *Geology* the inclination of the axis of an anticline or syncline or of a stratum or vein from the horizontal. 32 another name for **seven-up.** 33 the act or manner of pitching a ball, as in cricket. 34 *Chiefly Brit* a vendor's station, esp on a pavement. 35 *Slang* a persuasive sales talk, esp one routinely repeated. 36 *Chiefly Brit* (in many sports) the field of play. 37 Also called: **pitch shot.** *Golf* an approach shot in which the ball is struck in a high arc. 38 **make a pitch for.** *US and Canadian slang* **a** to give verbal support to. **b** to attempt to attract (someone) sexually or romantically. 39 **queer someone's pitch.** *Brit informal* to upset someone's plans. ◆ See also **pitch in, pitch into, pitch on.**
▷HISTORY C13 *picchen;* possibly related to PICK¹

pitch² (pɪtʃ) NOUN 1 any of various heavy dark viscid substances obtained as a residue from the distillation of tars. See also **coal-tar pitch.** 2 any of various similar substances, such as asphalt, occurring as natural deposits. 3 any of various similar substances obtained by distilling certain organic substances so that they are incompletely carbonized. 4 crude turpentine obtained as sap from pine trees. ◆ Related adjective: **piceous.** ◆ VERB 5 (*tr*) to apply pitch to (something).
▷HISTORY Old English *pic,* from Latin *pix*

pitch accent NOUN (in languages such as Ancient Greek or modern Swedish) an accent in which emphatic syllables are pronounced on a higher musical pitch relative to other syllables. Also called: **tonic accent.**

pitch and putt NOUN a type of miniature golf in which the holes are usually between 50 to 100 metres in length.

pitch-and-toss NOUN a game of skill and chance in which the player who pitches a coin nearest to a mark has the first chance to toss all the coins, winning those that land heads up.

pitchbend ('pɪtʃˌbɛnd) NOUN an electronic device that enables a player to bend the pitch of a note being sounded on a synthesizer, usually with a pitch wheel, strip, or lever.

pitch-black ADJECTIVE 1 extremely dark; unlit: *the room was pitch-black.* 2 of a deep black colour.

pitchblende ('pɪtʃˌblɛnd) NOUN a blackish mineral that is a type of uraninite and occurs in veins, frequently associated with silver: the principal source of uranium and radium. Formula: UO_2.
▷HISTORY C18: partial translation of German *Pechblende,* from *Pech* PITCH² (from its black colour) + BLENDE

pitch circle NOUN an imaginary circle passing through the teeth of a gearwheel, concentric with the gearwheel, and having a radius that would enable it to be in contact with a similar circle around a mating gearwheel.

pitch-cone angle NOUN (in a bevel gear) the apex angle of the truncated cone (pitch cone) which forms the reference surface on which the teeth of a bevel gear are cut.

pitch cylinder NOUN an imaginary cylinder

passing through, and coaxial with, the threads of a screw so that its intersection with opposite flanks of any groove is equal to half the thread pitch.

pitch-dark ADJECTIVE extremely or completely dark.

pitched battle NOUN 1 a battle ensuing from the deliberate choice of time and place, engaging all the planned resources. 2 any fierce encounter, esp one with large numbers.

pitcher¹ ('pɪtʃə) NOUN 1 a large jug, usually rounded with a narrow neck and often of earthenware, used mainly for holding water. 2 *Botany* any of the urn-shaped leaves of the pitcher plant.
▷HISTORY C13: from Old French *pichier,* from Medieval Latin *picārium,* variant of *bicārium* BEAKER

pitcher² ('pɪtʃə) NOUN 1 *Baseball* the player on the fielding team who pitches the ball to the batter. 2 a granite stone or sett used in paving.

pitcher plant NOUN any of various insectivorous plants of the genera *Sarracenia, Darlingtonia, Nepenthes,* and *Cephalotus,* having leaves modified to form pitcher-like organs that attract and trap insects, which are then digested. See also **huntsman's-cup.**

pitchfork ('pɪtʃˌfɔːk) NOUN 1 a long-handled fork with two or three long curved tines for lifting, turning, or tossing hay. ◆ VERB (*tr*) 2 to use a pitchfork on (something). 3 to thrust (someone) unwillingly into a position.

pitch in VERB (*intr, adverb*) 1 to cooperate or contribute. 2 to begin energetically.

pitching tool NOUN a masonry chisel for rough work.

pitching wedge NOUN *Golf* a club with a face angle of more than 50°, used for short, lofted pitch shots.

pitch into VERB (*intr, preposition*) *Informal* 1 to assail physically or verbally. 2 to get on with doing (something).

Pitch Lake NOUN a deposit of natural asphalt in the Caribbean, in SW Trinidad. Area: 46 hectares (114 acres).

pitchman ('pɪtʃmən) NOUN, *plural* **-men.** *US and Canadian* 1 an itinerant pedlar of small merchandise who operates from a stand at a fair, etc. 2 any high-pressure salesman or advertiser.

pitchometer (pɪtʃ'ɒmɪtə) NOUN an instrument embodying a clinometer, for measuring the pitch of a ship's propeller.

pitch on *or* **upon** VERB (*intr, preposition*) to determine or decide.

pitch pine NOUN 1 any of various coniferous trees of the genus *Pinus, esp P. rigida,* of North America, having red-brown bark and long lustrous light brown cones: valued as a source of turpentine and pitch. 2 the wood of any of these trees.

pitch pipe NOUN a small pipe, esp one having a reed like a harmonica, that sounds a note or notes of standard frequency. It is used for establishing the correct starting note for unaccompanied singing.

pitchstone ('pɪtʃˌstəʊn) NOUN a dark glassy acid volcanic rock similar in composition to granite, usually intruded as dykes, sills, etc.
▷HISTORY C18: translation of German *Pechstein*

pitchy ('pɪtʃɪ) ADJECTIVE **pitchier, pitchiest.** 1 full of or covered with pitch. 2 resembling pitch.
▸'**pitchiness** NOUN

piteous ('pɪtɪəs) ADJECTIVE 1 exciting or deserving pity. 2 *Archaic* having or expressing pity.
▸'**piteously** ADVERB ▸'**piteousness** NOUN

pitfall ('pɪtˌfɔːl) NOUN 1 an unsuspected difficulty or danger. 2 a trap in the form of a concealed pit, designed to catch men or wild animals.
▷HISTORY Old English *pytt* PIT¹ + *fealle* trap

pith (pɪθ) NOUN 1 the soft fibrous tissue lining the inside of the rind in fruits such as the orange and grapefruit. 2 the essential or important part, point, etc. 3 weight; substance. 4 Also called: **medulla.** *Botany* the central core of unspecialized cells surrounded by conducting tissue in stems. 5 the soft central part of a bone, feather, etc. ◆ VERB (*tr*) 6 to destroy the brain and spinal cord of (a laboratory animal) by piercing or severing. 7 to kill (animals) by severing the spinal cord. 8 to remove the pith from (a plant).
▷HISTORY Old English *pitha;* compare Middle Low German *pedik,* Middle Dutch *pitt(e)*

pithead ('pɪtˌhɛd) NOUN the top of a mine shaft and the buildings, hoisting gear, etc., situated around it.

pithecanthropus (ˌpɪθɪkæn'θrəʊpəs, -'kænθrə-) NOUN, *plural* **-pi** (-ˌpaɪ). any primitive apelike man of the former genus *Pithecanthropus,* now included in the genus *Homo.* See **Java man, Peking man.**
▷HISTORY C19: New Latin, from Greek *pithēkos* ape + *anthrōpos* man
▸ˌ**pithe'canthroˌpine** *or* ˌ**pithe'canthroˌpoid** ADJECTIVE

pith helmet NOUN a lightweight hat made of pith that protects the wearer from the sun. Also called: **topee, topi.**

pithos ('pɪθɒs, 'paɪ-) NOUN, *plural* **-thoi** (-θɔɪ). a large ceramic container for oil or grain.
▷HISTORY from Greek

pithy ('pɪθɪ) ADJECTIVE **pithier, pithiest.** 1 terse and full of meaning or substance. 2 of, resembling, or full of pith.
▸'**pithily** ADVERB ▸'**pithiness** NOUN

pitiable ('pɪtɪəbᵊl) ADJECTIVE exciting or deserving pity or contempt.
▸'**pitiableness** NOUN ▸'**pitiably** ADVERB

pitiful ('pɪtɪfʊl) ADJECTIVE 1 arousing or deserving pity. 2 arousing or deserving contempt. 3 *Archaic* full of pity or compassion.
▸'**pitifully** ADVERB ▸'**pitifulness** NOUN

pitiless ('pɪtɪlɪs) ADJECTIVE having or showing little or no pity or mercy.
▸'**pitilessly** ADVERB ▸'**pitilessness** NOUN

Pitjantjatjara (ˌpɪtʃəntʃə'tʃærə) *or* **Pitjantjara** (ˌpɪtʃən'dʒærə) NOUN 1 (*plural* **-ra** *or* **-ras**) an Aboriginal people of the desert area of South Australia. 2 the language of this people.

pitman ('pɪtmən) NOUN, *plural* **-men.** *Chiefly Scot and northern English* a person who works down a mine, esp a coal miner.

piton ('piːtɒn; *French* pitɔ̃) NOUN *Mountaineering* a metal spike that may be driven into a crevice of rock or into ice and used to secure a rope.
▷HISTORY C20: from French: ringbolt

Pitot-static tube ('piːtəʊ'stætɪk) NOUN combined Pitot and static pressure tubes placed in a fluid flow to measure the total and static pressures. The difference in pressures, as recorded on a manometer or airspeed indicator, indicates the fluid velocity. Also called: **Pitot tube.**

Pitot tube ('piːtəʊ) NOUN 1 a small tube placed in a fluid with its open end upstream and the other end connected to a manometer. It measures the total pressure of the fluid. 2 short for **Pitot-static tube,** esp one fitted to an aircraft
▷HISTORY C18: named after its inventor, Henri Pitot (1695–1771), French physicist

pits (pɪts) PLURAL NOUN *Slang* **the.** the worst possible person, place, or thing.
▷HISTORY C20: perhaps shortened from *armpits*

pitsaw ('pɪtˌsɔː) NOUN a large saw formerly used for cutting logs into planks, operated by two men, one standing on top of the log and the other in a pit underneath it.

pit-sawn ADJECTIVE (of timber, esp formerly) sawn into planks by hand in a saw-pit.

pit stop NOUN 1 *Motor racing* a brief stop made at a pit by a racing car for repairs, refuelling, etc. 2 *Informal* any stop made during a car journey for refreshment, rest, or refuelling.

pitta¹ ('pɪtə) NOUN another name for **pitta bread.**

pitta² ('pɪtə) NOUN any of various small brightly coloured ground-dwelling tropical birds of the genus *Pitta.*
▷HISTORY C19: from Telugu

pitta bread *or* **pitta** ('pɪtə) NOUN a flat rounded slightly leavened bread, originally from the Middle East, with a hollow inside like a pocket, which can be filled with food. Also called: **Arab bread, Greek bread.**
▷HISTORY from Modern Greek: a cake

pittance ('pɪtᵊns) NOUN a small amount or portion, esp a meagre allowance of money.
▷HISTORY C16: from Old French *pietance* ration, ultimately from Latin *pietās* duty

pitter-patter ('pɪtəˌpætə) NOUN 1 the sound of light rapid taps or pats, as of raindrops. ◆ VERB 2 (*intr*) to make such a sound. ◆ ADVERB 3 with such a sound: *the rain fell pitter-patter on the window.*

pittosporum (pɪ'tɒspərəm) NOUN any of various trees and shrubs of the *Pittosporum* genus of Australasia, Asia, and Africa, having small fragrant flowers.
▷HISTORY New Latin, from Greek *pitta* pitch (from the resinous coating of the seeds) + *spora* seed

Pittsburgh ('pɪtsbɜːg) NOUN a port in SW Pennsylvania, at the confluence of the Allegheny and Monongahela Rivers, which form the Ohio River: settled around Fort Pitt in 1758; developed rapidly with the discovery of iron deposits and one of the world's richest coalfields; the largest river port in the US and an important industrial centre, formerly with large steel mills. Pop.: 334 563 (2000).

Pitt Street Farmer NOUN *Austral slang* another name for **Collins Street Farmer.**
▷HISTORY C20: after a principal business street in Sydney, Australia

pituitary (pɪ'tjuːɪtərɪ, -trɪ) NOUN, *plural* **-taries.** 1 See **pituitary gland, pituitary extract.** ◆ ADJECTIVE 2 of or relating to the pituitary gland. 3 *Archaic* of or relating to phlegm or mucus.
▷HISTORY C17: from Late Latin *pītuītārius* slimy, from *pītuīta* phlegm

pituitary extract NOUN a preparation of the pituitary gland, used in medicine for the therapeutic effects of its hormones.

pituitary gland *or* **body** NOUN the master endocrine gland, attached by a stalk to the base of the brain. Its two lobes (see **adenohypophysis** and **neurohypophysis**) secrete hormones affecting skeletal growth, development of the sex glands, and the functioning of the other endocrine glands. Also called: **hypophysis, hypophysis cerebri.**

pituri ('pɪtʃərɪ) NOUN, *plural* **-ris.** an Australian solanaceous shrub, *Duboisia hopwoodii,* the leaves of which are the source of a narcotic used by the native Australians.
▷HISTORY C19: from a native Australian name

pit viper NOUN any venomous snake of the New World family *Crotalidae,* having a heat-sensitive organ in a pit on each side of the head: includes the rattlesnakes.

pity ('pɪtɪ) NOUN, *plural* **pities.** 1 sympathy or sorrow felt for the sufferings of another. 2 **have** (*or* **take**) **pity on.** to have sympathy or show mercy for. 3 something that causes regret or pity. 4 an unfortunate chance: *what a pity you can't come.* 5 **more's the pity.** it is highly regrettable (that). ◆ VERB **pities, pitying, pitied.** 6 (*tr*) to feel pity for.
▷HISTORY C13: from Old French *pité,* from Latin *pietās* duty
▸'**pitying** ADJECTIVE ▸'**pityingly** ADVERB

pityriasis (ˌpɪtə'raɪəsɪs) NOUN 1 any of a group of skin diseases characterized by the shedding of dry flakes of skin. 2 a similar skin disease of certain domestic animals.
▷HISTORY C17: via New Latin from Greek *pituriasis* scurfiness, from *pituron* bran

più (pjuː) ADVERB *Music* (*in combination*) more (quickly, softly, etc.): *più allegro,; più mosso,; più lento.*
▷HISTORY Italian, from Latin *plus* more

piupiu ('piːuːˌpiːuː) NOUN a skirt made from the leaves of the New Zealand flax, worn by Maoris on ceremonial occasions.
▷HISTORY Maori

Piura (*Spanish* 'pjura) NOUN a city in NW Peru: the oldest colonial city in Peru, founded by Pizarro in 1532; commercial centre of an agricultural district. Pop.: 308 155 (1998 est.).

Piute ('paɪˌuːt, paɪ'juːt) NOUN a variant spelling of **Paiute.**

pivot ('pɪvət) NOUN 1 a short shaft or pin supporting something that turns; fulcrum. 2 the end of a shaft or arbor that terminates in a bearing. 3 a person or thing upon which progress, success, etc., depends. 4 the person or position from which a military formation takes its reference, as when altering position. ◆ VERB 5 (*tr*) to mount on or provide with a pivot or pivots. 6 (*intr*) to turn on or as if on a pivot.
▷HISTORY C17: from Old French; perhaps related to Old Provençal *pua* tooth of a comb

pivotal ('pɪvətəl) ADJECTIVE [1] of, involving, or acting as a pivot. [2] of crucial importance.
▸**'pivotally** ADVERB

pivot bridge NOUN another name for **swing bridge**.

pivot grammar NOUN *Psychol* a loose grammar said to govern two-word utterances by children.

pix[1] (pɪks) PLURAL NOUN *Informal* photographs; prints.

pix[2] (pɪks) NOUN a less common spelling of **pyx**.

pixel ('pɪksəl) NOUN any of a number of very small picture elements that make up a picture, as on a visual display unit.
▹HISTORY C20: from *pix* pictures + *el(ement)*

pixelation (ˌpɪksɪ'leɪʃən) NOUN a video technique in which an image is blurred by being overlaid with a grid of squares, usually to disguise the identity of a person.

pixie *or* **pixy** ('pɪksɪ) NOUN, *plural* **pixies**. (in folklore) a fairy or elf.
▹HISTORY C17: of obscure origin

pixilated *or* **pixillated** ('pɪksɪˌleɪtɪd) ADJECTIVE *Chiefly US* [1] eccentric or whimsical. [2] *Slang* drunk.
▹HISTORY C20: from PIXIE + *-lated,* as in *stimulated, titillated,* etc.
▸ˌ**pixi'lation** *or* ˌ**pixil'lation** NOUN

pize (paɪz) VERB (*tr*) *Yorkshire dialect* to strike (someone a blow).
▹HISTORY of obscure origin

pizz. *Music* ABBREVIATION FOR pizzicato.

pizza ('piːtsə) NOUN a dish of Italian origin consisting of a baked disc of dough covered with cheese and tomatoes, usually with the addition of mushrooms, anchovies, sausage, or ham.
▹HISTORY C20: from Italian, perhaps from Vulgar Latin *picea* (unattested), from Latin *piceus* relating to PITCH[2]; perhaps related to Modern Greek *pitta* cake

pizzazz *or* **pizazz** (pə'zæz) NOUN *Informal* an attractive combination of energy and style; sparkle, vitality, glamour. Also called: **pazzazz, pazazz, pzazz.**
▹HISTORY C20: origin obscure

pizzeria (ˌpiːtsə'riːə) NOUN a place where pizzas are made, sold, or eaten.
▹HISTORY C20: from Italian, from PIZZA + *-eria* -ERY

pizzicato (ˌpɪtsɪ'kɑːtəʊ) *Music* ◆ ADJECTIVE, ADVERB [1] (in music for the violin family) to be plucked with the finger. ◆ NOUN [2] the style or technique of playing a normally bowed stringed instrument in this manner.
▹HISTORY C19: from Italian: pinched, from *pizzicare* to twist, twang

pizzle ('pɪzəl) NOUN *Archaic or dialect* the penis of an animal, esp a bull.
▹HISTORY C16: of Germanic origin; compare Low German *pēsel,* Flemish *pēzel,* Middle Dutch *pēze* sinew

pk *plural* **pks** ABBREVIATION FOR: [1] pack. [2] park. [3] peak.

pk THE INTERNET DOMAIN NAME FOR Pakistan.

PK [1] ABBREVIATION FOR psychokinesis. ◆ [2] INTERNATIONAL CAR REGISTRATION FOR Pakistan.

pkg. *plural* **pkgs** ABBREVIATION FOR package.

pkt ABBREVIATION FOR packet.

PKU ABBREVIATION FOR phenylketonuria.

pl ABBREVIATION FOR: [1] place. [2] plate. [3] plural.

pl THE INTERNET DOMAIN NAME FOR Poland.

PL [1] (in transformational grammar) ABBREVIATION FOR plural. ◆ [2] INTERNATIONAL CAR REGISTRATION FOR Poland.

Pl. (in street names) ABBREVIATION FOR Place.

PL/1 NOUN programming language 1: a high-level computer programming language designed for mathematical and scientific purposes.
▹HISTORY C20: *p(rogramming) l(anguage) 1*

PLA ABBREVIATION FOR Port of London Authority.

plaas (plɑːs) NOUN *South African* a farm.
▹HISTORY Afrikaans

placable ('plækəbəl) ADJECTIVE easily placated or appeased.
▹HISTORY C15: via Old French from Latin *plācābilis,* from *plācāre* to appease; related to *placēre* to please
▸ˌ**placa'bility** *or* **'placableness** NOUN ▸**'placably** ADVERB

placard ('plækɑːd) NOUN [1] a printed or written notice for public display; poster. [2] a small plaque or card. ◆ VERB (*tr*) [3] to post placards on or in. [4] to publicize or advertise by placards. [5] to display as a placard.
▹HISTORY C15: from Old French *plaquart,* from *plaquier* to plate, lay flat; see PLAQUE

placate (plə'keɪt) VERB (*tr*) to pacify or appease.
▹HISTORY C17: from Latin *plācāre;* see PLACABLE
▸**pla'cation** NOUN

placatory (plə'keɪtərɪ, 'plækətərɪ, -trɪ) *or less commonly* **placative** (plə'keɪtɪv, 'plækətɪv) ADJECTIVE placating or intended to placate.

place (pleɪs) NOUN [1] a particular point or part of space or of a surface, esp that occupied by a person or thing. [2] a geographical point, such as a town, city, etc. [3] a position or rank in a sequence or order. [4] **a** an open square lined with houses of a similar type in a city or town. **b** (*capital when part of a street name*): *Grosvenor Place.* [5] space or room. [6] a house or living quarters. [7] a country house with grounds. [8] any building or area set aside for a specific purpose. [9] a passage in a book, play, film, etc.: *to lose one's place.* [10] proper or appropriate position or time: *he still thinks a woman's place is in the home.* [11] right or original position: *put it back in its place.* [12] suitable, appropriate, or customary surroundings (esp in the phrases **out of place, in place**). [13] right, prerogative, or duty: *it is your place to give a speech.* [14] appointment, position, or job: *a place at college.* [15] position, condition, or state: *if I were in your place.* [16] **a** a space or seat, as at a dining table. **b** (*as modifier*): *place mat.* [17] *Maths* the relative position of a digit in a number. See also **decimal place.** [18] any of the best times in a race. [19] *Horse racing* **a** *Brit* the first, second, or third position at the finish. **b** *US and Canadian* the first or usually the second position at the finish. **c** (*as modifier*): *a place bet.* [20] *Theatre* one of the three unities. See **unity** (sense 8). [21] *Archaic* an important position, rank, or role. [22] **all over the place.** in disorder or disarray. [23] **another place.** *Brit parliamentary procedure* **a** (in the House of Commons) the House of Lords. **b** (in the House of Lords) the House of Commons. [24] **give place (to).** to make room (for) or be superseded (by). [25] **go places.** *Informal* **a** to travel. **b** to become successful. [26] **in place of. a** instead of; in lieu of: *go in place of my sister.* **b** in exchange for: *he gave her it in place of her ring.* [27] **know one's place.** to be aware of one's inferior position. [28] **pride of place.** the highest or foremost position. [29] **put someone in his** (*or* **her**) **place.** to humble someone who is arrogant, conceited, forward, etc. [30] **take one's place.** to take up one's usual or specified position. [31] **take the place of.** to be a substitute for. [32] **take place.** to happen or occur. [33] **the other place.** *Facetious* **a** (at Oxford University) Cambridge University. **b** (at Cambridge University) Oxford University. ◆ VERB (*mainly tr*) [34] to put or set in a particular or appropriate place. [35] to find or indicate the place of. [36] to identify or classify by linking with an appropriate context: *to place a face.* [37] to regard or view as being: *to place prosperity above sincerity.* [38] to make (an order, a bet, etc.). [39] to find a home or job for (someone). [40] to appoint to an office or position. [41] (often foll by *with*) to put under the care (of). [42] to direct or aim carefully. [43] (*passive*) *Brit* to cause (a racehorse, greyhound, athlete, etc.) to arrive in first, second, third, or sometimes fourth place. [44] (*intr*) *US and Canadian* (of a racehorse, greyhound, etc.) to finish among the first three in a contest, esp in second position. [45] to invest (funds). [46] to sing (a note) with accuracy of pitch. [47] to insert (an advertisement) in a newspaper, journal, etc.
▹HISTORY C13: via Old French from Latin *platēa* courtyard, from Greek *plateia,* from *platus* broad; compare French *plat* flat

placebo (plə'siːbəʊ) NOUN, *plural* **-bos** *or* **-boes.** [1] *Med* an inactive substance or other sham form of therapy administered to a patient usually to compare its effects with those of a real drug or treatment, but sometimes for the psychological benefit to the patient through his believing he is receiving treatment. See also **control group, placebo effect.** [2] something said or done to please or humour another. [3] *RC Church* a traditional name for the vespers of the office for the dead.
▹HISTORY C13 (in the ecclesiastical sense): from Latin *Placebo Domino* I shall please the Lord (from the opening of the office for the dead); C19 (in the medical sense)

placebo effect NOUN *Med* a positive therapeutic effect claimed by a patient after receiving a placebo believed by him to be an active drug. See **control group.**

place card NOUN a card placed on a dinner table before a seat, as at a formal dinner, indicating who is to sit there.

place kick *Football* ◆ NOUN [1] a kick in which the ball is placed in position before it is kicked. ◆ VERB **place-kick.** [2] to kick (a ball) using a place kick. ◆ Compare **drop kick, punt**[2].

placeless ('pleɪsˌlɪs) ADJECTIVE not rooted in a specific place or community.

placeman ('pleɪsmən) NOUN, *plural* **-men.** *Brit derogatory* a person who holds a public office, esp for private profit and as a reward for political support.

placement ('pleɪsmənt) NOUN [1] the act of placing or the state of being placed. [2] arrangement or position. [3] the process or business of finding employment.

place name NOUN the name of a geographical location, such as a town or area.

placenta (plə'sɛntə) NOUN, *plural* **-tas** *or* **-tae** (-tiː). [1] the vascular organ formed in the uterus during pregnancy, consisting of both maternal and embryonic tissues and providing oxygen and nutrients for the fetus and transfer of waste products from the fetal to the maternal blood circulation. See also **afterbirth.** [2] the corresponding organ or part in certain mammals. [3] *Botany* **a** the part of the ovary of flowering plants to which the ovules are attached. **b** the mass of tissue in nonflowering plants that bears the sporangia or spores.
▹HISTORY C17: via Latin from Greek *plakoeis* flat cake, from *plax* flat

placental (plə'sɛntəl) *or* **placentate** ADJECTIVE (esp of animals) having a placenta: *placental mammals.* See also **eutherian.**

placentation (ˌplæsɛn'teɪʃən) NOUN [1] *Botany* the way in which ovules are attached in the ovary. [2] *Zoology* **a** the way in which the placenta is attached in the uterus. **b** the process of formation of the placenta.

place of safety order NOUN *Social welfare, law* (in Britain) under the Children and Young Persons Act 1969, an order granted by a justice to a person or agency granting authority to detain a child or young person and take him or her to a place of safety for not more than 28 days, because of the child's actual or likely ill-treatment or neglect, etc.

placer ('plæsə) NOUN **a** a surface sediment containing particles of gold or some other valuable mineral. **b** (*in combination*): *placer-mining.*
▹HISTORY C19: from American Spanish: deposit, from Spanish *plaza* PLACE

place setting NOUN the set of items of cutlery, crockery, and glassware laid for one person at a dining table.

placet ('pleɪsɛt) NOUN a vote or expression of assent by saying the word *placet.*
▹HISTORY C16: from Latin, literally: it pleases

place-value ADJECTIVE denoting a series in which successive digits represent successive powers of the base.

placid ('plæsɪd) ADJECTIVE having a calm appearance or nature.
▹HISTORY C17: from Latin *placidus* peaceful; related to *placēre* to please
▸**placidity** (plə'sɪdɪtɪ) *or* **'placidness** NOUN ▸**'placidly** ADVERB

placing ('pleɪsɪŋ) NOUN *Stock Exchange* a method of issuing securities to the public using an intermediary, such as a stockbroking firm.

placket ('plækɪt) NOUN *Dressmaking* [1] a piece of cloth sewn in under a closure with buttons, hooks and eyes, zips, etc. [2] the closure itself.
▹HISTORY C16: perhaps from Middle Dutch *plackaet* breastplate, from Medieval Latin *placca* metal plate

placoderm ('plækəˌdɜːm) NOUN any extinct bony-plated fishlike vertebrate of the class *Placodermi,* of Silurian to Permian times: thought to have been the earliest vertebrates with jaws.
▹HISTORY C19: from Greek *plac-, plax* a flat plate + -DERM

placoid ('plækɔɪd) ADJECTIVE [1] platelike or flattened. [2] (of the scales of sharks and other

elasmobranchs) toothlike; composed of dentine with an enamel tip and basal pulp cavity.
▷HISTORY C19: from Greek *plac-, plax* flat

plafond (plə'fɒn; *French* plafɔ̃) NOUN [1] a ceiling, esp one having ornamentation. [2] a card game, a precursor of contract bridge.
▷HISTORY C17: from French, literally: ceiling, maximum, from *plat* flat + *fond* bottom, from Latin *fundus* bottom

plagal ('pleɪgᵊl) ADJECTIVE [1] (of a cadence) progressing from the subdominant to the tonic chord, as in the *Amen* of a hymn. [2] (of a mode) commencing upon the dominant of an authentic mode, but sharing the same final as the authentic mode. Plagal modes are designated by the prefix *Hypo-* before the name of their authentic counterparts: *the Hypodorian mode.* ◆ Compare **authentic** (sense 5).
▷HISTORY C16: from Medieval Latin *plagālis,* from *plaga,* perhaps from Greek *plagos* side

plage (plɑːʒ) NOUN *Astronomy* a bright patch in the sun's chromosphere.
▷HISTORY French, literally: beach, strand

plagiarism ('pleɪdʒəˌrɪzəm) NOUN [1] the act of plagiarizing. [2] something plagiarized.
▸ **'plagiarist** NOUN ▸ **ˌplagia'ristic** ADJECTIVE

plagiarize *or* **plagiarise** ('pleɪdʒəˌraɪz) VERB to appropriate (ideas, passages, etc.) from (another work or author).
▸ **'plagiaˌrizer** *or* **'plagiaˌriser** NOUN

plagiary ('pleɪdʒərɪ) NOUN, *plural* **-ries.** *Archaic* a person who plagiarizes or a piece of plagiarism.
▷HISTORY C16: from Latin *plagiārus* plunderer, from *plagium* kidnapping; related to *plaga* snare

plagio- COMBINING FORM slanting, inclining, or oblique: *plagiotropism.*
▷HISTORY from Greek *plagios,* from *plagos* side

plagioclase ('pleɪdʒɪəʊˌkleɪz) NOUN a series of feldspar minerals consisting of a mixture of sodium and calcium aluminium silicates in triclinic crystalline form: includes albite, oligoclase, and labradorite.
▸ **plagioclastic** (ˌpleɪdʒɪəʊ'klæstɪk) ADJECTIVE

plagioclimax (ˌpleɪdʒɪəʊ'klaɪmæks) NOUN *Ecology* the climax stage of a community, influenced by man or some other outside factor.

plagiotropism (ˌpleɪdʒɪəʊ'trəʊˌpɪzəm) NOUN the growth of a plant at an angle to the vertical in response to a stimulus.
▸ **ˌplagio'tropic** ADJECTIVE

plague (pleɪg) NOUN [1] any widespread and usually highly contagious disease with a high fatality rate. [2] an infectious disease of rodents, esp rats, transmitted to man by the bite of the rat flea (*Xenopsylla cheopis*). [3] See **bubonic plague.** [4] something that afflicts or harasses. [5] *Informal* an annoyance or nuisance. [6] a pestilence, affliction, or calamity on a large scale, esp when regarded as sent by God. [7] *Archaic* used to express annoyance, disgust, etc.: *a plague on you.* ◆ VERB **plagues, plaguing, plagued.** (*tr*) [8] to afflict or harass. [9] to bring down a plague upon. [10] *Informal* to annoy.
▷HISTORY C14: from Late Latin *plāga* pestilence, from Latin: a blow; related to Greek *plēgē* a stroke, Latin *plangere* to strike
▸ **'plaguer** NOUN

plaguy *or* **plaguey** ('pleɪgɪ) *Archaic, informal* ◆ ADJECTIVE [1] disagreeable or vexing. ◆ ADVERB [2] disagreeably or annoyingly.
▸ **'plaguily** ADVERB

plaice (pleɪs) NOUN, *plural* **plaice** *or* **plaices.** [1] a European flatfish, *Pleuronectes platessa,* having an oval brown body marked with red or orange spots and valued as a food fish: family *Pleuronectidae.* [2] *US and Canadian* any of various other fishes of the family *Pleuronectidae, esp Hippoglossoides platessoides.*
▷HISTORY C13: from Old French *plaïz,* from Late Latin *platessa* flatfish, from Greek *platus* flat

plaid (plæd, pleɪd) NOUN [1] a long piece of cloth of a tartan pattern, worn over the shoulder as part of Highland costume. [2] **a** a crisscross weave or cloth. **b** (*as modifier*): *a plaid scarf.*
▷HISTORY C16: from Scottish Gaelic *plaide,* of obscure origin

Plaid Cymru (ˌplaɪd 'kʌmrɪ) NOUN the Welsh nationalist party.
▷HISTORY C20: Welsh, literally: party of Wales

plain[1] (pleɪn) ADJECTIVE [1] flat or smooth; level. [2] not complicated; clear: *the plain truth.* [3] not difficult; simple or easy: *a plain task.* [4] honest or straightforward. [5] lowly, esp in social rank or education. [6] without adornment or show: *a plain coat.* [7] (of fabric) without pattern or of simple untwilled weave. [8] not attractive. [9] not mixed; simple: *plain vodka.* [10] *Knitting* of or done in plain. ◆ NOUN [11] a level or almost level tract of country, esp an extensive treeless region. [12] a simple stitch in knitting made by putting the right needle into a loop on the left needle, passing the wool round the right needle, and pulling it through the loop, thus forming a new loop. [13] (in billiards) **a** the unmarked white ball, as distinguished from the spot balls. **b** the player using this ball. [14] (in Ireland) short for **plain porter**, a light porter *two pints of plain, please.* ◆ ADVERB [15] (intensifier): *just plain tired.* ◆ See also **plains.**
▷HISTORY C13: from Old French: simple, from Latin *plānus* level, distinct, clear
▸ **'plainly** ADVERB ▸ **'plainness** NOUN

plain[2] (pleɪn) VERB a dialect or poetic word for **complain.**
▷HISTORY C14 *pleignen,* from Old French *plaindre* to lament, from Latin *plangere* to beat

plainchant ('pleɪnˌtʃɑːnt) NOUN another name for **plainsong.**
▷HISTORY C18: from French, rendering Medieval Latin *cantus plānus;* see PLAIN[1]

plain chocolate NOUN chocolate with a slightly bitter flavour and dark colour. Compare **milk chocolate.**

plain clothes PLURAL NOUN **a** ordinary clothes, as distinguished from uniform, as worn by a police detective on duty. **b** (*as modifier*): *a plain-clothes policeman.*

plain flour NOUN flour to which no raising agent has been added.

plain-laid ADJECTIVE (of a cable or rope) made of three strands twisted together from left to right.

plains (pleɪnz) PLURAL NOUN *Chiefly US* extensive tracts of level or almost level treeless countryside; prairies.

plain sailing NOUN [1] *Informal* smooth or easy progress. [2] *Nautical* sailing in a body of water that is unobstructed; clear sailing. Compare **plane sailing.**

Plains Indian NOUN a member of any of the North American Indian peoples formerly living in the Great Plains of the US and Canada.

plainsman ('pleɪnzmən) NOUN, *plural* **-men.** a person who lives in a plains region, esp in the Great Plains of North America.

Plains of Abraham NOUN (*functioning as singular*) a field in E Canada between Quebec City and the St Lawrence River: site of an important British victory (1759) in the Seven Years' War, which cost the French their possession of Canada.

plainsong ('pleɪnˌsɒŋ) NOUN the style of unison unaccompanied vocal music used in the medieval Church, esp in Gregorian chant. Also called: **plainchant.**
▷HISTORY C16: translation of Medieval Latin *cantus plānus*

plain-spoken ADJECTIVE candid; frank; blunt.

plaint (pleɪnt) NOUN [1] *Archaic* a complaint or lamentation. [2] *Law* a statement in writing of grounds of complaint made to a court of law and asking for redress of the grievance.
▷HISTORY C13: from Old French *plainte,* from Latin *planctus* lamentation, from *plangere* to beat

plain text NOUN *Telecomm* a message set in a directly readable form rather than in coded groups.

plaintiff ('pleɪntɪf) NOUN (formerly) a person who brings a civil action in a court of law. Now replaced by **claimant.** Compare **defendant** (sense 1).
▷HISTORY C14: from legal French *plaintif,* from Old French *plaintif* (adj) complaining, from *plainte* PLAINT

plaintive ('pleɪntɪv) ADJECTIVE expressing melancholy; mournful.
▷HISTORY C14: from Old French *plaintif* grieving, from *plainte* PLAINT
▸ **'plaintively** ADVERB ▸ **'plaintiveness** NOUN

plain turkey NOUN *Austral* a bustard.

plaister ('pleɪstə) NOUN *Scot* plaster.

plait (plæt) NOUN [1] a length of hair, ribbon, etc., that has been plaited. [2] (in Britain) a loaf of bread of several twisting or intertwining parts. [3] a rare spelling of **pleat.** ◆ VERB [4] (*tr*) to intertwine (strands or strips) in a pattern.
▷HISTORY C15 *pleyt,* from Old French *pleit,* from Latin *plicāre* to fold; see PLY[2]

plan (plæn) NOUN [1] a detailed scheme, method, etc., for attaining an objective. [2] (*sometimes plural*) a proposed, usually tentative idea for doing something. [3] a drawing to scale of a horizontal section through a building taken at a given level; a view from above an object or an area in orthographic projection. Compare **ground plan** (sense 1), **elevation** (sense 5). [4] an outline, sketch, etc. [5] (in perspective drawing) any of several imaginary planes perpendicular to the line of vision and between the eye and object depicted. ◆ VERB **plans, planning, planned.** [6] to form a plan (for) or make plans (for). [7] (*tr*) to make a plan of (a building). [8] (*tr; takes a clause as object or an infinitive*) to have in mind as a purpose; intend.
▷HISTORY C18: via French from Latin *plānus* flat; compare PLANE[1], PLAIN[1]

planar ('pleɪnə) ADJECTIVE [1] of or relating to a plane. [2] lying in one plane; flat.
▷HISTORY C19: from Late Latin *plānāris* on level ground, from Latin *plānus* flat
▸ **planarity** (pleɪ'nærɪtɪ) NOUN

planarian (plə'nɛərɪən) NOUN any free-living turbellarian flatworm of the mostly aquatic suborder *Tricladida,* having a three-branched intestine.
▷HISTORY C19: from New Latin *Plānāria* type genus, from Late Latin *plānārius* level, flat; see PLANE[1]

planar process NOUN a method of producing diffused junctions in semiconductor devices. A pattern of holes is etched into an oxide layer formed on a silicon substrate, into which impurities are diffused through the holes.

planation (pleɪ'neɪʃən) NOUN the erosion of a land surface until it is basically flat.

planchet ('plɑːntʃɪt) NOUN a piece of metal ready to be stamped as a coin, medal, etc.; flan.
▷HISTORY C17: from French: little board, from *planche* PLANK[1]

planchette (plɑːn'ʃet) NOUN a heart-shaped board on wheels, on which messages are written under supposed spirit guidance.
▷HISTORY C19: from French: little board, from *planche* PLANK[1]

Planck constant *or* **Planck's constant** NOUN a fundamental constant equal to the energy of any quantum of radiation divided by its frequency. It has a value of $6.62606876 \times 10^{-34}$ joule seconds. Symbol: *h.* See also **Dirac constant.**
▷HISTORY C20: after Max *Planck* (1858–1947), German physicist

Planck's law NOUN *Physics* a law that is the basis of quantum theory, which states that the energy of electromagnetic radiation is confined to indivisible packets (quanta), each of which has an energy equal to the product of the Planck constant and the frequency of the radiation.
▷HISTORY C20: after Max *Planck* (1858–1947), German physicist

plane[1] (pleɪn) NOUN [1] *Maths* a flat surface in which a straight line joining any two of its points lies entirely on that surface. [2] a flat or level surface. [3] a level of existence, performance, attainment, etc. [4] **a** short for **aeroplane. b** a wing or supporting surface of an aircraft or hydroplane. ◆ ADJECTIVE [5] level or flat. [6] *Maths* (of a curve, figure, etc.) lying entirely in one plane. ◆ VERB (*intr*) [7] to fly without moving wings or using engines; glide. [8] (of a boat) to rise partly and skim over the water when moving at a certain speed. [9] to travel by aeroplane.
▷HISTORY C17: from Latin *plānum* level surface
▸ **'planeness** NOUN

plane[2] (pleɪn) NOUN [1] a tool with an adjustable sharpened steel blade set obliquely in a wooden or iron body, for levelling or smoothing timber surfaces, cutting mouldings or grooves, etc. [2] a flat tool, usually metal, for smoothing the surface of clay or plaster in a mould. ◆ VERB (*tr*) [3] to level, smooth, or cut (timber, wooden articles, etc.) using a plane or similar tool. [4] (often foll by *off*) to remove using a plane.

▷**HISTORY** C14: via Old French from Late Latin *plāna* plane, from *plānāre* to level

plane³ (pleɪn) NOUN See **plane tree**.

plane angle NOUN an angle between two intersecting lines.

plane chart NOUN a chart used in plane sailing, in which the lines of latitude and longitude are straight and parallel.

plane geometry NOUN the study of the properties of and relationships between plane curves, figures, etc.

plane polarization NOUN a type of polarization in which the electric vector of waves of light or other electromagnetic radiation is restricted to vibration in a single plane.

planer (ˈpleɪnə) NOUN 1 a machine with a cutting tool that makes repeated horizontal strokes across the surface of a workpiece: used to cut flat surfaces into metal. 2 a machine for planing wood, esp one in which the cutting blades are mounted on a rotating drum. 3 *Printing* a flat piece of wood used to level type in a chase. 4 any person or thing that planes.

plane sailing NOUN *Nautical* navigation without reference to the earth's curvature. Compare **plain sailing**.

plane spotter NOUN a person who observes, photographs, and catalogues aircraft as a hobby.

plane surveying NOUN the surveying of areas of limited size, making no corrections for the earth's curvature.

planet (ˈplænɪt) NOUN 1 Also called: **major planet**. any of the nine celestial bodies, Mercury, Venus, Earth, Mars, Jupiter, Saturn, Uranus, Neptune, or Pluto, that revolve around the sun in elliptical orbits and are illuminated by light from the sun. 2 Also called: **extrasolar planet**. any other celestial body revolving around a star, illuminated by light from that star. 3 *Astrology* any of the planets of the solar system, excluding the earth but including the sun and moon, each thought to rule one or sometimes two signs of the zodiac. See also **house** (sense 9).
▷**HISTORY** C12: via Old French from Late Latin *planēta*, from Greek *planētēs* wanderer, from *planaein* to wander

plane table NOUN 1 a surveying instrument consisting of a drawing board mounted on adjustable legs, and used in the field for plotting measurements directly. ◆ VERB **plane-table**. 2 to survey (a plot of land) using a plane table.

planetarium (ˌplænɪˈtɛərɪəm) NOUN, *plural* **-iums** *or* **-ia** (-ɪə). 1 an instrument for simulating the apparent motions of the sun, moon, and planets against a background of stars by projecting images of these bodies onto the inside of a domed ceiling. 2 a building in which such an instrument is housed. 3 a model of the solar system, sometimes mechanized to show the relative motions of the planets.

planetary (ˈplænɪtərɪ, -trɪ) ADJECTIVE 1 of or relating to a planet. 2 mundane; terrestrial. 3 wandering or erratic. 4 *Astrology* under the influence of one of the planets. 5 (of a gear, esp an epicyclic gear) having an axis that rotates around that of another gear. 6 (of an electron) having an orbit around the nucleus of an atom. ◆ NOUN, *plural* **-taries**. 7 a train of planetary gears.

planetary nebula NOUN an expanding shell of gas surrounding a dying star, formed from matter ejected from the star's outer layers; the gas is ionized by the remaining hot stellar core, emitting light in the process.
▷**HISTORY** C18: named from its (occasional) resemblance to a planetary disc

planetesimal hypothesis (ˌplænɪˈtɛsɪməl) NOUN the discredited theory that the close passage of a star to the sun caused many small bodies (**planetesimals**) to be drawn from the sun, eventually coalescing to form the planets.
▷**HISTORY** C20: *planetesimal*, from PLANET + INFINITESIMAL

planetoid (ˈplænɪˌtɔɪd) NOUN another name for **asteroid** (sense 1).
▸ˌ**planeˈtoidal** ADJECTIVE

planetology (ˌplænɪˈtɒlədʒɪ) NOUN *Astronomy* the study of the origin, composition, and distribution of matter in the planets.

plane tree *or* **plane** NOUN any tree of the genus *Platanus*, having ball-shaped heads of fruits and leaves with pointed lobes: family *Platanaceae*. The hybrid *P.* × *acerifolia* (**London plane**) is frequently planted in towns. Also called: **platan**.
▷**HISTORY** C14 *plane*, from Old French, from Latin *platanus*, from Greek *platanos*, from *platos* wide, referring to the leaves

planet-struck *or* **planet-stricken** ADJECTIVE *Astrology* affected by the influence of a planet, esp malignly.

planet wheel *or* **gear** NOUN any one of the wheels of an epicyclic gear train that orbits the central axis of the train.

planet Zog NOUN *Brit informal* a place or situation that is far removed from reality or what is currently happening: *those of you who've been on planet Zog for the last ten years*.

planform (ˈplænˌfɔːm) NOUN the outline or silhouette of an object, esp an aircraft, as seen from above.

plangent (ˈplændʒənt) ADJECTIVE 1 having a loud deep sound. 2 resonant and mournful in sound.
▷**HISTORY** C19: from Latin *plangere* to beat (esp the breast, in grief); see PLAIN²
▸ˈ**plangency** NOUN ▸ˈ**plangently** ADVERB

planimeter (plæˈnɪmɪtə) NOUN a mechanical integrating instrument for measuring the area of an irregular plane figure, such as the area under a curve, by moving a point attached to an arm around the perimeter of the figure.

planimetry (plæˈnɪmɪtrɪ) NOUN the measurement of plane areas.
▸**planimetric** (ˌplænɪˈmɛtrɪk) *or* ˌ**planiˈmetrical** ADJECTIVE

planish (ˈplænɪʃ) VERB (*tr*) to give a final finish to (metal) by hammering or rolling to produce a smooth surface.
▷**HISTORY** C16: from Old French *planir* to smooth out, from Latin *plānus* flat, PLAIN¹
▸ˈ**planisher** NOUN

planisphere (ˈplænɪˌsfɪə) NOUN a projection or representation of all or part of a sphere on a plane surface, such as a polar projection of the celestial sphere onto a chart.
▷**HISTORY** C14: from Medieval Latin *plānisphaerium*, from Latin *plānus* flat + Greek *sphaira* globe
▸**planispheric** (ˌplænɪˈsfɛrɪk) ADJECTIVE

plank¹ (plæŋk) NOUN 1 a stout length of sawn timber. 2 something that supports or sustains. 3 one of the policies in a political party's programme. 4 **walk the plank**. to be forced by pirates to walk to one's death off the end of a plank jutting out over the water from the side of a ship. ◆ VERB (*tr*) 5 to cover or provide (an area) with planks. 6 to beat (meat) to make it tender. 7 *Chiefly US and Canadian* to cook or serve (meat or fish) on a special wooden board.
▷**HISTORY** C13: from Old Norman French *planke*, from Late Latin *planca* board, from *plancus* flat-footed; probably related to Greek *plax* flat surface

plank² (plæŋk) VERB (*tr*) *Scot* to hide; cache.
▷**HISTORY** C19: a variant of *plant*

planking (ˈplæŋkɪŋ) NOUN 1 a number of planks. 2 the act of covering or furnishing with planks.

plank-sheer NOUN *Nautical* a plank or timber covering the upper ends of the frames of a wooden vessel.
▷**HISTORY** C14 *plancher*, from Old French *planchier*, from *planche* plank, from Latin *planca*; spelling influenced by PLANK¹, SHEER¹

plankton (ˈplæŋktən) NOUN the organisms inhabiting the surface layer of a sea or lake, consisting of small drifting plants and animals, such as diatoms. Compare **nekton**.
▷**HISTORY** C19: via German from Greek *planktos* wandering, from *plazesthai* to roam
▸**planktonic** (plæŋkˈtɒnɪk) ADJECTIVE

planned economy NOUN another name for **command economy**.

planned obsolescence NOUN the policy of deliberately limiting the life of a product in order to encourage the purchaser to replace it. Also called: **built-in obsolescence**.

planner (ˈplænə) NOUN 1 a person who makes plans, esp for the development of a town, building, etc. 2 a chart for recording future appointments, tasks, goals, etc.

planning blight NOUN the harmful effects of uncertainty about likely restrictions on the types and extent of future development in a particular area on the quality of life of its inhabitants and the normal growth of its business and community enterprises.

planning permission NOUN (in Britain) formal permission that must be obtained from a local authority before development or a change of use of land or buildings.

plano- *or sometimes before a vowel* **plan-** COMBINING FORM indicating flatness or planeness: *plano-concave*.
▷**HISTORY** from Latin *plānus* flat, level

plano-concave (ˌpleɪnəʊˈkɒnkeɪv) ADJECTIVE (of a lens) having one side concave and the other side plane.

plano-convex (ˌpleɪnəʊˈkɒnvɛks) ADJECTIVE (of a lens) having one side convex and the other side plane.

planogamete (ˈplænəgəˌmiːt) NOUN a motile gamete, such as a spermatozoon.
▷**HISTORY** C19: from Greek *planos* wandering (see PLANET) + GAMETE

planography (pləˈnɒgrəfɪ) NOUN *Printing* any process, such as lithography, for printing from a flat surface.
▸**planographic** (ˌpleɪnəˈgræfɪk) ADJECTIVE
▸ˌ**planoˈgraphically** ADVERB

planometer (plæˈnɒmɪtə) NOUN a flat metal plate used for directly testing the flatness of metal surfaces in accurate metalwork.
▸**planometric** (ˌpleɪnəˈmɛtrɪk) ADJECTIVE
▸ˌ**planoˈmetrically** ADVERB ▸**plaˈnometry** NOUN

planosol (ˈpleɪnəˌsɒl) NOUN a type of intrazonal soil of humid or subhumid uplands having a strongly leached upper layer overlying a clay hardpan.
▷**HISTORY** C20: from Latin PLANO- + *solum* soil

plant¹ (plɑːnt) NOUN 1 any living organism that typically synthesizes its food from inorganic substances, possesses cellulose cell walls, responds slowly and often permanently to a stimulus, lacks specialized sense organs and nervous system, and has no powers of locomotion. 2 such an organism that is green, terrestrial, and smaller than a shrub or tree; a herb. 3 a cutting, seedling, or similar structure, esp when ready for transplantation. 4 *Informal* a thing positioned secretly for discovery by another, esp in order to incriminate an innocent person. 5 *Billiards, snooker* a position in which the cue ball can be made to strike an intermediate which then pockets another ball. ◆ VERB (*tr*) 6 (often foll by *out*) to set (seeds, crops, etc.) into (ground) to grow. 7 to place firmly in position. 8 to establish; found. 9 to implant in the mind. 10 *Slang* to deliver (a blow). 11 *Informal* to position or hide, esp in order to deceive or observe. 12 to place (young fish, oysters, spawn, etc.) in (a lake, river, etc.) in order to stock the water. ◆ See also **plant out**.
▷**HISTORY** Old English, from Latin *planta* a shoot, cutting
▸ˈ**plantable** ADJECTIVE ▸ˈ**plantˌlike** ADJECTIVE

plant² (plɑːnt) NOUN 1 **a** the land, buildings, and equipment used in carrying on an industrial, business, or other undertaking or service. **b** (*as modifier*): *plant costs*. 2 a factory or workshop. 3 mobile mechanical equipment for construction, road-making, etc.
▷**HISTORY** C20: special use of PLANT¹

plant agreement NOUN a collective agreement at plant level within industry.

plantain¹ (ˈplæntɪn) NOUN any of various N temperate plants of the genus *Plantago, esp P. major* (**great plantain**), which has a rosette of broad leaves and a slender spike of small greenish flowers: family *Plantaginaceae*. See also **ribwort**.
▷**HISTORY** C14 *plauntein*, from Old French *plantein*, from Latin *plantāgō*, from *planta* sole of the foot

plantain² (ˈplæntɪn) NOUN 1 a large tropical musaceous plant, *Musa paradisiaca*. 2 the green-skinned banana-like fruit of this plant, eaten as a staple food in many tropical regions.
▷**HISTORY** C16: from Spanish *platano* plantain, PLANE TREE

plantain-eater NOUN another name for **touraco**.

plantain lily NOUN any of several Asian plants of the liliaceous genus *Hosta,* having broad ribbed leaves and clusters of white, blue, or lilac flowers. Also called: **day lily.**

plantar ('plæntə) ADJECTIVE of, relating to, or occurring on the sole of the foot or a corresponding part: *plantar warts.*
▷HISTORY C18: from Latin *plantāris,* from *planta* sole of the foot

plantation (plæn'teɪʃən) NOUN 1 an estate, esp in tropical countries, where cash crops such as rubber, oil palm, etc., are grown on a large scale. 2 a group of cultivated trees or plants. 3 (formerly) a colony or group of settlers. 4 *Rare* the planting of seeds, shoots, etc.

planter ('plɑːntə) NOUN 1 the owner or manager of a plantation. 2 a machine designed for rapid, uniform, and efficient planting of seeds in the ground. 3 a colonizer or settler. 4 a decorative pot or stand for house plants.

planter's punch NOUN a cocktail consisting of rum with lime or lemon juice and sugar.

plantigrade ('plæntɪˌɡreɪd) ADJECTIVE 1 walking with the entire sole of the foot touching the ground, as, for example, man and bears. ◆ NOUN 2 a plantigrade animal.
▷HISTORY C19: via French from New Latin *plantigradus,* from Latin *planta* sole of the foot + *gradus* a step

plant kingdom NOUN a category of living organisms comprising all plants but excluding the algae, fungi, and bacteria. Compare **animal kingdom, mineral kingdom.**

plant louse NOUN 1 another name for an **aphid.** 2 **jumping plant louse.** any small active cicada-like insect of the homopterous family *Psyllidae* (or *Chermidae*), having hind legs adapted for leaping, and feeding on plant juices.

plantocracy (plɑːn'tɒkrəsɪ) NOUN, *plural* **-cies.** a ruling social class composed of planters.

plant out VERB (*tr, adverb*) to set (a seedling that has been raised in a greenhouse, frame, or other sheltered place) to grow out in open ground.

plantsman ('plɑːntsmən) *or feminine* **plantswoman** NOUN, *plural* **-men** *or* **-women.** an experienced gardener who specializes in collecting rare or interesting plants.

planula ('plænjʊlə) NOUN, *plural* **-lae** (-ˌliː). the ciliated free-swimming larva of hydrozoan coelenterates such as the hydra.
▷HISTORY C19: from New Latin: a little plane, from Latin *plānum* level ground
▸'**planular** ADJECTIVE

plaque (plæk, plɑːk) NOUN 1 an ornamental or commemorative inscribed tablet or plate of porcelain, wood, etc. 2 a small flat brooch or badge, as of a club, etc. 3 *Pathol* any small abnormal patch on or within the body, such as the typical lesion of psoriasis. 4 short for **dental plaque.** 5 *Bacteriol* a clear area within a bacterial or tissue culture caused by localized destruction of the cells by a bacteriophage or other virus.
▷HISTORY C19: from French, from *plaquier* to plate, from Middle Dutch *placken* to beat (metal) into a thin plate

plash[1] (plæʃ) VERB, NOUN a less common word for **splash.**
▷HISTORY Old English *plæsc,* probably imitative; compare Dutch *plas*

plash[2] (plæʃ) VERB another word for **pleach.**
▷HISTORY C15: from Old French *plassier,* from *plais* hedge, woven fence, from Latin *plectere* to plait; compare PLEACH

plashy ('plæʃɪ) ADJECTIVE **plashier, plashiest.** 1 wet or marshy. 2 splashing or splashy.

-plasia *or* **-plasy** NOUN COMBINING FORM indicating growth, development, or change: *hypoplasia.*
▷HISTORY from New Latin, from Greek *plasis* a moulding, from *plassein* to mould

plasm ('plæzəm) NOUN 1 protoplasm of a specified type: *germ plasm.* 2 a variant of **plasma.**

-plasm NOUN COMBINING FORM (in biology) indicating the material forming cells: *protoplasm; cytoplasm.*
▷HISTORY from Greek *plasma* something moulded; see PLASMA
▸**-plasmic** ADJECTIVE COMBINING FORM

plasma ('plæzmə) *or* **plasm** NOUN 1 the clear yellowish fluid portion of blood or lymph in which the red blood cells, white blood cells, and platelets are suspended. 2 short for **blood plasma.** 3 a former name for **protoplasm** or **cytoplasm.** 4 *Physics* **a** a hot ionized material consisting of nuclei and electrons. It is sometimes regarded as a fourth state of matter and is the material present in the sun, most stars, and fusion reactors. **b** the ionized gas in an electric discharge or spark, containing positive ions and electrons and a small number of negative ions together with un-ionized material. 5 a green slightly translucent variety of chalcedony, used as a gemstone. 6 a less common term for **whey.**
▷HISTORY C18: from Late Latin: something moulded, from Greek, from *plassein* to mould
▸**plasmatic** (plæz'mætɪk) *or* '**plasmic** ADJECTIVE

plasma engine NOUN an engine that generates thrust by reaction to the emission of a jet of plasma.

plasmagel ('plæzməˌdʒɛl) NOUN another name for **ectoplasm** (sense 1).

plasmagene ('plæzməˌdʒiːn) NOUN *Biology* any gene other than those carried in the nucleus of a eukaryotic cell, such as a mitochondrial gene.
▸**plasmagenic** (ˌplæzmə'dʒɛnɪk) ADJECTIVE

plasmalemma (ˌplæzmə'lɛmə) *or* **plasma membrane** NOUN other names for **cell membrane.**

plasmapheresis (ˌplæzmə'fɛrəsəs) NOUN (in blood transfusion) a technique for removing healthy or infected plasma by separating it from the red blood cells by settling or using a centrifuge and retransfusing the red blood cells into the donor or patient.
▷HISTORY C20: from PLASM + Greek *aphairesis* taking away

plasmasol ('plæzməˌsɒl) NOUN another name for **endoplasm.**

plasma torch NOUN an electrical device for converting a gas into a plasma, used for melting metal.

plasmid ('plæzmɪd) NOUN a small circle of bacterial DNA that is independent of the main bacterial chromosome. Plasmids often contain genes for drug resistances and can be transmitted between bacteria of the same and different species: used in genetic engineering.
▷HISTORY C20: from PLASM + -ID[1]

plasmin ('plæzmɪn) NOUN a proteolytic enzyme that causes fibrinolysis in blood clots.

plasminogen (plæz'mɪnədʒən) NOUN *Biochem* a zymogen found in blood that gives rise to plasmin on activation.

plasmo- *or before a vowel* **plasm-** COMBINING FORM of, relating to, or resembling plasma: *plasmolysis.*
▷HISTORY from Greek *plasma;* see PLASMA

plasmodesma (ˌplæzmə'dɛzmə) *or* **plasmodesm** ('plæzməˌdɛzəm) NOUN, *plural* **-desmata** (-'dɛzmətə) *or* **-desms.** *Botany* any of various very fine cytoplasmic threads connecting the cytoplasm of adjacent cells via minute holes in the cell walls.
▷HISTORY C20: from PLASMO- + Greek *desma* bond

plasmodium (plæz'məʊdɪəm) NOUN, *plural* **-dia** (-dɪə). 1 an amoeboid mass of protoplasm, containing many nuclei: a stage in the life cycle of certain organisms, esp the nonreproductive stage of the slime moulds. 2 any parasitic sporozoan protozoan of the genus *Plasmodium,* such as *P. falciparum* and *P. vivax,* which cause malaria.
▷HISTORY C19: New Latin; see PLASMA, -ODE[1]
▸**plas'modial** ADJECTIVE

plasmoid ('plæzˌmɔɪd) NOUN *Physics* a section of a plasma having a characteristic shape.

plasmolyse *or US* **plasmolyze** ('plæzməˌlaɪz) VERB to subject (a cell) to plasmolysis or (of a cell) to undergo plasmolysis.

plasmolysis (plæz'mɒlɪsɪs) NOUN the shrinkage of protoplasm away from the cell walls that occurs as a result of excessive water loss, esp in plant cells (see **exosmosis**).
▸**plasmolytic** (ˌplæzmə'lɪtɪk) ADJECTIVE
▸ˌ**plasmo'lytically** ADVERB

plasmon ('plæzmɒn) NOUN *Genetics* the sum total of plasmagenes in a cell.
▷HISTORY C20: from German, from Greek *plasma.* See PLASMA

plasmosome ('plæzməˌsəʊm) NOUN another name for **nucleolus.**

Plassey ('plæsɪ) NOUN a village in NE India, in W Bengal: scene of Clive's victory (1757) over Siraj-ud-daula, which established British supremacy over India.

-plast NOUN COMBINING FORM indicating an organized living cell or particle of living matter: *protoplast.*
▷HISTORY from Greek *plastos* formed, from *plassein* to form

plaster ('plɑːstə) NOUN 1 a mixture of lime, sand, and water, sometimes stiffened with hair or other fibres, that is applied to the surface of a wall or ceiling as a soft paste that hardens when dry. 2 *Brit, Austral, and NZ* an adhesive strip of material, usually medicated, for dressing a cut, wound, etc. 3 short for **mustard plaster** or **plaster of Paris.** ◆ VERB 4 to coat (a wall, ceiling, etc.) with plaster. 5 (*tr*) to apply like plaster: *she plastered make-up on her face.* 6 (*tr*) to cause to lie flat or to adhere. 7 (*tr*) to apply a plaster cast to. 8 (*tr*) *Slang* to strike or defeat with great force.
▷HISTORY Old English, from Medieval Latin *plastrum* medicinal salve, building plaster, via Latin from Greek *emplastron* curative dressing, from EM- + *plassein* to form
▸'**plasterer** NOUN ▸'**plastery** ADJECTIVE

plasterboard ('plɑːstəˌbɔːd) NOUN a thin rigid board, in the form of a layer of plaster compressed between two layers of fibreboard, used to form or cover walls.

plaster cast NOUN 1 *Surgery* a cast made of plaster of Paris. See **cast** (sense 40). 2 a copy or mould of a sculpture or other object cast in plaster of Paris.

plastered ('plɑːstəd) ADJECTIVE *Slang* intoxicated; drunk.

plastering ('plɑːstərɪŋ) NOUN a coating or layer of plaster.

plaster of Paris NOUN 1 a white powder that sets to a hard solid when mixed with water, used for making sculptures and casts, as an additive for lime plasters, and for making casts for setting broken limbs. It is usually the hemihydrate of calcium sulphate, $2CaSO_4.H_2O$. 2 the hard plaster produced when this powder is mixed with water: a fully hydrated form of calcium sulphate. ◆ Sometimes shortened to: **plaster.**
▷HISTORY C15: from Medieval Latin *plastrum parisiense,* originally made from the gypsum of *Paris*

plastic ('plæstɪk, 'plɑːs-) NOUN 1 any one of a large number of synthetic usually organic materials that have a polymeric structure and can be moulded when soft and then set, esp such a material in a finished state containing plasticizer, stabilizer, filler, pigments, etc. Plastics are classified as thermosetting (such as Bakelite) or thermoplastic (such as PVC) and are used in the manufacture of many articles and in coatings, artificial fibres, etc. Compare **resin** (sense 2). 2 short for **plastic money.** ◆ ADJECTIVE 3 made of plastic. 4 easily influenced; impressionable: *the plastic minds of children.* 5 capable of being moulded or formed. 6 *Fine arts* **a** of or relating to moulding or modelling: *the plastic arts.* **b** produced or apparently produced by moulding: *the plastic draperies of Giotto's figures.* 7 having the power to form or influence: *the plastic forces of the imagination.* 8 *Biology* of or relating to any formative process; able to change, develop, or grow: *plastic tissues.* 9 of or relating to plastic surgery. 10 *Slang* superficially attractive yet unoriginal or artificial: *plastic food.*
▷HISTORY C17: from Latin *plasticus* relating to moulding, from Greek *plastikos,* from *plassein* to form
▸'**plastically** ADVERB

-plastic ADJECTIVE COMBINING FORM growing or forming: *neoplastic.*
▷HISTORY from Greek *plastikos;* see PLASTIC

plastic bomb NOUN a bomb consisting of a putty-like explosive charge fitted with a detonator and timing device.

plastic bullet NOUN a solid PVC cylinder, 10 cm long and 38 mm in diameter, fired by police or military forces to regain control in riots. Formal name: **baton round.**

Plasticine ('plæstɪˌsiːn) NOUN *Trademark* a soft

coloured material used, esp by children, for modelling.

plasticity (plæ'stɪsɪtɪ) NOUN 1 the quality of being plastic or able to be moulded. 2 (in pictorial art) the quality of depicting space and form so that they appear three-dimensional.

plasticize *or* **plasticise** ('plæstɪ,saɪz) VERB to make or become plastic, as by the addition of a plasticizer.
▸ **,plastici'zation** *or* **,plastici'sation** NOUN

plasticizer *or* **plasticiser** ('plæstɪ,saɪzə) NOUN any of a number of substances added to materials in order to modify their physical properties. Their uses include softening and improving the flexibility of plastics and preventing dried paint coatings from becoming too brittle.

plasticky ('plæ,stɪkɪ) ADJECTIVE made of or resembling plastic.

plastic money NOUN credit cards, used instead of cash.
▷HISTORY C20: from the cards being made of plastic

plastic surgery NOUN the branch of surgery concerned with therapeutic or cosmetic repair or re-formation of missing, injured, or malformed tissues or parts. Also called: **anaplasty.**
▸ **plastic surgeon** NOUN

plastid ('plæstɪd) NOUN any of various small particles in the cytoplasm of the cells of plants and some animals that contain pigments (see **chromoplast**), starch, oil, protein, etc.
▷HISTORY C19: via German from Greek *plastēs* sculptor, from *plassein* to form

plastometer (plæ'stɒmɪtə) NOUN an instrument for measuring plasticity.
▸ **plastometric** (,plæstəʊ'mɛtrɪk) ADJECTIVE
▸ **plas'tometry** NOUN

plastron ('plæstrən) NOUN the bony plate forming the ventral part of the shell of a tortoise or turtle.
▷HISTORY C16: via French from Italian *piastrone*, from *piastra* breastplate, from Latin *emplastrum* PLASTER
▸ **'plastral** ADJECTIVE

-plasty NOUN COMBINING FORM indicating plastic surgery involving a bodily part, tissue, or a specified process: *rhinoplasty; neoplasty*.
▷HISTORY from Greek *-plastia;* see -PLAST

plat¹ (plæt) NOUN a small area of ground; plot.
▷HISTORY C16 (also occurring in Middle English in place names): originally variant of PLOT²

plat² (plæt) NOUN, VERB **plats, platting, platted.** *Dialect* a variant spelling of **plait.**
▷HISTORY C16: variant of PLAIT

Plata (*Spanish* 'plata) NOUN **Río de la** ('rio de la). an estuary on the SE coast of South America, between Argentina and Uruguay, formed by the Uruguay and Paraná Rivers. Length: 275 km (171 miles). Width: (at its mouth) 225 km (140 miles). Also called: **La Plata.** English name: (River) **Plate.**

Plataea (plə'ti:ə) NOUN an ancient city in S Boeotia, traditionally an ally of Athens: scene of the defeat of a great Persian army by the Greeks in 479 B.C.

platan ('plætᵊn) NOUN another name for **plane tree.**
▷HISTORY C14: from Latin *platanus*, from Greek *platanos;* see PLANE TREE

plat du jour ('plɑ: də 'ʒʊə; *French* pla dy ʒur) NOUN, *plural* **plats du jour** ('plɑ:z də 'ʒʊə; *French* pla dy ʒur). the specially prepared or recommended dish of the day on a restaurant's menu.
▷HISTORY French, literally: dish of the day

plate (pleɪt) NOUN 1 **a** a shallow usually circular dish made of porcelain, earthenware, glass, etc., on which food is served or from which food is eaten. **b** (*as modifier*): *a plate rack*. 2 **a** Also called: **plateful.** the contents of a plate or the amount a plate will hold. **b** *Austral and NZ* a plate of cakes, sandwiches, etc., brought by a guest to a party: *everyone was asked to bring a plate*. 3 an entire course of a meal: *a cold plate*. 4 any shallow or flat receptacle, esp for receiving a collection in church. 5 flat metal of uniform thickness obtained by rolling, usually having a thickness greater than about three millimetres. 6 a thin coating of metal usually on another metal, as produced by electrodeposition, chemical action, etc. 7 metal or metalware that has been coated in this way, esp with gold or silver: *Sheffield plate*. 8 dishes, cutlery, etc., made of gold or silver. 9 a sheet of metal, plastic, rubber, etc., having a printing surface produced by a process such as stereotyping, moulding, or photographic deposition. 10 a print taken from such a sheet or from a woodcut, esp when appearing in a book. 11 a thin flat sheet of a substance, such as metal or glass. 12 armour made of overlapping or articulated pieces of thin metal. 13 *Photog* **a** a sheet of glass, or sometimes metal, coated with photographic emulsion on which an image can be formed by exposure to light. **b** (*as modifier*): *a plate camera*. 14 an orthodontic device, esp one used for straightening children's teeth. 15 an informal word for **denture** (sense 1). 16 *Anatomy* any flat platelike structure or part. 17 **a** a cup or trophy awarded to the winner of a sporting contest, esp a horse race. **b** a race or contest for such a prize. 18 any of the rigid layers of the earth's lithosphere of which there are believed to be at least 15. See also **plate tectonics.** 19 *Electronics* **a** *Chiefly US* the anode in an electronic valve. **b** an electrode in an accumulator or capacitor. 20 a horizontal timber joist that supports rafters or studs. 21 a light horseshoe for flat racing. 22 a thin cut of beef from the brisket. 23 See **plate rail.** 24 Also called: **Communion plate.** *RC Church* a flat plate held under the chin of a communicant in order to catch any fragments of the consecrated Host. 25 *Archaic* a coin, esp one made of silver. 26 **on a plate.** in such a way as to be acquired without further trouble: *he was handed the job on a plate*. 27 **on one's plate.** waiting to be done or dealt with: *he has a lot on his plate at the moment*. ◆ VERB (*tr*) 28 to coat (a surface, usually metal) with a thin layer of other metal by electrolysis, chemical reaction, etc. 29 to cover with metal plates, as for protection. 30 *Printing* to make a stereotype or electrotype from (type or another plate). 31 to form (metal) into plate, esp by rolling. 32 to give a glossy finish to (paper) by calendering. 33 to grow (microorganisms) in a culture medium. ◆ See also **plate up.**
▷HISTORY C13: from Old French: thin metal sheet, something flat, from Vulgar Latin *plattus* (unattested); related to Greek *platus* flat

Plate (pleɪt) NOUN **River.** the English name for the (Río de la) **Plata.**

plate armour NOUN armour made of thin metal plates, which superseded mail during the 14th century.

plateau ('plætəʊ) NOUN, *plural* **-eaus** *or* **-eaux** (-əʊz). 1 a wide mainly level area of elevated land. 2 a relatively long period of stability; levelling off: *the rising prices reached a plateau*. ◆ VERB (*intr*) 3 to remain at a stable level for a relatively long period.
▷HISTORY C18: from French, from Old French *platel* something flat, from *plat* flat; see PLATE

Plateau ('plætəʊ) NOUN a state of central Nigeria, formed in 1976 from part of Benue-Plateau State: tin mining. Capital: Jos. Pop. (including Nassarawa state): 3 671 498 (1995 est.). Area (including Nassarawa state): 58 030 sq. km (22 405 sq. miles).

plated ('pleɪtɪd) ADJECTIVE 1 **a** coated with a layer of metal. **b** (*in combination*): *gold-plated*. 2 (of a fabric) knitted in two different yarns so that one appears on the face and the other on the back.

plate glass NOUN glass formed into a thin sheet by rolling, used for windows.

platelayer ('pleɪt,leɪə) NOUN *Brit* a workman who lays and maintains railway track. US equivalent: **trackman.**

platelet ('pleɪtlɪt) NOUN a minute cell occurring in the blood of vertebrates and involved in clotting of the blood. Formerly called: **thrombocyte.**
▷HISTORY C19: a small PLATE

platemark ('pleɪt,mɑ:k) NOUN, VERB another name for **hallmark** (senses 1, 4).

platen ('plætᵊn) NOUN 1 a flat plate in a printing press that presses the paper against the type. 2 the roller on a typewriter, against which the keys strike. 3 the worktable of a machine tool, esp one that is slotted to enable T-bolts to be used.
▷HISTORY C15: from Old French *platine*, from *plat* flat; see PLATE

plater ('pleɪtə) NOUN 1 a person or thing that plates. 2 *Horse racing* **a** a mediocre horse entered chiefly for minor races. **b** a blacksmith who shoes racehorses with the special type of light shoe used for racing.

plate rail NOUN *Railways* an early flat rail with an extended flange on its outer edge to retain wheels on the track. Sometimes shortened to: **plate.**

plate tectonics NOUN (*functioning as singular*) *Geology* the study of the structure of the earth's crust and mantle with reference to the theory that the earth's lithosphere is divided into large rigid blocks (**plates**) that are floating on semifluid rock and are thus able to interact with each other at their boundaries, and to the associated theories of continental drift and seafloor spreading.

plate up VERB (*adverb*) to put food on a plate, ready for serving.

platform ('plætfɔ:m) NOUN 1 a raised floor or other horizontal surface, such as a stage for speakers. 2 a raised area at a railway station, from which passengers have access to the trains. 3 See **drilling platform, production platform.** 4 the declared principles, aims, etc., of a political party, an organization, or an individual. 5 a level raised area of ground. 6 **a** the thick raised sole of some high-heeled shoes. **b** (*as modifier*): *platform shoes*. 7 a vehicle or level place on which weapons are mounted and fired. 8 a specific type of computer hardware or computer operating system.
▷HISTORY C16: from French *plateforme*, from *plat* flat + *forme* form, layout

platform game NOUN a type of computer game that is played by moving a figure on the screen through a series of obstacles and problems.

platform rocker NOUN *US and Canadian* a rocking chair supported on a stationary base.

platform ticket NOUN a ticket for admission to railway platforms but not for travel.

platina ('plætɪnə, plə'ti:nə) NOUN an alloy of platinum and several other metals, including palladium, osmium, and iridium.
▷HISTORY C18: from Spanish: silvery element, from *plata* silver, from Provençal: silver plate

plating ('pleɪtɪŋ) NOUN 1 a coating or layer of material, esp metal. 2 a layer or covering of metal plates.

platinic (plə'tɪnɪk) ADJECTIVE of or containing platinum, esp in the tetravalent state.

platiniferous (,plætɪ'nɪfərəs) ADJECTIVE platinum-bearing.

platiniridium (,plætɪnɪ'rɪdɪəm) NOUN any alloy of platinum and iridium: used in jewellery, electrical contacts, and hypodermic needles.

platinize *or* **platinise** ('plætɪ,naɪz) VERB (*tr*) to coat with platinum.
▸ **,platini'zation** *or* **,platini'sation** NOUN

platino-, platini-, *or before a vowel* **platin-** COMBINING FORM of, relating to, containing, or resembling platinum: *platinotype*.

platinocyanic acid (,plætɪnəʊsaɪ'ænɪk) NOUN a hypothetical tetrabasic acid known only in the form of platinocyanide salts. Formula: $H_2Pt(CN)_4$.

platinocyanide (,plætɪnəʊ'saɪə,naɪd, -nɪd) NOUN any salt containing the divalent complex cation $[Pt(CN)_4]^{2-}$.

platinoid ('plætɪ,nɔɪd) ADJECTIVE containing or resembling platinum: *a platinoid metal*.

platinotype ('plætɪnəʊ,taɪp) NOUN an obsolete process for producing photographic prints using paper coated with an emulsion containing platinum salts, the resulting image in platinum black being more permanent and of a richer tone than the usual silver image.

platinous ('plætɪnəs) ADJECTIVE of or containing platinum, esp in the divalent state.

platinum ('plætɪnəm) NOUN 1 a ductile malleable silvery-white metallic element, very resistant to heat and chemicals. It occurs free and in association with other platinum metals, esp in osmiridium: used in jewellery, laboratory apparatus, electrical contacts, dentistry, electroplating, and as a catalyst. Symbol: Pt; atomic no.: 78; atomic wt.: 195.08; valency: 1–4; relative density: 21.45; melting pt.: 1769°C; boiling pt.: 3827±100°C. 2 **a** a medium to light grey colour. **b** (*as adjective*): *a platinum carpet*.
▷HISTORY C19: New Latin, from PLATINA, on the model of other metals with the suffix *-um*

platinum black NOUN *Chem* a black powder consisting of very finely divided platinum metal. It is used as a catalyst, esp in hydrogenation reactions.

platinum-blond *or feminine* **platinum-blonde** ADJECTIVE 1 (of hair) of a pale silver-blond colour. 2 **a** having hair of this colour. **b** (*as noun*): *she was a platinum blonde.*

platinum disc NOUN **a** (in Britain) an album certified to have sold 300 000 copies or a single certified to have sold 600 000 copies. **b** (in the US) an album or single certified to have sold one million copies. Compare **gold disc, silver disc.**

platinum metal NOUN any of the group of precious metallic elements consisting of ruthenium, rhodium, palladium, osmium, iridium, and platinum.

platitude ('plætɪˌtjuːd) NOUN 1 a trite, dull, or obvious remark or statement; a commonplace. 2 staleness or insipidity of thought or language; triteness.
▷HISTORY C19: from French, literally: flatness, from *plat* flat
▸ˌplatiˈtudinous ADJECTIVE

platitudinize *or* **platitudinise** (ˌplætɪˈtjuːdɪˌnaɪz) VERB (*intr*) to speak or write in platitudes.
▸ˌplatiˈtudiˌnizer *or* ˌplatiˈtudiˌniser NOUN

Plato ('pleɪtəʊ) NOUN a crater in the NW quadrant of the moon, about 100 km in diameter, that has a conspicuous dark floor.

Platonic (pləˈtɒnɪk) ADJECTIVE 1 of or relating to the Greek philosopher Plato (?427–?347 B.C.) or his teachings. 2 (*often not capital*) free from physical desire: *Platonic love.*
▸Plaˈtonically ADVERB

Platonic solid NOUN any of the five possible regular polyhedra: cube, tetrahedron, octahedron, icosahedron, and dodecahedron. Also called (esp formerly): **Platonic body.**
▷HISTORY C17: named after Plato (?427–?347 B.C.), Greek philosopher, who was the first to list them

Platonism ('pleɪtəˌnɪzəm) NOUN 1 the teachings of the Greek philosopher Plato (?427–?347 B.C.) and his followers, esp the philosophical theory that the meanings of general words are real existing abstract entities (Forms) and that particular objects have properties in common by virtue of their relationship with these Forms. Compare **nominalism, conceptualism, intuitionism.** 2 the realist doctrine that mathematical entities have real existence and that mathematical truth is independent of human thought. 3 See **Neo-Platonism.**
▸ˈPlatonist NOUN

platoon (pləˈtuːn) NOUN 1 *Military* a subunit of a company usually comprising three sections of ten to twelve men: commanded by a lieutenant. 2 a group or unit of people, esp one sharing a common activity, characteristic, etc.
▷HISTORY C17: from French *peloton* little ball, group of men, from *pelote* ball; see PELLET

Plattdeutsch (*German* 'platdɔytʃ) NOUN another name for **Low German.**
▷HISTORY literally: flat (that is, low) German

Platte (plæt) NOUN a river system of the central US, formed by the confluence of the **North Platte** and **South Platte** at North Platte, Nebraska: flows generally east to the Missouri River. Length: 499 km (310 miles).

platteland ('plataˌlant) NOUN **the.** (in South Africa) the country districts or rural areas.
▷HISTORY C20: from Afrikaans, from Dutch *plat* flat + *land* country

platter ('plætə) NOUN 1 a large shallow usually oval dish or plate, used for serving food. 2 a course of a meal, usually consisting of several different foods served on the same plate: *a seafood platter.*
▷HISTORY C14: from Anglo-Norman *plater,* from *plat* dish, from Old French *plat* flat; see PLATE

platy[1] ('pleɪtɪ) ADJECTIVE **platier, platiest.** of, relating to, or designating rocks the constituents of which occur in flaky layers: *platy fracture.*
▷HISTORY C19: from PLATE + -Y[1]

platy[2] ('plætɪ) NOUN, *plural* **platy, platys** *or* **platies.** any of various small brightly coloured freshwater cyprinodont fishes of the Central American genus *Xiphophorus, esp X. maculatus.*
▷HISTORY C20: shortened from New Latin *Platypoecilus* former genus name, from PLATY- + *-poecilus,* from Greek *poikilos* spotted

platy- COMBINING FORM indicating something flat: *platyhelminth.*
▷HISTORY from Greek *platus* flat

platyhelminth (ˌplætɪˈhelmɪnθ) NOUN any invertebrate of the phylum *Platyhelminthes* (the flatworms).
▷HISTORY C19: from New Latin *Platyhelmintha* flatworm, from PLATY- + Greek *helmins* worm
▸ˌplatyhelˈminthic ADJECTIVE

platykurtic (ˌplætɪˈkɜːtɪk) ADJECTIVE *Statistics* (of a distribution) having kurtosis B_2 less than 3, less heavily concentrated about the mean than a normal distribution. Compare **leptokurtic, mesokurtic.**
▷HISTORY C20: from PLATY- + Greek *kurtos* arched, bulging + -IC

platypus ('plætɪpəs) NOUN, *plural* **-puses.** See **duck-billed platypus.**
▷HISTORY C18: New Latin, from PLATY- + *-pus,* from Greek *pous* foot

platyrrhine ('plætɪˌraɪn) *or* **platyrrhinian** (ˌplætɪˈrɪnɪən) ADJECTIVE 1 (esp of New World monkeys) having widely separated nostrils opening to the side of the face. 2 (of humans) having an unusually short wide nose. ◆ NOUN 3 an animal or person with this characteristic. ◆ Compare **catarrhine.**
▷HISTORY C19: from New Latin *platyrrhinus,* from PLATY- + *-rrhinus,* from Greek *rhis* nose

plaudit ('plɔːdɪt) NOUN (*usually plural*) 1 an expression of enthusiastic approval or approbation. 2 a round of applause.
▷HISTORY C17: shortened from earlier *plauditē,* from Latin: applaud!, from *plaudere* to APPLAUD

Plauen (*German* 'plauən) NOUN a city in E central Germany, in Saxony: textile centre. Pop.: 70 860 (1991).

plausible ('plɔːzəbᵊl) ADJECTIVE 1 apparently reasonable, valid, truthful, etc.: *a plausible excuse.* 2 apparently trustworthy or believable: *a plausible speaker.*
▷HISTORY C16: from Latin *plausibilis* worthy of applause, from *plaudere* to APPLAUD
▸ˌplausiˈbility *or* ˈplausibleness NOUN ▸ˈplausibly ADVERB

plausive ('plɔːsɪv) ADJECTIVE 1 expressing praise or approval; applauding. 2 *Obsolete* plausible.

play (pleɪ) VERB 1 to occupy oneself in (a sport or diversion); amuse oneself in (a game). 2 (*tr*) to contend against (an opponent) in a sport or game: *Ed played Tony at chess and lost.* 3 to fulfil or cause to fulfil (a particular role) in a team game: *he plays defence; he plays in the defence.* 4 (*tr*) to address oneself to (a ball) in a game: *play the ball not the man.* 5 (*intr;* often foll by *about* or *around*) to behave carelessly, esp in a way that is unconsciously cruel or hurtful; trifle or dally (with): *to play about with a young girl's affections.* 6 (when *intr,* often foll by *at*) to perform or act the part (of) in or as in a dramatic production; assume or simulate the role (of): *to play the villain; just what are you playing at?* 7 to act out or perform (a dramatic production). 8 to give a performance in (a place) or (of a performance) to be given in a place. 9 to have the ability to perform on (a musical instrument): *David plays the harp.* 10 to perform (on a musical instrument) as specified: *he plays out of tune.* 11 (*tr*) **a** to reproduce (a tune, melody, piece of music, note, etc.) on an instrument. **b** to perform works by (a specific composer): *to play Brahms.* 12 to discharge or cause to discharge: *he played the water from the hose onto the garden.* 13 to operate, esp to cause (a record player, radio, etc.) to emit sound or (of a record player, radio, etc.) to emit (sound): *he played a record; the radio was playing loudly.* 14 to move or cause to move freely, quickly, or irregularly: *lights played on the scenery.* 15 (*tr*) *Stock Exchange* to speculate or operate aggressively for gain in (a market). 16 (*tr*) *Angling* to attempt to tire (a hooked fish) by alternately letting out and reeling in line and by using the rod's flexibility. 17 to put (a card, counter, piece, etc.) into play. 18 to gamble (money) on a game. 19 **play ball.** *Informal* to cooperate. 20 **play fair** (*or* **false**). (often foll by *with*) to prove oneself fair (or unfair) in one's dealings. 21 **play by ear.** See **ear**[1] (sense 19). 22 **play for time.** to delay the outcome of some activity so as to gain time to one's own advantage. 23 **play into the hands of.** to act directly to the advantage of (an opponent). 24 **play the fool.** See **fool**[1] (sense 7). 25 **play the game.** See **game**[1] (sense 22). ◆ NOUN 26 a dramatic composition written for performance by actors on a stage, on television, etc.; drama. 27 **a** the performance of a dramatic composition. **b** (*in combination*): *playreader.* 28 **a** games, exercise, or other activity undertaken for pleasure, diversion, etc., esp by children. **b** (*in combination*): *playroom.* **c** (*as modifier*): *play dough.* 29 manner of action, conduct, or playing: *fair play.* 30 the playing or conduct of a game or the period during which a game is in progress: *rain stopped play.* 31 *US and Canadian* a move or manoeuvre in a game: *a brilliant play.* 32 the situation of a ball that is within the defined area and being played according to the rules (in the phrases **in play, out of play**). 33 a turn to play: *it's my play.* 34 the act of playing for stakes; gambling. 35 action, activity, or operation: *the play of the imagination.* 36 freedom of or scope or space for movement: *too much play in the rope.* 37 light, free, or rapidly shifting motion: *the play of light on the water.* 38 fun, jest, or joking: *I only did it in play.* 39 **make a play for.** *Informal* **a** to make an obvious attempt to gain. **b** to attempt to attract or seduce. ◆ See also **play along, playback, play down, play off, play on, play out, play up, play with.**
▷HISTORY Old English *plega* (n), *plegan* (vb); related to Middle Dutch *pleyen*
▸ˈplayable ADJECTIVE

playa ('plɑːjə; *Spanish* 'plaja) NOUN (in the US) a temporary lake, or its dry often salty bed, in a desert basin.
▷HISTORY Spanish: shore, from Late Latin *plagia,* from Greek *plagios* slanting, from *plagos* side; compare French *plage* beach

playable ('pleɪəbᵊl) ADJECTIVE able to be played or played up: *a simple bagatelle, playable by anybody; I doubt if our pitch is playable.*
▸ˌplayaˈbility NOUN

play-act VERB 1 (*intr*) to pretend or make believe. 2 (*intr*) to behave in an overdramatic or affected manner. 3 to act in or as in (a play).
▸ˈplay-ˌacting NOUN ▸ˈplay-ˌactor NOUN

play along VERB (*adverb*) 1 (*intr;* usually foll by *with*) to cooperate (with), esp as a temporary measure. 2 (*tr*) to manipulate as if in a game, esp for one's own advantage: *he played the widow along until she gave him her money.*

playback ('pleɪˌbæk) NOUN 1 the act or process of reproducing a recording, esp on magnetic tape. 2 the part of a tape recorder serving to reproduce or used for reproducing recorded material. 3 (*modifier*) of or relating to the reproduction of signals from a recording: *the playback head of a tape recorder.* ◆ VERB **play back.** (*adverb*) 4 to reproduce (recorded material) on (a magnetic tape) by means of a tape recorder.

playbill ('pleɪˌbɪl) NOUN 1 a poster or bill advertising a play. 2 the programme of a play.

playbook ('pleɪˌbʊk) NOUN 1 a book containing a range of possible set plays. 2 a notional range of possible tactics in any sphere of activity.

playboy ('pleɪˌbɔɪ) NOUN a man, esp one of private means, who devotes himself to the pleasures of nightclubs, expensive holiday resorts, female company, etc.

play-centre NOUN the NZ name for **playgroup.**

play down VERB (*tr, adverb*) to make little or light of; minimize the importance of.

player ('pleɪə) NOUN 1 a person who participates in or is skilled at some game or sport. 2 a person who plays a game or sport professionally. 3 a person who plays a musical instrument. 4 an actor. 5 *Informal* a participant, esp a powerful one, in a particular field of activity: *a leading city player.* 6 See **record player.** 7 the playing mechanism in a Pianola.

player piano NOUN a mechanical piano; Pianola.

playful ('pleɪfʊl) ADJECTIVE 1 full of high spirits and fun: *a playful kitten.* 2 good-natured and humorous: *a playful remark.*
▸ˈplayfully ADVERB ▸ˈplayfulness NOUN

playgoer ('pleɪˌgəʊə) NOUN a person who goes to theatre performances, esp frequently.

playground ('pleɪˌgraʊnd) NOUN 1 an outdoor area for children's play, esp one having swings, slides, etc., or adjoining a school. 2 a place or region particularly popular as a sports or holiday resort. 3 a sphere of activity: *reading was his private playground.*

playgroup ('pleɪˌgru:p) NOUN a regular meeting of small children arranged by their parents or a welfare agency to give them an opportunity of supervised creative play. See also **preschool, playschool.**

playhouse ('pleɪˌhaʊs) NOUN 1 a theatre where live dramatic performances are given. 2 a toy house, small room, etc., for children to play in.

playing card NOUN one of a pack of 52 rectangular stiff cards, used for playing a variety of games, each card having one or more symbols of the same kind (diamonds, hearts, clubs, or spades) on the face, but an identical design on the reverse. See also **suit** (sense 4).

playing field NOUN *Chiefly Brit* a field or open space used for sport.

playlet ('pleɪlɪt) NOUN a short play.

playlist ('pleɪˌlɪst) NOUN 1 a list of records chosen for playing, as on a radio station. ◆ VERB 2 (*tr*) to put (a song or record) on a playlist.

play-lunch NOUN *NZ* a schoolchild's mid-morning snack.

playmaker ('pleɪˌmeɪkə) NOUN *Sport* a player whose role is to create scoring opportunities for his or her team-mates.

playmate ('pleɪˌmeɪt) *or* **playfellow** NOUN a friend or partner in play or recreation: *childhood playmates.*

play off VERB (*adverb*) 1 (*tr; usually foll by against*) to deal with or manipulate as if in playing a game: *to play one person off against another.* 2 (*intr*) to take part in a play-off. ◆ NOUN **play-off.** 3 *Sport* an extra contest to decide the winner when two or more competitors are tied. 4 *Chiefly US and Canadian* a contest or series of games to determine a championship, as between the winners of two competitions.

play on VERB (*intr*) 1 (*adverb*) to continue to play. 2 (*preposition*) Also: **play upon.** to exploit or impose upon (the feelings or weakness of another) to one's own advantage. 3 (*adverb*) *Cricket* to hit the ball into one's own wicket.

play on words NOUN another term for **pun**[1] (sense 1).

play out VERB (*adverb*) 1 (*tr*) to finish: *let's play the game out if we aren't too late.* 2 (*tr; often passive*) *Informal* to use up or exhaust. 3 (*tr*) to release gradually: *he played the rope out.* 4 (*intr*) to happen or turn out: *Let's wait and see how things play out.*

playpen ('pleɪˌpɛn) NOUN a small enclosure, usually portable, in which a young child can be left to play in safety.

playroom ('pleɪˌru:m, -ˌrʊm) NOUN a recreation room, esp for children.

playschool ('pleɪˌsku:l) NOUN an informal nursery group taking preschool children in half-day sessions. Also called: **playgroup.**

playsuit ('pleɪˌsu:t, -ˌsju:t) NOUN a woman's or child's outfit, usually comprising shorts and a top.

play-the-ball NOUN *Rugby League* a method for bringing the ball back into play after a tackle, in which the tackled player is allowed to stand up and kick or heel the ball behind him or her to a team-mate.

plaything ('pleɪˌθɪŋ) NOUN 1 a toy. 2 a person regarded or treated as a toy: *he thinks she is just his plaything.*

playtime ('pleɪˌtaɪm) NOUN a time for play or recreation, esp the school break.

play up VERB (*adverb*) 1 (*tr*) to emphasize or highlight: *to play up one's best features.* 2 *Brit informal* to behave irritatingly (towards). 3 (*intr*) *Brit informal* (of a machine, car, etc.) to function erratically: *the car is playing up again.* 4 *Brit informal* to hurt; give (one) pain or trouble: *my back's playing me up again.* 5 **play up to. a** to support (another actor) in a performance. **b** to try to gain favour with by flattery.

play with VERB (*intr, preposition*) 1 to consider without giving deep thought to or coming to a conclusion concerning: *we're playing with the idea of emigrating.* 2 to behave carelessly with: *to play with a girl's affections.* 3 to fiddle or mess about with: *he's just playing with his food.*

playwright ('pleɪˌraɪt) NOUN a person who writes plays.

plaza ('plɑ:zə; *Spanish* 'plaθa) NOUN 1 an open space or square, esp in Spain or a Spanish-speaking country. 2 *Chiefly US and Canadian* **a** a modern complex of shops, buildings, and parking areas. **b** (*capital when part of a name*): *Rockefeller Plaza.*
▷**HISTORY** C17: from Spanish, from Latin *platēa* courtyard, from Greek *plateia;* see PLACE

plc *or* **PLC** ABBREVIATION FOR public limited company. See also **limited** (sense 5).

plea (pli:) NOUN 1 an earnest entreaty or request: *a plea for help.* 2 **a** *Law* something alleged or pleaded by or on behalf of a party to legal proceedings in support of his claim or defence. **b** *Criminal law* the answer made by an accused to the charge: *a plea of guilty.* **c** (in Scotland and formerly in England) a suit or action at law. 3 an excuse, justification, or pretext: *he gave the plea of a previous engagement.*
▷**HISTORY** C13: from Anglo-Norman *plai,* from Old French *plaid* lawsuit, from Medieval Latin *placitum* court order (literally: what is pleasing), from Latin *placēre* to please

plea bargaining NOUN an agreement between the prosecution and defence, sometimes including the judge, in which the accused agrees to plead guilty to a lesser charge in return for more serious charges being dropped.

pleach (pli:tʃ) VERB *Chiefly Brit* to interlace the stems or boughs of (a tree or hedge). Also: **plash.**
▷**HISTORY** C14 *plechen,* from Old North French *plechier,* from Latin *plectere* to weave, plait; compare PLASH[2]

plead (pli:d) VERB **pleads, pleading; pleaded, plead** (plɛd) *or esp Scot and US* **pled** (plɛd). 1 (when *intr,* often foll by *with*) to appeal earnestly or humbly (to). 2 (*tr; may take a clause as object*) to give as an excuse; offer in justification or extenuation: *to plead ignorance; he pleaded that he was insane.* 3 (*intr; often foll by for*) to provide an argument or appeal (for): *her beauty pleads for her.* 4 *Law* to declare oneself to be (guilty or not guilty) in answer to the charge. 5 *Law* to advocate (a case) in a court of law. 6 (*intr*) *Law* **a** to file pleadings. **b** to address a court as an advocate.
▷**HISTORY** C13: from Old French *plaidier,* from Medieval Latin *placitāre* to have a lawsuit, from Latin *placēre* to please; see PLEA
▸'**pleadable** ADJECTIVE ▸'**pleader** NOUN

pleading ('pli:dɪŋ) NOUN *Law* 1 the act of presenting a case in court, as by a lawyer on behalf of his client. 2 the art or science of preparing the formal written statements of the parties to a legal action. See also **pleadings.**

pleadings ('pli:dɪŋz) PLURAL NOUN *Law* (formerly) the formal written statements presented alternately by the claimant and defendant in a lawsuit setting out the respective matters relied upon. Official name: **statements of case.**

pleasance ('plɛzəns) NOUN 1 a secluded part of a garden laid out with trees, walks, etc. 2 *Archaic* enjoyment or pleasure.
▷**HISTORY** C14 *plesaunce,* from Old French *plaisance,* from *plaisant* pleasant, from *plaisir* to PLEASE

pleasant ('plɛzᵊnt) ADJECTIVE 1 giving or affording pleasure; enjoyable. 2 having pleasing or agreeable manners, appearance, habits, etc. 3 *Obsolete* merry and lively.
▷**HISTORY** C14: from Old French *plaisant,* from *plaisir* to PLEASE
▸'**pleasantly** ADVERB ▸'**pleasantness** NOUN

Pleasant Island NOUN the former name of **Nauru.**

pleasantry ('plɛzᵊntrɪ) NOUN, *plural* **-ries.** 1 (*often plural*) an agreeable or amusing remark, often one made in order to be polite: *they exchanged pleasantries.* 2 an agreeably humorous manner or style. 3 *Rare* enjoyment; pleasantness: *a pleasantry of life.*
▷**HISTORY** C17: from French *plaisanterie,* from *plaisant* PLEASANT

please (pli:z) VERB 1 to give satisfaction, pleasure, or contentment to (a person); make or cause (a person) to be glad. 2 to be the will of or have the will (to): *if it pleases you; the court pleases.* 3 **if you please.** if you will or wish, sometimes used in ironic exclamation. 4 **pleased with.** happy because of. 5 **please oneself.** to do as one likes. ◆ ADVERB 6 (*sentence modifier*) used in making polite requests and in pleading, asking for a favour, etc.: *please don't tell the police where I am.* 7 **yes please.** a polite formula for accepting an offer, invitation, etc.
▷**HISTORY** C14 *plese,* from Old French *plaisir,* from Latin *placēre* to please, satisfy
▸'**pleasable** ADJECTIVE ▸**pleased** ADJECTIVE ▸**pleasedly** ('pli:zɪdlɪ) ADVERB ▸'**pleaser** NOUN

pleasing ('pli:zɪŋ) ADJECTIVE giving pleasure; likable or gratifying.
▸'**pleasingly** ADVERB ▸'**pleasingness** NOUN

pleasurable ('plɛʒərəbᵊl) ADJECTIVE enjoyable, agreeable, or gratifying.
▸'**pleasurableness** NOUN ▸'**pleasurably** ADVERB

pleasure ('plɛʒə) NOUN 1 an agreeable or enjoyable sensation or emotion: *the pleasure of hearing good music.* 2 something that gives or affords enjoyment or delight: *his garden was his only pleasure.* 3 **a** amusement, recreation, or enjoyment. **b** (*as modifier*): *a pleasure boat; pleasure ground.* 4 *Euphemistic* sexual gratification or enjoyment: *he took his pleasure of her.* 5 a person's preference or choice. ◆ VERB 6 (when *intr,* often foll by *in*) to give pleasure to or take pleasure (in).
▷**HISTORY** C14 *plesir,* from Old French; related to Old French *plaisir* to PLEASE
▸'**pleasureful** ADJECTIVE ▸'**pleasureless** ADJECTIVE

pleasure principle NOUN *Psychoanal* the idea that psychological processes and actions are governed by the gratification of needs. It is seen as the governing process of the id, whereas the reality principle is the governing process of the ego. See also **hedonism.**

pleat (pli:t) NOUN 1 any of various types of fold formed by doubling back fabric and pressing, stitching, or steaming into place. See also **box pleat, inverted pleat, kick pleat, knife pleat, sunburst pleats.** ◆ VERB 2 (*tr*) to arrange (material, part of a garment, etc.) in pleats.
▷**HISTORY** C16: variant of PLAIT

pleater ('pli:tə) NOUN an attachment on a sewing machine that makes pleats.

pleb (plɛb) NOUN 1 short for **plebeian.** 2 *Brit informal, often derogatory* a common vulgar person. ◆ See also **plebs.**

plebby ('plɛbɪ) ADJECTIVE **-bier, -biest.** *Brit informal, often derogatory* common or vulgar: *a plebby party.*
▷**HISTORY** C20: shortened from PLEBEIAN

plebe (pli:b) NOUN *Informal* a member of the lowest class at the US Naval Academy or Military Academy; freshman.
▷**HISTORY** C19: shortened from PLEBEIAN

plebeian (plə'bi:ən) ADJECTIVE 1 of, relating to, or characteristic of the common people, esp those of Rome. 2 lacking refinement; vulgar: *plebeian tastes.* ◆ NOUN 3 one of the common people, esp one of the Roman plebs. 4 a person who is coarse or lacking in discernment.
▷**HISTORY** C16: from Latin *plēbēius* belonging to the people, from *plēbs* the common people of ancient Rome
▸**ple'beian,ism** NOUN

plebiscite ('plɛbɪˌsaɪt, -sɪt) NOUN 1 a direct vote by the electorate of a state, region, etc., on some question of usually national importance, such as union with another state or acceptance of a government programme. 2 any expression or determination of public opinion on some matter. ◆ See also **referendum.**
▷**HISTORY** C16: from Old French *plēbiscite,* from Latin *plēbiscītum* decree of the people, from *plēbs* the populace + *scītum,* from *scīscere* to decree, approve, from *scīre* to know
▸**plebiscitary** (plə'bɪsɪtərɪ) ADJECTIVE

plebs (plɛbz) NOUN 1 (*functioning as plural*) the common people; the masses. 2 (*functioning as singular or plural*) common people of ancient Rome. Compare **patrician.**
▷**HISTORY** C17: from Latin: the common people of ancient Rome

plectognath ('plɛktɒgˌnæθ) NOUN 1 any spiny-finned marine fish of the mainly tropical order *Plectognathi* (or *Tetraodontiformes*), having a small mouth, strong teeth, and small gill openings: includes puffers, triggerfish, trunkfish, sunfish, etc.

◆ ADJECTIVE [2] of, relating to, or belonging to the order *Plectognathi*.
▷HISTORY C19: via New Latin from Greek *plektos* twisted + *gnathos* jaw

plectrum ('plɛktrəm) NOUN, *plural* **-trums** *or* **-tra** (-trə). any implement for plucking a string, such as a small piece of plastic, wood, etc., used to strum a guitar, or the quill that plucks the string of a harpsichord.
▷HISTORY C17: from Latin *plēctrum* quill, plectrum, from Greek *plektron,* from *plessein* to strike

pled (plɛd) VERB *US or (esp in legal usage) Scot* a past tense and past participle of **plead**.

pledge (plɛdʒ) NOUN [1] a formal or solemn promise or agreement, esp to do or refrain from doing something. [2] **a** collateral for the payment of a debt or the performance of an obligation. **b** the condition of being collateral (esp in the phrase **in pledge**). [3] a sign, token, or indication: *the gift is a pledge of their sincerity*. [4] an assurance of support or goodwill, conveyed by drinking to a person, cause, etc.; toast: *we drank a pledge to their success*. [5] a person who binds himself, as by becoming bail or surety for another. [6] **take** *or* **sign the pledge**. to make a vow to abstain from alcoholic drink. ◆ VERB [7] to promise formally or solemnly: *he pledged allegiance*. [8] (*tr*) to bind or secure by or as if by a pledge: *they were pledged to secrecy*. [9] to give, deposit, or offer (one's word, freedom, property, etc.) as a guarantee, as for the repayment of a loan. [10] to drink a toast to (a person, cause, etc.).
▷HISTORY C14: from Old French *plege,* from Late Latin *plebium* gage, security, from *plebīre* to pledge, of Germanic origin; compare Old High German *pflegan* to look after, care for
▸**'pledgable** ADJECTIVE

pledgee (plɛdʒ'i:) NOUN [1] a person to whom a pledge is given. [2] a person to whom property is delivered as a pledge.

pledget ('plɛdʒɪt) NOUN a small flattened pad of wool, cotton, etc., esp for use as a pressure bandage to be applied to wounds or sores.
▷HISTORY C16: of unknown origin

pledgor, pledgeor (plɛdʒ'ɔ:), *or* **pledger** ('plɛdʒə) NOUN a person who gives or makes a pledge.

-plegia NOUN COMBINING FORM indicating a specified type of paralysis: *paraplegia*.
▷HISTORY from Greek, from *plēgē* stroke, from *plēssein* to strike
▸**-plegic** ADJECTIVE AND NOUN COMBINING FORM

pleiad ('plaɪəd) NOUN a brilliant or talented group, esp one with seven members.
▷HISTORY C16: originally French *Pléiade,* name given by Pierre de Ronsard (1524–85) to himself and six other poets after a group of Alexandrian Greek poets who were called this after the PLEIADES[1]

Pleiad ('plaɪəd) NOUN one of the Pleiades (stars or daughters of Atlas).

Pleiades[1] ('plaɪə,di:z) PLURAL NOUN *Greek myth* the seven daughters of Atlas, placed as stars in the sky either to save them from the pursuit of Orion or, in another account, after they had killed themselves for grief over the death of their half-sisters the Hyades.

Pleiades[2] ('plaɪə,di:z) PLURAL NOUN a young conspicuous open star cluster approximately 370 light years away in the constellation Taurus, containing several thousand stars only six or seven of which are visible to the naked eye. Compare **Hyades[1]**.

plein-air (,pleɪn'ɛə; *French* plɛnɛr) ADJECTIVE of or in the manner of various French 19th-century schools of painting, esp impressionism, concerned with the observation of light and atmosphere effects outdoors.
▷HISTORY C19: from French phrase *en plein air* in the open (literally: full) air
▸**plein-airist** (,pleɪn'ɛərɪst) NOUN

pleio- COMBINING FORM a variant of **plio-**.

Pleiocene ('plaɪəʊ,si:n) ADJECTIVE, NOUN a variant spelling of **Pliocene**.

pleiotropism (plaɪ'ɒtrə,pɪzəm) NOUN *Genetics* the condition of a gene of affecting more than one characteristic of the phenotype.

Pleistocene ('plaɪstə,si:n) ADJECTIVE [1] of, denoting, or formed in the first epoch of the Quaternary period, which lasted for about 1 600 000 years. It was characterized by extensive glaciations of the N hemisphere and the evolutionary development of man. ◆ NOUN [2] **the.** the Pleistocene epoch or rock series.
▷HISTORY C19: from Greek *pleistos* most + *kainos* recent

plenary ('pli:nərɪ, 'plɛn-) ADJECTIVE [1] full, unqualified, or complete: *plenary powers; plenary indulgence*. [2] (of assemblies, councils, etc.) attended by all the members. ◆ NOUN, *plural* **-ries**. [3] a book of the gospels or epistles and homilies read at the Eucharist.
▷HISTORY C15: from Late Latin *plēnārius,* from Latin *plēnus* full; related to Middle English *plener;* see PLENUM
▸**'plenarily** ADVERB

plenipotent (plə'nɪpətənt) ADJECTIVE a less common word for **plenipotentiary**.

plenipotentiary (,plɛnɪpə'tɛnʃərɪ) ADJECTIVE [1] (esp of a diplomatic envoy) invested with or possessing full power or authority. [2] conferring full power or authority. [3] (of power or authority) full; absolute. ◆ NOUN, *plural* **-aries**. [4] a person invested with full authority to transact business, esp a diplomat authorized to represent a country. See also **envoy[1]** (sense 1).
▷HISTORY C17: from Medieval Latin *plēnipotentiārius,* from Latin *plēnus* full + *potentia* POWER

plenish ('plɛnɪʃ) VERB (*tr*) *Scot* to fill, stock, or resupply.
▷HISTORY C15: from Old French *pleniss-,* from *plenir,* from Latin *plēnus* full
▸**'plenisher** NOUN ▸**'plenishment** NOUN

plenitude ('plɛnɪ,tju:d) NOUN [1] abundance; copiousness. [2] the condition of being full or complete.
▷HISTORY C15: via Old French from Latin *plēnitūdō,* from *plēnus* full

plenteous ('plɛntɪəs) ADJECTIVE [1] ample; abundant: *a plenteous supply of food*. [2] producing or yielding abundantly: *a plenteous grape harvest*.
▷HISTORY C13 *plenteus,* from Old French *plentivous,* from *plentif* abundant, from *plenté* PLENTY
▸**'plenteously** ADVERB ▸**'plenteousness** NOUN

plentiful ('plɛntɪfʊl) ADJECTIVE [1] ample; abundant. [2] having or yielding an abundance: *a plentiful year*.
▸**'plentifully** ADVERB ▸**'plentifulness** NOUN

plenty ('plɛntɪ) NOUN, *plural* **-ties**. [1] (often foll by *of*) a great number, amount, or quantity; lots: *plenty of time; there are plenty of cars on display here*. [2] generous or ample supplies of wealth, produce, or resources: *the age of plenty*. [3] **in plenty**. existing in abundance: *food in plenty*. ◆ DETERMINER [4] **a** very many; ample: *plenty of people believe in ghosts*. **b** (*as pronoun*): *there's plenty more; that's plenty, thanks*. ◆ ADVERB [5] *Not standard, chiefly US* (intensifier): *he was plenty mad*. [6] *Informal* more than adequately; abundantly: *the water's plenty hot enough*.
▷HISTORY C13: from Old French *plenté,* from Late Latin *plēnitās* fullness, from Latin *plēnus* full

Plenty ('plɛntɪ) NOUN **Bay of**. a large bay of the Pacific on the NE coast of the North Island, New Zealand.

plenum ('pli:nəm) NOUN, *plural* **-nums** *or* **-na** (-nə). [1] an enclosure containing gas at a higher pressure than the surrounding environment. [2] a fully attended meeting or assembly, esp of a legislative body. [3] (esp in the philosophy of the Stoics) space regarded as filled with matter. Compare **vacuum** (sense 1). [4] the condition or quality of being full.
▷HISTORY C17: from Latin: space filled by matter, from *plēnus* full

plenum system NOUN a type of air-conditioning system in which air is passed into a room at a pressure greater than atmospheric pressure.

pleo- COMBINING FORM a variant of **plio-**: *pleochroism; pleomorphism*.

pleochroism (plɪ'ɒkrəʊ,ɪzəm) NOUN a property of certain crystals of absorbing light to an extent that depends on the orientation of the electric vector of the light with respect to the optic axes of the crystal. The effect occurs in uniaxial crystals (**dichroism**) and esp in biaxial crystals (**trichroism**).
▷HISTORY C19: PLEO- + *-chroism,* from Greek *khrōs* skin colour
▸**pleochroic** (,pli:ə'krəʊɪk) ADJECTIVE

pleomorphism (,pli:ə'mɔ:,fɪzəm) *or* **pleomorphy** ('pli:ə,mɔ:fɪ) NOUN [1] the occurrence of more than one different form in the life cycle of a plant or animal. [2] the occurrence of more than one different form of crystal of one chemical compound; polymorphism.
▸**,pleo'morphic** ADJECTIVE

pleonasm ('pli:ə,næzəm) NOUN *Rhetoric* [1] the use of more words than necessary or an instance of this, such as *a tiny little child*. [2] a word or phrase that is superfluous.
▷HISTORY C16: from Latin *pleonasmus,* from Greek *pleonasmos* excess, from *pleonazein* to be redundant
▸**,pleo'nastic** ADJECTIVE ▸**,pleo'nastically** ADVERB

pleopod ('pli:ə,pɒd) NOUN another name for **swimmeret**.
▷HISTORY C19: from Greek *plein* to swim + *pous* foot

plerion ('plɪərɪən) NOUN a filled-centre supernova remnant in which radiation is emitted by the centre as well as the shell.
▷HISTORY from New Latin, from Greek *plerome* a filling + -ION

plesiosaur ('pli:sɪə,sɔ:) NOUN any of various extinct marine reptiles of the order *Sauropterygia, esp any of the suborder Plesiosauria,* of Jurassic and Cretaceous times, having a long neck, short tail, and paddle-like limbs. See also **ichthyosaur**. Compare **dinosaur, pterosaur**.
▷HISTORY C19: from New Latin *plēsiosaurus,* from Greek *plēsios* near + *sauros* a lizard

plessor ('plɛsə) NOUN another name for **plexor**.

plethora ('plɛθərə) NOUN [1] superfluity or excess; overabundance. [2] *Pathol, obsolete* a condition caused by dilation of superficial blood vessels, characterized esp by a reddish face.
▷HISTORY C16: via Medieval Latin from Greek *plēthōrē* fullness, from *plēthein* to grow full
▸**plethoric** (plɛ'θɒrɪk) ADJECTIVE ▸**ple'thorically** ADVERB

plethysmograph (plə'θɪzmə,grɑ:f, -,græf, -'θɪs-) NOUN a device for measuring the fluctuations in volume of a bodily organ or part, such as those caused by variations in the amount of blood it contains.
▷HISTORY C19: from Greek *plēthusmos* enlargement + *graphein* to write

pleugh *or* **pleuch** (plu:, plu:x) NOUN, VERB a Scot word for **plough**.

pleura ('plʊərə) NOUN, *plural* **pleurae** ('plʊəri:). [1] the thin transparent serous membrane enveloping the lungs and lining the walls of the thoracic cavity. [2] the plural of **pleuron**.
▷HISTORY C17: via Medieval Latin from Greek: side, rib
▸**'pleural** ADJECTIVE

pleurisy ('plʊərɪsɪ) NOUN inflammation of the pleura, characterized by pain that is aggravated by deep breathing or coughing.
▷HISTORY C14: from Old French *pleurisie,* from Late Latin *pleurisis,* from Greek *pleuritis,* from *pleura* side
▸**pleuritic** (plʊ'rɪtɪk) ADJECTIVE, NOUN

pleurisy root NOUN [1] the root of the butterfly weed, formerly used as a cure for pleurisy. [2] another name for **butterfly weed**.

pleuro- *or before a vowel* **pleur-** COMBINING FORM [1] of or relating to the side: *pleurodont; pleurodynia*. [2] indicating the pleura: *pleurotomy*.
▷HISTORY from Greek *pleura* side

pleurocarpous ('plʊərəʊ,kɑ:pəs) ADJECTIVE (of mosses) having mainly horizontal trailing stems and the reproductive parts borne laterally. ◆ Compare **acrocarpous**.

pleurocentesis (,plʊərəʊsen'ti:sɪs) NOUN another name for **thoracentesis**.

pleurodont ('plʊərəʊ,dɒnt) ADJECTIVE [1] (of the teeth of some reptiles) having no roots and being fused by their lateral sides only to the inner surface of the jawbone. See also **acrodont** (sense 1). [2] having pleurodont teeth: *pleurodont lizards*. ◆ NOUN [3] an animal having pleurodont teeth.

pleurodynia (,plʊərəʊ'daɪnɪə) NOUN pain in the muscles between the ribs.
▷HISTORY C19: from New Latin, from PLEURO- + Greek *-odynia,* from *odynē* pain

pleuron ('plʊərɒn) NOUN, *plural* **pleura** ('plʊərə). the part of the cuticle of arthropods that covers the lateral surface of a body segment.

▷HISTORY C18: from Greek: side

pleuropneumonia (ˌpluərəʊnjuːˈməʊnɪə) NOUN the combined disorder of pleurisy and pneumonia.

pleurotomy (plʊˈrɒtəmɪ) NOUN, *plural* **-mies.** surgical incision into the pleura, esp to drain fluid, as in pleurisy.

pleuston (ˈpluːstən, -stɒn) NOUN a mass of small organisms, esp algae, floating at the surface of shallow pools.
▷HISTORY C20: from Greek *pleusis* sailing, from *plein* to sail; for form, compare PLANKTON

pleustonic (pluːˈstɒnɪk) ADJECTIVE [1] of or relating to pleuston. [2] denoting a marine organism held at the surface of the water by a float, such as the Portuguese man-of-war.

Pleven (*Bulgarian* ˈplɛvɛn) *or* **Plevna** (*Bulgarian* ˈplɛvna) NOUN a town in N Bulgaria: taken by Russia from the Turks in 1877 after a siege of 143 days. Pop.: 121 952 (1999 est.).

plew, plu, *or* **plue** (pluː) NOUN (formerly in Canada) a beaver skin used as a standard unit of value in the fur trade.
▷HISTORY from Canadian French *pelu* (adj) hairy, from French *poilu,* from *poil* hair, from Latin *pilus*

plexiform (ˈplɛksɪˌfɔːm) ADJECTIVE like or having the form of a network or plexus; intricate or complex.

Plexiglas (ˈplɛksɪˌglɑːs) NOUN *Trademark US* a transparent plastic, polymethylmethacrylate, used for combs, plastic sheeting, etc.

plexor (ˈplɛksə) *or* **plessor** NOUN *Med* a small hammer with a rubber head for use in percussion of the chest and testing reflexes.
▷HISTORY C19: from Greek *plēxis* a stroke, from *plēssein* to strike

plexus (ˈplɛksəs) NOUN, *plural* **-uses** *or* **-us.** [1] any complex network of nerves, blood vessels, or lymphatic vessels. [2] an intricate network or arrangement.
▷HISTORY C17: New Latin, from Latin *plectere* to braid, PLAIT

pliable (ˈplaɪəbᵊl) ADJECTIVE easily moulded, bent, influenced, or altered.
▶ **ˌpliaˈbility** *or* **ˈpliableness** NOUN ▶ **ˈpliably** ADVERB

pliant (ˈplaɪənt) ADJECTIVE [1] easily bent; supple: *a pliant young tree.* [2] easily modified; adaptable; flexible: *a pliant system.* [3] yielding readily to influence; compliant.
▷HISTORY C14: from Old French, from *plier* to fold, bend; see PLY[2]
▶ **ˈpliancy** *or* **ˈpliantness** NOUN ▶ **ˈpliantly** ADVERB

plica (ˈplaɪkə) NOUN, *plural* **plicae** (ˈplaɪsiː). [1] Also called: **fold.** *Anatomy* a folding over of parts, such as a fold of skin, muscle, peritoneum, etc. [2] *Pathol* a condition of the hair characterized by matting, filth, and the presence of parasites.
▷HISTORY C17: from Medieval Latin: a fold, from Latin *plicāre* to fold; see PLY[2]
▶ **ˈplical** ADJECTIVE

plicate (ˈplaɪkeɪt) *or* **plicated** ADJECTIVE having or arranged in parallel folds or ridges; pleated: *a plicate leaf; plicate rock strata.*
▷HISTORY C18: from Latin *plicātus* folded, from *plicāre* to fold
▶ **ˈplicately** ADVERB ▶ **ˈplicateness** NOUN

plication (plaɪˈkeɪʃən) *or* **plicature** (ˈplɪkətʃə) NOUN [1] the act of folding or the condition of being folded or plicate. [2] a folded part or structure, esp a fold in a series of rock strata. [3] *Surgery* the act or process of suturing together the walls of a hollow organ or part to reduce its size.

plié (ˈpliːeɪ) NOUN a classic ballet practice posture with back erect and knees bent.
▷HISTORY French: bent, from *plier* to bend

plier (ˈplaɪə) NOUN a person who plies a trade.

pliers (ˈplaɪəz) PLURAL NOUN a gripping tool consisting of two hinged arms with usually serrated jaws that close on the workpiece.
▷HISTORY C16: from PLY[1]

plight¹ (plaɪt) NOUN a condition of extreme hardship, danger, etc.
▷HISTORY C14 *plit,* from Old French *pleit* fold, PLAIT; probably influenced by Old English *pliht* peril, PLIGHT[2]

plight² (plaɪt) VERB (*tr*) [1] to give or pledge (one's word): *he plighted his word to attempt it.* [2] to promise formally or pledge (allegiance, support, etc.): *to plight aid.* [3] **plight one's troth. a** to make a promise of marriage. **b** to give one's solemn promise. ◆ NOUN [4] *Archaic or dialect* a solemn promise, esp of engagement; pledge.
▷HISTORY Old English *pliht* peril; related to Old High German, German *Pflicht* duty
▶ **ˈplighter** NOUN

plimsoll *or* **plimsole** (ˈplɪmsəl) NOUN *Brit* a light rubber-soled canvas shoe worn for various sports. Also called: **gym shoe, sandshoe.**
▷HISTORY C20: so called because of the resemblance of the rubber sole to a Plimsoll line

Plimsoll line (ˈplɪmsəl) NOUN another name for **load line.**
▷HISTORY C19: named after Samuel *Plimsoll* (1824–98), MP, who advocated its adoption

Plinian (ˈplɪnɪən) ADJECTIVE *Geology* (of a volcanic eruption) characterized by repeated explosions.
▷HISTORY C20: named after Pliny the Younger (Latin name *Gaius Plinius Caecilius Secundus.* ?62–?113 A.D.), Roman writer and administrator, who described such eruptions

plink (plɪŋk) NOUN [1] a short sharp often metallic sound as of a string on a musical instrument being plucked or a bullet striking metal. ◆ VERB [2] (*intr*) to make such a noise. [3] to hit (a target, such as a tin can) by shooting or to shoot at such a target.
▷HISTORY C20: of imitative origin
▶ **ˈplinking** NOUN, ADJECTIVE

plinth (plɪnθ) NOUN [1] Also called: **socle.** the rectangular slab or block that forms the lowest part of the base of a column, statue, pedestal, or pier. [2] Also called: **plinth course.** the lowest part of the wall of a building that appears above ground level, esp one that is formed of a course of stone or brick. [3] a flat block on either side of a doorframe, where the architrave meets the skirting. [4] a flat base on which a structure or piece of equipment is placed.
▷HISTORY C17: from Latin *plinthus,* from Greek *plinthos* brick, shaped stone

plio-, pleo-, *or* **pleio-** COMBINING FORM greater in size, extent, degree, etc.; more: *Pliocene.*
▷HISTORY from Greek *pleiōn* more, from *polus* much, many

Pliocene *or* **Pleiocene** (ˈplaɪəʊˌsiːn) ADJECTIVE [1] of, denoting, or formed in the last epoch of the Tertiary period, which lasted for three million years, during which many modern mammals appeared. ◆ NOUN [2] **the.** the Pliocene epoch or rock series.
▷HISTORY C19: PLIO- + *-cene,* from Greek *kainos* recent

plissé (ˈpliːseɪ, ˈplɪs-) NOUN [1] fabric with a wrinkled finish, achieved by treatment involving caustic soda: *cotton plissé.* [2] such a finish on a fabric.
▷HISTORY French *plissé* pleated, from *plisser* to pleat; see PLY[2]

PLO ABBREVIATION FOR **Palestine Liberation Organization.**

ploat (pləʊt) VERB (*tr*) *Northeastern English dialect* [1] to thrash; beat soundly. [2] to pluck (a fowl).
▷HISTORY from Dutch or Flemish *ploten* to pluck the feathers or fur from

Płock (plɒk) NOUN a town in central Poland, on the River Vistula: several Polish kings are buried in the cathedral: oil refining, petrochemical works. Pop.: 131 011 (1999 est.).

plod (plɒd) VERB **plods, plodding, plodded.** [1] to make (one's way) or walk along (a path, road, etc.) with heavy usually slow steps. [2] (*intr*) to work slowly and perseveringly. ◆ NOUN [3] the act of plodding. [4] the sound of slow heavy steps. [5] *Brit slang* a policeman.
▷HISTORY C16: of imitative origin
▶ **ˈplodding** ADJECTIVE ▶ **ˈploddingly** ADVERB
▶ **ˈploddingness** NOUN

plodder (ˈplɒdə) NOUN a person who plods, esp one who works in a slow and persevering but uninspired manner.

plodge (plɒdʒ) *Northeastern English dialect* ◆ VERB [1] (*intr*) to wade in water, esp the sea. ◆ NOUN [2] the act of wading.
▷HISTORY of imitative origin; related to PLOD

Ploești (*Romanian* ploˈjeʃtj) NOUN a city in SE central Romania: centre of the Romanian petroleum industry. Pop.: 253 414 (1997 est.).

-ploid ADJECTIVE AND NOUN COMBINING FORM indicating a specific multiple of a single set of chromosomes: *diploid.*
▷HISTORY from Greek *-pl(oos)* -fold + -OID
▶ **-ploidy** NOUN COMBINING FORM

plonk¹ (plɒŋk) VERB [1] (often foll by *down*) to drop or be dropped, esp heavily or suddenly: *he plonked the money on the table.* ◆ NOUN [2] the act or sound of plonking. ◆ INTERJECTION [3] an exclamation imitative of this sound.

plonk² (plɒŋk) NOUN *Brit, Austral, and NZ informal* alcoholic drink, usually wine, esp of inferior quality.
▷HISTORY C20: perhaps from French *blanc* white, as in *vin blanc* white wine

plonker (ˈplɒŋkə) NOUN *Slang* a stupid person.
▷HISTORY C20: from PLONK[1]

plonking (ˈplɒŋkɪŋ) ADJECTIVE foolish, clumsy, or inept: *his plonking response to the princess's death.*

plonko (ˈplɒŋkəʊ) NOUN, *plural* **plonkos.** *Austral slang* an alcoholic, esp one who drinks wine.
▷HISTORY C20: from PLONK[2]

plook (pluk) NOUN *Scot* a variant spelling of **plouk.**

plop (plɒp) NOUN [1] the characteristic sound made by an object dropping into water without a splash. ◆ VERB **plops, plopping, plopped.** [2] to fall or cause to fall with the sound of a plop: *the stone plopped into the water.* ◆ INTERJECTION [3] an exclamation imitative of this sound: *to go plop.*
▷HISTORY C19: imitative of the sound

plosion (ˈpləʊʒən) NOUN *Phonetics* the sound of an abrupt break or closure, esp the audible release of a stop. Also called: **explosion.**

plosive (ˈpləʊsɪv) *Phonetics* ◆ ADJECTIVE [1] articulated with or accompanied by plosion. ◆ NOUN [2] a plosive consonant; stop.
▷HISTORY C20: from French, from *explosif* EXPLOSIVE

plot¹ (plɒt) NOUN [1] a secret plan to achieve some purpose, esp one that is illegal or underhand: *a plot to overthrow the government.* [2] the story or plan of a play, novel, etc. [3] *Military* a graphic representation of an individual or tactical setting that pinpoints an artillery target. [4] *Chiefly US* a diagram or plan, esp a surveyor's map. [5] **lose the plot.** *Informal* to lose one's ability or judgment in a given situation. ◆ VERB **plots, plotting, plotted.** [6] to plan secretly (something illegal, revolutionary, etc.); conspire. [7] (*tr*) to mark (a course, as of a ship or aircraft) on a map. [8] (*tr*) to make a plan or map of. [9] **a** to locate and mark (one or more points) on a graph by means of coordinates. **b** to draw (a curve) through these points. [10] (*tr*) to construct the plot of (a literary work).
▷HISTORY C16: from PLOT[2], influenced in use by COMPLOT

plot² (plɒt) NOUN [1] a small piece of land: *a vegetable plot.* ◆ VERB **plots, plotting, plotted.** [2] (*tr*) to arrange or divide (land) into plots.
▷HISTORY Old English: piece of land, plan of an area

plotter (ˈplɒtə) NOUN [1] an instrument for plotting lines or angles on a chart. [2] a person who plots; conspirator.

plough *or esp US* **plow** (plaʊ) NOUN [1] an agricultural implement with sharp blades, attached to a horse, tractor, etc., for cutting or turning over the earth. [2] any of various similar implements, such as a device for clearing snow. [3] a plane with a narrow blade for cutting grooves in wood. [4] (in agriculture) ploughed land. [5] **put one's hand to the plough.** to begin or undertake a task. ◆ VERB [6] to till (the soil) with a plough. [7] to make (furrows or grooves) in (something) with or as if with a plough. [8] (when *intr,* usually foll by *through*) to move (through something) in the manner of a plough: *the ship ploughed the water.* [9] (*intr;* foll by *through*) to work at slowly or perseveringly. [10] (*intr;* foll by *into* or *through*) (of a vehicle) to run uncontrollably into something in its path: *the plane ploughed into the cottage roof.* [11] (*tr;* foll by *in, up, under,* etc.) to turn over (a growing crop, manure, etc.) into the earth with a plough. [12] (*intr*) *Brit slang* to fail an examination.
▷HISTORY Old English *plōg* plough land; related to Old Norse *plogr,* Old High German *pfluoc*
▶ **ˈplougher** *or* (*esp US*) **ˈplower** NOUN

Plough (plaʊ) NOUN **the.** the group of the seven brightest stars in the constellation Ursa Major. Also called: **Charles's Wain.** Usual US name: **the Big Dipper.**

plough back VERB (*tr, adverb*) to reinvest (the profits of a business) in the same business.

ploughboy *or esp US* **plowboy** (ˈplaʊˌbɔɪ) NOUN 1 a boy who guides the animals drawing a plough. 2 any country boy.

ploughman *or esp US* **plowman** (ˈplaʊmən) NOUN, *plural* **-men**. 1 a man who ploughs, esp using horses. 2 any farm labourer.
▸ ˈ**ploughmanship** *or* (*esp US*) ˈ**plowmanship** NOUN

ploughman's lunch NOUN a snack lunch, served esp in a pub, consisting of bread and cheese with pickle.

ploughman's spikenard NOUN a European plant, *Inula conyza*, with tubular yellowish flower heads surrounded by purple bracts: family *Asteraceae* (composites). Also called: **fleawort**.

Plough Monday NOUN the first Monday after Epiphany, which in N and E England used to be celebrated with a procession of ploughmen drawing a plough from house to house.

ploughshare *or esp US* **plowshare** (ˈplaʊˌʃɛə) NOUN the horizontal pointed cutting blade of a mouldboard plough.

ploughstaff *or esp US* **plowstaff** (ˈplaʊˌstɑːf) NOUN 1 Also called: **ploughtail**. one of the handles of a plough. 2 a spade-shaped tool used to clean the ploughshare and mouldboard.

plouk *or* **plook** (plʊk) NOUN *Scot* a pimple.
▷ HISTORY C15: of uncertain origin
▸ ˈ**plouky** *or* ˈ**plooky** ADJECTIVE

Plovdiv (*Bulgarian* ˈplɔvdif) NOUN a city in S Bulgaria on the Maritsa River: the second largest town in Bulgaria; conquered by Philip II of Macedonia in 341 B.C.; capital of Roman Thracia; commercial centre of a rich agricultural region. Pop.: 342 584 (1999 est.). Greek name: **Philippopolis**.

plover (ˈplʌvə) NOUN 1 any shore bird of the family *Charadriidae*, typically having a round head, straight bill, and large pointed wings: order *Charadriiformes*. 2 any of similar and related birds, such as the Egyptian plover (see **crocodile bird**) and the upland plover. 3 **green plover**. another name for **lapwing**.
▷ HISTORY C14: from Old French *plovier* rainbird, from Latin *pluvia* rain

plow (plaʊ) NOUN, VERB the usual US spelling of **plough**.
▸ ˈ**plower** NOUN

plowter *or* **plouter** (ˈplaʊtər) *Scot* ◆ VERB (*intr*) 1 to work or play in water or mud; dabble. 2 to potter. ◆ NOUN 3 the act of plowtering.
▷ HISTORY C19: of uncertain origin

ploy (plɔɪ) NOUN 1 a manoeuvre or tactic in a game, conversation, etc.; stratagem; gambit. 2 any business, job, hobby, etc., with which one is occupied: *angling is his latest ploy*. 3 *Chiefly Brit* a frolic, escapade, or practical joke.
▷ HISTORY C18: originally Scot and northern English, perhaps from obsolete n sense of EMPLOY meaning an occupation

PLP (in Britain) ABBREVIATION FOR Parliamentary Labour Party.

PLR ABBREVIATION FOR **Public Lending Right**.

plu *or* **plue** (pluː) NOUN variant spellings of **plew**.

PLU *Text messaging* ABBREVIATION FOR people like us.

pluck (plʌk) VERB 1 (*tr*) to pull off (feathers, fruit, etc.) from (a fowl, tree, etc.). 2 (when *intr*, foll by *at*) to pull or tug. 3 (*tr; foll by off, away,* etc.) *Archaic* to pull (something) forcibly or violently (from something or someone). 4 (*tr*) to sound (the strings) of (a musical instrument) with the fingers, a plectrum, etc. 5 (*tr*) another word for **strip**[1] (sense 7). 6 (*tr*) *Slang* to fleece or swindle. ◆ NOUN 7 courage, usually in the face of difficulties or hardship. 8 a sudden pull or tug. 9 the heart, liver, and lungs, esp of an animal used for food.
▷ HISTORY Old English *pluccian, plyccan;* related to German *pflücken*
▸ ˈ**plucker** NOUN

pluck up VERB (*tr, adverb*) 1 to pull out; uproot. 2 to muster (courage, one's spirits, etc.).

plucky (ˈplʌkɪ) ADJECTIVE **pluckier, pluckiest**. having or showing courage in the face of difficulties, danger, etc.
▸ ˈ**pluckily** ADVERB ▸ ˈ**pluckiness** NOUN

plug (plʌg) NOUN 1 a piece of wood, cork, or other material, often cylindrical in shape, used to stop up holes and gaps or as a wedge for taking a screw or nail. 2 such a stopper used esp to close the waste pipe of a bath, basin, or sink while it is in use and removed to let the water drain away. 3 a device having one or more pins to which an electric cable is attached: used to make an electrical connection when inserted into a socket. 4 Also called: **volcanic plug**. a mass of solidified magma filling the neck of an extinct volcano. 5 See **sparking plug**. 6 **a** a cake of pressed or twisted tobacco, esp for chewing. **b** a small piece of such a cake. 7 *Angling* a weighted artificial lure with one or more sets of hooks attached, used in spinning. 8 a seedling with its roots encased in potting compost, grown in a tray with compartments for each individual plant. 9 *Informal* a recommendation or other favourable mention of a product, show, etc., as on television, on radio, or in newspapers. 10 *Slang* a shot, blow, or punch (esp in the phrase **take a plug at**). 11 *Informal* the mechanism that releases water to flush a lavatory (esp in the phrase **pull the plug**). 12 *Chiefly US* an old horse. 13 **pull the plug on**. *Informal* to put a stop to. ◆ VERB **plugs, plugging, plugged**. 14 (*tr*) to stop up or secure (a hole, gap, etc.) with or as if with a plug. 15 (*tr*) to insert or use (something) as a plug: *to plug a finger into one's ear*. 16 (*tr*) *Informal* to make favourable and often-repeated mentions of (a song, product, show, etc.), esp on television, on radio, or in newspapers. 17 (*tr*) *Slang* to shoot with a gun: *he plugged six rabbits*. 18 (*tr*) *Slang* to punch or strike. 19 (*intr; foll by along, away,* etc.) *Informal* to work steadily or persistently.
▷ HISTORY C17: from Middle Dutch *plugge;* related to Middle Low German *plugge,* German *Pflock*
▸ ˈ**plugger** NOUN

plug-and-play ADJECTIVE *Computing* capable of detecting the addition of a new input or output device and automatically activating the appropriate control software.

plugboard (ˈplʌgˌbɔːd) NOUN another name for **patch board**.

plug compatible ADJECTIVE *Computing* (of peripheral devices) designed to be plugged into computer systems produced by different manufacturers.

plug gauge NOUN *Engineering* an accurately machined plug used for checking the diameter of a hole. Compare **ring gauge**.

plugged-in ADJECTIVE *Slang* up-to-date; abreast of the times.

plughole (ˈplʌgˌhəʊl) NOUN a hole, esp in a bath, basin, or sink, through which waste water drains and which can be closed with a plug.

plug in VERB 1 (*tr, adverb*) to connect (an electrical appliance) with a power source by means of an electrical plug. ◆ NOUN **plug-in**. 2 a device that can be connected by means of a plug. 3 **a** *Computing* a module or piece of software that can be added to a system to provide extra functions or features. **b** (*as modifier*): *plug-in memory cards*.

plug-ugly ADJECTIVE 1 *Informal* extremely ugly. ◆ NOUN, *plural* **-lies**. 2 *US slang* a city tough; ruffian.
▷ HISTORY C19: origin obscure; originally applied to ruffians in New York who attempted to exert political pressure

plum[1] (plʌm) NOUN 1 a small rosaceous tree, *Prunus domestica*, with white flowers and an edible oval fruit that is purple, yellow, or green and contains an oval stone. See also **greengage, damson**. 2 the fruit of this tree. 3 a raisin, as used in a cake or pudding. 4 **a** a dark reddish-purple colour. **b** (*as adjective*): *a plum carpet*. 5 *Informal* **a** something of a superior or desirable kind, such as a financial bonus. **b** (*as modifier*): *a plum job*.
▷ HISTORY Old English *plūme;* related to Latin *prunum,* German *Pflaume*
▸ ˈ**plumˌlike** ADJECTIVE

plum[2] (plʌm) ADJECTIVE, ADVERB a variant spelling of **plumb** (senses 3–6).

plumage (ˈpluːmɪdʒ) NOUN the layer of feathers covering the body of a bird.
▷ HISTORY C15: from Old French, from *plume* feather, from Latin *plūma* down

plumate (ˈpluːmeɪt, -mɪt) *or* **plumose** ADJECTIVE *Zoology, botany* 1 of, relating to, or possessing one or more feathers or plumes. 2 resembling a plume; covered with small hairs: *a plumate seed*.
▷ HISTORY C19: from Latin *plumātus* covered with feathers; see PLUME

plumb (plʌm) NOUN 1 a weight, usually of lead, suspended at the end of a line and used to determine water depth or verticality. 2 the perpendicular position of a freely suspended plumb line (esp in the phrases **out of plumb, off plumb**). ◆ ADJECTIVE *also* **plum**. 3 (*prenominal*) *Informal, chiefly US* (intensifier): *a plumb nuisance*. ◆ ADVERB *also* **plum**. 4 in a vertical or perpendicular line. 5 *Informal, chiefly US* (intensifier): *plumb stupid*. 6 *Informal* exactly; precisely (also in the phrase **plumb on**). ◆ VERB 7 (*tr; often foll by up*) to test the alignment of or adjust to the vertical with a plumb line. 8 (*tr*) to undergo or experience (the worst extremes of misery, sadness, etc.): *to plumb the depths of despair*. 9 (*tr*) to understand or master (something obscure): *to plumb a mystery*. 10 to connect or join (a device such as a tap) to a water pipe or drainage system.
▷ HISTORY C13: from Old French *plomb* (unattested) lead line, from Old French *plon* lead, from Latin *plumbum* lead
▸ ˈ**plumbable** ADJECTIVE

plumbaginaceous (plʌmˌbædʒɪˈneɪʃəs) ADJECTIVE of, relating to, or belonging to the *Plumbaginaceae*, a family of typically coastal plants having flowers with a brightly coloured calyx and five styles: includes leadwort, thrift, and sea lavender.

plumbago (plʌmˈbeɪgəʊ) NOUN, *plural* **-gos**. 1 any plumbaginaceous plant of the genus *Plumbago*, of warm regions, having clusters of blue, white, or red flowers. See also **leadwort**. 2 another name for **graphite**.
▷ HISTORY C17: from Latin: lead ore, leadwort, translation of Greek *polubdaina* lead ore, from *polubdos* lead

plumb bob NOUN the weight, usually of lead, at the end of a plumb line; plummet.

plumbeous (ˈplʌmbɪəs) ADJECTIVE made of or relating to lead or resembling lead in colour.
▷ HISTORY C16: from Latin *plumbeus* leaden, from *plumbum* lead

plumber (ˈplʌmə) NOUN a person who installs and repairs pipes, fixtures, etc., for water, drainage, and gas.
▷ HISTORY C14: from Old French *plommier* worker in lead, from Late Latin *plumbārius,* from Latin *plumbum* lead

plumbery (ˈplʌmərɪ) NOUN, *plural* **-eries**. 1 the workshop of a plumber. 2 another word for **plumbing** (sense 1).

plumbic (ˈplʌmbɪk) ADJECTIVE of or containing lead in the tetravalent state.

Plumbicon (ˈplʌmbɪˌkɒn) NOUN *Trademark* a development of the vidicon television camera tube in which the photosensitive material is lead oxide.

plumbiferous (plʌmˈbɪfərəs) ADJECTIVE (of ores, rocks, etc.) containing or yielding lead.

plumbing (ˈplʌmɪŋ) NOUN 1 Also called: **plumbery**. the trade or work of a plumber. 2 the pipes, fixtures, etc., used in a water, drainage, or gas installation. 3 the act or procedure of using a plumb to gauge depth, a vertical, etc.

plumbism (ˈplʌmˌbɪzəm) NOUN chronic lead poisoning.
▷ HISTORY C19: from Latin *plumbum* lead

plumb line NOUN 1 a string with a metal weight at one end that, when suspended, points directly towards the earth's centre of gravity and so is used to determine verticality, the depth of water, etc. 2 another name for **plumb rule**.

plumbous (ˈplʌmbəs) ADJECTIVE of or containing lead in the divalent state.
▷ HISTORY C17: from Late Latin *plumbōsus* full of lead, from Latin *plumbum* lead

plumb rule NOUN a plumb line attached to a narrow board, used by builders, surveyors, etc.

plumbum (ˈplʌmbəm) NOUN an obsolete name for **lead**[2] (the metal).
▷ HISTORY from Latin

plume (pluːm) NOUN 1 a feather, esp one that is large or ornamental. 2 a feather or cluster of feathers worn esp formerly as a badge or ornament in a headband, hat, etc. 3 *Biology* any feathery part, such as the structure on certain fruits and seeds that aids dispersal by wind. 4 something

that resembles a plume: *a plume of smoke.* 5 a token or decoration of honour; prize. 6 *Geology* a rising column of hot, low viscosity material within the earth's mantle, which is believed to be responsible for linear oceanic island chains and flood basalts. also called **mantle plume.** ◆ VERB (*tr*) 7 to adorn or decorate with feathers or plumes. 8 (of a bird) to clean or preen (itself or its feathers). 9 (foll by *on* or *upon*) to pride or congratulate (oneself).
▷HISTORY C14: from Old French, from Latin *plūma* downy feather
▸**'plumeless** ADJECTIVE ▸**'plume,like** ADJECTIVE

plume moth NOUN 1 one of a family (*Pterophoridae*) of slender-bodied micro moths with narrow wings, each usually divided into two, three, or four "plumes". The type is the white *Pterophorus pentadactylus.* 2 **many-plumed moth.** an unrelated species, *Alucita hexadactyla.*

plummer block ('plʌmə) NOUN another name for **pillow block.**

plummet ('plʌmɪt) VERB **-mets, -meting, -meted.** 1 (*intr*) to drop down; plunge. ◆ NOUN 2 another word for **plumb bob.** 3 a lead plumb used by anglers to determine the depth of water.
▷HISTORY C14: from Old French *plommet* ball of lead, from *plomb* lead, from Latin *plumbum*

plummy ('plʌmɪ) ADJECTIVE **-mier, -miest.** 1 of, full of, or resembling plums. 2 *Brit informal* (of speech) having a deep tone and a refined and somewhat drawling articulation. 3 *Brit informal* choice; desirable.

plumose ('plu:məʊs, -məʊz) ADJECTIVE another word for **plumate.**
▷HISTORY C17: from Latin *plūmōsus* feathery
▸**'plumosely** ADVERB ▸**plumosity** (plu:'mɒsɪtɪ) NOUN

plump[1] (plʌmp) ADJECTIVE 1 well filled out or rounded; fleshy or chubby: *a plump turkey.* 2 bulging, as with contents; full: *a plump wallet.* 3 (of amounts of money) generous; ample: *a plump cheque.* ◆ VERB 4 (often foll by *up* or *out*) to make or become plump: *to plump up a pillow.*
▷HISTORY C15 (meaning: dull, rude), C16 (in current senses): perhaps from Middle Dutch *plomp* dull, blunt
▸**'plumply** ADVERB ▸**'plumpness** NOUN

plump[2] (plʌmp) VERB 1 (often foll by *down, into,* etc.) to drop or fall suddenly and heavily: *to plump down on the sofa.* 2 (*intr;* foll by *for*) to give support (to) or make a choice (of) one out of a group or number. ◆ NOUN 3 a heavy abrupt fall or the sound of this. ◆ ADVERB 4 suddenly or heavily: *he ran plump into the old lady.* 5 straight down; directly: *the helicopter landed plump in the middle of the field.* ◆ ADJECTIVE, ADVERB 6 in a blunt, direct, or decisive manner.
▷HISTORY C14: probably of imitative origin; compare Middle Low German *plumpen,* Middle Dutch *plompen*

plump[3] (plʌmp) NOUN *Archaic or dialect* a group of people, animals, or things; troop; cluster.
▷HISTORY C15: of uncertain origin

plumper ('plʌmpə) NOUN a pad carried in the mouth by actors to round out the cheeks.

plum pudding NOUN (in Britain) a dark brown rich boiled or steamed pudding made with flour, suet, sugar, and dried fruit.

plumule ('plu:mju:l) NOUN 1 the embryonic shoot of seed-bearing plants. 2 a down feather of young birds that persists in some adults.
▷HISTORY C18: from Late Latin *plūmula* a little feather

plumy ('plu:mɪ) ADJECTIVE **plumier, plumiest.** 1 plumelike; feathery. 2 consisting of, covered with, or adorned with feathers.

plunder ('plʌndə) VERB 1 to steal (valuables, goods, sacred items, etc.) from (a town, church, etc.) by force, esp in time of war; loot. 2 (*tr*) to rob or steal (choice or desirable things) from (a place): *to plunder an orchard.* ◆ NOUN 3 anything taken by plundering or theft; booty. 4 the act of plundering; pillage.
▷HISTORY C17: probably from Dutch *plunderen* (originally: to plunder household goods); compare Middle High German *plunder* bedding, household goods
▸**'plunderable** ADJECTIVE ▸**'plunderer** NOUN ▸**'plunderous** ADJECTIVE

plunderage ('plʌndərɪdʒ) NOUN 1 *Maritime law* **a** the embezzlement of goods on board a ship. **b** the goods embezzled. 2 the act of plundering.

plunge (plʌndʒ) VERB 1 (usually foll by *into*) to thrust or throw (something, oneself, etc.): *they plunged into the sea.* 2 to throw or be thrown into a certain state or condition: *the room was plunged into darkness.* 3 (usually foll by *into*) to involve or become involved deeply (in): *he plunged himself into a course of Sanskrit.* 4 (*intr*) to move or dash violently or with great speed or impetuosity. 5 (*intr*) to descend very suddenly or steeply: *the ship plunged in heavy seas; a plunging neckline.* 6 (*intr*) *Informal* to speculate or gamble recklessly, for high stakes, etc. ◆ NOUN 7 a leap or dive as into water. 8 *Informal* a swim; dip. 9 *Chiefly US* a place where one can swim or dive, such as a swimming pool. 10 a headlong rush: *a plunge for the exit.* 11 a pitching or tossing motion. 12 **take the plunge.** *Informal* **a** to resolve to do something dangerous or irrevocable. **b** to get married.
▷HISTORY C14: from Old French *plongier,* from Vulgar Latin *plumbicāre* (unattested) to sound with a plummet, from Latin *plumbum* lead

plunge bath NOUN a bath large enough to immerse the whole body or to dive into.

plunger ('plʌndʒə) NOUN 1 a rubber suction cup fixed to the end of a rod, used to clear blocked drains. 2 a device or part of a machine that has a plunging or thrusting motion; piston. 3 *Informal* a reckless gambler.

plunk (plʌŋk) VERB 1 to pluck (the strings) of (a banjo, harp, etc.) or (of such an instrument) to give forth a sound when plucked. 2 (often foll by *down*) to drop or be dropped, esp heavily or suddenly. ◆ NOUN 3 the act or sound of plunking. 4 *Informal* a hard blow. ◆ INTERJECTION 5 an exclamation imitative of the sound of something plunking. ◆ ADVERB 6 *Informal* exactly; squarely: *plunk into his lap.*
▷HISTORY C20: imitative

Plunket baby ('plʌŋkət) NOUN *NZ informal* a baby brought up in infancy under the dietary recommendations of the Plunket Society.

Plunket nurse NOUN *NZ* a child-care nurse appointed by the Plunket Society.

Plunket Society NOUN the Royal New Zealand Society for the Health of Women and Children.
▷HISTORY named after Sir William Lee *Plunket* (1864–1920), Governor General of New Zealand at the time of its founding (1907)

pluperfect (plu:'pɜ:fɪkt) ADJECTIVE, NOUN *Grammar* another term for **past perfect.**
▷HISTORY C16: from the Latin phrase *plūs quam perfectum* more than perfect

plur. ABBREVIATION FOR: 1 plural. 2 plurality.

plural ('plʊərəl) ADJECTIVE 1 containing, involving, or composed of more than one person, thing, item, etc.: *a plural society.* 2 denoting a word indicating that more than one referent is being referred to or described. ◆ NOUN 3 *Grammar* **a** the plural number. **b** a plural form.
▷HISTORY C14: from Old French *plurel,* from Late Latin *plūrālis* concerning many, from Latin *plūs* more
▸**'plurally** ADVERB

pluralism ('plʊərə,lɪzəm) NOUN 1 the holding by a single person of more than one ecclesiastical benefice or office. 2 *Sociol* a theory of society as several autonomous but interdependent groups which either share power or continuously compete for power. 3 the existence in a society of groups having distinctive ethnic origin, cultural forms, religions, etc. 4 a theory that views the power of employers as being balanced by the power of trade unions in industrial relations such that the interests of both sides can be catered for. 5 *Philosophy* **a** the metaphysical doctrine that reality consists of more than two basic types of substance. Compare **monism** (sense 1), **dualism** (sense 2). **b** the metaphysical doctrine that reality consists of independent entities rather than one unchanging whole. Compare **monism** (sense 1), **absolutism** (sense 2b).
▸**'pluralist** NOUN, ADJECTIVE ▸**,plural'istic** ADJECTIVE

plurality (plʊə'rælɪtɪ) NOUN, *plural* **-ties.** 1 the state of being plural or numerous. 2 *Maths* a number greater than one. 3 the US and Canadian term for **relative majority.** 4 a large number. 5 the greater number; majority. 6 another word for **pluralism** (sense 1).

pluralize *or* **pluralise** ('plʊərə,laɪz) VERB 1 (*intr*) to hold more than one ecclesiastical benefice or office at the same time. 2 to make or become plural.
▸**,plurali'zation** *or* **,plurali'sation** NOUN ▸**'plural,izer** *or* **'plural,iser** NOUN

plural voting NOUN 1 a system that enables an elector to vote more than once in an election. 2 (in Britain before 1948) a system enabling certain electors to vote in more than one constituency.

pluri- COMBINING FORM denoting several: *pluriliteral; pluripresence.*
▷HISTORY from Latin *plur-, plus* more, *plures* several

pluriliteral (,plʊrɪ'lɪtərəl) ADJECTIVE (in Hebrew grammar) containing more than three letters in the root.

pluripresence (,plʊrɪ'prɛzəns) NOUN *Theol* presence in more than one place at the same time.

plurry ('plʌrɪ) ADJECTIVE *Austral slang* a euphemism for **bloody**[6].

plus (plʌs) PREPOSITION 1 increased by the addition of: *four plus two* (written 4 + 2). 2 with or with the addition of: *a good job, plus a new car.* ◆ ADJECTIVE 3 (*prenominal*) Also: **positive.** indicating or involving addition: *a plus sign.* 4 another word for **positive** (senses 8, 9). 5 on the positive part of a scale or coordinate axis: *a value of +x.* 6 indicating the positive side of an electrical circuit. 7 involving positive advantage or good: *a plus factor.* 8 (*postpositive*) *Informal* having a value above that which is stated or expected: *she had charm plus.* 9 (*postpositive*) slightly above a specified standard on a particular grade or percentage: *he received a B+ rating on his essay.* 10 *Botany* designating the strain of fungus that can only undergo sexual reproduction with a minus strain. ◆ NOUN 11 short for **plus sign.** 12 a positive quantity. 13 *Informal* something positive or to the good. 14 a gain, surplus, or advantage. ◆ Mathematical symbol: +.
▷HISTORY C17: from Latin: more; compare Greek *pleiōn,* Old Norse *fleiri* more, German *viel* much

Language note *Plus, together with,* and *along with* do not create compound subjects in the way that *and* does: the number of the verb depends on that of the subject to which *plus, together with,* or *along with* is added: *this task, plus all the others, was* (not *were*) *undertaken by the government; the doctor, together with the nurses, was* (not *were*) *waiting for the patient.*

plus fours PLURAL NOUN men's baggy knickerbockers reaching below the knee, now only worn for hunting, golf, etc.
▷HISTORY C20: so called because the trousers are made with four inches of material to hang over at the knee

plush (plʌʃ) NOUN 1 **a** a fabric with a cut pile that is longer and softer than velvet. **b** (*as modifier*): *a plush chair.* ◆ ADJECTIVE 2 Also: **plushy.** *Informal* lavishly appointed; rich; costly.
▷HISTORY C16: from French *pluche,* from Old French *peluchier* to pluck, ultimately from Latin *pilus* a hair, PILE[3]
▸**'plushly** ADVERB ▸**'plushness** NOUN

plus sign NOUN the symbol +, indicating addition or positive quantity.

plus size NOUN **a** a clothing size designed for people who are above the average size. **b** (*as modifier*): *plus-size underwear.*

Pluto[1] ('plu:təʊ) NOUN *Classical myth* the god of the underworld; Hades.

Pluto[2] ('plu:təʊ) NOUN the smallest planet and the farthest known from the sun. Discovered in 1930 by Clyde Tombaugh (1906–97), it has one known satellite, Charon. Mean distance from sun: 5907 million km; period of revolution around sun: 248.6 years; period of axial rotation: 6.4 days; diameter and mass: 18 and 0.3 per cent that of earth respectively.
▷HISTORY Latin, from Greek *Ploutōn,* literally: the rich one

PLUTO ('plu:təʊ) NOUN the code name of pipelines laid under the English Channel to supply fuel to the Allied forces landing in Normandy in 1944.

▷HISTORY C20: from *p(ipe)l(ine) u(nder) t(he) o(cean)*

plutocracy (plu:ˈtɒkrəsɪ) NOUN, *plural* **-cies.** [1] the rule or control of society by the wealthy. [2] a state or government characterized by the rule of the wealthy. [3] a class that exercises power by virtue of its wealth.
▷HISTORY C17: from Greek *ploutokratia* government by the rich, from *ploutos* wealth + *-kratia* rule, power
▸**plutocratic** (ˌplu:təˈkrætɪk) *or* ˌ**plutoˈcratical** ADJECTIVE
▸ˌ**plutoˈcratically** ADVERB

plutocrat (ˈplu:təˌkræt) NOUN a member of a plutocracy.

pluton (ˈplu:tɒn) NOUN any mass of igneous rock that has solidified below the surface of the earth.
▷HISTORY C20: back formation from PLUTONIC

Plutonian (plu:ˈtəʊnɪən) ADJECTIVE of or relating to Pluto (the god) or the underworld; infernal.

plutonic (plu:ˈtɒnɪk) ADJECTIVE (of igneous rocks) derived from magma that has cooled and solidified below the surface of the earth. Also: **abyssal.**
▷HISTORY C20: named after PLUTO[1]

plutonium (plu:ˈtəʊnɪəm) NOUN a highly toxic metallic transuranic element. It occurs in trace amounts in uranium ores and is produced in a nuclear reactor by neutron bombardment of uranium-238. The most stable and important isotope, **plutonium-239**, readily undergoes fission and is used as a reactor fuel in nuclear power stations and in nuclear weapons. Symbol: Pu; atomic no.: 94; half-life of ^{239}Pu: 24 360 years; valency: 3, 4, 5, or 6; relative density (alpha modification): 19.84; melting pt.: 640°C; boiling pt.: 3230°C.
▷HISTORY C20: named after the planet *Pluto* because Pluto lies beyond Neptune and plutonium was discovered soon after NEPTUNIUM

Plutus (ˈplu:tʊs) NOUN the Greek god of wealth.
▷HISTORY from Greek *ploutos* wealth

pluvial (ˈplu:vɪəl) ADJECTIVE [1] of, characterized by, or due to the action of rain; rainy: *pluvial insurance.* ♦ NOUN [2] *Geology* of or relating to rainfall or precipitation. [3] a climate characterized by persistent heavy rainfall, esp one occurring in unglaciated regions during the Pleistocene epoch.
▷HISTORY C17: from Latin *pluviālis* rainy, from *pluvia* rain

pluviometer (ˌplu:vɪˈɒmɪtə) NOUN an obsolete word for **rain gauge.**
▸**pluviometric** (ˌplu:vɪəˈmɛtrɪk) ADJECTIVE
▸ˌ**pluvioˈmetrically** ADVERB ▸ˌ**pluviˈometry** NOUN

Pluviôse *French* (plyvjoz) NOUN the rainy month: the fifth month of the French revolutionary calendar, extending from Jan. 21 to Feb. 19.
▷HISTORY C19 *pluviose,* C15 *pluvious;* see PLUVIOUS

pluvious (ˈplu:vɪəs) *or* **pluviose** ADJECTIVE of or relating to rain; rainy.
▷HISTORY C15: from Late Latin *pluviōsus* full of rain, from *pluvia* rain, from *pluere* to rain

ply[1] (plaɪ) VERB **plies, plying, plied.** (*mainly tr*) [1] to carry on, pursue, or work at (a job, trade, etc.). [2] to manipulate or wield (a tool). [3] to sell (goods, wares, etc.), esp at a regular place. [4] (usually foll by *with*) to provide (with) or subject (to) repeatedly or persistently: *he plied us with drink the whole evening; to ply a horse with a whip; he plied the speaker with questions.* [5] (*intr*) to perform or work steadily or diligently: *to ply with a spade.* [6] (*also intr*) (esp of a ship) to travel regularly along (a route) or in (an area): *to ply between Dover and Calais; to ply the trade routes.*
▷HISTORY C14 *plye,* short for *aplye* to APPLY

ply[2] (plaɪ) NOUN, *plural* **plies.** [1] **a** a layer, fold, or thickness, as of cloth, wood, yarn, etc. **b** (*in combination*): *four-ply.* [2] a thin sheet of wood glued to other similar sheets to form plywood. [3] one of the strands twisted together to make rope, yarn, etc. ♦ VERB (*tr*) [4] to twist together (two or more single strands) to make yarn.
▷HISTORY C15: from Old French *pli* fold, from *plier* to fold, from Latin *plicāre*

Plymouth (ˈplɪməθ) NOUN [1] a port in SW England, in Plymouth unitary authority, SW Devon, on **Plymouth Sound** (an inlet of the English Channel): Britain's chief port in Elizabethan times; the last port visited by the Pilgrim Fathers in the *Mayflower* before sailing to America; naval base; university (1992). Pop.: 245 991 (1991). [2] a unitary authority in SW England, in Devon. Pop.: 240 718 (2001). Area: 76 sq. km (30 sq. miles). [3] a city in SE Massachusetts, on **Plymouth Bay:** the first permanent European settlement in New England; founded by the Pilgrim Fathers. Pop.: 45 608 (1990).

Plymouth Brethren PLURAL NOUN a religious sect founded *c.* 1827, strongly Puritanical in outlook and prohibiting many secular occupations for its members. It combines elements of Calvinism, Pietism, and millenarianism, and has no organized ministry.

Plymouth Colony NOUN the Puritan colony founded by the Pilgrim Fathers in SE Massachusetts (1620). See also **Mayflower.**

Plymouth Rock NOUN [1] a heavy American breed of domestic fowl bred for meat and laying. [2] a boulder on the coast of Massachusetts: traditionally thought to be the landing place of the Pilgrim Fathers (1620). See also **Mayflower.**

plywood (ˈplaɪˌwʊd) NOUN a structural board consisting of an odd number of thin layers of wood glued together under pressure, with the grain of one layer at right angles to the grain of the adjoining layer.

Plzeň (*Czech* ˈplzɛnj) NOUN an industrial city in the Czech Republic. Pop.: 167 534 (2000 est.). German name: **Pilsen.**

pm ABBREVIATION FOR premium.

pm THE INTERNET DOMAIN NAME FOR St. Pierre and Miquelon.

Pm THE CHEMICAL SYMBOL FOR promethium.

PM ABBREVIATION FOR: [1] Prime Minister. [2] Past Master (of a fraternity). [3] Paymaster. [4] Postmaster. [5] *Military* Provost Marshal.

p.m., P.M., pm, *or* **PM** ABBREVIATION FOR: [1] (indicating the time period from midday to midnight) post meridiem. Compare **a.m.** [Latin: after noon] [2] post-mortem (examination).

PMG ABBREVIATION FOR: [1] Paymaster General. [2] Postmaster General. [3] *Military* Provost Marshal General.

PMI ABBREVIATION FOR private medical insurance.

PMS ABBREVIATION FOR **premenstrual syndrome.**

PMT ABBREVIATION FOR: [1] **photomechanical transfer.** [2] premenstrual tension.

pn THE INTERNET DOMAIN NAME FOR Pitcairn Island.

PN, P/N, *or* **pn** ABBREVIATION FOR **promissory note.**

PNdB ABBREVIATION FOR **perceived noise decibel.**

pneuma (ˈnju:mə) NOUN *Philosophy* a person's vital spirit, soul, or creative energy. Compare **psyche.**
▷HISTORY C19: from Greek: breath, spirit, wind; related to *pnein* to blow, breathe

pneumatic (njuˈmætɪk) ADJECTIVE [1] of or concerned with air, gases, or wind. Compare **hydraulic.** [2] (of a machine or device) operated by compressed air or by a vacuum: *a pneumatic drill; pneumatic brakes.* [3] containing compressed air: *a pneumatic tyre.* [4] of or concerned with pneumatics. [5] *Theol* **a** of or relating to the soul or spirit. **b** of or relating to the Holy Ghost or other spiritual beings. [6] (of the bones of birds) containing air spaces which reduce their weight as an adaptation to flying. [7] *Informal* (of a woman) well rounded, esp with a large bosom. ♦ NOUN [8] short for **pneumatic tyre.**
▷HISTORY C17: from Late Latin *pneumaticus* of air or wind, from Greek *pneumatikos* of air or breath, from PNEUMA
▸**pneuˈmatically** ADVERB

pneumatic conveyor NOUN *Engineering* a tube through which powdered or granular material, such as cement, grain, etc. is transported by a flow of air.

pneumatics (njuˈmætɪks) NOUN (*functioning as singular*) the branch of physics concerned with the mechanical properties of gases, esp air. Also called: **aerometry, pneumodynamics.**

pneumatic trough NOUN *Chem* a shallow dishlike vessel filled with a liquid, usually water, and used in collecting gases by displacement of liquid from a filled jar held with its open end under the surface of the liquid.

pneumatic tyre NOUN a rubber tyre filled with air under pressure, used esp on motor vehicles.

pneumato- COMBINING FORM air; breath or breathing; spirit: *pneumatophore; pneumatology.*
▷HISTORY from Greek *pneuma, pneumat-,* breath; see PNEUMA

pneumatology (ˌnju:məˈtɒlədʒɪ) NOUN [1] the branch of theology concerned with the Holy Ghost and other spiritual beings. [2] an obsolete name for **psychology** (the science). [3] an obsolete term for **pneumatics.**
▸**pneumatological** (ˌnju:mətəˈlɒdʒɪkᵊl) ADJECTIVE
▸ˌ**pneumaˈtologist** NOUN

pneumatolysis (ˌnju:məˈtɒlɪsɪs) NOUN a type of metamorphism in which hot gases from solidifying magma react with surrounding rock.

pneumatometer (ˌnju:məˈtɒmɪtə) NOUN an instrument for measuring the pressure exerted by air being inhaled or exhaled during a single breath. Compare **spirometer.**
▸ˌ**pneumaˈtometry** NOUN

pneumatophore (nju:ˈmætəʊˌfɔ:) NOUN [1] a specialized root of certain swamp plants, such as the mangrove, that branches upwards, rising above ground, and undergoes gaseous exchange with the atmosphere. [2] a polyp in coelenterates of the order *Siphonophora,* such as the Portuguese man-of-war, that is specialized as a float.

pneumectomy (nju:ˈmɛktəmɪ) NOUN, *plural* **-mies.** *Surgery* another word for **pneumonectomy.**

pneumo-, pneumono-, *or before a vowel* **pneum-, pneumon-** COMBINING FORM of or related to a lung or the lungs; respiratory: *pneumoconiosis; pneumonitis.*
▷HISTORY from Greek *pneumōn* lung or *pneuma* breath

pneumobacillus (ˌnju:məʊbəˈsɪləs) NOUN, *plural* **-li** (-laɪ). a rod-shaped bacterium that occurs in the respiratory tract, esp the Gram-negative *Klebsiella pneumoniae,* which causes pneumonia.

pneumococcus (ˌnju:məʊˈkɒkəs) NOUN, *plural* **-cocci** (-ˈkɒkaɪ). a spherical bacterium that occurs in the respiratory tract, esp the Gram-positive *Diplococcus pneumoniae,* which causes pneumonia.
▸ˌ**pneumoˈcoccal** ADJECTIVE

pneumoconiosis (ˌnju:məʊˌkəʊnɪˈəʊsɪs) *or* **pneumonoconiosis** (ˌnju:mənəʊˌkəʊnɪˈəʊsɪs) NOUN any disease of the lungs or bronchi caused by the inhalation of metallic or mineral particles: characterized by inflammation, cough, and fibrosis.
▷HISTORY C19: shortened from *pneumonoconiosis,* from PNEUMO- + *-coniosis,* from Greek *konis* dust

pneumocystis (ˌnju:məʊˈsɪstɪs) NOUN any protozoan of the genus *Pneumocystis, esp P. carinii,* which is a cause of pneumonia in people whose immune defences have been lowered by drugs or a disease.

pneumodynamics (ˌnju:məʊdaɪˈnæmɪks) NOUN (*functioning as singular*) another name for **pneumatics.**

pneumoencephalogram (ˌnju:məʊɛnˈsɛfələˌgræm) NOUN See **encephalogram.**
▸**pneumoencephalography** (ˌnju:məʊɛnˌsɛfəˈlɒgrəfɪ) NOUN

pneumogastric (ˌnju:məʊˈgæstrɪk) ADJECTIVE *Anatomy* [1] of or relating to the lungs and stomach. [2] a former term for **vagus.**

pneumograph (ˈnju:məˌgrɑ:f, -ˌgræf) NOUN *Med* an instrument for making a record (**pneumogram**) of respiratory movements.

pneumonectomy (ˌnju:məʊˈnɛktəmɪ) *or* **pneumectomy** (nju:ˈmɛktəmɪ) NOUN, *plural* **-mies.** the surgical removal of a lung or part of a lung.
▷HISTORY C20: from Greek *pneumōn* lung + -ECTOMY

pneumonia (nju:ˈməʊnɪə) NOUN inflammation of one or both lungs, in which the air sacs (alveoli) become filled with liquid, which renders them useless for breathing. It is usually caused by bacterial (esp pneumococcal) or viral infection.
▷HISTORY C17: New Latin from Greek from *pneumōn* lung

pneumonic (nju:ˈmɒnɪk) ADJECTIVE [1] of, relating to, or affecting the lungs; pulmonary. [2] of or relating to pneumonia.
▷HISTORY C17: from New Latin *pneumonicus,* from Greek, from *pneumon* lung

pneumonitis (ˌnju:mɒnˈaɪtɪs) NOUN inflammation of the lungs.

pneumothorax (ˌnju:məʊˈθɔ:ræks) NOUN [1] the abnormal presence of air between the lung and the wall of the chest (pleural cavity), resulting in collapse of the lung. [2] *Med* the introduction of air into the pleural cavity to collapse the lung: a former treatment for tuberculosis.

PNG INTERNATIONAL CAR REGISTRATION FOR Papua New Guinea.

PNI ABBREVIATION FOR psychoneuroimmunology.

p-n junction NOUN *Electronics* a boundary between a p-type and n-type semiconductor that functions as a rectifier and is used in diodes and junction transistors.

Pnom Penh (ˈnɒm ˈpɛn) NOUN a variant spelling of **Phnom Penh.**

po (pəʊ) NOUN, *plural* **pos.** *Brit* an informal word for **chamber pot.**
▷HISTORY C19: from POT[1]

Po[1] THE CHEMICAL SYMBOL FOR polonium.

Po[2] (pəʊ) NOUN a river in N Italy, rising in the Cottian Alps and flowing northeast to Turin, then east to the Adriatic: the longest river in Italy. Length: 652 km (405 miles). Latin name: **Padus.**

PO ABBREVIATION FOR: 1 Post Office. 2 Personnel Officer. 3 petty officer. 4 Pilot Officer. 5 Also: **p.o.** postal order.

poaceous (pəʊˈeɪʃəs) ADJECTIVE of, relating to, or belonging to the plant family *Poaceae* (grasses).
▷HISTORY C18: via New Latin from Greek *poa* grass

poach[1] (pəʊtʃ) VERB 1 to catch (game, fish, etc.) illegally by trespassing on private property. 2 to encroach on or usurp (another person's rights, duties, etc.) or steal (an idea, employee, etc.). 3 *Tennis, badminton* to take or play (shots that should belong to one's partner). 4 to break up (land) into wet muddy patches, as by riding over it, or (of land) to become broken up in this way. 5 (*intr*) (of the feet, shoes, etc.) to sink into heavy wet ground.
▷HISTORY C17: from Old French *pocher,* of Germanic origin; compare Middle Dutch *poken* to prod; see POKE[1]

poach[2] (pəʊtʃ) VERB to simmer (eggs, fish, etc.) very gently in water, milk, stock, etc.
▷HISTORY C15: from Old French *pochier* to enclose in a bag (as the yolks are enclosed by the whites); compare POKE[2]

poacher[1] (ˈpəʊtʃə) NOUN 1 a person who illegally hunts game, fish, etc., on someone else's property. 2 **poacher turned gamekeeper.** someone whose occupation or behaviour is the opposite of what it previously was, such as a burglar who now advises on home security.

poacher[2] (ˈpəʊtʃə) NOUN a metal pan with individual cups for poaching eggs.

POB ABBREVIATION FOR Post Office Box.

pochard (ˈpəʊtʃəd) NOUN, *plural* **-chards** *or* **-chard.** any of various diving ducks of the genera *Aythya* and *Netta, esp A. ferina* of Europe, the male of which has a grey-and-black body and a reddish head.
▷HISTORY C16: of unknown origin

pochette (pɒˈʃɛt) NOUN an envelope-shaped handbag used by women and men.
▷HISTORY C20: from French: little pocket

pock (pɒk) NOUN 1 any pustule resulting from an eruptive disease, esp from smallpox. 2 another word for **pockmark** (sense 1).
▷HISTORY Old English *pocc;* related to Middle Dutch *pocke,* perhaps to Latin *bucca* cheek
▸ˈ**pocky** ADJECTIVE

pocket (ˈpɒkɪt) NOUN 1 a small bag or pouch in a garment for carrying small articles, money, etc. 2 any bag or pouch or anything resembling this. 3 **a** a cavity or hollow in the earth, etc., such as one containing gold or other ore. **b** the ore in such a place. 4 a small enclosed or isolated area: *a pocket of resistance.* 5 *Billiards, snooker* any of the six holes with pouches or nets let into the corners and sides of a billiard table. 6 a position in a race in which a competitor is hemmed in. 7 *Australian Rules football* a player in one of two side positions at the ends of the ground: *back pocket; forward pocket.* 8 *South African* a bag or sack of vegetables or fruit. 9 **in one's pocket.** under one's control. 10 **in** *or* **out of pocket.** having made a profit or loss, as after a transaction. 11 **line one's pockets.** to make money, esp by dishonesty when in a position of trust. 12 (*modifier*) suitable for fitting in a pocket; small: *a pocket edition.* ◆ VERB **-ets, -eting, -eted.** (*tr*) 13 to put into one's pocket. 14 to take surreptitiously or unlawfully; steal. 15 (*usually passive*) to enclose or confine in or as if in a pocket. 16 to receive (an insult, injury, etc.) without retaliating. 17 to conceal or keep back (feelings): *he pocketed his pride and accepted help.* 18 *Billiards, snooker* to drive (a ball) into a pocket. 19 *US* (esp of the President) to retain (a bill) without acting on it in order to prevent it from becoming law. See also **pocket veto.** 20 to hem in (an opponent), as in racing.
▷HISTORY C15: from Anglo-Norman *poket* a little bag, from *poque* bag, from Middle Dutch *poke* POKE[2], bag; related to French *poche* pocket
▸ˈ**pocketable** ADJECTIVE ▸ˈ**pocketless** ADJECTIVE

pocket battleship NOUN a small heavily armoured and armed battle cruiser specially built to conform with treaty limitations on tonnage and armament, esp any of those built by Germany in the 1930s.

pocket billiards NOUN (*functioning as singular*) *Billiards* 1 another name for **pool**[2] (sense 5). 2 any game played on a table in which the object is to pocket the balls, esp snooker and pool.

pocketbook (ˈpɒkɪtˌbʊk) NOUN *US and Canadian* a small bag or case for money, papers, etc., carried by a handle or in the pocket.

pocket borough NOUN (before the Reform Act of 1832) an English borough constituency controlled by one person or family who owned the land. Compare **rotten borough.**

pocketful (ˈpɒkɪtfʊl) NOUN, *plural* **-fuls.** 1 as much as a pocket will hold. 2 *Informal* a large amount: *it cost him a pocketful of money.*

pocket gopher NOUN the full name for **gopher** (sense 1).

pocketknife (ˈpɒkɪtˌnaɪf) NOUN, *plural* **-knives.** a small knife with one or more blades that fold into the handle; penknife.

pocket money NOUN 1 *Brit* a small weekly sum of money given to children by parents as an allowance. 2 money for day-to-day spending, incidental expenses, etc.

pocket mouse NOUN any small mouselike rodent with cheek pouches, of the genus *Perognathus,* of desert regions of W North America: family *Heteromyidae.*

pocket veto NOUN *US* 1 the action of the President in retaining unsigned a bill passed by Congress within the last ten days of a session and thus causing it to die. 2 any similar action by a state governor or other chief executive.

pockies (ˈpɒkɪz) PLURAL NOUN *Scot dialect* woollen mittens.

pockmark (ˈpɒkˌmɑːk) NOUN 1 Also called: **pock.** a pitted scar left on the skin after the healing of a smallpox or similar pustule. 2 any pitting of a surface that resembles or suggests such scars. ◆ VERB 3 (*tr*) to scar or pit (a surface) with pockmarks.

pockmarked (ˈpɒkˌmɑːkd) ADJECTIVE abounding in pockmarks.

poco (ˈpəʊkəʊ; *Italian* ˈpɔːko) *or* **un poco** ADJECTIVE, ADVERB *Music* (*in combination*) a little; to a small degree: *poco rit; un poco meno mosso.*
▷HISTORY from Italian: little, from Latin *paucus* few, scanty

poco a poco ADVERB (*in combination*) *Music* little by little: *poco a poco rall.*
▷HISTORY Italian

pococurante (ˌpəʊkəʊkjʊˈræntɪ) NOUN 1 a person who is careless or indifferent. ◆ ADJECTIVE 2 indifferent or apathetic.
▷HISTORY C18: from Italian, from *poco* little + *curante* caring
▸ˌ**pococuˈranteism** *or* ˌ**pococuˈrantism** NOUN

pod[1] (pɒd) NOUN 1 **a** the fruit of any leguminous plant, consisting of a long two-valved case that contains seeds and splits along both sides when ripe. **b** the seedcase as distinct from the seeds. 2 any similar fruit. 3 a streamlined structure attached by a pylon to an aircraft and used to house a jet engine (**podded engine**), fuel tank, armament, etc. 4 an enclosed cabin suspended from a cable or a big wheel, for carrying passengers. ◆ VERB **pods, podding, podded.** 5 (*tr*) to remove the pod or shell from (peas, beans, etc.). 6 (*intr*) (of a plant) to produce pods.
▷HISTORY C17: perhaps back formation from earlier *podware* bagged vegetables, probably from *pod,* variant of COD[2] + WARE[1]

pod[2] (pɒd) NOUN a small group of animals, esp seals, whales, or birds.
▷HISTORY C19: of unknown origin

pod[3] (pɒd) NOUN 1 a straight groove along the length of certain augers and bits. 2 the socket that holds the bit in a boring tool.
▷HISTORY C16: of unknown origin

POD ABBREVIATION FOR pay on delivery.

-pod *or* **-pode** NOUN COMBINING FORM indicating a certain type or number of feet: *arthropod; tripod.*
▷HISTORY from Greek *-podos* footed, from *pous* foot

podagra (pəˈdæɡrə) NOUN gout of the foot or big toe.
▷HISTORY C15: via Latin from Greek, from *pous* foot + *agra* a trap
▸**poˈdagral** *or* **poˈdagric** *or* **poˈdagrical** *or* **poˈdagrous** ADJECTIVE

poddle (ˈpɒdᵊl) VERB (*intr*) *Informal* (often foll by *along, round,* etc.) to move or travel in a leisurely manner; amble.
▷HISTORY C19: variant of PADDLE[2]

poddy (ˈpɒdɪ) NOUN, *plural* **-dies.** *Austral* 1 a handfed calf or lamb. 2 any creature at an early stage of growth: *poddy mullet.*
▷HISTORY perhaps from *poddy* (adj) fat

poddy-dodger (ˈpɒdɪˌdɒdʒə) NOUN *Austral informal* a cattle thief who steals unbranded calves.

podesta (pɒˈdɛstə; *Italian* podeˈsta) NOUN 1 (in modern Italy) a subordinate magistrate in some towns. 2 (in Fascist Italy) the chief magistrate of a commune. 3 (in medieval Italy) **a** any of the governors of the Lombard cities appointed by Frederick Barbarossa. **b** a chief magistrate in any of various republics, such as Florence.
▷HISTORY C16: from Italian: power, from Latin *potestās* ability, power, from *posse* to be able

podge (pɒdʒ) *or* **pudge** (pʌdʒ) NOUN *Informal* a short chubby person.

Podgorica *or* **Podgoritsa** (*Russian* ˈpɔdɡɔˌriːtsa) NOUN a city in Serbia and Montenegro, the capital of Montenegro: under Turkish rule (1474–1878). Pop.: 130 875 (2000 est.). Former name (1946–92): **Titograd.**

podgy (ˈpɒdʒɪ) ADJECTIVE **podgier, podgiest.** short and fat; chubby.
▸ˈ**podgily** ADVERB ▸ˈ**podginess** NOUN

podiatry (pɒˈdiːətrɪ) NOUN another word for **chiropody.**
▷HISTORY C20: from Greek *pous* foot
▸**podiatric** (ˌpəʊdɪˈætrɪk) ADJECTIVE ▸**poˈdiatrist** NOUN

podium (ˈpəʊdɪəm) NOUN, *plural* **-diums** *or* **-dia** (-dɪə). 1 a small raised platform used by lecturers, orchestra conductors, etc.; dais. 2 a plinth that supports a colonnade or wall. 3 a low wall surrounding the arena of an ancient amphitheatre. 4 *Zoology* **a** the terminal part of a vertebrate limb. **b** any footlike organ, such as the tube foot of a starfish.
▷HISTORY C18: from Latin: platform, balcony, from Greek *podion* little foot, from *pous* foot

-podium NOUN COMBINING FORM a part resembling a foot: *pseudopodium.*
▷HISTORY from New Latin: footlike; see PODIUM

Podolsk (*Russian* paˈdɔljsk) NOUN an industrial city in W Russia, near Moscow. Pop.: 195 900 (1999 est.).

podophyllin *or* **podophylin resin** (ˌpɒdəʊˈfɪlɪn) NOUN a bitter yellow resin obtained from the dried underground stems of the May apple and mandrake: used to treat warts and formerly as a cathartic.
▷HISTORY C19: from New Latin *Podophyllum* genus of herbs including the May apple, from *podo-,* from Greek *pous* foot + *phullon* leaf

-podous ADJECTIVE COMBINING FORM having feet of a certain kind or number: *cephalopodous.*

pod person NOUN, *plural* **pod people.** *Informal* a person who behaves in a strange esp mechanical way, as if not fully human.
▷HISTORY C20: from the science-fiction film *Invasion of the Body Snatchers (1956;* remade *1978)* in which individual humans are replaced by alien replicas grown in giant pods

podzol (ˈpɒdzɒl) *or* **podsol** (ˈpɒdsɒl) NOUN a type of soil characteristic of coniferous forest regions having a greyish-white colour in its upper leached layers.
▷HISTORY C20: from Russian: ash ground, from *pod* ground + *zola* ashes
▸**podˈzolic** *or* **podˈsolic** ADJECTIVE

podzolization (ˌpɒdzɒlaɪˈzeɪʃən), **podsolization** (ˌpɒdsɒlaɪˈzeɪʃən), **podzolisation,** *or* **podsolisation** NOUN the process by which the upper layer of a soil becomes acidic through the leaching of bases which are deposited in the lower horizons.

podzolize (ˈpɒdzɒˌlaɪz), **podsolize** (ˈpɒdsɒˌlaɪz), **podzolise,** *or* **podsolise** VERB (*usually passive*) to make into or form a podzol.

POE ABBREVIATION FOR: [1] *Military* port of embarkation. [2] **port of entry.**

poem (ˈpəʊɪm) NOUN [1] a composition in verse, usually characterized by concentrated and heightened language in which words are chosen for their sound and suggestive power as well as for their sense, and using such techniques as metre, rhyme, and alliteration. [2] a literary composition that is not in verse but exhibits the intensity of imagination and language common to it: *a prose poem.* [3] anything resembling a poem in beauty, effect, etc.
▷HISTORY C16: from Latin *poēma,* from Greek, variant of *poiēma* something composed, created, from *poiein* to make

poenology (piːˈnɒlədʒɪ) NOUN a variant spelling of **penology.**

poep (pʊp) NOUN *South African slang* [1] an emission of intestinal gas from the anus. [2] a mean or despicable person.

poesy (ˈpəʊɪzɪ) NOUN, *plural* **-sies.** [1] an archaic word for **poetry.** [2] *Poetic* the art of writing poetry. [3] *Archaic or poetic* a poem or verse, esp one used as a motto.
▷HISTORY C14: via Old French from Latin *poēsis,* from Greek, from *poiēsis* poetic art, creativity, from *poiein* to make

poet (ˈpəʊɪt) *or sometimes when feminine* **poetess** NOUN [1] a person who writes poetry. [2] a person with great imagination and creativity.
▷HISTORY C13: from Latin *poēta,* from Greek *poiētēs* maker, poet, from *poiein* to make

poetaster (ˌpəʊɪˈtæstə, -ˈteɪ-) NOUN a writer of inferior verse.
▷HISTORY C16: from Medieval Latin; see POET, -ASTER

poetic (pəʊˈɛtɪk) *or* **poetical** ADJECTIVE [1] of or relating to poetry. [2] characteristic of poetry, as in being elevated, sublime, etc. [3] characteristic of a poet. [4] recounted in verse.
▸**poˈetically** ADVERB

poeticize (pəʊˈɛtɪˌsaɪz), **poetize** (ˈpəʊɪˌtaɪz), **poeticise,** *or* **poetise** VERB [1] (*tr*) to put into poetry or make poetic. [2] (*intr*) to speak or write poetically.

poetic justice NOUN fitting retribution; just deserts.

poetic licence NOUN justifiable departure from conventional rules of form, fact, logic, etc., as in poetry.

poetics (pəʊˈɛtɪks) NOUN (*usually functioning as singular*) [1] the principles and forms of poetry or the study of these, esp as a form of literary criticism. [2] a treatise on poetry.

poet laureate NOUN, *plural* **poets laureate.** *Brit* the poet appointed as court poet of Britain who is given a post as an officer of the Royal Household. The first was Ben Jonson in 1616.

poetry (ˈpəʊɪtrɪ) NOUN [1] literature in metrical form; verse. [2] the art or craft of writing verse. [3] poetic qualities, spirit, or feeling in anything. [4] anything resembling poetry in rhythm, beauty, etc.
▷HISTORY C14: from Medieval Latin *poētria,* from Latin *poēta* POET

po-faced ADJECTIVE (of a person) wearing a disapproving stern expression.
▷HISTORY C20: possibly from PO + POKER-FACED

pogey *or* **pogy** (ˈpəʊgɪ) NOUN, *plural* **pogeys** *or* **pogies.** *Canadian slang* [1] financial or other relief given to the unemployed by the government; dole. [2] unemployment insurance. [3] **a** the office distributing relief to the unemployed. **b** (*as modifier*): *pogey clothes.*
▷HISTORY C20: from earlier *pogie* workhouse, of unknown origin

pogge (pɒg) NOUN [1] Also called: **armed bullhead.** a European marine scorpaenoid fish, *Agonus cataphractus,* of northern European waters, with a large head, long thin tail, and body completely covered with bony plates: family *Agonidae.* [2] any other fish of the family *Agonidae.*
▷HISTORY C18: of unknown origin

pogo (ˈpəʊgəʊ) VERB **pogos, pogoing, pogoed.** (*intr*) to jump up and down in one spot, as in a punk dance of the 1970s.
▷HISTORY C20: from POGO STICK; from the motion
▸**ˈpogoer** NOUN

pogonia (pəˈgəʊnɪə) NOUN any orchid of the chiefly American genus *Pogonia, esp the snakesmouth, having pink or white fragrant* flowers.
▷HISTORY C19: New Latin, from Greek *pōgōnias* bearded, from *pōgōn* a beard

pogo stick NOUN a stout pole with a handle at the top, steps for the feet and a spring at the bottom, so that the user can spring up, down, and along on it.
▷HISTORY C20: of uncertain origin

pogrom (ˈpɒgrəm) NOUN an organized persecution or extermination of an ethnic group, esp of Jews.
▷HISTORY C20: via Yiddish from Russian: destruction, from *po-* like + *grom* thunder

Pogson ratio (ˈpɒdʒsən) NOUN the brightness ratio of two celestial objects that differ by one magnitude. On the Pogson scale a difference of 5 magnitudes is defined as a difference of 100 in the intensities of two stars; therefore a difference of 1 magnitude is equal to the fifth root of 100, i.e. 2.512.
▷HISTORY C19: named after N. R. *Pogson* (1829–91), British astronomer

pogy (ˈpəʊgɪ, ˈpɒgɪ) NOUN [1] (*plural* **pogies** *or* **pogy**) another name for the **porgy.** [2] (*plural* **pogies**) a variant spelling of **pogey.**
▷HISTORY C19: perhaps from Algonquian *pohegan* menhaden

Pohai (ˌpəʊˈhaɪ) NOUN a variant transliteration of the Chinese name for **Bohai.**

pohutukawa (pəˌhuːtəˈkɑːwə) NOUN a myrtaceous New Zealand tree, *Metrosideros excelsa,* with red flowers and hard red wood.
▷HISTORY from Maori

poi[1] (pɔɪ, ˈpəʊɪ) NOUN a Hawaiian dish made of the root of the taro baked, pounded to a paste, and fermented.
▷HISTORY C19: from Hawaiian

poi[2] (pɔɪ) NOUN *NZ* a ball of woven flax swung rhythmically in poi dances.
▷HISTORY Maori

poi dance NOUN *NZ* a women's formation dance that involves singing and manipulating a poi.

-poiesis NOUN COMBINING FORM indicating the act of making or producing something specified: *haematopoiesis.*
▷HISTORY from Greek, from *poiēsis* a making; see POESY
▸**-poietic** ADJECTIVE COMBINING FORM

poignant (ˈpɔɪnjənt, -nənt) ADJECTIVE [1] sharply distressing or painful to the feelings. [2] to the point; cutting or piercing: *poignant wit.* [3] keen or pertinent in mental appeal: *a poignant subject.* [4] pungent in smell.
▷HISTORY C14: from Old French, from Latin *pungens* pricking, from *pungere* to sting, pierce, grieve
▸**ˈpoignancy** *or* **ˈpoignance** NOUN ▸**ˈpoignantly** ADVERB

poikilocyte (ˈpɔɪkɪləʊˌsaɪt) NOUN an abnormally shaped red blood cell.
▷HISTORY C19: from Greek *poikilos* various + -CYTE

poikilothermic (ˌpɔɪkɪləʊˈθɜːmɪk) *or* **poikilothermal** (ˌpɔɪkɪləʊˈθɜːməl) ADJECTIVE (of all animals except birds and mammals) having a body temperature that varies with the temperature of the surroundings. Compare **homoiothermic.**
▷HISTORY C19: from Greek *poikilos* various + THERMAL
▸**ˌpoikiloˈthermism** *or* **ˌpoikiloˈthermy** NOUN

poilu (ˈpwɑːluː; *French* pwaly) NOUN an infantryman in the French Army, esp one in the front lines in World War I.
▷HISTORY C20: from French, literally: hairy (that is, virile), from *poil* hair, from Latin *pilus* a hair

poinciana (ˌpɔɪnsɪˈɑːnə) NOUN any tree of the tropical leguminous genera *Caesalpinia* (formerly *Poinciana*) having large orange or red flowers. See **royal poinciana.**
▷HISTORY C17: New Latin, named after M. de *Poinci,* 17th-century governor of the French Antilles

poind (pɪnd) VERB (*tr*) *Scots law* [1] to take (property of a debtor) in execution or by way of distress; distrain. [2] to impound (stray cattle, etc.).
▷HISTORY C15: from Scots, variant of Old English *pyndan* to impound

poinsettia (pɔɪnˈsɛtɪə) NOUN a euphorbiaceous shrub, *Euphorbia* (or *Poinsettia*) *pulcherrima,* of Mexico and Central America, widely cultivated for its showy scarlet bracts, which resemble petals.
▷HISTORY C19: New Latin, from the name of J. P. *Poinsett* (1799–1851), US Minister to Mexico, who introduced it to the US

point (pɔɪnt) NOUN [1] a dot or tiny mark. [2] a location, spot, or position. [3] any dot or mark used in writing or printing, such as a decimal point or a full stop. [4] short for **vowel point.** [5] the sharp tapered end of a pin, knife, etc. [6] a pin, needle, or other object having such a point. [7] *Maths* **a** a geometric element having no dimensions and whose position in space is located by means of its coordinates. **b** a location: *point of inflection.* [8] a promontory, usually smaller than a cape. [9] a specific condition or degree. [10] a moment: *at that point he left the room.* [11] an important or fundamental reason, aim, etc.: *the point of this exercise is to train new teachers.* [12] an essential element or thesis in an argument: *you've made your point; I take your point.* [13] a suggestion or tip. [14] a detail or item. [15] an important or outstanding characteristic, physical attribute, etc.: *he has his good points.* [16] a distinctive characteristic or quality of an animal, esp one used as a standard in judging livestock. [17] (*often plural*) any of the extremities, such as the tail, ears, or feet, of a domestic animal. [18] *Ballet* (*often plural*) the tip of the toes. [19] a single unit for measuring or counting, as in the scoring of a game. [20] *Australian Rules football* an informal name for **behind** (sense 11). [21] *Printing* a unit of measurement equal to one twelfth of a pica, or approximately 0.01384 inch. There are approximately 72 points to the inch. [22] *Finance* **a** a unit of value used to quote security and commodity prices and their fluctuations. **b** a percentage unit sometimes payable by a borrower as a premium on a loan. [23] *Navigation* **a** one of the 32 marks on the circumference of a compass card indicating direction. **b** the angle of 11°15′ between two adjacent marks. **c** a point on the horizon indicated by such a mark. [24] *Cricket* **a** a fielding position at right angles to the batsman on the off side and relatively near the pitch. **b** a fielder in this position. [25] any of the numbers cast in the first throw in craps with which one neither wins nor loses by throwing them: 4, 5, 6, 8, 9, or 10. [26] either of the two electrical contacts that make or break the current flow in the distributor of an internal-combustion engine. [27] *Brit* (*often plural*) a junction of railway tracks in which a pair of rails can be moved so that a train can be directed onto either of two lines. US and Canadian equivalent: **switch.** [28] (*often plural*) a piece of ribbon, cord, etc., with metal tags at the end: used during the 16th and 17th centuries to fasten clothing. [29] *Backgammon* a place or position on the board. [30] *Brit* **a** short for **power point. b** an informal name for **socket** (sense 2). [31] an aggressive position adopted in bayonet or sword drill. [32] *Military* the position at the head of a body of troops, or a person in this position. [33] the position of the body of a pointer or setter when it discovers game. [34] *Boxing* a mark awarded for a scoring blow, knockdown, etc. [35] any diacritic used in a writing system, esp in a phonetic transcription, to indicate modifications of vowels or consonants. [36] *Jewellery* a unit of weight equal to 0.01 carat. [37] the act of pointing. [38] *Ice hockey* the position just inside the opponents' blue line. [39] **beside the point.** not pertinent; irrelevant. [40] **case in point.** a specific, appropriate, or relevant instance or example. [41] **in point of.** in the matter of; regarding. [42] **make a point of. a** to make (something) one's regular habit. **b** to do (something) because one thinks it important. [43] **not to put too fine a point on it.** to speak plainly and bluntly. [44] **on** (*or* **at**) **the point of.** at the moment immediately before a specified condition, action, etc., is expected to begin: *on the point of leaving the room.* [45] **score points off.** to gain an advantage at someone else's expense. [46] **stretch a point. a** to make a concession or

exception not usually made. **b** to exaggerate. 47 **to the point.** pertinent; relevant. 48 **up to a point.** not completely. ◆ VERB 49 (usually foll by *at* or *to*) to indicate the location or direction of by or as by extending (a finger or other pointed object) towards it: *he pointed to the front door; don't point that gun at me.* 50 (*intr;* usually foll by *at* or *to*) to indicate or identify a specific person or thing among several: *he pointed at the bottle he wanted; all evidence pointed to Donald as the murderer.* 51 (*tr*) to direct or cause to go or face in a specific direction or towards a place or goal: *point me in the right direction.* 52 (*intr*) to sharpen or taper. 53 (*intr*) (of gun dogs) to indicate the place where game is lying by standing rigidly with the muzzle turned in its direction. 54 (*tr*) to finish or repair the joints of (brickwork, masonry, etc.) with mortar or cement. 55 (*tr*) *Music* to mark (a psalm text) with vertical lines to indicate the points at which the music changes during chanting. 56 to steer (a sailing vessel) close to the wind or (of a sailing vessel) to sail close to the wind. 57 (*tr*) *Phonetics* to provide (a letter or letters) with diacritics. 58 (*tr*) to provide (a Hebrew or similar text) with vowel points. ◆ See also **point off, point out, point up.**
▷**HISTORY** C13: from Old French: spot, from Latin *punctum* a point, from *pungere* to pierce; also influenced by Old French *pointe* pointed end, from Latin *pungere*

point after NOUN *American football* a score given for a successful kick between the goalposts and above the crossbar, following a touchdown.

point-blank ADJECTIVE 1 **a** aimed or fired at a target so close that it is unnecessary to make allowance for the drop in the course of the projectile. **b** permitting such aim or fire without loss of accuracy: *at point-blank range.* 2 plain or blunt: *a point-blank question.* ◆ ADVERB 3 directly or straight. 4 plainly or bluntly.
▷**HISTORY** C16: from POINT + BLANK (in the sense: centre spot of an archery target)

point d'appui *French* (pwɛ̃ dapwi) NOUN, *plural* ***points d'appui*** (pwɛ̃ dapwi). 1 a support or prop. 2 (formerly) the base or rallying point for a military unit.

point defect NOUN an imperfection in a crystal, characterized by one unoccupied lattice position or one interstitial atom, molecule, or ion.

Point de Galle (pɔɪnt də ˈɡɑːlə) NOUN a former name of **Galle.**

point-device *Obsolete* ◆ ADJECTIVE 1 very correct or perfect; precise. ◆ ADVERB 2 to perfection; perfectly; precisely.
▷**HISTORY** C14: perhaps from old French *à point devis* to the point arranged

point duty NOUN 1 the stationing of a policeman or traffic warden at a road junction to control and direct traffic. 2 the position at the head of a military patrol, regarded as being the most dangerous.

pointe (pɔɪnt) NOUN *Ballet* the tip of the toe (esp in the phrase **on pointes**).
▷**HISTORY** from French: point

Pointe-à-Pitre (*French* pwɛ̃tapitrə) NOUN the chief port of Guadeloupe, on SW Grande Terre Island in the Caribbean. Pop.: 26 029 (1990).

pointed (ˈpɔɪntɪd) ADJECTIVE 1 having a point. 2 cutting or incisive: *a pointed wit.* 3 obviously directed at or intended for a particular person or aspect: *pointed criticism.* 4 emphasized or made conspicuous: *pointed ignorance.* 5 (of an arch or style of architecture employing such an arch) Gothic. 6 *Music* (of a psalm text) marked to show changes in chanting. 7 (of Hebrew text) with vowel points marked.
▸ˈ**pointedly** ADVERB ▸ˈ**pointedness** NOUN

pointed arch NOUN another name for **lancet arch.**

Pointe-Noire (*French* pwɛ̃tnwar) NOUN a port in S Congo-Brazzaville, on the Atlantic: the country's chief port and former capital (1950–58). Pop.: 576 206 (1995 est.).

pointer (ˈpɔɪntə) NOUN 1 a person or thing that points. 2 an indicator on a measuring instrument. 3 a long rod or cane used by a lecturer to point to parts of a map, blackboard, etc. 4 one of a breed of large swift smooth-coated dogs, usually white with black, liver, or lemon markings: when on shooting expeditions it points to the bird with its nose, body, and tail in a straight line. 5 a helpful piece of information or advice.

Pointers (ˈpɔɪntəz) PLURAL NOUN **the.** the two brightest stars in the Plough (Dubhe and Merak), which lie in the direction pointing towards the Pole Star and are therefore used to locate it.

point estimate NOUN *Statistics* a specific value assigned to a parameter of a population on the basis of sampling statistics. Compare **interval estimate.**

point group NOUN *Crystallog* another term for **crystal class.**

point guard NOUN *Basketball* **a** the position of the player responsible for directing the team's attacking play. **b** a player in this position.

pointillism (ˈpwæntɪˌlɪzəm, -tiːˌɪzəm, ˈpɔɪn-) NOUN the technique of painting elaborated from impressionism, in which dots of unmixed colour are juxtaposed on a white ground so that from a distance they fuse in the viewer's eye into appropriate intermediate tones. Also called: **divisionism.**
▷**HISTORY** C19: from French, from *pointiller* to mark with tiny dots, from *pointille* little point, from Italian *puntiglio,* from *punto* POINT
▸ˈ**pointillist** NOUN, ADJECTIVE

pointing (ˈpɔɪntɪŋ) NOUN 1 the act or process of repairing or finishing joints in brickwork, masonry, etc., with mortar. 2 **a** the insertion of marks to indicate the chanting of a psalm or the vowels in a Hebrew text. **b** the sequence of marks so inserted.

point lace NOUN lace made by a needle with buttonhole stitch on a paper pattern. Also called: **needlepoint.** Compare **pillow lace.**

pointless (ˈpɔɪntlɪs) ADJECTIVE 1 without a point. 2 without meaning, relevance, or force. 3 *Sport* without a point scored.
▸ˈ**pointlessly** ADVERB ▸ˈ**pointlessness** NOUN

point man NOUN *Chiefly US* 1 *Military* a soldier who walks at the front of an infantry patrol in combat. 2 the leader or spokesperson of a campaign or organization.

point off VERB (*tr, adverb*) to mark off from the right-hand side (a number of decimal places) in a whole number to create a mixed decimal: *point off three decimal places in 12345 and you get 12.345.*

point of honour NOUN, *plural* **points of honour.** a circumstance, event, etc., that involves the defence of one's principles, social honour, etc.

point of inflection NOUN, *plural* **points of inflection.** *Maths* a stationary point on a curve at which the tangent is horizontal or vertical and where tangents on either side have the same sign.

point of no return NOUN 1 a point at which an irreversible commitment must be made to an action, progression, etc. 2 a point in a journey at which, if one continues, supplies will be insufficient for a return to the starting place.

point of order NOUN, *plural* **points of order.** a question raised in a meeting or deliberative assembly by a member as to whether the rules governing procedures are being breached.

point of sale NOUN (in retail distribution) the place at which a sale is made. Abbreviation: **POS.**

point-of-sale terminal NOUN (in retail distribution) a device used to record and process information relating to sales. Abbreviation: **POST.**

point of view NOUN, *plural* **points of view.** 1 a position from which someone or something is observed. 2 a mental viewpoint or attitude. 3 the mental position from which a story is observed or narrated: *the omniscient point of view.*

point out VERB (*tr, adverb*) to indicate or specify.

pointsman (ˈpɔɪntsˌmæn, -mən) NOUN, *plural* **-men.** 1 a person who operates railway points. US and Canadian equivalent: **switchman.** 2 a policeman or traffic warden on point duty.

point source NOUN *Optics* a source of light or other radiation that can be considered to have negligible dimensions.

points system NOUN *Brit* a system used to assess applicants' eligibility for local authority housing, based on (points awarded for) such factors as the length of time the applicant has lived in the area, how many children are in the family, etc.

point system NOUN 1 *Printing* a system of measurement using the **point** (see sense 21) as its unit. 2 a system for evaluation of achievement, as in education or industry, based on awarding points. 3 any system of writing or printing, such as Braille, that uses protruding dots.

point-to-point NOUN 1 *Brit* **a** a steeplechase organized by a recognized hunt or other body, usually restricted to amateurs riding horses that have been regularly used in hunting. **b** (*as modifier*): *a point-to-point race.* ◆ ADJECTIVE 2 (of a route) from one place to the next. 3 (of a radiocommunication link) from one point to another, rather than broadcast.

point up VERB (*tr, adverb*) to emphasize, esp by identifying: *he pointed up the difficulties we would encounter.*

pointy (ˈpɔɪntɪ) ADJECTIVE **pointier, pointiest.** having a sharp point or points; pointed.

poise[1] (pɔɪz) NOUN 1 composure or dignity of manner. 2 physical balance or assurance in movement or bearing. 3 the state of being balanced or stable; equilibrium; stability. 4 the position of hovering. 5 suspense or indecision. ◆ VERB 6 to be or cause to be balanced or suspended. 7 (*tr*) to hold, as in readiness: *to poise a lance.* 8 (*tr*) a rare word for **weigh**[1].
▷**HISTORY** C16: from Old French *pois* weight, from Latin *pēnsum,* from *pendere* to weigh

poise[2] (pwɑːz, pɔɪz) NOUN the cgs unit of viscosity; the viscosity of a fluid in which a tangential force of 1 dyne per square centimetre maintains a difference in velocity of 1 centimetre per second between two parallel planes 1 centimetre apart. It is equivalent to 0.1 newton second per square metre. Symbol: P.
▷**HISTORY** C20: named after Jean Louis Marie *Poiseuille* (1799–1869), French physician

poised (pɔɪzd) ADJECTIVE 1 self-possessed; dignified; exhibiting composure. 2 balanced and prepared for action: *a skier poised at the top of the slope.*

poison (ˈpɔɪzᵊn) NOUN 1 any substance that can impair function, cause structural damage, or otherwise injure the body. Related adjective: **toxic.** 2 something that destroys, corrupts, etc.: *the poison of fascism.* 3 a substance that retards a chemical reaction or destroys or inhibits the activity of a catalyst. 4 a substance that absorbs neutrons in a nuclear reactor and thus slows down the reaction. It may be added deliberately or formed during fission. 5 **what's your poison?** *Informal* what would you like to drink? ◆ VERB (*tr*) 6 to give poison to (a person or animal) esp with intent to kill. 7 to add poison to. 8 to taint or infect with or as if with poison. 9 (foll by *against*) to turn (a person's mind) against: *he poisoned her mind against me.* 10 to retard or stop (a chemical or nuclear reaction) by the action of a poison. 11 to inhibit or destroy (the activity of a catalyst) by the action of a poison.
▷**HISTORY** C13: from Old French *puison* potion, from Latin *pōtiō* a drink, esp a poisonous one, from *pōtāre* to drink
▸ˈ**poisoner** NOUN

poison dogwood *or* **elder** NOUN other names for **poison sumach.**

poison gas NOUN a gaseous substance, such as chlorine, phosgene, or lewisite, used in warfare to kill or harm.

poison hemlock NOUN the US name for **hemlock** (sense 1).

poison ivy NOUN any of several North American anacardiaceous shrubs or vines of the genus *Rhus* (or *Toxicodendron*), esp *R. radicans,* which has small green flowers and whitish berries that cause an itching rash on contact. See also **sumach** (sense 1).

poison oak NOUN 1 either of two North American anacardiaceous shrubs, *Rhus toxicodendron* or *R. diversiloba,* that are related to the poison ivy and cause a similar rash. See also **sumach** (sense 1). 2 (*not in technical use*) another name for **poison ivy.**

poisonous (ˈpɔɪzənəs) ADJECTIVE 1 having the effects or qualities of a poison. 2 capable of killing or inflicting injury; venomous. 3 corruptive or malicious.
▸ˈ**poisonously** ADVERB ▸ˈ**poisonousness** NOUN

poison-pen letter NOUN a letter written in malice, usually anonymously, and intended to abuse, frighten, or insult the recipient.

poison pill NOUN *Finance* a tactic used by a company fearing an unwelcome takeover bid, in which the value of the company is automatically reduced, as by the sale of an issue of shares having an option unfavourable to the bidders, if the bid is successful.

poison sumach NOUN an anacardiaceous swamp shrub, *Rhus* (or *Toxicodendron*) *vernix* of the southeastern US, that has greenish-white berries and causes an itching rash on contact with the skin. Also called: **poison dogwood, poison elder.** See also **sumach.**

Poisson distribution ('pwɑːsᵊn) NOUN *Statistics* a distribution that represents the number of events occurring randomly in a fixed time at an average rate λ; symbol $P_0(\lambda)$. For large *n* and small *p* with *np* = λ it approximates to the binomial distribution *Bi(n,p)*.
▷HISTORY C19: named after Siméon Denis *Poisson* (1781–1840), French mathematician

Poisson's ratio NOUN a measure of the elastic properties of a material expressed as the ratio of the fractional contraction in breadth to the fractional increase in length when the material is stretched. Symbol: μ *or* ν.

Poitiers (*French* pwatje) NOUN a city in S central France: capital of the former province of Poitou until 1790; scene of the battle (1356) in which the English under the Black Prince defeated the French; university (1432). Pop.: 78 894 (1990).

poitín ('pɒtiːn) NOUN the Irish Gaelic spelling of **poteen.**

Poitou (*French* pwatu) NOUN a former province of W central France, on the Atlantic. Chief town: Poitiers.

Poitou-Charentes (*French* pwatuʃarɑ̃t) NOUN a region of W central France, on the Bay of Biscay: mainly low-lying.

poitrine (ˌpwa'triːn) NOUN a woman's bosom.
▷HISTORY French, literally: breast, chest

poke¹ (pəʊk) VERB 1 (*tr*) to jab or prod, as with the elbow, the finger, a stick, etc. 2 (*tr*) to make (a hole, opening, etc.) by or as by poking. 3 (when *intr,* often foll by *at*) to thrust (at). 4 (*tr*) *Informal* to hit with the fist; punch. 5 (usually foll by *in, out, out of, through,* etc.) to protrude or cause to protrude: *don't poke your arm out of the window.* 6 (*tr*) to stir (a fire, pot, etc.) by poking. 7 (*intr*) to meddle or intrude. 8 (*intr;* often foll by *about* or *around*) to search or pry. 9 (*intr;* often foll by *along*) to loiter, potter, dawdle, etc. 10 (*tr*) *Slang* (of a man) to have sexual intercourse with. 11 **poke fun at.** to mock or ridicule. 12 **poke one's nose into.** See **nose** (sense 17). ◆ NOUN 13 a jab or prod. 14 short for **slowpoke.** 15 *Informal* a blow with one's fist; punch. 16 *Slang* sexual intercourse.
▷HISTORY C14: from Low German and Middle Dutch *poken* to thrust, prod, strike

poke² (pəʊk) NOUN 1 *Dialect* a pocket or bag. 2 **a pig in a poke.** See **pig** (sense 9).
▷HISTORY C13: from Old Northern French *poque,* of Germanic origin; related to Old English *pocca* bag, Old Norse *poki* POUCH, Middle Dutch *poke* bag; compare POACH²

poke³ (pəʊk) NOUN 1 Also called: **poke bonnet.** a woman's bonnet with a brim that projects at the front, popular in the 18th and 19th centuries. 2 the brim itself.
▷HISTORY C18: from POKE¹ (in the sense: to thrust out, project)

poke⁴ (pəʊk) NOUN short for **pokeweed.**

pokeberry ('pəʊkbərɪ) NOUN, *plural* **-berries.** 1 Also called: **inkberry.** the berry of the pokeweed. 2 another name for the **pokeweed.**

pokelogan ('pəʊkˌləʊgən) NOUN *Canadian* another name for **bogan.**
▷HISTORY C19: from Ojibwa *pokenogun*

poker¹ ('pəʊkə) NOUN 1 a metal rod, usually with a handle, for stirring a fire. 2 a person or thing that pokes.

poker² ('pəʊkə) NOUN a card game of bluff and skill in which bets are made on the hands dealt, the highest-ranking hand (containing the most valuable combinations of sequences and sets of cards) winning the pool.
▷HISTORY C19: probably from French *poque* similar card game

poker dice NOUN 1 a dice marked on its six faces with the pictures of the playing cards from ace to nine. 2 a gambling game, based on poker hands, played with five such dice.

poker face NOUN *Informal* a face without expression, as that of a poker player attempting to conceal the value of his cards.

poker-faced ADJECTIVE *Informal* having a deliberately expressionless face.

poker machine NOUN *Austral and NZ* a fruit machine. Often shortened to: **pokie.**

pokerwork ('pəʊkəˌwɜːk) NOUN 1 the art of decorating wood or leather by burning a design with a heated metal point; pyrography. 2 artefacts decorated in this way.

pokeweed ('pəʊkˌwiːd), **pokeberry,** *or* **pokeroot** NOUN a tall North American plant, *Phytolacca americana,* that has small white flowers, juicy purple berries, and a poisonous purple root used medicinally: family *Phytolaccaceae.* Sometimes shortened to: **poke.** Also called: **inkberry.**
▷HISTORY C18 *poke,* shortened from Algonquian *puccoon* plant used in dyeing, from *pak* blood

pokie *or* **pokey** ('pəʊkɪ) NOUN *Austral and NZ informal* short for **poker machine.**

poky *or* **pokey** ('pəʊkɪ) ADJECTIVE **pokier, pokiest.** 1 *Informal* (esp of rooms) small and cramped. 2 without speed or energy; slow. ◆ NOUN 3 **the.** *Chiefly US and Canadian slang* prison.
▷HISTORY C19: from POKE¹ (in slang sense: to confine)
▸**'pokily** ADVERB ▸**'pokiness** NOUN

POL *Military* ABBREVIATION FOR petroleum, oil, and lubricants.

Pol. ABBREVIATION FOR: 1 Poland. 2 Polish.

Pola ('pɔːla) NOUN the Italian name for **Pula.**

Polack ('pəʊlæk) NOUN *Derogatory slang* a Pole or a person of Polish descent.
▷HISTORY C16: from Polish *Polak* Pole

polacre (pəʊ'lɑːkə) *or* **polacca** (pəʊ'lækə) NOUN a three-masted sailing vessel used in the Mediterranean.
▷HISTORY C17: from either French *polacre* or Italian *polacca* Pole or Polish; origin unknown

Poland ('pəʊlənd) NOUN a republic in central Europe, on the Baltic: first united in the 10th century; dissolved after the third partition effected by Austria, Russia, and Prussia in 1795; re-established independence in 1918; invaded by Germany in 1939; ruled by a Communist government from 1947 to 1989, when a multiparty system was introduced. It consists chiefly of a low undulating plain in the north, rising to a low plateau in the south, with the Sudeten and Carpathian Mountains along the S border. Official language: Polish. Religion: Roman Catholic majority. Currency: zloty. Capital: Warsaw. Pop.: 38 647 000 (2001 est.). Area: 311 730 sq. km (120 359 sq. miles). Polish name: **Polska.**

polar ('pəʊlə) ADJECTIVE 1 situated at or near, coming from, or relating to either of the earth's poles or the area inside the Arctic or Antarctic Circles: *polar regions.* 2 having or relating to a pole or poles. 3 pivotal or guiding in the manner of the Pole Star. 4 directly opposite, as in tendency or character. 5 *Chem* **a** (of a molecule or compound) being or having a molecule in which there is an uneven distribution of electrons and thus a permanent dipole moment: *water has polar molecules.* **b** (of a crystal or substance) being or having a crystal that is bound by ionic bonds: *sodium chloride forms polar crystals.*

polar axis NOUN the fixed line in a system of polar coordinates from which the polar angle, θ, is measured anticlockwise.

polar bear NOUN a white carnivorous bear, *Thalarctos maritimus,* of coastal regions of the North Pole.

polar body NOUN *Physiol* a tiny cell containing little cytoplasm that is produced with the ovum during oogenesis when the oocyte undergoes meiosis.

polar circle NOUN a term for either the **Arctic Circle** or **Antarctic Circle.**

polar coordinates PLURAL NOUN a pair of coordinates for locating a point in a plane by means of the length of a radius vector, *r,* which pivots about the origin to establish the angle, θ, that the position of the point makes with a fixed line. Usually written (*r*, θ). See also **Cartesian coordinates, spherical coordinates.**

polar distance NOUN the angular distance of a star, planet, etc., from the celestial pole; the complement of the declination. Also called: **codeclination.**

polar equation NOUN an equation in polar coordinates.

polar front NOUN *Meteorol* a front dividing cold polar air from warmer temperate or tropical air.

Polari (pə'lɑːrɪ) *or* **Parlyaree** (pɑː'ljɑːrɪ) NOUN an English slang that is derived from the Lingua Franca of Mediterranean ports; brought to England by sailors from the 16th century onwards. A few words survive, esp in male homosexual slang.
▷HISTORY C19: from Italian *parlare* to speak

polarimeter (ˌpəʊlə'rɪmɪtə) NOUN 1 an instrument for measuring the amount of polarization of light. 2 an instrument for measuring the rotation of the plane of polarization of light as a result of its passage through a liquid or solution. See **optical activity.**
▸**polarimetric** (ˌpəʊlərɪ'mɛtrɪk) ADJECTIVE ▸**ˌpolar'imetry** NOUN

Polaris (pə'lɑːrɪs) NOUN 1 Also called: **the Pole Star, the North Star.** the brightest star in the constellation Ursa Minor, situated slightly less than 1° from the north celestial pole. It is a Cepheid variable, with a period of four days. Visual magnitude: 2.08–2.17; spectral type: F8Ib. 2 **a** a type of US two-stage intermediate-range ballistic missile, usually fired by a submerged submarine. **b** (*as modifier*): *a Polaris submarine.*
▷HISTORY shortened from Medieval Latin *stella polāris* polar star

polariscope (pəʊ'lærɪˌskəʊp) NOUN an instrument for detecting polarized light or for observing objects under polarized light, esp for detecting strain in transparent materials. See **photoelasticity.**

polarity (pəʊ'lærɪtɪ) NOUN, *plural* **-ties.** 1 the condition of having poles. 2 the condition of a body or system in which it has opposing physical properties at different points, esp magnetic poles or electric charge. 3 the particular state of a part of a body or system that has polarity: *an electrode with positive polarity.* 4 the state of having or expressing two directly opposite tendencies, opinions, etc.

polarization *or* **polarisation** (ˌpəʊləraɪ'zeɪʃən) NOUN 1 the condition of having or giving polarity. 2 *Physics* the process or phenomenon in which the waves of light or other electromagnetic radiation are restricted to certain directions of vibration, usually specified in terms of the electric field vector.

polarize *or* **polarise** ('pəʊləˌraɪz) VERB 1 to acquire or cause to acquire polarity. 2 to acquire or cause to acquire polarization: *to polarize light.* 3 to cause people to adopt extreme opposing positions: *to polarize opinion.*
▸**'polarˌizable** *or* **'polarˌisable** ADJECTIVE

polarizer *or* **polariser** ('pəʊləˌraɪzə) NOUN a person or a device that causes polarization.

polar lights PLURAL NOUN the aurora borealis in the N hemisphere or the aurora australis in the S hemisphere.

polarography (ˌpəʊlə'rɒgrəfɪ) NOUN a technique for analysing and studying ions in solution by using an electrolytic cell with a very small cathode and obtaining a graph (**polarogram**) of the current against the potential to determine the concentration and nature of the ions. Because the cathode is small, polarization occurs and each type of anion is discharged at a different potential. The apparatus (**polarograph**) usually employs a dropping-mercury cathode.
▸**polarographic** (ˌpəʊlərə'græfɪk) ADJECTIVE

Polaroid ('pəʊləˌrɔɪd) *Trademark* ◆ NOUN 1 a type of plastic sheet that can polarize a transmitted beam of normal light because it is composed of long parallel molecules. It only transmits plane-polarized light if these molecules are parallel to the plane of polarization and, since reflected light is partly polarized, it is often used in sunglasses to eliminate glare. 2 **Polaroid Land Camera.** any of several types of camera yielding a finished print by means of a special developing and processing technique that occurs inside the camera and takes only a few seconds to complete. 3 (*plural*) sunglasses with lenses made from Polaroid plastic. ◆ ADJECTIVE 4 of, relating to, using, or used in a Polaroid Land Camera: *Polaroid film*.

polar orbit NOUN the orbit of a satellite that passes over the poles of a planet.

polar sequence NOUN *Astronomy* a series of stars in the vicinity of the N celestial pole whose accurately determined magnitudes serve as the standard for visual and photographic magnitudes of stars.

polar wander NOUN *Geology* the movement of the earth's magnetic poles with respect to the geographic poles.

polder ('pəʊldə, 'pɒl-) NOUN a stretch of land reclaimed from the sea or a lake, esp in the Netherlands.
▷HISTORY C17: from Middle Dutch *polre*

pole[1] (pəʊl) NOUN 1 a long slender usually round piece of wood, metal, or other material. 2 the piece of timber on each side of which a pair of carriage horses are hitched. 3 another name for **rod** (sense 7). 4 *Horse racing, chiefly US and Canadian* **a** the inside lane of a racecourse. **b** (*as modifier*): *the pole position*. **c** one of a number of markers placed at intervals of one sixteenth of a mile along the side of a racecourse. 5 *Nautical* **a** any light spar. **b** the part of a mast between the head and the attachment of the uppermost shrouds. 6 **under bare poles.** *Nautical* (of a sailing vessel) with no sails set. 7 **up the pole.** *Brit, Austral, and NZ informal* **a** slightly mad. **b** mistaken; on the wrong track. ◆ VERB 8 (*tr*) to strike or push with a pole. 9 (*tr*) **a** to set out (an area of land or garden) with poles. **b** to support (a crop, such as hops or beans) on poles. 10 (*tr*) to deoxidize (a molten metal, esp copper) by stirring it with green wood. 11 to punt (a boat).
▷HISTORY Old English *pāl*, from Latin *pālus* a stake, prop; see PALE[2]

pole[2] (pəʊl) NOUN 1 either of the two antipodal points where the earth's axis of rotation meets the earth's surface. See also **North Pole, South Pole.** 2 *Astronomy* short for **celestial pole.** 3 *Physics* **a** either of the two regions at the extremities of a magnet to which the lines of force converge or from which they diverge. **b** either of two points or regions in a piece of material, system, etc., at which there are opposite electric charges, as at the two terminals of a battery. 4 *Maths* an isolated singularity of an analytical function. 5 *Biology* **a** either end of the axis of a cell, spore, ovum, or similar body. **b** either end of the spindle formed during the metaphase of mitosis and meiosis. 6 *Physiol* the point on a neuron from which the axon or dendrites project from the cell body. 7 either of two mutually exclusive or opposite actions, opinions, etc. 8 *Geometry* the origin in a system of polar or spherical coordinates. 9 any fixed point of reference. 10 **poles apart** (*or* **asunder**). having widely divergent opinions, tastes, etc. 11 **from pole to pole.** throughout the entire world.
▷HISTORY C14: from Latin *polus* end of an axis, from Greek *polos* pivot, axis, pole; related to Greek *kuklos* circle

Pole (pəʊl) NOUN a native, inhabitant, or citizen of Poland or a speaker of Polish.

poleaxe *or US* **poleax** ('pəʊl,æks) NOUN 1 another term for **battle-axe** (sense 1). 2 a former naval weapon with an axe blade on one side of the handle and a spike on the other. 3 an axe used by butchers to slaughter animals. ◆ VERB 4 (*tr*) to hit or fell with or as if with a poleaxe.
▷HISTORY C14 *pollax* battle-axe, from POLL + AXE

polecat ('pəʊl,kæt) NOUN, *plural* **-cats** *or* **-cat.** 1 Also called (formerly): **foumart.** a dark brown musteline mammal, *Mustela putorius*, of woodlands of Europe, Asia, and N Africa, that is closely related to but larger than the weasel and gives off an unpleasant smell. See also **sweet marten.** 2 any of various related animals, such as the **marbled polecat**, *Vormela peregusna*. 3 *US* a nontechnical name for **skunk** (sense 1).
▷HISTORY C14 *polcat*, perhaps from Old French *pol* cock, from Latin *pullus*, + CAT[1]; from its habit of preying on poultry

pole horse NOUN a horse harnessed alongside the shaft (pole) of a vehicle. Also called: **poler.**

pole house NOUN *NZ* a timber house built on a steep section and supported by heavy debarked logs in long piles.

poleis ('pɒlaɪs) NOUN the plural of **polis**[1].

polemarch ('pɒlɪ,mɑːk) NOUN (in ancient Greece) a civilian official, originally a supreme general.
▷HISTORY C16: from Greek *polemarchos*, from *polemos* war + *archos* ruler

polemic (pə'lɛmɪk) ADJECTIVE *also* **po'lemical.** 1 of or involving dispute or controversy. ◆ NOUN 2 an argument or controversy, esp over a doctrine, belief, etc. 3 a person engaged in such an argument or controversy.
▷HISTORY C17: from Medieval Latin *polemicus*, from Greek *polemikos* relating to war, from *polemos* war
▸**po'lemically** ADVERB ▸**polemicist** (pə'lɛmɪsɪst) *or* **polemist** ('pɒlɪmɪst) NOUN

polemics (pə'lɛmɪks) NOUN (*functioning as singular*) the art or practice of dispute or argument, as in attacking or defending a doctrine or belief.

polemoniaceous (,pɒlɪ,məʊnɪ'eɪʃəs) ADJECTIVE of, relating to, or belonging to the *Polemoniaceae*, a chiefly North American family of plants that includes phlox and Jacob's ladder.
▷HISTORY C19: from New Latin *Polemōnium* type genus, from Greek *polemōnion* a plant, perhaps valerian

polenta (pəʊ'lɛntə) NOUN a thick porridge made in Italy, usually from maize.
▷HISTORY C16: via Italian from Latin: pearl barley, perhaps from Greek *palē* pollen

pole piece NOUN *Electrical engineering* a piece of ferromagnetic material forming an extension of the magnetic circuit in an electric motor, etc., used to concentrate the magnetic field where it will be most effective.

pole position NOUN 1 (in motor racing) the starting position on the inside of the front row, generally considered the best one. 2 an advantageous starting position.

poler ('pəʊlə) NOUN 1 another name for **pole horse.** 2 a person or thing that poles, esp a punter.

pole star NOUN a guiding principle, rule, standard, etc.

Pole Star NOUN **the.** the star closest to the N celestial pole at any particular time. At present this is Polaris, but it will eventually be replaced by some other star owing to precession of the earth's axis.

pole vault NOUN 1 **the.** a field event in which competitors attempt to clear a high bar with the aid of an extremely flexible long pole. 2 a single attempt in the pole vault. ◆ VERB **pole-vault.** 3 (*intr*) to perform a pole vault or compete in the pole vault.
▸**'pole-,vaulter** NOUN

poley ('pəʊlɪ) ADJECTIVE *Austral* (of cattle) hornless or polled.

poley cup ('pəʊlɪ,kʌp) NOUN *Austral informal* a cup which has lost its handle.
▷HISTORY from *poley* (of cattle) hornless or polled

poleyn ('pəʊleɪn) NOUN a piece of armour for protecting the knee. Also called: **kneecap.**
▷HISTORY from Old French *polain*

Polglish ('pəʊlglɪʃ) NOUN informal Polish containing a high proportion of words of English origin.
▷HISTORY C20: from a blend of POLISH + ENGLISH

police (pə'liːs) NOUN 1 **a** (often preceded by *the*) the organized civil force of a state, concerned with maintenance of law and order, the detection and prevention of crime, etc. **b** (*as modifier*): *a police inquiry*. 2 (*functioning as plural*) the members of such a force collectively. 3 any organized body with a similar function: *security police*. 4 *Archaic* **a** the regulation and control of a community, esp in regard to the enforcement of law, the prevention of crime, etc. **b** the department of government concerned with this. ◆ VERB (*tr*) 5 to regulate, control, or keep in order by means of a police or similar force. 6 to observe or record the activity or enforcement of: *a committee was set up to police the new agreement on picketing*. 7 *US* to make or keep (a military camp, etc.) clean and orderly.
▷HISTORY C16: via French from Latin *polītīa* administration, government; see POLITY

police court NOUN 1 another name for **magistrates' court.** 2 (in Scotland, formerly) a burgh court with limited jurisdiction, presided over by lay magistrates or a stipendiary magistrate: replaced in 1975 by the **district court.**

police dog NOUN a dog, often an Alsatian, trained to help the police, as in tracking.

policeman (pə'liːsmən) *or feminine* **policewoman** NOUN, *plural* **-men** *or* **-women.** a member of a police force, esp one holding the rank of constable.

policeman's helmet NOUN a Himalayan balsaminaceous plant, *Impatiens glandulifera*, with large purplish-pink flowers, introduced into Britain.

Police Motu NOUN a pidginized version of the Motu language, used as a lingua franca in Papua, originally chiefly by the police. Also called: **Hiri Motu.**

police officer NOUN a member of a police force, esp a constable; policeman. Often (esp as form of address) shortened to: **officer.**

police procedural NOUN a novel, film, or television drama that deals realistically with police work.

police state NOUN a state or country in which a repressive government maintains control through the police.

police station NOUN the office or headquarters of the police force of a district.

police wagon NOUN *US* another term for **patrol wagon.**

policy[1] ('pɒlɪsɪ) NOUN, *plural* **-cies.** 1 a plan of action adopted or pursued by an individual, government, party, business, etc. 2 wisdom, prudence, shrewdness, or sagacity. 3 *Scot* (*often plural*) the improved grounds surrounding a country house.
▷HISTORY C14: from Old French *policie*, from Latin *polītīa* administration, POLITY

policy[2] ('pɒlɪsɪ) NOUN, *plural* **-cies.** a document containing a contract of insurance.
▷HISTORY C16: from Old French *police* certificate, from Old Italian *polizza*, from Latin *apodixis* proof, from Greek *apodeixis* demonstration, proof

policyholder ('pɒlɪsɪ,həʊldə) NOUN a person or organization in whose name an insurance policy is registered.

policy science NOUN a branch of the social sciences concerned with the formulation and implementation of policy in bureaucracies, etc.

polio ('pəʊlɪəʊ) NOUN short for **poliomyelitis.**

poliomyelitis (,pəʊlɪəʊ,maɪə'laɪtɪs) NOUN an acute infectious viral disease, esp affecting children. In its paralytic form (**acute anterior poliomyelitis**) the brain and spinal cord are involved, causing weakness, paralysis, and wasting of muscle. Often shortened to: **polio.** Also called: **infantile paralysis.**
▷HISTORY C19: New Latin, from Greek *polios* grey + *muelos* marrow

polis[1] ('pɒlɪs) NOUN, *plural* **poleis** ('pɒlaɪs). an ancient Greek city-state.
▷HISTORY from Greek: city

polis[2] ('pɒlɪs) NOUN *Scot and Irish* the police or a police officer.
▷HISTORY C19: a variant pronunciation of *police*

polish ('pɒlɪʃ) VERB 1 to make or become smooth and shiny by rubbing, esp with wax or an abrasive. 2 (*tr*) to make perfect or complete. 3 to make or become elegant or refined. ◆ NOUN 4 a finish or gloss. 5 the act of polishing or the condition of having been polished. 6 a substance used to produce a smooth and shiny, often protective surface. 7 elegance or refinement, esp in style, manner, etc. ◆ See also **polish off, polish up.**
▷HISTORY C13 *polis*, from Old French *polir*, from Latin *polīre* to polish
▸**'polishable** ADJECTIVE ▸**'polisher** NOUN

Polish ('pəʊlɪʃ) ADJECTIVE 1 of, relating to, or characteristic of Poland, its people, or their language. ◆ NOUN 2 the official language of Poland, belonging to the West Slavonic branch of the Indo-European family.

Polish Corridor NOUN the strip of land through E Pomerania providing Poland with access to the sea (1919–39), given to her in 1919 in the Treaty of Versailles, and separating East Prussia from the rest of Germany. It is now part of Poland.

polished ('pɒlɪʃt) ADJECTIVE 1 accomplished: *a*

polished actor. [2] impeccably or professionally done: *a polished performance.* [3] (of rice) having had the outer husk removed by milling.

Polish Lowland sheepdog NOUN a strongly-built medium-sized sheepdog of a Polish breed with a long thick shaggy coat that covers the eyes.

Polish notation NOUN a logical notation that dispenses with the need for brackets by writing the logical constants as operators preceding their arguments.

polish off VERB *(tr, adverb) Informal* [1] to finish or process completely. [2] to dispose of or kill; eliminate.

polish up VERB *(adverb)* [1] to make or become smooth and shiny by polishing. [2] (when *intr,* foll by *on)* to study or practise until adept at; improve: *polish up your spelling; he's polishing up on his German.*

Politburo ('pɒlɪtˌbjʊərəʊ) NOUN [1] the executive and policy-making committee of a Communist Party. [2] the supreme policy-making authority in most Communist countries.
▷HISTORY C20: from Russian: contraction of *Politicheskoe Buro* political bureau

polite (pə'laɪt) ADJECTIVE [1] showing regard for others, in manners, speech, behaviour, etc.; courteous. [2] cultivated or refined: *polite society.* [3] elegant or polished: *polite letters.*
▷HISTORY C15: from Latin *polītus* polished; see POLISH
▸**po'litely** ADVERB ▸**po'liteness** NOUN

politesse (ˌpɒlɪ'tɛs) NOUN formal or genteel politeness.
▷HISTORY C18: via French from Italian *politezza,* ultimately from Latin *polīre* to POLISH

politic ('pɒlɪtɪk) ADJECTIVE [1] artful or shrewd; ingenious: *a politic manager.* [2] crafty or unscrupulous; cunning: *a politic old scoundrel.* [3] sagacious, wise, or prudent, esp in statesmanship: *a politic choice.* [4] an archaic word for **political.** ◆ See also **body politic, politics.**
▷HISTORY C15: from Old French *politique,* from Latin *polīticus* concerning civil administration, from Greek *politikos,* from *politēs* citizen, from *polis* city
▸**'politicly** ADVERB

political (pə'lɪtɪkᵊl) ADJECTIVE [1] of or relating to the state, government, the body politic, public administration, policy-making, etc. [2] **a** of, involved in, or relating to government policy-making as distinguished from administration or law. **b** of or relating to the civil aspects of government as distinguished from the military. [3] of, dealing with, or relating to politics: *a political person.* [4] of, characteristic of, or relating to the parties and the partisan aspects of politics. [5] organized or ordered with respect to government: *a political unit.*
▸**po'litically** ADVERB

political economy NOUN the former name for **economics** (sense 1).

politically correct ADJECTIVE demonstrating progressive ideals, esp by avoiding vocabulary that is considered offensive, discriminatory, or judgmental, esp concerning race and gender. Abbreviation: **PC.**
▸**political correctness** NOUN

political prisoner NOUN someone imprisoned for holding, expressing, or acting in accord with particular political beliefs.

political science NOUN (esp as an academic subject) the study of the state, government, and politics: one of the social sciences.
▸**political scientist** NOUN

politician (ˌpɒlɪ'tɪʃən) NOUN [1] a person actively engaged in politics, esp a full-time professional member of a deliberative assembly. [2] a person who is experienced or skilled in the art or science of politics, government, or administration; statesman. [3] *Disparaging, chiefly US* a person who engages in politics out of a wish for personal gain, as realized by holding a public office.

politicize *or* **politicise** (pə'lɪtɪˌsaɪz) VERB [1] *(tr)* to render political in tone, interest, or awareness. [2] *(intr)* to participate in political discussion or activity.
▸**poˌliticiˈzation** *or* **poˌliticiˈsation** NOUN

politicking ('pɒlɪˌtɪkɪŋ) NOUN [1] political activity, esp seeking votes. [2] activity directed towards acquiring power and influence, achieving one's own goals, etc.
▸**'poliˌticker** NOUN

politico (pə'lɪtɪˌkəʊ) NOUN, *plural* **-cos.** an informal word for a **politician** (senses 1, 3).
▷HISTORY C17: from Italian or Spanish

politico- COMBINING FORM denoting political or politics: *politicoeconomic.*

politics ('pɒlɪtɪks) NOUN [1] *(functioning as singular)* the practice or study of the art and science of forming, directing, and administrating states and other political units; the art and science of government; political science. [2] *(functioning as singular)* the complex or aggregate of relationships of people in society, esp those relationships involving authority or power. [3] *(functioning as plural)* political activities or affairs: *party politics.* [4] *(functioning as singular)* the business or profession of politics. [5] *(functioning as singular or plural)* any activity concerned with the acquisition of power, gaining one's own ends, etc.: *company politics are frequently vicious.* [6] *(functioning as plural)* opinions, principles, sympathies, etc., with respect to politics: *his conservative politics.* [7] *(functioning as plural)* **a** the policy-formulating aspects of government as distinguished from the administrative, or legal. **b** the civil functions of government as distinguished from the military.

polity ('pɒlɪtɪ) NOUN, *plural* **-ties.** [1] a form of government or organization of a state, church, society, etc.; constitution. [2] a politically organized society, state, city, etc. [3] the management of public or civil affairs. [4] political organization.
▷HISTORY C16: from Latin *polītīa,* from Greek *politeia* citizenship, civil administration, from *politēs* citizen, from *polis* city

polje ('pəʊljɛ) NOUN *Geography* a large elliptical depression in karst regions, sometimes containing a marsh or small lake.
▷HISTORY Serbo-Croat, literally: field; related to FLOOR

polka ('pɒlkə) NOUN, *plural* **-kas.** [1] a 19th-century Bohemian dance with three steps and a hop, in fast duple time. [2] a piece of music composed for or in the rhythm of this dance. ◆ VERB **-kas, -kaing, -kaed.** [3] *(intr)* to dance a polka.
▷HISTORY C19: via French from Czech *pulka* half-step, from *pul* half

polka dot NOUN [1] one of a pattern of small circular regularly spaced spots on a fabric. [2] **a** a fabric or pattern with such spots. **b** *(as modifier): a polka-dot dress.*
▷HISTORY C19: of uncertain origin

poll (pəʊl) NOUN [1] the casting, recording, or counting of votes in an election; a voting. [2] the result or quantity of such a voting: *a heavy poll.* [3] Also called: **opinion poll. a** a canvassing of a representative sample of a large group of people on some question in order to determine the general opinion of the group. **b** the results or record of such a canvassing. [4] any counting or enumeration: *a poll of the number of men with long hair.* [5] short for **poll tax.** [6] a list or enumeration of people, esp for taxation or voting purposes. [7] the striking face of a hammer. [8] the occipital or back part of the head of an animal. ◆ VERB *(mainly tr)* [9] to receive (a vote or quantity of votes): *he polled 10 000 votes.* [10] to receive, take, or record the votes of: *he polled the whole town.* [11] to canvass (a person, group, area, etc.) as part of a survey of opinion. [12] *Chiefly US* to take the vote, verdict, opinion, etc., individually of each member (of a jury, conference, etc.). [13] *(sometimes intr)* to cast (a vote) in an election. [14] *Computing* (in data transmission when several terminals share communications channels) to check each channel rapidly to establish which are free, or to call for data from each terminal in turn. [15] to clip or shear. [16] to remove or cut short the horns of (cattle).
▷HISTORY C13 (in the sense: a human head) and C17 (in the modern sense: a counting of heads, votes): from Middle Low German *polle* hair of the head, head, top of a tree; compare Swedish *pull* crown of the head

pollack *or* **pollock** ('pɒlək) NOUN, *plural* **-lacks, -lack** *or* **-locks, -lock.** a gadoid food fish, *Pollachius pollachius,* that has a dark green back and a projecting lower jaw and occurs in northern seas, esp the North Atlantic Ocean.
▷HISTORY C17: from earlier Scottish *podlok,* of obscure origin

pollan ('pɒlən) NOUN any of several varieties of the whitefish *Coregonus pollan* that occur in lakes in Northern Ireland.
▷HISTORY C18: probably from Irish *poll* lake

pollard ('pɒləd) NOUN [1] an animal, such as a sheep or deer, that has either shed its horns or antlers or has had them removed. [2] a tree that has had its top cut off to encourage the formation of a crown of branches. ◆ VERB [3] *(tr)* to convert into a pollard; poll.
▷HISTORY C16: hornless animal; see POLL

polled (pəʊld) ADJECTIVE [1] (of animals, esp cattle) having the horns cut off or being naturally hornless. [2] *Archaic* shorn of hair; bald.

pollen ('pɒlən) NOUN a fine powdery substance produced by the anthers of seed-bearing plants, consisting of numerous fine grains containing the male gametes.
▷HISTORY C16: from Latin: powder; compare Greek *palē* pollen
▸**pollinic** (pə'lɪnɪk) ADJECTIVE

pollen analysis NOUN another name for **palynology.**

pollen basket NOUN the part of the hind leg of a bee that is specialized for carrying pollen, typically consisting of a trough bordered by long hairs. Technical name: **corbicula.**

pollen count NOUN a measure of the pollen present in the air over a 24-hour period, often published to enable sufferers from hay fever to predict the severity of their attacks.

pollen tube NOUN a hollow tubular outgrowth that develops from a pollen grain after pollination, grows down the style to the ovule, and conveys male gametes to the egg cell.

pollex ('pɒlɛks) NOUN, *plural* **-lices** (-lɪˌsiːz). the first digit of the forelimb of amphibians, reptiles, birds, and mammals, such as the thumb of man and other primates.
▷HISTORY C19: from Latin: thumb, big toe
▸**pollical** ('pɒlɪkᵊl) ADJECTIVE

pollinate ('pɒlɪˌneɪt) VERB *(tr)* to transfer pollen from the anthers to the stigma of (a flower).
▸**ˌpolliˈnation** NOUN ▸**'polliˌnator** NOUN

polling ('pəʊlɪŋ) NOUN [1] **a** the casting or registering of votes at an election. **b** *(as modifier): polling day.* [2] the conducting of a public opinion poll. [3] *Computing* the automatic interrogation of terminals by a central controlling machine to determine if they are ready to receive or transmit messages.

polling booth NOUN a semienclosed space in which a voter stands to mark a ballot paper during an election.

polling station NOUN a building, such as a school, designated as the place to which voters go during an election to cast their votes.

polliniferous *or* **polleniferous** (ˌpɒlɪ'nɪfərəs) ADJECTIVE [1] producing pollen: *polliniferous plants.* [2] specialized for carrying pollen: *the polliniferous legs of bees.*

pollinium (pə'lɪnɪəm) NOUN, *plural* **-ia** (-ɪə). a mass of cohering pollen grains, produced by plants such as orchids and transported as a whole during pollination.
▷HISTORY C19: New Latin; see POLLEN

pollinosis *or* **pollenosis** (ˌpɒlɪ'nəʊsɪs) NOUN *Pathol* a technical name for **hay fever.**

polliwog *or* **pollywog** ('pɒlɪˌwɒg) NOUN [1] *Brit dialect US, and Canadian* another name for **tadpole.** [2] *Informal* a sailor who has not crossed the equator. Compare **shellback.**
▷HISTORY C15 *polwygle;* see POLL, WIGGLE

pollster ('pəʊlstə) NOUN a person who conducts opinion polls.

poll tax NOUN [1] a tax levied per head of adult population. [2] an informal name for (the former) **community charge.**

pollucite ('pɒljʊˌsaɪt, pə'luːˌsaɪt) NOUN a colourless rare mineral consisting of a hydrated caesium aluminium silicate, often containing some rubidium. It occurs in coarse granite, esp in

Manitoba, and is an important source of caesium. Formula: $CsAlSi_2O_6.½H_2O$.
▷**HISTORY** C19: from Latin *polluc-*, stem of *Pollux* + -ITE[1]; originally called *pollux*, alluding to Castor and Pollux, since it was associated with another mineral called *castor* or *castorite*

pollutant (pəˈluːtᵊnt) NOUN a substance that pollutes, esp a chemical or substance that is produced as a waste product of an industrial process.

pollute (pəˈluːt) VERB (*tr*) [1] to contaminate, as with poisonous or harmful substances. [2] to make morally corrupt or impure; sully. [3] to desecrate or defile.
▷**HISTORY** C14 *polute*, from Latin *polluere* to defile
▸**polˈluter** NOUN

polluted (pəˈluːtɪd) ADJECTIVE [1] made unclean or impure; contaminated. [2] *US slang* intoxicated; drunk.

pollution (pəˈluːʃən) NOUN [1] the act of polluting or the state of being polluted. [2] harmful or poisonous substances introduced into an environment.

Pollux (ˈpɒləks) NOUN [1] the brightest star in the constellation Gemini, lying close to the star **Castor**. Visual magnitude: 1.15; spectral type: K0III; distance: 34 light years. [2] *Classical myth* See **Castor and Pollux.**

polly (ˈpɒlɪ) NOUN, *plural* **-lies**. an informal word for **politician.**

Pollyanna (ˌpɒlɪˈænə) NOUN a person who is constantly or excessively optimistic.
▷**HISTORY** C20: after the chief character in *Pollyanna* (1913), a novel by Eleanor Porter (1868–1920), US writer

polo (ˈpəʊləʊ) NOUN [1] a game similar to hockey played on horseback using long-handled mallets (**polo sticks**) and a wooden ball. [2] any of several similar games, such as one played on bicycles. [3] short for **water polo.** [4] Also called: **polo neck. a** a collar on a garment, worn rolled over to fit closely round the neck. **b** a garment, esp a sweater, with such a collar.
▷**HISTORY** C19: from Balti (dialect of Kashmir): ball, from Tibetan *pulu*

polonaise (ˌpɒləˈneɪz) NOUN [1] a ceremonial marchlike dance in three-four time from Poland. [2] a piece of music composed for or in the rhythm of this dance. [3] a woman's costume with a tight bodice and an overskirt drawn back to show a decorative underskirt.
▷**HISTORY** C18: from French *danse polonaise* Polish dance

polonium (pəˈləʊnɪəm) NOUN a very rare radioactive element that occurs in trace amounts in uranium ores. The isotope **polonium-210** is produced artificially and is used as a lightweight power source in satellites and to eliminate static electricity in certain industries. Symbol: Po; atomic no.: 84; half-life of most stable isotope, ^{209}Po: 103 years; valency: –2, 0, 2, 4, or 6; relative density (alpha modification): 9.32; melting pt.: 254°C; boiling pt.: 962°C.
▷**HISTORY** C19: New Latin, from Medieval Latin *Polōnia* Poland; named in honour of the Polish nationality of its discoverer, Marie Curie

polony (pəˈləʊnɪ) NOUN, *plural* **-nies**. *Brit* another name for **bologna sausage.**
▷**HISTORY** C16: perhaps from BOLOGNA

polo shirt NOUN a knitted cotton short-sleeved shirt with a collar and three-button opening at the neck.

Polska (ˈpɔlska) NOUN the Polish name for **Poland.**

Poltava (*Russian* palˈtavə) NOUN a city in the E Ukraine: scene of the victory (1709) of the Russians under Peter the Great over the Swedes under Charles XII; centre of an agricultural region. Pop.: 317 300 (1998 est.).

poltergeist (ˈpɒltəˌɡaɪst) NOUN a spirit believed to manifest its presence by rappings and other noises and also by acts of mischief, such as throwing furniture about.
▷**HISTORY** C19: from German, from *poltern* to be noisy + *Geist* GHOST

poltroon (pɒlˈtruːn) NOUN [1] an abject or contemptible coward. ◆ ADJECTIVE [2] a rare word for **cowardly.**
▷**HISTORY** C16: from Old French *poultron*, from Old Italian *poltrone* lazy good-for-nothing, apparently from *poltrire* to lie indolently in bed, from *poltro* bed

poly (ˈpɒlɪ) NOUN, *plural* **polys**. *Informal* short for **polytechnic.**

poly- COMBINING FORM [1] more than one; many or much: *polyhedron.* [2] having an excessive or abnormal number or amount: *polycythaemia.*
▷**HISTORY** from Greek *polus* much, many; related to Old English *fela* many

polyadelphous (ˌpɒlɪəˈdɛlfəs) ADJECTIVE [1] (of stamens) having united filaments so that they are arranged in three or more groups. [2] (of flowers) having polyadelphous stamens.
▷**HISTORY** C19: from New Latin, from POLY- + *-adelphous* from Greek *adelphos* brother

polyadic (ˌpɒlɪˈædɪk) ADJECTIVE *Logic, maths* (of a relation, operation, etc.) having several argument places, as … *moves* … *from* … *to* …, which might be represented as $Mpox_1y_1z_1t_1x_2y_2z_2t_2$ where *p* names a person, *o* an object, and each *t* a time, and each *<x,y,z>* the coordinates of a place.
▷**HISTORY** C20: modelled on MONADIC

polyamide (ˌpɒlɪˈæmaɪd, -mɪd) NOUN any one of a class of synthetic polymeric materials containing recurring -CONH- groups. See also **nylon.**

polyandry (ˈpɒlɪˌændrɪ) NOUN [1] the practice or condition of being married to more than one husband at the same time. Compare **polygamy.** [2] the practice in animals of a female mating with more than one male during one breeding season. [3] the condition in flowers of having a large indefinite number of stamens. ◆ Compare **polygyny.**
▷**HISTORY** C18: from Greek *poluandria*, from POLY- + *-andria* from *anēr* man
▸ **ˌpolyˈandrous** ADJECTIVE

polyanthus (ˌpɒlɪˈænθəs) NOUN, *plural* **-thuses.** [1] any of several hybrid garden primroses, esp *Primula polyantha*, which has brightly coloured flowers. [2] **polyanthus narcissus.** a Eurasian amaryllidaceous plant, *Narcissus tazetta*, having clusters of small yellow or white fragrant flowers.
▷**HISTORY** C18: New Latin, Greek: having many flowers

polyarchy (ˈpɒlɪˌɑːkɪ) NOUN, *plural* **-chies.** a political system in which power is dispersed.
▷**HISTORY** C17: from POLY- + -ARCHY

polyatomic (ˌpɒlɪəˈtɒmɪk) ADJECTIVE (of a molecule) containing more than two atoms.

poly bag (ˈpɒlɪ) NOUN *Brit informal* a polythene bag, esp one used to store or protect food or household articles.

polybasic (ˌpɒlɪˈbeɪsɪk) ADJECTIVE (of an acid) having two or more replaceable hydrogen atoms per molecule.

polybasite (ˌpɒlɪˈbeɪsaɪt, pəˈlɪbəˌsaɪt) NOUN a grey to black mineral consisting of a sulphide of silver, antimony, and copper in the form of platelike monoclinic crystals. It occurs in veins of silver ore. Formula: $(Ag,Cu)_{16}Sb_2S_{11}$.
▷**HISTORY** C19: from POLY- + BASE[1] + -ITE[1]

polycarbonate (ˌpɒlɪˈkɑːbəˌneɪt, -nɪt) NOUN any of a class of strong transparent thermoplastic resins used in moulding materials, laminates, etc.

polycarboxylate (ˌpɒlɪˈkɑːbɒkˌsɪleɪt) NOUN a salt or ester of a polycarboxylic acid. Polycarboxylate esters are used in certain detergents.

polycarboxylic acid (ˌpɒlɪˈkɑːbɒkˌsɪlɪk) NOUN a type of carboxylic acid containing two or more carboxyl groups.

polycarpellary (ˌpɒlɪkɑːˈpɛlərɪ) ADJECTIVE (of a plant gynoecium) having or consisting of many carpels.

polycarpic (ˌpɒlɪˈkɑːpɪk) *or* **polycarpous** ADJECTIVE (of a plant) able to produce flowers and fruit several times in successive years or seasons.
▸ **ˈpolyˌcarpy** NOUN

polycarpous (ˌpɒlɪˈkɑːpəs) *or* **polycarpic** ADJECTIVE (of a plant) having a gynoecium consisting of many distinct carpels.

polycentrism (ˌpɒlɪˈsɛntrɪzəm) NOUN (formerly) the fact, principle, or advocacy of the existence of more than one guiding or predominant ideological or political centre in a political system, alliance, etc., in the Communist world.

polychaete (ˈpɒlɪˌkiːt) NOUN [1] any marine annelid worm of the class *Polychaeta*, having a distinct head and paired fleshy appendages (parapodia) that bear bristles (chaetae or setae) and are used in swimming: includes the lugworms, ragworms, and sea mice. ◆ ADJECTIVE *also* **polychaetous.** [2] of, relating to, or belonging to the class *Polychaeta*.
▷**HISTORY** C19: from New Latin, from Greek *polukhaitēs*: having much hair; see CHAETA

polychasium (ˌpɒlɪˈkeɪzɪəm) NOUN, *plural* **-sia** (-zɪə). *Botany* a cymose inflorescence in which three or more branches arise from each node.
▷**HISTORY** C20: from New Latin, from POLY- + *-chasium* as in DICHASIUM

polychlorinated biphenyl (ˌpɒlɪˈklɔːrɪˌneɪtɪd) NOUN any of a group of compounds in which chlorine atoms replace the hydrogen atoms in biphenyl: used in industry in electrical insulators and in the manufacture of plastics; a toxic pollutant that can become concentrated in animal tissue. Abbreviation: **PCB.**

polychromatic (ˌpɒlɪkrəʊˈmætɪk), **polychromic** (ˌpɒlɪˈkrəʊmɪk), *or* **polychromous** ADJECTIVE [1] having various or changing colours. [2] (of light or other electromagnetic radiation) containing radiation with more than one wavelength.
▸**polychromatism** (ˌpɒlɪˈkrəʊməˌtɪzəm) NOUN

polychrome (ˈpɒlɪˌkrəʊm) ADJECTIVE [1] having various or changing colours; polychromatic. [2] made with or decorated in various colours. ◆ NOUN [3] a work of art or artefact in many colours.

polychromy (ˈpɒlɪˌkrəʊmɪ) NOUN decoration in many colours, esp in architecture or sculpture.

polyclinic (ˌpɒlɪˈklɪnɪk) NOUN a hospital or clinic able to treat a wide variety of diseases: general hospital.

polyconic projection (ˌpɒlɪˈkɒnɪk) NOUN a type of conic projection in which the parallels are not concentric and all meridians except the central one are curved lines. It is neither equal-area nor conformal, but is suitable for maps of areas or countries of great longitudinal extent.

polycotton (ˈpɒlɪkɒtᵊn) NOUN a fabric made from a mixture of polyester and cotton.

polycotyledon (ˌpɒlɪˌkɒtɪˈliːdᵊn) NOUN any of various plants, esp gymnosperms, that have or appear to have more than two cotyledons.
▸ **ˌpolyˌcotyˈledonous** ADJECTIVE

polycrystal (ˈpɒlɪˌkrɪstᵊl) NOUN an object composed of randomly orient crystals, formed by rapid solidification.

polycyclic (ˌpɒlɪˈsaɪklɪk) ADJECTIVE [1] (of a molecule or compound) containing or having molecules that contain two or more closed rings of atoms. [2] *Biology* having two or more rings or whorls: *polycyclic shells; a polycyclic stele.* ◆ NOUN [3] a polycyclic compound: *anthracene is a polycyclic.*

polycystic (ˌpɒlɪˈsɪstɪk) ADJECTIVE *Med* containing many cysts: *a polycystic ovary.*

polycystic ovary syndrome NOUN a hormonal disorder in which the Graafian follicles in the ovary fail to develop completely so that they are unable to ovulate, remaining as multiple cysts that distend the ovary. The result is infertility, obesity, and hirsutism. Abbreviation: **POS.**

polycythaemia *or esp US* **polycythemia** (ˌpɒlɪsaɪˈθiːmɪə) NOUN an abnormal condition of the blood characterized by an increase in the number of red blood cells. It can occur as a primary disease of unknown cause (**polycythaemia vera** or **erythraemia**) or in association with respiratory or circulatory diseases.
▷**HISTORY** C19: from POLY- + CYTO- + -HAEMIA

polydactyl (ˌpɒlɪˈdæktɪl) ADJECTIVE *also* **polydactylous.** [1] (of man and other vertebrates) having more than the normal number of digits. ◆ NOUN [2] a human or other vertebrate having more than the normal number of digits.
▷**HISTORY** C19: via French from Greek *poludaktulos* many-toed; see DACTYL

polydemic (ˌpɒlɪˈdɛmɪk) ADJECTIVE *Ecology, rare* growing in or inhabiting more than two regions.
▷**HISTORY** C20: from POLY- + ENDEMIC

Polydeuces (ˌpɒlɪˈdjuːsiːz) NOUN the Greek name of **Pollux.** See **Castor and Pollux.**

polydipsia (ˌpɒlɪˈdɪpsɪə) NOUN *Pathol* excessive thirst.

▷HISTORY C18: New Latin, from POLY- + *-dipsia,* from Greek *dipsa* thirst
▸ˌ**poly'dipsic** ADJECTIVE

poly-drug ADJECTIVE involving or taking more than one kind of illegal drug: *a poly-drug user.*

polyembryony (ˌpɒlɪ'ɛmbrɪənɪ) NOUN the production of more than one embryo from a single fertilized egg cell: occurs in certain plants and parasitic hymenopterous insects.
▸**polyembryonic** (ˌpɒlɪˌɛmbrɪ'ɒnɪk) ADJECTIVE

polyene ('pɒlɪˌiːn) NOUN a chemical compound containing a chain of alternating single and double carbon-carbon bonds.

polyester (ˌpɒlɪ'ɛstə) NOUN any of a large class of synthetic materials that are polymers containing recurring -COO- groups: used as plastics, textile fibres, and adhesives.

polyethene (ˌpɒlɪ'ɛθiːn) NOUN the systematic name for **polythene.**

polyethylene (ˌpɒlɪ'ɛθɪˌliːn) NOUN another name for **polythene.**

polygala (pə'lɪgələ) NOUN any herbaceous plant or small shrub of the polygalaceous genus *Polygala.* See also **milkwort.**
▷HISTORY C18: New Latin, from Greek *polugalon,* from POLY- + *gala* milk

polygalaceous (ˌpɒlɪgə'leɪʃəs, pəˌlɪg-) ADJECTIVE of, relating to, or belonging to the *Polygalaceae,* a family of plants having flowers with two large outer petal-like sepals, three small sepals, and three to five petals: includes milkwort.

polygamy (pə'lɪgəmɪ) NOUN [1] the practice of having more than one wife or husband at the same time. Compare **polyandry, polygyny.** [2] **a** the condition of having male, female, and hermaphrodite flowers on the same plant. **b** the condition of having these different types of flower on separate plants of the same species. [3] the practice in male animals of having more than one mate during one breeding season.
▷HISTORY C16: via French from Greek *polugamia* from POLY- + -GAMY
▸**po'lygamist** NOUN ▸**po'lygamous** ADJECTIVE
▸**po'lygamously** ADVERB

polygene ('pɒlɪˌdʒiːn) NOUN any of a group of genes that each produce a small quantitative effect on a particular characteristic of the phenotype, such as height.

polygenesis (ˌpɒlɪ'dʒɛnɪsɪs) NOUN [1] *Biology* evolution of a polyphyletic organism or group. [2] the hypothetical descent of the different races of man from different ultimate ancestors. ◆ Compare **monogenesis.**
▸**polygenetic** (ˌpɒlɪdʒɪ'nɛtɪk) ADJECTIVE
▸ˌ**polyge'netically** ADVERB

polygenic (ˌpɒli'dʒenik) ADJECTIVE of, relating to, or controlled by polygenes: *polygenic inheritance.*

polyglot ('pɒlɪˌglɒt) ADJECTIVE [1] having a command of many languages. [2] written in, composed of, or containing many languages. ◆ NOUN [3] a person with a command of many languages. [4] a book, esp a Bible, containing several versions of the same text written in various languages. [5] a mixture or confusion of languages.
▷HISTORY C17: from Greek *poluglōttos* literally: many-tongued, from POLY- + *glōtta* tongue
▸'**polyˌglotism** *or* '**polyˌglottism** NOUN

polygon ('pɒlɪˌgɒn) NOUN a closed plane figure bounded by three or more straight sides that meet in pairs in the same number of vertices, and do not intersect other than at these vertices. The sum of the interior angles is $(n-2) \times 180°$ for n sides; the sum of the exterior angles is 360°. A **regular polygon** has all its sides and angles equal. Specific polygons are named according to the number of sides, such as triangle, pentagon, etc.
▷HISTORY C16: via Latin from Greek *polugōnon* figure with many angles
▸**polygonal** (pə'lɪgənᵊl) ADJECTIVE ▸**po'lygonally** ADVERB

polygonaceous (ˌpɒlɪgə'neɪʃəs, pəˌlɪgə-) ADJECTIVE of, relating to, or belonging to the *Polygonaceae,* a chiefly N temperate family of plants having a sheathing stipule (ocrea) clasping the stem and small inconspicuous flowers: includes dock, sorrel, buckwheat, knotgrass, and rhubarb.

polygonum (pə'lɪgənəm) NOUN any polygonaceous plant of the genus *Polygonum,* having stems with knotlike joints and spikes of small white, green, or pink flowers. See also **knotgrass, bistort, prince's-feather** (sense 2).
▷HISTORY C18: New Latin, from Greek *polugonon* knotgrass, from *polu-* POLY- + *-gonon,* from *gonu* knee

polygraph ('pɒlɪˌgrɑːf, -ˌgræf) NOUN [1] an instrument for the simultaneous electrical or mechanical recording of several involuntary physiological activities, including blood pressure, skin resistivity, pulse rate, respiration, and sweating, used esp as a would-be lie detector. [2] a device for producing copies of written, printed, or drawn matter.
▷HISTORY C18: from Greek *polugraphos* writing copiously
▸**polygraphic** (ˌpɒlɪ'græfɪk) ADJECTIVE ▸ˌ**poly'graphically** ADVERB

polygyny (pə'lɪdʒɪnɪ) NOUN [1] the practice or condition of being married to more than one wife at the same time. Compare **polygamy.** [2] the practice in animals of a male mating with more than one female during one breeding season. [3] the condition in flowers of having many carpels. ◆ Compare **polyandry.**
▷HISTORY C18: from POLY- + *-gyny,* from Greek *gunē* a woman
▸**po'lygynist** NOUN ▸**po'lygynous** ADJECTIVE

polyhedral angle (ˌpɒlɪ'hiːdrəl) NOUN a geometric configuration formed by the intersection of three or more planes, such as the faces of a polyhedron, that have a common vertex. See also **solid angle.**

polyhedron (ˌpɒlɪ'hiːdrən) NOUN, *plural* **-drons** *or* **-dra** (-drə). a solid figure consisting of four or more plane faces (all polygons), pairs of which meet along an edge, three or more edges meeting at a vertex. In a **regular polyhedron** all the faces are identical regular polygons making equal angles with each other. Specific polyhedrons are named according to the number of faces, such as tetrahedron, icosahedron, etc.
▷HISTORY C16: from Greek *poluedron,* from POLY- + *hedron* side, base
▸ˌ**poly'hedral** ADJECTIVE

polyhydric (ˌpɒlɪ'haɪdrɪk) ADJECTIVE another word for **polyhydroxy,** esp when applied to alcohols

polyhydroxy (ˌpɒlɪhaɪ'drɒksɪ) ADJECTIVE (of a chemical compound) containing two or more hydroxyl groups per molecule. Also: **polyhydric.**

Polyhymnia (ˌpɒlɪ'hɪmnɪə) NOUN *Greek myth* the Muse of singing, mime, and sacred dance.
▷HISTORY Latin, from Greek *Polumnia* full of songs; see POLY-, HYMN

polyisoprene (ˌpɒlɪ'aɪsəˌpriːn) NOUN any of various polymeric forms of isoprene, occurring in rubbers.

polymath ('pɒlɪˌmæθ) NOUN a person of great and varied learning.
▷HISTORY C17: from Greek *polumathēs* having much knowledge
▸ˌ**poly'mathic** ADJECTIVE ▸**polymathy** (pə'lɪməθɪ) NOUN

polymer ('pɒlɪmə) NOUN a naturally occurring or synthetic compound, such as starch or Perspex, that has large molecules made up of many relatively simple repeated units. Compare **copolymer, oligomer.**
▸**polymerism** (pə'lɪməˌrɪzəm, 'pɒlɪmə-) NOUN

polymerase (pə'lɪməreɪz) NOUN any enzyme that catalyses the synthesis of a polymer, esp the synthesis of DNA or RNA.

polymeric (ˌpɒlɪ'mɛrɪk) ADJECTIVE of, concerned with, or being a polymer: *a polymeric compound.*
▷HISTORY C19: from Greek *polumerēs* having many parts

polymerization *or* **polymerisation** (pəˌlɪməraɪ'zeɪʃən, ˌpɒlɪməraɪ-) NOUN the act or process of forming a polymer or copolymer, esp a chemical reaction in which a polymer is formed.

polymerize *or* **polymerise** ('pɒlɪməˌraɪz, pə'lɪmə-) VERB to react or cause to react to form a polymer.

polymerous (pə'lɪmərəs) ADJECTIVE [1] (of flowers) having the petals, sepals, and other parts arranged in whorls of many parts. [2] *Biology* having or being composed of many parts.

polymorph ('pɒlɪˌmɔːf) NOUN [1] a species of animal or plant that exhibits polymorphism. [2] any of the crystalline forms of a chemical compound that exhibits polymorphism. [3] Also called: **polymorphonuclear leucocyte.** any of a group of white blood cells that have lobed nuclei and granular cytoplasm and function as phagocytes; they include neutrophils, basophils, and eosinophils.
▷HISTORY C19: from Greek *polumorphos* having many forms

polymorphic function NOUN *Computing* a function in a computer program that can deal with a number of different types of data.

polymorphism (ˌpɒlɪ'mɔːfɪzəm) NOUN [1] *Biology* **a** the occurrence of more than one form of individual in a single species within an interbreeding population. **b** the occurrence of more than one form in the individual polyps of a coelenterate colony. [2] the existence or formation of different types of crystal of the same chemical compound.

polymorphonuclear (ˌpɒlɪˌmɔːfəʊ'njuːklɪə) ADJECTIVE (of a leucocyte) having a lobed or segmented nucleus. See also **polymorph** (sense 3).

polymorphous (ˌpɒlɪ'mɔːfəs) *or* **polymorphic** ADJECTIVE [1] having, taking, or passing through many different forms or stages. [2] (of a substance) exhibiting polymorphism. [3] (of an animal or plant) displaying or undergoing polymorphism.

polymyxin (ˌpɒlɪ'mɪksɪn) NOUN any of several polypeptide antibiotics active against Gram-negative bacteria, obtained from the soil bacterium *Bacillus polymyxa.*
▷HISTORY C20: from New Latin *Bacillus polymyxa;* see POLY-, MYXO-, -IN

Polynesia (ˌpɒlɪ'niːʒə, -ʒɪə) NOUN one of the three divisions of islands in the Pacific, the others being Melanesia and Micronesia: includes Samoa, Society, Marquesas, Mangareva, Tuamotu, Cook, and Tubuai Islands, and Tonga.
▷HISTORY C18: via French from POLY- + Greek *nēsos* island

Polynesian (ˌpɒlɪ'niːʒən, -ʒɪən) ADJECTIVE [1] of or relating to Polynesia, its people, or any of their languages. ◆ NOUN [2] a member of the people that inhabit Polynesia, generally of Caucasoid features with light skin and wavy hair. [3] a branch of the Malayo-Polynesian family of languages, including Maori and Hawaiian and a number of other closely related languages of the S and central Pacific.

polyneuritis (ˌpɒlɪnjʊ'raɪtɪs) NOUN inflammation of many nerves at the same time.

Polynices (ˌpɒlɪ'naɪsiːz) NOUN *Greek myth* a son of Oedipus and Jocasta, for whom the Seven Against Thebes sought to regain Thebes. He and his brother Eteocles killed each other in single combat before its walls.

polynomial (ˌpɒlɪ'nəʊmɪəl) ADJECTIVE [1] of, consisting of, or referring to two or more names or terms. ◆ NOUN [2] **a** a mathematical expression consisting of a sum of terms each of which is the product of a constant and one or more variables raised to a positive or zero integral power. For one variable, x, the general form is given by: $a_0x^n + a_1x^{n-1} + \ldots + a_{n-1}x + a_n$, where a_0, a_1, etc., are real numbers. **b** Also called: **multinomial.** any mathematical expression consisting of the sum of a number of terms. [3] *Biology* a taxonomic name consisting of more than two terms, such as *Parus major minor* in which *minor* designates the subspecies.

polynuclear (ˌpɒlɪ'njuːklɪə) *or* **polynucleate** ADJECTIVE having many nuclei; multinuclear.

polynucleotide (ˌpɒlɪ'njuːklɪəˌtaɪd) NOUN *Biochem* a molecular chain of nucleotides chemically bonded by a series of ester linkages between the phosphoryl group of one nucleotide and the hydroxyl group of the sugar in the adjacent nucleotide. Nucleic acids consist of long chains of polynucleotides.

polynya ('pɒlənˌjɑː) NOUN a stretch of open water surrounded by ice, esp near the mouths of large rivers, in arctic seas.
▷HISTORY C19: from Russian, from *poly* open, hollowed-out

polyonymous (ˌpɒlɪ'ɒnɪməs) ADJECTIVE having or known by several different names.

polyp ('pɒlɪp) NOUN [1] *Zoology* one of the two forms of individual that occur in coelenterates. It

usually has a hollow cylindrical body with a ring of tentacles around the mouth. Compare **medusa** (sense 2). [2] Also called: **polypus.** *Pathol* a small vascularized growth arising from the surface of a mucous membrane, having a rounded base or a stalklike projection.
▷HISTORY C16 *polip*, from French *polype* nasal polyp, from Latin *pōlypus* sea animal, nasal polyp, from Greek *polupous* having many feet
▸**ˈpolypous** *or* **ˈpolypoid** ADJECTIVE

polypary (ˈpɒlɪpərɪ) *or* **polyparium** (ˌpɒlɪˈpɛərɪəm) NOUN, *plural* **-paries** *or* **-paria** (-ˈpɛərɪə). the common base and connecting tissue of a colony of coelenterate polyps, esp coral.
▷HISTORY C18: from New Latin *polypārium;* see POLYP

polypeptide (ˌpɒlɪˈpeptaɪd) NOUN any of a group of natural or synthetic polymers made up of amino acids chemically linked together; this class includes the proteins. See also **peptide.**

polypetalous (ˌpɒlɪˈpetələs) ADJECTIVE (of flowers) having many distinct or separate petals. Compare **gamopetalous.**

polyphagia (ˌpɒlɪˈfeɪdʒə) NOUN [1] **a** an abnormal desire to consume excessive amounts of food, esp as the result of a neurological disorder. **b** an insatiable appetite. [2] the habit of certain animals, esp certain insects, of feeding on many different types of food.
▷HISTORY C17: New Latin, from Greek, from *poluphagos* eating much; see POLY-, -PHAGY
▸**polyphagous** (pəˈlɪfəgəs) ADJECTIVE

polyphase (ˈpɒlɪˌfeɪz) ADJECTIVE [1] Also: **multiphase.** (of an electrical system, circuit, or device) having, generating, or using two or more alternating voltages of the same frequency, the phases of which are cyclically displaced by fractions of a period. See also **single-phase, two-phase, three-phase.** [2] having more than one phase.

Polyphemus (ˌpɒlɪˈfiːməs) NOUN *Greek myth* a cyclops who imprisoned Odysseus and his companions in his cave. To effect his escape, Odysseus blinded him.

polyphone (ˈpɒlɪˌfəʊn) NOUN a letter or character having more than one phonetic value, such as English *c*, pronounced (k) before *a, o,* or *u* or (s) before *e* or *i.*

polyphonic (ˌpɒlɪˈfɒnɪk) ADJECTIVE [1] *Music* composed of relatively independent melodic lines or parts; contrapuntal. [2] many-voiced. [3] *Phonetics* of, relating to, or denoting a polyphone.
▸**ˌpolyˈphonically** ADVERB

polyphonic prose NOUN a rhythmically free prose employing poetic devices, such as assonance and alliteration.

polyphony (pəˈlɪfənɪ) NOUN, *plural* **-nies.** [1] polyphonic style of composition or a piece of music utilizing it. [2] the use of polyphones in a writing system.
▷HISTORY C19: from Greek *poluphōnia* diversity of tones, from POLY- + *phōnē* speech, sound
▸**poˈlyphonous** ADJECTIVE ▸**poˈlyphonously** ADVERB

polyphosphoric acid (ˌpɒlɪfɒsˈfɒrɪk) NOUN [1] any one of a series of oxyacids of phosphorus with the general formula $H_{n+2}P_nO_{3n+1}$. The first member is pyrophosphoric acid ($n = 2$) and the series includes the highly polymeric metaphosphoric acid. The higher acids exist in an equilibrium mixture. [2] a glassy or liquid mixture of orthophosphoric and polyphosphoric acids: used industrially as a dehydrating agent, catalyst, and oxidizing agent.

polyphyletic (ˌpɒlɪfaɪˈletɪk) ADJECTIVE *Biology* relating to or characterized by descent from more than one ancestral group of animals or plants.
▷HISTORY C19: from POLY- + PHYLETIC
▸**ˌpolyphyˈletically** ADVERB

polyphyodont (ˌpɒlɪˈfaɪəʊˌdɒnt) ADJECTIVE having many successive sets of teeth, as fishes and other lower vertebrates. Compare **diphyodont.**
▷HISTORY C19: from Greek *poluphuēs* manifold (from *polu-* POLY- + *phuē* growth) + -ODONT

polyploid (ˈpɒlɪˌplɔɪd) ADJECTIVE [1] (of cells, organisms, etc.) having more than twice the basic (haploid) number of chromosomes. ◆ NOUN [2] an individual or cell of this type.
▸**ˌpolyˈploidal** *or* **ˌpolyˈploidic** ADJECTIVE ▸**ˈpolyˌploidy** NOUN

polypod (ˈpɒlɪˌpɒd) ADJECTIVE *also* **polypodous** (pəˈlɪpədəs). [1] (esp of insect larvae) having many legs or similar appendages. ◆ NOUN [2] an animal of this type.

polypody (ˈpɒlɪˌpəʊdɪ) NOUN, *plural* **-dies.** [1] any of various ferns of the genus *Polypodium, esp P. vulgare,* having deeply divided leaves and round naked sori: family *Polypodiaceae.* [2] any fern of the family *Polypodiaceae,* all having opaque leaves that are divided in most species.
▷HISTORY C15: from Latin *polypodium,* from Greek, from POLY- + *pous* foot

polypoid (ˈpɒlɪˌpɔɪd) ADJECTIVE [1] of, relating to, or resembling a polyp. [2] (of a coelenterate) having the body in the form of a polyp.

polypropylene (ˌpɒlɪˈprəʊpɪˌliːn) NOUN any of various tough flexible synthetic thermoplastic materials made by polymerizing propylene and used for making moulded articles, laminates, bottles, pipes, and fibres for ropes, bristles, upholstery, and carpets. Systematic name: **polypropene.**

polyprotodont (ˌpɒlɪˈprəʊtəʊˌdɒnt) NOUN any marsupial of the group *Polyprotodontia,* characterized by four or more upper incisor teeth on each side of the jaw: includes the opossums and bandicoots. Compare **diprotodont.**
▷HISTORY C19: from POLY- + PROTO- + -ODONT

polyptych (ˈpɒlɪptɪk) NOUN an altarpiece consisting of more than three panels, set with paintings or carvings, and usually hinged for folding. Compare **diptych, triptych.**
▷HISTORY C19: via Late Latin from Greek *poluptuchon* something folded many times, from POLY- + *ptuchē* a fold

polypus (ˈpɒlɪpəs) NOUN, *plural* **-pi** (-paɪ). *Pathol* another word for **polyp** (sense 2).
▷HISTORY C16: via Latin from Greek: POLYP

polyrhythm (ˈpɒlɪˌrɪðəm) NOUN *Music* a style of composition in which each part exhibits different rhythms.

polyrhythmic (ˌpɒlɪˈrɪðmɪk) ADJECTIVE *Music* of or relating to polyrhythm; characterized by different rhythms.

polyribosome (ˌpɒlɪˈraɪbəˌsəʊm) NOUN *Biochem* an assemblage of ribosomes associated with a messenger RNA molecule, involved in peptide synthesis. Also called: **polysome.**

polysaccharide (ˌpɒlɪˈsækəˌraɪd, -rɪd) *or* **polysaccharose** (ˌpɒlɪˈsækəˌrəʊz, -ˌrəʊs) NOUN any one of a class of carbohydrates whose molecules contain linked monosaccharide units: includes starch, inulin, and cellulose. General formula: $(C_6H_{10}O_5)_n$. See also **oligosaccharide.**

polysemy (ˌpɒlɪˈsiːmɪ, pəˈlɪsəmɪ) NOUN the existence of several meanings in a single word. Compare **monosemy.**
▷HISTORY C20: from New Latin *polysēmia,* from Greek *polusēmos* having many meanings, from POLY- + *sēma* a sign
▸**ˌpolyˈsemous** ADJECTIVE

polysepalous (ˌpɒlɪˈsepələs) ADJECTIVE (of flowers) having distinct separate sepals. Compare **gamosepalous.**

polysome (ˈpɒlɪˌsəʊm) NOUN another name for **polyribosome.**

polysomic (ˌpɒlɪˈsəʊmɪk) ADJECTIVE of, relating to, or designating a basically diploid chromosome complement, in which some but not all the chromosomes are represented more than twice.
▷HISTORY C20: from POLY- + -SOME^3 + -IC

polystichous (ˌpɒlɪˈstaɪkəs) ADJECTIVE (of plant parts) arranged in a number of rows.

polystyrene (ˌpɒlɪˈstaɪriːn) NOUN a synthetic thermoplastic material obtained by polymerizing styrene; used as a white rigid foam (**expanded polystyrene**) for insulating and packing and as a glasslike material in light fittings and water tanks.

polysulphide (ˌpɒlɪˈsʌlfaɪd) NOUN any sulphide of a metal containing divalent anions in which there are chains of sulphur atoms, as in the polysulphides of sodium, Na_2S_2, Na_2S_3, Na_2S_4, etc.

polysyllabic (ˌpɒlɪsɪˈlæbɪk) ADJECTIVE consisting of more than two syllables. ◆ ADJECTIVE
▸**ˌpolysylˈlabically** ADVERB

polysyllable (ˈpɒlɪˌsɪləbᵊl) NOUN a word consisting of more than two syllables.

polysyllogism (ˌpɒlɪˈsɪləˌdʒɪzəm) NOUN a chain of syllogisms in which the conclusion of one syllogism serves as a premise for the next.

polysyndeton (ˌpɒlɪˈsɪndɪtən) NOUN [1] *Rhetoric* the use of several conjunctions in close succession, esp where some might be omitted, as in *he ran and jumped and laughed for joy.* [2] Also called: **syndesis.** *Grammar* a sentence containing more than two coordinate clauses.
▷HISTORY C16: POLY- + *-syndeton,* from Greek *sundetos* bound together

polysynthetic (ˌpɒlɪsɪnˈθetɪk) ADJECTIVE denoting languages, such as Eskimo, in which single words may express the meaning of whole phrases or clauses by virtue of multiple affixes. Compare **synthetic** (sense 3), **analytic** (sense 3), **agglutinative** (sense 2).
▸**polysynthesis** (ˌpɒlɪˈsɪnθɪsɪs) NOUN ▸**ˌpolyˈsynthesism** NOUN ▸**ˌpolysynˈthetically** ADVERB

polytechnic (ˌpɒlɪˈteknɪk) NOUN [1] *Brit* a college offering advanced full- and part-time courses, esp vocational courses, in many fields at and below degree standard. ◆ ADJECTIVE [2] of or relating to technical instruction and training.
▷HISTORY C19: via French from Greek *polutekhnos* skilled in many arts. See TECHNIC

polytene (ˈpɒlɪˌtiːn) ADJECTIVE denoting a type of giant-size chromosome consisting of many replicated genes in parallel, found esp in *Drosophila* larvae.
▷HISTORY C20: from POLY- + Greek *taenia* band

polytetrafluoroethylene (ˌpɒlɪˌtetrəˌfluərəʊˈeθɪˌliːn) NOUN a white thermoplastic material with a waxy texture, made by polymerizing tetrafluoroethylene. It is nonflammable, resists chemical action and radiation, and has a high electrical resistance and an extremely low coefficient of friction. It is used for making gaskets, hoses, insulators, bearings, and for coating metal surfaces in chemical plants and in nonstick cooking vessels. Abbreviation: **PTFE.** Also called (trademark): **Teflon.**

polytheism (ˈpɒlɪθiːˌɪzəm, ˌpɒlɪˈθiːɪzəm) NOUN the worship of or belief in more than one god.
▸**ˈpolyˌtheist** NOUN ▸**ˌpolytheˈistic** ADJECTIVE ▸**ˌpolytheˈistically** ADVERB

polythene (ˈpɒlɪˌθiːn) NOUN any one of various light thermoplastic materials made from ethylene with properties depending on the molecular weight of the polymer. The common forms are a waxy flexible plastic (**low-density polythene**) and a tougher rigid more crystalline form (**high-density polythene**). Polythene is used for packaging, moulded articles, pipes and tubing, insulation, textiles, and coatings on metal. Systematic name: **polyethene.** Also called: **polyethylene.**

polytonality (ˌpɒlɪtəʊˈnælɪtɪ) *or* **polytonalism** NOUN *Music* the simultaneous use of more than two different keys or tonalities.
▸**ˌpolyˈtonal** ADJECTIVE ▸**ˌpolyˈtonally** ADVERB ▸**ˌpolyˈtonalist** NOUN

polytrophic (ˌpɒlɪˈtrɒfɪk) ADJECTIVE (esp of bacteria) obtaining food from several different organic sources.

polytunnel (ˈpɒlɪˌtʌnᵊl) NOUN a large tunnel made of polythene and used as a greenhouse.

polytypic (ˌpɒlɪˈtɪpɪk) *or* **polytypical** ADJECTIVE [1] existing in, consisting of, or incorporating several different types or forms. [2] *Biology* (of a taxonomic group) having many subdivisions, esp (of a species) having many subspecies and geographical races.

polyunsaturated (ˌpɒlɪʌnˈsætʃəˌreɪtɪd) ADJECTIVE of or relating to a class of animal and vegetable fats, the molecules of which consist of long carbon chains with many double bonds. Polyunsaturated compounds are less likely to be converted into cholesterol in the body. They are widely used in margarines and in the manufacture of paints and varnishes. See also **monounsaturated.**

polyurethane (ˌpɒlɪˈjʊərəˌθeɪn) *or* **polyurethan** (ˌpɒlɪˈjʊərəˌθæn) NOUN a class of synthetic materials made by copolymerizing an isocyanate and a polyhydric alcohol and commonly used as a foam (**polyurethane foam**) for insulation and packing, as fibres and hard inert coatings, and in a flexible form (**polyurethane rubber**) for diaphragms and seals.

polyuria (ˌpɒlɪˈjʊərɪə) NOUN *Pathol, physiol* the state or condition of discharging abnormally large

quantities of urine, often accompanied by a need to urinate frequently.
▸ ˌpolyˈuric ADJECTIVE

polyvalent (ˌpɒlɪˈveɪlənt, pəˈlɪvələnt) ADJECTIVE [1] *Chem* having more than one valency. [2] (of a vaccine) **a** effective against several strains of the same disease-producing microorganism, antigen, or toxin. **b** produced from cultures containing several strains of the same microorganism.
▸ ˌpolyˈvalency NOUN

polyvinyl (ˌpɒlɪˈvaɪnɪl, -ˈvaɪnᵊl) NOUN (*modifier*) designating a plastic or resin formed by polymerization of a vinyl derivative.

polyvinyl acetate NOUN a colourless odourless tasteless resin used in emulsion paints, adhesives, sealers, a substitute for chicle in chewing gum, and for sealing porous surfaces. Abbreviation: **PVA**.

polyvinyl chloride NOUN the full name of **PVC**.

polyvinylidene chloride (ˌpɒlɪvaɪˈnɪlɪˌdiːn) NOUN any one of a class of thermoplastic materials formed by the polymerization of vinylidene chloride: used in packaging and for making pipes and fittings for chemical equipment. Also called: **saran**.

polyvinyl resin NOUN any of a class of thermoplastic resins that are made by polymerizing or copolymerizing a vinyl compound. The commonest type is PVC.

Polyxena (pɒˈlɪksɪnə) NOUN *Greek myth* a daughter of King Priam of Troy, who was sacrificed on the command of Achilles' ghost.

polyzoan (ˌpɒlɪˈzəʊən) NOUN, ADJECTIVE another word for **bryozoan**.
▹ HISTORY C19: from New Latin, *Polyzoa* class name, from POLY- + *-zoan*, from Greek *zōion* an animal

polyzoarium (ˌpɒlɪzəʊˈeərɪəm) NOUN, *plural* **-ia** (-ɪə). a colony of bryozoan animals or its supporting skeletal framework.
▸ ˌpolyzoˈarial ADJECTIVE

polyzoic (ˌpɒlɪˈzəʊɪk) ADJECTIVE *Zoology* [1] (of certain colonial animals) having many zooids or similar polyps. [2] producing or containing many sporozoites.

pom (pɒm) NOUN *Slang, Austral and NZ* short for **pommy**.

POM ABBREVIATION FOR prescription-only medicine *or* medication. Compare **OTC**.

pomace (ˈpʌmɪs) NOUN [1] the pulpy residue of apples or similar fruit after crushing and pressing, as in cider-making. [2] any pulpy substance left after crushing, mashing, etc.
▹ HISTORY C16: from Medieval Latin *pōmācium* cider, from Latin *pōmum* apple

pomaceous (pɒˈmeɪʃəs) ADJECTIVE of, relating to, or bearing pomes, such as the apple, pear, and quince trees.
▹ HISTORY C18: from New Latin *pōmāceus*, from Latin *pōmum* apple

pomade (pəˈmɑːd, -ˈmeɪd) NOUN [1] a perfumed oil or ointment put on the hair, as to make it smooth and shiny. ◆ VERB [2] (*tr*) to put pomade on. ◆ Also: **pomatum** (pəˈmeɪtəm).
▹ HISTORY C16: from French *pommade*, from Italian *pomato* (originally made partly from apples), from Latin *pōmum* apple

pomander (pəʊˈmændə) NOUN [1] a mixture of aromatic substances in a sachet or an orange, formerly carried as scent or as a protection against disease. [2] a container for such a mixture.
▹ HISTORY C15: from Old French *pome d'ambre*, from Medieval Latin *pōmum ambrae* apple of amber

pombe (ˈpɔmbɛ) NOUN *E African* any alcoholic drink.
▹ HISTORY Swahili

pome (pəʊm) NOUN the fleshy fruit of the apple and related plants, consisting of an enlarged receptacle enclosing the ovary and seeds.
▹ HISTORY C15: from Old French, from Late Latin *pōma* apple, pl (assumed to be sing) of Latin *pōmum* apple

pomegranate (ˈpɒmɪˌɡrænɪt, ˈpɒmˌɡrænɪt) NOUN [1] an Asian shrub or small tree, *Punica granatum*, cultivated in semitropical regions for its edible fruit: family *Punicaceae*. [2] the many-chambered globular fruit of this tree, which has tough reddish rind, juicy red pulp, and many seeds.
▹ HISTORY C14: from Old French *pome grenate*, from Latin *pōmum* apple + *grenate*, from Latin *grānātum*, from *grānātus* full of seeds

pomelo (ˈpɒmɪˌləʊ) NOUN, *plural* **-los**. [1] a tropical rutaceous tree, *Citrus maxima* (or *C. decumana*), grown widely in oriental regions for its large yellow grapefruit-like edible fruit. [2] the fruit of this tree. [3] *Chiefly US* another name for **grapefruit**. ◆ Also called: **shaddock**.
▹ HISTORY C19: from Dutch *pompelmoes*, perhaps from *pompoen* big + Portuguese *limão* a lemon

Pomerania (ˌpɒməˈreɪnɪə) NOUN a region of N central Europe, extending along the S coast of the Baltic Sea from Stralsund to the Vistula River: now chiefly in Poland, with a small area in NE Germany. German name: **Pommern**. Polish name: **Pomorze**.

Pomeranian (ˌpɒməˈreɪnɪən) ADJECTIVE [1] of or relating to Pomerania or its inhabitants. ◆ NOUN [2] a native or inhabitant of Pomerania, esp a German. [3] a breed of toy dog of the spitz type with a long thick straight coat.

pomfret[1] (ˈpʌmfrɪt, ˈpɒm-) *or* **pomfret-cake** NOUN a small black rounded confection of liquorice. Also called: **Pontefract cake**.
▹ HISTORY C19: from *Pomfret*, earlier form of PONTEFRACT, where the cake was originally made

pomfret[2] (ˈpɒmfrɪt) NOUN [1] any of various fishes of the genus *Stromateidae* of the Indian and Pacific oceans: valued as food fishes. [2] any of various scombroid fishes, esp *Brama raii*, of northern oceans: valued as food fishes.
▹ HISTORY C18: perhaps from a diminutive form of Portuguese *pampo*

pomiculture (ˈpɒmɪˌkʌltʃə) NOUN the cultivation of fruit.
▹ HISTORY C19: from Latin *pōmum* apple, fruit + CULTURE

pomiferous (pɒˈmɪfərəs) ADJECTIVE (of the apple, pear, etc.) producing pomes or pomelike fruits.
▹ HISTORY C17: from Latin *pomifer* fruit-bearing

pommel (ˈpʌməl, ˈpɒm-) NOUN [1] the raised part on the front of a saddle. [2] a knob at the top of a sword or similar weapon. ◆ VERB **-mels, -melling, -melled** *or US* **-mels, -meling, -meled**. [3] a less common word for **pummel**.
▹ HISTORY C14: from Old French *pomel* knob, from Vulgar Latin *pōmellum* (unattested) little apple, from Latin *pōmum* apple

Pommern (ˈpɔmərn) NOUN the German name for **Pomerania**.

pommy (ˈpɒmɪ) NOUN, *plural* **-mies**. (*sometimes capital*) *Slang* a mildly offensive word used by Australians and New Zealanders for an English person. Sometimes shortened to: **pom**.
▹ HISTORY C20: of uncertain origin. Among a number of explanations are: (1) based on a blend of IMMIGRANT and POMEGRANATE (alluding to the red cheeks of English immigrants); (2) from the abbreviation *POME*, Prisoner of Mother England (referring to convicts)

pomology (pɒˈmɒlədʒɪ) NOUN the branch of horticulture that is concerned with the study and cultivation of fruit.
▹ HISTORY C19: from New Latin *pōmologia*, from Latin *pōmum* apple, fruit
▸ pomological (ˌpɒməˈlɒdʒɪkᵊl) ADJECTIVE
▸ ˌpomoˈlogically ADVERB ▸ pomˈologist NOUN

Pomona[1] (pəˈməʊnə) NOUN another name for **Mainland** (in the Orkneys).

Pomona[2] (pəˈməʊnə) NOUN the Roman goddess of fruit trees.

Pomorze (pɔˈmɔʒɛ) NOUN the Polish name for **Pomerania**.

pomp (pɒmp) NOUN [1] stately or magnificent display; ceremonial splendour. [2] vain display, esp of dignity or importance. [3] *Obsolete* a procession or pageant.
▹ HISTORY C14: from Old French *pompe*, from Latin *pompa* procession, from Greek *pompē*; related to Greek *pompein* to send

pompadour (ˈpɒmpəˌdʊə) NOUN an early 18th-century hairstyle for women, having the front hair arranged over a pad to give it greater height and bulk.
▹ HISTORY C18: named after its originator Jeanne Antoinette Poisson, the Marquise de *Pompadour* (1721–64), mistress of Louis XV of France

pompano (ˈpɒmpəˌnəʊ) NOUN, *plural* **-no** *or* **-nos**. [1] any of several deep-bodied carangid food fishes of the genus *Trachinotus*, *esp T. carolinus*, of American coastal regions of the Atlantic. [2] a spiny-finned food fish, *Palometa simillima*, of North American coastal regions of the Pacific: family *Stromateidae* (butterfish, etc.).
▹ HISTORY C19: from Spanish *pámpano* type of fish, of uncertain origin

Pompeii (pɒmˈpeɪiː) NOUN an ancient city in Italy, southeast of Naples: buried by an eruption of Vesuvius (79 A.D.); excavation of the site, which is extremely well preserved, began in 1748.

Pompeiian (pɒmˈpeɪən, -ˈpiː-) ADJECTIVE [1] of or relating to Pompeii or its inhabitants. ◆ NOUN [2] a native or inhabitant of Pompeii.

Pompey (ˈpɒmpɪ) NOUN an informal name for **Portsmouth**.

pompilid (ˈpɒmpɪlɪd) NOUN another name for the **spider-hunting wasp**.
▹ HISTORY C20: from New Latin *pompilus*, from Greek *pompilos* a fish that accompanies ships, from *pempein* to send, escort

pompom (ˈpɒmpɒm) *or* **pompon** NOUN [1] a ball of tufted silk, wool, feathers, etc., worn on a hat for decoration. [2] **a** the small globelike flower head of certain cultivated varieties of dahlia and chrysanthemum. **b** (*as modifier*): *pompom dahlia*.
▹ HISTORY C18: from French, from Old French *pompe* knot of ribbons, of uncertain origin

pom-pom (ˈpɒmpɒm) NOUN an automatic rapid-firing, small-calibre cannon, esp a type of anti-aircraft cannon used in World War II. Also called: **pompom**.
▹ HISTORY C19: of imitative origin

pomposity (pɒmˈpɒsɪtɪ) NOUN, *plural* **-ties**. [1] vain or ostentatious display of dignity or importance. [2] the quality of being pompous. [3] ostentatiously lofty style, language, etc. [4] a pompous action, remark, etc.

pompous (ˈpɒmpəs) ADJECTIVE [1] exaggeratedly or ostentatiously dignified or self-important. [2] ostentatiously lofty in style: *a pompous speech*. [3] *Rare* characterized by ceremonial pomp or splendour.
▸ ˈpompously ADVERB ▸ ˈpompousness NOUN

'pon (pɒn) PREPOSITION *Poetic or archaic* ◆ CONTRACTION OF upon.

ponce (pɒns) *Derogatory slang, chiefly Brit* ◆ NOUN [1] a man given to ostentatious or effeminate display in manners, speech, dress, etc. [2] another word for **pimp**[1]. ◆ VERB [3] (*intr*; often foll by *around* or *about*) to act like a ponce.
▹ HISTORY C19: from Polari, from Spanish *pu(n)to* male prostitute or French *pront* prostitute

Ponce (*Spanish* ˈponθe) NOUN a port in S Puerto Rico, on the Caribbean: the second largest town on the island; settled in the 16th century. Pop.: 155 038 (2000).

poncey *or* **poncy** (ˈpɒnsɪ) *Derogatory slang, chiefly Brit* ADJECTIVE **-cier, -ciest**. ostentatious, pretentious, or effeminate.

poncho (ˈpɒntʃəʊ) NOUN, *plural* **-chos**. a cloak of a kind originally worn in South America, made of a rectangular or circular piece of cloth, esp wool, with a hole in the middle to put the head through.
▹ HISTORY C18: from American Spanish, from Araucanian *pantho* woollen material

pond (pɒnd) NOUN **a** a pool of still water, often artificially created. **b** (*in combination*): *a fishpond*.
▹ HISTORY C13 *ponde* enclosure; related to POUND[3]

ponder (ˈpɒndə) VERB (when *intr*, sometimes foll by *on* or *over*) to give thorough or deep consideration (to); meditate (upon).
▹ HISTORY C14: from Old French *ponderer*, from Latin *ponderāre* to weigh, consider, from *pondus* weight; related to *pendere* to weigh

ponderable (ˈpɒndərəbᵊl) ADJECTIVE [1] able to be evaluated or estimated; appreciable. [2] capable of being weighed or measured. ◆ NOUN [3] (*often plural*) something that can be evaluated or appreciated; a substantial thing.
▸ ˌponderaˈbility NOUN ▸ ˈponderably ADVERB

ponderous (ˈpɒndərəs) ADJECTIVE [1] of great weight; heavy; huge. [2] (esp of movement) lacking ease or lightness; awkward, lumbering, or graceless. [3] dull or laborious: *a ponderous oration*.

▷HISTORY C14: from Latin *ponderōsus* of great weight, from *pondus* weight
▸ˈ**ponderously** ADVERB ▸ˈ**ponderousness** *or* **ponderosity** (ˌpɒndəˈrɒsɪtɪ) NOUN

pond hockey NOUN *Canadian* ice hockey played on a frozen pond.

Pondicherry (ˌpɒndɪˈtʃɛrɪ) NOUN **1** a Union Territory of SE India: transferred from French to Indian administration in 1954 and made a Union Territory in 1962. Capital: Pondicherry. Pop.: 973 829 (2001 est.). Area: 479 sq. km (185 sq. miles). **2** a port in SE India, capital of the Union Territory of Pondicherry, on the Coromandel Coast. Pop.: 203 065 (1991).

pond life NOUN **1** the animals that live in ponds. **2** stupid or despicable people.

pond lily NOUN another name for **water lily.**

Pondo (ˈpɒndəʊ) NOUN **1** (*plural* **-do** *or* **-dos**) a member of a Negroid people of southern Africa, living chiefly in Pondoland. **2** the language of this people, belonging to the Bantu grouping of the Niger-Congo family, and closely related to Xhosa.

pondok (ˈpɒndɒk) *or* **pondokkie** (pɒnˈdɒkɪ) NOUN (in southern Africa) a crudely made house built of tin sheet, reeds, etc.
▷HISTORY C20: from Malay *pondók* leaf house

Pondoland (ˈpɒndəʊˌlænd) NOUN an area in SE central South Africa: inhabited chiefly by the Pondo people.

pond scum NOUN a greenish layer floating on the surface of stagnant waters, consisting of various freshwater algae.

pond-skater NOUN any of various heteropterous insects of the family *Gerrididae, esp Gerris lacustris* (**common pond-skater**), having a slender hairy body and long hairy legs with which they skim about on the surface of ponds. Also called: **water strider, water skater.**

pond snail NOUN a general term for the freshwater snails: often specifically for the **great pond snail** (*Limnaea stagnalis*) and others of that genus. *L. truncatula* is a host of the liver fluke.

pondweed (ˈpɒndˌwiːd) NOUN **1** any of various water plants of the genus *Potamogeton,* which grow in ponds and slow streams: family *Potamogetonaceae*. **2** Also called: **waterweed.** *Brit* any of various unrelated water plants, such as Canadian pondweed, mare's-tail, and water milfoil, that have thin or much divided leaves.

pone[1] (pəʊn) NOUN *Southern US* **1** Also called: **pone bread, corn pone.** bread made of maize. **2** a loaf or cake of this.
▷HISTORY C17: from Algonquian; compare Delaware *apán* baked

pone[2] (pəʊn, ˈpəʊnɪ) NOUN *Cards* the player to the right of the dealer, or the nondealer in two-handed games.
▷HISTORY C19: from Latin: put!, that is, play, from *ponere* to put

pong (pɒŋ) *Brit informal* ◆ NOUN **1** a disagreeable or offensive smell; stink. ◆ VERB **2** (*intr*) to give off an unpleasant smell; stink.
▷HISTORY C20: perhaps from Romany *pan* to stink
▸ˈ**pongy** ADJECTIVE

ponga (ˈpɒŋə) NOUN a tall tree fern, *Cyathea dealbata,* of New Zealand, with large feathery leaves.
▷HISTORY Maori

pongee (pɒnˈdʒiː, ˈpɒndʒiː) NOUN **1** a thin plain-weave silk fabric from China or India, left in its natural colour. **2** a cotton or rayon fabric similar to or in imitation of this, but not necessarily in the natural colour.
▷HISTORY C18: from Mandarin Chinese (Peking) *pen-chī* woven at home, on one's own loom, from *pen* own + *chi* loom

pongid (ˈpɒŋgɪd, ˈpɒndʒɪd) NOUN **1** any primate of the family *Pongidae,* which includes the gibbons and the great apes. ◆ ADJECTIVE **2** of, relating to, or belonging to the family *Pongidae*.
▷HISTORY from New Latin *Pongo* type genus, from Kongo *mpongi* ape

pongo (ˈpɒŋgəʊ) NOUN, *plural* **-gos. 1** an anthropoid ape, esp an orang-utan or (formerly) a gorilla. **2** *Military, slang* a soldier or marine.
▷HISTORY C17: from Kongo *mpongo*

poniard (ˈpɒnjəd) NOUN **1** a small dagger with a slender blade. ◆ VERB **2** (*tr*) to stab with a poniard.
▷HISTORY C16: from Old French *poignard* dagger, from *poing* fist, from Latin *pugnus;* related to Latin *pugnāre* to fight

pons (pɒnz) NOUN, *plural* **pontes** (ˈpɒntiːz). **1** a bridge of connecting tissue. **2** short for **pons Varolii.**
▷HISTORY Latin: bridge

pons asinorum (ˌæsɪˈnɔːrəm) NOUN the geometric proposition that the angles opposite the two equal sides of an isosceles triangle are equal.
▷HISTORY Latin: bridge of asses, referring originally to the fifth proposition of the first book of Euclid, which was considered difficult for students to learn

pons Varolii (vəˈrəʊlɪˌaɪ) NOUN, *plural* **pontes Varolii** (ˈpɒntiːz). a broad white band of connecting nerve fibres that bridges the hemispheres of the cerebellum in mammals. Sometimes shortened to: **pons.**
▷HISTORY C16: New Latin, literally: bridge of Varoli, after Costanzo *Varoli* (?1543–75), Italian anatomist

pont (pɒnt) NOUN (in South Africa) a river ferry, esp one that is guided by a cable from one bank to the other.
▷HISTORY C17: from Dutch: ferryboat, PUNT[1]; reintroduced through Afrikaans in 19th or 20th century

Ponta Delgada (*Portuguese* ˈpontə ðɛlˈgaðə) NOUN a port in the E Azores, on S São Miguel Island: chief commercial centre of the archipelago. Pop.: 22 200 (latest est.).

Pontchartrain (ˈpɒntʃəˌtreɪn) NOUN **Lake.** a shallow lagoon in SE Louisiana, linked with the Gulf of Mexico by a narrow channel, the **Rigolets:** resort and fishing centre. Area: 1620 sq. km (625 sq. miles).

Pontefract (ˈpɒntɪˌfrækt) NOUN an industrial town in N England, in Wakefield unitary authority, West Yorkshire: castle (1069), in which Richard II was imprisoned and murdered (1400). Pop.: 28 358 (1991).

Pontefract cake NOUN another name for **pomfret**[1].

Pontevedra (*Spanish* pɔnteˈβeðra) NOUN a port in NW Spain: takes its name from a 12-arched Roman bridge, the Pons Vetus. Pop.: 74 850 (1991).

pontianak (ˌpɒntɪˈɑːnæk) NOUN (in Malay folklore) a female vampire; the ghost of a woman who has died in childbirth.
▷HISTORY from Malay

Pontianak (ˌpɒntɪˈɑːnæk) NOUN a port in Indonesia, on W coast of Borneo almost exactly on the equator. Pop.: 409 632 (1995 est.).

Pontic (ˈpɒntɪk) ADJECTIVE denoting or relating to the Black Sea.
▷HISTORY C15: from Latin *Ponticus,* from Greek, from *Pontos* PONTUS

pontifex (ˈpɒntɪˌfɛks) NOUN, *plural* **pontifices** (pɒnˈtɪfɪˌsiːz). (in ancient Rome) any of the senior members of the Pontifical College, presided over by the **Pontifex Maximus.**
▷HISTORY C16: from Latin, perhaps from Etruscan but influenced by folk etymology as if meaning literally: bridge-maker, from *pons* bridge + *-fex* from *facere* to make

pontiff (ˈpɒntɪf) NOUN a former title of the pagan high priest at Rome, later used of popes and occasionally of other bishops, and now confined exclusively to the pope.
▷HISTORY C17: from French *pontife,* from Latin PONTIFEX

pontifical (pɒnˈtɪfɪkᵊl) ADJECTIVE **1** of, relating to, or characteristic of a pontiff, the pope, or a bishop. **2** having an excessively authoritative manner; pompous. ◆ NOUN **3** *RC Church, Church of England* a book containing the prayers and ritual instructions for ceremonies restricted to a bishop. ◆ See also **pontificals.**
▸**ponˈtifically** ADVERB

Pontifical College NOUN *RC Church* **1** a major theological college under the direct control of the Roman Curia. **2** the council of priests, being the chief hieratic body of the Church.

Pontifical Mass NOUN *RC Church, Church of England* a solemn celebration of Mass by a bishop.

pontificals (pɒnˈtɪfɪkᵊlz) PLURAL NOUN *Chiefly RC Church* the insignia and special vestments worn by a bishop, esp when celebrating High Mass.

pontificate VERB (pɒnˈtɪfɪˌkeɪt) (*intr*) **1** Also (less commonly): **pontify** (ˈpɒntɪˌfaɪ). to speak or behave in a pompous or dogmatic manner. **2** to serve or officiate as a pontiff, esp in celebrating a Pontifical Mass. ◆ NOUN (pɒnˈtɪfɪkɪt) **3** the office or term of office of a pontiff, now usually the pope.

pontil (ˈpɒntɪl) NOUN a less common word for **punty.**
▷HISTORY C19: from French, apparently from Italian *puntello;* see PUNTY

pontine (ˈpɒntaɪn) ADJECTIVE **1** of or relating to bridges. **2** of or relating to the pons Varolii.
▷HISTORY C19: from Latin *pons* bridge

Pontine Marshes (ˈpɒntaɪn) PLURAL NOUN an area of W Italy, southeast of Rome: formerly malarial swamps, drained in 1932–34 after numerous attempts since 160 B.C. had failed. Italian name: **Agro Pontino** (ˈɑːgro ponˈtiːno).

pontonier (ˌpɒntəˈnɪə) NOUN *Military, obsolete* a person in charge of or involved in building a pontoon bridge.
▷HISTORY C19: from French *pontonnier,* from Latin *pontō* ferry boat, PONTOON[1]

pontoon[1] (pɒnˈtuːn) NOUN **1 a** a watertight float or vessel used where buoyancy is required in water, as in supporting a bridge, in salvage work, or where a temporary or mobile structure is required in military operations. **b** (*as modifier*): *a pontoon bridge.* **2** *Nautical* a float, often inflatable, for raising a vessel in the water.
▷HISTORY C17: from French *ponton,* from Latin *pontō* punt, floating bridge, from *pōns* bridge

pontoon[2] (pɒnˈtuːn) NOUN **1** Also called: (esp US) **twenty-one, vingt-et-un.** a gambling game in which players try to obtain card combinations worth 21 points. **2** (in this game) the combination of an ace with a ten or court card when dealt to a player as his first two cards.
▷HISTORY C20: probably an alteration of French *vingt-et-un,* literally: twenty-one

Pontus (ˈpɒntəs) NOUN an ancient region of NE Asia Minor, on the Black Sea: became a kingdom in the 4th century B.C.; at its height under Mithridates VI (about 115–63 B.C.), when it controlled all Asia Minor; defeated by the Romans in the mid-1st century B.C.

Pontus Euxinus (juːkˈsaɪnəs) NOUN the Latin name of the **Black Sea.**

Pontypool (ˌpɒntɪˈpuːl) NOUN an industrial town in E Wales, in Torfaen county borough: famous for lacquered ironware in the 18th century. Pop.: 35 564 (1991).

Pontypridd (ˌpɒntɪˈpriːð) NOUN an industrial town in S Wales, in Rhondda Cynon Taff county borough. Pop.: 28 487 (1991).

pony (ˈpəʊnɪ) NOUN, *plural* **ponies. 1** any of various breeds of small horse, usually under 14.2 hands. **2 a** a small drinking glass, esp for liqueurs. **b** the amount held by such a glass. **3** anything small of its kind. **4** *Brit slang* a sum of £25, esp in bookmaking. **5** Also called: **trot.** *US slang* a literal translation used by students, often illicitly, in preparation for foreign language lessons or examinations; crib. ◆ See also **pony up.**
▷HISTORY C17: from Scottish *powney,* perhaps from obsolete French *poulenet* a little colt, from *poulain* colt, from Latin *pullus* young animal, foal

pony express NOUN (in the American West) a system of mail transport that employed relays of riders and mounts, esp that operating from Missouri to California in 1860–61.

ponytail (ˈpəʊnɪˌteɪl) NOUN a hairstyle in which the hair is pulled tightly into a band or ribbon at the back of the head into a loose hanging fall.

pony trekking NOUN the act of riding ponies cross-country, esp as a pastime.

pony up VERB (*adverb*) *US informal* to give the money required.

pooch (puːtʃ) NOUN a slang word for **dog** (sense 1).
▷HISTORY of unknown origin

pood (puːd) NOUN a unit of weight, used in Russia, equal to 36.1 pounds or 16.39 kilograms.
▷HISTORY C16: from Russian *pud,* probably from Old Norse *pund* POUND[2]

poodle (ˈpuːdᵊl) NOUN **1** a breed of dog, with varieties of different sizes, having curly hair, which is often clipped from ribs to tail for showing:

originally bred to hunt waterfowl. [2] a person who is servile; lackey.
▷HISTORY C19: from German *Pudel,* short for *Pudelhund,* from *pudeln* to splash + *Hund* dog; the dogs were formerly trained as water dogs; see PUDDLE, HOUND[1]

poodle-faker NOUN *Slang, old-fashioned* a young man or newly commissioned officer who makes a point of socializing with women; ladies' man.

poof (pʊf, puːf) *or* **poove** NOUN *Brit derogatory slang* a male homosexual.
▷HISTORY C20: from French *pouffe* puff
▸ **'poofy** ADJECTIVE

poofter ('pʊftə, 'puːf-) NOUN *Derogatory slang* [1] a man who is considered effeminate or homosexual. [2] *NZ* a contemptible person.
▷HISTORY C20: expanded form of POOF

pooh (puː) INTERJECTION [1] an exclamation of disdain, contempt, or disgust. ◆ NOUN, VERB [2] a childish word for **faeces** or **defecate.**

Pooh-Bah ('puː'bɑː) NOUN a pompous self-important official holding several offices at once and fulfilling none of them.
▷HISTORY C19: after the character, the Lord-High-Everything-Else, in *The Mikado* (1885), a light opera by Gilbert and Sullivan

pooh-pooh ('puː'puː) VERB *(tr)* to express disdain or scorn for; dismiss or belittle.

pook (pʊk) NOUN *Southwest English dialect* a haycock.

pool[1] (puːl) NOUN [1] a small body of still water, usually fresh; small pond. [2] a small isolated collection of liquid spilt or poured on a surface; puddle: *a pool of blood.* [3] a deep part of a stream or river where the water runs very slowly. [4] an underground accumulation of oil or gas, usually forming a reservoir in porous sedimentary rock. [5] See **swimming pool.**
▷HISTORY Old English *pōl;* related to Old Frisian *pōl,* German *Pfuhl*

pool[2] (puːl) NOUN [1] any communal combination of resources, funds, etc.: *a typing pool.* [2] the combined stakes of the betters in many gambling sports or games; kitty. [3] *Commerce* a group of producers who conspire to establish and maintain output levels and high prices, each member of the group being allocated a maximum quota; price ring. [4] *Finance, chiefly US* **a** a joint fund organized by security-holders for speculative or manipulative purposes on financial markets. **b** the persons or parties involved in such a combination. [5] any of various billiard games in which the object is to pot all the balls with the cue ball, esp that played with 15 coloured and numbered balls; pocket billiards. ◆ VERB *(tr)* [6] to combine (investments, money, interests, etc.) into a common fund, as for a joint enterprise. [7] *Commerce* to organize a pool of (enterprises). [8] *Austral informal* to inform on or incriminate (someone). ◆ See also **pools.**
▷HISTORY C17: from French *poule,* literally: hen used to signify stakes in a card game, from Medieval Latin *pulla* hen, from Latin *pullus* young animal

Poole (puːl) NOUN [1] a port and resort in S England, in Poole unitary authority, Dorset, on **Poole Harbour**; seat of Bournemouth University (1992). Pop.: 138 479 (1991). [2] a unitary authority in S England, in Dorset. Pop.: 138 299 (2001). Area: 37 sq. km (14 sq. miles).

Pool Malebo ('puːl mə'liːbəʊ) NOUN the Congolese name for **Stanley Pool.**

poolroom ('puːlˌruːm, -ˌrʊm) NOUN *US and Canadian* a hall or establishment where pool, billiards, etc., are played.

pools (puːlz) PLURAL NOUN *Brit* an organized nationwide principally postal gambling pool betting on the result of football matches. Also called: **football pools.**
▷HISTORY C20: from POOL[2] (in the sense: a gambling kitty)

pool table NOUN a billiard table on which pool is played.

poon[1] (puːn) NOUN [1] any of several trees of the SE Asian genus *Calophyllum* having lightweight hard wood and shiny leathery leaves: family *Clusiaceae.* [2] the wood of any of these trees, used to make masts and spars.
▷HISTORY C17: from Singhalese *pūna*

poon[2] (puːn) NOUN *Austral slang* a stupid or ineffectual person.
▷HISTORY C20: from English dialect

Poona *or* **Pune** ('puːnə) NOUN a city in W India, in W Maharashtra: under British rule served as the seasonal capital of the Bombay Presidency. Pop.: 1 566 651 (1991).

poonce (puːns) *Austral slang* ◆ NOUN [1] a male homosexual. ◆ VERB *(intr)* [2] to behave effeminately.
▷HISTORY C20: perhaps a blend of POOF and PONCE

poop[1] (puːp) *Nautical* ◆ NOUN [1] a raised structure at the stern of a vessel, esp a sailing ship. [2] See **poop deck.** ◆ VERB [3] *(tr)* (of a wave or sea) to break over the stern of (a vessel). [4] *(intr)* (of a vessel) to ship a wave or sea over the stern, esp repeatedly.
▷HISTORY C15: from Old French *pupe,* from Latin *puppis* poop, ship's stern

poop[2] (puːp) VERB *US and Canadian slang* [1] *(tr; usually passive)* to cause to become exhausted; tire: *he was pooped after the race.* [2] *(intr; usually foll by out)* to give up or fail, esp through tiredness: *he pooped out of the race.*
▷HISTORY C14 *poupen* to blow, make a sudden sound, perhaps of imitative origin

poop[3] (puːp) NOUN *US and Canadian slang* **a** information; the facts. **b** *(as modifier): a poop sheet.*
▷HISTORY of unknown origin

poop[4] (puːp) *Informal* ◆ VERB *(intr)* [1] to defecate. ◆ NOUN [2] faeces; excrement.
▷HISTORY perhaps related to POOP[2]

poop deck NOUN *Nautical* the deck on top of the poop.

pooper-scooper NOUN a device used to remove dogs' excrement from public areas.
▷HISTORY C20: POOP[4] + -ER[1] + SCOOPER

Poopó *(Spanish* poo'po) NOUN **Lake.** a lake in SW Bolivia, at an altitude of 3688 m (12 100 ft.): fed by the Desaguadero River. Area: 2540 sq. km (980 sq. miles).

poor (pʊə, pɔː) ADJECTIVE [1] **a** lacking financial or other means of subsistence; needy. **b** *(as collective noun;* preceded by *the): the poor.* [2] characterized by or indicating poverty: *the country had a poor economy.* [3] deficient in amount; scanty or inadequate: *a poor salary.* [4] (when *postpositive,* usually foll by *in)* badly supplied (with resources, materials, etc.): *a region poor in wild flowers.* [5] lacking in quality; inferior. [6] giving no pleasure; disappointing or disagreeable: *a poor play.* [7] *(prenominal)* deserving of pity; unlucky: *poor John is ill again.* [8] **poor man's (something).** a (cheaper) substitute for (something).
▷HISTORY C13: from Old French *povre,* from Latin *pauper;* see PAUPER, POVERTY
▸ **'poorness** NOUN

poor box NOUN a box, esp one in a church, used for the collection of alms or money for the poor.

poorhouse ('pʊəˌhaʊs, 'pɔː-) NOUN (formerly) a publicly maintained institution offering accommodation to the poor.

poor law NOUN *English history* a law providing for the relief or support of the poor from public, esp parish, funds.

poorly ('pʊəlɪ, 'pɔː-) ADVERB [1] in a poor way or manner; badly. ◆ ADJECTIVE [2] *(usually postpositive) Informal* in poor health; rather ill: *she's poorly today.*

poor man's orange NOUN *NZ informal, obsolete* a grapefruit.

poor mouth *Irish* ◆ NOUN [1] unjustified complaining, esp to excite sympathy: *she always has the poor mouth.* ◆ VERB **poor-mouth.** *(tr)* [2] *Informal* to speak of disparagingly; decry.

poor rate NOUN *English history* a rate or tax levied by parishes for the relief or support of the poor.

poor relation NOUN a person or thing considered inferior to another or others: *plastic is a poor relation of real leather.*

poort (pʊət) NOUN (in South Africa) a steep narrow mountain pass, usually following a river or stream.
▷HISTORY C19: from Afrikaans, from Dutch: gateway; see PORT[4]

poortith ('puːrˌtɪθ) NOUN *Scot* a variant of **puirtith.**

poor White NOUN *Often offensive* **a** a poverty-stricken and underprivileged White person, esp in the southern US and South Africa. **b** *(as modifier): poor White trash.*

Pooterish ('puːtərɪʃ) ADJECTIVE characteristic of or resembling the fictional character Pooter, esp in being bourgeois, genteel, or self-important.
▷HISTORY C20: from Charles *Pooter,* the hero of *Diary of a Nobody* (1892), by George and Weedon Grossmith

pootle ('puːtᵊl) VERB *(intr) Brit informal* to travel or go in a relaxed or leisurely manner.
▷HISTORY C20: from *p(oodle)* to travel + (T)OOTLE[2]

poove (puːv) NOUN *Brit derogatory slang* a variant of **poof.**

pop[1] (pɒp) VERB **pops, popping, popped.** [1] to make or cause to make a light sharp explosive sound. [2] to burst open or cause to burst open with such a sound. [3] *(intr; often foll by in, out, etc.) Informal* to come (to) or go (from) rapidly or suddenly; to pay a brief or unexpected visit (to). [4] *(intr)* (esp of the eyes) to protrude: *her eyes popped with amazement.* [5] to shoot or fire at (a target) with a firearm. [6] *(tr)* to place or put with a sudden movement: *she popped some tablets into her mouth.* [7] *(tr) Informal* to pawn: *he popped his watch yesterday.* [8] *(tr) Slang* to take (a drug) in pill form or as an injection: *pill popping.* [9] **pop one's clogs.** See **clog** (sense 9). [10] **pop the question.** *Informal* to propose marriage. ◆ NOUN [11] a light sharp explosive sound; crack. [12] *Informal* a flavoured nonalcoholic carbonated beverage. [13] *Informal* a try; attempt: *have a pop at goal.* [14] *Informal* an instance of criticism: *Townsend has had a pop at modern bands.* [15] **a pop.** *Informal* each: *30 million shares at 7 dollars a pop.* ◆ ADVERB [16] with a popping sound. ◆ INTERJECTION [17] an exclamation denoting a sharp explosive sound. ◆ See also **pop off, pop-up.**
▷HISTORY C14: of imitative origin

pop[2] (pɒp) NOUN [1] **a** music of general appeal, esp among young people, that originated as a distinctive genre in the 1950s. It is generally characterized by a heavy rhythmic element and the use of electrical amplification. **b** *(as modifier): pop music; a pop record; a pop group.* [2] *Informal* a piece of popular or light classical music. ◆ ADJECTIVE [3] *Informal* short for **popular.**

pop[3] (pɒp) NOUN [1] an informal word for **father.** [2] *Informal* a name used in addressing an old or middle-aged man.

POP ABBREVIATION FOR Post Office Preferred (size of envelopes, etc.).

pop. ABBREVIATION FOR: [1] popular. [2] popularly. [3] population.

pop art NOUN a movement in modern art that imitates the methods, styles, and themes of popular culture and mass media, such as comic strips, advertising, and science fiction.

popcorn ('pɒpˌkɔːn) NOUN [1] a variety of maize having hard pointed kernels that puff up when heated. [2] the puffed edible kernels of this plant.
▷HISTORY C19: so called because of the noise the grains make when they swell up and burst on heating

popcorn movie NOUN a film that appeals to a mass audience.

pope[1] (pəʊp) NOUN [1] *(often capital)* the bishop of Rome as head of the Roman Catholic Church. Related adjective: **papal.** [2] *Eastern Orthodox Churches* **a** a title sometimes given to a parish priest. **b** a title sometimes given to the Greek Orthodox patriarch of Alexandria. [3] a person assuming or having a status or authority resembling that of a pope.
▷HISTORY Old English *papa,* from Church Latin: bishop, esp of Rome, from Late Greek *papas* father-in-God, from Greek *pappas* father

pope[2] (pəʊp) NOUN another name for **ruffe** (the fish).

popedom ('pəʊpdəm) NOUN [1] the office or dignity of a pope. [2] the tenure of office of a pope. [3] the dominion of a pope; papal government.

Popemobile ('pəʊpməˌbiːl) NOUN *Informal* a small open-top car used by the Pope to move amongst crowds.
▷HISTORY C20: POPE + -MOBILE

popery ('pəʊpərɪ) NOUN a derogatory name for **Roman Catholicism.**

pope's eye NOUN [1] (in sheep and cows) a gland in the middle of the thigh surrounded by fat. ◆ ADJECTIVE **popeseye.** [2] (in Scotland) denoting a cut of steak.

pope's nose NOUN another name for **parson's nose.**

popette (pɒ'pet) NOUN *Informal* a young female fan or performer of pop music.
▷HISTORY C20: POP[2] + -ETTE (sense 2)

popeyed ('pɒpˌaɪd) ADJECTIVE 1 having bulging prominent eyes. 2 staring in astonishment; amazed.

popgun ('pɒpˌgʌn) NOUN a toy gun that fires a pellet or cork by means of compressed air and makes a popping sound.

popinjay ('pɒpɪnˌdʒeɪ) NOUN 1 a conceited, foppish, or excessively talkative person. 2 an archaic word for **parrot.** 3 the figure of a parrot used as a target.
▷HISTORY C13 *papeniai,* from Old French *papegay* a parrot, from Spanish *papagayo,* from Arabic *babaghā*

popish ('pəʊpɪʃ) ADJECTIVE *Derogatory* belonging to or characteristic of Roman Catholicism.
▸'**popishly** ADVERB

Popish Plot NOUN a supposed conspiracy (1678) to murder Charles II of England and replace him with his Catholic brother James: in reality a fabrication by the informer Titus Oates.

poplar ('pɒplə) NOUN 1 any tree of the salicaceous genus *Populus,* of N temperate regions, having triangular leaves, flowers borne in catkins, and light soft wood. See also **aspen, balsam poplar, Lombardy poplar, white poplar.** 2 any of various trees resembling the true poplars, such as the tulip tree. 3 the wood of any of these trees.
▷HISTORY C14: from Old French *poplier,* from *pouple,* from Latin *pōpulus*

poplin ('pɒplɪn) NOUN **a** a strong fabric, usually of cotton, in plain weave with fine ribbing, used for dresses, children's wear, etc. **b** (*as modifier*): *a poplin shirt.*
▷HISTORY C18: from French *papeline,* perhaps from *Poperinge,* a centre of textile manufacture in Flanders

popliteal (pɒp'lɪtɪəl, ˌpɒplɪ'tiːəl) ADJECTIVE of, relating to, or near the part of the leg behind the knee.
▷HISTORY C18: from New Latin *popliteus* the muscle behind the knee joint, from Latin *poples* the ham of the knee

popmobility (ˌpɒpməʊ'bɪlɪtɪ) NOUN a form of exercise that combines aerobics in a continuous dance routine, performed to pop music.
▷HISTORY C20: POP[2] + MOBILITY

Popocatépetl (ˌpɒpə'kætəpetᵊl, -ˌkætə'pɛtᵊl; *Spanish* popoka'tepetl) NOUN a volcano in SE central Mexico, southeast of Mexico City. Height: 5452 m (17 887 ft.).

pop off VERB (*intr, adverb*) *Informal* 1 to depart suddenly or unexpectedly. 2 to die, esp suddenly or unexpectedly: *he popped off at the age of sixty.* 3 to speak out angrily or indiscreetly: *he popped off at his boss and got fired.*

popover ('pɒpˌəʊvə) NOUN 1 *Brit* an individual Yorkshire pudding, often served with roast beef. 2 *US and Canadian* a light puffy hollow muffin made from a batter mixture. 3 a simple garment for women or girls that is put on by being slipped over the head.

poppadom *or* **poppadum** ('pɒpədəm) NOUN a thin round crisp Indian bread, fried or roasted and served with curry, etc.
▷HISTORY from Hindi

popper ('pɒpə) NOUN 1 a person or thing that pops. 2 *Brit* an informal name for **press stud.** 3 *Chiefly US and Canadian* a container for cooking popcorn in. 4 *Slang* an amyl nitrite capsule, which is crushed and its contents inhaled by drug users as a stimulant.

poppet ('pɒpɪt) NOUN 1 a term of affection for a small child or sweetheart. 2 Also called: **poppet valve.** a mushroom-shaped valve that is lifted from its seating against a spring by applying an axial force to its stem: commonly used as an exhaust or inlet valve in an internal-combustion engine. 3 *Nautical* a temporary supporting brace for a vessel hauled on land or in a dry dock.
▷HISTORY C14: early variant of PUPPET

poppet head NOUN the framework above a mining shaft that supports the winding mechanism.

poppied ('pɒpɪd) ADJECTIVE 1 covered with poppies. 2 of or relating to the effects of poppies, esp in inducing drowsiness or sleep.

popping crease NOUN *Cricket* a line four feet in front of and parallel with the bowling crease, at or behind which the batsman stands.
▷HISTORY C18: from POP[1] (in the obsolete or dialect sense: to hit) + CREASE[1]

popple ('pɒpᵊl) VERB (*intr*) 1 (of boiling water or a choppy sea) to heave or toss; bubble. 2 (often foll by *along*) (of a stream or river) to move with an irregular tumbling motion: *the small rivulet poppled along over rocks and stones for half a mile.*
▷HISTORY C14: of imitative origin; compare Middle Dutch *popelen* to bubble, throb

poppy ('pɒpɪ) NOUN, *plural* **-pies.** 1 any of numerous papaveraceous plants of the temperate genus *Papaver,* having red, orange, or white flowers and a milky sap: see **corn poppy, Iceland poppy, opium poppy.** 2 any of several similar or related plants, such as the California poppy, prickly poppy, horned poppy, and Welsh poppy. 3 *Obsolete* any of the drugs, such as opium, that are obtained from these plants. 4 **a** a strong red to reddish-orange colour. **b** (*as adjective*): *a poppy dress.* 5 a less common name for **poppyhead** (sense 2). 6 an artificial red poppy flower worn to mark Remembrance Sunday.
▷HISTORY Old English *popæg,* ultimately from Latin *papāver*

poppycock ('pɒpɪˌkɒk) NOUN *Informal* senseless chatter; nonsense.
▷HISTORY C19: from Dutch dialect *pappekak,* literally: soft excrement, from *pap* soft + *kak* dung; see PAP[1]

Poppy Day NOUN an informal name for **Remembrance Sunday.**

poppyhead ('pɒpɪˌhed) NOUN 1 the hard dry seed-containing capsule of a poppy. See also **capsule** (sense 3a). 2 a carved ornament, esp one used on the top of the end of a pew or bench in Gothic church architecture.

poppy seed NOUN the small grey seeds of one type of poppy flower, used esp on loaves and as a cake filling.

pop shop NOUN a slang word for a **pawnshop.**

Popsicle ('pɒpsɪkᵊl) NOUN *Trademark US and Canadian* an ice lolly.

popster ('pɒpstə) NOUN *Informal* a pop star.
▷HISTORY C20: POP[2] + -STER

popsy ('pɒpsɪ) NOUN, *plural* **-sies.** *Old-fashioned, Brit slang* an attractive young woman.
▷HISTORY C19: diminutive formed from *pop,* shortened from POPPET; originally a nursery term

populace ('pɒpjʊləs) NOUN (*sometimes functioning as plural*) 1 the inhabitants of an area. 2 the common people; masses.
▷HISTORY C16: via French from Italian *popolaccio* the common herd, from *popolo* people, from Latin *populus*

popular ('pɒpjʊlə) ADJECTIVE 1 appealing to the general public; widely favoured or admired. 2 favoured by an individual or limited group: *I'm not very popular with her.* 3 connected with, representing, or prevailing among the general public; common: *popular discontent.* 4 appealing to or comprehensible to the layman: *a popular lecture on physics.* ◆ NOUN 5 (*usually plural*) cheap newspapers with mass circulation; the popular press. Also shortened to: **pops.**
▷HISTORY C15: from Latin *populāris* belonging to the people, democratic, from *populus* people
▸**popularity** (ˌpɒpjʊ'lærɪtɪ) NOUN

popular etymology NOUN *Linguistics* another name for **folk etymology.**

popular front NOUN (*often capital*) any of the left-wing groups or parties that were organized from 1935 onwards to oppose the spread of fascism.

popularize *or* **popularise** ('pɒpjʊləˌraɪz) VERB (*tr*) 1 to make popular; make attractive to the general public. 2 to make or cause to become easily understandable or acceptable.
▸ˌ**populari'zation** *or* ˌ**populari'sation** NOUN ▸'**popularˌizer** *or* '**popularˌiser** NOUN

popularly ('pɒpjʊləlɪ) ADVERB 1 by the public as a whole; generally or widely. 2 usually; commonly: *his full name is Robert, but he is popularly known as Bob.* 3 in a popular manner.

popular music NOUN music having wide appeal, esp characterized by lightly romantic or sentimental melodies. See also **pop[2].**

popular sovereignty NOUN (in the pre-Civil War US) the doctrine that the inhabitants of a territory should be free from federal interference in determining their own domestic policy, esp in deciding whether or not to allow slavery.

populate ('pɒpjʊˌleɪt) VERB (*tr*) 1 (*often passive*) to live in; inhabit. 2 to provide a population for; colonize or people.
▷HISTORY C16: from Medieval Latin *populāre* to provide with inhabitants, from Latin *populus* people

population (ˌpɒpjʊ'leɪʃən) NOUN 1 (*sometimes functioning as plural*) all the persons inhabiting a country, city, or other specified place. 2 the number of such inhabitants. 3 (*sometimes functioning as plural*) all the people of a particular race or class in a specific area: *the Chinese population of San Francisco.* 4 the act or process of providing a place with inhabitants; colonization. 5 *Ecology* a group of individuals of the same species inhabiting a given area. 6 *Astronomy* either of two main groups of stars classified according to age and location. **Population I** consists of younger metal-rich hot white stars, many occurring in galactic clusters and forming the arms of spiral galaxies. Stars of **population II** are older, the brightest being red giants, and are found in the centre of spiral and elliptical galaxies in globular clusters. 7 Also called: **universe.** *Statistics* the entire finite or infinite aggregate of individuals or items from which samples are drawn.

population control NOUN a policy of attempting to limit the growth in numbers of a population, esp in poor or densely populated parts of the world, by programmes of contraception or sterilization.

population explosion NOUN a rapid increase in the size of a population caused by such factors as a sudden decline in infant mortality or an increase in life expectancy.

population pyramid NOUN a pyramid-shaped diagram illustrating the age distribution of a population: the youngest are represented by a rectangle at the base, the oldest by one at the apex.

populism ('pɒpjʊˌlɪzəm) NOUN a political strategy based on a calculated appeal to the interests or prejudices of ordinary people.

populist ('pɒpjʊlɪst) ADJECTIVE 1 appealing to the interests or prejudices of ordinary people. ◆ NOUN 2 a person, esp a politician, who appeals to the interests or prejudices of ordinary people.

Populist ('pɒpjʊlɪst) NOUN 1 *US history* a member of the People's Party, formed largely by agrarian interests to contest the 1892 presidential election. The movement gradually dissolved after the 1904 election. ◆ ADJECTIVE *also* **Populistic.** 2 of, characteristic of, or relating to the People's Party, the Populists, or any individual or movement with similar aims.
▸'**Populism** NOUN

populist shop steward NOUN a shop steward who operates in a delegate role, putting the immediate interests of his members before union principles and policies.

populous ('pɒpjʊləs) ADJECTIVE containing many inhabitants; abundantly populated.
▷HISTORY C15: from Late Latin *populōsus*
▸'**populously** ADVERB ▸'**populousness** NOUN

pop-up ADJECTIVE 1 (of an appliance) characterized by or having a mechanism that pops up: *a pop-up toaster.* 2 (of a book) having pages that rise when opened to simulate a three-dimensional form. ◆ VERB **pop up.** 3 (*intr, adverb*) to appear suddenly from below. ◆ NOUN 4 *Computing* something that appears over or above the open window on a computer screen.

porangi ('pɔːræŋɪ) ADJECTIVE *NZ informal* crazy; mad.
▷HISTORY Maori

porbeagle ('pɔːˌbiːgᵊl) NOUN any of several voracious sharks of the genus *Lamna, esp L. nasus,* of northern seas: family *Isuridae.* Also called: **mackerel shark.**
▷HISTORY C18: from Cornish *porgh-bugel,* of obscure origin

porcelain ('pɔːslɪn, -leɪn, 'pɔːsə-) NOUN [1] a more or less translucent ceramic material, the principal ingredients being kaolin and petuntse (hard paste) or other clays, ground glassy substances, soapstone, bone ash, etc. [2] an object made of this or such objects collectively. [3] (*modifier*) of, relating to, or made from this material: *a porcelain cup*.
▷HISTORY C16: from French *porcelaine*, from Italian *porcellana* cowrie shell, porcelain (from its shell-like finish), literally: relating to a sow (from the resemblance between a cowrie shell and a sow's vulva), from *porcella* little sow, from *porca* sow, from Latin; see PORK
▸**porcellaneous** (ˌpɔːsə'leɪnɪəs) ADJECTIVE

porcelain clay NOUN another name for **kaolin**.

porch (pɔːtʃ) NOUN [1] a low structure projecting from the doorway of a house and forming a covered entrance. [2] *US and Canadian* an exterior roofed gallery, often partly enclosed; veranda.
▷HISTORY C13: from French *porche*, from Latin *porticus* portico

porcine ('pɔːsaɪn) ADJECTIVE of, connected with, or characteristic of pigs.
▷HISTORY C17: from Latin *porcīnus*, from *porcus* pig

porcino (pɔː'tʃiːnəʊ) NOUN, *plural* **porcini** (pɔː'tʃiːnɪ). an edible saprotrophic basidiomycetous woodland fungus, *Boletus edulis*, with a brown shining cap covering white spore-bearing tubes and having a rich nutty flavour: family *Boletineae*. Also called: **cep**.
▷HISTORY Italian, from Latin *porcīnus*, from *porcus* pig

porcupine ('pɔːkjʊˌpaɪn) NOUN any of various large hystricomorph rodents of the families *Hystricidae*, of Africa, Indonesia, S Europe, and S Asia, and *Erethizontidae*, of the New World. All species have a body covering of protective spines or quills.
▷HISTORY C14 *porc despyne* pig with spines, from Old French *porc espin*; see PORK, SPINE
▸**'porcuˌpinish** ADJECTIVE ▸**'porcuˌpiny** ADJECTIVE

porcupine fish NOUN any of various plectognath fishes of the genus *Diodon* and related genera, of temperate and tropical seas, having a body that is covered with sharp spines and can be inflated into a globe: family *Diodontidae*. Also called: **globefish**.

porcupine grass NOUN *Austral* another name for **spinifex** (sense 2).

porcupine provisions PLURAL NOUN *Finance* provisions, such as poison pills or staggered directorships, made in the bylaws of a company to deter takeover bids. Also called: **shark repellents**.

pore[1] (pɔː) VERB (*intr*) [1] (foll by *over*) to make a close intent examination or study (of a book, map, etc.): *he pored over the documents for several hours*. [2] (foll by *over, on,* or *upon*) to think deeply (about): *he pored on the question of their future*. [3] (foll by *over, on,* or *upon*) *Rare* to look earnestly or intently (at); gaze fixedly (upon).
▷HISTORY C13 *pouren*; perhaps related to PEER[2]

> **Language note** See at **pour**.

pore[2] (pɔː) NOUN [1] *Anatomy, zoology* any small opening in the skin or outer surface of an animal. [2] *Botany* any small aperture, esp that of a stoma through which water vapour and gases pass. [3] any other small hole, such as a space in a rock, soil, etc.
▷HISTORY C14: from Late Latin *porus*, from Greek *poros* passage, pore

porgy ('pɔːgɪ) NOUN, *plural* **-gy** *or* **-gies**. [1] Also called: **pogy**. any of various sparid fishes, many of which occur in American Atlantic waters. See also **scup, sheepshead**. [2] any of various similar or related fishes.
▷HISTORY C18: from Spanish *pargo*, from Latin *phager* type of fish, from Greek *phagros* sea bream

Pori (*Finnish* 'pɔri) NOUN a port in SW Finland, on the Gulf of Bothnia. Pop.: 76 561 (1994). Swedish name: **Björneborg**.

poriferan (pɔː'rɪfərən) NOUN [1] any invertebrate of the phylum *Porifera*, which comprises the sponges. ◆ ADJECTIVE *also* **poriferous**. [2] of, relating to, or belonging to the phylum *Porifera*.
▷HISTORY C19: from New Latin *porifer* bearing pores

poriferous (pɔː'rɪfərəs) ADJECTIVE [1] *Biology* having many pores. [2] another word for **poriferan** (sense 2).

porina (pɒ'raɪnə) NOUN *NZ* **a** the larva of a moth which causes damage to grassland. **b** (*as modifier*): *porina infestation*.
▷HISTORY from New Latin

Porirua (ˌpɔːrɪ'ruːə) NOUN a city in New Zealand, on the North Island just north of Wellington. Pop.: 46 601 (1991).

porism ('pɔːrɪzəm) NOUN a type of mathematical proposition considered by Euclid, the 3rd century B.C. Greek mathematician, the meaning of which is now obscure. It is thought to be a proposition affirming the possibility of finding such conditions as will render a certain problem indeterminate or capable of innumerable solutions.
▷HISTORY C14: from Late Latin *porisma*, from Greek: deduction, from *porizein* to deduce, carry; related to Greek *poros* passage
▸**porismatic** (ˌpɔːrɪz'mætɪk) ADJECTIVE

pork (pɔːk) NOUN the flesh of pigs used as food.
▷HISTORY C13: from Old French *porc*, from Latin *porcus* pig

pork barrel NOUN *Slang, chiefly US* a bill or project requiring considerable government spending in a locality to the benefit of the legislator's constituents who live there.
▷HISTORY C20: term originally applied to the Federal treasury considered as a source of lucrative grants

porker ('pɔːkə) NOUN a pig, esp a young one weighing between 40 and 67 kg, fattened to provide meat such as pork chops.

pork pie NOUN [1] a pie filled with minced seasoned pork. [2] See **porky**[2].

porkpie hat ('pɔːkˌpaɪ) NOUN a hat with a round flat crown and a brim that can be turned up or down.

pork pig NOUN a pig, typically of a lean type, bred and used principally for pork.

pork scratchings PLURAL NOUN small pieces of crisply cooked pork crackling, eaten cold as an appetizer with drinks.

porky[1] ('pɔːkɪ) ADJECTIVE **porkier, porkiest**. [1] belonging to or characteristic of pork: *a porky smell*. [2] *Informal* fat; obese.
▸**'porkiness** NOUN

porky[2] ('pɔːkɪ) NOUN, *plural* **porkies**. *Brit slang* a lie. Also called: **pork pie**.
▷HISTORY from rhyming slang *pork pie* lie

porn (pɔːn) *or* **porno** ('pɔːnəʊ) NOUN, ADJECTIVE *Informal* short for **pornography** or **pornographic**.

pornocracy (pɔː'nɒkrəsɪ) NOUN government or domination of government by whores.
▷HISTORY C19: from Greek, from *pornē* a prostitute, harlot + -CRACY

pornography (pɔː'nɒgrəfɪ) NOUN [1] writings, pictures, films, etc., designed to stimulate sexual excitement. [2] the production of such material. ◆ Sometimes (informal) shortened to: **porn** *or* **porno**.
▷HISTORY C19: from Greek *pornographos* writing of harlots, from *pornē* a harlot + *graphein* to write
▸**por'nographer** NOUN ▸**pornographic** (ˌpɔːnə'græfɪk) ADJECTIVE ▸**ˌporno'graphically** ADVERB

poromeric (ˌpɔːrə'merɪk) ADJECTIVE [1] (of a plastic) permeable to water vapour. ◆ NOUN [2] a substance having this characteristic, esp one based on polyurethane and used in place of leather in making shoe uppers.
▷HISTORY C20: from PORO(SITY) + (POLY)MER + -IC

porosity (pɔː'rɒsɪtɪ) NOUN, *plural* **-ties**. [1] the state or condition of being porous. [2] *Geology* the ratio of the volume of space to the total volume of a rock.
▷HISTORY C14: from Medieval Latin *porōsitās*, from Late Latin *porus* PORE[2]

porous ('pɔːrəs) ADJECTIVE [1] permeable to water, air, or other fluids. [2] *Biology, geology* having pores; poriferous. [3] easy to cross or penetrate: *the porous border into Thailand; the most porous defence in the league*.
▷HISTORY C14: from Medieval Latin *porōsus*, from Late Latin *porus* PORE[2]
▸**'porously** ADVERB ▸**'porousness** NOUN

porphyria (pɔː'fɪrɪə) NOUN a hereditary disease of body metabolism, producing abdominal pain, mental confusion, etc.
▷HISTORY C19: from New Latin, from *porphyrin* a purple substance excreted by patients suffering from this condition, from Greek *porphura* purple

porphyrin ('pɔːfɪrɪn) NOUN any of a group of pigments occurring widely in animal and plant tissues and having a heterocyclic structure formed from four pyrrole rings linked by four methylene groups.
▷HISTORY C20: from Greek *porphura* purple, referring to its colour

porphyritic (ˌpɔːfɪ'rɪtɪk) ADJECTIVE [1] (of rocks) having large crystals in a fine groundmass of minerals. [2] consisting of porphyry.

porphyrogenite (ˌpɔːfə'rɒdʒɪˌnaɪt) NOUN (*sometimes capital*) a prince born after his father has succeeded to the throne.
▷HISTORY C17: via Medieval Latin from Late Greek *porphurogennētos* born in the purple, from Greek *porphuros* purple

porphyroid ('pɔːfɪˌrɔɪd) ADJECTIVE [1] (of metamorphic rocks) having a texture characterized by large crystals set in a finer groundmass. ◆ NOUN [2] a metamorphic rock having this texture.

porphyropsin (ˌpɔːfɪ'rɒpsɪn) NOUN a purple pigment occurring in the retina of the eye of certain freshwater fishes.
▷HISTORY C20: from Greek *porphura* purple + -OPSIS + -IN, on the model of RHODOPSIN

porphyry ('pɔːfɪrɪ) NOUN, *plural* **-ries**. [1] any igneous rock with large crystals embedded in a finer groundmass of minerals. [2] *Obsolete* a reddish-purple rock consisting of large crystals of feldspar in a finer groundmass of feldspar, hornblende, etc.
▷HISTORY C14 *porfurie*, from Late Latin *porphyrītēs*, from Greek *porphuritēs* (*lithos*) purple (stone), from *porphuros* purple

porpoise ('pɔːpəs) NOUN, *plural* **-poises** *or* **-poise**. [1] any of various small cetacean mammals of the genus *Phocaena* and related genera, having a blunt snout and many teeth: family *Delphinidae* (or *Phocaenidae*). [2] (*not in technical use*) any of various related cetaceans, esp the dolphin.
▷HISTORY C14: from French *pourpois*, from Medieval Latin *porcopiscus* (from Latin *porcus* pig + *piscis* fish), replacing Latin *porcus marīnus* sea pig

porrect (pə'rekt) ADJECTIVE *Botany* extended forwards.
▷HISTORY C20: from Latin *porrectus*, from *porrigere* to stretch out

porridge ('pɒrɪdʒ) NOUN [1] a dish made from oatmeal or another cereal, cooked in water or milk to a thick consistency. [2] *Slang* a term in prison (esp in the phrase **do porridge**).
▷HISTORY C16: variant (influenced by Middle English *porray* pottage) of POTTAGE

porringer ('pɒrɪndʒə) NOUN a small dish, often with a handle, for soup, porridge, etc.
▷HISTORY C16: changed from Middle English *potinger, poteger*, from Old French *potager*, from *potage* soup, contents of a pot; see POTTAGE

Porsena ('pɔːsɪnə) *or* **Porsenna** (pɔː'senə) NOUN **Lars** (lɑːz). 6th century B.C., a legendary Etruscan king, alleged to have besieged Rome in a vain attempt to reinstate Tarquinius Superbus on the throne.

port[1] (pɔːt) NOUN [1] a town or place alongside navigable water with facilities for the loading and unloading of ships. [2] See **port of entry**.
▷HISTORY Old English, from Latin *portus* harbour, port

port[2] (pɔːt) NOUN [1] Also called (formerly): **larboard**. **a** the left side of an aircraft or vessel when facing the nose or bow. **b** (*as modifier*): *the port bow*. Compare **starboard** (sense 1). ◆ VERB [2] to turn or be turned towards the port.
▷HISTORY C17: origin uncertain

port[3] (pɔːt) NOUN a sweet fortified dessert wine.
▷HISTORY C17: after *Oporto*, Portugal, from where it came originally

port[4] (pɔːt) NOUN [1] *Nautical* **a** an opening in the side of a ship, fitted with a watertight door, for access to the holds. **b** See **porthole** (sense 1). [2] a small opening in a wall, armoured vehicle, etc., for firing through. [3] an aperture, esp one controlled by a valve, by which fluid enters or leaves the cylinder head of an engine, compressor, etc. [4] *Electronics* a logic circuit for the input and ouput of data. [5] *Chiefly Scot* a gate or portal in a town or fortress.
▷HISTORY Old English, from Latin *porta* gate

port[5] (pɔːt) *Military* ◆ VERB [1] (*tr*) to carry (a rifle, etc.) in a position diagonally across the body with the muzzle near the left shoulder. ◆ NOUN [2] this position.
▷HISTORY C14: from Old French, from *porter* to carry, from Latin *portāre*

port[6] (pɔːt) VERB (*tr*) *Computing* to change (programs) from one system to another.
▷HISTORY C20: probably from PORT[4]

port[7] (pɔːt) NOUN *Austral* (esp in Queensland) a suitcase or school case.
▷HISTORY C20: shortened from PORTMANTEAU

Port. ABBREVIATION FOR: [1] Portugal. [2] Portuguese.

porta (ˈpɔːtə) NOUN *Anatomy* an aperture in an organ, such as the liver, esp one providing an opening for blood vessels.
▷HISTORY C14: from Latin: gate, entrance

portable (ˈpɔːtəbᵊl) ADJECTIVE [1] able to be carried or moved easily, esp by hand. [2] (of software, files, etc.) able to be transferred from one type of computer system to another. [3] *Archaic* able to be endured; bearable. ◆ NOUN [4] an article designed to be readily carried by hand, such as a television, typewriter, etc.
▷HISTORY C14: from Late Latin *portābilis*, from Latin *portāre* to carry
▸ **ˌportaˈbility** NOUN ▸ **ˈportably** ADVERB

Port Adelaide NOUN the chief port of South Australia, near Adelaide on St Vincent Gulf. Pop.: 39 000 (latest est.).

Portadown (ˌpɔːtəˈdaʊn) NOUN a town in S Northern Ireland, in the district of Armagh. Pop.: 21 299 (1991).

portage (ˈpɔːtɪdʒ; *French* pɔrtaʒ) NOUN [1] the act of carrying; transport. [2] the cost of carrying or transporting. [3] the act or process of transporting boats, supplies, etc., overland between navigable waterways. [4] the route overland used for such transport. ◆ VERB [5] to transport (boats, supplies, etc.) overland between navigable waterways.
▷HISTORY C15: from French, from Old French *porter* to carry

Portakabin (ˈpɔːtəˌkæbɪn) NOUN *Trademark* a portable building quickly set up for use as a temporary office, etc.

portal (ˈpɔːtᵊl) NOUN [1] an entrance, gateway, or doorway, esp one that is large and impressive. [2] any entrance or access to a place. ◆ ADJECTIVE [3] *Computing* an Internet site providing links to other sites. [4] *Anatomy* **a** of or relating to a portal vein: *hepatic portal system*. **b** of or relating to a porta.
▷HISTORY C14: via Old French from Medieval Latin *portāle*, from Latin *porta* gate, entrance

portal frame NOUN *Civil engineering, building trades* a frame, usually of steel, consisting of two uprights and a cross beam at the top: the simplest structural unit in a framed building or a doorway.

portal-to-portal ADJECTIVE of or relating to the period between the actual times workers enter and leave their mine, factory, etc.: *portal-to-portal pay*.

portal vein NOUN any vein connecting two capillary networks, esp in the liver (**hepatic portal vein**).

portamento (ˌpɔːtəˈmɛntəʊ) NOUN, *plural* **-ti** (-tɪ). *Music* a smooth slide from one note to another in which intervening notes are not separately discernible. Compare **glissando**.
▷HISTORY C18: from Italian: a carrying, from Latin *portāre* to carry

Port Arthur NOUN [1] a former penal settlement (1833–70) in Australia, on the S coast of the Tasman Peninsula, Tasmania. [2] the former name of **Lüshun**.

portative (ˈpɔːtətɪv) ADJECTIVE [1] a less common word for **portable**. [2] concerned with the act of carrying.
▷HISTORY C14: from French, from Latin *portāre* to carry

portative organ NOUN *Music* a small portable organ with arm-operated bellows popular in medieval times.

Port-au-Prince (ˈpɔːtəʊˈprɪns; *French* pɔrtoprɛ̃s) NOUN the capital and chief port of Haiti, in the south on the Gulf of Gonaïves: founded in 1749 by the French; university (1944). Pop.: 917 112 (1997 est.).

Port Blair (blɛə) NOUN the capital of the Indian Union Territory of the Andaman and Nicobar Islands, a port on the SE coast of South Andaman Island: a former penal colony. Pop.: 74 955 (1991).

portcullis (pɔːtˈkʌlɪs) NOUN an iron or wooden grating suspended vertically in grooves in the gateway of a castle or fortified town and able to be lowered so as to bar the entrance.
▷HISTORY C14 *port colice*, from Old French *porte coleïce* sliding gate, from *porte* door, entrance + *coleïce*, from *couler* to slide, flow, from Late Latin *cōlāre* to filter

Porte (pɔːt) NOUN short for **Sublime Porte**; the court or government of the Ottoman Empire.
▷HISTORY C17: shortened from French *Sublime Porte* High Gate, rendering the Turkish title *Babi Ali*, the imperial gate, which was regarded as the seat of government

porte-cochere (ˌpɔːtkɒˈʃɛə) NOUN [1] a large covered entrance for vehicles leading into a courtyard. [2] a large roof projecting over a drive to shelter travellers entering or leaving vehicles.
▷HISTORY C17: from French: carriage entrance, from *porte* gateway + *coche* coach

Port Elizabeth NOUN a port in S South Africa, on Algoa Bay: motor-vehicle manufacture, fruit canning; resort. Pop. (urban area): 749 921 (1996).

portend (pɔːˈtɛnd) VERB (*tr*) [1] to give warning of; predict or foreshadow. [2] *Obsolete* to indicate or signify; mean.
▷HISTORY C15: from Latin *portendere* to indicate, foretell; related to *prōtendere* to stretch out

portent (ˈpɔːtɛnt) NOUN [1] a sign or indication of a future event, esp a momentous or calamitous one; omen. [2] momentous or ominous significance: *a cry of dire portent*. [3] a miraculous occurrence; marvel.
▷HISTORY C16: from Latin *portentum* sign, omen, from *portendere* to PORTEND

portentous (pɔːˈtɛntəs) ADJECTIVE [1] of momentous or ominous significance. [2] miraculous, amazing, or awe-inspiring; prodigious. [3] self-important or pompous.
▸ **porˈtentously** ADVERB ▸ **porˈtentousness** NOUN

porter[1] (ˈpɔːtə) NOUN [1] a person employed to carry luggage, parcels, supplies, etc., esp at a railway station or hotel. [2] (in hospitals) a person employed to move patients from place to place. [3] *US and Canadian* a railway employee who waits on passengers, esp in a sleeper. [4] *E African* a manual labourer.
▷HISTORY C14: from Old French *portour*, from Late Latin *portātōr*, from Latin *portāre* to carry

porter[2] (ˈpɔːtə) NOUN [1] *Chiefly Brit* a person in charge of a gate or door; doorman or gatekeeper. [2] a person employed by a university or college as a caretaker and doorkeeper who also answers enquiries. [3] a person in charge of the maintenance of a building, esp a block of flats. [4] Also called: **ostiary**. *RC Church* a person ordained to what was formerly the lowest in rank of the minor orders.
▷HISTORY C13: from Old French *portier*, from Late Latin *portārius* doorkeeper, from Latin *porta* door

porter[3] (ˈpɔːtə) NOUN *Brit* a dark sweet ale brewed from black malt.
▷HISTORY C18: shortened from *porter's ale*, apparently because it was a favourite beverage of porters

porterage (ˈpɔːtərɪdʒ) NOUN [1] the work of carrying supplies, goods, etc., done by porters. [2] the charge made for this.

portered (ˈpɔːtəd) ADJECTIVE (of an apartment block) serviced by a caretaker.

porterhouse (ˈpɔːtəˌhaʊs) NOUN [1] Also called: **porterhouse steak**. a thick choice steak of beef cut from the middle ribs or sirloin. [2] (formerly) a place in which porter, beer, etc., and sometimes chops and steaks, were served.
▷HISTORY C19 (sense 1): said to be named after a porterhouse or chophouse in New York

portfire (ˈpɔːtˌfaɪə) NOUN (formerly) a slow-burning fuse used for firing rockets and fireworks and, in mining, for igniting explosives.
▷HISTORY C17: from French *porte-feu*, from *porter* to carry + *feu* fire

portfolio (pɔːtˈfəʊlɪəʊ) NOUN, *plural* **-os**. [1] a flat case, esp of leather, used for carrying maps, drawings, etc. [2] the contents of such a case, such as drawings, paintings, or photographs, that demonstrate recent work: *an art student's portfolio*. [3] such a case used for carrying ministerial or state papers. [4] the responsibilities or role of the head of a government department: *the portfolio for foreign affairs*. [5] **Minister without portfolio**. a cabinet minister who is not responsible for any government department. [6] the complete investments held by an individual investor or by a financial organization.
▷HISTORY C18: from Italian *portafoglio*, from *portāre* to carry + *foglio* leaf, paper, from Latin *folium* leaf

portfolio employment NOUN the practice of working for several employers simultaneously rather than working full-time for a single employer.

portfolio worker NOUN a person in portfolio employment.

Port-Gentil (*French* pɔrʒɑ̃ti) NOUN the chief port of Gabon, in the west near the mouth of the Ogooué River: oil refinery. Pop.: 80 841 (1993).

Port Harcourt (ˈhɑːkət, -kɔːt) NOUN a port in S Nigeria, capital of Rivers state on the Niger delta: the nation's second largest port; industrial centre. Pop.: 410 000 (1996 est.).

porthole (ˈpɔːtˌhəʊl) NOUN [1] a small aperture in the side of a vessel to admit light and air, usually fitted with a watertight glass or metal cover, or both. Sometimes shortened to: **port**. [2] an opening in a wall or parapet through which a gun can be fired; embrasure.

portico (ˈpɔːtɪkəʊ) NOUN, *plural* **-coes** *or* **-cos**. [1] a covered entrance to a building; porch. [2] a covered walkway in the form of a roof supported by columns or pillars, esp one built on to the exterior of a building.
▷HISTORY C17: via Italian from Latin *porticus* PORCH

portière (ˌpɔːtɪˈɛə; *French* pɔrtjɛr) NOUN a curtain hung in a doorway.
▷HISTORY C19: via French from Medieval Latin *portāria*, from Latin *porta* door
▸ **ˌportiˈèred** ADJECTIVE

Porţile de Fier (pɔrˈtsiːlɛ dɛ ˈfjɛr) NOUN the Romanian name for the **Iron Gate**.

portion (ˈpɔːʃən) NOUN [1] a part of a whole; fraction. [2] a part allotted or belonging to a person or group. [3] an amount of food served to one person; helping. [4] *Law* **a** a share of property, esp one coming to a child from the estate of his parents. **b** the property given by a woman to her husband at marriage; dowry. [5] a person's lot or destiny. ◆ VERB (*tr*) [6] to divide up; share out. [7] to give a share to (a person); assign or allocate. [8] *Law* to give a dowry or portion to (a person); endow.
▷HISTORY C13: via Old French from Latin *portiō* portion, allocation; related to *pars* PART
▸ **ˈportionless** ADJECTIVE

Port Jackson NOUN an inlet of the Pacific on the coast of SE Australia, forming a fine natural harbour: site of the city of Sydney, spanned by Sydney Harbour Bridge.

Port Jackson willow *or* **wattle** NOUN an Australian acacia tree, *Acacia cyanophylla*, introduced in the 19th century into South Africa, where it is now regarded as a pest.

Portland (ˈpɔːtlənd) NOUN [1] **Isle of**. a rugged limestone peninsula in SW England, in Dorset, connected to the mainland by a narrow isthmus and by Chesil Bank: the lighthouse of **Portland Bill** lies at the S tip; famous for the quarrying of **Portland stone**, a fine building material. Pop. (town): 12 000 (latest est.). [2] an inland port in NW Oregon, on the Willamette River: the largest city in the state; shipbuilding and chemical industries. Pop.: 529 121 (2000). [3] a port in SW Maine, on Casco Bay: the largest city in the state; settled by the English in 1632, destroyed successively by French, Indian, and British attacks, and rebuilt; capital of Maine (1820–32). Pop.: 64 358 (1990).

Portland cement NOUN a cement that hardens under water and is made by heating a slurry of clay and crushed chalk or limestone to clinker in a kiln.
▷HISTORY C19: named after the Isle of PORTLAND, because its colour resembles that of the stone quarried there

Portlaoise (ˌpɔːtˈliːʃə) NOUN a town in central Republic of Ireland, county town of Laois: site of a top-security prison. Pop.: 9500 (1990 est.).

Port Louis (ˈluːɪs, ˈluːɪ) NOUN the capital and chief

port of Mauritius, on the NW coast on the Indian Ocean. Pop.: 147 648 (1999 est.).

portly ('pɔːtlɪ) ADJECTIVE **-lier, -liest.** 1 stout or corpulent. 2 *Archaic* stately; impressive.
▷HISTORY C16: from PORT⁵ (in the sense: deportment, bearing)
▸ **'portliness** NOUN

Port Lyautey (ljəʊ'teɪ) NOUN the former name (1932–56) of **Mina Hassan Tani.**

portmanteau (pɔːt'mæntəʊ) NOUN, *plural* **-teaus** *or* **-teaux** (-təʊz). 1 (formerly) a large travelling case made of stiff leather, esp one hinged at the back so as to open out into two compartments. 2 (*modifier*) embodying several uses or qualities: *the heroine is a portmanteau figure of all the virtues.*
▷HISTORY C16: from French: cloak carrier, from *porter* to carry + *manteau* cloak, MANTLE

portmanteau word NOUN another name for **blend** (sense 7).
▷HISTORY C19: from the idea that two meanings are packed into one word

Port Moresby ('mɔːzbɪ) NOUN the capital and chief port of Papua New Guinea, on the SE coast on the Gulf of Papua: important Allied base in World War II. Pop. (urban area): 298 145 (1999 est.).

Portnet ('pɔːtnet) NOUN *South African* the South African Port Authority.

Port Nicholson NOUN 1 the first British settlement in New Zealand, established on Wellington Harbour in 1840: grew into Wellington. 2 the former name for Wellington Harbour.
▷HISTORY C19: named after Capt. John *Nicholson,* Australian naval officer

Pôrto ('portu) NOUN the Portuguese name for **Oporto.**

Pôrto Alegre (*Portuguese* 'portu a'lɛgri) NOUN a port in S Brazil, capital of the Rio Grande do Sul state: the country's chief inland port; the chief commercial centre of S Brazil, with two universities (1936 and 1948). Pop.: 1 320 000 (2000), with a conurbation of 3 349 000 (1995).

Portobello (ˌpɔːtəʊ'bɛləʊ) NOUN a small port in Panama, on the Caribbean northeast of Colón: the most important port in South America in colonial times; declined with the opening of the Panama Canal. Pop.: 3026 (1990 est.).

port of call NOUN 1 any port where a ship stops, excluding its home port. 2 any place visited on a traveller's itinerary.

port of entry NOUN *Law* an airport, harbour, etc., where customs officials are stationed to supervise the entry into and exit from a country of persons and merchandise.

Port of Spain NOUN the capital and chief port of Trinidad and Tobago, on the W coast of Trinidad. Pop.: 43 396 (1996 est.).

Porto Novo ('pɔːtəʊ 'nəʊvəʊ) NOUN the capital of Benin, in the southwest on a coastal lagoon: formerly a centre of Portuguese settlement and the slave trade. Pop.: 200 000 (1994 est.).

Porto Rican ('pɔːtə 'riːkən) ADJECTIVE, NOUN a former name for **Puerto Rican.**

Porto Rico ('pɔːtə 'riːkəʊ) NOUN the former name (until 1932) of **Puerto Rico.**

Pôrto Velho (*Portuguese* 'portu 'vɛʎu) NOUN a city in W Brazil, capital of the federal territory of Rondônia on the Madeira River. Pop.: 273 496 (2000).

Port Phillip Bay *or* **Port Phillip** NOUN a bay in SE Australia, which forms the harbour of Melbourne.

portrait ('pɔːtrɪt, -treɪt) NOUN 1 **a** a painting, drawing, sculpture, photograph, or other likeness of an individual, esp of the face. **b** (*as modifier*): *a portrait gallery.* 2 a verbal description or picture, esp of a person's character. ◆ ADJECTIVE 3 *Printing* (of a publication or an illustration in a publication) of greater height than width. Compare **landscape** (sense 5a).

portraitist ('pɔːtrɪtɪst, -treɪ-) NOUN an artist, photographer, etc., who specializes in portraits.

portraiture ('pɔːtrɪtʃə) NOUN 1 the practice or art of making portraits. 2 **a** another term for **portrait** (sense 1). **b** portraits collectively. 3 a verbal description.

portray (pɔː'treɪ) VERB (*tr*) 1 to represent in a painting, drawing, sculpture, etc.; make a portrait of. 2 to make a verbal picture of; depict in words. 3 to play the part of (a character) in a play or film.
▷HISTORY C14: from Old French *portraire* to depict, from Latin *prōtrahere* to drag forth, bring to light, from PRO-¹ + *trahere* to drag
▸ **por'trayable** ADJECTIVE ▸ **por'trayal** NOUN ▸ **por'trayer** NOUN

portress ('pɔːtrɪs) NOUN a female porter, esp a doorkeeper.

Port Royal NOUN 1 a fortified town in SE Jamaica, at the entrance to Kingston harbour: capital of Jamaica in colonial times. 2 the former name (until 1710) of **Annapolis Royal.** 3 (*French* pɔr rwajal) an educational institution about 27 km (17 miles) west of Paris that flourished from 1638 to 1704, when it was suppressed by papal bull as it had become a centre of Jansenism. Its teachers were noted esp for their work on linguistics: their *Grammaire générale et raisonnée* exercised much influence.

Port Said ('sɑːiːd, saɪd) NOUN a port in NE Egypt, at the N end of the Suez Canal: founded in 1859 when the Suez Canal was begun; became the largest coaling station in the world and later an oil-bunkering port; damaged in the Arab-Israeli wars of 1967 and 1973. Pop.: 469 533 (1996).

Port-Salut ('pɔː sə'luː; *French* pɔrsaly) NOUN a mild semihard whole-milk cheese of a round flat shape. Also called: **Port du Salut.**
▷HISTORY C19: named after the Trappist monastery at *Port du Salut* in NW France where it was first made

Portsmouth ('pɔːtsməθ) NOUN 1 a port in S England, in Portsmouth unitary authority, Hampshire, on the English Channel: Britain's chief naval base; university (1992). Pop.: 174 690 (1991). Informal name: **Pompey.** 2 a unitary authority in S England, in Hampshire. Pop.: 186 704 (2001). Area: 37 sq. km (14 sq. miles). 3 a port in SE Virginia, on the Elizabeth River: naval base; shipyards. Pop.: 100 565 (2000).

Port Sudan NOUN the chief port of the Sudan, in the NE on the Red Sea. Pop.: 305 385 (1993).

Port Talbot ('tɔːlbət, 'tæl-) NOUN a port in SE Wales, in Neath Port Talbot county borough on Swansea Bay: established as a coal port in the mid-19th century; large steelworks; ore terminal. Pop.: 37 647 (1991).

Portugal ('pɔːtjugᵊl) NOUN a republic in SW Europe, on the Atlantic: became an independent monarchy in 1139 and expelled the Moors in 1249 after more than four centuries of Muslim rule; became a republic in 1910; under the dictatorship of Salazar from 1932 until 1968, when he was succeeded by Dr Caetano, who was overthrown by a junta in 1974; constitutional government restored in 1976. Portugal is a member of the European Union. Official language: Portuguese. Religion: Roman Catholic majority. Currency: euro. Capital: Lisbon. Pop.: 10 328 000 (2001 est.). Area: 91 831 sq. km (35 456 sq. miles).

Portuguese (ˌpɔːtju'giːz) NOUN 1 the official language of Portugal, its overseas territories, and Brazil: the native language of approximately 110 million people. It belongs to the Romance group of the Indo-European family and is derived from the Galician dialect of Vulgar Latin. 2 (*plural* **-guese**) a native, citizen, or inhabitant of Portugal. ◆ ADJECTIVE 3 relating to, denoting, or characteristic of Portugal, its inhabitants, or their language.

Portuguese East Africa NOUN a former name (until 1975) of **Mozambique.**

Portuguese Guinea NOUN the former name (until 1974) of **Guinea-Bissau.**

Portuguese Guinean ADJECTIVE 1 of or relating to Portuguese Guinea, a former name for Guinea-Bissau, or its inhabitants. ◆ NOUN 2 a native or inhabitant of Portuguese Guinea.

Portuguese India NOUN a former Portuguese overseas province on the W coast of India, consisting of Goa, Daman, and Diu: established between 1505 and 1510; annexed by India in 1961.

Portuguese man-of-war NOUN any of several large complex colonial hydrozoans of the genus *Physalia, esp P. physalis,* having an aerial float and long stinging tentacles: order *Siphonophora.* Sometimes shortened to: **man-of-war.**

Portuguese water dog NOUN a robust dog of a Portuguese breed that has a wavy coat, often with the hindquarters and tail clipped, and is an excellent swimmer and diver.

Portuguese Timor NOUN a former name for **East Timor.**

Portuguese West Africa NOUN a former name (until 1975) of **Angola.**

portulaca (ˌpɔːtju'lækə, -'leɪkə) NOUN any portulacaceous plant of the genus *Portulaca,* such as rose moss and purslane, of tropical and subtropical America, having yellow, pink, or purple showy flowers.
▷HISTORY C16: from Latin: PURSLANE

portulacaceous (ˌpɔːtjʊlə'keɪʃəs) ADJECTIVE of, relating to, or belonging to the *Portulacaceae,* a cosmopolitan family of mainly fleshy-leaved flowering plants common in the US.

port wine stain NOUN a type of haemangioma, seen as a purplish birthmark, often large and on the face or neck.

POS ABBREVIATION FOR: 1 polycystic ovary syndrome. 2 **point of sale.** 3 **part of speech.**

pos. ABBREVIATION FOR: 1 position. 2 positive.

posada *Spanish* (po'saða) NOUN, *plural* **-das** (-ðas). an inn in a Spanish-speaking country.
▷HISTORY literally: place for stopping

pose¹ (pəʊz) VERB 1 to assume or cause to assume a physical attitude, as for a photograph or painting. 2 (*intr; often foll by* as) to pretend to be or present oneself (as something one is not). 3 (*intr*) to affect an attitude or play a part in order to impress others. 4 (*tr*) to put forward, ask, or assert: *to pose a question.* ◆ NOUN 5 a physical attitude, esp one deliberately adopted for or represented by an artist or photographer. 6 a mode of behaviour that is adopted for effect.
▷HISTORY C14: from Old French *poser* to set in place, from Late Latin *pausāre* to cease, put down (influenced by Latin *pōnere* to place)

pose² (pəʊz) VERB (*tr*) 1 *Rare* to puzzle or baffle. 2 *Archaic* to question closely.
▷HISTORY C16: from obsolete *appose,* from Latin *appōnere* to put to, set against; see OPPOSE

Poseidon (pɒ'saɪdᵊn) NOUN 1 *Greek myth* the god of the sea and of earthquakes; brother of Zeus, Hades, and Hera. He is generally depicted in art wielding a trident. Roman counterpart: **Neptune.** 2 a US submarine-launched ballistic missile.

Posen ('poːzən) NOUN the German name for **Poznań.**

poser¹ ('pəʊzə) NOUN 1 a person who poses. 2 *Informal* a person who likes to be seen in trendsetting clothes in fashionable bars, discos, etc.

poser² ('pəʊzə) NOUN a baffling or insoluble question.

poseur (pəʊ'zɜː) NOUN a person who strikes an attitude or assumes a pose in order to impress others.
▷HISTORY C19: from French, from *poser* to POSE¹

posey ('pəʊzɪ) *or* **poserish** ('pəʊzərɪʃ) ADJECTIVE *Informal* (of a place) for, characteristic of, or full of posers; affectedly trendy.

posh (pɒʃ) *Informal, chiefly Brit* ◆ ADJECTIVE 1 smart, elegant, or fashionable; exclusive: *posh clothes.* 2 upper-class or genteel. ◆ ADVERB 3 in a manner associated with the upper class: *to talk posh.*
▷HISTORY C19: often said to be an acronym of the phrase *port out, starboard home,* the most desirable location for a cabin in British ships sailing to and from the East, being the north-facing or shaded side; but more likely to be a development of obsolete slang *posh* a dandy

posho ('pɒʃɔ) NOUN *E African* 1 corn meal. 2 payment of workers in foodstuffs rather than money.
▷HISTORY from Swahili

posit ('pɒzɪt) VERB (*tr*) 1 to assume or put forward as fact or the factual basis for an argument; postulate. 2 to put in position. ◆ NOUN 3 a fact, idea, etc., that is posited; assumption.
▷HISTORY C17: from Latin *pōnere* to place, position

positif ('pɒsɪtɪf) NOUN (on older organs) a manual controlling soft stops.
▷HISTORY from French: positive

position (pə'zɪʃən) NOUN 1 the place, situation,

or location of a person or thing: *he took up a position to the rear.* [2] the appropriate or customary location: *the telescope is in position for use.* [3] the arrangement or disposition of the body or a part of the body: *the corpse was found in a sitting position.* [4] the manner in which a person or thing is placed; arrangement. [5] *Military* an area or point occupied for tactical reasons. [6] mental attitude; point of view; stand: *what's your position on this issue?* [7] social status or standing, esp high social standing. [8] a post of employment; job. [9] the act of positing a fact or viewpoint. [10] something posited, such as an idea, proposition, etc. [11] *Sport* the part of a field or playing area where a player is placed or where he generally operates. [12] *Music* **a** the vertical spacing or layout of the written notes in a chord. Chords arranged with the three upper voices close together are in **close position**. Chords whose notes are evenly or widely distributed are in **open position**. See also **root position**. **b** one of the points on the fingerboard of a stringed instrument, determining where a string is to be stopped. [13] (in classical prosody) **a** the situation in which a short vowel may be regarded as long, that is, when it occurs before two or more consonants. **b make position**. (of a consonant, either on its own or in combination with other consonants, such as x in Latin) to cause a short vowel to become metrically long when placed after it. [14] *Finance* the market commitment of a dealer in securities, currencies, or commodities: *a long position; a short position.* [15] **in a position**. (foll by an infinitive) able (to): *I'm not in a position to reveal these figures.* ◆ VERB (*tr*) [16] to put in the proper or appropriate place; locate. [17] *Sport* to place (oneself or another player) in a particular part of the field or playing area. [18] to put (someone or something) in a position (esp in relation to others) that confers a strategic advantage: *he's trying to position himself for a leadership bid.* [19] *Marketing* to promote (a product or service) by tailoring it to the needs of a specific market or by clearly differentiating it from its competitors (e.g. in terms of price or quality). [20] *Rare* to locate or ascertain the position of.
▷HISTORY C15: from Late Latin *positiō* a positioning, affirmation, from *pōnere* to place, lay down
▸**po'sitional** ADJECTIVE

positional notation NOUN the method of denoting numbers by the use of a finite number of digits, each digit having its value multiplied by its place value, as in 936 = (9 × 100) + (3 × 10) + 6.

position angle NOUN the direction in which one object lies relative to another on the celestial sphere, measured in degrees from north in an easterly direction.

position audit NOUN *Commerce* a systematic assessment of the current strengths and weaknesses of an organization as a prerequisite for future strategic planning.

position effect NOUN the effect on the phenotype of interacting genes when their relative positions on the chromosome are altered, as by inversion.

positioning (pə'zɪʃᵊnɪŋ) NOUN the position held by a product brand in the opinion of consumers, in comparison with its competitors' brands.

positive ('pɒzɪtɪv) ADJECTIVE [1] characterized by or expressing certainty or affirmation: *a positive answer.* [2] composed of or possessing actual or specific qualities; real: *a positive benefit.* [3] tending to emphasize what is good or laudable; constructive: *he takes a very positive attitude when correcting pupils' mistakes.* [4] tending towards progress or improvement; moving in a beneficial direction. [5] *Philosophy* **a** constructive rather than sceptical. **b** (of a concept) denoting the presence rather than the absence of some property. [6] independent of circumstances; absolute or unqualified. [7] (*prenominal*) *Informal* (intensifier): *a positive delight.* [8] *Maths* **a** having a value greater than zero: *a positive number.* **b** designating, consisting of, or graduated in one or more quantities greater than zero: *positive direction.* [9] *Maths* **a** measured in a direction opposite to that regarded as negative. **b** having the same magnitude as but opposite sense to an equivalent negative quantity. [10] *Grammar* denoting the usual form of an adjective as opposed to its comparative or superlative form. [11] *Biology* indicating movement or growth towards a particular stimulus. [12] *Physics* **a** (of an electric charge) having an opposite polarity to the charge of an electron and the same polarity as the charge of a proton. **b** (of a body, system, ion, etc.) having a positive electric charge; having a deficiency of electrons: *a positive ion.* **c** (of a point in an electric circuit) having a higher electric potential than some other point with an assigned zero potential. [13] short for **electropositive.** [14] (of a lens) capable of causing convergence of a parallel beam of light. [15] *Med* (of the results of an examination or test) indicating the existence or presence of a suspected disorder or pathogenic organism. [16] *Med* (of the effect of a drug or therapeutic regimen) beneficial or satisfactory. [17] short for **Rh positive.** [18] (of a machine part) having precise motion with no hysteresis or backlash. [19] *Chiefly US* (of a government) directly involved in activities beyond the minimum maintenance of law and order, such as social welfare or the organization of scientific research. [20] *Economics* of or denoting an analysis that is free of ethical, political, or value judgments. [21] *Astrology* of, relating to, or governed by the group of signs of the zodiac that belong to the air and fire classifications, which are associated with a self-expressive spontaneous nature. ◆ NOUN [22] something that is positive. [23] *Maths* a quantity greater than zero. [24] *Photog* a print or slide showing a photographic image whose colours or tones correspond to those of the original subject. [25] *Grammar* the positive degree of an adjective or adverb. [26] a positive object, such as a terminal or plate in a voltaic cell. [27] *Music* **a** Also called: **positive organ.** a medieval nonportable organ with one manual and no pedals. Compare **portative organ. b** a variant spelling of **positif.** ◆ Compare **negative.**
▷HISTORY C13: from Late Latin *positīvus* positive, agreed on an arbitrary basis, from *pōnere* to place
▸**'positiveness** *or* **,posi'tivity** NOUN

positive discrimination *or* **action** NOUN the provision of special opportunities in employment, training, etc. for a disadvantaged group, such as women, ethnic minorities, etc. US equivalent: **affirmative action.**

positive feedback NOUN See **feedback** (sense 1).

positively ('pɒzɪtɪvlɪ) ADVERB [1] in a positive manner. [2] (intensifier): *he disliked her: in fact, he positively hated her.* ◆ SENTENCE SUBSTITUTE [3] unquestionably; absolutely.

positive polarity NOUN *Grammar* the grammatical characteristic of a word or phrase, such as *delicious* or *rather,* that may normally only be used in a semantically or syntactically positive or affirmative context.

positive vetting NOUN the checking of a person's background, political affiliation, etc., to assess his suitability for a position that may involve national security.

positivism ('pɒzɪtɪ,vɪzəm) NOUN [1] a strong form of empiricism, esp as established in the philosophical system of Auguste Comte, the French mathematician and philosopher (1798–1857), that rejects metaphysics and theology as seeking knowledge beyond the scope of experience, and holds that experimental investigation and observation are the only sources of substantial knowledge. See also **logical positivism.** [2] Also called: **legal positivism.** the jurisprudential doctrine that the legitimacy of a law depends on its being enacted in proper form, rather than on its content. Compare **natural law** (sense 3). [3] the quality of being definite, certain, etc.
▸**'positivist** NOUN, ADJECTIVE ▸**,positiv'istic** ADJECTIVE
▸**,positiv'istically** ADVERB

positron ('pɒzɪ,trɒn) NOUN *Physics* the antiparticle of the electron, having the same mass but an equal and opposite charge. It is produced in certain decay processes and in pair production, annihilation occurring when it collides with an electron.
▷HISTORY C20: from *posi(tive + elec)tron*

positron emission tomography NOUN a technique for assessing brain activity and function by recording the emission of positrons from radioactively labelled substances, such as glucose or dopamine.

positronium (,pɒzɪ'trəʊnɪəm) NOUN *Physics* a short-lived entity consisting of a positron and an electron bound together. It decays by annihilation to produce two or three photons.
▷HISTORY C20: from POSITRON + -IUM

posology (pə'sɒlədʒɪ) NOUN the branch of medicine concerned with the determination of appropriate doses of drugs or agents.
▷HISTORY C19: from French *posologie,* from Greek *posos* how much
▸**posological** (,pɒsə'lɒdʒɪkᵊl) ADJECTIVE

poss (pɒs) VERB (*tr*) to wash (clothes) by agitating them with a long rod, pole, etc.
▷HISTORY of uncertain origin

poss. ABBREVIATION FOR: [1] possession. [2] possessive. [3] possible. [4] possibly.

posse ('pɒsɪ) NOUN [1] *US* short for **posse comitatus**, the able-bodied men of a district assembled together and forming a group upon whom the sheriff may call for assistance in maintaining law and order. [2] *Law* possibility (esp in the phrase **in posse**). [3] *Slang* a Jamaican street gang in the US. [4] *Informal* a group of friends or associates.
▷HISTORY C16: from Medieval Latin (n): power, strength, from Latin (vb): to be able, have power

posse comitatus (,kɒmɪ'tɑːtəs) NOUN the formal legal term for **posse** (sense 1).
▷HISTORY Medieval Latin: strength (manpower) of the county

posser ('pɒsə) NOUN a short stick used for stirring clothes in a washtub.

possess (pə'zɛs) VERB (*tr*) [1] to have as one's property; own. [2] to have as a quality, faculty, characteristic, etc.: *to possess good eyesight.* [3] to have knowledge or mastery of: *to possess a little French.* [4] to gain control over or dominate: *whatever possessed you to act so foolishly?* [5] (foll by *of*) to cause to be the owner or possessor: *I am possessed of the necessary information.* [6] (often foll by *with*) to cause to be influenced or dominated (by): *the news possessed him with anger.* [7] to have sexual intercourse with. [8] *Now rare* to keep control over or maintain (oneself or one's feelings) in a certain state or condition: *possess yourself in patience until I tell you the news.* [9] *Archaic* to gain or seize.
▷HISTORY C15: from Old French *possesser,* from Latin *possidēre* to own, occupy; related to Latin *sedēre* to sit
▸**pos'sessor** NOUN

possessed (pə'zɛst) ADJECTIVE [1] (foll by *of*) owning or having. [2] (*usually postpositive*) under the influence of a powerful force, such as a spirit or strong emotion. [3] a less common word for **self-possessed.**

possession (pə'zɛʃən) NOUN [1] the act of possessing or state of being possessed: *in possession of the crown.* [2] anything that is owned or possessed. [3] (*plural*) wealth or property. [4] the state of being controlled or dominated by or as if by evil spirits. [5] the physical control or occupancy of land, property, etc., whether or not accompanied by ownership: *to take possession of a house.* [6] a territory subject to a foreign state or to a sovereign prince: *colonial possessions.* [7] *Sport* control of the ball, puck, etc., as exercised by a player or team: *he got possession in his own half.*

possession order NOUN (in Britain) a court order that entitles a landlord legally to evict a tenant or squatter and regain possession of the property.

possessive (pə'zɛsɪv) ADJECTIVE [1] of or relating to possession or ownership. [2] having or showing an excessive desire to possess, control, or dominate: *a possessive mother.* [3] *Grammar* **a** another word for **genitive** (sense 1). **b** denoting an inflected form of a noun or pronoun used to convey the idea of possession, association, etc., as *my* or *Harry's.* ◆ NOUN [4] *Grammar* **a** the possessive case. **b** a word or speech element in the possessive case.
▸**pos'sessively** ADVERB ▸**pos'sessiveness** NOUN

possessory (pə'zɛsərɪ) ADJECTIVE [1] of, relating to, or having possession. [2] *Law* arising out of, depending upon, or concerned with possession: *a possessory title.*

posset ('pɒsɪt) NOUN a drink of hot milk curdled with ale, beer, etc., flavoured with spices, formerly used as a remedy for colds.
▷HISTORY C15 *poshoote,* of unknown origin

possibility (,pɒsɪ'bɪlɪtɪ) NOUN, *plural* **-ties.** [1] the state or condition of being possible. [2] anything that is possible. 3 a competitor, candidate, etc., who has a moderately good chance of winning, being chosen, etc. 4 (*often plural*) a future prospect or potential: *my new house has great possibilities.*

possible ('pɒsɪbᵊl) ADJECTIVE 1 capable of existing, taking place, or proving true without contravention of any natural law. 2 capable of being achieved: *it is not possible to finish in three weeks.* 3 having potential or capabilities for favourable use or development: *the idea is a possible money-spinner.* 4 that may or may not happen or have happened; feasible but less than probable: *it is possible that man will live on Mars.* 5 *Logic* (of a statement, formula, etc.) capable of being true under some interpretation, or in some circumstances. Usual symbol: *Mp* or ◇*p*, where *p* is the given expression. ◆ NOUN 6 another word for **possibility** (sense 3).
▷HISTORY C14: from Latin *possibilis* that may be, from *posse* to be able, have power

> **Language note** Although it is very common to talk about something being *very possible* or *more possible,* these uses are generally thought to be incorrect, since *possible* describes an absolute state, and therefore something can only be *possible* or *not possible: it is very likely* (not *very possible*) *that he will resign; it has now become easier* (not *more possible*) *to obtain an entry visa.*

possible world NOUN *Logic* (in modal logic) a semantic device formalizing the notion of what the world might have been like. A statement is necessarily true if and only if it is true in every possible world.

possibly ('pɒsɪblɪ) SENTENCE SUBSTITUTE, ADVERB 1 **a** perhaps or maybe. **b** (*as sentence modifier*): *possibly he'll come.* ◆ ADVERB 2 by any chance; at all: *he can't possibly come.*

possie *or* **pozzy** ('pɒzɪ) NOUN *Austral and NZ informal* a place; position: *if we're early for the film we'll get a good possie at the back.*

possum ('pɒsəm) NOUN 1 an informal name for **opossum** (sense 1). 2 an Austral and NZ name for **phalanger.** 3 **play possum.** to pretend to be dead, ignorant, asleep, etc., in order to deceive an opponent.

post¹ (pəʊst) NOUN 1 a length of wood, metal, etc., fixed upright in the ground to serve as a support, marker, point of attachment, etc. 2 *Horse racing* **a** either of two upright poles marking the beginning (**starting post**) and end (**winning post**) of a racecourse. **b** the finish of a horse race. 3 any of the main upright supports of a piece of furniture, such as a four-poster bed. ◆ VERB (*tr*) 4 (sometimes foll by *up*) to fasten or put up (a notice) in a public place. 5 to announce by means of or as if by means of a poster: *to post banns.* 6 to publish (a name) on a list.
▷HISTORY Old English, from Latin *postis;* related to Old High German *first* ridgepole, Greek *pastas* colonnade

post² (pəʊst) NOUN 1 a position to which a person is appointed or elected; appointment; job. 2 a position or station to which a person, such as a sentry, is assigned for duty. 3 a permanent military establishment. 4 *Brit* either of two military bugle calls (**first post** and **last post**) ordering or giving notice of the time to retire for the night. 5 See **trading post** (senses 1, 2). ◆ VERB 6 (*tr*) to assign to or station at a particular place or position. 7 *Chiefly Brit* to transfer to a different unit or ship on taking up a new appointment, etc.
▷HISTORY C16: from French *poste,* from Italian *posto,* ultimately from Latin *pōnere* to place

post³ (pəʊst) NOUN 1 *Chiefly Brit* letters, packages, etc., that are transported and delivered by the Post Office; mail. 2 *Chiefly Brit* a single collection or delivery of mail. 3 *Brit* an official system of mail delivery. 4 an item of electronic mail made publicly available. 5 (formerly) any of a series of stations furnishing relays of men and horses to deliver mail over a fixed route. 6 a rider who carried mail between such stations. 7 *Brit* another word for **pillar box.** 8 *Brit* short for **post office.** 9 a size of writing or printing paper, 15¼ by 19 inches or 16½ by 21 inches (**large post**). 10 any of various book sizes, esp 5¼ by 8¼ inches (**post octavo**) and 8¼ by 10¼ inches (**post quarto**). 11 **by return of post.** *Brit* by the next mail in the opposite direction. ◆ VERB 12 (*tr*) *Chiefly Brit* to send by post. US and Canadian word: **mail.** 13 (*tr*) to make (electronic mail) publicly available. 14 (*tr*) *Book-keeping* **a** to enter (an item) in a ledger. **b** (often foll by *up*) to compile or enter all paper items in (a ledger). 15 (*tr*) to inform of the latest news (esp in the phrase **keep someone posted**). 16 (*intr*) (of a rider) to rise from and reseat oneself in a saddle in time with the motions of a trotting horse; perform a rising trot. 17 (*intr*) (formerly) to travel with relays of post horses. 18 *Archaic* to travel or dispatch with speed; hasten. ◆ ADVERB 19 with speed; rapidly. 20 by means of post horses.
▷HISTORY C16: via French from Italian *poste,* from Latin *posita* something placed, from *pōnere* to put, place

POST ABBREVIATION FOR point of sales terminal.

post- PREFIX 1 after in time or sequence; following; subsequent: *postgraduate.* 2 behind; posterior to: *postorbital.*
▷HISTORY from Latin, from *post* after, behind

postage ('pəʊstɪdʒ) NOUN **a** the charge for delivering a piece of mail. **b** (*as modifier*): *postage charges.*

postage due stamp NOUN a stamp affixed by a Post Office to a letter, parcel, etc., indicating that insufficient or no postage has been prepaid and showing the amount to be paid by the addressee on delivery.

postage meter NOUN *Chiefly US and Canadian* a postal franking machine. Also called: **postal meter.**

postage stamp NOUN 1 a printed paper label with a gummed back for attaching to mail as an official indication that the required postage has been paid. 2 a mark directly printed or embossed on an envelope, postcard, etc., serving the same function.

postal ('pəʊstᵊl) ADJECTIVE of or relating to a Post Office or to the mail-delivery service.
▸ **'postally** ADVERB

postal card NOUN *US* another term for **postcard.**

postal code NOUN a Canadian term for **postcode.**

postal note NOUN *Austral and NZ* the usual name for **postal order.**

postal order NOUN a written order for the payment of a sum of money, to a named payee, obtainable and payable at a post office.

post-and-rail fence NOUN a fence constructed of upright wooden posts with horizontal timber slotted through it.

post-and-rail tea NOUN *Austral informal* (in the 19th century) a coarse tea in which floating particles resembled a post-and-rail fence.

postaxial (pəʊst'æksɪəl) ADJECTIVE *Anatomy* 1 situated or occurring behind the axis of the body. 2 of or relating to the posterior part of a vertebrate limb.

postbag ('pəʊst,bæg) NOUN 1 *Chiefly Brit* another name for **mailbag.** 2 the mail received by a magazine, radio programme, public figure, etc.

post-bellum ('pəʊst'bɛləm) ADJECTIVE (*prenominal*) of or during the period after a war, esp the American Civil War.
▷HISTORY C19: Latin *post* after + *bellum* war

postbox ('pəʊst,bɒks) NOUN *Chiefly Brit* a box into which mail is put for collection by the postal service. Also called: **letter box.**

postboy ('pəʊst,bɔɪ) NOUN 1 a man or boy who brings the post round to offices. 2 another name for **postilion.**

postbus ('pəʊst,bʌs) NOUN (in Britain, esp in rural districts) a vehicle carrying the mail that also carries passengers.

post captain NOUN *History* (formerly) a naval officer holding a commission as a captain, as distinct from an officer with the courtesy title of captain.

postcard ('pəʊst,kɑːd) NOUN a card, often bearing a photograph, picture, etc., on one side, (**picture postcard**), for sending a message by post without an envelope. Also called (US): **postal card.**

postcava (pəʊst'kɑːvə, -'keɪvə) NOUN *Anatomy* the inferior vena cava.
▷HISTORY C19: New Latin; see POST-, VENA CAVA
▸ **post'caval** ADJECTIVE

post chaise NOUN a closed four-wheeled horse-drawn coach used as a rapid means for transporting mail and passengers in the 18th and 19th centuries.
▷HISTORY C18: from POST³ + CHAISE

postcode ('pəʊst,kəʊd) NOUN *Brit and Austral* a code of letters and digits used as part of a postal address to aid the sorting of mail. Also called: **postal code.** US equivalent: **zip code.**

postcode discrimination NOUN discrimination on the basis of the area where someone lives, with relation to employment, credit rating, etc.

postcode lottery NOUN *Brit* a situation in which the standard of medical care, education, etc., received by the public varies from area to area, depending on the funding policies of various health boards, local authorities, etc.

postcode prescribing NOUN *Brit* the practice of prescribing more or less expensive and effective medical treatments to patients depending on where they live in a country, and which treatments their health board is willing and able to provide.

postcoital (pəʊst'kəʊɪtəl) ADJECTIVE of or relating to the period after sexual intercourse.

post-colonial ADJECTIVE existing or occurring since a colony gained independence: *post-colonial Nigeria.*

Postcomm ('pəʊst,kɒm) NOUN (in Britain) the Postal Services Commission, a body set up to look after the interests of postal service users.

post-consumer ADJECTIVE **a** (of a consumer item) having been discarded for disposal or recovery. **b** having been recycled.

post-cyclic ADJECTIVE *Transformational grammar* denoting rules that apply only after the transformations of a whole cycle. Compare **cyclic** (sense 6), **last-cyclic.**

postdate (pəʊst'deɪt) VERB (*tr*) 1 to write a future date on (a document), as on a cheque to prevent it being paid until then. 2 to assign a date to (an event, period, etc.) that is later than its previously assigned date of occurrence. 3 to be or occur at a later date than.

postdiluvian (,pəʊstdɪ'luːvɪən, -daɪ-) ADJECTIVE *also* **postdiluvial.** 1 existing or occurring after the biblical Flood. ◆ NOUN 2 a person or thing existing after the biblical Flood.
▷HISTORY C17: from POST- + *diluvian,* from Latin *diluvium* deluge, flood

postdoctoral (pəʊst'dɒktərəl) ADJECTIVE of, relating to, or designating studies, research, or professional work above the level of a doctorate.

postelection (,pəʊstɪ'lɛkʃən) ADJECTIVE happening or existing after an election.

poster ('pəʊstə) NOUN 1 a large printed picture, used for decoration. 2 a placard or bill posted in a public place as an advertisement.

poster boy *or* **poster girl** NOUN 1 a person who appears on a poster. 2 a person who typifies or represents a particular characteristic, cause, opinion, etc.: *a poster girl for late motherhood.* ◆ Also called: **poster child.**

poste restante ('pəʊst rɪ'stænt; *French* pɔst rɛstɑ̃t) NOUN 1 (not in the US and Canada) an address on mail indicating that it should be kept at a specified post office until collected by the addressee. 2 the mail-delivery service or post-office department that handles mail having this address. ◆ US and Canadian equivalent: **general delivery.**
▷HISTORY French, literally: mail remaining

posterior (pɒ'stɪərɪə) ADJECTIVE 1 situated at the back of or behind something. 2 coming after or following another in a series. 3 coming after in time. 4 *Zoology* (of animals) of or near the hind end. 5 *Botany* (of a flower) situated nearest to the main stem. 6 *Anatomy* dorsal or towards the spine. ◆ Compare **anterior.** ◆ NOUN 7 the buttocks; rump. 8 *Statistics* a posterior probability.
▷HISTORY C16: from Latin: latter, from *posterus* coming next, from *post* after
▸ **pos'teriorly** ADVERB

posterior probability NOUN *Statistics* the probability assigned to some parameter or to an event on the basis of its observed frequency in a sample, and calculated from a prior probability by

Bayes' theorem. Compare **prior probability.** See also **empirical** (sense 5).

posterity (pɒˈsterɪtɪ) NOUN 1 future or succeeding generations. 2 all of one's descendants.
▷HISTORY C14: from French *postérité,* from Latin *posteritās* future generations, from *posterus* coming after, from *post* after

postern (ˈpɒstən) NOUN 1 a back door or gate, esp one that is for private use. ◆ ADJECTIVE 2 situated at the rear or the side.
▷HISTORY C13: from Old French *posterne,* from Late Latin *posterula (jānua)* a back (entrance), from *posterus* coming behind; see POSTERIOR, POSTERITY

poster paint *or* **colour** NOUN a gum-based opaque watercolour paint used for writing posters, etc.

post exchange NOUN *US* a government-subsidized shop operated mainly for military personnel. Abbreviation: **PX.**

postexilian (ˌpəʊstɪgˈzɪlɪən) *or* **postexilic** ADJECTIVE *Old Testament* existing or occurring after the Babylonian exile of the Jews (587–539 B.C.).

post-fascist ADJECTIVE 1 of or relating to various right-wing political parties in Europe which espouse a modified form of fascism and which take part in constitutional politics. ◆ NOUN 2 a member or supporter of such a party.

postfeminist (pəʊstˈfɛmɪnɪst) ADJECTIVE 1 resulting from or including the beliefs and ideas of feminism. 2 differing from or showing moderation of these beliefs and ideas. ◆ NOUN 3 a person who believes in or advocates any of the ideas that have developed from the feminist movement.

postfix VERB (pəʊstˈfɪks) 1 *(tr)* to add or append at the end of something; suffix. ◆ NOUN (ˈpəʊstˌfɪks) 2 a less common word for **suffix.**

post-Fordism (ˌpəʊstˈfɔːdɪzəm) NOUN the idea that modern industrial production has moved away from mass production in huge factories, as pioneered by Henry Ford, the US car manufacturer (1863–1947), towards specialized markets based on small flexible manufacturing units.
▸ **ˌpost-ˈFordist** ADJECTIVE

post-free ADVERB, ADJECTIVE 1 *Brit* with the postage prepaid; post-paid. 2 free of postal charge.

postglacial (pəʊstˈgleɪsɪəl) ADJECTIVE formed or occurring after a glacial period, esp after the Pleistocene epoch.

postgraduate (pəʊstˈgrædjʊɪt) NOUN 1 a student who has obtained a degree from a university, etc., and is pursuing studies for a more advanced qualification. 2 *(modifier)* of or relating to such a student or to his studies. ◆ Also (US and Canadian): **graduate.**

posthaste (ˈpəʊstˈheɪst) ADVERB 1 with great haste; as fast as possible. ◆ NOUN 2 *Archaic* great haste.

post hoc (ˈpəʊst ˈhɒk) NOUN *Logic* the fallacy of assuming that temporal succession is evidence of causal relation.
▷HISTORY from Latin, short for *Post hoc ergo propter hoc* after this, therefore on account of this

post horn NOUN a simple valveless natural horn consisting of a long tube of brass or copper, either straight or coiled; formerly often used to announce the arrival of a mailcoach.

post horse NOUN (formerly) a horse kept at an inn or post house for use by postriders or for hire to travellers.

post house NOUN (formerly) a house or inn where horses were kept for postriders or for hire to travellers.

posthumous (ˈpɒstjʊməs) ADJECTIVE 1 happening or continuing after one's death. 2 (of a book, etc.) published after the author's death. 3 (of a child) born after the father's death.
▷HISTORY C17: from Latin *postumus* the last, but modified as though from Latin *post* after + *humus* earth, that is, after the burial
▸ **ˈposthumously** ADVERB

posthypnotic suggestion (ˌpəʊsthɪpˈnɒtɪk) NOUN a suggestion made to the subject while in a hypnotic trance, to be acted upon at some time after emerging from the trance.

postical (ˈpɒstiːkəl) *or* **posticous** (pɒˈstiːkəs, -ˈstaɪ-) ADJECTIVE (of the position of plant parts) behind another part; posterior. ◆ Compare **antical.**
▷HISTORY C19: from Latin *postīcus* that is behind, from *post* after

postiche (pɒˈstiːʃ) ADJECTIVE 1 (of architectural ornament) inappropriately applied; sham. 2 false or artificial; spurious. ◆ NOUN 3 another term for **hairpiece** (sense 2). 4 an imitation, counterfeit, or substitute. 5 anything that is false; sham or pretence.
▷HISTORY C19: from French, from Italian *apposticcio* (n), from Late Latin *appositīcius* (adj); see APPOSITE

postie (ˈpəʊstɪ) NOUN *Scot, Austral, and NZ informal* a postman.

postil (ˈpɒstɪl) NOUN 1 a commentary or marginal note, as in a Bible. 2 a homily or collection of homilies. ◆ VERB **-tils, -tiling, -tiled** *or* **-tils, -tilling, -tilled.** 3 *Obsolete* to annotate (a biblical passage).
▷HISTORY C15 *(postille)*: from Old French *postille* from Medieval Latin *postilla,* perhaps from *post illa (verba textus),* after these words in the text, often the opening phrase of such an annotation

postilion *or* **postillion** (pɒˈstɪljən) NOUN a person who rides the near horse of the leaders in order to guide a team of horses drawing a coach.
▷HISTORY C16: from French *postillon,* from Italian *postiglione,* from *posta* POST[3]

postimpressionism (ˌpəʊstɪmˈprɛʃəˌnɪzəm) NOUN a movement in painting in France at the end of the 19th century, begun by Paul Cézanne (1839–1906) and exemplified by Paul Gauguin (1848–1903), Vincent Van Gogh (1853–90), and Henri Matisse (1869–1954), which rejected the naturalism and momentary effects of impressionism but adapted its use of pure colour to paint subjects with greater subjective emotion.
▸ **ˌpostimˈpressionist** NOUN, ADJECTIVE
▸ **ˌpostimˌpressionˈistic** ADJECTIVE

postindustrial (ˌpəʊstɪnˈdʌstrɪəl) ADJECTIVE characteristic of, relating to, or denoting work or a society that is no longer based on heavy industry.

posting[1] (ˈpəʊstɪŋ) NOUN a wrestling attack in which the opponent is hurled at the post in one of the corners of the ring.

posting[2] (ˈpəʊstɪŋ) NOUN 1 an appointment to a position or post, usually in another town or country. 2 an electronic mail message sent to a bulletin board, website, etc., and intended for access by every user.

Post-it Note NOUN *Trademark* a small square of sticky paper on which notes can be written.

postliminy (pəʊstˈlɪmɪnɪ) *or* **postliminium** (ˌpəʊstlɪˈmɪnɪəm) NOUN, *plural* **-inies** *or* **-inia** (-ɪnɪə). *International law* the right by which persons and property seized in war are restored to their former status on recovery.
▷HISTORY C19: (in this sense): from Latin *postlīminium* a return behind one's threshold, from *līmen* threshold

postlude (ˈpəʊstluːd) NOUN 1 *Music* a final or concluding piece or movement. 2 a voluntary played at the end of a Church service.
▷HISTORY C19: from POST- + *-lude,* from Latin *lūdus* game; compare PRELUDE

postman (ˈpəʊstmən) *or feminine* **postwoman** NOUN, *plural* **-men** *or* **-women.** a person who carries and delivers mail as a profession.

postman's knock NOUN a children's party game in which a kiss is exchanged for a pretend letter.

postmark (ˈpəʊstˌmɑːk) NOUN 1 any mark stamped on mail by postal officials, such as a simple obliteration, date mark, or indication of route. See also **cancellation.** ◆ VERB 2 *(tr)* to put such a mark on mail.

postmaster (ˈpəʊstˌmɑːstə) NOUN 1 Also (feminine): **postmistress.** an official in charge of a local post office. 2 the person responsible for managing the electronic mail at a site.

postmaster general NOUN, *plural* **postmasters general.** the executive head of the postal service in certain countries.

postmenopausal (ˌpəʊstmɛnəʊˈpɔːzəl) ADJECTIVE existing or taking place after the menopause.

postmeridian (ˌpəʊstməˈrɪdɪən) ADJECTIVE after noon; in the afternoon or evening.
▷HISTORY C17: from Latin *postmerīdiānus* in the afternoon; see POST-, MERIDIAN

post meridiem (ˈpəʊst məˈrɪdɪəm) the full form of **p.m.**
▷HISTORY C17: Latin: after noon

post mill NOUN a windmill built round a central post on which the whole mill can be turned so that the sails catch the wind.

postmillennial (ˌpəʊstmɪˈlɛnɪəl) ADJECTIVE existing or taking place after the millennium.

postmillennialism (ˌpəʊstmɪˈlɛnɪəˌlɪzəm) NOUN the doctrine or belief that the Second Coming of Christ will be preceded by the millennium.
▸ **ˌpostmilˈlennialist** NOUN

postmodern (pəʊstˈmɒdən) ADJECTIVE (in the arts, architecture, etc.) characteristic of a style and school of thought that rejects the dogma and practices of any form of modernism; in architecture, contrasting with international modernism and featuring elements from several periods, esp the Classical, often with ironic use of decoration.
▸ **postˈmoderˌnism** NOUN ▸ **postˈmodernist** NOUN, ADJECTIVE

postmortem (pəʊstˈmɔːtəm) ADJECTIVE 1 *(prenominal)* occurring after death. ◆ NOUN 2 analysis or study of a recently completed event: *a postmortem on a game of chess.* 3 See **postmortem examination.**
▷HISTORY C18: from Latin, literally: after death

postmortem examination NOUN dissection and examination of a dead body to determine the cause of death. Also called: **autopsy, necropsy.**

postnasal drip (pəʊstˈneɪzəl) NOUN *Med* a mucus secretion from the rear part of the nasal cavity into the nasopharynx, usually as the result of a cold or an allergy.

postnatal (pəʊstˈneɪtəl) ADJECTIVE existing or taking place after giving birth.

Postnet (ˈpəʊstnet) NOUN *South African* an official postal service in South Africa.

post-obit (pəʊstˈəʊbɪt, -ˈɒbɪt) *Chiefly law* ◆ NOUN 1 Also called: **post-obit bond.** a bond given by a borrower, payable after the death of a specified person, esp one given to a moneylender by an expectant heir promising to repay when his interest falls into possession. ◆ ADJECTIVE 2 taking effect after death.
▷HISTORY C18: from Latin *post obitum* after death

post office NOUN a building or room where postage stamps are sold and other postal business is conducted.

Post Office NOUN a government department or authority in many countries responsible for postal services and often telecommunications.

post office box NOUN a private numbered place in a post office, in which letters received are kept until called for.

postoperative (pəʊstˈɒpərətɪv, -ˈɒprətɪv) ADJECTIVE of, relating to, or occurring in the period following a surgical operation.
▸ **postˈoperatively** ADVERB

postorbital (pəʊstˈɔːbɪtəl) ADJECTIVE *Anatomy* situated behind the eye or the eye socket.

post-paid ADVERB, ADJECTIVE with the postage prepaid.

postpartum (pəʊstˈpɑːtəm) ADJECTIVE *Med* following childbirth.
▷HISTORY Latin: after the act of giving birth

postpone (pəʊstˈpəʊn, pəˈspəʊn) VERB *(tr)* 1 to put off or delay until a future time. 2 to put behind in order of importance; defer.
▷HISTORY C16: from Latin *postpōnere* to put after, neglect, from POST- + *ponere* to place
▸ **postˈponable** ADJECTIVE ▸ **postˈponement** NOUN
▸ **postˈponer** NOUN

postposition (ˌpəʊstpəˈzɪʃən) NOUN 1 placement of a modifier or other speech element after the word that it modifies or to which it is syntactically related. 2 a word or speech element so placed.
▸ **ˌpostpoˈsitional** ADJECTIVE ▸ **ˌpostpoˈsitionally** ADVERB

postpositive (pəʊstˈpɒzɪtɪv) ADJECTIVE 1 (of an adjective or other modifier) placed after the word modified, either immediately after, as in *two men abreast,* or as part of a complement, as in *those men are bad.* ◆ NOUN 2 a postpositive modifier.
▸ **postˈpositively** ADVERB

postprandial (pəʊstˈprændɪəl) ADJECTIVE of or

relating to the period immediately after lunch or dinner: *a postprandial nap.*

postproduction (ˌpəʊstprəˈdʌkʃən) NOUN **a** the work on a film or a television programme, such as editing, dubbing, etc., that takes place after shooting or videotaping is completed. **b** (*as modifier*): *postproduction costs.*

post-Reformation ADJECTIVE happening or existing in the period or age after the Reformation.

post-Revolutionary ADJECTIVE of or relating to the period or age after a revolution.

postrider (ˈpəʊstˌraɪdə) NOUN (formerly) a person who delivered post on horseback.

post road NOUN a road or route over which post is carried and along which post houses were formerly sited.

post-rock NOUN 1 a type of music that often varies from traditional rock in terms of form and instrumentation. ◆ ADJECTIVE 2 of or relating to this type of music.

postscript (ˈpəʊsˌskrɪpt, ˈpəʊst-) NOUN 1 a message added at the end of a letter, after the signature. 2 any supplement, as to a document or book.
▷ HISTORY C16: from Late Latin *postscribere* to write after, from POST- + *scribere* to write

postseason (pəʊstˈsiːzᵊn) *Chiefly US* ◆ ADJECTIVE 1 of or relating to the period after the end of a regular sporting season. ◆ NOUN 2 the period after the end of a regular sporting season: *home run drought in the postseason.*

poststructuralism (pəʊstˈstrʌktʃərəˌlɪzəm) NOUN an approach to literature that, proceeding from the tenets of structuralism, maintains that, as words have no absolute meaning, any text is open to an unlimited range of interpretations.
▸ **postˈstructuralist** NOUN, ADJECTIVE

post town NOUN a town having a main Post Office branch.

post-traumatic stress disorder NOUN a psychological condition, characterized by anxiety, withdrawal, and a proneness to physical illness, that may follow a traumatic experience. Abbreviation: **PTSD.**

postulant (ˈpɒstjʊlənt) NOUN a person who makes a request or application, esp a candidate for admission to a religious order.
▷ HISTORY C18: from Latin *postulāns* asking, from *postulāre* to ask, demand
▸ **ˈpostulancy** *or* **ˈpostulantˌship** NOUN

postulate VERB (ˈpɒstjʊˌleɪt) (*tr; may take a clause as object*) 1 to assume to be true or existent; take for granted. 2 to ask, demand, or claim. 3 to nominate (a person) to a post or office subject to approval by a higher authority. ◆ NOUN (ˈpɒstjʊlɪt) 4 something taken as self-evident or assumed as the basis of an argument. 5 a necessary condition or prerequisite. 6 a fundamental principle. 7 *Logic, maths* an unproved and indemonstrable statement that should be taken for granted: used as an initial premise or underlying hypothesis in a process of reasoning.
▷ HISTORY C16: from Latin *postulāre* to ask for, require; related to *pōscere* to request
▸ **ˌpostuˈlation** NOUN

postulator (ˈpɒstjʊˌleɪtə) NOUN *RC Church* a person, usually a priest, deputed to prepare and present a plea for the beatification or canonization of some deceased person.

posture (ˈpɒstʃə) NOUN 1 a position or attitude of the limbs or body. 2 a characteristic manner of bearing the body; carriage: *to have good posture.* 3 the disposition of the parts of a visible object. 4 a mental attitude or frame of mind. 5 a state, situation, or condition. 6 a false or affected attitude; pose. ◆ VERB 7 to assume or cause to assume a bodily position or attitude. 8 (*intr*) to assume an affected or unnatural bodily or mental posture; pose.
▷ HISTORY C17: via French from Italian *postura,* from Latin *positūra,* from *pōnere* to place
▸ **ˈpostural** ADJECTIVE ▸ **ˈposturer** NOUN

posturize *or* **posturise** (ˈpɒstʃəˌraɪz) VERB a less common word for **posture** (senses 7, 8).

postviral syndrome (ˌpəʊstˈvaɪrəl) NOUN another name for **chronic fatigue syndrome.** Abbreviation: **PVS.**

postvocalic (ˌpəʊstvəˈkælɪk) ADJECTIVE *Phonetics* following a vowel.

post-war ADJECTIVE happening or existing after a war: *the early post-war years.*

posy (ˈpəʊzɪ) NOUN, *plural* **-sies.** 1 a small bunch of flowers or a single flower; nosegay. 2 *Archaic* a brief motto or inscription, esp one on a trinket or a ring.
▷ HISTORY C16: variant of POESY

pot¹ (pɒt) NOUN 1 a container made of earthenware, glass, or similar material; usually round and deep, often having a handle and lid, used for cooking and other domestic purposes. 2 short for **flowerpot, teapot.** 3 the amount that a pot will hold; potful. 4 a chamber pot, esp a small one designed for a baby or toddler. 5 a handmade piece of pottery. 6 a large mug or tankard, as for beer. 7 *Austral* any of various measures used for serving beer. 8 *Informal* a cup or trophy, esp of silver, awarded as a prize in a competition. 9 the money or stakes in the pool in gambling games, esp poker. 10 (*often plural*) *Informal* a large amount, esp of money. 11 a wicker trap for catching fish, esp crustaceans: *a lobster pot.* 12 *Billiards, snooker* a shot by which a ball is pocketed. 13 *Chiefly Brit* short for **chimneypot.** 14 *US informal* a joint fund created by a group of individuals or enterprises and drawn upon by them for specified purposes. 15 *Hunting* See **pot shot.** 16 See **potbelly.** 17 **go to pot.** to go to ruin; deteriorate. ◆ VERB **pots, potting, potted.** (*mainly tr*) 18 to set (a plant) in a flowerpot to grow. 19 to put or preserve (goods, meat, etc.) in a pot. 20 to cook (food) in a pot. 21 to shoot (game) for food rather than for sport. 22 to shoot (game birds or animals) while they are on the ground or immobile rather than flying or running. 23 (*also intr*) to shoot casually or without careful aim at (an animal, etc.). 24 to sit (a baby or toddler) on a chamber pot. 25 (*also intr*) to shape clay as a potter. 26 *Billiards, snooker* to pocket (a ball). 27 *Informal* to capture or win; secure. ◆ See also **pot on.**
▷ HISTORY Late Old English *pott,* from Medieval Latin *pottus* (unattested), perhaps from Latin *pōtus* a drink; compare Middle Low German *pot,* Old Norse *pottr*

pot² (pɒt) NOUN **a** *Scot and northern English dialect* a deep hole or pothole. **b** (*capital when part of a name*): *Pen-y-Ghent Pot.*
▷ HISTORY C14: perhaps identical with POT¹ but possibly of Scandinavian origin; compare Swedish dialect *putt* water hole, pit

pot³ (pɒt) NOUN *Slang* cannabis used as a drug in any form, such as leaves (marijuana or hemp) or resin (hashish).
▷ HISTORY C20: perhaps shortened from Mexican Indian *potiguaya*

pot⁴ (pɒt) NOUN *Informal* short for **potentiometer.**

potable (ˈpəʊtəbᵊl) ADJECTIVE 1 a less common word for **drinkable.** ◆ NOUN 2 something fit to drink; a beverage.
▷ HISTORY C16: from Late Latin *pōtābilis* drinkable, from Latin *pōtāre* to drink
▸ **ˌpotaˈbility** NOUN

potae (ˈpɔtaɪ) NOUN *NZ* a hat.
▷ HISTORY Maori

potage *French* (pɔtaʒ; *English* pəʊˈtɑːʒ) NOUN any thick soup.
▷ HISTORY C16: from Old French; see POTTAGE

potager (ˈpɒtɪdʒə) NOUN a small kitchen garden.
▷ HISTORY C17: from French *potagère* vegetable garden

potamic (pəˈtæmɪk) ADJECTIVE of or relating to rivers.
▷ HISTORY C19: from Greek *potamos* river

potamology (ˌpɒtəˈmɒlədʒɪ) NOUN *Obsolete* the scientific study of rivers.
▷ HISTORY C19: from Greek *potamos* river + -LOGY

potash (ˈpɒtˌæʃ) NOUN 1 another name for **potassium carbonate,** esp the form obtained by leaching wood ash 2 another name for **potassium hydroxide.** 3 potassium chemically combined in certain compounds: *chloride of potash.*
▷ HISTORY C17 *pot ashes,* translation of obsolete Dutch *potaschen;* so called because originally obtained by evaporating the lye of wood ashes in pots

potash alum NOUN the full name for **alum** (sense 1).

potassium (pəˈtæsɪəm) NOUN a light silvery element of the alkali metal group that is highly reactive and rapidly oxidizes in air; occurs principally in carnallite and sylvite. It is used when alloyed with sodium as a cooling medium in nuclear reactors and its compounds are widely used, esp in fertilizers. Symbol: K; atomic no.: 19; atomic wt.: 39.0983; valency: 1; relative density: 0.862; melting pt.: 63.71°C; boiling pt.: 759°C.
▷ HISTORY C19: New Latin *potassa* potash
▸ **poˈtassic** ADJECTIVE

potassium-argon dating NOUN a technique for determining the age of minerals based on the occurrence in natural potassium of a small fixed amount of radioisotope ^{40}K that decays to the stable argon isotope ^{40}Ar with a half-life of 1.28×10^9 years. Measurement of the ratio of these isotopes thus gives the age of the mineral. Compare **radiocarbon dating, rubidium-strontium dating.**

potassium bitartrate NOUN another name (not in technical usage) for **potassium hydrogen tartrate.**

potassium bromide NOUN a white crystalline soluble substance with a bitter saline taste used in making photographic papers and plates and in medicine as a sedative. Formula: KBr.

potassium carbonate NOUN a white odourless substance used in making glass and soft soap and as an alkaline cleansing agent. Formula: K_2CO_3.

potassium chlorate NOUN a white crystalline soluble substance used in fireworks, matches, and explosives, and as a disinfectant and bleaching agent. Formula: $KClO_3$.

potassium chloride NOUN a white soluble crystalline substance used as a fertilizer and in medicine to prevent potassium deficiency. Formula: KCl.

potassium cyanide NOUN a white poisonous granular soluble solid substance used in photography and in extracting gold from its ores. Formula: KCN.

potassium dichromate NOUN an orange-red crystalline soluble solid substance that is a good oxidizing agent and is used in making chrome pigments and as a bleaching agent. Formula: $K_2Cr_2O_7$.

potassium ferricyanide NOUN a bright red soluble crystalline substance used in making dyes, pigments, and light-sensitive paper. Formula: $K_3Fe(CN)_6$. Also called: **red prussiate of potash.**

potassium ferrocyanide NOUN a yellow soluble crystalline compound used in case-hardening steel and making dyes and pigments. Formula: $K_4Fe(CN)_6$. Also called: **yellow prussiate of potash.**

potassium hydrogen tartrate NOUN a colourless or white soluble crystalline salt used in baking powders, soldering fluxes, and laxatives. Formula: $KHC_4H_4O_6$. Also called (not in technical usage): **potassium bitartrate, cream of tartar.**

potassium hydroxide NOUN a white deliquescent alkaline solid used in the manufacture of soap, liquid shampoos, and detergents. Formula: KOH. Also called: **caustic potash.** See also **lye.**

potassium nitrate NOUN a colourless or white crystalline compound used in gunpowders, pyrotechnics, fertilizers, and as a preservative for foods, esp as a curing salt for ham, sausages, etc. (**E252**). Formula: KNO_3. Also called: **saltpetre, nitre.**

potassium permanganate NOUN a dark purple poisonous odourless soluble crystalline solid, used as a bleach, disinfectant, and antiseptic. Formula: $KMnO_4$. Systematic name: **potassium manganate(VII).**

potassium sulphate NOUN a soluble substance usually obtained as colourless crystals of the decahydrate: used in making glass and as a fertilizer. Formula: K_2SO_4.

potation (pəʊˈteɪʃən) NOUN 1 the act of drinking. 2 a drink or draught, esp of alcoholic drink.
▷ HISTORY C15: from Latin *pōtātiō* a drinking, from *pōtāre* to drink

potato (pəˈteɪtəʊ) NOUN, *plural* **-toes.** 1 Also called: **Irish potato, white potato. a** a solanaceous plant, *Solanum tuberosum,* of South America: widely cultivated for its edible tubers. **b** the starchy oval tuber of this plant, which has a brown or red skin and is cooked and eaten as a vegetable. 2 any of

various similar plants, esp the sweet potato. [3] **hot potato.** *Slang* a delicate or awkward matter.
▷HISTORY C16: from Spanish *patata* white potato, from Taino *batata* sweet potato

potato beetle NOUN another name for the **Colorado beetle.**

potato blight NOUN a devastating disease of potatoes produced by the oomycete *Phytophthora infestans* and the cause of the Irish potato famine of the mid 19th century.

potato chip NOUN [1] (*usually plural*) another name for **chip** (sense 4). [2] (*usually plural*) the US and Canadian term for **crisp** (sense 10).

potato crisp NOUN (*usually plural*) another name for **crisp** (sense 10).

potatory ('pəʊtətərɪ, -trɪ) ADJECTIVE *Rare* of, relating to, or given to drinking.
▷HISTORY C19: from Late Latin *pōtātōrius* concerning drinking, from Latin *pōtāre* to drink

pot-au-feu (*French* pɔtofø) NOUN [1] a traditional French stew of beef and vegetables. [2] the large earthenware casserole in which this is cooked.
▷HISTORY literally: pot on the fire

potbelly ('pɒtˌbɛlɪ) NOUN, *plural* **-lies.** [1] a protruding or distended belly. [2] a person having such a belly. [3] *US and Canadian* a small bulbous stove in which wood or coal is burned.
▸'**potˌbellied** ADJECTIVE

potboiler ('pɒtˌbɔɪlə) NOUN *Informal* a literary or artistic work of little merit produced quickly in order to make money.

pot-bound ADJECTIVE (of a pot plant) having grown to fill all the available root space and therefore lacking room for continued growth.

potboy ('pɒtˌbɔɪ) *or* **potman** ('pɒtmən) NOUN, *plural* **-boys** *or* **-men.** *Chiefly Brit* (esp formerly) a youth or man employed at a public house to serve beer, etc.

potch (pɒtʃ) NOUN *Chiefly Austral slang* inferior quality opal used in jewellery for mounting precious opals.
▷HISTORY C20: of uncertain origin

pot cheese NOUN *US* a type of coarse dry cottage cheese.

poteen *or* **poitín** ('pɒtiːn) NOUN (in Ireland) illicit spirit, often distilled from potatoes.
▷HISTORY C19: from Irish *poitín* little pot, from *pota* pot

Potemkin (pɒ'tɛmkɪn) ADJECTIVE apparently impressive but actually sham or artificial: *North Korea's Potemkin hospital.*
▷HISTORY C20: after the Russian statesman Grigori Aleksandrovich *Potemkin* (1739–91), who is reputed to have erected sham villages along the route of the Empress Catherine II's 1787 tour of the Crimea

potency ('pəʊtᵊnsɪ) *or* **potence** NOUN, *plural* **-tencies** *or* **-tences.** [1] the state or quality of being potent. [2] latent or inherent capacity for growth or development.
▷HISTORY C16: from Latin *potentia* power, from *posse* to be able

potent[1] ('pəʊtᵊnt) ADJECTIVE [1] possessing great strength; powerful. [2] (of arguments, etc.) persuasive or forceful. [3] influential or authoritative. [4] tending to produce violent physical or chemical effects: *a potent poison.* [5] (of a male) capable of having sexual intercourse.
▷HISTORY C15: from Latin *potēns* able, from *posse* to be able
▸'**potently** ADVERB ▸'**potentness** NOUN

potent[2] ('pəʊtᵊnt) ADJECTIVE *Heraldry* (of a cross) having flat bars across the ends of the arms.
▷HISTORY C17: from obsolete *potent* a crutch, from Latin *potentia* power

potentate ('pəʊtᵊnˌteɪt) NOUN a person who possesses great power or authority, esp a ruler or monarch.
▷HISTORY C14: from Late Latin *potentātus* ruler, from Latin: rule, command, from *potens* powerful, from *posse* to be able

potential (pə'tɛnʃəl) ADJECTIVE [1] **a** possible but not yet actual. **b** (*prenominal*) capable of being or becoming but not yet in existence; latent. [2] *Grammar* (of a verb or form of a verb) expressing possibility, as English *may* and *might.* [3] an archaic word for **potent**[1]. ◆ NOUN [4] latent but unrealized ability or capacity: *Jones has great potential as a sales manager.* [5] *Grammar* a potential verb or verb form. [6] short for **electric potential.**
▷HISTORY C14: from Old French *potencial,* from Late Latin *potentiālis,* from Latin *potentia* power
▸**po'tentially** ADVERB

potential difference NOUN the difference in electric potential between two points in an electric field; the work that has to be done in transferring unit positive charge from one point to the other, measured in volts. Symbol: *U,* Δ*V or* Δϕ. Abbreviation: **pd.** Compare **electromotive force.**

potential divider NOUN a tapped or variable resistor or a chain of fixed resistors in series, connected across a source of voltage and used to obtain a desired fraction of the total voltage. Also called: **voltage divider.**

potential energy NOUN the energy of a body or system as a result of its position in an electric, magnetic, or gravitational field. It is measured in joules (SI units), electronvolts, ergs, etc. Symbol: E_p, *V, U or* ϕ. Abbreviation: **PE.**

potentiality (pəˌtɛnʃɪ'ælɪtɪ) NOUN, *plural* **-ties.** [1] latent or inherent capacity or ability for growth, fulfilment, etc. [2] a person or thing that possesses such a capacity.

potential well NOUN *Physics* a localized region in a field of force in which the potential has a deep minimum.

potentiate (pə'tɛnʃɪˌeɪt) VERB (*tr*) [1] to cause to be potent. [2] *Med* to increase (the individual action or effectiveness) of two drugs by administering them in combination with each other.

potentilla (ˌpəʊtᵊn'tɪlə) NOUN any rosaceous plant or shrub of the N temperate genus *Potentilla,* having five-petalled flowers. See also **cinquefoil** (sense 1), **silverweed** (sense 1), **tormentil.**
▷HISTORY C16: New Latin, from Medieval Latin: garden valerian, from Latin *potēns* powerful, POTENT[1]

potentiometer (pəˌtɛnʃɪ'ɒmɪtə) NOUN [1] an instrument for determining a potential difference or electromotive force by measuring the fraction of it that balances a standard electromotive force. [2] a device with three terminals, two of which are connected to a resistance wire and the third to a brush moving along the wire, so that a variable potential can be tapped off: used in electronic circuits, esp as a volume control. Sometimes shortened to: **pot.**
▸**poˌtenti'ometry** NOUN

potentiometric (pəˌtɛnʃɪə'mɛtrɪk) ADJECTIVE *Chem* (of a titration) having the end point determined by a change in potential of an electrode immersed in the solution.

potful ('pɒtfʊl) NOUN the amount held by a pot.

pothead ('pɒtˌhɛd) NOUN *Slang* a habitual user of cannabis.

pothecary ('pɒθɪkərɪ) NOUN, *plural* **-caries.** an archaic or Brit dialect variant of **apothecary.**

potheen ('pɒtiːn, 'pɒθiːn) NOUN a rare variant of **poteen.**

pother ('pɒðə) NOUN [1] a commotion, fuss, or disturbance. [2] a choking cloud of smoke, dust, etc. ◆ VERB [3] to make or be troubled or upset.
▷HISTORY C16: of unknown origin

potherb ('pɒtˌhɜːb) NOUN any plant having leaves, flowers, stems, etc., that are used in cooking for seasoning and flavouring or are eaten as a vegetable.

pothole ('pɒtˌhəʊl) NOUN [1] *Geography* **a** a deep hole in limestone areas resulting from action by running water. See also **sinkhole** (sense 1). **b** a circular hole in the bed of a river produced by abrasion. [2] a deep hole, esp one produced in a road surface by wear or weathering.

potholing ('pɒtˌhəʊlɪŋ) NOUN *Brit* a sport in which participants explore underground caves.
▸'**potˌholer** NOUN

pothook ('pɒtˌhʊk) NOUN [1] a curved or S-shaped hook used for suspending a pot over a fire. [2] a long hook used for lifting hot pots, lids, etc. [3] an S-shaped mark, often made by children when learning to write.

pothouse ('pɒtˌhaʊs) NOUN *Brit* (formerly) a small tavern or pub.

pothunter ('pɒtˌhʌntə) NOUN [1] a person who hunts for food or for profit without regard to the rules of sport. [2] *Informal* a person who enters competitions for the sole purpose of winning prizes.
▸'**potˌhunting** NOUN, ADJECTIVE

potiche (pɒ'tiːʃ) NOUN, *plural* **-tiches** (-'tiːʃɪz, -'tiːʃ). a tall vase or jar, as of porcelain, with a round or polygonal body that narrows towards the neck and a detached lid or cover.
▷HISTORY French, from *pot* pot; compare POTTAGE

potion ('pəʊʃən) NOUN [1] a drink, esp of medicine, poison, or some supposedly magic beverage. [2] a rare word for **beverage.**
▷HISTORY C13: via Old French from Latin *pōtiō* a drink, especially a poisonous one, from *pōtāre* to drink

Potiphar ('pɒtɪfə) NOUN *Old Testament* one of Pharaoh's officers, who bought Joseph as a slave (Genesis 37:36).

potlatch ('pɒtˌlætʃ) NOUN [1] *Anthropol* a competitive ceremonial activity among certain North American Indians, esp the Kwakiutl, involving a lavish distribution of gifts and the destruction of property to emphasize the wealth and status of the chief or clan. [2] *US and Canadian informal* a wild party or revel.
▷HISTORY C19: from Chinook, from Nootka *patshatl* a giving, present

pot liquor NOUN *Chiefly US* the broth in which meat, esp pork or bacon, and vegetables have been cooked.

pot luck NOUN *Informal* [1] **a** whatever food happens to be available without special preparation. **b** (*as modifier*): *a pot-luck dinner.* [2] whatever is available (esp in the phrase **take pot luck**).

potman ('pɒtmən) NOUN, *plural* **-men.** *Chiefly Brit* another word for **potboy.**

pot marigold NOUN a Central European and Mediterranean plant, *Calendula officinalis,* grown for its rayed orange-and-yellow showy flowers, the petals of which were formerly used to colour food: family *Asteraceae* (composites). See also **calendula.**

Potomac (pə'təʊmək) NOUN a river in the E central US, rising in the Appalachian Mountains of West Virginia: flows northeast, then generally southeast to Chesapeake Bay. Length (from the confluence of headstreams): 462 km (287 miles).

potometer (pəˌtɒmɪtə) NOUN an apparatus that measures the rate of water uptake by a plant or plant part.
▷HISTORY from Latin *pōtāre* to drink + -METER

pot on VERB (*tr, adverb*) to transfer (a plant) to a larger flowerpot.

potoroo (ˌpɒtə'ruː) NOUN another name for **kangaroo rat.**
▷HISTORY from a native Australian language

Potosí (*Spanish* poto'si) NOUN a city in S Bolivia, at an altitude of 4066 m (13 340 ft.): one of the highest cities in the world; developed with the discovery of local silver in 1545; tin mining; university (1571). Pop.: 147 351 (2000 est.).

potpie ('pɒtˌpaɪ) NOUN a meat and vegetable stew with a pie crust on top.

pot plant NOUN a plant grown in a flowerpot, esp indoors.

potpourri (ˌpəʊ'pʊərɪ) NOUN, *plural* **-ris.** [1] a collection of mixed flower petals dried and preserved in a pot to scent the air. [2] a collection of unrelated or disparate items; miscellany. [3] a medley of popular tunes. [4] a stew of meat and vegetables.
▷HISTORY C18: from French, literally: rotten pot, translation of Spanish *olla podrida* miscellany

pot roast NOUN meat, esp beef, that is browned and cooked slowly in a covered pot with very little water, often with vegetables added.

Potsdam ('pɒtsdæm; *German* 'pɔtsdam) NOUN a city in Germany, the capital of Brandenburg on the Havel River: residence of Prussian kings and German emperors and scene of the **Potsdam Conference** of 1945, at which the main Allied powers agreed on a plan to occupy Germany at the end of the Second World War. Pop.: 129 500 (1999 est.).

potsherd ('pɒtˌʃɜːd) *or* **potshard** ('pɒtˌʃɑːd) NOUN a broken fragment of pottery.
▷HISTORY C14: from POT[1] + *schoord* piece of broken crockery; see SHARD

pot shot NOUN [1] a chance shot taken casually,

hastily, or without careful aim. **2** a shot fired to kill game in disregard of the rules of sport. **3** a shot fired at quarry within easy range, often from an ambush.

pot still NOUN a type of still used in distilling whisky in which heat is applied directly to the pot in which the wash is contained.

potstone (ˈpɒtˌstəʊn) NOUN an impure massive variety of soapstone, formerly used for making cooking vessels.

pottage (ˈpɒtɪdʒ) NOUN a thick meat or vegetable soup.
▷HISTORY C13: from Old French *potage* contents of a pot, from *pot* POT[1]

potted (ˈpɒtɪd) ADJECTIVE **1** placed or grown in a pot. **2** cooked or preserved in a pot: *potted shrimps.* **3** *Informal* summarized or abridged: *a potted version of a novel.*

potter[1] (ˈpɒtə) NOUN a person who makes pottery.

potter[2] (ˈpɒtə) *or esp US and Canadian* **putter** *Chiefly Brit* ◆ VERB **1** (*intr; often foll by about or around*) to busy oneself in a desultory though agreeable manner. **2** (*intr; often foll by along or about*) to move with little energy or direction: *to potter about town.* **3** (*tr; usually foll by away*) to waste (time): *to potter the day away.* ◆ NOUN **4** the act of pottering.
▷HISTORY C16 (in the sense: to poke repeatedly): from Old English *potian* to thrust; see PUT
▸ **ˈpotterer** *or (esp US and Canadian)* **ˈputterer** NOUN

Potteries (ˈpɒtərɪz) PLURAL NOUN (*sometimes functioning as singular*) **the.** a region of W central England, in Staffordshire, in which the china and earthenware industries are concentrated.

potter's field NOUN **1** *US* a cemetery where the poor or unidentified are buried at the public expense. **2** *New Testament* the land bought by the Sanhedrin with the money paid for the betrayal of Jesus (which Judas had returned to them) to be used as a burial place for strangers and the friendless poor (Acts 1:19; Matthew 27:7).

potter's wheel NOUN a device with a horizontal rotating disc, on which clay is shaped into pots, bowls, etc., by hand.

potter wasp NOUN any of various solitary wasps of the genus *Eumenes,* which construct vaselike cells of mud or clay, in which they lay their eggs: family *Vespidae.*

pottery (ˈpɒtərɪ) NOUN, *plural* **-teries. 1** articles, vessels, etc., made from earthenware and dried and baked in a kiln. **2** a place where such articles are made. **3** the craft or business of making such articles. ◆ Related adjective: **fictile.**
▷HISTORY C15: from Old French *poterie,* from *potier* potter, from *pot* POT[1]

potting shed (ˈpɒtɪŋ) NOUN a building in which plants are set in flowerpots and in which empty pots, potting compost, etc., are stored.

pottle (ˈpɒtᵊl) NOUN **1** *Archaic* a liquid measure equal to half a gallon. **2** *NZ* a plastic or cardboard container for foods such as yoghurt, fruit salad, or cottage cheese.
▷HISTORY C14: *potel,* from Old French: a small POT[1]

potto (ˈpɒtəʊ) NOUN, *plural* **-tos. 1** Also called: **kinkajou.** a short-tailed prosimian primate, *Perodicticus potto,* having vertebral spines protruding through the skin in the neck region: family *Lorisidae.* **2** **golden potto.** another name for **angwantibo. 3** another name for **kinkajou** (sense 1).
▷HISTORY C18: of West African origin; compare Wolof *pata* type of tail-less monkey

Pott's disease (pɒts) NOUN a disease of the spine, usually caused by tubercular infection and characterized by weakening and gradual disintegration of the vertebrae and the intervertebral discs.
▷HISTORY C18: named after Percivall *Pott* (1714–88), English surgeon

Pott's fracture NOUN a fracture of the lower part of the fibula, usually with dislocation of the ankle.
▷HISTORY C18: see POTT'S DISEASE

potty[1] (ˈpɒtɪ) ADJECTIVE **-tier, -tiest.** *Brit informal* **1** foolish or slightly crazy. **2** trivial or insignificant. **3** (foll by *about* or *on*) very keen (about).
▷HISTORY C19: perhaps from POT[1]
▸ **ˈpottiness** NOUN

potty[2] (ˈpɒtɪ) NOUN, *plural* **-ties.** a child's word for **chamber pot.**

pottymouth (ˈpɒtɪˌmaʊθ) NOUN *Informal* a person who habitually uses foul language.

pot-walloper *or* **potwaller** (ˈpɒtˌwɒlə) NOUN (in some English boroughs) a man entitled to the franchise before 1832 by virtue of possession of his own fireplace.
▷HISTORY C18: from POT[1] + *wallop* to boil furiously, from Old English *weallan* to boil

pouch (paʊtʃ) NOUN **1** a small flexible baglike container: *a tobacco pouch.* **2** a saclike structure in any of various animals, such as the abdominal receptacle marsupium in marsupials or the cheek fold in rodents. **3** *Anatomy* any sac, pocket, or pouchlike cavity or space in an organ or part. **4** another word for **mailbag. 5** a Scot word for **pocket.** ◆ VERB **6** (*tr*) to place in or as if in a pouch. **7** to arrange or become arranged in a pouchlike form. **8** (*tr*) (of certain birds and fishes) to swallow.
▷HISTORY C14: from Old Norman French *pouche,* from Old French *poche* bag; see POKE[2]
▸ **ˈpouchy** ADJECTIVE

pouched (paʊtʃt) ADJECTIVE having a pouch or pouches.

pouf *or* **pouffe** (puːf) NOUN **1** a large solid cushion, usually cylindrical or cubic in shape, used as a seat. **2** **a** a woman's hair style, fashionable esp in the 18th century, in which the hair is piled up in rolled puffs. **b** a pad set in the hair to make such puffs. **3** a stuffed pad worn under panniers. **4** (pʊf, puːf) *Brit derogatory slang* less common spellings of **poof.**
▷HISTORY C19: from French; see PUFF

Poujadism (ˈpuːʒɑːdɪzəm) NOUN a conservative reactionary movement to protect the business interests of small traders.
▷HISTORY C20: named after Pierre *Poujade* (born 1920), French publisher and bookseller who founded such a movement in 1954
▸ **ˈPoujadist** NOUN, ADJECTIVE

poulard *or* **poularde** (ˈpuːlɑːd) NOUN a hen that has been spayed for fattening. Compare **capon.**
▷HISTORY C18: from Old French *pollarde,* from *polle* hen; see PULLET

poult[1] (pəʊlt) NOUN the young of a gallinaceous bird, esp of domestic fowl.
▷HISTORY C15: syncopated variant of *poulet* PULLET

poult[2] (pʊlt) NOUN a fine plain-weave fabric of silk, rayon, nylon, etc., with slight ribs across it. Also called: **poult-de-soie.**
▷HISTORY C20: from French; of unknown origin; compare PADUASOY

poulterer (ˈpəʊltərə) NOUN *Brit* another word for a **poultryman.**
▷HISTORY C17: from obsolete *poulter,* from Old French *pouletier,* from *poulet* PULLET

poultice (ˈpəʊltɪs) NOUN **1** Also called: **cataplasm.** *Med* a local moist and often heated application for the skin consisting of substances such as kaolin, linseed, or mustard, used to improve the circulation, treat inflamed areas, etc. **2** *Austral slang* a large sum of money, esp a debt.
▷HISTORY C16: from earlier *pultes,* from Latin *puls* a thick porridge

poultry (ˈpəʊltrɪ) NOUN domestic fowls collectively.
▷HISTORY C14: from Old French *pouletrie,* from *pouletier* poultry-dealer

poultryman (ˈpəʊltrɪmən) *or* **poulterer** NOUN, *plural* **-trymen** *or* **-terers. 1** Also called: **chicken farmer.** a person who rears domestic fowls, esp chickens, for their eggs or meat. **2** a dealer in poultry, esp one who sells the dressed carcasses.

pounce[1] (paʊns) VERB **1** (*intr; often foll by on or upon*) to spring or swoop, as in capturing prey. ◆ NOUN **2** the act of pouncing; a spring or swoop. **3** the claw of a bird of prey.
▷HISTORY C17: apparently from Middle English *punson* pointed tool; see PUNCHEON[2]
▸ **ˈpouncer** NOUN

pounce[2] (paʊns) VERB (*tr*) to emboss (metal) by hammering from the reverse side.
▷HISTORY C15 *pounsen,* from Old French *poinçonner* to stamp; perhaps the same as POUNCE[1]

pounce[3] (paʊns) NOUN **1** a very fine resinous powder, esp of cuttlefish bone, formerly used to dry ink or sprinkled over parchment or unsized writing paper to stop the ink from running. **2** a fine powder, esp of charcoal, that is tapped through perforations in paper corresponding to the main lines of a design in order to transfer the design to another surface. **3** (*as modifier*): *a pounce box.* ◆ VERB (*tr*) **4** to dust (paper) with pounce. **5** to transfer (a design) by means of pounce.
▷HISTORY C18: from Old French *ponce,* from Latin *pūmex* PUMICE
▸ **ˈpouncer** NOUN

pouncet box (ˈpaʊnsɪt) NOUN a box with a perforated top used for containing perfume.
▷HISTORY C16 *pouncet,* perhaps alteration of *pounced* punched, perforated; see POUNCE[1]

pound[1] (paʊnd) VERB **1** (when *intr,* often foll by *on* or *at*) to strike heavily and often. **2** (*tr*) to beat to a pulp; pulverize. **3** (*tr*) to instil by constant drilling: *to pound Latin into him.* **4** (*tr;* foll by *out*) to produce, as by typing heavily. **5** to walk (the pavement, street, etc.) repeatedly: *he pounded the pavement looking for a job.* **6** (*intr*) to throb heavily. ◆ NOUN **7** a heavy blow; thump. **8** the act of pounding.
▷HISTORY Old English *pūnian;* related to Dutch *puin* rubble
▸ **ˈpounder** NOUN

pound[2] (paʊnd) NOUN **1** an avoirdupois unit of weight that is divided into 16 ounces and is equal to 0.453 592 kilograms. Abbreviation: **lb. 2** a troy unit of weight divided into 12 ounces equal to 0.373 242 kilograms. Abbreviation: **lb tr** *or* **lb t. 3** an apothecaries' unit of weight, used in the US, that is divided into 5760 grains and is equal to one pound troy. **4** (*not in technical usage*) a unit of force equal to the mass of 1 pound avoirdupois where the acceleration of free fall is 32.174 feet per second per second. Abbreviation: **lbf. 5** **a** the standard monetary unit of the United Kingdom, the Channel Islands, the Isle of Man, and various UK overseas territories, divided into 100 pence. Official name: **pound sterling. b** (*as modifier*): *a pound coin.* **6** the standard monetary unit of the following countries. **a** Cyprus: divided into 100 cents. **b** Egypt: divided into 100 piastres. **c** Lebanon: divided into 100 piastres. **d** Syria: divided into 100 piastres. **7** another name for **lira** (sense 2). **8** Also called: **pound Scots.** a former Scottish monetary unit originally worth an English pound but later declining in value to 1 shilling 8 pence. **9** the former standard monetary unit of the Republic of Ireland, divided into 100 pence; replaced by the euro in 2002. Also called: **punt. 10** a former monetary unit of the Sudan, replaced by the dinar in 1992.
▷HISTORY Old English *pund,* from Latin *pondō* pound; related to German *Pfund* pound, Latin *pondus* weight

pound[3] (paʊnd) NOUN **1** an enclosure, esp one maintained by a public authority, for keeping officially removed vehicles or distrained goods or animals, esp stray dogs. **2** a place where people are confined. **3** **a** a trap for animals. **b** a trap or keepnet for fish. See **pound net.** ◆ VERB **4** (*tr*) to confine in or as if in a pound; impound, imprison, or restrain.
▷HISTORY C14: from Late Old English *pund-* as in *pundfeald* PINFOLD

poundage[1] (ˈpaʊndɪdʒ) NOUN **1** a tax, charge, or other payment of so much per pound of weight. **2** a tax, charge, or other payment of so much per pound sterling. **3** a weight expressed in pounds.

poundage[2] (ˈpaʊndɪdʒ) NOUN *Agriculture* **a** confinement of livestock within a pound. **b** the fee required for freeing a head of livestock from a pound.

poundal (ˈpaʊndᵊl) NOUN the fps unit of force; the force that imparts an acceleration of 1 foot per second per second to a mass of 1 pound. 1 poundal is equivalent to 0.1382 newton or 1.382×10^4 dynes. Abbreviation: **pdl.**
▷HISTORY C19: from POUND[2] + QUINTAL

pound cake NOUN a rich fruit cake originally made with a pound each of butter, sugar, and flour.

pound cost averaging NOUN *Stock Exchange* a method of accumulating capital by investing a fixed sum in a particular security at regular intervals, in order to achieve an average purchase price below the arithmetic average of the market prices on the purchase dates.

-pounder ('paʊndə) NOUN (*in combination*) 1 something weighing a specified number of pounds: *a 200-pounder.* 2 something worth a specified number of pounds: *a ten-pounder.* 3 a gun that discharges a shell weighing a specified number of pounds: *a two-pounder.*

pound net NOUN a fishing trap having an arrangement of standing nets directing the fish into an enclosed net.

pound of flesh NOUN something that is one's legal right but is an unreasonable demand (esp in the phrase **to have one's pound of flesh**).
▷HISTORY from Shakespeare's *The Merchant of Venice* (1596), Act IV, scene i

pound sterling NOUN the official name for the standard monetary unit of the United Kingdom. See **pound**[2] (sense 5).

pour (pɔː) VERB 1 to flow or cause to flow in a stream. 2 (*tr*) to issue, emit, etc., in a profuse way. 3 (*intr; often foll by down*) Also: **pour with rain.** to rain heavily: *it's pouring down outside.* 4 (*intr*) to move together in large numbers; swarm. 5 (*intr*) to serve tea, coffee, etc.: *shall I pour?* 6 **it never rains but it pours.** events, esp unfortunate ones, come together or occur in rapid succession. 7 **pour cold water on.** *Informal* to be unenthusiastic about or discourage. 8 **pour oil on troubled waters.** to try to calm a quarrel, etc. ◆ NOUN 9 a pouring, downpour, etc.
▷HISTORY C13: of unknown origin
▸'**pourer** NOUN

> **Language note** The verbs *pour* and *pore* are sometimes confused: *she poured cream over her strudel; she pored* (not *poured*) *over the manuscript.*

pourboire *French* (purbwar) NOUN a tip; gratuity.
▷HISTORY literally: for drinking

pour encourager les autres *French* (pur ɑ̃kuraʒe lez otrə) in order to encourage the others: often used ironically.

pourparler *French* (purparle; *English* pʊə'pɑːleɪ) NOUN an informal or preliminary conference.
▷HISTORY literally: for speaking

pourpoint ('pʊəˌpɔɪnt) NOUN a man's stuffed quilted doublet of a kind worn between the Middle Ages and the 17th century.
▷HISTORY C15: from Old French, from *pourpoindre* to stick, from *pour-* variant of *par-*, from Latin *per* through + *poindre* to pierce, from Latin *pungere* to puncture

pour point NOUN *Chem* the lowest temperature at which a mineral oil will flow under specified conditions.

pousse-café *French* (puskafe) NOUN 1 a drink of liqueurs of different colours in unmixed layers. 2 any liqueur taken with coffee at the end of a meal.
▷HISTORY literally: coffee-pusher

poussette (puː'set) NOUN 1 a figure in country dancing in which couples hold hands and move up or down the set to change positions. ◆ VERB 2 (*intr*) to perform such a figure.
▷HISTORY C19: from French, from *pousser* to push

poussin (*French* pusɛ̃) NOUN a young chicken reared for eating.
▷HISTORY from French

pou sto ('puː 'stəʊ) NOUN, *plural* **pou stos.** *Literary* 1 a place upon which to stand. 2 a basis of operation.
▷HISTORY Greek: where I may stand, from Archimedes' saying that he could move the earth if given a place to stand

pout[1] (paʊt) VERB 1 to thrust out (the lips), as when sullen, or (of the lips) to be thrust out. 2 (*intr*) to swell out; protrude. 3 (*tr*) to utter with a pout. ◆ NOUN 4 (*sometimes* **the pouts**) a fit of sullenness. 5 the act or state of pouting.
▷HISTORY C14: of uncertain origin; compare Swedish dialect *puta* inflated, Danish *pude* PILLOW
▸'**poutingly** ADVERB ▸'**pouty** ADJECTIVE

pout[2] (paʊt) NOUN, *plural* **pout** *or* **pouts.** 1 short for **horned pout** or **eelpout.** 2 any of various gadoid food fishes, esp the bib (also called **whiting pout**). 3 any of certain other stout-bodied fishes.
▷HISTORY Old English *-pūte* as in *ǣlepūte* eelpout; related to Dutch *puit* frog

pouter ('paʊtə) NOUN 1 a person or thing that pouts. 2 a breed of domestic pigeon with a large crop capable of being greatly puffed out.

poutine (puː'tiːn) NOUN *Canadian* a dish of chipped potatoes topped with curd cheese and a tomato-based sauce.
▷HISTORY from Canadian French

poverty ('pɒvətɪ) NOUN 1 the condition of being without adequate food, money, etc. 2 scarcity or dearth: *a poverty of wit.* 3 a lack of elements conducive to fertility in land or soil.
▷HISTORY C12: from Old French *poverté*, from Latin *paupertās* restricted means, from *pauper* POOR

poverty-stricken ADJECTIVE suffering from extreme poverty.

poverty trap NOUN the situation of being unable to escape poverty because of being dependent on state benefits, which are reduced by the same amount as any extra income gained.

pow[1] (paʊ) INTERJECTION an exclamation imitative of a collision, explosion, etc.

pow[2] (paʊ) NOUN *Scot* the head or a head of hair.
▷HISTORY a Scot variant of POLL

pow[3] (paʊ) NOUN *Scot* a creek or slow stream.
▷HISTORY C15: from earlier Scots *poll*

POW ABBREVIATION FOR prisoner of war.

powan ('paʊən) NOUN 1 a freshwater whitefish, *Coregonus clupeoides*, occurring in some Scottish lakes. 2 any of certain similar related fishes, such as the vendace. ◆ Also called: **lake herring.**
▷HISTORY C17: Scottish variant of POLLAN

powder ('paʊdə) NOUN 1 a solid substance in the form of tiny loose particles. 2 any of various preparations in this form, such as gunpowder, face powder, or soap powder. 3 fresh loose snow, esp when considered as skiing terrain. 4 **take a powder.** *US and Canadian slang* to run away or disappear. ◆ VERB 5 to turn into powder; pulverize. 6 (*tr*) to cover or sprinkle with or as if with powder.
▷HISTORY C13: from Old French *poldre*, from Latin *pulvis* dust
▸'**powderer** NOUN ▸'**powdery** ADJECTIVE

powder blue NOUN **a** a dusty pale blue colour. **b** (*as adjective*): *a powder-blue coat.*

powder burn NOUN a superficial burn of the skin caused by a momentary intense explosion, esp of gunpowder.

powder compact NOUN See **compact** (sense 11).

powder flask NOUN a small flask or case formerly used to carry gunpowder.

powder horn NOUN a powder flask consisting of the hollow horn of an animal.

powder keg NOUN 1 a small barrel used to hold gunpowder. 2 *Informal* a potential source or scene of violence, disaster, etc.

powder metallurgy NOUN the science and technology of producing solid metal components from metal powder by compaction and sintering.

powder monkey NOUN (formerly) a boy who carried powder from the magazine to the guns on warships.

powder puff NOUN a soft pad or ball of fluffy material used for applying cosmetic powder to the skin.

powder room NOUN *Euphemistic* a lavatory for women in a restaurant, department store, etc.

powdery mildew NOUN 1 a plant disease characterized by a superficial white powdery growth on stems and leaves, caused by parasitic ascomycetous fungi of the family *Erysiphaceae*: affects the rose, aster, apple, vine, oak, etc. 2 any of the fungi causing this disease. ◆ Compare **downy mildew.**

power ('paʊə) NOUN 1 ability or capacity to do something. 2 (*often plural*) a specific ability, capacity, or faculty. 3 political, financial, social, etc., force or influence. 4 control or dominion or a position of control, dominion, or authority. 5 a state or other political entity with political, industrial, or military strength. 6 a person who exercises control, influence, or authority: *he's a power in the state.* 7 a prerogative, privilege, or liberty. 8 **a** legal authority to act, esp in a specified capacity, for another. **b** the document conferring such authority. 9 **a** a military force. **b** military potential. 10 *Maths* **a** the value of a number or quantity raised to some exponent. **b** another name for **exponent** (sense 4). 11 *Statistics* the probability of rejecting the null hypothesis in a test when it is false. The power of a test of a given null depends on the particular alternative hypothesis against which it is tested. 12 *Physics, engineering* a measure of the rate of doing work expressed as the work done per unit time. It is measured in watts, horsepower, etc. Symbol: *P.* 13 **a** the rate at which electrical energy is fed into or taken from a device or system. It is expressed, in a direct-current circuit, as the product of current and voltage and, in an alternating-current circuit, as the product of the effective values of the current and voltage and the cosine of the phase angle between them. It is measured in watts. **b** (*as modifier*): *a power amplifier.* 14 the ability to perform work. 15 **a** mechanical energy as opposed to manual labour. **b** (*as modifier*): *a power mower.* 16 a particular form of energy: *nuclear power.* 17 **a** a measure of the ability of a lens or optical system to magnify an object, equal to the reciprocal of the focal length. It is measured in dioptres. **b** another word for **magnification.** 18 *Informal* a large amount or quantity: *a power of good.* 19 (*plural*) the sixth of the nine orders into which the angels are traditionally divided in medieval angelology. 20 **in one's power.** (*often foll by an infinitive*) able or allowed (to). 21 **in (someone's) power.** under the control or sway of (someone). 22 **the powers that be.** the established authority or administration. ◆ VERB (*tr*) 23 to give or provide power to. 24 to fit (a machine) with a motor or engine. 25 (*intr*) *Slang* to travel with great speed or force. ◆ See also **power down, power up.**
▷HISTORY C13: from Anglo-Norman *poer*, from Vulgar Latin *potēre* (unattested), from Latin *posse* to be able

power amplifier NOUN *Electronics* an amplifier that is usually the final amplification stage in a device and is designed to give the required power output.

power-assisted ADJECTIVE (of the steering or brakes in a motor vehicle) helped by mechanical power.

powerboat ('paʊəˌbəʊt) NOUN a boat propelled by an inboard or outboard motor.

powerboating ('paʊəˌbəʊtɪŋ) NOUN the sport of driving powerboats in racing competitions.

power brand NOUN a brand of product that is a household name associated with a successful company.

power broker NOUN a person with power and influence, esp one who operates behind the scenes.

power cut NOUN a temporary interruption or reduction in the supply of electrical power to a particular area. Sometimes shortened to: **cut.**

power dive NOUN 1 a steep dive by an aircraft with its engines at high power. ◆ VERB **power-dive.** 2 to cause (an aircraft) to perform a power dive or (of an aircraft) to perform a power dive.

power down VERB (*tr, adverb*) to shut down (a computer system) in a methodical way, concluding by switching the power off.

power dressing NOUN a style of dressing in severely tailored suits, adopted by some women executives to project an image of efficiency.

power drill NOUN a hand tool with a rotating chuck driven by an electric motor and designed to take an assortment of tools for drilling, grinding, polishing, etc.

power factor NOUN (in an electrical circuit) the ratio of the power dissipated to the product of the input volts times amps.

power forward NOUN *Basketball* **a** the position of one of the two players responsible for blocking shots and catching rebounds. **b** a player in this position.

powerful ('paʊəfʊl) ADJECTIVE 1 having great power, force, potency, or effect. 2 extremely effective or efficient in action: *a powerful drug; a powerful lens.* 3 *Dialect* large or great: *a powerful amount of trouble.* ◆ ADVERB 4 *Dialect* extremely; very: *he ran powerful fast.*
▸'**powerfully** ADVERB ▸'**powerfulness** NOUN

powerhouse ('paʊəˌhaʊs) NOUN 1 an electrical generating station or plant. 2 *Informal* a forceful or powerful person or thing.

powerless ('paʊəlɪs) ADJECTIVE without power or authority.
▸ **'powerlessly** ADVERB ▸ **'powerlessness** NOUN

power line NOUN a set of conductors used to transmit and distribute electrical energy. Sometimes shortened to: **line.**

power lunch NOUN a high-powered business meeting conducted over lunch.

power nap NOUN a short sleep taken during the working day with the intention of improving the quality of work later in the day.

power of appointment NOUN *Property law* authority to appoint persons either from a particular class (**special power**) or selected by the donee of the power (**general power**) to take an estate or interest in property.

power of attorney NOUN [1] legal authority to act for another person in certain specified matters. [2] the document conferring such authority. ◆ Also called: **letter of attorney.**

power pack NOUN a device for converting the current from a supply into direct or alternating current at the voltage required by a particular electrical or electronic device.

power plant NOUN [1] the complex, including machinery, associated equipment, and the structure housing it, that is used in the generation of power, esp electrical power. [2] the equipment supplying power to a particular machine or for a particular operation or process.

power point NOUN [1] an electrical socket mounted on or recessed into a wall. [2] such a socket, esp one installed before the introduction of 13 ampere ring mains, that is designed to provide a current of up to 15 amperes for supplying heaters, etc., rather than lights.

power politics NOUN (*functioning as singular*) (in international affairs) the threat or use of force as an instrument of national policy.

power series NOUN a mathematical series whose terms contain ascending positive integral powers of a variable, such as $a_0 + a_1x + a_2x^2 + \ldots$.

power set NOUN *Maths, logic* a set the elements of which are all the subsets of a given set.

power-sharing NOUN a political arrangement in which opposing groups in a society participate in government.

power station NOUN an electrical generating station.

power steering NOUN a form of steering used on vehicles, where the torque applied to the steering wheel is augmented by engine power. Also called: **power-assisted steering.**

power structure NOUN [1] the structure or distribution of power and authority in a community. [2] the people and groups who are part of such a structure.

power tool NOUN a tool powered by electricity.

power up VERB [1] (*tr, adverb*) to switch on the power to (a computer system). [2] to begin to make good use of or take full advantage of.

power walking NOUN walking at a brisk pace while pumping the arms as part of an aerobic exercise routine.

power yoga NOUN a form of yoga involving aerobic exercises and constant strenuous movement.

powfagged ('paʊˌfægd) ADJECTIVE *Northern English dialect* exhausted.

powhiri (ˌpəʊ'fiːrɪ) NOUN *NZ* a Maori ceremony of welcome, esp to a marae.
▷ HISTORY Maori

powwow ('paʊˌwaʊ) NOUN [1] a talk, conference, or meeting. [2] a magical ceremony of certain North American Indians, usually accompanied by feasting and dancing. [3] (among certain North American Indians) a medicine man. [4] a meeting of or negotiation with North American Indians. ◆ VERB [5] (*intr*) to hold a powwow.
▷ HISTORY C17: from Algonquian; related to Natick *pauwau* one who practises magic, Narraganset *powwaw*

Powys ('paʊɪs) NOUN a county in E Wales, formed in 1974 from most of Breconshire, Montgomeryshire, and Radnorshire. Administrative centre: Llandrindod Wells. Pop.: 126 344 (2001). Area: 5077 sq. km (1960 sq. miles).

pox (pɒks) NOUN [1] any disease characterized by the formation of pustules on the skin that often leave pockmarks when healed. [2] (usually preceded by *the*) an informal name for **syphilis.** [3] **a pox on (someone** *or* **something).** (*interjection*) *Archaic* an expression of intense disgust or aversion for (someone or something).
▷ HISTORY C15: changed from *pocks,* plural of POCK

poxy ('pɒksɪ) ADJECTIVE **poxier, poxiest.** *Slang* [1] having or having had syphilis. [2] rotten; lousy.

Poyang *or* **P'o-yang** ('pɔː'jæŋ) NOUN a lake in E China, in N Jiangxi province, connected by canal with the Yangtze River: the second largest lake in China. Area (at its greatest): 2780 sq. km (1073 sq. miles).

Poynting theorem ('pɔɪntɪŋ) NOUN the theorem that the rate of flow of electromagnetic energy through unit area is equal to the **Poynting vector,** i.e. the cross product of the electric and magnetic field intensities.
▷ HISTORY C19: named after John Henry *Poynting* (1852–1914), English physicist

Poznań (*Polish* 'pɔznajn) NOUN a city in W Poland, on the Warta River: the centre of Polish resistance to German rule (1815–1918, 1939–45). Pop.: 578 235 (1999 est.). German name: **Posen.**

Pozsony ('poʒonj) NOUN the Hungarian name for **Bratislava.**

pozzuolana (ˌpɒtswə'lɑːnə) *or* **pozzolana** (ˌpɒtsə'lɑːnə) NOUN [1] a type of porous volcanic ash used in making hydraulic cements. [2] any of various artificial substitutes for this ash used in cements. ◆ Also called: **puzzolana.**
▷ HISTORY C18: from Italian: of POZZUOLI

Pozzuoli (*Italian* pot'tswɔːli) NOUN a port in SW Italy, in Campania on the **Gulf of Pozzuoli** (an inlet of the Bay of Naples): in a region of great volcanic activity; founded in the 6th century B.C. by the Greeks. Pop.: 65 025 (1987 est.).

pozzy ('pɒzɪ) NOUN, *plural* **pozzies.** a variant spelling of **possie.**

pp ABBREVIATION FOR: [1] past participle. [2] (in formal correspondence) per pro. [Latin *per procurationem:* by delegation to] [3] privately printed. [4] *Music* ◆ SYMBOL FOR pianissimo: an instruction to play very quietly.

> **Language note** In formal correspondence, when Brenda Smith is signing on behalf of Peter Jones, she should write *Peter Jones pp* (or *per pro*) *Brenda Smith,* not the other way about.

pp *or* **PP** ABBREVIATION FOR: [1] parcel post. [2] prepaid. [3] post-paid. [4] (in prescriptions) post prandium.
▷ HISTORY Latin: after a meal

PP ABBREVIATION FOR: [1] Parish Priest. [2] past President.

P2P ABBREVIATION FOR **peer-to-peer.**

pp. ABBREVIATION FOR pages.

PPARC (in Britain) ABBREVIATION FOR Particle Physics and Astronomy Research Council.

ppd ABBREVIATION FOR: [1] post-paid. [2] prepaid.

PPE ABBREVIATION FOR: [1] philosophy, politics, and economics: a university course. [2] personal protective equipment: clothing and equipment used to ensure personal safety in the workplace.

ppm ABBREVIATION FOR: [1] *Chem* parts per million. [2] Also: **PPM.** peak programme meter.

PPP ABBREVIATION FOR: [1] purchasing power parity: a rate of exchange between two currencies that gives them equal purchasing powers in their own economies. [2] private-public partnership: an agreement in which a private company commits skills or capital to a public-sector project for a financial return.

ppr *or* **p.pr.** ABBREVIATION FOR present participle.

PPS ABBREVIATION FOR: [1] **parliamentary private secretary.** [2] Also: **pps.** post postscriptum.
▷ HISTORY (for sense 2) Latin: after postscript; additional postscript

PPTA (in New Zealand) ABBREVIATION FOR Post-primary Teachers Association.

pq ABBREVIATION FOR previous question.

PQ (in Canada) ABBREVIATION FOR: [1] (esp in postal addresses) Province of Quebec. [2] **Parti Québécois.**

pr ABBREVIATION FOR: [1] (*plural* **prs**) pair. [2] paper. [3] (in prescriptions) per rectum. [Latin: through the rectum; to be inserted into the anus] [4] power.

pr THE INTERNET DOMAIN NAME FOR Puerto Rico.

Pr THE CHEMICAL SYMBOL FOR praseodymium.

PR ABBREVIATION FOR: [1] **proportional representation.** [2] public relations. [3] Puerto Rico.

Pr. ABBREVIATION FOR: [1] Priest. [2] Prince.

pracharak (prə'tʃɑːrək) NOUN (in India) a person appointed to propagate a cause through personal contact, meetings, public lectures, etc.
▷ HISTORY Hindi

practicable ('præktɪkəbᵊl) ADJECTIVE [1] capable of being done; feasible. [2] usable.
▷ HISTORY C17: from French *praticable,* from *pratiquer* to practise; see PRACTICAL
▸ ˌ**practica'bility** *or* **'practicableness** NOUN ▸ **'practicably** ADVERB
See at **practical.**

practical ('præktɪkᵊl) ADJECTIVE [1] of, involving, or concerned with experience or actual use; not theoretical. [2] of or concerned with ordinary affairs, work, etc. [3] adapted or adaptable for use. [4] of, involving, or trained by practice. [5] being such for all useful or general purposes; virtual. ◆ NOUN [6] an examination in the practical skills of a subject: *a science practical.*
▷ HISTORY C17: from earlier *practic,* from French *pratique,* via Late Latin from Greek *praktikos,* from *prassein* to experience, negotiate, perform
▸ ˌ**practi'cality** *or* **'practicalness** NOUN

> **Language note** A distinction is usually made between *practical* and *practicable. Practical* refers to a person, idea, project, etc., as being more concerned with or relevant to practice than theory: *he is a very practical person; the idea had no practical application. Practicable* refers to a project or idea as being capable of being done or put into effect: *the plan was expensive, yet practicable.*

practical joke NOUN a prank or trick usually intended to make the victim appear foolish.
▸ **practical joker** NOUN

practically ('præktɪkəlɪ, -klɪ) ADVERB [1] virtually; almost: *it has rained practically every day.* [2] in actuality rather than in theory: *what can we do practically to help?*

practical reason *or* **reasoning** NOUN *Philosophy, logic* [1] the faculty by which human beings determine how to act. [2] reasoning concerning the relative merits of actions. [3] the principles governing arguments which issue in actions or intentions to act.

practice ('præktɪs) NOUN [1] a usual or customary action or proceeding: *it was his practice to rise at six; he made a practice of stealing stamps.* [2] repetition or exercise of an activity in order to achieve mastery and fluency. [3] the condition of having mastery of a skill or activity through repetition (esp in the phrases **in practice, out of practice**). [4] the exercise of a profession: *he set up practice as a lawyer.* [5] the act of doing something: *he put his plans into practice.* [6] the established method of conducting proceedings in a court of law. ◆ VERB [7] the US spelling of **practise.**
▷ HISTORY C16: from Medieval Latin *practicāre* to practise, from Greek *praktikē* practical science, practical work, from *prattein* to do, act

practise *or US* **practice** ('præktɪs) VERB [1] to do or cause to do repeatedly in order to gain skill. [2] (*tr*) to do (something) habitually or frequently: *they practise ritual murder.* [3] to observe or pursue (something, such as a religion): *to practise Christianity.* [4] to work at (a profession, job, etc.): *he practises medicine.* [5] (foll by *on* or *upon*) to take advantage of (someone, someone's credulity, etc.).
▷ HISTORY C15: see PRACTICE

practised *or US* **practiced** ('præktɪst) ADJECTIVE [1] expert; skilled; proficient. [2] acquired or perfected by practice.

practitioner (præk'tɪʃənə) NOUN [1] a person who

practises a profession or art. 2 *Christian Science* a person authorized to practise spiritual healing.
▷HISTORY C16: from *practician,* from Old French *praticien,* from *pratiquer* to PRACTISE

Prader-Willi syndrome (ˌprɑːdəˈvɪlɪ) NOUN a congenital condition characterized by obsessive eating, obesity, mental retardation, and small genitalia.
▷HISTORY C20: after Andreas *Prader* (born 1919) and H. *Willi* (born 1920), Swiss paediatricians

Pradesh (prəˈdeɪʃ) NOUN *Indian* a state, esp a state in the Union of India.
▷HISTORY Hindi

Prado (ˈprɑːdəʊ) NOUN an art gallery in Madrid housing an important collection of Spanish paintings.

prae- PREFIX an archaic variant of **pre-**.

praedial *or* **predial** (ˈpriːdɪəl) ADJECTIVE 1 of or relating to land, farming, etc. 2 attached to or occupying land.
▷HISTORY C16: from Medieval Latin *praediālis,* from Latin *praedium* farm, estate
▸ˌ**praediˈality** *or* ˌ**prediˈality** NOUN

praefect (ˈpriːfɛkt) NOUN a variant spelling of **prefect** (senses 4–7).
▸**praefectorial** (ˌpriːfɛkˈtɔːrɪəl) ADJECTIVE

praemunire (ˌpriːmjʊˈnaɪərɪ) NOUN *English history* 1 a writ charging with the offence of resorting to a foreign jurisdiction, esp to that of the Pope, in a matter determinable in a royal court. 2 the statute of Richard II defining this offence.
▷HISTORY C14: from the Medieval Latin phrase (in the text of the writ) *praemūnīre faciās,* literally: that you cause (someone) to be warned in advance, from Latin *praemūnīre* to fortify or protect in front, from *prae* in front + *mūnīre* to fortify; in Medieval Latin the verb was confused with Latin *praemonēre* to forewarn

praenomen (priːˈnəʊmɛn) NOUN, *plural* **-nomina** (-ˈnɒmɪnə) *or* **-nomens.** an ancient Roman's first or given name. See also **agnomen, cognomen, nomen.**
▷HISTORY C18: from Latin, from *prae-* before + *nōmen* NAME
▸**praenominal** (priːˈnɒmɪnᵊl) ADJECTIVE ▸**praeˈnominally** ADVERB

Praesepe (praɪˈsiːpɪ) NOUN an open cluster of several hundred stars in the constellation Cancer, visible to the naked eye as a hazy patch of light.

praesidium (prɪˈsɪdɪəm) NOUN a variant spelling of **presidium.**

praetor *or* **pretor** (ˈpriːtə, -tɔː) NOUN (in ancient Rome) any of several senior magistrates ranking just below the consuls.
▷HISTORY C15: from Latin: one who leads the way, probably from *praeīre,* from *prae-* before + *īre* to go
▸**praeˈtorial** *or* **preˈtorial** ADJECTIVE ▸ˈ**praetorship** *or* ˈ**pretorship** NOUN

praetorian *or* **pretorian** (priːˈtɔːrɪən) ADJECTIVE 1 of or relating to a praetor. ◆ NOUN 2 a person holding praetorian rank; a praetor or ex-praetor.

Praetorian *or* **Pretorian** (priːˈtɔːrɪən) ADJECTIVE 1 of or relating to the Praetorian Guard. 2 (*sometimes not capital*) resembling the Praetorian Guard, esp with regard to corruption. ◆ NOUN 3 a member of the Praetorian Guard.

Praetorian Guard NOUN 1 the bodyguard of the Roman emperors, noted for its political corruption, which existed from 27 B.C. to 312 A.D. 2 a member of this bodyguard.

pragmatic (præɡˈmætɪk) ADJECTIVE 1 advocating behaviour that is dictated more by practical consequences than by theory or dogma. 2 *Philosophy* of or relating to pragmatism. 3 involving everyday or practical business. 4 of or concerned with the affairs of a state or community. 5 *Rare* interfering or meddlesome; officious. ◆ Also (for senses 3, 5): **pragmatical.**
▷HISTORY C17: from Late Latin *prāgmaticus,* from Greek *prāgmatikos* from *pragma* act, from *prattein* to do
▸**pragˌmatiˈcality** NOUN ▸**pragˈmatically** ADVERB

pragmatics (præɡˈmætɪks) NOUN (*functioning as singular*) 1 the study of those aspects of language that cannot be considered in isolation from its use. 2 the study of the relation between symbols and those who use them.

pragmatic sanction NOUN an edict, decree, or ordinance issued with the force of fundamental law by a sovereign.

pragmatism (ˈpræɡməˌtɪzəm) NOUN 1 action or policy dictated by consideration of the immediate practical consequences rather than by theory or dogma. 2 *Philosophy* **a** the doctrine that the content of a concept consists only in its practical applicability. **b** the doctrine that truth consists not in correspondence with the facts but in successful coherence with experience. See also **instrumentalism.**
▸ˈ**pragmatist** NOUN, ADJECTIVE ▸ˌ**pragmaˈtistic** ADJECTIVE

Prague (prɑːɡ) NOUN the capital and largest city of the Czech Republic, on the Vltava River: a rich commercial centre during the Middle Ages; site of Charles University (1348) and a technical university (1707); scene of defenestrations (1419 and 1618) that contributed to the outbreak of the Hussite Wars and the Thirty Years' War respectively. Pop.: 1 186 855 (2000 est.). Czech name: **Praha.**

Praha (ˈpraha) NOUN the Czech name for **Prague.**

Praia (praɪə) NOUN the capital of Cape Verde; a port and submarine cable station. Pop.: 94 757 (2000).

Prairial *French* (prɛrial) NOUN the month of meadows: the ninth month of the French Revolutionary calendar, extending from May 21 to June 19.
▷HISTORY C18: from French *prairie* meadow

prairie (ˈprɛərɪ) NOUN (*often plural*) a treeless grassy plain of the central US and S Canada. Compare **pampas, steppe, savanna.**
▷HISTORY C18: from French, from Old French *praierie,* from Latin *prātum* meadow

prairie chicken, fowl, grouse, *or* **hen** NOUN either of two mottled brown-and-white grouse, *Tympanuchus cupido* or *T. pallidicinctus,* of North America.

prairie crocus NOUN *Canadian* a spring flower of the buttercup family.

prairie dog NOUN any of several gregarious sciurine rodents of the genus *Cynomys,* such as *C. ludovicianus,* that live in large complex burrows in the prairies of North America. Also called: **prairie marmot.**

prairie-dogging NOUN *Informal* (in an open-plan office) the practice of looking over the top of one's partition in order to discover the source of or reason for a commotion.
▷HISTORY C20: after the actions of a PRAIRIE DOG, which stands on its hind legs to get a better view of something

prairie oyster NOUN 1 a drink consisting of raw unbeaten egg, vinegar or Worcester sauce (**Worcester oyster**), salt, and pepper: a supposed cure for a hangover. 2 the testicles of a bull calf cooked and eaten.

Prairie Provinces PLURAL NOUN the Canadian provinces of Manitoba, Saskatchewan, and Alberta, which lie in the N Great Plains region of North America: the chief wheat and petroleum producing area of Canada.

prairie schooner NOUN *Chiefly US* a horse-drawn covered wagon similar to but smaller than a Conestoga wagon, used in the 19th century to cross the prairies of North America.

prairie soil NOUN a soil type occurring in temperate areas formerly under prairie grasses and characterized by a black A horizon, rich in plant foods.

prairie turnip NOUN another name for **breadroot.**

prairie wolf NOUN another name for **coyote** (sense 1).

praise (preɪz) NOUN 1 the act of expressing commendation, admiration, etc. 2 the extolling of a deity or the rendering of homage and gratitude to a deity. 3 the condition of being commended, admired, etc. 4 *Archaic* the reason for praise. 5 **sing someone's praises.** to commend someone highly. ◆ VERB (*tr*) 6 to express commendation, admiration, etc., for. 7 to proclaim or describe the glorious attributes of (a deity) with homage and thanksgiving.
▷HISTORY C13: from Old French *preisier,* from Late Latin *pretiāre* to esteem highly, from Latin *pretium* prize; compare PRIZE², PRECIOUS
▸ˈ**praiser** NOUN

praiseworthy (ˈpreɪzˌwɜːðɪ) ADJECTIVE deserving of praise; commendable.
▸ˈ**praiseˌworthily** ADVERB ▸ˈ**praiseˌworthiness** NOUN

prajna (ˈprʊdʒnə, -njɑː) NOUN wisdom or understanding considered as the goal of Buddhist contemplation.
▷HISTORY from Sanskrit *prajñā,* from *prajānāti* he knows

Prakrit (ˈprɑːkrɪt) NOUN any of the vernacular Indic languages as distinguished from Sanskrit: spoken from about 300 B.C. to the Middle Ages. See also **Pali.**
▷HISTORY C18: from Sanskrit *prākrta* original, from *pra-* before + *kr* to do, make + *-ta* indicating a participle
▸**Praˈkritic** ADJECTIVE

praline (ˈprɑːliːn) NOUN 1 a confection of nuts with caramelized sugar, used in desserts and as a filling for chocolates. 2 Also called: **sugared almond.** a sweet consisting of an almond encased in sugar.
▷HISTORY C18: from French, named after César de Choiseul, comte de Plessis-*Praslin* (1598–1675), French field marshal whose chef first concocted it

pralltriller (ˈprɑːlˌtrɪlə) NOUN 1 an ornament used in 18th-century music consisting of an inverted mordent with an added initial upper note. 2 another word for **inverted mordent.**
▷HISTORY German: bouncing trill

pram¹ (præm) NOUN *Brit* a cotlike four-wheeled carriage for a baby. US and Canadian term: **baby carriage.**
▷HISTORY C19: shortened and altered from PERAMBULATOR

pram² (prɑːm) NOUN *Nautical* a light tender with a flat bottom and a bow formed from the ends of the side and bottom planks meeting in a small raised transom.
▷HISTORY C16: from Middle Dutch *prame;* related to Old Frisian *prām*

prana (ˈpranə) NOUN (in Oriental medicine, martial arts, etc.) cosmic energy believed to come from the sun and connecting the elements of the universe.
▷HISTORY from Sanskrit, literally: life-force

prance (prɑːns) VERB 1 (*intr*) to swagger or strut. 2 (*intr*) to caper, gambol, or dance about. 3 (*intr*) **a** (of a horse) to move with high lively springing steps. **b** to ride a horse that moves in this way. 4 (*tr*) to cause to prance. ◆ NOUN 5 the act or an instance of prancing.
▷HISTORY C14 *prauncen;* perhaps related to German *prangen* to be in full splendour; compare Danish (dialect) *pransk* lively, spirited, used of a horse
▸ˈ**prancer** NOUN ▸ˈ**prancingly** ADVERB

prandial (ˈprændɪəl) ADJECTIVE *Facetious* of or relating to a meal.
▷HISTORY C19: from Latin *prandium* meal, luncheon
▸ˈ**prandially** ADVERB

prang (præŋ) *Chiefly Brit slang* ◆ NOUN 1 an accident or crash in an aircraft, car, etc. 2 an aircraft bombing raid. 3 an achievement. ◆ VERB 4 to crash or damage (an aircraft, car, etc.). 5 to damage (a town, etc.) by bombing.
▷HISTORY C20: possibly imitative of an explosion; perhaps related to Malay *perang* war, fighting

prank¹ (præŋk) NOUN a mischievous trick or joke, esp one in which something is done rather than said.
▷HISTORY C16: of unknown origin
▸ˈ**prankish** ADJECTIVE

prank² (præŋk) VERB 1 (*tr*) to dress or decorate showily or gaudily. 2 (*intr*) to make an ostentatious display.
▷HISTORY C16: from Middle Dutch *pronken;* related to German *Prunk* splendour, *prangen* to be in full splendour

prankster (ˈpræŋkstə) NOUN a practical joker.

prase (preɪz) NOUN a light green translucent variety of chalcedony.
▷HISTORY C14: from French, from Latin *prasius* a leek-green stone, from Greek *prasios,* from *prason* a leek

praseodymium (ˌpreɪzɪəʊˈdɪmɪəm) NOUN a malleable ductile silvery-white element of the lanthanide series of metals. It occurs principally in monazite and bastnaesite and is used with other rare earths in carbon-arc lights and as a pigment in glass. Symbol: Pr; atomic no.: 59; atomic wt.:

140.90765; valency: 3; relative density: 6.773; melting pt.: 931°C; boiling pt.: 3520°C.
▷HISTORY C20: New Latin, from Greek *prasios* of a leek-green colour + DIDYMIUM

prat (præt) NOUN *Slang* an incompetent or ineffectual person: often used as a term of abuse.
▷HISTORY C20: probably special use of C16 *prat* buttocks, of unknown origin

prate (preɪt) VERB [1] (*intr*) to talk idly and at length; chatter. [2] (*tr*) to utter in an idle or empty way. ◆ NOUN [3] idle or trivial talk; prattle; chatter.
▷HISTORY C15: of Germanic origin; compare Middle Dutch *prāten*, Icelandic and Norwegian *prata*, Danish *prate*
▸ˈ**prater** NOUN ▸ˈ**pratingly** ADVERB

pratfall (ˈpræt,fɔːl) NOUN *US and Canadian slang* a fall upon one's buttocks.
▷HISTORY C20: from C16 *prat* buttocks (of unknown origin) + FALL

pratincole (ˈprætɪŋ,kəʊl, ˈpreɪ-) NOUN any of various swallow-like shore birds of the southern Old World genus *Glareola* and related genera, esp *G. pratincola*, having long pointed wings, short legs, and a short bill: family *Glareolidae*, order *Charadriiformes*.
▷HISTORY C18: from New Latin *pratincola* field-dwelling, from Latin *prātum* meadow + *incola* inhabitant

pratique (ˈprætiːk, præˈtiːk) NOUN formal permission given to a vessel to use a foreign port upon satisfying the requirements of local health authorities.
▷HISTORY C17: from French, from Medieval Latin *practica* PRACTICE

Prato (*Italian* ˈpraːto) NOUN a walled city in central Italy, in Tuscany: woollen industry. Pop.: 172 473 (2000 est.). Official name: **Prato in Toscana** (in tosˈkaːna).

prattle (ˈprætᵊl) VERB [1] (*intr*) to talk in a foolish or childish way; babble. [2] (*tr*) to utter in a foolish or childish way. ◆ NOUN [3] foolish or childish talk.
▷HISTORY C16: from Middle Low German *pratelen* to chatter; see PRATE
▸ˈ**prattler** NOUN ▸ˈ**prattlingly** ADVERB

prau (praʊ) NOUN another word for **proa.**

prawn (prɔːn) NOUN [1] any of various small edible marine decapod crustaceans of the genera *Palaemon*, *Penaeus*, etc., having a slender flattened body with a long tail and two pairs of pincers. [2] **come the raw prawn.** *Austral informal* to attempt deception.
▷HISTORY C15: of obscure origin
▸ˈ**prawner** NOUN

prawn cracker NOUN a puffy savoury crisp made from rice flour and prawn flavouring, served with Chinese food.

praxis (ˈpræksɪs) NOUN, *plural* **praxises** *or* **praxes** (ˈpræksiːz). [1] the practice and practical side of a profession or field of study, as opposed to the theory. [2] a practical exercise. [3] accepted practice or custom.
▷HISTORY C16: via Medieval Latin from Greek: deed, action, from *prassein* to do

pray (preɪ) VERB [1] (when *intr*, often foll by *for;* when *tr, usually takes a clause as object*) to utter prayers (to God or other object of worship): *we prayed to God for the sick child.* [2] (when *tr, usually takes a clause as object or an infinitive*) to make an earnest entreaty (to or for); beg or implore: *she prayed to be allowed to go; leave, I pray you.* [3] (*tr*) *Rare* to accomplish or bring by praying: *to pray a soul into the kingdom.* ◆ INTERJECTION [4] *Archaic* I beg you; please: *pray, leave us alone.*
▷HISTORY C13: from Old French *preier*, from Latin *precārī* to implore, from *prex* an entreaty; related to Old English *fricgan*, Old High German *frāgēn* to ask, Old Norse *fregna* to enquire

prayer¹ (prɛə) NOUN [1] **a** a personal communication or petition addressed to a deity, esp in the form of supplication, adoration, praise, contrition, or thanksgiving. **b** any other form of spiritual communion with a deity. [2] a similar personal communication that does not involve adoration, addressed to beings venerated as being closely associated with a deity, such as angels or saints. [3] the practice of praying: *prayer is our solution to human problems.* [4] (*often plural*) a form of devotion, either public or private, spent mainly or wholly praying: *morning prayers.* [5] (*capital when part of a recognized name*) a form of words used in praying: *the Lord's Prayer.* [6] an object or benefit prayed for. [7] an earnest request, petition, or entreaty. [8] *Law* a request contained in a petition to a court for the relief sought by the petitioner. [9] *Slang* a chance or hope: *she doesn't have a prayer of getting married.*
▷HISTORY C13 *preiere*, from Old French, from Medieval Latin *precāria*, from Latin *precārius* obtained by begging, from *prex* prayer
▸ˈ**prayerless** ADJECTIVE

prayer² (ˈpreɪə) NOUN a person who prays.

prayer beads (prɛə) PLURAL NOUN *RC Church* the beads of the rosary.

prayer book (prɛə) NOUN [1] *Ecclesiast* a book containing the prayers used at church services or recommended for private devotions. [2] *Church of England (often capitals)* another name for **Book of Common Prayer.**

prayerful (ˈprɛəfʊl) ADJECTIVE inclined to or characterized by prayer.
▸ˈ**prayerfully** ADVERB ▸ˈ**prayerfulness** NOUN

prayer meeting (prɛə) NOUN *Chiefly Protestantism* a religious meeting at which the participants offer up prayers to God.

prayer rug (prɛə) NOUN the small carpet on which a Muslim kneels and prostrates himself while saying his prayers. Also called: **prayer mat.**

prayer shawl (prɛə) NOUN *Judaism* another word for **tallit.**

prayer wheel (prɛə) NOUN *Buddhism* (esp in Tibet) a wheel or cylinder inscribed with or containing prayers, each revolution of which is counted as an uttered prayer, so that such prayers can be repeated by turning it.

praying mantis *or* **mantid** NOUN another name for **mantis.**

PRB ABBREVIATION FOR (after the signatures of Pre-Raphaelite painters) Pre-Raphaelite Brotherhood.

pre- PREFIX before in time, rank, order, position, etc.: *predate; pre-eminent; premeditation; prefrontal; preschool.*
▷HISTORY from Latin *prae-*, from *prae* before, beforehand, in front

preach (priːtʃ) VERB [1] to make known (religious truth) or give religious or moral instruction or exhortation in (sermons). [2] to advocate (a virtue, action, etc.), esp in a moralizing way.
▷HISTORY C13: from Old French *prechier*, from Church Latin *praedicāre*, from Latin: to proclaim in public; see PREDICATE
▸ˈ**preachable** ADJECTIVE

preacher (ˈpriːtʃə) NOUN [1] a person who has the calling and function of preaching the Christian Gospel, esp a Protestant clergyman. [2] a person who preaches.

Preacher (ˈpriːtʃə) NOUN **the.** *Bible* the author of Ecclesiastes or the book of Ecclesiastes.

preachify (ˈpriːtʃɪ,faɪ) VERB **-fies, -fying, -fied.** (*intr*) *Informal* to preach or moralize in a tedious manner.
▸ˈ**preachi,fying** NOUN

preachment (ˈpriːtʃmənt) NOUN [1] the act of preaching. [2] a tedious or pompous sermon or discourse.

preachy (ˈpriːtʃɪ) ADJECTIVE **preachier, preachiest.** *Informal* inclined to or marked by preaching.

preacquisition profit (,priːækwɪˈzɪʃən) NOUN the retained profit of a company earned before a takeover and therefore not eligible for distribution as a dividend to the shareholders of the acquiring company.

preadamite (priːˈædə,maɪt) NOUN [1] a person who believes that there were people on earth before Adam. [2] a person assumed to have lived before Adam. ◆ ADJECTIVE *also* **preadamic** (,priːəˈdæmɪk). [3] of or relating to a preadamite.

preadaptation (,priːædæpˈteɪʃən) NOUN *Biology* the possession by a species or other group of characteristics that may favour survival in a changed environment, such as the limblike fins of crossopterygian fishes, which are preadaptation to terrestrial life.

preadolescent (,priːædəˈlɛsᵊnt) NOUN [1] a person who has not yet reached adolescence. ◆ ADJECTIVE [2] of or relating to the period before adolescence.

preamble (priːˈæmbᵊl) NOUN [1] a preliminary or introductory statement, esp attached to a statute or constitution setting forth its purpose. [2] a preliminary or introductory conference, event, fact, etc.
▷HISTORY C14: from Old French *préambule*, from Late Latin *praeambulum* walking before, from Latin *prae-* before + *ambulāre* to walk

preamplifier (priːˈæmplɪ,faɪə) NOUN an electronic amplifier used to improve the signal-to-noise ratio of an electronic device. It boosts a low-level signal to an intermediate level before it is transmitted to the main amplifier. Sometimes shortened to: **preamp.**

prearranged (,priːəˈreɪndʒd) ADJECTIVE having been arranged beforehand: *a pre-arranged meeting.*

preaxial (priːˈæksɪəl) ADJECTIVE *Anatomy* [1] situated or occurring in front of the axis of the body. [2] of or relating to the anterior part of a vertebrate limb.
▸**preˈaxially** ADVERB

prebend (ˈprɛbənd) NOUN [1] the stipend assigned by a cathedral or collegiate church to a canon or member of the chapter. [2] the land, tithe, or other source of such a stipend. [3] a less common word for **prebendary.** [4] *Church of England* the office, formerly with an endowment, of a prebendary.
▷HISTORY C15: from Old French *prébende*, from Medieval Latin *praebenda* pension, stipend, from Latin *praebēre* to offer, supply, from *prae* forth + *habēre* to have, offer
▸**prebendal** (prɪˈbɛndᵊl) ADJECTIVE

prebendary (ˈprɛbəndərɪ, -drɪ) NOUN, *plural* **-daries.** [1] a canon or member of the chapter of a cathedral or collegiate church who holds a prebend. [2] *Church of England* an honorary canon with the title of prebendary.

prebuttal (priːˈbʌtəl) NOUN *Informal* a prepared response to an anticipated criticism.
▷HISTORY C20: PRE- + (RE)BUTTAL

Precambrian *or* **Pre-Cambrian** (priːˈkæmbrɪən) ADJECTIVE [1] of, denoting, or formed in the earliest geological era, which lasted for about 4 000 000 000 years before the Cambrian period. ◆ NOUN [2] **the.** the Precambrian era. See **Archaeozoic, Proterozoic.**

precancel (priːˈkænsᵊl) VERB **-cels, -celling, -celled** *or US* **-cels, -celing, -celed.** [1] (*tr*) to cancel (postage stamps) before placing them on mail. ◆ NOUN [2] a precancelled stamp.
▸**pre,cancelˈlation** NOUN

precancerous ADJECTIVE (esp of cells) displaying characteristics that may develop into cancer.

precarious (prɪˈkɛərɪəs) ADJECTIVE [1] liable to failure or catastrophe; insecure; perilous. [2] *Archaic* dependent on another's will.
▷HISTORY C17: from Latin *precārius* obtained by begging (hence, dependent on another's will), from *prex* PRAYER¹
▸**preˈcariously** ADVERB ▸**preˈcariousness** NOUN

precast ADJECTIVE (ˈpriː,kɑːst) [1] (esp of concrete when employed as a structural element in building) cast in a particular form before being used. ◆ VERB (priːˈkɑːst) **-casts, -casting, -cast.** [2] (*tr*) to cast (concrete) in a particular form before use.

precatory (ˈprɛkətərɪ, -trɪ) ADJECTIVE *Rare* of, involving, or expressing entreaty; supplicatory. Also: **precative** (ˈprɛkətɪv).
▷HISTORY C17: from Late Latin *precātōrius* relating to petitions, from Latin *precārī* to beg, PRAY

precaution (prɪˈkɔːʃən) NOUN [1] an action taken to avoid a dangerous or undesirable event. [2] caution practised beforehand; circumspection.
▷HISTORY C17: from French, from Late Latin *praecautiō*, from Latin *praecavēre* to guard against, from *prae* before + *cavēre* to beware
▸**preˈcautionary** *or* **preˈcautional** ADJECTIVE ▸**preˈcautious** ADJECTIVE

precede (prɪˈsiːd) VERB [1] to go or be before (someone or something) in time, place, rank, etc. [2] (*tr*) to preface or introduce.
▷HISTORY C14: via Old French from Latin *praecēdere* to go before, from *prae* before + *cēdere* to move

precedence (ˈprɛsɪdəns) *or* **precedency** NOUN [1] the act of preceding or the condition of being precedent. [2] the ceremonial order or priority to be observed by persons of different stations on formal occasions: *the officers are seated according to* *precedence.* 3 a right to preferential treatment: *I take precedence over you.*

precedent NOUN ('prɛsɪdənt) 1 *Law* a judicial decision that serves as an authority for deciding a later case. 2 an example or instance used to justify later similar occurrences. ◆ ADJECTIVE (prɪ'siːdᵊnt, 'prɛsɪdənt) 3 preceding.

precedented ('presɪˌdɛntɪd) ADJECTIVE (of a decision, etc.) supported by having a precedent.

precedential (ˌprɛsɪ'dɛnʃəl) ADJECTIVE 1 of, involving, or serving as a precedent. 2 having precedence.
▸ **ˌprece'dentially** ADVERB

preceding (prɪ'siːdɪŋ) ADJECTIVE (*prenominal*) going or coming before; former.

precentor (prɪ'sɛntə) NOUN 1 a cleric who directs the choral services in a cathedral. 2 a person who leads a congregation or choir in the sung parts of church services.
▹HISTORY C17: from Late Latin *praecentor* leader of the music, from *prae* before + *canere* to sing
▸ **precentorial** (ˌpriːsɛn'tɔːrɪəl) ADJECTIVE
▸ **pre'centorˌship** NOUN

precept ('priːsɛpt) NOUN 1 a rule or principle for action. 2 a guide or rule for morals; maxim. 3 a direction, esp for a technical operation. 4 *Law* **a** a writ or warrant. **b** a written order to a sheriff to arrange an election, the empanelling of a jury, etc. **c** (in England) an order to collect money under a rate.
▹HISTORY C14: from Latin *praeceptum* maxim, injunction, from *praecipere* to admonish, from *prae* before + *capere* to take

preceptive (prɪ'sɛptɪv) ADJECTIVE 1 of, resembling, or expressing a precept or precepts. 2 didactic.
▸ **pre'ceptively** ADVERB

preceptor (prɪ'sɛptə) NOUN 1 *US* a practising physician giving practical training to a medical student. 2 the head of a preceptory. 3 *Rare* a tutor or instructor.
▸ **pre'ceptorate** NOUN ▸ **preceptorial** (ˌpriːsɛp'tɔːrɪəl) *or* **pre'ceptoral** ADJECTIVE ▸ **pre'ceptorˌship** NOUN
▸ **pre'ceptress** FEMININE NOUN

preceptory (prɪ'sɛptərɪ) NOUN, *plural* **-ries.** (formerly) a subordinate house or community of the Knights Templars.

precess (prɪ'sɛs) VERB to undergo or cause to undergo precession.

precession (prɪ'sɛʃən) NOUN 1 the act of preceding. 2 See **precession of the equinoxes.** 3 the motion of a spinning body, such as a top, gyroscope, or planet, in which it wobbles so that the axis of rotation sweeps out a cone.
▹HISTORY C16: from Late Latin *praecessiō* a going in advance, from Latin *praecēdere* to PRECEDE
▸ **pre'cessional** ADJECTIVE ▸ **pre'cessionally** ADVERB

precession of the equinoxes NOUN the slightly earlier occurrence of the equinoxes each year due to the slow continuous westward shift of the equinoctial points along the ecliptic by 50 seconds of arc per year. It is caused by the precession of the earth's axis around the ecliptic pole, with a period of 25 800 years.

pre-Christian ADJECTIVE of or referring to the period of history prior to the establishment of Christianity.

pre-Christmas ADJECTIVE of or relating to the period prior to Christmas: *the pre-Christmas rush.*

precinct ('priːsɪŋkt) NOUN 1 **a** an enclosed area or building marked by a fixed boundary such as a wall. **b** such a boundary. 2 an area in a town, often closed to traffic, that is designed or reserved for a particular purpose: *a shopping precinct; pedestrian precinct.* 3 *US* **a** a district of a city for administrative or police purposes. **b** the police responsible for such a district. 4 *US* a polling or electoral district.
▹HISTORY C15: from Medieval Latin *praecinctum* (something) surrounded, from Latin *praecingere* to gird around, from *prae* before, around + *cingere* to gird

precincts ('priːsɪŋkts) PLURAL NOUN the surrounding region or area.

preciosity (ˌprɛʃɪ'ɒsɪtɪ) NOUN, *plural* **-ties.** fastidiousness or affectation, esp in speech or manners.

precious ('prɛʃəs) ADJECTIVE 1 beloved; dear; cherished. 2 very costly or valuable. 3 held in high esteem, esp in moral or spiritual matters. 4 very fastidious or affected, as in speech, manners, etc. 5 *Informal* worthless: *you and your precious ideas!* ◆ ADVERB 6 *Informal* (intensifier): *there's precious little left.*
▹HISTORY C13: from Old French *precios*, from Latin *pretiōsus* valuable, from *pretium* price, value
▸ **'preciously** ADVERB ▸ **'preciousness** NOUN

precious coral NOUN another name for **red coral.**

precious metal NOUN any of the metals gold, silver, or platinum.

precious stone NOUN any of certain rare minerals, such as diamond, ruby, sapphire, emerald, or opal, that are highly valued as gemstones.

precipice ('prɛsɪpɪs) NOUN 1 **a** the steep sheer face of a cliff or crag. **b** the cliff or crag itself. 2 a precarious situation.
▹HISTORY C16: from Latin *praecipitium* steep place, from *praeceps* headlong
▸ **'precipiced** ADJECTIVE

precipitant (prɪ'sɪpɪtənt) ADJECTIVE 1 hasty or impulsive; rash. 2 rushing or falling rapidly or without heed. 3 abrupt or sudden. ◆ NOUN 4 *Chem* a substance or agent that causes a precipitate to form.
▸ **pre'cipitance** *or* **pre'cipitancy** NOUN ▸ **pre'cipitantly** ADVERB

precipitate VERB (prɪ'sɪpɪˌteɪt) 1 (*tr*) to cause to happen too soon or sooner than expected; bring on. 2 to throw or fall from or as from a height. 3 to cause (moisture) to condense and fall as snow, rain, etc., or (of moisture, rain, etc.) to condense and fall thus. 4 *Chem* to undergo or cause to undergo a process in which a dissolved substance separates from solution as a fine suspension of solid particles. ◆ ADJECTIVE (prɪ'sɪpɪtɪt) 5 rushing ahead. 6 done rashly or with undue haste. 7 sudden and brief. ◆ NOUN (prɪ'sɪpɪtɪt) 8 *Chem* a precipitated solid in its suspended form or after settling or filtering.
▹HISTORY C16: from Latin *praecipitāre* to throw down headlong, from *praeceps* headlong, steep, from *prae* before, in front + *caput* head
▸ **pre'cipitable** ADJECTIVE ▸ **preˌcipita'bility** NOUN
▸ **pre'cipitately** ADVERB ▸ **pre'cipitateness** NOUN
▸ **pre'cipitative** ADJECTIVE ▸ **pre'cipiˌtator** NOUN

precipitation (prɪˌsɪpɪ'teɪʃən) NOUN 1 *Meteorol* **a** rain, snow, sleet, dew, etc., formed by condensation of water vapour in the atmosphere. **b** the deposition of these on the earth's surface. **c** the amount precipitated. 2 the production or formation of a chemical precipitate. 3 the act of precipitating or the state of being precipitated. 4 rash or undue haste. 5 *Spiritualism* the appearance of a spirit in bodily form; materialization.

precipitation hardening NOUN *Metallurgy* a process in which alloys are strengthened by the formation, in their lattice, of a fine dispersion of one component when the metal is quenched from a high temperature and aged at an intermediate temperature.

precipitin (prɪ'sɪpɪtɪn) NOUN *Immunol* an antibody that causes precipitation when mixed with its specific antigen.

precipitous (prɪ'sɪpɪtəs) ADJECTIVE 1 resembling a precipice or characterized by precipices. 2 very steep. 3 hasty or precipitate.
▸ **pre'cipitously** ADVERB ▸ **pre'cipitousness** NOUN

> **Language note** The use of *precipitous* to mean *hasty* is thought by some people to be incorrect.

precis *or* **précis** ('preɪsiː) NOUN, *plural* **precis** *or* **précis** ('preɪsiːz). 1 a summary of the essentials of a text; abstract. ◆ VERB 2 (*tr*) to make a precis of.
▹HISTORY C18: from French: PRECISE

precise (prɪ'saɪs) ADJECTIVE 1 strictly correct in amount or value: *a precise sum.* 2 designating a certain thing and no other; particular: *this precise location.* 3 using or operating with total accuracy: *precise instruments.* 4 strict in observance of rules, standards, etc.: *a precise mind.*
▹HISTORY C16: from French *précis*, from Latin *praecīdere* to curtail, from *prae* before + *caedere* to cut
▸ **pre'ciseness** NOUN

precisely (prɪ'saɪslɪ) ADVERB 1 in a precise manner. ◆ SENTENCE SUBSTITUTE 2 exactly: used to confirm a statement by someone else.

precisian (prɪ'sɪʒən) NOUN a punctilious observer of rules or forms, esp in the field of religion.
▸ **pre'cisianism** NOUN

precision (prɪ'sɪʒən) NOUN 1 the quality of being precise; accuracy. 2 (*modifier*) characterized by or having a high degree of exactness: *precision grinding; a precision instrument.*
▹HISTORY C17: from Latin *praecīsiō* a cutting off; see PRECISE
▸ **pre'cisionism** NOUN ▸ **pre'cisionist** NOUN

preclinical (priː'klɪnɪkᵊl) ADJECTIVE *Med* 1 of, relating to, or occurring during the early phases of a disease before accurate diagnosis is possible. 2 of, relating to, or designating an early period of scientific study by a medical student before practical experience with patients.
▸ **pre'clinically** ADVERB

preclude (prɪ'kluːd) VERB (*tr*) 1 to exclude or debar. 2 to make impossible, esp beforehand.
▹HISTORY C17: from Latin *praeclūdere* to shut up, from *prae* in front, before + *claudere* to close
▸ **pre'cludable** ADJECTIVE ▸ **preclusion** (prɪ'kluːʒən) NOUN
▸ **preclusive** (prɪ'kluːsɪv) ADJECTIVE ▸ **pre'clusively** ADVERB

precocial (prɪ'kəʊʃəl) ADJECTIVE 1 (of the young of some species of birds after hatching) covered with down, having open eyes, and capable of leaving the nest within a few days of hatching. ◆ NOUN 2 a precocial bird. ◆ Compare **altricial.**
▹HISTORY C19: see PRECOCIOUS

precocious (prɪ'kəʊʃəs) ADJECTIVE 1 ahead in development, such as the mental development of a child. 2 *Botany* (of plants, fruit, etc.) flowering or ripening early.
▹HISTORY C17: from Latin *praecox* early maturing, from *prae* early + *coquere* to ripen
▸ **pre'cociously** ADVERB ▸ **pre'cociousness** *or* **precocity** (prɪ'kɒsɪtɪ) NOUN

precognition (ˌpriːkɒg'nɪʃən) NOUN *Psychol* the alleged ability to foresee future events. See also **clairvoyance, clairaudience.**
▹HISTORY C17: from Late Latin *praecognitiō* foreknowledge, from *praecognoscere* to foresee, from *prae* before + *cognoscere* to know, ascertain
▸ **precognitive** (priː'kɒgnɪtɪv) ADJECTIVE

pre-Columbian ADJECTIVE of or relating to the Americas before they were discovered by Columbus.

preconceive (ˌpriːkən'siːv) VERB (*tr*) to form an idea of beforehand; conceive of ahead in time.

preconception (ˌpriːkən'sɛpʃən) NOUN 1 an idea or opinion formed beforehand. 2 a bias; prejudice.

preconcert (ˌpriːkɒn'sɜːt, -kɒn'sət) ADJECTIVE of or relating to the period immediately before a performance or concert.

precondition (ˌpriːkən'dɪʃən) NOUN 1 a necessary or required condition; prerequisite. ◆ VERB 2 (*tr*) *Psychol* to present successively two stimuli to (an organism) without reinforcement so that they become associated; if a response is then conditioned to the second stimulus on its own, the same response will be evoked by the first stimulus.

preconize *or* **preconise** ('priːkəˌnaɪz) VERB (*tr*) 1 to announce or commend publicly. 2 to summon publicly. 3 (of the pope) to approve the appointment of (a nominee) to one of the higher dignities in the Roman Catholic Church.
▹HISTORY C15: from Medieval Latin *praecōnīzāre* to make an announcement, from Latin *praecō* herald
▸ **ˌpreconi'zation** *or* **ˌpreconi'sation** NOUN

preconscious (priː'kɒnʃəs) ADJECTIVE 1 *Psychol* prior to the development of consciousness. ◆ NOUN 2 *Psychoanal* mental contents or activity not immediately in consciousness but readily brought there. ◆ Compare **subconscious, unconscious.**
▸ **pre'consciously** ADVERB ▸ **pre'consciousness** NOUN

precontract NOUN (priː'kɒntrækt) 1 a contract or arrangement made beforehand, esp a betrothal. ◆ VERB (ˌpriːkən'trækt) 2 to betroth or enter into a betrothal by previous agreement. 3 to make (an agreement, etc.) by prior arrangement.

precook (priː'kʊk) VERB (*tr*) to cook (food) beforehand.

precritical (priː'krɪtɪkᵊl) ADJECTIVE of, relating to,

or occurring during the period preceding a crisis or a critical state or condition: *a precritical phase of a disease.*

precursor (prɪˈkɜːsə) NOUN [1] a person or thing that precedes and shows or announces someone or something to come; harbinger. [2] a predecessor or forerunner. [3] a chemical substance that gives rise to another more important substance.
▷HISTORY C16: from Latin *praecursor* one who runs in front, from *praecurrere,* from *prae* in front + *currere* to run

precursory (prɪˈkɜːsərɪ) *or* **precursive** ADJECTIVE [1] serving as a precursor. [2] preliminary or introductory.

pred. ABBREVIATION FOR predicate.

predacious *or* **predaceous** (prɪˈdeɪʃəs) ADJECTIVE [1] (of animals) habitually hunting and killing other animals for food. [2] preying on others.
▷HISTORY C18: from Latin *praeda* plunder; compare PREDATORY
▸**preˈdaciousness** *or* **preˈdaceousness** *or* **predacity** (prɪˈdæsɪtɪ) NOUN

predate (priːˈdeɪt) VERB (*tr*) [1] to affix a date to (a document, paper, etc.) that is earlier than the actual date. [2] to assign a date to (an event, period, etc.) that is earlier than the actual or previously assigned date of occurrence. [3] to be or occur at an earlier date than; precede in time.

predation (prɪˈdeɪʃən) NOUN a relationship between two species of animal in a community, in which one (the predator) hunts, kills, and eats the other (the prey).

predator (ˈprɛdətə) NOUN [1] any carnivorous animal. [2] a predatory person or thing.

predatory (ˈprɛdətərɪ, -trɪ) ADJECTIVE [1] *Zoology* another word for **predacious** (sense 1). [2] of, involving, or characterized by plundering, robbing, etc.
▷HISTORY C16: from Latin *praedātōrius* rapacious, from *praedārī* to pillage, from *praeda* booty
▸ˈ**predatorily** ADVERB ▸ˈ**predatoriness** NOUN

predatory pricing NOUN *Commerce* offering goods or services at such a low price that competitors are forced out of the market.

predecease (ˌpriːdɪˈsiːs) VERB [1] to die before (some other person). ◆ NOUN [2] *Rare* earlier death.

predecessor (ˈpriːdɪˌsɛsə) NOUN [1] a person who precedes another, as in an office. [2] something that precedes something else. [3] an ancestor; forefather.
▷HISTORY C14: via Old French from Late Latin *praedēcessor,* from *prae* before + *dēcēdere* to go away, from *dē* away + *cēdere* to go

predella (prɪˈdɛlə; *Italian* preˈdɛlla) NOUN, *plural* **-le** (-liː; *Italian* -le). [1] a painting or sculpture or a series of small paintings or sculptures in a long narrow strip forming the lower edge of an altarpiece or the face of an altar step or platform. [2] a platform in a church upon which the altar stands.
▷HISTORY C19: from Italian: stool, step, probably from Old High German *bret* board

predeposit (ˌpriːdɪˈpɒzɪt) VERB (*tr*) to deposit beforehand or for future use.

predestinarian (ˌpriːdɛstɪˈnɛərɪən) *Theol* ◆ NOUN [1] a person who believes in divine predestination. ◆ ADJECTIVE [2] of or relating to predestination or characterizing those who believe in it.
▸ˌ**predestiˈnarianism** NOUN

predestinate VERB (priːˈdɛstɪˌneɪt) [1] (*tr*) another word for **predestine.** ◆ ADJECTIVE (priːˈdɛstɪnɪt, -ˌneɪt) [2] predestined or foreordained. [3] *Theol* subject to predestination; decided by God from all eternity.

predestination (priːˌdɛstɪˈneɪʃən) NOUN [1] *Theol* **a** the act of God foreordaining every event from eternity. **b** the doctrine or belief, esp associated with Calvin, that the final salvation of some of mankind is foreordained from eternity by God. [2] the act of predestining or the state of being predestined.

predestine (priːˈdɛstɪn) *or* **predestinate** VERB (*tr*) [1] to foreordain; determine beforehand. [2] *Theol* (of God) to decree from eternity (any event, esp the final salvation of individuals).
▷HISTORY C14: from Latin *praedestināre* to resolve beforehand, from *destināre* to determine, DESTINE
▸**preˈdestinable** ADJECTIVE

predeterminate (ˌpriːdɪˈtɜːmɪnɪt, -ˌneɪt) ADJECTIVE determined beforehand; predetermined.
▸ˌ**predeˈterminately** ADVERB

predetermine (ˌpriːdɪˈtɜːmɪn) VERB (*tr*) [1] to determine beforehand. [2] to influence or incline towards an opinion beforehand; bias.
▸ˌ**predeˌtermiˈnation** NOUN ▸ˌ**predeˈterminative** ADJECTIVE ▸ˌ**predeˈterminer** NOUN

predial (ˈpriːdɪəl) ADJECTIVE a variant spelling of **praedial.**

predicable (ˈprɛdɪkəbᵊl) ADJECTIVE [1] capable of being predicated or asserted. ◆ NOUN [2] a quality, attribute, etc., that can be predicated. [3] *Logic, obsolete* one of the five Aristotelian classes of predicates (**the five heads of predicables**), namely genus, species, difference, property, and relation.
▷HISTORY C16: from Latin *praedicābilis,* from *praedicāre* to assert publicly; see PREDICATE, PREACH
▸ˌ**predicaˈbility** *or* ˈ**predicableness** NOUN

predicament (prɪˈdɪkəmənt) NOUN [1] a perplexing, embarrassing, or difficult situation. [2] (ˈprɛdɪkəmənt) *Logic, obsolete* one of Aristotle's ten categories of being. [3] *Archaic* a specific condition, circumstance, state, position, etc.
▷HISTORY C14: from Late Latin *praedicāmentum* what is predicated, from *praedicāre* to announce, assert; see PREDICATE

predicant (ˈprɛdɪkənt) ADJECTIVE [1] of or relating to preaching. ◆ NOUN [2] a member of a religious order founded for preaching, esp a Dominican. [3] (ˌprɛdɪˈkænt) a variant spelling of **predikant.**
▷HISTORY C17: from Latin *praedicāns* preaching, from *praedicāre* to say publicly; see PREDICATE

predicate VERB (ˈprɛdɪˌkeɪt) (*mainly tr*) [1] (*also intr; when tr, may take a clause as object*) to proclaim, declare, or affirm. [2] to imply or connote. [3] (foll by *on* or *upon*) to base or found (a proposition, argument, etc.). [4] *Logic* **a** to assert or affirm (a property, characteristic, or condition) of the subject of a proposition. **b** to make (a term, expression, etc.) the predicate of a proposition. ◆ NOUN (ˈprɛdɪkɪt) [5] *Grammar* **a** the part of a sentence in which something is asserted or denied of the subject of a sentence; one of the two major components of a sentence, the other being the subject. **b** (*as modifier*): *a predicate adjective.* [6] *Logic* **a** an expression that is derived from a sentence by the deletion of a name. **b** a property, characteristic, or attribute that may be affirmed or denied of something. The categorial statement *all men are mortal* relates two predicates, *is a man* and *is mortal.* **c** the term of a categorial proposition that is affirmed or denied of its subject. In this example *all men* is the subject, and *mortal* is the predicate. **d** a function from individuals to truth values, the truth set of the function being the extension of the predicate. ◆ ADJECTIVE (ˈprɛdɪkɪt) [7] of or relating to something that has been predicated.
▷HISTORY C16: from Latin *praedicāre* to assert publicly, from *prae* in front, in public + *dīcere* to say
▸ˌ**prediˈcation** NOUN

predicate calculus NOUN the system of symbolic logic concerned not only with relations between propositions as wholes but also with the representation by symbols of individuals and predicates in propositions and with quantification over individuals. Also called: **functional calculus.** See also **propositional calculus.**

predicative (prɪˈdɪkətɪv) ADJECTIVE [1] *Grammar* relating to or occurring within the predicate of a sentence: *a predicative adjective.* Compare **attributive.** [2] *Logic* (of a definition) given in terms that do not require quantification over entities of the same type as that which is thereby defined. Compare **impredicative.**
▸**preˈdicatively** ADVERB

predicator (ˈprɛdɪˌkeɪtə) NOUN (in systemic grammar) the part of a sentence or clause containing the verbal group; one of the four or five major components into which clauses can be divided, the others being subject, object, adjunct, and (in some versions of the grammar) complement.

predicatory (ˈprɛdɪˌkeɪtərɪ, ˌprɛdɪˈkeɪtərɪ) ADJECTIVE of, relating to, or characteristic of preaching or a preacher.
▷HISTORY C17: from Late Latin *praedicātōrius,* from *praedicāre* to proclaim

predict (prɪˈdɪkt) VERB (*tr; may take a clause as object*) to state or make a declaration about in advance, esp on a reasoned basis; foretell.
▷HISTORY C17: from Latin *praedīcere* to mention beforehand, from *prae* before + *dīcere* to say
▸**preˈdictable** ADJECTIVE ▸**preˌdictaˈbility** *or* **preˈdictableness** NOUN ▸**preˈdictably** ADVERB

prediction (prɪˈdɪkʃən) NOUN [1] the act of predicting. [2] something predicted; a forecast, prophecy, etc.

predictive (prɪˈdɪktɪv) ADJECTIVE of, relating to, or making predictions.
▸**preˈdictively** ADVERB

predictor (prɪˈdɪktə) NOUN [1] a person or thing that predicts. [2] an instrument, used in conjunction with an anti-aircraft gun, that determines the speed, distance, height, and direction of hostile aircraft. [3] *Statistics* a more modern term for **independent variable.**

predigest (ˌpriːdaɪˈdʒɛst, -dɪ-) VERB (*tr*) to treat (food) artificially to aid subsequent digestion in the body.
▸ˌ**prediˈgestion** NOUN

predikant *or* **predicant** (ˌprɛdɪˈkænt) NOUN a minister in the Dutch Reformed Church, esp in South Africa.
▷HISTORY from Dutch, from Old French *predicant,* from Late Latin *praedicans* preaching, from *praedicāre* to PREACH

predilection (ˌpriːdɪˈlɛkʃən) NOUN a predisposition, preference, or bias.
▷HISTORY C18: from French *prédilection,* from Medieval Latin *praedīligere* to prefer, from Latin *prae* before + *dīligere* to love

predispose (ˌpriːdɪˈspəʊz) VERB (*tr*) [1] (often foll by *to* or *towards*) to incline or make (someone) susceptible to something beforehand. [2] *Chiefly law* to dispose of (property, etc.) beforehand; bequeath.
▸ˌ**predisˈposal** NOUN

predisposition (ˌpriːdɪspəˈzɪʃən) NOUN [1] the condition of being predisposed. [2] *Med* susceptibility to a specific disease. Compare **diathesis.**

prednisolone (prɛdˈnɪsəˌləʊn) NOUN a steroid drug derived from prednisone and having the same uses as cortisone.
▷HISTORY C20: altered from PREDNISONE

prednisone (ˈprɛdnɪˌsəʊn) NOUN a steroid drug derived from cortisone and having the same uses.
▷HISTORY C20: perhaps from PRE(GNANT) + -D(IE)N(E) + (CORT)ISONE

predominant (prɪˈdɒmɪnənt) ADJECTIVE [1] having superiority in power, influence, etc., over others. [2] prevailing; prominent.
▸**preˈdominance** *or* **preˈdominancy** NOUN

predominantly (prɪˈdɒmɪnəntlɪ) ADVERB for the most part; mostly; mainly.

predominate (prɪˈdɒmɪˌneɪt) VERB [1] (*intr;* often foll by *over*) to have power, influence, or control. [2] (*intr*) to prevail or preponderate. [3] (*tr*) *Rare* to dominate or have control over. ◆ ADJECTIVE (prɪˈdɒmɪnɪt) [4] another word for **predominant.**
▷HISTORY C16: from Medieval Latin *praedominārī,* from Latin *prae* before + *dominārī* to bear rule, domineer
▸**preˈdominately** ADVERB ▸**preˌdomiˈnation** NOUN ▸**preˈdomiˌnator** NOUN

pre-echo (priːˈɛkəʊ) NOUN [1] something that has preceded and anticipated something else; precursor. [2] a fault in an audio recording in which a sound that is to come is heard too early: on tape sometimes caused by print-through.

pre-eclampsia (ˌpriːɪˈklæmpsɪə) NOUN *Pathol* a toxic condition of pregnancy characterized by high blood pressure, protein in the urine, abnormal weight gain, and oedema. Compare **eclampsia.**

pre-election NOUN (*modifier*) existing or occurring before an election.

pre-embryo (priːˈɛmbrɪəʊ) NOUN the structure formed after fertilization of an ovum but before differentiation of embryonic tissue.

preemie *or* **premie** (ˈpriːmɪ) NOUN *Slang, chiefly US and Canadian* a premature infant.
▷HISTORY C20: altered from PREMATURE

pre-eminent (prɪˈɛmɪnənt) ADJECTIVE extremely eminent or distinguished; outstanding.
▸**pre-ˈeminence** NOUN ▸**pre-ˈeminently** ADVERB

pre-empt (prɪˈɛmpt) VERB 1 (*tr*) to acquire in advance of or to the exclusion of others; appropriate. 2 (*tr*) *Chiefly US* to occupy (public land) in order to acquire a prior right to purchase. 3 (*intr*) *Bridge* to make a high opening bid, often on a weak hand, to shut out opposition bidding.
▸**pre-ˈemptor** NOUN ▸**pre-ˈemptory** ADJECTIVE

pre-emption (prɪˈɛmpʃən) NOUN 1 *Law* the purchase of or right to purchase property in advance of or in preference to others. 2 *International law* the right of a government to intercept and seize for its own purposes goods or property of the subjects of another state while in transit, esp in time of war.
▷HISTORY C16: from Medieval Latin *praeemptiō*, from *praeemere* to buy beforehand, from *emere* to buy

pre-emptive (prɪˈɛmptɪv) ADJECTIVE 1 of, involving, or capable of pre-emption. 2 *Bridge* (of a high bid) made to shut out opposition bidding. 3 *Military* designed to reduce or destroy an enemy's attacking strength before it can use it: *a pre-emptive strike*.
▸**pre-ˈemptively** ADVERB

preen[1] (priːn) VERB 1 (of birds) to maintain (feathers) in a healthy condition by arrangement, cleaning, and other contact with the bill. 2 to dress or array (oneself) carefully; primp. 3 (usually foll by *on*) to pride or congratulate (oneself).
▷HISTORY C14 *preinen*, probably from *prunen* to PRUNE[3], influenced by *prenen* to prick, pin (see PREEN[2]); suggestive of the pricking movement of the bird's beak
▸**ˈpreener** NOUN

preen[2] (priːn) NOUN *Scot* a pin, esp a decorative one.
▷HISTORY Old English *prēon* a pin; related to Middle High German *pfrieme* awl, Dutch *priem* bodkin

pre-exilian (ˌpriːɪgˈzɪlɪən) *or* **pre-exilic** ADJECTIVE *Old Testament* prior to the Babylonian exile of the Jews (586–538 B.C.).

pre-exist ADJECTIVE occuring or existing previously.
▸**ˌpre-exˈistence** NOUN

pref. ABBREVIATION FOR: 1 preface. 2 preference. 3 preferred. 4 prefix.

prefab (ˈpriːˌfæb) NOUN **a** a building that is prefabricated, esp a small house. **b** (*as modifier*): *a prefab house*.

prefabricate (priːˈfæbrɪˌkeɪt) VERB (*tr*) to manufacture sections of (a building), esp in a factory, so that they can be easily transported to and rapidly assembled on a building site.
▸**preˈfabriˌcated** ADJECTIVE ▸**preˌfabriˈcation** NOUN

preface (ˈprɛfɪs) NOUN 1 a statement written as an introduction to a literary or other work, typically explaining its scope, intention, method, etc.; foreword. 2 anything introductory. 3 *RC Church* a prayer of thanksgiving and exhortation serving as an introduction to the canon of the Mass. ◆ VERB (*tr*) 4 to furnish with a preface. 5 to serve as a preface to.
▷HISTORY C14: from Medieval Latin *praefātia*, from Latin *praefātiō* a saying beforehand, from *praefārī* to utter in advance, from *prae* before + *fārī* to say
▸**ˈprefacer** NOUN

prefatory (ˈprɛfətərɪ, -trɪ) *or* **prefatorial** (ˌprɛfəˈtɔːrɪəl) ADJECTIVE of, involving, or serving as a preface; introductory.
▷HISTORY C17: from Latin *praefārī* to say in advance; see PREFACE
▸**ˈprefatorily** *or* **ˌprefaˈtorially** ADVERB

prefect (ˈpriːfɛkt) NOUN 1 (in France, Italy, etc.) the chief administrative officer in a department. 2 (in France, etc.) the head of a police force. 3 *Brit* a schoolchild appointed to a position of limited power over his fellows. 4 (in ancient Rome) any of several magistrates or military commanders. 5 Also called: **prefect apostolic.** *RC Church* an official having jurisdiction over a missionary district that has no ordinary. 6 *RC Church* one of two senior masters in a Jesuit school or college (the **prefect of studies** and the **prefect of discipline** or **first prefect**). 7 *RC Church* a cardinal in charge of a congregation of the Curia. ◆ Also (for senses 4–7): **praefect.**
▷HISTORY C14: from Latin *praefectus* one put in charge, from *praeficere* to place in authority over, from *prae* before + *facere* to do, make

▸**prefectorial** (ˌpriːfɛkˈtɔːrɪəl) ADJECTIVE

prefecture (ˈpriːfɛkˌtjʊə) NOUN 1 the office, position, or area of authority of a prefect. 2 the official residence of a prefect in France, Italy, etc.
▸**preˈfectural** ADJECTIVE

prefer (prɪˈfɜː) VERB **-fers, -ferring, -ferred.** 1 (when *tr, may take a clause as object or an infinitive*) to like better or value more highly: *I prefer to stand.* 2 *Law* to give preference, esp to one creditor over others. 3 (esp of the police) to put (charges) before a court, judge, magistrate, etc., for consideration and judgment. 4 (*tr; often passive*) to advance in rank over another or others; promote.
▷HISTORY C14: from Latin *praeferre* to carry in front, prefer, from *prae* in front + *ferre* to bear
▸**preˈferrer** NOUN

> **Language note** Normally, *to* is used after *prefer* and *preferable*, not *than*: *I prefer Brahms to Tchaikovsky; a small income is preferable to no income at all*. However, *than* or *rather than* should be used to link infinitives: *I prefer to walk than/rather than to catch the train.*

preferable (ˈprɛfərəb(ə)l, ˈprɛfrəb(ə)l) ADJECTIVE preferred or more desirable.
▸**ˌpreferaˈbility** *or* **ˈpreferableness** NOUN

> **Language note** Since *preferable* already means *more desirable*, one should not say something is *more preferable* or *most preferable*. See also at **prefer**.

preferably (ˈprɛfərəblɪ, ˈprɛfrəblɪ) ADVERB ideally; by preference; if one had a choice.

preference (ˈprɛfərəns, ˈprɛfrəns) NOUN 1 the act of preferring. 2 something or someone preferred. 3 *Law* **a** the settling of the claims of one or more creditors before or to the exclusion of the others. **b** a prior right to payment, as of a dividend or share in the assets of a company in the event of liquidation. 4 *Commerce* the granting of favour or precedence to particular foreign countries, as by levying differential tariffs.

preference shares PLURAL NOUN *Brit and Austral* shares representing part of the capital issued by a company and entitling their holders to priority with respect to both net profit and net assets. Preference shares usually carry a definite rate of dividend that is generally lower than that declared on ordinary shares. US and Canadian name: **preferred stock.** Compare **ordinary shares, preferred ordinary shares.**

preferential (ˌprɛfəˈrɛnʃəl) ADJECTIVE 1 showing or resulting from preference. 2 giving, receiving, or originating from preference in international trade.
▸**preferentiality** (ˌprɛfəˌrɛnʃɪˈælɪtɪ) NOUN
▸**ˌpreferˈentially** ADVERB

preferential voting NOUN a system of voting in which the electors signify their choices, as of candidates, in order of preference.

preferment (prɪˈfɜːmənt) NOUN 1 the act of promoting or advancing to a higher position, office, etc. 2 the state of being preferred for promotion or social advancement. 3 the act of preferring.

preferred ordinary shares PLURAL NOUN *Brit* shares issued by a company that rank between preference shares and ordinary shares in the payment of dividends. Compare **preference shares.**

preferred stock NOUN the US and Canadian name for **preference shares.**

prefiguration (ˌpriːfɪgəˈreɪʃən) NOUN 1 the act of prefiguring. 2 something that prefigures, such as a prototype.
▸**preˈfigurative** ADJECTIVE ▸**preˈfiguratively** ADVERB
▸**preˈfigurativeness** NOUN

prefigure (priːˈfɪgə) VERB (*tr*) 1 to represent or suggest in advance. 2 to imagine or consider beforehand.
▸**preˈfigurement** NOUN

prefix NOUN (ˈpriːfɪks) 1 *Grammar* an affix that precedes the stem to which it is attached, as for example *un-* in *unhappy*. Compare **suffix** (sense 1). 2 something coming or placed before. ◆ VERB (priːˈfɪks, ˈpriːfɪks) (*tr*) 3 to put or place before. 4 *Grammar* to add (a morpheme) as a prefix to the beginning of a word.
▸**prefixal** (ˈpriːfɪksəl, priːˈfɪks-) ADJECTIVE ▸**ˈprefixally** ADVERB ▸**prefixion** (priːˈfɪkʃən) NOUN

preflight (ˈpriːˈflaɪt) ADJECTIVE of or relating to the period just prior to a plane taking off.

preformation (ˌpriːfɔːˈmeɪʃən) NOUN 1 the act of forming in advance; previous formation. 2 *Biology* the theory, now discredited, that an individual develops by simple enlargement of a fully differentiated egg cell. Compare **epigenesis** (sense 1).

prefrontal (priːˈfrʌnt(ə)l) ADJECTIVE situated in, involving, or relating to the foremost part of the frontal lobe of the brain.

preggers (ˈprɛgəz) ADJECTIVE *Chiefly Brit* an informal word for **pregnant** (sense 1).

preggy (ˈprɛgɪ) ADJECTIVE *NZ* an informal word for **pregnant** (sense 1).

preglacial (priːˈgleɪsɪəl) ADJECTIVE formed or occurring before a glacial period, esp before the Pleistocene epoch.

pregnable (ˈprɛgnəb(ə)l) ADJECTIVE capable of being assailed or captured.
▷HISTORY C15 *prenable*, from Old French *prendre* to take, from Latin *prehendere* to lay hold of, catch
▸**ˌpregnaˈbility** NOUN

pregnancy (ˈprɛgnənsɪ) NOUN, *plural* **-cies.** 1 the state or condition of being pregnant. 2 the period from conception to childbirth.

pregnant (ˈprɛgnənt) ADJECTIVE 1 carrying a fetus or fetuses within the womb. 2 full of meaning or significance. 3 inventive or imaginative. 4 prolific or fruitful.
▷HISTORY C16: from Latin *praegnāns* with child, from *prae* before + *(g)nascī* to be born
▸**ˈpregnantly** ADVERB

preheat (priːˈhiːt) VERB (*tr*) to heat (an oven, grill, pan, etc.) beforehand.

prehensile (prɪˈhɛnsaɪl) ADJECTIVE adapted for grasping, esp by wrapping around a support: *a prehensile tail*.
▷HISTORY C18: from French *préhensile*, from Latin *prehendere* to grasp
▸**prehensility** (ˌpriːhɛnˈsɪlɪtɪ) NOUN

prehension (prɪˈhɛnʃən) NOUN 1 the act of grasping. 2 apprehension by the senses or the mind.

prehistoric (ˌpriːhɪˈstɒrɪk) *or* **prehistorical** ADJECTIVE of or relating to man's development before the appearance of the written word.
▸**ˌprehisˈtorically** ADVERB

prehistory (priːˈhɪstərɪ) NOUN, *plural* **-ries.** 1 the prehistoric period. 2 the study of this period, relying entirely on archaeological evidence.
▸**prehistorian** (ˌpriːhɪˈstɔːrɪən) NOUN

prehominid (priːˈhɒmɪnɪd) NOUN any of various extinct manlike primates. See **australopithecine.**

pre-ignition (ˌpriːɪgˈnɪʃən) NOUN ignition of all or part of the explosive charge in an internal-combustion engine before the exact instant necessary for correct operation.

preindustrial (ˌpriːɪnˈdʌstrɪəl) ADJECTIVE of or relating to a society, age, etc., before industrialization.

prejudge (priːˈdʒʌdʒ) VERB (*tr*) to judge beforehand, esp without sufficient evidence.
▸**preˈjudger** NOUN ▸**preˈjudgment** *or* **preˈjudgement** NOUN

prejudice (ˈprɛdʒʊdɪs) NOUN 1 an opinion formed beforehand, esp an unfavourable one based on inadequate facts. 2 the act or condition of holding such opinions. 3 intolerance of or dislike for people of a specific race, religion, etc. 4 disadvantage or injury resulting from prejudice. 5 **in** (*or* **to**) **the prejudice of.** to the detriment of. 6 **without prejudice.** *Law* without dismissing or detracting from an existing right or claim. ◆ VERB (*tr*) 7 to cause to be prejudiced. 8 to disadvantage or injure by prejudice.
▷HISTORY C13: from Old French *préjudice*, from Latin *praejūdicium* a preceding judgment, disadvantage, from *prae* before + *jūdicium* trial, sentence, from *jūdex* a judge

prejudicial (ˌprɛdʒʊˈdɪʃəl) ADJECTIVE causing prejudice; detrimental or damaging.
▸**ˌprejuˈdicially** ADVERB

prelacy (ˈprɛləsɪ) NOUN, *plural* **-cies.** 1 Also called:

prelature ('prɛlɪtʃə). **a** the office or status of a prelate. **b** prelates collectively. 2 Also called: **prelatism** ('prɛləˌtɪzəm). *Often derogatory* government of the Church by prelates.

prelapsarian (ˌpri:læp'sɛərɪən) ADJECTIVE characteristic of or relating to the human state or time before the Fall: *prelapsarian innocence.*

prelate ('prɛlɪt) NOUN a Church dignitary of high rank, such as a cardinal, bishop, or abbot.
▷HISTORY C13: from Old French *prélat,* from Church Latin *praelātus,* from Latin *praeferre* to hold in special esteem, PREFER
▸**prelatic** (prɪ'lætɪk) *or* **pre'latical** ADJECTIVE

prelatism ('prɛləˌtɪzəm) NOUN government of the Church by prelates; episcopacy.
▸**'prelatist** NOUN

prelect (prɪ'lɛkt) VERB (*intr*) *Rare* to lecture or discourse in public.
▷HISTORY C17: from Late Latin *praelegere* to instruct by reading, lecture, from *prae* in front of, in public + *legere* to read, choose
▸**pre'lection** NOUN ▸**pre'lector** NOUN

prelexical (pri:'lɛksɪkᵊl) ADJECTIVE *Transformational grammar* denoting or applicable at a stage in the formation of a sentence at which words and phrases have not yet replaced all of the underlying grammatical and semantic material of that sentence in the speaker's mind.

prelibation (ˌpri:laɪ'beɪʃən) NOUN *Rare* an advance taste or sample; foretaste.
▷HISTORY C16: from Late Latin *praelībātiō* a tasting beforehand, offering of the first fruits, from Latin *prae* before + *lībāre* to taste

prelim. ABBREVIATION FOR preliminary.

preliminaries (prɪ'lɪmɪnərɪz) PLURAL NOUN the full word for **prelims.**

preliminary (prɪ'lɪmɪnərɪ) ADJECTIVE 1 (*usually prenominal*) occurring before or in preparation; introductory. ◆ NOUN, *plural* **-naries.** 2 a preliminary event or occurrence. 3 an eliminating contest held before the main competition.
▷HISTORY C17: from New Latin *praelīmināris,* from Latin *prae* before + *līmen* threshold
▸**pre'liminarily** ADVERB

prelims ('pri:lɪmz, prə'lɪmz) PLURAL NOUN 1 Also called: **front matter.** the pages of a book, such as the title page and contents, before the main text. 2 the first public examinations taken for the bachelor's degree in some universities. 3 (in Scotland) the school examinations taken as practice before public examinations.
▷HISTORY C19: a contraction of PRELIMINARIES

prelingually deaf (pri:'lɪŋgwəlɪ) ADJECTIVE **a** deaf from birth or having acquired deafness before learning to speak. **b** (*as collective noun; preceded by the*): *the prelingually deaf.*

preliterate (pri:'lɪtərɪt) ADJECTIVE relating to a society that has not developed a written language.
▸**preliteracy** (pri:'lɪtərəsɪ) NOUN

preloved ('pri:ˌlʌvd) ADJECTIVE *Austral informal* previously owned or used; second-hand.

prelude ('prɛlju:d) NOUN 1 **a** a piece of music that precedes a fugue, or forms the first movement of a suite, or an introduction to an act in an opera, etc. **b** (esp for piano) a self-contained piece of music. 2 something serving as an introduction or preceding event, occurrence, etc. ◆ VERB 3 to serve as a prelude to (something). 4 (*tr*) to introduce by a prelude.
▷HISTORY C16: (n) from Medieval Latin *praelūdium,* from *prae* before + *-lūdium* entertainment, from Latin *lūdus* play; (vb) from Late Latin *praelūdere* to play beforehand, rehearse, from *lūdere* to play
▸**preluder** (prɪ'lju:də, 'prɛljudə) NOUN ▸**pre'ludial** ADJECTIVE ▸**prelusion** (prɪ'lju:ʒən) NOUN ▸**prelusive** (prɪ'lju:sɪv) *or* **prelusory** (prɪ'lju:sərɪ) ADJECTIVE
▸**pre'lusively** *or* **pre'lusorily** ADVERB

prem (prɛm) NOUN *Informal* a premature infant.

prem. ABBREVIATION FOR premium.

premarital (pri:'mærɪtᵊl) ADJECTIVE (esp of sexual relations) occurring before marriage. Compare **extramarital.**

premature (ˌprɛmə'tjʊə, 'prɛməˌtjʊə) ADJECTIVE 1 occurring or existing before the normal or expected time. 2 impulsive or hasty: *a premature judgment.* 3 (of an infant) weighing less than 2500 g (5½ lbs) and usually born before the end of the full period of gestation.
▷HISTORY C16: from Latin *praemātūrus,* very early, from *prae* in advance + *mātūrus* ripe
▸ˌ**prema'turely** ADVERB ▸ˌ**prema'tureness** *or* ˌ**prema'turity** NOUN

premaxilla (ˌpri:mæk'sɪlə) NOUN, *plural* **-lae** (-li:). either of two bones situated in the upper jaw between the maxillary bones.
▸ˌ**premax'illary** ADJECTIVE

premed (pri:'mɛd) *Informal* ◆ ADJECTIVE 1 short for **premedical.** ◆ NOUN *also* **premedic.** 2 short for **premedication.** 3 a premedical student.

premedical (pri:'mɛdɪkᵊl) ADJECTIVE 1 of or relating to a course of study prerequisite for entering medical school. 2 of or relating to a person engaged in such a course of study: *a premedical student.*
▸**pre'medically** ADVERB

premedication (ˌpri:mɛdɪ'keɪʃən) NOUN *Surgery* any drugs administered to sedate and otherwise prepare a patient for general anaesthesia.

premeditate (prɪ'mɛdɪˌteɪt) VERB to plan or consider (something, such as a violent crime) beforehand.
▸**pre'mediˌtatedly** ADVERB ▸**pre'mediˌtative** ADJECTIVE
▸**pre'mediˌtator** NOUN

premeditation (prɪˌmɛdɪ'teɪʃən) NOUN 1 *Law* prior resolve to do some act or to commit a crime. 2 the act of premeditating.

premenstrual (pri:'mɛnstrʊəl) ADJECTIVE 1 of or occurring before a menstrual period. 2 of or occuring before the menarche.

premenstrual syndrome *or* **tension** NOUN a group of symptoms, including nervous tension and fluid retention, any of which may be experienced as a result of hormonal changes in the days before a menstrual period starts. Abbreviations: **PMS, PMT.**

premie ('pri:mɪ) NOUN a variant spelling of **preemie.**

premier ('prɛmjə) NOUN 1 another name for **prime minister.** 2 any of the heads of governments of the Canadian provinces and the Australian states. 3 (*plural*) *Austral* the winners of a premiership. ◆ ADJECTIVE (*prenominal*) 4 first in importance, rank, etc. 5 first in occurrence; earliest.
▷HISTORY C15: from Old French: first, from Latin *prīmārius* principal, from *prīmus* first

premier danseur *French* (prəmje dɑ̃sœr) *or feminine* ***première danseuse*** (prəmjɛr dɑ̃søz) NOUN, *plural* ***premiers danseurs*** *or feminine* ***premières danseuses.*** the principal dancer in a ballet company.
▷HISTORY C19: literally: first dancer

premiere ('prɛmɪˌɛə, 'prɛmɪə) NOUN 1 the first public performance of a film, play, opera, etc. 2 the leading lady in a theatre company. ◆ VERB 3 to give or be the first public performance of.
▷HISTORY C19: from French, feminine of *premier* first

premiership ('prɛmjəʃɪp) NOUN 1 the office of premier. 2 **a** a championship competition held among a number of sporting clubs. **b** a victory in such a championship.

premillenarian (ˌpri:mɪlɪ'nɛərɪən) NOUN 1 a believer in or upholder of the doctrines of premillennialism. ◆ ADJECTIVE 2 of or relating to premillennialism.
▸ˌ**premille'narianism** NOUN

premillennial (ˌpri:mɪ'lɛnɪəl) ADJECTIVE of or relating to the period preceding the millennium.

premillennialism (ˌpri:mɪ'lɛnɪəˌlɪzəm) NOUN the doctrine or belief that the millennium will be preceded by the Second Coming of Christ.
▸ˌ**premil'lennialist** NOUN

premise NOUN ('prɛmɪs) 1 Also: **premiss.** *Logic* a statement that is assumed to be true for the purpose of an argument from which a conclusion is drawn. ◆ VERB (prɪ'maɪz, 'prɛmɪs) 2 (when *tr, may take a clause as object*) to state or assume (a proposition) as a premise in an argument, theory, etc.
▷HISTORY C14: from Old French *prémisse,* from Medieval Latin *praemissa* sent on before, from Latin *praemittere* to dispatch in advance, from *prae* before + *mittere* to send

premises ('prɛmɪsɪz) PLURAL NOUN 1 a piece of land together with its buildings, esp considered as a place of business. 2 *Law* **a** (in a deed, etc.) the matters referred to previously; the aforesaid; the foregoing. **b** the introductory part of a grant, conveyance, etc. 3 *Law* (in the US) the part of a bill in equity that states the names of the parties, details of the plaintiff's claims, etc.

premium ('pri:mɪəm) NOUN 1 an amount paid in addition to a standard rate, price, wage, etc.; bonus. 2 the amount paid or payable, usually in regular instalments, for an insurance policy. 3 the amount above nominal or par value at which something sells. 4 **a** an offer of something free or at a specially reduced price as an inducement to buy a commodity or service. **b** (*as modifier*): *a premium offer.* 5 a prize given to the winner of a competition; award. 6 *US* an amount sometimes charged for a loan of money in addition to the interest. 7 great value or regard: *to put a premium on someone's services.* 8 a fee, now rarely required, for instruction or apprenticeship in a profession or trade. 9 **at a premium. a** in great demand or of high value, usually because of scarcity. **b** above par.
▷HISTORY C17: from Latin *praemium* prize, booty, reward

Premium Savings Bonds PLURAL NOUN (in Britain) bonds issued by the Treasury since 1956 for purchase by the public. No interest is paid but there is a monthly draw for cash prizes of various sums. Also called: **premium bonds.**

premolar (pri:'məʊlə) ADJECTIVE 1 situated before a molar tooth. ◆ NOUN 2 any one of eight bicuspid teeth in the human adult, two situated on each side of both jaws between the first molar and the canine.

premonish (prɪ'mɒnɪʃ) VERB (*tr*) *Rare* to admonish beforehand; forewarn.

premonition (ˌprɛmə'nɪʃən) NOUN 1 an intuition of a future, usually unwelcome, occurrence; foreboding. 2 an early warning of a future event; forewarning.
▷HISTORY C16: from Late Latin *praemonitiō,* from Latin *praemonēre* to admonish beforehand, from *prae* before + *monēre* to warn, advise
▸**premonitory** (prɪ'mɒnɪtərɪ, -trɪ) ADJECTIVE

Premonstratensian (ˌpri:ˌmɒnstrə'tɛnsɪən) NOUN **a** a member of a religious order founded at Prémontré in N France in 1120 by St Norbert (about 1080–1134). **b** (*as modifier*): *a Premonstratensian canon.*
▷HISTORY C17: from Medieval Latin *(locus) praemonstrātus* the place foreshown, because it was said to have been prophetically pointed out by St Norbert

premorse (prɪ'mɔ:s) ADJECTIVE *Biology* appearing as though the end had been bitten off: *a premorse leaf.*
▷HISTORY C18: from Latin *praemorsus* bitten off in front, from *praemordēre,* from *prae* in front + *mordēre* to bite

premunition (ˌpri:mju'nɪʃən) NOUN *Med* a state of immunity acquired as the result of a persistent latent infection.
▷HISTORY C15 (in the sense: to protect beforehand): from Latin *praemūnītiō,* from *praemūnīre,* from *prae* before + *mūnīre* to fortify

prenatal (pri:'neɪtᵊl) ADJECTIVE 1 occurring or present before birth; during pregnancy. ◆ NOUN 2 *Informal* a prenatal examination. ◆ Also: **antenatal.**
▸**pre'natally** ADVERB

prenomen (pri:'nəʊmɛn) NOUN, *plural* **-nomina** (-'nɒmɪnə) *or* **-nomens.** *US* a less common spelling of **praenomen.**

prenominal (pri:'nɒmɪnᵊl) ADJECTIVE 1 placed before a noun, esp (of an adjective or sense of an adjective) used only before a noun. 2 of or relating to a praenomen.

prenotion (pri:'nəʊʃən) NOUN a rare word for **preconception.**

prentice ('prɛntɪs) NOUN an archaic word for **apprentice.**

prenup ('pri:ˌnʌp) NOUN *Informal* a prenuptial agreement.

prenuptial (pri:'nʌpʃəl, -tʃəl) ADJECTIVE occurring or existing before marriage: *a prenuptial agreement.*

prenuptial agreement NOUN a contract made between a man and woman before they marry, agreeing on the distribution of their assets in the event of divorce.

preoccupation (priːˌɒkjʊˈpeɪʃən) *or* **preoccupancy** (priːˈɒkjʊpənsɪ) NOUN 1 the state of being preoccupied, esp mentally. 2 something that holds the attention or preoccupies the mind.

preoccupied (priːˈɒkjʊˌpaɪd) ADJECTIVE 1 engrossed or absorbed in something, esp one's own thoughts. 2 already or previously occupied. 3 *Biology* (of a taxonomic name) already used to designate a genus, species, etc.

preoccupy (priːˈɒkjʊˌpaɪ) VERB **-pies, -pying, -pied.** (*tr*) 1 to engross the thoughts or mind of. 2 to occupy before or in advance of another.
▷HISTORY C16: from Latin *praeoccupāre* to capture in advance, from *prae* before + *occupāre* to seize, take possession of

preordain (ˌpriːɔːˈdeɪn) VERB (*tr*) to ordain, decree, or appoint beforehand.
▸**preordination** (ˌpriːɔːdɪˈneɪʃən) NOUN

prep (prɛp) NOUN 1 *Informal* short for **preparation** (sense 5) or (chiefly US) **preparatory school** ◆ VERB **preps, prepping, prepped.** 2 (*tr*) to prepare (a patient) for a medical operation or procedure.

prep. ABBREVIATION FOR: 1 preparation. 2 preparatory. 3 preposition.

prepacked (priːˈpækt) ADJECTIVE (of food, grain, etc.) packed in advance of sale.

preparation (ˌprɛpəˈreɪʃən) NOUN 1 the act or process of preparing. 2 the state of being prepared; readiness. 3 (*often plural*) a measure done in order to prepare for something; provision: *to make preparations for something.* 4 something that is prepared, esp a medicinal formulation. 5 (esp in a boarding school) **a** homework. **b** the period reserved for this. Usually shortened to: **prep.** 6 *Music* **a** the anticipation of a dissonance so that the note producing it in one chord is first heard in the preceding chord as a consonance. **b** a note so employed. 7 (*often capital*) the preliminary prayers at Mass or divine service.

preparative (prɪˈpærətɪv) ADJECTIVE 1 serving to prepare; preparatory. ◆ NOUN 2 something that prepares.
▸**preˈparatively** ADVERB

preparatory (prɪˈpærətərɪ, -trɪ) ADJECTIVE 1 serving to prepare. 2 introductory or preliminary. 3 occupied in preparation. 4 **preparatory to.** as a preparation to; before: *a drink preparatory to eating.*
▸**preˈparatorily** ADVERB

preparatory school NOUN 1 (in Britain) a private school, usually single-sex and for children between the ages of 6 and 13, generally preparing pupils for public school. 2 (in the US) a private secondary school preparing pupils for college. ◆ Often shortened to: **prep school.**

prepare (prɪˈpɛə) VERB 1 to make ready or suitable in advance for a particular purpose or for some use, event, etc.: *to prepare a meal; to prepare to go.* 2 to put together using parts or ingredients; compose or construct. 3 (*tr*) to equip or outfit, as for an expedition. 4 (*tr*) *Music* to soften the impact of (a dissonant note) by the use of preparation. 5 **be prepared.** (*foll by an infinitive*) to be willing and able (to do something): *I'm not prepared to reveal these figures.*
▷HISTORY C15: from Latin *praeparāre,* from *prae* before + *parāre* to make ready
▸**preˈparer** NOUN

preparedness (prɪˈpɛərɪdnɪs) NOUN the state of being prepared or ready, esp militarily ready for war.
▸**preˈparedly** ADVERB

prepared piano NOUN a piano in which some strings have been damped by having objects placed between them or tuned differently from the rest for specific tonal effect. This process was pioneered by US composer John Cage (1912–92).

prepay (priːˈpeɪ) VERB **-pays, -paying, -paid.** (*tr*) to pay for in advance.
▸**preˈpayable** ADJECTIVE ▸**preˈpayment** NOUN

prepense (prɪˈpɛns) ADJECTIVE (*postpositive*) (usually in legal contexts) arranged in advance; premeditated (esp in the phrase **malice prepense**).
▷HISTORY C18: from Anglo-Norman *purpensé,* from Old French *purpenser* to consider in advance, from *penser* to think, from Latin *pēnsāre* to weigh, consider

preponderant (prɪˈpɒndərənt) ADJECTIVE greater in weight, force, influence, etc.
▸**preˈponderance** *or* **preˈponderancy** NOUN
▸**preˈponderantly** ADVERB

preponderate (prɪˈpɒndəˌreɪt) VERB (*intr*) 1 (often foll by *over*) to be more powerful, important, numerous, etc. (than). 2 to be of greater weight than something else.
▷HISTORY C17: from Late Latin *praeponderāre* to be of greater weight, from *pondus* weight
▸**preˈponderately** ADVERB ▸**preˈponderˌating** ADJECTIVE
▸**preˌponderˈation** NOUN

prepone (priːˈpəʊn) VERB (*tr*) *Indian* to bring forward to an earlier time.
▷HISTORY C20: PRE- + (POST)PONE

preposition (ˌprɛpəˈzɪʃən) NOUN a word or group of words used before a noun or pronoun to relate it grammatically or semantically to some other constituent of a sentence. Abbreviation: **prep.**
▷HISTORY C14: from Latin *praepositiō* a putting before, from *pōnere* to place
▸ˌ**prepoˈsitional** ADJECTIVE ▸ˌ**prepoˈsitionally** ADVERB

> **Language note** The practice of ending a sentence with a preposition (*Venice is a place I should like to go to*) was formerly regarded as incorrect, but is now acceptable and is the preferred form in many contexts.

prepositive (priːˈpɒzɪtɪv) ADJECTIVE 1 (of a word or speech element) placed before the word governed or modified. ◆ NOUN 2 a prepositive element.
▸**preˈpositively** ADVERB

prepositor (priːˈpɒzɪtə) *or* **prepostor** (priːˈpɒstə) NOUN *Brit rare* a prefect in any of certain public schools.
▷HISTORY C16: from Latin *praepositus* placed before

prepossess (ˌpriːpəˈzɛs) VERB (*tr*) 1 to preoccupy or engross mentally. 2 to influence in advance for or against a person or thing; prejudice; bias. 3 to make a favourable impression on beforehand.

prepossessing (ˌpriːpəˈzɛsɪŋ) ADJECTIVE creating a favourable impression; attractive.
▸ˌ**preposˈsessingly** ADVERB ▸ˌ**preposˈsessingness** NOUN

prepossession (ˌpriːpəˈzɛʃən) NOUN 1 the state or condition of being prepossessed. 2 a prejudice or bias, esp a favourable one.

preposterous (prɪˈpɒstərəs) ADJECTIVE contrary to nature, reason, or sense; absurd; ridiculous.
▷HISTORY C16: from Latin *praeposterus* reversed, from *prae* in front, before + *posterus* following
▸**preˈposterously** ADVERB ▸**preˈposterousness** NOUN

prepotency (prɪˈpəʊtᵊnsɪ) NOUN 1 the state or condition of being prepotent. 2 *Genetics* the ability of one parent to transmit more characteristics to its offspring than the other parent. 3 *Botany* the ability of pollen from one source to bring about fertilization more readily than that from other sources.

prepotent (prɪˈpəʊtᵊnt) ADJECTIVE 1 greater in power, force, or influence. 2 *Biology* showing prepotency.
▷HISTORY C15: from Latin *praepotens* very powerful, from *posse* to be able
▸**preˈpotently** ADVERB

preppy (ˈprɛpɪ) *Informal* ◆ ADJECTIVE 1 characteristic of or denoting a fashion style of neat, understated, and often expensive clothes; young but classic: suggesting that the wearer is well off, upper class, and conservative. ◆ NOUN, *plural* **-pies.** 2 a person exhibiting such style.
▷HISTORY C20: originally US, from *preppy* a person who attends or has attended a preparatory school before college

preprandial (priːˈprændɪəl) ADJECTIVE of or relating to the period immediately before lunch or dinner: *enjoy a preprandial drink.*

preproduction (ˌpriːprəˈdʌkʃən) NOUN 1 preliminary work on or trial production of a play, industrial prototype, etc. ◆ ADJECTIVE 2 (of a period, model, etc.) preliminary; trial.

prep school NOUN *Informal* See **preparatory school.**

prepubescent (ˌpriːpjuːˈbɛsᵊnt) NOUN 1 a person who has not yet reached puberty. ◆ ADJECTIVE 2 not yet having reached puberty.

prepublication (ˌpriːpʌblɪˈkeɪʃən) ADJECTIVE of or relating to the time, processes, sales, etc., before publication of a book, newspaper, etc.

prepuce (ˈpriːpjuːs) NOUN 1 the retractable fold of skin covering the tip of the penis. Nontechnical name: **foreskin.** 2 a similar fold of skin covering the tip of the clitoris.
▷HISTORY C14: from Latin *praepūtium*
▸**preputial** (priːˈpjuːʃəl) ADJECTIVE

prequel (ˈpriːkwəl) NOUN a film or book about an earlier stage of a story or a character's life, released because the later part of it has already been successful.
▷HISTORY C20: from PRE- + (*se*)*quel*

Pre-Raphaelite (ˌpriːˈræfəlaɪt) NOUN 1 a member of the **Pre-Raphaelite Brotherhood,** an association of British painters and writers including Dante Gabriel Rossetti (1828–82), Holman Hunt (1827–1910), and Sir John Everett Millais (1829–96), founded in 1848 to combat the shallow conventionalism of academic painting and revive the fidelity to nature and the vivid realistic colour that they considered typical of Italian painting before Raphael (1483–1520). ◆ ADJECTIVE 2 of, in the manner of, or relating to Pre-Raphaelite painting and painters.
▸ˌ**Pre-ˈRaphaelˌitism** NOUN

prereading (priːˈriːdɪŋ) ADJECTIVE 1 of or relating to the period before reading a text, book, etc.

prerecorded (ˌpriːrɪˈkɔːdᵊd) ADJECTIVE having been recorded (on tape, video, etc.) beforehand: *a pre-recorded message.*

prerequisite (priːˈrɛkwɪzɪt) ADJECTIVE 1 required as a prior condition. ◆ NOUN 2 something required as a prior condition.

prerogative (prɪˈrɒgətɪv) NOUN 1 an exclusive privilege or right exercised by a person or group of people holding a particular office or hereditary rank. 2 any privilege or right. 3 a power, privilege, or immunity restricted to a sovereign or sovereign government. ◆ ADJECTIVE 4 having or able to exercise a prerogative.
▷HISTORY C14: from Latin *praerogātīva* privilege, earlier: group with the right to vote first, from *prae* before + *rogāre* to ask, beg for

pre-Roman ADJECTIVE of or relating to the period before the founding of ancient Rome.

Pres. ABBREVIATION FOR President.

presa (ˈprɛsɑː) NOUN, *plural* **-se** (-seɪ). *Music* a sign or symbol used in a canon, round, etc., to indicate the entry of each part. Usual signs: **+, :S:** *or* ※
▷HISTORY Italian, literally: a taking up, from *prendere* to take, from Latin *prehendere* to grasp

presage NOUN (ˈprɛsɪdʒ) 1 an intimation or warning of something about to happen; portent; omen. 2 a sense of what is about to happen; foreboding. 3 *Archaic* a forecast or prediction. ◆ VERB (ˈprɛsɪdʒ, prɪˈseɪdʒ) 4 (*tr*) to have a presentiment of. 5 (*tr*) to give a forewarning of; portend. 6 (*intr*) to make a prediction.
▷HISTORY C14: from Latin *praesāgium* presentiment, from *praesāgīre* to perceive beforehand, from *sāgīre* to perceive acutely
▸**preˈsageful** ADJECTIVE ▸**preˈsagefully** ADVERB
▸**preˈsager** NOUN

presale (ˈpriːseɪl) NOUN the practice of arranging the sale of a product before it is available.

Presb. ABBREVIATION FOR Presbyterian.

presbyopia (ˌprɛzbɪˈəʊpɪə) NOUN a progressively diminishing ability of the eye to focus, noticeable from middle to old age, caused by loss of elasticity of the crystalline lens.
▷HISTORY C18: New Latin, from Greek *presbus* old man + *ōps* eye
▸**presbyopic** (ˌprɛzbɪˈɒpɪk) ADJECTIVE

presbyter (ˈprɛzbɪtə) NOUN 1 **a** an elder of a congregation in the early Christian Church. **b** (in some Churches having episcopal politics) an official who is subordinate to a bishop and has administrative, teaching, and sacerdotal functions. 2 (in some hierarchical Churches) another name for **priest.** 3 (in the Presbyterian Church) **a** a teaching elder. **b** a ruling elder.
▷HISTORY C16: from Late Latin, from Greek *presbuteros* an older man, from *presbus* old man

presbyterate (prɛzˈbɪtərɪt, -ˌreɪt) NOUN 1 the

status or office of a presbyter. [2] a group of presbyters.

presbyterial (ˌprɛzbɪˈtɪərɪəl) ADJECTIVE of or relating to a presbyter or presbytery. Also: **presbyteral** (prɛzˈbɪtərəl).
▸ **ˌpresbyˈterially** ADVERB

presbyterian (ˌprɛzbɪˈtɪərɪən) ADJECTIVE [1] of, relating to, or designating Church government by presbyters or lay elders. ◆ NOUN [2] an upholder of this type of Church government.
▸ **ˌpresbyˈterianism** NOUN ▸ **ˌpresbyˌterianˈistic** ADJECTIVE

Presbyterian (ˌprɛzbɪˈtɪərɪən) ADJECTIVE [1] of or relating to any of various Protestant Churches governed by presbyters or lay elders and adhering to various modified forms of Calvinism. ◆ NOUN [2] a member of a Presbyterian Church.
▸ **ˌPresbyˈterianism** NOUN

presbytery (ˈprɛzbɪtərɪ, -trɪ) NOUN, *plural* **-teries.** [1] *Presbyterian Church* **a** a local Church court composed of ministers and elders. **b** the congregations or churches within the jurisdiction of any such court. [2] the part of a cathedral or church east of the choir, in which the main altar is situated; sanctuary. [3] presbyters or elders collectively. [4] government of a church by presbyters or elders. [5] *RC Church* the residence of a parish priest.
▷HISTORY C15: from Old French *presbiterie,* from Church Latin *presbyterium,* from Greek *presbyterion;* see PRESBYTER

preschool *or* **pre-school** (priːˈskuːl) ADJECTIVE **a** (of a child) under the age at which compulsory education begins. **b** (of services) for or relating to preschool children.

prescience (ˈprɛsɪəns) NOUN knowledge of events before they take place; foreknowledge.
▷HISTORY C14: from Latin *praescīre* to foreknow, from *prae* before + *scīre* to know
▸ **ˈprescient** ADJECTIVE ▸ **ˈpresciently** ADVERB

prescientific (ˌpriːsaɪənˈtɪfɪk) ADJECTIVE of or relating to the period before the development of modern science and its methods.

prescind (prɪˈsɪnd) VERB *Rare* [1] (*intr;* usually foll by *from*) to withdraw attention (from something). [2] (*tr*) to isolate, remove, or separate, as for special consideration.
▷HISTORY C17: from Late Latin *praescindere* to cut off in front, from Latin *prae* before + *scindere* to split

prescribe (prɪˈskraɪb) VERB [1] to lay down as a rule or directive. [2] *Law* to claim or acquire (a right, title, etc.) by prescription. [3] *Law* to make or become invalid or unenforceable by lapse of time. [4] *Med* to recommend or order the use of (a drug or other remedy).
▷HISTORY C16: from Latin *praescrībere* to write previously, from *prae* before + *scrībere* to write
▸ **preˈscriber** NOUN

prescript NOUN (ˈpriːskrɪpt) [1] something laid down or prescribed. ◆ ADJECTIVE (prɪˈskrɪpt, ˈpriːskrɪpt) [2] prescribed as a rule.
▷HISTORY C16: from Latin *praescriptum* something written down beforehand, from *praescrībere* to PRESCRIBE

prescriptible (prɪˈskrɪptəbᵊl) ADJECTIVE [1] subject to prescription. [2] depending on or derived from prescription.
▸ **preˌscriptiˈbility** NOUN

prescription (prɪˈskrɪpʃən) NOUN [1] **a** written instructions from a physician, dentist, etc., to a pharmacist stating the form, dosage strength, etc., of a drug to be issued to a specific patient. **b** the drug or remedy prescribed. [2] (*modifier*) (of drugs) available legally only with a doctor's prescription. [3] **a** written instructions from an optician specifying the lenses needed to correct defects of vision. **b** (*as modifier*): *prescription glasses.* [4] the act of prescribing. [5] something that is prescribed. [6] a long established custom or a claim based on one. [7] *Law* **a** the uninterrupted possession of property over a stated period of time, after which a right or title is acquired (**positive prescription**). **b** the barring of adverse claims to property, etc., after a specified period of time has elapsed, allowing the possessor to acquire title (**negative prescription**). **c** the right or title acquired in either of these ways.
▷HISTORY C14: from legal Latin *praescriptiō* an order, prescription; see PRESCRIBE

prescriptive (prɪˈskrɪptɪv) ADJECTIVE [1] making or giving directions, rules, or injunctions. [2] sanctioned by long-standing usage or custom. [3] derived from or based upon legal prescription: *a prescriptive title.*
▸ **preˈscriptively** ADVERB ▸ **preˈscriptiveness** NOUN

prescriptivism (prɪˈskrɪptɪˌvɪzəm) NOUN *Ethics* the theory that moral utterances have no truth value but prescribe attitudes to others and express the conviction of the speaker. Compare **descriptivism, emotivism.**

presell (priːˈsɛl) VERB (*tr*) **-sells, -selling, -sold** [1] to promote (a product, entertainment, etc.) with publicity in advance of its appearance. [2] to prepare (the public) for a product, entertainment, etc., with advance publicity. [3] to agree a sale of (a product) before it is available. [4] to sell (a book) before its publication date.

presence (ˈprɛzəns) NOUN [1] the state or fact of being present. [2] the immediate proximity of a person or thing. [3] personal appearance or bearing, esp of a dignified nature. [4] an imposing or dignified personality. [5] an invisible spirit felt to be nearby. [6] *Electronics* a recording control that boosts mid-range frequencies. [7] (of a recording) a quality that gives the impression that the listener is in the presence of the original source of the sound. [8] *Obsolete* assembly or company. [9] *Obsolete* short for **presence chamber.**
▷HISTORY C14: via Old French from Latin *praesentia* a being before, from *praeesse* to be before, from *prae* before + *esse* to be

presence chamber NOUN the room in which a great person, such as a monarch, receives guests, assemblies, etc.

presence of mind NOUN the ability to remain calm and act constructively during times of crisis.

presenile dementia (priːˈsiːnaɪl) NOUN a form of dementia, of unknown cause, starting before a person is old.

present[1] (ˈprɛzᵊnt) ADJECTIVE [1] (*prenominal*) in existence at the moment in time at which an utterance is spoken or written. [2] (*postpositive*) being in a specified place, thing, etc.: *the murderer is present in this room.* [3] (*prenominal*) now in consideration or under discussion: *the present topic; the present author.* [4] *Grammar* denoting a tense of verbs used when the action or event described is occurring at the time of utterance or when the speaker does not wish to make any explicit temporal reference. [5] *Archaic* readily available; instant: *present help is at hand.* [6] *Archaic* mentally alert; attentive. ◆ NOUN [7] **the present.** the time being; now. [8] *Grammar* **a** the present tense. **b** a verb in this tense. [9] **at present.** at the moment; now. [10] **for the present.** for the time being; temporarily. ◆ See also **presents.**
▷HISTORY C13: from Latin *praesens,* from *praeesse* to be in front of, from *prae-* before, in front + *esse* to be

present[2] VERB (prɪˈzɛnt) (*mainly tr*) [1] to introduce (a person) to another, esp to someone of higher rank. [2] to introduce to the public: *to present a play.* [3] to introduce and compere (a radio or television show). [4] to show; exhibit: *he presented a brave face to the world.* [5] to put forward; submit: *she presented a proposal for a new book.* [6] to bring or suggest to the mind: *to present a problem.* [7] to give or award: *to present a prize.* [8] to endow with or as if with a gift or award: *to present a university with a foundation scholarship.* [9] to offer formally: *to present one's compliments.* [10] to offer or hand over for action or settlement: *to present a bill.* [11] to represent or depict in a particular manner: *the actor presented Hamlet as a very young man.* [12] to salute someone with (one's weapon) (usually in the phrase **present arms**). [13] to aim or point (a weapon). [14] to nominate (a clergyman) to a bishop for institution to a benefice in his diocese. [15] to lay (a charge, etc.) before a court, magistrate, etc., for consideration or trial. [16] to bring a formal charge or accusation against (a person); indict. [17] *Chiefly US* (of a grand jury) to take notice of (an offence) from personal knowledge or observation, before any bill of indictment has been drawn up. [18] (*intr*) *Med* to seek treatment for a particular symptom or problem: *she presented with postnatal depression.* [19] (*intr*) *Informal* to produce a favourable, etc. impression: *she presents well in public; he presents as harmless but has poisoned his family.* [20] **present oneself.** to appear, esp at a specific time and place. ◆ NOUN (ˈprɛzᵊnt) [21] anything that is presented; a gift. [22] **make someone a present of something.** to give someone something: *I'll make you a present of a new car.*
▷HISTORY C13: from Old French *presenter,* from Latin *praesentāre* to exhibit, offer, from *praesens* PRESENT[1]

presentable (prɪˈzɛntəbᵊl) ADJECTIVE [1] fit to be presented or introduced to other people. [2] fit to be displayed or offered.
▸ **preˈsentableness** *or* **preˌsentaˈbility** NOUN ▸ **preˈsentably** ADVERB

presentation (ˌprɛzənˈteɪʃən) NOUN [1] the act of presenting or state of being presented. [2] the manner of presenting, esp the organization of visual details to create an overall impression: *the presentation of the project is excellent but the content poor.* [3] the method of presenting: *his presentation of the facts was muddled.* [4] a verbal report presented with illustrative material, such as slides, graphs, etc.: *a presentation on the company results.* [5] **a** an offering or bestowal, as of a gift. **b** (*as modifier*): *a presentation copy of a book.* [6] a performance or representation, as of a play. [7] the formal introduction of a person, as into society or at court; debut. [8] the act or right of nominating a clergyman to a benefice. [9] *Med* the position of a baby relative to the birth canal at the time of birth. [10] *Commerce* another word for **presentment** (sense 4). [11] *Television* linking material between programmes, such as announcements, trailers, or weather reports. [12] an archaic word for **gift.** [13] *Philosophy* a sense datum. [14] (*often capital*) another name for (feast of) **Candlemas.**
▸ **ˌpresenˈtational** ADJECTIVE

presentationism (ˌprɛzənˈteɪʃəˌnɪzəm) NOUN *Philosophy* the theory that objects are identical with our perceptions of them. Compare **representationalism.**
▸ **ˌpresenˈtationist** NOUN, ADJECTIVE

presentative (prɪˈzɛntətɪv) ADJECTIVE [1] *Philosophy* **a** able to be known or perceived immediately. **b** capable of knowing or perceiving in this way. [2] subject to or conferring the right of ecclesiastical presentation.
▸ **preˈsentativeness** NOUN

present-day NOUN (*modifier*) of the modern day; current: *I don't like present-day fashions.*

presentee (ˌprɛzənˈtiː) NOUN [1] a person who is presented, as at court. [2] a person to whom something is presented.

presenteeism (ˌprɛzənˈtiːɪzəm) NOUN the practice of persistently working longer hours and taking fewer holidays than the terms of one's employment demand, esp as a result of fear of losing one's job.
▷HISTORY C20: a play on ABSENTEEISM

presenter (prɪˈzɛntə) NOUN [1] a person who presents something or someone. [2] *Radio, television* a person who introduces a show, links items, interviews guests, etc.; compere.

presentient (prɪˈsɛnʃənt, -ˈzɛn-, priː-) ADJECTIVE characterized by or experiencing a presentiment.
▷HISTORY C19: from Latin *praesentiens* present participle of *praesentire,* from *prae-* PRE- + *sentire* to feel

presentiment (prɪˈzɛntɪmənt) NOUN a sense of something about to happen; premonition.
▷HISTORY C18: from obsolete French, from *pressentir* to sense beforehand; see PRE-, SENTIMENT

presently (ˈprɛzəntlɪ) ADVERB [1] in a short while; soon. [2] at the moment. [3] an archaic word for **immediately.**

presentment (prɪˈzɛntmənt) NOUN [1] the act of presenting or state of being presented; presentation. [2] something presented, such as a picture, play, etc. [3] *Law, chiefly US* a statement on oath by a grand jury of something within their own knowledge or observation, esp the commission of an offence when the indictment has been laid before them. [4] *Commerce* the presenting of a bill of exchange, promissory note, etc.

present participle NOUN a participial form of verbs used adjectivally when the action it describes is contemporaneous with that of the main verb of a sentence and also used in the formation of certain compound tenses. In English this form ends in *-ing.* Compare **gerund.**

present perfect ADJECTIVE, NOUN *Grammar* another term for **perfect** (senses 8, 11).

presents ('prɛzənts) PLURAL NOUN *Law* used in a deed or document to refer to itself: *know all men by these presents.*

present value NOUN the current capital value of a future income or outlay or of a series of such incomes or outlays. It is computed by the process of discounting at a predetermined rate of interest.

preservative (prɪ'zɜːvətɪv) NOUN [1] something that preserves or tends to preserve, esp a chemical added to foods to inhibit decomposition. ◆ ADJECTIVE [2] tending or intended to preserve.

preserve (prɪ'zɜːv) VERB (*mainly tr*) [1] to keep safe from danger or harm; protect. [2] to protect from decay or dissolution; maintain: *to preserve old buildings.* [3] to maintain possession of; keep up: *to preserve a façade of indifference.* [4] to prevent from decomposition or chemical change. [5] to prepare (food), as by freezing, drying, or salting, so that it will resist decomposition. [6] to make preserves of (fruit, etc.). [7] to rear and protect (game) in restricted places for hunting or fishing. [8] (*intr*) to maintain protection and favourable conditions for game in preserves. ◆ NOUN [9] something that preserves or is preserved. [10] a special area or domain: *archaeology is the preserve of specialists.* [11] (*usually plural*) fruit, etc., prepared by cooking with sugar. [12] areas where game is reared for private hunting or fishing.
▷HISTORY C14: via Old French, from Late Latin *praeservāre* literally: to keep safe in advance, from Latin *prae-* before + *servāre* to keep safe
▸**pre'servable** ADJECTIVE ▸**pre,serva'bility** NOUN ▸**pre'servably** ADVERB ▸**preservation** (,prɛzə'veɪʃən) NOUN ▸**pre'server** NOUN

preset (priː'sɛt) VERB **-sets, -setting, -set.** (*tr*) [1] to set (a timing device) so that something begins to operate at the time specified. ◆ NOUN [2] *Electronics* a control, such as a variable resistor, that is not as accessible as the main controls and is used to set initial conditions.

preshrunk (priː'ʃrʌŋk) ADJECTIVE (of fabrics, garments, etc.) having undergone a shrinking process during manufacture so that further shrinkage will not occur.

preside (prɪ'zaɪd) VERB (*intr*) [1] to sit in or hold a position of authority, as over a meeting. [2] to exercise authority; control. [3] to occupy a position as an instrumentalist: *he presided at the organ.*
▷HISTORY C17: via French from Latin *praesidēre* to superintend, from *prae* before + *sedēre* to sit
▸**pre'sider** NOUN

presidency ('prɛzɪdənsɪ) NOUN, *plural* **-cies.** [1] **a** the office, dignity, or term of a president. **b** (*often capital*) the office of president of a republic, esp the office of the President of the US. [2] *Mormon Church* **a** a local administrative council consisting of a president and two executive members. **b** (*often capital*) the supreme administrative body composed of the Prophet and two councillors.

president ('prɛzɪdənt) NOUN [1] (*often capital*) the chief executive or head of state of a republic, esp of the US. [2] (in the US) the chief executive officer of a company, corporation, etc. [3] a person who presides over an assembly, meeting, etc. [4] the chief executive officer of certain establishments of higher education.
▷HISTORY C14: via Old French from Late Latin *praesidens* ruler; see PRESIDE
▸**presidential** (,prɛzɪ'dɛnʃəl) ADJECTIVE ▸**,presi'dentially** ADVERB ▸**'president,ship** NOUN

president-elect NOUN a person who has been elected president but has not yet entered office.

presidio (prɪ'sɪdɪ,əʊ; *Spanish* pre'siðjo) NOUN, *plural* **-sidios** (-'sɪdɪ,əʊz; *Spanish* -'siðjos). a military post or establishment, esp in countries under Spanish control.
▷HISTORY C19: from Spanish: garrison, from Latin *praesidium* a guard, protection; see PRESIDE

presidium *or* **praesidium** (prɪ'sɪdɪəm) NOUN, *plural* **-iums** *or* **-ia** (-ɪə). [1] (*often capital*) (in Communist countries) a permanent committee of a larger body, such as a legislature, that acts for it when it is in recess. [2] a collective presidency, esp of a nongovernmental organization.
▷HISTORY C20: from Russian *prezidium*, from Latin *praesidium*, from *praesidēre* to superintend; see PRESIDE

presignify (priː'sɪgnɪ,faɪ) VERB **-fies, -fying, -fied.** (*tr*) to signify beforehand; foreshadow; foretell.

press[1] (prɛs) VERB [1] to apply or exert weight, force, or steady pressure on: *he pressed the button on the camera.* [2] (*tr*) to squeeze or compress so as to alter in shape or form. [3] to apply heat or pressure to (clothing) so as to smooth out or mark with creases; iron. [4] to make (objects) from soft material by pressing with a mould, form, etc., esp to make gramophone records from plastic. [5] (*tr*) to hold tightly or clasp, as in an embrace. [6] (*tr*) to extract or force out (juice) by pressure (from). [7] (*tr*) *Weightlifting* to lift (a weight) successfully with a press: *he managed to press 280 pounds.* [8] (*tr*) to force, constrain, or compel. [9] to importune or entreat (a person) insistently; urge: *they pressed for an answer.* [10] to harass or cause harassment. [11] (*tr*) to plead or put forward strongly or importunately: *to press a claim.* [12] (*intr*) to be urgent. [13] (*tr; usually passive*) to have little of: *we're hard pressed for time.* [14] (when *intr*, often foll by *on* or *forward*) to hasten or advance or cause to hasten or advance in a forceful manner. [15] (*intr*) to crowd; throng; push. [16] (*tr*) (formerly) to put to death or subject to torture by placing heavy weights upon. [17] (*tr*) *Archaic* to trouble or oppress. [18] **press charges.** to bring charges against a person. ◆ NOUN [19] any machine that exerts pressure to form, shape, or cut materials or to extract liquids, compress solids, or hold components together while an adhesive joint is formed. [20] See **printing press.** [21] the art or process of printing. [22] **at** *or* **in (the) press.** being printed. [23] **to (the) press.** to be printed: *when is this book going to press?* [24] **the press. a** news media and agencies collectively, esp newspapers. **b** (*as modifier*): *a press matter; press relations.* [25] **the press.** those who work in the news media, esp newspaper reporters and photographers. [26] the opinions and reviews in the newspapers, etc.: *the play received a poor press.* [27] the act of pressing or state of being pressed. [28] the act of crowding, thronging, or pushing together. [29] a closely packed throng of people; crowd; multitude. [30] urgency or hurry in business affairs. [31] a cupboard, esp a large one used for storing clothes or linen. [32] a wood or metal clamp or vice to prevent tennis rackets, etc., from warping when not in use. [33] *Weightlifting* a lift in which the weight is raised to shoulder level and then above the head.
▷HISTORY C14 *pressen*, from Old French *presser*, from Latin *pressāre*, from *premere* to press

press[2] (prɛs) VERB (*tr*) [1] to recruit (men) by forcible measures for military service. [2] to use for a purpose other than intended, (esp in the phrase **press into service**). ◆ NOUN [3] recruitment into military service by forcible measures, as by a press gang.
▷HISTORY C16: back formation from *prest* to recruit soldiers; see PREST[2]; also influenced by PRESS[1]

press agency NOUN another name for **news agency.**

press agent NOUN a person employed to obtain favourable publicity, such as notices in newspapers, for an organization, actor, etc. Abbreviation: **PA.**

press box NOUN an area reserved for reporters, as in a sports stadium.

Pressburg ('prɛsbʊrk) NOUN the German name for **Bratislava.**

press conference NOUN an interview for press and television reporters given by a politician, film star, etc.

press fit NOUN *Engineering* a type of fit for mating parts, usually tighter than a sliding fit, used when the parts do not have to move relative to each other.

press gallery NOUN an area set apart for newspaper reporters, esp in a legislative assembly.

press gang NOUN [1] (formerly) a detachment of men used to press civilians for service in the navy or army. ◆ VERB **press-gang.** (*tr*) [2] to force (a person) to join the navy or army by a press gang. [3] to induce (a person) to perform a duty by forceful persuasion: *his friends press-ganged him into joining the committee.*

pressie *or* **prezzie** ('prɛzɪ) NOUN an informal word for **present**[2] (sense 21).

pressing ('prɛsɪŋ) ADJECTIVE [1] demanding immediate attention. [2] persistent or importunate. ◆ NOUN [3] a large specified number of gramophone records produced at one time from a master record. [4] a component formed in a press. [5] *Football* the tactic of trying to stay very close to the opposition when they are in possession of the ball.
▸**'pressingly** ADVERB ▸**'pressingness** NOUN

pressman ('prɛsmən, -,mæn) NOUN, *plural* **-men.** [1] a person who works for the press. [2] a person who operates a printing press.

pressmark ('prɛs,mɑːk) NOUN *Library science* a location mark on a book indicating a specific bookcase.
▷HISTORY C19: from PRESS[1] (in the sense: cupboard) + MARK[1]

press of sail NOUN *Nautical* the most sail a vessel can carry under given conditions. Also called: **press of canvas.**

pressor ('prɛsə, -sɔː) ADJECTIVE *Physiol* relating to or producing an increase in blood pressure.
▷HISTORY C19: from Latin *premere* to press

press release NOUN an official announcement or account of a news item circulated to the press.

pressroom ('prɛs,ruːm, -,rʊm) NOUN the room in a printing establishment that houses the printing presses.

press stud NOUN a fastening device consisting of one part with a projecting knob that snaps into a hole on another like part, used esp in closures in clothing. Also called: **popper, snap fastener.**

press-up NOUN an exercise in which the body is alternately raised from and lowered to the floor by the arms only, the trunk being kept straight with the toes and hands resting on the floor. Also called (US and Canadian): **push-up.**

pressure ('prɛʃə) NOUN [1] the state of pressing or being pressed. [2] the exertion of force by one body on the surface of another. [3] a moral force that compels: *to bring pressure to bear.* [4] an urgent claim or demand or series of urgent claims or demands: *to work under pressure.* [5] a burdensome condition that is hard to bear: *the pressure of grief.* [6] the normal force applied to a unit area of a surface, usually measured in pascals (newtons per square metre), millibars, torr, or atmospheres. Symbol: *p* or *P.* [7] short for **atmospheric pressure** or **blood pressure.** ◆ VERB [8] (*tr*) to constrain or compel, as by the application of moral force. [9] another word for **pressurize.**
▷HISTORY C14: from Late Latin *pressūra* a pressing, from Latin *premere* to press
▸**'pressureless** ADJECTIVE

pressure cabin NOUN the pressurized cabin of an aircraft or spacecraft.

pressure-cook VERB to cook (food) in a pressure cooker.

pressure cooker NOUN [1] a strong hermetically sealed pot in which food may be cooked quickly under pressure at a temperature above the normal boiling point of water. [2] *NZ informal* a trainee student attending a shortened qualifying course.

pressure drag NOUN the part of the total drag of a body moving through a gas or liquid caused by the components of the pressures at right angles to the surface of the body.

pressure gauge NOUN any instrument for measuring fluid pressure. See also **Bourdon gauge, manometer.**

pressure gradient NOUN [1] the change of pressure per unit distance. See **adverse pressure gradient, favourable pressure gradient.** [2] *Meteorol* the decrease in atmospheric pressure per unit of horizontal distance, shown on a synoptic chart by the spacing of the isobars.

pressure group NOUN a group of people who seek to exert pressure on legislators, public opinion, etc., in order to promote their own ideas or welfare.

pressure head NOUN *Physics* a more formal name for **head** (sense 24a).

pressure point NOUN any of several points on the body above an artery that, when firmly pressed, will control bleeding from the artery at a point farther away from the heart.

pressure suit NOUN an inflatable suit worn by a person flying at high altitudes or in space, to provide protection from low pressure.

pressure vessel NOUN *Engineering* a vessel designed for containing substances, reactions, etc., at pressures above atmospheric pressure.

pressurize *or* **pressurise** (ˈprɛʃəˌraɪz) VERB (*tr*) 1 to increase the pressure in (an enclosure, such as an aircraft cabin) in order to maintain approximately atmospheric pressure when the external pressure is low. 2 to increase pressure on (a fluid). 3 to make insistent demands of (someone); coerce.
▸ **ˌpressuriˈzation** *or* **ˌpressuriˈsation** NOUN ▸ **ˈpressurˌizer** *or* **ˈpressurˌiser** NOUN

pressurized-water reactor NOUN a nuclear reactor using water as coolant and moderator at a pressure that is too high to allow boiling to take place inside the reactor. The fuel is enriched uranium oxide cased in zirconium. Abbreviation: **PWR**.

presswork (ˈprɛsˌwɜːk) NOUN 1 the operation of a printing press. 2 the matter printed by a printing press.

prest[1] (prɛst) ADJECTIVE *Obsolete* prepared for action or use; ready.
▷HISTORY C13: via Old French from Late Latin *praestus* ready to hand; see PRESTO

prest[2] (prɛst) NOUN *Obsolete* a loan of money.
▷HISTORY C16: originally, loan money offered as an inducement to recruits, from Old French: advance pay in the army, from *prester* to lend, from Latin *praestāre* to provide, from *prae* before + *stāre* to stand

Prestel (ˈprɛsˌtɛl) NOUN *Trademark* the Viewdata service operated by British Telecom. See **Viewdata**.

Prester John (ˈprɛstə) NOUN a legendary Christian priest and king, believed in the Middle Ages to have ruled in the Far East, but identified in the 14th century with the king of Ethiopia.
▷HISTORY C14 *Prestre Johan,* from Medieval Latin *presbyter Iohannes* Priest John

prestidigitation (ˌprɛstɪˌdɪdʒɪˈteɪʃən) NOUN another name for **sleight of hand.**
▷HISTORY C19: from French: quick-fingeredness, from Latin *praestigiae* feats of juggling, tricks, probably influenced by French *preste* nimble, and Latin *digitus* finger; see PRESTIGE
▸ **ˌprestiˈdigiˌtator** NOUN

prestige (prɛˈstiːʒ) NOUN 1 high status or reputation achieved through success, influence, wealth, etc.; renown. 2 **a** the power to influence or impress; glamour. **b** (*modifier*) *a prestige car.*
▷HISTORY C17: via French from Latin *praestigiae* feats of juggling, tricks; apparently related to Latin *praestringere* to bind tightly, blindfold, from *prae* before + *stringere* to draw tight, bind

prestige pricing NOUN 1 *Marketing* the practice of giving a product a high price to convey the idea that it must be of high quality or status.

prestigious (prɛˈstɪdʒəs) ADJECTIVE 1 having status or glamour; impressive or influential. 2 *Rare* characterized by or using deceit, cunning, or illusion; fraudulent.
▸ **presˈtigiously** ADVERB ▸ **presˈtigiousness** NOUN

prestissimo (prɛˈstɪsɪˌməʊ) *Music* ◆ ADJECTIVE, ADVERB 1 to be played as fast as possible. ◆ NOUN, *plural* **-mos**. 2 a piece or passage directed to be played in this way.
▷HISTORY C18: from Italian: very quickly, from *presto* fast

presto (ˈprɛstəʊ) ADJECTIVE, ADVERB 1 *Music* to be played very fast. ◆ ADVERB 2 immediately, suddenly, or at once (esp in the phrase **hey presto**). ◆ NOUN, *plural* **-tos**. 3 *Music* a movement or passage directed to be played very quickly.
▷HISTORY C16: from Italian: fast, from Late Latin *praestus* (adj) ready to hand, Latin *praestō* (adv) present

Preston (ˈprɛstən) NOUN a city in NW England, administrative centre of Lancashire, on the River Ribble: developed as a weaving centre (17th–18th centuries); university (1992). Pop.: 177 660 (1991).

Prestonpans (ˌprɛstənˈpænz) NOUN a small town and resort in SE Scotland, in East Lothian on the Firth of Forth: scene of the battle (1745) in which the Jacobite army of Prince Charles Edward defeated government forces under Sir John Cope. Pop.: 7014 (1991).

prestress (ˌpriːˈstrɛs) VERB (*tr*) to apply tensile stress to (the steel cables, wires, etc., of a precast concrete part) before the load is applied.

prestressed concrete NOUN concrete that contains steel wires, cables, etc., that are prestressed within their elastic limit to counteract the stresses that will occur under load.

Prestwich (ˈprɛstwɪtʃ) NOUN a town in NW England, in Bury unitary authority, Greater Manchester. Pop.: 31 801 (1991).

Prestwick (ˈprɛstwɪk) NOUN a town in SW Scotland, in South Ayrshire on the Firth of Clyde; international airport, golf course: tourism. Pop.: 13 705 (1991).

presumable (prɪˈzjuːməbᵊl) ADJECTIVE able to be presumed or taken for granted.

presumably (prɪˈzjuːməblɪ) ADVERB (*sentence modifier*) one presumes or supposes that: *presumably he won't see you, if you're leaving tomorrow.*

presume (prɪˈzjuːm) VERB 1 (when *tr, often takes a clause as object*) to take (something) for granted; assume. 2 (when *tr, often foll by an infinitive*) to take upon oneself (to do something) without warrant or permission; dare: *do you presume to copy my work?* 3 (*intr; foll by on or upon*) to rely or depend: *don't presume on his agreement.* 4 *Law* to take as proved until contrary evidence is produced.
▷HISTORY C14: via Old French from Latin *praesūmere* to take in advance, from *prae* before + *sūmere* to ASSUME
▸ **presumedly** (prɪˈzjuːmɪdlɪ) ADVERB ▸ **preˈsumer** NOUN ▸ **preˈsuming** ADJECTIVE ▸ **preˈsumingly** ADVERB

presumption (prɪˈzʌmpʃən) NOUN 1 the act of presuming. 2 bold or insolent behaviour or manners. 3 a belief or assumption based on reasonable evidence. 4 a ground or basis on which to presume. 5 *Law* an inference of the truth of a fact from other facts proved, admitted, or judicially noticed.
▷HISTORY C13: via Old French from Latin *praesumptiō* a using in advance, anticipation, from *praesūmere* to take beforehand; see PRESUME

presumptive (prɪˈzʌmptɪv) ADJECTIVE 1 based on presumption or probability. 2 affording reasonable ground for belief. 3 of or relating to embryonic tissues that become differentiated into a particular tissue or organ: *presumptive epidermis.*
▸ **preˈsumptively** ADVERB ▸ **preˈsumptiveness** NOUN

presumptuous (prɪˈzʌmptjʊəs) ADJECTIVE 1 characterized by presumption or tending to presume; bold; forward. 2 an obsolete word for **presumptive.**
▸ **preˈsumptuously** ADVERB ▸ **preˈsumptuousness** NOUN

presuppose (ˌpriːsəˈpəʊz) VERB (*tr*) 1 to take for granted; assume. 2 to require or imply as a necessary prior condition. 3 *Philosophy, logic, linguistics* to require (a condition) to be satisfied as a precondition for a statement to be either true or false or for a speech act to be felicitous. *Have you stopped beating your wife?* presupposes that the person addressed has a wife and has beaten her.
▸ **presupposition** (ˌpriːsʌpəˈzɪʃən) NOUN

preteen (priːˈtiːn) NOUN a boy or girl approaching his or her teens.

pretence *or US* **pretense** (prɪˈtɛns) NOUN 1 the act of pretending. 2 a false display; affectation. 3 a claim, esp a false one, to a right, title, or distinction. 4 make-believe or feigning. 5 a false claim or allegation; pretext. 6 a less common word for **pretension** (sense 3).

pretend (prɪˈtɛnd) VERB 1 (when *tr, usually takes a clause as object or an infinitive*) to claim or allege (something untrue). 2 (*tr; may take a clause as object or an infinitive*) to make believe, as in a play: *you pretend to be Ophelia.* 3 (*intr;* foll by *to*) to present a claim, esp a dubious one: *to pretend to the throne.* 4 (*intr;* foll by *to*) *Obsolete* to aspire as a candidate or suitor (for). ◆ ADJECTIVE 5 fanciful; make-believe; simulated: *a pretend gun.*
▷HISTORY C14: from Latin *praetendere* to stretch forth, feign, from *prae* in front + *tendere* to stretch

pretender (prɪˈtɛndə) NOUN 1 a person who pretends or makes false allegations. 2 a person who mounts a claim, as to a throne or title.

pretension (prɪˈtɛnʃən) NOUN 1 (*often plural*) a false or unsupportable claim, esp to merit, worth, or importance. 2 a specious or unfounded allegation; pretext. 3 the state or quality of being pretentious.

pretensive (prɪˈtɛnsɪv) ADJECTIVE *Caribbean* pretentious.

pretentious (prɪˈtɛnʃəs) ADJECTIVE 1 making claim to distinction or importance, esp undeservedly. 2 having or creating a deceptive outer appearance of great worth; ostentatious.
▸ **preˈtentiously** ADVERB ▸ **preˈtentiousness** NOUN

preter- PREFIX beyond, more than, or exceeding: *preternatural.*
▷HISTORY from Latin *praeter-*, from *praeter*

preterhuman (ˌpriːtəˈhjuːmən) ADJECTIVE *Rare* beyond what is human.

preterite *or US* **preterit** (ˈprɛtərɪt) *Grammar* ◆ NOUN 1 a tense of verbs used to relate past action, formed in English by inflection of the verb, as *jumped, swam.* 2 a verb in this tense. ◆ ADJECTIVE 3 denoting this tense.
▷HISTORY C14: from Late Latin *praeteritum (tempus)* past (time, tense), from Latin *praeterīre* to go by, from PRETER- + *īre* to go

preterition (ˌprɛtəˈrɪʃən) NOUN 1 the act of passing over or omitting. 2 *Roman law* the failure of a testator to name one of his children in his will, thus invalidating it. 3 (in Calvinist theology) the doctrine that God passed over or left unpredestined those not elected to final salvation.
▷HISTORY C17: from Late Latin *praeteritiō* a passing over

preteritive (prɪˈtɛrɪtɪv) ADJECTIVE (of a verb) having only past tense forms.

preterm (ˌpriːˈtɜːm) ADJECTIVE 1 (of a baby) born prematurely. ◆ ADVERB 2 prematurely.

pretermit (ˌpriːtəˈmɪt) VERB **-mits, -mitting, -mitted.** (*tr*) *Rare* 1 to overlook intentionally; disregard. 2 to fail to do; neglect; omit.
▷HISTORY C16: from Latin *praetermittere* to let pass, from PRETER- + *mittere* to send, release
▸ **pretermission** (ˌpriːtəˈmɪʃən) NOUN ▸ **ˌpreterˈmitter** NOUN

preternatural (ˌpriːtəˈnætʃrəl) ADJECTIVE 1 beyond what is ordinarily found in nature; abnormal. 2 another word for **supernatural.**
▷HISTORY C16: from Medieval Latin *praeternātūrālis,* from Latin *praeter natūram* beyond the scope of nature
▸ **ˌpreterˈnaturally** ADVERB ▸ **ˌpreterˈnaturalism** NOUN ▸ **ˌpreterˈnaturalness** *or* **ˌpreterˌnatuˈrality** NOUN

pretest (priːˈtɛst) VERB (*tr*) 1 to test (something) before presenting it to its intended public or client. ◆ NOUN (ˈpriːtɛst) 2 the act or instance of pretesting.

pretext (ˈpriːtɛkst) NOUN 1 a fictitious reason given in order to conceal the real one. 2 a specious excuse; pretence.
▷HISTORY C16: from Latin *praetextum* disguise, from *praetexere* to weave in front, disguise; see TEXTURE

pretonic (priːˈtɒnɪk) ADJECTIVE denoting or relating to the syllable before the one bearing the primary stress in a word.

pretor (ˈpriːtə) NOUN a variant spelling of **praetor.**

Pretoria (prɪˈtɔːrɪə) NOUN a city in N South Africa, the administrative capital of South Africa; formerly capital of Transvaal province: two universities (1873, 1930); large steelworks. Pop. (urban area): 1 104 479 (1996).

prettify (ˈprɪtɪˌfaɪ) VERB **-fies, -fying, -fied.** (*tr*) to make pretty, esp in a trivial fashion; embellish.
▸ **ˌprettifiˈcation** NOUN ▸ **ˈprettiˌfier** NOUN

pretty (ˈprɪtɪ) ADJECTIVE **-tier, -tiest.** 1 pleasing or appealing in a delicate or graceful way. 2 dainty, neat, or charming. 3 *Informal, often ironic* excellent, grand, or fine: *here's a pretty mess!* 4 *Informal* lacking in masculinity; effeminate; foppish. 5 *Scot* vigorous or brave. 6 an archaic word for **elegant.** 7 **a pretty penny.** *Informal* a large sum of money. 8 **sitting pretty.** *Informal* well placed or established financially, socially, etc. ◆ NOUN, *plural* **-ties.** 9 a pretty person or thing. ◆ ADVERB 10 *Informal* fairly or moderately; somewhat. 11 *Informal* quite or very. ◆ VERB **-ties, -tying, -tied.** 12 (*tr;* often foll by *up*) to make pretty; adorn.
▷HISTORY Old English *prættig* clever; related to Middle Low German *prattich* obstinate, Dutch *prettig* glad, Old Norse *prettugr* cunning
▸ **ˈprettily** ADVERB ▸ **ˈprettiness** NOUN

pretty-pretty ADJECTIVE *Informal* excessively or ostentatiously pretty.

pretzel (ˈprɛtsəl) NOUN a brittle savoury biscuit, in the form of a knot or stick, glazed and salted on the outside, eaten esp in Germany and the US.

▷HISTORY C19: from German, from Old High German *brezitella;* perhaps related to Medieval Latin *bracellus* bracelet, from Latin *bracchium* arm

Preussen ('prɔysən) NOUN the German name for **Prussia.**

prevail (prɪ'veɪl) VERB *(intr)* 1 (often foll by *over* or *against*) to prove superior; gain mastery: *skill will prevail.* 2 to be or appear as the most important feature; be prevalent. 3 to exist widely; be in force. 4 (often foll by *on* or *upon*) to succeed in persuading or inducing.
▷HISTORY C14: from Latin *praevalēre* to be superior in strength, from *prae* beyond + *valēre* to be strong
▸**pre'vailer** NOUN

prevailing (prɪ'veɪlɪŋ) ADJECTIVE 1 generally accepted; widespread: *the prevailing opinion.* 2 most frequent or conspicuous; predominant: *the prevailing wind is from the north.*
▸**pre'vailingly** ADVERB

prevalent ('prɛvələnt) ADJECTIVE 1 widespread or current. 2 superior in force or power; predominant.
▷HISTORY C16 (in the sense: powerful): from Latin *praevalens* very strong, from *praevalēre:* see PREVAIL
▸**'prevalence** *or* **'prevalentness** NOUN ▸**'prevalently** ADVERB

prevaricate (prɪ'værɪˌkeɪt) VERB *(intr)* to speak or act falsely or evasively with intent to deceive.
▷HISTORY C16: from Latin *praevāricārī* to walk crookedly, from *prae* beyond + *vāricare* to straddle the legs; compare Latin *vārus* bent
▸**preˌvari'cation** NOUN ▸**pre'variˌcator** NOUN

prevenient (prɪ'viːnɪənt) ADJECTIVE coming before; anticipating or preceding.
▷HISTORY C17: from Latin *praevenīre* to precede, PREVENT
▸**pre'veniently** ADVERB

prevent (prɪ'vɛnt) VERB 1 *(tr)* to keep from happening, esp by taking precautionary action. 2 *(tr; often foll by from)* to keep (someone from doing something); hinder; impede. 3 *(intr)* to interpose or act as a hindrance. 4 *(tr) Archaic* to anticipate or precede.
▷HISTORY C15: from Latin *praevenīre,* from *prae* before + *venīre* to come
▸**pre'ventable** *or* **pre'ventible** ADJECTIVE ▸**preˌventa'bility** *or* **preˌventi'bility** NOUN ▸**pre'ventably** *or* **pre'ventibly** ADVERB

preventer (prɪ'vɛntə) NOUN 1 a person or thing that prevents. 2 *Nautical* a rope or other piece of gear rigged to prevent a sail from gybing.

prevention (prɪ'vɛnʃən) NOUN 1 the act of preventing. 2 a hindrance, obstacle, or impediment.

preventive (prɪ'vɛntɪv) ADJECTIVE 1 tending or intended to prevent or hinder. 2 *Med* **a** tending to prevent disease; prophylactic. **b** of or relating to the branch of medicine concerned with prolonging life and preventing disease. 3 (in Britain) of, relating to, or belonging to the customs and excise service or the coastguard. ◆ NOUN 4 something that serves to prevent or hinder. 5 *Med* any drug or agent that tends to prevent or protect against disease. 6 another name for **contraceptive.** ◆ Also (except for sense 3): **preventative** (prɪ'vɛntətɪv).
▸**pre'ventively** ADVERB ▸**pre'ventiveness** NOUN

preverbal (ˌpriː'vɜːbᵊl) ADJECTIVE 1 being before the development of speech: *preverbal infants.* 2 *Grammar* coming before the verb.

preview *or US* **prevue** ('priːvjuː) NOUN 1 an advance or preliminary view or sight. 2 an advance showing before public presentation of a film, art exhibition, etc., usually before an invited audience of celebrities and journalists. 3 a public performance of a play before the official first night. ◆ VERB 4 *(tr)* to view in advance.

preview monitor NOUN (in a television studio control room) a picture monitor used for inspecting a picture source before it is switched to transmission.

previous ('priːvɪəs) ADJECTIVE 1 *(prenominal)* existing or coming before something else in time or position; prior. 2 *(postpositive) Informal* taking place or done too soon; premature. 3 **previous to.** before; prior to.
▷HISTORY C17: from Latin *praevius* leading the way, from *prae* before + *via* way
▸**'previously** ADVERB ▸**'previousness** NOUN

previous question NOUN 1 (in the House of Commons) a motion to drop the present topic under debate, put in order to prevent a vote. 2 (in the House of Lords and US legislative bodies) a motion to vote on a bill or other question without delay. ◆ See also **closure** (sense 4).

previse (prɪ'vaɪz) VERB *(tr) Rare* 1 to predict or foresee. 2 to notify in advance.
▷HISTORY C16: from Latin *praevidēre* to foresee, from *prae* before + *vidēre* to see

prevision (prɪ'vɪʒən) NOUN *Rare* 1 the act or power of foreseeing; prescience. 2 a prophetic vision or prophecy.

prevocalic (ˌpriːvəʊ'kælɪk) ADJECTIVE (of a consonant) coming immediately before a vowel.
▸**ˌprevo'calically** ADVERB

prewar (ˌpriː'wɔː, 'priːˌwɔː) ADJECTIVE of or occurring in the period before a war, esp before World War I or II.

prewash (priː'wɒʃ) VERB 1 to give a preliminary wash to (clothes), esp in a washing machine. ◆ NOUN ('priːwɒʃ) 2 a preliminary wash, esp in a washing machine.

prey (preɪ) NOUN 1 an animal hunted or captured by another for food. 2 a person or thing that becomes the victim of a hostile person, influence, etc. 3 **bird** *or* **beast of prey.** a bird or animal that preys on others for food. 4 an archaic word for **booty.** ◆ VERB *(intr;* often foll by *on* or *upon)* 5 to hunt or seize food by killing other animals. 6 to make a victim (of others), as by profiting at their expense. 7 to exert a depressing or obsessive effect (on the mind, spirits, etc.); weigh heavily (upon).
▷HISTORY C13: from Old French *preie,* from Latin *praeda* booty; see PREDATORY
▸**'preyer** NOUN

prezzie ('prɛzɪ) NOUN a variant of **pressie,** an informal word for **present²** (sense 21).

Priam ('praɪəm) NOUN *Greek myth* the last king of Troy, killed at its fall. He was father by Hecuba of Hector, Paris, and Cassandra.

priapic (praɪ'æpɪk, -'eɪ-) *or* **priapean** (ˌpraɪə'piːən) ADJECTIVE 1 *(sometimes capital)* of or relating to Priapus. 2 a less common word for **phallic.**

priapism ('praɪəˌpɪzəm) NOUN *Pathol* prolonged painful erection of the penis, caused by neurological disorders, obstruction of the penile blood vessels, etc.
▷HISTORY C17: from Late Latin *priāpismus,* ultimately from Greek PRIAPUS

Priapus (praɪ'eɪpəs) NOUN 1 (in classical antiquity) the god of the male procreative power and of gardens and vineyards. 2 *(often not capital)* a representation of the penis.

Pribilof Islands ('prɪbɪləf) PLURAL NOUN a group of islands in the Bering Sea, off SW Alaska, belonging to the US: the breeding ground of the northern fur seal. Area: about 168 sq. km (65 sq. miles). Also called: **Fur Seal Islands.**

price (praɪs) NOUN 1 the sum in money or goods for which anything is or may be bought or sold. 2 the cost at which anything is obtained. 3 the cost of bribing a person. 4 a sum of money offered or given as a reward for a capture or killing. 5 value or worth, esp high worth. 6 *Gambling* another word for **odds.** 7 **at any price.** whatever the price or cost. 8 **at a price.** at a high price. 9 **beyond** *(or* **without) price.** invaluable or priceless. 10 **the price of (one).** *Irish* what (one) deserves, esp a fitting punishment: *it's just the price of him.* 11 **what price (something)?** what are the chances of (something) happening now? ◆ VERB *(tr)* 12 to fix or establish the price of. 13 to ascertain or discover the price of. 14 **price out of the market.** to charge so highly for as to prevent the sale, hire, etc., of.
▷HISTORY C13 *pris,* from Old French, from Latin *pretium* price, value, wage
▸**'pricer** NOUN

price break NOUN a reduction in price, esp for bulk purchase.

Price Commission NOUN (in Britain) a commission established by the government in 1973 with authority to control prices as a measure against inflation. It was abolished in 1980.

price control NOUN the establishment and maintenance of maximum price levels for basic goods and services by a government, esp during periods of war or inflation.

price discrimination NOUN *Economics* the setting of different prices to be charged to different consumers or in different markets for the same goods or services.

price-dividend ratio NOUN the ratio of the price of a share on a stock exchange to the dividends per share paid in the previous year, used as a measure of a company's potential as an investment. Abbreviations: **P-D ratio, PDR.**

price-earnings ratio NOUN the ratio of the price of a share on a stock exchange to the earnings per share, used as a measure of a company's future profitability. Abbreviation: **P/E ratio.**

price-fixing NOUN 1 the setting of prices by agreement among producers and distributors. 2 another name for **price control** or **resale price maintenance.**

price leadership NOUN *Marketing* the setting of the price of a product or service by a dominant firm at a level that competitors can match, in order to avoid a price war.

priceless ('praɪslɪs) ADJECTIVE 1 of inestimable worth; beyond valuation; invaluable. 2 *Informal* extremely amusing or ridiculous.
▸**'pricelessly** ADVERB ▸**'pricelessness** NOUN

price ring NOUN a group of traders formed to maintain the prices of their goods.

prices and incomes policy NOUN voluntary or statutory regulation of the level of increases in prices and incomes.

price-sensitive ADJECTIVE likely to affect the price of property, esp shares and securities: *price-sensitive information.*

price support NOUN government maintenance of specified price levels at a minimum above market equilibrium by subsidy or by purchase of the market surplus at the guaranteed levels.

price tag NOUN 1 a ticket or label on an article for sale showing its price. 2 the cost, esp of something not usually priced: *the price tag on a top footballer.*

price war NOUN a period of intense competition among enterprises, esp retail enterprises, in the same market, characterized by repeated price reductions rather than advertising, brand promotion, etc.

pricey *or* **pricy** ('praɪsɪ) ADJECTIVE **pricier, priciest.** an informal word for **expensive.**

prick (prɪk) VERB *(mainly tr)* 1 **a** to make (a small hole) in (something) by piercing lightly with a sharp point. **b** to wound in this manner. 2 *(intr)* to cause or have a piercing or stinging sensation. 3 to cause to feel a sharp emotional pain: *knowledge of such poverty pricked his conscience.* 4 to puncture or pierce. 5 to mark, delineate, or outline by dots or punctures. 6 *(also intr;* usually foll by *up)* to rise or raise erect; point: *the dog pricked his ears up at his master's call.* 7 (usually foll by *out* or *off)* to transplant (seedlings) into a larger container. 8 (often foll by *off) Navigation* to measure or trace (a course, distance, etc.) on a chart with dividers. 9 *Archaic* to rouse or impel; urge on. 10 *(intr) Archaic* to ride fast on horseback; spur a horse on. 11 **prick up one's ears.** to start to listen attentively; become interested. ◆ NOUN 12 the act of pricking or the condition or sensation of being pricked. 13 a mark made by a sharp point; puncture. 14 a sharp emotional pain resembling the physical pain caused by being pricked: *a prick of conscience.* 15 a taboo slang word for **penis.** 16 *Slang, derogatory* an obnoxious or despicable man. 17 an instrument or weapon with a sharp point, such as a thorn, goad, bee sting, etc. 18 the footprint or track of an animal, esp a hare. 19 *Obsolete* a small mark caused by pricking a surface; dot; point. 20 **kick against the pricks.** to hurt oneself by struggling against something in vain.
▷HISTORY Old English *prica* point, puncture; related to Dutch *prik,* Icelandic *prik* short stick, Swedish *prick* point, stick

pricker ('prɪkə) NOUN 1 a person or thing that pricks. 2 *US* a thorn; prickle.

pricket ('prɪkɪt) NOUN 1 a male deer in the second year of life having unbranched antlers. 2 a

sharp metal spike on which to stick a candle. [3] a candlestick having such a spike.
▷HISTORY C14 *priket,* from *prik* PRICK

prickle (ˈprɪkᵊl) NOUN [1] *Botany* a pointed process arising from the outer layer of a stem, leaf, etc., and containing no woody or conducting tissue. Compare **thorn** (sense 1). [2] a pricking or stinging sensation. ◆ VERB [3] to feel or cause to feel a stinging sensation. [4] (*tr*) to prick, as with a thorn.
▷HISTORY Old English *pricel;* related to Middle Low German *prekel,* German *Prickel*

prickly (ˈprɪklɪ) ADJECTIVE **-lier, -liest.** [1] having or covered with prickles. [2] stinging or tingling. [3] bad-tempered or irritable. [4] full of difficulties; knotty: *a prickly problem.*
▸ˈ**prickliness** NOUN

prickly ash NOUN a North American rutaceous shrub or small tree, *Zanthoxylum americanum,* having prickly branches, feathery aromatic leaves, and bark used as a remedy for toothache. Also called: **toothache tree.**

prickly heat NOUN a nontechnical name for **miliaria.**

prickly pear NOUN [1] any of various tropical cacti of the genus *Opuntia,* having flattened or cylindrical spiny joints and oval fruit that is edible in some species. See also **cholla, nopal** (sense 2). [2] the fruit of any of these plants.

prickly poppy NOUN an annual papaveraceous plant, *Argemone mexicana,* of tropical America, having prickly stems and leaves and large yellow or white flowers.

prick song NOUN *Obsolete* **a** a piece of written vocal music. **b** vocal music sung from a copy.
▷HISTORY C16: from *pricked song, prickt song,* from PRICK (in the sense: to mark out, notate)

pride (praɪd) NOUN [1] a feeling of honour and self-respect; a sense of personal worth. [2] excessive self-esteem; conceit. [3] a source of pride. [4] satisfaction or pleasure taken in one's own or another's success, achievements, etc. (esp in the phrase **take (a) pride in**). [5] the better or most superior part of something; flower. [6] the most flourishing time. [7] a group (of lions). [8] the mettle of a horse; courage; spirit. [9] *Archaic* sexual desire, esp in a female animal. [10] *Archaic* display, pomp, or splendour. [11] **pride of place.** the most important position. ◆ VERB [12] (*tr;* foll by *on* or *upon*) to take pride in (oneself) for. [13] (*intr*) to glory or revel (in).
▷HISTORY Old English *prȳda;* related to Latin *prodesse* to be useful, Old Norse *prūthr* stately; see PROUD
▸ˈ**prideful** ADJECTIVE ▸ˈ**pridefully** ADVERB

Pride's Purge (praɪd) NOUN the expulsion from the Long Parliament of members hostile to the army by Thomas Pride (died 1658) in 1648.

prie-dieu (priːˈdjɜː) NOUN a piece of furniture consisting of a low surface for kneeling upon and a narrow front surmounted by a rest for the elbows or for books, for use when praying.
▷HISTORY C18: from French, from *prier* to pray + *Dieu* God

prier *or* **pryer** (ˈpraɪə) NOUN a person who pries.

priest (priːst) *or feminine* **priestess** NOUN [1] *Christianity* a person ordained to act as a mediator between God and man in administering the sacraments, preaching, blessing, guiding, etc. [2] (in episcopal Churches) a minister in the second grade of the hierarchy of holy orders, ranking below a bishop but above a deacon. [3] a minister of any religion. [4] *Judaism* a descendant of the family of Aaron who has certain privileges in the synagogue service. [5] (in some non-Christian religions) an official who offers sacrifice on behalf of the people and performs other religious ceremonies. [6] (*sometimes capital*) a variety of fancy pigeon having a bald pate with a crest or peak at the back of the head. [7] *Angling* a small club used to kill fish caught. ◆ VERB (*tr*) [8] to make a priest; ordain. ◆ Related adjective: **hieratic.**
▷HISTORY Old English *prēost,* apparently from PRESBYTER; related to Old High German *prēster,* Old French *prestre*
▸ˈ**priestˌlike** ADJECTIVE

priestcraft (ˈpriːstˌkrɑːft) NOUN [1] the art and skills involved in the work of a priest. [2] *Derogatory* the influence of priests upon politics or the use by them of secular power.

priest-hole *or* **priest's hole** NOUN a secret chamber in certain houses in England, built as a hiding place for Roman Catholic priests when they were proscribed in the 16th and 17th centuries.

priesthood (ˈpriːstˌhʊd) NOUN [1] the state, order, or office of a priest. [2] priests collectively.

priestly (ˈpriːstlɪ) ADJECTIVE **-lier, -liest.** of, relating to, characteristic of, or befitting a priest.
▸ˈ**priestliness** NOUN

priest-ridden ADJECTIVE dominated or governed by or excessively under the influence of priests.

prig[1] (prɪg) NOUN a person who is smugly self-righteous and narrow-minded.
▷HISTORY C18: of unknown origin
▸ˈ**priggery** *or* ˈ**priggishness** NOUN ▸ˈ**priggish** ADJECTIVE
▸ˈ**priggishly** ADVERB ▸ˈ**priggism** NOUN

prig[2] (prɪg) *Brit slang, archaic* ◆ VERB **prigs, prigging, prigged.** [1] another word for **steal.** ◆ NOUN [2] another word for **thief.**
▷HISTORY C16: of unknown origin

prill (prɪl) VERB [1] (*tr*) to convert (a material) into a granular free-flowing form. ◆ NOUN [2] prilled material.
▷HISTORY C18: originally a Cornish copper-mining term, of obscure origin

prim (prɪm) ADJECTIVE **primmer, primmest.** [1] affectedly proper, precise, or formal. ◆ VERB **prims, primming, primmed.** [2] (*tr*) to make prim. [3] to purse (the mouth) primly or (of the mouth) to be so pursed.
▷HISTORY C18: of unknown origin
▸ˈ**primly** ADVERB ▸ˈ**primness** NOUN

prima ballerina (ˈpriːmə) NOUN a leading female ballet dancer.
▷HISTORY from Italian, literally: first ballerina

primacy (ˈpraɪməsɪ) NOUN, *plural* **-cies.** [1] the state of being first in rank, grade, etc. [2] *Christianity* the office, rank, or jurisdiction of a primate or senior bishop or (in the Roman Catholic Church) the pope.

prima donna (ˈpriːmə ˈdɒnə) NOUN, *plural* **prima donnas.** [1] a female operatic star; diva. [2] *Informal* a temperamental person.
▷HISTORY C19: from Italian: first lady

primaeval (praɪˈmiːvᵊl) ADJECTIVE a variant spelling of **primeval.**

prima facie (ˈpraɪmə ˈfeɪʃɪ) at first sight; as it seems at first.
▷HISTORY C15: from Latin, from *prīmus* first + *faciēs* FACE

prima-facie evidence NOUN *Law* evidence that is sufficient to establish a fact or to raise a presumption of the truth of a fact unless controverted.

primage (ˈpraɪmɪdʒ) NOUN *NZ* tax added to customs duty.

primal (ˈpraɪməl) ADJECTIVE [1] first or original. [2] chief or most important.
▷HISTORY C17: from Medieval Latin *prīmālis,* from Latin *prīmus* first

primal therapy NOUN *Psychol* a form of psychotherapy in which patients are encouraged to scream abusively about their parents and agonizingly about their own suffering in infancy. Also called: **primal scream therapy, scream therapy.**
▷HISTORY C20: from the book *The Primal Scream* (1970) by Arthur Janov, US psychologist, who originated the treatment

primaquine (ˈpraɪməˌkwiːn) NOUN a synthetic drug used in the treatment of malaria. Formula: $C_{15}H_{21}N_3O$.
▷HISTORY C20: from *prima-,* from Latin *prīmus* first + QUIN(OLIN)E

primarily (ˈpraɪmərəlɪ) ADVERB [1] principally; chiefly; mainly. [2] at first; originally.

primary (ˈpraɪmərɪ) ADJECTIVE [1] first in importance, degree, rank, etc. [2] first in position or time, as in a series. [3] fundamental; basic. [4] being the first stage; elementary. [5] (*prenominal*) of or relating to the education of children up to the age of 11. [6] (of the flight feathers of a bird's wing) growing from the manus. [7] **a** being the part of an electric circuit, such as a transformer or induction coil, in which a changing current induces a current in a neighbouring circuit: *a primary coil.* **b** (of a current) flowing in such a circuit. Compare **secondary.** [8] **a** (of a product) consisting of a natural raw material; unmanufactured. **b** (of production or industry) involving the extraction or winning of such products. Agriculture, fishing, forestry, hunting, and mining are primary industries. Compare **secondary** (sense 7), **tertiary** (sense 2). [9] *Chem* **a** (of an organic compound) having a functional group attached to a carbon atom that is attached to at least two hydrogen atoms. **b** (of an amine) having only one organic group attached to the nitrogen atom; containing the group NH_2. **c** (of a salt) derived from a tribasic acid by replacement of one acidic hydrogen atom with a metal atom or electropositive group. [10] *Linguistics* **a** derived from a word that is not a derivation but the ultimate form itself. *Lovable* is a primary derivative of *love.* **b** (of Latin, Greek, or Sanskrit tenses) referring to present or future time. Compare **historic** (sense 3). [11] *Geology* relating to magmas that have not experienced fractional crystallization or crystal contamination. ◆ NOUN, *plural* **-ries.** [12] a person or thing that is first in rank, occurrence, etc. [13] (in the US) **a** a preliminary election in which the voters of a state or region choose a party's convention delegates, nominees for office, etc. See also **closed primary, direct primary, open primary. b** a local meeting of voters registered with one party to nominate candidates, select convention delegates, etc. Full name: **primary election.** [14] See **primary colour.** [15] any of the flight feathers growing from the manus of a bird's wing. [16] a primary coil, winding, inductance, or current in an electric circuit. [17] *Astronomy* a celestial body around which one or more specified secondary bodies orbit: *the sun is the primary of the earth.*
▷HISTORY C15: from Latin *prīmārius* of the first rank, principal, from *prīmus* first

primary accent *or* **stress** NOUN *Linguistics* the strongest accent in a word or breath group, as that on the first syllable of *agriculture.* Compare **secondary accent.**

primary cell NOUN an electric cell that generates an electromotive force by the direct and usually irreversible conversion of chemical energy into electrical energy. It cannot be recharged efficiently by an electric current. Also called: **voltaic cell.** Compare **secondary cell.**

primary colour NOUN [1] Also called: **additive primary.** any of three spectral colours (usually red, green, and blue) that can be mixed to match any other colour, including white light but excluding black. [2] Also called: **subtractive primary.** any one of the spectral colours cyan, magenta, or yellow that can be subtracted from white light to match any other colour. An equal mixture of the three produces a black pigment. [3] Also called: **psychological primary.** any one of the colours red, yellow, green, or blue. All other colours look like a mixture of two or more of these colours and they play a unique role in the processing of colour by the visual system. ◆ See also **secondary colour, complementary colour.**

primary effect NOUN *Psychol* the process whereby the first few items on a list are learnt more rapidly than the middle items.

primary election NOUN See **primary** (sense 13).

primary mirror NOUN the mirror that collects and focuses the incoming light in a reflecting telescope.

primary processes PLURAL NOUN *Psychoanal* unconscious, irrational thought processes, such as condensation or displacement, governed by the pleasure principle. Compare **secondary processes.**

primary qualities PLURAL NOUN (in empiricist philosophy) those properties of objects that are directly known by experience, such as size, shape, and number.

primary school NOUN [1] (in Britain) a school for children below the age of 11. It is usually divided into an infant and a junior section. [2] (in the US and Canada) a school equivalent to the first three or four grades of elementary school, sometimes including a kindergarten.

primary stress NOUN *Linguistics* another term for **primary accent.**

primate[1] (ˈpraɪmeɪt) NOUN [1] any placental mammal of the order *Primates,* typically having

flexible hands and feet with opposable first digits, good eyesight, and, in the higher apes, a highly developed brain: includes lemurs, lorises, monkeys, apes, and man. ◆ ADJECTIVE [2] of, relating to, or belonging to the order *Primates.*
▷HISTORY C18: from New Latin *primates,* plural of *prīmās* principal, from *prīmus* first
▸**primatial** (praɪˈmeɪʃəl) ADJECTIVE

primate² (ˈpraɪmeɪt) NOUN [1] another name for **archbishop.** [2] **Primate of all England.** the Archbishop of Canterbury. [3] **Primate of England.** the Archbishop of York.
▷HISTORY C13: from Old French, from Latin *prīmās* principal, from *prīmus* first

primatology (ˌpraɪməˈtɒlədʒɪ) NOUN the branch of zoology that is concerned with the study of primates.
▸**ˌprimaˈtologist** NOUN

prime (praɪm) ADJECTIVE [1] (*prenominal*) first in quality or value; first-rate. [2] (*prenominal*) fundamental; original. [3] (*prenominal*) first in importance, authority, etc.; chief. [4] *Maths* **a** having no factors except itself or one: $x^2 + x + 3$ *is a prime polynomial.* **b** (foll by *to*) having no common factors (with): *20 is prime to 21.* [5] *Finance* having the best credit rating: *prime investments.* ◆ NOUN [6] the time when a thing is at its best. [7] a period of power, vigour, etc., usually following youth (esp in the phrase **the prime of life**). [8] the beginning of something, such as the spring. [9] *Maths* short for **prime number.** [10] *Linguistics* a semantically indivisible element; minimal component of the sense of a word. [11] *Music* **a** unison. **b** the tonic of a scale. [12] *Chiefly RC Church* the second of the seven canonical hours of the divine office, originally fixed for the first hour of the day, at sunrise. [13] the first of eight basic positions from which a parry or attack can be made in fencing. ◆ VERB [14] to prepare (something); make ready. [15] (*tr*) to apply a primer, such as paint or size, to (a surface). [16] (*tr*) to fill (a pump) with its working fluid before starting, in order to improve the sealing of the pump elements and to expel air from it before starting. [17] (*tr*) to increase the quantity of fuel in the float chamber of (a carburettor) in order to facilitate the starting of an engine. [18] (*tr*) to insert a primer into (a gun, mine, charge, etc.) preparatory to detonation or firing. [19] (*intr*) (of a steam engine or boiler) to operate with or produce steam mixed with large amounts of water. [20] (*tr*) to provide with facts, information, etc., beforehand; brief.
▷HISTORY (adj) C14: from Latin *prīmus* first; (n) C13: from Latin *prīma* (*hora*) the first (hour); (vb) C16: of uncertain origin, probably connected with n
▸**ˈprimely** ADVERB ▸**ˈprimeness** NOUN

prime cost NOUN the portion of the cost of a commodity that varies directly with the amount of it produced, principally comprising materials and labour. Also called: **variable cost.** Compare **overheads.**

prime focus NOUN the focal point of the objective lens or primary mirror of a telescope.

prime meridian NOUN the 0° meridian from which the other meridians or lines of longitude are calculated, usually taken to pass through Greenwich.

prime minister NOUN [1] the head of a parliamentary government. [2] the chief minister of a sovereign or a state.
▸**prime ministership** *or* **prime ministry** NOUN

prime mover NOUN [1] the original or primary force behind an idea, enterprise, etc. [2] **a** the source of power, such as fuel, wind, electricity, etc., for a machine. **b** the means of extracting power from such a source, such as a steam engine, electric motor, etc. [3] (in the philosophy of Aristotle) that which is the cause of all movement.

Prime Mover NOUN (usually preceded by *the*) *Philosophy* God, esp when considered as a first cause.

prime number NOUN an integer that cannot be factorized into other integers but is only divisible by itself or 1, such as 2, 3, 5, 7, and 11. Sometimes shortened to: **prime.** Compare **composite number.**

primer¹ (ˈpraɪmə) NOUN [1] an introductory text, such as a school textbook. [2] *Printing* See **long primer, great primer.**
▷HISTORY C14: via Anglo-Norman from Medieval Latin *primārius* (*liber*) a first (book), from Latin *prīmārius* PRIMARY

primer² (ˈpraɪmə) NOUN [1] a person or thing that primes. [2] a device, such as a tube containing explosive, for detonating the main charge in a gun, mine, etc. [3] a substance, such as paint, applied to a surface as a base, sealer, etc. Also called (for senses 2, 3): **priming.**
▷HISTORY C15: see PRIME (vb)

prime rate NOUN the lowest commercial interest rate charged by a bank at a particular time.

primero (prɪˈmeərəʊ) NOUN *Chiefly Brit* a 16th- and 17th-century card game.
▷HISTORY C16: from Spanish *primera* card game, from *primero* first, from Latin *prīmārius* chief

primers (ˈprɪməz) PLURAL NOUN *NZ informal* the youngest class in a primary school.

prime time NOUN [1] the peak viewing time on television, for which advertising rates are the highest. ◆ ADJECTIVE **primetime.** [2] occurring during or designed for prime time: *a primetime drama.*

primeval *or* **primaeval** (praɪˈmiːvᵊl) ADJECTIVE of or belonging to the first age or ages, esp of the world.
▷HISTORY C17: from Latin *prīmaevus* youthful, from *prīmus* first + *aevum* age
▸**priˈmevally** *or* **priˈmaevally** ADVERB

prime vertical NOUN *Astronomy* the great circle passing through the observer's zenith and meeting the horizon due east and west.

primigravida (ˌpraɪmɪˈgrævɪdə) NOUN, *plural* **-das** *or* **-dae** (-ˌdiː). *Obstetrics* a woman who is pregnant for the first time.
▷HISTORY C19: New Latin, from Latin *prima* first + *gravida* GRAVID (woman)

primine (ˈpraɪmɪn) NOUN *Botany, now rare* the integument surrounding an ovule or the outer of two such integuments. Compare **secundine.**
▷HISTORY C19: via French from Latin *prīmus* first

priming (ˈpraɪmɪŋ) NOUN [1] something used to prime. [2] a substance, used to ignite an explosive charge.

primipara (praɪˈmɪpərə) NOUN, *plural* **-ras** *or* **-rae** (-ˌriː). *Obstetrics* a woman who has borne only one child. Also written: **Para I.**
▷HISTORY C19: from Latin, from *prīmus* first + *parere* to bring forth
▸**primiparity** (ˌpraɪmɪˈpærɪtɪ) NOUN ▸**priˈmiparous** ADJECTIVE

primitive (ˈprɪmɪtɪv) ADJECTIVE [1] of or belonging to the first or beginning; original. [2] characteristic of an early state, esp in being crude or uncivilized: *a primitive dwelling.* [3] *Anthropol* denoting or relating to a preliterate and nonindustrial social system. [4] *Biology* **a** of, relating to, or resembling an early stage in the evolutionary development of a particular group of organisms: *primitive amphibians.* **b** another word for **primordial** (sense 3). [5] showing the characteristics of primitive painters; untrained, childlike, or naive. [6] *Geology* pertaining to magmas that have experienced only small degrees of fractional crystallization or crystal contamination. [7] *Obsolete* Of, relating to, or denoting rocks formed in or before the Palaeozoic era. [8] *Obsolete* denoting a word from which another word is derived, as for example *hope,* from which *hopeless* is derived. [9] *Protestant theol* of, relating to, or associated with a minority group that breaks away from a sect, denomination, or Church in order to return to what is regarded as the original simplicity of the Gospels. ◆ NOUN [10] a primitive person or thing. [11] **a** an artist whose work does not conform to traditional, academic, or avant-garde standards of Western painting, such as a painter from an African or Oceanic civilization. **b** a painter of the pre-Renaissance era in European painting. **c** a painter of any era whose work appears childlike or untrained. Also called (for senses 11a, 11c): **naive.** [12] a work by such an artist. [13] a word or concept from which another word or concept is derived. [14] *Maths* a curve, function, or other form from which another is derived.
▷HISTORY C14: from Latin *prīmitīvus* earliest of its kind, primitive, from *prīmus* first
▸**ˈprimitively** ADVERB ▸**ˈprimitiveness** NOUN

primitivism (ˈprɪmɪtɪˌvɪzəm) NOUN [1] the condition of being primitive. [2] the notion that the value of primitive cultures is superior to that of the modern world. [3] the principles, characteristics, etc., of primitive art and artists.
▸**ˈprimitivist** NOUN, ADJECTIVE ▸**ˌprimitivˈistic** ADJECTIVE

primo (ˈpriːməʊ) NOUN, *plural* **-mos** *or* **-mi** (-mɪ). *Music* the upper or right-hand part in a piano duet. Compare **secondo.**
▷HISTORY Italian: first, from Latin *prīmus*

primogenitor (ˌpraɪməʊˈdʒenɪtə) NOUN [1] a forefather; ancestor. [2] an earliest parent or ancestor, as of a race.
▷HISTORY C17: alteration of PROGENITOR after PRIMOGENITURE

primogeniture (ˌpraɪməʊˈdʒenɪtʃə) NOUN [1] the state of being a first-born. [2] *Law* the right of an eldest son to succeed to the estate of his ancestor to the exclusion of all others. Compare **ultimogeniture.**
▷HISTORY C17: from Medieval Latin *prīmōgenitūra* birth of a first child, from Latin *prīmō* at first + Late Latin *genitūra* a birth
▸**primogenitary** (ˌpraɪməʊˈdʒenɪtərɪ, -trɪ) ADJECTIVE

primordial (praɪˈmɔːdɪəl) ADJECTIVE [1] existing at or from the beginning; earliest; primeval. [2] constituting an origin; fundamental. [3] *Biology* of or relating to an early stage of development: *primordial germ cells.* ◆ NOUN [4] an elementary or basic principle.
▷HISTORY C14: from Late Latin *prīmōrdiālis* original, from Latin *prīmus* first + *ōrdīrī* to begin
▸**priˌmordiˈality** NOUN ▸**priˈmordially** ADVERB

primordium (praɪˈmɔːdɪəm) NOUN, *plural* **-dia** (-dɪə). *Biology* an organ or part in the earliest stage of development.

primp (prɪmp) VERB to dress (oneself), esp in fine clothes; prink.
▷HISTORY C19: probably from PRIM

primrose (ˈprɪmˌrəʊz) NOUN [1] any of various temperate primulaceous plants of the genus *Primula, esp P. vulgaris* of Europe, which has pale yellow flowers. [2] short for **evening primrose.** [3] Also called: **primrose yellow.** a light to moderate yellow, sometimes with a greenish tinge. ◆ ADJECTIVE [4] of, relating to, or abounding in primroses. [5] of the colour primrose. [6] pleasant or gay.
▷HISTORY C15: from Old French *primerose,* from Medieval Latin *prīma rosa* first rose

primrose path NOUN (often preceded by *the*) a pleasurable way of life.

primula (ˈprɪmjʊlə) NOUN any primulaceous plant of the N temperate genus *Primula,* having white, yellow, pink, or purple funnel-shaped flowers with five spreading petals: includes the primrose, oxlip, cowslip, and polyanthus.
▷HISTORY C18: New Latin, from Medieval Latin *prīmula* (*vēris*) little first one (of the spring)

primulaceous (ˌprɪmjʊˈleɪʃəs) ADJECTIVE of, relating to, or belonging to the *Primulaceae,* a family of plants having funnel-shaped or bell-shaped flowers: includes primrose, moneywort, pimpernel, and loosestrife.

primum mobile *Latin* (ˈpraɪmʊm ˈməʊbɪlɪ) NOUN [1] a prime mover. [2] *Astronomy* the outermost empty sphere in the Ptolemaic system that was thought to revolve around the earth from east to west in 24 hours carrying with it the inner spheres of the planets, sun, moon, and fixed stars.
▷HISTORY C15: from Medieval Latin: first moving (thing)

primus (ˈpraɪməs) NOUN *Scottish Episcopal Church* the presiding bishop in the Synod.
▷HISTORY from Latin: first

Primus (ˈpraɪməs) NOUN *Trademark* a portable paraffin cooking stove, used esp by campers. Also called: **Primus stove.**

primus inter pares *Latin* (ˈpraɪməs ɪntə ˈpɑːriːz) first among equals.

prince (prɪns) NOUN [1] (in Britain) a son of the sovereign or of one of the sovereign's sons. [2] a nonreigning male member of a sovereign family. [3] the monarch of a small territory, such as Monaco, usually called a principality, that was at some time subordinate to an emperor or king. [4] any sovereign; monarch. [5] a nobleman in various countries, such as Italy and Germany. [6] an outstanding member of a specified group: *a merchant prince.* [7] *US and Canadian informal* a generous and charming man.

▷HISTORY C13: via Old French from Latin *princeps* first man, ruler, chief
▸ **'prince,like** ADJECTIVE

Prince Albert NOUN a man's double-breasted frock coat worn esp in the early 20th century.

prince consort NOUN the husband of a female sovereign, who is himself a prince.

princedom ('prɪnsdəm) NOUN [1] the dignity, rank, or position of a prince. [2] a land ruled by a prince; principality.

princedoms ('prɪnsdəmz) PLURAL NOUN (*often capital*) another term for: **principalities.**

Prince Edward Island NOUN an island in the Gulf of St Lawrence that constitutes the smallest Canadian province. Capital: Charlottetown. Pop.: 138 500 (2001 est.). Area: 5656 sq. km (2184 sq. miles). Abbreviations: **PE, PEI.**

Prince Edward Islander NOUN a native or inhabitant of Prince Edward Island.

princeling ('prɪnslɪŋ) NOUN [1] Also called: **princekin.** a young prince. [2] Also called: **princelet.** the ruler of an insignificant territory; petty or minor prince.

princely ('prɪnslɪ) ADJECTIVE **-lier, -liest.** [1] generous or lavish. [2] of, belonging to, or characteristic of a prince. ◆ ADVERB [3] in a princely manner.
▸ **'princeliness** NOUN

Prince of Darkness NOUN another name for **Satan.**

Prince of Peace NOUN *Bible* the future Messiah (Isaiah 9:6): held by Christians to be Christ.

Prince of Wales[1] NOUN the eldest son and heir apparent of the British sovereign.

Prince of Wales[2] NOUN **Cape.** a cape in W Alaska, on the Bering Strait opposite the coast of the extreme northeast of Russia: the westernmost point of North America.

Prince of Wales Island NOUN [1] an island in N Canada, in Nunavut. Area: about 36 000 sq. km (14 000 sq. miles). [2] an island in SE Alaska, the largest island in the Alexander Archipelago. Area: about 4000 sq. km (1500 sq. miles). [3] an island in NE Australia, in N Queensland in the Torres Strait. [4] the former name (until about 1867) of the island of **Penang.**

prince regent NOUN a prince who acts as regent during the minority, disability, or absence of the legal sovereign.

prince royal NOUN the eldest son of a monarch.

Prince Rupert ('ru:pət) NOUN a port in W Canada, on the coast of British Columbia: one of the W termini of the Canadian National transcontinental railway. Pop.: 16 620 (1991).

prince's feather NOUN [1] an amaranthaceous garden plant, *Amaranthus hybridus hypochondriacus,* with spikes of bristly brownish-red flowers. [2] a tall tropical polygonaceous plant, *Polygonum orientale,* with hanging spikes of pink flowers.

princess (prɪn'sɛs) NOUN [1] (in Britain) a daughter of the sovereign or of one of the sovereign's sons. [2] a nonreigning female member of a sovereign family. [3] the wife and consort of a prince. [4] any very attractive or outstanding woman. [5] Also called: **princess dress, princess line.** a style of dress with a fitted bodice and an A-line skirt that is shaped by seams from shoulder to hem without a seam at the waistline.

princess royal NOUN [1] the eldest daughter of a British or (formerly) a Prussian sovereign: a title not always conferred. [2] (*capitals*) the title of Princess Anne.

Princeton ('prɪnstən) NOUN a town in central New Jersey: settled by Quakers in 1696; an important educational centre, seat of Princeton University (founded at Elizabeth in 1747 and moved here in 1756); scene of the battle (1777) during the War of American Independence in which Washington's troops defeated the British on the university campus. Pop.: 12 016 (1990).

principal ('prɪnsɪpᵊl) ADJECTIVE (*prenominal*) [1] first in importance, rank, value, etc.; chief. [2] denoting or relating to capital or property as opposed to interest, etc. ◆ NOUN [3] a person who is first in importance or directs some event, action, organization, etc. [4] (in Britain) a civil servant of an executive grade who is in charge of a section. [5] *Law* **a** a person who engages another to act as his agent. **b** an active participant in a crime. **c** the person primarily liable to fulfil an obligation. [6] the head of a school or other educational institution. [7] (in Scottish schools) a head of department. [8] *Finance* **a** capital or property, as contrasted with the income derived from it. **b** the original amount of a debt on which interest is calculated. [9] a main roof truss or rafter. [10] *Music* **a** the chief instrumentalist in a section of the orchestra. **b** one of the singers in an opera company. **c** either of two types of open diapason organ stops, one of four-foot length and pitch and the other of eight-foot length and pitch. [11] the leading performer in a play.
▷HISTORY C13: via Old French from Latin *principālis* chief, from *princeps* chief man, PRINCE
▸ **'principalship** NOUN

> **Language note** See at **principle.**

principal axis NOUN [1] the line passing through the optical centre and centres of curvature of the faces of a lens or a curved mirror. [2] any of three mutually perpendicular axes about which the moment of inertia of a body is maximum.

principal boy NOUN the leading male role in a pantomime, played by a woman.

principal focus NOUN another name for **focal point.**

principalities (,prɪnsɪ'pælɪtɪz) PLURAL NOUN (*often capital*) the seventh of the nine orders into which the angels are divided in medieval angelology. Also called: **princedoms.**

principality (,prɪnsɪ'pælɪtɪ) NOUN, *plural* **-ties.** [1] **a** a territory ruled by a prince. **b** a territory from which a prince draws his title. [2] the dignity or authority of a prince.
▷HISTORY C14 (in the sense: pre-eminence): via Old French from Latin *principālis* PRINCIPAL

principally ('prɪnsɪpᵊlɪ) ADVERB mainly or most importantly.

principal nursing officer NOUN a grade of nurse concerned with administration in the British National Health Service.

principal parts PLURAL NOUN [1] *Grammar* the main inflected forms of a verb, from which all other inflections may be deduced. In English they are generally considered to consist of the third person present singular, present participle, past tense, and past participle. [2] the sides and interior angles of a triangle.

principate ('prɪnsɪ,peɪt) NOUN [1] a state ruled by a prince. [2] a form of rule in the early Roman Empire in which some republican forms survived.

Principe ('prɪnsɪpi:; *Portuguese* 'prĩsipə) NOUN an island in the Gulf of Guinea, off the W coast of Africa: part of São Tomé e Principe. Area: 150 sq. km (58 sq. miles).

principium (prɪn'sɪpɪəm) NOUN, *plural* **-ia** (-ɪə). (*ususually plural*) a principle, esp a fundamental one.
▷HISTORY C17: Latin: an origin, beginning

principle ('prɪnsɪpᵊl) NOUN [1] a standard or rule of personal conduct: *a man of principle.* [2] (*often plural*) a set of such moral rules: *he'd stoop to anything; he has no principles.* [3] adherence to such a moral code; morality: *it's not the money but the principle of the thing; torn between principle and expediency.* [4] a fundamental or general truth or law: *first principles.* [5] the essence of something: *the male principle.* [6] a source or fundamental cause; origin: *principle of life.* [7] a rule or law concerning a natural phenomenon or the behaviour of a system: *the principle of the conservation of mass.* [8] an underlying or guiding theory or belief: *the hereditary principle; socialist principles.* [9] *Chem* a constituent of a substance that gives the substance its characteristics and behaviour: *bitter principle.* [10] **in principle.** in theory or essence. [11] **on principle.** because of or in demonstration of a principle.
▷HISTORY C14: from Latin *principium* beginning, basic tenet

> **Language note** *Principle* and *principal* are often confused: *the principal* (not *principle*) *reason for his departure; the plan was approved in principle* (not *in principal*).

Principle ('prɪnsɪpᵊl) NOUN *Christian Science* another word for **God.**

principled ('prɪnsɪpᵊld) ADJECTIVE **a** having high moral principles. **b** (*in combination*): *high-principled.*

principle of economy NOUN **the.** another name for **Ockham's razor.**

principle of indifference NOUN the principle that, in the absence of any reason to expect one event rather than another, all the possible events should be assigned the same probability. See **mathematical probability.**

principle of least action NOUN the principle that motion between any two points in a conservative dynamical system is such that the action has a minimum value with respect to all paths between the points that correspond to the same energy. Also called: **Maupertuis principle.**

prink (prɪŋk) VERB [1] to dress (oneself, etc.) finely; deck out. [2] (*intr*) to preen oneself.
▷HISTORY C16: probably changed from PRANK[2] (to adorn, decorate)
▸ **'prinker** NOUN

print (prɪnt) VERB [1] to reproduce (text, pictures, etc.), esp in large numbers, by applying ink to paper or other material by one of various processes. [2] to produce or reproduce (a manuscript, a book, data, etc.) in print, as for publication. [3] to write (letters, etc.) in the style of printed matter. [4] to mark or indent (a surface) by pressing (something) onto it. [5] to produce a photographic print from (a negative). [6] (*tr*) to implant or fix in the mind or memory. [7] (*tr*) to make (a mark or indentation) by applying pressure. ◆ NOUN [8] printed matter such as newsprint. [9] a printed publication such as a newspaper or book. [10] **in print. a** in printed or published form. **b** (of a book, etc.) offered for sale by the publisher. [11] **out of print.** no longer available from a publisher. [12] a design or picture printed from an engraved plate, wood block, or other medium. [13] printed text, esp with regard to the typeface used: *small print.* [14] a positive photographic image in colour or black and white produced, usually on paper, from a negative image on film. Compare **slide** (sense 13). [15] **a** a fabric with a printed design. **b** (*as modifier*): *a print dress.* [16] **a** a mark or indentation made by pressing something onto a surface. **b** a stamp, die, etc., that makes such an impression. **c** the surface subjected to such an impression. [17] See **fingerprint.** ◆ See also **print out.**
▷HISTORY C13 *priente,* from Old French: something printed, from *preindre* to make an impression, from Latin *premere* to press

printable ('prɪntəbᵊl) ADJECTIVE [1] capable of being printed or of producing a print. [2] suitable for publication.
▸ **,printa'bility** *or* **'printableness** NOUN

printed circuit NOUN an electronic circuit in which certain components and the connections between them are formed by etching a metallic coating or by electrodeposition on one or both sides of a thin insulating board. Also called: **printed circuit board** *or* **card.**

printer ('prɪntə) NOUN [1] a person or business engaged in printing. [2] a machine or device that prints. [3] *Computing* an output device for printing results on paper.

printer's devil NOUN an apprentice or errand boy in a printing establishment.

printery ('prɪntərɪ) NOUN, *plural* **-eries.** [1] *Chiefly US* an establishment in which printing is carried out. [2] an establishment in which fabrics are printed.

printhead ('prɪnt,hɛd) NOUN *Computing* a component in a printer that forms a printed character.

printing ('prɪntɪŋ) NOUN [1] **a** the process, business, or art of producing printed matter. **b** (*as modifier*): *printing ink.* [2] printed text. [3] Also called: **impression.** all the copies of a book or other publication printed at one time. [4] a form of writing in which letters resemble printed letters.

printing press NOUN any of various machines used for printing.

printmaker ('prɪnt,meɪkə) NOUN a person who makes print, esp a craftsman or artist in this field.

print out VERB (*tr, adverb*) [1] (of a computer

output device, such as a line printer) to produce (printed information). ◆ NOUN **print-out.** 2 such printed information.

print shop NOUN a place in which printing is carried out.

print-through NOUN the unwanted transfer of a recorded magnetic field pattern from one turn of magnetic tape to the preceding or succeeding turn on a reel, causing distortion.

print unions PLURAL NOUN the trade unions within the printing industry.

printwheel (ˈprɪntˌwiːl) NOUN another name for **daisywheel.**

prion[1] (ˈpraɪən) NOUN any of various dovelike petrels of the genus *Pachyptila* of the southern oceans that have a serrated bill.
▷HISTORY C19: New Latin, from Greek *priōn* a saw

prion[2] (ˈpriːɒn) NOUN a protein in the brain, an abnormal form of which is thought to be the transmissable agent responsible for certain spongiform encephalopathies, such as BSE, scrapie, Creutzfeldt-Jakob disease, and kuru.
▷HISTORY C20: altered from *pro(teinaceous) in(fectious particle)*

prior[1] (ˈpraɪə) ADJECTIVE 1 (*prenominal*) previous; preceding. 2 **prior to.** before; until. ◆ NOUN 3 *Statistics* a prior probability.
▷HISTORY C18: from Latin: previous

prior[2] (ˈpraɪə) NOUN 1 the superior of a house and community in certain religious orders. 2 the deputy head of a monastery or abbey, ranking immediately below the abbot. 3 (formerly) a chief magistrate in medieval Florence and other Italian republics.
▷HISTORY C11: from Late Latin: head, from Latin (adj): previous, from Old Latin *pri* before

priorate (ˈpraɪərɪt) NOUN the office, status, or term of office of a prior.

prioress (ˈpraɪərɪs) NOUN a nun holding an office in her convent corresponding to that of a prior in a male religious order.

prioritize *or* **prioritise** (praɪˈɒrɪˌtaɪz) VERB (*tr*) 1 to arrange (items to be attended to) in order of their relative importance. 2 to give priority to or establish as a priority.
▸ˌ**prioritiˈzation** *or* ˌ**prioritiˈsation** NOUN

priority (praɪˈɒrɪtɪ) NOUN, *plural* **-ties.** 1 the condition of being prior; antecedence; precedence. 2 the right of precedence over others. 3 something given specified attention: *my first priority.*

prior probability NOUN *Statistics* the probability assigned to a parameter or to an event in advance of any empirical evidence, often subjectively or on the assumption of the principle of indifference. Compare **posterior probability.**

priory (ˈpraɪərɪ) NOUN, *plural* **-ories.** a religious house governed by a prior, sometimes being subordinate to an abbey.
▷HISTORY C13: from Medieval Latin *priōria;* see PRIOR[2]

Pripet (ˈpriːpɪt) NOUN a river in E Europe, rising in the NW Ukraine and flowing northeast into Belarus across the **Pripet Marshes** (the largest swamp in Europe), then east into the Dnieper River. Length: about 800 km (500 miles). Russian name: **Pripyat** (ˈprɪpjətj).

prisage (ˈpraɪzɪdʒ) NOUN a customs duty levied until 1809 upon wine imported into England.
▷HISTORY C16: from Anglo-French, from Old French *prise* a taking or requisitioning, duty, from *prendre* to take; see PRISE

prise *or* **prize** (praɪz) VERB (*tr*) 1 to force open by levering. 2 to extract or obtain with difficulty: *they had to prise the news out of him.* ◆ NOUN 3 *Rare or dialect* a tool involving leverage in its use or the leverage so employed. ◆ US and Canadian equivalent: **pry.**
▷HISTORY C17: from Old French *prise* a taking, from *prendre* to take, from Latin *prehendere;* see PRIZE[1]

prisere (ˈpraɪˌsɪə) NOUN *Ecology* a primary sere or succession from bare ground to the community climax.
▷HISTORY C20: PRI(MARY) + SERE[2]

prism (ˈprɪzəm) NOUN 1 a transparent polygonal solid, often having triangular ends and rectangular sides, for dispersing light into a spectrum or for reflecting and deviating light. They are used in spectroscopes, binoculars, periscopes, etc. 2 a form of crystal with faces parallel to the vertical axis. 3 *Maths* a polyhedron having parallel, polygonal, and congruent bases and sides that are parallelograms.
▷HISTORY C16: from Medieval Latin *prisma,* from Greek: something shaped by sawing, from *prizein* to saw

prismatic (prɪzˈmætɪk) ADJECTIVE 1 concerned with, containing, or produced by a prism. 2 exhibiting bright spectral colours: *prismatic light.* 3 *Crystallog* another word for **orthorhombic.**
▸**prisˈmatically** ADVERB

prismatoid (ˈprɪzməˌtɔɪd) NOUN a polyhedron whose vertices lie in either one of two parallel planes. Compare **prism** (sense 3), **prismoid.**
▷HISTORY C19: from Greek *prismatoeidēs* shaped like a prism; see PRISM, -OID
▸ˌ**prismaˈtoidal** ADJECTIVE

prismoid (ˈprɪzmɔɪd) NOUN a prismatoid having an equal number of vertices in each of the two parallel planes and whose sides are trapeziums or parallelograms.
▷HISTORY C18: from French *prismoïde;* see PRISM, -OID
▸**prisˈmoidal** ADJECTIVE

prison (ˈprɪzᵊn) NOUN 1 a public building used to house convicted criminals and accused persons remanded in custody and awaiting trial. See also **jail, penitentiary, reformatory.** 2 any place of confinement or seeming confinement.
▷HISTORY C12: from Old French *prisun,* from Latin *prēnsiō* a capturing, from *prehendere* to lay hold of

prisoner (ˈprɪzənə) NOUN 1 a person deprived of liberty and kept in prison or some other form of custody as a punishment for a crime, while awaiting trial, or for some other reason. 2 a person confined by any of various restraints: *we are all prisoners of time.* 3 **take no prisoners.** *Informal* to be uncompromising and determined in one's actions. 4 **take (someone) prisoner.** to capture and hold (someone) as a prisoner, esp as a prisoner of war.

prisoner of war NOUN a person, esp a serviceman, captured by an enemy in time of war. Abbreviation: **POW.**

prisoner's base NOUN a children's game involving two teams, members of which chase and capture each other to increase the number of children in their own base.

prissy (ˈprɪsɪ) ADJECTIVE **-sier, -siest.** fussy and prim, esp in a prudish way.
▷HISTORY C20: probably from PRIM + SISSY
▸ˈ**prissily** ADVERB ▸ˈ**prissiness** NOUN

Priština (*Serbo-Croat* ˈpriːʃtina) NOUN a city in S Serbia and Montenegro, the capital of Kosovo: under Turkish control until 1912; severely damaged in the Kosovo conflict of 1999; nearby is the 14th-century Gračanica monastery. Pop.: 186 611 (2000 est.).

pristine (ˈprɪstaɪn, -tiːn) ADJECTIVE 1 of or involving the earliest period, state, etc.; original. 2 pure; uncorrupted. 3 fresh, clean, and unspoiled: *his pristine new car.*
▷HISTORY C15: from Latin *pristinus* primitive; related to *prīmus* first, PRIME

> **Language note** The use of *pristine* to mean *fresh, clean, and unspoiled* is considered by some people to be incorrect.

prithee (ˈprɪðɪ) INTERJECTION *Archaic* pray thee; please.
▷HISTORY C16: shortened from *I pray thee*

prittle-prattle (ˈprɪtᵊlˌprætᵊl) NOUN foolish or idle talk; babble.
▷HISTORY C16: reduplication of PRATTLE

priv. ABBREVIATION FOR: 1 private. 2 privative.

privacy (ˈpraɪvəsɪ, ˈprɪvəsɪ) NOUN 1 the condition of being private or withdrawn; seclusion. 2 the condition of being secret; secrecy. 3 *Philosophy* the condition of being necessarily restricted to a single person.

Privatdocent (*German* priˈvaːtdoˈtsɛnt) NOUN (esp in German-speaking countries) a university lecturer who formerly received fees from his students rather than a university salary.
▷HISTORY German, from *privat* PRIVATE + *docent* (for *Dozent* lecturer) from Latin *docēre* to teach

private (ˈpraɪvɪt) ADJECTIVE 1 not widely or publicly known: *they had private reasons for the decision.* 2 confidential; secret: *a private conversation.* 3 not for general or public use: *a private bathroom.* 4 (*prenominal*) individual; special: *my own private recipe.* 5 (*prenominal*) having no public office, rank, etc.: *a private man.* 6 (*prenominal*) denoting a soldier of the lowest military rank: *a private soldier.* 7 of, relating to, or provided by a private individual or organization, rather than by the state or a public body: *the private sector; private housing.* 8 (of a place) retired; sequestered; not overlooked. 9 (of a person) reserved; uncommunicative. 10 **in private.** in secret; confidentially. ◆ NOUN 11 a soldier of the lowest rank, sometimes separated into qualification grades, in many armies and marine corps: *private first class.*
▷HISTORY C14: from Latin *prīvātus* belonging to one individual, withdrawn from public life, from *prīvāre* to deprive, bereave
▸ˈ**privately** ADVERB

private bar NOUN *Brit* the saloon or lounge bar of a public house. Also called: **the private.** Compare **public bar.**

private bill NOUN a bill presented to Parliament or Congress on behalf of a private individual, corporation, etc.

private company NOUN a limited company that does not issue shares for public subscription and whose owners do not enjoy an unrestricted right to transfer their shareholdings. Compare **public company.**

private detective NOUN an individual privately employed to investigate a crime, keep watch on a suspected person, or make other inquiries. Also called: **private investigator.**

private enterprise NOUN 1 economic activity undertaken by private individuals or organizations under private ownership. Compare **public enterprise.** 2 another name for **capitalism.**

privateer (ˌpraɪvəˈtɪə) NOUN 1 an armed, privately owned vessel commissioned for war service by a government. 2 Also called: **privateersman.** a commander or member of the crew of a privateer. ◆ VERB 3 a competitor, esp in motor racing, who is privately financed rather than sponsored by a manufacturer. 4 (*intr*) to serve as a privateer.

private eye NOUN *Informal* a private detective.

Private Finance Initiative NOUN (in Britain) a government scheme to encourage private investment in public projects. Abbreviation: **PFI.**

private health insurance NOUN insurance against the need for medical treatment as a private patient.

private hotel NOUN 1 a residential hotel or boarding house in which the proprietor has the right to refuse to accept a person as a guest, esp a person arriving by chance. 2 *Austral and NZ* a hotel not having a licence to sell alcoholic liquor.

private income NOUN an income from sources other than employment, such as investment. Also called: **private means.**

private language NOUN *Philosophy* a language that is not merely secret or accidentally limited to one user, but that cannot in principle be communicated to another.

private law NOUN the branch of law that deals with the rights and duties of private individuals and the relations between them. Compare **public law.**

private life NOUN the social or family life or personal relationships of an individual, esp of a person in the public eye, such as a politician or celebrity.

private member NOUN a member of a legislative assembly, such as the House of Commons, not having an appointment in the government.

private member's bill NOUN a public bill introduced in the House of Commons or the legislative assemblies of Canada, Australia, or New Zealand by a private member.

private parts *or* **privates** (ˈpraɪvɪts) PLURAL NOUN euphemistic terms for **genitals.**

private patient NOUN *Brit* a patient receiving

medical treatment not paid for by the National Health Service.

private pay bed NOUN (in Britain) a bed in a National Health Service hospital, reserved for private patients who pay a consultant acting privately for treatment and who are charged by the health service for use of hospital facilities. Often shortened to: **pay bed.** Compare **amenity bed.**

private practice NOUN *Brit* medical practice that is not part of the National Health Service.

private press NOUN a printing establishment primarily run as a pastime.

private property NOUN land or belongings owned by a person or group and kept for their exclusive use.

private school NOUN a school under the financial and managerial control of a private body or charitable trust, accepting mostly fee-paying pupils.

private secretary NOUN 1 a secretary entrusted with the personal and confidential matters of a business executive. 2 a civil servant who acts as aide to a minister or senior government official. Compare **parliamentary private secretary.**

private sector NOUN the part of a country's economy that consists of privately owned enterprises. Compare **public sector.**

private treaty NOUN a sale of property for a price agreed directly between seller and buyer.

private view NOUN a preview, esp of an art exhibition, for specially invited guests.

private viewdata NOUN an interactive video text system with restricted access.

privation (praɪˈveɪʃən) NOUN 1 loss or lack of the necessities of life, such as food and shelter. 2 hardship resulting from this. 3 the state of being deprived. 4 *Logic, obsolete* the absence from an object of what ordinarily or naturally belongs to such objects.
▷HISTORY C14: from Latin *prīvātiō* deprivation

privative (ˈprɪvətɪv) ADJECTIVE 1 causing privation. 2 expressing lack or negation, as for example the English suffix *-less* and prefix *un-*. 3 *Logic, obsolete* (of a proposition) that predicates a logical privation.
▷HISTORY C16: from Latin *prīvātīvus* indicating loss, negative
▸ˈ**privatively** ADVERB

privatization issue NOUN an issue of shares available for purchase by members of the public when a publicly owned organization is transferred to the private sector.

privatize *or* **privatise** (ˈpraɪvɪˌtaɪz) VERB (*tr*) to transfer (the production of goods or services) from the public sector of an economy into private ownership and operation.
▸ˌ**privatiˈzation** *or* ˌ**privatiˈsation** NOUN

privet (ˈprɪvɪt) NOUN **a** any oleaceous shrub of the genus *Ligustrum, esp L. vulgare* or *L. ovalifolium*, having oval dark green leaves, white flowers, and purplish-black berries. **b** (*as modifier*): *a privet hedge.*
▷HISTORY C16: of unknown origin

privet hawk NOUN a hawk moth, *Sphinx ligustri*, with a mauve-and-brown striped body: frequents privets.

privilege (ˈprɪvɪlɪdʒ) NOUN 1 a benefit, immunity, etc., granted under certain conditions. 2 the advantages and immunities enjoyed by a small usually powerful group or class, esp to the disadvantage of others: *one of the obstacles to social harmony is privilege.* 3 any of the fundamental rights guaranteed to the citizens of a country by its constitution. 4 **a** the right of a lawyer to refuse to divulge information obtained in confidence from a client. **b** the right claimed by any of certain other functionaries to refuse to divulge information: *executive privilege.* 5 the rights and immunities enjoyed by members of most legislative bodies, such as freedom of speech, freedom from arrest in civil cases during a session, etc. 6 *US stock Exchange* a speculative contract permitting its purchaser to make optional purchases or sales of securities at a specified time over a limited period of time. See also **call** (sense 61), **put** (sense 20), **spread** (sense 24c), **straddle** (sense 9). ◆ VERB (*tr*) 7 to bestow a privilege or privileges upon. 8 (foll by *from*) to free or exempt.
▷HISTORY C12: from Old French *privilēge,* from Latin *prīvilēgium* law relevant to rights of an individual, from *prīvus* an individual + *lēx* law

privileged (ˈprɪvɪlɪdʒd) ADJECTIVE 1 enjoying or granted as a privilege or privileges. 2 *Law* **a** not actionable as a libel or slander. **b** (of a communication, document, etc.) that a witness cannot be compelled to divulge. 3 *Nautical* (of a vessel) having the right of way.

privily (ˈprɪvɪlɪ) ADVERB *Archaic or literary* in a secret way.

privity (ˈprɪvɪtɪ) NOUN, *plural* **-ties.** 1 a legally recognized relationship existing between two parties, such as that between lessor and lessee and between the parties to a contract: *privity of estate; privity of contract.* 2 secret knowledge that is shared.
▷HISTORY C13: from Old French *priveté*

privy (ˈprɪvɪ) ADJECTIVE **privier, priviest.** 1 (*postpositive;* foll by *to*) participating in the knowledge of something secret. 2 *Archaic* secret, hidden, etc. 3 *Archaic* of or relating to one person only. ◆ NOUN, *plural* **privies.** 4 a lavatory, esp an outside one. 5 *Law* a person in privity with another. See **privity** (sense 1).
▷HISTORY C13: from Old French *privé* something private, from Latin *prīvātus* PRIVATE

privy chamber NOUN 1 a private apartment inside a royal residence. 2 *Archaic* a private room reserved for the use of a specific person or group.

privy council NOUN 1 the council of state of a monarch or noble, esp formerly. 2 *Archaic* a private or secret council.

Privy Council NOUN the private council of the British sovereign, consisting of all current and former ministers of the Crown and other distinguished subjects, all of whom are appointed for life. See also **Judicial Committee of the Privy Council.**
▸**Privy Counsellor** NOUN

privy purse NOUN (*often capitals*) 1 **a** (in Britain) an allowance voted by Parliament for the private expenses of the monarch: part of the civil list. **b** (in other countries) a similar sum of money for the monarch. 2 an official of the royal household responsible for dealing with the monarch's private expenses. Full name: **Keeper of the Privy Purse.**

privy seal NOUN (*often capitals*) (in Britain) a seal affixed to certain documents issued by royal authority: of less rank and importance than the great seal.

prix fixe (*French* pri fiks) NOUN, *plural* **prix fixes** (fiks). a fixed price charged for one of a set number of meals offered on a menu. Compare **à la carte, table d'hôte.**

Prix Goncourt (*French* gɔ̃kur) NOUN an annual prize for a work of French fiction.
▷HISTORY C20: after the Académie *Goncourt*, which awards the prizes, founded by the will of Edmond Goncourt (1822–96), French writer

prize[1] (praɪz) NOUN 1 **a** a reward or honour for victory or for having won a contest, competition, etc. **b** (*as modifier*): *prize jockey; prize essay.* 2 something given to the winner of any game of chance, lottery, etc. 3 something striven for. 4 any valuable property captured in time of war, esp a vessel.
▷HISTORY C14: from Old French *prise* a capture, from Latin *prehendere* to seize; influenced also by Middle English *prise* reward; see PRICE

prize[2] (praɪz) VERB (*tr*) to esteem greatly; value highly.
▷HISTORY C15 *prise,* from Old French *preisier* to PRAISE

prize[3] (praɪz) VERB, NOUN a variant spelling of **prise.**

prize court NOUN *Law* a court having jurisdiction to determine how property captured at sea in wartime is to be distributed.

prizefight (ˈpraɪzˌfaɪt) NOUN a boxing match for a prize or purse, esp one of the fights popular in the 18th and 19th centuries.
▸ˈ**prizeˌfighter** NOUN ▸ˈ**prizeˌfighting** NOUN

prize money NOUN 1 any money offered, paid, or received as a prize. 2 (formerly) a part of the money realized from the sale of a captured vessel.

prize ring NOUN 1 the enclosed area or ring used by prizefighters. 2 **the prize ring.** the sport of prizefighting.

prizewinner (ˈpraɪzˌwɪnə) NOUN a person, animal, or thing that wins a prize.
▸ˈ**prizeˌwinning** ADJECTIVE

prn (in prescriptions) ABBREVIATION FOR pro re nata.
▷HISTORY Latin: as the situation demands; whenever needed

pro[1] (prəʊ) ADVERB 1 in favour of a motion, issue, course of action, etc. Compare **anti.** ◆ PREPOSITION 2 in favour of. ◆ NOUN, *plural* **pros.** 3 (*usually plural*) an argument or vote in favour of a proposal or motion. See also **pros and cons.** 4 (*usually plural*) a person who votes in favour of a proposal, motion, etc. ◆ Compare **con**[2].
▷HISTORY from Latin *prō* (prep) in favour of

pro[2] (prəʊ) NOUN, *plural* **pros,** ADJECTIVE 1 *Informal* short for **professional.** ◆ 2 AN INTERNET DOMAIN NAME FOR a professional practitioner. 3 *Slang* a prostitute.
▷HISTORY C19: by shortening

PRO ABBREVIATION FOR: 1 Public Records Office. 2 public relations officer.

pro-[1] PREFIX 1 in favour of; supporting: *pro-Chinese.* 2 acting as a substitute for: *proconsul; pronoun.*
▷HISTORY from Latin *prō* (adv and prep). In compound words borrowed from Latin, *prō-* indicates: forward, out (*project*); forward and down (*prostrate*); away from a place (*prodigal*); onward in time or space (*proceed*); extension outwards (*propagate*); before in time or place (*provide, protect*); on behalf of (*procure*); acting as a substitute for (*pronominal*); and sometimes intensive force (*promiscuous*)

pro-[2] PREFIX before in time or position; anterior; forward: *prophase; procephalic; prognathous.*
▷HISTORY from Greek *pro* (prep) before (in time, position, rank, etc.)

proa (ˈprəʊə) *or* **prau** NOUN any of several kinds of canoe-like boats used in the South Pacific, esp one equipped with an outrigger and sails.
▷HISTORY C16: from Malay *parāhū* a boat

proabortion (ˌprəʊəˈbɔːʃən) ADJECTIVE in favour of the medical provision of abortion.

proaction (prəʊˈækʃən) NOUN action that initiates change as opposed to reaction to events.
▷HISTORY C20: from PRO-[2] + (RE)ACTION

proactive (prəʊˈæktɪv) ADJECTIVE 1 tending to initiate change rather than reacting to events. 2 *Psychol* of or denoting a mental process that affects a subsequent process.
▷HISTORY C20: from PRO-[2] + (RE)ACTIVE

proactive inhibition *or* **interference** NOUN *Psychol* the tendency for earlier memories to interfere with the retrieval of material learned later. Compare **retroactive inhibition.**

pro-am (ˈprəʊˈæm) ADJECTIVE 1 (of a golf tournament, snooker tournament, etc.) involving both professional and amateur players. ◆ NOUN 2 a sporting tournament involving both professional and amateur players.

pro-American ADJECTIVE 1 in favour of or supporting America, its people, culture, etc. ◆ NOUN 2 a person who is in favour of or supports America, its people, culture, etc.

prob. ABBREVIATION FOR: 1 probable. 2 probably.

probabilism (ˈprɒbəbɪˌlɪzəm) NOUN 1 *Philosophy* the doctrine that although certainty is impossible, probability is a sufficient basis for belief and action. 2 the principle of Roman Catholic moral theology that in a situation in which authorities differ as to what is the right course of action it is permissible to follow any course which has the support of some authority.
▸ˈ**probabilist** NOUN, ADJECTIVE ▸ˌ**probabilˈistic** ADJECTIVE ▸ˌ**probabilˈistically** ADVERB

probability (ˌprɒbəˈbɪlɪtɪ) NOUN, *plural* **-ties.** 1 the condition of being probable. 2 an event or other thing that is probable. 3 *Statistics* a measure or estimate of the degree of confidence one may have in the occurrence of an event, measured on a scale from zero (impossibility) to one (certainty). It may be defined as the proportion of favourable outcomes to the total number of possibilities if these are indifferent (**mathematical probability**), or the proportion observed in a sample (**empirical probability**), or the limit of this as the sample size tends to infinity (**relative frequency**), or by more subjective criteria (**subjective probability**).

probability density function NOUN *Statistics* a function representing the relative distribution of frequency of a continuous random variable from which parameters such as its mean and variance can be derived and having the property that its integral from *a* to *b* is the probability that the variable lies in this interval. Its graph is the limiting case of a histogram as the amount of data increases and the class intervals decrease in size. Also called: **density function.** Compare **cumulative distribution function, frequency distribution.**

probability function NOUN *Statistics* the function the values of which are probabilities of the distinct outcomes of a discrete random variable.

probable ('prɒbəbᵊl) ADJECTIVE [1] likely to be or to happen but not necessarily so. [2] most likely: *the probable cause of the accident.* ◆ NOUN [3] a person who is probably to be chosen for a team, event, etc.
▷**HISTORY** C14: via Old French from Latin *probābilis* that may be proved, from *probāre* to prove

probable cause NOUN *Law* reasonable grounds for holding a belief, esp such as will justify bringing legal proceedings against a person or will constitute a defence to a charge of malicious prosecution.

probably ('prɒbəblɪ) ADVERB [1] (*sentence modifier; not used with a negative or in a question*) in all likelihood or probability: *I'll probably see you tomorrow.* ◆ SENTENCE SUBSTITUTE [2] I believe such a thing or situation may be the case.

proband ('prəʊbænd) NOUN another name (esp US) for **propositus** (sense 2).
▷**HISTORY** C20: from Latin *probandus,* gerundive of *probāre* to test

probang ('prəʊbæŋ) NOUN *Surgery* a long flexible rod, often with a small sponge at one end, for inserting into the oesophagus, as to apply medication.
▷**HISTORY** C17: variant, apparently by association with PROBE, of *provang,* name coined by W. Rumsey (1584–1660), Welsh judge, its inventor; of unknown origin

probate ('prəʊbɪt, -beɪt) NOUN [1] the act or process of officially proving the authenticity and validity of a will. [2] **a** the official certificate stating a will to be genuine and conferring on the executors power to administer the estate. **b** the probate copy of a will. [3] (in the US) all matters within the jurisdiction of a probate court. [4] (*modifier*) of, relating to, or concerned with probate: *probate value; a probate court.* ◆ VERB [5] (*tr*) *Chiefly US and Canadian* to establish officially the authenticity and validity of (a will).
▷**HISTORY** C15: from Latin *probāre* to inspect

probation (prə'beɪʃən) NOUN [1] a system of dealing with offenders by placing them under the supervision of a probation officer. [2] **on probation. a** under the supervision of a probation officer. **b** undergoing a test period. [3] a trial period, as for a teacher, religious novitiate, etc. [4] the act of proving or testing. [5] a period during which a new employee may have his employment terminated on the grounds of unsuitability.
▸**pro'bational** *or* **pro'bationary** ADJECTIVE ▸**pro'bationally** ADVERB

probationary assistant NOUN *NZ* a teacher in the first probationary years. Abbreviation: **PA.**

probationer (prə'beɪʃənə) NOUN a person on probation.

probation officer NOUN an officer of a court who supervises offenders placed on probation and assists and befriends them.

probative ('prəʊbətɪv) *or* **probatory** ('prəʊbətərɪ, -trɪ) ADJECTIVE [1] serving to test or designed for testing. [2] providing proof or evidence.
▷**HISTORY** C15: from Late Latin *probātīvus* concerning proof
▸**'probatively** ADVERB

probe (prəʊb) VERB [1] (*tr*) to search into or question closely. [2] to examine (something) with or as if with a probe. ◆ NOUN [3] something that probes, examines, or tests. [4] *Surgery* a slender and usually flexible instrument for exploring a wound, sinus, etc. [5] a thorough inquiry, such as one by a newspaper into corrupt practices. [6] *Electronics* a lead connecting to or containing a measuring or monitoring circuit used for testing. [7] *Electronics* a conductor inserted into a waveguide or cavity resonator to provide coupling to an external circuit. [8] any of various devices that provide a coupling link, esp a flexible tube extended from an aircraft to link it with another so that it can refuel. [9] See **space probe.**
▷**HISTORY** C16: from Medieval Latin *proba* investigation, from Latin *probāre* to test
▸**'probeable** ADJECTIVE ▸**'prober** NOUN

probiotic (ˌprəʊbaɪ'ɒtɪk) NOUN [1] a harmless bacterium that helps to protect the body from harmful bacteria. ◆ ADJECTIVE [2] of or relating to probiotics: *probiotic yogurt.*
▷**HISTORY** C20: from PRO-[1] + (ANTI)BIOTIC

probity ('prəʊbɪtɪ) NOUN confirmed integrity; uprightness.
▷**HISTORY** C16: from Latin *probitās* honesty, from *probus* virtuous

problem ('prɒbləm) NOUN [1] **a** any thing, matter, person, etc., that is difficult to deal with, solve, or overcome. **b** (*as modifier*): *a problem child.* [2] a puzzle, question, etc., set for solution. [3] *Maths* a statement requiring a solution usually by means of one or more operations or geometric constructions. [4] (*modifier*) designating a literary work that deals with difficult moral questions: *a problem play.*
▷**HISTORY** C14: from Late Latin *problēma,* from Greek: something put forward; related to *proballein* to throw forwards, from PRO-[2] + *ballein* to throw

problematic (ˌprɒblə'mætɪk) *or* **problematical** ADJECTIVE [1] having the nature or appearance of a problem; questionable. [2] *Logic, obsolete* (of a proposition) asserting that a property may or may not hold. Compare **apodeictic** (sense 2), **assertoric.**
▸**ˌproblem'atically** ADVERB

pro bono publico *Latin* ('prəʊ 'bəʊnəʊ 'pʊblɪkəʊ) for the public good.

proboscidean *or* **proboscidian** (ˌprəʊbɒ'sɪdɪən) ADJECTIVE [1] of, relating to, or belonging to the *Proboscidea,* an order of massive herbivorous placental mammals having tusks and a long trunk: contains the elephants. ◆ NOUN [2] any proboscidean animal.

proboscis (prəʊ'bɒsɪs) NOUN, *plural* **-cises** *or* **-cides** (-sɪˌdiːz). [1] a long flexible prehensile trunk or snout, as of an elephant. [2] the elongated mouthparts of certain insects, adapted for piercing or sucking food. [3] any similar part or organ. [4] *Informal, facetious* a person's nose, esp if large.
▷**HISTORY** C17: via Latin from Greek *proboskis* trunk of an elephant, from *boskein* to feed

proboscis monkey NOUN an Old World monkey, *Nasalis larvatus,* of Borneo, with an elongated bulbous nose.

pro-British ADJECTIVE in favour of or supporting Britain, its people, culture, etc.

probusiness (prəʊ'bɪznɪs) ADJECTIVE in favour of or supporting the practices of business.

proc. ABBREVIATION FOR: [1] procedure. [2] proceedings.

procaine ('prəʊkeɪn, prəʊ'keɪn) NOUN a colourless or white crystalline water-soluble substance used, as the hydrochloride, as a local anaesthetic; 2-diethylaminoethyl-4-amino benzoate. Formula: $NH_2C_6H_4COOC_2H_4N(C_2H_5)_2$. See also **Novocaine.**
▷**HISTORY** C20: from PRO-[1] + (CO)CAINE

procambium (prəʊ'kæmbɪəm) NOUN undifferentiated plant tissue, just behind the growing tip in stems and roots, that develops into conducting tissues.
▷**HISTORY** C19: from PRO-[2] + CAMBIUM
▸**pro'cambial** ADJECTIVE

procapitalist (prəʊ'kæpɪtəlɪst) ADJECTIVE in favour of or supporting capitalist policies and ideologies.

procarp ('prəʊkɑːp) NOUN a female reproductive organ in red algae.
▷**HISTORY** C19: from New Latin *procarpium,* from PRO-[2] + *-carpium,* from Greek *karpos* fruit

procaryote (prəʊ'kærɪɒt) NOUN a variant spelling of **prokaryote.**

procathedral (ˌprəʊkə'θiːdrəl) NOUN a church serving as a cathedral.

procedural agreement NOUN regulations agreed between the parties to collective bargaining, defining the bargaining units, bargaining scope, procedures for collective bargaining, and the facilities to be provided to trade union representatives.

procedure (prə'siːdʒə) NOUN [1] a way of acting or progressing in a course of action, esp an established method. [2] the established mode or form of conducting the business of a legislature, the enforcement of a legal right, etc. [3] *Computing* another name for **subroutine.**
▸**pro'cedural** ADJECTIVE ▸**pro'cedurally** ADVERB

proceed (prə'siːd) VERB (*intr*) [1] (often foll by *to*) to advance or carry on, esp after stopping. [2] (often foll by *with*) to undertake and continue (something or to do something): *he proceeded with his reading.* [3] (often foll by *against*) to institute or carry on a legal action. [4] to emerge or originate; arise: *evil proceeds from the heart.* ◆ See also **proceeds.**
▷**HISTORY** C14: from Latin *prōcēdere* to advance, from PRO-[1] + *cēdere* to go
▸**pro'ceeder** NOUN

proceeding (prə'siːdɪŋ) NOUN [1] an act or course of action. [2] **a** the institution of a legal action. **b** any step taken in a legal action. [3] (*plural*) the minutes of the meetings of a club, society, etc. [4] (*plural*) legal action; litigation. [5] (*plural*) the events of an occasion, meeting, etc.

proceeds ('prəʊsiːdz) PLURAL NOUN [1] the profit or return derived from a commercial transaction, investment, etc. [2] the result, esp the revenue or total sum, accruing from some undertaking or course of action, as in commerce.

proceleusmatic (ˌprɒsɪluːs'mætɪk) *Prosody* ◆ ADJECTIVE [1] denoting or consisting of a metrical foot of four short syllables. ◆ NOUN [2] a proceleusmatic metrical foot.
▷**HISTORY** C18: from Late Latin *proceleusmaticus,* from Greek *prokeleusmatikos,* from *prokeleuein* to drive on, from PRO-[2] + *keleuein* to give orders

procephalic (ˌprəʊsɪ'fælɪk) ADJECTIVE *Anatomy* of or relating to the anterior part of the head.

process[1] ('prəʊses) NOUN [1] a series of actions that produce a change or development: *the process of digestion.* [2] a method of doing or producing something. [3] a forward movement. [4] the course of time. [5] **a** a summons, writ, etc., commanding a person to appear in court. **b** the whole proceedings in an action at law. [6] a natural outgrowth or projection of a part, organ, or organism. [7] a distinct subtask of a computer system which can be regarded as proceeding in parallel with other subtasks of the system. [8] (*modifier*) relating to the general preparation of a printing forme or plate by the use, at some stage, of photography. [9] (*modifier*) denoting a film, film scene, shot, etc., made by techniques that produce unusual optical effects. ◆ VERB (*tr*) [10] to subject to a routine procedure; handle. [11] to treat or prepare by a special method, esp to treat (food) in order to preserve it: *to process cheese.* [12] **a** to institute legal proceedings against. **b** to serve a process on. [13] *Photog* **a** to develop, rinse, fix, wash, and dry (exposed film, etc.). **b** to produce final prints or slides from (undeveloped film). [14] *Computing* to perform mathematical and logical operations on (data) according to programmed instructions in order to obtain the required information. [15] to prepare (food) using a food processor.
▷**HISTORY** C14: from Old French *procès,* from Latin *prōcessus* an advancing, from *prōcēdere* to PROCEED

process[2] (prə'ses) VERB (*intr*) to proceed in or as if in a procession.
▷**HISTORY** C19: back formation from PROCESSION

process camera NOUN *Printing* a large camera used in the photographic processes involved in the printing industry.

process colour NOUN *Printing* any of the four colours (cyan, magenta, yellow, and black) used in process printing.

process engineering NOUN the branch of engineering concerned with industrial processes, esp continuous ones, such as the production of petrochemicals.
▸**process engineer** NOUN

procession (prə'seʃən) NOUN [1] the act of proceeding in a regular formation. [2] a group of people or things moving forwards in an orderly, regular, or ceremonial manner. [3] a hymn, litany, etc., sung in a procession. [4] *Christianity* the emanation of the Holy Spirit. ◆ VERB [5] (*intr*) *Rare* to go in procession.

▷HISTORY C12: via Old French from Latin *prōcessiō* a marching forwards

processional (prəˈsɛʃənəl) ADJECTIVE 1 of, relating to, or suitable for a procession. ◆ NOUN 2 *Christianity* **a** a book containing the prayers, hymns, litanies, and liturgy prescribed for processions. **b** a hymn, litany, etc., used in a procession.
▸**proˈcessionally** ADVERB

processionary (prəˈsɛʃənərɪ) ADJECTIVE 1 of, relating to, or moving in a procession. ◆ NOUN 2 a processionary moth.

processionary moth NOUN a moth of the family *Thaumetopoeidae, esp the* **oak processionary moth** (*Thaumetopoea processionea*), the larvae of which leave the communal shelter nightly for food in a V-shaped procession.

processor (ˈprəʊsɛsə) NOUN 1 *Computing* another name for **central processing unit.** 2 a person or thing that carries out a process.

process printing NOUN a method of making reproductions of a coloured picture, usually by using four halftone plates for different coloured inks.

process-server NOUN a sheriff's officer who serves legal documents such as writs for appearance in court.

procès-verbal *French* (prɔsɛvɛrbal) NOUN, *plural* **-baux** (-bo). a written record of an official proceeding; minutes.
▷HISTORY C17: from French: see PROCESS[1], VERBAL

pro-Chinese ADJECTIVE in favour of or supporting China, its people, culture, etc.

pro-choice ADJECTIVE (of an organization, pressure group, etc.) supporting the right of a woman to have an abortion. Compare **pro-life.**

prochronism (ˈprəʊkrəˌnɪzəm) NOUN an error in dating that places an event earlier than it actually occurred. Compare **parachronism.**
▷HISTORY C17: from PRO-[2] + Greek *khronos* time + -ISM, by analogy with ANACHRONISM

proclaim (prəˈkleɪm) VERB (*tr*) 1 (*may take a clause as object*) to announce publicly; declare. 2 (*may take a clause as object*) to show or indicate plainly. 3 to praise or extol.
▷HISTORY C14: from Latin *prōclāmāre* to shout aloud
▸**proˈclaimer** NOUN ▸**proclamation** (ˌprɒkləˈmeɪʃən) NOUN ▸**proclamatory** (prəˈklæmətərɪ, -trɪ) ADJECTIVE

proclitic (prəʊˈklɪtɪk) ADJECTIVE 1 **a** relating to or denoting a monosyllabic word or form having no stress or accent and pronounced as a prefix of the following word, as in English *'t* for *it* in *'twas*. **b** (in classical Greek) relating to or denoting a word that throws its accent onto the following word. ◆ NOUN 2 a proclitic word or form. ◆ Compare **enclitic.**
▷HISTORY C19: from New Latin *proclīticus,* from Greek *proklinein* to lean forwards; formed on the model of ENCLITIC

proclivity (prəˈklɪvɪtɪ) NOUN, *plural* **-ties.** a tendency or inclination.
▷HISTORY C16: from Latin *prōclīvitās,* from *prōclīvis* steep, from PRO-[1] + *clīvus* a slope

Procne (ˈprɒknɪ) NOUN *Greek myth* a princess of Athens, who punished her husband for raping her sister Philomela by feeding him the flesh of their son. She was changed at her death into a swallow. See **Philomela.**

pro-Communist ADJECTIVE 1 in favour of or supporting Communist policies and ideologies etc. ◆ NOUN 2 a person who is pro-Communist.

proconsul (prəʊˈkɒnsəl) NOUN 1 an administrator or governor of a colony, occupied territory, or other dependency. 2 (in ancient Rome) the governor of a senatorial province.
▷HISTORY C14: from Latin, from *prō consule* (someone acting) for the consul. See PRO-[2], CONSUL
▸**proconsular** (prəʊˈkɒnsjʊlə) ADJECTIVE ▸**proˈconsulate** *or* **proˈconsulship** NOUN

procrastinate (prəʊˈkræstɪˌneɪt, prə-) VERB (*usually intr*) to put off or defer (an action) until a later time; delay.
▷HISTORY C16: from Latin *prōcrāstināre* to postpone until tomorrow, from PRO-[1] + *crās* tomorrow
▸**proˌcrastiˈnation** NOUN ▸**proˈcrastiˌnator** NOUN

procreate (ˈprəʊkrɪˌeɪt) VERB 1 to beget or engender (offspring). 2 (*tr*) to bring into being.
▷HISTORY C16: from Latin *prōcreāre,* from PRO-[1] + *creāre* to create
▸**ˈprocreant** *or* **ˈprocreˌative** ADJECTIVE ▸**ˌprocreˈation** NOUN ▸**ˈprocreˌator** NOUN

Procrustean (prəʊˈkrʌstɪən) ADJECTIVE tending or designed to produce conformity by violent or ruthless methods.

Procrustes (prəʊˈkrʌstiːz) NOUN *Greek myth* a robber, who put travellers in his bed, stretching or lopping off their limbs so that they fitted it.
▷HISTORY C16: from Greek *Prokroustēs* the stretcher, from *prokrouein* to extend by hammering out

procryptic (prəʊˈkrɪptɪk) ADJECTIVE (of animals) having protective coloration.
▷HISTORY C19: from PRO-[2] + Greek *kruptein* to conceal
▸**proˈcryptically** ADVERB

procto- *or before a vowel* **proct-** COMBINING FORM indicating the anus or rectum: *proctology.*
▷HISTORY from Greek *prōktos*

proctology (prɒkˈtɒlədʒɪ) NOUN the branch of medical science concerned with the rectum.
▸**proctological** (ˌprɒktəˈlɒdʒɪkəl) ADJECTIVE ▸**procˈtologist** NOUN

proctor (ˈprɒktə) NOUN 1 a member of the teaching staff of any of certain universities having the duties of enforcing discipline. 2 *US* (in a college or university) a supervisor or monitor who invigilates examinations, enforces discipline, etc. 3 (formerly) an agent, esp one engaged to conduct another's case in a court. 4 (formerly) an agent employed to collect tithes. 5 *Church of England* one of the elected representatives of the clergy in Convocation and the General Synod. ◆ VERB 6 (*tr*) *US* to invigilate (an examination).
▷HISTORY C14: syncopated variant of PROCURATOR
▸**proctorial** (prɒkˈtɔːrɪəl) ADJECTIVE ▸**procˈtorially** ADVERB

proctoscope (ˈprɒktəˌskəʊp) NOUN a medical instrument for examining the rectum.
▸**proctoscopic** (ˌprɒktəˈskɒpɪk) ADJECTIVE ▸**proctoscopy** (prɒkˈtɒskəpɪ) NOUN

procumbent (prəʊˈkʌmbənt) ADJECTIVE 1 Also: **prostrate.** (of stems) growing along the ground. 2 leaning forwards or lying on the face.
▷HISTORY C17: from Latin *prōcumbere* to fall forwards; compare INCUMBENT

procuration (ˌprɒkjʊˈreɪʃən) NOUN 1 the act of procuring. 2 *Law* **a** the appointment of an agent, procurator, or attorney. **b** the office, function, or authority of such an official. **c** the formal written authority given to such an official. See also **power of attorney.** 3 *Criminal law* the offence of procuring women for immoral purposes. 4 *Archaic* the management of another person's affairs.

procurator (ˈprɒkjʊˌreɪtə) NOUN 1 (in ancient Rome) a civil official of the emperor's administration, often employed as the governor of a minor province or as a financial agent. 2 *Rare* a person engaged and authorized by another to manage his affairs.
▷HISTORY C13: from Latin: a manager, from *prōcūrāre* to attend to
▸**procuracy** (ˈprɒkjʊrəsɪ) *or* **ˈprocuˌratorship** NOUN ▸**procuratorial** (ˌprɒkjʊrəˈtɔːrɪəl) *or* **procuratory** (ˈprɒkjʊrətərɪ, -trɪ) ADJECTIVE

procurator fiscal NOUN (in Scotland) a legal officer who performs the functions of public prosecutor and coroner.

procuratory (ˈprɒkjʊrətərɪ) NOUN *Law* authorization to act on behalf of someone else.

procure (prəˈkjʊə) VERB 1 (*tr*) to obtain or acquire; secure. 2 to obtain (women or girls) to act as prostitutes.
▷HISTORY C13: from Latin *prōcūrāre* to look after, from PRO-[1] + *cūrāre* to care for
▸**proˈcurable** ADJECTIVE ▸**proˈcurance** *or* **proˈcural** NOUN

procurement (prəˈkjʊəmənt) NOUN 1 the act or an instance of procuring. 2 *Commerce* **a** the act of buying. **b** (*as modifier*): *procurement cost; procurement budget.*

procurer (prəˈkjʊərə) *or feminine* **procuress** (prəˈkjʊərɪs) NOUN a person who procures, esp one who procures women or girls as prostitutes.

Procyon (ˈprəʊsɪən) NOUN the brightest star in the constellation Canis Minor, a binary with a very faint companion. Visual magnitude: 0.34; spectral type: F5IV; distance: 114 light years.
▷HISTORY C17: via Latin from Greek *Prokuōn* literally: before the Dog, from PRO-[2] + *kuōn* dog; so named because it rises just before Sirius, the Dog Star

prod (prɒd) VERB **prods, prodding, prodded.** 1 to poke or jab with or as if with a pointed object. 2 (*tr*) to rouse or urge to action. ◆ NOUN 3 the act or an instance of prodding. 4 a sharp or pointed object. 5 a stimulus or reminder.
▷HISTORY C16: of uncertain origin
▸**ˈprodder** NOUN

Prod (prɒd) NOUN *Derogatory slang* another word for **Protestant.**

prod. ABBREVIATION FOR: 1 produce. 2 produced. 3 product.

prodigal (ˈprɒdɪgəl) ADJECTIVE 1 recklessly wasteful or extravagant, as in disposing of goods or money. 2 lavish in giving or yielding: *prodigal of compliments.* ◆ NOUN 3 a person who spends lavishly or squanders money.
▷HISTORY C16: from Medieval Latin *prōdigālis* wasteful, from Latin *prōdigus* lavish, from *prōdigere* to squander, from PRO-[1] + *agere* to drive
▸**ˌprodiˈgality** NOUN ▸**ˈprodigally** ADVERB

prodigious (prəˈdɪdʒəs) ADJECTIVE 1 vast in size, extent, power, etc. 2 wonderful or amazing. 3 *Obsolete* threatening.
▷HISTORY C16: from Latin *prōdigiōsus* marvellous, from *prōdigium,* see PRODIGY
▸**proˈdigiously** ADVERB ▸**proˈdigiousness** NOUN

prodigy (ˈprɒdɪdʒɪ) NOUN, *plural* **-gies.** 1 a person, esp a child, of unusual or marvellous talents. 2 anything that is a cause of wonder and amazement. 3 something monstrous or abnormal. 4 an archaic word for **omen.**
▷HISTORY C16: from Latin *prōdigium* an unnatural happening, from PRO-[1] + *-igium,* probably from *āio* I say

prodrome (ˈprəʊdrəʊm) NOUN *Med* any symptom that signals the impending onset of a disease.
▷HISTORY C19: via French from New Latin *prodromus,* from Greek *prodromos* forerunner, from PRO-[2] + *dramein* to run
▸**proˈdromal** *or* **prodromic** (prəʊˈdrɒmɪk) ADJECTIVE

prodrug (ˈprəʊˌdrʌg) NOUN a compound that is itself biologically inactive but is metabolized in the body to produce an active therapeutic drug.

produce VERB (prəˈdjuːs) 1 to bring (something) into existence; yield. 2 to bring forth (a product) by mental or physical effort; make: *she produced a delicious dinner for us.* 3 (*tr*) to give birth to. 4 (*tr*) to manufacture (a commodity): *this firm produces cartons.* 5 (*tr*) to give rise to: *her joke produced laughter.* 6 (*tr*) to present to view: *to produce evidence.* 7 to bring before the public: *he produced two plays and a film last year.* 8 to conceive and create the overall sound of (a record) and supervise its arrangement, recording, and mixing. 9 (*tr*) *Geometry* to extend (a line). ◆ NOUN (ˈprɒdjuːs) 10 anything that is produced; product. 11 agricultural products regarded collectively: *farm produce.*
▷HISTORY C15: from Latin *prōdūcere* to bring forward, from PRO-[1] + *dūcere* to lead
▸**proˈducible** ADJECTIVE ▸**proˌduciˈbility** NOUN

producer (prəˈdjuːsə) NOUN 1 a person or thing that produces. 2 *Brit* a person responsible for the artistic direction of a play, including interpretation of the script, preparation of the actors, and overall design. 3 *US and Canadian* a person who organizes the stage production of a play, including the finance, management, etc. 4 the person who takes overall administrative responsibility for a film or television programme. Compare **director** (sense 4). 5 the person who supervises the arrangement, recording, and mixing of a record. 6 *Economics* a person or business enterprise that generates goods or services for sale. Compare **consumer** (sense 1). 7 *Chem* an apparatus or plant for making producer gas. 8 (*often plural*) *Ecology* an organism, esp a green plant, that builds up its own tissues from simple inorganic compounds. See also **consumer** (sense 3), **decomposer.**

producer gas NOUN a mixture of carbon monoxide and nitrogen produced by passing air over hot coke, used mainly as a fuel. Also called: **air gas.** See also **water gas.**

producer goods *or* **producer's goods** PLURAL NOUN other terms for **capital goods.**

product (ˈprɒdʌkt) NOUN 1 something produced by effort, or some mechanical or industrial process. 2 the result of some natural process. 3 a result or consequence. 4 a substance formed in a chemical reaction. 5 *Maths* **a** the result of the multiplication of two or more numbers, quantities, etc. **b** Also called: **set product.** another name for **intersection** (sense 3). 6 See **Cartesian product.**
▷HISTORY C15: from Latin *prōductum* (something) produced, from *prōdūcere* to bring forth

product differentiation NOUN *Commerce* the real or illusory distinction between competing products in a market.

production (prəˈdʌkʃən) NOUN 1 the act of producing. 2 anything that is produced; product. 3 the amount produced or the rate at which it is produced. 4 *Economics* the creation or manufacture for sale of goods and services with exchange value. 5 any work created as a result of literary or artistic effort. 6 the organization and presentation of a film, play, opera, etc. 7 *Brit* the artistic direction of a play. 8 **a** the supervision of the arrangement, recording, and mixing of a record. **b** the overall sound quality or character of a recording: *the material is very strong but the production is poor.* 9 (*modifier*) manufactured by a mass-production process: *a production model of a car.* 10 **make a production (out) of.** *Informal* to make an unnecessary fuss about.
▸**proˈductional** ADJECTIVE

production line NOUN a factory system in which parts or components of the end product are transported by a conveyor through a number of different sites at each of which a manual or machine operation is performed on them without interrupting the flow of production.

production platform NOUN (in the oil industry) a platform from which development wells are drilled that also houses a processing plant and other equipment necessary to keep an oilfield in production.

productive (prəˈdʌktɪv) ADJECTIVE 1 producing or having the power to produce; fertile. 2 yielding favourable or effective results. 3 *Economics* **a** producing or capable of producing goods and services that have monetary or exchange value: *productive assets.* **b** of or relating to such production: *the productive processes of an industry.* 4 (*postpositive*; foll by *of*) resulting in: *productive of good results.* 5 denoting an affix or combining form used to produce new words.
▸**proˈductively** ADVERB ▸**proˈductiveness** NOUN

productivity (ˌprɒdʌkˈtɪvɪtɪ) NOUN 1 the output of an industrial concern in relation to the materials, labour, etc., it employs. 2 the state of being productive.

productivity bargaining NOUN the process of reaching an agreement (**productivity agreement**) through collective bargaining whereby the employees of an organization agree to changes which are intended to improve productivity in return for an increase in pay or other benefits.

product liability NOUN the liability to the public of a manufacturer or trader for selling a faulty product.

product life cycle NOUN *Marketing* the four stages (introduction, growth, maturity, and decline) into one of which the sales of a product fall during its market life.

product line NOUN *Marketing* a group of related products marketed by the same company.

product placement NOUN the practice of a company paying for its product to be placed in a prominent position in a film or television programme as a form of advertising.

proem (ˈprəʊɛm) NOUN an introduction or preface, such as to a work of literature.
▷HISTORY C14: from Latin *prooemium* introduction, from Greek *prooimion*, from PRO-[2] + *hoimē* song
▸**proemial** (prəʊˈiːmɪəl) ADJECTIVE

proenzyme (prəʊˈɛnzaɪm) NOUN the inactive form of an enzyme; zymogen.

proestrus (prəʊˈɛstrəs, -ˈiːstrəs) NOUN the usual US spelling of **pro-oestrus.**

pro-European ADJECTIVE 1 having enthusiasm or admiration for the European Union. ◆ NOUN 2 a person who admires the European Union.

prof (prɒf) NOUN *Informal* short for **professor.**

Prof. ABBREVIATION FOR Professor.

profane (prəˈfeɪn) ADJECTIVE 1 having or indicating contempt, irreverence, or disrespect for a divinity or something sacred. 2 not designed or used for religious purposes; secular. 3 not initiated into the inner mysteries or sacred rites. 4 vulgar, coarse, or blasphemous: *profane language.* ◆ VERB (*tr*) 5 to treat or use (something sacred) with irreverence. 6 to put to an unworthy or improper use.
▷HISTORY C15: from Latin *profānus* outside the temple, from PRO-[1] + *fānum* temple
▸**profanation** (ˌprɒfəˈneɪʃən) NOUN ▸**profanatory** (prəˈfænətərɪ, -trɪ) ADJECTIVE ▸**proˈfanely** ADVERB ▸**proˈfaneness** NOUN ▸**proˈfaner** NOUN

profanity (prəˈfænɪtɪ) NOUN, *plural* **-ties.** 1 the state or quality of being profane. 2 vulgar or irreverent action, speech, etc.

profascist (prəʊˈfæʃɪst) ADJECTIVE in favour of or supporting Fascism.

profeminist (prəʊˈfɛmɪnɪst) ADJECTIVE in favour of or supporting feminism.

profess (prəˈfɛs) VERB 1 to affirm or announce (something, such as faith); acknowledge: *to profess ignorance; to profess a belief in God.* 2 (*tr*) to claim (something, such as a feeling or skill, or to be or do something), often insincerely or falsely: *to profess to be a skilled driver.* 3 to receive or be received into a religious order, as by taking vows.
▷HISTORY C14: from Latin *prōfitērī* to confess openly, from PRO-[1] + *fatērī* to confess

professed (prəˈfɛst) ADJECTIVE (*prenominal*) 1 avowed or acknowledged. 2 alleged or pretended. 3 professing to be qualified as: *a professed philosopher.* 4 having taken vows of a religious order.
▸**professedly** (prəˈfɛsɪdlɪ) ADVERB

profession (prəˈfɛʃən) NOUN 1 an occupation requiring special training in the liberal arts or sciences, esp one of the three learned professions, law, theology, or medicine. 2 the body of people in such an occupation. 3 the act of professing; avowal; declaration. 4 **a** Also called: **profession of faith.** a declaration of faith in a religion, esp as made on entering the Church of that religion or an order belonging to it. **b** the faith or the religion that is the subject of such a declaration.
▷HISTORY C13: from Medieval Latin *professiō* the taking of vows upon entering a religious order, from Latin: public acknowledgment; see PROFESS

professional (prəˈfɛʃənᵊl) ADJECTIVE 1 of, relating to, suitable for, or engaged in as a profession. 2 engaging in an activity for gain or as a means of livelihood. 3 extremely competent in a job, etc. 4 undertaken or performed for gain or by people who are paid. ◆ NOUN 5 a person who belongs to or engages in one of the professions. 6 a person who engages for his livelihood in some activity also pursued by amateurs. 7 a person who engages in an activity with great competence. 8 an expert player of a game who gives instruction, esp to members of a club by whom he is hired.
▸**proˈfessionally** ADVERB

professional association NOUN a body of persons engaged in the same profession, formed usually to control entry into the profession, maintain standards, and represent the profession in discussions with other bodies.

professional foul NOUN *Football* a deliberate foul committed as a last-ditch tactic to prevent an opponent from scoring.

professionalism (prəˈfɛʃənəˌlɪzəm) NOUN 1 the methods, character, status, etc., of a professional. 2 the pursuit of an activity for gain or livelihood.
▸**proˈfessionalist** NOUN, ADJECTIVE

professionalize *or* **professionalise** (prəˈfɛʃənəˌlaɪz) VERB (*tr*) to impose a professional structure or status on (something).
▸**proˌfessionaliˈzation** *or* **proˌfessionaliˈsation** NOUN

professor (prəˈfɛsə) NOUN 1 the principal lecturer or teacher in a field of learning at a university or college; a holder of a university chair. 2 *Chiefly US and Canadian* any teacher in a university or college. See also **associate professor, assistant professor, full professor.** 3 a person who claims skill and instructs others in some sport, occupation, etc. 4 a person who professes his opinions, beliefs, etc.
▷HISTORY C14: from Medieval Latin: one who has made his profession in a religious order, from Latin: a public teacher; see PROFESS
▸**professorial** (ˌprɒfɪˈsɔːrɪəl) ADJECTIVE ▸**ˌprofesˈsorially** ADVERB

professoriate (ˌprɒfɪˈsɔːrɪɪt) *or* **professorate** (prəˈfɛsərɪt) NOUN 1 a group of professors. 2 Also called (esp Brit): **professorship** (prəˈfɛsəʃɪp). the rank or position of university professor.

proffer (ˈprɒfə) VERB 1 (*tr*) to offer for acceptance; tender. ◆ NOUN 2 the act of proffering.
▷HISTORY C13: from Old French *proffrir*, from PRO-[1] + *offrir* to offer
▸**ˈprofferer** NOUN

proficient (prəˈfɪʃənt) ADJECTIVE 1 having great facility (in an art, occupation, etc.); skilled. ◆ NOUN 2 an archaic word for an **expert.**
▷HISTORY C16: from Latin *prōficere* to make progress, from PRO-[1] + *facere* to make
▸**proˈficiency** NOUN ▸**proˈficiently** ADVERB

profile (ˈprəʊfaɪl) NOUN 1 a side view, outline, or representation of an object, esp of a human face or head. 2 a view or representation of an object, esp a building, in contour or outline. 3 a short biographical sketch of a subject. 4 a graph, table, or list of scores representing the extent to which a person, field, or object exhibits various tested characteristics or tendencies: *a population profile.* 5 a vertical section of soil from the ground surface to the parent rock showing the different horizons. 6 **a** a vertical section of part of the earth's crust showing the layers of rock. **b** a representation of such a section. 7 the outline of the shape of a river valley either from source to mouth (**long profile**) or at right angles to the flow of the river (**cross profile**). ◆ VERB (*tr*) 8 to draw, write, or make a profile of. 9 to cut out a shape from a blank (as of steel) with a cutter.
▷HISTORY C17: from Italian *profilo*, from *profilare* to sketch lightly, from PRO-[1] + Latin *filum* thread
▸**profilist** (ˈprəʊfɪlɪst) NOUN

profile component NOUN *Brit education* attainment targets in different subjects brought together for the general assessment of a pupil.

profile drag NOUN the sum of the surface friction drag and the form drag for a body moving subsonically through a fluid.

profiler (ˈprəʊfaɪlə) NOUN a person or device that creates a profile, esp someone with psychological training who assists police investigations by identifying the likely characteristics of the perpetrator of a particular crime.

profit (ˈprɒfɪt) NOUN 1 (*often plural*) excess of revenues over outlays and expenses in a business enterprise over a given period of time, usually a year. 2 the monetary gain derived from a transaction. 3 **a** income derived from property or an investment, as contrasted with capital gains. **b** the ratio of this income to the investment or principal. 4 *Economics* **a** the income or reward accruing to a successful entrepreneur and held to be the motivating factor of all economic activity in a capitalist economy. **b** (*as modifier*): *the profit motive.* 5 a gain, benefit, or advantage. ◆ VERB 6 to gain or cause to gain profit.
▷HISTORY C14: from Latin *prōfectus* advance, from *prōficere* to make progress; see PROFICIENT
▸**ˈprofiter** NOUN ▸**ˈprofitless** ADJECTIVE

profitable (ˈprɒfɪtəbᵊl) ADJECTIVE affording gain, benefit, or profit.
▸**ˈprofitably** ADVERB ▸**ˈprofitableness** *or* **ˌprofitaˈbility** NOUN

profit and loss NOUN *Book-keeping* an account compiled at the end of a financial year showing that year's revenue and expense items and indicating gross and net profit or loss.

profit centre NOUN a unit or department of a company that is responsible for its costs and its profits.

profiteer (ˌprɒfɪˈtɪə) NOUN 1 a person who makes excessive profits, esp by charging exorbitant prices for goods in short supply. ◆ VERB 2 (*intr*) to make excessive profits.
▸**ˌprofiˈteering** NOUN

profiterole (ˌprɒfɪtəˈrəʊl, ˈprɒfɪtəˌrəʊl,

prəˈfɪtəˌrəʊl) NOUN a small case of choux pastry with a sweet or savoury filling.
▷HISTORY C16: from French, literally: a small profit, (related to the gifts, etc., given to a servant), from *profiter* to PROFIT

profit-sharing NOUN a system in which a portion of the net profit of a business is distributed to its employees, usually in proportion to their wages or their length of service.

profit taking NOUN selling commodities, securities, etc., at a profit after a rise in market values or before an expected fall in values.

profit warning NOUN a public announcement made by a company to shareholders and others warning that profits for a stated period will be much lower than had been expected.

profligate (ˈprɒflɪgɪt) ADJECTIVE 1 shamelessly immoral or debauched. 2 wildly extravagant or wasteful. ◆ NOUN 3 a profligate person.
▷HISTORY C16: from Latin *prōflīgātus* corrupt, from *prōflīgāre* to overthrow, from PRO-[1] + *flīgere* to beat
▸**profligacy** (ˈprɒflɪgəsɪ) NOUN ▸**ˈprofligately** ADVERB

profluent (ˈprɒflʊənt) ADJECTIVE flowing smoothly or abundantly.
▷HISTORY C15: from Latin *prōfluere* to flow along

pro-form NOUN a word having grammatical function but assuming the meaning of an antecedent word or phrase for which it substitutes: *the word "does" is a pro-form for "understands Greek" in "I can't understand Greek but he does."*

pro forma (ˈprəʊ ˈfɔːmə) ADJECTIVE 1 prescribing a set form or procedure. ◆ ADVERB 2 performed in a set manner.
▷HISTORY Latin: for form's sake

pro forma invoice NOUN an invoice issued before an order is placed or before the goods are delivered giving all the details and the cost of the goods.

profound (prəˈfaʊnd) ADJECTIVE 1 penetrating deeply into subjects or ideas: *a profound mind.* 2 showing or requiring great knowledge or understanding: *a profound treatise.* 3 situated at or extending to a great depth. 4 reaching to or stemming from the depths of one's nature: *profound regret.* 5 intense or absolute: *profound silence.* 6 thoroughgoing; extensive: *profound changes.* ◆ NOUN 7 *Archaic or literary* a great depth; abyss.
▷HISTORY C14: from Old French *profund,* from Latin *profundus* deep, from PRO-[1] + *fundus* bottom
▸**proˈfoundly** ADVERB ▸**proˈfoundness** *or* **profundity** (prəˈfʌndɪtɪ) NOUN

profuse (prəˈfjuːs) ADJECTIVE 1 plentiful, copious, or abundant: *profuse compliments.* 2 (often foll by *in*) free or generous in the giving (of): *profuse in thanks.*
▷HISTORY C15: from Latin *profundere* to pour lavishly
▸**proˈfusely** ADVERB ▸**proˈfuseness** *or* **proˈfusion** NOUN

prog[1] (prɒg) VERB **progs, progging, progged.** 1 (*intr*) *Brit slang or dialect* to prowl about for or as if for food or plunder. ◆ NOUN 2 *Brit slang or dialect* food obtained by begging. 3 *Canadian dialect* a Newfoundland word for **food.**
▷HISTORY C17: of unknown origin

prog[2] (prɒg) *Brit slang, archaic* ◆ NOUN 1 short for **proctor** (sense 1). ◆ VERB **progs, progging, progged.** 2 (*tr*) (of a proctor) to discipline (a student).

prog[3] (prɒg) NOUN *Informal* short for **programme**, esp a television programme

prog. ABBREVIATION FOR: 1 programme. 2 progress. 3 progressive.

Prog. ABBREVIATION FOR Progressive (Party, movement, etc.).

progenitive (prəʊˈdʒɛnɪtɪv) ADJECTIVE capable of bearing offspring.
▸**proˈgenitiveness** NOUN

progenitor (prəʊˈdʒɛnɪtə) NOUN 1 a direct ancestor. 2 an originator or founder of a future development; precursor.
▷HISTORY C14: from Latin: ancestor, from PRO-[1] + *genitor* parent, from *gignere* to beget

progeny (ˈprɒdʒɪnɪ) NOUN, *plural* **-nies.** 1 the immediate descendant or descendants of a person, animal, etc. 2 a result or outcome.
▷HISTORY C13: from Latin *prōgeniēs* lineage; see PROGENITOR

progeria (prəʊˈdʒɪərɪə) NOUN *Med* premature old age, a rare condition occurring in children and characterized by small stature, absent or greying hair, wrinkled skin, and other signs of old age.
▷HISTORY C20: from PRO-[2] + Greek *gēras* old age

pro-German ADJECTIVE in favour of or supporting Germany, its people, culture, etc.: *pro-German sentiment in Britain.*

progestational (ˌprəʊdʒɛˈsteɪʃənᵊl) ADJECTIVE *Physiol* 1 of or relating to the phase of the menstrual cycle, lasting approximately 14 days, during which the uterus is prepared for pregnancy by the secretion of progesterone from the corpus luteum. 2 preceding gestation; before pregnancy.

progesterone (prəʊˈdʒɛstəˌrəʊn) NOUN a steroid hormone, secreted mainly by the corpus luteum in the ovary, that prepares and maintains the uterus for pregnancy. Formula: $C_{21}H_{30}O_2$. Also called: **corpus luteum hormone.**
▷HISTORY C20: from PRO-[1] + GE(STATION) + STER(OL) + -ONE

progestogen (prəʊˈdʒɛstədʒən) *or* **progestin** (prəˈdʒɛstɪn) NOUN any of a group of steroid hormones that have progesterone-like activity, used in oral contraceptives and in treating gynaecological disorders.
▷HISTORY C20: from PROGEST(ERONE) + -O- + -GEN

proglottis (prəʊˈglɒtɪs) *or* **proglottid** NOUN, *plural* **-glottides** (-ˈglɒtɪˌdiːz). any of the segments that make up the body of a tapeworm. Each contains reproductive organs and separates from the worm when filled with fertilized eggs.
▷HISTORY C19: from Greek *proglōssis, proglōttis* point of the tongue, from PRO-[2] + *glōssa, glōtta* (so called because of its shape)
▸**proˈglottic** *or* ˌ**proglotˈtidean** ADJECTIVE

prognathous (prɒgˈneɪθəs) *or* **prognathic** (prɒgˈnæθɪk) ADJECTIVE having a projecting lower jaw.
▷HISTORY C19: from PRO-[2] + Greek *gnathos* jaw
▸**prognathism** (ˈprɒgnəˌθɪzəm) NOUN

prognosis (prɒgˈnəʊsɪs) NOUN, *plural* **-noses** (-ˈnəʊsiːz). 1 *Med* **a** a prediction of the course or outcome of a disease or disorder. **b** the chances of recovery from a disease. 2 any forecast or prediction.
▷HISTORY C17: via Latin from Greek: knowledge beforehand

prognostic (prɒgˈnɒstɪk) ADJECTIVE 1 of, relating to, or serving as a prognosis. 2 foretelling or predicting. ◆ NOUN 3 *Med* any symptom or sign used in making a prognosis. 4 a sign or forecast of some future occurrence.
▷HISTORY C15: from Old French *pronostique,* from Latin *prognōsticum,* from Greek *prognōstikon,* from *progignōskein* to know in advance

prognosticate (prɒgˈnɒstɪˌkeɪt) VERB 1 to foretell (future events) according to present signs or indications; prophesy. 2 (*tr*) to foreshadow or portend.
▷HISTORY C16: from Medieval Latin *prognōsticāre* to predict
▸**progˌnostiˈcation** NOUN ▸**progˈnosticative** ADJECTIVE ▸**progˈnostiˌcator** NOUN

program *or sometimes* **programme** (ˈprəʊgræm) NOUN 1 a sequence of coded instructions fed into a computer, enabling it to perform specified logical and arithmetical operations on data. ◆ VERB **-grams, -gramming, -grammed** *or* **-grammes, -gramming, -grammed.** 2 (*tr*) to feed a program into (a computer). 3 (*tr*) to arrange (data) into a suitable form so that it can be processed by a computer. 4 (*intr*) to write a program.

program generator NOUN a computer program that can be used to help to create other computer programs.

programmable *or* **programable** (prəʊˈgræməbᵊl) ADJECTIVE (esp of a device or operation) capable of being programmed for automatic operation or computer processing.
▸**proˌgrammaˈbility** NOUN

programmatic (ˌprəʊgrəˈmætɪk) ADJECTIVE 1 of or relating to programme music. 2 of or relating to a programme.

programme *or US* **program** (ˈprəʊgræm) NOUN 1 a written or printed list of the events, performers, etc., in a public performance. 2 a performance or series of performances, often presented at a scheduled time, esp on radio or television. 3 a specially arranged selection of things to be done: *what's the programme for this afternoon?* 4 a plan, schedule, or procedure. 5 a syllabus or curriculum. ◆ VERB **-grammes, -gramming, -grammed** *or US* **-grams, -graming, -gramed.** 6 to design or schedule (something) as a programme. ◆ NOUN, VERB 7 *Computing* a variant spelling of **program.**
▷HISTORY C17: from Late Latin *programma,* from Greek: written public notice, from PRO-[2] + *graphein* to write

programmed camera NOUN *Photog* a camera with electronic facilities for setting both aperture and shutter speed automatically on the basis of a through-the-lens light value and a given film speed.

programmed cell death NOUN another name for **apoptosis.**

programmed learning NOUN a teaching method in which the material to be learnt is broken down into easily understandable parts on which the pupil is able to test himself.

programme evaluation and review technique NOUN a method of planning, controlling, and checking the times taken to finish important parts of complex operations, such as making aircraft, ships, or bridges. Acronym: **PERT.** Compare **critical path analysis.**

programme music NOUN music that is intended to depict or evoke a scene or idea. Compare **absolute music.**

programme of study NOUN *Brit education* the prescribed syllabus that pupils must be taught at each key stage in the National Curriculum.

programmer (ˈprəʊgræmə) NOUN a person who writes a program so that data may be processed by a computer.

programming language NOUN a simple language system designed to facilitate the writing of computer programs. See **high-level language, low-level language, machine code.**

program statement NOUN a single instruction in a computer program.

program trading NOUN trading on international stock exchanges using a computer program to exploit differences between stock index futures and actual share prices on world equity markets.

progress NOUN (ˈprəʊgrɛs) 1 movement forwards, esp towards a place or objective. 2 satisfactory development, growth, or advance: *she is making progress in maths.* 3 advance towards completion, maturity, or perfection: *the steady onward march of progress.* 4 (*modifier*) of or relating to progress: *a progress report.* 5 *Biology* increasing complexity, adaptation, etc., during the development of an individual or evolution of a group. 6 *Brit* a stately royal journey. 7 **in progress.** taking place; under way. ◆ VERB (prəˈgrɛs) 8 (*intr*) to move forwards or onwards, as towards a place or objective. 9 to move towards or bring nearer to completion, maturity, or perfection.
▷HISTORY C15: from Latin *prōgressus* a going forwards, from *prōgredī* to advance, from PRO-[1] + *gradī* to step

progress chaser NOUN a person employed to make sure at each stage, esp of a manufacturing process, that a piece of work is on schedule and is delivered to the customer on time.
▸**progress chasing** NOUN

progression (prəˈgrɛʃən) NOUN 1 the act of progressing; advancement. 2 the act or an instance of moving from one thing or unit in a sequence to the next. 3 *Maths* a sequence of numbers in which each term differs from the succeeding term by a constant relation. See also **arithmetic progression, geometric progression, harmonic progression.** 4 *Music* movement, esp of a logical kind, from one note to the next (**melodic progression**) or from one chord to the next (**harmonic progression**). 5 *Astrology* one of several calculations, based on the movement of the planets, from which it is supposed that one can find the expected developments in a person's birth chart and the probable trends of circumstances for a year in his life.
▸**proˈgressional** ADJECTIVE ▸**proˈgressionally** ADVERB

progressionist (prəˈgrɛʃənɪst) *or* **progressist** (prəˈgrɛsɪst) NOUN *Rare* an advocate of social, political, or economic progress; a member of a progressive political party.
▸**proˈgressionism** NOUN

progressive (prəˈgrɛsɪv) ADJECTIVE [1] of or relating to progress. [2] proceeding or progressing by steps or degrees. [3] (*often capital*) favouring or promoting political or social reform through government action, or even revolution, to improve the lot of the majority: *a progressive policy.* [4] denoting or relating to an educational system that allows flexibility in learning procedures, based on activities determined by the needs and capacities of the individual child, the aim of which is to integrate academic with social development. [5] (of a tax or tax system) graduated so that the rate increases relative to the amount taxed. Compare **regressive** (sense 2). [6] (esp of a disease) advancing in severity, complexity, or extent. [7] (of a dance, card game, etc.) involving a regular change of partners after one figure, one game, etc. [8] denoting an aspect of verbs in some languages, including English, used to express prolonged or continuous activity as opposed to momentary or habitual activity: *a progressive aspect of the verb "to walk" is "is walking."* ◆ NOUN [9] a person who advocates progress, as in education, politics, etc. [10] **a** the progressive aspect of a verb. **b** a verb in this aspect.
▸**proˈgressively** ADVERB ▸**proˈgressiveness** NOUN ▸**proˈgressivism** NOUN ▸**proˈgressivist** NOUN

Progressive (prəˈgrɛsɪv) NOUN [1] *US history* a member or supporter of a Progressive Party. [2] *Canadian history* a member or supporter of a chiefly agrarian reform movement advocating the nationalization of railways, low tariffs, an end to party politics, and similar measures: important in the early 1920s. ◆ ADJECTIVE [3] of, relating to, or characteristic of a Progressive Party, Progressive movement, or Progressives.

Progressive Conservative NOUN (in Canada) a member or supporter of the Progressive Conservative Party.

Progressive Conservative Party NOUN (in Canada) a major political party with conservative policies.

progressive dinner NOUN *Austral and NZ* a meal in which each course is served at the home of a different person.

Progressive Federal Party NOUN *South African* a political party, formed in 1977 by a merger between the Progressive Party and members of the United Party, supporting qualified franchise for all South Africans irrespective of race, colour, or creed. See also **National Party, United Party.**

Progressive Party NOUN [1] a US political party, made up chiefly of dissident Republicans, that nominated Theodore Roosevelt as its presidential candidate in 1912 and supported primaries, progressive labour legislation, and other reforms. [2] a US political party, composed mostly of farmers, socialists, and unionists, that nominated Robert La Follette for president in 1924 and supported public ownership of railways and of public utilities and other reforms. [3] a US political party, composed chiefly of dissident Democrats, that nominated Henry Wallace for president in 1948 and supported the nationalization of key industries, advocated social reforms, and opposed the Cold War. [4] (in South Africa) the former name for the **Progressive Federal Party.**

progress payment NOUN an instalment of a larger payment made to a contractor for work carried out up to a specified stage of the job.

prog rock *or* **progressive rock** NOUN a style of rock music originating in the 1970s and characterized by large-scale compositions, often on epic themes, in which musicians display instrumental virtuosity.

prohibit (prəˈhɪbɪt) VERB (*tr*) [1] to forbid by law or other authority. [2] to hinder or prevent.
▷HISTORY C15: from Latin *prohibēre* to prevent, from PRO-[1] + *habēre* to hold
▸**proˈhibiter** *or* **proˈhibitor** NOUN

prohibition (ˌprəʊɪˈbɪʃən) NOUN [1] the act of prohibiting or state of being prohibited. [2] an order or decree that prohibits. [3] (*sometimes capital*) (esp in the US) a policy of legally forbidding the manufacture, transportation, sale, or consumption of alcoholic beverages except for medicinal or scientific purposes. [4] *Law* an order of a superior court (in Britain the High Court) forbidding an inferior court to determine a matter outside its jurisdiction.
▸**ˌprohiˈbitionary** ADJECTIVE

Prohibition (ˌprəʊɪˈbɪʃən) NOUN the period (1920–33) when the manufacture, sale, and transportation of intoxicating liquors was banned by constitutional amendment in the US.
▸**ˌProhiˈbitionist** NOUN

prohibitionist (ˌprəʊɪˈbɪʃənɪst) NOUN (*sometimes capital*) a person who favours prohibition, esp of alcoholic beverages.
▸**ˌprohiˈbitionism** NOUN

prohibitive (prəˈhɪbɪtɪv) *or less commonly* **prohibitory** (prəˈhɪbɪtərɪ, -trɪ) ADJECTIVE [1] prohibiting or tending to prohibit. [2] (esp of prices) tending or designed to discourage sale or purchase.
▸**proˈhibitively** ADVERB ▸**proˈhibitiveness** NOUN

project NOUN (ˈprɒdʒɛkt) [1] a proposal, scheme, or design. [2] **a** a task requiring considerable or concerted effort, such as one by students. **b** the subject of such a task. [3] *US* short for **housing project.** ◆ VERB (prəˈdʒɛkt) [4] (*tr*) to propose or plan. [5] (*tr*) to predict; estimate; extrapolate: *we can project future needs on the basis of the current birth rate.* [6] (*tr*) to throw or cast forwards. [7] to jut or cause to jut out. [8] (*tr*) to send forth or transport in the imagination: *to project oneself into the future.* [9] (*tr*) to cause (an image) to appear on a surface. [10] to cause (one's voice) to be heard clearly at a distance. [11] *Psychol* **a** (*intr*) (esp of a child) to believe that others share one's subjective mental life. **b** to impute to others (one's hidden desires and impulses), esp as a means of defending oneself. Compare **introject.** [12] (*tr*) *Geometry* to draw a projection of. [13] (*intr*) to communicate effectively, esp to a large gathering.
▷HISTORY C14: from Latin *prōicere* to throw down, from PRO-[1] + *iacere* to throw

projectile (prəˈdʒɛktaɪl) NOUN [1] an object or body thrown forwards. [2] any self-propelling missile, esp one powered by a rocket or the rocket itself. [3] any object that can be fired from a gun, such as a bullet or shell. ◆ ADJECTIVE [4] capable of being or designed to be hurled forwards. [5] projecting or thrusting forwards. [6] *Zoology* another word for **protrusile.**
▷HISTORY C17: from New Latin *prōjectilis* jutting forwards

projection (prəˈdʒɛkʃən) NOUN [1] the act of projecting or the state of being projected. [2] an object or part that juts out. [3] See **map projection.** [4] the representation of a line, figure, or solid on a given plane as it would be seen from a particular direction or in accordance with an accepted set of rules. [5] a scheme or plan. [6] a prediction based on known evidence and observations. [7] **a** the process of showing film on a screen. **b** the image or images shown. [8] *Psychol* **a** the belief, esp in children, that others share one's subjective mental life. **b** the process of projecting one's own hidden desires and impulses. See also **defence mechanism.** [9] the mixing by alchemists of powdered philosopher's stone with molten base metals in order to transmute them into gold.
▸**proˈjectional** ADJECTIVE

projectionist (prəˈdʒɛkʃənɪst) NOUN a person responsible for the operation of film projection machines.

projection room NOUN a small room in a cinema in which the film projectors are operated.

projection television NOUN a television receiver in which a very bright picture on a small cathode-ray tube screen is optically projected onto a large screen.

projective (prəˈdʒɛktɪv) ADJECTIVE relating to or concerned with projection: *projective geometry.*
▸**proˈjectively** ADVERB

projective geometry NOUN the branch of geometry concerned with the properties of solids that are invariant under projection and section.

projective test NOUN any psychological test, such as the Rorschach test, in which the subject is asked to respond to vague material. It is thought that unconscious ideas are thus projected, which, when the responses are interpreted, reveal hidden aspects of the subject's personality.

projector (prəˈdʒɛktə) NOUN [1] an optical instrument that projects an enlarged image of individual slides onto a screen or wall. Full name: **slide projector.** [2] an optical instrument in which a strip of film is wound past a lens at a fixed speed so that the frames can be viewed as a continuously moving sequence on a screen or wall. Full name: **film** *or* **cine projector.** [3] a device for projecting a light beam. [4] a person who devises projects.

projet (ˈprɒʒeɪ) NOUN *Diplomacy* a draft of a proposed treaty; plan or proposition.
▷HISTORY C19: via French from Latin *prōjectum* something projecting

prokaryon (prəʊˈkærɪɒn) NOUN the nucleus of a prokaryote.

prokaryote *or* **procaryote** (prəʊˈkærɪɒt) NOUN any organism having cells in each of which the genetic material is in a single DNA chain, not enclosed in a nucleus. Bacteria and archaeans are prokaryotes. Compare **eukaryote.**
▷HISTORY from PRO-[2] + KARYO- + *-ote* as in *zygote*
▸**prokaryotic** *or* **procaryotic** (prəʊˌkærɪˈɒtɪk) ADJECTIVE

Prokopyevsk (*Russian* praˈkɔpjɪfsk) NOUN a city in S Russia: the chief coal-mining centre of the Kuznetsk Basin. Pop.: 240 500 (1999 est.).

prolactin (prəʊˈlæktɪn) NOUN a gonadotrophic hormone secreted by the anterior lobe of the pituitary gland. In mammals it stimulates the secretion of progesterone by the corpus luteum and initiates and maintains lactation. Also called: **luteotrophin, luteotrophic hormone.** See also **follicle-stimulating hormone, luteinizing hormone.**

prolamine (ˈprəʊləˌmiːn, -mɪn, prəʊˈlæmiːn) NOUN any of a group of simple plant proteins, including gliadin, hordein, and zein.
▷HISTORY C20: from PROL(INE) + AM(MONIA) + -INE[2]

prolapse (ˈprəʊlæps, prəʊˈlæps) *Pathol* ◆ NOUN [1] Also called: **prolapsus** (prəʊˈlæpsəs). the sinking or falling down of an organ or part, esp the womb. Compare **proptosis.** ◆ VERB (*intr*) [2] (of an organ, etc.) to sink from its normal position.
▷HISTORY C17: from Latin *prōlābi* to slide along, from PRO-[1] + *lābī* to slip

prolate (ˈprəʊleɪt) ADJECTIVE having a polar diameter of greater length than the equatorial diameter. Compare **oblate**[1].
▷HISTORY C17: from Latin *prōferre* to enlarge
▸**ˈprolately** ADVERB ▸**ˈprolateness** NOUN

prole (prəʊl) NOUN, ADJECTIVE *Derogatory slang, chiefly Brit* short for **proletarian.**

proleg (ˈprəʊˌlɛg) NOUN any of the short paired unjointed appendages on each abdominal segment of a caterpillar and any of certain other insect larvae.
▷HISTORY C19: from PRO-[1] + LEG

prolegomenon (ˌprəʊlɛˈgɒmɪnən) NOUN, *plural* **-na** (-nə). (*often plural*) a preliminary discussion, esp a formal critical introduction to a lengthy text.
▷HISTORY C17: from Greek, from *prolegein,* from PRO-[2] + *legein* to say
▸**ˌproleˈgomenal** ADJECTIVE

prolepsis (prəʊˈlɛpsɪs) NOUN, *plural* **-ses** (-siːz). [1] a rhetorical device by which objections are anticipated and answered in advance. [2] use of a word after a verb in anticipation of its becoming applicable through the action of the verb, as *flat* in *hammer it flat.*
▷HISTORY C16: via Late Latin from Greek: anticipation, from *prolambanein* to anticipate, from PRO-[2] + *lambanein* to take
▸**proˈleptic** ADJECTIVE

proletarian (ˌprəʊlɪˈtɛərɪən) *or less commonly* **proletary** (ˈprəʊlɪtərɪ, -trɪ) ADJECTIVE [1] of, relating, or belonging to the proletariat. ◆ NOUN, *plural* **-tarians** *or* **-taries.** [2] a member of the proletariat.
▷HISTORY C17: from Latin *prōlētārius* one whose only contribution to the state was his offspring, from *prōlēs* offspring
▸**ˌproleˈtarianism** NOUN ▸**ˌproleˈtarianness** NOUN

proletariat (ˌprəʊlɪˈtɛərɪət) NOUN [1] all wage-earners collectively. [2] the lower or working class. [3] (in Marxist theory) the class of wage-earners, esp industrial workers, in a capitalist society, whose only possession of significant material value is their labour. [4] (in ancient Rome) the lowest class of citizens, who had no property.
▷HISTORY C19: via French from Latin *prōlētārius* PROLETARIAN

pro-life ADJECTIVE (of an organization, pressure group, etc.) supporting the right to life of the unborn; against abortion, experiments on embryos, etc.
▸ **ˌpro-ˈlifer** NOUN

proliferate (prəˈlɪfəˌreɪt) VERB [1] to grow or reproduce (new parts, cells, etc.) rapidly. [2] to grow or increase or cause to grow or increase rapidly.
▷HISTORY C19: from Medieval Latin *prōlifer* having offspring, from Latin *prōlēs* offspring + *ferre* to bear
▸ **proˈliferative** ADJECTIVE

proliferation (prəˌlɪfəˈreɪʃən) NOUN [1] rapid growth or reproduction of new parts, cells, etc. [2] rapid growth or increase in numbers. [3] a great number: *done up in a proliferation of fancy frills.*

proliferous (prəˈlɪfərəs) ADJECTIVE [1] (of plants) producing many side branches or offshoots and normally reproducing vegetatively by buds or by plantlets produced in the inflorescence. [2] (of certain animals) reproducing by means of buds, etc.
▷HISTORY C17: from Medieval Latin *prōlifer* having offspring

prolific (prəˈlɪfɪk) ADJECTIVE [1] producing fruit, offspring, etc., in abundance. [2] producing constant or successful results. [3] (often foll by *in* or *of*) rich or fruitful.
▷HISTORY C17: from Medieval Latin *prōlificus,* from Latin *prōlēs* offspring
▸ **proˈlifically** ADVERB ▸ **proˈlificness** *or* **proˈlificacy** NOUN

proline (ˈprəʊliːn, -lɪn) NOUN a nonessential amino acid that occurs in protein.
▷HISTORY C20: from PYRROLIDINE

prolix (ˈprəʊlɪks, prəʊˈlɪks) ADJECTIVE [1] (of a speech, book, etc.) so long as to be boring; verbose. [2] indulging in prolix speech or writing; long-winded.
▷HISTORY C15: from Latin *prōlixus* stretched out widely, from PRO-[1] + *līquī* to flow
▸ **proˈlixity** *or (less commonly)* **proˈlixness** NOUN
▸ **proˈlixly** ADVERB

prolocutor (prəʊˈlɒkjʊtə) NOUN a chairman, esp of the lower house of clergy in a convocation of the Anglican Church.
▷HISTORY C15: from Latin: advocate, from PRO-[1] + *loquī* to speak
▸ **proˈlocutorˌship** NOUN

PROLOG *or* **Prolog** (ˈprəʊlɒg) NOUN a computer programming language based on mathematical logic.
▷HISTORY C20: from *pro(gramming in) log(ic)*

prologue *or often US* **prolog** (ˈprəʊlɒg) NOUN [1] **a** the prefatory lines introducing a play or speech. **b** the actor speaking these lines. [2] a preliminary act or event. [3] (in early opera) **a** an introductory scene in which a narrator summarizes the main action of the work. **b** a brief independent play preceding the opera, esp one in honour of a patron. ◆ VERB **-logues, -loguing, -logued** *or US* **-logs, -loging, -loged.** [4] (*tr*) to introduce or preface with or as if with a prologue.
▷HISTORY C13: from Latin *prologus,* from Greek *prologos,* from PRO-[2] + *logos* discourse

prolong (prəˈlɒŋ) VERB (*tr*) to lengthen in duration or space; extend.
▷HISTORY C15: from Late Latin *prōlongāre* to extend, from Latin PRO-[1] + *longus* long
▸ **prolongation** (ˌprəʊlɒŋˈgeɪʃən) NOUN ▸ **proˈlonger** NOUN
▸ **proˈlongment** NOUN

prolonge (prəˈlɒndʒ) NOUN (formerly) a specially fitted rope used as part of the towing equipment of a gun carriage.
▷HISTORY C19: from French, from *prolonger* to PROLONG

prolusion (prəˈluːʒən) NOUN [1] a preliminary written exercise. [2] an introductory essay, sometimes of a slight or tentative nature.
▷HISTORY C17: from Latin *prōlūsiō* preliminary exercise, from *prōlūdere* to practise beforehand, from PRO-[1] + *lūdere* to play
▸ **prolusory** (prəˈluːzərɪ) ADJECTIVE

prom (prɒm) NOUN [1] *Brit* short for **promenade** (sense 1) or **promenade concert.** [2] *US and Canadian informal* short for **promenade** (sense 3).

PROM (prɒm) NOUN *Computing* ◆ ACRONYM FOR programmable read only memory.

promenade (ˌprɒməˈnɑːd) NOUN [1] *Chiefly Brit* a public walk, esp at a seaside resort. [2] a leisurely walk, esp one in a public place for pleasure or display. [3] *US and Canadian* a ball or formal dance at a high school or college. [4] a marchlike step in dancing. [5] a marching sequence in a square or country dance. ◆ VERB [6] to take a promenade in or through (a place). [7] (*intr*) *Dancing* to perform a promenade. [8] (*tr*) to display or exhibit (someone or oneself) on or as if on a promenade.
▷HISTORY C16: from French, from *promener* to lead out for a walk, from Late Latin *prōmināre* to drive (cattle) along, from PRO-[1] + *mināre* to drive, probably from *minārī* to threaten
▸ **ˌpromeˈnader** NOUN

promenade concert NOUN a concert at which some of the audience stand rather than sit. Often shortened to: **prom.**

promenade deck NOUN an upper covered deck of a passenger ship for the use of the passengers.

promethazine (prəʊˈmɛθəˌziːn) NOUN an antihistamine drug used to treat allergies and to prevent vomiting, esp in motion sickness.
▷HISTORY C20: from PRO(PYL) + *(di)meth(ylamine)* + (PHENOTHI)AZINE

Promethean (prəˈmiːθɪən) ADJECTIVE [1] of or relating to Prometheus. [2] creative, original, or life-enhancing. ◆ NOUN [3] a person who resembles Prometheus.

Prometheus (prəˈmiːθɪəs) NOUN *Greek myth* a Titan, who stole fire from Olympus to give to mankind and in punishment was chained to a rock, where an eagle tore at his liver until Hercules freed him.

promethium (prəˈmiːθɪəm) NOUN a radioactive element of the lanthanide series artificially produced by the fission of uranium. Symbol: Pm; atomic no.: 61; half-life of most stable isotope, ^{145}Pm: 17.7 years; valency: 3; melting pt.: 1042°C; boiling pt.: 2460°C (approx.).
▷HISTORY C20: New Latin from PROMETHEUS

promilitary (prəʊˈmɪlɪtərɪ, -ˈmɪlɪtrɪ) ADJECTIVE in favour of or supporting military organizations, operations, or action.

prominence (ˈprɒmɪnəns) NOUN [1] the state or quality of being prominent. [2] something that is prominent, such as a protuberance. [3] relative importance or consequence. [4] *Astronomy* an eruption of incandescent gas from the sun's surface that can reach an altitude of several hundred thousand kilometres. Prominences are visible during a total eclipse. When viewed in front of the brighter solar disc, they are called filaments.

prominent (ˈprɒmɪnənt) ADJECTIVE [1] jutting or projecting outwards. [2] standing out from its surroundings; noticeable. [3] widely known; eminent.
▷HISTORY C16: from Latin *prōminēre* to jut out, from PRO-[1] + *ēminēre* to project
▸ **ˈprominently** ADVERB ▸ **ˈprominentness** NOUN

prominent moth NOUN any moth of the family *Notodontidae* characterized by tufts of scales on the back edge of the forewing that stand up prominently at rest and give the group its name. It includes the puss moth and buff-tip as well as those with *prominent* in the name.

promiscuity (ˌprɒmɪˈskjuːɪtɪ) NOUN [1] promiscuous sexual behaviour. [2] indiscriminate mingling, mixture, or confusion, as of parts or elements.

promiscuous (prəˈmɪskjʊəs) ADJECTIVE [1] indulging in casual and indiscriminate sexual relationships. [2] consisting of a number of dissimilar parts or elements mingled in a confused or indiscriminate manner. [3] indiscriminate in selection. [4] casual or heedless.
▷HISTORY C17: from Latin *prōmiscuus* indiscriminate, from PRO-[1] + *miscēre* to mix
▸ **proˈmiscuously** ADVERB ▸ **proˈmiscuousness** NOUN

promise (ˈprɒmɪs) VERB [1] (often foll by *to;* when *tr, may take a clause as object or an infinitive*) to give an assurance of (something to someone); undertake (to do something) in the future: *I promise that I will come.* [2] (*tr*) to undertake to give (something to someone): *he promised me a car for my birthday.* [3] (when *tr, takes an infinitive*) to cause one to expect that in the future one is likely (to be or do something): *she promises to be a fine soprano.* [4] (*usually passive*) to engage to be married; betroth: *I'm promised to Bill.* [5] (*tr*) to assure (someone) of the authenticity or inevitability of something (often in the parenthetic phrase **I promise you,** used to emphasize a statement): *there'll be trouble, I promise you.* ◆ NOUN [6] an undertaking or assurance given by one person to another agreeing or guaranteeing to do or give something, or not to do or give something, in the future. [7] indication of forthcoming excellence or goodness: *a writer showing considerable promise.* [8] the thing of which an assurance is given.
▷HISTORY C14: from Latin *prōmissum* a promise, from *prōmittere* to send forth
▸ **ˈpromiser** NOUN

Promised Land NOUN [1] *Old Testament* the land of Canaan, promised by God to Abraham and his descendants as their heritage (Genesis 12:7). [2] heaven, esp when considered as the goal towards which Christians journey in their earthly lives. [3] any longed-for place where one expects to find greater happiness or fulfilment.

promisee (ˌprɒmɪˈsiː) NOUN *Contract law* a person to whom a promise is made. Compare **promisor.**

promising (ˈprɒmɪsɪŋ) ADJECTIVE showing promise of favourable development or future success.
▸ **ˈpromisingly** ADVERB

promisor (ˌprɒmɪˈsɔː, ˈprɒmɪˌsɔː) NOUN *Contract law* a person who makes a promise. Compare **promisee.**

promissory (ˈprɒmɪsərɪ) ADJECTIVE [1] containing, relating to, or having the nature of a promise. [2] *Insurance* stipulating how the provisions of an insurance contract will be fulfilled after it has been signed.

promissory note NOUN *Chiefly US commerce* a document, usually negotiable, containing a signed promise to pay a stated sum of money to a specified person at a designated date or on demand. Also called: **note, note of hand.**

promo (ˈprəʊməʊ) NOUN, *plural* **-mos.** *Informal* something that is used to promote a product, esp a videotape film used to promote a pop record.
▷HISTORY C20: shortened from *promotion*

promonarchist (prəʊˈmɒnəkɪst) ADJECTIVE in favour of or supporting the monarchy.

promontory (ˈprɒməntərɪ, -trɪ) NOUN, *plural* **-ries.** [1] a high point of land, esp of rocky coast, that juts out into the sea. [2] *Anatomy* any of various projecting structures.
▷HISTORY C16: from Latin *prōmunturium* headland; related to *prōminēre;* see PROMINENT

promote (prəˈməʊt) VERB (*tr*) [1] to further or encourage the progress or existence of. [2] to raise to a higher rank, status, degree, etc. [3] to advance (a pupil or student) to a higher course, class, etc. [4] to urge the adoption of; work for: *to promote reform.* [5] to encourage the sale of (a product) by advertising or securing financial support. [6] *Chess* to exchange (a pawn) for any piece other than a king when the pawn reaches the 8th rank.
▷HISTORY C14: from Latin *prōmovēre* to push onwards, from PRO-[1] + *movēre* to move
▸ **proˈmotable** ADJECTIVE ▸ **proˈmotion** NOUN
▸ **proˈmotional** ADJECTIVE

promoter (prəˈməʊtə) NOUN [1] a person or thing that promotes. [2] a person who helps to organize, develop, or finance an undertaking. [3] a person who organizes and finances a sporting event, esp a boxing match. [4] *Chem* a substance added in small amounts to a catalyst to increase its activity. [5] *Genetics* a sequence of nucleotides, associated with a structural gene, that must bind with messenger RNA polymerase before transcription can proceed.

promotive (prəˈməʊtɪv) ADJECTIVE tending to promote.
▸ **proˈmotiveness** NOUN

prompt (prɒmpt) ADJECTIVE [1] performed or executed without delay. [2] quick or ready to act or respond. ◆ ADVERB [3] *Informal* punctually. ◆ VERB [4] (*tr*) to urge (someone to do something). [5] to remind (an actor, singer, etc.) of lines forgotten during a performance. [6] (*tr*) to refresh the memory of. [7] (*tr*) to give rise to by suggestion: *his affairs will prompt discussion.* ◆ NOUN [8] *Commerce* **a** the time limit allowed for payment of the debt incurred by purchasing goods or services on credit. **b** the contract specifying this time limit. **c** Also called: **prompt note.** a memorandum sent to a purchaser to remind him of the time limit and the sum due. [9] the act of prompting. [10] anything that serves to remind. [11] an aid to the operator of a computer in

the form of a question or statement that appears on the screen showing that the equipment is ready to proceed and indicating the options available.
▷HISTORY C15: from Latin *promptus* evident, from *prōmere* to produce, from PRO-[1] + *emere* to buy
▸**'promptly** ADVERB ▸**'promptness** NOUN

promptbook ('prɒmpt,bʊk) NOUN the production script of a play containing notes, cues, etc.

prompter ('prɒmptə) NOUN 1 a person offstage who reminds the actors of forgotten lines or cues. 2 a person, thing, etc., that prompts.

promptitude ('prɒmptɪ,tjuːd) NOUN the quality of being prompt; punctuality.

prompt side NOUN *Theatre* the side of the stage where the prompter is, usually to the actor's left in Britain and to his right in the United States.

promulgate ('prɒməl,geɪt) VERB (*tr*) 1 to put into effect (a law, decree, etc.), esp by formal proclamation. 2 to announce or declare officially. 3 to make widespread. ♦ Also (archaic): **promulge** (prəʊ'mʌldʒ).
▷HISTORY C16: from Latin *prōmulgāre* to bring to public knowledge; probably related to *provulgāre* to publicize, from PRO-[1] + *vulgāre* to make common, from *vulgus* the common people
▸**,promul'gation** NOUN ▸**'promul,gator** NOUN

promycelium (,prəʊmaɪ'siːlɪəm) NOUN, *plural* **-lia** (-lɪə). *Botany* a short tubular outgrowth from certain germinating fungal spores that produces spores itself and then dies.
▷HISTORY C19: New Latin from PRO-[1] + MYCELIUM
▸**,promy'celial** ADJECTIVE

pron. ABBREVIATION FOR: 1 pronominal. 2 pronoun. 3 pronounced. 4 pronunciation.

pronate (prəʊ'neɪt) VERB (*tr*) to turn (a limb, hand, or foot) so that the palm or sole is directed downwards.
▷HISTORY C19: from Late Latin *prōnāre* to bend forwards, bow
▸**pro'nation** NOUN

pronator (prəʊ'neɪtə) NOUN any muscle whose contractions produce or affect pronation.

prone (prəʊn) ADJECTIVE 1 lying flat or face downwards; prostrate. 2 sloping or tending downwards. 3 having an inclination to do something.
▷HISTORY C14: from Latin *prōnus* bent forward, from PRO-[1]
▸**'pronely** ADVERB ▸**'proneness** NOUN

-prone ADJECTIVE COMBINING FORM liable or disposed to suffer: *accident-prone*.

pronephros (prəʊ'nɛfrɒs) NOUN, *plural* **-roi** (-rɔɪ) *or* **-ra** (-rə). the first-formed anterior part of the embryonic kidney in vertebrates, which remains functional in the larvae of the lower vertebrates. See also **mesonephros, metanephros.**
▷HISTORY C19: New Latin, from PRO-[2] + Greek *nephros* kidney
▸**pro'nephric** ADJECTIVE

prong (prɒŋ) NOUN 1 a sharply pointed end of an instrument, such as on a fork. 2 any pointed projecting part. ♦ VERB 3 (*tr*) to prick or spear with or as if with a prong.
▷HISTORY C15: related to Middle Low German *prange* a stake, Gothic *anaprangan* to afflict
▸**pronged** ADJECTIVE

pronghorn ('prɒŋ,hɔːn) NOUN a ruminant mammal, *Antilocapra americana*, inhabiting rocky deserts of North America and having small branched horns: family *Antilocapridae*. Also called: **American antelope.**

prong key NOUN a key or spanner with two prongs or projections which engage corresponding holes in the face of a nut or component to be turned for tightening, adjustment, etc.

pronominal (prəʊ'nɒmɪnᵊl) ADJECTIVE relating to or playing the part of a pronoun.
▷HISTORY C17: from Late Latin *prōnōminālis*, from *prōnōmen* a PRONOUN
▸**pro'nominally** ADVERB

pronominalize *or* **pronominalise** (prəʊ'nɒmɪnə,laɪz) VERB (*tr*) to make (a word) into or treat as a pronoun.
▸**pro,nominali'zation** *or* **pro,nominali'sation** NOUN

pronotum (prəʊ'nəʊtəm) NOUN the notum of the prothorax of an insect.
▷HISTORY C19: PRO-[2] + NOTUM

pronoun ('prəʊ,naʊn) NOUN one of a class of words that serves to replace a noun phrase that has already been or is about to be mentioned in the sentence or context. Abbreviation: **pron.**
▷HISTORY C16: from Latin *prōnōmen*, from PRO-[1] + *nōmen* noun

pronounce (prə'naʊns) VERB 1 to utter or articulate (a sound or sequence of sounds). 2 (*tr*) to utter or articulate (sounds or words) in the correct way. 3 (*tr; may take a clause as object*) to proclaim officially and solemnly: *I now pronounce you man and wife*. 4 (when *tr, may take a clause as object*) to declare as one's judgment: *to pronounce the death sentence upon someone*. 5 (*tr*) to make a phonetic transcription of (sounds or words).
▷HISTORY C14: from Latin *prōnuntiāre* to announce, from PRO-[1] + *nuntiāre* to announce
▸**pro'nounceable** ADJECTIVE ▸**pro'nouncer** NOUN

pronounced (prə'naʊnst) ADJECTIVE 1 strongly marked or indicated. 2 (of a sound) articulated with vibration of the vocal cords; voiced.
▸**pronouncedly** (prə'naʊnsɪdlɪ) ADVERB

pronouncement (prə'naʊnsmənt) NOUN 1 an official or authoritative statement or announcement. 2 the act of pronouncing, declaring, or uttering formally.

pronto ('prɒntəʊ) ADVERB *Informal* at once; promptly.
▷HISTORY C20: from Spanish: quick, from Latin *promptus* PROMPT

pronuclear[1] (,prəʊ'njuːklɪə) ADJECTIVE in favour of or supporting the use of nuclear power.
▸**,pro'nuclearist** NOUN, ADJECTIVE

pronuclear[2] (,prəʊ'njuːklɪə) ADJECTIVE of or relating to a pronucleus.

pronucleus (,prəʊ'njuːklɪəs) NOUN, *plural* **-clei** (-klɪ,aɪ). the nucleus of a mature ovum or spermatozoan before fertilization.

pronunciamento (prə,nʌnsɪə'mɛntəʊ) NOUN, *plural* **-tos.** 1 an edict, proclamation, or manifesto, esp one issued by rebels in a Spanish-speaking country. 2 an authoritarian announcement.
▷HISTORY C19: from Spanish: pronouncement

pronunciation (prə,nʌnsɪ'eɪʃən) NOUN 1 the act, instance, or manner of pronouncing sounds. 2 the supposedly correct manner of pronouncing sounds in a given language. 3 a phonetic transcription of a word.

pro-oestrus (prəʊ'iːstrəs, -'ɛstrəs) *or US* **proestrus** NOUN the period in the oestrous cycle that immediately precedes oestrus.

proof (pruːf) NOUN 1 any evidence that establishes or helps to establish the truth, validity, quality, etc., of something. 2 *Law* the whole body of evidence upon which the verdict of a court is based. 3 *Maths, logic* a sequence of steps or statements that establishes the truth of a proposition. See also **direct** (sense 17), **induction** (senses 4, 8). 4 the act of testing the truth of something (esp in the phrase **put to the proof**). 5 *Scots law* trial before a judge without a jury. 6 *Printing* a trial impression made from composed type, or a print-out (from a laser printer, etc.) for the correction of errors. 7 (in engraving, etc.) a print made by an artist or under his supervision for his own satisfaction before he hands the plate over to a professional printer. 8 *Photog* a trial print from a negative. 9 **a** the alcoholic strength of proof spirit. **b** the strength of a beverage or other alcoholic liquor as measured on a scale in which the strength of proof spirit is 100 degrees. ♦ ADJECTIVE 10 (*usually postpositive;* foll by *against*) able to resist; impervious (to): *the roof is proof against rain*. 11 having the alcoholic strength of proof spirit. 12 of proved strength or impenetrability: *proof armour*. ♦ VERB 13 (*tr*) to take a proof from (type matter, a plate, etc.). 14 to proofread (text) or inspect (a print, etc.), as for approval. 15 to render (something) proof, esp to waterproof.
▷HISTORY C13: from Old French *preuve* a test, from Late Latin *proba*, from Latin *probāre* to test

-proof ADJECTIVE, VERB COMBINING FORM secure against (damage by); (make) impervious to: *waterproof; mothproof; childproof*.
▷HISTORY from PROOF (adj)

proofread ('pruːf,riːd) VERB **-reads, -reading, -read** (-,rɛd). to read (copy or printer's proofs) to detect and mark errors to be corrected.
▸**'proof,reader** NOUN

proof spirit NOUN 1 (in Britain and Canada) a mixture of alcohol and water or an alcoholic beverage that contains 49.28 per cent of alcohol by weight, 57.1 per cent by volume at 51°F: up until 1980 used as a standard of alcoholic liquids. 2 (in the US) a similar standard mixture containing 50 per cent of alcohol by volume at 60°F.

proof stress NOUN *Engineering* the equivalent of yield stress in materials which have no clearly defined yield point.

proof theory NOUN the branch of logic that studies the syntactic properties of formal theories, esp the syntactic characterization of deductive validity.

prop[1] (prɒp) VERB **props, propping, propped.** (when *tr*, often foll by *up*) 1 (*tr*) to support with a rigid object, such as a stick. 2 (*tr;* usually also foll by *against*) to place or lean. 3 (*tr*) to sustain or support. 4 (*intr*) *Austral and NZ* to stop suddenly or unexpectedly. ♦ NOUN 5 something that gives rigid support, such as a stick. 6 a person or thing giving support, as of a moral or spiritual nature. 7 *Rugby* either of the forwards at either end of the front row of a scrum.
▷HISTORY C15: related to Middle Dutch *proppe* vine prop; compare Old High German *pfropfo* shoot, German *Pfropfen* stopper

prop[2] (prɒp) NOUN short for **property** (sense 8).

prop[3] (prɒp) NOUN an informal word for **propeller.**

propaedeutic (,prəʊpɪ'djuːtɪk) NOUN 1 (*often plural*) preparatory instruction basic to further study of an art or science. ♦ ADJECTIVE *also* **propaedeutical.** 2 of, relating to, or providing such instruction.
▷HISTORY C19: from Greek *propaideuein* to teach in advance, from PRO-[2] + *paideuein* to rear

propagable ('prɒpəgəbᵊl) ADJECTIVE capable of being propagated.
▸**,propaga'bility** *or* **'propagableness** NOUN

propaganda (,prɒpə'gændə) NOUN 1 the organized dissemination of information, allegations, etc., to assist or damage the cause of a government, movement, etc. 2 such information, allegations, etc.
▷HISTORY C18: from Italian, use of *propāgandā* in the New Latin title *Sacra Congregatio de Propaganda Fide* Sacred Congregation for Propagating the Faith
▸**,propa'gandism** NOUN ▸**,propa'gandist** NOUN, ADJECTIVE

Propaganda (,prɒpə'gændə) NOUN *RC Church* a congregation responsible for directing the work of the foreign missions and the training of priests for these.

propagandize *or* **propagandise** (,prɒpə'gændaɪz) VERB 1 (*tr*) to spread by propaganda. 2 (*tr*) to subject to propaganda. 3 (*intr*) to spread or organize propaganda.

propagate ('prɒpə,geɪt) VERB 1 *Biology* to reproduce or cause to reproduce; breed. 2 (*tr*) *Horticulture* to produce (plants) by layering, grafting, cuttings, etc. 3 (*tr*) to promulgate; disseminate. 4 *Physics* to move through, cause to move through, or transmit, esp in the form of a wave: *to propagate sound*. 5 (*tr*) to transmit (characteristics) from one generation to the next.
▷HISTORY C16: from Latin *propāgāre* to increase (plants) by cuttings, from *propāgēs* a cutting, from *pangere* to fasten
▸**,propa'gation** NOUN ▸**,propa'gational** ADJECTIVE
▸**'propagative** ADJECTIVE

propagator ('prɒpə,geɪtə) NOUN 1 a person or thing that propagates. 2 a shallow box with a heating element and cover used for germinating seeds or rooting cuttings.

propagule ('prɒpə,gjuːl) *or* **propagulum** (prəʊ'pægjʊləm) NOUN a plant part, such as a bud, that becomes detached from the rest of the plant and grows into a new plant.
▷HISTORY C20: from PROPAG(ATE) + -ULE

propane ('prəʊpeɪn) NOUN a colourless flammable gaseous alkane found in petroleum and used as a fuel. Formula: $CH_3CH_2CH_3$.
▷HISTORY C19: from PROPIONIC ACID + -ANE

propanedioic acid (,prəʊpeɪndaɪ'əʊɪk) NOUN a colourless crystalline compound occurring in sugar beet. Formula: $C_3H_4O_4$,$CH_2(COOH)_2$. Also called: **malonic acid.**
▷HISTORY C20: from PROPANE + DI-[1] + -O- + -IC

propanoic acid (ˌprəʊpəˈnəʊɪk) NOUN a colourless liquid carboxylic acid used in inhibiting the growth of moulds in bread. Formula: CH_3CH_2COOH. Former name: **propionic acid.**
▷HISTORY C20: from PROPANE + -O- + -IC

proparoxytone (ˌprəʊpəˈrɒksɪˌtəʊn) ADJECTIVE [1] (in Ancient Greek) of, relating to, or denoting words having an acute accent on the third syllable from the end. ◆ NOUN [2] a proparoxytone word. ◆ Compare **paroxytone.**
▷HISTORY C18: from Greek *proparoxutonos;* see PRO-[2], PAROXYTONE

pro patria *Latin* (ˈprəʊ ˈpætrɪˌɑː) for one's country.

propel (prəˈpɛl) VERB **-pels, -pelling, -pelled.** (*tr*) to impel, drive, or cause to move forwards.
▷HISTORY C15: from Latin *prōpellere* to drive onwards, from PRO-[1] + *pellere* to drive

propellant *or* **propellent** (prəˈpɛlənt) NOUN [1] something that provides or causes propulsion, such as the explosive charge in a gun or the fuel in a rocket. [2] the gas used to carry the liquid droplets in an aerosol spray.

propellent (prəˈpɛlənt) ADJECTIVE able or tending to propel.

propeller (prəˈpɛlə) NOUN [1] a device having blades radiating from a central hub that is rotated to produce thrust to propel a ship, aircraft, etc. [2] a person or thing that propels.

propeller shaft NOUN the shaft that transmits power from the gearbox to the differential gear in a motor vehicle or from the engine to the propeller in a ship or aircraft.

propelling pencil NOUN a pencil consisting of a metal or plastic case containing a replaceable lead. As the point is worn away the lead can be extended, usually by turning part of the case.

propend (prəʊˈpɛnd) VERB (*intr*) *Obsolete* to be inclined or disposed.
▷HISTORY C16: from Latin *prōpendēre* to hang forwards

propene (ˈprəʊpiːn) NOUN a colourless gaseous alkene obtained by cracking petroleum: used in synthesizing many organic compounds. Formula: $CH_3CH{:}CH_2$. Also called: **propylene.**

propensity (prəˈpɛnsɪtɪ) NOUN, *plural* **-ties.** [1] a natural tendency or disposition. [2] *Obsolete* partiality.
▷HISTORY C16: from Latin *prōpensus* inclined to, from *prōpendēre* to PROPEND

proper (ˈprɒpə) ADJECTIVE [1] (*usually prenominal*) appropriate or suited for some purpose: *in its proper place.* [2] correct in behaviour or conduct. [3] excessively correct in conduct; vigorously moral. [4] up to a required or regular standard. [5] (*immediately postpositive*) (of an object, quality, etc.) referred to or named specifically so as to exclude anything not directly connected with it: *his claim is connected with the deed proper.* [6] (*postpositive;* foll by *to*) belonging to or characteristic of a person or thing. [7] (*prenominal*) *Brit informal* (intensifier): *I felt a proper fool.* [8] (*usually postpositive*) (of heraldic colours) considered correct for the natural colour of the object or emblem depicted: *three martlets proper.* [9] *Maths, logic* (of a relation) distinguished from a weaker relation by excluding the case where the relata are identical. For example, every set is a subset of itself, but a **proper subset** must exclude at least one member of the containing set. See also **strict** (sense 6). [10] *Archaic* pleasant or good. ◆ ADVERB [11] *Brit dialect* (intensifier): *he's proper stupid.* [12] **good and proper.** *Informal* thoroughly: *to get drunk good and proper.* ◆ NOUN [13] the parts of the Mass that vary according to the particular day or feast on which the Mass is celebrated. Compare **ordinary** (sense 10).
▷HISTORY C13: via Old French from Latin *prōprius* special
▸ˈ**properly** ADVERB ▸ˈ**properness** NOUN

properdin (ˈprəʊpədɪn) NOUN *Immunol* a protein present in blood serum that, acting with complement, is involved in the destruction of alien cells, such as bacteria.

proper fraction NOUN a fraction in which the numerator has a lower absolute value than the denominator, as ½ or $x/(3 + x^2)$.

proper motion NOUN the very small continuous change in the direction of motion of a star relative to the sun. It is determined from its radial and tangential motion.

proper noun *or* **name** NOUN the name of a person, place, or object, as for example *Iceland, Patrick,* or *Uranus.* Compare **common noun.** Related adjective: **onomastic.**

propertied (ˈprɒpətɪd) ADJECTIVE owning land or property.

proper time NOUN time measured by a clock that has the same motion as the observer. Any clock in motion relative to the observer, or in a different gravitational field, will not, according to the theory of relativity, measure proper time.

property (ˈprɒpətɪ) NOUN, *plural* **-ties.** [1] something of value, either tangible, such as land, or intangible, such as patents, copyrights, etc. [2] *Law* the right to possess, use, and dispose of anything. [3] possessions collectively or the fact of owning possessions of value. [4] **a** a piece of land or real estate, esp used for agricultural purposes. **b** (*as modifier*): *property rights.* [5] *Chiefly Austral* a ranch or station, esp a small one. [6] a quality, attribute, or distinctive feature of anything, esp a characteristic attribute such as the density or strength of a material. [7] *Logic, obsolete* another name for **proprium.** [8] any movable object used on the set of a stage play or film. Usually shortened to: **prop.**
▷HISTORY C13: from Old French *propriété,* from Latin *proprietās* something personal, from *proprius* one's own

property bond NOUN a bond issued by a life-assurance company, the premiums for which are invested in a property-owning fund.

property centre NOUN a service for buying and selling property, including conveyancing, provided by a group of local solicitors. In full: **solicitors' property centre.**

property man NOUN a member of the stage crew in charge of the stage properties. Usually shortened to: **propman.**

prophage (ˈprəʊfeɪdʒ) NOUN a virus that exists in a bacterial cell and undergoes division with its host without destroying it. Compare **bacteriophage.**
▷HISTORY C20: by contraction from French *probactériophage;* see PRO-[2], BACTERIOPHAGE

prophase (ˈprəʊˌfeɪz) NOUN [1] the first stage of mitosis, during which the nuclear membrane disappears and the nuclear material resolves itself into chromosomes. See also **metaphase, anaphase, telophase.** [2] the first stage of meiosis, divided into leptotene, zygotene, pachytene, diplotene, and diakinesis phases.

prophecy (ˈprɒfɪsɪ) NOUN, *plural* **-cies.** [1] **a** a message of divine truth revealing God's will. **b** the act of uttering such a message. [2] a prediction or guess. [3] the function, activity, or charismatic endowment of a prophet or prophets.
▷HISTORY C13: ultimately from Greek *prophētēs* PROPHET

prophesy (ˈprɒfɪˌsaɪ) VERB **-sies, -sying, -sied.** [1] to reveal or foretell (something, esp a future event) by or as if by divine inspiration. [2] (*intr*) *Archaic* to give instruction in religious subjects.
▷HISTORY C14 *prophecien,* from PROPHECY
▸ˈ**propheˌsiable** ADJECTIVE ▸ˈ**propheˌsier** NOUN

prophet (ˈprɒfɪt) NOUN [1] a person who supposedly speaks by divine inspiration, esp one through whom a divinity expresses his will. Related adjective: **vatic.** [2] a person who predicts the future: *a prophet of doom.* [3] a spokesman for a movement, doctrine, etc. [4] *Christian Science* **a** a seer in spiritual matters. **b** the vanishing of material sense to give way to the conscious facts of spiritual truth.
▷HISTORY C13: from Old French *prophète,* from Latin *prophēta,* from Greek *prophētēs* one who declares the divine will, from PRO-[2] + *phanai* to speak
▸ˈ**prophetess** FEMININE NOUN ▸ˈ**prophet-ˌlike** ADJECTIVE

Prophet (ˈprɒfɪt) NOUN **the.** [1] the principal designation of Mohammed as the founder of Islam. [2] a name for Joseph Smith as founder of the Mormon Church.

prophetic (prəˈfɛtɪk) ADJECTIVE [1] of or relating to a prophet or prophecy. [2] containing or of the nature of a prophecy; predictive.
▸**proˈphetically** ADVERB

Prophets (ˈprɒfɪts) PLURAL NOUN the books constituting the second main part of the Hebrew Bible, which in Jewish tradition is subdivided into the **Former Prophets,** Joshua, Judges, I-II Samuel, and I-II Kings, and the **Latter Prophets,** comprising those books which in Christian tradition are alone called the **Prophets** and which are divided into **Major Prophets** and **Minor Prophets.** Compare **Law of Moses, Hagiographa.**

prophylactic (ˌprɒfɪˈlæktɪk) ADJECTIVE [1] protecting from or preventing disease. [2] protective or preventive. ◆ NOUN [3] a prophylactic drug or device, esp a condom.
▷HISTORY C16: via French from Greek *prophulaktikos,* from *prophulassein* to guard by taking advance measures, from PRO-[2] + *phulax* a guard

prophylaxis (ˌprɒfɪˈlæksɪs) NOUN the prevention of disease or control of its possible spread.

propinquity (prəˈpɪŋkwɪtɪ) NOUN [1] nearness in place or time. [2] nearness in relationship.
▷HISTORY C14: from Latin *propinquitās* closeness, from *propinquus* near, from *prope* near by

propionate (ˈprəʊpɪəˌneɪt) NOUN any ester or salt of propionic acid.

propionic acid (ˌprəʊpɪˈɒnɪk) NOUN the former name for **propanoic acid.**
▷HISTORY C19: from Greek *pro-* first + *pionic* from *piōn* fat, because it is first in order of the fatty acids

propitiate (prəˈpɪʃɪˌeɪt) VERB (*tr*) to appease or make well disposed; conciliate.
▷HISTORY C17: from Latin *propitiāre* to appease, from *propitius* gracious
▸**proˈpitiable** ADJECTIVE ▸**proˌpitiˈation** NOUN
▸**proˌpitiˈatious** ADJECTIVE ▸**proˈpitiative** ADJECTIVE
▸**proˈpitiˌator** NOUN

propitiatory (prəˈpɪʃɪətərɪ) ADJECTIVE [1] designed or intended to propitiate; conciliatory; expiatory. ◆ NOUN [2] the mercy seat.
▸**proˈpitiatorily** ADVERB

propitious (prəˈpɪʃəs) ADJECTIVE [1] favourable; auguring well. [2] gracious or favourably inclined.
▷HISTORY C15: from Latin *propitius* well disposed, from *prope* close to
▸**proˈpitiously** ADVERB ▸**proˈpitiousness** NOUN

propjet (ˈprɒpˌdʒɛt) NOUN another name for **turboprop.**

propman (ˈprɒpˌmæn) NOUN, *plural* **-men.** short for **property man.**

propolis (ˈprɒpəlɪs) NOUN a greenish-brown resinous aromatic substance collected by bees from the buds of trees for use in the construction of hives. Also called: **bee glue, hive dross.**
▷HISTORY C17: via Latin from Greek: suburb, bee glue, from *pro-* before + *polis* city

propone (prəˈpon, -ˈpəʊn) VERB *Scot* to propose or put forward, esp before a court.
▷HISTORY C14: from Latin *prōpōnere* to PROPOSE

proponent (prəˈpəʊnənt) NOUN [1] a person who argues in favour of something. [2] *Law* a person who seeks probate of a will.
▷HISTORY C16: from Latin *prōpōnere* to PROPOSE

Propontis (prəˈpɒntɪs) NOUN the ancient name for (the Sea of) **Marmara.**

proportion (prəˈpɔːʃən) NOUN [1] the relationship between different things or parts with respect to comparative size, number, or degree; relative magnitude or extent; ratio. [2] the correct or desirable relationship between parts of a whole; balance or symmetry. [3] a part considered with respect to the whole. [4] (*plural*) dimensions or size: *a building of vast proportions.* [5] a share, part, or quota. [6] *Maths* a relationship that maintains a constant ratio between two variable quantities: *x increases in direct proportion to y.* [7] *Maths* a relationship between four numbers or quantities in which the ratio of the first pair equals the ratio of the second pair. ◆ VERB (*tr*) [8] to adjust in relative amount, size, etc. [9] to cause to be harmonious in relationship of parts.
▷HISTORY C14: from Latin *prōportiō* (a translation of Greek *analogia*), from phrase *prō portione,* literally: for (its, his, one's) PORTION
▸**proˈportionable** ADJECTIVE ▸**proˌportionaˈbility** NOUN
▸**proˈportionably** ADVERB ▸**proˈportionment** NOUN

proportional (prəˈpɔːʃənᵊl) ADJECTIVE [1] of, involving, or being in proportion. [2] *Maths* having or related by a constant ratio. ◆ NOUN [3] *Maths* an unknown term in a proportion: *in a/b = c/x, x is the fourth proportional.*
▸**proˌportionˈality** NOUN ▸**proˈportionally** ADVERB

proportional counter NOUN an instrument for detecting and measuring the intensity of ionizing radiation. It is similar to a Geiger counter but operates at a lower potential difference such that the magnitude of the discharge is directly proportional to the number of gas molecules ionized by the detected particle. This may permit the identification of the particle or the determination of its energy.

proportional representation NOUN representation of parties in an elective body in proportion to the votes they win. Abbreviation: **PR.** Compare **first-past-the-post.** See also **Additional Member System, Alternative Vote, party list, Single Transferable Vote.**

proportional spacing NOUN a feature of some typewriters and other output devices whereby the space allotted to each character is determined by the width of the character.

proportionate ADJECTIVE (prə'pɔːʃənɪt) [1] being in proper proportion. ◆ VERB (prə'pɔːʃəˌneɪt) [2] (*tr*) to make proportionate.
▸**pro'portionately** ADVERB ▸**pro'portionateness** NOUN

proposal (prə'pəuzᵊl) NOUN [1] the act of proposing. [2] something proposed, as a plan. [3] an offer, esp of marriage.

propose (prə'pəuz) VERB [1] (when *tr, may take a clause as object*) to put forward (a plan, motion, etc.) for consideration or action. [2] (*tr*) to nominate, as for a position. [3] (*tr*) to plan or intend (to do something): *I propose to leave town now.* [4] (*tr*) to announce the drinking of (a toast) to (the health of someone, etc.). [5] (*intr;* often foll by *to*) to make an offer of marriage (to someone).
▹HISTORY C14: from Old French *proposer,* from Latin *prōpōnere* to display, from PRO-[1] + *pōnere* to place
▸**pro'posable** ADJECTIVE ▸**pro'poser** NOUN

proposition (ˌprɒpə'zɪʃən) NOUN [1] a proposal or topic presented for consideration. [2] *Philosophy* **a** the content of a sentence that affirms or denies something and is capable of being true or false. **b** the meaning of such a sentence: *I am warm* always expresses the same proposition whoever the speaker is. Compare **statement** (sense 8). [3] *Maths* a statement or theorem, usually containing its proof. [4] *Informal* a person or matter to be dealt with: *he's a difficult proposition.* [5] an invitation to engage in sexual intercourse. ◆ VERB [6] (*tr*) to propose a plan, deal, etc., to, esp to engage in sexual intercourse.
▹HISTORY C14 *proposicioun,* from Latin *prōpositiō* a setting forth; see PROPOSE
▸**ˌpropo'sitional** ADJECTIVE ▸**ˌpropo'sitionally** ADVERB

propositional attitude NOUN *Logic, philosophy* a relation between a person and a proposition, such as belief, desire, intention, etc.

propositional calculus NOUN the system of symbolic logic concerned only with the relations between propositions as wholes, taking no account of their internal structure. Compare **predicate calculus.**

propositional function NOUN another name for **open sentence.**

propositus (prə'pɒzɪtəs) *or feminine* **proposita** (prə'pɒzɪtə) NOUN, *plural* **-ti** (-ˌtaɪ) *or feminine* **-tae** (-tiː). [1] *Law* the person from whom a line of descent is traced. [2] *Med* Also called (esp US): **proband.** the first patient to be investigated in a family study, to whom all relationships are referred.
▹HISTORY from New Latin, from Latin *prōpōnere* to set forth; see PROPOUND

propound (prə'paund) VERB (*tr*) [1] to suggest or put forward for consideration. [2] *English law* **a** to produce (a will or similar instrument) to the proper court or authority in order for its validity to be established. **b** (of an executor) to bring (an action to obtain probate) in solemn form.
▹HISTORY C16 *propone,* from Latin *prōpōnere* to set forth, from PRO-[1] + *pōnere* to place
▸**pro'pounder** NOUN

propr ABBREVIATION FOR proprietor.

propraetor *or* **propretor** (prəu'priːtə) NOUN (in ancient Rome) a citizen, esp an ex-praetor, granted a praetor's imperium to be exercised outside Rome, esp in the provinces.
▹HISTORY Latin, from *prō praetōre* one who acts for a praetor

propranolol (prəu'prænəˌlɒl) NOUN a drug used in the treatment of angina pectoris, arrhythmia, hypertension, and some forms of tremor. Formula: $C_{16}H_{21}NO_2$.
▹HISTORY C20: from PRO(PYL) + *pr(op)anol* (from PROPANE + -OL) + -OL

proprietary (prə'praɪɪtərɪ, -trɪ) ADJECTIVE [1] of, relating to, or belonging to property or proprietors. [2] privately owned and controlled. [3] *Med* of or denoting a drug or agent manufactured and distributed under a trade name. Compare **ethical** (sense 3). ◆ NOUN, *plural* **-taries.** [4] *Med* a proprietary drug or agent. [5] a proprietor or proprietors collectively. [6] **a** a right to property. **b** property owned. [7] Also called: **lord proprietary.** (in Colonial America) an owner, governor, or grantee of a proprietary colony.
▹HISTORY C15: from Late Latin *proprietārius* an owner, from *proprius* one's own
▸**pro'prietarily** ADVERB

proprietary colony NOUN *US history* any of various colonies, granted by the Crown in the 17th century to a person or group of people with full governing rights.

proprietary name NOUN a name that is a trademark.

proprietor (prə'praɪətə) NOUN [1] an owner of an unincorporated business enterprise. [2] a person enjoying exclusive right of ownership to some property. [3] *US history* a governor or body of governors of a proprietary colony.
▸**pro'prietorship** NOUN ▸**proprietorial** (prəˌpraɪə'tɔːrɪəl) ADJECTIVE ▸**pro'prietress** *or* **pro'prietrix** FEMININE NOUN

propriety (prə'praɪətɪ) NOUN, *plural* **-ties.** [1] the quality or state of being appropriate or fitting. [2] conformity to the prevailing standard of behaviour, speech, etc. [3] (*plural*) **the proprieties.** the standards of behaviour considered correct by polite society.
▹HISTORY C15: from Old French *propriété,* from Latin *proprietās* a peculiarity, from *proprius* one's own

proprioceptor (ˌprəuprɪə'sɛptə) NOUN *Physiol* any receptor (as in the gut, blood vessels, muscles, etc.) that supplies information about the state of the body. Compare **exteroceptor, interoceptor.**
▹HISTORY C20: from *proprio-,* from Latin *proprius* one's own + RECEPTOR
▸**ˌproprio'ceptive** ADJECTIVE

proprium ('prəuprɪəm) NOUN *Logic, obsolete* Also called: **property.** an attribute that is not essential to a species but is common and peculiar to it.
▹HISTORY C16: Latin, neuter sing of *proprius* proper, own

prop root NOUN a root that grows from and supports the stem above the ground in plants such as mangroves.

proptosis (prɒp'təusɪs) NOUN, *plural* **-ses** (-siːz). *Pathol* the forward displacement of an organ or part, such as the eyeball. See also **exophthalmos.** Compare **prolapse.**
▹HISTORY C17: via Late Latin from Greek, from *propiptein* to fall forwards

propulsion (prə'pʌlʃən) NOUN [1] the act of propelling or the state of being propelled. [2] a propelling force.
▹HISTORY C15: from Latin *prōpellere* to PROPEL
▸**propulsive** (prə'pʌlsɪv) *or* **pro'pulsory** ADJECTIVE

propyl ('prəupɪl) NOUN (*modifier*) of, consisting of, or containing the monovalent group of atoms C_3H_7-: *a propyl group or radical.*
▹HISTORY C19: from PROP(IONIC ACID) + -YL

propylaeum (ˌprɒpɪ'liːəm) *or* **propylon** ('prɒpɪˌlɒn) NOUN, *plural* **-laea** (-'liːə) *or* **-lons, -la.** a portico, esp one that forms the entrance to a temple.
▹HISTORY C18: via Latin from Greek *propulaion* before the gate, from PRO-[2] + *pulē* gate

propylene ('prəupɪˌliːn) NOUN another name for **propene.**
▹HISTORY C19: from PROPYL + -ENE

propylene glycol NOUN a colourless viscous hygroscopic sweet-tasting compound used as an antifreeze and brake fluid. Formula: $CH_3CH(OH)CH_2OH$. Systematic name: **1,2-dihydroxypropane.**

propylite ('prɒpɪˌlaɪt) NOUN *Geology* an altered andesite or similar rock containing calcite, chlorite, etc., produced by the action of hot water.
▹HISTORY C20: from *propylon* (see PROPYLAEUM) + -ITE[1]; so named because it is associated with the start of the Tertiary volcanic era

propylthiouracil (ˌprəupɪlˌθaɪəu'juərəsɪl) NOUN a white crystalline water-insoluble substance with an intensely bitter taste, used in medicine to treat hyperthyroidism. Formula: $C_7H_2N_2OS$.
▹HISTORY from PROPYL + THIO- + *uracil* (URO-[1] + AC(ETIC) + *-il* -ILE)

pro rata ('prəu 'rɑːtə) in proportion.
▹HISTORY Medieval Latin

prorate (prəu'reɪt, 'prəureɪt) VERB *Chiefly US and Canadian* to divide, assess, or distribute (something) proportionately.
▹HISTORY C19: from PRO RATA
▸**pro'ratable** ADJECTIVE ▸**pro'ration** NOUN

proreform (ˌprəurɪ'fɔːm) ADJECTIVE in favour of or supporting reform, esp within politics.

prorogue (prə'rəug) VERB to discontinue the meetings of (a legislative body) without dissolving it.
▹HISTORY C15: from Latin *prorogāre* literally: to ask publicly, from *prō-* in public + *rogāre* to ask
▸**prorogation** (ˌprəurə'geɪʃən) NOUN

prosaic (prəu'zeɪɪk) ADJECTIVE [1] lacking imagination. [2] having the characteristics of prose.
▹HISTORY C16: from Late Latin *prōsaicus,* from Latin *prōsa* PROSE
▸**pro'saically** ADVERB ▸**pro'saicness** NOUN

prosaism (prəu'zeɪɪzəm) *or* **prosaicism** (prəu'zeɪɪˌsɪzəm) NOUN [1] prosaic quality or style. [2] a prosaic expression, thought, etc.
▸**pro'saist** NOUN

pros and cons PLURAL NOUN the various arguments in favour of and against a motion, course of action, etc.
▹HISTORY C16: from Latin *prō* for + *con,* from *contrā* against

proscenium (prə'siːnɪəm) NOUN, *plural* **-nia** (-nɪə) *or* **-niums.** [1] the arch or opening separating the stage from the auditorium together with the area immediately in front of the arch. [2] (in ancient theatres) the stage itself.
▹HISTORY C17: via Latin from Greek *proskēnion,* from *pro-* before + *skēnē* scene

prosciutto (prəu'ʃuːtəu; *Italian* pro'ʃutto) NOUN cured ham from Italy: usually served as an hors d'oeuvre.
▹HISTORY Italian, literally: dried beforehand, from *pro-* PRE- + *asciutto* dried

proscribe (prəu'skraɪb) VERB (*tr*) [1] to condemn or prohibit. [2] to outlaw; banish; exile. [3] (in ancient Rome) to outlaw (a citizen) by posting his name in public.
▹HISTORY C16: from Latin *prōscrībere* to put up a written public notice, from *prō-* in public + *scrībere* to write
▸**pro'scriber** NOUN

proscription (prəu'skrɪpʃən) NOUN [1] the act of proscribing or the state of being proscribed. [2] denunciation, prohibition, or exclusion. [3] outlawry or ostracism.
▹HISTORY C14: from Latin *prōscriptiō;* see PROSCRIBE
▸**pro'scriptive** ADJECTIVE ▸**pro'scriptively** ADVERB
▸**pro'scriptiveness** NOUN

prose (prəuz) NOUN [1] spoken or written language as in ordinary usage, distinguished from poetry by its lack of a marked metrical structure. [2] a passage set for translation into a foreign language. [3] commonplace or dull discourse, expression, etc. [4] *RC Church* a hymn recited or sung after the gradual at Mass. [5] (*modifier*) written in prose. [6] (*modifier*) matter-of-fact. ◆ VERB [7] to write or say (something) in prose. [8] (*intr*) to speak or write in a tedious style.
▹HISTORY C14: via Old French from Latin phrase *prōsa ōrātiō* straightforward speech, from *prorsus* prosaic, from *prōvertere* to turn forwards, from PRO-[1] + *vertere* to turn
▸**'proseˌlike** ADJECTIVE

prosector (prəu'sɛktə) NOUN a person who prepares or dissects anatomical subjects for demonstration.
▹HISTORY C19: from Latin, from *prōsecare* to cut up; probably on the model of French *prosecteur*

prosecute ('prɒsɪˌkjuːt) VERB [1] (*tr*) to bring a criminal action against (a person) for some offence. [2] (*intr*) **a** to seek redress by legal proceedings. **b** to institute or conduct a prosecution. [3] (*tr*) to engage

in or practise (a profession or trade). [4] (*tr*) to continue to do (a task, etc.).
▷HISTORY C15: from Latin *prōsequī* to follow, from *prō-* forward + *sequī* to follow
▸ˈ**prose,cutable** ADJECTIVE

prosecuting attorney NOUN *US law* (in some states) an officer in a judicial district appointed to conduct criminal prosecutions on behalf of the state and people.

prosecution (ˌprɒsɪˈkjuːʃən) NOUN [1] the act of prosecuting or the state of being prosecuted. [2] **a** the institution and conduct of legal proceedings against a person. **b** the proceedings brought in the name of the Crown to put an accused on trial. [3] the lawyers acting for the Crown to put the case against a person. Compare **defence** (sense 6). [4] the following up or carrying on of something begun, esp with a view to its accomplishment or completion.

prosecutor (ˈprɒsɪˌkjuːtə) NOUN a person who institutes or conducts legal proceedings, esp in a criminal court.

proselyte (ˈprɒsɪˌlaɪt) NOUN [1] a person newly converted to a religious faith or sect; a convert, esp a gentile converted to Judaism. ◆ VERB [2] a less common word for **proselytize.**
▷HISTORY C14: from Church Latin *prosēlytus,* from Greek *prosēlutos* recent arrival, convert, from *proserchesthai* to draw near
▸**proselytism** (ˈprɒsɪlɪˌtɪzəm) NOUN ▸**proselytic** (ˌprɒsɪˈlɪtɪk) ADJECTIVE

proselytize *or* **proselytise** (ˈprɒsɪlɪˌtaɪz) VERB to convert (someone) from one religious faith to another.
▸ˌ**proselytiˈzation** *or* ˌ**proselytiˈsation** NOUN ▸ˈ**proselyt,izer** *or* ˈ**proselyt,iser** NOUN

prosencephalon (ˌprɒsenˈsɛfəlɒn) NOUN, *plural* **-la** (-lə). the part of the brain that develops from the anterior portion of the neural tube. Compare **mesencephalon, rhombencephalon.** Nontechnical name: **forebrain.**
▷HISTORY C19: from New Latin, from Greek *prosō* forward + *enkephalos* brain
▸**prosencephalic** (ˌprɒsensɪˈfælɪk) ADJECTIVE

prosenchyma (prɒsˈɛŋkɪmə) NOUN a plant tissue consisting of long narrow cells with pointed ends: occurs in conducting tissue.
▷HISTORY C19: from New Latin, from Greek *pros-* towards + *enkhuma* infusion; compare PARENCHYMA
▸**prosenchymatous** (ˌprɒsɛnˈkaɪmətəs) ADJECTIVE

prose poem NOUN a prose composition characterized by a poetic style.

Proserpina (prəʊˈsɜːpɪnə) NOUN the Roman goddess of the underworld. Greek counterpart: **Persephone.**

prosimian (prəʊˈsɪmɪən) NOUN [1] any primate of the primitive suborder *Prosimii,* including lemurs, lorises, and tarsiers. ◆ ADJECTIVE [2] of, relating to, or belonging to the *Prosimii.* ◆ Compare **anthropoid** (sense 4).
▷HISTORY C19: via New Latin from PRO-^{2} + Latin *sīmia* ape

prosit *German* (ˈproːzɪt) INTERJECTION good health! cheers!
▷HISTORY German, from Latin, literally: may it prove beneficial

proslavery (ˌprəʊˈsleɪvərɪ) ADJECTIVE in favour of or supporting slavery.

prosody (ˈprɒsədɪ) NOUN [1] the study of poetic metre and of the art of versification, including rhyme, stanzaic forms, and the quantity and stress of syllables. [2] a system of versification. [3] the patterns of stress and intonation in a language.
▷HISTORY C15: from Latin *prosōdia* accent of a syllable, from Greek *prosōidia* song set to music, from *pros* towards + *ōidē,* from *aoidē* song; see ODE
▸**prosodic** (prəˈsɒdɪk) ADJECTIVE ▸ˈ**prosodist** NOUN

prosoma (prəʊˈsəʊmə) NOUN, *plural* **-mas** *or* **-mata** (-mətə). *Zoology* the head and thorax of an arachnid.

prosopagnosia (ˌprɒsəpægˈnəʊzɪə) NOUN an inability to recognize faces.
▷HISTORY C20: from Greek *prosōpon* face + AGNOSIA

prosopography (ˌprɒsəˈpɒgrəfɪ) NOUN [1] a description of a person's life and career. [2] the study of such descriptions as part of history, esp Roman history.
▷HISTORY C16: from New Latin *prosopographia,* from Greek *prosōpon* face, person + -GRAPHY
▸ˌ**prosoˈpographer** NOUN ▸**prosopographical** (ˌprɒsəpəˈgræfɪkᵊl) ADJECTIVE ▸ˌ**prosopoˈgraphically** ADVERB

prosopopoeia *or* **prosopopeia** (ˌprɒsəpəˈpiːə) NOUN [1] *Rhetoric* another word for **personification.** [2] a figure of speech that represents an imaginary, absent, or dead person speaking or acting.
▷HISTORY C16: via Latin from Greek *prosōpopoiia* dramatization, from *prosōpon* face + *poiein* to make
▸ˌ**prosopoˈpoeial** *or* ˌ**prosopoˈpeial** ADJECTIVE

pro-Soviet ADJECTIVE in favour of or supporting anything of, characteristic of, or relating to the former Soviet Union, its people, or its government.

prospect NOUN (ˈprɒspɛkt) [1] (*sometimes plural*) a probability or chance for future success, esp as based on present work or aptitude: *a good job with prospects.* [2] a vision of the future; what is foreseen; expectation: *she was excited at the prospect of living in London; unemployment presents a grim prospect.* [3] a view or scene, esp one offering an extended outlook. [4] a prospective buyer, project, etc. [5] a survey or observation. [6] *Mining* **a** a known or likely deposit of ore. **b** the location of a deposit of ore. **c** a sample of ore for testing. **d** the yield of mineral obtained from a sample of ore. ◆ VERB (prəˈspɛkt) [7] (when *intr,* often foll by *for*) to explore (a region) for gold or other valuable minerals. [8] (*tr*) to work (a mine) to discover its profitability. [9] (*intr;* often foll by *for*) to search (for).
▷HISTORY C15: from Latin *prōspectus* distant view, from *prōspicere* to look into the distance, from *prō-* forward + *specere* to look
▸ˈ**prospectless** ADJECTIVE

prospective (prəˈspɛktɪv) ADJECTIVE [1] looking towards the future. [2] (*prenominal*) anticipated or likely.
▸**proˈspectively** ADVERB

prospector (prəˈspɛktə) NOUN a person who searches for the natural occurrence of gold, petroleum, etc.

prospectus (prəˈspɛktəs) NOUN, *plural* **-tuses.** [1] a formal statement giving details of a forthcoming event, such as the publication of a book or an issue of shares. [2] a pamphlet or brochure giving details of courses, as at a college or school.
▷HISTORY C18: Latin, literally: distant view; see PROSPECT

prosper (ˈprɒspə) VERB (*usually intr*) to thrive, succeed, etc., or cause to thrive, succeed, etc. in a healthy way.
▷HISTORY C15: from Latin *prosperāre* to succeed, from *prosperus* fortunate, from PRO-^{1} + *spēs* hope

prosperity (prɒˈspɛrɪtɪ) NOUN the condition of prospering; success or wealth.

prosperity gospel NOUN a modern version or, according to some, perversion of the gospel according to which the full blessings of God available to those who approach Him in faith and obedience include wealth, health and power.

prosperous (ˈprɒspərəs) ADJECTIVE [1] flourishing; prospering. [2] rich; affluent; wealthy. [3] favourable or promising.
▸ˈ**prosperously** ADVERB ▸ˈ**prosperousness** NOUN

prostaglandin (ˌprɒstəˈglændɪn) NOUN any of a group of potent hormone-like compounds composed of essential fatty acids and found in all mammalian tissues, esp human semen. Prostaglandins stimulate the muscles of the uterus and affect the blood vessels; they are used to induce abortion or birth.
▷HISTORY C20: from *prosta(te) gland* + -IN; it was originally believed to be secreted by the prostate gland

prostate (ˈprɒsteɪt) NOUN [1] Also called: **prostate gland.** a gland in male mammals that surrounds the neck of the bladder and urethra and secretes a liquid constituent of the semen. ◆ ADJECTIVE [2] Also: **prostatic** (prɒˈstætɪk). of or relating to the prostate gland. See also **PSA.**
▷HISTORY C17: via Medieval Latin from Greek *prostatēs* something standing in front (of the bladder), from *pro-* in front + *histanai* to cause to stand

prostatectomy (ˌprɒstəˈtɛktəmɪ) NOUN, *plural* **-mies.** surgical removal of all or a part of the prostate gland.

prostatitis (ˌprɒstəˈtaɪtɪs) NOUN inflammation of the prostate gland.

prosternum (prəʊˈstɜːnəm) NOUN, *plural* **-na** (-nə) *or* **-nums.** the sternum of the prothorax of an insect.

prosthesis (ˈprɒsθɪsɪs, prɒsˈθiːsɪs) NOUN, *plural* **-ses** (-ˌsiːz). [1] *Surgery* **a** the replacement of a missing bodily part with an artificial substitute. **b** an artificial part such as a limb, eye, or tooth. [2] *Linguistics* another word for **prothesis.**
▷HISTORY C16: via Late Latin from Greek: an addition, from *prostithenai* to add, from *pros-* towards + *tithenai* to place
▸**prosthetic** (prɒsˈθɛtɪk) ADJECTIVE ▸**prosˈthetically** ADVERB

prosthetic group NOUN the nonprotein component of a conjugated protein, such as the lipid group in a lipoprotein.

prosthetics (prɒsˈθɛtɪks) NOUN (*functioning as singular*) the branch of surgery concerned with prosthesis.

prosthodontics (ˌprɒsθəˈdɒntɪks) NOUN (*functioning as singular*) the branch of dentistry concerned with the artificial replacement of missing teeth.
▷HISTORY C20: from PROSTH(ESIS) + -ODONT + -ICS
▸ˌ**prosthoˈdontist** NOUN

prostitute (ˈprɒstɪˌtjuːt) NOUN [1] a woman who engages in sexual intercourse for money. [2] a man who engages in such activity, esp in homosexual practices. [3] a person who offers his talent or work for unworthy purposes. ◆ VERB (*tr*) [4] to offer (oneself or another) in sexual intercourse for money. [5] to offer (a person, esp oneself, or a person's talent) for unworthy purposes.
▷HISTORY C16: from Latin *prōstituere* to expose to prostitution, from *prō-* in public + *statuere* to cause to stand
▸ˌ**prostiˈtution** NOUN ▸ˈ**prosti,tutor** NOUN

prostomium (prəʊˈstəʊmɪəm) NOUN, *plural* **-mia** (-mɪə). the lobe at the head end of earthworms and other annelids: bears tentacles, palps, etc., or forms part of a sucker or proboscis.
▷HISTORY via New Latin from Greek *prostomion* mouth
▸**proˈstomial** ADJECTIVE

prostrate ADJECTIVE (ˈprɒstreɪt) [1] lying with the face downwards, as in submission. [2] exhausted physically or emotionally. [3] helpless or defenceless. [4] (of a plant) growing closely along the ground. ◆ VERB (prɒˈstreɪt) (*tr*) [5] to bow or cast (oneself) down, as in submission. [6] to lay or throw down flat, as on the ground. [7] to make helpless or defenceless. [8] to make exhausted.
▷HISTORY C14: from Latin *prōsternere* to throw to the ground, from *prō-* before + *sternere* to lay low
▸**prosˈtration** NOUN

prostyle (ˈprəʊstaɪl) ADJECTIVE [1] (of a building) having a row of columns in front, esp as in the portico of a Greek temple. ◆ NOUN [2] a prostyle building, portico, etc.
▷HISTORY C17: from Latin *prostȳlos,* from Greek: with pillars in front, from PRO-^{2} + *stulos* pillar

prosy (ˈprəʊzɪ) ADJECTIVE **prosier, prosiest.** [1] of the nature of or similar to prose. [2] dull, tedious, or long-winded.
▸ˈ**prosily** ADVERB ▸ˈ**prosiness** NOUN

Prot. ABBREVIATION FOR Protestant.

prot- COMBINING FORM a variant of **proto-** before a vowel.

protactinium (ˌprəʊtækˈtɪnɪəm) NOUN a toxic radioactive metallic element that occurs in uranium ores and is produced by neutron irradiation of thorium. Symbol: Pa; atomic no.: 91; half-life of the most stable isotope, ^{231}Pa: 32 500 years; valency: 4 or 5; relative density: 15.37 (calc.); melting pt.: 1572°C. Former name: **protoactinium.**

protagonist (prəʊˈtægənɪst) NOUN [1] the principal character in a play, story, etc. [2] a supporter, esp when important or respected, of a cause, political party, etc.
▷HISTORY C17: from Greek *prōtagōnistēs,* from *prōtos* first + *agōnistēs* actor
▸**proˈtagonism** NOUN

protamine (ˈprəʊtəˌmiːn) NOUN any of a group of basic simple proteins that occur, in association with nucleic acids, in the sperm of some fish.
▷HISTORY C19: from German: see PROTO-, AMINE

protandrous (prəʊˈtændrəs) ADJECTIVE [1] (of hermaphrodite or monoecious plants) maturing the anthers before the stigma. [2] (of hermaphrodite animals) producing male gametes before female gametes. Compare **protogynous.**
▸**pro'tandry** NOUN

protanopia (ˌprəʊtəˈnəʊpɪə) NOUN a form of colour blindness characterized by a tendency to confuse reds and greens and by a loss of sensitivity to red light.
▷HISTORY C20: New Latin, from PROTO- + AN- + -OPIA
▸**protanopic** (ˌprəʊtəˈnɒpɪk) ADJECTIVE

protasis (ˈprɒtəsɪs) NOUN, *plural* **-ses** (-siːz). [1] *Logic, grammar* the antecedent of a conditional statement, such as *it rains* in *if it rains the game will be cancelled*. Compare **apodosis.** [2] (in classical drama) the introductory part of a play.
▷HISTORY C17: via Latin from Greek: a proposal, from *pro-* before + *teinein* to extend
▸**protatic** (prɒˈtætɪk) ADJECTIVE

protea (ˈprəʊtɪə) NOUN any shrub or small tree of the genus *Protea*, of tropical and southern Africa, having flowers with coloured bracts arranged in showy heads: family *Proteaceae*.
▷HISTORY C20: from New Latin, from PROTEUS, referring to the large number of different forms of the plant
▸**proteaceous** (ˌprəʊtɪˈeɪʃəs) ADJECTIVE

protean (prəʊˈtiːən, ˈprəʊtɪən) ADJECTIVE readily taking on various shapes or forms; variable.
▷HISTORY C16: from PROTEUS

protease (ˈprəʊtɪˌeɪs) NOUN any enzyme involved in proteolysis.
▷HISTORY C20: from PROTEIN + -ASE

protease inhibitor NOUN any one of a class of antiviral drugs that impair the growth and replication of HIV by inhibiting the action of protease produced by the virus: used in the treatment of AIDS.

protect (prəˈtɛkt) VERB (*tr*) [1] to defend from trouble, harm, attack, etc. [2] *Economics* to assist (domestic industries) by the imposition of protective tariffs on imports. [3] *Commerce* to provide funds in advance to guarantee payment of (a note, draft, etc.).
▷HISTORY C16: from Latin *prōtegere* to cover before, from PRO-[1] + *tegere* to cover

protectant (prəˈtɛktənt) NOUN a chemical substance that affords protection, as against frost, rust, insects, etc.

protection (prəˈtɛkʃən) NOUN [1] the act of protecting or the condition of being protected. [2] something that protects. [3] **a** the imposition of duties or quotas on imports, designed for the protection of domestic industries against overseas competition, expansion of domestic employment, etc. **b** Also called: **protectionism.** the system, policy, or theory of such restrictions. Compare **free trade.** [4] a document that grants protection or immunity from arrest or harassment to a person, esp a traveller. [5] *Mountaineering* security on a climb provided by running belays, etc. [6] *Informal* **a** Also called: **protection money.** money demanded by gangsters for freedom from molestation. **b** freedom from molestation purchased in this way.
▸**pro'tection,ism** NOUN ▸**pro'tectionist** NOUN, ADJECTIVE

protection ratio NOUN the minimum acceptable ratio between the amplitudes of a wanted radio or television broadcast signal and any interfering signal.

protective (prəˈtɛktɪv) ADJECTIVE [1] giving or capable of giving protection. [2] *Economics* of, relating to, or intended for protection of domestic industries. ◆ NOUN [3] something that protects. [4] a condom.
▸**pro'tectively** ADVERB ▸**pro'tectiveness** NOUN

protective coloration NOUN the coloration of an animal that enables it to blend with its surroundings and therefore escape the attention of predators.

protective tariff NOUN a tariff levied on imports to protect the domestic economy rather than to raise revenue.

protector (prəˈtɛktə) NOUN [1] a person or thing that protects. [2] *History* a person who exercised royal authority during the minority, absence, or incapacity of the monarch.
▸**pro'tectoral** ADJECTIVE ▸**pro'tectress** FEMININE NOUN

Protector (prəˈtɛktə) NOUN short for **Lord Protector**, the title borne by Oliver Cromwell (1653–58) and by Richard Cromwell (1658–59) as heads of state during the period known as the **Protectorate**

protectorate (prəˈtɛktərɪt) NOUN [1] **a** a territory largely controlled by but not annexed to a stronger state. **b** the relation of a protecting state to its protected territory. [2] the office or period of office of a protector.

protectory (prəˈtɛktərɪ) NOUN, *plural* **-ries**. an institution for the care of homeless, delinquent, or destitute children.

protégé *or feminine* **protégée** (ˈprəʊtɪˌʒeɪ) NOUN a person who is protected and aided by the patronage of another person.
▷HISTORY C18: from French *protéger* to PROTECT

protein (ˈprəʊtiːn) NOUN any of a large group of nitrogenous compounds of high molecular weight that are essential constituents of all living organisms. They consist of one or more chains of amino acids linked by peptide bonds and are folded into a specific three-dimensional shape maintained by further chemical bonding.
▷HISTORY C19: via German from Greek *prōteios* primary, from *protos* first + -IN
▸**ˌprotein'aceous** *or* **pro'teinic** *or* **pro'teinous** ADJECTIVE

proteinase (ˈprəʊtɪˌneɪs, -ˌneɪz) NOUN another name for **endopeptidase.**

proteinuria (ˌprəʊtɪˈnjʊərɪə) NOUN *Med* another name for **albuminuria.**

pro tempore *Latin* (ˈprəʊ ˈtɛmpərɪ) ADVERB, ADJECTIVE for the time being. Often shortened to: **pro tem** (ˈprəʊ ˈtɛm).

proteolysis (ˌprəʊtɪˈɒlɪsɪs) NOUN the hydrolysis of proteins into simpler compounds by the action of enzymes: occurs esp during digestion.
▷HISTORY C19: from New Latin, from *proteo-* (from PROTEIN) + -LYSIS
▸**proteolytic** (ˌprəʊtɪəˈlɪtɪk) ADJECTIVE

proteome (ˈprəʊtɪˌəʊm) NOUN the full complement of proteins that occur within a cell, tissue, or organism.
▷HISTORY C20: from PROTE[IN] + -OME

proteomics (ˌprəʊtɪˈɒmɪks) NOUN (*functioning as singular*) the branch of biochemistry concerned with the structure and analysis of the proteins occurring in living organisms.

proteose (ˈprəʊtɪˌəʊs, -ˌəʊz) NOUN *Now rare* any of a group of compounds formed during proteolysis that are less complex than metaproteins but more so than peptones. Also called (esp US): **albumose.**
▷HISTORY C20: from PROTEIN + -OSE[2]

protero- COMBINING FORM anterior or former in time, place, order, etc.: *proterozoic*.
▷HISTORY from Greek *proteros* fore

Proterozoic (ˌprəʊtərəʊˈzəʊɪk) NOUN [1] the later of two divisions of the Precambrian era, during which the earliest plants and animals are assumed to have lived. Compare **Archaeozoic.** ◆ ADJECTIVE [2] of or formed in the late Precambrian era.

protest NOUN (ˈprəʊtɛst) [1] **a** public, often organized, dissent or manifestation of such dissent. **b** (*as modifier*): *a protest march*. [2] a declaration or objection that is formal or solemn. [3] an expression of disagreement or complaint: *without a squeak of protest*. [4] **a** a formal notarial statement drawn up on behalf of a creditor and declaring that the debtor has dishonoured a bill of exchange or promissory note. **b** the action of drawing up such a statement. **c** a formal declaration by a taxpayer disputing the legality or accuracy of his assessment. [5] a statement made by the master of a vessel attesting to the circumstances in which his vessel was damaged or imperilled. [6] the act of protesting. [7] **under protest.** having voiced objections; unwillingly. ◆ VERB (prəˈtɛst) [8] (when *intr*, foll by *against, at, about*, etc.; when *tr, may take a clause as object*) to make a strong objection (to something, esp a supposed injustice or offence). [9] (when *tr, may take a clause as object*) to assert or affirm in a formal or solemn manner. [10] (when *tr, may take a clause as object*) to put up arguments against; disagree; complain; object: *"I'm okay," she protested; he protested that it was not his turn to wash up*. [11] (*tr*) *Chiefly US* to object forcefully to: *leaflets protesting Dr King's murder*. [12] (*tr*) to declare formally that (a bill of exchange or promissory note) has been dishonoured.
▷HISTORY C14: from Latin *prōtestārī* to make a formal declaration, from *prō-* before + *testārī* to assert
▸**pro'testant** ADJECTIVE, NOUN ▸**pro'tester** *or* **pro'testor** NOUN ▸**pro'testingly** ADVERB

Protestant (ˈprɒtɪstənt) NOUN **a** an adherent of Protestantism. **b** (*as modifier*): *the Protestant Church*.

Protestant Episcopal Church NOUN the full title of the **Episcopal Church.**

Protestantism (ˈprɒtɪstənˌtɪzəm) NOUN [1] the religion or religious system of any of the Churches of Western Christendom that are separated from the Roman Catholic Church and adhere substantially to principles established by Luther, Calvin, etc., in the Reformation. [2] the Protestant Churches collectively. [3] adherence to the principles of the Reformation.

protestation (ˌprəʊtɛsˈteɪʃən) NOUN [1] the act of protesting. [2] something protested about. [3] a strong declaration.

Proteus (ˈprəʊtɪəs) NOUN *Greek myth* a prophetic sea god capable of changing his shape at will.

Proteus syndrome NOUN *Pathol* a condition caused by malfunction in cell growth, in which bone and flesh tissue overgrow in localized areas of the body.

prothalamion (ˌprəʊθəˈleɪmɪən) *or* **prothalamium** NOUN, *plural* **-mia** (-mɪə). a song or poem in celebration of a marriage.
▷HISTORY C16: from Greek *pro-* before + *thalamos* marriage; coined by Edmund Spenser, on the model of EPITHALAMION

prothallus (prəʊˈθæləs) *or* **prothallium** (prəʊˈθælɪəm) NOUN, *plural* **-li** (-laɪ) *or* **-lia** (-lɪə). *Botany* the small flat free-living gametophyte that bears the reproductive organs of ferns, horsetails, and club mosses. It is either a green disc on the soil surface or it is colourless and subterranean.
▷HISTORY C19: from New Latin, from *pro-* before + Greek *thallus* a young shoot
▸**pro'thallic** *or* **pro'thallial** ADJECTIVE

prothesis (ˈprɒθɪsɪs) NOUN [1] a process in the development of a language by which a phoneme or syllable is prefixed to a word to facilitate pronunciation: *Latin "scala" gives Spanish "escala" by prothesis*. [2] *Eastern Orthodox Church* the solemn preparation of the Eucharistic elements before consecration.
▷HISTORY C16: via Late Latin from Greek: a setting out in public, from *pro-* forth + *thesis* a placing
▸**prothetic** (prəˈθɛtɪk) ADJECTIVE ▸**pro'thetically** ADVERB

prothonotary (ˌprəʊθəˈnəʊtərɪ, -trɪ, prəʊˈθɒnə-) *or* **protonotary** NOUN, *plural* **-taries**. (formerly) a chief clerk in certain law courts.
▷HISTORY C15: from Medieval Latin *prōthonotārius*, from *prōtho-* PROTO- + Late Latin *notārius* NOTARY
▸**prothonotarial** (prəʊˌθɒnəˈtɛərɪəl) *or* **proˌtono'tarial** ADJECTIVE

prothorax (prəʊˈθɔːræks) NOUN, *plural* **-thoraxes** *or* **-thoraces** (-ˈθɔːrəˌsiːz). the first segment of the thorax of an insect, which bears the first pair of walking legs. See also **mesothorax, metathorax.**

prothrombin (prəʊˈθrɒmbɪn) NOUN *Biochem* a zymogen found in blood that gives rise to thrombin on activation. See also **phylloquinone.**

protist (ˈprəʊtɪst) NOUN (in some classification systems) any organism belonging to the kingdom *Protista*, originally including bacteria, protozoans, algae, and fungi, regarded as distinct from plants and animals. It was later restricted to protozoans, unicellular algae, and simple fungi. See also **protoctist.**
▷HISTORY C19: from New Latin *Protista* most primitive organisms, from Greek *prōtistos* the very first, from *prōtos* first

protium (ˈprəʊtɪəm) NOUN the most common isotope of hydrogen, having a mass number of 1.
▷HISTORY C20: New Latin, from PROTO- + -IUM

proto- *or sometimes before a vowel* **prot-** COMBINING FORM [1] indicating the first in time, order, or rank: *protomartyr*. [2] primitive, ancestral, or original: *prototype*. [3] indicating the reconstructed earliest stage of a language: *Proto-Germanic*. [4] indicating the first in a series of chemical compounds: *protoxide*. [5] indicating the parent of a chemical compound or an element: *protactinium*.
▷HISTORY from Greek *prōtos* first, from *pro* before; see PRO-[2]

protoactinium (ˌprəʊtəʊækˈtɪnɪəm) NOUN the former name of **protactinium.**

protochordate (ˌprəʊtəʊˈkɔːdeɪt) NOUN 1 any chordate animal of the subphyla *Hemichordata* (acorn worms), *Urochordata* (tunicates), and *Cephalochordata* (lancelets). ◆ ADJECTIVE 2 of or relating to protochordates.

protocol (ˈprəʊtəˌkɒl) NOUN 1 the formal etiquette and code of behaviour, precedence, and procedure for state and diplomatic ceremonies. 2 a memorandum or record of an agreement, esp one reached in international negotiations, a meeting, etc. 3 **a** an amendment to a treaty or convention. **b** an annexe appended to a treaty to deal with subsidiary matters or to render the treaty more lucid. **c** a formal international agreement or understanding on some matter. 4 *Philosophy* In full: **protocol statement.** a statement that is immediately verifiable by experience. See **logical positivism.** 5 *Computing* the set form in which data must be presented for handling by a particular computer configuration, esp in the transmission of information between different computer systems.
▷HISTORY C16: from Medieval Latin *prōtocollum,* from Late Greek *prōtokollon* sheet glued to the front of a manuscript, from PROTO- + *kolla* glue

protoctist (prəʊˈtɒktɪst) NOUN (in modern biological classifications) any unicellular or simple multicellular organism belonging to the kingdom *Protoctista,* which includes protozoans, algae, and slime moulds.
▷HISTORY C19: from New Latin *protoctista,* perhaps from Greek *prototokos* first born

protogalaxy (ˌprəʊtəʊˈɡæləksɪ) NOUN, *plural* **-axies.** a cloud of gas in the early stages of its evolution into a galaxy.

protogenic (ˌprəʊtəˈdʒɛnɪk) ADJECTIVE *Chem* (of a compound) able to donate a hydrogen ion (proton) in a chemical reaction.

Proto-Germanic NOUN the prehistoric unrecorded language that was the ancestor of all Germanic languages.

protogynous (prəʊˈtɒdʒɪnəs) ADJECTIVE (of plants and hermaphrodite animals) producing female gametes before male ones. Compare **protandrous.**
▸**proˈtogyny** NOUN

protohistory (ˌprəʊtəʊˈhɪstərɪ, -ˈhɪstrɪ) NOUN the period or stage of human development or of a particular culture immediately prior to the emergence of writing.
▸**protohistoric** (ˌprəʊtəʊhɪˈstɒrɪk) ADJECTIVE

protohuman (ˌprəʊtəʊˈhjuːmən) NOUN 1 any of various prehistoric primates that resembled modern man. ◆ ADJECTIVE 2 of or relating to any of these primates.

Proto-Indo-European NOUN the prehistoric unrecorded language that was the ancestor of all Indo-European languages.

protolanguage (ˌprəʊtəʊˈlæŋɡwɪdʒ) NOUN an extinct and unrecorded language reconstructed by comparison of its recorded or living descendants. Also called: **Ursprache.**

protolithic (ˌprəʊtəʊˈlɪθɪk) ADJECTIVE of or referring to the earliest Stone Age.

protomartyr (ˌprəʊtəʊˈmɑːtə) NOUN 1 St Stephen as the first Christian martyr. 2 the first martyr to lay down his life in any cause.

protomorphic (ˌprəʊtəʊˈmɔːfɪk) ADJECTIVE *Biology* primitive in structure; primordial.

proton (ˈprəʊtɒn) NOUN a stable, positively charged elementary particle, found in atomic nuclei in numbers equal to the atomic number of the element. It is a baryon with a charge of $1.602176462 \times 10^{-19}$ coulomb, a rest mass of $1.672\ 62159 \times 10^{-27}$ kilogram, and spin ½.
▷HISTORY C20: from Greek *prōtos* first

protonema (ˌprəʊtəˈniːmə) NOUN, *plural* **-nemata** (-ˈniːmətə). a branched threadlike structure that grows from a moss spore and eventually develops into the moss plant.
▷HISTORY C19: from New Latin, from PROTO- + Greek *nema* thread
▸ˌ**protoˈnemal** *or* **protonematal** (ˌprəʊtəˈniːmətᵊl, -ˈnɛmətᵊl) ADJECTIVE

protonic (prəʊˈtɒnɪk) ADJECTIVE *Chem* (of a solvent, such as water) able to donate hydrogen ions to solute molecules.

proton microscope NOUN a powerful type of microscope that uses a beam of protons, giving high resolution and sharp contrast.

proton number NOUN another name for **atomic number.** Symbol: *Z.*

Proto-Norse NOUN the North Germanic language of Scandinavia up to about 700 A.D. See also **Old Norse.**

proton-pump inhibitor NOUN any of a group of drugs used to treat excessive secretion of acid in the stomach and any resulting ulcers. They block the enzyme (proton pump) in the cells of the gastric glands that secrete hydrochloric acid.

protopathic (ˌprəʊtəˈpæθɪk) ADJECTIVE *Physiol* 1 of or relating to a sensory nerve that perceives only coarse stimuli, such as pain. 2 of or relating to such perception.
▷HISTORY C20: from PROTO- + Greek *pathos* suffering, disease + -IC
▸**protopathy** (prəʊˈtɒpəθɪ) NOUN

protophilic (ˌprəʊtəˈfɪlɪk) ADJECTIVE *Chem* having or involving an affinity for hydrogen ions (protons).

protoplanet (ˌprəʊtəʊˈplænɪt) NOUN a planet in its early stages of evolution by the process of accretion.

protoplasm (ˈprəʊtəˌplæzəm) NOUN *Biology* the living contents of a cell, differentiated into cytoplasm and nucleoplasm.
▷HISTORY C19: from New Latin, from PROTO- + Greek *plasma* form
▸ˌ**protoˈplasmic** ADJECTIVE

protoplast (ˈprəʊtəˌplæst) NOUN a unit consisting of the living parts of a cell, including the protoplasm and cell membrane but not the vacuoles or (in plants) the cell wall.
▷HISTORY C16: from Late Latin *prōtoplastus* the first-formed, from Greek *prōtoplastos,* from PROTO- + *plassein* to shape
▸ˌ**protoˈplastic** ADJECTIVE

protoporphyrin (ˌprəʊtəʊˈpɔːfɪrɪn) NOUN a type of porphyrin that, when combined with an iron atom, forms haem, the oxygen-bearing prosthetic group of the red blood pigment haemoglobin.

Protosemitic (ˌprəʊtəʊsɪˈmɪtɪk) NOUN the hypothetical parent language of the Semitic group of languages.

protostar (ˈprəʊtəʊˌstɑː) NOUN a cloud of interstellar gas and dust that gradually collapses, forming a hot dense core, and evolves into a star once nuclear fusion can occur in the core.

protostele (ˈprəʊtəˌstiːl, -ˌstiːlɪ) NOUN a simple type of stele with a central core of xylem surrounded by a cylinder of phloem: occurs in most roots and the stems of ferns, etc.
▸ˌ**protoˈstelic** ADJECTIVE

prototherian (ˌprəʊtəʊˈθɪərɪən) ADJECTIVE 1 of, relating to, or belonging to the *Prototheria,* a subclass of mammals that includes the monotremes. ◆ NOUN 2 any prototherian mammal; a monotreme. ◆ Compare **eutherian, metatherian.**
▷HISTORY C19: New Latin, from PROTO- + Greek *theria* wild animals

prototrophic (ˌprəʊtəˈtrɒfɪk) ADJECTIVE 1 (esp of bacteria) feeding solely on inorganic matter. 2 (of cultured bacteria, fungi, etc.) having no specific nutritional requirements.

prototype (ˈprəʊtəˌtaɪp) NOUN 1 one of the first units manufactured of a product, which is tested so that the design can be changed if necessary before the product is manufactured commercially. 2 a person or thing that serves as an example of a type. 3 *Biology* the ancestral or primitive form of a species or other group; an archetype.
▸ˌ**protoˈtypal** *or* **prototypic** (ˌprəʊtəˈtɪpɪk) *or* ˌ**protoˈtypical** ADJECTIVE

protoxide (prəʊˈtɒksaɪd) NOUN the oxide of an element that contains the smallest amount of oxygen of any of its oxides.

protoxylem (ˌprəʊtəˈzaɪləm) NOUN the first-formed xylem tissue, consisting of extensible thin-walled cells thickened with rings or spirals of lignin. Compare **metaxylem.**

protozoan (ˌprəʊtəˈzəʊən) NOUN, *plural* **-zoa** (-ˈzəʊə) *or* **-zoans.** 1 Also called: **protozoon** (ˌprəʊtəˈzəʊɒn). ◆ PLURAL **-zoa.** any of various minute unicellular organisms formerly regarded as invertebrates of the phylum *Protozoa* but now usually classified in certain phyla of protoctists. Protozoans include flagellates, ciliates, sporozoans, amoebas, and foraminifers. ◆ ADJECTIVE *also* ˌ**protoˈzoic.** 2 of or relating to protozoans.
▷HISTORY C19: via New Latin from Greek PROTO- + *zoion* animal

protozoology (ˌprəʊtəʊzəʊˈɒlədʒɪ) NOUN the branch of biology concerned with the study of protozoans.
▸**protozoological** (ˌprəʊtəʊˌzəʊəˈlɒdʒɪkᵊl) ADJECTIVE
▸ˌ**protozoˈologist** NOUN

protract (prəˈtrækt) VERB (*tr*) 1 to lengthen or extend (a speech, etc.); prolong in time. 2 (of a muscle) to draw, thrust, or extend (a part, etc.) forwards. 3 to plot or draw using a protractor and scale.
▷HISTORY C16: from Latin *prōtrahere* to prolong, from PRO-[1] + *trahere* to drag
▸**proˈtractedly** ADVERB ▸**proˈtractedness** NOUN
▸**proˈtractive** ADJECTIVE

protractile (prəˈtræktaɪl) *or less commonly* **protractible** ADJECTIVE able to be extended or protruded: *protractile muscle.*

protraction (prəˈtrækʃən) NOUN 1 the act or process of protracting. 2 the state or condition of being protracted. 3 a prolongation or protrusion. 4 an extension of something in time or space. 5 something that is extended in time or space. 6 the irregular lengthening of a syllable that is usually short.

protractor (prəˈtræktə) NOUN 1 an instrument for measuring or drawing angles on paper, usually a flat semicircular transparent plastic sheet graduated in degrees. 2 a person or thing that protracts. 3 a surgical instrument for removing a bullet from the body. 4 *Anatomy* a former term for **extensor.**

protrude (prəˈtruːd) VERB 1 to thrust or cause to thrust forwards or outwards. 2 to project or cause to project from or as if from a surface.
▷HISTORY C17: from Latin, from PRO-[2] + *trudere* to thrust
▸**proˈtrudable** ADJECTIVE ▸**proˈtrudent** ADJECTIVE

protrusile (prəˈtruːsaɪl) ADJECTIVE *Zoology* capable of being thrust forwards: *protrusile jaws.* Also: **projectile.**

protrusion (prəˈtruːʒən) NOUN 1 something that protrudes. 2 the state or condition of being protruded. 3 the act or process of protruding.

protrusive (prəˈtruːsɪv) ADJECTIVE 1 tending to project or jut outwards. 2 a less common word for **obtrusive.** 3 *Archaic* causing propulsion.
▸**proˈtrusively** ADVERB ▸**proˈtrusiveness** NOUN

protuberant (prəˈtjuːbərənt) ADJECTIVE swelling out from the surrounding surface; bulging.
▷HISTORY C17: from Late Latin *prōtūberāre* to swell, from PRO-[1] + *tūber* swelling
▸**proˈtuberance** *or* **proˈtuberancy** NOUN ▸**proˈtuberantly** ADVERB

protuberate (prəˈtjuːbəˌreɪt) VERB (*intr*) *Rare* to swell out or project from the surrounding surface; bulge out.

protyle (ˈprəʊtaɪl) *or* **protyl** (ˈprəʊtɪl) NOUN a hypothetical primitive substance from which the chemical elements were supposed to have been formed.
▷HISTORY C19: from Greek *prōt-* PROTO- + *hylē* substance

proud (praʊd) ADJECTIVE 1 (foll by *of,* an infinitive, or a clause) pleased or satisfied, as with oneself, one's possessions, achievements, etc, or with another person, his or her achievements, qualities, etc. 2 feeling honoured or gratified by or as if by some distinction. 3 having an inordinately high opinion of oneself; arrogant or haughty. 4 characterized by or proceeding from a sense of pride: *a proud moment.* 5 having a proper sense of self-respect. 6 stately or distinguished. 7 bold or fearless. 8 (of a surface, edge, etc.) projecting or protruding from the surrounding area. 9 (of animals) restive or excited, esp sexually; on heat. ◆ ADVERB 10 **do (someone) proud. a** to entertain (someone) on a grand scale: *they did us proud at the hotel.* **b** to honour or distinguish (a person): *his honesty did him proud.*
▷HISTORY Late Old English *prūd,* from Old French *prud, prod* brave, from Late Latin *prōde* useful, from

Latin *prōdesse* to be of value, from *prōd-*, variant of *prō-* for + *esse* to be
▸ 'proudly ADVERB ▸ 'proudness NOUN

proud flesh NOUN a non-technical name for **granulation tissue.**
▷HISTORY C14: from PROUD (in the sense: swollen, protruding)

prounion (prəʊ'juːnjən) ADJECTIVE 1 in favour of or supporting the constitutional union between two or more countries. 2 in favour of or supporting the trades union movement.

Proustian ('pruːstɪən) ADJECTIVE 1 of or relating to Marcel Proust, the French novelist (1871–1922), his works, or his style. ◆ NOUN 2 an admirer of Marcel Proust's works.

proustite ('pruːstaɪt) NOUN a red mineral consisting of silver arsenic sulphide in hexagonal crystalline form. Formula: Ag_3AsS_3.
▷HISTORY C19: from French, named after Joseph Louis Proust (1754–1826), French chemist

prov. ABBREVIATION FOR: 1 province. 2 provincial. 3 provisional.

Prov. 1 *Bible* Proverbs. 2 Province. 3 Provost.

prove (pruːv) VERB **proves, proving, proved; proved** *or* **proven.** (*mainly tr*) 1 (*may take a clause as object or an infinitive*) to establish or demonstrate the truth or validity of; verify, esp by using an established sequence of procedures or statements. 2 to establish the quality of, esp by experiment or scientific analysis. 3 *Law* to establish the validity and genuineness of (a will). 4 to show (oneself) able or courageous. 5 (*copula*) to be found or shown (to be): *this has proved useless; he proved to be invaluable.* 6 *Printing* to take a trial impression of (type, etc.). 7 (*intr*) (of dough) to rise in a warm place before baking. 8 *Archaic* to undergo.
▷HISTORY C12: from Old French *prover,* from Latin *probāre* to test, from *probus* honest
▸ 'provable ADJECTIVE ▸ ˌprova'bility NOUN ▸ 'provably ADVERB

proven ('pruːvᵊn) VERB 1 a past participle of **prove.** 2 See **not proven.** ◆ ADJECTIVE 3 tried; tested: *a proven method.*
▸ 'provenly ADVERB

provenance ('prɒvɪnəns) *or chiefly US* **provenience** (prəʊ'viːnɪəns) NOUN a place of origin, esp that of a work of art or archaeological specimen.
▷HISTORY C19: from French, from *provenir,* from Latin *prōvenīre* to originate, from *venīre* to come

Provençal (ˌprɒvɒn'sɑːl; *French* prɔvɑ̃sal) ADJECTIVE 1 relating to, denoting, or characteristic of Provence, its inhabitants, their dialect of French, or their Romance language. ◆ NOUN 2 a language of Provence, closely related to Catalan, French, and Italian, belonging to the Romance group of the Indo-European family. It was important in the Middle Ages as a literary language, and attempts have been made since the 19th century to revive its literary status. See also **langue d'oc.** 3 a native or inhabitant of Provence.

Provençale (ˌprɒvɒn'sɑːl; *French* prɔvɑ̃sal) ADJECTIVE (of dishes) prepared with garlic, oil, and often tomatoes.

Provence (*French* prɔvɑ̃s) NOUN a former province of SE France, on the Mediterranean, and the River Rhône: forms part of the administrative region of Provence-Alpes-Côte d'Azur.

provender ('prɒvɪndə) NOUN 1 any dry feed or fodder for domestic livestock. 2 food in general.
▷HISTORY C14: from Old French *provendre,* from Late Latin *praebenda* grant, from Latin *praebēre* to proffer; influenced also by Latin *prōvidēre* to look after

proventriculus (ˌprəʊvɛn'trɪkjʊləs) NOUN, *plural* **-triculi** (-'trɪkjʊˌlaɪ). 1 the first part of the stomach of birds, the gizzard. 2 the thick muscular stomach of crustaceans and insects; gizzard.
▷HISTORY C19: from New Latin, from Latin PRO-[1] + *ventriculus* little belly, from *venter* belly
▸ ˌproven'tricular ADJECTIVE

proverb ('prɒvɜːb) NOUN 1 a short, memorable, and often highly condensed saying embodying, esp with bold imagery, some commonplace fact or experience. 2 a person or thing exemplary in respect of a characteristic: *Antarctica is a proverb for extreme cold.* 3 *Ecclesiast* a wise saying or admonition providing guidance. ◆ VERB (*tr*) 4 to utter or describe (something) in the form of a proverb. 5 to make (something) a proverb.
▷HISTORY C14: via Old French from Latin *prōverbium,* from *verbum* word

proverbial (prə'vɜːbɪəl) ADJECTIVE 1 (*prenominal*) commonly or traditionally referred to, esp as being an example of some peculiarity, characteristic, etc. 2 of, connected with, embodied in, or resembling a proverb.
▸ pro'verbially ADVERB

Proverbs ('prɒvɜːbz) NOUN (*functioning as singular*) a book of the Old Testament consisting of the proverbs of various Israelite sages including Solomon.

provide (prə'vaɪd) VERB (*mainly tr*) 1 to put at the disposal of; furnish or supply. 2 to afford; yield: *this meeting provides an opportunity to talk.* 3 (*intr; often foll by for or against*) to take careful precautions (over): *he provided against financial ruin by wise investment.* 4 (*intr; foll by for*) to supply means of support (to), esp financially: *he provides for his family.* 5 (in statutes, documents, etc.) to determine (what is to happen in certain contingencies), esp by including a proviso condition. 6 to confer and induct into ecclesiastical offices. 7 *Now rare* to have or get in store: *in summer many animals provide their winter food.*
▷HISTORY C15: from Latin *prōvidēre* to provide for, from *prō-* beforehand + *vidēre* to see
▸ pro'vider NOUN

providence ('prɒvɪdəns) NOUN 1 **a** *Christianity* God's foreseeing protection and care of his creatures. **b** such protection and care as manifest by some other force. 2 a supposed manifestation of such care and guidance. 3 the foresight or care exercised by a person in the management of his affairs or resources.

Providence[1] ('prɒvɪdəns) NOUN *Christianity* God, esp as showing foreseeing care and protection of his creatures.
▷HISTORY C14: via French from Latin *prōvidentia,* from *prōvidēre* to provide; see PROVIDE, -ENCE

Providence[2] ('prɒvɪdəns) NOUN a port in NE Rhode Island, capital of the state, at the head of Narragansett Bay: founded by Roger Williams in 1636. Pop.: 173 618 (2000).

provident ('prɒvɪdənt) ADJECTIVE 1 providing for future needs. 2 exercising foresight in the management of one's affairs or resources. 3 characterized by or proceeding from foresight.
▷HISTORY C15: from Latin *prōvidens* foreseeing, from *prōvidēre* to PROVIDE
▸ 'providently ADVERB

provident club NOUN *Brit* a hire-purchase system offered by some large retail organizations.

providential (ˌprɒvɪ'dɛnʃəl) ADJECTIVE relating to, characteristic of, or presumed to proceed from or as if from divine providence.
▸ ˌprovi'dentially ADVERB

provident society NOUN another name for **friendly society.**

providing (prə'vaɪdɪŋ) *or* **provided** CONJUNCTION (*subordinating;* sometimes foll by *that*) on the condition or understanding (that): *I'll play, providing you pay me.*

province ('prɒvɪns) NOUN 1 a territory governed as a unit of a country or empire. 2 a district, territory, or region. 3 (*plural;* usually preceded by *the*) those parts of a country lying outside the capital and other large cities and regarded as outside the mainstream of sophisticated culture. 4 *Ecology* a subdivision of a region, characterized by a particular fauna and flora. 5 an area or branch of learning, activity, etc. 6 the field or extent of a person's activities or office. 7 *RC Church, Church of England* an ecclesiastical territory, usually consisting of several dioceses, and having an archbishop or metropolitan at its head. 8 a major administrative and territorial subdivision of a religious order. 9 *History* a region of the Roman Empire outside Italy ruled by a governor from Rome.
▷HISTORY C14: from Old French, from Latin *prōvincia* conquered territory

Provincetown ('prɒvɪnsˌtaʊn) NOUN a village in SE Massachusetts, at the tip of Cape Cod: scene of the first landing place of the Pilgrims (1620) and of the signing of the Mayflower Compact (1620). Pop.: 3374 (1990).

provincewide ('prɒvɪnsˌwaɪd) *Canadian* ◆ ADJECTIVE 1 covering or available to the whole of a province: *a provincewide referendum.* ◆ ADVERB 2 throughout a province: *an advertising campaign to go provincewide.*

provincial (prə'vɪnʃəl) ADJECTIVE 1 of or connected with a province. 2 characteristic of or connected with the provinces; local. 3 having attitudes and opinions supposedly common to people living in the provinces; rustic or unsophisticated; limited. 4 *NZ* denoting a football team representing a province, one of the historical administrative areas of New Zealand. ◆ NOUN 5 a person lacking the sophistications of city life; rustic or narrow-minded individual. 6 a person coming from or resident in a province or the provinces. 7 the head of an ecclesiastical province. 8 the head of a major territorial subdivision of a religious order.
▸ provinciality (prəˌvɪnʃɪ'ælɪtɪ) NOUN ▸ pro'vincially ADVERB

Provincial Council NOUN (formerly) a council administering any of the New Zealand provinces.

provincialism (prə'vɪnʃəˌlɪzəm) NOUN 1 narrowness of mind or outlook; lack of sophistication. 2 a word or attitude characteristic of a provincial. 3 attention to the affairs of one's province rather than the whole nation. 4 the state or quality of being provincial. ◆ Also called: **localism.**

provincial police NOUN (in Canada) the police force of a province, esp Ontario or Quebec.

proving ground NOUN a place or situation in which something new, such as equipment or a theory, can be tested.

provirus ('prəʊˌvaɪrəs) NOUN the inactive form of a virus in a host cell.

provision (prə'vɪʒən) NOUN 1 the act of supplying or providing food, etc. 2 something that is supplied or provided. 3 preparations made beforehand (esp in the phrase **make provision for**). 4 (*plural*) food and other necessities, esp for an expedition. 5 (*plural*) food obtained for a household. 6 a demand, condition, or stipulation formally incorporated in a document; proviso. 7 the conferring of and induction into ecclesiastical offices. ◆ VERB 8 (*tr*) to supply with provisions.
▷HISTORY C14: from Latin *prōvīsiō* a providing; see PROVIDE
▸ pro'visioner NOUN

provisional (prə'vɪʒənᵊl) *or less commonly* **provisionary** (prə'vɪʒənərɪ) ADJECTIVE 1 subject to later alteration; temporary or conditional: *a provisional decision.* ◆ NOUN 2 a postage stamp surcharged during an emergency to alter the stamp's denomination or significance until a new or regular issue is printed.
▸ pro'visionally ADVERB

Provisional (prə'vɪʒənᵊl) ADJECTIVE 1 of, designating, or relating to the unofficial factions of the IRA and Sinn Féin that became increasingly dominant following a split in 1969. The Provisional movement remained committed to a policy of terrorism until its ceasefires of the mid-1990s. ◆ NOUN 2 Also called: **Provo.** a member of the Provisional IRA or Sinn Féin. ◆ Compare **Official.**

proviso (prə'vaɪzəʊ) NOUN, *plural* **-sos** *or* **-soes.** 1 a clause in a document or contract that embodies a condition or stipulation. 2 a condition or stipulation.
▷HISTORY C15: from Medieval Latin phrase *prōvīsō quod* it being provided that, from Latin *prōvīsus* provided

provisory (prə'vaɪzərɪ) ADJECTIVE 1 containing a proviso; conditional. 2 another word for **provisional.**
▸ pro'visorily ADVERB

provitamin (prəʊ'vɪtəmɪn) NOUN a substance, such as carotene, that is converted into a vitamin in animal tissues.

Provo ('prəʊvəʊ) NOUN, *plural* **-vos.** another name for a **Provisional** (sense 2).

provocation (ˌprɒvə'keɪʃən) NOUN 1 the act of provoking or inciting. 2 something that causes indignation, anger, etc. 3 *English criminal law* words or conduct that incite a person to attack another.

provocative (prə'vɒkətɪv) ADJECTIVE acting as a stimulus or incitement, esp to anger or sexual desire; provoking: *a provocative look; a provocative remark*.
▸**pro'vocatively** ADVERB ▸**pro'vocativeness** NOUN

provoke (prə'vəʊk) VERB (*tr*) 1 to anger or infuriate. 2 to cause to act or behave in a certain manner; incite or stimulate. 3 to promote (certain feelings, esp anger, indignation, etc.) in a person. 4 *Obsolete* to summon.
▷HISTORY C15: from Latin *prōvocāre* to call forth, from *vocāre* to call
▸**pro'voking** ADJECTIVE ▸**pro'vokingly** ADVERB

provolone (ˌprəʊvə'ləʊnɪ) NOUN a mellow, pale yellow, soft, and sometimes smoked cheese, made of cow's milk: usually moulded in the shape of a pear.
▷HISTORY Italian, from *provola,* apparently from Medieval Latin *probula* cheese made from buffalo milk

provost ('prɒvəst) NOUN 1 an appointed person who superintends or presides. 2 the head of certain university colleges or schools. 3 (in Scotland) the chairman and civic head of certain district councils or (formerly) of a burgh council. Compare **convener** (sense 2). 4 *Church of England* the senior dignitary of one of the more recent cathedral foundations. 5 *RC Church* **a** the head of a cathedral chapter in England and some other countries. **b** (formerly) the member of a monastic community second in authority under the abbot. 6 (in medieval times) an overseer, steward, or bailiff in a manor. 7 *Obsolete* a prison warder. 8 (prə'vəʊ) *Brit and Canadian military* a military policeman.
▷HISTORY Old English *profost,* from Medieval Latin *prōpositus* placed at the head (of), from Latin *praepōnere* to place first, from *prae-* before + *pōnere* to put

provost court (prə'vəʊ) NOUN a military court for trying people charged with minor offences in an occupied area.

provost guard (prə'vəʊ) NOUN (esp in the US) a detachment under command of the provost marshal.

provost marshal (prə'vəʊ) NOUN the officer in charge of military police and thus responsible for military discipline in a large camp, area, or city.

prow (praʊ) NOUN the bow of a vessel.
▷HISTORY C16: from Old French *proue,* from Latin *prora,* from Greek *prōra;* related to Latin *pro* in front

prowar ('prəʊ'wɔː) ADJECTIVE in favour of or supporting war.

prowess ('praʊɪs) NOUN 1 outstanding or superior skill or ability. 2 bravery or fearlessness, esp in battle.
▷HISTORY C13: from Old French *proesce,* from *prou* good; see PROUD

prowl (praʊl) VERB 1 (when *intr,* often foll by *around* or *about*) to move stealthily around (a place) as if in search of prey or plunder. ◆ NOUN 2 the act of prowling. 3 **on the prowl. a** moving around stealthily. **b** zealously pursuing members of the opposite sex.
▷HISTORY C14 *prollen,* of unknown origin
▸**'prowler** NOUN

prox. ABBREVIATION FOR proximo (next month).

proxemics (prɒk'siːmɪks) NOUN (*functioning as singular*) the study of spatial interrelationships in humans or in populations of animals of the same species.

Proxima ('prɒksɪmə) NOUN a flare star in the constellation Centaurus that is the nearest star to the sun. It is a red dwarf of very low magnitude. Distance: 4.3 light years. Also called: **Proxima Centauri.** See also **Rigil Kent.**

proximal ('prɒksɪməl) ADJECTIVE 1 *Anatomy* situated close to the centre, median line, or point of attachment or origin. Compare **distal.** 2 another word for **proximate.**
▸**'proximally** ADVERB

proximate ('prɒksɪmɪt) *or* **proximal** ADJECTIVE 1 next or nearest in space or time. 2 very near; close. 3 immediately preceding or following in a series. 4 a less common word for **approximate.**
▷HISTORY C16: from Late Latin *proximāre* to draw near, from Latin *proximus* next, from *prope* near
▸**'proximately** ADVERB ▸**'proximateness** NOUN
▸**ˌproxi'mation** NOUN

proxime accessit ('prɒksɪmɪ æk'sɛsɪt) NOUN the person coming next after the winner in a competitive examination or an academic prize giving; runner-up.
▷HISTORY Latin: he came next

proximity (prɒk'sɪmɪtɪ) NOUN 1 nearness in space or time. 2 nearness or closeness in a series.
▷HISTORY C15: from Latin *proximitās* closeness; see PROXIMATE

proximity fuse NOUN an electronically triggered device designed to detonate an explosive charge in a missile, etc., at a predetermined distance from the target.

proximity talks PLURAL NOUN a diplomatic process whereby an impartial representative acts as go-between for two opposing parties who are willing to attend the same conference but unwilling to meet face to face.

proximo ('prɒksɪməʊ) ADVERB *Now rare except when abbreviated in formal correspondence* in or during the next or coming month: *a letter of the seventh proximo.* Abbreviation: **prox.** Compare **instant, ultimo.**
▷HISTORY C19: from Latin: in or on the next, from *proximus* next

proxy ('prɒksɪ) NOUN, *plural* **proxies.** 1 a person authorized to act on behalf of someone else; agent: *to vote by proxy.* 2 the authority, esp in the form of a document, given to a person to act on behalf of someone else.
▷HISTORY C15: *prokesye,* contraction of *procuracy,* from Latin *prōcūrātiō* procuration; see PROCURE

Prozac ('prəʊzæk) NOUN *Trademark* fluoxetine; a drug that prolongs the action of serotonin in the brain; used as an antidepressant.

PRP ABBREVIATION FOR: 1 performance-related pay. 2 profit-related pay.

prs ABBREVIATION FOR pairs.

PRT *Text messaging* ◆ ABBREVIATION FOR: 1 party. 2 personal rapid transit. 3 petroleum revenue tax.

prude (pruːd) NOUN a person who affects or shows an excessively modest, prim, or proper attitude, esp regarding sex.
▷HISTORY C18: from French, from *prudefemme,* from Old French *prode femme* respectable woman; see PROUD
▸**'prudish** ADJECTIVE ▸**'prudishly** ADVERB ▸**'prudishness** *or* **'prudery** NOUN

prudence ('pruːdəns) NOUN 1 caution in practical affairs; discretion or circumspection. 2 care taken in the management of one's resources. 3 consideration for one's own interests. 4 the condition or quality of being prudent.

prudent ('pruːdᵊnt) ADJECTIVE 1 discreet or cautious in managing one's activities; circumspect. 2 practical and careful in providing for the future. 3 exercising good judgment or common sense.
▷HISTORY C14: from Latin *prūdēns* far-sighted, contraction of *prōvidens* acting with foresight; see PROVIDENT
▸**'prudently** ADVERB

prudential (pruː'dɛnʃəl) ADJECTIVE 1 characterized by or resulting from prudence. 2 exercising prudence or sound judgment.
▸**pru'dentially** ADVERB

pruinose ('pruːɪˌnəʊs, -ˌnəʊz) ADJECTIVE *Botany* coated with a powdery or waxy bloom.
▷HISTORY C19: from Latin *pruīnōsus* frost-covered, from *pruīna* hoarfrost

prune[1] (pruːn) NOUN 1 a purplish-black partially dried fruit of any of several varieties of plum tree. 2 *Slang, chiefly Brit* a dull, uninteresting, or foolish person.
▷HISTORY C14: from Old French *prune,* from Latin *prūnum* plum, from Greek *prounon*

prune[2] (pruːn) VERB 1 to remove (dead or superfluous twigs, branches, etc.) from (a tree, shrub, etc.), esp by cutting off. 2 to remove (anything undesirable or superfluous) from (a book, etc.).
▷HISTORY C15: from Old French *proignier* to clip, probably from *provigner* to prune vines, from *provain* layer (of a plant), from Latin *propāgo* a cutting
▸**'prunable** ADJECTIVE ▸**'pruner** NOUN

prune[3] (pruːn) VERB an archaic word for **preen**[1].

prunella[1] (pruː'nɛlə), **prunelle** (pruː'nɛl), *or* **prunello** (pruː'nɛləʊ) NOUN a strong fabric, esp a twill-weave worsted, used for gowns and the upper of some shoes.
▷HISTORY C17: perhaps from PRUNELLE, with reference to the colour of the cloth

prunella[2] (pruː'nɛlə) NOUN See **selfheal.**
▷HISTORY New Latin, altered from *brunella,* from German *Braüne* quinsy, which it was thought to cure

prunelle (pruː'nɛl) NOUN a green French liqueur made from sloes.
▷HISTORY C18: from French: a little plum, from *prune* PRUNE[1]

pruning hook NOUN a tool with a curved steel blade terminating in a hook, used for pruning.

prurient ('prʊərɪənt) ADJECTIVE 1 unusually or morbidly interested in sexual thoughts or practices 2 exciting or encouraging lustfulness; erotic.
▷HISTORY C17: from Latin *prūrīre* to itch, to lust after
▸**'prurience** NOUN ▸**'pruriently** ADVERB

prurigo (prʊə'raɪgəʊ) NOUN a chronic inflammatory disease of the skin characterized by the formation of papules and intense itching.
▷HISTORY C19: from Latin: an itch
▸**pruriginous** (prʊə'rɪdʒɪnəs) ADJECTIVE

pruritus (prʊə'raɪtəs) NOUN *Pathol* 1 any intense sensation of itching. 2 any of various conditions characterized by intense itching.
▷HISTORY C17: from Latin: an itching; see PRURIENT
▸**pruritic** (prʊə'rɪtɪk) ADJECTIVE

prusik ('prʌsɪk) NOUN *Mountaineering* 1 Also: **prusik knot.** a sliding knot that locks under pressure and can be used to form a loop (**prusik loop**) in which a climber can place his foot in order to stand or ascend a rope. ◆ VERB **-siks, -siking, -siked.** (*intr*) 2 to climb (up a standing rope) using prusik loops.
▷HISTORY C20: named after Dr *Prusik,* Austrian climber who devised the knot

Prussia ('prʌʃə) NOUN a former German state in N and central Germany, extending from France and the Low Countries to the Baltic Sea and Poland: developed as the chief military power of the Continent, leading the North German Confederation from 1867–71, when the German Empire was established; dissolved in 1947 and divided between East and West Germany, Poland, and the former Soviet Union. Area: (in 1939) 294 081 sq. km (113 545 sq. miles). German name: **Preussen.**

Prussian ('prʌʃən) ADJECTIVE 1 of, relating to, or characteristic of Prussia or its people, esp of the Junkers and their formal military tradition. ◆ NOUN 2 a German native or inhabitant of Prussia. 3 a member of a Baltic people formerly inhabiting the coastal area of the SE Baltic. 4 See **Old Prussian.**

Prussian blue NOUN 1 any of a number of blue pigments containing ferrocyanide or ferricyanide complexes. 2 **a** the blue or deep greenish-blue colour of this pigment. **b** (*as adjective*): *a Prussian-blue carpet.*

Prussianism ('prʌʃəˌnɪzəm) NOUN the ethos of the Prussian state and aristocracy, esp militarism and stern discipline.

Prussianize *or* **Prussianise** ('prʌʃəˌnaɪz) VERB (*tr*) to make Prussian in character, esp with respect to military matters.
▸**ˌPrussiani'zation** *or* **ˌPrussiani'sation** NOUN

prussiate ('prʌʃɪɪt) NOUN any cyanide, ferrocyanide, or ferricyanide.

prussic acid ('prʌsɪk) NOUN the weakly acidic extremely poisonous aqueous solution of hydrogen cyanide.
▷HISTORY C18: from French *acide prussique* Prussian acid, so called because obtained from Prussian blue

Prut (*Russian* prut) NOUN a river in E Europe, rising in the SW Ukraine and flowing generally southeast, forming part of the border between Romania and Moldova, to join the River Danube. Length: 853 km (530 miles).

PRW *Text messaging* ABBREVIATION FOR parents are watching.

pry[1] (praɪ) VERB **pries, prying, pried.** 1 (*intr;* often foll by *into*) to make an impertinent or uninvited inquiry (about a private matter, topic, etc.). ◆ NOUN,

plural **pries.** [2] the act of prying. [3] a person who pries.
▷HISTORY C14: of unknown origin

pry² (praɪ) VERB **pries, prying, pried.** the US and Canadian word for **prise.**
▷HISTORY C14: of unknown origin

pryer ('praɪə) NOUN a variant spelling of **prier.**

prytaneum (ˌprɪtə'niːəm) NOUN, *plural* **-nea** (-'niːə). the public hall of a city in ancient Greece.
▷HISTORY Latin, from Greek *prutaneion,* from *prutanis, prutaneus*

Przemyśl (*Polish* 'pʃɛmiʃl) NOUN a city in SE Poland, near the border with the Ukraine on the San River: a fortress in the early Middle Ages; belonged to Austria (1722–1918). Pop.: 67 000 (latest est.).

Przewalski's horse (ˌpɜːʒə'vælskɪz) NOUN a wild horse, *Equus przewalskii,* of W Mongolia, having an erect mane and no forelock: extinct in the wild, only a few survive in captivity.
▷HISTORY C19: named after the Russian explorer Nikolai Mikhailovich *Przewalski* (1839–88), who discovered it

ps THE INTERNET DOMAIN NAME FOR Palestinian Territories.

PS ABBREVIATION FOR: [1] Passenger Steamer. [2] phrase structure. [3] Police Sergeant. [4] Also: **ps.** postscript. [5] private secretary. [6] prompt side.

Ps. *or* **Psa.** *Bible* ABBREVIATION FOR Psalm.

PSA [1] prostatic specific antigen: an enzyme secreted by the prostate gland, increased levels of which are found in the blood of patients with cancer of the prostate. [2] (in New Zealand) Public Service Association.

psalm (sɑːm) NOUN [1] (*often capital*) any of the 150 sacred songs, lyric poems, and prayers that together constitute a book (Psalms) of the Old Testament. [2] a musical setting of one of these poems. [3] any sacred song or hymn.
▷HISTORY Old English, from Late Latin *psalmus,* from Greek *psalmos* song accompanied on the harp, from *psallein* to play (the harp)
▸**'psalmic** ADJECTIVE

psalmist ('sɑːmɪst) NOUN the composer of a psalm or psalms, esp (when *capital* and preceded by *the*) David, traditionally regarded as the author of The Book of Psalms.

psalmody ('sɑːmədɪ, 'sæl-) NOUN, *plural* **-dies.** [1] the act of singing psalms or hymns. [2] the art or practice of the setting to music or singing of psalms.
▷HISTORY C14: via Late Latin from Greek *psalmōdia* singing accompanied by a harp, from *psalmos* (see PSALM) + *ōidē* ODE
▸**'psalmodist** NOUN ▸**psalmodic** (sɑː'mɒdɪk, sæl-) ADJECTIVE

Psalms (sɑːmz) NOUN (*functioning as singular*) the collection of 150 psalms in the Old Testament, the full title of which is **The Book of Psalms.**

Psalter ('sɔːltə) NOUN [1] another name for **Psalms,** esp in the version in the Book of Common Prayer [2] a translation, musical, or metrical version of the Psalms. [3] a devotional or liturgical book containing a version of Psalms, often with a musical setting.
▷HISTORY Old English *psaltere,* from Late Latin *psaltērium,* from Greek *psaltērion* stringed instrument, from *psallein* to play a stringed instrument

psalterium (sɔːl'tɪərɪəm) NOUN, *plural* **-teria** (-'tɪərɪə). the third compartment of the stomach of ruminants, between the reticulum and abomasum. Also called: **omasum.**
▷HISTORY C19: from Latin *psaltērium* PSALTER; from the similarity of its folds to the pages of a book

psaltery ('sɔːltərɪ) NOUN, *plural* **-teries.** *Music* an ancient stringed instrument similar to the lyre, but having a trapezoidal sounding board over which the strings are stretched.
▷HISTORY Old English: see PSALTER

psammite ('sæmaɪt) NOUN a rare name for **sandstone.**
▷HISTORY C19: from Greek *psammos* sand
▸**psammitic** (sæ'mɪtɪk) ADJECTIVE

p's and q's PLURAL NOUN behaviour within social conventions; manners (esp in the phrase **to mind one's p's and q's**).
▷HISTORY altered from *p(lea)se and (than)k-you's*

PSBR (in Britain) ABBREVIATION FOR public sector borrowing requirement: the excess of government expenditure over receipts (mainly from taxation) that has to be financed by borrowing from the banks or the public.

psephite ('siːfaɪt) NOUN any rock, such as a breccia, that consists of large fragments embedded in a finer matrix.
▷HISTORY C19: via French from Greek *psēphos* a pebble
▸**psephitic** (siː'fɪtɪk) ADJECTIVE

psephology (sɛ'fɒlədʒɪ) NOUN the statistical and sociological study of elections.
▷HISTORY C20: from Greek *psephos* pebble, vote + -LOGY, from the ancient Greeks' custom of voting with pebbles
▸**psephological** (ˌsɛfə'lɒdʒɪkᵊl) ADJECTIVE
▸**ˌpsepho'logically** ADVERB ▸**pse'phologist** NOUN

pseud (sjuːd) NOUN [1] *Informal* a false, artificial, or pretentious person. ◆ ADJECTIVE [2] another word for **pseudo.**

pseud. ABBREVIATION FOR pseudonym.

pseudaxis (sjuː'dæksɪs) NOUN *Botany* another name for **sympodium.**

Pseudepigrapha (ˌsjuːdɪ'pɪgrəfə) PLURAL NOUN various Jewish writings from the first century B.C. to the first century A.D. that claim to have been divinely revealed but which have been excluded from the Greek canon of the Old Testament. Also called (in the Roman Catholic Church): **Apocrypha.**
▷HISTORY C17: from Greek *pseudepigraphos* falsely entitled, from PSEUDO- + *epigraphein* to inscribe
▸**Pseudepigraphic** (ˌsjuːdepɪ'græfɪk) *or* ˌ**Pseudepi'graphical** *or* ˌ**Pseude'pigraphous** ADJECTIVE

pseudo ('sjuːdəʊ) ADJECTIVE *Informal* not genuine; pretended.

pseudo- *or sometimes before a vowel* **pseud-** COMBINING FORM [1] false, pretending, or unauthentic: *pseudo-intellectual.* [2] having a close resemblance to: *pseudopodium.*
▷HISTORY from Greek *pseudēs* false, from *pseudein* to lie

pseudoarthrosis (ˌsjuːdəʊɑː'θrəʊsɪs) *or* **pseudarthrosis** (ˌsjuːdɑː'θrəʊsɪs) NOUN, *plural* **-ses** (-siːz). a joint formed by fibrous tissue bridging the gap between the two fragments of bone of an old fracture that have not united. Nontechnical names: **false joint, false ankylosis.** Also called: **nearthrosis.**

pseudocarp ('sjuːdəʊˌkɑːp) NOUN a fruit, such as the strawberry or apple, that includes parts other than the ripened ovary. Also called: **false fruit, accessory fruit.**
▸ˌ**pseudo'carpous** ADJECTIVE

pseudo-colour NOUN an artificial colour.

pseudocopulation (ˌsjuːdəʊˌkɒpjʊ'leɪʃən) NOUN *Botany* pollination of plants, esp orchids, by male insects while attempting to mate with flowers that resemble the female insect.

pseudocyesis (ˌsjuːdəʊsaɪ'iːsɪs) NOUN, *plural* **-ces** (-siːz). the technical name for **phantom pregnancy.**

pseudoephedrine (ˌsjuːdəʊ'ɛfɪˌdriːn, -ˌdrɪn) NOUN a drug similar in action to ephedrine, used extensively as a decongestant.

pseudohermaphroditism (ˌsjuːdəʊhɜː'mæfrədaɪˌtɪzəm) NOUN the congenital condition of having the organs of reproduction of one sex and the external genitalia, usually malformed, of the opposite sex. Compare **hermaphroditism.**

pseudo-intransitive ADJECTIVE denoting an occurrence of a normally transitive verb in which a direct object is not explicitly stated or forms the subject of the sentence, as in *Margaret is cooking* or *these apples cook well.*

pseudomonas (sjuː'dɒmənəs) NOUN, *plural* **pseudomonades** (ˌsjuːdəʊ'mɒnədiːz). any of a genus of rodlike Gram-negative bacteria that live in soil and decomposing organic matter: many species are pathogenic to plants and a few are pathogenic to man.
▷HISTORY C20: from New Latin, from PSEUDO- + Greek *monas* unit

pseudomorph ('sjuːdəʊˌmɔːf) NOUN a mineral that has an uncharacteristic crystalline form as a result of assuming the shape of another mineral that it has replaced.
▸ˌ**pseudo'morphic** *or* ˌ**pseudo'morphous** ADJECTIVE
▸ˌ**pseudo'morphism** NOUN

pseudomutuality (ˌsjuːdəʊˌmjuːtjʊ'ælɪtɪ) NOUN, *plural* **-ties.** *Psychol* a relationship between two persons in which conflict of views or opinions is solved by simply ignoring it.

pseudonym ('sjuːdəˌnɪm) NOUN a fictitious name adopted, esp by an author.
▷HISTORY C19: via French from Greek *pseudōnumon*
▸ˌ**pseudo'nymity** NOUN

pseudonymous (sjuː'dɒnɪməs) ADJECTIVE [1] having or using a false or assumed name. [2] writing or having been written under a pseudonym.
▸**pseu'donymously** ADVERB

pseudopodium (ˌsjuːdəʊ'pəʊdɪəm) NOUN, *plural* **-dia** (-dɪə). a temporary projection from the cell of an amoeboid protozoan, leucocyte, etc., used for feeding and locomotion.

pseudopregnancy ('sjuːdəʊˌpregnənsɪ) NOUN another name for **phantom pregnancy.**

pseudoscalar (ˌsjuːdəʊ'skeɪlə) NOUN *Maths* a variable quantity that has magnitude but not direction and is an odd function of the coordinates. Compare **pseudovector, scalar** (sense 1), **tensor** (sense 2), **vector** (sense 1).

pseudoscience (ˌsjuːdəʊ'saɪəns) NOUN a discipline or approach that pretends to be or has a close resemblance to science.
▸ˌ**pseudoˌscien'tific** ADJECTIVE

pseudovector (ˌsjuːdəʊ'vɛktə) NOUN *Maths* a variable quantity, such as angular momentum, that has magnitude and orientation with respect to an axis. The components are even functions of the coordinates. Also called: **axial vector.** Compare **pseudoscalar, scalar** (sense 1), **tensor** (sense 2), **vector** (sense 1).

psf ABBREVIATION FOR pounds per square foot.

PSG ABBREVIATION FOR phrase-structure grammar.

pshaw (pʃɔː) INTERJECTION *Becoming rare* an exclamation of disgust, impatience, disbelief, etc.

psi¹ ABBREVIATION FOR pounds per square inch.

psi² (psaɪ) NOUN [1] the 23rd letter of the Greek alphabet (Ψ, ψ), a composite consonant, transliterated as *ps.* [2] **a** paranormal or psychic phenomena collectively. **b** (*as modifier*): *psi powers.*

psia ABBREVIATION FOR pounds per square inch, absolute.

psid ABBREVIATION FOR pounds per square inch, differential.

psig ABBREVIATION FOR pounds per square inch, gauge.

psilocybin (ˌsɪlə'saɪbɪn, ˌsaɪlə-) NOUN a crystalline phosphate ester that is the active principle of the hallucinogenic fungus *Psilocybe mexicana.* Formula: $C_{12}H_{17}N_2O_4P$.
▷HISTORY C20: from New Latin *Psilocybe* (from Greek *psilos* bare + *kubē* head) + -IN

psilomelane (sɪ'lɒmɪˌleɪn) NOUN a common black to grey secondary mineral consisting of hydrated basic oxide of manganese and barium: a source of manganese. Formula: $BaMn_9O_{16}(OH)_4$. also called **romanechite.**
▷HISTORY C19: from Greek *psilos* bare + *melas* black

psi particle NOUN See **J/psi particle.**

PSIS (in New Zealand) ABBREVIATION FOR Public Service Investment Society, New Zealand's largest credit union.

psittacine ('sɪtəˌsaɪn, -sɪn) ADJECTIVE of, relating to, or resembling a parrot.
▷HISTORY C19: from Late Latin *psittacīnus,* from Latin *psittacus* a parrot

psittacosis (ˌsɪtə'kəʊsɪs) NOUN a disease of parrots, caused by the obligate intracellular parasite *Chlamydia psittaci,* that can be transmitted to man, in whom it produces inflammation of the lungs and pneumonia. Also called: **parrot fever, ornithosis.**
▷HISTORY C19: from New Latin, from Latin *psittacus* a parrot, from Greek *psittakos;* see -OSIS

PSK ABBREVIATION FOR phase shift keying: a digital data modulation system in which binary data signals switch the phase of a radio frequency carrier.

Pskov (*Russian* pskɔf) NOUN [1] a city in NW Russia, on the Velikaya River: one of the oldest Russian cities, at its height in the 13th and 14th centuries. Pop.: 202 900 (1999 est.). [2] **Lake.** the S part of Lake Peipus in NW Russia, linked to the main part by a channel 24 km (15 miles) long. Area: about 1000 sq. km (400 sq. miles).

PSL ABBREVIATION FOR private sector liquidity: a measure of the money supply. See **M4, M5.**

PSNI ABBREVIATION FOR Police Service of Northern Ireland, established in 2000.

psoas ('səʊəs) NOUN either of two muscles of the loins that aid in flexing and rotating the thigh.
▷HISTORY C17: from New Latin, from Greek *psoai* (pl)

psoralea (sə'reɪlɪə) NOUN any plant of the tropical and subtropical leguminous genus *Psoralea,* having curly leaves, white or purple flowers, and short one-seeded pods. See **breadroot.**
▷HISTORY C19: via New Latin from Greek *psōraleos* mangy, from *psōra* mange, an allusion to the glandular dots of the plant

psoriasis (sə'raɪəsɪs) NOUN a skin disease characterized by the formation of reddish spots and patches covered with silvery scales: tends to run in families.
▷HISTORY C17: via New Latin from Greek: itching disease, from *psōra* itch
▸**psoriatic** (ˌsɔːrɪ'ætɪk) ADJECTIVE

PSS *or* **pss.** ABBREVIATION FOR postscripts.

psst (pst) INTERJECTION an exclamation of beckoning, esp one made surreptitiously.

PST (in the US and Canada) ABBREVIATION FOR **Pacific Standard Time.**

PSTN ABBREVIATION FOR public switched telephone network: the conventional message switched telephone network.

PSV (in Britain) ABBREVIATION FOR public service vehicle (now called passenger carrying vehicle).

psych *or* **psyche** (saɪk) VERB (*tr*) *Informal* to psychoanalyse. See also **psych out, psych up.**
▷HISTORY C20: shortened from PSYCHOANALYSE

psyche ('saɪkɪ) NOUN the human mind or soul.
▷HISTORY C17: from Latin, from Greek *psukhē* breath, soul; related to Greek *psukhein* to breathe

Psyche ('saɪkɪ) NOUN *Greek myth* a beautiful girl loved by Eros (Cupid), who became the personification of the soul.

psychedelia (ˌsaɪkə'dɛlɪə, -'diːlɪə) NOUN (*functioning as singular or plural*) psychedelic objects, dress, music, etc.

psychedelic *or* **psychodelic** (ˌsaɪkɪ'dɛlɪk) ADJECTIVE 1 relating to or denoting new or altered perceptions or sensory experiences, as through the use of hallucinogenic drugs. 2 denoting any of the drugs, esp LSD, that produce these effects. 3 *Informal* (of painting, fabric design, etc.) having the vivid colours and complex patterns popularly associated with the visual effects of psychedelic states.
▷HISTORY C20: from PSYCHE + Greek *delos* visible
▸ˌ**psyche'delically** *or* ˌ**psycho'delically** ADVERB

psychiatric (ˌsaɪkɪ'ætrɪk) *or* **psychiatrical** ADJECTIVE of or relating to mental disorders or psychiatry.
▸ˌ**psychi'atrically** ADVERB

psychiatric social worker NOUN *Social welfare* (in Britain) a qualified person who works with mentally disordered people and their families, based in a psychiatric hospital, child guidance clinic, or social services department area team, and who may also be an approved social worker.

psychiatry (saɪ'kaɪətrɪ) NOUN the branch of medicine concerned with the diagnosis and treatment of mental disorders.
▸**psy'chiatrist** NOUN

psychic ('saɪkɪk) ADJECTIVE 1 **a** outside the possibilities defined by natural laws, as mental telepathy. **b** (of a person) sensitive to forces not recognized by natural laws. 2 mental as opposed to physical; psychogenic. 3 *Bridge* (of a bid) based on less strength than would normally be required to make the bid. ◆ NOUN 4 a person who is sensitive to parapsychological forces or influences.
▷HISTORY C19: from Greek *psukhikos* of the soul or life
▸'**psychical** ADJECTIVE ▸'**psychically** ADVERB

psychic determinism NOUN *Psychol* the assumption, made esp by Sigmund Freud, the Austrian psychiatrist (1856–1939), that mental processes do not occur by chance but that a cause can always be found for them.

psycho ('saɪkəʊ) NOUN, *plural* **-chos,** ADJECTIVE an informal word for **psychopath** or **psychopathic.**

psycho- *or sometimes before a vowel* **psych-** COMBINING FORM indicating the mind or psychological or mental processes: *psychology; psychogenesis; psychosomatic.*
▷HISTORY from Greek *psukhē* spirit, breath

psychoacoustics (ˌsaɪkəʊə'kuːstɪks) NOUN (*functioning as singular*) *Psychol* the study of the relationship between sounds and their physiological and psychological effects.

psychoactive (ˌsaɪkəʊ'æktɪv) ADJECTIVE capable of affecting mental activity: *a psychoactive drug.*

psychoanal. ABBREVIATION FOR psychoanalysis.

psychoanalyse *or US* **psychoanalyze** (ˌsaɪkəʊ'ænəˌlaɪz) VERB (*tr*) to examine or treat (a person) by psychoanalysis.
▸ˌ**psycho'anaˌlyser** *or US* ˌ**psycho'anaˌlyzer** NOUN

psychoanalysis (ˌsaɪkəʊə'nælɪsɪs) NOUN a method of studying the mind and treating mental and emotional disorders based on revealing and investigating the role of the unconscious mind.
▸**psychoanalyst** (ˌsaɪkəʊ'ænəlɪst) NOUN ▸**psychoanalytic** (ˌsaɪkəʊˌænə'lɪtɪk) *or* ˌ**psychoˌana'lytical** ADJECTIVE
▸ˌ**psychoˌana'lytically** ADVERB

psychobabble ('saɪkəʊˌbæbᵊl) NOUN *Informal* the jargon of psychology, esp as used and popularized in various types of psychotherapy.

psychobilly ('saɪkəˌbɪlɪ) NOUN, *plural* **-lies. a** loud frantic rockabilly music. **b** (*as modifier*): *a psychobilly track.*

psychobiography (ˌsaɪkəʊbaɪ'ɒgrəfɪ) NOUN a biography that pays particular attention to a person's psychological development.
▸**psychobiographical** (ˌsaɪkəʊbaɪəʊ'græfɪkᵊl) ADJECTIVE

psychobiology (ˌsaɪkəʊbaɪ'ɒlədʒɪ) NOUN *Psychol* the attempt to understand the psychology of organisms in terms of their biological functions and structures.
▸**psychobiological** (ˌsaɪkəʊˌbaɪə'lɒdʒɪkᵊl) ADJECTIVE
▸ˌ**psychobio'logically** ADVERB ▸ˌ**psychobi'ologist** NOUN

psychochemical (ˌsaɪkəʊ'kɛmɪkᵊl) NOUN 1 any of various chemical compounds whose primary effect is the alteration of the normal state of consciousness. ◆ ADJECTIVE 2 of or relating to such chemical compounds.

psychodrama ('saɪkəʊˌdrɑːmə) NOUN 1 *Psychiatry* a form of group therapy in which individuals act out, before an audience, situations from their past. 2 a film, television drama, etc., in which the psychological development of the characters is emphasized.
▸**psychodramatic** (ˌsaɪkəʊdrə'mætɪk) ADJECTIVE

psychodynamics (ˌsaɪkəʊdaɪ'næmɪks) NOUN (*functioning as singular*) *Psychol* the study of interacting motives and emotions.
▸ˌ**psychody'namic** ADJECTIVE ▸ˌ**psychody'namically** ADVERB

psychogalvanic response (ˌsaɪkəʊgəl'vænɪk) NOUN another name for **galvanic skin response.** Abbreviation: **PGR.**

psychogenesis (ˌsaɪkəʊ'dʒɛnɪsɪs) NOUN *Psychol* the study of the origin and development of personality, human behaviour, and mental processes.
▸**psychogenetic** (ˌsaɪkəʊdʒɪ'nɛtɪk) ADJECTIVE
▸ˌ**psychoge'netically** ADVERB

psychogenic (ˌsaɪkəʊ'dʒɛnɪk) ADJECTIVE *Psychol* (esp of disorders or symptoms) of mental, rather than organic, origin.
▸ˌ**psycho'genically** ADVERB

psychogeriatric (ˌsaɪkəʊdʒɛrɪ'ætrɪk) ADJECTIVE 1 *Med* (of an old person) no longer in touch with everyday realities; exhibiting delusions; mentally incompetent. ◆ NOUN 2 **a** *Derogatory* a confused old person. **b** an impersonal label for a patient, as a unit, requiring institutional services appropriate for a mentally disordered old person. ◆ See also **confused elderly, geriatric, senile.**

psychogeriatrics (ˌsaɪkəʊdʒɛrɪ'ætrɪks) NOUN (*functioning as singular*) *Med* the branch of health care concerned with the study, diagnosis, and sometimes treatment of mentally disordered old people. Compare **geriatrics.**

psychognosis (saɪ'kɒgnəsɪs) NOUN *Psychol* 1 the use of hypnosis to study mental phenomena. 2 the study of personality by observation of outward bodily signs.
▸**psychognostic** (ˌsaɪkɒg'nɒstɪk) ADJECTIVE

psychographics (ˌsaɪkəʊ'græfɪks) PLURAL NOUN (*functioning as singular*) the study and grouping of people according to their attitudes and tastes, esp for market research.

psychohistory (ˌsaɪkəʊ'hɪstərɪ, -'hɪstrɪ) NOUN, *plural* **-ries.** biography based on psychological theories of personality development.

psychokinesis (ˌsaɪkəʊkɪ'niːsɪs, -kaɪ-) NOUN 1 (in parapsychology) alteration of the state of an object by mental influence alone, without any physical intervention. 2 *Psychiatry* a state of violent uncontrolled motor activity.
▷HISTORY C20: from PSYCHO- + Greek *kinēsis* motion
▸**psychokinetic** (ˌsaɪkəʊkɪ'nɛtɪk) ADJECTIVE

psychol. ABBREVIATION FOR: 1 psychological. 2 psychology.

psycholinguistics (ˌsaɪkəʊlɪŋ'gwɪstɪks) NOUN (*functioning as singular*) the psychology of language, including language acquisition by children, the mental processes underlying adult comprehension and production of speech, language disorders, etc.
▸ˌ**psycho'linguist** NOUN ▸ˌ**psycholin'guistic** ADJECTIVE

psychological (ˌsaɪkə'lɒdʒɪkᵊl) ADJECTIVE 1 of or relating to psychology. 2 of or relating to the mind or mental activity. 3 having no real or objective basis; arising in the mind: *his backaches are all psychological.* 4 affecting the mind.
▸ˌ**psycho'logically** ADVERB

psychological block NOUN See **block** (sense 21).

psychological moment NOUN the most appropriate time for producing a desired effect: *he proposed to her at the psychological moment.*

psychological operations PLURAL NOUN another term for **psychological warfare.**

psychological primary NOUN one of a set of perceived colours (red, yellow, blue, green, black, and white) that can be used to characterize all other perceived colours.

psychological warfare NOUN the military application of psychology, esp to propaganda and attempts to influence the morale of enemy and friendly groups in time of war.

psychologism (saɪ'kɒləˌdʒɪzəm) NOUN 1 the belief in the importance and relevance of psychology for other sciences. 2 the belief that psychology is the basis for all other natural and social sciences.
▸**psyˌcholo'gistic** ADJECTIVE

psychologize *or* **psychologise** (saɪ'kɒləˌdʒaɪz) VERB (*intr*) 1 to make interpretations of behaviour and mental processes. 2 to carry out investigation in the field of psychology.

psychology (saɪ'kɒlədʒɪ) NOUN, *plural* **-gies.** 1 the scientific study of all forms of human and animal behaviour, sometimes concerned with the methods through which behaviour can be modified. See also **analytical psychology, clinical psychology, comparative psychology, educational psychology, experimental psychology.** 2 *Informal* the mental make-up or structure of an individual that causes him or her to think or act in the way he or she does.
▸**psy'chologist** NOUN

psychomachia (ˌsaɪkəʊ'mækɪə) *or* **psychomachy** ('saɪkəʊməkɪ) NOUN conflict of the soul.
▷HISTORY C17: from Late Latin *psȳchomachia,* title of a poem by Prudentius (about 400), from Greek *psukhē* spirit + *makhē* battle

psychometric (ˌsaɪkəʊ'mɛtrɪk) *or* **psychometrical** ADJECTIVE of or relating to psychometrics or psychometry.
▸ˌ**psycho'metrically** ADVERB

psychometrics (ˌsaɪkəʊ'mɛtrɪks) NOUN (*functioning as singular*) 1 the branch of psychology concerned with the design and use of psychological tests. 2 the application of statistical and mathematical techniques to psychological testing.

psychometry (saɪ'kɒmɪtrɪ) NOUN *Psychol* 1 measurement and testing of mental states and processes. See also **psychometrics.** 2 (in parapsychology) the supposed ability to deduce facts about events by touching objects related to them.

▸**psychometrician** (ˌsaɪkəʊməˈtrɪʃən) *or* **psyˈchometrist** NOUN

psychomotor (ˌsaɪkəʊˈməʊtə) ADJECTIVE of, relating to, or characterizing movements of the body associated with mental activity.

psychoneuroimmunology (ˌsaɪkəʊˌnjʊərəʊˌɪmjʊˈnɒlədʒɪ) NOUN the study of the effects of psychological factors on the immune system. Abbreviation: **PNI.**

psychoneurosis (ˌsaɪkəʊnjʊˈrəʊsɪs) NOUN, *plural* **-roses** (-ˈrəʊsiːz). another word for **neurosis.**
▸**psychoneurotic** (ˌsaɪkəʊnjʊˈrɒtɪk) ADJECTIVE

psychopath (ˈsaɪkəʊˌpæθ) NOUN a person afflicted with a personality disorder characterized by a tendency to commit antisocial and sometimes violent acts and a failure to feel guilt for such acts. Also called: **sociopath.**
▸ˌ**psychoˈpathic** ADJECTIVE ▸ˌ**psychoˈpathically** ADVERB

psychopathic disorder NOUN *Law* (in England, according to the Mental Health Act 1983) a persistent disorder or disability of mind which results in abnormally aggressive or seriously irresponsible conduct on the part of the person concerned. See also **mental disorder.**

psychopathic personality NOUN *Psychiatry* an antisocial personality characterized by the failure to develop any sense of moral responsibility and the capability of performing violent or antisocial acts.

psychopathology (ˌsaɪkəʊpəˈθɒlədʒɪ) NOUN the scientific study of mental disorders.
▸**psychopathological** (ˌsaɪkəʊˌpæθəˈlɒdʒɪkəl) ADJECTIVE
▸ˌ**psychopaˈthologist** NOUN

psychopathy (saɪˈkɒpəθɪ) NOUN *Psychiatry* 1 another name for **psychopathic personality.** 2 any mental disorder or disease.

psychopharmacology (ˌsaɪkəʊˌfɑːməˈkɒlədʒɪ) NOUN the study of drugs that affect the mind.
▸**psychopharmacological** (ˌsaɪkəʊˌfɑːməkəˈlɒdʒɪkəl) ADJECTIVE ▸ˌ**psychoˌpharmaˈcologist** NOUN

psychophysics (ˌsaɪkəʊˈfɪzɪks) NOUN (*functioning as singular*) the branch of psychology concerned with the relationship between physical stimuli and the effects they produce in the mind.
▸ˌ**psychoˈphysical** ADJECTIVE

psychophysiology (ˌsaɪkəʊˌfɪzɪˈɒlədʒɪ) NOUN the branch of psychology concerned with the physiological basis of mental processes.
▸**psychophysiological** (ˌsaɪkəʊˌfɪzɪəˈlɒdʒɪkəl) ADJECTIVE
▸ˌ**psychoˌphysiˈologist** NOUN

psychoprophylaxis (ˌsaɪkəʊˌprəʊfɪˈlæksɪs) NOUN a method of preparing women for natural childbirth by means of special breathing and relaxation.

psychosexual (ˌsaɪkəʊˈsɛksjʊəl) ADJECTIVE of or relating to the mental aspects of sex, such as sexual fantasies.
▸ˌ**psychoˌsexuˈality** NOUN ▸ˌ**psychoˈsexually** ADVERB

psychosis (saɪˈkəʊsɪs) NOUN, *plural* **-choses** (-ˈkəʊsiːz). any form of severe mental disorder in which the individual's contact with reality becomes highly distorted. Compare **neurosis.**
▷HISTORY C19: New Latin, from PSYCHO- + -OSIS

psychosocial (ˌsaɪkəʊˈsəʊʃəl) ADJECTIVE of or relating to processes or factors that are both social and psychological in origin.

psychosomatic (ˌsaɪkəʊsəˈmætɪk) ADJECTIVE of or relating to disorders, such as stomach ulcers, thought to be caused or aggravated by psychological factors such as stress.

psychosurgery (ˌsaɪkəʊˈsɜːdʒərɪ) NOUN any surgical procedure on the brain, such as a frontal lobotomy, to relieve serious mental disorders.
▸**psychosurgical** (ˌsaɪkəʊˈsɜːdʒɪkəl) ADJECTIVE

psychosynthesis (ˌsaɪkəʊˈsɪnθɪsɪs) a form of psychotherapy intended to release the patient's full potential by focusing on the positive rather than the negative.

psychotherapy (ˌsaɪkəʊˈθɛrəpɪ) *or less commonly* **psychotherapeutics** (ˌsaɪkəʊˌθɛrəˈpjuːtɪks) NOUN the treatment of nervous disorders by psychological methods.
▸ˌ**psychoˌtheraˈpeutic** ADJECTIVE
▸ˌ**psychoˌtheraˈpeutically** ADVERB ▸ˌ**psychoˈtherapist** NOUN

psychotic (saɪˈkɒtɪk) *Psychiatry* ◆ ADJECTIVE 1 of, relating to, or characterized by psychosis. ◆ NOUN 2 a person suffering from psychosis.
▸**psyˈchotically** ADVERB

psychotomimetic (saɪˌkɒtəʊmɪˈmɛtɪk) ADJECTIVE (of drugs such as LSD and mescaline) capable of inducing psychotic symptoms.

psychotropic (ˌsaɪkəʊˈtrɒpɪk) ADJECTIVE another word for **psychoactive.**

psych out VERB (*mainly tr, adverb*) *Informal* 1 to guess correctly the intentions of (another); outguess. 2 to analyse or solve (a problem, etc.) psychologically. 3 to intimidate or frighten. 4 (*intr, adverb*) to lose control psychologically; break down.

psychro- COMBINING FORM cold: *psychrometer.*
▷HISTORY from Greek *psukhros*

psychrometer (saɪˈkrɒmɪtə) NOUN a type of hygrometer consisting of two thermometers, one of which has a dry bulb and the other a bulb that is kept moist and ventilated. The difference between the readings of the thermometers gives an indication of atmospheric humidity. Also called: **wet-and-dry-bulb thermometer.**

psychrophilic (ˌsaɪkrəʊˈfɪlɪk) ADJECTIVE (esp of bacteria) showing optimum growth at low temperatures.

psych up VERB (*tr, adverb*) *Informal* to get (oneself or another) into a state of psychological readiness for an action, performance, etc.

psyllid (ˈsɪlɪd) *or* **psylla** (ˈsɪlə) NOUN any homopterous insect of the family *Psyllidae,* which comprises the jumping plant lice. See **plant louse** (sense 2).
▷HISTORY C19: from Greek *psulla* flea

psyllium (ˈsɪlɪəm) NOUN a grain, *Plantago psafra,* the husks of which are used medicinally as a laxative and to reduce blood cholesterol levels.
▷HISTORY C16: Latin, from Greek *psulla* flea, due to the resemblance of the seeds to fleas

psyops (ˈsaɪˌɒps) PLURAL NOUN short for **psychological operations.**

pt ABBREVIATION FOR: 1 part. 2 past tense. 3 patient. 4 payment. 5 point. 6 port. ◆ 7 THE INTERNET DOMAIN NAME FOR Portugal. 8 pro tempore.

Pt (in place names) ABBREVIATION FOR: 1 Point. 2 Port. ◆ 3 THE CHEMICAL SYMBOL FOR platinum.

PT ABBREVIATION FOR: 1 physical therapy. 2 physical training. 3 postal telegraph. 4 pupil teacher. 5 (in Britain, formerly) purchase tax. 6 prothrombin time.

pt. ABBREVIATION FOR pint.

pta SYMBOL FOR peseta.

PTA ABBREVIATION FOR Parent-Teacher Association.

Ptah (ptɑː, tɑː) NOUN (in ancient Egypt) a major god worshipped as the creative power, esp at Memphis.

ptarmigan (ˈtɑːmɪɡən) NOUN, *plural* **-gans** *or* **-gan.** 1 any of several arctic and subarctic grouse of the genus *Lagopus, esp L. mutus,* which has a white winter plumage. 2 (*sometimes capital*) a created domestic fancy pigeon with ruffled or curled feathers on the wings and back.
▷HISTORY C16: changed (perhaps influenced by Greek *pteron* wing) from Scottish Gaelic *tarmachan,* diminutive of *tarmach,* of obscure origin

PT boat NOUN patrol torpedo boat, the former US term for an **MTB.**

Pte *Military* ABBREVIATION FOR private.

pteridology (ˌtɛrɪˈdɒlədʒɪ) NOUN the branch of botany concerned with the study of ferns and related plants.
▷HISTORY C19: from *pterido-,* from Greek *pteris* fern + -LOGY
▸**pteridological** (ˌtɛrɪdəʊˈlɒdʒɪkəl) ADJECTIVE
▸ˌ**pteriˈdologist** NOUN

pteridophyte (ˈtɛrɪdəʊˌfaɪt) NOUN (in traditional classification) any plant of the division *Pteridophyta,* reproducing by spores and having vascular tissue, roots, stems, and leaves: includes the ferns, horsetails, and club mosses. In modern classifications these plants are placed in separate phyla.
▷HISTORY C19: from *pterido-,* from Greek *pteris* fern + -PHYTE
▸**pteridophytic** (ˌtɛrɪdəʊˈfɪtɪk) *or* **pteridophytous** (ˌtɛrɪˈdɒfɪtəs) ADJECTIVE

pteridosperm (ˈtɛrɪdəˌspɜːm) NOUN any extinct seed-producing fernlike plant of the group *Pteridospermae.* Also called: **seed fern.**
▷HISTORY C19: from Greek *pteris* a fern + -SPERM

ptero- COMBINING FORM wing, feather, or a part resembling a wing: *pterodactyl.*
▷HISTORY from Greek *pteron* wing, feather

pterodactyl (ˌtɛrəˈdæktɪl) NOUN any extinct flying reptile of the genus *Pterodactylus* and related genera, having membranous wings supported on an elongated fourth digit. See also **pterosaur.**
▷HISTORY C19: from PTERO- + Greek *daktulos* finger

pteropod (ˈtɛrəˌpɒd) NOUN any small marine gastropod mollusc of the group or order *Pteropoda,* in which the foot is expanded into two winglike lobes for swimming and the shell is absent or thin-walled. Also called: **sea butterfly.**

pterosaur (ˈtɛrəˌsɔː) NOUN any extinct flying reptile of the order *Pterosauria,* of Jurassic and Cretaceous times: included the pterodactyls. Compare **dinosaur, plesiosaur.**

-pterous *or* **-pteran** ADJECTIVE COMBINING FORM indicating a specified number or type of wings: *dipterous.*
▷HISTORY from Greek *-pteros,* from *pteron* wing

pterygial (təˈrɪdʒɪəl) ADJECTIVE *Zoology* of or relating to a fin or wing.
▷HISTORY from Greek *pterux* wing

pterygoid process (ˈtɛrɪˌɡɔɪd) NOUN *Anatomy* either of two long bony plates extending downwards from each side of the sphenoid bone within the skull.
▷HISTORY C18 *pterygoid,* from Greek *pterugoeidēs,* from *pterux* wing; see -OID

pteryla (ˈtɛrɪlə) NOUN, *plural* **-lae** (-ˌliː). *Ornithol* any of the tracts of skin that bear contour feathers, arranged in lines along the body of a bird.
▷HISTORY C19: from New Latin, from Greek *pteron* feather + *hulē* wood, forest

PTFE ABBREVIATION FOR polytetrafluoroethylene.

ptg ABBREVIATION FOR printing.

ptisan (tɪˈzæn) NOUN 1 grape juice drained off without pressure. 2 a variant spelling of **tisane.**
▷HISTORY C14: from Old French *tisane,* from Latin *ptisana,* from Greek *ptisanē* barley groats

PTN ABBREVIATION FOR public telephone network: the telephone network provided in Britain by British Telecom.

PTO *or* **pto** ABBREVIATION FOR please turn over.

ptochocracy (təʊˈkɒkrəsɪ) NOUN, *plural* **-cies.** government by the poor.
▷HISTORY C18: from Greek, from *ptochos* poor + -CRACY

Ptolemaeus (ˌtɒlɪˈmiːəs) NOUN a crater in the SE quadrant of the moon, about 140 kilometres (90 miles) in diameter.

Ptolemaic (ˌtɒlɪˈmeɪɪk) ADJECTIVE 1 of or relating to the 2nd century A.D. Greek astronomer, mathematician and geographer Ptolemy (Latin name *Claudius Ptolemaeus*) or to his conception of the universe. 2 of or relating to the Macedonian dynasty that ruled Egypt from the death of Alexander the Great (323 B.C.) to the death of Cleopatra (30 B.C.).

Ptolemaic system NOUN the theory of planetary motion developed by Ptolemy from the hypotheses of earlier philosophers, stating that the earth lay at the centre of the universe with the sun, the moon, and the known planets revolving around it in complicated orbits. Beyond the largest of these orbits lay a sphere of fixed stars. See also **epicycle** (sense 1). Compare **Copernican system.**

Ptolemaist (ˌtɒlɪˈmeɪɪst) NOUN a believer in or adherent of the Ptolemaic system of the universe.

ptomaine *or* **ptomain** (ˈtəʊmeɪn) NOUN any of a group of amines, such as cadaverine or putrescine, formed by decaying organic matter.
▷HISTORY C19: from Italian *ptomaina,* from Greek *ptoma* corpse, from *piptein* to fall

ptomaine poisoning NOUN a popular term for **food poisoning.** Ptomaines were once erroneously thought to be a cause of food poisoning.

ptosis (ˈtəʊsɪs) NOUN, *plural* **ptoses** (ˈtəʊsiːz). prolapse or drooping of a part, esp the eyelid.
▷HISTORY C18: from Greek: a falling
▸**ptotic** (ˈtɒtɪk) ADJECTIVE

pts ABBREVIATION FOR: [1] parts. [2] payments. [3] points. [4] ports.

PTSD ABBREVIATION FOR **post-traumatic stress disorder**.

Pty *Austral, NZ, and South African* ABBREVIATION FOR proprietary: used to denote a private limited company.

ptyalin ('taɪəlɪn) NOUN *Biochem* an amylase secreted in the saliva of man and other animals.
▷**HISTORY** C19: from Greek *ptualon* saliva, from *ptuein* to spit

ptyalism ('taɪəˌlɪzəm) NOUN excessive secretion of saliva.
▷**HISTORY** C17: from Greek *ptualismos*, from *ptualizein* to produce saliva, from *ptualon* saliva

p-type ADJECTIVE [1] (of a semiconductor) having a density of mobile holes in excess of that of conduction electrons. [2] associated with or resulting from the movement of holes in a semiconductor: *p-type conductivity*. Compare **n-type**.

Pu THE CHEMICAL SYMBOL FOR plutonium.

pub (pʌb) NOUN [1] *Chiefly Brit* a building with a bar and one or more public rooms licensed for the sale and consumption of alcoholic drink, often also providing light meals. Formal name: **public house.** [2] *Austral and NZ* a hotel. ◆ VERB **pubs, pubbing, pubbed.** [3] *(intr) Informal* to visit a pub or pubs (esp in the phrase **go pubbing**).

pub. ABBREVIATION FOR: [1] public. [2] publication. [3] published. [4] publisher. [5] publishing.

pub-crawl *Informal, chiefly Brit* ◆ NOUN [1] drinking tour of a number of pubs or bars. ◆ VERB [2] *(intr)* to make such a tour.
▸**'pubˌcrawler** NOUN

pube ('pju:b) NOUN *Informal* a pubic hair.

puberty ('pju:bətɪ) NOUN the period at the beginning of adolescence when the sex glands become functional and the secondary sexual characteristics emerge. Also called: **pubescence.** Related adjective: **hebetic.**
▷**HISTORY** C14: from Latin *pūbertās* maturity, from *pūber* adult
▸**'pubertal** ADJECTIVE

puberulent (pjʊ'bɛrjʊlənt) ADJECTIVE *Biology* covered with very fine down; finely pubescent.
▷**HISTORY** C19: from Latin *pūber*

pubes ('pju:bi:z) NOUN, *plural* **pubes** ('pju:bi:z). [1] the region above the external genital organs, covered with hair from the time of puberty. [2] the pubic bones. [3] the plural of **pubis.** ◆ PLURAL NOUN ('pju:bz) [4] *Informal* pubic hair.
▷**HISTORY** from Latin

pubescent (pju:'bɛsᵊnt) ADJECTIVE [1] arriving or having arrived at puberty. [2] (of certain plants and animals or their parts) covered with a layer of fine short hairs or down.
▷**HISTORY** C17: from Latin *pūbēscere* to reach manhood, from *pūber* adult
▸**pu'bescence** NOUN

pub grub NOUN *Informal* food served in a pub.

pubic ('pju:bɪk) ADJECTIVE of or relating to the pubes or pubis: *pubic hair.*

pubis ('pju:bɪs) NOUN, *plural* **-bes** (-bi:z). one of the three sections of the hipbone that forms part of the pelvis.
▷**HISTORY** C16: shortened from New Latin *os pūbis* bone of the PUBES

public ('pʌblɪk) ADJECTIVE [1] of, relating to, or concerning the people as a whole. [2] open or accessible to all: *public gardens.* [3] performed or made openly or in the view of all: *public proclamation.* [4] *(prenominal)* well-known or familiar to people in general: *a public figure.* [5] *(usually prenominal)* maintained at the expense of, serving, or for the use of a community: *a public library.* [6] open, acknowledged, or notorious: *a public scandal.* [7] **go public. a** (of a private company) to issue shares for subscription by the public. **b** to reveal publicly hitherto confidential information. ◆ NOUN [8] the community or people in general. [9] a part or section of the community grouped because of a common interest, activity, etc.: *the racing public.*
▷**HISTORY** C15: from Latin *pūblicus*, changed from *pōplicus* of the people, from *populus* people

public-address system NOUN a system of one or more microphones, amplifiers, and loudspeakers for increasing the sound level of speech or music, used in auditoriums, public gatherings, etc. Sometimes shortened to: **PA system.**

publican ('pʌblɪkən) NOUN [1] (in Britain) a person who keeps a public house. [2] (in ancient Rome) a public contractor, esp one who farmed the taxes of a province.
▷**HISTORY** C12: from Old French *publicain*, from Latin *pūblicānus* tax gatherer, from *pūblicum* state revenues

public assistance NOUN *US* payment given to individuals by government agencies on the basis of need.

publication (ˌpʌblɪ'keɪʃən) NOUN [1] the act or process of publishing a printed work. [2] any printed work offered for sale or distribution. [3] the act or an instance of making information public. [4] the act of disseminating defamatory matter, esp by communicating it to a third person. See **libel, slander.** Archaic word: **publishment.**
▷**HISTORY** C14: via Old French from Latin *pūblicātiō* confiscation of an individual's property, from *pūblicāre* to seize and assign to public use

public bar NOUN *Brit* a bar in a public house usually serving drinks at a cheaper price than in the saloon bar. Also called: **the public.** Compare **private bar.**

public bill NOUN (in Parliament) a bill dealing with public policy that usually applies to the whole country. Compare **private bill, hybrid bill.**

public company NOUN a limited company whose shares may be purchased by the public and traded freely on the open market and whose share capital is not less than a statutory minimum; public limited company. Compare **private company.**

public convenience NOUN a public lavatory, esp one in a public place.

public corporation NOUN (in Britain) an organization established to run a nationalized industry or state-owned enterprise. The chairman and board members are appointed by a government minister, and the government has overall control.

public debt NOUN *Chiefly US* [1] the total financial obligations incurred by all governmental bodies of a nation. [2] another name for **national debt.**

public defender NOUN (in the US) a lawyer engaged at public expense to represent indigent defendants.

public domain NOUN [1] *US* lands owned by a state or by the federal government. [2] the status of a published work or invention upon which the copyright or patent has expired or which has not been patented or subject to copyright. It may thus be freely used by the public. [3] **in the public domain.** able to be discussed and examined freely by the general public.

public enemy NOUN a notorious person, such as a criminal, who is regarded as a menace to the public.

public enterprise NOUN economic activity by governmental organizations. Compare **private enterprise** (sense 1).

public expenditure NOUN spending by central government, local authorities, and public corporations.

public footpath NOUN a footpath along which the public has right of way.

public gallery NOUN the gallery in a chamber of Parliament reserved for members of the public who wish to listen to the proceedings. Also called: **strangers' gallery.**

public health inspector NOUN (in Britain) a former name for **Environmental Health Officer.**

public holiday NOUN a holiday observed over the whole country.

public house NOUN [1] *Brit* the formal name for **pub.** [2] *US and Canadian* an inn, tavern, or small hotel.

publicist ('pʌblɪsɪst) NOUN [1] a person who publicizes something, esp a press or publicity agent. [2] a journalist. [3] *Rare* a person learned in public or international law.

publicity (pʌ'blɪsɪtɪ) NOUN [1] **a** the technique or process of attracting public attention to people, products, etc., as by the use of the mass media. **b** *(as modifier)*: *a publicity agent.* [2] public interest resulting from information supplied by such a technique or process. [3] information used to draw public attention to people, products, etc. [4] the state of being public.
▷**HISTORY** C18: via French from Medieval Latin *pūblicitās*; see PUBLIC

publicize *or* **publicise** ('pʌblɪˌsaɪz) VERB *(tr)* to bring to public notice; advertise.

public law NOUN [1] a law that applies to the public of a state or nation. [2] the branch of law that deals with relations between a state and its individual members. Compare **private law.**

Public Lending Right NOUN the right of authors to receive payment when their books are borrowed from public libraries. Abbreviation: **PLR.**

public-liability insurance NOUN (in Britain) a form of insurance, compulsory for any business in contact with the public, which pays compensation to a member of the public suffering injury or damage as a result of the policyholder or his employees failing to take reasonable care.

public limited company NOUN another name for **public company.** Abbreviation: **plc** *or* **PLC.**

publicly ('pʌblɪklɪ) ADVERB [1] in a public manner; without concealment; openly. [2] in the name or with the consent of the public.

public nuisance NOUN [1] *Law* an illegal act causing harm to members of a particular community rather than to any individual. [2] *Informal* a person who is generally considered objectionable.

public opinion NOUN the attitude of the public, esp as a factor in determining the actions of government.

public ownership NOUN ownership by the state; nationalization.

public prosecutor NOUN *Law* an official in charge of prosecuting important cases.

Public Record Office NOUN an institution in which official records are stored and kept available for inspection by the public.

public relations NOUN *(functioning as singular or plural)* [1] **a** the practice of creating, promoting, or maintaining goodwill and a favourable image among the public towards an institution, public body, etc. **b** the methods and techniques employed. **c** *(as modifier)*: *the public relations industry.* [2] the condition of the relationship between an organization and the public. [3] the professional staff employed to create, promote, or maintain a favourable relationship between an organization and the public. Abbreviation: **PR.**

public school NOUN [1] (in England and Wales) a private independent fee-paying secondary school. [2] (in the US) any school that is part of a free local educational system.

public sector NOUN the part of an economy that consists of state-owned institutions, including nationalized industries and services provided by local authorities. Compare **private sector.**

public servant NOUN [1] an elected or appointed holder of a public office. [2] the Austral and NZ name for **civil servant.**

public service NOUN [1] **a** government employment. **b** the management and administration of the affairs of a political unit, esp the civil service. [2] **a** a service provided for the community: *buses provide a public service.* **b** *(as modifier)*: *a public-service announcement.* [3] the Austral and NZ name for the **civil service.**

public-service corporation NOUN *US* a private corporation that provides services to the community, such as telephone service, public transport.

public speaking NOUN the art or practice of making speeches to large audiences.
▸**public speaker** NOUN

public spending NOUN expenditure by central government, local authorities, and public enterprises.

public-spirited ADJECTIVE having or showing active interest in public welfare or the good of the community.

public transport NOUN a system of buses, trains, etc., running on fixed routes, on which the public may travel.

public utility NOUN an enterprise concerned with the provision to the public of essentials, such as electricity or water. Also called (US): **public-service corporation.**

public works PLURAL NOUN engineering projects and other constructions, financed and undertaken by a government for the community.

publish (ˈpʌblɪʃ) VERB 1 to produce and issue (printed or electronic matter) for distribution and sale. 2 (*intr*) to have one's written work issued for publication. 3 (*tr*) to announce formally or in public. 4 (*tr*) to communicate (defamatory matter) to someone other than the person defamed: *to publish a libel.*
▷HISTORY C14: from Old French *puplier,* from Latin *pūblicāre* to make PUBLIC
▸ˈ**publishable** ADJECTIVE ▸ˈ**publishing** NOUN

publisher (ˈpʌblɪʃə) NOUN 1 a company or person engaged in publishing periodicals, books, music, etc. 2 *US and Canadian* the proprietor of a newspaper or his representative.

púcán (ˈpuːkɑːn) NOUN *Irish* a traditional Connemara open sailing boat.
▷HISTORY Irish Gaelic

puccoon (pəˈkuːn) NOUN 1 Also called: **alkanet.** any of several North American boraginaceous plants of the genus *Lithospermum, esp L. canescens,* that yield a red dye. See also **gromwell.** 2 any of several other plants that yield a reddish dye, esp the bloodroot (**red puccoon**). 3 the dye from any of these plants.
▷HISTORY C17: of Algonquian origin; see POKEWEED

puce (pjuːs) NOUN **a** a colour varying from deep red to dark purplish-brown. **b** (*as adjective*): *a puce carpet.*
▷HISTORY C18: shortened from French *couleur puce* flea colour, from Latin *pūlex* flea

puck¹ (pʌk) NOUN 1 a small disc of hard rubber used in ice hockey. 2 a stroke at the ball in hurling. 3 *Irish slang* a sharp blow. ◆ VERB (*tr*) 4 to strike (the ball) in hurling. 5 *Irish slang* to strike hard; punch.
▷HISTORY C19: of unknown origin

puck² (pʌk) NOUN (*often capital*) a mischievous or evil spirit. Also called: **Robin Goodfellow.**
▷HISTORY Old English *pūca,* of obscure origin
▸ˈ**puckish** ADJECTIVE

pucka (ˈpʌkə) ADJECTIVE a less common spelling of **pukka.**

pucker (ˈpʌkə) VERB 1 to gather or contract (a soft surface such as the skin of the face) into wrinkles or folds, or (of such a surface) to be so gathered or contracted. ◆ NOUN 2 a wrinkle, crease, or irregular fold.
▷HISTORY C16: perhaps related to POKE², from the creasing into baglike wrinkles

puckerood (ˌpʌkəˈruːd) ADJECTIVE *NZ informal* ruined; exhausted.
▷HISTORY from Maori *pakaru* to shatter

pud (pʊd) NOUN *Brit informal* short for **pudding.**

pudding (ˈpʊdɪŋ) NOUN 1 a sweetened usually cooked dessert made in many forms and of various ingredients, such as flour, milk, and eggs, with fruit, etc. 2 a savoury dish, usually soft and consisting partially of pastry or batter: *steak-and-kidney pudding.* 3 the dessert course in a meal. 4 a sausage-like mass of seasoned minced meat, oatmeal, etc., stuffed into a prepared skin or bag and boiled.
▷HISTORY C13 *poding;* compare Old English *puduc* a wart, Low German *puddek* sausage
▸ˈ**puddingy** ADJECTIVE

pudding club NOUN *Slang* the state of being pregnant (esp in the phrase **in the pudding club**).

pudding stone NOUN a conglomerate rock in which there is a difference in colour or composition between the pebbles and the matrix.

puddle (ˈpʌdᵊl) NOUN 1 a small pool of water, esp of rain. 2 a small pool of any liquid. 3 a worked mixture of wet clay and sand that is impervious to water and is used to line a pond or canal. 4 *Rowing* the patch of eddying water left by the blade of an oar after completion of a stroke. ◆ VERB 5 (*tr*) to make (clay, etc.) into puddle. 6 (*tr*) to subject (iron) to puddling. 7 (*intr*) to dabble or wade in puddles, mud, or shallow water. 8 (*intr*) to mess about.
▷HISTORY C14 *podel,* diminutive of Old English *pudd* ditch, of obscure origin
▸ˈ**puddler** NOUN ▸ˈ**puddly** ADJECTIVE

puddling (ˈpʌdlɪŋ) NOUN 1 a process for converting pig iron into wrought iron by heating it with ferric oxide in a furnace to oxidize the carbon. 2 *Building trades* the process of making a puddle.

puddock (ˈpʌdək) NOUN a Scot variant of **paddock²**.

pudency (ˈpjuːdᵊnsɪ) NOUN modesty, shame, or prudishness.
▷HISTORY C17: from Late Latin *pudentia,* from Latin *pudēre* to feel shame

pudendum (pjuːˈdɛndəm) NOUN, *plural* **-da** (-də). (*often plural*) the human external genital organs collectively, esp of a female.
▷HISTORY C17: from Late Latin, from Latin *pudenda* the shameful (parts), from *pudēre* to be ashamed
▸**puˈdendal** *or* **pudic** (ˈpjuːdɪk) ADJECTIVE

pudge (pʌdʒ) NOUN *Informal* a variant of **podge.**
▷HISTORY C19: of uncertain origin; see PUDGY

pudgy (ˈpʌdʒɪ) ADJECTIVE **pudgier, pudgiest.** a variant spelling (esp US) of **podgy.**
▷HISTORY C19: of uncertain origin; compare earlier *pudsy* plump, perhaps from Scottish *pud* stomach, plump child
▸ˈ**pudgily** ADVERB ▸ˈ**pudginess** NOUN

Pudsey (ˈpʌdzɪ) NOUN a town in N England, in Leeds unitary authority, West Yorkshire. Pop.: 31 636 (1991).

pudu (ˈpuːˌduː) NOUN a diminutive Andean antelope, *Pudu pudu,* some 35 cm (13 to 14 in.) tall at the shoulder, with short straight horns and reddish-brown spotted coat.
▷HISTORY C19: its native name

Puebla (*Spanish* ˈpweβla) NOUN 1 an inland state of S central Mexico, situated on the Anáhuac Plateau. Capital: Puebla. Pop.: 5 070 346 (2000 est.). Area: 33 919 sq. km (13 096 sq. miles). 2 a city in S Mexico, capital of Puebla state: founded in 1532; university (1537). Pop.: 1 270 989 (2000 est.). Full name: **Puebla de Zaragoza** (de θaraˈɣoθa).

pueblo (ˈpwɛbləʊ; *Spanish* ˈpweβlo) NOUN, *plural* **-los** (-ləʊz; *Spanish* -los). 1 a communal village, built by certain Indians of the southwestern US and parts of Latin America, consisting of one or more flat-roofed stone or adobe houses. 2 (in Spanish America) a village or town. 3 (in the Philippines) a town or township.
▷HISTORY C19: from Spanish: people, from Latin *populus*

Pueblo¹ (ˈpwɛbləʊ) NOUN, *plural* **-lo** *or* **-los.** a member of any of the North American Indian peoples who live in pueblos, including the Tanoans, Zuñi, and Hopi.

Pueblo² (ˈpwɛbləʊ) NOUN a city in the US, in Colorado: a centre of the steel industry. Pop.: 102 121 (2000).

puerile (ˈpjʊəraɪl) ADJECTIVE 1 exhibiting silliness; immature; trivial. 2 of or characteristic of a child.
▷HISTORY C17: from Latin *puerīlis* childish, from *puer* a boy
▸ˈ**puerilely** ADVERB ▸**puerility** (pjʊəˈrɪlɪtɪ) NOUN

puerilism (ˈpjʊərɪˌlɪzəm) NOUN *Psychiatry* immature or childish behaviour by an adult.

puerperal (pjuːˈɜːpərəl) ADJECTIVE of, relating to, or occurring during the puerperium.
▷HISTORY C18: from New Latin *puerperālis* relating to childbirth; see PUERPERIUM

puerperal fever NOUN a serious, formerly widespread, form of blood poisoning caused by infection contracted during childbirth.

puerperal psychosis NOUN a mental disorder sometimes occurring in women after childbirth, characterized by deep depression, delusions of the child's death, and homicidal feelings towards the child.

puerperium (pjʊəˈpɪərɪəm) NOUN the period following childbirth, lasting approximately six weeks, during which the uterus returns to its normal size and shape.
▷HISTORY C17: from Latin: childbirth, from *puerperus* relating to a woman in labour, from *puer* boy + *parere* to bear

Puerto Rican (ˈpwɜːtəʊ ˈriːkən, ˈpwɛə-) ADJECTIVE 1 of or relating to Puerto Rico or its inhabitants. ◆ NOUN 2 a native or inhabitant of Puerto Rico.

Puerto Rico (ˈpwɜːtəʊ ˈriːkəʊ, ˈpwɛə-) NOUN an autonomous commonwealth (in association with the US) occupying the smallest and easternmost of the Greater Antilles in the Caribbean: one of the most densely populated areas in the world; ceded by Spain to the US in 1899. Currency: US dollar. Capital: San Juan. Pop.: 3 829 000 (2001 est.). Area: 9104 sq. km (3515 sq. miles). Former name (until 1932): **Porto Rico.** Abbreviation: **PR.**

puff (pʌf) NOUN 1 a short quick draught, gust, or emission, as of wind, smoke, air, etc., esp a forceful one. 2 the amount of wind, smoke, etc., released in a puff. 3 the sound made by or associated with a puff. 4 an instance of inhaling and expelling the breath as in smoking. 5 a swelling. 6 a light aerated pastry usually filled with cream, jam, etc. 7 a powder puff. 8 exaggerated praise, as of a book, product, etc., esp through an advertisement. 9 a piece of clothing fabric gathered up so as to bulge in the centre while being held together at the edges. 10 a loose piece of hair wound into a cylindrical roll, usually over a pad, and pinned in place in a coiffure. 11 a less common word for **quilt** (sense 1). 12 one's breath (esp in the phrase **out of puff**). 13 *Derogatory slang* a male homosexual. 14 a dialect word for **puffball.** ◆ VERB 15 to blow or breathe or cause to blow or breathe in short quick draughts or blasts. 16 (*tr; often foll by out; usually passive*) to cause to be out of breath. 17 to take puffs or draws at (a cigarette, cigar, or pipe). 18 to move with or by the emission of puffs: *the steam train puffed up the incline.* 19 (often foll by *up, out,* etc.) to swell, as with air, pride, etc. 20 (*tr*) to praise with exaggerated empty words, often in advertising. 21 (*tr*) to apply (cosmetic powder) from a powder puff to (the face). 22 to increase the price of (a lot in an auction) artificially by having an accomplice make false bids.
▷HISTORY Old English *pyffan;* related to Dutch German *puffen,* Swiss *pfuffen,* Norwegian *puffa,* all of imitative origin

puff adder NOUN 1 a large venomous African viper, *Bitis arietans,* that is yellowish-grey with brown markings and inflates its body when alarmed. 2 another name for **hognose snake.**

puffball (ˈpʌfˌbɔːl) NOUN any of various basidiomycetous saprotrophic fungi of the genera *Calvatia* and *Lycoperdon,* having a round fruiting body that discharges a cloud of brown spores when mature.

puffbird (ˈpʌfˌbɜːd) NOUN any of various brownish tropical American birds of the family *Bucconidae,* having a large head: order *Piciformes* (woodpeckers, etc.).
▷HISTORY C19: so called because of its habit of puffing out its feathers

puffer (ˈpʌfə) NOUN 1 a person or thing that puffs. 2 Also called: **globefish.** any marine plectognath fish of the family *Tetraodontidae,* having an elongated spiny body that can be inflated to form a globe.

puffery (ˈpʌfərɪ) NOUN, *plural* **-eries.** *Informal* exaggerated praise, esp in publicity or advertising.

puffin (ˈpʌfɪn) NOUN any of various northern diving birds of the family Alcidae (auks, etc.), esp *Fratercula arctica* (**common** or **Atlantic puffin**), having a black-and-white plumage and a brightly coloured vertically flattened bill: order *Charadriiformes.*
▷HISTORY C14: perhaps of Cornish origin

puffin crossing NOUN a UK pedestrian crossing with traffic lights signalling red to stop the traffic flow when pedestrians are seen on the crossing by infrared detectors. The green signal reappears when no pedestrians are seen on the crossing.
▷HISTORY C20: *p(edestrian) u(ser) f(riendly) in(telligent) crossing*

puff pastry *or US* **puff paste** NOUN a dough rolled in thin layers incorporating fat to make a rich flaky pastry for pies, rich pastries, etc.

puff piece NOUN a flattering newspaper or magazine article about a person or an organization.

puff-puff NOUN *Brit* a children's name for a steam locomotive or railway train.

puffy (ˈpʌfɪ) ADJECTIVE **puffier, puffiest.** 1 short of breath. 2 swollen or bloated: *a puffy face.* 3 pompous or conceited. 4 blowing in gusts.
▸ˈ**puffily** ADVERB ▸ˈ**puffiness** NOUN

pug¹ (pʌg) NOUN 1 Also called: **carlin.** a small compact breed of dog with a smooth coat, lightly

curled tail, and a short wrinkled nose. 2 any of several small geometrid moths, mostly of the genus *Eupithecia,* with slim forewings held outstretched at rest.
▷HISTORY C16: of uncertain origin
▸ˈ**puggish** ADJECTIVE

pug² (pʌg) VERB **pugs, pugging, pugged.** (*tr*) 1 to mix or knead (clay) with water to form a malleable mass or paste, often in a **pug mill.** 2 to fill or stop with clay or a similar substance. 3 (of cattle) to trample (the ground) into consolidated mud.
▷HISTORY C19: of uncertain origin

pug³ (pʌg) NOUN a slang name for **boxer** (sense 1).
▷HISTORY C20: shortened from PUGILIST

Puget Sound (ˈpjuːdʒɪt) NOUN an inlet of the Pacific in NW Washington. Length: about 130 km (80 miles).

pugging (ˈpʌgɪŋ) NOUN material such as clay, mortar, sawdust, sand, etc., inserted between wooden flooring and ceiling to reduce the transmission of sound. Also called: **pug.**

puggree, pugree (ˈpʌgrɪ), **puggaree,** *or* **pugaree** (ˈpʌgərɪ) NOUN 1 the usual Indian word for **turban.** 2 a scarf, usually pleated, around the crown of some hats, esp sun helmets.
▷HISTORY C17: from Hindi *pagrī,* from Sanskrit *parikara*

puggy (ˈpʌgɪ) ADJECTIVE **-gier, -giest.** *NZ* sticky, claylike.
▷HISTORY probably from PUG²

pugilism (ˈpjuːdʒɪˌlɪzəm) NOUN the art, practice, or profession of fighting with the fists; boxing.
▷HISTORY C18: from Latin *pugil* a boxer; related to *pugnus* fist, *pugna* a fight
▸ˈ**pugilist** NOUN ▸ˌ**pugiˈlistic** ADJECTIVE ▸ˌ**pugiˈlistically** ADVERB

Puglia (ˈpuʎʎa) NOUN the Italian name for **Apulia.**

pugnacious (pʌgˈneɪʃəs) ADJECTIVE readily disposed to fight; belligerent.
▷HISTORY C17: from Latin *pugnāx*
▸**pugˈnaciously** ADVERB ▸**pugnacity** (pʌgˈnæsɪtɪ) *or* **pugˈnaciousness** NOUN

pug nose NOUN a short stubby upturned nose.
▷HISTORY C18: from PUG¹
▸ˈ**pug-ˌnosed** ADJECTIVE

Pugwash conferences (ˈpʌgˌwɒʃ) PLURAL NOUN international peace conferences of scientists held regularly to discuss world problems: Nobel peace prize 1995 awarded to Joseph Rotblat, one of the founders of the conferences, secretary-general (1957–73), and president from 1988.
▷HISTORY C20: from *Pugwash,* Nova Scotia, where the first conference was held

puha (ˈpuːhɑː) NOUN *NZ* another name for **sow thistle.**
▷HISTORY Maori

puh-leeze (ˌpəˈliːz) INTERJECTION a humorous spelling of the emphatic pronunciation of *please,* suggesting the speaker's exasperation.

puir (puːr, pyr) ADJECTIVE a Scot word for **poor.**

puirtith *or* **poortith** (ˈpuːrˌtɪθ, ˈpyr-) NOUN *Scot* poverty.
▷HISTORY C16: from Old French *pouerteit, poverteit;* compare POVERTY

puisne (ˈpjuːnɪ) ADJECTIVE (esp of a subordinate judge) of lower rank.
▷HISTORY C16: from Anglo-French, from Old French *puisné* born later, from *puis* at a later date, from Latin *posteā* afterwards + *né* born, from *naistre* to be born, from Latin *nascī*

puissance (ˈpjuːɪsᵊns, ˈpwiːsɑːns) NOUN 1 a competition in showjumping that tests a horse's ability to jump a limited number of large obstacles. 2 *Archaic or poetic* power.
▷HISTORY C15: from Old French; see PUISSANT

puissant (ˈpjuːɪsᵊnt) ADJECTIVE *Archaic or poetic* powerful.
▷HISTORY C15: from Old French, ultimately from Latin *potēns* mighty, from *posse* to have power
▸ˈ**puissantly** ADVERB

puja (ˈpuːdʒɑː) NOUN *Hinduism* a ritual in honour of the gods, performed either at home or in the mandir (temple).
▷HISTORY from Sanskrit: worship

puke (pjuːk) *Slang* ◆ VERB 1 to vomit. ◆ NOUN 2 the act of vomiting. 3 the matter vomited.
▷HISTORY C16: probably of imitative origin; compare German *spucken* to spit

pukeko (ˈpʊkəkəʊ) NOUN, *plural* **-kos.** a wading bird, *Porphyrio melanotus,* of New Zealand, with a brightly coloured plumage.
▷HISTORY Maori

pukka *or* **pucka** (ˈpʌkə) ADJECTIVE (esp in India) 1 properly or perfectly done, constructed, etc.: *a pukka road.* 2 genuine: *pukka sahib.*
▷HISTORY C17: from Hindi *pakkā* firm, from Sanskrit *pakva*

pul (puːl) NOUN, *plural* **puls** *or* **puli** (ˈpuːlɪ). an Afghan monetary unit worth one hundredth of an afghani.
▷HISTORY via Persian from Turkish: small coin, from Late Greek *phollis* bag for money, from Latin *follis* bag

pula (ˈpʊlə) NOUN the standard monetary unit of Botswana, divided into 100 thebe.

Pula (*Serbo-Croat* ˈpuːla) NOUN a port in NW Croatia at the S tip of the Istrian Peninsula: made a Roman military base in 178 B.C.; became the main Austro-Hungarian naval station and passed to Italy in 1919, to Yugoslavia in 1947, and is now in independent Croatia. Pop.: 62 300 (1991). Latin name: **Pietas Julia** (paɪˈɛɪtæs ˈjuːlɪə). Italian name: **Pola.**

Pulau Pinang (ˈpʊlaʊ pɪˈnæŋ) NOUN another name for **Penang.**

pulchritude (ˈpʌlkrɪˌtjuːd) NOUN *Formal or literary* physical beauty.
▷HISTORY C15: from Latin *pulchritūdō,* from *pulcher* beautiful
▸ˌ**pulchriˈtudinous** ADJECTIVE

pule (pjuːl) VERB (*intr*) to cry plaintively; whimper.
▷HISTORY C16: perhaps of imitative origin
▸ˈ**puler** NOUN

puli (ˈpjuːlɪ, ˈpʊlɪ) NOUN a breed of Hungarian sheepdog having a very long dense coat, usually black, that hangs in strands with a ropey or corded appearance.
▷HISTORY Hungarian, literally: leader

Pulitzer prize (ˈpʊlɪtsə) NOUN one of a group of prizes established by Hungarian-born US newspaper publisher Joseph Pulitzer (1847–1911) and awarded yearly since 1917 for excellence in American journalism, literature, and music.

pull (pʊl) VERB (*mainly tr*) 1 (*also intr*) to exert force on (an object) so as to draw it towards the source of the force. 2 to exert force on so as to remove; extract: *to pull a tooth.* 3 to strip of feathers, hair, etc.; pluck. 4 to draw the entrails from (a fowl). 5 to rend or tear. 6 to strain (a muscle, ligament, or tendon) injuriously. 7 (usually foll by *off*) *Informal* to perform or bring about: *to pull off a million-pound deal.* 8 (often foll by *on*) *Informal* to draw out (a weapon) for use: *he pulled a knife on his attacker.* 9 *Informal* to attract: *the pop group pulled a crowd.* 10 (*also intr*) *Slang* to attract (a sexual partner). 11 (*intr;* usually foll by *on* or *at*) to drink or inhale deeply: *to pull at one's pipe; pull on a bottle of beer.* 12 to put on or make (a grimace): *to pull a face.* 13 (*also intr;* foll by *away, out, over,* etc.) to move (a vehicle) or (of a vehicle) be moved in a specified manner: *he pulled his car away from the roadside.* 14 *Printing* to take (a proof) from type. 15 to withdraw or remove: *the board decided to pull their support.* 16 *Sport* to hit (a ball) so that it veers away from the direction in which the player intended to hit it (to the left for a right-handed player). 17 *Cricket* to hit (a ball pitched straight or on the off side) to the leg side. 18 *Hurling* to strike (a fast-moving ball) in the same direction as it is already moving. 19 (*also intr*) to row (a boat) or take a stroke of (an oar) in rowing. 20 to be rowed by: *a racing shell pulls one, two, four, or eight oars.* 21 (of a rider) to restrain (a horse), esp to prevent it from winning a race. 22 (*intr*) (of a horse) to resist strongly the attempts of a rider to rein in or check it. 23 **pull a fast one.** *Slang* to play a sly trick. 24 **pull apart** *or* **to pieces.** to criticize harshly. 25 **pull your head in.** *Austral informal* be quiet! 26 **pull (one's) punches. a** *Informal* to restrain the force of one's criticisms or actions. **b** *Boxing* to restrain the force of one's blows, esp when deliberately losing after being bribed, etc. 27 **pull one's weight.** *Informal* to do one's fair or proper share of a task. 28 **pull strings.** *Informal* to exercise personal influence, esp secretly or unofficially. 29 **pull (someone's) leg.** *Informal* to make fun of, fool, or tease (someone). ◆ NOUN 30 an act or an instance of pulling or being pulled. 31 the force or effort used in pulling: *the pull of the moon affects the tides on earth.* 32 the act or an instance of taking in drink or smoke. 33 something used for pulling, such as a knob or handle. 34 *Informal* special advantage or influence: *his uncle is chairman of the company, so he has quite a lot of pull.* 35 *Informal* the power to attract attention or support. 36 a period of rowing. 37 a single stroke of an oar in rowing. 38 the act of pulling the ball in golf, cricket, etc. 39 the act of checking or reining in a horse. 40 the amount of resistance in a bowstring, trigger, etc. ◆ See also **pull about, pull back, pull down, pull in, pull off, pull on, pull out, pull through. pull together, pull up.**
▷HISTORY Old English *pullian;* related to Icelandic *pūla* to beat
▸ˈ**puller** NOUN

pull about VERB (*tr, adverb*) to handle roughly: *the thugs pulled the old lady about.*

pull back VERB (*adverb*) 1 to return or be returned to a rearward position by pulling: *the army pulled back.* ◆ NOUN **pullback.** 2 the act of pulling back. 3 a device for restraining the motion of a mechanism, etc., or for returning it to its original position.

pull down VERB (*tr, adverb*) to destroy or demolish: *the old houses were pulled down.*

pullet (ˈpʊlɪt) NOUN a young hen of the domestic fowl, less than one year old.
▷HISTORY C14: from Old French *poulet* chicken, from Latin *pullus* a young animal or bird

pulley (ˈpʊlɪ) NOUN 1 a wheel with a grooved rim in which a rope, chain, or belt can run in order to change the direction or point of application of a force applied to the rope, etc. 2 a number of such wheels pivoted in parallel in a block, used to raise heavy loads. 3 a wheel with a flat, convex, or grooved rim mounted on a shaft and driven by or driving a belt passing around it.
▷HISTORY C14 *poley,* from Old French *polie,* from Vulgar Latin *polidium* (unattested), apparently from Late Greek *polidion* (unattested) a little pole, from Greek *polos* axis

pull in VERB (*adverb*) 1 (*intr;* often foll by *to*) to reach a destination: *the train pulled in at the station.* 2 (*intr*) Also: **pull over.** (of a motor vehicle, driver, etc.) **a** to draw in to the side of the road in order to stop or to allow another vehicle to pass. **b** to stop (at a café, lay-by, etc.). 3 (*tr*) to draw or attract: *his appearance will pull in the crowds.* 4 (*tr*) *Slang* to arrest. 5 (*tr*) to earn or gain (money). ◆ NOUN **pull-in.** 6 *Brit* a roadside café, esp for lorry drivers.

Pullman (ˈpʊlmən) NOUN, *plural* **-mans.** a luxurious railway coach, esp a sleeping car. Also called: **Pullman car.**
▷HISTORY C19: named after George M. *Pullman* (1831–97), the US inventor who first manufactured such coaches

pull off VERB (*tr*) 1 to remove (clothing) forcefully. 2 (*adverb*) to succeed in performing (a difficult feat).

pull on VERB (*tr, adverb*) to don (clothing).

pullorum disease (pʊˈlɔːrəm) NOUN an acute serious bacterial disease of very young birds, esp chickens, characterized by a whitish diarrhoea: caused by *Salmonella pullorum,* transmitted during egg production. Also called: **bacillary white diarrhoea.**
▷HISTORY Latin *pullōrum* of chickens, from *pullus* chicken

pull out VERB (*adverb*) 1 (*tr*) to extract. 2 (*intr*) to depart: *the train pulled out of the station.* 3 *Military* to withdraw or escape or be withdrawn or rescued, as from a difficult situation: *the troops were pulled out of the ruined city.* 4 (*intr*) (of a motor vehicle, driver, etc.) **a** to draw away from the side of the road. **b** to draw out from behind another vehicle to overtake. 5 (*intr*) to abandon a position or situation, esp a dangerous or embarrassing one. 6 (foll by *of*) to level out or cause to level out (from a dive). ◆ NOUN **pull-out.** 7 an extra leaf of a book that folds out. 8 a removable section of a magazine, etc. 9 a flight manoeuvre during which an aircraft levels out after a dive. 10 a withdrawal from a position or situation, esp a dangerous or embarrassing one.

pullover (ˈpʊlˌəʊvə) NOUN a garment, esp a sweater, that is pulled on over the head.

pull through VERB 1 Also: **pull round.** to survive or recover or cause to survive or recover, esp after a serious illness or crisis. ◆ NOUN **pull-through.** 2 a weighted cord with a piece of cloth at the end used to clean the bore of a firearm.

pull together VERB 1 (*intr, adverb*) to cooperate or work harmoniously. 2 **pull oneself together.** *Informal* to regain one's self-control or composure.

pullulate ('pʌljʊˌleɪt) VERB (*intr*) 1 (of animals, etc.) to breed rapidly or abundantly; teem; swarm. 2 (of plants or plant parts) to sprout, bud, or germinate.
▷HISTORY C17: from Latin *pullulāre* to sprout, from *pullulus* a baby animal, from *pullus* young animal
▸**ˌpulluˈlation** NOUN

pull up VERB (*adverb*) 1 (*tr*) to remove by the roots. 2 (often foll by *with* or *on*) to move level (with) or ahead (of) or cause to move level (with) or ahead (of), esp in a race. 3 to stop: *the car pulled up suddenly.* 4 (*tr*) to rebuke. ◆ NOUN **pull-up.** 5 an exercise in which the body is raised up by the arms pulling on a horizontal bar fixed above the head. 6 *Brit old-fashioned* a roadside café; pull-in.

pullus ('pʊləs) NOUN a technical term for a chick or young bird.
▷HISTORY C18: from Latin, from *pullulāre* to sprout

pulmonary ('pʌlmənərɪ, -mənrɪ, 'pʊl-) ADJECTIVE 1 of, or relating to or affecting the lungs. 2 having lungs or lunglike organs.
▷HISTORY C18: from Latin *pulmōnārius,* from *pulmō* a lung; related to Greek *pleumōn* a lung

pulmonary artery NOUN either of the two arteries that convey oxygen-depleted blood from the heart to the lungs.

pulmonary vein NOUN any one of the four veins that convey oxygen-rich blood from the lungs to the heart.

pulmonate ('pʌlmənɪt, 'pʊl-) ADJECTIVE 1 having lungs or lunglike organs. 2 of, relating to, or belonging to the *Pulmonata,* a mostly terrestrial subclass or order of gastropod molluscs, including snails and slugs, in which the mantle is adapted as a lung. ◆ NOUN 3 any pulmonate mollusc.
▷HISTORY C19: from New Latin *pulmōnātus*

pulmonic (pʌl'mɒnɪk, pʊl-) ADJECTIVE 1 of or relating to the lungs; pulmonary. ◆ NOUN 2 *Rare* **a** a person with lung disease. **b** a drug or remedy for lung disease.
▷HISTORY C17: from French *pulmonique,* from Latin *pulmō* a lung; see PULMONARY

Pulmotor ('pʌlˌməʊtə, 'pʊl-) NOUN *Trademark* an apparatus for pumping oxygen into the lungs during artificial respiration.

pulp (pʌlp) NOUN 1 soft or fleshy plant tissue, such as the succulent part of a fleshy fruit. 2 a moist mixture of cellulose fibres, as obtained from wood, from which paper is made. 3 **a** a magazine or book containing trite or sensational material, and usually printed on cheap rough paper. **b** (*as modifier*): *a pulp novel.* 4 *Dentistry* the soft innermost part of a tooth, containing nerves and blood vessels. 5 any soft soggy mass or substance. 6 *Mining* pulverized ore, esp when mixed with water. ◆ VERB 7 to reduce (a material or solid substance) to pulp or (of a material or solid substance) to be reduced to pulp. 8 (*tr*) to remove the pulp from (fruit).
▷HISTORY C16: from Latin *pulpa*
▸**ˈpulper** NOUN

pulpit ('pʊlpɪt) NOUN 1 a raised platform, usually surrounded by a barrier, set up in churches as the appointed place for preaching, leading in prayer, etc. 2 any similar raised structure, such as a lectern. 3 a medium for expressing an opinion, such as a column in a newspaper. 4 (usually preceded by *the*) **a** the preaching of the Christian message. **b** the clergy or their message and influence.
▷HISTORY C14: from Latin *pulpitum* a platform

pulpwood ('pʌlpˌwʊd) NOUN pine, spruce, or any other soft wood used to make paper.

pulpy ('pʌlpɪ) ADJECTIVE **pulpier, pulpiest.** having a soft or soggy consistency.
▸**ˈpulpily** ADVERB ▸**ˈpulpiness** NOUN

pulque ('pʊlkɪ; *Spanish* 'pulke) NOUN a light alcoholic drink from Mexico made from the juice of various agave plants, esp the maguey.
▷HISTORY C17: from Mexican Spanish, apparently from Nahuatl, from *puliuhqui* decomposed, since it will only keep for a day

pulsar ('pʌlˌsɑː) NOUN any of a number of very small extremely dense objects first observed in 1967, which rotate very rapidly and emit very regular pulses of polarized radiation, esp radio waves. They are thought to be neutron stars formed following supernova explosions.
▷HISTORY C20: from *puls(ating st)ar,* on the model of QUASAR

pulsate (pʌl'seɪt) VERB (*intr*) 1 to expand and contract with a rhythmic beat; throb. 2 *Physics* to vary in intensity, magnitude, size, etc.: *the current was pulsating.* 3 to quiver or vibrate.
▷HISTORY C18: from Latin *pulsāre* to push
▸**pulsative** ('pʌlsətɪv) ADJECTIVE ▸**ˈpulsatively** ADVERB

pulsatile ('pʌlsəˌtaɪl) ADJECTIVE beating rhythmically; pulsating or throbbing.
▸**pulsatility** (ˌpʌlsə'tɪlɪtɪ) NOUN

pulsatilla (ˌpʌlsə'tɪlə) NOUN another name for **pasqueflower.**
▷HISTORY C16: from Medieval Latin, from *pulsāta* beaten (by the wind)

pulsating star NOUN a type of variable star, the variation in brightness resulting from expansion and subsequent contraction of the star.

pulsation (pʌl'seɪʃən) NOUN 1 the act of pulsating. 2 *Physiol* a rhythmic beating or pulsing esp of the heart or an artery.

pulsator (pʌl'seɪtə) NOUN 1 a device that stimulates rhythmic motion of a body; a vibrator. 2 any pulsating machine, device, or part.

pulsatory ('pʌlsətərɪ, -trɪ) ADJECTIVE 1 of or relating to pulsation. 2 throbbing or pulsating.

pulse¹ (pʌls) NOUN 1 *Physiol* **a** the rhythmic contraction and expansion of an artery at each beat of the heart, often discernible to the touch at points such as the wrists. **b** a single pulsation of the heart or arteries. 2 *Physics, electronics* **a** a transient sharp change in voltage, current, or some other quantity normally constant in a system. **b** one of a series of such transient disturbances, usually recurring at regular intervals and having a characteristic geometric shape. **c** (*as modifier*): *a pulse generator.* Less common name: **impulse.** 3 **a** a recurrent rhythmic series of beats, waves, vibrations, etc. **b** any single beat, wave, etc., in such a series. 4 bustle, vitality, or excitement: *the pulse of a city.* 5 the feelings or thoughts of a group or society as they can be measured: *the pulse of the voters.* 6 **keep one's finger on the pulse.** to be well-informed about current events. ◆ VERB 7 (*intr*) to beat, throb, or vibrate.
▷HISTORY C14 *pous,* from Latin *pulsus* a beating, from *pellere* to beat
▸**ˈpulseless** ADJECTIVE

pulse² (pʌls) NOUN 1 the edible seeds of any of several leguminous plants, such as peas, beans, and lentils. 2 the plant producing any of these seeds.
▷HISTORY C13 *pols,* from Old French, from Latin *puls* pottage of pulse

pulse code modulation NOUN *Electronics* a form of pulse modulation in which the information is carried by coded groups of pulses. Abbreviation: **pcm.**

pulse height analyser NOUN *Electronics* a multichannel analyser that sorts pulses into selected amplitude ranges.

pulsejet ('pʌlsˌdʒɛt) NOUN a type of ramjet engine in which air is admitted through movable vanes that are closed by the pressure resulting from each intermittent explosion of the fuel in the combustion chamber, thus causing a pulsating thrust. Also called: **pulsejet engine, pulsojet** ('pʌlsəʊˌdʒɛt).

pulse modulation NOUN *Electronics* 1 a type of modulation in which a train of pulses is used as the carrier wave, one or more of its parameters, such as amplitude, being modulated or modified in order to carry information. 2 the modulation of a continuous carrier wave by means of pulses.

pulsimeter (pʌl'sɪmɪtə) NOUN *Med* an instrument for measuring the strength and rate of the pulse. Also called: **pulsometer.**

pulsometer (pʌl'sɒmɪtə) NOUN 1 another name for **pulsimeter.** 2 a vacuum pump that operates by steam being condensed and water admitted alternately in two chambers.

pulverable ('pʌlvərəbᵊl) ADJECTIVE able to be pulverized.

pulverize *or* **pulverise** ('pʌlvəˌraɪz) VERB 1 to reduce (a substance) to fine particles, as by crushing or grinding, or (of a substance) to be so reduced. 2 (*tr*) to destroy completely; defeat or injure seriously.
▷HISTORY C16: from Late Latin *pulverizare* or French *pulvériser,* from Latin *pulverum,* from *pulvis* dust
▸**ˈpulverˌizable** *or* **ˈpulverˌisable** ADJECTIVE ▸**ˌpulveriˈzation** *or* **ˌpulveriˈsation** NOUN ▸**ˈpulverˌizer** *or* **ˈpulverˌiser** NOUN

pulverulent (pʌl'vɛrʊlənt) ADJECTIVE consisting of, covered with, or crumbling to dust or fine particles.
▷HISTORY C17: from Latin *pulverulentus,* from *pulvis* dust
▸**pulˈverulence** NOUN

pulvillus (pʌl'vɪləs) NOUN, *plural* **-li** (-laɪ). a small pad between the claws at the end of an insect's leg.
▷HISTORY C18: from Latin, from *pulvīnulus,* diminutive of *pulvīnus* cushion

pulvinate ('pʌlvɪˌneɪt) *or* **pulvinated** ADJECTIVE 1 *Architect* (of a frieze) curved convexly; having a swelling. 2 *Botany* **a** shaped like a cushion. **b** (of a leafstalk) having a pulvinus.
▷HISTORY C19: from Latin *pulvīnātus* cushion-shaped

pulvinus (pʌl'vaɪnəs) NOUN, *plural* **-ni** (-naɪ). a swelling at the base of a leafstalk: changes in its turgor pressure cause changes in the position of the leaf.
▷HISTORY C19: from Latin: cushion

puma ('pjuːmə) NOUN a large American feline mammal, *Felis concolor,* that resembles a lion, having a plain greyish-brown coat and long tail. Also called: **cougar, mountain lion.**
▷HISTORY C18: via Spanish from Quechuan

pumice ('pʌmɪs) NOUN 1 Also called: **pumice stone.** a light porous acid volcanic rock having the composition of rhyolite, used for scouring and, in powdered form, as an abrasive and for polishing. ◆ VERB 2 (*tr*) to rub or polish with pumice.
▷HISTORY C15 *pomys,* from Old French *pomis,* from Latin *pūmex*
▸**pumiceous** (pjuː'mɪʃəs) ADJECTIVE

pumice country NOUN *NZ* volcanic farmland in the North Island.

pummel ('pʌməl) VERB **-mels, -melling, -melled** *or US* **-mels, -meling, -meled.** (*tr*) to strike repeatedly with or as if with the fists. Also (less commonly): **pommel.**
▷HISTORY C16: see POMMEL

pump¹ (pʌmp) NOUN 1 any device for compressing, driving, raising, or reducing the pressure of a fluid, esp by means of a piston or set of rotating impellers. 2 *Biology* a mechanism for the active transport of ions, such as protons, calcium ions, and sodium ions, across cell membranes: *a sodium pump.* ◆ VERB 3 (when *tr,* usually foll by *from, out, into, away,* etc.) to raise or drive (air, liquid, etc., esp into or from something) with a pump or similar device. 4 (*tr;* usually foll by *in* or *into*) to supply in large amounts: *to pump capital into a project.* 5 (*tr*) to deliver (shots, bullets, etc.) repeatedly with great force. 6 to operate (something, esp a handle or lever) in the manner of a pump or (of something) to work in this way: *to pump the pedals of a bicycle.* 7 (*tr*) to obtain (information) from (a person) by persistent questioning. 8 (*intr;* usually foll by *from* or *out of*) (of liquids) to flow freely in large spurts: *oil pumped from the fissure.*
▷HISTORY C15: from Middle Dutch *pumpe* pipe, probably from Spanish *bomba,* of imitative origin

pump² (pʌmp) NOUN 1 a low-cut low-heeled shoe without fastenings, worn esp for dancing. 2 a type of shoe with a rubber sole, used in games such as tennis; plimsoll.
▷HISTORY C16: of unknown origin

pump-action ADJECTIVE 1 (of a shotgun or other repeating firearm) operated by a slide-action mechanism feeding ammunition from a magazine under the barrel into the breech. 2 spraying or dispensing liquid by means of a pump rather than using a propellant.

pumped storage NOUN (in hydroelectric systems) a method of using power at a period of low demand to pump water back up to a high storage reservoir so that it can be released to generate electricity at a period of peak demand.

pumpernickel (ˈpʌmpəˌnɪkəl) NOUN a slightly sour black bread, originating in Germany, made of coarse rye flour.
▷HISTORY C18: from German, of uncertain origin

pump gun NOUN a repeating gun operated by a slide-action mechanism feeding ammunition from a magazine under the barrel into the breech.

pump iron VERB (*intr*) *Slang* to exercise with weights; do body-building exercises.

pumpkin (ˈpʌmpkɪn) NOUN 1 any of several creeping cucurbitaceous plants of the genus *Cucurbita, esp C. pepo* of North America and *C. maxima* of Europe. 2 **a** the large round fruit of any of these plants, which has a thick orange rind, pulpy flesh, and numerous seeds. **b** (*as modifier*): *pumpkin pie*.
▷HISTORY C17: from earlier *pumpion,* from Old French *pompon,* from Latin *pepo,* from Greek *pepōn,* from *pepōn* ripe, from *peptein* to ripen

pumpkinseed (ˈpʌmpkɪnˌsiːd) NOUN 1 the seed of the pumpkin. 2 a common North American freshwater sunfish, *Lepomis gibbosus,* with brightly coloured markings: family *Centrarchidae*.

pump priming NOUN 1 the act or process of introducing fluid into a pump to improve the sealing of the pump parts on starting and to expel air from it. 2 *US* government expenditure designed to stimulate economic activity in stagnant or depressed areas. 3 another term for **deficit financing.**

pump room NOUN a building or room at a spa in which the water from a mineral spring may be drunk.

pun¹ (pʌn) NOUN 1 the use of words or phrases to exploit ambiguities and innuendoes in their meaning, usually for humorous effect; a play on words. An example is: *"Ben Battle was a soldier bold, And used to war's alarms: But a cannonball took off his legs, So he laid down his arms."* (Thomas Hood). ◆ VERB **puns, punning, punned.** 2 (*intr*) to make puns.
▷HISTORY C17: possibly from Italian *puntiglio* point of detail, wordplay; see PUNCTILIO

pun² (pʌn) VERB **puns, punning, punned.** (*tr*) *Brit* to pack (earth, rubble, etc.) by pounding.
▷HISTORY C16: dialectal variant of POUND¹
▸ˈ**punner** NOUN

puna *Spanish* (ˈpuna) NOUN 1 a high cold dry plateau, esp in the Andes. 2 another name for **mountain sickness.**
▷HISTORY C17: from American Spanish, from Quechuan

Punakha *or* **Punaka** (ˈpuːnəkə) NOUN a town in W central Bhutan: a former capital of the country.

punce (pʌns) *Northern English dialect* ◆ NOUN 1 a kick. ◆ VERB **punce, puncing, punced.** 2 to kick.

punch¹ (pʌntʃ) VERB 1 to strike blows (at), esp with a clenched fist. 2 (*tr*) *Western US* to herd or drive (cattle), esp for a living. 3 (*tr*) to poke or prod with a stick or similar object. 4 **punch above one's weight.** to do something that is considered to be beyond one's ability. ◆ NOUN 5 a blow with the fist. 6 *Informal* telling force, point, or vigour: *his arguments lacked punch.* 7 **pull (one's) punches.** See **pull** (sense 26).
▷HISTORY C15: perhaps a variant of POUNCE²
▸ˈ**puncher** NOUN

punch² (pʌntʃ) NOUN 1 a tool or machine for piercing holes in a material. 2 any of various tools used for knocking a bolt, rivet, etc., out of a hole. 3 a tool or machine used for stamping a design on something or shaping it by impact. 4 the solid die of a punching machine for cutting, stamping, or shaping material. 5 *Computing* a device, such as a card punch or tape punch, used for making holes in a card or paper tape. 6 See **centre punch.** ◆ VERB 7 (*tr*) to pierce, cut, stamp, shape, or drive with a punch.
▷HISTORY C14: shortened from *puncheon,* from Old French *ponçon;* see PUNCHEON²

punch³ (pʌntʃ) NOUN any mixed drink containing fruit juice and, usually, alcoholic liquor, generally hot and spiced.
▷HISTORY C17: perhaps from Hindi *pānch,* from Sanskrit *pañca* five; the beverage originally included five ingredients

Punch (pʌntʃ) NOUN the main character in the traditional children's puppet show **Punch and Judy.**

punchbag (ˈpʌntʃˌbæg) NOUN Also called (US and Canadian): **punching bag.** a suspended stuffed bag that is punched for exercise, esp boxing training.

punchball (ˈpʌntʃˌbɔːl) NOUN 1 a stuffed or inflated ball, supported by a flexible rod, that is punched for exercise, esp boxing training. 2 *US* a game resembling baseball in which a light ball is struck with the fist.

punchboard (ˈpʌntʃˌbɔːd) NOUN a board full of holes containing slips of paper, used in a gambling game in which a player attempts to push out a slip marked with a winning number.

punchbowl (ˈpʌntʃˌbəʊl) NOUN 1 a large bowl for serving punch, lemonade, etc., usually with a ladle and often having small drinking glasses hooked around the rim. 2 *Brit* a bowl-shaped depression in the land.

punch-drunk ADJECTIVE 1 demonstrating or characteristic of the behaviour of a person who has suffered repeated blows to the head, esp a professional boxer. 2 dazed; stupefied.

punched card *or esp US* **punch card** NOUN (formerly) a card on which data can be coded in the form of punched holes. In computing, there were usually 80 columns and 12 rows, each column containing a pattern of holes representing one character. Sometimes shortened to: **card.**

punched tape *or sometimes US* **perforated tape** NOUN other terms for **paper tape.**

puncheon¹ (ˈpʌntʃən) NOUN 1 a large cask of variable capacity, usually between 70 and 120 gallons. 2 the volume of such a cask used as a liquid measure.
▷HISTORY C15 *poncion,* from Old French *ponchon,* of uncertain origin

puncheon² (ˈpʌntʃən) NOUN 1 a short wooden post that is used as a vertical strut. 2 a less common name for **punch²** (sense 1).
▷HISTORY C14 *ponson,* from Old French *ponçon,* from Latin *punctiō* a puncture, from *pungere* to prick

Punchinello (ˌpʌntʃɪˈnɛləʊ) NOUN, *plural* **-los** *or* **-loes.** 1 a type of clown from Italian burlesque or puppet shows, the prototype of Punch. 2 (*sometimes not capital*) any grotesque or absurd character.
▷HISTORY C17: from earlier *Polichinello,* from Italian (Neapolitan dialect) *Polecenella,* from Italian *pulcino* chicken, ultimately from Latin *pullus* young animal

punch line NOUN the culminating part of a joke, funny story, etc., that gives it its humorous or dramatic point.

punch-up NOUN *Brit informal* a fight, brawl, or violent argument.

punchy (ˈpʌntʃɪ) ADJECTIVE **punchier, punchiest.** 1 an informal word for **punch-drunk.** 2 *Informal* incisive or forceful: *a punchy article.*
▸ˈ**punchily** ADVERB ▸ˈ**punchiness** NOUN

punctate (ˈpʌŋkteɪt) *or* **punctated** ADJECTIVE having or marked with minute spots, holes, or depressions.
▷HISTORY C18: from New Latin *punctātus,* from Latin *punctum* a point
▸**puncˈtation** NOUN

punctilio (pʌŋkˈtɪlɪˌəʊ) NOUN, *plural* **-os.** 1 strict attention to minute points of etiquette. 2 a petty formality or fine point of etiquette.
▷HISTORY C16: from Italian *puntiglio* small point, from *punto* point, from Latin *punctum* point

punctilious (pʌŋkˈtɪlɪəs) ADJECTIVE 1 paying scrupulous attention to correctness in etiquette. 2 attentive to detail.
▸**puncˈtiliously** ADVERB ▸**puncˈtiliousness** NOUN

punctual (ˈpʌŋktjʊəl) ADJECTIVE 1 arriving or taking place at an arranged time; prompt. 2 (of a person) having the characteristic of always keeping to arranged times, as for appointments, meetings, etc. 3 *Obsolete* precise; exact; apposite. 4 *Maths* consisting of or confined to a point in space.
▷HISTORY C14: from Medieval Latin *punctuālis* concerning detail, from Latin *punctum* point
▸ˌ**punctuˈality** NOUN ▸ˈ**punctually** ADVERB

punctuate (ˈpʌŋktjʊˌeɪt) VERB (*mainly tr*) 1 (*also intr*) to insert punctuation marks into (a written text). 2 to interrupt or insert at frequent intervals: *a meeting punctuated by heckling.* 3 to give emphasis to.
▷HISTORY C17: from Medieval Latin *punctuāre* to prick, from Latin *punctum* a prick, from *pungere* to puncture
▸ˈ**punctuˌator** NOUN

punctuation (ˌpʌŋktjʊˈeɪʃən) NOUN 1 the use of symbols not belonging to the alphabet of a writing system to indicate aspects of the intonation and meaning not otherwise conveyed in the written language. 2 the symbols used for this purpose. 3 the act or an instance of punctuating.

punctuation mark NOUN any of the signs used in punctuation, such as a comma or question mark.

puncture (ˈpʌŋktʃə) NOUN 1 a small hole made by a sharp object. 2 a perforation and loss of pressure in a pneumatic tyre, made by sharp stones, glass, etc. 3 the act of puncturing or perforating. ◆ VERB 4 (*tr*) to pierce (a hole) in (something) with a sharp object. 5 to cause (something pressurized, esp a tyre) to lose pressure by piercing, or (of a tyre, etc.) to be pierced and collapse in this way. 6 (*tr*) to depreciate (a person's self-esteem, pomposity, etc.).
▷HISTORY C14: from Latin *punctūra,* from *pungere* to prick
▸ˈ**puncturable** ADJECTIVE ▸ˈ**puncturer** NOUN

pundit (ˈpʌndɪt) NOUN 1 an expert. 2 (formerly) a learned person. 3 Also called: **pandit.** a Brahman learned in Sanskrit and, esp in Hindu religion, philosophy or law.
▷HISTORY C17: from Hindi *pandit,* from Sanskrit *pandita* learned man, from *pandita* learned

punditry (ˈpʌndɪtrɪ) NOUN the expressing of expert opinions.

Pune (ˈpuːnə) NOUN another name for **Poona.**

pung (pʌŋ) NOUN *Eastern US and Canadian* a horse-drawn sleigh with a boxlike body on runners.
▷HISTORY C19: shortened from Algonquian *tom-pung;* compare TOBOGGAN

punga (ˈpʌŋə) NOUN a variant spelling of **ponga.**

pungent (ˈpʌndʒənt) ADJECTIVE 1 having an acrid smell or sharp bitter flavour. 2 (of wit, satire, etc.) biting; caustic. 3 *Biology* ending in a sharp point: *a pungent leaf.*
▷HISTORY C16: from Latin *pungens* piercing, from *pungere* to prick
▸ˈ**pungency** NOUN ▸ˈ**pungently** ADVERB

Punic (ˈpjuːnɪk) ADJECTIVE 1 of or relating to ancient Carthage or the Carthaginians. 2 characteristic of the treachery of the Carthaginians. ◆ NOUN 3 the language of the ancient Carthaginians; a late form of Phoenician.
▷HISTORY C15: from Latin *Pūnicus,* variant of *Poenicus* Carthaginian, from Greek *Phoinix*

Punic Wars PLURAL NOUN three wars (264–241 B.C., 218–201 B.C., and 149–146 B.C.), in which Rome crushed Carthaginian power, destroying Carthage itself.

punish (ˈpʌnɪʃ) VERB 1 to force (someone) to undergo a penalty or sanction, such as imprisonment, fines, death, etc., for some crime or misdemeanour. 2 (*tr*) to inflict punishment for (some crime, etc.). 3 (*tr*) to use or treat harshly or roughly, esp as by overexertion: *to punish a horse.* 4 (*tr*) *Informal* to consume (some commodity) in large quantities: *to punish the bottle.*
▷HISTORY C14 *punisse,* from Old French *punir,* from Latin *pūnīre* to punish, from *poena* penalty
▸ˈ**punisher** NOUN ▸ˈ**punishing** ADJECTIVE ▸ˈ**punishingly** ADVERB

punishable (ˈpʌnɪʃəbəl) ADJECTIVE liable to be punished or deserving of punishment.
▸ˌ**punishaˈbility** NOUN

punishment (ˈpʌnɪʃmənt) NOUN 1 a penalty or sanction given for any crime or offence. 2 the act of punishing or state of being punished. 3 *Informal* rough treatment. 4 *Psychol* any aversive stimulus administered to an organism as part of training.

punitive (ˈpjuːnɪtɪv) *or less commonly* **punitory** (ˈpjuːnɪtərɪ, -trɪ) ADJECTIVE relating to, involving, or with the intention of inflicting punishment: *a punitive expedition.*
▷HISTORY C17: from Medieval Latin *pūnītīvus* concerning punishment, from Latin *pūnīre* to punish
▸ˈ**punitively** ADVERB ▸ˈ**punitiveness** NOUN

Punjab (pʌnˈdʒɑːb, ˈpʌndʒɑːb) NOUN 1 (formerly) a province in NW British India: divided between India and Pakistan in 1947. 2 a state of NW India: reorganized in 1966 as a Punjabi-speaking state, a large part forming the new state of Haryana; mainly agricultural. Capital: Chandigarh. Pop.: 24 289 296 (2001). Area: 50 255 sq. km (19 403 sq. miles). 3 a province of W Pakistan: created in 1947. Capital: Lahore. Pop.: 72 585 000 (1998). Area: 205 344 sq. km (127 595 sq. miles).

Punjabi *or* **Panjabi** (pʌnˈdʒɑːbɪ) NOUN 1 a member of the chief people of the Punjab. 2 the state language of the Punjab, belonging to the Indic branch of the Indo-European family. ◆ ADJECTIVE 3 of or relating to the Punjab, its people, or their language.

Punjab States PLURAL NOUN (formerly) a group of states in NW India, amalgamated in 1956 with Punjab state.

punk[1] (pʌŋk) NOUN 1 **a** a youth movement of the late 1970s, characterized by anti-Establishment slogans and outrageous clothes and hairstyles. **b** an adherent of punk. **c** short for **punk rock**. **d** (*as modifier*): *a punk record*. 2 an inferior, rotten, or worthless person or thing. 3 worthless articles collectively. 4 a petty criminal or hoodlum. 5 *Obsolete* a young male homosexual; catamite. 6 *Obsolete* a prostitute. ◆ ADJECTIVE 7 inferior, rotten, or worthless.
▷HISTORY C16: via Polari from Spanish *pu(n)ta* prostitute, *pu(n)to* male prostitute
▸ˈ**punkish** ADJECTIVE

punk[2] (pʌŋk) NOUN 1 dried decayed wood that smoulders when ignited: used as tinder. 2 any of various other substances that smoulder when ignited, esp one used to light fireworks.
▷HISTORY C18: of uncertain origin

punka *or* **punkah** (ˈpʌŋkə) NOUN a fan made of a palm leaf or leaves.
▷HISTORY C17: from Hindi *pankhā*, from Sanskrit *paksaka* fan, from *paksa* wing

punk rock NOUN a fast abrasive style of rock music of the late 1970s, characterized by aggressive or offensive lyrics and performance. Sometimes shortened to: **punk**.
▸**punk rocker** NOUN

punnet (ˈpʌnɪt) NOUN *Chiefly Brit* a small basket for fruit, such as strawberries.
▷HISTORY C19: perhaps diminutive of dialect *pun* POUND[2]

punster (ˈpʌnstə) NOUN a person who is fond of making puns, esp one who makes a tedious habit of this.

punt[1] (pʌnt) NOUN 1 an open flat-bottomed boat with square ends, propelled by a pole. See **quant[1]**. ◆ VERB 2 to propel (a boat, esp a punt) by pushing with a pole on the bottom of a river, etc.
▷HISTORY Old English *punt* shallow boat, from Latin *pontō* punt, PONTOON[1]

punt[2] (pʌnt) NOUN 1 a kick in certain sports, such as rugby, in which the ball is released and kicked before it hits the ground. 2 any long high kick. ◆ VERB 3 to kick (a ball, etc.) using a punt.
▷HISTORY C19: perhaps a variant of English dialect *bunt* to push, perhaps a nasalized variant of BUTT[3]

punt[3] (pʌnt) *Chiefly Brit* ◆ VERB 1 (*intr*) to gamble; bet. ◆ NOUN 2 a gamble or bet, esp against the bank, as in roulette, or on horses. 3 Also called: **punter**. a person who bets. 4 **take a punt at**. *Austral and NZ informal* to have an attempt or try at (something).
▷HISTORY C18: from French *ponter* to punt, from *ponte* bet laid against the banker, from Spanish *punto* point, from Latin *punctum*

punt[4] (pʊnt) NOUN (formerly) the Irish pound.
▷HISTORY Irish Gaelic: pound

Punta Arenas (*Spanish* ˈpunta aˈrenas) NOUN a port in S Chile, on the Strait of Magellan: the southernmost city in the world. Pop.: 120 148 (1999 est.). Former name: **Magallanes**.

punter[1] (ˈpʌntə) NOUN a person who punts a boat.

punter[2] (ˈpʌntə) NOUN a person who kicks a ball.

punter[3] (ˈpʌntə) NOUN 1 a person who places a bet. 2 *Informal* any member of the public, esp when a customer: *the punters flock into the sales*. 3 *Slang* a prostitute's client. 4 *Slang* a victim of a con man.

punty (ˈpʌntɪ) NOUN, *plural* **-ties**. a long iron rod used in the finishing process of glass-blowing. Also called: **pontil**.
▷HISTORY C17: see PONTIL

puny (ˈpjuːnɪ) ADJECTIVE **-nier, -niest**. 1 having a small physique or weakly constitution. 2 paltry; insignificant.
▷HISTORY C16: from Old French *puisne* PUISNE
▸ˈ**punily** ADVERB ▸ˈ**puniness** NOUN

pup (pʌp) NOUN 1 **a** a young dog, esp when under one year of age; puppy. **b** the young of various other animals, such as the seal. 2 **in pup**. (of a bitch) pregnant. 3 *Informal, chiefly Brit contemptuous* a conceited young man (esp in the phrase **young pup**). 4 **sell (someone) a pup**. to swindle (someone) by selling him something worthless. 5 **the night's a pup**. *Austral slang* it's early yet. ◆ VERB **pups, pupping, pupped**. 6 (of dogs, seals, etc.) to give birth to (young).
▷HISTORY C18: back formation from PUPPY

pupa (ˈpjuːpə) NOUN, *plural* **-pae** (-piː) *or* **-pas**. an insect at the immobile nonfeeding stage of development between larva and adult, when many internal changes occur. See **coarctate, exarate, obtect**.
▷HISTORY C19: via New Latin, from Latin: a doll, puppet
▸ˈ**pupal** ADJECTIVE

puparium (pjuːˈpɛərɪəm) NOUN, *plural* **-ia** (-ɪə). a hard barrel-shaped case enclosing the pupae of the housefly and other dipterous insects.
▸**puˈparial** ADJECTIVE

pupate (pjuːˈpeɪt) VERB (*intr*) (of an insect larva) to develop into a pupa.
▸**puˈpation** NOUN

pupil[1] (ˈpjuːpᵊl) NOUN 1 a student who is taught by a teacher, esp a young student. 2 *Civil and Scots law* a boy under 14 or a girl under 12 who is in the care of a guardian.
▷HISTORY C14: from Latin *pupillus* an orphan, from *pūpus* a child

pupil[2] (ˈpjuːpᵊl) NOUN the dark circular aperture at the centre of the iris of the eye, through which light enters.
▷HISTORY C16: from Latin *pūpilla*, diminutive of *pūpa* girl, puppet; from the tiny reflections in the eye

pupillage *or US* **pupilage** (ˈpjuːpɪlɪdʒ) NOUN 1 the condition of being a pupil or duration for which one is a pupil. 2 (in England) the period spent by a newly called barrister in the chambers of a member of the bar.

pupillary[1] *or* **pupilary** (ˈpjuːpɪlərɪ) ADJECTIVE of or relating to a pupil or a legal ward.
▷HISTORY C17: from PUPIL[1] + -ARY
▸ˌ**pupilˈlarity** *or* ˌ**pupiˈlarity** NOUN

pupillary[2] *or* **pupilary** (ˈpjuːpɪlərɪ) ADJECTIVE of or relating to the pupil of the eye.
▷HISTORY C18: from Latin *pūpilla* PUPIL[2]

pupiparous (pjuːˈpɪpərəs) ADJECTIVE (of certain dipterous flies) producing young that have already reached the pupa stage at the time of hatching.
▷HISTORY C19: from New Latin *pupiparus*, from PUPA + *parere* to bring forth

puppet (ˈpʌpɪt) NOUN 1 **a** a small doll or figure of a person or animal moved by strings attached to its limbs or by the hand inserted in its cloth body. **b** (*as modifier*): *a puppet theatre*. 2 **a** a person, group, state, etc., that appears independent but is in fact controlled by another. **b** (*as modifier*): *a puppet government*.
▷HISTORY C16 *popet*, perhaps from Old French *poupette* little doll, ultimately from Latin *pūpa* girl, doll

puppeteer (ˌpʌpɪˈtɪə) NOUN a person who manipulates puppets.

puppetry (ˈpʌpɪtrɪ) NOUN 1 the art of making and manipulating puppets and presenting puppet shows. 2 unconvincing or specious presentation.

Puppis (ˈpʌpɪs) NOUN, *Latin genitive* **Puppis**. a constellation in the S hemisphere lying between Vela and Canis Major, a section of which is crossed by the Milky Way.
▷HISTORY Latin: the ship, the POOP of a ship

puppy (ˈpʌpɪ) NOUN, *plural* **-pies**. 1 a young dog; pup. 2 *Informal, contemptuous* a brash or conceited young man; pup.
▷HISTORY C15 *popi*, from Old French *popée* doll; compare PUPPET
▸ˈ**puppyˌhood** NOUN ▸ˈ**puppyish** ADJECTIVE

puppy fat NOUN fatty tissue that develops in childhood or adolescence and usually disappears by maturity.

puppy love NOUN another term for **calf love**.

pup tent NOUN another name for **shelter tent**.

Purana (pʊˈrɑːnə) NOUN any of a class of Sanskrit writings not included in the Vedas, characteristically recounting the birth and deeds of Hindu gods and the creation, destruction, or recreation of the universe.
▷HISTORY C17: from Sanskrit: ancient, from *purā* formerly
▸**Puˈranic** ADJECTIVE

Purbeck marble *or* **stone** (ˈpɜːbɛk) NOUN a fossil-rich limestone that takes a high polish: used for building, etc.
▷HISTORY C15: named after *Purbeck*, Dorset, where it is quarried

purblind (ˈpɜːˌblaɪnd) ADJECTIVE 1 partly or nearly blind. 2 lacking in insight or understanding; obtuse.
▷HISTORY C13: see PURE, BLIND; compare PARBOIL

purchasable (ˈpɜːtʃɪsəbᵊl) ADJECTIVE 1 able to be bribed or corrupted. 2 able to be bought.
▸ˌ**purchasaˈbility** NOUN

purchase (ˈpɜːtʃɪs) VERB (*tr*) 1 to obtain (goods, etc.) by payment. 2 to obtain by effort, sacrifice, etc.: *to purchase one's freedom*. 3 to draw, haul, or lift (a load) with the aid of mechanical apparatus. 4 to acquire (an estate) other than by inheritance. ◆ NOUN 5 something that is purchased, esp an article bought with money. 6 the act of buying. 7 acquisition of an estate by any lawful means other than inheritance. 8 a rough measure of the mechanical advantage achieved by a lever. 9 a firm foothold, grasp, etc., as for climbing or levering something. 10 a means of achieving some influence, advantage, etc.
▷HISTORY C13: from Old French *porchacier* to strive to obtain, from *por-* for + *chacier* to CHASE[1]
▸ˈ**purchaser** NOUN

purchase ledger NOUN *Commerce* a record of a company's purchases of goods and services showing the amounts paid and due.

purchase tax NOUN *Brit* a tax levied on nonessential consumer goods and added to selling prices by retailers.

purdah *or* **purda** (ˈpɜːdə) NOUN 1 the custom in some Muslim and Hindu communities of keeping women in seclusion, with clothing that conceals them completely when they go out. 2 a screen in a Hindu house used to keep the women out of view. 3 a veil worn by Hindu women of high caste. 4 *Informal* hiding or isolation: *the Treasury is currently locked in pre-budget purdah*.
▷HISTORY C19: from Hindi *parda* veil, from Persian *pardah*

purdonium (pɜːˈdəʊnɪəm) NOUN a type of coal scuttle having a slanted cover that is raised to open it, and an inner removable metal container for the coal.
▷HISTORY C19: named after its inventor, a Mr *Purdon*

pure (pjʊə) ADJECTIVE 1 not mixed with any extraneous or dissimilar materials, elements, etc.: *pure nitrogen*. 2 free from tainting or polluting matter; clean; wholesome: *pure water*. 3 free from moral taint or defilement: *pure love*. 4 (*prenominal*) (intensifier): *pure stupidity; a pure coincidence*. 5 (of a subject, etc.) studied in its theoretical aspects rather than for its practical applications: *pure mathematics; pure science*. Compare **applied**. 6 (of a vowel) pronounced with more or less unvarying quality without any glide; monophthongal. 7 (of a consonant) not accompanied by another consonant. 8 of supposedly unmixed racial descent. 9 *Genetics, biology* breeding true for one or more characteristics; homozygous. 10 *Music* **a** (of a sound) composed of a single frequency without overtones. **b** (of intervals in the system of just intonation) mathematically accurate in respect to the ratio of one frequency to another.
▷HISTORY C13: from Old French *pur*, from Latin *pūrus* unstained
▸ˈ**pureness** NOUN

purebred ADJECTIVE (ˈpjʊəˈbrɛd) 1 denoting a pure strain obtained through many generations of controlled breeding for desirable traits. ◆ NOUN ('pjʊəˌbrɛd) [2] a purebred animal. Compare **grade** (sense 9), **crossbred** (sense 2).

pure culture NOUN *Bacteriol* a culture containing a single species of microorganism.

puree *or* **puri** ('puːrɪ) NOUN an unleavened flaky Indian bread, that is deep-fried in ghee and served hot.
▷HISTORY Hindi

purée ('pjʊəreɪ) NOUN [1] a smooth thick pulp of cooked and sieved fruit, vegetables, meat, or fish. ◆ VERB **-rées, -réeing, -réed.** [2] (*tr*) to make (cooked foods) into a purée.
▷HISTORY C19: from French *purer* to PURIFY

pure laine (pjʊə 'lɛn) NOUN (in Quebec) a person belonging to a long-established family of French descent.
▷HISTORY French, literally: pure wool

Pure Land sects PLURAL NOUN Mahayana Buddhist sects venerating the Buddha as the compassionate saviour.

pure line NOUN a breed or strain of animals or plants in which certain characters appear in successive generations as a result of inbreeding or self-fertilization.

purely ('pjʊəlɪ) ADVERB [1] in a pure manner. [2] entirely: *purely by chance.* [3] in a chaste or innocent manner.

purfle ('pɜːfᵊl) NOUN *also* **purfling.** [1] a ruffled or curved ornamental band, as on clothing, furniture, etc. ◆ VERB [2] (*tr*) to decorate with such a band or bands.
▷HISTORY C14: from Old French *purfiler* to decorate with a border, from *filer* to spin, from *fil* thread, from Latin *fīlum*

purgation (pɜː'geɪʃən) NOUN the act of purging or state of being purged; purification.

purgative ('pɜːgətɪv) *Med* ◆ NOUN [1] a drug or agent for purging the bowels. ◆ ADJECTIVE [2] causing evacuation of the bowels; cathartic.
▸**'purgatively** ADVERB

purgatorial (ˌpɜːgə'tɔːrɪəl) ADJECTIVE [1] serving to purify from sin. [2] of, relating to, or like purgatory.
▸**ˌpurga'torially** ADVERB

purgatory ('pɜːgətərɪ, -trɪ) NOUN [1] *Chiefly RC Church* a state or place in which the souls of those who have died in a state of grace are believed to undergo a limited amount of suffering to expiate their venial sins and become purified of the remaining effects of mortal sin. [2] a place or condition of suffering or torment, esp one that is temporary.
▷HISTORY C13: from Old French *purgatoire,* from Medieval Latin *pūrgātōrium,* literally: place of cleansing, from Latin *pūrgāre* to PURGE

purge (pɜːdʒ) VERB [1] (*tr*) to rid (something) of (impure or undesirable elements). [2] (*tr*) to rid (a state, political party, etc.) of (dissident or troublesome people). [3] (*tr*) **a** to empty (the bowels) by evacuation of faeces. **b** to cause (a person) to evacuate his bowels. [4] **a** to clear (a person) of a charge. **b** to free (oneself) of guilt, as by atonement: *to purge contempt.* [5] (*intr*) to be cleansed or purified. ◆ NOUN [6] the act or process of purging. [7] the elimination of opponents or dissidents from a state, political party, etc. [8] a purgative drug or agent; cathartic.
▷HISTORY C14: from Old French *purger,* from Latin *pūrgāre* to purify
▸**'purger** NOUN

Puri ('pʊəriː, pʊə'riː) NOUN a port in E India, in Orissa on the Bay of Bengal: 12th-century temple of Jagannath. Pop.: 125 199 (1991).

Purification of the Virgin Mary NOUN **the.** *Christianity* [1] the presentation of Jesus in the Temple after the completion of Mary's purification (Luke 2:22). [2] Also called: **Candlemas.** the feast commemorating this (Feb. 2).

purificator ('pjʊərɪfɪˌkeɪtə) NOUN *Christianity* a small white linen cloth used to wipe the chalice and paten and also the lips and fingers of the celebrant at the Eucharist.

purifier ('pjʊərɪˌfaɪə) NOUN a device or substance that frees something of extraneous, contaminating, or debasing matter.

purify ('pjʊərɪˌfaɪ) VERB **-fies, -fying, -fied.** [1] to free (something) of extraneous, contaminating, or debasing matter. [2] (*tr*) to free (a person, etc.) from sin or guilt. [3] (*tr*) to make clean, as in a ritual, esp the churching of women after childbirth.
▷HISTORY C14: from Old French *purifier,* from Late Latin *pūrificāre* to cleanse, from *pūrus* pure + *facere* to make
▸**ˌpurifi'cation** NOUN ▸**purificatory** ('pjʊərɪfɪˌkeɪtərɪ) ADJECTIVE

Purim ('pʊərɪm; *Hebrew* puː'riːm) NOUN a Jewish holiday celebrated on Adar 14, in February or March, and in Adar Sheni in leap years, to commemorate the deliverance of the Jews from the massacre planned for them by Haman (Esther 9).
▷HISTORY Hebrew *pūrīm,* plural of *pūr* lot; from the casting of lots by Haman

purine ('pjʊəriːn) *or* **purin** ('pjʊərɪn) NOUN [1] a colourless crystalline solid that can be prepared from uric acid. Formula: $C_5H_4N_4$. [2] Also called: **purine base.** any of a number of nitrogenous bases, such as guanine and adenine, that are derivatives of purine and constituents of nucleic acids and certain coenzymes.
▷HISTORY C19: from German *Purin;* see PURE, URIC, -INE[2]

puriri (puː'riːriː) NOUN, *plural* **-ris.** a forest tree, *Vitex lucens,* of New Zealand, having red berries and glossy green leaves and yielding a durable dark brown timber.

purism ('pjʊəˌrɪzəm) NOUN insistence on traditional canons of correctness of form or purity of style or content, esp in language, art, or music.
▸**'purist** ADJECTIVE, NOUN ▸**pu'ristic** ADJECTIVE
▸**pu'ristically** ADVERB

puritan ('pjʊərɪtᵊn) NOUN [1] a person who adheres to strict moral or religious principles, esp one opposed to luxury and sensual enjoyment. ◆ ADJECTIVE [2] characteristic of a puritan.
▷HISTORY C16: from Late Latin *pūritās* PURITY
▸**'puritanˌism** NOUN

Puritan ('pjʊərɪtᵊn) (in the late 16th and 17th centuries) NOUN [1] any of the more extreme English Protestants, most of whom were Calvinists, who wished to purify the Church of England of most of its ceremony and other aspects that they deemed to be Catholic. ◆ ADJECTIVE [2] of, characteristic of, or relating to the Puritans.
▸**'Puritanˌism** NOUN

puritanical (ˌpjʊərɪ'tænɪkᵊl) *or less commonly* **puritanic** ADJECTIVE [1] *Usually disparaging* strict in moral or religious outlook, esp in shunning sensual pleasures. [2] (*sometimes capital*) of or relating to a puritan or the Puritans.
▸**ˌpuri'tanically** ADVERB ▸**ˌpuri'tanicalness** NOUN

purity ('pjʊərɪtɪ) NOUN [1] the state or quality of being pure. [2] *Physics* a measure of the amount of a single-frequency colour in a mixture of spectral and achromatic colours.

purl[1] (pɜːl) NOUN [1] Also called: **purl stitch.** a knitting stitch made by doing a plain stitch backwards. [2] a decorative border, as of lace. [3] gold or silver wire thread. ◆ VERB [4] to knit (a row or garment) in purl stitch. [5] to edge (something) with a purl. ◆ Also (for senses 2, 3, 5): **pearl.**
▷HISTORY C16: from dialect *pirl* to twist into a cord

purl[2] (pɜːl) VERB [1] (*intr*) (of a stream, etc.) to flow with a gentle curling or rippling movement and a murmuring sound. ◆ NOUN [2] a curling movement of water; eddy. [3] a murmuring sound, as of a shallow stream.
▷HISTORY C16: related to Norwegian *purla* to bubble

purler[1] ('pɜːlə) NOUN *Informal* a headlong or spectacular fall (esp in the phrase **come a purler**).

purler[2] ('pɜːlə) NOUN *Austral slang* something outstanding in its class.
▷HISTORY of unknown origin

purlieu ('pɜːljuː) NOUN [1] *English history* land on the edge of a forest that was once included within the bounds of the royal forest but was later separated although still subject to some of the forest laws, esp regarding hunting. [2] (*usually plural*) a neighbouring area; outskirts. [3] (*often plural*) a place one frequents; haunt. [4] *Rare* a district or suburb, esp one that is poor or squalid.
▷HISTORY C15 *purlewe,* from Anglo-French *puralé* a going through (influenced also by Old French *lieu* place), from Old French *puraler* to traverse, from *pur* through + *aler* to go

purlin *or* **purline** ('pɜːlɪn) NOUN a horizontal beam that provides intermediate support for the common rafters of a roof construction.
▷HISTORY C15: of uncertain origin

purloin (pɜː'lɔɪn) VERB to take (something) dishonestly; steal.
▷HISTORY C15: from Old French *porloigner* to put at a distance, from *por-* for + *loin* distant, from Latin *longus* long
▸**pur'loiner** NOUN

purple ('pɜːpᵊl) NOUN [1] any of various colours with a hue lying between red and blue and often highly saturated; a nonspectral colour. [2] a dye or pigment producing such a colour. [3] cloth of this colour, often used to symbolize royalty or nobility. [4] (usually preceded by *the*) high rank; nobility. [5] **a** the official robe of a cardinal. **b** the rank, office, or authority of a cardinal as signified by this. [6] **the purple.** bishops collectively. ◆ ADJECTIVE [7] of the colour purple. [8] (of writing) excessively elaborate or full of imagery: *purple prose.* [9] noble or royal.
▷HISTORY Old English, from Latin *purpura* purple dye, from Greek *porphura* the purple fish (*Murex*)
▸**'purpleness** NOUN ▸**'purplish** ADJECTIVE ▸**'purply** ADJECTIVE

purple emperor NOUN any of several Old World nymphalid butterflies of the genus *Apatura, esp A. iris,* having mottled purple-and-brown wings.

purple-fringed orchid *or* **orchis** NOUN either of two North American orchids, *Habenaria psychodes* or *H. fimbriata,* having purple fringed flowers.

purple gallinule NOUN a long-toed purple aquatic bird, *Porphyrio porphyrio* (or *Porphyrula martinica*), of the southern US and Europe, with red legs and red bill: family *Rallidae* (rails, etc.).

purple heart NOUN [1] any of several tropical American leguminous trees of the genus *Peltogyne.* [2] the decorative purple heartwood of any of these trees. [3] *Informal, chiefly Brit* a heart-shaped purple tablet consisting mainly of amphetamine.

Purple Heart NOUN a decoration awarded to members of the US Armed Forces for a wound incurred in action.

purple medic NOUN another name for **alfalfa.**

purple patch NOUN [1] Also called: **purple passage.** a section in a piece of writing characterized by rich, fanciful, or ornate language. [2] *Slang* a period of success, good fortune, etc.

purport VERB (pɜː'pɔːt) (*tr*) [1] to claim (to be a certain thing, etc.) by manner or appearance, esp falsely. [2] (esp of speech or writing) to signify or imply. ◆ NOUN ('pɜːpɔːt) [3] meaning; significance; import. [4] purpose; object; intention.
▷HISTORY C15: from Anglo-French: contents, from Old French *porporter* to convey, from *por-* forth + *porter* to carry, from Latin *portāre*

purported (pɜː'pɔːtɪd) ADJECTIVE alleged; supposed; rumoured: *a purported two million dollar deal.*
▸**pur'portedly** ADVERB

purpose ('pɜːpəs) NOUN [1] the reason for which anything is done, created, or exists. [2] a fixed design, outcome, or idea that is the object of an action or other effort. [3] fixed intention in doing something; determination: *a man of purpose.* [4] practical advantage or use: *to work to good purpose.* [5] that which is relevant or under consideration (esp in the phrase **to** or **from the purpose**). [6] *Archaic* purport. [7] **on purpose.** intentionally. ◆ VERB (*tr*) [8] to intend or determine to do (something).
▷HISTORY C13: from Old French *porpos,* from *porposer* to plan, from Latin *prōpōnere* to PROPOSE

purpose-built ADJECTIVE made to serve a specific purpose.

purposeful ('pɜːpəsfʊl) ADJECTIVE [1] having a definite purpose in view. [2] fixed in one's purpose; determined.
▸**'purposefully** ADVERB ▸**'purposefulness** NOUN

> **Language note** *Purposefully* is sometimes wrongly used where *purposely* is meant: *he had purposely* (not *purposefully*) *left the door unlocked.*

purposeless ('pɜːpəslɪs) ADJECTIVE having no fixed plan or intention.

▸ˈ**purposelessly** ADVERB ▸ˈ**purposelessness** NOUN

purposely (ˈpɜːpəslɪ) ADVERB for a definite reason; on purpose.

Language note See at **purposeful**.

purposive (ˈpɜːpəsɪv) ADJECTIVE 1 relating to, having, or indicating conscious intention. 2 serving a purpose; useful.
▸ˈ**purposively** ADVERB ▸ˈ**purposiveness** NOUN

purpura (ˈpɜːpjʊrə) NOUN *Pathol* any of several blood diseases causing purplish spots or patches on the skin due to subcutaneous bleeding.
▷HISTORY C18: via Latin from Greek *porphura* a shellfish yielding purple dye
▸ˈ**purpuric** ADJECTIVE

purpure (ˈpɜːpjʊə) NOUN, ADJECTIVE (*usually postpositive*) *Heraldry* purple.
▷HISTORY Old English from Latin *purpura* PURPLE

purpurin (ˈpɜːpjʊrɪn) NOUN a red crystalline compound used as a stain for biological specimens; 1,2,4-trihydroxyanthraquinone. Formula: $C_{14}H_5O_2(OH)_3$.
▷HISTORY C19: from Latin *purpura* PURPLE + -IN

purr (pɜː) VERB 1 (*intr*) (esp of cats) to make a low vibrant sound, usually considered as expressing pleasure, etc. 2 (*tr*) to express (pleasure, etc.) by this sound. ◆ NOUN 3 a purring sound.
▷HISTORY C17: of imitative origin; compare French *ronronner* to purr, German *schnurren,* Dutch *snorren*

purse (pɜːs) NOUN 1 a small bag or pouch, often made of soft leather, for carrying money, esp coins. 2 *US and Canadian* a woman's handbag. 3 anything resembling a small bag or pouch in form or function. 4 wealth; funds; resources. 5 a sum of money that is offered, esp as a prize. ◆ VERB 6 (*tr*) to contract (the mouth, lips, etc.) into a small rounded shape.
▷HISTORY Old English *purs,* probably from Late Latin *bursa* bag, ultimately from Greek: leather

purser (ˈpɜːsə) NOUN an officer aboard a passenger ship, merchant ship, or aircraft who keeps the accounts and attends to the welfare of the passengers.

purse seine NOUN a large net towed, usually by two boats, that encloses a school of fish and is then closed at the bottom by means of a line resembling the string formerly used to draw shut the neck of a money pouch or purse.

purse strings PLURAL NOUN control of finance or expenditure (esp in such phrases as **hold** or **control the purse strings**).

purslane (ˈpɜːslɪn, -leɪn) NOUN 1 a weedy portulacaceous plant, *Portulaca oleracea,* with small yellow flowers and fleshy leaves, which are used in salads and as a potherb. 2 any of various similar or related plants, such as sea purslane and water purslane.
▷HISTORY C14 *purcelane,* from Old French *porcelaine,* from Late Latin *porcillāgō,* from Latin *porcillāca,* variant of *portulāca*

pursuance (pəˈsjuːəns) NOUN the carrying out or pursuing of an action, plan, etc.

pursuant (pəˈsjuːənt) ADJECTIVE 1 (*usually postpositive;* often foll by *to*) *Chiefly law* in agreement or conformity. 2 *Archaic* pursuing.
▷HISTORY C17: related to Middle English *poursuivant* following after, from Old French; see PURSUE
▸**purˈsuantly** ADVERB

pursue (pəˈsjuː) VERB **-sues, -suing, -sued.** (*mainly tr*) 1 (*also intr*) to follow (a fugitive, etc.) in order to capture or overtake. 2 (esp of something bad or unlucky) to follow closely or accompany: *ill health pursued her.* 3 to seek or strive to attain (some object, desire, etc.). 4 to follow the precepts of (a plan, policy, etc.). 5 to apply oneself to (one's studies, hobbies, interests, etc.). 6 to follow persistently or seek to become acquainted with. 7 to continue to discuss or argue (a point, subject, etc.).
▷HISTORY C13: from Anglo-Norman *pursiwer,* from Old French *poursivre,* from Latin *prōsequī* to follow after
▸**purˈsuer** NOUN

pursuit (pəˈsjuːt) NOUN 1 **a** the act of pursuing, chasing, or striving after. **b** (*as modifier*): *a pursuit plane.* 2 an occupation, hobby, or pastime. 3 (in cycling) a race in which the riders set off at intervals along the track and attempt to overtake each other.
▷HISTORY C14: from Old French *poursieute,* from *poursivre* to prosecute, PURSUE

pursuivant (ˈpɜːsɪvənt) NOUN 1 the lowest rank of heraldic officer. 2 *History* a state or royal messenger. 3 *History* a follower or attendant.
▷HISTORY C14: from Old French, from *poursivre* to PURSUE

pursy (ˈpɜːsɪ) ADJECTIVE 1 short-winded. 2 *Archaic* fat; overweight.
▷HISTORY C15: alteration of earlier *pursive,* from Anglo-French *porsif,* ultimately from Latin *pulsāre* to PULSATE

purtenance (ˈpɜːtɪnəns) NOUN *Archaic* the inner organs, viscera.
▷HISTORY C14: from Old French *pertinance* something that belongs; see APPURTENANCE

purulent (ˈpjʊərʊlənt) ADJECTIVE of, relating to, or containing pus.
▷HISTORY C16: from Latin *pūrulentus,* from PUS
▸ˈ**purulence** *or* ˈ**purulency** NOUN ▸ˈ**purulently** ADVERB

Purús (*Spanish* (*Portuguese* puˈrus)) NOUN a river in NW central South America, rising in SE Peru and flowing northeast to the Amazon. Length: about 3200 km (2000 miles).

purvey (pəˈveɪ) VERB (*tr*) 1 to sell or provide (commodities, esp foodstuffs) on a large scale. 2 to publish or make available (lies, scandal, etc.). ◆ NOUN (ˈpɜːvɪ) 3 *Scot* the food and drink laid on at a wedding reception, etc.
▷HISTORY C13: from Old French *porveeir,* from Latin *prōvidēre* to PROVIDE

purveyance (pəˈveɪəns) NOUN 1 *History* the collection or requisition of provisions for a sovereign. 2 *Rare* the act of purveying. 3 *Rare* that which is purveyed.

purveyor (pəˈveɪə) NOUN 1 (*often plural*) a person, organization, etc., that supplies food and provisions. 2 a person who spreads, repeats, or sells (information, lies, etc.). 3 a person or thing that habitually provides or supplies a particular thing or quality: *a purveyor of humour.* 4 *History* an officer providing or exacting provisions, lodging, etc., for a sovereign.

purview (ˈpɜːvjuː) NOUN 1 the scope of operation or concern of something. 2 the breadth or range of outlook or understanding. 3 *Law* the body of a statute, containing the enacting clauses.
▷HISTORY C15: from Anglo-Norman *purveu,* from *porveeir* to furnish; see PURVEY

pus (pʌs) NOUN the yellow or greenish fluid product of inflammation, composed largely of dead leucocytes, exuded plasma, and liquefied tissue cells.
▷HISTORY C16: from Latin *pūs;* related to Greek *puon* pus

Pusan (ˈpuːˈsæn) NOUN a port in SE South Korea, on the Korea Strait: the second largest city and chief port of the country; industrial centre; two universities. Pop.: 3 813 814 (1995).

Puseyism (ˈpjuːzɪˌɪzəm) NOUN a derogatory term for the **Oxford Movement**, used by its contemporary opponents
▷HISTORY C19: after Edward Bouverie *Pusey* (1800–82), British ecclesiastic, a leader of the Oxford Movement
▸ˈ**Puseyite** NOUN, ADJECTIVE

push (pʊʃ) VERB 1 (when *tr,* often foll by *off, away,* etc.) to apply steady force to (something) in order to move it. 2 to thrust (one's way) through something, such as a crowd, by force. 3 (when *intr,* often foll by *for*) to apply oneself vigorously (to achieving a task, plan, etc.). 4 (*tr*) to encourage or urge (a person) to some action, decision, etc. 5 (when *intr,* often foll by *for*) to be an advocate or promoter (of): *to push for acceptance of one's theories.* 6 (*tr*) to use one's influence to help (a person): *to push one's own candidate.* 7 to bear upon (oneself or another person) in order to achieve more effort, better results, etc.: *she was a woman who liked to push her husband.* 8 **a** (*tr*) to take undue risks, esp through overconfidence, thus risking failure: *to push one's luck.* **b** (*intr*) to act overconfidently. 9 *Sport* to hit (a ball) with a stiff pushing stroke. 10 (*tr*) *Informal* to sell (narcotic drugs) illegally. 11 (*intr;* foll by *out, into,* etc.) (esp of geographical features) to reach or extend: *the cliffs pushed out to the sea.* 12 (*tr*) to overdevelop (a photographic film), usually by the equivalent of up to two stops, to compensate for underexposure or increase contrast. 13 **push up (the) daisies.** *Slang* to be dead and buried. ◆ NOUN 14 the act of pushing; thrust. 15 a part or device that is pressed to operate some mechanism. 16 *Informal* ambitious or enterprising drive, energy, etc. 17 *Informal* a special effort or attempt to advance, as of an army in a war: *to make a push.* 18 *Informal* a number of people gathered in one place, such as at a party. 19 *Austral slang* a group or gang, esp one considered to be a clique. 20 *Sport* a stiff pushing stroke. 21 **at a push.** *Informal* with difficulty; only just. 22 **the push.** *Informal, chiefly Brit* dismissal, esp from employment. 23 **when push comes to shove.** *Informal* when matters become critical; when a decision needs to be made. ◆ See also **push about, push along, push in, push off, push on, push through.**
▷HISTORY C13: from Old French *pousser,* from Latin *pulsāre,* from *pellere* to drive

push about *or* **around** VERB (*tr, adverb*) *Slang* to bully; keep telling (a person) what to do in a bossy manner.

push along VERB (*intr, adverb*) *Informal* to go away; leave.

pushball (ˈpʊʃˌbɔːl) NOUN *Chiefly US and Canadian* a game in which two teams try to push a heavy ball towards opposite goals.

push-bike NOUN *Brit* an informal name for **bicycle.**

push button NOUN 1 an electrical switch operated by pressing a button, which closes or opens a circuit. 2 (*modifier*) **push-button. a** operated by a push button: *a push-button radio.* **b** initiated as simply as by pressing a button: *push-button warfare.*

pushcart (ˈpʊʃˌkɑːt) NOUN another name (esp US and Canadian) for **barrow**[1] (sense 3).

pushchair (ˈpʊʃˌtʃɛə) NOUN a usually collapsible chair-shaped carriage in which a small child may be wheeled. Also called: **baby buggy, buggy.** US and Canadian word: **stroller.** Austral words: **pusher, stroller.**

pushed (pʊʃt) ADJECTIVE (often foll by *for*) *Informal* short (of) or in need (of time, money, etc.).

pusher (ˈpʊʃə) NOUN 1 *Informal* a person who sells illegal drugs, esp narcotics such as heroin and morphine. 2 *Informal* an actively or aggressively ambitious person. 3 **a** a type of aircraft propeller placed behind the engine. **b** a type of aircraft using such a propeller. 4 a person or thing that pushes. 5 *Brit* a rakelike implement used by small children to push food onto a spoon. 6 *Austral* the usual name for **pushchair.**

push fit NOUN *Engineering* another name for **sliding fit.**

push in VERB (*intr, adverb*) to force one's way into a group of people, queue, etc.

pushing (ˈpʊʃɪŋ) ADJECTIVE 1 enterprising, resourceful, or aggressively ambitious. 2 impertinently self-assertive. ◆ ADVERB 3 almost or nearly (a certain age, speed, etc.): *pushing fifty.*
▸ˈ**pushingly** ADVERB ▸ˈ**pushingness** NOUN

Pushkin (ˈpʊʃkɪn) NOUN a town in NW Russia: site of the imperial summer residence and Catherine the Great's palace. Pop.: 97 000 (latest est.). Former name: **Tsarskoye Selo** (1708–1937).

push money NOUN a cash inducement provided by a manufacturer or distributor for a retailer or his staff, to reward successful selling.

push off VERB (*adverb*) 1 Also: **push out.** to move into open water, as by being cast off from a mooring. 2 (*intr*) *Informal* to go away; leave.

push on VERB (*intr, adverb*) to resume one's course; carry on one's way steadily; press on.

pushover (ˈpʊʃˌəʊvə) NOUN *Informal* 1 something that is easily achieved or accomplished. 2 a person, team, etc., that is easily taken advantage of or defeated.

pushpin (ˈpʊʃˌpɪn) NOUN *US and Canadian* a pin with a small ball-shaped head.

push polling NOUN the use of loaded questions in a supposedly objective telephone opinion poll during a political campaign in order to bias voters against an opposing candidate.

push-pull NOUN (*modifier*) using two similar

electronic devices, such as matched valves, made to operate 180° out of phase with each other. The outputs are combined to produce a signal that replicates the input waveform: *a push-pull amplifier.*

pushrod ('pʊʃˌrɒd) NOUN a metal rod transmitting the reciprocating motion that operates the valves of an internal-combustion engine having the camshaft in the crankcase.

push-start VERB (*tr*) 1 to start (a motor vehicle) by pushing it while it is in gear, thus turning the engine. ◆ NOUN 2 the act or process of starting a vehicle in this way.

push through VERB (*tr*) to compel to accept: *the bill was pushed through Parliament.*

Pushto ('pʌʃtəʊ) *or* **Pushtu** ('pʌʃtuː) NOUN, ADJECTIVE variant spellings of **Pashto.**

push-up NOUN the US and Canadian term for **press-up.**

pushy ('pʊʃɪ) ADJECTIVE **pushier, pushiest.** *Informal* 1 offensively assertive or forceful. 2 aggressively or ruthlessly ambitious.
▸ **'pushily** ADVERB ▸ **'pushiness** NOUN

pusillanimous (ˌpjuːsɪ'lænɪməs) ADJECTIVE characterized by a lack of courage or determination.
▷ **HISTORY** C16: from Late Latin *pusillanimis* from Latin *pusillus* weak + *animus* courage
▸ **pusillanimity** (ˌpjuːsɪlə'nɪmɪtɪ) NOUN
▸ **ˌpusil'lanimously** ADVERB

puss[1] (pʊs) NOUN 1 an informal name for a **cat.** See also **pussy**[1] (sense 1). 2 *Slang* a girl or woman. 3 an informal name for a **hare.**
▷ **HISTORY** C16: related to Middle Low German *pūs,* Dutch *poes,* Lithuanian *puz*

puss[2] (pʊs) NOUN *Slang* 1 the face. 2 *Irish* a gloomy or sullen expression.
▷ **HISTORY** C17: from Irish *pus*

puss moth NOUN a large pale prominent moth, *Cerura vinula,* whose larvae feed on willow and poplar, and are bright green with a masklike red head and claspers modified as "tails" that are protruded and raised in a state of alarm: family *Notodontidae.*

pussy[1] ('pʊsɪ) NOUN, *plural* **pussies.** 1 Also called: **puss, pussycat** ('pʊsɪˌkæt). an informal name for a **cat.** 2 a furry catkin, esp that of the pussy willow. 3 a rare word for **tipcat.** 4 *Taboo slang* the female pudenda. 5 *Taboo slang* a woman considered as a sexual object. 6 *Taboo slang, chiefly US* an ineffectual or timid person.
▷ **HISTORY** C18: from PUSS[1]

> **Language note** Though possibly not quite as taboo for most people as the c... word, many still consider this item out of bounds in normal conversation and writing.

pussy[2] ('pʌsɪ) ADJECTIVE **-sier, -siest.** containing or full of pus.

pussycat ('pʊsɪˌkæt) NOUN 1 an informal or child's name for a **cat**[1] (sense 1). 2 *Brit informal* an endearing or gentle person.

pussyfoot ('pʊsɪˌfʊt) *Informal* ◆ VERB (*intr*) 1 to move about stealthily or warily like a cat. 2 to avoid committing oneself. ◆ NOUN, *plural* **-foots.** 3 a person who pussyfoots.

pussy willow ('pʊsɪ) NOUN 1 a willow tree that produces silvery silky catkins, esp *Salix caprea* or *S. cinerea* in Britain or *S. discolor* in North America. 2 any of various similar willows.

pustulant ('pʌstjʊlənt) ADJECTIVE 1 causing the formation of pustules. ◆ NOUN 2 an agent causing such formation.

pustulate VERB ('pʌstjʊˌleɪt) 1 to form or cause to form into pustules. ◆ ADJECTIVE ('pʌstjʊlɪt, -ˌleɪt) 2 covered with pustules.
▸ **ˌpustu'lation** NOUN

pustule ('pʌstjuːl) NOUN 1 a small inflamed elevated area of skin containing pus. 2 any small distinct spot resembling a pimple or blister.
▷ **HISTORY** C14: from Latin *pustula* a blister, variant of *pūsula;* compare Greek *phusallis* bladder, *phusa* bellows
▸ **pustular** ('pʌstjʊlə) ADJECTIVE

put (pʊt) VERB **puts, putting, put.** (*mainly tr*) 1 to cause to be (in a position or place): *to put a book on the table.* 2 to cause to be (in a state, relation, etc.): *to put one's things in order.* 3 (foll by *to*) to cause (a person) to experience the endurance or suffering (of): *to put to death; to put to the sword.* 4 to set or commit (to an action, task, or duty), esp by force: *he put him to work.* 5 to render, transform, or translate: *to put into English.* 6 to set (words) in a musical form (esp in the phrase **put to music**). 7 (foll by *at*) to estimate: *he put the distance at fifty miles.* 8 (foll by *to*) to utilize (for the purpose of): *he put his knowledge to good use.* 9 (foll by *to*) to couple a female animal (with a male) for the purpose of breeding: *the farmer put his heifer to the bull.* 10 to state; express: *to put it bluntly.* 11 to set or make (an end or limit): *he put an end to the proceedings.* 12 to present for consideration in anticipation of an answer or vote; propose: *he put the question to the committee; I put it to you that one day you will all die.* 13 to invest (money) in; give (support) to: *he put five thousand pounds into the project.* 14 to impart: *to put zest into a party.* 15 to throw or cast. 16 **not know where to put oneself.** to feel awkward or embarrassed. 17 **put paid to.** to destroy irrevocably and utterly: *the manager's disfavour put paid to their hopes for promotion.* 18 **stay put.** to refuse to leave; keep one's position. ◆ NOUN 19 a throw or cast, esp in putting the shot. 20 Also called: **put option.** *Stock Exchange* an option to sell a stated amount of securities at a specified price during a specified limited period. Compare **call** (sense 58). ◆ See also **put about, put across, put aside, put away, put back, put by, put down, put forth, put forward, put in, put off, put on, put on to, put out, put over, put through, put up, put upon.**
▷ **HISTORY** C12 *puten* to push; related to Old English *potian* to push, Norwegian, Icelandic *pota* to poke

put about VERB (*adverb*) 1 *Nautical* to change course or cause to change course: *we put about and headed for home.* 2 (*tr*) to make widely known: *he put about the news of the air disaster.* 3 (*tr; usually passive*) to disconcert or disturb: *she was quite put about by his appearance.*

put across VERB (*tr*) 1 (*adverb*) to communicate in a comprehensible way: *he couldn't put things across very well.* 2 **put one across.** *Informal* to get (someone) to accept or believe a claim, excuse, etc., by deception: *they put one across their teacher.*

putamen (pjuː'teɪmɛn) NOUN, *plural* **-tamina** (-'tæmɪnə). the hard endocarp or stone of fruits such as the peach, plum, and cherry.
▷ **HISTORY** C19: from Latin: clippings, from *putāre* to prune

put aside VERB (*tr, adverb*) 1 to move (an object, etc.) to one side, esp in rejection. 2 to store up; save: *to put money aside for a rainy day.* 3 to ignore or disregard: *let us put aside our differences.*

putative ('pjuːtətɪv) ADJECTIVE 1 (*prenominal*) commonly regarded as being: *the putative father.* 2 (*prenominal*) considered to exist or have existed; inferred. 3 *Grammar* denoting a mood of the verb in some languages used when the speaker does not have direct evidence of what he is asserting, but has inferred it on the basis of something else.
▷ **HISTORY** C15: from Late Latin *putātīvus* supposed, from Latin *putāre* to consider
▸ **'putatively** ADVERB

put away VERB (*tr, adverb*) 1 to return (something) to the correct or proper place: *he put away his books.* 2 to save: *to put away money for the future.* 3 to lock up in a prison, mental institution, etc.: *they put him away for twenty years.* 4 to eat or drink, esp in large amounts. 5 to put to death, because of old age or illness: *the dog had to be put away.*

put back VERB (*tr, adverb*) 1 to return to its former place. 2 to move to a later time or date: *the wedding was put back a fortnight.* 3 to delay or impede the progress of: *the strike put back production severely.*

put by VERB (*tr, adverb*) to set aside (money, goods, etc.) to be kept for the future; store; save.

put down VERB (*tr, adverb*) 1 to make a written record of. 2 to repress: *to put down a rebellion.* 3 to consider; account: *they put him down for an ignoramus.* 4 to attribute: *I put the mistake down to his inexperience.* 5 to put to death, because of old age or illness: *the vet put the cat down.* 6 to table on the agenda: *the MPs put down a motion on the increase in crime.* 7 to put (a baby) to bed. 8 to dismiss, reject, or humiliate. ◆ NOUN **put-down.** 9 a cruelly crushing remark.

put forth VERB (*tr, adverb*) *Formal* 1 to present; propose. 2 (of a plant) to produce or bear (leaves, branches, shoots, etc.).

put forward VERB (*tr, adverb*) 1 to propose; suggest. 2 to offer the name of; nominate.

put in VERB (*adverb*) 1 (*intr*) *Nautical* to bring a vessel into port, esp for a brief stay: *we put in for fresh provisions.* 2 (often foll by *for*) to apply or cause to apply (for a job, in a competition, etc.). 3 (*tr*) to submit: *he put in his claims form.* 4 to intervene with (a remark) during a conversation. 5 (*tr*) to devote (time, effort, etc.) to a task: *he put in three hours overtime last night.* 6 (*tr*) to establish or appoint: *he put in a manager.* 7 (*tr*) *Cricket* to cause (a team, esp the opposing one) to bat: *England won the toss and put the visitors in to bat.* ◆ NOUN **put-in.** 8 *Rugby* the act of throwing the ball into a scrum.

putlog ('pʌtˌlɒg) *or* **putlock** NOUN a short horizontal beam that with others supports the floor planks of a scaffold.
▷ **HISTORY** C17: changed (through influence of LOG[1]) from earlier *putlock,* probably from PUT (past participle) + LOCK[1]

put off VERB 1 (*tr, adverb*) to postpone or delay: *they have put off the dance until tomorrow.* 2 (*tr, adverb*) to evade (a person) by postponement or delay: *they tried to put him off, but he came anyway.* 3 (*tr, adverb*) to confuse; disconcert: *he was put off by her appearance.* 4 (*tr, preposition*) to cause to lose interest in or enjoyment of: *the accident put him off driving.* 5 (*intr, adverb*) *Nautical* to be launched off from shore or from a ship: *we put off in the lifeboat towards the ship.* 6 (*tr, adverb*) *Archaic* to remove (clothes). ◆ NOUN **putoff.** 7 *Chiefly US* a pretext or delay.

put on VERB (*tr, mainly adverb*) 1 to clothe oneself in: *to put on a coat.* 2 (*usually passive*) to adopt (an attitude or feeling) insincerely: *his misery was just put on.* 3 to present or stage (a play, show, etc.). 4 to increase or add: *she put on weight; the batsman put on fifty runs before lunch.* 5 to cause (an electrical device) to function. 6 (*also preposition*) to wager (money) on a horse race, game, etc.: *he put ten pounds on the favourite.* 7 (*also preposition*) to impose as a burden or levy: *to put a tax on cars.* 8 *Cricket* to cause (a bowler) to bowl. 9 **put (someone) on. a** to connect (a person) by telephone. **b** *Slang* to mock or tease. ◆ NOUN **put-on.** *Slang, chiefly US and Canadian.* 10 a hoax or piece of mockery. 11 an affected manner or mode of behaviour.

put on to VERB (*tr, preposition*) 1 to connect by telephone. 2 to inform (someone) of (a person's location or activities): *I'll put the police on to you if you don't stop.* 3 to tell (a person) about (someone or something beneficial): *can you put me on to a cheap supermarket?*

put out VERB (*tr, adverb*) 1 (*often passive*) **a** to annoy; anger. **b** to confound or disturb; confuse. 2 to extinguish or douse (a fire, light, etc.): *he put out the fire.* 3 to poke forward: *to put out one's tongue.* 4 to be or present a source of inconvenience or annoyance to (a person): *I hope I'm not putting you out.* 5 to issue or publish; broadcast: *the authorities put out a leaflet.* 6 to render unconscious. 7 to dislocate: *he put out his shoulder in the accident.* 8 to show or exert: *the workers put out all their energy in the campaign.* 9 to pass, give out (work to be done) at different premises. 10 to lend (money) at interest. 11 *Cricket* to dismiss (a player or team). 12 *Baseball* to cause (a batter or runner) to be out by a fielding play. ◆ NOUN **putout.** 13 *Baseball* a play in which the batter or runner is put out.

put over VERB (*tr, adverb*) 1 *Informal* to communicate (facts, information, etc.) comprehensibly: *he puts his thoughts over badly.* 2 *Chiefly US* to postpone; defer: *the match was put over a week.* Brit equivalent: **put off.** 3 **put (a fast) one over on.** *Informal* to get (someone) to accept or believe a claim, excuse, etc., by deception: *he put one over on his boss.*

put-put ('pʌtˌpʌt) *Informal* ◆ NOUN 1 a light chugging or popping sound, as made by a petrol engine. 2 a vehicle powered by an engine making such a sound. ◆ VERB **-puts, -putting, -putted.** 3 (*intr*) to make or travel along with such a sound.

Putrajaya ('puːtrəˌdʒeɪə) NOUN the capital of Malaysia since 1999, in the SW Malay Peninsula; a high-tech garden city, construction of which began in 1995 and is expected to be complete in 2010, when the population will be over 300 000.

putrefy ('pju:trɪˌfaɪ) VERB **-fies, -fying, -fied.** (of organic matter) to decompose or rot with an offensive smell.
▷HISTORY C15: from Old French *putrefier* + Latin *putrefacere,* from *puter* rotten + *facere* to make
▸**putrefaction** (ˌpju:trɪ'fækʃən) NOUN ▸**ˌputre'factive** *or* **putrefacient** (ˌpju:trɪ'feɪʃənt) ADJECTIVE ▸**'putreˌfiable** ADJECTIVE ▸**'putreˌfier** NOUN

putrescent (pju:'trɛsᵊnt) ADJECTIVE [1] becoming putrid; rotting. [2] characterized by or undergoing putrefaction.
▷HISTORY C18: from Latin *putrescere* to become rotten
▸**pu'trescence** NOUN

putrescible (pju:'trɛsɪbᵊl) ADJECTIVE [1] liable to become putrid. ◆ NOUN [2] a putrescible substance.
▷HISTORY C18: from Latin *putrescere* to decay
▸**puˌtresci'bility** NOUN

putrescine (pju:'trɛsi:n, -ɪn) NOUN a colourless crystalline amine produced by decaying animal matter; 1,4-diaminobutane. Formula: $H_2N(CH_2)_4NH_2$.
▷HISTORY C20: from Latin *putrescere* + -INE²

putrid ('pju:trɪd) ADJECTIVE [1] (of organic matter) in a state of decomposition, usually giving off a foul smell: *putrid meat.* [2] morally corrupt or worthless. [3] sickening; foul: *a putrid smell.* [4] *Informal* deficient in quality or value: *a putrid film.*
▷HISTORY C16: from Latin *putridus* rotten, from *putrēre* to be rotten
▸**pu'tridity** *or* **'putridness** NOUN ▸**'putridly** ADVERB

putsch (putʃ) NOUN a violent and sudden uprising; political revolt, esp a coup d'état.
▷HISTORY C20: from German: from Swiss German: a push, of imitative origin

putt (pʌt) *Golf* ◆ NOUN [1] a stroke on the green with a putter to roll the ball into or near the hole. ◆ VERB [2] to strike (the ball) in this way.
▷HISTORY C16: of Scottish origin; related to PUT

puttee *or* **putty** ('pʌtɪ) NOUN, *plural* **-tees** *or* **-ties.** (*usually plural*) a strip of cloth worn wound around the legs from the ankle to the knee, esp as part of a military uniform in World War I.
▷HISTORY C19: from Hindi *paṭṭī,* from Sanskrit *paṭṭikā,* from *paṭṭa* cloth

putter¹ ('pʌtə) NOUN *Golf* [1] a club for putting, usually having a solid metal head. [2] a golfer who putts: *he is a good putter.*

putter² ('pʌtə) VERB the usual US and Canadian word for **potter²**.
▸**'putterer** NOUN

putter³ ('putə) NOUN [1] a person who puts: *the putter of a question.* [2] a person who puts the shot.

put through VERB (*tr, mainly adverb*) [1] to carry out to a conclusion: *he put through his plan.* [2] (*also preposition*) to organize the processing of: *she put through his application to join the organization.* [3] to connect by telephone. [4] to make (a telephone call).

putting green ('pʌtɪŋ) NOUN [1] (on a golf course) the area of closely mown grass at the end of a fairway where the hole is. [2] an area of smooth grass with several holes for putting games.

putto ('putəu) NOUN, *plural* **-ti** (-tɪ). a representation of a small boy, a cherub or cupid, esp in baroque painting or sculpture. See also **amoretto.**
▷HISTORY from Italian, from Latin *putus* boy

putty ('pʌtɪ) NOUN, *plural* **-ties.** [1] a stiff paste made of whiting and linseed oil that is used to fix glass panes into frames and to fill cracks or holes in woodwork, etc. [2] any substance with a similar consistency, function, or appearance. [3] a mixture of lime and water with sand or plaster of Paris used on plaster as a finishing coat. [4] (*as modifier*): *a putty knife.* [5] See **putty powder.** [6] a person who is easily influenced or persuaded: *he's putty in her hands.* [7] **a** a colour varying from a greyish-yellow to a greyish-brown or brownish-grey. **b** (*as adjective*): *putty-coloured.* [8] **up to putty.** *Austral informal* worthless or useless. ◆ VERB **-ties, -tying, -tied.** [9] (*tr*) to fix, fill, or coat with putty.
▷HISTORY C17: from French *potée* a potful

putty powder NOUN a powder, either tin oxide or tin and lead oxide, used for polishing glassware, metal, etc.

Putumayo (*Spanish* putu'majo) NOUN a river in NW South America, rising in S Colombia and flowing southeast as most of the border between Colombia and Peru, entering the Amazon in Brazil: scene of the Putumayo rubber scandal (1910–11) during the rubber boom, in which many Indians were enslaved and killed by rubber exploiters. Length: 1578 km (980 miles). Brazilian name: **Içá.**

put up VERB (*adverb, mainly tr*) [1] to build; erect: *to put up a statue.* [2] to accommodate or be accommodated at: *can you put me up for tonight?* [3] to increase (prices). [4] to submit or present (a plan, case, etc.). [5] to offer: *to put a house up for sale.* [6] to provide or supply; give: *to put up a good fight.* [7] to provide (money) for; invest in: *they put up five thousand for the new project.* [8] to preserve or can (jam, etc.). [9] to pile up (long hair) on the head in any of several styles. [10] (*also intr*) to nominate or be nominated as a candidate, esp for a political or society post: *he put his wife up as secretary; he put up for president.* [11] *Archaic* to return (a weapon) to its holder, as a sword to its sheath: *put up your pistol!* [12] **put up to. a** to inform or instruct (a person) about (tasks, duties, etc.). **b** to urge or goad (a person) on to; incite to. [13] **put up with.** *Informal* to endure; tolerate. ◆ ADJECTIVE **put-up.** [14] dishonestly or craftily prearranged or conceived (esp in the phrase **put-up job**).

put upon VERB (*intr, preposition, usually passive*) [1] to presume on (a person's generosity, good nature, etc.); take advantage of: *he's always being put upon.* [2] to impose hardship on; maltreat: *he was sorely put upon.*

putz (pʌts) NOUN *US slang* a despicable or stupid person.
▷HISTORY from Yiddish *puts* ornament

Puy de Dôme (pwi də dom) NOUN [1] a department of central France in Auvergne region. Capital: Clermont-Ferrand. Pop.: 604 266 (1999). Area: 8016 sq. km (3094 sq. miles). [2] a mountain in central France, in the Auvergne Mountains: a volcanic plug. Height: 1485 m (4872 ft.).

Puy de Sancy (*French* pwi də sɑ̃si) NOUN a mountain in S central France: highest peak of the Monts Dore. Height: 1886 m (6188 ft.).

puzzle ('pʌzᵊl) VERB [1] to perplex or be perplexed. [2] (*intr; foll by over*) to attempt the solution (of); ponder (about): *he puzzled over her absence.* [3] (*tr; usually foll by out*) to solve by mental effort: *he puzzled out the meaning of the inscription.* ◆ NOUN [4] a person or thing that puzzles. [5] a problem that cannot be easily or readily solved. [6] the state or condition of being puzzled. [7] a toy, game, or question presenting a problem that requires skill or ingenuity for its solution. See **jigsaw puzzle, Chinese puzzle.**
▷HISTORY C16: of unknown origin
▸**'puzzling** ADJECTIVE

puzzlement ('pʌzᵊlmənt) NOUN the state or condition of being puzzled; perplexity.

puzzler ('pʌzlə) NOUN a person or thing that puzzles.

puzzolana (ˌputsə'lɑ:nə) NOUN a variant of **pozzuolana.**

PVA ABBREVIATION FOR polyvinyl acetate.

PVC ABBREVIATION FOR polyvinyl chloride; a synthetic thermoplastic material made by polymerizing vinyl chloride. The properties depend on the added plasticizer. The flexible forms are used in hosepipes, insulation, shoes, garments, etc. Rigid PVC is used for moulded articles.

PVR ABBREVIATION FOR personal(ized) video recorder: a device for recording and replaying television programmes and films etc. that uses a hard disk rather than videocassettes or DVDs and has various computer functions.

PVS ABBREVIATION FOR: [1] persistent vegetative state. [2] postviral syndrome.

Pvt. *Military* ABBREVIATION FOR private.

pw THE INTERNET DOMAIN NAME FOR Palau.

PW ABBREVIATION FOR policewoman.

PWA ABBREVIATION FOR person with AIDS.

PWR ABBREVIATION FOR pressurized-water reactor.

pwt ABBREVIATION FOR pennyweight.

PX *US military* ABBREVIATION FOR Post Exchange.

py THE INTERNET DOMAIN NAME FOR Paraguay.

PY INTERNATIONAL CAR REGISTRATION FOR Paraguay.

py- COMBINING FORM variant of **pyo-** before a vowel.

pya (pjɑ:, pɪ'ɑ:) NOUN a monetary unit of Myanmar worth one hundredth of a kyat.
▷HISTORY from Burmese

pyaemia *or* **pyemia** (paɪ'i:mɪə) NOUN blood poisoning characterized by pus-forming microorganisms in the blood.
▷HISTORY C19: from New Latin, from Greek *puon* pus + *haima* blood
▸**py'aemic** *or* **py'emic** ADJECTIVE

pyat, pyot, *or* **pyet** ('paɪət) *Scot* ◆ NOUN [1] the magpie. ◆ ADJECTIVE [2] pied.
▷HISTORY Middle English *piot,* from PIE²

pycnidium (pɪk'nɪdɪəm) NOUN, *plural* **-ia** (-ɪə). a small flask-shaped structure containing spores that occurs in ascomycetes and certain other fungi.
▷HISTORY C19: from New Latin, from Greek *puknos* thick

pycno- *or before a vowel* **pycn-** COMBINING FORM indicating thickness or density: *pycnometer.*
▷HISTORY via New Latin from Greek *puknos* thick

pycnometer (pɪk'nɒmɪtə) NOUN a small glass bottle of known volume for determining the relative density of liquids and solids by weighing.
▸**pycnometric** (ˌpɪknə'mɛtrɪk) ADJECTIVE

Pydna ('pɪdnə) NOUN a town in ancient Macedonia: site of a major Roman victory over the Macedonians, resulting in the downfall of their kingdom (168 B.C.).

pye (paɪ) NOUN a variant spelling of **pie⁵**.

pye-dog, pie-dog, *or* **pi-dog** NOUN an ownerless half-wild Asian dog.
▷HISTORY C19: Anglo-Indian *pye, paë,* from Hindi *pāhī* outsider

pyelitis (ˌpaɪə'laɪtɪs) NOUN inflammation of the pelvis of the kidney. Compare **pyelonephritis.**
▸**pyelitic** (ˌpaɪə'lɪtɪk) ADJECTIVE

pyelo- *or before a vowel* **pyel-** COMBINING FORM denoting the renal pelvis: *pyelonephritis.*
▷HISTORY from Greek *puelos* trough, pan; in the sense: pelvis

pyelography (ˌpaɪə'lɒgrəfɪ) NOUN *Med* the branch of radiology concerned with examination of the kidney and associated structures by means of an X-ray picture called a **pyelogram** ('paɪələuˌgræm). Also called: **urography.**
▸**pyelographic** (ˌpaɪələu'græfɪk) ADJECTIVE

pyelonephritis (ˌpaɪələunɪ'fraɪtɪs) NOUN inflammation of the kidney and renal pelvis. Compare **pyelitis.**

pygidium (paɪ'dʒɪdɪəm, -'gɪd-) NOUN, *plural* **-ia** (-ɪə). the terminal segment, division, or other structure in certain annelids, arthropods, and other invertebrates.
▷HISTORY C19: from New Latin, from Greek *pugē* rump
▸**py'gidial** ADJECTIVE

Pygmalion (pɪg'meɪlɪən) NOUN *Greek myth* a king of Cyprus, who fell in love with the statue of a woman he had sculpted and which his prayers brought to life as Galatea.

pygmy *or* **pigmy** ('pɪgmɪ) NOUN, *plural* **-mies.** [1] an abnormally undersized person. [2] something that is a very small example of its type. [3] a person of little importance or significance. [4] (*modifier*) of very small stature or size.
▷HISTORY C14 *pigmeis* the Pygmies, from Latin *Pygmaeus* a Pygmy, from Greek *pugmaios* undersized, from *pugmē* fist
▸**pygmaean** *or* **pygmean** (pɪg'mi:ən) ADJECTIVE

Pygmy *or* **Pigmy** ('pɪgmɪ) NOUN, *plural* **-mies.** a member of one of the dwarf peoples of Equatorial Africa, noted for their hunting and forest culture.

pygmy chimpanzee NOUN another name for **bonobo.**

pygmy glider NOUN a small arboreal marsupial, *Acrobates pygmaeus,* of Australia and New Guinea moving with gliding leaps using folds of skin between the hind limbs and forelimbs.

pygmy possum NOUN any of various small Australasian marsupials, esp the burramys.

pyinkado (pjɪŋ'kɑ:dəu) NOUN [1] a leguminous tree, *Xylia xylocarpa* (or *dolabriformis*), native to India and Myanmar. [2] the heavy durable timber of this tree, used for construction.

▷**HISTORY** C19: from Burmese

pyjama *or US* **pajama** (pəˈdʒɑːmə) NOUN *(modifier)* 1 of or forming part of pyjamas: *pyjama top.* 2 requiring pyjamas to be worn: *a pyjama party.* ◆ See also **pyjamas.**
▷**HISTORY** C19: via Persian or Urdu from Persian *pāē, pāy* foot, leg + *jāmah* clothing, garment

pyjamas *or US* **pajamas** (pəˈdʒɑːməz) PLURAL NOUN 1 loose-fitting nightclothes comprising a jacket or top and trousers. 2 full loose-fitting ankle-length trousers worn by either sex in various Eastern countries. 3 women's flared trousers or trouser suit used esp for leisure wear.

pyknic (ˈpɪknɪk) ADJECTIVE (of a physical type) characterized by a broad squat fleshy physique with a large chest and abdomen.
▷**HISTORY** C20: from Greek *puknos* thick

pylon (ˈpaɪlən) NOUN 1 a large vertical steel tower-like structure supporting high-tension electrical cables. 2 a post or tower for guiding pilots or marking a turning point in a race. 3 a streamlined aircraft structure for attaching an engine pod, external fuel tank, etc., to the main body of the aircraft. 4 a monumental gateway, such as one at the entrance to an ancient Egyptian temple. 5 a temporary artificial leg.
▷**HISTORY** C19: from Greek *pulōn* a gateway

pylorectomy (ˌpaɪlɔːˈrɛktəmɪ) NOUN, *plural* **-mies.** the surgical removal of all or part of the pylorus, often including the adjacent portion of the stomach (**partial gastrectomy**).

pylorus (paɪˈlɔːrəs) NOUN, *plural* **-ri** (-raɪ). the small circular opening at the base of the stomach through which partially digested food (chyme) passes to the duodenum.
▷**HISTORY** C17: via Late Latin from Greek *pulōrus* gatekeeper, from *pulē* gate + *ouros* guardian
▸**pyˈloric** ADJECTIVE

Pylos (ˈpaɪlɒs) NOUN a port in SW Greece, in the SW Peloponnese; scene of a defeat of the Spartans by the Athenians (425 B.C.) during the Peloponnesian War and of the Battle of Navarino (see **Navarino**). Italian name: **Navarino.** Modern Greek name: **Pílos.**

pyo- *or before a vowel* **py-** COMBINING FORM denoting pus: *pyosis.*
▷**HISTORY** from Greek *puon*

pyoderma (ˌpaɪəʊˈdɜːmə) NOUN *Pathol* any skin eruption characterized by pustules or the formation of pus.

pyogenesis (ˌpaɪəʊˈdʒɛnɪsɪs) NOUN *Pathol* the formation of pus.
▸**ˌpyoˈgenic** ADJECTIVE

pyoid (ˈpaɪɔɪd) ADJECTIVE resembling pus.

Pyongyang *or* **P'yŏng-yang** (ˈpjɒŋˈjæŋ) NOUN the capital of North Korea, in the southwest on the Taedong River: industrial centre; university (1946). Pop.: 2 355 000 (latest est.).

pyorrhoea *or esp US* **pyorrhea** (ˌpaɪəˈrɪə) NOUN inflammation of the gums characterized by the discharge of pus and loosening of the teeth; periodontal disease.
▸**ˌpyorˈrhoeal** *or* **ˌpyorˈrhoeic** *or (esp US)* **ˌpyorˈrheal** *or* **ˌpyorˈrheic** ADJECTIVE

pyosis (paɪˈəʊsɪs) NOUN *Pathol* the formation of pus.

pyr- COMBINING FORM a variant of **pyro-** before a vowel.

pyracantha (ˌpaɪrəˈkænθə) NOUN any rosaceous shrub of the genus *Pyracantha, esp the* firethorn, widely cultivated for ornament.
▷**HISTORY** C17: from Greek *purakantha* name of a shrub, from PYRO- + *akantha* thorn

pyralid (ˈpɪrəlɪd) NOUN 1 any moth of the mostly tropical family *Pyralidae,* typically having narrow forewings and broad fringed hind wings: includes the bee moths and the corn borer. ◆ ADJECTIVE 2 of, relating to, or belonging to the family *Pyralidae.*
▷**HISTORY** C19: via New Latin from Greek *puralis:* a mythical winged insect believed to live in fire, from *pur* fire

pyramid (ˈpɪrəmɪd) NOUN 1 a huge masonry construction that has a square base and, as in the case of the ancient Egyptian royal tombs, four sloping triangular sides. 2 an object, formation, or structure resembling such a construction. 3 *Maths* a solid having a polygonal base and triangular sides that meet in a common vertex. 4 *Crystallog* a crystal form in which three planes intersect all three axes of the crystal. 5 *Anatomy* any pointed or cone-shaped bodily structure or part. 6 *Finance* a group of enterprises containing a series of holding companies structured so that the top holding company controls the entire group with a relatively small proportion of the total capital invested. 7 *Chiefly US* the series of transactions involved in pyramiding securities. 8 *(plural)* a game similar to billiards with fifteen coloured balls. ◆ VERB 9 to build up or be arranged in the form of a pyramid. 10 *Chiefly US* to speculate in (securities or property) by increasing purchases on additional margin or collateral derived from paper profits associated with high prices of securities and property in a boom. 11 *Finance* to form (companies) into a pyramid.
▷**HISTORY** C16 (earlier *pyramis*): from Latin *pyramis,* from Greek *puramis,* probably from Egyptian
▸**pyramidal** (pɪˈræmɪdᵊl) *or* **ˌpyraˈmidical** *or* **ˌpyraˈmidic** ADJECTIVE ▸**pyˈramidally** *or* **ˌpyraˈmidically** ADVERB

pyramidal orchid NOUN a chalk-loving orchid, *Anacamptis pyramidalis,* bearing a dense cone-shaped spike of purplish-pink flowers with a long curved spur.

pyramidal peak NOUN *Geology* a sharp peak formed where the ridges separating three or more cirques intersect; horn.

pyramid selling NOUN a practice adopted by some manufacturers of advertising for distributors and selling them batches of goods. The first distributors then advertise for more distributors who are sold subdivisions of the original batches at an increased price. This process continues until the final distributors are left with a stock that is unsaleable except at a loss.

Pyramus and Thisbe (ˈpɪrəməs, ˈθɪzbɪ) NOUN (in Greek legend) two lovers of Babylon: Pyramus, wrongly supposing Thisbe to be dead, killed himself and she, encountering him in his death throes, did the same.

pyran (ˈpaɪræn, paɪˈræn) NOUN an unsaturated heterocyclic compound having a ring containing five carbon atoms and one oxygen atom and two double bonds. It has two isomers depending on the position of the saturated carbon atom relative to the oxygen.
▷**HISTORY** C20: from PYRO- + -AN

pyranometer (ˌpaɪrəˈnɒmɪtə) NOUN *Physics* another name for **solarimeter.**

pyrargyrite (paɪˈrɑːdʒɪˌraɪt) NOUN a dark red to black mineral consisting of silver antimony sulphide in hexagonal crystalline form: occurs in silver veins and is an important ore of silver. Formula: Ag_3SbS_3.
▷**HISTORY** C19: from German *Pyrargyrit,* from PYRO- + Greek *arguros* silver

pyrazole (ˈpaɪrəˌzəʊl) NOUN a crystalline soluble basic heterocyclic compound; 1,2-diazole. Formula: $C_3H_4N_2$.
▷**HISTORY** C19: from German, from PYRROLE + inserted *-az-* (see AZO-)

pyre (paɪə) NOUN a heap or pile of wood or other combustible material, esp one used for cremating a corpse.
▷**HISTORY** C17: from Latin *pyra,* from Greek *pura* hearth, from *pur* fire

pyrene[1] (ˈpaɪriːn) NOUN a solid polynuclear aromatic hydrocarbon extracted from coal tar. Formula: $C_{16}H_{10}$.
▷**HISTORY** C19: from PYRO- + -ENE

pyrene[2] (ˈpaɪriːn) NOUN *Botany* any of several small hard stones that occur in a single fruit and contain a single seed each.
▷**HISTORY** C19: from New Latin *pyrena,* from Greek *purēn*

Pyrenean (ˌpɪrəˈniːən) ADJECTIVE of or relating to the Pyrenees or their inhabitants.

Pyrenean mountain dog NOUN a large heavily built dog of an ancient breed originally used to protect sheep from wild animals: it has a long thick white coat with a dense ruff. Also called: **Great Pyrenees.**

Pyrenees (ˌpɪrəˈniːz) PLURAL NOUN a mountain range between France and Spain, extending from the Bay of Biscay to the Mediterranean. Highest peak: Pico de Aneto, 3404 m (11 168 ft.).
▸**ˌPyreˈnean** ADJECTIVE

Pyrénées *or* **Pyrénées-Atlantiques** *(French* pirenez-atlɑ̃tik) NOUN a department of SW France in Aquitaine region. Capital: Pau. Pop.: 600 018 (1999). Area: 7712 sq. km (3008 sq. miles). Former name: **Basses-Pyrénées.**

Pyrénées-Orientales *(French* pirenezɔrjɑ̃tal) NOUN a department of S France, in Languedoc-Roussillon region. Capital: Perpignan. Pop.: 392 803 (1999). Area: 4144 sq. km (1616 sq. miles).

pyrenoid (ˈpaɪrəˌnɔɪd) NOUN any of various small protein granules that occur in certain algae, mosses, and protozoans and are involved in the synthesis of starch.
▷**HISTORY** C19: from PYRENE[2] + -OID

pyrethrin (paɪˈriːθrɪn) NOUN 1 Also called: **pyrethrin I.** an oily water-insoluble compound used as an insecticide. Formula: $C_{21}H_{28}O_3$. 2 Also called: **pyrethrin II.** a compound of similar chemical structure and action, also found in pyrethrum. Formula: $C_{22}H_{28}O_5$.
▷**HISTORY** C19: from PYRETHRUM + -IN

pyrethroid (paɪˈriːθrɔɪd) NOUN 1 any of various chemical compounds having similar insecticidal properties to pyrethrin. ◆ ADJECTIVE 2 of or relating to such compounds.

pyrethrum (paɪˈriːθrəm) NOUN 1 any of several cultivated Eurasian chrysanthemums, such as *Chrysanthemum coccineum* and *C. roseum,* with white, pink, red, or purple flowers. 2 any insecticide prepared from the dried flowers of any of these plants, esp *C. roseum.*
▷**HISTORY** C16: via Latin from Greek *purethron* feverfew, probably from *puretos* fever; see PYRETIC

pyretic (paɪˈrɛtɪk) ADJECTIVE *Pathol* of, relating to, or characterized by fever. Compare **antipyretic.**
▷**HISTORY** C18: from New Latin *pyreticus,* from Greek *puretos* fever, from *pur* fire

Pyrex (ˈpaɪrɛks) NOUN *Trademark* **a** any of a variety of borosilicate glasses that have low coefficients of expansion, making them suitable for heat-resistant glassware used in cookery and chemical apparatus. **b** *(as modifier): a Pyrex dish.*

pyrexia (paɪˈrɛksɪə) NOUN a technical name for **fever.**
▷**HISTORY** C18: from New Latin, from Greek *purexis,* from *puressein* to be feverish, from *pur* fire
▸**pyˈrexial** *or* **pyˈrexic** ADJECTIVE

pyrgeometer (ˌpɜːdʒɪˈɒmɪtə) NOUN *Physics* an instrument for measuring the loss of heat by radiation from the earth's surface.

pyrheliometer (pəˌhiːlɪˈɒmɪtə) NOUN an instrument for measuring the intensity of the sun's radiant energy.
▸**pyrheliometric** (pəˌhiːlɪəʊˈmɛtrɪk) ADJECTIVE

pyridine (ˈpɪrɪˌdiːn) NOUN a colourless hygroscopic liquid with a characteristic odour. It is a basic heterocyclic compound containing one nitrogen atom and five carbon atoms in its molecules and is used as a solvent and in preparing other organic chemicals. Formula: C_5H_5N.
▷**HISTORY** C19: from PYRO- + -ID[3] + -INE[2]

pyridoxal (ˌpɪrɪˈdɒksəl) NOUN *Biochem* a naturally occurring derivative of pyridoxine that is a precursor of a coenzyme (**pyridoxal phosphate**) involved in several enzymic reactions. Formula: $(CH_2OH)(CHO)C_5HN(OH)(CH_3)$.

pyridoxamine (ˌpɪrɪˈdɒksəmiːn) NOUN *Biochem* a metabolic form of pyridoxine.

pyridoxine (ˌpɪrɪˈdɒksiːn) NOUN *Biochem* a derivative of pyridine that is a precursor of the compounds pyridoxal and pyridoxamine. Also called: **vitamin B_6.**
▷**HISTORY** C20: from PYRID(INE) + OX(YGEN) + -INE[2]

pyriform (ˈpɪrɪˌfɔːm) ADJECTIVE (esp of organs of the body) pear-shaped.
▷**HISTORY** C18: from New Latin *pyriformis,* from *pyri-,* erroneously from Latin *pirum* pear + *-formis* -FORM

pyrimidine (paɪˈrɪmɪˌdiːn) NOUN 1 a liquid or crystalline organic compound with a penetrating odour; 1,3-diazine. It is a weakly basic soluble heterocyclic compound and can be prepared from barbituric acid. Formula: $C_4H_4N_2$. 2 Also called: **pyrimidine base.** any of a number of similar compounds having a basic structure that is derived

from pyrimidine, including cytosine, thymine, and uracil, which are constituents of nucleic acids.
▷HISTORY C20: variant of PYRIDINE

pyrite (ˈpaɪraɪt) NOUN a yellow mineral, found in igneous and metamorphic rocks and in veins. It is a source of sulphur and is used in the manufacture of sulphuric acid. Composition: iron sulphide. Formula: FeS_2. Crystal structure: cubic. Also called: **iron pyrites, pyrites.** Nontechnical name: **fool's gold.**
▷HISTORY C16: from Latin *pyrites* flint, from Greek *puritēs* (*lithos*) fire (stone), that is, capable of withstanding or striking fire, from *pur* fire
▸**pyritic** (paɪˈrɪtɪk) *or* **pyˈritous** ADJECTIVE

pyrites (paɪˈraɪtiːz; *in combination* ˈpaɪraɪts) NOUN, *plural* **-tes.** [1] another name for **pyrite.** [2] any of a number of other disulphides of metals, esp of copper and tin.

pyro- *or before a vowel* **pyr-** COMBINING FORM [1] denoting fire, heat, or high temperature: *pyromania; pyrometer.* [2] caused or obtained by fire or heat: *pyroelectricity.* [3] *Chem* **a** denoting a new substance obtained by heating another: *pyroboric acid is obtained by heating boric acid.* **b** denoting an acid or salt with a water content intermediate between that of the ortho- and meta- compounds: *pyro-phosphoric acid.* [4] *Mineralogy* **a** having a property that changes upon the application of heat: *pyromorphite.* **b** having a flame-coloured appearance: *pyroxylin.*

pyrocatechol (ˌpaɪrəʊˈkætɪˌtʃɒl, -kɒl) *or* **pyrocatechin** (ˌpaɪrəʊˈkætɪkɪn) NOUN another name for **catechol.**

pyrochemical (ˌpaɪrəʊˈkɛmɪkᵊl) ADJECTIVE of, concerned with, being, producing, or resulting from chemical changes at high temperatures.
▸**ˌpyroˈchemically** ADVERB

pyroclastic (ˌpaɪrəʊˈklæstɪk) ADJECTIVE (of rocks) formed from the solid fragments ejected during a volcanic eruption.

pyroconductivity (ˌpaɪrəʊˌkɒndʌkˈtɪvɪtɪ) NOUN conductivity that can be induced in certain solids by heating them.

pyroelectric (ˌpaɪrəʊɪˈlɛktrɪk) ADJECTIVE [1] of, concerned with, or exhibiting pyroelectricity. ◆ NOUN [2] a pyroelectric substance.

pyroelectricity (ˌpaɪrəʊɪlɛkˈtrɪsɪtɪ, -ˌiːlɛk-) NOUN the development of opposite charges at the ends of the axis of certain hemihedral crystals, such as tourmaline, as a result of a change in temperature.

pyrogallate (ˌpaɪrəʊˈgæleɪt) NOUN any salt or ester of pyrogallol.

pyrogallol (ˌpaɪrəʊˈgælɒl) NOUN a white lustrous crystalline soluble phenol with weakly acidic properties; 1,2,3-trihydroxybenzene: used as a photographic developer and for absorbing oxygen. Formula: $C_6H_3(OH)_3$.
▷HISTORY C20: from PYRO- + GALL(IC)² + -OL¹
▸**ˌpyroˈgallic** ADJECTIVE

pyrogen (ˈpaɪrəʊˌdʒɛn) NOUN any of a group of substances that cause a rise in temperature in an animal body.

pyrogenic (ˌpaɪrəʊˈdʒɛnɪk) *or* **pyrogenous** (paɪˈrɒdʒɪnəs) ADJECTIVE [1] produced by or producing heat. [2] *Pathol* causing or resulting from fever. [3] *Geology* less common words for **igneous.**

pyrognostics (ˌpaɪrɒgˈnɒstɪks) PLURAL NOUN the characteristics of a mineral, such as fusibility and flame coloration, that are revealed by the application of heat.
▷HISTORY C19: from PYRO- + *-gnostics,* from Greek *gnōsis* knowledge

pyrography (paɪˈrɒgrəfɪ) NOUN, *plural* **-phies.** [1] the art or process of burning designs on wood or leather with heated tools or a flame. [2] a design made by this process.
▸**pyˈrographer** NOUN ▸**pyrographic** (ˌpaɪrəʊˈgræfɪk) ADJECTIVE

pyroligneous (ˌpaɪrəʊˈlɪgnɪəs) *or* **pyrolignic** ADJECTIVE (of a substance) produced by the action of heat on wood, esp by destructive distillation.
▷HISTORY C18: from French *pyroligneux,* from PYRO- + *ligneux* LIGNEOUS

pyroligneous acid NOUN the crude reddish-brown acidic liquid obtained by the distillation of wood and containing acetic acid, methanol, and acetone. Also called: **wood vinegar.**

pyrolusite (ˌpaɪrəʊˈluːsaɪt) NOUN a blackish fibrous or soft powdery mineral consisting of manganese dioxide in tetragonal crystalline form. It occurs in association with other manganese ores and is an important source of manganese. Formula: MnO_2.
▷HISTORY C19: from PYRO- + Greek *lousis* a washing + -ITE¹, from its use in purifying glass

pyrolyse *or US* **pyrolyze** (ˈpaɪrəʊˌlaɪz) VERB (*tr*) to subject to pyrolysis.
▸**ˈpyroˌlyser** *or* **ˈpyroˌlyzer** NOUN

pyrolysis (paɪˈrɒlɪsɪs) NOUN [1] the application of heat to chemical compounds in order to cause decomposition. [2] chemical decomposition of compounds caused by high temperatures.
▸**pyrolytic** (ˌpaɪrəʊˈlɪtɪk) ADJECTIVE

pyromagnetic (ˌpaɪrəʊmægˈnɛtɪk) ADJECTIVE a former term for **thermomagnetic.**

pyromancy (ˈpaɪrəʊˌmænsɪ) NOUN divination by fire or flames.
▸**ˈpyroˌmancer** NOUN ▸**ˌpyroˈmantic** ADJECTIVE

pyromania (ˌpaɪrəʊˈmeɪnɪə) NOUN *Psychiatry* the uncontrollable impulse and practice of setting things on fire.
▸**ˌpyroˈmaniˌac** NOUN ▸**pyromaniacal** (ˌpaɪrəʊməˈnaɪəkᵊl) ADJECTIVE

pyrometallurgy (ˌpaɪrəʊmɛˈtælədʒɪ, -ˈmɛtəˌlɜːdʒɪ) NOUN the branch of metallurgy involving processes performed at high temperatures, including sintering, roasting, smelting, casting, refining, alloying, and heat treatment.

pyrometer (paɪˈrɒmɪtə) NOUN an instrument for measuring high temperatures, esp by measuring the brightness (**optical pyrometer**) or total quantity (**radiation pyrometer**) of the radiation produced by the source. Other types include the resistance thermometer and the thermocouple.
▸**pyrometric** (ˌpaɪrəʊˈmɛtrɪk) *or* **ˌpyroˈmetrical** ADJECTIVE
▸**ˌpyroˈmetrically** ADVERB ▸**pyˈrometry** NOUN

pyromorphite (ˌpaɪrəʊˈmɔːfaɪt) NOUN a green, yellow, brown, or grey secondary mineral that consists of lead chloro-phosphate in the form of hexagonal crystals. Formula: $Pb_5Cl(PO_4)_3$.
▷HISTORY C19: from German *Pyromorphit,* from PYRO- + Greek *morphē* form + -ITE¹, an allusion to the fact that it assumes a crystalline form when heated

pyrone (ˈpaɪrəʊn, paɪˈrəʊn) NOUN [1] either of two heterocyclic compounds that have a ring containing five carbon atoms and one oxygen atom with two double bonds and a second oxygen atom attached to a carbon atom in either the *ortho*-position (**alpha pyrone**) or the *para*-position (**gamma pyrone**). [2] any one of a class of compounds that are substituted derivatives of a pyrone.

pyrope (ˈpaɪrəʊp) NOUN a deep yellowish-red garnet that consists of magnesium aluminium silicate and is used as a gemstone. Formula: $Mg_3Al_2(SiO_4)_3$.
▷HISTORY C14 (used loosely of a red gem; modern sense C19): from Old French *pirope,* from Latin *pyrōpus* bronze, from Greek *purōpus* fiery-eyed, from *pur* fire + *ōps* eye

pyrophoric (ˌpaɪrəʊˈfɒrɪk) ADJECTIVE [1] (of a chemical) igniting spontaneously on contact with air. [2] (of an alloy) producing sparks when struck or scraped: *lighter flints are made of pyrophoric alloy.*
▷HISTORY C19: from New Latin *pyrophorus,* from Greek *purophoros* fire-bearing, from *pur* fire + *pherein* to bear

pyrophosphate (ˌpaɪrəʊˈfɒsfeɪt) NOUN any salt or ester of pyrophosphoric acid.

pyrophosphoric acid (ˌpaɪrəʊfɒsˈfɒrɪk) NOUN a crystalline soluble solid acid formed by the reaction between one molecule of phosphorus pentoxide and two water molecules. Formula: $H_4P_2O_7$. See also **polyphosphoric acid.**

pyrophotometer (ˌpaɪrəʊfəʊˈtɒmɪtə) NOUN a type of pyrometer in which the temperature of an incandescent body is determined by photometric measurement of the light it emits.
▸**ˌpyrophoˈtometry** NOUN

pyrophyllite (ˌpaɪrəʊˈfɪlaɪt) NOUN a white, silvery, or green micaceous mineral that consists of hydrated aluminium silicate in monoclinic crystalline form and occurs in metamorphic rocks. Formula: $Al_2Si_4O_{10}(OH)_2$.

pyrosis (paɪˈrəʊsɪs) NOUN *Pathol* a technical name for **heartburn.**
▷HISTORY C18: from New Latin, from Greek: a burning, from *puroun* to burn, from *pur* fire

pyrostat (ˈpaɪrəʊˌstæt) NOUN [1] a device that activates an alarm or extinguisher in the event of a fire. [2] a thermostat for use at high temperatures.
▸**ˌpyroˈstatic** ADJECTIVE

pyrosulphate (ˌpaɪrəʊˈsʌlfeɪt) NOUN any salt of pyrosulphuric acid. Also called: **disulphate.**

pyrosulphuric acid (ˌpaɪrəʊsʌlˈfjʊərɪk) NOUN a fuming liquid acid made by adding sulphur trioxide to concentrated sulphuric acid. Formula: $H_2S_2O_7$. Also called: **disulphuric acid.** See also **fuming sulphuric acid.**

pyrotechnics (ˌpaɪrəʊˈtɛknɪks) NOUN [1] (*functioning as singular*) the art or craft of making fireworks. [2] (*functioning as singular or plural*) a firework display. [3] (*functioning as singular or plural*) brilliance of display, as in the performance of music. ◆ Also called: **pyrotechny.**
▸**ˌpyroˈtechnic** *or* **ˌpyroˈtechnical** ADJECTIVE

pyroxene (paɪˈrɒksiːn) NOUN any of a group of silicate minerals having the general formula $ABSi_2O_6$, where A is usually calcium, sodium, magnesium, or iron, and B is usually magnesium, iron, chromium, manganese, or aluminium. Pyroxenes occur in basic igneous rocks and some metamorphic rocks, and have colours ranging from white to dark green or black. They may be monoclinic (clinopyroxenes) or orthorhombic (orthopyroxenes) in crystal structure. Examples are augite (the most important pyroxene), diopside, enstatite, hypersthene, and jadeite.
▷HISTORY C19: PYRO- + *-xene* from Greek *xenos* foreign, because it was mistakenly thought to have originated elsewhere when found in igneous rocks
▸**pyroxenic** (ˌpaɪrɒkˈsɛnɪk) ADJECTIVE

pyroxenite (paɪˈrɒksɪˌnaɪt) NOUN a very dark coarse-grained ultrabasic rock consisting entirely of pyroxene minerals.

pyroxylin (paɪˈrɒksɪlɪn) NOUN a yellow substance obtained by nitrating cellulose with a mixture of nitric and sulphuric acids; guncotton: used to make collodion, plastics, lacquers, and adhesives.
▷HISTORY C19: from PYRO- + XYL(O)- + -IN

Pyrrha (ˈpɪrə) NOUN *Greek myth* the wife of Deucalion, saved with him from the flood loosed upon mankind by Zeus.

pyrrhic¹ (ˈpɪrɪk) *Prosody* ◆ NOUN [1] a metrical foot of two short or unstressed syllables. ◆ ADJECTIVE [2] of or relating to such a metrical foot. [3] (of poetry) composed in pyrrhics.
▷HISTORY C16: via Latin, from Greek *purrhikhē,* traditionally said to be named after its inventor *Purrhikhos*

pyrrhic² (ˈpɪrɪk) NOUN [1] a war dance of ancient Greece. ◆ ADJECTIVE [2] of or relating to this dance.
▷HISTORY C17: Latin from Greek *purrhikhios* belonging to the *purrhikhē* war dance performed in armour; see PYRRHIC¹

Pyrrhic victory NOUN a victory in which the victor's losses are as great as those of the defeated. Also called: **Cadmean victory.**
▷HISTORY named after *Pyrrhus* (319–272 B.C.), king of Epirus (306–272), who defeated the Romans at Asculum in 279 B.C. but suffered heavy losses

Pyrrhonism (ˈpɪrəˌnɪzəm) NOUN the sceptical philosophy of Pyrrho, the Greek philosopher (?365–?275 B.C.).
▸**ˈPyrrhonist** NOUN, ADJECTIVE

pyrrhotite (ˈpɪrəˌtaɪt) *or* **pyrrhotine** (ˈpɪrəˌtiːn, -ˌtaɪn, -tɪn) NOUN a common bronze-coloured magnetic mineral consisting of ferrous sulphide in hexagonal crystalline form. Formula: FeS.
▷HISTORY C19: from Greek *purrhotēs* redness, from *purrhos* fiery, from *pur* fire

pyrrhuloxia (ˌpɪrəˈlɒksɪə) NOUN a grey-and-pink crested bunting, *Pyrrhuloxia sinuata,* of Central and SW North America, with a short parrot-like bill.
▷HISTORY from New Latin *Pyrrhula* genus of the finches (from Greek *purrhoulas* a flame-coloured bird, from *purrhos* red, from *pur* fire) + *Loxia* genus of the crossbills, from Greek *loxos* oblique

pyrrole (ˈpɪrəʊl, pɪˈrəʊl) NOUN a colourless insoluble toxic liquid having a five-membered ring containing one nitrogen atom, found in many naturally occurring compounds, such as chlorophyll. Formula: C_4H_5N. Also called: **azole.**

▷HISTORY C19: from Greek *purrhos* red, from *pur* fire + -OLE[1]

▸**pyrrolic** (pɪˈrɒlɪk) ADJECTIVE

pyrrolidine (pɪˈrɒlɪˌdiːn) NOUN an almost colourless liquid occurring in tobacco leaves and made commercially by hydrogenating pyrrole. It is a strongly alkaline heterocyclic base with molecules that contain a ring of four carbon atoms and one nitrogen atom. Formula: C_4H_9N.

pyruvic acid (paɪˈruːvɪk) NOUN a colourless pleasant-smelling liquid formed as an intermediate in the metabolism of proteins and carbohydrates, helping to release energy to the body; 2-oxopropanoic acid. Formula: $CH_3COCOOH$.
▷HISTORY C19: *pyruvic* from PYRO- + Latin *ūva* grape

Pythagoras (paɪˈθæɡərəs) NOUN a deep crater in the NE quadrant of the moon, 136 kilometres in diameter.

Pythagoras' theorem NOUN the theorem that in a right-angled triangle the square of the length of the hypotenuse equals the sum of the squares of the other two sides.

Pythagorean (paɪˌθæɡəˈriːən) ADJECTIVE 1 of or relating to Pythagoras, the Greek philosopher and mathematician (?580–?500 B.C.). 2 *Music* denoting the diatonic scale of eight notes arrived at by Pythagoras and based on a succession of fifths. ◆ NOUN 3 a follower of Pythagoras.

Pythagoreanism (paɪˌθæɡəˈriːəˌnɪzəm) NOUN the teachings of Pythagoras and his followers, esp that the universe is essentially a manifestation of mathematical relationships.

Pythia (ˈpɪθɪə) NOUN *Greek myth* the priestess of Apollo at Delphi, who transmitted the oracles.

Pythian (ˈpɪθɪən) ADJECTIVE *also* **Pythic.** 1 of or relating to Delphi or its oracle. ◆ NOUN 2 the priestess of Apollo at the oracle of Delphi. 3 an inhabitant of ancient Delphi.
▷HISTORY C16: via Latin *Pȳthius* from Greek *Puthios* of Delphi

Pythian Games PLURAL NOUN (in ancient Greece) the second most important Panhellenic festival, celebrated in the third year of each Olympiad near Delphi. The four-year period between celebrations was known as a **Pythiad** (ˈpɪθɪˌæd).

Pythias (ˈpɪθɪˌæs) NOUN See **Damon and Pythias.**

python (ˈpaɪθən) NOUN any large nonvenomous snake of the family *Pythonidae* of Africa, S Asia, and Australia, such as *Python reticulatus* (**reticulated python**). They can reach a length of more than 20 feet and kill their prey by constriction.
▷HISTORY C16: New Latin, after PYTHON

▸**pythonic** (paɪˈθɒnɪk) ADJECTIVE

Python (ˈpaɪθən) NOUN *Greek myth* a dragon, killed by Apollo at Delphi.

Pythonesque (ˌpaɪθəˈnɛsk) ADJECTIVE denoting a kind of humour that is absurd and unpredictable; zany; surreal.
▷HISTORY C20: named after the British television show *Monty Python's Flying Circus,* first broadcast in 1969

pythoness (ˈpaɪθəˌnɛs) NOUN 1 a woman, such as Apollo's priestess at Delphi, believed to be possessed by an oracular spirit. 2 a female soothsayer.
▷HISTORY C14 *phitonesse,* ultimately from Greek *Puthōn* PYTHON

pyuria (paɪˈjʊərɪə) NOUN *Pathol* any condition characterized by the presence of pus in the urine.
▷HISTORY C19: from New Latin, from Greek *puon* pus + *ouron* urine

pyx *or less commonly* **pix** (pɪks) NOUN 1 Also called: **pyx chest.** the chest in which coins from the British mint are placed to be tested for weight, etc. 2 *Christianity* any receptacle in which the Eucharistic Host is kept.
▷HISTORY C14: from Latin *pyxis* small box, from Greek, from *puxos* box tree

pyxidium (pɪkˈsɪdɪəm) *or* **pyxis** (ˈpɪksɪs) NOUN, *plural* **-ia** (-ɪə) *or* **pyxides** (ˈpɪksɪˌdiːz). the dry fruit of such plants as the plantain: a capsule whose upper part falls off when mature so that the seeds are released.
▷HISTORY C19: via New Latin from Greek *puxidion* a little box, from *puxis* box, PYX

pyxie (ˈpɪksɪ) NOUN a creeping evergreen shrub, *Pyxidanthera barbulata,* of the eastern US with small white or pink star-shaped flowers: family *Diapensiaceae.*
▷HISTORY C19: shortened from New Latin *Pyxidanthera,* from PYXIS + ANTHER

pyxis (ˈpɪksɪs) NOUN, *plural* **pyxides** (ˈpɪksɪˌdiːz). 1 a small box used by the ancient Greeks and Romans to hold medicines, etc. 2 a rare word for **pyx.** 3 another name for **pyxidium.**
▷HISTORY C14: via Latin from Greek: box

Pyxis (ˈpɪksɪs) NOUN, *Latin genitive* **Pyxidis** (ˈpɪksɪdɪs). an inconspicuous constellation close to Puppis that was originally considered part of the more extensive constellation Argo.

pzazz (pəˈzæz) NOUN *Informal* a variant of **pizzazz.**

Qq

q *or* **Q** (kjuː) NOUN, *plural* **q's, Q's** *or* **Qs.** **1** the 17th letter and 13th consonant of the modern English alphabet. **2** a speech sound represented by this letter, in English usually a voiceless velar stop, as in *unique* and *quick*.

q SYMBOL FOR quintal.

Q SYMBOL FOR: **1** *Chess* queen. **2** question. **3** *Physics* heat. ◆ *Text messaging* ABBREVIATION FOR **4** queue.

q. ABBREVIATION FOR: **1** quart. **2** quarter. **3** quarterly.

Q. ABBREVIATION FOR: **1** quartermaster. **2** (*plural* **Qq, qq**) Also: **q.** quarto. **3** Queen. **4** question.

qa THE INTERNET DOMAIN NAME FOR Qatar.

QA INTERNATIONAL CAR REGISTRATION FOR Qatar.

Qabis (ˈkɑːbɪs) NOUN the Arabic name for **Gabès.**

Qaddish (ˈkædɪʃ) NOUN, *plural* **Qaddishim.** a variant spelling of **Kaddish.**

qadi (ˈkɑːdɪ, ˈkeɪdɪ) NOUN, *plural* **-dis.** a variant spelling of **cadi.**

Qairwan (kaɪəˈwɑːn) NOUN a variant of **Kairouan.**

QANTAS (ˈkwɒntəs) NOUN the Australian national airline.
▷HISTORY acronym of *Q*ueensland *and N*orthern *T*erritory *A*erial *S*ervices, its original name: founded 1920

Qaraghandy (*Kazakh* kɑrɑγɑnˈdɪ) NOUN a variant transliteration of the Kazakh name for **Karaganda.**

QARANC ABBREVIATION FOR Queen Alexandra's Royal Army Nursing Corps.

qat (kæt, kɑːt) NOUN a variant spelling of **khat.**

Qatar *or* **Katar** (kæˈtɑː) NOUN a state in E Arabia, occupying a peninsula in the Persian Gulf: under Persian rule until the 19th century; became a British protectorate in 1916; declared independence in 1971; exports petroleum and natural gas. Official language: Arabic. Official religion: (Sunni) Muslim. Currency: riyal. Capital: Doha. Pop.: 596 000 (2001 est.). Area: about 11 000 sq. km (4250 sq. miles).

Qatari *or* **Katari** (kæˈtɑːrɪ) ADJECTIVE **1** of or relating to Qatar or its inhabitants. ◆ NOUN **2** a native or inhabitant of Qatar.

Qattara Depression (kəˈtɑːrə) NOUN an arid basin in the Sahara, in NW Egypt, impassable to vehicles. Area: about 18 000 sq. km (7000 sq. miles). Lowest point: 133 m (435 ft.) below sea level.

qawwali (kəˈvɑːlɪ) NOUN an Islamic religious song, esp in Asia.

QB **1** ABBREVIATION FOR Queen's Bench. ◆ **2** *Chess* SYMBOL FOR queen's bishop.

QBP *Chess* SYMBOL FOR queen's bishop's pawn.

QC ABBREVIATION FOR: **1** **Queen's Counsel.** **2** (esp in postal addresses) Quebec.

QCA (in Britain) ABBREVIATION FOR Qualifications and Curriculum Authority.

QCD ABBREVIATION FOR **quantum chromodynamics.**

q.e. ABBREVIATION FOR quod est.
▷HISTORY Latin: which is

QED ABBREVIATION FOR: **1** quod erat demonstrandum. [Latin: which was to be shown or proved] **2** **quantum electrodynamics.**

QEF ABBREVIATION FOR quod erat faciendum.
▷HISTORY Latin: which was to be done

Qeshm (ˈkɛʃəm) *or* **Qishm** NOUN **1** the largest island in the Persian Gulf: part of Iran. Area: 1336 sq. km (516 sq. miles). **2** the chief town of this island.

QF ABBREVIATION FOR quick-firing.

Q factor NOUN **1** a measure of the relationship between stored energy and rate of energy dissipation in certain electrical components, devices, etc., thus indicating their efficiency. **2** Also called: **Q value.** the heat released in a nuclear reaction, usually expressed in millions of electronvolts for each individual reaction. Symbol: Q.
▷HISTORY C20: short for *quality factor*

QFD ABBREVIATION FOR **quantum flavourdynamics.**

Q fever NOUN an acute disease characterized by fever and pneumonia, transmitted to man by the rickettsia *Coxiella burnetii.*
▷HISTORY C20: from *q(uery) fever* (the cause being unknown when it was named)

qi (tʃiː) NOUN a variant of **chi**[2].

qibla (ˈkɪblə) NOUN a variant of **kiblah.**

qigong (ˈtʃiːˈgɒŋ) *or* **chi kung** NOUN a system of breathing and exercise designed to benefit both physical and mental health.
▷HISTORY C20: from Chinese *qi* energy + *gong* exercise

qindar (ˈkɪntɑː) *or* **qintar** (kɪnˈtɑː) NOUN, *plural* **qindarka** (-ˈdɑːkə) *or* **-tarka** (-ˈtɑːkə). an Albanian monetary unit worth one hundredth of a lek.

Qingdao (ˈtʃɪŋˈdaʊ), **Tsingtao,** *or* **Chingtao** NOUN a port in E China, in E Shandong province on Jiazhou Bay, developed as a naval base and fort in 1891. Shandong university (1926). Pop.: 1 702 108 (1999 est.).

Qinghai, Tsinghai, *or* **Chinghai** (ˈtʃɪŋˈhaɪ) NOUN **1** a province of NW China: consists largely of mountains and high plateaus. Capital: Xining. Pop.: 5 180 000 (2000 est.). Area: 721 000 sq. km (278 400 sq. miles). **2** the Pinyin transliteration of the Chinese name for **Koko Nor.**

qintar (kɪnˈtɑː) NOUN a variant spelling of **qindar.**

Qiqihar, Chichihaerh, Ch'i-ch'i-haerh, *or* **Tsitsihar** (ˈtʃiːˌtʃiːˈhɑː) NOUN a city in NE China, in Heilongjiang province on the Nonni River. Pop.: 1 115 766 (1999 est.).

Qishm (ˈkɪʃəm) NOUN a variant of **Qeshm.**

QKt *Chess* SYMBOL FOR queen's knight.

QKtP *Chess* SYMBOL FOR queen's knight's pawn.

ql ABBREVIATION FOR quintal.

q.l. (in prescriptions) ABBREVIATION FOR quantum libet.
▷HISTORY Latin: as much as you please

Qld *or* **QLD** ABBREVIATION FOR Queensland.

q.m. (in prescriptions) ABBREVIATION FOR quaque mane.
▷HISTORY Latin: every morning

QM ABBREVIATION FOR Quartermaster.

QMC ABBREVIATION FOR Quartermaster Corps.

Q-methodology NOUN a statistical methodology used by psychologists to identify alternative world-views, opinions, interpretations, etc. in terms of statistically independent patterns of response recognized by clustering together individuals whose orderings of items, typically attitude statements, are similar. Compare **R-methodology.**

QMG ABBREVIATION FOR Quartermaster General.

QMS ABBREVIATION FOR Quartermaster Sergeant.

QMV ABBREVIATION FOR **Qualified Majority Voting.**

qn (in prescriptions) ABBREVIATION FOR quaque nocte.
▷HISTORY Latin: every night

QN *Chess* SYMBOL FOR queen's knight.

QNP *Chess* SYMBOL FOR queen's knight's pawn.

Qom (kɒm), **Qum,** *or* **Kum** NOUN a city in NW central Iran: a place of pilgrimage for Shiite Muslims. Pop.: 777 677 (1996).

qoph (kʊf, kɒf; *Hebrew* kɔf) NOUN a variant of **koph.**

qorma (ˈkɔːmə) NOUN a variant spelling of **korma.**

QP *Chess* SYMBOL FOR queen's pawn.

qqv ABBREVIATION FOR quae vide (denoting a cross-reference to more than one item). Compare **qv.**
▷HISTORY New Latin: which (words, items, etc.) see

QR[1] ABBREVIATION FOR Queen's Regulations.

QR[2] *Chess* SYMBOL FOR queen's rook.

qr. *plural* **qrs** ABBREVIATION FOR: **1** quarter. **2** quarterly. **3** quire.

QRP *Chess* SYMBOL FOR queen's rook's pawn.

qs ABBREVIATION FOR: **1** (in prescriptions) quantum sufficit. [Latin: as much as will suffice] **2** quarter section (of land).

QS ABBREVIATION FOR **quarter sessions.**

Q-ship NOUN a merchant ship with concealed guns, used to decoy enemy ships into the range of its weapons.
▷HISTORY named from *q(uery)*

QSM (in New Zealand) ABBREVIATION FOR Queen's Service Medal.

QSO ABBREVIATION FOR: **1** *Astronomy* **quasi-stellar object.** **2** (in New Zealand) Queen's Service Order.

Q-sort NOUN a psychological test requiring subjects to sort items relative to one another along a dimension such as "agree"/"disagree" for analysis by Q-methodological statistics.

qt *plural* **qt** *or* **qts** ABBREVIATION FOR quart.

q.t. *Informal* **1** ABBREVIATION FOR quiet. **2** **on the q.t.** secretly.

qto ABBREVIATION FOR quarto.

QTS (in Britain) ABBREVIATION FOR Qualified Teacher Status.

qty ABBREVIATION FOR quantity.

qua (kweɪ, kwɑː) PREPOSITION in the capacity of; by virtue of being.
▷HISTORY C17: from Latin, ablative singular (feminine) of *qui* who

quack[1] (kwæk) VERB (*intr*) **1** (of a duck) to utter a harsh guttural sound. **2** to make a noise like a duck. ◆ NOUN **3** the harsh guttural sound made by a duck.
▷HISTORY C17: of imitative origin; related to Dutch *kwakken,* German *quacken*

quack[2] (kwæk) NOUN **1** **a** an unqualified person who claims medical knowledge or other skills. **b** (*as modifier*): *a quack doctor.* **2** *Brit, Austral, and NZ informal* a doctor; physician or surgeon. ◆ VERB **3** (*intr*) to act in the manner of a quack.
▷HISTORY C17: short for QUACKSALVER
▶ˈ**quackish** ADJECTIVE

quackery (ˈkwækərɪ) NOUN, *plural* **-eries.** the activities or methods of a quack.

quack grass NOUN another name for **couch grass.**
▷HISTORY C19: a variant of QUICK GRASS

quacksalver (ˈkwækˌsælvə) NOUN an archaic word for **quack**[2].
▷HISTORY C16: from Dutch, from *quack,* apparently: to hawk + *salf* SALVE[1]

quad[1] (kwɒd) NOUN short for **quadrangle** (sense 2).

quad[2] (kwɒd) NOUN *Printing* a block of type metal used for spacing.

quad[3] (kwɒd) NOUN a variant spelling of **quod** (prison).

quad[4] (kwɒd) NOUN short for **quadruplet** (sense 1).

quad[5] (kwɒd) ADJECTIVE, NOUN **1** short for **quadraphonic** or **quadraphonics.** ◆ NOUN **2** *Anatomy* short for **quadriceps.**

quad. ABBREVIATION FOR: **1** quadrangle. **2** quadrilateral.

quad bike *or* **quad** NOUN a vehicle like a motorcycle with four large wheels, designed for agricultural, sporting, and other off-road uses.

quadr- COMBINING FORM a variant of **quadri-** before a vowel.

quadragenarian (ˌkwɒdrədʒɪˈnɛərɪən) NOUN **1** a person who is between 40 and 49 years old. ◆ ADJECTIVE **2** being from 40 to 49 years old.
▷HISTORY C19: from Latin *quadrāgēnārius* consisting of forty, from *quādrāgintā* forty

Quadragesima (ˌkwɒdrəˈdʒɛsɪmə) NOUN **1** Also called: **Quadragesima Sunday.** the first Sunday in Lent. **2** *Obsolete* the forty days of Lent.

▷HISTORY C16: from Medieval Latin *quadrāgēsima dies* the fortieth day

Quadragesimal (ˌkwɒdrəˈdʒɛsɪməl) ADJECTIVE of, relating to, or characteristic of Lent or the season of Lent.

quadrangle (ˈkwɒdˌræŋgᵊl) NOUN [1] *Geometry* a plane figure consisting of four points connected by four lines. In a **complete quadrangle,** six lines connect all pairs of points. [2] a rectangular courtyard, esp one having buildings on all four sides. Often shortened to: **quad.** [3] the building surrounding such a courtyard.
▷HISTORY C15: from Late Latin *quadrangulum* figure having four corners
▸**quadrangular** (kwɒˈdræŋgjʊlə) ADJECTIVE

quadrant (ˈkwɒdrənt) NOUN [1] *Geometry* **a** a quarter of the circumference of a circle. **b** the area enclosed by two perpendicular radii of a circle and its circumference. **c** any of the four sections into which a plane is divided by two coordinate axes. [2] a piece of a mechanism in the form of a quarter circle, esp one used as a cam or a gear sector. [3] an instrument formerly used in astronomy and navigation for measuring the altitudes of stars, consisting of a graduated arc of 90° and a sighting mechanism attached to a movable arm.
▷HISTORY C14: from Latin *quadrāns* a quarter
▸**quadrantal** (kwɒˈdræntᵊl) ADJECTIVE

Quadrantid (ˈkwɒˌdræntɪd) NOUN any member of a meteor shower occurring annually around Jan. 3 and appearing to radiate from a point in the constellation Boötes.

quadraphonics *or* **quadrophonics** (ˌkwɒdrəˈfɒnɪks) NOUN (*functioning as singular*) a system of sound recording and reproduction that uses four independent loudspeakers to give directional sources of sound. The speakers are fed by four separate amplified signals.
▸**ˌquadraˈphonic** *or* **ˌquadroˈphonic** ADJECTIVE
▸**quadraphony** *or* **quadrophony** (kwɒdˈrɒfənɪ) NOUN

quadrat (ˈkwɒdrət) NOUN [1] *Ecology* an area of vegetation, often one square metre, marked out for study of the plants in the surrounding area. [2] the frame used to mark out such an area.
▷HISTORY C14 (meaning "a square"): variant of QUADRATE

quadrate NOUN (ˈkwɒdrɪt, -reɪt) [1] a cube, square, or a square or cubelike object. [2] one of a pair of bones of the upper jaw of fishes, amphibians, reptiles, and birds that articulates with the lower jaw. In mammals it forms the incus. ◆ ADJECTIVE (ˈkwɒdrɪt, -reɪt) [3] of or relating to this bone. [4] square or rectangular. ◆ VERB (kwɒˈdreɪt) [5] (*tr*) to make square or rectangular. [6] (often foll by *with*) to conform or cause to conform.
▷HISTORY C14: from Latin *quadrāre* to make square

quadratic (kwɒˈdrætɪk) *Maths* ◆ NOUN [1] Also called: **quadratic equation.** an equation containing one or more terms in which the variable is raised to the power of two, but no terms in which it is raised to a higher power. ◆ ADJECTIVE [2] of or relating to the second power.

quadrature (ˈkwɒdrətʃə) NOUN [1] *Maths* the process of determining a square having an area equal to that of a given figure or surface. [2] the process of making square or dividing into squares. [3] *Astronomy* a configuration in which two celestial bodies, usually the sun and the moon or a planet, form an angle of 90° with a third body, usually the earth. [4] *Electronics* the relationship between two waves that are 90° out of phase.

quadrella (kwɒˈdrɛlə) NOUN *Austral* four nominated horseraces in which the punter bets on selecting the four winners.

quadrennial (kwɒˈdrɛnɪəl) ADJECTIVE [1] occurring every four years. [2] relating to or lasting four years. ◆ NOUN [3] a period of four years.
▸**quadˈrennially** ADVERB

quadrennium (kwɒˈdrɛnɪəm) NOUN, *plural* **-niums** *or* **-nia** (-nɪə). a period of four years.
▷HISTORY C17: from Latin *quadriennium,* from QUADRI- + *annus* year

quadri- *or before a vowel* **quadr-** COMBINING FORM four: *quadrilateral; quadrilingual; quadrisyllabic.*
▷HISTORY from Latin; compare *quattuor* four

quadric (ˈkwɒdrɪk) *Maths* ◆ ADJECTIVE [1] having or characterized by an equation of the second degree, usually in two or three variables. [2] of the second degree. ◆ NOUN [3] a quadric curve, surface, or function.

quadricentennial (ˌkwɒdrɪsɛnˈtɛnɪəl) NOUN [1] a 400th anniversary. ◆ ADJECTIVE [2] of, relating to, or celebrating a 400th anniversary.

quadriceps (ˈkwɒdrɪˌsɛps) NOUN, *plural* **-cepses** (-ˌsɛpsɪz) *or* **-ceps.** *Anatomy* a large four-part muscle of the front of the thigh, which extends the leg.
▷HISTORY C19: New Latin, from QUADRI- + *-ceps* as in BICEPS
▸**quadricipital** (ˌkwɒdrɪˈsɪpɪtᵊl) ADJECTIVE

quadrifid (ˈkwɒdrɪfɪd) ADJECTIVE *Botany* divided into four lobes or other parts: *quadrifid leaves.*

quadriga (kwɒˈdriːgə) NOUN, *plural* **-gas** *or* **-gae** (-dʒiː). (in the classical world) a two-wheeled chariot drawn by four horses abreast.
▷HISTORY C18: from Latin, from earlier *quadrijugae* a team of four, from QUADRI- + *jugum* yoke

quadrilateral (ˌkwɒdrɪˈlætərəl) ADJECTIVE [1] having or formed by four sides. ◆ NOUN [2] Also called: **tetragon.** a polygon having four sides. A **complete quadrilateral** consists of four lines and their six points of intersection.

quadrille[1] (kwɒˈdrɪl, kwə-) NOUN [1] a square dance of five or more figures for four or more couples. [2] a piece of music for such a dance, alternating between simple duple and compound duple time.
▷HISTORY C18: via French from Spanish *cuadrilla,* diminutive of *cuadro* square, from Latin *quadra*

quadrille[2] (kwɒˈdrɪl, kwə-) NOUN an old card game for four players.
▷HISTORY C18: from French, from Spanish *cuartillo,* from *cuarto* fourth, from Latin *quartus,* influenced by QUADRILLE[1]

quadrillion (kwɒˈdrɪljən) NOUN [1] (in Britain) the number represented as one followed by 24 zeros (10^{24}). US and Canadian word: **septillion.** [2] (in the US and Canada) the number represented as one followed by 15 zeros (10^{15}). ◆ DETERMINER [3] (preceded by *a* or a numeral) **a** amounting to this number: *a quadrillion atoms.* **b** (*as pronoun*): *a quadrillion.*
▷HISTORY C17: from French *quadrillon,* from QUADRI- + *-illion,* on the model of *million*
▸**quadˈrillionth** ADJECTIVE

quadrinomial (ˌkwɒdrɪˈnəʊmɪəl) NOUN an algebraic expression containing four terms.

quadripartite (ˌkwɒdrɪˈpɑːtaɪt) ADJECTIVE [1] divided into or composed of four parts. [2] maintained by or involving four participants or groups of participants.

quadriplegia (ˌkwɒdrɪˈpliːdʒɪə, -dʒə) NOUN *Pathol* paralysis of all four limbs, usually as the result of injury to the spine. Also called: **tetraplegia.** Compare **hemiplegia, paraplegia.**
▷HISTORY C20: from QUADRI- + Greek *plēgē* a blow, from *plēssein* to strike

quadriplegic (ˌkwɒdrɪˈpliːdʒɪk) ADJECTIVE [1] *Pathol* of, relating to, or afflicted with quadriplegia. ◆ NOUN [2] *Pathol* a person afflicted with quadriplegia.

quadripole (ˈkwɒdrɪˌpəʊl) NOUN *Physics* an electric circuit with two input and two output terminals.

quadrisect (ˈkwɒdrɪˌsɛkt) VERB to divide into four parts, esp into four equal parts.
▸**ˌquadriˈsection** NOUN

quadrivalent (ˌkwɒdrɪˈveɪlənt) ADJECTIVE *Chem* another word for **tetravalent.**
▸**ˌquadriˈvalency** *or* **ˌquadriˈvalence** NOUN

quadrivial (kwɒˈdrɪvɪəl) ADJECTIVE [1] having or consisting of four roads meeting at a point. [2] (of roads or ways) going in four directions. [3] of or relating to the quadrivium.

quadrivium (kwɒˈdrɪvɪəm) NOUN, *plural* **-ia** (-ɪə). (in medieval learning) the higher division of the seven liberal arts, consisting of arithmetic, geometry, astronomy, and music. Compare **trivium.**
▷HISTORY from Medieval Latin, from Latin: crossroads, meeting of four ways, from QUADRI- + *via* way

quadroon (kwɒˈdruːn) NOUN the offspring of a Mulatto and a White; a person who is one-quarter Black.
▷HISTORY C18: from Spanish *cuarterón,* from *cuarto* quarter, from Latin *quartus*

quadrophonics (ˌkwɒdrəˈfɒnɪks) NOUN a variant spelling of **quadraphonics.**

quadrumanous (kwɒˈdruːmənəs) ADJECTIVE (of monkeys and apes) having all four feet specialized for use as hands.
▷HISTORY C18: from New Latin *quadrumanus,* from QUADRI- + Latin *manus* hand

quadruped (ˈkwɒdrʊˌpɛd) NOUN [1] an animal, esp a mammal, that has all four limbs specialized for walking. ◆ ADJECTIVE [2] having four feet.
▷HISTORY C17: from Latin *quadrupēs,* from *quadru-* (see QUADRI-) + *pēs* foot
▸**quadrupedal** (kwɒˈdruːpɪdᵊl, ˌkwɒdrʊˈpɛdᵊl) ADJECTIVE

quadruple (ˈkwɒdrʊpᵊl, kwɒˈdruːpᵊl) VERB [1] to multiply by four or increase fourfold. ◆ ADJECTIVE [2] four times as much or as many; fourfold. [3] consisting of four parts. ◆ NOUN [4] a quantity or number four times as great as another.
▷HISTORY C16: via Old French from Latin *quadruplus,* from *quadru-* (see QUADRI-) + *-plus* -fold
▸**ˈquadruply** ADVERB

quadruplet (ˈkwɒdrʊplɪt, kwɒˈdruːplɪt) NOUN [1] one of four offspring born at one birth. Often shortened to: **quad.** [2] a group or set of four similar things. [3] *Music* a group of four notes to be played in a time value of three.

quadruple time NOUN musical time in which there are four beats in each bar.

quadruplex (ˈkwɒdrʊˌplɛks, kwɒˈdruːplɛks) ADJECTIVE [1] consisting of four parts; fourfold. [2] denoting a type of television video tape recorder having four transversely rotating heads.
▷HISTORY C19: from Latin, from *quadru-* (see QUADRI-) + *-plex* -fold
▸**quadruplicity** (ˌkwɒdrʊˈplɪsɪtɪ) NOUN

quadruplicate ADJECTIVE (kwɒˈdruːplɪkɪt, -ˌkeɪt) [1] fourfold or quadruple. ◆ VERB (kwɒˈdruːplɪˌkeɪt) [2] to multiply or be multiplied by four. ◆ NOUN (kwɒˈdruːplɪkɪt, -ˌkeɪt) [3] a group or set of four things.
▷HISTORY C17: from Latin *quadruplicāre* to increase fourfold
▸**quadˌrupliˈcation** NOUN

quadrupole (ˈkwɒdrʊˌpəʊl) NOUN *Physics* a set of four associated positive and negative electric charges or two associated magnetic dipoles.

quaere (ˈkwɪərɪ) *Rare* ◆ NOUN [1] a query or question. ◆ INTERJECTION [2] ask or inquire: used esp to introduce a question.
▷HISTORY C16: Latin, imperative of *quaerere* to inquire

quaestor (ˈkwiːstə, -tɔː) *or sometimes US* **questor** (ˈkwɛstə) NOUN any of several magistrates of ancient Rome, usually a financial administrator.
▷HISTORY C14: from Latin, from *quaerere* to inquire
▸**quaestorial** (kwɛˈstɔːrɪəl) ADJECTIVE ▸**ˈquaestorˌship** NOUN

quaff (kwɒf, kwɑːf) VERB to drink heartily or in one draught.
▷HISTORY C16: perhaps of imitative origin; compare Middle Low German *quassen* to eat or drink excessively
▸**ˈquaffable** ADJECTIVE ▸**ˈquaffer** NOUN

quag (kwæg, kwɒg) NOUN another word for **quagmire.**
▷HISTORY C16: perhaps related to QUAKE; compare Middle Low German *quabbe*

quagga (ˈkwægə) NOUN, *plural* **-gas** *or* **-ga.** a recently extinct member of the horse family (*Equidae*), *Equus quagga,* of southern Africa: it had a sandy brown colouring with zebra-like stripes on the head and shoulders.
▷HISTORY C18: from obsolete Afrikaans, from Khoikhoi *quăgga;* compare Xhosa *i-qwara* something striped

quaggy (ˈkwægɪ, ˈkwɒgɪ) ADJECTIVE **-gier, -giest.** [1] resembling a marsh or quagmire; boggy. [2] yielding, soft, or flabby.
▸**ˈquagginess** NOUN

quagmire (ˈkwægˌmaɪə, ˈkwɒg-) NOUN [1] a soft wet area of land that gives way under the feet; bog. [2] an awkward, complex, or embarrassing situation.
▷HISTORY C16: from QUAG + MIRE

quahog (ˈkwɑːˌhɒg) NOUN an edible clam, *Venus* (or *Mercenaria*) *mercenaria,* native to the Atlantic coast of North America, having a large heavy

rounded shell. Also called: **hard-shell clam, hard-shell, round clam.** Compare **soft-shell clam.**
▷HISTORY C18: from Narraganset, short for *poquauhock,* from *pohkeni* dark + *hogki* shell

quaich *or* **quaigh** (kwex, kweɪx) NOUN, *plural* **quaichs** *or* **quaighs.** *Scot* a small shallow drinking cup, usually with two handles.
▷HISTORY from Scottish Gaelic *cuach* cup

Quai d'Orsay (*French* ke dɔrsɛ) NOUN the quay along the S bank of the Seine, Paris, where the French foreign office is situated.

quail[1] (kweɪl) NOUN, *plural* **quails** *or* **quail.** 1 any small Old World gallinaceous game bird of the genus *Coturnix* and related genera, having a rounded body and small tail: family *Phasianidae* (pheasants). 2 any of various similar and related American birds, such as the bobwhite.
▷HISTORY C14: from Old French *quaille,* from Medieval Latin *quaccula,* probably of imitative origin

quail[2] (kweɪl) VERB (*intr*) to shrink back with fear; cower.
▷HISTORY C15: perhaps from Old French *quailler,* from Latin *coāgulāre* to curdle

quaint (kweɪnt) ADJECTIVE 1 attractively unusual, esp in an old-fashioned style: *a quaint village.* 2 odd, peculiar, or inappropriate: *a quaint sense of duty.*
▷HISTORY C13 (in the sense: clever): from Old French *cointe,* from Latin *cognitus* known, from *cognoscere* to ascertain
▸ **ˈquaintly** ADVERB ▸ **ˈquaintness** NOUN

quair (kwer, kwɛə) NOUN *Scot* a book.
▷HISTORY a variant of QUIRE[1]

quake (kweɪk) VERB (*intr*) 1 to shake or tremble with or as with fear. 2 to convulse or quiver, as from instability. ◆ NOUN 3 the act or an instance of quaking. 4 *Informal* short for **earthquake.**
▷HISTORY Old English *cwacian;* related to Old English *cweccan* to shake, Old Irish *bocaim,* German *wackeln*

Quaker (ˈkweɪkə) NOUN 1 a member of the Religious Society of Friends, a Christian sect founded by the English religious leader George Fox (1624–91) about 1650, whose central belief is the doctrine of the Inner Light. Quakers reject sacraments, ritual, and formal ministry, hold meetings at which any member may speak, and have promoted many causes for social reform. ◆ ADJECTIVE 2 of, relating to, or designating the Religious Society of Friends or its religious beliefs or practices.
▷HISTORY C17: originally a derogatory nickname, alluding either to their alleged ecstatic fits, or to George Fox's injunction to "*quake* at the word of the Lord"
▸ **ˈQuakeress** FEMININE NOUN ▸ **ˈQuakerish** ADJECTIVE
▸ **ˈQuakerism** NOUN

Quaker gun NOUN a dummy gun, as of wood.
▷HISTORY alluding to the Quakers' traditional pacifism

Quaker meeting NOUN a gathering of the Quakers for worship, characterized by periods of silence and by members speaking as moved by the Spirit.

quaking (ˈkweɪkɪŋ) ADJECTIVE unstable or unsafe to walk on, as a bog or quicksand: *a quaking bog; quaking sands.*

quaking grass NOUN any grass of the genus *Briza,* of N temperate regions and South America, having delicate flower branches that shake in the wind.

quaky (ˈkweɪkɪ) ADJECTIVE **quakier, quakiest.** inclined to quake; shaky; tremulous.
▸ **ˈquakily** ADVERB ▸ **ˈquakiness** NOUN

quale (ˈkwɑːlɪ, ˈkweɪ-) NOUN, *plural* **-lia** (-lɪə). *Philosophy* an essential property or quality.
▷HISTORY C17: Latin, neuter singular of *qualis* of what kind

qualification (ˌkwɒlɪfɪˈkeɪʃən) NOUN 1 an ability, quality, or attribute, esp one that fits a person to perform a particular job or task: *he has no qualifications to be a teacher.* 2 a condition that modifies or limits; restriction. 3 the act of qualifying or state of being qualified.

qualified (ˈkwɒlɪˌfaɪd) ADJECTIVE 1 having the abilities, qualities, attributes, etc., necessary to perform a particular job or task. 2 limited, modified, or restricted; not absolute.

Qualified Majority Voting NOUN a voting system, used by the EU Council of Ministers, enabling certain resolutions to be passed without unanimity. Abbreviation: **QMV.**

qualifier (ˈkwɒlɪˌfaɪə) NOUN 1 a person or thing that qualifies, esp a contestant in a competition who wins a preliminary heat or contest and so earns the right to take part in the next round. 2 a preliminary heat or contest. 3 *Grammar* another word for **modifier** (sense 1).

qualify (ˈkwɒlɪˌfaɪ) VERB **-fies, -fying, -fied.** 1 to provide or be provided with the abilities or attributes necessary for a task, office, duty, etc.: *his degree qualifies him for the job; he qualifies for the job, but would he do it well?* 2 (*tr*) to make less strong, harsh, or violent; moderate or restrict. 3 (*tr*) to modify or change the strength or flavour of. 4 (*tr*) *Grammar* another word for **modify** (sense 3). 5 (*tr*) to attribute a quality to; characterize. 6 (*intr*) to progress to the final stages of a competition, as by winning preliminary contests.
▷HISTORY C16: from Old French *qualifier,* from Medieval Latin *quālificāre* to characterize, from Latin *quālis* of what kind + *facere* to make
▸ **ˈqualiˌfiable** ADJECTIVE ▸ **qualificatory** (ˈkwɒlɪfɪkətərɪ, -ˌkeɪ-) ADJECTIVE

qualitative (ˈkwɒlɪtətɪv, -ˌteɪ-) ADJECTIVE involving or relating to distinctions based on quality or qualities. Compare **quantitative.**
▸ **ˈqualitatively** ADVERB

qualitative analysis NOUN See **analysis** (sense 4).

qualitative identity NOUN *Logic* the relation that holds between two relata that have properties in common. This term is used to distinguish many uses of the words *identical* or *same* in ordinary language from strict identity or numerical identity.

quality (ˈkwɒlɪtɪ) NOUN, *plural* **-ties.** 1 a distinguishing characteristic, property, or attribute. 2 the basic character or nature of something. 3 a trait or feature of personality. 4 degree or standard of excellence, esp a high standard. 5 (formerly) high social status or the distinction associated with it. 6 musical tone colour; timbre. 7 *Logic* the characteristic of a proposition that is dependent on whether it is affirmative or negative. 8 *Phonetics* the distinctive character of a vowel, determined by the configuration of the mouth, tongue, etc., when it is articulated and distinguished from the pitch and stress with which it is uttered. 9 (*modifier*) having or showing excellence or superiority: *a quality product.*
▷HISTORY C13: from Old French *qualité,* from Latin *quālitās* state, nature, from *quālis* of what sort

quality control NOUN control of the relative quality of a manufactured product, usually by statistical sampling techniques.

quality factor NOUN a property of ionizing radiations that affects their ability to cause biological effects. For weakly ionizing radiations such as gamma rays it has value 1 whilst for alpha rays it is about 20. Former name: **relative biological effectiveness.**

qualm (kwɑːm) NOUN 1 a sudden feeling of sickness or nausea. 2 a pang or sudden feeling of doubt, esp concerning moral conduct; scruple. 3 a sudden sensation of misgiving or unease.
▷HISTORY Old English *cwealm* death or plague; related to Old High German *qualm* despair, Dutch *kwalm* smoke, stench
▸ **ˈqualmish** ADJECTIVE ▸ **ˈqualmishly** ADVERB
▸ **ˈqualmishness** NOUN

quamash (ˈkwɒmæʃ, kwəˈmæʃ) NOUN another name for **camass** (sense 1).

quandary (ˈkwɒndrɪ, -dərɪ) NOUN, *plural* **-ries.** a situation or circumstance that presents problems difficult to solve; predicament; dilemma.
▷HISTORY C16: of uncertain origin; perhaps related to Latin *quandō* when

quandong, quandang (ˈkwɒnˌdɒŋ), *or* **quantong** (ˈkwɒnˌtɒŋ) NOUN 1 Also called: **native peach. a** a small Australian santalaceous tree, *Eucarya acuminata* (or *Fusanus acuminatus*). **b** the edible fruit or nut of this tree, used in preserves. 2 **silver quandong. a** an Australian tree, *Elaeocarpus grandis*: family *Elaeocarpaceae*. **b** the pale easily worked timber of this tree. 3 *Austral informal* a person who takes advantage of other people's generosity.
▷HISTORY from a native Australian language

quango (ˈkwæŋgəʊ) NOUN, *plural* **-gos.** a semipublic government-financed administrative body whose members are appointed by the government.
▷HISTORY C20: *qu(asi-)a(utonomous) n(on)g(overnmental) o(rganization)*

quangocracy (kwæŋˈgɒkrəsɪ) NOUN, *plural* **-cies.** 1 the control or influence ascribed to quangos. 2 quangos collectively.

quant[1] (kwɒnt) NOUN 1 a long pole for propelling a boat, esp a punt, by pushing on the bottom of a river or lake. ◆ VERB 2 to propel (a boat) with a quant.
▷HISTORY C15: probably from Latin *contus* a pole, from Greek *kontos*

quant[2] (kwɒnt) NOUN *Informal* a highly paid computer specialist with a degree in a quantitative science, employed by a financial house to predict the future price movements of securities, commodities, currencies, etc.
▷HISTORY C20: from QUANTITATIVE

quanta (ˈkwɒntə) NOUN the plural of **quantum.**

quantic (ˈkwɒntɪk) NOUN a homogeneous function of two or more variables in a rational and integral form, as in $x^2 + 3xy + y^2$.
▷HISTORY C19: from Latin *quantus* how great

quantifier (ˈkwɒntɪˌfaɪə) NOUN 1 *Logic* **a** a symbol including a variable that indicates the degree of generality of the expression in which that variable occurs, as (∃*x*) in (∃*x*)*Fx*, rendered "something is an F", (*x*) in (*x*)(*Fx*→*Gx*), rendered "all Fs are Gs". **b** any other symbol with an analogous interpretation: *the existential quantifier,* (∃*x*), *corresponds to the words "there is something, x, such that ...".* 2 *Grammar* a word or phrase in a natural language having this role, such as *some, all,* or *many* in English.

quantify (ˈkwɒntɪˌfaɪ) VERB **-fies, -fying, -fied.** (*tr*) 1 to discover or express the quantity of. 2 *Logic* to specify the quantity of (a term) by using a quantifier, such as *all, some,* or *no.*
▷HISTORY C19: from Medieval Latin *quantificāre,* from Latin *quantus* how much + *facere* to make
▸ **ˈquantifiable** ADJECTIVE ▸ **ˌquantifiˈcation** NOUN

quantitative (ˈkwɒntɪtətɪv, -ˌteɪ-) *or* **quantitive** ADJECTIVE 1 involving or relating to considerations of amount or size. Compare **qualitative.** 2 capable of being measured. 3 *Prosody* denoting or relating to a metrical system, such as that in Latin and Greek verse, that is based on the relative length rather than stress of syllables.
▸ **ˈquantitatively** *or* **ˈquantitively** ADVERB

quantitative analysis NOUN See **analysis** (sense 4).

quantity (ˈkwɒntɪtɪ) NOUN, *plural* **-ties.** 1 **a** a specified or definite amount, weight, number, etc. **b** (*as modifier*): *a quantity estimate.* 2 the aspect or property of anything that can be measured, weighed, counted, etc. 3 a large or considerable amount. 4 *Maths* an entity having a magnitude that may be denoted by a numerical expression. 5 *Physics* a specified magnitude or amount; the product of a number and a unit. 6 *Logic* the characteristic of a proposition dependent on whether it is a universal or particular statement, considering all or only part of a class. 7 *Prosody* the relative duration of a syllable or the vowel in it.
▷HISTORY C14: from Old French *quantité,* from Latin *quantitās* extent, amount, from *quantus* how much

> **Language note** The use of a plural noun after *quantity of* as in *a large quantity of bananas* was formerly considered incorrect, but is now acceptable.

quantity surveyor NOUN a person who estimates the cost of the materials and labour necessary for a construction job.

quantity theory NOUN *Economics* a theory stating that the general price level varies directly with the quantity of money in circulation and the velocity with which it is circulated, and inversely with the volume of production expressed by the total number of money transactions.

quantize *or* **quantise** (ˈkwɒntaɪz) VERB (*tr*) 1

Physics to restrict (a physical quantity) to one of a set of values characterized by quantum numbers. 2 *Maths* to limit (a variable) to values that are integral multiples of a basic unit.
▸ **ˌquantiˈzation** *or* **ˌquantiˈsation** NOUN

quantometer (kwɒnˈtɒmɪtə) NOUN *Engineering* a spectroscopic instrument for measuring the percentage of different metals present in a sample.

quantum (ˈkwɒntəm) NOUN, *plural* **-ta** (-tə). 1 *Physics* **a** the smallest quantity of some physical property, such as energy, that a system can possess according to the quantum theory. **b** a particle with such a unit of energy. 2 amount or quantity, esp a specific amount. 3 (*often used with a negative*) the least possible amount that can suffice: *there is not a quantum of evidence for your accusation.* 4 something that can be quantified or measured. 5 (*modifier*) loosely, sudden, spectacular, or vitally important: *a quantum improvement.*
▷ HISTORY C17: from Latin *quantus* (adj) how much

quantum chromodynamics NOUN *Physics* a theory describing the strong interaction in terms of quarks and gluons, with the colour of quarks used as an analogue of charge and the gluon as an analogue of the photon. Abbreviation: **QCD.**
▷ HISTORY C20: *chromodynamics* from CHROMO- (referring to quark colour) + DYNAMICS, modelled on QUANTUM ELECTRODYNAMICS

quantum cryptography NOUN a method of coding information based on quantum mechanics, which is said to be unbreakable.

quantum efficiency NOUN 1 *Physics* the number of electrons released by a photocell per photon of incident radiation of a given energy. 2 *Chem* the number of chemical species that undergo reaction per photon of absorbed radiation of a given energy.

quantum electrodynamics NOUN *Physics* a relativistic quantum mechanical theory concerned with electromagnetic interactions. Abbreviation: **QED.**

quantum electronics NOUN the application of quantum mechanics and quantum optics to the study and design of electronic devices.

quantum field theory NOUN *Physics* quantum mechanical theory concerned with elementary particles, which are represented by fields whose normal modes of oscillation are quantized.

quantum flavourdynamics NOUN a gauge theory of the electromagnetic and weak interactions. Also called: **electroweak theory.** Abbreviation: **QFD.**
▷ HISTORY C20: *flavourdynamics* from FLAVOUR (referring to quark flavour) + DYNAMICS, modelled on QUANTUM ELECTRODYNAMICS

quantum gravity NOUN *Physics* a theory of the gravitational interaction that involves quantum mechanics to explain the force.

quantum leap *or* **jump** NOUN a sudden highly significant advance; breakthrough.
▷ HISTORY C20: from its use in physics meaning the sudden jump of an electron, atom, etc. from one energy level to another

quantum mechanics NOUN (*functioning as singular*) the branch of mechanics, based on the quantum theory used for interpreting the behaviour of elementary particles and atoms, which do not obey Newtonian mechanics.

quantum meruit *Latin* (ˈmɛruːɪt) as much as he has earned: denoting a payment for goods or services in partial fulfilment of a contract or for those supplied when no price has been agreed.

quantum number NOUN *Physics* one of a set of integers or half-integers characterizing the energy states of a particle or system of particles. A function of the number multiplied by a fixed quantity gives the observed value of some specified physical quantity possessed by the system.

quantum state NOUN *Physics* a state of a system characterized by a set of quantum numbers and represented by an eigenfunction. The energy of each state is precise within the limits imposed by the uncertainty principle but may be changed by applying a field of force. States that have the same energy are called **degenerate.** See also **energy level.**

quantum statistics NOUN (*functioning as singular*) *Physics* statistics concerned with the distribution of a number of identical elementary particles, atoms, ions, or molecules among possible quantum states.

quantum theory NOUN a theory concerning the behaviour of physical systems based on Planck's idea that they can only possess certain properties, such as energy and angular momentum, in discrete amounts (quanta). The theory later developed in several equivalent mathematical forms based on De Broglie's theory (see **wave mechanics**) and on the Heisenberg uncertainty principle.

quaquaversal (ˌkwɑːkwəˈvɜːsəl) ADJECTIVE *Geology* directed outwards in all directions from a common centre: *the quaquaversal dip of a pericline.*
▷ HISTORY C18: from Latin *quāquā* in every direction + *versus* towards

quarantine (ˈkwɒrənˌtiːn) NOUN 1 a period of isolation or detention, esp of persons or animals arriving from abroad, to prevent the spread of disease, usually consisting of the maximum known incubation period of the suspected disease. 2 the place or area where such detention is enforced. 3 any period or state of enforced isolation. ◆ VERB 4 (*tr*) to isolate in or as if in quarantine.
▷ HISTORY C17: from Italian *quarantina* period of forty days, from *quaranta* forty, from Latin *quadrāgintā*

quarantine flag NOUN *Nautical* the yellow signal flag for the letter Q, flown alone from a vessel to indicate that there is no disease aboard and to request pratique or, with a second signal flag, to indicate that there is disease aboard. Also called: **yellow flag, yellow jack.**

quare (kweə) ADJECTIVE *Irish dialect* 1 remarkable or strange: *a quare fellow.* 2 great or good: *you're in a quare mess.*
▷ HISTORY probably variant of QUEER

quark¹ (kwɑːk) NOUN *Physics* any of a set of six hypothetical elementary particles together with their antiparticles thought to be fundamental units of all baryons and mesons but unable to exist in isolation. The magnitude of their charge is either two thirds or one third of that of the electron.
▷ HISTORY C20: coined by James Joyce (1882–1941), Irish novelist and short-story writer, in the novel *Finnegans Wake,* and given special application in physics

quark² (kwɑːk) NOUN a type of low-fat soft cheese.
▷ HISTORY from German

quarrel¹ (ˈkwɒrəl) NOUN 1 an angry disagreement; argument. 2 a cause of disagreement or dispute; grievance. ◆ VERB **-rels, -relling, -relled** *or US* **-rels, -reling, -reled.** (*intr;* often foll by *with*) 3 to engage in a disagreement or dispute; argue. 4 to find fault; complain.
▷ HISTORY C14: from Old French *querele,* from Latin *querēlla* complaint, from *querī* to complain
▸ **ˈquarreller** *or US* **ˈquarreler** NOUN

quarrel² (ˈkwɒrəl) NOUN 1 an arrow having a four-edged head, fired from a crossbow. 2 a small square or diamond-shaped pane of glass, usually one of many in a fixed or casement window and framed with lead.
▷ HISTORY C13: from Old French *quarrel* pane, from Medieval Latin *quadrellus,* diminutive of Latin *quadrus* square

quarrelsome (ˈkwɒrəlsəm) ADJECTIVE inclined to quarrel or disagree; belligerent.
▸ **ˈquarrelsomely** ADVERB ▸ **ˈquarrelsomeness** NOUN

quarrian *or* **quarrion** (ˈkwɒrɪən) NOUN a cockatiel, *Leptolophus hollandicus,* of scrub and woodland regions of inland Australia, that feeds on seeds and grasses.
▷ HISTORY C20: probably from a native Australian language

quarrier (ˈkwɒrɪə) NOUN another word for **quarryman.**

quarry¹ (ˈkwɒrɪ) NOUN, *plural* **-ries.** 1 an open surface excavation for the extraction of building stone, slate, marble, etc., by drilling, blasting, or cutting. 2 a copious source of something, esp information. ◆ VERB **-ries, -rying, -ried.** 3 to extract (stone, slate, etc.) from or as if from a quarry. 4 (*tr*) to excavate a quarry in. 5 to obtain (something, esp information) diligently and laboriously: *he was quarrying away in the reference library.*
▷ HISTORY C15: from Old French *quarriere,* from *quarre* (unattested) square-shaped stone, from Latin *quadrāre* to make square

quarry² (ˈkwɒrɪ) NOUN, *plural* **-ries.** 1 an animal, bird, or fish that is hunted, esp by other animals; prey. 2 anything pursued or hunted.
▷ HISTORY C14 *quirre* entrails offered to the hounds, from Old French *cuirée* what is placed on the hide, from *cuir* hide, from Latin *corium* leather; probably also influenced by Old French *coree* entrails, from Latin *cor* heart

quarry³ (ˈkwɒrɪ) NOUN, *plural* **-ries.** 1 a square or diamond shape. 2 something having this shape. 3 another word for **quarrel².**
▷ HISTORY C16: from Old French *quarré;* see QUARREL²

quarryman (ˈkwɒrɪmən) NOUN, *plural* **-men.** a man who works in or manages a quarry.

quarry tile NOUN a square or diamond-shaped unglazed floor tile.
▷ HISTORY C20: from QUARRY³

quart¹ (kwɔːt) NOUN 1 a unit of liquid measure equal to a quarter of a gallon or two pints. 1 US quart (0.946 litre) is equal to 0.8326 UK quart. 1 UK quart (1.136 litres) is equal to 1.2009 US quarts. 2 a unit of dry measure equal to 2 pints or one eighth of a peck.
▷ HISTORY C14: from Old French *quarte,* from Latin *quartus* fourth

quart² NOUN 1 (kɑːt) *Piquet* a sequence of four cards in the same suit. 2 (kart) *Fencing* a variant spelling of **quarte.**
▷ HISTORY C17: from French *quarte* fourth

quartan (ˈkwɔːtᵊn) ADJECTIVE (esp of a malarial fever) occurring every third day.
▷ HISTORY C13: from Latin *febris quartāna* fever occurring every fourth day, reckoned inclusively

quarte *French* (kart) NOUN the fourth of eight basic positions from which a parry or attack can be made in fencing.
▷ HISTORY C18: from French, fem of *quart* a quarter

quarter (ˈkwɔːtə) NOUN 1 one of four equal or nearly equal parts of an object, quantity, amount, etc. 2 Also called: **fourth.** the fraction equal to one divided by four (1/4). 3 *US and Canadian* a quarter of a dollar; 25-cent piece. 4 a unit of weight equal to a quarter of a hundredweight. 1 US quarter is equal to 25 pounds; 1 Brit quarter is equal to 28 pounds. 5 short for **quarter-hour.** 6 a fourth part of a year; three months. 7 *Astronomy* **a** one fourth of the moon's period of revolution around the earth. **b** either of two phases of the moon, **first quarter** or **last quarter** when half of the lighted surface is visible from the earth. 8 *Informal* a unit of weight equal to a quarter of a pound or 4 ounces. 9 *Brit* a unit of capacity for grain, etc., usually equal to 8 UK bushels. 10 *Sport* one of the four periods into which certain games are divided. 11 *Nautical* the part of a vessel's side towards the stern, usually aft of the aftermost mast: *the port quarter.* 12 *Nautical* the general direction along the water in the quadrant between the beam of a vessel and its stern: *the wind was from the port quarter.* 13 a region or district of a town or city: *the Spanish quarter.* 14 a region, direction, or point of the compass. 15 (*sometimes plural*) an unspecified person or group of people: *to get word from the highest quarter.* 16 mercy or pity, as shown to a defeated opponent (esp in the phrases **ask for** or **give quarter**). 17 any of the four limbs, including the adjacent parts, of the carcass of a quadruped or bird: *a hind quarter of beef.* 18 *Vet science* the side part of the wall of a horse's hoof. 19 the part of a shoe or boot covering the heel and joining the vamp. 20 *Heraldry* one of four more or less equal quadrants into which a shield may be divided. 21 *Military, slang* short for **quartermaster.** ◆ VERB 22 (*tr*) to divide into four equal or nearly equal parts. 23 (*tr*) to divide into any number of parts. 24 (*tr*) (esp formerly) to dismember (a human body): *to be drawn and quartered.* 25 to billet or be billeted in lodgings, esp (of military personnel) in civilian lodgings. 26 (*intr*) (of gun dogs or hounds) to range over an area of ground in search of game or the scent of quarry. 27 (*intr*) *Nautical* (of the wind) to blow onto a vessel's quarter: *the wind began to quarter.* 28 (*tr*) *Heraldry* **a** to divide (a shield) into four separate bearings with a cross. **b** to place (one set of arms) in diagonally opposite quarters to another. ◆ ADJECTIVE 29 being or consisting of one of four equal parts: *a quarter pound of butter.* ◆ See also **quarters.**

▷HISTORY C13: from Old French *quartier,* from Latin *quartārius* a fourth part, from *quartus* fourth

quarterage (ˈkwɔːtərɪdʒ) NOUN 1 an allowance or payment made quarterly. 2 *Rare* shelter or lodging.

quarterback (ˈkwɔːtəˌbæk) NOUN *US and Canadian* 1 a player in American or Canadian football, positioned usually behind the centre, who directs attacking play. 2 **Monday-morning quarterbacking.** wisdom after the event, esp by spectators.

quarter-bound ADJECTIVE (of a book) having a binding consisting of two types of material, the better type being used on the spine.

quarter crack NOUN *Vet science* a sand crack on the inside of the forefoot of a horse.

quarter day NOUN any of four days in the year when certain payments become due. In England, Wales, and Northern Ireland these are Lady Day, Midsummer's Day, Michaelmas, and Christmas. In Scotland they are Candlemas, Whit Sunday, Lammas, and Martinmas.

quarterdeck (ˈkwɔːtəˌdɛk) NOUN *Nautical* the after part of the weather deck of a ship, traditionally the deck on a naval vessel for official or ceremonial use.

quartered (ˈkwɔːtəd) ADJECTIVE 1 *Heraldry* (of a shield) divided into four sections, each having contrasting arms or having two sets of arms, each repeated in diagonally opposite corners. 2 (of a log) sawn into four equal parts along two diameters at right angles to each other; quartersawn.

quarterfinal (ˈkwɔːtəˌfaɪnᵊl) NOUN the round before the semifinal in a competition.

quarter grain NOUN the grain of quartersawn timber.

quarter horse NOUN a small powerful breed of horse, originally bred for sprinting in quarter-mile races in Virginia in the late 18th century.

quarter-hour NOUN 1 a period of 15 minutes. 2 any of the points on the face of a timepiece that mark 15 minutes before or after the hour, and sometimes 30 minutes after.
▸ **ˌquarter-ˈhourly** ADVERB, ADJECTIVE

quartering (ˈkwɔːtərɪŋ) NOUN 1 *Military* the allocation of accommodation to service personnel. 2 *Heraldry* **a** the marshalling of several coats of arms on one shield, usually representing intermarriages. **b** any coat of arms marshalled in this way.

quarterlife crisis (ˈkwɔːtəˌlaɪf) NOUN a crisis that may be experienced in one's twenties, involving anxiety over the direction and quality of one's life.

quarterlight (ˈkwɔːtəˌlaɪt) NOUN *Brit* a small pivoted window in the door of a car for ventilation.

quarterly (ˈkwɔːtəlɪ) ADJECTIVE 1 occurring, done, paid, etc., at intervals of three months. 2 of, relating to, or consisting of a quarter. ◆ NOUN, *plural* **-lies.** 3 a periodical issued every three months. ◆ ADVERB 4 once every three months. 5 *Heraldry* into or in quarters: *a shield divided quarterly.*

quartermaster (ˈkwɔːtəˌmɑːstə) NOUN 1 an officer responsible for accommodation, food, and equipment in a military unit. 2 a rating in the navy, usually a petty officer, with particular responsibility for steering a ship and other navigational duties.

quarter-miler NOUN an athlete who specializes in running the quarter mile or the 400 metres.

quartern (ˈkwɔːtən) NOUN 1 a fourth part of certain weights or measures, such as a peck or a pound. 2 Also called: **quartern loaf.** *Brit* **a** a type of loaf 4 inches square, used esp for making sandwiches. **b** any loaf weighing 1600 g when baked.
▷HISTORY C13: from Old French *quarteron,* from *quart* a quarter

quarter note NOUN the usual US and Canadian name for **crotchet** (sense 1).

quarter-phase ADJECTIVE another term for **two-phase.**

quarter plate NOUN a photographic plate measuring 3¼ × 4¼ inches (8.3 × 10.8 cm).

quarter round NOUN *Architect* another name for **ovolo.**

quarters (ˈkwɔːtəz) PLURAL NOUN 1 housing or accommodation, esp as provided for military personnel and their families. 2 the stations assigned to military personnel, esp to each crew member of a warship: *general quarters.* 3 (in India) housing provided by an employer or by the government. 4 (*functioning as singular*) *Military, slang* short for **quartermaster.**

quartersaw (ˈkwɔːtəˌsɔː) VERB **-saws, -sawing, -sawed, -sawed** *or* **-sawn.** (*tr*) to saw (timber) into quarters along two diameters of a log at right angles to each other.

quarter section NOUN *US and Canadian* a land measure, used in surveying, with sides half a mile long; 160 acres.

quarter sessions NOUN (*functioning as singular or plural*) 1 (in England and Wales, formerly) a criminal court held four times a year before justices of the peace or a recorder, empowered to try all but the most serious offences and to hear appeals from petty sessions. Replaced in 1972 by **crown courts.** Compare **assizes.** 2 (in Scotland, formerly) a court held by justices of the peace four times a year, empowered to hear appeals from justice of the peace courts and to deal with some licensing matters: abolished in 1975.

quarterstaff (ˈkwɔːtəˌstɑːf) NOUN, *plural* **-staves** (-ˌsteɪvz, -ˌstɑːvz). 1 a stout iron-tipped wooden staff about 6ft. long, formerly used in England as a weapon. 2 the use of such a staff in fighting, sport, or exercise.
▷HISTORY C16: of uncertain origin

quarter tone NOUN *Music* a quarter of a whole tone; a pitch interval corresponding to 50 cents measured on the well-tempered scale.

quartet *or* **quartette** (kwɔːˈtɛt) NOUN 1 a group of four singers or instrumentalists or a piece of music composed for such a group. See **string quartet.** 2 any group of four.
▷HISTORY C18: from Italian *quartetto,* diminutive of *quarto* fourth

quartic (ˈkwɔːtɪk) ADJECTIVE, NOUN another word for **biquadratic.**
▷HISTORY C19: from Latin *quartus* fourth

quartile (ˈkwɔːtaɪl) NOUN 1 *Statistics* one of three actual or notional values of a variable dividing its distribution into four groups with equal frequencies. ◆ ADJECTIVE 2 *Statistics* denoting or relating to a quartile. 3 *Astrology* denoting an aspect of two heavenly bodies when their longitudes differ by 90°. 4 a quarter part of a distribution.
▷HISTORY C16: from Medieval Latin *quartīlis,* from Latin *quartus* fourth

quarto (ˈkwɔːtəʊ) NOUN, *plural* **-tos.** 1 a book size resulting from folding a sheet of paper, usually crown or demy, into four leaves or eight pages, each one quarter the size of the sheet. Often written: **4to, 4°.** 2 (formerly) a size of cut paper 10 in. by 8 in. (25.4 cm by 20.3 cm).
▷HISTORY C16: from New Latin phrase *in quartō* in quarter

quartz (kwɔːts) NOUN 1 a colourless mineral often tinted by impurities, found in igneous, sedimentary, and metamorphic rocks. It is used in the manufacture of glass, abrasives, and cement, and also as a gemstone; the violet-purple variety is amethyst, the brown variety is cairngorm, the yellow variety is citrine, and the pink variety is rose quartz. Composition: silicon dioxide. Formula: SiO_2. Crystal structure: hexagonal. 2 short for **quartz glass.**
▷HISTORY C18: from German *Quarz,* of Slavic origin

quartz clock *or* **watch** NOUN a clock or watch that is operated by the vibrations of a quartz crystal controlled by a microcircuit.

quartz crystal NOUN a thin plate or rod cut in certain directions from a piece of piezoelectric quartz and accurately ground so that it vibrates at a particular frequency.

quartz glass NOUN a colourless glass composed of almost pure silica, resistant to very high temperatures and transparent to near-ultraviolet radiation. Sometimes shortened to: **quartz.**

quartziferous (kwɔːtˈsɪfərəs) ADJECTIVE containing or composed of quartz.

quartz-iodine lamp *or* **quartz lamp** NOUN a type of tungsten-halogen lamp containing small amounts of iodine and having a quartz envelope, operating at high temperature and producing an intense light for use in car headlamps, etc.

quartzite (ˈkwɔːtsaɪt) NOUN 1 a very hard metamorphic rock consisting of a mosaic of intergrown quartz crystals. 2 a white or grey sandstone composed of quartz.

quasar (ˈkweɪzɑː, -sɑː) NOUN any of a class of extragalactic objects that emit an immense amount of energy in the form of light, infrared radiation, etc., from a compact source. They are extremely distant and their energy generation is thought to involve a supermassive black hole located in the centre of a galaxy.
▷HISTORY C20: *quas(i-stell)ar (object)*

quash (kwɒʃ) VERB (*tr*) 1 to subdue forcefully and completely; put down; suppress. 2 to annul or make void (a law, decision, etc.). 3 to reject (an indictment, writ, etc.) as invalid.
▷HISTORY C14: from Old French *quasser,* from Latin *quassāre* to shake

Quashi *or* **Quashie** (ˈkwɑːʃɪ) NOUN *Caribbean* an unsophisticated or gullible male Black peasant: *I'm not a Quashi that anyone can fool.*
▷HISTORY from Twi

quasi (ˈkweɪzaɪ, -saɪ, ˈkwɑːzɪ) ADVERB as if; as it were.
▷HISTORY from Latin, literally: as if

quasi- COMBINING FORM 1 almost but not really; seemingly: *a quasi-religious cult.* 2 resembling but not actually being; so-called: *a quasi-scholar.*

quasi-contract NOUN an implied contract which arises without the express agreement of the parties.

quasi-judicial ADJECTIVE denoting or relating to powers and functions similar to those of a judge, such as those exercised by an arbitrator, administrative tribunal, etc.

quasi-quotation NOUN *Logic* a metalinguistic device for referring to the form of an expression containing variables without referring to the symbols for those variables. Thus while *"not p"* refers to the expression consisting of the word *not* followed by the letter *p,* the quasi-quotation ⌈not p⌉ refers to the form of any expression consisting of the word *not* followed by any value of the variable *p.* Usual symbol: ⌈ ⌉ (**corners**).

quasi-stellar object NOUN a member of any of several classes of astronomical bodies, including **quasars** (strong radio sources) and **quasi-stellar galaxies** (no traceable radio emission), both of which have exceptionally large red shifts. Abbreviation: **QSO.**

quass (kvɑːs, kwɑːs) NOUN a variant of **kvass.**

quassia (ˈkwɒʃə) NOUN 1 any tree of the tropical American simaroubaceous genus *Quassia,* having bitter bark and wood. 2 the bark and wood of *Quassia amara* and of a related tree, *Picrasma excelsa,* used in furniture making. 3 a bitter compound extracted from this bark and wood, formerly used as a tonic and anthelmintic, now used in insecticides.
▷HISTORY C18: from New Latin, named after Graman *Quassi,* a slave who discovered (1730) the medicinal value of the root

quatercentenary (ˌkwætəsɛnˈtiːnərɪ) NOUN, *plural* **-naries.** a 400th anniversary or the year or celebration marking it.
▷HISTORY C19: from Latin *quater* four times + CENTENARY
▸ **ˌquatercenˈtennial** ADJECTIVE, NOUN

quaternary (kwəˈtɜːnərɪ) ADJECTIVE 1 consisting of fours or by fours. 2 fourth in a series. 3 *Chem* containing or being an atom bound to four other atoms or groups: *a quaternary ammonium compound.* 4 *Maths* having four variables. ◆ NOUN, *plural* **-naries.** 5 the number four or a set of four.
▷HISTORY C15: from Latin *quaternārius* each containing four, from *quaternī* by fours, distributive of *quattuor* four

Quaternary (kwəˈtɜːnərɪ) ADJECTIVE 1 of, denoting, or formed in the most recent period of geological time, which succeeded the Tertiary period nearly two million years ago. ◆ NOUN 2 **the.** the Quaternary period or rock system, divided into Pleistocene and Holocene (Recent) epochs or series.

quaternary ammonium compound NOUN a type of ionic compound that can be regarded as derived from ammonium compounds by replacing the hydrogen atoms with organic groups.

quaternion (kwəˈtɜːnɪən) NOUN 1 *Maths* a

generalized complex number consisting of four components, $x = x_0 + x_1i + x_2j + x_3k$, where x, $x_0 \ldots x_3$ are real numbers and $i^2 = j^2 = k^2 = -1$, $ij = -ji = k$, etc. 2 another word for **quaternary** (sense 5).
▷**HISTORY** C14: from Late Latin *quaterniōn,* from Latin *quaternī* four at a time

quaternity (kwə'tɜːnɪtɪ) NOUN, *plural* **-ties.** a group of four, esp a concept of God as consisting of four persons.
▷**HISTORY** C16: from Late Latin *quaternitās,* from Latin *quaternī* by fours; see QUATERNARY

Quathlamba (kwɑːt'lɑːmbɑː) NOUN the Sotho name for the **Drakensberg.**

quatrain ('kwɒtreɪn) NOUN a stanza or poem of four lines, esp one having alternate rhymes.
▷**HISTORY** C16: from French, from *quatre* four, from Latin *quattuor*

quatre ('kætrə; *French* katrə) NOUN a playing card with four pips.
▷**HISTORY** French: four

Quatre Bras (*French* katrə bra) NOUN a village in Belgium near Brussels; site of a battle in June 1815 where Wellington defeated the French under Marshal Ney, immediately preceding the battle of Waterloo.

quatrefoil ('kætrəˌfɔɪl) NOUN 1 a leaf composed of four leaflets. 2 *Architect* a carved ornament having four foils arranged about a common centre, esp one used in tracery.
▷**HISTORY** C15: from Old French, from *quatre* four + *-foil* leaflet; compare TREFOIL

quattrocento (ˌkwætrəʊ'tʃɛntəʊ; *Italian* kwattro'tʃɛnto) NOUN the 15th century, esp in reference to Renaissance Italian art and literature.
▷**HISTORY** Italian, shortened from *milquattrocento* 1400

quaver ('kweɪvə) VERB 1 to say or sing (something) with a trembling voice. 2 (*intr*) (esp of the voice) to quiver, tremble, or shake. 3 (*intr*) *Rare* to sing or play quavers or ornamental trills. ◆ NOUN 4 *Music* a note having the time value of an eighth of a semibreve. Usual US and Canadian name: **eighth note.** 5 a tremulous sound or note.
▷**HISTORY** C15 (in the sense: to vibrate, QUIVER[1]): from *quaven* to tremble, of Germanic origin; compare Low German *quabbeln* to tremble
▸ **'quaverer** NOUN ▸ **'quavering** ADJECTIVE ▸ **'quaveringly** ADVERB ▸ **'quavery** ADJECTIVE

quay (kiː) NOUN a wharf, typically one built parallel to the shoreline. Compare **pier** (sense 1).
▷**HISTORY** C14 *keye,* from Old French *kai,* of Celtic origin; compare Cornish *kē* hedge, fence, Old Breton *cai* fence

quayage ('kiːɪdʒ) NOUN 1 a system of quays. 2 a charge for the use of a quay.

quayside ('kiːˌsaɪd) NOUN the edge of a quay along the water.

quazzy ('kwæzɪ) ADJECTIVE **quazzier, quazziest.** *Southwest English dialect* unwell.

Que. ABBREVIATION FOR Quebec.

quean (kwiːn) NOUN 1 *Archaic* **a** a boisterous, impudent, or disreputable woman. **b** a prostitute; whore. 2 *Scot* a young unmarried woman or girl.
▷**HISTORY** Old English *cwene;* related to Old Saxon, Old High German *quena,* Gothic *qino,* Old Norse *kona,* Greek *gunē* woman. Compare QUEEN

queasy ('kwiːzɪ) ADJECTIVE **-sier, -siest.** 1 having the feeling that one is about to vomit; nauseous. 2 feeling or causing uneasiness: *a queasy conscience.*
▷**HISTORY** C15: of uncertain origin
▸ **'queasily** ADVERB ▸ **'queasiness** NOUN

Quebec (kwɪ'bɛk, kə-, kɛ-) NOUN 1 a province of E Canada: the largest Canadian province; a French colony from 1608 to 1763, when it passed to Britain; lying mostly on the Canadian Shield, it has vast areas of forest and extensive tundra and is populated mostly in the plain around the St Lawrence River. Capital: Quebec. Pop.: 7 410 500 (2001 est.). Area: 1 540 680 sq. km (594 860 sq. miles). Abbreviation: **PQ.** 2 a port in E Canada, capital of the province of Quebec, situated on the St Lawrence River: founded in 1608 by Champlain; scene of the battle of the Plains of Abraham (1759), by which the British won Canada from the French. Pop.: 167 264 (1996). 3 *Communications* a code word for the letter *q.*

Quebecker *or* **Quebecer** (kwɪ'bɛkə, kə-, kɛ-) NOUN a native or inhabitant of the province of Quebec.

Québecois (*French* kebɛkwa) NOUN, *plural* **-cois** (-kwa). a native or inhabitant of the province of Quebec, esp a French-speaking one.

quebracho (keɪ'brɑːtʃəʊ; *Spanish* ke'βratʃo) NOUN, *plural* **-chos** (-tʃəʊz; *Spanish* -tʃos). 1 either of two anacardiaceous South American trees, *Schinopsis lorentzii* or *S. balansae,* having a tannin-rich hard wood used in tanning and dyeing. 2 an apocynaceous South American tree, *Aspidosperma quebrachoblanco,* whose bark yields alkaloids used in medicine and tanning. 3 the wood or bark of any of these trees. 4 any of various other South American trees having hard wood.
▷**HISTORY** C19: from American Spanish, from *quiebracha,* from *quebrar* to break (from Latin *crepāre* to rattle) + *hacha* axe (from French *hache*)

Quechua, Kechua ('kɛtʃwə), *or* **Quichua** NOUN 1 (*plural* **-uas** *or* **-ua**) a member of any of a group of South American Indian peoples of the Andes, including the Incas. 2 the language or family of languages spoken by these peoples, possibly distantly related to the Tupi-Guarani family.
▸ **'Quechuan** *or* **'Kechuan** *or* **'Quichuan** ADJECTIVE, NOUN

queen (kwiːn) NOUN 1 a female sovereign who is the official ruler or head of state. 2 the wife or widow of a king. 3 a woman or a thing personified as a woman considered the best or most important of her kind: *a beauty queen; the queen of ocean liners.* 4 *Slang* an effeminate male homosexual. 5 **a** the only fertile female in a colony of social insects, such as bees, ants, and termites, from the eggs of which the entire colony develops. **b** (*as modifier*): *a queen bee.* 6 an adult female cat. 7 one of four playing cards in a pack, one for each suit, bearing the picture of a queen. 8 a chess piece, theoretically the most powerful piece, able to move in a straight line in any direction or diagonally, over any number of squares. ◆ VERB 9 *Chess* to promote (a pawn) to a queen when it reaches the eighth rank. 10 (*tr*) to crown as queen. 11 (*intr*) *Informal* (of a gay man) to flaunt one's homosexuality. 12 (*intr*) to reign as queen. 13 **queen it.** (often foll by *over*) *Informal* to behave in an overbearing manner.
▷**HISTORY** Old English *cwēn;* related to Old Saxon *quān* wife, Old Norse *kvæn,* Gothic *qēns* wife

Queen-Anne NOUN 1 a style of furniture popular in England about 1700–20 and in America about 1720–70, characterized by the use of unencumbered curves, walnut veneer, and the cabriole leg. ◆ ADJECTIVE 2 in or of this style. 3 denoting or relating to a style of architecture popular in England during the early 18th century, characterized by red-brick construction with classical ornamentation.

Queen Anne's Bounty NOUN *Church of England* 1 a fund formed by Queen Anne in 1704 for the augmentation of the livings of the poorer Anglican clergy. In 1948 the administrators of the fund were replaced by the Church Commissioners for England. 2 the office or board administering this fund.

Queen Anne's lace NOUN another name for **cow parsley.**

Queen Anne's War NOUN those conflicts (1702–13) of the War of the Spanish Succession that were fought in North America.

queen bee NOUN 1 the fertile female bee in a hive. 2 *Informal* a woman in a position of dominance or ascendancy over her peers or associates.

Queenborough in Sheppey ('kwiːnbərə, 'ʃɛpɪ) NOUN a town in SE England, in Kent: formed in 1968 by the amalgamation of Queenborough, Sheerness, and Sheppey. Pop.: 30 790 (1991).

queencake ('kwiːnˌkeɪk) NOUN a small light cake containing currants.

Queen Charlotte Islands PLURAL NOUN a group of about 150 islands off the W coast of Canada: part of British Columbia. Pop.: 5316 (1991). Area: 9596 sq. km (3705 sq. miles).

queen consort NOUN the wife of a reigning king.

queendom ('kwiːndəm) NOUN a territory, state, people, or community ruled over by a queen.

queen dowager NOUN the widow of a king.

Queen Elizabeth Islands PLURAL NOUN a group of islands off the N coast of Canada: the northernmost islands of the Canadian Arctic archipelago, lying N of latitude 74°N; part of Nunavut. Area: about 390 000 sq. km (150 000 sq. miles).

queenly ('kwiːnlɪ) ADJECTIVE **-lier, -liest.** 1 resembling or appropriate to a queen. 2 having the rank of queen. ◆ ADVERB 3 in a manner appropriate to a queen.
▸ **'queenliness** NOUN

Queen Mab (mæb) NOUN (in British folklore) a bewitching fairy who rules over men's dreams.

Queen Maud Land (mɔːd) NOUN the large section of Antarctica between Coats Land and Enderby Land: claimed by Norway in 1939.

Queen Maud Range NOUN a mountain range in Antarctica, in S Ross Dependency, extending for about 800 km (500 miles).

queen mother NOUN the widow of a former king who is also the mother of the reigning sovereign.

queen of puddings NOUN a pudding made of moist but firm breadcrumb and custard mixture topped with jam and meringue.

queen olive NOUN a variety of olive having large fleshy fruit suitable for pickling, esp one from around Seville in Spain.

queen post NOUN one of a pair of vertical posts that connect the tie beam of a truss to the principal rafters. Compare **king post.**

queen regent NOUN a queen who acts as regent.

queen regnant NOUN a queen who reigns on her own behalf.

Queens (kwiːnz) NOUN a borough of E New York City, on Long Island. Pop.: 1 951 598 (1990).

Queen's Award NOUN either of two awards instituted by royal warrant (1976) for a sustained increase in export earnings by a British firm (**Queen's Award for Export Achievement**) or for an advance in technology (**Queen's Award for Technological Achievement**).

Queen's Bench Division NOUN (in England when the sovereign is female) one of the divisions of the High Court of Justice. Also called (when the sovereign is male): **King's Bench.**

Queensberry rules ('kwiːnzbərɪ, -brɪ) PLURAL NOUN 1 the code of rules followed in modern boxing, requiring the use of padded gloves, rounds of three minutes, and restrictions on the types of blows allowed. 2 *Informal* gentlemanly or polite conduct, esp in a dispute.
▷**HISTORY** C19: named after the ninth Marquess of *Queensberry,* who originated the rules in 1869

Queen's Counsel NOUN (in England when the sovereign is female) a barrister or advocate appointed Counsel to the Crown on the recommendation of the Lord Chancellor, entitled to sit within the bar of the court and to wear a silk gown. Also called (when the sovereign is male): **King's Counsel.**

Queen's County NOUN the former name of **Laois.**

queen's English NOUN (when the British sovereign is female) standard Southern British English.

queen's evidence NOUN *English law* (when the sovereign is female) evidence given for the Crown against his or her former associates in crime by an accomplice (esp in the phrase **turn queen's evidence**). Also called (when the sovereign is male): **king's evidence.** US equivalent: **state's evidence.**

Queen's Guide NOUN (in Britain and the Commonwealth when the sovereign is female) a Guide who has passed the highest tests of proficiency.

queen's highway NOUN (in Britain when the sovereign is female) any public road or right of way.

Queen's House NOUN **the.** a Palladian mansion in Greenwich, London: designed (1616–35) by Inigo Jones; now part of the National Maritime Museum; restored 1984–90.

queen-size *or* **queen-sized** ADJECTIVE (of a bed, etc.) larger or longer than normal size but smaller or shorter than king-size.

Queensland ('kwiːnzˌlænd, -lənd) NOUN a state of NE Australia: fringed on the Pacific side by the Great Barrier Reef; the Great Dividing Range lies in the east, separating the coastal lowlands from the dry Great Artesian Basin in the south. Capital: Brisbane. Pop.: 3 512 360 (1999 est.). Area: 1 727 500 sq. km (667 000 sq. miles).

Queensland arrowroot NOUN another name for **tous-les-mois** (sense 2).

Queensland blue NOUN *Austral* a pumpkin with a bluish skin.

Queensland cane toad NOUN *Austral* a toad, *Bufo marinus,* introduced into Queensland from Hawaii to control insect pests, becoming a pest itself.

Queenslander (ˈkwiːnzˌlændə, -ləndə) NOUN a native or inhabitant of Queensland.

Queensland lungfish NOUN a lungfish, *Neoceratodus forsteri,* reaching a length of six feet: occurs in Queensland rivers but introduced elsewhere.

Queensland nut NOUN another name for **macadamia.**

Queen's proctor NOUN (in England when the sovereign is female) an official empowered to intervene in divorce and certain other cases when it is alleged that material facts are being suppressed.

Queen's Regulations PLURAL NOUN (in Britain and certain other Commonwealth countries when the sovereign is female) the code of conduct for members of the armed forces. Abbreviation: **QR.**

Queen's Scout NOUN (in Britain and the Commonwealth when the sovereign is female) a Scout who has passed the highest tests of endurance, proficiency, and skill. US equivalent: **Eagle Scout.**

queen's shilling *or when the sovereign was male* **king's shilling** NOUN [1] (until 1879) a shilling paid to new recruits to the British army. [2] **take the queen's shilling.** *Brit archaic* to enlist in the army.

Queen's speech NOUN (in Britain and the Commonwealth when the sovereign is female) another name for the **speech from the throne.**

Queenstown (ˈkwiːnzˌtaʊn) NOUN the former name (1849–1922) of **Cóbh.**

Queen Street Farmer NOUN *NZ* a businessman who runs a farm, often for a tax loss.
▷HISTORY from *Queen Street,* the main business street in Auckland

queen substance NOUN a pheromone secreted by queen honeybees and consumed by the workers, in whom it causes suppression of egg-laying.

Queensware (ˈkwiːnzˌwɛə) *or* **Queen's ware** NOUN a type of light white earthenware with a brilliant glaze developed from creamware by Josiah Wedgwood and named in honour of his patroness, Queen Charlotte.

queer (kwɪə) ADJECTIVE [1] differing from the normal or usual in a way regarded as odd or strange. [2] suspicious, dubious, or shady. [3] faint, giddy, or queasy. [4] *Informal, derogatory* homosexual. [5] *Informal* odd or unbalanced mentally; eccentric or slightly mad. [6] *Slang* worthless or counterfeit. ◆ NOUN [7] *Informal, derogatory* a homosexual, usually a male. ◆ VERB *(tr)* *Informal* [8] to spoil or thwart (esp in the phrase **queer someone's pitch**). [9] to put in a difficult or dangerous position.
▷HISTORY C16: perhaps from German *quer* oblique, ultimately from Old High German *twërh*
▸ˈ**queerish** ADJECTIVE ▸ˈ**queerly** ADVERB ▸ˈ**queerness** NOUN

> **Language note** Although the term *queer* meaning homosexual is still considered derogatory when used by non-homosexuals, it is now being used by homosexuals of themselves as a positive term, as in *queer politics, queer cinema.*

queer-bashing NOUN *Brit slang* the activity of making vicious and unprovoked verbal or physical assaults upon homosexuals or supposed homosexuals.
▸ˈ**queer-ˌbasher** NOUN

queer fish NOUN *Brit informal* an eccentric or odd person.

queer street NOUN *(sometimes capitals)* *Informal* a difficult situation, such as debt or bankruptcy (in the phrase **in queer street**).

quell (kwɛl) VERB *(tr)* [1] to suppress or beat down (rebellion, disorder, etc.); subdue. [2] to overcome or allay: *to quell pain; to quell grief.*
▷HISTORY Old English *cwellan* to kill; related to Old Saxon *quellian,* Old High German *quellen,* Old Norse *kvelja* to torment
▸ˈ**queller** NOUN

Quelpart (ˈkwɛlˌpɑːt) NOUN another name for **Cheju.**

quelquechose (ˈkɛlkəˈʃəʊz) NOUN an insignificant thing; mere trifle.
▷HISTORY French, literally: something

Quemoy (kɛˈmɔɪ) NOUN an island in Formosa Strait, off the SE coast of China: administratively part of Taiwan. Pop. (with associated islets): 53 237 (1996 est.). Area: 130 sq. km (50 sq. miles).

quench (kwɛntʃ) VERB *(tr)* [1] to satisfy (one's thirst, desires, etc.); slake. [2] to put out (a fire, flame, etc.); extinguish. [3] to put down or quell; suppress: *to quench a rebellion.* [4] to cool (hot metal) by plunging it into cold water. [5] *Physics* to reduce the degree of (luminescence or phosphorescence) in (excited molecules or a material) by adding a suitable substance. [6] *Electronics* **a** to suppress (sparking) when the current is cut off in an inductive circuit. **b** to suppress (an oscillation or discharge) in a component or device.
▷HISTORY Old English *ācwencan* to extinguish; related to Old Frisian *quinka* to vanish
▸ˈ**quenchable** ADJECTIVE ▸ˈ**quencher** NOUN ▸ˈ**quenchless** ADJECTIVE

quenelle (kəˈnɛl) NOUN a finely sieved mixture of cooked meat or fish, shaped into various forms and cooked in stock or fried as croquettes.
▷HISTORY C19: from French, from German *Knödel* dumpling, from Old High German *knodo* knot

quercetin *or* **quercitin** (ˈkwɜːsɪtɪn) NOUN a yellow crystalline pigment found naturally in the rind and bark of many plants. It is used in medicine to treat fragile capillaries. Formula: $C_{15}H_{10}O_7$; melting pt: 316–7°C. Also called: **flavin.**
▷HISTORY C19: from Latin *quercētum* an oak forest (from *quercus* an oak) + -IN
▸**quercetic** (kwɜːˈsɛtɪk, -ˈsiː-) ADJECTIVE

Querétaro (*Spanish* keˈretaro) NOUN [1] an inland state of central Mexico: economy based on agriculture and mining. Capital: Querétaro. Pop.: 1 402 010 (2000). Area: 11 769 sq. km (4544 sq. miles). [2] a city in central Mexico, capital of Querétaro state: scene of the signing (1848) of the treaty ending the US-Mexican War and of the execution of Emperor Maximilian (1867). Pop.: 535 468 (2000 est.).

querist (ˈkwɪərɪst) NOUN a person who makes inquiries or queries; questioner.

quern (kwɜːn) NOUN a stone hand mill for grinding corn.
▷HISTORY Old English *cweorn;* related to Old Frisian *quern,* Old High German *kurn,* Old Norse *kverna,* Gothic *quairnus* millstone

quernstone (ˈkwɜːnˌstəʊn) NOUN [1] another name for **millstone** (sense 1). [2] one of the two small circular stones used in a quern.

querulous (ˈkwɛrʊləs, ˈkwɛrjʊ-) ADJECTIVE [1] inclined to make whining or peevish complaints. [2] characterized by or proceeding from a complaining fretful attitude or disposition: *a querulous tone.*
▷HISTORY C15: from Latin *querulus* from *querī* to complain
▸ˈ**querulously** ADVERB ▸ˈ**querulousness** NOUN

query (ˈkwɪərɪ) NOUN, *plural* **-ries.** [1] a question, esp one expressing doubt, uncertainty, or an objection. [2] a less common name for **question mark.** ◆ VERB **-ries, -rying, -ried.** *(tr)* [3] to express uncertainty, doubt, or an objection concerning (something). [4] to express as a query: *"What's up now?" she queried.* [5] *US* to put a question to (a person); ask.
▷HISTORY C17: from earlier *quere,* from Latin *quaere* ask!, from *quaerere* to seek, inquire

query language NOUN *Computing* the instructions and procedures used to retrieve information from a database.

quest (kwɛst) NOUN [1] the act or an instance of looking for or seeking; search: *a quest for diamonds.* [2] (in medieval romance) an expedition by a knight or company of knights to accomplish some prescribed task, such as finding the Holy Grail. [3] the object of a search; goal or target: *my quest is the treasure of the king.* [4] *Rare* a collection of alms. ◆ VERB *(mainly intr)* [5] (foll by *for* or *after*) to go in search (of). [6] to go on a quest. [7] (of gun dogs or hounds) **a** to search for game. **b** to bay when in pursuit of game. [8] *Rare* to collect alms. [9] *(also tr)* *Archaic* to go in search of (a thing); seek or pursue.
▷HISTORY C14: from Old French *queste,* from Latin *quaesita* sought, from *quaerere* to seek
▸ˈ**quester** NOUN ▸ˈ**questing** ADJECTIVE ▸ˈ**questingly** ADVERB

question (ˈkwɛstʃən) NOUN [1] a form of words addressed to a person in order to elicit information or evoke a response; interrogative sentence. [2] a point at issue: *it's only a question of time until she dies; the question is how long they can keep up the pressure.* [3] a difficulty or uncertainty; doubtful point: *a question of money; there's no question about it.* [4] **a** an act of asking. **b** an investigation into some problem or difficulty. [5] a motion presented for debate by a deliberative body. [6] **put the question.** to require members of a deliberative assembly to vote on a motion presented. [7] *Law* a matter submitted to a court or other tribunal for judicial or quasi-judicial decision. [8] **question of fact.** (in English law) that part of the issue before a court that is decided by the jury. [9] **question of law.** (in English law) that part of the issue before a court that is decided by the judge. [10] **beg the question. a** to avoid giving a direct answer by posing another question. **b** to assume the truth of that which is intended to be proved. See **petitio principii.** [11] **beyond (all) question.** beyond (any) dispute or doubt. [12] **call in** *or* **into question. a** to make (something) the subject of disagreement. **b** to cast doubt upon the validity, truth, etc., of (something). [13] **in question.** under discussion: *this is the man in question.* [14] **out of the question.** beyond consideration; unthinkable or impossible: *the marriage is out of the question.* [15] **pop the question.** *Informal* to propose marriage. ◆ VERB *(mainly tr)* [16] to put a question or questions to (a person); interrogate. [17] to make (something) the subject of dispute or disagreement. [18] to express uncertainty about the validity, truth, etc., of (something); doubt.
▷HISTORY C13: via Old French from Latin *quaestiō,* from *quaerere* to seek
▸ˈ**questioner** NOUN

> **Language note** *The question whether* should be used rather than *the question of whether* or *the question as to whether: this leaves open the question whether he acted correctly.*

questionable (ˈkwɛstʃənəbᵊl) ADJECTIVE [1] (esp of a person's morality or honesty) admitting of some doubt; dubious. [2] of disputable value or authority: *a questionable text.*
▸ˈ**questionableness** *or* ˌ**questionaˈbility** NOUN
▸ˈ**questionably** ADVERB

questioning (ˈkwɛstʃənɪŋ) ADJECTIVE [1] proceeding from or characterized by a feeling of doubt or uncertainty. [2] enthusiastic or eager for philosophical or other investigations; intellectually stimulated: *an alert and questioning mind.*
▸ˈ**questioningly** ADVERB

questionless (ˈkwɛstʃənlɪs) ADJECTIVE [1] blindly adhering, as to a principle or course of action; unquestioning. [2] a less common word for **unquestionable.**
▸ˈ**questionlessly** ADVERB

question mark NOUN [1] the punctuation mark **?**, used at the end of questions and in other contexts where doubt or ignorance is implied. [2] this mark used for any other purpose, as to draw attention to a possible mistake, as in a chess commentary. [3] an element of doubt or uncertainty.

question master NOUN *Brit* the chairman of a quiz or panel game.

questionnaire (ˌkwɛstʃəˈnɛə, ˌkɛs-) NOUN a set of questions on a form, submitted to a number of people in order to collect statistical information.
▷HISTORY C20: from French, from *questionner* to ask questions

question time NOUN (in parliamentary bodies of the British type) a period of time set aside each day for members to question government ministers.

questor (ˈkwɛstə) NOUN *US* a variant of **quaestor.**
▸**questorial** (kwɛˈstɔːrɪəl) ADJECTIVE ▸ˈ**questorˌship** NOUN

Quetta ('kwɛtə) NOUN a city in W central Pakistan, at an altitude of 1650 m (5500 ft.): a summer resort, military station, and trading centre. Pop.: 560 387 (1998).

quetzal ('kɛtsəl) *or* **quezal** (kɛ'sɑ:l) NOUN, *plural* **-zals** *or* **-zales** (-'sɑ:lɛs). [1] Also called: **resplendent trogon.** a crested bird, *Pharomachrus mocinno,* of Central and N South America, which has a brilliant green, red, and white plumage and, in the male, long tail feathers: family *Trogonidae,* order *Trogoniformes* (trogons). [2] the standard monetary unit of Guatemala, divided into 100 centavos.
▷HISTORY via American Spanish from Nahuatl *quetzalli* brightly coloured tail feather

Quetzalcoatl (ˌkɛtsəlkəʊ'ætəl) NOUN a god of the Aztecs and Toltecs, represented as a feathered serpent.

queue (kju:) *Chiefly Brit* ◆ NOUN [1] a line of people, vehicles, etc., waiting for something: *a queue at the theatre.* [2] *Computing* a list in which entries are deleted from one end and inserted at the other. [3] a pigtail. [4] **jump the queue.** See **queue-jump.** ◆ VERB **queues, queuing** *or* **queueing, queued.** [5] (*intr;* often foll by *up*) to form or remain in a line while waiting. [6] *Computing* to arrange (a number of programs) in a predetermined order for accessing by a computer. ◆ US and Canadian word: **line.**
▷HISTORY C16 (in the sense: tail); C18 (in the sense: pigtail): via French from Latin *cauda*tail

queue-jump VERB (*intr*) [1] to take a place in a queue ahead of those already queuing; push in. [2] to obtain prior consideration or some other advantage out of turn or unfairly. Also: **jump the queue.**
▸**queue-jumper** NOUN

queuing theory NOUN a mathematical approach to the rate at which components queue to be processed by a machine, instructions are accessed by a computer, orders need to be serviced, etc., to achieve the optimum flow.

Quezon City ('keɪzɒn) NOUN a city in the Philippines, on central Luzon adjoining Manila: capital of the Philippines from 1948 to 1976; seat of the University of the Philippines (1908). Pop.: 2 173 831 (2000).

quibble ('kwɪbəl) VERB (*intr*) [1] to make trivial objections; prevaricate. [2] *Archaic* to play on words; pun. ◆ NOUN [3] a trivial objection or equivocation, esp one used to avoid an issue. [4] *Archaic* a pun.
▷HISTORY C17: probably from obsolete *quib,* perhaps from Latin *quibus* (from *quī* who, which), as used in legal documents, with reference to their obscure phraseology
▸'**quibbler** NOUN ▸'**quibbling** ADJECTIVE, NOUN
▸'**quibblingly** ADVERB

Quiberon (*French* kibrɔ̃) NOUN a peninsula of NW France, on the S coast of Brittany: a naval battle was fought off its coast in 1759 during the Seven Years' War, in which the British defeated the French.

quiche (ki:ʃ) NOUN an open savoury tart with a rich custard filling to which bacon, onion, cheese, etc., are added: *quiche Lorraine.*
▷HISTORY French, from German *Kuchen* cake

Quichua ('kɪtʃwə) NOUN, *plural* **-uas** *or* **-ua.** a variant of **Quechua.**

quick (kwɪk) ADJECTIVE [1] (of an action, movement, etc.) performed or occurring during a comparatively short time: *a quick move.* [2] lasting a comparatively short time; brief: *a quick flight.* [3] accomplishing something in a time that is shorter than normal: *a quick worker.* [4] characterized by rapidity of movement; swift or fast: *a quick walker.* [5] immediate or prompt: *a quick reply.* [6] (*postpositive*) eager or ready to perform (an action): *quick to criticize.* [7] responsive to stimulation; perceptive or alert; lively: *a quick eye.* [8] eager or enthusiastic for learning: *a quick intelligence.* [9] easily excited or aroused: *a quick temper.* [10] skilfully swift or nimble in one's movements or actions; deft: *quick fingers.* [11] *Archaic* **a** alive; living. **b** (*as noun*) living people (esp in the phrase **the quick and the dead**). [12] *Archaic or dialect* lively or eager: *a quick dog.* [13] (of a fire) burning briskly. [14] composed of living plants: *a quick hedge.* [15] *Dialect* (of sand) lacking firmness through being wet. [16] **quick with child.** *Archaic* pregnant, esp being in an advanced state of pregnancy, when the movements of the fetus can be felt. ◆ NOUN [17] any area of living flesh that is highly sensitive to pain or touch, esp that under a toenail or fingernail or around a healing wound. [18] the vital or most important part (of a thing). [19] short for **quickset** (sense 1). [20] **cut (someone) to the quick.** to hurt (someone's) feelings deeply; offend gravely. ◆ ADVERB *Informal* [21] in a rapid or speedy manner; swiftly. [22] soon: *I hope he comes quick.* ◆ INTERJECTION [23] a command requiring the hearer to perform an action immediately or in as short a time as possible.
▷HISTORY Old English *cwicu* living; related to Old Saxon *quik,* Old High German *queck,* Old Norse *kvikr* alive, Latin *vīvus* alive, Greek *bios* life
▸'**quickly** ADVERB ▸'**quickness** NOUN

quick assets PLURAL NOUN *Accounting* assets readily convertible into cash; liquid current assets.

quick-change artist NOUN an actor or entertainer who undertakes several rapid changes of costume during his performance.

quicken ('kwɪkən) VERB [1] to make or become faster; accelerate: *he quickened his walk; her heartbeat quickened with excitement.* [2] to impart to or receive vigour, enthusiasm, etc.; stimulate or be stimulated: *science quickens man's imagination.* [3] to make or become alive; revive. [4] **a** (of an unborn fetus) to begin to show signs of life. **b** (of a pregnant woman) to reach the stage of pregnancy at which movements of the fetus can be felt.

quick fire NOUN [1] rapid continuous gunfire, esp at a moving target. ◆ ADJECTIVE **quick-fire.** [2] Also: **quick-firing.** capable of or designed for quick fire. [3] *Informal* rapid or following one another in rapid succession: *quick-fire questions.*

quick-freeze VERB **-freezes, -freezing, -froze, -frozen.** (*tr*) to preserve (food) by subjecting it to rapid refrigeration at temperatures of 0°C or lower.

quick grass NOUN another name for **couch grass.**
▷HISTORY C17: Scot and northern English variant of *couch grass,* from the earlier *quick* living; compare QUITCH GRASS

quickie ('kwɪkɪ) NOUN *Informal* [1] Also called (esp Brit): **quick one.** a speedily consumed alcoholic drink. [2] **a** anything made, done, produced, or consumed rapidly or in haste. **b** (*as modifier*): *a quickie divorce.*

quicklime ('kwɪkˌlaɪm) NOUN another name for **calcium oxide.**
▷HISTORY C15: from QUICK (in the archaic sense: living) + LIME[1]

quick march NOUN [1] a march at quick time or the order to proceed at such a pace. ◆ INTERJECTION [2] a command to commence such a march.

quick response NOUN *Marketing* the rapid replenishment of a customer's stock by a supplier with direct access to data from the customer's point of sale.

quicksand ('kwɪkˌsænd) NOUN a deep mass of loose wet sand that submerges anything on top of it.

quickset ('kwɪkˌsɛt) *Chiefly Brit* ◆ NOUN [1] **a** a plant or cutting, esp of hawthorn, set so as to form a hedge. **b** such plants or cuttings collectively. [2] a hedge composed of such plants. ◆ ADJECTIVE [3] composed of such plants.
▷HISTORY C15: from *quick* in the archaic sense live, growing + *set* to plant, set in the ground

quicksilver ('kwɪkˌsɪlvə) NOUN [1] another name for **mercury** (sense 1). ◆ ADJECTIVE [2] rapid or unpredictable in movement or change: *a quicksilver temper.*
▷HISTORY Old English, from *cwicu* alive (see QUICK) + *seolfor* silver

quickstep ('kwɪkˌstɛp) NOUN [1] a modern ballroom dance in rapid quadruple time. [2] a piece of music composed for or in the rhythm of this dance. ◆ VERB **-steps, -stepping, -stepped.** [3] (*intr*) to perform this dance.

quick-tempered ADJECTIVE readily roused to anger; irascible.

quickthorn ('kwɪkˌθɔ:n) NOUN hawthorn, esp when planted as a hedge.
▷HISTORY C17: probably from *quick* in the sense "fast-growing": compare QUICKSET

quick time NOUN *Military* the normal marching rate of 120 paces to the minute. Compare **double time** (senses 3, 4).

quick trick NOUN *Bridge* a high card almost certain to win a trick, usually an ace or a king: the unit in one of the systems of hand valuation.

quick-witted ADJECTIVE having a keenly alert mind, esp as used to avert danger, make effective reply, etc.
▸ˌ**quick-'wittedly** ADVERB ▸ˌ**quick-'wittedness** NOUN

quid[1] (kwɪd) NOUN a piece of tobacco, suitable for chewing.
▷HISTORY Old English *cwidu* chewing resin; related to Old High German *quiti* glue, Old Norse *kvātha* resin; see CUD

quid[2] (kwɪd) NOUN, *plural* **quid.** [1] *Brit* a slang word for **pound** (sterling). [2] (**be**) **quids in.** *Brit slang* to be in a very favourable or advantageous position. [3] **not the full quid.** *Austral and NZ slang* mentally subnormal.
▷HISTORY C17: of obscure origin

quidditch ('kwɪdɪtʃ) an imaginary game in which players fly on broomsticks.
▷HISTORY C20: coined by the British novelist J.K. Rowling (born 1965) in the novel *Harry Potter and the Philosopher's Stone*

quiddity ('kwɪdɪtɪ) NOUN, *plural* **-ties.** [1] *Philosophy* the essential nature of something. Compare **haecceity.** [2] a petty or trifling distinction; quibble.
▷HISTORY C16: from Medieval Latin *quidditās,* from Latin *quid* what

quidnunc ('kwɪdˌnʌŋk) NOUN a person eager to learn news and scandal; gossipmonger.
▷HISTORY C18: from Latin, literally: what now

quid pro quo ('kwɪd prəʊ 'kwəʊ) NOUN, *plural* **quid pro quos.** [1] a reciprocal exchange. [2] something given in compensation, esp an advantage or object given in exchange for another.
▷HISTORY C16: from Latin: something for something

quiescent (kwɪ'ɛsənt) ADJECTIVE quiet, inactive, or dormant.
▷HISTORY C17: from Latin *quiescere* to rest
▸**qui'escence** *or* **qui'escency** NOUN ▸**qui'escently** ADVERB

quiescent tank NOUN a tank, usually for sewage sludge, in which the sludge is allowed to remain for a time so that sedimentation can occur.

quiet ('kwaɪət) ADJECTIVE [1] characterized by an absence or near absence of noise: *a quiet street.* [2] characterized by an absence of turbulent motion or disturbance; peaceful, calm, or tranquil: *a quiet glade; the sea is quiet tonight.* [3] free from activities, distractions, worries, etc.; untroubled: *a quiet life; a quiet day at work.* [4] marked by an absence of work, orders, etc.; not busy: *the factory is very quiet at the moment.* [5] private; not public; secret: *a quiet word with someone.* [6] free from anger, impatience, or other extreme emotion: *a quiet disposition.* [7] free from pretentiousness or vain display; modest or reserved: *quiet humour.* [8] *Astronomy* (of the sun) exhibiting a very low number of sunspots, solar flares, and other surface phenomena; inactive. Compare **active** (sense 8). ◆ NOUN [9] the state of being silent, peaceful, or untroubled. [10] **on the quiet.** without other people knowing; secretly. ◆ VERB [11] a less common word for **quieten.**
▷HISTORY C14: from Latin *quiētus,* past participle of *quiēscere* to rest, from *quiēs* repose, rest
▸'**quietness** NOUN

quieten ('kwaɪətən) VERB *Chiefly Brit* [1] (often foll by *down*) to make or become calm, silent, etc.; pacify or become peaceful. [2] (*tr*) to allay (fear, doubts, etc.).

quietism ('kwaɪəˌtɪzəm) NOUN [1] a form of religious mysticism originating in Spain in the late 17th century, requiring withdrawal of the spirit from all human effort and complete passivity to God's will. [2] a state of passivity and calmness of mind towards external events.
▸'**quietist** NOUN, ADJECTIVE

quietly ('kwaɪətlɪ) ADVERB [1] in a quiet manner. [2] **just quietly.** *Austral* between you and me; confidentially.

quietude ('kwaɪəˌtju:d) NOUN the state or condition of being quiet, peaceful, calm, or tranquil.

quietus (kwaɪ'i:təs, -'eɪtəs) NOUN, *plural* **-tuses.** [1] anything that serves to quash, eliminate, or kill: *to give the quietus to a rumour.* [2] a release from life; death. [3] the discharge or settlement of debts, duties, etc.

▷HISTORY C16: from Latin *quiētus est,* literally: he is at rest, QUIET

quiff (kwɪf) NOUN *Brit* a prominent tuft of hair, esp one brushed up above the forehead.
▷HISTORY C19: of unknown origin

quill (kwɪl) NOUN [1] **a** any of the large stiff feathers of the wing or tail of a bird. **b** the long hollow central part of a bird's feather; calamus. [2] a bird's feather made into a pen for writing. [3] any of the stiff hollow spines of a porcupine or hedgehog. [4] a device, formerly usually made from a crow quill, for plucking a harpsichord string. [5] *Angling* a length of feather barb stripped of barbules and used for the body of some artificial flies. [6] a small roll of bark, esp one of dried cinnamon. [7] (in weaving) a bobbin or spindle. [8] a fluted fold, as in a ruff. [9] a hollow shaft that rotates upon an inner spindle or concentrically about an internal shaft. ◆ VERB (*tr*) [10] to wind (thread, yarn, etc.) onto a spool or bobbin. [11] to make or press fluted folds in (a ruff).
▷HISTORY C15 (in the sense: hollow reed or pipe): of uncertain origin; compare Middle Low German *quiele* quill

quillai (kɪˈlaɪ) NOUN another name for **soapbark** (sense 1).
▷HISTORY C19: via American Spanish from Araucanian

quillet (ˈkwɪlɪt) NOUN *Archaic* a quibble or subtlety.
▷HISTORY C16: from earlier *quillity,* perhaps an alteration of QUIDDITY

quilling (ˈkwɪlɪŋ) NOUN decorative craftwork in which a material such as glass, fabric, or paper is formed into small bands or rolls that form the basis of a design.

quillon (*French* kijɔ̃) NOUN (*often plural*) either half of the extended crosspiece of a sword or dagger.
▷HISTORY C19: from French, diminutive of *quille* bowling pin, ultimately from Old High German *kegil* club, stake

quill pen NOUN another name for **quill** (sense 2).

quillwort (ˈkwɪl,wɜːt) NOUN any aquatic tracheophyte plant of the genus *Isoetes,* with quill-like leaves at the bases of which are spore-producing structures: family *Isoetaceae,* phylum *Lycopodophyta* (club mosses, etc.).

Quilmes (*Spanish* ˈkilmes) NOUN a city in E Argentina: a resort and suburb of Buenos Aires. Pop.: 550 069 (1999 est.).

quilt (kwɪlt) NOUN [1] a thick warm cover for a bed, consisting of a soft filling sewn between two layers of material, usually with crisscross seams. [2] a bedspread or counterpane. [3] anything quilted or resembling a quilt. ◆ VERB (*tr*) [4] to stitch together (two pieces of fabric) with (a thick padding or lining) between them: *to quilt cotton and wool.* [5] to create (a garment, covering, etc.) in this way. [6] to pad with material. [7] *Austral informal* to strike; clout.
▷HISTORY C13: from Old French *coilte* mattress, from Latin *culcita* stuffed item of bedding
▸ˈ**quilter** NOUN

quilting (ˈkwɪltɪŋ) NOUN [1] material used for making a quilt. [2] the act or process of making a quilt. [3] quilted work.

quim (kwɪm) NOUN *Brit taboo* the female genitals.
▷HISTORY C19: of uncertain origin

Quimper (*French* kɛ̃pɛr) NOUN a city in NW France: capital of Finistère department. Pop.: 62 540 (1990).

quin (kwɪn) NOUN *Brit* short for **quintuplet** (sense 2). US and Canadian word: **quint.**

quinacrine (ˈkwɪnə,kriːn) NOUN [1] another name for **mepacrine.** [2] **quinacrine mustard.** a nitrogen mustard derived from mepacrine and used as a stain for chromosomes.
▷HISTORY C20: from QUIN(INE) + ACR(ID) + -INE[2]

quinary (ˈkwaɪnərɪ) ADJECTIVE [1] consisting of fives or by fives. [2] fifth in a series. [3] (of a number system) having a base of five. ◆ NOUN, *plural* **-ries.** [4] a set of five.
▷HISTORY C17: from Latin *quīnārius* containing five, from *quīnī* five each

quinate (ˈkwaɪneɪt) ADJECTIVE *Botany* arranged in or composed of five parts: *quinate leaflets.*
▷HISTORY C19: from Latin *quīnī* five each

quince (kwɪns) NOUN [1] a small widely cultivated Asian rosaceous tree, *Cydonia oblonga,* with pinkish-white flowers and edible pear-shaped fruits. [2] the acid-tasting fruit of this tree, much used in preserves. [3] **Japanese** *or* **flowering quince.** another name for **japonica.**
▷HISTORY C14 *qwince* plural of *quyn* quince, from Old French *coin,* from Latin *cotōneum,* from Greek *kudōnion* quince, Cydonian (apple)

quincentenary (,kwɪnsɛnˈtiːnərɪ) NOUN, *plural* **-naries.** a 500th anniversary or the year or celebration marking it.
▷HISTORY C19: irregularly from Latin *quinque* five + CENTENARY
▸**quincentennial** (,kwɪnsɛnˈtɛnɪəl) ADJECTIVE, NOUN

quincuncial (kwɪnˈkʌnʃəl) ADJECTIVE [1] consisting of or having the appearance of a quincunx. [2] (of the petals or sepals of a five-membered corolla or calyx in the bud) arranged so that two members overlap another two completely and the fifth overlaps on one margin and is itself overlapped on the other.
▸**quinˈcuncially** ADVERB

quincunx (ˈkwɪnkʌŋks) NOUN [1] a group of five objects arranged in the shape of a rectangle with one at each of the four corners and the fifth in the centre. [2] *Botany* a quincuncial arrangement of sepals or petals in the bud. [3] *Astrology* an aspect of 150° between two planets.
▷HISTORY C17: from Latin: five twelfths, from *quinque* five + *uncia* twelfth; in ancient Rome, this was a coin worth five twelfths of an AS[2] and marked with five spots

quindecagon (kwɪnˈdɛkəgən) NOUN a geometric figure having 15 sides and 15 angles.
▷HISTORY C16: from Latin *quindecim* fifteen + *-agon,* as in *decagon*

quindecaplet (kwɪnˈdɛkə,plɛt) NOUN [1] a group of 15. [2] one of a group of 15.
▷HISTORY C20: irregularly formed on the models of *quadruplet, quintuplet,* etc.

quindecennial (,kwɪndɪˈsɛnɪəl) ADJECTIVE ◆ [1] NOUN occurring once every 15 years or over a period of 15 years. [2] a 15th anniversary.
▷HISTORY C20: from Latin *quindecim* fifteen + *annus* year, on the model of *biennial*

quine (kwəɪn) NOUN *Scot* a variant of **quean** (sense 2).

quinella (kwɪˈnɛlə) NOUN *Austral and NZ* a form of betting on a horse race in which the punter bets on selecting the first and second place-winners in any order.
▷HISTORY from American Spanish *quiniela* a game of chance

Qui Nhong (ˈkwiː ˈnjɒŋ) NOUN a port in SE Vietnam, on the South China Sea. Pop.: 163 385 (1992 est.).

quinic acid (ˈkwɪnɪk) NOUN a white crystalline soluble optically active carboxylic acid, found in cinchona bark, bilberries, coffee beans, and the leaves of certain other plants; 1,3,4,5-tetrahydroxycyclohexanecarboxylic acid. Formula: $C_6H_7(OH)_4COOH$.

quinidine (ˈkwɪnɪ,diːn) NOUN a crystalline alkaloid drug that is an optically active diastereoisomer of quinine: used to treat heart arrhythmias. Formula: $C_{20}H_{24}N_2O_2$.

quinine (kwɪˈniːn; *US* ˈkwaɪnaɪn) NOUN a bitter crystalline alkaloid extracted from cinchona bark, the salts of which are used as a tonic, antipyretic, analgesic, etc., and in malaria therapy. Formula: $C_{20}H_{24}N_2O_2$.
▷HISTORY C19: from Spanish *quina* cinchona bark, from Quechua *kina* bark

quinnat salmon (ˈkwɪnæt) NOUN another name for **Chinook salmon.**
▷HISTORY C19: from Salish *tʼkwinnat*

quino- *or before a vowel* **quin-** COMBINING FORM indicating cinchona, cinchona bark, or quinic acid: *quinidine; quinol; quinoline.*
▷HISTORY see QUININE

quinol (ˈkwɪnɒl) NOUN another name for **hydroquinone.**

quinoline (ˈkwɪnə,liːn, -lɪn) NOUN [1] an oily colourless insoluble basic heterocyclic compound synthesized by heating aniline, nitrobenzene, glycerol, and sulphuric acid: used as a food preservative and in the manufacture of dyes and antiseptics. Formula: C_9H_7N. [2] any substituted derivative of quinoline.

quinolone (ˈkwɪnə,ləʊn) NOUN any of a group of synthetic antibiotics, including ciprofloxacin, that inactivate an enzyme required for the replication of certain microorganisms.

quinone (kwɪˈnəʊn, ˈkwɪnəʊn) NOUN another name for **benzoquinone.**

quinonoid (ˈkwɪnə,nɔɪd, kwɪˈnəʊnɔɪd) *or* **quinoid** ADJECTIVE of, resembling, or derived from quinone.

quinquagenarian (,kwɪŋkwədʒɪˈnɛərɪən) NOUN [1] a person between 50 and 59 years old. ◆ ADJECTIVE [2] being between 50 and 59 years old. [3] of or relating to a quinquagenarian.
▷HISTORY C16: from Latin *quinquāgēnārius* containing fifty, from *quinquāgēnī* fifty each

Quinquagesima (,kwɪŋkwəˈdʒɛsɪmə) NOUN the Sunday preceding Ash Wednesday, the beginning of Lent. Also called: **Quinquagesima Sunday.**
▷HISTORY C14: via Medieval Latin from Latin *quinquāgēsima diēs* fiftieth day

quinque- COMBINING FORM five: *quinquevalent.*
▷HISTORY from Latin *quinque*

quinquecentenary (,kwɪŋkwɪsɛnˈtiːnərɪ) NOUN, *plural* **-naries.** another name for **quincentenary.**

quinquefoliate (,kwɪŋkwɪˈfəʊlɪɪt, -,eɪt) ADJECTIVE (of leaves) having or consisting of five leaflets.

quinquennial (kwɪnˈkwɛnɪəl) ADJECTIVE [1] occurring once every five years or over a period of five years. ◆ NOUN [2] another word for **quinquennium.** [3] a fifth anniversary.
▸**quinˈquennially** ADVERB

quinquennium (kwɪnˈkwɛnɪəm) NOUN, *plural* **-nia** (-nɪə). a period or cycle of five years.
▷HISTORY C17: from Latin *quinque* five + *annus* year

quinquepartite (,kwɪŋkwɪˈpɑːtaɪt) ADJECTIVE [1] divided into or composed of five parts. [2] maintained by or involving five participants or groups of participants.

quinquereme (,kwɪŋkwɪˈriːm) NOUN an ancient Roman galley with five banks of oars on each side.
▷HISTORY C16: from Latin *quinquerēmis,* from QUINQUE- + *rēmus* oar

quinquevalent (,kwɪŋkwɪˈveɪlənt, kwɪnˈkwɛvələnt) ADJECTIVE *Chem* another word for **pentavalent.**
▸,**quinqueˈvalency** *or* **quinquevalence** (,kwɪŋkwɪˈveɪləns, kwɪnˈkwɛvələns) NOUN

quinsy (ˈkwɪnzɪ) NOUN inflammation of the tonsils and surrounding tissues with the formation of abscesses.
▷HISTORY C14: via Old French and Medieval Latin from Greek *kunankhē,* from *kuōn* dog + *ankhein* to strangle

quint[1] NOUN [1] (kwɪnt) an organ stop sounding a note a fifth higher than that normally produced by the key depressed. [2] (kɪnt) *Piquet* a sequence of five cards in the same suit.
▷HISTORY C17: from French *quinte,* from Latin *quintus* fifth

quint[2] (kwɪnt) NOUN the US and Canadian word for **quin.**

quinta (ˈkɪntə) NOUN *Winemaking* a Portuguese vineyard where grapes for wine or port are grown.
▷HISTORY C20: from Portuguese, literally: a country estate, farm

quintain (ˈkwɪntɪn) NOUN (esp in medieval Europe) [1] a post or target set up for tilting exercises for mounted knights or foot soldiers. [2] the exercise of tilting at such a target.
▷HISTORY C14: from Old French *quintaine,* from Latin: street in a Roman camp between the fifth and sixth maniples, from *quintus* fifth

quintal (ˈkwɪntᵊl) NOUN [1] a unit of weight equal to 100 pounds. [2] a unit of weight equal to 100 kilograms.
▷HISTORY C15: via Old French from Arabic *qintār,* possibly from Latin *centēnārius* consisting of a hundred

quintan (ˈkwɪntən) ADJECTIVE (of a fever) occurring every fourth day.
▷HISTORY C17: from Latin *febris quintāna* fever occurring every fifth day, reckoned inclusively

Quintana Roo (*Spanish* kinˈtana ˈrɔo) NOUN a state of SE Mexico, on the E Yucatán Peninsula: hot, humid, forested, and inhabited chiefly by Maya Indians. Capital: Chetumal. Pop.: 873 804 (2000). Area: 50 350 sq. km (19 463 sq. miles).

quinte *French* (kɛ̃t) NOUN the fifth of eight basic positions from which a parry or attack can be made in fencing.
▷HISTORY C18: French, from Latin *quinta,* fem of *quintus* fifth, from *quinque* five

quintessence (kwɪn'tɛsəns) NOUN [1] the most typical representation of a quality, state, etc. [2] an extract of a substance containing its principle in its most concentrated form. [3] (in ancient and medieval philosophy) ether, the fifth and highest essence or element after earth, water, air, and fire, which was thought to be the constituent matter of the heavenly bodies and latent in all things.
▷HISTORY C15: via French from Medieval Latin *quinta essentia* the fifth essence, translation of Greek *pemptē ousia*

quintessential (ˌkwɪntɪ'sɛnʃəl) ADJECTIVE most typically representative of a quality, state, etc.; perfect.
▸ **ˌquintes'sentially** ADVERB

quintet *or* **quintette** (kwɪn'tɛt) NOUN [1] a group of five singers or instrumentalists or a piece of music composed for such a group. [2] any group of five.
▷HISTORY C19: from Italian *quintetto,* from *quinto* fifth

quintic ('kwɪntɪk) ADJECTIVE *Maths* of or relating to the fifth degree: *a quintic equation.*

quintile ('kwɪntaɪl) NOUN *Astrology* [1] an aspect of 72° between two heavenly bodies. [2] a fifth part of a distribution.
▷HISTORY C17: from Latin *quintus* fifth

quintillion (kwɪn'tɪljən) NOUN, *plural* **-lions** *or* **-lion.** [1] (in Britain, France, and Germany) the number represented as one followed by 30 zeros (10^{30}). US and Canadian word: **nonillion.** [2] (in the US and Canada) the number represented as one followed by 18 zeros (10^{18}). Brit word: **trillion.**
▷HISTORY C17: from Latin *quintus* fifth + *-illion,* as in MILLION
▸ **quin'tillionth** ADJECTIVE

quintuple ('kwɪntjʊpᵊl, kwɪn'tju:pᵊl) VERB [1] to multiply by five. ◆ ADJECTIVE [2] five times as much or as many; fivefold. [3] consisting of five parts. ◆ NOUN [4] a quantity or number five times as great as another.
▷HISTORY C16: from French, from Latin *quintus,* on the model of QUADRUPLE

quintuplet ('kwɪntjʊplɪt, kwɪn'tju:plɪt) NOUN [1] a group or set of five similar things. [2] one of five offspring born at one birth. Often shortened to: **quin.** [3] *Music* a group of five notes to be played in a time value of three, four, or some other value.

quintuplicate ADJECTIVE (kwɪn'tju:plɪkɪt) [1] fivefold or quintuple. ◆ VERB (kwɪn'tju:plɪˌkeɪt) [2] to multiply or be multiplied by five. ◆ NOUN (kwɪn'tju:plɪkɪt) [3] a group or set of five things.
▸ **quinˌtupli'cation** NOUN

quinze (*French* kɛ̃z) NOUN a card game with rules similar to those of vingt-et-un, except that the score aimed at is 15 rather than 21.
▷HISTORY French: fifteen

quip (kwɪp) NOUN [1] a sarcastic or cutting remark; gibe. [2] a witty or clever saying: *a merry quip.* [3] *Archaic* another word for **quibble.** ◆ VERB **quips, quipping, quipped.** [4] (*intr*) to make a quip.
▷HISTORY C16: from earlier *quippy,* probably from Latin *quippe* indeed, to be sure

quipster ('kwɪpstə) NOUN a person inclined to make sarcastic or witty remarks.

quipu *or* **quippu** ('ki:pu:, 'kwɪpu:) NOUN a device of the Incas of Peru used to record information, consisting of an arrangement of variously coloured and knotted cords attached to a base cord.
▷HISTORY C17: from Spanish *quipo,* from Quechua *quipu,* literally: knot

quire¹ (kwaɪə) NOUN [1] a set of 24 or 25 sheets of paper; a twentieth of a ream. [2] **a** four sheets of paper folded once to form a section of 16 pages. **b** a section or gathering. [3] a set of all the sheets in a book.
▷HISTORY C15 *quayer,* from Old French *quaier,* from Latin *quaternī* four at a time, from *quater* four times

quire² (kwaɪə) NOUN an obsolete spelling of **choir.**

Quirinal ('kwɪrɪnᵊl) NOUN one of the seven hills on which ancient Rome was built.

Quirinus (kwɪ'raɪnəs) NOUN *Roman myth* a god of war, who came to be identified with the deified Romulus.

Quirites (kwɪ'raɪti:z) PLURAL NOUN the citizens of ancient Rome.
▷HISTORY from Latin: inhabitants of *Cures,* later applied generally to Roman citizens

quirk (kwɜ:k) NOUN [1] an individual peculiarity of character; mannerism or foible. [2] an unexpected twist or turn: *a quirk of fate.* [3] a continuous groove in an architectural moulding. [4] a flourish, as in handwriting.
▷HISTORY C16: of unknown origin
▸ **'quirky** ADJECTIVE ▸ **'quirkily** ADVERB ▸ **'quirkiness** NOUN

quirt (kwɜ:t) *US and South African* ◆ NOUN [1] a whip with a leather thong at one end. ◆ VERB (*tr*) [2] to strike with a quirt.
▷HISTORY C19: from Spanish *cuerda* CORD

quis custodiet ipsos custodes? *Latin* (kwɪs kʊs'təʊdɪˌɛt 'ɪpsɒs kʊs'təʊdi:z) who will guard the guards?

quisling ('kwɪzlɪŋ) NOUN a traitor who aids an occupying enemy force; collaborator.
▷HISTORY C20: after Major Vidkun *Quisling* (1887–1945), Norwegian collaborator with the Nazis

quist (kwɪst) NOUN, *plural* **quists** *or* **quist.** *West Midland and southwestern English dialect* a wood pigeon.
▷HISTORY of obscure origin

quit (kwɪt) VERB **quits, quitting, quitted** *or chiefly US* **quit.** [1] (*tr*) to depart from; leave: *he quitted the place hastily.* [2] to resign; give up (a job): *he quitted his job today.* [3] (*intr*) (of a tenant) to give up occupancy of premises and leave them: *they received notice to quit.* [4] to desist or cease from (something or doing something); break off: *quit laughing.* [5] (*tr*) to pay off (a debt); discharge or settle. [6] (*tr*) *Archaic* to conduct or acquit (oneself); comport (oneself): *he quits himself with great dignity.* ◆ ADJECTIVE [7] (*usually predicative; foll by of*) free (from); released (from): *he was quit of all responsibility for their safety.*
▷HISTORY C13: from Old French *quitter,* from Latin *quiētus* QUIET; see QUIETUS

quitch grass (kwɪtʃ) NOUN another name for **couch grass.** Sometimes shortened to: **quitch.**
▷HISTORY Old English *cwice;* perhaps related to *cwicu* living, QUICK (with the implication that the grass cannot be killed); compare Dutch *kweek,* Norwegian *kvike,* German *Queckengras*

quitclaim ('kwɪtˌkleɪm) *Law* ◆ NOUN [1] a formal renunciation of any claim against a person or of a right to land. ◆ VERB [2] (*tr*) **a** to renounce (a claim) formally. **b** to declare (a person) free from liability.
▷HISTORY C14: from Anglo-French *quiteclame,* from *quite* QUIT + *clamer* to declare (from Latin *clāmāre* to shout)

quite (kwaɪt) ADVERB [1] to the greatest extent; completely or absolutely: *you're quite right; quite the opposite.* [2] (*not used with a negative*) to a noticeable or partial extent; somewhat: *she's quite pretty.* [3] in actuality; truly: *he thought the bag was heavy, but it was quite light; it's quite the thing to do.* [4] **quite a** *or* **an.** (*not used with a negative*) of an exceptional, considerable, or noticeable kind: *quite a girl; quite a long walk.* [5] **quite something.** a remarkable or noteworthy thing or person. ◆ SENTENCE SUBSTITUTE [6] Also: **quite so.** an expression used to indicate agreement or assent.
▷HISTORY C14: adverbial use of *quite* (adjective) QUIT

Language note See at **very.**

Quito ('ki:təʊ; *Spanish* 'kito) NOUN the capital of Ecuador, in the north at an altitude of 2850 m (9350 ft.), just south of the equator: the oldest capital in South America, existing many centuries before the Incan conquest in 1487; a cultural centre since the beginning of Spanish rule (1534); two universities. Pop.: 1 487 513 (1997 est.).

quitrent ('kwɪtˌrɛnt) NOUN (formerly) a rent payable by a freeholder or copyholder to his lord that released him from liability to perform services.

quits (kwɪts) *Informal* ◆ ADJECTIVE (*postpositive*) [1] on an equal footing; even: *now we are quits.* [2] **call it quits.** to agree to end a dispute, contest, etc., agreeing that honours are even. ◆ INTERJECTION [3] an exclamation indicating willingness to give up.

quittance ('kwɪtᵊns) NOUN [1] release from debt or other obligation. [2] a receipt or other document certifying this.
▷HISTORY C13: from Old French, from *quitter* to release from obligation; see QUIT

quitter ('kwɪtə) NOUN a person who gives up easily; defeatist, deserter, or shirker.

quittor ('kwɪtə) NOUN *Vet science* infection of the cartilages on the side of a horse's foot, characterized by inflammation and the formation of pus.
▷HISTORY C13: perhaps from Old French *cuiture* a boiling, from Latin *coctūra* a cooking, from *coquere* to cook

quiver¹ ('kwɪvə) VERB [1] (*intr*) to shake with a rapid tremulous movement; tremble. ◆ NOUN [2] the state, process, or noise of shaking or trembling.
▷HISTORY C15: from obsolete *cwiver* quick, nimble; compare QUAVER
▸ **'quiverer** NOUN ▸ **'quivering** ADJECTIVE ▸ **'quiveringly** ADVERB ▸ **'quivery** ADJECTIVE

quiver² ('kwɪvə) NOUN a case for arrows.
▷HISTORY C13: from Old French *cuivre;* related to Old English *cocer,* Old Saxon *kokari,* Old High German *kohhari,* Medieval Latin *cucurum*

quiverful ('kwɪvəfʊl) NOUN [1] the amount that a quiver can hold. [2] *Literary* a fair number or full complement: *a quiverful of children.*

qui vive (ˌki: 'vi:v) NOUN **on the qui vive.** on the alert; attentive.
▷HISTORY C18: from French, literally: long live who?, sentry's challenge (equivalent to "To whose party do you belong?" or "Whose side do you support?")

Quixote ('kwɪksət; *Spanish* ki'xote) NOUN See **Don Quixote.**

quixotic (kwɪk'sɒtɪk) ADJECTIVE preoccupied with an unrealistically optimistic or chivalrous approach to life; impractically idealistic.
▷HISTORY C18: after DON QUIXOTE
▸ **quix'otically** ADVERB ▸ **quixotism** ('kwɪksəˌtɪzəm) NOUN

quiz (kwɪz) NOUN, *plural* **quizzes.** [1] **a** an entertainment in which the general or specific knowledge of the players is tested by a series of questions, esp as a radio or television programme. **b** (*as modifier*): *a quiz programme.* [2] any set of quick questions designed to test knowledge. [3] an investigation by close questioning; interrogation. [4] *Obsolete* a practical joke; hoax. [5] *Obsolete* a puzzling or eccentric individual. [6] *Obsolete* a person who habitually looks quizzically at others, esp through a small monocle. ◆ VERB **quizzes, quizzing, quizzed.** (*tr*) [7] to investigate by close questioning; interrogate. [8] *US and Canadian informal* to test or examine the knowledge of (a student or class). [9] (*tr*) *Obsolete* to look quizzically at, esp through a small monocle.
▷HISTORY C18: of unknown origin
▸ **'quizzer** NOUN

quizmaster ('kwɪzˌmɑ:stə) NOUN a person who puts questions to contestants on a quiz programme.

quizzical ('kwɪzɪkᵊl) ADJECTIVE questioning and mocking or supercilious: *a quizzical look.*
▸ **ˌquizzi'cality** NOUN ▸ **'quizzically** ADVERB

Qum (kʊm) NOUN a variant of **Qom.**

Qumran ('kʊmrɑ:n) NOUN See **Khirbet Qumran.**

Qungur ('kʊŋgʊə) NOUN a variant transliteration of the Chinese name for **Kongur Shan.**

quod (kwɒd) NOUN *Chiefly Brit* a slang word for **jail.**
▷HISTORY C18: of uncertain origin; perhaps changed from *quad,* short for *quadrangle*

quod erat demonstrandum *Latin* ('kwɒd 'ɛræt ˌdɛmən'strændʊm) (at the conclusion of a proof, esp of a theorem in Euclidean geometry) which was to be proved. Abbreviation: **QED.**

quodlibet ('kwɒdlɪˌbɛt) NOUN [1] a light piece of music based on two or more popular tunes. [2] a subtle argument, esp one prepared as an exercise on a theological topic.
▷HISTORY C14: from Latin, from *quod* what + *libet* pleases, that is, whatever you like
▸ **ˌquodli'betical** ADJECTIVE ▸ **ˌquodli'betically** ADVERB

quoin, coign, *or* **coigne** (kwɔɪn, kɔɪn) NOUN [1] an external corner of a wall. [2] Also called: **cornerstone.** a stone forming the external corner of a wall. [3] another name for **keystone** (sense 1). [4] *Printing* a metal or wooden wedge or an expanding mechanical device used to lock type up in a chase. [5] a wedge used for any of various other purposes,

such as (formerly) to adjust elevation in muzzle-loading cannon.
▷HISTORY C16: variant of COIN (corner)

quoin post NOUN the vertical post at the side of a lock gate, about which the gate swings.

quoit (kɔɪt) NOUN 1 a ring of iron, plastic, rope, etc., used in the game of quoits. 2 *Austral slang* a variant spelling of **coit**.
▷HISTORY C15: of unknown origin

quoits (kɔɪts) PLURAL NOUN (*usually functioning as singular*) a game in which quoits are tossed at a stake in the ground in attempts to encircle it.

quokka (ˈkwɒkə) NOUN a small wallaby, *Setonix brachyurus*, of Western Australia, occurring mostly on offshore islands.
▷HISTORY from a native Australian language

quoll (ˈkwɒl) NOUN *Austral* another name for **native cat**.
▷HISTORY C18: from a native Australian language

quondam (ˈkwɒndæm) ADJECTIVE (*prenominal*) of an earlier time; former: *her quondam lover*.
▷HISTORY C16: from Latin adv: formerly

Quonset hut (ˈkwɒnsɪt) NOUN *Trademark, US* a military shelter made of corrugated steel sheet, having a semicircular cross section. Brit equivalent: **Nissen hut**.

quorate (ˈkwɔːˌreɪt) ADJECTIVE *Brit* constituting or having a quorum.

Quorn (kwɔːn) NOUN *Trademark* a vegetable protein developed from a type of fungus and used in cooking as a meat substitute.

quorum (ˈkwɔːrəm) NOUN a minimum number of members in an assembly, society, board of directors, etc., required to be present before any valid business can be transacted: *the quorum is forty*.
▷HISTORY C15: from Latin, literally: of whom, occurring in Latin commissions in the formula *quorum vos…duos* (etc.) *volumus* of whom we wish that you be…two

quot. ABBREVIATION FOR quotation.

quota (ˈkwəʊtə) NOUN 1 the proportional share or part of a whole that is due from, due to, or allocated to a person or group. 2 a prescribed number or quantity, as of items to be manufactured, imported, or exported, immigrants admitted to a country, or students admitted to a college.
▷HISTORY C17: from Latin *quota pars* how big a share?, from *quotus* of what number

quotable (ˈkwəʊtəbᵊl) ADJECTIVE apt or suitable for quotation: *his remarks are not quotable in mixed company*.
► ˌ**quotaˈbility** NOUN

quota-hopping NOUN (in the EU) the practice of obtaining the right to catch a part of a country's national quota for fish in European waters by buying licences from its fishermen.
► ˈ**quota-ˌhopper** NOUN

quota sampling NOUN *Marketing* a method of conducting marketing research in which the sample is selected according to a quota-system based on such factors as age, sex, social class, etc.

quotation (kwəʊˈteɪʃən) NOUN 1 a phrase or passage from a book, poem, play, etc., remembered and spoken, esp to illustrate succinctly or support a point or an argument. 2 the act or habit of quoting from books, plays, poems, etc. 3 *Commerce* a statement of the current market price of a security or commodity. 4 an estimate of costs submitted by a contractor to a prospective client; tender. 5 *Stock Exchange* registration granted to a company or governmental body, enabling the shares and other securities of the company or body to be officially listed and traded. 6 *Printing* a large block of type metal that is less than type-high and is used to fill up spaces in type pages.

quotation mark NOUN either of the punctuation marks used to begin or end a quotation, respectively " and " or ' and ' in English printing and writing. When double marks are used, single marks indicate a quotation within a quotation, and vice versa. Also called: **inverted comma**.

quote (kwəʊt) VERB 1 to recite a quotation (from a book, play, poem, etc.), esp as a means of illustrating or supporting a statement. 2 (*tr*) to put quotation marks round (a word, phrase, etc.). 3 *Stock Exchange* to state (a current market price) of (a security or commodity). ◆ NOUN 4 an informal word for **quotation** (senses 1–4). 5 (*often plural*) an informal word for **quotation mark**: *put it in quotes*. ◆ INTERJECTION 6 an expression used parenthetically to indicate that the words that follow it form a quotation: *the president said, quote, I shall not run for office in November, unquote*.
▷HISTORY C14: from Medieval Latin *quotāre* to assign reference numbers to passages, from Latin *quot* how many

quote-driven ADJECTIVE denoting an electronic market system, esp for stock exchanges, in which prices are determined by quotations made by market makers or dealers. Compare **order-driven**.

quoth (kwəʊθ) VERB *Archaic* (used with all pronouns except *thou* and *you*, and with nouns) another word for **said**[1] (sense 2).
▷HISTORY Old English *cwæth*, third person singular of *cwethan* to say; related to Old Frisian *quetha* to say, Old Saxon, Old High German *quethan;* see BEQUEATH

quotha (ˈkwəʊθə) INTERJECTION *Archaic* an expression of mild sarcasm, used in picking up a word or phrase used by someone else: *Art thou mad? Mad, quotha! I am more sane than thou.*
▷HISTORY C16: from *quoth a* quoth he

quotidian (kwəʊˈtɪdɪən) ADJECTIVE 1 (esp of attacks of malarial fever) recurring daily. 2 everyday; commonplace. ◆ NOUN 3 a malarial fever characterized by attacks that recur daily.
▷HISTORY C14: from Latin *quotīdiānus*, variant of *cottīdiānus* daily

quotient (ˈkwəʊʃənt) NOUN 1 **a** the result of the division of one number or quantity by another. **b** the integral part of the result of division. 2 a ratio of two numbers or quantities to be divided.
▷HISTORY C15: from Latin *quotiens* how often

quo vadis (ˈkwəʊ ˈvɑːdɪs) where are you going?
▷HISTORY Latin: from the Vulgate version of John 16:5

quo warranto (ˈkwəʊ wɒˈræntəʊ) NOUN *Law* a proceeding initiated to determine or (formerly) a writ demanding by what authority a person claims an office, franchise, or privilege.
▷HISTORY from Medieval Latin: by what warrant

Qur'an (kʊˈrɑːn, -ˈræn) NOUN a variant of **Koran**.

qv (denoting a cross reference) ABBREVIATION FOR quod vide.
▷HISTORY New Latin: which (word, item, etc.) see

Qwaqwa (ˈkwɑːkwə) NOUN (formerly, in South Africa) a Bantu homeland in N South Africa; the only Bantu homeland without exclaves: abolished in 1994. Also called: **Basotho-Qwaqwa**. Former name (until 1972): **Basotho-Ba-Borwa**.

qwerty *or* **QWERTY keyboard** (ˈkwɜːtɪ) NOUN the standard English language typewriter keyboard layout with the characters q, w, e, r, t, and y positioned on the top row of alphabetic characters at the left side of the keyboard.

qy ABBREVIATION FOR query.

Rr

r *or* **R** (ɑː) NOUN, *plural* **r's, R's** *or* **Rs.** [1] the 18th letter and 14th consonant of the modern English alphabet. [2] a speech sound represented by this letter, in English usually an alveolar semivowel, as in *red.* [3] See **three Rs.**

R SYMBOL FOR: [1] *Chem* radical. [2] *Currency* **a** rand. **b** rupee. [3] Réaumur temperature (scale). [4] *Physics, electronics* resistance. [5] roentgen *or* röntgen. [6] *Chess* rook. [7] Royal. [8] *Chem* gas constant. [9] (in the US and Australia) **a** restricted exhibition (used to describe a category of film certified as unsuitable for viewing by anyone under the age of 18). **b** (*as modifier*): *an R film.*

r. ABBREVIATION FOR: [1] rare. [2] recto. [3] Also: **r.** rod (unit of length). [4] ruled. [5] *Cricket, baseball* run(s).

R. ABBREVIATION FOR: [1] rabbi. [2] rector. [3] Regina. [Latin: Queen] [4] Republican. [5] response (in Christian liturgy). [6] Rex. [Latin: King] [7] River. [8] Royal.

R. *or* **r.** ABBREVIATION FOR: [1] registered (trademark). [2] right. [3] river. [4] rouble.

Ra[1] THE CHEMICAL SYMBOL FOR radium.

Ra[2] (rɑː) *or* **Re** NOUN the ancient Egyptian sun god, depicted as a man with a hawk's head surmounted by a solar disc and serpent.

RA ABBREVIATION FOR: [1] rear admiral. [2] *Astronomy* **right ascension.** [3] (in Britain) Royal Academician *or* Academy. [4] (in Britain) Royal Artillery. ◆ [5] INTERNATIONAL CAR REGISTRATION FOR Argentina (officially Argentine Republic).

RAAF ABBREVIATION FOR Royal Australian Air Force.

Rabat (rəˈbɑːt) NOUN the capital of Morocco, in the northwest on the Atlantic coast, served by the port of Salé: became a military centre in the 12th century and a Corsair republic in the 17th century. Pop. (with Salé): 1 386 000 (1994 est.).

rabato *or* **rebato** (rəˈbɑːtəʊ) NOUN, *plural* **-tos.** a wired or starched collar, often of intricate lace, that stood up at the back and sides: worn in the 17th century.
▷HISTORY C16: from French *rabat* collar, with the ending *-o* added as if the word were from Italian

Rabaul (rɑːˈbaʊl) NOUN a port in Papua New Guinea, on NE New Britain Island, in the Bismarck Archipelago: capital of the Territory of New Guinea until 1941; almost surrounded by volcanoes. Pop.: 17 022 (1990).

Rabbath Ammon (ˈræbəθ ˈæmən) NOUN *Old Testament* the ancient royal city of the Ammonites, on the site of modern Amman.

rabbet (ˈræbɪt) *or* **rebate** NOUN [1] a recess, groove, or step, usually of rectangular section, cut into a surface or along the edge of a piece of timber to receive a mating piece. [2] a joint made between two pieces of timber using a rabbet. ◆ VERB (*tr*) [3] to cut or form a rabbet in (timber). [4] to join (pieces of timber) using a rabbet.
▷HISTORY C15: from Old French *rabattre* to beat down

rabbi (ˈræbaɪ) NOUN, *plural* **-bis.** [1] (in Orthodox Judaism) a man qualified in accordance with traditional religious law to expound, teach, and rule in accordance with this law. [2] the religious leader of a congregation; the minister of a synagogue. [3] **the Rabbis.** the early Jewish scholars whose teachings are recorded in the Talmud. ◆ See also **Rav.**
▷HISTORY Hebrew, from *rabh* master + *-ī* my

rabbinate (ˈræbɪnɪt) NOUN [1] the position, function, or tenure of office of a rabbi. [2] rabbis collectively.

rabbinic (rəˈbɪnɪk) *or* **rabbinical** ADJECTIVE of or relating to the rabbis, their teachings, writings, views, language, etc.
▸**rabˈbinically** ADVERB

Rabbinic (rəˈbɪnɪk) *or* **Rabbinical Hebrew** NOUN the form of the Hebrew language used by the rabbis of the Middle Ages.

rabbinics (rəˈbɪnɪks) NOUN (*functioning as singular*) the study of rabbinic literature of the post-Talmudic period.

rabbinism (ˈræbɪˌnɪzəm) NOUN the teachings and traditions of the rabbis of the Talmudic period.
▸**ˈrabbinist** NOUN, ADJECTIVE ▸**ˌrabbiˈnistic** ADJECTIVE

rabbit (ˈræbɪt) NOUN, *plural* **-bits** *or* **-bit.** [1] any of various common gregarious burrowing leporid mammals, esp *Oryctolagus cuniculus* of Europe and North Africa and the cottontail of America. They are closely related and similar to hares but are smaller and have shorter ears. [2] the fur of such an animal. [3] *Brit informal* a novice or poor performer at a game or sport. ◆ VERB [4] (*intr*; often foll by *on* or *away*) *Brit informal* to talk inconsequentially; chatter.
▷HISTORY C14: perhaps from Walloon *robett*, diminutive of Flemish *robbe* rabbit, of obscure origin: C20 in sense 4, from rhyming slang *rabbit and pork* talk

rabbiter (ˈræbɪtə) NOUN *Chiefly Austral* a person who traps and sells rabbits.

rabbit fever NOUN *Pathol* another name for **tularaemia.**

rabbitfish (ˈræbɪtˌfɪʃ) NOUN, *plural* **-fish** *or* **-fishes.** [1] a large chimaera, *Chimaera monstrosa*, common in European seas, with separate caudal and anal fins and a long whiplike tail. [2] any of the spiny-finned tropical marine fishes of the family *Siganidae* of Indo-Pacific waters. They have a rabbit-like snout and spines on the pelvic or ventral fins.

rabbiting (ˈræbɪtɪŋ) NOUN the activity of hunting rabbits.

rabbitoh *or* **rabbito** (ˈræbɪtˌəʊ) NOUN *Austral informal* (formerly) an itinerant seller of rabbits for eating.
▷HISTORY C20: from such a seller's cry

rabbit-proof fence NOUN **a** a fence through which rabbits are unable to pass. **b** *Austral informal* a boundary between certain Australian states, marked by such a fence.

rabbit punch NOUN a sharp blow to the back of the neck that can cause loss of consciousness or even death. Austral name: **rabbit killer.**

rabbitry (ˈræbɪtrɪ) NOUN, *plural* **-ries.** [1] a place where tame rabbits are kept and bred. [2] the rabbits kept in such a place.

rabble[1] (ˈræbᵊl) NOUN [1] a disorderly crowd; mob. [2] **the.** *Contemptuous* the common people.
▷HISTORY C14 (in the sense: a pack of animals): of uncertain origin; perhaps related to Middle Dutch *rabbelen* to chatter, rattle

rabble[2] (ˈræbᵊl) NOUN [1] Also called: **rabbler.** an iron tool or mechanical device for stirring, mixing, or skimming a molten charge in a roasting furnace. ◆ VERB [2] (*tr*) to stir, mix, or skim (the molten charge) in a roasting furnace.
▷HISTORY C17: from French *râble*, from Latin *rutābulum* rake for a furnace, from *ruere* to rake, dig up

rabble-rouser NOUN a person who manipulates the passions of the mob; demagogue.
▸**ˈrabble-ˌrousing** ADJECTIVE, NOUN

Rabelaisian (ˌræbəˈleɪzɪən, -ʒən) ADJECTIVE [1] of, relating to, or resembling the work of François Rabelais, the French writer (?1494–1553), esp by broad, often bawdy humour and sharp satire. ◆ NOUN [2] a student or admirer of Rabelais.
▸**ˌRabeˈlaisianism** NOUN

rabi (ˈrʌbɪ) NOUN (in Pakistan, India, etc.) a crop that is harvested at the end of winter. Compare **kharif.**
▷HISTORY Urdu: spring crop, from Arabic *rabī'* spring

Rabia (rəˈbɪə) NOUN either the third or the fourth month of the Muslim year, known as **Rabia I** and **Rabia II** respectively; the Muslim spring.

rabid (ˈræbɪd, ˈreɪ-) ADJECTIVE [1] relating to or having rabies. [2] zealous; fanatical; violent; raging.
▷HISTORY C17: from Latin *rabidus* frenzied, mad, from *rabere* to be mad
▸**rabidity** (rəˈbɪdɪtɪ) *or* **ˈrabidness** NOUN ▸**ˈrabidly** ADVERB

rabies (ˈreɪbiːz) NOUN *Pathol* an acute infectious viral disease of the nervous system transmitted by the saliva of infected animals, esp dogs. It is characterized by excessive salivation, aversion to water, convulsions, and paralysis. Also called: **hydrophobia, lyssa.**
▷HISTORY C17: from Latin: madness, from *rabere* to rave
▸**rabic** (ˈræbɪk) *or* **rabietic** (ˌreɪbɪˈɛtɪk) ADJECTIVE

RAC ABBREVIATION FOR: [1] Royal Automobile Club. [2] Royal Armoured Corps.

raccoon *or* **racoon** (rəˈkuːn) NOUN, *plural* **-coons** *or* **-coon.** [1] any omnivorous mammal of the genus *Procyon*, esp *P. lotor* (**North American raccoon**), inhabiting forests of North and Central America and the Caribbean: family *Procyonidae*, order *Carnivora* (carnivores). Raccoons have a pointed muzzle, long tail, and greyish-black fur with black bands around the tail and across the face. [2] the fur of the North American raccoon.
▷HISTORY C17: from Algonquian *ärähkun*, from *ärähkuněm* he scratches with his hands

raccoon dog NOUN [1] a canine mammal, *Nyctereutes procyonoides*, inhabiting woods and forests near rivers in E Asia. It has long yellowish-brown black-tipped hair and facial markings resembling those of a raccoon. [2] Also called: **coonhound.** an American breed of dog having a short smooth black coat with tan markings, bred to hunt raccoons.

race[1] (reɪs) NOUN [1] a contest of speed, as in running, swimming, driving, riding, etc. [2] any competition or rivalry: *the race for the White House.* [3] rapid or constant onward movement: *the race of time.* [4] a rapid current of water, esp one through a narrow channel that has a tidal range greater at one end than the other. [5] a channel of a stream, esp one for conducting water to or from a water wheel or other device for utilizing its energy: *a mill race.* [6] **a** a channel or groove that contains ball bearings or roller bearings or that restrains a sliding component. **b** the inner or outer cylindrical ring in a ball bearing or roller bearing. [7] *Austral and NZ* a narrow passage or enclosure in a sheep yard through which sheep pass individually, as to a sheep dip. [8] *Austral* a wire tunnel through which footballers pass from the changing room onto a football field. [9] *NZ* a line of containers coupled together, used in mining to transport coal. [10] another name for **slipstream** (sense 1). [11] *Archaic* the span or course of life. [12] **not in the race.** *Austral informal* given or having no chance. ◆ VERB [13] to engage in a contest of speed with (another). [14] to engage (oneself or one's representative) in a race, esp as a profession or pastime: *to race pigeons.* [15] to move or go as fast as possible. [16] to run (an engine, shaft, propeller, etc.) or (of an engine, shaft, propeller, etc.) to run at high speed, esp after reduction of the load or resistance. ◆ See also **race off, races.**
▷HISTORY C13: from Old Norse *rās* running; related to Old English *rǣs* attack

race[2] (reɪs) NOUN [1] a group of people of common ancestry, distinguished from others by physical characteristics, such as hair type, colour of eyes and skin, stature, etc. Principal races are Caucasoid, Mongoloid, and Negroid. [2] **the human race.** human beings collectively. [3] a group of animals or plants having common characteristics that distinguish them from other members of the same species, usually forming a geographically isolated group; subspecies. [4] a group of people sharing the same interests, characteristics, etc.: *the race of authors.*
▷HISTORY C16: from French, from Italian *razza*, of uncertain origin

race[3] (reɪs) NOUN a ginger root.
▷HISTORY C15: from Old French *rais*, from Latin *rādīx* a root

Race (reɪs) NOUN **Cape.** a cape at the SE extremity of Newfoundland, Canada.

racecard ('reɪsˌkɑːd) NOUN a card or booklet at a race meeting with the times of the races, names of the runners, etc., printed on it.

racecourse ('reɪsˌkɔːs) NOUN a long broad track, usually of grass, enclosed between rails, and with starting and finishing points marked upon it, over which horses are raced. Also called (esp US and Canadian): **racetrack.**

racegoer ('reɪsˌɡəʊə) NOUN one who attends a race meeting, esp a habitual frequenter of race meetings.

racehorse ('reɪsˌhɔːs) NOUN a horse specially bred for racing.

raceme (rə'siːm) NOUN an inflorescence in which the flowers are borne along the main stem, with the oldest flowers at the base. It can be simple, as in the foxglove, or compound (see **panicle**).
▷HISTORY C18: from Latin *racēmus* bunch of grapes

race meeting NOUN a prearranged fixture for racing horses (or sometimes greyhounds) over a set course at set times.

racemic (rə'siːmɪk, -'sɛm-) ADJECTIVE *Chem* of, concerned with, or being a mixture of equal amounts of enantiomers and consequently having no optical activity.
▷HISTORY C19: from RACEME (as in *racemic acid*) + -IC
▸**racemism** ('ræsɪˌmɪzəm, rə'siːmɪzəm) NOUN

racemic acid NOUN the optically inactive form of tartaric acid that is sometimes found in grape juice.

racemize *or* **racemise** ('ræsɪˌmaɪz) VERB to change or cause to change into a racemic mixture.
▸**ˌracemiˈzation** *or* **ˌracemiˈsation** NOUN

racemose ('ræsɪˌməʊs, -ˌməʊz) *or* **racemous** ADJECTIVE being or resembling a raceme.
▷HISTORY C17: from Latin *racēmōsus* clustering
▸**ˈraceˌmosely** *or* **ˈracemously** ADVERB

race off VERB (*tr, adverb*) *Austral informal* to entice (a person) away with a view to seduction.

racer ('reɪsə) NOUN [1] a person, animal, or machine that races. [2] a turntable used to traverse a heavy gun. [3] any of several long slender nonvenomous North American snakes of the colubrid genus *Coluber* and related genera, such as *C. lateralis* (**striped racer**).

race relations NOUN [1] (*functioning as plural*) the relations between members of two or more human races, esp within a single community. [2] (*functioning as singular*) the branch of sociology concerned with such relations.

race riot NOUN a riot among members of different races in the same community.

races ('reɪsɪz) PLURAL NOUN **the.** a series of contests of speed between horses (or sometimes greyhounds) over a set course at prearranged times; a race meeting.

racetrack ('reɪsˌtræk) NOUN [1] a circuit or course, esp an oval one, used for motor racing, speedway, etc. [2] the usual US and Canadian word for a **racecourse.**

raceway ('reɪsˌweɪ) NOUN [1] another word for **race**[1] (sense 5). [2] a racetrack, esp one for banger racing. [3] another word (esp US) for **race**[1] (sense 6).

rachilla *or* **rhachilla** (rə'kɪlə) NOUN (in grasses) the short stem of a spikelet that bears the florets.
▷HISTORY C19: from New Latin, diminutive of RACHIS

rachiotomy (ˌreɪkɪ'ɒtəmɪ) NOUN another name for **laminectomy.**

rachis *or* **rhachis** ('reɪkɪs) NOUN, *plural* **rachises, rhachises** *or* **rachides, rhachides** ('rækɪˌdiːz, 'reɪ-). [1] *Botany* the main axis or stem of an inflorescence or compound leaf. [2] *Ornithol* the shaft of a feather, esp the part that carries the barbs. [3] another name for **vertebral column.**
▷HISTORY C17: via New Latin from Greek *rhakhis* ridge
▸**rachial** *or* **rhachial** ('reɪkɪəl) *or* **rachidial** *or* **rhachidial** (rə'kɪdɪəl) ADJECTIVE

rachitis (rə'kaɪtɪs) NOUN *Pathol* another name for **rickets.**
▷HISTORY C18: New Latin, from Greek *rhakitis*; see RACHIS
▸**rachitic** (rə'kɪtɪk) ADJECTIVE

Rachmanism ('rækməˌnɪzəm) NOUN extortion or exploitation by a landlord of tenants of dilapidated or slum property, esp when involving intimidation or use of racial fears to drive out sitting tenants whose rent is fixed at a low rate.
▷HISTORY C20: after Perec *Rachman* (1920–62), British property-owner born in Poland

racial ('reɪʃəl) ADJECTIVE [1] denoting or relating to the division of the human species into races on grounds of physical characteristics. [2] characteristic of any such group. [3] relating to or arising from differences between the races: *racial harmony.* [4] of or relating to a subspecies.
▸**ˈracially** ADVERB

racialize *or* **racialise** ('reɪʃəˌlaɪz) VERB (*tr*) to render racial in tone or content.

racial unconscious NOUN *Psychol* another term for **collective unconscious.**

racing ('reɪsɪŋ) ADJECTIVE [1] denoting or associated with horse races: *the racing fraternity; a racing man.* ◆ NOUN [2] the practice of engaging horses (or sometimes greyhounds) in contests of speed.

racism ('reɪsɪzəm) *or* **racialism** ('reɪʃəˌlɪzəm) NOUN [1] the belief that races have distinctive cultural characteristics determined by hereditary factors and that this endows some races with an intrinsic superiority over others. [2] abusive or aggressive behaviour towards members of another race on the basis of such a belief.
▸**ˈracist** *or* **racialist** NOUN, ADJECTIVE

rack[1] (ræk) NOUN [1] a framework for holding, carrying, or displaying a specific load or object: *a plate rack; a hat rack; a hay rack; a luggage rack.* [2] a toothed bar designed to engage a pinion to form a mechanism that will interconvert rotary and rectilinear motions. [3] a framework fixed to an aircraft for carrying bombs, rockets, etc. [4] (usually preceded by *the*) an instrument of torture that stretched the body of the victim. [5] a cause or state of mental or bodily stress, suffering, etc.; anguish; torment (esp in the phrase **on the rack**). [6] *US and Canadian* (in pool, snooker, etc.) **a** the triangular frame used to arrange the balls for the opening shot. **b** the balls so grouped. Brit equivalent: **frame.** ◆ VERB (*tr*) [7] to torture on the rack. [8] Also: **wrack.** to cause great stress or suffering to: *guilt racked his conscience.* [9] Also: **wrack.** to strain or shake (something) violently, as by great physical force: *the storm racked the town.* [10] to place or arrange in or on a rack: *to rack bottles of wine.* [11] to move (parts of machinery or a mechanism) using a toothed rack. [12] to raise (rents) exorbitantly; rack-rent. [13] **rack one's brains.** to strain in mental effort, esp to remember something or to find the solution to a problem. ◆ See also **rack up.**
▷HISTORY C14 *rekke*, probably from Middle Dutch *rec* framework; related to Old High German *recchen* to stretch, Old Norse *rekja* to spread out
▸**ˈracker** NOUN

Language note See at **wrack**[1].

rack[2] (ræk) NOUN destruction; wreck (obsolete except in the phrase **go to rack and ruin**).
▷HISTORY C16: variant of WRACK[1]

rack[3] (ræk) NOUN another word for **single-foot**, a gait of the horse
▷HISTORY C16: perhaps based on ROCK[2]

rack[4] (ræk) NOUN [1] a group of broken clouds moving in the wind. ◆ VERB [2] (*intr*) (of clouds) to be blown along by the wind.
▷HISTORY Old English *wrǣc* what is driven; related to Gothic *wraks* persecutor, Swedish *vrak* wreckage

rack[5] (ræk) VERB (*tr*) [1] to clear (wine, beer, etc.) as by siphoning it off from the dregs. [2] to fill a container with (beer, wine, etc.).
▷HISTORY C15: from Old Provençal *arraca*, from *raca* dregs of grapes after pressing

rack[6] (ræk) NOUN the neck or rib section of mutton, pork, or veal.
▷HISTORY Old English *hrace*; related to Old High German *rahho*, Danish *harke*, Swedish *harkla* to clear one's throat

rack-and-pinion NOUN [1] a device for converting rotary into linear motion and vice versa, in which a gearwheel (the pinion) engages with a flat toothed bar (the rack). ◆ ADJECTIVE [2] (of a type of steering gear in motor vehicles) having a track rod with a rack along part of its length that engages with a pinion attached to the steering column.

racket[1] ('rækɪt) NOUN [1] a noisy disturbance or loud commotion; clamour; din. [2] gay or excited revelry, dissipation, etc. [3] an illegal enterprise carried on for profit, such as extortion, fraud, prostitution, drug peddling, etc. [4] *Slang* a business or occupation: *what's your racket?* [5] *Music* **a** a medieval woodwind instrument of deep bass pitch. **b** a reed stop on an organ of deep bass pitch. ◆ VERB [6] (*intr*; often foll by *about*) *Now rare* to go about gaily or noisily, in search of pleasure, excitement, etc.
▷HISTORY C16: probably of imitative origin; compare RATTLE[1]

racket[2] *or* **racquet** ('rækɪt) NOUN [1] a bat consisting of an open network of nylon or other strings stretched in an oval frame with a handle, used to strike the ball in tennis, badminton, etc. [2] a snowshoe shaped like a tennis racket. ◆ VERB [3] (*tr*) to strike (a ball, shuttlecock, etc.) with a racket. ◆ See also **rackets.**
▷HISTORY C16: from French *raquette*, from Arabic *rāhat* palm of the hand

racketeer (ˌrækɪ'tɪə) NOUN [1] a person engaged in illegal enterprises for profit. ◆ VERB [2] (*intr*) to operate a racket.
▸**ˌrackeˈteering** NOUN

racket press NOUN a device consisting of a frame closed by a spring mechanism, for keeping taut the strings of a tennis racket, squash racket, etc.

rackets ('rækɪts) NOUN (*functioning as singular*) **a** a game similar to squash played in a large four-walled court by two or four players using rackets and a small hard ball. **b** (*as modifier*): *a rackets court; a rackets championship.*

racket-tail NOUN any of several birds with a racket-shaped tail, such as certain hummingbirds and kingfishers.

rackety ('rækɪtɪ) ADJECTIVE [1] noisy, rowdy, or boisterous. [2] socially lively and, sometimes, mildly dissolute: *a rackety life.*

rack off VERB (*intr, adverb; usually imperative*) *Austral and NZ slang* to go away; depart.

rack railway NOUN a steep mountain railway having a middle rail fitted with a rack that engages a pinion on the locomotive to provide traction. Also called: **cog railway.**

rack-rent NOUN [1] a high rent that annually equals or nearly equals the value of the property upon which it is charged. [2] any extortionate rent. ◆ VERB [3] to charge an extortionate rent for (property, land, etc.).
▷HISTORY C17: from RACK[1] (sense 12) + RENT[1]
▸**ˈrack-ˌrenter** NOUN

rack saw NOUN *Building trades* a wide-toothed saw.

rack up VERB (*tr, adverb*) [1] to accumulate (points). [2] Also: **rack down.** to adjust the vertical alignment of (the picture from a film projector or telecine machine) so that the upper or lower edges of the frame do not show.

racon ('reɪkɒn) NOUN another name for **radar beacon.**
▷HISTORY C20: from *ra*(*dar*) + (*bea*)*con*

raconteur (ˌrækɒn'tɜː) NOUN a person skilled in telling stories.
▷HISTORY C19: French, from *raconter* to tell

racoon (rə'kuːn) NOUN, *plural* **-coons** *or* **-coon.** a variant spelling of **raccoon.**

RACQ (in Australia) ABBREVIATION FOR Royal Automobile Club of Queensland.

racquet ('rækɪt) NOUN a variant spelling of **racket**[2].

racy ('reɪsɪ) ADJECTIVE **racier, raciest.** [1] (of a person's manner, literary style, etc.) having a distinctively lively and spirited quality; fresh. [2] having a characteristic or distinctive flavour: *a racy wine.* [3] suggestive; slightly indecent; risqué: *a racy comedy.*
▸**ˈracily** ADVERB ▸**ˈraciness** NOUN

rad[1] (ræd) NOUN a former unit of absorbed ionizing radiation dose equivalent to an energy absorption per unit mass of 0.01 joule per kilogram of irradiated material. 1 rad is equivalent to 0.01 gray.
▷HISTORY C20: shortened from RADIATION

rad[2] SYMBOL FOR radian.

rad. ABBREVIATION FOR: [1] radical. [2] radius.

RADA ('rɑːdə) NOUN (in Britain) ACRONYM FOR Royal Academy of Dramatic Art.

radar ('reɪdɑː) NOUN [1] a method for detecting the position and velocity of a distant object, such as an aircraft. A narrow beam of extremely high-frequency radio pulses is transmitted and reflected by the object back to the transmitter, the signal being displayed on a radarscope. The direction of the reflected beam and the time between transmission and reception of a pulse determine the position of the object. Former name: **radiolocation.** [2] the equipment used in such detection.
▷HISTORY C20 *ra(dio) d(etecting) a(nd) r(anging)*

radar astronomy NOUN the use of radar to map the surfaces of the planets, their satellites, and other bodies.

radar beacon NOUN a device for transmitting a coded radar signal in response to a signal from an aircraft or ship. The coded signal is then used by the navigator to determine his position. Also called: **racon.**

radarscope ('reɪdɑːˌskəʊp) NOUN a cathode-ray oscilloscope on which radar signals can be viewed. In a **plan position indicator**, the target is represented by a blip on a radial line that rotates around a point, representing the antenna.

radar trap NOUN See **speed trap.**

raddle[1] ('ræd^əl) VERB (*tr*) another word for **interweave.**
▷HISTORY C17: from obsolete noun sense of *raddle* meaning a rod, wattle, or lath, from Old French *redalle* a stick, pole; of obscure origin

raddle[2] ('ræd^əl) VERB [1] (*tr*) *Chiefly Brit* to paint (the face) with rouge. ◆ NOUN, VERB [2] another word for **ruddle.**
▷HISTORY C16: variant of RUDDLE

raddled ('ræd^əld) ADJECTIVE (esp of a person) unkempt or run-down in appearance.
▷HISTORY C17: from RADDLE[2]

radge (rædʒ) *Scot dialect* ◆ ADJECTIVE [1] angry or uncontrollable. ◆ NOUN [2] a person acting in such a way. [3] a rage.
▷HISTORY variant of RAGE; perhaps influenced by Romany *raj*

radial ('reɪdɪəl) ADJECTIVE [1] (of lines, bars, beams of light, etc.) emanating from a common central point; arranged like the radii of a circle. [2] of, like, or relating to a radius or ray. [3] spreading out or developing uniformly on all sides. [4] of or relating to the arms of a starfish or similar radiating structures. [5] *Anatomy* of or relating to the radius or forearm. [6] *Astronomy* (of velocity) in a direction along the line of sight of a celestial object and measured by means of the red shift (or blue shift) of the spectral lines of the object. Compare **tangential** (sense 2). ◆ NOUN [7] a radial part or section. [8] *Zoology* **a** any of the basal fin rays of most bony fishes. **b** a radial or radiating structure, such as any of the ossicles supporting the oral disc of a sea star. [9] short for **radial tyre** or **radial drilling machine.**
▷HISTORY C16: from Medieval Latin *radiālis* from RADIUS
▸ **'radially** ADVERB

radial drilling machine NOUN a machine in which the drilling head is mounted to slide along a radial arm which can be rotated, raised, or lowered on a vertical mast to adjust the position of the drill above the workpiece. Often shortened to: **radial.**

radial engine NOUN an internal-combustion engine having a number of cylinders arranged about a central crankcase.

radial keratotomy (ˌkɛrə'tɒtəmɪ) NOUN an operation designed to improve short-sightedness in which a number of cuts are made around the cornea to change the shape of it.
▷HISTORY C20: from KERATO- + -TOMY

radial paralysis NOUN *Vet science* paralysis of a forelimb as a result of loss of function of the radial nerve, usually following traumatic injury.

radial-ply ADJECTIVE (of a motor tyre) having the fabric cords in the outer casing running radially to enable the sidewalls to be flexible. Compare **cross-ply.**

radial symmetry NOUN a type of structure of an organism or part of an organism in which a vertical cut through the axis in any of two or more planes produces two halves that are mirror images of each other. Compare **bilateral symmetry.**

radial tyre NOUN a motor-vehicle tyre having a radial-ply casing. Often shortened to: **radial.**

radial velocity NOUN the component of the velocity of an object, esp a celestial body, directed along a line from the observer to the object.

radian ('reɪdɪən) NOUN an SI unit of plane angle; the angle between two radii of a circle that cut off on the circumference an arc equal in length to the radius. 1 radian is equivalent to 57.296 degrees and $\pi/2$ radians equals a right angle. Symbol: rad.
▷HISTORY C19: from RADIUS

radiance ('reɪdɪəns) *or* **radiancy** NOUN, *plural* **-ances** *or* **-ancies.** [1] the quality or state of being radiant. [2] a measure of the amount of electromagnetic radiation leaving or arriving at a point on a surface. It is the radiant intensity in a given direction of a small element of surface area divided by the orthogonal projection of this area onto a plane at right angles to the direction. Symbol: L_e.

radiant ('reɪdɪənt) ADJECTIVE [1] sending out rays of light; bright; shining. [2] characterized by health, intense joy, happiness, etc.: *a radiant countenance.* [3] emitted or propagated by or as radiation; radiated: *radiant heat.* [4] sending out heat by radiation: *a radiant heater.* [5] *Physics* (of a physical quantity in photometry) evaluated by absolute energy measurements: *radiant flux; radiant efficiency.* Compare **luminous.** ◆ NOUN [6] a point or object that emits radiation, esp the part of a heater that gives out heat. [7] *Astronomy* the point in space from which a meteor shower appears to emanate.
▷HISTORY C15: from Latin *radiāre* to shine, from *radius* ray of light, RADIUS
▸ **'radiantly** ADVERB

radiant efficiency NOUN the ratio of the power emitted by a source of radiation to the power consumed by it. Symbol: η_e.

radiant energy NOUN energy that is emitted or propagated in the form of particles or electromagnetic radiation. It is measured in joules. Symbol: Q_e.

radiant exitance NOUN the ability of a surface to emit radiation expressed as the radiant flux emitted per unit area at a specified point on the surface. Symbol: M_e.

radiant flux NOUN the rate of flow of energy as radiation. It is measured in watts. Symbol: Φ_e.

radiant heat NOUN heat transferred in the form of electromagnetic radiation rather than by conduction or convection; infrared radiation.

radiant heating NOUN a system of heating a building by radiant heat emitted from panels containing electrical conductors, hot water, etc.

radiant intensity NOUN a measure of the amount of radiation emitted from a point expressed as the radiant flux per unit solid angle leaving this source. Symbol: I_e.

radiata pine (ˌreɪdɪ'ɑːtə) NOUN a pine tree, *Pinus radiata*, native to the western USA. but grown in Australia, New Zealand, and elsewhere to produce building timber. Often shortened to: **radiata.**
▷HISTORY from New Latin

radiate VERB ('reɪdɪˌeɪt) [1] Also: **eradiate.** to emit (heat, light, or some other form of radiation) or (of heat, light, etc.) to be emitted as radiation. [2] (*intr*) (of lines, beams, etc.) to spread out or be arranged in a radial pattern. [3] (*tr*) (of a person) to show (happiness, health, etc.) to a great degree. ◆ ADJECTIVE ('reɪdɪɪt, -ˌeɪt) [4] having rays; radiating. [5] (of a capitulum) consisting of ray florets. [6] (of animals or their parts) showing radial symmetry. [7] adorned or decorated with rays: *a radiate head on a coin.*
▷HISTORY C17: from Latin *radiāre* to emit rays

radiation (ˌreɪdɪ'eɪʃən) NOUN [1] *Physics* **a** the emission or transfer of radiant energy as particles, electromagnetic waves, sound, etc. **b** the particles, etc., emitted, esp the particles and gamma rays emitted in nuclear decay. [2] Also called: **radiation therapy.** *Med* treatment using a radioactive substance. [3] *Anatomy* a group of nerve fibres that diverge from their common source. [4] See **adaptive radiation.** [5] the act, state, or process of radiating or being radiated. [6] *Surveying* the fixing of points around a central plane table by using an alidade and measuring tape.
▸ ˌ**radi'ational** ADJECTIVE

radiation belt NOUN a region in the magnetosphere of a planet in which charged particles are trapped by the planet's magnetic field, an example being the earth's Van Allen belts.

radiation pattern NOUN the graphic representation of the strength and direction of electromagnetic radiation in the vicinity of a transmitting aerial. Also called: **antenna pattern.**

radiation pyrometer NOUN See **pyrometer.**

radiation resistance NOUN the resistive component of the impedance of a radio transmitting aerial that arises from the radiation of power.

radiation sickness NOUN *Pathol* illness caused by overexposure of the body or a part of the body to ionizing radiations from radioactive material or X-rays. It is characterized by vomiting, diarrhoea, and in severe cases by sterility and cancer.

radiative ('reɪdɪətɪv) *or* **radiatory** ('reɪdɪətərɪ, -trɪ) ADJECTIVE *Physics* emitting or causing the emission of radiation: *a radiative collision.*

radiator ('reɪdɪˌeɪtə) NOUN [1] a device for heating a room, building, etc., consisting of a series of pipes through which hot water or steam passes. [2] a device for cooling an internal-combustion engine, consisting of thin-walled tubes through which water passes. Heat is transferred from the water through the walls of the tubes to the airstream, which is created either by the motion of the vehicle or by a fan. [3] *Austral and NZ* an electric fire. [4] *Electronics* the part of an aerial or transmission line that radiates electromagnetic waves. [5] an electric space heater.

radical ('rædɪk^əl) ADJECTIVE [1] of, relating to, or characteristic of the basic or inherent constitution of a person or thing; fundamental: *a radical fault.* [2] concerned with or tending to concentrate on fundamental aspects of a matter; searching or thoroughgoing: *radical thought; a radical re-examination.* [3] favouring or tending to produce extreme or fundamental changes in political, economic, or social conditions, institutions, habits of mind, etc: *a radical party.* [4] *Med* (of treatment) aimed at removing the source of a disease: *radical surgery.* [5] *Slang, chiefly US* very good; excellent. [6] of, relating to, or arising from the root or the base of the stem of a plant: *radical leaves.* [7] *Maths* of, relating to, or containing roots of numbers or quantities. [8] *Linguistics* of or relating to the root of a word. ◆ NOUN [9] a person who favours extreme or fundamental change in existing institutions or in political, social, or economic conditions. [10] *Maths* a root of a number or quantity, such as $\sqrt[3]{5}$, $\sqrt{x}$. [11] *Chem* **a** short for **free radical. b** another name for **group** (sense 10). [12] *Linguistics* another word for **root**[1] (sense 9). [13] (in logographic writing systems such as that used for Chinese) a part of a character conveying lexical meaning.
▷HISTORY C14: from Late Latin *rādīcālis* having roots, from Latin *rādix* a root
▸ **'radicalness** NOUN

radical axis NOUN a line from any point of which tangents to two given circles are of equal length. It is the line joining the points of intersection of two circles.

radicalism ('rædɪkəˌlɪzəm) NOUN [1] the principles, desires, or practices of political radicals. [2] a radical movement, esp in politics. [3] the state or nature of being radical, esp in politics.
▸ ˌ**radical'istic** ADJECTIVE ▸ ˌ**radical'istically** ADVERB

radically ('rædɪkəlɪ) ADVERB thoroughly; completely; fundamentally: *to alter radically.*

radical sign NOUN the symbol √ placed before a number or quantity to indicate the extraction of a root, esp a square root. The value of a higher root is indicated by a raised digit in front of the symbol, as in $\sqrt[3]{}$.

radicand ('rædɪˌkænd, ˌrædɪ'kænd) NOUN a number or quantity from which a root is to be extracted, usually preceded by a radical sign: 3 *is the radicand of* $\sqrt{3}$.
▷HISTORY C20: from Latin *rādīcandum*, literally: that which is to be rooted, from *rādīcāre* to take root, from *rādīx* root

radicchio (ræ'diːkɪəʊ) NOUN, *plural* **-chios.** an

Italian variety of chicory, having purple leaves streaked with white that are eaten raw in salads.

radicel (ˈrædɪˌsɛl) NOUN a very small root; radicle.
▷HISTORY C19: from New Latin *radicella* a little root, from Latin *rādix* root

radices (ˈreɪdɪˌsiːz) NOUN a plural of **radix**.

radicle (ˈrædɪk^{ə}l) NOUN [1] *Botany* **a** part of the embryo of seed-bearing plants that develops into the main root. **b** a very small root or rootlike part. [2] *Anatomy* any bodily structure resembling a rootlet, esp one of the smallest branches of a vein or nerve. [3] *Chem* a variant spelling of **radical** (sense 11).
▷HISTORY C18: from Latin *rādīcula* a little root, from *rādīx* root

radii (ˈreɪdɪˌaɪ) NOUN a plural of **radius**.

radio (ˈreɪdɪəʊ) NOUN, *plural* **-os.** [1] the use of electromagnetic waves, lying in the radio-frequency range, for broadcasting, two-way communications, etc. [2] an electronic device designed to receive, demodulate, and amplify radio signals from sound broadcasting stations, etc. [3] a similar device permitting both transmission and reception of radio signals for two-way communications. [4] the broadcasting, content, etc., of sound radio programmes: *he thinks radio is poor these days.* [5] **a** the occupation or profession concerned with any aspect of the broadcasting of sound radio programmes: *he's in radio.* **b** (*modifier*) relating to, produced for, or transmitted by sound radio: *radio drama.* [6] short for **radiotelegraph, radiotelegraphy** or **radiotelephone.** [7] (*modifier*) **a** of, relating to, employed in, or sent by radio signals: *a radio station.* **b** of, concerned with, using, or operated by radio frequencies: *radio spectrum.* [8] (*modifier*) (of a motor vehicle) equipped with a radio for communication: *radio car.* ◆ VERB **-os, -oing, -oed.** [9] to transmit (a message) to (a person, radio station, etc.) by means of radio waves. ◆ Also called (esp Brit): **wireless.**
▷HISTORY C20: short for *radiotelegraphy*

radio- COMBINING FORM [1] denoting radio, broadcasting, or radio frequency: *radiogram.* [2] indicating radioactivity or radiation: *radiochemistry; radiolucent.* [3] indicating a radioactive isotope or substance: *radioactinium; radiothorium; radioelement.*
▷HISTORY from French, from Latin *radius* ray; see RADIUS

radioactivate (ˌreɪdɪəʊˈæktɪˌveɪt) VERB (*tr*) to make radioactive.
▸ **ˌradioˌactiˈvation** NOUN

radioactive (ˌreɪdɪəʊˈæktɪv) ADJECTIVE exhibiting, using, or concerned with radioactivity.
▸ **ˌradioˈactively** ADVERB

radioactive dating NOUN another term for **radiometric dating.**

radioactive decay NOUN disintegration of a nucleus that occurs spontaneously or as a result of electron capture. One or more different nuclei are formed and usually particles and gamma rays are emitted. Sometimes shortened to: **decay.** Also called: **disintegration.**

radioactive series NOUN *Physics* a series of nuclides each of which undergoes radioactive decay into the next member of the series, ending with a stable element, usually lead. See **uranium series, neptunium series, thorium series, actinium series.**

radioactive tracer NOUN *Med* See **tracer** (sense 3).

radioactive waste NOUN any waste material containing radionuclides. Also called: **nuclear waste.**

radioactivity (ˌreɪdɪəʊækˈtɪvɪtɪ) NOUN the spontaneous emission of radiation from atomic nuclei. The radiation can consist of alpha, beta, and gamma radiation.

radio astronomy NOUN a branch of astronomy in which a radio telescope is used to detect and analyse radio signals received on earth from radio sources in space.

radioautograph (ˌreɪdɪəʊˈɔːtəˌgrɑːf, -ˌgræf) NOUN another name for **autoradiograph.**

radio beacon NOUN a fixed radio transmitting station that broadcasts a characteristic signal by means of which a vessel or aircraft can determine its bearing or position. Sometimes shortened to: **beacon.**

radio beam NOUN a narrow beam of radio signals transmitted by a radio or radar beacon, radio telescope, or some other directional aerial, used for communications, navigation, etc. Sometimes shortened to: **beam.**

radiobiology (ˌreɪdɪəʊbaɪˈɒlədʒɪ) NOUN the branch of biology concerned with the effects of radiation on living organisms and the study of biological processes using radioactive substances as tracers.
▸ **radiobiological** (ˌreɪdɪəʊˌbaɪəˈlɒdʒɪk^{ə}l) ADJECTIVE
▸ **ˌradioˌbioˈlogically** ADVERB ▸ **ˌradiobiˈologist** NOUN

radiocarbon (ˌreɪdɪəʊˈkɑːb^{ə}n) NOUN a radioactive isotope of carbon, esp carbon-14. See **carbon** (sense 1).

radiocarbon dating NOUN a technique for determining the age of organic materials, such as wood, based on their content of the radioisotope ^{14}C acquired from the atmosphere when they formed part of a living plant. The ^{14}C decays to the nitrogen isotope ^{14}N with a half-life of 5730 years. Measurement of the amount of radioactive carbon remaining in the material thus gives an estimate of its age. Also called: **carbon-14 dating.**

radiochemistry (ˌreɪdɪəʊˈkɛmɪstrɪ) NOUN the chemistry of radioactive elements and their compounds.
▸ **ˌradioˈchemical** ADJECTIVE ▸ **ˌradioˈchemist** NOUN

radiocommunication (ˌreɪdɪəʊkəˌmjuːnɪˈkeɪʃən) NOUN communication by means of radio waves.

radio compass NOUN any navigational device that gives a bearing by determining the direction of incoming radio waves transmitted from a particular radio station or beacon. See also **goniometer** (sense 2).

radio control NOUN remote control by means of radio signals from a transmitter.

radio-controlled ADJECTIVE controlled remotely using radio signals from a transmitter.

radioelement (ˌreɪdɪəʊˈɛlɪmənt) NOUN an element that is naturally radioactive.

radio frequency NOUN [1] **a** a frequency or band of frequencies that lie in the range 10 kilohertz to 300 000 megahertz and can be used for radio communications and broadcasting. Abbreviations: **rf, RF.** See also **frequency band. b** (*as modifier*): *a radio-frequency amplifier.* [2] the frequency transmitted by a particular radio station.

radio galaxy NOUN a galaxy that is a strong emitter of radio waves.

radiogenic (ˌreɪdɪəʊˈdʒɛnɪk) ADJECTIVE produced or caused by radioactive decay: *a radiogenic element; radiogenic heat.*

radiogoniometer (ˌreɪdɪəʊˌgəʊnɪˈɒmɪtə) NOUN a device used to detect the direction of radio waves, consisting of a coil that is free to rotate within two fixed coils at right angles to each other.

radiogram (ˈreɪdɪəʊˌgræm) NOUN [1] *Brit* a unit comprising a radio and record player. [2] a message transmitted by radiotelegraphy. [3] another name for **radiograph.**

radiograph (ˈreɪdɪəʊˌgrɑːf, -ˌgræf) NOUN an image produced on a specially sensitized photographic film or plate by radiation, usually by X-rays or gamma rays. Also called: **radiogram, shadowgraph.**

radiography (ˌreɪdɪˈɒgrəfɪ) NOUN the production of radiographs of opaque objects for use in medicine, surgery, industry, etc.
▸ **ˌradiˈographer** NOUN ▸ **radiographic** (ˌreɪdɪəʊˈgræfɪk) ADJECTIVE ▸ **ˌradioˈgraphically** ADVERB

radioimmunoassay (ˈreɪdɪəʊˌɪmjʊnəʊˈæseɪ) NOUN a sensitive immunological assay, making use of antibodies and radioactive labelling, for the detection and quantification of biologically important substances, such as hormone concentrations in the blood.

radio interferometer NOUN a type of radio telescope in which two or more aerials connected to the same receiver produce interference patterns that can be analysed to provide an image of the source of the radio waves.

radioisotope (ˌreɪdɪəʊˈaɪsətəʊp) NOUN an isotope that is radioactive.
▸ **radioisotopic** (ˌreɪdɪəʊˌaɪsəˈtɒpɪk) ADJECTIVE

radiolarian (ˌreɪdɪəʊˈlɛərɪən) NOUN any of various marine protozoans constituting the order *Radiolaria*, typically having a siliceous shell and stiff radiating cytoplasmic projections: phylum *Actinopoda* (actinopods).
▷HISTORY C19: from New Latin *Radiolaria*, from Late Latin *radiolus* little sunbeam, from Latin *radius* ray, RADIUS

radiolocation (ˌreɪdɪəʊləˈkeɪʃən) NOUN a former name for **radar.**
▸ **ˌradioloˈcational** ADJECTIVE

radiological (ˌreɪdɪəˈlɒdʒɪk^{ə}l) ADJECTIVE [1] of, relating to, or concerning radiology or the equipment used in radiology. [2] of, relating to, or involving radioactive materials: *radiological warfare.*
▸ **ˌradioˈlogically** ADVERB

radiology (ˌreɪdɪˈɒlədʒɪ) NOUN the use of X-rays and radioactive substances in the diagnosis and treatment of disease.
▸ **ˌradiˈologist** NOUN

radiolucent (ˌreɪdɪəʊˈluːs^{ə}nt) ADJECTIVE almost transparent to electromagnetic radiation, esp X-rays.

radioluminescence (ˌreɪdɪəʊˌluːmɪˈnɛsəns) NOUN *Physics* luminescence that is induced by radiation from a radioactive material.
▸ **ˌradioˌlumiˈnescent** ADJECTIVE

radiolysis (ˌreɪdɪˈɒlɪsɪs) NOUN chemical decomposition caused by radiation, such as a beam of electrons or X-rays.
▸ **radiolytic** (ˌreɪdɪəʊˈlɪtɪk) ADJECTIVE

radiometeorograph (ˌreɪdɪəʊˈmiːtɪərəˌgrɑːf, -ˌgræf) NOUN another name for **radiosonde.**

radiometer (ˌreɪdɪˈɒmɪtə) NOUN any instrument for the detection or measurement of radiant energy.
▸ **radiometric** (ˌreɪdɪəʊˈmɛtrɪk) ADJECTIVE ▸ **ˌradiˈometry** NOUN

radiometric dating NOUN any method of dating material based on the decay of its constituent radioactive atoms, such as potassium-argon dating or rubidium-strontium dating. Also called: **radioactive dating.**

radiomicrometer (ˌreɪdɪəʊmaɪˈkrɒmɪtə) NOUN an instrument for detecting and measuring small amounts of radiation, usually by a sensitive thermocouple.

radio microphone NOUN a microphone incorporating a radio transmitter so that the user can move around freely.

radiomimetic (ˌreɪdɪəʊmɪˈmɛtɪk) ADJECTIVE (of drugs) producing effects similar to those produced by X-rays.

radionics (ˌreɪdɪˈɒnɪks) NOUN (*functioning as singular*) a dowsing technique using a pendulum to detect the energy fields that are emitted by all forms of matter.

radionuclide (ˌreɪdɪəʊˈnjuːklaɪd) NOUN a nuclide that is radioactive.

radiopager (ˈreɪdɪəʊˌpeɪdʒə) NOUN a small radio receiver fitted with a buzzer to alert a person to telephone their home, office, etc., to receive a message.
▸ **ˈradioˌpaging** NOUN

radiopaque (ˌreɪdɪəʊˈpeɪk) *or* **radio-opaque** ADJECTIVE not permitting X-rays or other radiation to pass through.
▸ **radiopacity** (ˌreɪdɪəʊˈpæsɪtɪ) *or* **ˌradio-oˈpacity** NOUN

radiophone (ˈreɪdɪəʊˌfəʊn) NOUN another name for **radiotelephone** (sense 1).

radiophonic (ˌreɪdɪəʊˈfɒnɪk) ADJECTIVE denoting or relating to music produced by electronic means.
▸ **ˌradioˈphonically** ADVERB ▸ **radiophony** (ˌreɪdɪˈɒfənɪ) NOUN

radio receiver NOUN an apparatus that receives incoming modulated radio waves and converts them into sound.

radioresistant (ˌreɪdɪəʊrɪˈsɪstənt) ADJECTIVE *Med* resistant to the effects of radiation.

radioscope (ˈreɪdɪəʊˌskəʊp) NOUN an instrument, such as a fluoroscope, capable of detecting radiant energy.

radioscopy (ˌreɪdɪˈɒskəpɪ) NOUN another word for **fluoroscopy.**
▸ **radioscopic** (ˌreɪdɪəʊˈskɒpɪk) ADJECTIVE
▸ **ˌradioˈscopically** ADVERB

radiosensitive (ˌreɪdɪəʊˈsɛnsɪtɪv) ADJECTIVE affected by or sensitive to radiation.
▸ **ˌradioˈsensitively** ADVERB ▸ **ˌradioˌsensiˈtivity** NOUN

radiosonde (ˈreɪdɪəʊˌsɒnd) NOUN an airborne

instrument to send meteorological information back to earth by radio. Also called: **radiometeorograph.**
▷HISTORY C20: RADIO- + French *sonde* sounding line

radio source NOUN a celestial object, such as a supernova remnant or quasar, that is a source of radio waves.

radio spectrum NOUN the range of electromagnetic frequencies used in radio transmission, lying between 10 kilohertz and 300 000 megahertz.

radio star NOUN a former name for **radio source.**

radio station NOUN 1 an installation consisting of one or more transmitters or receivers, etc., used for radiocommunications. 2 a broadcasting organization.

radiotelegram (ˌreɪdɪəʊˈtɛlɪˌɡræm) NOUN a message transmitted by radiotelegraphy. Also called: **radiogram.**

radiotelegraph (ˌreɪdɪəʊˈtɛlɪˌɡrɑːf, -ˌɡræf) VERB 1 to send (a message) by radiotelegraphy. ◆ NOUN 2 a message sent by radiotelegraphy.

radiotelegraphy (ˌreɪdɪəʊtɪˈlɛɡrəfɪ) NOUN a type of telegraphy in which messages (usually in Morse code) are transmitted by radio waves; its use is no longer widespread as it has been superseded by satellite technology. Also called: **wireless telegraphy.**
▸**radiotelegraphic** (ˌreɪdɪəʊˌtɛlɪˈɡræfɪk) ADJECTIVE
▸**ˌradioˌteleˈgraphically** ADVERB

radiotelemetry (ˌreɪdɪəʊtɪˈlɛmɪtrɪ) NOUN the use of radio waves for transmitting information from a distant instrument to a device that indicates or records the measurements. Sometimes shortened to: **telemetry.**

radiotelephone (ˌreɪdɪəʊˈtɛlɪˌfəʊn) NOUN 1 Also called: **radiophone, wireless telephone.** a device for communication by means of radio waves rather than by transmitting along wires or cables. ◆ VERB 2 to telephone (a person) by radiotelephone. ◆ Sometimes shortened to: **radio.**
▸**radiotelephonic** (ˌreɪdɪəʊˌtɛlɪˈfɒnɪk) ADJECTIVE
▸**radiotelephony** (ˌreɪdɪəʊtɪˈlɛfənɪ) NOUN

radio telescope NOUN an instrument consisting of an antenna or system of antennas connected to one or more radio receivers, used in radio astronomy to detect and analyse radio waves from space.

radioteletype (ˌreɪdɪəʊˈtɛlɪˌtaɪp) NOUN 1 a teleprinter that transmits or receives information by means of radio waves rather than by cable or wire. 2 a network of such devices widely used for communicating news, messages, information, etc. Abbreviations: **RTT, RTTY.**

radiotherapy (ˌreɪdɪəʊˈθɛrəpɪ) NOUN the treatment of disease, esp cancer, by means of alpha or beta particles emitted from an implanted or ingested radioisotope, or by means of a beam of high-energy radiation. Compare **chemotherapy.**
▸**radiotherapeutic** (ˌreɪdɪəʊˌθɛrəˈpjuːtɪk) ADJECTIVE
▸**ˌradioˌtheraˈpeutically** ADVERB ▸**ˌradioˈtherapist** NOUN

radiothermy (ˈreɪdɪəʊˌθɜːmɪ) NOUN *Med* the treatment of disease by means of heat generated by electromagnetic radiation.

radiotoxic (ˌreɪdɪəʊˈtɒksɪk) ADJECTIVE of or denoting the toxic effects of radiation or radioactive substances.

radio valve NOUN another name for **valve** (sense 3).

radio wave NOUN an electromagnetic wave of radio frequency.

radio window NOUN a gap in ionospheric reflection that allows radio waves, with frequencies in the range 10 000 to 40 000 megahertz, to pass from or into space.

radish (ˈrædɪʃ) NOUN 1 any of various plants of the genus *Raphanus*, esp *R. sativus* of Europe and Asia, cultivated for its edible root: family *Brassicaceae* (crucifers). 2 the root of this plant, which has a pungent taste and is eaten raw in salads. 3 **wild radish.** another name for **white charlock.** See **charlock** (sense 2).
▷HISTORY Old English *rǣdīc*, from Latin *rādīx* root

radium (ˈreɪdɪəm) NOUN **a** a highly radioactive luminescent white element of the alkaline earth group of metals. It occurs in pitchblende, carnotite, and other uranium ores, and is used in radiotherapy and in luminous paints. Symbol: Ra; atomic no.: 88; half-life of most stable isotope, ^{226}Ra: 1620 years; valency: 2; relative density: 5; melting pt.: 700°C; boiling pt.: 1140°C. **b** (*as modifier*): *radium needle.*
▷HISTORY C20: from Latin *radius* ray

radium therapy NOUN treatment of disease, esp cancer, by exposing affected tissues to radiation from radium.

radius (ˈreɪdɪəs) NOUN, *plural* **-dii** (-dɪˌaɪ) *or* **-diuses.** 1 a straight line joining the centre of a circle or sphere to any point on the circumference or surface. 2 the length of this line, usually denoted by the symbol *r*. 3 the distance from the centre of a regular polygon to a vertex (**long radius**) or the perpendicular distance to a side (**short radius**). 4 *Anatomy* the outer and slightly shorter of the two bones of the human forearm, extending from the elbow to the wrist. 5 a corresponding bone in other vertebrates. 6 any of the veins of an insect's wing. 7 a group of ray florets, occurring in such plants as the daisy. 8 **a** any radial or radiating part, such as a spoke. **b** (*as modifier*): *a radius arm.* 9 the lateral displacement of a cam or eccentric wheel. 10 a circular area of a size indicated by the length of its radius: *the police stopped every lorry within a radius of four miles.* 11 the operational limit of a ship, aircraft, etc.
▷HISTORY C16: from Latin: rod, ray, spoke

radius of action NOUN *Military* the maximum distance that a ship, aircraft, or land vehicle can travel from its base and return without refuelling.

radius of curvature NOUN the absolute value of the reciprocal of the curvature of a curve at a given point; the radius of a circle the curvature of which is equal to that of the given curve at that point. See also **centre of curvature.**

radius of gyration NOUN a length that represents the distance in a rotating system between the point about which it is rotating and the point to or from which a transfer of energy has the maximum effect. Symbol: *k* or *r*. In a system with a moment of inertia *I* and mass *m*, $k^2 = I/m$.

radius vector NOUN 1 *Maths* a line joining a point in space to the origin of polar or spherical coordinates. 2 *Astronomy* an imaginary line joining a satellite to the planet or star around which it is orbiting.

radix (ˈreɪdɪks) NOUN, *plural* **-dices** (-dɪˌsiːz) *or* **-dixes.** 1 *Maths* any number that is the base of a number system or of a system of logarithms: *10 is the radix of the decimal system.* 2 *Biology* the root or point of origin of a part or organ. 3 *Linguistics* a less common word for **root**[1] (sense 9).
▷HISTORY C16: from Latin *rādīx* root; compare Greek *rhadix* small branch, *rhiza* root

radix point NOUN a point, such as the decimal point in the decimal system, separating the integral part of a number from the fractional part.

Radnorshire (ˈrædnəˌʃɪə, -ʃə) *or* **Radnor** NOUN (until 1974) a county of E Wales, now part of Powys.

Radom (*Polish* ˈradɔm) NOUN a city in E Poland: under Austria from 1795 to 1815 and Russia from 1815 to 1918. Pop.: 232 262 (1999 est.).

radome (ˈreɪdəʊm) NOUN a protective housing for a radar antenna made from a material that is transparent to radio waves.
▷HISTORY C20: RA(DAR) + DOME

radon (ˈreɪdɒn) NOUN a colourless radioactive element of the rare gas group, the most stable isotope of which, radon-222, is a decay product of radium. It is used as an alpha particle source in radiotherapy. Symbol: Rn; atomic no.: 86; half-life of ^{222}Rn: 3.82 days; valency: 0; density: 9.73 kg/m^3; melting pt.: –71°C; boiling pt.: –61.7°C.
▷HISTORY C20: from RADIUM + -ON

radula (ˈrædjʊlə) NOUN, *plural* **-lae** (-ˌliː). a horny tooth-bearing strip on the tongue of molluscs that is used for rasping food.
▷HISTORY C19: from Late Latin: a scraping iron, from Latin *rādere* to scrape
▸**ˈradular** ADJECTIVE

RAE (in Britain) ABBREVIATION FOR Royal Aircraft Establishment.

RAEC ABBREVIATION FOR Royal Army Educational Corps.

RAF (*Not standard* ræf) ABBREVIATION FOR Royal Air Force.

raff (ræf) NOUN *Archaic or dialect* 1 rubbish; refuse. 2 rabble or riffraff.
▷HISTORY C14: perhaps from Old French *rafle* a snatching up; compare RAFFLE, RIFFRAFF

Rafferty (ˈræfətɪ) *or* **Rafferty's rules** PLURAL NOUN *Austral and NZ slang* no rules at all.
▷HISTORY C20: of uncertain origin

raffia *or* **raphia** (ˈræfɪə) NOUN 1 Also called: **raffia palm.** a palm tree, *Raphia ruffia*, native to Madagascar, that has large plumelike leaves, the stalks of which yield a useful fibre. 2 the fibre obtained from this plant, used for tying, weaving, etc. 3 any of several related palms or the fibre obtained from them.
▷HISTORY C19: from Malagasy

raffinate (ˈræfɪˌneɪt) NOUN the liquid left after a solute has been extracted by solvent extraction.
▷HISTORY C20: from French *raffiner* to refine + -ATE[1]

raffinose (ˈræfɪˌnəʊz, -ˌnəʊs) NOUN *Biochem* a trisaccharide of fructose, glucose, and galactose that occurs in sugar beet, cotton seed, certain cereals, etc. Formula: $C_{18}H_{32}O_{16}$.
▷HISTORY C19: from French *raffiner* to refine + -OSE[2]

raffish (ˈræfɪʃ) ADJECTIVE 1 careless or unconventional in dress, manners, etc.; rakish. 2 tawdry; flashy; vulgar.
▷HISTORY C19: see RAFF
▸**ˈraffishly** ADVERB ▸**ˈraffishness** NOUN

raffle (ˈræfᵊl) NOUN 1 **a** a lottery in which the prizes are goods rather than money. **b** (*as modifier*): *a raffle ticket.* ◆ VERB 2 (*tr*; often foll by *off*) to dispose of (goods) in a raffle.
▷HISTORY C14 (a dice game): from Old French, of obscure origin
▸**ˈraffler** NOUN

rafflesia (ræˈfliːzɪə) NOUN any of various tropical Asian parasitic leafless plants constituting the genus *Rafflesia*, esp *R. arnoldi*, the flowers of which grow up to 45 cm (18 inches) across, smell of putrid meat, and are pollinated by carrion flies: family *Rafflesiaceae*.
▷HISTORY C19: New Latin, named after Sir Stamford *Raffles* (1781–1826), British colonial administrator, who discovered it

raft[1] (rɑːft) NOUN 1 a buoyant platform of logs, planks, etc., used as a vessel or moored platform. 2 a thick slab of reinforced concrete laid over soft ground to provide a foundation for a building. ◆ VERB 3 to convey on or travel by raft, or make a raft from.
▷HISTORY C15: from Old Norse *raptr* RAFTER
▸**ˈrafting** NOUN

raft[2] (rɑːft) NOUN *Informal* a large collection or amount: *a raft of old notebooks discovered in a cupboard.*
▷HISTORY C19: from RAFF

rafter (ˈrɑːftə) NOUN any one of a set of sloping beams that form the framework of a roof.
▷HISTORY Old English *ræfter*; related to Old Saxon *rehter*, Old Norse *raptr*, Old High German *rāvo*; see RAFT[1]

RAFVR ABBREVIATION FOR Royal Air Force Volunteer Reserve.

rag[1] (ræɡ) NOUN 1 **a** a small piece of cloth, such as one torn from a discarded garment, or such pieces of cloth collectively. **b** (*as modifier*): *a rag doll; a rag book; rag paper.* 2 a fragmentary piece of any material; scrap; shred. 3 *Informal* a newspaper or other journal, esp one considered as worthless, sensational, etc. 4 *Informal* an item of clothing. 5 *Informal* a handkerchief. 6 *Brit slang, esp naval* a flag or ensign. 7 **lose one's rag.** to lose one's temper suddenly. ◆ See also **rags.**
▷HISTORY C14: probably back formation from RAGGED, from Old English *raggig*; related to Old Norse *rögg* tuft

rag[2] (ræɡ) VERB **rags, ragging, ragged.** (*tr*) 1 to draw attention facetiously and persistently to the shortcomings or alleged shortcomings of (a person). 2 *Brit* to play rough practical jokes on. ◆ NOUN 3 *Brit* a boisterous practical joke, esp one on a fellow student. 4 (in British universities) **a** a period, usually a week, in which various events are organized to raise money for charity, including a procession of decorated floats and tableaux. **b** (*as modifier*): *rag day.*

▷HISTORY C18: of uncertain origin

rag[3] (ræg) *Jazz* ♦ NOUN [1] a piece of ragtime music. ♦ VERB **rags, ragging, ragged.** [2] (*tr*) to compose or perform in ragtime.
▷HISTORY C20: shortened from RAGTIME

rag[4] (ræg) NOUN a roofing slate that is rough on one side.
▷HISTORY C13: of obscure origin

raga (ˈrɑːɡə) NOUN (in Indian music) [1] any of several conventional patterns of melody and rhythm that form the basis for freely interpreted compositions. Each pattern is associated with different aspects of religious devotion. [2] a composition based on one of these patterns.
▷HISTORY C18: from Sanskrit *rāga* tone, colour

ragamuffin (ˈræɡəˌmʌfɪn) NOUN [1] a ragged unkempt person, esp a child. [2] another name for **ragga.**
▷HISTORY C14 *Ragamoffyn*, name of a demon in the poem *Piers Plowman* (1393); probably based on RAG[1]

rag-and-bone man NOUN *Brit* a man who buys and sells discarded clothing, furniture, etc. Also called: **ragman, ragpicker.** US equivalent: **junkman.**

ragbag (ˈræɡˌbæɡ) NOUN [1] a bag for storing odd rags. [2] a confused assortment; jumble: *a ragbag of ideas.* [3] *Informal* a scruffy or slovenly person.
▷HISTORY C19

ragbolt (ˈræɡˌbəʊlt) NOUN a bolt that has angled projections on it to prevent it working loose once it has been driven home.

Ragdoll (ˈræɡˌdɒl) NOUN a breed of large long-haired cat with blue eyes.

rage (reɪdʒ) NOUN [1] intense anger; fury. [2] violent movement or action, esp of the sea, wind, etc. [3] great intensity of hunger, sexual desire, or other feelings. [4] aggressive behaviour associated with a specified environment or activity: *road rage; school rage.* [5] a fashion or craze (esp in the phrase **all the rage**). [6] *Austral and NZ informal* a dance or party. ♦ VERB (*intr*) [7] to feel or exhibit intense anger. [8] (esp of storms, fires, etc.) to move or surge with great violence. [9] (esp of a disease or epidemic) to spread rapidly and uncontrollably. [10] *Austral and NZ informal* to have a good time.
▷HISTORY C13: via Old French from Latin *rabiēs* madness

ragga (ˈræɡə) NOUN a dance-orientated style of reggae. Also called: **ragamuffin.**
▷HISTORY C20: shortened from RAGAMUFFIN

ragged (ˈræɡɪd) ADJECTIVE [1] (of clothes) worn to rags; tattered. [2] (of a person) dressed in shabby tattered clothes. [3] having a neglected or unkempt appearance: *ragged weeds.* [4] having a loose, rough, or uneven surface or edge; jagged. [5] uneven or irregular: *a ragged beat; a ragged shout.*
▷HISTORY C13: probably from *ragge* RAG[1]
▸ˈ**raggedly** ADVERB ▸ˈ**raggedness** NOUN

ragged robin NOUN a caryophyllaceous plant, *Lychnis floscuculi*, native to Europe and Asia, that has pink or white flowers with ragged petals. Also called: **cuckooflower.** See also **catchfly.**

ragged school NOUN (in Britain, formerly) a free elementary school for poor children.

raggedy (ˈræɡɪdɪ) ADJECTIVE *Informal* somewhat ragged; tattered: *a raggedy doll.*

raggle (ˈræɡᵊl) NOUN *Chiefly Scot* a thin groove cut in stone or brickwork, esp to hold the edge of a roof.
▷HISTORY C19: of obscure origin

raggle-taggle (ˈræɡᵊlˈtæɡᵊl) ADJECTIVE motley or unkempt: *a raggle-taggle Gypsy.*
▷HISTORY augmented form of RAGTAG

ragi, raggee, *or* **raggy** (ˈræɡɪ) NOUN a cereal grass, *Eleusine coracana*, cultivated in Africa and Asia for its edible grain.
▷HISTORY C18: from Hindi

raglan (ˈræɡlən) NOUN [1] a coat with sleeves that continue to the collar instead of having armhole seams. ♦ ADJECTIVE [2] cut in this design: *a raglan sleeve.*
▷HISTORY C19: named after Fitzroy James Henry Somerset, 1st Baron *Raglan* (1788–1855), British field marshal, diplomatist, and politician

ragman (ˈræɡˌmæn) NOUN, *plural* **-men.** another name for **rag-and-bone man.**

Ragman rolls (ˈræɡmən) PLURAL NOUN *History* a set of parchment rolls of 1296 enumerating the Scottish nobles who owed allegiance to Edward I of England, important as the only full list of the nobility of Scotland in the later 13th century.
▷HISTORY C18: from obsolete *ragman* in the sense: statute, roll, list

Ragnarök *or* **Ragnarok** (ˈrɑːɡnəˌrɒk) NOUN *Norse myth* the ultimate destruction of the gods in a cataclysmic battle with evil, out of which a new order will arise. German equivalent: **Götterdämmerung.**
▷HISTORY Old Norse *ragnarökkr*, from *regin* the gods + *rökkr* twilight

ragout (ræˈɡuː) NOUN [1] a richly seasoned stew of meat or poultry and vegetables. ♦ VERB **-gouts** (-ˈɡuːz), **-gouting** (-ˈɡuːɪŋ), **-gouted** (-ˈɡuːd). [2] (*tr*) to make into a ragout.
▷HISTORY C17: from French, from *ragoûter* to stimulate the appetite again, from *ra-* RE- + *goûter* from Latin *gustāre* to taste

rag-rolling NOUN a decorating technique in which paint is applied with a roughly folded cloth in order to create a marbled effect.

rags (ræɡz) PLURAL NOUN [1] torn, old, or shabby clothing. [2] cotton or linen cloth waste used in the manufacture of rag paper. [3] **glad rags.** *Informal* best clothes; finery. [4] **from rags to riches.** *Informal* **a** from poverty to great wealth. **b** (*as modifier*): *a rags-to-riches tale.*

ragstone (ˈræɡˌstəʊn) NOUN a hard sandstone or limestone, esp when used for building. Also called: **rag** *or* **ragg.**
▷HISTORY C14: from RAG[4] + STONE

ragtag (ˈræɡˌtæɡ) NOUN *Disparaging* the common people; rabble (esp in the phrase **ragtag and bobtail**).
▷HISTORY C19

ragtime (ˈræɡˌtaɪm) NOUN a style of jazz piano music, developed by Scott Joplin around 1900, having a two-four rhythm base and a syncopated melody.
▷HISTORY C20: probably from RAGGED + TIME

rag trade NOUN *Informal* the clothing business, esp the aspects concerned with the manufacture and sale of dresses.

Ragusa (*Italian* raˈɡuːza) NOUN [1] an industrial town in SE Sicily. Pop.: 68 850 (1990). [2] the Italian name (until 1918) for **Dubrovnik.**

ragweed (ˈræɡˌwiːd) NOUN any plant of the chiefly North American genus *Ambrosia*, such as *A. artemisiifolia* (**common ragweed**): family *Asteraceae* (composites). Their green tassel-like flowers produce large amounts of pollen, which causes hay fever. Also called: **ambrosia.**

ragworm (ˈræɡˌwɜːm) NOUN any polychaete worm of the genus *Nereis*, living chiefly in burrows in sand or mud and having a flattened body with a row of fleshy parapodia along each side. US name: **clamworm.**

ragwort (ˈræɡˌwɜːt) NOUN any of several plants of the genus *Senecio*, esp *S. jacobaea* of Europe, that have yellow daisy-like flowers: family *Asteraceae* (composites). See also **groundsel** (sense 1).

rah (rɑː) INTERJECTION *Informal, chiefly US* short for **hurrah.**

rah-rah (ˈrɑːˌrɑː) ADJECTIVE *Informal, chiefly US* like or marked by boisterous and uncritical enthusiasm and excitement.
▷HISTORY C20: a reduplication of RAH

rahui (ˌrɑːˈhuːɪ) NOUN *NZ* a Maori prohibition.
▷HISTORY Maori

rai (raɪ) NOUN a type of Algerian popular music based on traditional Algerian music influenced by modern Western pop.
▷HISTORY C20: Arabic, literally: opinion

raia (ˈrɑːjə, ˈraɪə) NOUN a less common variant of **rayah.**

raid (reɪd) NOUN [1] a sudden surprise attack: *an air raid.* [2] a surprise visit by police searching for criminals or illicit goods: *a fraud-squad raid.* ♦ See also **bear raid, dawn raid.** ♦ VERB [3] to make a raid against (a person, thing, etc.). [4] to sneak into (a place) in order to take something, steal, etc.: *raiding the larder.*
▷HISTORY C15: Scottish dialect, from Old English *rād* military expedition; see ROAD
▸ˈ**raider** NOUN

rail[1] (reɪl) NOUN [1] a horizontal bar of wood, metal, etc., supported by vertical posts, functioning as a fence, barrier, handrail, etc. [2] a horizontal bar fixed to a wall on which to hang things: *a picture rail.* [3] a horizontal framing member in a door or piece of panelling. Compare **stile**[2]. [4] short for **railing.** [5] one of a pair of parallel bars laid on a prepared track, roadway, etc., that serve as a guide and running surface for the wheels of a railway train, tramcar, etc. [6] **a** short for **railway. b** (*as modifier*): *rail transport.* [7] *Nautical* a trim for finishing the top of a bulwark. [8] **off the rails. a** into or in a state of dysfunction or disorder. **b** eccentric or mad. ♦ VERB (*tr*) [9] to provide with a rail or railings. [10] (usually foll by *in* or *off*) to fence (an area) with rails.
▷HISTORY C13: from Old French *raille* rod, from Latin *rēgula* ruler, straight piece of wood
▸ˈ**railless** ADJECTIVE

rail[2] (reɪl) VERB (*intr*; foll by *at* or *against*) to complain bitterly or vehemently: *to rail against fate.*
▷HISTORY C15: from Old French *railler* to mock, from Old Provençal *ralhar* to chatter, joke, from Late Latin *ragere* to yell, neigh
▸ˈ**railer** NOUN

rail[3] (reɪl) NOUN any of various small wading birds of the genus *Rallus* and related genera: family *Rallidae*, order *Gruiformes* (cranes, etc.). They have short wings, long legs, and dark plumage.
▷HISTORY C15: from Old French *raale*, perhaps from Latin *rādere* to scrape

railcar (ˈreɪlˌkɑː) NOUN a passenger-carrying railway vehicle consisting of a single coach with its own power unit.

railcard (ˈreɪlˌkɑːd) NOUN *Brit* an identity card that young people or pensioners in Britain can buy, which allows them to buy train tickets more cheaply.

rail gauge NOUN See **gauge** (sense 11).

railhead (ˈreɪlˌhɛd) NOUN [1] a terminal of a railway. [2] the farthest point reached by completed track on an unfinished railway. [3] *Military* the point at which material and personnel are transferred from rail to another conveyance. [4] the upper part of a railway rail, on which the traffic wheels run.

railing (ˈreɪlɪŋ) NOUN [1] (*often plural*) a fence, balustrade, or barrier that consists of rails supported by posts. [2] rails collectively or material for making rails.

raillery (ˈreɪlərɪ) NOUN, *plural* **-leries.** [1] light-hearted satire or ridicule; banter. [2] an example of this, esp a bantering remark.
▷HISTORY C17: from French, from *railler* to tease, banter; see RAIL[2]

rail rage NOUN a sense of extreme frustration experienced by rail users when subjected to delays, cancellations, etc., sometimes resulting in aggressive behaviour towards railway employees.

railroad (ˈreɪlˌrəʊd) NOUN [1] the usual US word for **railway.** ♦ VERB [2] (*tr*) *Informal* to force (a person) into (an action) with haste or by unfair means.

railway (ˈreɪlˌweɪ) *or US* **railroad** NOUN [1] a permanent track composed of a line of parallel metal rails fixed to sleepers, for transport of passengers and goods in trains. [2] any track on which the wheels of a vehicle may run: *a cable railway.* [3] the entire equipment, rolling stock, buildings, property, and system of tracks used in such a transport system. [4] the organization responsible for operating a railway network. [5] (*modifier*) of, relating to, or used on a railway or railways: *a railway engine; a railway strike.*

railwayman (ˈreɪlˌweɪmən) NOUN, *plural* **-men.** a worker on a railway, esp one other than a driver.

raiment (ˈreɪmənt) NOUN *Archaic or poetic* attire; clothing; garments.
▷HISTORY C15: shortened from *arrayment*, from Old French *areement*; see ARRAY

rain (reɪn) NOUN [1] **a** precipitation from clouds in the form of drops of water, formed by the condensation of water vapour in the atmosphere. **b** a fall of rain; shower. **c** (*in combination*): *a raindrop.* Related adjectives: **hyetal, pluvious.** [2] a large quantity of anything falling rapidly or in quick succession: *a rain of abuse.* [3] (**come**) **rain or shine. a** regardless of the weather. **b** regardless of circumstances. [4] **right as rain.** *Brit informal* perfectly all right; perfectly fit. ♦ VERB [5] (*intr*; with *it* as subject) to be the case that rain is falling. [6] (often

with *it* as subject) to fall or cause to fall like rain: *the lid flew off and popcorn rained on everyone.* 7 (*tr*) to bestow in large measure: *to rain abuse on someone.* 8 **rain cats and dogs.** *Informal* to rain heavily; pour. 9 **rained off.** cancelled or postponed on account of rain. US and Canadian term: **rained out.** ◆ See also **rains.**
▷HISTORY Old English *regn*; related to Old Frisian *rein*, Old High German *regan*, Gothic *rign*
▸**'rainless** ADJECTIVE

rainband ('reɪn,bænd) NOUN a dark band in the solar spectrum caused by water in the atmosphere.

rainbird ('reɪn,bɜːd) NOUN any of various birds, such as (in Britain) the green woodpecker, whose cry is supposed to portend rain.

rainbow ('reɪn,bəʊ) NOUN 1 a bow-shaped display in the sky of the colours of the spectrum, caused by the refraction and reflection of the sun's rays through rain or mist. 2 **a** any similar display of bright colours. **b** (*as modifier*): *a rainbow pattern.* 3 an illusory hope: *to chase rainbows.* 4 (*modifier*) of or relating to a political grouping together by several minorities, esp of different races: *the rainbow coalition.*

Rainbow ('reɪn,bəʊ) NOUN a member of the Rainbow Guides, the youngest group of girls (aged 5-7 years) in The Guide Association.

rainbow bird NOUN an Australian bee-eater, *Merops ornatus*, with a brightly-coloured plumage. It feeds in flight and nests in sandy burrows.

Rainbow Bridge NOUN a natural stone bridge over a creek in SE Utah. Height: 94 m (309 ft.). Span: 85 m (278 ft.).

rainbow lorikeet NOUN a small Australasian parrot, *Trichoglossus haematodus*, with brightly-coloured plumage.

rainbow nation NOUN *South African* an epithet, alluding to its multiracial population, of **South Africa.**
▷HISTORY C20: coined by Nelson Mandela (born 1918), South African statesman, following the end of apartheid

rainbow quartz NOUN *Mineralogy* another name for **iris** (sense 3).

rainbow trout NOUN a freshwater trout of North American origin, *Salmo gairdneri*, having a body marked with many black spots and two longitudinal red stripes.

rain check NOUN 1 *US and Canadian* a ticket stub for a baseball or other game that allows readmission on a future date if the event is cancelled because of rain. 2 the deferral of acceptance of an offer, esp, a voucher issued to a customer wishing to purchase a sale item that is temporarily out of stock, enabling him to buy it at the special price when next the item is available. 3 **take a rain check.** *Informal* to accept the postponement of an offer.

raincoat ('reɪn,kəʊt) NOUN a coat made of a waterproof material.

rainfall ('reɪn,fɔːl) NOUN 1 precipitation in the form of raindrops. 2 *Meteorol* the amount of precipitation in a specified place and time.

rainforest ('reɪn,fɒrɪst) NOUN dense forest found in tropical areas of heavy rainfall. The trees are broad-leaved and evergreen, and the vegetation tends to grow in three layers (undergrowth, intermediate trees and shrubs, and very tall trees, which form a canopy). Also called: **selva.**

rain gauge NOUN an instrument for measuring rainfall or snowfall, consisting of a cylinder covered by a funnel-like lid. Also called: **pluviometer.**

Rainier ('reɪnɪə, reɪ'nɪə, rə-) NOUN **Mount.** a mountain in W Washington State: the highest mountain in the state and in the Cascade Range. Height: 4392 m (14 410 ft.).

rainmaker ('reɪn,meɪkə) NOUN 1 (among American Indians) a professional practitioner of ritual incantations or other actions intended to cause rain to fall. 2 *Informal, chiefly US* an influential employee who creates a great deal of business or revenue for his or her firm.
▸**'rain,making** NOUN

rainout ('reɪn,aʊt) NOUN radioactive fallout or atmospheric pollution carried to the earth by rain.

rainproof ('reɪn,pruːf) ADJECTIVE 1 Also: **raintight.** (of garments, materials, buildings, etc.) impermeable to rainwater. ◆ VERB 2 (*tr*) to make rainproof.

rains (reɪnz) PLURAL NOUN **the.** the season of heavy rainfall, esp in the tropics.

rain shadow NOUN the relatively dry area on the leeward side of high ground in the path of rain-bearing winds.

rainstorm ('reɪn,stɔːm) NOUN a storm with heavy rain.

rain tree NOUN a leguminous tree, *Samanea saman*, native to Central America and widely planted in the tropics for ornament. It has red-and-yellow feathery flowers and pinnate leaves whose leaflets close at the approach of rain.

rainwater ('reɪn,wɔːtə) NOUN water from rain (as distinguished from spring water, tap water, etc.).

rainwater pipe NOUN *Brit* another name for **downpipe.**

rainy ('reɪnɪ) ADJECTIVE **rainier, rainiest.** 1 characterized by a large rainfall: *a rainy climate.* 2 wet or showery; bearing rain.
▸**'rainily** ADVERB ▸**'raininess** NOUN

rainy day NOUN a future time of need, esp financial.

raise (reɪz) VERB (*mainly tr*) 1 to move, cause to move, or elevate to a higher position or level; lift. 2 to set or place in an upright position. 3 to construct, build, or erect: *to raise a barn.* 4 to increase in amount, size, value, etc.: *to raise prices.* 5 to increase in degree, strength, intensity, etc.: *to raise one's voice.* 6 to advance in rank or status; promote. 7 to arouse or awaken from or as if from sleep or death. 8 to stir up or incite; activate: *to raise a mutiny.* 9 **raise Cain** (*or* **the devil, hell, the roof** etc.). **a** to create a boisterous disturbance. **b** to react or protest heatedly. 10 to give rise to; cause or provoke: *to raise a smile.* 11 to put forward for consideration: *to raise a question.* 12 to cause to assemble or gather together; collect: *to raise an army.* 13 to grow or cause to grow: *to raise a crop.* 14 to bring up; rear: *to raise a family.* 15 to cause to be heard or known; utter or express: *to raise a shout; to raise a protest.* 16 to bring to an end; remove: *to raise a siege; raise a ban.* 17 to cause (dough, bread, etc.) to rise, as by the addition of yeast. 18 *Poker* to bet more than (the previous player). 19 *Bridge* to bid (one's partner's suit) at a higher level. 20 *Nautical* to cause (something) to seem to rise above the horizon by approaching: *we raised land after 20 days.* 21 to establish radio communications with: *we managed to raise Moscow last night.* 22 to obtain (money, funds, capital, etc.). 23 to bring (a surface, a design, etc.) into relief; cause to project. 24 to cause (a blister, welt, etc.) to form on the skin. to expel (phlegm) by coughing. 26 *Phonetics* to modify the articulation of (a vowel) by bringing the tongue closer to the roof of the mouth. 27 *Maths* to multiply (a number) by itself a specified number of times: *8 is 2 raised to the power 3.* 28 **a** to institute (a suit or action at law). **b** to draw up (a summons). 29 *Chiefly US and Canadian* to increase the amount payable on (a cheque, money order, etc.) fraudulently. 30 *Curling* to push (a stone) towards the tee with another stone. 31 **raise an eyebrow. a** Also: **raise one's eyebrows.** to look quizzical or surprised. **b** to give rise to doubt or disapproval. 32 **raise one's glass** (**to**). to drink the health of (someone); drink a toast (to). 33 **raise one's hat.** *Old-fashioned* to take one's hat briefly off one's head as a greeting or mark of respect. ◆ NOUN 34 the act or an instance of raising. 35 *Chiefly US and Canadian* an increase, esp in salary, wages, etc.; rise.
▷HISTORY C12: from Old Norse *reisa*; related to Old English *rǣran* to REAR[2]
▸**'raisable** *or* **'raiseable** ADJECTIVE ▸**'raiser** NOUN

raised beach NOUN a wave-cut platform raised above the shoreline by a relative fall in the water level.

raised bog NOUN *Ecology* a bog of convex shape produced by growth of sphagnum and other bog plants in acid conditions and the subsequent build up of acid peat.

raisin ('reɪzᵊn) NOUN a dried grape.
▷HISTORY C13: from Old French: grape, ultimately from Latin *racēmus* cluster of grapes; compare Greek *rhax* berry, grape
▸**'raisiny** ADJECTIVE

raising ('reɪzɪŋ) NOUN *Transformational grammar* a rule that moves a constituent from an embedded clause into the main clause. See also **subject-raising, negative-raising.**

raison d'être *French* (rɛzɔ̃ dɛtrə) NOUN, *plural* ***raisons d'être*** (rɛzɔ̃ dɛtrə). reason or justification for existence.

raita ('reɪtə, raɪ'iːtə) NOUN an Indian dish of finely chopped cucumber, peppers, mint, etc., in yoghurt, served with curries.
▷HISTORY C20: from Hindi

raj (rɑːdʒ) NOUN (in India) government; rule.
▷HISTORY C19: from Hindi, from Sanskrit *rājya*, from *rājati* he rules

Raj (rɑːdʒ) NOUN **the.** the British government in India before 1947.

Rajab (rə'dʒæb) NOUN the seventh month of the Muslim year.

rajah *or* **raja** ('rɑːdʒə) NOUN 1 (in India, formerly) a ruler or landlord: sometimes used as a form of address or as a title preceding a name. 2 a Malayan or Javanese prince or chieftain.
▷HISTORY C16: from Hindi *rājā*, from Sanskrit *rājan* king; see RAJ; compare Latin *rex* king

RAJAR ('reɪdʒɑː) NOUN ACRONYM FOR Radio Joint Audience Research.

Rajasthan (,rɑːdʒə'stɑːn) NOUN a state of NW India, bordering on Pakistan: formed in 1958; contains the Thar Desert in the west; now the largest state in India. Capital: Jaipur. Pop.: 56 473 122 (2001). Area: 342 239 sq. km (132 111 sq. miles).

raja yoga ('rɑːdʒə) NOUN (*sometimes capitals*) a form of yoga chiefly concerned with controlling and using the energy of the mind by meditation. Compare **hatha yoga.**
▷HISTORY C19: from Sanskrit *rājan* king + YOGA

Rajkot ('rɑːdʒkəʊt) NOUN a city in W India, in S Gujarat. Pop.: 559 407 (1991).

Rajput *or* **Rajpoot** ('rɑːdʒpʊt) NOUN *Hinduism* one of a Hindu military caste claiming descent from the Kshatriya, the original warrior caste.
▷HISTORY C16: from Hindi, from Sanskrit *rājan* king; see RAJ

Rajputana (,rɑːdʒpʊ'tɑːnə) NOUN a former group of princely states in NW India: now mostly part of Rajasthan.

Rajya Sabha ('rɑːdʒjə 'sʌbə) NOUN the upper chamber of India's Parliament. Compare **Lok Sabha.**
▷HISTORY C20: Hindi, *rajya* state + *sabha* assembly

Rakata (rə'kɑːtə) NOUN another name for **Krakatoa.**

rake[1] (reɪk) NOUN 1 a hand implement consisting of a row of teeth set in a headpiece attached to a long shaft and used for gathering hay, straw, leaves, etc., or for smoothing loose earth. 2 any of several mechanical farm implements equipped with rows of teeth or rotating wheels mounted with tines and used to gather hay, straw, etc. 3 any of various implements similar in shape or function, such as a tool for drawing out ashes from a furnace. 4 the act of raking. 5 *NZ* a line of wagons coupled together as one unit, used on railways. ◆ VERB 6 to scrape, gather, or remove (leaves, refuse, etc.) with or as if with a rake. 7 to level or prepare (a surface, such as a flower bed) with a rake or similar implement. 8 (*tr*; sometimes foll by *out*) to clear (ashes, clinker, etc.) from (a fire or furnace). 9 (*tr*; foll by *up* or *together*) to gather (items or people) with difficulty, as from a scattered area or limited supply. 10 (*tr*; often foll by *through, over* etc.) to search or examine carefully. 11 (when *intr*, foll by *against, along* etc.) to scrape or graze: *the ship raked the side of the quay.* 12 (*tr*) to direct (gunfire) along the length of (a target): *machine-guns raked the column.* 13 (*tr*) to sweep (one's eyes) along the length of (something); scan. ◆ See also **rake in, rake-off, rake up.**
▷HISTORY Old English *raca*; related to Old Norse *raka*, Old High German *rehho* a rake, Gothic *rikan* to heap up, Latin *rogus* funeral pile

rake[2] (reɪk) NOUN a dissolute man, esp one in fashionable society; roué.
▷HISTORY C17: short for RAKEHELL

rake[3] (reɪk) VERB (*mainly intr*) 1 to incline from the vertical by a perceptible degree, esp (of a ship's mast or funnel) towards the stern. 2 (*tr*) to construct with a backward slope. ◆ NOUN 3 the degree to which an object, such as a ship's mast,

inclines from the perpendicular, esp towards the stern. [4] *Theatre* the slope of a stage from the back towards the footlights. [5] *Aeronautics* **a** the angle between the wings of an aircraft and the line of symmetry of the aircraft. **b** the angle between the line joining the centroids of the section of a propeller blade and a line perpendicular to the axis. [6] the angle between the working face of a cutting tool and a plane perpendicular to the surface of the workpiece. [7] a slanting ledge running across a crag in the Lake District.
▷HISTORY C17: of uncertain origin; perhaps related to German *ragen* to project, Swedish *raka*

rake⁴ (reɪk) VERB (*intr*) [1] (of gun dogs or hounds) to hunt with the nose to the ground. [2] (of hawks) **a** to pursue quarry in full flight. **b** (often foll by *away*) to fly wide of the quarry, esp beyond the control of the falconer.
▷HISTORY Old English *racian* to go forward, of uncertain origin

rakehell ('reɪk,hel) *Archaic* ◆ NOUN [1] a dissolute man; rake. ◆ ADJECTIVE *also* **rakehelly**. [2] profligate; dissolute.
▷HISTORY C16: from RAKE[1] + HELL; but compare Middle English *rakel* rash

rake in VERB (*tr, adverb*) *Informal* to acquire (money) in large amounts.

rake-off *Slang* ◆ NOUN [1] a share of profits, esp one that is illegal or given as a bribe. ◆ VERB **rake off**. [2] (*tr, adverb*) to take or receive (such a share of profits).

raker ('reɪkə) NOUN [1] a person who rakes. [2] a raking implement. [3] *Midland English dialect* a large lump of coal.

rake up VERB (*tr, adverb*) to revive, discover, or bring to light (something forgotten): *to rake up an old quarrel*.

raki *or* **rakee** (rɑː'kiː, 'rækɪ) NOUN a strong spirit distilled in Turkey, the former Yugoslavia, etc., from grain, usually flavoured with aniseed or other aromatics.
▷HISTORY C17: from Turkish *rāqī*

raking ('reɪkɪŋ) NOUN *Rugby* the offence committed when a player deliberately scrapes an opponent's leg, arm, etc. with the studs of his or her boots.

rakish¹ ('reɪkɪʃ) ADJECTIVE dissolute; profligate.
▷HISTORY C18: from RAKE[2] + -ISH
▸'**rakishly** ADVERB ▸'**rakishness** NOUN

rakish² ('reɪkɪʃ) ADJECTIVE [1] dashing; jaunty: *a hat set at a rakish angle*. [2] *Nautical* (of a ship or boat) having lines suggestive of speed.
▷HISTORY C19: probably from RAKE[3] (sense 1), with reference to the sloping masts of pirate ships

rale *or* **râle** (rɑːl) NOUN *Med* an abnormal coarse crackling sound heard on auscultation of the chest, usually caused by the accumulation of fluid in the lungs.
▷HISTORY C19: from French *râle*, from *râler* to breathe with a rattling sound; compare RAIL[3]

Raleigh ('rɔːlɪ, 'rɑː-) NOUN a city in E central North Carolina, capital of the state. Pop.: 276 093 (2000).

rall. *Music* ABBREVIATION FOR rallentando.

rallentando (,rælɛn'tændəʊ) ADJECTIVE, ADVERB *Music* becoming slower. Abbreviation: **rall.** Also: **ritardando, ritenuto.**
▷HISTORY C19: Italian, from *rallentare* to slow down

ralline ('rælaɪn, -ɪn) ADJECTIVE of, relating to, or belonging to the *Rallidae*, a family of birds that includes the rails, crakes, and coots.
▷HISTORY C19: from New Latin *Rallus* RAIL[3]

rally¹ ('rælɪ) VERB **-lies, -lying, -lied.** [1] to bring (a group, unit, etc.) into order, as after dispersal, or (of such a group) to reform and come to order: *the troops rallied for a final assault*. [2] (when *intr*, foll by *to*) to organize (supporters, etc.) for a common cause or (of such people) to come together for a purpose. [3] to summon up (one's strength, spirits, etc.) or (of a person's health, strength, or spirits) to revive or recover. [4] (*intr*) *Stock Exchange* to increase sharply after a decline: *steels rallied after a bad day*. [5] (*intr*) *Tennis, squash, badminton* to engage in a rally. ◆ NOUN, *plural* **-lies**. [6] a large gathering of people for a common purpose, esp for some political cause: *the Nuremberg Rallies*. [7] a marked recovery of strength or spirits, as during illness. [8] a return to order after dispersal or rout, as of troops, etc. [9] *Stock Exchange* a sharp increase in price or trading activity after a decline. [10] *Tennis, squash, badminton* an exchange of several shots before one player wins the point. [11] a type of motoring competition over public and closed roads.
▷HISTORY C16: from Old French *rallier*, from RE- + *alier* to unite; see ALLY
▸'**rallier** NOUN

rally² ('rælɪ) VERB **-lies, -lying, -lied.** to mock or ridicule (someone) in a good-natured way; chaff; tease.
▷HISTORY C17: from Old French *railler* to tease; see RAIL[2]

rallycross ('rælɪ,krɒs) NOUN a form of motor sport in which cars race over a one-mile circuit of rough grass with some hard-surfaced sections. See also **autocross, motocross.**

rally round VERB (*intr*) to come to the aid of (someone); offer moral or practical support.

ram (ræm) NOUN [1] an uncastrated adult sheep. [2] a piston or moving plate, esp one driven hydraulically or pneumatically. [3] the falling weight of a pile driver or similar device. [4] short for **battering ram.** [5] Also called: **rostrum, beak.** a pointed projection in the stem of an ancient warship for puncturing the hull of enemy ships. [6] a warship equipped with a ram. [7] *Slang* a sexually active man. ◆ VERB **rams, ramming, rammed.** [8] (*tr*; usually foll by *into*) to force or drive, as by heavy blows: *to ram a post into the ground*. [9] (of a moving object) to crash with force (against another object) or (of two moving objects) to collide in this way: *the ships rammed the enemy*. [10] (*tr*; often foll by *in* or *down*) to stuff or cram (something into a hole, etc.). [11] (*tr*; foll by *onto, against* etc.) to thrust violently: *he rammed the books onto the desk*. [12] (*tr*) to present (an idea, argument, etc.) forcefully or aggressively (esp in the phrase **ram (something) down someone's throat**). [13] (*tr*) to drive (a charge) into a firearm.
▷HISTORY Old English *ramm*; related to Old High German *ram* ram, Old Norse *ramr* fierce, *rimma* to fight
▸'**rammer** NOUN

Ram (ræm) NOUN **the**. the constellation Aries, the first sign of the zodiac.

RAM¹ (ræm) NOUN *Computing* ◆ ACRONYM FOR random access memory: semiconductor memory in which all storage locations can be rapidly accessed in the same amount of time. It forms the main memory of a computer, used by applications to perform tasks while the device is operating.

RAM² ABBREVIATION FOR Royal Academy of Music.

r.a.m. ABBREVIATION FOR relative atomic mass.

Rama ('rɑːmə) NOUN (in Hindu mythology) any of Vishnu's three incarnations (the heroes Balarama, Parashurama, or Ramachandra).
▷HISTORY from Sanskrit *Rāma* black, dark

Ramachandra (,rɑːmə'tʃʌndrə) NOUN (in Hindu mythology) an incarnation of Vishnu; the hero of the *Ramayana* and a character in the *Mahabharata*. See also **Rama.**

Ramadan, Rhamadhan (,ræmə'dɑːn), *or* **Ramazan** (,ræmə'zɑːn) NOUN [1] the ninth month of the Muslim year, lasting 30 days, during which strict fasting is observed from sunrise to sunset. [2] the fast itself.
▷HISTORY C16: from Arabic, literally: the hot month, from *ramad* dryness

ram-air turbine NOUN a small air-driven turbine fitted to an aircraft to provide power in the event of a failure of the normal systems.

Raman effect ('rɑːmən) NOUN a change in wavelength of light that is scattered by electrons within a material. The effect is used in **Raman spectroscopy** for studying molecules.
▷HISTORY C20: named after Sir Chandrasekhara *Raman* (1888–1970), Indian physicist

Ramat Gan (rɑː'mɑːt 'gɑːn) NOUN a city in Israel, E of Tel Aviv. Pop.: 126 900 (1999 est.).

Ramayana (rɑː'maɪənə) NOUN a Sanskrit epic poem, composed about 300 B.C., recounting the feats of Ramachandra.

ramble ('ræmbᵊl) VERB (*intr*) [1] to stroll about freely, as for relaxation, with no particular direction. [2] (of paths, streams, etc.) to follow a winding course; meander. [3] (of plants) to grow in a random fashion. [4] (of speech, writing, etc.) to lack organization. ◆ NOUN [5] a leisurely stroll, esp in the countryside.
▷HISTORY C17: probably related to Middle Dutch *rammelen* to ROAM (of animals); see RAM

rambler ('ræmblə) NOUN [1] a weak-stemmed plant, esp any of various cultivated hybrid roses that straggle over other vegetation. [2] a person who rambles, esp one who takes country walks. [3] a person who lacks organization in his speech or writing.

rambling ('ræmblɪŋ) ADJECTIVE [1] straggling or sprawling haphazardly; unplanned: *a rambling old house*. [2] (of speech or writing) lacking a coherent plan; diffuse and disconnected. [3] (of a plant, esp a rose) profusely climbing and straggling. [4] nomadic; wandering.

Ramboesque (,ræmbəʊ'ɛsk) ADJECTIVE looking or behaving like, or characteristic of, Rambo, a fictional film character noted for his mindless brutality.
▷HISTORY C20: after *Rambo, First Blood II*, released in Britain 1985
▸'**Rambo,ism** NOUN

Rambouillet¹ (*French* rɑ̃bujɛ) NOUN a town in N France, in the Yvelines department: site of the summer residence of French presidents. Pop.: 25 300 (1990).

Rambouillet² ('rɒmbʊ,jeɪ, 'ræmbʊ,leɪ; *French* rɑ̃bujɛ) NOUN a fine-woolled merino-like breed of sheep.
▷HISTORY C19: from RAMBOUILLET[1]

rambunctious (ræm'bʌŋkʃəs) ADJECTIVE *Informal* boisterous; unruly.
▷HISTORY C19: probably from Icelandic *ram-* (intensifying prefix) + *-bunctious*, from BUMPTIOUS
▸**ram'bunctiously** ADVERB ▸**ram'bunctiousness** NOUN

rambutan (ræm'buːtᵊn) NOUN [1] a sapindaceous tree, *Nephelium lappaceum*, native to SE Asia, that has bright red edible fruit. [2] the fruit of this tree.
▷HISTORY C18: from Malay, from *rambut* hair

RAMC ABBREVIATION FOR Royal Army Medical Corps.

ramekin *or* **ramequin** ('ræmɪkɪn) NOUN [1] a savoury dish made from a cheese mixture baked in a fireproof container. [2] the container itself.
▷HISTORY C18: French *ramequin*, of Germanic origin

ramen ('rɑːmən) NOUN [1] a Japanese dish consisting of a clear broth containing thin white noodles and sometimes vegetables, meat, etc. ◆ PLURAL NOUN [2] thin white noodles served in such a broth.
▷HISTORY Japanese, from Chinese *la* to pull + *mian* noodles

ramentum (rə'mɛntəm) NOUN, *plural* **-ta** (-tə). any of the thin brown scales that cover the stems and leaves of young ferns.
▷HISTORY C17: from Latin *rādere* to scrape
▸**ramentaceous** (,ræmɛn'teɪʃəs) ADJECTIVE

rami ('reɪmaɪ) NOUN the plural of **ramus.**

ramie *or* **ramee** ('ræmɪ) NOUN [1] a woody urticaceous shrub of Asia, *Boehmeria nivea*, having broad leaves and a stem that yields a flaxlike fibre. [2] the fibre from this plant, used in making fabrics, cord, etc.
▷HISTORY C19: from Malay *rami*

ramification (,ræmɪfɪ'keɪʃən) NOUN [1] the act or process of ramifying or branching out. [2] an offshoot or subdivision. [3] (*often plural*) a subsidiary consequence, esp one that complicates. [4] a structure of branching parts.

ramiform ('ræmɪ,fɔːm) ADJECTIVE having a branchlike shape.
▷HISTORY C19: from Latin *rāmus* branch + -FORM

ramify ('ræmɪ,faɪ) VERB **-fies, -fying, -fied.** [1] to divide into branches or branchlike parts. [2] (*intr*) to develop complicating consequences; become complex.
▷HISTORY C16: from French *ramifier*, from Latin *rāmus* branch + *facere* to make

Ramillies ('ræmɪliːz; *French* ramiji) NOUN a village in central Belgium where the Duke of Marlborough defeated the French in 1706.

ramjet *or* **ramjet engine** ('ræm,dʒɛt) NOUN **a** a type of jet engine in which fuel is burned in a duct using air compressed by the forward speed of the aircraft. **b** an aircraft powered by such an engine. Also called: **athodyd.**

rammel ('ræməl) NOUN *Northern English dialect* discarded or waste matter.

rammish ('ræmɪʃ) ADJECTIVE like a ram, esp in being lustful or foul-smelling.
▸ **'rammishly** ADVERB ▸ **'rammishness** NOUN

rammle ('ræməl) NOUN *Midland English dialect* a collection of items saved in case they become useful.

rammy ('ræmɪ) NOUN, *plural* **-mies**. *Scot* a noisy disturbance or free-for-all.
▷ HISTORY C20: perhaps from earlier Scottish *rammle* row, uproar

ramose ('reɪməʊs, ræ'məʊs) *or* **ramous** ('reɪməs) ADJECTIVE having branches.
▷ HISTORY C17: from Latin *rāmōsus*, from *rāmus* branch
▸ **'ramosely** *or* **'ramously** ADVERB ▸ **ramosity** (ræ'mɒsɪtɪ) NOUN

ramp (ræmp) NOUN 1 a sloping floor, path, etc., that joins two surfaces at different levels. 2 a movable stairway by which passengers enter and leave an aircraft. 3 the act of ramping. 4 *Brit slang* a swindle, esp one involving exorbitant prices. 5 an NZ name for **sleeping policeman**. ◆ VERB 6 (*intr*; often foll by *about* or *around*) (esp of animals) to rush around in a wild excited manner. 7 to act in a violent or threatening manner, as when angry (esp in the phrase **ramp and rage**). 8 (*tr*) *Finance* to buy (a security) in the market with the object of raising its price and enhancing the image of the company behind it for financial gain. ◆ See also **ramp down, ramp up**.
▷ HISTORY C18 (n): from C13 *rampe*, from Old French *ramper* to crawl or rear, probably of Germanic origin; compare Middle Low German *ramp* cramp

rampage VERB (ræm'peɪdʒ) 1 (*intr*) to rush about in an angry, violent, or agitated fashion. ◆ NOUN ('ræmpeɪdʒ, ræm'peɪdʒ) 2 angry or destructive behaviour. 3 **on the rampage**. behaving violently or destructively.
▷ HISTORY C18: from Scottish, of uncertain origin; perhaps based on RAMP
▸ **ram'pageous** ADJECTIVE ▸ **ram'pageously** ADVERB
▸ **ram'pageousness** NOUN ▸ **'rampager** NOUN

rampant ('ræmpənt) ADJECTIVE 1 unrestrained or violent in behaviour, desire, opinions, etc. 2 growing or developing unchecked. 3 (*postpositive*) *Heraldry* (of a beast) standing on the hind legs, the right foreleg raised above the left. 4 (of an arch) having one abutment higher than the other.
▷ HISTORY C14: from Old French *ramper* to crawl, rear; see RAMP
▸ **'rampancy** NOUN ▸ **'rampantly** ADVERB

rampart ('ræmpɑːt) NOUN 1 the surrounding embankment of a fort, often including any walls, parapets, walks, etc., that are built on the bank. 2 anything resembling a rampart in form or function, esp in being a defence or bulwark. 3 *Canadian* a steep rock wall in a river gorge. ◆ VERB 4 (*tr*) to provide with a rampart; fortify.
▷ HISTORY C16: from Old French, from *remparer*, from RE- + *emparer* to take possession of, from Old Provençal *antparar*, from Latin *ante* before + *parāre* to prepare

ramp down VERB (*adverb*) 1 to decrease or cause to decrease. 2 (*intr*) to decrease the effort involved in a process.

rampion ('ræmpɪən) NOUN 1 a campanulaceous plant, *Campanula rapunculus*, native to Europe and Asia, that has clusters of bluish flowers and an edible white tuberous root used in salads. 2 any of several plants of the related genus *Phyteuma* that are native to Europe and Asia and have heads of blue flowers.
▷ HISTORY C16: probably from Old French *raiponce*, from Old Italian *raponzo*, from *rapa* turnip, from Latin *rāpum* turnip; see RAPE[2]

ramp up VERB (*adverb*) 1 to increase or cause to increase. 2 (*intr*) to increase the effort involved in a process.

Rampur ('ræmpʊə) NOUN a city in N India, in N Uttar Pradesh. Pop.: 243 742 (1991).

ram raid NOUN *Informal* a raid in which a stolen car is driven through a shop window in order to steal goods from the shop.
▸ **ram raiding** NOUN ▸ **ram raider** NOUN

ramrod ('ræmˌrɒd) NOUN 1 a rod for cleaning the barrel of a rifle or other small firearms. 2 a rod for ramming in the charge of a muzzle-loading firearm.

Ramsgate ('ræmzˌgeɪt) NOUN a port and resort in SE England, in E Kent on the North Sea coast. Pop.: 37 895 (1991).

ramshackle ('ræmˌʃækəl) ADJECTIVE (esp of buildings) badly constructed or maintained; rickety, shaky, or derelict.
▷ HISTORY C17 *ramshackled*, from obsolete *ransackle* to RANSACK

ramshorn snail ('ræmzˌhɔːn) NOUN any of various freshwater snails of the genus *Planorbis* that are widely used in aquariums.

ramsons ('ræmzənz, -sənz) PLURAL NOUN (*usually functioning as singular*) 1 a broad-leaved garlic, *Allium ursinum*, native to Europe and Asia. 2 the bulbous root of this plant, eaten as a relish.
▷ HISTORY Old English *hramesa*; related to Middle Low German *ramese* Norwegian *rams*

ramstam ('ræm'stæm) *Scot* ◆ ADVERB 1 headlong; hastily. ◆ ADJECTIVE 2 headlong; precipitate.
▷ HISTORY C18: perhaps from RAM + dialect *stam* to stamp

ramtil ('ræmtɪl) NOUN 1 an African plant, *Guizotia abyssinica*, grown in India: family *Asteraceae* (composites). 2 Also called: **Niger seed**. the seed of this plant, used as a source of oil and a bird food.
▷ HISTORY C19: from Hindi, from Sanskrit *rāma* black + *tila* sesame

ramulose ('ræmjʊˌləʊs) *or* **ramulous** ('ræmjʊləs) ADJECTIVE (of the parts or organs of animals and plants) having many small branches.
▷ HISTORY C18: from Latin *rāmulōsus* full of branching veins, from *rāmulus* twig, from *rāmus* branch

ramus ('reɪməs) NOUN, *plural* **-mi** (-maɪ). 1 the barb of a bird's feather. 2 either of the two parts of the lower jaw of a vertebrate. 3 any part or organ that branches from another part.
▷ HISTORY C19: from Latin: branch

ran (ræn) VERB the past tense of **run**.

RAN ABBREVIATION FOR Royal Australian Navy.

Rancagua (*Spanish* raŋ'kaɣwa) NOUN a city in central Chile. Pop.: 202 067 (1999 est.).

rance (rɑːns) NOUN a type of red marble, often with white or blue graining, that comes from Belgium.
▷ HISTORY C19: apparently from French *ranche* rod, pole

ranch (rɑːntʃ) NOUN 1 a large tract of land, esp one in North America, together with the necessary personnel, buildings, and equipment, for rearing livestock, esp cattle. 2 **a** any large farm for the rearing of a particular kind of livestock or crop: *a mink ranch*. **b** the buildings, land, etc., connected with it. ◆ VERB 3 (*intr*) to manage or run a ranch. 4 (*tr*) to raise (animals) on or as if on a ranch.
▷ HISTORY C19: from Mexican Spanish *rancho* small farm; see RANCHO

rancher ('rɑːntʃə) NOUN a person who owns, manages, or works on a ranch.

rancherie ('rɑːntʃərɪ) NOUN (in British Columbia, Canada) a settlement of North American Indians, esp on a reserve.
▷ HISTORY from Spanish *rancheria*

ranchero (rɑːn'tʃɛərəʊ) NOUN, *plural* **-ros**. *Southwestern US* another word for **rancher**.
▷ HISTORY C19: from American Spanish

Ranchi ('ræntʃɪ) NOUN an industrial city in E India, between the coal and iron belts of the Chota Nagpur Plateau; the capital of Jharkand from 2000. Pop.: 599 306 (1991).

rancho ('rɑːntʃəʊ) NOUN, *plural* **-chos**. *Southwestern US* 1 a hut or group of huts for housing ranch workers. 2 another word for **ranch**.
▷ HISTORY C17: from Mexican Spanish: camp, from Old Spanish *ranchar* to be billeted, from Old French *ranger* to place

rancid ('rænsɪd) ADJECTIVE 1 (of butter, bacon, etc.) having an unpleasant stale taste or smell as the result of decomposition. 2 (of a taste or smell) rank or sour; stale.
▷ HISTORY C17: from Latin *rancidus* rank, from *rancēre* to stink
▸ **rancidity** (ræn'sɪdɪtɪ) *or* **'rancidness** NOUN

rancour *or US* **rancor** ('ræŋkə) NOUN malicious resentfulness or hostility; spite.
▷ HISTORY C14: from Old French, from Late Latin *rancor* rankness
▸ **'rancorous** ADJECTIVE ▸ **'rancorously** ADVERB
▸ **'rancorousness** NOUN

rand[1] (rænd, rɒnt) NOUN the standard monetary unit of the Republic of South Africa, divided into 100 cents.
▷ HISTORY C20: from Afrikaans, shortened from WITWATERSRAND, referring to the gold-mining there; related to RAND[2]

rand[2] (rænd) NOUN 1 *Shoemaking* a leather strip put in the heel of a shoe before the lifts are put on. 2 *Dialect* **a** a strip or margin; border. **b** a strip of cloth; selvage.
▷ HISTORY Old English; related to Old High German *rant* border, rim of a shield, Old Norse *rönd* shield, rim

Rand (rænd) NOUN **the**. short for **Witwatersrand**.

R & A ABBREVIATION FOR Royal and Ancient (Golf Club, St Andrews).

randan[1] (ræn'dæn, 'rændæn) NOUN a boat rowed by three people, in which the person in the middle uses two oars and the people fore and aft use one oar each.
▷ HISTORY C19: of uncertain origin

randan[2] (ˌræn'dæn, 'rænˌdæn) NOUN rowdy behaviour; a spree.
▷ HISTORY C18: perhaps changed from RANDOM

R & B ABBREVIATION FOR rhythm and blues.

R & D ABBREVIATION FOR research and development.

randem ('rændɛm) ADVERB 1 with three horses harnessed together as a team. ◆ NOUN 2 a carriage or team of horses so driven.
▷ HISTORY C19: probably from RANDOM + TANDEM

Randers (*Danish* 'randərs) NOUN a port and industrial centre in Denmark, in E Jutland on **Randers Fjord** (an inlet of the Kattegat). Pop.: 61 435 (1995).

randlord ('rændˌlɔːd) NOUN *South African* a mining magnate during the 19th-century gold boom in Johannesburg.

random ('rændəm) ADJECTIVE 1 lacking any definite plan or prearranged order; haphazard: *a random selection*. 2 *Statistics* **a** having a value which cannot be determined but only described probabilistically: *a random variable*. **b** chosen without regard to any characteristics of the individual members of the population so that each has an equal chance of being selected: *random sampling*. 3 *Informal* (of a person) unknown: *some random guy waiting for a bus*. ◆ NOUN 4 **at random**. in a purposeless fashion; not following any prearranged order.
▷ HISTORY C14: from Old French *randon*, from *randir* to gallop, of Germanic origin; compare Old High German *rinnan* to run
▸ **'randomly** ADVERB ▸ **'randomness** NOUN

random access NOUN another name for **direct access**.

random access memory NOUN See **RAM**.

randomize *or* **randomise** ('rændəˌmaɪz) VERB (*tr*) to set up (a selection process, sample, etc.) in a deliberately random way in order to enhance the statistical validity of any results obtained.
▸ **ˌrandomi'zation** *or* **ˌrandomi'sation** NOUN ▸ **'randomˌizer** *or* **'randomˌiser** NOUN

random numbers PLURAL NOUN a sequence of numbers that do not form any progression, used to facilitate unbiased sampling of a population. A **random-number generator** is part of the software of most computers and many calculators.

random rubble NOUN masonry in which untooled stones are set without coursing.

random variable NOUN *Statistics* a quantity that may take any of a range of values, either continuous or discrete, which cannot be predicted with certainty but only described probabilistically. Abbreviation: **rv**.

random walk NOUN 1 a mathematical model used to describe physical processes, such as diffusion, in which a particle moves in straight-line steps of constant length but random direction. 2 *Statistics* a route consisting of successive and connected steps in which each step is chosen by a random mechanism uninfluenced by any previous step.

random walk theory NOUN *Stock Exchange* the

theory that the future movement of share prices does not reflect past movements and therefore will not follow a discernible pattern.

R and R *US military* ABBREVIATION FOR rest and recreation.

randy (ˈrændɪ) ADJECTIVE **randier, randiest.** 1 *Informal, chiefly Brit* **a** sexually excited or aroused. **b** sexually eager or lustful. 2 *Chiefly Scot* lacking any sense of propriety or restraint; reckless. ◆ NOUN, *plural* **randies.** 3 *Chiefly Scot* **a** a rude or reckless person. **b** a coarse rowdy woman.
▷HISTORY C17: probably from obsolete *rand* to RANT
▸ˈ**randily** ADVERB ▸ˈ**randiness** NOUN

ranee (ˈrɑːnɪ) NOUN a variant spelling of **rani.**

Ranelagh Gardens (ˈrænɪlə) PLURAL NOUN a public garden in Chelsea opened in 1742: a centre for members of fashionable society to meet and promenade. The gardens were closed in 1804. Also called: **Ranelagh.**
▷HISTORY named after the Earl of *Ranelagh*, in whose grounds they were sited

Ranfurly Shield (rænˈfɜːlɪ) NOUN (in New Zealand) the premier rugby trophy, competed for annually by provincial teams.
▷HISTORY C20: named after the Earl of *Ranfurly* (1856–1933), 15th Governor of New Zealand (1897–1904), who presented it to the New Zealand Rugby Football Union in 1902

rang (ræŋ) VERB the past tense of **ring**[2].

Language note See at **ring**[2].

rangatira (ˌrʌŋgəˈtɪərə) NOUN *NZ* a Maori chief of either sex.
▷HISTORY Maori

rangatiratanga (ˌrʌŋgətɪərəˈtʌŋgə) NOUN *NZ* the condition of being a Maori chief; sovereignty.
▷HISTORY Maori

range (reɪndʒ) NOUN 1 the limits within which a person or thing can function effectively: *the range of vision.* 2 the limits within which any fluctuation takes place: *a range of values.* 3 the total products of a manufacturer, designer, or stockist: *the new autumn range.* 4 **a** the maximum effective distance of a projectile fired from a weapon. **b** the distance between a target and a weapon. 5 an area set aside for shooting practice or rocket testing. 6 the total distance which a ship, aircraft, or land vehicle is capable of covering without taking on fresh fuel: *the range of this car is about 160 miles.* 7 *Physics* the distance that a particle of ionizing radiation, such as an electron or proton, can travel through a given medium, esp air, before ceasing to cause ionization. 8 *Maths, logic* **a** (of a function) the set of values that the function takes for all possible arguments. Compare **domain** (sense 7a). **b** (of a variable) the set of values that a variable can take. **c** (of a quantifier) the set of values that the variable bound by the quantifier can take. 9 *Statistics* a measure of dispersion obtained by subtracting the smallest from the largest sample values. 10 the extent of pitch difference between the highest and lowest notes of a voice, instrument, etc. 11 *US and Canadian* **a** an extensive tract of open land on which livestock can graze. **b** (*as modifier*): *range cattle.* 12 the geographical region in which a species of plant or animal normally grows or lives. 13 a rank, row, or series of items. 14 a series or chain of mountains. 15 a large stove with burners and one or more ovens, usually heated by solid fuel. 16 the act or process of ranging. 17 *Nautical* a line of sight taken from the sea along two or more navigational aids that mark a navigable channel. 18 the extension or direction of a survey line, established by marking two or more points. 19 a double-faced bookcase, as in a library. 20 **range of significance.** *Philosophy, logic* the set of subjects for which a given predicate is intelligible. ◆ VERB 21 to establish or be situated in a line, row, or series. 22 (*tr; often reflexive*, foll by *with*) to put into a specific category; classify: *she ranges herself with the angels.* 23 (foll by *on*) to aim or point (a telescope, gun, etc.) or (of a gun, telescope, etc.) to be pointed or aimed. 24 to establish the distance of (a target) from (a weapon). 25 (*intr*) (of a gun or missile) to have a specified range. 26 (when *intr*, foll by *over*) to wander about (in) an area; roam (over). 27 (*intr*; foll by *over*) (of an animal or plant) to live or grow in its normal habitat. 28 (*tr*) to put (cattle) to graze on a range. 29 (*intr*) to fluctuate within specific limits: *their ages range from 18 to 21.* 30 (*intr*) to extend or run in a specific direction. 31 (*tr*) *Nautical* to coil (an anchor rope or chain) so that it will pay out smoothly. 32 (*intr*) *Nautical* (of a vessel) to swing back and forth while at anchor. 33 (*tr*) to make (lines of printers' type) level or even at the margin.
▷HISTORY C13: from Old French: row, from *ranger* to position, from *renc* line

rangefinder (ˈreɪndʒˌfaɪndə) NOUN 1 an instrument for determining the distance of an object from the observer, esp in order to sight a gun or focus a camera. 2 another word for **tacheometer.**

rangeland (ˈreɪndʒˌlænd) NOUN (*often plural*) land that naturally produces forage plants suitable for grazing but where rainfall is too low or erratic for growing crops.

range light NOUN *Nautical* 1 one of a pattern of navigation lights, usually fixed ashore, used by vessels for manoeuvring in narrow channels at night. 2 one of a distinctive pattern of lights shown at night on the masts of a powered vessel, such as a tugboat, to aid in identifying its size, number of barges in tow, etc.

ranger (ˈreɪndʒə) NOUN 1 (*sometimes capital*) an official in charge of a forest, park, estate, nature reserve, etc. 2 *Chiefly US* a person employed to patrol a State or national park or forest. Brit equivalent: **warden.** 3 *US* one of a body of armed troops employed to police a State or district: *a Texas Ranger.* 4 (in the US and certain other armies) a commando specially trained in making raids. 5 a person who wanders about large areas of country; a rover.

Ranger[1] *or* **Ranger Guide** (ˈreɪndʒə) NOUN *Brit* a member of the senior branch of the Guides.

Ranger[2] (ˈreɪndʒə) NOUN any of a series of nine American lunar probes launched between 1961 and 1965, three of which transmitted to earth photographs of the moon.

ranging pole *or* **rod** NOUN a pole for marking positions in surveying. Also called: **range pole, rod.**

rangiora (ˌræŋgɪˈɔːrə, ˌræŋɪ-) NOUN an evergreen shrub or small tree, *Brachyglottis repanda*, of New Zealand, having large ovate leaves and small greenish-white flowers: family *Asteraceae* (composites).
▷HISTORY Maori

Rangoon (ræŋˈguːn) NOUN the former name (until 1989) of **Yangon.**

rangy (ˈreɪndʒɪ) ADJECTIVE **rangier, rangiest.** 1 (of animals or people) having long slender limbs. 2 adapted to wandering or roaming. 3 allowing considerable freedom of movement; spacious; roomy.
▷HISTORY C19: from RANGE + -Y[1]
▸ˈ**rangily** ADVERB ▸ˈ**ranginess** NOUN

rani *or* **ranee** (ˈrɑːnɪ) NOUN (in oriental countries, esp India) a queen or princess; the wife of a rajah.
▷HISTORY C17: from Hindi: queen, from Sanskrit *rājñī*, feminine of *rājan* RAJAH

rank[1] (ræŋk) NOUN 1 a position, esp an official one, within a social organization, esp the armed forces: *the rank of captain.* 2 high social or other standing; status. 3 a line or row of people or things. 4 the position of an item in any ordering or sequence. 5 *Brit* a place where taxis wait to be hired. 6 a line of soldiers drawn up abreast of each other. Compare **file**[1] (sense 5). 7 any of the eight horizontal rows of squares on a chessboard. 8 (in systemic grammar) one of the units of description of which a grammar is composed. Ranks of English grammar are sentence, clause, group, word, and morpheme. 9 *Music* a set of organ pipes controlled by the same stop. 10 *Maths* (of a matrix) the largest number of linearly independent rows or columns; the number of rows (or columns) of the nonzero determinant of greatest order that can be extracted from the matrix. 11 **break ranks.** *Military* to fall out of line, esp when under attack. 12 **close ranks.** to maintain discipline or solidarity, esp in anticipation of attack. 13 **pull rank.** to get one's own way by virtue of one's superior position or rank. ◆ VERB 14 (*tr*) to arrange (people or things) in rows or lines; range. 15 to accord or be accorded a specific position in an organization, society, or group. 16 (*tr*) to array (a set of objects) as a sequence, esp in terms of the natural arithmetic ordering of some measure of the elements: *to rank students by their test scores.* 17 (*intr*) to be important; rate: *money ranks low in her order of priorities.* 18 *Chiefly US* to take precedence or surpass in rank: *the colonel ranks at this camp.*
▷HISTORY C16: from Old French *ranc* row, rank, of Germanic origin; compare Old High German *hring* circle

rank[2] (ræŋk) ADJECTIVE 1 showing vigorous and profuse growth: *rank weeds.* 2 highly offensive or disagreeable, esp in smell or taste. 3 (*prenominal*) complete or absolute; utter: *a rank outsider.* 4 coarse or vulgar; gross: *his language was rank.*
▷HISTORY Old English *ranc* straight, noble; related to Old Norse *rakkr* upright, Dutch, Swedish *rank* tall and thin, weak
▸ˈ**rankly** ADVERB ▸ˈ**rankness** NOUN

rank and file NOUN 1 the ordinary soldiers of an army, excluding the officers. 2 the great mass or majority of any group or organization, as opposed to the leadership. 3 (*modifier*) of, relating to, or characteristic of the rank and file: *rank-and-file opinion; rank-and-file support.*
▸**rank and filer** NOUN

ranker (ˈræŋkə) NOUN 1 a soldier in the ranks. 2 a commissioned officer who entered service as a recruit, esp in the army.

Rankine cycle (ˈræŋkɪn) NOUN the thermodynamic cycle in steam engines by which water is pumped into a boiler at one end and the steam is condensed at the other.
▷HISTORY C19: named after W. J. M. *Rankine* (1820–72), Scottish physicist

Rankine scale NOUN an absolute scale of temperature in which the unit of temperature is equal to that on the Fahrenheit scale and the zero value of temperature is equal to –459.67°F. Compare **Kelvin scale.**

ranking (ˈræŋkɪŋ) ADJECTIVE 1 *Chiefly US and Canadian* prominent; high ranking. 2 *Caribbean slang* possessed of style; fashionable; exciting. ◆ NOUN 3 a position on a scale; rating: *a ranking in a tennis tournament.*

rankle (ˈræŋkᵊl) VERB (*intr*) to cause severe and continuous irritation, anger, or bitterness; fester: *his failure to win still rankles.*
▷HISTORY C14 *ranclen*, from Old French *draoncler* to fester, from *draoncle* ulcer, from Latin *dracunculus* small serpent, from *dracō* serpent; see DRAGON

rankshift (ˈræŋkˌʃɪft) (in systemic grammar) NOUN 1 a phenomenon in which a unit at one rank in the grammar has the function of a unit at a lower rank, as for example in the phrase *the house on the corner*, where the words *on the corner* shift down from the rank of group to the rank of word. ◆ VERB 2 to shift or be shifted from one linguistic rank to another.

ransack (ˈrænsæk) VERB (*tr*) 1 to search through every part of (a house, box, etc.); examine thoroughly. 2 to plunder; pillage.
▷HISTORY C13: from Old Norse *rann* house + *saka* to search, SEEK
▸ˈ**ransacker** NOUN

ransom (ˈrænsəm) NOUN 1 the release of captured prisoners, property, etc., on payment of a stipulated price. 2 the price demanded or stipulated for such a release. 3 rescue or redemption of any kind. 4 **hold to ransom. a** to keep (prisoners, property, etc.) in confinement until payment for their release is made or received. **b** to attempt to force (a person or persons) to comply with one's demands. 5 **a king's ransom.** a very large amount of money or valuables. ◆ VERB (*tr*) 6 to pay a stipulated price and so obtain the release of (prisoners, property, etc.). 7 to set free (prisoners, property, etc.) upon receiving the payment demanded. 8 to redeem; rescue: *Christ ransomed men from sin.*
▷HISTORY C14: from Old French *ransoun*, from Latin *redemptiō* a buying back, REDEMPTION
▸ˈ**ransomer** NOUN

rant (rænt) VERB 1 to utter (something) in loud, violent, or bombastic tones. 2 (*intr*) *Chiefly Scot* to make merry; frolic. ◆ NOUN 3 loud, declamatory, or extravagant speech; bombast. 4 *Chiefly Scot* a wild revel. 5 *Scot* an energetic dance or its tune.

▷HISTORY C16: from Dutch *ranten* to rave; related to German *ranzen* to gambol
▸ '**ranter** NOUN ▸ '**ranting** ADJECTIVE, NOUN ▸ '**rantingly** ADVERB

ranula ('rænjʊlə) a saliva-filled cyst that develops under the tongue.
▷HISTORY C17: from Latin *rana* frog + *-ula* from Latin *-ulus*, small

ranunculaceous (rəˌnʌŋkjʊ'leɪʃəs) ADJECTIVE of, relating to, or belonging to the *Ranunculaceae*, a N temperate family of flowering plants typically having flowers with five petals and numerous anthers and styles. The family includes the buttercup, clematis, hellebore, and columbine.

ranunculus (rə'nʌŋkjʊləs) NOUN, *plural* **-luses** *or* **-li** (-ˌlaɪ). any ranunculaceous plant of the genus *Ranunculus*, having finely divided leaves and typically yellow five-petalled flowers. The genus includes buttercup, crowfoot, spearwort, and lesser celandine.
▷HISTORY C16: from Latin: tadpole, from *rāna* a frog

RAOC ABBREVIATION FOR Royal Army Ordnance Corps.

rap[1] (ræp) VERB **raps, rapping, rapped.** 1 to strike (a fist, stick, etc.) against (something) with a sharp quick blow; knock: *he rapped at the door.* 2 (*intr*) to make a sharp loud sound, esp by knocking. 3 (*tr*) to rebuke or criticize sharply. 4 (*tr*; foll by *out*) to put (forth) in sharp rapid speech; utter in an abrupt fashion: *to rap out orders.* 5 (*intr*) *Slang* to talk, esp volubly. 6 (*intr*) to perform a rhythmic monologue with a musical backing. 7 **rap over the knuckles.** to reprimand. ◆ NOUN 8 a sharp quick blow or the sound produced by such a blow. 9 a sharp rebuke or criticism. 10 *Slang* voluble talk; chatter: *stop your rap.* 11 **a** a fast, rhythmic monologue over a prerecorded instrumental track. **b** (*as modifier*): *rap music.* 12 *Slang* a legal charge or case. 13 **beat the rap.** *US and Canadian slang* to escape punishment or be acquitted of a crime. 14 **take the rap.** *Slang* to suffer the consequences of a mistake, misdeed, or crime, whether guilty or not.
▷HISTORY C14: probably of Scandinavian origin; compare Swedish *rappa* to beat
▸ '**rapping** NOUN

rap[2] (ræp) NOUN (*used with a negative*) the least amount (esp in the phrase **not to care a rap**).
▷HISTORY C18: probably from *ropaire* counterfeit coin formerly current in Ireland

rap[3] (ræp) VERB, NOUN *Austral informal* a variant spelling of **wrap** (senses 8, 14).

rapacious (rə'peɪʃəs) ADJECTIVE 1 practising pillage or rapine. 2 greedy or grasping. 3 (of animals, esp birds) subsisting by catching living prey.
▷HISTORY C17: from Latin *rapāx* grasping, from *rapere* to seize
▸ **ra'paciously** ADVERB ▸ **rapacity** (rə'pæsɪtɪ) *or* **ra'paciousness** NOUN

Rapacki Plan (*Polish* ra'patski) NOUN the denuclearization of Poland, Czechoslovakia, East Germany, and West Germany, proposed by Adam *Rapacki* (1909–70), the Polish foreign minister, in 1957.

Rapallo (*Italian* ra'pallo) NOUN a port and resort in NW Italy, in Liguria on the **Gulf of Rapallo** (an inlet of the Ligurian Sea): scene of the signing of two treaties after World War I. Pop.: 30 000 (1990 est.).

Rapa Nui ('rɑːpɑː 'nuːɪ) NOUN another name for **Easter Island.**

rape[1] (reɪp) NOUN 1 the offence of forcing a person, esp a woman, to submit to sexual intercourse against that person's will. See also **statutory rape.** 2 the act of despoiling a country in warfare; rapine. 3 any violation or abuse: *the rape of justice.* 4 *Archaic* abduction: *the rape of the Sabine women.* ◆ VERB (*mainly tr*) 5 to commit rape upon (a person). 6 (*also intr*) to plunder or despoil (a place) in war. 7 *Archaic* to carry off by force; abduct.
▷HISTORY C14: from Latin *rapere* to seize

rape[2] (reɪp) NOUN a Eurasian plant, *Brassica napus*, that has bright yellow flowers and is cultivated for its seeds, which yield a useful oil, and as a fodder plant: family *Brassicaceae* (crucifers). Also called: **colza, cole.**
▷HISTORY C14: from Latin *rāpum* turnip

rape[3] (reɪp) NOUN (*often plural*) the skins and stalks of grapes left after wine-making: used in making vinegar.
▷HISTORY C17: from French *râpe*, of Germanic origin; compare Old High German *raspōn* to scrape together

rapeseed ('reɪpˌsiːd) NOUN the seed of the rape plant.

rapeseed oil NOUN oil extracted from rapeseed, used as a lubricant, as a constituent of soaps, etc. Also called: **rape oil, colza oil.**

raphe ('reɪfɪ) NOUN, *plural* **-phae** (-fiː). 1 an elongated ridge of conducting tissue along the side of certain seeds. 2 a longitudinal groove on the valve of a diatom. 3 *Anatomy* a connecting ridge, such as that between the two halves of the medulla oblongata.
▷HISTORY C18: via New Latin from Greek *rhaphē* a seam, from *rhaptein* to sew together

raphia ('ræfɪə) NOUN a variant spelling of **raffia.**

raphide ('reɪfaɪd) *or* **raphis** ('reɪfɪs) NOUN, *plural* **raphides** ('ræfɪˌdiːz). any of numerous needle-shaped crystals, usually of calcium oxalate, that occur in many plant cells as a metabolic product.
▷HISTORY C18: from French, from Greek *rhaphis* needle

rapid ('ræpɪd) ADJECTIVE 1 (of an action or movement) performed or occurring during a short interval of time; quick: *a rapid transformation.* 2 characterized by high speed: *rapid movement.* 3 acting or moving quickly; fast: *a rapid worker.* ◆ See also **rapids.**
▷HISTORY C17: from Latin *rapidus* tearing away, from *rapere* to seize; see RAPE[1]
▸ '**rapidly** ADVERB ▸ **rapidity** (rə'pɪdɪtɪ) *or* '**rapidness** NOUN

rapid eye movement NOUN movement of the eyeballs under closed eyelids during paradoxical sleep, which occurs while the sleeper is dreaming. Abbreviation: **REM.**

rapid fire NOUN 1 a fast rate of gunfire. ◆ ADJECTIVE **rapid-fire.** 2 **a** firing shots rapidly. **b** denoting medium-calibre mounted guns designed for rapid fire. 3 done, delivered, or occurring in rapid succession.

rapids ('ræpɪdz) PLURAL NOUN part of a river where the current is very fast and turbulent.

rapid transit chess NOUN the US name for **lightning chess.**
▷HISTORY from the name of the New York City underground railway system

rapier ('reɪpɪə) NOUN 1 a long narrow two-edged sword with a guarded hilt, used as a thrusting weapon, popular in the 16th and 17th centuries. 2 a smaller single-edged 18th-century sword, used principally in France.
▷HISTORY C16: from Old French *espee rapiere*, literally: rasping sword; see RASP[1]
▸ '**rapier-ˌlike** ADJECTIVE

rapine ('ræpaɪn) NOUN the seizure of property by force; pillage.
▷HISTORY C15: from Latin *rapīna* plundering, from *rapere* to snatch

rapist ('reɪpɪst) NOUN a person who commits rape.

rap jumping NOUN the sport of descending high buildings, attached to ropes and a pulley.

rapparee (ˌræpə'riː) NOUN 1 an Irish irregular soldier of the late 17th century. 2 *Obsolete* any plunderer or robber.
▷HISTORY C17: from Irish *rapairidhe* pike, probably from English RAPIER

rappee (ræ'piː) NOUN a moist English snuff of the 18th and 19th centuries.
▷HISTORY C18: from French *tabac râpé*, literally: scraped tobacco, from *râper* to scrape; see RAPE[3], RASP[1]

rappel (ræ'pɛl) VERB **-pels, -pelling, -pelled,** NOUN 1 another word for **abseil.** ◆ NOUN 2 (formerly) a drumbeat to call soldiers to arms.
▷HISTORY C19: from French, from *rappeler* to call back, from Latin *appellāre* to summon

rappé pie *or* **rappe** ('ræpeɪ) NOUN *Canadian* an Acadian dish of grated potatoes and pork or chicken.
▷HISTORY from Acadian French *tarte râpée* grated pie

rapper ('ræpə) NOUN 1 something used for rapping, such as a knocker on a door. 2 a performer of rap music.

rapport (ræ'pɔː) NOUN (often foll by *with*) a sympathetic relationship or understanding. See also **en rapport.**
▷HISTORY C15: from French, from *rapporter* to bring back, from RE- + *aporter*, from Latin *apportāre*, from *ad*to + *portāre* to carry

rapporteur (ˌræpɔː'tɜː) NOUN a person appointed by a committee to prepare reports of meetings or carry out an investigation.
▷HISTORY C18: from French, literally: recorder, reporter

rapprochement *French* (raprɔʃmɑ̃) NOUN a resumption of friendly relations, esp between two countries.
▷HISTORY C19: literally: bringing closer

rapscallion (ræp'skæljən) NOUN a disreputable person; rascal or rogue.
▷HISTORY C17: from earlier *rascallion*; see RASCAL

rapt[1] (ræpt) ADJECTIVE 1 totally absorbed; engrossed; spellbound, esp through or as if through emotion: *rapt with wonder.* 2 characterized by or proceeding from rapture: *a rapt smile.*
▷HISTORY C14: from Latin *raptus* carried away, from *rapere* to seize; see RAPE[1]
▸ '**raptly** ADVERB

rapt[2] (ræpt) ADJECTIVE Also: **wrapped.** *Austral and NZ informal* very pleased; delighted.

raptor ('ræptə) NOUN 1 another name for **bird of prey.** 2 *Informal* a carnivorous bipedal dinosaur of the late Cretaceous period.
▷HISTORY C17: from Latin: plunderer, from *rapere* to take by force

raptorial (ræp'tɔːrɪəl) ADJECTIVE *Zoology* 1 (of the feet of birds) adapted for seizing prey. 2 (esp of birds) feeding on prey; predatory. 3 of or relating to birds of prey.
▷HISTORY C19: from Latin *raptor* a robber, from *rapere* to snatch

rapture ('ræptʃə) NOUN 1 the state of mind resulting from feelings of high emotion; joyous ecstasy. 2 (*often plural*) an expression of ecstatic joy. 3 the act of transporting a person from one sphere of existence to another, esp from earth to heaven. ◆ VERB 4 (*tr*) *Archaic or literary* to entrance; enrapture.
▷HISTORY C17: from Medieval Latin *raptūra*, from Latin *raptus* RAPT[1]

rapturous ('ræptʃərəs) ADJECTIVE experiencing or manifesting ecstatic joy or delight.
▸ '**rapturously** ADVERB ▸ '**rapturousness** NOUN

RAR ABBREVIATION FOR Royal Australian Regiment.

rara avis ('rɛərə 'eɪvɪs) NOUN, *plural* **rarae aves** ('rɛəriː 'eɪviːz). an unusual, uncommon, or exceptional person or thing.
▷HISTORY Latin: rare bird

rare[1] (rɛə) ADJECTIVE 1 not widely known; not frequently used or experienced; uncommon or unusual: *a rare word.* 2 occurring seldom: *a rare appearance.* 3 not widely distributed; not generally occurring: *a rare herb.* 4 (of a gas, esp the atmosphere at high altitudes) having a low density; thin; rarefied. 5 uncommonly great; extreme: *kind to a rare degree.* 6 exhibiting uncommon excellence; superlatively good or fine: *rare skill.* 7 highly valued because of its uncommonness: *a rare prize.*
▷HISTORY C14: from Latin *rārus* sparse
▸ '**rareness** NOUN

rare[2] (rɛə) ADJECTIVE (of meat, esp beef) very lightly cooked.
▷HISTORY Old English *hrēr*; perhaps related to *hreaw* RAW

rarebit ('rɛəbɪt) NOUN another term for **Welsh rabbit.**
▷HISTORY C18: by folk etymology from (WELSH) RABBIT; see RARE[2], BIT[1]

rare earth NOUN 1 any oxide of a lanthanide. 2 Also called: **rare-earth element.** another name for **lanthanide.**

raree show ('rɛəriː) NOUN 1 a street show or carnival. 2 another name for **peepshow.**
▷HISTORY C17: *raree* from RARE[1]

rarefaction (ˌrɛərɪ'fækʃən) *or* **rarefication** (ˌrɛərɪfɪ'keɪʃən) NOUN the act or process of making less dense or the state of being less dense.
▸ ˌ**rare'factional** *or* ˌ**rarefi'cational** *or* ˌ**rare'factive** ADJECTIVE

rarefied ('rɛərɪˌfaɪd) ADJECTIVE 1 exalted in nature

or character; lofty: *a rarefied spiritual existence*. [2] current within only a small group; esoteric or exclusive. [3] (of a gas, esp the atmosphere at high altitudes) having a low density; thin.

rarefy ('rɛərɪˌfaɪ) VERB **-fies, -fying, -fied**. to make or become rarer or less dense; thin out.
▷HISTORY C14: from Old French *raréfier*, from Latin *rārēfacere*, from *rārus* RARE[1] + *facere* to make
▸**'rareˌfiable** ADJECTIVE ▸**'rareˌfier** NOUN

rare gas NOUN another name for **inert gas** (sense 1).

rarely ('rɛəlɪ) ADVERB [1] hardly ever; seldom: *I'm rarely in town these days*. [2] to an unusual degree; exceptionally. [3] *Dialect* uncommonly well; excellently: *he did rarely at market yesterday*.

> **Language note** Since *rarely* means *hardly ever*, one should not say something *rarely ever* happens.

rareripe ('rɛəˌraɪp) *US* ◆ ADJECTIVE [1] ripening early. ◆ NOUN [2] a fruit or vegetable that ripens early.
▷HISTORY C18 *rare*, variant of RATHE + RIPE

raring ('rɛərɪŋ) ADJECTIVE ready; willing; enthusiastic (esp in the phrase **raring to go**).
▷HISTORY C20: from *rare*, variant of REAR[2]

rarity ('rɛərɪtɪ) NOUN, *plural* **-ties**. [1] a rare person or thing, esp something interesting or valued because it is uncommon. [2] the state or quality of being rare.

rark up VERB (*tr, adverb*) *NZ informal* to give (someone) a severe reprimand.

Rarotonga (ˌrɛərə'tɒŋgə) NOUN an island in the S Pacific, in the SW Cook Islands: the chief island of the group. Chief settlement: Avarua. Pop.: 9281 (1986). Area: 67 sq. km (26 sq. miles).

RAS ABBREVIATION FOR: [1] Royal Agricultural Society. [2] Royal Astronomical Society.

rasbora (ræz'bɔːrə) NOUN any of the small cyprinid fishes constituting the genus *Rasbora* of tropical Asia and East Africa. Many species are brightly coloured and are popular aquarium fishes.
▷HISTORY from New Latin, from an East Indian language

RASC ABBREVIATION FOR (the former) Royal Army Service Corps, now called Royal Corps of Transport.

rascal ('rɑːskᵊl) NOUN [1] a disreputable person; villain. [2] a mischievous or impish rogue. [3] an affectionate or mildly reproving term for a child or old man: *you little rascal; the wicked old rascal kissed her*. [4] *Obsolete* a person of lowly birth. ◆ ADJECTIVE [5] (*prenominal*) *Obsolete* **a** belonging to the mob or rabble. **b** dishonest; knavish.
▷HISTORY C14: from Old French *rascaille* rabble, perhaps from Old Norman French *rasque* mud, filth

rascality (rɑː'skælɪtɪ) NOUN, *plural* **-ties**. mischievous, disreputable, or dishonest character, behaviour, or action.

rascally ('rɑːskəlɪ) ADJECTIVE [1] dishonest or mean; base. [2] *Archaic* (esp of places) wretchedly unpleasant; miserable. ◆ ADVERB [3] in a dishonest or mean fashion.

rase (reɪz) VERB a variant spelling of **raze**.

rash[1] (ræʃ) ADJECTIVE [1] acting without due consideration or thought; impetuous. [2] characterized by or resulting from excessive haste or impetuosity: *a rash word*.
▷HISTORY C14: from Old High German *rasc* hurried, clever; related to Old Norse *roskr* brave
▸**'rashly** ADVERB ▸**'rashness** NOUN

rash[2] (ræʃ) NOUN [1] *Pathol* any skin eruption. [2] a series of unpleasant and unexpected occurrences: *a rash of forest fires*.
▷HISTORY C18: from Old French *rasche*, from *raschier* to scratch, from Latin *rādere* to scrape
▸**'rashˌlike** ADJECTIVE

rasher ('ræʃə) NOUN a thin slice of bacon or ham.
▷HISTORY C16: of unknown origin

Rashid (ræ'ʃiːd) NOUN a town in N Egypt, on the Nile delta. Pop.: 52 015 (latest est.). Former name: **Rosetta**.

Rasht (ræʃt) *or* **Resht** NOUN a city in NW Iran, near the Caspian Sea: agricultural and commercial centre in a rice-growing area. Pop.: 417 748 (1996).

rasorial (rə'sɔːrɪəl) ADJECTIVE (of birds such as domestic poultry) adapted for scratching the ground for food.
▷HISTORY C19: from New Latin *Rasores* such birds, from Latin *rādere* to scrape

rasp[1] (rɑːsp) NOUN [1] a harsh grating noise. [2] a coarse file with rows of raised teeth. ◆ VERB [3] (*tr*) to scrape or rub (something) roughly, esp with a rasp; abrade. [4] to utter with or make a harsh grating noise. [5] to irritate (one's nerves or senses); grate (upon).
▷HISTORY C16: from Old French *raspe*, of Germanic origin; compare Old High German *raspōn* to scrape
▸**'rasper** NOUN ▸**'raspish** ADJECTIVE

rasp[2] (rɑːsp) NOUN another name, now Scottish or informal, for **raspberry**.

raspatory ('rɑːspətərɪ, -trɪ) NOUN, *plural* **-ies**. a surgical instrument for abrading; surgeon's rasp.
▷HISTORY C16: from Medieval Latin *raspatorium*

raspberry ('rɑːzbərɪ, -brɪ) NOUN, *plural* **-ries**. [1] any of the prickly shrubs of the rosaceous genus *Rubus*, such as *R. strigosus* of E North America and *R. idaeus* of Europe, that have pinkish-white flowers and typically red berry-like fruits (drupelets). See also **bramble**. [2] **a** the fruit of any such plant. **b** (*as modifier*): *raspberry jelly*. [3] **black raspberry**. Popular name: **blackcap**. **a** a related plant, *Rubus occidentalis*, of E North America, that has black berry-like fruits. **b** the fruit of this plant. [4] **a** a dark purplish-red colour. **b** (*as adjective*): *a raspberry dress*. [5] a spluttering noise made with the tongue and lips to express contempt (esp in the phrase **blow a raspberry**).
▷HISTORY C17: from earlier *raspis* raspberry, of unknown origin + BERRY: C19 in sense 5, from rhyming slang *raspberry tart* fart

rasping ('rɑːspɪŋ) *or* **raspy** ADJECTIVE (esp of a noise) harsh or grating; rough.

raspings ('rɑːspɪŋz) PLURAL NOUN browned breadcrumbs for coating fish and other foods before frying, baking, etc.

rasse ('ræsɪ, ræs) NOUN a small civet, *Viverricula indica*, of S and SE Asia.
▷HISTORY C19: from Javanese *rase*

Rasta ('ræstə) NOUN, ADJECTIVE short for **Rastafarian**.

Rastafarian (ˌræstə'fɛərɪən) NOUN [1] a member of an originally Jamaican religion that regards **Ras Tafari** (the former emperor of Ethiopia, Haile Selassie (1892–1975)) as God. ◆ ADJECTIVE [2] of, characteristic of, or relating to the Rastafarians.

raster ('ræstə) NOUN a pattern of horizontal scanning lines traced by an electron beam, esp on a television screen.
▷HISTORY C20: via German from Latin: rake, from *rādere* to scrape

rat (ræt) NOUN [1] any of numerous long-tailed murine rodents, esp of the genus *Rattus*, that are similar to but larger than mice and are now distributed all over the world. See also **brown rat, black rat**. [2] *Informal* a person who deserts his friends or associates, esp in time of trouble. [3] *Informal* a worker who works during a strike; blackleg; scab. [4] *Slang, chiefly US* an informer; stool pigeon. [5] *Informal* a despicable person. [6] **smell a rat**. to detect something suspicious. ◆ VERB **rats, ratting, ratted**. [7] (*intr*; usually foll by *on*) *Informal* **a** to divulge secret information (about); betray the trust (of). **b** to default (on); abandon: *he ratted on the project at the last minute*. [8] to hunt and kill rats. ◆ See also **rats**.
▷HISTORY Old English *rætt*; related to Old Saxon *ratta*, Old High German *rato*
▸**'ratˌlike** ADJECTIVE

rata ('rɑːtə) NOUN either of two New Zealand myrtaceous forest trees, *Metrosideros robusta* or *M. lucida*, having crimson flowers and hard wood.
▷HISTORY C19: from Maori

ratable *or* **rateable** ('reɪtəbᵊl) ADJECTIVE [1] able to be rated or evaluated. [2] *Brit* (of property) liable to payment of rates.
▸**ˌrata'bility** *or* **ˌratea'bility** *or* **'ratableness** *or* **'rateableness** NOUN ▸**'ratably** *or* **'rateably** ADVERB

ratable value *or* **rateable value** NOUN *Brit* (formerly) a fixed value assigned to a property by a local authority, on the basis of which variable annual rates are charged.

ratafia (ˌrætə'fɪə) *or* **ratafee** (ˌrætə'fiː) NOUN [1] any liqueur made from fruit or from brandy with added fruit. [2] a flavouring essence made from almonds. [3] *Chiefly Brit* Also called: **ratafia biscuit**. a small macaroon flavoured with almonds.
▷HISTORY C17: from West Indian Creole French

ratal ('reɪtᵊl) *Brit* ◆ NOUN [1] the amount on which rates are assessed; ratable value. ◆ ADJECTIVE [2] of or relating to rates (local taxation).
▷HISTORY C19: see RATE[1]

ratan (ræ'tæn) NOUN a variant spelling of **rattan**.

rataplan (ˌrætə'plæn) NOUN a drumming sound.
▷HISTORY from French, of imitative origin

rat-arsed ADJECTIVE *Brit slang* drunk.

rat-a-tat-tat ('rætəˌtæt'tæt) *or* **rat-a-tat** ('rætə'tæt) NOUN the sound of knocking on a door.

ratatouille (ˌrætə'twiː) NOUN a vegetable casserole made of tomatoes, aubergines, peppers, etc., fried in oil and stewed slowly.
▷HISTORY C19: from French, from *touiller* to stir, from Latin *tudiculāre*, from *tudes* hammer

ratbag ('rætˌbæg) NOUN *Slang* a despicable person.
▷HISTORY C20: from RAT + BAG

ratbaggery ('rætˌbægərɪ) NOUN *Austral slang* nonsense, eccentricity.

ratbite fever *or* **disease** ('rætˌbaɪt) NOUN *Pathol* an acute infectious febrile disease caused by the bite of a rat infected with either of two pathogenic bacteria (*Streptobacillus moniliformis* or *Spirillum minus*).

rat-catcher NOUN a person whose job is to destroy or drive away vermin, esp rats.

ratchet ('rætʃɪt) NOUN [1] a device in which a toothed rack or wheel is engaged by a pawl to permit motion in one direction only. [2] the toothed rack or wheel forming part of such a device.
▷HISTORY C17: from French *rochet*, from Old French *rocquet* blunt head of a lance, of Germanic origin: compare Old High German *rocko* distaff

ratchet effect NOUN *Economics* an effect that occurs when a price or wage increases as a result of temporary pressure but fails to fall back when the pressure is removed.

rate[1] (reɪt) NOUN [1] a quantity or amount considered in relation to or measured against another quantity or amount: *a rate of 70 miles an hour*. [2] **a** a price or charge with reference to a standard or scale: *rate of interest; rate of discount*. **b** (*as modifier*): *a rate card*. [3] a charge made per unit for a commodity, service, etc. [4] See **rates**. [5] the relative speed of progress or change of something variable; pace: *he works at a great rate; the rate of production has doubled*. [6] **a** relative quality; class or grade. **b** (*in combination*): *first-rate ideas*. [7] *Statistics* a measure of the frequency of occurrence of a given event, such as births and deaths, usually expressed as the number of times the event occurs for every thousand of the total population considered. [8] a wage calculated against a unit of time. [9] the amount of gain or loss of a timepiece. [10] **at any rate**. in any case; at all events; anyway. ◆ VERB (*mainly tr*) [11] (*also intr*) to assign or receive a position on a scale of relative values; rank: *he is rated fifth in the world*. [12] to estimate the value of; evaluate: *we rate your services highly*. [13] to be worthy of; deserve: *this hotel does not rate four stars*. [14] to consider; regard: *I rate him among my friends*. [15] *Brit* to assess the value of (property) for the purpose of local taxation. [16] *Slang* to think highly of: *the clients do not rate the new system*.
▷HISTORY C15: from Old French, from Medieval Latin *rata*, from Latin *prō ratā parte* according to a fixed proportion, from *ratus* fixed, from *rērī* to think, decide

rate[2] (reɪt) VERB (*tr*) to scold or criticize severely; rebuke harshly.
▷HISTORY C14: perhaps related to Swedish *rata* to chide

rateable ('reɪtəbᵊl) ADJECTIVE a variant spelling of **ratable**.

rate-cap ('reɪtˌkæp) VERB (*tr*) **-caps, -capping, -capped** (formerly in Britain) to impose on (a local authority) an upper limit on the level of the rate it may levy.
▸**'rate-ˌcapping** NOUN

rateen (ræ'tiːn) NOUN a variant spelling of **ratine**.

ratel ('reɪtᵊl) NOUN [1] a musteline mammal, *Mellivora capensis*, inhabiting wooded regions of Africa and S Asia. It has a massive body, strong

claws, and a thick coat that is paler on the back and it feeds on honey and small animals. Also called: **honey badger.** [2] *South African* a six-wheeled armoured vehicle.
▷HISTORY C18: from Afrikaans

rate of exchange NOUN See **exchange rate.**

rate of return NOUN *Finance* the ratio of the annual income from an investment to the original investment, often expressed as a percentage.

ratepayer (ˈreɪtˌpeɪə) NOUN a person who pays local rates, esp a householder.

rates (reɪts) PLURAL NOUN (in some countries) a tax levied on property by a local authority.

ratfink (ˈrætˌfɪŋk) NOUN *Slang, chiefly US and Canadian* a contemptible or undesirable person.
▷HISTORY C20: from RAT + FINK

ratfish (ˈrætˌfɪʃ) NOUN, *plural* **-fish** *or* **-fishes.** [1] another name for **rabbitfish** (sense 1). [2] a chimaera, *Hydrolagus colliei*, of the North Pacific Ocean, which has a long narrow tail.

rath (rɑθ) NOUN *Irish history* a circular enclosure surrounded by an earthen wall: used as a dwelling and stronghold in former times.
▷HISTORY C16: from Irish Gaelic

ratha (rʌt) NOUN (in India) a four-wheeled carriage drawn by horses or bullocks; chariot.
▷HISTORY Hindi

rathe (reɪð) *or* **rath** (rɑːθ) ADJECTIVE *Archaic or literary* [1] blossoming or ripening early in the season. [2] eager or prompt.
▷HISTORY Old English *hrathe*; related to Old High German *hrado*, Old Norse *hrathr*

rather (ˈrɑːðə) ADVERB (*in senses 1-4, not used with a negative*) [1] relatively or fairly; somewhat: *it's rather dull.* [2] to a significant or noticeable extent; quite: *she's rather pretty.* [3] to a limited extent or degree: *I rather thought that was the case.* [4] with better or more just cause: *this text is rather to be deleted than rewritten.* [5] more readily or willingly; sooner: *I would rather not see you tomorrow.* ◆ SENTENCE CONNECTOR [6] on the contrary: *it's not cold. Rather, it's very hot indeed.* ◆ SENTENCE SUBSTITUTE (ˈrɑːˈðɜː) [7] an expression of strong affirmation, often in answer to a question: *Is it worth seeing? Rather!*
▷HISTORY Old English *hrathor* comparative of *hræth* READY, quick; related to Old Norse *hrathr*

> **Language note** Both *would* and *had* are used with *rather* in sentences such as *I would rather* (or *had rather*) *go to the film than to the play. Had rather* is less common and is now widely regarded as slightly old-fashioned.

rathouse (ˈræthaʊs) NOUN *Austral slang* a psychiatric hospital or asylum.

ratify (ˈrætɪˌfaɪ) VERB **-fies, -fying, -fied.** (*tr*) to give formal approval or consent to.
▷HISTORY C14: via Old French from Latin *ratus* fixed (see RATE[1]) + *facere* to make
▸ˈ**ratiˌfiable** ADJECTIVE ▸ˌ**ratifiˈcation** NOUN ▸ˈ**ratiˌfier** NOUN

ratine, rateen, ratteen (ræˈtiːn), *or* **ratiné** (ˈrætɪˌneɪ) NOUN a coarse loosely woven cloth.
▷HISTORY C17: from French, from *ratine*, of obscure origin

rating[1] (ˈreɪtɪŋ) NOUN [1] a classification according to order or grade; ranking. [2] (in certain navies) a sailor who holds neither commissioned nor warrant rank; an ordinary seaman. [3] *Sailing* a handicap assigned to a racing boat based on its dimensions, sail area, weight, draught, etc. [4] the estimated financial or credit standing of a business enterprise or individual. [5] *Radio, television* a figure based on statistical sampling indicating what proportion of the total listening and viewing audience tune in to a specific programme or network.

rating[2] (ˈreɪtɪŋ) NOUN a sharp scolding or rebuke.

ratio (ˈreɪʃɪˌəʊ) NOUN, *plural* **-tios.** [1] a measure of the relative size of two classes expressible as a proportion: *the ratio of boys to girls is 2 to 1.* [2] *Maths* a quotient of two numbers or quantities. See also **proportion** (sense 6).
▷HISTORY C17: from Latin: a reckoning, from *rērī* to think; see REASON

ratiocinate (ˌrætɪˈɒsɪˌneɪt) VERB (*intr*) to think or argue logically and methodically; reason.
▷HISTORY C17: from Latin *ratiōcinārī* to calculate, from *ratiō* REASON
▸ˌ**ratiˌociˈnation** NOUN ▸ˌ**ratiˈocinative** ADJECTIVE ▸ˌ**ratiˈociˌnator** NOUN

ration (ˈræʃən) NOUN [1] **a** a fixed allowance of food, provisions, etc., esp a statutory one for civilians in time of scarcity or soldiers in time of war: *a tea ration.* **b** (*as modifier*): *a ration book.* [2] a sufficient or adequate amount: *you've had your ration of television for today.* ◆ VERB (*tr*) [3] (often foll by *out*) to distribute (provisions), esp to an army. [4] to restrict the distribution or consumption of (a commodity) by (people): *the government has rationed sugar; sugar is short, so I'll have to ration you.* ◆ See also **rations.**
▷HISTORY C18: via French from Latin *ratiō* calculation; see REASON

rational (ˈræʃənᵊl) ADJECTIVE [1] using reason or logic in thinking out a problem. [2] in accordance with the principles of logic or reason; reasonable. [3] of sound mind; sane: *the patient seemed quite rational.* [4] endowed with the capacity to reason; capable of logical thought: *man is a rational being.* [5] *Maths* expressible as a ratio of two integers or polynomials: *a rational number; a rational function.* ◆ NOUN [6] *Maths* a rational number.
▷HISTORY C14: from Latin *ratiōnālis*, from *ratiō* REASON
▸ˈ**rationally** ADVERB ▸ˈ**rationalness** NOUN

rationale (ˌræʃəˈnɑːl) NOUN a reasoned exposition, esp one defining the fundamental reasons for a course of action, belief, etc.
▷HISTORY C17: from New Latin, from Latin *ratiōnālis*

rationalism (ˈræʃənəˌlɪzəm) NOUN [1] reliance on reason rather than intuition to justify one's beliefs or actions. [2] *Philosophy* **a** the doctrine that knowledge about reality can be obtained by reason alone without recourse to experience. **b** the doctrine that human knowledge can all be encompassed within a single, usually deductive, system. **c** the school of philosophy initiated by René Descartes, the French philosopher and mathematician (1596–1650), which held both the above doctrines. [3] the belief that knowledge and truth are ascertained by rational thought and not by divine or supernatural revelation.
▸ˈ**rationalist** NOUN ▸ˌ**rationalˈistic** ADJECTIVE ▸ˌ**rationalˈistically** ADVERB

rationality (ˌræʃəˈnælɪtɪ) NOUN, *plural* **-ties.** [1] the state or quality of being rational or logical. [2] the possession or utilization of reason or logic. [3] a reasonable or logical opinion. [4] *Economics* the assumption that an individual will compare all possible combinations of goods and their prices when making purchases.

rationalize *or* **rationalise** (ˈræʃənəˌlaɪz) VERB [1] to justify (one's actions, esp discreditable actions, or beliefs) with plausible reasons, esp after the event. [2] *Psychol* to indulge, often unchallenged, in excuses for or explanations of (behaviour about which one feels uncomfortable or guilty). [3] to apply logic or reason to (something). [4] (*tr*) to eliminate unnecessary equipment, personnel, or processes from (a group of businesses, factory, etc.), in order to make it more efficient. [5] (*tr*) *Maths* to eliminate one or more radicals without changing the value of (an expression) or the roots of (an equation).
▸ˌ**rationaliˈzation** *or* ˌ**rationaliˈsation** NOUN ▸ˈ**rationalˌizer** *or* ˈ**rationalˌiser** NOUN

rational number NOUN any real number of the form *a*/*b*, where *a* and *b* are integers and *b* is not zero, as 7 or 7/3.

rations (ˈræʃənz) PLURAL NOUN (*sometimes singular*) a fixed daily allowance of food, esp to military personnel or when supplies are limited. See also **iron rations.**

ratio scale NOUN *Statistics* a scale of measurement of data which permits the comparison of differences of values; a scale having a fixed zero value. The distances travelled by a projectile, for instance, are measured on a ratio scale since it makes sense to talk of one projectile travelling twice as far as another. Compare **ordinal scale, interval scale, nominal scale.**

Ratisbon (ˈrætɪzˌbɒn) NOUN the former English name for **Regensburg.**

ratite (ˈrætaɪt) ADJECTIVE [1] (of flightless birds) having a breastbone that lacks a keel for the attachment of flight muscles. [2] of or denoting the flightless birds, formerly classified as a group (the *Ratitae*), that have a flat breastbone, feathers lacking vanes, and reduced wings. ◆ NOUN [3] a bird, such as an ostrich, kiwi, or rhea, that belongs to this group; a flightless bird.
▷HISTORY C19: from Latin *ratis* raft

rat kangaroo NOUN any of several ratlike kangaroos of the genera *Bettongia, Potorous, Aepyprymnus*, etc., found on the Australian mainland and in Tasmania.

ratline *or* **ratlin** (ˈrætlɪn) NOUN *Nautical* any of a series of light lines tied across the shrouds of a sailing vessel for climbing aloft.
▷HISTORY C15: of unknown origin

RATO (ˈreɪtəʊ) NOUN ACRONYM FOR rocket-assisted takeoff.

ratoon *or* **rattoon** (ræˈtuːn) NOUN [1] a new shoot that grows from near the root or crown of crop plants, esp the sugar cane, after the old growth has been cut back. ◆ VERB [2] to propagate or cause to propagate by such a growth.
▷HISTORY C18: from Spanish *retoño* young shoot, from RE- + *otoñar* to sprout in autumn, from *otoño* AUTUMN

ratpack (ˈrætˌpæk) NOUN *Derogatory slang* those members of the press who give wide, often intrusive, coverage of the private lives of celebrities: *the royal ratpack.*

rat race NOUN a continual routine of hectic competitive activity: *working in the City is a real rat race.*

rat-running NOUN the practice of driving through residential side streets to avoid congested main roads.
▸ˈ**rat-ˌrun** NOUN ▸ˈ**rat-ˌrunner** NOUN

rats (ræts) INTERJECTION [1] an exclamation of rejection or disdain. ◆ ADJECTIVE [2] *Austral slang* deranged; insane.

ratsbane (ˈrætsˌbeɪn) NOUN rat poison, esp arsenic oxide.

Ratskeller *German* (ˈraːtskɛlər) NOUN [1] the cellar of a town hall, esp one used as a beer hall or restaurant. [2] any similar establishment, esp in the US.
▷HISTORY German: from *Rat*(*haus*) town hall + *Keller* cellar

rat snake NOUN any of various nonvenomous rodent-eating colubrid snakes, such as *Elaphe obsoleta* of North America and *Ptyas mucosus* of Asia.

rat-tail NOUN [1] another name for **grenadier** (the fish). [2] **a** a horse's tail that has no hairs. **b** a horse having such a tail. [3] a style of spoon in which the line of the handle is prolonged in a tapering moulding along the back of the bowl. [4] a kind of woodworking or metalworking file.

rat tamer NOUN *Austral* an informal name for **psychologist** or **psychiatrist.**

rattan *or* **ratan** (ræˈtæn) NOUN [1] any of the climbing palms of the genus *Calamus* and related genera, having tough stems used for wickerwork and canes. [2] the stems of such plants collectively. [3] a stick made from one of these stems.
▷HISTORY C17: from Malay *rōtan*

rat-tat (ˈrætˌtæt) NOUN a variant of **rat-a-tat-tat.**

ratteen (ræˈtiːn) NOUN a variant spelling of **ratine.**

ratter (ˈrætə) NOUN [1] a dog or cat that catches and kills rats. [2] another word for **rat** (senses 3, 4).

rattish (ˈrætɪʃ) ADJECTIVE of, resembling, or infested with rats.

rattle[1] (ˈrætᵊl) VERB [1] to make or cause to make a rapid succession of short sharp sounds, as of loose pellets colliding when shaken in a container. [2] to shake or cause to shake with such a sound: *the explosion rattled the windows.* [3] to send, move, drive, etc., with such a sound: *the car rattled along the country road.* [4] (*intr*; foll by *on*) to chatter idly; talk, esp at length: *he rattled on about his work.* [5] (*tr*; foll by *off, out* etc.) to recite perfunctorily or rapidly. [6] (*tr*) *Informal* to disconcert; make frightened or anxious. ◆ NOUN [7] a rapid succession of short sharp sounds. [8] an object, esp a baby's toy, filled with small pellets that rattle when shaken. [9] a series of loosely connected horny segments on the tail of a rattlesnake, vibrated to produce a rattling

sound. **10** any of various European scrophulariaceous plants having a capsule in which the seeds rattle, such as *Pedicularis palustris* (**red rattle**) and *Rhinanthus minor* (**yellow rattle**). **11** idle chatter. **12** an idle chatterer. **13** *Med* another name for **rale**.
▷HISTORY C14: from Middle Dutch *ratelen*; related to Middle High German *razzen*, of imitative origin

rattle[2] ('rætəl) VERB (*tr*; *often foll by down*) to fit (a vessel or its rigging) with ratlines.
▷HISTORY C18: back formation from *rattling*, variant of RATLINE

rattlebox ('rætəlˌbɒks) NOUN any of various tropical and subtropical leguminous plants that have inflated pods within which the seeds rattle.

rattler ('rætlə) NOUN **1** something that rattles. **2** *Chiefly US and Canadian* an informal name for **rattlesnake**.

rattlesnake ('rætəlˌsneɪk) NOUN any of the venomous New World snakes constituting the genera *Crotalus* and *Sistrurus*, such as *C. horridus* (**black** or **timber rattlesnake**): family *Crotalidae* (pit vipers). They have a series of loose horny segments on the tail that are vibrated to produce a buzzing or whirring sound.

rattlesnake plantain NOUN any of various small temperate and tropical orchids of the genus *Goodyera*, having mottled or striped leaves and spikes of yellowish-white flowers.

rattletrap ('rætəlˌtræp) NOUN *Informal* a broken-down old vehicle, esp an old car.

rattling ('rætlɪŋ) ADVERB *Informal* (intensifier qualifying something good, fine, pleasant, etc.): *a rattling good lunch*.

rattly ('rætlɪ) ADJECTIVE **-tlier, -tliest.** having a rattle; rattling.

rattoon (ræ'tuːn) NOUN, VERB a variant spelling of **ratoon**.

rat-trap NOUN **1** a device for catching rats. **2** *Informal* a type of bicycle pedal having serrated steel foot pads and a toe clip.

ratty ('rætɪ) ADJECTIVE **-tier, -tiest.** **1** *Brit and NZ informal* irritable; annoyed. **2** *Informal* (of the hair) unkempt or greasy. **3** *US and Canadian slang* shabby; dilapidated. **4** *Austral slang* **a** angry. **b** mad. **5** of, like, or full of rats.
▸ **'rattily** ADVERB ▸ **'rattiness** NOUN

raucous ('rɔːkəs) ADJECTIVE (of voices, cries, etc.) harshly or hoarsely loud.
▷HISTORY C18: from Latin *raucus* hoarse
▸ **'raucously** ADVERB ▸ **'raucousness** *or* (*less commonly*) **raucity** ('rɔːsɪtɪ) NOUN

raunch (rɔːntʃ) NOUN *Slang* **1** lack of polish or refinement; crudeness. **2** *Chiefly US* slovenliness or untidiness.

raunchy ('rɔːntʃɪ) ADJECTIVE **-chier, -chiest.** *Slang* **1** openly sexual; lusty; earthy. **2** *Chiefly US* slovenly or untidy.
▷HISTORY C20: of unknown origin
▸ **'raunchily** ADVERB ▸ **'raunchiness** NOUN

raupatu (ˌraʊ'pɑːtuː) NOUN *NZ* the confiscation or seizure of land.
▷HISTORY Maori

rauriki ('raʊrəkiː) NOUN, *plural* **-kis.** *NZ* another name for **sow thistle**.
▷HISTORY Maori

rauwolfia (rɔː'wʊlfɪə, raʊ-) NOUN **1** any tropical tree or shrub of the apocynaceous genus *Rauwolfia*, esp *R. serpentina* of SE Asia. **2** the powdered root of *R. serpentina*: a source of various drugs, esp reserpine.
▷HISTORY C19: New Latin, named after Leonhard *Rauwolf* (died 1596), German botanist

Rav (ræv; *Hebrew* rav) NOUN *Judaism* **1** a rabbi who is a person's religious mentor, or one to whom questions are addressed for authoritative decision. **2** the title preferred by many orthodox rabbis to distinguish them from the clergy of other brands of Judaism.

ravage ('rævɪdʒ) VERB **1** to cause extensive damage to. ◆ NOUN **2** (*often plural*) destructive action: *the ravages of time*.
▷HISTORY C17: from French, from Old French *ravir* to snatch away, RAVISH
▸ **'ravagement** NOUN

RAVC ABBREVIATION FOR Royal Army Veterinary Corps.

rave[1] (reɪv) VERB **1** to utter (something) in a wild or incoherent manner, as when mad or delirious. **2** (*intr*) to speak in an angry uncontrolled manner. **3** (*intr*) (of the sea, wind, etc.) to rage or roar. **4** (*intr*; *foll by over or about*) *Informal* to write or speak (about) with great enthusiasm. **5** (*intr*) *Brit slang* to enjoy oneself wildly or uninhibitedly. ◆ NOUN **6** *Informal* **a** enthusiastic or extravagant praise. **b** (*as modifier*): *a rave review*. **7** *Brit slang* **a** Also called: **rave-up.** a party. **b** a professionally organized party for young people, with electronic dance music, sometimes held in a field or disused building. **8** *Brit slang* a fad or fashion: *the latest rave*. **9** a name given to various types of dance music, such as techno, that feature fast electronic rhythm.
▷HISTORY C14 *raven*, apparently from Old French *resver* to wander

rave[2] (reɪv) NOUN a vertical sidepiece on a wagon.
▷HISTORY C16: modification of dialect *rathe*, of uncertain origin

ravel ('rævəl) VERB **-els, -elling, -elled** *or US* **-els, -eling, -eled.** **1** to tangle (threads, fibres, etc.) or (of threads, fibres, etc.) to become entangled. **2** (often foll by *out*) to tease or draw out (the fibres of a fabric or garment) or (of a garment or fabric) to fray out in loose ends; unravel. **3** (*tr*; *usually foll by out*) to disentangle or resolve: *to ravel out a complicated story*. **4** to break up (a road surface) in patches or (of a road surface) to begin to break up; fret; scab. **5** *Archaic* to make or become confused or complicated. ◆ NOUN **6** a tangle or complication.
▷HISTORY C16: from Middle Dutch *ravelen*
▸ **'raveller** NOUN ▸ **'ravelly** ADJECTIVE

ravelin ('rævlɪn) NOUN *Fortifications* an outwork having two embankments at a salient angle.
▷HISTORY C16: from Italian *ravellino* a little bank, from *riva* bank, from Latin *rīpa*

ravelment ('rævəlmənt) NOUN *Rare* a ravel or tangle.

raven[1] ('reɪvən) NOUN **1** a large passerine bird, *Corvus corax*, having a large straight bill, long wedge-shaped tail, and black plumage: family *Corvidae* (crows). It has a hoarse croaking cry. **2** **a** a shiny black colour. **b** (*as adjective*): *raven hair*.
▷HISTORY Old English *hræfn*; related to Old High German *hraban*, Old Norse *hrafn*

raven[2] ('rævən) VERB **1** to seize or seek (plunder, prey, etc.). **2** to eat (something) voraciously or greedily; be ravenous in eating.
▷HISTORY C15: from Old French *raviner* to attack impetuously; see RAVENOUS
▸ **'ravener** NOUN

Raven ('reɪvən) NOUN a traditional trickster hero among the native peoples of the Canadian Pacific Northwest.
▷HISTORY from RAVEN[1]

ravening ('rævənɪŋ) ADJECTIVE (esp of animals such as wolves) voracious; predatory.
▸ **'raveningly** ADVERB

Ravenna (rə'venə; *Italian* ra'venna) NOUN a city and port in NE Italy, in Emilia-Romagna: capital of the Western Roman Empire from 402 to 476, of the Ostrogoths from 493 to 526, and of the Byzantine exarchate from 584 to 751; famous for its ancient mosaics. Pop.: 138 418 (2000 est.).

ravenous ('rævənəs) ADJECTIVE **1** famished; starving. **2** rapacious; voracious.
▷HISTORY C16: from Old French *ravineux*, from Latin *rapīna* plunder, from *rapere* to seize
▸ **'ravenously** ADVERB ▸ **'ravenousness** NOUN

raver ('reɪvə) NOUN **1** *Brit slang* a person who leads a wild or uninhibited social life. **2** *Slang* a person who enjoys rave music, esp one who frequents raves.

ravin ('rævɪn) VERB an archaic spelling of **raven**[2].

ravine (rə'viːn) NOUN a deep narrow steep-sided valley, esp one formed by the action of running water.
▷HISTORY C15: from Old French: torrent, from Latin *rapīna* robbery, influenced by Latin *rapidus* RAPID, both from *rapere* to snatch

raving ('reɪvɪŋ) ADJECTIVE **1** **a** delirious; frenzied. **b** (*as adv.*): *raving mad*. **2** *Informal* (intensifier): *a raving beauty*. ◆ NOUN **3** (*usually plural*) frenzied, irrational, or wildly extravagant talk or utterances.
▸ **'ravingly** ADVERB

ravioli (ˌrævɪ'əʊlɪ) NOUN small squares of pasta containing a savoury mixture of meat, cheese, etc.

▷HISTORY C19: from Italian dialect, literally: little turnips, from Italian *rava* turnip, from Latin *rāpa*

ravish ('rævɪʃ) VERB (*tr*) **1** (*often passive*) to give great delight to; enrapture. **2** to rape. **3** *Archaic* to carry off by force.
▷HISTORY C13: from Old French *ravir*, from Latin *rapere* to seize
▸ **'ravisher** NOUN ▸ **'ravishment** NOUN

ravishing ('rævɪʃɪŋ) ADJECTIVE delightful; lovely; entrancing.
▸ **'ravishingly** ADVERB

raw (rɔː) ADJECTIVE **1** (of food) not cooked: *raw onion*. **2** (*prenominal*) in an unfinished, natural, or unrefined state; not treated by manufacturing or other processes: *raw materials for making steel*; *raw brick*. **3** (of the skin, a wound, etc.) having the surface exposed or abraded, esp painfully. **4** ignorant, inexperienced, or immature: *a raw recruit*. **5** (*prenominal*) not selected or modified: *raw statistics*. **6** frank or realistic: *a raw picture of the breakdown of a marriage*. **7** (of spirits) undiluted. **8** *Chiefly US* coarse, vulgar, or obscene. **9** *Chiefly US* recently done; fresh: *raw paintwork*. **10** (of the weather) harshly cold and damp. **11** *Informal* unfair; unjust (esp in the phrase **a raw deal**). ◆ NOUN **12** **the raw.** *Brit informal* a sensitive point: *his criticism touched me on the raw*. **13** **in the raw.** **a** *Informal* without clothes; naked. **b** in a natural or unmodified state: *life in the raw*.
▷HISTORY Old English *hreaw*; related to Old High German *hrao*, Old Norse *hrār* raw, Latin *cruor* thick blood, Greek *kreas* meat
▸ **'rawish** ADJECTIVE ▸ **'rawly** ADVERB ▸ **'rawness** NOUN

Rawalpindi (rɔːl'pɪndɪ) NOUN an ancient city in N Pakistan: interim capital of Pakistan (1959–67) during the building of Islamabad. Pop.: 1 406 214 (1998).

rawboned ('rɔː'bəʊnd) ADJECTIVE having a lean bony physique.

rawhide ('rɔːˌhaɪd) NOUN **1** untanned hide. **2** a whip or rope made of strips cut from such a hide.

rawhide hammer NOUN a hammer, used to avoid damaging a surface, having a head consisting of a metal tube from each end of which a tight roll of hide protrudes.

rawinsonde ('reɪwɪnˌsɒnd) NOUN a hydrogen balloon carrying meteorological instruments and a radar target, enabling the velocity of winds in the atmosphere to be measured.
▷HISTORY C20: blend of *radar* + *wind* + *radiosonde*

Rawlplug ('rɔːlplʌg) NOUN *Trademark* a short fibre or plastic tube used to provide a fixing in a wall for a screw.

raw material NOUN **1** material on which a particular manufacturing process is carried out. **2** a person or thing regarded as suitable for some particular purpose: *raw material for the army*.

raw milk NOUN unpasteurized milk.

raw silk NOUN **1** untreated silk fibres reeled from the cocoon. **2** fabric woven from such fibres.

rax (ræks) *Scot* ◆ VERB **1** (*tr*) to stretch or extend. **2** (*intr*) to reach out. **3** (*tr*) to pass or give (something to a person) with the outstretched hand; reach: *rax me the salt*. **4** (*tr*) to strain or sprain. ◆ NOUN **5** the act of stretching or straining.
▷HISTORY Old English *raxan*

ray[1] (reɪ) NOUN **1** a narrow beam of light; gleam. **2** a slight indication, esp of something anticipated or hoped for: *a ray of solace*. **3** *Maths* a straight line extending from a point. **4** a thin beam of electromagnetic radiation or particles. **5** any of the bony or cartilaginous spines of the fin of a fish that form the support for the soft part of the fin. **6** any of the arms or branches of a starfish or other radiate animal. **7** *Astronomy* any of a number of bright streaks that radiate from the youngest lunar craters, such as Tycho; they are composed of crater ejecta not yet darkened, and extend considerable distances. **8** *Botany* any strand of tissue that runs radially through the vascular tissue of some higher plants. See **medullary ray.** ◆ VERB **9** (of an object) to emit (light) in rays or (of light) to issue in the form of rays. **10** (*intr*) (of lines, etc.) to extend in rays or on radiating paths. **11** (*tr*) to adorn (an ornament, etc.) with rays or radiating lines.
▷HISTORY C14: from Old French *rai*, from Latin *radius* spoke, RADIUS

ray[2] (reɪ) NOUN any of various marine selachian

fishes typically having a flattened body, greatly enlarged winglike pectoral fins, gills on the undersurface of the fins, and a long whiplike tail. They constitute the orders *Torpediniformes* (**electric rays**) and *Rajiformes*.
▷HISTORY C14: from Old French *raie*, from Latin *raia*

ray³ (reɪ) NOUN *Music* (in tonic sol-fa) the second degree of any major scale; supertonic.
▷HISTORY C14: see GAMUT

Ray (reɪ) NOUN **Cape.** a promontory in SW Newfoundland, Canada.

rayah ('rɑːjə, 'raɪə) NOUN (formerly) a non-Muslim subject of the Ottoman Empire. Also (less common): **raia.**
▷HISTORY C19: from Turkish *raiyye*, from Arabic *ra'iyah* herd, flock

Raybans ('reɪˌbænz) PLURAL NOUN *Trademark* a brand of sunglasses.

ray floret *or* **flower** NOUN any of the small strap-shaped flowers in the flower head of certain composite plants, such as the daisy. Compare **disc floret.**

ray gun NOUN (in science fiction) a gun that emits rays to paralyse, stun, or destroy.

Rayleigh disc ('reɪlɪ) NOUN a small light disc suspended in the path of a sound wave, used to measure the intensity of the sound by analysing the resulting deflection of the disc.
▷HISTORY named after John William Strutt (1842–1919), Lord *Rayleigh*, British physicist

Rayleigh scattering NOUN a process in which electromagnetic radiation is elastically deflected by particles of matter, without a change of frequency but with a phase change.

rayless ('reɪlɪs) ADJECTIVE [1] dark; gloomy. [2] lacking rays: *a rayless flower.*
▸ **'raylessly** ADVERB ▸ **'raylessness** NOUN

raylet ('reɪlɪt) NOUN a small ray.

Raynaud's disease ('reɪnəʊz) NOUN a disease, mainly affecting women, in which spasms in the blood vessels of the fingers or toes restrict blood flow to the affected part, which becomes pale, numb, and sometimes painful. Often shortened to: **Raynaud's.**
▷HISTORY named after Maurice *Raynaud* (1834–81), French physician who first described it

rayon ('reɪɒn) NOUN [1] any of a number of textile fibres made from wood pulp or other forms of cellulose. [2] any fabric made from such a fibre. [3] (*modifier*) consisting of or involving rayon: *a rayon shirt.*
▷HISTORY C20: from French, from Old French *rai* RAY¹

raze *or* **rase** (reɪz) VERB (*tr*) [1] to demolish (a town, buildings, etc.) completely; level (esp in the phrase **raze to the ground**). [2] to delete; erase. [3] *Archaic* to graze.
▷HISTORY C16: from Old French *raser* from Latin *rādere* to scrape
▸ **'razer** *or* **'raser** NOUN

razee (ræ'ziː) *History* ◆ NOUN, *plural* **razees.** [1] a sailing ship that has had its upper deck or decks removed. ◆ VERB **razees, razeeing, razeed.** (*tr*) [2] to remove the upper deck or decks of (a sailing ship).
▷HISTORY C19: from French *rasée* shaved close, from *raser* to RAZE

razoo (rə'zuː) NOUN *Austral and NZ informal* an imaginary coin: *not a brass razoo; they took every last razoo.*
▷HISTORY C20: of uncertain origin

razor ('reɪzə) NOUN [1] a sharp implement used esp by men for shaving the face. [2] **on a razor's edge** *or* **razor-edge.** in an acute dilemma. ◆ VERB [3] (*tr*) to cut or shave with a razor.
▷HISTORY C13: from Old French *raseor*, from *raser* to shave; see RAZE

razorback ('reɪzəˌbæk) NOUN [1] Also called: **finback.** another name for the **common rorqual** (see **rorqual**). [2] a semiwild or wild pig of the southeastern US, having a narrow body, long legs, and a ridged back.

razorbill ('reɪzəˌbɪl) *or* **razor-billed auk** NOUN a common auk, *Alca torda*, of the North Atlantic, having a thick laterally compressed bill with white markings.

razor blade NOUN a small rectangular piece of metal sharpened on one or both long edges for use in a razor for shaving.

razor-cut VERB **-cuts, -cutting, -cut.** [1] (*tr*) to trim or shape (the hair) with a razor. ◆ NOUN **razor cut.** [2] a fluffy hairstyle, usually tapering at the neck, trimmed by a razor.

razor-shell NOUN any of various sand-burrowing bivalve molluscs of the genera *Ensis* and *Solen*, which have a long tubular shell. US name: **razor clam.**

razor wire NOUN strong wire with pieces of sharp metal set across it at close intervals, used to make fences or barriers.

razz (ræz) *US and Canadian slang* ◆ VERB [1] (*tr*) to make fun of; deride. ◆ NOUN [2] short for **raspberry** (sense 5).

razzia ('ræzɪə) NOUN, *plural* **-zias.** *History* a raid for plunder or slaves, esp one carried out by Moors in North Africa.
▷HISTORY C19: from French, from Arabic *ghaziah* war

Razzie ('ræzɪ) any of several gold-plated ornamental raspberries awarded annually in the United States by the Golden Raspberry Award Foundation for films or acting performances in films considered to be the worst of the year.

razzle ('ræzᵊl) NOUN **on the razzle** *or* **razz.** *Brit informal* out enjoying oneself or celebrating, esp while drinking freely.
▷HISTORY C20: from RAZZLE-DAZZLE

razzle-dazzle ('ræzᵊl'dæzᵊl) *or* **razzmatazz** ('ræzmə'tæz) NOUN *Slang* noisy or showy fuss or activity.
▷HISTORY C19: rhyming compound based on DAZZLE

Rb THE CHEMICAL SYMBOL FOR rubidium.

RB INTERNATIONAL CAR REGISTRATION FOR (Republic of) Botswana.

RB- ABBREVIATION FOR reconnaissance bomber: *RB-57.*

RBE ABBREVIATION FOR relative biological effectiveness (of radiation).

rc ABBREVIATION FOR reinforced concrete.

RC ABBREVIATION FOR: [1] Red Cross. [2] Reserve Corps. [3] Also: **R.C.** Roman Catholic. ◆ [4] INTERNATIONAL CAR REGISTRATION FOR (Republic of) China.

RCA ABBREVIATION FOR: [1] (formerly) Radio Corporation of America. [2] Royal Canadian Academy. [3] Royal College of Art. ◆ [4] INTERNATIONAL CAR REGISTRATION FOR Central African Republic.

RCAF ABBREVIATION FOR Royal Canadian Air Force.

RCB(CG) INTERNATIONAL CAR REGISTRATION FOR (Republic of) Congo-Brazzaville.

rcd ABBREVIATION FOR received.

RCD ABBREVIATION FOR **residual current device.**

RCH INTERNATIONAL CAR REGISTRATION FOR (Republic of) Chile.

RCL ABBREVIATION FOR Royal Canadian Legion.

RCM ABBREVIATION FOR Royal College of Music.

RCMP ABBREVIATION FOR Royal Canadian Mounted Police.

RCN ABBREVIATION FOR: [1] Royal Canadian Navy. [2] Royal College of Nursing.

RCO ABBREVIATION FOR Royal College of Organists.

r-colour *or* **r-colouring** NOUN *Phonetics* an (r) quality imparted to certain vowels, usually by retroflexion.
▸ **'r-ˌcoloured** ADJECTIVE

RCP ABBREVIATION FOR Royal College of Physicians.

rcpt ABBREVIATION FOR receipt.

RCS ABBREVIATION FOR: [1] Royal College of Science. [2] Royal College of Surgeons.

rct *Military* ABBREVIATION FOR recruit.

RCT ABBREVIATION FOR Royal Corps of Transport.

RCVS ABBREVIATION FOR Royal College of Veterinary Surgeons.

rd ABBREVIATION FOR: [1] rendered. [2] rod (unit of length). [3] road. [4] round. [5] *Physics* rutherford.

rd *or* **RD** (on a cheque) ABBREVIATION FOR refer to drawer.

Rd ABBREVIATION FOR Road.

RD (in New Zealand) ABBREVIATION FOR Rural Delivery.

RDA ABBREVIATION FOR: [1] Recommended Daily *or* Dietary Amount *or* Allowance. [2] (in England) Regional Development Agency.

RDC (formerly, in Britain) ABBREVIATION FOR Rural District Council.

RDS ABBREVIATION FOR radio data system: a system in which digital signals are transmitted with normal radio programme to effect automatic tuning of receivers and other functions.

RDX ABBREVIATION FOR Research Department Explosive; another name for **cyclonite.**

re¹ (reɪ, riː) NOUN *Music* a variant spelling of **ray³.**

re² (riː) PREPOSITION with reference to.
▷HISTORY C18: from Latin *rē*, ablative case of *rēs* thing

> **Language note** *Re*, in contexts such as *re your letter, your remarks have been noted* or *he spoke to me re your complaint*, is common in business or official correspondence. In general English *with reference to* is preferable in the former case and *about* or *concerning* in the latter. Even in business correspondence, the use of *re* is often restricted to the letter heading.

re³ THE INTERNET DOMAIN NAME FOR Reunion Island.

Re¹ (reɪ) NOUN another name for **Ra².**

Re² THE CHEMICAL SYMBOL FOR rhenium.

Re³ *or* **re** SYMBOL FOR rupee.

RE ABBREVIATION FOR: [1] Reformed Episcopal. [2] Religious Education. [3] Right Excellent. [4] Royal Engineers.

re- PREFIX [1] indicating return to a previous condition, restoration, withdrawal, etc.: *rebuild; renew; retrace; reunite.* [2] indicating repetition of an action: *recopy; remarry.*
▷HISTORY from Latin

> **Language note** Verbs beginning with *re-* indicate repetition or restoration. It is unnecessary to add an adverb such as *back* or *again*: *This must not occur again* (not *recur again*); *we recounted the votes* (not *recounted the votes again*, which implies that the votes were counted three times, not twice).

're CONTRACTION OF are: *we're; you're; they're.*

reach (riːtʃ) VERB [1] (*tr*) to arrive at or get to (a place, person, etc.) in the course of movement or action: *to reach the office.* [2] to extend as far as (a point or place): *to reach the ceiling; can you reach?* [3] (*tr*) to come to (a certain condition, stage, or situation): *to reach the point of starvation.* [4] (*intr*) to extend in influence or operation: *the Roman conquest reached throughout England.* [5] (*tr*) *Informal* to pass or give (something to a person) with the outstretched hand: *to reach someone a book.* [6] (*intr*; foll by *out, for,* or *after*) to make a movement (towards), as if to grasp or touch: *to reach for something on a shelf.* [7] (*intr*; foll by *for* or *after*) to strive or yearn: *to reach for the impossible.* [8] (*tr*) to make contact or communication with (someone): *we tried to reach him all day.* [9] (*tr*) to strike, esp in fencing or boxing. [10] (*tr*) to amount to (a certain sum): *to reach the five million mark.* [11] (*intr*) *Nautical* to sail on a tack with the wind on or near abeam. ◆ NOUN [12] the act of reaching. [13] the extent or distance of reaching: *within reach of safety; beyond her reach.* [14] the range of influence, power, jurisdiction, etc. [15] an open stretch of water, esp on a river. [16] *Nautical* the direction or distance sailed by a vessel on one tack. [17] a bar on the rear axle of a vehicle connecting it with some part at the front end. [18] *Television, radio* the percentage of the population selecting a broadcast programme or channel for more than a specified time during a day or week. [19] *Marketing* the proportion of a market that an advertiser hopes to reach at least once in a campaign.
▷HISTORY Old English *rǣcan*; related to Old Frisian *rēka*, Old High German *reihhen*
▸ **'reachable** ADJECTIVE ▸ **'reacher** NOUN

reach-me-down NOUN *Informal* [1] **a** (*often plural*) a garment that is cheaply ready-made or second-hand. **b** (*as modifier*): *reach-me-down finery.* [2]

(*plural*) trousers. 3 (*modifier*) not original; derivative; stale: *a stock of reach-me-down ideas.*

reacquire (ˌriːəˈkwaɪə) VERB (*tr*) to get or gain (something) again which one has owned.

react (rɪˈækt) VERB 1 (*intr*; foll by *to, upon* etc.) (of a person or thing) to act in response to another person, a stimulus, etc. or (of two people or things) to act together in a certain way. 2 (*intr*; foll by *against*) to act in an opposing or contrary manner. 3 (*intr*) *Physics* to exert an equal force in the opposite direction to an acting force. 4 *Chem* to undergo or cause to undergo a chemical reaction.
▷HISTORY C17: from Late Latin *reagere*, from RE- + Latin *agere* to drive, do

re-act (riːˈækt) VERB (*tr*) to act or perform again.

reactance (rɪˈæktəns) NOUN 1 the opposition to the flow of alternating current by the capacitance or inductance of an electrical circuit; the imaginary part of the impedance *Z*, $Z = R + iX$, where *R* is the resistance, $i = \sqrt{-1}$, and *X* is the reactance. It is expressed in ohms. Compare **resistance** (sense 3). 2 the opposition to the flow of an acoustic or mechanical vibration, usually due to inertia or stiffness. It is the magnitude of the imaginary part of the acoustic or mechanical impedance.

reactant (rɪˈæktənt) NOUN a substance that participates in a chemical reaction, esp a substance that is present at the start of the reaction. Compare **product** (sense 4).

reaction (rɪˈækʃən) NOUN 1 a response to some foregoing action or stimulus. 2 the reciprocal action of two things acting together. 3 opposition to change, esp political change, or a desire to return to a former condition or system. 4 a response indicating a person's feelings or emotional attitude. 5 *Med* **a** any effect produced by the action of a drug, esp an adverse effect. Compare **side effect. b** any effect produced by a substance (allergen) to which a person is allergic. the simultaneous equal and opposite force that acts on a body whenever it exerts a force on another body. 7 short for **chemical reaction** or **nuclear reaction.** 8 *Stock Exchange* a sharp fall in price interrupting a general rise.
▸**reˈactional** ADJECTIVE

> **Language note** *Reaction* is used to refer both to an instant response (*her reaction was one of amazement*) and to a considered response in the form of a statement (*the Minister gave his reaction to the court's decision*). Some people think this second use is incorrect.

reactionary (rɪˈækʃənərɪ, -ʃənrɪ) *or* **reactionist** ADJECTIVE 1 of, relating to, or characterized by reaction, esp against radical political or social change. ◆ NOUN, *plural* **-aries** *or* **-ists.** 2 a person opposed to radical change.
▸**reˈactionism** NOUN

reaction chamber NOUN *Engineering* the chamber in a rocket engine in which the reaction or combustion of fuel occurs.

reaction engine *or* **motor** NOUN an engine, such as a jet or rocket engine, that ejects gas at high velocity and develops its thrust from the ensuing reaction.

reaction formation NOUN *Psychoanal* a defence mechanism by which a person at a conscious level condemns a repressed wish: thus, a latent homosexual may denounce homosexuality.

reaction time NOUN *Physiol* another name for **latent time.**

reaction turbine NOUN a turbine in which the working fluid is accelerated by expansion in both the static nozzles and the rotor blades. Torque is produced by the momentum changes in the rotor and by reaction from fluid accelerating out of the rotor. Compare **impulse turbine.**

reactivate (rɪˈæktɪˌveɪt) VERB (*tr*) to make (something) active or functional again.
▸**reˌactiˈvation** NOUN

reactive (rɪˈæktɪv) ADJECTIVE 1 readily partaking in chemical reactions: *sodium is a reactive metal; free radicals are very reactive.* 2 of, concerned with, or having a reactance. 3 responsive to stimulus. 4 (of mental illnesses) precipitated by an external cause: *reactive depression.*
▸**reˈactively** ADVERB ▸**reactivity** (ˌriːækˈtɪvɪtɪ) *or* **reˈactiveness** NOUN

reactor (rɪˈæktə) NOUN 1 *Chem* a substance, such as a reagent, that undergoes a reaction. 2 short for **nuclear reactor.** 3 a vessel, esp one in industrial use, in which a chemical reaction takes place. 4 a coil of low resistance and high inductance that introduces reactance into a circuit. 5 *Med* a person sensitive to a particular drug or agent.

read[1] (riːd) VERB **reads, reading, read** (rɛd). 1 to comprehend the meaning of (something written or printed) by looking at and interpreting the written or printed characters. 2 to be occupied in such an activity: *he was reading all day.* 3 (when *tr*, often foll by *out*) to look at, interpret, and speak aloud (something written or printed): *he read to us from the Bible.* 4 (*tr*) to interpret the significance or meaning of through scrutiny and recognition: *he read the sky and predicted rain; to read a map.* 5 (*tr*) to interpret or understand the meaning of (signs, characters, etc.) other than by visual means: *to read Braille.* 6 (*tr*) to have sufficient knowledge of (a language) to understand the written or printed word: *do you read German?* 7 (*tr*) to discover or make out the true nature or mood of: *to read someone's mind.* 8 to interpret or understand (something read) in a specified way, or (of something read) to convey a particular meaning or impression: *I read this speech as satire; this book reads well.* 9 (*tr*) to adopt as a reading in a particular passage: *for "boon" read "bone".* 10 (*intr*) to have or contain a certain form or wording: *the sentence reads as follows.* 11 to undertake a course of study in (a subject): *to read history; read for the bar.* 12 to gain knowledge by reading: *he read about the war.* 13 (*tr*) to register, indicate, or show: *the meter reads 100.* 14 (*tr*) to bring or put into a specified condition by reading: *to read a child to sleep.* 15 (*tr*) to hear and understand, esp when using a two-way radio: *we are reading you loud and clear.* 16 *Computing* to obtain (data) from a storage device, such as magnetic tape. Compare **write** (sense 17). 17 (*tr*) to understand (written or printed music) by interpretation of the notes on the staff and to be able to reproduce the musical sounds represented by these notes. 18 **read a lesson** *or* **lecture.** *Informal* to censure or reprimand, esp in a long-winded manner. 19 **read between the lines.** to perceive or deduce a meaning that is hidden or implied rather than being openly stated. 20 **you wouldn't read about it.** *Austral informal* an expression of dismay, disgust, or disbelief. ◆ NOUN 21 matter suitable for reading: *this new book is a very good read.* 22 the act of reading. ◆ See also **read in, read into, read out, read up.**
▷HISTORY Old English *rǣdan* to advise, explain; related to Old Frisian *rēda*, Old High German *rātan*, Gothic *garēdan*

read[2] (rɛd) VERB 1 the past tense and past participle of **read**[1]. ◆ ADJECTIVE 2 having knowledge gained from books (esp in the phrases **widely read, well-read**). 3 **take (something) as read.** to take (something) for granted as a fact; understand or presume.

readable (ˈriːdəbᵊl) ADJECTIVE 1 (of handwriting, etc.) able to be read or deciphered; legible. 2 (of style of writing) interesting, easy, or pleasant to read.
▸**ˌreadaˈbility** *or* **ˈreadableness** NOUN ▸**ˈreadably** ADVERB

readdress (ˌriːəˈdrɛs) VERB (*tr*) 1 to look at or discuss (an issue, situation, etc.) from a new or different point of view. 2 to put a forwarding address onto (a letter received).

reader (ˈriːdə) NOUN 1 a person who reads. 2 a person who is fond of reading. 3 **a** *Chiefly Brit* at a university, a member of staff having a position between that of a senior lecturer and a professor. **b** *US* a teaching assistant in a faculty who grades papers, examinations, etc., on behalf of a professor. 4 **a** a book that is part of a planned series for those learning to read. **b** a standard textbook, esp for foreign-language learning. 5 a person who reads aloud in public. 6 a person who reads and assesses the merit of manuscripts submitted to a publisher. 7 a person employed to read proofs and indicate errors by comparison with the original copy; proofreader. 8 short for **lay reader.** 9 *Judaism chiefly Brit* another word for **cantor** (sense 1).

readership (ˈriːdəʃɪp) NOUN 1 all the readers collectively of a particular publication or author: *a readership of five million; Dickens's readership.* 2 *Chiefly Brit* the office, position, or rank of university reader.

readies (ˈrɛdɪz) PLURAL NOUN *Informal* a variant of **ready** (sense 8): see **ready money.**

readily (ˈrɛdɪlɪ) ADVERB 1 promptly; eagerly; willingly. 2 without difficulty or delay; easily or quickly.

read in (riːd) VERB (*adverb*) 1 to read (data) into a computer memory or storage device. 2 **read oneself in.** *Church of England* to assume possession of a benefice by publicly reading the Thirty-nine Articles.

readiness (ˈrɛdɪnɪs) NOUN 1 the state of being ready or prepared, as for use or action. 2 **in readiness. a** prepared and waiting: *all was in readiness for the guests' arrival.* **b** in preparation for: *he tidied the house in readiness for the guests' arrival.* 3 willingness or eagerness to do something. 4 ease or promptness.

reading (ˈriːdɪŋ) NOUN 1 **a** the act of a person who reads. **b** (*as modifier*): *a reading room; a reading lamp.* 2 **a** ability to read. **b** (*as modifier*): *the reading public; a child of reading age.* 3 any matter that can be read; written or printed text. 4 a public recital or rendering of a literary work. 5 the form of a particular word or passage in a given text, esp where more than one version exists. 6 an interpretation, as of a piece of music, a situation, or something said or written. 7 knowledge gained from books: *a person of little reading.* 8 a measurement indicated by a gauge, dial, scientific instrument, etc. 9 *Parliamentary procedure* **a** the formal recital of the body or title of a bill in a legislative assembly in order to begin one of the stages of its passage. **b** one of the three stages in the passage of a bill through a legislative assembly. See **first reading, second reading, third reading.** 10 the formal recital of something written, esp a will.

Reading (ˈrɛdɪŋ) NOUN 1 a town in S England, in Reading unitary authority, Berkshire, on the River Thames: university (1892). Pop.: 134 600 (1991). 2 a unitary authority in S England, in Berkshire. Pop.: 143 124 (2001). Area: 37 sq. km (14 sq. miles).

reading group NOUN a group of people who meet regularly to discuss a book that they have all read.

read into (riːd) VERB (*tr, preposition*) to discern in or infer from a statement (meanings not intended by the speaker or writer).

readjust (ˌriːəˈdʒʌst) VERB to adjust or adapt (oneself or something) again, esp after an initial failure.
▸**ˌreadˈjustable** ADJECTIVE ▸**ˌreadˈjuster** NOUN
▸**ˌreadˈjustment** NOUN

readmission (ˌriːədˈmɪʃən) NOUN the act or an instance of readmitting or being readmitted.

readmit (ˌriːədˈmɪt) VERB **-mits, -mitting, -mitted.** (*tr*) to allow (someone) to enter or be admitted again.

read only memory NOUN See **ROM.**

read out (riːd) VERB (*adverb*) 1 (*tr*) to read (something) aloud. 2 to retrieve information from a computer memory or storage device. 3 (*tr*) *US and Canadian* to expel (someone) from a political party or other society. ◆ NOUN **read-out.** 4 **a** the act of retrieving information from a computer memory or storage device. **b** the information retrieved.

read up (riːd) VERB (*adverb*; when intr, often foll by *on*) to acquire information about (a subject) by reading intensively.

read-write head (ˈriːdˈraɪt) NOUN *Computing* an electromagnet that can both read and write information on a magnetic medium such as magnetic tape or disk.

ready (ˈrɛdɪ) ADJECTIVE **readier, readiest.** 1 in a state of completion or preparedness, as for use or action. 2 willing or eager: *ready helpers.* 3 prompt or rapid: *a ready response.* 4 (*prenominal*) quick in perceiving; intelligent: *a ready mind.* 5 (*postpositive*; foll by *to*) on the point (of) or liable (to): *ready to collapse.* 6 (*postpositive*) conveniently near (esp in the phrase **ready to hand**). 7 **make** *or* **get ready.** to prepare (oneself or something) for use or action. ◆ NOUN 8 *Informal* (often preceded by *the*) short for **ready money.** 9 **at** *or* **to the ready. a** poised for use or action: *with pen at the ready.* **b** (of a rifle) in the position normally adopted immediately prior to

aiming and firing. ◆ VERB [10] (*tr*) to put in a state of readiness; prepare.
▷HISTORY Old English (*ge*)*rǣde*; related to Old Frisian *rēde*, Old High German *reiti*, Old Norse *reithr* ready

ready-made ADJECTIVE [1] made for purchase and immediate use by any customer: *a ready-made jacket*. [2] extremely convenient or ideally suited: *a ready-made solution*. [3] unoriginal or conventional: *ready-made phrases*. ◆ NOUN [4] a ready-made article, esp a garment.

ready-mix NOUN [1] (*modifier*) consisting of ingredients blended in advance, esp of food that is ready to cook or eat after addition of milk or water: *a ready-mix cake*. [2] concrete that is mixed before or during delivery to a building site.

ready money *or* **cash** NOUN funds for immediate use; cash. Also called: **the ready, the readies.**

ready reckoner NOUN a table of numbers used to facilitate simple calculations, esp one for applying rates of discount, interest, charging, etc. to different sums.

ready-to-wear ADJECTIVE (**ready to wear** when postpositive) [1] (of clothes) not tailored for the wearer; of a standard size. ◆ NOUN [2] an article or suit of such clothes.

ready-witted ADJECTIVE quick to learn or perceive.

reaffirm (ˌriːəˈfɜːm) VERB (*tr*) to affirm (a claim, etc.) again; reassert.
▸ **ˌreaffirˈmation** NOUN

reafforest (ˌriːəˈfɒrɪst) *or* **reforest** VERB (*tr*) to replant (an area that was formerly forested).
▸ **ˌreafˌforestˈation** *or* **ˌreforestˈation** NOUN

reagent (riːˈeɪdʒənt) NOUN a substance for use in a chemical reaction, esp for use in chemical synthesis and analysis.

reagin (ˈrɪədʒɪn) NOUN *Immunol* a type of antibody that is formed against an allergen and is attached to the cells of a tissue. The antigen–antibody reaction that occurs on subsequent contact with the allergen causes tissue damage, leading to the release of histamine and other substances responsible for an allergic reaction.
▷HISTORY C20: from German *reagieren* to react + -IN

real[1] (ˈrɪəl) ADJECTIVE [1] existing or occurring in the physical world; not imaginary, fictitious, or theoretical; actual. [2] (*prenominal*) true; actual; not false: *the real reason*. [3] (*prenominal*) deserving the name; rightly so called: *a real friend; a real woman*. [4] not artificial or simulated; genuine: *real sympathy; real fur*. [5] (of food, etc.) traditionally made and having a distinct flavour: *real ale; real cheese*. [6] *Philosophy* existent or relating to actual existence (as opposed to nonexistent, potential, contingent, or apparent). [7] (*prenominal*) *Economics* (of prices, incomes, wages, etc.) considered in terms of purchasing power rather than nominal currency value. [8] (*prenominal*) denoting or relating to immovable property such as land and tenements: *real property*. Compare **personal.** [9] *Physics* See **image** (sense 2). [10] *Maths* involving or containing real numbers alone; having no imaginary part. [11] *Music* **a** (of the answer in a fugue) preserving the intervals as they appear in the subject. **b** denoting a fugue as having such an answer. Compare **tonal** (sense 3). [12] *Informal* (intensifier): *a real fool; a real genius*. [13] **the real thing.** the genuine article, not an inferior or mistaken substitute. ◆ NOUN [14] short for **real number.** [15] **the real.** that which exists in fact; reality. [16] **for real.** *Slang* not as a test or trial; in earnest.
▷HISTORY C15: from Old French *réel*, from Late Latin *reālis*, from Latin *rēs* thing
▸ **ˈrealness** NOUN

real[2] (reɪˈɑːl; *Spanish* reˈal) NOUN, *plural* **reals** *or* **reales** (*Spanish* reˈales). a former small Spanish or Spanish-American silver coin.
▷HISTORY C17: from Spanish, literally: royal, from Latin *rēgālis*; see REGAL[1]

real[3] (*Portuguese* reˈal) NOUN, *plural* **reis** (rəjʃ). [1] the standard monetary unit of Brazil, divided into 100 centavos. [2] a former coin of Portugal.
▷HISTORY ultimately from Latin *rēgālis* REGAL[1]

real ale *or* **beer** NOUN any beer which is allowed to ferment in the cask and which when served is pumped up without using carbon dioxide.

real estate NOUN another term for **real property.**

realgar (rɪˈælgə) NOUN a rare orange-red soft mineral consisting of arsenic sulphide in monoclinic crystalline form. It occurs in Utah and Romania and as a deposit from hot springs. It is an important ore of arsenic and is also used as a pigment. Formula: AsS.
▷HISTORY C14: via Medieval Latin from Arabic *rahj al-ghar* powder of the mine

realia (rɪˈeɪlɪə) PLURAL NOUN real-life facts and material used in teaching.
▷HISTORY C20: from neuter pl of Late Latin *reālis*; see REAL[1]

realign (ˌriːəˈlaɪn) VERB (*tr*) to change or put back to a new or former place or position.

realignment (ˌriːəˈlaɪnmənt) NOUN the act or instance of restoring or changing to a previous or different position.

realism (ˈrɪəˌlɪzəm) NOUN [1] awareness or acceptance of the physical universe, events, etc., as they are, as opposed to the abstract or ideal. [2] awareness or acceptance of the facts and necessities of life; a practical rather than a moral or dogmatic view of things. [3] a style of painting and sculpture that seeks to represent the familiar or typical in real life, rather than an idealized, formalized, or romantic interpretation of it. [4] any similar school or style in other arts, esp literature. [5] *Philosophy* the thesis that general terms such as common nouns refer to entities that have a real existence separate from the individuals which fall under them. See also **universal** (sense 11b). Compare **Platonism, nominalism, conceptualism, naive realism.** [6] *Philosophy* the theory that physical objects continue to exist whether they are perceived or not. Compare **idealism, phenomenalism.** [7] *Logic, philosophy* the theory that the sense of a statement is given by a specification of its truth conditions, or that there is a reality independent of the speaker's conception of it that determines the truth or falsehood of every statement.

realist (ˈrɪəlɪst) NOUN [1] a person who is aware of and accepts the physical universe, events, etc., as they are; pragmatist. [2] an artist or writer who seeks to represent the familiar or typical in real life rather than an idealized, formalized, or romantic interpretation. [3] *Philosophy* a person who accepts realism. [4] (*modifier*) of, relating to, or characteristic of realism or realists in the arts, philosophy, etc.: *a realist school*.

realistic (ˌrɪəˈlɪstɪk) ADJECTIVE [1] showing awareness and acceptance of reality. [2] practical or pragmatic rather than ideal or moral. [3] (of a book, film, etc.) depicting or emphasizing what is real and actual rather than abstract or ideal. [4] of or relating to philosophical realism.
▸ **ˌrealˈistically** ADVERB

reality (rɪˈælɪtɪ) NOUN, *plural* **-ties.** [1] the state of things as they are or appear to be, rather than as one might wish them to be. [2] something that is real. [3] the state of being real. [4] *Philosophy* **a** that which exists, independent of human awareness. **b** the totality of facts as they are independent of human awareness of them. See also **conceptualism.** Compare **appearance** (sense 6). [5] **in reality.** actually; in fact.

reality check NOUN an occasion or opportunity to consider a matter realistically or honestly.

reality fiction NOUN a satirical parody of a reality TV show.

reality principle NOUN *Psychoanal* control of behaviour by the ego to meet the conditions imposed by the external world.

reality show NOUN a television show in which members of the public or celebrities are filmed living their everyday lives or undertaking specific challenges.

reality TV NOUN television programmes focusing on members of the public living in conditions created especially by the programme makers.

realize *or* **realise** (ˈrɪəˌlaɪz) VERB [1] (when *tr, may take a clause as object*) to become conscious or aware of (something). [2] (*tr, often passive*) to bring (a plan, ambition, etc.) to fruition; make actual or concrete. [3] (*tr*) to give (something, such as a drama or film) the appearance of reality. [4] (*tr*) (of goods, property, etc.) to sell for or make (a certain sum): *this table realized £800*. [5] (*tr*) to convert (property or goods) into cash. [6] (*tr*) (of a musicologist or performer) **a** to expand or complete (a thorough-bass part in a piece of baroque music) by supplying the harmonies indicated in the figured bass. **b** to reconstruct (a composition) from an incomplete set of parts. [7] to sound or utter (a phoneme or other speech sound) in actual speech; articulate.
▸ **ˈrealˌizable** *or* **ˈrealˌisable** ADJECTIVE ▸ **ˈrealˌizably** *or* **ˈrealˌisably** ADVERB ▸ **ˌrealiˈzation** *or* **ˌrealiˈsation** NOUN ▸ **ˈrealˌizer** *or* **ˈrealˌiser** NOUN

real life NOUN **a** actual human life, as lived by real people, esp contrasted with the lives of fictional or fantasy characters: *miracles don't happen in real life*. **b** (*as modifier*): *a real-life mystery*.

reallocate (riːˈæləkeɪt) VERB (*tr*) to assign or allot to a different purpose or person from the one originally intended.
▸ **ˌralloˈcation** NOUN

really (ˈrɪəlɪ) ADVERB [1] in reality; in actuality; assuredly: *it's really quite harmless*. [2] truly; genuinely: *really beautiful*. ◆ INTERJECTION [3] an exclamation of dismay, disapproval, doubt, surprise, etc. [4] **not really?** an exclamation of surprise or polite doubt.

Language note See at **very**.

realm (rɛlm) NOUN [1] a royal domain; kingdom (now chiefly in such phrases as **Peer of the Realm**). [2] a field of interest, study, etc.: *the realm of the occult*.
▷HISTORY C13: from Old French *reialme*, from Latin *regimen* rule, influenced by Old French *reial* royal, from Latin *rēgālis* REGAL[1]

real number NOUN a number expressible as a limit of rational numbers. See **number** (sense 1).

real part NOUN the term *a* in a complex number $a + ib$, where $i = \sqrt{-1}$.

realpolitik (reɪˈɑːlpɒlɪˈtiːk) NOUN a ruthlessly realistic and opportunist approach to statesmanship, rather than a moralistic one, esp as exemplified by Bismarck.
▷HISTORY C19: German: politics of realism

real presence NOUN the doctrine that the body of Christ is actually present in the Eucharist.

real property NOUN immovable property, esp land and buildings, including proprietary rights over land, such as mineral rights. Compare **personal property.** Also called: **real estate.**

real tennis NOUN an ancient form of tennis played in a four-walled indoor court with various openings, a sloping-roofed corridor along three sides, and a buttress on the fourth side. Also called: **royal tennis.**

real-time ADJECTIVE denoting or relating to a data-processing system in which a computer receives constantly changing data, such as information relating to air-traffic control, travel booking systems, etc., and processes it sufficiently rapidly to be able to control the source of the data.

realtor (ˈrɪəltə, -ˌtɔː) NOUN a US and Canadian word for an **estate agent**, esp an accredited one.
▷HISTORY C20: from a trademark

realty (ˈrɪəltɪ) NOUN another term for **real property.**

real wages PLURAL NOUN *Economics* wages evaluated with reference to their purchasing power rather than to the money actually paid. Compare **money wages.**

ream[1] (riːm) NOUN [1] a number of sheets of paper, formerly 480 sheets (**short ream**), now 500 sheets (**long ream**) or 516 sheets (**printer's ream** or **perfect ream**). One ream is equal to 20 quires. [2] (*often plural*) *Informal* a large quantity, esp of written matter: *he wrote reams*.
▷HISTORY C14: from Old French *raime*, from Spanish *rezma*, from Arabic *rizmah* bale

ream[2] (riːm) VERB (*tr*) [1] to enlarge (a hole) by use of a reamer. [2] *US* to extract (juice) from (a citrus fruit) using a reamer.
▷HISTORY C19: perhaps from C14 *remen* to open up, from Old English *rȳman* to widen

reamer (ˈriːmə) NOUN [1] a steel tool with a cylindrical or tapered shank around which longitudinal teeth are ground, used for smoothing the bores of holes accurately to size. [2] *US* a utensil with a conical projection used for extracting juice from citrus fruits; lemon squeezer.

rean (ri:n) NOUN a variant spelling of **reen.**

reanalysis (ˌri:əˈnælɪsɪs) NOUN the act or an instance of analysing again.

reanimate (ri:ˈænɪmeɪt) VERB (*tr*) 1 to refresh or enliven (something) again: *to reanimate their enervated lives*. 2 to bring back to life.

reap (ri:p) VERB 1 to cut or harvest (a crop), esp corn, from (a field or tract of land). 2 (*tr*) to gain or get (something) as a reward for or result of some action or enterprise.
▷HISTORY Old English *riopan*; related to Norwegian *ripa* to scratch, Middle Low German *repen* to card, ripple (flax)
▸ˈ**reapable** ADJECTIVE

reaper (ˈri:pə) NOUN 1 a person who reaps or a machine for reaping. 2 **the grim reaper.** death.

reappear (ˌri:əˈpɪə) VERB to appear again.
▸ˌ**reapˈpearance** NOUN

reapply (ˌri:əˈplaɪ) VERB **-plies, -plying, -plied.** 1 (*tr*) to put or spread (something) on again: *reapply sunscreen frequently*. 2 (*intr*; often followed by *for*) to put in an application or request again.

reappoint (ˌri:əˈpɔɪnt) VERB (*tr*) to assign (a person, committee, etc.) to a post or role again.
▸ˌ**reapˈpointment** NOUN

reappraisal (ˌri:əˈpreɪzᵊl) NOUN the assessment or estimation again of the worth, value, or quality of a person or thing.

reappraise (ˌri:əˈpreɪz) VERB (*tr*) to assess the worth, value, or quality of (someone or something) again.

rear[1] (rɪə) NOUN 1 the back or hind part. 2 the area or position that lies at the back: *a garden at the rear of the house*. 3 the section of a military force or procession farthest from the front. 4 an informal word for **buttocks** (see **buttock**). 5 **bring up the rear.** to be at the back in a procession, race, etc. 6 **in the rear.** at the back. 7 (*modifier*) of or in the rear: *the rear legs; the rear side*.
▷HISTORY C17: probably abstracted from REARWARD or REARGUARD

rear[2] (rɪə) VERB 1 (*tr*) to care for and educate (children) until maturity; bring up; raise. 2 (*tr*) to breed (animals) or grow (plants). 3 (*tr*) to place or lift (a ladder, etc.) upright. 4 (*tr*) to erect (a monument, building, etc.); put up. 5 (*intr*; often foll by *up*) (esp of horses) to lift the front legs in the air and stand nearly upright. 6 (*intr*; often foll by *up* or *over*) (esp of tall buildings) to rise high; tower. 7 (*intr*) to start with anger, resentment, etc.
▷HISTORY Old English *rǣran*; related to Old High German *rēren* to distribute, Old Norse *reisa* to RAISE
▸ˈ**rearer** NOUN

rear admiral NOUN an officer holding flag rank in any of certain navies, junior to a vice admiral.

rearguard (ˈrɪəˌgɑ:d) NOUN 1 a detachment detailed to protect the rear of a military formation, esp in retreat. 2 an entrenched or conservative element, as in a political party. 3 **rearguard action. a** an action fought by a rearguard. **b** a defensive action undertaken to try to stop something happening or continuing.
▷HISTORY C15: from Old French *rereguarde* (modern French *arrière-garde*), from *rer*, from Latin *retro* back + *guarde* GUARD; compare VANGUARD

rear light *or* **lamp** NOUN a red light, usually one of a pair, attached to the rear of a motor vehicle. Also called: **tail-light, tail lamp.**

rearm (ri:ˈɑ:m) VERB 1 to arm again. 2 (*tr*) to equip (an army, a nation, etc.) with better weapons.
▸**reˈarmament** NOUN

rearmost (ˈrɪəˌməʊst) ADJECTIVE nearest the rear; coming last.

rearmouse (ˈrɪəˌmaʊs) NOUN, *plural* **-mice.** an archaic or dialect word for **bat** (the animal).
▷HISTORY See REREMOUSE

rearrange (ˌri:əˈreɪndʒ) VERB (*tr*) 1 to put (something) into a new order: *to rearrange the lighting*. 2 to put (something) back in its original order after it has been displaced. 3 to fix a new date or time for (something postponed): *to rearrange a match*.
▸ˌ**rearˈranger** NOUN ▸ˌ**rearˈrangement** NOUN

rear sight NOUN the sight of a gun nearest to the breech.

rear-view mirror NOUN a mirror on a motor vehicle enabling the driver to see traffic coming behind him or her.

rearward (ˈrɪəwəd) ADJECTIVE, ADVERB 1 Also (for adverb only): **rearwards.** towards or in the rear. ◆ NOUN 2 a position in the rear, esp the rear division of a military formation.
▷HISTORY C14 (as a noun: the part of an army positioned behind the main body of troops): from Anglo-French *rerewarde*, variant of *reregarde*; see REARGUARD

Rea Silvia (ˈrɪə ˈsɪlvɪə) NOUN a variant spelling of **Rhea Silvia.**

reason (ˈri:zᵊn) NOUN 1 the faculty of rational argument, deduction, judgment, etc. 2 sound mind; sanity. 3 a cause or motive, as for a belief, action, etc. 4 an argument in favour of or a justification for something. 5 *Philosophy* the intellect regarded as a source of knowledge, as contrasted with experience. 6 *Logic* grounds for a belief; a premise of an argument supporting that belief. 7 **by reason of.** because of. 8 **in** *or* **within reason.** within moderate or justifiable bounds. 9 **it stands to reason.** it is logical or obvious: *it stands to reason that he will lose*. 10 **listen to reason.** to be persuaded peaceably. 11 **reasons of State.** political justifications for an immoral act. ◆ VERB 12 (when *tr, takes a clause as object*) to think logically or draw (logical conclusions) from facts or premises. 13 (*intr*; usually foll by *with*) to urge or seek to persuade by reasoning. 14 (*tr*; often foll by *out*) to work out or resolve (a problem) by reasoning.
▷HISTORY C13: from Old French *reisun*, from Latin *ratiō* reckoning, from *rērī* to think
▸ˈ**reasoner** NOUN

Language note The expression *the reason is because...* should be avoided. Instead one should say either *this is because...* or *the reason is that...*

reasonable (ˈri:zənəbᵊl) ADJECTIVE 1 showing reason or sound judgment. 2 having the ability to reason. 3 having modest or moderate expectations; not making unfair demands. 4 moderate in price; not expensive. 5 fair; average: *reasonable weather*.
▸ˈ**reasonably** ADVERB ▸ˈ**reasonableness** NOUN

reasoned (ˈri:zᵊnd) ADJECTIVE well thought-out or well presented: *a reasoned explanation*.
▸ˈ**reasonedly** ADVERB

reasoning (ˈri:zənɪŋ) NOUN 1 the act or process of drawing conclusions from facts, evidence, etc. 2 the arguments, proofs, etc., so adduced.

reassemble (ˌri:əˈsɛmbᵊl) VERB 1 to come or bring together again: *parliament is due to reassemble*. 2 to fit or join (something) together again.
▸ˌ**reasˈsembly** NOUN

reassert (ˌri:əˈsɜ:t) VERB (*tr*) to assert (rights, claims, etc.) again: *he reasserted his belief*.

reassess (ˌri:əˈsɛs) VERB (*tr*) to assess (something) again; re-evaluate.

reassessment (ˌri:əˈsɛsmənt) NOUN the act or an instance of assessing again.

reassign (ˌri:əˈsaɪn) VERB (*tr*) to move (personnel, resources, etc.) to a new post, department, location, etc.
▸ˌ**reasˈsignment** NOUN

reassure (ˌri:əˈʃʊə) VERB (*tr*) 1 to relieve (someone) of anxieties; restore confidence to. 2 another term for **reinsure.**
▸ˌ**reasˈsurance** NOUN ▸ˌ**reasˈsurer** NOUN ▸ˌ**reasˈsuringly** ADVERB

reast (ri:st) VERB a variant spelling of **reest.**

Réaum. ABBREVIATION FOR Réaumur (scale).

Réaumur (ˈreɪəˌmjʊə) ADJECTIVE indicating measurement on the Réaumur scale of temperature.

Réaumur scale NOUN a scale of temperature in which the freezing point of water is taken as 0° and the boiling point is 80°.
▷HISTORY C18: named after René Antoine Ferchault de *Réaumur* (1683–1757), French physicist, who introduced it

reave[1] (ri:v) VERB **reaves, reaving, reaved** *or* **reft** (rɛft). *Archaic* 1 to carry off (property, prisoners, etc.) by force. 2 (*tr*; foll by *of*) to deprive; strip. See also **reive.**
▷HISTORY Old English *reāfian*; related to Old High German *roubōn* to rob, Old Norse *raufa* to break open

reave[2] (ri:v) VERB **reaves, reaving, reaved** *or* **reft** (rɛft). *Archaic* to break or tear (something) apart; cleave.
▷HISTORY C13 *reven*, probably from REAVE[1] and influenced in meaning by RIVE

reawaken (ˌri:əˈweɪkən) VERB 1 to emerge or rouse from sleep. 2 to become or make aware of (something) again.

reb (rɛb) NOUN (*sometimes capital*) *US informal* a Confederate soldier in the American Civil War (1861–65). Also called: **Johnny Reb.**
▷HISTORY short for REBEL

Reb (rɛb) NOUN *Judaism* an honorific title, corresponding to *Mr*, for those who do not have rabbinic qualifications: usually followed by the person's forename: *Reb Dovid*.
▷HISTORY Yiddish, from Hebrew *rabbī* rabbi, master

rebadge (ri:ˈbædʒ) VERB (*tr*) to relaunch (a product) under a new name, brand, or logo.

rebarbative (rɪˈbɑ:bətɪv) ADJECTIVE fearsome; forbidding.
▷HISTORY C19: from French *rébarbatif*, from Old French *rebarber* to repel (an enemy), to withstand (him) face to face, from RE- + *barbe* beard, from Latin *barba*

rebate[1] NOUN (ˈri:beɪt) 1 a refund of a fraction of the amount payable or paid, as for goods purchased in quantity; discount. ◆ VERB (rɪˈbeɪt) (*tr*) 2 to deduct (a part) of a payment from (the total). 3 *Archaic* to reduce or diminish (something or the effectiveness of something).
▷HISTORY C15: from Old French *rabattre* to beat down, hence reduce, deduct, from RE- + *abatre* to put down; see ABATE
▸**reˈbatable** *or* **reˈbateable** ADJECTIVE ▸ˈ**rebater** NOUN

rebate[2] (ˈri:beɪt, ˈræbɪt) NOUN, VERB another word for **rabbet.**

rebato (rəˈbɑ:təʊ) NOUN, *plural* **-tos.** a variant spelling of **rabato.**

Rebbe (ˈrɛbə) NOUN *Judaism* 1 the usually dynastic leader of a Chassidic sect. 2 an individual's chosen spiritual mentor.
▷HISTORY Yiddish, from Hebrew *rabbī* rabbi

rebbetzin (ˈrɛbətsən) NOUN *Judaism* the wife of a rabbi.
▷HISTORY from Yiddish

rebec *or* **rebeck** (ˈri:bɛk) NOUN a medieval stringed instrument resembling the violin but having a lute-shaped body.
▷HISTORY C16: from Old French *rebebe*, from Arabic *rebāb*; perhaps also influenced by Old French *bec* beak

Rebecca (rɪˈbɛkə) NOUN *Old Testament* the sister of Laban, who became the wife of Isaac and the mother of Esau and Jacob (Genesis 24–27). Douay spelling: **Rebekah.**

rebel VERB (rɪˈbɛl) **-bels, -belling, -belled.** (*intr*; often foll by *against*) 1 to resist or rise up against a government or other authority, esp by force of arms. 2 to dissent from an accepted moral code or convention of behaviour, dress, etc. 3 to show repugnance (towards). ◆ NOUN (ˈrɛbᵊl) 4 **a** a person who rebels. **b** (*as modifier*): *a rebel soldier; a rebel leader*. 5 a person who dissents from some accepted moral code or convention of behaviour, dress, etc.
▷HISTORY C13: from Old French *rebelle*, from Latin *rebellis* insurgent, from RE- + *bellum* war
▸ˈ**rebeldom** NOUN

rebellion (rɪˈbɛljən) NOUN 1 organized resistance or opposition to a government or other authority. 2 dissent from an accepted moral code or convention of behaviour, dress, etc.
▷HISTORY C14: via Old French from Latin *rebelliō* revolt (of those conquered); see REBEL

rebellious (rɪˈbɛljəs) ADJECTIVE 1 showing a tendency towards rebellion. 2 (of a problem, etc.) difficult to overcome; refractory.
▸**reˈbelliously** ADVERB ▸**reˈbelliousness** NOUN

rebellow (rɪˈbɛləʊ) VERB *Archaic or literary* to re-echo loudly.

rebirth (ri:ˈbɜ:θ) NOUN 1 a revival or renaissance: *the rebirth of learning*. 2 a second or new birth; reincarnation.

rebirthing (ri:ˈbɜ:θɪŋ) NOUN a form of

psychotherapy in which the subject supposedly "relives" the experience of being born, in order to confront and overcome traumas and anxieties stemming from birth.

reboot VERB (riːˈbuːt), VERB to shut down and restart (a computer system) or (of a computer system) to shut down and restart.

rebore NOUN (ˈriːˌbɔː) 1 the process of boring out the cylinders of a worn reciprocating engine and fitting oversize pistons. ♦ VERB (riːˈbɔː) 2 (*tr*) to carry out this process.

reborn (riːˈbɔːn) ADJECTIVE born or as if born again, esp in having undergone spiritual regeneration.

rebound VERB (rɪˈbaʊnd) (*tr*) 1 to spring back, as from a sudden impact. 2 to misfire, esp so as to hurt the perpetrator: *the plan rebounded.* ♦ NOUN (ˈriːbaʊnd) 3 the act or an instance of rebounding. 4 **on the rebound. a** in the act of springing back. **b** *Informal* in a state of recovering from rejection, disappointment, etc.: *he married her on the rebound from an unhappy love affair.*
▷HISTORY C14: from Old French *rebondir*, from RE- + *bondir* to BOUND[2]

rebozo (rɪˈbəʊzəʊ; *Spanish* reˈβoθo) NOUN, *plural* **-zos** (-zəʊz; *Spanish* -θos). a long wool or linen scarf covering the shoulders and head, worn by Latin American women.
▷HISTORY C19: from Spanish: shawl, from *rebozar* to muffle

rebrand (riːˈbrænd) VERB (*tr*) to change or update the image of (an organization or product).

rebuff (rɪˈbʌf) VERB (*tr*) 1 to snub, reject, or refuse (a person offering help or sympathy, an offer of help, etc.) abruptly or out of hand. 2 to beat back (an attack); repel. ♦ NOUN 3 a blunt refusal or rejection; snub. 4 any sudden check to progress or action.
▷HISTORY C16: from Old French *rebuffer*, from Italian *ribuffare*, from *ribuffo* a reprimand, from *ri-* RE- + *buffo* puff, gust, apparently of imitative origin

rebuild (riːˈbɪld) VERB **-builds, -building, -built.** 1 to make, construct, or form again: *the cost of rebuilding the house.* 2 (*tr*) to restore (a system or situation) to a previous condition: *his struggle to rebuild his life.*

rebuke (rɪˈbjuːk) VERB 1 (*tr*) to scold or reprimand (someone). ♦ NOUN 2 a reprimand or scolding.
▷HISTORY C14: from Old Norman French *rebuker*, from RE- + Old French *buchier* to hack down, from *busche* log, of Germanic origin
▸**reˈbukable** ADJECTIVE ▸**reˈbuker** NOUN

rebus (ˈriːbəs) NOUN, *plural* **-buses.** 1 a puzzle consisting of pictures representing syllables and words; in such a puzzle the word *hear* might be represented by H followed by a picture of an ear. 2 a heraldic emblem or device that is a pictorial representation of or pun on the name of the bearer.
▷HISTORY C17: from French *rébus*, from the Latin *rēbus* by things, from RES

rebut (rɪˈbʌt) VERB **-buts, -butting, -butted.** (*tr*) to refute or disprove, esp by offering a contrary contention or argument.
▷HISTORY C13: from Old French *reboter*, from RE- + *boter* to thrust, BUTT[3]
▸**reˈbuttable** ADJECTIVE ▸**reˈbuttal** NOUN

rebutter (rɪˈbʌtə) NOUN 1 *Law* a defendant's pleading in reply to a claimant's surrejoinder. 2 a person who rebuts.

rec (rɛk) NOUN *Informal* short for **recreation** (ground).

recalcitrant (rɪˈkælsɪtrənt) ADJECTIVE 1 not susceptible to control or authority; refractory. ♦ NOUN 2 a recalcitrant person.
▷HISTORY C19: via French from Latin *recalcitrāre*, from RE- + *calcitrāre* to kick, from *calx* heel
▸**reˈcalcitrance** NOUN

recalculate (riːˈkælkjʊˌleɪt) VERB (*tr*) to calculate (a total, sum, etc.) again.

recalesce (ˌriːkəˈlɛs) VERB (*intr*) to undergo recalescence.

recalescence (ˌriːkəˈlɛsəns) NOUN a sudden spontaneous increase in the temperature of cooling iron resulting from an exothermic change in crystal structure occurring at a particular temperature.
▷HISTORY C19: from Latin *recalēscere* to grow warm again, from RE- + *calēscere*, from *calēre* to be hot
▸**ˌrecaˈlescent** ADJECTIVE

recall (rɪˈkɔːl) VERB (*tr*) 1 (*may take a clause as object*) to bring back to mind; recollect; remember. 2 to order to return; call back permanently or temporarily: *to recall an ambassador.* 3 to revoke or take back. 4 to cause (one's thoughts, attention, etc.) to return from a reverie or digression. 5 *Poetic* to restore or revive. ♦ NOUN 6 the act of recalling or state of being recalled. 7 revocation or cancellation. 8 the ability to remember things; recollection. 9 *Military* (esp formerly) a signal to call back troops, etc., usually a bugle call: *to sound the recall.* 10 *US* the process by which elected officials may be deprived of office by popular vote.
▸**reˈcallable** ADJECTIVE

recant (rɪˈkænt) VERB to repudiate or withdraw (a former belief or statement), esp formally in public.
▷HISTORY C16: from Latin *recantāre* to sing again, from RE- + *cantāre* to sing; see CHANT
▸**recantation** (ˌriːkænˈteɪʃən) NOUN ▸**reˈcanter** NOUN

recap VERB (ˈriːˌkæp, riːˈkæp) **-caps, -capping, -capped**, NOUN (ˈriːˌkæp) 1 *Informal* short for **recapitulate** or **recapitulation.** ♦ NOUN (ˈriːˌkæp) 2 *Austral and NZ* another name for **retread.**
▸**reˈcappable** ADJECTIVE

recapitulate (ˌriːkəˈpɪtjʊˌleɪt) VERB 1 to restate the main points of (an argument, speech, etc.); summarize. 2 (*tr*) (of an animal) to repeat (stages of its evolutionary development) during the embryonic stages of its life. 3 to repeat at some point during a piece of music (material used earlier in the same work).
▷HISTORY C16: from Late Latin *recapitulāre*, literally: to put back under headings; see CAPITULATE
▸**ˌrecaˈpitulative** *or* **ˌrecaˈpitulatory** ADJECTIVE

recapitulation (ˌriːkəˌpɪtjʊˈleɪʃən) NOUN 1 the act of recapitulating, esp summing up, as at the end of a speech. 2 Also called: **palingenesis.** *Biology* the apparent repetition in the embryonic development of an animal of the changes that occurred during its evolutionary history. Compare **caenogenesis.** 3 *Music* the repeating of earlier themes, esp when forming the final section of a movement in sonata form.

recaption (riːˈkæpʃən) NOUN *Law* the process of taking back one's own wife, child, property, etc., without causing a breach of the peace.
▷HISTORY C17: from RE- + CAPTION (in the sense: seizure)

recapture (riːˈkæptʃə) VERB (*tr*) 1 to capture or take again. 2 to recover, renew, or repeat (a lost or former ability, sensation, etc.): *she soon recaptured her high spirits.* 3 *US* (of the government) to take lawfully (a proportion of the profits of a public-service undertaking). ♦ NOUN 4 the act of recapturing or fact of being recaptured. 5 *US* the seizure by the government of a proportion of the profits of a public-service undertaking.

recast (riːˈkɑːst) VERB **-casts, -casting, -cast.** (*tr*) 1 (often foll by *as*) to give (someone or something) a new role, function, or character: *recast themselves as moderate and kind.* 2 (often foll by *as*) to cast (an actor or actress) again or in a different part. 3 to cast new actors or actresses for a production of (a play, film, etc.).

recce (ˈrɛkɪ) NOUN, VERB **-ces, -ceing, -ced** *or* **-ceed.** a slang word for **reconnaissance** or **reconnoitre.**

recd *or* **rec'd** ABBREVIATION FOR received.

recede (rɪˈsiːd) VERB (*intr*) 1 to withdraw from a point or limit; go back: *the tide receded.* 2 to become more distant: *hopes of rescue receded.* 3 to slope backwards: *apes have receding foreheads.* 4 **a** (of a man's hair) to cease to grow at the temples and above the forehead. **b** (of a man) to start to go bald in this way. 5 to decline in value or character. 6 (usually foll by *from*) to draw back or retreat, as from a promise.
▷HISTORY C15: from Latin *recēdere* to go back, from RE- + *cēdere* to yield, CEDE

re-cede (riːˈsiːd) VERB (*tr*) to restore to a former owner.

receipt (rɪˈsiːt) NOUN 1 a written acknowledgment by a receiver of money, goods, etc., that payment or delivery has been made. 2 the act of receiving or fact of being received. 3 (*usually plural*) an amount or article received. 4 *Archaic* another word for **recipe.** ♦ VERB 5 (*tr*) to acknowledge payment of (a bill), as by marking it. 6 *Chiefly US* to issue a receipt for (money, goods, etc.).
▷HISTORY C14: from Old Norman French *receite*, from Medieval Latin *recepta*, from Latin *recipere* to RECEIVE

receiptor (rɪˈsiːtə) NOUN *Chiefly US* a person who receipts.

receivable (rɪˈsiːvəbᵊl) ADJECTIVE 1 suitable for or capable of being received, esp as payment or legal tender. 2 (of a bill, etc.) awaiting payment: *accounts receivable.* ♦ NOUN 3 (*usually plural*) the part of the assets of a business represented by accounts due for payment.

receive (rɪˈsiːv) VERB (*mainly tr*) 1 to take (something offered) into one's hand or possession. 2 to have (an honour, blessing, etc.) bestowed. 3 to accept delivery or transmission of (a letter, telephone call, etc.). 4 to be informed of (news or information). 5 to hear and consent to or acknowledge (an oath, confession, etc.). 6 (of a vessel or container) to take or hold (a substance, commodity, or certain amount). 7 to support or sustain (the weight of something); bear. 8 to apprehend or perceive (ideas, etc.). 9 to experience, undergo, or meet with: *to receive a crack on the skull.* 10 (*also intr*) to be at home to (visitors). 11 to greet or welcome (visitors or guests), esp in formal style. 12 to admit (a person) to a place, society, condition, etc.: *he was received into the priesthood.* 13 to accept or acknowledge (a precept or principle) as true or valid. 14 to convert (incoming radio signals) into sounds, pictures, etc., by means of a receiver. 15 (*also intr*) *Tennis* to play at the other end from the server; be required to return (service). 16 (*also intr*) to partake of (the Christian Eucharist). 17 (*intr*) *Chiefly Brit* to buy and sell stolen goods.
▷HISTORY C13: from Old French *receivre*, from Latin *recipere* to take back, from RE- + *capere* to take

received (rɪˈsiːvd) ADJECTIVE generally accepted or believed: *received wisdom.*

Received Pronunciation NOUN the accent of standard Southern British English. Abbreviation: **RP.**

receiver (rɪˈsiːvə) NOUN 1 a person who receives something; recipient. 2 a person appointed by a court to manage property pending the outcome of litigation, during the infancy of the owner, or after the owner has been declared bankrupt or of unsound mind. 3 *Chiefly Brit* a person who receives stolen goods knowing that they have been stolen. 4 the equipment in a telephone, radio, or television that receives incoming electrical signals or modulated radio waves and converts them into the original audio or video signals. 5 the part of a telephone containing the earpiece and mouthpiece that is held by the telephone user. 6 the equipment in a radar system, radio telescope, etc., that converts incoming radio signals into a useful form, usually displayed on the screen of a cathode-ray oscilloscope. 7 an obsolete word for **receptacle.** 8 *Chem* a vessel in which the distillate is collected during distillation. 9 *US sport* a player whose function is to receive the ball, esp a footballer who catches long passes. 10 the metallic frame situated behind the breech of a gun to guide the round into the chamber.

receivership (rɪˈsiːvəʃɪp) NOUN *Law* 1 the office or function of a receiver. 2 the condition of being administered by a receiver.

receiving order NOUN *Brit, obsolete* a court order appointing a receiver to manage the property of a debtor or bankrupt. Official name: **bankruptcy order.**

recency effect (ˈriːsənsɪ) NOUN *Psychol* the phenomenon that when people are asked to recall in any order the items on a list, those that come at the end of the list are more likely to be recalled than the others.

recension (rɪˈsɛnʃən) NOUN 1 a critical revision of a literary work. 2 a text revised in this way.
▷HISTORY C17: from Latin *recēnsiō*, from *recēnsēre* to survey, from RE- + *cēnsēre* to assess

recent (ˈriːsᵊnt) ADJECTIVE having appeared, happened, or been made not long ago; modern, fresh, or new.
▷HISTORY C16: from Latin *recens* fresh; related to Greek *kainos* new
▸**ˈrecently** ADVERB ▸**ˈrecentness** *or* **ˈrecency** NOUN

Recent (ˈriːsᵊnt) ADJECTIVE, NOUN *Geology* another word for **Holocene.**

recept (ˈriːsɛpt) NOUN *Psychol* an idea or image

formed in the mind by repeated experience of a particular pattern of sensory stimulation.
▷HISTORY C20: from RE- + (CON)CEPT

receptacle (rɪˈsɛptək^əl) NOUN [1] an object that holds something; container. [2] *Botany* **a** the enlarged or modified tip of the flower stalk that bears the parts of the flower. **b** the shortened flattened stem bearing the florets of the capitulum of composite flowers such as the daisy. **c** the part of lower plants that bears the reproductive organs or spores.
▷HISTORY C15: from Latin *receptāculum* a store-place, from *receptāre* to receive again, from *recipere* to RECEIVE

reception (rɪˈsɛpʃən) NOUN [1] the act of receiving or state of being received. [2] the manner in which something, such as a guest or a new idea, is received: *a cold reception.* [3] a formal party for guests, such as one after a wedding. [4] an area in an office, hotel, etc., where visitors or guests are received and appointments or reservations dealt with. [5] short for **reception room.** [6] the quality or fidelity of a received radio or television broadcast: *the reception was poor.* [7] *Brit* **a** the first class in an infant school. **b** a class in a school designed to receive new immigrants, esp those whose knowledge of English is poor. **c** (*as modifier*): *a reception teacher.*
▷HISTORY C14: from Latin *receptiō* a receiving, from *recipere* to RECEIVE

reception centre NOUN *Social welfare* (in Britain) [1] a place to which distressed people, such as vagrants, addicts, victims of a disaster, refugees, etc., go pending more permanent arrangements. [2] a local-authority home where children are looked after in a family crisis or where long-term placement is arranged for a child whose family cannot provide a home.

receptionist (rɪˈsɛpʃənɪst) NOUN a person employed in an office, hotel, doctor's surgery, etc., to receive clients, guests, or patients, answer the telephone, and arrange appointments, etc.

reception room NOUN [1] a room in a private house suitable for entertaining guests, esp a lounge or dining room. [2] a room in a hotel suitable for large parties, receptions, etc.

receptive (rɪˈsɛptɪv) ADJECTIVE [1] able to apprehend quickly. [2] tending to receive new ideas or suggestions favourably. [3] able to hold or receive.
▸**reˈceptively** ADVERB ▸**receptivity** (ˌriːsɛpˈtɪvɪtɪ) *or* **reˈceptiveness** NOUN

receptor (rɪˈsɛptə) NOUN [1] *Physiol* a sensory nerve ending that changes specific stimuli into nerve impulses. [2] any of various devices that receive information, signals, etc.

recess NOUN (rɪˈsɛs, ˈriːsɛs) [1] a space, such as a niche or alcove, set back or indented. [2] (*often plural*) a secluded or secret place: *recesses of the mind.* [3] a cessation of business, such as the closure of Parliament during a vacation. [4] *Anatomy* a small cavity or depression in a bodily organ, part, or structure. [5] *US and Canadian* a break between classes at a school. ◆ VERB (rɪˈsɛs) [6] (*tr*) to place or set (something) in a recess. [7] (*tr*) to build a recess or recesses in (a wall, building, etc.).
▷HISTORY C16: from Latin *recessus* a retreat, from *recēdere* to RECEDE

recession¹ (rɪˈsɛʃən) NOUN [1] a temporary depression in economic activity or prosperity. [2] the withdrawal of the clergy and choir in procession from the chancel at the conclusion of a church service. [3] the act of receding. [4] a part of a building, wall, etc., that recedes.
▷HISTORY C17: from Latin *recessio*; see RECESS

recession² (riːˈsɛʃən) NOUN the act of restoring possession to a former owner.
▷HISTORY C19: from RE- + CESSION

recessional (rɪˈsɛʃən^əl) ADJECTIVE [1] of or relating to recession. ◆ NOUN [2] a hymn sung as the clergy and choir withdraw from the chancel at the conclusion of a church service.

recessionary (rɪˈsɛʃənərɪ) ADJECTIVE of, caused by, or undergoing economic recession.

recessive (rɪˈsɛsɪv) ADJECTIVE [1] tending to recede or go back; receding. [2] *Genetics* **a** (of a gene) capable of producing its characteristic phenotype in the organism only when its allele is identical. **b** (of a character) controlled by such a gene. Compare **dominant** (sense 4). [3] *Linguistics* (of stress) tending to be placed on or near the initial syllable of a polysyllabic word. ◆ NOUN [4] *Genetics* **a** a recessive gene or character. **b** an organism having such a gene or character.
▸**reˈcessively** ADVERB ▸**reˈcessiveness** NOUN

Rechabite (ˈrɛkəˌbaɪt) NOUN a total abstainer from alcoholic drink, esp a member of the **Independent Order of Rechabites**, a society devoted to abstention.
▷HISTORY C14: via Medieval Latin from Hebrew *Rēkābīm* descendants of *Rēkāb*. See Jeremiah 35:6

RECHAR (ˈriːtʃɑː) NOUN an EU funding programme providing grants for the reconversion or development of depressed mining areas.
▷HISTORY C20: from French *Re*conversion de Bassins *Char*bonniers, literally: reconversion of coal fields

recharge (riːˈtʃɑːdʒ) VERB (*tr*) [1] to cause (an accumulator, capacitor, etc.) to take up and store electricity again. [2] to revive or renew (one's energies) (esp in **recharge one's batteries**).
▸**reˈchargeable** ADJECTIVE

réchauffé *French* (reʃofe) NOUN [1] warmed-up leftover food. [2] old, stale, or reworked material.
▷HISTORY C19: from French *réchauffer* to reheat, from RE- + *chauffer* to warm; see CHAFE

recherché (rəˈʃɛəʃeɪ; *French* rəʃɛrʃe) ADJECTIVE [1] known only to connoisseurs; choice or rare. [2] studiedly refined or elegant.
▷HISTORY C18: from French: past participle of *rechercher* to make a thorough search for; see RESEARCH

recidivism (rɪˈsɪdɪˌvɪzəm) NOUN habitual relapse into crime.
▷HISTORY C19: from Latin *recidīvus* falling back, from RE- + *cadere* to fall
▸**reˈcidivist** NOUN, ADJECTIVE ▸**reˌcidiˈvistic** *or* **reˈcidivous** ADJECTIVE

Recife (rɛˈsiːfə) NOUN a port at the easternmost point of Brazil on the Atlantic: capital of Pernambuco state; built partly on an island, with many waterways and bridges. Pop. (city): 1 421 947 (2000), with a conurbation of 3 168 000 (1995 est.). Former name: **Pernambuco.**

recipe (ˈrɛsɪpɪ) NOUN [1] a list of ingredients and directions for making something, esp a food preparation. [2] *Med* (formerly) a medical prescription. [3] a method for achieving some desired objective: *a recipe for success.*
▷HISTORY C14: from Latin, literally: take (it)! from *recipere* to take, RECEIVE

recipience (rɪˈsɪpɪəns) NOUN [1] the act of receiving. [2] the quality of being receptive; receptiveness.

recipient (rɪˈsɪpɪənt) NOUN [1] a person who or thing that receives. ◆ ADJECTIVE [2] a less common word for **receptive.**
▷HISTORY C16: via French from Latin *recipiēns*, from *recipere* to RECEIVE

reciprocal (rɪˈsɪprək^əl) ADJECTIVE [1] of, relating to, or designating something given by each of two people, countries, etc., to the other; mutual: *reciprocal friendship; reciprocal trade.* [2] given or done in return: *a reciprocal favour.* [3] (of a pronoun) indicating that action is given and received by each subject; for example, *each other* in the sentence *they started to shout at each other.* [4] *Maths* of or relating to a number or quantity divided into one. [5] *Navigation* denoting a course or bearing that is 180° from the previous or assumed one. ◆ NOUN [6] something that is reciprocal. [7] Also called: **inverse.** *Maths* a number or quantity that when multiplied by a given number or quantity gives a product of one: *the reciprocal of 2 is 0.5.*
▷HISTORY C16: from Latin *reciprocus* alternating
▸**reˌciproˈcality** NOUN ▸**reˈciprocally** ADVERB

reciprocate (rɪˈsɪprəˌkeɪt) VERB [1] to give or feel in return. [2] to move or cause to move backwards and forwards. [3] (*intr*) to be correspondent or equivalent.
▷HISTORY C17: from Latin *reciprocāre*, from *reciprocus* RECIPROCAL
▸**reˌciproˈcation** NOUN ▸**reˈciprocative** *or* **reˈciproˌcatory** ADJECTIVE ▸**reˈciproˌcator** NOUN

reciprocating engine NOUN an engine in which one or more pistons move backwards and forwards inside a cylinder or cylinders.

reciprocity (ˌrɛsɪˈprɒsɪtɪ) NOUN, *plural* **-ities.** [1] reciprocal action or relation. [2] a mutual exchange of commercial or other privileges.
▷HISTORY C18: via French from Latin *reciprocus* RECIPROCAL

reciprocity failure NOUN *Photog* a failure of the two exposure variables, light intensity and exposure time, to behave in a reciprocal fashion at very high or very low values.

recision (rɪˈsɪʒən) NOUN the act of cancelling or rescinding; annulment: *the recision of a treaty.*
▷HISTORY C17: from Latin *recīsiō*, from *recīdere* to cut back

recital (rɪˈsaɪt^əl) NOUN [1] a musical performance by a soloist or soloists. Compare **concert** (sense 1). [2] the act of reciting or repeating something learned or prepared. [3] an account, narration, or description. [4] a detailed statement of facts, figures, etc. [5] (*often plural*) *Law* the preliminary statement in a deed showing the reason for its existence and leading up to and explaining the operative part.
▸**reˈcitalist** NOUN

recitation (ˌrɛsɪˈteɪʃən) NOUN [1] the act of reciting from memory, or a formal reading of verse before an audience. [2] something recited.

recitative¹ (ˌrɛsɪtəˈtiːv) NOUN a passage in a musical composition, esp the narrative parts in an oratorio, set for one voice with either continuo accompaniment only or full accompaniment, reflecting the natural rhythms of speech.
▷HISTORY C17: from Italian *recitativo*; see RECITE

recitative² (rɪˈsaɪtətɪv) ADJECTIVE of or relating to recital.

recite (rɪˈsaɪt) VERB [1] to repeat (a poem, passage, etc.) aloud from memory before an audience, teacher, etc. [2] (*tr*) to give a detailed account of. [3] (*tr*) to enumerate (examples, etc.).
▷HISTORY C15: from Latin *recitāre* to cite again, from RE- + *citāre* to summon; see CITE
▸**reˈcitable** ADJECTIVE ▸**reˈciter** NOUN

reck (rɛk) VERB *Archaic* (*used mainly with a negative*) [1] to mind or care about (something): *to reck nought.* [2] (*usually impersonal*) to concern or interest (someone).
▷HISTORY Old English *reccan*; related to Old High German *ruohhen* to take care, Old Norse *rækja*, Gothic *rakjan*

reckless (ˈrɛklɪs) ADJECTIVE having or showing no regard for danger or consequences; heedless; rash: *a reckless driver; a reckless attempt.*
▷HISTORY Old English *recceleās* (see RECK, -LESS); related to Middle Dutch *roekeloos*, Old High German *ruahhalōs*
▸**ˈrecklessly** ADVERB ▸**ˈrecklessness** NOUN

Recklinghausen (*German* rɛklɪŋˈhauzən) NOUN an industrial city in NW Germany, in North Rhine-Westphalia on the N edge of the Ruhr. Pop.: 126 241 (1999 est.).

reckon (ˈrɛkən) VERB [1] to calculate or ascertain by calculating; compute. [2] (*tr*) to include; count as part of a set or class: *I reckon her with the angels.* [3] (*usually passive*) to consider or regard: *he is reckoned clever.* [4] (when *tr*, *takes a clause as object*) to think or suppose; be of the opinion: *I reckon you don't know where to go next.* [5] (*intr*; foll by *with*) to settle accounts (with). [6] (*intr*; foll by *with* or *without*) to take into account or fail to take into account: *the bully reckoned without John's big brother.* [7] (*intr*; foll by *on* or *upon*) to rely or depend: *I reckon on your support in this crisis.* [8] (*tr*) *Slang* to regard as good: *I don't reckon your chances of success.* [9] (*tr*) *Informal* to have a high opinion of: *she was sensitive to bad reviews, even from people she did not reckon.* [10] **to be reckoned with.** of considerable importance or influence.
▷HISTORY Old English *(ge)recenian* recount; related to Old Frisian *rekenia*, Old High German *rehhanōn* to count

reckoner (ˈrɛkənə) NOUN any of various devices or tables used to facilitate reckoning, esp a ready reckoner.

reckoning (ˈrɛkənɪŋ) NOUN [1] the act of counting or calculating. [2] settlement of an account or bill. [3] a bill or account. [4] retribution for one's actions (esp in the phrase **day of reckoning**). [5] *Navigation* short for **dead reckoning.**

reclaim (rɪˈkleɪm) VERB (*tr*) [1] to claim back: *to*

reclaim baggage. 2 to convert (desert, marsh, waste ground, etc.) into land suitable for growing crops. 3 to recover (useful substances) from waste products. 4 to convert (someone) from sin, folly, vice, etc. 5 *Falconry* to render (a hawk or falcon) tame. ◆ NOUN 6 the act of reclaiming or state of being reclaimed.
▷HISTORY C13: from Old French *réclamer*, from Latin *reclāmāre* to cry out, protest, from RE- + *clāmāre* to shout
▸**re'claimable** ADJECTIVE ▸**re'claimant** *or* **re'claimer** NOUN

reclamation (ˌrɛkləˈmeɪʃən) NOUN 1 the conversion of desert, marsh, or other waste land into land suitable for cultivation. 2 the recovery of useful substances from waste products. 3 the act of reclaiming or state of being reclaimed.

réclame *French* (reklam) NOUN 1 public acclaim or attention; publicity. 2 the capacity for attracting publicity.

reclinate (ˈrɛklɪˌneɪt) ADJECTIVE (esp of a leaf or stem) naturally curved or bent backwards so that the upper part rests on the ground.
▷HISTORY C18: from Latin *reclīnātus* bent back

recline (rɪˈklaɪn) VERB to rest or cause to rest in a leaning position.
▷HISTORY C15: from Old French *recliner*, from Latin *reclīnāre* to lean back, from RE- + *clīnāre* to LEAN[1]
▸**re'clinable** ADJECTIVE ▸**reclination** (ˌrɛklɪˈneɪʃən) NOUN

recliner (rɪˈklaɪnə) NOUN a type of armchair having a back that can be adjusted to slope at various angles and, usually, a leg rest.

recluse (rɪˈkluːs) NOUN 1 a person who lives in seclusion. 2 a person who lives in solitude to devote himself to prayer and religious meditation; a hermit, anchorite, or anchoress. ◆ ADJECTIVE 3 solitary; retiring.
▷HISTORY C13: from Old French *reclus*, from Late Latin *reclūdere* to shut away, from Latin RE- + *claudere* to close
▸**reclusion** (rɪˈkluːʒən) NOUN ▸**re'clusive** ADJECTIVE

recognition (ˌrɛkəgˈnɪʃən) NOUN 1 the act of recognizing or fact of being recognized. 2 acceptance or acknowledgment of a claim, duty, fact, truth, etc. 3 a token of thanks or acknowledgment. 4 formal acknowledgment of a government or of the independence of a country. 5 *Chiefly US and Canadian* an instance of a chairman granting a person the right to speak in a deliberative body, debate, etc.
▷HISTORY C15: from Latin *recognitiō*, from *recognoscere* to know again, from RE- + *cognoscere* to know, ascertain
▸**recognitive** (rɪˈkɒgnɪtɪv) *or* **re'cognitory** ADJECTIVE

recognizance *or* **recognisance** (rɪˈkɒgnɪzəns) NOUN 1 *Law* **a** a bond entered into before a court or magistrate by which a person binds himself to do a specified act, as to appear in court on a stated day, keep the peace, or pay a debt. **b** a monetary sum pledged to the performance of such an act. 2 an obsolete word for **recognition.**
▷HISTORY C14: from Old French *reconoissance*, from *reconoistre* to RECOGNIZE
▸**re'cognizant** *or* **re'cognisant** ADJECTIVE

recognize *or* **recognise** (ˈrɛkəgˌnaɪz) VERB *(tr)* 1 to perceive (a person, creature, or thing) to be the same as or belong to the same class as something previously seen or known; know again. 2 to accept or be aware of (a fact, duty, problem, etc.): *to recognize necessity.* 3 to give formal acknowledgment of the status or legality of (a government, an accredited representative, etc.). 4 *Chiefly US and Canadian* to grant (a person) the right to speak in a deliberative body, debate, etc. 5 to give a token of thanks for (a service rendered, etc.). 6 to make formal acknowledgment of (a claim, etc.). 7 to show approval or appreciation of (something good or pleasing). 8 to acknowledge or greet (a person), as when meeting by chance. 9 *(intr) Chiefly US* to enter into a recognizance.
▷HISTORY C15: from Latin *recognoscere* to know again, from RE- + *cognoscere* to know, ascertain
▸**'recogˌnizable** *or* **'recogˌnisable** ADJECTIVE ▸**ˌrecogˌnizaˈbility** *or* **ˌrecogˌnisaˈbility** NOUN ▸**'recogˌnizably** *or* **'recogˌnisably** ADVERB ▸**'recogˌnizer** *or* **'recogˌniser** NOUN

recognizee *or* **recognisee** (rɪˌkɒgnɪˈziː) NOUN *Law* the person to whom one entering into a recognizance is bound.

recognizor *or* **recognisor** (rɪˌkɒgnɪˈzɔː) NOUN *Law* a person who enters into a recognizance.

recoil VERB (rɪˈkɔɪl) *(intr)* 1 to jerk back, as from an impact or violent thrust. 2 (often foll by *from*) to draw back in fear, horror, or disgust: *to recoil from the sight of blood.* 3 (foll by *on* or *upon*) to go wrong, esp so as to hurt the perpetrator. 4 (of a nucleus, atom, molecule, or elementary particle) to change momentum as a result of the emission of a photon or particle. ◆ NOUN (rɪˈkɔɪl, ˈriːkɔɪl) 5 **a** the backward movement of a gun when fired. **b** the distance moved. 6 the motion acquired by a particle as a result of its emission of a photon or other particle. 7 the act of recoiling.
▷HISTORY C13: from Old French *reculer*, from RE- + *cul* rump, from Latin *cūlus*
▸**re'coiler** NOUN

recoilless (rɪˈkɔɪllɪs) ADJECTIVE denoting a gun, esp an antitank weapon, in which the blast is vented to the rear so as to eliminate or reduce recoil.

recollect (ˌrɛkəˈlɛkt) VERB (when *tr, often takes a clause as object*) to recall from memory; remember.
▷HISTORY C16: from Latin *recolligere* to gather again, from RE- + *colligere* to COLLECT[1]
▸**ˌrecol'lective** ADJECTIVE ▸**ˌrecol'lectively** ADVERB

recollection (ˌrɛkəˈlɛkʃən) NOUN 1 the act of recalling something from memory; the ability to remember. 2 something remembered; a memory.

recombinant (riːˈkɒmbɪnənt) *Genetics* ◆ ADJECTIVE 1 produced by the combining of genetic material from more than one origin. ◆ NOUN 2 a chromosome, cell, organism, etc., the genetic makeup of which results from recombination.

recombinant DNA NOUN DNA molecules that are extracted from different sources and chemically joined together; for example DNA comprising an animal gene may be recombined with DNA from a bacterium.

recombination (ˌriːkɒmbɪˈneɪʃən) NOUN 1 *Genetics* any of several processes by which genetic material of different origins becomes combined. It most commonly occurs between two sets of parental chromosomes during production of germ cells. 2 *Physics* the union of free electrons and holes in a semiconductor or of free ions and electrons in a plasma.

recombine (ˌriːkəmˈbaɪn) VERB to join together again.

recommence (ˌriːkəˈmɛns) VERB to begin or commence again.
▸**ˌrecom'mencement** NOUN

recommend (ˌrɛkəˈmɛnd) VERB *(tr)* 1 *(may take a clause as object or an infinitive)* to advise as the best course or choice; counsel: *to recommend prudence.* 2 to praise or commend: *to recommend a new book.* 3 to make attractive or advisable: *the trip has little to recommend it.* 4 *Archaic* to entrust (a person or thing) to someone else's care; commend.
▷HISTORY C14: via Medieval Latin from Latin RE- + *commendāre* to COMMEND
▸**ˌrecom'mendable** ADJECTIVE ▸**ˌrecom'mender** NOUN

recommendation (ˌrɛkəmɛnˈdeɪʃən) NOUN 1 the act of recommending. 2 something that recommends, esp a letter presenting someone as suitable for a job, etc. 3 something that is recommended, such as a course of action.

recommendatory (ˌrɛkəˈmɛndətərɪ, -trɪ) ADJECTIVE intended to or serving to recommend.

recommit (ˌriːkəˈmɪt) VERB **-mits, -mitting, -mitted.** *(tr)* 1 to send (a bill) back to a committee for further consideration. 2 to commit again.
▸**ˌrecom'mitment** *or* **ˌrecom'mittal** NOUN

recompense (ˈrɛkəmˌpɛns) VERB 1 *(tr)* to pay or reward for service, work, etc. 2 *(tr)* to compensate for loss, injury, etc. ◆ NOUN 3 compensation for loss, injury, etc.: *to make recompense.* 4 reward, remuneration, or repayment.
▷HISTORY C15: from Old French *recompenser*, from Latin RE- + *compensāre* to balance in weighing; see COMPENSATE
▸**'recomˌpensable** ADJECTIVE ▸**'recomˌpenser** NOUN

recompose (ˌriːkəmˈpəʊz) VERB *(tr)* 1 to restore to composure or calmness. 2 to arrange or compose again; reform.
▸**recomposition** (ˌriːkɒmpəˈzɪʃən) NOUN

reconcilable (ˈrɛkənˌsaɪləbᵊl, ˌrɛkənˈsaɪ-) ADJECTIVE able or willing to be reconciled.
▸**ˌreconˌcilaˈbility** *or* **'reconˌcilableness** NOUN ▸**'reconˌcilably** ADVERB

reconcile (ˈrɛkənˌsaɪl) VERB *(tr)* 1 *(often passive; usually foll by to)* to make (oneself or another) no longer opposed; cause to acquiesce in something unpleasant: *she reconciled herself to poverty.* 2 to become friendly with (someone) after estrangement or to re-establish friendly relations between (two or more people). 3 to settle (a quarrel or difference). 4 to make (two apparently conflicting things) compatible or consistent with each other. 5 to reconsecrate (a desecrated church, etc.).
▷HISTORY C14: from Latin *reconciliāre* to bring together again, from RE- + *conciliāre* to make friendly, CONCILIATE
▸**'reconˌcilement** NOUN ▸**'reconˌciler** NOUN ▸**reconciliation** (ˌrɛkənˌsɪlɪˈeɪʃən) NOUN ▸**reconciliatory** (ˌrɛkənˈsɪlɪətərɪ, -trɪ) ADJECTIVE

Reconciliation (ˌrɛkənˌsɪlɪˈeɪʃən) NOUN *RC Church* a sacrament in which repentant sinners are absolved and gain reconciliation with God and the Church, on condition of confession of their sins to a priest and of performing a penance.

recondite (rɪˈkɒndaɪt, ˈrɛkənˌdaɪt) ADJECTIVE 1 requiring special knowledge to be understood; abstruse. 2 dealing with abstruse or profound subjects.
▷HISTORY C17: from Latin *reconditus* hidden away, from RE- + *condere* to conceal
▸**re'conditely** ADVERB ▸**re'conditeness** NOUN

recondition (ˌriːkənˈdɪʃən) VERB *(tr)* to restore to good condition or working order: *to recondition an engine.*

reconfirm (ˌriːkənˈfɜːm) VERB *(tr)* to confirm (an arrangement, agreement, etc.) again: *reconfirm your return flight on arrival.*

reconnaissance *or* **reconnoissance** (rɪˈkɒnɪsəns) NOUN 1 the act of reconnoitring. 2 the process of obtaining information about the position, activities, resources, etc., of an enemy or potential enemy. 3 a preliminary inspection of an area of land before an engineering survey is made.
▷HISTORY C18: from French, from Old French *reconoistre* to explore, RECOGNIZE

reconnect (ˌriːkəˈnɛkt) VERB to link or be linked together again.
▸**ˌrecon'nection** NOUN

reconnoitre *or US* **reconnoiter** (ˌrɛkəˈnɔɪtə) VERB 1 to survey or inspect (an enemy's position, region of land, etc.); make a reconnaissance (of). ◆ NOUN 2 the act or process of reconnoitring; a reconnaissance.
▷HISTORY C18: from obsolete French *reconnoître* to inspect, explore; see RECOGNIZE
▸**ˌrecon'noitrer** *or US* **ˌrecon'noiterer** NOUN

reconsider (ˌriːkənˈsɪdə) VERB 1 to consider (something) again, with a view to changing one's policy or course of action. 2 (in a legislative assembly or similar body) to consider again (a bill or other matter) that has already been voted upon.
▸**ˌreconˌsiderˈation** NOUN

reconstitute (riːˈkɒnstɪˌtjuːt) VERB *(tr)* 1 to restore (food, etc.) to its former or natural state or a semblance of it, as by the addition of water to a concentrate: *reconstituted lemon juice.* 2 to reconstruct; form again.
▸**reconstituent** (ˌriːkənˈstɪtjʊənt) ADJECTIVE, NOUN ▸**ˌreconstiˈtution** NOUN

reconstruct (ˌriːkənˈstrʌkt) VERB *(tr)* 1 to construct or form again; rebuild: *to reconstruct a Greek vase from fragments.* 2 to form a picture of (a crime, past event, etc.) by piecing together evidence or acting out a version of what might have taken place.
▸**ˌrecon'structible** ADJECTIVE ▸**ˌrecon'struction** NOUN ▸**ˌrecon'structive** *or* **ˌrecon'structional** ADJECTIVE ▸**ˌrecon'structor** NOUN

Reconstruction (ˌriːkənˈstrʌkʃən) NOUN *US history* the period after the Civil War when the South was reorganized and reintegrated into the Union (1865–77).

reconvene (ˌriːkənˈviːn) VERB to gather, call together, or summon again, esp for a formal meeting.

reconvert (ˌriːkənˈvɜːt) VERB *(tr)* 1 to change (something) back to a previous state or form. 2 to bring (someone) back to his or her former religion. 3 *Property law* to convert back (property previously

converted) into its original form, as land into money and vice versa. See also **conversion** (sense 5).
▸**reconversion** (ˌriːkənˈvɜːʃən) NOUN

record NOUN (ˈrɛkɔːd) 1 an account in permanent form, esp in writing, preserving knowledge or information about facts or events. 2 a written account of some transaction that serves as legal evidence of the transaction. 3 a written official report of the proceedings of a court of justice or legislative body, including the judgments given or enactments made. 4 anything serving as evidence or as a memorial: *the First World War is a record of human folly.* 5 (*often plural*) information or data on a specific subject collected methodically over a long period: *weather records.* 6 **a** the best or most outstanding amount, rate, height, etc., ever attained, as in some field of sport: *an Olympic record; a world record; to break the record for the long jump.* **b** (*as modifier*): *a record time.* 7 the sum of one's recognized achievements, career, or performance: *the officer has an excellent record.* 8 a list of crimes of which an accused person has previously been convicted, which are known to the police but may only be disclosed to a court in certain circumstances. 9 **have a record.** to be a known criminal; have a previous conviction or convictions. 10 Also called: **gramophone record, disc.** a thin disc of a plastic material upon which sound has been recorded. Each side has a spiral groove, which undulates in accordance with the frequency and amplitude of the sound. Records were formerly made from a shellac-based compound but were later made from vinyl plastics. 11 the markings made by a recording instrument such as a seismograph. 12 *Computing* a group of data or piece of information preserved as a unit in machine-readable form. 13 (in some computer languages) a data structure designed to allow the handling of groups of related pieces of information as though the group was a single entity. 14 **for the record.** for the sake of a strict factual account. 15 **go on record.** to state one's views publicly. 16 See **off the record.** 17 **on record. a** stated in a public document. **b** publicly known. 18 **set** *or* **put the record straight.** to correct an error or misunderstanding. ◆ VERB (rɪˈkɔːd) (*mainly tr*) 19 to set down in some permanent form so as to preserve the true facts of: *to record the minutes of a meeting.* 20 to contain or serve to relate (facts, information, etc.). 21 to indicate, show, or register: *his face recorded his disappointment.* 22 to remain as or afford evidence of: *these ruins record the life of the Romans in Britain.* 23 (*also intr*) to make a recording of (music, speech, etc.) for reproduction, or for later broadcasting. 24 (*also intr*) (of an instrument) to register or indicate (information) on a scale: *the barometer recorded a low pressure.*
▷**HISTORY** C13: from Old French *recorder* to call to mind, from Latin *recordārī* to remember, from RE- + *cor* heart
▸**reˈcordable** ADJECTIVE

record-changer NOUN a device in a record player for changing records automatically.

recorded delivery NOUN a Post Office service by which an official record of posting and delivery is obtained for a letter or package. Compare **registered post.**

recorder (rɪˈkɔːdə) NOUN 1 a person who records, such as an official or historian. 2 something that records, esp an apparatus that provides a permanent record of experiments, etc. 3 short for **tape recorder.** 4 *Music* a wind instrument of the flute family, blown through a fipple in the mouth end, having a reedlike quality of tone. There are four usual sizes: bass, tenor, treble, and descant. 5 (in England) a barrister or solicitor of at least ten years' standing appointed to sit as a part-time judge in the crown court.
▷**HISTORY** sense 4 probably from *record* (*vb*) in the archaic sense "to sing"
▸**reˈcorderˌship** NOUN

recording (rɪˈkɔːdɪŋ) NOUN 1 **a** the act or process of making a record, esp of sound on a gramophone record or magnetic tape. **b** (*as modifier*): *recording studio; recording head.* 2 the record or tape so produced. 3 something that has been recorded, esp a radio or television programme.

Recording Angel NOUN an angel who supposedly keeps a record of every person's good and bad acts.

record of achievement NOUN *Brit* a statement of the personal and educational development of each pupil.

record player NOUN a device for reproducing the sounds stored on a record, consisting of a turntable, usually electrically driven, that rotates the record at a fixed speed of 33, 45, or (esp formerly) 78 revolutions a minute. A stylus vibrates in accordance with undulations in the groove in the record: these vibrations are converted into electric currents, which, after amplification, are recreated in the form of sound by one or more loudspeakers. See also **monophonic, quadraphonics, stereophonic.**

reco-reco (ˈrɛkəʊˈrɛkəʊ) NOUN, *plural* **reco-recos.** a percussion instrument consisting of a ridged gourd or bamboo cane that is scraped with a piece of wood or metal.
▷**HISTORY** C20: from a native Brazilian language

recount (rɪˈkaʊnt) VERB (*tr*) to tell the story or details of; narrate.
▷**HISTORY** C15: from Old French *reconter,* from RE- + *conter* to tell, relate; see COUNT[1]
▸**reˈcountal** NOUN

re-count VERB (riːˈkaʊnt) 1 to count (votes, etc.) again. ◆ NOUN (ˈriːˌkaʊnt) 2 a second or further count, esp of votes in a closely contested election.

recoup (rɪˈkuːp) VERB 1 to regain or make good (a financial or other loss). 2 (*tr*) to reimburse or compensate (someone), as for a loss. 3 *Law* to keep back (something due), having rightful claim to do so; withhold; deduct.
▷**HISTORY** C15: from Old French *recouper* to cut back, from RE- + *couper* to cut, from *coper* to behead; see COUP[1]
▸**reˈcoupable** ADJECTIVE ▸**reˈcoupment** NOUN

recourse (rɪˈkɔːs) NOUN 1 the act of resorting to a person, course of action, etc., in difficulty or danger (esp in the phrase **have recourse to**). 2 a person, organization, or course of action that is turned to for help, protection, etc. 3 the right to demand payment, esp from the drawer or endorser of a bill of exchange or other negotiable instrument when the person accepting it fails to pay. 4 **without recourse.** a qualified endorsement on such a negotiable instrument, by which the endorser protects himself from liability to subsequent holders.
▷**HISTORY** C14: from Old French *recours,* from Late Latin *recursus* a running back, from RE- + *currere* to run

recover (rɪˈkʌvə) VERB 1 (*tr*) to find again or obtain the return of (something lost). 2 to regain (loss of money, position, time, etc.); recoup. 3 (of a person) to regain (health, spirits, composure, etc.), as after illness, a setback, or a shock, etc. 4 to regain (a former and usually better condition): *industry recovered after the war.* 5 *Law* **a** (*tr*) to gain (something) by the judgment of a court of law: *to recover damages.* **b** (*intr*) to succeed in a lawsuit. 6 (*tr*) to obtain (useful substances) from waste. 7 (*intr*) (in fencing, swimming, rowing, etc.) to make a recovery.
▷**HISTORY** C14: from Old French *recoverer,* from Latin *recuperāre* RECUPERATE
▸**reˈcoverable** ADJECTIVE ▸**reˌcoveraˈbility** NOUN
▸**reˈcoverer** NOUN

re-cover (riːˈkʌvə) VERB (*tr*) 1 to cover again. 2 to provide (a piece of furniture, book, etc.) with a new cover.

recovered memory NOUN the alleged recollection of traumatic events from childhood by a person undergoing psychotherapy. See also **false memory syndrome.**

recovery (rɪˈkʌvərɪ) NOUN, *plural* **-eries.** 1 the act or process of recovering, esp from sickness, a shock, or a setback; recuperation. 2 restoration to a former or better condition. 3 the regaining of something lost. 4 the extraction of useful substances from waste. 5 *Law* **a** the obtaining of a right, etc., by the judgment of a court. **b** (in the US) the final judgment or verdict in a case. 6 *Fencing* a return to the position of guard after making an attack. 7 *Swimming, rowing* the action of bringing the arm, oar, etc., forward for another stroke. 8 *Golf* a stroke played from the rough or a bunker to the fairway or green.

recovery stock NOUN *Stock Exchange* a security that has fallen in price but is believed to have the ability to recover.

recreant (ˈrɛkrɪənt) *Archaic* ◆ ADJECTIVE 1 cowardly; faint-hearted. 2 disloyal. ◆ NOUN 3 a disloyal or cowardly person.
▷**HISTORY** C14: from Old French, from *recroire* to surrender, from RE- + Latin *crēdere* to believe; compare MISCREANT
▸**ˈrecreance** *or* **ˈrecreancy** NOUN ▸**ˈrecreantly** ADVERB

recreate (ˈrɛkrɪˌeɪt) VERB *Rare* to amuse (oneself or someone else).
▷**HISTORY** C15: from Latin *recreāre* to invigorate, renew, from RE- + *creāre* to CREATE
▸**ˈrecreative** ADJECTIVE ▸**ˈrecreatively** ADVERB ▸**ˈrecreˌator** NOUN

re-create (ˌriːkrɪˈeɪt) VERB to create anew; reproduce.
▸**ˌre-creˈator** NOUN

recreation (ˌrɛkrɪˈeɪʃən) NOUN 1 refreshment of health or spirits by relaxation and enjoyment. 2 an activity or pastime that promotes this. 3 **a** an interval of free time between school lessons. **b** (*as modifier*): *recreation period.*

re-creation NOUN 1 the state or instance of creating again or anew: *the re-creation of the Russian Empire.* 2 a simulation or re-enactment of a scene, place, time, etc.: *a re-creation of a vineyard kitchen.*

recreational (ˌrɛkrɪˈeɪʃənᵊl) ADJECTIVE 1 of, relating to, or used for recreation: *recreational facilities.* 2 (of a drug) taken for pleasure rather than for medical reasons or because of an addiction.

recreational vehicle NOUN *Chiefly US* a large vanlike vehicle equipped to be lived in. Abbreviation: **RV.**

recreation ground NOUN an open space for public recreation, esp one in a town, with swings and slides, etc., for children. Often (informal) shortened to: **rec.**

recreation room NOUN *US and Canadian* 1 the full name for **rec room.** 2 a room in a hotel, hospital, etc., for entertainment and social gatherings.

recrement (ˈrɛkrɪmənt) NOUN 1 *Physiol* any substance, such as bile, that is secreted from a part of the body and later reabsorbed instead of being excreted. 2 waste matter; refuse; dross.
▷**HISTORY** C16: via Old French from Latin *recrēmentum* slag, filth, from RE- + *cernere* to sift
▸**ˌrecreˈmental** ADJECTIVE

recriminate (rɪˈkrɪmɪˌneɪt) VERB (*intr*) to return an accusation against someone or engage in mutual accusations.
▷**HISTORY** C17: from Medieval Latin *recrīmināre,* from Latin *crīminārī* to accuse, from *crīmen* an accusation; see CRIME
▸**reˈcriminative** *or* **reˈcriminatory** ADJECTIVE
▸**reˈcrimiˌnator** NOUN

recrimination (rɪˌkrɪmɪˈneɪʃən) NOUN 1 the act or an instance of recriminating. 2 *Law* a charge made by an accused against his accuser; countercharge.

rec room NOUN *US and Canadian* a room in a house used by the family for relaxation and entertainment. In full: **recreation room.**

recross (riːˈkrɒs) VERB (*tr*) to move or go across (something) again: *recross the river at the Ponte Solferino.*

recrudesce (ˌriːkruːˈdɛs) VERB (*intr*) (of a disease, trouble, etc.) to break out or appear again after a period of dormancy; recur.
▷**HISTORY** C19: from Latin *recrūdēscere* to become raw again, from RE- + *crūdēscere* to grow worse, from *crūdus* bloody, raw; see CRUDE
▸**ˌrecruˈdescence** NOUN ▸**ˌrecruˈdescent** ADJECTIVE

recruit (rɪˈkruːt) VERB 1 **a** to enlist (men) for military service. **b** to raise or strengthen (an army, navy, etc.) by enlistment. 2 (*tr*) to enrol or obtain (members, support, etc.). 3 to furnish or be furnished with a fresh supply; renew. 4 *Archaic* to recover (health, strength, spirits, etc.). ◆ NOUN 5 a newly joined member of a military service. 6 any new member or supporter.
▷**HISTORY** C17: from French *recrute* literally: new growth, from *recroître* to grow again, from Latin *recrēscere* from RE- + *crēscere* to grow

▸re'cruitable ADJECTIVE ▸re'cruiter NOUN ▸re'cruitment NOUN

recrystallize *or* **recrystallise** (riːˈkrɪstəˌlaɪz) VERB 1 *Chem* to dissolve and subsequently crystallize (a substance) from the solution, as in purifying chemical compounds, or (of a substance) to crystallize in this way. 2 to undergo or cause to undergo the process in which a deformed metal forms a new set of undeformed crystal grains.
▸reˌcrystalliˈzation *or* reˌcrystalliˈsation NOUN

rect *or* **rec't** ABBREVIATION FOR receipt.

recta (ˈrɛktə) NOUN a plural of **rectum.**

rectal (ˈrɛktəl) ADJECTIVE of or relating to the rectum.
▸ˈrectally ADVERB

rectangle (ˈrɛkˌtæŋgəl) NOUN a parallelogram having four right angles. Compare **rhombus.**
▹HISTORY C16: from Medieval Latin *rectangulum,* from Latin *rectus* straight + *angulus* angle

rectangular (rɛkˈtæŋgjʊlə) ADJECTIVE 1 shaped like a rectangle. 2 having or relating to right angles. 3 mutually perpendicular: *rectangular coordinates.* 4 having a base or section shaped like a rectangle.
▸recˌtanguˈlarity NOUN ▸recˈtangularly ADVERB

rectangular coordinates PLURAL NOUN the Cartesian coordinates in a system of mutually perpendicular axes.

rectangular hyperbola NOUN a hyperbola with perpendicular asymptotes.

recti (ˈrɛktaɪ) NOUN the plural of **rectus.**

recti- *or before a vowel* **rect-** COMBINING FORM straight or right: *rectilinear; rectangle.*
▹HISTORY from Latin *rectus*

rectified spirit NOUN *Chem* a constant-boiling mixture of ethanol and water, containing 95.6 per cent ethanol.

rectifier (ˈrɛktɪˌfaɪə) NOUN 1 an electronic device, such as a semiconductor diode or valve, that converts an alternating current to a direct current by suppression or inversion of alternate half cycles. 2 *Chem* an apparatus for condensing a hot vapour to a liquid in distillation; condenser. 3 a thing or person that rectifies.

rectify (ˈrɛktɪˌfaɪ) VERB **-fies, -fying, -fied.** (*tr*) 1 to put right; correct; remedy. 2 to separate (a substance) from a mixture or refine (a substance) by fractional distillation. 3 to convert (alternating current) into direct current. 4 *Maths* to determine the length of (a curve). 5 to cause (an object) to assume a linear motion or characteristic.
▹HISTORY C14: via Old French from Medieval Latin *rectificāre* to adjust, from Latin *rectus* straight + *facere* to make
▸ˈrectiˌfiable ADJECTIVE ▸ˌrectifiˈcation NOUN

rectilinear (ˌrɛktɪˈlɪnɪə) *or* **rectilineal** ADJECTIVE 1 in, moving in, or characterized by a straight line or lines: *the rectilinear propagation of light.* 2 consisting of, bounded by, or formed by a straight line or lines.
▸ˌrectiˈlinearly *or* ˌrectiˈlineally ADVERB

rectitude (ˈrɛktɪˌtjuːd) NOUN 1 moral or religious correctness. 2 correctness of judgment.
▹HISTORY C15: from Late Latin *rectitūdō,* from Latin *rectus* right, straight, from *regere* to rule

recto (ˈrɛktəʊ) NOUN, *plural* **-tos.** 1 the front of a sheet of printed paper. 2 the right-hand pages of a book, bearing the odd numbers. Compare **verso** (sense 1b).
▹HISTORY C19: from Latin *rectus* right, in *rectō foliō* on the right-hand page

rectocele (ˈrɛktəʊˌsiːl) NOUN *Pathol* a protrusion or herniation of the rectum into the vagina.
▹HISTORY C19: New Latin, from RECTUM + -CELE

rector (ˈrɛktə) NOUN 1 *Church of England* a clergyman in charge of a parish in which, as its incumbent, he would formerly have been entitled to the whole of the tithes. Compare **vicar.** 2 *RC Church* a cleric in charge of a college, religious house, or congregation. 3 *Protestant Episcopal Church, Scottish Episcopal Church* a clergyman in charge of a parish. 4 *Chiefly Brit* the head of certain schools or colleges. 5 (in Scotland) a high-ranking official in a university: now a public figure elected for three years by the students.
▹HISTORY C14: from Latin: director, ruler, from *regere* to rule
▸ˈrectorate NOUN ▸rectorial (rɛkˈtɔːrɪəl) ADJECTIVE ▸ˈrectorship NOUN

rectory (ˈrɛktərɪ) NOUN, *plural* **-ries.** 1 the official house of a rector. 2 *Church of England* the office and benefice of a rector.

rectrix (ˈrɛktrɪks) NOUN, *plural* **rectrices** (ˈrɛktrɪˌsiːz, rɛkˈtraɪsiːz). any of the large stiff feathers of a bird's tail, used in controlling the direction of flight.
▹HISTORY C17: from Late Latin, feminine of *rector* governor, RECTOR
▸rectricial (rɛkˈtrɪʃəl) ADJECTIVE

rectum (ˈrɛktəm) NOUN, *plural* **-tums** *or* **-ta** (-tə). the lower part of the alimentary canal, between the sigmoid flexure of the colon and the anus.
▹HISTORY C16: shortened from New Latin *rectum intestinum* the straight intestine

rectus (ˈrɛktəs) NOUN, *plural* **-ti** (-taɪ). *Anatomy* a straight muscle, esp either of two muscles of the anterior abdominal wall (**rectus abdominis**).
▹HISTORY C18: from New Latin *rectus musculus*

recumbent (rɪˈkʌmbənt) ADJECTIVE 1 lying down; reclining. 2 (of a part or organ) leaning or resting against another organ or the ground: *a recumbent stem.* 3 (of a fold in a rock formation) in which the axial plane is nearly horizontal.
▹HISTORY C17: from Latin *recumbere* to lie back, from RE- + *cumbere* to lie
▸reˈcumbence *or* reˈcumbency NOUN ▸reˈcumbently ADVERB

recumbent bicycle NOUN a type of bicycle that is ridden in a reclining position.

recuperate (rɪˈkuːpəˌreɪt, -ˈkjuː-) VERB 1 (*intr*) to recover from illness or exhaustion. 2 to recover (losses of money, etc.).
▹HISTORY C16: from Latin *recuperāre* to recover, from RE- + *capere* to gain, take
▸reˌcuperˈation NOUN ▸reˈcuperative ADJECTIVE

recuperator (rɪˈkuːpəˌreɪtə, -ˈkjuː-) NOUN 1 a person that recuperates. 2 a device employing springs or pneumatic power to return a gun to the firing position after the recoil. 3 *Chemical engineering* a system of flues that transfers heat from the hot gases leaving a furnace to the incoming air.

recur (rɪˈkɜː) VERB **-curs, -curring, -curred.** (*intr*) 1 to happen again, esp at regular intervals. 2 (of a thought, idea, etc.) to come back to the mind. 3 (of a problem, etc.) to come up again. 4 *Maths* (of a digit or group of digits) to be repeated an infinite number of times at the end of a decimal fraction.
▹HISTORY C15: from Latin *recurrere,* from RE- + *currere* to run
▸reˈcurring ADJECTIVE ▸reˈcurringly ADVERB

recurrent (rɪˈkʌrənt) ADJECTIVE 1 happening or tending to happen again or repeatedly. 2 *Anatomy* (of certain nerves, branches of vessels, etc.) turning back, so as to run in the opposite direction.
▸reˈcurrently ADVERB ▸reˈcurrence NOUN

recurrent fever NOUN another name for **relapsing fever.**

recurring decimal NOUN a rational number that contains a pattern of digits repeated indefinitely after the decimal point. Also called: **circulating decimal, repeating decimal.**

recursion (rɪˈkɜːʃən) NOUN 1 the act or process of returning or running back. 2 *Logic, maths* the application of a function to its own values to generate an infinite sequence of values. The **recursion formula** or **clause** of a definition specifies the progression from one term to the next, as given the base clause $f(0) = 0$, $f(n + 1) = f(n) + 3$ specifies the successive terms of the sequence $f(n) = 3n$.
▹HISTORY C17: from Latin *recursio,* from *recurrere* RECUR
▸reˈcursive ADJECTIVE

recursive function NOUN *Logic, maths* a function defined in terms of the repeated application of a number of simpler functions to their own values, by specifying a base clause and a recursion formula.

recursive subroutine NOUN *Computing* a subroutine that can call itself as part of its execution.

recurvate (rɪˈkɜːvɪt, -veɪt) ADJECTIVE *Rare* bent back.

recurve (rɪˈkɜːv) VERB to curve or bend (something) back or down or (of something) to be so curved or bent.
▹HISTORY C16: from Latin *recurvāre* from RE- + *curvāre* to CURVE

recusant (ˈrɛkjʊzənt) NOUN 1 (in 16th to 18th century England) a Roman Catholic who did not attend the services of the Church of England, as was required by law. 2 any person who refuses to submit to authority. ◆ ADJECTIVE 3 (formerly, of Catholics) refusing to attend services of the Church of England. 4 refusing to submit to authority.
▹HISTORY C16: from Latin *recūsāns* refusing, from *recūsāre* from RE- + *causārī* to dispute, from *causa* a CAUSE
▸ˈrecusance *or* ˈrecusancy NOUN

recycle (riːˈsaɪkəl) VERB (*tr*) 1 to pass (a substance) through a system again for further treatment or use. 2 to reclaim (packaging or products with a limited useful life) for further use. 3 to institute a different cycle of processes or events in (a machine, system, etc.). 4 to repeat (a series of operations). ◆ NOUN 5 the repetition of a fixed sequence of events.
▸reˈcyclable *or* reˈcycleable ADJECTIVE

red[1] (rɛd) NOUN 1 any of a group of colours, such as that of a ripe tomato or fresh blood, that lie at one end of the visible spectrum, next to orange, and are perceived by the eye when light in the approximate wavelength range 740–620 nanometres falls on the retina. Red is the complementary colour of cyan and forms a set of primary colours with blue and green. Related adjectivess: **rubicund, ruddy.** 2 a pigment or dye of or producing these colours. 3 red cloth or clothing: *dressed in red.* 4 a red ball in snooker, billiards, etc. 5 (in roulette and other gambling games) one of two colours on which players may place even bets, the other being black. 6 Also called: **inner.** *Archery* a red ring on a target, between the blue and the gold, scoring seven points. 7 **in the red.** *Informal* in debit; owing money. 8 **see red.** *Informal* to become very angry. ◆ ADJECTIVE **redder, reddest.** 9 of the colour red. 10 reddish in colour or having parts or marks that are reddish: *red hair; red deer.* 11 having the face temporarily suffused with blood, being a sign of anger, shame, etc. 12 (of the complexion) rosy; florid. 13 (of the eyes) bloodshot. 14 (of the hands) stained with blood, as after committing murder. 15 bloody or violent: *red revolution.* 16 (of wine) made from black grapes and coloured by their skins. 17 denoting the highest degree of urgency in an emergency; used by the police and the army and informally (esp in the phrase **red alert**). ◆ VERB **reds, redding, redded.** 18 another word for **redden.**
▹HISTORY Old English *rēad;* compare Old High German *rōt,* Gothic *rauths,* Latin *ruber,* Greek *eruthros,* Sanskrit *rohita*
▸ˈredly ADVERB ▸ˈredness NOUN

red[2] (rɛd) VERB **reds, redding, red** *or* **redded.** (*tr*) a variant spelling of **redd**[1].

Red (rɛd) *Informal* ◆ ADJECTIVE 1 Communist, Socialist, or Soviet. 2 radical, leftist, or revolutionary. ◆ NOUN 3 a member or supporter of a Communist or Socialist Party or a national of a state having such a government, esp the former Soviet Union. 4 a radical, leftist, or revolutionary.
▹HISTORY C19: from the colour chosen to symbolize revolutionary socialism

redact (rɪˈdækt) VERB (*tr*) 1 to compose or draft (an edict, proclamation, etc.). 2 to put (a literary work, etc.) into appropriate form for publication; edit.
▹HISTORY C15: from Latin *redigere* to bring back, from *red-* RE- + *agere* to drive
▸reˈdaction NOUN ▸reˈdactional ADJECTIVE ▸reˈdactor NOUN

red admiral NOUN a nymphalid butterfly, *Vanessa atalanta,* of temperate Europe and Asia, having black wings with red and white markings. See also **white admiral.**

red algae PLURAL NOUN the numerous algae that constitute the phylum *Rhodophyta,* which contain a red pigment in addition to chlorophyll. The group includes carrageen, dulse, and laver. Also called: **red seaweed.**

redan (rɪˈdæn) NOUN a fortification of two parapets at a salient angle.
▹HISTORY C17: from French, from earlier *redent* notching of a saw edge, from RE- + *dent* tooth, from Latin *dēns*

Red Army Faction NOUN another name for the **Baader-Meinhof Gang.**

red-backed shrike NOUN a common Eurasian shrike, *Lanius collurio*, the male of which has a grey crown and rump, brown wings and back, and a black-and-white face.

redback *or* **redback spider** NOUN a small venomous Australian spider, *Latrodectus hasselti*, having long thin legs and, in the female, a red stripe on the back of its globular abdomen.

red bag NOUN (in Britain) a fabric bag for a barrister's robes, presented by a Queen's Counsel to a junior in appreciation of good work in a case. See also **blue bag.**

red bark NOUN a kind of cinchona containing a high proportion of alkaloids.

red beds PLURAL NOUN sequences of red sedimentary rocks, usually sandstones or shales, coloured by the oxidization of the iron in them.

red-bellied black snake NOUN a highly venomous Australian black snake, *Pseudechis porphyriacus*, with a reddish underside.

red biddy NOUN *Informal* cheap red wine fortified with methylated spirits.

red blood cell *or* **corpuscle** NOUN another name for **erythrocyte.**

red-blooded ADJECTIVE *Informal* vigorous; virile.
▸ **ˌred-ˈbloodedness** NOUN

red book NOUN *Brit* (*sometimes capitals*) a government publication bound in red, esp the Treasury's annual forecast of revenue, expenditure, growth, and inflation.

redbreast (ˈrɛdˌbrɛst) NOUN any of various birds having a red breast, esp the Old World robin (see **robin** (sense 1)).

redbrick (ˈrɛdˌbrɪk) NOUN (*modifier*) denoting, relating to, or characteristic of a provincial British university of relatively recent foundation, esp as distinguished from Oxford and Cambridge.

Redbridge (ˈrɛdˌbrɪdʒ) NOUN a borough of NE Greater London: includes part of Epping Forest. Pop.: 238 628 (2001). Area: 56 sq. km (22 sq. miles).

Red Brigades PLURAL NOUN **the.** a group of urban guerrillas, based in Italy, who kidnapped and murdered the former Italian prime minister Aldo Moro in 1978.

redbud (ˈrɛdˌbʌd) NOUN an American leguminous tree, *Cercis canadensis*, that has heart-shaped leaves and small budlike pink flowers. Also called: **American Judas tree.**

redbug (ˈrɛdˌbʌg) NOUN *US* another name for **chigger** (sense 1).

redcap (ˈrɛdˌkæp) NOUN 1 *Brit informal* a military policeman. 2 *US and Canadian* a porter at an airport or station.

Redcar and Cleveland (ˈrɛdkɑː) NOUN a unitary authority in NE England, in North Yorkshire: formerly (1975–96) part of Cleveland county. Pop.: 139 141 (2001). Area: 240 sq. km (93 sq. miles).

red card *Sport* ◆ NOUN 1 a card of a red colour displayed by a referee to indicate that a player has been sent off. ◆ VERB **red-card.** 2 (*tr*) to send off (a player).

red carpet NOUN 1 a strip of red carpeting laid for important dignitaries to walk on when arriving or departing. 2 **a** deferential treatment accorded to a person of importance. **b** (*as modifier*): *the returning hero had a red-carpet reception.*

red cedar NOUN 1 any of several North American coniferous trees, esp *Juniperus virginiana*, a juniper that has fragrant reddish wood used for making pencils, and *Thuja plicata*, an arbor vitae. 2 the wood of any of these trees.

red cent NOUN (*used with a negative*) *Informal, chiefly US* a cent considered as a trivial amount of money (esp in the phrases **not have a red cent, not worth a red cent,** etc.).

Red China NOUN an unofficial name for (the People's Republic of) **China.**

red clover NOUN a leguminous plant, *Trifolium pratense*, native to Europe and Asia, frequently planted as a forage crop. It has fragrant red flowers and three-lobed compound leaves.

redcoat (ˈrɛdˌkəʊt) NOUN (formerly) a British soldier.
▷ HISTORY C16: from the colour of the uniform jacket

red cod NOUN a deep-sea fish, *Physiculus bachus*, of Australia and New Zealand, with a grey-and-pink body that turns red when it is removed from water.

red coral NOUN any of several corals of the genus *Corallium*, the skeletons of which are pinkish red in colour and used to make ornaments, etc. Also called: **precious coral.**

red corpuscle *or* **blood cell** NOUN another name for **erythrocyte.**

Red Crescent NOUN a national branch of or the emblem of the Red Cross Society in a Muslim country.

Red Cross NOUN 1 an international humanitarian organization (**Red Cross Society**) formally established by the Geneva Convention of 1864. It was originally limited to providing medical care for war casualties, but its services now include liaison between prisoners of war and their families, relief to victims of natural disasters, etc. 2 any national branch of this organization. 3 the emblem of this organization, consisting of a red cross on a white background.

redcurrant (ˈrɛdˈkʌrənt) NOUN 1 a N temperate shrub, *Ribes rubrum*, having greenish flowers and small edible rounded red berries: family *Grossulariaceae*. 2 **a** the fruit of this shrub. **b** (*as modifier*): *redcurrant jelly.*

redd[1] *or* **red** (rɛd) *Scot and northern English dialect* ◆ VERB **redds, redding, redd** *or* **redded.** 1 (*tr*; often foll by *up*) to bring order to; tidy (up). ◆ NOUN 2 the act or an instance of redding.
▷ HISTORY C15 *redden* to clear, perhaps a variant of RID
▸ **ˈredder** NOUN

redd[2] (rɛd) NOUN a hollow in sand or gravel on a river bed, scooped out as a spawning place by salmon, trout, or other fish.
▷ HISTORY C17 (originally: spawn): of obscure origin

red deer NOUN a large deer, *Cervus elaphus*, formerly widely distributed in the woodlands of Europe and Asia. The coat is reddish brown in summer and the short tail is surrounded by a patch of light-coloured hair.

Red Deer NOUN 1 a town in S Alberta on the Red Deer River: trade centre for mixed farming, dairying region, and natural gas processing. Pop: 58 134 (1991). 2 a river in W Canada, in SW Alberta, flowing southeast into the South Saskatchewan River. Length: about 620 km (385 miles). 3 a river in W Canada, flowing east through **Red Deer Lake** into Lake Winnipegosis. Length: about 225 km (140 miles).

redden (ˈrɛd^{ə}n) VERB 1 to make or become red. 2 (*intr*) to flush with embarrassment, anger, etc.; blush.

reddish (ˈrɛdɪʃ) ADJECTIVE somewhat red.
▸ **ˈreddishly** ADVERB ▸ **ˈreddishness** NOUN

Redditch (ˈrɛdɪtʃ) NOUN a town in W central England, in N Worcestershire: designated a new town in the mid-1960s; metal-working industries. Pop.: 73 372 (1991).

reddle (ˈrɛd^{ə}l) NOUN, VERB a variant spelling of **ruddle.**

red duster NOUN *Brit* an informal name for the **Red Ensign.**

red dwarf NOUN one of a class of small cool main-sequence stars.

rede (riːd) *Archaic* ◆ NOUN 1 advice or counsel. 2 an explanation. ◆ VERB (*tr*) 3 to advise; counsel. 4 to explain.
▷ HISTORY Old English *rǣdan* to rule; see READ[1]

red earth NOUN a clayey zonal soil of tropical savanna lands, formed by extensive chemical weathering, coloured by iron compounds, and less strongly leached than laterite.

redecorate (riːˈdɛkəˌreɪt) VERB to paint or wallpaper (a room, house, etc.) again.
▸ **reˌdecoˈration**

redeem (rɪˈdiːm) VERB (*tr*) 1 to recover possession or ownership of by payment of a price or service; regain. 2 to convert (bonds, shares, etc.) into cash. 3 to pay off (a promissory note, loan, etc.). 4 to recover (something pledged, mortgaged, or pawned). 5 to convert (paper money) into bullion or specie. 6 to fulfil (a promise, pledge, etc.). 7 to exchange (trading stamps, coupons, etc.) for goods. 8 to reinstate in someone's estimation or good opinion; restore to favour: *he redeemed himself by his altruistic action.* 9 to make amends for. 10 to recover from captivity, esp by a money payment. 11 *Christianity* (of Christ as Saviour) to free (mankind) from sin by his death on the Cross.
▷ HISTORY C15: from Old French *redimer*, from Latin *redimere* to buy back, from *red-* RE- + *emere* to buy
▸ **reˈdeemer** NOUN

redeemable (rɪˈdiːməb^{ə}l) *or* **redemptible** (rɪˈdɛmptəb^{ə}l) ADJECTIVE (of bonds, shares, etc.) 1 subject to cancellation by repayment at a specified date or under specified conditions. 2 payable in or convertible into cash.
▸ **reˌdeemaˈbility** NOUN ▸ **reˈdeemably** ADVERB

Redeemer (rɪˈdiːmə) NOUN **The.** Jesus Christ as having brought redemption to mankind.

redeeming (rɪˈdiːmɪŋ) ADJECTIVE serving to compensate for faults or deficiencies in quality, etc.: *one redeeming feature.*

redefine (ˌriːdɪˈfaɪn) VERB (*tr*) to define (something) again or differently.

red emperor NOUN *Austral* a brightly-coloured marine food fish, *Lutjanus sebae*, of the Great Barrier Reef.

redemption (rɪˈdɛmpʃən) NOUN 1 the act or process of redeeming. 2 the state of being redeemed. 3 *Christianity* **a** deliverance from sin through the incarnation, sufferings, and death of Christ. **b** atonement for guilt. 4 conversion of paper money into bullion or specie. 5 **a** removal of a financial obligation by paying off a note, bond, etc. **b** (*as modifier*): *redemption date.*
▷ HISTORY C14: via Old French from Latin *redemptiō* a buying back; see REDEEM
▸ **reˈdemptional** *or* **reˈdemptive** *or* **reˈdemptory** ADJECTIVE
▸ **reˈdemptively** ADVERB

redemptioner (rɪˈdɛmpʃənə) NOUN *History* an emigrant to Colonial America who paid for his passage by becoming an indentured servant.

redemption yield NOUN *Stock Exchange* the yield produced by a redeemable gilt-edged security taking into account the annual interest it pays and an annualized amount to account for any profit or loss when it is redeemed.

Redemptorist (rɪˈdɛmptərɪst) NOUN *RC Church* a member of a religious congregation founded in 1732 to do missionary work among the poor.
▷ HISTORY C19: from French *rédemptoriste*, from Old French or Latin *redemptor*, from Latin *redimere*, see REDEEM

Red Ensign NOUN the ensign of the British Merchant Navy, having the Union Jack on a red background at the upper corner of the vertical edge alongside the hoist. Compare **White Ensign, Blue Ensign.**

redeploy (ˌriːdɪˈplɔɪ) VERB to assign new positions or tasks to (labour, troops, etc.).
▸ **ˌredeˈployment** NOUN

redesign (ˌriːdɪˈzaɪn) VERB (*tr*) 1 to change the design of (something). ◆ NOUN 2 something that has been redesigned.

redevelop (ˌriːdɪˈvɛləp) VERB (*tr*) 1 to rebuild or replan (a building, area, etc.). 2 *Photog* to develop (a negative or print) for a second time, in order to improve the contrast, colour, etc. 3 to develop (something) again.
▸ **ˌredeˈveloper** NOUN ▸ **ˌredeˈvelopment** NOUN

redevelopment area NOUN an urban area in which all or most of the buildings are demolished and rebuilt.

redeye (ˈrɛdˌaɪ) NOUN 1 *US slang* inferior whiskey. 2 *Canadian slang* a drink incorporating beer and tomato juice. 3 another name for **rudd.**

red-eye NOUN *Informal* **a** an aeroplane flight leaving late at night or arriving early in the morning. **b** (*as modifier*): *a red-eye flight.*

red eye NOUN *Photog* an undesirable effect that sometimes appears in flashlight portraits when light from the flash enters the eye and is reflected from the retina on to the film, producing a red colour.

red-faced ADJECTIVE 1 flushed with embarrassment or anger. 2 having a florid complexion.
▸ **red-facedly** (ˌrɛdˈfeɪsɪdlɪ, -ˈfeɪstlɪ) ADVERB

redfin (ˈrɛdˌfɪn) NOUN any of various small cyprinid fishes of the genus *Notropis*, esp *N. cornutus*. They have reddish fins and are popular aquarium fishes.

red fir NOUN 1 a North American coniferous tree, *Abies magnifica*, having reddish wood valued as timber: family *Pinaceae*. 2 any of various other pinaceous trees that have reddish wood. 3 the wood of any of these trees.

red fire NOUN any combustible material that burns with a bright red flame: used in flares and fireworks. The colour is usually produced by strontium salts.

redfish (ˈrɛdˌfɪʃ) NOUN, *plural* **-fish** *or* **-fishes.** 1 a male salmon that has recently spawned. Compare **blackfish** (sense 2). 2 any of several red European scorpaenid fishes of the genus *Sebastes*, esp *S. marinus*, valued as a food fish.

red flag NOUN 1 a symbol of socialism, communism, or revolution. 2 a warning of danger or a signal to stop.

Red Flag NOUN **the.** a socialist song, written by James Connell in 1889.

redfoot (ˈrɛdˌfʊt) NOUN *Vet science* a fatal disease of newborn lambs of unknown cause in which the horny layers of the feet become separated, exposing the red laminae below.

red fox NOUN the common fox, *Vulpes vulpes*, which has a reddish-brown coat: family *Canidae*, order *Carnivora* (carnivores).

red giant NOUN a giant star towards the end of its life, with a relatively low temperature of 2000–4000 K, that emits red light.

red grouse NOUN a reddish-brown grouse, *Lagopus scoticus*, of upland moors of Great Britain: an important game bird.

Red Guard NOUN a member of a Chinese youth movement that attempted to effect the Cultural Revolution (1965–71).

red gum NOUN 1 any of several Australian myrtaceous trees of the genus *Eucalyptus*, esp *E. camaldulensis*, which has reddish wood. See also **blue gum.** 2 the hard red wood from this tree, used for making railway sleepers, posts, etc. 3 another name for **sweet gum.**

red-handed ADJECTIVE (*postpositive*) in the act of committing a crime or doing something wrong or shameful (esp in the phrase **catch red-handed**).
▷HISTORY C19 (earlier, C15 *red hand*)
▸ **ˌred-ˈhandedly** ADVERB ▸ **ˌred-ˈhandedness** NOUN

red hat NOUN 1 the broad-brimmed crimson hat given to cardinals as the symbol of their rank and office. 2 the rank and office of a cardinal.

redhead (ˈrɛdˌhɛd) NOUN 1 a person with red hair. 2 a diving duck, *Aythya americana*, of North America, the male of which has a grey-and-black body and a reddish-brown head.

red-headed ADJECTIVE 1 (of a person) having red hair. 2 (of an animal) having a red head.

red heat NOUN 1 the temperature at which a substance is red-hot. 2 the state or condition of being red-hot.

red herring NOUN 1 anything that diverts attention from a topic or line of inquiry. 2 a herring cured by salting and smoking.

red-hot ADJECTIVE 1 (esp of metal) heated to the temperature at which it glows red: *iron is red-hot at about 500°C.* 2 extremely hot: *the stove is red-hot, so don't touch it.* 3 keen, excited, or eager; enthusiastic. 4 furious; violent: *red-hot anger.* 5 very recent or topical: *red-hot information.* 6 *Austral slang* extreme, unreasonable, or unfair: *the charges are red-hot.*

red-hot poker NOUN See **kniphofia.**

redia (ˈriːdɪə) NOUN, *plural* **-diae** (-dɪˌiː). a parasitic larva of flukes that has simple locomotory organs, pharynx, and intestine and gives rise either to other rediae or to a different larva (the cercaria).
▷HISTORY C19: from New Latin, named after Francesco *Redi* (1629–97), Italian naturalist

redial (riːˈdaɪəl, -daɪl) VERB **-dials, -dialling, -dialled.** to dial (a telephone number) again.

Rediffusion (ˌriːdɪˈfjuːʒən) NOUN *Trademark Brit* a system by which radio or television programmes are relayed to subscribers from a receiver via cables.

Red Indian NOUN, ADJECTIVE another name, now considered offensive, for **American Indian.**
▷HISTORY see REDSKIN

redingote (ˈrɛdɪŋˌɡəʊt) NOUN 1 a woman's coat with a close-fitting top and a full skirt. 2 a man's or woman's full-skirted outer coat of the 18th and 19th centuries. 3 a woman's light dress or coat of the 18th century, with an open-fronted skirt, revealing a decorative underskirt.
▷HISTORY C19: from French, from English *riding coat*

redintegrate (rɛˈdɪntɪˌɡreɪt) VERB 1 (*tr*) to make whole or complete again; restore to a perfect state; renew. 2 (*intr*) *Psychol* to engage in the process of redintegration.
▷HISTORY C15: from Latin *redintegrāre* to renew, from *red-* RE- + *integer* complete
▸ **redˈinteˌgrative** ADJECTIVE

redintegration (rɛˌdɪntɪˈɡreɪʃən) NOUN 1 the act or process of making whole again; renewal. 2 *Psychol* the process of responding to a part of a situation in the same manner as one has responded to the whole situation, as in the case of a souvenir reminding one of a holiday.

redirect (ˌriːdɪˈrɛkt, ˌriːdaɪ-) VERB (*tr*) to direct (someone or something) to a different place or by a different route.
▸ **ˌrediˈrection** NOUN

rediscover (ˌriːdɪˈskʌvə) VERB (*tr*) to discover (something) again: *rediscover the joys of life.*

rediscovery (ˌriːdɪˈskʌvərɪ) NOUN, *plural* **-ies.** the act, process, or an instance of discovering (something) again.

redistribute (ˌriːdɪˈstrɪbjuːt) VERB (*tr*) to distribute (something) again or differently.
▸ **ˌredisˈtributive** ADJECTIVE

redistribution (ˌriːdɪstrɪˈbjuːʃən) NOUN the act or instance of distributing or the state or manner of being distributed again.

redivivus (ˌrɛdɪˈvaɪvəs) ADJECTIVE *Rare* returned to life; revived.
▷HISTORY C17: from Late Latin, from Latin *red-* RE- + *vīvus* alive

red kangaroo NOUN a large Australian kangaroo, *Macropus rufus*, the male of which has a reddish coat.

red kowhai NOUN another name for **kaka beak.**

red lead (lɛd) NOUN a bright-red poisonous insoluble oxide of lead usually obtained as a powder by heating litharge in air. It is used as a pigment in paints. Formula: Pb_3O_4. Also called: **minium.**

red-lead ore (ˈrɛdˈlɛd) NOUN another name for **crocoite.**

redleg (ˈrɛdˌlɛɡ) NOUN *Caribbean derogatory* a poor White.

red-legged partridge NOUN a partridge, *Alectoris rufa*, having a reddish tail, red legs and bill, and flanks barred with chestnut, black, and white: common on farmlands and heaths in SW Europe, including Britain.

red-letter day NOUN a memorably important or happy occasion.
▷HISTORY C18: from the red letters used in ecclesiastical calendars to indicate saints' days and feasts

red light NOUN 1 a signal to stop, esp a red traffic signal in a system of traffic lights. 2 a danger signal. 3 an instruction to stop or discontinue. 4 **a** a red lamp in a window of or outside a house indicating that it is a brothel. **b** (*as modifier*): *a red-light district.*

redline (ˈrɛdˌlaɪn) VERB (*tr*) 1 (esp of a bank or group of banks) to refuse a loan to (a person or country) because of the presumed risks involved. 2 to restrict people's access to goods or services on the basis of the area in which they live.

red line NOUN a point beyond which a person or group is not prepared to negotiate.

red man NOUN *Archaic* a North American Indian.
▷HISTORY C18: see REDSKIN

red meat NOUN any meat that is dark in colour, esp beef and lamb. Compare **white meat.**

red mist NOUN *Informal* a feeling of extreme anger that clouds one's judgment temporarily.

red mullet NOUN any of the marine percoid fishes constituting the family *Mullidae*, esp *Mullus surmuletus*, a food fish of European waters. They have a pair of long barbels beneath the chin and a reddish coloration. US name: **goatfish.**

redneck (ˈrɛdˌnɛk) NOUN *Disparaging* 1 (in the southwestern US) a poor uneducated White farm worker. 2 a person or institution that is extremely reactionary. ◆ ADJECTIVE 3 reactionary and bigoted: *redneck laws.*

red ned (nɛd) NOUN *Austral slang* any cheap red wine.

redo (riːˈduː) VERB **-does, -doing, -did, -done.** (*tr*) 1 to do over again. 2 *Informal* to redecorate, esp thoroughly: *we redid the house last summer.*

red oak NOUN 1 any of several deciduous oak trees, esp *Quercus borealis*, native to North America, having bristly leaves with triangular lobes and acorns with small cups. 2 the hard cross-grained reddish wood of this tree.

red ochre NOUN any of various natural red earths containing ferric oxide: used as pigments.

redolent (ˈrɛdəʊlənt) ADJECTIVE 1 having a pleasant smell; fragrant. 2 (*postpositive*; foll by *of* or *with*) having the odour or smell (of); scented (with): *a room redolent of country flowers.* 3 (*postpositive*; foll by *of* or *with*) reminiscent or suggestive (of): *a picture redolent of the 18th century.*
▷HISTORY C14: from Latin *redolens* smelling (of), from *redolēre* to give off an odour, from *red-* RE + *olēre* to smell
▸ **ˈredolence** *or* (*less commonly*) **ˈredolency** NOUN
▸ **ˈredolently** ADVERB

red osier NOUN any of several willow trees that have red twigs used for basketwork.

red-osier dogwood NOUN a North American shrub, *Cornus stolonifera*, having bright or dark red wood, white flowers, and whitish fruit.

redouble (rɪˈdʌbᵊl) VERB 1 to make or become much greater in intensity, number, etc.: *to redouble one's efforts.* 2 to send back (sounds) or (of sounds) to be sent back; echo or re-echo. 3 *Bridge* to double (an opponent's double). ◆ NOUN 4 the act of redoubling.

redoubt (rɪˈdaʊt) NOUN 1 an outwork or detached fieldwork defending a pass, hilltop, etc. 2 a temporary defence work built inside a fortification as a last defensive position.
▷HISTORY C17: via French from obsolete Italian *ridotta*, from Medieval Latin *reductus* shelter, from Latin *redūcere* to withdraw, from RE- + *dūcere* to lead

redoubtable (rɪˈdaʊtəbᵊl) ADJECTIVE 1 to be feared; formidable. 2 worthy of respect.
▷HISTORY C14: from Old French, from *redouter* to dread, from RE- + *douter* to be afraid, DOUBT
▸ **reˈdoubtableness** NOUN ▸ **reˈdoubtably** ADVERB

redound (rɪˈdaʊnd) VERB 1 (*intr*; foll by *to*) to have an advantageous or disadvantageous effect (on): *brave deeds redound to your credit.* 2 (*intr*; foll by *on* or *upon*) to recoil or rebound. 3 (*intr*) *Archaic* to arise; accrue: *wealth redounding from wise investment.* 4 (*tr*) *Archaic* to reflect; bring: *his actions redound dishonour upon him.*
▷HISTORY C14: from Old French *redonder*, from Latin *redundāre* to stream over, from *red-* RE + *undāre* to rise in waves, from *unda* a wave

redowa (ˈrɛdəvə, -wə) NOUN a Bohemian folk dance similar to the waltz.
▷HISTORY C19: via French and German from Czech *rejdovák*, from *rejdovati* to guide around

redox (ˈriːdɒks) NOUN (*modifier*) another term for **oxidation-reduction.**
▷HISTORY C20: from RED(UCTION) + OX(IDATION)

red packet NOUN (in Hong Kong, Malaysia, etc.) 1 a sum of money folded inside red paper and given at the Chinese New Year to unmarried younger relatives. 2 such a gift given at Chinese weddings by the parents to the bride and groom and by the bride and groom to unmarried younger relatives.

red-pencil VERB **-cils, -cilling, -cilled** *or US* **-cils, -ciling, -ciled.** (*tr*) to revise or correct (a book, manuscript, etc.).

red pepper NOUN 1 any of several varieties of the pepper plant *Capsicum frutescens*, cultivated for their hot pungent red podlike fruits. 2 the fruit of any of these plants. 3 the ripe red fruit of the sweet pepper. 4 another name for **cayenne pepper.**

red pine NOUN a coniferous tree, *Dacrydium cupressinum*, of New Zealand, having narrow sharp pointed leaves: family *Podocarpaceae*. Also called: **rimu.**

Red Planet NOUN **the.** an informal name for **Mars**[2] (sense 1).

redpoll ('rɛd,pɒl) NOUN either of two widely distributed finches, *Acanthis flammea* or *A. hornemanni* (**arctic** *or* **hoary redpoll**), having a greyish-brown plumage with a red crown and pink breast.

Red Poll *or* **Polled** NOUN a red hornless short-haired breed of beef and dairy cattle.

redraft NOUN ('ri:,drɑ:ft) 1 a second draft. 2 a bill of exchange drawn on the drawer or endorser of a protested bill by the holder for the amount of the protested bill plus costs and charges. 3 a re-exported commodity. ◆ VERB (ri:'drɑ:ft) (*intr*) 4 to make a second copy of; draft again: *to redraft proposals for a project.*

red rag NOUN a provocation; something that infuriates.
▷HISTORY so called because red objects supposedly infuriate bulls

red rattle NOUN See **rattle** (sense 10).

redraw (ri:'drɔ:) VERB **-draws, -drawing, -drew, -drawn.** (*tr*) to draw or draw up (something) again or differently.

redress (rɪ'drɛs) VERB (*tr*) 1 to put right (a wrong), esp by compensation; make reparation for: *to redress a grievance.* 2 to correct or adjust (esp in the phrase **redress the balance**). 3 to make compensation to (a person) for a wrong. ◆ NOUN 4 the act or an instance of setting right a wrong; remedy or cure: *to seek redress of grievances.* 5 compensation, amends, or reparation for a wrong, injury, etc. 6 relief from poverty or want.
▷HISTORY C14: from Old French *redrecier* to set up again, from RE- + *drecier* to straighten; see DRESS
▸**re'dressable** *or* **re'dressible** ADJECTIVE ▸**re'dresser** *or (less commonly)* **re'dressor** NOUN

re-dress (ri:'drɛs) VERB (*tr*) to dress (something) again.

Red River NOUN 1 Also called: **Red River of the South.** a river in the S central US, flowing east from N Texas through Arkansas into the Mississippi in Louisiana. Length: 1639 km (1018 miles). 2 a river in the northern US, flowing north as the border between North Dakota and Minnesota and into Lake Winnipeg, Canada. Length: 515 km (320 miles). 3 a river in SE Asia, rising in SW China in Yünnan province and flowing southeast across N Vietnam to the Gulf of Tongkin: the chief river of N Vietnam, with an extensive delta. Length: 500 km (310 miles). Vietnamese name: **Song Koi.**

red roman NOUN *South African* a marine food fish, *Chrisoblephus laticeps.*

redroot ('rɛd,ru:t) NOUN 1 a bog plant, *Lachnanthes tinctoria*, of E North America, having woolly yellow flowers and roots that yield a red dye: family *Haemodoraceae*. 2 another name for **pigweed** (sense 1).

red rose NOUN *English history* the emblem of the House of Lancaster. See also **Wars of the Roses, white rose.**

red route NOUN an urban through route where the penalties for illegal parking are severe and are immediately enforced.

red run NOUN *Skiing* a run of some difficulty, suitable for intermediate skiers.

red salmon NOUN 1 any salmon having reddish flesh, esp the sockeye salmon. 2 the flesh of such a fish, esp canned.

Red Sea NOUN a long narrow sea between Arabia and NE Africa, linked with the Mediterranean in the north by the Suez Canal and with the Indian Ocean in the south: occasionally reddish in appearance through algae. Area: 438 000 sq. km (169 000 sq. miles).

red seaweed NOUN another term for **red algae.**

red setter NOUN a popular name for **Irish setter.**

redshank ('rɛd,ʃæŋk) NOUN either of two large common European sandpipers, *Tringa totanus* or *T. erythropus* (**spotted redshank**), having red legs.

red shank NOUN an annual polygonaceous plant, *Polygonum persicaria*, of N temperate regions, having red stems, narrow leaves, and oblong spikes of pink flowers. Also called: **persicaria, lady's-thumb.**

redshift ('rɛd,ʃɪft) NOUN a shift in the lines of the spectrum of an astronomical object towards a longer wavelength (the red end of an optical spectrum), relative to the wavelength of these lines in the terrestrial spectrum, usually as a result of the **Doppler effect** caused by the recession of the object. Compare: **blueshift.**

redskin ('rɛd,skɪn) NOUN an informal name, now considered offensive, for an **American Indian.**
▷HISTORY C17: so called because one particular tribe, the now extinct Beothuks of Newfoundland, painted themselves with red ochre

red snapper NOUN any of various marine percoid food fishes of the genus *Lutjanus*, esp *L. blackfordi*, having a reddish coloration, common in American coastal regions of the Atlantic: family *Lutjanidae* (snappers).

red spider NOUN short for **red spider mite** (see **spider mite**).

Red Spot See **Great Red Spot.**

red squirrel NOUN 1 a reddish-brown squirrel, *Sciurus vulgaris*, inhabiting woodlands of Europe and parts of Asia. 2 **American red squirrel.** Also called: **chickaree.** either of two reddish-brown squirrels, *Tamiasciurus hudsonicus* or *T. douglasii*, inhabiting forests of North America.

redstart ('rɛd,stɑ:t) NOUN 1 any European songbird of the genus *Phoenicurus*, esp *P. phoenicurus*, in which the male has a black throat, orange-brown tail and breast, and grey back: family *Muscicapidae* (thrushes, etc.). 2 any North American warbler of the genus *Setophaga*, esp *S. ruticilla*.
▷HISTORY Old English *rēad* RED[1] + *steort* tail; compare German *Rotsterz*

red tape NOUN obstructive official routine or procedure; time-consuming bureaucracy.
▷HISTORY C18: from the red tape used to bind official government documents

red tide NOUN a discoloration of sea water caused by an explosive growth in phytoplankton density: sometimes toxic to fish life and, through accumulation in shellfish, to humans.

red-top NOUN a tabloid newspaper characterized by sensationalism.
▷HISTORY C20: from the colour of the masthead on these publications

reduce (rɪ'dju:s) VERB (*mainly tr*) 1 (*also intr*) to make or become smaller in size, number, extent, degree, intensity, etc. 2 to bring into a certain state, condition, etc.: *to reduce a forest to ashes; to reduce someone to despair.* 3 (*also intr*) to make or become slimmer; lose or cause to lose excess weight. 4 to impoverish (esp in the phrase **in reduced circumstances**). 5 to bring into a state of submission to one's authority; subjugate: *the whole country was reduced after three months.* 6 to bring down the price of (a commodity): *the shirt was reduced in the sale.* 7 to lower the rank or status of; demote: *he was reduced from corporal to private; reduced to the ranks.* 8 to set out systematically as an aid to understanding; simplify: *his theories have been reduced in a popular treatise.* 9 *Maths* to modify or simplify the form of (an expression or equation), esp by substitution of one term by another. 10 *Cookery* to make (a sauce, stock, etc.) more concentrated by boiling away some of the water in it. 11 to thin out (paint) by adding oil, turpentine, etc.; dilute. 12 (*also intr*) *Chem* **a** to undergo or cause to undergo a chemical reaction with hydrogen or formation of a hydride. **b** to lose or cause to lose oxygen atoms. **c** to undergo or cause to undergo an increase in the number of electrons. Compare **oxidize.** 13 *Photog* to lessen the density of (a negative or print) by converting some of the blackened silver in the emulsion to soluble silver compounds by an oxidation process using a photographic reducer. 14 *Surgery* to manipulate or reposition (a broken or displaced bone, organ, or part) back to its normal site. 15 (*also intr*) *Biology* to undergo or cause to undergo meiosis.
▷HISTORY C14: from Latin *redūcere* to bring back, from RE- + *dūcere* to lead
▸**re'ducible** ADJECTIVE ▸**re,duci'bility** NOUN ▸**re'ducibly** ADVERB

reduced level NOUN *Surveying* calculated elevation in relation to a particular datum.

reducer (rɪ'dju:sə) NOUN 1 *Photog* a chemical solution used to lessen the density of a negative or print by oxidizing some of the blackened silver to soluble silver compounds. Compare **intensifier** (sense 3). 2 a pipe fitting connecting two pipes of different diameters. 3 a person or thing that reduces.

reducing agent NOUN *Chem* a substance that reduces another substance in a chemical reaction, being itself oxidized in the process. Compare **oxidizing agent.**

reducing glass NOUN a lens or curved mirror that produces an image smaller than the object observed.

reductase (rɪ'dʌkteɪz) NOUN any enzyme that catalyses a biochemical reduction reaction.
▷HISTORY C20: from REDUCTION + -ASE

reductio ad absurdum (rɪ'dʌktɪəʊ æd æb'sɜ:dəm) NOUN 1 a method of disproving a proposition by showing that its inevitable consequences would be absurd. 2 a method of indirectly proving a proposition by assuming its negation to be true and showing that this leads to an absurdity. 3 application of a principle or proposed principle to an instance in which it is absurd.
▷HISTORY Latin, literally: reduction to the absurd

reduction (rɪ'dʌkʃən) NOUN 1 the act or process or an instance of reducing. 2 the state or condition of being reduced. 3 the amount by which something is reduced. 4 a form of an original resulting from a reducing process, such as a copy on a smaller scale. 5 a simplified form, such as an orchestral score arranged for piano. 6 *Maths* **a** the process of converting a fraction into its decimal form. **b** the process of dividing out the common factors in the numerator and denominator of a fraction; cancellation.
▸**re'ductive** ADJECTIVE

reduction division NOUN another name for **meiosis.**

reduction formula NOUN *Maths* a formula, such as $\sin (90° \pm A) = \cos A$, expressing the values of a trigonometric function of any angle greater than 90° in terms of a function of an acute angle.

reductionism (rɪ'dʌkʃə,nɪzəm) NOUN 1 the analysis of complex things, data, etc., into less complex constituents. 2 *Often disparaging* any theory or method that holds that a complex idea, system, etc., can be completely understood in terms of its simpler parts or components.
▸**re'ductionist** NOUN, ADJECTIVE ▸**re,duction'istic** ADJECTIVE

redundancy (rɪ'dʌndənsɪ) NOUN, *plural* **-cies.** 1 **a** the state or condition of being redundant or superfluous, esp superfluous in one's job. **b** (*as modifier*): *a redundancy payment.* 2 excessive proliferation or profusion, esp of superfluity. 3 duplication of components in electronic or mechanical equipment so that operations can continue following failure of a part. 4 repetition of information or inclusion of additional information to reduce errors in telecommunication transmissions and computer processing.

redundancy payment NOUN a sum of money given by an employer to an employee who has been made redundant: usually calculated on the basis of the employee's rate of pay and length of service.

redundant (rɪ'dʌndənt) ADJECTIVE 1 surplus to requirements; unnecessary or superfluous. 2 verbose or tautological. 3 deprived of one's job because it is no longer necessary for efficient operation: *he has been made redundant.* 4 (of components, information, etc.) duplicated or added as a precaution against failure, error, etc.
▷HISTORY C17: from Latin *redundans* overflowing, from *redundāre* to run back, stream over; see REDOUND
▸**re'dundantly** ADVERB

red underwing NOUN a large noctuid moth, *Catocala nupta*, having dull forewings and hind wings coloured red and black.

reduplicate VERB (rɪ'dju:plɪ,keɪt) 1 to make or become double; repeat. 2 to repeat (a sound or syllable) in a word or (of a sound or syllable) to be repeated, esp in forming inflections in certain languages. ◆ ADJECTIVE (rɪ'dju:plɪkɪt) 3 doubled or

repeated. [4] (of petals or sepals) having the margins curving outwards.
▸ **re'duplicative** ADJECTIVE

reduplication (rɪˌdjuːplɪˈkeɪʃən) NOUN [1] the process or an instance of redoubling. [2] the state, condition, or quality of being redoubled. [3] a thing that has been redoubled. [4] repetition of a sound or syllable in a word, as in the formation of the Latin perfect *tetigi* from *tangere* "touch".

reduviid (rɪˈdjuːvɪɪd) NOUN [1] any hemipterous bug of the family *Reduviidae*, which includes the assassin bugs and the wheel bug. ◆ ADJECTIVE [2] of, relating to, or belonging to the family *Reduviidae*.
▹ HISTORY C19: from New Latin *Reduviidae*, from Latin *reduvia* a hangnail

redware (ˈrɛdˌwɛə) NOUN another name for **kelp** (the seaweed).

red water NOUN [1] a disease of cattle caused by the protozoan *Babesia* (or *Piroplasma*) *bovis*, which destroys the red blood cells, characterized by the passage of red or blackish urine. It is transmitted by tick bites. [2] any of various other animal diseases characterized by haematuria.

redwing (ˈrɛdˌwɪŋ) NOUN [1] a small European thrush, *Turdus iliacus*, having a speckled breast, reddish flanks, and brown back. [2] a North American oriole, *Agelaius phoeniceus*, the male of which has a black plumage with a red-and-yellow patch on each wing.

redwood (ˈrɛdˌwʊd) NOUN a giant coniferous tree, *Sequoia sempervirens*, of coastal regions of California, having reddish fibrous bark and durable timber: family *Taxodiaceae*. The largest specimen is over 120 metres (360 feet) tall. See also **sequoia**.

Redwood seconds NOUN (*functioning as singular*) a scale of measurement of viscosity based on the time in seconds taken for fluid to flow through a standard orifice: accepted as standard in the UK in 1886. See also **Saybolt universal seconds, Engler degrees.**
▹ HISTORY named after Sir B. *Redwood* (1846–1919), English chemist who proposed it

reebok (ˈriːbʌk, -bɒk) NOUN, *plural* **-boks** *or* **-bok**. a variant spelling of **rhebok**.

re-echo (riːˈɛkəʊ) VERB **-oes, -oing, -oed.** [1] to echo (a sound that is already an echo); resound. [2] (*tr*) to repeat like an echo.

reed (riːd) NOUN [1] any of various widely distributed tall grasses of the genus *Phragmites*, esp *P. communis*, that grow in swamps and shallow water and have jointed hollow stalks. [2] the stalk, or stalks collectively, of any of these plants, esp as used for thatching. [3] *Music* **a** a thin piece of cane or metal inserted into the tubes of certain wind instruments, which sets in vibration the air column inside the tube. **b** a wind instrument or organ pipe that sounds by means of a reed. [4] one of the several vertical parallel wires on a loom that may be moved upwards to separate the warp threads. [5] a small semicircular architectural moulding. See also **reeding.** [6] an ancient Hebrew unit of length equal to six cubits. [7] an archaic word for **arrow.** [8] **broken reed.** a weak, unreliable, or ineffectual person. ◆ VERB (*tr*) [9] to fashion into or supply with reeds or reeding. [10] to thatch using reeds.
▹ HISTORY Old English *hreod*; related to Old Saxon *hriod*, Old High German *hriot*

reedbird (ˈriːdˌbɜːd) NOUN any of several birds that frequent reed beds, esp (in the US and Canada) the bobolink.

reedbuck (ˈriːdˌbʌk) NOUN, *plural* **-bucks** *or* **-buck**. any antelope of the genus *Redunca*, of Africa south of the Sahara, having a buff-coloured coat and inward-curving horns.

reed bunting NOUN a common European bunting, *Emberiza schoeniclus*, that occurs near reed beds and has a brown streaked plumage with, in the male, a black head.

reed grass NOUN a tall perennial grass, *Glyceria maxima*, of rivers and ponds of Europe, Asia, and Canada.

reeding (ˈriːdɪŋ) NOUN [1] a set of small semicircular architectural mouldings. [2] the milling on the edges of a coin.

reedling (ˈriːdlɪŋ) NOUN a titlike Eurasian songbird, *Panurus biarmicus*, common in reed beds: family *Muscicapidae* (Old World flycatchers, etc.). It has a tawny back and tail and, in the male, a grey-and-black head. Also called: **bearded tit.**

reed mace NOUN [1] Also called: (popularly) **bulrush, false bulrush, cat's-tail.** a tall reedlike marsh plant, *Typha latifolia*, with straplike leaves and flowers in long brown sausage-shaped spikes: family *Typhaceae*. See also **bulrush** (sense 2). [2] a related and similar plant, *Typha angustifolia*.

reed organ NOUN [1] a wind instrument, such as the harmonium, accordion, or harmonica, in which the sound is produced by reeds, each reed producing one note only. [2] a type of pipe organ, such as the regal, in which all the pipes are fitted with reeds.

reed pipe NOUN [1] a wind instrument, such as a clarinet or oboe, whose sound is produced by a vibrating reed. [2] an organ pipe sounded by a vibrating reed.

reed stop NOUN an organ stop controlling a rank of reed pipes.

re-educate VERB (*tr*) to teach or show (someone) something new or in a different way.
▸ **ˌre-eduˈcation** NOUN

reed warbler NOUN any of various common Old World warblers of the genus *Acrocephalus*, esp *A. scirpaceus*, that inhabit marshy regions and have a brown plumage.

reedy (ˈriːdɪ) ADJECTIVE **reedier, reediest.** [1] (of a place, esp a marsh) abounding in reeds. [2] of or like a reed. [3] having a tone like a reed instrument; shrill or piping: *a reedy voice*.
▸ **ˈreedily** ADVERB ▸ **ˈreediness** NOUN

reef[1] (riːf) NOUN [1] a ridge of rock, sand, coral, etc., the top of which lies close to the surface of the sea. [2] a ridge- or mound-like structure built by sedentary calcareous organisms (esp corals) and consisting mainly of their remains. [3] a vein of ore, esp one of gold-bearing quartz.
▹ HISTORY C16: from Middle Dutch *ref*, from Old Norse *rif* RIB[1], REEF[2]

reef[2] (riːf) *Nautical* ◆ NOUN [1] the part gathered in when sail area is reduced, as in a high wind. ◆ VERB [2] to reduce the area of (sail) by taking in a reef. [3] (*tr*) to shorten or bring inboard (a spar).
▹ HISTORY C14: from Middle Dutch *rif*; related to Old Norse *rif* reef, RIB[1], German *reffen* to reef; see REEF[1]

Reef (riːf) NOUN **the.** [1] another name for the **Great Barrier Reef.** [2] another name for the **Witwatersrand.**

reefer[1] (ˈriːfə) NOUN [1] *Nautical* a person who reefs, such as a midshipman. [2] another name for **reefing jacket.** [3] *Slang* a hand-rolled cigarette, esp one containing cannabis.
▹ HISTORY C19: from REEF[2]; applied to the cigarette because of its resemblance to the rolled reef of a sail

reefer[2] (ˈriːfə) NOUN a ship, lorry, or other form of transport designed to carry refrigerated cargo.
▹ HISTORY C20: shortened and adapted from *refrigerator*

reefing jacket NOUN a man's short double-breasted jacket of sturdy wool. Also called: **reefer.**

reef knot NOUN a knot consisting of two overhand knots turned opposite ways. Also called: **square knot.**

reef point NOUN *Nautical* one of several short lengths of line stitched through a sail for tying a reef.

reek (riːk) VERB [1] (*intr*) to give off or emit a strong unpleasant odour; smell or stink. [2] (*intr*; often foll by *of*) to be permeated (by); be redolent (of): *the letter reeks of subservience*. [3] (*tr*) to treat with smoke; fumigate. [4] (*tr*) *Chiefly dialect* to give off or emit (smoke, fumes, vapour, etc.). ◆ NOUN [5] a strong offensive smell; stink. [6] *Chiefly dialect* smoke or steam; vapour.
▹ HISTORY Old English *rēocan*; related to Old Frisian *riāka* to smoke, Old High German *rouhhan*, Old Norse *rjūka* to smoke, steam
▸ **ˈreeking** ADJECTIVE ▸ **ˈreekingly** ADVERB ▸ **ˈreeky** ADJECTIVE

reel[1] (riːl, rɪəl) NOUN [1] any of various cylindrical objects or frames that turn on an axis and onto which film, magnetic tape, paper tape, wire, thread, etc., may be wound. US equivalent: **spool.** [2] *Angling* a device for winding, casting, etc., consisting of a revolving spool with a handle, attached to a fishing rod. [3] a roll of celluloid exhibiting a sequence of photographs to be projected. ◆ VERB (*tr*) [4] to wind (cotton, thread, etc.) onto a reel. [5] (foll by *in, out* etc) to wind or draw with a reel: *to reel in a fish*.
▹ HISTORY Old English *hrēol*; related to Old Norse *hræll* weaver's rod, Greek *krekein* to weave
▸ **ˈreelable** ADJECTIVE ▸ **ˈreeler** NOUN

reel[2] (riːl, rɪəl) VERB (*mainly intr*) [1] to sway, esp under the shock of a blow or through dizziness or drunkenness. [2] to whirl about or have the feeling of whirling about: *his brain reeled*. ◆ NOUN [3] a staggering or swaying motion or sensation.
▹ HISTORY C14 *relen*, probably from REEL[1]

reel[3] (riːl, rɪəl) NOUN [1] any of various lively Scottish dances, such as the **eightsome reel** and **foursome reel** for a fixed number of couples who combine in square and circular formations. [2] a piece of music having eight quavers to the bar composed for or in the rhythm of this dance.
▹ HISTORY C18: from REEL[2]

re-elect VERB (*tr*) to elect (a person, political party, etc.) to an official post for a further term.

re-election NOUN [1] the election of a person or persons for a further term of office: *his re-election as party leader*. [2] **a** the state of being elected again: *not seeking re-election*. **b** (*as modifier*): *a re-election campaign*.

reel-fed ADJECTIVE *Printing* involving or printing on a web of paper: *a reel-fed press*. Compare **sheet-fed.**

reel man NOUN *Austral and NZ* (formerly) the member of a beach life-saving team who controlled the reel on which the line was wound.

reel off VERB (*tr, adverb*) to recite or write fluently and without apparent effort: *to reel off items on a list*.

reel of three NOUN (in Scottish country dancing) a figure-of-eight movement danced by three people.

reel-to-reel ADJECTIVE [1] (of magnetic tape) wound from one reel to another in use. [2] (of a tape recorder) using magnetic tape wound from one reel to another, as opposed to cassettes.

re-emerge VERB (*intr:* often foll by *from*) to emerge or appear again; resurface: *to re-emerge as a threat*.

re-emergence NOUN the act or an instance of re-emerging.

re-employ VERB (*tr*) to take on (a previous employee) again.

re-employment NOUN the act or an instance of employing or being employed again.

reen *or* **rean** (riːn) NOUN *Southwest English dialect* a ditch, esp a drainage channel.
▹ HISTORY from earlier *rhine*, from Old English *ryne*

re-enact VERB (*tr*) to represent or perform (an event, etc.) that has happened before.

re-enactment NOUN the acting out or repetition of a past event or situation.

re-engage VERB [1] (*intr*) to take part in or participate again: *re-engaged in terrorism*. [2] (*tr*) to employ (someone) again.

re-engineering NOUN **a** the restructuring of a company or part of its operations, esp by utilizing information technology. **b** (*as modifier*): *a massive re-engineering programme*.

re-enter VERB (*tr*) to enter (something or somewhere) again.

re-entering angle NOUN an interior angle of a polygon that is greater than 180°. Also called: **re-entrant angle.**

re-entrant (riːˈɛntrənt) ADJECTIVE [1] (of an angle, esp in fortifications) pointing inwards. Compare **salient** (sense 2). [2] *Maths* (of an angle in a polygon) greater than 180° and thus pointing inwards. ◆ NOUN [3] an angle or part that points inwards.

re-entry (riːˈɛntrɪ) NOUN, *plural* **-tries.** [1] the act of retaking possession of land, etc., under a right reserved in an earlier transfer of the property, such as a lease. [2] the return of a spacecraft into the earth's atmosphere.

re-entry vehicle NOUN the portion of a ballistic missile that carries a nuclear warhead and re-enters the earth's atmosphere.

re-equip VERB **-quips, -quipping, -quipped.** (*tr*) to furnish (someone or something) with new supplies, equipment, etc.

reest *or* **reast** (riːst) VERB (*intr*) *Northern English dialect* (esp of horses) to be noisily uncooperative.

▷HISTORY probably from Scottish *arreest* ARREST; perhaps related to RESTIVE

re-establish VERB (*tr*) to establish (something) again: *a fight to re-establish his authority.*
▸ˌ**re-es'tablishment** NOUN

re-evaluate VERB (*tr*) to evaluate again or differently.
▸ˌ**re-eˌvalu'ation** NOUN

reeve¹ (riːv) NOUN 1 *English history* the local representative of the king in a shire (under the ealdorman) until the early 11th century. Compare **sheriff.** 2 (in medieval England) a manorial steward who supervised the daily affairs of the manor: often a villein elected by his fellows. 3 *Canadian government* (in certain provinces) a president of a local council, esp in a rural area. 4 (formerly) a minor local official in any of several parts of England and the US.
▷HISTORY Old English *gerēva*; related to Old High German *ruova* number, array

reeve² (riːv) VERB **reeves, reeving; reeved** *or* **rove** (rəʊv). (*tr*) *Nautical* 1 to pass (a rope or cable) through an eye or other narrow opening. 2 to fasten by passing through or around something.
▷HISTORY C17: perhaps from Dutch *rēven* REEF²

reeve³ (riːv) NOUN the female of the ruff (the bird).
▷HISTORY C17: of uncertain origin

re-examine (ˌriːɪg'zæmɪn) VERB (*tr*) 1 to examine again. 2 *Law* to examine (one's own witness) again upon matters arising out of his cross-examination.
▸ˌ**re-ex'aminable** ADJECTIVE ▸ˌ**re-exˌami'nation** NOUN
▸ˌ**re-ex'aminer** NOUN

re-experience VERB (*tr*) to participate in or undergo (an event or experience) again.

re-export VERB (ˌriːɪk'spɔːt, riː'ɛkspɔːt) 1 to export (imported goods, esp after processing). ◆ NOUN (riː'ɛkspɔːt) 2 the act of re-exporting. 3 a re-exported commodity.
▸ˌ**re-expor'tation** NOUN ▸ˌ**re-ex'porter** NOUN

ref (rɛf) NOUN *Informal* short for **referee.**

ref. ABBREVIATION FOR: 1 referee. 2 reference.

reface (riː'feɪs) VERB (*tr*) 1 to repair or renew the facing of (a wall). 2 to put a new facing on (a garment).

refashion (riː'fæʃən) VERB (*tr*) to give a new form to (something).

Ref. Ch. ABBREVIATION FOR Reformed Church.

refection (rɪ'fɛkʃən) NOUN refreshment with food and drink.
▷HISTORY C14: from Latin *refectiō* a restoring, from *reficere* to remake, from RE- + *facere* to make

refectory (rɪ'fɛktərɪ, -trɪ) NOUN, *plural* **-tories.** a communal dining hall in a religious, academic, or other institution.
▷HISTORY C15: from Late Latin *refectōrium*, from Latin *refectus* refreshed

refectory table NOUN a long narrow dining table supported by two trestles joined by a stretcher or set into a base.

refer (rɪ'fɜː) VERB **-fers, -ferring, -ferred.** (often foll by *to*) 1 (*intr*) to make mention (of). 2 (*tr*) to direct the attention of (someone) for information, facts, etc.: *the reader is referred to Chomsky, 1965.* 3 (*intr*) to seek information (from): *I referred to Directory Enquiries; he referred to his notes.* 4 (*intr*) to be relevant (to); pertain or relate (to): *this song refers to an incident in the Civil War.* 5 (*tr*) to assign or attribute: *Cromwell referred his victories to God.* 6 (*tr*) to hand over for consideration, reconsideration, or decision: *to refer a complaint to another department.* 7 (*tr*) to hand back to the originator as unacceptable or unusable. 8 (*tr*) *Brit* to fail (a student) in an examination. 9 (*tr*) *Brit* to send back (a thesis) to a student for improvement. 10 **refer to drawer.** a request by a bank that the payee consult the drawer concerning a cheque payable by that bank (usually because the drawer has insufficient funds in his account), payment being suspended in the meantime. 11 (*tr*) to direct (a patient) for treatment to another doctor, usually a specialist. 12 (*tr*) *Social welfare* to direct (a client) to another agency or professional for a service.
▷HISTORY C14: from Latin *referre* to carry back, from RE- + *ferre* to BEAR¹
▸**referable** ('rɛfərəbᵊl) *or* **referrable** (rɪ'fɜːrəbᵊl) ADJECTIVE ▸**re'ferral** NOUN ▸**re'ferrer** NOUN

> **Language note** The common practice of adding *back* to *refer* is tautologous, since this meaning is already contained in the *re-* of *refer: this refers to* (not *back to*) *what has already been said.* However, when *refer* is used in the sense of passing a document or question for further consideration to the person from whom it was received, it may be appropriate to say *he referred the matter back.*

referee (ˌrɛfə'riː) NOUN 1 a person to whom reference is made, esp for an opinion, information, or a decision. 2 the umpire or judge in any of various sports, esp football and boxing, responsible for ensuring fair play according to the rules. 3 a person who is willing to testify to the character or capabilities of someone. 4 *Law* See **Official Referee.** ◆ VERB **-ees, -eeing, -eed.** 5 to act as a referee (in); preside (over).

reference ('rɛfərəns, 'rɛfrəns) NOUN 1 the act or an instance of referring. 2 something referred, esp proceedings submitted to a referee in law. 3 a direction of the attention to a passage elsewhere or to another book, document, etc. 4 a book or passage referred to. 5 a mention or allusion: *this book contains several references to the Civil War.* 6 *Philosophy* **a** the relation between a word, phrase, or symbol and the object or idea to which it refers. **b** the object referred to by an expression. Compare **sense** (sense 13). 7 **a** a source of information or facts. **b** (*as modifier*): *a reference book; a reference library.* 8 a written testimonial regarding one's character or capabilities. 9 a person referred to for such a testimonial. 10 **a** (foll by *to*) relation or delimitation, esp to or by membership of a specific class or group; respect or regard: *all people, without reference to sex or age.* **b** (*as modifier*): *a reference group.* 11 **terms of reference.** the specific limits of responsibility that determine the activities of an investigating body, etc. 12 **point of reference.** a fact forming the basis of an evaluation or assessment; criterion. ◆ VERB (*tr*) 13 to furnish or compile a list of references for (an academic thesis, publication, etc.). 14 to make a reference to; refer to: *he referenced Chomsky, 1956.* ◆ PREPOSITION 15 *Business* with reference to: *reference your letter of the 9th inst.* Abbreviation: **re.**
▸**'referencer** NOUN ▸**referential** (ˌrɛfə'rɛnʃəl) ADJECTIVE

reference book NOUN 1 a book, such as an encyclopedia, dictionary, etc., from which information may be obtained. 2 *South African* another name for **passbook** (sense 4).

referendum (ˌrɛfə'rɛndəm) NOUN, *plural* **-dums** *or* **-da** (-də). 1 submission of an issue of public importance to the direct vote of the electorate. 2 a vote on such a measure. 3 a poll of the members of a club, union, or other group to determine their views on some matter. 4 a diplomatic official's note to his government requesting instructions. ◆ See also (for senses 1, 2) **plebiscite.**
▷HISTORY C19: from Latin: something to be carried back, from *referre* to REFER

referent ('rɛfərənt) NOUN the object or idea to which a word or phrase refers. Compare **sense** (sense 13).
▷HISTORY C19: from Latin *referens*, from *referre* to REFER

referred pain NOUN *Psychol* pain felt in the body at some place other than its actual place of origin.

reffo ('rɛfəʊ) NOUN, *plural* **reffos.** *Austral slang* an offensive name for a European refugee after World War II.

refill VERB (riː'fɪl) 1 to fill (something) again. ◆ NOUN ('riːfɪl) 2 a replacement for a consumable substance in a permanent container. 3 a second or subsequent filling: *a refill at the petrol station.* 4 *Informal* another drink to replace one already drunk.
▸**re'fillable** ADJECTIVE

refinancing (ˌriːfɪ'nænsɪŋ) NOUN a method of paying a debt by borrowing additional money thus creating a second debt in order to pay the first.

refine (rɪ'faɪn) VERB 1 to make or become free from impurities, sediment, or other foreign matter; purify. 2 (*tr*) to separate (a mixture) into pure constituents, as in an oil refinery. 3 to make or become free from coarse characteristics; make or become elegant or polished. 4 (*tr*; often foll by *out*) to remove (something impure or extraneous). 5 (*intr*; often foll by *on* or *upon*) to enlarge or improve (upon) by making subtle or fine distinctions. 6 (*tr*) to make (language) more subtle or polished.
▷HISTORY C16: from RE- + FINE¹
▸**re'finable** ADJECTIVE

refined (rɪ'faɪnd) ADJECTIVE 1 not coarse or vulgar; genteel, elegant, or polite. 2 subtle; discriminating. 3 freed from impurities; purified.

refinement (rɪ'faɪnmənt) NOUN 1 the act of refining or the state of being refined. 2 a fine or delicate point, distinction, or expression; a subtlety. 3 fineness or precision of thought, expression, manners, etc.; polish or cultivation. 4 a device, change, adaptation, etc., designed to improve performance or increase efficiency.

refiner (rɪ'faɪnə) NOUN a person, device, or substance that removes impurities, sediment, or other unwanted matter from something.

refinery (rɪ'faɪnərɪ) NOUN, *plural* **-eries.** a factory for the purification of some crude material, such as ore, sugar, oil, etc.

refit VERB (riː'fɪt) **-fits, -fitting, -fitted.** 1 to make or be made ready for use again by repairing, re-equipping, or resupplying. ◆ NOUN ('riːˌfɪt) 2 a repair or re-equipping, as of a ship, for further use.
▸**re'fitment** NOUN

reflate (riː'fleɪt) VERB to inflate or be inflated again.
▷HISTORY C20: back formation from REFLATION

reflation (riː'fleɪʃən) NOUN 1 an increase in economic activity. 2 an increase in the supply of money and credit designed to cause such an increase. ◆ Compare **inflation** (sense 2).
▷HISTORY C20: from RE- + *-flation*, as in INFLATION or DEFLATION

reflect (rɪ'flɛkt) VERB 1 to undergo or cause to undergo a process in which light, other electromagnetic radiation, sound, particles, etc., are thrown back after impinging on a surface. 2 (of a mirror, etc.) to form an image of (something) by reflection. 3 (*tr*) to show or express: *his tactics reflect his desire for power.* 4 (*tr*) to bring as a consequence: *the success of the project reflected great credit on all the staff.* 5 (*intr*; foll by *on* or *upon*) to cause to be regarded in a specified way: *her behaviour reflects well on her.* 6 (*intr*; foll by *on* or *upon*) to cast dishonour, discredit, etc. (on): *his conduct reflects on his parents.* 7 (*intr*; usually foll by *on*) to think, meditate, or ponder.
▷HISTORY C15: from Latin *reflectere* to bend back, from RE- + *flectere* to bend; see FLEX

reflectance (rɪ'flɛktəns) *or* **reflection factor** NOUN a measure of the ability of a surface to reflect light or other electromagnetic radiation, equal to the ratio of the reflected flux to the incident flux. Symbol: ρ. Compare **transmittance, absorptance.**

reflecting telescope NOUN a type of telescope in which the initial image is formed by a concave mirror. Also called: **reflector.** Compare **refracting telescope.**

reflection *or less commonly* **reflexion** (rɪ'flɛkʃən) NOUN 1 the act of reflecting or the state of being reflected. 2 something reflected or the image so produced, as by a mirror. 3 careful or long consideration or thought. 4 implicit or explicit attribution of discredit or blame. 5 *Maths* a transformation in which the direction of one axis is reversed or which changes the sign of one of the variables. 6 *Anatomy* the bending back of a structure or part upon itself.
▸**re'flectional** *or* **re'flexional** ADJECTIVE

reflection density NOUN *Physics* a measure of the extent to which a surface reflects light or other electromagnetic radiation, equal to the logarithm to base ten of the reciprocal of the reflectance. Symbol: *D*. Former name: **optical density.**

reflective (rɪ'flɛktɪv) ADJECTIVE 1 characterized by quiet thought or contemplation. 2 capable of reflecting: *a reflective surface.* 3 produced by reflection.
▸**re'flectively** ADVERB

reflectivity (ˌriːflɛk'tɪvɪtɪ) NOUN 1 *Physics* a measure of the ability of a surface to reflect radiation, equal to the reflectance of a layer of material sufficiently thick for the reflectance not to depend on the thickness. 2 Also called: **reflectiveness.** the quality or capability of being reflective.

reflectometer (ˌri:flɛkˈtɒmɪtə) NOUN *Physics* an instrument for measuring the ratio of the energy of a reflected wave to the incident wave in a system.

reflector (rɪˈflɛktə) NOUN [1] a person or thing that reflects. [2] a surface or object that reflects light, sound, heat, etc. [3] a small translucent red disc, strip, etc., with a reflecting backing on the rear of a road vehicle, which reflects the light of the headlights of a following vehicle. [4] another name for **reflecting telescope.** [5] part of an aerial placed so as to increase the forward radiation of the radiator and decrease the backward radiation.

reflet (rəˈfleɪ) NOUN an iridescent glow or lustre, as on ceramic ware.
▷HISTORY C19: from French: a reflection, from Italian *riflesso*, from Latin *reflexus*, from *reflectere* to REFLECT

reflex NOUN (ˈri:flɛks) [1] **a** an immediate involuntary response, esp one that is innate, such as coughing or removal of the hand from a hot surface, evoked by a given stimulus. **b** (*as modifier*): *a reflex action.* See also **reflex arc.** [2] **a** a mechanical response to a particular situation, involving no conscious decision. **b** (*as modifier*): *a reflex response.* [3] a reflection; an image produced by or as if by reflection. [4] a speech element derived from a corresponding form in an earlier state of the language: *"sorrow" is a reflex of Middle English "sorwe".*. ◆ ADJECTIVE (ˈri:flɛks) [5] *Maths* (of an angle) between 180° and 360°. [6] (*prenominal*) turned, reflected, or bent backwards. ◆ VERB (rɪˈflɛks) [7] (*tr*) to bend, turn, or reflect backwards.
▷HISTORY C16: from Latin *reflexus* bent back, from *reflectere* to reflect
▸**reˈflexible** ADJECTIVE ▸**reˌflexiˈbility** NOUN

reflex arc NOUN *Physiol* the neural pathway over which impulses travel to produce a reflex action, consisting of at least one afferent (receptor) and one efferent (effector) neuron.

reflex camera NOUN a camera in which the image is composed and focused on a large ground-glass viewfinder screen. In a **single-lens reflex** the light enters through the camera lens and falls on the film when the viewfinder mirror is retracted. In a **twin-lens reflex** the light enters through a separate lens and is deflected onto the viewfinder screen.

reflexion (rɪˈflɛkʃən) NOUN *Brit* a less common spelling of **reflection.**
▸**reˈflexional** ADJECTIVE

reflexive (rɪˈflɛksɪv) ADJECTIVE [1] denoting a class of pronouns that refer back to the subject of a sentence or clause. Thus, in the sentence *that man thinks a great deal of himself*, the pronoun *himself* is reflexive. [2] denoting a verb used transitively with the reflexive pronoun as its direct object, as the French *se lever* "to get up" (literally "to raise oneself") or English *to dress oneself.* [3] *Physiol* of or relating to a reflex. [4] *Logic, maths* (of a relation) holding between any member of its domain and itself: *"… is a member of the same family as …" is reflexive.* Compare **irreflexive, nonreflexive.** ◆ NOUN [5] a reflexive pronoun or verb.
▸**reˈflexively** ADVERB ▸**reˈflexiveness** *or* **reflexivity** (ˌri:flɛkˈsɪvɪtɪ) NOUN

reflexology (ˌri:flɛkˈsɒlədʒɪ) NOUN [1] a form of therapy practised as a treatment in alternative medicine in which the soles of the feet are massaged: designed to stimulate the blood supply and nerves and thus relieve tension. [2] *Psychol* the belief that behaviour can be understood in terms of combinations of reflexes.
▸**ˌreflexˈologist** NOUN

refluent (ˈrɛfluənt) ADJECTIVE *Rare* flowing back; ebbing.
▷HISTORY C18: from Latin *refluere* to flow back
▸**ˈrefluence** NOUN

reflux (ˈri:flʌks) VERB [1] *Chem* to boil or be boiled in a vessel attached to a condenser, so that the vapour condenses and flows back into the vessel. ◆ NOUN [2] *Chem* **a** an act of refluxing. **b** (*as modifier*): *a reflux condenser.* [3] the act or an instance of flowing back; ebb.
▷HISTORY C15: from Medieval Latin *refluxus*, from Latin *refluere* to flow back

reflux oesophagitis (i:ˌsɒfəˈdʒaɪtɪs) NOUN inflammation of the gullet caused by regurgitation of stomach acids, producing heartburn: may be associated with a hiatus hernia.

reforest (ri:ˈfɒrɪst) VERB (*tr*) another word for **reafforest.**

reform (rɪˈfɔ:m) VERB [1] (*tr*) to improve (an existing institution, law, practice, etc.) by alteration or correction of abuses. [2] to give up or cause to give up a reprehensible habit or immoral way of life. [3] *Chem* to change the molecular structure of (a hydrocarbon) to make it suitable for use as petrol by heat, pressure, and the action of catalysts. ◆ NOUN [4] an improvement or change for the better, esp as a result of correction of legal or political abuses or malpractices. [5] a principle, campaign, or measure aimed at achieving such change. [6] improvement of morals or behaviour, esp by giving up some vice.
▷HISTORY C14: via Old French from Latin *refōrmāre* to form again
▸**reˈformable** ADJECTIVE ▸**reˈformative** ADJECTIVE
▸**reˈformer** NOUN

re-form (ri:ˈfɔ:m) VERB to form anew.
▸**ˌre-forˈmation** NOUN

reformation (ˌrɛfəˈmeɪʃən) NOUN the act or an instance of reforming or the state of being reformed.
▸**ˌreforˈmational** ADJECTIVE

Reformation (ˌrɛfəˈmeɪʃən) NOUN a religious and political movement of 16th-century Europe that began as an attempt to reform the Roman Catholic Church and resulted in the establishment of the Protestant Churches.

reformatory (rɪˈfɔ:mətərɪ, -trɪ) NOUN, *plural* **-ries.** [1] Also called: **reform school.** (formerly) a place of instruction where young offenders were sent for corrective training. Compare **approved school.** ◆ ADJECTIVE [2] having the purpose or function of reforming.

Reform Bill *or* **Act** NOUN *Brit history* any of several bills or acts extending the franchise or redistributing parliamentary seats, esp the acts of 1832 and 1867.

Reformed (rɪˈfɔ:md) ADJECTIVE [1] of or designating a Protestant Church, esp the Calvinist as distinct from the Lutheran. [2] of or designating Reform Judaism.

reformism (rɪˈfɔ:mɪzəm) NOUN a doctrine or movement advocating reform, esp political or religious reform, rather than abolition.
▸**reˈformist** NOUN, ADJECTIVE

Reform Judaism NOUN a movement in Judaism originating in the 19th century, which does not require strict observance of the law, but adapts the historical forms of Judaism to the contemporary world. Compare **Orthodox Judaism, Conservative Judaism.**

reformulate (ri:ˈfɔ:mjuˌleɪt) VERB to change or update (an idea, plan, etc. already formulated).
▸**ˌreformuˈlation** NOUN

refract (rɪˈfrækt) VERB (*tr*) [1] to cause to undergo refraction. [2] to measure the refractive capabilities of (the eye, a lens, etc.).
▷HISTORY C17: from Latin *refractus* broken up, from *refringere*, from RE- + *frangere* to break
▸**reˈfractable** ADJECTIVE

refracting telescope NOUN a type of telescope in which the image is formed by a set of lenses. Also called: **refractor.** Compare **reflecting telescope.**

refraction (rɪˈfrækʃən) NOUN [1] *Physics* the change in direction of a propagating wave, such as light or sound, in passing from one medium to another in which it has a different velocity. [2] the amount by which a wave is refracted. [3] the ability of the eye to refract light. [4] the determination of the refractive condition of the eye. [5] *Astronomy* the apparent elevation in position of a celestial body resulting from the refraction of light by the earth's atmosphere.

refractive (rɪˈfræktɪv) ADJECTIVE [1] of or concerned with refraction. [2] (of a material or substance) capable of causing refraction.
▸**reˈfractively** ADVERB ▸**reˈfractiveness** *or* **refractivity** (ˌri:frækˈtɪvɪtɪ) NOUN

refractive index NOUN *Physics* a measure of the extent to which radiation is refracted on passing through the interface between two media. It is the ratio of the sine of the angle of incidence to the sine of the angle of refraction, which can be shown to be equal to the ratio of the phase speed in the first medium to that in the second. In the case of electromagnetic radiation, esp light, it is usual to give values of the **absolute refractive index** of a medium, that is for radiation entering the medium from free space. Symbol: ν, μ.

refractometer (ˌri:frækˈtɒmɪtə) NOUN any instrument for determining the refractive index of a substance.
▸**refractometric** (rɪˌfræktəˈmɛtrɪk) ADJECTIVE
▸**ˌrefracˈtometry** NOUN

refractor (rɪˈfræktə) NOUN [1] an object or material that refracts. [2] another name for **refracting telescope.**

refractory (rɪˈfræktərɪ) ADJECTIVE [1] unmanageable or obstinate. [2] *Med* not responding to treatment. [3] (of a material) able to withstand high temperatures without fusion or decomposition. ◆ NOUN, *plural* **-ries.** [4] a material, such as fireclay or alumina, that is able to withstand high temperatures: used to line furnaces, kilns, etc.
▷HISTORY C17: variant of obsolete *refractary*; see REFRACT
▸**reˈfractorily** ADVERB ▸**reˈfractoriness** NOUN

refractory period NOUN a period during which a nerve or muscle is incapable of responding to stimulation, esp immediately following a previous stimulation. In an **absolute refractory period** there is a total inability to respond; in an **effective** *or* **relative refractory period** there is a response to very large stimuli.

refrain[1] (rɪˈfreɪn) VERB (*intr*; usually foll by *from*) to abstain (from action); forbear.
▷HISTORY C14: from Latin *refrēnāre* to check with a bridle, from RE- + *frēnum* a bridle
▸**reˈfrainer** NOUN ▸**reˈfrainment** NOUN

refrain[2] (rɪˈfreɪn) NOUN [1] a regularly recurring melody, such as the chorus of a song. [2] a much repeated saying or idea.
▷HISTORY C14: via Old French, ultimately from Latin *refringere* to break into pieces

reframe (ri:ˈfreɪm) verb (*tr*) [1] to support or enclose (a picture, photograph, etc.) in a new or different frame. [2] to change the plans or basic details of (a policy, idea, etc.): *reframe policy issues and problems.* [3] to look at, present, or think of (beliefs, ideas, relationships, etc.) in a new or different way: *reframe masculinity from this new perspective.* [4] to change the focus or perspective of (a view) through a lens. [5] to say (something) in a different way: *reframe the question.*

refrangible (rɪˈfrændʒɪbᵊl) ADJECTIVE capable of being refracted.
▷HISTORY C17: from Latin *refringere* to break up, from RE- + *frangere* to break
▸**reˌfrangiˈbility** *or* **reˈfrangibleness** NOUN

refreeze (ri:ˈfri:z) VERB **-freezes, -freezing, -froze, -frozen.** to freeze or be frozen again after having defrosted.

refresh (rɪˈfrɛʃ) VERB [1] (*usually tr or reflexive*) to make or become fresh or vigorous, as through rest, drink, or food; revive or reinvigorate. [2] (*tr*) to enliven (something worn or faded), as by adding new decorations. [3] (*tr*) to stimulate (the memory). [4] (*tr*) to replenish, as with new equipment or stores.
▷HISTORY C14: from Old French *refreschir*; see RE-, FRESH
▸**reˈfreshful** ADJECTIVE

refresher (rɪˈfrɛʃə) NOUN [1] something that refreshes, such as a cold drink. [2] *English law* a fee, additional to that marked on the brief, paid to counsel in a case that lasts more than a day.

refresher course NOUN a short educational course for people to review their subject and developments in it.

refreshing (rɪˈfrɛʃɪŋ) ADJECTIVE [1] able to or tending to refresh; invigorating. [2] pleasantly different or novel.
▸**reˈfreshingly** ADVERB

refreshment (rɪˈfrɛʃmənt) NOUN [1] the act of refreshing or the state of being refreshed. [2] (*plural*) snacks and drinks served as a light meal.

refrigerant (rɪˈfrɪdʒərənt) NOUN [1] a fluid capable of changes of phase at low temperatures: used as the working fluid of a refrigerator. [2] a cooling substance, such as ice or solid carbon dioxide. 3 *Med* an agent that provides a sensation of coolness or reduces fever. ◆ ADJECTIVE 4 causing cooling or freezing.

refrigerate (rɪˈfrɪdʒəˌreɪt) VERB to make or become frozen or cold, esp for preservative purposes; chill or freeze.
▷HISTORY C16: from Latin *refrīgerāre* to make cold, from RE- + *frīgus* cold
▸**reˌfrigerˈation** NOUN ▸**reˈfrigerative** ADJECTIVE ▸**reˈfrigeratory** ADJECTIVE, NOUN

refrigerator (rɪˈfrɪdʒəˌreɪtə) NOUN a chamber in which food, drink, etc., are kept cool. Informal word: **fridge**.

refringent (rɪˈfrɪndʒənt) ADJECTIVE *Physics* of, concerned with, or causing refraction; refractive.
▷HISTORY C18: from Latin *refringere* to break up; see REFRACT
▸**reˈfringency** *or* **reˈfringence** NOUN

reft (rɛft) VERB a past tense and past participle of **reave**.

refuel (riːˈfjuːəl) VERB **-els, -elling, -elled** *or US* **-els, -eling, -eled**. to supply or be supplied with fresh fuel.

refuge (ˈrɛfjuːdʒ) NOUN 1 shelter or protection, as from the weather or danger. 2 any place, person, action, or thing that offers or appears to offer protection, help, or relief: *accused of incompetence, he took refuge in lying*. 3 another name for a traffic island. See **island** (sense 2). ◆ VERB 4 *Archaic* to take refuge or give refuge to.
▷HISTORY C14: via Old French from Latin *refugium*, from *refugere* to flee away, from RE- + *fugere* to escape

refugee (ˌrɛfjuˈdʒiː) NOUN **a** a person who has fled from some danger or problem, esp political persecution: *refugees from Rwanda*. **b** (*as modifier*): *a refugee camp; a refugee problem*.
▸**ˌrefuˈgeeism** NOUN

refugee capital NOUN *Finance* money from abroad invested, esp for a short term, in the country offering the highest interest rate.

refugium (rɪˈfjuːdʒɪəm) NOUN, *plural* **-gia** (-dʒɪə). a geographical region that has remained unaltered by a climatic change affecting surrounding regions and that therefore forms a haven for relict fauna and flora.
▷HISTORY C20: Latin: refuge

refulgent (rɪˈfʌldʒənt) ADJECTIVE *Literary* shining, brilliant, or radiant.
▷HISTORY C16: from Latin *refulgēre* to shine brightly, from RE- + *fulgēre* to shine
▸**reˈfulgence** *or* (*less commonly*) **reˈfulgency** NOUN ▸**reˈfulgently** ADVERB

refund VERB (rɪˈfʌnd) (*tr*) 1 to give back (money), as when an article purchased is unsatisfactory. 2 to reimburse (a person). ◆ NOUN (ˈriːˌfʌnd) 3 return of money to a purchaser or the amount so returned.
▷HISTORY C14: from Latin *refundere* to pour back, from RE- + *fundere* to pour
▸**reˈfundable** ADJECTIVE ▸**reˈfunder** NOUN

re-fund (riːˈfʌnd) VERB (*tr*) *Finance* 1 to discharge (an old or matured debt) by new borrowing, as by a new bond issue. 2 to replace (an existing bond issue) with a new one.
▷HISTORY C20: from RE- + FUND

refurbish (riːˈfɜːbɪʃ) VERB (*tr*) to make neat, clean, or complete, as by renovating, re-equipping, or restoring.
▸**reˈfurbishing** *or* **reˈfurbishment** NOUN

refusal (rɪˈfjuːzᵊl) NOUN 1 the act or an instance of refusing. 2 the opportunity to reject or accept; option.

refuse¹ (rɪˈfjuːz) VERB 1 (*tr*) to decline to accept (something offered): *to refuse a present; to refuse promotion*. 2 to decline to give or grant (something) to (a person, organization, etc.). 3 (*when tr, takes an infinitive*) to express determination not (to do something); decline: *he refuses to talk about it*. 4 (of a horse) to be unwilling to take (a jump), as by swerving or stopping. 5 (*tr*) (of a woman) to declare one's unwillingness to accept (a suitor) as a husband.
▷HISTORY C14: from Old French *refuser*, from Latin *refundere* to pour back; see REFUND
▸**reˈfusable** ADJECTIVE ▸**reˈfuser** NOUN

refuse² (ˈrɛfjuːs) NOUN **a** anything thrown away; waste; rubbish. **b** (*as modifier*): *a refuse collection*.
▷HISTORY C15: from Old French *refuser* to REFUSE¹

refusenik *or* **refusnik** (rɪˈfjuːznɪk) NOUN 1 (formerly) a Jew in the Soviet Union who had been refused permission to emigrate. 2 a person who refuses to cooperate with a system or comply with a law because of a moral conviction.
▷HISTORY C20: from REFUSE¹ + -NIK

refutation (ˌrɛfjʊˈteɪʃən) NOUN 1 the act or process of refuting. 2 something that refutes; disproof.

refute (rɪˈfjuːt) VERB 1 (*tr*) to prove (a statement, theory, charge, etc.) of (a person) to be false or incorrect; disprove. 2 to deny (a claim, charge, allegation, etc.).
▷HISTORY C16: from Latin *refūtāre* to rebut
▸**refutable** (ˈrɛfjʊtəbᵊl, rɪˈfjuː-) ADJECTIVE ▸**refutability** (ˌrɛfjʊtəˈbɪlɪtɪ, rɪˌfjuː-) NOUN ▸**ˈrefutably** ADVERB ▸**reˈfuter** NOUN

Language note The use of *refute* to mean *deny* is thought by many people to be incorrect.

Reg. ABBREVIATION FOR: 1 Regent. 2 Regina.

regain VERB (rɪˈɡeɪn) (*tr*) 1 to take or get back; recover. 2 to reach again. ◆ NOUN (ˈriːˌɡeɪn) 3 the process of getting something back, esp lost weight: *this regain was inevitable*.
▸**reˈgainable** ADJECTIVE ▸**reˈgainer** NOUN

regal¹ (ˈriːɡᵊl) ADJECTIVE of, relating to, or befitting a king or queen; royal.
▷HISTORY C14: from Latin *rēgālis* from *rēx* king
▸**ˈregally** ADVERB

regal² (ˈriːɡᵊl) NOUN (*sometimes plural*) a portable organ equipped only with small reed pipes, popular from the 15th century and recently revived for modern performance.
▷HISTORY C16: from French *régale*; of obscure origin

regale (rɪˈɡeɪl) VERB (*tr*; usually foll by *with*) 1 to give delight or amusement to: *he regaled them with stories of his youth*. 2 to provide with choice or abundant food or drink. ◆ NOUN 3 *Archaic* **a** a feast. **b** a delicacy of food or drink.
▷HISTORY C17: from French *régaler*, from *gale* pleasure; related to Middle Dutch *wale* riches; see also GALA
▸**reˈgalement** NOUN

regalia (rɪˈɡeɪlɪə) PLURAL NOUN (*sometimes functioning as singular*) 1 the ceremonial emblems or robes of royalty, high office, an order, etc. 2 any splendid or special clothes; finery.
▷HISTORY C16: from Medieval Latin: royal privileges, from Latin *rēgālis* REGAL¹

regality (riːˈɡælɪtɪ) NOUN, *plural* **-ties**. 1 the state or condition of being royal; kingship or queenship; royalty. 2 the rights or privileges of royalty. 3 *Scot history* **a** jurisdiction conferred by the sovereign on a powerful subject. **b** a territory under such jurisdiction.

regard (rɪˈɡɑːd) VERB 1 to look closely or attentively at (something or someone); observe steadily. 2 (*tr*) to hold (a person or thing) in respect, admiration, or affection: *we regard your work very highly*. 3 (*tr*) to look upon or consider in a specified way: *she regarded her brother as her responsibility*. 4 (*tr*) to relate to; concern; have a bearing on. 5 to take notice of or pay attention to (something); heed: *he has never regarded the conventions*. 6 **as regards**. (*preposition*) in respect of; concerning. ◆ NOUN 7 a gaze; look. 8 attention; heed: *he spends without regard to his bank balance*. 9 esteem, affection, or respect. 10 reference, relation, or connection (esp in the phrases **with regard to** *or* **in regard to**). 11 (*plural*) good wishes or greetings (esp in the phrase **with kind regards**, used at the close of a letter). 12 **in this regard**. on this point.
▷HISTORY C14: from Old French *regarder* to look at, care about, from RE- + *garder* to GUARD
▸**reˈgardable** ADJECTIVE

regardant (rɪˈɡɑːdᵊnt) ADJECTIVE (*usually postpositive*) *Heraldry* (of a beast) shown looking backwards over its shoulder.
▷HISTORY C15: from Old French; see REGARD

regardful (rɪˈɡɑːdfʊl) ADJECTIVE 1 (often foll by *of*) showing regard (for); heedful (of). 2 showing regard, respect, or consideration.
▸**reˈgardfully** ADVERB ▸**reˈgardfulness** NOUN

regarding (rɪˈɡɑːdɪŋ) PREPOSITION in respect of; on the subject of.

regardless (rɪˈɡɑːdlɪs) ADJECTIVE 1 (usually foll by *of*) taking no regard or heed; heedless. ◆ ADVERB 2 in spite of everything; disregarding drawbacks: *to carry on regardless*.
▸**reˈgardlessly** ADVERB ▸**reˈgardlessness** NOUN

regatta (rɪˈɡætə) NOUN an organized series of races of yachts, rowing boats, etc.
▷HISTORY C17: from obsolete Italian (Venetian dialect) *rigatta* contest, of obscure origin

regd ABBREVIATION FOR registered.

regelate (ˈriːdʒɪˌleɪt) VERB *Physics* to undergo or cause to undergo regelation.
▷HISTORY C19: from RE- + stem of participle of Latin *gelāre* to freeze

regelation (ˌriːdʒɪˈleɪʃən) NOUN the rejoining together of two pieces of ice as a result of melting under pressure at the interface between them and subsequent refreezing.

regency (ˈriːdʒənsɪ) NOUN, *plural* **-cies**. 1 government by a regent or a body of regents. 2 the office of a regent or body of regents. 3 a territory under the jurisdiction of a regent or body of regents.
▷HISTORY C15: from Medieval Latin *regentia*, from Latin *regere* to rule

Regency (ˈriːdʒənsɪ) NOUN (preceded by *the*) 1 (in the United Kingdom) the period (1811–20) during which the Prince of Wales (later George IV (1762–1830; king 1820–30)) acted as regent during his father's periods of insanity. 2 (in France) the period of the regency of Philip, Duke of Orleans, during the minority (1715–23) of Louis XV (1710–74; king 1715–74). ◆ ADJECTIVE 3 characteristic of or relating to the Regency periods in France or the United Kingdom or to the styles of architecture, furniture, art, literature, etc., produced in them.

regenerate VERB (rɪˈdʒɛnəˌreɪt) 1 to undergo or cause to undergo moral, spiritual, or physical renewal or invigoration. 2 to form or be formed again; come or bring into existence once again. 3 to replace (lost or damaged tissues or organs) by new growth, or to cause (such tissues) to be replaced. 4 *Chem* to restore or be restored to an original physical or chemical state. 5 (*tr*) *Electronics* (in a digital system) to reshape (distorted incoming pulses) for onward transmission. ◆ ADJECTIVE (rɪˈdʒɛnərɪt) 6 morally, spiritually, or physically renewed or reborn; restored or refreshed.
▸**reˈgenerable** ADJECTIVE ▸**reˈgeneracy** NOUN ▸**reˈgenerative** ADJECTIVE ▸**reˈgeneratively** ADVERB ▸**reˈgenerˌator** NOUN

regeneration (rɪˌdʒɛnəˈreɪʃən) NOUN 1 the act or process of regenerating or the state of being regenerated; rebirth or renewal. 2 the regrowth by an animal or plant of an organ, tissue, or part that has been lost or destroyed. 3 *Electronics* the use of positive feedback to increase the amplification of a radio frequency stage.

regenerative cooling NOUN the process of cooling the walls of the combustion chamber of a rocket by circulating the propellant around the chamber before combustion.

Regensburg (*German* ˈreːɡənsbʊrk) NOUN a city in SE Germany, in Bavaria on the River Danube: a free Imperial city from 1245 and the leading commercial city of S Germany in the 12th and 13th centuries; the Imperial Diet was held in the town hall from 1663 to 1806. Pop.: 125 200 (1999 est.). Former English name: **Ratisbon**.

regent (ˈriːdʒənt) NOUN 1 the ruler or administrator of a country during the minority, absence, or incapacity of its monarch. 2 (formerly) a senior teacher or administrator in any of certain universities. 3 *US and Canadian* a member of the governing board of certain schools and colleges. 4 *Rare* any person who governs or rules. ◆ ADJECTIVE 5 (*usually postpositive*) acting or functioning as a regent: *a queen regent*. 6 *Rare* governing, ruling, or controlling.
▷HISTORY C14: from Latin *regēns* ruling, from *regere* to rule
▸**ˈregental** ADJECTIVE ▸**ˈregentship** NOUN

regent bowerbird *or* **regent bird** NOUN an Australian bowerbird, *Sericulus chrysocephalus*, the male of which has a showy yellow and velvety-black plumage.
▷HISTORY after the Prince Regent, the title of George IV (1762–1830) as regent of Great Britain

and Ireland during the insanity of his father (1811–20)

regent honeyeater NOUN a large brightly-coloured Australian honeyeater, *Zanthomiza phrygia*.

Regent's Park NOUN a park in central London, laid out as Marylebone Park by John Nash; now known for the London Zoo, its open-air theatre, and Nash's curved terraces.

reggae ('rɛgeɪ) NOUN a type of West Indian popular music having four beats to the bar, the upbeat being strongly accented.
▷HISTORY C20: of West Indian origin

Reggio di Calabria (*Italian* 'reddʒo di ka'la:brja) NOUN a port in S Italy, in Calabria on the Strait of Messina: founded about 720 B.C. by Greek colonists. Pop.: 179 617 (2000 est.).

Reggio nell'Emilia (*Italian* 'reddʒo nɛlle'mi:lja) NOUN a city in N central Italy, in Emilia-Romagna: founded in the 2nd century B.C. by Marcus Aemilius Lepidus; ruled by the Este family in the 15th–18th centuries. Pop.: 143 664 (2000 est.).

regicide ('rɛdʒɪˌsaɪd) NOUN 1 the killing of a king. 2 a person who kills a king.
▷HISTORY C16: from Latin *rēx* king + -CIDE
▸ˌregi'cidal ADJECTIVE

regime *or* **régime** (reɪ'ʒi:m) NOUN 1 a system of government or a particular administration: *a fascist regime; the regime of Fidel Castro.* 2 a social system or order. 3 *Med* another word for **regimen** (sense 1).
▷HISTORY C18: from French, from Latin *regimen* guidance, from *regere* to rule

regime change NOUN the transition from one political regime to another, esp through concerted political or military action.

regimen ('rɛdʒɪˌmɛn) NOUN 1 Also called: **regime**. a systematic way of life or course of therapy, often including exercise and a recommended diet. 2 administration or rule.
▷HISTORY C14: from Latin: guidance

regiment NOUN ('rɛdʒɪmənt) 1 a military formation varying in size from a battalion to a number of battalions. 2 a large number in regular or organized groups: *regiments of beer bottles.* ◆ VERB ('rɛdʒɪˌmɛnt) (*tr*) 3 to force discipline or order on, esp in a domineering manner. 4 to organize into a regiment or regiments. 5 to form into organized groups. 6 to assign to a regiment.
▷HISTORY C14: via Old French from Late Latin *regimentum* government, from Latin *regere* to rule
▸ˌregi'mental ADJECTIVE ▸ˌregi'mentally ADVERB
▸ˌregimen'tation NOUN

regimentals (ˌrɛdʒɪ'mɛntəlz) PLURAL NOUN 1 the uniform and insignia of a regiment. 2 military dress.

regimental sergeant major NOUN *Military* the senior Warrant Officer I in a British or Commonwealth regiment or battalion, responsible under the adjutant for all aspects of duty and discipline of the warrant officers, NCOs, and men. Abbreviation: **RSM**. Compare **company sergeant major**. See also **warrant officer**.

Regin ('reɪgɪn) NOUN *Norse myth* a dwarf smith, tutor of Sigurd, whom he encouraged to kill Fafnir for the gold he guarded.

Regina[1] (rɪ'dʒaɪnə) NOUN queen: now used chiefly in documents, inscriptions, etc. Compare **Rex**.

Regina[2] (rɪ'dʒaɪnə) NOUN a city in W Canada, capital and largest city of Saskatchewan: founded in 1882 as Pile O'Bones. Pop.: 180 400 (1996).

region ('ri:dʒən) NOUN 1 any large, indefinite, and continuous part of a surface or space. 2 an area considered as a unit for geographical, functional, social, or cultural reasons. 3 an administrative division of a country: *Tuscany is one of the regions of the Italian Republic.* 4 a realm or sphere of activity or interest. 5 range, area, or scope: *in what region is the price likely to be?* 6 (in Scotland from 1975 until 1996) any of the nine territorial divisions into which the mainland of Scotland was divided for purposes of local government; replaced in 1996 by council areas. See also **islands council**.
▷HISTORY C14: from Latin *regiō*, from *regere* to govern

regional ('ri:dʒənəl) ADJECTIVE of, characteristic of, or limited to a region: *the regional dialects of English.*
▸'regionally ADVERB

regional enteritis NOUN another name for **Crohn's disease**.

regionalism ('ri:dʒənəˌlɪzəm) NOUN 1 division of a country into administrative regions having partial autonomy. 2 advocacy of such division. 3 loyalty to one's home region; regional patriotism. 4 the common interests of national groups, people, etc., living in the same part of the world. 5 a word, custom, accent, or other characteristic associated with a specific region.
▸'regionalist NOUN, ADJECTIVE

régisseur *French* (reʒisœr) NOUN an official in a dance company with varying duties, usually including directing productions.
▷HISTORY from *régir* to manage

register ('rɛdʒɪstə) NOUN 1 an official or formal list recording names, events, or transactions. 2 the book in which such a list is written. 3 an entry in such a list. 4 a recording device that accumulates data, totals sums of money, etc.: *a cash register.* 5 a movable plate that controls the flow of air into a furnace, chimney, room, etc. 6 *Computing* one of a set of word-sized locations in the central processing unit in which items of data are placed temporarily before they are operated on by program instructions. 7 *Music* **a** the timbre characteristic of a certain manner of voice production. See **head voice, chest voice**. **b** any of the stops on an organ as classified in respect of its tonal quality: *the flute register.* 8 *Printing* **a** the correct alignment of the separate plates in colour printing. **b** the exact correspondence of lines of type, columns, etc., on the two sides of a printed sheet of paper. 9 a form of a language associated with a particular social situation or subject matter, such as obscene slang, legal language, or journalese. 10 the act or an instance of registering. ◆ VERB 11 (*tr*) to enter or cause someone to enter (an event, person's name, ownership, etc.) on a register; formally record. 12 to show or be shown on a scale or other measuring instrument: *the current didn't register on the meter.* 13 to show or be shown in a person's face, bearing, etc.: *his face registered surprise.* 14 (*intr*) to have an effect; make an impression: *the news of her uncle's death just did not register.* 15 to send (a letter, package, etc.) by registered post. 16 (*tr*) *Printing* to adjust (a printing press, forme, etc.) to ensure that the printed matter is in register. 17 (*intr; often foll by with*) (of a mechanical part) to align (with another part). 18 *Military* to bring (a gun) to bear on its target by adjustment according to the accuracy of observed single rounds.
▷HISTORY C14: from Medieval Latin *registrum*, from Latin *regerere* to transcribe, from RE- + *gerere* to bear
▸'registerer NOUN ▸'registrable ADJECTIVE

registered disabled ADJECTIVE *Social welfare* (in Britain) 1 (of a handicapped person) on a local authority register under the Chronically Sick and Disabled Persons Act 1970. 2 on a register kept by the Manpower Services Commission for employment purposes, and holding a green identity card, thus qualifying for special services. ◆ Also called: **registered handicapped**. See also **green card** (sense 3), **handicap register**.

Registered General Nurse NOUN (in Britain) a nurse who has completed a three-year training course in all aspects of nursing care to enable the nurse to be registered with the United Kingdom Central Council for Nursing, Midwifery, and Health Visiting. Abbreviation: **RGN**.

registered post NOUN 1 a Post Office service by which compensation is paid for loss or damage to mail for which a registration fee has been paid. Compare **recorded delivery**. 2 mail sent by this service.

Registered Trademark NOUN See **trademark** (sense 1).

register mark NOUN *Printing* any of several marks incorporated on to printing plates to assist in the accurate positioning of images during printing.

register office NOUN *Brit* a government office where civil marriages are performed and births, marriages, and deaths are recorded. Often called: **registry office**.

register ton NOUN the full name for **ton**[1] (sense 7).

registrant ('rɛdʒɪstrənt) NOUN a person who registers a trademark or patent.

registrar (ˌrɛdʒɪ'strɑ:, 'rɛdʒɪˌstrɑ:) NOUN 1 a person who keeps official records. 2 an administrative official responsible for student records, enrolment procedure, etc., in a school, college, or university. 3 *Brit and NZ* a hospital doctor senior to a houseman but junior to a consultant, specializing in either medicine (**medical registrar**) or surgery (**surgical registrar**). 4 *Chiefly US* a person employed by a company to maintain a register of its security issues.
▸'registrarship NOUN

registration (ˌrɛdʒɪ'streɪʃən) NOUN 1 **a** the act of registering or state of being registered. **b** (*as modifier*): *a registration number.* 2 an entry in a register. 3 a group of people, such as students, who register at a particular time. 4 a combination of organ or harpsichord stops used in the performance of a piece of music.
▸ˌregis'trational ADJECTIVE

registration document NOUN *Brit* a document giving identification details of a motor vehicle, including its manufacturer, date of registration, engine and chassis numbers, and owner's name. Compare **logbook** (sense 2).

registration number NOUN a sequence of letters and numbers assigned to a motor vehicle when it is registered, usually indicating the year and place of registration, displayed on numberplates at the front and rear of the vehicle, and by which the vehicle may be identified.

registration plate NOUN the Austral and NZ name for **numberplate**.

registry ('rɛdʒɪstrɪ) NOUN, *plural* **-tries**. 1 a place where registers are kept, such as the part of a church where the bride and groom sign a register after a wedding. 2 the registration of a ship's country of origin: *a ship of Liberian registry.* 3 another word for **registration**.

registry office NOUN *Brit* a name often used for a **register office**.

Regius professor ('ri:dʒɪəs) NOUN *Brit* a person appointed by the Crown to a university chair founded by a royal patron.
▷HISTORY C17: *regius*, from Latin: royal, from *rex* king

reglet ('rɛglɪt) NOUN 1 a flat narrow architectural moulding. 2 *Printing* a strip of oiled wood used for spacing between lines of hot metal type. Compare **lead**[2] (sense 7).
▷HISTORY C16: from Old French, literally: a little rule, from *regle* rule, from Latin *rēgula*

regmaker ('rɛxˌmɑ:kə) NOUN *South African* a drink taken to relieve the symptoms of a hangover; a pick-me-up.
▷HISTORY Afrikaans

regnal ('rɛgnəl) ADJECTIVE 1 of a sovereign, reign, or kingdom. 2 designating a year of a sovereign's reign calculated from the date of his or her accession.
▷HISTORY C17: from Medieval Latin *rēgnālis*, from Latin *rēgnum* sovereignty; see REIGN

regnant ('rɛgnənt) ADJECTIVE 1 (*postpositive*) reigning. 2 prevalent; current.
▷HISTORY C17: from Latin *regnāre* to REIGN
▸'regnancy NOUN

rego ('rɛdʒəʊ) NOUN *Austral slang* **a** the registration of a motor vehicle. **b** a fee paid for this.

regolith ('rɛgəlɪθ) NOUN the layer of loose material covering the bedrock of the earth and moon, etc., comprising soil, sand, rock fragments, volcanic ash, glacial drift, etc.
▷HISTORY C20: from Greek *rhēgos* covering, blanket + *lithos* stone

regorge (rɪ'gɔ:dʒ) VERB 1 (*tr*) to vomit up; disgorge. 2 (*intr*) (esp of water) to flow or run back.
▷HISTORY C17: from French *regorger*; see GORGE

regosol ('rɛgəˌsɒl) NOUN a type of azonal soil consisting of unconsolidated material derived from freshly deposited alluvium or sands.
▷HISTORY C20: from Greek *rhēgos* covering, blanket + Latin *solum* soil

Reg. prof. ABBREVIATION FOR Regius professor.

regrate (rɪ'greɪt) VERB (*tr*) 1 to buy up (commodities) in advance so as to raise their price for profitable resale. 2 to resell (commodities so

purchased); retail. 3 *Building trades* to redress the surface of (hewn stonework).
▷HISTORY C15: from Old French *regrater* perhaps from RE- + *grater* to scratch
▸**reˈgrater** NOUN

regress VERB (rɪˈgrɛs) 1 *(intr)* to return or revert, as to a former place, condition, or mode of behaviour. 2 *(tr) Statistics* to measure the extent to which (a dependent variable) is associated with one or more independent variables. ◆ NOUN (ˈriːgrɛs) 3 the act of regressing. 4 movement in a backward direction; retrogression. 5 *Logic* a supposed explanation each stage of which requires to be similarly explained, as saying that knowledge requires a justification in terms of propositions themselves known to be true.
▷HISTORY C14: from Latin *regressus* a retreat, from *regredī* to go back, from RE- + *gradī* to go
▸**reˈgressor** NOUN

regression (rɪˈgrɛʃən) NOUN 1 *Psychol* the adoption by an adult or adolescent of behaviour more appropriate to a child, esp as a defence mechanism to avoid anxiety. 2 *Statistics* **a** the analysis or measure of the association between one variable (the dependent variable) and one or more other variables (the independent variables), usually formulated in an equation in which the independent variables have parametric coefficients, which may enable future values of the dependent variable to be predicted. **b** *(as modifer)*: *regression curve*. 3 *Astronomy* the slow movement around the ecliptic of the two points at which the moon's orbit intersects the ecliptic. One complete revolution occurs about every 19 years. 4 *Geology* the retreat of the sea from the land. 5 the act of regressing.

regressive (rɪˈgrɛsɪv) ADJECTIVE 1 regressing or tending to regress. 2 (of a tax or tax system) levied or graduated so that the rate decreases as the amount taxed increases. Compare **progressive** (sense 5). 3 of, relating to, or characteristic of regression.
▸**reˈgressively** ADVERB ▸**reˈgressiveness** NOUN

regret (rɪˈgrɛt) VERB **-grets, -gretting, -gretted.** *(tr)* 1 *(may take a clause as object or an infinitive)* to feel sorry, repentant, or upset about. 2 to bemoan or grieve the death or loss of. ◆ NOUN 3 a sense of repentance, guilt, or sorrow, as over some wrong done or an unfulfilled ambition. 4 a sense of loss or grief. 5 *(plural)* a polite expression of sadness, esp in a formal refusal of an invitation.
▷HISTORY C14: from Old French *regrete*, of Scandinavian origin; compare Old Norse *grāta* to weep
▸**reˈgretful** ADJECTIVE ▸**reˈgretfully** ADVERB ▸**reˈgretfulness** NOUN ▸**reˈgrettable** ADJECTIVE ▸**reˈgrettably** ADVERB ▸**reˈgretter** NOUN

> **Language note** *Regretful* and *regretfully* are sometimes wrongly used where *regrettable* and *regrettably* are meant: *he gave a regretful smile; he smiled regretfully; this is a regrettable* (not *regretful*) *mistake; regrettably* (not *regretfully*), *I shall be unable to attend.*

regroup (riːˈgruːp) VERB 1 to reorganize (military forces), esp after an attack or a defeat. 2 *(tr)* to rearrange into a new grouping or groupings. 3 *(intr)* to consider using different tactics after a setback in a contest or argument.

regrow (riːˈgrəʊ) VERB **-grows, -growing, -grew, -grown.** to grow or be grown again after having been cut or having died or withered.

regrowth (riːˈgrəʊθ) NOUN 1 the growing back of hair, plants, etc. 2 the resurgence of an industry, economy, etc.

Regt ABBREVIATION FOR: 1 Regent. 2 Regiment.

regulable (ˈrɛgjʊləbəl) ADJECTIVE able to be regulated.

regular (ˈrɛgjʊlə) ADJECTIVE 1 normal, customary, or usual. 2 according to a uniform principle, arrangement, or order: *trees planted at regular intervals*. 3 occurring at fixed or prearranged intervals: *to make a regular call on a customer*. 4 following a set rule or normal practice; methodical or orderly. 5 symmetrical in appearance or form; even: *regular features*. 6 *(prenominal)* organized, elected, conducted, etc., in a proper or officially prescribed manner. 7 *(prenominal)* officially qualified or recognized: *he's not a regular doctor*. 8 *(prenominal)* (intensifier): *a regular fool*. 9 *US and Canadian informal* likable, dependable, or nice (esp in the phrase **a regular guy**). 10 denoting or relating to the personnel or units of the permanent military services: *a regular soldier; the regular army*. 11 (of flowers) having any of their parts, esp petals, alike in size, shape, arrangement, etc.; symmetrical. 12 (of the formation, inflections, etc., of a word) following the usual pattern of formation in a language. 13 *Maths* **a** (of a polygon) equilateral and equiangular. **b** (of a polyhedron) having identical regular polygons as faces that make identical angles with each other. **c** (of a prism) having regular polygons as bases. **d** (of a pyramid) having a regular polygon as a base and the altitude passing through the centre of the base. **e** another name for **analytic** (sense 5). 14 *Botany* another word for **actinomorphic**. 15 *(postpositive)* subject to the rule of an established religious order or community: *canons regular*. 16 *US politics* of, selected by, or loyal to the leadership or platform of a political party: *a regular candidate; regular policies*. 17 *Crystallog* another word for **cubic** (sense 4). ◆ NOUN 18 a professional long-term serviceman in a military unit. 19 *Informal* a person who does something regularly, such as attending a theatre or patronizing a shop. 20 a member of a religious order or congregation, as contrasted with a secular. 21 *US politics* a party member loyal to the leadership, platform, etc., of his party.
▷HISTORY C14: from Old French *reguler*, from Latin *rēgulāris* of a bar of wood or metal, from *rēgula* ruler, model
▸**ˌreguˈlarity** NOUN ▸**ˈregularly** ADVERB

regularize *or* **regularise** (ˈrɛgjʊləˌraɪz) VERB *(tr)* to make regular; cause to conform.
▸**ˌregulariˈzation** *or* **ˌregulariˈsation** NOUN

regulate (ˈrɛgjʊˌleɪt) VERB *(tr)* 1 to adjust (the amount of heat, sound, etc., of something) as required; control. 2 to adjust (an instrument or appliance) so that it operates correctly. 3 to bring into conformity with a rule, principle, or usage.
▷HISTORY C17: from Late Latin *rēgulāre* to control, from Latin *rēgula* a ruler
▸**ˈregulative** *or* **ˈregulatory** ADJECTIVE ▸**ˈregulatively** ADVERB

regulated tenancy NOUN *Social welfare* (in Britain) the letting of a dwelling by a nonresident private landlord, usually at a registered fair rent, from which the landlord cannot evict the tenant without a possession order from a court. Compare **assured tenancy.**

regulation (ˌrɛgjʊˈleɪʃən) NOUN 1 the act or process of regulating. 2 a rule, principle, or condition that governs procedure or behaviour. 3 a governmental or ministerial order having the force of law. 4 *Embryol* the ability of an animal embryo to develop normally after its structure has been altered or damaged in some way. 5 *(modifier)* as required by official rules or procedure: *regulation uniform*. 6 *(modifier)* normal; usual; conforming to accepted standards: *a regulation haircut*. 7 *Electrical engineering* the change in voltage occurring when a load is connected across a power supply, caused by internal resistance (for direct current) or internal impedance (alternating current).

regulator (ˈrɛgjʊˌleɪtə) NOUN 1 a person or thing that regulates. 2 the mechanism, including the hairspring and the balance wheel, by which the speed of a timepiece is regulated. 3 a timepiece, known to be accurate, by which others are timed and regulated. 4 any of various mechanisms or devices, such as a governor valve, for controlling fluid flow, pressure, temperature, voltage, etc. 5 Also called: **regulator gene.** a gene the product of which controls the synthesis of a product from another gene.

regulo (ˈrɛgjʊləʊ) NOUN any of a number of temperatures to which a gas oven may be set: *cook at regulo 4 for 40 minutes*.
▷HISTORY C20: from *Regulo*, trademark for a type of thermostatic control on gas ovens

regulus (ˈrɛgjʊləs) NOUN, *plural* **-luses** *or* **-li** (-ˌlaɪ). impure metal forming beneath the slag during the smelting of ores.
▷HISTORY C16: from Latin: a petty king, from *rēx* king; formerly used for *antimony*, because it combines readily with gold, thought of as the king of metals
▸**ˈreguline** ADJECTIVE

Regulus (ˈrɛgjʊləs) NOUN the brightest star in the constellation Leo. Visual magnitude: 1.3; spectral type: B8; distance: 69 light years.

regurgitate (rɪˈgɜːdʒɪˌteɪt) VERB 1 to vomit forth (partially digested food). 2 (of some birds and certain other animals) to bring back to the mouth (undigested or partly digested food with which to feed the young). 3 *(intr)* to be cast up or out, esp from the mouth. 4 *(intr) Med* (of blood) to flow backwards, in a direction opposite to the normal one, esp through a defective heart valve.
▷HISTORY C17: from Medieval Latin *regurgitāre*, from RE- + *gurgitāre* to flood, from Latin *gurges* gulf, whirlpool
▸**reˈgurgitant** NOUN, ADJECTIVE ▸**reˌgurgiˈtation** NOUN

rehab (ˈriːhæb) NOUN 1 short for **rehabilitation.** 2 *NZ informal* short for **Rehabilitation Department.**

rehabilitate (ˌriːəˈbɪlɪˌteɪt) VERB *(tr)* 1 to help (a person who has acquired a disability or addiction or who has just been released from prison) to readapt to society or a new job, as by vocational guidance, retraining, or therapy. 2 to restore to a former position or rank. 3 to restore the good reputation of.
▷HISTORY C16: from Medieval Latin *rehabilitāre* to restore, from RE- + Latin *habilitās* skill, ABILITY
▸**ˌrehaˈbilitative** ADJECTIVE

rehabilitation (ˌriːəˌbɪlɪˈteɪʃən) NOUN 1 the act or process of rehabilitating. 2 *Med* **a** the treatment of physical disabilities by massage, electrotherapy, or exercises. **b** *(as modifier)*: *rehabilitation centre*.

Rehabilitation Department NOUN *NZ* a government department set up after World War II to assist ex-servicemen. Often shortened to: **rehab.**

rehash VERB (riːˈhæʃ) 1 *(tr)* to rework, reuse, or make over (old or already used material). ◆ NOUN (ˈriːˌhæʃ) 2 something consisting of old, reworked, or reused material.
▷HISTORY C19: from RE- + HASH^1 (to chop into pieces)

rehearsal (rɪˈhɜːsəl) NOUN 1 a session of practising a play, concert, speech etc., in preparation for public performance. 2 the act of going through or recounting; recital: *rehearsal of his own virtues was his usual occupation*. 3 **in rehearsal.** being prepared for public performance.

rehearse (rɪˈhɜːs) VERB 1 to practise (a play, concert, etc.), in preparation for public performance. 2 *(tr)* to run through; recount; recite: *the official rehearsed the grievances of the committee*. 3 *(tr)* to train or drill (a person or animal) for the public performance of a part in a play, show, etc.
▷HISTORY C16: from Anglo-Norman *rehearser*, from Old French *rehercier* to harrow a second time, from RE- + *herce* harrow
▸**reˈhearser** NOUN

reheat VERB (riːˈhiːt) 1 to heat or be heated again: *to reheat yesterday's soup*. 2 *(tr)* to add fuel to (the exhaust gases of an aircraft jet engine) to produce additional heat and thrust. ◆ NOUN (ˈriːˌhiːt) *also* **reheating.** 3 *Aeronautics* another name (esp Brit) for **afterburning** (sense 1).
▸**reˈheater** NOUN

rehoboam (ˌriːəˈbəʊəm) NOUN a wine bottle holding the equivalent of six normal bottles (approximately 156 ounces).
▷HISTORY C19: named after *Rehoboam*, a son of King Solomon, from Hebrew, literally: the nation is enlarged

rehouse (riːˈhaʊz) VERB *(tr)* to accommodate (someone or something) in a new house or building.

Reich (raɪk; *German* raiç) NOUN 1 the Holy Roman Empire (**First Reich**). 2 the Hohenzollern empire from 1871 to 1919 (**Second Reich**). 3 the Weimar Republic from 1919 to 1933. 4 the Nazi dictatorship from 1933 to 1945 (**Third Reich**).
▷HISTORY German: kingdom

Reichenberg (ˈraiçənbɛrk) NOUN the German name for **Liberec.**

Reichsmark (ˈraɪksˌmɑːk; *German* ˈraiçsmark) NOUN, *plural* **-marks** *or* **-mark.** the standard monetary unit of Germany between 1924 and 1948, divided into 100 **Reichspfennigs.**

Reichsrat (*German* ˈraiçsrat) NOUN 1 the bicameral parliament of the Austrian half of

Austria-Hungary (1867–1918). [2] the council of representatives of state governments within Germany from 1919 to 1934.

Reichstag ('raiks,tɑ:g; *German* 'raiçstak) NOUN [1] Also called: **diet.** (in medieval Germany) the estates or a meeting of the estates. [2] the legislative assembly representing the people in the North German Confederation (1867–71) and in the German empire (1871–1919). [3] the sovereign assembly of the Weimar Republic (1919–33). [4] the building in Berlin in which this assembly met and from 1999 in which the German government meets: its destruction by fire on Feb. 27, 1933 (probably by agents of the Nazi government) marked the end of Weimar democracy. It was restored in the 1990s following German reunification.

reify ('ri:ɪ,faɪ) VERB **-fies, -fying, -fied.** (*tr*) to consider or make (an abstract idea or concept) real or concrete.
▷HISTORY C19: from Latin *rēs* thing; compare DEIFY
▸,**reifi'cation** NOUN ▸,**reifi'catory** ADJECTIVE ▸'**rei,fier** NOUN

Reigate ('raɪgɪt, -geɪt) NOUN a town in S England, in Surrey at the foot of the North Downs. Pop.: 47 602 (1991).

reign (reɪn) NOUN [1] the period during which a monarch is the official ruler of a country. [2] a period during which a person or thing is dominant, influential, or powerful: *the reign of violence is over.* ◆ VERB (*intr*) [3] to exercise the power and authority of a sovereign. [4] to be accorded the rank and title of a sovereign without having ruling authority, as in a constitutional monarchy. [5] to predominate; prevail: *a land where darkness reigns.* [6] (*usually present participle*) to be the most recent winner of a competition, contest, etc.: *the reigning heavyweight champion.*
▷HISTORY C13: from Old French *reigne*, from Latin *rēgnum* kingdom, from *rēx* king

> **Language note** *Reign* is sometimes wrongly written for *rein* in certain phrases: *he gave full rein* (not *reign*) *to his feelings; it will be necessary to rein in* (not *reign in*) *public spending.*

reignite (,ri:ɪg'naɪt) VERB [1] to catch fire or cause to catch fire again: *the burners reignited.* [2] to flare up or cause to flare up again: *to reignite the war.*

Reign of Terror NOUN the period of Jacobin rule during the French Revolution, during which thousands of people were executed for treason (Oct. 1793–July 1794).

reiki ('reɪkɪ) NOUN a form of therapy in which the practitioner is believed to channel energy into the patient in order to encourage healing or restore wellbeing.
▷HISTORY Japanese, from *rei* universal + *ki* life force

reimburse (,ri:ɪm'bɜ:s) VERB (*tr*) to repay or compensate (someone) for (money already spent, losses, damages, etc.): *your fare will be reimbursed after your interview.*
▷HISTORY C17: from RE- + *imburse*, from Medieval Latin *imbursāre* to put in a moneybag, from *bursa* PURSE
▸,**reim'bursable** ADJECTIVE ▸,**reim'bursement** NOUN ▸,**reim'burser** NOUN

reimport VERB (,ri:ɪm'pɔ:t, ri:'ɪmpɔ:t) [1] (*tr*) to import (goods manufactured from exported raw materials). ◆ NOUN (ri:'ɪmpɔ:t) [2] the act of reimporting. [3] a reimported commodity.
▸,**reimpor'tation** NOUN ▸,**reim'porter** NOUN

reimpose (,ri:ɪm'pəʊz) VERB (*tr*) to establish previously imposed laws, controls, etc., again.
▸,**reimpo'sition** NOUN

reimpression (,ri:ɪm'prɛʃən) NOUN a reprinting of a book without editorial changes or additions.

Reims *or* **Rheims** (ri:mz; *French* rɛ̃s) NOUN a city in NE France: scene of the coronation of most French monarchs. Pop.: 187 206 (1999).

rein (reɪn) NOUN [1] (*often plural*) one of a pair of long straps, usually connected together and made of leather, used to control a horse, running from the side of the bit or the headstall to the hand of the rider, driver, or trainer. [2] a similar device used to control a very young child. [3] any form or means of control: *to take up the reins of government.* [4] the direction in which a rider turns (in phrases such as **on a left** (*or* **right**) **rein, change the rein**). [5] something that restrains, controls, or guides. [6] **give** (**a**) **free rein.** to allow considerable freedom; remove restraints. [7] **keep a tight rein on.** to control carefully; limit: *we have to keep a tight rein on expenditure.* [8] **on a long rein.** with the reins held loosely so that the horse is relatively unconstrained. [9] **shorten the reins.** to take up the reins so that the distance between hand and bit is lessened, in order that the horse may be more collected. ◆ VERB [10] (*tr*) to check, restrain, hold back, or halt with or as if with reins. [11] to control or guide (a horse) with a rein or reins: *they reined left.* ◆ See also **rein in.**
▷HISTORY C13: from Old French *resne*, from Latin *retinēre* to hold back, from RE- + *tenēre* to hold; see RESTRAIN

> **Language note** See at **reign.**

reincarnate VERB (ri:'ɪnkɑ:neɪt) (*tr; often passive*) [1] to cause to undergo reincarnation; be born again. ◆ ADJECTIVE (,ri:ɪn'kɑ:nɪt) [2] born again in a new body.

reincarnation (,ri:ɪnkɑ:'neɪʃən) NOUN [1] the belief that on the death of the body the soul transmigrates to or is born again in another body. [2] the incarnation or embodiment of a soul in a new body after it has left the old one at physical death. [3] embodiment again in a new form, as of a principle or idea.
▸,**reincar'nationist** NOUN, ADJECTIVE

reindeer ('reɪn,dɪə) NOUN, *plural* **-deer** *or* **-deers.** a large deer, *Rangifer tarandus*, having large branched antlers in the male and female and inhabiting the arctic regions of Greenland, Europe, and Asia. It also occurs in North America, where it is known as a caribou.
▷HISTORY C14: from Old Norse *hreindȳri*, from *hreinn* reindeer + *dyr* animal; related to Dutch *rendier*, German *Rentier*; see DEER

Reindeer Lake NOUN a lake in W Canada, in Saskatchewan and Manitoba: drains into the Churchill River via the **Reindeer River**. Area: 6390 sq. km (2467 sq. miles).

reindeer moss NOUN any of various lichens of the genus *Cladonia*, esp *C. rangiferina*, which occur in arctic and subarctic regions, providing food for reindeer.

reinfect (,ri:ɪn'fɛkt) VERB (*mainly tr*) to infect or contaminate again.
▸,**rein'fection** NOUN

reinforce (,ri:ɪn'fɔ:s) VERB (*tr*) [1] to give added strength or support to. [2] to give added emphasis to; stress, support, or increase: *his rudeness reinforced my determination.* [3] to give added support to (a military force) by providing more men, supplies, etc. [4] *Psychol* to reward an action or response of (a human or animal) so that it becomes more likely to occur again.
▷HISTORY C17: from obsolete *renforce*, from French *renforcer*; see RE- + *inforce* ENFORCE
▸,**rein'forcement** NOUN

reinforced concrete NOUN concrete with steel bars, mesh, etc., embedded in it to enable it to withstand tensile and shear stresses.

reinforced plastic NOUN plastic with fibrous matter, such as carbon fibre, embedded in it to confer additional strength.

rein in VERB (*adverb*) to stop (a horse) by pulling on the reins.

reins (reɪnz) PLURAL NOUN *Archaic* the kidneys or loins.
▷HISTORY C14: from Old French, from Latin *rēnēs* the kidneys

reinsman ('reɪnzmən) NOUN, *plural* **-men.** *Austral and NZ* the driver in a trotting race.

reinstall *or* **reinstal** (,ri:ɪn'stɔ:l) VERB **-stalls, -stalling, -stalled** *or* **-stals, -stalling, -stalled.** (*tr*) [1] to put in place and connect (machinery, equipment, etc.) again. [2] to install (computer software) again, usually to solve a technical problem. [3] to put (someone) back in a position, rank, etc.: *Trinidad reinstalled him against Honduras.*

reinstate (,ri:ɪn'steɪt) VERB (*tr*) to restore to a former rank or condition.
▸,**rein'statement** NOUN ▸,**rein'stator** NOUN

reinsure (,ri:ɪn'ʃʊə, -ʃɔ:) VERB (*tr*) [1] to insure again. [2] (of an insurer) to obtain partial or complete insurance coverage from another insurer for (a risk on which a policy has already been issued).
▸,**rein'surance** NOUN ▸,**rein'surer** NOUN

reintegrate (ri:'ɪntɪ,greɪt) VERB [1] (*tr*) to make or be made into a whole again: *to reintegrate inner divisions.* [2] (often followed by *into*) to amalgamate or help to amalgamate (a group) with an existing community: *reintegrate young homeless people into society.*
▸,**reinte'gration** NOUN

reinterpret (,ri:ɪn'tɜ:prɪt) VERB (*tr*) to interpret (an idea, etc.) in a new or different way.
▸,**rein,terpre'tation** NOUN

reintroduce (,ri:ɪntrə'dju:s) VERB (*tr*) to introduce (something) again.
▸,**reintro'duction** NOUN

reinvent (,ri:ɪn'vɛnt) VERB (*tr*) [1] to replace (a product, etc.) with an entirely new version. [2] to duplicate (something that already exists) in what is therefore a wasted effort (esp in the phrase **reinvent the wheel**).

reinvest (,ri:ɪn'vɛst) VERB to put back profits from a previous investment into the same enterprise.

reinvestigate (,ri:ɪn'vɛstɪ,geɪt) VERB to investigate (a crime, murder, problem, etc.) again.
▸,**rein,vesti'gation** NOUN

reinvigorate (,ri:ɪn'vɪgə,reɪt) VERB (*tr*) to put vitality and vigour back into (someone or something).
▸,**rein,vigo'ration** NOUN

reissue (,ri:'ɪʃju:) VERB (*tr*) [1] to issue (a recording, book, etc.) again. ◆ NOUN [2] something, esp a recording or book, which has been issued again.

reiterate (ri:'ɪtə,reɪt) VERB (*tr; may take a clause as object*) to say or do again or repeatedly.
▷HISTORY C16: from Latin *reiterāre* to repeat, from RE- + *iterāre* to do again, from *iterum* again
▸**re'iterant** ADJECTIVE ▸**re,iter'ation** NOUN ▸**re'iterative** ADJECTIVE ▸**re'iteratively** ADVERB

Reithian *or* **Reithean** ('ri:θɪən) ADJECTIVE of or relating to John, 1st Baron Reith, the British public servant and first director general of the BBC (1889–1971).

reive (ri:v) VERB (*intr*) *Scot and northern English dialect* to go on a plundering raid.
▷HISTORY variant of REAVE[1]
▸'**reiver** NOUN

reject VERB (rɪ'dʒɛkt) (*tr*) [1] to refuse to accept, acknowledge, use, believe, etc. [2] to throw out as useless or worthless; discard. [3] to rebuff (a person). [4] (of an organism) to fail to accept (a foreign tissue graft or organ transplant) because of immunological incompatibility. ◆ NOUN ('ri:dʒɛkt) [5] something rejected as imperfect, unsatisfactory, or useless.
▷HISTORY C15: from Latin *rēicere* to throw back, from RE- + *jacere* to hurl
▸**re'jectable** ADJECTIVE ▸**re'jecter** *or* **re'jector** NOUN ▸**re'jection** NOUN ▸**re'jective** ADJECTIVE

rejig (ri:'dʒɪg) VERB **-jigs, -jigging, -jigged.** (*tr*) [1] to re-equip (a factory or plant). [2] to rearrange, alter, or manipulate, sometimes in a slightly unscrupulous way. ◆ NOUN [3] the act or process of rejigging.
▸**re'jigger** NOUN

rejoice (rɪ'dʒɔɪs) VERB [1] (when *tr, takes a clause as object or an infinitive*; when *intr*, often foll by *in*) to feel or express great joy or happiness. [2] (*tr*) *Archaic* to cause to feel joy.
▷HISTORY C14: from Old French *resjoir*, from RE- + *joir* to be glad, from Latin *gaudēre* to rejoice
▸**re'joicer** NOUN ▸**re'joicing** NOUN

rejoin[1] (ri:'dʒɔɪn) VERB [1] to come again into company with (someone or something). [2] (*tr*) to put or join together again; reunite.

rejoin[2] (rɪ'dʒɔɪn) VERB (*tr*) [1] to say (something) in reply; answer, reply, or retort. [2] *Law* to answer (a claimant's reply).
▷HISTORY C15: from Old French *rejoign-*, stem of *rejoindre*; see RE-, JOIN

rejoinder (rɪ'dʒɔɪndə) NOUN [1] a reply or response to a question or remark, esp a quick witty one;

retort. 2 *Law* (in pleading) the answer made by a defendant to the claimant's reply.
▷HISTORY C15: from Old French *rejoindre* to REJOIN[2]

rejuvenate (rɪ'dʒuːvɪˌneɪt) VERB (*tr*) 1 to give new youth, restored vitality, or youthful appearance to. 2 (*usually passive*) *Geography* **a** to cause (a river) to begin eroding more vigorously to a new lower base level, usually because of uplift of the land. **b** to cause (a land surface) to develop youthful features.
▷HISTORY C19: from RE- + Latin *juvenis* young
▸**reˌjuve'nation** NOUN ▸**re'juveˌnator** NOUN

rejuvenesce (rɪˌdʒuːvə'nɛs) VERB 1 to make or become youthful or restored to vitality. 2 *Biology* to convert (cells) or (of cells) to be converted into a more active form.
▸**reˌjuve'nescence** NOUN ▸**reˌjuve'nescent** ADJECTIVE

rekindle (riː'kɪndᵊl) VERB 1 to arouse or cause to be aroused again: *rekindle the romance in your relationship*. 2 to set alight or start to burn again.

rel. ABBREVIATION FOR: 1 relating. 2 relative(ly).

relapse VERB (rɪ'læps) (*intr*) 1 to lapse back into a former state or condition, esp one involving bad habits. 2 to become ill again after apparent recovery. ◆ NOUN (rɪ'læps, 'riːˌlæps) 3 the act or an instance of relapsing. 4 the return of ill health after an apparent or partial recovery.
▷HISTORY C16: from Latin *relabī* to slip back, from RE- + *labī* to slip, slide
▸**re'lapser** NOUN

relapsing fever NOUN any of various infectious diseases characterized by recurring fever, caused by the bite of body lice or ticks infected with spirochaetes of the genus *Borrelia*. Also called: **recurrent fever.**

relata (rɪ'leɪtə) NOUN the plural of **relatum.**

relate (rɪ'leɪt) VERB 1 (*tr*) to tell or narrate (a story, information, etc.). 2 (often foll by *to*) to establish association (between two or more things) or (of something) to have relation or reference (to something else). 3 (*intr*; often foll by *to*) to form a sympathetic or significant relationship (with other people, things, etc.).
▷HISTORY C16: from Latin *relātus* brought back, from *referre* to carry back, from RE- + *ferre* to bear; see REFER
▸**re'latable** ADJECTIVE ▸**re'later** NOUN

related (rɪ'leɪtɪd) ADJECTIVE 1 connected; associated. 2 connected by kinship or marriage. 3 (in diatonic music) denoting or relating to a key that has notes in common with another key or keys.
▸**re'latedness** NOUN

relation (rɪ'leɪʃən) NOUN 1 the state or condition of being related or the manner in which things are related. 2 connection by blood or marriage; kinship. 3 a person who is connected by blood or marriage; relative; kinsman. 4 reference or regard (esp in the phrase **in** *or* **with relation to**). 5 the position, association, connection, or status of one person or thing with regard to another or others. 6 the act of relating or narrating. 7 an account or narrative. 8 *Law* the principle by which an act done at one time is regarded in law as having been done antecedently. 9 *Law* the statement of grounds of complaint made by a relator. 10 *Logic, maths* **a** an association between ordered pairs of objects, numbers, etc., such as ... *is greater than* .... **b** the set of ordered pairs whose members have such an association. 11 *Philosophy* **a internal relation.** a relation that necessarily holds between its relata, as *4 is greater than 2*. **b external relation.** a relation that does not so hold. ◆ See also **relations.**
▷HISTORY C14: from Latin *relātiō* a narration, a relation (between philosophical concepts)

relational (rɪ'leɪʃənᵊl) ADJECTIVE 1 *Grammar* indicating or expressing syntactic relation, as for example the case endings in Latin. 2 having relation or being related. 3 *Computing* based on data stored in a tabular form: *a relational database*.

relations (rɪ'leɪʃənz) PLURAL NOUN 1 social, political, or personal connections or dealings between or among individuals, groups, nations, etc.: *to enjoy good relations*. 2 family or relatives. 3 *Euphemistic* sexual intercourse.

relationship (rɪ'leɪʃənʃɪp) NOUN 1 the state of being connected or related. 2 association by blood or marriage; kinship. 3 the mutual dealings, connections, or feelings that exist between two parties, countries, people, etc.: *a business relationship*. 4 an emotional or sexual affair or liaison. 5 *Logic, maths* another name for **relation** (sense 10).

relationship marketing NOUN a marketing strategy in which a company seeks to build long-term relationships with its customers by providing consistent satisfaction.

relative ('rɛlətɪv) ADJECTIVE 1 having meaning or significance only in relation to something else; not absolute: *a relative value*. 2 (*prenominal*) (of a scientific quantity) being measured or stated relative to some other substance or measurement: *relative humidity; relative density*. Compare **absolute** (sense 10). 3 (*prenominal*) comparative or respective: *the relative qualities of speed and accuracy*. 4 (*postpositive*; foll by *to*) in proportion (to); corresponding (to): *earnings relative to production*. 5 having reference (to); pertinent (to): *matters not relative to the topic under discussion*. 6 *Grammar* denoting or belonging to a class of words that function as subordinating conjunctions in introducing relative clauses. In English, relative pronouns and determiners include *who, which,* and *that*. Compare **demonstrative** (sense 5), **interrogative** (sense 3). 7 *Grammar* denoting or relating to a clause (**relative clause**) that modifies a noun or pronoun occurring earlier in the sentence. 8 (of a musical key or scale) having the same key signature as another key or scale: *C major is the relative major of A minor*. ◆ NOUN 9 a person who is related by blood or marriage; relation. 10 a relative pronoun, clause, or grammatical construction.
▷HISTORY C16: from Late Latin *relātīvus* referring
▸**'relatively** ADVERB ▸**'relativeness** NOUN

relative aperture NOUN *Photog* the ratio of the equivalent focal length of a lens to the effective aperture of the lens; written as *f/n*, *f:n*, or *fn*, where *n* is the numerical value of this ratio and is equivalent to the f-number.

relative atomic mass NOUN the ratio of the average mass per atom of the naturally occurring form of an element to one-twelfth the mass of an atom of carbon-12. Symbol: A_r. Abbreviation: **r.a.m.** Former name: **atomic weight.**

relative density NOUN the ratio of the density of a substance to the density of a standard substance under specified conditions. For liquids and solids the standard is usually water at 4°C or some other specified temperature. For gases the standard is often air or hydrogen at the same temperature and pressure as the substance. Symbol: *d*. See also **specific gravity, vapour density.**

relative frequency NOUN **a** the ratio of the actual number of favourable events to the total possible number of events; often taken as an estimate of probability. **b** the proportion of the range of a random variable taking a given value or lying in a given interval.

relative humidity NOUN the mass of water vapour present in the air expressed as a percentage of the mass that would be present in an equal volume of saturated air at the same temperature. Compare **absolute humidity.**

relatively ('rɛlətɪvlɪ) ADVERB in comparison or relation to something else; not absolutely.

relative majority NOUN *Brit* the excess of votes or seats won by the winner of an election over the runner-up when no candidate or party has more than 50 per cent. Compare **absolute majority.**

relative molecular mass NOUN the sum of all the relative atomic masses of the atoms in a molecule; the ratio of the average mass per molecule of a specified isotopic composition of a substance to one-twelfth the mass of an atom of carbon-12. Symbol: M_r. Abbreviation: **r.m.m.** Former name: **molecular weight.**

relative permeability NOUN the ratio of the permeability of a medium to that of free space. Symbol: μ_r.

relative permittivity NOUN the ratio of the permittivity of a substance to that of free space. Symbol: ε_r. Also called: **dielectric constant.**

relativism ('rɛlətɪˌvɪzəm) NOUN any theory holding that truth or moral or aesthetic value, etc., is not universal or absolute but may differ between individuals or cultures. See also **historicism.**
▸**'relativist** NOUN, ADJECTIVE

relativistic (ˌrɛlətɪ'vɪstɪk) ADJECTIVE 1 *Physics* having or involving a speed close to that of light so that the behaviour is described by the theory of relativity rather than by Newtonian mechanics: *a relativistic electron; a relativistic velocity*. 2 *Physics* of, concerned with, or involving relativity. 3 of or relating to relativism.
▸**ˌrelativ'istically** ADVERB

relativity (ˌrɛlə'tɪvɪtɪ) NOUN 1 either of two theories developed by Albert Einstein, the **special theory of relativity**, which requires that the laws of physics shall be the same as seen by any two different observers in uniform relative motion, and the **general theory of relativity** which considers observers with relative acceleration and leads to a theory of gravitation. 2 *Philosophy* dependence upon some variable factor such as the psychological, social, or environmental context. See **relativism.** 3 the state or quality of being relative.

relativize *or* **relativise** ('rɛlətɪvaɪz) VERB 1 to make or become relative. 2 (*tr*) to apply the theory of relativity to.
▸**ˌrelativi'zation** *or* **ˌrelativi'sation** NOUN

relator (rɪ'leɪtə) NOUN 1 a person who relates a story; narrator. 2 *English law* a person who gives information upon which the attorney general brings an action. 3 *US law* a person who institutes proceedings by criminal information or quo warranto.

relatum (rɪ'leɪtəm) NOUN, *plural* **-ta** (-tə). *Logic* one of the objects between which a relation is said to hold.

relaunch VERB (riː'lɔːntʃ) (*tr*) 1 to launch again. 2 to start, set in motion, or make available again. ◆ NOUN ('riːˌlɔːntʃ) 3 another launching, or something that is relaunched.

relax (rɪ'læks) VERB 1 to make (muscles, a grip, etc.) less tense or rigid or (of muscles, a grip, etc.) to become looser or less rigid. 2 (*intr*) to take rest or recreation, as from work or effort: *on Sundays, she just relaxes; she relaxes by playing golf*. 3 to lessen the force of (effort, concentration, etc.) or (of effort) to become diminished. 4 to make (rules or discipline) less rigid or strict or (of rules, etc.) to diminish in severity. 5 (*intr*) (of a person) to become less formal; unbend.
▷HISTORY C15: from Latin *relaxāre* to loosen, from RE- + *laxāre* to loosen, from *laxus* loose, LAX
▸**re'laxable** ADJECTIVE ▸**re'laxed** ADJECTIVE ▸**relaxedly** (rɪ'læksɪdlɪ) ADVERB

relaxant (rɪ'læksᵊnt) NOUN 1 *Med* a drug or agent that relaxes, esp one that relaxes tense muscles. ◆ ADJECTIVE 2 of, relating to, or tending to produce relaxation.

relaxation (ˌriːlæk'seɪʃən) NOUN 1 rest or refreshment, as after work or effort; recreation. 2 a form of rest or recreation: *his relaxation is cricket*. 3 a partial lessening of a punishment, duty, etc. 4 the act of relaxing or state of being relaxed. 5 *Physics* the return of a system to equilibrium after a displacement from this state. 6 *Maths* a method by which errors resulting from an approximation are reduced by using new approximations.

relaxation oscillator NOUN *Electronics* a nonsinusoidal oscillator, the timing of which is controlled by the charge and discharge time constants of resistance and capacitance components.

relaxer (rɪ'læksə) NOUN a person or thing that relaxes, esp a substance used to straighten curly hair.

relaxin (rɪ'læksɪn) NOUN 1 a mammalian polypeptide hormone secreted by the corpus luteum during pregnancy, which relaxes the pelvic ligaments. 2 a preparation of this hormone, used to facilitate childbirth.
▷HISTORY C20: from RELAX + -IN

relay NOUN ('riːleɪ) 1 a person or team of people relieving others, as on a shift. 2 a fresh team of horses, dogs, etc., posted at intervals along a route to relieve others. 3 the act of relaying or process of being relayed. 4 **a** short for **relay race. b** one of the sections of a relay race. 5 an automatic device that controls the setting of a valve, switch, etc., by means of an electric motor, solenoid, or pneumatic mechanism. 6 *Electronics* an electrical device in which a small change in current or voltage controls the switching on or off of circuits or other devices. 7 *Radio* **a** a combination of a receiver and

transmitter designed to receive radio signals and retransmit them, in order to extend their range. **b** (*as modifier*): *a relay station.* ♦ VERB (rɪˈleɪ) (*tr*) 8 to carry or spread (something, such as news or information) by relays. 9 to supply or replace with relays. 10 to retransmit (a signal) by means of a relay. 11 *Brit* to broadcast (a performance) by sending out signals through a transmitting station: *this concert is being relayed from the Albert Hall.*
▷HISTORY C15 *relaien*, from Old French *relaier* to leave behind, from RE- + *laier* to leave, ultimately from Latin *laxāre* to loosen; see RELAX

relay fast NOUN (esp in India) a form of protest in which a number of persons go without food by turns. Also called: **relay hunger strike.**

relay language NOUN a language, usually an internationally dominant one, which acts as a medium to translate other usually little-spoken languages.

relay race NOUN a race between two or more teams of contestants in which each contestant covers a specified portion of the distance.

relearn (riːˈlɜːn) VERB **-learns, -learning, -learned** *or* **-learnt.** (*tr*) to learn (something previously known) again.

release (rɪˈliːs) VERB (*tr*) 1 to free (a person, animal, etc.) from captivity or imprisonment. 2 to free (someone) from obligation or duty. 3 to free (something) from (one's grip); let go or fall. 4 to issue (a record, film, book, etc.) for sale or circulation. 5 to make (news or information) known or allow (news, information, etc.) to be made known: *to release details of an agreement.* 6 *Law* to relinquish (a right, claim, title, etc.) in favour of someone else. 7 *Ethology* to evoke (a response) through the presentation of a stimulus that produces the response innately. ♦ NOUN 8 the act of freeing or state of being freed, as from captivity, imprisonment, duty, pain, life, etc. 9 the act of issuing for sale or publication. 10 something issued for sale or public showing, esp a film or a record: *a new release from Bob Dylan.* 11 a news item, document, etc., made available for publication, broadcasting, etc. 12 *Law* the surrender of a claim, right, title, etc., in favour of someone else. 13 a control mechanism for starting or stopping an engine. 14 **a** the opening of the exhaust valve of a steam engine near the end of the piston stroke. **b** the moment at which this valve opens. 15 the electronic control regulating how long a note sounds after a synthesizer key has been released. 16 the control mechanism for the shutter in a camera.
▷HISTORY C13: from Old French *relesser*, from Latin *relaxāre* to slacken; see RELAX
▸**reˈleaser** NOUN

relegate (ˈrɛlɪˌɡeɪt) VERB (*tr*) 1 to move to a position of less authority, importance, etc.; demote. 2 (*usually passive*) *Chiefly Brit* to demote (a football team, etc.) to a lower division. 3 to assign or refer (a matter) to another or others, as for action or decision. 4 (foll by *to*) to banish or exile. 5 to assign (something) to a particular group or category.
▷HISTORY C16: from Latin *relēgāre* to send away, from RE- + *lēgāre* to send
▸**ˈreleˌgatable** ADJECTIVE ▸**ˌreleˈgation** NOUN

relent (rɪˈlɛnt) VERB (*intr*) 1 to change one's mind about some decided course, esp a harsh one; become more mild or amenable. 2 (of the pace or intensity of something) to slacken. 3 (of the weather) to become more mild.
▷HISTORY C14: from RE- + Latin *lentāre* to bend, from *lentus* flexible, tenacious

relentless (rɪˈlɛntlɪs) ADJECTIVE 1 (of an enemy, hostile attitude, etc.) implacable; inflexible; inexorable. 2 (of pace or intensity) sustained; unremitting.
▸**reˈlentlessly** ADVERB ▸**reˈlentlessness** NOUN

Relenza (rɪˈlɛnzə) NOUN *Trademark* a preparation of an antiviral drug, zanamivir, used in the treatment of influenza to reduce the duration and severity of the illness.

relevant (ˈrɛlɪvənt) ADJECTIVE 1 having direct bearing on the matter in hand; pertinent. 2 *Linguistics* another word for **distinctive** (sense 2).
▷HISTORY C16: from Medieval Latin *relevans*, from Latin *relevāre* to lighten, from RE- + *levāre* to raise, RELIEVE
▸**ˈrelevance** *or* **ˈrelevancy** NOUN ▸**ˈrelevantly** ADVERB

reliable (rɪˈlaɪəbᵊl) ADJECTIVE able to be trusted; predictable or dependable.
▸**reˌliaˈbility** *or* (*less commonly*) **reˈliableness** NOUN
▸**reˈliably** ADVERB

reliance (rɪˈlaɪəns) NOUN 1 dependence, confidence, or trust. 2 something or someone upon which one relies.
▸**reˈliant** ADJECTIVE ▸**reˈliantly** ADVERB

relic (ˈrɛlɪk) NOUN 1 something that has survived from the past, such as an object or custom. 2 something kept as a remembrance or treasured for its past associations; keepsake. 3 (*usually plural*) a remaining part or fragment. 4 *RC Church, Eastern Church* part of the body of a saint or something supposedly used by or associated with a saint, venerated as holy. 5 *Informal* an old or old-fashioned person or thing. 6 (*plural*) *Archaic* the remains of a dead person; corpse. 7 *Ecology* a less common term for **relict** (sense 1).
▷HISTORY C13: from Old French *relique*, from Latin *reliquiae* remains, from *relinquere* to leave behind, RELINQUISH

relict (ˈrɛlɪkt) NOUN 1 *Ecology* **a** a group of animals or plants that exists as a remnant of a formerly widely distributed group in an environment different from that in which it originated. **b** (*as modifier*): *a relict fauna.* 2 *Geology* **a** a mountain, lake, glacier, etc., that is a remnant of a pre-existing formation after a destructive process has occurred. **b** a mineral that remains unaltered after metamorphism of the rock in which it occurs. 3 an archaic word for **widow** (sense 1). 4 an archaic word for **relic** (sense 6).
▷HISTORY C16: from Latin *relictus* left behind, from *relinquere* to RELINQUISH

relief (rɪˈliːf) NOUN 1 a feeling of cheerfulness or optimism that follows the removal of anxiety, pain, or distress. 2 deliverance from or alleviation of anxiety, pain, distress, etc. 3 **a** help or assistance, as to the poor, needy, or distressed. **b** (*as modifier*): *relief work.* 4 short for **tax relief.** 5 something that affords a diversion from monotony. 6 a person who replaces or relieves another at some task or duty. 7 a bus, shuttle plane, etc., that carries additional passengers when a scheduled service is full. 8 a road (**relief road**) carrying traffic round an urban area; bypass. 9 **a** the act of freeing a beleaguered town, fortress, etc.: *the relief of Mafeking.* **b** (*as modifier*): *a relief column.* 10 Also called: **relievo, rilievo.** *Sculpture, architect* **a** the projection of forms or figures from a flat ground, so that they are partly or wholly free of it. **b** a piece of work of this kind. 11 a printing process, such as engraving, letterpress, etc., that employs raised surfaces from which ink is transferred to the paper. 12 any vivid effect resulting from contrast: *comic relief.* 13 variation in altitude in an area; difference between highest and lowest level: *a region of low relief.* 14 *Mechanical engineering* the removal of the surface material of a bearing area to allow the access of lubricating fluid. 15 *Law* redress of a grievance or hardship: *to seek relief through the courts.* 16 *European history* a succession of payments made by an heir to a fief to his lord: the size of the relief was determined by the lord within bounds set by custom. 17 **on relief.** *US and Canadian* (of people) in receipt of government aid because of personal need.
▷HISTORY C14: from Old French, from *relever* to raise up; see RELIEVE

relief map NOUN a map that shows the configuration and height of the land surface, usually by means of contours.

relieve (rɪˈliːv) VERB (*tr*) 1 to bring alleviation of (pain, distress, etc.) to (someone). 2 to bring aid or assistance to (someone in need, a disaster area, etc.). 3 to take over the duties or watch of (someone). 4 to bring aid or a relieving force to (a besieged town, city, etc.). 5 to free (someone) from an obligation. 6 to make (something) less unpleasant, arduous, or monotonous. 7 to bring into relief or prominence, as by contrast. 8 (foll by *of*) *Informal* to take from: *the thief relieved him of his watch.* 9 **relieve oneself.** to urinate or defecate.
▷HISTORY C14: from Old French *relever*, from Latin *relevāre* to lift up, relieve, from RE- + *levāre* to lighten
▸**reˈlievable** ADJECTIVE ▸**reˈliever** NOUN

relieved (rɪˈliːvd) ADJECTIVE 1 (*postpositive; often foll by at, about,* etc.) experiencing relief, esp from worry or anxiety. 2 *Mechanical engineering* having part of the surface cut away to avoid friction or wear.

relievo (rɪlˈjeɪvəʊ, rɪˈliːvəʊ) NOUN, *plural* **-vos.** another name for **relief** (sense 9).
▷HISTORY from Italian, literally: raised work

relight (riːˈlaɪt) VERB **-lights, -lighting, -lighted** *or* **-lit.** to ignite or cause to ignite again.

religieuse *French* (rəliʒjøz) NOUN a nun.
▷HISTORY C18: feminine of RELIGIEUX

religieux *French* (rəliʒjø) NOUN, *plural* ***-gieux*** (-ʒjø). a member of a monastic order or clerical body.
▷HISTORY C17: from Latin *religiōsus* religious

religion (rɪˈlɪdʒən) NOUN 1 belief in, worship of, or obedience to a supernatural power or powers considered to be divine or to have control of human destiny. 2 any formal or institutionalized expression of such belief: *the Christian religion.* 3 the attitude and feeling of one who believes in a transcendent controlling power or powers. 4 *Chiefly RC Church* the way of life determined by the vows of poverty, chastity, and obedience entered upon by monks, friars, and nuns: *to enter religion.* 5 something of overwhelming importance to a person: *football is his religion.* 6 *Archaic* **a** the practice of sacred ritual observances. **b** sacred rites and ceremonies.
▷HISTORY C12: via Old French from Latin *religiō* fear of the supernatural, piety, probably from *religāre* to tie up, from RE- + *ligāre* to bind

religionism (rɪˈlɪdʒəˌnɪzəm) NOUN extreme religious fervour.
▸**reˈligionist** NOUN, ADJECTIVE

religiose (rɪˈlɪdʒɪˌəʊs) ADJECTIVE affectedly or extremely pious; sanctimoniously religious.
▸**reˈligiˌosely** ADVERB ▸**religiosity** (rɪˌlɪdʒɪˈɒsɪtɪ) NOUN

religious (rɪˈlɪdʒəs) ADJECTIVE 1 of, relating to, or concerned with religion. 2 **a** pious; devout; godly. **b** (*as collective noun;* preceded by *the*): *the religious.* 3 appropriate to or in accordance with the principles of a religion. 4 scrupulous, exact, or conscientious. 5 *Christianity* of or relating to a way of life dedicated to religion by the vows of poverty, chastity, and obedience, and defined by a monastic rule. ♦ NOUN 6 *Christianity* a member of an order or congregation living by such a rule; a monk, friar, or nun.
▸**reˈligiously** ADVERB ▸**reˈligiousness** NOUN

Religious Society of Friends NOUN the official name for the **Quakers.**

relinquish (rɪˈlɪŋkwɪʃ) VERB (*tr*) 1 to give up (a task, struggle, etc.); abandon. 2 to surrender or renounce (a claim, right, etc.). 3 to release; let go.
▷HISTORY C15: from French *relinquir*, from Latin *relinquere* to leave behind, from RE- + *linquere* to leave
▸**reˈlinquisher** NOUN ▸**reˈlinquishment** NOUN

reliquary (ˈrɛlɪkwərɪ) NOUN, *plural* **-quaries.** a receptacle or repository for relics, esp relics of saints.
▷HISTORY C17: from Old French *reliquaire*, from *relique* RELIC

relique (rəˈliːk, ˈrɛlɪk) NOUN an archaic spelling of **relic.**

reliquiae (rɪˈlɪkwɪˌiː) PLURAL NOUN *Archaic* fossil remains of animals or plants.
▷HISTORY C19: from Latin: remains

relish (ˈrɛlɪʃ) VERB (*tr*) 1 to savour or enjoy (an experience) to the full. 2 to anticipate eagerly; look forward to. 3 to enjoy the taste or flavour of (food, etc.); savour. 4 to give appetizing taste or flavour to (food), by or as if by the addition of pickles or spices. ♦ NOUN 5 liking or enjoyment, as of something eaten or experienced (esp in the phrase **with relish**). 6 pleasurable anticipation: *he didn't have much relish for the idea.* 7 an appetizing or spicy food added to a main dish to enhance its flavour. 8 an appetizing taste or flavour. 9 a zestful trace or touch: *there was a certain relish in all his writing.* 10 *Music* (in English lute, viol, and keyboard music of the 16th and 17th centuries) a trilling ornament, used esp at cadences.
▷HISTORY C16: from earlier *reles* aftertaste, from Old French: something remaining, from *relaisser* to leave behind; see RELEASE
▸**ˈrelishable** ADJECTIVE

relive (riːˈlɪv) VERB (*tr*) to experience (a sensation, event, etc.) again, esp in the imagination.
▸**reˈlivable** ADJECTIVE

rellies ('rɛlɪz) PLURAL NOUN *Austral and NZ informal* relatives or relations.

reload (riː'ləʊd) VERB [1] (*tr*) to place (cargo, goods, etc.) back on (a ship. lorry, etc.). [2] to put ammunition into a firearm after having discharged it.

relocate (ˌriːləʊ'keɪt) VERB [1] to move or be moved to a new place, esp (of an employee, a business, etc.) to a new area or place of employment. [2] (*intr*) (of an employee, a business, etc.) to move for reasons of business to a new area or place of employment.
▸**ˌrelo'cation** NOUN

relocation costs *or* **expenses** PLURAL NOUN payment made by an employer or a government agency to cover removal expenses and other costs incurred by an employee who is required to take up employment elsewhere.

relucent (rɪ'luːsᵊnt) ADJECTIVE *Archaic* bright; shining.
▹HISTORY C16: from Latin *relūcēre* to shine out, from RE- + *lūcēre* to shine, from *lūx* light

reluct (rɪ'lʌkt) VERB (*intr*) *Archaic* [1] (often foll by *against*) to struggle or rebel. [2] to object; show reluctance.
▹HISTORY C16: from Latin *reluctārī* to resist, from RE- + *luctārī* to struggle

reluctance (rɪ'lʌktəns) *or less commonly* **reluctancy** NOUN [1] lack of eagerness or willingness; disinclination. [2] *Physics* a measure of the resistance of a closed magnetic circuit to a magnetic flux, equal to the ratio of the magnetomotive force to the magnetic flux.

reluctant (rɪ'lʌktənt) ADJECTIVE [1] not eager; unwilling; disinclined. [2] *Archaic* offering resistance or opposition.
▹HISTORY C17: from Latin *reluctārī* to resist; see RELUCT
▸**re'luctantly** ADVERB

reluctivity (ˌrɛlʌk'tɪvɪtɪ) NOUN, *plural* **-ties**. *Physics* a specific or relative reluctance of a magnetic material.
▹HISTORY C19: RELUCT + *-ivity* on the model of *conductivity*

relume (rɪ'luːm) *or* **relumine** (rɪ'luːmɪn) VERB (*tr*) *Archaic* to light or brighten again; rekindle.
▹HISTORY C17: from Late Latin *relūmināre*, from Latin RE- + *illūmināre* to ILLUMINE

rely (rɪ'laɪ) VERB **-lies, -lying, -lied**. (*intr*; foll by *on* or *upon*) [1] to be dependent (on): *he relies on his charm*. [2] to have trust or confidence (in): *you can rely on us*.
▹HISTORY C14: from Old French *relier* to fasten together, repair, from Latin *religāre* to tie back, from RE- + *ligāre* to tie

REM[1] ABBREVIATION FOR **rapid eye movement**.

REM[2] *or* **rem** (rɛm) NOUN ACRONYM FOR roentgen equivalent man.

remain (rɪ'meɪn) VERB (*mainly intr*) [1] to stay behind or in the same place: *to remain at home; only Tom remained*. [2] (*copula*) to continue to be: *to remain cheerful*. [3] to be left, as after use, consumption, the passage of time, etc: *a little wine still remained in the bottle*. [4] to be left to be done, said, etc.: *it remains to be pointed out*. See also **remains**.
▹HISTORY C14: from Old French *remanoir*, from Latin *remanēre* to be left, from RE- + *manēre* to stay

remainder (rɪ'meɪndə) NOUN [1] a part or portion that is left, as after use, subtraction, expenditure, the passage of time, etc.: *the remainder of the milk; the remainder of the day*. [2] *Maths* **a** the amount left over when one quantity cannot be exactly divided by another: *for 10 ÷ 3, the remainder is 1*. **b** another name for **difference** (sense 7b). [3] *Property law* a future interest in property; an interest in a particular estate that will pass to one at some future date, as on the death of the current possessor. [4] a number of copies of a book left unsold when demand slows or ceases, which are sold at a reduced price by the publisher. ◆ VERB [5] (*tr*) to sell (copies of a book) as a remainder.
▹HISTORY C15: from Anglo-French, from Old French *remaindre* (infinitive used as noun), variant of *remanoir*; see REMAIN

remainderman (rɪ'meɪndəˌmæn) NOUN, *plural* **-men**. *Property law* the person entitled to receive a particular estate on its determination. Compare **reversioner**.

remains (rɪ'meɪnz) PLURAL NOUN [1] any pieces, scraps, fragments, etc., that are left unused or still extant, as after use, consumption, the passage of time, etc.: *the remains of a meal; archaeological remains*. [2] the body of a dead person; corpse. [3] Also called: **literary remains**. the unpublished writings of an author at the time of his death.

remake NOUN ('riːˌmeɪk) [1] something that is made again, esp a new version of an old film. [2] the act of making again or anew. ◆ VERB (riː'meɪk) **-makes, -making, -made**. [3] (*tr*) to make again or anew.

remand (rɪ'mɑːnd) VERB (*tr*) [1] *Law* (of a court or magistrate) to send (a prisoner or accused person) back into custody or admit him to bail, esp on adjourning a case for further inquiries to be made. [2] to send back. ◆ NOUN [3] the sending of a prisoner or accused person back into custody (or sometimes admitting him to bail) to await trial or continuation of his trial. [4] the act of remanding or state of being remanded. [5] **on remand**. in custody or on bail awaiting trial or completion of one's trial.
▹HISTORY C15: from Medieval Latin *remandāre* to send back word, from Latin RE- + *mandāre* to command, confine; see MANDATE
▸**re'mandment** NOUN

remand centre NOUN (in Britain) an institution to which accused persons are sent for detention while awaiting appearance before a court. Until 1967 remand centres were for young people between 14 and 21 years of age.

remand home NOUN (no longer in technical use) an institution to which juvenile offenders between 8 and 14 years may be remanded or committed for detention. See also **community home**.

remanence ('rɛmənəns) NOUN *Physics* the ability of a material to retain magnetization, equal to the magnetic flux density of the material after the removal of the magnetizing field. Also called: **retentivity**.
▹HISTORY C17: from Latin *remanēre* to stay behind, REMAIN

remanent ('rɛmənənt) ADJECTIVE *Rare* remaining or left over.

remark (rɪ'mɑːk) VERB [1] (when *intr*, often foll by *on* or *upon*; when *tr, may take a clause as object*) to pass a casual comment (about); reflect in informal speech or writing. [2] (*tr; may take a clause as object*) to perceive; observe; notice. ◆ NOUN [3] a brief casually expressed thought or opinion; observation. [4] notice, comment, or observation: *the event passed without remark*. [5] *Engraving* a variant spelling of **remarque**.
▹HISTORY C17: from Old French *remarquer* to observe, from RE- + *marquer* to note, MARK[1]
▸**re'marker** NOUN

remarkable (rɪ'mɑːkəbᵊl) ADJECTIVE [1] worthy of note or attention: *a remarkable achievement*. [2] unusual, striking, or extraordinary: *a remarkable sight*.
▸**re'markableness** *or* **reˌmarka'bility** NOUN ▸**re'markably** ADVERB

remarque *or* **remark** (rɪ'mɑːk) NOUN [1] a mark in the margin of an engraved plate to indicate the stage of production of the plate. It is removed before the plate is finished. [2] a plate so marked. [3] a print or proof from a plate so marked.
▹HISTORY C19: from French; see REMARK

remarry (riː'mærɪ) VERB **-ries, -rying, -ried**. to marry again.
▸**re'marriage** NOUN

remaster (riː'mɑːstə) VERB (*tr*) to make a new master audio recording, now usually digital, from (an earlier recording), to produce compact discs or stereo records with improved sound reproduction.

rematch NOUN ('riːˌmætʃ) [1] *Sport* a second or return match between contestants. ◆ VERB (riː'mætʃ) [2] (*tr*) to match (two contestants) again.

remblai (*French* rɑ̃blɛ) NOUN earth used for an embankment or rampart.
▹HISTORY C18: from French, from *remblayer* to embank, from *emblayer* to pile up

Rembrandtesque (ˌrɛmbrænt'ɛsk) ADJECTIVE reminiscent of Rembrandt (full name *Rembrandt Harmensz van Rijn*) the Dutch painter (1606–69).

REME ('riːmiː) NOUN ACRONYM FOR Royal Electrical and Mechanical Engineers.

remedial (rɪ'miːdɪəl) ADJECTIVE [1] affording a remedy; curative. [2] denoting or relating to special teaching, teaching methods, or material for backward and slow learners: *remedial education*.
▸**re'medially** ADVERB

remediation (rɪˌmiːdɪ'eɪʃən) NOUN the action of remedying something, esp the reversal or stopping of damage to the environment.

remedy ('rɛmɪdɪ) NOUN, *plural* **-dies**. [1] (usually foll by *for* or *against*) any drug or agent that cures a disease or controls its symptoms. [2] (usually foll by *for* or *against*) anything that serves to put a fault to rights, cure defects, improve conditions, etc.: *a remedy for industrial disputes*. [3] the legally permitted variation from the standard weight or quality of coins; tolerance. ◆ VERB (*tr*) [4] to relieve or cure (a disease, illness, etc.) by or as if by a remedy. [5] to put to rights (a fault, error, etc.); correct.
▹HISTORY C13: from Anglo-Norman *remedie*, from Latin *remedium* a cure, from *remedērī* to heal again, from RE- + *medērī* to heal; see MEDICAL
▸**remediable** (rɪ'miːdɪəbᵊl) ADJECTIVE ▸**re'mediably** ADVERB ▸**'remediless** ADJECTIVE

remember (rɪ'mɛmbə) VERB [1] to become aware of (something forgotten) again; bring back to one's consciousness; recall. [2] to retain (an idea, intention, etc.) in one's conscious mind: *to remember Pythagoras' theorem; remember to do one's shopping*. [3] (*tr*) to give money, etc., to (someone), as in a will or in tipping. [4] (*tr*; foll by *to*) to mention (a person's name) to another person, as by way of greeting or friendship: *remember me to your mother*. [5] (*tr*) to mention (a person) favourably, as in prayer. [6] (*tr*) to commemorate (a person, event, etc.): *to remember the dead of the wars*. [7] **remember oneself**. to recover one's good manners after a lapse; stop behaving badly.
▹HISTORY C14: from Old French *remembrer*, from Late Latin *rememorārī* to recall to mind, from Latin RE- + *memor* mindful; see MEMORY
▸**re'memberer** NOUN

remembrance (rɪ'mɛmbrəns) NOUN [1] the act of remembering or state of being remembered. [2] something that is remembered; reminiscence. [3] a memento or keepsake. [4] the extent in time of one's power of recollection. [5] **a** the act of honouring some past event, person, etc. **b** (*as modifier*): *a remembrance service*.

remembrancer (rɪ'mɛmbrənsə) NOUN *Archaic* a reminder, memento, or keepsake.

Remembrancer (rɪ'mɛmbrənsə) NOUN (in Britain) [1] any of several officials of the Exchequer esp one (**Queen's** *or* **King's Remembrancer**) whose duties include collecting debts due to the Crown. [2] an official (**City Remembrancer**) appointed by the Corporation of the City of London to represent its interests to Parliament and elsewhere.

Remembrance Sunday NOUN *Brit* the second Sunday in November, which is the Sunday closest to November 11, the anniversary of the armistice of 1918 that ended World War I, on which the dead of both World Wars are commemorated. Also called: **Remembrance Day**.

remex ('riːmɛks) NOUN, *plural* **remiges** ('rɛmɪˌdʒiːz). any of the large flight feathers of a bird's wing.
▹HISTORY C18: from Latin: a rower, from *rēmus* oar
▸**remigial** (rɪ'mɪdʒɪəl) ADJECTIVE

remind (rɪ'maɪnd) VERB (*tr*; usually foll by *of; may take a clause as object or an infinitive*) to cause (a person) to remember (something or to do something); make (someone) aware (of something he may have forgotten): *remind me to phone home; flowers remind me of holidays*.

reminder (rɪ'maɪndə) NOUN [1] something that recalls the past. [2] a note to remind a person of something not done.

remindful (rɪ'maɪndfʊl) ADJECTIVE [1] serving to remind. [2] (*postpositive*) bearing in mind; mindful.

reminisce (ˌrɛmɪ'nɪs) VERB (*intr*) to talk or write about old times, past experiences, etc.

reminiscence (ˌrɛmɪ'nɪsəns) NOUN [1] the act of recalling or narrating past experiences. [2] (*often plural*) some past experience, event, etc., that is recalled or narrated; anecdote. [3] an event, phenomenon, or experience that reminds one of something else. [4] (in the philosophy of Plato) the doctrine that perception and recognition of particulars is possible because the mind has seen the universal forms of all things in a previous disembodied existence. 5 *Psychol* the ability to perform a task better when tested some time after the task has been learnt than when tested immediately after learning it.

reminiscent (ˌrɛmɪˈnɪsᵊnt) ADJECTIVE 1 (*postpositive*; foll by *of*) stimulating memories (of) or comparisons (with). 2 characterized by reminiscence. 3 (of a person) given to reminiscing.
▷HISTORY C18: from Latin *reminiscī* to call to mind, from RE- + *mēns* mind
▸ˌ**remiˈniscently** ADVERB

remise (rɪˈmaɪz) VERB 1 (*tr*) *Law* to give up or relinquish (a right, claim, etc.); surrender. 2 *Fencing* to make a renewed thrust on the same lunge after the first has missed. ◆ NOUN 3 *Fencing* a second thrust made on the same lunge after the first has missed. 4 *Obsolete* a hired carriage. 5 *Obsolete* a coach house.
▷HISTORY C17: from French *remettre* to put back, from Latin *remittere* to send back, from RE- + *mittere* to send

remiss (rɪˈmɪs) ADJECTIVE (*postpositive*) 1 lacking in care or attention to duty; negligent. 2 lacking in energy; dilatory.
▷HISTORY C15: from Latin *remissus* from *remittere* to release, from RE- + *mittere* to send
▸**reˈmissly** ADVERB ▸**reˈmissness** NOUN

remissible (rɪˈmɪsəbᵊl) ADJECTIVE able to be remitted.
▷HISTORY C16: from Latin *remissibilis*; see REMIT
▸**reˌmissiˈbility** *or* **reˈmissibleness** NOUN

remission (rɪˈmɪʃən) *or less commonly* **remittal** (rɪˈmɪtᵊl) NOUN 1 the act of remitting or state of being remitted. 2 a reduction of the term of a sentence of imprisonment, as for good conduct: *he got three years' remission.* 3 forgiveness for sin. 4 discharge or release from penalty, obligation, etc. 5 lessening of intensity; abatement, as in the severity of symptoms of a disease.
▸**reˈmissive** ADJECTIVE ▸**reˈmissively** ADVERB

remit VERB (rɪˈmɪt) **-mits, -mitting, -mitted**. (*mainly tr*) 1 (*also intr*) to send (money, payment, etc.), as for goods or service, esp by post. 2 *Law* (esp of an appeal court) to send back (a case or proceeding) to an inferior court for further consideration or action. 3 to cancel or refrain from exacting (a penalty or punishment). 4 (*also intr*) to relax (pace, intensity, etc.) or (of pace or the like) to slacken or abate. 5 to postpone; defer. 6 *Archaic* to pardon or forgive (crime, sins, etc.). ◆ NOUN (ˈriːmɪt, rɪˈmɪt) 7 the area of authority or responsibility of an individual or a group: *by taking that action, the committee has exceeded its remit.* 8 *Law* the transfer of a case from one court or jurisdiction to another, esp from an appeal court to an inferior tribunal. 9 the act of remitting. 10 something remitted. 11 *NZ* a proposal from a branch of an organization put forward for discussion at the annual general meeting.
▷HISTORY C14: from Latin *remittere* to send back, release, RE- + *mittere* to send
▸**reˈmittable** ADJECTIVE ▸**reˈmittal** NOUN

remittance (rɪˈmɪtəns) NOUN 1 payment for goods or services received or as an allowance, esp when sent by post. 2 the act of remitting.

remittance man NOUN a man living abroad on money sent from home, esp in the days of the British Empire.

remittee (rɪˌmɪtˈiː) NOUN the recipient of a remittance; one to whom payment is sent.

remittent (rɪˈmɪtᵊnt) ADJECTIVE (of a fever or the symptoms of a disease) characterized by periods of diminished severity.
▸**reˈmittence** *or* **reˈmittency** NOUN ▸**reˈmittently** ADVERB

remitter (rɪˈmɪtə) NOUN 1 Also called: **remittor.** a person who remits. 2 *Property law* the principle by which a person out of possession of land to which he had a good title is adjudged to regain this when he again enters into possession of the land.

remix VERB (riːˈmɪks) 1 to change the balance and separation of (a recording), usually to emphasize the rhythm section. ◆ NOUN (ˈriːˌmɪks) 2 a remixed version of a recording.

remnant (ˈrɛmnənt) NOUN 1 (*often plural*) a part left over after use, processing, etc. 2 a surviving trace or vestige, as of a former era: *a remnant of imperialism.* 3 a piece of material from the end of a roll, sold at a lower price. ◆ ADJECTIVE 4 remaining; left over.
▷HISTORY C14: from Old French *remenant* remaining, from *remanoir* to REMAIN

remodel VERB (riːˈmɒdᵊl) **-els, -elling, -elled** *or US* **-els, -eling, -eled.** (*tr*) 1 to change or alter the structure, style, or form of (something): *expand and remodel the kitchen.* 2 to model again in clay, wax, etc.; remould. ◆ NOUN (ˈriːˌmɒdᵊl) 3 something that has been remodelled.

remonetize *or* **remonetise** (riːˈmʌnɪˌtaɪz) VERB (*tr*) to reinstate as legal tender: *to remonetize silver.*
▸**reˌmonetiˈzation** *or* **reˌmonetiˈsation** NOUN

remonstrance (rɪˈmɒnstrəns) NOUN 1 the act of remonstrating; protestation. 2 a protest or reproof, esp a petition presented in protest against something.

Remonstrance (rɪˈmɒnstrəns) NOUN *History* 1 See **Grand Remonstrance.** 2 the statement of Arminian principles drawn up in 1610 in Gouda in the Netherlands.

remonstrant (rɪˈmɒnstrənt) NOUN 1 a person who remonstrates, esp one who signs a remonstrance. ◆ ADJECTIVE 2 *Rare* remonstrating or protesting.

Remonstrant (rɪˈmɒnstrənt) NOUN a Dutch supporter of the Arminian Remonstrance of 1610.

remonstrate (ˈrɛmənˌstreɪt) VERB (*intr*) 1 (usually foll by *with, against,* etc.) to argue in protest or objection: *to remonstrate with the government.* 2 *Archaic* to show or point out.
▷HISTORY C16: from Medieval Latin *remonstrāre* to point out (errors), from Latin RE- + *monstrāre* to show
▸ˌ**remonˈstration** NOUN ▸**remonstrative** (rɪˈmɒnstrətɪv) ADJECTIVE ▸ˈ**remonˌstrator** NOUN

remontant (rɪˈmɒntənt) ADJECTIVE 1 (esp of cultivated roses) flowering more than once in a single season. ◆ NOUN 2 a rose having such a growth.
▷HISTORY C19: from French: coming up again, from *remonter*; see REMOUNT

remontoir *or* **remontoire** (ˌrɛmənˈtwɑː) NOUN any of various devices used in watches, clocks, etc., to compensate for errors arising from the changes in the force driving the escapement.
▷HISTORY C19: from French: winding mechanism, from *remonter* to wind; see REMOUNT

remora (ˈrɛmərə) NOUN any of the marine spiny-finned fishes constituting the family *Echeneidae.* They have a flattened elongated body and attach themselves to larger fish, rocks, etc., by a sucking disc on the top of the head.
▷HISTORY C16: from Latin, from RE- + *mora* delay; an allusion to its alleged habit of delaying ships

remorse (rɪˈmɔːs) NOUN 1 a sense of deep regret and guilt for some misdeed. 2 compunction; pity; compassion.
▷HISTORY C14: from Medieval Latin *remorsus* a gnawing, from Latin *remordēre* to bite again, from RE- + *mordēre* to bite
▸**reˈmorseful** ADJECTIVE ▸**reˈmorsefully** ADVERB
▸**reˈmorsefulness** NOUN

remorseless (rɪˈmɔːslɪs) ADJECTIVE 1 without compunction, pity, or compassion. 2 not abating in intensity; relentless: *a remorseless wind.*
▸**reˈmorselessly** ADVERB ▸**reˈmorselessness** NOUN

remortgage (riːˈmɔːɡɪdʒ) VERB to take out a new or different mortgage on a property.

remote (rɪˈməʊt) ADJECTIVE 1 located far away; distant. 2 far from any centre of population, society, or civilization; out-of-the-way. 3 distant in time. 4 distantly related or connected: *a remote cousin.* 5 removed, as from the source or point of action. 6 slight or faint (esp in the phrases **not the remotest idea, a remote chance**). 7 (of a person's manner) aloof or abstracted. 8 operated from a distance; remote-controlled: *a remote monitor.*
▷HISTORY C15: from Latin *remōtus* far removed, from *removēre,* from RE- + *movēre* to move
▸**reˈmotely** ADVERB ▸**reˈmoteness** NOUN

remote access NOUN *Computing* access to a computer from a physically separate terminal.

remote control NOUN control of a system or activity by a person at a different place, usually by means of radio or ultrasonic signals or by electrical signals transmitted by wire.
▸**reˈmote-conˈtrolled** ADJECTIVE

remote sensing NOUN the use of an instrument, such as a radar device or camera, to scan the earth or another planet from space in order to collect data about some aspect of it.
▸**remote-sensing** ADJECTIVE

remote sensor NOUN any instrument, such as a radar device or camera, that scans the earth or another planet from space in order to collect data about some aspect of it.

rémoulade (ˌrɛməˈleɪd; *French* remulad) NOUN a mayonnaise sauce flavoured with herbs, mustard, and capers, served with salads, cold meat, etc.
▷HISTORY C19: from French, from Picard dialect *ramolas* horseradish, from Latin *armoracea*

remould VERB (riːˈməʊld) (*tr*) 1 to mould again. 2 to bond a new tread onto the casing of (a worn pneumatic tyre). ◆ NOUN (ˈriːˌməʊld) 3 a tyre made by this process. ◆ Also (for senses 2, 3): **retread.**

remount VERB (riːˈmaʊnt) 1 to get on (a horse, bicycle, etc.) again. 2 (*tr*) to mount (a picture, jewel, exhibit, etc.) again. ◆ NOUN (ˈriːˌmaʊnt) 3 a fresh horse, esp (formerly) to replace one killed or injured in battle.

removal (rɪˈmuːvᵊl) NOUN 1 the act of removing or state of being removed. 2 **a** a change of residence. **b** (*as modifier*): *a removal company.* 3 dismissal from office. 4 *South African* the forced displacement of a community for political or social reasons.

removalist (rɪˈmuːvəlɪst) NOUN *Austral* a person or company that transports household effects to a new home.

remove (rɪˈmuːv) VERB (*mainly tr*) 1 to take away and place elsewhere. 2 to displace (someone) from office; dismiss. 3 to do away with (a grievance, cause of anxiety, etc.); abolish. 4 to cause (dirt, stains, or anything unwanted) to disappear; get rid of. 5 *Euphemistic* to assassinate; kill. 6 (*intr*) *Formal* to change the location of one's home or place of business: *the publishers have removed to Mayfair.* ◆ NOUN 7 the act of removing, esp (formal) a removal of one's residence or place of work. 8 the degree of difference separating one person, thing, or condition from another: *only one remove from madness.* 9 *Brit* (in certain schools) a class or form, esp one for children of about 14 years, designed to introduce them to the greater responsibilities of a more senior position in the school. 10 (at a formal dinner, formerly) a dish to be changed while the rest of the course remains on the table.
▷HISTORY C14: from Old French *removoir,* from Latin *removēre*; see MOVE
▸**reˈmovable** ADJECTIVE ▸**reˌmovaˈbility** *or* **reˈmovableness** NOUN ▸**reˈmovably** ADVERB ▸**reˈmover** NOUN

removed (rɪˈmuːvd) ADJECTIVE 1 separated by distance or abstract distinction. 2 (*postpositive*) separated by a degree of descent or kinship: *the child of a person's first cousin is his first cousin once removed.*
▸**removedness** (rɪˈmuːvɪdnɪs) NOUN

Remscheid (*German* ˈrɛmʃait) NOUN an industrial city in W Germany, in North Rhine-Westphalia. Pop.: 119 500 (1999 est.).

Remuera tractor (ˌrɛmuˈɛərə) NOUN *NZ informal* a four-wheel drive recreational vehicle.
▷HISTORY from the name of a wealthy suburb of Auckland

remunerate (rɪˈmjuːnəˌreɪt) VERB (*tr*) to reward or pay for work, service, etc.
▷HISTORY C16: from Latin *remūnerārī* to reward, from RE- + *mūnerāre* to give, from *mūnus* a gift; see MUNIFICENT
▸**reˌmuneraˈbility** NOUN ▸**reˈmunerable** ADJECTIVE
▸**reˈmunerˌator** NOUN

remuneration (rɪˌmjuːnəˈreɪʃən) NOUN 1 the act of remunerating. 2 pay; recompense.

remunerative (rɪˈmjuːnərətɪv) ADJECTIVE earning money or rewards; paying.
▸**reˈmuneratively** ADVERB ▸**reˈmunerativeness** NOUN

Remus (ˈriːməs) NOUN *Roman myth* the brother of Romulus.

renaissance (rəˈneɪsəns; *US also* ˈrɛnəˌsɒns) *or* **renascence** NOUN a revival or rebirth, esp of culture and learning.
▷HISTORY C19: from French, from Latin RE- + *nascī* to be born

Renaissance (rəˈneɪsəns; *US also* ˈrɛnəˌsɒns) NOUN

1 **the.** the period of European history marking the waning of the Middle Ages and the rise of the modern world: usually considered as beginning in Italy in the 14th century. 2 **a** the spirit, culture, art, science, and thought of this period. Characteristics of the Renaissance are usually considered to include intensified classical scholarship, scientific and geographical discovery, a sense of individual human potentialities, and the assertion of the active and secular over the religious and contemplative life. **b** (*as modifier*): *Renaissance writers*. See also **Early Renaissance, High Renaissance.** ◆ ADJECTIVE 3 of, characteristic of, or relating to the Renaissance, its culture, etc.

Renaissance man NOUN a man of any period who has a broad range of intellectual interests.

renal ('ri:nᵊl) ADJECTIVE of, relating to, resembling, or situated near the kidney.
▷HISTORY C17: from French, from Late Latin *rēnālis*, from Latin *rēnēs* kidneys, of obscure origin

renal pelvis NOUN a small funnel-shaped cavity of the kidney into which urine is discharged before passing into the ureter.

rename (ri:'neɪm) VERB (*tr*) to change the name of (someone or something).

renascence (rɪ'næsəns, -'neɪ-) NOUN a variant of **renaissance.**

renascent (rɪ'næsᵊnt, -'neɪ-) ADJECTIVE becoming active or vigorous again; reviving: *renascent nationalism*.
▷HISTORY C18: from Latin *renascī* to be born again

rencounter (rɛn'kaʊntə) *Archaic* ◆ NOUN *also* **rencontre** (rɛn'kɒntə). 1 an unexpected meeting. 2 a hostile clash, as of two armies, adversaries, etc.; skirmish. ◆ VERB 3 to meet (someone) unexpectedly.
▷HISTORY C16: from French *rencontre*, from *rencontrer*; see ENCOUNTER

rend (rɛnd) VERB **rends, rending, rent.** 1 to tear with violent force or to be torn in this way; rip. 2 (*tr*) to tear or pull (one's clothes, etc.), esp as a manifestation of rage or grief. 3 (*tr*) (of a noise or cry) to disturb (the air, silence, etc.) with a shrill or piercing tone. 4 (*tr*) to pain or distress (the heart, conscience, etc.).
▷HISTORY Old English *rendan*; related to Old Frisian *renda*
▸**'rendible** ADJECTIVE

render ('rɛndə) VERB (*tr*) 1 to present or submit (accounts, etc.) for payment, approval, or action. 2 to give or provide (aid, charity, a service, etc.). 3 to show (obedience), as due or expected. 4 to give or exchange, as by way of return or requital: *to render blow for blow*. 5 to cause to become: *grief had rendered him simple-minded*. 6 to deliver (a verdict or opinion) formally. 7 to portray or depict (something), as in painting, music, or acting. 8 *Computing* to use colour and shading to make a digital image look three-dimensional and solid. 9 to translate (something) into another language or form. 10 (sometimes foll by *up*) to yield or give: *the tomb rendered up its secret*. 11 (often foll by *back*) to return (something); give back. 12 to cover the surface of (brickwork, stone, etc.) with a coat of plaster. 13 (often foll by *down*) to extract (fat) from (meat) by melting. 14 *Nautical* **a** to reeve (a line). **b** to slacken (a rope, etc.). 15 *History* (of a feudal tenant) to make (payment) in money, goods, or services to one's overlord. ◆ NOUN 16 a first thin coat of plaster applied to a surface. 17 *History* a payment in money, goods, or services made by a feudal tenant to his lord.
▷HISTORY C14: from Old French *rendre*, from Latin *reddere* to give back (influenced by Latin *prendere* to grasp), from RE- + *dare* to give
▸**'renderable** ADJECTIVE ▸**'renderer** NOUN

rendering ('rɛndərɪŋ) NOUN 1 the act or an instance of performing a play, piece of music, etc. 2 a translation of a text from a foreign language. 3 Also called: **rendering coat, render.** a coat of plaster or cement mortar applied to a surface. 4 a perspective drawing showing an architect's idea of a finished building, interior, etc.

rendezvous ('rɒndɪˌvu:) NOUN, *plural* **-vous** (-ˌvu:z). 1 a meeting or appointment to meet at a specified time and place. 2 a place where people meet. 3 an arranged meeting of two spacecraft. ◆ VERB 4 to meet or cause to meet at a specified time or place.
▷HISTORY C16: from French, from *rendez-vous!* present yourselves! from *se rendre* to present oneself; see RENDER

rendition (rɛn'dɪʃən) NOUN 1 a performance of a musical composition, dramatic role, etc. 2 a translation of a text. 3 the act of rendering. 4 *Archaic* surrender.
▷HISTORY C17: from obsolete French, from Late Latin *redditiō* see RENDER

rendzina (rɛn'dzi:nə) NOUN a dark interzonal type of soil found in grassy or formerly grassy areas of moderate rainfall, esp on chalklands.
▷HISTORY C20: from Polish

renegade ('rɛnɪˌgeɪd) NOUN 1 **a** a person who deserts his cause or faith for another; apostate; traitor. **b** (*as modifier*): *a renegade priest*. 2 any outlaw or rebel.
▷HISTORY C16: from Spanish *renegado*, from Medieval Latin *renegāre* to renounce, from Latin RE- + *negāre* to deny

renegado (ˌrɛnɪ'gɑ:dəʊ) NOUN, *plural* **-dos.** an archaic word for **renegade.**

renege *or* **renegue** (rɪ'ni:g, -'neɪg) VERB 1 (*intr*; often foll by *on*) to go back (on one's promise, etc.). ◆ VERB, NOUN 2 *Cards* other words for **revoke.**
▷HISTORY C16 (in the sense: to deny, renounce): from Medieval Latin *renegāre* to renounce; see RENEGADE
▸**re'neger** *or* **re'neguer** NOUN

renegotiate (ˌri:nɪ'gəʊʃɪˌeɪt) VERB to negotiate again in order to alter or change previously agreed terms.
▸**ˌreneˌgoti'ation** NOUN

renew (rɪ'nju:) VERB (*mainly tr*) 1 to take up again. 2 (*also intr*) to begin (an activity) again; recommence: *to renew an attempt*. 3 to restate or reaffirm (a promise, etc.). 4 (*also intr*) to make (a lease, licence, or contract) valid or effective for a further period. 5 to extend the period of loan of (a library book). 6 to regain or recover (vigour, strength, activity, etc.). 7 to restore to a new or fresh condition. 8 to replace (an old or worn-out part or piece). 9 to replenish (a supply, etc.).
▸**re'newable** ADJECTIVE ▸**reˌnewa'bility** NOUN ▸**re'newer** NOUN

renewable energy NOUN another name for **alternative energy.**

renewables PLURAL NOUN sources of alternative energy, such as wind and wave power.

renewal (rɪ'nju:əl) NOUN 1 the act of renewing or state of being renewed. 2 something that is renewed.

Renfrew ('rɛnfru:) NOUN an industrial town in W central Scotland, in Renfrewshire, W of Glasgow. Pop.: 20 764 (1991).

Renfrewshire ('rɛnfru:ʃɪə, -ʃə) NOUN 1 a council area of W central Scotland, on the River Clyde W of Glasgow: corresponds to part of the historical county of Renfrewshire; part of Strathclyde region from 1975 to 1996: agricultural and residential, with clothing and manufacturing industries in Paisley. Administrative centre: Paisley. Pop.: 172 867 (2001 est.). Area: 261 sq. km (101 sq. miles). 2 a former county of W central Scotland, on the Firth of Clyde: became part of Strathclyde region in 1975; now covered by the council areas of Renfrewshire, East Renfrewshire, and Inverclyde.

reni- COMBINING FORM kidney or kidneys: *reniform*.
▷HISTORY from Latin *rēnēs*

reniform ('rɛnɪˌfɔ:m) ADJECTIVE having the shape or profile of a kidney: *a reniform leaf*; *a reniform mass of haematite*.

renin ('ri:nɪn) NOUN a proteolytic enzyme secreted by the kidneys, which plays an important part in the maintenance of blood pressure.
▷HISTORY C20: from RENI- + -IN

renitent (rɪ'naɪtᵊnt, 'rɛnɪtənt) ADJECTIVE *Rare* 1 reluctant; recalcitrant. 2 not flexible.
▷HISTORY C18: from Latin *renītī* to strive afresh, from RE- + *nītī* to endeavour
▸**re'nitence** *or* **re'nitency** NOUN

renk (rɛŋk) ADJECTIVE *Northern English dialect* unpleasant; horrible.

renminbi *or* **renminbi yuan** (ˌrɛnˌmɪn'bi:) NOUN, *plural* **renminbi.** another name for the Chinese **yuan.**
▷HISTORY Chinese *renminbi* people + *bi* currency

Rennes (*French* rɛn) NOUN a city in NW France: the ancient capital of Brittany. Pop.: 206 229 (1999).

rennet ('rɛnɪt) NOUN 1 **a** the membrane lining the fourth stomach (abomasum) of a young calf. **b** the stomach of certain other young animals. 2 a substance, containing the enzyme rennin, prepared esp from the stomachs of calves and used for curdling milk in making cheese and junket.
▷HISTORY C15: related to Old English *gerinnan* to curdle, RUN

rennin ('rɛnɪn) NOUN an enzyme that occurs in gastric juice and is a constituent of rennet. It coagulates milk by converting caseinogen to casein. Also called: **chymosin.**
▷HISTORY C20: from RENNET + -IN

Reno ('ri:nəʊ) NOUN a city in W Nevada, at the foot of the Sierra Nevada: noted as a divorce, wedding, and gambling centre by reason of its liberal laws. Pop.: 180 480 (2000).

renounce (rɪ'naʊns) VERB 1 (*tr*) to give up (a claim or right), esp by formal announcement: *to renounce a title*. 2 (*tr*) to repudiate: *to renounce Christianity*. 3 (*tr*) to give up (some habit, pursuit, etc.) voluntarily: *to renounce smoking*. 4 (*intr*) *Cards* to fail to follow suit because one has no cards of the suit led. ◆ NOUN 5 *Rare* a failure to follow suit in a card game.
▷HISTORY C14: from Old French *renoncer*, from Latin *renuntiāre* to disclaim, from RE- + *nuntiāre* to announce, from *nuntius* messenger
▸**re'nouncement** NOUN ▸**re'nouncer** NOUN

renovate ('rɛnəˌveɪt) VERB (*tr*) 1 to restore (something) to good condition: *to renovate paintings*. 2 to revive or refresh (one's spirits, health, etc.).
▷HISTORY C16: from Latin *renovāre*, from RE- + *novāre* to make new, from *novus* NEW
▸**ˌreno'vation** NOUN ▸**'renoˌvative** ADJECTIVE ▸**'renoˌvator** NOUN

renown (rɪ'naʊn) NOUN widespread reputation, esp of a good kind; fame.
▷HISTORY C14: from Anglo-Norman *renoun*, from Old French *renom*, from *renomer* to celebrate, from RE- + *nomer* to name, from Latin *nōmināre*

renowned (rɪ'naʊnd) ADJECTIVE having a widespread, esp good, reputation; famous.

rensselaerite ('rɛnsələˌraɪt, ˌrɛnsə'lɛəraɪt) NOUN a white or yellow compact variety of talc, used for ornaments.
▷HISTORY C19: named after Stephen Van *Rensselaer* (1764–1839), American army officer and politician

rent[1] (rɛnt) NOUN 1 a payment made periodically by a tenant to a landlord or owner for the occupation or use of land, buildings, or by a user for the use of other property, such as a telephone. 2 *Economics* **a** that portion of the national income accruing to owners of land and real property. **b** the return derived from the cultivation of land in excess of production costs. **c** See **economic rent.** 3 **for rent.** *Chiefly US and Canadian* available for use and occupation subject to the payment of rent. ◆ VERB 4 (*tr*) to grant (a person) the right to use one's property in return for periodic payments. 5 (*tr*) to occupy or use (property) in return for periodic payments. 6 (*intr*; often foll by *at*) to be let or rented (for a specified rental).
▷HISTORY C12: from Old French *rente* revenue, from Vulgar Latin *rendere* (unattested) to yield; see RENDER
▸**ˌrenta'bility** NOUN ▸**'rentable** ADJECTIVE

rent[2] (rɛnt) NOUN 1 a slit or opening made by tearing or rending; tear. 2 a breach or division, as in relations. ◆ VERB 3 the past tense and past participle of **rend.**

rent-a- PREFIX 1 denoting a rental service. 2 *Derogatory or facetious* denoting a person or group that performs a function as if hired from a rental service: *rent-a-mob*.

rental ('rɛntᵊl) NOUN 1 **a** the amount paid by a tenant as rent. **b** the amount paid by a user for the use of property: *telephone rental*. **c** an income derived from rents received. 2 property available for renting. 3 a less common name for **rent-roll.** ◆ ADJECTIVE 4 of or relating to rent or renting.

rent boy NOUN a young male prostitute.

rent control NOUN regulation by law of the rent a landlord can charge for domestic accommodation and of his right to evict tenants.

rente *French* (rɑ̃t) NOUN 1 annual income from capital investment; annuity. 2 government securities of certain countries, esp France. [3] the interest on such securities.

renter (ˈrɛntə) NOUN [1] a person who lets his property in return for rent, esp a landlord. [2] a person who rents property from another; tenant. [3] a distributor of films to cinemas for commercial showing.

rent-free ADJECTIVE, ADVERB without payment of rent.

rentier *French* (rɑ̃tje) NOUN **a** a person whose income consists primarily of fixed unearned amounts, such as rent or bond interest. **b** (*as modifier*): *the rentier class.*
▷HISTORY from *rente*; see RENT[1]

rent-roll NOUN [1] a register of lands and buildings owned by a person, company, etc., showing the rent due and total amount received from each tenant. [2] the total income arising from rented property.

renunciation (rɪˌnʌnsɪˈeɪʃən) NOUN [1] the act or an instance of renouncing. [2] a formal declaration renouncing something. [3] *Stock Exchange* the surrender to another of the rights to buy new shares in a rights issue.
▷HISTORY C14: from Latin *renunciātiō* a declaration, from *renuntiāre* to report, RENOUNCE
▸**reˈnunciative** *or* **reˈnunciatory** ADJECTIVE

renvoi (rɛnˈvɔɪ) NOUN the referring of a dispute or other legal question to a jurisdiction other than that in which it arose.
▷HISTORY C17: from French: a sending back, from *renvoyer*, from RE- + *envoyer* to send; see ENVOY[1]

reo (ˈriːəʊ) NOUN *NZ* a language.
▷HISTORY Maori

reoccupy (riːˈɒkjʊˌpaɪ) VERB **-pies, -pying, -pied.** (*tr*) to occupy (a building, area, etc.) again.
▸ˌ**reoccuˈpation** NOUN

reoccur (ˌriːəˈkɜː) VERB **-curs, -curring, -curred.** (*intr*) to happen, take place, or come about again.
▸ˌ**reocˈcurrence** NOUN

reopen (riːˈəʊpən) VERB to open or cause to open again.

reorder (riːˈɔːdə) VERB (*tr*) [1] to request (something) to be supplied again or differently. [2] to arrange, regulate, or dispose (articles) in their proper places again.

reorganization *or* **reorganisation** (ˌriːɔːgənaɪˈzeɪʃən) NOUN the act of organizing or the state of being organized again.

reorganize *or* **reorganise** (riːˈɔːgəˌnaɪz) VERB (*tr*) to change the way (something) is organized.

reorient (riːˈɔːrɪənt) VERB (*tr*) to adjust or align (something) in a new or different way.
▸ˌ**reorienˈtation** NOUN

rep[1] *or* **repp** (rɛp) NOUN a silk, wool, rayon, or cotton fabric with a transversely corded surface.
▷HISTORY C19: from French *reps*, perhaps from English *ribs*; see RIB[1]
▸**repped** ADJECTIVE

rep[2] (rɛp) NOUN *Theatre* short for **repertory (company).**

rep[3] (rɛp) NOUN short for **representative** (senses 2, 5).

rep[4] (rɛp) NOUN *Informal* short for **reputation.**

Rep. ABBREVIATION FOR: [1] *US* Representative. [2] *US* Republican. [3] Republic.

repack (riːˈpæk) VERB (*tr*) to place or arrange (articles) in (a container) again or in a different way.

repackage (riːˈpækɪdʒ) VERB (*tr*) to wrap or put (something) in a package again.

repaint (riːˈpeɪnt) VERB to apply a new or fresh coat of paint.

repair[1] (rɪˈpɛə) VERB (*tr*) [1] to restore (something damaged or broken) to good condition or working order. [2] to heal (a breach or division) in (something): *to repair a broken marriage.* [3] to make good or make amends for (a mistake, injury, etc.). ◆ NOUN [4] the act, task, or process of repairing. [5] a part that has been repaired. [6] state or condition: *in good repair.*
▷HISTORY C14: from Old French *reparer*, from Latin *reparāre*, from RE- + *parāre* to make ready
▸**reˈpairable** ADJECTIVE ▸**reˈpairer** NOUN

repair[2] (rɪˈpɛə) VERB (*intr*) [1] (usually foll by *to*) to go (to a place): *to repair to the country.* [2] (usually foll by *to*) to have recourse (to) for help, etc.: *to repair to one's lawyer.* [3] (usually foll by *from*) *Archaic* to come back; return. ◆ NOUN *Archaic* [4] the act of going or returning. [5] a haunt or resort.
▷HISTORY C14: from Old French *repairier*, from Late Latin *repatriāre* to return to one's native land, from Latin RE- + *patria* fatherland; compare REPATRIATE

repairman (rɪˈpɛəˌmæn) NOUN, *plural* **-men.** a man whose job it is to repair machines, appliances, etc.

repand (rɪˈpænd) ADJECTIVE *Botany* having a wavy margin: *a repand leaf.*
▷HISTORY C18: from Latin *repandus* bent backwards, from RE- + *pandus* curved
▸**reˈpandly** ADVERB

reparable (ˈrɛpərəbəl, ˈrɛprə-) ADJECTIVE able to be repaired, recovered, or remedied: *a reparable loss.*
▷HISTORY C16: from Latin *reparābilis*, from *reparāre* to REPAIR[1]
▸ˌ**reparaˈbility** NOUN ▸ˈ**reparably** ADVERB

reparation (ˌrɛpəˈreɪʃən) NOUN [1] the act or process of making amends: *an injury admitting of no reparation.* [2] (*usually plural*) compensation exacted as an indemnity from a defeated nation by the victors: esp the compensation demanded of Germany by the Treaty of Versailles after World War I. [3] the act or process of repairing or state of having been repaired.
▷HISTORY C14 *reparacioun*, ultimately from Latin *reparāre* to REPAIR[1]
▸**reparative** (rɪˈpærətɪv) *or* **reˈparatory** ADJECTIVE

repartee (ˌrɛpɑːˈtiː) NOUN [1] a sharp, witty, or aphoristic remark made as a reply. [2] terse rapid conversation consisting of such remarks. [3] skill in making sharp witty replies or conversation.
▷HISTORY C17: from French *repartie*, from *repartir* to retort, from RE- + *partir* to go away

repartition (ˌriːpɑːˈtɪʃən) NOUN [1] distribution or allotment. [2] the act or process of distributing afresh. ◆ VERB [3] (*tr*) to divide up again; reapportion or reallocate.

repast (rɪˈpɑːst) NOUN [1] a meal or the food provided at a meal: *a light repast.* [2] *Archaic* **a** food in general; nourishment. **b** the act of taking food or refreshment. ◆ VERB [3] (*intr*) *Archaic* to feed (on).
▷HISTORY C14: from Old French, from *repaistre* to feed, from Late Latin *repāscere* to nourish again, from Latin RE- + *pāscere* to feed, pasture (of animals)

repatriate VERB (*tr*) (riːˈpætrɪˌeɪt) [1] to send back (a refugee, prisoner of war, etc.) to the country of his birth or citizenship. [2] to send back (a sum of money previously invested abroad) to its country of origin. ◆ NOUN (riːˈpætrɪɪt) [3] a person who has been repatriated.
▷HISTORY C17: from Late Latin *repatriāre* from Latin RE- + *patria* fatherland; compare REPAIR[2]
▸**reˌpatriˈation** NOUN

repay (rɪˈpeɪ) VERB **-pays, -paying, -paid.** [1] to pay back (money) to (a person); refund or reimburse. [2] to make a return for (something) by way of compensation: *to repay kindness.*
▸**reˈpayable** ADJECTIVE ▸**reˈpayment** NOUN

repeal (rɪˈpiːl) VERB (*tr*) [1] to annul or rescind officially (something previously ordered); revoke: *these laws were repealed.* [2] *Obsolete* to call back (a person) from exile. ◆ NOUN [3] an instance or the process of repealing; annulment.
▷HISTORY C14: from Old French *repeler*, from RE- + *apeler* to call, APPEAL
▸**reˈpealable** ADJECTIVE ▸**reˈpealer** NOUN

Repeal (rɪˈpiːl) NOUN (esp in the 19th century) the proposed dissolution of the Union between Great Britain and Ireland.

repeat (rɪˈpiːt) VERB [1] (when *tr, may take a clause as object*) to say or write (something) again, either once or several times; restate or reiterate. [2] to do or experience (something) again once or several times. [3] (*intr*) to occur more than once: *the last figure repeats.* [4] (*tr; may take a clause as object*) to reproduce (the words, sounds, etc.) uttered by someone else; echo. [5] (*tr*) to utter (a poem, speech, etc.) from memory; recite. [6] (*intr*) **a** (of food) to be tasted again after ingestion as the result of belching or slight regurgitation. **b** to belch. [7] (*tr; may take a clause as object*) to tell to another person (the words, esp secrets, imparted to one by someone else). [8] (*intr*) (of a clock) to strike the hour or quarter-hour just past, when a spring is pressed. [9] (*intr*) *US* to vote (illegally) more than once in a single election. [10] **repeat oneself.** to say or do the same thing more than once, esp so as to be tedious. ◆ NOUN [11] **a** the act or an instance of repeating. **b** (*as modifier*): *a repeat performance.* [12] a word, action, etc., that is repeated. [13] an order made out for goods, provisions, etc., that duplicates a previous order. [14] a duplicate copy of something; reproduction. [15] *Radio, television* a further broadcast of a programme, film, etc., which has been broadcast before. [16] *Music* a passage that is an exact restatement of the passage preceding it.
▷HISTORY C14: from Old French *repeter*, from Latin *repetere* to seek again, from RE- + *petere* to seek
▸**reˌpeataˈbility** NOUN ▸**reˈpeatable** ADJECTIVE

Language note Since *again* is part of the meaning of *repeat*, one should not say something is *repeated again*.

repeated (rɪˈpiːtɪd) ADJECTIVE done, made, or said again and again; continual or incessant.
▸**reˈpeatedly** ADVERB

repeater (rɪˈpiːtə) NOUN [1] a person or thing that repeats. [2] Also called: **repeating firearm.** a firearm capable of discharging several shots without reloading. [3] a timepiece having a mechanism enabling it to strike the hour or quarter-hour just past, when a spring is pressed. [4] *Electrical engineering* a device that amplifies or augments incoming electrical signals and retransmits them, thus compensating for transmission losses. [5] Also called: **substitute.** *Nautical* one of three signal flags hoisted with others to indicate that one of the top three is to be repeated.

repeating decimal NOUN another name for **recurring decimal.**

repechage (ˌrɛpɪˈʃɑːʒ) NOUN a heat of a competition, esp in rowing or fencing, in which eliminated contestants have another chance to qualify for the next round or the final.
▷HISTORY C19: from French *repêchage* literally: fishing out again, from RE- + *pêcher* to fish + -AGE

repel (rɪˈpɛl) VERB **-pels, -pelling, -pelled.** (*mainly tr*) [1] to force or drive back (something or somebody, esp an attacker). [2] (*also intr*) to produce a feeling of aversion or distaste in (someone or something); be disgusting (to). [3] to push aside; dismiss: *he repelled the suggestion as wrong and impossible.* [4] to be effective in keeping away, controlling, or resisting: *an aerosol spray that repels flies.* [5] to have no affinity for; fail to mix with or absorb: *water and oil repel each other.* [6] to disdain to accept (something); turn away from or spurn: *she repelled his advances.* [7] (*also intr*) to exert an opposing force on (something): *an electric charge repels another charge of the same sign.*
▷HISTORY C15: from Latin *repellere*, from RE- + *pellere* to push, drive
▸**reˈpeller** NOUN

Language note See at **repulse.**

repellent (rɪˈpɛlənt) ADJECTIVE [1] giving rise to disgust or aversion; distasteful or repulsive. [2] driving or forcing away or back; repelling. ◆ NOUN *also* **repellant.** [3] something, esp a chemical substance, that repels: *insect repellent.* [4] a substance with which fabrics are treated to increase their resistance to water.
▸**reˈpellence** *or* **reˈpellency** NOUN ▸**reˈpellently** ADVERB

repent[1] (rɪˈpɛnt) VERB to feel remorse (for); be contrite (about); show penitence (for): *he repents of his extravagance; he repented his words.*
▷HISTORY C13: from Old French *repentir* from RE- + *pentir* to be contrite, from Latin *paenitēre* to repent
▸**reˈpenter** NOUN

repent[2] (ˈriːpənt) ADJECTIVE *Botany* lying or creeping along the ground; reptant: *repent stems.*
▷HISTORY C17: from Latin *rēpere* to creep

repentance (rɪˈpɛntəns) NOUN [1] remorse or contrition for one's past actions or sins. [2] an act or the process of being repentant; penitence.

repentant (rɪˈpɛntənt) ADJECTIVE [1] reproaching oneself for one's past actions or sins; contrite. [2] characterized by or proceeding from a sense of contrition: *a repentant heart; his repentant words.*
▸**reˈpentantly** ADVERB

repercussion (ˌriːpəˈkʌʃən) NOUN [1] (*often plural*)

a result or consequence, esp one that is somewhat removed from the action or event which precipitated it: *the repercussions of the war are still keenly felt.* [2] a recoil after impact; a rebound. [3] a reflection, esp of sound; echo or reverberation. [4] *Music* the reappearance of a fugal subject and answer after an episode.
▷**HISTORY** C16: from Latin *repercussiō*, from *repercutere* to strike back; see PERCUSSION
▸**ˌreperˈcussive** ADJECTIVE

repertoire (ˈrɛpəˌtwɑː) NOUN [1] all the plays, songs, operas, or other works collectively that a company, actor, singer, dancer, etc., has prepared and is competent to perform. [2] the entire stock of things available in a field or of a kind: *the comedian's repertoire of jokes was becoming stale.* [3] **in repertoire.** denoting the performance of two or more plays, ballets, etc., by the same company in the same venue on different evenings over a period of time: *"Nutcracker" returns to Covent Garden over Christmas in repertoire with "Giselle".*
▷**HISTORY** C19: from French, from Late Latin *repertōrium* inventory; see REPERTORY

repertory (ˈrɛpətərɪ, -trɪ) NOUN, *plural* **-ries.** [1] the entire stock of things available in a field or of a kind; repertoire. [2] a building or place where a stock of things is kept; repository. [3] short for **repertory company.**
▷**HISTORY** C16: from Late Latin *repertōrium* storehouse, from Latin *reperīre* to obtain, from RE- + *parere* to bring forth
▸**ˌreperˈtorial** ADJECTIVE

repertory company NOUN a theatrical company that performs plays from a repertoire, esp at its own theatre. US name: **stock company.**

repertory society NOUN *NZ* a group that supports amateur performances of plays by its members.

repetend (ˈrɛpɪˌtɛnd, ˌrɛpɪˈtɛnd) NOUN [1] *Maths* the digit or series of digits in a recurring decimal that repeats itself. [2] anything repeated.
▷**HISTORY** C18: from Latin *repetendum* what is to be repeated, from *repetere* to REPEAT

répétiteur *French* (repetitœr) NOUN a member of an opera company who accompanies rehearsals on the piano and coaches the singers.
▸***répétiteuse*** (repetitøz) FEMININE NOUN

repetition (ˌrɛpɪˈtɪʃən) NOUN [1] the act or an instance of repeating; reiteration. [2] a thing, word, action, etc., that is repeated. [3] a replica or copy. [4] *Civil and Scots law* the recovery or repayment of money paid or received by mistake, as when the same bill has been paid twice.

repetitious (ˌrɛpɪˈtɪʃəs) ADJECTIVE characterized by unnecessary repetition.
▸**ˌrepeˈtitiously** ADVERB ▸**ˌrepeˈtitiousness** NOUN

repetitive (rɪˈpɛtɪtɪv) ADJECTIVE characterized by or given to unnecessary repetition; boring: *dull, repetitive work.*
▸**reˈpetitively** ADVERB ▸**reˈpetitiveness** NOUN

repetitive strain *or* **stress injury** NOUN a condition, characterized by arm or wrist pains, that can affect musicians, computer operators, etc., who habitually perform awkward hand movements. Abbreviation: **RSI.**

rephrase (riːˈfreɪz) VERB (*tr*) to phrase again, esp so as to express more clearly.

repine (rɪˈpaɪn) VERB (*intr*) to be fretful or low-spirited through discontent.
▷**HISTORY** C16: from RE- + PINE²

repique (rɪˈpiːk) *Piquet* ◆ NOUN [1] a score of 30 points made from the cards held by a player before play begins. ◆ VERB [2] to score a repique against (someone).
▷**HISTORY** from French *repiq*

replace (rɪˈpleɪs) VERB (*tr*) [1] to take the place of; supersede: *the manual worker is being replaced by the machine.* [2] to substitute a person or thing for (another which has ceased to fulfil its function); put in place of: *to replace an old pair of shoes.* [3] to put back or return; restore to its rightful place.
▸**reˈplaceable** ADJECTIVE ▸**reˌplaceaˈbility** NOUN ▸**reˈplacer** NOUN

replacement (rɪˈpleɪsmənt) NOUN [1] the act or process of replacing. [2] a person or thing that replaces another. [3] *Geology* the growth of a mineral within another of different chemical composition by gradual simultaneous deposition and removal. [4] a process of fossilization by gradual substitution of mineral matter for the original organic matter. Also called **petrification.**

replant (riːˈplɑːnt) VERB (*tr*) [1] to plant again: *she replanted the bulbs that the dog had dug up.* [2] to reattach (a severed limb or part) by surgery.

replantation (ˌriːplænˈteɪʃən) NOUN the reattachment of (severed limbs or parts) by surgery.

replay NOUN (ˈriːˌpleɪ) [1] Also called: **action replay.** *Television* a showing again of a sequence of action, esp of part of a sporting contest immediately after it happens either in slow motion (a **slow-motion replay**) or at normal speed. [2] a rematch. ◆ VERB (riːˈpleɪ) [3] to play again (a record, television sequence, sporting contest, etc.).

replenish (rɪˈplɛnɪʃ) VERB (*tr*) [1] to make full or complete again by supplying what has been used up or is lacking. [2] to put fresh fuel on (a fire).
▷**HISTORY** C14: from Old French *replenir*, from RE- + *plenir* to fill, from Latin *plēnus* full
▸**reˈplenisher** NOUN ▸**reˈplenishment** NOUN

replete (rɪˈpliːt) ADJECTIVE (*usually postpositive*) [1] (often foll by *with*) copiously supplied (with); abounding (in). [2] having one's appetite completely or excessively satisfied by food and drink; stuffed; gorged; satiated.
▷**HISTORY** C14: from Latin *replētus*, from *replēre* to refill, from RE- + *plēre* to fill
▸**reˈpletely** ADVERB ▸**reˈpleteness** NOUN

repletion (rɪˈpliːʃən) NOUN [1] the state or condition of being replete; fullness, esp excessive fullness due to overeating. [2] the satisfaction of a need or desire.

replevin (rɪˈplɛvɪn) *Law* ◆ NOUN [1] the recovery of goods unlawfully taken, made subject to establishing the validity of the recovery in a legal action and returning the goods if the decision is adverse. [2] (formerly) a writ of replevin. ◆ VERB [3] another word for **replevy.**
▷**HISTORY** C15: from Anglo-French, from Old French *replevir* to give security for, from RE- + *plevir* to PLEDGE

replevy (rɪˈplɛvɪ) *Law* ◆ VERB **-plevies, -plevying, -plevied.** (*tr*) [1] to recover possession of (goods) by replevin. ◆ NOUN, *plural* **-plevies.** [2] another word for **replevin.**
▷**HISTORY** C15: from Old French *replevir*; see REPLEVIN
▸**reˈpleviable** *or* **reˈplevisable** ADJECTIVE

replica (ˈrɛplɪkə) NOUN an exact copy or reproduction, esp on a smaller scale.
▷**HISTORY** C19: from Italian, literally: a reply, from *replicare* to repeat, from Latin: to bend back, repeat

replicate VERB (ˈrɛplɪˌkeɪt) (*mainly tr*) [1] (*also intr*) to make or be a copy of; reproduce. [2] to fold (something) over on itself; bend back. [3] to reply to. ◆ ADJECTIVE (ˈrɛplɪkɪt) [4] folded back on itself: *a replicate leaf.*
▷**HISTORY** C19: from Latin *replicātus* bent back; see REPLICA
▸**ˈreplicative** ADJECTIVE

replication (ˌrɛplɪˈkeɪʃən) NOUN [1] a reply or response. [2] *Law* (formerly) the plaintiff's reply to a defendant's answer or plea. [3] *Biology* the production of exact copies of complex molecules, such as DNA molecules, that occurs during growth of living organisms. [4] repetition of a procedure, such as a scientific experiment, in order to reduce errors. [5] a less common word for **replica.**
▷**HISTORY** C14: via Old French from Latin *replicātiō* a folding back, from *replicāre* to unroll; see REPLY

replicon (ˈrɛplɪˌkɒn) NOUN *Genetics* a region of a DNA molecule that is replicated from a single origin.
▷**HISTORY** C20: from REPLIC(ATION) + -ON

reply (rɪˈplaɪ) VERB **-plies, -plying, -plied.** (*mainly intr*) [1] to make answer (to) in words or writing or by an action; respond: *he replied with an unexpected move.* [2] (*tr; takes a clause as object*) to say (something) in answer: *he replied that he didn't want to come.* [3] *Law* to answer a defendant's plea. [4] to return (a sound); echo. ◆ NOUN, *plural* **-plies.** [5] an answer made in words or writing or through an action; response. [6] the answer made by a plaintiff or petitioner to a defendant's case.
▷**HISTORY** C14: from Old French *replier* to fold again, reply, from Latin *replicāre* to fold back, from RE- + *plicāre* to fold
▸**reˈplier** NOUN

repo (ˈriːpəʊ) NOUN *Informal* short for: [1] repurchase agreement. [2] **a** repossession of property. **b** (*as modifier*): *a repo car.*

repoint (ˌriːˈpɔɪnt) VERB (*tr*) to repair the joints of (brickwork, masonry, etc.) with mortar or cement.

repone (rɪˈpəʊn) VERB (*tr*) *Scots law* to restore (someone) to his former status, office, etc.; rehabilitate.
▷**HISTORY** C16: from Latin *repōnere* to put back, replace

repopulate (riːˈpɒpjʊˌleɪt) VERB (*tr*) to provide a new population for (an area in which the population has declined).

report (rɪˈpɔːt) NOUN [1] an account prepared for the benefit of others, esp one that provides information obtained through investigation and published in a newspaper or broadcast. [2] a statement made widely known; rumour: *according to report, he is not dead.* [3] an account of the deliberations of a committee, body, etc.: *a report of parliamentary proceedings.* [4] *Brit* a statement on the progress, academic achievement, etc., of each child in a school, written by teachers and sent to the parents or guardian annually or each term. [5] a written account of a case decided at law, giving the main points of the argument on each side, the court's findings, and the decision reached. [6] comment on a person's character or actions; reputation: *he is of good report here.* [7] a sharp loud noise, esp one made by a gun. ◆ VERB (when *tr, may take a clause as object;* when *intr*, often foll by *on*) [8] to give an account (of); describe. [9] to give an account of the results of an investigation (into): *to report on housing conditions.* [10] (of a committee, legislative body, etc.) to make a formal report on (a bill). [11] (*tr*) to complain about (a person), esp to a superior: *I'll report you to the teacher.* [12] (*tr*) to reveal information about (a fugitive, escaped prisoner, etc.) esp concerning his whereabouts. [13] (*intr*) to present oneself or be present at an appointed place or for a specific purpose: *report to the manager's office.* [14] (*intr*) to say or show that one is (in a certain state): *to report fit.* [15] (*intr*; foll by *to*) to be responsible to and under the authority of: *the plant manager reports to the production controller.* [16] (*intr*) to act as a reporter for a newspaper or for radio or television. [17] *Law* to take down in writing details of (the proceedings of a court of law) as a record or for publication.
▷**HISTORY** C14: from Old French, from *reporter* to carry back, from Latin *reportāre*, from RE- + *portāre* to carry
▸**reˈportable** ADJECTIVE

reportage (rɪˈpɔːtɪdʒ, ˌrɛpɔːˈtɑːʒ) NOUN [1] the act or process of reporting news or other events of general interest. [2] a journalist's style of reporting. [3] a technique of documentary film or photo journalism that tells a story entirely through pictures.

reported clause NOUN *Grammar* a bound clause that reports what someone has said or thought, bound to a main clause that contains a verb of saying or thinking.

reportedly (rɪˈpɔːtɪdlɪ) ADVERB according to rumour or report: *he is reportedly living in Australia.*

reported speech NOUN another term for **indirect speech.**

reporter (rɪˈpɔːtə) NOUN [1] a person who reports, esp one employed to gather news for a newspaper, news agency, or broadcasting organization. [2] a person, esp a barrister, authorized to write official accounts of judicial proceedings. [3] a person authorized to report the proceedings of a legislature. [4] (in Scotland) *Social welfare* an official who arranges and conducts children's panel hearings and who may investigate cases and decide on the action to be taken.

reportorial (ˌrɛpɔːˈtɔːrɪəl) ADJECTIVE *Chiefly US* of or relating to a newspaper reporter.
▷**HISTORY** C20: from REPORTER, influenced by EDITORIAL
▸**reporˈtorially** ADVERB

report stage NOUN the stage preceding the third reading in the passage of a bill through Parliament, at which the bill, as amended in committee, is reported back to the chamber considering it.

repose¹ (rɪˈpəʊz) NOUN [1] a state of quiet restfulness; peace or tranquillity. [2] dignified

calmness of manner; composure. ◆ VERB [3] to place (oneself or one's body) in a state of quiet relaxation; lie or lay down at rest. [4] *(intr)* to lie when dead, as in the grave. [5] *(intr; foll by on, in, etc.) Formal* to take support (from) or be based (on): *your plan reposes on a fallacy.*
▷HISTORY C15: from Old French *reposer*, from Late Latin *repausāre* from RE- + *pausāre* to stop; see PAUSE
▸**re'posal** NOUN ▸**re'poser** NOUN ▸**re'poseful** ADJECTIVE ▸**re'posefully** ADVERB ▸**re'posefulness** NOUN

repose² (rɪ'pəʊz) VERB *(tr)* [1] to put (trust or confidence) in a person or thing. [2] to place or put (an object) somewhere.
▷HISTORY C15: from Latin *repōnere* to store up, from RE- + *pōnere* to put
▸**re'posal** NOUN

reposit (rɪ'pɒzɪt) VERB *(tr)* to put away, deposit, or store up.
▷HISTORY C17: from Latin *repositus* replaced, from *repōnere*; see REPOSE², POSIT

reposition (ˌriːpə'zɪʃən) NOUN [1] the act or process of depositing or storing. [2] *Surgery* the return of a broken or displaced organ, or part to its normal site. [3] *Archaic* the reinstatement of a person in a post or office. ◆ VERB *(tr)* [4] to place in a new position. [5] to target (a product or brand) at a new market by changing its image.

repository (rɪ'pɒzɪtərɪ, -trɪ) NOUN, *plural* **-ries.** [1] a place or container in which things can be stored for safety. [2] a place where things are kept for exhibition; museum. [3] a place where commodities are kept before being sold; warehouse. [4] a place of burial; sepulchre. [5] a receptacle containing the relics of the dead. [6] a person to whom a secret is entrusted; confidant.
▷HISTORY C15: from Latin *repositōrium*, from *repōnere* to place

repossess (ˌriːpə'zɛs) VERB *(tr)* [1] to take back possession of (property), esp for nonpayment of money due under a hire-purchase agreement. [2] to restore ownership of (something) to someone.
▸**repossession** (ˌriːpə'zɛʃən) NOUN ▸ˌ**repos'sessor** NOUN

repot (riː'pɒt) VERB **-pots, -potting, -potted.** *(tr)* to put (a house plant) into a new usually larger pot.

repoussé (rə'puːseɪ) ADJECTIVE [1] raised in relief, as a design on a thin piece of metal hammered through from the underside. [2] decorated with such designs. ◆ NOUN [3] a design or surface made in this way. [4] the technique of hammering designs in this way.
▷HISTORY C19: from French, from *repousser* to push back, from RE- + *pousser* to PUSH

repp (rɛp) NOUN a variant spelling of **rep¹**.

reprehend (ˌrɛprɪ'hɛnd) VERB *(tr)* to find fault with; criticize.
▷HISTORY C14: from Latin *reprehendere* to hold fast, rebuke, from RE- + *prendere* to grasp
▸ˌ**repre'hendable** ADJECTIVE ▸ˌ**repre'hender** NOUN

reprehensible (ˌrɛprɪ'hɛnsəbᵊl) ADJECTIVE open to criticism or rebuke; blameworthy.
▷HISTORY C14: from Late Latin *reprehensibilis*, from Latin *reprehendere* to hold back, reprove; see REPREHEND
▸ˌ**repreˌhensi'bility** *or* ˌ**repre'hensibleness** NOUN
▸ˌ**repre'hensibly** ADVERB

reprehension (ˌrɛprɪ'hɛnʃən) NOUN the act or an instance of reprehending; reproof or rebuke.
▸ˌ**repre'hensive** *or (rarely)* ˌ**repre'hensory** ADJECTIVE
▸ˌ**repre'hensively** ADVERB

represent (ˌrɛprɪ'zɛnt) VERB *(tr)* [1] to stand as an equivalent of; correspond to: *our tent represents home to us when we go camping.* [2] to act as a substitute or proxy (for). [3] to act as or be the authorized delegate or agent for (a person, country, etc.): *an MP represents his constituency.* [4] to serve or use as a means of expressing: *letters represent the sounds of speech.* [5] to exhibit the characteristics of; exemplify; typify: *romanticism in music is represented by Beethoven.* [6] to present an image of through the medium of a picture or sculpture; portray. [7] to bring clearly before the mind. [8] to set forth in words; state or explain. [9] to describe as having a specified character or quality; make out to be: *he represented her as a saint.* [10] to act out the part of on stage; portray. [11] to perform or produce (a play); stage.
▷HISTORY C14: from Latin *repraesentāre* to exhibit, from RE- + *praesentāre* to PRESENT²
▸ˌ**repre'sentable** ADJECTIVE ▸ˌ**repreˌsenta'bility** NOUN

re-present (ˌriːprɪ'zɛnt) VERB *(tr)* to present again.
▸**re-presentation** (ˌriːprɛzən'teɪʃən) NOUN

representation (ˌrɛprɪzɛn'teɪʃən) NOUN [1] the act or an instance of representing or the state of being represented. [2] anything that represents, such as a verbal or pictorial portrait. [3] anything that is represented, such as an image brought clearly to mind. [4] the principle by which delegates act for a constituency. [5] a body of representatives. [6] *Contract law* a statement of fact made by one party to induce another to enter into a contract. [7] an instance of acting for another, on his authority, in a particular capacity, such as executor or administrator. [8] a dramatic production or performance. [9] *(often plural)* a statement of facts, true or alleged, esp one set forth by way of remonstrance or expostulation. [10] *Linguistics* an analysis of a word, sentence, etc., into its constituents: *phonetic representation.*

representational (ˌrɛprɪzɛn'teɪʃənᵊl) ADJECTIVE [1] *Fine arts* depicting or attempting to depict objects, scenes, figures, etc., directly as seen; naturalistic. [2] of or relating to representation.

representationalism (ˌrɛprɪzɛn'teɪʃənəˌlɪzəm) *or* **representationism** NOUN [1] *Philosophy* the doctrine that in perceptions of objects what is before the mind is not the object but a representation of it. Compare **presentationism, naive realism.** See also **barrier of ideas.** [2] *Fine arts* the practice or advocacy of attempting to depict objects, scenes, figures, etc., directly as seen.
▸ˌ**representˌtational'istic** ADJECTIVE ▸ˌ**represen'tationist** NOUN, ADJECTIVE

representative (ˌrɛprɪ'zɛntətɪv) NOUN [1] a person or thing that represents another or others. [2] a person who represents and tries to sell the products or services of a firm, esp a travelling salesman. Often shortened to: **rep.** [3] a typical example. [4] a person representing a constituency in a deliberative, legislative, or executive body, esp *(cap)* a member of the **House of Representatives** (the lower house of Congress). [5] *NZ* a rugby player, football player, etc., chosen to represent a province in interprovincial sports. ◆ ADJECTIVE [6] serving to represent; symbolic. [7] **a** exemplifying a class or kind; typical: *a representative example of the species.* **b** containing or including examples of all the interests, types, etc., in a group: *a representative collection.* [8] acting as deputy or proxy for another or others. [9] acting for or representing a constituency or the whole people in the process of government: *a representative council.* [10] of, characterized by, or relating to the political principle of representation of the people: *representative government.* [11] of or relating to a mental picture or representation.
▸ˌ**repre'sentatively** ADVERB ▸ˌ**repre'sentativeness** NOUN

repress (rɪ'prɛs) VERB *(tr)* [1] to keep (feelings, etc.) under control; suppress or restrain: *to repress a desire.* [2] to put into a state of subjugation: *to repress a people.* [3] *Psychoanal* to banish (thoughts and impulses that conflict with conventional standards of conduct) from one's conscious mind.
▷HISTORY C14: from Latin *reprimere* to press back, from RE- + *premere* to PRESS¹
▸**re'presser** NOUN ▸**re'pressible** ADJECTIVE

repressed (rɪ'prɛst) ADJECTIVE (of a person) repressing feelings, instincts, desires, etc.

repression NOUN [1] the act or process of repressing or the condition of being repressed. [2] *Psychoanal* the subconscious rejection of thoughts and impulses that conflict with conventional standards of conduct. Compare **suppression** (sense 2).

repressive (rɪ'prɛsɪv) ADJECTIVE [1] acting to control, suppress, or restrain. [2] subjecting people, a society, etc. to a state of subjugation.
▸**re'pressively** ADVERB ▸**re'pressiveness** NOUN

repressor (rɪ'prɛsə) NOUN *Biochem* a protein synthesized under the control of a repressor gene, which has the capacity to bind to the operator gene and thereby shut off the expression of the structural genes of an operon.

reprieve (rɪ'priːv) VERB *(tr)* [1] to postpone or remit the punishment of (a person, esp one condemned to death). [2] to give temporary relief to (a person or thing), esp from otherwise irrevocable harm: *the government has reprieved the company with a huge loan.* ◆ NOUN [3] a postponement or remission of punishment, esp of a person condemned to death. [4] a warrant granting a postponement. [5] a temporary relief from pain or harm; respite. [6] the act of reprieving or the state of being reprieved.
▷HISTORY C16: from Old French *repris* (something) taken back, from *reprendre* to take back, from Latin *reprehendere*; perhaps also influenced by obsolete English *repreve* to reprove
▸**re'prievable** ADJECTIVE ▸**re'priever** NOUN

reprimand ('rɛprɪˌmɑːnd) NOUN [1] a reproof or formal admonition; rebuke. ◆ VERB [2] *(tr)* to admonish or rebuke, esp formally; reprove.
▷HISTORY C17: from French *réprimande*, from Latin *reprimenda* (things) to be repressed; see REPRESS

reprint NOUN ('riːˌprɪnt) [1] a reproduction in print of any matter already published; offprint. [2] a reissue of a printed work using the same type, plates, etc., as the original. ◆ VERB (riː'prɪnt) [3] *(tr)* to print again.
▸**re'printer** NOUN

reprisal (rɪ'praɪzᵊl) NOUN [1] *(often plural)* retaliatory action against an enemy in wartime, such as the execution of prisoners of war, destruction of property, etc. [2] the act or an instance of retaliation in any form. [3] (formerly) the forcible seizure of the property or subjects of one nation by another.
▷HISTORY C15: from Old French *reprisaille*, from Old Italian *ripresaglia*, from *riprendere* to recapture, from Latin *reprehendere* to hold fast; see REPREHEND

reprise (rɪ'priːz) *Music* ◆ NOUN [1] the repeating of an earlier theme. ◆ VERB [2] to repeat (an earlier theme).
▷HISTORY C14: from Old French, from *reprendre* to take back, from Latin *reprehendere*; see REPREHEND

repro ('riːprəʊ) NOUN, *plural* **-pros.** [1] short for **reproduction** (sense 2): *repro furniture.* [2] short for **reproduction proof.**

reproach (rɪ'prəʊtʃ) VERB *(tr)* [1] to impute blame to (a person) for an action or fault; rebuke. [2] *Archaic* to bring disgrace or shame upon. ◆ NOUN [3] the act of reproaching. [4] rebuke or censure; reproof: *words of reproach.* [5] disgrace or shame: *to bring reproach upon one's family.* [6] something that causes or merits blame, rebuke, or disgrace. [7] **above** *or* **beyond reproach.** perfect; beyond criticism.
▷HISTORY C15: from Old French *reprochier*, from Latin RE- + *prope* near
▸**re'proachable** ADJECTIVE ▸**re'proachableness** NOUN
▸**re'proachably** ADVERB ▸**re'proacher** NOUN

reproachful (rɪ'prəʊtʃfʊl) ADJECTIVE [1] full of or expressing reproach. [2] *Archaic* deserving of reproach; disgraceful.
▸**re'proachfully** ADVERB ▸**re'proachfulness** NOUN

reprobate ('rɛprəʊˌbeɪt) ADJECTIVE [1] morally unprincipled; depraved. [2] *Christianity* destined or condemned to eternal punishment in hell. ◆ NOUN [3] an unprincipled, depraved, or damned person. [4] a disreputable or roguish person: *the old reprobate.* ◆ VERB *(tr)* [5] to disapprove of; condemn. [6] (of God) to destine, consign, or condemn to eternal punishment in hell.
▷HISTORY C16: from Late Latin *reprobātus* held in disfavour, from Latin RE- + *probāre* to APPROVE¹
▸**reprobacy** ('rɛprəbəsɪ) NOUN ▸'**reproˌbater** NOUN

reprobation (ˌrɛprəʊ'beɪʃən) NOUN [1] disapproval, blame, or censure. [2] *Christianity* condemnation to eternal punishment in hell; rejection by God.
▸**reprobative** ('rɛprəbətɪv) *or* ˌ**repro'bationary** ADJECTIVE
▸'**reprobatively** ADVERB

reprocess (riː'prəʊsɛs) VERB *(tr)* [1] to treat or prepare (something) by a special method again. [2] to subject to a routine procedure again.

reprocessing (riː'prəʊsɛsɪŋ) ADJECTIVE of or relating to the treatment of materials in order to make them reusable: *reprocessing plant.*

reproduce (ˌriːprə'djuːs) VERB *(mainly tr)* [1] to make a copy, representation, or imitation of; duplicate. [2] *(also intr) Biology* to undergo or cause to undergo a process of reproduction. [3] to produce or exhibit again. [4] to bring back into existence again; re-create. [5] to bring before the mind again (a scene, event, etc.) through memory or imagination. [6] *(intr)* to come out (well, badly, etc.), when copied. [7] to replace (damaged parts or organs) by a process of natural growth; regenerate.

8 to cause (a sound or television recording) to be heard or seen.
▸ˌrepro'ducible ADJECTIVE ▸ˌrepro'ducibly ADVERB ▸ˌreproˌduci'bility NOUN

reproducer (ˌri:prə'dju:sə) NOUN 1 a person or thing that makes reproductions. 2 a complete sound reproduction system. 3 another name for **loudspeaker.**

reproduction (ˌri:prə'dʌkʃən) NOUN 1 *Biology* any of various processes, either sexual or asexual, by which an animal or plant produces one or more individuals similar to itself. 2 **a** an imitation or facsimile of a work of art, esp of a picture made by photoengraving. **b** (*as modifier*): *a reproduction portrait.* Sometimes shortened to: **repro.** 3 the quality of sound from an audio system: *this amplifier gives excellent reproduction.* 4 the act or process of reproducing. 5 the state of being reproduced. 6 a revival of an earlier production, as of a play.

reproduction proof NOUN *Printing* a proof of very good quality used for photographic reproduction to make a printing plate. Sometimes shortened to: **repro** *or* **repro proof.**

reproductive (ˌri:prə'dʌktɪv) ADJECTIVE of, relating to, characteristic of, or taking part in reproduction.
▸ˌrepro'ductively ADVERB ▸ˌrepro'ductiveness NOUN

reprography (rɪ'prɒgrəfɪ) NOUN the art or process of copying, reprinting, or reproducing printed material.
▸reprographic (ˌrɛprə'græfɪk) ADJECTIVE
▸ˌrepro'graphically ADVERB

reproof (rɪ'pru:f) NOUN an act or expression of rebuke or censure. Also called: **reproval** (rɪ'pru:vᵊl).
▷HISTORY C14 *reproffe*, from Old French *reprove*, from Late Latin *reprobāre* to disapprove of; see REPROBATE

re-proof (ri:'pru:f) VERB (*tr*) 1 to treat (a coat, jacket, etc.) so as to renew its texture, waterproof qualities, etc. 2 to provide a new proof of (a book, galley, etc.).

reprove (rɪ'pru:v) VERB (*tr*) to speak disapprovingly to (a person); rebuke or scold.
▷HISTORY C14: from Old French *reprover*, from Late Latin *reprobāre*, from Latin RE- + *probāre* to examine, APPROVE[1]
▸re'provable ADJECTIVE ▸re'prover NOUN ▸re'proving ADJECTIVE ▸re'provingly ADVERB

rept ABBREVIATION FOR: 1 receipt. 2 report.

reptant ('rɛptənt) ADJECTIVE *Biology* creeping, crawling, or lying along the ground. Also: **repent.**
▷HISTORY C17: from Latin *reptāre* to creep

reptile ('rɛptaɪl) NOUN 1 any of the cold-blooded vertebrates constituting the class *Reptilia*, characterized by lungs, an outer covering of horny scales or plates, and young produced in amniotic eggs. The class today includes the tortoises, turtles, snakes, lizards, and crocodiles; in Mesozoic times it was the dominant group, containing the dinosaurs and related forms. 2 a grovelling insignificant person: *you miserable little reptile!* ◆ ADJECTIVE 3 creeping, crawling, or squirming. 4 grovelling or insignificant; mean; contemptible.
▷HISTORY C14: from Late Latin *reptilis* creeping, from Latin *rēpere* to crawl

reptilian (rɛp'tɪlɪən) ADJECTIVE 1 of, relating to, resembling, or characteristic of reptiles. 2 mean or treacherous; contemptible: *reptilian behaviour.* ◆ NOUN 3 a less common name for **reptile.**

Repub. ABBREVIATION FOR: 1 Republic. 2 Republican.

republic (rɪ'pʌblɪk) NOUN 1 a form of government in which the people or their elected representatives possess the supreme power. 2 a political or national unit possessing such a form of government. 3 a constitutional form in which the head of state is an elected or nominated president. 4 any community or group that resembles a political republic in that its members or elements exhibit a general equality, shared interests, etc: *the republic of letters.*
▷HISTORY C17: from French *république*, from Latin *rēspublica* literally: the public thing, from *rēs* thing + *publica* PUBLIC

republican (rɪ'pʌblɪkən) ADJECTIVE 1 of, resembling, or relating to a republic. 2 supporting or advocating a republic. ◆ NOUN 3 a supporter or advocate of a republic.

Republican (rɪ'pʌblɪkən) ADJECTIVE 1 of, belonging to, or relating to a Republican Party. 2 of, belonging to, or relating to the Irish Republican Army. ◆ NOUN 3 a member or supporter of a Republican Party. 4 a member or supporter of the Irish Republican Army.

republicanism (rɪ'pʌblɪkəˌnɪzəm) NOUN 1 the principles or theory of republican government. 2 support for a republic. 3 (*often capital*) support for a Republican Party or for the Irish Republican Army.

republicanize *or* **republicanise** (rɪ'pʌblɪkəˌnaɪz) VERB (*tr*) to make republican.
▸reˌpublicani'zation *or* reˌpublicani'sation NOUN

Republican Party NOUN 1 the more conservative of the two major political parties in the US: established around 1854. Compare **Democratic Party.** 2 any of a number of political parties in other countries, usually so named to indicate their opposition to monarchy. 3 *US history* another name for the **Democratic-Republican Party.**

Republic of Ireland NOUN See **Ireland**[1] (sense 2).

repudiate (rɪ'pju:dɪˌeɪt) VERB (*tr*) 1 to reject the authority or validity of; refuse to accept or ratify: *Congress repudiated the treaty that the President had negotiated.* 2 to refuse to acknowledge or pay (a debt). 3 to cast off or disown (a son, lover, etc.).
▷HISTORY C16: from Latin *repudiāre* to put away, from *repudium* a separation, divorce, from RE- + *pudēre* to be ashamed
▸re'pudiable ADJECTIVE ▸reˌpudi'ation NOUN ▸re'pudiative ADJECTIVE ▸re'pudiˌator NOUN

repugn (rɪ'pju:n) VERB *Archaic* to oppose or conflict (with).
▷HISTORY C14: from Old French *repugner*, from Latin *repugnāre* to fight against, from RE- + *pugnāre* to fight

repugnant (rɪ'pʌgnənt) ADJECTIVE 1 repellent to the senses; causing aversion. 2 distasteful; offensive; disgusting. 3 contradictory; inconsistent or incompatible.
▷HISTORY C14: from Latin *repugnāns* resisting; see REPUGN
▸re'pugnance *or* (*now rarely*) re'pugnancy NOUN
▸re'pugnantly ADVERB

repulse (rɪ'pʌls) VERB (*tr*) 1 to drive back or ward off (an attacking force); repel; rebuff. 2 to reject with coldness or discourtesy: *she repulsed his advances.* 3 to produce a feeling of aversion or distaste. ◆ NOUN 4 the act or an instance of driving back or warding off; rebuff. 5 a cold discourteous rejection or refusal.
▷HISTORY C16: from Latin *repellere* to drive back, REPEL
▸re'pulser NOUN

> **Language note** Some people think that the use of *repulse* in sentences such as *he was repulsed by what he saw* is incorrect and that the correct word is *repel.*

repulsion (rɪ'pʌlʃən) NOUN 1 a feeling of disgust or aversion. 2 *Physics* a force tending to separate two objects, such as the force between two like electric charges or magnetic poles.

repulsive (rɪ'pʌlsɪv) ADJECTIVE 1 causing or occasioning repugnance; loathsome; disgusting or distasteful: *a repulsive sight.* 2 tending to repel, esp by coldness and discourtesy. 3 *Physics* concerned with, producing, or being a repulsion.
▸re'pulsively ADVERB ▸re'pulsiveness NOUN

repurchase (ri:'pɜ:tʃɪs) VERB (*tr*) 1 to buy back or buy again goods, securities, assets, etc. ◆ NOUN 2 an act or instance of repurchasing.

repurchase agreement NOUN an agreement in which a security or asset is sold and later repurchased at an agreed price to raise ready money. Sometimes shortened to: **repo.**

reputable ('rɛpjʊtəbᵊl) ADJECTIVE 1 having a good reputation; honoured, trustworthy, or respectable. 2 (of words) acceptable as good usage; standard.
▸ˌreputa'bility NOUN ▸'reputably ADVERB

reputation (ˌrɛpjʊ'teɪʃən) NOUN 1 the estimation in which a person or thing is generally held; opinion. 2 a high opinion generally held about a person or thing; esteem. 3 notoriety or fame, esp for some specified characteristic. 4 **have a reputation.** to be known or notorious, esp for promiscuity, excessive drinking, or the like.
▷HISTORY C14: from Latin *reputātiō* a reckoning, from *reputāre* to calculate, meditate; see REPUTE
▸ˌrepu'tationless ADJECTIVE

repute (rɪ'pju:t) VERB 1 (*tr; usually passive*) to consider (a person or thing) to be as specified: *he is reputed to be intelligent.* ◆ NOUN 2 public estimation; reputation: *a writer of little repute.*
▷HISTORY C15: from Old French *reputer*, from Latin *reputāre* to think over, from RE- + *putāre* to think

reputed (rɪ'pju:tɪd) ADJECTIVE (*prenominal*) generally reckoned or considered; supposed or alleged: *he is the reputed writer of a number of romantic poems.*

reputedly (rɪ'pju:tɪdlɪ) ADVERB according to general belief or supposition: *the reputedly excellent food.*

request (rɪ'kwɛst) VERB (*tr*) 1 to express a desire for, esp politely; ask for or demand: *to request a bottle of wine.* ◆ NOUN 2 **a** the act or an instance of requesting, esp in the form of a written statement; petition or solicitation: *a request for a song.* **b** (*as modifier*): *a request programme.* 3 **at the request of.** in accordance with the specific demand or wish of (someone). 4 **by request.** in accordance with someone's desire. 5 **in request.** in demand; popular: *he is in request in concert halls all over the world.* 6 **on request.** on the occasion of a demand or request: *application forms are available on request.*
▷HISTORY C14: from Old French *requeste*, from Vulgar Latin *requaerere* (unattested) to seek after; see REQUIRE, QUEST
▸re'quester NOUN

request stop NOUN a point on a route at which a bus will stop only if signalled to do so. US equivalent: **flag stop.**

Requiem ('rɛkwɪˌɛm) NOUN 1 *RC Church* a Mass celebrated for the dead. 2 a musical setting of this Mass. 3 any piece of music composed or performed as a memorial to a dead person or persons.
▷HISTORY C14: from Latin *requiēs* rest, from the opening of the introit, *Requiem aeternam dona eis* Rest eternal grant unto them

requiem shark NOUN any shark of the family *Carcharhinidae*, occurring mostly in tropical seas and characterized by a nictitating membrane and a heterocercal tail. The family includes the tiger shark and the soupfin.
▷HISTORY C17: French *requiem* probably assimilated from a native name

requiescat (ˌrɛkwɪ'ɛskæt) NOUN a prayer for the repose of the souls of the dead.
▷HISTORY Latin, from *requiescat in pace* may he rest in peace

require (rɪ'kwaɪə) VERB (*mainly tr; may take a clause as object or an infinitive*) 1 to have need of; depend upon; want. 2 to impose as a necessity; make necessary: *this work requires precision.* 3 (*also intr*) to make formal request (for); insist upon or demand, esp as an obligation. 4 to call upon or oblige (a person) authoritatively; order or command: *to require someone to account for his actions.*
▷HISTORY C14: from Old French *requerre*, from Vulgar Latin *requaerere* (unattested) to seek after, from Latin *requīrere* to seek to know, but also influenced by *quaerere* to seek
▸re'quirable ADJECTIVE ▸re'quirer NOUN

> **Language note** The use of *require to* as in *I require to see the manager* or *you require to complete a special form* is thought by many people to be incorrect: *I need to see the manager; you are required to complete a special form.*

requirement (rɪ'kwaɪəmənt) NOUN 1 something demanded or imposed as an obligation: *Latin is no longer a requirement for entry to university.* 2 a thing desired or needed. 3 the act or an instance of requiring.

requisite ('rɛkwɪzɪt) ADJECTIVE 1 absolutely essential; indispensable. ◆ NOUN 2 something indispensable; necessity.
▷HISTORY C15: from Latin *requīsītus* sought after, from *requīrere* to seek for, REQUIRE
▸'requisitely ADVERB ▸'requisiteness NOUN

requisition (ˌrɛkwɪˈzɪʃən) NOUN 1 a request or demand, esp an authoritative or formal one. 2 an official form on which such a demand is made. 3 the act of taking something over, esp temporarily for military or public use in time of emergency. 4 a necessary or essential condition; requisite. 5 a formal request by one government to another for the surrender of a fugitive from justice. ◆ VERB (*tr*) 6 to demand and take for use or service, esp by military or public authority. 7 (*may take an infinitive*) to require (someone) formally to do (something): *to requisition a soldier to drive a staff officer's car.*
▸ ˌ**requiˈsitionary** ADJECTIVE

requital (rɪˈkwaɪtᵊl) NOUN 1 the act or an instance of requiting. 2 a return or compensation for a good or bad action.

requite (rɪˈkwaɪt) VERB (*tr*) to make return to (a person for a kindness or injury); repay with a similar action.
▷ HISTORY C16: RE- + obsolete *quite* to discharge, repay; see QUIT
▸ **reˈquitable** ADJECTIVE ▸ **reˈquitement** NOUN ▸ **reˈquiter** NOUN

reradiation (ˌriːreɪdɪˈeɪʃən) NOUN radiation resulting from the previous absorption of primary radiation.

rerailing (riːˈreɪlɪŋ) NOUN the replacement of existing rails on a railway line.

reread (riːˈriːd) VERB **-reads, -reading, -read.** (*tr*) to read (something) again.

re-record VERB (*tr*) to make a recording of (something recorded before) again: *they had to re-record it in the studio.*

re-recording NOUN a new or different version of a piece of music recorded previously: *a re-recording of the song.*

reredorter (ˈrɪəˌdɔːtə) NOUN *History* a privy at the back of a monastic dormitory.

reredos (ˈrɪədɒs) NOUN 1 a screen or wall decoration at the back of an altar, in the form of a hanging, tapestry, painting, or piece of metalwork or sculpture. 2 another word for **fireback** (sense 1).
▷ HISTORY C14: from Old French *areredos*, from *arere* behind + *dos* back, from Latin *dorsum*

reremouse *or* **rearmouse** (ˈrɪəˌmaʊs) NOUN, *plural* **-mice.** an archaic or dialect word for **bat** (the animal).
▷ HISTORY Old English *hrēremūs*, probably from *hrēran* to move + *mūs* MOUSE

re-route VERB (*tr*) 1 to route or direct (traffic, a road, a river, etc.) in a different direction. 2 to change the direction of (a project, funds, etc.).

rerun VERB (riːˈrʌn) **-runs, -running, -ran.** (*tr*) 1 to broadcast or put on (a film, play, series, etc.) again. 2 to run (a race, etc.) again. ◆ NOUN (ˈriːˌrʌn) 3 a film, play, series, etc., that is broadcast or put on again; repeat. 4 a race that is run again. 5 *Computing* the repeat of a part of a computer program.

res *Latin* (reɪs) NOUN, *plural* ***res.*** a thing, matter, or object.

res. 1 residence. 2 resides. 3 resigned. 4 resolution.

res adjudicata (ˈreɪs əˌdʒuːdɪˈkɑːtə) NOUN another term for **res judicata.**

resale (ˈriːˌseɪl, riːˈseɪl) NOUN the selling again of something purchased.
▸ **reˈsalable** *or* **reˈsaleable** ADJECTIVE

resale price maintenance NOUN the practice by which a manufacturer establishes a fixed or minimum price for the resale of a brand product by retailers or other distributors. US equivalent: **fair trade.** Abbreviation: **rpm.**

reschedule (riːˈʃɛdjuːl; *also, esp US* -ˈskɛdʒuəl) VERB (*tr*) 1 to change the time, date, or schedule of. 2 to arrange a revised schedule for repayment of (a debt).

rescind (rɪˈsɪnd) VERB (*tr*) to annul or repeal.
▷ HISTORY C17: from Latin *rescindere* to cut off, from *re-* (intensive) + *scindere* to cut
▸ **reˈscindable** ADJECTIVE ▸ **reˈscinder** NOUN ▸ **reˈscindment** NOUN

rescissible (rɪˈsɪsəbᵊl) ADJECTIVE able to be rescinded.

rescission (rɪˈsɪʒən) NOUN 1 the act of rescinding. 2 *Law* the right to have a contract set aside if it has been entered into mistakenly, as a result of misrepresentation, undue influence, etc.

rescissory (rɪˈsɪsərɪ) ADJECTIVE having the power to rescind.

rescript (ˈriːˌskrɪpt) NOUN 1 (in ancient Rome) an ordinance taking the form of a reply by the emperor to a question on a point of law. 2 any official announcement or edict; a decree. 3 something rewritten. 4 the act or process of rewriting.
▷ HISTORY C16: from Latin *rēscriptum* a reply, from *rēscribere* to write back

rescue (ˈrɛskjuː) VERB **-cues, -cuing, -cued.** (*tr*) 1 to bring (someone or something) out of danger, attack, harm, etc.; deliver or save. 2 to free (a person) from legal custody by force. 3 *Law* to seize (goods or property) by force. ◆ NOUN 4 **a** the act or an instance of rescuing. **b** (*as modifier*): *a rescue party.* 5 the forcible removal of a person from legal custody. 6 *Law* the forcible seizure of goods or property.
▷ HISTORY C14: *rescowen*, from Old French *rescourre*, from RE- + *escourre* to pull away, from Latin *excutere* to shake off, from *quatere* to shake
▸ **ˈrescuable** ADJECTIVE ▸ **ˈrescuer** NOUN

reseal (riːˈsiːl) VERB (*tr*) to close (something) tightly or securely again.
▸ **reˈsealable** ADJECTIVE

research (rɪˈsɜːtʃ, ˈriːsɜːtʃ) NOUN 1 systematic investigation to establish facts or principles or to collect information on a subject. ◆ VERB 2 to carry out investigations into (a subject, problem, etc.).
▷ HISTORY C16: from Old French *recercher* to seek, search again, from RE- + *cercher* to SEARCH
▸ **reˈsearchable** ADJECTIVE ▸ **reˈsearcher** NOUN

research and development NOUN the part of a commercial company's activity concerned with applying the results of scientific research to develop new products and improve existing ones. Abbreviation: **R & D.**

reseat (riːˈsiːt) VERB (*tr*) 1 to show (a person) to a new seat. 2 to put a new seat on (a chair, etc.). 3 to provide new seats for (a hall, theatre, etc.). 4 to re-form the seating of (a valve).

reseau (ˈrɛzəʊ) NOUN, *plural* **-seaux** (-zəʊ, -zəʊz) *or* **-seaus.** 1 a mesh background to a lace or other pattern. 2 *Astronomy* a network of fine lines cut into a glass plate used as a reference grid on star photographs. 3 *Photog* a screen covered in a regular pattern of minute coloured dots or lines, formerly used in colour photography.
▷ HISTORY C19: from French, from Old French *resel* a little net, from *rais* net, from Latin *rēte*

resect (rɪˈsɛkt) VERB (*tr*) *Surgery* to cut out part of (a bone, an organ, or other structure or part).
▷ HISTORY C17: from Latin *resecāre* to cut away, from RE- + *secāre* to cut

resection (rɪˈsɛkʃən) NOUN 1 *Surgery* excision of part of a bone, organ, or other part. 2 *Surveying* a method of fixing the position of a point by making angular observations to three fixed points.
▸ **reˈsectional** ADJECTIVE

reseda (ˈrɛsɪdə) NOUN 1 any plant of the European genus *Reseda*, including mignonette and dyer's rocket, which has small spikes of grey-green flowers. ◆ ADJECTIVE 2 of a greyish-green colour; mignonette.
▷ HISTORY C18: from New Latin, from Latin: heal! from *resēdāre* to assuage, from RE- + *sēdāre* to soothe; see SEDATE²

reselect (ˌriːsɪˈlɛkt) VERB (*tr*) to choose (someone or something) again, esp to choose an existing office-holder as candidate for re-election.
▸ ˌ**reseˈlection** NOUN

resell (riːˈsɛl) VERB **-sells, -selling, -sold.** (*tr*) to sell (something) one has previously bought; sell on.

resemblance (rɪˈzɛmbləns) NOUN 1 the state or quality of resembling; likeness or similarity in nature, appearance, etc. 2 the degree or extent to which or the respect in which a likeness exists. 3 something resembling something else; semblance; likeness.
▸ **reˈsemblant** ADJECTIVE

resemble (rɪˈzɛmbᵊl) VERB (*tr*) to possess some similarity to; be like.
▷ HISTORY C14: from Old French *resembler*, from RE- + *sembler* to look like, from Latin *similis* like
▸ **reˈsembler** NOUN

resent (rɪˈzɛnt) VERB (*tr*) to feel bitter, indignant, or aggrieved at.
▷ HISTORY C17: from French *ressentir*, from RE- + *sentir* to feel, from Latin *sentīre* to perceive; see SENSE

resentful (rɪˈzɛntfʊl) ADJECTIVE feeling or characterized by resentment.
▸ **reˈsentfully** ADVERB ▸ **reˈsentfulness** NOUN

resentment (rɪˈzɛntmənt) NOUN anger, bitterness, or ill will.

reserpine (ˈrɛsəpɪn) NOUN an insoluble alkaloid, extracted from the roots of the plant *Rauwolfia serpentina*, used medicinally to lower blood pressure and as a sedative and tranquillizer. Its main adverse effect is mental depression. Formula: $C_{33}H_{40}N_2O_9$.
▷ HISTORY C20: from German *Reserpin*, probably from the New Latin name of the plant

reservation (ˌrɛzəˈveɪʃən) NOUN 1 the act or an instance of reserving. 2 something reserved, esp hotel accommodation, a seat on an aeroplane, in a theatre, etc. 3 (*often plural*) a stated or unstated qualification of opinion that prevents one's wholehearted acceptance of a proposal, claim, statement, etc. 4 an area of land set aside, esp (in the US) for American Indian peoples. 5 *Brit* the strip of land between the two carriageways of a dual carriageway. 6 the act or process of keeping back, esp for oneself; withholding. 7 *Law* a right or interest retained by the grantor in property granted, conveyed, leased, etc., to another: *a reservation of rent.*

reserve (rɪˈzɜːv) VERB (*tr*) 1 to keep back or set aside, esp for future use or contingency; withhold. 2 to keep for oneself; retain: *I reserve the right to question these men later.* 3 to obtain or secure by advance arrangement: *I have reserved two tickets for tonight's show.* 4 to delay delivery of (a judgment), esp in order to allow time for full consideration of the issues involved. ◆ NOUN 5 **a** something kept back or set aside, esp for future use or contingency. **b** (*as modifier*): *a reserve stock.* 6 the state or condition of being reserved: *I have plenty in reserve.* 7 a tract of land set aside for the protection and conservation of wild animals, flowers, etc.: *a nature reserve.* 8 the usual Canadian name for **reservation** (sense 4). 9 *Austral and NZ* an area of publicly owned land set aside for sport, recreation, etc. 10 the act of reserving; reservation. 11 a member of a team who only plays if a playing member drops out; a substitute. 12 (*often plural*) **a** a part of an army or formation not committed to immediate action in a military engagement. **b** that part of a nation's armed services not in active service. 13 coolness or formality of manner; restraint, silence, or reticence. 14 *Finance* **a** a portion of capital not invested (a **capital reserve**) or a portion of profits not distributed (a **revenue** or **general reserve**) by a bank or business enterprise and held to meet legal requirements, future liabilities, or contingencies. **b** (*often plural*) liquid assets held by an organization, government, etc., to meet expenses and liabilities. 15 **without reserve.** without reservations; fully; wholeheartedly.
▷ HISTORY C14: from Old French *reserver*, from Latin *reservāre* to save up, from RE- + *servāre* to keep
▸ **reˈservable** ADJECTIVE ▸ **reˈserver** NOUN

re-serve (riːˈsɜːv) VERB (*tr*) to serve again.

reserve bank NOUN one of the twelve banks forming part of the US Federal Reserve System.

reserve currency NOUN foreign currency that is acceptable as a medium of international payments and that is therefore held in reserve by many countries.

reserved (rɪˈzɜːvd) ADJECTIVE 1 set aside for use by a particular person or people: *this table is reserved.* 2 cool or formal in manner; restrained, silent, or reticent. 3 destined; fated: *reserved for great things.*
▸ **reservedly** (rɪˈzɜːvɪdlɪ) ADVERB ▸ **reˈservedness** NOUN

reserved list NOUN *Brit* a list of retired naval, army, or air-force officers available for recall to active service in an emergency.

reserved occupation NOUN *Brit* in time of war, an occupation from which one will not be called up for military service.

reserved word NOUN a word in a programming language or computer system that has a fixed meaning and therefore cannot be redefined by a programmer.

reserve-grade ADJECTIVE *Austral* denoting a sporting team of the second rank in a club.

reserve price NOUN *Brit* the minimum price acceptable to the owner of property being auctioned or sold. Also called (esp Scot and US): **upset price.**

reserve tranche NOUN the quota of 25 per cent to which a member of the IMF has unconditional access. Prior to 1978 it was paid in gold and known as the **gold tranche.**

reservist (rɪˈzɜːvɪst) NOUN one who serves in the reserve formations of a nation's armed forces.

reservoir (ˈrɛzəˌvwɑː) NOUN 1 a natural or artificial lake or large tank used for collecting and storing water, esp for community water supplies or irrigation. 2 a receptacle for storing gas, esp one attached to a stove. 3 *Biology* a vacuole or cavity in an organism, containing a secretion or some other fluid. 4 *Anatomy* another name for **cisterna.** 5 a place where a great stock of anything is accumulated. 6 a large supply of something; reserve: *a reservoir of talent.*
▷HISTORY C17: from French *réservoir*, from *réserver* to RESERVE

reset[1] VERB (riːˈsɛt) **-sets, -setting, -set.** (*tr*) 1 to set again (a broken bone, matter in type, a gemstone, etc.). 2 to restore (a gauge, dial, etc.) to zero. 3 Also: **clear.** to restore (the contents of a register or similar device) in a computer system to zero. ◆ NOUN (ˈriːˌsɛt) 4 the act or an instance of setting again. 5 a thing that is set again. 6 a plant that has been recently transplanted. 7 a device for resetting instruments, controls, etc.
▸**reˈsetter** NOUN

reset[2] *Scot* ◆ VERB (riːˈsɛt) **-sets, -setting, -set.** 1 to receive or handle goods knowing they have been stolen. ◆ NOUN (ˈriːˌsɛt) 2 the receiving of stolen goods.
▷HISTORY C14: from Old French *receter*, from Latin *receptāre*, from *recipere* to receive
▸**reˈsetter** NOUN

resettle (riːˈsɛtᵊl) VERB to settle or cause to settle in a new or different place.

resettlement (riːˈsetᵊlmənt) NOUN **a** the act or instance of settling or being settled in another place. **b** (*as modifier*): *resettlement procedures.*

res gestae (ˈreɪs ˈdʒɛstiː) PLURAL NOUN 1 things done or accomplished; achievements. 2 *Law* incidental facts and circumstances that are admissible in evidence because they introduce or explain the matter in issue.
▷HISTORY Latin

resh (reɪʃ; *Hebrew* reʃ) NOUN the 20th letter in the Hebrew alphabet (ר), transliterated as *r.*
▷HISTORY from Hebrew, from *rōsh* head

reshape (riːˈʃeɪp) VERB (*tr*) to shape (something) again or differently.

Resht (rɛʃt) NOUN a variant of **Rasht.**

reshuffle (riːˈʃʌfᵊl) NOUN 1 an act of shuffling again. 2 a reorganization, esp of jobs within a government or cabinet. ◆ VERB 3 to carry out a reshuffle (on).

reside (rɪˈzaɪd) VERB (*intr*) *Formal* 1 to live permanently or for a considerable time (in a place); have one's home (in): *he now resides in London.* 2 (of things, qualities, etc.) to be inherently present (in); be vested (in): *political power resides in military strength.*
▷HISTORY C15: from Latin *residēre* to sit back, from RE- + *sedēre* to sit
▸**reˈsider** NOUN

residence (ˈrɛzɪdəns) NOUN 1 the place in which one resides; abode or home. 2 a large imposing house; mansion. 3 the fact of residing in a place or a period of residing. 4 the official house of the governor of any of various countries. 5 the state of being officially present. 6 **in residence. a** actually resident: *the royal standard indicates that the Queen is in residence.* **b** designating a creative artist resident for a set period at a university, college, etc., whose role is to stimulate an active interest in the subject: *composer in residence.* 7 the seat of some inherent quality, characteristic, etc.

residency (ˈrɛzɪdənsɪ) NOUN, *plural* **-cies.** 1 a variant of **residence.** 2 a regular series of concerts by a band or singer at one venue. 3 *US and Canadian* the period, following internship, during which a physician undergoes further clinical training, usually in one medical speciality. 4 (in India, formerly) the official house of the governor general at the court of a native prince.

resident (ˈrɛzɪdənt) NOUN 1 a person who resides in a place. 2 *Social welfare* an occupant of a welfare agency home. Former name: **inmate.** 3 (esp formerly) a representative of the British government in a British protectorate. 4 (esp in the 17th century) a diplomatic representative ranking below an ambassador. 5 (in India, formerly) a representative of the British governor general at the court of a native prince. 6 a bird or other animal that does not migrate. 7 *US and Canadian* a physician who lives in the hospital where he works while undergoing specialist training after completing his internship. Compare **house physician.** 8 *Brit and NZ* a junior doctor, esp a house officer, who lives in the hospital in which he works. ◆ ADJECTIVE 9 living in a place; residing. 10 living or staying at a place in order to discharge a duty, etc. 11 (of qualities, characteristics, etc.) existing or inherent (in). 12 (of birds and other animals) not in the habit of migrating.
▸**ˈresidentˌship** NOUN

resident commissioner NOUN the representative of Puerto Rico in the US House of Representatives. He may speak but has no vote.

residential (ˌrɛzɪˈdɛnʃəl) ADJECTIVE 1 suitable for or allocated for residence: *a residential area.* 2 relating to or having residence.
▸**ˌresiˈdentially** ADVERB

residential care NOUN *Social welfare* the provision by a welfare agency of a home with social-work supervision for people who need more than just housing accommodation, such as children in care or mentally handicapped adults.

residential school NOUN (in Canada) a boarding school maintained by the Canadian government for Indian and Inuit children from sparsely populated settlements.

residentiary (ˌrɛzɪˈdɛnʃərɪ) ADJECTIVE 1 residing in a place, esp officially; resident. 2 subject to an obligation to reside in an official residence: *a residentiary benefice.* ◆ NOUN, *plural* **-tiaries.** 3 a clergyman obliged to reside in the place of his official appointment.

residents association NOUN an organization composed of voluntary members living in a particular neighbourhood, which aims to improve the social and communal facilities of the neighbourhood and to conserve or improve its environmental advantages. See also **community association, tenants association.**

residual (rɪˈzɪdjʊəl) ADJECTIVE 1 of, relating to, or designating a residue or remainder; remaining; left over. 2 (of deposits, soils, etc.) formed by the weathering of pre-existing rocks and the removal of disintegrated material. 3 of or relating to the payment of residuals. ◆ NOUN 4 something left over as a residue; remainder. 5 *Statistics* **a** the difference between the mean of a set of observations and one particular observation. **b** the difference between the numerical value of one particular observation and the theoretical result. 6 (*often plural*) payment made to an actor, actress, musician, etc., for subsequent use of film in which the person appears.
▸**reˈsidually** ADVERB

residual current device ADVERB, NOUN a circuit-breaking device installed in electrical equipment to protect the operator from electrocution. Abbreviation: **RCD.**

residual unemployment NOUN the unemployment that remains in periods of full employment, as a result of those mentally, physically, or emotionally unfit to work.

residuary (rɪˈzɪdjʊərɪ) ADJECTIVE 1 of, relating to, or constituting a residue; residual. 2 *Law* entitled to the residue of an estate after payment of debts and distribution of specific gifts.

residue (ˈrɛzɪˌdjuː) NOUN 1 matter remaining after something has been removed. 2 *Law* what is left of an estate after the discharge of debts and distribution of specific gifts.
▷HISTORY C14: from Old French *residu*, from Latin *residuus* remaining over, from *residēre* to stay behind, RESIDE

residuum (rɪˈzɪdjʊəm) NOUN, *plural* **-ua** (-jʊə). a more formal word for **residue.**

resign (rɪˈzaɪn) VERB 1 (when *intr*, often foll by *from*) to give up tenure of (a job, office, etc.). 2 (*tr*) to reconcile (oneself) to; yield: *to resign oneself to death.* 3 (*tr*) to give up (a right, claim, etc.); relinquish: *he resigned his claim to the throne.*
▷HISTORY C14: from Old French *resigner*, from Latin *resignāre* to unseal, invalidate, destroy, from RE- + *signāre* to seal; see SIGN
▸**reˈsigner** NOUN

re-sign (riːˈsaɪn) VERB to sign (a document, etc.) again.

resignation (ˌrɛzɪgˈneɪʃən) NOUN 1 the act of resigning. 2 a formal document stating one's intention to resign. 3 a submissive unresisting attitude; passive acquiescence.

resigned (rɪˈzaɪnd) ADJECTIVE characteristic of or proceeding from an attitude of resignation; acquiescent or submissive.
▸**resignedly** (rɪˈzaɪnɪdlɪ) ADVERB ▸**reˈsignedness** NOUN

resile (rɪˈzaɪl) VERB (*intr*) to spring or shrink back; recoil or resume original shape.
▷HISTORY C16: from Old French *resilir*, from Latin *resilīre* to jump back, from RE- + *salīre* to jump
▸**reˈsilement** NOUN

resilience (rɪˈzɪlɪəns) NOUN 1 Also called: **resiliency.** the state or quality of being resilient. 2 *Ecology* the ability of an ecosystem to return to its original state after being disturbed. 3 *Physics* the amount of potential energy stored in an elastic material when deformed.

resilient (rɪˈzɪlɪənt) ADJECTIVE 1 (of an object or material) capable of regaining its original shape or position after bending, stretching, compression, or other deformation; elastic. 2 (of a person) recovering easily and quickly from shock, illness, hardship, etc.; irrepressible.
▸**reˈsiliently** ADVERB

resin (ˈrɛzɪn) NOUN 1 any of a group of solid or semisolid amorphous compounds that are obtained directly from certain plants as exudations. They are used in medicine and in varnishes. 2 any of a large number of synthetic, usually organic, materials that have a polymeric structure, esp such a substance in a raw state before it is moulded or treated with plasticizer, stabilizer, filler, etc. Compare **plastic** (sense 1). ◆ VERB 3 (*tr*) to treat or coat with resin.
▷HISTORY C14: from Old French *resine*, from Latin *rēsīna*, from Greek *rhētinē* resin from a pine
▸**ˈresinous** ADJECTIVE ▸**ˈresinously** ADVERB ▸**ˈresinousness** NOUN

resinate (ˈrɛzɪˌneɪt) VERB (*tr*) to impregnate with resin.

resiniferous (ˌrɛzɪˈnɪfərəs) ADJECTIVE yielding or producing resin.

resinoid (ˈrɛzɪˌnɔɪd) ADJECTIVE 1 resembling, characteristic of, or containing resin. ◆ NOUN 2 any resinoid substance, esp a synthetic compound.

resipiscence (ˌrɛsɪˈpɪsəns) NOUN *Literary* acknowledgment that one has been mistaken.
▷HISTORY C16: from Late Latin *resipiscentia*, from *resipiscere* to recover one's senses, from Latin *sapere* to know
▸**ˌresiˈpiscent** ADJECTIVE

res ipsa loquitur (reɪs ˌɪpsɑː ˈlɒkwɪtə) *Law* the thing or matter speaks for itself.
▷HISTORY Latin

resist (rɪˈzɪst) VERB 1 to stand firm (against); not yield (to); fight (against). 2 (*tr*) to withstand the deleterious action of; be proof against: *to resist corrosion.* 3 (*tr*) to oppose; refuse to accept or comply with: *to resist arrest; to resist the introduction of new technology.* 4 (*tr*) to refrain from, esp in spite of temptation (esp in the phrases **cannot** *or* **could not resist (something)**). ◆ NOUN 5 a substance used to protect something, esp a coating that prevents corrosion.
▷HISTORY C14: from Latin *resistere* to stand still, oppose, from RE- + *sistere* to stand firm
▸**reˈsister** NOUN ▸**reˈsistible** ADJECTIVE ▸**reˌsistiˈbility** NOUN ▸**reˈsistibly** ADVERB

resistance (rɪˈzɪstəns) NOUN 1 the act or an instance of resisting. 2 the capacity to withstand something, esp the body's natural capacity to withstand disease. 3 **a** the opposition to a flow of electric current through a circuit component, medium, or substance. It is the magnitude of the real part of the impedance and is measured in ohms. Symbol: *R*. Compare **reactance** (sense 1). **b** (*as modifier*): *resistance coupling; a resistance thermometer.* 4 any force that tends to retard or oppose motion: *air resistance; wind resistance.* 5 (in psychoanalytical theory) the tendency of a person to prevent the translation of repressed thoughts and ideas from the unconscious to the conscious and esp to resist the analyst's attempt to bring this about. 6 *Physics* the magnitude of the real part of the acoustic or mechanical impedance. 7 **line of least resistance.** the easiest, but not necessarily the best or most honourable, course of action. 8 See **passive resistance.**

Resistance (rɪˈzɪstəns) NOUN **the.** an illegal organization fighting for national liberty in a country under enemy occupation, esp in France during World War II.

resistance thermometer NOUN an accurate type of thermometer in which temperature is calculated from the resistance of a coil of wire (usually of platinum) or of a semiconductor placed at the point at which the temperature is to be measured.

resistance welding NOUN a welding technique in which the parts to be joined are held together under pressure and heat is produced by passing a current through the contact resistance formed between the two surfaces.

resistant (rɪˈzɪstənt) ADJECTIVE 1 characterized by or showing resistance; resisting. 2 **a** impervious to the action of corrosive substances, heat, etc: *a highly resistant surface.* **b** (*in combination*): *a heat-resistant surface.* ◆ NOUN 3 a person or thing that resists.

Resistencia (*Spanish* resisˈtenθja) NOUN a city in NE Argentina, on the Paraná River. Pop.: 280 000 (1999 est.).

resistive (rɪˈzɪstɪv) ADJECTIVE 1 another word for **resistant.** 2 exhibiting electrical resistance.

resistivity (ˌriːzɪsˈtɪvɪtɪ) NOUN 1 the electrical property of a material that determines the resistance of a piece of given dimensions. It is equal to *RA/l*, where *R* is the resistance, *A* the cross-sectional area, and *l* the length, and is the reciprocal of conductivity. It is measured in ohms. Symbol: ρ. Former name: **specific resistance.** 2 the power or capacity to resist; resistance.

resistless (rɪˈzɪstlɪs) ADJECTIVE *Archaic* 1 unresisting. 2 irresistible.
▸**reˈsistlessly** ADVERB

resistor (rɪˈzɪstə) NOUN an electrical component designed to introduce a known value of resistance into a circuit.

resit VERB (riːˈsɪt) **-sits, -sitting, -sat.** (*tr*) 1 to sit (an examination) again. ◆ NOUN (ˈriːsɪt) 2 an examination taken again by a person who has not been successful in a previous attempt.

res judicata (ˈreɪs ˌdʒuːdɪˈkɑːtə) *or* **res adjudicata** NOUN *Law* a matter already adjudicated upon that cannot be raised again.
▷**HISTORY** Latin

reskill (riːˈskɪl) VERB (*tr*) to train (workers) to acquire new or improved skills.
▸**reˈskilling** NOUN

resnatron (ˈreznəˌtrɒn) NOUN a tetrode used to generate high power at high frequencies.
▷**HISTORY** C20: from RESONATOR + -TRON

resoluble (rɪˈzɒljʊbᵊl, ˈrezəl-) ADJECTIVE another word for **resolvable.**

re-soluble (riːˈsɒljʊbᵊl) ADJECTIVE capable of being dissolved again.
▸**re-ˈsolubleness** *or* **re-ˌsoluˈbility** NOUN ▸**re-ˈsolubly** ADVERB

resolute (ˈrezəˌluːt) ADJECTIVE 1 firm in purpose or belief; steadfast. 2 characterized by resolution; determined: *a resolute answer.*
▷**HISTORY** C16: from Latin *resolutus*, from *resolvere* to RESOLVE
▸**ˈresoˌlutely** ADVERB ▸**ˈresoˌluteness** NOUN

resolution (ˌrezəˈluːʃən) NOUN 1 the act or an instance of resolving. 2 the condition or quality of being resolute; firmness or determination. 3 something resolved or determined; decision. 4 a formal expression of opinion by a meeting, esp one agreed by a vote. 5 a judicial decision on some matter; verdict; judgment. 6 the act or process of separating something into its constituent parts or elements. 7 *Med* **a** return from a pathological to a normal condition. **b** subsidence of the symptoms of a disease, esp the disappearance of inflammation without the formation of pus. 8 *Music* the process in harmony whereby a dissonant note or chord is followed by a consonant one. 9 the ability of a television or film image to reproduce fine detail. 10 *Physics* another word for **resolving power.**
▸**ˌresoˈlutioner** *or* **ˌresoˈlutionist** NOUN

resolutive (rɪˈzɒljʊtɪv) ADJECTIVE 1 capable of dissolving; causing disintegration. 2 *Law* denoting a condition the fulfilment of which terminates a contract or other legal obligation.

resolvable (rɪˈzɒlvəbᵊl) *or* **resoluble** ADJECTIVE able to be resolved or analysed.
▸**reˌsolvaˈbility** *or* **reˌsoluˈbility** *or* **reˈsolvableness** *or* **reˈsolubleness** NOUN

resolve (rɪˈzɒlv) VERB (*mainly tr*) 1 (*takes a clause as object or an infinitive*) to decide or determine firmly. 2 to express (an opinion) formally, esp (of a public meeting) one agreed by a vote. 3 (*also intr*; usually foll by *into*) to separate or cause to separate (into) (constituent parts or elements). 4 (*usually reflexive*) to change, alter, or appear to change or alter: *the ghost resolved itself into a tree.* 5 to make up the mind of; cause to decide: *the tempest resolved him to stay at home.* 6 to find the answer or solution to; solve: *to resolve a problem.* 7 to explain away or dispel: *to resolve a doubt.* 8 to bring to an end; conclude: *to resolve an argument.* 9 *Med* to cause (a swelling or inflammation) to subside, esp without the formation of pus. 10 (*also intr*) to follow (a dissonant note or chord) or (of a dissonant note or chord) to be followed by one producing a consonance. 11 *Chem* to separate (a racemic mixture) into its optically active constituents. 12 *Physics* **a** to distinguish between (separate parts) of (an image) as in a microscope, telescope, or other optical instrument. **b** to separate (two adjacent peaks) in a spectrum by means of a spectrometer. 13 *Maths* to split (a vector) into its components in specified directions. 14 an obsolete word for **dissolve.** ◆ NOUN 15 something determined or decided; resolution: *he had made a resolve to work all day.* 16 firmness of purpose; determination: *nothing can break his resolve.*
▷**HISTORY** C14: from Latin *resolvere* to unfasten, reveal, from RE- + *solvere* to loosen; see SOLVE
▸**reˈsolver** NOUN

resolved (rɪˈzɒlvd) ADJECTIVE fixed in purpose or intention; determined.
▸**resolvedly** (rɪˈzɒlvɪdlɪ) ADVERB ▸**reˈsolvedness** NOUN

resolvent (rɪˈzɒlvənt) ADJECTIVE 1 serving to dissolve or separate something into its elements; resolving. ◆ NOUN 2 something that resolves; solvent. 3 a drug or agent able to reduce swelling or inflammation.

resolving power NOUN 1 Also called: **resolution.** *Physics* **a** the ability of a microscope, telescope, or other optical instrument to produce separate images of closely placed objects. **b** the ability of a spectrometer to separate two adjacent peaks in a spectrum. 2 *Photog* the ability of an emulsion to show up fine detail in an image.

resonance (ˈrezənəns) NOUN 1 the condition or quality of being resonant. 2 sound produced by a body vibrating in sympathy with a neighbouring source of sound. 3 the condition of a body or system when it is subjected to a periodic disturbance of the same frequency as the natural frequency of the body or system. At this frequency the system displays an enhanced oscillation or vibration. 4 amplification of speech sounds by sympathetic vibration in the bone structure of the head and chest, resounding in the cavities of the nose, mouth, and pharynx. 5 *Electronics* the condition of an electrical circuit when the frequency is such that the capacitive and inductive reactances are equal in magnitude. In a series circuit there is then maximum alternating current whilst in a parallel circuit there is minimum alternating current. 6 *Med* the sound heard when percussing a hollow bodily structure, esp the chest or abdomen. Change in the quality of the sound often indicates an underlying disease or disorder. 7 *Chem* the phenomenon in which the electronic structure of a molecule can be represented by two or more hypothetical structures involving single, double, and triple chemical bonds. The true structure is considered to be an average of these theoretical structures. 8 *Physics* **a** the condition of a system in which there is a sharp maximum probability for the absorption of electromagnetic radiation or capture of particles. **b** a type of elementary particle of extremely short lifetime. Resonances are regarded as excited states of more stable particles. **c** a highly transient atomic state formed during a collision process.
▷**HISTORY** C16: from Latin *resonāre* to RESOUND

resonant (ˈrezənənt) ADJECTIVE 1 (of sound) resounding or re-echoing. 2 producing or enhancing resonance, as by sympathetic vibration. 3 characterized by resonance.
▸**ˈresonantly** ADVERB

resonant cavity NOUN another name for **cavity resonator.**

resonate (ˈrezəˌneɪt) VERB 1 to resound or cause to resound; reverberate. 2 (of a mechanical system, electrical circuit, chemical compound, etc.) to exhibit or cause to exhibit resonance.
▷**HISTORY** C19: from Latin *resonāre*
▸**ˌresoˈnation** NOUN

resonator (ˈrezəˌneɪtə) NOUN any body or system that displays resonance, esp a tuned electrical circuit or a conducting cavity in which microwaves are generated by a resonant current.

resorb (rɪˈsɔːb) VERB (*tr*) to absorb again.
▷**HISTORY** C17: from Latin *resorbēre*, from RE- + *sorbēre* to suck in; see ABSORB
▸**reˈsorbent** ADJECTIVE ▸**reˈsorptive** ADJECTIVE

resorcinol (rɪˈzɔːsɪˌnɒl) NOUN a colourless crystalline phenol with a sweet taste, used in making dyes, drugs, resins, and adhesives. Formula: $C_6H_4(OH)_2$; relative density: 1.27; melting pt.: 111°C; boiling pt. at 1 atm.: 276°C.
▷**HISTORY** C19: New Latin, from RESIN + ORCINOL
▸**reˈsorcinal** ADJECTIVE

resorption (rɪˈsɔːpʃən) NOUN 1 the process of resorbing or the state of being resorbed. 2 *Geology* the partial or complete remelting or dissolution of a mineral by magma, resulting from changes in temperature, pressure, or magma composition.

resort (rɪˈzɔːt) VERB (*intr*) 1 (usually foll by *to*) to have recourse (to) for help, use, etc.: *to resort to violence.* 2 to go, esp often or habitually; repair: *to resort to the beach.* ◆ NOUN 3 a place to which many people go for recreation, rest, etc.: *a holiday resort.* 4 the use of something as a means, help, or recourse. 5 the act of going to a place, esp for recreation, rest, etc. 6 **last resort.** the last possible course of action open to one.
▷**HISTORY** C14: from Old French *resortir* to come out again, from RE- + *sortir* to emerge
▸**reˈsorter** NOUN

re-sort (riːˈsɔːt) VERB (*tr*) to sort again.

resound (rɪˈzaʊnd) VERB (*intr*) 1 to ring or echo with sound; reverberate: *the hall resounded with laughter.* 2 to make a prolonged echoing noise: *the trumpet resounded.* 3 (of sounds) to echo or ring. 4 to be widely famous: *his achievements resounded throughout India.*
▷**HISTORY** C14: from Old French *resoner*, from Latin *resonāre* to sound again

re-sound (riːˈsaʊnd) VERB to sound or cause to sound again.

resounding (rɪˈzaʊndɪŋ) ADJECTIVE 1 clear and emphatic; unmistakable: *a resounding vote of confidence.* 2 full of or characterized by resonance; reverberating: *a resounding slap.*
▸**reˈsoundingly** ADVERB

resource (rɪˈzɔːs, -ˈsɔːs) NOUN 1 capability, ingenuity, and initiative; quick-wittedness: *a man of resource.* 2 (*often plural*) a source of economic wealth, esp of a country (mineral, land, labour, etc.) or business enterprise (capital, equipment, personnel, etc.). 3 a supply or source of aid or support; something resorted to in time of need. 4 a means of doing something; expedient.
▷**HISTORY** C17: from Old French *ressourse* relief, from *resourdre* to rise again, from Latin *resurgere*, from RE- + *surgere* to rise
▸**reˈsourceless** ADJECTIVE ▸**reˈsourcelessness** NOUN

resourceful (rɪˈzɔːsfʊl, -ˈsɔːs-) ADJECTIVE ingenious,

capable, and full of initiative, esp in dealing with difficult situations.
▸re'sourcefully ADVERB ▸re'sourcefulness NOUN

respect (rɪ'spɛkt) NOUN [1] an attitude of deference, admiration, or esteem; regard. [2] the state of being honoured or esteemed. [3] a detail, point, or characteristic; particular: *he differs in some respects from his son.* [4] reference or relation (esp in the phrases **in respect of, with respect to**). [5] polite or kind regard; consideration: *respect for people's feelings.* [6] (*often plural*) an expression of esteem or regard (esp in the phrase **pay one's respects**). ◆ VERB (*tr*) [7] to have an attitude of esteem towards; show or have respect for: *to respect one's elders.* [8] to pay proper attention to; not violate: *to respect Swiss neutrality.* [9] to show consideration for; treat courteously or kindly. [10] *Archaic* to concern or refer to.
▷HISTORY C14: from Latin *rēspicere* to look back, pay attention to, from RE- + *specere* to look

respectable (rɪ'spɛktəbᵊl) ADJECTIVE [1] having or deserving the respect of other people; estimable; worthy. [2] having good social standing or reputation. [3] having socially or conventionally acceptable morals, standards, etc.: *a respectable woman.* [4] relatively or fairly good; considerable: *a respectable salary.* [5] fit to be seen by other people; presentable.
▸re,specta'bility *or* (*less commonly*) re'spectableness NOUN ▸re'spectably ADVERB

respecter (rɪ'spɛktə) NOUN [1] a person who respects someone or something. [2] **no respecter of persons.** a person whose attitude and behaviour is uninfluenced by consideration of another's rank, power, wealth, etc.

respectful (rɪ'spɛktfʊl) ADJECTIVE full of, showing, or giving respect.
▸re'spectfully ADVERB ▸re'spectfulness NOUN

respecting (rɪ'spɛktɪŋ) PREPOSITION concerning; regarding.

respective (rɪ'spɛktɪv) ADJECTIVE [1] belonging or relating separately to each of several people or things; several: *we took our respective ways home.* [2] an archaic word for **respectful.**
▸re'spectiveness NOUN

respectively (rɪ'spɛktɪvlɪ) ADVERB (in listing a number of items or attributes that refer to another list) separately in the order given: *he gave Janet and John a cake and a chocolate respectively.*

respirable ('rɛspɪrəbᵊl) ADJECTIVE [1] able to be breathed. [2] suitable or fit for breathing.
▸,respira'bility NOUN

respiration (,rɛspə'reɪʃən) NOUN [1] the process in living organisms of taking in oxygen from the surroundings and giving out carbon dioxide (**external respiration**). In terrestrial animals this is effected by breathing air. [2] the chemical breakdown of complex organic substances, such as carbohydrates and fats, that takes place in the cells and tissues of animals and plants, during which energy is released and carbon dioxide produced (**internal respiration**).

respirator ('rɛspə,reɪtə) NOUN [1] an apparatus for providing long-term artificial respiration. [2] Also called: **gas mask.** a device worn over the mouth and nose to prevent inhalation of noxious fumes or to warm cold air before it is breathed.

respiratory ('rɛspərətərɪ, -trɪ) *or rarely* **respirational** (,rɛspə'reɪʃənᵊl) of, relating to, or affecting respiration or the organs used in respiration.

respiratory failure NOUN a condition in which the respiratory system is unable to provide an adequate supply of oxygen or to remove carbon dioxide efficiently.

respiratory quotient NOUN *Biology* the ratio of the volume of carbon dioxide expired to the volume of oxygen consumed by an organism, tissue, or cell in a given time.

respiratory syncytial virus NOUN a myxovirus causing infections of the nose and throat, esp in young children. It is thought to be involved in some cot deaths. Abbreviation: **RSV.**

respiratory system NOUN the specialized organs, collectively, concerned with external respiration: in humans and other mammals it includes the trachea, bronchi, bronchioles, lungs, and diaphragm.

respire (rɪ'spaɪə) VERB [1] to inhale and exhale (air); breathe. [2] (*intr*) to undergo the process of respiration. [3] *Literary* to breathe again in a relaxed or easy manner, as after stress or exertion.
▷HISTORY C14: from Latin *rēspīrāre* to exhale, from RE- + *spīrāre* to breathe; see SPIRIT[1]

respite ('rɛspɪt, -paɪt) NOUN [1] a pause from exertion; interval of rest. [2] a temporary delay. [3] a temporary stay of execution; reprieve. ◆ VERB [4] (*tr*) to grant a respite to; reprieve.
▷HISTORY C13: from Old French *respit*, from Latin *respectus* a looking back; see RESPECT
▸'respiteless ADJECTIVE

respite care NOUN *Social welfare* occasional usually planned residential care for dependent old or handicapped people, to provide relief for their permanent carers.

resplendent (rɪ'splɛndənt) ADJECTIVE having a brilliant or splendid appearance.
▷HISTORY C15: from *rēsplendēre* to shine brightly, from RE- + *splendēre* to shine; see SPLENDOUR
▸re'splendence *or* re'splendency NOUN ▸re'splendently ADVERB

respond (rɪ'spɒnd) VERB [1] to state or utter (something) in reply. [2] (*intr*) to act in reply; react: *to respond by issuing an invitation.* [3] (*intr*; foll by *to*) to react favourably: *this patient will respond to treatment.* [4] an archaic word for **correspond.** ◆ NOUN [5] *Architect* a pilaster or an engaged column that supports an arch or a lintel. [6] *Christianity* a choral anthem chanted in response to a lesson read at a church service.
▷HISTORY C14: from Old French *respondre*, from Latin *rēspondēre* to return like for like, from RE- + *spondēre* to pledge; see SPOUSE, SPONSOR
▸re'spondence *or* re'spondency NOUN ▸re'sponder NOUN

respondent (rɪ'spɒndənt) NOUN [1] *Law* a person against whom a petition, esp in a divorce suit, or appeal is brought. ◆ ADJECTIVE [2] a less common word for **responsive.**

responsa (rɪ'spɒnsə) NOUN *Judaism* [1] the plural of **responsum.** [2] that part of rabbinic literature concerned with written rulings in answer to questions.

response (rɪ'spɒns) NOUN [1] the act of responding; reply or reaction. [2] *Bridge* a bid replying to a partner's bid or double. [3] (*usually plural*) *Christianity* a short sentence or phrase recited or sung by the choir or congregation in reply to the officiant at a church service. [4] *Electronics* the ratio of the output to the input level, at a particular frequency, of a transmission line or electrical device. [5] any pattern of glandular, muscular, or electrical reactions that arises from stimulation of the nervous system.
▷HISTORY C14: from Latin *rēsponsum* answer, from *rēspondēre* to RESPOND
▸re'sponseless ADJECTIVE

responser *or* **responsor** (rɪ'spɒnsə) NOUN a radio or radar receiver used in conjunction with an interrogator to receive and display signals from a transponder.

response time NOUN *Computing* the length of time taken by a system to respond to an instruction.

response variable NOUN *Statistics* a more modern term for **dependent variable** (sense 2).

responsibility (rɪ,spɒnsə'bɪlɪtɪ) NOUN, *plural* **-ties.** [1] the state or position of being responsible. [2] a person or thing for which one is responsible. [3] the ability or authority to act or decide on one's own, without supervision.

responsible (rɪ'spɒnsəbᵊl) ADJECTIVE [1] (*postpositive*; usually foll by *for*) having control or authority (over). [2] (*postpositive*; foll by *to*) being accountable for one's actions and decisions (to): *to be responsible to one's commanding officer.* [3] (of a position, duty, etc.) involving decision and accountability. [4] (often foll by *for*) being the agent or cause (of some action): *to be responsible for a mistake.* [5] able to take rational decisions without supervision; accountable for one's own actions: *a responsible adult.* [6] able to meet financial obligations; of sound credit.
▷HISTORY C16: from Latin *rēsponsus*, from *rēspondēre* to RESPOND
▸re'sponsibleness NOUN ▸re'sponsibly ADVERB

responsive (rɪ'spɒnsɪv) ADJECTIVE [1] reacting or replying quickly or favourably, as to a suggestion, initiative, etc. [2] (of an organism) reacting to a stimulus.
▸re'sponsively ADVERB ▸re'sponsiveness NOUN

responsory (rɪ'spɒnsərɪ) NOUN, *plural* **-ries.** *Christianity* an anthem or chant consisting of versicles and responses and recited or sung after a lesson in a church service.
▷HISTORY C15: from Late Latin *rēsponsōrium*, from Latin *rēspondēre* to answer

responsum (rɪ'spɒnsəm) NOUN, *plural* **-sa** (-sə). *Judaism* a written answer from a rabbinic authority to a question submitted.
▷HISTORY Latin, literally: reply, RESPONSE

respray VERB (riː'spreɪ) (*tr*) [1] to spray (a car, wheels, etc.) with a new coat of paint. ◆ NOUN ('riː,spreɪ) [2] the act or an instance of respraying.

res publica ('reɪs 'pʊblɪ,kɑː) NOUN the state, republic, or commonwealth.
▷HISTORY Latin, literally: the public thing

rest[1] (rɛst) NOUN [1] a relaxation from exertion or labour. **b** (*as modifier*): *a rest period.* [2] repose; sleep. [3] any relief or refreshment, as from worry or something troublesome. [4] calm; tranquillity. [5] death regarded as repose: *eternal rest.* [6] cessation from motion. [7] **at rest. a** not moving; still. **b** calm; tranquil. **c** dead. **d** asleep. [8] a pause or interval. [9] a mark in a musical score indicating a pause of specific duration. [10] *Prosody* a pause in or at the end of a line; caesura. [11] a shelter or lodging: *a seaman's rest.* [12] a thing or place on which to put something for support or to steady it; prop. [13] *Billiards, snooker* any of various special poles used as supports for the cue in shots that cannot be made using the hand as a support. [14] **come to rest.** to slow down and stop. [15] **lay to rest.** to bury (a dead person). [16] **set (someone's mind) at rest.** to reassure (someone) or settle (someone's mind). ◆ VERB [17] to take or give rest, as by sleeping, lying down, etc. [18] to place or position (oneself, etc.) for rest or relaxation. [19] (*tr*) to place or position for support or steadying: *to rest one's elbows on the table.* [20] (*intr*) to be at ease; be calm. [21] to cease or cause to cease from motion or exertion; halt. [22] to lie dead and buried. [23] (*intr*) to remain without further attention or action: *let the matter rest.* [24] to direct (one's eyes) or (of one's eyes) to be directed: *her eyes rested on the sleeping child.* [25] to depend or cause to depend; base; rely: *the whole argument rests on one crucial fact.* [26] to place or be placed, as blame, censure, etc. [27] (*intr*; foll by *with, on, upon,* etc.) to be a responsibility (of): *it rests with us to apportion blame.* [28] *Law* to finish the introduction of evidence in (a case). [29] **rest on one's laurels.** See **laurel** (sense 9). [30] **rest on one's oars. a** to stop rowing for a time. **b** to stop doing anything for a time.
▷HISTORY Old English *ræst, reste*, of Germanic origin; related to Gothic *rasta* a mile, Old Norse *röst* mile
▸'rester NOUN

rest[2] (rɛst) NOUN (usually preceded by *the*) [1] something left or remaining; remainder. [2] the others: *the rest of the world.* ◆ VERB [3] (*copula*) to continue to be (as specified); remain: *rest assured.*
▷HISTORY C15: from Old French *rester* to remain, from Latin *restāre*, from RE- + *stāre* to STAND

restage (riː'steɪdʒ) VERB (*tr*) [1] to produce or perform a new production of (a play). [2] to organize or carry out (an event) again, esp if it has been cancelled: *attempts have been made to restage the race.*

rest area NOUN *Austral and NZ* a motorists' stopping place, usually off a highway, equipped with tables, seats, etc.

restart VERB (riː'stɑːt) [1] to start again. ◆ NOUN ('riː,stɑːt) [2] **a** the act or an instance of starting again: *the restart of the lap.* **b** (*as modifier*): *a restart device.*

restate (riː'steɪt) VERB (*tr*) to state or affirm again or in a new way.
▸re'statement NOUN

restaurant ('rɛstə,rɒŋ, 'rɛstrɒŋ, -rɒnt) NOUN a commercial establishment where meals are prepared and served to customers.
▷HISTORY C19: from French, from *restaurer* to RESTORE

restaurant car NOUN *Brit* a railway coach in which meals are served. Also called: **dining car.**

restaurateur (ˌrɛstərəˈtɜː) NOUN a person who owns or runs a restaurant.
▷HISTORY C18: via French from Late Latin *restaurātor* one who restores, from Latin *restaurāre* to RESTORE

> **Language note** Although the spelling *restauranteur* occurs frequently, it is a misspelling and should be avoided.

rest-cure NOUN 1 a rest taken as part of a course of medical treatment, as for stress, anxiety, etc. 2 an easy undemanding time or assignment: usually used with a negative: *it's no rest-cure, I can assure you.*

restful (ˈrɛstfʊl) ADJECTIVE 1 giving or conducive to rest. 2 being at rest; tranquil; calm.
▸ˈ**restfully** ADVERB ▸ˈ**restfulness** NOUN

restharrow (ˈrɛstˌhærəʊ) NOUN any of several Eurasian leguminous plants of the genus *Ononis*, such as *O. repens* and *O. spinosa*, with tough stems and roots.
▷HISTORY C16: from *rest* variant of ARREST (to hinder, stop) + HARROW[1]

rest-home NOUN an old people's home.

restiform (ˈrɛstɪˌfɔːm) ADJECTIVE (esp of bundles of nerve fibres) shaped like a cord or rope; cordlike.
▷HISTORY C19: from New Latin *restiformis*, from Latin *restis* a rope + *forma* shape

resting (ˈrɛstɪŋ) ADJECTIVE 1 not moving or working; at rest. 2 *Euphemistic* (of an actor) out of work. 3 (esp of plant spores) undergoing a period of dormancy before germination. 4 (of cells) not undergoing mitosis.

resting place NOUN a place where someone or something rests, esp (**last resting place**) the grave.

restitution (ˌrɛstɪˈtjuːʃən) NOUN 1 the act of giving back something that has been lost or stolen. 2 *Law* the act of compensating for loss or injury by reverting as far as possible to the position before such injury occurred. 3 the return of an object or system to its original state, esp a restoration of shape after elastic deformation.
▷HISTORY C13: from Latin *rēstitūtiō*, from *rēstituere* to rebuild, from RE- + *statuere* to set up
▸ˈ**restiˌtutive** *or* ˌ**restiˈtutory** ADJECTIVE

restive (ˈrɛstɪv) ADJECTIVE 1 restless, nervous, or uneasy. 2 impatient of control or authority.
▷HISTORY C16: from Old French *restif* balky, from *rester* to remain
▸ˈ**restively** ADVERB ▸ˈ**restiveness** NOUN

restless (ˈrɛstlɪs) ADJECTIVE 1 unable to stay still or quiet. 2 ceaselessly active or moving: *the restless wind.* 3 worried; anxious; uneasy. 4 not restful; without repose: *a restless night.*
▸ˈ**restlessly** ADVERB ▸ˈ**restlessness** NOUN

rest mass NOUN the mass of an object that is at rest relative to an observer. It is the mass used in Newtonian mechanics.

resto (ˈrɛstəʊ) NOUN, *plural* **restos.** *Austral informal* a restored antique, vintage car, etc.

restock (riːˈstɒk) VERB to replenish stores or supplies.

restoration (ˌrɛstəˈreɪʃən) NOUN 1 the act of restoring or state of being restored, as to a former or original condition, place, etc. 2 the replacement or giving back of something lost, stolen, etc. 3 something restored, replaced, or reconstructed. 4 a model or representation of an extinct animal, landscape of a former geological age, etc.

Restoration (ˌrɛstəˈreɪʃən) NOUN *Brit history* **a** the re-establishment of the monarchy in 1660 or the reign of Charles II (1660–85). **b** (*as modifier*): *Restoration drama.*

restorationism (ˌrɛstəˈreɪʃəˌnɪzəm) NOUN belief in a future life in which human beings will be restored to a state of perfection and happiness.
▸ˌ**restoˈrationist** NOUN, ADJECTIVE

restorative (rɪˈstɒrətɪv) ADJECTIVE 1 tending to revive or renew health, spirits, etc. ◆ NOUN 2 anything that restores or revives, esp a drug or agent that promotes health or strength.

restorative justice NOUN a method of dealing with convicted criminals in which they are urged to accept responsibility for their offences through meeting victims, making amends to victims or the community, etc.

restore (rɪˈstɔː) VERB (*tr*) 1 to return (something, esp a work of art or building) to an original or former condition. 2 to bring back to health, good spirits, etc. 3 to return (something lost, stolen, etc.) to its owner. 4 to reintroduce or re-enforce: *to restore discipline.* 5 to reconstruct (an extinct animal, former landscape, etc.).
▷HISTORY C13: from Old French, from Latin *rēstaurāre* to rebuild, from RE- + *-staurāre*, as in *instaurāre* to renew
▸**reˈstorable** ADJECTIVE ▸**reˈstorableness** NOUN ▸**reˈstorer** NOUN

restrain (rɪˈstreɪn) VERB (*tr*) 1 to hold (someone) back from some action, esp by force. 2 to deprive (someone) of liberty, as by imprisonment. 3 to limit or restrict.
▷HISTORY C14 *restreyne*, from Old French *restreindre*, from Latin *rēstringere* to draw back tightly, from RE- + *stringere* to draw, bind; see STRAIN[1]
▸**reˈstrainable** ADJECTIVE

restrained (rɪˈstreɪnd) ADJECTIVE 1 (of a person or person's manner) calm and unemotional. 2 (of clothes, décor, etc.) subtle and tasteful.
▸**restrainedly** (rɪˈstreɪnɪdlɪ) ADVERB

restrainer (rɪˈstreɪnə) NOUN 1 a person who restrains. 2 a chemical, such as potassium bromide, added to a photographic developer in order to reduce the amount of fog on a film and to retard the development.

restraint (rɪˈstreɪnt) NOUN 1 the ability to control or moderate one's impulses, passions, etc: *to show restraint.* 2 the act of restraining or the state of being restrained. 3 something that restrains; restriction.
▷HISTORY C15: from Old French *restreinte*, from *restreindre* to RESTRAIN

restraint of trade NOUN action tending to interfere with the freedom to compete in business.

restraint order NOUN *Law* another name for **freezing injunction.**

restrict (rɪˈstrɪkt) VERB (often foll by *to*) to confine or keep within certain often specified limits or selected bounds: *to restrict one's drinking to the evening.*
▷HISTORY C16: from Latin *rēstrictus* bound up, from *rēstringere*; see RESTRAIN

restricted (rɪˈstrɪktɪd) ADJECTIVE 1 limited or confined. 2 not accessible to the general public or (*esp US*) out of bounds to military personnel. 3 *Brit* denoting or in a zone in which a speed limit or waiting restrictions for vehicles apply.
▸**reˈstrictedly** ADVERB ▸**reˈstrictedness** NOUN

restricted users group NOUN a group of people who, with knowledge of a secret password, or by some other method, have access to restricted information stored in a computer. Abbreviation: **RUG.**

restriction (rɪˈstrɪkʃən) NOUN 1 something that restricts; a restrictive measure, law, etc. 2 the act of restricting or the state of being restricted. 3 *Logic, maths* a condition that imposes a constraint on the possible values of a variable or on the domain of arguments of a function.
▸**reˈstrictionist** NOUN, ADJECTIVE

restriction enzyme NOUN any of several enzymes produced by bacteria as a defence against viral infection and commonly used to cut DNA for genetic manipulation or diagnosis.

restriction fragment NOUN *Genetics* a fragment of a DNA molecule cleaved by a restriction enzyme. See also **RFLP.**

restrictive (rɪˈstrɪktɪv) ADJECTIVE 1 restricting or tending to restrict. 2 *Grammar* denoting a relative clause or phrase that restricts the number of possible referents of its antecedent. The relative clause in *Americans who live in New York* is restrictive; the relative clause in *Americans, who are generally extrovert*, is nonrestrictive.
▸**reˈstrictively** ADVERB ▸**reˈstrictiveness** NOUN

restrictive covenant NOUN *Law* a covenant imposing a restriction on the use of land for the purpose of preserving the enjoyment or value of adjoining land.

restrictive practice NOUN *Brit* 1 a trading agreement against the public interest. 2 a practice of a union or other group tending to limit the freedom of other workers or employers.

rest room NOUN a room in a public building having lavatories, washing facilities, and sometimes couches.

restructure (riːˈstrʌktʃə) VERB (*tr*) to organize (a system, business, society, etc.) in a different way: *radical attempts to restructure the economy.*
▸**reˈstructuring** NOUN

rest stop NOUN the US name for **lay-by** (sense 1).

resubmit (ˌriːsəbˈmɪt) VERB **-mits, -mitting, -mitted.** to submit again: *to rework and resubmit her designs.*

result (rɪˈzʌlt) NOUN 1 something that ensues from an action, policy, course of events, etc.; outcome; consequence. 2 a number, quantity, or value obtained by solving a mathematical problem. 3 *US* a decision of a legislative body. 4 (*often plural*) the final score or outcome of a sporting contest. 5 a favourable result, esp a victory or success. ◆ VERB (*intr*) 6 (often foll by *from*) to be the outcome or consequence (of). 7 (foll by *in*) to issue or terminate (in a specified way, state, etc.); end: *to result in tragedy.* 8 *Property law* (of an undisposed or partially disposed of interest in land) to revert to a former owner when the prior interests come to an end.
▷HISTORY C15: from Latin *resultāre* to rebound, spring from, from RE- + *saltāre* to leap

resultant (rɪˈzʌltənt) ADJECTIVE 1 that results; resulting. ◆ NOUN 2 *Maths, physics* a single vector that is the vector sum of two or more other vectors.

resultant tone NOUN a musical sound sometimes heard when two loud notes are sounded together, either lower in pitch than either (**differential tone**) or higher (**summational tone**).

resume (rɪˈzjuːm) VERB 1 to begin again or go on with (something adjourned or interrupted). 2 (*tr*) to occupy again, take back, or recover: *to resume one's seat; to resume possession.* 3 (*tr*) to assume (a title, office, etc.) again: *to resume the presidency.* 4 *Archaic* to summarize; make a résumé of.
▷HISTORY C15: from Latin *resūmere* to take up again, from RE- + *sūmere* to take up
▸**reˈsumable** ADJECTIVE ▸**reˈsumer** NOUN

résumé (ˈrɛzjuˌmeɪ) NOUN 1 a short descriptive summary, as of events. 2 *US and Canadian* another name for **curriculum vitae.**
▷HISTORY C19: from French, from *résumer* to RESUME

resumption (rɪˈzʌmpʃən) NOUN the act of resuming or beginning again.
▷HISTORY C15: via Old French from Late Latin *resumptiō*, from Latin *resūmere* to RESUME
▸**reˈsumptive** ADJECTIVE ▸**reˈsumptively** ADVERB

resupinate (rɪˈsjuːpɪnɪt) ADJECTIVE *Botany* (of plant parts, esp the flowers of many orchids) reversed or inverted in position, so as to appear to be upside down.
▷HISTORY C18: from Latin *resupīnātus* bent back, from *resupīnāre*, from RE- + *supīnāre* to place on the back; see SUPINE
▸**reˌsupiˈnation** NOUN

resupine (rɪˈsjuːpaɪn) ADJECTIVE *Rare* lying on the back; supine.
▷HISTORY C17: from Latin *resupīnus* lying on the back

resupply (ˌriːsəˈplaɪ) VERB **-plies, -plying, -plied.** (*tr*) to provide (with something) again.

resurface (riːˈsɜːfɪs) VERB 1 (*intr*) to arise or occur again: *the problem resurfaced.* 2 (*intr*) to rise or cause to rise again to the surface. 3 (*tr*) to supply (something) with a new surface.

resurge (rɪˈsɜːdʒ) VERB (*intr*) *Rare* to rise again from or as if from the dead.
▷HISTORY C16: from Latin *resurgere* to rise again, reappear, from RE- + *surgere* to lift, arise, SURGE

resurgent (rɪˈsɜːdʒənt) ADJECTIVE rising again, as to new life, vigour, etc.: *resurgent nationalism.*
▸**reˈsurgence** NOUN

resurrect (ˌrɛzəˈrɛkt) VERB 1 to rise or raise from the dead; bring or be brought back to life. 2 (*tr*) to bring back into use or activity; revive: *to resurrect an ancient law.* 3 (*tr*) to renew (one's hopes, etc.). 4 (*tr*) *Facetious* (formerly) to exhume and steal (a body) from its grave, esp in order to sell it.

resurrection (ˌrɛzəˈrɛkʃən) NOUN 1 a supposed act or instance of a dead person coming back to life. 2 belief in the possibility of this as part of a religious or mystical system. 3 the condition of

those who have risen from the dead: *we shall all live in the resurrection.*
▷HISTORY C13: via Old French from Late Latin *resurrectiō*, from Latin *resurgere* to rise again; see RESURGE
▸**ˌresurˈrectional** *or* **ˌresurˈrectionary** ADJECTIVE

Resurrection (ˌrɛzəˈrɛkʃən) NOUN *Christian theol* [1] the rising again of Christ from the tomb three days after his death. [2] the rising again from the dead of all mankind at the Last Judgment.

resurrectionism (ˌrɛzəˈrɛkʃəˌnɪzəm) NOUN [1] belief that men will rise again from the dead, esp the Christian doctrine of the Resurrection of Christ and of all mankind at the Last Judgment. [2] *Facetious* (formerly) body snatching.

resurrectionist (ˌrɛzəˈrɛkʃənɪst) NOUN [1] *Facetious* (formerly) a body snatcher. [2] a member of an Anglican religious community founded in 1892. [3] a person who believes in the Resurrection.

resurrection plant NOUN any of several unrelated desert plants that form a tight ball when dry and unfold and bloom when moistened. The best-known examples are the crucifer *Anastatica hierochuntica* (also called **rose of Jericho**), club mosses of the genus *Selaginella*, and the composite *Asteriscus pygmoeus*.

resuscitate (rɪˈsʌsɪˌteɪt) VERB (*tr*) to restore to consciousness; revive.
▷HISTORY C16: from Latin *resuscitāre*, from RE- + *suscitāre* to raise, from *sub-* up from below + *citāre* to rouse, from *citus* quick
▸**reˈsuscitable** ADJECTIVE ▸**reˌsusciˈtation** NOUN ▸**reˈsuscitative** ADJECTIVE

resuscitator (rɪˈsʌsɪˌteɪtə) NOUN [1] an apparatus for forcing oxygen or a mixture containing oxygen into the lungs. [2] a person who resuscitates.

ret (rɛt) VERB **rets, retting, retted.** (*tr*) to moisten or soak (flax, hemp, jute, etc.) to promote bacterial action in order to facilitate separation of the fibres from the woody tissue by beating.
▷HISTORY C15: of Germanic origin; related to Middle Dutch *reeten*, Swedish *röta*, German *rösten*; see ROT[1]

retable (rɪˈteɪbəl) NOUN an ornamental screenlike structure above and behind an altar, esp one used as a setting for a religious picture or carving.
▷HISTORY C19: from French, from Spanish *retablo*, from Latin *retrō* behind + *tabula* board; see REAR[1], TABLE

retail (ˈriːteɪl) NOUN [1] the sale of goods individually or in small quantities to consumers. Compare **wholesale** (sense 1). ◆ ADJECTIVE [2] of, relating to, or engaged in such selling: *retail prices.* ◆ ADVERB [3] in small amounts or at a retail price. ◆ VERB [4] to sell or be sold in small quantities to consumers. [5] (rɪˈteɪl) (*tr*) to relate (gossip, scandal, etc.) in detail, esp persistently.
▷HISTORY C14: from Old French *retaillier* to cut off, from RE- + *taillier* to cut; see TAILOR
▸**ˈretailer** NOUN

retail price index NOUN (in Britain) a list, based on government figures and usually published monthly, that shows the extent of change in the prices of a range of goods selected as being essential items in the budget of a normal household. Abbreviation: **RPI.**

retail therapy NOUN *Jocular* the action of shopping for clothes, etc. in order to cheer oneself up.

retain (rɪˈteɪn) VERB (*tr*) [1] to keep in one's possession. [2] to be able to hold or contain: *soil that retains water.* [3] (of a person) to be able to remember (information, facts, etc.) without difficulty. [4] to hold in position. [5] to keep for one's future use, as by paying a retainer or nominal charge: *to retain one's rooms for the holidays.* [6] *Law* to engage the services of (a barrister) by payment of a preliminary fee. [7] (in selling races) to buy back a winner that one owns when it is auctioned after the race. [8] (of racehorse trainers) to pay an advance fee to (a jockey) so as to have prior or exclusive claims upon his services throughout the season.
▷HISTORY C14: from Old French *retenir*, from Latin *retinēre* to hold back, from RE- + *tenēre* to hold
▸**reˈtainable** ADJECTIVE ▸**reˈtainment** NOUN

retained object NOUN *Grammar* a direct or indirect object of a passive verb. The phrase *the drawings* in the sentence *Harry was given the drawings* is a retained object.

retainer (rɪˈteɪnə) NOUN [1] *History* a supporter or dependant of a person of rank, esp a soldier. [2] a servant, esp one who has been with a family for a long time. [3] a clip, frame, or similar device that prevents a part of a machine, engine, etc., from moving. [4] a dental appliance for holding a loose tooth or prosthetic device in position. [5] a fee paid in advance to secure first option on the services of a barrister, jockey, etc. [6] a reduced rent paid for a flat, room, etc., during absence to reserve it for future use.

retaining ring NOUN another name for **circlip.**

retaining wall NOUN a wall constructed to hold back earth, loose rock, etc. Also called: **revetment.**

retake VERB (riːˈteɪk) **-takes, -taking, -took, -taken.** (*tr*) [1] to take back or capture again: *to retake a fortress.* [2] *Films* to shoot again (a shot or scene). [3] to tape again (a recording). ◆ NOUN (ˈriːˌteɪk) [4] *Films* a rephotographed shot or scene. [5] a retaped recording.
▸**reˈtaker** NOUN

retaliate (rɪˈtælɪˌeɪt) VERB [1] (*intr*) to take retributory action, esp by returning some injury or wrong in kind. [2] (*tr*) *Rare* to avenge (an injury, wrong, etc.).
▷HISTORY C17: from Late Latin *retāliāre*, from Latin RE- + *tālis* of such kind
▸**reˌtaliˈation** NOUN ▸**reˈtaliative** *or* **reˈtaliatory** ADJECTIVE ▸**reˈtaliˌator** NOUN

retard (rɪˈtɑːd) VERB (*tr*) to delay or slow down (the progress, speed, or development) of (something).
▷HISTORY C15: from Old French *retarder*, from Latin *retardāre*, from RE- + *tardāre* to make slow, from *tardus* sluggish; see TARDY

retardant (rɪˈtɑːdənt) NOUN [1] a substance that reduces the rate of a chemical reaction. ◆ ADJECTIVE [2] having a slowing effect.

retardate (rɪˈtɑːdeɪt) NOUN *Psychol* a person who is retarded.

retardation (ˌriːtɑːˈdeɪʃən) *or less commonly* **retardment** (rɪˈtɑːdmənt) NOUN [1] the act of retarding or the state of being retarded. [2] something that retards; hindrance. [3] the rate of deceleration. [4] *Psychiatry* the slowing down of mental functioning and bodily movement.
▸**reˈtardative** *or* **reˈtardatory** ADJECTIVE

retarded (rɪˈtɑːdɪd) ADJECTIVE underdeveloped, esp mentally and esp having an IQ of 70 to 85. See also **ESN, mental handicap, subnormal** (sense 2).

retarder (rɪˈtɑːdə) NOUN [1] a person or thing that retards. [2] a substance added to slow down the rate of a chemical change, such as one added to cement to delay its setting.

retch (rɛtʃ, riːtʃ) VERB [1] (*intr*) to undergo an involuntary spasm of ineffectual vomiting; heave. [2] to vomit. ◆ NOUN [3] an involuntary spasm of ineffectual vomiting.
▷HISTORY Old English *hrǣcan*; related to Old Norse *hrǣkja* to spit

retd ABBREVIATION FOR: [1] retired. [2] retained. [3] returned.

rete (ˈriːtɪ) NOUN, *plural* **retia** (ˈriːʃɪə, -tɪə). *Anatomy* any network of nerves or blood vessels; plexus.
▷HISTORY C14 (referring to a metal network used with an astrolabe): from Latin *rēte* net
▸**ˈretial** ADJECTIVE

retell (riːˈtɛl) VERB **-tells, -telling, -told.** (*tr*) to relate (a story, etc.) again or differently.

retene (ˈriːtiːn, ˈrɛt-) NOUN a yellow crystalline hydrocarbon found in tar oils from pine wood and in certain fossil resins. Formula: $C_{18}H_{18}$.
▷HISTORY C19: from Greek *rhētinē* resin

retention (rɪˈtɛnʃən) NOUN [1] the act of retaining or state of being retained. [2] the capacity to hold or retain liquid. [3] the capacity to remember. [4] *Pathol* the abnormal holding within the body of urine, faeces, etc., that are normally excreted. [5] *Commerce* a sum of money owed to a contractor but not paid for an agreed period as a safeguard against any faults found in the work carried out. [6] (*plural*) *Accounting* profits earned by a company but not distributed as dividends; retained earnings.
▷HISTORY C14: from Latin *retentiō*, from *retinēre* to RETAIN

retentionist (rɪˈtɛnʃənɪst) NOUN a person who advocates the retention of something, esp capital punishment.

retentive (rɪˈtɛntɪv) ADJECTIVE having the capacity to retain or remember.
▸**reˈtentively** ADVERB ▸**reˈtentiveness** NOUN

retentivity (ˌriːtɛnˈtɪvɪtɪ) NOUN [1] the state or quality of being retentive. [2] *Physics* another name for **remanence.**

retest (riːˈtɛst) VERB (*tr*) to test (something) again or differently.

rethink VERB (riːˈθɪŋk) **-thinks, -thinking, -thought.** [1] to think about (something) again, esp with a view to changing one's tactics or opinions. ◆ NOUN (ˈriːˌθɪŋk) [2] the act or an instance of thinking again.

retiarius (ˌriːtɪˈɛərɪəs, ˌriːʃɪ-) NOUN, *plural* **-arii** (-ˈɛərɪˌaɪ). (in ancient Rome) a gladiator armed with a net and trident.
▷HISTORY Latin, from *rēte* net

retiary (ˈriːtɪərɪ, -ʃɪə-) ADJECTIVE *Rare* of, relating to, or resembling a net or web.
▷HISTORY C17: from Latin RETIARIUS

reticent (ˈrɛtɪsənt) ADJECTIVE not open or communicative; not saying all that one knows; taciturn; reserved.
▷HISTORY C19: from Latin *reticēre* to keep silent, from RE- + *tacēre* to be silent
▸**ˈreticence** NOUN ▸**ˈreticently** ADVERB

reticle (ˈrɛtɪkəl) *or less commonly* **reticule** NOUN a network of fine lines, wires, etc., placed in the focal plane of an optical instrument to assist measurement of the size or position of objects under observation. Also called: **graticule.**
▷HISTORY C17: from Latin *rēticulum* a little net, from *rēte* net

reticulate (rɪˈtɪkjʊlɪt) ADJECTIVE *also* **reticular** (rɪˈtɪkjʊlə). [1] in the form of a network or having a network of parts: *a reticulate leaf.* [2] resembling, covered with, or having the form of a net. ◆ VERB (rɪˈtɪkjʊˌleɪt) [3] to form or be formed into a net.
▷HISTORY C17: from Late Latin *rēticulātus* made like a net
▸**reˈticulately** ADVERB ▸**reˌticuˈlation** NOUN

reticule (ˈrɛtɪˌkjuːl) NOUN [1] (in the 18th and 19th centuries) a woman's small bag or purse, usually in the form of a pouch with a drawstring and made of net, beading, brocade, etc. [2] a variant of **reticle.**
▷HISTORY C18: from French *réticule*, from Latin *rēticulum* RETICLE

reticulocyte (rɪˈtɪkjʊləˌsaɪt) NOUN an immature red blood cell containing a network of granules or filaments.
▷HISTORY C20: from RETICULUM + -CYTE

reticuloendothelial (rɪˌtɪkjʊləʊˌɛndəʊˈθiːlɪəl) ADJECTIVE *Physiol* denoting or relating to a bodily system that consists of all the cells able to ingest bacteria, colloidal particles, etc., with the exception of the leucocytes; it includes the lymphatic system and the spleen. See also **macrophage.**
▷HISTORY C20: from RETICULUM + ENDOTHELIAL

reticulum (rɪˈtɪkjʊləm) NOUN, *plural* **-la** (-lə). [1] any fine network, esp one in the body composed of cells, fibres, etc. [2] the second compartment of the stomach of ruminants, situated between the rumen and psalterium.
▷HISTORY C17: from Latin: little net, from *rēte* net

Reticulum (rɪˈtɪkjʊləm) NOUN, *Latin genitive* **Reticuli** (rɪˈtɪkjʊˌlaɪ). a small constellation in the S hemisphere lying between Dorado and Hydrus.

retiform (ˈriːtɪˌfɔːm, ˈrɛt-) ADJECTIVE *Rare* netlike; reticulate.
▷HISTORY C17: from Latin *rēte* net + *forma* shape

retina (ˈrɛtɪnə) NOUN, *plural* **-nas, -nae** (-ˌniː). the light-sensitive membrane forming the inner lining of the posterior wall of the eyeball, composed largely of a specialized terminal expansion of the optic nerve. Images focused here by the lens of the eye are transmitted to the brain as nerve impulses.
▷HISTORY C14: from Medieval Latin, perhaps from Latin *rēte* net
▸**ˈretinal** ADJECTIVE

retinaculum (ˌrɛtɪˈnækjʊləm) NOUN, *plural* **-la** (-lə). [1] connection or retention or something that connects or retains. [2] *Zoology* a small hook that joins the forewing and hind wing of a moth during flight.

▷HISTORY C18 (a surgical instrument used in castration): Latin, from *rētinēre* to hold back
▸**ˌretiˈnacular** ADJECTIVE

retinal rivalry NOUN *Psychol* another name for **binocular rivalry.**

retinene (ˈrɛtɪˌniːn) *or* **retinal** (ˈrɛtɪnəl) NOUN the aldehyde form of the polyene retinol (vitamin A) that associates with the protein opsin to form the visual purple pigment rhodopsin.
▷HISTORY C20: from RETINA + -ENE

retinite (ˈrɛtɪˌnaɪt) NOUN any of various resins of fossil origin, esp one derived from lignite.
▷HISTORY C19: from French *rétinite*, from Greek *rhētinē* resin + -ITE[1]

retinitis (ˌrɛtɪˈnaɪtɪs) NOUN inflammation of the retina.
▷HISTORY C20: from New Latin, from RETINA + -ITIS

retinol (ˈrɛtɪˌnɒl) NOUN another name for **vitamin A** and **rosin oil.**
▷HISTORY C19: from Greek *rhētinē* resin + -OL[1]

retinoscopy (ˌrɛtɪˈnɒskəpɪ) NOUN *Ophthalmol* a procedure for detecting errors of refraction in the eye by means of an instrument (**retinoscope**) that reflects a beam of light from a mirror into the eye. Diagnosis is made by observing the areas of shadow and the direction in which the light moves when the mirror is rotated. Also called: **skiascopy, shadow test.**
▸**retinoscopic** (ˌrɛtɪnəˈskɒpɪk) ADJECTIVE
▸**ˌretinoˈscopically** ADVERB ▸**ˌretiˈnoscopist** NOUN

retinue (ˈrɛtɪˌnjuː) NOUN a body of aides and retainers attending an important person, royalty, etc.
▷HISTORY C14: from Old French *retenue*, from *retenir* to RETAIN
▸**ˈretiˌnued** ADJECTIVE

retiral (rɪˈtaɪərᵊl) NOUN *Scot* the act of retiring from office, one's work, etc.; retirement.

retire (rɪˈtaɪə) VERB (*mainly intr*) [1] (*also tr*) to give up or to cause (a person) to give up his work, a post, etc., esp on reaching pensionable age (in Britain and Australia usually 65 for men, 60 for women). [2] to go away, as into seclusion, for recuperation, etc. [3] to go to bed. [4] to recede or disappear: *the sun retired behind the clouds.* [5] to withdraw from a sporting contest, esp because of injury. [6] (*also tr*) to pull back (troops, etc.) from battle or an exposed position or (of troops, etc.) to fall back. [7] (*tr*) **a** to remove (bills, bonds, shares, etc.) from circulation by taking them up and paying for them. **b** to remove (money) from circulation.
▷HISTORY C16: from French *retirer*, from Old French RE- + *tirer* to pull, draw
▸**reˈtirer** NOUN

retired (rɪˈtaɪəd) ADJECTIVE [1] **a** having given up one's work, office, etc., esp on completion of the normal period of service: *a retired headmistress.* **b** (*as collective noun*; preceded by *the*): *the retired.* [2] withdrawn; secluded: *a retired life; a retired cottage in the woods.*

retiree (rɪˌtaɪəˈriː) NOUN *Chiefly US* a person who has retired from work.

retirement (rɪˈtaɪəmənt) NOUN [1] **a** the act of retiring from one's work, office, etc. **b** (*as modifier*): *retirement age.* [2] the period of being retired from work: *she had many plans for her retirement.* [3] seclusion from the world; privacy. [4] the act of going away or retreating.

retirement pension NOUN a pension given to a person who has retired from regular employment, whether paid by the state, arising from the person's former employment, or the product of investment in a personal or stakeholder pension scheme.

retirement relief NOUN (formerly in Britain) relief from capital-gains tax given to persons at or over 50 when disposing of business assets.

retiring (rɪˈtaɪərɪŋ) ADJECTIVE shunning contact with others; shy; reserved.
▸**reˈtiringly** ADVERB

retool (riːˈtuːl) VERB [1] to replace, re-equip, or rearrange the tools in (a factory, etc.). [2] *Chiefly US and Canadian* to revise or reorganize.

retorsion (rɪˈtɔːʃən) NOUN *Rare* retaliatory action taken by a state whose citizens have been mistreated by a foreign power by treating the subjects of that power similarly; reprisal.
▷HISTORY C17: from French; see RETORT[1]

retort[1] (rɪˈtɔːt) VERB [1] (when *tr, takes a clause as object*) to utter (something) quickly, sharply, wittily, or angrily, in response. [2] to use (an argument) against its originator; turn the tables by saying (something). ◆ NOUN [3] a sharp, angry, or witty reply. [4] an argument used against its originator.
▷HISTORY C16: from Latin *retorquēre* to twist back, from RE- + *torquēre* to twist, wrench
▸**reˈtorter** NOUN

retort[2] (rɪˈtɔːt) NOUN [1] a glass vessel with a round bulb and long tapering neck that is bent down, used esp in a laboratory for distillation. [2] a vessel in which large quantities of material may be heated, esp one used for heating ores in the production of metals or heating coal to produce gas. ◆ VERB [3] (*tr*) to heat in a retort.
▷HISTORY C17: from French *retorte*, from Medieval Latin *retorta*, from Latin *retorquēre* to twist back; see RETORT[1]

retortion (rɪˈtɔːʃən) NOUN [1] the act of retorting. [2] a variant spelling of **retorsion.**

retouch (riːˈtʌtʃ) VERB (*tr*) [1] to restore, correct, or improve (a painting, make-up, etc.) with new touches. [2] *Photog* to alter (a negative or print) by painting over blemishes or adding details. [3] to make small finishing improvements to. [4] *Archaeol* to detach small flakes from (a blank) in order to make a tool. ◆ NOUN [5] the art or practice of retouching. [6] a detail that is the result of retouching. [7] a photograph, painting, etc., that has been retouched. [8] *Archaeol* fine percussion to shape flakes of stone into usable tools.
▸**reˈtouchable** ADJECTIVE ▸**reˈtoucher** NOUN

retrace (rɪˈtreɪs) VERB (*tr*) [1] to go back over (one's steps, a route, etc.) again: *we retraced the route we took last summer.* [2] to go over (a past event) in the mind; recall. [3] to go over (a story, account, etc.) from the beginning.
▸**reˈtraceable** ADJECTIVE ▸**reˈtracement** NOUN

re-trace (riːˈtreɪs) VERB (*tr*) to trace (a map, drawing, etc.) again.

retract (rɪˈtrækt) VERB [1] (*tr*) to draw in (a part or appendage): *a snail can retract its horns; to retract the landing gear of an aircraft.* [2] to withdraw (a statement, opinion, charge, etc.) as invalid or unjustified. [3] to go back on (a promise or agreement). [4] (*intr*) to shrink back, as in fear. [5] *Phonetics* to modify the articulation of (a vowel) by bringing the tongue back away from the lips.
▷HISTORY C16: from Latin *retractāre* to withdraw, from *tractāre* to pull, from *trahere* to drag
▸**reˈtractable** *or* **reˈtractible** ADJECTIVE ▸**reˌtractaˈbility** *or* **reˌtractibility** NOUN ▸**retractation** (ˌriːtrækˈteɪʃən) NOUN
▸**reˈtractive** ADJECTIVE

retractile (rɪˈtræktaɪl) ADJECTIVE capable of being drawn in: *the retractile claws of a cat.*
▸**retractility** (ˌriːtrækˈtɪlɪtɪ) NOUN

retraction (rɪˈtrækʃən) NOUN [1] the act of retracting or state of being retracted. [2] the withdrawal of a statement, charge, etc.

retractor (rɪˈtræktə) NOUN [1] *Anatomy* any of various muscles that retract an organ or part. [2] *Surgery* an instrument for holding back the edges of a surgical incision or organ or part. [3] a person or thing that retracts.

retrain (riːˈtreɪn) VERB [1] (*tr*) to teach (someone) a new skill so that he or she can do a job or find employment. [2] (*intr*) to learn a new skill with a view to doing a job or finding employment.

retral (ˈriːtrəl, ˈrɛtrəl) ADJECTIVE *Rare* at, near, or towards the back.
▷HISTORY C19: from Latin *retrō* backwards
▸**ˈretrally** ADVERB

retread VERB (riːˈtrɛd) **-treads, -treading, -treaded.** [1] (*tr*) another word for **remould** (sense 2). ◆ NOUN (ˈriːˌtrɛd) [2] another word for **remould** (sense 3). [3] *Austral & NZ informal* a pensioner who has resumed employment, esp in a former profession. [4] a film, piece of music, etc. which is a superficially altered version of an earlier original.

re-tread (riːˈtrɛd) VERB **-treads, -treading, -trod, -trodden** *or* **-trod.** (*tr*) to tread or walk over (one's steps) again.

retreat (rɪˈtriːt) VERB (*mainly intr*) [1] *Military* to withdraw or retire in the face of or from action with an enemy, either due to defeat or in order to adopt a more favourable position. [2] to retire or withdraw, as to seclusion or shelter. [3] (of a person's features) to slope back; recede. [4] (*tr*) *Chess* to move (a piece) back. ◆ NOUN [5] the act of retreating or withdrawing. [6] *Military* **a** a withdrawal or retirement in the face of the enemy. **b** a bugle call signifying withdrawal or retirement, esp (formerly) to within a defended fortification. [7] retirement or seclusion. [8] a place, such as a sanatorium or monastery, to which one may retire for refuge, quiet, etc. [9] a period of seclusion, esp for religious contemplation. [10] an institution, esp a private one, for the care and treatment of the mentally ill, infirm, elderly, etc.
▷HISTORY C14: from Old French *retret*, from *retraire* to withdraw, from Latin *retrahere* to pull back; see RETRACT

retrench (rɪˈtrɛntʃ) VERB [1] to reduce or curtail (costs); economize. [2] (*tr*) to shorten, delete, or abridge. [3] (*tr*) to protect by a retrenchment.
▷HISTORY C17: from Old French *retrenchier*, from RE- + *trenchier* to cut, from Latin *truncāre* to lop; see TRENCH
▸**reˈtrenchable** ADJECTIVE

retrenchment (rɪˈtrɛntʃmənt) NOUN [1] the act of reducing expenditure in order to improve financial stability. [2] an extra interior fortification to reinforce outer walls.

retrial (riːˈtraɪəl) NOUN a second or new trial, esp of a case that has already been adjudicated upon.

retribution (ˌrɛtrɪˈbjuːʃən) NOUN [1] the act of punishing or taking vengeance for wrongdoing, sin, or injury. [2] punishment or vengeance.
▷HISTORY C14: via Old French from Church Latin *retribūtiō*, from Latin *retribuere* to repay, from RE- + *tribuere* to pay; see TRIBUTE
▸**retributive** (rɪˈtrɪbjʊtɪv) *or* (*less commonly*) **reˈtributory** ADJECTIVE ▸**reˈtributively** ADVERB

retrieval (rɪˈtriːvᵊl) NOUN [1] the act or process of retrieving. [2] the possibility of recovery, restoration, or rectification (esp in the phrase **beyond retrieval**). [3] a computer filing operation that recalls records or other data from a file.

retrieve (rɪˈtriːv) VERB (*mainly tr*) [1] to get or fetch back again; recover: *he retrieved his papers from various people's drawers.* [2] to bring back to a more satisfactory state; revive. [3] to extricate from trouble or danger; rescue or save. [4] to recover or make newly available (stored information) from a computer system. [5] (*also intr*) (of dogs) to find and fetch (shot game). [6] *Tennis, squash, badminton* to return successfully (a shot difficult to reach). [7] to recall; remember. ◆ NOUN [8] the act of retrieving. [9] the chance of being retrieved.
▷HISTORY C15: from Old French *retrover*, from RE- + *trouver* to find, perhaps from Vulgar Latin *tropāre* (unattested) to compose; see TROVER, TROUBADOUR
▸**reˈtrievable** ADJECTIVE ▸**reˌtrievaˈbility** NOUN
▸**reˈtrievably** ADVERB

retriever (rɪˈtriːvə) NOUN [1] one of a breed of large gun dogs that can be trained to retrieve game: see **golden retriever, labrador retriever, Chesapeake Bay retriever, curly-coated retriever, flat-coated retriever.** [2] any dog used to retrieve shot game. [3] a person or thing that retrieves.

retro (ˈrɛtrəʊ) NOUN, *plural* **-ros.** [1] short for **retrorocket.** ◆ ADJECTIVE [2] denoting something associated with or revived from the past: *retro dressing; retro fashion.*

retro- PREFIX [1] back or backwards: *retroactive.* [2] located behind: *retrolental.*
▷HISTORY from Latin *retrō* behind, backwards

retroact (ˈrɛtrəʊˌækt) VERB (*intr*) [1] to act in opposition. [2] to influence or have reference to past events.

retroaction (ˌrɛtrəʊˈækʃən) NOUN [1] an action contrary or reciprocal to a preceding action. [2] a retrospective action, esp a law affecting events prior to its enactment.

retroactive (ˌrɛtrəʊˈæktɪv) ADJECTIVE [1] applying or referring to the past: *retroactive legislation.* [2] effective or operative from a date or for a period in the past.
▸**ˌretroˈactively** ADVERB ▸**ˌretroˈactiveness** *or* **ˌretroacˈtivity** NOUN

retroactive inhibition *or* **interference** NOUN *Psychol* the tendency for the retention of learned material or skills to be impaired by subsequent learning, esp by learning of a similar kind. Compare **proactive inhibition.**

retrocede (ˌrɛtrəʊˈsiːd) VERB [1] (tr) to give back; return. [2] (intr) to go back or retire; recede. ▸**retrocession** (ˌrɛtrəʊˈsɛʃən) *or* **ˌretroˈcedence** NOUN ▸**ˌretroˈcessive** *or* **ˌretroˈcedent** ADJECTIVE

retrochoir (ˈrɛtrəʊˌkwaɪə) NOUN the space in a large church or cathedral behind the high altar.

retrofire (ˈrɛtrəʊˌfaɪə) NOUN [1] the act of firing a retrorocket. [2] the moment at which it is fired.

retrofit (ˈrɛtrəʊˌfɪt) VERB **-fits, -fitting, -fitted.** (tr) to equip (a vehicle, piece of equipment, etc.) with new parts, safety devices, etc., after manufacture.

retroflex (ˈrɛtrəʊˌflɛks) *or* **retroflexed** ADJECTIVE [1] bent or curved backwards. [2] *Phonetics* of, relating to, or involving retroflexion.
▷HISTORY C18: from Latin *retrōflexus*, from *retrōflectere*, from RETRO- + *flectere* to bend

retroflexion *or* **retroflection** (ˌrɛtrəʊˈflɛkʃən) NOUN [1] the act or condition of bending or being bent backwards. [2] *Phonetics* the act of turning the tip of the tongue upwards and backwards towards the hard palate in the articulation of a vowel or a consonant.

retrograde (ˈrɛtrəʊˌɡreɪd) ADJECTIVE [1] moving or bending backwards. [2] (esp of order) reverse or inverse. [3] tending towards an earlier worse condition; declining or deteriorating. [4] *Astronomy* **a** occurring or orbiting in a direction opposite to that of the earth's motion around the sun. Compare **direct** (sense 18). **b** occurring or orbiting in a direction around a planet opposite to the planet's rotational direction: *the retrograde motion of the satellite Phoebe around Saturn.* **c** appearing to move in a clockwise direction due to the rotational period exceeding the period of revolution around the sun: *Venus has retrograde rotation.* [5] *Biology* tending to retrogress; degenerate. [6] *Music* of, concerning, or denoting a melody or part that is played backwards. [7] *Obsolete* opposed, contrary, or repugnant to. ◆ VERB (intr) [8] to move in a retrograde direction; retrogress. [9] *US military* another word for **retreat** (sense 1).
▷HISTORY C14: from Latin *retrōgradī* to go backwards, from *gradi* to walk, go
▸**ˌretrograˈdation** NOUN ▸**ˈretroˌgradely** ADVERB

retrograde amnesia NOUN amnesia caused by a trauma such as concussion, in which the memory loss relates to material learnt before the trauma. Compare **anterograde amnesia.**

retrogress (ˌrɛtrəʊˈɡrɛs) VERB (intr) [1] to go back to an earlier, esp worse, condition; degenerate or deteriorate. [2] to move backwards; recede. [3] *Biology* to develop characteristics or features of lower or simpler organisms; degenerate.
▷HISTORY C19: from Latin *retrōgressus* having moved backwards, from *retrōgradī*; see RETROGRADE
▸**ˌretroˈgression** NOUN ▸**ˌretroˈgressive** ADJECTIVE ▸**ˌretroˈgressively** ADVERB

retroject (ˌrɛtrəʊˈdʒɛkt) VERB (tr) to throw backwards (opposed to *project*).
▷HISTORY C19: from RETRO- + *-ject* as in PROJECT
▸**ˌretroˈjection** NOUN

retrolental (ˌrɛtrəʊˈlɛntᵊl) ADJECTIVE behind a lens, esp of the eye.
▷HISTORY C20: from RETRO- + *-lental*, from New Latin: LENS

retro-operative ADJECTIVE affecting or operating on past events; retroactive.

retropack (ˈrɛtrəʊˌpæk) NOUN a system of retrorockets on a spacecraft.

retropulsion (ˌrɛtrəʊˈpʌlʃən) NOUN *Med* an abnormal tendency to walk backwards: a symptom of Parkinson's disease.

retrorocket (ˈrɛtrəʊˌrɒkɪt) NOUN a small auxiliary rocket engine on a larger rocket, missile, or spacecraft, that produces thrust in the opposite direction to the direction of flight in order to decelerate the vehicle or make it move backwards. Often shortened to: **retro.**

retrorse (rɪˈtrɔːs) ADJECTIVE (esp of plant parts) pointing backwards or in a direction opposite to normal.
▷HISTORY C19: from Latin *retrōrsus*, shortened form of *retrōversus* turned back, from RETRO- + *vertere* to turn
▸**reˈtrorsely** ADVERB

retrospect (ˈrɛtrəʊˌspɛkt) NOUN [1] the act of surveying things past (often in the phrase **in retrospect**). ◆ VERB *Archaic* [2] to contemplate (anything past); look back on (something). [3] (intr; often foll by *to*) to refer.
▷HISTORY C17: from Latin *retrōspicere* to look back, from RETRO- + *specere* to look

retrospection (ˌrɛtrəʊˈspɛkʃən) NOUN the act of recalling things past, esp in one's personal experience.

retrospective (ˌrɛtrəʊˈspɛktɪv) ADJECTIVE [1] looking or directed backwards, esp in time; characterized by retrospection. [2] applying to the past; retroactive. ◆ NOUN [3] an exhibition of an artist's life's work or a representative selection of it.
▸**ˌretroˈspectively** ADVERB ▸**ˌretroˈspectiveness** NOUN

retroussé (rəˈtruːseɪ; *French* rətruse) ADJECTIVE (of a nose) turned up.
▷HISTORY C19: from French *retrousser* to tuck up; see TRUSS

retroversion (ˌrɛtrəʊˈvɜːʃən) NOUN [1] the act of turning or condition of being turned backwards. [2] the condition of a part or organ, esp the uterus, that is turned or tilted backwards.
▸**ˈretroˌverse** ADJECTIVE ▸**ˈretroˌverted** ADJECTIVE

Retrovir (ˈrɛtrəʊˌvɪə) NOUN *Trademark* a brand of the drug zidovudine.

retrovirus (ˈrɛtrəʊˌvaɪrəs) NOUN any of several viruses whose genetic specification is encoded in RNA rather than DNA and that are able to reverse the normal flow of genetic information from DNA to RNA by transcribing RNA into DNA: many retroviruses are known to cause cancer in animals.
▸**ˈretroˌviral** ADJECTIVE

retry (riːˈtraɪ) VERB **-tries, -trying, -tried.** (tr) to try again (a case already determined); give a new trial to.

retsina (rɛtˈsiːnə, ˈrɛtsɪnə) NOUN a Greek wine flavoured with resin.
▷HISTORY Modern Greek, from Italian *resina* RESIN

retune (riːˈtjuːn) VERB (tr) [1] to tune (a musical instrument) differently or again. [2] to tune (a radio, television, etc.) to a different frequency.

return (rɪˈtɜːn) VERB [1] (intr) to come back to a former place or state. [2] (tr) to give, take, or carry back; replace or restore. [3] (tr) to repay or recompense, esp with something of equivalent value: *return the compliment.* [4] (tr) to earn or yield (profit or interest) as an income from an investment or venture. [5] (intr) to come back or revert in thought or speech: *I'll return to that later.* [6] (intr) to recur or reappear: *the symptoms have returned.* [7] to answer or reply. [8] (tr) to vote into office; elect. [9] (tr) *Law* (of a jury) to deliver or render (a verdict). [10] (tr) to send back or reflect (light or sound): *the canyon returned my shout.* [11] (tr) to submit (a report, etc.) about (someone or something) to someone in authority. [12] (tr) *Cards* to lead back (the suit led by one's partner). [13] (tr) *Ball games* to hit, throw, or play (a ball) back. [14] (tr) *Architect* to turn (a part, decorative moulding, etc.) away from its original direction. [15] **return thanks.** (of Christians) to say grace before a meal. ◆ NOUN [16] the act or an instance of coming back. [17] something that is given or sent back, esp unsatisfactory merchandise returned to the maker or supplier or a theatre ticket sent back by a purchaser for resale. [18] the act or an instance of putting, sending, or carrying back; replacement or restoration. [19] (*often plural*) the yield, revenue, or profit accruing from an investment, transaction, or venture. [20] the act or an instance of reciprocation or repayment (esp in the phrase **in return for**). [21] a recurrence or reappearance. [22] an official report, esp of the financial condition of a company. [23] **a** a form (a **tax return**) on which a statement concerning one's taxable income is made. **b** the statement itself. [24] (*often plural*) a statement of the votes counted at an election or poll. [25] an answer or reply. [26] *Brit* short for **return ticket.** [27] *NZ informal* a second helping of food served at a table. [28] *Architect* **a** a part of a building that forms an angle with the façade. **b** any part of an architectural feature that forms an angle with the main part. [29] *Law* a report by a bailiff or other officer on the outcome of a formal document such as a claim, summons, etc., issued by a court. [30] *Cards* a lead of a card in the suit that one's partner has previously led. [31] *Ball games* the act of playing or throwing a ball back. [32] **by return (of post).** *Brit* by the next post back to the sender. [33] **many happy returns (of the day).** a conventional greeting to someone on his or her birthday. [34] **the point of no return.** the point at which a person's commitment is irrevocable. ◆ ADJECTIVE [35] of, relating to, or characterized by a return: *a return visit; a return performance.* [36] denoting a second, reciprocated occasion: *a return match.*
▷HISTORY C14: from Old French *retorner*; see RE-, TURN

returnable (rɪˈtɜːnəbᵊl) ADJECTIVE [1] able to be taken, given, or sent back. [2] required to be returned by law, as a claim to the court from which it issued.
▸**reˌturnaˈbility** NOUN

return crease NOUN *Cricket* one of two lines marked at right-angles to each bowling crease, from inside which a bowler must deliver the ball.

returned soldier NOUN *Austral and NZ* a soldier who has served abroad. Also: (Austral) **returned man.**

returnee (rɪˈtɜːˌniː) NOUN *Chiefly US and Canadian* a person who returns to his native country, esp after war service.

returner (rɪˈtɜːnə) NOUN [1] a person or thing that returns. [2] a person who goes back to work after a break, esp a woman who has had children.

returning officer NOUN (in Britain, Canada, Australia, etc.) an official in charge of conducting an election in a constituency or electoral district, who supervises the counting of votes and announces the results.

return ticket NOUN *Brit* a ticket entitling a passenger to travel to his destination and back again. US and Canadian equivalent: **round-trip ticket.**

retuse (rɪˈtjuːs) ADJECTIVE *Botany* having a rounded apex and a central depression: *retuse leaves.*
▷HISTORY C18: from Latin *retundere* to make blunt, from RE- + *tundere* to pound

Reuben (ˈruːbɪn) NOUN *Old Testament* [1] the eldest son of Jacob and Leah: one of the 12 patriarchs of Israel (Genesis 29:30). [2] the Israelite tribe descended from him. [3] the territory of this tribe, lying to the northeast of the Dead Sea. Douay spelling: **Ruben.**

reunify (riːˈjuːnɪˌfaɪ) VERB **-fies, -fying, -fied.** (tr) to bring together again (something, esp a country previously divided).
▸**ˌreunifiˈcation** NOUN

reunion (riːˈjuːnjən) NOUN [1] the act or process of coming together again. [2] the state or condition of having been brought together again. [3] a gathering of relatives, friends, or former associates.

Réunion (riːˈjuːnjən; *French* reynjɔ̃) NOUN an island in the Indian Ocean, in the Mascarene Islands: an overseas region of France, having been in French possession since 1642. Capital: Saint-Denis. Pop.: 733 000 (2001 est.). Area: 2510 sq. km (970 sq. miles).

reunionist (riːˈjuːnjənɪst) NOUN a person who desires or works for reunion between the Roman Catholic Church and the Church of England.
▸**reˈunionism** NOUN ▸**reˌunionˈistic** ADJECTIVE

reunite (ˌriːjuːˈnaɪt) VERB to bring or come together again.
▸**ˌreuˈnitable** ADJECTIVE ▸**ˌreuˈniter** NOUN

Reus (*Spanish* reus) NOUN a city in NE Spain, northwest of Tarragona: became commercially important after the establishment of an English colony (about 1750). Pop.: 86 864 (1991).

reusable (riːˈjuːzəbᵊl) ADJECTIVE able to be used more than once.

reuse VERB (riːˈjuːz) (tr) [1] to use again. ◆ NOUN (riːˈjuːs) [2] the act or process of using again.

Reutlingen (*German* ˈrɔytlɪŋən) NOUN a city in SW Germany, in Baden-Württemberg: founded in the 11th century; an Imperial free city from 1240 until 1802; textile industry. Pop.: 109 882 (1999 est.).

rev (rɛv) *Informal* ◆ NOUN [1] revolution per minute: *the engine was doing 5000 revs.* ◆ VERB **revs, revving, revved.** [2] (often foll by *up*) to increase the speed of revolution of (an engine).

rev. ABBREVIATION FOR: [1] revenue. [2] reverse(d). [3] review. [4] revise(d). [5] revision. [6] revolution. [7] revolving.

Rev. ABBREVIATION FOR: [1] *Bible* Revelation. [2] Reverend.

Reval ('re:val) NOUN the German name for **Tallinn.**

revalorize *or* **revalorise** (ri:'vælə,raɪz) VERB (*tr*) [1] to change the valuation of (assets). [2] to replace (a currency unit) by another.
▸**re,valori'zation** *or* **re,valori'sation** NOUN

revalue (ri:'vælju:) *or US* **revaluate** VERB [1] to adjust the exchange value of (a currency), esp upwards. Compare **devalue.** [2] (*tr*) to make a fresh valuation or appraisal of.
▸**re,valu'ation** NOUN

revamp (ri:'væmp) VERB (*tr*) [1] to patch up or renovate; repair or restore. ◆ NOUN [2] something that has been renovated or revamped. [3] the act or process of revamping.
▷HISTORY C19: from RE- + VAMP[2]
▸**re'vamper** NOUN ▸**re'vamping** NOUN

revanchism (rɪ'væntʃɪzəm) NOUN [1] a foreign policy aimed at revenge or the regaining of lost territories. [2] desire or support for such a policy.
▷HISTORY C20: from French *revanche* REVENGE
▸**re'vanchist** NOUN, ADJECTIVE

rev counter NOUN *Brit* an informal name for **tachometer.**

Revd ABBREVIATION FOR Reverend.

reveal (rɪ'vi:l) VERB (*tr*) [1] (*may take a clause as object or an infinitive*) to disclose (a secret); divulge. [2] to expose to view or show (something concealed). [3] (of God) to disclose (divine truths) either directly or through the medium of prophets, etc. ◆ NOUN [4] *Architect* the vertical side of an opening in a wall, esp the side of a window or door between the frame and the front of the wall.
▷HISTORY C14: from Old French *reveler*, from Latin *revēlāre* to unveil, from RE- + *vēlum* a VEIL
▸**re'vealable** ADJECTIVE ▸**re,veala'bility** NOUN ▸**re'vealer** NOUN ▸**re'vealment** NOUN

revealed religion NOUN [1] religion based on the revelation by God to man of ideas that he would not have arrived at by his natural reason alone. [2] religion in which the existence of God depends on revelation.

revealing (rɪ'vi:lɪŋ) ADJECTIVE [1] of significance or import: *a very revealing experience.* [2] showing or designed to show more of the body than is usual or conventional: *a revealing costume.*
▸**re'vealingly** ADVERB ▸**re'vealingness** NOUN

revegetate (ri:'vedʒɪ,teɪt) VERB (*intr*) (of plants) to grow again and produce new tissue, esp to produce new growth on bare ground.
▸**re,vege'tation** NOUN

reveille (rɪ'vælɪ) NOUN [1] a signal, given by a bugle, drum, etc., to awaken soldiers or sailors in the morning. [2] the hour at which this takes place. ◆ Also called (esp US): **rouse.**
▷HISTORY C17: from French *réveillez!* awake! from RE- + Old French *esveillier* to be wakeful, ultimately from Latin *vigilāre* to keep watch; see VIGIL

revel ('rev[ə]l) VERB **-els, -elling, -elled** *or US* **-els, -eling, -eled.** (*intr*) [1] (foll by *in*) to take pleasure or wallow: *to revel in success.* [2] to take part in noisy festivities; make merry. ◆ NOUN [3] (*often plural*) an occasion of noisy merrymaking. [4] a less common word for **revelry.**
▷HISTORY C14: from Old French *reveler* to be merry, noisy, from Latin *rebellāre* to revolt, REBEL
▸**'reveller** NOUN ▸**'revelment** NOUN

revelation (,revə'leɪʃən) NOUN [1] the act or process of disclosing something previously secret or obscure, esp something true. [2] a fact disclosed or revealed, esp in a dramatic or surprising way. [3] *Christianity* **a** God's disclosure of his own nature and his purpose for mankind, esp through the words of human intermediaries. **b** something in which such a divine disclosure is contained, such as the Bible.
▷HISTORY C14: from Church Latin *revēlātiō* from Latin *revēlāre* to REVEAL
▸**,reve'lational** ADJECTIVE

Revelation (,revə'leɪʃən) NOUN (*popularly, often plural*) the last book of the New Testament, containing visionary descriptions of heaven, of conflicts between good and evil, and of the end of the world. Also called: the **Apocalypse**, the **Revelation of Saint John the Divine**.

revelationist (,revə'leɪʃənɪst) NOUN a person who believes that God has revealed certain truths to man.

revelry ('rev[ə]lrɪ) NOUN, *plural* **-ries.** noisy or unrestrained merrymaking.

revenant ('revɪnənt) NOUN something, esp a ghost, that returns.
▷HISTORY C19: from French: ghost, from *revenir* to come back, from Latin *revenīre*, from RE- + *venīre* to come

revenge (rɪ'vendʒ) NOUN [1] the act of retaliating for wrongs or injury received; vengeance. [2] something done as a means of vengeance. [3] the desire to take vengeance or retaliate. [4] a return match, regarded as a loser's opportunity to even the score. ◆ VERB (*tr*) [5] to inflict equivalent injury or damage for (injury received); retaliate in return for. [6] to take vengeance for (oneself or another); avenge.
▷HISTORY C14: from Old French *revenger*, from Late Latin *revindicāre*, from RE- + *vindicāre* to VINDICATE
▸**re'vengeless** ADJECTIVE ▸**re'venger** NOUN ▸**re'venging** ADJECTIVE ▸**re'vengingly** ADVERB

revengeful (rɪ'vendʒfʊl) ADJECTIVE full of or characterized by desire for vengeance; vindictive.
▸**re'vengefully** ADVERB ▸**re'vengefulness** NOUN

revenue ('revɪ,nju:) NOUN [1] the income accruing from taxation to a government during a specified period of time, usually a year. [2] **a** a government department responsible for the collection of government revenue. **b** (*as modifier*): *revenue men.* [3] the gross income from a business enterprise, investment, property, etc. [4] a particular item of income. [5] something that yields a regular financial return; source of income.
▷HISTORY C16: from Old French, from *revenir* to return, from Latin *revenīre*; see REVENANT
▸**'reve,nued** ADJECTIVE

revenue cutter NOUN a small lightly armed boat used to enforce customs regulations and catch smugglers.

revenuer ('revɪ,nju:ə) NOUN *US slang* a revenue officer or cutter.

revenue tariff NOUN a tariff for the purpose of producing public revenue. Compare **protective tariff.**

reverb ('ri:vɜ:b) NOUN an electronic device that creates artificial acoustics.

reverberate (rɪ'vɜ:bə,reɪt) VERB [1] (*intr*) to resound or re-echo: *the explosion reverberated through the castle.* [2] to reflect or be reflected many times. [3] (*intr*) to rebound or recoil. [4] (*intr*) (of the flame or heat in a reverberatory furnace) to be deflected onto the metal or ore on the hearth. [5] (*tr*) to heat, melt, or refine (a metal or ore) in a reverberatory furnace.
▷HISTORY C16: from Latin *reverberāre* to strike back, from RE- + *verberāre* to beat, from *verber* a lash
▸**re'verberant** *or (less commonly)* **re'verberative** ADJECTIVE ▸**re'verberantly** ADVERB ▸**re'verber'ation** NOUN

reverberation time NOUN a measure of the acoustic properties of a room, equal to the time taken for a sound to fall in intensity by 60 decibels. It is usually measured in seconds.

reverberator (rɪ'vɜ:bə,reɪtə) NOUN [1] anything that produces or undergoes reverberation. [2] another name for **reverberatory furnace.**

reverberatory (rɪ'vɜ:bərətərɪ, -trɪ) ADJECTIVE [1] characterized by, utilizing, or produced by reverberation. ◆ NOUN, *plural* **-ries.** [2] short for **reverberatory furnace.**

reverberatory furnace NOUN a metallurgical furnace having a curved roof that deflects heat onto the charge so that the fuel is not in direct contact with the ore.

revere (rɪ'vɪə) VERB (*tr*) to be in awe of and respect deeply; venerate.
▷HISTORY C17: from Latin *reverērī*, from RE- + *verērī* to fear, be in awe of
▸**re'verable** ADJECTIVE ▸**re'verer** NOUN

reverence ('revərəns) NOUN [1] a feeling or attitude of profound respect, usually reserved for the sacred or divine; devoted veneration. [2] an outward manifestation of this feeling, esp a bow or act of obeisance. [3] the state of being revered or commanding profound respect. [4] **saving your reverence.** *Archaic* a form of apology for using an obscene or taboo expression. ◆ VERB [5] (*tr*) to revere or venerate.
▸**'reverencer** NOUN

Reverence ('revərəns) NOUN (preceded by *Your* or *His*) a title sometimes used to address or refer to a Roman Catholic priest.

reverend ('revərənd) ADJECTIVE [1] worthy of reverence. [2] relating to or designating a clergyman or the clergy. ◆ NOUN [3] *Informal* a clergyman.
▷HISTORY C15: from Latin *reverendus* fit to be revered; see REVERE

Reverend ('revərənd) ADJECTIVE a title of respect for a clergyman. Abbrevs: **Rev, Revd.** See also **Very Reverend, Right Reverend, Most Reverend.**

> **Language note** *Reverend* with a surname alone (*Reverend Smith*), as a term of address (*"Yes, Reverend"*), or in the salutation of a letter (*Dear Rev. Mr Smith*) are all generally considered to be wrong usage. Preferred are (*the*) *Reverend John Smith* or *Reverend Mr Smith* and *Dear Mr Smith.*

Reverend Mother NOUN a title of respect or form of address for the Mother Superior of a convent.

reverent ('revərənt, 'revrənt) ADJECTIVE feeling, expressing, or characterized by reverence.
▷HISTORY C14: from Latin *reverēns* respectful
▸**'reverently** ADVERB ▸**'reverentness** NOUN

reverential (,revə'renʃəl) ADJECTIVE resulting from or showing reverence: *a pilgrimage is a reverential act, performed by reverent people.*
▸**,rever'entially** ADVERB

reverie *or* **revery** ('revərɪ) NOUN, *plural* **-eries.** [1] an act or state of absent-minded daydreaming: *to fall into a reverie.* [2] a piece of instrumental music suggestive of a daydream. [3] *Archaic* a fanciful or visionary notion; daydream.
▷HISTORY C14: from Old French *resverie* wildness, from *resver* to behave wildly, of uncertain origin; see RAVE[1]

revers (rɪ'vɪə) NOUN, *plural* **-vers** (-'vɪəz). (*usually plural*) the turned-back lining of part of a garment, esp of a lapel or cuff.
▷HISTORY C19: from French, literally: REVERSE

reversal (rɪ'vɜ:s[ə]l) NOUN [1] the act or an instance of reversing. [2] a change for the worse; reverse: *a reversal of fortune.* [3] the state of being reversed. [4] the annulment of a judicial decision, esp by an appeal court on grounds of error or irregularity.

reversal film NOUN photographic film that can be processed to produce a positive transparent image for direct projection, rather than a negative for printing.

reverse (rɪ'vɜ:s) VERB (*mainly tr*) [1] to turn or set in an opposite direction, order, or position. [2] to change into something different or contrary; alter completely: *reverse one's policy.* [3] (*also intr*) to move or cause to move backwards or in an opposite direction: *to reverse a car.* [4] to run (machinery, etc.) in the opposite direction to normal. [5] to turn inside out. [6] *Law* to revoke or set aside (a judgment, decree, etc.); annul. [7] (often foll by *out*) to print from plates so made that white lettering or design of (a page, text, display, etc.) appears on a black or coloured background. [8] **reverse arms.** *Military* to turn one's arms upside down, esp as a token of mourning. [9] **reverse the charge(s).** to make a telephone call at the recipient's expense. ◆ NOUN [10] the opposite or contrary of something. [11] the back or rear side of something. [12] a change to an opposite position, state, or direction. [13] a change for the worse; setback or defeat. [14] **a** the mechanism or gears by which machinery, a vehicle, etc., can be made to reverse its direction. **b** (*as modifier*): *reverse gear.* [15] the side of a coin bearing a secondary design. Compare **obverse** (sense 5). [16] **a** printed matter in which normally black or coloured areas, esp lettering, appear white, and vice versa. **b** (*as modifier*): *reverse plates.* [17] **in reverse.** in an opposite or backward direction. [18] **the reverse of.** emphatically not; not at all: *he was the reverse of polite when I called.* ◆ ADJECTIVE [19] opposite or contrary in direction, position, order, nature, etc.; turned backwards. [20] back to front; inverted. [21] operating or moving in a manner contrary to that which is usual. [22] denoting or relating to a mirror image.
▷HISTORY C14: from Old French, from Latin *reversus*, from *revertere* to turn back
▸**re'versely** ADVERB ▸**re'verser** NOUN

reverse-charge ADJECTIVE (*prenominal*) (of a telephone call) made at the recipient's expense. US equivalent: **collect.**

reverse osmosis NOUN a technique for purifying water, in which pressure is applied to force liquid through a semipermeable membrane in the opposite direction to that in normal osmosis.

reverse takeover NOUN *Finance* the purchase of a larger company by a smaller company, esp of a public company by a private company.

reverse transcriptase (træn'skrɪpteɪz) NOUN an enzyme present in retroviruses that copies RNA into DNA, thus reversing the usual flow of genetic information in which DNA is copied into RNA.

reverse video NOUN *Computing* a highlighting feature achieved by reversing the colours of normal characters and background on a visual display unit.

reversi (rɪ'vɜːsɪ) NOUN a game played on a draughtboard with 64 pieces, black on one side and white on the other. When pieces are captured they are turned over to join the capturing player's forces; the winner is the player who fills the board with pieces of his colour.
▷**HISTORY** C19: from French; see REVERSE

reversible (rɪ'vɜːsəbᵊl) ADJECTIVE 1 capable of being reversed: *a reversible decision.* 2 capable of returning to an original condition. 3 *Chem, physics* capable of assuming or producing either of two possible states and changing from one to the other: *a reversible reaction.* 4 *Thermodynamics* (of a change, process, etc.) occurring through a number of intermediate states that are all in thermodynamic equilibrium. 5 (of a fabric or garment) woven, printed, or finished so that either side may be used as the outer side. ◆ NOUN 6 a reversible garment, esp a coat.
▸**re,versi'bility** NOUN ▸**re'versibly** ADVERB

reversing light NOUN a light on the rear of a motor vehicle to warn others that the vehicle is being reversed.

reversion (rɪ'vɜːʃən) NOUN 1 a return to or towards an earlier condition, practice, or belief; act of reverting. 2 the act of reversing or the state of being reversed; reversal. 3 *Biology* **a** the return of individuals, organs, etc., to a more primitive condition or type. **b** the reappearance of primitive characteristics in an individual or group. 4 *Property law* **a** an interest in an estate that reverts to the grantor or his heirs at the end of a period, esp at the end of the life of a grantee. **b** an estate so reverting. **c** the right to succeed to such an estate. 5 the benefit payable on the death of a life-insurance policyholder.
▸**re'versionally** ADVERB ▸**re'versionary** *or* **re'versional** ADJECTIVE

reversionary bonus NOUN *Insurance* a bonus added to the sum payable on death or at the maturity of a with-profits assurance policy.

reversioner (rɪ'vɜːʃənə) NOUN *Property law* a person entitled to an estate in reversion. Compare **remainderman.**

reverso (rɪ'vɜːsəʊ) NOUN, *plural* **-sos.** another name for **verso.**

revert VERB (rɪ'vɜːt) (*intr*; foll by *to*) 1 to go back to a former practice, condition, belief, etc.: *she reverted to her old wicked ways.* 2 to take up again or come back to a former topic. 3 *Biology* (of individuals, organs, etc.) to return to a more primitive, earlier, or simpler condition or type. 4 *Property law* (of an estate or interest in land) to return to its former owner or his heirs when a grant, esp a grant for the lifetime of the grantee, comes to an end. 5 **revert to type.** to resume characteristics that were thought to have disappeared. ◆ NOUN ('riːˌvɜːt) 6 a person who, having been converted, has returned to his former beliefs or Church.
▷**HISTORY** C13: from Latin *revertere* to return, from RE- + *vertere* to turn
▸**re'verter** NOUN ▸**re'vertible** ADJECTIVE

> **Language note** Since *back* is part of the meaning of *revert*, one should not say that someone *reverts back* to a certain type of behaviour.

revest (riː'vɛst) VERB (often foll by *in*) to restore (former power, authority, status, etc., to a person) or (of power, authority, etc.) to be restored.
▷**HISTORY** C16: from Old French *revestir* to clothe again, from Latin RE- + *vestīre* to clothe; see VEST

revet (rɪ'vɛt) VERB **-vets, -vetting, -vetted.** to face (a wall or embankment) with stones.
▷**HISTORY** C19: from French *revêt*, from Old French *revestir* to reclothe; see REVEST

revetment (rɪ'vɛtmənt) NOUN 1 a facing of stones, sandbags, etc., to protect a wall, embankment, or earthworks. 2 another name for **retaining wall.**
▷**HISTORY** C18: from French *revêtement* literally: a reclothing, from *revêtir*; see REVEST

review (rɪ'vjuː) VERB (*mainly tr*) 1 to look at or examine again: *to review a situation.* 2 to look back upon (a period of time, sequence of events, etc.); remember: *he reviewed his achievements with pride.* 3 to inspect, esp formally or officially: *the general reviewed his troops.* 4 to read through or go over in order to correct. 5 *Law* to re-examine (a decision) judicially. 6 to write a critical assessment of (a book, film, play, concert, etc.), esp as a profession. ◆ NOUN 7 Also called: **reviewal.** the act or an instance of reviewing. 8 a general survey or report: *a review of the political situation.* 9 a critical assessment of a book, film, play, concert, etc., esp one printed in a newspaper or periodical. 10 **a** a publication containing such articles. **b** (*capital when part of a name*): *the Saturday Review.* 11 a second consideration; re-examination. 12 a retrospective survey. 13 a formal or official inspection. 14 a US and Canadian word for **revision** (sense 2). 15 *Law* judicial re-examination of a case, esp by a superior court. 16 a less common spelling of **revue.**
▷**HISTORY** C16: from French, from *revoir* to see again, from Latin *re-* RE- + *vidēre* to see
▸**re'viewable** ADJECTIVE ▸**re'viewer** NOUN

review copy NOUN a copy of a book sent by a publisher to a journal, newspaper, etc., to enable it to be reviewed.

revile (rɪ'vaɪl) VERB to use abusive or scornful language against (someone or something).
▷**HISTORY** C14: from Old French *reviler*, from RE- + *vil* VILE
▸**re'vilement** NOUN ▸**re'viler** NOUN

revise (rɪ'vaɪz) VERB 1 (*tr*) to change, alter, or amend: *to revise one's opinion.* 2 *Brit* to reread (a subject or notes on it) so as to memorize it, esp in preparation for an examination. 3 (*tr*) to prepare a new version or edition of (a previously printed work). ◆ NOUN 4 the act, process, or result of revising; revision.
▷**HISTORY** C16: from Latin *revīsere* to look back at, from RE- + *vīsere* to inspect, from *vidēre* to see; see REVIEW, VISIT
▸**re'visable** ADJECTIVE ▸**re'visal** NOUN ▸**re'viser** NOUN

Revised Standard Version NOUN a revision by American scholars of the American Standard Version of the Bible. The New Testament was published in 1946 and the entire Bible in 1953.

Revised Version NOUN a revision of the Authorized Version of the Bible prepared by two committees of British scholars, the New Testament being published in 1881 and the Old in 1885.

revision (rɪ'vɪʒən) NOUN 1 the act or process of revising. 2 *Brit* the process of rereading a subject or notes on it, esp in preparation for an examination. 3 a corrected or new version of a book, article, etc.

revisionary (rɪ'vɪʒənərɪ) ADJECTIVE of or relating to a new or different version of something.

revisionism (rɪ'vɪʒəˌnɪzəm) NOUN 1 (*sometimes capital*) **a** a moderate, nonrevolutionary version of Marxism developed in Germany around 1900. **b** (in Marxist-Leninist ideology) any dangerous departure from the true interpretation of the teachings of Karl Marx, the German founder of modern Communism (1818–83). 2 the advocacy of revision of some political theory, religious doctrine, historical or critical interpretation, etc. 3 (*usually capital*) an ultra-nationalist form of Zionism that arose in Palestine in the 1940s.
▸**re'visionist** NOUN, ADJECTIVE

revisit (riː'vɪzɪt) VERB (*tr*) 1 to visit again. 2 to re-examine (a topic or theme) after an interval, with a view to making a fresh appraisal.

revisory (rɪ'vaɪzərɪ) ADJECTIVE of, relating to, or having the power to revise.

revitalize *or* **revitalise** (riː'vaɪtᵊˌlaɪz) VERB (*tr*) to restore vitality or animation to.
▸**re,vitali'zation** *or* **re,vitali'sation** NOUN

revival (rɪ'vaɪvᵊl) NOUN 1 the act or an instance of reviving or the state of being revived. 2 an instance of returning to life or consciousness; restoration of vigour or vitality. 3 a renewed use, acceptance of, or interest in (past customs, styles, etc.): *a revival of learning; the Gothic revival.* 4 a new production of a play that has not been recently performed. 5 a reawakening of faith or renewal of commitment to religion. 6 an evangelistic meeting or service intended to effect such a reawakening in those present. 7 the re-establishment of legal validity, as of a judgment, contract, etc.

revivalism (rɪ'vaɪvəˌlɪzəm) NOUN 1 a movement, esp an evangelical Christian one, that seeks to reawaken faith. 2 the tendency or desire to revive former customs, styles, etc.

revivalist (rɪ'vaɪvəlɪst) NOUN 1 a person who holds, promotes, or presides over religious revivals. 2 a person who revives customs, institutions, ideas, etc. ◆ ADJECTIVE 3 of, relating to, or characterizing revivalism or religious revivals: *a revivalist meeting.*
▸**re,vival'istic** ADJECTIVE

revive (rɪ'vaɪv) VERB 1 to bring or be brought back to life, consciousness, or strength; resuscitate or be resuscitated: *revived by a drop of whisky.* 2 to give or assume new vitality; flourish again or cause to flourish again. 3 to make or become operative or active again: *the youth movement was revived.* 4 to bring or come into use or currency again: *to revive a language.* 5 (*tr*) to take up again: *he revived his old hobby.* 6 to bring or come back to mind. 7 (*tr*) *Theatre* to mount a new production of (an old play).
▷**HISTORY** C15: from Old French *revivre* to live again, from Latin *revīvere*, from RE- + *vīvere* to live; see VIVID
▸**re'vivable** ADJECTIVE ▸**re,viva'bility** NOUN ▸**re'vivably** ADVERB ▸**re'viver** NOUN ▸**re'viving** ADJECTIVE ▸**re'vivingly** ADVERB

revivify (rɪ'vɪvɪˌfaɪ) VERB **-fies, -fying, -fied.** (*tr*) to give new life or spirit to; revive.
▸**re,vivifi'cation** NOUN

reviviscence (ˌrɛvɪ'vɪsəns, rɪ'vɪvɪsəns) NOUN *Rare* restoration to life or animation; revival.
▷**HISTORY** C17: from Latin, from *revīviscere* come back to life, related to *vīvere* to live; see REVIVE
▸**ˌrevi'viscent** ADJECTIVE

revocable ('rɛvəkəbᵊl) *or* **revokable** (rɪ'vəʊkəbᵊl) ADJECTIVE capable of being revoked; able to be cancelled.
▸**ˌrevoca'bility** *or* **re,voka'bility** NOUN ▸**'revocably** *or* **re'vokably** ADVERB

revocation (ˌrɛvə'keɪʃən) NOUN 1 the act of revoking or state of being revoked; cancellation. 2 **a** the cancellation or annulment of a legal instrument, esp a will. **b** the withdrawal of an offer, power of attorney, etc.
▸**revocatory** ('rɛvəkətərɪ, -trɪ) ADJECTIVE

revoice (riː'vɔɪs) VERB (*intr*) 1 to utter again; echo. 2 to adjust the design of (an organ pipe or wind instrument) as after disuse or to conform with modern pitch.

revoke (rɪ'vəʊk) VERB 1 (*tr*) to take back or withdraw; cancel; rescind: *to revoke a law.* 2 (*intr*) *Cards* to break a rule of play by failing to follow suit when able to do so; renege. ◆ NOUN 3 *Cards* the act of revoking; a renege.
▷**HISTORY** C14: from Latin *revocāre* to call back, withdraw, from RE- + *vocāre* to call
▸**re'voker** NOUN

revolt (rɪ'vəʊlt) NOUN 1 a rebellion or uprising against authority. 2 **in revolt.** in the process or state of rebelling. ◆ VERB 3 (*intr*) to rise up in rebellion against authority. 4 (*usually passive*) to feel or cause to feel revulsion, disgust, or abhorrence.
▷**HISTORY** C16: from French *révolter* to revolt, from Old Italian *rivoltare* to overturn, ultimately from Latin *revolvere* to roll back, REVOLVE
▸**re'volter** NOUN

revolting (rɪ'vəʊltɪŋ) ADJECTIVE 1 causing revulsion; nauseating, disgusting, or repulsive. 2 *Informal* unpleasant or nasty: *that dress is revolting.*
▸**re'voltingly** ADVERB

revolute ('rɛvəˌluːt) ADJECTIVE (esp of the margins of a leaf) rolled backwards and downwards.
▷**HISTORY** C18: from Latin *revolūtus* rolled back; see REVOLVE

revolution (ˌrɛvəˈluːʃən) NOUN 1 the overthrow or repudiation of a regime or political system by the governed. 2 (in Marxist theory) the violent and historically necessary transition from one system of production in a society to the next, as from feudalism to capitalism. 3 a far-reaching and drastic change, esp in ideas, methods, etc. 4 **a** movement in or as if in a circle. **b** one complete turn in such a circle: *a turntable rotating at 33 revolutions per minute.* 5 **a** the orbital motion of one body, such as a planet or satellite, around another. Compare **rotation** (sense 5a). **b** one complete turn in such motion. 6 a cycle of successive events or changes. 7 *Geology, obsolete* a profound change in conditions over a large part of the earth's surface, esp one characterized by mountain building: *an orogenic revolution.*
▷HISTORY C14: via Old French from Late Latin *revolūtiō*, from Latin *revolvere* to REVOLVE

revolutionary (ˌrɛvəˈluːʃənərɪ) NOUN, *plural* **-aries.** 1 a person who advocates or engages in revolution. ◆ ADJECTIVE 2 relating to or characteristic of a revolution. 3 advocating or engaged in revolution. 4 radically new or different: *a revolutionary method of making plastics.* 5 rotating or revolving.
▸ **ˌrevoˈlutionarily** ADVERB

Revolutionary (ˌrɛvəˈluːʃənərɪ) ADJECTIVE 1 *Chiefly US* of or relating to the conflict or period of the War of American Independence (1775–83). 2 of or relating to any of various other Revolutions, esp the **Russian Revolution** (1917) or the **French Revolution** (1789).

Revolutionary calendar NOUN the calendar adopted by the French First Republic in 1793 and abandoned in 1805. Dates were calculated from Sept. 22, 1792. The months were called Vendémiaire, Brumaire, Frimaire, Nivôse, Pluviôse, Ventôse, Germinal, Floréal, Prairial, Messidor, Thermidor, and Fructidor.

Revolutionary Wars PLURAL NOUN the series of wars (1792–1802) fought against Revolutionary France by a combination of other powers, esp Britain, Austria, and Prussia.

revolutionist (ˌrɛvəˈluːʃənɪst) NOUN 1 a less common word for a **revolutionary.** ◆ ADJECTIVE 2 of, characteristic of, or relating to revolution or revolutionaries.

revolutionize *or* **revolutionise** (ˌrɛvəˈluːʃəˌnaɪz) VERB (*tr*) 1 to bring about a radical change in: *science has revolutionized civilization.* 2 to inspire or infect with revolutionary ideas: *they revolutionized the common soldiers.* 3 to cause a revolution in (a country, etc.).
▸ **ˌrevoˈlutionˌizer** *or* **ˌrevoˈlutionˌiser** NOUN

revolve (rɪˈvɒlv) VERB 1 to move or cause to move around a centre or axis; rotate. 2 (*intr*) to occur periodically or in cycles. 3 to consider or be considered. 4 (*intr*; foll by *around* or *about*) to be centred or focused (upon): *Juliet's thoughts revolved around Romeo.* ◆ NOUN 5 *Theatre* a circular section of a stage that can be rotated by electric power to provide a scene change.
▷HISTORY C14: from Latin *revolvere*, from RE- + *volvere* to roll, wind
▸ **reˈvolvable** ADJECTIVE ▸ **reˈvolvably** ADVERB

revolver (rɪˈvɒlvə) NOUN a pistol having a revolving multichambered cylinder that allows several shots to be discharged without reloading.

revolving (rɪˈvɒlvɪŋ) ADJECTIVE denoting or relating to an engine, such as a radial aero engine, in which the cylinders revolve about a fixed shaft.
▸ **reˈvolvingly** ADVERB

revolving credit NOUN a letter of credit for a fixed sum, specifying that the beneficiary may make repeated use of the credit provided that the fixed sum is never exceeded.

revolving door NOUN 1 a door that rotates about a central vertical axis, esp one with four leaves arranged at right angles to each other, thereby excluding draughts. 2 **a** *Informal* a tendency to change personnel on a frequent basis. **b** (*as modifier*): *a revolving-door band.* 3 **a** *Informal* the hiring of former government employees by private companies with which they had dealings when they worked for the government. **b** (*as modifier*): *revolving-door consultancies.*

revolving fund NOUN a fund set up for a specific purpose and constantly added to by income from its investments.

revue *or less commonly* **review** (rɪˈvjuː) NOUN a form of light entertainment consisting of a series of topical sketches, songs, dancing, comic turns, etc.
▷HISTORY C20: from French; see REVIEW

revulsion (rɪˈvʌlʃən) NOUN 1 a sudden and unpleasant violent reaction in feeling, esp one of extreme loathing. 2 the act or an instance of drawing back or recoiling from something. 3 *Obsolete* the diversion of disease or congestion from one part of the body to another by cupping, counterirritants, etc.
▷HISTORY C16: from Latin *revulsiō* a pulling away, from *revellere*, from RE- + *vellere* to pull, tear
▸ **reˈvulsionary** ADJECTIVE

revulsive (rɪˈvʌlsɪv) ADJECTIVE 1 of or causing revulsion. ◆ NOUN 2 *Med* a counterirritant.
▸ **reˈvulsively** ADVERB

Rev. Ver. ABBREVIATION FOR Revised Version (of the Bible).

reward (rɪˈwɔːd) NOUN 1 something given or received in return for a deed or service rendered. 2 a sum of money offered, esp for help in finding a criminal or for the return of lost or stolen property. 3 profit or return. 4 something received in return for good or evil; deserts. 5 *Psychol* any pleasant event that follows a response and therefore increases the likelihood of the response recurring in the future. ◆ VERB 6 (*tr*) to give (something) to (someone), esp in gratitude for a service rendered; recompense.
▷HISTORY C14: from Old Norman French *rewarder* to regard, from RE- + *warder* to care for, guard, of Germanic origin; see WARD
▸ **reˈwardable** ADJECTIVE ▸ **reˈwarder** NOUN ▸ **reˈwardless** ADJECTIVE

reward claim NOUN *Austral history* a claim granted to a miner who discovered gold in a new area.

rewarding (rɪˈwɔːdɪŋ) ADJECTIVE giving personal satisfaction; gratifying: *caring for the elderly is rewarding.*

rewa-rewa (ˈreɪwəˈreɪwə) NOUN a tall proteaceous tree of New Zealand, *Knightia excelsa*, yielding a beautiful reddish timber.
▷HISTORY C19: from Maori

rewind VERB (riːˈwaɪnd) **-winds, -winding, -wound.** 1 (*tr*) to wind back, esp a film or tape onto the original reel. ◆ NOUN (ˈriːˌwaɪnd, riːˈwaɪnd) 2 something rewound. 3 the act of rewinding.
▸ **reˈwinder** NOUN

rewire (riːˈwaɪə) VERB (*tr*) to provide (a house, engine, etc.) with new wiring.
▸ **reˈwirable** ADJECTIVE

reword (riːˈwɜːd) VERB (*tr*) to alter the wording of; express differently.

rework (riːˈwɜːk) VERB (*tr*) 1 to use again in altered form: *the theme has been reworked in countless well-known poems.* 2 to rewrite or revise. 3 to reprocess for use again.

reworked fossil (riːˈwɜːkt) NOUN a fossil eroded from sediment and redeposited in younger sediment. Also called: **derived fossil.**

rewrite VERB (riːˈraɪt) **-writes, -writing, -wrote, -written.** (*tr*) 1 to write (written material) again, esp changing the words or form. 2 *Computing* to return (data) to a store when it has been erased during reading. ◆ NOUN (ˈriːˌraɪt) 3 something rewritten.

rewrite rule NOUN *Generative grammar* another name for **phrase-structure rule.**

Rex (rɛks) NOUN king: part of the official title of a king, now used chiefly in documents, legal proceedings, inscriptions on coins, etc. Compare **Regina**^{1}.
▷HISTORY Latin

Rexine (ˈrɛksiːn) NOUN *Trademark* a form of artificial leather.

Reye's syndrome (raɪz, reɪz) NOUN a rare metabolic disease in children that can be fatal, involving damage to the brain, liver, and kidneys.
▷HISTORY C20: named after R. D. K. *Reye* (1912–78) Australian paediatrician

Reykjavik (ˈreɪkjəˌviːk) NOUN the capital and chief port of Iceland, situated in the southwest: its buildings are heated by natural hot water. Pop.: 109 184 (1999 est.).

Reynard (ˈrɛnəd, ˈrɛnɑːd, ˈreɪnəd, ˈreɪnɑːd) NOUN a name for a fox, used in medieval tales, fables, etc.
▷HISTORY from earlier *Renard, Renart*, hero of the French bestiary *Roman de Renart*: ultimately from the Old High German name *Reginhart*, literally: strong in counsel

Reynolds number NOUN a dimensionless number, $v\rho l/\eta$, where v is the fluid velocity, ρ the density, η the viscosity and l a dimension of the system. The value of the number indicates the type of fluid flow.
▷HISTORY C19: named after Osborne *Reynolds* (1842–1912), British physicist

Reynosa (*Spanish* reˈnosa) NOUN a city in E Mexico, in Tamaulipas state on the Rio Grande. Pop.: 398 000 (2000 est.).

rf *Music* ABBREVIATION FOR rinforzando. Also: **rfz.**

Rf THE CHEMICAL SYMBOL FOR rutherfordium.

RF ABBREVIATION FOR **radio frequency.**

RF- (in the US Air Force) ABBREVIATION FOR reconnaissance fighter: *RF-4E.*

RFC ABBREVIATION FOR: 1 Rugby Football Club. 2 Royal Flying Corps.

RFID ABBREVIATION FOR radio-frequency identity (*or* identification): a method of security tagging used in shops, etc.

RFLP ABBREVIATION FOR restriction fragment length polymorphism: any variation in DNA between individuals revealed by restriction enzymes that cut DNA into fragments of different lengths in consequence of such variations. It is used forensically and in the diagnosis of hereditary disease.

RG INTERNATIONAL CAR REGISTRATION FOR (Republic of) Guinea.

RGB ABBREVIATION FOR red, green, blue: *RGB components of a colour; RGB signal.*

RGN (in Britain) ABBREVIATION FOR **Registered General Nurse.**

RGS ABBREVIATION FOR Royal Geographical Society.

Rgt ABBREVIATION FOR regiment.

rh *or* **RH** ABBREVIATION FOR right hand.

Rh 1 THE CHEMICAL SYMBOL FOR rhodium. ◆ 2 ABBREVIATION FOR rhesus (esp in **Rh factor**).

RH 1 ABBREVIATION FOR Royal Highness. ◆ 2 INTERNATIONAL CAR REGISTRATION FOR (Republic of) Haiti.

RHA ABBREVIATION FOR: 1 Regional Health Authority. 2 Royal Horse Artillery.

rhabdomancy (ˈræbdəˌmænsɪ) NOUN divination for water or mineral ore by means of a rod or wand; dowsing; divining.
▷HISTORY C17: via Late Latin from Late Greek *rhabdomanteia*, from *rhabdos* a rod + *manteia* divination
▸ **ˈrhabdoˌmantist** *or* **ˈrhabdoˌmancer** NOUN

rhabdomyoma (ˌræbdəʊmaɪˈəʊmə) NOUN, *plural* **-mas** *or* **-mata** (-mətə). *Pathol* a benign tumour of striated muscle.
▷HISTORY C19: from New Latin, from Greek *rhabdos* a rod + MYOMA

rhachilla (rəˈkɪlə) NOUN a variant spelling of **rachilla.**

rhachis (ˈreɪkɪs) NOUN, *plural* **rhachises** *or* **rhachides** (ˈrækɪˌdiːz, ˈreɪ-). a variant spelling of **rachis.**

Rhadamanthus *or* **Rhadamanthys** (ˌrædəˈmænθəs) NOUN *Greek myth* one of the judges of the dead in the underworld.
▸ **ˌRhadaˈmanthine** ADJECTIVE

Rhaetia (ˈriːʃɪə) NOUN an Alpine province of ancient Rome including parts of present-day Tyrol and E Switzerland.

Rhaetian (ˈriːʃən) NOUN 1 Also called: **Rhaeto-Romanic** (ˈriːtəʊrəʊˈmænɪk). a group of Romance languages or dialects spoken in certain valleys of the Alps, including Romansch, Ladin, and Friulian. ◆ ADJECTIVE 2 denoting or relating to this group of languages. 3 of or relating to Rhaetia.

Rhaetian Alps PLURAL NOUN a section of the central Alps along E Switzerland's borders with Austria and Italy. Highest peak: Piz Bernina, 4049 m (13 284 ft.).

Rhaetic *or* **Rhetic** (ˈriːtɪk) ADJECTIVE 1 of or relating to a series of rocks formed in the late Triassic period. ◆ NOUN 2 **the.** the Rhaetic series.

Rhamadhan (ˌræmə'dɑːn) NOUN a variant spelling of **Ramadan.**

rhamnaceous (ræm'neɪʃəs) ADJECTIVE of, relating to, or belonging to the *Rhamnaceae*, a widely distributed family of trees and shrubs having small inconspicuous flowers. The family includes the buckthorns.
▷HISTORY C19: from New Latin *Rhamnaceae*, from Greek *rhamnos* a thorn

rhapsodic (ræp'sɒdɪk) ADJECTIVE 1 of or like a rhapsody. 2 lyrical or romantic.
▸**rhap'sodically** ADVERB

rhapsodist ('ræpsədɪst) NOUN 1 a person who speaks or writes rhapsodies. 2 a person who speaks with extravagant enthusiasm. 3 Also called: **rhapsode** ('ræpsəʊd). (in ancient Greece) a professional reciter of poetry, esp of Homer.
▸ˌ**rhapso'distic** ADJECTIVE

rhapsodize *or* **rhapsodise** ('ræpsəˌdaɪz) VERB 1 to speak or write (something) with extravagant enthusiasm. 2 (*intr*) to recite or write rhapsodies.

rhapsody ('ræpsədɪ) NOUN, *plural* **-dies.** 1 *Music* a composition free in structure and highly emotional in character. 2 an expression of ecstatic enthusiasm. 3 (in ancient Greece) an epic poem or part of an epic recited by a rhapsodist. 4 a literary work composed in an intense or exalted style. 5 rapturous delight or ecstasy. 6 *Obsolete* a medley.
▷HISTORY C16: via Latin from Greek *rhapsōidia*, from *rhaptein* to sew together + *ōidē* song

rhatany ('rætənɪ) NOUN, *plural* **-nies.** 1 either of two South American leguminous shrubs, *Krameria triandra* or *K. argentea*, that have thick fleshy roots. 2 the dried roots of such shrubs used as an astringent. ◆ Also called: **krameria.**
▷HISTORY C19: from New Latin *rhatānia*, ultimately from Quechua *ratánya*

rhd ABBREVIATION FOR right-hand drive.

rhea ('rɪə) NOUN either of two large fast-running flightless birds, *Rhea americana* or *Pterocnemia pennata*, inhabiting the open plains of S South America: order *Rheiformes* (see **ratite**). They are similar to but smaller than the ostrich, having three-toed feet and a completely feathered body.
▷HISTORY C19: New Latin; arbitrarily named after RHEA[1]

Rhea[1] ('rɪə) NOUN *Greek myth* a Titaness, wife of Cronus and mother of several of the gods, including Zeus: a fertility goddess. Roman counterpart: **Ops.**

Rhea[2] ('rɪə) NOUN the second largest satellite of the planet Saturn.

Rhea Silvia *or* **Rea Silvia** ('sɪlvɪə) NOUN *Roman myth* the mother of Romulus and Remus by Mars. See also **Ilia.**

rhebok *or* **reebok** ('riːbʌk, -bɒk) NOUN, *plural* **-boks** *or* **-bok.** an antelope, *Pelea capreolus*, of southern Africa, having woolly brownish-grey hair.
▷HISTORY C18: Afrikaans, from Dutch *reebok* ROEBUCK

Rheims (riːmz; *French* rɛ̃s) NOUN a variant spelling of **Reims.**

Rhein (rain) NOUN the German name for the **Rhine.**

Rheinland ('rainlant) NOUN the German name for the **Rhineland.**

Rheinland-Pfalz ('raɪnlant'pfalts) NOUN the German name for **Rhineland-Palatinate.**

rheme (riːm) NOUN *Linguistics* the constituent of a sentence that adds most new information, in addition to what has already been said in the discourse. The rheme is usually, but not always, associated with the subject. Compare **theme** (sense 5).
▷HISTORY C20: from Greek *rhēma* that which is said

Rhemish ('riːmɪʃ) ADJECTIVE of, relating to, or originating in Reims.

Rhenish ('rɛnɪʃ, 'riː-) ADJECTIVE 1 of or relating to the River Rhine or the lands adjacent to it, esp the Rhineland-Palatinate. ◆ NOUN 2 another word for **hock** (the wine).

rhenium ('riːnɪəm) NOUN a dense silvery-white metallic element that has a high melting point. It occurs principally in gadolinite and molybdenite and is used, alloyed with tungsten or molybdenum, in high-temperature thermocouples. Symbol: Re; atomic no.: 75; atomic wt.: 186.207; valency: –1 or 1–7; relative density: 21.02; melting pt.: 3186°C; boiling pt.: 5596°C (est.).
▷HISTORY C19: New Latin, from *Rhēnus* the Rhine

rheo. ABBREVIATION FOR rheostat.

rheo- COMBINING FORM indicating stream, flow, or current: *rheometer; rheoscope.*
▷HISTORY from Greek *rheos* stream, anything flowing, from *rhein* to flow

rheobase ('riːəʊˌbeɪs) NOUN *Physiol* the minimum nerve impulse required to elicit a response from a tissue.

rheology (rɪ'ɒlədʒɪ) NOUN the branch of physics concerned with the flow and change of shape of matter.
▸**rheological** (ˌriːə'lɒdʒɪkᵊl) ADJECTIVE ▸**rhe'ologist** NOUN

rheometer (rɪ'ɒmɪtə) NOUN 1 *Med* an instrument for measuring the velocity of the blood flow. 2 another word for **galvanometer.**
▸**rheometric** (ˌriːə'mɛtrɪk) ADJECTIVE ▸**rhe'ometry** NOUN

rheomorphism (ˌriːə'mɔːfɪzəm) NOUN *Geology* the liquefaction of rock, which results in its flowing and intruding into surrounding rocks.
▸ˌ**rheo'morphic** ADJECTIVE

rheoreceptor ('riːərɪˌsɛptə) NOUN *Zoology* a receptor in fish and some amphibians that responds to water currents.

rheostat ('riːəˌstæt) NOUN a variable resistance, usually consisting of a coil of wire with a terminal at one end and a sliding contact that moves along the coil to tap off the current.
▸ˌ**rheo'static** ADJECTIVE

rheotaxis (ˌriːə'tæksɪs) NOUN movement of an organism towards or away from a current of water.
▸**rheotactic** (ˌriːə'tæktɪk) ADJECTIVE

rheotropism (rɪ'ɒtrəˌpɪzəm) NOUN growth of a plant or sessile animal in the direction of a current of water.
▸**rheotropic** (ˌriːə'trɒpɪk) ADJECTIVE

Rhesus ('riːsəs) NOUN *Greek myth* a king of Thrace, who arrived in the tenth year of the Trojan War to aid Troy. Odysseus and Diomedes stole his horses because an oracle had said that if these horses drank from the River Xanthus, Troy would not fall.

rhesus baby ('riːsəs) NOUN a baby suffering from haemolytic disease at birth as its red blood cells (which are Rh positive) have been attacked in the womb by antibodies from its Rh negative mother. Technical name: **erythroblastosis fetalis.**
▷HISTORY C20: see RH FACTOR

rhesus factor NOUN See **Rh factor.**

rhesus monkey NOUN a macaque monkey, *Macaca mulatta*, of S Asia: used extensively in medical research.
▷HISTORY C19: New Latin, arbitrarily from Greek *Rhesos* RHESUS

Rhetic ('riːtɪk) ADJECTIVE, NOUN a variant spelling of **Rhaetic.**

rhetor ('riːtə) NOUN 1 a teacher of rhetoric. 2 (in ancient Greece) an orator.
▷HISTORY C14: via Latin from Greek *rhētōr*; related to *rhēma* word

rhetoric ('rɛtərɪk) NOUN 1 the study of the technique of using language effectively. 2 the art of using speech to persuade, influence, or please; oratory. 3 excessive use of ornamentation and contrivance in spoken or written discourse; bombast. 4 speech or discourse that pretends to significance but lacks true meaning: *all the politician says is mere rhetoric.*
▷HISTORY C14: via Latin from Greek *rhētorikē* (*tekhnē*) (the art of) rhetoric, from *rhētōr* RHETOR

rhetorical (rɪ'tɒrɪkᵊl) ADJECTIVE 1 concerned with effect or style rather than content or meaning; bombastic. 2 of or relating to rhetoric or oratory.
▸**rhe'torically** ADVERB

rhetorical question NOUN a question to which no answer is required: used esp for dramatic effect. An example is *Who knows?* (with the implication *Nobody knows*).

rhetorician (ˌrɛtə'rɪʃən) NOUN 1 a teacher of the art of rhetoric. 2 a stylish or eloquent writer or speaker. 3 a person whose speech is pompous or extravagant.

rheum (ruːm) NOUN a watery discharge from the eyes or nose.
▷HISTORY C14: from Old French *reume*, ultimately from Greek *rheuma* bodily humour, stream, from *rhein* to flow

rheumatic (ruː'mætɪk) ADJECTIVE 1 of, relating to, or afflicted with rheumatism. ◆ NOUN 2 a person afflicted with rheumatism.
▷HISTORY C14: ultimately from Greek *rheumatikos*, from *rheuma* a flow; see RHEUM
▸**rheu'matically** ADVERB

rheumatic fever NOUN a disease characterized by sore throat, fever, inflammation, and pain in the joints.

rheumatics (ruː'mætɪks) NOUN (*functioning as singular*) *Informal* rheumatism.

rheumatism ('ruːməˌtɪzəm) NOUN any painful disorder of joints, muscles, or connective tissue. Compare **arthritis, fibrositis.**
▷HISTORY C17: from Latin *rheumatismus* catarrh, from Greek *rheumatismos*; see RHEUM

rheumatoid ('ruːməˌtɔɪd) ADJECTIVE (of the symptoms of a disease) resembling rheumatism.
▸ˌ**rheuma'toidally** ADVERB

rheumatoid arthritis NOUN a chronic disease of the musculoskeletal system, characterized by inflammation and swelling of the joints (esp joints in the hands, wrists, knees, and feet), muscle weakness, and fatigue.

rheumatology (ˌruːmə'tɒlədʒɪ) NOUN the branch of medicine concerned with the study of rheumatic diseases.
▸**rheumatological** (ˌruːmətə'lɒdʒɪkᵊl) ADJECTIVE
▸ˌ**rheuma'tologist** NOUN

rheumy ('ruːmɪ) ADJECTIVE 1 of the nature of rheum. 2 *Literary* damp and unhealthy: *the rheumy air.*

rhexis ('rɛksɪs) NOUN *Med* the rupture of an organ or blood vessel.
▷HISTORY C17: from Greek *rhēxis* a bursting

Rh factor NOUN an agglutinogen commonly found in human blood: it may cause a haemolytic reaction, esp during pregnancy or following transfusion of blood that does not contain this agglutinogen. Full name: **rhesus factor.** See also **Rh positive, Rh negative.**
▷HISTORY C20: named after the rhesus monkey, in which it was first discovered

RHG ABBREVIATION FOR Royal Horse Guards.

rhigolene ('rɪgəʊˌliːn) NOUN a volatile liquid obtained from petroleum and used as a local anaesthetic.
▷HISTORY C19: from Greek *rhigos* cold; see -OLE, -ENE

rhinal ('raɪnᵊl) ADJECTIVE of or relating to the nose; nasal.
▷HISTORY C19: from Greek *rhis, rhin*

Rhine (raɪn) NOUN a river in central and W Europe, rising in SE Switzerland: flows through Lake Constance north through W Germany and west through the Netherlands to the North Sea. Length: about 1320 km (820 miles). Dutch name: **Rijn.** French name: **Rhin** (rɛ̃). German name: **Rhein.**

Rhineland ('raɪnˌlænd, -lənd) NOUN the region of Germany surrounding the Rhine. German name: **Rheinland.**

Rhineland-Palatinate NOUN a state of W Germany: formed in 1946 from the S part of the Prussian Rhine province, the Palatinate, and parts of Rhine-Hesse and Hesse-Nassau; part of West Germany until 1990: agriculture (with extensive vineyards) and tourism are important. Capital: Mainz. Pop.: 4 030 800 (2000 est.). Area: 19 832 sq. km (7657 sq. miles). German name: **Rheinland-Pfalz.**

rhinencephalon (ˌraɪnɛn'sɛfəˌlɒn) NOUN, *plural* **-lons** *or* **-la** (-lə). *Anatomy* the parts of the brain, in both cerebal hemispheres, that in the early stages of evolution were concerned with the sense of smell. It includes the olefactory bulb and tract and the regions of the limbic system.
▷HISTORY C19: from RHINO- + ENCEPHALON
▸**rhinencephalic** (ˌraɪnɛnsɪ'fælɪk) ADJECTIVE

Rhine Palatinate NOUN See **Palatinate.**

rhinestone ('raɪnˌstəʊn) NOUN an imitation gem made of paste.
▷HISTORY C19: translation of French *caillou du Rhin*, referring to Strasbourg, where such gems were made

Rhine wine NOUN any of several wines produced along the banks of the Rhine, characteristically a white table wine such as riesling.

rhinitis (raɪˈnaɪtɪs) NOUN inflammation of the mucous membrane that lines the nose.
▸**rhinitic** (raɪˈnɪtɪk) ADJECTIVE

rhino[1] (ˈraɪnəʊ) NOUN, *plural* **-nos** *or* **-no.** short for **rhinoceros.**

rhino[2] (ˈraɪnəʊ) NOUN *Brit* a slang word for **money.**
▷HISTORY C17: of unknown origin

rhino- *or before a vowel* **rhin-** COMBINING FORM indicating the nose or nasal: *rhinology.*
▷HISTORY from Greek *rhis, rhin*

rhinoceros (raɪˈnɒsərəs, -ˈnɒsrəs) NOUN, *plural* **-oses** *or* **-os.** any of several perissodactyl mammals constituting the family *Rhinocerotidae* of SE Asia and Africa and having either one horn on the nose, like the **Indian rhinoceros** (*Rhinoceros unicornis*), or two horns, like the African **white rhinoceros** (*Diceros simus*) They have a very thick skin, massive body, and three digits on each foot.
▷HISTORY C13: via Latin from Greek *rhinokerōs,* from *rhis* nose + *keras* horn
▸**rhinocerotic** (ˌraɪnəʊsɪˈrɒtɪk) ADJECTIVE

rhinoceros beetle NOUN any of various scarabaeid beetles having one or more horns on the head, esp *Oryctes rhinoceros,* a serious pest on coconut plantations.

rhinoceros bird NOUN another name for the **oxpecker.**

rhinology (raɪˈnɒlədʒɪ) NOUN the branch of medical science concerned with the nose and its diseases.
▸**rhinological** (ˌraɪnəˈlɒdʒɪkəl) ADJECTIVE ▸**rhiˈnologist** NOUN

rhinoplasty (ˈraɪnəʊˌplæstɪ) NOUN plastic surgery of the nose.
▸**ˌrhinoˈplastic** ADJECTIVE

rhinoscopy (raɪˈnɒskəpɪ) NOUN *Med* examination of the nasal passages, esp with a special instrument called a **rhinoscope** (ˈraɪnəʊˌskəʊp).
▸**rhinoscopic** (ˌraɪnəʊˈskɒpɪk) ADJECTIVE

rhizo- *or before a vowel* **rhiz-** COMBINING FORM root: *rhizomorphous.*
▷HISTORY from Greek *rhiza*

rhizobium (raɪˈzəʊbɪəm) NOUN, *plural* **-bia** (-bɪə). any rod-shaped bacterium of the genus *Rhizobium,* typically occurring in the root nodules of leguminous plants and able to fix atmospheric nitrogen. See also **nitrogen fixation.**
▷HISTORY C20: from RHIZO- + Greek *bios* life

rhizocarpous (ˌraɪzəʊˈkɑːpəs) ADJECTIVE [1] (of plants) producing subterranean flowers and fruit. [2] (of perennial plants) having roots that persist throughout the year but stems and leaves that wither at the end of the growing season.

rhizocephalan (ˌraɪzəʊˈsɛfələn) NOUN [1] any parasitic crustacean of the order *Rhizocephala,* esp *Sacculina carcini,* which has a saclike body and sends out absorptive processes into the body of its host, the crab: subclass *Cirripedia* (barnacles). ◆ ADJECTIVE *also* **rhizocephalous.** [2] of, relating to, or belonging to the order *Rhizocephala.*
▷HISTORY C19: from New Latin *Rhizocephala* (literally: root-headed), from RHIZO- + *-cephala* from Greek *kephalē* head

rhizogenic (ˌraɪzəʊˈdʒɛnɪk), **rhizogenetic** (ˌraɪzəʊdʒəˈnɛtɪk), *or* **rhizogenous** (raɪˈzɒdʒənəs) ADJECTIVE (of cells and tissues) giving rise to roots.

rhizoid (ˈraɪzɔɪd) NOUN any of various slender hairlike structures that function as roots in the gametophyte generation of mosses, ferns, and related plants.
▸**rhiˈzoidal** ADJECTIVE

rhizome (ˈraɪzəʊm) NOUN a thick horizontal underground stem of plants such as the mint and iris whose buds develop new roots and shoots. Also called: **rootstock, rootstalk.**
▷HISTORY C19: from New Latin *rhizoma,* from Greek, from *rhiza* a root
▸**rhizomatous** (raɪˈzɒmətəs, -ˈzəʊ-) ADJECTIVE

rhizomorph (ˈraɪzəʊˌmɔːf) NOUN a rootlike structure of certain fungi, such as the honey fungus *Armillaria mellea,* consisting of a dense mass of hyphae.

rhizomorphous (ˌraɪzəʊˈmɔːfəs) ADJECTIVE *Botany* having the appearance of a root.

rhizopod (ˈraɪzəʊˌpɒd) NOUN [1] any protozoan of the phylum *Rhizopoda,* characterized by naked protoplasmic processes (pseudopodia). The group includes the amoebas. ◆ ADJECTIVE [2] of, relating to, or belonging to the *Rhizopoda.*
▸**rhizopodan** (raɪˈzɒpədən) ADJECTIVE, NOUN
▸**rhiˈzopodous** ADJECTIVE

rhizopus (ˈraɪzəʊpəs) NOUN any zygomycetous fungus of the genus *Rhizopus,* esp *R. nigricans,* a bread mould.
▷HISTORY C19: New Latin, from RHIZO- + Greek *pous* foot

rhizosphere (ˈraɪzəʊˌsfɪə) NOUN the region of the soil in contact with the roots of a plant. It contains many microorganisms and its composition is affected by root activities.

rhizotomy (raɪˈzɒtəmɪ) NOUN, *plural* **-mies.** surgical incision into the roots of spinal nerves, esp for the relief of pain.

Rh negative NOUN [1] blood that does not contain the Rh factor. [2] a person having such blood.

rho (rəʊ) NOUN, *plural* **rhos.** the 17th letter in the Greek alphabet (Ρ, ρ), a consonant transliterated as *r* or *rh.*

rhodamine (ˈrəʊdəˌmiːn, -mɪn) NOUN any one of a group of synthetic red or pink basic dyestuffs used for wool and silk. They are made from phthalic anhydride and aminophenols.
▷HISTORY C20: from RHODO- + AMINE

Rhode Island (rəʊd) NOUN a state of the northeastern US, bordering on the Atlantic: the smallest state in the US; mainly low-lying and undulating, with an indented coastline in the east and uplands in the northwest. Capital: Providence. Pop.: 1 048 319 (2000). Area: 2717 sq. km (1049 sq. miles). Abbreviations: **R.I.,** (with zip code) **RI.**

Rhode Island Red NOUN a breed of domestic fowl, originating in America, characterized by a dark reddish-brown plumage and the production of brown eggs.

Rhodes (rəʊdz) NOUN [1] a Greek island in the SE Aegean Sea, about 16 km (10 miles) off the Turkish coast: the largest of the Dodecanese and the most easterly island in the Aegean. Capital: Rhodes. Pop.: 40 390 (latest est.). Area: 1400 sq. km (540 sq. miles). [2] a port on this island, in the NE: founded in 408 B.C.; of great commercial and political importance in the 3rd century B.C.; suffered several earthquakes, notably in 225, when the Colossus was destroyed. Pop.: 41 000 (latest est.). ◆ Ancient Greek name: **Rhodos.** Modern Greek name: **Ródhos.**

Rhodes grass NOUN a perennial grass, *Chloris gayana,* native to Africa but widely cultivated in dry regions for forage.
▷HISTORY C19: named after Cecil John *Rhodes* (1853–1902), British colonial financier and statesman

Rhodesia (rəʊˈdiːʃə, -zɪə) NOUN a former name (1964–79) for **Zimbabwe.**

Rhodesian (rəʊˈdiːʃən, -zɪən) ADJECTIVE [1] of or relating to the former Rhodesia (now Zimbabwe) or its inhabitants. ◆ NOUN [2] a native or inhabitant of the former Rhodesia.

Rhodesian Front NOUN the governing party in Zimbabwe (then called Rhodesia) 1962–78.

Rhodesian man NOUN a type of early man, *Homo rhodesiensis* (or *H. sapiens rhodesiensis*), occurring in Africa in late Pleistocene times and resembling Neanderthal man in many features.

Rhodesian ridgeback (ˈrɪdʒˌbæk) NOUN a large short-haired breed of dog characterized by a ridge of hair growing along the back in the opposite direction to the rest of the coat. It was originally a hunting dog from South Africa.

Rhodesoid (rəʊˈdiːzɔɪd) ADJECTIVE relating to or resembling Rhodesian man.

Rhodes scholarship NOUN one of 72 scholarships founded by Cecil Rhodes, awarded annually on merit to Commonwealth and US students to study for two or sometimes three years at Oxford University.
▸**Rhodes scholar** NOUN

Rhodian (ˈrəʊdɪən) ADJECTIVE [1] of or relating to the island of Rhodes. ◆ NOUN [2] a native or inhabitant of Rhodes.

rhodic (ˈrəʊdɪk) ADJECTIVE of or containing rhodium, esp in the tetravalent state.

rhodinal (ˈrəʊdɪˌnæl) NOUN another name for **citronellal.**

rhodium (ˈrəʊdɪəm) NOUN a hard corrosion-resistant silvery-white element of the platinum metal group, occurring free with other platinum metals in alluvial deposits and in nickel ores. It is used as an alloying agent to harden platinum and palladium. Symbol: Rh; atomic no.: 45; atomic wt.: 102.90550; valency: 2–6; relative density: 12.41; melting pt.: 1963±3°C; boiling pt.: 3697±100°C.
▷HISTORY C19: New Latin, from Greek *rhodon* rose, from the pink colour of its compounds

rhodo- *or before a vowel* **rhod-** COMBINING FORM rose or rose-coloured: *rhododendron; rhodolite.*
▷HISTORY from Greek *rhodon* rose

rhodochrosite (ˌrəʊdəʊˈkrəʊsaɪt) NOUN a pink, red, grey, or brown mineral that consists of manganese carbonate in hexagonal crystalline form and occurs in ore veins. Formula: $MnCO_3$.
▷HISTORY C19: from Greek *rhodokhrōs* of a rosy colour, from *rhodon* rose + *khrōs* colour

rhododendron (ˌrəʊdəˈdɛndrən) NOUN any ericaceous shrub of the genus *Rhododendron,* native to S Asia but widely cultivated in N temperate regions. They are mostly evergreen and have clusters of showy red, purple, pink, or white flowers. Also called (US): **rosebay.** See also **azalea.**
▷HISTORY C17: from Latin: oleander, from Greek, from *rhodon* rose + *dendron* tree

rhododendron bug NOUN See **lace bug.**

rhodolite (ˈrɒdəˌlaɪt) NOUN a pale violet or red variety of garnet, used as a gemstone.

rhodonite (ˈrɒdəˌnaɪt) NOUN a brownish translucent mineral consisting of manganese silicate in triclinic crystalline form with calcium, iron, or magnesium sometimes replacing the manganese. It occurs in metamorphic rocks, esp in New Jersey and Russia, and is used as an ornamental stone, glaze, and pigment. Formula: $MnSiO_3$.
▷HISTORY C19: from German *Rhodonit,* from Greek *rhodon* rose + -ITE

Rhodope Mountains (ˈrɒdəpɪ, rɒˈdəʊ-) PLURAL NOUN a mountain range in SE Europe, in the Balkan Peninsula extending along the border between Bulgaria and Greece. Highest peak: Golyam Perelik (Bulgaria), 2191 m (7188 ft.).

rhodopsin (rəʊˈdɒpsɪn) NOUN a red pigment in the rods of the retina in vertebrates. It is dissociated by light into retinene, the light energy being converted into nerve signals, and is re-formed in the dark. Also called: **visual purple.** See also **iodopsin.**
▷HISTORY C20: from RHODO- + -OPSIS + -IN

Rhodos (ˈrɔðɔs) NOUN the Ancient Greek name for **Rhodes.**

rhoicissus (ˌrəʊɪˈsɪsəs) NOUN any plant of the climbing genus *Rhoicissus,* related to and resembling cissus, esp *R. rhomboidea* (grape ivy), grown for its shiny evergreen foliage: family *Vitaceae.*
▷HISTORY New Latin, from Greek *rhoia* pomegranate + CISSUS

rhomb (rɒm) NOUN another name for **rhombus.**

rhombencephalon (ˌrɒmbɛnˈsɛfəˌlɒn) NOUN the part of the brain that develops from the posterior portion of the embryonic neural tube and comprises the cerebellum, pons, and the medulla oblongata. Compare **mesencephalon, prosencephalon.** Nontechnical name: **hindbrain.**
▷HISTORY C20: from RHOMBUS + ENCEPHALON

rhombic (ˈrɒmbɪk) ADJECTIVE [1] relating to or having the shape of a rhombus. [2] *Crystallog* another word for **orthorhombic.**

rhombic aerial NOUN a directional travelling-wave aerial, usually horizontal, consisting of two conductors each forming a pair of adjacent sides of a rhombus.

rhombohedral (ˌrɒmbəʊˈhiːdrəl) ADJECTIVE [1] of or relating to a rhombohedron. [2] *Crystallog* another term for **trigonal** (sense 2).

rhombohedron (ˌrɒmbəʊˈhiːdrən) NOUN a six-sided prism whose sides are parallelograms.
▷HISTORY C19: from RHOMBUS + -HEDRON

rhomboid (ˈrɒmbɔɪd) NOUN [1] a parallelogram having adjacent sides of unequal length. ◆ ADJECTIVE *also* **rhomˈboidal.** [2] having such a shape.
▷HISTORY C16: from Late Latin *rhomboides,* from Greek *rhomboeidēs* shaped like a RHOMBUS

rhomboideus (rɒmˈbɔɪdɪəs) NOUN, *plural* **-dei**

(-dɪˌaɪ). *Anatomy* either of two muscles that connect the spinal vertebrae to the scapulae.
▷HISTORY C19: New Latin, from Late Latin *rhomboides*: see RHOMBOID

rhombus (ˈrɒmbəs) NOUN, *plural* **-buses** *or* **-bi** (-baɪ). an oblique-angled parallelogram having four equal sides. Also called: **rhomb.** Compare **square** (sense 1).
▷HISTORY C16: from Greek *rhombos* something that spins; related to *rhembein* to whirl

rhonchus (ˈrɒŋkəs) NOUN, *plural* **-chi** (-kaɪ). a rattling or whistling respiratory sound resembling snoring, caused by secretions in the trachea or bronchi.
▷HISTORY C19: from Latin, from Greek *rhenkhos* snoring
▸ **ˈrhonchal** *or* **ˈrhonchial** ADJECTIVE

Rhondda (ˈrɒndə) NOUN an urban area in S Wales, in Rhondda Cynon Taff county borough on two branches of the **Rhondda Valley**: developed into a major coal-mining centre after 1807 and grew to a population of 167 900 in 1924: the last coal mine closed in 1990. Pop.: 59 947 (1991).

Rhondda Cynon Taff (ˈrɒndə ˈkʊnən ˈtæf) NOUN a county borough in S Wales, created from part of Mid Glamorgan in 1996. Pop.: 231 952 (2001). Area: 558 sq. km (215 sq. miles).

Rhône (rəʊn) NOUN [1] a river in W Europe, rising in S Switzerland in the **Rhône glacier** and flowing to Lake Geneva, then into France through gorges between the Alps and Jura and south to its delta on the Gulf of Lions: important esp for hydroelectricity and for wine production along its valley. Length: 812 km (505 miles). [2] a department of E central France, in the Rhône-Alpes region. Capital: Lyons. Pop.: 1 578 869 (1999). Area: 3233 sq. km (1261 sq. miles).

Rhône-Alpes (*French* ronalp) NOUN a region of E France: mainly mountainous, rising to the edge of the Massif Central in the west and the French Alps in the east; drained by the Rivers Rhône, Saône, and Isère.

rhotacism (ˈrəʊtəˌsɪzəm) NOUN excessive use or idiosyncratic pronunciation of *r*.
▷HISTORY C19: from New Latin *rhōtacismus*, from Greek *rhōtakizein* (verb) from the letter *rho*
▸ **ˈrhotacist** NOUN ▸ **ˌrhotaˈcistic** ADJECTIVE

rhotic (ˈrəʊtɪk) ADJECTIVE *Phonetics* denoting or speaking a dialect of English in which postvocalic *r*s are pronounced.
▷HISTORY from Greek *rho*, the letter *r*
▸ **rhoticity** (rəʊˈtɪsɪtɪ) NOUN

Rh positive NOUN [1] blood containing the Rh factor. [2] a person having such blood.

RHS ABBREVIATION FOR: [1] Royal Historical Society. [2] Royal Horticultural Society. [3] Royal Humane Society.

rhubarb (ˈruːbɑːb) NOUN [1] any of several temperate and subtropical plants of the polygonaceous genus *Rheum*, esp *R. rhaponticum* (**common garden rhubarb**), which has long green and red acid-tasting edible leafstalks, usually eaten sweetened and cooked. [2] the leafstalks of this plant. [3] a related plant, *Rheum officinale*, of central Asia, having a bitter-tasting underground stem that can be dried and used medicinally as a laxative or astringent. [4] *US and Canadian slang* a heated discussion or quarrel. ◆ INTERJECTION, NOUN, VERB [5] the noise made by actors to simulate conversation, esp by repeating the word *rhubarb* at random.
▷HISTORY C14: from Old French *reubarbe*, from Medieval Latin *reubarbum*, probably a variant of *rha barbarum* barbarian rhubarb, from *rha* rhubarb (from Greek, perhaps from *Rha* ancient name of the Volga) + Latin *barbarus* barbarian

rhumb (rʌm) NOUN short for **rhumb line.**

rhumba (ˈrʌmbə, ˈrʊm-) NOUN, *plural* **-bas.** a variant spelling of **rumba.**

rhumbatron (ˈrʌmbəˌtrɒn) NOUN another name for **cavity resonator.**
▷HISTORY C20: from RHUMBA + TRON, from the rhythmic variation of the waves

rhumb line NOUN [1] an imaginary line on the surface of a sphere, such as the earth, that intersects all meridians at the same angle. [2] the course navigated by a vessel or aircraft that maintains a uniform compass heading. ◆ Often shortened to: **rhumb.**
▷HISTORY C16: from Old Spanish *rumbo*, apparently from Middle Dutch *ruum* space, ship's hold, but also influenced by Latin RHOMBUS

rhus (rʊs) NOUN any shrub or small tree of the anacardiaceous genus *Rhus*, several species of which are cultivated as ornamentals for their foliage, which assumes brilliant colours in autumn. ◆ See also **sumach.**

rhyme *or archaic* **rime** (raɪm) NOUN [1] identity of the terminal sounds in lines of verse or in words. [2] a word that is identical to another in its terminal sound: *"while" is a rhyme for "mile".* [3] a verse or piece of poetry having corresponding sounds at the ends of the lines: *the boy made up a rhyme about his teacher.* [4] any verse or piece of poetry. [5] **rhyme or reason.** sense, logic, or meaning: *this proposal has no rhyme or reason.* ◆ VERB [6] to use (a word) or (of a word) to be used so as to form a rhyme; be or make identical in sound. [7] to render (a subject) into rhyme. [8] to compose (verse) in a metrical structure. ◆ See also **masculine rhyme, feminine rhyme, eye rhyme.**
▷HISTORY C12: from Old French *rime*, from *rimer* to rhyme, from Old High German *rīm* a number; spelling influenced by RHYTHM
▸ **ˈrhymeless** *or* **ˈrimeless** ADJECTIVE

rhyme royal NOUN *Prosody* a stanzaic form introduced into English verse by Chaucer, consisting of seven lines of iambic pentameter rhyming a b a b b c c.

rhymester, rimester (ˈraɪmstə), **rhymer,** *or* **rimer** NOUN a poet, esp one considered to be mediocre or mechanical in diction; poetaster or versifier.

rhyming slang NOUN slang in which a word is replaced by another word or phrase that rhymes with it; for example, *apples and pears* meaning *stairs.*

rhynchocephalian (ˌrɪŋkəʊsɪˈfæliən) ADJECTIVE [1] of, relating to, or belonging to the *Rhyncocephalia*, an order of lizard-like reptiles common in the Mesozoic era but today represented only by the tuatara. ◆ NOUN [2] any reptile belonging to the order *Rhyncocephalia.*
▷HISTORY C19: from New Latin *Rhynchocephalia*, from Greek *rhunkhos* a snout + *kephalē* head

rhynchophore (ˈrɪŋkəˌfɔː) NOUN a member of the *Rhynchophora*, a former name for the superfamily of beetles (*Curculionoidea*) that comprises the weevils and bark beetles.
▷HISTORY C19: New Latin *rhyncophora*, from Greek *rhunkhos* a snout + *-phoros* bearing

rhyolite (ˈraɪəˌlaɪt) NOUN a fine-grained igneous rock consisting of quartz, feldspars, and mica or amphibole. It is the volcanic equivalent of granite.
▷HISTORY C19: *rhyo-* from Greek *rhuax* a stream of lava + LITE
▸ **rhyolitic** (ˌraɪəˈlɪtɪk) ADJECTIVE

rhythm (ˈrɪðəm) NOUN [1] **a** the arrangement of the relative durations of and accents on the notes of a melody, usually laid out into regular groups (**bars**) of beats, the first beat of each bar carrying the stress. **b** any specific arrangement of such groupings; time: *quadruple rhythm.* [2] (in poetry) **a** the arrangement of words into a more or less regular sequence of stressed and unstressed or long and short syllables. **b** any specific such arrangement; metre. [3] (in painting, sculpture, architecture, etc.) a harmonious sequence or pattern of masses alternating with voids, of light alternating with shade, of alternating colours, etc. [4] any sequence of regularly recurring functions or events, such as the regular recurrence of certain physiological functions of the body, as the cardiac rhythm of the heartbeat.
▷HISTORY C16: from Latin *rhythmus*, from Greek *rhuthmos*; related to *rhein* to flow
▸ **ˈrhythmless** ADJECTIVE

rhythm and blues NOUN (*functioning as singular*) any of various kinds of popular music derived from or influenced by the blues. Abbreviation: **R & B.**

rhythmic (ˈrɪðmɪk) *or* **rhythmical** (ˈrɪðmɪkəl) ADJECTIVE of, relating to, or characterized by rhythm, as in movement or sound; metrical, periodic, or regularly recurring.
▸ **ˈrhythmically** ADVERB ▸ **rhythmicity** (rɪðˈmɪsɪtɪ) NOUN

rhythmic gymnastics NOUN (*functioning as singular or plural*) a form of gymnastics involving movements using hand apparatus such as balls, hoops, and ribbons.

rhythmics (ˈrɪðmɪks) NOUN (*functioning as singular*) the study of rhythmic movement.

rhythmist (ˈrɪðmɪst) NOUN *Rare* a person who has a good sense of rhythm.

rhythm method NOUN a method of controlling conception without the aid of a contraceptive device, by restricting sexual intercourse to those days in a woman's menstrual cycle on which conception is considered least likely to occur. See also **safe period.**

rhythm section NOUN those instruments in a band or group (usually piano, double bass, and drums) whose prime function is to supply the rhythm.

rhyton (ˈraɪtɒn) NOUN, *plural* **-ta** (-tə). (in ancient Greece) a horn-shaped drinking vessel with a hole in the pointed end through which to drink.
▷HISTORY C19: from Greek *rhuton*, from *rhutos* flowing; related to *rhein* to flow

RI ABBREVIATION FOR [1] Regina et Imperatrix. [Latin: Queen and Empress] [2] Rex et Imperator. [Latin: King and Emperor] [3] Rhode Island. [4] Royal Institution. [5] religious instruction. ◆ [6] INTERNATIONAL CAR REGISTRATION FOR (Republic of) Indonesia.

ria (ˈrɪə) NOUN a long narrow inlet of the seacoast, being a former valley that was submerged by a rise in the level of the sea. Rias are found esp on the coasts of SW Ireland and NW Spain.
▷HISTORY C19: from Spanish, from *rio* river

RIA ABBREVIATION FOR Royal Irish Academy.

RIAA curve NOUN *Electronics* a graphical representation, adopted as a worldwide standard, of the amplitude in relation to frequency response required for correct reproduction of microgroove disc recordings, compensating for the characteristics of the recording process.
▷HISTORY C20: *R*ecord *I*ndustry *A*ssociation of *A*merica

rial (ˈraɪəl) NOUN [1] the standard monetary unit of Iran. [2] the standard monetary unit of Oman, divided into 1000 baizas. [3] another name for **riyal.**
▷HISTORY C14: from Persian, from Arabic *riyāl* RIYAL

rialto (rɪˈæltəʊ) NOUN, *plural* **-tos.** a market or exchange.
▷HISTORY C19: after the RIALTO

Rialto (rɪˈæltəʊ) NOUN an island in Venice, Italy, linked with San Marco Island by the **Rialto Bridge** (1590) over the Grand Canal: the business centre of medieval and renaissance Venice.

riant (ˈraɪənt) ADJECTIVE *Rare* laughing; smiling; cheerful.
▷HISTORY C16: from French, from *rire* to laugh, from Latin *rīdēre*
▸ **ˈriantly** ADVERB

rib¹ (rɪb) NOUN [1] any of the 24 curved elastic arches of bone that together form the chest wall in man. All are attached behind to the thoracic part of the spinal column. Technical name: **costa.** Compare **true rib, false ribs, floating rib.** [2] the corresponding bone in other vertebrates. [3] a cut of meat including one or more ribs. [4] a part or element similar in function or appearance to a rib, esp a structural or supporting member or a raised strip or ridge. [5] a structural member in a wing that extends from the leading edge to the trailing edge and maintains the shape of the wing surface. [6] a projecting moulding or band on the underside of a vault or ceiling, which may be structural or ornamental. [7] one of a series of raised rows in knitted fabric. See also **ribbing** (sense 3). [8] a raised ornamental line on the spine of a book where the stitching runs across it. [9] any of the transverse stiffening timbers or joists forming the frame of a ship's hull. [10] any of the larger veins of a leaf. [11] a metal strip running along the top of the barrel of a shotgun or handgun and guiding the alignment of the sights. [12] a vein of ore in rock. [13] a projecting ridge of a mountain; spur. ◆ VERB **ribs, ribbing, ribbed.** (*tr*) [14] to furnish or support with a rib or ribs. [15] to mark with or form into ribs or ridges. [16] to knit plain and purl stitches alternately in order to make raised rows in (knitting). [17] *Archaic* to enclose with or as if with ribs.
▷HISTORY Old English *ribb*; related to Old High German *rippi*, Old Norse *rif* REEF¹
▸ **ˈribless** ADJECTIVE ▸ **ˈribˌlike** ADJECTIVE

rib^{2} (rɪb) *Informal* ◆ VERB **ribs, ribbing, ribbed.** [1] (*tr*) to tease or ridicule. ◆ NOUN [2] a joke or hoax.
▷HISTORY C20: short for *rib-tickle* (vb)

RIBA ABBREVIATION FOR Royal Institute of British Architects.

ribald (ˈrɪbᵊld) ADJECTIVE [1] coarse, obscene, or licentious, usually in a humorous or mocking way. ◆ NOUN [2] a ribald person.
▷HISTORY C13: from Old French *ribauld*, from *riber* to live licentiously, of Germanic origin
▸ ˈ**ribaldly** ADVERB

ribaldry (ˈrɪbᵊldrɪ) NOUN ribald language or behaviour.

riband *or* **ribband** (ˈrɪbənd) NOUN [1] a ribbon, esp one awarded for some achievement. See also **blue riband.** [2] a flat rail attached to posts in a palisade.
▷HISTORY C14: variant of RIBBON

ribbed and smoked sheet NOUN another name for **smoked rubber.**

ribbing (ˈrɪbɪŋ) NOUN [1] a framework or structure of ribs. [2] ribs collectively. [3] a raised pattern in woven or knitted material, made in knitting by doing purl and plain stitches alternately.

Ribble (ˈrɪbᵊl) NOUN a river in NW England, flowing south and west through Lancashire to the Irish Sea. Length: 121 km (75 miles).

ribbon (ˈrɪbᵊn) NOUN [1] a narrow strip of fine material, esp silk, used for trimming, tying, etc. [2] something resembling a ribbon; a long strip: *a ribbon of land.* [3] a long thin flexible band of metal used as a graduated measure, spring, etc. [4] a long narrow strip of ink-impregnated cloth for making the impression of type characters on paper in a typewriter or similar device. [5] (*plural*) ragged strips or shreds (esp in the phrase **torn to ribbons**). [6] a small strip of coloured cloth signifying membership of an order or award of military decoration, prize, or other distinction. [7] a small, usually looped, strip of coloured cloth worn to signify support for a charity or cause: *a red AIDS ribbon.* ◆ VERB (*tr*) [8] to adorn with a ribbon or ribbons. [9] to mark with narrow ribbon-like marks. [10] to reduce to ribbons; tear into strips.
▷HISTORY C14 *ryban*, from Old French *riban*, apparently of Germanic origin; probably related to RING^{1}, BAND^{2}
▸ ˈ**ribbon-ˌlike** *or* ˈ**ribbony** ADJECTIVE

ribbon development NOUN *Brit* the building of houses in a continuous row along a main road: common in England between the two World Wars.

ribbonfish (ˈrɪbᵊnˌfɪʃ) NOUN, *plural* **-fish** *or* **-fishes.** any of various soft-finned deep-sea teleost fishes, esp *Regalecus glesne* (see **oarfish**), that have an elongated compressed body. They are related to the opah and dealfishes.

ribbon microphone NOUN a type of microphone in which the conductor is a thin ribbon of aluminium alloy moving perpendicularly in a magnetic field. It is strongly directional and can be used to reduce unwanted side noise.

ribbon strip NOUN another name for **ledger board** (sense 2).

ribbonwood (ˈrɪbᵊnˌwʊd) NOUN a small evergreen malvaceous tree, *Hoheria populnea*, of New Zealand. Its wood is used in furniture making and the tough bark for making cord. Also called: **lacebark.**

ribbon worm NOUN another name for **nemertean** (sense 1).

ribcage (ˈrɪbˌkeɪdʒ) NOUN the bony structure consisting of the ribs and their connective tissue that encloses and protects the lungs, heart, etc.

Ribeirão Prêto (*Portuguese* riβeiˈrɐ̃u ˈpretu) NOUN a city in SE Brazil, in São Paulo state. Pop.: 416 186 (1991).

ribgrass (ˈrɪbˌgrɑːs) NOUN another name for **ribwort.**

riboflavin *or* **riboflavine** (ˌraɪbəʊˈfleɪvɪn) NOUN a yellow water-soluble vitamin of the B complex that occurs in green vegetables, germinating seeds, and in milk, fish, egg yolk, liver, and kidney. It is essential for the carbohydrate metabolism of cells. It is used as a permitted food colour, yellow or orange-yellow (**E101**). Formula: $C_{17}H_{20}N_4O_6$. Also called: **vitamin B_2, lactoflavin.**
▷HISTORY C20: from RIBOSE + FLAVIN

ribonuclease (ˌraɪbəʊˈnjuːkliːˌeɪs, -ˌeɪz) NOUN any of a group of enzymes that catalyse the hydrolysis of RNA.
▷HISTORY C20: from RIBONUCLE(IC ACID) + -ASE

ribonucleic acid (ˌraɪbəʊnjuːˈkliːɪk, -ˈkleɪ-) NOUN the full name of **RNA.**
▷HISTORY C20: from RIBO(SE) + NUCLEIC ACID

ribose (ˈraɪbəʊz, -bəʊs) NOUN *Biochem* a pentose sugar that is an isomeric form of arabinose and that occurs in RNA and riboflavin. Formula: $CH_2OH(CHOH)_3CHO$.
▷HISTORY C20: changed from ARABINOSE

ribosomal RNA NOUN *Biochem* a type of RNA thought to be transcribed from DNA in the nucleoli of cell nuclei, subsequently forming the component of ribosomes on which the translation of messenger RNA into protein chains is accomplished. Sometimes shortened to: **rRNA.**

ribosome (ˈraɪbəˌsəʊm) NOUN any of numerous minute particles in the cytoplasm of cells, either free or attached to the endoplasmic reticulum, that contain RNA and protein and are the site of protein synthesis.
▷HISTORY C20: from RIBO(NUCLEIC ACID) + -SOME^{3}
▸ ˌ**riboˈsomal** ADJECTIVE

ribozyme (ˈraɪbəʊˌzaɪm) NOUN an RNA molecule capable of catalysing a chemical reaction, usually the cleavage of another RNA molecule.
▷HISTORY C20: from RIBO(NUCLEIC ACID) + (EN)ZYME

rib-tickler NOUN a very amusing joke or story.

rib-tickling ADJECTIVE very amusing; causing laughter.

ribwort (ˈrɪbˌwɜːt) NOUN a Eurasian plant, *Plantago lanceolata*, that has lancelike ribbed leaves, which form a rosette close to the ground, and a dense spike of small white flowers: family *Plantaginaceae.* Also called: **ribgrass.** See also **plantain^{1}.**

RIC ABBREVIATION FOR Royal Institute of Chemistry.

Ricardian (rɪˈkɑːdɪən) ADJECTIVE of or relating to David Ricardo, the British economist (1772–1823).

rice (raɪs) NOUN [1] an erect grass, *Oryza sativa*, that grows in East Asia on wet ground and has drooping flower spikes and yellow oblong edible grains that become white when polished. [2] the grain of this plant. ◆ VERB [3] (*tr*) *US and Canadian* to sieve (potatoes or other vegetables) to a coarse mashed consistency, esp with a ricer. ◆ See also **Indian rice.**
▷HISTORY C13 *rys*, via French, Italian, and Latin from Greek *orūza*, of Oriental origin

RICE (raɪs) NOUN ACRONYM FOR rest, ice, compression, elevation: the recommended procedure for controlling inflammation in injured limbs or joints.

ricebird (ˈraɪsˌbɜːd) NOUN any of various birds frequenting rice fields, esp the Java sparrow.

rice bowl NOUN [1] a small bowl for eating rice out of, esp a decorative one made of china or porcelain. [2] a fertile rice-producing region.

rice grass NOUN another name for **cord grass.**

rice paper NOUN [1] a thin semitransparent edible paper made from the straw of rice, on which macaroons and similar cakes are baked. [2] a thin delicate Chinese paper made from an araliaceous plant, *Tetrapanax papyriferum* (**rice-paper plant**) of Taiwan, the pith of which is pared and flattened into sheets.

ricer (ˈraɪsə) NOUN *US and Canadian* a kitchen utensil with small holes through which cooked potatoes and similar soft foods are pressed to form a coarse mash.

ricercare (ˌriːtʃəˈkɑːreɪ) *or* **ricercar** (ˈriːtʃəˌkɑː) NOUN, *plural* **-cari** (-ˈkɑːriː) *or* **-cars.** (in music of the 16th and 17th centuries) [1] an elaborate polyphonic composition making extensive use of contrapuntal imitation and usually very slow in tempo. [2] an instructive composition to illustrate instrumental technique; étude.
▷HISTORY Italian, literally: to seek again

rich (rɪtʃ) ADJECTIVE [1] **a** well supplied with wealth, property, etc.; owning much. **b** (*as collective noun; preceded by the*): *the rich.* [2] (when *postpositive*, usually foll by *in*) having an abundance of natural resources, minerals, etc.: *a land rich in metals.* [3] producing abundantly; fertile: *rich soil.* [4] (when *postpositive*, usually foll by *in* or *with*) well supplied (with desirable qualities); abundant (in): *a country rich with cultural interest.* [5] of great worth or quality; valuable: *a rich collection of antiques.* [6] luxuriant or prolific: *a rich growth of weeds.* [7] expensively elegant, elaborate, or fine; costly: *a rich display.* [8] (of food) having a large proportion of flavoursome or fatty ingredients, such as spices, butter, or cream. [9] having a full-bodied flavour: *a rich ruby port.* [10] (of a smell) pungent or fragrant. [11] (of colour) intense or vivid; deep: *a rich red.* [12] (of sound or a voice) full, mellow, or resonant. [13] (of a fuel-air mixture) containing a relatively high proportion of fuel. Compare **weak** (sense 12). [14] very amusing, laughable, or ridiculous: *a rich joke; a rich situation.* ◆ NOUN [15] See **riches.**
▷HISTORY Old English *rīce* (originally of persons: great, mighty), of Germanic origin, ultimately from Celtic (compare Old Irish *rī* king)

Richelieu River (ˈrɪʃəˌljɜ, *French* riʃəljø) NOUN a river in E Canada, in S Quebec, rising in Lake Champlain and flowing north to the St Lawrence River. Length: 338 km (210 miles).

riches (ˈrɪtʃɪz) PLURAL NOUN wealth; an abundance of money, valuable possessions, or property.

richly (ˈrɪtʃlɪ) ADVERB [1] in a rich or elaborate manner: *a richly decorated carving.* [2] fully and appropriately: *he was richly rewarded for his service.*

Richmond (ˈrɪtʃmənd) NOUN [1] a borough of Greater London, on the River Thames: formed in 1965 by the amalgamation of Barnes, Richmond, and Twickenham; site of Hampton Court Palace and the Royal Botanic Gardens at Kew. Pop.: 172 327 (2001). Area: 55 sq. km (21 sq. miles). Official name: **Richmond-upon-Thames.** [2] a town in N England, in North Yorkshire: Norman castle. Pop.: 7862 (1991). [3] a port in E Virginia, the state capital, at the falls of the James River: developed after the establishment of a trading post (1637); scene of the Virginia Conventions of 1774 and 1775; Confederate capital in the American Civil War. Pop.: 197 790 (2000). [4] a county of SW New York City: coextensive with Staten Island borough; consists of Staten Island and several smaller islands.

richness (ˈrɪtʃnɪs) NOUN [1] the state or quality of being rich. [2] *Ecology* the number of individuals of a species in a given area.

rich rhyme NOUN *Prosody* another term for **rime riche.**

richt (rɪxt) ADJECTIVE, ADVERB, NOUN a Scottish word for **right.**

Richter scale (ˈrɪxtə) NOUN a scale for expressing the magnitude of an earthquake in terms of the logarithm of the amplitude of the ground wave; values range from 0 to over 9. Compare **Mercalli scale.** See also **magnitude** (sense 5).
▷HISTORY C20: named after Charles *Richter* (1900–85) US seismologist

ricin (ˈraɪsɪn, ˈrɪs-) NOUN *Biochem* a highly toxic protein, a lectin, derived from castor-oil seeds: used in experimental cancer therapy.
▷HISTORY C19: from New Latin *Ricinus* genus name, from Latin: castor-oil plant

ricinoleic acid (ˌrɪsɪnəʊˈliːɪk, -ˈnəʊlɪɪk) NOUN [1] an oily unsaturated carboxylic acid found, as the glyceride, in castor oil and used in the manufacture of soap and in finishing textiles; 12-hydroxy-9-octadecanoic acid. Formula: $C_{18}H_{34}O_3$. [2] the mixture of fatty acids obtained by hydrolysing castor oil.
▷HISTORY C19: from RICIN + OLEIC ACID

rick^{1} (rɪk) NOUN [1] a large stack of hay, corn, peas, etc., built in the open in a regular-shaped pile, esp one with a thatched top. ◆ VERB [2] (*tr*) to stack or pile into ricks.
▷HISTORY Old English *hrēac*; related to Old Norse *hraukr*

rick^{2} (rɪk) NOUN [1] a wrench or sprain, as of the back. ◆ VERB [2] (*tr*) to wrench or sprain (a joint, a limb, the back, etc.).
▷HISTORY C18: see WRICK

ricker (ˈrɪkə) NOUN a young kauri tree of New Zealand.
▷HISTORY from earlier use of the trunks as ships' rigging

rickets (ˈrɪkɪts) NOUN (*functioning as singular or plural*) *Pathol* a disease mainly of children, characterized by softening of developing bone, and hence bow legs, malnutrition, and enlargement of the liver and spleen, caused by a deficiency of vitamin D.
▷HISTORY C17: of unknown origin

rickettsia (rɪˈketsɪə) NOUN, *plural* **-siae** (-sɪˌiː) *or* **-sias.** any of a group of parasitic bacteria that live in the tissues of ticks, mites, and other arthropods, and cause disease when transmitted to man and other animals.
▷**HISTORY** C20: named after Howard T. *Ricketts* (1871–1910), US pathologist
▸**rickˈettsial** ADJECTIVE

rickettsial disease NOUN any of several acute infectious diseases caused by ticks, mites, or body lice infected with rickettsiae. The main types include typhus, spotted fever, Q fever, trench fever, and tsutsugamushi disease.

rickety (ˈrɪkɪtɪ) ADJECTIVE 1 (of a structure, piece of furniture, etc.) likely to collapse or break; shaky. 2 feeble with age or illness; infirm. 3 relating to, resembling, or afflicted with rickets.
▷**HISTORY** C17: from RICKETS
▸**ˈricketiness** NOUN

rickey (ˈrɪkɪ) NOUN a cocktail consisting of gin or vodka, lime juice, and soda water, served iced (esp in the phrase **a gin rickey**).
▷**HISTORY** C19: of uncertain origin

rickle (ˈrɪkᵊl) NOUN *Scot* 1 an unsteady or shaky structure, esp a dilapidated building. 2 a loose or disorganized heap.
▷**HISTORY** C16: perhaps of Scandinavian origin

rickrack *or* **ricrac** (ˈrɪkˌræk) NOUN a zigzag braid used for trimming.
▷**HISTORY** C20: dissimilated reduplication of RACK[1]

rickshaw (ˈrɪkʃɔː) *or* **ricksha** (ˈrɪkʃə) NOUN 1 Also called: **jinrikisha.** a small two-wheeled passenger vehicle drawn by one or two men, used in parts of Asia. 2 Also called: **trishaw.** a similar vehicle with three wheels, propelled by a man pedalling as on a tricycle. ◆ See also **autorickshaw.**
▷**HISTORY** C19: shortened from JINRIKISHA

ricochet (ˈrɪkəˌʃeɪ, ˈrɪkəˌʃet) VERB **-chets, -cheting** (-ˌʃeɪɪŋ), **-cheted** (-ˌʃeɪd) *or* **-chets, -chetting** (-ˌʃetɪŋ), **-chetted** (-ˌʃetɪd). 1 (*intr*) (esp of a bullet) to rebound from a surface or surfaces, usually with a characteristic whining or zipping sound. ◆ NOUN 2 the motion or sound of a rebounding object, esp a bullet. 3 an object, esp a bullet, that ricochets.
▷**HISTORY** C18: from French, of unknown origin

ricotta (rɪˈkɒtə) NOUN a soft white unsalted cheese made from sheep's milk, used esp in making ravioli and gnocchi.
▷**HISTORY** C19: Italian, from Latin *recocta* recooked, from *recoquere*, from RE- + *coquere* to COOK

RICS ABBREVIATION FOR Royal Institution of Chartered Surveyors.

rictus (ˈrɪktəs) NOUN, *plural* **-tus** *or* **-tuses.** 1 the GAPE or cleft of an open mouth or beak. 2 a fixed or unnatural grin or grimace, as in horror or death.
▷**HISTORY** C18: from Latin, from *ringī* to gape
▸**ˈrictal** ADJECTIVE

rid (rɪd) VERB **rids, ridding, rid** *or* **ridded.** (*tr*) 1 (foll by *of*) to relieve or deliver from something disagreeable or undesirable; make free (of): *to rid a house of mice.* 2 **get rid of.** to relieve or free oneself of (something or someone unpleasant or undesirable).
▷**HISTORY** C13 (meaning: to clear land): from Old Norse *rythja*; related to Old High German *riutan* to clear land
▸**ˈridder** NOUN

riddance (ˈrɪdᵊns) NOUN the act of getting rid of something undesirable or unpleasant; deliverance or removal (esp in the phrase **good riddance**).

ridden (ˈrɪdᵊn) VERB 1 the past participle of **ride.** ◆ ADJECTIVE 2 (*in combination*) afflicted, affected, or dominated by something specified: *damp-ridden; disease-ridden.*

riddle[1] (ˈrɪdᵊl) NOUN 1 a question, puzzle, or verse so phrased that ingenuity is required for elucidation of the answer or meaning; conundrum. 2 a person or thing that puzzles, perplexes, or confuses; enigma. ◆ VERB 3 to solve, explain, or interpret (a riddle or riddles). 4 (*intr*) to speak in riddles.
▷**HISTORY** Old English *rǣdelle, rǣdelse*, from *rǣd* counsel; related to Old Saxon *rādislo*, German *Rätsel*
▸**ˈriddler** NOUN

riddle[2] (ˈrɪdᵊl) VERB (*tr*) 1 (usually foll by *with*) to pierce or perforate with numerous holes: *riddled with bullets.* 2 to damage or impair. 3 to put through a sieve; sift. ◆ NOUN 4 a sieve, esp a coarse one used for sand, grain, etc.
▷**HISTORY** Old English *hriddel* a sieve, variant of *hridder*; related to Latin *crībrum* sieve
▸**ˈriddler** NOUN

ride (raɪd) VERB **rides, riding, rode, ridden.** 1 to sit on and control the movements of (a horse or other animal). 2 (*tr*) to sit on and propel (a bicycle or similar vehicle). 3 (*intr*; often foll by *on* or *in*) to be carried along or travel on or in a vehicle: *she rides to work on the bus.* 4 (*tr*) to travel over or traverse: *they rode the countryside in search of shelter.* 5 (*tr*) to take part in by riding: *to ride a race.* 6 to travel through or be carried across (sea, sky, etc.): *the small boat rode the waves; the moon was riding high.* 7 (*tr*) *US and Canadian* to cause to be carried: *to ride someone out of town.* 8 (*intr*) to be supported as if floating: *the candidate rode to victory on his new policies.* 9 (*intr*) (of a vessel) to lie at anchor. 10 (*tr*) (of a vessel) to be attached to (an anchor). 11 (esp of a bone) to overlap or lie over (another structure or part). 12 *South African informal* **a** (*intr*) to drive a car. **b** (*tr*) to transport (goods, farm produce, etc.) by motor vehicle or cart. 13 (*tr*) (esp of a male animal) to copulate with; mount. 14 (*tr; usually passive*) to tyrannize over or dominate: *ridden by fear.* 15 (*tr*) *Informal* to persecute, esp by constant or petty criticism: *don't ride me so hard over my failure.* 16 (*intr*) *Informal* to continue undisturbed: *I wanted to change something, but let it ride.* 17 (*tr*) to endure successfully; ride out. 18 (*tr*) to yield slightly to (a blow or punch) in order to lessen its impact. 19 (*intr*; often foll by *on*) (of a bet) to remain placed: *let your winnings ride on the same number.* 20 (*intr*) *Jazz* to play well, esp in freely improvising at perfect tempo. 21 **ride roughshod over.** to domineer over or act with complete disregard for. 22 **ride to hounds.** to take part in a fox hunt on horseback. 23 **ride for a fall.** to act in such a way as to invite disaster. 24 **ride again.** *Informal* to return to a former activity or scene of activity. 25 **riding high.** confident, popular, and successful. ◆ NOUN 26 a journey or outing on horseback or in a vehicle. 27 a path specially made for riding on horseback. 28 transport in a vehicle, esp when given freely to a pedestrian; lift: *can you give me a ride to the station?* 29 a device or structure, such as a roller coaster at a fairground, in which people ride for pleasure or entertainment. 30 **take for a ride.** *Informal* **a** to cheat, swindle, or deceive. **b** to take (someone) away in a car and murder him. ◆ See also **ride down, ride out, ride up.**
▷**HISTORY** Old English *rīdan*; related to Old High German *rītan*, Old Norse *rītha*
▸**ˈridable** *or* **ˈrideable** ADJECTIVE

Rideau Hall (ˈriːdəʊ) NOUN (in Canada) the official residence of the Governor General, in Ottawa.

ride down VERB (*tr, adverb*) 1 to trample under the hooves of a horse. 2 to catch up with or overtake by riding.

rident (ˈraɪdᵊnt) ADJECTIVE *Rare* laughing, smiling, or gay.
▷**HISTORY** C17: from Latin *rīdēre* to laugh; see RIANT

ride out VERB (*tr, adverb*) to endure successfully; survive (esp in the phrase **ride out the storm**).

rider (ˈraɪdə) NOUN 1 a person or thing that rides, esp a person who rides a horse, a bicycle, or a motorcycle. 2 an additional clause, amendment, or stipulation added to a legal or other document, esp (in Britain) a legislative bill at its third reading. 3 *Brit* a statement made by a jury in addition to its verdict, such as a recommendation for mercy. 4 any of various objects or devices resting on, surmounting, or strengthening something else. 5 a small weight that can be slid along one arm of a chemical balance to make fine adjustments during weighing. 6 *Geology* a thin seam, esp of coal or mineral ore, overlying a thicker seam.
▸**ˈriderless** ADJECTIVE

ride up VERB (*intr, adverb*) to move or work away from the proper place or position: *her new skirt rode up uncomfortably.*

ridge (rɪdʒ) NOUN 1 a long narrow raised land formation with sloping sides esp one formed by the meeting of two faces of a mountain or of a mountain buttress or spur. 2 any long narrow raised strip or elevation, as on a fabric or in ploughed land. 3 *Anatomy* any elongated raised margin or border on a bone, tooth, tissue membrane, etc. 4 **a** the top of a roof at the junction of two sloping sides. **b** (*as modifier*): *a ridge tile.* 5 the back or backbone of an animal, esp a whale. 6 *Meteorol* an elongated area of high pressure, esp an extension of an anticyclone. Compare **trough** (sense 4). ◆ VERB 7 to form into a ridge or ridges.
▷**HISTORY** Old English *hrycg*; related to Old High German *hrucki*, Old Norse *hryggr*
▸**ˈridgeˌlike** ADJECTIVE ▸**ˈridgy** ADJECTIVE

ridgeling, ridgling (ˈrɪdʒlɪŋ), *or* **ridgel** (ˈrɪdʒəl) NOUN 1 a domestic male animal with one or both testicles undescended, esp a horse. 2 an imperfectly castrated male domestic animal.
▷**HISTORY** C16: perhaps from RIDGE, from the belief that the undescended testicles were near the animal's ridge or back

ridgepole (ˈrɪdʒˌpəʊl) NOUN 1 a timber laid along the ridge of a roof, to which the upper ends of the rafters are attached. 2 the horizontal pole at the apex of a tent.

ridgetree (ˈrɪdʒˌtriː) NOUN another name for **ridgepole** (sense 1).

ridgeway (ˈrɪdʒˌweɪ) NOUN *Brit* a road or track along a ridge, esp one of great antiquity.

ridicule (ˈrɪdɪˌkjuːl) NOUN 1 language or behaviour intended to humiliate or mock; derision. ◆ VERB 2 (*tr*) to make fun of, mock, or deride.
▷**HISTORY** C17: from French, from Latin *rīdiculus*, from *rīdēre* to laugh
▸**ˈridiˌculer** NOUN

ridiculous (rɪˈdɪkjʊləs) ADJECTIVE worthy of or exciting ridicule; absurd, preposterous, laughable, or contemptible.
▷**HISTORY** C16: from Latin *rīdiculōsus*, from *rīdēre* to laugh
▸**riˈdiculously** ADVERB ▸**riˈdiculousness** NOUN

riding[1] (ˈraɪdɪŋ) NOUN **a** the art or practice of horsemanship. **b** (*as modifier*): *a riding school; riding techniques.*

riding[2] (ˈraɪdɪŋ) NOUN 1 (*capital when part of a name*) any of the three former administrative divisions of Yorkshire: **North Riding, East Riding** and **West Riding.** 2 (in Canada) a parliamentary constituency. 3 (in New Zealand) a rural electorate for local government.
▷**HISTORY** from Old English *thriding*, from Old Norse *thrithjungr* a third. The *th-* was lost by assimilation to the *-t* or *-th* that preceded it, as in *west thriding*, etc.

riding breeches PLURAL NOUN tough breeches with padding inside the knees, worn for riding horses.

riding crop NOUN a short whip with a thong at one end and a handle for opening gates at the other.

riding habit NOUN a woman's dress worn for riding, usually with a full or a divided skirt.

riding lamp *or* **light** NOUN a light on a boat or ship showing that it is at anchor.

ridotto (rɪˈdɒtəʊ) NOUN, *plural* **-tos.** an entertainment with music and dancing, often in masquerade: popular in 18th-century England.
▷**HISTORY** C18: from Italian: retreat, from Latin *reductus*, from *redūcere* to lead back

riel (ˈriːəl) NOUN the standard monetary unit of Cambodia, divided into 100 sen.

Riemannian (*German* riːˈmænɪən) ADJECTIVE of or relating to Georg Friedrich Bernhard Riemann, the German mathematician (1826–66).

Riemannian geometry NOUN a branch of non-Euclidean geometry in which a line may have many parallels through a given point. It has a model on the surface of a sphere, with lines represented by great circles. Also called: **elliptic geometry.**

riempie (ˈrɪmpɪ) NOUN *South African* a leather thong or lace used mainly to make chair seats.
▷**HISTORY** C19 (earlier *riem*): from Afrikaans, diminutive of *riem*, from Dutch: RIM

riesling (ˈriːzlɪŋ, ˈraɪz-) NOUN 1 a white wine from the Rhine valley in Germany and from certain districts in other countries. 2 the grape used to make this wine.
▷**HISTORY** C19: from German, from earlier *Rüssling*, of obscure origin

Rievaulx Abbey (ˈriːvəʊ) NOUN a ruined Cistercian abbey near Helmsley in Yorkshire: built in the 12th century and abandoned at the dissolution of the monasteries; landscaped in the 18th century.

Rif, Riff (rɪf), *or* **Rifi** (ˈrɪfɪ) NOUN **1** (*plural* **Rifs, Riffs, Rifis** *or* **Rif, Riff, Rifi**) a member of a Berber people, inhabiting the Atlas Mountains in Morocco. **2** Also called: **Rifian, Riffian** (ˈrɪfɪən). the dialect of Berber spoken by this people. **3** See **Er Rif**.

rifampicin (rɪˈfæmpɪsɪn) *or US* **rifampin** (rɪˈfæmpɪn) NOUN a drug used in the treatment of tuberculosis, meningitis, and leprosy.
▷**HISTORY** C20: from *rifam(y)cin*, from *Rififi*, nickname of the original culture, + -MYCIN, + inserted PI(PERAZINE)

rife (raɪf) ADJECTIVE (*postpositive*) **1** of widespread occurrence; prevalent or current: *rumour was rife in the village*. **2** very plentiful; abundant. **3** (foll by *with*) abounding (in): *a land rife with poverty*.
▷**HISTORY** Old English *rīfe*; related to Old Norse *rīfr* generous, Middle Dutch *rīve*
▸ˈ**rifely** ADVERB ▸ˈ**rifeness** NOUN

riff (rɪf) *Music* ◆ NOUN **1** (in jazz or rock music) a short series of chords. ◆ VERB **2** (*intr*) to play or perform riffs in jazz or rock music.
▷**HISTORY** C20: probably altered and shortened from REFRAIN[2]

riffle (ˈrɪfᵊl) VERB **1** (when *intr*, often foll by *through*) to flick rapidly through (the pages of a book, magazine, etc.), esp in a desultory manner. **2** to shuffle (playing cards) by halving the pack and flicking the adjacent corners together. **3** to make or become a riffle. ◆ NOUN **4** *US and Canadian* **a** a rapid in a stream. **b** a rocky shoal causing a rapid. **c** a ripple on water. **5** *Mining* a contrivance on the bottom of a sluice, containing transverse grooves for trapping particles of gold. **6** the act or an instance of riffling.
▷**HISTORY** C18: probably from RUFFLE[1], influenced by RIPPLE[1]

riffler (ˈrɪflə) NOUN a file with a curved face for filing concave surfaces.
▷**HISTORY** C18: from French *rifloir*, from *rifler* to scratch

riffola (ˌrɪˈfəʊlə) NOUN *Informal* the use of an abundance of dominant riffs.

riffraff (ˈrɪfˌræf) NOUN (*sometimes functioning as plural*) **1** worthless people, esp collectively; rabble. **2** *Dialect* worthless rubbish.
▷**HISTORY** C15 *rif and raf*, from Old French *rif et raf*; related to *rifler* to plunder, and *rafle* a sweeping up; see RIFLE[2], RAFFLE

rifle[1] (ˈraɪfᵊl) NOUN **1** **a** a firearm having a long barrel with a spirally grooved interior, which imparts to the bullet spinning motion and thus greater accuracy over a longer range. **b** (*as modifier*): *rifle fire*. **2** (formerly) a large cannon with a rifled bore. **3** one of the grooves in a rifled bore. **4** (*plural*) **a** a unit of soldiers equipped with rifles. **b** (*capital when part of a name*): *the Rifle Brigade*. ◆ VERB (*tr*) **5** to cut or mould spiral grooves inside the barrel of (a gun). **6** to throw or hit (a ball) with great speed.
▷**HISTORY** C18: from Old French *rifler* to scratch; related to Low German *rifeln* from *riefe* groove, furrow

rifle[2] (ˈraɪfᵊl) VERB (*tr*) **1** to search (a house, safe, etc.) and steal from it; ransack. **2** to steal and carry off: *to rifle goods from a shop*.
▷**HISTORY** C14: from Old French *rifler* to plunder, scratch, of Germanic origin
▸ˈ**rifler** NOUN

riflebird (ˈraɪfᵊlˌbɜːd) NOUN any of various birds of paradise of the genera *Ptiloris* and *Craspedophora*, such as *C. magnifica* (**magnificent riflebird**).
▷**HISTORY** from its call, compared to a whistling bullet

rifle green NOUN *Brit* **a** a dark olive green, as in the uniforms of certain rifle regiments. **b** (*as adjective*): *rifle-green cloth*.

rifle grenade NOUN a grenade fired from a rifle.

rifleman (ˈraɪfᵊlmən) NOUN, *plural* **-men**. **1** a person skilled in the use of a rifle, esp a soldier. **2** a wren, *Acanthisitta chloris*, of New Zealand: family *Xenicidae*. See also **bush wren**.

rifle range NOUN an area used for target practice with rifles.

riflery (ˈraɪfᵊlrɪ) NOUN *US* **1** rifle shots. **2** the practice or skill of rifle marksmanship.

rifling (ˈraɪflɪŋ) NOUN **1** the cutting of spiral grooves on the inside of a firearm's barrel. **2** the series of grooves so cut.

rift[1] (rɪft) NOUN **1** a gap or space made by cleaving or splitting; fissure. **2** *Geology* a long narrow zone of faulting resulting from tensional stress in the earth's crust. **3** a gap between two cloud masses; break or chink: *he saw the sun through a rift in the clouds*. **4** a break in friendly relations between people, nations, etc. ◆ VERB **5** to burst or cause to burst open; split.
▷**HISTORY** C13: from Old Norse; related to Danish *rift* cleft, Icelandic *ript* breach of contract

rift[2] (rɪft) NOUN *US* **1** a shallow or rocky part in a stream. **2** the backwash from a wave that has just broken.
▷**HISTORY** C14: from Old Norse *rypta*; related to Icelandic *ropa* to belch

rift valley NOUN a long narrow valley resulting from the subsidence of land between two parallel faults, often associated with volcanism. The East African Rift Valley is an example.

rig[1] (rɪg) VERB **rigs, rigging, rigged**. (*tr*) **1** *Nautical* to equip (a vessel, mast, etc.) with (sails, rigging, etc.). **2** *Nautical* to set up or prepare ready for use. **3** to put the components of (an aircraft, etc.) into their correct positions. **4** to manipulate in a fraudulent manner, esp for profit: *to rig prices; to rig an election*. ◆ NOUN **5** *Nautical* the distinctive arrangement of the sails, masts, and other spars of a vessel. **6** In full: **drilling rig**. the installation used in drilling for and exploiting natural oil and gas deposits: *an oil rig*. **7** apparatus or equipment; gear. **8** an amateur radio operator's transmitting and receiving set. **9** *US and Canadian* a carriage together with one or more horses. **10** *Chiefly US and Canadian* an articulated lorry. ◆ See also **rig down, rig out, rig up**.
▷**HISTORY** C15: from Scandinavian; related to Norwegian *rigga* to wrap

rig[2] (rɪg) NOUN *Scot and northern English dialect* a ridge or raised strip of unploughed land in a ploughed field.
▷**HISTORY** a variant of RIDGE

Riga (ˈriːgə) NOUN the capital of Latvia, on the **Gulf of Riga** at the mouth of the Western Dvina on the Baltic Sea: a port and major trading centre since Viking times. Pop.: 788 283 (2000 est.).

rigadoon (ˌrɪgəˈduːn) *or* **rigaudon** (*French* rigodɔ̃) NOUN **1** an old Provençal couple dance, light and graceful, in lively duple time. **2** a piece of music for or in the rhythm of this dance.
▷**HISTORY** C17: from French, allegedly from its inventor *Rigaud*, a dancing master at Marseille

rigamarole (ˈrɪgəməˌrəʊl) NOUN a variant of **rigmarole**.

rigatoni (ˌrɪgəˈtəʊnɪ) NOUN macaroni in the form of short ridged often slightly curved pieces.
▷**HISTORY** C20: Italian, plural of *rigato*, from *rigare* to draw lines, make stripes, from *riga* a line, of Germanic origin

rig down VERB (*adverb*) *Nautical* to disassemble and stow.

Rigel (ˈraɪdʒəl, ˈraɪgᵊl) NOUN the brightest star, Beta Orionis, in the constellation Orion: a very luminous and extremely remote bluish-white supergiant, a double star. Visual magnitude: 0.12; spectral type: B8I.
▷**HISTORY** C16: from Arabic *rijl* foot; from its position in Orion's foot

-rigged ADJECTIVE (*in combination*) (of a sailing vessel) having a rig of a certain kind: *ketch-rigged; schooner-rigged*.

rigger (ˈrɪgə) NOUN **1** a workman who rigs vessels, etc. **2** *Rowing* a bracket on a racing shell or other boat to support a projecting rowlock. **3** a person skilled in the use of pulleys, lifting gear, cranes, etc.

rigging (ˈrɪgɪŋ) NOUN **1** the shrouds, stays, halyards, etc., of a vessel. **2** the bracing wires, struts, and lines of a biplane, balloon, etc. **3** any form of lifting gear, tackle, etc.

rigging loft NOUN **1** a loft or gallery in a boatbuilder's yard from which rigging can be fitted. **2** a loft in a theatre from which scenery, etc., is raised and lowered.

right (raɪt) ADJECTIVE **1** in accordance with accepted standards of moral or legal behaviour, justice, etc.: *right conduct*. **2** in accordance with fact, reason, or truth; correct or true: *the right answer*. **3** appropriate, suitable, fitting, or proper: *the right man for the job*. **4** most favourable or convenient; preferred: *the right time to act*. **5** in a satisfactory condition; orderly: *things are right again now*. **6** indicating or designating the correct time: *the clock is right*. **7** correct in opinion or judgment. **8** sound in mind or body; healthy or sane. **9** (*usually prenominal*) of, designating, or located near the side of something or someone that faces east when the front is turned towards the north. Related adjective: **dextral**. **10** (*usually prenominal*) worn on a right hand, foot, etc. **11** (*sometimes capital*) of, designating, supporting, belonging to, or relating to the political or intellectual right (see sense 39). **12** (*sometimes capital*) conservative or reactionary: *the right wing of the party*. **13** *Geometry* **a** formed by or containing a line or plane perpendicular to another line or plane. **b** having the axis perpendicular to the base: *a right circular cone*. **c** straight: *a right line*. **14** relating to or designating the side of cloth worn or facing outwards. **15** *Informal* (intensifier): *a right idiot*. **16** **in one's right mind**. sane. **17** **she'll be right**. *Austral and NZ informal* that's all right; not to worry. **18** **the right side of**. **a** in favour with: *you'd better stay on the right side of him*. **b** younger than: *she's still on the right side of fifty*. ◆ ADVERB **19** **too right**. *Austral and NZ informal* an exclamation of agreement. **20** in accordance with correctness or truth; accurately: *to guess right*. **21** in the appropriate manner; properly: *do it right next time!* **22** in a straight line; directly: *right to the top*. **23** in the direction of the east from the point of view of a person or thing facing north. **24** absolutely or completely; utterly: *he went right through the floor*. **25** all the way: *the bus goes right to the city centre*. **26** without delay; immediately or promptly: *I'll be right over*. **27** exactly or precisely: *right here*. **28** in a manner consistent with a legal or moral code; justly or righteously: *do right by me*. **29** in accordance with propriety; fittingly or suitably: *it serves you right*. **30** to good or favourable advantage; well: *it all came out right in the end*. **31** (esp in religious titles) most or very: *right reverend*. **32** *Informal or dialect* (intensifier): *I'm right glad to see you*. **33** **right, left, and centre**. on all sides; from every direction. **34** **right off the bat**. *Informal* as the first in a series; to begin with. ◆ NOUN **35** any claim, title, etc., that is morally just or legally granted as allowable or due to a person: *I know my rights*. **36** anything that accords with the principles of legal or moral justice. **37** the fact or state of being in accordance with reason, truth, or accepted standards (esp in the phrase **in the right**). **38** *Irish* an obligation or duty: *you had a right to lock the door*. **39** the right side, direction, position, area, or part: *the right of the army; look to the right*. **40** (*often capital* and preceded by *the*) the supporters or advocates of social, political, or economic conservatism or reaction, based generally on a belief that things are better left unchanged (opposed to *radical* or *left*). **41** *Boxing* **a** a punch with the right hand. **b** the right hand. **42** *Finance* **a** (*often plural*) the privilege of a company's shareholders to subscribe for new issues of the company's shares on advantageous terms. **b** the negotiable certificate signifying this privilege. **43** **by right** (*or* **rights**). properly; justly: *by rights you should be in bed*. **44** **in one's own right**. having a claim or title oneself rather than through marriage or other connection: *a peeress in her own right*. **45** **to rights**. consistent with justice, correctness, or orderly arrangement: *he put the matter to rights*. ◆ VERB (*mainly tr*) **46** (*also intr*) to restore to or attain a normal, esp an upright, position: *the raft righted in a few seconds*. **47** to make (something) accord with truth or facts; correct. **48** to restore to an orderly state or condition; put right. **49** to make reparation for; compensate for or redress (esp in the phrase **right a wrong**). ◆ SENTENCE SUBSTITUTE **50** **a** indicating that a statement has been understood. **b** asking whether a statement has been understood. **c** indicating a subdividing point within a discourse. ◆ INTERJECTION **51** an expression of agreement or compliance.
▷**HISTORY** Old English *riht, reoht*; related to Old High German *reht*, Gothic *raihts*, Latin *rēctus*
▸ˈ**righter** NOUN

rightable (ˈraɪtəbᵊl) ADJECTIVE capable of being righted.
▸ˈ**rightably** ADVERB ▸ˈ**rightableness** NOUN

right about NOUN **1** a turn executed through

180°. ◆ ADJECTIVE, ADVERB [2] in the opposite direction.

right angle NOUN [1] the angle between two radii of a circle that cut off on the circumference an arc equal in length to one quarter of the circumference; an angle of 90° or π/2 radians. [2] **at right angles.** perpendicular or perpendicularly. Related adjective: **orthogonal.**
▸ **'right-,angled** ADJECTIVE

right-angled triangle NOUN a triangle one angle of which is a right angle. US and Canadian name: **right triangle.**

right ascension NOUN *Astronomy* the angular distance measured eastwards along the celestial equator from the vernal equinox to the point at which the celestial equator intersects a great circle passing through the celestial pole and the heavenly object in question. Symbol: α. Compare **declination** (sense 1).

right away ADVERB without delay; immediately or promptly.

right-down ADVERB, ADJECTIVE a variant of **downright.**

righten ('raɪtᵊn) VERB [1] (*tr*) to set right. [2] to restore to or attain a normal or upright position.

righteous ('raɪtʃəs) ADJECTIVE [1] **a** characterized by, proceeding from, or in accordance with accepted standards of morality, justice, or uprightness; virtuous: *a righteous man.* **b** (*as collective noun*; preceded by *the*): *the righteous.* [2] morally justifiable or right, esp from one's own point of view: *righteous indignation.*
▹ **HISTORY** Old English *rīhtwīs*, from RIGHT + WISE[2]
▸ **'righteously** ADVERB ▸ **'righteousness** NOUN

right-footer NOUN *Informal* (esp in Ireland) a Protestant.
▹ **HISTORY** See LEFT-FOOTER

rightful ('raɪtfʊl) ADJECTIVE [1] in accordance with what is right; proper or just. [2] (*prenominal*) having a legally or morally just claim: *the rightful owner.* [3] (*prenominal*) held by virtue of a legal or just claim: *my rightful property.*
▸ **'rightfully** ADVERB ▸ **'rightfulness** NOUN

right-hand ADJECTIVE (*prenominal*) [1] of, relating to, located on, or moving towards the right: *a right-hand bend; this car has right-hand drive.* [2] for use by the right hand; right-handed. [3] **right-hand man.** one's most valuable assistant or supporter.

right-handed ADJECTIVE [1] using the right hand with greater skill or ease than the left. [2] performed with the right hand: *right-handed writing.* [3] made for use by the right hand. [4] worn on the right hand. [5] turning from left to right; clockwise.
▸ **,right-'handedly** ADVERB ▸ **,right-'handedness** NOUN

right-hander NOUN [1] a blow with the right hand. [2] a person who is right-handed.

Right Honourable ADJECTIVE [1] (in Britain and certain Commonwealth countries) a title of respect for a Privy Councillor or an appeal-court judge. [2] (in Britain) a title of respect for an earl, a viscount, a baron, or the Lord Mayor or Lord Provost of any of certain cities.

rightish ('raɪtɪʃ) ADJECTIVE somewhat right, esp politically.

rightist ('raɪtɪst) ADJECTIVE [1] of, tending towards, or relating to the political right or its principles; conservative, traditionalist, or reactionary. ◆ NOUN [2] a person who supports or belongs to the political right.
▸ **'rightism** NOUN

rightly ('raɪtlɪ) ADVERB [1] in accordance with the facts; correctly. [2] in accordance with principles of justice or morality. [3] with good reason; justifiably: *he was rightly annoyed with her.* [4] properly or suitably; appropriately: *rightly dressed for a wedding.* [5] (*used with a negative*) *Informal* with certainty; positively or precisely (usually in the phrases **I don't rightly know, I can't rightly say**).

right-minded ADJECTIVE holding opinions or principles that accord with what is right or with the opinions of the speaker.
▸ **,right-'mindedly** ADVERB ▸ **,right-'mindedness** NOUN

rightness ('raɪtnɪs) NOUN the state or quality of being right.

righto *or* **right oh** ('raɪt'əʊ) SENTENCE SUBSTITUTE *Brit informal* an expression of agreement or compliance.

right off ADVERB immediately; right away.

right of search NOUN the right of a belligerent to stop and search neutral merchant ships on the high seas in wartime.

right of way NOUN, *plural* **rights of way.** [1] the right of one vehicle or vessel to take precedence over another, as laid down by law or custom. [2] **a** the legal right of someone to pass over another's land, acquired by grant or by long usage. **b** the path or road used by this right. [3] *US* the strip of land over which a power line, railway line, road, etc., extends.

right on INTERJECTION [1] *Slang, chiefly US and Canadian* an exclamation of full agreement, concurrence, or compliance with the wishes, words, or actions of another. ◆ ADJECTIVE [2] *Informal* modern, trendy, and socially aware or relevant: *right-on green politics.*

Right Reverend ADJECTIVE (in Britain) a title of respect for an Anglican or Roman Catholic bishop.

rights issue NOUN *Stock Exchange* an issue of new shares offered by a company to its existing shareholders on favourable terms. Also called: **capitalization issue.**

rightsize ('raɪt,saɪz) VERB to restructure (an organization) to cut costs and improve effectiveness without ruthlessly downsizing.

right-thinking ('raɪt,θɪŋkɪŋ) ADJECTIVE possessing reasonable and generally acceptable opinions.

right triangle NOUN US and Canadian name for **right-angled triangle.**

rightward ('raɪtwəd) ADJECTIVE [1] situated on or directed towards the right. ◆ ADVERB [2] a variant of **rightwards.**

rightwards ('raɪtwədz) *or* **rightward** ADVERB towards or on the right.

right whale NOUN any large whalebone whale of the family *Balaenidae.* They are grey or black, have a large head, and, in most, no dorsal fin, and are hunted as a source of whalebone and oil. See also **bowhead.**
▹ **HISTORY** C19: perhaps so named because it was *right* for hunting

right wing NOUN [1] (*often capitals*) the conservative faction of an assembly, party, etc. [2] the part of an army or field of battle on the right from the point of view of one facing the enemy. [3] **a** the right-hand side of the field of play from the point of view of a team facing its opponent's goal. **b** a player positioned in this area in any of various games. **c** the position occupied by such a player. ◆ ADJECTIVE **right-wing.** [4] of, belonging to, or relating to the right wing.
▸ **'right-'winger** NOUN

Rigi ('ri:gɪ) NOUN a mountain in the Alps of N central Switzerland, between Lakes Lucerne, Zug, and Lauerz.

rigid ('rɪdʒɪd) ADJECTIVE [1] not bending; physically inflexible or stiff: *a rigid piece of plastic.* [2] unbending; rigorously strict; severe: *rigid rules.* ◆ ADVERB [3] completely or excessively: *the lecture bored him rigid.*
▹ **HISTORY** C16: from Latin *rigidus*, from *rigēre* to be stiff
▸ **'rigidly** ADVERB ▸ **ri'gidity** *or* **'rigidness** NOUN

rigid designator NOUN *Logic* an expression that identifies the same individual in every possible world: for example, "Shakespeare" is a rigid designator since it is possible that Shakespeare might not have been a playwright but not that he might not have been Shakespeare.

rigidify (rɪ'dʒɪdɪ,faɪ) VERB **-fies, -fying, -fied.** to make or become rigid.

Rigil Kent ('raɪdʒɪl 'kɛnt) NOUN *Astronomy* the star Alpha Centauri. Often shortened to: **Rigil.**
▹ **HISTORY** from *Rigil Kentaurus*, from Arabic *al Rigil al Kentaurus* the Centaur's foot

rigmarole ('rɪgmə,rəʊl) *or* **rigamarole** NOUN [1] any long complicated procedure. [2] a set of incoherent or pointless statements; garbled nonsense.
▹ **HISTORY** C18: from earlier *ragman roll* a list, probably a roll used in a medieval game, wherein various characters were described in verse, beginning with *Ragemon le bon* Ragman the good

rigor ('raɪgɔ:, 'rɪgə) NOUN [1] *Med* a sudden feeling of chilliness, often accompanied by shivering: it sometimes precedes a fever. [2] ('rɪgə) *Pathol* rigidity of a muscle; muscular cramp. [3] a state of rigidity assumed by some animals in reaction to sudden shock. [4] the inertia assumed by some plants in conditions unfavourable to growth.
▹ **HISTORY** see RIGOUR

rigorism ('rɪgə,rɪzəm) NOUN [1] strictness in judgment or conduct. [2] the religious cult of extreme self-denial. [3] *RC theol* the doctrine that in cases of doubt in moral matters the stricter course must always be followed.
▸ **'rigorist** NOUN ▸ **,rigor'istic** ADJECTIVE

rigor mortis ('rɪgə 'mɔ:tɪs) NOUN *Pathol* the stiffness of joints and muscular rigidity of a dead body, caused by depletion of ATP in the tissues. It begins two to four hours after death and lasts up to about four days, after which the muscles and joints relax.
▹ **HISTORY** C19: Latin, literally: rigidity of death

rigorous ('rɪgərəs) ADJECTIVE [1] characterized by or proceeding from rigour; harsh, strict, or severe: *rigorous discipline.* [2] severely accurate; scrupulous: *rigorous book-keeping.* [3] (esp of weather) extreme or harsh. [4] *Maths, logic* (of a proof) making the validity of the successive steps completely explicit.
▸ **'rigorously** ADVERB ▸ **'rigorousness** NOUN

rigour *or US* **rigor** ('rɪgə) NOUN [1] harsh but just treatment or action. [2] a severe or cruel circumstance; hardship: *the rigours of famine.* [3] strictness, harshness, or severity of character. [4] strictness in judgment or conduct; rigorism. [5] *Maths, logic* logical validity or accuracy. [6] *Obsolete* rigidity.
▹ **HISTORY** C14: from Latin *rigor*

rig out VERB [1] (*tr, adverb*; often foll by *with*) to equip or fit out (with): *his car is rigged out with gadgets.* [2] to dress or be dressed: *rigged out smartly.* ◆ NOUN **rigout.** [3] *Informal* a person's clothing or costume, esp a bizarre outfit.

rigsdaler ('rɪgz,dɑ:lə) NOUN another word for **rix-dollar.**

rig up VERB (*tr, adverb*) to erect or construct, esp as a temporary measure: *cameras were rigged up to televise the event.*

Rig-Veda (rɪg'veɪdə, -'vi:də) NOUN a compilation of 1028 Hindu poems dating from 2000 B.C. or earlier.
▹ **HISTORY** C18: from Sanskrit *rigveda*, from *ric* song of praise + VEDA

Rijeka (rɪ'ɛkə; *Serbo-Croat* ri'jɛka) NOUN a port in Croatia: an ancient town, changing hands many times before passing to Yugoslavia in 1947 until Croatia became independent in 1991. Pop.: 147 709 (2001). Italian name: **Fiume.**

rijksdaaler ('raɪks,dɑ:lə) NOUN a variant of **rix-dollar.**

Rijksmuseum ('raɪxsmju:,zɪəm) NOUN a museum in Amsterdam housing the national art collection of the Netherlands.

Rijn (rɛjn) NOUN the Dutch name for the **Rhine.**

rijsttafel ('raɪs,tɑ:fəl) NOUN an Indonesian food consisting of a selection of rice dishes to which are added small pieces of a variety of other foods, such as meat, fish, fruit, pickles, and curry.
▹ **HISTORY** from Dutch *rijst* rice + *tafel* table

Rijswijk ('raɪsvaɪk; *Dutch* 'rɛjswɛjk) NOUN a town in the SW Netherlands, in South Holland province on the SE outskirts of The Hague: scene of the signing (1697) of the **Treaty of Rijswijk** ending the War of the Grand Alliance. Pop.: 48 000 (1991). English name: **Ryswick.**

rikishi (rɪ'kɪʃɪ) NOUN, *plural* **rikishi.** a sumo wrestler.
▹ **HISTORY** Japanese, literally: strong man

Riksdag (*Swedish* 'ri:ksdag) NOUN the Swedish parliament.

Riksmål (*Norwegian* 'riksmɔl) NOUN a former name for **Bokmål.**
▹ **HISTORY** literally: language of the kingdom

rile (raɪl) VERB (*tr*) [1] to annoy or anger; irritate. [2] *US and Canadian* to stir up or agitate (water, etc.); roil or make turbid.
▹ **HISTORY** C19: variant of ROIL

Riley ('raɪlɪ) NOUN **the life of Riley.** a luxurious and carefree existence.
▹ **HISTORY** C20: origin unknown

rilievo *Italian* (ri'ljevo; *English* ,rɪlɪ'eɪvəʊ) NOUN, *plural* ***-vi*** (-vi; *English* -viː). another name for **relief** (sense 9).

rill (rɪl) NOUN [1] a brook or stream; rivulet. [2] a small channel or gulley, such as one formed during soil erosion. [3] Also: **rille.** one of many winding cracks on the moon.
▷HISTORY C15: from Low German *rille*; related to Dutch *ril*

rillet (ˈrɪlɪt) NOUN a little rill.

rim (rɪm) NOUN [1] the raised edge of an object, esp of something more or less circular such as a cup or crater. [2] the peripheral part of a wheel, to which the tyre is attached. [3] *Basketball* the hoop from which the net is suspended. ◆ VERB **rims, rimming, rimmed.** (*tr*) [4] to put a rim on (a pot, cup, wheel, etc.). [5] *Slang* to lick, kiss, or suck the anus of (one's sexual partner). [6] *Ball games* (of a ball) to run around the edge of (a hole, basket, etc.).
▷HISTORY Old English *rima*; related to Old Saxon *rimi*, Old Norse *rimi* ridge

RIM INTERNATIONAL CAR REGISTRATION FOR (Islamic Republic of) Mauritania.

rimaye (rɪˈmeɪ) NOUN another name for **bergschrund.**
▷HISTORY C20: French, from Latin *rima* cleft

rime^1 (raɪm) NOUN [1] frost formed by the freezing of supercooled water droplets in fog onto solid objects. ◆ VERB [2] (*tr*) to cover with rime or something resembling rime.
▷HISTORY Old English *hrīm*; related to Dutch *rijm*, Middle High German *rīmeln* to coat with frost

rime^2 (raɪm) NOUN, VERB an archaic spelling of **rhyme.**

rimer (ˈraɪmə) NOUN another name for **rhymester.**

rime riche (ˈriːm ˈriːʃ) NOUN, *plural* **rimes riches** (ˈriːmˈriːʃ). rhyme between words or syllables that are identical in sound, as in *command/demand, pair/pear.*
▷HISTORY French, literally: rich rhyme

rimester (ˈraɪmstə) NOUN a variant spelling of **rhymester.**

rim-fire ADJECTIVE [1] (of a cartridge) having the primer in the rim of the base. [2] (of a firearm) adapted for such cartridges. ◆ Compare **centre-fire.**

Rimini (ˈrɪmɪnɪ) NOUN a port and resort in NE Italy, in Emilia-Romagna on the N Adriatic coast. Pop.: 131 062 (2000 est.). Ancient name: **Ariminum.**

rimose (raɪˈməʊs, -ˈməʊz) ADJECTIVE (esp of plant parts) having the surface marked by a network of intersecting cracks.
▷HISTORY C18: from Latin *rīmōsus*, from *rīma* a split, crack
▸**ˈrimosely** ADVERB ▸**rimosity** (raɪˈmɒsɪtɪ) NOUN

rimrock (ˈrɪmˌrɒk) NOUN rock forming the boundaries of a sandy or gravelly alluvial deposit.

rimu (ˈriːmuː) NOUN another name for **red pine.**
▷HISTORY from Maori

rimy (ˈraɪmɪ) ADJECTIVE **rimier, rimiest.** coated with rime.

rind (raɪnd) NOUN [1] a hard outer layer or skin on bacon, cheese, etc. [2] the outer layer of a fruit or of the spore-producing body of certain fungi. [3] the outer layer of the bark of a tree.
▷HISTORY Old English *rinde*; Old High German *rinta*, German *Rinde*

rinderpest (ˈrɪndəˌpɛst) NOUN an acute contagious viral disease of cattle, characterized by severe inflammation of the intestinal tract and diarrhoea.
▷HISTORY C19: German: cattle pest

rinforzando (ˌriːnfɔːˈtsændəʊ) a less common term for **sforzando.**
▷HISTORY Italian, literally: reinforcing

ring^1 (rɪŋ) NOUN [1] a circular band usually of a precious metal, esp gold, often set with gems and worn upon the finger as an adornment or as a token of engagement or marriage. [2] any object or mark that is circular in shape. [3] a circular path or course: *to run around in a ring.* [4] a group of people or things standing or arranged so as to form a circle: *a ring of spectators.* [5] an enclosed space, usually circular in shape, where circus acts are performed. [6] a square apron or raised platform, marked off by ropes, in which contestants box or wrestle. [7] **the ring.** the sport of boxing. [8] the field of competition or rivalry. [9] **throw one's hat in the ring.** to announce one's intention to be a candidate or contestant. [10] a group of people usually operating illegally and covertly: *a drug ring; a paedophile ring; a ring of antique dealers.* [11] (esp at country fairs) an enclosure, often circular, where horses, cattle, and other livestock are paraded and auctioned. [12] an area reserved for betting at a racecourse. [13] a circular strip of bark cut from a tree or branch, esp in order to kill it. [14] a single turn in a spiral. [15] *Geometry* the area of space lying between two concentric circles. [16] *Maths* a set that is subject to two binary operations, addition and multiplication, such that the set is an Abelian group under addition and is closed under multiplication, this latter operation being associative. [17] *Botany* short for **annual ring.** [18] Also called: **closed chain.** *Chem* a closed loop of atoms in a molecule. [19] *Astronomy* any of the thin circular bands of small bodies orbiting a giant planet, esp Saturn. See also **Saturn**^{2} (sense 1). [20] **run rings around.** *Informal* to be greatly superior to; outclass completely. ◆ VERB **rings, ringing, ringed.** (*tr*) [21] to surround with or as if with or form a ring; encircle. [22] to mark (a bird) with a ring or clip for subsequent identification. [23] to fit a ring in the nose of (a bull, pig, etc.) so that it can be led easily. [24] Also: **ringbark. a** to cut away a circular strip of bark from (a tree or branch) in order to kill it. **b** to cut a narrow or partial ring from (the trunk of a tree) in order to check or prevent vigorous growth. [25] *Austral and NZ* to be the fastest shearer in a shearing shed (esp in the phrase **ring the shed**).
▷HISTORY Old English *hring*; related to Old Norse *hringr*

ring^2 (rɪŋ) VERB **rings, ringing, rang, rung.** [1] to emit or cause to emit a sonorous or resonant sound, characteristic of certain metals when struck. [2] to cause (a bell) to emit a ringing sound by striking it once or repeatedly or (of a bell) to emit such a sound. [3] **a** (*tr*) to cause (a large bell, esp a church bell) to emit a ringing sound by pulling on a rope that is attached to a wheel on which the bell swings back and forth, being sounded by a clapper inside it. Compare **chime**^{1} (sense 6). **b** (*intr*) (of a bell) to sound by being swung in this way. [4] (*intr*) (of a building, place, etc.) to be filled with sound; echo: *the church rang with singing.* [5] (*intr*; foll by *for*) to call by means of a bell, buzzer, etc.: *to ring for the butler.* [6] Also: **ring up.** *Chiefly Brit* to call (a person) by telephone. [7] (*tr*) to strike or tap (a coin) in order to assess its genuineness by the sound produced. [8] (*intr*) (of the ears) to have or give the sensation of humming or ringing. [9] (*intr*) *Electronics* (of an electric circuit) to produce a damped oscillatory wave after the application of a sharp input transition. [10] *Slang* to change the identity of (a stolen vehicle) by using the licence plate, serial number, etc., of another, usually disused, vehicle. [11] **ring a bell.** to sound familiar; remind one of something, esp indistinctly. [12] **ring down the curtain. a** to lower the curtain at the end of a theatrical performance. **b** (foll by *on*) to put an end (to). [13] **ring false.** to give the impression of being false. [14] **ring the bell. a** to do, say, or be the right thing. **b** to reach the pinnacle of success or happiness. [15] **ring the changes.** to vary the manner or performance of an action that is often repeated. [16] **ring true.** to give the impression of being true: *that story doesn't ring true.* ◆ NOUN [17] the act of or a sound made by ringing. [18] a sound produced by or suggestive of a bell. [19] any resonant or metallic sound, esp one sustained or re-echoed: *the ring of trumpets.* [20] *Informal, chiefly Brit* a telephone call: *he gave her a ring last night.* [21] the complete set of bells in a tower or belfry: *a ring of eight bells.* See **peal**^{1} (sense 3). [22] an inherent quality or characteristic: *his explanation has the ring of sincerity.* [23] *Electronics* the damped oscillatory wave produced by a circuit that rings. ◆ See also **ring back, ring in, ring off, ring out, ring up.**
▷HISTORY Old English *hringan*; related to Old High German *hringen* Old Norse *hringja*

> **Language note** *Rang* and *sang* are the correct forms of the past tenses of *ring* and *sing*, although *rung* and *sung* are still heard informally and dialectally: *he rung (rang) the bell.*

ring back VERB (*adverb*) to return a telephone call (to).

ringbark (ˈrɪŋˌbɑːk) VERB another term for **ring**^{1} (sense 24).

ring binder NOUN a loose-leaf binder fitted with metal rings that can be opened to allow perforated paper to be inserted.

ringbolt (ˈrɪŋˌbəʊlt) NOUN a bolt with a ring fitted through an eye attached to the bolt head.

ringbone (ˈrɪŋˌbəʊn) NOUN an abnormal bony growth affecting the pastern of a horse, often causing lameness.

ring circuit NOUN an electrical system in which distribution points are connected to the main supply in a continuous closed circuit.

ringdove (ˈrɪŋˌdʌv) NOUN [1] another name for **wood pigeon.** [2] an Old World turtledove, *Streptopelia risoria*, having a greyish plumage with a black band around the neck.

ring-dyke NOUN a dyke having an approximately circular outcrop of rock.

ringed (rɪŋd) ADJECTIVE [1] displaying ringlike markings. [2] having or wearing a ring. [3] formed by rings; annular.

ringed plover NOUN a European shorebird, *Charadrius hiaticula*, with a greyish-brown back, white underparts with a black throat band, and orange legs: family *Charadriidae* (plovers).

ringent (ˈrɪndʒənt) ADJECTIVE (of the corolla of plants such as the snapdragon) consisting of two distinct gaping lips.
▷HISTORY C18: from Latin *ringī* to open the mouth wide

ringer (ˈrɪŋə) NOUN [1] a person or thing that rings a bell. [2] Also called: **dead ringer.** *Slang* a person or thing that is almost identical to another. [3] *Slang* a stolen vehicle the identity of which has been changed by the use of the licence plate, serial number, etc., of another, usually disused, vehicle. [4] *US* a contestant, esp a horse, entered in a competition under false representations of identity, record, or ability. [5] *Austral and NZ* the fastest shearer in a shed. [6] *Austral informal* the fastest or best at anything. [7] a quoit thrown so as to encircle a peg. [8] such a throw.

Ringer's solution (ˈrɪŋəz) NOUN a solution containing the chlorides of sodium, potassium, and calcium, used to correct dehydration and, in physiological experiments, as a medium for in vitro preparations.

ring-fence VERB [1] to assign (money, a grant, fund, etc.) to one particular purpose, so as to restrict its use: *to ring-fence a financial allowance.* [2] to oblige (a person or organization) to use money for a particular purpose: *to ring-fence a local authority.* ◆ NOUN **ring fence.** [3] an agreement, contract, etc., in which the use of money is restricted to a particular purpose.

ring finger NOUN the third finger, esp of the left hand, on which a wedding ring is traditionally worn.

ring flash NOUN *Photog* a type of electronic flash in which the light source is arranged in a ring around the lens in order to produce a light without shadows.

ring gauge NOUN *Engineering* a ring having an internal diameter of a specified size used for checking the diameter of a cylindrical object or part. Compare **plug gauge.**

ringgit (ˈrɪŋgɪt) NOUN the standard monetary unit of Malaysia, divided into 100 sen.
▷HISTORY from Malay

ring in VERB (*adverb*) [1] (*intr*) *Chiefly Brit* to report to someone by telephone. [2] (*tr*) to accompany the arrival of with bells (esp in the phrase **ring in the new year**). [3] (*tr*) *Austral* to substitute (a horse) fraudulently for another horse in a race. [4] (*tr*) *Austral and NZ informal* to recruit or include (a person). ◆ NOUN **ring-in.** [5] *Austral informal* a horse that serves as a substitute. [6] *Austral and NZ informal* a person or thing that is not normally a member of a particular group; outsider.

ringing tone NOUN *Brit* a sequence of pairs of tones heard by the dialler on a telephone when the number dialled is ringing. Compare **engaged tone, dialling tone.**

ringleader (ˈrɪŋˌliːdə) NOUN a person who leads others in any kind of unlawful or mischievous activity.

ringlet (ˈrɪŋlɪt) NOUN 1 a lock of hair hanging down in a spiral curl. 2 any of numerous butterflies of the genus *Erebia*, most of which occur in S Europe and have dark brown wings marked with small black-and-white eyespots: family *Satyridae*.
▸ **ˈringleted** ADJECTIVE

ring main NOUN a domestic electrical supply in which outlet sockets are connected to the mains supply through a ring circuit.

ringmaster (ˈrɪŋˌmɑːstə) NOUN the master of ceremonies in a circus.

ring-necked ADJECTIVE (of animals, esp certain birds and snakes) having a band of distinctive colour around the neck.

ring-necked pheasant NOUN a common pheasant, *Phasianus colchicus*, originating in Asia. The male has a bright plumage with a band of white around the neck and the female is mottled brown.

ring off VERB (*intr, adverb*) *Chiefly Brit* to terminate a telephone conversation by replacing the receiver; hang up.

Ring of the Nibelung NOUN 1 *German myth* a magic ring on which the dwarf Alberich placed a curse after it was stolen from him. 2 the four operas by Wagner, *Das Rheingold* (1869), *Die Walküre* (1870), *Siegfried* (1876), and *Götterdämmerung* (1876), based on this myth. often shortened to: **The Ring.**

ring out VERB (*adverb*) 1 (*tr*) to accompany the departure of with bells (esp in the phrase **ring out the old year**). 2 (*intr*) to send forth a loud resounding noise.

ring ouzel NOUN a European thrush, *Turdus torquatus*, common in rocky areas. The male has a blackish plumage with a white band around the neck and the female is brown.

ring road NOUN a main road that bypasses a town or town centre. US names: **belt, beltway.**

ring-shout NOUN a West African circle dance that has influenced jazz, surviving in the Black churches of the southern US.

ringside (ˈrɪŋˌsaɪd) NOUN 1 the area immediately surrounding an arena, esp the row of seats nearest a boxing or wrestling ring. 2 **a** any place affording a close uninterrupted view. **b** (*as modifier*): *a ringside seat.*

ringster (ˈrɪŋstə) NOUN a member of a ring controlling a market in antiques, art treasures, etc.

ringtail (ˈrɪŋˌteɪl) NOUN 1 Also called: **ring-tailed cat.** another name for **cacomistle.** 2 *Austral* any of several possums having curling prehensile tails used to grasp branches while climbing. Also called: **ring-tailed possum.**

ring-tailed ADJECTIVE (of an animal) having a tail marked with rings of a distinctive colour.

ring taw NOUN a game of marbles in which players attempt to knock other players' marbles out of a ring.

ring up VERB (*adverb*) 1 *Chiefly Brit* to make a telephone call (to). 2 (*tr*) to record on a cash register. 3 (*tr*) to chronicle; record: *to ring up another success.* 4 **ring up the curtain. a** to begin a theatrical performance. **b** (often foll by *on*) to make a start (on).

ringwomb (ˈrɪŋˌwuːm) NOUN *Vet science* a complication at lambing resulting from failure of the cervix to open.

ringworm (ˈrɪŋˌwɜːm) NOUN any of various fungal infections of the skin (esp the scalp) or nails, often appearing as itching circular patches. Also called: **tinea.**

rink (rɪŋk) NOUN 1 an expanse of ice for skating on, esp one that is artificially prepared and under cover. 2 an area for roller skating on. 3 a building or enclosure for ice skating or roller skating. 4 *Bowls* a strip of the green, usually about 5–7 metres wide, on which a game is played. 5 *Curling* the strip of ice on which the game is played, usually 41 by 4 metres. 6 (in bowls and curling) the players on one side in a game.
▹HISTORY C14 (Scots): from Old French *renc* row, RANK[1]

rinkhals (ˈrɪŋkˌhals) NOUN, *plural* **-hals** *or* **-halses.** a venomous elapid snake, *Hemachatus hemachatus* of southern Africa, which spits venom at its enemies from a distance. Also called: **spitting snake.**
▹HISTORY Afrikaans, literally: ring neck

rink rat NOUN *Canadian informal* a young person who carries out chores at an ice-hockey rink in return for free skating time.

rinse (rɪns) VERB (*tr*) 1 to remove soap from (clothes, etc.) by applying clean water in the final stage in washing. 2 to wash lightly, esp without using soap: *to rinse one's hands.* 3 to give a light tint to (hair). ◆ NOUN 4 the act or an instance of rinsing. 5 *Hairdressing* a liquid preparation put on the hair when wet to give a tint to it: *a blue rinse.*
▹HISTORY C14: from Old French *rincer*, from Latin *recens* fresh, new
▸ **ˈrinsable** *or* **ˈrinsible** ADJECTIVE ▸ **ˌrinsaˈbility** *or* **ˌrinsiˈbility** NOUN ▸ **ˈrinser** NOUN

rinsin' (ˈrɪnsɪn) ADJECTIVE *Slang* excellent; wonderful.

Rinzai (ˈrɪnzaɪ) NOUN a Zen Buddhist school of Japan, characterized by the use of koans to lead to moments of insight and enlightenment.

Rio Branco (*Portuguese* ˈriu ˈbrɐŋku) NOUN 1 a city in W Brazil, capital of Acre state. Pop.: 226 054 (2000). 2 a river in Brazil, flowing south to the Rio Negro. Length: 644 km (400 miles).

Río Bravo (*Spanish* ˈrio ˈbraβo) NOUN the Mexican name for the **Rio Grande.**

Rio de Janeiro (ˈriːəʊ də dʒəˈnɪərəʊ) *or* **Rio** NOUN 1 a port in SE Brazil, on Guanabara Bay: the country's chief port and its capital from 1763 to 1960; backed by mountains, notably Sugar Loaf Mountain; founded by the French in 1555 and taken by the Portuguese in 1567. Pop.: 5 850 544 (2000), with a conurbation of 9 888 000 (1995 est.). Related noun: **Cariocan.** 2 a state of E Brazil. Capital: Rio de Janeiro. Pop.: 14 367 225 (2000). Area: 42 911 sq. km (16 568 sq. miles).

Río de la Plata (ˈriːəʊ də lɑː ˈplɑːtə) NOUN See **Plata.**

Río de Oro (*Spanish* ˈrio ðe ˈoro) NOUN a former region of W Africa: comprised the S part of the Spanish Sahara (now Western Sahara).

Rio Grande NOUN 1 (ˈriːəʊ ˈgrænd, ˈgrændɪ) a river in North America, rising in SW Colorado and flowing southeast to the Gulf of Mexico, forming the border between the US and Mexico. Length: about 3030 km (1885 miles). Mexican name: **Río Bravo.** 2 (*Portuguese* ˈriu ˈgrɐndi) a port in SE Brazil, in SE Rio Grande do Sul state: serves as the port for Pôrto Alegre. Pop.: 179 422 (2000).

Rio Grande do Norte (*Portuguese* ˈriu ˈgrɐndi du ˈnɔrti) NOUN a state of NE Brazil, on the Atlantic: much of it is semiarid plateau. Capital: Natal. Pop.: 2 770 730 (2000 est.). Area: 53 014 sq. km (20 469 sq. miles).

Rio Grande do Sul (*Portuguese* ˈriu ˈgrɐndi du ˈsul) NOUN a state of S Brazil, on the Atlantic. Capital: Pôrto Alegre. Pop.: 10 178 970 (2000). Area: 282 183 sq. km (108 951 sq. miles).

rioja (riːˈəʊxə) NOUN a red or white wine, with a distinctive vanilla bouquet and flavour, produced around the Ebro river in central N Spain.
▹HISTORY C20: from *La Rioja*, the area where it is produced

Río Negro (ˈriːəʊ ˈneɪgrəʊ, ˈnɛg-; *Spanish* ˈrio ˈneγro) NOUN See **Negro**[2].

riot (ˈraɪət) NOUN 1 **a** a disturbance made by an unruly mob or (in law) three or more persons; tumult or uproar. **b** (*as modifier*): *a riot gun; riot police; a riot shield.* 2 boisterous activity; unrestrained revelry. 3 an occasion of boisterous merriment. 4 *Slang* a person who occasions boisterous merriment. 5 a dazzling or arresting display: *a riot of colour.* 6 *Hunting* the indiscriminate following of any scent by hounds. 7 *Archaic* wanton lasciviousness. 8 **run riot. a** to behave wildly and without restraint. **b** (of plants) to grow rankly or profusely. ◆ VERB 9 (*intr*) to take part in a riot. 10 (*intr*) to indulge in unrestrained revelry or merriment. 11 (*tr*; foll by *away*) to spend (time or money) in wanton or loose living: *he has rioted away his life.*
▹HISTORY C13: from Old French *riote* dispute, from *ruihoter* to quarrel, probably from *ruir* to make a commotion, from Latin *rugīre* to roar
▸ **ˈrioter** NOUN ▸ **ˈrioting** NOUN

Riot Act NOUN 1 *Criminal law* (formerly in England) a statute of 1715 by which persons committing a riot had to disperse within an hour of the reading of the act by a magistrate. 2 **read the riot act (to).** to warn or reprimand severely.

riotous (ˈraɪətəs) ADJECTIVE 1 proceeding from or of the nature of riots or rioting. 2 inciting to riot. 3 characterized by wanton or lascivious revelry: *riotous living.* 4 characterized by boisterous or unrestrained merriment: *riotous laughter.*
▸ **ˈriotously** ADVERB ▸ **ˈriotousness** NOUN

riot shield NOUN a large oblong curved transparent shield used by police controlling crowds.

rip[1] (rɪp) VERB **rips, ripping, ripped.** 1 to tear or be torn violently or roughly; split or be rent. 2 (*tr*; foll by *off* or *out*) to remove hastily, carelessly, or roughly: *they ripped out all the old kitchen units.* 3 (*intr*) *Informal* to move violently or precipitously; rush headlong. 4 (*intr*; foll by *into*) *Informal* to pour violent abuse (on); make a verbal attack (on). 5 (*tr*) to saw or split (wood) in the direction of the grain. 6 **let rip.** to act or speak without restraint. ◆ NOUN 7 the place where something is torn; a tear or split. 8 short for **ripsaw.** See also **rip off, rip on, rip up.**
▹HISTORY C15: perhaps from Flemish *rippen*; compare Middle Dutch *rippen* to pull
▸ **ˈrippable** ADJECTIVE

rip[2] (rɪp) NOUN short for **riptide** (sense 1).
▹HISTORY C18: perhaps from RIP[1]

rip[3] (rɪp) NOUN *Informal, archaic* 1 something or someone of little or no value. 2 an old worn-out horse. 3 a dissolute character; reprobate.
▹HISTORY C18: perhaps altered from *rep*, shortened from REPROBATE

RIP ABBREVIATION FOR requiescat *or* requiescant in pace.
▹HISTORY Latin: may he, she, *or* they rest in peace

riparian (raɪˈpɛərɪən) ADJECTIVE 1 of, inhabiting, or situated on the bank of a river. 2 denoting or relating to the legal rights of the owner of land on a river bank, such as fishing or irrigation. ◆ NOUN 3 *Property law* a person who owns land on a river bank.
▹HISTORY C19: from Latin *rīpārius*, from *rīpa* a river bank

ripcord (ˈrɪpˌkɔːd) NOUN 1 a cord that when pulled opens a parachute from its pack. 2 a cord on the gas bag of a balloon that when pulled opens a panel, enabling gas to escape and the balloon to descend.

ripe (raɪp) ADJECTIVE 1 (of fruit, grain, etc.) mature and ready to be eaten or used; fully developed. 2 mature enough to be eaten or used: *ripe cheese.* 3 fully developed in mind or body. 4 resembling ripe fruit, esp in redness or fullness: *a ripe complexion.* 5 (*postpositive*; foll by *for*) ready or eager (to undertake or undergo an action). 6 (*postpositive*; foll by *for*) suitable; right or opportune: *the time is not yet ripe.* 7 mature in judgment or knowledge. 8 advanced but healthy (esp in the phrase **a ripe old age**). 9 *Slang* **a** complete; thorough. **b** excessive; exorbitant. 10 *Slang* slightly indecent; risqué.
▹HISTORY Old English *rīpe*; related to Old Saxon *rīpi*, Old High German *rīfi*, German *reif*
▸ **ˈripely** ADVERB ▸ **ˈripeness** NOUN

ripen (ˈraɪpᵊn) VERB to make or become ripe.
▸ **ˈripener** NOUN

ripieno (rɪˈpjɛnəʊ; *Italian* riˈpjeːno) NOUN, *plural* **-ni** (-niː) *or* **-nos.** (in baroque concertos and concerti grossi) the full orchestra, as opposed to the instrumental soloists. Also called: **concerto.** Compare **concertino** (sense 1).
▹HISTORY C18: from Italian: from *ri-* RE- + *pieno*, from Latin *plēnus* full

rip off VERB 1 (*tr*) to tear violently or roughly (from). 2 (*adverb*) *Slang* to steal from or cheat (someone). ◆ NOUN **rip-off.** 3 *Slang* an article or articles stolen. 4 *Slang* a grossly overpriced article. 5 *Slang* the act of stealing or cheating.

rip on VERB (*adverb*) *US slang* to insult or criticize (someone) playfully; tease.

Ripon (ˈrɪpᵊn) NOUN a city in N England, in North Yorkshire: cathedral (12th–16th centuries). Pop.: 13 806 (1991 est.).

riposte *or* **ripost** (rɪˈpɒst, rɪˈpəʊst) NOUN 1 a swift sharp reply in speech or action. 2 *Fencing* a counterattack made immediately after a successful parry. ◆ VERB 3 (*intr*) to make a riposte.
▹HISTORY C18: from French, from Italian *risposta*, from *rispondere* to reply, RESPOND

ripper (ˈrɪpə) NOUN 1 a person who rips. 2 a murderer who dissects or mutilates his victims' bodies. 3 *Informal, chiefly Austral and NZ* a fine or excellent person or thing.

ripping (ˈrɪpɪŋ) ADJECTIVE *Archaic Brit slang* excellent; splendid.
▸ **ˈrippingly** ADVERB

ripple¹ (ˈrɪpᵊl) NOUN 1 a slight wave or undulation on the surface of water. 2 a small wave or undulation in fabric, hair, etc. 3 a sound reminiscent of water flowing quietly in ripples: *a ripple of laughter.* 4 *Electronics* an oscillation of small amplitude superimposed on a steady value. 5 *US and Canadian* another word for **riffle** (sense 4). 6 another word for **ripple mark.** ◆ VERB 7 (*intr*) to form ripples or flow with a rippling or undulating motion. 8 (*tr*) to stir up (water) so as to form ripples. 9 (*tr*) to make ripple marks. 10 (*intr*) (of sounds) to rise and fall gently: *her laughter rippled through the air.*
▹ HISTORY C17: perhaps from RIP¹
▸ **ˈrippler** NOUN ▸ **ˈrippling** ADJECTIVE ▸ **ˈripplingly** ADVERB
▸ **ˈripply** ADJECTIVE

ripple² (ˈrɪpᵊl) NOUN 1 a special kind of comb designed to separate the seed from the stalks in flax, hemp, or broomcorn. ◆ VERB 2 (*tr*) to comb with this tool.
▹ HISTORY C14: of Germanic origin; compare Middle Dutch *repelen*, Middle High German *reffen* to ripple
▸ **ˈrippler** NOUN

ripple control NOUN the remote control of a switch by electrical impulses.

ripple effect NOUN the repercussions of an event or situation experienced far beyond its immediate location.

ripple mark NOUN one of a series of small wavy ridges of sand formed by waves on a beach, by a current in a sandy riverbed, or by wind on land: sometimes found fossilized on bedding planes of sedimentary rock.

ripplet (ˈrɪplɪt) NOUN a tiny ripple.

rip-rap NOUN *Civil engineering* broken stones loosely deposited in water or on a soft bottom to provide a foundation and protect a riverbed or river banks from scour: used for revetments, embankments, breakwaters, etc.
▹ HISTORY C19: reduplication of RAP¹

rip-roaring ADJECTIVE *Informal* characterized by excitement, intensity, or boisterous behaviour.

ripsaw (ˈrɪpˌsɔː) NOUN a handsaw for cutting along the grain of timber.

ripsnorter (ˈrɪpˌsnɔːtə) NOUN *Slang* a person or thing noted for intensity or excellence.
▹ HISTORY C19: from RIP¹ + SNORTER
▸ **ˈripˌsnorting** ADJECTIVE

riptide (ˈrɪpˌtaɪd) NOUN 1 Also called: **rip, tide-rip.** a stretch of turbulent water in the sea, caused by the meeting of currents or abrupt changes in depth. 2 Also called: **rip current.** a strong current, esp one flowing outwards from the shore, causing disturbance on the surface.

Ripuarian (ˌrɪpjʊˈɛərɪən) ADJECTIVE 1 **a** of or relating to the group of Franks who lived during the 4th century near Cologne along the Rhine. **b** of or designating their code of laws. ◆ NOUN 2 a Ripuarian Frank.
▹ HISTORY C18: from Medieval Latin *Ripuārius*, perhaps from Latin *rīpa* a river bank

rip up VERB (*tr, adverb*) 1 to tear (paper) into small pieces. 2 to annul, cancel, or unilaterally disregard. 3 to dig up, dig into, or remove (a surface): *they are ripping up the street.*

Rip Van Winkle (rɪp væn ˈwɪŋkᵊl) NOUN *Informal* 1 a person who is oblivious to changes, esp in social attitudes or thought. 2 a person who sleeps a lot.
▹ HISTORY C19: from a character who slept for 20 years, in a story (1819) by Washington Irving

riroriro (ˈriːrəʊˌriːrəʊ) NOUN, *plural* **-ros.** another name for the **grey warbler.**
▹ HISTORY Maori

RISC (rɪsk) NOUN ACRONYM FOR reduced instruction set computer: a computer in which the set of instructions which it can perform has been reduced to the minimum, resulting in very fast data processing.

rise (raɪz) VERB **rises, rising, rose** (rəʊz), **risen** (ˈrɪzᵊn). (*mainly intr*) 1 to get up from a lying, sitting, kneeling, or prone position. 2 to get out of bed, esp to begin one's day: *he always rises early.* 3 to move from a lower to a higher position or place; ascend. 4 to ascend or appear above the horizon: *the sun is rising.* 5 to increase in height or level: *the water rose above the normal level.* 6 to attain higher rank, status, or reputation: *he will rise in the world.* 7 to be built or erected: *those blocks of flats are rising fast.* 8 to become apparent; appear: *new troubles rose to afflict her.* 9 to increase in strength, degree, intensity, etc.: *her spirits rose; the wind is rising.* 10 to increase in amount or value: *house prices are always rising.* 11 to swell up: *dough rises.* 12 to become erect, stiff, or rigid: *the hairs on his neck rose in fear.* 13 (of one's stomach or gorge) to manifest or feel nausea; retch. 14 to become actively rebellious; revolt: *the people rose against their oppressors.* 15 to slope upwards: *the ground rises beyond the lake.* 16 to return from the dead; be resurrected. 17 to originate; come into existence: *that river rises in the mountains.* 18 (of a session of a court, legislative assembly, etc.) to come to an end; adjourn. 19 *Angling* (of fish) to come to the surface of the water, as when taking flies. 20 (*tr*) *Nautical* another term for **raise** (sense 20). 21 (often foll by *to*) *Informal* to respond (to teasing, etc.) or fall into a trap prepared for one. ◆ NOUN 22 the act or an instance of rising; ascent. 23 an increase in height; elevation. 24 an increase in rank, status, or position. 25 an increase in amount, cost, or value. 26 an increase in degree or intensity. 27 *Brit* an increase in salary or wages. US and Canadian word: **raise.** 28 a piece of rising ground. 29 an upward slope or incline. 30 the appearance of the sun, moon, or other celestial body above the horizon. 31 the vertical height of a step or of a flight of stairs. 32 the vertical height of a roof above the walls or columns. 33 the height of an arch above the impost level. 34 *Angling* the act or instance of fish coming to the surface of the water to take flies, etc. 35 the beginning, origin, or source; derivation. 36 *Slang* an erection of the penis. 37 **get** *or* **take a rise out of.** to provoke an angry or petulant reaction from. 38 **give rise to.** to cause the development of; produce. ◆ See also **rise above, rise to.**
▹ HISTORY Old English *rīsan*; related to Old Saxon *rīsan*, Gothic *reisan*

rise above VERB (*intr, preposition*) to overcome or be unaffected by (something mean or contemptible).

risen (ˈrɪzᵊn) VERB 1 the past participle of **rise.** ◆ ADJECTIVE 2 restored from death; ascended into glory: *the risen Christ.*

riser (ˈraɪzə) NOUN 1 a person who rises, esp from bed: *an early riser.* 2 the vertical part of a stair or step. 3 a vertical pipe, esp one within a building.

rise to VERB (*intr, preposition*) to respond adequately to (the demands of something, esp a testing challenge).

risibility (ˌrɪzɪˈbɪlɪtɪ) NOUN, *plural* **-ties.** 1 a tendency to laugh. 2 hilarity; laughter.

risible (ˈrɪzɪbᵊl) ADJECTIVE 1 having a tendency to laugh. 2 causing laughter; ridiculous.
▹ HISTORY C16: from Late Latin *rīsibilis*, from Latin *rīdēre* to laugh
▸ **ˈrisibly** ADVERB

rising (ˈraɪzɪŋ) NOUN 1 an insurrection or rebellion; revolt. 2 the yeast or leaven used to make dough rise in baking. ◆ ADJECTIVE (*prenominal*) 3 increasing in rank, status, or reputation: *a rising young politician.* 4 increasing in maturity; growing up to adulthood: *the rising generation.* ◆ ADVERB 5 *Informal* approaching the age of; nearly: *she's rising 40.*

rising damp NOUN capillary movement of moisture from the ground into the walls of buildings. It results in structural damage up to a level of three feet.

rising trot NOUN a horse's trot in which the rider rises from the saddle every second beat. Compare **sitting trot.**

risk (rɪsk) NOUN 1 the possibility of incurring misfortune or loss; hazard. 2 *Insurance* **a** chance of a loss or other event on which a claim may be filed. **b** the type of such an event, such as fire or theft. **c** the amount of the claim should such an event occur. **d** a person or thing considered with respect to the characteristics that may cause an insured event to occur. 3 **at risk. a** vulnerable; likely to be lost or damaged. **b** *Social welfare* vulnerable to personal damage, to the extent that a welfare agency might take protective responsibility. 4 **no risk.** *Austral informal* an expression of assent. 5 **take** *or* **run a risk.** to proceed in an action without regard to the possibility of danger involved in it. ◆ VERB (*tr*) 6 to expose to danger or loss; hazard. 7 to act in spite of the possibility of (injury or loss): *to risk a fall in climbing.*
▹ HISTORY C17: from French *risque*, from Italian *risco*, from *rischiare* to be in peril, from Greek *rhiza* cliff (from the hazards of sailing along rocky coasts)
▸ **ˈrisker** NOUN

risk aversion NOUN a strong disinclination to take risks.

risk capital NOUN *Chiefly Brit* capital invested in an issue of ordinary shares, esp of a speculative enterprise. Also called: **venture capital.**

risk factor NOUN *Med* a factor, such as a habit or an environmental condition, that predisposes an individual to develop a particular disease.

risky (ˈrɪskɪ) ADJECTIVE **riskier, riskiest.** involving danger; perilous.
▸ **ˈriskily** ADVERB ▸ **ˈriskiness** NOUN

Risorgimento (rɪˌsɔːdʒɪˈmɛntəʊ) NOUN the period of and the movement for the political unification of Italy in the 19th century.
▹ HISTORY Italian, from *risorgere* to rise again, from Latin *resurgere*, from RE- + *surgere* to rise

risotto (rɪˈzɒtəʊ) NOUN, *plural* **-tos.** a dish of rice cooked in stock and served variously with tomatoes, cheese, chicken, etc.
▹ HISTORY C19: from Italian, from *riso* RICE

risqué (ˈrɪskeɪ) ADJECTIVE bordering on impropriety or indecency: *a risqué joke.*
▹ HISTORY C19: from French *risquer* to hazard, RISK

Riss (rɪs) NOUN the third major Pleistocene glaciation in Alpine Europe. See also **Günz, Mindel, Würm.**
▹ HISTORY C20: named after the river *Riss*, a tributary of the Danube in Germany

rissole (ˈrɪsəʊl) NOUN a mixture of minced cooked meat coated in egg and breadcrumbs and fried. Compare **croquette.**
▹ HISTORY C18: from French, probably ultimately from Latin *russus* red; see RUSSET

risus sardonicus (ˈriːsəs sɑːˈdɒnɪkəs) NOUN *Pathol* fixed contraction of the facial muscles resulting in a peculiar distorted grin, caused esp by tetanus. Also called: **trismus cynicus** (ˈtrɪzməs ˈsɪnɪkəs).
▹ HISTORY C17: New Latin, literally: sardonic laugh

rit. *Music* ◆ ABBREVIATION FOR: 1 ritardando. 2 ritenuto.

Ritalin (ˈrɪtəlɪn) NOUN *Trademark* a preparation of methylphenidate, a drug related to amphetamine, used to treat attention deficit disorder in children.

ritardando (ˌrɪtɑːˈdændəʊ) ADJECTIVE, ADVERB another term for **rallentando.** Abbreviation: **rit.**
▹ HISTORY C19: from Italian, from *ritardare* to slow down

rite (raɪt) NOUN 1 a formal act or procedure prescribed or customary in religious ceremonies: *fertility rites; the rite of baptism.* 2 a particular body of such acts or procedures, esp of a particular Christian Church: *the Latin rite.* 3 a Christian Church: *the Greek rite.*
▹ HISTORY C14: from Latin *rītus* religious ceremony

ritenuto (ˌrɪtəˈnuːtəʊ) ADJECTIVE, ADVERB *Music* 1 held back momentarily. 2 another term for **rallentando.** Abbreviation: **rit.**
▹ HISTORY C19: from Italian, from past participle of *ritenere*, from Latin *retinēre* to hold back

rite of passage *or* **rite de passage** (*French* rit də pɑsaʒ) NOUN 1 a ceremony performed in some cultures at times when an individual changes his status, as at puberty and marriage. 2 a significant event in a transitional period of someone's life.

ritornello (ˌrɪtəˈnɛləʊ) NOUN, *plural* **-los** *or* **-li** (-liː). *Music* 1 an orchestral passage between verses of an aria or song. 2 a ripieno passage in a concerto grosso.
▹ HISTORY C17: from Italian, literally: a little return, from *ritorno* a RETURN

ritual (ˈrɪtjʊəl) NOUN 1 the prescribed or

established form of a religious or other ceremony. [2] such prescribed forms in general or collectively. [3] stereotyped activity or behaviour. [4] *Psychol* any repetitive behaviour, such as hand-washing, performed by a person with a compulsive personality disorder. [5] any formal act, institution, or procedure that is followed consistently: *the ritual of the law*. ◆ ADJECTIVE [6] of, relating to, or characteristic of religious, social, or other rituals.
▷HISTORY C16: from Latin *rītuālis*, from *rītus* RITE
▸'**ritually** ADVERB

ritualism ('rɪtjʊəˌlɪzəm) NOUN [1] emphasis, esp exaggerated emphasis, on the importance of rites and ceremonies. [2] the study of rites and ceremonies, esp magical or religious ones.
▸'**ritualist** NOUN

ritualistic (ˌrɪtjʊə'lɪstɪk) ADJECTIVE of, relating to, or suggestive of ritualism.
▸ˌ**ritual'istically** ADVERB

ritualize *or* **ritualise** ('rɪtjʊəˌlaɪz) VERB [1] (*intr*) to engage in ritualism or devise rituals. [2] (*tr*) to make (something) into a ritual.

Ritz (rɪts) NOUN [1] any very luxurious and expensive establishment: usually used with a negative: *this isn't the Ritz, you know*. [2] **put on the Ritz**. (*sometimes not capital*) to assume a superior air or make an ostentatious display.
▷HISTORY from the luxury hotels created by the Swiss César *Ritz* (1850–1918)

ritzy ('rɪtsɪ) ADJECTIVE **ritzier, ritziest**. *Slang* luxurious or elegant.
▸'**ritzily** ADVERB ▸'**ritziness** NOUN

rivage ('rɪvɪdʒ) NOUN *Archaic* a bank, shore, or coast.
▷HISTORY C14: from Old French, from *rive* river bank, from Latin *rīpa*

rival ('raɪvᵊl) NOUN [1] **a** a person, organization, team, etc., that competes with another for the same object or in the same field. **b** (*as modifier*): *rival suitors; a rival company*. [2] a person or thing that is considered the equal of another or others: *she is without rival in the field of economics*. ◆ VERB **-vals, -valling, -valled** *or US* **-vals, -valing, -valed**. (*tr*) [3] to be the equal or near equal of: *an empire that rivalled Rome*. [4] to try to equal or surpass; compete with in rivalry.
▷HISTORY C16: from Latin *rīvalis*, literally: one who shares the same brook, from *rīvus* a brook

rivalry ('raɪvəlrɪ) NOUN, *plural* **-ries**. [1] the act of rivalling; competition. [2] the state of being a rival or rivals.
▸'**rivalrous** ADJECTIVE

rive (raɪv) VERB **rives, riving, rived, rived** *or* **riven** ('rɪvᵊn). (*usually passive*) [1] to split asunder: *a tree riven by lightning*. [2] to tear apart: *riven to shreds*. [3] *Archaic* to break (the heart) or (of the heart) to be broken.
▷HISTORY C13: from Old Norse *rīfa*; related to Old Frisian *rīva*

river ('rɪvə) NOUN [1] **a** a large natural stream of fresh water flowing along a definite course, usually into the sea, being fed by tributary streams. **b** (*as modifier*): *river traffic; a river basin*. **c** (*in combination*): *riverside; riverbed*. Related adjectives: **fluvial, potamic**. [2] any abundant stream or flow: *a river of blood*. [3] **sell down the river**. *Informal* to deceive or betray.
▷HISTORY C13: from Old French *riviere*, from Latin *rīpārius* of a river bank, from *rīpa* bank
▸'**riverless** ADJECTIVE

river blindness NOUN another name for **onchocerciasis**.

river horse NOUN an informal name for the **hippopotamus**.

riverine ('rɪvəˌraɪn) ADJECTIVE [1] of, like, relating to, or produced by a river. [2] located or dwelling near a river; riparian.

river red gum NOUN a large Australian red gum tree, *Eucalyptus camaldulensis*, growing along river banks.

Rivers ('rɪvəz) NOUN a state of S Nigeria, in the Niger River Delta on the Gulf of Guinea. Capital: Port Harcourt. Pop.: 4 103 372 (1995 est.). Area: 21 850 sq. km (8436 sq. miles).

Riverside ('rɪvəˌsaɪd) NOUN a city in SW California. Pop.: 255 166 (2000).

rivet ('rɪvɪt) NOUN [1] a short metal pin for fastening two or more pieces together, having a head at one end, the other end being hammered flat after being passed through holes in the pieces. ◆ VERB **-ets, -eting, -eted**. (*tr*) [2] to join by riveting. [3] to hammer in order to form into a head. [4] (*often passive*) to cause to be fixed or held firmly, as in fascinated attention, horror, etc.: *to be riveted to the spot*.
▷HISTORY C14: from Old French, from *river* to fasten, fix, of unknown origin
▸'**riveter** NOUN

riveting ('rɪvətɪŋ) ADJECTIVE absolutely fascinating; enthralling.

Riviera (ˌrɪvɪ'ɛərə) NOUN the Mediterranean coastal region between Cannes, France, and La Spezia, Italy: contains some of Europe's most popular resorts.
▷HISTORY C18: from Italian literally: shore, ultimately from Latin *rīpa* bank, shore

rivière (ˌrɪvɪ'ɛə) NOUN a necklace the diamonds or other precious stones of which gradually increase in size up to a large centre stone.
▷HISTORY C19: from French: brook, RIVER

rivulet ('rɪvjʊlɪt) NOUN a small stream.
▷HISTORY C16: from Italian *rivoletto*, from Latin *rīvulus*, from *rīvus* stream

rix-dollar ('rɪksˌdɒlə) NOUN any of various former Scandinavian or Dutch small silver coins. Also called: **rijksdaaler, rigsdaler**.
▷HISTORY C16: partial translation of obsolete Dutch *rijksdaler; rijk* realm, kingdom

Riyadh (rɪ'jɑːd) NOUN the joint capital (with Mecca) of Saudi Arabia, situated in a central oasis: the largest city in the country. Pop.: 2 800 000 (1996 est.).

riyal (rɪ'jɑːl) NOUN the standard monetary unit of Qatar, divided into 100 dirhams; Saudi Arabia, divided into 100 halala; and Yemen, divided into 100 fils.
▷HISTORY from Arabic *riyāl*, from Spanish *real* REAL²

Rizal (*Spanish* ri'θal) NOUN another name for **Pasay**.

RL [1] ABBREVIATION FOR Rugby League. ◆ [2] INTERNATIONAL CAR REGISTRATION FOR (Republic of) Lebanon.

rly ABBREVIATION FOR railway.

rm ABBREVIATION FOR: [1] ream. [2] room.

RM ABBREVIATION FOR: [1] Royal Mail. [2] Royal Marines. ◆ [3] INTERNATIONAL CAR REGISTRATION FOR (Republic of) Madagascar.

RMA ABBREVIATION FOR Royal Military Academy (Sandhurst).

RME ABBREVIATION FOR: [1] religious and moral education. [2] rape *or* rapeseed methyl ester: a fuel derived from rapeseed oil.

R-methodology NOUN any statistical methodology in psychology that is contrasted with Q-methodology.

RMM INTERNATIONAL CAR REGISTRATION FOR (Republic of) Mali.

r.m.m. ABBREVIATION FOR relative molecular mass.

rms ABBREVIATION FOR root mean square.

RMS ABBREVIATION FOR: [1] Royal Mail Service. [2] Royal Mail Steamer.

RMT ABBREVIATION FOR National Union of Rail, Maritime and Transport Workers.

Rn THE CHEMICAL SYMBOL FOR radon.

RN [1] ABBREVIATION FOR Royal Navy. ◆ [2] INTERNATIONAL CAR REGISTRATION FOR (Republic of) Niger.

RNA NOUN *Biochem* ribonucleic acid; any of a group of nucleic acids, present in all living cells, that play an essential role in the synthesis of proteins. On hydrolysis they yield the pentose sugar ribose, the purine bases adenine and guanine, the pyrimidine bases cytosine and uracil, and phosphoric acid. See also **messenger RNA, transfer RNA, ribosomal RNA, DNA**.

RNAS ABBREVIATION FOR: [1] Royal Naval Air Service(s). [2] Royal Naval Air Station.

RNIB *Brit* ABBREVIATION FOR Royal National Institute for the Blind.

RNID *Brit* ABBREVIATION FOR Royal National Institute for Deaf People.

RNLI ABBREVIATION FOR Royal National Lifeboat Institution.

RNR ABBREVIATION FOR Royal Naval Reserve.

RNVR ABBREVIATION FOR Royal Naval Volunteer Reserve.

RNWMP (in Canada) ABBREVIATION FOR Royal Northwest Mounted Police: a former name for the Royal Canadian Mounted Police.

RNZ ABBREVIATION FOR Radio New Zealand.

RNZAF ABBREVIATION FOR Royal New Zealand Air Force.

RNZN ABBREVIATION FOR Royal New Zealand Navy.

ro THE INTERNET DOMAIN NAME FOR Romania.

RO INTERNATIONAL CAR REGISTRATION FOR Romania.

roach¹ (rəʊtʃ) NOUN, *plural* **roaches** *or* **roach**. [1] a European freshwater cyprinid food fish, *Rutilus rutilus*, having a deep compressed body and reddish ventral and tail fins. [2] any of various similar fishes.
▷HISTORY C14: from Old French *roche*, of obscure origin

roach² (rəʊtʃ) NOUN [1] short for **cockroach**. [2] *Slang* the butt of a cannabis cigarette.

roach³ (rəʊtʃ) NOUN *Nautical* [1] the amount by which the leech of a fore-and-aft sail projects beyond an imaginary straight line between the clew and the head. [2] the curve at the foot of a square sail.
▷HISTORY C18: of unknown origin

roach clip NOUN *Slang* a small clip resembling tweezers, used to hold the butt of a cannabis cigarette, in order to prevent burning one's fingers.

roached (rəʊtʃt) ADJECTIVE arched convexly, as the back of certain breeds of dog, such as the whippet.
▷HISTORY C19: from ROACH³ or *roach* (vb) to cut (a sail) into a roach

road (rəʊd) NOUN [1] **a** an open way, usually surfaced with tarmac or concrete, providing passage from one place to another. **b** (*as modifier*): *road traffic; a road map; a road sign*. **c** (*in combination*): *the roadside*. [2] **a** a street. **b** (*capital when part of a name*): *London Road*. [3] **a** *US* short for **railroad**. **b** *Brit* one of the tracks of a railway. [4] a way, path, or course: *the road to fame*. [5] (*often plural*) Also called: **roadstead**. *Nautical* a partly sheltered anchorage. [6] a drift or tunnel in a mine, esp a level one. [7] **hit the road**. *Slang* to start or resume travelling. [8] **on the road**. **a** travelling, esp as a salesman. **b** (of a theatre company, pop group, etc.) on tour. **c** leading a wandering life. [9] **take (to) the road**. to begin a journey or tour. [10] **one for the road**. *Informal* a last alcoholic drink before leaving.
▷HISTORY Old English *rād*; related to *rīdan* to RIDE, and to Old Saxon *rēda*, Old Norse *reith*
▸'**roadless** ADJECTIVE

road agent NOUN *US* (formerly) a bandit who robbed stagecoaches; highwayman.

road allowance NOUN *Canadian* land reserved by the government to be used for public roads.

roadbed ('rəʊdˌbɛd) NOUN [1] the material used to make a road. [2] a layer of ballast that supports the sleepers of a railway track.

roadblock ('rəʊdˌblɒk) NOUN [1] a barrier set up across a road by the police or military, in order to stop a fugitive, inspect traffic, etc. [2] a difficulty or obstacle to progress.

road book NOUN a book of maps, sometimes including a gazetteer.

road-fund licence NOUN *Brit* a licence showing that the tax payable in respect of a motor vehicle has been paid.
▷HISTORY C20: from the former *road fund* for the maintenance of public highways

road hog NOUN *Informal* a selfish or aggressive driver.

roadholding ('rəʊdˌhəʊldɪŋ) NOUN the extent to which a motor vehicle is stable and does not skid, esp at high speeds, or on sharp bends or wet roads.

roadhouse ('rəʊdˌhaʊs) NOUN a pub, restaurant, etc., that is situated at the side of a road, esp a country road.

road hump NOUN the official name for **sleeping policeman**.

roadie ('rəʊdɪ) NOUN *Informal* a person who transports and sets up equipment for a band or group.

roadkill ('rəʊdˌkɪl) NOUN *Chiefly US* the remains of an animal or animals killed on the road by motor vehicles.

road map NOUN 1 a map intended for drivers, showing roads, distances, etc. in a country or area. 2 a plan or guide for future actions.

road metal NOUN crushed rock, broken stone, etc., used to construct a road.

road movie NOUN a genre of film in which the chief character is on the run or travelling in search of, or to escape from, himself.

road pricing NOUN the practice of charging motorists for using certain stretches of road, in order to reduce congestion.

road rage NOUN aggressive behaviour by a motorist in response to the actions of another road user.

roadroller (ˈrəʊdˌrəʊlə) NOUN a motor vehicle with heavy rollers for compressing road surfaces during road-making.

roadrunner (ˈrəʊdˌrʌnə) NOUN a terrestrial crested bird, *Geococcyx californianus*, of Central and S North America, having a streaked plumage and long tail: family *Cuculidae* (cuckoos). Also called: **chaparral cock**.

road show NOUN 1 **a** a radio show broadcast live from one of a number of towns or venues being visited by a disc jockey who is touring an area. **b** the touring disc jockey and the personnel and equipment needed to present such a show: *the Radio 1 road show will be in Brighton next week*. 2 a group of entertainers, esp pop musicians, on tour. 3 any occasion when an organization attracts publicity while touring or visiting: *an antiques road show; a royal road show*.

roadstead (ˈrəʊdˌstɛd) NOUN *Nautical* another word for **road** (sense 5).

roadster (ˈrəʊdstə) NOUN 1 an open car, esp one seating only two. 2 a kind of bicycle.

road tax NOUN a tax paid, usually annually, on motor vehicles in use on the roads.

road test NOUN 1 a test to ensure that a vehicle is roadworthy, esp after repair or servicing, by driving it on roads. 2 a test of something in actual use. ◆ VERB **road-test**. (*tr*) 3 to test (a vehicle) in this way. 4 to test (something) in a real and appropriate context.

road train NOUN *Austral* a line of linked trailers pulled by a truck, used for transporting stock, etc.

roadway (ˈrəʊdˌweɪ) NOUN 1 the surface of a road. 2 the part of a road that is used by vehicles.

roadwork (ˈrəʊdˌwɜːk) NOUN sports training by running along roads.

roadworks (ˈrəʊdˌwɜːks) PLURAL NOUN repairs to a road or cable under a road, esp when forming a hazard or obstruction to traffic.

roadworthy (ˈrəʊdˌwɜːðɪ) ADJECTIVE 1 (of a motor vehicle) mechanically sound; fit for use on the roads. ◆ NOUN, *plural* **-ies**. 2 *South African* a certificate of roadworthiness for a motor vehicle.
▸ **ˈroadˌworthiness** NOUN

roam (rəʊm) VERB 1 to travel or walk about with no fixed purpose or direction; wander. ◆ NOUN 2 the act of roaming.
▷HISTORY C13: origin unknown
▸ **ˈroamer** NOUN

roan (rəʊn) ADJECTIVE 1 (of a horse) having a bay (**red roan**), chestnut (**strawberry roan**), or black (**blue roan**) coat sprinkled with white hairs. ◆ NOUN 2 a horse having such a coat. 3 a soft unsplit sheepskin leather with a close tough grain, used in bookbinding, etc.
▷HISTORY C16: from Old French, from Spanish *roano*, probably from Gothic *rauths* red

Roanoke Island (ˈrəʊəˌnəʊk) NOUN an island off the coast of North Carolina: site of the first attempted English settlement in America. Length: 19 km (12 miles). Average width: 5 km (3 miles).

roar (rɔː) VERB (*mainly intr*) 1 (of lions and other animals) to utter characteristic loud growling cries. 2 (*also tr*) (of people) to utter (something) with a loud deep cry, as in anger or triumph. 3 to laugh in a loud hearty unrestrained manner. 4 (of horses) to breathe with laboured rasping sounds. See **roaring** (sense 6). 5 (of the wind, waves, etc.) to blow or break loudly and violently, as during a storm. 6 (of a fire) to burn fiercely with a roaring sound. 7 (of a machine, gun, etc.) to operate or move with a loud harsh noise. 8 (*tr*) to bring (oneself) into a certain condition by roaring: *to roar oneself hoarse*. ◆ NOUN 9 a loud deep cry, uttered by a person or crowd, esp in anger or triumph. 10 a prolonged loud cry of certain animals, esp lions. 11 any similar noise made by a fire, the wind, waves, artillery, an engine, etc. ◆ See also **roar up**.
▷HISTORY Old English *rārian*; related to Old High German *rērēn*, Middle Dutch *reren*
▸ **ˈroarer** NOUN

roaring (ˈrɔːrɪŋ) ADJECTIVE 1 *Informal* very brisk and profitable (esp in the phrase **a roaring trade**). 2 **the roaring days.** *Austral* the period of the Australian goldrushes. 3 *Irish derogatory informal* (intensifier): *a roaring communist*. ◆ ADVERB 4 noisily or boisterously (esp in the phrase **roaring drunk**). ◆ NOUN 5 a loud prolonged cry. 6 a debilitating breathing defect of horses characterized by rasping sounds with each breath: caused by inflammation of the respiratory tract or obstruction of the larynx. Compare **whistling**.
▸ **ˈroaringly** ADVERB

Roaring Forties **the.** *Nautical* the areas of ocean between 40° and 50° latitude in the S Hemisphere, noted for gale-force winds.

roarming (ˈrɔːmɪŋ) ADJECTIVE *Midland English dialect* severe: *a roarming cold*.

roar up VERB (*tr, adverb*) *Austral informal* to rebuke or reprimand (a person).

roast (rəʊst) VERB (*mainly tr*) 1 to cook (meat or other food) by dry heat, usually with added fat and esp in an oven. 2 to brown or dry (coffee, etc.) by exposure to heat. 3 *Metallurgy* to heat (an ore) in order to produce a concentrate that is easier to smelt. 4 to heat (oneself or something) to an extreme degree, as when sunbathing, sitting before the fire, etc. 5 (*intr*) to be excessively and uncomfortably hot. 6 *Informal* to criticize severely. ◆ NOUN 7 something that has been roasted, esp meat.
▷HISTORY C13: from Old French *rostir*, of Germanic origin; compare Middle Dutch *roosten* to roast
▸ **ˈroaster** NOUN

roasting (ˈrəʊstɪŋ) *Informal* ◆ ADJECTIVE 1 extremely hot. ◆ NOUN 2 severe criticism.

rob (rɒb) VERB **robs, robbing, robbed**. 1 to take something from (someone) illegally, as by force or threat of violence. (*tr*) 2 to plunder (a house, shop, etc.). 3 (*tr*) to deprive unjustly: *to be robbed of an opportunity*.
▷HISTORY C13: from Old French *rober*, of Germanic origin; compare Old High German *roubōn* to rob
▸ **ˈrobber** NOUN

robalo (ˈrɒbəˌləʊ, ˈrəʊ-) NOUN, *plural* **-los** *or* **-lo**. any percoid fish of the family *Centropomidae*, occurring in warm and tropical (mostly marine) waters. Some of the larger species, such as the snooks, are important food fishes and many of the smaller ones are aquarium fishes.
▷HISTORY Spanish, probably changed from *lobaro* (unattested), from *lobo* wolf, from Latin *lupus*

roband (ˈrɒbənd, ˈrəʊbənd) *or* **robbin** NOUN *Nautical* a piece of marline used for fastening a sail to a spar.
▷HISTORY C18: probably related to Middle Dutch *rabant*, from *ra* sailyard + *bant* band

Robben Island (ˈrɒbᵊn) NOUN a small island in South Africa, 11 km (7 miles) off the Cape Peninsula: formerly used by the South African government to house political prisoners.

robber crab NOUN a terrestrial crab, *Birgus latro*, of the Indo-Pacific region, known for its habit of climbing coconut palms to feed on the nuts.

robber fly NOUN any of the predatory dipterous flies constituting the family *Asilidae*, which have a strong bristly body with piercing mouthparts and which prey on other insects. Also called: **bee killer, assassin fly**.

robber trench NOUN *Archaeol* a trench that originally contained the foundations of a wall, the stones of which have been taken away.

robbery (ˈrɒbərɪ) NOUN, *plural* **-beries**. 1 *Criminal law* the stealing of property from a person by using or threatening to use force. 2 the act or an instance of robbing.

robbin (ˈrɒbɪn) NOUN *Nautical* another word for **roband**.

robe (rəʊb) NOUN 1 any loose flowing garment, esp the official vestment of a peer, judge, or academic. 2 a dressing gown or bathrobe. 3 *Austral informal* a wardrobe. ◆ VERB 4 to put a robe, etc., on (oneself or someone else); dress.
▷HISTORY C13: from Old French: of Germanic origin; compare Old French *rober* to ROB, Old High German *roub* booty

robe-de-chambre *French* (rɔbdəʃɑ̃brə) NOUN, *plural* ***robes-de-chambre*** (rɔbdəʃɑ̃brə). a dressing gown or bathrobe.

Robertson screw (ˈrɒbətsᵊn) NOUN *Trademark* a screw having a square hole in the head into which a screwdriver with a square point (**Robertson screwdriver** (*Trademark*)) fits.
▷HISTORY C20: after its inventor P. L. *Robertson* (1896–1951), a Canadian industrialist

robin (ˈrɒbɪn) NOUN 1 Also called: **robin redbreast.** a small Old World songbird, *Erithacus rubecula*, related to the thrushes: family *Muscicapidae*. The male has a brown back, orange-red breast and face, and grey underparts. 2 a North American thrush, *Turdus migratorius*, similar to but larger than the Old World robin. 3 any of various similar birds having a reddish breast.
▷HISTORY C16: arbitrary use of given name

Robin Goodfellow (ˈrɒbɪn ˈgʊdˌfɛləʊ) NOUN another name for **puck**².

robing room NOUN a room in a palace, court, legislature, etc., where official robes of office are put on.

Robin Hood NOUN a legendary English outlaw of the reign of Richard I, who according to tradition lived in Sherwood Forest and robbed the rich to give to the poor.

robinia (rəˈbɪnɪə) NOUN any tree of the leguminous genus *Robinia*, esp the locust tree (see **locust** (sense 2)).

robin's-egg blue NOUN *Chiefly US* **a** a light greenish-blue colour. **b** (*as adjective*): *a robin's-egg-blue dress*.

Robinson Crusoe NOUN the hero of Daniel Defoe's novel *Robinson Crusoe* (1719), who survived being shipwrecked on a desert island The character is supposedly based on the Scottish sailor Alexander Selkirk (1676–1721), who was marooned on one of the islets of Juan Fernández.

roble (ˈrəʊbleɪ) NOUN 1 Also called: **white oak.** an oak tree, *Quercus lobata*, of California, having leathery leaves and slender pointed acorns. 2 any of several similar or related trees.
▷HISTORY C19: from Spanish: from Latin *rōbur* oak, strength

roborant (ˈrəʊbərənt, ˈrɒb-) ADJECTIVE 1 tending to fortify or increase strength. ◆ NOUN 2 a drug or agent that increases strength.
▷HISTORY C17: from Latin *rōborāre* to strengthen, from *rōbur* an oak

robot (ˈrəʊbɒt) NOUN 1 any automated machine programmed to perform specific mechanical functions in the manner of a man. 2 (*modifier*) not controlled by man; automatic: *a robot pilot*. 3 a person who works or behaves like a machine; automaton. 4 *South African* a set of traffic lights.
▷HISTORY C20: (used in *R.U.R.*, a play by Karel Čapek) from Czech *robota* work; related to Old Slavonic *rabota* servitude, German *Arbeit* work
▸ **roˈbotic** ADJECTIVE ▸ **ˈrobotism** *or* **ˈrobotry** NOUN
▸ **ˈrobot-ˌlike** ADJECTIVE

robot bomb NOUN another name for the **V-1**.

robot dancing, robotics, *or* **robotic dancing** NOUN a dance of the 1980s characterized by jerky mechanical movements.

robotics (rəʊˈbɒtɪks) NOUN (*functioning as singular*) 1 the science or technology of designing, building, and using robots. 2 another name for **robot dancing**.

robotize *or* **robotise** (ˈrəʊbəˌtaɪz) VERB (*tr*) 1 *Chiefly US* to automate: *robotized assembly lines*. 2 to cause (a person) to be or become mechanical and lifeless, like a robot.

Robson (ˈrɒbsən) NOUN **Mount.** a mountain in SW Canada, in E British Columbia: the highest peak in the Canadian Rockies. Height: 3954 m (12 972 ft.).

robust (rəʊˈbʌst, ˈrəʊbʌst) ADJECTIVE 1 strong in constitution; hardy; vigorous. 2 sturdily built: *a robust shelter*. 3 requiring or suited to physical strength: *a robust sport*. 4 (esp of wines) having a rich full-bodied flavour. 5 rough or boisterous. 6

(of thought, intellect, etc.) straightforward and imbued with common sense.
▷HISTORY C16: from Latin *rōbustus,* from *rōbur* an oak, strength
▸**ro'bustly** ADVERB

robusta (rəʊ'bʌstə) NOUN 1 a species of coffee tree, *Coffea canephora.* 2 coffee or coffee beans obtained from this plant.
▷HISTORY from Latin *rōbustus* strong

robustious (rəʊ'bʌstʃəs) ADJECTIVE *Archaic* 1 rough; boisterous. 2 strong, robust, or stout.
▸**ro'bustiously** ADVERB ▸**ro'bustiousness** NOUN

robustness (rəʊ'bʌstnɪs) NOUN 1 the quality of being robust. 2 *Computing* the ability of a computer system to cope with errors during execution.

roc (rɒk) NOUN (in Arabian legend) a bird of enormous size and power.
▷HISTORY C16: from Arabic *rukhkh,* from Persian *rukh*

ROC ABBREVIATION FOR Royal Observer Corps.

Roca ('rəʊkə) NOUN **Cape.** a cape in SW central Portugal, near Lisbon: the westernmost point of continental Europe.

rocaille (rɒ'kaɪ) NOUN decorative rock or shell work, esp as ornamentation in a rococo fountain, grotto, or interior.
▷HISTORY from French, from *roc* ROCK[1]

rocambole ('rɒkəm,bəʊl) NOUN a variety of sand leek whose garlic-like bulb is used for seasoning.
▷HISTORY C17: from French, from German *Rockenbolle,* literally: distaff bulb (with reference to its shape)

Rochdale ('rɒtʃ,deɪl) NOUN 1 a town in NW England, in Rochdale unitary authority, Greater Manchester: former centre of the textile industry. Pop.: 94 313 (1991). 2 a unitary authority in NW England, in Greater Manchester. Pop.: 205 233 (2001). Area: 159 sq. km (61 sq. miles).

Roche limit (rɒʃ) NOUN *Astronomy* the distance from the centre of a body, such as a planet, at which the tidal forces are stronger than the mutual gravitational attraction between two adjacent orbiting objects.
▷HISTORY C19: named after E. A. *Roche* (1820–83), French mathematician

Rochelle powder (rɒ'ʃɛl) NOUN another name for **Seidlitz powder.**
▷HISTORY C18: named after *La Rochelle,* French port

Rochelle salt NOUN a white crystalline double salt, sodium potassium tartrate, used in Seidlitz powder. Formula: $KNaC_4H_4O_6.4H_2O$.

roche moutonnée ('rəʊʃ ,muːtə'neɪ) NOUN, *plural* **roches moutonnées** ('rəʊʃ ,muːtə'neɪz). a rounded mass of rock smoothed and striated by ice that has flowed over it.
▷HISTORY C19: French, literally: fleecy rock, from *mouton* sheep

Rochester ('rɒtʃɪstə) NOUN 1 a city in SE England, in Medway unitary authority, Kent, on the River Medway. Pop.: 23 971 (1991). 2 a city in NW New York State, on Lake Ontario. Pop.: 219 773 (2000). 3 a city in the US, in Minnesota: site of the Mayo Clinic. Pop.: 85 806 (2000).

rochet ('rɒtʃɪt) NOUN a white surplice with tight sleeves, worn by bishops, abbots, and certain other Church dignitaries.
▷HISTORY C14: from Old French, from *roc* coat, outer garment, of Germanic origin; compare Old High German *roc* coat

rock[1] (rɒk) NOUN 1 *Geology* any aggregate of minerals that makes up part of the earth's crust. It may be unconsolidated, such as a sand, clay, or mud, or consolidated, such as granite, limestone, or coal. See also **igneous, sedimentary, metamorphic.** 2 any hard mass of consolidated mineral matter, such as a boulder. 3 *Chiefly US, Canadian, and Austral* a stone. 4 a person or thing suggesting a rock, esp in being dependable, unchanging, or providing firm foundation. 5 *Brit* a hard sweet, typically a long brightly-coloured peppermint-flavoured stick, sold esp in holiday resorts. 6 *Slang* a jewel, esp a diamond. 7 short for **rock salmon.** 8 *(plural) Slang* the testicles. 9 *Slang* another name for **crack** (sense 29). 10 **between a rock and a hard place.** having to choose between two equally unpleasant alternatives. 11 **on the rocks. a** in a state of ruin or destitution. **b** (of drinks, esp whisky) served with ice.
▷HISTORY C14: from Old French *roche,* of unknown origin

rock[2] (rɒk) VERB 1 to move or cause to move from side to side or backwards and forwards. 2 to reel or sway or cause (someone) to reel or sway, as with a violent shock or emotion. 3 *(tr)* to shake or move (something) violently. 4 *(intr)* to dance in the rock-and-roll style. 5 *Mining* to wash (ore) or (of ore) to be washed in a cradle. 6 *(tr)* to roughen (a copper plate) with a rocker before engraving a mezzotint. 7 **rock the boat.** *Informal* to create a disturbance in the existing situation. ◆ NOUN 8 a rocking motion. 9 short for **rock and roll.** 10 Also called: **rock music.** any of various styles of pop music having a heavy beat, derived from rock and roll.
◆ See also **rock up.**
▷HISTORY Old English *roccian;* related to Middle Dutch, Old High German *rocken,* German *rücken*

Rock (rɒk) NOUN 1 **the.** an informal name for **Gibraltar.** 2 **the.** a Canadian informal name for **Newfoundland.**

rockabilly ('rɒkə,bɪlɪ) NOUN **a** a fast, spare style of White rock music which originated in the mid-1950s in the US South. **b** *(as modifier): a rockabilly number.*
▷HISTORY C20: from ROCK (AND ROLL) + (HILL)BILLY

Rockall ('rɒkɔːl) NOUN an uninhabited British island in the N Atlantic, 354 km (220 miles) W of the Outer Hebrides. Area: 0.07 ha (0.18 acres).

rock and roll *or* **rock'n'roll** NOUN 1 **a** a type of pop music originating in the 1950s as a blend of rhythm and blues and country and western. It is generally based upon the twelve-bar blues, the first and third beats in each bar being heavily accented. **b** *(as modifier): the rock-and-roll era.* 2 dancing performed to such music, with exaggerated body movements stressing the beat. ◆ VERB 3 *(intr)* to perform this dance.
▸**rock and roller** *or* **rock'n'roller** NOUN

rockaway ('rɒkə,weɪ) NOUN *US* a four-wheeled horse-drawn carriage, usually with two seats and a hard top.

rock bass (bæs) NOUN 1 a North American freshwater percoid fish, *Ambloplites rupestris*: an important food fish; family *Centrarchidae* (sunfishes, etc.). 2 any similar or related fish.

rock boot NOUN a tight-fitting rock-climbing boot with a canvas or suede upper and smooth rubber sole, designed to give good grip on small holds.

rock borer NOUN any of various sea creatures that bore into rock, such as some sea urchins, sponges, annelid worms, barnacles, isopods, and molluscs.

rock bottom NOUN **a** the lowest possible level. **b** *(as modifier): rock-bottom prices.*

rock-bound ADJECTIVE hemmed in or encircled by rocks. Also (poetic): **rock-girt.**

rock brake NOUN any of various ferns of the genera *Pellaea* and *Cryptogramma,* which grow on rocky ground and have sori at the ends of the veins.

rock cake NOUN a small cake containing dried fruit and spice, with a rough surface supposed to resemble a rock.

rock candy NOUN the usual US and Canadian name for **rock**[1] (sense 5).

rock chopper NOUN *Austral slang* a Roman Catholic.
▷HISTORY from the initials RC

rock climb NOUN 1 an instance of rock climbing or the route followed. ◆ VERB **rock-climb.** *(intr)* 2 to practise rock climbing.

rock climbing NOUN the technique and sport of climbing on steep rock faces, usually with ropes and other equipment and as part of a team or pair.

rock cod NOUN 1 *Austral* any of various marine fishes found in rocky habitats in Australian waters. 2 *NZ* another name for **blue cod.**

rock cress NOUN another name for **arabis.**

rock crystal NOUN a pure transparent colourless quartz, used in electronic and optical equipment. Formula: SiO_2.

rock cycle NOUN another name for **geological cycle.**

rock dove *or* **pigeon** NOUN a common dove, *Columba livia,* from which domestic and feral pigeons are descended. It has a pale grey plumage with black-striped wings.

rocker ('rɒkə) NOUN 1 any of various devices that transmit or operate with a rocking motion. See also **rocker arm.** 2 another word for **rocking chair.** 3 either of two curved supports on the legs of a chair or other article of furniture on which it may rock. 4 a steel tool with a curved toothed cage, used to roughen the copper plate in engraving a mezzotint. 5 *Mining* another word for **cradle** (sense 9). 6 **a** an ice skate with a curved blade. **b** the curve itself. 7 *Skating* **a** a figure consisting of three interconnecting circles. **b** a half turn in which the skater turns through 180°, so facing about while continuing to move in the same direction. 8 a rock-music performer, fan, or song. 9 *Brit* an adherent of a youth movement rooted in the 1950s, characterized by motorcycle trappings. Compare **mod**[1]. 10 **off one's rocker.** *Slang* crazy; demented.

rocker arm NOUN a lever that rocks about a pivot, esp a lever in an internal-combustion engine that transmits the motion of a pushrod or cam to a valve.

rockery ('rɒkərɪ) NOUN, *plural* **-eries.** a garden constructed with rocks, esp one where alpine plants are grown. Also called: **rock garden.**

rocket[1] ('rɒkɪt) NOUN 1 a self-propelling device, esp a cylinder containing a mixture of solid explosives, used as a firework, distress signal, line carrier, etc. 2 **a** any vehicle propelled by a rocket engine, esp one used to carry a warhead, spacecraft, etc. **b** *(as modifier): rocket propulsion; rocket launcher.* 3 *Brit and NZ informal* a severe reprimand. ◆ VERB **-ets, -eting, -eted.** 4 *(tr)* to propel (a missile, spacecraft, etc.) by means of a rocket. 5 *(intr;* foll by *off, away,* etc.) to move off at high speed. 6 *(intr)* to rise rapidly: *he rocketed to the top.*
▷HISTORY C17: from Old French *roquette,* from Italian *rochetto* a little distaff, from *rocca* distaff, of Germanic origin

rocket[2] ('rɒkɪt) NOUN 1 Also called: **arugula.** a Mediterranean plant, *Eruca sativa,* having yellowish-white flowers and leaves used as a salad: family *Brassicaceae* (crucifers). 2 any of several plants of the related genus *Sisymbrium,* esp *S. irio* (**London rocket**), which grow on waste ground and have pale yellow flowers. 3 **yellow rocket.** any of several yellow-flowered plants of the related genus *Barbarea,* esp *B. vulgaris.* 4 **sea rocket.** any of several plants of the related genus *Cakile,* esp *C. maritima,* which grow along the seashores of Europe and North America and have mauve, pink, or white flowers. 5 **dame's rocket.** another name for **dame's violet.** ◆ See also **dyer's rocket, wall rocket.**
▷HISTORY C16: from French *roquette,* from Italian *rochetta,* from Latin *ērūca* a caterpillar, hairy plant

rocketeer (,rɒkɪ'tɪə) NOUN an engineer or scientist concerned with the design, operation, or launching of rockets.

rocket engine NOUN a reaction engine in which a fuel and oxidizer are burnt in a combustion chamber, the products of combustion expanding through a nozzle and producing thrust. Also called: **rocket motor.**

rocketry ('rɒkɪtrɪ) NOUN the science and technology of the design, operation, maintenance, and launching of rockets.

rocket science NOUN *Informal* an activity requiring considerable intelligence and ability (esp in the phrase **not exactly rocket science**).
▸**rocket scientist** NOUN

rockfish ('rɒk,fɪʃ) NOUN, *plural* **-fish** *or* **-fishes.** 1 any of various fishes that live among rocks, esp scorpaenid fishes of the genus *Sebastodes* and related genera, such as *S. caurinus* (**copper rockfish**) of North American Pacific coastal waters. 2 *Brit* any of several coarse fishes when used as food, esp the dogfish or wolffish. Formerly called: **rock salmon.**

rock flour NOUN very finely powdered rock, produced when rocks are ground together (as along the faces of a moving fault or during the motion of glaciers) and are thus chemically unweathered.

Rockford ('rɒkfəd) NOUN a city in N Illinois, on the Rock River. Pop.: 150 115 (2000).

rock garden NOUN a garden featuring rocks or rockeries.

Rockhampton (rɒk'hæmptən, -'hæmtən) NOUN a port in Australia, in E Queensland on the Fitzroy River. Pop.: 65 868 (1993).

rockhopper ('rɒk,hɒpə) NOUN 1 a small penguin, *Eudyptes crestatus*, of Antarctica, the Falkland Islands, and New Zealand, with a yellow crest on each side of its head. 2 *Austral informal* a fisherman who fishes from the rocks on the sea coast.

Rockies ('rɒkɪz) PLURAL NOUN another name for the **Rocky Mountains.**

rocking chair NOUN a chair set on curving supports so that the sitter may rock backwards and forwards.

rocking horse NOUN a toy horse mounted on a pair of rockers on which a child can rock to and fro in a seesaw movement.

rocking stone NOUN a boulder so delicately poised that it can be rocked. Also called: **logan, logan-stone.**

rockling ('rɒklɪŋ) NOUN, *plural* **-lings** *or* **-ling**. any small gadoid fish of the genera *Gaidropsarus, Ciliata*, etc. (formerly all included in *Motella*), which have an elongated body with barbels around the mouth and occur mainly in the North Atlantic Ocean.
▷HISTORY C17: from ROCK[1] + -LING[1]

rock lobster NOUN another name for the **spiny lobster.**

rock mechanics NOUN (*functioning as singular*) the study of the mechanical behaviour of rocks, esp their strength, elasticity, permeability, porosity, density, and reaction to stress.

rock melon NOUN *US, Austral, and NZ* another name for **cantaloupe.**

rock'n'roll NOUN a variant spelling of **rock and roll.**
▸**rock'n'roller** NOUN

rock oil NOUN another name for **petroleum.**

rockoon (rɒ'ku:n) NOUN a rocket carrying scientific equipment for studying the upper atmosphere, fired from a balloon at high altitude.
▷HISTORY C20: from ROCKET[1] + BALLOON

rock pigeon NOUN another name for **rock dove.**

rock plant NOUN any plant that grows on rocks or in rocky ground.

rock rabbit NOUN *South African* another name for the **dassie.**

rockrose ('rɒk,rəʊz) NOUN any of various cistaceous shrubs or herbaceous plants of the Eurasian genera *Helianthemum, Tuberaria*, and *Cistus*, cultivated for their yellow-white or reddish roselike flowers.

rock salmon NOUN *Brit* (formerly) any of several coarse fishes when used as food, esp the dogfish or wolffish: now known as **catfish** or **rockfish.**

rock salt NOUN another name for **halite.**

rockshaft ('rɒk,ʃɑ:ft) NOUN a shaft that rotates backwards and forwards rather than continuously, esp one used in the valve gear of a steam engine.

rock snake *or* **python** NOUN any large Australasian python of the genus *Liasis*.

rock steady NOUN a type of slow Jamaican dance music of the 1960s.

rock tripe NOUN *Canadian* any of various edible lichens, esp of the genus *Umbilicaria*, that grow on rocks and are used in the North as a survival food.

rock up VERB (*intr, adverb*) *South African* to arrive late or unannounced.

rockweed ('rɒk,wi:d) NOUN any of various seaweeds that grow on rocks exposed at low tide.

rock wool NOUN another name for **mineral wool.**

rocky[1] ('rɒkɪ) ADJECTIVE **rockier, rockiest.** 1 consisting of or abounding in rocks: *a rocky shore.* 2 hard or unyielding: *rocky determination.* 3 hard like rock: *rocky muscles.*
▸**'rockily** ADVERB ▸**'rockiness** NOUN

rocky[2] ('rɒkɪ) ADJECTIVE **rockier, rockiest.** 1 weak, shaky, or unstable. 2 *Informal* (of a person) dizzy; sickly; nauseated.
▸**'rockily** ADVERB ▸**'rockiness** NOUN

Rocky Mountain goat NOUN a sure-footed goat antelope, *Oreamnos americanus*, inhabiting the Rocky Mountains. It has thick white hair and black backward-curving horns.

Rocky Mountains *or* **Rockies** PLURAL NOUN the chief mountain system of W North America, extending from British Columbia to New Mexico: forms the Continental Divide. Highest peak: Mount Elbert, 4399 m (14 431 ft.). Mount McKinley (6194 m (20 320 ft.)), in the Alaska Range, is not strictly part of the Rocky Mountains.

Rocky Mountain spotted fever NOUN an acute rickettsial disease characterized by high fever, chills, pain in muscles and joints, skin rash, etc. It is caused by the bite of a tick infected with the microorganism *Rickettsia rickettsii.*

rococo (rə'kəʊkəʊ) NOUN (*often capital*) 1 a style of architecture and decoration that originated in France in the early 18th century, characterized by elaborate but graceful, light, ornamentation, often containing asymmetrical motifs. 2 an 18th-century style of music characterized by petite prettiness, a decline in the use of counterpoint, and extreme use of ornamentation. 3 any florid or excessively ornamental style. ◆ ADJECTIVE 4 denoting, being in, or relating to the rococo. 5 florid or excessively elaborate.
▷HISTORY C19: from French, from ROCAILLE, from *roc* ROCK[1]

rod (rɒd) NOUN 1 a slim cylinder of metal, wood, etc.; stick or shaft. 2 a switch or bundle of switches used to administer corporal punishment. 3 any of various staffs of insignia or office. 4 power, esp of a tyrannical kind: *a dictator's iron rod.* 5 a straight slender shoot, stem, or cane of a woody plant. 6 See **fishing rod.** 7 Also called: **pole, perch. a** a unit of length equal to 5½ yards. **b** a unit of square measure equal to 30¼ square yards. 8 a straight narrow board marked with the dimensions of a piece of joinery, as the spacing of steps on a staircase. 9 a metal shaft that transmits power in axial reciprocating motion: *piston rod, con(necting) rod.* Compare **shaft** (sense 5). 10 *Surveying* another name (esp US) for **staff[1]** (sense 8). 11 Also called: **retinal rod.** any of the elongated cylindrical cells in the retina of the eye, containing the visual purple (rhodopsin), which are sensitive to dim light but not to colour. Compare **cone** (sense 5). 12 any rod-shaped bacterium. 13 a slang word for **penis.** 14 *US* slang name for **pistol** (sense 1). 15 short for **hot rod.**
▷HISTORY Old English *rodd*; related to Old Norse *rudda* club, Norwegian *rudda, rydda* twig
▸**'rod,like** ADJECTIVE

rode[1] (rəʊd) VERB the past tense of **ride.**

rode[2] (rəʊd) NOUN *Nautical* an anchor rope or chain.
▷HISTORY C17: of unknown origin

rode[3] (rəʊd) VERB (*intr*) (of the male woodcock) to perform a display flight at dusk during the breeding season.
▷HISTORY C18: in the sense "(of birds) to fly homeward in the evening"; of uncertain origin
▸**'roding** NOUN

rodent ('rəʊdənt) NOUN **a** any of the relatively small placental mammals that constitute the order *Rodentia*, having constantly growing incisor teeth specialized for gnawing. The group includes porcupines, rats, mice, squirrels, marmots, etc. **b** (*as modifier*): *rodent characteristics.*
▷HISTORY C19: from Latin *rōdere* to gnaw, corrode
▸**'rodent-,like** ADJECTIVE

rodenticide (rəʊ'dɛntɪ,saɪd) NOUN a substance used for killing rats, mice, and other rodents.

rodent operative NOUN *Brit* a name sometimes used for an official (operative) employed by a local authority to destroy vermin.

rodeo ('rəʊdɪ,əʊ) NOUN, *plural* **-os.** *Chiefly US and Canadian* 1 a display of the skills of cowboys, including bareback riding, steer wrangling, etc. 2 the rounding up of cattle for branding, counting, inspection, etc. 3 an enclosure for cattle that have been rounded up.
▷HISTORY C19: from Spanish, from *rodear* to go around, from *rueda* a wheel, from Latin *rota*

Ródhos ('rɔðɔs) NOUN transliteration of the Modern Greek name for **Rhodes.**

rodomontade (,rɒdəmɒn'teɪd, -'tɑ:d) *Literary* ◆ NOUN 1 **a** boastful words or behaviour; bragging. **b** (*as modifier*): *rodomontade behaviour.* ◆ VERB 2 (*intr*) to boast, bluster, or rant.
▷HISTORY C17: from French, from Italian *rodomonte* a boaster, from *Rodomonte* the name of a braggart king of Algiers in epic poems by Boiardo and Ariosto

roe[1] (rəʊ) NOUN 1 Also called: **hard roe.** the ovary of a female fish filled with mature eggs. 2 Also called: **soft roe.** the testis of a male fish filled with mature sperm. 3 the ripe ovary of certain crustaceans, such as the lobster.
▷HISTORY C15: from Middle Dutch *roge*, from Old High German *roga*; related to Old Norse *hrogn*

roe[2] (rəʊ) NOUN, *plural* **roes** *or* **roe.** short for **roe deer.**
▷HISTORY Old English *rā(ha)*, related to Old High German *rēh(o)*, Old Norse *rā*

Roe (rəʊ) NOUN **Richard.** *Law* (formerly) the defendant in a fictitious action, Doe versus Roe, to test a point of law. See also **Doe** (sense 1).

roebuck ('rəʊ,bʌk) NOUN, *plural* **-bucks** *or* **-buck.** the male of the roe deer.

roe deer NOUN a small graceful deer, *Capreolus capreolus*, of woodlands of Europe and Asia. The antlers are small and the summer coat is reddish-brown.

roentgen *or* **röntgen** ('rɒntgən, -tjən, 'rɛnt-) NOUN a unit of dose of electromagnetic radiation equal to the dose that will produce in air a charge of 0.258×10^{-3} coulomb on all ions of one sign, when all the electrons of both signs liberated in a volume of air of mass one kilogram are stopped completely. Symbol: R *or* r.
▷HISTORY C20: named after the German physicist W.K. *Roentgen* or *Röntgen* (1845–1923), who discovered X-rays

roentgen equivalent man NOUN the dose of ionizing radiation that produces the same effect in man as one roentgen of x- or gamma-radiation. Abbreviation: **REM** *or* **rem.**

roentgenize, roentgenise, röntgenize, *or* **röntgenise** ('rɒntgə,naɪz, -tjə-, 'rɛnt-) VERB (*tr*) to bombard with X-rays.
▸**,roentgeni'zation** *or* **,roentgeni'sation** *or* **,röntgeni'zation** *or* **,röntgeni'sation** NOUN

roentgeno- *or* **röntgeno-** COMBINING FORM indicating X-rays: *roentgenogram.*
▷HISTORY from ROENTGEN

roentgenogram, röntgenogram ('rɒntgənə,græm, -tjə-, 'rɛnt-), **roentgenograph,** *or* **röntgenograph** NOUN *Chiefly US* an X-ray.

roentgenology *or* **röntgenology** (,rɒntgə'nɒlədʒɪ, -tjə-, ,rɛnt-) NOUN an obsolete name for **radiology.**
▸**roentgenological** *or* **röntgenological** (,rɒntgənə'lɒdʒɪkəl, -tjə-, ,rɛnt-) ADJECTIVE
▸**,roentgeno'logically** *or* **,röntgeno'logically** ADVERB
▸**,roentgen'ologist** *or* **,röntgen'ologist** NOUN

roentgenopaque *or* **röntgenopaque** (,rɒntgənəʊ'peɪk, -tjən-, ,rɛnt-) ADJECTIVE (of a material) not allowing the transmission of X-rays.

roentgenoscope *or* **röntgenoscope** ('rɒntgənəʊ,skəʊp, -tjə-, 'rɛnt-) NOUN a less common name for **fluoroscope.**
▸**roentgenoscopic** *or* **röntgenoscopic** (,rɒntgənəʊ'skɒpɪk, -tjə-,,rɛnt-) ADJECTIVE
▸**roentgenoscopy** *or* **röntgenoscopy** (,rɒntgə'nɒskəpɪ, -tjə-, ,rɛnt-) NOUN

roentgenotherapy *or* **röntgenotherapy** (,rɒntgənə'θɛrəpɪ, -tjə-, ,rɛnt-) NOUN the therapeutic use of X-rays.

roentgen ray NOUN a former name for **X-ray.**

Roeselare ('ru:səla:rə) NOUN the Flemish name for **Roulers.**

ROFL(OL) *Text messaging* ABBREVIATION FOR rolling on floor laughing (out loud).

rogallo (rə'gæləʊ) NOUN, *plural* **-los.** a flexible fabric delta wing, originally designed as a possible satellite retrieval vehicle but actually developed in the 1960s as the first successful hang-glider.
▷HISTORY C20: after Francis M. *Rogallo*, the US engineer who designed it

rogation (rəʊ'geɪʃən) NOUN (*usually plural*) *Christianity* a solemn supplication, esp in a form of ceremony prescribed by the Church.
▷HISTORY C14: from Latin *rogātiō*, from *rogāre* to ask, make supplication

Rogation Days PLURAL NOUN April 25 (the **Major Rogation**) and the Monday, Tuesday, and Wednesday before Ascension Day, observed by Christians as days of solemn supplication for the harvest and marked by processions, special prayers, and blessing of the crops.

rogatory ('rɒgətərɪ, -trɪ) ADJECTIVE (esp in legal

ontexts) seeking or authorized to seek information.
>HISTORY C19: from Medieval Latin *rogātōrius*, from atin *rogāre* to ask

oger ('rɒdʒə) INTERJECTION **1** (used in signalling, elecommunications, etc.) message received and nderstood. Compare **wilco.** **2** an expression of greement. ◆ VERB **3** *Slang* (of a man) to copulate with).
>HISTORY C20: from the name *Roger*, representing *R* or *received*

> **Language note** The verb sense of this word was formerly considered to be taboo, and it was labelled as such in previous editions of *Collins English Dictionary*. However, it has now become acceptable in speech, although some older or more conservative people may object to its use.

ognon *French* (rɔɲɔ̃) NOUN *Mountaineering* an solated rock outcrop on a glacier.
>HISTORY C20: literally: kidney

ogue (rəʊg) NOUN **1** a dishonest or unprincipled erson, esp a man; rascal; scoundrel. **2** *Often jocular* mischievous or wayward person, often a child; camp. **3** a crop plant which is inferior, diseased, r of a different, unwanted variety. **4** **a** any nferior or defective specimen. **b** (*as modifier*): *rogue eroin.* **5** *Archaic* a vagrant. **6** **a** an animal of icious character that has separated from the main erd and leads a solitary life. **b** (*as modifier*): *a rogue lephant.* ◆ VERB **7** **a** (*tr*) to rid (a field or crop) of lants that are inferior, diseased, or of an unwanted ariety. **b** to identify and remove such plants.
>HISTORY C16: of unknown origin; perhaps related o Latin *rogāre* to beg

oguery ('rəʊgərɪ) NOUN, *plural* **-gueries.** **1** ehaviour characteristic of a rogue. **2** a roguish or nischievous act.

ogues' gallery NOUN **1** a collection of hotographs of known criminals kept by the police or identification purposes. **2** a group of ndesirable people.

ogue state NOUN a state that conducts its policy n a dangerously unpredictable way, disregarding nternational law or diplomacy.

oguish ('rəʊgɪʃ) ADJECTIVE **1** dishonest or nprincipled. **2** mischievous or arch.
▸**'roguishly** ADVERB ▸**'roguishness** NOUN

Rohypnol (ˌrəʊ'hɪpnɒl) NOUN *Trademark* a brand of he drug flunitrazepam used as a hypnotic: its bility to render someone unconscious and lisoriented on awakening has been exploited by apists.

oil (rɔɪl) VERB **1** (*tr*) to make (a liquid) cloudy or urbid by stirring up dregs or sediment. **2** (*intr*) esp of a liquid) to be agitated or disturbed. **3** (*intr*) *Dialect* to be noisy or boisterous. **4** (*tr*) another vord (now rare) for **rile** (sense 1).
>HISTORY C16: of unknown origin; compare RILE

oily ('rɔɪlɪ) ADJECTIVE **roilier, roiliest.** *Rare* cloudy or nuddy.

oister ('rɔɪstə) VERB (*intr*) **1** to engage in noisy nerrymaking; revel. **2** to brag, bluster, or swagger.
>HISTORY C16: from Old French *rustre* lout, from *uste* uncouth, from Latin *rusticus* rural; see RUSTIC
▸**'roisterer** NOUN ▸**'roisterous** ADJECTIVE ▸**'roisterously** ADVERB

ojak ('rodʒak) NOUN (in Malaysia) a salad dish erved in chilli sauce.
>HISTORY from Malay

ROK INTERNATIONAL CAR REGISTRATION FOR South Korea Republic of Korea).

ole *or* **rôle** (rəʊl) NOUN **1** a part or character in a lay, film, etc., to be played by an actor or actress. **2** *Psychol* the part played by a person in a articular social setting, influenced by his xpectation of what is appropriate. **3** usual or ustomary function: *what is his role in the rganization?*
>HISTORY C17: from French *rôle* ROLL, an actor's cript

ole model NOUN a person regarded by others, esp ounger people, as a good example to follow.

ole-playing NOUN *Psychol* activity in which a erson imitates, consciously or unconsciously, a role uncharacteristic of himself. See also **psychodrama.**

role-playing game NOUN a game in which players assume the roles of fantasy characters.

roll (rəʊl) VERB **1** to move or cause to move along by turning over and over. **2** to move or cause to move along on wheels or rollers. **3** to flow or cause to flow onwards in an undulating movement: *billows of smoke rolled over the ground.* **4** (*intr*) to extend in undulations: *the hills roll down to the sea.* **5** (*intr*; usually foll by *around*) to move or occur in cycles. **6** (*intr*) (of a planet, the moon, etc.) to revolve in an orbit. **7** (*intr*; foll by *on, by,* etc.) to pass or elapse: *the years roll by.* **8** to rotate or cause to rotate wholly or partially: *to roll one's eyes.* **9** to curl, cause to curl, or admit of being curled, so as to form a ball, tube, or cylinder; coil. **10** to make or form by shaping into a ball, tube, or cylinder: *to roll a cigarette.* **11** (often foll by *out*) to spread or cause to spread out flat or smooth under or as if under a roller: *to roll the lawn; to roll pastry.* **12** to emit, produce, or utter with a deep prolonged reverberating sound: *the thunder rolled continuously.* **13** to trill or cause to be trilled: *to roll one's r's.* **14** (*intr*) (of a vessel, aircraft, rocket, etc.) to turn from side to side around the longitudinal axis. Compare **pitch**[1] (sense 11), **yaw** (sense 1). **15** to cause (an aircraft) to execute a roll or (of an aircraft) to execute a roll (sense 40). **16** (*intr*) to walk with a swaying gait, as when drunk; sway. **17** (*intr*; often foll by *over*) (of an animal, esp a dog) to lie on its back and wriggle while kicking its legs in the air, without moving along. **18** (*intr*) to wallow or envelop oneself (in). **19** (*tr*) to apply ink to (type, etc.) with a roller or rollers. **20** to throw (dice). **21** (*intr*) to operate or begin to operate: *the presses rolled.* **22** (*intr*) *Informal* to make progress; move or go ahead: *let the good times roll.* **23** (*tr*) *Informal, chiefly US and NZ* to rob (a helpless person, such as someone drunk or asleep). **24** (*tr*) *Slang* to have sexual intercourse or foreplay with (a person). **25** **start** *or* **set the ball rolling.** to open or initiate (an action, discussion, movement, etc.). ◆ NOUN **26** the act or an instance of rolling. **27** anything rolled up in a cylindrical form: *a roll of newspaper.* **28** an official list or register, esp of names: *an electoral roll.* **29** a rounded mass: *rolls of flesh.* **30** a strip of material, esp leather, fitted with pockets or pouches for holding tools, toilet articles, needles and thread, etc. **31** a cylinder used to flatten something; roller. **32** a small loaf of bread for one person: eaten plain, with butter, or as a light meal when filled with meat, cheese, etc. **33** a flat pastry or cake rolled up with a meat (**sausage roll**), jam (**jam roll**), or other filling. See also **swiss roll.** **34** a swell, ripple, or undulation on a surface: *the roll of the hills.* **35** a swaying, rolling, or unsteady movement or gait. **36** a deep prolonged reverberating sound: *the roll of thunder.* **37** a rhythmic cadenced flow of words. **38** a trilling sound; trill. **39** a very rapid beating of the sticks on a drum. **40** a flight manoeuvre in which an aircraft makes one complete rotation about its longitudinal axis without loss of height or change in direction. **41** the angular displacement of a vessel, rocket, missile, etc., caused by rolling. **42** a throw of dice. **43** a bookbinder's tool having a brass wheel, used to impress a line or repeated pattern on the cover of a book. **44** *Slang* an act of sexual intercourse or petting (esp in the phrase **a roll in the hay**). **45** *US slang* an amount of money, esp a wad of paper money. **46** **on a roll.** *Slang* experiencing continued good luck or success. **47** **strike off the roll(s).** **a** to expel from membership. **b** to debar (a solicitor) from practising, usually because of dishonesty. ◆ See also **roll in, roll off, roll on, roll out, roll over, roll up.**
▷HISTORY C14 *rollen*, from Old French *roler*, from Latin *rotulus* a little wheel, from *rota* a wheel

rollaway ('rəʊləˌweɪ) NOUN (*modifier*) mounted on rollers so as to be easily moved, esp to be stored away after use.

rollbar ('rəʊlˌbɑː) NOUN a bar that reinforces the frame of a car, esp one used for racing, rallying, etc., to protect the driver if the car should turn over.

roll call NOUN **1** the reading aloud of an official list of names, those present responding when their names are read out. **2** the time or signal for such a reading.

rolled gold NOUN a metal, such as brass, coated with a thin layer of gold, usually of above 9 carat purity. It is used in inexpensive jewellery. Also called (US): **filled gold.**

rolled paperwork NOUN a form of decoration on small objects, such as boxes, in which a design is made up of tiny rolls of paper cut crossways and laid together: popular in the 18th and 19th centuries. Also called: **curled paperwork, paper filigree.**

rolled-steel joist NOUN a steel beam, esp one with a cross section in the form of a letter *H* or *I*. Abbreviation: **RSJ.**

roller ('rəʊlə) NOUN **1** a cylinder having an absorbent surface and a handle, used for spreading paint. **2** Also called: **garden roller.** a heavy cast-iron cylinder or pair of cylinders on an axle to which a handle is attached; used for flattening lawns. **3** a long heavy wave of the sea, advancing towards the shore. Compare **breaker**[1] (sense 2). **4** a hardened cylinder of precision-ground steel that forms one of the rolling components of a roller bearing or of a linked driving chain. **5** a cylinder fitted on pivots, used to enable heavy objects to be easily moved; castor. **6** *Printing* a cylinder, usually of hard rubber, used to ink a forme or plate before impression. **7** a cylindrical tube or barrel onto which material is rolled for transport or storage. **8** any of various other cylindrical devices that rotate about a cylinder, used for any of various purposes. **9** a small cylinder, esp one that is heated, onto which a woman's hair may be rolled to make it curl. **10** *Med* a bandage consisting of a long strip of muslin or cheesecloth rolled tightly into a cylindrical form before application. **11** a band fastened around a horse's belly to keep a blanket in position. **12** any of various Old World birds of the family *Coraciidae*, such as *Coracias garrulus* (**European roller**), that have a blue, green, and brown plumage, a slightly hooked bill, and an erratic flight: order *Coraciiformes* (kingfishers, etc.). **13** (*often capital*) a variety of tumbler pigeon that performs characteristic backward somersaults in flight. **14** a breed of canary that has a soft trilling song in which the notes are run together. **15** a person or thing that rolls. **16** *Austral* a man who rolls and trims fleeces after shearing. **17** short for **roadroller** or **steamroller.** **18** short for **roller caption.**

rollerball ('rəʊləˌbɔːl) NOUN a pen having a small moving nylon, plastic, or metal ball as a writing point.

roller bearing NOUN a bearing in which a shaft runs on a number of hardened-steel rollers held within a cage.

Rollerblade ('rəʊləˌbleɪd) NOUN *Trademark* a type of roller skate in which the wheels are set in a single straight line under the boot.

roller caption NOUN *Television* caption lettering that moves progressively up or across the picture, as for showing the credits at the end of a programme. Often shortened to: **roller.**

roller chain NOUN *Engineering* a chain for transmitting power in which each link consists of two free-moving rollers held in position by pins connected to sideplates.

roller coaster NOUN another term for **big dipper.**

roller derby NOUN a race on roller skates, esp one involving aggressive tactics.

roller skate NOUN **1** a device having clamps and straps for fastening to a boot or shoe and four small wheels that enable the wearer to glide swiftly over a floor or other surface. ◆ VERB **roller-skate.** **2** (*intr*) to move on roller skates.
▸**roller skater** NOUN

roller towel NOUN **1** a towel with the two ends sewn together, hung on a roller. **2** a continuous towel wound inside a roller enabling a clean section to be pulled out when required.

roll film NOUN a length of photographic film backed with opaque paper and rolled on a spool.

rollick ('rɒlɪk) VERB **1** (*intr*) to behave in a carefree, frolicsome, or boisterous manner. ◆ NOUN **2** a boisterous or carefree escapade or event.
▷HISTORY C19: of Scottish dialect origin, probably from ROMP + FROLIC

rollicking[1] ('rɒlɪkɪŋ) ADJECTIVE boisterously carefree and swaggering.

rollicking² ('rɒlɪkɪŋ) NOUN *Brit informal* a very severe telling-off; dressing-down.
▷HISTORY C20: from ROLLICK (vb) (in former sense: to be angry, make a fuss); perhaps influenced by BOLLOCKING

roll in VERB (*mainly intr*) [1] (*adverb*) to arrive in abundance or in large numbers. [2] (*adverb*) *Informal* to arrive at one's destination. [3] (*preposition*) *Informal* to abound or luxuriate in (wealth, money, etc.). [4] (*adverb; also tr*) *Hockey* to return (the ball) to play after it has crossed the touchline.

rolling ('rəʊlɪŋ) ADJECTIVE [1] having gentle rising and falling slopes; undulating: *rolling country.* [2] progressing or spreading by stages or by occurrences in different places in succession, with continued or increasing effectiveness: *three weeks of rolling strikes disrupted schools.* [3] subject to regular review and updating: *a rolling plan for overseas development.* [4] deeply resounding; reverberating: *rolling thunder.* [5] *Slang* extremely rich. [6] that may be turned up or down: *a rolling hat brim.* ◆ ADVERB [7] *Slang* swaying or staggering (in the phrase **rolling drunk**).

rolling bearing NOUN any bearing in which the antifriction action depends on the rolling action of balls or rollers.

rolling friction NOUN *Engineering* frictional resistance to rotation or energy losses in rolling bearings. Compare **sliding friction.**

rolling hitch NOUN a knot used for fastening one rope to another or to a spar, being easily released but jamming when the rope is pulled.

rolling launch NOUN *Marketing* the process of introducing a new product into a market gradually. Compare **roll out** (sense 3).

rolling mill NOUN [1] a mill or factory where ingots of heated metal are passed between rollers to produce sheets or bars of a required cross section and form. [2] a machine having rollers that may be shaped to reduce ingots, etc., to a required cross section and form.

rolling pin NOUN a cylinder with handles at both ends, often of wood, used for rolling dough, pastry, etc., out flat.

rolling stock NOUN the wheeled vehicles collectively used on a railway, including the locomotives, passenger coaches, freight wagons, guard's vans, etc.

rolling stone NOUN a restless or wandering person.

rollmop ('rəʊl,mɒp) NOUN a herring fillet rolled, usually around onion slices, and pickled in spiced vinegar.
▷HISTORY C20: from German *Rollmops*, from *rollen* to ROLL + *Mops* pug dog

rollneck ('rəʊl,nɛk) ADJECTIVE [1] (of a garment) having a high neck that may be rolled over. ◆ NOUN [2] a rollneck sweater or other garment.

roll off VERB (*intr, adverb*) *Electronics* to exhibit gradually reduced response at the upper or lower ends of the working frequency range.

roll of honour NOUN a list of those who have died in war for their country, esp those from a particular locality or organization.

roll on VERB [1] *Brit* used to express the wish that an eagerly anticipated event or date will come quickly: *roll on Saturday.* ◆ ADJECTIVE **roll-on.** [2] (of a deodorant, lip gloss, etc.) dispensed by means of a revolving ball fitted into the neck of the container. ◆ NOUN **roll-on.** [3] a woman's foundation garment, made of elasticized material and having no fastenings. [4] a liquid cosmetic, esp a deodorant, packed in a container having an applicator consisting of a revolving ball.

roll-on/roll-off ADJECTIVE denoting a cargo ship or ferry designed so that vehicles can be driven straight on and straight off.

roll out VERB (*tr, adverb*) [1] to cause (pastry) to become flatter and thinner by pressure with a rolling pin. [2] to show (a new type of aircraft) to the public for the first time. [3] to launch (a new film, product, etc.) in a series of stages over an area, each stage involving an increased number of outlets. ◆ NOUN **roll-out.** [4] a presentation to the public of a new aircraft, product, etc.; a launch.

roll over VERB (*adverb*) [1] (*intr*) to overturn. [2] See **roll** (sense 17). [3] *Slang* to surrender. [4] (*tr*) to allow (a loan, prize, etc.) to continue in force for a further period. ◆ NOUN **rollover.** [5] **a** an instance of such continuance of a loan, prize, etc. **b** (*as modifier*): *a rollover jackpot.*

Rolls-Royce (,rəʊlz'rɔɪs) NOUN *Trademark* [1] Also called (informal): **Rolls.** a make of very high-quality, luxurious, and prestigious British car. The Rolls-Royce company is no longer British-owned. [2] anything considered to be the very best of its kind.
▷HISTORY named after its designers, Charles Stewart *Rolls* (1877–1910), English pioneer motorist and aviator, and Sir (Frederick) Henry *Royce* (1863–1933), English engineer, who founded the Rolls-Royce Company (1906)

roll-top desk NOUN a desk having a slatted wooden panel that can be pulled down over the writing surface when not in use. Also called: **roll-top.**

roll up VERB (*adverb*) [1] to form or cause to form a cylindrical shape. [2] (*tr*) to wrap (an object) round on itself or on an axis: *to roll up a map.* [3] (*intr*) *Informal* to arrive, esp in a vehicle. ◆ NOUN **roll-up.** [4] (*intr*) to proceed or develop. [5] *Brit informal* a cigarette made by hand from loose tobacco and cigarette paper. [6] *Austral* (in the 19th century) a mass meeting of workers on an issue of common concern. [7] *Austral archaic* the attendance at any fixture: *they had a good roll-up.*

rollway ('rəʊl,weɪ) NOUN [1] an incline down which logs are rolled for transportation. [2] a series of rollers laid parallel to each other, over which heavy loads may be moved.

roll-your-own NOUN *Informal* a hand-rolled cigarette.

Rolodex ('rəʊlə,dɛks) NOUN *Trademark Chiefly US* a small file for holding names, addresses, and telephone numbers, consisting of cards attached horizontally to a rotatable central cylinder.

roly-poly ('rəʊlɪ'pəʊlɪ) ADJECTIVE [1] plump, buxom, or rotund. ◆ NOUN, *plural* **-lies.** [2] *Brit* a strip of suet pastry spread with jam, fruit, or a savoury mixture, rolled up, and baked or steamed as a pudding. [3] a plump, buxom, or rotund person. [4] *Austral* an informal name for **tumbleweed.**
▷HISTORY C17: apparently by reduplication from *roly*, from ROLL

Rom (rɒm) NOUN, *plural* **Roma** ('rɒmə). a male Gypsy.
▷HISTORY Romany

ROM (rɒm) NOUN *Computing* ACRONYM FOR read only memory: a storage device that holds data permanently and cannot in normal circumstances be altered by the programmer.

rom. *Printing* ABBREVIATION FOR roman (type).

Rom. ABBREVIATION FOR: [1] Roman. [2] Romance (languages). [3] *Bible* Romans. [4] Romania(n).

Roma¹ ('ro:ma) NOUN the Italian name for **Rome.**

Roma² ('rəʊmə) NOUN [1] **a** another name for **Gypsy.** **b** (*as modifier*): *Roma gypsy musicians.* [2] another name for **Romany.**

Romagna (*Italian* ro'maɲɲa) NOUN an area of N Italy: part of the Papal States up to 1860.

Romaic (rəʊ'meɪɪk) *Obsolete* ◆ NOUN [1] the modern Greek vernacular, esp Demotic. ◆ ADJECTIVE [2] of or relating to Greek, esp Demotic.
▷HISTORY C19: from Greek *Rhōmaikos* Roman, with reference to the Eastern Roman Empire

romaine (rəʊ'meɪn) NOUN the usual US and Canadian name for **cos¹** (lettuce).
▷HISTORY C20: from French, from *romain* Roman

romaji ('rəʊmɑ:dʒɪ) NOUN the Roman alphabet as used to write Japanese.

roman¹ ('rəʊmən) ADJECTIVE [1] of, relating to, or denoting a vertical style of printing type: the usual form of type for most printed matter. Compare **italic.** ◆ NOUN [2] roman type or print.
▷HISTORY C16: so called because the style of letters is that used in ancient Roman inscriptions

roman² (*French* rɔmɑ̃) NOUN a metrical narrative in medieval French literature derived from the *chansons de geste.*

Roman ('rəʊmən) ADJECTIVE [1] of or relating to Rome or its inhabitants in ancient or modern times. [2] of or relating to Roman Catholicism or the Roman Catholic Church. [3] denoting, relating to, or having the style of architecture used by the ancient Romans, characterized by large-scale masonry domes, barrel vaults, and semicircular arches. ◆ NOUN [4] a citizen or inhabitant of ancient or modern Rome. [5] *Informal* short for **Roman Catholic.**

roman à clef *French* (rɔmɑ̃ a kle) NOUN, *plural* ***romans à clef*** (rɔmɑ̃ a kle). a novel in which real people are depicted under fictitious names.
▷HISTORY literally: novel with a key

Roman alphabet NOUN the alphabet evolved by the ancient Romans for the writing of Latin, based upon an Etruscan form derived from the Greeks and ultimately from the Phoenicians. The alphabet serves for writing most of the languages of W Europe and many other languages.

Roman arch NOUN another name for **Norman arch.**

Roman blind NOUN a window blind consisting of a length of material which, when drawn up, gathers into horizontal folds from the bottom.

Roman calendar NOUN the lunar calendar of ancient Rome, replaced in 45 B.C. by the Julian calendar. It originally consisted of 10 months, with a special month intercalated between Feb. 23 and 24.

Roman candle NOUN a firework that produces a continuous shower of sparks punctuated by coloured balls of fire.
▷HISTORY C19: so called from its having been originated in Italy

Roman Catholic ADJECTIVE [1] of or relating to the Roman Catholic Church. ◆ NOUN [2] a member of this Church. ◆ Often shortened to: **Catholic.**

Roman Catholic Church NOUN the Christian Church over which the pope presides, with administrative headquarters in the Vatican. Also called: **Catholic Church, Church of Rome.**

Roman Catholicism NOUN the beliefs, practices and system of government of the Roman Catholic Church.

romance NOUN (rə'mæns, 'rəʊmæns) [1] a love affair, esp an intense and happy but short-lived affair involving young people. [2] love, esp romantic love idealized for its purity or beauty. [3] a spirit of or inclination for adventure, excitement, or mystery. [4] a mysterious, exciting, sentimental, or nostalgic quality, esp one associated with a place. [5] a narrative in verse or prose, written in a vernacular language in the Middle Ages, dealing with strange and exciting adventures of chivalrous heroes. [6] any similar narrative work dealing with events and characters remote from ordinary life. [7] the literary genre represented by works of these kinds. [8] (in Spanish literature) a short narrative poem, usually an epic or historical ballad. [9] a story, novel, film, etc., dealing with love, usually in an idealized or sentimental way. [10] an extravagant, absurd, or fantastic account or explanation. [11] a lyrical song or short instrumental composition having a simple melody. ◆ VERB (rə'mæns) [12] (*intr*) to tell, invent, or write extravagant or romantic fictions. [13] (*intr*) to tell extravagant or improbable lies. [14] (*intr*) to have romantic thoughts. [15] (*intr*) (of a couple) to indulge in romantic behaviour. [16] (*tr*) to be romantically involved with.
▷HISTORY C13: *romauns*, from Old French *romans*, ultimately from Latin *Rōmānicus* Roman
▸**ro'mancer** NOUN

Romance (rə'mæns, 'rəʊmæns) ADJECTIVE [1] denoting, relating to, or belonging to the languages derived from Latin, including Italian, Spanish, Portuguese, French, and Romanian. [2] denoting a word borrowed from a Romance language: *there are many Romance words in English.* ◆ NOUN [3] this group of languages; the living languages that belong to the Italic branch of the Indo-European family.

Roman collar NOUN another name for **clerical collar.**

Roman Empire NOUN [1] the territories ruled by ancient Rome. At its height under Trajan, the Roman Empire included W and S Europe, Africa north of the Sahara, and SW Asia. In 395 A.D. it was divided by Theodosius into the **Eastern Roman Empire** whose capital was Byzantium and which lasted until 1453, and the **Western Roman Empire** which lasted until the sack of Rome in 476. [2] the government of Rome and its dominions by the emperors from 27 B.C. [3] the Byzantine Empire. [4] the Holy Roman Empire.

Romanes (ˈrɒmənɪs) NOUN Romany; the language of the Gypsies.
▷HISTORY from Romany

Romanesque (ˌrəʊməˈnɛsk) ADJECTIVE 1 denoting, relating to, or having the style of architecture used in W and S Europe from the 9th to the 12th century, characterized by the rounded arch, the groin vault, massive-masonry wall construction, and a restrained use of mouldings. See also **Norman** (sense 6). 2 denoting or relating to a corresponding style in painting, sculpture, etc.
▷HISTORY C18: see ROMAN, -ESQUE

roman-fleuve *French* (rɔmɑ̃flœv) NOUN, *plural* ***romans-fleuves*** (rɔmɑ̃flœv). a novel or series of novels dealing with a family or other group over several generations.
▷HISTORY literally: stream novel

Roman holiday NOUN entertainment or pleasure that depends on the suffering of others.
▷HISTORY C19: from Byron's poem *Childe Harold* (IV, 141)

Romani (ˈrɒmənɪ, ˈrəʊ-) NOUN, *plural* **-nis.** a variant spelling of **Romany.**

Romania (rəʊˈmeɪnɪə), **Rumania,** *or* **Roumania** NOUN a republic in SE Europe, bordering on the Black Sea: united in 1861; became independent in 1878; Communist government set up in 1945; became a socialist republic in 1965; a more democratic regime was installed after a revolution in 1989. It consists chiefly of a great central arc of the Carpathian Mountains and Transylvanian Alps, with the plains of Walachia, Moldavia, and Dobriya on the south and east and the Pannonian Plain in the west. Official language: Romanian. Religion: Romanian Orthodox (Christian) majority. Currency: leu. Capital: Bucharest. Pop.: 22 413 000 (2001 est.). Area: 237 500 sq. km (91 699 sq. miles).

Romanian (rəʊˈmeɪnɪən), **Rumanian,** *or* **Roumanian** NOUN 1 the official language of Romania, belonging to the Romance group of the Indo-European family. 2 a native, citizen, or inhabitant of Romania. ◆ ADJECTIVE 3 relating to, denoting, or characteristic of Romania, its people, or their language.

Romanic (rəʊˈmænɪk) ADJECTIVE another word for **Roman** or **Romance.**

romanicite (rəʊˈmænɪˌsaɪt) NOUN another name for **psilomelane.**

Romanism (ˈrəʊməˌnɪzəm) NOUN Roman Catholicism, esp when regarded as excessively or superstitiously ritualistic.

Romanist (ˈrəʊmənɪst) NOUN 1 a member of a Church, esp the Church of England, who favours or is influenced by Roman Catholicism. 2 a Roman Catholic. 3 a student of classical Roman civilization or law.
▸ˌ**Romanˈistic** ADJECTIVE

Romanize *or* **Romanise** (ˈrəʊməˌnaɪz) VERB 1 (*tr*) to impart a Roman Catholic character to (a ceremony, practice, etc.). 2 (*intr*) to be converted to Roman Catholicism. 3 (*tr*) to transcribe or transliterate (a language) into the Roman alphabet. 4 to make Roman in character, allegiance, style, etc.
▸ˌ**Romaniˈzation** *or* ˌ**Romaniˈsation** NOUN

Roman law NOUN 1 the system of jurisprudence of ancient Rome, codified under Justinian and forming the basis of many modern legal systems. 2 another term for **civil law.**

Roman mile NOUN a unit of length used in ancient Rome, equivalent to about 1620 yards or 1481 metres.

Roman nose NOUN a nose having a high prominent bridge.

Roman numerals PLURAL NOUN the letters used by the Romans for the representation of cardinal numbers, still used occasionally today. The integers are represented by the following letters: I (= 1), V (= 5), X (= 10), L (= 50), C (= 100), D (= 500), and M (= 1000). If a numeral is followed by another numeral of lower denomination, the two are added together; if it is preceded by one of lower denomination, the smaller numeral is subtracted from the greater. Thus VI = 6 (V + I), but IV = 4 (V – I). Other examples are XC (= 90), CL (= 150), XXV (= 25), XLIV (= 44). Multiples of a thousand are indicated by a superior bar: thus, $\bar{V}$ = 5000, $\bar{X}$ = 10 000, $\overline{XD}$ = 490 000, etc.

Romano (rəʊˈmɑːnəʊ) NOUN a hard light-coloured sharp-tasting cheese, similar to Parmesan.

Roman pace NOUN an ancient Roman measure of length, equal to 5 Roman feet or about 58 inches (147 centimetres). See also **geometric pace.**

Romans (ˈrəʊmənz) NOUN (*functioning as singular*) a book of the New Testament (in full **The Epistle of Paul the Apostle to the Romans**), containing one of the fullest expositions of the doctrines of Saint Paul, written in 58 A.D.

Romansch *or* **Romansh** (rəʊˈmænʃ) NOUN a group of Rhaetian dialects spoken in the Swiss canton of Graubünden; an official language of Switzerland since 1938. See also **Friulian, Ladin.**
▷HISTORY C17: from Romansch, literally: Romance language, from Latin *Rōmānicus* ROMANIC

Roman snail NOUN a large edible European snail, *Helix pomatia*, the usual *escargot* of menus, erroneously thought to have been introduced to northern Europe by the Romans.

romantic (rəʊˈmæntɪk) ADJECTIVE 1 of, relating to, imbued with, or characterized by romance. 2 evoking or given to thoughts and feelings of love, esp idealized or sentimental love: *a romantic woman; a romantic setting.* 3 impractical, visionary, or idealistic: *a romantic scheme.* 4 *Often euphemistic* imaginary or fictitious: *a romantic account of one's war service.* 5 (*often capital*) of or relating to a movement in European art, music, and literature in the late 18th and early 19th centuries, characterized by an emphasis on feeling and content rather than order and form, on the sublime, supernatural, and exotic, and the free expression of the passions and individuality. ◆ NOUN 6 a person who is romantic, as in being idealistic, amorous, or soulful. 7 a person whose tastes in art, literature, etc., lie mainly in romanticism; romanticist. 8 (*often capital*) a poet, composer, etc., of the romantic period or whose main inspiration or interest is romanticism.
▷HISTORY C17: from French *romantique*, from obsolete *romant* story, romance, from Old French *romans* ROMANCE
▸**roˈmantically** ADVERB

romanticism (rəʊˈmæntɪˌsɪzəm) NOUN 1 (*often capital*) the theory, practice, and style of the romantic art, music, and literature of the late 18th and early 19th centuries, usually opposed to classicism. 2 romantic attitudes, ideals, or qualities.
▸**roˈmanticist** NOUN

romanticize *or* **romanticise** (rəʊˈmæntɪˌsaɪz) VERB 1 (*intr*) to think or act in a romantic way. 2 (*tr*) to interpret according to romantic precepts. 3 to make or become romantic, as in style.
▸**roˌmanticiˈzation** *or* **roˌmanticiˈsation** NOUN

Romany *or* **Romani** (ˈrɒmənɪ, ˈrəʊ-) NOUN 1 (*plural* **-nies** *or* **-nis**) **a** another name for a **Gypsy. b** (*as modifier*): *Romany customs.* 2 the language of the Gypsies, belonging to the Indic branch of the Indo-European family, but incorporating extensive borrowings from local European languages. Most of its 250 000 speakers are bilingual. It is extinct in Britain.
▷HISTORY C19: from Romany *romani* (adj) Gypsy, ultimately from Sanskrit *domba* man of a low caste of musicians, of Dravidian origin

romanza (rəˈmænzə) NOUN *Music* a short instrumental piece of song-like character.
▷HISTORY from Italian

romaunt (rəˈmɔːnt) NOUN *Archaic* a verse romance.
▷HISTORY C16: from Old French; see ROMANTIC

Rom. Cath. ABBREVIATION FOR Roman Catholic.

romcom (ˈrɒmˌkɒm) NOUN *Informal* a film or television comedy based around the romantic relationships of the characters.
▷HISTORY C20: ROM(ANTIC) + COM(EDY)

Rome (rəʊm) NOUN 1 the capital of Italy, on the River Tiber: includes the independent state of the Vatican City; traditionally founded by Romulus on the Palatine Hill in 753 B.C., later spreading to six other hills east of the Tiber; capital of the Roman Empire; a great cultural and artistic centre, esp during the Renaissance. Pop.: 2 643 581 (2000 est.). Italian name: **Roma.** 2 the Roman Empire. 3 the Roman Catholic Church or Roman Catholicism.

Romeo (ˈrəʊmɪəʊ) NOUN 1 (*plural* **-os**) an ardent male lover. 2 *Communications* a code word for the letter *r.*
▷HISTORY from the hero of Shakespeare's *Romeo and Juliet* (1594)

Romish (ˈrəʊmɪʃ) ADJECTIVE *Usually derogatory* of, relating to, or resembling Roman Catholic beliefs or practices.

Romney Marsh (ˈrɒmnɪ, ˈrʌm-) NOUN 1 a marshy area of SE England, on the Kent coast between New Romney and Rye: includes Dungeness. 2 a type of hardy British sheep from this area, with long wool, bred for mutton.

romp (rɒmp) VERB (*intr*) 1 to play or run about wildly, boisterously, or joyfully. 2 **romp home** (*or* **in**). to win a race easily. ◆ NOUN 3 a noisy or boisterous game or prank. 4 an instance of sexual activity between two or more people that is entered into light-heartedly and without emotional commitment: *naked sex romps.* 5 Also called: **romper.** *Archaic* a playful or boisterous child, esp a girl. 6 an easy victory.
▷HISTORY C18: probably variant of RAMP, from Old French *ramper* to crawl, climb
▸ˈ**rompish** ADJECTIVE

rompers (ˈrɒmpəz) PLURAL NOUN 1 a one-piece baby garment consisting of trousers and a bib with straps. 2 *NZ* a type of costume worn by schoolgirls for games and gymnastics.

romp through VERB (*intr, preposition*) *Informal* to progress quickly and easily through something: *he romped through the work.*

Romulus (ˈrɒmjʊləs) NOUN *Roman myth* the founder of Rome, suckled with his twin brother Remus by a she-wolf after they were abandoned in infancy. Their parents were Rhea Silvia and Mars. Romulus later killed Remus in an argument over the new city.

Roncesvalles (ˈrɒnsəˌvælz; *Spanish* rɔnθezˈβaʎes) NOUN a village in N Spain, in the Pyrenees: a nearby pass was the scene of the defeat of Charlemagne and death of Roland in 778. French name: **Roncevaux** (rɔ̃svo).

rondavel (ˈrɒndɑːvəl) NOUN *South African* a circular often thatched building with a conical roof.
▷HISTORY of uncertain origin

rondeau (ˈrɒndəʊ) NOUN, *plural* **-deaux** (-dəʊ, -dəʊz). a poem consisting of 13 or 10 lines with two rhymes and having the opening words of the first line used as an unrhymed refrain. See also **roundel.**
▷HISTORY C16: from Old French, from *rondel* a little round, from *rond* ROUND

rondel (ˈrɒndᵊl) NOUN 1 a rondeau consisting of three stanzas of 13 or 14 lines with a two-line refrain appearing twice or three times. 2 a figure in Scottish country dancing by means of which couples change position in the set.
▷HISTORY C14: from Old French, literally: a little circle, from *rond* ROUND

rondelet (ˈrɒndəˌlɛt) NOUN a brief rondeau, having five or seven lines and a refrain taken from the first line.
▷HISTORY C16: from Old French: a little RONDEL

rondo (ˈrɒndəʊ) NOUN, *plural* **-dos.** a piece of music in which a refrain is repeated between episodes: often constitutes the form of the last movement of a sonata or concerto.
▷HISTORY C18: from Italian, from French RONDEAU

Rondônia (*Portuguese* rõˈdonja) NOUN a state of W Brazil: consists chiefly of tropical rainforest; a centre of the Amazon rubber boom until about 1912. Capital: Pôrto Velho. Pop.: 1 377 792 (2000). Area: 243 043 sq. km (93 839 sq. miles). Former name (until 1956): **Guaporé.**

rondure (ˈrɒndjʊə) NOUN *Literary* 1 a circle or curve. 2 roundness or curvature.
▷HISTORY C17: from French *rondeur*, from *rond* ROUND

rone (rəʊn; *Scot* ron) *or* **ronepipe** (ˈrəʊnˌpaɪp; *Scot* ˈronˌpəɪp) NOUN *Scot* a drainpipe or gutter for carrying rainwater from a roof.
▷HISTORY C19: origin unknown

Roneo (ˈrəʊnɪəʊ) *Trademark* ◆ VERB **-neos, -neoing, -neoed.** (*tr*) 1 to duplicate (a document) from a stencil. ◆ NOUN, *plural* **-neos.** 2 a document reproduced by this process.

ronggeng ('rɒŋgɛŋ) NOUN a Malay traditional dance.
▷HISTORY Malay

ronin ('rəʊnɪn) NOUN *Japanese history* 1 a lordless samurai, esp one whose feudal lord had been deprived of his territory. 2 such samurai collectively.
▷HISTORY Japanese

röntgen ('rɒntgən, -tjən, 'rɛnt-) NOUN a variant spelling of **roentgen**.

ronz (rɒnz) ABBREVIATION FOR *NZ* rest of New Zealand (in relation to Auckland).
▸ **'ronzer** NOUN

roo (ru:) NOUN *Austral informal* a kangaroo.

rood (ru:d) NOUN 1 **a** a crucifix, esp one set on a beam or screen at the entrance to the chancel of a church. **b** (*as modifier*): *rood beam; rood arch; rood screen.* 2 the Cross on which Christ was crucified. 3 a unit of area equal to one quarter of an acre or 0.10117 hectares. 4 a unit of area equal to 40 square rods.
▷HISTORY Old English *rōd*; related to Old Saxon *rōda*, Old Norse *rōtha*

Roodepoort-Maraisburg ('ru:də,puət mə'reɪsbɜ:g) NOUN an industrial city in NE South Africa, on the Witwatersrand. Pop.: 162 632 (1991).

rood screen NOUN a partition of stone or wood, often richly carved and decorated, that separates the chancel from the main part of a church: it is surmounted by a crucifix (rood), and was an important feature of medieval churches, though in England many rood screens were destroyed at the Reformation.

roof (ru:f) NOUN, *plural* **roofs** (ru:fs, ru:vz). 1 **a** a structure that covers or forms the top of a building. **b** (*in combination*): *the rooftop.* **c** (*as modifier*): *a roof garden.* 2 the top covering of a vehicle, oven, or other structure: *the roof of a car.* 3 *Anatomy* any structure that covers an organ or part: *the roof of the mouth.* 4 a highest or topmost point or part: *Mount Everest is the roof of the world.* 5 a house or other shelter: *a poor man's roof.* 6 *Mountaineering* the underside of a projecting overhang. 7 **hit** (*or* **go through**) **the roof.** *Informal* **a** to get extremely angry; become furious. **b** to rise or increase steeply. 8 **raise the roof. a** to create a boisterous disturbance. **b** to react or protest heatedly. ◆ VERB 9 (*tr*) to provide or cover with a roof or rooflike part.
▷HISTORY Old English *hrōf*; related to Middle Dutch, Old Norse *hrōf*
▸ **'roofer** NOUN ▸ **'roofless** ADJECTIVE ▸ **'roof,like** ADJECTIVE

roof garden NOUN a garden on a flat roof of a building.

roofing ('ru:fɪŋ) NOUN 1 material used to construct a roof. 2 the act of constructing a roof.

roof rack NOUN a rack attached to the roof of a motor vehicle for carrying luggage, skis, etc.

roofscape ('ru:f,skeɪp) NOUN a view of the rooftops of a town, city, etc.

rooftop ('ru:f,tɒp) NOUN 1 the outside part of the roof of a building. 2 **shout from the rooftops.** to proclaim (something) publicly.

rooftree ('ru:f,tri:) NOUN another name for **ridgepole.**

rooibos tea ('rɔɪbɒs) NOUN *South African* tea prepared from any of several species of *Borbonia* or *Aspalanthus*, believed to have tonic properties.
▷HISTORY from Afrikaans *rooi* red + *bos* bush

rooikat ('rɔɪ,kæt) NOUN a South African lynx, *Felis caracal*.
▷HISTORY Afrikaans *rooi* red + *kat* cat

rooinek ('rɔɪnɛk, 'rɔɪ-) NOUN *South African* a contemptuous name for an Englishman.
▷HISTORY C19: Afrikaans, literally: red neck

rook¹ (rʊk) NOUN 1 a large Eurasian passerine bird, *Corvus frugilegus*, with a black plumage and a whitish base to its bill: family *Corvidae* (crows). 2 *Slang* a swindler or cheat, esp one who cheats at cards. ◆ VERB 3 (*tr*) *Slang* to overcharge, swindle, or cheat.
▷HISTORY Old English *hrōc*; related to Old High German *hruoh*, Old Norse *hrōkr*

rook² (rʊk) NOUN a chesspiece that may move any number of unoccupied squares in a straight line, horizontally or vertically. Also called: **castle.**
▷HISTORY C14: from Old French *rok*, ultimately from Arabic *rukhkh*

rookery ('rʊkərɪ) NOUN, *plural* **-eries.** 1 a group of nesting rooks. 2 a clump of trees containing rooks' nests. 3 **a** a breeding ground or communal living area of certain other species of gregarious birds or mammals, esp penguins or seals. **b** a colony of any such creatures. 4 *Archaic* an overcrowded slum tenement building or area of housing.

rookie ('rʊkɪ) NOUN *Informal* an inexperienced person or newcomer, esp a raw recruit in the army.
▷HISTORY C20: changed from RECRUIT

rooky ('rʊkɪ) ADJECTIVE **rookier, rookiest.** *Literary* abounding in rooks.

room (ru:m, rʊm) NOUN 1 space or extent, esp unoccupied or unobstructed space for a particular purpose: *is there room to pass?* 2 an area within a building enclosed by a floor, a ceiling, and walls or partitions. 3 (*functioning as singular or plural*) the people present in a room: *the whole room was laughing.* 4 (foll by *for*) opportunity or scope: *room for manoeuvre.* 5 (*plural*) a part of a house, hotel, etc. that is rented out as separate accommodation; lodgings: *she got rooms quite easily in Dulwich Road.* 6 a euphemistic word for **lavatory** (sense 1). ◆ VERB 7 (*intr*) *Chiefly US* to occupy or share a room or lodging: *where does he room?*
▷HISTORY Old English *rūm*; related to Gothic, Old High German *rūm*
▸ **'roomer** NOUN

roomette (ru:'mɛt, rʊ'mɛt) NOUN *US and Canadian* a self-contained compartment in a railway sleeping car.

roomful ('ru:mfʊl, 'rʊm-) NOUN, *plural* **-fuls.** a number or quantity sufficient to fill a room: *a roomful of furniture.*

rooming house NOUN *US and Canadian* a house having self-contained furnished rooms or flats for renting.

roommate ('ru:m,meɪt, 'rʊm-) NOUN a person with whom one shares a room or lodging.

room service NOUN service in a hotel providing meals, drinks, etc., in guests' rooms.

room temperature NOUN the normal temperature of a living room, usually taken as being around 20°C.

roomy ('ru:mɪ, 'rʊmɪ) ADJECTIVE **roomier, roomiest.** having ample room; spacious.
▸ **'roomily** ADVERB ▸ **'roominess** NOUN

roorback ('rʊə,bæk) NOUN *US* a false or distorted report or account, used to obtain political advantage.
▷HISTORY C19: after Baron von *Roorback*, invented author of an imaginary *Tour through the Western and Southern States* (1844), which contained a passage defaming James K. Polk

roost (ru:st) NOUN 1 a place, perch, branch, etc., where birds, esp domestic fowl, rest or sleep. 2 a temporary place to rest or stay. 3 **rule the roost.** See **rule** (sense 20). ◆ VERB 4 (*intr*) to rest or sleep on a roost. 5 (*intr*) to settle down or stay. 6 **come home to roost.** to have unfavourable repercussions.
▷HISTORY Old English *hrōst*; related to Old Saxon *hrost* loft, German *Rost* grid

Roost (ru:st) NOUN **the.** a powerful current caused by conflicting tides around the Shetland and Orkney Islands.
▷HISTORY C16: from Old Norse *röst*

rooster ('ru:stə) NOUN *Chiefly US and Canadian* the male of the domestic fowl; a cock.

root¹ (ru:t) NOUN 1 **a** the organ of a higher plant that anchors the rest of the plant in the ground, absorbs water and mineral salts from the soil, and does not bear leaves or buds. **b** (loosely) any of the branches of such an organ. 2 any plant part, such as a rhizome or tuber, that is similar to a root in structure, function, or appearance. 3 **a** the essential, fundamental, or primary part or nature of something: *your analysis strikes at the root of the problem.* **b** (*as modifier*): *the root cause of the problem.* 4 *Anatomy* the embedded portion of a tooth, nail, hair, etc. 5 origin or derivation, esp as a source of growth, vitality, or existence. 6 (*plural*) a person's sense of belonging in a community, place, etc., esp the one in which he was born or brought up. 7 an ancestor or antecedent. 8 *Bible* a descendant. 9 the form of a word that remains after removal of all affixes; a morpheme with lexical meaning that is not further subdivisible into other morphemes with lexical meaning. Compare **stem¹** (sense 9). 10 *Maths* a number or quantity that when multiplied by itself a certain number of times equals a given number or quantity: *3 is a cube root of 27.* 11 Also called: **solution.** *Maths* a number that when substituted for the variable satisfies a given equation: *2 is a root of* $x^3 - 2x - 4 = 0$. 12 *Music* (in harmony) the note forming the foundation of a chord. 13 *Austral and NZ slang* sexual intercourse. 14 **root and branch. a** (*adverb*) entirely; completely; utterly. **b** (*adjective*) thorough; radical; complete. ◆ Related adjective: **radical.** ◆ VERB 15 (*intr*) Also: **take root.** to put forth or establish a root and begin to grow. 16 (*intr*) Also: **take root.** to become established, embedded, or effective. 17 (*tr*) to fix or embed with or as if with a root or roots. 18 *Austral and NZ slang* to have sexual intercourse (with). ◆ See also **root out, roots, root up.**
▷HISTORY Old English *rōt*, from Old Norse; related to Old English *wyrt* WORT
▸ **'rooter** NOUN ▸ **'root,like** ADJECTIVE ▸ **'rooty** ADJECTIVE
▸ **'rootiness** NOUN

root² (ru:t) VERB (*intr*) 1 (of a pig) to burrow in or dig up the earth in search of food, using the snout. 2 (foll by *about, around, in* etc.) *Informal* to search vigorously but unsystematically.
▷HISTORY C16: changed (through influence of ROOT¹) from earlier *wroot*, from Old English *wrōtan*; related to Old English *wrōt* snout, Middle Dutch *wrōte* mole
▸ **'rooter** NOUN

root³ VERB (*intr*; usually foll by *for*) *Informal* to give support to (a contestant, team, etc.), as by cheering.
▷HISTORY C19: perhaps a variant of Scottish *rout* to make a loud noise, from Old Norse *rauta* to roar
▸ **'rooter** NOUN

root-and-branch ADJECTIVE 1 on a large scale or without discrimination; wholesale: *root-and-branch reforms.* ◆ ADVERB **root and branch.** 2 entirely; completely; utterly: *Brazil needs reform root and branch.*

root beer NOUN *US and Canadian* an effervescent drink made from extracts of various roots and herbs.

root canal NOUN the passage in the root of a tooth through which its nerves and blood vessels enter the pulp cavity.

root-canal therapy NOUN another name for **root treatment.**

root cap NOUN a hollow cone of loosely arranged cells that covers the growing tip of a root and protects it during its passage through the soil.

root climber NOUN any of various climbing plants, such as the ivy, that adhere to a supporting structure by means of small roots growing from the side of the stem.

root crop NOUN a crop, as of turnips or beets, cultivated for the food value of its roots.

rooted ('ru:tɪd) ADJECTIVE 1 having roots. 2 deeply felt: *rooted objections.* 3 *Austral slang* tired or defeated. 4 **get rooted!** *Austral taboo slang* an exclamation of contemptuous anger or annoyance, esp against another person.

root ginger NOUN the raw underground stem of the ginger plant used finely chopped or grated, esp in Chinese dishes.

root hair NOUN any of the hollow hairlike outgrowths of the outer cells of a root, just behind the tip, that absorb water and salts from the soil.

rooting compound NOUN *Horticulture* a substance, usually a powder, containing auxins in which plant cuttings are dipped in order to promote root growth.

rootle ('ru:tᵊl) VERB (*intr*) *Brit* another word for **root².**

rootless ('ru:tlɪs) ADJECTIVE having no roots, esp (of a person) having no ties with a particular place or community.

rootlet ('ru:tlɪt) NOUN a small root or branch of a root.

root mean square NOUN the square root of the average of the squares of a set of numbers or quantities: *the root mean square of* 1, 2, *and* 4 *is* $\sqrt{[(1^2 + 2^2 + 4^2)/3]} = \sqrt{7}$. Abbreviation: **rms.**

root nodule NOUN a swelling on the root of a leguminous plant, such as the pea or clover, that contains bacteria of the genus *Rhizobium*, capable of nitrogen fixation.

root out VERB (*tr, adverb*) to remove or eliminate completely: *we must root out inefficiency.*

root position NOUN *Music* the vertical distribution of the written notes of a chord in which the root of the chord is in the bass. See **position** (sense 12a), **inversion** (sense 5a).

roots (ru:ts) ADJECTIVE (of popular music) going back to the origins of a style, esp in being genuine and unpretentious: *roots rock.*
▸ **'rootsy** ADJECTIVE

rootserver ('ru:tˌsɜ:və) NOUN any of a small number of important large servers on the Internet that match addresses at the top-domain level.

roots music NOUN [1] another name for **world music.** [2] reggae, esp when regarded as authentic and uncommercialized.

rootstock ('ru:tˌstɒk) NOUN [1] another name for **rhizome.** [2] another name for **stock** (sense 7). [3] *Biology* a basic structure from which offshoots have developed.

root treatment NOUN *Dentistry* a procedure, used for treating an abscess at the tip of the root of a tooth, in which the pulp is removed and a filling (**root filling**) inserted in the root canal. Also called: **root-canal therapy.**

root up VERB (*tr, adverb*) to tear or dig up by the roots.

ropable *or* **ropeable** ('rəʊpəbᵊl) ADJECTIVE [1] capable of being roped. [2] *Austral and NZ informal* **a** angry. **b** wild or intractable: *a ropable beast.*

rope (rəʊp) NOUN [1] **a** a fairly thick cord made of twisted and intertwined hemp or other fibres or of wire or other strong material. **b** (*as modifier*): *a rope bridge; a rope ladder.* [2] a row of objects fastened or united to form a line: *a rope of pearls; a rope of onions.* [3] a quantity of material twisted or wound in the form of a cord. [4] anything in the form of a filament or strand, esp something viscous or glutinous: *a rope of slime.* [5] **the rope. a** a rope, noose, or halter used for hanging. **b** death by hanging, strangling, etc. [6] **give (someone) enough rope to hang himself.** to allow (someone) to accomplish his own downfall by his own foolish acts. [7] **know the ropes. a** to have a thorough understanding of a particular sphere of activity. **b** to be experienced in the ways of the world. [8] **on the ropes. a** *Boxing* driven against the ropes enclosing the ring by an opponent's attack. **b** in a defenceless or hopeless position. ◆ VERB [9] (*tr*) to bind or fasten with or as if with a rope. [10] (*tr*; usually foll by *off*) to enclose or divide by means of a rope. [11] (*intr*) to become extended in a long filament or thread. [12] (when *intr*, foll by *up*) *Mountaineering* to tie (climbers) together with a rope. ◆ See also **rope in.**
▷ **HISTORY** Old English *rāp*; related to Old Saxon *rēp*, Old High German *reif*

rope-a-dope NOUN **a** a method of tiring out a boxing opponent by pretending to be trapped on the ropes while the opponent expends energy on punches that are blocked. **b** (*as modifier*): *rope-a-dope strategy.*
▷ **HISTORY** C20: coined by US boxer Muhammad Ali (born 1942)

rope dancer NOUN another name for a **tightrope walker.**

rope in VERB (*tr, adverb*) [1] *Brit* to persuade to take part in some activity. [2] *US and Canadian* to trick or entice into some activity.

rope's end NOUN a short piece of rope, esp as formerly used for flogging sailors.

ropewalk ('rəʊpˌwɔ:k) NOUN a long narrow usually covered path or shed where ropes are made.

ropey *or* **ropy** ('rəʊpɪ) ADJECTIVE **ropier, ropiest.** [1] *Brit informal* **a** inferior or inadequate. **b** slightly unwell; below par. [2] (of a viscous or sticky substance) forming strands or filaments. [3] resembling a rope: *ropey muscles.*
▸ **'ropily** ADVERB ▸ **'ropiness** NOUN

rope yarn NOUN the natural or synthetic fibres out of which rope is made.

roque (rəʊk) NOUN *US* a game developed from croquet, played on a hard surface with a resilient surrounding border from which the ball can rebound.
▷ **HISTORY** C19: variant of CROQUET

Roquefort ('rɒkfɔ:) NOUN a blue-veined cheese with a strong flavour, made from ewe's and goat's milk: matured in caves.
▷ **HISTORY** C19: named after *Roquefort*, village in S France

roquelaure ('rɒkəˌlɔ:) NOUN a man's hooded knee-length cloak of the 18th and 19th centuries.
▷ **HISTORY** C18: from French, named after the Duc de *Roquelaure* (1656–1738), French marshal

roquet ('rəʊkɪ) *Croquet* ◆ VERB **-quets** (-kɪz), **-queting** (-kɪɪŋ), **-queted** (-kɪd). [1] to drive one's ball against (another person's ball) in order to be allowed to croquet. ◆ NOUN [2] the act of roqueting.
▷ **HISTORY** C19: variant of CROQUET

Roraima (*Portuguese* rɔ'raima) NOUN a state of N Brazil: chiefly rainforest. Capital: Boa Vista. Pop.: 324 152 (2000). Area: 230 104 sq. km (89 740 sq. miles).

ro-ro ('rəʊrəʊ) ADJECTIVE ACRONYM FOR **roll-on/roll-off.**

rorqual ('rɔ:kwəl) NOUN any of several whalebone whales of the genus *Balaenoptera*, esp *B. physalus*: family *Balaenopteridae*. They have a dorsal fin and a series of grooves along the throat and chest. Also called: **finback.**
▷ **HISTORY** C19: from French, from Norwegian *rörhval*, from Old Norse *reytharhvalr*, from *reythr* (from *rauthr* red) + *hvalr* whale

Rorschach test ('rɔ:ʃɑ:k; *German* 'rɔrʃax) NOUN *Psychol* a personality test consisting of a number of unstructured ink blots presented for interpretation.
▷ **HISTORY** C20: named after Hermann *Rorschach* (1884–1922), Swiss psychiatrist

rort (rɔ:t) *Austral informal* ◆ NOUN [1] a rowdy party or celebration. [2] a dishonest scheme. ◆ VERB [3] to take unfair advantage of something.
▷ **HISTORY** C20: back formation from *rorty* (in the sense: good, splendid)
▸ **'rorty** ADJECTIVE

rorter ('rɔ:tə) NOUN *Austral informal* a small-scale confidence trickster.

Rosa ('rəʊzə; *Italian* 'rɔ:za) NOUN **Monte** ('mɒntɪ; *Italian* 'monte). a mountain between Italy and Switzerland: the highest in the Pennine Alps. Height: 4634 m (15 204 ft.).

rosace ('rəʊzeɪs) NOUN [1] another name for **rose window.** [2] another name for **rosette.**
▷ **HISTORY** C19: from French, from Latin *rosāceus* ROSACEOUS

rosacea (rəʊ'zeɪʃə) NOUN a chronic inflammatory disease causing the skin of the face to become abnormally flushed and sometimes pustular. Also called: **acne rosacea.**

rosaceous (rəʊ'zeɪʃəs) ADJECTIVE [1] of, relating to, or belonging to the *Rosaceae*, a family of flowering plants typically having white, yellow, pink, or red five-petalled flowers. The family includes the rose, strawberry, blackberry, and many fruit trees such as apple, cherry, and plum. [2] of the colour rose; rose-coloured; rosy.
▷ **HISTORY** C18: from Latin *rosāceus* composed of roses, from *rosa* ROSE[1]

rosaniline (rəʊ'zænɪˌli:n, -lɪn) *or* **rosanilin** NOUN a reddish-brown crystalline insoluble derivative of aniline used, in the form of its soluble hydrochloride, as a red dye. See also **fuchsin.**
▷ **HISTORY** C19: from ROSE[1] + ANILINE

rosarian (rəʊ'zɛərɪən) NOUN a person who cultivates roses, esp professionally.

Rosario (rəʊ'sɑ:rɪəʊ; *Spanish* rɔ'sarjo) NOUN an inland port in E Argentina, on the Paraná River: the second largest city in the country; industrial centre. Pop.: 1 000 000 (1999 est.).

rosarium (rəʊ'zɛərɪəm) NOUN, *plural* **-sariums** *or* **-saria** (-'zɛərɪə). a rose garden.
▷ **HISTORY** C19: New Latin

rosary ('rəʊzərɪ) NOUN, *plural* **-saries.** [1] *RC Church* **a** a series of prayers counted on a string of beads, usually consisting of five or 15 decades of Aves, each decade beginning with a Paternoster and ending with a Gloria. **b** a string of 55 or 165 beads used to count these prayers as they are recited. [2] (in other religions) a similar string of beads used in praying. [3] a bed or garden of roses. [4] an archaic word for a **garland** (of flowers, leaves, etc.).
▷ **HISTORY** C14: from Latin *rosārium* rose garden, from *rosārius* of roses, from *rosa* ROSE[1]

rosbif (ˌrəʊs'bi:f; *French* rɔsbif) NOUN a term used in France for an English person.
▷ **HISTORY** from French, from English *roast beef*, considered as being typically English

Roscius ('rɒskɪəs, -sɪəs) NOUN any actor.
▷ **HISTORY** from Quintus Roscius Gallus (died 62 B.C.), Roman actor
▸ **'Roscian** ADJECTIVE

Roscommon (rɒs'kɒmən) NOUN [1] an inland county of N central Republic of Ireland, in Connacht: economy based on cattle and sheep farming. County town: Roscommon. Pop.: 51 975 (1996). Area: 2463 sq. km (951 sq. miles). [2] a former name for **Galway** (sense 3).

rose[1] (rəʊz) NOUN [1] **a** any shrub or climbing plant of the rosaceous genus *Rosa*, typically having prickly stems, compound leaves, and fragrant flowers. **b** (*in combination*): *rosebush; rosetree.* [2] the flower of any of these plants. [3] any of various similar plants, such as the rockrose and Christmas rose. [4] **a** a moderate purplish-red colour; purplish pink. **b** (*as adjective*): *rose paint.* [5] a rose, or a representation of one, as the national emblem of England. [6] *Jewellery* **a** a cut for a diamond or other gemstone, having a hemispherical faceted crown and a flat base. **b** a gem so cut. [7] a perforated cap fitted to the spout of a watering can or the end of a hose, causing the water to issue in a spray. [8] a design or decoration shaped like a rose; rosette. [9] Also called: **ceiling rose.** *Electrical engineering* a circular boss attached to a ceiling through which the flexible lead of an electric-light fitting passes. [10] *History* See **red rose, white rose.** [11] **bed of roses.** a situation of comfort or ease. [12] **under the rose.** in secret; privately; sub rosa. ◆ VERB [13] (*tr*) to make rose-coloured; cause to blush or redden.
▷ **HISTORY** Old English, from Latin *rosa*, probably from Greek *rhodon* rose
▸ **'roseˌlike** ADJECTIVE

rose[2] (rəʊz) VERB the past tense of **rise.**

rosé ('rəʊzeɪ) NOUN any pink wine, made either by removing the skins of red grapes after only a little colour has been extracted or by mixing red and white wines.
▷ **HISTORY** C19: from French, literally: pink, from Latin *rosa* ROSE[1]

rose acacia NOUN a leguminous shrub, *Robinia hispida*, of the southern US, having prickly branches bearing clusters of red scentless flowers. See also **locust** (sense 2).

rose apple NOUN an ornamental myrtaceous tree, *Syzygium jambos*, of the East Indies, cultivated in the tropics for its edible fruit.

roseate ('rəʊzɪˌeɪt) ADJECTIVE [1] of the colour rose or pink. [2] excessively or idealistically optimistic.
▸ **'roseˌately** ADVERB

Roseau (rəʊ'zəʊ) NOUN the capital of Dominica, a port on the SW coast: botanical gardens. Pop.: 15 853 (1991).

rosebay ('rəʊzˌbeɪ) NOUN [1] *US* any of several rhododendrons, esp *Rhododendron maximum* of E North America. [2] **rosebay willowherb.** a perennial onagraceous plant, *Chamerion* (formerly *Epilobium*) *angustifolium*, that has spikes of deep pink flowers and is widespread in open places throughout N temperate regions. [3] another name for **oleander.**

rosebud ('rəʊzˌbʌd) NOUN [1] the bud of a rose. [2] *Literary* a pretty young woman.

rose campion NOUN a European caryophyllaceous plant, *Lychnis coronaria*, widely cultivated for its pink flowers. Its stems and leaves are covered with white woolly down. Also called: **dusty miller.**

rose chafer *or* **beetle** NOUN a British scarabaeid beetle, *Cetonia aurata*, that has a greenish-golden body with a metallic lustre and feeds on plants.

rose-coloured ADJECTIVE [1] of the colour rose; rosy. [2] See **rose-tinted.** [3] **see through rose-coloured** (*or* **rose-tinted**) **glasses** (*or* **spectacles**). to view in an excessively optimistic light.

rose-cut ADJECTIVE (of a gemstone) cut with a hemispherical faceted crown and a flat base.

rosefish ('rəʊzˌfɪʃ) NOUN, *plural* **-fish** *or* **-fishes.** [1] a red scorpaenid food fish, *Sebastes marinus*, of North Atlantic coastal waters. [2] any of various other red fishes.

rose geranium NOUN a small geraniaceous shrub, *Pelargonium graveolens*, grown in North

America for its pink flowers and fragrant leaves, used for scenting perfumes and cosmetics.

rosehip ('rəʊz,hɪp) NOUN the berry-like fruit of a rose plant. See **hip**[2].

rosella (rəʊ'zɛlə) NOUN any of various Australian parrots of the genus *Platycercus*, such as *P. elegans* (**crimson rosella**), often kept as cage birds.
▷HISTORY C19: probably alteration of *Rose-hiller*, after *Rose Hill*, Parramatta, near Sydney

rosemaling ('rəʊzə,mɑːlɪŋ, -sə-) NOUN a type of painted or carved decoration in Scandinavian peasant style consisting of floral motifs.
▷HISTORY C20: from Norwegian, literally: rose painting

rose mallow NOUN [1] Also called (US and Canadian): **marsh mallow**. any of several malvaceous marsh plants of the genus *Hibiscus*, such as *H. moscheutos*, of E North America, having pink or white flowers and downy leaves. [2] *US* another name for the **hollyhock**.

rosemary ('rəʊzmərɪ) NOUN, *plural* **-maries**. an aromatic European shrub, *Rosmarinus officinalis*, widely cultivated for its grey-green evergreen leaves, which are used in cookery for flavouring and yield a fragrant oil used in the manufacture of perfumes: family *Lamiaceae* (labiates). It is the traditional flower of remembrance.
▷HISTORY C15: earlier *rosmarine*, from Latin *rōs* dew + *marīnus* marine; modern form influenced by folk etymology, as if ROSE[1] + MARY

rose moss NOUN a low-growing portulacaceous plant, *Portulaca grandiflora*, native to Brazil but widely cultivated as a garden plant for its brightly coloured flowers.

rose of Jericho NOUN another name for the **resurrection plant**.

rose of Sharon NOUN [1] Also called: **Aaron's beard**. a creeping shrub, *Hypericum calycinum*, native to SE Europe but widely cultivated, having large yellow flowers: family *Hypericaceae*. [2] Also called: **althaea**. a Syrian malvaceous shrub, *Hibiscus syriacus* (or *Althaea frutex*), cultivated for its red or purplish flowers.

roseola (rəʊ'ziːələ) NOUN *Pathol* [1] a feverish condition of young children that lasts for some five days during the last two of which the patient has a rose-coloured rash. It is caused by the human herpes virus. [2] any red skin eruption or rash.
▷HISTORY C19: from New Latin, diminutive of Latin *roseus* rosy
▸**ro'seolar** ADJECTIVE

rose quartz NOUN a rose-pink often translucent variety of quartz that is used for ornaments.

rose-root NOUN a Eurasian crassulaceous mountain plant, *Sedum rosea*, with fleshy pink-tipped leaves, a thick fleshy pinkish underground stem, and a cluster of yellow flowers. Also called: **midsummer-men**.

rosery ('rəʊzərɪ) NOUN, *plural* **-series**. a bed or garden of roses.

rose-tinted ADJECTIVE [1] Also: **rose-coloured**. excessively optimistic. [2] **see through rose-tinted** (*or* **rose-coloured**) **glasses** (*or* **spectacles**). to view in an excessively optimistic light.

rose topaz NOUN a rose-pink form of topaz produced by heating yellow-brown topaz.

Rosetta (rəʊ'zɛtə) NOUN the former name of **Rashid**.

Rosetta stone NOUN a basalt slab discovered in 1799 at Rosetta, dating to the reign of Ptolemy V (196 B.C.) and carved with parallel inscriptions in Egyptian hieroglyphics, demotic characters, and Greek, which provided the key to the decipherment of ancient Egyptian texts.

rosette (rəʊ'zɛt) NOUN [1] a decoration or pattern resembling a rose, esp an arrangement of ribbons or strips formed into a rose-shaped design and worn as a badge or presented as a prize. [2] another name for **rose window**. [3] a rose-shaped patch of colour, such as one of the clusters of spots marking a leopard's fur. [4] *Botany* a circular cluster of leaves growing from the base of a stem. [5] any of various plant diseases characterized by abnormal leaf growth.
▷HISTORY C18: from Old French: a little ROSE[1]

rose-water NOUN [1] **a** scented water used as a perfume and in cooking, made by the distillation of rose petals or by impregnation with oil of roses. **b** (*as modifier*): *rose-water scent*. [2] (*modifier*) elegant or delicate, esp excessively so.

rose window NOUN a circular window, esp one that has ornamental tracery radiating from the centre to form a symmetrical roselike pattern. Also called: **wheel window, rosette**.

rosewood ('rəʊz,wʊd) NOUN [1] the hard dark wood of any of various tropical and subtropical leguminous trees, esp of the genus *Dalbergia*. It has a roselike scent and is used in cabinetwork. [2] any of the trees yielding this wood.

Rosh Chodesh (rɒʃ 'xɔdəʃ) NOUN *Judaism* the first day of a new month, coinciding usually with the new moon, and also the preceding day if the previous month has 30 days, observed as a minor festival. See also **Jewish calendar**.
▷HISTORY from Hebrew, literally: the beginning of the new moon

Rosh Hashanah *or* **Rosh Hashana** ('rɒʃ hə'ʃɑːnə; *Hebrew* 'rɔʃ haʃa'na) NOUN the festival marking the Jewish New Year, celebrated on the first and second days of Tishri, and marked by penitential prayers and by the blowing of the shofar.
▷HISTORY from Hebrew *rōsh hasshānāh*, literally: beginning of the year, from *rōsh* head + *hash-shānāh* year

Rosicrucian (,rəʊzɪ'kruːʃən) NOUN [1] a member of a society professing esoteric religious doctrines, venerating the emblems of the rose and Cross as symbols of Christ's Resurrection and Redemption, and claiming various occult powers. ◆ ADJECTIVE [2] of, relating to, or designating the Rosicrucians or Rosicrucianism.
▷HISTORY C17: from Latin *Rosae Crucis* Rose of the Cross, translation of the German name Christian *Rosenkreuz*, supposed founder of the society in the 15th century
▸**,Rosi'crucianism** NOUN

Rosie Lee ('rəʊzɪ 'liː) NOUN *Cockney rhyming slang* tea.

rosin ('rɒzɪn) NOUN [1] Also called: **colophony**. a translucent brittle amber substance produced in the distillation of crude turpentine oleoresin and used esp in making varnishes, printing inks, and sealing waxes and for treating the bows of stringed instruments. [2] (not in technical usage) another name for **resin** (sense 1). ◆ VERB [3] (*tr*) to treat or coat with rosin.
▷HISTORY C14: variant of RESIN
▸**'rosiny** ADJECTIVE

Rosinante (,rɒzɪ'næntɪ) NOUN a worn-out emaciated old horse.
▷HISTORY C18: from Spanish, the name of Don Quixote's horse, from *rocín* old horse

rosiner ('rɒzənə) NOUN *Austral slang* a strong alcoholic drink.
▷HISTORY from English dialect sense of *rosin* to supply with liquor

rosin oil NOUN a yellowish fluorescent oily liquid obtained from certain resins, used in the manufacture of carbon black, varnishes, and lacquers. Also called: **'rosinol, retinol**.

rosinweed ('rɒzɪn,wiːd) NOUN any of several North American plants of the genus *Silphium* and related genera, esp the compass plant, having resinous juice, sticky foliage, and a strong smell: family *Asteraceae* (composites).

Roskilde (*Danish* 'rɔskilə) NOUN a city in Denmark, on NE Sjælland west of Copenhagen: capital of Denmark from the 10th century to 1443; scene of the signing (1658) of the **Peace of Roskilde** between Denmark and Sweden. Pop.: 49 080 (1990).

ROSPA ('rɒspə) NOUN (in Britain) ACRONYM FOR Royal Society for the Prevention of Accidents.

Ross and Cromarty (rɒs ənd 'krɒmətɪ) NOUN (until 1975) a county of N Scotland, including the island of Lewis and many islets: now split between the Highland and Western Isles council areas.

Ross Dependency NOUN a section of Antarctica administered by New Zealand: includes the coastal regions of Victoria Land and King Edward VII Land, the Ross Sea and islands, and the Ross Ice Shelf. Area: about 414 400 sq. km (160 000 sq. miles).

Ross Ice Shelf NOUN the ice shelf forming the S part of the Ross Sea, between Victoria Land and Byrd Land. Also called: **Ross Barrier, Ross Shelf Ice**.

Ross Island NOUN an island in the W Ross Sea: contains the active volcano Mount Erebus.

Rossiya (ra'siːjə) NOUN transliteration of the Russian name for **Russia**.

Ross Sea NOUN a large arm of the S Pacific in Antarctica, incorporating the Ross Ice Shelf and lying between Victoria Land and the Edward VII Peninsula.

rostellum (rɒ'stɛləm) NOUN, *plural* **-la** (-lə). *Biology* a small beaklike process, such as the hooked projection from the top of the head in tapeworms or the outgrowth from the stigma of an orchid.
▷HISTORY C18: from Latin: a little beak, from *rōstrum* a beak
▸**ros'tellate** *or* **ros'tellar** ADJECTIVE

roster[1] ('rɒstə) NOUN [1] a list or register, esp one showing the order of people enrolled for duty. ◆ VERB [2] *Marketing* the list of advertising agencies regularly used by a particular company. [3] (*tr*) to place on a roster.
▷HISTORY C18: from Dutch *rooster* grating or list (the lined paper looking like a grid)

roster[2] ('rɒstə) NOUN *Northern English dialect* a rascal.

Rostock ('rɒstɒk) NOUN a port in NE Germany, in Mecklenburg-West Pomerania on the Warnow estuary 13 km (8 miles) from the Baltic and its outport, Warnemünde: formerly the chief port of East Germany; university (1419). Pop.: 205 900 (1999 est.).

Rostov *or* **Rostov-on-Don** ('rɒstɒv) NOUN a port in S Russia, on the River Don 48 km (30 miles) from the Sea of Azov: industrial centre. Pop.: 1 017 300 (1999 est.).

rostral ('rɒstrəl) ADJECTIVE [1] *Biology* of or like a beak or snout. [2] adorned with the prows of ships: *a rostral column*.

rostrate ('rɒs,treɪt) ADJECTIVE *Biology* having a beak or beaklike process.

rostrum ('rɒstrəm) NOUN, *plural* **-trums** *or* **-tra** (-trə). [1] any platform, stage, or dais on which public speakers stand to address an audience. [2] a platform or dais in front of an orchestra on which the conductor stands. [3] another word for **ram** (sense 5). [4] the prow of an ancient Roman ship. [5] *Biology, zoology* a beak or beaklike part.
▷HISTORY C16: from Latin *rōstrum* beak, ship's prow, from *rōdere* to nibble, gnaw; in plural, *rōstra*, orator's platform, because this platform in the Roman forum was adorned with the prows of captured ships

rosy ('rəʊzɪ) ADJECTIVE **rosier, rosiest**. [1] of the colour rose or pink. [2] having a healthy pink complexion: *rosy cheeks*. [3] optimistic, esp excessively so: *a rosy view of social improvements*. [4] full of health, happiness, or joy: *rosy slumbers*. [5] resembling, consisting of, or abounding in roses.
▸**'rosily** ADVERB ▸**'rosiness** NOUN

rosy finch NOUN any of several finches of the genus *Leucosticte*, occurring in mountainous regions of North America and Asia. They have brown or grey plumage with pink patches on the wings, rump, and tail.

rot[1] (rɒt) VERB **rots, rotting, rotted**. [1] to decay or cause to decay as a result of bacterial or fungal action. [2] (*intr*; usually foll by *off* or *away*) to fall or crumble (off) or break (away), as from natural decay, corrosive action, or long use. [3] (*intr*) to become weak, debilitated, or depressed through inertia, confinement, etc.; languish: *rotting in prison*. [4] to become or cause to become morally corrupt or degenerate. [5] (*tr*) *Textiles* another word for **ret**. ◆ NOUN [6] the process of rotting or the state of being rotten. [7] something decomposed, disintegrated, or degenerate. Related adjective: **putrid**. [8] short for **dry rot**. [9] *Pathol* any putrefactive decomposition of tissues. [10] a condition in plants characterized by breakdown and decay of tissues, caused by bacteria, fungi, etc. [11] *Vet science* a contagious fungal disease of the feet of sheep characterized by inflammation, swelling, a foul-smelling discharge, and lameness. [12] (*also interjection*) nonsense; rubbish.
▷HISTORY Old English *rotian* (verb); related to Old Norse *rotna*. C13 (noun), from Scandinavian

rot[2] ABBREVIATION FOR rotation (of a mathematical function).

rota (ˈrəʊtə) NOUN *Chiefly Brit* a register of names showing the order in which people take their turn to perform certain duties.
▷**HISTORY** C17: from Latin: a wheel

Rota (ˈrəʊtə) NOUN *RC Church* the supreme ecclesiastical tribunal for judging cases brought before the Holy See.

rota bed NOUN *Social welfare* a bed in an old people's home, reserved for the regular respite care of dependent old people.

rotachute (ˈrəʊtəˌʃuːt) NOUN a device serving the same purpose as a parachute, in which the canopy is replaced by freely revolving rotor blades, used for the delivery of stores or recovery of missiles.

Rotameter (ˈrəʊtəˌmiːtə) NOUN *Trademark* a device used for measuring the flow of a fluid. It consists of a small float supported in a tapering glass by the flow of the fluid, the height of the float indicating the rate of flow.

rotan (rəʊˈtæn) (in Indonesia and Malaysia) NOUN another name for **rattan** (sense 1).

rotaplane (ˈrəʊtəˌpleɪn) NOUN an aircraft that derives its lift from freely revolving rotor blades.

Rotarian (rəʊˈtɛərɪən) NOUN 1 a member of a Rotary Club. ◆ ADJECTIVE 2 of or relating to Rotary Clubs or their members.
▸**Roˈtarianism** NOUN

rotary (ˈrəʊtərɪ) ADJECTIVE 1 of, relating to, or operating by rotation. 2 turning or able to turn; revolving. ◆ NOUN, *plural* **-ries.** 3 a part of a machine that rotates about an axis. 4 *US and Canadian* another term for **roundabout** (for road traffic).
▷**HISTORY** C18: from Medieval Latin *rotārius*, from Latin *rota* a wheel

rotary clothesline *or* **clothes dryer** NOUN an apparatus of radiating spokes that support lines on which clothes are hung to dry.

Rotary Club NOUN any of the local clubs that form **Rotary International**, an international association of professional and businessmen founded in the US in 1905 to promote community service.

rotary engine NOUN 1 an internal-combustion engine having radial cylinders that rotate about a fixed crankshaft. 2 an engine, such as a turbine or wankel engine, in which power is transmitted directly to rotating components.

rotary plough *or* **tiller** NOUN an implement with a series of blades mounted on a power-driven shaft, used to break up soil or weeds.

rotary press NOUN a machine for printing from a revolving cylinder, or a plate attached to one, usually onto a continuous strip of paper.

rotary pump NOUN *Engineering* a pump in which a liquid is displaced through a shaped stator by a shaped rotor.

rotate VERB (rəʊˈteɪt) 1 to turn or cause to turn around an axis, line, or point; revolve or spin. 2 to follow or cause to follow a set order or sequence. 3 to replace one group of personnel with another. ◆ ADJECTIVE (ˈrəʊteɪt) 4 *Botany* designating a corolla the united petals of which radiate from a central point like the spokes of a wheel.
▸**roˈtatable** ADJECTIVE

rotation (rəʊˈteɪʃən) NOUN 1 the act of rotating; rotary motion. 2 a regular cycle of events in a set order or sequence. 3 a planned sequence of cropping according to which the crops grown in successive seasons on the same land are varied so as to make a balanced demand on its resources of fertility. 4 *Maths* **a** a circular motion of a configuration about a given point or line, without a change in shape. **b** a transformation in which the coordinate axes are rotated by a fixed angle about the origin. **c** another name for **curl** (sense 11). Abbreviation (for sense 4c): **rot.** 5 **a** the spinning motion of a body, such as a planet, about an internal axis. Compare **revolution** (sense 5a). **b** one complete turn in such motion.
▸**roˈtational** ADJECTIVE

rotator (rəʊˈteɪtə) NOUN 1 a person, device, or part that rotates or causes rotation. 2 *Anatomy* any of various muscles that revolve a part on its axis.

rotatory (ˈrəʊtətərɪ, -trɪ) *or less commonly* **rotative** (ˈrəʊtətɪv) ADJECTIVE of, relating to, possessing, or causing rotation.
▸ˈ**rotatively** ADVERB

Rotavator *or* **Rotovator** (ˈrəʊtəˌveɪtə) NOUN *Trademark* a type of machine with rotating blades that will break up soil.
▷**HISTORY** C20: original form *Rotavator*, from *rota(ry)* *(culti)vator*

rotavirus (ˈrəʊtəˌvaɪrəs) NOUN any member of a genus of viruses that cause worldwide endemic infections. They occur in birds and mammals, cause diarrhoea in children, and are usually transmitted in food prepared with unwashed hands.

rote[1] (rəʊt) NOUN 1 a habitual or mechanical routine or procedure. 2 **by rote.** by repetition; by heart (often in the phrase **learn by rote**).
▷**HISTORY** C14: origin unknown

rote[2] (rəʊt) NOUN an ancient violin-like musical instrument; crwth.
▷**HISTORY** C13: from Old French *rote*, of Germanic origin; related to Old High German *rotta*, Middle Dutch *rotte*

rotenone (ˈrəʊtɪˌnəʊn) NOUN a white odourless crystalline substance extracted from the roots of derris: a powerful insecticide. Formula: $C_{23}H_{22}O_6$; relative density: 1.27; melting pt.: 163°C.
▷**HISTORY** C20: from Japanese *rōten* derris + -ONE

rotgut (ˈrɒtˌgʌt) NOUN *Facetious slang* alcoholic drink, esp spirits, of inferior quality.

Rotherham (ˈrɒðərəm) NOUN 1 an industrial town in N England, in Rotherham unitary authority, South Yorkshire. Pop.: 121 380 (1991). 2 a unitary authority in N England, in South Yorkshire. Pop.: 248 176 (2001). Area: 283 sq. km (109 sq. miles).

Rothesay (ˈrɒθsɪ) NOUN a town in SW Scotland, in Argyll and Bute, on the E coast of Bute Island. Pop.: 5264 (1991).

roti (ˈrəʊtɪ, ˈrʊtɪ) NOUN (in India and the Caribbean) a type of unleavened bread.
▷**HISTORY** from Hindi: bread

rotifer (ˈrəʊtɪfə) NOUN any minute aquatic multicellular invertebrate of the phylum *Rotifera*, having a ciliated wheel-like organ used in feeding and locomotion: common constituents of freshwater plankton. Also called: **wheel animalcule.**
▷**HISTORY** C18: from New Latin *Rotifera*, from Latin *rota* wheel + *ferre* to bear
▸**rotiferal** (rəʊˈtɪfərəl) *or* **roˈtiferous** ADJECTIVE

rotisserie (rəʊˈtɪsərɪ) NOUN 1 a rotating spit on which meat, poultry, etc., can be cooked. 2 a shop or restaurant where meat is roasted to order.
▷**HISTORY** C19: from French, from Old French *rostir* to ROAST

rotl (ˈrɒtᵊl) NOUN, *plural* **rotls** *or* **artal** (ˈɑːtɑːl). a unit of weight used in Muslim countries, varying in value between about one and five pounds.
▷**HISTORY** C17: from Arabic *ratl*, perhaps from Greek *litra* a pound

rotogravure (ˌrəʊtəʊgrəˈvjʊə) NOUN 1 a printing process using a cylinder etched with many small recesses, from which ink is transferred to a moving web of paper, plastic, etc., in a rotary press. 2 printed material produced in this way, esp magazines. ◆ Often shortened to: **roto.**
▷**HISTORY** C20: from Latin *rota* wheel + GRAVURE

roton (ˈrəʊtɒn) NOUN *Physics* a quantum of vortex motion.

rotor (ˈrəʊtə) NOUN 1 the rotating member of a machine or device, esp the armature of a motor or generator or the rotating assembly of a turbine. Compare **stator.** 2 a device having blades radiating from a central hub that is rotated to produce thrust to lift and propel a helicopter. 3 the revolving arm of the distributor of an internal-combustion engine. 4 a violent rolling wave of air occurring in the lee of a mountain or hill, in which the air rotates about a horizontal axis.
▷**HISTORY** C20: shortened form of ROTATOR

Rotorua (ˌrəʊtəˈruːə) NOUN a city in New Zealand, on N central North Island at the SW end of Lake Rotorua: centre of forestry; noted for volcanic activity. Pop.: 54 700 (1994).

rotovate *or* **rotavate** (ˈrəʊtəˌveɪt) VERB *(tr)* to break up (the surface of the earth, or an area of ground) using a Rotavator.

rotten (ˈrɒtᵊn) ADJECTIVE 1 affected with rot; decomposing, decaying, or putrid. 2 breaking up, esp through age or hard use; disintegrating: *rotten ironwork.* 3 morally despicable or corrupt. 4 untrustworthy, disloyal, or treacherous. 5 *Informal* unpleasant, unfortunate, or nasty: *rotten luck; rotten weather.* 6 *Informal* unsatisfactory or poor: *rotten workmanship.* 7 *Informal* miserably unwell. 8 *Informal* distressed, uncomfortable, and embarrassed: *I felt rotten when I told him to go.* 9 (of rocks, soils, etc.) soft and crumbling, esp as a result of weathering. 10 *Slang, chiefly Austral and NZ* intoxicated; drunk. ◆ ADVERB *Informal* 11 extremely; very much: *men fancy her rotten.*
▷**HISTORY** C13: from Old Norse *rottin*; related to Old English *rotian* to ROT[1]
▸ˈ**rottenly** ADVERB ▸ˈ**rottenness** NOUN

rotten borough NOUN (before the Reform Act of 1832) any of certain English parliamentary constituencies with only a very few electors. Compare **pocket borough.**

rottenstone (ˈrɒtᵊnˌstəʊn) NOUN a much-weathered limestone, rich in silica: used in powdered form for polishing metal.

rotter (ˈrɒtə) NOUN *Slang, chiefly Brit* a worthless, unpleasant, or despicable person.

Rotterdam (ˈrɒtəˌdæm) NOUN a port in the SW Netherlands, in South Holland province: the second largest city of the Netherlands and one of the world's largest ports; oil refineries, shipbuilding yards, etc. Pop.: 592 665 (1999 est.).

Rottweiler (ˈrɒtˌvaɪlə) NOUN a breed of large robustly built dog with a smooth coat of black with dark tan markings on the face, chest, and legs. It was previously a docked breed.
▷**HISTORY** German, named after *Rottweil*, German city where the dog was originally bred

rotund (rəʊˈtʌnd) ADJECTIVE 1 rounded or spherical in shape. 2 plump. 3 sonorous or grandiloquent; full in tone, style of speaking, etc.
▷**HISTORY** C18: from Latin *rotundus* wheel-shaped, round, from *rota* wheel
▸**roˈtundity** *or* **roˈtundness** NOUN ▸**roˈtundly** ADVERB

rotunda (rəʊˈtʌndə) NOUN a building or room having a circular plan, esp one that has a dome.
▷**HISTORY** C17: from Italian *rotonda*, from Latin *rotundus* round, from *rota* a wheel

ROU INTERNATIONAL CAR REGISTRATION FOR (Republic of) Uruguay.

Roubaix (*French* rubɛ) NOUN a city in N France near the Belgian border: forms, with Tourcoing, a large industrial conurbation. Pop.: 97 746 (1990).

rouble *or* **ruble** (ˈruːbᵊl) NOUN 1 the standard monetary unit of Belarus and Russia, divided into 100 kopecks. 2 the former standard monetary unit of Tajikistan, divided into 100 tanga.
▷**HISTORY** C16: from Russian *rubl* silver bar, from Old Russian *rublĭ* bar, block of wood, from *rubiti* to cut up

rouche (ruːʃ) NOUN a variant spelling of **ruche.**

roucou (ˈruːˌkuː) NOUN another name for **annatto.**
▷**HISTORY** C17: via French from Tupi *urucú*

roué (ˈruːeɪ) NOUN a debauched or lecherous man.
▷**HISTORY** C19: from French, literally: one broken on the wheel, from *rouer*, from Latin *rotāre* to revolve, from *rota* a wheel; with reference to the fate deserved by a debauchee

Rouen (*French* rwɑ̃) NOUN a city in N France, on the River Seine: the chief river port of France; became capital of the duchy of Normandy in 912; scene of the burning of Joan of Arc (1431); university (1964). Pop.: 106 035 (1999).

rouge (ruːʒ) NOUN 1 a red powder, used as a cosmetic for adding redness to the cheeks. 2 short for **jeweller's rouge.** ◆ VERB *(tr)* 3 to apply rouge to.
▷**HISTORY** C18: from French: red, from Latin *rubeus*

Rouge Croix (ˌruːʒ ˈkrwɑː) NOUN a pursuivant at the English college of arms.

Rouge Dragon (ˌruːʒ ˈdrægən) NOUN a pursuivant at the English college of arms.

rouge et noir (ˈruːʒ eɪ ˈnwɑː; *French* ruʒ e nwar) NOUN a card game in which the players put their stakes on any of two red and two black diamond-shaped spots marked on the table. Also called: **trente et quarante.**
▷**HISTORY** French, literally: red and black

rough (rʌf) ADJECTIVE 1 (of a surface) not smooth; uneven or irregular. 2 (of ground) covered with

scrub, boulders, etc. 3 denoting or taking place on uncultivated ground: *rough grazing; rough shooting.* 4 shaggy or hairy. 5 turbulent; agitated: *a rough sea.* 6 (of the performance or motion of something) uneven; irregular: *a rough engine.* 7 (of behaviour or character) rude, coarse, ill mannered, inconsiderate, or violent. 8 harsh or sharp: *rough words.* 9 *Informal* severe or unpleasant: *a rough lesson.* 10 (of work, a task, etc.) requiring physical rather than mental effort. 11 *Informal* ill or physically upset: *he felt rough after an evening of heavy drinking.* 12 unfair or unjust: *rough luck.* 13 harsh or grating to the ear. 14 harsh to the taste. 15 without refinement, luxury, etc. 16 not polished or perfected in any detail; rudimentary; not elaborate: *rough workmanship; rough justice.* 17 not prepared or dressed: *rough gemstones.* 18 (of a guess, estimate, etc.) approximate. 19 *Austral informal* (of a chance) not good. 20 having the sound of *h*; aspirated. 21 **rough on.** *Informal, chiefly Brit* **a** severe towards. **b** unfortunate for (a person). 22 **the rough side of one's tongue.** harsh words; a reprimand, rebuke, or verbal attack. ◆ NOUN 23 rough ground. 24 a sketch or preliminary piece of artwork. 25 an unfinished or crude state (esp in the phrase **in the rough**). 26 **the rough.** *Golf* the part of the course bordering the fairways where the grass is untrimmed. 27 *Tennis, squash, badminton* the side of a racket on which the binding strings form an uneven line. 28 *Informal* a rough or violent person; thug. 29 the unpleasant side of something (esp in the phrase **take the rough with the smooth**). ◆ ADVERB 30 in a rough manner; roughly. 31 **sleep rough.** to spend the night in the open; be without a home or without shelter. ◆ VERB 32 (*tr*) to make rough; roughen. 33 (*tr*; foll by *out, in,* etc.) to prepare (a sketch, report, piece of work, etc.) in preliminary form. 34 **rough it.** *Informal* to live without the usual comforts or conveniences of life. ◆ See also **rough out, rough up.**
▷HISTORY Old English *rūh*; related to Old Norse *ruksa*, Middle Dutch *rūge, rūwe*, German *rauh*
▸ ˈ**roughness** NOUN

roughage (ˈrʌfɪdʒ) NOUN 1 the coarse indigestible constituents of food or fodder, which provide bulk to the diet and promote normal bowel function. See also **dietary fibre.** 2 any rough or coarse material.

rough-and-ready ADJECTIVE 1 crude, unpolished, or hastily prepared, but sufficient for the purpose. 2 (of a person) without formality or refinement; rudely vigorous.
▸ ˈ**rough-and-ˈreadiness** NOUN

rough-and-tumble NOUN 1 a fight or scuffle without rules. ◆ ADJECTIVE 2 characterized by roughness, disorderliness, and disregard for rules or conventions.

rough breathing NOUN (in Greek) the sign (ʽ) placed over an initial letter, or a second letter if the word begins with a diphthong, indicating that (in ancient Greek) it was pronounced with an *h*. Compare **smooth breathing.**

roughcast (ˈrʌfˌkɑːst) NOUN 1 a coarse plaster used to cover the surface of an external wall. 2 any rough or preliminary form, model, etc. ◆ ADJECTIVE 3 covered with or denoting roughcast. ◆ VERB **-casts, -casting, -cast.** 4 to apply roughcast to (a wall, etc.). 5 to prepare in rough. 6 (*tr*) another word for **rough-hew.**
▸ ˈ**roughˌcaster** NOUN

rough collie NOUN a large long-haired collie having a distinctive ruff and a long narrow head without a pronounced stop.

rough-cut NOUN a first edited version of a film with the scenes in sequence and the soundtrack synchronized.

rough diamond NOUN 1 an unpolished diamond. 2 an intrinsically trustworthy or good person with uncouth manners or dress.

rough-dry ADJECTIVE 1 (of clothes or linen) dried ready for pressing. ◆ VERB **-dries, -drying, -dried.** 2 (*tr*) to dry (clothes or linen) without smoothing or pressing.

roughen (ˈrʌfᵊn) VERB to make or become rough.

rough fish NOUN a fish that is neither a sport fish nor useful as food or bait for sport fish.

rough-hew VERB **-hews, -hewing, -hewed, -hewed** *or* **-hewn.** (*tr*) 1 to cut or hew (timber, stone, etc.) roughly without finishing the surface. 2 Also: **roughcast.** to shape roughly or crudely.

roughhouse (ˈrʌfˌhaʊs) *Slang* ◆ NOUN 1 rough, disorderly, or noisy behaviour. ◆ VERB 2 to treat (someone) in a boisterous or rough way.

roughie[1] (ˈrʌfɪ) NOUN a small food fish of the family *Arripididae*, found in southern and western Australian waters. Also called: **orange roughie, ruff, tommy rough.**

roughie[2] NOUN *Austral slang* 1 something unfair, esp a trick: *he put a roughie over.* 2 (in horse racing) an outsider that wins.

roughish (ˈrʌfɪʃ) ADJECTIVE somewhat rough.

rough-legged buzzard NOUN a buzzard, *Buteo lagopus*, of Europe, Asia, and North America, having feathers covering its legs.

roughly (ˈrʌflɪ) ADVERB 1 without being exact or fully authenticated; approximately: *roughly half the candidates were successful.* 2 in a clumsy, coarse, or violent manner: *his captors did not treat him roughly.* 3 in a crude or primitive manner: *a slab of roughly hewn stone.*

rough music NOUN (formerly) a loud cacophony created with tin pans, drums, etc., esp as a protest or demonstration of indignation outside someone's house.

roughneck (ˈrʌfˌnɛk) NOUN *Slang* 1 a rough or violent person; thug. 2 a worker in an oil-drilling operation.

rough out VERB (*tr, adverb*) 1 See **rough** (sense 33). 2 *Engineering* to machine (a workpiece, such as a casting or forging) with heavy cuts leaving a rough surface to be finished.

rough passage NOUN 1 a stormy sea journey. 2 a difficult or testing time.

rough puff pastry NOUN a rich flaky pastry made with butter and used for pie-crusts, flans, etc.

roughrider (ˈrʌfˌraɪdə) NOUN a rider of wild or unbroken horses.

roughshod (ˈrʌfˌʃɒd) ADJECTIVE 1 (of a horse) shod with rough-bottomed shoes to prevent sliding. ◆ ADVERB 2 **ride roughshod over.** to domineer over or act with complete disregard for.

rough sleeper NOUN a homeless person who sleeps rough.

rough spin NOUN *NZ informal* hard or unfair treatment.

rough-spoken ADJECTIVE rude or uncouth in speech; blunt.

rough stuff NOUN *Informal* violence.

rough trade NOUN *Slang* (in homosexual use) a tough or violent sexual partner, esp a lorry driver, construction worker, or docker, casually picked up.

rough up VERB (*tr, adverb*) 1 *Informal* to treat violently; beat up. 2 to cause (feathers, hair, etc.) to stand up by rubbing against the grain.

roulade (ruːˈlɑːd) NOUN 1 a slice of meat rolled, esp around a stuffing, and cooked. 2 an elaborate run in vocal music.
▷HISTORY C18: from French, literally: a rolling, from *rouler* to ROLL

rouleau (ˈruːləʊ) NOUN, *plural* **-leaux** (-ləʊ, -ləʊz) *or* **-leaus.** 1 a roll of paper containing coins. 2 (*often plural*) a roll of ribbon.
▷HISTORY C17: from French, from *role* ROLL

Roulers (ruːˈlɛəz; *French* rulɛrs) NOUN a city in NW Belgium, in West Flanders province: electronics. Pop.: 53 617 (1995 est.). Flemish name: **Roeselare.**

roulette (ruːˈlɛt) NOUN 1 a gambling game in which a ball is dropped onto a spinning horizontal wheel divided into 37 or 38 coloured and numbered slots, with players betting on the slot into which the ball will fall. 2 **a** a toothed wheel for making a line of perforations. **b** a tiny slit made by such a wheel on a sheet of stamps as an aid to tearing it apart. 3 a curve generated by a point on one curve rolling on another. ◆ VERB (*tr*) 4 to use a roulette on (something), as in engraving, making stationery, etc.
▷HISTORY C18: from French, from *rouelle* a little wheel, from *roue* a wheel, from Latin *rota*

Roumania (ruːˈmeɪnɪə) NOUN a variant of **Romania.**

Roumanian (ruːˈmeɪnɪən) NOUN, ADJECTIVE a variant of **Romanian.**

Roumelia (ruːˈmiːlɪə) NOUN a variant spelling of **Rumelia.**

round (raʊnd) ADJECTIVE 1 having a flat circular shape, as a disc or hoop. 2 having the shape of a sphere or ball. 3 curved; not angular. 4 involving or using circular motion. 5 (*prenominal*) complete; entire: *a round dozen.* 6 *Maths* **a** forming or expressed by an integer or whole number, with no fraction. **b** expressed to the nearest ten, hundred, or thousand: *in round figures.* 7 (of a sum of money) considerable; ample. 8 fully depicted or developed, as a character in a book. 9 full and plump: *round cheeks.* 10 (of sound) full and sonorous. 11 (of pace) brisk; lively. 12 (*prenominal*) (of speech) candid; straightforward; unmodified: *a round assertion.* 13 (of a vowel) pronounced with rounded lips. ◆ NOUN 14 a round shape or object. 15 **in the round. a** in full detail. **b** *Theatre* with the audience all round the stage. 16 a session, as of a negotiation: *a round of talks.* 17 a series, cycle, or sequence: *a giddy round of parties.* 18 **the daily round.** the usual activities of one's day. 19 a stage of a competition: *he was eliminated in the first round.* 20 (*often plural*) a series of calls, esp in a set order: *a doctor's rounds; a milkman's round.* 21 a playing of all the holes on a golf course. 22 a single turn of play by each player, as in a card game. 23 one of a number of periods constituting a boxing, wrestling, or other match, each usually lasting three minutes. 24 *Archery* a specified number of arrows shot from a specified distance. 25 a single discharge by a number of guns or a single gun. 26 a bullet, blank cartridge, or other charge of ammunition. 27 a number of drinks bought at one time for a group of people. 28 a single slice of bread or toast or two slices making a single serving of sandwiches. 29 a general outburst of applause, cheering, etc. 30 movement in a circle or around an axis. 31 *Music* a part song in which the voices follow each other at equal intervals at the same pitch. 32 a sequence of bells rung in order of treble to tenor. Compare **change** (sense 29). 33 a dance in which the dancers move in a circle. 34 a cut of beef from the thigh between the rump and the shank. 35 **go** *or* **make the rounds. a** to go from place to place, as in making deliveries or social calls. **b** (of information, rumour, etc.) to be passed around, so as to be generally known. ◆ PREPOSITION 36 surrounding, encircling, or enclosing: *a band round her head.* 37 on all or most sides of: *to look round one.* 38 on or outside the circumference or perimeter of: *the stands round the racecourse.* 39 situated at various points in: *a lot of shelves round the house.* 40 from place to place in: *driving round Ireland.* 41 somewhere in or near: *to stay round the house.* 42 making a circuit or partial circuit about: *the ring road round the town.* 43 reached by making a partial circuit about something: *the shop round the corner.* 44 revolving round a centre or axis: *the earth's motion round its axis.* 45 so as to have a basis in: *the story is built round a good plot.* ◆ ADVERB 46 on all or most sides: *the garden is fenced all round; the crowd gathered round.* 47 on or outside the circumference or perimeter: *the racing track is two miles round.* 48 in all directions from a point of reference: *he owns the land for ten miles round.* 49 to all members of a group: *pass the food round.* 50 in rotation or revolution: *the wheels turn round.* 51 by a circuitous route: *the road to the farm goes round by the pond.* 52 to a specific place: *she came round to see me.* 53 **all year round.** throughout the year; in every month. ◆ VERB 54 to make or become round. 55 (*tr*) to encircle; surround. 56 to move or cause to move with circular motion: *to round a bend.* 57 (*tr*) **a** to pronounce (a speech sound) with rounded lips. **b** to purse (the lips). ◆ See also **round down, round off, round on, round out, round up.**
▷HISTORY C13: from Old French *ront*, from Latin *rotundus* round, from *rota* a wheel
▸ ˈ**roundness** NOUN

roundabout (ˈraʊndəˌbaʊt) NOUN 1 *Brit* a revolving circular platform provided with wooden animals, seats, etc., on which people ride for amusement; merry-go-round. 2 a road junction in which traffic streams circulate around a central island. US and Canadian name: **traffic circle.** 3 an informal name for **boring mill.** ◆ ADJECTIVE 4 indirect or circuitous; devious. ◆ ADVERB, PREPOSITION **round about.** 5 on all sides: *spectators standing round about.* 6 approximately: *at round about 5 o'clock.*

round and round ADVERB, PREPOSITION following a

circuitous or circular course for a comparatively long time, esp vainly.

round angle NOUN another name for **perigon**.

round-arm ADJECTIVE, ADVERB *Cricket* denoting or using bowling with the arm held more or less horizontal.

round clam NOUN another name for the **quahog**.

round dance NOUN 1 a dance in which the dancers form a circle. 2 a ballroom dance, such as the waltz, in which couples revolve.

round down VERB (*tr, adverb*) to lower (a number) to the nearest whole number or ten, hundred, or thousand below it. Compare **round up** (sense 2).

rounded ('raʊndɪd) ADJECTIVE 1 round or curved. 2 having been made round or curved. 3 full, mature, or complete. 4 (of the lips) pursed, as in pronouncing the sound (u:). 5 (of a speech sound) articulated with rounded lips.
▸ **'roundedly** ADVERB ▸ **'roundedness** NOUN

roundel ('raʊndᵊl) NOUN 1 a form of rondeau consisting of three stanzas each of three lines with a refrain after the first and the third. 2 a circular identifying mark in national colours on military aircraft. 3 a small ornamental circular window, panel, medallion, plate, disc, etc. 4 a round plate of armour used to protect the armpit. 5 *Heraldry* a charge in the shape of a circle. 6 another word for **roundelay** (sense 1).
▷ HISTORY C13: from Old French *rondel* a little circle; see RONDEL

roundelay ('raʊndɪˌleɪ) NOUN 1 Also called: **roundel**. a slow medieval dance performed in a circle. 2 a song in which a line or phrase is repeated as a refrain.
▷ HISTORY C16: from Old French *rondelet* a little rondel, from *rondel*; also influenced by LAY[4]

rounder ('raʊndə) NOUN 1 a run round all four bases after one hit in rounders. 2 a tool or machine for rounding edges or surfaces.

rounders ('raʊndəz) NOUN (*functioning as singular*) *Brit* a ball game in which players run between posts after hitting the ball, scoring a **rounder** if they run round all four before the ball is retrieved.

round file *Slang* ◆ NOUN 1 a wastepaper basket. ◆ VERB **round-file**. 2 (*tr*) to throw into a wastepaper basket; discard; reject.

round hand NOUN a style of handwriting with large rounded curves. Compare **italic, copperplate** (sense 3).

Roundhead ('raʊndˌhɛd) NOUN *English history* a supporter of Parliament against Charles I during the Civil War. Compare **Cavalier**.
▷ HISTORY referring to their short-cut hair

roundhouse ('raʊndˌhaʊs) NOUN 1 a circular building in which railway locomotives are serviced or housed, radial tracks being fed by a central turntable. 2 *Boxing, slang* **a** a swinging punch or style of punching. **b** (*as modifier*): *a roundhouse style*. 3 *Pinochle US* a meld of all four kings and queens. 4 an obsolete word for **jail**. 5 *Obsolete* a cabin on the quarterdeck of a sailing ship.

rounding ('raʊndɪŋ) NOUN *Computing* a process in which a number is approximated as the closest number that can be expressed using the number of bits or digits available.

rounding error NOUN *Computing* an error introduced into a computation by the need to perform rounding.

roundish ('raʊndɪʃ) ADJECTIVE somewhat round.

roundlet ('raʊndlɪt) NOUN *Literary* a small circle.
▷ HISTORY C14: from Old French *rondelet*, from Old French RONDEL

roundly ('raʊndlɪ) ADVERB 1 frankly, bluntly, or thoroughly: *to be roundly criticized*. 2 in a round manner or so as to be round.

round off VERB (*tr, adverb*) 1 (often foll by *with*) to bring to a satisfactory conclusion; complete, esp agreeably: *we rounded off the evening with a brandy*. 2 to make round or less jagged.

round on VERB (*intr, preposition*) to attack or reply to (someone) with sudden irritation or anger.

round out VERB (*tr, adverb*) 1 to make or become bigger or plumper; fill out, esp so as to be symmetrical. 2 to round up (a number).

round robin NOUN 1 a letter, esp a petition or protest, having the signatures in a circle in order to disguise the order of signing. 2 any letter or petition signed by a number of people. 3 *US and Canadian* a tournament, as in a competitive game or sport, in which each player plays against every other player.

round-shouldered ADJECTIVE denoting a faulty posture characterized by drooping shoulders and a slight forward bending of the back.

roundsman ('raʊndzmən) NOUN, *plural* **-men**. 1 *Brit* a person who makes rounds, as for inspection or to deliver goods. 2 *Austral and NZ* a reporter covering a particular district or topic.

round table NOUN **a** a meeting of parties or people on equal terms for discussion. **b** (*as modifier*): *a round-table conference*.

Round Table NOUN **the**. 1 (in Arthurian legend) the table of King Arthur, shaped so that his knights could sit around it without any having precedence. 2 Arthur and his knights collectively. 3 one of an organization of clubs of young business and professional men who meet in order to further social and business activities and charitable work. 4 (in New Zealand) an organization of businessmen supporting policies of the New Right.

round-the-clock ADJECTIVE (*or as adverb* **round the clock**) throughout the day and night.

round top NOUN a platform round the masthead of a sailing ship.

round tower NOUN a freestanding circular stone belfry built in Ireland from the 10th century beside a monastery and used as a place of refuge.

round trip NOUN a trip to a place and back again, esp returning by a different route.

roundtripping ('raʊndˌtrɪpɪŋ) NOUN *Finance* a form of trading in which a company borrows a sum of money from one source and takes advantage of a short-term rise in interest rates to make a profit by lending it to another.

round-trip ticket NOUN the usual US and Canadian name for **return ticket**.

round up VERB (*tr, adverb*) 1 to gather (animals, suspects, etc.) together: *to round ponies up*. 2 to raise (a number) to the nearest whole number or ten, hundred, or thousand above it. Compare **round down**. ◆ NOUN **roundup**. 3 the act of gathering together livestock, esp cattle, so that they may be branded, counted, or sold. 4 a collection of suspects or criminals by the police, esp in a raid. 5 any similar act of collecting or bringing together: *a roundup of today's news*.

roundwood ('raʊndˌwʊd) NOUN *Forestry* small pieces of timber (about 5–15 cm, or 2–6 in.) in diameter; small logs.

roundworm ('raʊndˌwɜːm) NOUN any nematode worm, esp *Ascaris lumbricoides*, a common intestinal parasite of man and pigs.

roup[1] (ruːp) NOUN *Vet science* any of various chronic respiratory diseases of birds, esp poultry.
▷ HISTORY C16: of unknown origin
▸ **'roupy** ADJECTIVE

roup[2] (raʊp) *Scot and northern English dialect* ◆ VERB (*tr*) 1 to sell by auction. ◆ NOUN 2 an auction.
▷ HISTORY C16 (originally: to shout): of Scandinavian origin; compare Icelandic *raupa* to boast

rouse[1] (raʊz) VERB 1 to bring (oneself or another person) out of sleep, unconsciousness, etc., or (of a person) to come to consciousness in this way. 2 (*tr*) to provoke, stir, or excite: *to rouse someone's anger*. 3 **rouse oneself**. to become active or energetic. 4 *Hunting* to start or cause to start from cover: *to rouse game birds*. 5 (*intr*) *Falconry* (of hawks) to ruffle the feathers and cause them to stand briefly on end (a sign of contentment). 6 (raʊs) (*intr*; foll by *on*) *Austral* to speak scoldingly or rebukingly (to). ◆ NOUN 7 *Chiefly US* another term for **reveille**.
▷ HISTORY C15 (in sense 5): origin obscure
▸ **rousedness** ('raʊzɪdnɪs) NOUN

rouse[2] (raʊz) NOUN *Archaic* 1 an alcoholic drink, esp a full measure. 2 another word for **carousal**.
▷ HISTORY C17: probably a variant of CAROUSE (as in the phrase *drink a rouse*, erroneous for *drink carouse*); compare Danish *drikke en rus* to become drunk, German *Rausch* drunkenness

rouseabout ('raʊsəˌbaʊt) NOUN *Austral and NZ* an unskilled labourer in a shearing shed. Also called: **roustabout**.

rouser ('raʊzə) NOUN **a** a person or thing that rouses people, such as a stirring speech or compelling rock song. **b** (*in combination*) *rabble-rouser*.

rousing ('raʊzɪŋ) ADJECTIVE tending to rouse or excite; lively, brisk, or vigorous: *a rousing chorus*.
▸ **'rousingly** ADVERB

Roussillon (*French* rusijɔ̃) NOUN a former province of S France: united with Aragon in 1172; passed to the French crown in 1659; now forms part of the region of Languedoc-Roussillon.

roust (raʊst) VERB (*tr*; often foll by *out*) to rout or stir, as out of bed.
▷ HISTORY C17: perhaps an alteration of ROUSE[1]

roustabout ('raʊstəˌbaʊt) NOUN 1 an unskilled labourer on an oil rig. 2 *Austral* another word for **rouseabout**. 3 *US and Canadian* a labourer in a circus or fairground.

rout[1] (raʊt) NOUN 1 an overwhelming defeat. 2 a disorderly retreat. 3 a noisy rabble. 4 *Law* a group of three or more people proceeding to commit an illegal act. 5 *Archaic* a large party or social gathering. ◆ VERB 6 (*tr*) to defeat and cause to flee in confusion.
▷ HISTORY C13: from Anglo-Norman *rute*, from Old French: disorderly band, from Latin *ruptus* broken, from *rumpere* to burst; see ROUTE

rout[2] (raʊt) VERB 1 to dig over or turn up (something), esp (of an animal) with the snout; root. 2 (*tr*; usually foll by *out* or *up*) to get or find by searching. 3 (*tr*; usually foll by *out*) to force or drive out: *they routed him out of bed at midnight*. 4 (*tr*; often foll by *out*) to hollow or gouge out. 5 (*intr*) to search, poke, or rummage.
▷ HISTORY C16: variant of ROOT[2]

route (ruːt) NOUN 1 the choice of roads taken to get to a place. 2 a regular journey travelled. 3 (*capital*) *US* a main road between cities: *Route 66*. 4 *Mountaineering* the direction or course taken by a climb. 5 *Med* the means by which a drug or agent is administered or enters the body, such as by mouth or by injection: *oral route*. ◆ VERB **routes, routing** *or* **routeing, routed**. (*tr*) 6 to plan the route of; send by a particular route.
▷ HISTORY C13: from Old French *rute*, from Vulgar Latin *rupta via* (unattested), literally: a broken (established) way, from Latin *ruptus* broken, from *rumpere* to break, burst

> **Language note** When forming the present participle or verbal noun from the verb *to route* it is preferable to retain the *e* in order to distinguish the word from *routing*, the present participle or verbal noun from *rout*[1], to defeat or *rout*[2], to dig, rummage: *the routeing of buses from the city centre to the suburbs*. The spelling *routing* in this sense is, however, sometimes encountered, esp in American English.

routemarch ('ruːtˌmɑːtʃ) NOUN 1 *Military* a long training march. 2 *Informal* any long exhausting walk. ◆ VERB 3 to go or send on a routemarch.

router[1] ('raʊtə) NOUN any of various tools or machines for hollowing out, cutting grooves, etc.

router[2] ('ruːtə) NOUN *Computing* a device that allows packets of data to be moved efficiently between two points on a network.

routh *or* **rowth** (raʊθ) *Scot* ◆ NOUN 1 abundance. ◆ ADJECTIVE 2 abundant; plentiful.
▷ HISTORY C18: of uncertain origin

routine (ruːˈtiːn) NOUN 1 a usual or regular method of procedure, esp one that is unvarying. 2 *Computing* a program or part of a program performing a specific function: *an input routine; an output routine*. 3 a set sequence of dance steps. 4 *Informal* a hackneyed or insincere speech. ◆ ADJECTIVE 5 of, relating to, or characteristic of routine.
▷ HISTORY C17: from Old French, from *route* a customary way, ROUTE
▸ **rou'tinely** ADVERB

roux (ruː) NOUN, *plural* **roux**. a mixture of equal amounts of fat and flour, heated, blended, and used as a basis for sauces.
▷ HISTORY C19: from French: brownish, from Latin *russus* RUSSET

rove[1] (rəʊv) VERB 1 to wander about (a place) with

no fixed direction; roam. [2] (*intr*) (of the eyes) to look around; wander. [3] **have a roving eye.** to show a widespread amorous interest in the opposite sex. [4] (*intr*) *Australian Rules football* to play as a rover. ◆ NOUN [5] the act of roving.
▷HISTORY C15 *roven* (in archery) to shoot at a target chosen at random (C16: to wander, stray), from Scandinavian; compare Icelandic *rāfa* to wander

rove² (rəʊv) VERB [1] (*tr*) to pull out and twist (fibres of wool, cotton, etc.) lightly, as before spinning or in carding. ◆ NOUN [2] wool, cotton, etc., thus prepared.
▷HISTORY C18: of obscure origin

rove³ (rəʊv) NOUN a metal plate through which a rivet is passed and then clenched over.
▷HISTORY C15: from Scandinavian; compare Icelandic *ro*

rove⁴ (rəʊv) VERB a past tense and past participle of **reeve²**.

rove beetle NOUN any beetle of the family *Staphylinidae*, characterized by very short elytra and an elongated body: typically they are of carnivorous or scavenging habits.

rove-over ADJECTIVE *Prosody* (in sprung rhythm) denoting a metrical foot left incomplete at the end of one line and completed in the next.

rover¹ (ˈrəʊvə) NOUN [1] a person who roves; wanderer. [2] *Archery* a mark selected at random for use as a target. [3] *Croquet* a ball that has been driven through all the hoops but has not yet hit the winning peg. [4] *Australian Rules football* one of the three players in the ruck, usually smaller than the other two, selected for his agility in play.
▷HISTORY C15: from ROVE¹

rover² (ˈrəʊvə) NOUN a pirate or pirate ship.
▷HISTORY C14: probably from Middle Dutch or Middle Low German, from *roven* to rob

rover³ (ˈrəʊvə) NOUN a machine for roving wool, cotton, etc., or a person who operates such a machine.
▷HISTORY C18: from ROVE²

Rover *or* **Rover Scout** (ˈrəʊvə) NOUN *Brit* the former name for **Venture Scout**.

roving commission NOUN authority or power given in a general area, without precisely defined terms of reference.

row¹ (rəʊ) NOUN [1] an arrangement of persons or things in a line: *a row of chairs*. [2] **a** *Chiefly Brit* a street, esp a narrow one lined with identical houses. **b** (*capital when part of a street name*): *Church Row*. [3] a line of seats, as in a cinema, theatre, etc. [4] *Maths* a horizontal linear arrangement of numbers, quantities, or terms, esp in a determinant or matrix. [5] a horizontal rank of squares on a chessboard or draughtboard. [6] **in a row.** in succession; one after the other: *he won two gold medals in a row*. [7] **a hard row to hoe.** a difficult task or assignment.
▷HISTORY Old English *rāw*, *rǣw*; related to Old High German *rīga* line, Lithuanian *raiwe* strip

row² (rəʊ) VERB [1] to propel (a boat) by using oars. [2] (*tr*) to carry (people, goods, etc.) in a rowing boat. [3] to be propelled by means of (oars or oarsmen). [4] (*intr*) to take part in the racing of rowing boats as a sport, esp in eights, in which each member of the crew pulls one oar. Compare **scull** (sense 6). [5] (*tr*) to race against in a boat propelled by oars: *Oxford row Cambridge every year*. ◆ NOUN [6] an act, instance, period, or distance of rowing. [7] an excursion in a rowing boat. ◆ See also **row over**.
▷HISTORY Old English *rōwan*; related to Middle Dutch *roien*, Middle High German *rüejen*, Old Norse *rōa*, Latin *rēmus* oar
▸ˈ**rower** NOUN ▸ˈ**rowing** NOUN

row³ (raʊ) NOUN [1] a noisy quarrel or dispute. [2] a noisy disturbance; commotion: *we couldn't hear the music for the row next door*. [3] a reprimand. [4] **give (someone) a row.** *Informal* to scold (someone); tell off. ◆ VERB [5] (*intr*; often foll by *with*) to quarrel noisily. [6] (*tr*) *Archaic* to reprimand.
▷HISTORY C18: origin unknown

rowan (ˈrəʊən, ˈraʊ-) NOUN another name for the (European) **mountain ash**.
▷HISTORY C16: from Scandinavian; compare Norwegian *rogn*, *raun*, Old Norse *reynir*

rowboat (ˈrəʊˌbəʊt) NOUN the usual US and Canadian word for **rowing boat**.

rowdy (ˈraʊdɪ) ADJECTIVE **-dier, -diest.** [1] tending to create noisy disturbances; rough, loud, or disorderly: *a rowdy gang of football supporters*. ◆ NOUN, *plural* **-dies.** [2] a person who behaves in a rough disorderly fashion.
▷HISTORY C19: originally US slang, perhaps related to ROW³
▸ˈ**rowdily** ADVERB ▸ˈ**rowdiness** NOUN

rowdyism (ˈraʊdɪɪzəm) NOUN rowdy behaviour or tendencies or a habitual pattern of rowdy behaviour: *the problem of rowdyism at football matches*.

rowel (ˈraʊəl) NOUN [1] a small spiked wheel attached to a spur. [2] *Vet science, obsolete* a piece of leather or other material inserted under the skin of a horse to act as a seton and allow drainage. ◆ VERB **-els, -elling, -elled** *or US* **-els, -eling, -eled.** (*tr*) [3] to goad (a horse) using a rowel. [4] *Vet science, obsolete* to insert a rowel in (the skin of a horse) to allow drainage.
▷HISTORY C14: from Old French *roel* a little wheel, from *roe* a wheel, from Latin *rota*

rowen (ˈraʊən) NOUN another word for **aftermath** (sense 2).
▷HISTORY C14 *reywayn*, corresponding to Old French *regaïn*, from RE- + *gaïn* rowen, from *gaignier* to till, earn; see GAIN¹

row house (rəʊ) NOUN a US and Canadian term for **terraced house**.

rowing boat (ˈrəʊɪŋ) NOUN *Chiefly Brit* a small boat propelled by one or more pairs of oars. Usual US and Canadian word: **rowboat**.

rowing machine NOUN a device with oars and a sliding seat resembling a sculling boat, used to provide exercise.

rowlock (ˈrɒlək) NOUN a swivelling device attached to the gunwale of a boat that holds an oar in place and acts as a fulcrum during rowing. Usual US and Canadian word: **oarlock**.

row over (rəʊ) VERB (*intr, adverb*) [1] to win a rowing race unopposed, by rowing the course. ◆ NOUN **rowover.** [2] the act of doing this.

rowth (raʊθ) NOUN, ADJECTIVE *Scot* a variant spelling of **routh**.

Roxburghshire (ˈrɒksbərəʃɪə, -ʃə) NOUN (until 1975) a county of SE Scotland, now part of Scottish Borders council area.

Roy (rɔɪ) NOUN *Austral slang* a trendy Australian male.

royal (ˈrɔɪəl) ADJECTIVE [1] of, relating to, or befitting a king, queen, or other monarch; regal. [2] (*prenominal; often capital*) established, chartered by, under the patronage or in the service of royalty: *the Royal Society of St George*. [3] being a member of a royal family. [4] above the usual or normal in standing, size, quality, etc. [5] *Informal* unusually good or impressive; first-rate. [6] *Nautical* just above the topgallant (in the phrase **royal mast**). ◆ NOUN [7] (*sometimes capital*) *Informal* a member of a royal family. [8] Also called: **royal stag.** a stag with antlers having 12 or more branches. [9] *Nautical* a sail set next above the topgallant, on a royal mast. [10] a size of printing paper, 20 by 25 inches. [11] Also called: **small royal.** *Chiefly Brit* a size of writing paper, 19 by 24 inches. [12] any of various book sizes, esp 6¼ by 10 inches (**royal octavo**), 6¾ by 10¼ inches (**super royal octavo**), and (chiefly Brit) 10 by 12½ inches (**royal quarto**) and 10¼ by 13½ inches (**super royal quarto**).
▷HISTORY C14: from Old French *roial*, from Latin *rēgālis*, fit for a king, from *rēx* king; compare REGAL¹
▸ˈ**royally** ADVERB

Royal Academy NOUN a society founded by George III in 1768 to foster a national school of painting, sculpture, and design in England. Full name: **Royal Academy of Arts**.

Royal Air Force NOUN the air force of the United Kingdom. Abbreviation: **RAF**.

Royal Air Force List NOUN *Brit* an official list of all serving commissioned officers of the RAF and reserve officers liable for recall.

Royal and Ancient Club NOUN **the.** a golf club, headquarters of the sport's ruling body, based in St Andrews, Scotland. Abbreviation: **R&A**.

royal assent NOUN (in Britain) the formal signing of an act of Parliament by the sovereign, by which it becomes law.

royal blue NOUN **a** a deep blue colour. **b** (*as adjective*): *a royal-blue carpet*.

Royal British Legion NOUN *Brit* an organization founded in 1921 to provide services and assistance for former members of the armed forces.

royal burgh NOUN (in Scotland) a burgh that was established by a royal charter granted directly by the sovereign.

Royal Canadian Mounted Police NOUN the federal police force of Canada. Abbreviation: **RCMP**.

Royal Commission NOUN (in Britain) a body set up by the monarch on the recommendation of the prime minister to gather information about the operation of existing laws or to investigate any social, educational, or other matter. The commission has prescribed terms of reference and reports to the government on how any change might be achieved.

royal duke NOUN a duke who is also a royal prince, being a member of the royal family.

Royal Engineers PLURAL NOUN a branch of the British army that undertakes the building of fortifications, mines, bridges, and other engineering works. Abbreviation: **RE**.

royal fern NOUN a fern, *Osmunda regalis*, of damp regions, having large fronds up to 2 metres (7 feet) in height, some of which are modified for bearing spores: family *Osmundaceae*.

royal flush NOUN *Poker* a hand made up of the five top honours of a suit.

Royal Highness NOUN a title of honour used in addressing or referring to a member of a royal family.

royal icing NOUN *Brit* a hard white icing made from egg whites and icing sugar, used for coating and decorating cakes, esp fruit cakes.

Royal Institution NOUN a British society founded in 1799 for the dissemination of scientific knowledge.

royalist (ˈrɔɪəlɪst) NOUN [1] a supporter of a monarch or monarchy, esp a supporter of the Stuarts during the English Civil War. [2] *Informal* an extreme reactionary or conservative: *an economic royalist*. ◆ ADJECTIVE *also (less commonly)* **royalistic.** [3] of, characteristic of, or relating to royalists.
▸ˈ**royalism** NOUN

royal jelly NOUN a substance secreted by the pharyngeal glands of worker bees and fed to all larvae when very young and to larvae destined to become queens throughout their development.

Royal Leamington Spa NOUN the official name of **Leamington Spa**.

Royal Marines PLURAL NOUN *Brit* a corps of soldiers specially trained in amphibious warfare. Abbreviation: **RM**.

Royal Mint NOUN a British organization having the sole right to manufacture coins since the 16th century. In 1968 it moved from London to Llantrisant in Wales.

Royal National Theatre NOUN a theatre complex in London, on the S bank of the Thames (opened 1976). The prefix Royal was added in 1988. It houses the Royal National Theatre Company.

Royal Navy NOUN the navy of the United Kingdom. Abbreviation: **RN**.

royal palm NOUN any of several palm trees of the genus *Roystonea*, esp *R. regia*, of tropical America, having a tall trunk with a tuft of feathery pinnate leaves.

royal poinciana NOUN a leguminous tree, *Delonix regia*, that is native to Madagascar but widely cultivated elsewhere, having clusters of large scarlet flowers and long pods. Also called: **flamboyant**.

royal purple NOUN **a** a deep reddish-purple colour, sometimes approaching a strong violet. **b** (*as adjective*): *a royal-purple dress*.

royal road NOUN an easy or direct way of achieving a desired end: *the royal road to success*.

Royal Scots Greys PLURAL NOUN **the.** a British cavalry regiment, the Second Dragoons. Also called: **Greys, Scots Greys**.
▷HISTORY C17: from their grey uniforms

Royal Society NOUN an association founded in England by Charles II in 1660 to promote research in the sciences.

royal stag NOUN See **royal** (sense 8).

Royal Standard NOUN a flag bearing the arms of the British sovereign, flown only when she (or he) is present.

royal tennis NOUN another name for **real tennis**.

royalty ('rɔɪəltɪ) NOUN, *plural* **-ties**. 1 the rank, power, or position of a king or queen. 2 **a** royal persons collectively. **b** one who belongs to the royal family. 3 any quality characteristic of a monarch; kingliness or regal dignity. 4 a percentage of the revenue from the sale of a book, performance of a theatrical work, use of a patented invention or of land, etc., paid to the author, inventor, or proprietor.

Royal Victorian Order NOUN (in Britain) an order of chivalry founded by Queen Victoria in 1896, membership of which is conferred for special services to the sovereign. Abbreviation: **VO**.

royal warrant NOUN an authorization to a tradesman to supply goods to a royal household.

Royal Worcester NOUN Worcester china made after 1862.

rozzer ('rɒzə) NOUN *Cockney slang* a policeman.
▷HISTORY C19: of unknown origin

RP ABBREVIATION FOR: 1 **Received Pronunciation**. 2 Reformed Presbyterian. 3 Regius Professor. ◆ 4 INTERNATIONAL CAR REGISTRATION FOR (Republic of the) Philippines.

RPC ABBREVIATION FOR Royal Pioneer Corps.

RPG ABBREVIATION FOR: 1 report program generator: a business-oriented computer programming language. 2 rocket propelled grenade. 3 role-playing game.

RPI (in Britain) ABBREVIATION FOR **retail price index**.

rpm ABBREVIATION FOR: 1 revolutions per minute. 2 resale price maintenance.

rps ABBREVIATION FOR revolutions per second.

RPS (in Britain) ABBREVIATION FOR Royal Photographic Society.

rpt ABBREVIATION FOR report.

RPV ABBREVIATION FOR remotely piloted vehicle.

RQ ABBREVIATION FOR **respiratory quotient**.

RR ABBREVIATION FOR: 1 Right Reverend. 2 (in the US and Canada) railroad. 3 (in the US and Canada) rural route.

-rrhagia NOUN COMBINING FORM (in pathology) an abnormal discharge or flow: *menorrhagia*.
▷HISTORY from Greek *-rrhagia* a bursting forth, from *rhēgnunai* to burst, break

-rrhoea *or esp US* **-rrhea** NOUN COMBINING FORM (in pathology) a discharge or flow: *diarrhoea*.
▷HISTORY from New Latin, from Greek *-rrhoia*, from *rhoia* a flowing, from *rhein* to flow

rRNA ABBREVIATION FOR ribosomal RNA.

RRP ABBREVIATION FOR recommended retail price.

RRSP (in Canada) ABBREVIATION FOR Registered Retirement Savings Plan.

Rs SYMBOL FOR rupees.

RS (in Britain) ABBREVIATION FOR Royal Society.

RSA ABBREVIATION FOR: 1 Republic of South Africa. 2 Royal Scottish Academy. 3 Royal Scottish Academician. 4 Royal Society of Arts. 5 (in New Zealand) Returned Services Association.

RSC ABBREVIATION FOR: 1 Royal Shakespeare Company. 2 Royal Society of Chemistry.

RSFSR ABBREVIATION FOR (formerly) Russian Soviet Federative Socialist Republic.

RSG (in Britain) ABBREVIATION FOR: 1 rate support grant. 2 *Civil defence* Regional Seat of Government.

RSGB ABBREVIATION FOR Radio Society of Great Britain (amateur radio operators).

RSI ABBREVIATION FOR **repetitive strain** *or* **stress injury**.

RSJ ABBREVIATION FOR rolled-steel joist.

RSL ABBREVIATION FOR: 1 Royal Society of Literature. 2 (in Australia) Returned Services League.

RSM ABBREVIATION FOR: 1 **regimental sergeant major**. 2 Royal School of Music. 3 Royal Society of Medicine. ◆ 4 INTERNATIONAL CAR REGISTRATION FOR (Republic of) San Marino.

RSNO ABBREVIATION FOR Royal Scottish National Orchestra.

RSNZ ABBREVIATION FOR Royal Society of New Zealand.

RSPB (in Britain) ABBREVIATION FOR Royal Society for the Protection of Birds.

RSPCA (in Britain and Australia) ABBREVIATION FOR Royal Society for the Prevention of Cruelty to Animals.

RSV ABBREVIATION FOR: 1 Revised Standard Version (of the Bible). 2 respiratory syncytial virus.

RSVP ABBREVIATION FOR répondez s'il vous plaît.
▷HISTORY French: please reply

rt ABBREVIATION FOR right.

RT ABBREVIATION FOR radio telegraphy *or* radio telephony.

RTA ABBREVIATION FOR road traffic accident.

RTC (in India) ABBREVIATION FOR: 1 Road Transport Corporation. 2 Round Table Conference.

RTE ABBREVIATION FOR Radio Telefis Éireann.
▷HISTORY Irish Gaelic: Irish Radio and Television

RTF *Computing* ABBREVIATION FOR rich text format: a standard file format allowing file transfer between different applications and operating systems.

Rt Hon. ABBREVIATION FOR Right Honourable.

RTR ABBREVIATION FOR Royal Tank Regiment.

Rt Revd *or* **Rt Rev.** ABBREVIATION FOR Right Reverend.

RTT *or* **RTTY** ABBREVIATION FOR radioteletype.

ru THE INTERNET DOMAIN NAME FOR Russian Federation.

Ru THE CHEMICAL SYMBOL FOR ruthenium.

RU 1 ABBREVIATION FOR Rugby Union. ◆ 2 INTERNATIONAL CAR REGISTRATION FOR Burundi.

Ruanda-Urundi (ru'ændəʊ'rʊndɪ) NOUN a former territory of central Africa: part of German East Africa from 1890; a League of Nations mandate under Belgian administration from 1919; a United Nations trusteeship from 1946; divided into the independent states of Rwanda and Burundi in 1962.

rub (rʌb) VERB **rubs, rubbing, rubbed**. 1 to apply pressure and friction to (something) with a circular or backward and forward motion. 2 to move (something) with pressure along, over, or against (a surface). 3 to chafe or fray. 4 (*tr*) to bring into a certain condition by rubbing: *rub it clean*. 5 (*tr*) to spread with pressure, esp in order to cause to be absorbed: *he rubbed ointment into his back*. 6 (foll by *off, out, away*, etc.) to remove or be removed by rubbing. 7 *Bowls* (of a bowl) to be slowed or deflected by an uneven patch on the green. 8 (*tr*; often foll by *together*) to move against each other with pressure and friction (esp in the phrases **rub one's hands**, often a sign of glee, anticipation, or satisfaction, and **rub noses**, a greeting among Eskimos). 9 **rub (someone's) nose in it**. *Informal* to remind (someone) unkindly of his failing or error. 10 **rub (up) the wrong way**. to arouse anger (in); annoy. 11 **rub shoulders** (*or* **elbows**) **with**. *Informal* to mix with socially or associate with. ◆ NOUN 12 the act of rubbing. 13 (preceded by *the*) an obstacle or difficulty (esp in the phrase **there's the rub**). 14 something that hurts the feelings or annoys; rebuke. 15 *Bowls* an uneven patch in the green. 16 any roughness or unevenness of surface. 17 **a** *Golf* an incident of accidental interference with the ball. **b** *Informal* a piece of good or bad luck. ◆ See also **rub along, rub down, rub in, rub off, rub out, rub up**.
▷HISTORY C15: perhaps from Low German *rubben*, of obscure origin

rubaboo ('rʌbə,buː) NOUN *Canadian* a soup or stew made by boiling pemmican with, if available, flour and vegetables.
▷HISTORY C19: from Canadian French *rababou*, from Algonquian

rubáiyát ('ruːbaɪ,jæt) NOUN *Prosody* (in Persian poetry) a verse form consisting of four-line stanzas.
▷HISTORY C19: from Arabic *rubā'īyah*, from *rubā'ī* consisting of four elements

Rub' al Khali ('rʊb æl 'kɑːlɪ) NOUN a desert in S Arabia, mainly in Saudi Arabia, extending southeast from Nejd to Hadramaut and northeast from Yemen to the United Arab Emirates. Area: about 777 000 sq. km (300 000 sq. miles). English names: **Great Sandy Desert, Empty Quarter**. Also called: **Ar Rimal, Dahna**.

rub along VERB (*intr, adverb*) *Brit* 1 to continue in spite of difficulties. 2 to maintain an amicable relationship; not quarrel.

rubato (ruː'bɑːtəʊ) *Music* ◆ NOUN, *plural* **-tos**. 1 flexibility of tempo in performance. ◆ ADJECTIVE, ADVERB 2 to be played with a flexible tempo.
▷HISTORY C19: from the Italian phrase *tempo rubato*, literally: stolen time, from *rubare* to ROB

rubber[1] ('rʌbə) NOUN 1 Also called: **India rubber, gum elastic, caoutchouc**. a cream to dark brown elastic material obtained by coagulating and drying the latex from certain plants, esp the tree *Hevea brasiliensis*. 2 any of a large variety of elastomers produced by improving the properties of natural rubber or by synthetic means. 3 *Chiefly Brit* a piece of rubber or felt used for erasing something written, typed, etc.; eraser. 4 a coarse file. 5 a cloth, pad, etc., used for polishing or buffing. 6 a person who rubs something in order to smooth, polish, or massage. 7 (*often plural*) *Chiefly US and Canadian* a rubberized waterproof article, such as a mackintosh or overshoe. 8 *Slang* a male contraceptive; condom. 9 (*modifier*) made of or producing rubber: *a rubber ball; a rubber factory*.
▷HISTORY C17: from RUB + -ER[1]; the tree was so named because its product was used for rubbing out writing

rubber[2] ('rʌbə) NOUN 1 *Bridge, whist* **a** a match of three games. **b** the deal that wins such a match. 2 a series of matches or games in any of various sports.
▷HISTORY C16: origin unknown

rubber band NOUN a continuous loop of thin rubber, used to hold papers, etc., together. Also called: **elastic band**.

rubber bridge NOUN a form of bridge in which fresh hands are dealt for each round and the aim is to win a rubber. Compare **duplicate bridge**.

rubber cement NOUN any of a number of adhesives made by dissolving rubber in a solvent such as benzene.

rubber cheque NOUN *Facetious* a cheque that bounces.

rubber goods PLURAL NOUN *Euphemistic* contraceptives; condoms.

rubberize *or* **rubberise** ('rʌbə,raɪz) VERB (*tr*) to coat or impregnate with rubber.

rubber jaw NOUN *Vet science* a condition in which the mandible becomes demineralized and excessively mobile in animals with advanced renal disease.

rubberneck ('rʌbə,nɛk) *Slang* ◆ NOUN 1 a person who stares or gapes inquisitively, esp in a naive or foolish manner. 2 a sightseer or tourist. ◆ VERB 3 (*intr*) to stare in a naive or foolish manner.

rubber plant NOUN 1 a moraceous plant, *Ficus elastica*, with glossy leathery leaves: a tall tree in India and Malaya, it is cultivated as a house plant in Europe and America. 2 any of several tropical trees, the sap of which yields rubber. See also **rubber tree**.

rubber stamp NOUN 1 a device used for imprinting dates or commonly used phrases on forms, invoices, etc. 2 automatic authorization of a payment, proposal, etc., without challenge. 3 a person who makes such automatic authorizations; a cipher or person of little account. ◆ VERB **rubber-stamp**. (*tr*) 4 to imprint (forms, invoices, etc.) with a rubber stamp. 5 *Informal* to approve automatically.

rubber tree NOUN a tropical American euphorbiaceous tree, *Hevea brasiliensis*, cultivated throughout the tropics, esp in Malaya, for the latex of its stem, which is the major source of commercial rubber. See also **Pará rubber**.

rubbery ('rʌbərɪ) ADJECTIVE having the texture of or resembling rubber, esp in flexibility or toughness.

rubbing ('rʌbɪŋ) NOUN an impression taken of an incised or raised surface, such as a brass plate on a tomb, by laying paper over it and rubbing with wax, graphite, etc.

rubbing alcohol NOUN a liquid usually consisting of 70 per cent denatured ethyl alcohol, used by external application as an antiseptic or rubefacient.

rubbish ('rʌbɪʃ) NOUN 1 worthless, useless, or unwanted matter. 2 discarded or waste matter; refuse. 3 foolish words or speech; nonsense. ◆ VERB 4 (*tr*) *Informal* to criticize; attack verbally.
▷HISTORY C14 *robys*, of uncertain origin

rubbish bin NOUN a container for rubbish. NZ equivalent: **rubbish tin.**

rubbishy ('rʌbɪʃɪ) ADJECTIVE worthless, of poor quality, or useless.

rubbity ('rʌbətɪ) *or* **rubbidy** ('rʌbədɪ) NOUN, *plural* **-ties** *or* **-dies.** a pub.
▷**HISTORY** from rhyming slang *rubbity dub*

rubble ('rʌbᵊl) NOUN 1 fragments of broken stones, bricks, etc. 2 any fragmented solid material. 3 *Quarrying* the weathered surface layer of rock. 4 Also called: **rubblework.** masonry constructed of broken pieces of rock, stone, etc.
▷**HISTORY** C14 *robyl;* perhaps related to Middle English *rubben* to rub, or to RUBBISH
▸'**rubbly** ADJECTIVE

rubby ('rʌbɪ) NOUN, *plural* **-bies.** *Canadian slang* 1 rubbing alcohol, esp when mixed with cheap wine for drinking. 2 a person who drinks such mixtures, esp a derelict alcoholic.

rub down VERB *(adverb)* 1 to dry or clean (a horse, athlete, oneself, etc.) vigorously, esp after exercise. 2 to make or become smooth by rubbing. 3 *(tr)* to prepare (a surface) for painting by rubbing it with sandpaper. ◆ NOUN **rubdown.** 4 the act of rubbing down. 5 the Hong Kong term for **dressing-down.**

rube (ru:b) NOUN *US and Canadian slang* an unsophisticated countryman.
▷**HISTORY** C20: probably from the name *Reuben*

rubefy ('ru:bɪˌfaɪ) VERB **-fies, -fying, -fied.** *(tr)* to make red, esp (of a counterirritant) to make the skin go red.
▷**HISTORY** C19: from Latin *rubefacere,* from *rubeus* red + *facere* to make
▸**rubefacient** (ˌru:bɪ'feɪʃənt) ADJECTIVE, NOUN
▸**rubefaction** (ˌru:bɪ'fækʃən) NOUN

rubella (ru:'bɛlə) NOUN a mild contagious viral disease, somewhat similar to measles, characterized by cough, sore throat, skin rash, and occasionally vomiting. It can cause congenital defects if caught during the first three months of pregnancy. Also called: **German measles.**
▷**HISTORY** C19: from New Latin, from Latin *rubellus* reddish, from *rubeus* red

rubellite ('ru:bɪˌlaɪt, ru:'bɛl-) NOUN a red transparent variety of tourmaline, used as a gemstone.
▷**HISTORY** C18: from Latin *rubellus* reddish

Rubenesque (ˌru:bəˌnɛsk) ADJECTIVE (of a woman) having the physique associated with portraits of women by Sir Peter Paul Rubens (1577–1640), the Flemish painter; plump and attractive.

rubeola (ru:'bi:ələ) NOUN technical name for **measles.** Compare **rubella.**
▷**HISTORY** C17: from New Latin, from Latin *rubeus* reddish, from *ruber* red
▸**ru'beolar** ADJECTIVE

rubescent (ru:'bɛsᵊnt) ADJECTIVE *Literary* reddening; blushing.
▷**HISTORY** C18: from Latin *rubescere* to grow red, from *ruber* red
▸**ru'bescence** NOUN

rubiaceous (ˌru:bɪ'eɪʃəs) ADJECTIVE of, relating to, or belonging to the *Rubiaceae,* a widely distributed family of trees, shrubs, and herbaceous plants that includes the coffee and cinchona trees, gardenia, madder, and bedstraws.
▷**HISTORY** C19: from New Latin *Rubiaceae,* from Latin *rubia* madder, from *rubeus* red

Rubicon ('ru:bɪkən) NOUN 1 a stream in N Italy: in ancient times the boundary between Italy and Cisalpine Gaul. By leading his army across it and marching on Rome in 49 B.C., Julius Caesar broke the law that a general might not lead an army out of the province to which he was posted and so committed himself to civil war with the senatorial party. 2 *(sometimes not capital)* a point of no return. 3 a penalty in piquet by which the score of a player who fails to reach 100 points in six hands is added to his opponent's. 4 **cross** (*or* **pass**) **the Rubicon.** to commit oneself irrevocably to some course of action.

rubicund ('ru:bɪkənd) ADJECTIVE of a reddish colour; ruddy; rosy.
▷**HISTORY** C16: from Latin *rubicundus,* from *rubēre* to be ruddy, from *ruber* red
▸**rubicundity** (ˌru:bɪ'kʌndɪtɪ) NOUN

rubidium (ru:'bɪdɪəm) NOUN a soft highly reactive radioactive element of the alkali metal group; the 16th most abundant element in the earth's crust (310 parts per million), occurring principally in pollucite, carnallite, and lepidolite. It is used in electronic valves, photocells, and special glass. Symbol: Rb; atomic no.: 37; atomic wt.: 85.4678; half-life of ^{87}Rb: 5×10^{11} years; valency: 1, 2, 3, or 4; relative density: 1.532 (solid), 1.475 (liquid); melting pt.: 39.48°C; boiling pt.: 688°C.
▷**HISTORY** C19: from New Latin, from Latin *rubidus* dark red, with reference to the two red lines in its spectrum
▸**ru'bidic** ADJECTIVE

rubidium-strontium dating NOUN a technique for determining the age of minerals based on the occurrence in natural rubidium of a fixed amount of the radioisotope ^{87}Rb which decays to the stable strontium isotope ^{87}Sr with a half-life of 4.7×10^{11} years. Measurement of the ratio of these isotopes thus gives the age of a mineral, for ages of up to about 4×10^{9} years.

rubiginous (ru:'bɪdʒɪnəs) ADJECTIVE rust-coloured.
▷**HISTORY** C17: from Latin *rūbīginōsus,* from *rūbīgō* rust, from *ruber* red

Rubik cube ('ru:bɪk) *or* **Rubik's cube** NOUN *Trademark* a puzzle consisting of a cube of six colours, each face of which is made up of nine squares, eight of which are individually rotatable. The aim is to swivel the squares until each face of the cube shows one colour only.
▷**HISTORY** C20: named after Professor Erno *Rubik* (born 1944), its Hungarian inventor

rub in VERB *(tr, adverb)* 1 to spread with pressure, esp in order to cause to be absorbed. 2 **rub it in.** *Informal* to harp on (something distasteful to a person, of which he does not wish to be reminded).

rubious ('ru:bɪəs) ADJECTIVE *Literary* of the colour ruby; dark red.
▷**HISTORY** C17: from RUBY + -OUS

ruble ('ru:bᵊl) NOUN a variant spelling of **rouble.**

rub off VERB 1 to remove or be removed by rubbing. 2 *(intr;* often foll by *on* or *onto)* to have an effect through close association or contact, esp so as to make similar: *her crude manners have rubbed off on you.* ◆ NOUN **rub-off.** 3 a resulting effect on something else; consequences: *a positive rub-off.*

rub out VERB *(tr, adverb)* 1 to remove or be removed with a rubber. 2 *US slang* to murder. 3 *Australian Rules football* to suspend (a player).

rubric ('ru:brɪk) NOUN 1 a title, heading, or initial letter in a book, manuscript, or section of a legal code, esp one printed or painted in red ink or in some similarly distinguishing manner. 2 a set of rules of conduct or procedure. 3 a set of directions for the conduct of Christian church services, often printed in red in a prayer book or missal. 4 instructions to a candidate at the head of the examination paper. 5 an obsolete name for **red ochre.** ◆ ADJECTIVE 6 written, printed, or marked in red.
▷**HISTORY** C15 *rubrike* red ochre, red lettering, from Latin *rubrīca* *(terra)* red (earth), ruddle, from *ruber* red
▸'**rubrical** ADJECTIVE ▸'**rubrically** ADVERB

rubricate ('ru:brɪˌkeɪt) VERB *(tr)* 1 to print (a book or manuscript) with red titles, headings, etc. 2 to mark in red. 3 to supply with or regulate by rubrics.
▷**HISTORY** C16: from Latin *rubricāre* to colour red, from *rubrīca* red earth; see RUBRIC
▸ˌ**rubri'cation** NOUN ▸'**rubriˌcator** NOUN

rubrician (ru:'brɪʃən) NOUN an authority on liturgical rubrics.

rubstone ('rʌbˌstəʊn) NOUN a stone used for sharpening or smoothing, esp a whetstone.

rub up VERB *(adverb) Chiefly Brit* 1 (when *intr,* foll by *on)* to refresh one's memory (of). 2 *(tr)* to smooth or polish.

ruby ('ru:bɪ) NOUN, *plural* **-bies.** 1 a deep red transparent precious variety of corundum: occurs naturally in Myanmar and Sri Lanka but is also synthesized. It is used as a gemstone, in lasers, and for bearings and rollers in watchmaking. Formula: Al_2O_3. 2 **a** the deep-red colour of a ruby. **b** *(as adjective): ruby lips.* 3 **a** something resembling, made of, or containing a ruby. **b** *(as modifier): ruby necklace.* 4 *(modifier)* denoting a fortieth anniversary: *our ruby wedding.* 5 (formerly) a size of printer's type approximately equal to 5½ point.
▷**HISTORY** C14: from Old French *rubi,* from Latin *rubeus* reddish, from *ruber* red
▸'**ruby-ˌlike** ADJECTIVE

ruby glass NOUN glass that has a deep rich red colour produced from oxides of various minerals, such as lead, copper, and iron.

ruby silver NOUN another name for **proustite** or **pyrargyrite.**

ruby spinel NOUN a red transparent variety of spinel, used as a gemstone.

ruby-tail wasp NOUN any of various brightly coloured wasps of the family *Chrysididae,* having a metallic sheen, which parasitize bees and other solitary wasps.

RUC ABBREVIATION FOR (the former) Royal Ulster Constabulary, now superseded by the Police Service of Northern Ireland.

ruche *or* **rouche** (ru:ʃ) NOUN a strip of pleated or frilled lawn, lace, etc., used to decorate blouses, dresses, etc., or worn around the neck like a small ruff as in the 16th century.
▷**HISTORY** C19: from French, literally: beehive, from Medieval Latin *rūsca* bark of a tree, of Celtic origin

ruching ('ru:ʃɪŋ) NOUN 1 material used for a ruche. 2 a ruche or ruches collectively.

ruck[1] (rʌk) NOUN 1 a large number or quantity; mass, esp of ordinary or undistinguished people or things. 2 (in a race) a group of competitors who are well behind the leaders at the finish. 3 *Rugby* a loose scrum that forms around the ball when it is on the ground. 4 *Australian Rules football* the three players, two ruckmen and a rover, that do not have fixed positions but follow the ball closely. ◆ VERB 5 *(intr) Rugby* to try to win the ball by mauling and scrummaging.
▷**HISTORY** C13 (meaning "heap of firewood"): perhaps from Scandinavian; compare Old Norse *hraukr* RICK[1]

ruck[2] (rʌk) NOUN 1 a wrinkle, crease, or fold. ◆ VERB 2 (usually foll by *up)* to become or make wrinkled, creased, or puckered.
▷**HISTORY** C18: from Scandinavian; related to Old Norse *hrukka*

ruck[3] (rʌk) NOUN *Prison slang* a fight.
▷**HISTORY** C20: short for RUCKUS

ruckle ('rʌkᵊl) NOUN, VERB *Brit* another word for **ruck**[2].

ruckman ('rʌkˌmæn, -mən) NOUN, *plural* **-men.** *Australian Rules football* a person who plays in the ruck.

rucksack ('rʌkˌsæk) NOUN a large bag, usually having two straps and a supporting frame, carried on the back and often used by climbers, campers, etc. US and Canadian name: **backpack.**
▷**HISTORY** C19: from German, literally: back sack

ruckus ('rʌkəs) NOUN, *plural* **-uses.** *Informal* an uproar; ruction.
▷**HISTORY** C20: from RUCTION + RUMPUS

ruction ('rʌkʃən) NOUN *Informal* 1 an uproar; noisy or quarrelsome disturbance. 2 *(plural)* a violent and unpleasant row; trouble: *there'll be ructions when she hears about it.*
▷**HISTORY** C19: perhaps changed from INSURRECTION

rudaceous (ru:'deɪʃəs) ADJECTIVE (of conglomerate, breccia, and similar rocks) composed of coarse-grained material. Compare **arenaceous** (sense 1), **argillaceous.**
▷**HISTORY** C20: from Latin *rudis* coarse, rough + -ACEOUS

Ruda Śląska ('ru:də 'ʃlɔnskə) NOUN a town in SW Poland: coalmining. Pop.: 159 665 (1999 est.).

rudbeckia (rʌd'bɛkɪə) NOUN any plant of the North American genus *Rudbeckia,* cultivated for their showy flowers, which have golden-yellow rays and green or black conical centres: family *Asteraceae* (composites). See also **coneflower, black-eyed Susan.**
▷**HISTORY** C18: New Latin, named after Olaus *Rudbeck* (1630–1702), Swedish botanist

rudd (rʌd) NOUN a European freshwater cyprinid fish, *Scardinius erythrophthalmus,* having a compressed dark greenish body and reddish ventral and tail fins.
▷**HISTORY** C17: probably from dialect *rud* red colour, from Old English *rudu* redness

rudder ('rʌdə) NOUN 1 *Nautical* a pivoted vertical

vane that projects into the water at the stern of a vessel and can be controlled by a tiller, wheel, or other apparatus to steer the vessel. 2 a vertical control surface attached to the rear of the fin used to steer an aircraft, in conjunction with the ailerons. 3 anything that guides or directs.
▷HISTORY Old English *rōther*; related to Old French *rōther*, Old High German *ruodar*, Old Norse *rōthr*. See ROW[2]
▸ **'rudderless** ADJECTIVE

rudderhead ('rʌdəˌhɛd) NOUN *Nautical* the top of the rudderpost, to which the steering apparatus may be fixed.

rudderpost ('rʌdəˌpəʊst) NOUN *Nautical* 1 Also called: **rudderstock** ('rʌdəˌstɒk). a postlike member at the forward edge of a rudder. 2 the part of the stern frame of a vessel to which a rudder is fitted.

ruddle ('rʌdᵊl), **raddle,** *or* **reddle** NOUN 1 a red ochre, used esp to mark sheep. ◆ VERB 2 (*tr*) to mark (sheep) with ruddle.
▷HISTORY C16: diminutive formed from Old English *rudu* redness; see RUDD

ruddock ('rʌdək) NOUN *Brit* a dialect name for the **robin** (sense 1).
▷HISTORY Old English *rudduc*; related to *rudu* redness; see RUDD

ruddy ('rʌdɪ) ADJECTIVE **-dier, -diest.** 1 (of the complexion) having a healthy reddish colour, usually resulting from an outdoor life. 2 coloured red or pink: *a ruddy sky*. ◆ ADVERB, ADJECTIVE *Informal, chiefly Brit* 3 (intensifier) bloody; damned: *a ruddy fool*.
▷HISTORY Old English *rudig*, from *rudu* redness (see RUDD); related to Old High German *rot* RED[1], Swedish *rod*, Old Norse *rythga* to make rusty
▸ **'ruddily** ADVERB ▸ **'ruddiness** NOUN

ruddy duck NOUN a small duck, *Oxyura jamaicensis*, that inhabits marshes, ponds, etc., in North America and N South America and has a stiff upright tail. The male has a reddish-brown body and blue bill in the breeding season.

rude (ruːd) ADJECTIVE 1 insulting or uncivil; discourteous; impolite: *he was rude about her hairstyle*. 2 lacking refinement; coarse or uncouth. 3 vulgar or obscene: *a rude joke*. 4 unexpected and unpleasant: *a rude awakening to the facts of economic life*. 5 roughly or crudely made: *we made a rude shelter on the island*. 6 rough or harsh in sound, appearance, or behaviour. 7 humble or lowly. 8 (*prenominal*) robust or sturdy: *in rude health*. 9 (*prenominal*) approximate or imprecise: *a rude estimate*.
▷HISTORY C14: via Old French from Latin *rudis* coarse, unformed
▸ **'rudely** ADVERB ▸ **'rudeness** *or* (*informal*) **'rudery** NOUN

rude awakening NOUN an occurrence of being made to face an unpleasant fact.

ruderal ('ruːdərəl) NOUN 1 a plant that grows on waste ground. ◆ ADJECTIVE 2 growing in waste places.
▷HISTORY C19: from New Latin *rūderālis*, from Latin *rūdus* rubble

Rudesheimer ('ruːdəsˌhaɪmə) NOUN a white Rhine wine: named after the town of Rüdesheim on the Rhine.

rudiment ('ruːdɪmənt) NOUN 1 (*often plural*) the first principles or elementary stages of a subject. 2 (*often plural*) a partially developed version of something. 3 *Biology* an organ or part in its earliest recognizable form, esp one in an embryonic or vestigial state.
▷HISTORY C16: from Latin *rudīmentum* a beginning, from *rudis* unformed; see RUDE

rudimentary (ˌruːdɪ'mɛntərɪ) *or less commonly* **rudimental** ADJECTIVE 1 basic; fundamental; not elaborated or perfected. 2 incompletely developed; vestigial: *rudimentary leaves*.
▸ **ˌrudi'mentarily** *or* (*less commonly*) **ˌrudi'mentally** ADVERB

rudish ('ruːdɪʃ) ADJECTIVE somewhat rude.

Rudolf ('ruːdɒlf) NOUN **Lake.** the former name (until 1979) of (Lake) **Turkana**.

rue[1] (ruː) VERB **rues, ruing, rued.** 1 to feel sorrow, remorse, or regret for (one's own wrongdoing, past events with unpleasant consequences, etc.). ◆ NOUN 2 *Archaic* sorrow, pity, or regret.
▷HISTORY Old English *hrēowan*; related to Old Saxon *hreuwan*, Old High German *hriuwan*
▸ **'ruer** NOUN

rue[2] (ruː) NOUN any rutaceous plant of the genus *Ruta*, esp *R. graveolens*, an aromatic Eurasian shrub with small yellow flowers and evergreen leaves which yield an acrid volatile oil, formerly used medicinally as a narcotic and stimulant. Archaic name: **herb of grace.** Compare **goat's-rue, meadow rue, wall rue.**
▷HISTORY C14: from Old French, from Latin *rūta*, from Greek *rhutē*

rueful ('ruːfʊl) ADJECTIVE 1 feeling or expressing sorrow or repentance: *a rueful face*. 2 inspiring sorrow or pity.
▸ **'ruefully** ADVERB ▸ **'ruefulness** NOUN

rufescent (ruː'fɛsᵊnt) ADJECTIVE *Botany* tinged with red or becoming red.
▷HISTORY C19: from Latin *rūfescere* to grow reddish, from *rūfus* red, auburn
▸ **ru'fescence** NOUN

ruff[1] (rʌf) NOUN 1 a circular pleated, gathered, or fluted collar of lawn, muslin, etc., often starched or wired, worn by both men and women in the 16th and 17th centuries. 2 a natural growth of long or coloured hair or feathers around the necks of certain animals or birds. 3 **a** an Old World shore bird, *Philomachus pugnax*, the male of which has a large erectile ruff of feathers in the breeding season: family *Scolopacidae* (sandpipers, etc.), order *Charadriiformes*. **b** the male of this bird. Compare **reeve[3]**.
▷HISTORY C16: back formation from RUFFLE[1]
▸ **'ruffˌlike** ADJECTIVE

ruff[2] (rʌf) NOUN *Cards* 1 (*also verb*) another word for **trump[1]**. 2 an old card game similar to whist.
▷HISTORY C16: from Old French *roffle*; perhaps changed from Italian *trionfa* TRUMP[1]

ruff[3] (rʌf) NOUN another name for **roughie[1]**.

ruffe *or* **ruff[4]** (rʌf) NOUN a European freshwater teleost fish, *Acerina cernua*, having a single spiny dorsal fin: family *Percidae* (perches). Also called: **pope.**
▷HISTORY C15: perhaps an alteration of ROUGH (referring to its scales)

ruffed grouse NOUN a large North American grouse, *Bonasa umbellus*, having brown plumage with darker markings around the neck and a black-tipped fan-shaped tail.

ruffian ('rʌfɪən) NOUN a violent or lawless person; hoodlum or villain.
▷HISTORY C16: from Old French *rufien*, from Italian *ruffiano*, perhaps related to Langobardic *hruf* scurf, scabbiness
▸ **'ruffianism** NOUN ▸ **'ruffianly** ADJECTIVE

ruffle[1] ('rʌfᵊl) VERB 1 to make, be, or become irregular or rumpled: *to ruffle a child's hair; a breeze ruffling the water*. 2 to annoy, irritate, or be annoyed or irritated. 3 (*tr*) to make into a ruffle; pleat. 4 (of a bird) to erect (its feathers) in anger, display, etc. 5 (*tr*) to flick (cards, pages, etc.) rapidly with the fingers. ◆ NOUN 6 an irregular or disturbed surface. 7 a strip of pleated material used for decoration or as a trim. 8 *Zoology* another name for **ruff[1]** (sense 2). 9 annoyance or irritation.
▷HISTORY C13: of Germanic origin; compare Middle Low German *ruffelen* to crumple, Old Norse *hrufla* to scratch

ruffle[2] ('rʌfᵊl) NOUN 1 a low continuous drumbeat. ◆ VERB 2 (*tr*) to beat (a drum) with a low repetitive beat.
▷HISTORY C18: from earlier *ruff*, of imitative origin

ruffle[3] ('rʌfᵊl) VERB (*intr*) *Archaic* to behave riotously or arrogantly; swagger.
▷HISTORY C15: of obscure origin

ruffler ('rʌflə) NOUN 1 a person or thing that ruffles. 2 an attachment on a sewing machine used for making frills.

rufiyaa (ruː'fiːjɑː) NOUN the standard monetary unit of the Maldives, divided into 100 laari.

rufous ('ruːfəs) ADJECTIVE reddish-brown.
▷HISTORY C18: from Latin *rūfus*

rug (rʌg) NOUN 1 a floor covering, smaller than a carpet and made of thick wool or of other material, such as an animal skin. 2 *Chiefly Brit* a blanket, esp one used as a wrap or lap robe for travellers. 3 *Slang* a wig. 4 **pull the rug out from under.** to betray, expose, or leave defenceless.
▷HISTORY C16: from Scandinavian; compare Norwegian *rugga*, Swedish *rugg* coarse hair. See RAG[1]
▸ **'rugˌlike** ADJECTIVE

RUG *Computing* ABBREVIATION FOR **restricted users group.**

ruga ('ruːgə) NOUN, *plural* **-gae** (-dʒiː). (*usually plural*) *Anatomy* a fold, wrinkle, or crease.
▷HISTORY C18: Latin

Rugbeian ('rʌgbɪən) ADJECTIVE 1 of or relating to Rugby School. ◆ NOUN 2 a person educated at Rugby School.

rugby *or* **rugby football** ('rʌgbɪ) NOUN 1 a form of football played with an oval ball in which the handling and carrying of the ball is permitted. Also called: **rugger.** 2 *Canadian* another name for **Canadian football.** ◆ See also **rugby league, rugby union.**
▷HISTORY C19: named after the public school at Rugby, where it was first played

Rugby ('rʌgbɪ) NOUN a town in central England, in E Warwickshire: famous public school, founded in 1567. Pop.: 61 106 (1991).

rugby head NOUN *NZ derogatory slang* a male follower of rugby culture.

rugby league NOUN a form of rugby football played between teams of 13 players.

rugby union NOUN a form of rugby football played between teams of 15 players.

rugged ('rʌgɪd) ADJECTIVE 1 having an uneven or jagged surface. 2 rocky or steep: *rugged scenery*. 3 (of the face) strong-featured or furrowed. 4 rough, severe, or stern in character. 5 without refinement or culture; rude: *rugged manners*. 6 involving hardship; harsh: *he leads a rugged life in the mountains*. 7 difficult or hard: *a rugged test*. 8 (of equipment, machines, etc.) designed to withstand rough treatment or use in rough conditions: *a handheld rugged computer which can survive being submerged in water*. 9 *Chiefly US and Canadian* sturdy or strong; robust.
▷HISTORY C14: from Scandinavian; compare Swedish *rugga* to make rough
▸ **'ruggedly** ADVERB ▸ **'ruggedness** NOUN

ruggedize *or* **ruggedise** ('rʌgɪˌdaɪz) VERB (*tr*) to make durable, as for military use.

rugger ('rʌgə) NOUN *Chiefly Brit* an informal name for **rugby.**

rugger bugger NOUN *Derogatory slang* a male follower of rugby culture.

rugose ('ruːgəʊs, -gəʊz), **rugous,** *or* **rugate** ('ruːgeɪt, -gɪt) ADJECTIVE wrinkled: *rugose leaves*.
▷HISTORY C18: from Latin *rūgōsus*, from *rūga* a wrinkle
▸ **'rugosely** ADVERB ▸ **rugosity** (ruː'gɒsɪtɪ) NOUN

rug rat NOUN *US and Canadian informal* a child not yet walking.

Ruhr (rʊə; *German* ruːr) NOUN the chief coalmining and industrial region of Germany: in North Rhine-Westphalia around the valley of the **River Ruhr** (a tributary of the Rhine 235 km (146 miles) long). German name: **Ruhrgebiet** ('ruːrgəˌbiːt).

ruin ('ruːɪn) NOUN 1 destroyed or decayed building or town. 2 the state or condition of being destroyed or decayed. 3 loss of wealth, position, etc., or something that causes such loss; downfall. 4 something that is severely damaged: *his life was a ruin*. 5 a person who has suffered a downfall, bankruptcy, etc. 6 loss of value or usefulness. 7 *Archaic* loss of her virginity by a woman outside marriage. ◆ VERB 8 (*tr*) to bring to ruin; destroy. 9 (*tr*) to injure or spoil: *the town has been ruined with tower blocks*. 10 (*intr*) *Archaic or poetic* to fall into ruins; collapse.
▷HISTORY C14: from Old French *ruine*, from Latin *ruīna* a falling down, from *ruere* to fall violently
▸ **'ruinable** ADJECTIVE ▸ **'ruiner** NOUN

ruination (ˌruːɪ'neɪʃən) NOUN 1 the act of ruining or the state of being ruined. 2 something that causes ruin.

ruinous ('ruːɪnəs) ADJECTIVE causing, tending to cause, or characterized by ruin or destruction: *a ruinous course of action*.
▸ **'ruinously** ADVERB ▸ **'ruinousness** NOUN

rule (ruːl) NOUN 1 an authoritative regulation or direction concerning method or procedure, as for a court of law, legislative body, game, or other human institution or activity: *judges' rules; play according to the rules*. 2 the exercise of governmental authority or control: *the rule of Caesar*. 3 the period of time in which a monarch or government has power: *his rule lasted 100 days*. 4

a customary form or procedure; regular course of action: *he made a morning swim his rule.* **5** (usually preceded by *the*) the common order of things; normal condition: *violence was the rule rather than the exception.* **6** a prescribed method or procedure for solving a mathematical problem, or one constituting part of a computer program, usually expressed in an appropriate formalism. **7** a formal expression of a grammatical regularity in a linguistic description of a language. **8** any of various devices with a straight edge for guiding or measuring; ruler: *a carpenter's rule.* **9** **a** a printed or drawn character in the form of a long thin line. **b** another name for **dash**[1] (sense 13): *en rule; em rule.* **c** a strip of brass or other metal used to print such a line. **10** *Christianity* a systematic body of prescriptions defining the way of life to be followed by members of a religious order. **11** *Law* an order by a court or judge. **12** **as a rule.** normally or ordinarily. ◆ VERB **13** to exercise governing or controlling authority over (a people, political unit, individual, etc.): *he ruled for 20 years; his passion for her ruled his life.* **14** (when *tr, often takes a clause as object*) to decide authoritatively; decree: *the chairman ruled against the proposal.* **15** (*tr*) to mark with straight parallel lines or make one straight line, as with a ruler: *to rule a margin.* **16** (*tr*) to restrain or control: *to rule one's temper.* **17** (*intr*) to be customary or prevalent: *chaos rules in this school.* **18** (*intr*) to be pre-eminent or superior: *football rules in the field of sport.* **19** (*tr*) *Astrology* (of a planet) to have a strong affinity with certain human attributes, activities, etc., associated with (one or sometimes two signs of the zodiac): *Mars rules Aries.* **20** **rule the roost** (*or* **roast**). to be pre-eminent; be in charge.
▷HISTORY C13: from Old French *riule*, from Latin *rēgula* a straight edge; see REGULATE
▸'**rulable** ADJECTIVE

rule of three NOUN a mathematical rule asserting that the value of one unknown quantity in a proportion is found by multiplying the denominator of each ratio by the numerator of the other.

rule of thumb NOUN **a** a rough and practical approach, based on experience, rather than a scientific or precise one based on theory. **b** (*as modifier*): *a rule-of-thumb decision.*

rule out VERB (*tr, adverb*) **1** to dismiss from consideration. **2** to make impossible; preclude or prevent: *the rain ruled out outdoor games.*

ruler ('ruːlə) NOUN **1** a person who rules or commands. **2** Also called: **rule.** a strip of wood, metal, or other material, having straight edges graduated usually in millimetres or inches, used for measuring and drawing straight lines.

Rules (ruːlz) PLURAL NOUN **1** short for **Australian Rules** (football). **2** **the Rules.** *English history* the neighbourhood around certain prisons (esp the Fleet and King's Bench prison) in which trusted prisoners were allowed to live under specified restrictions.

ruling ('ruːlɪŋ) NOUN **1** a decision of someone in authority, such as a judge. **2** one or more parallel ruled lines. ◆ ADJECTIVE **3** controlling or exercising authority: *the ruling classes.* **4** prevalent or predominant.

ruly ('ruːlɪ) ADJECTIVE *Facetious* orderly; well-behaved; tidy.
▷HISTORY C20: back-formation from UNRULY

rum[1] (rʌm) NOUN spirit made from sugar cane, either coloured brownish-red by the addition of caramel or by maturation in oak containers, or left white.
▷HISTORY C17: perhaps shortened from C16 *rumbullion*, of uncertain origin

rum[2] (rʌm) ADJECTIVE **rummer, rummest.** *Brit slang* strange; peculiar; odd.
▷HISTORY C19: perhaps from Romany *rom* man
▸'**rumly** ADVERB ▸'**rumness** NOUN

rum[3] (rʌm) NOUN short for **rummy**[1].

Rumania (ruː'meɪnɪə) NOUN a variant of **Romania.**

Rumanian (ruː'meɪnɪən) ADJECTIVE, NOUN a variant of **Romanian.**

rumba *or* **rhumba** ('rʌmbə, 'rum-) NOUN **1** a rhythmic and syncopated Cuban dance in duple time. **2** a ballroom dance derived from this. **3** a piece of music composed for or in the rhythm of this dance.
▷HISTORY C20: from Spanish: lavish display, of uncertain origin

rumble ('rʌmb^əl) VERB **1** to make or cause to make a deep resonant sound: *thunder rumbled in the sky.* **2** to move with such a sound: *the train rumbled along.* **3** (*tr*) to utter with a rumbling sound: *he rumbled an order.* **4** (*tr*) to tumble (metal components, gemstones, etc.) in a barrel of smooth stone in order to polish them. **5** (*tr*) *Brit informal* to find out about (someone or something); discover (something): *the police rumbled their plans.* **6** (*intr*) *US slang* to be involved in a gang fight. ◆ NOUN **7** a deep resonant sound. **8** a widespread murmur of discontent. **9** another name for **tumbler** (sense 4). **10** *US, Canadian, and NZ slang* a gang fight.
▷HISTORY C14: perhaps from Middle Dutch *rummelen*; related to German *rummeln, rumpeln*
▸'**rumbler** NOUN ▸'**rumbling** ADJECTIVE ▸'**rumblingly** ADVERB

rumble seat NOUN *US and Canadian* a folding outside seat at the rear of some early cars; dicky.

rumble strip NOUN one of a set of roughly surfaced strips set in a road on the approach to a junction or hazard, to alert drivers by means of a change in tyre noise.

rumbustious (rʌm'bʌstjəs) ADJECTIVE boisterous or unruly.
▷HISTORY C18: probably a variant of ROBUSTIOUS
▸**rum'bustiously** ADVERB ▸**rum'bustiousness** NOUN

Rumelia (ruː'miːlɪə) NOUN *History* the possessions of the Ottoman Empire in the Balkan peninsula: including Macedonia, Albania, Thrace, and an autonomous province (**Eastern Rumelia**) ceded in 1885 to Bulgaria.

rumen ('ruːmen) NOUN, *plural* **-mens** *or* **-mina** (-mɪnə). the first compartment of the stomach of ruminants, behind the reticulum, in which food is partly digested before being regurgitated as cud.
▷HISTORY C18: from Latin: throat, gullet

ruminant ('ruːmɪnənt) NOUN **1** any artiodactyl mammal of the suborder *Ruminantia*, the members of which chew the cud and have a stomach of four compartments, one of which is the rumen. The group includes deer, antelopes, cattle, sheep, and goats. **2** any other animal that chews the cud, such as a camel. ◆ ADJECTIVE **3** of, relating to, or belonging to the suborder *Ruminantia.* **4** (of members of this suborder and related animals, such as camels) chewing the cud; ruminating. **5** meditating or contemplating in a slow quiet way.

ruminate ('ruːmɪˌneɪt) VERB **1** (of ruminants) to chew (the cud). **2** (when *intr*, often foll by *upon, on,* etc.) to meditate or ponder (upon).
▷HISTORY C16: from Latin *rūmināre* to chew the cud, from RUMEN
▸ˌ**rumi'nation** NOUN ▸'**ruminative** ADJECTIVE ▸'**ruminatively** ADVERB ▸'**rumiˌnator** NOUN

rummage ('rʌmɪdʒ) VERB **1** (when *intr*, often foll by *through*) to search (through) while looking for something, often causing disorder or confusion. ◆ NOUN **2** an act of rummaging. **3** a jumble of articles. **4** *Obsolete* confusion or bustle.
▷HISTORY C14 (in the sense: to pack a cargo): from Old French *arrumage*, from *arrumer* to stow in a ship's hold, probably of Germanic origin
▸'**rummager** NOUN

rummage out *or* **up** VERB (*tr*) to find by searching vigorously; turn out.

rummage sale NOUN **1** the US and Canadian term for **jumble sale.** **2** *US* a sale of unclaimed property or unsold stock.

rummer ('rʌmə) NOUN a drinking glass, typically having an ovoid bowl on a short stem.
▷HISTORY C17: from Dutch *roemer* a glass for drinking toasts, from *roemen* to praise

rummy[1] ('rʌmɪ) *or* **rum** NOUN a card game based on collecting sets and sequences.
▷HISTORY C20: perhaps from RUM[2]

rummy[2] ('rʌmɪ) ADJECTIVE another word for **rum**[2].

rummy[3] ('rʌmɪ) NOUN, *plural* **-mies.** **1** *US and Canadian* a slang word for **drunkard.** ◆ ADJECTIVE **2** of or like rum in taste or smell.

rumour *or US* **rumor** ('ruːmə) NOUN **1** **a** information, often a mixture of truth and untruth, passed around verbally. **b** (*in combination*): *a rumour-monger.* **2** gossip or hearsay. **3** *Archaic* din or clamour. **4** *Obsolete* fame or reputation. ◆ VERB **5** (*tr; usually passive*) to pass around or circulate in the form of a rumour: *it is rumoured that the Queen is coming.* **6** *Literary* to make or cause to make a murmuring noise.
▷HISTORY C14: via Old French from Latin *rūmor* common talk; related to Old Norse *rymja* to roar, Sanskrit *rāut* he cries

rump (rʌmp) NOUN **1** the hindquarters of a mammal, not including the legs. **2** the rear part of a bird's back, nearest to the tail. **3** a person's buttocks. **4** Also called: **rump steak.** a cut of beef from behind the loin and above the round. **5** an inferior remnant.
▷HISTORY C15: from Scandinavian; compare Danish *rumpe*, Icelandic *rumpr*, German *Rumpf* trunk of the body
▸'**rumpless** ADJECTIVE

Rumpelstiltskin (ˌrʌmp^əl'stɪltskɪn) NOUN a dwarf in a German folktale who aids the king's bride on condition that she give him her first child or guess the dwarf's name. She guesses correctly and in his rage he destroys himself.

rumple ('rʌmp^əl) VERB **1** to make or become wrinkled, crumpled, ruffled, or dishevelled. ◆ NOUN **2** a wrinkle, fold, or crease.
▷HISTORY C17: from Middle Dutch *rompelen*; related to Old English *gerumpen* creased, wrinkled
▸'**rumply** ADJECTIVE

Rump Parliament *or* **the Rump** NOUN *English history* the remainder of the Long Parliament after Pride's Purge. It sat from 1648–53.

rumpus ('rʌmpəs) NOUN, *plural* **-puses.** a noisy, confused, or disruptive commotion.
▷HISTORY C18: of unknown origin

rumpus room NOUN *US, Canadian, and NZ* a room used for noisy activities, such as parties or children's games.

rumpy-pumpy ('rʌmpɪ'pʌmpɪ) NOUN *Informal* sexual intercourse.

Rum Rebellion NOUN *Austral* the deposition of Governor William Bligh in 1808 by officers of the New South Wales Corps, caused by his interference in their trading activities, esp in the trafficking of rum.

run (rʌn) VERB **runs, running, ran, run.** **1** (*intr*) **a** (of a two-legged creature) to move on foot at a rapid pace so that both feet are off the ground together for part of each stride. **b** (of a four-legged creature) to move at a rapid gait; gallop or canter. **2** (*tr*) to pass over (a distance, route, etc.) in running: *to run a mile; run a race.* **3** (*intr*) to run in or finish a race as specified, esp in a particular position: *John is running third.* **4** (*tr*) to perform or accomplish by or as if by running: *to run an errand.* **5** (*intr*) to flee; run away: *they took to their heels and ran.* **6** (*tr*) to bring into a specified state or condition by running: *to run oneself to a standstill.* **7** (*tr*) to track down or hunt (an animal): *to run a fox to earth.* **8** (*intr*) to move about freely and without restraint: *the children are running in the garden.* **9** (*intr*; usually foll by *to*) to go or have recourse, as for aid, assistance, etc: *he's always running to his mother when he's in trouble.* **10** (*tr*) to set (animals) loose on (a field or tract of land) so as to graze freely. **11** (*intr*; often foll by *over, round* or *up*) to make a short trip or brief informal visit: *I'll run over to your house this afternoon.* **12** to move quickly and easily on wheels by rolling, or in any of certain other ways: *a ball running along the ground; a sledge running over snow.* **13** to move or cause to move with a specified result or in a specified manner: *to run a ship aground; to run into a tree.* **14** (often foll by *over*) to move or pass or cause to move or pass quickly: *to run a vacuum cleaner over the carpet; to run one's eyes over a page.* **15** (*tr*; foll by *into, out of, through,* etc.) to force, thrust, or drive: *she ran a needle into her finger.* **16** (*tr*) to drive or maintain and operate (a vehicle). **17** (*tr*) to give a lift to (someone) in a vehicle; transport: *he ran her to the railway station.* **18** to ply or cause to ply between places on a route: *the bus runs from Piccadilly to Golders Green.* **19** to operate or be operated; function or cause to function: *the engine is running smoothly; to run a program on a computer.* **20** (*tr*) to be in charge of; manage: *to run a company.* **21** to extend or continue or cause to extend or continue in a particular direction, for a particular duration or distance, etc.: *the road runs* *north; the play ran for two years; the months ran into years.* 22 (*intr*) *Law* **a** to have legal force or effect: *the lease runs for two more years.* **b** to accompany; be an integral part of or adjunct to: *an easement runs with the land.* 23 (*tr*) to be subjected to, be affected by, or incur: *to run a risk; run a temperature.* 24 (*intr; often foll by to*) to be characterized (by); tend or incline: *her taste runs to extravagant hats; to run to fat.* 25 (*intr*) to recur persistently or be inherent: *red hair runs in my family.* 26 to cause or allow (liquids) to flow or (of liquids) to flow, esp in a manner specified: *water ran from the broken pipe; the well has run dry.* 27 (*intr*) to melt and flow: *the wax grew hot and began to run.* 28 *Metallurgy* **a** to melt or fuse. **b** (*tr*) to mould or cast (molten metal): *to run lead into ingots.* 29 (*intr*) (of waves, tides, rivers, etc.) to rise high, surge, or be at a specified height: *a high sea was running that night.* 30 (*intr*) to be diffused: *the colours in my dress ran when I washed it.* 31 (*intr*) (of stitches) to unravel or come undone or (of a garment) to have stitches unravel or come undone: *if you pull that thread the whole seam will run.* 32 to sew (an article) with continuous stitches. 33 (*intr*) (of growing vines, creepers, etc.) to trail, spread, or climb: *ivy running over a cottage wall.* 34 (*intr*) to spread or circulate quickly: *a rumour ran through the town.* 35 (*intr*) to be stated or reported: *his story runs as follows.* 36 to publish or print or be published or printed in a newspaper, magazine, etc: *they ran his story in the next issue.* 37 (often foll by *for*) *Chiefly US and Canadian* to be a candidate or present as a candidate for political or other office: *Anderson is running for president.* 38 (*tr*) to get past or through; evade: *to run a blockade.* 39 (*tr*) to deal in (arms, etc.), esp by importing illegally: *he runs guns for the rebels.* 40 *Nautical* to sail (a vessel, esp a sailing vessel) or (of such a vessel) to be sailed with the wind coming from astern. 41 (*intr*) (of fish) **a** to migrate upstream from the sea, esp in order to spawn. **b** to swim rapidly in any area of water, esp during migration. 42 (*tr*) *Cricket* to score (a run or number of runs) by hitting the ball and running between the wickets. 43 (*tr*) *Billiards, snooker* to make (a number of successful shots) in sequence. 44 (*tr*) *Golf* to hit (the ball) so that it rolls along the ground. 45 (*tr*) *Bridge* to cash (all one's winning cards in a long suit) successively. 46 **run a bath.** to turn on the taps to fill a bath with water for bathing oneself. 47 **run close.** to compete closely with; present a serious challenge to: *he got the job, but a younger man ran him close.* 48 **run for it.** *Informal* to attempt to escape from arrest, etc., by running. 49 **be run off one's feet.** to be extremely busy. ◆ NOUN 50 an act, instance, or period of running. 51 a gait, pace, or motion faster than a walk: *she went off at a run.* 52 a distance covered by running or a period of running: *a run of ten miles.* 53 an act, instance, or period of travelling in a vehicle, esp for pleasure: *to go for a run in the car.* 54 free and unrestricted access: *we had the run of the house and garden for the whole summer.* 55 **a** a period of time during which a machine, computer, etc., operates. **b** the amount of work performed in such a period. 56 a continuous or sustained period: *a run of good luck.* 57 a continuous sequence of performances: *the play had a good run.* 58 *Cards* a sequence of winning cards in one suit, usually more than five: *a run of spades.* 59 tendency or trend: *the run of the market.* 60 type, class, or category: *the usual run of graduates.* 61 (usually foll by *on*) a continuous and urgent demand: *a run on butter; a run on the dollar.* 62 a series of unravelled stitches, esp in stockings or tights; ladder. 63 the characteristic pattern or direction of something: *the run of the grain on a piece of wood.* 64 **a** a continuous vein or seam of ore, coal, etc. **b** the direction in which it lies. 65 **a** a period during which water or other liquid flows. **b** the amount of such a flow. 66 a pipe, channel, etc., through which water or other liquid flows. 67 *US* a small stream. 68 a steeply inclined pathway or course, esp a snow-covered one used for skiing and bobsleigh racing. See also **green run, blue run, red run, black run.** 69 an enclosure for domestic fowls or other animals, in which they have free movement: *a chicken run.* 70 (esp in Australia and New Zealand) a tract of land for grazing livestock. 71 a track or area frequented by animals: *a deer run; a rabbit run.* 72 a group of animals of the same species moving together. 73 the migration of fish upstream in order to spawn. 74 *Nautical* **a** the tack of a sailing vessel in which the wind comes from astern. **b** part of the hull of a vessel near the stern where it curves upwards and inwards. 75 *Military* **a** a mission in a warplane. **b** short for **bombing run.** 76 the movement of an aircraft along the ground during takeoff or landing. 77 *Music* a rapid scalelike passage of notes. 78 *Cricket* a score of one, normally achieved by both batsmen running from one end of the wicket to the other after one of them has hit the ball. Compare **extra** (sense 6), **boundary** (sense 2c). 79 *Baseball* an instance of a batter touching all four bases safely, thereby scoring. 80 *Golf* the distance that a ball rolls after hitting the ground. 81 **a run for (one's) money.** *Informal* **a** a strong challenge or close competition. **b** pleasure derived from an activity. 82 **in the long run.** as the eventual outcome of a sequence of events, actions, etc.; ultimately. 83 **in the short run.** as the immediate outcome of a series of events, etc. 84 **on the run. a** escaping from arrest; fugitive. **b** in rapid flight; retreating: *the enemy is on the run.* **c** hurrying from place to place: *she's always on the run.* 85 **the runs.** *Slang* diarrhoea. ◆ See also **run about, run across, run after, run along, run around, run away, run down, run in, run into, run off, run on, run out, run over, run through, run to, run up, run with.**

▷HISTORY Old English *runnen*, past participle of *(ge)rinnan*; related to Old Frisian, Old Norse *rinna*, Old Saxon, Gothic, Old High German *rinnan*

runabout (ˈrʌnəˌbaut) NOUN 1 a small car, esp one for use in a town. 2 a light aircraft. 3 a light motorboat. 4 a person who moves about constantly or busily. ◆ VERB **run about.** 5 (*intr, adverb*) to move busily from place to place.

run across VERB (*intr, preposition*) to meet unexpectedly; encounter by chance.

run after VERB (*intr, preposition*) *Informal* 1 to pursue (a member of the opposite sex) with persistent attention. 2 to pursue (anything) persistently. 3 to care for in an excessively attentive or servile way: *she runs after her three grown sons as if they were babies.*

runagate (ˈrʌnəˌgeɪt) NOUN *Archaic* **a** a vagabond, fugitive, or renegade. **b** (*as modifier*): *a runagate priest.*

▷HISTORY C16: variant (influenced by RUN) of RENEGADE

run along VERB (*intr, adverb*) (often said patronizingly) to go away; leave.

run around VERB (*intr, adverb*) *Informal* 1 (often foll by *with*) to associate habitually (with). 2 to behave in a fickle or promiscuous manner. ◆ NOUN **run-around.** 3 *Informal* deceitful or evasive treatment of a person (esp in the phrase **give** *or* **get the run-around**). 4 *Printing* an arrangement of printed matter in which the column width is narrowed to accommodate an illustration.

run away VERB (*intr, adverb*) 1 to take flight; escape. 2 to go away; depart. 3 (of a horse) to gallop away uncontrollably. 4 **a** to abscond or elope with: *he ran away with his boss's daughter.* **b** to make off with; steal. **c** to escape from the control of: *his enthusiasm ran away with him.* **d** to win easily or be assured of victory in (a competition): *he ran away with the race.* ◆ NOUN **runaway.** 5 **a** a person or animal that runs away. **b** (*as modifier*): *a runaway horse.* 6 the act or an instance of running away. 7 (*modifier*) occurring as a result of the act of eloping: *a runaway wedding.* 8 (*modifier*) (of a race, victory, etc.) easily won.

runch (rʌntʃ) NOUN *Scot and northern English* another name for **white charlock.** See **charlock** (sense 2).

▷HISTORY C16: of obscure origin

runcible spoon (ˈrʌnsɪbᵊl) NOUN a forklike utensil with two broad prongs and one sharp curved prong.

▷HISTORY *runcible* coined by Edward Lear in a nonsense poem (1871)

runcinate (ˈrʌnsɪnɪt, -ˌneɪt) ADJECTIVE (of a leaf) having a saw-toothed margin with the teeth or lobes pointing backwards.

▷HISTORY C18: from New Latin *runcīnātus*, from Latin *runcīnāre* to plane off, from *runcīna* a carpenter's plane

Runcorn (ˈrʌŋˌkɔːn) NOUN a town in NW England, in Halton unitary authority, N Cheshire, on the Manchester Ship Canal: port and industrial centre; designated a new town in 1964. Pop.: 64 154 (1991).

rundale (ˈrʌnˌdeɪl) NOUN (formerly) the name given, esp in Ireland and earlier in Scotland, to the system of land tenure in which each land-holder had several strips of land that were not contiguous. Also called (in Scotland): **runrig.**

▷HISTORY C16 *ryndale*, from RUN (vb) + *dale*, a northern variant of DOLE[1], in the sense "a portion"

rundle (ˈrʌndᵊl) NOUN 1 a rung of a ladder. 2 a wheel, esp of a wheelbarrow.

▷HISTORY C14: variant of ROUNDEL

rundlet (ˈrʌndlɪt) NOUN *Obsolete* a liquid measure, generally about 15 gallons.

▷HISTORY C14: see ROUNDLET

run down VERB (*mainly adverb*) 1 to cause or allow (an engine, battery, etc.) to lose power gradually and cease to function or (of an engine, battery, etc.) to do this. 2 to decline or reduce in number or size: *the firm ran down its sales force.* 3 (*tr, usually passive*) to tire, sap the strength of, or exhaust: *he was thoroughly run down and needed a holiday.* 4 (*tr*) to criticize adversely; denigrate; decry. 5 (*tr*) to hit and knock to the ground with a moving vehicle. 6 *Nautical* **a** (*tr*) to collide with and cause to sink. **b** (*intr, preposition*) to navigate so as to move parallel to (a coast). 7 (*tr*) to pursue and find or capture: *to run down a fugitive.* 8 (*tr*) to read swiftly or perfunctorily: *he ran down their list of complaints.* ◆ ADJECTIVE **run-down.** 9 tired; exhausted. 10 worn-out, shabby, or dilapidated. ◆ NOUN **rundown.** 11 a brief review, résumé, or summary. 12 the process of a motor or mechanism coming gradually to a standstill after the source of power is removed. 13 a reduction in number or size.

rune (ruːn) NOUN 1 any of the characters of an ancient Germanic alphabet, derived from the Roman alphabet, in use, esp in Scandinavia, from the 3rd century A.D. to the end of the Middle Ages. Each character was believed to have a magical significance. 2 any obscure piece of writing using mysterious symbols. 3 a kind of Finnish poem or a stanza in such a poem.

▷HISTORY Old English *rūn*, from Old Norse *rūn* secret; related to Old Saxon, Old High German, Gothic *runa*

▸ˈ**runic** ADJECTIVE

rung[1] (rʌŋ) NOUN 1 one of the bars or rods that form the steps of a ladder. 2 a crosspiece between the legs of a chair, etc. 3 *Nautical* a spoke on a ship's wheel or a handle projecting from the periphery. 4 *Dialect* a cudgel or staff.

▷HISTORY Old English *hrung*; related to Old High German *runga*, Gothic *hrugga*

▸ˈ**rungless** ADJECTIVE

rung[2] (rʌŋ) VERB the past participle of **ring**[2].

Language note See at **ring**[2].

run in VERB (*adverb*) 1 to run (an engine) gently, usually for a specified period when it is new, in order that the running surfaces may become polished. 2 (*tr*) to insert or include. 3 (*intr*) (of an aircraft) to approach a point or target. 4 (*tr*) *Informal* to take into custody; arrest: *he was run in for assault.* ◆ NOUN **run-in.** 5 *Informal* an argument or quarrel: *he had a run-in with the boss yesterday.* 6 an approach to the end of an event, etc: *the run-in to the championship.* 7 *Printing* matter inserted in an existing paragraph.

run into VERB (*preposition; mainly intr*) 1 (*also tr*) to collide with or cause to collide with: *her car ran into a tree.* 2 to encounter unexpectedly. 3 (*also tr*) to be beset by or cause to be beset by: *the project ran into financial difficulties.* 4 to extend to; be of the order of: *debts running into thousands.*

runlet (ˈrʌnlɪt) NOUN *Archaic* a cask for wine, beer, etc.

▷HISTORY C14: from Old French *rondelet* ROUNDLET

runnel (ˈrʌnᵊl) NOUN *Literary* a small stream.

▷HISTORY C16: from Old English *rynele*; related to RUN

runner (ˈrʌnə) NOUN 1 a person who runs, esp an athlete. 2 a messenger for a bank or brokerage firm. 3 an employee of an art or antique dealer who visits auctions to bid on desired lots. 4 a person engaged in the solicitation of business. 5 a person on the run; fugitive. 6 **a** a person or vessel engaged in smuggling; smuggler. **b** (*in combination*):

a rum-runner. 7 a person who operates, manages, or controls something. 8 **a** either of the strips of metal or wood on which a sledge runs. **b** the blade of an ice skate. 9 a roller or guide for a sliding component. 10 a channel through which molten material enters a casting or moulding. 11 the rotating element of a water turbine. 12 another name for **running belay.** 13 any of various carangid fishes of temperate and tropical seas, such as *Caranx crysos* (**blue runner**) of American Atlantic waters. 14 *Botany* **a** a slender stem with very long internodes, as of the strawberry, that arches down to the ground and propagates by producing roots and shoots at the nodes or tip. **b** a plant that propagates in this way. 15 a strip of lace, linen, etc., placed across a table, dressing table, etc. for protection and decoration. 16 a narrow rug or carpet, as for a passage. 17 another word for **rocker** (on a rocking chair). 18 **do a runner.** *Slang* to run away in order to escape trouble or to avoid paying for something.

runner bean NOUN another name for **scarlet runner.**

runner-up NOUN, *plural* **runners-up**. a contestant finishing a race or competition in second place.

running ('rʌnɪŋ) ADJECTIVE 1 maintained continuously; incessant: *a running battle; running commentary.* 2 (*postpositive*) without interruption; consecutive: *he lectured for two hours running.* 3 denoting or relating to the scheduled operation of a public vehicle: *the running time of a train.* 4 accomplished at a run: *a running jump.* 5 (of a knot) sliding along the rope from which it is made, so as to form a noose which becomes smaller when the rope is pulled. 6 (of a wound, sore, etc.) discharging pus or a serous fluid. 7 denoting or relating to operations for maintenance: *running repairs.* 8 prevalent; current: *running prices.* 9 repeated or continuous: *a running design.* 10 (of certain plants, plant stems, etc.) creeping along the ground. 11 flowing: *running water.* 12 (of handwriting) having the letters run together. ◆ NOUN 13 management or organization: *the running of a company.* 14 operation or maintenance: *the running of a machine.* 15 competition or a competitive situation (in the phrases **in the running, out of the running**). 16 **make the running.** to set the pace in a competition or race. 17 *Rare* the power or ability to run.

running belay NOUN *Mountaineering* the clipping of the rope through a karabiner attached to a sling, piton, nut, etc., secured to the mountain: used by a leading climber of a team to reduce the length of a possible fall. Also called: **runner.**

running board NOUN a footboard along the side of a vehicle, esp an early motorcar.

running commentary NOUN a continuous spoken description of an event while it is happening.

running head *or* **title** NOUN *Printing* a heading printed at the top of every page or every other page of a book.

running light NOUN *Nautical* one of several white, red, or green lights displayed by vessels operating at night.

running mate NOUN 1 *US* a candidate for the subordinate of two linked positions, esp a candidate for the vice-presidency. 2 a horse that pairs another in a team.

running repairs PLURAL NOUN repairs, as to a machine or vehicle, that are minor and can be made with little or no interruption in the use of the item.

running rigging NOUN *Nautical* the wires and ropes used to control the operations of a sailing vessel. Compare **standing rigging.**

running stitch NOUN a simple form of hand stitching, consisting of small stitches that look the same on both sides of the fabric, usually used for gathering. Sometimes called: **gathering stitch.**

runny ('rʌnɪ) ADJECTIVE **-nier, -niest.** 1 tending to flow; liquid. 2 (of the nose or nasal passages) exuding mucus.

Runnymede ('rʌnɪˌmiːd) NOUN a meadow on the S bank of the Thames near Windsor, where King John met his rebellious barons in 1215 and acceded to Magna Carta.

run off VERB (*adverb*) 1 (*intr*) to depart in haste. 2 (*tr*) to produce quickly, as copies on a duplicating machine. 3 to drain (liquid) or (of liquid) to be drained. 4 (*tr*) to decide (a race) by a runoff. 5 (*tr*) to get rid of (weight, etc.) by running. 6 (*intr*) (of a flow of liquid) to begin to dry up; cease to run. 7 **run off with. a** to steal; purloin. **b** to elope with. ◆ NOUN **runoff.** 8 **a** an extra race to decide the winner after a tie. **b** a contest or election held after a previous one has failed to produce a clear victory for any one person. 9 that portion of rainfall that runs into streams as surface water rather than being absorbed into ground water or evaporating. 10 the overflow of a liquid from a container. 11 *NZ* grazing land for store cattle.

run-of-paper ADJECTIVE (of a story, advertisement, etc.) placed anywhere in a newspaper, at the discretion of the editor.

run-of-the-mill ADJECTIVE ordinary, average, or undistinguished in quality, character, or nature; not special or excellent.

run on VERB (*adverb*) 1 (*intr*) to continue without interruption. 2 to write with linked-up characters. 3 *Printing* to compose text matter without indentation or paragraphing. ◆ NOUN **run-on.** 4 *Printing* **a** text matter composed without indenting. **b** (*as modifier*): *run-on text matter.* 5 **a** a word added at the end of a dictionary entry whose meaning can be easily inferred from the definition of the headword. **b** (*as modifier*): *a run-on entry.*

run out VERB (*adverb*) 1 (*intr*; often foll by *of*) to exhaust (a supply of something) or (of a supply) to become exhausted. 2 **run out on.** *Informal* to desert or abandon. 3 (*tr*) *Cricket* to dismiss (a running batsman) by breaking the wicket with the ball, or with the ball in the hand, while he is out of his ground. ◆ NOUN **run-out.** 4 *Cricket* dismissal of a batsman by running him out. 5 *Mechanical engineering* an imperfection of a rotating component so that not all parts revolve about their intended axes relative to each other.

run over VERB 1 (*tr, adverb*) to knock down (a person) with a moving vehicle. 2 (*intr*) to overflow the capacity of (a container). 3 (*intr, preposition*) to examine hastily or make a rapid survey of. 4 (*intr, preposition*) to exceed (a limit): *we've run over our time.*

runt (rʌnt) NOUN 1 the smallest and weakest young animal in a litter, esp the smallest piglet in a litter. 2 *Derogatory* an undersized or inferior person. 3 a large pigeon, originally bred for eating.
▷ **HISTORY** C16: origin unknown
▸ **'runtish** ADJECTIVE ▸ **'runty** ADJECTIVE ▸ **'runtiness** NOUN

run through VERB 1 (*tr, adverb*) to transfix with a sword or other weapon. 2 (*intr, preposition*) to exhaust (money) by wasteful spending; squander. 3 (*intr, preposition*) to practise or rehearse: *let's run through the plan.* 4 (*intr, preposition*) to examine hastily. ◆ NOUN **run-through.** 5 a practice or rehearsal. 6 a brief survey.

run time NOUN *Computing* the time during which a computer program is executed.

run to VERB (*intr, preposition*) to be sufficient for: *my income doesn't run to luxuries.*

run up VERB (*tr, adverb*) 1 to amass or accumulate; incur: *to run up debts.* 2 to make by sewing together quickly: *to run up a dress.* 3 to hoist: *to run up a flag.* ◆ NOUN **run-up.** 4 an approach run by an athlete for a long jump, pole vault, etc. 5 a preliminary or preparatory period: *the run-up to the election.*

runway ('rʌnˌweɪ) NOUN 1 a hard level roadway or other surface from which aircraft take off and on which they land. 2 an enclosure for domestic animals; run. 3 *Forestry US and Canadian* a chute for sliding logs down. 4 a narrow ramp extending from the stage into the audience in a theatre, nightclub, etc., esp as used by models in a fashion show.

run with VERB (*intr, preposition*) 1 to associate with habitually: *run with the pack.* 2 to proceed with or put into action: *possible for us to run with this proposal.*

RUOK *Text messaging* ABBREVIATION FOR are you OK?

rupee (ruːˈpiː) NOUN the standard monetary unit of India, Nepal, and Pakistan (divided into 100 paise), Sri Lanka, Mauritius, and the Seychelles (divided into 100 cents).
▷ **HISTORY** C17: from Hindi *rupaīyā*, from Sanskrit *rūpya* coined silver, from *rūpa* shape, beauty

Rupert ('ruːpət) NOUN *Military, derogatory slang* a junior army officer.

Rupert's Land NOUN (formerly, in Canada) the territories granted by Charles II to the Hudson's Bay Company in 1670 and ceded to the Canadian Government in 1870, comprising all the land watered by rivers flowing into Hudson Bay.

rupiah (ruːˈpiːə) NOUN, *plural* **-ah** *or* **-ahs**. the standard monetary unit of Indonesia, divided into 100 sen.
▷ **HISTORY** from Hindi: RUPEE

rupicolous (ruːˈpɪkələs) ADJECTIVE *Biology* living or growing on or among rocks.
▷ **HISTORY** C19: from Latin *rūp(ēs)* crag + -I- + -COLOUS

rupture ('rʌptʃə) NOUN 1 the act of breaking or bursting or the state of being broken or burst. 2 a breach of peaceful or friendly relations. 3 *Pathol* **a** the breaking or tearing of a bodily structure or part. **b** another word for **hernia.** ◆ VERB 4 to break or burst or cause to break or burst. 5 to affect or be affected with a rupture or hernia. 6 to undergo or cause to undergo a breach in relations or friendship.
▷ **HISTORY** C15: from Latin *ruptūra* a breaking, from *rumpere* to burst forth; see ERUPT
▸ **'rupturable** ADJECTIVE

rural ('rʊərəl) ADJECTIVE 1 of, relating to, or characteristic of the country or country life. 2 living in or accustomed to the country. 3 of, relating to, or associated with farming. ◆ Compare **urban.**
▷ **HISTORY** C15: via Old French from Latin *rūrālis*, from *rūs* the country
▸ **'ruralism** NOUN ▸ **'ruralist** NOUN ▸ **ru'rality** NOUN
▸ **'rurally** ADVERB

rural dean NOUN *Chiefly Brit* a clergyman having authority over a group of parishes.

rural delivery NOUN *NZ* a mail service in a country area, often run by contractors for the Post Office.

rural district NOUN (in England and Wales from 1888 to 1974 and Northern Ireland from 1898 to 1973) a rural division of a county.

ruralize *or* **ruralise** ('rʊərəˌlaɪz) VERB 1 (*tr*) to make rural in character, appearance, etc. 2 (*intr*) to go into the country to live.
▸ **ˌrurali'zation** *or* **ˌrurali'sation** NOUN

rural science *or* **studies** NOUN *Brit* the study and theory of agriculture, biology, ecology, and associated fields.

Ruritania (ˌrʊərɪˈteɪnɪə, -njə) NOUN 1 an imaginary kingdom of central Europe: setting of several novels by Anthony Hope, esp *The Prisoner of Zenda* (1894). 2 any setting of adventure, romance, and intrigue.

Ruritanian (ˌrʊərɪˈteɪnɪən, -njən) ADJECTIVE 1 of or relating to Ruritania. 2 involving adventure, romance, and intrigue. ◆ NOUN 3 a native or inhabitant of Ruritania.

ruru ('ruːruː) NOUN *NZ* another name for **mopoke.**
▷ **HISTORY** Maori

RUS INTERNATIONAL CAR REGISTRATION FOR Russia.

ruse (ruːz) NOUN an action intended to mislead, deceive, or trick; stratagem.
▷ **HISTORY** C15: from Old French: trick, esp to evade capture, from *ruser* to retreat, from Latin *recūsāre* to refuse

Ruse ('ruːseɪ) NOUN a city in NE Bulgaria, on the River Danube: the chief river port and one of the largest industrial centres in Bulgaria. Pop.: 166 467 (1999 est.).

rush¹ (rʌʃ) VERB 1 to hurry or cause to hurry; hasten. 2 to make a sudden attack upon (a fortress, position, person, etc.). 3 (when *intr*, often foll by *at, in* or *into*) to proceed or approach in a reckless manner. 4 **rush one's fences.** to proceed with precipitate haste. 5 (*intr*) to come, flow, swell, etc., quickly or suddenly: *tears rushed to her eyes.* 6 *Slang* to cheat, esp by grossly overcharging. 7 (*tr*) *US and Canadian* to make a concerted effort to secure the agreement, participation, etc., of (a person). 8 (*intr*) *American football* to gain ground by running forwards with the ball. ◆ NOUN 9 the act or condition of rushing. 10 a sudden surge towards someone or something: *a gold rush.* 11 a sudden surge of sensation, esp produced by a drug. 12 a sudden demand. ◆ ADJECTIVE (*prenominal*) 13 requiring speed or urgency: *a rush job.* 14 characterized by much movement, business, etc: *a rush period.*

▷HISTORY C14 *ruschen*, from Old French *ruser* to put to flight, from Latin *recūsāre* to refuse, reject
▸'**rusher** NOUN

rush[2] (rʌʃ) NOUN 1 any annual or perennial plant of the genus *Juncus*, growing in wet places and typically having grasslike cylindrical leaves and small green or brown flowers: family *Juncaceae* Many species are used to make baskets. 2 any of various similar or related plants, such as the woodrush, scouring rush, and spike-rush. 3 something valueless; a trifle; straw: *not worth a rush*. 4 short for **rush light**.
▷HISTORY Old English *risce, rysce*; related to Middle Dutch *risch*, Norwegian *rusk*, Old Slavonic *rozga* twig, rod
▸'**rush,like** ADJECTIVE

rushes (rʌʃɪz) PLURAL NOUN (*sometimes singular*) (in film-making) the initial prints of a scene or scenes before editing, usually prepared daily.

rush hour NOUN a period at the beginning and end of the working day when large numbers of people are travelling to or from work.

rush light *or* **candle** NOUN a narrow candle, formerly in use, made of the pith of various types of rush dipped in tallow.

Rushmore ('rʌʃmɔː) NOUN **Mount**. a mountain in W South Dakota, in the Black Hills: a national memorial, with the faces of Washington, Lincoln, Jefferson, and Roosevelt carved into its side by Gutzon Borglum between 1927 and 1941. Height: 1841 m (6040 ft.).

rushy ('rʌʃɪ) ADJECTIVE **rushier, rushiest**. abounding in, covered with, or made of rushes.
▸'**rushiness** NOUN

rus in urbe *Latin* (rʊs ɪn 'ɜːbɪ) the country in the town.

rusk (rʌsk) NOUN a light bread dough, sweet or plain, baked twice until it is brown, hard, and crisp: often given to babies.
▷HISTORY C16: from Spanish or Portuguese *rosca* screw, bread shaped in a twist, of unknown origin

Russ (rʌs) NOUN, *plural* **Russ** *or* **Russes**, ADJECTIVE an archaic word for **Russian** (person or language).

Russ. ABBREVIATION FOR Russia(n).

RUSS INTERNATIONAL CAR REGISTRATION FOR Russia.

Russborough House ('rʌsbərə) NOUN a mansion near Blessington in Co. Wicklow, Republic of Ireland: built by Richard Castle and Francis Bindon for the 1st Earl of Miltown from 1740.

Russell's paradox NOUN *Logic* the paradox discovered by the British philosopher and mathematician Bertrand Russell (1872–1970) in the work of Gottlob Frege, that the class of all classes that are not members of themselves is a member of itself only if it is not, and is not only if it is. This undermines the notion of an all-inclusive universal class.

russet ('rʌsɪt) NOUN 1 brown with a yellowish or reddish tinge. 2 **a** a rough homespun fabric, reddish-brown in colour, formerly in use for clothing. **b** (*as modifier*): *a russet coat*. 3 any of various apples with rough brownish-red skins. 4 abnormal roughness on fruit, caused by parasites, pesticides, or frost. ◆ ADJECTIVE 5 (of tanned hide leather) dressed ready for staining. 6 *Archaic* simple; homely; rustic: *a russet life*. 7 of the colour russet: *russet hair*.
▷HISTORY C13: from Anglo-Norman, from Old French *rosset*, from *rous*, from Latin *russus*; related to Latin *ruber* red
▸'**russety** ADJECTIVE

Russia ('rʌʃə) NOUN (full name **Russian Federation**) 1 the largest country in the world, covering N Eurasia and bordering on the Pacific and Arctic Oceans and the Baltic, Black, and Caspian Seas: originating from the principality of Muscovy in the 17th century, it expanded to become the Russian Empire; the Tsar was overthrown in 1917 and the Communist Russian Soviet Federative Socialist Republic was created; this merged with neighbouring Soviet Republics in 1922 to form the Soviet Union; on the disintegration of the Soviet Union in 1991 the Russian Federation was established as an independent state. Official language: Russian. Religion: nonreligious and Russian orthodox Christian. Currency: rouble. Capital: Moscow. Pop.: 144 417 000 (2001 est.). Area: 17 074 984 sq. km (6 592 658 sq. miles). 2 another name for the **Russian Empire**. 3 another name for the former **Soviet Union**. 4 another name for the former **Russian Soviet Federative Socialist Republic**. ◆ Russian name: **Rossiya**.

Russia leather NOUN a smooth dyed leather made from calfskin and scented with birch tar oil, originally produced in Russia.

Russian ('rʌʃən) NOUN 1 the official language of Russia: an Indo-European language belonging to the East Slavonic branch. 2 the official language of the former Soviet Union. 3 a native or inhabitant of Russia. ◆ ADJECTIVE 4 of, relating to, or characteristic of Russia, its people, or their language.

Russian doll NOUN any of a set of hollow wooden figures, each of which splits in half to contain the next smallest figure, down to the smallest. Also called: **matryoshka, matrioshka**.

Russian dressing NOUN mayonnaise or vinaigrette with chilli sauce, chopped gherkins, etc.

Russian Empire NOUN the tsarist empire in Asia and E Europe, overthrown by the Russian Revolution of 1917.

Russian Federation NOUN See **Russia**.

Russianize *or* **Russianise** ('rʌʃə,naɪz) VERB to make or become Russian in style, character, etc.
▸,**Russiani'zation** *or* ,**Russiani'sation** NOUN

Russian Orthodox Church NOUN the national Church of Russia, constituting a branch of the Eastern Church presided over by the Patriarch of Moscow.

Russian Revolution NOUN 1 Also called (reckoned by the Julian calendar): **February Revolution**. the uprising in Russia in March 1917, during which the tsar abdicated and a provisional government was set up. 2 Also called (reckoned by the Julian calendar): **October Revolution**. the seizure of power by the Bolsheviks under Lenin in November 1917, transforming the uprising into a socialist revolution. This was followed by a period of civil war against counter-revolutionary armies (1918–22), which ended in eventual victory for the Bolsheviks.

Russian roulette NOUN 1 a game of chance in which each player in turn spins the cylinder of a revolver loaded with only one cartridge and presses the trigger with the barrel against his own head. 2 any act which, if repeated several times, is likely to have disastrous consequences.

Russian salad NOUN a salad of cold diced cooked vegetables mixed with Russian dressing.

Russian Soviet Federative Socialist Republic NOUN (formerly) the largest administrative division of the Soviet Union. Abbreviation: **RSFSR**.

Russian Turkestan NOUN See **Turkestan**.

Russian wolfhound NOUN a less common name for **borzoi**.

Russian Zone NOUN another name for the **Soviet Zone**.

Russify ('rʌsɪ,faɪ) VERB **-fies, -fying, -fied**. (*tr*) to cause to become Russian in character.
▸,**Russifi'cation** NOUN

Russky *or* **Russki** ('rʌskɪ) NOUN, *plural* **-kies** *or* **-kis**, ADJECTIVE *Chiefly US* a slang word for **Russian**.
▷HISTORY C20

Russo- ('rʌsəʊ-) COMBINING FORM Russia or Russian: *Russo-Japanese*.

Russo-Japanese War NOUN a war (1904–05) between Russia and Japan, caused largely by rivalry over Korea and Manchuria. Russia suffered a series of major defeats.

Russophile ('rʌsəʊ,faɪl) *or* **Russophil** NOUN 1 an admirer of Russia or the former Soviet Union, its customs, political system, etc. ◆ ADJECTIVE 2 marked by or possessing admiration of Russia or the former Soviet Union.

Russophobe ('rʌsəʊ,fəʊb) NOUN a person who feels intense and often irrational hatred (**Russophobia**) for Russia, or esp the former Soviet Union, its political system, etc.
▸,**Russo'phobic** ADJECTIVE

russula ('rʌsjʊlə) NOUN, *plural* **-lae** (-liː) *or* **-las**. any fungus of the large basidiomycetous genus *Russula*, of typical toadstool shape and often brightly coloured, such as the yellow *R. ochroleuca* and *R. lutea*, the green *R. aeruginea*, the violet-pink *R. fragilis*, and the purple *R. atropurpurea*.

rust (rʌst) NOUN 1 a reddish-brown oxide coating formed on iron or steel by the action of oxygen and moisture. 2 Also called: **rust fungus**. *Plant pathol* **a** any basidiomycetous fungus of the order *Uredinales*, parasitic on cereal plants, conifers, etc. **b** any of various plant diseases characterized by reddish-brown discoloration of the leaves and stem, esp that caused by the rust fungi. 3 **a** a strong brown colour, sometimes with a reddish or yellowish tinge. **b** (*as adjective*): *a rust carpet*. 4 any corrosive or debilitating influence, esp lack of use. ◆ VERB 5 to become coated with a layer of rust. 6 to deteriorate or cause to deteriorate through some debilitating influence or lack of use: *he allowed his talent to rust over the years*.
▷HISTORY Old English *rūst*; related to Old Saxon, Old High German *rost*
▸'**rustless** ADJECTIVE

rust belt NOUN an area where heavy industry is in decline, esp in the Midwest of the US.

rust bucket NOUN 1 *Slang* something that is run-down or dilapidated, esp a very badly rusted car. ◆ ADJECTIVE **rustbucket**. 2 *Informal* run-down or dilapidated: *rustbucket factories*.

rustic ('rʌstɪk) ADJECTIVE 1 of, characteristic of, or living in the country; rural. 2 having qualities ascribed to country life or people; simple; unsophisticated: *rustic pleasures*. 3 crude, awkward, or uncouth. 4 made of untrimmed branches: *a rustic seat*. 5 denoting or characteristic of a style of furniture popular in England in the 18th and 19th centuries, in which the legs and feet of chairs, tables, etc., were made to resemble roots, trunks, and branches of trees. 6 (of masonry) having a rusticated finish. ◆ NOUN 7 a person who comes from or lives in the country. 8 an unsophisticated, simple, or clownish person from the country. 9 Also called: **rusticwork**. brick or stone having a rough finish.
▷HISTORY C16: from Old French *rustique*, from Latin *rūsticus*, from *rūs* the country
▸'**rustically** ADVERB ▸**rusticity** (rʌ'stɪsɪtɪ) NOUN

rusticana (,rʌstɪ'kaːnə) PLURAL NOUN objects, such as agricultural implements, garden furniture, etc., relating to the countryside or made in imitation of rustic styles.

rusticate ('rʌstɪ,keɪt) VERB 1 to banish or retire to the country. 2 to make or become rustic in style, behaviour, etc. 3 (*tr*) *Architect* to finish (an exterior wall) with large blocks of masonry that are separated by deep joints and decorated with a bold, usually textured, design. 4 (*tr*) *Brit* to send down from university for a specified time as a punishment.
▷HISTORY C17: from Latin *rūsticārī*, from *rūs* the country
▸,**rusti'cation** NOUN ▸'**rusti,cator** NOUN

rusticating ('rʌstɪ,keɪtɪŋ) NOUN (in New Zealand) a wide type of weatherboarding used in older houses. Also called: **rusticated**.

rustle[1] ('rʌsᵊl) VERB 1 to make or cause to make a low crisp whispering or rubbing sound, as of dry leaves or paper. 2 to move with such a sound. ◆ NOUN 3 such a sound or sounds.
▷HISTORY Old English *hrūxlian*; related to Gothic *hrukjan* to CROW[2], Old Norse *hraukr* raven, CROW[1]
▸'**rustling** ADJECTIVE, NOUN ▸'**rustlingly** ADVERB

rustle[2] ('rʌsᵊl) VERB 1 *Chiefly US and Canadian* to steal (cattle, horses, etc.). 2 *US and Canadian informal* to move swiftly and energetically.
▷HISTORY C19: probably special use of RUSTLE[1] (in the sense: to move with quiet sound)

rustler ('rʌslə) NOUN 1 *Chiefly US and Canadian* a cattle or horse thief. 2 *US and Canadian informal* an energetic or vigorous person.

rustle up VERB (*tr, adverb*) *Informal* 1 to prepare (a meal, snack, etc.) rapidly, esp at short notice. 2 to forage for and obtain.

rustproof ('rʌst,pruːf) ADJECTIVE treated against rusting.

rusty ('rʌstɪ) ADJECTIVE **rustier, rustiest**. 1 covered with, affected by, or consisting of rust: *a rusty machine; a rusty deposit*. 2 of the colour rust. 3 discoloured by age: *a rusty coat*. 4 (of the voice) tending to croak. 5 old-fashioned in appearance; seemingly antiquated: *a rusty old gentleman*. 6 out

of practice; impaired in skill or knowledge by inaction or neglect. [7] (of plants) affected by the rust fungus.
▸ **'rustily** ADVERB ▸ **'rustiness** NOUN

rut[1] (rʌt) NOUN [1] a groove or furrow in a soft road, caused by wheels. [2] any deep mark, hole, or groove. [3] a narrow or predictable way of life, set of attitudes, etc.; dreary or undeviating routine (esp in the phrase **in a rut**). ◆ VERB **ruts, rutting, rutted.** [4] (*tr*) to make a rut or ruts in.
▹HISTORY C16: probably from French *route* road

rut[2] (rʌt) NOUN [1] a recurrent period of sexual excitement and reproductive activity in certain male ruminants, such as the deer, that corresponds to the period of oestrus in females. [2] another name for **oestrus.** ◆ VERB **ruts, rutting, rutted.** [3] (*intr*) (of male ruminants) to be in a period of sexual excitement and activity.
▹HISTORY C15: from Old French *rut* noise, roar, from Latin *rugītus*, from *rugīre* to roar

rutabaga (ˌruːtəˈbeɪɡə) NOUN the US and Canadian name for **swede.**
▹HISTORY C18: from Swedish dialect *rotabagge*, literally: root bag

rutaceous (ruːˈteɪʃəs) ADJECTIVE of, relating to, or belonging to the *Rutaceae*, a family of tropical and temperate flowering plants many of which have aromatic leaves. The family includes rue and citrus trees.
▹HISTORY C19: from New Latin *Rutaceae*, from Latin *rūta* RUE[2]

ruth (ruːθ) NOUN *Archaic* [1] pity; compassion. [2] repentance; remorse. [3] grief or distress.
▹HISTORY C12: from *rewen* to RUE[1]

Ruthenia (ruːˈθiːnɪə) NOUN a region of E Europe on the south side of the Carpathian Mountains: belonged to Hungary from the 14th century, to Czechoslovakia from 1918 to 1939, and was ceded to the former Soviet Union in 1945; in 1991 it became part of the newly independent Ukraine. Also called: **Carpatho-Ukraine.**

Ruthenian (ruːˈθiːnɪən) ADJECTIVE [1] of or relating to Ruthenia, its people, or their dialect of Ukrainian. ◆ NOUN [2] a dialect of Ukrainian. [3] a native or inhabitant of Ruthenia.

ruthenic (ruːˈθɛnɪk) ADJECTIVE of or containing ruthenium, esp in a high valency state.

ruthenious (ruːˈθiːnɪəs) ADJECTIVE of or containing ruthenium in a divalent state.

ruthenium (ruːˈθiːnɪəm) NOUN a hard brittle white element of the platinum metal group. It occurs free with other platinum metals in pentlandite and other ores and is used to harden platinum and palladium. Symbol: Ru; atomic no.: 44; atomic wt.: 101.07; valency: 0–8; relative density: 12.41; melting pt.: 2334°C; boiling pt.: 4150°C.
▹HISTORY C19: from Medieval Latin *Ruthenia* Russia, where it was first discovered

rutherford (ˈrʌðəfəd) NOUN a unit of activity equal to the quantity of a radioactive nuclide required to produce one million disintegrations per second. Abbreviation: **rd.**
▹HISTORY C20: named after Ernest *Rutherford*, 1st Baron Rutherford (1871–1937), New Zealand-born British physicist

rutherfordium (ˌrʌðəˈfɔːdɪəm) NOUN a transactinide element produced by bombarding californium-249 nuclei with carbon-12 nuclei. Symbol: Rf; atomic number.: 104; atomic wt.: 261. Name in the former Soviet Union: **kurchatovium.**
▹HISTORY C20: named after Ernest *Rutherford*, 1st Baron Rutherford (1871–1937), New Zealand-born British physicist

ruthful (ˈruːθfʊl) ADJECTIVE *Archaic* full of or causing sorrow or pity.
▸ **'ruthfully** ADVERB ▸ **'ruthfulness** NOUN

ruthless (ˈruːθlɪs) ADJECTIVE feeling or showing no mercy; hardhearted.
▸ **'ruthlessly** ADVERB ▸ **'ruthlessness** NOUN

rutilant (ˈruːtɪlənt) ADJECTIVE *Rare* of a reddish colour or glow.
▹HISTORY C15: from Latin *rutilāns* having a red glow, from *rutilāre*, from *rutilus* ruddy, red

rutilated (ˈruːtɪˌleɪtɪd) ADJECTIVE (of minerals, esp quartz) containing needles of rutile.

rutile (ˈruːtaɪl) NOUN a black, yellowish, or reddish-brown mineral, found in igneous rocks, metamorphosed limestones, and quartz veins. It is a source of titanium. Composition: titanium dioxide. Formula: TiO_2. Crystal structure: tetragonal.
▹HISTORY C19: via French from German *Rutil*, from Latin *rutilus* red, glowing

Rutland (ˈrʌtlənd) NOUN an inland county of central England: the smallest of the historical English counties, it became part of Leicestershire in 1974 but was reinstated as an independent unitary authority in 1997: mainly agricultural. Administrative centre: Oakham. Pop.: 34 560 (2001). Area: 394 sq. km (152 sq. miles).

ruttish (ˈrʌtɪʃ) ADJECTIVE [1] (of an animal) in a condition of rut. [2] lascivious or salacious.
▸ **'ruttishly** ADVERB ▸ **'ruttishness** NOUN

rutty (ˈrʌtɪ) ADJECTIVE **-tier, -tiest.** full of ruts or holes: *a rutty track.*
▸ **'ruttily** ADVERB ▸ **'ruttiness** NOUN

Ruwenzori (ˌruːwɛnˈzɔːrɪ) NOUN a mountain range in central Africa, on the border between Uganda and the Democratic Republic of Congo (formerly Zaïre) between Lakes Edward and Albert: generally thought to be Ptolemy's "Mountains of the Moon". Highest peak: Mount Stanley, 5109 m (16 763 ft.).

rv *Statistics* ABBREVIATION FOR random variable.

RV ABBREVIATION FOR: [1] Revised Version (of the Bible). [2] *Chiefly US* recreational vehicle.

rw THE INTERNET DOMAIN NAME FOR Rwanda.

RW ABBREVIATION FOR: [1] Right Worshipful. [2] Right Worthy.

RWA INTERNATIONAL CAR REGISTRATION FOR Rwanda.

Rwanda[1] (rʊˈændə) NOUN a republic in central Africa: part of German East Africa from 1899 until 1917, when Belgium took over the administration; became a republic in 1961 after the successful Hutu revolt against the Tutsi (1959); fighting between the ethnic groups has broken out repeatedly since independence, culminating in the genocide of Tutsis by Hutus in 1994. Official languages: Rwanda, French, and English. Religion: Roman Catholic, African Protestant, Muslim, and animist. Currency: Rwanda franc. Capital: Kigali. Pop.: 7 313 000 (2001 est.). Area: 26 338 sq. km (10 169 sq. miles). Former name (until 1962): **Ruanda.**

Rwanda[2] (rʊˈændə) NOUN one of the official languages of Rwanda, belonging to the Bantu group of the Niger-Congo family and closely related to Kirundi. Also called: **Kinyarwanda.**

Rwandan (rʊˈændən) ADJECTIVE [1] of or relating to Rwanda or its inhabitants. ◆ NOUN [2] a native or inhabitant of Rwanda.

rwd ABBREVIATION FOR rear-wheel drive.

Rwy *or* **Ry** ABBREVIATION FOR railway.

-ry SUFFIX FORMING NOUNS a variant of **-ery**: *dentistry.*

Ryazan (*Russian* rɪˈzanj) NOUN a city in W central Russia: capital of a medieval principality; oil refineries and engineering industries. Pop.: 531 300 (1999 est.).

Rybinsk (*Russian* ˈribinsk) NOUN a city in W central Russia, on the River Volga: an important river port, terminal of the Mariinsk Waterway (between Saint Petersburg and the Volga) at the SE end of the **Rybinsk Reservoir** (area: 4700 sq. km (1800 sq. miles)). Pop.: 241 800 (1999 est.). Former names: **Shcherbakov** (from the Revolution until 1957), **Andropov** (1984–91).

Rydal (ˈraɪdᵊl) NOUN a village in NW England, in Cumbria on **Rydal Water** (a small lake). **Rydal Mount**, home of Wordsworth from 1813 to 1850, is situated here.

Ryder Cup (raɪdə) NOUN **the.** the trophy awarded in a professional golfing competition between teams representing Europe and the US.
▹HISTORY C20: named after Samuel *Ryder* (1859–1936), British businessman and golf patron

rye[1] (raɪ) NOUN [1] a tall hardy widely cultivated annual grass, *Secale cereale*, having soft bluish-green leaves, bristly flower spikes, and light brown grain. See also **wild rye.** [2] the grain of this grass, used in making flour and whiskey, and as a livestock food. [3] Also called: **rye whiskey.** whiskey distilled from rye. US whiskey must by law contain not less than 51 per cent rye. [4] *US* short for **rye bread.**
▹HISTORY Old English *ryge*; related to Old Norse *rugr*, Old Frisian *rogga*, Old Saxon *roggo*

rye[2] (raɪ) NOUN *Gypsy dialect* a gentleman.
▹HISTORY from Romany *rai*, from Sanskrit *rājan* king; see RAJAH

Rye (raɪ) NOUN a resort in SE England, in East Sussex: one of the Cinque Ports. Pop.: 3708 (1991).

rye bread NOUN any of various breads made entirely or partly from rye flour, often with caraway seeds.

rye-brome NOUN a grass, *Bromus secalinus*, native to Europe and Asia, having rough leaves and wheatlike ears. US names: **cheat, chess.**

rye-grass NOUN any of various grasses of the genus *Lolium*, esp *L. perenne*, native to Europe, N Africa, and Asia and widely cultivated as forage crops. They have a flattened flower spike and hairless leaves.

Ryeland (ˈraɪlənd) NOUN a breed of large hornless sheep having fine wool, originating from Herefordshire, England.

Ryobu Shinto (riːˈəʊbuː) NOUN a fusion of Shinto and Buddhism, which flourished in Japan in the 13th century.
▹HISTORY from Japanese *ryō bu* literally: two parts

ryokan (rɪˈəʊkən) NOUN a traditional Japanese inn.
▹HISTORY Japanese

ryot (ˈraɪət) NOUN (in India) a peasant or tenant farmer.
▹HISTORY C17: from Hindi *ra'īyat*, from Arabic *ra'īyah* flock, peasants, from *ra'ā* pasture

Ryswick (ˈrɪzwɪk) NOUN the English name for **Rijswijk.**

Ryukyu Islands (rɪˈuːkjuː) PLURAL NOUN a chain of 55 islands in the W Pacific, extending almost 650 km (400 miles) from S Japan to N Taiwan: an ancient kingdom, under Chinese rule from the late 14th century, invaded by Japan in the early 17th century, under full Japanese sovereignty from 1879 to 1945, and US control from 1945 to 1972; now part of Japan again. They are subject to frequent typhoons. Chief town: Naha City (on Okinawa). Pop.: 1 318 000 (2000 est.). Area: 2196 sq. km (849 sq. miles).

Ss

s *or* **S** (ɛs) NOUN, *plural* **s's, S's** *or* **Ss.** [1] the 19th letter and 15th consonant of the modern English alphabet. [2] a speech sound represented by this letter, usually an alveolar fricative, either voiceless, as in *sit,* or voiced, as in *dogs.* [3] **a** something shaped like an S. **b** (*in combination*): *an S-bend in a road.*

s SYMBOL FOR second (of time).

S SYMBOL FOR: [1] satisfactory. [2] Society. [3] small (size). [4] South. [5] *Chem* sulphur. [6] *Physics* **a** entropy. **b** siemens. **c** strangeness. [7] *Currency* **a** (the former) schilling. **b** sol. **c** (the former) sucre. ◆ [8] INTERNATIONAL CAR REGISTRATION FOR Sweden.

s. ABBREVIATION FOR: [1] see. [2] semi-. [3] shilling. [4] singular. [5] son. [6] succeeded.

S. ABBREVIATION FOR: [1] (*plural* **SS**) Saint. [2] school. [3] Sea. [4] Signor. [5] Society.
▷**HISTORY** Latin *socius*

-s^{1} *or* **-es** SUFFIX forming the plural of most nouns: *boys; boxes.*
▷**HISTORY** from Old English *-as,* plural nominative and accusative ending of some masculine nouns

-s^{2} *or* **-es** SUFFIX forming the third person singular present indicative tense of verbs: *he runs; she washes.*
▷**HISTORY** from Old English (northern dialect) *-es, -s,* originally the ending of the second person singular

-s^{3} SUFFIX OF NOUNS forming nicknames and names expressing affection or familiarity: *Fats; Fingers; ducks.*
▷**HISTORY** special use of *-s*^{1}

-'s SUFFIX [1] forming the possessive singular of nouns and some pronouns: *man's; one's.* [2] forming the possessive plural of nouns whose plurals do not end in *-s*: *children's.* [3] forming the plural of numbers, letters, or symbols: *20's; p's and q's.* [4] *Informal* contraction of *is* or *has*: *he's here; John's coming; it's gone.* [5] *Informal* contraction of *us* with *let*: *let's.* [6] *Informal* contraction of *does* in some questions: *where's he live?; what's he do?*
▷**HISTORY** senses 1, 2: assimilated contraction from Middle English *-es,* from Old English, masculine and neuter genitive singular; sense 3, equivalent to *-s*^{1}

-s' SUFFIX forming the possessive of plural nouns ending in the sound *s* or *z* and of some singular nouns: *girls'; for goodness' sake.*

sa THE INTERNET DOMAIN NAME FOR Saudi Arabia.

Sa A FORMER CHEMICAL SYMBOL FOR samarium.

SA ABBREVIATION FOR: [1] Salvation Army. [2] Sociedad Anónima. [Spanish: limited company] [3] Société anonyme. [French: limited company] [4] South Africa. [5] South America. [6] South Australia. [7] *Sturmabteilung:* the Nazi terrorist militia, organized around 1924. ◆ [8] INTERNATIONAL CAR REGISTRATION FOR Saudi Arabia.

s.a. ABBREVIATION FOR: [1] semiannual. [2] sex appeal. [3] sine anno.
▷**HISTORY** Latin: without date

Saar (sɑː; *German* zaːr) NOUN [1] a river in W Europe, rising in the Vosges Mountains and flowing north to the Moselle River in Germany. Length: 246 km (153 miles). French name: **Sarre.** [2] **the Saar.** another name for **Saarland.**

Saarbrücken (*German* zaːrˈbrykən) NOUN an industrial city in W Germany, capital of Saarland state, on the Saar River. Pop.: 186 402 (1999 est.).

SAARC ABBREVIATION FOR South Asian Association for Regional Cooperation.

Saarland (*German* ˈzaːrlant) NOUN a state of W Germany: formed in 1919; under League of Nations administration until 1935; occupied by France (1945–57); part of West Germany (1957–90): contains rich coal deposits and is a major industrial region. Capital: Saarbrücken. Pop.: 1 071 500 (2000 est.). Area: 2567 sq. km (991 sq. miles).

sab (sæb) NOUN *Informal* a person engaged in direct action to prevent a targeted activity, esp fox hunting, taking place.
▷**HISTORY** C20: shortened from SABOTEUR

Saba (ˈsɑːbə) NOUN [1] an island in the NE Caribbean, in the Netherlands Antilles. Pop.: 1704 (2000 est.). Area: 13 sq. km (5 sq. miles). [2] another name for **Sheba**^{1} (sense 1).

Sabadell (*Spanish* saβaˈðel) NOUN a town in NE Spain, near Barcelona: textile manufacturing. Pop.: 184 859 (1998 est.).

sabadilla (ˌsæbəˈdɪlə) NOUN [1] a tropical American liliaceous plant, *Schoenocaulon officinale.* [2] the bitter brown seeds of this plant, which contain the alkaloids veratrine and veratridine and are used in insecticides.
▷**HISTORY** C19: from Spanish *cebadilla,* diminutive of *cebada* barley, from Latin *cibāre* to feed, from *cibus* food

Sabaean *or* **Sabean** (səˈbiːən) NOUN [1] an inhabitant or native of ancient Saba. [2] the ancient Semitic language of Saba. ◆ ADJECTIVE [3] of or relating to ancient Saba, its inhabitants, or their language.
▷**HISTORY** C16: from Latin *Sabaeus,* from Greek *Sabaios* belonging to Saba (Sheba)

Sabah (ˈsɑːbɑː) NOUN a state of Malaysia, occupying N Borneo and offshore islands in the South China and Sulu Seas: became a British protectorate in 1888; gained independence and joined Malaysia in 1963. Capital: Kota Kinabalu. Pop.: 2 449 389 (2000). Area: 76 522 sq. km (29 545 sq. miles). Former name (until 1963): **North Borneo.**

Sabaoth (sæˈbeɪɒθ, ˈsæbeɪɒθ) NOUN *Bible* hosts, armies (esp in the phrase **the Lord of Sabaoth** in Romans 9:29).
▷**HISTORY** C14: via Latin and Greek from Hebrew *ç'bāōth,* from *çābā*

sabayon (ˌsæbaɪˈjɒn; *French* sabajɔ̃) NOUN a dessert or sweet sauce made with egg yolks, sugar, and wine beaten together over heat till thick: served either hot or cold.
▷**HISTORY** C20: from French, alteration of Italian *zabione* ZABAGLIONE

sabbat (ˈsæbæt, -ət) NOUN another word for **Sabbath** (sense 4).

Sabbatarian (ˌsæbəˈtɛərɪən) NOUN [1] a person advocating the strict religious observance of Sunday. [2] a person who observes Saturday as the Sabbath. ◆ ADJECTIVE [3] of or relating to the Sabbath or its observance.
▷**HISTORY** C17: from Late Latin *sabbatārius* a Sabbath-keeper
▸ **ˌSabbaˈtarianism** NOUN

Sabbath (ˈsæbəθ) NOUN [1] the seventh day of the week, Saturday, devoted to worship and rest from work in Judaism and in certain Christian Churches. [2] Sunday, observed by Christians as the day of worship and rest from work in commemoration of Christ's Resurrection. [3] (*not capital*) a period of rest. [4] Also called: **sabbat, witches' Sabbath.** a midnight meeting or secret rendezvous for practitioners of witchcraft, sorcery, or devil worship.
▷**HISTORY** Old English *sabbat,* from Latin *sabbatum,* from Greek *sabbaton,* from Hebrew *shabbāth,* from *shābath* to rest

sabbath school NOUN (*sometimes capitals*) *Chiefly US* a school for religious instruction held on the Sabbath.

sabbatical (səˈbætɪkᵊl) ADJECTIVE [1] denoting a period of leave granted to university staff, teachers, etc., esp approximately every seventh year: *a sabbatical year; sabbatical leave.* [2] denoting a post that renders the holder eligible for such leave. ◆ NOUN [3] any sabbatical period.
▷**HISTORY** C16: from Greek *sabbatikos;* see SABBATH

Sabbatical (səˈbætɪkᵊl) ADJECTIVE *also* **Sabbatic.** [1] of, relating to, or appropriate to the Sabbath as a day of rest and religious observance. ◆ NOUN [2] short for **sabbatical year.**

sabbatical year NOUN (*often capitals*) *Bible* a year during which the land was to be left uncultivated, debts annulled, etc., supposed to be observed every seventh year by the ancient Israelites according to Leviticus 25.

SABC ABBREVIATION FOR South African Broadcasting Corporation.

Sabellian (səˈbelɪən) NOUN [1] an extinct language or group of languages of ancient Italy, surviving only in a few inscriptions belonging to the Osco-Umbrian group. [2] a member of any of the ancient peoples speaking this language, including the Sabines. ◆ ADJECTIVE [3] of or relating to this language or its speakers.
▷**HISTORY** C17: from Latin *Sabellī* group of Italian tribes

saber (ˈseɪbə) NOUN, VERB the US spelling of **sabre.**

sabin (ˈsæbɪn, ˈseɪ-) NOUN *Physics* a unit of acoustic absorption equal to the absorption resulting from one square foot of a perfectly absorbing surface.
▷**HISTORY** C20: introduced by Wallace C. *Sabine* (1868–1919), US physicist

Sabine (ˈsæbaɪn) NOUN [1] a member of an ancient Oscan-speaking people who lived in central Italy northeast of Rome. ◆ ADJECTIVE [2] of, characteristic of, or relating to this people or their language.

Sabin vaccine (ˈseɪbɪn) NOUN a vaccine taken orally to immunize against poliomyelitis, developed by Albert Bruce Sabin (1906–93) in 1955.

sabkha (ˈsæbxə, -kə) NOUN a flat coastal plain with a salt crust, common in Arabia.
▷**HISTORY** C19: from Arabic

sable (ˈseɪbᵊl) NOUN, *plural* **-bles** *or* **-ble.** [1] a marten, *Martes zibellina,* of N Asian forests, with dark brown luxuriant fur. Related adjective: **zibeline.** [2] **a** the highly valued fur of this animal. **b** (*as modifier*): *a sable coat.* [3] **American sable.** the brown, slightly less valuable fur of the American marten, *Martes americana.* [4] the colour of sable fur: a dark brown to yellowish-brown colour. ◆ ADJECTIVE [5] of the colour of sable fur. [6] black; dark; gloomy. [7] (*usually postpositive*) *Heraldry* of the colour black.
▷**HISTORY** C15: from Old French, from Old High German *zobel,* of Slavic origin; related to Russian *sobol',* Polish *sobol*

Sable (ˈseɪbᵊl) NOUN **Cape.** [1] a cape at the S tip of Florida: the southernmost point of continental US. [2] the southernmost point of Nova Scotia, Canada.

sable antelope NOUN a large black E African antelope, *Hippotragus niger,* with long backward-curving horns.

Sable Island pony NOUN a variety of wild pony found on Sable Island, Nova Scotia.

sabot (ˈsæbəʊ; *French* sabo) NOUN [1] a shoe made from a single block of wood. [2] a shoe with a wooden sole and a leather or cloth upper. [3] a lightweight sleeve in which a subcalibre round is enclosed in order to make it fit the rifling of a firearm. After firing the sabot drops away. [4] *Austral* a small sailing boat with a shortened bow.
▷**HISTORY** C17: from French, probably from Old French *savate* an old shoe, also influenced by *bot* BOOT^{1}; related to Italian *ciabatta* old shoe, Old Provençal *sabata*

sabotage (ˈsæbəˌtɑːʒ) NOUN [1] the deliberate destruction, disruption, or damage of equipment, a public service, etc., as by enemy agents, dissatisfied employees, etc. [2] any similar action or behaviour. ◆ VERB [3] (*tr*) to destroy, damage, or disrupt, esp by secret means.
▷**HISTORY** C20: from French, from *saboter* to spoil through clumsiness (literally: to clatter in sabots)

saboteur (ˌsæbəˈtɜː) NOUN a person who commits sabotage.
▷**HISTORY** C20: from French; see SABOTAGE

sabra (ˈsɑːbrə) NOUN a native-born Israeli Jew.

▷HISTORY from Hebrew *Sabēr* prickly pear, common plant in the coastal areas of the country

sabre *or US* **saber** ('seɪbə) NOUN [1] a stout single-edged cavalry sword, having a curved blade. [2] a sword used in fencing, having a narrow V-shaped blade, a semicircular guard, and a slightly curved hand. [3] a cavalry soldier. ◆ VERB [4] (*tr*) to injure or kill with a sabre.
▷HISTORY C17: via French from German (dialect) *Sabel,* from Middle High German *sebel,* perhaps from Magyar *szablya;* compare Russian *sablya* sabre

sabre-rattling NOUN, ADJECTIVE *Informal* seeking to intimidate by an aggressive display of military power.

sabretache ('sæbəˌtæʃ) NOUN a leather case suspended from a cavalryman's saddle.
▷HISTORY C19: via French from German *Säbeltasche* sabre pocket

sabre-toothed tiger *or* **cat** NOUN any of various extinct Tertiary felines of the genus *Smilodon* and related genera, with long curved upper canine teeth.

SABS ABBREVIATION FOR South African Bureau of Standards.

sabulous ('sæbjʊləs) *or* **sabulose** ('sæbjʊləʊs) ADJECTIVE [1] like sand in texture; gritty. [2] Also: **sabuline** ('sæbjʊliːn). (of plants) growing in sand.
▷HISTORY C17: from Latin *sabulōsus,* from *sabulum* SAND
▸**sabulosity** (ˌsæbjʊ'lɒsɪtɪ) NOUN

sac (sæk) NOUN a pouch, bag, or pouchlike part in an animal or plant.
▷HISTORY C18: from French, from Latin *saccus;* see SACK[1]
▸**'sacˌlike** ADJECTIVE

SAC (in Britain) ABBREVIATION FOR Special Area of Conservation.

sacaton (ˌsækə'təʊn) NOUN a coarse grass, *Sporobolus wrightii,* of the southwestern US and Mexico, grown for hay and pasture.
▷HISTORY American Spanish *zacatón,* from *zacate* coarse grass, from Nahuatl *zacatl*

SACC ABBREVIATION FOR South African Council of Churches.

saccade (sə'kɑːd, -'keɪd) NOUN [1] the movement of the eye when it makes a sudden change of fixation, as in reading. [2] a sudden check given to a horse.
▷HISTORY C18: from French: a jerk on the reins of a horse

saccate ('sækeɪt) ADJECTIVE *Botany* in the form of a sac; pouched.
▷HISTORY C19: from New Latin *saccatus,* from *saccus:* see SACK[1]

saccharase ('sækəˌreɪs) NOUN another name for **invertase.**

saccharate ('sækəˌreɪt) NOUN any salt or ester of saccharic acid.

saccharic acid (sæ'kærɪk) NOUN a white soluble solid dicarboxylic acid obtained by the oxidation of cane sugar or starch; 2,3,4,5-tetrahydroxyhexanedioic acid. Formula: $COOH(CHOH)_4COOH$.

saccharide ('sækəˌraɪd, -rɪd) NOUN any sugar or other carbohydrate, esp a simple sugar.

saccharify (sæ'kærɪˌfaɪ), **saccharize,** *or* **saccharise** ('sækəˌraɪz) VERB **-fies, -fying, -fied.** (*tr*) to convert (starch) into sugar.
▸**sacˌcharifi'cation** *or* ˌ**sacchari'zation** *or* ˌ**sacchari'sation** NOUN

saccharimeter (ˌsækə'rɪmɪtə) NOUN any instrument for measuring the strength of sugar solutions, esp a type of polarimeter for determining the concentration from the extent to which the solution rotates the plane of polarized light.
▸ˌ**saccha'rimetry** NOUN

saccharin ('sækərɪn) NOUN a very sweet white crystalline slightly soluble powder used as a nonfattening sweetener. Formula: $C_7H_5NO_3S$.
▷HISTORY C19: from SACCHARO- + -IN

saccharine ('sækəˌraɪn, -ˌriːn) ADJECTIVE [1] excessively sweet; sugary: *a saccharine smile.* [2] of, relating to, of the nature of, or containing sugar or saccharin.
▸**'saccharinely** ADVERB ▸**saccharinity** (ˌsækə'rɪnɪtɪ) NOUN

saccharo- *or before a vowel* **sacchar-** COMBINING FORM sugar: *saccharomycete.*
▷HISTORY via Latin from Greek *sakkharon,* ultimately from Sanskrit *śarkarā* sugar

saccharoid ('sækəˌrɔɪd) ADJECTIVE [1] Also: **saccharoidal.** *Geology* having or designating a texture resembling that of loaf sugar: *saccharoid marble.* ◆ NOUN [2] *Biochem* any of a group of polysaccharides that remotely resemble sugars, but are not sweet and are often insoluble.

saccharometer (ˌsækə'rɒmɪtə) NOUN a hydrometer used to measure the strengths of sugar solutions. It is usually calibrated directly to give a reading of concentration.

saccharose ('sækəˌrəʊz, -ˌrəʊs) NOUN a technical name for **sugar** (sense 1).

saccular ('sækjʊlə) ADJECTIVE of or resembling a sac.

sacculate ('sækjʊlɪt, -ˌleɪt) *or* **sacculated** ADJECTIVE of, relating to, or possessing a saccule, saccules, or a sacculus.
▸ˌ**saccu'lation** NOUN

saccule ('sækjuːl) *or* **sacculus** ('sækjʊləs) NOUN, *plural* **-cules** *or* **-li** (liː). [1] a small sac. [2] the smaller of the two parts of the membranous labyrinth of the internal ear. Compare **utricle** (sense 1).
▷HISTORY C19: from Latin *sacculus* diminutive of *saccus* SACK[1]

sacculiform (sæ'kjʊlɪˌfɔːm) ADJECTIVE *Biology* (of plant parts, etc.) shaped like a small sac.

sacerdotal (ˌsæsə'dəʊtᵊl) ADJECTIVE of, relating to, or characteristic of priests.
▷HISTORY C14: from Latin *sacerdōtālis,* from *sacerdōs* priest, from *sacer* sacred
▸ˌ**sacer'dotally** ADVERB

sacerdotalism (ˌsæsə'dəʊtᵊˌlɪzəm) NOUN [1] the principles, methods, etc., of the priesthood. [2] the belief that ordained priests are endowed with sacramental and sacrificial powers. [3] exaggerated respect for priests. [4] *Derogatory* power over people's opinions and actions achieved by priests through sophistry or guile.
▸ˌ**sacer'dotalist** NOUN

sachem ('seɪtʃəm) NOUN [1] *US* a leader of a political party or organization, esp of Tammany Hall. [2] another name for **sagamore.**
▷HISTORY C17: from Narraganset *săchim* chief
▸**sachemic** (seɪ'tʃemɪk, 'seɪtʃə-) ADJECTIVE

sachet ('sæʃeɪ) NOUN [1] a small sealed envelope, usually made of plastic or paper, for containing sugar, salt, shampoo, etc. [2] **a** a small soft bag containing perfumed powder, placed in drawers to scent clothing. **b** the powder contained in such a bag.
▷HISTORY C19: from Old French: a little bag, from *sac* bag; see SACK[1]

Sachsen ('zaksən) NOUN the German name for **Saxony.**

sack[1] (sæk) NOUN [1] a large bag made of coarse cloth, thick paper, etc., used as a container. [2] Also called: **sackful.** the amount contained in a sack, sometimes used as a unit of measurement. [3] **a** a woman's loose tube-shaped dress. **b** Also called: **sacque.** a woman's full loose hip-length jacket, worn in the 18th and mid-20th centuries. [4] short for **rucksack.** [5] *Cricket* the Austral word for **bye[1]**. [6] **the sack.** *Informal* dismissal from employment. [7] a slang word for **bed.** [8] **hit the sack.** *Slang* to go to bed. [9] **rough as sacks.** *NZ* uncouth. ◆ VERB (*tr*) [10] *Informal* to dismiss from employment. [11] to put into a sack or sacks.
▷HISTORY Old English *sacc,* from Latin *saccus* bag, from Greek *sakkos;* related to Hebrew *saq*
▸**'sackˌlike** ADJECTIVE

sack[2] (sæk) NOUN [1] the plundering of a place by an army or mob, usually involving destruction, slaughter, etc. [2] *American football* a tackle on a quarterback which brings him down before he has passed the ball. ◆ VERB [3] (*tr*) to plunder and partially destroy (a place). [4] *American football* to tackle and bring down a quarterback before he has passed the ball.
▷HISTORY C16: from French phrase *mettre à sac,* literally: to put (loot) in a sack, from Latin *saccus* SACK[1]
▸**'sacker** NOUN

sack[3] (sæk) NOUN *Archaic except in trademarks* any dry white wine formerly imported into Britain from SW Europe.
▷HISTORY C16 *wyne seck,* from French *vin sec* dry wine, from Latin *siccus* dry

sackable ('sækəbᵊl) ADJECTIVE of or denoting an offence, infraction of rules, etc., that is sufficently serious to warrant dismissal from an employment.

sackbut ('sækˌbʌt) NOUN a medieval form of trombone.
▷HISTORY C16: from French *saqueboute,* from Old French *saquer* to pull + *bouter* to push; see BUTT[3]: used in the Bible (Daniel 3) as a mistranslation of Aramaic *sabb'ka* stringed instrument

sackcloth ('sækˌklɒθ) NOUN [1] coarse cloth such as sacking. [2] garments made of such cloth, worn formerly to indicate mourning or penitence. [3] **sackcloth and ashes.** a public display of extreme grief, remorse, or repentance.

sacking ('sækɪŋ) NOUN coarse cloth used for making sacks, woven from flax, hemp, jute, etc.

sack race NOUN a race in which the competitors' legs and often bodies are enclosed in sacks.
▸**sack racing** NOUN

SACP ABBREVIATION FOR South African Communist Party.

sacral[1] ('seɪkrəl) ADJECTIVE of, relating to, or associated with sacred rites.
▷HISTORY C19: from Latin *sacrum* sacred object

sacral[2] ('seɪkrəl) ADJECTIVE of or relating to the sacrum.
▷HISTORY C18: from New Latin *sacrālis* of the SACRUM

sacrament ('sækrəmənt) NOUN [1] an outward sign combined with a prescribed form of words and regarded as conferring some specific grace upon those who receive it. The Protestant sacraments are baptism and the Lord's Supper. In the Roman Catholic and Eastern Churches they are baptism, penance, confirmation, the Eucharist, holy orders, matrimony, and the anointing of the sick (formerly extreme unction). [2] (*often capital*) the Eucharist. [3] the consecrated elements of the Eucharist, esp the bread. [4] something regarded as possessing a sacred or mysterious significance. [5] a symbol; pledge.
▷HISTORY C12: from Church Latin *sacrāmentum* vow, from Latin *sacrāre* to consecrate

sacramental (ˌsækrə'mɛntᵊl) ADJECTIVE [1] of, relating to, or having the nature of a sacrament. [2] bound by or as if by a sacrament. ◆ NOUN [3] *RC Church* a sacrament-like ritual action, such as the sign of the cross or the use of holy water.
▸ˌ**sacra'mentally** ADVERB ▸**sacramentality** (ˌsækrəmɛn'tælɪtɪ) *or* ˌ**sacra'mentalness** NOUN

sacramentalism (ˌsækrə'mentᵊˌlɪzəm) NOUN belief in or special emphasis upon the efficacy of the sacraments for conferring grace.
▸ˌ**sacra'mentalist** NOUN

Sacramentarian (ˌsækrəmɛn'tɛərɪən) NOUN [1] any Protestant theologian, such as the Swiss Reformation leader Ulrich Zwingli (1484–1531), who maintained that the bread and wine of the Eucharist were the body and blood of Christ only in a figurative sense and denied His real presence in these elements. [2] one who believes in sacramentalism. ◆ ADJECTIVE [3] of or relating to Sacramentarians. [4] (*not capital*) of or relating to sacraments.
▸ˌ**Sacramen'tarianism** NOUN

Sacramento (ˌsækrə'mɛntəʊ) NOUN [1] an inland port in N central California, capital of the state at the confluence of the American and Sacramento Rivers: became a boom town in the gold rush of the 1850s. Pop.: 407 018 (2000). [2] a river in N California, flowing generally south to San Francisco Bay. Length: 615 km (382 miles).

sacrarium (sæ'krɛərɪəm) NOUN, *plural* **-craria** (-'krɛərɪə). [1] the sanctuary of a church. [2] *RC Church* a place near the altar of a church, similar in function to the piscina, where materials used in the sacred rites are deposited or poured away.
▷HISTORY C18: from Latin *sacrārium,* from *sacer* SACRED

sacred ('seɪkrɪd) ADJECTIVE [1] exclusively devoted to a deity or to some religious ceremony or use; holy; consecrated. [2] worthy of or regarded with reverence, awe, or respect. [3] protected by superstition or piety from irreligious actions. [4]

connected with or intended for religious use: *sacred music.* 5 dedicated to; in honour of.
▷HISTORY C14: from Latin *sacrāre* to set apart as holy, from *sacer* holy
▸'**sacredly** ADVERB ▸'**sacredness** NOUN

Sacred College NOUN the collective body of the cardinals of the Roman Catholic Church.

sacred cow NOUN *Informal* a person, institution, custom, etc., unreasonably held to be beyond criticism.
▷HISTORY alluding to the Hindu belief that cattle are sacred

Sacred Heart NOUN *RC Church* 1 the heart of Jesus Christ, a symbol of His love and sacrifice. 2 a representation of this, usually bleeding, as an aid to devotion.

sacred mushroom NOUN 1 any of various hallucinogenic mushrooms, esp species of *Psilocybe* and *Amanita,* that have been eaten in rituals in various parts of the world. 2 a mescal button, used in a similar way.

sacred site NOUN *Austral informal* a place of great significance.

sacrifice ('sækrɪˌfaɪs) NOUN 1 a surrender of something of value as a means of gaining something more desirable or of preventing some evil. 2 a ritual killing of a person or animal with the intention of propitiating or pleasing a deity. 3 a symbolic offering of something to a deity. 4 the person, animal, or object surrendered, destroyed, killed, or offered. 5 a religious ceremony involving one or more sacrifices. 6 loss entailed by giving up or selling something at less than its value. 7 *Chess* the act or an instance of sacrificing a piece. ◆ VERB 8 to make a sacrifice (of); give up, surrender, or destroy (a person, thing, etc.). 9 *Chess* to permit or force one's opponent to capture (a piece) freely, as in playing a combination or gambit: *he sacrificed his queen and checkmated his opponent on the next move.*
▷HISTORY C13: via Old French from Latin *sacrificium,* from *sacer* holy + *facere* to make
▸'**sacriˌficeable** ADJECTIVE ▸'**sacriˌficer** NOUN

sacrifice paddock NOUN *NZ* a grassed area allowed to be grazed completely, to be cultivated and resown later.

sacrificial (ˌsækrɪ'fɪʃəl) ADJECTIVE used in or connected with a sacrifice.
▸ˌ**sacri'ficially** ADVERB

sacrificial anode NOUN *Metallurgy* an electropositive metal, such as zinc, that protects a more important electronegative part by corroding when attacked by electrolytic action.

sacrilege ('sækrɪlɪdʒ) NOUN 1 the misuse or desecration of anything regarded as sacred or as worthy of extreme respect: *to play Mozart's music on a kazoo is sacrilege.* 2 the act or an instance of taking anything sacred for secular use.
▷HISTORY C13: from Old French *sacrilège,* from Latin *sacrilegium,* from *sacrilegus* temple-robber, from *sacra* sacred things + *legere* to take
▸**sacrilegist** (ˌsækrɪ'liːdʒɪst) NOUN

sacrilegious (ˌsækrɪ'lɪdʒəs) ADJECTIVE 1 of, relating to, or involving sacrilege; impious. 2 guilty of sacrilege.
▸ˌ**sacri'legiously** ADVERB ▸ˌ**sacri'legiousness** NOUN

sacring ('seɪkrɪŋ) NOUN *Archaic* the act or ritual of consecration, esp of the Eucharist or of a bishop.
▷HISTORY C13: from obsolete *sacren* to consecrate, from Latin *sacrāre;* see SACRED

sacring bell NOUN *Chiefly RC Church* a small bell rung at the elevation of the Host and chalice during Mass.

sacristan ('sækrɪstən) *or* **sacrist** ('sækrɪst, 'seɪ-) NOUN 1 a person who has charge of the contents of a church, esp the sacred vessels, vestments, etc. 2 a less common word for **sexton** (sense 1).
▷HISTORY C14: from Medieval Latin *sacristānus,* from *sacrista,* from Latin *sacer* holy

sacristy ('sækrɪstɪ) NOUN, *plural* **-ties.** a room attached to a church or chapel where the sacred vessels, vestments, etc., are kept and where priests attire themselves.
▷HISTORY C17: from Medieval Latin *sacristia;* see SACRISTAN

sacroiliac (ˌseɪkrəʊ'ɪlɪˌæk, ˌsæk-) *Anatomy* ◆ ADJECTIVE 1 of or relating to the sacrum and ilium, their articulation, or their associated ligaments. ◆ NOUN 2 the joint where these bones meet.

sacrosanct ('sækrəʊˌsæŋkt) ADJECTIVE very sacred or holy; inviolable.
▷HISTORY C17: from Latin *sacrōsanctus* made holy by sacred rite, from *sacrō* by sacred rite, from *sacer* holy + *sanctus,* from *sancīre* to hallow
▸ˌ**sacro'sanctity** *or* '**sacroˌsanctness** NOUN

sacrum ('seɪkrəm, 'sækrəm) NOUN, *plural* **-cra** (-krə). 1 (in man) the large wedge-shaped bone, consisting of five fused vertebrae, in the lower part of the back. 2 the corresponding part in some other vertebrates.
▷HISTORY C18: from Latin *os sacrum* holy bone, because it was used in sacrifices, from *sacer* holy

sad (sæd) ADJECTIVE **sadder, saddest.** 1 feeling sorrow; unhappy. 2 causing, suggestive, or expressive of such feelings: *a sad story.* 3 unfortunate; unsatisfactory; shabby; deplorable: *her clothes were in a sad state.* 4 *Brit informal* ludicrously contemptible; pathetic: *he's a sad, boring little wimp.* 5 (of pastry, cakes, etc.) not having risen fully; heavy. 6 (of a colour) lacking brightness; dull or dark. 7 *Archaic* serious; grave. ◆ VERB 8 *NZ* to express sadness or displeasure strongly.
▷HISTORY Old English *sæd* weary; related to Old Norse *sathr,* Gothic *saths,* Latin *satur, satis* enough
▸'**sadly** ADVERB ▸'**sadness** NOUN

SAD ABBREVIATION FOR **seasonal affective disorder.**

sad case NOUN *Informal* a person considered to be ludicrously contemptible or pathetic.

sadden ('sædᵊn) VERB to make or become sad.

saddle ('sædᵊl) NOUN 1 a seat for a rider, usually made of leather, placed on a horse's back and secured with a girth under the belly. 2 a similar seat on a bicycle, tractor, etc., made of leather or steel. 3 a back pad forming part of the harness of a packhorse. 4 anything that resembles a saddle in shape, position, or function. 5 a cut of meat, esp mutton, consisting of part of the backbone and both loins. 6 the part of a horse or similar animal on which a saddle is placed. 7 the part of the back of a domestic chicken that is nearest to the tail. 8 *Civil engineering* a block on top of one of the towers of a suspension bridge that acts as a bearing surface over which the cables or chains pass. 9 *Engineering* the carriage that slides on the bed of a lathe and supports the slide rest, tool post, or turret. 10 the nontechnical name for **clitellum.** 11 another name for **col** (sense 1). 12 a raised piece of wood or metal for covering a doorsill. 13 **in the saddle.** in a position of control. ◆ VERB 14 (sometimes foll by *up*) to put a saddle on (a horse). 15 (*intr*) to mount into the saddle. 16 (*tr*) to burden; charge: *I didn't ask to be saddled with this job.*
▷HISTORY Old English *sadol, sædel;* related to Old Norse *sothull,* Old High German *satul*
▸'**saddleless** ADJECTIVE ▸'**saddle-ˌlike** ADJECTIVE

saddleback ('sædᵊlˌbæk) NOUN 1 a marking resembling a saddle on the backs of various animals. 2 a breed of black pig with a white band across its back. 3 a rare bird of New Zealand, *Philesturnus carunculatus,* having a chestnut-coloured saddle-shaped marking across its back and wings. 4 another name for **saddle roof.** 5 another name for **col** (sense 1).

saddle-backed ADJECTIVE 1 having the back curved in shape or concave like a saddle. 2 having a saddleback.

saddlebag ('sædᵊlˌbæg) NOUN 1 a pouch or small bag attached to the saddle of a horse, bicycle, etc. 2 (*plural*) *Informal* rolls of fat protruding from the sides of a person's thighs.

saddlebill ('sædᵊlˌbɪl) NOUN a large black-and-white stork, *Ephippiorhynchus senegalensis,* of tropical Africa, having a heavy red bill with a black band around the middle and a yellow patch at the base. Also called: **jabiru.**
▷HISTORY C19 (as *saddle-bill stork*): so called because of the appearance of its bill

saddle block NOUN *Surgery* a type of spinal anaesthesia producing sensory loss in the buttocks, inner sides of the thighs, and perineum.

saddlebow ('sædᵊlˌbəʊ) NOUN the pommel of a saddle.

saddlecloth ('sædᵊlˌklɒθ) NOUN a light cloth put under a horse's saddle, so as to prevent rubbing.

saddle gall NOUN *Vet science* a raw area of skin, with loss of hair, on the back or behind the elbow of a horse caused by uneven pressure by the saddle or girth.

saddle horse NOUN a lightweight horse kept for riding only. Compare **carthorse.** Also called: **saddler.**

saddler ('sædlə) NOUN a person who makes, deals in, or repairs saddles and other leather equipment for horses.

saddle roof NOUN a roof that has a ridge and two gables. Also called: **saddleback.**

saddlery ('sædlərɪ) NOUN, *plural* **-dleries.** 1 saddles, harness, and other leather equipment for horses collectively. 2 the business, work, or place of work of a saddler.

saddle soap NOUN a soft soap containing neat's-foot oil used to preserve and clean leather.

saddle-sore ADJECTIVE 1 sore after riding a horse. 2 (of a horse or rider) having sores caused by the chafing of the saddle. ◆ NOUN **saddle sore.** 3 such a sore.

saddle stitching NOUN a method of binding in which the sections of a publication are inserted inside each other and secured through the middle fold with thread, or wire staples.

saddletree ('sædᵊlˌtriː) NOUN the frame of a saddle.

saddo ('sædəʊ) NOUN, *plural* **-dos** *or* **-does.** *Brit slang* a socially inadequate or pathetic person.
▷HISTORY C20: from SAD (sense 4) + -O

Sadducee ('sædjʊˌsiː) NOUN *Judaism* a member of an ancient Jewish sect that was opposed to the Pharisees, denying the resurrection of the dead, the existence of angels, and the validity of oral tradition.
▷HISTORY Old English *saddūcēas,* via Latin and Greek from Late Hebrew *ṣāddūqi,* probably from *Ṣadoq* Zadok, high priest and supposed founder of the sect
▸ˌ**Saddu'cean** ADJECTIVE ▸'**Sadduˌceeism** NOUN

sadhana ('sɑːdʌnə) NOUN *Hinduism* one of a number of spiritual practices or disciplines which lead to perfection, these being contemplation, asceticism, worship of a god, and correct living.
▷HISTORY from Sanskrit: effective

sadhe, sade, *or* **tsade** ('sɑːdiː, 'tsɑːdiː; *Hebrew* 'tsadiː) NOUN the 18th letter in the Hebrew alphabet (צ or, at the end of a word ץ), transliterated as *s* or *ts* and pronounced more or less like English *s* or *ts* with pharyngeal articulation.

sadhu *or* **saddhu** ('sɑːduː) NOUN a Hindu wandering holy man.
▷HISTORY Sanskrit, from *sādhu* good

sadiron ('sædˌaɪən) NOUN a heavy iron pointed at both ends, for pressing clothes.
▷HISTORY C19: from SAD (in the obsolete sense: heavy) + IRON

sadism ('seɪdɪzəm, 'sæ-) NOUN the gaining of pleasure or sexual gratification from the infliction of pain and mental suffering on another person. See also **algolagnia.** Compare **masochism.**
▷HISTORY C19: from French, named after Comte Donatien Alphonse François de Sade, known as the *Marquis de Sade* (1740–1814), French soldier and writer of works describing sexual perversion
▸'**sadist** NOUN ▸**sadistic** (sə'dɪstɪk) ADJECTIVE
▸**sa'distically** ADVERB

Sadler's Wells ('sædləz wɛlz) NOUN (*functioning as singular*) a theatre in London. It was renovated in 1931 by Lilian Bayliss and became the home of the Sadler's Wells Opera Company and the Sadler's Wells Ballet (now the Royal Ballet).
▷HISTORY named after the medicinal *wells* on the site and its owner Thomas *Sadler,* who founded the original theatre on the site

sado ('sɑːdəʊ) NOUN a variant of **chado.**

sadomasochism (ˌseɪdəʊ'mæsəˌkɪzəm, ˌsædəʊ-) NOUN 1 the combination of sadistic and masochistic elements in one person, characterized by both aggressive and submissive periods in relationships with others. 2 sexual practice in which one partner adopts a sadistic role and the other a masochistic one. Abbreviation: **SM.** Compare **sadism, masochism.**
▸ˌ**sadomaso'chistic** ADJECTIVE

Sadowa ('sɑːdəvə) NOUN a village in the Czech Republic, in NE Bohemia: scene of the decisive battle of the Austro-Prussian war (1866) in which the Austrians were defeated by the Prussians. Czech name: **Sadová** ('sadɔva:).

SADS (sædz) NOUN ACRONYM FOR sudden adult death syndrome: the sudden death of an apparently healthy adult, for which no cause can be found at postmortem.
▷HISTORY late C20: by analogy with SIDS (sudden infant death syndrome)

sad sack NOUN *US slang* an inept person who makes mistakes despite good intentions.
▷HISTORY C20: from a cartoon character created by G. Baker, US cartoonist

sae (se) ADVERB a Scot word for **so**[1] (sense 1).

SAE (in the US) ABBREVIATION FOR Society of Automotive Engineers.

s.a.e. ABBREVIATION FOR stamped addressed envelope.

Safar *or* **Saphar** (sə'fɑ:) NOUN the second month of the Muslim year.
▷HISTORY from Arabic

safari (sə'fɑ:rɪ) NOUN, *plural* **-ris.** 1 an overland journey or hunting expedition, esp in Africa. 2 the people, animals, etc., that go on the expedition.
▷HISTORY C19: from Swahili: journey, from Arabic *safarīya,* from *safara* to travel

safari jacket NOUN another name for **bush jacket.**

safari park NOUN an enclosed park in which lions and other wild animals are kept uncaged in the open and can be viewed by the public from cars, etc.

safari suit NOUN an outfit made of tough cotton, denim, etc., consisting of a bush jacket with matching trousers, shorts, or skirt.

safe (seɪf) ADJECTIVE 1 affording security or protection from harm: *a safe place.* 2 (*postpositive*) free from danger: *you'll be safe here.* 3 secure from risk; certain; sound: *a safe investment; a safe bet.* 4 worthy of trust; prudent: *a safe companion.* 5 tending to avoid controversy or risk: *a safe player.* 6 unable to do harm; not dangerous: *a criminal safe behind bars; water safe to drink.* 7 *Brit informal* excellent. 8 **on the safe side.** as a precaution. ◆ ADVERB 9 in a safe condition: *the children are safe in bed now.* 10 **play safe.** to act in a way least likely to cause danger, controversy, or defeat. ◆ NOUN 11 a strong container, usually of metal and provided with a secure lock, for storing money or valuables. 12 a small ventilated cupboard-like container for storing food. 13 *US and Canadian* a slang word for **condom.**
▷HISTORY C13: from Old French *salf,* from Latin *salvus;* related to Latin *salus* safety
▸**'safely** ADVERB ▸**'safeness** NOUN

safe-blower NOUN a person who uses explosives to open safes and rob them.

safe-breaker NOUN a person who breaks open and robs safes. Also called: **safe-cracker.**

safe-conduct NOUN 1 a document giving official permission to travel through a region, esp in time of war. 2 the protection afforded by such a document. ◆ VERB (*tr*) 3 to conduct (a person) in safety. 4 to give a safe-conduct to.

safe-deposit *or* **safety-deposit** NOUN **a** a place or building with facilities for the safe storage of money or valuables. **b** (*as modifier*): *a safe-deposit box.*

safeguard ('seɪf,gɑ:d) NOUN 1 a person or thing that ensures protection against danger, damage, injury, etc. 2 a document authorizing safe-conduct. ◆ VERB 3 (*tr*) to defend or protect.

safe house NOUN a place used secretly by undercover agents, terrorists, etc., as a meeting place or refuge.

safekeeping ('seɪf'ki:pɪŋ) NOUN the act of keeping or state of being kept in safety.

safelight ('seɪf,laɪt) NOUN *Photog* a light that can be used in a room in which photographic material is handled, transmitting only those colours to which a particular type of film, plate, or paper is relatively insensitive.

safe period NOUN *Informal* the period during the menstrual cycle when conception is considered least likely to occur. See also **rhythm method.**

safe seat NOUN a Parliamentary seat that at an election is sure to be held by the same party as held it before.

safe sex *or* **safer sex** NOUN sexual intercourse using physical protection, such as a condom, or nonpenetrative methods to prevent the spread of such diseases as AIDS.

safe surfing NOUN the practice of using security measures to protect one's computer while surfing the Internet.

safety ('seɪftɪ) NOUN, *plural* **-ties.** 1 the quality of being safe. 2 freedom from danger or risk of injury. 3 a contrivance or device designed to prevent injury. 4 *American football* **a** Also called: **safetyman.** either of two players who defend the area furthest back in the field. **b** a play in which the offensive team causes the ball to cross its own goal line and then grounds the ball behind that line, scoring two points for the opposing team. Compare **touchback.**

safety belt NOUN 1 another name for **seat belt.** 2 a belt or strap worn by a person working at a great height and attached to a fixed object to prevent him from falling.

safety catch NOUN a device to prevent the accidental operation of a mechanism, e.g. in a firearm or lift.

safety chain NOUN a chain on the fastening of a bracelet, watch, etc., to ensure that it cannot open enough to fall off accidentally. Also called: **guard.**

safety curtain NOUN a curtain made of fireproof material that can be lowered to separate the auditorium and stage in a theatre to prevent the spread of a fire.

safety factor NOUN another name for **factor of safety.**

safety film NOUN photographic film consisting of a nonflammable cellulose acetate or polyester base.

safety fuse NOUN 1 a slow-burning fuse for igniting detonators from a distance. 2 an electrical fuse that protects a circuit from overloading.

safety glass NOUN glass made by sandwiching a layer of plastic or resin between two sheets of glass so that if broken the fragments will not shatter.

Safety Islands PLURAL NOUN a group of three small French islands in the Atlantic, off the coast of French Guiana. French name: **Îles du Salut.**

safety lamp NOUN an oil-burning miner's lamp in which the flame is surrounded by a metal gauze to prevent it from igniting combustible gas. Also called: **Davy lamp.**

safety match NOUN a match that will light only when struck against a specially prepared surface.

safety net NOUN 1 a net used in a circus to catch high-wire and trapeze artistes if they fall. 2 any means of protection from hardship or loss, such as insurance.

safety pin NOUN 1 a spring wire clasp with a covering catch, made so as to shield the point when closed and to prevent accidental unfastening. 2 another word for **pin** (sense 9).

safety razor NOUN a razor with a guard or guards fitted close to the cutting edge or edges so that deep cuts are prevented and the risk of accidental cuts reduced.

safety touch NOUN *Canadian football* a two-point play.

safety valve NOUN 1 a valve in a pressure vessel that allows fluid to escape when a predetermined level of pressure has been reached. 2 a harmless outlet for emotion, energy, etc.

saffian ('sæfɪən) NOUN leather tanned with sumach and usually dyed a bright colour.
▷HISTORY C16: via Russian and Turkish from Persian *sakhtiyān* goatskin, from *sakht* hard

safflower ('sæflauə) NOUN 1 a thistle-like Eurasian annual plant, *Carthamus tinctorius,* having large heads of orange-yellow flowers and yielding a dye and an oil used in paints, medicines, etc.: family *Asteraceae* (composites). 2 a red dye used for cotton and for colouring foods and cosmetics, or a drug obtained from the florets of this plant. ◆ Also called: **false saffron.**
▷HISTORY C16: via Dutch *saffloer* or German *safflor* from Old French *saffleur,* from Early Italian *saffiore,* of uncertain origin. Influenced by SAFFRON, FLOWER

saffron ('sæfrən) NOUN 1 an Old World crocus, *Crocus sativus,* having purple or white flowers with orange stigmas. 2 the dried stigmas of this plant, used to flavour or colour food. 3 **meadow saffron.** another name for **autumn crocus.** 4 **false saffron.** another name for **safflower.** 5 **a** an orange to orange-yellow colour. **b** (*as adjective*): *a saffron dress.*
▷HISTORY C13: from Old French *safran,* from Medieval Latin *safranum,* from Arabic *za'farān*

Safi (*French* safi) NOUN a port in W Morocco, 170 km (105 miles) northwest of Marrakech, to which it is the nearest port. Pop.: 364 648 (1994).

Safid Rud (sæ'fi:d 'ru:d) NOUN a river in N Iran, flowing northeast to a delta on the Caspian Sea. Length: about 785 km (490 miles).

S.Afr. ABBREVIATION FOR South Africa(n).

safranine *or* **safranin** ('sæfrənɪn, -,ni:n) NOUN any of a class of azine dyes, used for textiles and biological stains.
▷HISTORY C19: from French *safran* SAFFRON + -INE[2]

safrole ('sæfrəul) NOUN a colourless or yellowish oily water-insoluble liquid present in sassafras and camphor oils and used in soaps and perfumes. Formula: $C_{10}H_{10}O_2$.
▷HISTORY C19: from (SAS)SAFR(AS) + -OLE[1]

saft (sæft) ADJECTIVE a Scot word for **soft.**

sag (sæg) VERB (*mainly intr*) **sags, sagging, sagged** 1 (*also tr*) to sink or cause to sink in parts, as under weight or pressure: *the bed sags in the middle.* 2 to fall in value: *prices sagged to a new low.* 3 to hang unevenly; droop. 4 (of courage, spirits, etc.) to weaken; flag. ◆ NOUN 5 the act or an instance of sagging: *a sag in profits.* 6 *Nautical* the extent to which a vessel's keel sags at the centre. Compare **hog** (sense 6), **hogged.** 7 **a** a marshy depression in an area of glacial till, chiefly in the US Middle West. **b** (*as modifier*): *sag and swell topography.*
▷HISTORY C15: from Scandinavian; compare Swedish *sacka,* Dutch *zakken,* Norwegian dialect *sakka* to subside, Danish *sakke* to lag behind

saga ('sɑ:gə) NOUN 1 any of several medieval prose narratives written in Iceland and recounting the exploits of a hero or a family. 2 any similar heroic narrative. 3 Also called: **saga novel.** a series of novels about several generations or members of a family. 4 any other artistic production said to resemble a saga. 5 *Informal* a series of events or a story stretching over a long period.
▷HISTORY C18: from Old Norse: a narrative; related to Old English *secgan* to SAY[1]

sagacious (sə'geɪʃəs) ADJECTIVE 1 having or showing sagacity; wise. 2 *Obsolete* (of hounds) having an acute sense of smell.
▷HISTORY C17: from Latin *sagāx,* from *sāgīre* to be astute
▸**sa'gaciously** ADVERB ▸**sa'gaciousness** NOUN

sagacity (sə'gæsɪtɪ) NOUN foresight, discernment, or keen perception; ability to make good judgments.

sagamore ('sægə,mɔ:) NOUN (among some North American Indians) a chief or eminent man. Also called: **sachem.**
▷HISTORY C17: from Abnaki *sāgimau,* literally: he overcomes

sag bag NOUN another name for **bean bag** (sense 2).

sage[1] (seɪdʒ) NOUN 1 a man revered for his profound wisdom. ◆ ADJECTIVE 2 profoundly wise or prudent. 3 *Obsolete* solemn.
▷HISTORY C13: from Old French, from Latin *sapere* to be sensible; see SAPIENT
▸**'sagely** ADVERB ▸**'sageness** NOUN

sage[2] (seɪdʒ) NOUN 1 a perennial Mediterranean plant, *Salvia officinalis,* having grey-green leaves and purple, blue, or white flowers: family *Lamiaceae* (labiates). 2 the leaves of this plant, used in cooking for flavouring. 3 short for **sagebrush.**
▷HISTORY C14: from Old French *saulge,* from Latin *salvia,* from *salvus* safe, in good health (from the curative properties attributed to the plant)

sagebrush ('seɪdʒ,brʌʃ) NOUN any of several aromatic plants of the genus *Artemisia,* esp *A. tridentata,* a shrub of W North America, having silver-green leaves and large clusters of small white flowers: family *Asteraceae* (composites).

sage Derby NOUN See **Derby**[2] (sense 4).

sage grouse NOUN a large North American grouse, *Centrocercus urophasianus,* the males of which perform elaborate courtship displays.
▷HISTORY C19: so named because it lives among, and eats, SAGEBRUSH

saggar *or* **sagger** ('sægə) NOUN a clay box in which fragile ceramic wares are placed for protection during firing.
▷HISTORY C17: perhaps alteration of SAFEGUARD

sagging moment NOUN a bending moment that produces concave bending at the middle of a simple supported beam. Also called: **positive bending moment.**

Saghalien (sə'gɑːljən) NOUN a variant of **Sakhalin.**

Sagitta (sə'gɪtə) NOUN, *Latin genitive* **Sagittae** (sə'gɪtiː). a small constellation in the N hemisphere lying between Cygnus and Aquila and crossed by the Milky Way.
▷HISTORY C16: from Latin, literally: an arrow

sagittal ('sædʒɪtəl) ADJECTIVE [1] resembling an arrow; straight. [2] of or relating to the sagittal suture. [3] situated in a plane parallel to the sagittal suture.
▸ **'sagittally** ADVERB

sagittal suture NOUN a serrated line on the top of the skull that marks the junction of the two parietal bones.

Sagittarius (ˌsædʒɪ'tɛərɪəs) NOUN, *Latin genitive* **Sagittarii** (ˌsædʒɪ'tɛərɪˌaɪ). [1] *Astronomy* a large conspicuous zodiacal constellation in the S hemisphere lying between Scorpius and Capricornus on the ecliptic and crossed by the Milky Way and containing the galactic centre. [2] Also called: **the Archer.** *Astrology* **a** the ninth sign of the zodiac, symbol ♐, having a mutable fire classification and ruled by the planet Jupiter. The sun is in this sign between Nov. 22 and Dec. 21. **b** a person born when the sun is in this sign. ◆ ADJECTIVE [3] *Astrology* born under or characteristic of Sagittarius. ◆ Also (for senses 2b, 3): **Sagittarian** (ˌsædʒɪ'tɛərɪən).
▷HISTORY C14: from Latin: an archer, from *sagitta* an arrow

sagittate ('sædʒɪˌteɪt) *or* **sagittiform** (sə'dʒɪtɪˌfɔːm, 'sædʒ-) ADJECTIVE (esp of leaves) shaped like the head of an arrow.
▷HISTORY C18: from New Latin *sagittātus,* from Latin *sagitta* arrow

sago ('seɪgəʊ) NOUN a starchy cereal obtained from the powdered pith of a sago palm, used for puddings and as a thickening agent.
▷HISTORY C16: from Malay *sāgū*

sago grass NOUN *Austral* a tall tough grass, *Paspalidum globoideum,* grown as forage for cattle.

sago palm NOUN [1] any of various tropical Asian palm trees, esp any of the genera *Metroxylon, Arenga,* and *Caryota,* the trunks of which yield sago. [2] any of several palmlike cycads that yield sago, esp *Cycas revoluta.*

saguaro (sə'gwɑːrəʊ, sə'wɑː-) *or* **sahuaro** (sə'wɑːrəʊ) NOUN, *plural* **-ros.** a giant cactus, *Carnegiea gigantea,* of desert regions of Arizona, S California, and Mexico, having white nocturnal flowers and edible red pulpy fruits.
▷HISTORY Mexican Spanish, variant of *sahuaro,*an Indian name

Saguenay (ˌsægə'neɪ) NOUN a river in SE Canada in S Quebec, rising as the Péribonca River on the central plateau and flowing south, then east to the St. Lawrence. Length: 764 km (475 miles).

Sagunto (*Spanish* sa'γunto) NOUN an industrial town in E Spain, near Valencia: allied to Rome and made a heroic resistance to the Carthaginian attack led by Hannibal (219–218 B.C.). Pop.: 57 300 (latest est.). Ancient name: **Saguntum** (sə'guːntəm).

Sahaptin (sɑː'hæptɪn), **Sahaptan** (sɑː'hæptən), *or* **Sahaptian** (sɑː'hæptɪən) NOUN [1] (*plural* **-tins, -tans, -tians** *or* **-tin, -tan, -tian**) a member of a North American Indian people of Oregon and Washington, including the Nez Percé. [2] the language of this people. ◆ Also: **Shahaptin** (ʃə'hæptɪn).

Sahara (sə'hɑːrə) NOUN a desert in N Africa, extending from the Atlantic to the Red Sea and from the Mediterranean to central Mali, Niger, Chad, and the Sudan: the largest desert in the world, occupying over a quarter of Africa; rises to over 3300 m (11 000 ft.) in the central mountain system of the Ahaggar and Tibesti massifs; large reserves of iron ore, oil, and natural gas. Area: 9 100 000 sq. km (3 500 000 sq. miles). Average annual rainfall: less than 254 mm (10 in.). Highest recorded temperature: 58°C (136.4°F).

Saharan (sə'hɑːrən) NOUN [1] a group of languages spoken in parts of Chad and adjacent countries, now generally regarded as forming a branch of the Nilo-Saharan family. ◆ ADJECTIVE [2] relating to or belonging to this group of languages. [3] of or relating to the Sahara.

sahib ('sɑːhɪb) *or* **saheb** ('sɑːhɛb) NOUN (in India) a form of address or title placed after a man's name or designation, used as a mark of respect.
▷HISTORY C17: from Urdu, from Arabic *çāhib,* literally: friend

Sahitya Akademi (sɑː'hɪtjə ə'kɑːdəmɪ) NOUN a body set up by the Government of India for cultivating literature in Indian languages and in English.

saice (saɪs) NOUN a variant spelling of **syce.**

said[1] (sɛd) ADJECTIVE [1] (*prenominal*) (in contracts, pleadings, etc.) named or mentioned previously; aforesaid. ◆ VERB [2] the past tense and past participle of **say.**

said[2] ('sɑːɪd) NOUN a variant of **sayyid.**

Saida ('sɑːɪdə) NOUN a port in SW Lebanon, on the Mediterranean: on the site of ancient Sidon; terminal of the Trans-Arabian pipeline from Saudi Arabia. Pop.: 100 000 (1991 est.).

saiga ('saɪgə) NOUN either of two antelopes, *Saiga tatarica* or *S. mongolica,* of the plains of central Asia, having an enlarged slightly elongated nose.
▷HISTORY C19: from Russian

Saigon (saɪ'gɒn) NOUN the former name (until 1976) of **Ho Chi Minh City.**

sail (seɪl) NOUN [1] an area of fabric, usually Terylene or nylon (formerly canvas), with fittings for holding it in any suitable position to catch the wind, used for propelling certain kinds of vessels, esp over water. [2] a voyage on such a vessel: *a sail down the river.* [3] a vessel with sails or such vessels collectively: *to travel by sail; we raised seven sail in the northeast.* [4] a ship's sails collectively. [5] something resembling a sail in shape, position, or function, such as the part of a windmill that is turned by the wind or the part of a Portuguese man-of-war that projects above the water. [6] the conning tower of a submarine. [7] **in sail.** having the sail set. [8] **make sail. a** to run up the sail or to run up more sail. **b** to begin a voyage. [9] **set sail. a** to embark on a voyage by ship. **b** to hoist sail. [10] **under sail. a** with sail hoisted. **b** under way. ◆ VERB (*mainly intr*) [11] to travel in a boat or ship: *we sailed to Le Havre.* [12] to begin a voyage; set sail: *we sail at 5 o'clock.* [13] (of a vessel) to move over the water: *the liner is sailing to the Caribbean.* [14] (*tr*) to manoeuvre or navigate a vessel: *he sailed the schooner up the channel.* [15] (*tr*) to sail over: *she sailed the Atlantic single-handed.* [16] (often foll by *over, through,* etc.) to move fast or effortlessly: *we sailed through customs; the ball sailed over the fence.* [17] to move along smoothly; glide. [18] (often foll by *in* or *into*) *Informal* **a** to begin (something) with vigour. **b** to make an attack (on) violently with words or physical force.
▷HISTORY Old English *segl;* related to Old Frisian *seil,* Old Norse *segl,* German *Segel*
▸ **'sailable** ADJECTIVE ▸ **'sailless** ADJECTIVE

sailboard ('seɪlˌbɔːd) NOUN the craft used for windsurfing, consisting of a moulded board like a surfboard, to which a mast bearing a single sail is attached by a swivel joint.

sailboarding ('seɪlˌbɔːdɪŋ) NOUN another name for **windsurfing.**

sailcloth ('seɪlˌklɒθ) NOUN [1] any of various fabrics from which sails are made. [2] a lighter cloth used for clothing, etc.

sailer ('seɪlə) NOUN a vessel, esp one equipped with sails, with specified sailing characteristics: *a good sailer.*

sailfish ('seɪlˌfɪʃ) NOUN, *plural* **-fish** *or* **-fishes.** [1] any of several large scombroid game fishes of the genus *Istiophorus,* such as *I. albicans* (**Atlantic sailfish**), of warm and tropical seas: family *Istiophoridae.* They have an elongated upper jaw and a long sail-like dorsal fin. [2] another name for **basking shark.**

sailing ('seɪlɪŋ) NOUN [1] the practice, art, or technique of sailing a vessel. [2] a method of navigating a vessel: *rhumb-line sailing.* [3] an instance of a vessel's leaving a port: *scheduled for a midnight sailing.*

sailing boat *or esp US and Canadian* **sailboat** ('seɪlˌbəʊt) NOUN a boat propelled chiefly by sail.

sailing ship NOUN a large sailing vessel.

sailor ('seɪlə) NOUN [1] any member of a ship's crew, esp one below the rank of officer. [2] a person who sails, esp with reference to the likelihood of his becoming seasick: *a good sailor.* [3] short for **sailor hat** or **sailor suit.**
▸ **'sailorly** ADJECTIVE

sailor hat NOUN a hat with a flat round crown and fairly broad brim that is rolled upwards.

sailor's-choice NOUN any of various small percoid fishes of American coastal regions of the Atlantic, esp the grunt *Haemulon parra* and the pinfish.

sailor suit NOUN a child's suit, usually navy and white, with a collar that is squared off at the back like a sailor's.

sailplane ('seɪlˌpleɪn) NOUN a high-performance glider.

sain (seɪn) VERB (*tr*) *Archaic* to make the sign of the cross over so as to bless or protect from evil or sin.
▷HISTORY Old English *segnian,* from Latin *signare* to SIGN (with the cross)

sainfoin ('sænfɔɪn) NOUN a Eurasian perennial leguminous plant, *Onobrychis viciifolia,* widely grown as a forage crop, having pale pink flowers and curved pods.
▷HISTORY C17: from French, from Medieval Latin *sānum faenum* wholesome hay, referring to its former use as a medicine

saint (seɪnt; *unstressed* sənt) NOUN [1] a person who after death is formally recognized by a Christian Church, esp the Roman Catholic Church, as having attained, through holy deeds or behaviour, a specially exalted place in heaven and the right to veneration. [2] a person of exceptional holiness or goodness. [3] (*plural*) *Bible* the collective body of those who are righteous in God's sight. ◆ VERB [4] (*tr*) to canonize; recognize formally as a saint.
▷HISTORY C12: from Old French, from Latin *sanctus* holy, from *sancīre* to hallow
▸ **'saintdom** NOUN ▸ **'saintless** ADJECTIVE ▸ **'saintlike** ADJECTIVE

Saint Agnes's Eve NOUN, *usually abbreviated to* **St Agnes's Eve.** the night of Jan. 20, when according to tradition a woman can discover the identity of her future husband by performing certain rites.

Saint Albans ('ɔːlbənz) NOUN, *usually abbreviated to* **St Albans.** a city in SE England, in W Hertfordshire: founded in 948 A.D. around the Benedictine abbey first built in Saxon times on the site of the martyrdom (about 303 A.D.) of St Alban; present abbey built in 1077; Roman ruins. Pop.: 80 376 (1991). Latin name: **Verulamium.**

Saint Andrews NOUN, *usually abbreviated to* **St Andrews.** a city in E Scotland, in Fife on the North Sea: the oldest university in Scotland (1411); famous golf links. Pop.: 11 136 (1991).

Saint Andrew's Cross NOUN, *usually abbreviated to* **St Andrew's Cross.** [1] a diagonal cross with equal arms. [2] a white diagonal cross on a blue ground.
▷HISTORY C18: so called because Saint Andrew, one of the twelve apostles of Jesus, is reputed to have been crucified on a cross of this shape

Saint Anthony's Cross NOUN, *usually abbreviated to* **St Anthony's Cross.** another name for **tau cross.**

Saint Anthony's fire NOUN, *usually abbreviated to* **St Anthony's fire.** *Pathol* another name for **ergotism** or **erysipelas.**
▷HISTORY C16: so named because praying to *St Anthony* was believed to effect a cure

Saint Augustine ('ɔːgəsˌtiːn) NOUN, *usually abbreviated to* **St Augustine.** a resort in NE Florida, on the Intracoastal Waterway: the oldest town in North America (1565); the northernmost outpost of the Spanish colonial empire for over 200 years. Pop.: 11 692 (1990).

Saint Austell ('ɔːstəl) NOUN, *usually abbreviated to* **St Austell.** a town in SW England, in S Cornwall on **St Austell Bay** (an inlet of the English Channel): centre for the now-declining china clay industry; the Eden Project, a rainforest environment in the world's largest greenhouse, is nearby; administratively part of St Austell with Fowey since 1968. Pop. (with Fowey): 21 622 (1991).

Saint Bartholomew's Day Massacre NOUN, *usually abbreviated to* **St Bartholomew's Day Massacre**. the murder of Huguenots in Paris that began on Aug. 24, 1572 on the orders of Charles IX, acting under the influence of his mother Catherine de' Medici.

Saint Bernard NOUN, *usually abbreviated to* **St Bernard**. a large breed of dog with a dense red-and-white coat, formerly used as a rescue dog in mountainous areas.
▷HISTORY C19: so called because they were kept by the monks of the hospice at the Great SAINT BERNARD PASS

Saint Bernard Pass NOUN, *usually abbreviated to* **St Bernard Pass**. either of two passes over the Alps: the **Great St Bernard Pass** 2472 m (8110 ft.) high, east of Mont Blanc between Italy and Switzerland, or the **Little St Bernard Pass** 2157 m (7077 ft.) high, south of Mont Blanc between Italy and France.

Saint-Brieuc (*French* sɛ̃briø) NOUN, *usually abbreviated to* **St-Brieuc**. a market town in NW France, near the N coast of Brittany. Pop.: 47 370 (1990).

Saint Catharines NOUN, *usually abbreviated to* **St Catharines**. an industrial city in S central Canada, in S Ontario on the Welland Canal. Pop.: 130 926 (1991).

Saint Christopher NOUN, *usually abbreviated to* **St Christopher**. another name for **Saint Kitts**.

Saint Christopher-Nevis NOUN, *usually abbreviated to* **St Christopher-Nevis**. the official name of **Saint Kitts-Nevis**.

Saint Clair (klɛə) NOUN, *usually abbreviated to* **St Clair. Lake.** a lake between SE Michigan and Ontario: linked with Lake Huron by the **St Clair River** and with Lake Erie by the Detroit River. Area: 1191 sq. km (460 sq. miles).

Saint-Cloud (*French* sɛ̃klu) NOUN, *usually abbreviated to* **St-Cloud**. a residential suburb of Paris: former royal palace; Sèvres porcelain factory. Pop.: 28 670 (1990).

Saint Croix (krɔɪ) NOUN, *usually abbreviated to* **St Croix**. an island in the Caribbean, the largest of the Virgin Islands of the US: purchased by the US in 1917. Chief town: Christiansted. Pop.: 53 234 (2000). Area: 207 sq. km (80 sq. miles). Also called: **Santa Cruz** ('sæntə 'kru:z).

Saint Croix River NOUN, *usually abbreviated to* **St Croix River**. a river on the border between the northeast US and SE Canada, flowing from the Chiputneticook Lakes to Passamaquoddy Bay, forming the border between Maine, US, and New Brunswick, Canada. Length: 121 km (75 miles).

Saint David's NOUN, *usually abbreviated to* **St David's**. a town in SW Wales, in Pembrokeshire: its cathedral was a place of pilgrimage in medieval times. Pop.: 1627 (1991).

Saint-Denis (*French* sɛ̃dni) NOUN, *usually abbreviated to* **St-Denis**. 1 a town in N France, on the Seine: 12th-century Gothic abbey church, containing the tombs of many French monarchs; an industrial suburb of Paris. Pop.: 89 988 (1990). 2 the capital of the French overseas region of Réunion, a port on the N coast. Pop.: 131 557 (1999).

sainted ('seɪntɪd) ADJECTIVE 1 canonized. 2 like a saint in character or nature. 3 hallowed or holy.

Sainte Foy (seɪnt 'fɔɪ, sənt) NOUN, *usually abbreviated to* **Ste Foy**. a SW suburb of Quebec, on the St Lawrence River. Pop.: 71 133 (1991).

Saint Elias Mountains PLURAL NOUN, *usually abbreviated to* **St Elias Mountains**. a mountain range between SE Alaska and the SW Yukon, Canada. Highest peak: Mount Logan, 6050 m (19 850 ft.).

Saint Elmo's fire ('ɛlməʊz) NOUN, *usually abbreviated to* **St Elmo's fire**. (not in technical usage) a luminous region that sometimes appears around church spires, the masts of ships, etc. It is a corona discharge in the air caused by atmospheric electricity. Also called: **corposant**.
▷HISTORY C16: so called because it was associated with *Saint Elmo* (a corruption, via *Sant'Ermo,* of *Saint Erasmus,* died 303) the patron saint of Mediterranean sailors

Saint-Émilion (*French* sɛ̃temiljɔ̃) NOUN a full-bodied red wine, similar to a Burgundy, produced around the town of Saint-Émilion in Bordeaux.

Saint-Étienne (*French* sɛ̃tetjɛn) NOUN, *usually abbreviated to* **St-Étienne**. a town in E central France: a major producer of textiles and armaments. Pop.: 179 755 (1999).

Saint Gall (*French* sɛ̃ gal) NOUN, *usually abbreviated to* **St Gall**. 1 a canton of NE Switzerland. Capital: St Gall. Pop.: 447 600 (2000 est.). Area: 2012 sq. km (777 sq. miles). 2 a town in NE Switzerland, capital of St Gall canton: an important educational centre in the Middle Ages. Pop.: 75 541 (1994). German name: **Sankt Gallen** (zaŋkt 'galən).

Saint George's NOUN, *usually abbreviated to* **St George's**. the capital of Grenada, a port in the southwest. Pop.: 4621 (1991).

Saint George's Channel NOUN, *usually abbreviated to* **St George's Channel**. a strait between Wales and Ireland, linking the Irish Sea with the Atlantic. Length: about 160 km (100 miles). Width: up to 145 km (90 miles).

Saint George's Cross NOUN, *usually abbreviated to* **St George's Cross**. a red Greek cross on a white background.

Saint George's mushroom NOUN an edible whitish basidiomycetous fungus, *Tricholoma gambosum,* with a floury smell.
▷HISTORY so named because it appears earlier than most fungi, around St George's day (23 April)

Saint Gotthard ('gɒtəd) NOUN, *usually abbreviated to* **St Gotthard**. 1 a range of the Lepontine Alps in SE central Switzerland. 2 a pass over the St Gotthard mountains, in S Switzerland. Height: 2114 m (6935 ft.).

Saint Helena (ˌsɛntɪ'li:nə) NOUN, *usually abbreviated to* **St Helena**. a volcanic island in the SE Atlantic, forming (with its dependencies Tristan da Cunha and Ascension) a UK Overseas Territory: discovered by the Portuguese in 1502 and annexed by England in 1651; scene of Napoleon's exile and death. Capital: Jamestown. Pop.: 5157 (1994 est.). Area: 122 sq. km (47 sq. miles).

Saint Helens NOUN, *usually abbreviated to* **St Helens**. 1 a town in NW England, in St Helens unitary authority, Merseyside: glass industry. Pop.: 176 845 (2001). 2 a unitary authority in NW England, in Merseyside. Pop.: 181 000 (1994 est.). Area: 130 sq. km (50 sq. miles). 3 a volcanic peak in S Washington state; it erupted in 1980 after lying dormant from 1857.

Saint Helier ('hɛlɪə) NOUN, *usually abbreviated to* **St Helier**. a market town and resort in the Channel Islands, on the S coast of Jersey. Pop.: 27 523 (1996).

sainthood ('seɪnthʊd) NOUN 1 the state or character of being a saint. 2 saints collectively.

Saint James's Palace NOUN, *usually abbreviated to* **St James's Palace**. a palace in Pall Mall, London: residence of British monarchs from 1697 to 1837.

Saint John NOUN, *usually abbreviated to* **St John**. 1 a port in E Canada, at the mouth of the St John River: the largest city in New Brunswick. Pop.: 90 457 (1991). 2 an island in the Caribbean, in the Virgin Islands of the US. Pop.: 4197 (2000). Area: 49 sq. km (19 sq. miles). 3 **Lake.** a lake in Canada, in S Quebec: drained by the Saguenay River. Area: 971 sq. km (375 sq. miles). 4 a river in E North America, rising in Maine, US, and flowing northeast to New Brunswick, Canada, then generally southeast to the Bay of Fundy. Length: 673 km (418 miles).

Saint John's NOUN, *usually abbreviated to* **St John's**. 1 a port in Canada, capital of Newfoundland, on the E coast of the Avalon Peninsula. Pop.: 101 936 (1996). 2 the capital of Antigua and Barbuda: a port on the NW coast of the island of Antigua. Pop.: 21 514 (1991).

Saint John's bread NOUN, *usually abbreviated to* **St John's bread**. another name for **carob** (sense 2).
▷HISTORY C16: so called because its beans were thought to be the "locusts" that JOHN THE BAPTIST ate in the desert

Saint John's wort NOUN, *usually abbreviated to* **St John's wort**. any of numerous shrubs or herbaceous plants of the temperate genus *Hypericum,* such as *H. perforatum,* having yellow flowers and glandular leaves: family *Hypericaceae*. See also **rose of Sharon** (sense 1), **tutsan**.
▷HISTORY C15: so named because it was traditionally gathered on *Saint John's Eve* (June 23rd) as a protection against evil spirits

Saint Kilda ('kɪldə) NOUN, *usually abbreviated to* **St Kilda**. 1 a group of volcanic islands in the Atlantic, in the Outer Hebrides: uninhabited since 1930; bird sanctuary. 2 Also called: **Hirta**. the main island of this group.

Saint Kitts (kɪts) NOUN, *usually abbreviated to* **St Kitts**. an island in the E Caribbean, in the Leeward Islands: part of the state of St Kitts-Nevis. Capital: Basseterre. Pop.: 35 340 (1995 est.). Area: 168 sq. km (65 sq. miles). Also called: **Saint Christopher**.

Saint Kitts-Nevis NOUN, *usually abbreviated to* **St Kitts-Nevis**. an independent state in the E Caribbean; comprises the two islands of St Kitts and Nevis: with the island of Anguilla formed a colony (1882–1967) and a British associated state (1967–83); Anguilla formally separated from the group in 1983; gained full independence in 1983 as a member of the Commonwealth. Official language: English. Religion: Protestant majority. Currency: E Caribbean dollar. Capital: Basseterre. Pop.: 42 300 (1998 est.). Area: 262 sq. km (101 sq. miles).

Saint Laurent (*French* sɛ̃ lɔrɑ̃) NOUN, *usually abbreviated to* **St Laurent**. a W suburb of Montreal, Canada. Pop.: 72 402 (1991).

Saint Lawrence NOUN, *usually abbreviated to* **St Lawrence**. 1 a river in SE Canada, flowing northeast from Lake Ontario, forming part of the border between Canada and the US, to the Gulf of St Lawrence: commercially one of the most important rivers in the world as the easternmost link of the St Lawrence Seaway. Length: 1207 km (750 miles). Width at mouth: 145 km (90 miles). 2 **Gulf of.** a deep arm of the Atlantic off the E coast of Canada between Newfoundland and the mainland coasts of Quebec, New Brunswick, and Nova Scotia.

Saint Lawrence Seaway NOUN, *usually abbreviated to* **St Lawrence Seaway**. an inland waterway of North America, passing through the Great Lakes, the St Lawrence River, and connecting canals and locks: one of the most important waterways in the world. Length: 3993 km (2480 miles).

Saint Leger ('lɛdʒə) NOUN, *usually abbreviated to* **St Leger. the.** an annual horse race run at Doncaster since 1776: one of the classics of the flat-racing season.

Saint Leonard ('lɛnəd) NOUN, *usually abbreviated to* **St Leonard**. a N suburb of Montreal, Canada. Pop.: 82 200 (latest est.).

Saint-Lô (*French* sɛ̃lo) NOUN, *usually abbreviated to* **St-Lô**. a market town in NW France: a Calvinist stronghold in the 16th century. Pop.: 22 819 (1990).

Saint Louis ('lʊɪs) NOUN, *usually abbreviated to* **St Louis**. a port in E Missouri, on the Mississippi River near its confluence with the Missouri: the largest city in the state; university; major industrial centre. Pop.: 348 189 (2000).

Saint-Louis (*French* sɛ̃lwi) NOUN, *usually abbreviated to* **St-Louis**. a port in NW Senegal, on an island at the mouth of the Senegal River: the first French settlement in W Africa (1689); capital of Senegal until 1958. Pop.: 180 000 (1998 est.).

Saint Lucia ('lu:ʃə) NOUN, *usually abbreviated to* **St Lucia**. an island state in the Caribbean, in the Windward Islands group of the Lesser Antilles: a volcanic island; gained self-government in 1967 as a British Associated State; attained full independence within the Commonwealth in 1979. Official language: English. Religion: Roman Catholic majority. Currency: E Caribbean dollar. Capital: Castries. Pop.: 158 000 (2001 est.). Area: 616 sq. km (238 sq. miles).

Saint Luke's summer NOUN, *usually abbreviated to* **St Luke's summer**. a period of unusually warm weather in the autumn.
▷HISTORY referring to St Luke's feast-day, Oct. 7 in the pre-Gregorian calendar (now Oct. 18)

saintly ('seɪntlɪ) ADJECTIVE **-lier, -liest**. like, relating to, or suitable for a saint.
▸'**saintlily** ADVERB ▸'**saintliness** NOUN

Saint Martin NOUN, *usually abbreviated to* **St Martin**. an island in the E Caribbean, in the Leeward

Islands: administratively divided since 1648, the north belonging to France (as a dependency of Guadeloupe) and the south belonging to the Netherlands (as part of the Netherlands Antilles); salt industry. Pop.: (French) 29 078 (1999); (Dutch) 41 718 (2000 est.). Areas: (French) 52 sq. km (20 sq. miles); (Dutch) 33 sq. km (13 sq. miles). Dutch name: **Sint Maarten**.

Saint Martin's summer NOUN, *usually abbreviated to* **St Martin's summer**. a period of unusually warm weather in the late autumn, esp early November.
▷HISTORY referring to St Martin's feast-day, Oct. 31 in the pre-Gregorian calendar (now Nov. 11)

Saint-Maur-des-Fossés (*French* sɛ̃mɔrdefose) NOUN, *usually abbreviated to* **St-Maur-des-Fossés**. a town in N France, on the River Marne: a residential suburb of SE Paris. Pop.: 77 492 (1990).

Saint-Mihiel (*French* sɛ̃mjɛl) NOUN, *usually abbreviated to* **St-Mihiel**. a village in NE France, on the River Meuse: site of a battle in World War I, in which the American army launched its first offensive in France.

Saint Moritz (mə'rɪts) NOUN, *usually abbreviated to* **St Moritz**. a village in E Switzerland, in Graubünden canton in the Upper Engadine, at an altitude of 1856 m (6089 ft.): sports and tourist centre. Pop.: 5335 (1990 est.).

Saint-Nazaire (*French* sɛ̃nazɛr) NOUN, *usually abbreviated to* **St-Nazaire**. a port in NW France, at the mouth of the River Loire: German submarine base in World War II; shipbuilding. Pop.: 64 812 (1990).

Saint-Ouen (*French* sɛ̃twɛ̃) NOUN, *usually abbreviated to* **St-Ouen**. a town in N France, on the Seine: an industrial suburb of Paris; famous flea market. Pop.: 42 611 (1990).

Saint Paul NOUN, *usually abbreviated to* **St Paul**. a port in SE Minnesota, capital of the state, at the head of navigation of the Mississippi: now contiguous with Minneapolis (the Twin Cities). Pop.: 287 151 (2000).

saintpaulia (sənt'pɔːlɪə) NOUN another name for **African violet**.
▷HISTORY C20: New Latin, named after Baron W. von *Saint Paul,* German soldier (died 1910), who discovered it

Saint Paul's NOUN, *usually abbreviated to* **St Paul's**. a cathedral in central London, built between 1675 and 1710 to replace an earlier cathedral destroyed during the Great Fire (1666): regarded as Wren's masterpiece.

Saint Peter's NOUN, *usually abbreviated to* **St Peter's**. the basilica of the Vatican City, built between 1506 and 1615 to replace an earlier church: the largest church in the world, 188 m (615 ft.) long, and chief pilgrimage centre of Europe; designed by many architects, notably Bramante, Raphael, Sangallo, Michelangelo, and Bernini.

Saint Petersburg ('piːtəzˌbɜːg) NOUN, *usually abbreviated to* **St Petersburg**. [1] a city and port in Russia, on the Gulf of Finland at the mouth of the Neva River: founded by Peter the Great in 1703 and built on low-lying marshes subject to frequent flooding; capital of Russia from 1712 to 1918; a cultural and educational centre, with a university (1819); a major industrial centre, with engineering, shipbuilding, chemical, textile, and printing industries. Pop.: 4 169 400 (1999 est.). Former names: **Petrograd** (1914–24), **Leningrad** (1924–91). [2] a city and resort in W Florida, on Tampa Bay. Pop.: 235 988 (1996 est.).

Saint Pierre (*French* sɛ̃ pjɛr) NOUN, *usually abbreviated to* **St Pierre**. a former town on the coast of the French island of Martinique, destroyed by the eruption of Mont Pelée in 1902.

Saint Pierre and Miquelon (ˌmɪkə'lɒn; *French* miklɔ̃) NOUN, *usually abbreviated to* **St Pierre and Miquelon**. an archipelago in the Atlantic, off the S coast of Newfoundland: an overseas department of France, the only remaining French possession in North America; consists of the islands of St Pierre, with most of the population, and Miquelon, about ten times as large; fishing industries. Capital: St Pierre. Pop.: 6392 (1990). Area: 242 sq. km (94 sq. miles).

Saint Pölten ('pɜːltən) NOUN See **Sankt Pölten**.

Saint-Quentin (*French* sɛ̃kɑ̃tɛ̃) NOUN, *usually abbreviated to* **St-Quentin**. a town in N France, on the River Somme: textile industry. Pop.: 62 085 (1990).

saint's day NOUN *Christianity* a day in the church calendar commemorating a saint.

Saint-Simonianism (səntsɪ'məʊnɪəˌnɪzəm) *or* **Saint-Simonism** (sənt'saɪmənɪzəm) NOUN the socialist system advocated by the Comte de Saint-Simon (1760–1825), the French social philosopher.
▸**Saint-Si'monian** NOUN, ADJECTIVE

Saint Swithin's Day NOUN, *usually abbreviated to* **St Swithin's Day**. July 15, observed as a Church festival commemorating Saint Swithin. It is popularly supposed that if it rains on this day the rain will persist for the next 40 days.

Saint Thomas NOUN, *usually abbreviated to* **St Thomas**. [1] an island in the E Caribbean, in the Virgin Islands of the US. Capital: Charlotte Amalie. Pop.: 51 181 (2000). Area: 83 sq. km (28 sq. miles). [2] the former name (1921–37) of **Charlotte Amalie**.

Saint Valentine's Day NOUN, *usually abbreviated to* **St Valentine's Day**. Feb. 14, the day on which valentines are exchanged, originally connected with the pagan festival of Lupercalia.

Saint Vincent NOUN, *usually abbreviated to* **St Vincent**. [1] **Cape**. a headland at the SW extremity of Portugal: scene of several important naval battles, notably in 1797, when the British defeated the French and Spanish. [2] **Gulf**. a shallow inlet of SE South Australia, to the east of the Yorke Peninsula: salt industry.

Saint Vincent and the Grenadines NOUN, *usually abbreviated to* **St Vincent and the Grenadines**. an island state in the Caribbean, in the Windward Islands of the Lesser Antilles: comprises the island of St Vincent and the Northern Grenadines; formerly a British associated state (1969–79); gained full independence in 1979 as a member of the Commonwealth. Official language: English. Religion: Protestant majority. Currency: Caribbean dollar. Capital: Kingstown. Pop.: 113 000 (2001 est.). Area: 389 sq. km (150 sq. miles).

Saint Vitus's dance ('vaɪtəsɪz) NOUN, *usually abbreviated to* **St Vitus's dance**. *Pathol* a nontechnical name for **Sydenham's chorea**.
▷HISTORY C17: so called because sufferers traditionally prayed to *Saint Vitus* (3rd-century child martyr) for relief and were said to be cured by a visit to his shrine

Saipan (saɪ'pæn) NOUN an island in the W Pacific, administrative centre of the US associated territory of the Northern Mariana Islands; captured by the Americans and used as an air base until the end of World War II. Pop.: 62 392 (2000). Area: 180 sq. km (70 sq. miles).

sair (ser) ADJECTIVE, ADVERB a Scot word for **sore**.

Saïs ('seɪɪs) NOUN (in ancient Egypt) a city in the W Nile delta; the royal capital of the 24th dynasty (about 730–715 B.C.) and the 26th dynasty (about 664–525 B.C.).

Saite ('seɪaɪt) NOUN a native or inhabitant of the ancient Egyptian city of Saïs.

saith (sɛθ) VERB (used with *he, she,* or *it*) *Archaic* a form of the present tense (indicative mood) of **say**.

saithe (seɪθ) NOUN *Brit* another name for **coalfish**.
▷HISTORY C19: from Old Norse *seithr* coalfish; compare Gaelic *saigh, saighean* coalfish, Irish *saoidhean* young of fish

Saitic (seɪ'ɪtɪk) ADJECTIVE of or relating to the ancient Egyptian city of Saïs or its inhabitants.

Saiva ('saɪvə, 'ʃaɪ-) NOUN [1] a member of a branch of Hinduism devoted to the worship of Siva, but rejecting the notion of his incarnations. ◆ ADJECTIVE [2] of or relating to Saivism or Saivites.
▸**'Saivism** NOUN ▸**'Saivite** NOUN

sakai ('sakaɪ) NOUN (in Malaysia) [1] a Malaysian aborigine. [2] a wild or uncouth person.
▷HISTORY from Malay

Sakai (sɑː'kaɪ) NOUN a port in S Japan, on S Honshu on Osaka Bay: an industrial satellite of Osaka. Pop.: 802 965 (1995).

sake[1] (seɪk) NOUN [1] benefit or interest (esp in the phrase **for (someone's** *or* **one's own) sake**). [2] the purpose of obtaining or achieving (esp in the phrase **for the sake of (something)**). [3] used in various exclamations of impatience, urgency, etc.: *for heaven's sake; for pete's sake.*
▷HISTORY C13 (in the phrase *for the sake of,* probably from legal usage): from Old English *sacu* lawsuit (hence, a cause); related to Old Norse *sok,* German *Sache* matter

sake[2], **saké,** *or* **saki** ('sækɪ) NOUN a Japanese alcoholic drink made from fermented rice.
▷HISTORY C17: from Japanese

saker ('seɪkə) NOUN a large falcon, *Falco cherrug,* of E Europe and central Asia: used in falconry.
▷HISTORY C14 *sagre,* from Old French *sacre,* from Arabic *saqr*

Sakhalin (*Russian* səxa'lin) *or* **Saghalien** NOUN an island in the Sea of Okhotsk, off the SE coast of Russia north of Japan: fishing, forestry, and mineral resources (coal and petroleum). Capital: Yuzhno-Sakhalinsk. Pop.: 598 000 (2000 est.). Area: 76 000 sq. km (29 300 sq. miles). Japanese name (1905–24): **Karafuto**.

Sakha Republic (*Russian* 'saxa) NOUN an administrative division in E Russia, in NE Siberia on the Arctic Ocean: the coldest inhabited region of the world; it has rich mineral resources. Capital: Yakutsk. Pop.: 977 000 (2000 est.). Area: 3 103 200 sq. km (1 197 760 sq. miles). Former names: **Yakut Republic, Yakutia**.

saki ('sɑːkɪ) NOUN any of several small mostly arboreal New World monkeys of the genera *Pithecia* and *Chiropotes,* having long hair and a long bushy tail.
▷HISTORY C20: French, from Tupi *saqi*

Saktas ('sæktəs) NOUN a Hindu sect worshipping female goddesses represented by the vulva.
▷HISTORY C19: from Sanskrit. See SAKTI

Sakti ('sæktɪ) *or* **Shakti** ('ʃʌktɪ) NOUN *Hinduism* [1] the female principle or organ of reproduction and generative power in general. [2] this principle manifested in the consorts of the gods, esp Kali.
▷HISTORY C19: from Sanskrit *śákti* power

Sakyamuni (ˌsɑːkjə'muːnɪ) NOUN one of the titles of the Buddha, deriving from the name of Sakya where he was born.
▷HISTORY Sanskrit, literally: hermit of the *Sākya* tribe

sal (sæl) NOUN a pharmacological term for **salt** (sense 3).
▷HISTORY Latin

salaam (sə'lɑːm) NOUN [1] a Muslim form of salutation consisting of a deep bow with the right palm on the forehead. [2] a salutation signifying peace, used chiefly by Muslims. ◆ VERB [3] to make a salaam or salute (someone) with a salaam.
▷HISTORY C17: from Arabic *salām* peace, from the phrase *assalām 'alaikum* peace be to you

salable ('seɪləbᵊl) ADJECTIVE the US spelling of **saleable**.

salacious (sə'leɪʃəs) ADJECTIVE [1] having an excessive interest in sex. [2] (of books, magazines, etc.) erotic, bawdy, or lewd.
▷HISTORY C17: from Latin *salax* fond of leaping, from *salīre* to leap
▸**sa'laciously** ADVERB ▸**sa'laciousness** *or* **salacity** (sə'læsɪtɪ) NOUN

salad ('sæləd) NOUN [1] a dish of raw vegetables, such as lettuce, tomatoes, etc., served as a separate course with cold meat, eggs, etc., or as part of a main course. [2] any dish of cold vegetables or fruit: *potato salad; fruit salad.* [3] any green vegetable used in such a dish, esp lettuce.
▷HISTORY C15: from Old French *salade,* from Old Provençal *salada,* from *salar* to season with salt, from Latin *sal* salt

salad bar NOUN a counter in a restaurant or other place where food is sold at which a range of salads is displayed, often for self-service.

salad days PLURAL NOUN a period of youth and inexperience.
▷HISTORY allusion to *Antony and Cleopatra* (1.v.73) by William Shakespeare: "my salad days When I was green in judgment, cold in blood"

salad dressing NOUN a sauce for salad, such as oil and vinegar or mayonnaise.

salade (sə'lɑːd) NOUN another word for **sallet**.

salade niçoise (sæ'lɑːd niː'swɑːz) NOUN a cold dish consisting of hard-boiled eggs, anchovy filets, olives, tomatoes, tuna fish, etc.
▷HISTORY C20: from French, literally salad of or from *Nice,* S France

Salado (*Spanish* sa'laðo) NOUN [1] a river in N Argentina, rising in the Andes as the Juramento and flowing southeast to the Paraná River. Length: 2012 km (1250 miles). [2] a river in W Argentina, rising near the Chilean border as the Desaguadero and flowing south to the Colorado River. Length: about 1365 km (850 miles).

Salamanca (*Spanish* sala'maŋka) NOUN a city in W Spain: a leading cultural centre of Europe till the end of the 16th century; market town. Pop.: 158 457 (1998 est.).

salamander ('sælə,mændə) NOUN [1] any of various urodele amphibians, such as *Salamandra salamandra* (**European fire salamander**) of central and S Europe (family *Salamandridae*). They are typically terrestrial, have an elongated body, and only return to water to breed. [2] *Chiefly US and Canadian* any urodele amphibian. [3] a mythical reptile supposed to live in fire. [4] an elemental fire-inhabiting being. [5] any person or thing able to exist in fire or great heat. [6] *Metallurgy* a residue of metal and slag deposited on the walls of a furnace. [7] a portable stove used to dry out a building under construction.
▷HISTORY C14: from Old French *salamandre,* from Latin *salamandra,* from Greek
▸**salamandrine** (,sælə'mændrɪn) ADJECTIVE

Salambria (sə'læmbrɪə, ,sɑ:lɑ:m'brɪə) NOUN a river in N Greece, in Thessaly, rising in the Pindus Mountains and flowing southeast and east to the Gulf of Salonika. Length: about 200 km (125 miles). Ancient name: **Peneus.** Modern Greek name: **Piniós.**

salami (sə'lɑ:mɪ) NOUN a highly seasoned type of sausage, usually flavoured with garlic.
▷HISTORY C19: from Italian, plural of *salame,* from Vulgar Latin *salāre* (unattested) to salt, from Latin *sal* salt

Salamis ('sæləmɪs) NOUN an island in the Saronic Gulf, Greece: scene of the naval battle in 480 B.C., in which the Greeks defeated the Persians. Pop.: 20 000 (latest est.). Area: 95 sq. km (37 sq. miles).

sal ammoniac NOUN another name for **ammonium chloride.**

salaried ('sælərɪd) ADJECTIVE earning or yielding a salary: *a salaried worker; salaried employment.*

salary ('sælərɪ) NOUN, *plural* **-ries.** [1] a fixed regular payment made by an employer, often monthly, for professional or office work as opposed to manual work. Compare **wage** (sense 1). ◆ VERB **-ries, -rying, -ried.** [2] (*tr*) to pay a salary to.
▷HISTORY C14: from Anglo-Norman *salarie,* from Latin *salārium* the sum given to Roman soldiers to buy salt, from *sal* salt

salaryman ('sælərɪ,mæn) NOUN, *plural* **-men.** (in Japan) an office worker.

salchow ('sɔ:lkəʊ) NOUN a figure-skating jump made from the inner backward edge of one foot with one, two, or three full turns in the air, returning to the outer backward edge of the opposite foot.
▷HISTORY C20: named after Ulrich *Salchow* (1877–1949), Swedish figure skater, who originated it

Salduba (sæl'du:bə, 'sældəbə) NOUN the pre-Roman (Celtiberian) name for **Zaragoza.**

sale (seɪl) NOUN [1] the exchange of goods, property, or services for an agreed sum of money or credit. [2] the amount sold. [3] the opportunity to sell; market: *there was no sale for luxuries.* [4] the rate of selling or being sold: *a slow sale of synthetic fabrics.* [5] **a** an event at which goods are sold at reduced prices, usually to clear old stocks. **b** (*as modifier*): *sale bargains.* [6] an auction.
▷HISTORY Old English *sala,* from Old Norse *sala.* See also SELL

Sale (seɪl) NOUN [1] a town in NW England, in Trafford unitary authority, Greater Manchester: a residential suburb of Manchester. Pop.: 57 824 (1991). [2] a city in SE Australia, in SE Victoria: centre of an agricultural region. Pop.: 13 858 (1991).

Salé (*French* sale) NOUN a port in NW Morocco, on the Atlantic adjoining Rabat. Pop.: 504 420 (1994).

saleable *or US* **salable** ('seɪləbᵊl) ADJECTIVE fit for selling or capable of being sold.
▸**,salea'bility** *or* **'saleableness** *or US* **,sala'bility** *or* **'salableness** NOUN ▸**'saleably** *or US* **'salably** ADVERB

sale and lease back NOUN a system of raising capital for a business by selling the business property and then renting it from the new owner for an agreed period.

Salem ('seɪləm) NOUN [1] a city in S India, in Tamil Nadu: textile industries. Pop.: 366 712 (1991). [2] a city in NE Massachusetts, on the Atlantic: scene of the execution of 19 people after the witch hunts of 1692. Pop.: 38 091 (1990). [3] a city in the NW USA, the state capital of Oregon: food-processing. Pop.: 136 924 (2000). [4] an Old Testament name for **Jerusalem** (Genesis 14:18; Psalms 76:2).

sale of work NOUN *Brit* a sale of goods and handicrafts made by the members of a club, church congregation, etc., to raise money.

sale or return *or* **sale and return** NOUN an arrangement by which a retailer pays only for goods sold, returning those that are unsold to the wholesaler or manufacturer.

salep ('sælɛp) NOUN the dried ground starchy tubers of various orchids, used for food and formerly as drugs.
▷HISTORY C18: via French and Turkish from Arabic *sahlab,* shortened from *khusy ath-tha'lab,* literally: fox's testicles, name of an orchid

saleratus (,sælə'reɪtəs) NOUN another name for **sodium bicarbonate**, esp when used in baking powders
▷HISTORY C19: from New Latin *sal aerātus* aerated salt

Salerno (*Italian* sa'lɛrno) NOUN a port in SW Italy, in Campania on the **Gulf of Salerno**: first medical school of medieval Europe. Pop.: 142 055 (2000 est.).

saleroom ('seɪl,ru:m, -,rʊm) NOUN *Chiefly Brit* a room where objects are displayed for sale, esp by auction.

salesclerk ('seɪlz,klɜ:rk) NOUN *US and Canadian* a shop assistant. Sometimes shortened to: **clerk.**

sales forecast NOUN a prediction of future sales of a product, either judgmental or based on previous sales patterns.

Salesian (sə'li:zjən, -ʒjən) ADJECTIVE [1] of or relating to the French ecclesiastic and theologian St Francis of Sales (1567–1622) or to the religious orders founded by him or by St John Bosco in his name. See also **Visitation** (sense 2). ◆ NOUN [2] a member of a Salesian order, esp a member of the Society of St Francis of Sales founded in Turin by St John Bosco (1854), and dedicated to all types of educational work.
▷HISTORY C19: from *Sales*

salesman ('seɪlzmən) NOUN, *plural* **-men.** [1] Also called: (fem) **saleswoman,** (fem) **salesgirl,** (fem) **saleslady, salesperson.** a person who sells merchandise or services either in a shop or by canvassing in a designated area. [2] short for **travelling salesman.**

salesmanship ('seɪlzmənʃɪp) NOUN [1] the technique, skill, or ability of selling. [2] the work of a salesman.

sales pitch *or* **talk** NOUN an argument or other persuasion used in selling.

sales promotion NOUN activities or techniques intended to create consumer demand for a product or service.

sales resistance NOUN opposition of potential customers to selling, esp aggressive selling.

salesroom ('seɪlz,ru:m, -,rʊm) NOUN a room in which merchandise on sale is displayed.

sales tax NOUN a tax levied on retail sales receipts and added to selling prices by retailers.

sales trader NOUN *Stock Exchange* a person employed by a market maker, or his firm, to find clients.

salet ('sælɪt) NOUN a variant spelling of **sallet.**

saleyard ('seɪl,jɑ:d) NOUN *Austral and NZ* an area with pens for holding animals before auction.

Salford ('sɔ:lfəd, 'sɒl-) NOUN [1] a city in NW England in Salford unitary authority, Greater Manchester, on the Manchester Ship Canal: a major centre of the cotton industry in the 19th century; extensive dock area, now redeveloped, including the Lowry arts centre; university (1967). Pop.: 79 755 (1991). [2] a unitary authority in NW England, in Greater Manchester. Pop.: 216 119 (2001). Area: 97 sq. km (37 sq. miles).

Salian ('seɪlɪən) ADJECTIVE [1] denoting or relating to a group of Franks (the **Salii**) who settled in the Netherlands in the 4th century A.D. and later conquered large areas of Gaul, esp in the north. ◆ NOUN [2] a member of this group.

salic ('sælɪk, 'seɪ-) ADJECTIVE (of rocks and minerals) having a high content of silica and alumina.
▷HISTORY C20: from *s(ilica)* + *al(umina)* + -IC

Salic *or* **Salique** ('sælɪk, 'seɪlɪk) ADJECTIVE of or relating to the Salian Franks or the Salic law.

salicaceous (,sælɪ'keɪʃəs) ADJECTIVE of, relating to, or belonging to the *Salicaceae,* a chiefly N temperate family of trees and shrubs having catkins: includes the willows and poplars.
▷HISTORY C19: via New Latin from Latin *salix* a willow

salicin *or* **salicine** ('sælɪsɪn) NOUN a colourless or white crystalline water-soluble glucoside obtained from the bark of poplar trees and used as a medical analgesic. Formula: $C_{13}H_{18}O_7$.
▷HISTORY C19: from French *salicine,* from Latin *salix* willow

salicional (sə'lɪʃənəl) *or* **salicet** ('sælɪ,sɛt) NOUN a soft-toned organ stop with a reedy quality.
▷HISTORY C19: from German, from Latin *salix* willow

Salic law NOUN *History* [1] **a** the code of laws of the Salic Franks and other Germanic tribes. **b** a law within this code excluding females from inheritance. [2] a law excluding women from succession to the throne in certain countries, such as France and Spain.

salicornia (,sælɪ'kɔ:nɪə) NOUN any chenopodiaceous plant of the genus *Salicornia,* of seashores and salt marshes: includes glasswort.
▷HISTORY C19: from Late Latin, perhaps from Latin *sal* salt + *cornu* a horn

salicylate (sə'lɪsɪ,leɪt) NOUN any salt or ester of salicylic acid.

salicylic acid (,sælɪ'sɪlɪk) NOUN a white crystalline slightly water-soluble substance with a sweet taste and bitter aftertaste, used in the manufacture of aspirin, dyes, and perfumes, and as a fungicide. Formula: $C_6H_4(OH)(COOH)$.
▷HISTORY C19: from *salicyl* (via French from Latin *salix* a willow + -YL) + -IC

salient ('seɪlɪənt) ADJECTIVE [1] prominent, conspicuous, or striking: *a salient feature.* [2] (esp in fortifications) projecting outwards at an angle of less than 180°. Compare **re-entrant** (sense 1). [3] *Geometry* (of an angle) pointing outwards from a polygon and hence less than 180°. Compare **re-entrant** (sense 2). [4] (esp of animals) leaping. ◆ NOUN [5] *Military* a projection of the forward line into enemy-held territory. [6] a salient angle.
▷HISTORY C16: from Latin *salīre* to leap
▸**'salience** *or* **'saliency** NOUN ▸**'saliently** ADVERB

salientian (,seɪlɪ'ɛnʃɪən) NOUN, ADJECTIVE another word for **anuran.**
▷HISTORY C19: from New Latin *Salientia,* literally: leapers, from Latin *salīre* to leap

saliferous (sæ'lɪfərəs) ADJECTIVE (esp of rock strata) containing or producing salt.
▷HISTORY C19: from Latin *sal* SALT + *ferre* to bear

salify ('sælɪ,faɪ) VERB **-fies, -fying, -fied.** (*tr*) [1] to treat, mix with, or cause to combine with a salt. [2] to convert (a substance) into a salt: *to salify ammonia by treatment with hydrochloric acid.*
▷HISTORY C18: from French *salifier,* from New Latin *salificāre,* from Latin *sal* salt + *facere* to make
▸**'sali,fiable** ADJECTIVE ▸**,salifi'cation** NOUN

salimeter (sæ'lɪmɪtə) NOUN another word for **salinometer.**
▸**salimetric** (,sælɪ'mɛtrɪk) ADJECTIVE ▸**sal'imetry** NOUN

salina (sə'laɪnə) NOUN a salt marsh, lake, or spring.
▷HISTORY C17: from Spanish, from Medieval Latin: salt pit, from Late Latin *salīnus* SALINE

saline ('seɪlaɪn) ADJECTIVE [1] of, concerned with, consisting of, or containing common salt: *a saline taste.* [2] *Med* of or relating to a saline. [3] of, concerned with, consisting of, or containing any chemical salt, esp a metallic salt resembling sodium chloride. ◆ NOUN [4] *Med* an isotonic solution of sodium chloride in distilled water.
▷HISTORY C15: from Late Latin *salīnus,* from Latin *sal* salt
▸**salinity** (sə'lɪnɪtɪ) NOUN

salinometer (,sælɪ'nɒmɪtə) NOUN a hydrometer for determining the amount of salt in a solution,

usually calibrated to measure concentration. Also called: **salimeter.**
▸**salinometric** (ˌsælɪnəˈmɛtrɪk) ADJECTIVE ▸**ˌsaliˈnometry** NOUN

Salique (ˈsælɪk, ˈseɪlɪk) ADJECTIVE a variant spelling of **Salic.**

Salisbury (ˈsɔːlzbərɪ, -brɪ) NOUN 1 the former name (until 1982) of **Harare.** 2 a city in S Australia: an industrial suburb of N Adelaide. Pop.: 112 344 (1998 est.). 3 a city in S England, in SE Wiltshire: nearby Old Sarum was the site of an Early Iron Age hill fort; its cathedral (1220–58) has the highest spire in England. Pop.: 39 268 (1991). Ancient name: **Sarum.** Official name: **New Sarum.**

Salisbury Plain NOUN an open chalk plateau in S England, in Wiltshire: site of Stonehenge; military training area. Average height: 120 m (400 ft.).

Salish (ˈseɪlɪʃ) *or* **Salishan** (ˈseɪlɪʃən, ˈsæl-) NOUN 1 a family of North American Indian languages spoken in the northwestern US and W Canada. 2 **the Salish.** (*functioning as plural*) the peoples collectively who speak these languages, divided in Canada into the **Coast Salish** and the **Interior Salish.**

saliva (səˈlaɪvə) NOUN the secretion of salivary glands, consisting of a clear usually slightly acid aqueous fluid of variable composition. It moistens the oral cavity, prepares food for swallowing, and initiates the process of digestion. Related adjective: **sialoid.**
▷HISTORY C17: from Latin, of obscure origin
▸**salivary** (səˈlaɪvərɪ, ˈsælɪvərɪ) ADJECTIVE

salivary gland NOUN any of the glands in mammals that secrete saliva. In man the chief salivary glands are the **parotid, sublingual** and **submaxillary** glands.

salivate (ˈsælɪˌveɪt) VERB 1 (*intr*) to secrete saliva, esp an excessive amount. 2 (*tr*) to cause (a laboratory animal, etc.) to produce saliva, as by the administration of mercury.
▸**ˌsaliˈvation** NOUN

sallee *or* **sally** (ˈsælɪ) NOUN *Austral* 1 Also called: **snow gum.** a SE Australian eucalyptus tree, *Eucalyptus pauciflora,* with a pale grey bark. 2 any of various acacia trees.
▷HISTORY probably of native origin

sallenders (ˈsæləndəz) NOUN *Vet science* a disease of the skin behind the tarsus (hock) of a horse.

sallet, salet (ˈsælɪt), *or* **salade** NOUN a light round helmet extending over the back of the neck; replaced the basinet in the 15th century.
▷HISTORY C15: from French *salade,* probably from Old Italian *celata,* from *celare* to conceal, from Latin

sallow[1] (ˈsæləʊ) ADJECTIVE 1 (esp of human skin) of an unhealthy pale or yellowish colour. ◆ VERB 2 (*tr*) to make sallow.
▷HISTORY Old English *salu;* related to Old Norse *sol* seaweed (Icelandic *sōlr* yellowish), Old High German *salo,* French *sale* dirty
▸**ˈsallowish** ADJECTIVE ▸**ˈsallowly** ADVERB ▸**ˈsallowness** NOUN

sallow[2] (ˈsæləʊ) NOUN 1 any of several small willow trees, esp the Eurasian *Salix cinerea* (**common sallow**), which has large catkins that appear before the leaves. 2 a twig or the wood of any of these trees.
▷HISTORY Old English *sealh;* related to Old Norse *selja,* Old High German *salaha,* Middle Low German *salwīde,* Latin *salix*
▸**ˈsallowy** ADJECTIVE

sally[1] (ˈsælɪ) NOUN, *plural* **-lies.** 1 a sudden violent excursion, esp by besieged forces to attack the besiegers; sortie. 2 a sudden outburst or emergence into action, expression, or emotion. 3 an excursion or jaunt. 4 a jocular retort. ◆ VERB **-lies, -lying, -lied.** (*intr*) 5 to make a sudden violent excursion. 6 (often foll by *forth*) to go out on an expedition, etc. 7 to come, go, or set out in an energetic manner. 8 to rush out suddenly.
▷HISTORY C16: from Old French *saillie,* from *saillir* to dash forwards, from Latin *salīre* to leap
▸**ˈsallier** NOUN

sally[2] (ˈsælɪ) NOUN, *plural* **-lies.** the lower part of a bell rope, where it is caught at handstroke, into which coloured wool is woven to make a grip.
▷HISTORY C19: perhaps from an obsolete or dialect sense of SALLY[1] leaping movement

Sally (ˈsælɪ) NOUN, *plural* **-lies.** a member of the Salvation Army.

Sally Army NOUN *Brit informal* short for **Salvation Army.**

Sally Lunn (lʌn) NOUN a flat round cake made from a sweet yeast dough, usually served hot.
▷HISTORY C19: said to be named after an 18th-century English baker who invented it

sallyport (ˈsælɪˌpɔːt) NOUN an opening in a fortified place from which troops may make a sally.

salmagundi *or* **salmagundy** (ˌsælməˈgʌndɪ) NOUN 1 a mixed salad dish of cooked meats, eggs, beetroot, etc., popular in 18th-century England. 2 a miscellany; potpourri.
▷HISTORY C17: from French *salmigondis,* perhaps from Italian *salami conditi* pickled salami

Salmanazar (ˌsælməˈnæzə) NOUN a wine bottle holding the equivalent of twelve normal bottles (approximately 312 ounces).
▷HISTORY C19: humorous allusion to an Assyrian king mentioned in the Bible (II Kings 17:3); compare JEROBOAM

salmi *or* **salmis** (ˈsælmɪ) NOUN, *plural* **-mis** (-mɪ). a ragout of game stewed in a rich brown sauce.
▷HISTORY C18: from French, shortened form of *salmigondis* SALMAGUNDI

salmon (ˈsæmən) NOUN, *plural* **-ons** *or* **-on.** 1 any soft-finned fish of the family *Salmonidae,* esp *Salmo salar* of the Atlantic and *Oncorhynchus* species (sockeye, Chinook, etc.) of the Pacific, which are important food fishes. They occur in cold and temperate waters and many species migrate to fresh water to spawn. 2 *Austral* any of several unrelated fish, esp the Australian salmon. 3 short for **salmon pink.**
▷HISTORY C13: from Old French *saumon,* from Latin *salmō;* related to Late Latin *salar* trout

salmonberry (ˈsæmənbərɪ, -brɪ) NOUN, *plural* **-ries.** 1 a spineless raspberry bush, *Rubus spectabilis,* of North America, having reddish-purple flowers and large red or yellow edible fruits. 2 the fruit of this plant.
▷HISTORY C19: so called from the colour of the berries

salmonella (ˌsælməˈnɛlə) NOUN, *plural* **-lae** (-ˌliː). any Gram-negative rod-shaped aerobic bacterium of the genus *Salmonella,* including *S. typhosa,* which causes typhoid fever, and many species (notably *S. enteritidis*) that cause food poisoning (**salmonellosis**): family *Enterobacteriaceae.*
▷HISTORY C19: New Latin, named after Daniel E. *Salmon* (1850–1914), US veterinary surgeon

salmonid (ˈsælmənɪd) NOUN any fish of the family *Salmonidiae.*

salmon ladder NOUN a series of steps in a river designed to enable salmon to bypass a dam and move upstream to their breeding grounds.

salmonoid (ˈsælməˌnɔɪd) ADJECTIVE 1 of, relating to, or belonging to the *Salmonoidea,* a suborder of soft-finned teleost fishes having a fatty fin between the dorsal and tail fins: includes the salmon, whitefish, grayling, smelt, and char. 2 of, relating to, or resembling a salmon. ◆ NOUN 3 any fish belonging to the suborder *Salmonoidea,* esp any of the family *Salmonidae* (salmon, trout, char).

salmon pink NOUN **a** a yellowish-pink colour, sometimes with an orange tinge. **b** (*as adjective*): *a salmon-pink hat.* ◆ Sometimes shortened to: **salmon.**

salmon trout NOUN any of various large trout, esp the sea trout.

salol (ˈsælɒl) NOUN a white sparingly soluble crystalline compound with a slight aromatic odour, used as a preservative and to absorb light in sun-tan lotions, plastics, etc.; phenyl salicylate. Formula: $C_6H_4(OH)COOC_6H_5$.
▷HISTORY C19: from *salicyl* (see SALICYLIC ACID) + -OL

Salome (səˈləʊmɪ) NOUN *New Testament* the daughter of Herodias, at whose instigation she beguiled Herod by her seductive dancing into giving her the head of John the Baptist.

salon (ˈsælɒn) NOUN 1 a room in a large house in which guests are received. 2 an assembly of guests in a fashionable household, esp a gathering of major literary, artistic, and political figures from the 17th to the early 20th centuries. 3 a commercial establishment in which hairdressers, beauticians, etc., carry on their businesses: *beauty salon.* 4 **a** a hall for exhibiting works of art. **b** such an exhibition, esp one showing the work of living artists.
▷HISTORY C18: from French, from Italian *salone,* augmented form of *sala* hall, of Germanic origin; compare Old English *sele* hall, Old High German *sal,* Old Norse *salr* hall

Salonika *or* **Salonica** (səˈlɒnɪkə) NOUN the English name for **Thessaloníki.**

salon music NOUN *Sometimes derogatory* light classical music intended esp for domestic entertaining.

saloon (səˈluːn) NOUN 1 Also called: **saloon bar.** *Brit* another word for **lounge** (sense 5). 2 a large public room on a passenger ship. 3 any large public room used for a specific purpose: *a dancing saloon.* 4 *Chiefly US and Canadian* a place where alcoholic drink is sold and consumed. 5 a closed two-door or four-door car with four to six seats. US, Canadian, and NZ name: **sedan.** 6 an obsolete word for **salon** (sense 1).
▷HISTORY C18: from French SALON

saloop (səˈluːp) NOUN an infusion of aromatic herbs or other plant parts, esp salep, formerly used as a tonic or cure.
▷HISTORY C18: changed from SALEP

Salop (ˈsæləp) NOUN a former name (1974–80) of **Shropshire.**

salopettes (ˌsæləˈpɛts) PLURAL NOUN a garment worn for skiing, consisting of quilted trousers reaching to the chest and held up by shoulder straps.
▷HISTORY C20: from French

Salopian (səˈləʊpjən) NOUN 1 a native or inhabitant of Shropshire ◆ ADJECTIVE 2 of or relating to Shropshire or its inhabitants
▷HISTORY from *Salop,* a former name of Shropshire

salpa (ˈsælpə) NOUN, *plural* **-pas** *or* **-pae** (-piː). any of various minute floating animals of the genus *Salpa,* of warm oceans, having a transparent barrel-shaped body with openings at either end: class *Thaliacea,* subphylum *Tunicata* (tunicates).
▷HISTORY C19: from New Latin, from Latin: variety of stockfish, from Greek *salpē*
▸**salpiform** (ˈsælpɪˌfɔːm) ADJECTIVE

salpicon (ˈsælpɪkən) NOUN a mixture of chopped fish, meat, or vegetables in a sauce, used as fillings for croquettes, pastries, etc.
▷HISTORY C18: from French, from Spanish, from *salpicar* to sprinkle with salt

salpiglossis (ˌsælpɪˈglɒsɪs) NOUN any solanaceous plant of the Chilean genus *Salpiglossis,* some species of which are cultivated for their bright funnel-shaped flowers.
▷HISTORY C19: New Latin, from Greek *salpinx* trumpet + *glōssa* tongue

salpingectomy (ˌsælpɪnˈdʒɛktəmɪ) NOUN, *plural* **-mies.** surgical removal of a Fallopian tube.
▷HISTORY C20: from SALPINX + -ECTOMY

salpingitis (ˌsælpɪnˈdʒaɪtɪs) NOUN inflammation of a Fallopian tube.
▷HISTORY C19: from SALPINX + -ITIS
▸**salpingitic** (ˌsælpɪnˈdʒɪtɪk) ADJECTIVE

salpingo- ADJECTIVE, COMBINING FORM indicating the Fallopian tubes: *salpingo-oophorectomy.*
▷HISTORY C20: from SALPINX

salpinx (ˈsælpɪŋks) NOUN, *plural* **salpinges** (sælˈpɪndʒiːz). *Anatomy* another name for the **Fallopian tube** or the **Eustachian tube.**
▷HISTORY C19: from Greek: trumpet
▸**salpingian** (sælˈpɪndʒɪən) ADJECTIVE

salsa (ˈsælsə) NOUN 1 a type of Latin American big-band dance music. 2 a dance performed to this kind of music. 3 *Mexican cookery* a spicy tomato-based sauce.
▷HISTORY C20: from Spanish: sauce

salsify (ˈsælsɪfɪ) NOUN, *plural* **-fies.** 1 Also called: **oyster plant, vegetable oyster.** a Mediterranean plant, *Tragopogon porrifolius,* having grasslike leaves, purple flower heads, and a long white edible taproot: family *Asteraceae* (composites). 2 the root of this plant, which tastes of oysters and is eaten as a vegetable.
▷HISTORY C17: from French *salsifis,* from Italian *sassefrica,* from Late Latin *saxifrica,* from Latin *saxum* rock + *fricāre* to rub

sal soda NOUN the crystalline decahydrate of sodium carbonate.

salt (sɔːlt) NOUN 1 a white powder or colourless crystalline solid, consisting mainly of sodium chloride and used for seasoning and preserving food. 2 (*modifier*) preserved in, flooded with, containing, or growing in salt or salty water: *salt pork; salt marshes.* 3 *Chem* any of a class of usually crystalline solid compounds that are formed from, or can be regarded as formed from, an acid and a base by replacement of one or more hydrogen atoms in the acid molecules by positive ions from the base. 4 liveliness or pungency: *his wit added salt to the discussion.* 5 dry or laconic wit. 6 a sailor, esp one who is old and experienced. 7 short for **saltcellar.** 8 **rub salt into someone's wounds.** to make someone's pain, shame, etc., even worse. 9 **salt of the earth.** a person or group of people regarded as the finest of their kind. 10 **with a grain** (*or* **pinch**) **of salt.** with reservations; sceptically. 11 **worth one's salt.** efficient; worthy of one's pay. ◆ VERB (*tr*) 12 to season or preserve with salt. 13 to scatter salt over (an icy road, path, etc.) to melt the ice. 14 to add zest to. 15 (often foll by *down* or *away*) to preserve or cure with salt or saline solution. 16 *Chem* to treat with common salt or other chemical salt. 17 to provide (cattle, etc.) with salt. 18 to give a false appearance of value to, esp to introduce valuable ore fraudulently into (a mine, sample, etc.). ◆ ADJECTIVE 19 not sour, sweet, or bitter; salty. 20 *Obsolete* rank or lascivious (esp in the phrase **a salt wit**). ◆ See also **salt away, salt out, salts.**
▷HISTORY Old English *sealt;* related to Old Norse, Gothic *salt,* German *Salz,* Lettish *sāls,* Latin *sāl,* Greek *hals*
▸**'saltish** ADJECTIVE ▸**'saltless** ADJECTIVE ▸**'salt,like** ADJECTIVE ▸**'saltness** NOUN

SALT (sɔːlt) NOUN ACRONYM FOR Strategic Arms Limitation Talks *or* Treaty.

Salta (*Spanish* 'salta) NOUN a city in NW Argentina: thermal springs. Pop.: 457 223 (1999 est.).

saltant ('sæltənt) ADJECTIVE (of an organism) differing from others of its species because of a saltation.
▷HISTORY C17: from Latin *saltāns* dancing, from *saltāre,* from *salīre* to spring

saltarello (ˌsæltə'rεləʊ) NOUN, *plural* **-li** (-lɪ) *or* **-los.** 1 a traditional Italian dance, usually in compound duple time. 2 a piece of music composed for or in the rhythm of this dance.
▷HISTORY C18: from Italian, from *saltare* to dance energetically, from Latin; see SALTANT

saltation (sæl'teɪʃən) NOUN 1 *Biology* an abrupt variation in the appearance of an organism, species, etc., usually caused by genetic mutation. 2 *Geology* the leaping movement of sand or soil particles carried in water or by the wind. 3 a sudden abrupt movement or transition.
▷HISTORY C17: from Latin *saltātiō* a dance, from *saltāre* to leap about

saltatorial (ˌsæltə'tɔːrɪəl) *or* **saltatory** ADJECTIVE 1 *Biology* specialized for or characterized by jumping: *the saltatorial legs of a grasshopper.* 2 of or relating to saltation.
▷HISTORY C17 *saltatory,* from Latin *saltātōrius* concerning dancing, from *saltātor* a dancer; see SALTANT

salt away *or less commonly* **down** VERB (*tr, adverb*) to hoard or save (money, valuables, etc.).

salt bath NOUN *Metallurgy* a bath of molten salts in which steel can be immersed to soak to a uniform and accurately maintained temperature as part of the process of heat treatment. Different salts are used for different temperatures.

saltbox ('sɔːltˌbɒks) NOUN 1 a box for salt with a sloping lid. 2 *US* a house that has two storeys in front and one storey at the back, with a gable roof that extends downwards over the rear.

saltbush ('sɔːltˌbʊʃ) NOUN any of various chenopodiaceous shrubs of the genus *Atriplex* that grow in alkaline desert regions.

salt cake NOUN an impure form of sodium sulphate obtained as a by-product in several industrial processes: used in the manufacture of detergents, glass, and ceramic glazes.

saltcellar ('sɔːltˌselə) NOUN 1 a small container for salt used at the table. 2 *Brit informal* either of the two hollows formed above the collarbones of very slim people.
▷HISTORY changed (through influence of cellar) from C15 *salt saler; saler* from Old French *saliere* container for salt, from Latin *salārius* belonging to salt, from *sal* salt

saltchuck ('sɔːltˌtʃʌk) NOUN *Canadian, chiefly W coast* any body of salt water.
▷HISTORY C20: from SALT + CHUCK[4]

saltchucker ('sɔːltˌtʃʌkə) NOUN *Canadian W coast informal* a saltwater angler.

salt dome *or* **plug** NOUN a domelike structure of stratified rocks containing a central core of salt: formed by the upward movement of a salt deposit.

Salteaux *or* **Saulteaux** ('səʊtəʊ) NOUN a member of a Native Canadian people of Manitoba.
▷HISTORY from Ojibwa

salted ('sɔːltɪd) ADJECTIVE 1 seasoned, preserved, or treated with salt. 2 *Informal* experienced in an occupation.

salter ('sɔːltə) NOUN 1 a person who deals in or manufactures salt. 2 a person who treats meat, fish, etc., with salt.

saltern ('sɔːltən) NOUN 1 another word for **saltworks.** 2 a place where salt is obtained from pools of evaporated sea water.
▷HISTORY Old English *saltærn,* from SALT + *ærn* house. Compare BARN[1], RANSACK

saltfish ('sɔːltfɪʃ) NOUN *Caribbean* salted cod.

salt flat NOUN a flat expanse of salt left by the total evaporation of a body of water.

saltie ('sɔːltɪ) NOUN *Austral informal* a saltwater crocodile.

saltigrade ('sæltɪˌgreɪd) ADJECTIVE (of animals) adapted for moving in a series of jumps.
▷HISTORY C19: from New Latin *Saltigradae,* name formerly applied to jumping spiders, from Latin *saltus* a leap + *gradī* to move

Saltillo (*Spanish* sal'tiʎo) NOUN a city in N Mexico, capital of Coahuila state: resort and commercial centre of a mining region. Pop.: 560 000 (2000 est.).

salting ('sɔːltɪŋ) NOUN (*often plural*) an area of low ground regularly inundated with salt water; often taken to include its halophyte vegetation; a salt marsh.

saltire *or less commonly* **saltier** ('sɔːlˌtaɪə) NOUN *Heraldry* an ordinary consisting of a diagonal cross on a shield.
▷HISTORY C14 *sawturoure,* from Old French *sauteour* cross-shaped barricade, from *saulter* to jump, from Latin *saltāre*

salt lake NOUN an inland lake of high salinity resulting from inland drainage in an arid area of high evaporation.

Salt Lake City NOUN a city in N central Utah, near the Great Salt Lake at an altitude of 1330 m (4300 ft.): state capital; founded in 1847 by the Mormons as world capital of the Mormon Church; University of Utah (1850). Pop.: 181 743 (2000).

salt lick NOUN 1 a place where wild animals go to lick naturally occurring salt deposits. 2 a block of salt or a salt preparation given to domestic animals to lick.

salt marsh NOUN an area of marshy ground that is intermittently inundated with salt water or that retains pools or rivulets of salt or brackish water, together with its characteristic halophytic vegetation.

Salto (*Spanish* 'salto) NOUN a port in NW Uruguay, on the Uruguay River: Uruguay's second largest city. Pop.: 77 400 (latest est.).

salt out VERB (*adverb*) *Chem* to cause (a dissolved substance) to come out of solution by adding an electrolyte.

saltpan ('sɔːltˌpæn) NOUN a shallow basin, usually in a desert region, containing salt, gypsum, etc., that was deposited from an evaporated salt lake.

saltpetre *or US* **saltpeter** (ˌsɔːlt'piːtə) NOUN 1 another name for **potassium nitrate.** 2 short for **Chile saltpetre.**
▷HISTORY C16: from Old French *salpetre,* from Latin *sal petrae* salt of rock

salt pork NOUN pork, esp the fat pork taken from the back, sides, and belly, that has been cured with salt.

salts (sɔːlts) PLURAL NOUN 1 *Med* any of various mineral salts, such as magnesium sulphate or sodium sulphate, for use as a cathartic. 2 short for **smelling salts.** 3 **like a dose of salts.** *Informal* very fast.

saltus ('sæltəs) NOUN, *plural* **-tuses.** a break in the continuity of a sequence, esp the omission of a necessary step in a logical argument.
▷HISTORY Latin: a leap

saltwater ('sɔːltˌwɔːtə) ADJECTIVE of, relating to, or inhabiting salt water, esp the sea: *saltwater fishes.*

saltworks ('sɔːltˌwɜːks) NOUN (*functioning as singular*) a place, building, or factory where salt is produced.

saltwort ('sɔːltˌwɜːt) NOUN 1 Also called: **glasswort, kali.** any of several chenopodiaceous plants of the genus *Salsola,* esp *S. kali,* of beaches and salt marshes, which has prickly leaves, striped stems, and small green flowers. See also **barilla.** 2 another name for **sea milkwort.**

salty ('sɔːltɪ) ADJECTIVE **saltier, saltiest.** 1 of, tasting of, or containing salt. 2 (esp of humour) sharp; piquant. 3 relating to life at sea.
▸**'saltily** ADVERB ▸**'saltiness** NOUN

salubrious (sə'luːbrɪəs) ADJECTIVE conducive or favourable to health; wholesome.
▷HISTORY C16: from Latin *salūbris,* from *salūs* health
▸**sa'lubriously** ADVERB ▸**sa'lubriousness** *or* **salubrity** (sə'luːbrɪtɪ) NOUN

Saluki (sə'luːkɪ) NOUN a tall breed of hound with a smooth coat and long fringes on the ears and tail. Also called: **gazehound, gazelle hound, Persian greyhound.**
▷HISTORY C19: from Arabic *salūqīy* of Saluq, name of an ancient Arabian city

salutary ('sæljʊtərɪ, -trɪ) ADJECTIVE 1 promoting or intended to promote an improvement or beneficial effect: *a salutary warning.* 2 promoting or intended to promote health.
▷HISTORY C15: from Latin *salūtāris* wholesome, from *salūs* safety
▸**'salutarily** ADVERB ▸**'salutariness** NOUN

salutation (ˌsælju'teɪʃən) NOUN 1 an act, phrase, gesture, etc., that serves as a greeting. 2 a form of words used as an opening to a speech or letter, such as *Dear Sir* or *Ladies and Gentlemen.* 3 the act of saluting.
▷HISTORY C14: from Latin *salūtātiō,* from *salūtāre* to greet; see SALUTE

salutatory (sə'luːtətərɪ, -trɪ) ADJECTIVE of, relating to, or resembling a salutation.
▸**sa'lutatorily** ADVERB

salute (sə'luːt) VERB 1 (*tr*) to address or welcome with friendly words or gestures of respect, such as bowing or lifting the hat; greet. 2 (*tr*) to acknowledge with praise or honour: *we salute your gallantry.* 3 *Military* to pay or receive formal respect, as by presenting arms or raising the right arm. ◆ NOUN 4 the act of saluting. 5 a formal military gesture of respect.
▷HISTORY C14: from Latin *salūtāre* to greet, from *salūs* wellbeing
▸**sa'luter** NOUN

salvable ('sælvəb[ə]l) ADJECTIVE capable of or suitable for being saved or salvaged.
▷HISTORY C17: from Late Latin *salvāre* to save, from Latin *salvus* safe
▸**ˌsalva'bility** *or* **'salvableness** NOUN ▸**'salvably** ADVERB

Salvador ('sælvəˌdɔː; *Portuguese* salva'dor) NOUN a port in E Brazil, capital of Bahia state: founded in 1549 as capital of the Portuguese colony, which it remained until 1763; a major centre of the African slave trade in colonial times. Pop.: 2 439 881 (2000). Former name: **Bahia.** Official name: **São Salvador da Bahia de Todos os Santos** (sãu salva'dor 'də: ba'ia 'də: 'to:duʃ uʃ 'səntuʃ).

Salvadorian[1], Salvadorean (ˌsælvə'dɔːrɪən), *or* **Salvadoran** (ˌsælvə'dɔːrən) NOUN 1 a native or inhabitant of El Salvador. ◆ ADJECTIVE 2 of or relating to El Salvador, or its people, culture, etc.

Salvadorian[2] (ˌsælvə'dɔːrɪən) NOUN 1 a native or inhabitant of Salvador. ◆ ADJECTIVE 2 of or relating to Salvador or its inhabitants.

salvage ('sælvɪdʒ) NOUN 1 the act, process, or business of rescuing vessels or their cargoes from loss at sea. 2 **a** the act of saving any goods or property in danger of damage or destruction. **b** (*as modifier*): *a salvage operation.* 3 the goods or property so saved. 4 compensation paid for the salvage of a vessel or its cargo. 5 the proceeds from the sale of salvaged goods or property. ◆ VERB (*tr*) 6 to save or rescue (goods or property) from fire,

shipwreck, etc. 7 to gain (something beneficial) from a failure: *she salvaged little from the broken marriage.*
▷HISTORY C17: from Old French, from Medieval Latin *salvāgium,* from *salvāre* to SAVE[1]
▸'**salvageable** ADJECTIVE ▸'**salvager** NOUN

salvation (sæl'veɪʃən) NOUN 1 the act of preserving or the state of being preserved from harm. 2 a person or thing that is the means of preserving from harm. 3 *Christianity* deliverance by redemption from the power of sin and from the penalties ensuing from it. 4 *Christian Science* the realization that Life, Truth, and Love are supreme and that they can destroy such illusions as sin, death, etc.
▷HISTORY C13: from Old French *sauvacion,* from Late Latin *salvātiō,* from Latin *salvātus* saved, from *salvāre* to SAVE[1]
▸**sal'vational** ADJECTIVE

Salvation Army NOUN **a** a Christian body founded in 1865 by William Booth and organized on quasi-military lines for evangelism and social work among the poor. **b** (*as modifier*): *the Salvation Army Hymn Book.*

salvationist (sæl'veɪʃənɪst) NOUN 1 a member of an evangelical sect emphasizing the doctrine of salvation. 2 (*often capital*) a member of the Salvation Army. ◆ ADJECTIVE 3 stressing the doctrine of salvation. 4 (*often capital*) of or relating to the Salvation Army.
▸**sal'vationism** NOUN

Salvation Jane (dʒeɪn) NOUN *Austral* another name, used in South Australia, for **viper's bugloss** (sense 2).

salva veritate *Latin* ('sælvə ˌverɪ'tɑːteɪ) ADVERB *Philosophy* without affecting truth-value.

salve[1] (sælv, sɑːv) NOUN 1 an ointment for wounds, sores, etc. 2 anything that heals or soothes. ◆ VERB (*tr*) 3 to apply salve to (a wound, sore, etc.). 4 to soothe, comfort, or appease.
▷HISTORY Old English *sealf;* related to Old High German *salba,* Greek *elpos* oil, Sanskrit *sarpis* lard

salve[2] (sælv) VERB 1 a less common word for **salvage.** 2 an archaic word for **save[1]** (sense 3).
▷HISTORY C18: from SALVAGE

salver ('sælvə) NOUN a tray, esp one of silver, on which food, letters, visiting cards, etc., are presented.
▷HISTORY C17: from French *salve,* from Spanish *salva* tray from which the king's taster sampled food, from Latin *salvāre* to SAVE[1]

salverform ('sælvəˌfɔːm) ADJECTIVE (of the corolla of the phlox and certain other flowers) consisting of a narrow tube with flat spreading terminal petals.

salvia ('sælvɪə) NOUN any herbaceous plant or small shrub of the genus *Salvia,* such as the sage, grown for their medicinal or culinary properties or for ornament: family *Lamiaceae* (labiates).
▷HISTORY C19: from Latin: SAGE[2]

salvo[1] ('sælvəʊ) NOUN, *plural* **-vos** *or* **-voes.** 1 a discharge of fire from weapons in unison, esp on a ceremonial occasion. 2 concentrated fire from many weapons, as in a naval battle. 3 an outburst, as of applause.
▷HISTORY C17: from Italian *salva,* from Old French *salve,* from Latin *salvē!* greetings! from *salvēre* to be in good health, from *salvus* safe

salvo[2] ('sælvəʊ) NOUN, *plural* **-vos.** *Rare* 1 an excuse or evasion. 2 an expedient to save a reputation or soothe hurt feelings. 3 (in legal documents) a saving clause; reservation.
▷HISTORY C17: from such Medieval Latin phrases as *salvō iurē* the right of keeping safe, from Latin *salvus* safe

Salvo ('sælvəʊ) NOUN, *plural* **-vos.** *Austral slang* a member of the Salvation Army.

sal volatile (vɒ'lætɪlɪ) NOUN 1 another name for **ammonium carbonate.** 2 Also called: **spirits of ammonia,** (archaic) **hartshorn.** a solution of ammonium carbonate in alcohol and aqueous ammonia, often containing aromatic oils, used as smelling salts.
▷HISTORY C17: from New Latin: volatile salt

salvor *or* **salver** ('sælvə) NOUN a person instrumental in salvaging a vessel or its cargo.
▷HISTORY C17: from SALVAGE + -OR[1]

salwar kameez ('sælwɑː ˌkæmiːz) NOUN a long tunic worn over a pair of baggy trousers, usually worn by women, esp in Pakistan.

Salween ('sælwiːn) NOUN a river in SW Asia, rising in the Tibetan Plateau and flowing east and south through SW China and Myanmar to the Gulf of Martaban. Length: 2400 km (1500 miles).

Salyut (sæl'juːt) NOUN any of a series of seven Soviet space stations. The first was launched into earth orbit in April 1971 and the last was launched in April 1982. The Salyut programme led to the Mir space station.
▷HISTORY C20: Russian: salute

Salzburg ('sæltsbɜːg; *German* 'zaltsbʊrk) NOUN 1 a city in W Austria, capital of Salzburg province: 7th-century Benedictine abbey; a centre of music since the Middle Ages and birthplace of Mozart; tourist centre. Pop.: 144 816 (2001). 2 a state of W Austria. Pop.: 518 580 (2001). Area: 7154 sq. km (2762 sq. miles).

Salzgitter (*German* zalts'gɪtər) NOUN an industrial city in central Germany, in SE Lower Saxony. Pop.: 113 700 (1999 est.).

sam (sæm) VERB (*tr*) **sams, samming, sammed.** *Northern English dialect* **sam hold of.** to collect; gather up.

SAM (sæm) NOUN ACRONYM FOR surface-to-air missile.

Sam. *Bible* ABBREVIATION FOR Samuel.

S.Am. ABBREVIATION FOR South America(n).

samadhi (sʌ'mɑːdi) NOUN *Buddhism, Hinduism* a state of deep meditative contemplation which leads to higher consciousness.
▷HISTORY from Sanskrit: concentration, from *samā* together + *dhi* mind

Samar ('sɑːmə) NOUN an island in the E central Philippines, separated from S Luzon by the San Bernardino Strait: the third largest island in the republic. Capital: Catbalogan. Pop.: 1 300 000 (latest est.). Area: 13 080 sq. km (5050 sq. miles).

samara (sə'mɑːrə, 'sæmərə) NOUN a dry indehiscent one-seeded fruit with a winglike extension to aid dispersal: occurs in the ash, maple, etc. Also called: **key fruit.**
▷HISTORY C16: from New Latin, from Latin: seed of an elm

Samara (*Russian* sa'marə) NOUN a port in SW Russia, on the River Volga: centre of an important industrial complex; oil refining. Pop.: 1 168 000 (1999 est.). Former name (1935–91): **Kuibyshev** *or* **Kuybyshev.**

Samarang (sə'mɑːrɑːŋ) NOUN a variant spelling of **Semarang.**

Samaria (sə'mɛərɪə) NOUN 1 the region of ancient Palestine that extended from Judaea to Galilee and from the Mediterranean to the River Jordan; the N kingdom of Israel. 2 the capital of this kingdom; constructed northwest of Shechem in the 9th century B.C.

samariform (sə'mɑːrɪˌfɔːm) ADJECTIVE *Botany* shaped like a samara; winged.

Samaritan (sə'mærɪtᵊn) NOUN 1 a native or inhabitant of Samaria. 2 short for **Good Samaritan.** 3 a member of a voluntary organization (**the Samaritans**) which offers counselling to people in despair, esp by telephone. 4 the dialect of Aramaic spoken in Samaria. ◆ ADJECTIVE 5 of or relating to Samaria.
▸**Sa'maritanism** NOUN

samarium (sə'mɛərɪəm) NOUN a silvery metallic element of the lanthanide series occurring chiefly in monazite and bastnaesite and used in carbon-arc lighting, as a doping agent in laser crystals, and as a neutron-absorber. Symbol: Sm; atomic no.: 62; atomic wt.: 150.36; valency: 2 or 3; relative density: 7.520; melting pt.: 1074°C; boiling pt.: 1794°C.
▷HISTORY C19: New Latin, from SAMARSKITE + -IUM

Samarkand ('sæməˌkænd; *Russian* səmar'kant) NOUN a city in E Uzbekistan: under Tamerlane it became the chief economic and cultural centre of central Asia, on trade routes from China and India (the "silk road"). Pop.: 388 000 (1998 est.). Ancient name: **Maracanda.**

samarskite (sə'mɑːskaɪt) NOUN a velvety black mineral of complex composition occurring in pegmatites: used as a source of uranium and certain rare earth elements.
▷HISTORY C19: named after Colonel von *Samarski,* 19th-century Russian inspector of mines

Sama-Veda ('sɑːmə'veɪdə) NOUN *Hinduism* the third Veda containing the rituals for sacrifices.
▷HISTORY C18: from Sanskrit *sāman* a chant + VEDA

samba ('sæmbə) NOUN, *plural* **-bas.** 1 a lively modern ballroom dance from Brazil in bouncy duple time. 2 a piece of music composed for or in the rhythm of this dance. ◆ VERB **-bas, -baing, -baed.** 3 (*intr*) to perform such a dance.
▷HISTORY Portuguese, of African origin

sambar *or* **sambur** ('sæmbə) NOUN, *plural* **-bars, -bar** *or* **-burs, -bur.** a S Asian deer, *Cervus unicolor,* with three-tined antlers.
▷HISTORY C17: from Hindi, from Sanskrit *śambarra,* of obscure origin

sambo[1] ('sæmbəʊ) NOUN, *plural* **-bos.** 1 *Slang* an offensive word for **Black[1]**: often used as a term of address. 2 the offspring of a Black and a member of another race or a mulatto.
▷HISTORY C18: from American Spanish *zambo* a person of Black descent; perhaps related to Bantu *nzambu* monkey

sambo[2] *or* **sambo wrestling** ('sæmbəʊ) NOUN a type of wrestling based on judo that originated in Russia and now features in international competitions.
▷HISTORY C20: from Russian *sam(ozashchita) b(ez) o(ruzhiya)* self-defence without weapons
▸**sambo wrestler** NOUN

Sambre (*French* sɑ̃brə) NOUN a river in W Europe, rising in N France and flowing east into Belgium to join the Meuse at Namur. Length: 190 km (118 miles).

Sam Browne belt NOUN a military officer's wide belt supported by a strap passing from the left side of the belt over the right shoulder.
▷HISTORY C20: named after Sir *Samuel J. Browne* (1824–1901), British general, who devised such a belt

same (seɪm) ADJECTIVE (usually preceded by *the*) 1 being the very one: *she is wearing the same hat she wore yesterday.* 2 **a** being the one previously referred to; aforesaid. **b** (*as noun*): *a note received about same.* 3 **a** identical in kind, quantity, etc.: *two girls of the same age.* **b** (*as noun*): *we'd like the same, please.* 4 unchanged in character or nature: *his attitude is the same as ever.* 5 **all the same. a** Also: **just the same.** nevertheless; yet. **b** immaterial: *it's all the same to me.* ◆ ADVERB 6 in an identical manner.
▷HISTORY C12: from Old Norse *samr;* related to Old English adverbial phrase *swā same* likewise, Gothic *sama,* Latin *similis,* Greek *homos* same

> **Language note** The use of *same* exemplified in *if you send us your order for the materials, we will deliver same tomorrow* is common in business and official English. In general English, however, this use of the word is avoided: *may I borrow your book? I'll return it* (not *same*) *tomorrow.*

samekh ('sɑːmək; *Hebrew* 'samɛx) NOUN the 15th letter in the Hebrew alphabet (ס) transliterated as *s.*
▷HISTORY Hebrew, literally: a support

sameness ('seɪmnɪs) NOUN 1 the state or quality of being the same. 2 lack of change; monotony.

samey ('seɪmɪ) ADJECTIVE *Informal* monotonous; repetitive; unvaried.

samfoo ('sæmfuː) NOUN a style of casual dress worn by Chinese women, consisting of a waisted blouse and trousers.
▷HISTORY from Chinese (Cantonese) *sam* dress + *foo* trousers

Samhain ('sɑːwɪn, 'saʊeɪn, 'saʊɪn) an ancient Celtic festival held on Nov. 1 to mark the beginning of winter and the beginning of a new year. It is also celebrated by modern pagans.
▷HISTORY from Irish, from Old Irish *samain*

Sami ('sɑːmɪ) NOUN 1 a member of the indigenous people of Lapland. 2 the language of this people, belonging to the Finno-Ugric family. ◆ ADJECTIVE 3 of or relating to this people or their language.

> **Language note** The indigenous people of Lapland prefer to be called *Sami,* although *Lapp* is still in widespread use.

Samian ('seɪmɪən) ADJECTIVE [1] of or relating to Samos or its inhabitants. ◆ NOUN [2] a native or inhabitant of Samos.

Samian ware NOUN [1] a fine earthenware pottery, reddish-brown or black in colour, found in large quantities on Roman sites. [2] Also called: **Arretine ware.** the earlier pottery from which this developed, an imitation of a type of Greek pottery, made during the first century B.C. at Arretium.
▷HISTORY C19: named after the island of SAMOS, source of a reddish-coloured earth resembling terra sigillata, similar to the earth from which the pottery was made

samiel ('sæmjel) NOUN another word for **simoom.**
▷HISTORY C17: from Turkish *samyeli,* from *sam* poisonous + *yel* wind

samisen ('sæmɪˌsɛn) NOUN a Japanese plucked stringed instrument with a long neck, an unfretted fingerboard, and a rectangular soundbox.
▷HISTORY Japanese, from Chinese *san-hsien,* from *san* three + *hsien* string

samite ('sæmaɪt, 'seɪ-) NOUN a heavy fabric of silk, often woven with gold or silver threads, used in the Middle Ages for clothing.
▷HISTORY C13: from Old French *samit,* from Medieval Latin *examitum,* from Greek *hexamiton,* from *hexamitos* having six threads, from *hex* six + *mitos* a thread

samiti *or* **samithi** ('sʌmɪtɪ) NOUN (in India) an association, esp one formed to organize political activity.
▷HISTORY Hindi

samizdat (*Russian* səmiz'dat) NOUN (in the former Soviet Union) **a** a system of clandestine printing and distribution of banned or dissident literature. **b** (*as modifier*): *a samizdat publication.*
▷HISTORY C20: from Russian, literally: self-published

Sammarinese (səˌmærɪ'ni:z) ADJECTIVE, NOUN a variant of **San Marinese.**

sammy ('sæmɪ) NOUN, *plural* **-mies.** *Informal* (in South Africa) an Indian fruit and vegetable vendor who goes from house to house.
▷HISTORY C20: from the forename *Sammy*

Samnite ('sæmnaɪt) (in ancient Italy) NOUN [1] a member of an Oscan-speaking people of the S Apennines, who clashed repeatedly with Rome between 350 B.C. and 200 B.C. ◆ ADJECTIVE [2] of or relating to this people.

Samnium ('sæmnɪəm) NOUN an ancient country of central Italy inhabited by Oscan-speaking Samnites: corresponds to the present-day regions of Abruzzi, Molise, and part of Campania.

Samoa (sə'məʊə) NOUN [1] an independent state occupying four inhabited islands and five uninhabited islands in the S Pacific archipelago of the Samoa Islands: established as a League of Nations mandate under New Zealand administration in 1920 and a UN trusteeship in 1946; gained independence as Western Samoa in 1962 as the first fully independent Polynesian state; officially changed its name to Samoa in 1997; a member of the Commonwealth. Languages: Samoan and English. Religion: Christian. Currency: tala. Capital: Apia. Pop.: 179 000 (2001 est.). Area 2841 sq. km (1097 sq. miles). [2] Also called: **Samoa Islands.** a group of islands in the S Pacific, northeast of Fiji: an independent kingdom until the mid 19th century, when it was divided administratively into **American Samoa** (in the east) and **German Samoa** (in the west); the latter was mandated to New Zealand in 1919 and gained full independence in 1962 as Western Samoa, now **Samoa** (sense 1). Area: 3038 sq. km (1173 sq. miles).

Samoan (sə'məʊən) ADJECTIVE [1] of or relating to Samoa, its people, or their language. ◆ NOUN [2] a member of the people that inhabit Samoa. [3] the language of Samoa, belonging to the Polynesian family of languages.

Samos ('seɪmɒs) NOUN a Greek island in the E Aegean Sea, off the SW coast of Turkey: a leading commercial centre of ancient Greece. Pop.: 41 965 (1991). Area: 492 sq. km (190 sq. miles).

samosa (sə'məʊsə) NOUN, *plural* **-sas** *or* **-sa.** (in Indian cookery) a small triangular pastry case containing spiced vegetables or meat and served fried.
▷HISTORY C20: from Hindi

Samothrace ('sæməˌθreɪs) NOUN a Greek island in the NE Aegean Sea: mountainous. Pop.: 4000 (latest est.).

samovar ('sæməˌvɑ:, ˌsæmə'vɑ:) NOUN (esp in Russia) a metal urn for making tea, in which the water is heated esp formerly by charcoal held in an inner container or nowadays more usually by electricity.
▷HISTORY C19: from Russian, from *samo-* self (related to SAME) + *varit'* to boil

Samoyed (ˌsæmə'jɛd) NOUN [1] (*plural* **-yed** *or* **-yeds**) a member of a group of peoples who migrated along the Russian Arctic coast and now live chiefly in the area of the N Urals: related to the Finns. [2] the languages of these peoples, related to Finno-Ugric within the Uralic family. [3] (sə'mɔɪɛd) a Siberian breed of dog of the spitz type, having a dense white or cream coat with a distinct ruff, and a tightly curled tail.
▷HISTORY C17: from Russian *Samoed*
▸ˌSamo'yedic ADJECTIVE

samp (sæmp) NOUN *South African* crushed maize used for porridge.
▷HISTORY C17: from Narragenset *nasaump* softened by water

sampan ('sæmpæn) NOUN any small skiff, widely used in the Orient, that is propelled by oars or a scull.
▷HISTORY C17: from Chinese *san pan,* from *san* three + *pan* board

samphire ('sæmˌfaɪə) NOUN [1] Also called: **rock samphire.** an umbelliferous plant, *Crithmum maritimum,* of Eurasian coasts, having fleshy divided leaves and clusters of small greenish-white flowers. [2] **golden samphire.** a Eurasian coastal plant, *Inula crithmoides,* with fleshy leaves and yellow flower heads: family *Asteraceae* (composites). [3] another name for **glasswort** (sense 1). [4] any of several other plants of coastal areas.
▷HISTORY C16 *sampiere,* from French *herbe de Saint Pierre* Saint Peter's herb; perhaps influenced by *camphire* CAMPHOR

sample ('sɑ:mpᵊl) NOUN [1] **a** a small part of anything, intended as representative of the whole; specimen. **b** (*as modifier*): *a sample bottle.* [2] Also called: **sampling.** *Statistics* **a** a set of individuals or items selected from a population for analysis to yield estimates of, or to test hypotheses about, parameters of the whole population. A **biased sample** is one in which the items selected share some property which influences their distribution, while a **random sample** is devised to avoid any such interference so that its distribution is affected only by, and so can be held to represent, that of the whole population. See also **matched sample. b** (*as modifier*): *sample distribution.* ◆ VERB [3] (*tr*) to take a sample or samples of. [4] *Music* **a** to take a short extract from (one record) and mix it into a different backing track. **b** to record (a sound) and feed it into a computerized synthesizer so that it can be reproduced at any pitch.
▷HISTORY C13: from Old French *essample,* from Latin *exemplum* EXAMPLE

sample point NOUN *Statistics* a single possible observed value of a variable; a member of the sample space of an experiment.

sampler ('sɑ:mplə) NOUN [1] a person who takes samples. [2] a piece of embroidery executed as an example of the embroiderer's skill in using a variety of stitches: often incorporating numbers, letters, and the name and age of the embroiderer in a decorative panel. [3] *Music* a piece of electronic equipment used for sampling. [4] a recording comprising a collection of tracks from other albums, intended to stimulate interest in the featured products.

sample space NOUN *Statistics* the set of possible outcomes of an experiment; the range of values of a random variable.

sampling ('sɑ:mplɪŋ) NOUN [1] the process of selecting a random sample. [2] a variant of **sample** (sense 2). [3] the process of taking a short extract from (a record) and mixing it into a different backing track. [4] a process in which a continuous electrical signal is approximately represented by a series of discrete values, usually regularly spaced.

sampling frame NOUN *Statistics* See **frame** (sense 13).

sampling statistic NOUN any function of observed data, esp one used to estimate the corresponding parameter of the underlying distribution, such as the sample mean, sample variance, etc. Compare **parameter** (sense 3).

samsara (səm'sɑ:rə) NOUN [1] *Hinduism* the endless cycle of birth, death, and rebirth. [2] *Buddhism* the transmigration or rebirth of a person.
▷HISTORY Sanskrit, literally: a passing through, from *sam* altogether + *sarati* it runs

samshu ('sæmʃu:, -sju:) NOUN an alcoholic drink from China that is made from fermented rice and resembles sake.
▷HISTORY C17: perhaps modification of Chinese *shao chiu* spirits that will burn, from *shao* to burn + *chiu* spirits

Samson ('sæmsən) NOUN [1] a judge of Israel, who performed herculean feats of strength against the Philistine oppressors until he was betrayed to them by his mistress Delilah (Judges 13–16). [2] any man of outstanding physical strength.

Samsun (*Turkish* 'sɑmsun) NOUN a port in N Turkey, on the Black Sea. Pop.: 338 387 (1997). Ancient name: **Amisus** (əmi:səs).

Samuel ('sæmjuəl) NOUN *Old Testament* [1] a Hebrew prophet, seer, and judge, who anointed the first two kings of the Israelites (I Samuel 1–3; 8–15). [2] either of the two books named after him, **I** and **II Samuel.**

samurai ('sæmʊˌraɪ, 'sæmjʊ-) NOUN, *plural* **-rai.** [1] the Japanese warrior caste that provided the administrative and fighting aristocracy from the 11th to the 19th centuries. [2] a member of this aristocracy.
▷HISTORY C19: from Japanese

samurai bond NOUN a bond issued in Japan and denominated in yen, available for purchase by nonresidents of Japan. Compare **shogun bond.**

san (sæn) NOUN *Old-fashioned informal* short for **sanatorium** (esp sense 3).

San[1] (sɑ:n) NOUN [1] an aboriginal people of southern Africa. [2] a group of the Khoisan languages, spoken mostly by Bushmen.

San[2] (sɑ:n) NOUN a river in E central Europe, rising in the W Ukraine and flowing northwest across SE Poland to the Vistula River. Length: about 450 km (280 miles).

San'a *or* **Sanaa** (sɑ:'nɑ:) NOUN the administrative capital of Yemen, on the central plateau at an altitude of 2350 m (7700 ft.): formerly the capital of North Yemen. Pop.: 972 000 (1995 est.).

San Antonian (sæn æn'təʊnɪˌən) ADJECTIVE [1] of or relating to San Antonio or its inhabitants. ◆ NOUN [2] a native or inhabitant of San Antonio.

San Antonio (sæn æn'təʊnɪˌəʊ) NOUN a city in S Texas: site of the Alamo; the leading town in Texas until about 1930. Pop.: 1 144 646 (2000).

Sanatana Dharma (saˌnɑtana 'dɑrma:) NOUN the name used by Hindus for Hinduism.
▷HISTORY from Sanskrit: the eternal way

sanative ('sænətɪv) ADJECTIVE a less common word for **curative.**
▷HISTORY C15: from Medieval Latin *sānātīvus,* from Latin *sānāre* to heal, from *sānus* healthy

sanatorium (ˌsænə'tɔ:rɪəm) *or US* **sanitarium** NOUN, *plural* **-riums** *or* **-ria** (-rɪə). [1] an institution for the medical care and recuperation of persons who are chronically ill. [2] a health resort. [3] *Brit* a room in a boarding school where sick pupils may be treated in isolation.
▷HISTORY C19: from New Latin, from Latin *sānāre* to heal

sanbenito (ˌsænbə'ni:təʊ) NOUN, *plural* **-tos.** [1] a yellow garment bearing a red cross, worn by penitent heretics in the Inquisition. [2] a black garment bearing flames and devils, worn by impenitent heretics at an auto-da-fé.
▷HISTORY C16: from Spanish *San Benito* Saint Benedict, an ironical allusion to its likeness to the Benedictine scapular

San Bernardino (sæn ˌbɜ:nə'di:nəʊ) NOUN a city in SE California: founded in 1851 by Mormons from Salt Lake City. Pop.: 185 401 (2000).

San Bernardino Pass NOUN a pass over the Lepontine Alps in SE Switzerland. Highest point: 2062 m (6766 ft.).

San Blas ('sɑ:n 'blɑ:s) NOUN [1] **Isthmus of.** the

narrowest part of the Isthmus of Panama. Width: about 50 km (30 miles). [2] **Gulf of.** an inlet of the Caribbean on the N coast of Panama.

Sancerre (sɒn'sɛə; *French* sɑ̃sɛr) NOUN a dry white wine produced in the Loire valley in France.
▷HISTORY French

San Cristóbal (*Spanish* saŋ kri'stoβal) NOUN [1] Also called: **Chatham Island.** an island in the Pacific, in the Galápagos Islands. Area: 505 sq. km (195 sq. miles). [2] a city in SW Venezuela: founded in 1561 by Spanish conquistadores. Pop.: 307 184 (2000 est.).

sanctified ('sæŋktɪˌfaɪd) ADJECTIVE [1] consecrated or made holy. [2] a less common word for **sanctimonious.**

sanctify ('sæŋktɪˌfaɪ) VERB **-fies, -fying, -fied.** (*tr*) [1] to make holy. [2] to free from sin; purify. [3] to sanction (an action or practice) as religiously binding: *to sanctify a marriage.* [4] to declare or render (something) productive of or conductive to holiness, blessing, or grace. [5] *Obsolete* to authorize to be revered.
▷HISTORY C14: from Late Latin *sanctificāre,* from Latin *sanctus* holy + *facere* to make
▸'**sanctiˌfiable** ADJECTIVE ▸ˌ**sanctifi'cation** NOUN
▸'**sanctiˌfier** NOUN

sanctimonious (ˌsæŋktɪ'məʊnɪəs) ADJECTIVE affecting piety or making a display of holiness.
▷HISTORY C17: from Latin *sanctimonia* sanctity, from *sanctus* holy
▸ˌ**sancti'moniously** ADVERB ▸ˌ**sancti'moniousness** NOUN
▸'**sanctimony** NOUN

sanction ('sæŋkʃən) NOUN [1] final permission; authorization. [2] aid or encouragement. [3] something, such as an ethical principle, that imparts binding force to a rule, oath, etc. [4] the penalty laid down in a law for contravention of its provisions. [5] (*often plural*) a coercive measure, esp one taken by one or more states against another guilty of violating international law. ◆ VERB (*tr*) [6] to give authority to; permit. [7] to make authorized; confirm.
▷HISTORY C16: from Latin *sanctiō* the establishment of an inviolable decree, from *sancīre* to decree
▸'**sanctionable** ADJECTIVE ▸'**sanctioner** NOUN
▸'**sanctionless** ADJECTIVE

sanction mark NOUN a mark on pieces of 19th-century French furniture signifying that the piece met the quality standards required by the Parisian guild of ebonists.

sanctitude ('sæŋktɪˌtjuːd) NOUN saintliness; holiness.

sanctity ('sæŋktɪtɪ) NOUN, *plural* **-ties.** [1] the condition of being sanctified; holiness. [2] anything regarded as sanctified or holy. [3] the condition of being inviolable; sacredness: *the sanctity of marriage.*
▷HISTORY C14: from Old French *saincteté,* from Latin *sanctitās,* from *sanctus* holy

sanctuary ('sæŋktjʊərɪ) NOUN, *plural* **-aries.** [1] a holy place. [2] a consecrated building or shrine. [3] *Old Testament* **a** the Israelite temple at Jerusalem, esp the holy of holies. **b** the tabernacle in which the Ark was enshrined during the wanderings of the Israelites. [4] the chancel, or that part of a sacred building surrounding the main altar. [5] **a** a sacred building where fugitives were formerly entitled to immunity from arrest or execution. **b** the immunity so afforded. [6] a place of refuge; asylum. [7] a place, protected by law, where animals, esp birds, can live and breed without interference.
▷HISTORY C14: from Old French *sainctuarie,* from Late Latin *sanctuārium* repository for holy things, from Latin *sanctus* holy

sanctuary lamp NOUN *Christianity* a lamp, usually red, placed in a prominent position in the sanctuary of a church, that when lit indicates the presence of the Blessed Sacrament.

sanctum ('sæŋktəm) NOUN, *plural* **-tums, -ta** (-tə). [1] a sacred or holy place. [2] a room or place of total privacy or inviolability.
▷HISTORY C16: from Latin, from *sanctus* holy

sanctum sanctorum (sæŋk'tɔːrəm) NOUN [1] *Bible* another term for the **holy of holies.** [2] *Often facetious* an especially private place.
▷HISTORY C14: from Latin, literally: holy of holies, rendering Hebrew *qōdesh haqqŏdāshīm*

Sanctus ('sæŋktəs) NOUN [1] *Liturgy* the hymn that occurs immediately after the preface in the celebration of the Eucharist. [2] a musical setting of this, usually incorporated into the Ordinary of the Roman Catholic Mass.
▷HISTORY C14: from the first word of the hymn, *Sanctus sanctus sanctus* Holy, holy, holy, from Latin *sancīre* to consecrate

Sanctus bell NOUN *Chiefly RC Church* a bell rung as the opening words of the Sanctus are pronounced and also at other important points during Mass.

sand (sænd) NOUN [1] loose material consisting of rock or mineral grains, esp rounded grains of quartz, between 0.05 and 2 mm in diameter. [2] (*often plural*) a sandy area, esp on the seashore or in a desert. [3] **a** a greyish-yellow colour. **b** (*as adjective*): *sand upholstery.* [4] the grains of sandlike material in an hourglass. [5] *US informal* courage; grit. [6] **draw a line in the sand.** to put a stop to or a limit on. [7] **the sands are running out.** there is not much time left before death or the end. ◆ VERB [8] (*tr*) to smooth or polish the surface of with sandpaper or sand: *to sand a floor.* [9] (*tr*) to sprinkle or cover with or as if with sand; add sand to. [10] to fill or cause to fill with sand: *the channel sanded up.*
▷HISTORY Old English; related to Old Norse *sandr,* Old High German *sant,* Greek *hamathos*
▸'**sandˌlike** ADJECTIVE

Sandakan (sɑːn'dɑːkɑːn) NOUN a port in Malaysia, on the NE coast of Sabah: capital (until 1947) of North Borneo. Pop.: 223 432 (1991).

sandal ('sænd^əl) NOUN [1] a light shoe consisting of a sole held on the foot by thongs, straps, etc. [2] a strap passing over the instep or around the ankle to keep a low shoe on the foot.
▷HISTORY C14: from Latin *sandalium,* from Greek *sandalion* a small sandal, from *sandalon* sandal
▸'**sandalled** ADJECTIVE

sandalwood ('sænd^əlˌwʊd) *or* **sandal** NOUN [1] any of several evergreen hemiparasitic trees of the genus *Santalum,* esp *S. album* (**white sandalwood**), of S Asia and Australia, having hard light-coloured heartwood: family *Santalaceae.* [2] the wood of any of these trees, which is used for carving, is burned as incense, and yields an aromatic oil used in perfumery. [3] any of various similar trees or their wood, esp *Pterocarpus santalinus* (**red sandalwood**), a leguminous tree of SE Asia having dark red wood used as a dye.
▷HISTORY C14 *sandal,* from Medieval Latin *sandalum,* from Late Greek *sandanon,* from Sanskrit *candana* sandalwood

Sandalwood Island NOUN the former name for **Sumba.**

sandarac *or* **sandarach** ('sændəˌræk) NOUN [1] Also called: **sandarac tree.** either of two coniferous trees, *Tetraclinis articulata* of N Africa or *Callistris endlicheri* of Australia, having hard fragrant dark wood: family *Cupressaceae.* [2] a brittle pale yellow transparent resin obtained from the bark of this tree and used in making varnish and incense. [3] Also called: **citron wood.** the wood of this tree, used in building.
▷HISTORY C16 *sandaracha,* from Latin *sandaraca* red pigment, from Greek *sandarakē*

sandbag ('sændˌbæg) NOUN [1] a sack filled with sand used for protection against gunfire, floodwater, etc., or as ballast in a balloon, ship, etc. [2] a bag filled with sand and used as a weapon. ◆ VERB **-bags, -bagging, -bagged.** (*tr*) [3] to protect or strengthen with sandbags. [4] to hit with or as if with a sandbag. [5] *Finance* to obstruct (an unwelcome takeover bid) by prolonging talks in the hope that an acceptable bidder will come forward.
▸'**sandˌbagger** NOUN

sandbank ('sændˌbæŋk) NOUN a submerged bank of sand in a sea or river, that may be exposed at low tide.

sand bar NOUN a ridge of sand in a river or sea, built up by the action of tides, currents, etc., and often exposed at low tide.

sandblast ('sændˌblɑːst) NOUN [1] a jet of sand or grit blown from a nozzle under air, water, or steam pressure. ◆ VERB (*tr*) [2] to clean, grind, or decorate (a surface) with a sandblast.
▸'**sandˌblaster** NOUN

sand-blind ADJECTIVE not completely blind; partially able to see. Compare **stone-blind.**
▷HISTORY C15: changed (through influence of SAND) from Old English *samblind* (unattested), from *sam-* half, SEMI- + BLIND
▸'**sand-ˌblindness** NOUN

sandbox ('sændˌbɒks) NOUN [1] a container on a railway locomotive from which sand is released onto the rails to assist the traction. [2] a box with sand shaped for moulding metal. [3] a container of sand for small children to play in.

sandbox tree NOUN a tropical American euphorbiaceous tree, *Hura crepitans,* having small woody seed capsules, which explode when ripe to scatter the seeds: formerly used to hold sand for blotting ink.

sandboy ('sændˌbɔɪ) NOUN **happy** (*or* **jolly**) **as a sandboy.** very happy; high-spirited.

sand-cast VERB **-casts, -casting, -cast.** (*tr*) to produce (a casting) by pouring molten metal into a mould of sand.
▸'**sand-ˌcasting** NOUN

sand castle NOUN a mass of sand moulded into a castle-like shape, esp as made by a child on the seashore.

sand colic NOUN *Vet science* a form of colic caused by the ingestion of sand or eating sand-contaminated feeds and subsequent collection of sand in the gastrointestinal tract.

sand crab NOUN *Austral* another name for **blue swimmer.**

sand crack NOUN *Vet science* a deep crack or fissure in the wall of a horse's hoof, often causing lameness. See also **toe crack, quarter crack.**

sand dab NOUN any of various small flatfishes of the genus *Citharichthys* that occur in American Pacific coastal waters and are important food fishes.

sand dollar NOUN any of various flattened disclike echinoderms of the order *Clypeasteroida,* of shallow North American coastal waters: class *Echinoidea* (sea urchins).

sand eel *or* **lance** NOUN any silvery eel-like marine spiny-finned fish of the family *Ammodytidae* found burrowing in sand or shingle. Popular name: **launce.**

sandek ('sɑnˌdɛk) NOUN *Judaism* a man who holds a baby being circumcised.
▷HISTORY Hebrew

sander ('sændə) NOUN [1] a power-driven tool for smoothing surfaces, esp wood, plastic, etc., by rubbing with an abrasive disc. [2] a person who uses such a device.

sanderling ('sændəlɪŋ) NOUN a small sandpiper, *Crocethia alba,* that frequents sandy shores.
▷HISTORY C17: perhaps from SAND + Old English *erthling, earthling* EARTHLING

sand flea NOUN another name for the **chigoe** (sense 1), **sand hopper.**

sandfly ('sændˌflaɪ) NOUN, *plural* **-flies.** [1] any of various small mothlike dipterous flies of the genus *Phlebotomus* and related genera: the bloodsucking females transmit diseases including leishmaniasis: family *Psychodidae.* [2] any of various similar and related flies.

sandglass ('sændˌglɑːs) NOUN a less common word for **hourglass.**

sandgrouse ('sændˌgraʊs) NOUN any bird of the family *Pteroclididae,* of dry regions of the Old World, having very short feet, a short bill, and long pointed wings and tail: order *Columbiformes.*

sandhi ('sændɪ) NOUN, *plural* **-dhis.** *Linguistics* modification of the form or sound of a word under the influence of an adjacent word.
▷HISTORY from Sanskrit *samdhi* a placing together, from *sam* together + *dadhāti* he puts

sandhog ('sændˌhɒg) NOUN *Chiefly US and Canadian* a person who works in underground or underwater construction projects.

sand hopper NOUN any of various small hopping amphipod crustaceans of the genus *Orchestia* and related genera, common in intertidal regions of seashores. Also called: **beach flea, sand flea.**

Sandhurst ('sændˌhɜːst) NOUN a village in S England, in Bracknell unitary authority, Berkshire: seat of the Royal Military Academy for the training of officer cadets in the British Army. Pop.: 19 153 (1991).

San Diego (ˌsæn dɪ'eɪgəʊ) NOUN a port in S

California, on the Pacific: naval base; two universities. Pop.: 1 223 400 (2000).

Sandinista (ˌsændɪˈniːstə) NOUN (in Nicaragua) **a** one of a left-wing group of revolutionaries who overthrew President Somoza in 1979 and formed a socialist coalition government. The Sandinistas were opposed militarily by the US-backed Contras during the 1980s and were defeated in a general election in 1990. **b** (*as modifier*): *the Sandinista revolution.*
▷HISTORY C20: from Spanish, named after Augusto César *Sandino* a Nicaraguan general and rebel leader, murdered in 1933

sand lance *or* **launce** NOUN another name for the **sand eel.**

sand leek NOUN a Eurasian alliaceous plant, *Allium scorodoprasum,* having reddish-pink flowers, purple bulbils, and a garlic-like bulb. See also **rocambole.**

sand lizard NOUN a small greyish-brown European lizard, *Lacerta agilis,* that has long clawed digits and, in the male, bright green underparts: family *Lacertidae.*

sandlot (ˈsændˌlɒt) NOUN *US* 1 an area of vacant ground used by children for playing baseball and other games. 2 (*modifier*) denoting a game or sport played on a sandlot: *sandlot baseball.*

sandman (ˈsændˌmæn) NOUN, *plural* **-men.** (in folklore) a magical person supposed to put children to sleep by sprinkling sand in their eyes.

sand martin NOUN a small brown European songbird, *Riparia riparia,* with white underparts: it nests in tunnels bored in sand, river banks, etc.: family *Hirundinidae* (swallows and martins).

sand painting NOUN a type of painting done by American Indians, esp in the healing ceremonies of the Navaho, using fine coloured sand on a neutral ground.

sandpaper (ˈsændˌpeɪpə) NOUN 1 (formerly) a strong paper coated with sand for smoothing and polishing. 2 a common name for **glasspaper.** ◆ VERB 3 (*tr*) to polish or grind (a surface) with or as if with sandpaper.

sandpiper (ˈsændˌpaɪpə) NOUN 1 any of numerous N hemisphere shore birds of the genera *Tringa, Calidris,* etc., typically having a long slender bill and legs and cryptic plumage: family *Scolopacidae,* order *Charadriiformes.* 2 any other bird of the family *Scolopacidae,* which includes snipes and woodcocks.

sandpit (ˈsændˌpɪt) NOUN 1 a shallow pit or container holding sand for children to play in. 2 a pit from which sand is extracted.

Sandringham (ˈsændrɪŋəm) NOUN a village in E England, in Norfolk near the E shore of the Wash: site of **Sandringham House,** a residence of the royal family.

sandshoe (ˈsændˌʃuː) NOUN *Brit and Austral* a light canvas shoe with a rubber sole; plimsoll.

sand shrimp NOUN See **shrimp** (sense 4).

sandsoap (ˈsændˌsəʊp) NOUN a gritty general-purpose soap.

sandstone (ˈsændˌstəʊn) NOUN any of a group of common sedimentary rocks consisting of sand grains consolidated with such materials as quartz, haematite, and clay minerals: used widely in building.

sandstorm (ˈsændˌstɔːm) NOUN a strong wind that whips up clouds of sand, esp in a desert.

sand table NOUN *Military* a surface on which sand can be modelled into a relief map on which to demonstrate tactics.

sand trap NOUN another name (esp US) for **bunker** (sense 2).

sand viper NOUN 1 a S European viper, *Vipera ammodytes,* having a yellowish-brown coloration with a zigzag pattern along the back. 2 another name for **horned viper.**

sand wasp NOUN a solitary wasp of the subfamily *Sphecinae,* a subgroup of the digger wasps most of which nest in sandy ground.

sand wedge NOUN *Golf* a club with a flanged sole and a face angle of more than 50°, used in bunker shots to cut through sand, get under the ball, and lift it clear.

Sandwell (ˈsændwɛl) NOUN a unitary authority in central England, in West Midlands. Pop.: 282 901 (2001). Area: 86 sq. km (33 sq. miles).

sandwich (ˈsænwɪdʒ, -wɪtʃ) NOUN 1 two or more slices of bread, usually buttered, with a filling of meat, cheese, etc. 2 anything that resembles a sandwich in arrangement. ◆ VERB (*tr*) 3 to insert tightly between two other things. 4 to put into a sandwich. 5 to place between two dissimilar things.
▷HISTORY C18: named after John Montagu, 4th Earl of *Sandwich* (1718–92), who ate sandwiches rather than leave the gambling table for meals

sandwich beam NOUN a composite beam in which a viscoelastic layer is sandwiched between two elastic layers.

sandwich board NOUN one of two connected boards, usually bearing advertisements, that are hung over the shoulders in front of and behind a person.

sandwich cake NOUN a cake that is made up of two or more layers with a jam or other filling. Also called: **layer cake.**

sandwich compound NOUN *Chem* any of a class of organometallic compounds whose molecules have a metal atom or ion bound between two plane parallel organic rings. See also **metallocene.**

sandwich course NOUN any of several courses consisting of alternate periods of study and industrial work.

Sandwich Islands PLURAL NOUN the former name of **Hawaii.**

sandwich man NOUN a man who carries sandwich boards.

sandwich tern NOUN a European tern, *Sterna sandvicensis,* that has a yellow-tipped bill, whitish plumage, and white forked tail, and nests in colonies on beaches, etc.
▷HISTORY C18: from the town of *Sandwich* in Kent

sandworm (ˈsændˌwɜːm) NOUN any of various polychaete worms that live in burrows on sandy shores, esp the lugworm.

sandwort (ˈsændˌwɜːt) NOUN 1 any of numerous caryophyllaceous plants of the genus *Arenaria,* which grow in dense tufts on sandy soil and have white or pink solitary flowers. 2 any of various related plants.

sandy (ˈsændɪ) ADJECTIVE **sandier, sandiest.** 1 consisting of, containing, or covered with sand. 2 (esp of hair) reddish-yellow. 3 resembling sand in texture.
▸ **ˈsandiness** NOUN

sand yacht NOUN a wheeled boat with sails, built to be propelled over sand, esp beaches, by the wind.

sandy blight NOUN *Austral* a nontechnical name for any of various eye inflammations.

sane (seɪn) ADJECTIVE 1 sound in mind; free from mental disturbance. 2 having or showing reason, good judgment, or sound sense. 3 *Obsolete* healthy.
▷HISTORY C17: from Latin *sānus* healthy
▸ **ˈsanely** ADVERB ▸ **ˈsaneness** NOUN

San Fernando (*Spanish* san fɛrˈnando) NOUN 1 a port in Trinidad and Tobago, on Trinidad on the Gulf of Paria: the second-largest town in the country. Pop.: 30 100 (1990). 2 an inland port in W Venezuela, on the Apure River. Pop.: 84 180 (latest est.). Official name: **San Fernando de Apure.** 3 a port in SW Spain, on the Isla de León SE of Cádiz; site of an arsenal (founded 1790) and of the most southerly observatory in Europe. Pop.: 85 191 (1991).

Sanforized *or* **Sanforised** (ˈsænfəˌraɪzd) ADJECTIVE *Trademark* (of a fabric) preshrunk using a patented process.

San Franciscan (ˌsæn frænˈsɪskən) NOUN 1 a native or inhabitant of San Francisco. ◆ ADJECTIVE 2 of or relating to San Francisco or its inhabitants.

San Francisco (ˌsæn frænˈsɪskəʊ) NOUN a port in W California, situated around the Golden Gate: developed rapidly during the California gold rush; a major commercial centre and one of the world's finest harbours. Pop.: 776 733 (2000).

San Francisco Bay NOUN an inlet of the Pacific in W California, linked with the open sea by the Golden Gate strait. Length: about 80 km (50 miles). Greatest width: 19 km (12 miles).

sang[1] (sæŋ) VERB the past tense of **sing.**

> **Language note** See at **ring**[2].

sang[2] (sæŋ) NOUN a Scot word for **song.**

sangar (ˈsʌŋgə) NOUN *Military* a breastwork of stone or sods.
▷HISTORY C19: from Pashto

sangaree (ˌsæŋgəˈriː) NOUN a spiced drink similar to sangria.
▷HISTORY C18: from Spanish *sangría* a bleeding, from *sangre* blood, from Latin *sanguis;* see SANGUINE

sanger (ˈsæŋə) NOUN *Austral slang* a sandwich. Also called: **sango.**

sang-froid (*French* sɑ̃frwa) NOUN composure; self-possession; calmness.
▷HISTORY C18: from French, literally: cold blood

Sangh (sʌŋg) NOUN (in India) an association or union, esp a political or labour organization.
▷HISTORY Hindi

Sangha (ˈsɑnˌgə) NOUN **a** the Buddhist community. **b** (in Theravada Buddhism) the monastic order.
▷HISTORY from Sanskrit: group, congregation

sanghat (sʌngʌt) NOUN *Sikhism* a fellowship or assembly, esp a local Sikh community or congregation.
▷HISTORY Punjabi

Sango (ˈsɑːŋgəʊ) NOUN a language used in Chad, the Central African Republic, N Democratic Republic of Congo (formerly Zaïre), and the Congo, belonging to the Adamawa branch of the Niger-Congo family.

sangoma (sæŋˈgəʊmə, -ˈgɔːmə) NOUN *South African* a witch doctor, healer, or herbalist.
▷HISTORY from Zulu *isangoma*

Sangrail, Sangraal (sæŋˈgreɪl), *or* **Sangreal** (ˈsæŋgrɪəl) NOUN another name for the **Holy Grail.**
▷HISTORY C15: from Old French *Saint Graal.* See SAINT, HOLY GRAIL

Sangre de Cristo Mountains (ˈsæŋgrɪ də ˈkrɪstəʊ) PLURAL NOUN a mountain range in S Colorado and N New Mexico: part of the Rocky Mountains. Highest peak: Blanca Peak, 4364 m (14 317 ft.).

sangria (sæŋˈgriːə) NOUN a Spanish drink of red wine, sugar, orange or lemon juice, and iced soda, sometimes laced with brandy.
▷HISTORY Spanish: a bleeding; see SANGAREE

sanguinaria (ˌsæŋgwɪˈnɛərɪə) NOUN 1 the dried rhizome of the bloodroot, used as an emetic. 2 another name for **bloodroot** (sense 1).
▷HISTORY C19: from New Latin *herba sanguināria,* literally: the bloody herb

sanguinary (ˈsæŋgwɪnərɪ) ADJECTIVE 1 accompanied by much bloodshed. 2 bloodthirsty. 3 consisting of, flowing, or stained with blood.
▷HISTORY C17: from Latin *sanguinārius*
▸ **ˈsanguinarily** ADVERB ▸ **ˈsanguinariness** NOUN

sanguine (ˈsæŋgwɪn) ADJECTIVE 1 cheerful and confident; optimistic. 2 (esp of the complexion) ruddy in appearance. 3 blood-red. 4 an obsolete word for **sanguinary** (sense 2). ◆ NOUN 5 Also called: **red chalk.** a red pencil containing ferric oxide, used in drawing.
▷HISTORY C14: from Latin *sanguineus* bloody, from *sanguis* blood
▸ **ˈsanguinely** ADVERB ▸ **ˈsanguineness** *or* **sanˈguinity** NOUN

sanguineous (sæŋˈgwɪnɪəs) ADJECTIVE 1 of, containing, relating to, or associated with blood. 2 a less common word for **sanguine** (senses 1–3).
▸ **sanˈguineousness** NOUN

sanguinolent (sæŋˈgwɪnələnt) ADJECTIVE containing, tinged with, or mixed with blood.
▷HISTORY C15: from Latin *sanguinolentus,* from *sanguis* blood
▸ **sanˈguinolency** NOUN

Sanhedrin (ˈsænɪdrɪn) NOUN *Judaism* 1 the supreme judicial, ecclesiastical, and administrative council of the Jews in New Testament times, having 71 members. 2 a similar tribunal of 23 members having less important functions and authority.
▷HISTORY C16: from Late Hebrew, from Greek *sunedrion* council, from *sun-* SYN- + *hedra* seat

sanicle (ˈsænɪkᵊl) NOUN any umbelliferous plant of the genus *Sanicula,* of most regions except Australia,

having clusters of small white flowers and oval fruits with hooked bristles: formerly thought to have healing powers.
▷HISTORY C15: via Old French from Medieval Latin *sānicula,* probably from Latin *sānus* healthy

sanidine ('sænɪˌdiːn, -dɪn) NOUN an alkali feldspar that is a high-temperature glassy form of orthoclase in flat, tabular crystals, found in lavas and dykes. Formula: $KAlSi_3O_8$.
▷HISTORY C19: from German, from Greek *sanis, sanidos* a board

sanies ('seɪnɪˌiːz) NOUN *Pathol* a thin greenish foul-smelling discharge from a wound, ulcer, etc., containing pus and blood.
▷HISTORY C16: from Latin, of obscure origin

San Ildefonso (*Spanish* san ilde'fɔnso) NOUN a town in central Spain, near Segovia: site of the 18th-century summer palace of the kings of Spain. Also called: **La Granja.**

sanitarian (ˌsænɪ'tɛərɪən) ADJECTIVE 1 of or relating to sanitation. ◆ NOUN 2 a sanitation expert.

sanitarium (ˌsænɪ'tɛərɪəm) NOUN, *plural* **-riums** *or* **-ria** (-rɪə). the US spelling of **sanatorium.**
▷HISTORY C19: from Latin *sānitās* health

sanitary ('sænɪtərɪ, -trɪ) ADJECTIVE 1 of or relating to health and measures for the protection of health. 2 conducive to or promoting health; free from dirt, germs, etc.; hygienic.
▷HISTORY C19: from French *sanitaire,* from Latin *sānitās* health
▸'**sanitarily** ADVERB ▸'**sanitariness** NOUN

sanitary belt NOUN a belt for supporting a sanitary towel.

sanitary engineering NOUN the branch of civil engineering associated with the supply of water, disposal of sewage, and other public health services.
▸**sanitary engineer** NOUN

sanitary inspector NOUN (in Britain) a former name for **Environmental Health Officer.**

sanitary protection NOUN sanitary towels and tampons, collectively.

sanitary towel *or esp US* **napkin** NOUN an absorbent pad worn externally by women during menstruation to absorb the menstrual flow.

sanitation (ˌsænɪ'teɪʃən) NOUN the study and use of practical measures for the preservation of public health.

sanitize *or* **sanitise** ('sænɪˌtaɪz) VERB (*tr*) 1 to make sanitary or hygienic, as by sterilizing. 2 to omit unpleasant details from (a news report, document, etc.) to make it more palatable to the recipients.
▸ˌ**saniti'zation** *or* ˌ**saniti'sation** NOUN

sanity ('sænɪtɪ) NOUN 1 the state of being sane. 2 good sense or soundness of judgment.
▷HISTORY C15: from Latin *sānitās* health, from *sānus* healthy

sanjak ('sændʒæk) NOUN (in the Turkish Empire) a subdivision of a vilayet.
▷HISTORY C16: from Turkish *sancàk,* literally: a flag

San Jose (ˌsæn həʊ'zeɪ) NOUN a city in W central California: a leading world centre of the fruit drying and canning industry. Pop.: 894 943 (2000).

San José (*Spanish* saŋ xo'se) NOUN the capital of Costa Rica, on the central plateau: a major centre of coffee production in the mid-19th century; University of Costa Rica (1843). Pop.: 344 349 (2000 est.).

San Jose scale NOUN a small E Asian homopterous insect, *Quadraspidiotus perniciosus,* introduced into the US and other countries, where it has become a serious pest of fruit trees: family *Diaspididae.*
▷HISTORY C20: from its first being seen in the United States at *San Jose,* California

San Juan (*Spanish* saŋ 'xwan) NOUN 1 the capital and chief port of Puerto Rico, on the NE coast; University of Puerto Rico; manufacturing centre. Pop.: 421 958 (2000). 2 a city in W Argentina: almost completely destroyed by an earthquake in 1944. Pop.: 120 000 (1999 est.).

San Juan Bautista (*Spanish* saŋ 'xwan bau'tista) NOUN the former name of **Villahermosa.**

San Juan Islands (sæn 'wɑːn, 'hwɑːn) PLURAL NOUN a group of islands between NW Washington, US, and SE Vancouver Island, Canada: administratively part of Washington.

San Juan Mountains PLURAL NOUN a mountain range in SW Colorado and N New Mexico: part of the Rocky Mountains. Highest peak: Uncompahgre Peak, 4363 m (14 314 ft.).

sank (sæŋk) VERB the past tense of **sink.**

Sankhya ('sæŋkjə) NOUN one of the six orthodox schools of Hindu philosophy, teaching an eternal interaction of spirit and matter.
▷HISTORY from Sanskrit *sāmkhya,* literally: based on calculation, from *samkhyāti* he reckons

Sankt Pölten (*German* zaŋkt 'pœltən) NOUN, *usually abbreviated to* **St Pölten.** a city in NE Austria, the capital of Lower Austria state. Pop.: 50 026 (1991).

San Luis Potosí (*Spanish* san 'lwis poto'si) NOUN 1 a state of central Mexico: mainly high plateau; economy based on mining (esp silver) and agriculture. Capital: San Luis Potosí. Pop.: 2 296 363 (2000). Area: 62 849 sq. km (24 266 sq. miles). 2 an industrial city in central Mexico, capital of San Luis Potosí state, at an altitude of 1850 m (6000 ft.). Pop.: 628 134 (2000 est.).

San Marinese (ˌsæn ˌmærɪ'niːz) *or* **Sammarinese** (səˌmærɪ'niːz) ADJECTIVE 1 of or relating to San Marino or its inhabitants. ◆ NOUN 2 a native or inhabitant of San Marino.

San Marino (ˌsæn mə'riːnəʊ) NOUN a republic in S central Europe in the Apennines, forming an enclave in Italy: the smallest republic in Europe, according to tradition founded by St Marinus in the 4th century. Official language: Italian. Religion: Roman Catholic majority. Currency: euro. Capital: San Marino. Pop.: 27 200 (2001 est.). Area: 62 sq. km (24 sq. miles).

sannyasi (sʌn'jɑːsɪ) *or* **sannyasin** (sʌn'jɑːsɪn) NOUN a Brahman who having attained the fourth and last stage of life as a beggar will not be reborn, but will instead be absorbed into the Universal Soul.
▷HISTORY from Hindi: abandoning, from Sanskrit *samnyāsin*

San Pedro Sula (*Spanish* san 'peðro 'sula) NOUN a city in NW Honduras: the country's chief industrial centre. Pop.: 452 100 (1999 est.).

sanpro ('sænˌprəʊ) NOUN *Advertising* sanitary-protection products, collectively.

San Remo (*Italian* san 'rɛːmo) NOUN a port and resort in NW Italy, in Liguria on the slopes of the Maritime Alps; flower market. Pop.: 60 800 (latest est.).

sans (sænz) PREPOSITION an archaic word for **without.**
▷HISTORY C13: from Old French *sanz,* from Latin *sine* without, but probably also influenced by Latin *absentiā* in the absence of

Sans. *or* **Sansk.** ABBREVIATION FOR Sanskrit.

San Salvador (sæn 'sælvəˌdɔː; *Spanish* san salβa'ðor) NOUN the capital of El Salvador, situated in the SW central part: became capital in 1841; ruined by earthquakes in 1854 and 1873; university (1841). Pop.: 422 570 (1992).

San Salvador Island NOUN an island in the central Bahamas: the first land in the New World seen by Christopher Columbus (1492). Area: 156 sq. km (60 sq. miles). Also called: **Watling Island.**

sans-culotte (ˌsænzkju'lɒt; *French* sɑ̃kylɔt) NOUN 1 (during the French Revolution) **a** (originally) a revolutionary of the poorer class. **b** (later) any revolutionary, esp one having extreme republican sympathies. 2 any revolutionary extremist.
▷HISTORY C18: from French, literally: without knee breeches, because the revolutionaries wore pantaloons or trousers rather than knee breeches
▸ˌ**sans-cu'lottism** NOUN ▸ˌ**sans-cu'lottist** NOUN

San Sebastián (ˌsæn sə'bæstjən; *Spanish* san seβas'tjan) NOUN a port and resort in N Spain on the Bay of Biscay: former summer residence of the Spanish court. Pop.: 169 933 (1991).

sansevieria (ˌsænsɪ'vɪərɪə) NOUN any herbaceous perennial plant of the liliaceous genus *Sansevieria,* of Old World tropical regions. Some are cultivated as house plants for their erect bayonet-like fleshy leaves of variegated green (mother-in-law's tongue); others yield useful fibre (bowstring hemp).
▷HISTORY New Latin, named after Raimondo di Sangro (1710–1771), Italian scholar and prince of *San Severo*

Sanskrit ('sænskrɪt) NOUN an ancient language of India, the language of the Vedas, of Hinduism, and of an extensive philosophical and scientific literature dating from the beginning of the first millennium B.C. It is the oldest recorded member of the Indic branch of the Indo-European family of languages; recognition of the existence of the Indo-European family arose in the 18th century from a comparison of Sanskrit with Greek and Latin. Although it is used only for religious purposes, it is one of the official languages of India.
▷HISTORY C17: from Sanskrit *samskrta* perfected, literally: put together
▸'**Sanskritist** NOUN

Sanskritic (sæn'skrɪtɪk) ADJECTIVE 1 of or relating to Sanskrit. 2 denoting or belonging to those Indic languages that developed directly from Sanskrit, such as Pali, Hindi, Punjabi, and Bengali. ◆ NOUN 3 this group of languages.

Sanson-Flamsteed projection ('sænsən'flæmstiːd) NOUN another name for **sinusoidal projection.**
▷HISTORY devised by the cartographer *Sanson* in 1650, adapted by *Flamsteed* in 1729

sans serif *or* **sanserif** (sæn'sɛrɪf) NOUN a style of printer's typeface in which the characters have no serifs.

San Stefano (ˌsæn stɪ'fɑːnəʊ) NOUN a village in NW Turkey, near Istanbul on the Sea of Marmara: scene of the signing (1878) of the treaty ending the Russo-Turkish War. Turkish name: **Yeşilköy.**

Santa ('sæntə) NOUN *Informal* short for **Santa Claus.**

Santa Ana NOUN 1 (*Spanish* 'santa 'ana) a city in NW El Salvador: the second largest city in the country; coffee-processing industry. Pop.: 202 337 (1992). 2 ('sæntə 'ænə) a city in SW California: commercial and processing centre of a rich agricultural region. Pop.: 337 977 (2000).

Santa Catalina ('sæntə ˌkætᵊ'liːnə) NOUN an island in the Pacific, off the coast of SW California: part of Los Angeles county: resort. Area: 181 sq. km (70 sq. miles). Also called: **Catalina Island.**

Santa Catarina (*Portuguese* 'santə kətə'rinə) NOUN a state of S Brazil, on the Atlantic: consists chiefly of the Great Escarpment. Capital: Florianópolis. Pop.: 5 333 284 (2000). Area: 95 985 sq. km (37 060 sq. miles).

Santa Clara (*Spanish* 'santa 'klara) NOUN a city in W central Cuba: sugar and tobacco industries. Pop.: 205 400 (1994 est.).

Santa Claus ('sæntə ˌklɔːz) NOUN the legendary patron saint of children, commonly identified with Saint Nicholas, who brings presents to children on Christmas Eve or, in some European countries, on Saint Nicholas' Day. Often shortened to: **Santa.** Also called: **Father Christmas.**

Santa Cruz ('sæntə 'kruːz; *Spanish* 'santa 'kruθ) NOUN 1 a province of S Argentina, on the Atlantic: consists of a large part of Patagonia, with the forested foothills of the Andes in the west. Capital: Río Gallegos. Pop.: 206 897 (2000 est.). Area: 243 940 sq. km (94 186 sq. miles). 2 a city in E Bolivia: the second largest town in Bolivia. Pop.: 1 016 137 (2000 est.). 3 another name for **Saint Croix.**

Santa Cruz de Tenerife ('sæntə 'kruːz də ˌtenə'riːf; *Spanish* 'santa 'kruθ de tene'rife) NOUN a port and resort in the W Canary Islands, on NE Tenerife: oil refinery. Pop.: 211 930 (1998 est.).

Santa Fe NOUN 1 ('sæntə 'feɪ) a city in N central New Mexico, capital of the state: one of the oldest European settlements in North America, founded in 1610 as the capital of the Kingdom of New Mexico; developed trade with the US by the Santa Fe Trail in the early 19th century. Pop.: 62 514 (1994 est.). 2 (*Spanish* 'santa 'fe) an inland port in E Argentina, on the Salado River: University of the Littoral (1920). Pop.: 400 000 (1999 est.).

Santa Fean ('sæntə 'feɪən) ADJECTIVE 1 of or relating to Santa Fe or its inhabitants. ◆ NOUN 2 a native or inhabitant of Santa Fe.

Santa Fe Trail ('sæntə 'feɪ) NOUN an important trade route in the western US from about 1821 to 1880, linking Independence, Missouri to Santa Fe, New Mexico.

Santa Gertrudis ('sæntə gə'tru:dɪs) NOUN one of a breed of large red beef cattle developed in Texas.

Santa Isabel (*Spanish* 'santa isa'βel) NOUN the former name (until 1973) of **Malabo.**

santalaceous (ˌsæntə'leɪʃəs) ADJECTIVE of, relating to, or belonging to the *Santalaceae,* a family of semiparasitic plants of Australia and Malaysia including sandalwood and quandong.
▷HISTORY C19: via New Latin from Late Greek *santalon* sandalwood

Santa Maria[1] ('sæntə mə'ri:ə) NOUN **the.** the flagship of Columbus on his first voyage to America (1492).

Santa Maria[2] NOUN 1 (*Portuguese* 'səntə ma'ria) a city in S Brazil, in Rio Grande do Sul state. Pop.: 230 464 (2000). 2 (*Spanish* 'santa ma'ria) an active volcano in SW Guatemala. Height: 3768 m (12 362 ft.).

Santa Marta (*Spanish* 'santa 'marta) NOUN a port in NW Colombia, on the Caribbean: the oldest city in Colombia, founded in 1525; terminus of the Atlantic railway from Bogotá (opened 1961). Pop.: 359 147 (1999 est.).

Santa Maura ('santa 'maura) NOUN the Italian name for **Levkás.**

Santander (*Spanish* santan'der) NOUN a port and resort in N Spain, on an inlet of the Bay of Biscay: noted for its prehistoric collection from nearby caves; shipyards and an oil refinery. Pop.: 184 165 (1998 est.).

Santarém (*Portuguese* sənta'rẽj) NOUN a port in N Brazil, in Pará state where the Tapajós River flows into the Amazon. Pop.: 186 518 (2000).

Santa Rosa de Copán (*Spanish* 'santa 'rɔsa de ko'pan) NOUN a village in W Honduras: noted for the ruined Mayan city of Copán, which lies to the west.

Santee (sæn'ti:) NOUN a river in SE central South Carolina, formed by the union of the Congaree and Wateree Rivers: flows southeast to the Atlantic; part of the **Santee-Wateree-Catawba River System** an inland waterway 866 km (538 miles) long. Length: 230 km (143 miles).

Santeria (ˌsæntə'rɪə) NOUN a Caribbean religion composed of elements from both traditional African religion and Roman Catholicism.
▷HISTORY American Spanish, literally: holiness

Santiago (ˌsæntɪ'ɑ:gəʊ; *Spanish* san'tjaɣo) NOUN 1 the capital of Chile, at the foot of the Andes: commercial and industrial centre; two universities. Pop. (urban area): 4 640 635 (1999 est.). Official name: **Santiago de Chile** (de 'tʃile). 2 a city in the N Dominican Republic. Pop.: 365 463 (1993). Official name: **Santiago de los Caballeros** (de los kaβa'ʎeros).

Santiago de Compostela (*Spanish* de kɔmpɔs'tela) NOUN a city in NW Spain: place of pilgrimage since the 9th century and the most visited (after Jerusalem and Rome) in the Middle Ages; cathedral built over the tomb of the apostle St. James. Pop.: 87 472 (1991). Latin name: **Campus Stellae** ('kæmpəs 'steli:).

Santiago de Cuba (*Spanish* de 'kuβa) NOUN a port in SE Cuba, on **Santiago Bay** (a large inlet of the Caribbean): capital of Cuba until 1589; university (1947); industrial centre. Pop.: 440 084 (1994 est.).

Santiago del Estero (*Spanish* del es'tero) NOUN a city in N Argentina: the oldest continuous settlement in Argentina, founded in 1553 by Spaniards from Peru. Pop.: 202 876 (1999 est.).

Santo Domingo ('sæntəʊ də'mɪŋgəʊ; *Spanish* 'santo ðo'miŋgo) NOUN 1 the capital and chief port of the Dominican Republic, on the S coast: the oldest continuous European settlement in the Americas, founded in 1496; university (1538). Pop. (capital district): 2 138 262 (1993). Former name (1936–61): **Ciudad Trujillo.** 2 the former name (until 1844) of the **Dominican Republic.** 3 another name (esp in colonial times) for **Hispaniola.**

santolina (ˌsæntə'li:nə) NOUN any plant of the evergreen Mediterranean genus *Santolina,* esp *S. chamaecyparissus,* grown for its silvery-grey felted foliage: family *Asteraceae* (composites).
▷HISTORY New Latin, altered from SANTONICA

santonica (sæn'tɒnɪkə) NOUN 1 an oriental wormwood plant, *Artemisia cina* (or *maritima*). 2 the dried flower heads of this plant, formerly used as a vermifuge. ◆ Also called: **wormseed.**
▷HISTORY C17: New Latin, from Late Latin *herba santonica* herb of the *Santones* (probably wormwood), from Latin *Santonī* a people of Aquitania

santonin ('sæntənɪn) NOUN a white crystalline soluble substance extracted from the dried flower heads of santonica and used in medicine as an anthelmintic. Formula: $C_{15}H_{18}O_3$.
▷HISTORY C19: from SANTONICA + -IN

Santos (*Portuguese* 'səntuʃ) NOUN a port in S Brazil, in São Paulo state: the world's leading coffee port. Pop.: 415 553 (2000).

SANZAR ('sænˌzə) NOUN ACRONYM FOR South African, New Zealand, and Australian Rugby: an agreement between the rugby unions of these nations under which various competitions are held.

São Francisco (*Portuguese* sə̃un frə̃'sisku) NOUN a river in E Brazil, rising in SW Minas Gerais state and flowing northeast, then southeast to the Atlantic northeast of Aracajú. Length: 3200 km (1990 miles).

São Luís (*Portuguese* sə̃un 'lwis) *or* **São Luíz** ('lwiʃ) NOUN a port in NE Brazil, capital of Maranhão state, on the W coast of São Luís Island: founded in 1612 by the French and taken by the Portuguese in 1615. Pop. (urban area): 834 968 (2000).

São Miguel (*Portuguese* sə̃un mi'ɣel) NOUN an island in the E Azores: the largest of the group. Pop.: 126 388 (1991 est.). Area: 854 sq. km (333 sq. miles).

Saône (*French* son) NOUN a river in E France, rising in Lorraine and flowing generally south to join the Rhône at Lyon, as its chief tributary: canalized for 375 km (233 miles) above Lyon; linked by canals with the Rhine, Marne, Seine, and Loire Rivers. Length: 480 km (298 miles).

Saône-et-Loire (*French* sonelwar) NOUN a department of central France, in Burgundy region. Capital: Mâcon. Pop.: 554 893 (1999). Area: 8627 sq. km (3365 sq. miles).

São Paulo (*Portuguese* sə̃un 'paulu) NOUN 1 a state of SE Brazil: consists chiefly of tableland draining west into the Paraná River. Capital: São Paulo. Pop.: 36 966 527 (2000). Area: 247 239 sq. km (95 459 sq. miles). 2 a city in S Brazil, capital of São Paulo state: the largest city and industrial centre in Brazil, with one of the busiest airports in the world; three universities; rapidly expanding population. Pop.: 25 000 (1874); 2 017 025 (1950); 9 785 640 (2000).

Saorstat Eireann ('seəstɑ:t 'ɛərən) NOUN the Gaelic name for the **Irish Free State.**

São Salvador (*Portuguese* sə̃un salva'dor) NOUN short for **São Salvador da Bahia de Todos os Santos,** the official name for **Salvador.**

São Tomé e Principe (*Portuguese* sə̃un tu'mɛ 'ɛ: 'prĩ:sipə) NOUN a republic in the Gulf of Guinea, off the W coast of Africa, on the Equator: consists of the islands of Principe and São Tomé; colonized by the Portuguese in the late 15th century; became independent in 1975. Official language: Portuguese. Religion: Roman Catholic majority. Currency: dobra. Capital: São Tomé. Pop.: 147 000 (2001 est.). Area: 1001 sq. km (386 sq. miles).

sap[1] (sæp) NOUN 1 a solution of mineral salts, sugars, etc., that circulates in a plant. 2 any vital body fluid. 3 energy; vigour. 4 *Slang* a gullible or foolish person. 5 another name for **sapwood.** ◆ VERB **saps, sapping, sapped.** (*tr*) 6 to drain of sap.
▷HISTORY Old English *sæp;* related to Old High German *sapf,* German *Saft* juice, Middle Low German *sapp,* Sanskrit *sabar* milk juice
▸'**sapless** ADJECTIVE

sap[2] (sæp) NOUN 1 a deep and narrow trench used to approach or undermine an enemy position, esp in siege warfare. ◆ VERB **saps, sapping, sapped.** 2 to undermine (a fortification, etc.) by digging saps. 3 (*tr*) to weaken.
▷HISTORY C16 *zappe,* from Italian *zappa* spade, of uncertain origin; perhaps from Old Italian (dialect) *zappo* a goat

SAP (sæp) (in Britain) ACRONYM FOR Standard Assessment Procedure, the recognized performance indicator for measuring energy efficiency in buildings.

sapajou ('sæpəˌdʒu:) NOUN another name for **capuchin** (monkey).
▷HISTORY C17: from French, of Tupi origin

sapanwood ('sæpənˌwʊd) NOUN a variant spelling of **sappanwood.**

sapele (sə'pi:lɪ) NOUN 1 any of several W African meliaceous trees of the genus *Entandrophragma,* esp *E. cylindricum,* yielding a hard timber resembling mahogany. 2 the timber obtained from such a tree, used to make furniture.
▷HISTORY C20: West African name

Saphar (sə'fɑ:) NOUN a variant spelling of **Safar.**

saphead[1] ('sæpˌhɛd) NOUN *Slang* a simpleton, idiot, or fool.
▸'**sapˌheaded** ADJECTIVE

saphead[2] ('sæpˌhɛd) NOUN *Military* the end of a sap nearest to the enemy.

saphena (sə'fi:nə) NOUN, *plural* **-nae** (-ni:). *Anatomy* either of two large superficial veins of the legs.
▷HISTORY C14: via Medieval Latin from Arabic *ṣāfin*
▸**sa'phenous** ADJECTIVE

sapid ('sæpɪd) ADJECTIVE 1 having a pleasant taste. 2 agreeable or engaging.
▷HISTORY C17: from Latin *sapidus,* from *sapere* to taste
▸**sapidity** (sə'pɪdɪtɪ) *or* '**sapidness** NOUN

sapient ('seɪpɪənt) ADJECTIVE *Often used ironically* wise or sagacious.
▷HISTORY C15: from Latin *sapere* to taste
▸'**sapience** NOUN ▸'**sapiently** ADVERB

sapiential (ˌseɪpɪ'ɛnʃəl, ˌsæpɪ-) ADJECTIVE showing, having, or providing wisdom.
▸ˌ**sapi'entially** ADVERB

sapindaceous (ˌsæpɪn'deɪʃəs) ADJECTIVE of, relating to, or belonging to the *Sapindaceae,* a tropical and subtropical family of trees, shrubs, and lianas including the soapberry, litchi, and supplejack.
▷HISTORY C19: via New Latin from Latin *sāpō* soap + *Indus* Indian

Sapir-Whorf hypothesis NOUN the theory that human languages determine the structure of the real world as perceived by human beings, rather than vice versa, and that this structure is different and incommensurable from one language to another.
▷HISTORY named after Edward *Sapir* (1884–1939), US anthropologist and linguist, and Benjamin Lee *Whorf* (1897–1943), US linguist

sapling ('sæplɪŋ) NOUN 1 a young tree. 2 *Literary* a youth.

sapodilla (ˌsæpə'dɪlə) NOUN 1 a large tropical American evergreen tree, *Achras zapota,* the latex of which yields chicle. 2 Also called: **sapodilla plum.** the edible brown rough-skinned fruit of this tree, which has a sweet yellowish pulp. ◆ Also called: **naseberry, sapota.**
▷HISTORY C17: from Spanish *zapotillo,* diminutive of *zapote* sapodilla fruit, from Nahuatl *tsapotl*

saponaceous (ˌsæpəʊ'neɪʃəs) ADJECTIVE resembling soap; soapy.
▷HISTORY C18: from New Latin *sāpōnāceus,* from Latin *sāpō* SOAP
▸ˌ**sapo'naceousness** NOUN

saponaria (ˌsæpə'nɛərɪə) NOUN See **soapwort.**
▷HISTORY New Latin, from Late Latin *saponarius* soapy

saponify (sə'pɒnɪˌfaɪ) VERB **-fies, -fying, -fied.** *Chem* 1 to undergo or cause to undergo a process in which a fat is converted into a soap by treatment with alkali. 2 to undergo or cause to undergo a reaction in which an ester is hydrolysed to an acid and an alcohol as a result of treatment with an alkali.
▷HISTORY C19: from French *saponifier,* from Latin *sāpō* SOAP
▸**sa'poniˌfiable** ADJECTIVE ▸**sa'poniˌfier** NOUN
▸**saˌponifi'cation** NOUN

saponin ('sæpənɪn) NOUN any of a group of plant glycosides with a steroid structure that foam when shaken and are used in detergents.
▷HISTORY C19: from French *saponine,* from Latin *sāpō* SOAP

saponite ('sæpəˌnaɪt) NOUN a clay mineral consisting of hydrated magnesium aluminium silicate and occurring in metamorphic rocks such as serpentine.
▷HISTORY C19: from Swedish *saponit* (a rendering of German *Seifenstein* soapstone), from Latin *sāpō* SOAP

sapor ('seɪpɔː, -pə) NOUN *Rare* the quality in a substance that is perceived by the sense of taste; flavour.
▷HISTORY C15: from Latin: SAVOUR
▸ˌ**sapoˈrific** *or* ˈ**saporous** ADJECTIVE

sapota (səˈpəʊtə) NOUN [1] (in tropical America) any of various different fruits. [2] another name for **sapodilla.**
▷HISTORY C16: from Spanish *zapote,* from Nahuatl *tsapotl;* see SAPODILLA

sapotaceous (ˌsæpəˈteɪʃəs) ADJECTIVE of, relating to, or belonging to the *Sapotaceae,* a family of leathery-leaved tropical plants: includes the gutta-percha and balata trees, sapodilla, and shea.
▷HISTORY C19: from New Latin *sapota* SAPOTA

sappanwood *or* **sapanwood** ('sæpənˌwʊd) NOUN [1] a small leguminous tree, *Caesalpinia sappan,* of S Asia producing wood that yields a red dye. [2] the wood of this tree.
▷HISTORY C16: *sapan,* via Dutch from Malay *sapang*

sapper ('sæpə) NOUN [1] a soldier who digs trenches. [2] (in the British Army) a private of the Royal Engineers.

Sapphic ('sæfɪk) ADJECTIVE [1] *Prosody* denoting a metre associated with Sappho, the 6th century B.C. Greek lyric poetess of Lesbos, consisting generally of a trochaic pentameter line with a dactyl in the third foot. [2] of or relating to Sappho or her poetry. [3] lesbian. ◆ NOUN [4] *Prosody* a verse, line, or stanza written in the Sapphic form.

Sapphic ode NOUN another term for **Horatian ode.**

sapphire ('sæfaɪə) NOUN [1] **a** any precious corundum gemstone that is not red, esp the highly valued transparent blue variety. A synthetic form is used in electronics and precision apparatus. Formula: Al_2O_3. **b** (*as modifier*): *a sapphire ring.* [2] **a** the blue colour of sapphire. **b** (*as adjective*): *sapphire eyes.*
▷HISTORY C13 *safir,* from Old French, from Latin *sapphīrus,* from Greek *sappheiros,* perhaps from Hebrew *sappīr,* ultimately perhaps from Sanskrit *śanipriya,* literally: beloved of the planet Saturn, from *śani* Saturn + *priya* beloved

sapphirine ('sæfəˌriːn, -rɪn) NOUN [1] a rare blue or bluish-green mineral that consists of magnesium aluminium silicate in monoclinic crystalline form and occurs as small grains in some metamorphic rocks. [2] a blue variety of spinel. ◆ ADJECTIVE [3] relating to or resembling sapphire.

sapphism ('sæfɪzəm) NOUN a less common word for **lesbianism.**
▷HISTORY C19: after Sappho, 6th century B.C., Greek lyric poetess of Lesbos, who is believed to have been a lesbian

Sapporo ('sɑːpəʊˌrəʊ) NOUN a city in N Japan, on W Hokkaido: commercial centre; university (1918). Pop.: 1 756 968 (1995).

sappy ('sæpɪ) ADJECTIVE **-pier, -piest.** [1] (of plants) full of sap. [2] full of energy or vitality. [3] *Slang* silly or fatuous.
▸ˈ**sappily** ADVERB ▸ˈ**sappiness** NOUN

sapraemia (sæˈpriːmɪə) NOUN *Pathol* blood poisoning caused by toxins of putrefactive bacteria.
▷HISTORY C19: New Latin, from SAPRO- + -EMIA
▸**saˈpraemic** ADJECTIVE

sapro- *or before a vowel* **sapr-** COMBINING FORM indicating dead or decaying matter: *saprogenic; saprolite.*
▷HISTORY from Greek *sapros* rotten

saprobe ('sæprəʊb) NOUN an organism, esp a fungus, that lives on decaying organisms; a saprotroph. ◆ See also **saprophyte.**
▷HISTORY C20: from Greek, from SAPRO- + *bios* life
▸**sapˈrobic** ADJECTIVE

saprobiont (ˌsæprəʊˈbaɪɒnt) NOUN another name for **saprotroph.**

saprogenic (ˌsæprəʊˈdʒɛnɪk) *or* **saprogenous** (sæˈprɒdʒɪnəs) ADJECTIVE [1] producing or resulting from decay: *saprogenic bacteria.* [2] growing on decaying matter.
▸**saprogenicity** (ˌsæprədʒəˈnɪsɪtɪ) NOUN

saprolite ('sæprəʊlɪt) NOUN a deposit of earth, clay, silt, etc., formed by decomposition of rocks that has remained in its original site.
▸ˌ**sapro'litic** ADJECTIVE

sapropel ('sæprəˌpel) NOUN an unconsolidated sludge consisting of the decomposed remains of aquatic organisms, esp algae, that accumulates at the bottoms of lakes and oceans.
▷HISTORY C20: from SAPRO- + *-pel* from Greek *pēlos* mud
▸ˌ**saproˈpelic** ADJECTIVE

saprophagous (sæˈprɒfəgəs) ADJECTIVE (of certain animals) feeding on dead or decaying organic matter.

saprophyte ('sæprəʊˌfaɪt) NOUN any plant that lives and feeds on dead organic matter using mycorrhizal fungi associated with its roots; a saprotrophic plant.
▸**saprophytic** (ˌsæprəʊˈfɪtɪk) ADJECTIVE ▸ˌ**saproˈphytically** ADVERB

saprotroph ('sæprəʊˌtrəʊf) NOUN any organism, esp a fungus or bacterium, that lives and feeds on dead organic matter. Also called: **saprobe, saprobiont.**
▸**saprotrophic** (ˌsæprəʊˈtrəʊfɪk) ADJECTIVE
▸ˌ**saproˈtrophically** ADVERB

saprozoic (ˌsæprəʊˈzəʊɪk) ADJECTIVE [1] (of animals or plants) feeding on dead organic matter. [2] of or relating to nutrition in which the nutrient substances are derived from dead organic matter.

sapsago ('sæpsəˌgəʊ) NOUN a hard greenish Swiss cheese made with sour skimmed milk and coloured and flavoured with clover.
▷HISTORY C19: changed from German *Schabziger,* from *schaben* to grate + dialect *Ziger* a kind of cheese

sapsucker ('sæpˌsʌkə) NOUN either of two North American woodpeckers, *Sphyrapicus varius* or *S. thyroideus,* that have white wing patches and feed on the sap from trees.

sapwood ('sæpˌwʊd) NOUN the soft wood, just beneath the bark in tree trunks, that consists of living tissue. Compare **heartwood.**

SAR ABBREVIATION FOR Special Administrative Region (of China).

sarabande *or* **saraband** ('særəˌbænd) NOUN [1] a decorous 17th-century courtly dance. [2] *Music* a piece of music composed for or in the rhythm of this dance, in slow triple time, often incorporated into the classical suite.
▷HISTORY C17: from French, from Spanish *zarabanda,* of uncertain origin

Saracen ('særəsᵊn) NOUN [1] *History* a member of one of the nomadic Arabic tribes, esp of the Syrian desert, that harassed the borders of the Roman Empire in that region. [2] **a** a Muslim, esp one who opposed the crusades. **b** (in later use) any Arab. ◆ ADJECTIVE [3] of or relating to Arabs of either of these periods, regions, or types. [4] designating, characterizing, or relating to Muslim art or architecture.
▷HISTORY C13: from Old French *Sarrazin,* from Late Latin *Saracēnus,* from Late Greek *Sarakēnos,* perhaps from Arabic *sharq* sunrise, from *shāraqa* to rise
▸**Saracenic** (ˌsærəˈsɛnɪk) *or* ˌ**Saraˈcenical** ADJECTIVE

Saragossa (ˌsærəˈgɒsə) NOUN the English name for **Zaragoza.**

Sarah ('sɛərə) NOUN *Old Testament* the wife of Abraham and mother of Isaac (Genesis 17:15–22).

Sarajevo (*Serbo-Croat* 'sarajɛvɔ) *or* **Serajevo** NOUN the capital of Bosnia-Herzegovina: developed as a Turkish town in the 15th century; capital of the Turkish and Austro-Hungarian administrations in 1850 and 1878 respectively; scene of the assassination of Archduke Franz Ferdinand in 1914, precipitating World War I; besieged by Bosnian Serbs (1992–95). Pop.: 360 000 (1997 est.).

saran (səˈræn) NOUN any one of a class of thermoplastic resins based on vinylidene chloride, used in fibres, moulded articles, and coatings.
▷HISTORY C20: after *Saran,* trademark coined by the Dow Chemical Co.

sarangi (sɑːˈrʌŋgɪ) NOUN *Music* a stringed instrument of India played with a bow.
▷HISTORY Hindi

Saransk (*Russian* saˈransk) NOUN a city in W central Russia, capital of the Mordovian Republic: university (1957). Pop.: 316 600 (1999 est.).

Sarasvati (sʌˈrʌsvətɪ) NOUN *Hinduism* a goddess of learning and eloquence.

Saratov (*Russian* saˈratəf) NOUN an industrial city in W Russia, on the River Volga: university (1919). Pop.: 881 000 (1999 est.).

Sarawak (səˈrɑːwək) NOUN a state of Malaysia, on the NW coast of Borneo on the South China Sea: granted to Sir James Brooke by the Sultan of Brunei in 1841 as a reward for helping quell a revolt; mainly agricultural. Capital: Kuching. Pop.: 2 012 616 (2000). Area: about 121 400 sq. km (48 250 sq. miles).

sarcasm ('sɑːkæzəm) NOUN [1] mocking, contemptuous, or ironic language intended to convey scorn or insult. [2] the use or tone of such language.
▷HISTORY C16: from Late Latin *sarcasmus,* from Greek *sarkasmos,* from *sarkazein* to rend the flesh, from *sarx* flesh

sarcastic (sɑːˈkæstɪk) ADJECTIVE [1] characterized by sarcasm. [2] given to the use of sarcasm.
▸**sarˈcastically** ADVERB

sarcenet *or* **sarsenet** ('sɑːsnɪt) NOUN a fine soft silk fabric formerly from Italy and used for clothing, ribbons, etc.
▷HISTORY C15: from Old French *sarzinet,* from *Sarrazin* SARACEN

sarco- *or before a vowel* **sarc-** COMBINING FORM indicating flesh: *sarcoma.*
▷HISTORY from Greek *sark-, sarx* flesh

sarcocarp ('sɑːkəʊˌkɑːp) NOUN *Botany* [1] the fleshy mesocarp of such fruits as the peach or plum. [2] any fleshy fruit.

sarcoid ('sɑːkɔɪd) ADJECTIVE [1] of, relating to, or resembling flesh. ◆ NOUN [2] a tumour resembling a sarcoma.

sarcolemma (ˌsɑːkəʊˈlɛmə) NOUN, *plural* **-mas, -mata** (-mətə). the membrane covering a muscle fibre.

sarcoma (sɑːˈkəʊmə) NOUN, *plural* **-mata** (-mətə) *or* **-mas.** *Pathol* a usually malignant tumour arising from connective tissue.
▷HISTORY C17: via New Latin from Greek *sarkōma* fleshy growth; see SARCO-, -OMA
▸**sarˈcomaˌtoid** *or* **sarˈcomatous** ADJECTIVE

sarcomatosis (sɑːˌkəʊməˈtəʊsɪs) NOUN *Pathol* a condition characterized by the development of several sarcomas at various bodily sites.
▷HISTORY C19: see SARCOMA, -OSIS

sarcomere ('sɑːkəʊˌmɪə) NOUN any of the units that together comprise skeletal muscle.

sarcophagus (sɑːˈkɒfəgəs) NOUN, *plural* **-gi** (-ˌgaɪ) *or* **-guses.** a stone or marble coffin or tomb, esp one bearing sculpture or inscriptions.
▷HISTORY C17: via Latin from Greek *sarkophagos* flesh-devouring; from the type of stone used, which was believed to destroy the flesh of corpses

sarcoplasm ('sɑːkəʊˌplæzəm) NOUN the cytoplasm of a muscle fibre.
▸ˌ**sarcoˈplasmic** ADJECTIVE

sarcous ('sɑːkəs) ADJECTIVE (of tissue) muscular or fleshy.
▷HISTORY C19: from Greek *sarx* flesh

sard (sɑːd) *or* **sardius** ('sɑːdɪəs) NOUN an orange, red, or brown variety of chalcedony, used as a gemstone. Formula: SiO_2. Also called: **sardine.**
▷HISTORY C14: from Latin *sarda,* from Greek *sardios* stone from Sardis

sardar *or* **sirdar** (səˈdɑː) NOUN (in India) [1] a title used before the name of Sikh men. [2] a leader.
▷HISTORY Hindi, from Persian

Sardegna (sarˈdeɲɲa) NOUN the Italian name for **Sardinia.**

sardine[1] (sɑːˈdiːn) NOUN, *plural* **-dines, -dine.** [1] any of various small marine food fishes of the herring family, esp a young pilchard. See also **sild.** [2] **like sardines.** very closely crowded together.
▷HISTORY C15: via Old French from Latin *sardīna,* diminutive of *sarda* a fish suitable for pickling

sardine[2] ('sɑːdiːn, -dᵊn) NOUN another name for **sard.**
▷HISTORY C14: from Late Latin *sardinus,* from Greek *sardinos lithos* Sardian stone, from *Sardeis* Sardis

Sardinia (sɑːˈdɪnɪə) NOUN the second-largest island in the Mediterranean: forms, with offshore islands, an administrative region of Italy; ceded to Savoy by Austria in 1720 in exchange for Sicily and formed the Kingdom of Sardinia with Piedmont; became part of Italy in 1861. Capital: Cagliari. Pop.: 1 651 888 (2000 est.). Area: 24 089 sq. km (9301 sq. miles). Italian name: **Sardegna.**

Sardinian (sɑːˈdɪnɪən) ADJECTIVE [1] of or relating to Sardinia, its inhabitants, or their language. ◆ NOUN [2] a native or inhabitant of Sardinia. [3] the spoken language of Sardinia, sometimes regarded as a dialect of Italian but containing many loan words from Spanish.

Sardis ('sɑːdɪs) *or* **Sardes** ('sɑːdiːz) NOUN an ancient city of W Asia Minor: capital of Lydia.

sardius ('sɑːdɪəs) NOUN 1 *Old Testament* a precious stone, probably a ruby, set in the breastplate of the high priest. 2 another name for **sard**.
▷HISTORY C14: via Late Latin from Greek *sardios*, from *Sardeis* Sardis

sardonic (sɑː'dɒnɪk) ADJECTIVE characterized by irony, mockery, or derision.
▷HISTORY C17: from French *sardonique*, from Latin *sardonius*, from Greek *sardonios* derisive, literally: of Sardinia, alteration of Homeric *sardanios* scornful (laughter or smile)
▸**sar'donically** ADVERB ▸**sar'donicism** NOUN

sardonyx ('sɑːdənɪks) NOUN a variety of chalcedony with alternating reddish-brown and white parallel bands, used as a gemstone. Formula: SiO_2.
▷HISTORY C14: via Latin from Greek *sardonux*, perhaps from *sardion* SARDINE[2] + *onux* nail

SARFU ABBREVIATION FOR South African Rugby Football Union.

sargasso *or* **sargasso weed** (sɑː'gæsəʊ) NOUN, *plural* **-sos**. another name for **gulfweed, sargassum**.
▷HISTORY C16: from Portuguese *sargaço*, of unknown origin

Sargasso Sea NOUN a calm area of the N Atlantic, between the Caribbean and the Azores, where there is an abundance of floating seaweed of the genus *Sargassum*.

sargassum (sɑː'gæsəm) *or* **sargasso** (sɑː'gæsəʊ) NOUN any floating brown seaweed of the genus *Sargassum*, such as gulfweed, of warm seas, having ribbon-like fronds containing air sacs.
▷HISTORY C18: from New Latin; see SARGASSO

sarge (sɑːdʒ) NOUN *Informal* sergeant: used esp as a term of address.

Sargodha (sɑː'gəʊdə) NOUN a city in NE Pakistan: grain market. Pop. (urban area): 455 300 (1998).

sari *or* **saree** ('sɑːrɪ) NOUN, *plural* **-ris** *or* **-rees**. the traditional dress of women of India, Pakistan, etc., consisting of a very long narrow piece of cloth elaborately swathed around the body.
▷HISTORY C18: from Hindi *sārī*, from Sanskrit *śāṭī*

Sarie Marais ('sɑːrɪ mɑː'reɪ) NOUN *South African* a popular Afrikaans song.

sarin ('særɪn) NOUN isopropyl methylphosphonofluoridate: used in chemical warfare as a lethal nerve gas producing asphyxia. Formula: $CH_3P(O)(F)OCH(CH_3)_2$.
▷HISTORY C20: from German, from the surnames of its inventors, *S(chrader), A(mbrose), R(udinger), and (van der L)in(de)*

sark (særk) NOUN *Scot* a shirt or (formerly) chemise.
▷HISTORY Old English *serc*; related to Old Norse *serkr*

Sark (sɑːk) NOUN an island in the English Channel in the Channel Islands, consisting of **Great Sark** and **Little Sark**, connected by an isthmus: ruled by a hereditary seigneur or dame. Pop.: 550 (1996). Area: 5 sq. km (2 sq. miles). French name: **Sercq**.

Sarka ('zɑːkə) NOUN a variant spelling of **Zarqa**.

sarking ('sɑːkɪŋ, 'særkɪŋ) NOUN *Scot, northern English, and NZ* a timber or felt cladding placed over the rafters of a roof before the tiles or slates are fixed in place.
▷HISTORY C15: from verbal use of SARK

sarky ('sɑːkɪ) ADJECTIVE **-kier, -kiest**. *Brit informal* sarcastic.

Sarmatia (sɑː'meɪʃɪə) NOUN the ancient name of a region between the Volga and Vistula Rivers now covering parts of Poland, Belarus, and SW Russia.

Sarmatian (sɑː'meɪʃɪən) NOUN 1 a native or inhabitant of Sarmatia, an ancient region of E Europe. ♦ ADJECTIVE 2 of or relating to Sarmatia or its inhabitants.

Sarmatic (sɑː'mætɪk) ADJECTIVE of or relating to Sarmatia or its inhabitants.

sarmentose (sɑː'mɛntəʊs), **sarmentous** (sɑː'mɛntəs), *or* **sarmentaceous** (ˌsɑːmən'teɪʃəs) ADJECTIVE (of plants such as the strawberry) having stems in the form of runners.
▷HISTORY C18: from Latin *sarmentōsus* full of twigs, from *sarmentum* brushwood, from *sarpere* to prune

sarmie ('sɑːmɪ) NOUN *South African children's slang* a sandwich.
▷HISTORY C20: from Northern English SARNIE

Sarnen (*German* 'zarnən) NOUN a town in central Switzerland, capital of Obwalden demicanton: resort. Pop.: 7200 (latest est.).

Sarnia ('sɑːnɪə) NOUN an inland port in S central Canada, in SW Ontario at the S end of Lake Huron: oil refineries. Pop.: 74 376 (1991).

sarnie ('sɑːnɪ) NOUN *Brit informal* a sandwich.
▷HISTORY C20: probably from Northern or dialect pronunciation of first syllable of *sandwich*

sarod (sæ'rəʊd) NOUN an Indian stringed musical instrument that may be played with a bow or plucked.
▷HISTORY C19: from Hindi

sarong (sə'rɒŋ) NOUN 1 a draped skirtlike garment worn by men and women in the Malay Archipelago, Sri Lanka, the Pacific islands, etc. 2 a fashionable Western adaptation of this garment.
▷HISTORY C19: from Malay, literally: sheath

Saronic Gulf (sə'rɒnɪk) NOUN an inlet of the Aegean on the SE coast of Greece. Length: about 80 km (50 miles). Width: about 48 km (30 miles). Also called: (Gulf of) **Aegina**.

saros ('seɪrɒs) NOUN a cycle of about 18 years 11 days (6585.32 days) in which eclipses of the sun and moon occur in the same sequence and at the same intervals as in the previous such cycle.
▷HISTORY C19: from Greek, from Babylonian *šāru* 3600 (years); modern astronomical use apparently based on mistaken interpretation of *šāru* as a period of 18½ years
▸**saronic** (sə'rɒnɪk) ADJECTIVE

Saros ('sɑːrɒs) NOUN **Gulf of**. an inlet of the Aegean in NW Turkey, north of the Gallipoli Peninsula. Length: 59 km (37 miles). Width: 35 km (22 miles).

sarpanch (sə'pʌntʃ) NOUN the head of a panchayat.
▷HISTORY Urdu, from *sar* head + Sanskrit *panch* five; see PANCHAYAT

Sarpedon (sɑː'piːdɒn) NOUN *Greek myth* a son of Zeus and Laodameia, or perhaps Europa, and king of Lycia. He was slain by Patroclus while fighting on behalf of the Trojans.

sarracenia (ˌsærə'siːnɪə) NOUN any American pitcher plant of the genus *Sarracenia*, having single nodding flowers and leaves modified as pitchers that trap and digest insects: family *Sarraceniaceae*.
▷HISTORY C18: New Latin, named after D. *Sarrazin*, 17th-century botanist of Quebec

sarraceniaceous (ˌsærəˌsiːnɪ'eɪʃəs) ADJECTIVE of, relating to, or belonging to the *Sarraceniaceae*, an American family of pitcher plants.

Sarre (sar) NOUN the French name for the **Saar**.

sarrusophone (sə'ruːzəˌfəʊn) NOUN a wind instrument resembling the oboe but made of brass.
▷HISTORY C19: named after *Sarrus*, French bandmaster, who invented it (1856)

SARS[1] (sɑːz) NOUN ACRONYM FOR severe acute respiratory syndrome; a severe viral infection of the lungs characterized by high fever, a dry cough, and breathing difficulties. It is contagious, having an airborne mode of transmission.

SARS[2] ABBREVIATION FOR South African Revenue Service.

sarsaparilla (ˌsɑːsəpə'rɪlə, ˌsɑːspə-) NOUN 1 any of various prickly climbing plants of the tropical American genus *Smilax* having large aromatic roots and heart-shaped leaves: family *Smilacaceae*. 2 the dried roots of any of these plants, formerly used as a medicine. 3 a nonalcoholic drink prepared from these roots. 4 any of various plants resembling true sarsaparilla, esp the araliaceous plant *Aralia nudicaulis* (**wild sarsaparilla**), of North America.
▷HISTORY C16: from Spanish *sarzaparrilla*, from *zarza* a bramble, (from Arabic *šaras*) + *-parrilla*, from Spanish *parra* a climbing plant

sarsen ('sɑːsᵊn) NOUN 1 *Geology* a boulder of silicified sandstone, probably of Tertiary age, found in large numbers in S England. 2 such a stone used in a megalithic monument. Also called: **greywether**.
▷HISTORY C17: probably a variant of SARACEN

sarsenet ('sɑːsnɪt) NOUN a variant spelling of **sarcenet**.

Sarthe (*French* sart) NOUN a department of NW France, in Pays de la Loire region. Capital: Le Mans. Pop.: 529 851 (1999). Area: 6245 sq. km (2436 sq. miles).

sartor ('sɑːtə) NOUN a humorous or literary word for **tailor**.
▷HISTORY C17: from Latin: a patcher, from *sarcīre* to patch

sartorial (sɑː'tɔːrɪəl) ADJECTIVE 1 of or relating to a tailor or to tailoring. 2 *Anatomy* of or relating to the sartorius.
▷HISTORY C19: from Late Latin *sartōrius* from SARTOR
▸**sar'torially** ADVERB

sartorius (sɑː'tɔːrɪəs) NOUN, *plural* **-torii** (-'tɔːrɪˌaɪ). *Anatomy* a long ribbon-shaped muscle that aids in flexing the knee.
▷HISTORY C18: New Latin, from *sartorius musculus*, literally: tailor's muscle, because it is used when one sits in the cross-legged position in which tailors traditionally sat while sewing

Sarum ('sɛərəm) NOUN the ancient name of **Salisbury** (sense 3).

Sarum use NOUN the distinctive local rite or system of rites used at Salisbury cathedral in late medieval times.

Sarvodaya (sə'vəʊdəjə) NOUN (in India) economic and social development and improvement of a community as a whole.
▷HISTORY Hindi, from *sarva* all + *udaya* rise

SAS ABBREVIATION FOR **Special Air Service**.

Sasebo ('sɑːsəˌbəʊ) NOUN a port in SW Japan, on NW Kyushu on Omura Bay: naval base. Pop.: 244 879 (1995).

saser ('seizə) NOUN a device for amplifying ultrasound, working on a similar principle to a laser.
▷HISTORY C20: *s(ound) a(mplification by) s(timulated) e(mission) of r(adiation)*

sash[1] (sæʃ) NOUN a long piece of ribbon, silk, etc., worn around the waist like a belt or over one shoulder, as a symbol of rank.
▷HISTORY C16: from Arabic *shāsh* muslin

sash[2] (sæʃ) NOUN 1 a frame that contains the panes of a window or door. ♦ VERB (*tr*) 2 to furnish with a sash, sashes, or sash windows.
▷HISTORY C17: originally plural *sashes*, variant of *shashes*, from CHASSIS

sashay (sæ'ʃeɪ) VERB (*intr*) *Informal* 1 to move, walk, or glide along casually. 2 to move or walk in a showy way; parade.
▷HISTORY C19: from an alteration of *chassé*, a gliding dance step

sash cord NOUN a strong cord connecting a sash weight to a sliding sash.

sashimi ('sæʃɪmɪ) NOUN a Japanese dish of thin fillets of raw fish.
▷HISTORY C19: from Japanese *sashi* pierce + *mi* flesh

sash saw NOUN a small tenon saw used for cutting sashes.

sash weight NOUN a weight used to counterbalance the weight of a sliding sash in a sash window and thus hold it in position at any height.

sash window NOUN a window consisting of two sashes placed one above the other so that one or each can be slid over the other to open the window.

sasin ('sæsɪn) NOUN another name for the **blackbuck**.
▷HISTORY C19: of unknown origin

sasine ('sesɪn, 'seɪ-) NOUN *Scots law* the granting of legal possession of feudal property.
▷HISTORY C17: Scots variant of SEISIN

Sask. ABBREVIATION FOR Saskatchewan.

Saskatchewan (sæs'kætʃɪwən) NOUN 1 a province of W Canada: consists of Canadian Shield in the north and open prairie in the south; economy based chiefly on agriculture and mineral resources. Capital: Regina. Pop.: 1 015 800 (2001 est.). Area: 651 900 sq. km (251 700 sq. miles). Abbreviations: **Sask, SK.** 2 a river in W Canada, formed by the confluence of the North and South Saskatchewan Rivers: flows east to Lake Winnipeg. Length: 596 km (370 miles).

Saskatchewanian (sæsˌkætʃə'wɒnɪən) NOUN 1

a native or inhabitant of Saskatchewan. ◆ ADJECTIVE [2] of or relating to Saskatchewan or its inhabitants.

saskatoon (ˌsæskəˈtuːn) NOUN a species of serviceberry, *Amelanchier alnifolia,* of W Canada: noted for its succulent purplish berries.
▷HISTORY from Cree *misaskwatomin,* from *misaskwat* tree of many branches + *min* fruit

Saskatoon (ˌsæskəˈtuːn) NOUN a city in W Canada, in S Saskatchewan on the South Saskatchewan River: oil refining; university (1907). Pop.: 193 647 (1996).

sasquatch (ˈsæsˌkwætʃ) NOUN (in Canadian folklore) in British Columbia, a hairy beast or manlike monster said to leave huge footprints.
▷HISTORY from Salish

sass (sæs) *US and Canadian informal* ◆ NOUN [1] insolent or impudent talk or behaviour. ◆ VERB (*intr*) [2] to talk or answer back in such a way.
▷HISTORY C20: back formation from SASSY[1]

sassaby (ˈsæsəbɪ) NOUN, *plural* **-bies.** an African antelope, *Damaliscus lunatus,* of grasslands and semideserts, having angular curved horns and an elongated muzzle: thought to be the swiftest hoofed mammal.
▷HISTORY C19: from Bantu *tshêsêbê*

sassafras (ˈsæsəˌfræs) NOUN [1] an aromatic deciduous lauraceous tree, *Sassafras albidum,* of North America, having three-lobed leaves and dark blue fruits. [2] the aromatic dried root bark of this tree, used as a flavouring, and yielding sassafras oil. [3] *Austral* any of several unrelated trees having a similar fragrant bark.
▷HISTORY C16: from Spanish *sasafras,* of uncertain origin

sassafras oil NOUN a clear volatile oil that is extracted from the root of the sassafras tree and contains camphor, pinene, and safrole.

Sassanid (ˈsæsənɪd) NOUN, *plural* **Sassanids** *or* **Sassanidae** (sæˈsænɪˌdiː). any member of the native dynasty that built and ruled an empire in Persia from 224 to 636 A.D.
▸**Sasˈsanian** ADJECTIVE

Sassari (*Italian* ˈsassari) NOUN a city in NW Sardinia, Italy: the second-largest city on the island; university (1565). Pop.: 120 803 (2000 est.).

Sassenach (ˈsæsəˌnæk; *Scot* -næx) NOUN *Scot and occasionally Irish* an English person or a Lowland Scot.
▷HISTORY C18: from Scot Gaelic *Sasunnach,* Irish *Sasanach,* from Late Latin *saxonēs* Saxons

sassy[1] (ˈsæsɪ) ADJECTIVE **-sier, -siest.** *US informal* insolent, impertinent.
▷HISTORY C19: variant of SAUCY
▸**ˈsassily** ADVERB ▸**ˈsassiness** NOUN

sassy[2] (ˈsæsɪ), **sasswood** (ˈsæsˌwʊd), *or* **sassy wood** NOUN [1] a W African leguminous tree, *Erythrophleum guineense,* with poisonous bark (**sassy bark**) and hard strong wood. [2] the bark or wood of this tree or the alkaloid derived from them, which is sometimes used in medicine.
▷HISTORY C19: probably from a language of the Kwa family: compare Twi *sese* plane tree, Ewe *sesewu* a kind of timber tree

sastra (ˈʃɑːstrə) NOUN a variant spelling of **shastra.**

sastruga (səˈstruːgə, sæ-) *or* **zastruga** NOUN one of a series of ridges on snow-covered plains, caused by the action of wind laden with ice particles.
▷HISTORY from Russian *zastruga* groove, from *za* by + *struga* deep place

sat (sæt) VERB the past tense and past participle of **sit.**

SAT ABBREVIATION FOR (in the US) Scholastic Aptitude Test.

Sat. ABBREVIATION FOR: [1] Saturday. [2] Saturn.

Satan (ˈseɪtᵊn) NOUN the devil, adversary of God, and tempter of mankind: sometimes identified with Lucifer (Luke 4:5–8).
▷HISTORY Old English, from Late Latin, from Greek, from Hebrew: plotter, from *sātan* to plot against

satang (sæˈtæŋ) NOUN, *plural* **-tang.** a monetary unit of Thailand worth one hundredth of a baht.
▷HISTORY from Thai *satān*

satanic (səˈtænɪk) *or now rarely* **satanical** ADJECTIVE [1] of or relating to Satan. [2] supremely evil or wicked; diabolic.
▸**saˈtanically** ADVERB ▸**saˈtanicalness** NOUN

Satanism (ˈseɪtᵊˌnɪzəm) NOUN [1] the worship of Satan. [2] a form of such worship which includes blasphemous or obscene parodies of Christian prayers, etc. [3] a satanic disposition or satanic practices.
▸**ˈSatanist** NOUN, ADJECTIVE

satay, satai, *or* **saté** (ˈsæteɪ) NOUN barbecued spiced meat cooked on skewers usually made from the stems of coconut leaves.
▷HISTORY from Malay

SATB ABBREVIATION FOR soprano, alto, tenor, bass: a combination of voices in choral music.

satchel (ˈsætʃəl) NOUN a rectangular bag, usually made of leather or cloth and provided with a shoulder strap, used for carrying books, esp school books.
▷HISTORY C14: from Old French *sachel* a little bag, from Late Latin *saccellus,* from Latin *saccus* SACK[1]
▸**ˈsatchelled** ADJECTIVE

sate[1] (seɪt) VERB (*tr*) [1] to satisfy (a desire or appetite) fully. [2] to supply beyond capacity or desire.
▷HISTORY Old English *sadian;* related to Old High German *satōn;* see SAD, SATIATE

sate[2] (sæt, seɪt) VERB *Archaic* a past tense and past participle of **sit.**

sateen (sæˈtiːn) NOUN a glossy linen or cotton fabric, woven in such a way that it resembles satin.
▷HISTORY C19: changed from SATIN, on the model of VELVETEEN

satellite (ˈsætᵊˌlaɪt) NOUN [1] a celestial body orbiting around a planet or star: *the earth is a satellite of the sun.* [2] Also called: **artificial satellite.** a man-made device orbiting around the earth, moon, or another planet transmitting to earth scientific information or used for communication. See also **communications satellite.** [3] a person, esp one who is obsequious, who follows or serves another. [4] a country or political unit under the domination of a foreign power. [5] a subordinate area or community that is dependent upon a larger adjacent town or city. [6] (*modifier*) subordinate to or dependent upon another: *a satellite nation.* [7] (*modifier*) of, used in, or relating to the transmission of television signals from a satellite to the house: *a satellite dish aerial.* ◆ VERB [8] (*tr*) to transmit by communications satellite.
▷HISTORY C16: from Latin *satelles* an attendant, probably of Etruscan origin

satellite broadcasting NOUN the transmission of television or radio programmes from an artificial satellite at a power suitable for direct reception in the home.

satellite dish aerial NOUN a parabolic aerial for reception from or transmission to an artificial satellite. Often shortened to: **dish aerial** *or* **dish.**

satellitium (ˌsætᵊˈlɪtɪəm, -ˈlɪʃɪəm) NOUN *Astrology* a group of three or more planets lying in one sign of the zodiac.
▷HISTORY C17: from Latin, literally: bodyguard, retinue, from *satelles* an attendant. See SATELLITE

satem (ˈsɑːtəm, ˈseɪ-) ADJECTIVE denoting or belonging to the group of Indo-European languages in which original velar stops became palatalized (k > s or ʃ). These languages belong to the Indic, Iranian, Armenian, Slavonic, Baltic, and Albanian branches and are traditionally regarded as the E group. Compare **centum.**
▷HISTORY from Avestan *satəm* hundred; chosen to exemplify the variation of initial *s* with initial *k* (as in *centum*) in Indo-European languages

satiable (ˈseɪʃɪəbᵊl, ˈseɪʃə-) ADJECTIVE capable of being satiated.
▸**ˌsatiaˈbility** NOUN ▸**ˈsatiably** ADVERB

satiate (ˈseɪʃɪˌeɪt) VERB (*tr*) [1] to fill or supply beyond capacity or desire, often arousing weariness. [2] to supply to satisfaction or capacity.
▷HISTORY C16: from Latin *satiāre* to satisfy, from *satis* enough
▸**ˌsatiˈation** NOUN

Saticon (ˈsætɪˌkɒn) NOUN *Trademark* a high-resolution television camera tube used when high definition is required.
▷HISTORY C20: from S(ELENIUM) + A(RSENIC) + T(ELLURIUM) (used in the tube screen) + ICON(OSCOPE)

satiety (səˈtaɪɪtɪ) NOUN the state of being satiated.
▷HISTORY C16: from Latin *satietās,* from *satis* enough

satin (ˈsætɪn) NOUN [1] a fabric of silk, rayon, etc., closely woven to show much of the warp, giving a smooth glossy appearance. [2] (*modifier*) of or like satin in texture: *a satin finish.*
▷HISTORY C14: via Old French from Arabic *zaitūnī* of *Zaytūn,* Arabic rendering of Chinese *Tseutung* (now *Tsinkiang*), port in southern China from which the cloth was probably first exported
▸**ˈsatin-ˌlike** ADJECTIVE ▸**ˈsatiny** ADJECTIVE

satin bowerbird NOUN the largest Australian bowerbird, *Ptilonorhynchus violaceus,* the male of which has lustrous blue plumage.

satinet *or* **satinette** (ˌsætɪˈnɛt) NOUN a thin or imitation satin.
▷HISTORY C18: from French: small satin

satinflower (ˈsætɪnˌflaʊə) NOUN another name for **greater stitchwort** (see **stitchwort**).

satinpod (ˈsætɪnˌpɒd) NOUN another name for **honesty** (the plant).

satin stitch NOUN an embroidery stitch consisting of rows of flat stitches placed close together.
▷HISTORY C17: so called from the satin-like appearance of embroidery using this stitch

satin walnut NOUN the brown heartwood of the sweet gum tree, used for furniture, fittings, and panelling.

satinwood (ˈsætɪnˌwʊd) NOUN [1] a rutaceous tree, *Chloroxylon swietenia,* that occurs in the East Indies and has hard wood with a satiny texture. [2] the wood of this tree, used in veneering, cabinetwork, marquetry, etc. [3] **West Indian Satinwood.** another name for **yellowwood** (sense 2).

satire (ˈsætaɪə) NOUN [1] a novel, play, entertainment, etc., in which topical issues, folly, or evil are held up to scorn by means of ridicule and irony. [2] the genre constituted by such works. [3] the use of ridicule, irony, etc., to create such an effect.
▷HISTORY C16: from Latin *satira* a mixture, from *satur* sated, from *satis* enough

satirical (səˈtɪrɪkᵊl) *or* **satiric** ADJECTIVE [1] of, relating to, or containing satire. [2] given to the use of satire.
▸**saˈtirically** ADVERB ▸**saˈtiricalness** NOUN

satirist (ˈsætərɪst) NOUN [1] a person who writes satire. [2] a person given to the use of satire.

satirize *or* **satirise** (ˈsætəˌraɪz) VERB to deride (a person or thing) by means of satire.
▸**ˌsatiriˈzation** *or* **ˌsatiriˈsation** NOUN ▸**ˈsatiˌrizer** *or* **ˈsatiˌriser** NOUN

satisfaction (ˌsætɪsˈfækʃən) NOUN [1] the act of satisfying or state of being satisfied. [2] the fulfilment of a desire. [3] the pleasure obtained from such fulfilment. [4] a source of fulfilment. [5] reparation or compensation for a wrong done or received. [6] *RC Church, Church of England* the performance by a repentant sinner of a penance. [7] *Christianity* the atonement for sin by the death of Christ.
▷HISTORY C15: via French from Latin *satisfactionem,* from *satisfacere* to SATISFY

satisfactory (ˌsætɪsˈfæktərɪ, -trɪ) ADJECTIVE [1] adequate or suitable; acceptable: *a satisfactory answer.* [2] giving satisfaction. [3] constituting or involving atonement, recompense, or expiation for sin.
▸**ˌsatisˈfactorily** ADVERB ▸**ˌsatisˈfactoriness** NOUN

satisfice (ˈsætɪsˌfaɪs) VERB [1] (*intr*) to act in such a way as to satisfy the minimum requirements for achieving a particular result. [2] (*tr*) *Obsolete* to satisfy.
▷HISTORY C16: altered from SATISFY
▸**ˈsatisˌficer** NOUN

satisficing behaviour (ˈsætɪsˌfaɪsɪŋ) NOUN *Economics* the form of behaviour demonstrated by firms who seek satisfactory profits and satisfactory growth rather than maximum profits.

satisfy (ˈsætɪsˌfaɪ) VERB **-fies, -fying, -fied.** (*mainly tr*) [1] (*also intr*) to fulfil the desires or needs of (a person). [2] to provide amply for (a need or desire). [3] to relieve of doubt; convince. [4] to dispel (a doubt). [5] to make reparation to or for. [6] to discharge or pay off (a debt) to (a creditor). [7] to fulfil the requirements of; comply with: *you must satisfy the terms of your lease.* [8] *Maths, logic* to fulfil the conditions of (a theorem, assumption, etc.); to

yield a truth by substitution of the given value: $x = 3$ *satisfies* $x^2 - 4x + 3 = 0$.
▷HISTORY C15: from Old French *satisfier,* from Latin *satisfacere,* from *satis* enough + *facere* to make, do
▸ **'satis,fiable** ADJECTIVE ▸ **'satis,fier** NOUN ▸ **'satis,fying** ADJECTIVE ▸ **'satis,fyingly** ADVERB

satori (sə'tɔːrɪ) NOUN *Zen Buddhism* the state of sudden indescribable intuitive enlightenment.
▷HISTORY from Japanese

satrap ('sætrəp) NOUN 1 (in ancient Persia) a provincial governor. 2 a subordinate ruler, esp a despotic one.
▷HISTORY C14: from Latin *satrapa,* from Greek *satrapēs,* from Old Persian *khshathrapāvan,* literally: protector of the land

satrapy ('sætrəpɪ) NOUN, *plural* **-trapies.** the province, office, or period of rule of a satrap.

SATs (sæts) PLURAL NOUN *Brit education* ◆ ACRONYM FOR **standard assessment tasks, standard assessment tests,** or **standard attainment tests** (now officially called **national tests**). See also **SAT.**

satsuma (sæt'suːmə) NOUN 1 a small citrus tree, *Citrus nobilis* var. *unshiu,* cultivated, esp in Japan, for its edible fruit. 2 the fruit of this tree, which has a loose rind and easily separable segments.
▷HISTORY C19: originally from the province of Satsuma, Japan

Satsuma ('sætsʊ,mɑː) NOUN a former province of SW Japan, on S Kyushu: famous for its porcelain.

Satsuma ware NOUN 1 simple pottery made in Satsuma, Japan, from the late 16th century. 2 ornamental glazed porcelain ware made in Satsuma, Japan, from the late 18th century.

saturable ('sætʃərəbᵊl) ADJECTIVE *Chem* capable of being saturated.
▸ **,satura'bility** NOUN

saturant ('sætʃərənt) *Chem* ◆ NOUN 1 the substance that causes a solution, etc., to be saturated. ◆ ADJECTIVE 2 (of a substance) causing saturation.
▷HISTORY C18: from Latin *saturāns*

saturate VERB ('sætʃə,reɪt) 1 to fill, soak, or imbue totally. 2 to make (a chemical compound, vapour, solution, magnetic material, etc.) saturated or (of a compound, vapour, etc.) to become saturated. 3 (*tr*) *Military* to bomb or shell heavily. ◆ ADJECTIVE ('sætʃərɪt, -,reɪt) 4 a less common word for **saturated.**
▷HISTORY C16: from Latin *saturāre,* from *satur* sated, from *satis* enough
▸ **,satu'rater** *or* **,satu'rator** NOUN

saturated ('sætʃə,reɪtɪd) ADJECTIVE 1 (of a solution or solvent) containing the maximum amount of solute that can normally be dissolved at a given temperature and pressure. See also **supersaturated.** 2 (of a colour) having a large degree of saturation. 3 (of a chemical compound) **a** containing no multiple bonds and thus being incapable of undergoing additional reactions: *a saturated hydrocarbon.* **b** containing no unpaired valence electrons. 4 (of a fat, esp an animal fat) containing a high proportion of fatty acids having single bonds. See also **polyunsaturated, unsaturated.** 5 (of a vapour) containing the equilibrium amount of gaseous material at a given temperature and pressure. See also **supersaturated.** 6 (of a magnetic material) fully magnetized. 7 extremely wet; soaked.

saturation (,sætʃə'reɪʃən) NOUN 1 the act of saturating or the state of being saturated. 2 *Chem* the state of a chemical compound, solution, or vapour when it is saturated. 3 *Meteorol* the state of the atmosphere when it can hold no more water vapour at its particular temperature and pressure, the relative humidity then being 100 per cent. 4 the attribute of a colour that enables an observer to judge its proportion of pure chromatic colour. See also **colour.** 5 *Physics* the state of a ferromagnetic material in which it is fully magnetized. The magnetic domains are then all fully aligned. 6 *Electronics* the state of a valve or semiconductor device that is carrying the maximum current of which it is capable and is therefore unresponsive to further increases of input signal. 7 the level beyond which demand for a product or service is not expected to increase. ◆ MODIFIER 8 denoting the maximum possible intensity of coverage of an area: *saturation bombing; a saturation release of a film.*

saturation diving NOUN a method of diving in which divers live in a complex of decompression chambers for up to 28 days, going to work via a diving bell, and only decompressing at the end of the period. Helium is substituted for nitrogen in the air supply to avoid the narcotic effects of nitrogen.

saturation point NOUN 1 the point at which no more (people, things, ideas, etc.) can be absorbed, accommodated, used, etc. 2 *Chem* the point at which no more solute can be dissolved in a solution or gaseous material absorbed in a vapour.

Saturday ('sætədɪ) NOUN the seventh and last day of the week: the Jewish Sabbath.
▷HISTORY Old English *sæternes dæg,* translation of Latin *Sāturnī diēs* day of Saturn; compare Middle Dutch *saterdach,* Dutch *zaterdag*

Saturday night special NOUN *US informal* a small handgun that is cheap and easy to buy.

Saturn[1] ('sætɜːn) NOUN the Roman god of agriculture and vegetation. Greek counterpart: **Cronus.**

Saturn[2] ('sætɜːn) NOUN 1 one of the **giant planets,** the sixth planet from the sun, around which revolve planar concentric rings (**Saturn's rings**) consisting of small frozen particles. The planet has at least 30 satellites. Mean distance from sun: 1425 million km; period of revolution around sun: 29.41 years; period of axial rotation: 10.23 hours; equatorial diameter and mass: 9.26 and 95.3 times that of the earth, respectively. See also **Titan**[2]. 2 a large US rocket used for launching various objects, such as a spaceprobe or an Apollo spacecraft, into space. 3 the alchemical name for **lead**[2].

Saturnalia (,sætə'neɪlɪə) NOUN, *plural* **-lia** *or* **-lias.** 1 an ancient Roman festival celebrated in December: renowned for its general merrymaking. 2 (*sometimes not capital*) a period or occasion of wild revelry.
▷HISTORY C16: from Latin *Sāturnālis* relating to SATURN[1]
▸ **,Satur'nalian** ADJECTIVE

Saturnian (sæ'tɜːnɪən) ADJECTIVE 1 of or connected with the Roman god Saturn, whose reign was thought of as a golden age. 2 of or relating to the planet Saturn. 3 *Prosody* denoting a very early verse form in Latin in which the accent was one of stress rather than quantity, there being an equal number of main stresses in each line, regardless of the number of unaccented syllables. ◆ NOUN 4 a line in Saturnian metre.

saturniid (sæ'tɜːnɪɪd) NOUN 1 any moth of the mainly tropical family *Saturniidae,* typically having large brightly coloured wings: includes the emperor, cecropia, and luna moths. ◆ ADJECTIVE 2 of, relating to, or belonging to the *Saturniidae.*

saturnine ('sætə,naɪn) ADJECTIVE 1 having a gloomy temperament; taciturn. 2 *Archaic* **a** of or relating to lead. **b** having or symptomatic of lead poisoning.
▷HISTORY C15: from French *saturnin,* from Medieval Latin *sāturnīnus* (unattested), from Latin *Sāturnus* Saturn, with reference to the gloomy influence attributed to the planet Saturn
▸ **'satur,ninely** ADVERB ▸ **saturninity** (,sætə'nɪnɪtɪ) NOUN

saturnism ('sætə,nɪzəm) NOUN *Pathol* another name for **lead poisoning.**
▷HISTORY C19: from New Latin *sāturnismus;* properties similar to those of lead were attributed to the planet

satyagraha ('sɑːtjɑː,grɔːhɑː) NOUN 1 the policy of nonviolent resistance adopted by Mahatma Gandhi from about 1919 to oppose British rule in India. 2 any movement of nonviolent resistance.
▷HISTORY via Hindi from Sanskrit, literally: insistence on truth, from *satya* truth + *agraha* fervour

satyagrahi ('sʌtjə,grʌhiː) NOUN an exponent of nonviolent resistance, esp as a form of political protest.

satyr ('sætə) NOUN 1 *Greek myth* one of a class of sylvan deities, represented as goatlike men who drank and danced in the train of Dionysus and chased the nymphs. 2 a man who has strong sexual desires. 3 a man who has satyriasis. 4 any of various butterflies of the genus *Satyrus* and related genera, having dark wings often marked with eyespots: family *Satyridae.*
▷HISTORY C14: from Latin *satyrus,* from Greek *saturos*
▸ **satyric** (sə'tɪrɪk) *or* **sa'tyrical** ADJECTIVE ▸ **'satyr-,like** ADJECTIVE

satyriasis (,sætɪ'raɪəsɪs) NOUN a neurotic condition in men in which the symptoms are a compulsion to have sexual intercourse with as many women as possible and an inability to have lasting relationships with them. Compare **nymphomania.**
▷HISTORY C17: via New Latin from Greek *saturiasis;* see SATYR, -IASIS

satyrid (sə'tɪərɪd) NOUN any butterfly of the family *Satyridae,* having typically brown or dark wings with paler markings: includes the graylings, satyrs, browns, ringlets, and gatekeepers.

satyr play NOUN (in ancient Greek drama) a ribald play with a chorus of satyrs, presented at the Dionysian festival.

sauce (sɔːs) NOUN 1 any liquid or semiliquid preparation eaten with food to enhance its flavour. 2 anything that adds piquancy. 3 *US and Canadian* stewed fruit. 4 *US dialect* vegetables eaten with meat. 5 *Informal* impudent language or behaviour. ◆ VERB (*tr*) 6 to prepare (food) with sauce. 7 to add zest to. 8 to make agreeable or less severe. 9 *Informal* to be saucy to.
▷HISTORY C14: via Old French from Latin *salsus* salted, from *salīre* to sprinkle with salt, from *sal* salt
▸ **'sauceless** ADJECTIVE

sauce boat NOUN another term for **gravy boat.**

saucebox ('sɔːs,bɒks) NOUN *Informal* a saucy person.

saucepan ('sɔːspən) NOUN a metal or enamel pan with a long handle and often a lid, used for cooking food.

saucer ('sɔːsə) NOUN 1 a small round dish on which a cup is set. 2 any similar dish.
▷HISTORY C14: from Old French *saussier* container for SAUCE
▸ **'saucerful** NOUN ▸ **'saucerless** ADJECTIVE

sauch *or* **saugh** (sɔːx) NOUN a sallow or willow.
▷HISTORY C15: from Old English *salh*

saucy ('sɔːsɪ) ADJECTIVE **saucier, sauciest.** 1 impertinent. 2 pert; jaunty: *a saucy hat.*
▸ **'saucily** ADVERB ▸ **'sauciness** NOUN

Saudi ('sɔːdɪ, 'saʊ-) *or* **Saudi Arabian** ADJECTIVE 1 of or relating to Saudi Arabia or its inhabitants. ◆ NOUN 2 a native or inhabitant of Saudi Arabia.

Saudi Arabia ('sɔːdɪ, 'saʊ-) NOUN a kingdom in SW Asia, occupying most of the Arabian peninsula between the Persian Gulf and the Red Sea: founded in 1932 by Ibn Saud, who united Hejaz and Nejd; consists mostly of desert plateau; large reserves of petroleum and natural gas. Official language: Arabic. Official religion: (Sunni) Muslim. Currency: riyal. Capital: Riyadh (royal), Jidda (administrative). Pop.: 22 757 000 (2001 est.). Area: 2 260 353 sq. km (872 722 sq. miles).

sauerbraten ('saʊə,brɑːtᵊn; *German* 'zauər,braːtən) NOUN beef marinated in vinegar, sugar, and seasonings, and then braised.
▷HISTORY German, from *sauer* SOUR + *Braten* roast

sauerkraut ('saʊə,kraʊt) NOUN finely shredded and pickled cabbage.
▷HISTORY German, from *sauer* SOUR + *Kraut* cabbage

sauger ('sɔːgə) NOUN a small North American pikeperch, *Stizostedion canadense,* with a spotted dorsal fin: valued as a food and game fish.
▷HISTORY C19: of unknown origin

Saul (sɔːl) NOUN 1 *Old Testament* the first king of Israel (?1020–1000 B.C.). He led Israel successfully against the Philistines, but was in continual conflict with the high priest Samuel. He became afflicted with madness and died by his own hand; succeeded by David. 2 *New Testament* the name borne by Paul prior to his conversion (Acts 9: 1–30).

Sault Sainte Marie ('suː seɪnt mə'riː) NOUN, *usually abbreviated to* **Sault Ste Marie.** 1 an inland port in central Canada, in Ontario on the St. Mary's River, which links Lake Superior and Lake Huron, opposite Sault Ste Marie, Michigan: canal bypassing the rapids completed in 1895. Pop.: 80 054 (1996). 2 an inland port in NE Michigan, opposite Sault Ste Marie, Ontario: canal around the rapids completed in 1855, enlarged and divided in 1896 and 1919 (popularly called **Soo Canals**). Pop.: 14 689 (1990).

sauna ('sɔːnə) NOUN 1 an invigorating bath

originating in Finland in which the bather is subjected to hot steam, usually followed by a cold plunge or by being lightly beaten with birch twigs. 2 the place in which such a bath is taken.
▷HISTORY C20: from Finnish

saunter (ˈsɔːntə) VERB (*intr*) 1 to walk in a casual manner; stroll. ◆ NOUN 2 a leisurely pace or stroll. 3 a leisurely old-time dance.
▷HISTORY C17 (meaning: to wander aimlessly), C15 (to muse): of obscure origin
► ˈ**saunterer** NOUN

-saur *or* **-saurus** NOUN COMBINING FORM lizard: *dinosaur.*
▷HISTORY from New Latin *saurus*

saurel (ˈsɔːrəl) NOUN a US name for **horse mackerel** (sense 1).
▷HISTORY C19: via French from Late Latin *saurus,* from Greek *sauros,* of obscure origin

saurian (ˈsɔːrɪən) ADJECTIVE 1 of, relating to, or resembling a lizard. 2 of, relating to, or belonging to the *Sauria,* a former suborder of reptiles (now called *Lacertilia*), which included the lizards. ◆ NOUN 3 a former name for **lizard.**
▷HISTORY C15: from New Latin *Sauria,* from Greek *sauros*

saurischian (sɔːˈrɪskɪən) ADJECTIVE 1 of, relating to, or belonging to the *Saurischia,* an order of late Triassic to Cretaceous dinosaurs including the theropods and sauropods. ◆ NOUN 2 any dinosaur belonging to the order *Saurischia*; a lizard-hipped dinosaur.
▷HISTORY C19: from New Latin *Saurischia,* from *saurus* + ISCHIUM

sauropod (ˈsɔːrəˌpɒd) NOUN any herbivorous quadrupedal saurischian dinosaur of the suborder *Sauropoda,* of Jurassic and Cretaceous times, including the brontosaurus, diplodocus, and titanosaurs. They had small heads and long necks and tails and were partly amphibious.
▷HISTORY C19: from New Latin *sauropoda,* from Greek *sauros* lizard + *pous* foot
► **sauropodous** (sɔːˈrɒpədəs) ADJECTIVE

saury (ˈsɔːrɪ) NOUN, *plural* **-ries.** any teleost fish, such as the Atlantic *Scomberesox saurus* of the family *Scomberesocidae* of tropical and temperate seas, having an elongated body and long toothed jaws. Also called: **skipper.**
▷HISTORY C18: perhaps from Late Latin *saurus;* see SAUREL

sausage (ˈsɒsɪdʒ) NOUN 1 finely minced meat, esp pork or beef, mixed with fat, cereal or bread, and seasonings (**sausage meat**), and packed into a tube-shaped animal intestine or synthetic casing. 2 an object shaped like a sausage. 3 *Aeronautics, informal* a captive balloon shaped like a sausage. 4 **not a sausage.** nothing at all.
▷HISTORY C15: from Old Norman French *saussiche,* from Late Latin *salsīcia,* from Latin *salsus* salted; see SAUCE
► ˈ**sausage-ˌlike** ADJECTIVE

sausage dog NOUN an informal name for **dachshund.**

sausage roll NOUN *Brit* a roll of sausage meat in pastry.

Saussurean (səʊsˈjʊərɪən) ADJECTIVE of or relating to Ferdinand de Saussure, the Swiss linguist (1857–1913).

saut (sɔːt) NOUN, VERB, ADJECTIVE a Scot word for **salt.**

sauté (ˈsəʊteɪ) VERB **-tés, -téing** *or* **-téeing, -téed.** 1 to fry (food) quickly in a little fat. ◆ NOUN 2 a dish of sautéed food, esp meat that is browned and then cooked in a sauce. ◆ ADJECTIVE 3 sautéed until lightly brown: *sauté potatoes.*
▷HISTORY C19: from French: tossed, from *sauter* to jump, from Latin *saltāre* to dance, from *salīre* to spring

Sauternes (səʊˈtɜːn) NOUN (*sometimes not capital*) a sweet white wine made in the southern Bordeaux district of France.
▷HISTORY C18: from *Sauternes,* the district where it is produced

sauve qui peut *French* (sov ki pø) NOUN a state of panic or disorder; rout.
▷HISTORY literally: save (himself) who can

Sauvignon Blanc (ˈsəʊvɪnjɒn ˈblɒŋk) NOUN 1 a white grape grown in the Bordeaux and Loire regions of France, New Zealand, and elsewhere, used for making wine. 2 any of various white wines made from this grape.

sav (sæv) NOUN *Austral and NZ informal* short for **saveloy.**

Sava (ˈsɑːvə) *or* **Save** (sɑːv) NOUN a river in SE Europe, rising in NW Slovenia and flowing east and south to the Danube at Belgrade. Length: 940 km (584 miles).

savage (ˈsævɪdʒ) ADJECTIVE 1 wild; untamed: *savage beasts of the jungle.* 2 ferocious in temper; vicious: *a savage dog.* 3 uncivilized; crude: *savage behaviour.* 4 (of peoples) nonliterate or primitive: *a savage tribe.* 5 (of terrain) rugged and uncultivated. 6 *Obsolete* far from human habitation. ◆ NOUN 7 a member of a nonliterate society, esp one regarded as primitive. 8 a crude or uncivilized person. 9 a fierce or vicious person or animal. ◆ VERB (*tr*) 10 to criticize violently. 11 to attack ferociously and wound: *the dog savaged the child.*
▷HISTORY C13: from Old French *sauvage,* from Latin *silvāticus* belonging to a wood, from *silva* a wood
► ˈ**savagedom** NOUN ► ˈ**savagely** ADVERB ► ˈ**savageness** NOUN

Savage Island NOUN another name for **Niue.**

savagery (ˈsævɪdʒrɪ) NOUN, *plural* **-ries.** 1 an uncivilized condition. 2 a savage act or nature. 3 savages collectively.

Savaii (sɑːˈvaɪiː) NOUN the largest island in Samoa: mountainous and volcanic. Pop.: 45 050 (1991). Area: 1174 sq. km (662 sq. miles).

savanna *or* **savannah** (səˈvænə) NOUN open grasslands, usually with scattered bushes or trees, characteristic of much of tropical Africa.
▷HISTORY C16: from Spanish *zavana,* from Taino *zabana*

Savannah (səˈvænə) NOUN 1 a port in the US, in E Georgia, near the mouth of the Savannah River: port of departure of the *Savannah* for Liverpool (1819), the first steamship to cross the Atlantic. Pop.: 131 510 (2000). 2 a river in the southeastern US, formed by the confluence of the Tugaloo and Seneca Rivers in NW South Carolina: flows southeast to the Atlantic. Length: 505 km (314 miles).

savant (ˈsævənt; *French* savɑ̃) NOUN a man of great learning; sage.
▷HISTORY C18: from French, from *savoir* to know, from Latin *sapere* to be wise; see SAPIENT
► ˈ**savante** FEMININE NOUN

savate (səˈvæt) NOUN a form of boxing in which blows may be delivered with the feet as well as the hands.
▷HISTORY C19: from French, literally: old worn-out shoe; related to SABOT

save[1] (seɪv) VERB 1 (*tr*) to rescue, preserve, or guard (a person or thing) from danger or harm. 2 to avoid the spending, waste, or loss of (money, possessions, etc.). 3 (*tr*) to deliver from sin; redeem. 4 (often foll by *up*) to set aside or reserve (money, goods, etc.) for future use. 5 (*tr*) to treat with care so as to avoid or lessen wear or degeneration: *use a good light to save your eyes.* 6 (*tr*) to prevent the necessity for; obviate the trouble of: *good work now will save future revision.* 7 (*tr*) *Sport* to prevent (a goal) by stopping (a struck ball or puck). 8 (*intr*) *Chiefly US* (of food) to admit of preservation; keep. ◆ NOUN 9 *Sport* the act of saving a goal. 10 *Computing* an instruction to write information from the memory onto a tape or disk.
▷HISTORY C13: from Old French *salver,* via Late Latin from Latin *salvus* safe
► ˈ**savable** *or* ˈ**saveable** ADJECTIVE ► ˈ**savableness** *or* ˈ**saveableness** NOUN ► ˈ**saver** NOUN

save[2] (seɪv) *Archaic or literary* ◆ PREPOSITION 1 (often foll by *for*) Also: **saving.** with the exception of. ◆ CONJUNCTION 2 but; except.
▷HISTORY C13 *sauf,* from Old French, from Latin *salvō,* from *salvus* safe

save-all NOUN 1 a device to prevent waste or loss. 2 *Nautical* **a** a net used while loading a ship. **b** a light sail set to catch wind spilling from another sail. 3 *Dialect* overalls or a pinafore. 4 *Brit* a dialect word for **miser.**

save as you earn NOUN (in Britain) a savings scheme operated by the government, in which monthly contributions earn tax-free interest. Abbreviation: **SAYE.**

saveloy (ˈsævɪˌlɔɪ) NOUN a smoked sausage made from salted pork, well seasoned and coloured red with saltpetre.
▷HISTORY C19: probably via French from Italian *cervellato,* from *cervello* brain, from Latin *cerebellum,* diminutive of *cerebrum* brain

savin *or* **savine** (ˈsævɪn) NOUN 1 a small spreading juniper bush, *Juniperus sabina,* of Europe, N Asia, and North America. 2 the oil derived from the shoots and leaves of this plant, formerly used in medicine to treat rheumatism, etc. 3 another name for **red cedar** (sense 1).
▷HISTORY C14: from Old French *savine,* from Latin *herba Sabīna* the Sabine plant

saving (ˈseɪvɪŋ) ADJECTIVE 1 tending to save or preserve. 2 redeeming or compensating (esp in the phrase **saving grace**). 3 thrifty or economical. 4 *Law* denoting or relating to an exception or reservation: *a saving clause in an agreement.* ◆ NOUN 5 preservation or redemption, esp from loss or danger. 6 economy or avoidance of waste. 7 reduction in cost or expenditure: *a saving of 20p.* 8 anything saved. 9 (*plural*) money saved for future use. 10 *Law* an exception or reservation. ◆ PREPOSITION 11 with the exception of. ◆ CONJUNCTION 12 except.
► ˈ**savingly** ADVERB

savings account NOUN an account at a bank that accumulates interest.

savings and loan association NOUN a US name for a **building society.**

savings bank NOUN 1 a bank that accepts the savings of depositors and pays interest on them. 2 a container, usually having a slot in the top, for saving coins.

savings ratio NOUN *Economics* the ratio of personal savings to disposable income, esp using the difference between national figures for disposable income and consumer spending as a measure of savings.

saviour *or US* **savior** (ˈseɪvjə) NOUN a person who rescues another person or a thing from danger or harm.
▷HISTORY C13 *saveour,* from Old French, from Church Latin *Salvātor* the Saviour; see SAVE[1]

Saviour *or US* **Savior** (ˈseɪvjə) NOUN *Christianity* Jesus Christ regarded as the saviour of men from sin.

Savoie (*French* savwa) NOUN 1 a department of E France, in Rhône-Alpes region. Capital: Chambéry. Pop.: 373 258 (1999). Area: 6188 sq. km (2413 sq. miles). 2 the French name for **Savoy.**

savoir-faire (ˈsævwɑːˈfɛə) NOUN the ability to do the right thing in any situation.
▷HISTORY French, literally: a knowing how to do

savoir-vivre (ˈsævwɑːˈviːvrə) NOUN familiarity with the customs of good society; breeding.
▷HISTORY French, literally: a knowing how to live

Savona (*Italian* saˈvoːna) NOUN a port in NW Italy, in Liguria on the Mediterranean: an important centre of the Italian iron and steel industry. Pop.: 69 806 (1990).

savory (ˈseɪvərɪ) NOUN, *plural* **-vories.** 1 any of numerous aromatic plants of the genus *Satureja,* esp *S. montana* (**winter savory**) and *S. hortensis* (**summer savory**), of the Mediterranean region, having narrow leaves and white, pink, or purple flowers: family *Lamiaceae* (labiates). 2 the leaves of any of these plants, used as a potherb.
▷HISTORY C14: probably from Old English *sætherie,* from Latin *saturēia,* of obscure origin

savour *or US* **savor** (ˈseɪvə) NOUN 1 the quality in a substance that is perceived by the sense of taste or smell. 2 a specific taste or smell: *the savour of lime.* 3 a slight but distinctive quality or trace. 4 the power to excite interest: *the savour of wit has been lost.* 5 *Archaic* reputation. ◆ VERB 6 (*intr;* often foll by *of*) to possess the taste or smell (of). 7 (*intr;* often foll by *of*) to have a suggestion (of). 8 (*tr*) to give a taste to; season. 9 (*tr*) to taste or smell, esp appreciatively. 10 (*tr*) to relish or enjoy.
▷HISTORY C13: from Old French *savour,* from Latin *sapor* taste, from *sapere* to taste
► ˈ**savourless** *or US* ˈ**savorless** ADJECTIVE ► ˈ**savorous** ADJECTIVE

savoury *or US* **savory** (ˈseɪvərɪ) ADJECTIVE 1 attractive to the sense of taste or smell. 2 salty or spicy; not sweet: *a savoury dish.* 3 pleasant. 4

respectable. ◆ NOUN, *plural* **-vouries.** [5] a savoury dish served as an hors d'oeuvre or dessert.
▷HISTORY C13 *savure,* from Old French *savouré,* from *savourer* to SAVOUR
▸ **'savourily** *or US* **'savorily** ADVERB ▸ **'savouriness** *or US* **'savoriness** NOUN

savoy (sə'vɔɪ) NOUN a cultivated variety of cabbage, *Brassica oleracea capitata,* having a compact head and wrinkled leaves.
▷HISTORY C16: named after the SAVOY region

Savoy (sə'vɔɪ) NOUN an area of SE France, bordering on Italy, mainly in the Savoy Alps: a duchy in the late Middle Ages and part of the Kingdom of Sardinia from 1720 to 1860, when it became part of France. French name: **Savoie.**

Savoy Alps PLURAL NOUN a range of the Alps in SE France. Highest peak: Mont Blanc, 4807 m (15 772 ft.).

Savoyard[1] (sə'vɔɪɑːd; *French* savwajar) NOUN [1] a native of Savoy. [2] the dialect of French spoken in Savoy. ◆ ADJECTIVE [3] of or relating to Savoy, its inhabitants, or their dialect.

Savoyard[2] (sə'vɔɪɑːd) NOUN [1] a person keenly interested in the operettas of Gilbert and Sullivan. [2] a person who takes part in these operettas.
▷HISTORY C20: from the *Savoy* Theatre, built in London in 1881 by Richard D'Oyly Carte for the presentation of operettas by Gilbert and Sullivan

savvy ('sævɪ) *Slang* ◆ VERB **-vies, -vying, -vied.** [1] to understand or get the sense of (an idea, etc.). [2] **no savvy.** I don't (he doesn't, etc.) understand. ◆ NOUN [3] comprehension. ◆ ADJECTIVE **-vier, -viest.** [4] *Chiefly US* shrewd; well-informed.
▷HISTORY C18: corruption of Spanish *sabe(usted)* (you) know, from *saber* to know, from Latin *sapere* to be wise

saw[1] (sɔː) NOUN [1] any of various hand tools for cutting wood, metal, etc., having a blade with teeth along one edge. [2] any of various machines or devices for cutting by use of a toothed blade, such as a power-driven circular toothed wheel or toothed band of metal. ◆ VERB **saws, sawing, sawed; sawed** *or* **sawn.** [3] to cut with a saw. [4] to form by sawing. [5] to cut as if wielding a saw: *to saw the air.* [6] to move (an object) from side to side as if moving a saw.
▷HISTORY Old English *sagu;* related to Old Norse *sog,* Old High German *saga,* Latin *secāre* to cut, *secūris* axe
▸ **'sawer** NOUN ▸ **'saw,like** ADJECTIVE

saw[2] (sɔː) VERB the past tense of **see.**

saw[3] (sɔː) NOUN a wise saying, maxim, or proverb.
▷HISTORY Old English *sagu* a saying; related to SAGA

SAW ABBREVIATION FOR **surface acoustic wave.**

sawbill ('sɔː,bɪl) NOUN [1] another name for **merganser** or **motmot.** [2] any of various hummingbirds of the genus *Ramphodon.*
▷HISTORY C19: so called because of their serrated bills

sawbones ('sɔː,bəʊnz) NOUN, *plural* **-bones** *or* **-boneses.** *Slang* a surgeon or doctor.

sawbuck ('sɔː,bʌk) NOUN [1] *US and Canadian* a sawhorse, esp one having an X-shaped supporting structure. [2] *Chiefly US and Canadian slang* a ten-dollar bill.
▷HISTORY C19: (in the sense: sawhorse) translated from Dutch *zaagbok;* (in the sense: ten-dollar bill) from the legs of a sawbuck forming the Roman numeral X

sawder ('sɔːdə) *Informal* ◆ NOUN [1] flattery; compliments (esp in the phrase **soft sawder**). ◆ VERB (*tr*) [2] to flatter.
▷HISTORY C19: metaphorical use of variant of SOLDER

saw doctor NOUN *NZ* a sawmill specialist who sharpens and services saw blades.

sawdust ('sɔː,dʌst) NOUN particles of wood formed by sawing.

sawfish ('sɔː,fɪʃ) NOUN, *plural* **-fish** *or* **-fishes.** any sharklike ray of the family *Pristidae* of subtropical coastal waters and estuaries, having a serrated bladelike mouth.

sawfly ('sɔː,flaɪ) NOUN, *plural* **-flies.** any of various hymenopterous insects of the family *Tenthredinidae* and related families, the females of which have a sawlike ovipositor.

sawhorse ('sɔː,hɔːs) NOUN a stand for timber during sawing.

sawmill ('sɔː,mɪl) NOUN [1] an industrial establishment where timber is sawn into planks, etc. [2] a large sawing machine.

sawn (sɔːn) VERB a past participle of **saw.**

Sawney ('sɔːnɪ) NOUN [1] a derogatory word for **Scotsman.** [2] (*also not capital*) *Informal* a fool.
▷HISTORY C18: a Scots variant of *Sandy,* short for *Alexander*

sawn-off *or esp US* **sawed-off** ADJECTIVE [1] (*prenominal*) (of a shotgun) having the barrel cut short, mainly to facilitate concealment of the weapon. [2] *Informal* (of a person) small in stature.

saw-off *or Canadian* NOUN [1] a deadlock or stalemate. [2] a compromise.

saw palmetto NOUN any of several dwarf prickly palms, esp any of the genus *Sabal,* of the southeastern US.

saw-pit NOUN (esp formerly) a pit above which a log is sawn into planks with a large pitsaw.

saw set NOUN a tool used for setting the teeth of a saw, consisting of a type of clamp used to bend each tooth in turn at a slight angle to the plane of the saw, alternate teeth being bent in the same direction.

sawtooth ('sɔː,tuːθ) ADJECTIVE [1] (of a waveform) having an amplitude that varies linearly with time between two values, the interval in one direction often being much greater than the other. [2] having or generating such a waveform.

saw-wort ('sɔː,wɜːt) NOUN a perennial Old World plant, *Serratula tinctoria,* having serrated leaves that yield a yellow dye: family *Asteraceae* (composites).

sawyer ('sɔːjə) NOUN a person who saws timber for a living.
▷HISTORY C14 *sawier,* from SAW[1] + *-ier,* variant of -ER[1]

sax[1] (sæks) NOUN a tool resembling a small axe, used for cutting roofing slate.
▷HISTORY Old English *seax* knife; related to Old Saxon *sahs,* Old Norse *sax*

sax[2] (sæks) NOUN *Informal* short for **saxophone.**

saxatile ('sæksə,taɪl; *as specific name* sæk'sætɪlɪ) ADJECTIVE growing on or living among rocks.
▷HISTORY C17: from Latin *saxitilis,* from *saxum* rock

Saxe (saks) NOUN the French name for **Saxony.**

saxe blue (sæks) NOUN **a** a light greyish-blue colour. **b** (*as adjective*): *a saxe-blue dress.*
▷HISTORY C19: from French *Saxe* Saxony, source of a dye of this colour

saxhorn ('sæks,hɔːn) NOUN a valved brass instrument used chiefly in brass and military bands, having a tube of conical bore and a brilliant tone colour. It resembles the tuba and constitutes a family of instruments related to the flugelhorn and cornet.
▷HISTORY C19: named after Adolphe *Sax* (see SAXOPHONE), who invented it (1845)

saxicolous (sæk'sɪkələs) ADJECTIVE living on or among rocks: *saxicolous plants.* Also: **saxicole, saxatile** ('sæksə,taɪl).
▷HISTORY C19: from New Latin *saxicolus,* from Latin *saxum* rock + *colere* to dwell

saxifragaceous (,sæksɪfrə'geɪʃəs) ADJECTIVE of, relating to, or belonging to the *Saxifragaceae,* a chiefly arctic and alpine family of plants having a basal rosette or cushion of leaves and small but showy flowers: includes saxifrage.

saxifrage ('sæksɪ,freɪdʒ) NOUN any saxifragaceous plant of the genus *Saxifraga,* having smallish white, yellow, purple, or pink flowers.
▷HISTORY C15: from Late Latin *saxifraga,* literally: rock-breaker (probably alluding to its ability to dissolve kidney stones), from Latin *saxum* rock + *frangere* to break

Saxon ('sæksən) NOUN [1] a member of a West Germanic people who in Roman times spread from Schleswig across NW Germany to the Rhine. Saxons raided and settled parts of S Britain in the fifth and sixth centuries A.D. In Germany they established a duchy and other dominions, which changed and shifted through the centuries, usually retaining the name Saxony. [2] a native or inhabitant of Saxony. [3] **a** the Low German dialect of Saxony. **b** any of the West Germanic dialects spoken by the ancient Saxons or their descendants. ◆ ADJECTIVE [4] of, relating to, or characteristic of the ancient Saxons, the Anglo-Saxons, or their descendants. [5] of, relating to, or characteristic of Saxony, its inhabitants, or their Low German dialect. ◆ See also **West Saxon, Anglo-Saxon.**
▷HISTORY C13 (replacing Old English *Seaxe*): via Old French from Late Latin *Saxon-, Saxo,* from Greek; of Germanic origin and perhaps related to the name of a knife used by the Saxons; compare SAW[1]

Saxon blue NOUN a dye made by dissolving indigo in a solution of sulphuric acid.
▷HISTORY C19: named after SAXONY, where it originated

saxony ('sæksənɪ) NOUN [1] a fine 3-ply yarn used for knitting and weaving. [2] a fine woollen fabric used for coats, etc.
▷HISTORY C19: named after SAXONY, where it was produced

Saxony ('sæksənɪ) NOUN [1] a state in E Germany, formerly part of East Germany. Pop.: 4 459 700 (2000 est.). [2] a former duchy and electorate in SE and central Germany, whose territory changed greatly over the centuries. [3] (in the early Middle Ages) any territory inhabited or ruled by Saxons. ◆ Compare **Saxony-Anhalt, Lower Saxony.** German name: **Sachsen.** French name: **Saxe.**

Saxony-Anhalt ('sæksənɪ 'ɑːnhɑːlt) NOUN a state of E Germany: created in 1947 from the state of Anhalt and those parts of Prussia formerly ruled by the duchy of Saxony: part of East Germany until 1990. Pop.: 2 648 700 (2000 est.).

saxophone ('sæksə,fəʊn) NOUN a keyed wind instrument of mellow tone colour, used mainly in jazz and dance music. It is made in various sizes, has a conical bore, and a single reed. Often shortened to: **sax.**
▷HISTORY C19: named after Adolphe *Sax* (1814–94), Belgian musical-instrument maker, who invented it (1846)
▸ **saxophonic** (,sæksə'fɒnɪk) ADJECTIVE ▸ **saxophonist** (sæk'sɒfənɪst) NOUN

say[1] (seɪ) VERB **says** (sɛz), **saying, said.** (*mainly tr*) [1] to speak, pronounce, or utter. [2] (*also intr*) to express (an idea) in words; tell: *we asked his opinion but he refused to say.* [3] (*also intr; may take a clause as object*) to state (an opinion, fact, etc.) positively; declare; affirm. [4] to recite: *to say grace.* [5] (*may take a clause as object*) to report or allege: *they say we shall have rain today.* [6] (*may take a clause as object*) to take as an assumption; suppose: *let us say that he is lying.* [7] (*may take a clause as object*) to convey by means of artistic expression: *the artist in this painting is saying that we should look for hope.* [8] to make a case for: *there is much to be said for either course of action.* [9] (*usually passive*) *Irish* to persuade or coax (someone) to do something: *If I hadn't been said by her I wouldn't be in this fix.* [10] **go without saying.** to be so obvious as to need no explanation. [11] **I say!** *Chiefly Brit informal* an exclamation of surprise. [12] **not to say.** even; and indeed. [13] **that is to say.** in other words; more explicitly. [14] **to say nothing of.** as well as; even disregarding: *he was warmly dressed in a shirt and heavy jumper, to say nothing of a thick overcoat.* [15] **to say the least.** without the slightest exaggeration; at the very least. ◆ ADVERB [16] approximately: *there were, say, 20 people present.* [17] for example: *choose a number, say, four.* ◆ NOUN [18] the right or chance to speak: *let him have his say.* [19] authority, esp to influence a decision: *he has a lot of say in the company's policy.* [20] a statement of opinion: *you've had your say, now let me have mine.* ◆ INTERJECTION [21] *US and Canadian informal* an exclamation to attract attention or express surprise, etc.
▷HISTORY Old English *secgan;* related to Old Norse *segja,* Old Saxon *seggian,* Old High German *sagēn*
▸ **'sayer** NOUN

say[2] (seɪ) NOUN *Archaic* a type of fine woollen fabric.
▷HISTORY C13: from Old French *saie,* from Latin *saga,* plural of *sagum* a type of woollen cloak

Sayan Mountains (sɑː'jæn) PLURAL NOUN a mountain range in S central Russia, in S Siberia. Highest peak: Munku-Sardyk, 3437 m (11 457 ft.).

Saybolt universal seconds ('seɪ,bəʊlt) NOUN (*functioning as singular*) a US measurement of viscosity similar in type to the British Redwood seconds.
▷HISTORY named after G. M. *Saybolt* (died 1924), US chemist, who proposed it

SAYE ABBREVIATION FOR **save as you earn.**

saying (ˈseɪɪŋ) NOUN a maxim, adage, or proverb.

say-so NOUN *Informal* [1] an arbitrary assertion. [2] an authoritative decision. [3] the authority to make a final decision.

sayyid, sayid (ˈsaɪɪd), *or* **said** NOUN [1] a Muslim claiming descent from Mohammed's grandson Husain. [2] a Muslim honorary title.
▷HISTORY C17: from Arabic: lord

sazerac (ˈsæzəˌræk) NOUN *US* a mixed drink of whisky, Pernod, syrup, bitters, and lemon.
▷HISTORY C20: of uncertain origin

sb THE INTERNET DOMAIN NAME FOR Solomon Islands.

Sb THE CHEMICAL SYMBOL FOR antimony.
▷HISTORY from New Latin *stibium*

sb. ABBREVIATION FOR substantive.

SBA ABBREVIATION FOR standard beam approach: a radar navigation system that gives lateral guidance to aircraft when landing.

SBE ABBREVIATION FOR Southern British English.

SBS ABBREVIATION FOR **Special Boat Service**.

SBU ABBREVIATION FOR strategic business unit: a division within an organization responsible for marketing its own range of products.

sc[1] *Printing* ABBREVIATION FOR small capitals.

sc[2] THE INTERNET DOMAIN NAME FOR Seychelles.

Sc THE CHEMICAL SYMBOL FOR scandium.

SC ABBREVIATION FOR: [1] Signal Corps. [2] South Carolina. [3] (in Canada) Star of Courage.

sc. ABBREVIATION FOR: [1] scene. [2] scilicet.

scab (skæb) NOUN [1] the dried crusty surface of a healing skin wound or sore. [2] a contagious disease of sheep, a form of mange, caused by a mite (*Psoroptes communis*). [3] a fungal disease of plants characterized by crusty spots on the fruits, leaves, etc. [4] *Derogatory* **a** Also called: **blackleg.** a person who refuses to support a trade union's actions, esp one who replaces a worker who is on strike. **b** (*as modifier*): *scab labour*. [5] a despicable person. ◆ VERB **scabs, scabbing, scabbed**. (*intr*) [6] to become covered with a scab. [7] (of a road surface) to become loose so that potholes develop. [8] to replace a striking worker.
▷HISTORY Old English *sceabb;* related to Old Norse *skabb*, Latin *scabiēs*, Middle Low German *schabbe* scoundrel, German *schäbig* SHABBY
▸ˈ**scabˌlike** ADJECTIVE

scabbard (ˈskæbəd) NOUN a holder for a bladed weapon such as a sword or bayonet; sheath.
▷HISTORY C13 *scauberc*, from Norman French *escaubers* (pl), of Germanic origin; related to Old High German *skār* blade and *bergan* to protect

scabbard fish NOUN any of various marine spiny-finned fishes of the family *Trichiuridae*, esp of the genus *Lepidopus*, having a long whiplike scaleless body and long sharp teeth: most common in warm waters.

scabble (ˈskæbᵊl) VERB (*tr*) to shape (stone) roughly.
▷HISTORY C17: from earlier *scapple*, from French *escapler* to shape (timber)

scabby (ˈskæbɪ) ADJECTIVE **-bier, -biest**. [1] *Pathol* having an area of the skin covered with scabs. [2] *Pathol, obsolete* having scabies. [3] *Informal* despicable.
▸ˈ**scabbily** ADVERB ▸ˈ**scabbiness** NOUN

scabies (ˈskeɪbiːz, -bɪˌiːz) NOUN a contagious skin infection caused by the mite *Sarcoptes scabiei*, characterized by intense itching, inflammation, and the formation of vesicles and pustules.
▷HISTORY C15: from Latin: scurf, from *scabere* to scratch; see SHAVE
▸**scabietic** (ˌskeɪbɪˈɛtɪk) ADJECTIVE

scabious[1] (ˈskeɪbɪəs) ADJECTIVE [1] having or covered with scabs. [2] of, relating to, or resembling scabies.
▷HISTORY C17: from Latin *scabiōsus*, from SCABIES

scabious[2] (ˈskeɪbɪəs) NOUN [1] any plant of the genus *Scabiosa*, esp *S. atropurpurea*, of the Mediterranean region, having blue, red, or whitish dome-shaped flower heads: family *Dipsacaceae*. [2] any of various similar plants of the related genus *Knautia*. [3] **devil's bit scabious.** a similar and related Eurasian marsh plant, *Succisa pratensis*.
▷HISTORY C14: from Medieval Latin *scabiōsa herba* the scabies plant, referring to its use in treating scabies

scablands (ˈskæbˌlændz) PLURAL NOUN a type of terrain, found for example in the NW US, consisting of bare rock surfaces, with little or no soil cover and scanty vegetation, that have been deeply channelled by glacial flood waters.

scabrid (ˈskæbrɪd) ADJECTIVE having a rough or scaly surface.
▷HISTORY C19: see SCABROUS
▸**scabridity** (skəˈbrɪdɪtɪ) NOUN

scabrous (ˈskeɪbrəs) ADJECTIVE [1] roughened because of small projections; scaly. [2] indelicate, indecent, or salacious: *scabrous humour*. [3] difficult to deal with; knotty.
▷HISTORY C17: from Latin *scaber* rough; related to SCABIES
▸ˈ**scabrously** ADVERB ▸ˈ**scabrousness** NOUN

scad (skæd) NOUN, *plural* **scad** *or* **scads**. any of various carangid fishes of the genus *Trachurus*, esp the horse mackerel.
▷HISTORY C17: of uncertain origin; compare Swedish *skädde* flounder

scads (skædz) PLURAL NOUN *Informal* a large amount or number.
▷HISTORY C19: of uncertain origin

Scafell Pike (skɔːˈfɛl) NOUN a mountain in NW England, in Cumbria in the Lake District: the highest peak in England. Height: 978 m (3209 ft.).

scaffold (ˈskæfəld, -fəʊld) NOUN [1] a temporary metal or wooden framework that is used to support workmen and materials during the erection, repair, etc., of a building or other construction. [2] a raised wooden platform on which plays are performed, tobacco, etc., is dried, or (esp formerly) criminals are executed. ◆ VERB (*tr*) [3] to provide with a scaffold. [4] to support by means of a scaffold.
▷HISTORY C14: from Old French *eschaffaut*, from Vulgar Latin *catafalicum* (unattested); see CATAFALQUE
▸ˈ**scaffolder** NOUN

scaffolding (ˈskæfəldɪŋ) NOUN [1] a scaffold or system of scaffolds. [2] the building materials used to make scaffolds.

scag[1] *or* **skag** (skæg) NOUN a slang name for **heroin.**

scag[2] (skæg) *South Wales and southwest English dialect* ◆ NOUN [1] a tear in a garment or piece of cloth. ◆ VERB **scags, scagging, scagged**. [2] (*tr*) to make a tear in (cloth).
▷HISTORY apparently related to Old Norse *skaga* to project

scagliola (skælˈjəʊlə) NOUN imitation marble made of glued gypsum with a polished surface of coloured stone or marble dust.
▷HISTORY C16: from Italian, diminutive of *scaglia* chip of marble, of Germanic origin; related to SHALE, SCALE[2]

Scala (ˈskaːla) NOUN **La**. See **La Scala.**

scalable (ˈskeɪləbᵊl) ADJECTIVE [1] capable of being scaled or climbed. [2] *Computing* (of a network) able to be expanded to cope with increased use.
▸ˈ**scalableness** NOUN ▸ˈ**scalably** ADVERB

scalade (skəˈleɪd) *or* **scalado** (skəˈleɪdəʊ) NOUN, *plural* **-lades** *or* **-lados**. short for **escalade.**
▷HISTORY C16: from Old Italian *scalada*, from *scala* a ladder; see SCALE[3]

scalage (ˈskeɪlɪdʒ) NOUN [1] *US* a percentage deducted from the price of goods liable to shrink or leak. [2] *Forestry, US and Canadian* the estimated amount of usable timber in a log.
▷HISTORY C19: from SCALE[3] + -AGE

scalar (ˈskeɪlə) NOUN [1] a quantity, such as time or temperature, that has magnitude but not direction. Compare **vector** (sense 1), **tensor** (sense 2), **pseudoscalar, pseudovector.** [2] *Maths* an element of a field associated with a vector space. ◆ ADJECTIVE [3] having magnitude but not direction.
▷HISTORY C17 (meaning: resembling a ladder): from Latin *scālāris*, from *scāla* ladder

scalare (skəˈlɛərɪ) NOUN another name for **angelfish** (sense 2).
▷HISTORY C19: from Latin *scālāris* of a ladder, SCALAR, referring to the runglike pattern on its body

scalariform (skəˈlærɪˌfɔːm) ADJECTIVE *Biology* resembling a ladder: *a scalariform cell.*
▷HISTORY C19: from New Latin *scālāriformis* from Latin *scālāris* of a ladder + -FORM

scalar multiplication NOUN *Maths* an operation used in the definition of a vector space in which the product of a scalar and a vector is a vector, the operation is distributive over the addition of both scalars and vectors, and is associative with multiplication of scalars.

scalar product NOUN the product of two vectors to form a scalar, whose value is the product of the magnitudes of the vectors and the cosine of the angle between them. Written: ***A.B*** or ***AB***. Compare **vector product.** Also called: **dot product.**

scalawag (ˈskæləˌwæg) NOUN a variant of **scallywag.**

scald[1] (skɔːld) VERB [1] to burn or be burnt with or as if with hot liquid or steam. [2] (*tr*) to subject to the action of boiling water, esp so as to sterilize. [3] (*tr*) to heat (a liquid) almost to boiling point. [4] (*tr*) to plunge (tomatoes, peaches, etc.) into boiling water briefly in order to skin them more easily. ◆ NOUN [5] the act or result of scalding. [6] an abnormal condition in plants, characterized by discoloration and wrinkling of the skin of the fruits, caused by exposure to excessive sunlight, gases, etc.
▷HISTORY C13: via Old Norman French from Late Latin *excaldāre* to wash in warm water, from *calida* (*aqua*) warm (water), from *calēre* to be warm
▸ˈ**scalder** NOUN

scald[2] (skɔːld) NOUN a variant spelling of **skald.**

scald[3] (skɔːld) *Obsolete* ◆ ADJECTIVE *also* **scalled.** [1] scabby. ◆ NOUN [2] a scab or a skin disease producing scabs.
▷HISTORY C16: from SCALL

scald-crow NOUN *Irish* another name for **hooded crow.**

scaldfish (ˈskɔːldˌfɪʃ, ˈskɑːld-) NOUN, *plural* **-fish** *or* **-fishes**. a small European flatfish, *Arnoglossus laterna*, covered with large fragile scales: family *Bothidae*.
▷HISTORY C19: from SCALD[3]

scale[1] (skeɪl) NOUN [1] any of the numerous plates, made of various substances resembling enamel or dentine, covering the bodies of fishes. [2] **a** any of the horny or chitinous plates covering a part or the entire body of certain reptiles and mammals. **b** any of the numerous minute structures covering the wings of lepidoptera. Related adjective: **squamous.** [3] a thin flat piece or flake. [4] a thin flake of dead epidermis shed from the skin: excessive shedding may be the result of a skin disease. [5] a specialized leaf or bract, esp the protective covering of a bud or the dry membranous bract of a catkin. [6] See **scale insect.** [7] a flaky black oxide of iron formed on the surface of iron or steel at high temperatures. [8] any oxide formed on a metal during heat treatment. [9] another word for **limescale.** ◆ VERB [10] (*tr*) to remove the scales or coating from. [11] to peel off or cause to peel off in flakes or scales. [12] (*intr*) to shed scales. [13] to cover or become covered with scales, incrustation, etc. [14] (*tr*) to throw (a disc or thin flat object) edgewise through the air or along the surface of water. [15] (*intr*) *Austral informal* to ride on public transport without paying a fare.
▷HISTORY C14: from Old French *escale*, of Germanic origin; compare Old English *scealu* SHELL
▸ˈ**scaleˌlike** ADJECTIVE

scale[2] (skeɪl) NOUN [1] (*often plural*) a machine or device for weighing. [2] one of the pans of a balance. [3] **tip the scales. a** to exercise a decisive influence. **b** (foll by *at*) to amount in weight (to). ◆ VERB (*tr*) [4] to weigh with or as if with scales. [5] to have a weight of.
▷HISTORY C13: from Old Norse *skāl* bowl, related to Old High German *scāla* cup, Old English *scealu* SHELL, SCALE[1]

scale[3] (skeɪl) NOUN [1] a sequence of marks either at regular intervals or else representing equal steps used as a reference in making measurements. [2] a measuring instrument having such a scale. [3] **a** the ratio between the size of something real and that of a model or representation of it: *the scale of the map was so large that we could find our house on it.* **b** (*as modifier*): *a scale model.* [4] a line, numerical ratio, etc., for showing this ratio. [5] a progressive or graduated table of things, wages, etc., in order of size, value, etc.: *a wage scale for carpenters.* [6] an established measure or standard. [7] a relative degree or extent: *he entertained on a grand scale.* [8] *Music* a group of notes taken in ascending or descending order, esp within the compass of one octave. [9] *Maths* the notation of a given number system: *the decimal scale.* [10] a graded series of tests

measuring mental development, etc. 11 *Obsolete* a ladder or staircase. ◆ VERB 12 to climb to the top of (a height) by or as if by a ladder. 13 (*tr*) to make or draw (a model, plan, etc.) according to a particular ratio of proportionate reduction. 14 (*tr; usually foll by up or down*) to increase or reduce proportionately in size, etc. 15 *US and Canadian* (in forestry) to estimate the board footage of (standing timber or logs). ◆ See also **scale back.**
▷HISTORY C15: via Italian from Latin *scāla* ladder; related to Old French *eschiele,* Spanish *escala*

scale back VERB (*adverb*) to reduce or make a reduction in the level of activity, extent, numbers, etc.

scaleboard ('skeɪl,bɔːd, 'skæbəd) NOUN a very thin piece of board, used for backing a picture, as a veneer, etc.

scale insect NOUN any small homopterous insect of the family *Coccidae* and related families, which typically live and feed on plants and secrete a protective scale around themselves. Many species, such as the San Jose scale, are important pests.

scale leaf NOUN 1 *Botany* a modified leaf, often small and membranous, protecting buds, etc. 2 any of the leaves of some conifers, such as cypresses, that are small and tightly pressed to the stem.

scale moss NOUN any of various leafy liverworts of the order *Jungermanniales,* which resemble mosses.

scalene ('skeɪliːn) ADJECTIVE 1 *Maths* (of a triangle) having all sides of unequal length. 2 *Anatomy* of or relating to any of the scalenus muscles.
▷HISTORY C17: from Late Latin *scalēnus* with unequal sides, from Greek *skalēnos*

scalenus (skəˈliːnəs, skeɪ-) NOUN, *plural* **-ni** (-naɪ). *Anatomy* any one of the three muscles situated on each side of the neck extending from the cervical vertebrae to the first or second pair of ribs.
▷HISTORY C18: from New Latin; see SCALENE

scaler ('skeɪlə) NOUN 1 a person or thing that scales. 2 Also called: **counter, scaling circuit.** an electronic device or circuit that aggregates electric pulses and gives a single output pulse for a predetermined number of input pulses.

Scales (skeɪlz) NOUN **the.** the constellation Libra, the seventh sign of the zodiac.

scaling ladder NOUN a ladder used to climb high walls, esp one used formerly to enter a besieged town, fortress, etc.

scall (skɔːl) NOUN *Pathol* a former term for any of various diseases of the scalp characterized by itching and scab formation.
▷HISTORY C14: from Old Norse *skalli* bald head. Compare SKULL
▸**scalled** ADJECTIVE

scallion ('skæljən) NOUN any of various onions or similar plants, such as the spring onion, that have a small bulb and long leaves and are eaten in salads. Also called: **green onion.**
▷HISTORY C14: from Anglo-French *scalun,* from Latin *Ascalōnia (caepa)* Ascalonian (onion), from *Ascalo* Ascalon, a Palestinian port

scallop ('skɒləp, 'skæl-) NOUN 1 any of various marine bivalves of the family *Pectinidae,* having a fluted fan-shaped shell: includes free-swimming species (genus *Pecten*) and species attached to a substratum (genus *Chlamys*). See also **pecten** (sense 3). 2 the edible adductor muscle of certain of these molluscs. 3 either of the shell valves of any of these molluscs. 4 a scallop shell or similarly shaped dish, in which fish, esp shellfish, is cooked and served. 5 one of a series of curves along an edge, esp an edge of cloth. 6 the shape of a scallop shell used as the badge of a pilgrim, esp in the Middle Ages. 7 *Chiefly Austral* a potato cake fried in batter. ◆ VERB 8 (*tr*) to decorate (an edge) with scallops. 9 to bake (food) in a scallop shell or similar dish. 10 (*intr*) to collect scallops.
▷HISTORY C14: from Old French *escalope* shell, of Germanic origin; see SCALP
▸**'scalloper** NOUN ▸**'scalloping** NOUN

scally ('skælɪ) NOUN, *plural* **-lies.** *Northwest English dialect* a rascal; rogue.
▷HISTORY C20: from SCALLYWAG

scallywag ('skælɪ,wæg) NOUN 1 *Informal* a scamp; rascal. 2 (after the US Civil War) a White Southerner who supported the Republican Party and its policy of Black emancipation. Scallywags were viewed as traitors by their fellow Southerners. ◆ Also: **scalawag, scallawag.**
▷HISTORY C19: (originally undersized animal) of uncertain origin

scaloppine *or* **scaloppini** (,skæləˈpiːnɪ) PLURAL NOUN escalopes of meat, esp veal, cooked in a rich sauce, usually of wine with seasonings.
▷HISTORY Italian: from *scaloppa* a fillet, probably from Old French *escalope* SCALLOP

scalp (skælp) NOUN 1 *Anatomy* the skin and subcutaneous tissue covering the top of the head. 2 (among North American Indians) a part of this removed as a trophy from a slain enemy. 3 a trophy or token signifying conquest. 4 *Hunting, chiefly US* a piece of hide cut from the head of a victim as a trophy or as proof of killing in order to collect a bounty. 5 *Informal, chiefly US* a small speculative profit taken in quick transactions. 6 *Scot dialect* a projection of bare rock from vegetation. ◆ VERB (*tr*) 7 to cut the scalp from. 8 *Informal, chiefly US* to purchase and resell (securities) quickly so as to make several small profits. 9 *Informal* to buy (tickets) cheaply and resell at an inflated price.
▷HISTORY C13: probably from Scandinavian; compare Old Norse *skalpr* sheath, Middle Dutch *schelpe,* Danish *skalp* husk
▸**'scalper** NOUN

scalpel ('skælpᵊl) NOUN a surgical knife with a short thin blade.
▷HISTORY C18: from Latin *scalpellum,* from *scalper* a knife, from *scalpere* to scrape
▸**scalpellic** (skælˈpɛlɪk) ADJECTIVE

scalping ('skælpɪŋ) NOUN a process in which the top portion of a metal ingot is machined away before use, thus removing the layer containing defects and impurities.

scalp lock NOUN a small tuft or plait of hair left on the shaven scalp by American Indian warriors as a challenge to enemies.

scaly ('skeɪlɪ) ADJECTIVE **scalier, scaliest.** 1 resembling or covered in scales. 2 peeling off in scales.
▸**'scaliness** NOUN

scaly anteater NOUN another name for **pangolin.**

scam (skæm) *Slang* ◆ NOUN 1 a stratagem for gain; a swindle. ◆ VERB **scams, scamming, scammed.** 2 (*tr*) to swindle (someone) by means of a trick.

Scamander (skəˈmændə) NOUN the ancient name for the **Menderes** (sense 2).

scammer ('skæmə) *or* **scamster** NOUN *Slang* a person who perpetrates a scam; swindler.

scammony ('skæmənɪ) NOUN, *plural* **-nies.** 1 a twining Asian convolvulus plant, *Convolvulus scammonia,* having arrow-shaped leaves, white or purple flowers, and tuberous roots. 2 a resinous juice obtained from the roots of this plant and having purgative properties. 3 any of various similar medicinal resins or the plants that yield them.
▷HISTORY Old English, via Latin from Greek *skammōnia,* of obscure origin
▸**scammoniate** (skæˈməʊnɪɪt) ADJECTIVE

scamp[1] (skæmp) NOUN 1 an idle mischievous person; rascal. 2 a mischievous child.
▷HISTORY C18: from *scamp* (vb) to be a highway robber, probably from Middle Dutch *schampen* to decamp, from Old French *escamper,* from *es-* EX-[1] + *-camper,* from Latin *campus* field
▸**'scampish** ADJECTIVE

scamp[2] (skæmp) VERB a less common word for **skimp.**
▸**'scamper** NOUN

scamper ('skæmpə) VERB (*intr*) 1 to run about playfully. 2 (often foll by *through*) to hurry quickly through (a place, task, book, etc.). ◆ NOUN 3 the act of scampering.
▷HISTORY C17: probably from *scamp* (vb); see SCAMP[1]
▸**'scamperer** NOUN

scampi ('skæmpɪ) NOUN (*usually functioning as singular*) large prawns, usually eaten fried in breadcrumbs.
▷HISTORY Italian: plural of *scampo* shrimp, of obscure origin

scamster ('skæmstə) NOUN *Slang* a variant of **scammer.**

scamto ('skæmtəʊ) NOUN *South African* the argot of urban South African Blacks.
▷HISTORY C20: of uncertain origin

scan (skæn) VERB **scans, scanning, scanned.** 1 (*tr*) to scrutinize minutely. 2 (*tr*) to glance over quickly. 3 (*tr*) *Prosody* to read or analyse (verse) according to the rules of metre and versification. 4 (*intr*) *Prosody* to conform to the rules of metre and versification. 5 (*tr*) *Electronics* to move a beam of light, electrons, etc., in a predetermined pattern over (a surface or region) to obtain information, esp either to sense and transmit or to reproduce a television image. 6 (*tr*) to examine data stored on (magnetic tape, etc.), usually in order to retrieve information. 7 to examine or search (a prescribed region) by systematically varying the direction of a radar or sonar beam. 8 *Physics* to examine or produce or be examined or produced by a continuous charge of some variable: *to scan a spectrum.* 9 *Med* to obtain an image of (a part of the body) by means of a scanner. ◆ NOUN 10 the act or an instance of scanning. 11 *Med* **a** the examination of a part of the body by means of a scanner: *a brain scan; ultrasound scan.* **b** the image produced by a scanner.
▷HISTORY C14: from Late Latin *scandere* to scan (verse), from Latin: to climb
▸**'scannable** ADJECTIVE

scandal ('skændᵊl) NOUN 1 a disgraceful action or event: *his negligence was a scandal.* 2 censure or outrage arising from an action or event. 3 a person whose conduct causes reproach or disgrace. 4 malicious talk, esp gossip about the private lives of other people. 5 *Law* a libellous action or statement. ◆ VERB (*tr*) *Obsolete* 6 to disgrace. 7 to scandalize.
▷HISTORY C16: from Late Latin *scandalum* stumbling block, from Greek *skandalon* a trap
▸**'scandalous** ADJECTIVE ▸**'scandalously** ADVERB
▸**'scandalousness** NOUN

scandalize *or* **scandalise** ('skændə,laɪz) VERB (*tr*) to shock, as by improper behaviour.
▸**,scandali'zation** *or* **,scandali'sation** NOUN ▸**'scandal,izer** *or* **'scandal,iser** NOUN

scandalmonger ('skændᵊl,mʌŋgə) NOUN a person who spreads or enjoys scandal, gossip, etc.

Scandaroon (,skændəˈruːn) NOUN a large variety of fancy pigeon having a long thin body and an elongated neck and head.
▷HISTORY from *Scandaroon* the former name of *Ishenderon* a seaport in Turkey

scandent ('skændənt) ADJECTIVE (of plants) having a climbing habit.
▷HISTORY C17: from Latin *scandere* to climb

Scandian ('skændɪən) NOUN another name for a **Scandinavian.**
▷HISTORY C17: from Latin *Scandia* Scandinavia

scandic ('skændɪk) ADJECTIVE of or containing scandium.

Scandinavia (,skændɪˈneɪvɪə) NOUN 1 Also called: **the Scandinavian Peninsula.** the peninsula of N Europe occupied by Norway and Sweden. 2 the countries of N Europe, esp considered as a cultural unit and including Norway, Sweden, Denmark, and often Finland, Iceland, and the Faeroe Islands.

Scandinavian (,skændɪˈneɪvɪən) ADJECTIVE 1 of, relating to, or characteristic of Scandinavia, its inhabitants, or their languages. ◆ NOUN 2 a native or inhabitant of Scandinavia. 3 Also called: **Norse.** the northern group of Germanic languages, consisting of Swedish, Danish, Norwegian, Icelandic, and Faeroese.

Scandinavian Shield NOUN another name for **Baltic Shield.**

scandium ('skændɪəm) NOUN a rare light silvery-white metallic element occurring in minute quantities in numerous minerals. Symbol: Sc; atomic no.: 21; atomic wt.: 44.955910; valency: 3; relative density: 2.989; melting pt.: 1541°C; boiling pt.: 2836°C.
▷HISTORY C19: from New Latin, from Latin *Scandia* Scandinavia, where it was discovered

scanner ('skænə) NOUN 1 a person or thing that scans. 2 a device, usually electronic, used to measure or sample the distribution of some quantity or condition in a particular system, region, or area. [3] an aerial or similar device designed to transmit or receive signals, esp radar signals, inside a given solid angle of space, thus allowing a particular region to be scanned. [4] any of various devices used in medical diagnosis to obtain an image of an internal organ or part. See **CAT scanner, nuclear magnetic resonance scanner, ultrasound scanner.** [5] *Informal* a television outside broadcast vehicle. [6] short for **optical scanner.** [7] *Printing* an electronic device which scans artwork and illustrations and converts the images to digital form for manipulation, and incorporation into printed publications.

scanning electron microscope NOUN a type of electron microscope that produces a three-dimensional image.

scansion ('skænʃən) NOUN the analysis of the metrical structure of verse. See **quantity** (sense 7), **stress** (sense 4).
▷HISTORY C17: from Latin: climbing up, from *scandere* to climb, SCAN

scansorial (skæn'sɔːrɪəl) ADJECTIVE *Zoology* specialized for, characterized by, or relating to climbing: *a scansorial bird.*
▷HISTORY C19: from Latin *scānsōrius,* from *scandere* to climb

scant (skænt) ADJECTIVE [1] scarcely sufficient; limited: *he paid her scant attention.* [2] *(prenominal)* slightly short of the amount indicated; bare: *a scant ten inches.* [3] *(postpositive; foll by of)* having a short supply (of). ◆ VERB *(tr)* [4] to limit in size or quantity. [5] to provide with a limited or inadequate supply of. [6] to treat in a slighting or inadequate manner. ◆ ADVERB [7] scarcely; barely.
▷HISTORY C14: from Old Norse *skamt,* from *skammr*/short; related to Old High German *scam*
▸ **'scantly** ADVERB ▸ **'scantness** NOUN

scantling ('skæntlɪŋ) NOUN [1] a piece of sawn timber, such as a rafter, that has a small cross section. [2] the dimensions of a piece of building material or the structural parts of a ship, esp those in cross section. [3] a building stone, esp one that is more than 6 feet in length. [4] a small quantity or amount.
▷HISTORY C16: changed (through influence of SCANT and -LING[1]) from earlier *scantillon,* a carpenter's gauge, from Old Norman French *escantillon,* ultimately from Latin *scandere* to climb; see SCAN

scantlings ('skæntlɪŋz) PLURAL NOUN the structural casings of the internal gas paths in an aeroengine.

scanty ('skæntɪ) ADJECTIVE **scantier, scantiest.** [1] limited; barely enough; meagre. [2] insufficient; inadequate. [3] lacking fullness; small.
▸ **'scantily** ADVERB ▸ **'scantiness** NOUN

Scapa Flow ('skæpə) NOUN an extensive landlocked anchorage off the N coast of Scotland, in the Orkney Islands: major British naval base in both World Wars. Length: about 24 km (15 miles). Width: 13 km (8 miles).

scape[1] (skeɪp) NOUN [1] a leafless stalk in plants that arises from a rosette of leaves and bears one or more flowers. [2] *Zoology* a stalklike part, such as the first segment of an insect's antenna.
▷HISTORY C17: from Latin *scāpus* stem, from (Doric) Greek *skapos;* see SHAFT
▸ **'scapose** ADJECTIVE

scape[2] *or* **'scape** (skeɪp) VERB, NOUN an archaic word for **escape.**

-scape SUFFIX FORMING NOUNS indicating a scene or view of something, esp a pictorial representation: *seascape.*
▷HISTORY abstracted from LANDSCAPE

scapegoat ('skeɪpˌgəʊt) NOUN [1] a person made to bear the blame for others. [2] *Old Testament* a goat used in the ritual of Yom Kippur (Leviticus 16); it was symbolically laden with the sins of the Israelites and sent into the wilderness to be destroyed. ◆ VERB [3] *(tr)* to make a scapegoat of.
▷HISTORY C16: from ESCAPE + GOAT, coined by William Tyndale to translate Biblical Hebrew *azāzēl* (probably) goat for Azazel, mistakenly thought to mean "goat that escapes"

scapegrace ('skeɪpˌgreɪs) NOUN an idle mischievous person.
▷HISTORY C19: from SCAPE[2] + GRACE, alluding to a person who lacks God's grace

scapewheel ('skeɪpˌwiːl) NOUN a less common name for **escape wheel.**

scaphocephalic (ˌskæfɪsɪ'fælɪk) ADJECTIVE [1] *Anatomy* having a head that is abnormally long and narrow as a result of the two parietal bones on the top of the skull closing prematurely. [2] an individual with such a head. Compare **dolichocephalic, brachycephalic.**
▸ **'scaphoˌcephaly** *or* **'scaphoˌcephalism** NOUN

scaphoid ('skæfɔɪd) ADJECTIVE *Anatomy* an obsolete word for **navicular.**
▷HISTORY C18: via New Latin from Greek *skaphoeidēs,* from *skaphē* boat

scaphopod ('skæfəˌpɒd) NOUN any marine mollusc of the class *Scaphopoda,* which includes the tusk (or tooth) shells.
▷HISTORY C20: from New Latin, from Greek *skaphē* boat + -POD

scapolite ('skæpəˌlaɪt) NOUN any of a group of colourless, white, grey, or violet fluorescent minerals consisting of sodium or calcium aluminium silicate, carbonate, and chloride in tetragonal crystalline form. They occur mainly in impure limestones and pegmatites. Also called: **wernerite.**
▷HISTORY C19: from German *Skapolith,* from Greek *skapos* rod + -LITE

scapula ('skæpjʊlə) NOUN, *plural* **-lae** (-liː) *or* **-las.** [1] either of two large flat triangular bones, one on each side of the back part of the shoulder in man. Nontechnical name: **shoulder blade.** [2] the corresponding bone in most vertebrates.
▷HISTORY C16: from Late Latin: shoulder

scapular ('skæpjʊlə) ADJECTIVE [1] *Anatomy* of or relating to the scapula. ◆ NOUN [2] part of the monastic habit worn by members of many Christian, esp Roman Catholic, religious orders, consisting of a piece of woollen cloth worn over the shoulders, and hanging down in front and behind to the ankles. [3] two small rectangular pieces of woollen cloth joined by tapes passing over the shoulders and worn under secular clothes in token of affiliation to a religious order. [4] any of the small feathers that are attached to the humerus of a bird and lie along the shoulder. ◆ Also called (for senses 2, 3): **scapulary.**

scar[1] (skɑː) NOUN [1] any mark left on the skin or other tissue following the healing of a wound. [2] a permanent change in a person's character resulting from emotional distress: *his wife's death left its scars on him.* [3] the mark on a plant indicating the former point of attachment of a part, esp the attachment of a leaf to a stem. [4] a mark of damage; blemish. ◆ VERB **scars, scarring, scarred.** [5] to mark or become marked with a scar. [6] *(intr)* to heal leaving a scar.
▷HISTORY C14: via Late Latin from Greek *eskhara* scab

scar[2] (skɑː) NOUN [1] an irregular enlongated trench-like feature on a land surface that often exposes bedrock. [2] a similar formation in a river or sea. Also called (Scot): **scaur.**
▷HISTORY C14: from Old Norse *sker* low reef, SKERRY

scarab ('skærəb) NOUN [1] any scarabaeid beetle, esp *Scarabaeus sacer* (**sacred scarab**), regarded by the ancient Egyptians as divine. [2] the scarab as represented on amulets, etc., of ancient Egypt, or in hieroglyphics as a symbol of the solar deity.
▷HISTORY C16: from Latin *scarabaeus;* probably related to Greek *karabos* horned beetle

scarabaeid (ˌskærə'biːɪd) *or* **scarabaean** (ˌskærə'biːən) NOUN [1] any beetle of the family *Scarabaeidae,* including the sacred scarab and other dung beetles, the chafers, goliath beetles, and rhinoceros beetles. ◆ ADJECTIVE [2] of, relating to, or belonging to the family *Scarabaeidae.*
▷HISTORY C19: from New Latin

scarabaeoid (ˌskærə'biːɔɪd) ADJECTIVE [1] Also: **scaraboid** ('skærəˌbɔɪd). of, relating to, or resembling a scarabaeid. [2] a former word for **lamellicorn.**

scarabaeus (ˌskærə'biːəs) NOUN, *plural* **-baeuses** *or* **-baei** (-'biːaɪ). a less common name for **scarab.**

Scaramouch *or* **Scaramouche** ('skærəˌmaʊtʃ, -ˌmuːtʃ) NOUN a stock character who appears as a boastful coward in commedia dell'arte and farce.
▷HISTORY C17: via French from Italian *Scaramuccia,* from *scaramuccia* a SKIRMISH

Scarborough ('skɑːbrə) NOUN a fishing port and resort in NE England, in North Yorkshire on the North Sea: developed as a spa after 1660; ruined 12th-century castle. Pop.: 38 809 (1991).

scarce (skɛəs) ADJECTIVE [1] rarely encountered. [2] insufficient to meet the demand. [3] **make oneself scarce.** *Informal* to go away, esp suddenly. ◆ ADVERB [4] *Archaic or literary* scarcely.
▷HISTORY C13: from Old Norman French *scars,* from Vulgar Latin *excarpsus* (unattested) plucked out, from Latin *excerpere* to select; see EXCERPT
▸ **'scarceness** NOUN

scarcely ('skɛəslɪ) ADVERB [1] hardly at all; only just. [2] *Often used ironically* probably not or definitely not: *that is scarcely justification for your actions.*

> Language note See at **hardly.**

scarcement ('skɛəsmənt) NOUN a ledge in a wall.
▷HISTORY C16: probably from obsolete sense of SCARCE to reduce + -MENT

scarcity ('skɛəsɪtɪ) NOUN, *plural* **-ties.** [1] inadequate supply; dearth; paucity. [2] rarity or infrequent occurrence.

scare (skɛə) VERB [1] to fill or be filled with fear or alarm. [2] *(tr; often foll by away or off)* to drive (away) by frightening. [3] *(tr) US and Canadian informal* (followed by *up*) **a** to produce (a meal) quickly from whatever is available. **b** to manage to find (something) quickly or with difficulty: *brewers need to scare up more sales.* ◆ NOUN [4] a sudden attack of fear or alarm. [5] a period of general fear or alarm. ◆ ADJECTIVE [6] causing (needless) fear or alarm: *a scare story.*
▷HISTORY C12: from Old Norse *skirra;* related to Norwegian *skjerra,* Swedish dialect *skjarra*
▸ **'scarer** NOUN

scarecrow ('skɛəˌkrəʊ) NOUN [1] an object, usually in the shape of a man, made out of sticks and old clothes to scare birds away from crops. [2] a person or thing that appears frightening but is not actually harmful. [3] *Informal* **a** an untidy-looking person. **b** a very thin person.

scaredy-cat ('skɛədɪˌkæt) NOUN *Informal* someone who is easily frightened.

scaremonger ('skɛəˌmʌŋgə) NOUN a person who delights in spreading rumours of disaster.
▸ **'scareˌmongering** NOUN

scare quotes PLURAL NOUN quotation marks placed around a word or phrase to indicate that it should not be taken literally or automatically accepted as true.

scarf[1] (skɑːf) NOUN, *plural* **scarves** (skɑːvz) *or* **scarfs.** [1] a rectangular, triangular, or long narrow piece of cloth worn around the head, neck, or shoulders for warmth or decoration. ◆ VERB *(tr) Rare* [2] to wrap with or as if with a scarf. [3] to use as or in the manner of a scarf.
▷HISTORY C16: of uncertain origin; compare Old Norman French *escarpe,* Medieval Latin *scrippum* pilgrim's pack; see SCRIP[2]

scarf[2] (skɑːf) NOUN, *plural* **scarfs.** [1] Also called: **scarf joint, scarfed joint.** a lapped joint between two pieces of timber made by notching or grooving the ends and strapping, bolting, or gluing the two pieces together. [2] the end of a piece of timber shaped to form such a joint. [3] *NZ* a wedge-shaped cut made in a tree before felling, to determine the direction of the fall. [4] *Whaling* an incision made along a whale's body before stripping off the blubber. ◆ VERB *(tr)* [5] to join (two pieces of timber) by means of a scarf. [6] to make a scarf on (a piece of timber). [7] to cut a scarf in (a whale).
▷HISTORY C14: probably from Scandinavian; compare Norwegian *skarv,* Swedish *skarf,* Low German, Dutch *scherf* SCARF[1]

scarfskin ('skɑːfˌskɪn) NOUN the outermost layer of the skin; epidermis or cuticle.
▷HISTORY C17: from SCARF[1] (in the sense: an outer covering)

scarificator ('skɛərɪfɪˌkeɪtə, 'skærɪ-) NOUN a surgical instrument for use in superficial puncturing of the skin or other tissue.

scarify[1] ('skɛərɪˌfaɪ, 'skærɪ-) VERB **-fies, -fying, -fied.** *(tr)* [1] *Surgery* to make tiny punctures or superficial incisions in (the skin or other tissue), as for inoculating. [2] *Agriculture* **a** to break up and loosen (soil) to a shallow depth. **b** to scratch or abrade the

outer surface of (seeds) to increase water absorption or hasten germination. [3] to wound with harsh criticism.
▷**HISTORY** C15: via Old French from Latin *scarīfāre* to scratch open, from Greek *skariphasthai* to draw, from *skariphos* a pencil
▸ ˌ**scarifiˈcation** NOUN ▸ ˈ**scariˌfier** NOUN

scarify² (ˈskɛərɪˌfaɪ) VERB **-fies, -fying, -fied.** (*tr*) *Informal* to make scared; frighten.
▷**HISTORY** C18: from SCARE + -IFY
▸ ˈ**scariˌfyingly** ADVERB

> **Language note** *Scarify* is sometimes wrongly thought to mean the same as *scare: a frightening* (not *scarifying*) *film.*

scarious (ˈskɛərɪəs) *or* **scariose** (ˈskɛərɪˌəʊs) ADJECTIVE (of plant parts) membranous, dry, and brownish in colour: *scarious bracts.*
▷**HISTORY** C19: from New Latin *scariōsus,* of uncertain origin

scarlatina (ˌskɑːləˈtiːnə) NOUN the technical name for **scarlet fever.**
▷**HISTORY** C19: from New Latin, from Italian *scarlattina,* diminutive of *scarlatto* SCARLET
▸ ˌ**scarlaˈtinal** ADJECTIVE

scarlet (ˈskɑːlɪt) NOUN [1] a vivid red colour, sometimes with an orange tinge. [2] cloth or clothing of this colour. ◆ ADJECTIVE [3] of the colour scarlet. [4] sinful or immoral, esp unchaste.
▷**HISTORY** C13: from Old French *escarlate* fine cloth, of unknown origin

scarlet fever NOUN an acute communicable disease characterized by fever, strawberry-coloured tongue, and a typical rash starting on the neck and chest and spreading to the abdomen and limbs, caused by all group A haemolytic *Streptococcus* bacteria. Technical name: **scarlatina.**

scarlet hat NOUN another term for **red hat.**

scarlet letter NOUN (esp among US Puritans) a scarlet letter *A* formerly worn by a person convicted of adultery.

scarlet pimpernel NOUN a weedy primulaceous plant, *Anagallis arvensis,* of temperate regions, having small red, purple, or white star-shaped flowers that close in bad weather. Also called: **shepherd's** (or **poor man's**) **weatherglass.**

scarlet runner NOUN a climbing perennial bean plant, *Phaseolus multiflorus* (or *P. coccineus*), of tropical America, having scarlet flowers: widely cultivated for its long green edible pods containing edible seeds. Also called: **runner bean, string bean.**

scarlet tanager NOUN an E North American tanager, *Piranga olivacea,* the male of which has a bright red head and body with black wings and tail.

scarlet woman NOUN [1] *New Testament* a sinful woman described in Revelation 17, interpreted as a figure either of pagan Rome or of the Roman Catholic Church regarded as typifying vice overlaid with gaudy pageantry. [2] any sexually promiscuous woman, esp a prostitute.

scarp (skɑːp) NOUN [1] a steep slope, esp one formed by erosion or faulting; escarpment. See also **cuesta.** [2] *Fortifications* the side of a ditch cut nearest to and immediately below a rampart. ◆ VERB [3] (*tr; often passive*) to wear or cut so as to form a steep slope.
▷**HISTORY** C16: from Italian *scarpa*

scarper (ˈskɑːpə) *Brit slang* ◆ VERB (*intr*) [1] to depart in haste. ◆ NOUN [2] a hasty departure.
▷**HISTORY** C19: probably an adaptation of Italian *scappare* to escape; perhaps influenced by folk etymology *Scapa Flow* Cockney rhyming slang for *go*

scart (skært) *Scot* ◆ VERB [1] to scratch or scrape. ◆ NOUN [2] a scratch or scrape. [3] a stroke of a pen. [4] a small amount; scraping.
▷**HISTORY** C14: from earlier *scrat*

Scart *or* **SCART** (skɑːt) NOUN *Electronics* **a** a 21-pin plug-and-socket system which carries picture, sound, and other signals, used especially in home entertainment systems. **b** (*as modifier*): *a Scart cable.*
▷**HISTORY** C20: after Syndicat des Constructeurs des Appareils Radiorécepteurs et Téléviseurs, the company that designed it

scarves (skɑːvz) NOUN a plural of **scarf.**

scary (ˈskɛərɪ) ADJECTIVE **scarier, scariest.** *Informal* [1] causing fear or alarm; frightening. [2] easily roused to fear; timid.

scat¹ (skæt) VERB **scats, scatting, scatted.** (*intr; usually imperative*) *Informal* to go away in haste.
▷**HISTORY** C19: perhaps from a hiss + the word *cat,* used to frighten away cats

scat² (skæt) NOUN [1] a type of jazz singing characterized by improvised vocal sounds instead of words. ◆ VERB **scats, scatting, scatted.** [2] (*intr*) to sing jazz in this way.
▷**HISTORY** C20: perhaps imitative

scat³ (skæt) NOUN any marine and freshwater percoid fish of the Asian family *Scatophagidae,* esp *Scatophagus argus,* which has a beautiful coloration.
▷**HISTORY** C20: shortened from *Scatophagus;* see SCATO-

scat⁴ (skæt) NOUN an animal dropping.
▷**HISTORY** C20: see SCATO-

scathe (skeɪð) VERB (*tr*) [1] *Rare* to attack with severe criticism. [2] *Archaic or dialect* to injure. ◆ NOUN [3] *Archaic or dialect* harm.
▷**HISTORY** Old English *sceatha;* related to Old Norse *skathi,* Old Saxon *scatho*
▸ ˈ**scatheless** ADJECTIVE

scathing (ˈskeɪðɪŋ) ADJECTIVE [1] harshly critical; scornful: *a scathing remark.* [2] damaging; painful.
▸ ˈ**scathingly** ADVERB

scato- *or before a vowel* **scat-** COMBINING FORM dung or excrement: *scatophagous.*
▷**HISTORY** from Greek *skōr, skat-* dung

scatological (ˌskætəˈlɒdʒɪkᵊl) *or less commonly* **scatologic** (ˌskætəˈlɒdʒɪk) ADJECTIVE [1] characterized by obscenity or preoccupation with obscenity, esp in the form of references to excrement. [2] of or relating to the scientific study of excrement.

scatology (skæˈtɒlədʒɪ) NOUN [1] the scientific study of excrement, esp in medicine for diagnostic purposes, and in palaeontology of fossilized excrement. [2] obscenity or preoccupation with obscenity, esp in the form of references to excrement.
▸ **scaˈtologist** NOUN

scatter (ˈskætə) VERB [1] (*tr*) to throw about in various directions; strew. [2] to separate and move or cause to separate and move in various directions; disperse. [3] to deviate or cause to deviate in many directions, as in the diffuse reflection or refraction of light. ◆ NOUN [4] the act of scattering. [5] a substance or a number of objects scattered about.
▷**HISTORY** C13: probably a variant of SHATTER
▸ ˈ**scatterable** ADJECTIVE ▸ ˈ**scatterer** NOUN

scatterbrain (ˈskætəˌbreɪn) NOUN a person who is incapable of serious thought or concentration.

scatterbrained (ˈskætəˌbreɪnd) ADJECTIVE exhibiting or characterized by lack of serious thought or concentration; disorganized; silly.

scatter diagram NOUN *Statistics* a graph that plots along two axes at right angles to each other the relationship between two variable quantities, such as height and weight.

scatter-gun NOUN a shotgun.

scattering (ˈskætərɪŋ) NOUN [1] a small amount. [2] *Physics* the process in which particles, atoms, etc., are deflected as a result of collision.

scatter pin NOUN a small decorative pin usually worn in groups of two or three.

scatter rug NOUN a small rug used to cover a limited area.

scatty (ˈskætɪ) ADJECTIVE **-tier, -tiest.** *Brit informal* [1] empty-headed, frivolous, or thoughtless. [2] distracted (esp in **drive someone scatty**).
▷**HISTORY** C20: from SCATTERBRAINED
▸ ˈ**scattily** ADVERB ▸ ˈ**scattiness** NOUN

scaud (skɔːd) VERB, NOUN a Scot word for **scald.**

scaup *or* **scaup duck** (skɔːp) NOUN either of two diving ducks, *Aythya marila* (**greater scaup**) or *A. affinis* (**lesser scaup**), of Europe and America, having a black-and-white plumage in the male. Also called (US): **bluebill, broadbill.**
▷**HISTORY** C16: Scottish variant of SCALP

scauper (ˈskɔːpə) NOUN a variant spelling of **scorper.**

scaur (skɔːr) NOUN a Scot variant of **scar.**

scavenge (ˈskævɪndʒ) VERB [1] to search for (anything usable) among discarded material. [2] (*tr*) to purify (a molten metal) by bubbling a suitable gas through it. The gas may be inert or may react with the impurities. [3] to clean up filth from (streets, etc.). [4] *Chem* to act as a scavenger for (atoms, molecules, ions, radicals, etc.).

scavenge pump NOUN *Engineering* an oil pump used in some internal-combustion engines to return oil from the crankcase to the oil tank.

scavenger (ˈskævɪndʒə) NOUN [1] a person who collects things discarded by others. [2] any animal that feeds on decaying organic matter, esp on refuse. [3] a substance added to a chemical reaction or mixture to counteract the effect of impurities. [4] a person employed to clean the streets.
▷**HISTORY** C16: from Anglo-Norman *scawager,* from Old Norman French *escauwage* examination, from *escauwer* to scrutinize, of Germanic origin; related to Flemish *scauwen*
▸ ˈ**scavengery** NOUN

scavenger beetle NOUN any beetle of the mostly aquatic family *Hydrophilidae,* having clubbed antennae and long palps, and usually feeding on decaying vegetation.

scavenger hunt NOUN a game in which players are required to collect an assortment of miscellaneous items: usually played outdoors.

scavenge stroke *or* **scavenging stroke** NOUN (in a reciprocating engine) the stroke of a piston in a four-stroke cycle that pushes the burnt gases out as exhaust. Also called: **exhaust stroke.**

ScD ABBREVIATION FOR Doctor of Science.

SCE (in Scotland) ABBREVIATION FOR Scottish Certificate of Education: either of two public examinations in specific subjects taken as school-leaving qualifications or as qualifying examinations for entry into a university, college, etc. See also **higher** (sense 2), **O grade.**

scena (ˈʃeɪnə) NOUN, *plural* **-ne** (-ˌneɪ). [1] a scene in an opera, usually longer than a single aria. [2] a dramatic vocal piece written in operatic style.

scenario (sɪˈnɑːrɪˌəʊ) NOUN, *plural* **-narios.** [1] a summary of the plot of a play, etc., including information about its characters, scenes, etc. [2] a predicted sequence of events: *let's try another scenario, involving the demise of democracy.*
▷**HISTORY** C19: via Italian from Latin *scēnārium,* from *scēna;* see SCENE
▸ **scenarist** (ˈsiːnərɪst, sɪˈnɑː-) NOUN

scend *or* **send** (sɛnd) *Nautical* ◆ VERB **scends, scending, scended** *or* **sends, sending, sent.** [1] (of a vessel) to surge upwards in a heavy sea. ◆ NOUN [2] the upward heaving of a vessel pitching. [3] the forward lift given a vessel by the sea.
▷**HISTORY** C17: perhaps from DESCEND or ASCEND

scene (siːn) NOUN [1] the place where an action or event, real or imaginary, occurs. [2] the setting for the action of a play, novel, etc. [3] an incident or situation, real or imaginary, esp as described or represented. [4] **a** a subdivision of an act of a play, in which the time is continuous and the setting fixed. **b** a single event, esp a significant one, in a play. [5] *Films* a shot or series of shots that constitutes a unit of the action. [6] the backcloths, stage setting, etc., for a play or film set; scenery. [7] the prospect of a place, landscape, etc. [8] a display of emotion, esp an embarrassing one to the onlookers. [9] *Informal* the environment for a specific activity: *the fashion scene.* [10] *Informal* interest or chosen occupation: *classical music is not my scene.* [11] *Rare* the stage, esp of a theatre in ancient Greece or Rome. [12] **behind the scenes.** out of public view; privately.
▷**HISTORY** C16: from Latin *scēna* theatrical stage, from Greek *skēnē* tent, stage

scene dock *or* **bay** NOUN a place in a theatre where scenery is stored, usually near the stage.

scenery (ˈsiːnərɪ) NOUN, *plural* **-eries.** [1] the natural features of a landscape. [2] *Theatre* the painted backcloths, stage structures, etc., used to represent a location in a theatre or studio.
▷**HISTORY** C18: from Italian SCENARIO

scenic (ˈsiːnɪk, ˈsɛn-) ADJECTIVE [1] of or relating to natural scenery. [2] having beautiful natural scenery: *a scenic drive.* [3] of or relating to the stage or stage scenery. [4] (in painting) representing a scene, such as a scene of action or a historical event.
▸ ˈ**scenically** ADVERB

scenic railway NOUN 1 a miniature railway used for amusement in a park, zoo, etc. 2 a roller coaster.

scenic reserve NOUN *NZ* an area of natural beauty, set aside for public recreation.

scenography (siːˈnɒɡrəfɪ) NOUN 1 the art of portraying objects or scenes in perspective. 2 scene painting, esp in ancient Greece.
▷HISTORY C17: via Latin from Greek *skēnographia* a drawing in perspective, from *skēnē* SCENE
▸**sceˈnographer** NOUN ▸**scenographic** (ˌsiːnəʊˈɡræfɪk) *or* ˌ**scenoˈgraphical** ADJECTIVE ▸ˌ**scenoˈgraphically** ADVERB

scent (sɛnt) NOUN 1 a distinctive smell, esp a pleasant one. 2 a smell left in passing, by which a person or animal may be traced. 3 a trail, clue, or guide. 4 an instinctive ability for finding out or detecting. 5 another word (esp Brit) for **perfume.** ♦ VERB 6 (*tr*) to recognize or be aware of by or as if by the smell. 7 (*tr*) to have a suspicion of; detect: *I scent foul play.* 8 (*tr*) to fill with odour or fragrance. 9 (*intr*) (of hounds, etc.) to hunt by the sense of smell. 10 to smell (at): *the dog scented the air.*
▷HISTORY C14: from Old French *sentir* to sense, from Latin *sentīre* to feel; see SENSE
▸ˈ**scented** ADJECTIVE ▸ˈ**scentless** ADJECTIVE
▸ˈ**scentlessness** NOUN

scented orchid NOUN a slender orchid, *Gymnadenia conopsea,* with fragrant pink flowers carried in a dense spike and having a three-lobed lip; found in calcareous turf. Also called: **fragrant orchid.**

sceptic *or archaic and US* **skeptic** (ˈskɛptɪk) NOUN 1 a person who habitually doubts the authenticity of accepted beliefs. 2 a person who mistrusts people, ideas, etc., in general. 3 a person who doubts the truth of religion, esp Christianity. ♦ ADJECTIVE 4 of or relating to sceptics; sceptical.
▷HISTORY C16: from Latin *scepticus,* from Greek *skeptikos* one who reflects upon, from *skeptesthai* to consider
▸ˈ**scepticism** *or (archaic and US)* ˈ**skepticism** NOUN

Sceptic *or archaic and US* **Skeptic** (ˈskɛptɪk) NOUN 1 a member of one of the ancient Greek schools of philosophy, esp that of Pyrrho (?365–?275 B.C.), who believed that real knowledge of things is impossible. ♦ ADJECTIVE 2 of or relating to the Sceptics.
▸ˈ**Scepticism** *or (archaic and US)* ˈ**Skepticism** NOUN

sceptical *or archaic and US* **skeptical** (ˈskɛptɪkəl) ADJECTIVE 1 not convinced that something is true; doubtful. 2 tending to mistrust people, ideas, etc., in general. 3 of or relating to sceptics; sceptic.
▸ˈ**sceptically** *or (archaic and US)* ˈ**skeptically** ADVERB

sceptre *or US* **scepter** (ˈsɛptə) NOUN 1 a ceremonial staff held by a monarch as the symbol of authority. 2 imperial authority; sovereignty. ♦ VERB 3 (*tr*) to invest with authority.
▷HISTORY C13: from Old French *sceptre,* from Latin *scēptrum,* from Greek *skeptron* staff
▸ˈ**sceptred** *or US* ˈ**sceptered** ADJECTIVE

SCG (in Australia) ABBREVIATION FOR Sydney Cricket Ground.

sch. ABBREVIATION FOR school.

Schadenfreude *German* (ˈʃaːdənfrɔydə) NOUN delight in another's misfortune.
▷HISTORY German: from *Schaden* harm + *Freude* joy

Schaerbeek (*Flemish* ˈsxaːrbeːk) NOUN a city in central Belgium: an industrial suburb of Brussels. Pop.: 105 692 (2000 est.).

Schaffhausen (*German* ʃaːfˈhauzən) NOUN 1 a small canton of N Switzerland. Pop.: 73 600 (2000 est.). Area: 298 sq. km (115 sq. miles). 2 a town in N Switzerland, capital of Schaffhausen canton, on the Rhine. Pop.: 35 000 (latest est.). French name: **Schaffhouse.**

schappe (ˈʃæpə) NOUN a yarn or fabric made from waste silk.
▷HISTORY from German

Schaumburg-Lippe (*German* ˈʃaumbʊrkˈlɪpə) NOUN a former state of NW Germany, between Westphalia and Hanover: part of Lower Saxony since 1946.

schedule (ˈʃɛdjuːl; *also, esp US* ˈskɛdʒʊəl) NOUN 1 a plan of procedure for a project, allotting the work to be done and the time for it. 2 a list of items: *a schedule of fixed prices.* 3 a list of times, esp of arrivals and departures; timetable. 4 a list of tasks to be performed, esp within a set period. 5 *Law* a list or inventory, usually supplementary to a contract, will, etc. 6 **on schedule.** at the expected or planned time. ♦ VERB (*tr*) 7 to make a schedule of or place in a schedule. 8 to plan to occur at a certain time.
▷HISTORY C14: earlier *cedule, sedule* via Old French from Late Latin *schedula* small piece of paper, from Latin *scheda* sheet of paper
▸ˈ**schedular** ADJECTIVE

scheduled (ˈʃɛdjuːld) ADJECTIVE 1 arranged or planned according to a programme, timetable, etc.: *a scheduled meeting; a change to the scheduled programmes on TV tonight.* 2 (of an aircraft or a flight) part of a regular service, not specially chartered. 3 *Brit* (of a building, place of historic interest, etc.) entered on a list of places to be preserved. See also **listed building.**

scheduled castes PLURAL NOUN certain classes in Indian society officially granted special concessions. See **Harijan.**

scheduled territories PLURAL NOUN **the.** another name for **sterling area.**

scheelite (ˈʃiːlaɪt) NOUN a white, brownish, or greenish mineral, usually fluorescent, consisting of calcium tungstate in tetragonal crystalline form with some tungsten often replaced by molybdenum: occurs principally in contact metamorphic rocks and quartz veins, and is an important source of tungsten and purified calcium tungstate. Formula: $CaWO_4$.
▷HISTORY C19: from German *Scheelit,* named after Karl Wilhelm Scheele (1742–86), Swedish chemist

Scheldt (ʃɛlt, skɛlt) NOUN a river in W Europe, rising in NE France and flowing north and northeast through W Belgium to Antwerp, then northwest to the North Sea in the SW Netherlands. Length: 435 km (270 miles). Flemish and Dutch name: **Schelde** (ˈsxɛldɛ). French name: **Escaut.**

schema (ˈskiːmə) NOUN, *plural* **-mata** (-mətə). 1 a plan, diagram, or scheme. 2 (in the philosophy of Kant) a rule or principle that enables the understanding to apply its categories and unify experience: *universal succession is the schema of causality.* 3 *Psychol* a mental model of aspects of the world or of the self that is structured in such a way as to facilitate the processes of cognition and perception. 4 *Logic* an expression using metavariables that may be replaced by object language expressions to yield a well-formed formula. Thus $A = A$ is an axiom schema for identity, representing the infinite number of axioms, $x = x$, $y = y$, $z = z$, etc.
▷HISTORY C19: from Greek: form

schematic (skɪˈmætɪk, skiː-) ADJECTIVE 1 of or relating to the nature of a diagram, plan, or schema. ♦ NOUN 2 a schematic diagram, esp of an electrical circuit.
▸**scheˈmatically** ADVERB

schematism (ˈskiːməˌtɪzəm) NOUN the general form, arrangement, or classification of something.

schematize *or* **schematise** (ˈskiːməˌtaɪz) VERB (*tr*) to form into or arrange in a scheme.
▸ˌ**schematiˈzation** *or* ˌ**schematiˈsation** NOUN

scheme (skiːm) NOUN 1 a systematic plan for a course of action. 2 a systematic arrangement of correlated parts; system. 3 a secret plot. 4 a visionary or unrealizable project. 5 a chart, diagram, or outline. 6 an astrological diagram giving the aspects of celestial bodies at a particular time. 7 *Chiefly Brit* a plan formally adopted by a commercial enterprise or governmental body, as for pensions, etc. 8 *Chiefly Scot* an area of housing that is laid out esp by a local authority; estate. ♦ VERB 9 (*tr*) to devise a system for. 10 to form intrigues (for) in an underhand manner.
▷HISTORY C16: from Latin *schema,* from Greek *skhēma* form
▸ˈ**schemer** NOUN

scheming (ˈskiːmɪŋ) ADJECTIVE 1 given to making plots; cunning. ♦ NOUN 2 intrigues.
▸ˈ**schemingly** ADVERB

Schengen Convention *or* **Agreement** (ˈʃɛŋən) NOUN an agreement, signed in 1985, but not implemented until 1995, to abolish border controls within Europe: ten countries had acceded by 1995; the UK is not a signatory.

scherzando (skɛəˈtsændəʊ) *Music* ♦ ADJECTIVE, ADVERB 1 to be performed in a light-hearted manner. ♦ NOUN, *plural* **-di** (-diː) *or* **-dos.** 2 a movement, passage, etc., directed to be performed in this way.
▷HISTORY Italian, literally: joking. See SCHERZO

scherzo (ˈskɛətsəʊ) NOUN, *plural* **-zos** *or* **-zi** (-tsiː). a brisk lively movement, developed from the minuet, with a contrastive middle section (a trio). See **minuet** (sense 2).
▷HISTORY Italian: joke, of Germanic origin; compare Middle High German *scherzen* to jest

Schickard (ˈʃɪkəd) NOUN a large crater in the SW quadrant of the moon, about 227 kilometres (141 miles) in diameter.

Schick test (ʃɪk) NOUN *Med* a skin test to determine immunity to diphtheria: a dilute diphtheria toxin is injected into the skin; within two or three days a red inflamed area will develop if no antibodies are present.
▷HISTORY C20: named after Bela *Schick* (1877–1967), US paediatrician

Schiedam (*Dutch* sxiːˈdɑm) NOUN a port in the SW Netherlands, in South Holland province west of Rotterdam: gin distilleries. Pop.: 72 515 (1994).

Schiff base (ʃɪf) NOUN the product of the chemical association of an aldehyde with a primary amine.
▷HISTORY C19: named after Hugo *Schiff* (1834–1915), German chemist

schiller (ˈʃɪlə) NOUN an unusual iridescent or metallic lustre in some minerals caused by internal reflection from certain inclusions such as gas cavities or mineral intergrowths. Formula: $NaFe_3B_3Al_3(Al_3Si_6O_{27})(OH)_4$.
▷HISTORY C19: from German *Schiller* iridescence, from Old High German *scilihen* to blink

schilling (ˈʃɪlɪŋ) NOUN 1 the former standard monetary unit of Austria, divided into 100 groschen; replaced by the euro in 2002. 2 an old German coin of low denomination.
▷HISTORY C18: from German: SHILLING

schipperke (ˈʃɪpəkɪ, ˈskɪp-) NOUN a small Dutch breed of tailless dog with a foxy head, pricked ears, and usually a black coat.
▷HISTORY C19: from Dutch, literally: little boatman (from its use as a guard dog on canal barges). See SKIPPER[1]

schism (ˈskɪz-, ˈsɪzəm) NOUN 1 the division of a group into opposing factions. 2 the factions so formed. 3 division within or separation from an established Church, esp the Roman Catholic Church, not necessarily involving differences in doctrine.
▷HISTORY C14: from Church Latin *schisma,* from Greek *skhisma* a cleft, from *skhizein* to split

schismatic (skɪzˈmætɪk, sɪz-) *or* **schismatical** ADJECTIVE 1 of, relating to, or promoting schism. ♦ NOUN 2 a person who causes schism or belongs to a schismatic faction.
▸**schisˈmatically** ADVERB ▸**schisˈmaticalness** NOUN

schist (ʃɪst) NOUN any metamorphic rock that can be split into thin layers because its micaceous minerals have become aligned in thin parallel bands.
▷HISTORY C18: from French *schiste,* from Latin *lapis schistos* stone that may be split, from Greek *skhizein* to split
▸ˈ**schistose** ADJECTIVE ▸**schistosity** (ʃɪˈstɒsɪtɪ) NOUN

schistosome (ˈʃɪstəˌsəʊm) NOUN any of various blood flukes of the chiefly tropical genus *Schistosoma,* which cause disease in man and domestic animals. Also called: **bilharzia.**
▷HISTORY C19: from New Latin *Schistosoma;* see SCHIST, -SOME[3]

schistosomiasis (ˌʃɪstəsəʊˈmaɪəsɪs) NOUN a disease caused by infestation of the body with blood flukes of the genus *Schistosoma.* Also called: **bilharziasis.**

schizanthus (skɪtˈsænθəs) NOUN any plant of the Chilean annual genus *Schizanthus,* some species of which are grown as pot or garden plants for their showy red, white, or yellow orchid-like flowers: family *Solanaceae.* Sometimes called: **poor man's orchid.**
▷HISTORY New Latin, from Greek *schizein* to cut + *anthos* flower (from the deeply divided corolla)

schizo (ˈskɪtsəʊ) *Offensive* ♦ ADJECTIVE 1

schizophrenic. ◆ NOUN, *plural* **-os.** [2] a schizophrenic person.

schizo- *or before a vowel* **schiz-** COMBINING FORM indicating a cleavage, split, or division: *schizocarp; schizophrenia.*
▷HISTORY from Greek *skhizein* to split

schizocarp (ˈskɪzəˌkɑːp) NOUN *Botany* a dry fruit that splits into two or more one-seeded portions at maturity.
▸ˌ**schizo'carpous** *or* ˌ**schizo'carpic** ADJECTIVE

schizogenesis (ˌskɪtsəʊˈdʒɛnɪsɪs) NOUN asexual reproduction by fission of the parent organism or part.
▸**schizogenetic** (ˌskɪtsəʊdʒɪˈnɛtɪk) ADJECTIVE

schizogony (skɪtˈsɒɡənɪ) NOUN asexual reproduction in protozoans that is characterized by multiple fission.

schizoid (ˈskɪtsɔɪd) ADJECTIVE [1] *Psychol* denoting a personality disorder characterized by extreme shyness and oversensitivity to others. [2] *Informal* characterized by or showing conflicting or contradictory attitudes, ideas, etc. ◆ NOUN [3] a person who has a schizoid personality.

schizomycete (ˌskɪtsəʊmaɪˈsiːt) NOUN (formerly) any microscopic organism of the now obsolete class *Schizomycetes,* which included the bacteria.
▸**schizomycetic** (ˌskɪtsəʊmaɪˈsɛtɪk) *or* ˌ**schizomy'cetous** ADJECTIVE

schizont (ˈskɪtsɒnt) NOUN a cell formed from a trophozoite during the asexual stage of the life cycle of sporozoan protozoans, such as the malaria parasite.
▷HISTORY C19: from SCHIZO- + *-ont* a being, from Greek *einai* to be

schizophrenia (ˌskɪtsəʊˈfriːnɪə) NOUN [1] any of a group of psychotic disorders characterized by progressive deterioration of the personality, withdrawal from reality, hallucinations, delusions, social apathy, emotional instability, etc. See **catatonia, hebephrenia, paranoia.** [2] *Informal* behaviour that appears to be motivated by contradictory or conflicting principles.
▷HISTORY C20: from SCHIZO- + Greek *phrēn* mind + -IA

schizophrenic (ˌskɪtsəʊˈfrɛnɪk) ADJECTIVE [1] exhibiting symptoms of schizophrenia. [2] *Informal* experiencing or maintaining contradictory attitudes, emotions, etc. ◆ NOUN [3] a person who is schizophrenic.

schizophrenogenic (ˌskɪtsəʊˌfriːnəʊˈdʒɛnɪk, -ˌfrɛnəʊ-) ADJECTIVE tending to cause schizophrenia.

schizopod (ˈskɪtsəʊˌpɒd) NOUN any of various shrimplike crustaceans of the former order *Schizopoda,* now separated into the orders *Mysidacea* (opossum shrimps) and *Euphausiacea.*

schizothymia (ˌskɪtsəʊˈθaɪmɪə) NOUN *Psychiatry* the condition of being schizoid or introverted. It encompasses elements of schizophrenia but does not involve the same depth of psychological disturbance.
▷HISTORY C20: New Latin, from SCHIZO- + *-thymia,* from Greek *thumos* spirit
▸ˌ**schizo'thymic** ADJECTIVE

schlemiel, schlemihl, *or* **shlemiel** (ʃləˈmiːl) NOUN *US slang* an awkward or unlucky person whose endeavours usually fail.
▷HISTORY Yiddish, from German, after the hero of a novel by Chamisso (1781–1838)

schlep (ʃlɛp) VERB **schleps, schlepping, schlepped.** [1] to drag or lug (oneself or an object) with difficulty. ◆ NOUN [2] a stupid or clumsy person. [3] an arduous journey or procedure.
▷HISTORY Yiddish, from German *schleppen*

Schlesien (ˈʃleːziən) NOUN the German name for **Silesia.**

Schleswig (*German* ˈʃleːsvɪç) NOUN [1] a fishing port in N Germany, in Schleswig-Holstein state: on an inlet of the Baltic. Pop.: 26 820 (latest est.). [2] a former duchy, in the S Jutland Peninsula: annexed by Prussia in 1864; N part returned to Denmark after a plebiscite in 1920; S part forms part of the German state of Schleswig-Holstein. Danish name: **Slesvig.**

Schleswig-Holstein (*German* ˈʃleːsvɪçˈhɔlʃtain) NOUN a state of N Germany, formerly in West Germany: drained chiefly by the River Elbe; mainly agricultural. Capital: Kiel. Pop.: 2 777 300 (1996 est.). Area: 15 658 sq. km (6045 sq. miles).

Schlieffen Plan (*German* ˈʃliːfən) NOUN a plan intended to ensure German victory over a Franco-Russian alliance by holding off Russia with minimal strength and swiftly defeating France by a massive flanking movement through the Low Countries, devised by Alfred, Count von Schlieffen (1833–1913) in 1905.

schlieren (ˈʃlɪərən) NOUN [1] *Physics* visible streaks produced in a transparent medium as a result of variations in the medium's density leading to variations in refractive index. They can be recorded by flash photography (**schlieren photography**). [2] streaks or platelike masses of mineral in a rock mass, that differ in texture or composition from the main mass.
▷HISTORY German, plural of *Schliere* streak
▸'**schlieric** ADJECTIVE

schlock (ʃlɒk) *Chiefly US slang* ◆ NOUN [1] goods or produce of cheap or inferior quality; trash. ◆ ADJECTIVE [2] cheap, inferior, or trashy.
▷HISTORY Yiddish: damaged merchandise, probably from German *Schlag* a blow; related to SLAY

schlong (ʃlɒŋ) NOUN *US* a slang word for **penis.**

schlub (ʃlʌb) NOUN *US slang* a coarse or contemptible person.
▷HISTORY Yiddish, of uncertain origin

schlumbergera (ʃləmˈbɜːɡərə) NOUN See **Christmas cactus.**

schmaltz *or* **schmalz** (ʃmælts, ʃmɔːlts) NOUN [1] excessive sentimentality, esp in music. [2] *US* animal fat used in cooking.
▷HISTORY C20: from German (*Schmalz*) and Yiddish: melted fat, from Old High German *smalz*

schmaltzy (ʃmæltsɪ, ʃmɔːltsɪ) ADJECTIVE **-ier, -iest.** excessively sentimental.

schmear *or* **schmeer** (ʃmɪə) NOUN *US informal* a situation, matter, or affair (esp in the phrase **the whole schmear**).
▷HISTORY C20: from Yiddish *shmirn* to smear or grease

Schmidt telescope *or* **camera** NOUN a catadioptric telescope designed to produce a very sharp image of a large area of sky in one photographic exposure. It incorporates a thin specially shaped glass plate at the centre of curvature of a short-focus spherical primary mirror so that the resulting image, which is focused on a photographic plate, is free from spherical aberration, coma, and astigmatism.
▷HISTORY C20: named after B. V. *Schmidt* (1879–1935), Estonian-born German inventor

Schmitt trigger NOUN *Electronics* a bistable circuit that gives a constant output when the input voltage is above a specified value.
▷HISTORY C20: named after O. H. *Schmitt* (born 1913), US scientist

schmo *or* **shmo** (ʃməʊ) NOUN, *plural* **schmoes** *or* **shmoes.** *US slang* a dull, stupid, or boring person.
▷HISTORY from Yiddish *shmok*

schmooze (ʃmuːz) *Slang* ◆ VERB [1] (*intr*) to chat or gossip. [2] (*tr*) to chat to (someone) for the purposes of self-promotion or to gain some advantage. ◆ NOUN [3] a trivial conversation; chat.
▷HISTORY Yiddish, from *schmues* a chat, from Hebrew *shemuoth* reports

schmuck (ʃmʌk) NOUN *US slang* a stupid or contemptible person; oaf.
▷HISTORY from Yiddish *schmuck* penis, from German *Schmuck* decoration, from Middle High German *smucken* to press into

schmutter (ˈʃmʌtə) NOUN *Slang* cloth or clothing.
▷HISTORY C20: from Yiddish *schmatte* rag, from Polish *szmata*

schnapper (ˈʃnæpə) NOUN a variant of **snapper** (senses 1, 2).

schnapps *or* **schnaps** (ʃnæps) NOUN [1] a Dutch spirit distilled from potatoes. [2] (in Germany) any strong spirit.
▷HISTORY C19: from German *Schnaps,* from *schnappen* to SNAP

schnauzer (ˈʃnaʊtsə) NOUN a wire-haired breed of dog of the terrier type, originally from Germany, having a greyish coat and distinctive beard, moustache, and eyebrows.
▷HISTORY C19: from German *Schnauze* SNOUT

schnecken (ˈʃnɛkən) PLURAL NOUN, *singular* **schnecke** (ˈʃnɛkə). *Chiefly US* a sweet spiral-shaped bread roll flavoured with cinnamon and nuts.
▷HISTORY German, plural of *Schnecke* SNAIL

Schneider Trophy (ˈʃnaɪdə) NOUN a trophy for air racing between seaplanes of any nation, first presented by Jacques Schneider in 1913; won outright by Britain in 1931.

schnitzel (ˈʃnɪtsəl) NOUN a thin slice of meat, esp veal. See also **Wiener schnitzel.**
▷HISTORY German: cutlet, from *schnitzen* to carve, *schnitzeln* to whittle

schnook (ʃnʊk) NOUN *US slang* a stupid or gullible person.
▷HISTORY from Yiddish *shnok,* variant of *shmok* SCHMO

schnorkel (ˈʃnɔːkᵊl) NOUN, VERB a less common variant of **snorkel.**

schnorrer (ˈʃnɔːrə) NOUN *US slang* a person who lives off the charity of others; professional beggar.
▷HISTORY Yiddish, from German *Schnurrer* beggar (who played an instrument), from Middle High German *snurren* to hum

schnozzle (ˈʃnɒzᵊl) NOUN *Chiefly US* a slang word for **nose** (sense 1).
▷HISTORY alteration of Yiddish *shnoitsl,* diminutive of *shnoits,* from German *Schnauze* SNOUT

schola cantorum (ˈskəʊlə kænˈtɔːrəm) NOUN, *plural* **scholae cantorum** (ˈskəʊliː). a choir or choir school maintained by a church.
▷HISTORY Medieval Latin: school of singers

scholar (ˈskɒlə) NOUN [1] a learned person, esp in the humanities. [2] a person, esp a child, who studies; pupil. [3] a student of merit at an educational establishment who receives financial aid, esp from an endowment given for such a purpose. [4] *South African* a school pupil.
▷HISTORY C14: from Old French *escoler,* via Late Latin from Latin *schola* SCHOOL[1]
▸'**scholarly** ADJECTIVE ▸'**scholarliness** NOUN

scholarship (ˈskɒləʃɪp) NOUN [1] academic achievement; erudition; learning. [2] **a** financial aid provided for a scholar because of academic merit. **b** the position of a student who gains this financial aid. **c** (*as modifier*): *a scholarship student.* [3] the qualities of a scholar.

scholar's mate NOUN *Chess* a simple mate by the queen on the f7 square, achievable by white's fourth move.

scholastic (skəˈlæstɪk) ADJECTIVE [1] of, relating to, or befitting schools, scholars, or education. [2] pedantic or precise. [3] (*often capital*) characteristic of or relating to the medieval Schoolmen. ◆ NOUN [4] a student or pupil. [5] a person who is given to quibbling or logical subtleties; pedant. [6] (*often capital*) a disciple or adherent of scholasticism; Schoolman. [7] **a** a Jesuit student who is undergoing a period of probation prior to commencing his theological studies. **b** the status and position of such a student. [8] a formalist in art.
▷HISTORY C16: via Latin from Greek *skholastikos* devoted to learning, ultimately from *skholē* SCHOOL[1]
▸**scho'lastically** ADVERB

scholasticate (skəˈlæstɪˌkeɪt, -kɪt) NOUN *RC Church* the state of being a scholastic, the period during which a Jesuit student is a scholastic, or an institution where scholastics pass this period.
▷HISTORY C19: from New Latin *scholasticātus,* from Latin *scholasticus* SCHOLASTIC

scholasticism (skəˈlæstɪˌsɪzəm) NOUN [1] (*sometimes capital*) the system of philosophy, theology, and teaching that dominated medieval western Europe and was based on the writings of the Church Fathers and (from the 12th century) Aristotle, the Greek philosopher (384–322 B.C.). [2] strict adherence to traditional doctrines.

scholiast (ˈskəʊlɪˌæst) NOUN a medieval annotator, esp of classical texts.
▷HISTORY C16: from Late Greek *skholiastēs,* from *skholiazein* to write a SCHOLIUM
▸ˌ**scholi'astic** ADJECTIVE

scholium (ˈskəʊlɪəm) NOUN, *plural* **-lia** (-lɪə). a commentary or annotation, esp on a classical text.
▷HISTORY C16: from New Latin, from Greek *skholion* exposition, from *skholē* SCHOOL[1]

school[1] (skuːl) NOUN [1] **a** an institution or building at which children and young people

usually under 19 receive education. **b** (*as modifier*): *school bus; school day.* **c** (*in combination*): *schoolroom; schoolwork.* [2] any educational institution or building. [3] a faculty, institution, or department specializing in a particular subject: *a law school.* [4] the staff and pupils of a school. [5] the period of instruction in a school or one session of this: *he stayed after school to do extra work.* [6] meetings held occasionally for members of a profession, etc. [7] a place or sphere of activity that instructs: *the school of hard knocks.* [8] a body of people or pupils adhering to a certain set of principles, doctrines, or methods. [9] a group of artists, writers, etc., linked by the same style, teachers, or aims: *the Venetian school of painting.* [10] a style of life: *a gentleman of the old school.* [11] *Informal* a group assembled for a common purpose, esp gambling or drinking. ◆ VERB (*tr*) [12] to train or educate in or as in a school. [13] to discipline or control. [14] an archaic word for **reprimand**.
▷HISTORY Old English *scōl,* from Latin *schola* school, from Greek *skholē* leisure spent in the pursuit of knowledge

school[2] (sku:l) NOUN [1] a group of porpoises or similar aquatic animals that swim together. ◆ VERB [2] (*intr*) to form such a group.
▷HISTORY Old English *scolu* SHOAL[2]

school attendance officer NOUN a former name for **Educational Welfare Officer**.

school board NOUN [1] (formerly in Britain) an elected board of ratepayers who provided local elementary schools between 1870 and 1902. [2] (in the US and Canada) a local board of education.

schoolboy ('sku:lˌbɔɪ) *or feminine* **schoolgirl** NOUN a child attending school.

School Certificate NOUN (in England and Wales between 1917 and 1951 and currently in New Zealand) a certificate awarded to school pupils who pass a public examination: the equivalent of O level. Abbreviation: **SC**.

School Committee NOUN (in New Zealand) a parent group selected to support a primary school.

school crossing patrol NOUN the official name for **lollipop man** or **lady**.

schoolhouse ('sku:lˌhaʊs) NOUN [1] a building used as a school, esp a rural school. [2] a house attached to a school.

schoolie ('sku:lɪ) NOUN *Austral slang* a schoolteacher or a high school student.

schooling ('sku:lɪŋ) NOUN [1] education, esp when received at school. [2] the process of teaching or being taught in a school. [3] the training of an animal, esp of a horse for dressage. [4] an archaic word for **reprimand**.

school-leaver NOUN a pupil who is about to leave or has recently left school, esp at the minimum school-leaving age.
▸**'school-ˌleaving** ADJECTIVE

schoolman ('sku:lmən) NOUN, *plural* **-men**. [1] (*sometimes capital*) a scholar versed in the learning of the Schoolmen. [2] *Rare, chiefly US* a professional educator or teacher.

Schoolman ('sku:lmən) NOUN, *plural* **-men**. (*sometimes not capital*) a master in one of the schools or universities of the Middle Ages who was versed in scholasticism; scholastic.

schoolmarm ('sku:lˌmɑ:m) NOUN *Informal* [1] a woman schoolteacher, esp when considered to be prim, prudish, or old-fashioned. [2] *Brit* any woman considered to be prim, prudish, or old-fashioned.
▷HISTORY C19: from SCHOOL[1] + *marm,* variant of MA'AM. See MADAM
▸**'schoolˌmarmish** ADJECTIVE

schoolmaster ('sku:lˌmɑ:stə) NOUN [1] a man who teaches in or runs a school. [2] a person or thing that acts as an instructor. [3] a food fish, *Lutjanus apodus,* of the warm waters of the Caribbean and Atlantic: family *Lutjanidae* (snappers). ◆ VERB (*intr*) [4] to be a schoolmaster.
▸**'schoolˌmastering** NOUN ▸**'schoolˌmasterish** ADJECTIVE ▸**'schoolˌmasterly** ADJECTIVE ▸**'schoolˌmastership** NOUN

schoolmate ('sku:lˌmeɪt) *or* **schoolfellow** NOUN a companion at school; fellow pupil.

school milk NOUN *Social welfare* (formerly, in Britain) a third of a pint of milk, originally provided free by the local education authority to all young pupils, then later given only to children who passed a needs or means test.

schoolmistress ('sku:lˌmɪstrɪs) NOUN a woman who teaches in or runs a school.
▸**'schoolˌmistressy** ADJECTIVE

school night NOUN [1] any night of the week that precedes a day of school. [2] *Jocular* any night of the week that precedes a day of work.

school of arts NOUN *Austral* a public building in a small town, originally one used for adult education.

school prawn NOUN *Austral* a common olive-gree prawn, *Metapenaeus macleayi.*

Schools (sku:lz) PLURAL NOUN [1] **the.** the medieval Schoolmen collectively. [2] (at Oxford University) **a** the Examination Schools, the University building in which examinations are held. **b** *Informal* the Second Public Examination for the degree of Bachelor of Arts; finals.

school shark NOUN *Austral* an Australian shark resembling the tope, *Notogaleus australis.*

school ship NOUN a ship for training young men in seamanship, for a career in the regular or merchant navy.

schoolteacher ('sku:lˌti:tʃə) NOUN a person who teaches in a school.
▸**'schoolˌteaching** NOUN

school welfare officer NOUN a former name for **Educational Welfare Officer**.

school year NOUN [1] a twelve-month period, (in Britain) usually starting in late summer and continuing for three terms until the following summer, during which pupils remain in the same class. [2] the time during this period when the school is open.

schooner ('sku:nə) NOUN [1] a sailing vessel with at least two masts, with all lower sails rigged fore-and-aft, and with the main mast stepped aft. [2] *Brit* a large glass for sherry. [3] *US, Canadian, Austral, and NZ* a large glass for beer.
▷HISTORY C18: origin uncertain

schooner rig NOUN *Nautical* a rig in which the mainmast is taller than the foremast.

schorl (ʃɔ:l) NOUN a black tourmaline consisting of a borosilicate of sodium, iron, and aluminium. Formula: $NaFe_3B_3Al_3(Al_3Si_6O_{27})(OH)_4$.
▷HISTORY C18: from German *Schörl,* origin unknown
▸**schor'laceous** ADJECTIVE

schottische (ʃɒ'ti:ʃ) NOUN [1] a 19th-century German dance resembling a slow polka. [2] a piece of music composed for or in the manner of this dance.
▷HISTORY C19: from German *der schottische Tanz* the Scottish dance

Schottky defect ('ʃɒtkɪ) NOUN *Physics* a crystal defect in which vacancies exist in the lattice.
▷HISTORY C20: named after Walter *Schottky* (1886–1976), German physicist

Schottky effect NOUN *Physics* a reduction in the energy required to remove an electron from a solid surface in a vacuum when an electric field is applied to the surface.

Schottky noise NOUN another name for **shot noise**.

Schouten Islands ('ʃaʊtᵊn) PLURAL NOUN a group of islands in the Pacific, off the N coast of Papua New Guinea. Pop.: 25 490 (latest est.). Area: 3185 sq. km (1230 sq. miles).

Schrödinger equation NOUN an equation used in wave mechanics to describe a physical system. For a particle of mass *m* and potential energy *V* it is written $(ih/2\pi).(\partial\psi/\partial t) = (-h^2/8\pi^2 m)\nabla^2\psi + V\psi$, where $i = \sqrt{-1}$, *h* is the Planck constant, *t* the time, ∇^2 the Laplace operator, and ψ the wave function.

schtick (ʃtɪk) NOUN a variant form of **shtick**.

schul (ʃu:l) NOUN a variant spelling of **shul**.

schuss (ʃʊs) *Skiing* ◆ NOUN [1] a straight high-speed downhill run. ◆ VERB [2] (*intr*) to perform a schuss.
▷HISTORY German: SHOT[1]

Schutzstaffel *German* ('ʃʊtsʃtafəl) NOUN, *plural* **-feln** (-fəln). See **SS**.

schwa *or* **shwa** (ʃwɑ:) NOUN [1] a central vowel represented in the International Phonetic Alphabet by (ə). The sound occurs in unstressed syllables in English, as in *around, mother,* and *sofa.* [2] the symbol (ə) used to represent this sound.
▷HISTORY C19: via German from Hebrew *shewā,* a diacritic indicating lack of a vowel sound

Schwaben ('ʃva:bən) NOUN the German name for **Swabia**.

Schwarzschild radius ('ʃwɔ:tsˌʃɪld; *German* 'ʃvartsʃɪlt) NOUN *Astronomy* the radius of a sphere (**Schwarzschild sphere**) surrounding a non-rotating uncharged black hole, from within which no information can escape because of gravitational forces.
▷HISTORY C20: named after Karl *Schwarzschild* (1873–1916), US astrophysicist

Schwarzwald ('ʃvartsvalt) NOUN the German name for the **Black Forest**.

Schweinfurt (*German* 'ʃvainfʊrt) NOUN a city in central Germany, in N Bavaria on the River Main. Pop.: 54 520 (1991).

Schweiz (ʃvaits) NOUN the German name for **Switzerland**.

Schwerin (*German* ʃve'ri:n) NOUN a city in N Germany, in Mecklenburg-West Pomerania on **Lake Schwerin**. Pop.: 104 200 (1999 est.).

Schwyz (*German* ʃvi:ts) NOUN [1] a canton of central Switzerland: played an important part in the formation of the Swiss confederation, to which it gave its name. Capital: Schwyz. Pop.: 128 200 (2000 est.). Area: 908 sq. km (351 sq. miles). [2] a town in E central Switzerland, capital of Schwyz canton: tourism. Pop.: 12 740 (1990).

sci. ABBREVIATION FOR: [1] science. [2] scientific.

sciaenid (saɪ'i:nɪd) *or* **sciaenoid** ADJECTIVE [1] of, relating to, or belonging to the *Sciaenidae,* a family of mainly tropical and subtropical marine percoid fishes that includes the drums, grunts, and croakers. ◆ NOUN [2] any sciaenid fish.
▷HISTORY C19: from Latin *sciaena* a type of fish, from Greek *skiaina*

sciamachy (saɪ'æməkɪ), **sciomachy,** *or* **skiamachy** (skaɪ'æməkɪ) NOUN, *plural* **-chies**. *Rare* a fight with an imaginary enemy.
▷HISTORY C17: from Greek *skiamakhia* a mock fight, from *skia* a shadow + *makhesthai* to fight

sciatic (saɪ'ætɪk) ADJECTIVE [1] *Anatomy* of or relating to the hip or the hipbone. [2] of, relating to, or afflicted with sciatica.
▷HISTORY C16: from French *sciatique,* from Late Latin *sciaticus,* from Latin *ischiadicus* relating to pain in the hip, from Greek *iskhiadikos,* from *iskhia* hip joint

sciatica (saɪ'ætɪkə) NOUN a form of neuralgia characterized by intense pain and tenderness along the course of the body's longest nerve (**sciatic nerve**), extending from the back of the thigh down to the calf of the leg.
▷HISTORY C15: from Late Latin *sciatica;* see SCIATIC

SCID ABBREVIATION FOR severe combined immune deficiency; a serious condition in which babies are born with reduced numbers of T- and B-lymphocytes, which impairs their immune systems and makes them susceptible to severe infections and cancer.

science ('saɪəns) NOUN [1] the systematic study of the nature and behaviour of the material and physical universe, based on observation, experiment, and measurement, and the formulation of laws to describe these facts in general terms. [2] the knowledge so obtained or the practice of obtaining it. [3] any particular branch of this knowledge: *the pure and applied sciences.* [4] any body of knowledge organized in a systematic manner. [5] skill or technique. [6] *Archaic* knowledge.
▷HISTORY C14: via Old French from Latin *scientia* knowledge, from *scīre* to know

science fiction NOUN **a** a literary genre that makes imaginative use of scientific knowledge or conjecture. **b** (*as modifier*): *a science fiction writer.*

Science Museum NOUN a museum in London, originating from 1852 and given its present name and site in 1899: contains collections relating to the history of science, technology, and industry.

science park NOUN an area usually linked with a university where scientific research and commercial development are carried on in cooperation.

scienter (saɪ'ɛntə) ADVERB *Law* knowingly; wilfully.
▷HISTORY from Latin

sciential (saɪ'ɛnʃəl) ADJECTIVE [1] of or relating to science. [2] skilful or knowledgeable.

scientific (ˌsaɪən'tɪfɪk) ADJECTIVE [1] (*prenominal*) of, relating to, derived from, or used in science: *scientific equipment.* [2] (*prenominal*) occupied in science: *scientific manpower.* [3] conforming with the principles or methods used in science: *a scientific approach.*
▸ˌscien'tifically ADVERB

scientific content analysis NOUN the close analysis of the content of statements made to the police by suspects in an attempt to identify innocence or guilt.

scientific method NOUN a method of investigation in which a problem is first identified and observations, experiments, or other relevant data are then used to construct or test hypotheses that purport to solve it.

scientific socialism NOUN Marxist socialism. Compare **utopian socialism.**

scientism ('saɪənˌtɪzəm) NOUN [1] the application of, or belief in, the scientific method. [2] the uncritical application of scientific or quasi-scientific methods to inappropriate fields of study or investigation.
▸ˌscien'tistic ADJECTIVE

scientist ('saɪəntɪst) NOUN a person who studies or practises any of the sciences or who uses scientific methods.

Scientist ('saɪəntɪst) NOUN [1] *Christian Science* Christ as supreme spiritual healer. [2] short for **Christian Scientist.**

Scientology (ˌsaɪən'tɒlədʒɪ) NOUN *Trademark* the philosophy of the Church of Scientology, a nondenominational movement founded in the US in the 1950s, which emphasizes self-knowledge as a means of realizing full spiritual potential.
▷HISTORY C20: from Latin *scient(ia)* SCIENCE + -LOGY
▸ˌScien'tologist NOUN

sci-fi ('saɪˌfaɪ) NOUN short for **science fiction.**

scilicet ('sɪlɪˌsɛt) ADVERB namely; that is: used esp in explaining an obscure text or supplying a missing word.
▷HISTORY Latin: shortened from *scīre licet* it is permitted to know

scilla ('sɪlə) NOUN any liliaceous plant of the genus *Scilla,* of Old World temperate regions, having small bell-shaped flowers. See also **squill** (sense 3).
▷HISTORY C19: via Latin from Greek *skilla;* compare SQUILL

Scillonian (sɪ'ləʊnɪən) ADJECTIVE [1] of or relating to the Scilly Isles or their inhabitants. ◆ NOUN [2] a native or inhabitant of the Scilly Isles.

Scilly Isles, Scilly Islands ('sɪlɪ), *or* **Scillies** ('sɪlɪz) PLURAL NOUN a group of about 140 small islands (only five inhabited) off the extreme SW coast of England: tourist centre. Capital: Hugh Town. Pop.: 2153 (2001). Area: 16 sq. km (6 sq. miles).

scimitar *or rarely* **simitar** ('sɪmɪtə) NOUN an oriental sword with a curved blade broadening towards the point.
▷HISTORY C16: from Old Italian *scimitarra,* probably from Persian *shimshīr,* of obscure origin

scincoid ('sɪŋkɔɪd) *or* **scincoidian** ADJECTIVE [1] of, relating to, or resembling a skink. ◆ NOUN [2] any animal, esp a lizard, resembling a skink.
▷HISTORY C18: from New Latin *scincoidēs,* from Latin *scincus* a SKINK

scindapsus (sɪn'dæpsəs) NOUN any plant of the tropical Asiatic climbing genus *Scindapsus,* typically stem rooting, esp *S. aureus* and *S. pictus,* grown as greenhouse or house plants for their leathery heart-shaped variegated leaves: family *Araceae.*
▷HISTORY New Latin, from Greek *skindapsos* an ivy-like plant

scintigraphy (ˌsɪn'tɪgrəfɪ) NOUN *Med* a diagnostic technique using a radioactive tracer and scintillation counter for producing pictures (**scintigrams**) of internal parts of the body.
▷HISTORY C20: from SCINTI(LLATION) + -GRAPHY

scintilla (sɪn'tɪlə) NOUN a minute amount; hint, trace, or particle.
▷HISTORY C17: from Latin: a spark

scintillate ('sɪntɪˌleɪt) VERB (*mainly intr*) [1] (*also tr*) to give off (sparks); sparkle; twinkle. [2] to be animated or brilliant. [3] *Physics* to give off flashes of light as a result of the impact of particles or photons.
▷HISTORY C17: from Latin *scintillāre,* from *scintilla* a spark
▸'scintillant ADJECTIVE ▸'scintillantly ADVERB

scintillating ('sɪntɪˌleɪtɪŋ) ADJECTIVE [1] sparkling; twinkling. [2] animated or brilliant.
▸'scintilˌlatingly ADVERB

scintillation (ˌsɪntɪ'leɪʃən) NOUN [1] the act of scintillating. [2] a spark or flash. [3] the twinkling of stars or radio sources, caused by rapid changes in the density of the earth's atmosphere, the interplanetary medium, or the interstellar medium producing uneven refraction of starlight. [4] *Physics* a flash of light produced when a material scintillates.

scintillation counter NOUN an instrument for detecting and measuring the intensity of high-energy radiation. It consists of a phosphor with which particles collide producing flashes of light that are detected by a photomultiplier and converted into pulses of electric current that are counted by electronic equipment.

scintillator ('sɪntɪˌleɪtə) NOUN *Physics* a phosphor that produces scintillations.

scintillometer (ˌsɪntɪ'lɒmɪtə) NOUN *Physics* a device for observing ionizing radiation by the scintillations it produces in a suitable material.

scintillon (sɪn'tɪlən) NOUN a luminescent body present in the cytoplasm of some dinoflagellates.

sciolism ('saɪəˌlɪzəm) NOUN *Rare* the practice of opinionating on subjects of which one has only superficial knowledge.
▷HISTORY C19: from Late Latin *sciolus* someone with a smattering of knowledge, from Latin *scīre* to know
▸'sciolist NOUN ▸ˌscio'listic ADJECTIVE

sciomachy (saɪ'ɒməkɪ) NOUN, *plural* **-chies.** a variant of **sciamachy.**

sciomancy ('saɪəˌmænsɪ) NOUN divination with the help of ghosts.
▷HISTORY C17: via Latin from Greek *skia* ghost + -MANCY
▸'sciomancer NOUN ▸ˌscio'mantic ADJECTIVE

scion ('saɪən) NOUN [1] a descendant, heir, or young member of a family. [2] a shoot or twig of a plant used to form a graft.
▷HISTORY C14: from Old French *cion,* of Germanic origin; compare Old High German *chīnan* to sprout

sciophyte ('saɪəˌfaɪt) NOUN *Now rare* any plant that grows best in the shade.
▷HISTORY C20: via Latin from Greek *skia* shade + -PHYTE
▸sciophytic (ˌsaɪə'fɪtɪk) ADJECTIVE

scire facias ('saɪərɪ 'feɪʃɪˌæs) NOUN *Law, rare* [1] a judicial writ founded upon some record, such as a judgment, letters patent, etc., requiring the person against whom it is brought to show cause why the record should not be enforced or annulled. [2] a proceeding begun by the issue of such a writ.
▷HISTORY C15: from legal Latin, literally: cause (him) to know

scirrhous ('sɪrəs) ADJECTIVE *Pathol* of or resembling a scirrhus; hard.
▸scirrhosity (sɪ'rɒsɪtɪ) NOUN

scirrhus ('sɪrəs) NOUN, *plural* **-rhi** (-raɪ) *or* **-rhuses.** *Pathol* a hard cancerous growth composed of fibrous tissues. Also called: **scirrhous carcinoma.**
▷HISTORY C17: from New Latin, from Latin *scirros,* from Greek *skirros,* from *skiros* hard
▸scirrhoid ('sɪrɔɪd) ADJECTIVE

scissel ('skɪsᵊl) NOUN the waste metal left over from sheet metal after discs have been punched out of it.
▷HISTORY C19: from French *cisaille,* from *cisailler* to clip

scissile ('sɪsaɪl) ADJECTIVE capable of being cut or divided.
▷HISTORY C17: from Latin *scissilis* that can be split, from *scindere* to cut

scission ('sɪʃən) NOUN the act or an instance of cutting, splitting, or dividing.
▷HISTORY C15: from Late Latin *scissiō,* from *scindere* to split

scissor ('sɪzə) VERB to cut (an object) with scissors.

scissors ('sɪzəz) PLURAL NOUN [1] Also called: **pair of scissors.** a cutting instrument used for cloth, hair, etc., having two crossed pivoted blades that cut by a shearing action, with ring-shaped handles at one end. [2] a wrestling hold in which a wrestler wraps his legs round his opponent's body or head, locks his feet together, and squeezes. [3] any gymnastic or athletic feat in which the legs cross and uncross in a scissor-like movement. [4] *Athletics* a technique in high-jumping, now little used, in which the legs perform a scissor-like movement in clearing the bar.
▷HISTORY C14 *sisoures,* from Old French *cisoires,* from Vulgar Latin *cīsōria* (unattested), ultimately from Latin *caedere* to cut; see CHISEL
▸'scissor-ˌlike ADJECTIVE

scissors kick NOUN [1] a type of swimming kick used esp in the sidestroke, in which one leg is moved forward and the other bent back and they are then brought together again in a scissor-like action. [2] *Football* a kick in which the player leaps into the air raising one leg and brings up his other leg to kick the ball.

scissure ('sɪʒə, 'sɪʃə) NOUN *Rare* a longitudinal cleft.
▷HISTORY C15: from Latin *scissūra* a rending, from Latin *scindere* to split

sciurine ('saɪjʊrɪn, -ˌraɪn) ADJECTIVE [1] of, relating to, or belonging to the *Sciuridae,* a family of rodents inhabiting most parts of the world except Australia and southern South America: includes squirrels, marmots, and chipmunks. ◆ NOUN [2] any sciurine animal.
▷HISTORY C19: from Latin *sciūrus,* from Greek *skiouros* squirrel, from *skia* a shadow + *oura* a tail

sciuroid ('saɪjʊrɔɪd, saɪ'jʊərɔɪd) ADJECTIVE [1] (of an animal) resembling a squirrel. [2] (esp of the spikes of barley) shaped like a squirrel's tail.
▷HISTORY C19: from Latin *sciūrus* squirrel + -OID

sclaff (sklæf) *Golf* ◆ VERB [1] to cause (the club) to hit (the ground behind the ball) when making a stroke. ◆ NOUN [2] a sclaffing stroke or shot. Also: **duff.**
▷HISTORY C19: from Scottish *sclaf* to shuffle
▸'sclaffer NOUN

sclera ('sklɪərə) NOUN the firm white fibrous membrane that forms the outer covering of the eyeball. Also called: **sclerotic.**
▷HISTORY C19: from New Latin, from Greek *sklēros* hard

sclere (sklɪə) NOUN *Zoology* a supporting anatomical structure, esp a sponge spicule.

sclerenchyma (sklɪə'rɛŋkɪmə) NOUN a supporting tissue in plants consisting of dead cells with very thick lignified walls.
▷HISTORY C19: from SCLERO- + PARENCHYMA
▸sclerenchymatous (ˌsklɪərɛŋ'kɪmətəs) ADJECTIVE

sclerite ('sklɪəraɪt) NOUN *Zoology* [1] any of the hard chitinous plates that make up the exoskeleton of an arthropod. [2] any calcareous or chitinous part, such as a spicule or plate.
▷HISTORY C19: from SCLERO- + -ITE[1]
▸scleritic (sklɪə'rɪtɪk) ADJECTIVE

scleritis (sklɪə'raɪtɪs) *or* **sclerotitis** (ˌsklɪərəʊ'taɪtɪs) NOUN *Pathol* inflammation of the sclera.

sclero- *or before a vowel* **scler-** COMBINING FORM [1] indicating hardness: *sclerosis.* [2] of or relating to the sclera: *sclerotomy.*
▷HISTORY from Greek *sklēros* hard

scleroderma (ˌsklɪərəʊ'dɜːmə), **sclerodermia** (ˌsklɪərəʊ'dɜːmɪə), *or* **scleriasis** (sklɪ'raɪəsɪs) NOUN a chronic progressive disease most common among women, characterized by a local or diffuse thickening and hardening of the skin.
▷HISTORY C19: from New Latin *sclerōdermus,* from Greek, from *sklēros* hard + *derma* skin

sclerodermatous (ˌsklɪərəʊ'dɜːmətəs) ADJECTIVE [1] (of animals) possessing a hard external covering of scales or plates. [2] of or relating to scleroderma.

scleroid ('sklɪərɔɪd) ADJECTIVE (of organisms and their parts) hard or hardened.

scleroma (sklɪə'rəʊmə) NOUN, *plural* **-mata** (-mətə) *or* **-mas.** *Pathol* any small area of abnormally hard tissue, esp in a mucous membrane.

▷HISTORY C17: from New Latin, from Greek, from *sklēroun* to harden, from *sklēros* hard

sclerometer (sklɪəˈrɒmɪtə) NOUN an instrument that determines the hardness of a mineral or metal by means of a diamond point.
▸**sclerometric** (ˌsklɪərəˈmɛtrɪk) ADJECTIVE

sclerophyll (ˈsklɛrəʊˌfɪl) NOUN a woody plant with small leathery evergreen leaves that is the dominant plant form in certain hot dry areas, esp the Mediterranean region.
▷HISTORY C20: from Greek *sklēros* hard + *phullon* a leaf
▸**sclerophyllous** (sklɛˈrɒfɪləs) ADJECTIVE

scleroprotein (ˌsklɪərəʊˈprəʊtiːn) NOUN any of a group of insoluble stable proteins such as keratin, elastin, and collagen that occur in skeletal and connective tissues. Also called: **albuminoid.**

sclerosed (ˈsklɪərəʊst) ADJECTIVE *Pathol* hardened; sclerotic.

sclerosis (sklɪəˈrəʊsɪs) NOUN, *plural* **-ses** (-siːz). [1] *Pathol* a hardening or thickening of organs, tissues, or vessels from chronic inflammation, abnormal growth of fibrous tissue, or degeneration of the myelin sheath of nerve fibres, or (esp on the inner walls of arteries) deposition of fatty plaques. Compare **arteriosclerosis, atherosclerosis, multiple sclerosis.** [2] the hardening of a plant cell wall or tissue by the deposition of lignin. [C14: via Medieval Latin from Greek *sklērōsis* a hardening] [3] a debilitating lack of progress or innovation within an institution or organization.
▸**scleˈrosal** ADJECTIVE

sclerotic (sklɪəˈrɒtɪk) ADJECTIVE [1] of or relating to the sclera. [2] of, relating to, or having sclerosis. [3] *Botany* characterized by the hardening and strengthening of cell walls. ◆ NOUN [4] another name for **sclera.**
▷HISTORY C16: from Medieval Latin *sclērōticus,* from Greek; see SCLEROMA

sclerotin (ˈsklɛrəʊtɪn) NOUN a protein in the cuticle of insects that becomes hard and dark.

sclerotium (sklɪəˈrəʊʃɪəm) NOUN, *plural* **-tia** (-ʃɪə). a compact mass of hyphae, that is formed by certain fungi and gives rise to new fungal growth or spore-producing structures.
▷HISTORY C18: from New Latin, from Greek *sklēros* hard
▸**scleˈrotioid** *or* **scleˈrotial** ADJECTIVE

sclerotize *or* **sclerotise** (ˈsklɛrəˌtaɪz) VERB (*tr; usually passive*) *Zoology* to harden and darken (an insect's cuticle).
▸**ˌscleroti'zation** *or* **ˌscleroti'sation** NOUN

sclerotomy (sklɪəˈrɒtəmɪ) NOUN, *plural* **-mies**. surgical incision into the sclera.

sclerous (ˈsklɪərəs) ADJECTIVE *Anatomy, pathol* hard; bony; indurated.
▷HISTORY C19: from Greek *sklēros* hard

SCM (in Britain) ABBREVIATION FOR: [1] State Certified Midwife. [2] Student Christian Movement.

scody (ˈskəʊdɪ) ADJECTIVE *NZ informal* unkempt; dirty: *they lived in a scody student flat.*

scoff[1] (skɒf) VERB [1] (*intr; often foll by at*) to speak contemptuously (about); express derision (for); mock. [2] (*tr*) *Obsolete* to regard with derision. ◆ NOUN [3] an expression of derision. [4] an object of derision.
▷HISTORY C14: probably from Scandinavian; compare Old Frisian *skof* mockery, Danish *skof, skuf* jest
▸**ˈscoffer** NOUN ▸**ˈscoffing** ADJECTIVE ▸**ˈscoffingly** ADVERB

scoff[2] (skɒf) *Informal, chiefly Brit* ◆ VERB [1] to eat (food) fast and greedily; devour. ◆ NOUN [2] food or rations.
▷HISTORY C19: variant of *scaff* food; related to Afrikaans, Dutch *schoft* quarter of the day, one of the four daily meals

scofflaw (ˈskɒflɔː) NOUN *US informal* a person who habitually flouts or violates the law, esp one who fails to pay debts or answer summonses.

scold (skəʊld) VERB [1] to find fault with or reprimand (a person) harshly; chide. [2] (*intr*) to use harsh or abusive language. ◆ NOUN [3] a person, esp a woman, who constantly finds fault.
▷HISTORY C13: from Old Norse SKALD
▸**ˈscoldable** ADJECTIVE ▸**ˈscolder** NOUN ▸**ˈscolding** NOUN ▸**ˈscoldingly** ADVERB

scolecite (ˈskɒlɪˌsaɪt, ˈskəʊl-) NOUN a white zeolite mineral consisting of hydrated calcium aluminium silicate in groups of radiating monoclinic crystals. Formula: $CaAl_2Si_3O_{10}.3H_2O$.
▷HISTORY C19: *scolec-* from Greek *skōlēx* SCOLEX + -ITE[1]

scolex (ˈskəʊlɛks) NOUN, *plural* **scoleces** (skəʊˈliːsiːz) *or* **scolices** (ˈskɒlɪˌsiːz, ˈskəʊ-). the headlike part of a tapeworm, bearing hooks and suckers by which the animal is attached to the tissues of its host.
▷HISTORY C19: from New Latin, from Greek *skōlēx* worm

scoliosis (ˌskɒlɪˈəʊsɪs) NOUN *Pathol* an abnormal lateral curvature of the spine, of congenital origin or caused by trauma or disease of the vertebrae or hipbones. Compare **kyphosis, lordosis.**
▷HISTORY C18: from New Latin, from Greek: a curving, from *skolios* bent
▸**scoliotic** (ˌskɒlɪˈɒtɪk) ADJECTIVE

scollop[1] (ˈskɒləp) NOUN, VERB a variant of **scallop.**

scollop[2] (ˈskɒləp) NOUN (in Ireland) a rod, pointed at both ends, used to pin down thatch.
▷HISTORY C19: from Irish Gaelic *scolb*

scolopendrid (ˌskɒləˈpɛndrɪd) NOUN any centipede of the family *Scolopendridae,* including some large and poisonous species.
▷HISTORY C19: from New Latin *Scolopendridae,* from Latin *scolopendra,* from Greek *skolopendra* legendary sea-fish
▸**scolopendrine** (ˌskɒləˈpɛndraɪn, -drɪn) ADJECTIVE

scolopendrium (skɒləˈpɛndrɪəm) NOUN another name for **hart's-tongue.**
▷HISTORY C17: from New Latin, from Greek *scolopendrion,* from a fancied resemblance of the fern and its sori to a centipede

scombroid (ˈskɒmbrɔɪd) ADJECTIVE [1] of, relating to, or belonging to the *Scombroidea,* a suborder of marine spiny-finned fishes having a spindle-shaped body and a forked powerful tail: includes the mackerels, tunnies, bonitos, swordfish, and sailfish. ◆ NOUN [2] any fish belonging to the suborder *Scombroidea.*
▷HISTORY C19: from Greek *skombros* a mackerel; see -OID

sconce[1] (skɒns) NOUN [1] a bracket fixed to a wall for holding candles or lights. [2] a flat candlestick with a handle.
▷HISTORY C14: from Old French *esconse* hiding place, lantern, or from Late Latin *sconsa,* from *absconsa* dark lantern

sconce[2] (skɒns) NOUN a small protective fortification, such as an earthwork.
▷HISTORY C16: from Dutch *schans,* from Middle High German *schanze* bundle of brushwood

sconce[3] (skɒns) (at Oxford and Cambridge Universities, esp formerly) VERB (*tr*) [1] to challenge (a fellow student) on the grounds of a social misdemeanour to drink a large quantity of beer without stopping. [2] *Obsolete* to fine (a student) for some minor misdemeanour. ◆ NOUN [3] the act of sconcing. [4] a mug or tankard used in sconcing.
▷HISTORY C17: of obscure origin

sconce[4] (skɒns) NOUN *Archaic* [1] the head or skull. [2] sense, brain, or wit.
▷HISTORY C16: probably jocular use of SCONCE[1]

scone NOUN [1] (skɒn, skəʊn) a light plain doughy cake made from flour with very little fat, cooked in an oven or (esp originally) on a griddle, usually split open and buttered. [2] (skɒn) *Austral* a slang word for **head** (sense 1). [3] *Austral slang* **a** angry. **b** insane.
▷HISTORY C16: Scottish, perhaps from Middle Low German *schonbrot,* Middle Dutch *schoonbrot* fine bread

Scone (skuːn) NOUN a parish in Perth and Kinross, E Scotland, consisting of the two villages of New Scone and Old Scone, formerly the site of the Pictish capital and the stone upon which medieval Scottish kings were crowned. The stone was removed to Westminster Abbey by Edward I in 1296; it was returned to Scotland in 1996 and placed in Edinburgh Castle. Scone Palace was rebuilt in the Neo-Gothic style in the 19th century.

scooby doo (ˌskuːbɪ ˈduː) NOUN *Rhyming slang* a clue: *I don't have a scooby doo what you're talking about.* Often shortened to: **scooby**
▷HISTORY C20: from *Scooby Doo,* a cartoon character on children's television

scoop (skuːp) NOUN [1] a utensil used as a shovel or ladle, esp a small shovel with deep sides and a short handle, used for taking up flour, corn, etc. [2] a utensil with a long handle and round bowl used for dispensing liquids. [3] a utensil with a round bowl and short handle, sometimes with a mechanical device to empty the bowl, for serving ice cream or mashed potato. [4] anything that resembles a scoop in action, such as the bucket on a dredge. [5] a spoonlike surgical instrument for scraping or extracting foreign matter, etc., from the body. [6] the quantity taken up by a scoop. [7] the act of scooping, dredging, etc. [8] a hollow cavity. [9] *Slang* a large quick gain, as of money. [10] a news story reported in one newspaper before all the others; an exclusive. [11] any sensational piece of news. ◆ VERB (*mainly tr*) [12] (often foll by *up*) to take up and remove (an object or substance) with or as if with a scoop. [13] (often foll by *out*) to hollow out with or as if with a scoop: *to scoop a hole in a hillside.* [14] to win (a prize, award, or large amount of money). [15] to beat (rival newspapers) in uncovering a news item. [16] *Sport* to hit (the ball) on its underside so that it rises into the air.
▷HISTORY C14: via Middle Dutch *schōpe* from Germanic; compare Old High German *scephan* to ladle, German *schöpfen, Schaufel* SHOVEL, Dutch *schoep* vessel for baling
▸**ˈscooper** NOUN ▸**ˈscoopˌful** NOUN

scoop neck NOUN a rounded low-cut neckline on a woman's garment.

scoosh (skuʃ) *Scot* ◆ VERB [1] to squirt. [2] (*intr*) (of liquid) to rush. ◆ NOUN [3] a squirt or rush of liquid. [4] any fizzy drink.
▷HISTORY C19: of imitative origin

scoot (skuːt) VERB [1] to go or cause to go quickly or hastily; dart or cause to dart off or away. [2] *Scot* to squirt. ◆ NOUN [3] the act of scooting. [4] *Scot* a squirt.
▷HISTORY C19 probably of Scandinavian origin; compare SHOOT

scooter (ˈskuːtə) NOUN [1] a child's vehicle consisting of a low footboard on wheels, steered by handlebars. It is propelled by pushing one foot against the ground. [2] See **motor scooter.** [3] (in the US and Canada) another term for **ice yacht.**
▸**ˈscooterist** NOUN

scop (skɒp) NOUN (in Anglo-Saxon England) a bard or minstrel.
▷HISTORY Old English: related to Old Norse *skop, skaup,* Old High German *scof, scopf* poem

scopa (ˈskəʊpə) NOUN, *plural* **-pae** (-ˌpiː). a tuft of hairs on the abdomen or hind legs of bees, used for collecting pollen.
▷HISTORY C19: from Latin, used only in pl *scopae* twigs, brush

SCOPA (ˈskəʊpə) (in South Africa) NOUN ACRONYM FOR Standing Committee on Public Accounts.

scope (skəʊp) NOUN [1] opportunity for exercising the faculties or abilities; capacity for action. [2] range of view, perception, or grasp; outlook. [3] the area covered by an activity, topic, etc.; range: *the scope of his thesis was vast.* [4] *Nautical* slack left in an anchor cable. [5] *Logic, linguistics* that part of an expression that is governed by a given operator: the scope of the negation in $PV\text{–}(q \wedge r)$ is $\text{–}(q \wedge r)$. [6] *Informal* short for **telescope, microscope, oscilloscope,** etc. [7] *Archaic* purpose or aim. ◆ VERB (*tr*) [8] *Informal* to look at or examine carefully. ◆ See also **scope out.**
▷HISTORY C16: from Italian *scopo* goal, from Latin *scopus,* from Greek *skopos* target; related to Greek *skopein* to watch

-scope NOUN COMBINING FORM indicating an instrument for observing, viewing, or detecting: *microscope; stethoscope.*
▷HISTORY from New Latin *-scopium,* from Greek *-skopion,* from *skopein* to look at
▸**-scopic** ADJECTIVE COMBINING FORM

scope out VERB (*tr*) to assess the potential of an opportunity or suggestion: *a scoping-out study.*

scopolamine (skəˈpɒləˌmiːn, -mɪn, ˌskəʊpəˈlæmɪn) NOUN a colourless viscous liquid alkaloid extracted from certain plants, such as henbane: used in preventing travel sickness and as an anticholinergic, sedative, and truth serum. Formula: $C_{17}H_{21}NO_4$. Also called: **hyoscine.** See also **atropine.**
▷HISTORY C20 *scopol-* from New Latin *scopolia Japonica* Japanese belladonna (from which the

alkaloid is extracted), named after G. A. *Scopoli* (1723–88), Italian naturalist, + AMINE

scopoline ('skəupəˌliːn, -lɪn) NOUN a soluble crystalline alkaloid obtained from the decomposition of scopolamine and used as a sedative. Formula: $C_8H_{13}NO_2$. Also called: **oscine.**
▷HISTORY C19: from *scopol-* (as in SCOPOLAMINE) + -INE[2]

scopula ('skɒpjʊlə) NOUN, *plural* **-las, -lae** (-ˌliː). a small tuft of dense hairs on the legs and chelicerae of some spiders.
▷HISTORY C19: from Late Latin: a broom-twig, from *scōpa* thin twigs
▸**scopulate** ('skɒpjʊˌleɪt, -lɪt) ADJECTIVE

Scopus ('skəupəs) NOUN **Mount.** a mountain in central Israel, east of Jerusalem: a N extension of the Mount of Olives; site of the Hebrew University (1925). Height: 834 m (2736 ft.).

-scopy NOUN COMBINING FORM indicating a viewing or observation: *microscopy.*
▷HISTORY from Greek *-skopia,* from *skopein* to look at

scorbutic (skɔː'bjuːtɪk) ADJECTIVE of, relating to, or having scurvy.
▷HISTORY C17: from New Latin *scorbūticus,* from Medieval Latin *scorbūtus,* probably of Germanic origin; compare Old English *sceorf* scurf, Middle Low German *scorbuk* scurvy
▸**scor'butically** ADVERB

scorch (skɔːtʃ) VERB [1] to burn or become burnt, so as to affect the colour, taste, etc., or to cause or feel pain. [2] to wither or parch or cause to wither from exposure to heat. [3] (*intr*) *Informal* to be very hot: *it is scorching outside.* [4] (*tr*) *Informal* to criticize harshly. [5] (*intr*) *Brit slang* to drive or ride very fast. ◆ NOUN [6] a slight burn. [7] a mark caused by the application of too great heat. [8] *Horticulture* a mark or series of marks on fruit, vegetables, etc., caused by pests or insecticides.
▷HISTORY C15: probably from Old Norse *skorpna* to shrivel up
▸**'scorching** ADJECTIVE

scorched earth policy NOUN [1] the policy in warfare of removing or destroying everything that might be useful to an invading enemy, esp by fire. [2] *Business* a manoeuvre by a company expecting an unwelcome takeover bid in which apparent profitability is greatly reduced by a reversible operation, such as borrowing at an exorbitant interest rate.

scorcher ('skɔːtʃə) NOUN [1] a person or thing that scorches. [2] something severe or caustic. [3] *Informal* a very hot day. [4] *Brit informal* something remarkable.

score (skɔː) NOUN [1] an evaluative usually numerical record of a competitive game or match. [2] the total number of points made by a side or individual in a game or match. [3] the act of scoring, esp a point or points. [4] **the score.** *Informal* the actual situation; the true facts: *to know the score.* [5] *US and Canadian* the result of a test or exam. [6] a group or set of twenty: *three score years and ten.* [7] (*usually plural; foll by of*) a great number; lots: *I have scores of things to do.* [8] *Music* **a** the written or printed form of a composition in which the instrumental or vocal parts appear on separate staves vertically arranged on large pages (**full score**) or in a condensed version, usually for piano (**short score**) or voices and piano (**vocal score**). **b** the incidental music for a film or play. **c** the songs, music, etc., for a stage or film musical. [9] a mark or notch, esp one made in keeping a tally. [10] an account of amounts due. [11] an amount recorded as due. [12] a reason or account: *the book was rejected on the score of length.* [13] a grievance. [14] **a** a line marking a division or boundary. **b** (*as modifier*): *score line.* [15] *Informal* the victim of a theft or swindle. [16] *Dancing* notation indicating a dancer's moves. [17] **over the score.** *Informal* excessive; unfair. [18] **settle** *or* **pay off a score. a** to avenge a wrong. **b** to repay a debt. ◆ VERB [19] to gain (a point or points) in a game or contest. [20] (*tr*) to make a total score of: *to score twelve.* [21] to keep a record of the score (of). [22] (*tr*) to be worth (a certain amount) in a game. [23] (*tr*) *US and Canadian* to evaluate (a test or exam) numerically; mark. [24] (*tr*) to record by making notches in. [25] to make (cuts, lines, etc.) in or on. [26] (*intr*) *Slang* to obtain something desired, esp to purchase an illegal drug. [27] (*intr*) *Slang* (of a man) to be successful in seducing a person. [28] (*tr*) **a** to set or arrange (a piece of music) for specific instruments or voices. **b** to write the music for (a film, play, etc.). [29] to achieve (success or an advantage): *your idea really scored with the boss.* [30] (*tr*) *Chiefly US and Canadian* to criticize harshly; berate. [31] to accumulate or keep a record of (a debt).
▷HISTORY Old English *scora;* related to Old Norse *skor* notch, tally, twenty
▸**'scorer** NOUN

scoreboard ('skɔːˌbɔːd) NOUN *Sport* a board for displaying the score of a game or match.

scorecard ('skɔːˌkɑːd) NOUN [1] a card on which scores are recorded in various games, esp golf. [2] a card identifying the players in a sports match, esp cricket or baseball.

score draw NOUN (esp in football) a result of a match in which both sides have scored an equal number of goals.

score off VERB (*intr, preposition*) to gain an advantage at someone else's expense.

score out VERB (*tr, adverb*) to delete or cancel by marking through with a line or lines; cross out.

scoria ('skɔːrɪə) NOUN, *plural* **-riae** (-rɪˌiː). [1] a rough cindery crust on top of solidified lava flows containing numerous vesicles. [2] refuse obtained from smelted ore; slag.
▷HISTORY C17: from Latin: dross, from Greek *skōria,* from *skōr* excrement
▸**scoriaceous** (ˌskɔːrɪ'eɪʃəs) ADJECTIVE

scorify ('skɔːrɪˌfaɪ) VERB **-fies, -fying, -fied.** to remove (impurities) from metals by forming scoria.
▸ˌ**scorifi'cation** NOUN ▸**'scoriˌfier** NOUN

scoring ('skɔːrɪŋ) NOUN [1] the act or practice of scoring. [2] another name for **orchestration** (see **orchestrate**).

scorn (skɔːn) NOUN [1] open contempt or disdain for a person or thing; derision. [2] an object of contempt or derision. [3] *Archaic* an act or expression signifying contempt. ◆ VERB [4] to treat with contempt or derision. [5] (*tr*) to reject with contempt.
▷HISTORY C12 *schornen,* from Old French *escharnir,* of Germanic origin; compare Old High German *scerōn* to behave rowdily, obsolete Dutch *schern* mockery
▸**'scorner** NOUN ▸**'scornful** ADJECTIVE ▸**'scornfully** ADVERB ▸**'scornfulness** NOUN

scorpaenid (skɔː'piːnɪd) NOUN [1] any spiny-finned marine fish of the family *Scorpaenidae,* having sharp spines on the fins and a heavy armoured head: includes the scorpion fishes, rockfishes, and redfishes. ◆ ADJECTIVE [2] of, relating to, or belonging to the family *Scorpaenidae.*
▷HISTORY via New Latin from Latin *scorpaena* a sea-scorpion; see SCORPION

scorpaenoid (skɔː'piːnɔɪd) ADJECTIVE [1] of, relating to, or belonging to the *Scorpaenoidea,* a suborder of spiny-finned fishes having bony plates covering the head: includes the scorpaenids, scorpion fishes, gurnards, etc. ◆ NOUN [2] any fish belonging to the suborder *Scorpaenoidea.*

scorper *or* **scauper** ('skɔːpə) NOUN a kind of fine chisel with a square or curved tip used in wood engraving for clearing away large areas of the block or clearing away lines.
▷HISTORY C19: erroneously for *scauper* scalper, from Latin *scalper* knife

Scorpio ('skɔːpɪˌəu) NOUN [1] Also called: **the Scorpion.** *Astrology* **a** the eighth sign of the zodiac, symbol ♏, having a fixed water classification and ruled by the planets Mars and Pluto. The sun is in this sign between about Oct. 23 and Nov. 21. **b** a person born during a period when the sun is in this sign. [2] *Astronomy* another name for **Scorpius.** ◆ ADJECTIVE [3] *Astrology* born under or characteristic of Scorpio. ◆ Also (for senses 1b, 3): **Scorpionic** (ˌskɔːpɪ'ɒnɪk).
▷HISTORY Latin: SCORPION

scorpioid ('skɔːpɪˌɔɪd) ADJECTIVE [1] of, relating to, or resembling scorpions or the order (*Scorpionida*) to which they belong. [2] *Botany* (esp of a cymose inflorescence) having the main stem coiled during development.

scorpion ('skɔːpɪən) NOUN [1] any arachnid of the order *Scorpionida,* of warm dry regions, having a segmented body with a long tail terminating in a venomous sting. [2] **false scorpion.** any small nonvenomous arachnid of the order *Pseudoscorpionida* (or *Chelonethida*), which superficially resemble scorpions but lack the long tail. See **book scorpion.** [3] any of various other similar arachnids, such as the whip scorpion, or other arthropods, such as the water scorpion. [4] *Old Testament* a barbed scourge (I Kings 12:11). [5] *History* a war engine for hurling stones; ballista.
▷HISTORY C13: via Old French from Latin *scorpiō,* from Greek *skorpios,* of obscure origin

Scorpion ('skɔːpɪən) NOUN **the.** the constellation Scorpio, the eighth sign of the zodiac.

scorpion fish NOUN any of various scorpaenid fishes of the genus *Scorpaena* and related genera, of temperate and tropical seas, having venomous spines on the dorsal and anal fins.

scorpion fly NOUN any of various insects of the family *Panorpidae,* of the N hemisphere, having a scorpion-like but nonvenomous tail in the males, long antennae, and a beaklike snout: order *Mecoptera.*

scorpion grass NOUN another name for **forget-me-not.**

Scorpius ('skɔːpɪəs) NOUN, *Latin genitive* **Scorpii** ('skɔːpɪˌaɪ). a large zodiacal constellation lying between Libra and Sagittarius and crossed by the Milky Way. It contains the first magnitude star Antares. Also called: **Scorpio.**

Scot (skɒt) NOUN [1] a native or inhabitant of Scotland. [2] a member of a tribe of Celtic raiders from the north of Ireland who carried out periodic attacks against the British mainland coast from the 3rd century A.D., eventually settling in N Britain during the 5th and 6th centuries.

Scot. ABBREVIATION FOR: [1] Scotch (whisky). [2] Scotland. [3] Scottish.

scot and lot NOUN *Brit history* a municipal tax paid by burgesses and others that came to be regarded as a qualification for the borough franchise in parliamentary elections (until the Reform Act of 1832).
▷HISTORY C13 *scot* tax, from Germanic; compare Old Norse *skot;* related to Old French *escot* (French *écot*) + LOT (in the obsolete sense: tax)

scotch[1] (skɒtʃ) VERB (*tr*) [1] to put an end to; crush: *bad weather scotched our plans.* [2] *Archaic* to injure so as to render harmless. [3] *Obsolete* to cut or score. ◆ NOUN [4] *Archaic* a gash; scratch. [5] a line marked down, as for hopscotch.
▷HISTORY C15: of obscure origin

scotch[2] (skɒtʃ) VERB [1] (*tr*) to block, prop, or prevent from moving with or as if with a wedge. ◆ NOUN [2] a block or wedge to prevent motion.
▷HISTORY C17: of obscure origin

Scotch[1] (skɒtʃ) ADJECTIVE [1] another word for **Scottish.** ◆ NOUN [2] the Scots or their language.

> **Language note** In the north of England and in Scotland, *Scotch* is not used outside fixed expressions such as *Scotch whisky.* The use of *Scotch* for *Scots* or *Scottish* is otherwise felt to be incorrect, esp when applied to people.

Scotch[2] (skɒtʃ) NOUN [1] Also called: **Scotch whisky.** whisky distilled esp from fermented malted barley and made in Scotland. [2] *Northeast English* a type of relatively mild beer.

Scotch broth NOUN *Brit* a thick soup made from mutton, lamb, or beef stock, vegetables, and pearl barley.

Scotch egg NOUN *Brit* a hard-boiled egg enclosed in a layer of sausage meat, covered in egg and crumbs, and fried.

Scotchman ('skɒtʃmən) NOUN, *plural* **-men.** (*regarded as bad usage by the Scots*) another word for **Scotsman.**

Scotch mist NOUN [1] a heavy wet mist. [2] drizzle.
▷HISTORY C16: so called because it is common on Scottish hills

Scotch pancake NOUN another name for **drop scone.**

Scotch snap NOUN *Music* a rhythmic pattern consisting of a short note followed by a long one. Also called: **Scotch catch.**

▷HISTORY C19: so named because it is characteristic of, though not exclusive to, Scottish dance music, esp that for strathspeys

Scotch tape NOUN *Trademark, chiefly US* a transparent or coloured adhesive tape made of cellulose or a similar substance.

Scotch terrier NOUN another name for **Scottish terrier**.

Scotchwoman (ˈskɒtʃˌwʊmən) NOUN, *plural* **-women**. (*regarded as bad usage by the Scots*) another word for **Scotswoman**.

Scotch woodcock NOUN hot toast spread with anchovies or anchovy paste and topped with creamy scrambled eggs.

scoter (ˈskəʊtə) NOUN, *plural* **-ters** *or* **-ter**. any sea duck of the genus *Melanitta,* such as *M. nigra* (**common scoter**), of northern regions. The male plumage is black with white patches around the head and eyes.
▷HISTORY C17: origin unknown

scot-free ADVERB, ADJECTIVE (*predicative*) without harm, loss, or penalty.
▷HISTORY C16: see SCOT AND LOT

scotia (ˈskəʊʃə) NOUN a deep concave moulding, esp one used on the base of an Ionic column between the two torus mouldings.
▷HISTORY C16: via Latin from Greek *skotia,* from *skotos* darkness (from the shadow in the cavity)

Scotism (ˈskəʊtɪzəm) NOUN the doctrines of John Duns Scotus, the Scottish scholastic theologian and Franciscan priest (?1265–1308), esp those holding that philosophy and theology are independent. See **haecceity**.
▸ **ˈScotist** NOUN, ADJECTIVE ▸ **Scoˈtistic** ADJECTIVE

Scotland (ˈskɒtlənd) NOUN a country that is part of the United Kingdom, occupying the north of Great Britain: the English and Scottish thrones were united under one monarch in 1603 and the parliaments in 1707: a separate Scottish parliament was established in 1999. Scotland consists of the Highlands in the north, the central Lowlands, and hilly uplands in the south; has a deeply indented coastline, about 800 offshore islands (mostly in the west), and many lochs. Capital: Edinburgh. Pop.: 5 062 011 (2001). Area: 78 768 sq. km (30 412 sq. miles). Related adjectives: **Scots, Caledonian, Scottish**.

Scotland Yard NOUN the headquarters of the police force of metropolitan London, controlled directly by the British Home Office and hence having certain national responsibilities. Official name: **New Scotland Yard**.

scotoma (skɒˈtəʊmə) NOUN, *plural* **-mas** *or* **-mata** (-mətə). [1] *Pathol* a blind spot; a permanent or temporary area of depressed or absent vision caused by lesions of the visual system, viewing the sun directly (**eclipse scotoma**), squinting, etc. [2] *Psychol* a mental blind spot; inability to understand or perceive certain matters.
▷HISTORY C16: via Medieval Latin from Greek *skotōma* giddiness, from *skotoun* to make dark, from *skotos* darkness
▸ **scotomatous** (skɒˈtɒmətəs) ADJECTIVE

scotopia (skəˈtəʊpɪə, skəʊ-) NOUN the ability of the eye to adjust for night vision.
▷HISTORY New Latin, from Greek *skotos* darkness + -OPIA
▸ **scotopic** (skəˈtɒpɪk, skəʊ-) ADJECTIVE

Scots (skɒts) ADJECTIVE [1] of, relating to, or characteristic of Scotland, its people, their English dialects, or their Gaelic language. ◆ NOUN [2] any of the English dialects spoken or written in Scotland. See also **Lallans**.

Scots Greys PLURAL NOUN **the**. another name for (the) **Royal Scots Greys**.

Scotsman (ˈskɒtsmən) NOUN, *plural* **-men**. a native or inhabitant of Scotland.

Scots pine *or* **Scotch pine** NOUN [1] a coniferous tree, *Pinus sylvestris,* of Europe and W and N Asia, having blue-green needle-like leaves and brown cones with a small prickle on each scale: a valuable timber tree. [2] the wood of this tree. ◆ Also called: **Scots** *or* **Scotch fir**.

Scotswoman (ˈskɒtsˌwʊmən) NOUN, *plural* **-women**. a woman who is a native or inhabitant of Scotland.

Scotticism (ˈskɒtɪˌsɪzəm) NOUN a Scottish idiom, word, etc.

Scottie *or* **Scotty** (ˈskɒtɪ) NOUN, *plural* **-ties**. [1] See **Scottish terrier**. [2] *Informal* a Scotsman.

Scottish (ˈskɒtɪʃ) ADJECTIVE [1] of, relating to, or characteristic of Scotland, its people, their Gaelic language, or their English dialect. ◆ NOUN [2] **the**. (*functioning as plural*) the Scots collectively.

Scottish Blackface NOUN a common breed of hardy mountain sheep having horns and a black face, kept chiefly on the mainland of Scotland.

Scottish Borders NOUN a council area in SE Scotland, on the English border: created in 1996, it has the same boundaries as the former Borders Region: it is mainly hilly, with agriculture (esp sheep farming) the chief economic activity. Administrative centre: Newtown St Boswells. Pop.: 106 764 (2001). Area: 4734 sq. km (1827 sq. miles).

Scottish Certificate of Education NOUN See **SCE**.

Scottish Fold NOUN a breed of medium-sized short-haired cat with folded ears.

Scottish Gaelic NOUN the Goidelic language of the Celts of Scotland, spoken in the Highlands and Western Isles.

Scottish National Party NOUN a political party advocating the independence of Scotland, founded in 1934. Abbreviation: **SNP**.
▸ **Scottish Nationalist** *or* (*informal*) **Scot Nat** (næt) NOUN, ADJECTIVE

Scottish terrier NOUN a small but sturdy breed of terrier, having short legs and erect ears and tail and a longish, wiry, usually black coat. Often shortened to: **Scottie**. Former name: **Aberdeen terrier**.

Scottish topaz NOUN a form of yellow transparent quartz.

scoundrel (ˈskaʊndrəl) NOUN a worthless or villainous person.
▷HISTORY C16: of unknown origin
▸ **ˈscoundrelly** ADJECTIVE

scour[1] (skaʊə) VERB [1] to clean or polish (a surface) by washing and rubbing, as with an abrasive cloth. [2] to remove dirt from or have the dirt removed from. [3] (*tr*) to clear (a channel) by the force of water; flush. [4] (*tr*) to remove by or as if by rubbing. [5] (*intr*) (of livestock, esp cattle) to have diarrhoea. [6] (*tr*) to cause (livestock) to purge their bowels. [7] (*tr*) to wash (wool) to remove wax, suint, and other impurities. ◆ NOUN [8] the act of scouring. [9] the place scoured, esp by running water. [10] something that scours, such as a cleansing agent. [11] (*often plural*) prolonged diarrhoea in livestock, esp cattle.
▷HISTORY C13: via Middle Low German *schūren,* from Old French *escurer,* from Late Latin *excūrāre* to cleanse, from *cūrāre;* see CURE
▸ **ˈscourer** NOUN

scour[2] (skaʊə) VERB [1] to range over (territory), as in making a search. [2] to move swiftly or energetically over (territory).
▷HISTORY C14: from Old Norse *skūr*

scourge (skɜːdʒ) NOUN [1] a person who harasses, punishes, or causes destruction. [2] a means of inflicting punishment or suffering. [3] a whip used for inflicting punishment or torture. ◆ VERB (*tr*) [4] to whip; flog. [5] to punish severely.
▷HISTORY C13: from Anglo-French *escorge,* from Old French *escorgier* (unattested) to lash, from *es-* EX-[1] + Latin *corrigia* whip
▸ **ˈscourger** NOUN

scouring rush NOUN any of several horsetails, esp *Equisetum hyemale,* that have rough-ridged stems and were formerly used for scouring and polishing.

scourings (ˈskaʊərɪŋz) PLURAL NOUN [1] the residue left after cleaning grain. [2] residue that remains after scouring.

scouse (skaʊs) NOUN *Liverpool dialect* a stew made from left-over meat.
▷HISTORY C19: shortened from LOBSCOUSE

Scouse (skaʊs) *Brit informal* ◆ NOUN [1] Also called: **Scouser**. a person who lives in or comes from Liverpool. [2] the dialect spoken by such a person. ◆ ADJECTIVE [3] of or from Liverpool; Liverpudlian.
▷HISTORY C20: from SCOUSE

scout[1] (skaʊt) NOUN [1] a person, ship, or aircraft sent out to gain information. [2] *Military* a person or unit despatched to reconnoitre the position of the enemy. [3] *Sport* a person employed by a club to seek new players. [4] the act or an instance of scouting. [5] (esp at Oxford University) a college servant. Compare **gyp**[3]. [6] *Obsolete* (in Britain) a patrolman of a motoring organization. [7] *Informal* a fellow or companion. ◆ VERB [8] to examine or observe (anything) in order to obtain information. [9] (*tr;* sometimes foll by *out* or *up*) to seek. [10] (*intr*) to act as a scout for a sports club. [11] (*intr;* foll by *about* or *around*) to go in search (for).
▷HISTORY C14: from Old French *ascouter* to listen to, from Latin *auscultāre* to AUSCULTATE
▸ **ˈscouter** NOUN

scout[2] (skaʊt) VERB *Archaic* to reject (a person or thing) with contempt.
▷HISTORY C17: from Old Norse *skūta* derision

Scout (skaʊt) NOUN (*sometimes not capital*) a boy or (in some countries) a girl who is a member of a worldwide movement (the **Scout Association**) founded as the Boy Scouts in England in 1908 by Lord Baden-Powell with the aim of developing character and responsibility. See also **Air Scout, Girl Scout, Guide, Sea Scout, Venture Scout**.

scout car NOUN a fast lightly armoured vehicle used for reconnaissance.

Scouting (ˈskaʊtɪŋ) NOUN **a** the activities, programmes, principles, etc., of the Scout Association. **b** (*as modifier*): *the international Scouting movement.*

Scout Leader NOUN the leader of a troop of Scouts.

scoutmaster (ˈskaʊtˌmɑːstə) NOUN a former name for **Scout Leader**.

scow (skaʊ) NOUN [1] an unpowered barge used for freight; lighter. [2] (esp in the midwestern US) a sailing yacht with a flat bottom, designed to plane.
▷HISTORY C18: via Dutch *schouw* from Low German *schalde,* related to Old Saxon *skaldan* to push (a boat) into the sea

scowl (skaʊl) VERB [1] (*intr*) to contract the brows in a threatening or angry manner. ◆ NOUN [2] a gloomy or threatening expression.
▷HISTORY C14: probably from Scandinavian; compare Danish *skule* to look down, Old English *scūlēgede* squint-eyed

scowler (ˈskaʊlə) NOUN [1] a person who scowls. [2] *Northern English dialect* a hooligan.

scozza (ˈskɒzə) NOUN *Austral slang* a rowdy person, esp one who drinks a lot of alcohol.

SCP ABBREVIATION FOR **single-cell protein**.

SCQF (in Scotland) ABBREVIATION FOR Scottish Credit and Qualifications Framework.

SCR ABBREVIATION FOR: [1] (in British universities) senior common room. [2] silicon controlled rectifier.

scr. ABBREVIATION FOR scruple (unit of weight).

scrabble (ˈskræbᵊl) VERB [1] (*intr;* often foll by *about* or *at*) to scrape (at) or grope (for), as with hands or claws. [2] to struggle (with). [3] (*intr;* often foll by *for*) to struggle to gain possession, esp in a disorderly manner. [4] to scribble. ◆ NOUN [5] the act or an instance of scrabbling. [6] a scribble. [7] a disorderly struggle.
▷HISTORY C16: from Middle Dutch *shrabbelen,* frequentative of *shrabben* to scrape
▸ **ˈscrabbler** NOUN

Scrabble (ˈskræbᵊl) NOUN *Trademark* a board game in which words are formed by placing lettered tiles in a pattern similar to a crossword puzzle.

scrag (skræg) NOUN [1] a thin or scrawny person or animal. [2] the lean end of a neck of veal or mutton. [3] *Informal* the neck of a human being. ◆ VERB **scrags, scragging, scragged**. (*tr*) [4] *Informal* to wring the neck of; throttle.
▷HISTORY C16: perhaps variant of CRAG; related to Norwegian *skragg,* German *Kragen* collar

scraggly (ˈskræglɪ) ADJECTIVE **-glier, -gliest**. untidy or irregular.

scraggy (ˈskrægɪ) ADJECTIVE **-gier, -giest**. [1] lean or scrawny. [2] rough; unkempt.
▸ **ˈscraggily** ADVERB ▸ **ˈscragginess** NOUN

scram[1] (skræm) VERB **scrams, scramming, scrammed**. (*intr; often imperative*) *Informal* to go away hastily; get out.
▷HISTORY C20: shortened from SCRAMBLE

scram[2] (skræm) NOUN [1] an emergency shutdown

of a nuclear reactor. ◆ VERB 2 (of a nuclear reactor) to shut down or be shut down in an emergency.
▷HISTORY C20: perhaps from SCRAM[1]

scramb *or* **scram** (skræm) VERB (*tr*) *Brit dialect* to scratch with nails or claws.
▷HISTORY from Dutch *schrammen*

scramble (ˈskræmbᵊl) VERB 1 (*intr*) to climb or crawl, esp by using the hands to aid movement. 2 (*intr*) to proceed hurriedly or in a disorderly fashion. 3 (*intr; often foll by for*) to compete with others, esp in a disordered manner: *to scramble for a prize.* 4 (*intr; foll by through*) to deal with hurriedly and unsystematically. 5 (*tr*) to throw together in a haphazard manner; jumble. 6 (*tr*) to collect in a hurried or disorganized manner. 7 (*tr*) to cook (eggs that have been whisked up with milk and seasoning) in a pan containing a little melted butter. 8 *Military* to order (a crew or aircraft) to take off immediately or (of a crew or aircraft) to take off immediately. 9 (*tr*) to render (speech) unintelligible during transmission by means of an electronic scrambler. ◆ NOUN 10 the act of scrambling. 11 a climb over rocks that involves the use of the hands but not ropes, etc. 12 a disorderly struggle, esp to gain possession. 13 *Military* an immediate preparation for action, as of crew, aircraft, etc. 14 *Brit* a motorcycle rally in which competitors race across rough open ground.
▷HISTORY C16: blend of SCRABBLE and RAMP

scrambled egg *or* **eggs** NOUN *Slang* gold embroidery on the peak of a high-ranking military officer's cap.

scrambler (ˈskræmblə) NOUN 1 a plant that produces long weak shoots by which it grows over other plants. 2 an electronic device that renders speech unintelligible during transmission, normal speech being restored at the receiving system.

scran (skræn) NOUN 1 *Slang* food; provisions. 2 **bad scran to.** *Irish dialect* bad luck to.
▷HISTORY C18: of unknown origin

scrannel (ˈskrænᵊl) ADJECTIVE *Archaic* 1 thin. 2 harsh.
▷HISTORY C17: probably from Norwegian *skran* lean. Compare SCRAWNY

Scranton (ˈskræntən) NOUN an industrial city in NE Pennsylvania: university (1888). Pop.: 77 189 (1996 est.).

scrap[1] (skræp) NOUN 1 a small piece of something larger; fragment. 2 an extract from something written. 3 **a** waste material or used articles, esp metal, often collected and reprocessed. **b** (*as modifier*): *scrap iron.* 4 (*plural*) pieces of discarded food. ◆ VERB **scraps, scrapping, scrapped**. (*tr*) 5 to make into scrap. 6 to discard as useless.
▷HISTORY C14: from Old Norse *skrap;* see SCRAPE

scrap[2] (skræp) *Informal* ◆ NOUN 1 a fight or argument. ◆ VERB **scraps, scrapping, scrapped**. 2 (*intr*) to quarrel or fight.
▷HISTORY C17: perhaps from SCRAPE

scrapbook (ˈskræpˌbʊk) NOUN a book or album of blank pages in which to mount newspaper cuttings, pictures, etc.

scrape (skreɪp) VERB 1 to move (a rough or sharp object) across (a surface), esp to smooth or clean. 2 (*tr; often foll by away or off*) to remove (a layer) by rubbing. 3 to produce a harsh or grating sound by rubbing against (an instrument, surface, etc.). 4 (*tr*) to injure or damage by rough contact: *to scrape one's knee.* 5 (*intr*) to be very economical or sparing in the use (of) (esp in the phrase **scrimp and scrape**). 6 (*intr*) to draw the foot backwards in making a bow. 7 (*tr*) to finish (a surface) by use of a scraper. 8 (*tr*) to make (a bearing, etc.) fit by scraping. 9 **bow and scrape.** to behave with excessive humility. ◆ NOUN 10 the act of scraping. 11 a scraped place. 12 a harsh or grating sound. 13 *Informal* an awkward or embarrassing predicament. 14 *Informal* a conflict or struggle.
▷HISTORY Old English *scrapian;* related to Old Norse *skrapa,* Middle Dutch *schrapen,* Middle High German *schraffen*
▸ˈ**scrapable** ADJECTIVE ▸ˈ**scraper** NOUN

scrape in VERB (*intr, adverb*) to succeed in entering with difficulty or by a narrow margin: *he only just scraped into university.* Also: **scrape into.**

scraperboard (ˈskreɪpəˌbɔːd) NOUN 1 thin card covered with a layer of white china clay and a black top layer of Indian ink, which can be scraped away with a special tool to leave a white line. 2 a picture or design produced in this way.

scrape through VERB (*adverb*) 1 (*intr*) to manage or survive with difficulty. 2 to succeed in with difficulty or by a narrow margin: *he scraped through by one mark.*

scrape together *or* **up** VERB (*tr, adverb*) to collect with difficulty: *to scrape together money for a new car.*

scrapheap (ˈskræpˌhiːp) NOUN 1 a pile of discarded material. 2 **on the scrapheap.** (of people or things) having outlived their usefulness.

scrapie (ˈskreɪpɪ) NOUN a disease of sheep and goats: one of a group of diseases (including BSE in cattle) that are caused by a protein prion, and result in spongiform encephalopathy.
▷HISTORY C20: from SCRAPE + -IE

scraping (ˈskreɪpɪŋ) NOUN 1 the act of scraping. 2 a sound produced by scraping. 3 (*often plural*) something scraped off, together, or up; a small amount.

scrapple (ˈskræpᵊl) NOUN *US* scraps of pork cooked with cornmeal and formed into a loaf.
▷HISTORY C19: from SCRAP[1]

scrappy[1] (ˈskræpɪ) ADJECTIVE **-pier, -piest.** fragmentary; disjointed.
▸ˈ**scrappily** ADVERB ▸ˈ**scrappiness** NOUN

scrappy[2] (ˈskræpɪ) ADJECTIVE **-pier, -piest.** *Informal* pugnacious.

scratch (skrætʃ) VERB 1 to mark or cut (the surface of something) with a rough or sharp instrument. 2 (often foll by *at, out, off,* etc.) to scrape (the surface of something), as with claws, nails, etc. 3 to scrape (the surface of the skin) with the nails, as to relieve itching. 4 to chafe or irritate (a surface, esp the skin). 5 to make or cause to make a grating sound; scrape. 6 (*tr; sometimes foll by out*) to erase by or as if by scraping. 7 (*tr*) to write or draw awkwardly. 8 (*intr; sometimes foll by along*) to earn a living, manage, etc., with difficulty. 9 to withdraw (an entry) from a race, match, etc. 10 (*intr*) *Billiards, snooker* **a** to make a shot resulting in a penalty. **b** to make a lucky shot. 11 (*tr*) *US* to cancel (the name of a candidate) from a party ticket in an election. 12 (*intr; often foll by for*) *Austral informal* to be struggling or in difficulty, esp in earning a living. 13 to treat (a subject) superficially. 14 **you scratch my back and I'll scratch yours.** if you will help me, I will help you. ◆ NOUN 15 the act of scratching. 16 a slight injury. 17 a mark made by scratching. 18 a slight grating sound. 19 (in a handicap sport) **a** a competitor or the status of a competitor who has no allowance or receives a penalty. **b** (*as modifier*): *a scratch player.* 20 the time, initial score, etc., of such a competitor. 21 **a** the line from which competitors start in a race. **b** (formerly) a line drawn on the floor of a prize ring at which the contestants stood to begin or continue fighting. 22 a withdrawn competitor in a race, etc. 23 *Billiards, snooker* **a** a shot that results in a penalty, as when the cue ball enters the pocket. **b** a lucky shot. 24 poultry food. 25 **from scratch.** *Informal* from the very beginning. 26 **up to scratch.** (*usually used with a negative*) *Informal* up to standard. ◆ ADJECTIVE 27 *Sport* (of a team) assembled hastily. 28 (in a handicap sport) with no allowance or penalty. 29 *Informal* rough or haphazard. ◆ See also **scratches, scratch together.**
▷HISTORY C15: via Old French *escrater* from Germanic; compare Old High German *krazzōn* (German *kratzen*); related to Old French *gratter* to GRATE[1]
▸ˈ**scratchy** ADJECTIVE ▸ˈ**scratchily** ADVERB ▸ˈ**scratchiness** NOUN

scratchcard (ˈskrætʃˌkɑːd) NOUN a ticket that reveals whether or not the holder is eligible for a prize when the surface is removed by scratching.

scratcher (ˈskrætʃə) NOUN a person, animal, or thing that scratches.

scratches (ˈskrætʃɪz) NOUN (*functioning as singular*) a disease of horses characterized by dermatitis in the region of the fetlock. Also called: **cracked heels, mud fever.**
▷HISTORY C16: so called because it makes the pastern appear to be scratched

scratch file NOUN *Computing* a temporary store for use during the execution of a program.

scratchie (ˈskrætʃɪ) NOUN *Austral informal* a scratchcard.

scratching (ˈskrætʃɪŋ) NOUN a percussive effect obtained by rotating a gramophone record manually: a disc-jockey and dub technique.

scratch pad NOUN 1 *Chiefly US and Canadian* a notebook, esp one with detachable leaves. 2 *Computing* a small semiconductor memory for temporary storage.

scratchplate (ˈskrætʃˌpleɪt) NOUN a plastic or metal plate attached to the front of a guitar to protect it from pick scratches.

scratch sheet NOUN *US and Canadian informal* another term for a **dope sheet.**

scratch test NOUN *Med* a skin test to determine allergic sensitivity to various substances by placing the allergen to be tested over an area of lightly scratched skin. A positive reaction is typically indicated by the formation of a weal.

scratch together *or* **up** VERB (*tr, adverb*) to assemble with difficulty: *he scratched up a team for the football match.*

scratch video NOUN the technique or practice of recycling images from films or television to make collages.

scraw (skrɑː) NOUN *Irish* a sod from the surface of a peat bog or from a field.
▷HISTORY from Irish Gaelic *scraith*

scrawl (skrɔːl) VERB 1 to write or draw (signs, words, etc.) carelessly or hastily; scribble. ◆ NOUN 2 careless or scribbled writing, drawing, or marks.
▷HISTORY C17: perhaps a blend of SPRAWL and CRAWL[1]
▸ˈ**scrawler** NOUN ▸ˈ**scrawly** ADJECTIVE

scrawny (ˈskrɔːnɪ) ADJECTIVE **scrawnier, scrawniest.** 1 very thin and bony; scraggy. 2 meagre or stunted: *scrawny vegetation.*
▷HISTORY C19: variant of dialect *scranny;* see SCRANNEL
▸ˈ**scrawnily** ADVERB ▸ˈ**scrawniness** NOUN

scrawp (skrɑːp) VERB *Midland English dialect* to scratch (the skin) to relieve itching.

screak (skriːk) *Dialect, chiefly US* ◆ VERB 1 (*intr*) to screech or creak. ◆ NOUN 2 a screech or creak.
▷HISTORY C16: from Old Norse *skrækja.* See SCREECH[1], SHRIEK
▸ˈ**screaky** ADJECTIVE

scream (skriːm) VERB 1 to utter or emit (a sharp piercing cry or similar sound or sounds), esp as of fear, pain, etc. 2 (*intr*) to laugh wildly. 3 (*intr*) to speak, shout, or behave in a wild or impassioned manner. 4 (*tr*) to bring (oneself) into a specified state by screaming: *she screamed herself hoarse.* 5 (*intr*) to be extremely conspicuous: *these orange curtains scream, you need more restful colours in a bedroom.* ◆ NOUN 6 a sharp piercing cry or sound, esp one denoting fear or pain. 7 *Informal* a person or thing that causes great amusement.
▷HISTORY C13: from Germanic; compare Middle Dutch *schreem,* West Frisian *skrieme* to weep

screamer (ˈskriːmə) NOUN 1 a person or thing that screams. 2 any goose-like aquatic bird, such as *Chauna torquata* (**crested screamer**), of the family *Anhimidae* of tropical and subtropical South America: order *Anseriformes* (ducks, geese, etc.). 3 someone or something that raises screams of laughter or astonishment. 4 *US and Canadian slang* a sensational headline. 5 *Austral slang* **a** a person or thing that is excellent of its kind. **b** See **two-pot screamer.**

scream therapy NOUN another name for **primal therapy.**

scree (skriː) NOUN an accumulation of weathered rock fragments at the foot of a cliff or hillside, often forming a sloping heap. Also called: **talus.**
▷HISTORY Old English *scrīthan* to slip; related to Old Norse *skrītha* to slide, German *schreiten* to walk

screech[1] (skriːtʃ) NOUN 1 a shrill, harsh, or high-pitched sound or cry. ◆ VERB 2 to utter with or produce a screech.
▷HISTORY C16: variant of earlier *scritch,* of imitative origin
▸ˈ**screecher** NOUN

screech[2] (skriːtʃ) NOUN *Canadian* (esp in Newfoundland) a dark rum.
▷HISTORY perhaps special use of SCREECH[1]

screech owl NOUN 1 a small North American owl, *Otus asio,* having ear tufts and a reddish-brown or grey plumage. 2 *Brit* any owl that utters a screeching cry.

screechy (ˈskriːtʃɪ) ADJECTIVE **-ier, -iest.** loud and shrill.

screed (skriːd) NOUN 1 a long or prolonged speech or piece of writing. 2 a strip of wood, plaster, or metal placed on a surface to act as a guide to the thickness of the cement or plaster coat to be applied. 3 a mixture of cement, sand, and water applied to a concrete slab, etc., to give a smooth surface finish. 4 *Scot* a rent or tear or the sound produced by this.
▷HISTORY C14: probably variant of Old English *scrēade* SHRED

screen (skriːn) NOUN 1 a light movable frame, panel, or partition serving to shelter, divide, hide, etc. 2 anything that serves to shelter, protect, or conceal. 3 a frame containing a mesh that is placed over a window or opening to keep out insects. 4 a decorated partition, esp in a church around the choir. See also **rood** (sense 1). 5 a sieve. 6 a system for selecting people, such as candidates for a job. 7 the wide end of a cathode-ray tube, esp in a television set, on which a visible image is formed. 8 a white or silvered surface, usually fabric, placed in front of a projector to receive the enlarged image of a film or of slides. 9 **the screen.** the film industry or films collectively. 10 *Photog* a plate of ground glass in some types of camera on which the image of a subject is focused before being photographed. 11 *Printing* a glass marked with fine intersecting lines, used in a camera for making half-tone reproductions. 12 men or ships deployed around and ahead of a larger military formation to warn of attack or protect from a specific threat. 13 *Sport, chiefly US and Canadian* a tactical ploy in which a player blocks an opponent's view. 14 *Psychoanal* anything that prevents a person from realizing his true feelings about someone or something. 15 *Electronics* See **screen grid.** ◆ VERB (*tr*) 16 (sometimes foll by *off*) to shelter, protect, or conceal. 17 to sieve or sort. 18 to test or check (an individual or group) so as to determine suitability for a task, etc. 19 to examine for the presence of a disease, weapons, etc.: *the authorities screened five hundred cholera suspects.* 20 to provide with a screen or screens. 21 to project (a film) onto a screen, esp for public viewing. 22 (*intr*) to be shown at a cinema or on the television. 23 *Printing* to photograph (a picture) through a screen to render it suitable for half-tone reproduction. 24 *Sport, chiefly US and Canadian* to block the view of (an opposing player).
▷HISTORY C15: from Old French *escren* (French *écran*); related to Old High German *skrank*, German *Schrank* cupboard
▸ˈ**screenable** ADJECTIVE ▸ˈ**screener** NOUN ▸ˈ**screenˌful** NOUN ▸ˈ**screenˌlike** ADJECTIVE

screenager (ˈskriːnˌeɪdʒə) NOUN *Informal* a teenager who is dully conversant with and skilled in the use of computers and other electronic devices.

screen grid NOUN *Electronics* an electrode placed between the control grid and anode of a valve and having a fixed positive potential relative to the grid. It acts as an electrostatic shield preventing capacitive coupling between grid and anode, thus increasing the stability of the device. Sometimes shortened to: **screen.** See also **suppressor grid.**

screenings (ˈskriːnɪŋz) PLURAL NOUN refuse separated by sifting.

screening test NOUN a simple test performed on a large number of people to identify those who have or are likely to develop a specified disease.

screen memory NOUN *Psychoanal* a memory that is tolerable but allied to a distressing event and which is unconsciously used to hide the distressing memory.

screenplay (ˈskriːnˌpleɪ) NOUN the script for a film, including instructions for sets and camera work.

screen process NOUN a method of printing using a fine mesh of silk, nylon, etc., treated with an impermeable coating except in the areas through which ink is subsequently forced onto the paper behind. Also called: **silk-screen printing.**

screensaver (ˈskriːnseɪvər) NOUN a computer program that reduces screen damage resulting from an unchanging display when a computer is switched on but not in use by blanking the screen or generating moving patterns, etc.

screen test NOUN 1 a filmed audition of a prospective actor or actress to test suitability. 2 the test film so made.

screen trading NOUN a form of trading on a market or exchange in which the visual display unit of a computer replaces personal contact as in floor trading.

screenwriter (ˈskriːnˌraɪtə) NOUN a person who writes screenplays.

screet (skriːt) *Midland English dialect* ◆ VERB 1 to shed tears; weep. ◆ NOUN 2 the act or sound of crying.

screigh *or* **screich** (skriːx) NOUN, VERB a Scot word for **screech** (sense 1).

screw (skruː) NOUN 1 a device used for fastening materials together, consisting of a threaded and usually tapered shank that has a slotted head by which it may be rotated so as to cut its own thread as it bores through the material. 2 Also called: **screw-bolt.** a threaded cylindrical rod that engages with a similarly threaded cylindrical hole; bolt. 3 a thread in a cylindrical hole corresponding with that on the bolt or screw with which it is designed to engage. 4 anything resembling a screw in shape or spiral form. 5 a twisting movement of or resembling that of a screw. 6 Also called: **screw-back.** *Billiards, snooker* **a** a stroke in which the cue ball recoils or moves backward after striking the object ball, made by striking the cue ball below its centre. **b** the motion resulting from this stroke. 7 another name for **propeller** (sense 1). 8 *Slang* a prison guard. 9 *Brit slang* salary, wages, or earnings. 10 *Brit* a small amount of salt, tobacco, etc., in a twist of paper. 11 *Slang* a person who is mean with money. 12 *Slang* an old, unsound, or worthless horse. 13 (*often plural*) *Slang* force or compulsion (esp in the phrase **put the screws on**). 14 *Slang* sexual intercourse. 15 **have a screw loose.** *Informal* to be insane. 16 **turn** *or* **tighten the screw.** *Slang* to increase the pressure. ◆ VERB 17 (*tr*) to rotate (a screw or bolt) so as to drive it into or draw it out of a material. 18 (*tr*) to cut a screw thread in (a rod or hole) with a tap or die or on a lathe. 19 to turn or cause to turn in the manner of a screw. 20 (*tr*) to attach or fasten with a screw or screws. 21 (*tr*) *Informal* to take advantage of; cheat. 22 (*tr; often foll by up*) to distort or contort: *he screwed his face into a scowl.* 23 Also: **screw back.** to impart a screw to (a ball). 24 (*tr, often foll by from* or *out of*) to coerce or force out of; extort. 25 *Slang* to have sexual intercourse (with). 26 (*tr*) *Slang* to burgle. 27 **have one's head screwed on (the right way).** *Informal* to be wise or sensible. ◆ See also **screw up.**
▷HISTORY C15: from French *escroe*, from Medieval Latin *scrōfa* screw, from Latin: sow, presumably because the thread of the screw is like the spiral of the sow's tail
▸ˈ**screwer** NOUN ▸ˈ**screwˌlike** ADJECTIVE

> **Language note** The use of this otherwise utilitarian word in a sexual sense, though recorded in an 18th century slang dictionary, does not appear to have really taken off until well into the 20th. Although a classic example of the anatomical metaphor for the sex act seen from the male point of view, it can be used as a transitive verb by women, which suggests that the metaphor is all but dead.

screwball (ˈskruːˌbɔːl) *Slang, chiefly US and Canadian* ◆ NOUN 1 an odd or eccentric person. ◆ ADJECTIVE 2 odd; zany; eccentric.

screw conveyor NOUN *Engineering* a duct along which material is conveyed by the rotational action of a spiral vane which lies along the length of the duct. Also called: **worm conveyor.**

screwdriver (ˈskruːˌdraɪvə) NOUN 1 a tool used for turning screws, usually having a handle of wood, plastic, etc., and a steel shank with a flattened square-cut tip that fits into a slot in the head of the screw. 2 an alcoholic beverage consisting of orange juice and vodka.

screwed (skruːd) ADJECTIVE 1 fastened by a screw or screws. 2 having spiral grooves like a screw; threaded. 3 twisted or distorted. 4 *Brit* a slang word for **drunk.**

screw eye NOUN a wood screw with its shank bent into a ring.

screw jack NOUN a lifting device utilizing the mechanical advantage of a screw thread, the effort being applied through a bevel drive. Also called: **jackscrew, jack.**

screw pile NOUN a pile with a threaded tip that is screwed into the ground by a winch or capstan.

screw pine NOUN any of various pandanaceous plants of the Old World tropical genus *Pandanus*, having a spiral mass of pineapple-like leaves and heavy conelike fruits.

screw plate NOUN a steel plate with threaded holes used for making male screws.

screw propeller NOUN an early form of ship's propeller in which an Archimedes' screw is used to produce thrust by accelerating a flow of water.
▸ˈ**screw-proˈpelled** ADJECTIVE

screw tap NOUN another name for **tap**[2] (sense 6).

screw thread NOUN the helical ridge on a screw formed by a die or lathe tool.

screw top NOUN 1 a lid with a threaded rim that is turned on the corresponding thread on the neck of a bottle or container to close it securely. 2 a bottle or container having such a lid.
▸ˈ**screw-ˌtop** *or* ˈ**screw-ˌtopped** ADJECTIVE

screw up VERB (*tr, adverb*) 1 to twist out of shape or distort. 2 to summon up or call upon: *to screw up one's courage.* 3 (*also intr*) *Informal* to mishandle or make a mess (of). 4 (*often passive*) *Informal* to cause to become very anxious, confused, or nervous: *he is really screwed up about his exams.* ◆ NOUN **screw-up.** 5 *Slang* something mishandled or done badly.

screwworm (ˈskruːˌwɜːm) NOUN 1 the larva of a dipterous fly, *Callitroga macellaria*, that develops beneath the skin of living mammals often causing illness or death. 2 the fly producing this larva: family *Calliphoridae.*

screwy (ˈskruːɪ) ADJECTIVE **screwier, screwiest.** *Informal* odd, crazy, or eccentric.

scribble[1] (ˈskrɪbᵊl) VERB 1 to write or draw in a hasty or illegible manner. 2 to make meaningless or illegible marks (on). 3 *Derogatory or facetious* to write poetry, novels, etc. ◆ NOUN 4 hasty careless writing or drawing. 5 writing, esp literary matter, of poor quality. 6 meaningless or illegible marks.
▷HISTORY C15: from Medieval Latin *scrībillāre* to write hastily, from Latin *scrībere* to write
▸ˈ**scribbly** ADJECTIVE

scribble[2] (ˈskrɪbᵊl) VERB (*tr*) to card (wool, etc.).
▷HISTORY C17: probably from Low German; compare *schrubben* SCRUB[1]

scribbler (ˈskrɪblə) NOUN *Derogatory or facetious* a writer of poetry, novels, journalism, etc.

scribbly gum (ˈskrɪbᵊlɪ) NOUN any species of the genus *Eucalyptus* with smooth white bark marked with random patterns made by wood-boring insects.

scribe (skraɪb) NOUN 1 a person who copies documents, esp a person who made handwritten copies before the invention of printing. 2 a clerk or public copyist. 3 *Old Testament* a recognized scholar and teacher of the Jewish Law. 4 *Judaism* a man qualified to write certain documents in accordance with religious requirements. 5 an author or journalist: used humorously. 6 another name for **scriber.** ◆ VERB 7 to score a line on (a surface) with a pointed instrument, as in metalworking.
▷HISTORY (in the senses: writer, etc.) C14: from Latin *scrība* clerk, from *scrībere* to write; C17 (vb): perhaps from INSCRIBE
▸ˈ**scribal** ADJECTIVE

scriber (ˈskraɪbə) NOUN a pointed steel tool used to score materials as a guide to cutting, etc. Also called: **scribe.**

scrim (skrɪm) NOUN an open-weave muslin or hessian fabric, used in upholstery, lining, building, and in the theatre to create the illusion of a solid wall or to suggest haziness, etc., according to the lighting.
▷HISTORY C18: origin unknown

scrimmage (ˈskrɪmɪdʒ) NOUN 1 a rough or disorderly struggle. 2 *American football* the clash of

opposing linemen at every down. ◆ VERB 3 (*intr*) to engage in a scrimmage. 4 (*tr*) to put (the ball) into a scrimmage.
▷HISTORY C15: from earlier *scrimish*, variant of SKIRMISH
▸**'scrimmager** NOUN

scrimp (skrɪmp) VERB 1 (when *intr*, sometimes foll by *on*) to be very economical or sparing in the use (of) (esp in the phrase **scrimp and save**). 2 (*tr*) to treat meanly: *he is scrimping his children.* 3 (*tr*) to cut too small. ◆ ADJECTIVE 4 a less common word for **scant.**
▷HISTORY C18: Scottish, origin unknown
▸**'scrimpy** ADJECTIVE ▸**'scrimpily** ADVERB ▸**'scrimpiness** NOUN

scrimshank ('skrɪm,ʃæŋk) VERB (*intr*) *Brit military slang* to shirk work.
▷HISTORY C19: of unknown origin

scrimshaw ('skrɪm,ʃɔː) NOUN 1 the art of decorating or carving shells, ivory, etc., done by sailors as a leisure activity. 2 **a** an article made in this manner. **b** such articles collectively. ◆ VERB 3 to produce scrimshaw (from).
▷HISTORY C19: origin uncertain, perhaps after a surname

scrip[1] (skrɪp) NOUN 1 a written certificate, list, etc. 2 a small scrap, esp of paper with writing on it. 3 *Finance* **a** a certificate representing a claim to part of a share of stock. **b** the shares allocated in a bonus issue.
▷HISTORY C18: in some senses, probably from SCRIPT; otherwise, short for *subscription receipt*

scrip[2] (skrɪp) NOUN *Archaic* a small bag or wallet, as carried by pilgrims.
▷HISTORY C14: from Old French *escreppe*, variant of *escarpe* SCARF[1]

scrip[3] (skrɪp) *or* **script** NOUN *Informal* a medical prescription.
▷HISTORY C20: short for PRESCRIPTION

scrip issue NOUN another name for **bonus issue.**

scripophily (skrɪ'pɒfɪlɪ) NOUN the hobby of collecting bonds and share certificates, esp those of historical interest.
▷HISTORY C20: from SCRIP[1] + -O- + *-phily*, from Greek *philos* loving
▸**scripophile** ('skrɪpəʊ,faɪl) NOUN

script (skrɪpt) NOUN 1 handwriting as distinguished from print, esp cursive writing. 2 the letters, characters, or figures used in writing by hand. 3 any system or style of writing. 4 written copy for the use of performers in films and plays. 5 *Law* **a** an original or principal document. **b** (esp in England) a will or codicil or the draft for one. 6 any of various typefaces that imitate handwriting. 7 an answer paper in an examination. 8 another word for **scrip**[3]. ◆ VERB 9 (*tr*) to write a script for.
▷HISTORY C14: from Latin *scriptum* something written, from *scrībere* to write

scripter ('skrɪptə) NOUN a person who writes scripts for films, play, or television dramas.

script kiddie NOUN *Slang* a child or teenager who gains illegal access to computer systems, often by using hacking programs downloaded from the Internet.

scriptorium (skrɪp'tɔːrɪəm) NOUN, *plural* **-riums** *or* **-ria** (-rɪə). a room, esp in a monastery, set apart for the writing or copying of manuscripts.
▷HISTORY from Medieval Latin

scriptural ('skrɪptʃərəl) ADJECTIVE 1 (*often capital*) of, in accordance with, or based on Scripture. 2 of or relating to writing.
▸**'scripturally** ADVERB

scripture ('skrɪptʃə) NOUN a sacred, solemn, or authoritative book or piece of writing.
▷HISTORY C13: from Latin *scriptūra* written material, from *scrībere* to write

Scripture ('skrɪptʃə) NOUN 1 Also called: **Holy Scripture, Holy Writ, the Scriptures.** *Christianity* the Old and New Testaments. 2 any book or body of writings, esp when regarded as sacred by a particular religious group.

scriptwriter ('skrɪpt,raɪtə) NOUN a person who prepares scripts, esp for a film.
▸**'script,writing** NOUN

scrivener ('skrɪvnə) NOUN *Archaic* 1 a person who writes out deeds, letters, etc.; copyist. 2 a notary.
▷HISTORY C14: from *scrivein* clerk, from Old French *escrivain*, ultimately from Latin *scrība* SCRIBE

scrobiculate (skrəʊ'bɪkjʊlɪt, -,leɪt) *or* **scrobiculated** ADJECTIVE *Biology* having a surface covered with small round pits or grooves.
▷HISTORY C19: from Latin *scrobiculus* diminutive of *scrobis* a ditch

scrod (skrɒd) NOUN *US* a young cod or haddock, esp one split and prepared for cooking.
▷HISTORY C19: perhaps from obsolete Dutch *schrood*, from Middle Dutch *schrode* SHRED (n); the name perhaps refers to the method of preparing the fish for cooking

scrofula ('skrɒfjʊlə) NOUN *Pathol* (*no longer in technical use*) tuberculosis of the lymphatic glands. Also called (formerly): **the king's evil.**
▷HISTORY C14: from Medieval Latin, from Late Latin *scrōfulae* swollen glands in the neck, literally: little sows (sows were thought to be particularly prone to the disease), from Latin *scrōfa* sow

scrofulous ('skrɒfjʊləs) ADJECTIVE 1 of, relating to, resembling, or having scrofula. 2 morally degraded.
▸**'scrofulously** ADVERB ▸**'scrofulousness** NOUN

scroggin ('skrɒgɪn) NOUN *NZ informal* a tramper's home-made high-calorie sweetmeat.

scroll (skrəʊl) NOUN 1 a roll of parchment, paper, etc., usually inscribed with writing. 2 an ancient book in the form of a roll of parchment, papyrus, etc. 3 **a** a decorative carving or moulding resembling a scroll. **b** (*as modifier*): *a scroll saw.* **c** (*in combination*): *scrollwork.* ◆ VERB 4 (*tr*) to saw into scrolls. 5 to roll up like a scroll. 6 *Computing* to move (text) from right to left or up and down on a screen in order to view text that cannot be contained within a single display image.
▷HISTORY C15 *scrowle*, from *scrowe*, from Old French *escroe* scrap of parchment, but also influenced by ROLL

scroll saw NOUN a saw with a narrow blade for cutting intricate ornamental curves in wood.

scrollwork ('skrəʊl,wɜːk) NOUN ornamental work in scroll-like patterns, esp when done with a scroll saw.

scrome (skrəʊm) VERB *Northern English dialect* **scromes, scroming, scromed** 1 (*intr*) to crawl or climb, esp using the hands to aid movement. 2 to wriggle.

scrooch (skruːtʃ) VERB *Midland English dialect* to scratch (the skin) to relieve itching.

Scrooge (skruːdʒ) NOUN a mean or miserly person.
▷HISTORY C19: after a character in Dickens' story *A Christmas Carol* (1843)

scroop (skruːp) *Dialect* ◆ VERB 1 (*intr*) to emit a grating or creaking sound. ◆ NOUN 2 such a sound.
▷HISTORY C18: of imitative origin

scrophulariaceous (,skrɒfjʊ,leərɪ'eɪʃəs) ADJECTIVE of, relating to, or belonging to the *Scrophulariaceae*, a family of plants including figwort, snapdragon, foxglove, toadflax, speedwell, and mullein.
▷HISTORY C19: from New Latin (*herba*) *scrophularia* scrofula (plant), from the use of such plants in treating scrofula

scrorp (skrɔp) NOUN *Midland English dialect* a deep scratch or weal.

scrotum ('skrəʊtəm) NOUN, *plural* **-ta** (-tə) *or* **-tums.** the pouch of skin containing the testes in most mammals.
▷HISTORY C16: from Latin
▸**'scrotal** ADJECTIVE

scrouge (skraʊdʒ, skruːdʒ) VERB (*tr*) *Dialect* to crowd or press.
▷HISTORY C18: alteration of C16 *scruze* to squeeze, perhaps blend of SCREW + SQUEEZE

scrounge (skraʊndʒ) VERB *Informal* 1 (when *intr*, sometimes foll by *around*) to search in order to acquire (something) without cost. 2 to obtain or seek to obtain (something) by cadging or begging.
▷HISTORY C20: variant of dialect *scrunge* to steal, of obscure origin
▸**'scrounger** NOUN

scrub[1] (skrʌb) VERB **scrubs, scrubbing, scrubbed.** 1 to rub (a surface) hard, with or as if with a brush, soap, and water, in order to clean it. 2 to remove (dirt), esp by rubbing with a brush and water. 3 (*intr; foll by up*) (of a surgeon) to wash the hands and arms thoroughly before operating. 4 (*tr*) to purify (a vapour or gas) by removing impurities. 5 (*tr*) *Informal* to delete or cancel. 6 (*intr*) *Horse racing, slang* (of jockeys) to urge a horse forwards by moving the arms and whip rhythmically forwards and backwards alongside its neck. ◆ NOUN 7 the act of or an instance of scrubbing. ◆ See also **scrub round.**
▷HISTORY C14: from Middle Low German *schrubben*, or Middle Dutch *schrobben*

scrub[2] (skrʌb) NOUN 1 **a** vegetation consisting of stunted trees, bushes, and other plants growing in an arid area. **b** (*as modifier*): *scrub vegetation.* 2 an area of arid land covered with such vegetation. 3 **a** an animal of inferior breeding or condition. **b** (*as modifier*): *a scrub bull.* 4 a small or insignificant person. 5 anything stunted or inferior. 6 *Sport, US and Canadian* a player not in the first team. 7 **the scrub.** *Austral informal* a remote place, esp one where contact with people can be avoided. ◆ ADJECTIVE prenominal. 8 small, stunted, or inferior. 9 *Sport US and Canadian* **a** (of a player) not in the first team. **b** (of a team) composed of such players. **c** (of a contest) between scratch or incomplete teams.
▷HISTORY C16: variation of SHRUB[1]

scrubber[1] ('skrʌbə) NOUN 1 a person or thing that scrubs. 2 an apparatus for purifying a gas. 3 *Brit and Austral derogatory slang* a promiscuous woman.

scrubber[2] ('skrʌbə) NOUN *Austral* a domestic animal, esp a bullock, that has run wild in the bush.
▷HISTORY C19: from SCRUB[2]

scrub bird NOUN either of two fast-running wren-like passerine birds, *Atrichornis clamosus* or *A. rufescens*, that constitute the Australian family *Atrichornithidae*.

scrubby ('skrʌbɪ) ADJECTIVE **-bier, -biest.** 1 covered with or consisting of scrub. 2 (of trees or vegetation) stunted in growth. 3 *Brit informal* messy.
▸**'scrubbiness** NOUN

scrub fowl *or* **turkey** NOUN another name for **megapode.**

scrubland ('skrʌb,lænd) NOUN an area of scrub vegetation.

scrub round VERB (*intr, preposition*) *Informal* to waive; avoid or ignore: *we can scrub round the rules.*

scrub turkey NOUN 1 another name for **megapode.** 2 *Austral* another name for **brush turkey.**

scrub typhus NOUN an acute febrile disease characterized by severe headache, skin rash, chills, and swelling of the lymph nodes, caused by the bite of mites infected with the microorganism *Rickettsia tsutsugamushi:* occurs mainly in Asia, Australia, and the islands of the western Pacific.

scruff[1] (skrʌf) NOUN the nape of the neck (esp in the phrase **by the scruff of the neck**).
▷HISTORY C18: variant of *scuft*, perhaps from Old Norse *skoft* hair; related to Old High German *scuft*

scruff[2] (skrʌf) NOUN 1 *Informal* an untidy scruffy person. 2 *Informal* a disreputable person, ruffian. 3 another name for **scum** (sense 3).

scruffy ('skrʌfɪ) ADJECTIVE **scruffier, scruffiest.** unkempt or shabby.

scrum (skrʌm) NOUN 1 *Rugby* the act or method of restarting play after an infringement when the two opposing packs of forwards group together with heads down and arms interlocked and push to gain ground while the scrum half throws the ball in and the hookers attempt to scoop it out to their own team. A scrum is usually called by the referee (**set scrum**) but may be formed spontaneously (**loose scrum**). 2 *Informal* a disorderly struggle. ◆ VERB **scrums, scrumming, scrummed.** 3 (*intr; usually followed by down*) *Rugby* to form a scrum.
▷HISTORY C19: shortened from SCRUMMAGE

scrum half NOUN *Rugby* 1 a player who puts in the ball at scrums and tries to get it away to his three-quarter backs. 2 this position in a team.

scrummage ('skrʌmɪdʒ) NOUN, VERB 1 *Rugby* another word for **scrum.** 2 a variant of **scrimmage.**
▷HISTORY C19: variant of SCRIMMAGE
▸**'scrummager** NOUN

scrummy ('skrʌmɪ) ADJECTIVE **-mier, -miest.** *Informal* delicious; lovely.
▷HISTORY C20: from SCRUMPTIOUS

scrump (skrʌmp) VERB *Dialect* to steal (apples) from an orchard or garden.
▷HISTORY dialect variant of SCRIMP

scrumple (ˈskrʌmpᵊl) VERB (usually foll by *up*) to crumple or crush (something, esp a piece of paper) or (esp of a piece of paper) to become crumpled or crushed.
▷HISTORY C16: variant of CRUMPLE

scrumptious (ˈskrʌmpʃəs) ADJECTIVE *Informal* very pleasing; delicious.
▷HISTORY C19: probably changed from SUMPTUOUS
▸**ˈscrumptiously** ADVERB ▸**ˈscrumptiousness** NOUN

scrumpy (ˈskrʌmpɪ) NOUN a rough dry cider, brewed esp in the West Country.
▷HISTORY from *scrump*, variant of SCRIMP (in obsolete sense: withered), referring to the apples used

scrunch (skrʌntʃ) VERB [1] to crumple, crush, or crunch or to be crumpled, crushed, or crunched. ◆ NOUN [2] the act or sound of scrunching.
▷HISTORY C19: variant of CRUNCH

scruncheon *or* **scrunchion** (ˈskrʌntʃən) NOUN *Canadian* (in Newfoundland) a small crisp piece of fried pork fat.
▷HISTORY origin unknown

scrunchie (ˈskrʌntʃɪ) NOUN a loop of elastic covered loosely with fabric, used to hold the hair in a ponytail, etc.

scruple (ˈskruːpᵊl) NOUN [1] (*often plural*) a doubt or hesitation as to what is morally right in a certain situation. [2] *Archaic* a very small amount. [3] a unit of weight equal to 20 grains (1.296 grams). [4] an ancient Roman unit of weight equivalent to approximately one twenty-fourth of an ounce. ◆ VERB [5] (*obsolete when tr*) to have doubts (about), esp for a moral reason.
▷HISTORY C16: from Latin *scrūpulus* a small weight, from *scrūpus* rough stone
▸**ˈscrupleless** ADJECTIVE

scrupulous (ˈskruːpjʊləs) ADJECTIVE [1] characterized by careful observation of what is morally right. [2] very careful or precise.
▷HISTORY C15: from Latin *scrūpulōsus* punctilious
▸**ˈscrupulously** ADVERB ▸**ˈscrupulousness** NOUN

scrutable (ˈskruːtəbᵊl) ADJECTIVE *Rare* open to or able to be understood by scrutiny.
▷HISTORY C17: from Latin *scrūtārī* to inspect closely; see SCRUTINY
▸**ˌscrutaˈbility** NOUN

scrutator (skruːˈteɪtə) NOUN a person who examines or scrutinizes.
▷HISTORY from Latin, from *scrūtārī* to search

scrutineer (ˌskruːtɪˈnɪə) NOUN a person who examines, esp one who scrutinizes the conduct of an election poll.

scrutinize *or* **scrutinise** (ˈskruːtɪˌnaɪz) VERB (*tr*) to examine carefully or in minute detail.
▸**ˈscrutiˌnizer** *or* **ˈscrutiˌniser** NOUN

scrutiny (ˈskruːtɪnɪ) NOUN, *plural* **-nies.** [1] close or minute examination. [2] a searching look. [3] **a** (in the early Christian Church) a formal testing that catechumens had to undergo before being baptized. **b** a similar examination of candidates for holy orders.
▷HISTORY C15: from Late Latin *scrūtinium* an investigation, from *scrūtārī* to search (originally referring to rag-and-bone men), from *scrūta* rubbish

scry (skraɪ) VERB **scries, scrying, scried.** (*intr*) to divine, esp by crystal gazing.
▷HISTORY C16: from DESCRY

SCSI (ˈskʌzɪ) Small Computer Systems Interface: a system for connecting a computer to peripheral devices.

scuba (ˈskjuːbə) NOUN **a** an apparatus used in skindiving, consisting of a cylinder or cylinders containing compressed air attached to a breathing apparatus. **b** (*as modifier*): *scuba diving.*
▷HISTORY C20: from the initials of *self-contained underwater breathing apparatus*

scud (skʌd) VERB **scuds, scudding, scudded.** [1] (*intr*) (esp of clouds) to move along swiftly and smoothly. [2] (*intr*) *Nautical* to run before a gale. [3] (*tr*) *Scot* to hit; slap. ◆ NOUN [4] the act of scudding. [5] *Meteorol* **a** a formation of low fractostratus clouds driven by a strong wind beneath rain-bearing clouds. **b** a sudden shower or gust of wind. [6] *Scot* a slap.
▷HISTORY C16: probably of Scandinavian origin; related to Norwegian *skudda* to thrust, Swedish *skudda* to shake

Scud (skʌd) NOUN *Informal* a Soviet-made surface-to-surface missile, originally designed to carry nuclear warheads and with a range of 300 km; later modified to achieve greater range: used by Iraq in the Iran-Iraq War and in the Gulf Wars.

scudo (ˈskuːdəʊ) NOUN, *plural* **-di** (-diː). any of several former Italian coins.
▷HISTORY C17: from Italian: shield, from Latin *scūtum*

scuff (skʌf) VERB [1] to scrape or drag (the feet) while walking. [2] to rub or scratch (a surface) or (of a surface) to become rubbed or scratched. [3] (*tr*) *US* to poke at (something) with the foot. ◆ NOUN [4] the act or sound of scuffing. [5] a rubbed place caused by scuffing. [6] a backless slipper.
▷HISTORY C19: probably of imitative origin

scuffle[1] (ˈskʌfᵊl) VERB (*intr*) [1] to fight in a disorderly manner. [2] to move by shuffling. [3] to move in a hurried or confused manner. ◆ NOUN [4] a disorderly struggle. [5] the sound made by scuffling or shuffling.
▷HISTORY C16: from Scandinavian; compare Swedish *skuff, skuffa* to push

scuffle[2] (ˈskʌfᵊl) NOUN *US* a type of hoe operated by pushing rather than pulling.
▷HISTORY C18: from Dutch *schoffel* SHOVEL

scull (skʌl) NOUN [1] a single oar moved from side to side over the stern of a boat to propel it. [2] one of a pair of short-handled oars, both of which are pulled by one oarsman, esp in a racing shell. [3] a racing shell propelled by an oarsman or oarsmen pulling two oars. [4] (*plural*) a race between racing shells, each propelled by one, two, or four oarsmen pulling two oars. [5] an act, instance, period, or distance of sculling. ◆ VERB [6] to propel (a boat) with a scull.
▷HISTORY C14: of unknown origin
▸**ˈsculler** NOUN

scullery (ˈskʌlərɪ) NOUN, *plural* **-leries.** *Chiefly Brit* a small room or part of a kitchen where washing up, vegetable preparation, etc. is done.
▷HISTORY C15: from Anglo-Norman *squillerie*, from Old French *escuelerie*, from *escuele* a bowl, from Latin *scutella*, from *scutra* a flat tray

scullion (ˈskʌljən) NOUN [1] a mean or despicable person. [2] *Archaic* a servant employed to do rough household work in a kitchen.
▷HISTORY C15: from Old French *escouillon* cleaning cloth, from *escouve* a broom, from Latin *scōpa* a broom

sculpin (ˈskʌlpɪn) NOUN, *plural* **-pin** *or* **-pins.** *US and Canadian* any of various fishes of the family *Cottidae* (bullheads and sea scorpions).
▷HISTORY C17: of unknown origin

sculpsit *Latin* (ˈskʌlpsɪt) he (or she) sculptured it: an inscription following the artist's name on a sculpture.

sculpt (skʌlpt) VERB [1] a variant of **sculpture** (senses 5–8). [2] (*intr*) to practise sculpture. ◆ Also: **sculp.**
▷HISTORY C19: from French *sculpter*, from Latin *sculpere* to carve

sculptor (ˈskʌlptə) *or feminine* **sculptress** NOUN a person who practises sculpture.

Sculptor (ˈskʌlptə) NOUN, *Latin genitive* **Sculptoris** (skʌlpˈtɔːrɪs). a faint constellation in the S hemisphere between Phoenix and Cetus.

sculpture (ˈskʌlptʃə) NOUN [1] the art of making figures or designs in relief or the round by carving wood, moulding plaster, etc., or casting metals, etc. [2] works or a work made in this way. [3] ridges or indentations as on a shell, formed by natural processes. [4] the gradual formation of the landscape by erosion. ◆ VERB (*mainly tr*) [5] (*also intr*) to carve, cast, or fashion (stone, bronze, etc.) three dimensionally. [6] to portray (a person, etc.) by means of sculpture. [7] to form in the manner of sculpture, esp to shape (landscape) by erosion. [8] to decorate with sculpture. ◆ Also (for senses 5–8): **sculpt.**
▷HISTORY C14: from Latin *sculptūra* a carving; see SCULPT
▸**ˈsculptural** ADJECTIVE ▸**ˈsculpturally** ADVERB

sculpturesque (ˌskʌlptʃəˈrɛsk) ADJECTIVE resembling sculpture.
▸**ˌsculpturˈesquely** ADVERB ▸**ˌsculpturˈesqueness** NOUN

scum (skʌm) NOUN [1] a layer of impure matter that forms on the surface of a liquid, often as the result of boiling or fermentation. [2] the greenish film of algae and similar vegetation surface of a stagnant pond. [3] Also called: **dross, scruff.** the skin of oxides or impurities on the surface of a molten metal. [4] waste matter. [5] a worthless person or group of people. ◆ VERB **scums, scumming, scummed.** [6] (*tr*) to remove scum from. [7] (*intr*) *Rare* to form a layer of or become covered with scum.
▷HISTORY C13: of Germanic origin; related to Old High German *scūm*, Middle Dutch *schūm*, Old French *escume;* see SKIM
▸**ˈscumˌlike** ADJECTIVE ▸**ˈscummer** NOUN

scumbag (ˈskʌmˌbæg) NOUN *Slang* an offensive or despicable person.
▷HISTORY C20: perhaps from earlier US sense: condom, from US slang *scum* semen + bag

scumble (ˈskʌmbᵊl) VERB [1] (in painting and drawing) to soften or blend (an outline or colour) with an upper coat of opaque colour, applied very thinly. ◆ NOUN [2] the upper layer of colour applied in this way. [3] the technique or effects of scumbling.
▷HISTORY C18: probably from SCUM

scummy (ˈskʌmɪ) ADJECTIVE **-mier, -miest.** [1] of, resembling, consisting of, or covered with scum. [2] dirty, unpleasant, or nasty.

scuncheon (ˈskʌntʃən) NOUN the inner part of a door jamb or window frame.
▷HISTORY C15: from Old French *escoinson*, from *coin* angle

scunge (skʌndʒ) *Austral and NZ slang* ◆ VERB [1] to borrow. ◆ NOUN [2] a dirty or worthless person. [3] a person who borrows, esp habitually.
▷HISTORY C20: of unknown origin

scungy (ˈskʌndʒɪ) ADJECTIVE **scungier, scungiest.** *Austral and NZ informal* miserable; sordid; dirty.
▷HISTORY C20: of uncertain origin

scunner (ˈskʌnə; *Scot* ˈskʌnər) *Dialect, chiefly Scot* ◆ VERB [1] (*intr*) to feel aversion. [2] (*tr*) to produce a feeling of aversion in. ◆ NOUN [3] a strong aversion (often in the phrase **take a scunner to**). [4] an object of dislike; nuisance.
▷HISTORY C14: from Scottish *skunner*, of unknown origin

Scunthorpe (ˈskʌnˌθɔːp) NOUN a town in E England, in North Lincolnshire unitary authority, Lincolnshire: developed rapidly after the discovery of local iron ore in the late 19th century; iron and steel industries have declined. Pop.: 75 982 (1991).

scup (skʌp) NOUN a common sparid fish, *Stenotomus chrysops*, of American coastal regions of the Atlantic. Also called: **northern porgy.**
▷HISTORY C19: from Narraganset *mishcup*, from *mishe* big + *kuppe* close together; from the form of the scales

scupper[1] (ˈskʌpə) NOUN [1] *Nautical* a drain or spout allowing water on the deck of a vessel to flow overboard. [2] an opening in the side of a building for draining off water. [3] a drain in a factory floor for running off the water from a sprinkler system.
▷HISTORY C15 *skopper*, of uncertain origin; perhaps related to SCOOP

scupper[2] (ˈskʌpə) VERB (*tr*) *Brit* [1] *Slang* to overwhelm, ruin, or disable. [2] to sink (one's ship) deliberately.
▷HISTORY C19: of unknown origin

scuppernong (ˈskʌpəˌnɒŋ) NOUN [1] a sweet American wine, slightly golden, made from a variety of muscadine grape. [2] another name for **muscadine** (sense 2), the variety from which this wine is made
▷HISTORY C19: named after *Scuppernong* River in North Carolina where the grape grows

scur (skɜː) NOUN *Vet science* a small unattached growth of horn at the site of a normal horn in cattle.

scurf (skɜːf) NOUN [1] another name for **dandruff.** [2] flaky or scaly matter adhering to or peeling off a surface.
▷HISTORY Old English *scurf;* related to Old Norse *skurfōttr* scurfy, Old High German *scorf*, Danish *skurv*
▸**ˈscurfy** ADJECTIVE

scurrilous (ˈskʌrɪləs) ADJECTIVE [1] grossly or obscenely abusive or defamatory. [2] characterized by gross or obscene humour.

▷HISTORY C16: from Latin *scurrīlis* derisive, from *scurra* buffoon
▸**scurrility** (skəˈrɪlɪtɪ) *or* ˈ**scurrilousness** NOUN
▸ˈ**scurrilously** ADVERB

scurry (ˈskʌrɪ) VERB **-ries, -rying, -ried.** 1 to move about or proceed hurriedly. 2 (*intr*) to whirl about. ◆ NOUN, *plural* **-ries.** 3 the act or sound of scurrying. 4 a brisk light whirling movement, as of snow. 5 *Horse racing* a short race or sprint.
▷HISTORY C19: probably shortened from *hurry-scurry*

scurvy (ˈskɜːvɪ) NOUN 1 a disease caused by a lack of vitamin C, characterized by anaemia, spongy gums, bleeding beneath the skin, and (in infants) malformation of bones and teeth. Related adjective: **scorbutic.** ◆ ADJECTIVE **-vier, -viest.** 2 mean or despicable.
▷HISTORY C16: see SCURF
▸ˈ**scurvily** ADVERB ▸ˈ**scurviness** NOUN

scurvy grass NOUN any of various plants of the genus *Cochlearia,* esp *C. officinalis,* of Europe and North America, formerly used to treat scurvy: family *Brassicaceae* (crucifers).

scut (skʌt) NOUN the short tail of animals such as the deer and rabbit.
▷HISTORY C15: probably of Scandinavian origin; compare Old Norse *skutr* end of a vessel, Icelandic *skott* tail

scuta (ˈskjuːtə) NOUN the plural of **scutum.**

scutage (ˈskjuːtɪdʒ) NOUN (in feudal society) a payment sometimes exacted by a lord from his vassal in lieu of military service.
▷HISTORY C15: from Medieval Latin *scūtāgium,* literally: shield dues, from Latin *scūtum* a shield

Scutari NOUN 1 (ˈskuːtərɪ, skuːˈtɑːrɪ) the former name of **Üsküdar.** 2 (skuˈtari) the Italian name for **Shkodër.**

scutate (ˈskjuːteɪt) ADJECTIVE 1 (of animals) having or covered with large bony or horny plates. 2 *Botany* shaped like a round shield or buckler: *a scutate leaf.*
▷HISTORY C19: from Latin *scūtātus* armed with a shield, from *scūtum* a shield
▸**scuˈtation** NOUN

scutch[1] (skʌtʃ) VERB 1 (*tr*) to separate the fibres from the woody part of (flax) by pounding. ◆ NOUN 2 the tool used for this. Also called: **scutcher.**
▷HISTORY C18: from obsolete French *escoucher,* from Vulgar Latin *excuticāre* (unattested) to beat out, from Latin EX-[1] + *quatere* to shake

scutch[2] (skʌtʃ) VERB (*tr*) *Northern English dialect* to strike with an open hand.

scutcheon (ˈskʌtʃən) NOUN 1 a variant of **escutcheon.** 2 any rounded or shield-shaped structure, esp a scute.
▸ˈ**scutcheonless** ADJECTIVE ▸ˈ**scutcheon-ˌlike** ADJECTIVE

scutch grass NOUN another name for **Bermuda grass** and **couch grass.** Sometimes shortened to: **scutch.**
▷HISTORY variant of COUCH GRASS

scute (skjuːt) NOUN *Zoology* a horny or chitinous plate that makes up part of the exoskeleton in armadillos, turtles, fishes, etc.
▷HISTORY C14 (the name of a French coin; C19 in zoological sense): from Latin *scūtum* shield

scutellation (ˌskjuːtɪˈleɪʃən) NOUN *Zoology* 1 the way in which scales or plates are arranged in an animal. 2 a covering of scales or scutella, as on a bird's leg.
▷HISTORY C19: New Latin, from *scutella,* plural of SCUTELLUM + -ATION

scutellum (skjuːˈtɛləm) NOUN, *plural* **-la** (-lə). *Biology* 1 the last of three plates into which the notum of an insect's thorax is divided. 2 one of the scales on the tarsus of a bird's leg. 3 an outgrowth from a germinating grass seed that probably represents the cotyledon. 4 any other small shield-shaped part or structure.
▷HISTORY C18: from New Latin: a little shield, from Latin *scūtum* a shield
▸**scuˈtellar** ADJECTIVE ▸**scutellate** (ˈskjuːtɪˌleɪt, -lɪt) ADJECTIVE

scutiform (ˈskjuːtɪˌfɔːm) ADJECTIVE (esp of plant parts) shaped like a shield.
▷HISTORY C17: from New Latin *scūtiformis,* from Latin *scūtum* a shield + *forma* shape

scutter (ˈskʌtə) VERB, NOUN *Brit* an informal word for **scurry.**
▷HISTORY C18: probably from SCUTTLE[2], with -ER[1] as in SCATTER

scuttle[1] (ˈskʌtᵊl) NOUN 1 See **coal scuttle.** 2 *Dialect, chiefly Brit* a shallow basket, esp for carrying vegetables. 3 the part of a motor-car body lying immediately behind the bonnet.
▷HISTORY Old English *scutel* trencher, from Latin *scutella* bowl, diminutive of *scutra* platter; related to Old Norse *skutill,* Old High German *scuzzila,* perhaps to Latin *scūtum* shield

scuttle[2] (ˈskʌtᵊl) VERB 1 (*intr*) to run or move about with short hasty steps. ◆ NOUN 2 a hurried pace or run.
▷HISTORY C15: perhaps from SCUD, influenced by SHUTTLE

scuttle[3] (ˈskʌtᵊl) VERB 1 (*tr*) *Nautical* to cause (a vessel) to sink by opening the seacocks or making holes in the bottom. 2 (*tr*) to give up (hopes, plans, etc.). ◆ NOUN 3 *Nautical* a small hatch or its cover.
▷HISTORY C15 (n): via Old French from Spanish *escotilla* a small opening, from *escote* opening in a piece of cloth, from *escotar* to cut out

scuttlebutt (ˈskʌtᵊlˌbʌt) NOUN *Nautical* 1 a drinking fountain. 2 (formerly) a cask of drinking water aboard a ship. 3 *Chiefly US slang* rumour or gossip.
▷HISTORY C19: from SCUTTLE[3] + BUTT[4]

scutum (ˈskjuːtəm) NOUN, *plural* **-ta** (-tə). 1 the middle of three plates into which the notum of an insect's thorax is divided. 2 another word for **scute.** 3 a large Roman shield.
▷HISTORY Latin: shield

Scutum (ˈskjuːtəm) NOUN, *Latin genitive* **Scuti** (ˈskjuːtaɪ). a small faint constellation in the S hemisphere lying between Sagittarius and Aquila and crossed by the Milky Way. Also called: **Scutum Sobieskii** (sɒˈbjɛskɪ).
▷HISTORY Latin, literally: the Shield

scuzzy (ˈskʌzɪ) ADJECTIVE **-zier, -ziest.** *Slang, chiefly US* unkempt, dirty, or squalid.
▷HISTORY C20: perhaps from *disgusting* or perhaps from a blend of *scum* and *fuzz*

Scylla (ˈsɪlə) NOUN 1 *Greek myth* a sea nymph transformed into a sea monster believed to drown sailors navigating the Strait of Messina. She was identified with a rock off the Italian coast. Compare **Charybdis.** 2 **between Scylla and Charybdis.** in a predicament in which avoidance of either of two dangers means exposure to the other.

scyphiform (ˈsaɪfɪˌfɔːm) ADJECTIVE shaped like a cup or goblet: *a scyphiform cell.*
▷HISTORY C19: from Greek *skuphos* cup + -FORM

scyphistoma (saɪˈfɪstəmə) NOUN, *plural* **-mae** (-ˌmiː) *or* **-mas.** a sessile hydra-like individual representing the polyp stage of scyphozoans. It produces forms which become free-swimming jellyfish.
▷HISTORY C19: from Greek *skuphos* cup + STOMA

scyphozoan (ˌsaɪfəˈzəʊən) NOUN 1 any marine medusoid coelenterate of the class *Scyphozoa;* a jellyfish. ◆ ADJECTIVE 2 of, relating to, or belonging to the *Scyphozoa.*
▷HISTORY C19: via New Latin from Greek *skuphos* bowl + *zōion* animal

scyphus (ˈsaɪfəs) NOUN, *plural* **-phi** (-faɪ). 1 an ancient Greek two-handled drinking cup without a footed base. 2 *Botany* a cuplike body formed at the end of the thallus in certain lichens.
▷HISTORY C18: from Latin: goblet, from Greek *skuphos*

Scyros (ˈskirɔs) NOUN a variant spelling of **Skyros.**

scythe (saɪð) NOUN 1 a manual implement for cutting grass, etc., having a long handle held with both hands and a curved sharpened blade that moves in a plane parallel to the ground. ◆ VERB 2 (*tr*) to cut (grass, etc.) with a scythe.
▷HISTORY Old English *sigthe;* related to Old Norse *sigthr,* Old High German *segansa*
▸ˈ**scytheˌlike** ADJECTIVE

Scythia (ˈsɪðɪə) NOUN an ancient region of SE Europe and Asia, north of the Black Sea: now part of the Ukraine.

Scythian (ˈsɪðɪən) ADJECTIVE 1 of or relating to ancient Scythia, its inhabitants, or their language. ◆ NOUN 2 a member of an ancient nomadic people of Scythia. 3 the extinct language of this people, belonging to the East Iranian branch of the Indo-European family.

sd[1] ABBREVIATION FOR: 1 sine die. 2 sound. 3 *Philosophy* sense datum.

sd[2] THE INTERNET DOMAIN NAME FOR Sudan.

SD ABBREVIATION FOR: 1 South Dakota. 2 Also: **sd.** *Statistics* **standard deviation.** ◆ 3 INTERNATIONAL CAR REGISTRATION FOR Swaziland.

S. Dak. ABBREVIATION FOR South Dakota.

SDI ABBREVIATION FOR Strategic Defense Initiative. See **Star Wars.**

SDLP (in Northern Ireland) ABBREVIATION FOR **Social Democratic and Labour Party.**

SDP ABBREVIATION FOR **Social Democratic Party.**

SDRs ABBREVIATION FOR **special drawing rights.**

se THE INTERNET DOMAIN NAME FOR Sweden.

Se THE CHEMICAL SYMBOL FOR selenium.

SE SYMBOL FOR southeast(ern).

sea (siː) NOUN 1 **a** (usually preceded by *the*) the mass of salt water on the earth's surface as differentiated from the land. Related adjectives: **marine, maritime, thalassic. b** (*as modifier*): *sea air.* 2 (*capital when part of place name*) **a** one of the smaller areas of ocean: *the Irish Sea.* **b** a large inland area of water: *the Caspian Sea.* 3 turbulence or swell, esp of considerable size: *heavy seas.* 4 (*capital when part of a name*) *Astronomy* any of many huge dry plains on the surface of the moon. See also **mare**[2]. 5 anything resembling the sea in size or apparent limitlessness. 6 the life or career of a sailor (esp in the phrase **follow the sea**). 7 **at sea. a** on the ocean. **b** in a state of confusion. 8 **go to sea.** to become a sailor. 9 **put (out) to sea.** to embark on a sea voyage.
▷HISTORY Old English *sǣ;* related to Old Norse *sǣr,* Old Frisian *sē,* Gothic *saiws,* Old High German *sēo*

sea anchor NOUN *Nautical* any device, such as a bucket or canvas funnel, dragged in the water to keep a vessel heading into the wind or reduce drifting.

sea anemone NOUN any of various anthozoan coelenterates, esp of the order *Actiniaria,* having a polypoid body with oral rings of tentacles. See also **actinia.**

sea aster NOUN a composite perennial plant of salt marshes, *Aster tripolium,* having yellow and purple flowers like those of the related Michaelmas daisy.

sea bag NOUN a canvas bag, closed by a line threaded through grommets at the top, used by a seaman for his belongings.

sea bass (bæs) NOUN any of various American coastal percoid fishes of the genus *Centropristes* and related genera, such as *C. striatus* (**black sea bass**), having an elongated body with a long spiny dorsal fin almost divided into two: family *Serranidae.*

Seabee (ˈsiːˌbiː) NOUN a member of the US Navy's Construction Battalions established to build airstrips.
▷HISTORY C20: from pronunciation of *CB,* for *Construction Battalion*

sea beet NOUN the wild form of *Beta vulgaris.* See **beet.**

sea bird NOUN a bird such as a gull, that lives on the sea.

sea biscuit NOUN another term for **hardtack.**

seablite (ˈsiːˌblaɪt) NOUN a prostrate annual plant of the goosefoot family, *Suaeda maritima,* of salt marshes, having fleshy alternate leaves and small green flowers.
▷HISTORY C18: SEA + *blite,* via Latin from Greek *bliton* ORACHE

seaboard (ˈsiːˌbɔːd) NOUN **a** land bordering on the sea; the seashore. **b** (*as modifier*): *seaboard towns.*

seaborgium (ˈsiːbɔːgɪəm) NOUN a synthetic transuranic element, synthesized and identified in 1974. Symbol: Sg; atomic no.: 106.
▷HISTORY C20: named after Glenn *Seaborg* (1912–99), US chemist and nuclear physicist

seaborne (ˈsiːˌbɔːn) ADJECTIVE 1 carried on or by the sea. 2 transported by ship.

sea bream NOUN any sparid fish, esp *Pagellus centrodontus,* of European seas, valued as a food fish.

sea breeze NOUN a wind blowing from the sea to

the land, esp during the day when the land surface is warmer.

sea buckthorn NOUN a thorny Eurasian shrub, *Hippophaë rhamnoides,* growing on sea coasts and having silvery leaves and orange fruits: family *Elaeagnaceae.*

sea butterfly NOUN another name for **pteropod.**

sea captain NOUN the master of a ship, usually a merchant ship.

sea change NOUN a seemingly magical change, as brought about by the action of the sea.
▷HISTORY coined by Shakespeare, in Ariel's song "Full Fathom Five" in *The Tempest* (1611)

sea chest NOUN a usually large firm chest used by a sailor for storing personal property.

seacoast ('siːˌkəʊst) NOUN land bordering on the sea; a coast.

seacock ('siːˌkɒk) NOUN *Nautical* a valve in the hull of a vessel below the water line for admitting sea water or for pumping out bilge water.

sea cow NOUN 1 any sirenian mammal, such as a dugong or manatee. 2 an archaic name for **walrus.**

sea cucumber NOUN any echinoderm of the class *Holothuroidea,* having an elongated body covered with a leathery skin and bearing a cluster of tentacles at the oral end. They usually creep on the sea bed or burrow in sand.
▷HISTORY C17: so named because of its cucumber-like shape

seadog ('siːˌdɒg) NOUN another word for **fogbow** or **fogdog.**

sea dog NOUN an experienced or old sailor.

Sea-Doo ('siːˌduː) NOUN *Trademark, Canadian* a small self-propelled watercraft for one person.

sea duck NOUN any of various large diving ducks, such as the eider and the scoter, that occur along coasts.

sea eagle NOUN any of various fish-eating eagles that live near the sea, esp *Haliaetus albicilla* (**European sea eagle** or **white-tailed eagle**) having a brown plumage and white tail.

sea-ear NOUN another name for the **ormer** (sense 1).

sea elephant NOUN another name for **elephant seal.**

sea fan NOUN any of various corals of the genus *Gorgonia* and related genera, having a treelike or fan-shaped horny skeleton: order *Gorgonacea* (gorgonians).

seafarer ('siːˌfɛərə) NOUN 1 a traveller who goes by sea. 2 a less common word for **sailor.**

seafaring ('siːˌfɛərɪŋ) ADJECTIVE (*prenominal*) 1 travelling by sea. 2 working as a sailor. ◆ NOUN 3 the act of travelling by sea. 4 the career or work of a sailor.

sea fir NOUN another name for **hydroid** (sense 3).

sea-floor spreading ('siːˌflɔː) NOUN a series of processes in which new oceanic lithosphere is created at oceanic ridges, spreads away from the ridges, and returns to the earth's interior along subduction zones. Also called: **ocean floor spreading.**

sea foam NOUN 1 foam formed on the surface of the sea. 2 a former name for **meerschaum** (sense 1).

seafood ('siːˌfuːd) NOUN edible saltwater fish or shellfish.

sea fret NOUN a wet mist or haze coming inland from the sea.

seafront ('siːˌfrʌnt) NOUN a built-up area facing the sea.

sea-girt ADJECTIVE *Literary* surrounded by the sea.

seagoing ('siːˌgəʊɪŋ) ADJECTIVE intended for or used at sea.

sea gooseberry NOUN any of various ctenophores of the genus *Pleurobrachia* and related genera, having a rounded body with longitudinal rows of cilia and hairlike tentacles.

sea green NOUN **a** a moderate green colour, sometimes with a bluish or yellowish tinge. **b** (*as adjective*): *a sea-green carpet.*

seagull ('siːˌgʌl) NOUN 1 a popular name for the **gull** (the bird). 2 *NZ* a casual wharf labourer who is not a trade-union member.

sea hare NOUN any of various marine gastropods of the order *Aplysiomorpha* (or *Anaspidea*), esp *Aplysia punctata,* having a soft body with an internal shell and two pairs of earlike tentacles.

sea heath NOUN a small tough perennial plant, *Frankenia laevis,* of Eurasian salt marshes, having minute leaves and pink flowers: family *Frankeniaceae.*

sea holly NOUN a European umbelliferous plant, *Eryngium maritimum,* of sandy shores, having spiny bluish-green stems and blue flowers.

sea horse NOUN 1 any marine teleost fish of the temperate and tropical genus *Hippocampus,* having a bony-plated body, a prehensile tail, and a horselike head and swimming in an upright position: family *Syngnathidae* (pipefishes). 2 an archaic name for the **walrus.** 3 a fabled sea creature with the tail of a fish and the front parts of a horse.

sea-island cotton NOUN 1 a cotton plant, *Gossypium barbadense,* of the Sea Islands, widely cultivated for its fine long fibres. 2 the fibre of this plant or the material woven from it.

Sea Islands PLURAL NOUN a chain of islands in the Atlantic off the coasts of South Carolina, Georgia, and Florida.

sea kale NOUN a European coastal plant, *Crambe maritima,* with broad fleshy leaves and white flowers, cultivated for its edible asparagus-like shoots: family *Brassicaceae* (crucifers). Compare **kale.**

seakale beet ('siːˌkeɪl) NOUN another name for **chard.**

sea king NOUN any of the greater Viking pirate chiefs who led raids on the coasts of early medieval Europe.

seal[1] (siːl) NOUN 1 a device impressed on a piece of wax, moist clay, etc., fixed to a letter, document, etc., as a mark of authentication. 2 a stamp, ring, etc., engraved with a device to form such an impression. 3 a substance, esp wax, so placed over an envelope, document, etc., that it must be broken before the object can be opened or used. 4 any substance or device used to close or fasten tightly. 5 a material, such as putty or cement, that is used to close an opening to prevent the passage of air, water, etc. 6 a small amount of water contained in the trap of a drain to prevent the passage of foul smells. 7 an agent or device for keeping something hidden or secret. 8 anything that gives a pledge or confirmation. 9 a decorative stamp often sold in aid of charity. 10 *RC Church* Also called: **seal of confession.** the obligation never to reveal anything said by a penitent in confession. 11 **set one's seal on** (*or* **to**). **a** to mark with one's sign or seal. **b** to endorse. ◆ VERB (*tr*) 12 to affix a seal to, as proof of authenticity. 13 to stamp with or as if with a seal. 14 to approve or authorize. 15 (sometimes foll by *up*) to close or secure with or as if with a seal: *to seal one's lips; seal up a letter.* 16 (foll by *off*) to enclose (a place) with a fence, wall, etc. 17 to decide irrevocably. 18 *Mormon Church* to make (a marriage or adoption) perpetually binding. 19 to close tightly so as to render airtight or watertight. 20 to paint (a porous material) with a nonporous coating. 21 *Austral and NZ* to consolidate (a road surface) with bitumen, tar, etc.
▷HISTORY C13 *seel,* from Old French, from Latin *sigillum* little figure, from *signum* a sign
▸ **'sealable** ADJECTIVE

seal[2] (siːl) NOUN 1 any pinniped mammal of the families *Otariidae* (see **eared seal**) and *Phocidae* (see **earless seal**) that are aquatic but come on shore to breed. Related adjectives: **otarid, phocine.** 2 any earless seal (family *Phocidae*), esp the common or harbour seal or the grey seal (*Halichoerus grypus*). 3 sealskin. ◆ VERB 4 (*intr*) to hunt for seals.
▷HISTORY Old English *seolh;* related to Old Norse *selr,* Old High German *selah,* Old Irish *selige* tortoise
▸ **'seal-ˌlike** ADJECTIVE

sea lace NOUN a brown seaweed, *Chorda filum,* that grows on stones under sandy bottoms and produces chordlike fronds up to 8.5 metres (28 ft.) long.

sea ladder NOUN a rope ladder, set of steps, etc., by which a boat may be boarded at sea.

sea lamprey NOUN a common anadromous lamprey, *Petromyzon marinus,* a form of which occurs in the Great Lakes of N America and causes great losses of fish.

sea lane NOUN an established route for ships.

sealant ('siːlənt) NOUN 1 any substance, such as wax, used for sealing documents, bottles, etc. 2 any of a number of substances used for stopping leaks, waterproofing wood, etc.

sea lavender NOUN any of numerous perennial plants of the plumbaginaceous genus *Limonium,* of temperate salt marshes, having spikes of white, pink, or mauve flowers, several species of which are grown as garden plants. See also **statice.**

sea lawyer NOUN *Nautical, slang* a contentious seaman.

seal brown NOUN **a** a dark brown colour often with a yellowish or greyish tinge. **b** (*as adjective*): *a seal-brown dress.*

sealed (siːld) VERB 1 the past participle of **seal[1]**. ◆ ADJECTIVE 2 *Austral and NZ* (of a road) having a hard surface; made-up.

sealed-beam ADJECTIVE (esp of a car headlight) having a lens and prefocused reflector sealed in the lamp vacuum.

sealed book NOUN another term for **closed book.**

sealed move NOUN *Chess* the last move before an adjournment, which is written down by the player making it, sealed in an envelope, and kept secret from his opponent until play is resumed.

sealed orders PLURAL NOUN written instructions that are not to be read until a specified time.

sealed unit NOUN a hard disk that is permanently sealed to prevent damage to the read/write head. See also **Winchester disk.**

sea legs PLURAL NOUN *Informal* 1 the ability to maintain one's balance on board ship, esp in rough weather. 2 the ability to resist seasickness, esp in rough weather.

sealer[1] ('siːlə) NOUN 1 a person or thing that seals. 2 (formerly in Britain and currently in the US) an official who examines the accuracy of weights and measures. 3 a coating of paint, varnish, etc., applied to a surface to prevent the absorption of subsequent coats.

sealer[2] ('siːlə) NOUN a person or ship occupied in hunting seals.

sealery ('siːlərɪ) NOUN, *plural* **-eries.** 1 the occupation of hunting seals. 2 any place where seals are regularly to be found, esp a seal rookery.

sea letter NOUN 1 Also called: **passport.** a document issued to a merchant vessel, esp in wartime, authorizing it to leave a port or proceed freely. 2 (formerly) a document issued to a vessel in port, describing its cargo, crew, etc.

sea lettuce NOUN any of various green seaweeds of the genus *Ulva,* which have edible wavy translucent fronds.

sea level NOUN the level of the surface of the sea with respect to the land, taken to be the mean level between high and low tide, and used as a standard base for measuring heights and depths.

sea lily NOUN any of various sessile echinoderms, esp of the genus *Ptilocrinus,* in which the body consists of a long stalk attached to a hard surface and bearing a central disc with delicate radiating arms: class *Crinoidea* (crinoids).

sealing wax NOUN a hard material made of shellac, turpentine, and pigment that softens when heated. It is used for sealing documents, parcels, letters, etc.

sea lion NOUN any of various large eared seals, such as *Zalophus californianus* (**Californian sea lion**), of the N Pacific, often used as a performing animal.

sea loch NOUN another name for **loch** (sense 2).

Sea Lord NOUN (in Britain) either of the two serving naval officers (**First** and **Second Sea Lords**) who sit on the admiralty board of the Ministry of Defence.

seal-point NOUN a popular variety of the Siamese cat, having a dark brown mask, paws, and tail, and a cream body.

seal ring NOUN another term for **signet ring.**

sealskin ('siːlˌskɪn) NOUN 1 **a** the skin or pelt of a fur seal, esp when dressed with the outer hair removed and the underfur dyed dark brown. **b** (*as modifier*): *a sealskin coat.* 2 a garment made of this skin.

Sealyham terrier ('siːlɪəm) NOUN a short-legged wire-haired breed of terrier with a medium-length white coat. Often shortened to: **Sealyham.**

▷**HISTORY** named after *Sealyham,* village in S Wales, where it was bred in the 19th century

seam (si:m) NOUN **1** the line along which pieces of fabric are joined, esp by stitching. **2** a ridge or line made by joining two edges. **3** a stratum of coal, ore, etc. **4** **in a good seam.** *Northern English dialect* doing well, esp financially. **5** a linear indentation, such as a wrinkle or scar. **6** *Surgery* another name for **suture** (sense 1b). **7** *(modifier) Cricket* of or relating to a style of bowling in which the bowler utilizes the stitched seam round the ball in order to make it swing in flight and after touching the ground: *a seam bowler.* **8** **bursting at the seams.** full to overflowing. ◆ VERB **9** *(tr)* to join or sew together by or as if by a seam. **10** *US* to make ridges in (knitting) using purl stitch. **11** to mark or become marked with or as if with a seam or wrinkle.
▷**HISTORY** Old English; related to Old Norse *saumr,* Old High German *soum*

seaman ('si:mən) NOUN, *plural* **-men. 1** a rating trained in seamanship as opposed to electrical engineering, etc. **2** a man who serves as a sailor. **3** a person skilled in seamanship.
▸**'seaman-,like** ADJECTIVE ▸**'seamanly** ADJECTIVE, ADVERB

seamanship ('si:mənʃɪp) NOUN skill in and knowledge of the work of navigating, maintaining, and operating a vessel.

seamark ('si:,mɑ:k) NOUN *Nautical* an aid to navigation, such as a conspicuous object on a shore used as a guide.

sea mat NOUN a popular name for a **bryozoan.**

seam bowler *or* **seamer** NOUN *Cricket* a fast bowler who makes the ball bounce on its seam so that it will change direction.
▸**seam bowling** NOUN

seamer ('si:mə) NOUN **1** a person or thing that seams. **2** another name for **seam bowler.**

sea mew NOUN another name for **mew** (sense 2).

sea mile NOUN a unit of distance used in navigation, defined as the length of one minute of arc, measured along the meridian, in the latitude of the position. Its actual length varies slightly with latitude but is about 1853 metres (6080 feet). Symbol: M. See also **nautical mile.**

sea milkwort NOUN a primulaceous plant, *Glaux maritima,* of estuary mud and seaside rocks of N temperate coasts, having trailing stems and small pink flowers. Also called: **saltwort, black saltwort.** Compare **milkwort.**

seamless ('si:mlɪs) ADJECTIVE **1** (of a garment) having no seams. **2** continuous or flowing: *seamless output; a seamless performance.*

seamount ('si:,maʊnt) NOUN a submarine mountain rising more than 1000 metres above the surrounding ocean floor. Compare **guyot.**

sea mouse NOUN any of several large polychaete worms of the genus *Aphrodite* and related genera, having a broad flattened body covered dorsally with a dense mat of iridescent hairlike chaetae.
▷**HISTORY** C16: so called because of its appearance

seamstress ('sɛmstrɪs) *or rarely* **sempstress** ('sɛmpstrɪs) NOUN a woman who sews and makes clothes, esp professionally.

seamy ('si:mɪ) ADJECTIVE **seamier, seamiest. 1** showing the least pleasant aspect; sordid. **2** (esp of the inner side of a garment) showing many seams.
▸**'seaminess** NOUN

Seanad Éireann ('ʃænəð 'e:rən) NOUN (in the Republic of Ireland) the upper chamber of parliament; the Senate.
▷**HISTORY** from Irish, literally: senate of Ireland

seance *or* **séance** ('seɪɑ̃ns, -ɑ:ns) NOUN **1** a meeting at which spiritualists attempt to receive messages from the spirits of the dead. **2** a meeting of a society.
▷**HISTORY** C19: from French, literally: a sitting, from Old French *seoir* to sit, from Latin *sedēre*

sea onion NOUN another name for **sea squill.**

sea otter NOUN a large marine otter, *Enhydra lutris,* of N Pacific coasts, formerly hunted for its thick dark brown fur.

sea pen NOUN any of various anthozoan coelenterates of the genus *Pennatula* and related genera, forming fleshy feather-like colonies in warm seas: order *Pennatulacea.*

sea perch NOUN **1** any of various marine serranid fishes, such as the bass and stone bass, that have an elongated body with a very spiny dorsal fin and occur in all except polar seas. **2** another name for **surfperch.**

sea pink NOUN another name for **thrift** (the plant).

seaplane ('si:,pleɪn) NOUN any aircraft that lands on and takes off from water. Also called (esp US): **hydroplane.**

seaport ('si:,pɔ:t) NOUN **1** a port or harbour accessible to seagoing vessels. **2** a town or city located at such a place.

sea power NOUN **1** a nation that possesses great naval strength. **2** the naval strength of a country or nation.

sea purse NOUN a tough horny envelope containing fertilized eggs, produced by the female of certain sharks and skates. Also called: **mermaid's purse.**

sea purslane NOUN a small chenopodiaceous shrub, *Halimione portulacoides,* of salt marshes in Eurasia and parts of Africa, having oval leaves and inconspicuous flowers.

SEAQ ('si:,æk) (in Britain) NOUN ACRONYM FOR Stock Exchange Automated Quotation: a computerized system that collects and displays the prices and transactions in securities.

seaquake ('si:,kweɪk) NOUN *Obsolete* an agitation and disturbance of the sea caused by an earthquake at the sea bed. It is now usually described as an earthquake.

sear[1] (sɪə) VERB *(tr)* **1** to scorch or burn the surface of. **2** to brand with a hot iron. **3** to cause to wither or dry up. **4** *Rare* to make callous or unfeeling. ◆ NOUN **5** a mark caused by searing. ◆ ADJECTIVE **6** *Poetic* dried up.
▷**HISTORY** Old English *sēarian* to become withered, from *sēar* withered; related to Old High German *sōrēn,* Greek *hauos* dry, Sanskrit *sōsa* drought

sear[2] (sɪə) NOUN the catch in the lock of a small firearm that holds the hammer or firing pin cocked.
▷**HISTORY** C16: probably from Old French *serre* a clasp, from *serrer* to hold firmly, from Late Latin *serāre* to bolt, from Latin *sera* a bar

sea ranger NOUN *Brit* a senior Guide training in seamanship. US equivalent: **mariner.**

sea raven NOUN a large fish, *Hemitripterus americanus,* of North American Atlantic coastal waters that inflates itself with air when caught: family *Cottidae* (bullheads and sea scorpions).

search (sɜ:tʃ) VERB **1** to look through (a place, records, etc.) thoroughly in order to find someone or something. **2** *(tr)* to examine (a person) for concealed objects by running one's hands over the clothing. **3** to look at or examine (something) closely: *to search one's conscience.* **4** *(tr; foll by out)* to discover by investigation. **5** *Surgery* **a** to explore (a bodily cavity) during a surgical procedure. **b** to probe (a wound). **6** *(tr) Military* to fire all over (an area). **7** *Computing* to review (a file) to locate specific information. **8** *Archaic* to penetrate. **9** **search me.** *Informal* I don't know. ◆ NOUN **10** the act or an instance of searching. **11** the examination of a vessel by the right of search. **12** *Computing* **a** a review of a file to locate specific information. **b** *(as modifier): a search routine.* **13** **right of search.** *International law* the right possessed by the warships of a belligerent state in time of war to board and search merchant vessels to ascertain whether ship or cargo is liable to seizure.
▷**HISTORY** C14: from Old French *cerchier,* from Late Latin *circāre* to go around, from Latin *circus* CIRCLE
▸**'searchable** ADJECTIVE ▸**'searcher** NOUN

search dog NOUN a dog trained to assist rescue workers in finding people buried under rubble by detection by smell.

search engine NOUN *Computing* a service provided on the Internet enabling users to search for items of interest.

searching ('sɜ:tʃɪŋ) ADJECTIVE keenly penetrating: *a searching look.*
▸**'searchingly** ADVERB ▸**'searchingness** NOUN

searchlight ('sɜ:tʃ,laɪt) NOUN **1** a device, consisting of a light source and a reflecting surface behind it, that projects a powerful beam of light in a particular direction. **2** the beam of light produced by such a device.

search order NOUN *Law* an injunction allowing a person to enter the premises of another to search for and take copies of evidence required for a court case, used esp in cases of infringement of copyright. Former name: **Anton Piller order.**

search party NOUN a group of people taking part in an organized search, as for a lost, missing, or wanted person.

search warrant NOUN a written order issued by a justice of the peace authorizing a constable or other officer to enter and search premises for stolen goods, drugs, etc.

sea robin NOUN any of various American gurnards of the genus *Prionotus* and related genera, such as *P. carolinus* (**northern sea robin**).

sea room NOUN sufficient space to manoeuvre a vessel.

sea salt NOUN salt obtained by evaporation of sea water.

seascape ('si:,skeɪp) NOUN a sketch, picture, etc., of the sea.

sea scorpion NOUN any of various northern marine scorpaenoid fishes of the family *Cottidae,* esp *Taurulus bubalis* (**long-spined sea scorpion**). They have a tapering body and a large head covered with bony plates and spines.

Sea Scout NOUN a Scout belonging to any of a number of Scout troops whose main activities are canoeing, sailing, etc., and who wear sailors' caps as part of their uniform.

sea serpent NOUN a huge legendary creature of the sea resembling a snake or dragon.

sea shanty NOUN same as **shanty**[2].

seashell ('si:,ʃɛl) NOUN the empty shell of a marine mollusc.

seashore ('si:,ʃɔ:) NOUN **1** land bordering on the sea. **2** the land between the marks of high and low water.

seasick ('si:,sɪk) ADJECTIVE suffering from nausea and dizziness caused by the motion of a ship at sea.
▸**'sea,sickness** NOUN

seaside ('si:,saɪd) NOUN **a** any area bordering on the sea, esp one regarded as a resort. **b** *(as modifier): a seaside hotel.*

sea slater NOUN a large (2.5 cm or 1 in.) nocturnal isopod, *Ligea oceanica,* that lives in cracks in rocks or walls around the high-water mark.

sea slug NOUN any of various shell-less marine gastropod molluscs, esp those of the order *Nudibranchia.* See **nudibranch.**

sea snail NOUN any small spiny-finned fish of the family *Liparidae,* esp *Liparis liparis,* of cold seas, having a soft scaleless tadpole-shaped body with the pelvic fins fused into a sucker. Also called: **snailfish.**

sea snake NOUN any venomous snake of the family *Hydrophiidae,* of tropical seas, that swims by means of a laterally compressed oarlike tail.

season ('si:z^{ə}n) NOUN **1** one of the four equal periods into which the year is divided by the equinoxes and solstices, resulting from the apparent movement of the sun north and south of the equator during the course of the earth's orbit around it. These periods (spring, summer, autumn, and winter) have their characteristic weather conditions in different regions, and occur at opposite times of the year in the N and S hemispheres. **2** a period of the year characterized by particular conditions or activities: *the rainy season.* **3** the period during which any particular species of animal, bird, or fish is legally permitted to be caught or killed: *open season on red deer.* **4** a period during which a particular entertainment, sport, etc., takes place: *a season at the National Theatre; the football season; the tourist season.* **5** (esp. formerly) a period of fashionable social events in a particular place: *the London season.* **6** any definite or indefinite period. **7** any of the major periods into which the ecclesiastical calendar is divided, such as Lent, Advent, or Easter. **8** *(sometimes capital)* Christmas (esp. in the phrases **compliments of the season, Season's greetings**). **9** a period or time that is considered proper, suitable, or natural for something. **10** **in good season.** early enough. **11** **in season. a** (of game) permitted to be caught or killed.

b (of fresh food) readily available. **c** Also: **in** *or* **on heat.** (of some female mammals) sexually receptive. **d** appropriate. ♦ VERB [12] (*tr*) to add herbs, salt, pepper, or spice to (food). [13] (*tr*) to add zest to. [14] (in the preparation of timber) to undergo or cause to undergo drying. [15] (*tr; usually passive*) to make or become mature or experienced: *seasoned troops.* [16] (*tr*) to mitigate or temper: *to season one's admiration with reticence.*
▷HISTORY C13: from Old French *seson,* from Latin *satiō* a sowing, from *serere* to sow
▸**'seasoned** ADJECTIVE ▸**'seasoner** NOUN ▸**'seasonless** ADJECTIVE

seasonable ('siːzənəbᵊl) ADJECTIVE [1] suitable for the season. [2] taking place at the appropriate time.
▸**'seasonableness** NOUN ▸**'seasonably** ADVERB

seasonal ('siːzənᵊl) ADJECTIVE of, relating to, or occurring at a certain season or certain seasons of the year: *seasonal labour.*
▸**'seasonally** ADVERB ▸**'seasonalness** NOUN

seasonal affective disorder NOUN a state of depression sometimes experienced by people in winter, thought to be related to lack of sunlight. Abbreviation: **SAD.**

seasoning ('siːzənɪŋ) NOUN [1] something that enhances the flavour of food, such as salt or herbs. [2] another term (not now in technical usage) for **drying** (sense 2).

season ticket NOUN a ticket for a series of events, number of journeys, etc., within a limited time, usually obtained at a reduced rate.

sea spider NOUN a small marine arachnid, having four pairs of legs and somewhat resembling a spider, unusual in that the male carries the eggs once they are laid and cares for the offspring.

sea squill *or* **onion** NOUN a Mediterranean liliaceous plant, *Urginea maritima,* having dense spikes of small white flowers, and yielding a bulb with medicinal properties.

sea squirt NOUN any minute primitive marine animal of the class *Ascidiacea,* most of which are sedentary, having a saclike body with openings through which water enters and leaves. See also **ascidian.**

sea steps PLURAL NOUN projecting metal bars attached to a ship's side, used for boarding.

sea swallow NOUN a popular name for **tern**[1].

seat (siːt) NOUN [1] a piece of furniture designed for sitting on, such as a chair or sofa. [2] the part of a chair, bench, etc., on which one sits. [3] a place to sit, esp one that requires a ticket: *I have two seats for the film tonight.* [4] another name for **buttocks** (see **buttock**). [5] the part of a garment covering the buttocks. [6] the part or area serving as the base of an object. [7] the part or surface on which the base of an object rests. [8] the place or centre in which something is located: *a seat of government.* [9] a place of abode, esp a country mansion that is or was originally the chief residence of a family. [10] a membership or the right to membership in a legislative or similar body. [11] *Chiefly Brit* a parliamentary constituency. [12] membership in a stock exchange. [13] the manner in which a rider sits on a horse. [14] **by the seat of one's pants.** by instinct rather than knowledge or experience. [15] **on seat.** *W African informal* (of officials) in the office rather than on tour or on leave: *the agricultural advisor will be on seat tomorrow.* ♦ VERB [16] (*tr*) to bring to or place on a seat; cause to sit down. [17] (*tr*) to provide with seats. [18] (*tr; often passive*) to place or centre: *the ministry is seated in the capital.* [19] (*tr*) to set firmly in place. [20] (*tr*) to fix or install in a position of power. [21] (*tr*) to put a seat on or in (an item of furniture, garment, etc.). [22] (*intr*) (of garments) to sag in the area covering the buttocks: *your thin skirt has seated badly.*
▷HISTORY Old English *gesete;* related to Old Norse *sæti,* Old High German *gasāzi,* Middle Dutch *gesaete*
▸**'seatless** ADJECTIVE

sea tangle NOUN any of various brown seaweeds, esp any of the genus *Laminaria.*

seat belt NOUN [1] Also called: **safety belt.** a belt or strap worn in a vehicle to restrain forward motion in the event of a collision. [2] a similar belt or strap worn in an aircraft at takeoff and landing and in rough weather.

-seater NOUN a settee, vehicle, cinema, etc., having a number of seats as specified: *a forty-seater coach.*

seating ('siːtɪŋ) NOUN [1] the act of providing with a seat or seats. [2] **a** the provision of seats, as in a theatre, cinema, etc. **b** (*as modifier*): *seating arrangements.* [3] material used for covering or making seats.

Seaton Valley ('siːtᵊn) NOUN a region in NE England, in SE Northumberland: consists of a group of former coal-mining villages. Pop.: 46 140 (latest est.).

sea trout NOUN [1] a silvery marine variety of the brown trout that migrates to fresh water to spawn. Compare **brown trout.** [2] any of several marine sciaenid fishes of the genus *Cynoscion,* such as *C. nebulosus* (**spotted sea trout**) and the weakfish, of North American coastal waters.

Seattle (sɪ'ætᵊl) NOUN a port in W Washington, on the isthmus between Lake Washington and Puget Sound: the largest city in the state and chief commercial centre of the Northwest; two universities. Pop.: 563 374 (2000).

sea urchin NOUN any echinoderm of the class *Echinoidea,* such as *Echinus esculentus* (**edible sea urchin**), typically having a globular body enclosed in a rigid spiny test and occurring in shallow marine waters.

sea vegetable NOUN an edible seaweed.

sea wall NOUN a wall or embankment built to prevent encroachment or erosion by the sea or to serve as a breakwater.
▸**'sea-,walled** ADJECTIVE

seawan *or* **sewan** ('siːwən) NOUN shell beads, usually unstrung, used by certain North American Indians as money; wampum.
▷HISTORY C18: from Narraganset *seawohn* loose

seaward ('siːwəd) ADVERB [1] a variant of **seawards.** ♦ ADJECTIVE [2] directed or moving towards the sea. [3] (esp of a wind) coming from the sea.

seawards ('siːwədz) *or* **seaward** ADVERB towards the sea.

seaware ('siːˌwɛə) NOUN any of numerous large coarse seaweeds, esp when cast ashore and used as fertilizer.
▷HISTORY Old English *sǣwār,* from *sǣ* SEA + *wār* seaweed

sea wasp NOUN *Austral* another name for **box jellyfish.**

seaway ('siːˌweɪ) NOUN [1] a waterway giving access to an inland port, navigable by ocean-going ships. [2] a vessel's progress. [3] a rough or heavy sea. [4] a route across the sea.

seaweed ('siːˌwiːd) NOUN [1] any of numerous multicellular marine algae that grow on the seashore, in salt marshes, in brackish water, or submerged in the ocean. [2] any of certain other plants that grow in or close to the sea.

seaworthy ('siːˌwɜːðɪ) ADJECTIVE in a fit condition or ready for a sea voyage.
▸**'sea,worthiness** NOUN

sea wrack NOUN any of various seaweeds found on the shore, esp any of the larger species.

sebaceous (sɪ'beɪʃəs) ADJECTIVE [1] of or resembling sebum, fat, or tallow; fatty. [2] secreting fat or a greasy lubricating substance.
▷HISTORY C18: from Late Latin *sēbāceus,* from SEBUM

sebaceous glands PLURAL NOUN the small glands in the skin that secrete sebum into hair follicles and onto most of the body surface except the soles of the feet and the palms of the hands.

sebacic acid (sɪ'bæsɪk, -'beɪ-) NOUN another name for **decanedioic acid.**

Sebastopol (sɪ'bæstəpəl) NOUN the English name for **Sevastopol.**

sebi- *or* **sebo-** COMBINING FORM fat or fatty matter: *sebiferous.*
▷HISTORY from Latin *sēbum* tallow

sebiferous (sɪ'bɪfərəs) ADJECTIVE *Biology* producing or carrying a fatty, oily, or waxlike substance.

seborrhoea *or esp US* **seborrhea** (ˌsɛbə'rɪə) NOUN any disease of the skin characterized by excessive secretion of sebum by the sebaceous glands and its accumulation on the skin surface.
▸**ˌsebor'rhoeal** *or* **ˌsebor'rhoeic** *or* (*esp US*) **ˌsebor'rheal** *or* **ˌsebor'rheic** ADJECTIVE

sebum ('siːbəm) NOUN the oily secretion of the sebaceous glands that acts as a lubricant for the hair and skin and provides some protection against bacteria.
▷HISTORY C19: from New Latin, from Latin: tallow

sec[1] (sɛk) ADJECTIVE [1] (of wines) dry. [2] (of champagne) of medium sweetness.
▷HISTORY C19: from French, from Latin *siccus*

sec[2] (sɛk) NOUN *Informal* short for **second:** *wait a sec.*

sec[3] (sɛk) ABBREVIATION FOR secant.

SEC ABBREVIATION FOR **Securities and Exchange Commission.**

sec. ABBREVIATION FOR: [1] second (of time). [2] secondary. [3] secretary. [4] section. [5] sector.

SECAM ('siːˌkæm) NOUN ACRONYM FOR séquentiel couleur à mémoire: a colour-television broadcasting system used in France, the former Soviet Union, and some other countries.

secant ('siːkənt) NOUN [1] (of an angle) a trigonometric function that in a right-angled triangle is the ratio of the length of the hypotenuse to that of the adjacent side; the reciprocal of cosine. Abbreviation: **sec.** [2] a line that intersects a curve.
▷HISTORY C16: from Latin *secāre* to cut
▸**'secantly** ADVERB

secateurs ('sɛkətəz, ˌsɛkə'tɜːz) PLURAL NOUN *Chiefly Brit* a small pair of shears for pruning, having a pair of pivoted handles, sprung so that they are normally open, and usually a single cutting blade that closes against a flat surface.
▷HISTORY C19: plural of French *sécateur,* from Latin *secāre* to cut

secco ('sɛkəʊ) NOUN, *plural* **-cos.** [1] wall painting done on dried plaster with tempera or pigments ground in limewater. Compare **fresco.** [2] any wall painting other than true fresco.
▷HISTORY C19: from Italian: dry, from Latin *siccus*

secede (sɪ'siːd) VERB (*intr; often foll by from*) (of a person, section, etc.) to make a formal withdrawal of membership, as from a political alliance, church, organization, etc.
▷HISTORY C18: from Latin *sēcēdere* to withdraw, from *sē-* apart + *cēdere* to go
▸**se'ceder** NOUN

secern (sɪ'sɜːn) VERB (*tr*) *Rare* [1] (of a gland or follicle) to secrete. [2] to distinguish or discriminate.
▷HISTORY C17: from Latin *sēcernere* to separate, from *sē-* apart + *cernere* to distinguish
▸**se'cernment** NOUN

secession (sɪ'sɛʃən) NOUN [1] the act of seceding. [2] (*often capital*) *Chiefly US* the withdrawal in 1860–61 of 11 Southern states from the Union to form the Confederacy, precipitating the American Civil War.
▷HISTORY C17: from Latin *sēcessiō* a withdrawing, from *sēcēdere* to SECEDE
▸**se'cessional** ADJECTIVE ▸**se'cession,ism** NOUN
▸**se'cessionist** NOUN, ADJECTIVE

sech (ʃɛk, sɛtʃ, 'sɛk'eɪtʃ) NOUN hyperbolic secant; a hyperbolic function that is the reciprocal of cosh.

seclude (sɪ'kluːd) VERB (*tr*) [1] to remove from contact with others. [2] to shut off or screen from view.
▷HISTORY C15: from Latin *sēclūdere* to shut off, from *sē-* + *claudere* to imprison

secluded (sɪ'kluːdɪd) ADJECTIVE [1] kept apart from the company of others: *a secluded life.* [2] sheltered; private.
▸**se'cludedly** ADVERB ▸**se'cludedness** NOUN

seclusion (sɪ'kluːʒən) NOUN [1] the act of secluding or the state of being secluded. [2] a secluded place.
▷HISTORY C17: from Medieval Latin *sēclūsiō;* see SECLUDE

seclusive (sɪ'kluːsɪv) ADJECTIVE [1] tending to seclude. [2] fond of seclusion.
▸**se'clusively** ADVERB ▸**se'clusiveness** NOUN

second[1] ('sɛkənd) ADJECTIVE (*usually prenominal*) [1] **a** coming directly after the first in numbering or counting order, position, time, etc.; being the ordinal number of *two:* often written 2nd. **b** (*as noun*): *the second in line.* [2] rated, graded, or ranked between the first and third levels. [3] alternate: *every second Thursday.* [4] additional; extra: *a second opportunity.* [5] resembling a person or event from an earlier period of history; unoriginal: *a second Wagner.* [6] of lower quality; inferior: *belonging to the second class.* [7] denoting the lowest but one forward

ratio of a gearbox in a motor vehicle. [8] *Music* **a** relating to or denoting a musical part, voice, or instrument lower in pitch than another part, voice, or instrument (the first): *the second tenors.* **b** of or relating to a part, instrument, or instrumentalist regarded as subordinate to another (the first): *the second flute.* [9] **at second hand.** by hearsay. ◆ NOUN [10] *Brit education* an honours degree of the second class, usually further divided into an upper and lower designation. Full term: **second-class honours degree.** [11] the lowest but one forward ratio of a gearbox in a motor vehicle: *he changed into second on the bend.* [12] (in boxing, duelling, etc.) an attendant who looks after a competitor. [13] a speech seconding a motion or the person making it. [14] *Music* **a** the interval between one note and another lying next above or below it in the diatonic scale. **b** one of two notes constituting such an interval in relation to the other. See also **minor** (sense 4), **major** (sense 14), **interval** (sense 5). [15] (*plural*) goods of inferior quality. [16] (*plural*) *Informal* a second helping of food. [17] (*plural*) the second course of a meal. ◆ VERB (*tr*) [18] to give aid or backing to. [19] (in boxing, etc.) to act as second to (a competitor). [20] to make a speech or otherwise express formal support for (a motion already proposed). ◆ ADVERB [21] Also: **secondly.** in the second place. ◆ SENTENCE CONNECTOR [22] Also: **secondly.** as the second point: linking what follows with the previous statement.
▷HISTORY C13: via Old French from Latin *secundus* coming next in order, from *sequī* to follow
▸ˈ**seconder** NOUN

second[2] (ˈsɛkənd) NOUN [1] **a** 1/60 of a minute of time. **b** the basic SI unit of time: the duration of 9 192 631 770 periods of radiation corresponding to the transition between two hyperfine levels of the ground state of caesium-133. Symbol: s. [2] 1/60 of a minute of angle. Symbol: ″. [3] a very short period of time; moment.
▷HISTORY C14: from Old French, from Medieval Latin *pars minūta secunda* the second small part (a minute being the first small part of an hour); see SECOND[1]

second[3] (sɪˈkɒnd) VERB (*tr*) *Brit* [1] to transfer (an employee) temporarily to another branch, etc. [2] *Military* to transfer (an officer) to another post, often retiring him to a staff or nonregimental position.
▷HISTORY C19: from French *en second* in second rank (or position)

Second Advent NOUN a less common term for the **Second Coming.**

secondary (ˈsɛkəndərɪ, -drɪ) ADJECTIVE [1] one grade or step after the first; not primary. [2] derived from or depending on what is primary, original, or first: *a secondary source.* [3] below the first in rank, importance, etc.; not of major importance. [4] (*prenominal*) of or relating to the education of young people between the ages of 11 and 18: *secondary education.* [5] (of the flight feathers of a bird's wing) growing from the ulna. [6] **a** being the part of an electric circuit, such as a transformer or induction coil, in which a current is induced by a changing current in a neighbouring coil: *a secondary coil.* **b** (of a current) flowing in such a circuit. Compare **primary** (sense 7). [7] (of an industry) involving the manufacture of goods from raw materials. Compare **primary** (sense 8b), **tertiary** (sense 2). [8] *Geology* (of minerals) formed by the alteration of pre-existing minerals. [9] *Chem* **a** (of an organic compound) having a functional group attached to a carbon atom that is attached to one hydrogen atom and two other groups. **b** (of an amine) having only two organic groups attached to a nitrogen atom; containing the group NH. **c** (of a salt) derived from a tribasic acid by replacement of two acidic hydrogen atoms with metal atoms or electropositive groups. [10] *Linguistics* **a** derived from a word that is itself a derivation from another word. Thus, *lovably* comes from *lovable* and is a secondary derivative from *love.* **b** (of a tense in Latin, Greek, or Sanskrit) another word for **historic** (sense 3). ◆ NOUN, *plural* **-aries.** [11] a person or thing that is secondary. [12] a subordinate, deputy, or inferior. [13] a secondary coil, winding, inductance, or current in an electric circuit. [14] *Ornithol* any of the flight feathers that grow from the ulna of a bird's wing. See **primary** (sense 6). [15] *Astronomy* a celestial body that orbits around a specified primary body: *the moon is the secondary of the earth.* [16] *Med* a cancerous growth in some part of the body away from the site of the original tumour. [17] *American football* **a** (usually preceded by *the*) cornerbacks and safeties collectively. **b** their area in the field. [18] short for **secondary colour.**
▸ˈ**secondarily** ADVERB ▸ˈ**secondariness** NOUN

secondary accent *or* **stress** NOUN *Phonetics* (in a system of transcribing utterances recognizing three levels of stress) the accent on a syllable of a word or breath group that is weaker than the primary accent but stronger than the lack of stress: *in the word "agriculture" the secondary accent falls on the third syllable.* Compare **primary accent.**

secondary cell NOUN an electric cell that can be recharged and can therefore be used to store electrical energy in the form of chemical energy. See also **accumulator** (sense 1). Compare **primary cell.**

secondary colour NOUN a colour formed by mixing two primary colours. Sometimes shortened to: **secondary.**

secondary emission NOUN *Physics* the emission of electrons (**secondary electrons**) from a solid as a result of bombardment with a beam of electrons, ions, or metastable atoms: used in electron multipliers.

secondary modern school NOUN *Brit* (formerly) a secondary school offering a more technical or practical and less academic education than a grammar school.

secondary picketing NOUN the picketing by strikers of a place of work that supplies goods to or distributes goods from their employer.
▸**secondary picket** NOUN

secondary processes PLURAL NOUN *Psychoanal* the logical conscious type of mental functioning, guided by external reality. Compare **primary processes.**

secondary qualities PLURAL NOUN (in empiricist philosophy) those properties of objects that are explained in terms of the primary properties of their parts, such as heat in terms of the motion of molecules.

secondary school NOUN a school for young people, usually between the ages of 11 and 18.

secondary sexual characteristic NOUN any of various features distinguishing individuals of different sex but not directly concerned in reproduction. Examples are the antlers of a stag and the beard of a man.

secondary stress NOUN another term for **secondary accent.**

second ballot NOUN an electoral procedure in which if no candidate emerges as a clear winner in a first ballot, candidates at the bottom of the poll are eliminated and another ballot is held among the remaining candidates.

second-best ADJECTIVE [1] next to the best. [2] **come off second best.** *Informal* to be defeated in competition. ◆ NOUN **second best.** [3] an inferior alternative.

second chamber NOUN the upper house of a bicameral legislative assembly.

second childhood NOUN dotage; senility (esp in the phrases **in his, her,** etc., **second childhood**).

second class NOUN [1] the class or grade next in value, quality, etc., to the first. ◆ ADJECTIVE **second-class** when prenominal. [2] of the class or grade next to the best in quality, etc. [3] shoddy or inferior. [4] of or denoting the class of accommodation in a hotel or on a train, etc., lower in quality and price than first class. [5] **a** (in Britain) of or relating to mail that is processed more slowly than first-class mail. **b** (in the US and Canada) of or relating to mail that consists mainly of newspapers, etc. [6] *Education* See **second**[1] (sense 10). ◆ ADVERB [7] by second-class mail, transport, etc.

second-class citizen NOUN a person whose rights and opportunities are treated as less important than those of other people in the same society.

Second Coming *or less commonly* **Second Advent** NOUN the prophesied return of Christ to earth at the Last Judgment.

second cousin NOUN the child of a first cousin of either of one's parents.

second-degree burn NOUN *Pathol* See **burn**[1] (sense 22).

seconde (sɪˈkɒnd; *French* səgɔ̃d) NOUN the second of eight positions from which a parry or attack can be made in fencing.
▷HISTORY C18: from French *seconde parade* the second parry

secondee (səˌkɒnˈdiː) NOUN a person who is seconded.

Second Empire NOUN [1] **a** the imperial government of France under Napoleon III. **b** the period during which this government functioned (1852–70). [2] the style of furniture and decoration of the Second Empire, reviving the Empire style, but with fussier ornamentation.

second estate NOUN *Rare* the nobility collectively.

second fiddle NOUN *Informal* [1] **a** the second violin in a string quartet or one of the second violins in an orchestra. **b** the musical part assigned to such an instrument. [2] a secondary status. [3] a person who has a secondary status.

second floor NOUN [1] *Brit* the storey of a building immediately above the first and two floors up from the ground. US and Canadian term: **third floor.** [2] the US and Canadian term for **first floor.**

second generation NOUN [1] offspring of parents born in a given country. ◆ MODIFIER [2] of an improved or refined stage of development in manufacture: *a second-generation robot.*

second growth *or* **secondary growth** NOUN natural regrowth of a forest after fire, cutting, or some other disturbance.

second-guess VERB *Informal* [1] to criticize or evaluate with hindsight. [2] to attempt to anticipate or predict (a person or thing).
▸ˈ**second-**ˈ**guesser** NOUN

second hand NOUN a pointer on the face of a timepiece that indicates the seconds. Compare **hour hand, minute hand.**

second-hand ADJECTIVE [1] previously owned or used. [2] not from an original source or experience. [3] dealing in or selling goods that are not new: *a second-hand car dealer.* ◆ ADVERB [4] from a source of previously owned or used goods: *he prefers to buy second-hand.* [5] not directly: *he got the news second-hand.*

second-homer NOUN a person who owns another house in addition to their main home, often in an area where they are not native and used as a holiday home.

Second International NOUN [1] **the.** an international association of socialist parties and trade unions that began in Paris in 1889 and collapsed during World War I. The right-wing elements reassembled at Berne in 1919. See also **Labour and Socialist International.** [2] another name for the **Labour and Socialist International.**

second language NOUN [1] a language other than the mother tongue that a person or community uses for public communication, esp in trade, higher education, and administration. [2] a non-native language officially recognized and adopted in a multilingual country as a means of public communication.

second lieutenant NOUN an officer holding the lowest commissioned rank in the armed forces of certain nations.

secondly (ˈsɛkəndlɪ) ADVERB another word for **second**[1], usually used to precede the second item in a list of topics

second man NOUN a person who assists the driver in crewing a locomotive.

second mate NOUN the next in command of a merchant vessel after the first mate. Also called: **second officer.**

secondment (sɪˈkɒndmənt) NOUN *Brit* a temporary transfer to another job or post within the same organization.
▷HISTORY C19: from French *en second* in second rank (or position)

second mortgage NOUN a mortgage incurred after a first mortgage and having second claim against the security.

second name NOUN another term for **surname** (sense 1).

second nature NOUN a habit, characteristic, etc.,

not innate but so long practised or acquired as to seem so.

secondo (sɛˈkɒndəʊ) NOUN, *plural* **-di** (-diː). the left-hand part in a piano duet. Compare **primo**.
▷HISTORY Italian: SECOND[1]

second person NOUN a grammatical category of pronouns and verbs used when referring to or describing the individual or individuals being addressed.

second-rate ADJECTIVE 1 not of the highest quality; mediocre. 2 second in importance, etc.
▸ **ˈsecond-ˈrater** NOUN

second reading NOUN the second presentation of a bill in a legislative assembly, as to approve its general principles (in Britain), or to discuss a committee's report on it (in the US).

Second Republic NOUN 1 the republican government of France from the deposition of Louis Philippe (1848) until the Second Empire (1852). 2 the period during which this form of government existed (1848–52).

second sight NOUN the alleged ability to foresee the future, see actions taking place elsewhere, etc.; clairvoyance.
▸ **ˈsecond-ˈsighted** ADJECTIVE ▸ **ˈsecond-ˈsightedness** NOUN

second-strike ADJECTIVE 1 (of a nuclear weapon) intended to be used in a counterattack in response to a nuclear attack. 2 (of a strategy) based on the concept of surviving an initial nuclear attack with enough nuclear weaponry to retaliate.

second string NOUN 1 *Chiefly Brit* an alternative course of action, etc., intended to come into use should the first fail (esp in the phrase **a second string to one's bow**). 2 a substitute or reserve player or team. ◆ ADJECTIVE **second-string.** *Chiefly US and Canadian.* 3 *Sport* **a** being a substitute player. **b** being the second-ranked player of a team in an individual sport. 4 second-rate or inferior.

second thought NOUN (*usually plural*) a revised opinion or idea on a matter already considered.

second wind (wɪnd) NOUN 1 the return of the ability to breathe at a comfortable rate, esp following a period of exertion. 2 renewed ability to continue in an effort.

Second World War NOUN another name for **World War II.**

secrecy (ˈsiːkrɪsɪ) NOUN, *plural* **-cies.** 1 the state or quality of being secret. 2 the state of keeping something secret. 3 the ability or tendency to keep things secret.

secret (ˈsiːkrɪt) ADJECTIVE 1 kept hidden or separate from the knowledge of others. Related adjective: **cryptic.** 2 known only to initiates: *a secret password.* 3 hidden from general view or use: *a secret garden.* 4 able or tending to keep things private or to oneself. 5 operating without the knowledge of outsiders: *a secret society.* 6 outside the normal range of knowledge. ◆ NOUN 7 something kept or to be kept hidden. 8 something unrevealed; mystery. 9 an underlying explanation, reason, etc., that is not apparent: *the secret of success.* 10 a method, plan, etc., known only to initiates. 11 *Liturgy* a variable prayer, part of the Mass, said by the celebrant after the offertory and before the preface. 12 in the secret. among the people who know a secret.
▷HISTORY C14: via Old French from Latin *sēcrētus* concealed, from *sēcernere* to sift; see SECERN
▸ **ˈsecretly** ADVERB

secret agent NOUN a person employed in espionage.

secretagogue (sɪˈkriːtəgɒg) NOUN *Med* a substance that stimulates secretion.
▸ **seˌcretaˈgogic** ADJECTIVE

secretaire (ˌsɛkrɪˈtɛə) NOUN an enclosed writing desk, usually having an upper cabinet section.
▷HISTORY C19: from French *secrétaire;* see SECRETARY

secretariat (ˌsɛkrɪˈtɛərɪət) NOUN 1 **a** an office responsible for the secretarial, clerical, and administrative affairs of a legislative body, executive council, or international organization. **b** the staff of such an office. **c** the building or rooms in which such an office is housed. 2 a body of secretaries. 3 a secretary's place of work; office. 4 the position of a secretary.
▷HISTORY C19: via French from Medieval Latin *sēcrētāriātus,* from *sēcrētārius* SECRETARY

secretary (ˈsɛkrətrɪ) NOUN, *plural* **-taries.** 1 a person who handles correspondence, keeps records, and does general clerical work for an individual, organization, etc. 2 the official manager of the day-to-day business of a society or board. 3 (in Britain) a senior civil servant who assists a government minister. 4 (in the US and New Zealand) the head of a government administrative department. 5 (in Britain) See **secretary of state.** 6 (in Australia) the head of a public service department. 7 *Diplomacy* the assistant to an ambassador or diplomatic minister of certain countries. 8 another name for **secretaire.**
▷HISTORY C14: from Medieval Latin *sēcrētārius,* from Latin *sēcrētum* something hidden; see SECRET
▸ **secretarial** (ˌsɛkrɪˈtɛərɪəl) ADJECTIVE ▸ **ˈsecretaryship** NOUN

secretary bird NOUN a large African long-legged diurnal bird of prey, *Sagittarius serpentarius,* having a crest and tail of long feathers and feeding chiefly on snakes: family *Sagittariidae,* order *Falconiformes* (hawks, falcons, etc.).
▷HISTORY C18: so called because its crest resembles a group of quill pens stuck behind the ear

secretary-general NOUN, *plural* **secretaries-general.** a chief administrative official, as of the United Nations.

secretary of state NOUN 1 (in Britain) the head of any of several government departments. 2 (in the US) the head of the government department in charge of foreign affairs (**State Department**). 3 (in certain US states) an official with various duties, such as keeping records.

secrete[1] (sɪˈkriːt) VERB (of a cell, organ, etc.) to synthesize and release (a secretion).
▷HISTORY C18: back formation from SECRETION
▸ **seˈcretor** NOUN

secrete[2] (sɪˈkriːt) VERB (*tr*) to put in a hiding place.
▷HISTORY C18: variant of obsolete *secret* to hide away; see SECRET (n)

secretin (sɪˈkriːtɪn) NOUN a peptic hormone secreted by the mucosae of the duodenum and jejunum when food passes from the stomach.
▷HISTORY C20: from SECRETION + -IN

secretion (sɪˈkriːʃən) NOUN 1 a substance that is released from a cell, esp a glandular cell, and is synthesized in the cell. 2 the process involved in producing and releasing such a substance from the cell.
▷HISTORY C17: from Medieval Latin *sēcrētiō,* from Latin: a separation; see SECERN
▸ **seˈcretionary** ADJECTIVE

secretive (ˈsiːkrɪtɪv, sɪˈkriːtɪv) ADJECTIVE 1 inclined to secrecy; reticent. 2 another word for **secretory.**
▸ **ˈsecretively** ADVERB ▸ **ˈsecretiveness** NOUN

secretory (sɪˈkriːtərɪ) ADJECTIVE of, relating to, or producing a secretion: *a secretory cell; secretory function.*

secret police NOUN a police force that operates relatively secretly to check subversion or political dissent.

secret service NOUN 1 a government agency or department that conducts intelligence or counterintelligence operations. 2 such operations.

Secret Service NOUN a US government agency responsible for the protection of the president, the suppression of counterfeiting, and certain other police activities.

secret society NOUN a society or organization that conceals its rites, activities, etc., from those who are not members.

sect (sɛkt) NOUN 1 a subdivision of a larger religious group (esp the Christian Church as a whole) the members of which have to some extent diverged from the rest by developing deviating beliefs, practices, etc. 2 *Often disparaging* **a** a schismatic religious body characterized by an attitude of exclusivity in contrast to the more inclusive religious groups called denominations or Churches. **b** a religious group regarded as extreme or heretical. 3 a group of people with a common interest, doctrine, etc.; faction.
▷HISTORY C14: from Latin *secta* faction, following, from the stem of *sequī* to follow

-sect VERB COMBINING FORM to cut or divide, esp into a specified number of parts: *trisect.*
▷HISTORY from Latin *sectus* cut, from *secāre* to cut; see SAW[1]

sectarian (sɛkˈtɛərɪən) ADJECTIVE 1 of, belonging or relating to, or characteristic of sects or sectaries. 2 adhering to a particular sect, faction, or doctrine. 3 narrow-minded, esp as a result of rigid adherence to a particular sect. ◆ NOUN 4 a member of a sect or faction, esp one who is bigoted in his adherence to its doctrines or in his intolerance towards other sects, etc.
▸ **secˈtarianˌism** NOUN

sectarianize *or* **sectarianise** (sɛkˈtɛərɪəˌnaɪz) VERB (*tr*) to render sectarian.

sectary (ˈsɛktərɪ) NOUN, *plural* **-taries.** 1 a member of a sect, esp a person who belongs to a religious sect that is regarded as heretical or schismatic. 2 a person excessively devoted to a particular sect. 3 a member of a Nonconformist denomination, esp one that is small.
▷HISTORY C16: from Medieval Latin *sectārius,* from Latin *secta* SECT

sectile (ˈsɛktaɪl) ADJECTIVE able to be cut smoothly.
▷HISTORY C18: from Latin *sectilis,* from *secāre* to cut
▸ **sectility** (sɛkˈtɪlɪtɪ) NOUN

section (ˈsɛkʃən) NOUN 1 a part cut off or separated from the main body of something. 2 a part or subdivision of a piece of writing, book, etc.: *the sports section of the newspaper.* 3 one of several component parts. 4 a distinct part or subdivision of a country, community, etc. 5 *US and Canadian* an area one mile square (640 acres) in a public survey, esp in the western parts of the US and Canada. 6 *NZ* a plot of land for building on, esp in a suburban area. 7 the section of a railway track that is maintained by a single crew or is controlled by a particular signal box. 8 the act or process of cutting or separating by cutting. 9 a representation of a portion of a building or object exposed when cut by an imaginary vertical plane so as to show its construction and interior. 10 *Geometry* **a** a plane surface formed by cutting through a solid. **b** the shape or area of such a plane surface. Compare **cross section** (sense 1). 11 *Surgery* any procedure involving the cutting or division of an organ, structure, or part, such as a Caesarian section. 12 a thin slice of biological tissue, mineral, etc., prepared for examination by a microscope. 13 a segment of an orange or other citrus fruit. 14 a small military formation, typically comprising two or more squads or aircraft. 15 *Austral and NZ* a fare stage on a bus, tram, etc. 16 *Music* **a** an extended division of a composition or movement that forms a coherent part of the structure: *the development section.* **b** a division in an orchestra, band, etc., containing instruments belonging to the same class: *the brass section.* 17 Also called: **signature, gathering, gather, quire.** a folded printing sheet or sheets ready for gathering and binding. ◆ VERB (*tr*) 18 to cut or divide into sections. 19 to cut through so as to reveal a section. 20 (in drawing, esp mechanical drawing) to shade so as to indicate sections. 21 *Surgery* to cut or divide (an organ, structure, or part). 22 *Brit social welfare* to have (a mentally disturbed person) confined in a mental hospital under an appropriate section of the mental health legislation.
▷HISTORY C16: from Latin *sectiō,* from *secāre* to cut

sectional (ˈsɛkʃənᵊl) ADJECTIVE 1 composed of several sections. 2 of or relating to a section.
▸ **ˈsectionally** ADVERB

sectionalism (ˈsɛkʃənəˌlɪzəm) NOUN excessive or narrow-minded concern for local or regional interests as opposed to the interests of the whole.
▸ **ˈsectionalist** NOUN, ADJECTIVE

sectionalize *or* **sectionalise** (ˈsɛkʃənəˌlaɪz) VERB (*tr*) 1 to render sectional. 2 to divide into sections, esp geographically.
▸ **ˌsectionaliˈzation** *or* **ˌsectionaliˈsation** NOUN

section mark NOUN *Printing* a mark (§) inserted into text matter to draw attention to a footnote or to indicate a section of a book, etc. Also called: **section.**

sector (ˈsɛktə) NOUN 1 a part or subdivision, esp of a society or an economy: *the private sector.* 2 *Geometry* either portion of a circle included between two radii and an arc. Area: $\frac{1}{2}r^2\theta$, where r is the radius and θ is the central angle subtended by the arc (in radians). 3 a measuring instrument consisting of two graduated arms hinged at one

end. [4] a part or subdivision of an area of military operations. [5] *Computing* the smallest addressable portion of the track on a magnetic tape, disk, or drum store.
▷HISTORY C16: from Late Latin: sector, from Latin: a cutter, from *secāre* to cut
▸'**sectoral** ADJECTIVE

sectorial (sɛk'tɔːrɪəl) ADJECTIVE [1] of or relating to a sector. [2] *Zoology* **a** adapted for cutting: *the sectorial teeth of carnivores.* **b** designating a vein in the wing of an insect that links certain branches of the radius vein.

secular ('sɛkjʊlə) ADJECTIVE [1] of or relating to worldly as opposed to sacred things; temporal. [2] not concerned with or related to religion. [3] not within the control of the Church. [4] (of an education, etc.) **a** having no particular religious affinities. **b** not including compulsory religious studies or services. [5] (of clerics) not bound by religious vows to a monastic or other order. [6] occurring or appearing once in an age or century. [7] lasting for a long time. [8] *Astronomy* occurring slowly over a long period of time: *the secular perturbation of a planet's orbit.* ◆ NOUN [9] a member of the secular clergy. [10] another word for **layman.**
▷HISTORY C13: from Old French *seculer,* from Late Latin *saeculāris* temporal, from Latin: concerning an age, from *saeculum* an age
▸'**secularly** ADVERB

secularism ('sɛkjʊlə,rɪzəm) NOUN [1] *Philosophy* a doctrine that rejects religion, esp in ethics. [2] the attitude that religion should have no place in civil affairs. [3] the state of being secular.
▸'**secularist** NOUN, ADJECTIVE ▸,**secular'istic** ADJECTIVE

secularity (,sɛkjʊ'lærɪtɪ) NOUN, *plural* **-ties.** [1] the state or condition of being secular. [2] interest in or adherence to secular things. [3] a secular concern or matter.

secularize *or* **secularise** ('sɛkjʊlə,raɪz) VERB *(tr)* [1] to change from religious or sacred to secular functions, etc. [2] to dispense from allegiance to a religious order. [3] *Law* to transfer (property) from ecclesiastical to civil possession or use. [4] *English legal history* to transfer (an offender) from the jurisdiction of the ecclesiastical courts to that of the civil courts for the imposition of a more severe punishment.
▸,**seculari'zation** *or* ,**seculari'sation** NOUN ▸'**secular,izer** *or* '**secular,iser** NOUN

secund (sɪ'kʌnd) ADJECTIVE *Botany* having or designating parts arranged on or turned to one side of the axis.
▷HISTORY C18: from Latin *secundus* following, from *sequī* to follow; see SECOND[1]
▸**se'cundly** ADVERB

Secunderabad (sə'kʌndərə,bæd, -,bɑːd) NOUN a former town in S central India, in N Andra Pradesh: one of the largest British military stations in India: now part of Hyderabad city.

secundine ('sɛkən,daɪn, -dɪn) NOUN *Botany, now rare* one of the two integuments surrounding the ovule of a plant.
▷HISTORY C17: from Late Latin *secundīnae,* from Latin *secundus* following + -INE. See SECOND[1]

secundines ('sɛkən,daɪnz, sɪ'kʌndɪnz) PLURAL NOUN *Physiol* a technical word for **afterbirth.**
▷HISTORY C14: from Late Latin *secundīnae,* from Latin *secundus* following; see SECOND[1]

secure (sɪ'kjʊə) ADJECTIVE [1] free from danger, damage, etc. [2] free from fear, care, etc. [3] in safe custody. [4] not likely to fail, become loose, etc. [5] able to be relied on; certain: *a secure investment.* [6] *Nautical* stowed away or made inoperative. [7] *Archaic* careless or overconfident. ◆ VERB [8] *(tr)* to obtain or get possession of: *I will secure some good seats.* [9] (when *intr,* often foll by *against*) to make or become free from danger, fear, etc. [10] *(tr)* to make fast or firm; fasten. [11] (when *intr,* often foll by *against*) to make or become certain; guarantee: *this plan will secure your happiness.* [12] *(tr)* to assure (a creditor) of payment, as by giving security. [13] *(tr)* to make (a military position) safe from attack. [14] *Nautical* to make (a vessel or its contents) safe or ready by battening down hatches, stowing gear, etc. [15] *(tr) Nautical* to stow or make inoperative: *to secure the radio.*
▷HISTORY C16: from Latin *sēcūrus* free from care, from *sē-* without + *cūra* care
▸**se'curable** ADJECTIVE ▸**se'curely** ADVERB ▸**se'curement** NOUN ▸**se'cureness** NOUN ▸**se'curer** NOUN

secure tenancy NOUN (in Britain) *Social welfare* the letting of a dwelling by a nonprivate landlord, usually a local council or housing association, under an agreement that allows security of tenure, subletting, improvements made to the property by the tenant without consequent rent increase, and the right to buy the dwelling at a discount after three years' occupancy.

secure unit NOUN an establishment providing secure accommodation, education and training, psychiatric help, etc. for offenders and people who are mentally ill.

Securities and Exchange Commission NOUN a US federal agency established in 1934 to supervise and regulate issues of and transactions in securities and to prosecute illegal stock manipulations. Abbreviation: **SEC.**

Securities and Investments Board NOUN (from 1986 to 1997) a British regulatory body that oversaw London's financial markets, each of which has its own self-regulatory organization: replaced by the Financial Services Authority. Abbreviation: **SIB.**

securitization *or* **securitisation** (sɪ,kjʊərɪtaɪ'zeɪʃən) NOUN *Finance* the use of such securities as eurobonds to enable investors to lend directly to borrowers with a minimum of risk but without using banks as intermediaries.

security (sɪ'kjʊərɪtɪ) NOUN, *plural* **-ties.** [1] the state of being secure. [2] assured freedom from poverty or want: *he needs the security of a permanent job.* [3] a person or thing that secures, guarantees, etc. [4] precautions taken to ensure against theft, espionage, etc.: *the security in the government offices was not very good.* [5] *(often plural)* **a** a certificate of creditorship or property carrying the right to receive interest or dividend, such as shares or bonds. **b** the financial asset represented by such a certificate. [6] the specific asset that a creditor can claim title to in the event of default on an obligation. [7] something given or pledged to secure the fulfilment of a promise or obligation. [8] a person who undertakes to fulfil another person's obligation. [9] the protection of data to ensure that only authorized personnel have access to computer files. [10] *Archaic* carelessness or overconfidence.

security blanket NOUN [1] a policy of temporary secrecy by police or those in charge of security, in order to protect a person, place, etc., threatened with danger, from further risk. [2] a baby's blanket, soft toy, etc., to which a baby or young child becomes very attached, using it as a comforter. [3] *Informal* anything used or thought of as providing reassurance.

Security Council NOUN a permanent organ of the United Nations established to maintain world peace. It consists of five permanent members (China, France, Russia, the UK, and the US) and ten nonpermanent members.

security guard NOUN a person employed to protect buildings, people, etc., and to collect and deliver large sums of money.

security of tenure NOUN (in Britain) the right of a tenant to continue to occupy a dwelling or site unless the landlord obtains a court order for possession of the property or termination of the tenancy agreement.

security risk NOUN a person deemed to be a threat to state security in that he could be open to pressure, have subversive political beliefs, etc.

securocrat (sɪ'kjʊərəʊ,kræt) NOUN a military or police officer who has the power to influence government policy.

secy *or* **sec'y** ABBREVIATION FOR secretary.

sedan (sɪ'dæn) NOUN [1] the US, Canadian, and NZ name for a **saloon** (sense 5). [2] short for **sedan chair.**
▷HISTORY C17: of uncertain origin; compare Latin *sēdēs* seat

Sedan (*French* sədɑ̃; *English* sɪ'dæn) NOUN a town in NE France, on the River Meuse: passed to France in 1642; a Protestant stronghold (16th–17th centuries); scene of a French defeat (1870) during the Franco-Prussian War and of a battle (1940) in World War II, which began the German invasion of France. Pop.: 22 400 (1990).

sedan chair NOUN a closed chair for one passenger, carried on poles by two bearers. It was commonly used in the 17th and 18th centuries. Sometimes shortened to: **sedan.**

sedate[1] (sɪ'deɪt) ADJECTIVE [1] habitually calm and composed in manner; serene. [2] staid, sober, or decorous.
▷HISTORY C17: from Latin *sēdāre* to soothe; related to *sedēre* to sit
▸**se'dately** ADVERB ▸**se'dateness** NOUN

sedate[2] (sɪ'deɪt) VERB *(tr)* to administer a sedative to.
▷HISTORY C20: back formation from SEDATIVE

sedation (sɪ'deɪʃən) NOUN [1] a state of calm or reduced nervous activity. [2] the administration of a sedative.

sedative ('sɛdətɪv) ADJECTIVE [1] having a soothing or calming effect. [2] of or relating to sedation. ◆ NOUN [3] *Med* a sedative drug or agent.
▷HISTORY C15: from Medieval Latin *sēdātīvus,* from Latin *sēdātus* assuaged; see SEDATE[1]

sedentary ('sɛdᵊntərɪ, -trɪ) ADJECTIVE [1] characterized by or requiring a sitting position: *sedentary work.* [2] tending to sit about without taking much exercise. [3] (of animals) moving about very little, usually because of attachment to a rock or other surface. [4] (of animals) not migratory.
▷HISTORY C16: from Latin *sedentārius,* from *sedēre* to sit
▸'**sedentarily** ADVERB ▸'**sedentariness** NOUN

Seder ('seɪdə) NOUN *Judaism* a ceremonial meal with prescribed ritual reading of the Haggadah observed in Jewish homes on the first night or first two nights of Passover.
▷HISTORY from Hebrew *sēdher* order

sederunt (sɪ'derʊnt, sɪ'dɛərənt) NOUN (in Scotland) [1] a sitting of an ecclesiastical assembly, court, etc. [2] the list of persons present.
▷HISTORY C17: from Latin *sēdērunt* they were sitting, from *sedēre* to sit

sedge (sɛdʒ) NOUN [1] any grasslike cyperaceous plant of the genus *Carex,* typically growing on wet ground and having rhizomes, triangular stems, and minute flowers in spikelets. [2] any other plant of the family *Cyperaceae.*
▷HISTORY Old English *secg;* related to Middle High German *segge* sedge, Old English *sagu* SAW[1]
▸'**sedgy** ADJECTIVE

sedge fly NOUN an angler's name for various caddis flies, notably the grey sedge, the murragh, and the cinnamon sedge.

Sedgemoor ('sɛdʒ,mʊə) NOUN a low-lying plain in SW England, in central Somerset: scene of the defeat (1685) of the Duke of Monmouth.

sedge warbler NOUN a European songbird, *Acrocephalus schoenobaenus,* of reed beds and swampy areas, having a streaked brownish plumage with white eye stripes: family *Muscicapidae* (Old World flycatchers, etc.).

sedilia (sɛ'daɪlɪə) NOUN *(functioning as singular)* the group of three seats, each called a **sedile** (sɛ'daɪlɪ), often recessed, on the south side of a sanctuary where the celebrant and ministers sit at certain points during High Mass.
▷HISTORY C18: from Latin, from *sedīle* a chair, from *sedēre* to sit

sediment ('sɛdɪmənt) NOUN [1] matter that settles to the bottom of a liquid. [2] material that has been deposited from water, ice, or wind.
▷HISTORY C16: from Latin *sedimentum* a settling, from *sedēre* to sit
▸**sedimentous** (,sɛdɪ'mɛntəs) ADJECTIVE

sedimentary (,sɛdɪ'mɛntərɪ) ADJECTIVE [1] characteristic of, resembling, or containing sediment. [2] (of rocks) formed by the accumulation and consolidation of mineral and organic fragments that have been deposited by water, ice, or wind. Compare **igneous, metamorphic.**
▸,**sedi'mentarily** ADVERB

sedimentation (,sɛdɪmɛn'teɪʃən) NOUN [1] the process of formation of sedimentary rocks. [2] the deposition or production of sediment. [3] *Chem, biochem* the process by which large molecules or macroscopic particles are concentrated in a centrifugal field in a centrifuge or ultracentrifuge.

sedimentation tank NOUN a tank into which

sewage is passed to allow suspended solid matter to separate out.

sedimentology (ˌsedɪmenˈtɒlədʒɪ) NOUN the branch of geology concerned with sedimentary rocks and deposits.
▸ **ˌsedimenˈtologist** NOUN

sedition (sɪˈdɪʃən) NOUN [1] speech or behaviour directed against the peace of a state. [2] an offence that tends to undermine the authority of a state. [3] an incitement to public disorder. [4] *Archaic* revolt.
▷HISTORY C14: from Latin *sēditiō* discord, from *sēd-* apart + *itiō* a going, from *īre* to go
▸ **seˈditionary** NOUN, ADJECTIVE

seditious (sɪˈdɪʃəs) ADJECTIVE [1] of, like, or causing sedition. [2] inclined to or taking part in sedition.
▸ **seˈditiously** ADVERB ▸ **seˈditiousness** NOUN

seduce (sɪˈdjuːs) VERB (*tr*) [1] to persuade to engage in sexual intercourse. [2] to lead astray, as from the right action. [3] to win over, attract, or lure.
▷HISTORY C15: from Latin *sēdūcere* to lead apart, from *sē-* apart + *dūcere* to lead
▸ **seˈducible** *or* **seˈduceable** ADJECTIVE

seducer (sɪˈdjuːsə) *or feminine* **seductress** (sɪˈdʌktrɪs) NOUN a person who entices, allures, or seduces, esp one who entices another to engage in sexual intercourse.

seduction (sɪˈdʌkʃən) NOUN [1] the act of seducing or the state of being seduced. [2] a means of seduction.

seductive (sɪˈdʌktɪv) ADJECTIVE tending to seduce or capable of seducing; enticing; alluring.
▸ **seˈductively** ADVERB ▸ **seˈductiveness** NOUN

sedulous (ˈsedjʊləs) ADJECTIVE constant or persistent in use or attention; assiduous; diligent.
▷HISTORY C16: from Latin *sēdulus*, of uncertain origin
▸ **sedulity** (sɪˈdjuːlɪtɪ) *or* **ˈsedulousness** NOUN
▸ **ˈsedulously** ADVERB

sedum (ˈsiːdəm) NOUN any crassulaceous rock plant of the genus *Sedum*, having thick fleshy leaves and clusters of white, yellow, or pink flowers. See also **stonecrop, rose-root, orpine.**
▷HISTORY C15: from Latin: houseleek

see¹ (siː) VERB **sees, seeing, saw, seen.** [1] to perceive with the eyes. [2] (when *tr, may take a clause as object*) to perceive (an idea) mentally; understand: *I explained the problem but he could not see it.* [3] (*tr*) to perceive with any or all of the senses: *I hate to see you so unhappy.* [4] (*tr; may take a clause as object*) to be aware of in advance; foresee: *I can see what will happen if you don't help.* [5] (when *tr, may take a clause as object*) to ascertain or find out (a fact); learn: *see who is at the door.* [6] (when *tr, takes a clause as object;* when *intr*, foll by *to*) to make sure (of something) or take care (of something): *see that he gets to bed early.* [7] (when *tr, may take a clause as object*) to consider, deliberate, or decide: *see if you can come next week.* [8] (*tr*) to have experience of; undergo: *he had seen much unhappiness in his life.* [9] (*tr*) to allow to be in a specified condition: *I cannot stand by and see a child in pain.* [10] (*tr*) to be characterized by: *this period of history has seen much unrest.* [11] (*tr*) to meet or pay a visit to: *to see one's solicitor.* [12] (*tr*) to receive, esp as a guest or visitor: *the Prime Minister will see the deputation now.* [13] (*tr*) to frequent the company of: *she is seeing a married man.* [14] (*tr*) to accompany or escort: *I saw her to the door.* [15] (*tr*) to refer to or look up: *for further information see the appendix.* [16] (in gambling, esp in poker) to match (another player's bet) or match the bet of (another player) by staking an equal sum. [17] **as far as I can see.** to the best of my judgment or understanding. [18] **see fit.** (*takes an infinitive*) to consider proper, desirable, etc.: *I don't see fit to allow her to come here.* [19] **see (someone) hanged** *or* **damned first.** *Informal* to refuse absolutely to do what one has been asked. [20] **see (someone) right.** *Brit informal* to ensure fair treatment of (someone): *if he has cheated you, I'll see you right.* [21] **see the light (of day).** See **light¹** (sense 24). [22] **see you, see you later,** *or* **be seeing you.** an expression of farewell. [23] **you see.** *Informal* a parenthetical filler phrase used to make a pause in speaking or add slight emphasis. ◆ See also **see about, see into, see of, see off, see out, see over, see through.**
▷HISTORY Old English *sēon;* related to Old Norse *sjā*, Gothic *saihwan*, Old Saxon *sehan*
▸ **ˈseeable** ADJECTIVE

see² (siː) NOUN the diocese of a bishop, or the place within it where his cathedral or procathedral is situated. See also **Holy See.**
▷HISTORY C13: from Old French *sed*, from Latin *sēdēs* a seat; related to *sedēre* to sit

see about VERB (*intr, preposition*) [1] to take care of; look after: *he couldn't see about the matter because he was ill.* [2] to investigate; enquire into: *to see about a new car.*

Seebeck (ˈsiːbɛk) NOUN *Philately* [1] any of a set of stamps issued (1890–99) in Nicaragua, Honduras, Ecuador, and El Salvador and named after Nicholas Frederick Seebeck, who provided them free to the respective governments. [2] any of the reprints issued later for personal gain by Seebeck.

Seebeck effect (ˈsiːbɛk; *German* ˈzeːbɛk) NOUN the phenomenon in which a current is produced in a circuit containing two or more different metals when the junctions between the metals are maintained at different temperatures. Also called: **thermoelectric effect.** Compare **Peltier effect.**
▷HISTORY C19: named after Thomas *Seebeck* (1770–1831), German physicist

seed (siːd) NOUN [1] *Botany* a mature fertilized plant ovule, consisting of an embryo and its food store surrounded by a protective seed coat (testa). Related adjective: **seminal.** [2] the small hard seedlike fruit of plants such as wheat. [3] (loosely) any propagative part of a plant, such as a tuber, spore, or bulb. [4] such parts collectively. [5] the source, beginning, or germ of anything: *the seeds of revolt.* [6] *Chiefly Bible* offspring or descendants: *the seed of Abraham.* [7] an archaic or dialect term for **sperm** or **semen.** [8] *Sport* a seeded player. [9] the egg cell or cells of the lobster and certain other animals. [10] See **seed oyster.** [11] *Chem* a small crystal added to a supersaturated solution or supercooled liquid to induce crystallization. [12] **go** *or* **run to seed. a** (of plants) to produce and shed seeds. **b** to lose vigour, usefulness, etc. ◆ VERB [13] to plant (seeds, grain, etc.) in (soil): *we seeded this field with oats.* [14] (*intr*) (of plants) to form or shed seeds. [15] (*tr*) to remove the seeds from (fruit, etc.). [16] (*tr*) *Chem* to add a small crystal to (a supersaturated solution or supercooled liquid) in order to cause crystallization. [17] (*tr*) to scatter certain substances, such as silver iodide, in (clouds) in order to cause rain. [18] (*tr*) **a** to arrange (the draw of a tournament) so that outstanding teams or players will not meet in the early rounds. **b** to distribute (players or teams) in this manner.
▷HISTORY Old English *sǣd;* related to Old Norse *sāth*, Gothic *sēths*, Old High German *sāt*
▸ **ˈseedˌlike** ADJECTIVE ▸ **ˈseedless** ADJECTIVE

SEED ABBREVIATION FOR Scottish Executive Education Department.

seedbed (ˈsiːdˌbed) NOUN [1] a plot of land in which seeds or seedlings are grown before being transplanted. [2] the place where something develops: *the seedbed of discontent.*

seedcake (ˈsiːdˌkeɪk) NOUN a sweet cake flavoured with caraway seeds and lemon rind or essence.

seed capital NOUN *Finance* a small amount of capital required to finance the research necessary to produce a business plan for a new company.

seed capsule *or* **seedcase** (ˈsiːdˌkeɪs) NOUN the part of a fruit enclosing the seeds; pericarp.

seed coat NOUN the nontechnical name for **testa.**

seed coral NOUN small pieces of coral used in jewellery, etc.

seed corn NOUN [1] the good quality ears or kernels of corn that are used as seed. [2] assets or investments that are expected to provide profits in the future.

seeder (ˈsiːdə) NOUN [1] a person or thing that seeds. [2] a device used to remove seeds, as from fruit, etc. [3] any of various devices for sowing grass seed or grain on the surface of the ground.

seed fern NOUN another name for **pteridosperm.**

seed leaf NOUN the nontechnical name for **cotyledon.**

seedling (ˈsiːdlɪŋ) NOUN a very young plant produced from a seed.

seed money NOUN money used for the establishment of an enterprise.

seed oyster NOUN a young oyster, esp a cultivated oyster, ready for transplantation.

seed pearl NOUN a tiny pearl weighing less than a quarter of a grain.

seed plant NOUN any plant that reproduces by means of seeds: a gymnosperm or angiosperm.

seed pod NOUN a carpel or pistil enclosing the seeds of a plant, esp a flowering plant.

seed potato NOUN a potato tuber used for planting.

seed vessel NOUN *Botany* a dry fruit, such as a capsule.

seedy (ˈsiːdɪ) ADJECTIVE **seedier, seediest.** [1] shabby or unseemly in appearance: *seedy clothes.* [2] (of a plant) at the stage of producing seeds. [3] *Informal* not physically fit; sickly.
▸ **ˈseedily** ADVERB ▸ **ˈseediness** NOUN

seeing (ˈsiːɪŋ) NOUN [1] the sense or faculty of sight; vision. [2] *Astronomy* the quality of the observing conditions (especially the turbulence of the atmosphere) during an astronomical observation. ◆ CONJUNCTION [3] (*subordinating;* often foll by *that*) in light of the fact (that); inasmuch as; since.

> **Language note** The use of *seeing as how* as in *seeing as (how) the bus is always late, I don't need any reason to hurry* is generally thought to be incorrect or non-standard.

seeing-eye dog NOUN the US name for **guide dog.**

see into VERB (*intr, preposition*) [1] to examine or investigate. [2] to discover the true nature of: *I can't see into your thoughts.*

seek (siːk) VERB **seeks, seeking, sought.** (*mainly tr*) [1] (when *intr*, often foll by *for* or *after*) to try to find by searching; look for: *to seek a solution.* [2] (*also intr*) to try to obtain or acquire: *to seek happiness.* [3] to attempt (to do something); try: *I'm only seeking to help.* [4] (*also intr*) to enquire about or request (something): *to seek help.* [5] to go or resort to: *to seek the garden for peace.* [6] an archaic word for **explore.**
▷HISTORY Old English *sēcan;* related to Old Norse *sōkja*, Gothic *sōkjan*, Old High German *suohhen*, Latin *sāgīre* to perceive by scent; see BESEECH
▸ **ˈseeker** NOUN

seek out VERB (*tr, adverb*) to search hard for a specific person or thing and find: *she sought out her friend from amongst the crowd.*

seel (siːl) VERB (*tr*) [1] to sew up the eyelids of (a hawk or falcon) so as to render it quiet and tame. [2] *Obsolete* to close up the eyes of, esp by blinding.
▷HISTORY C15 *silen*, from Old French *ciller*, from Medieval Latin *ciliāre*, from Latin *cilium* an eyelid

Seeland (ˈzeːlant) NOUN the German name for **Sjælland.**

seelie (ˈsiːlɪ) PLURAL NOUN **the.** [1] good benevolent fairies. ◆ ADJECTIVE [2] **a** of or belonging to the seelie. **b** good and benevolent like the seelie: *seelie wights.*
▷HISTORY an earlier form of SILLY

seem (siːm) VERB (may take an infinitive) [1] (*copula*) to appear to the mind or eye; look: *this seems nice; the car seems to be running well.* [2] to give the impression of existing; appear to be: *there seems no need for all this nonsense.* [3] used to diminish the force of a following infinitive to be polite, more noncommittal, etc.: *I can't seem to get through to you.*
▷HISTORY C12: perhaps from Old Norse *soma* to beseem, from *sœmr* befitting; related to Old English *sēman* to reconcile; see SAME
▸ **ˈseemer** NOUN

> **Language note** See at **like¹**.

seeming (ˈsiːmɪŋ) ADJECTIVE [1] (*prenominal*) apparent but not actual or genuine: *seeming honesty.* ◆ NOUN [2] outward or false appearance.
▸ **ˈseemingness** NOUN

seemingly (ˈsiːmɪŋlɪ) ADVERB [1] in appearance but not necessarily in actuality: *with seemingly effortless ease.* [2] (*sentence modifier*) apparently; as far as one knows: *seemingly, he had few friends left.*

seemly (ˈsiːmlɪ) ADJECTIVE **-lier, -liest.** [1] proper or fitting. [2] *Obsolete* pleasing or handsome in appearance. ◆ ADVERB [3] *Archaic* properly or decorously.
▷HISTORY C13: from Old Norse *sœmiligr*, from *sœmr* befitting
▸ **ˈseemliness** NOUN

seen (siːn) VERB the past participle of **see.**

see of VERB *(tr, preposition)* to meet; be in contact with: *we haven't seen much of him since he got married.*

see off VERB *(tr, adverb)* [1] to be present at the departure of (a person making a journey). [2] *Informal* to cause to leave or depart, esp by force.

see out VERB *(tr, adverb)* [1] to remain or endure until the end of: *we'll see the first half of the game out and then leave.* [2] to be present at the departure of (a person from a house, room, etc.).

see over *or* **round** VERB *(intr, preposition)* to inspect by making a tour of: *she said she'd like to see over the house.*

seep (siːp) VERB [1] *(intr)* to pass gradually or leak through or as if through small openings; ooze. ◆ NOUN [2] a small spring or place where water, oil, etc., has oozed through the ground. [3] another word for **seepage.**
▷HISTORY Old English *sīpian;* related to Middle High German *sīfen,* Swedish dialect *sipa*

seepage (ˈsiːpɪdʒ) NOUN [1] the act or process of seeping. [2] liquid or moisture that has seeped.

seer[1] (sɪə) NOUN [1] a person who can supposedly see into the future; prophet. [2] a person who professes supernatural powers. [3] a person who sees.
▸ **ˈseeress** FEMININE NOUN

seer[2] (sɪə) NOUN a variant spelling of **ser.**

seersucker (ˈsɪəˌsʌkə) NOUN a light cotton, linen, or other fabric with a crinkled surface and often striped.
▷HISTORY C18: from Hindi *śīrśakar,* from Persian *shīr o shakkar,* literally: milk and sugar

seesaw (ˈsiːˌsɔː) NOUN [1] a plank balanced in the middle so that two people seated on the ends can ride up and down by pushing on the ground with their feet. [2] the pastime of riding up and down on a seesaw. [3] **a** an up-and-down or back-and-forth movement. **b** *(as modifier): a seesaw movement.* ◆ VERB [4] *(intr)* to move up and down or back and forth in such a manner; oscillate.
▷HISTORY C17: reduplication of SAW[1], alluding to the movement from side to side, as in sawing

seethe (siːð) VERB [1] *(intr)* to boil or to foam as if boiling. [2] *(intr)* to be in a state of extreme agitation, esp through anger. [3] *(tr)* to soak in liquid. [4] *(tr) Archaic* to cook or extract the essence of (a food) by boiling. ◆ NOUN [5] the act or state of seething.
▷HISTORY Old English *sēothan;* related to Old Norse *sjōtha,* Old High German *siodan* to seethe

seething (ˈsiːðɪŋ) ADJECTIVE [1] boiling or foaming as if boiling. [2] crowded and full of restless activity. [3] in a state of extreme agitation, esp through anger.
▸ **ˈseethingly** ADVERB

see through VERB [1] *(tr)* to help out in time of need or trouble: *I know you're short of money, but I'll see you through.* [2] *(tr, adverb)* to remain with until the end or completion: *let's see the job through.* [3] *(intr, preposition)* to perceive the true nature of: *I can see through your evasion.* ◆ ADJECTIVE **see-through.** [4] partly or wholly transparent or translucent, esp (of clothes) in a titillating way: *a see-through nightie.*

sefer (ˈsɛfɛr, ˈseɪfɛr) NOUN *Judaism* [1] In full: **sefer torah.** the scrolls of the Law. [2] any book of Hebrew religious literature.
▷HISTORY from Hebrew, literally: book

Sefton (ˈsɛftᵊn) NOUN a unitary authority in NW England, in Merseyside. Pop.: 282 956 (2001). Area: 150 sq. km (58 sq. miles).

segment NOUN (ˈsɛɡmənt) [1] *Maths* **a** a part of a line or curve between two points. **b** a part of a plane or solid figure cut off by an intersecting line, plane, or planes, esp one between a chord and an arc of a circle. [2] one of several parts or sections into which an object is divided; portion. [3] *Zoology* any of the parts into which the body or appendages of an annelid or arthropod are divided. [4] *Linguistics* a speech sound considered in isolation. ◆ VERB (sɛɡˈmɛnt) [5] to cut or divide (a whole object) into segments.
▷HISTORY C16: from Latin *segmentum,* from *secāre* to cut
▸ **segmentary** (ˈsɛɡməntərɪ, -trɪ) ADJECTIVE

segmental (sɛɡˈmɛntᵊl) ADJECTIVE [1] of, like, or having the form of a segment. [2] divided into segments. [3] *Linguistics* of, relating to, or constituting an isolable speech sound.
▸ **segˈmentally** ADVERB

segmentation (ˌsɛɡmɛnˈteɪʃən) NOUN [1] the act or an instance of dividing into segments. [2] *Embryol* another name for **cleavage** (sense 4). [3] *Zoology* another name for **metamerism** (sense 1).

segmentation cavity NOUN another name for **blastocoel.**

segno (ˈsɛnjəʊ; *Italian* ˈseɲɲo) NOUN, *plural* **-gni** (-njiː; *Italian* -ɲɲi). *Music* a sign at the beginning or end of a section directed to be repeated. Symbol: 𝄋 *or* **:S:**.
▷HISTORY Italian: a sign, from Latin *signum*

Segovia (sɪˈɡəʊvɪə; *Spanish* seˈɣoβja) NOUN a town in central Spain: site of a Roman aqueduct, still in use, and the fortified palace of the kings of Castile (the Alcázar). Pop.: 58 060 (1991).

segregate (ˈsɛɡrɪˌɡeɪt) VERB [1] to set or be set apart from others or from the main group. [2] *(tr)* to impose segregation on (a racial or minority group). [3] *Genetics, metallurgy* to undergo or cause to undergo segregation.
▷HISTORY C16: from Latin *sēgregāre,* from *sē-* apart + *grex* a flock
▸ **segregable** (ˈsɛɡrɪɡəbᵊl) ADJECTIVE ▸ **ˈsegreˌgative** ADJECTIVE ▸ **ˈsegreˌgator** NOUN

segregation (ˌsɛɡrɪˈɡeɪʃən) NOUN [1] the act of segregating or state of being segregated. [2] *Sociol* the practice or policy of creating separate facilities within the same society for the use of a minority group. [3] *Genetics* the separation at meiosis of the two members of any pair of alleles into separate gametes. See also **Mendel's laws.** [4] *Metallurgy* the process in which a component of an alloy or solid solution separates in small regions within the solid or on the solid's surface.
▸ **ˌsegreˈgational** ADJECTIVE

segregationist (ˌsɛɡrɪˈɡeɪʃənɪst) NOUN a person who favours, advocates, or practises racial segregation.

segue (ˈsɛɡweɪ) VERB **segues, segueing, segued.** *(intr)* [1] (often foll by *into*) to proceed from one section or piece of music to another without a break. [2] *(imperative)* play on without pause: a musical direction. ◆ NOUN [3] the practice or an instance of playing music in this way.
▷HISTORY from Italian: follows, from *seguire* to follow, from Latin *sequī*

seguidilla (ˌsɛɡɪˈdiːljə) NOUN [1] a Spanish dance in a fast triple rhythm. [2] a piece of music composed for or in the rhythm of this dance. [3] *Prosody* a stanzaic form consisting of four to seven lines and marked by a characteristic rhythm.
▷HISTORY Spanish: a little dance, from *seguida* a dance, from *seguir* to follow, from Latin *sequī*

seicento *(Italian* seiˈtʃento) NOUN the 17th century with reference to Italian art and literature.
▷HISTORY Italian, shortened from *mille seicento* one thousand six hundred

seiche (seɪʃ) NOUN a periodic oscillation of the surface of an enclosed or semienclosed body of water (lake, inland sea, bay, etc.) caused by such phenomena as atmospheric pressure changes, winds, tidal currents, and earthquakes.
▷HISTORY C19: from Swiss French, first used to describe rise and fall of water in Lake Geneva; of obscure origin

Seidlitz powder *or* **powders** (ˈsɛdlɪts) NOUN a laxative consisting of two powders, tartaric acid and a mixture of sodium bicarbonate and Rochelle salt (sodium potassium tartrate). Also called: **Rochelle powder.**
▷HISTORY C19: named after *Seidlitz,* a village in Bohemia with mineral springs having similar laxative effects

seif dune (seɪf) NOUN (in deserts, esp the Sahara) a long ridge of blown sand, often several miles long.
▷HISTORY *seif,* from Arabic: sword, from the shape of the dune

seigneur (sɛˈnjɜː; *French* sɛɲœr) NOUN [1] a feudal lord, esp in France. [2] (in French Canada, until 1854) the landlord of an estate that was subdivided among peasants who held their plots by a form of feudal tenure.
▷HISTORY C16: from Old French, from Vulgar Latin *senior,* from Latin: an elderly man; see SENIOR
▸ **seiˈgneurial** ADJECTIVE

seigneury (ˈseɪnjərɪ) NOUN, *plural* **-gneuries.** the estate of a seigneur.

seignior (ˈseɪnjə) NOUN [1] a less common name for a **seigneur.** [2] (in England) the lord of a seigniory.
▷HISTORY C14: from Anglo-French *segnour;* see SEIGNEUR
▸ **seigniorial** (seɪˈnjɔːrɪəl) ADJECTIVE

seigniorage (ˈseɪnjərɪdʒ) NOUN [1] something claimed by a sovereign or superior as a prerogative, right, or due. [2] a fee payable to a government for coining bullion. [3] the difference in value between the cost of bullion and the face value of the coin made from it.

seigniory (ˈseɪnjərɪ) *or* **signory** (ˈsiːnjərɪ) NOUN, *plural* **-gniories** *or* **-gnories.** [1] less common names for a **seigneury.** [2] (in England) the fee or manor of a seignior; a feudal domain. [3] the authority of a seignior or the relationship between him and his tenants. [4] a body of lords.

seik (siːk) ADJECTIVE a Scot word for **sick.**

seine (seɪn) NOUN [1] a large fishing net that hangs vertically in the water by means of floats at the top and weights at the bottom. ◆ VERB [2] to catch (fish) using this net.
▷HISTORY Old English *segne,* from Latin *sagēna,* from Greek *sagēnē;* related to Old High German *segina,* Old French *saïne*

Seine (seɪn; *French* sɛn) NOUN a river in N France, rising on the Plateau de Langres and flowing northwest through Paris to the English Channel: the second longest river in France, linked by canal with the Rivers Somme, Scheldt, Meuse, Rhine, Saône, and Loire. Length: 776 km (482 miles).

Seine-et-Marne *(French* senemarn) NOUN a department of N central France, in Île-de-France region. Capital: Melun. Pop.: 1 193 767 (1999). Area: 5931 sq. km (2313 sq. miles).

Seine-Maritime *(French* senmaritim) NOUN a department of N France, in Haute-Normandie region. Capital: Rouen. Pop.: 1 239 138 (1999). Area: 6342 sq. km (2473 sq. miles).

Seine-Saint-Denis *(French* sensēdni) NOUN a department of N central France, in Île-de-France region. Capital: Bobigny. Pop.: 1 382 861 (1999). Area: 236 sq. km (92 sq. miles).

seise *or US* **seize** (siːz) VERB to put into legal possession of (property, etc.).
▷HISTORY variant of SEIZE
▸ **ˈseisable** ADJECTIVE ▸ **ˈseiser** NOUN

seisin *or US* **seizin** (ˈsiːzɪn) NOUN *Property law* feudal possession of an estate in land.
▷HISTORY C13: from Old French *seisine,* from *seisir* to SEIZE

seism (ˈsaɪzəm) NOUN a less common name for **earthquake.**
▷HISTORY C19: from Greek *seismos,* from *seiein* to shake

seismic (ˈsaɪzmɪk) ADJECTIVE [1] Also (less commonly): **seismical** (ˈsaɪzmɪkᵊl). relating to or caused by earthquakes or artificially produced earth tremors. [2] of enormous proportions or having highly significant consequences: *seismic social change.*
▸ **ˈseismically** ADVERB

seismic array NOUN a system of linked seismographs arranged in a regular geometric pattern to increase sensitivity to earthquake detection.

seismicity (saɪzˈmɪsɪtɪ) NOUN seismic activity; the phenomenon of earthquake activity or the occurrence of artificially produced earth tremors.

seismic wave NOUN an earth vibration generated by an earthquake or explosion.

seismo- *or before a vowel* **seism-** COMBINING FORM earthquake: *seismology.*
▷HISTORY from Greek *seismos*

seismograph (ˈsaɪzməˌɡrɑːf, -ˌɡræf) NOUN an instrument that registers and records the features of earthquakes. A **seismogram** (ˈsaɪzməˌɡræm) is the record from such an instrument. Also called: **seismometer.**
▸ **seismographic** (ˌsaɪzməˈɡræfɪk) ADJECTIVE ▸ **seismographer** (saɪzˈmɒɡrəfə) NOUN ▸ **seisˈmography** NOUN

seismology (saɪzˈmɒlədʒɪ) NOUN the branch of

geology concerned with the study of earthquakes and seismic waves.
▸**seismologic** (ˌsaɪzməˈlɒdʒɪk) ▸**ˌseismoˈlogical** ADJECTIVE ▸**ˌseismoˈlogically** ADVERB ▸**seisˈmologist** NOUN

seismonasty (ˈsaɪzməˌnæstɪ) NOUN *Botany* a nastic movement in response to shock, esp the rapid folding of the leaflets of the sensitive plant due to changes in turgor pressure caused by vibration.
▷**HISTORY** C20: from SEISMO- + -NASTY

seismoscope (ˈsaɪzməˌskəʊp) NOUN an obsolete instrument that indicates the occurrence of an earthquake. Compare **seismograph.**
▸**seismoscopic** (ˌsaɪzməˈskɒpɪk) ADJECTIVE

sei whale (seɪ) NOUN a rorqual, *Balaenoptera borealis.*
▷**HISTORY** C20: from Norwegian *seihval,* from *sei* coalfish (see SAITHE) + *hval* whale: so called because it follows coalfish in search of food

seize (si:z) VERB *(mainly tr)* [1] (also *intr,* foll by *on*) to take hold of quickly; grab: *she seized her hat and ran for the bus.* [2] (sometimes foll by *on* or *upon*) to grasp mentally, esp rapidly: *she immediately seized his idea.* [3] to take mental possession of: *alarm seized the crowd.* [4] to take possession of rapidly and forcibly: *the thief seized the woman's purse.* [5] to take legal possession of; take into custody. [6] to take by force or capture: *the army seized the undefended town.* [7] to take immediate advantage of: *to seize an opportunity.* [8] *Nautical* to bind (two ropes together or a piece of gear to a rope). See also **serve** (sense 19). [9] *(intr;* often foll by *up)* (of mechanical parts) to become jammed, esp because of excessive heat. [10] *(passive;* usually foll by *of)* to be apprised of; conversant with. [11] the usual US spelling of **seise.**
▷**HISTORY** C13 *saisen,* from Old French *saisir,* from Medieval Latin *sacīre* to position, of Germanic origin; related to Gothic *satjan* to SET[1]
▸**ˈseizable** ADJECTIVE

seizing (ˈsi:zɪŋ) NOUN *Nautical* a binding used for holding together two ropes, two spars, etc., esp by lashing with a separate rope.

seizure (ˈsi:ʒə) NOUN [1] the act or an instance of seizing or the state of being seized. [2] *Pathol* a sudden manifestation or recurrence of a disease, such as an epileptic convulsion.

sejant *or* **sejeant** (ˈsi:dʒənt) ADJECTIVE *(usually postpositive) Heraldry* (of a beast) shown seated.
▷**HISTORY** C16: variant of *seant,* from Old French, from *seoir* to sit, from Latin *sedēre*

Sejm (seɪm) NOUN the unicameral legislature of Poland.
▷**HISTORY** Polish: assembly

Sekondi (ˌsɛkənˈdi:) NOUN a port in SW Ghana, 8 km (5 miles) northeast of Takoradi: linked administratively with Takoradi in 1946. Pop. (with Takoradi): 103 600 (latest est.).

Sekt (zɛkt) NOUN any of various German sparkling wines.
▷**HISTORY** C20: from German, from Spanish *vino seco* dry wine

sel (sɛl) NOUN a Scot word for **self.**

selachian (sɪˈleɪkɪən) ADJECTIVE [1] of, relating to, or belonging to the *Selachii* (or *Elasmobranchii*), a large subclass of cartilaginous fishes including the sharks, rays, dogfish, and skates. ◆ NOUN [2] any fish belonging to the subclass *Selachii.* Also: **elasmobranch.**
▷**HISTORY** C19: from New Latin *Selachiī,* from Greek *selakhē* a shark; related to Greek *selas* brightness

selaginella (ˌsɛlədʒɪˈnɛlə) NOUN any club moss of the genus *Selaginella,* having stems covered in small pointed leaves and small spore-bearing cones: family *Selaginellaceae.* See also **resurrection plant.**
▷**HISTORY** C19: from New Latin, diminutive of Latin *selāgō* plant similar to the savin

selah (ˈsi:lə) NOUN a Hebrew word of unknown meaning occurring in the Old Testament psalms, and thought to be a musical direction.
▷**HISTORY** C16: from Hebrew

Selangor (səˈlæŋə) NOUN a state of Peninsular Malaysia, on the Strait of Malacca: established as a British protectorate in 1874, became a Federated Malay State in 1896 and part of Malaysia in 1946; tin producer. Capital: Shah Alam. Pop.: 3 617 527 (2000 est.). Area: 8203 sq. km (3167 sq. miles).

Selby (ˈsɛlbɪ) NOUN an inland port in N England, in North Yorkshire, on the River Ouse: centre for a coalfield since 1983: agricultural products. Pop.: 15 292 (1991).

seldom (ˈsɛldəm) ADVERB not often; rarely.
▷**HISTORY** Old English *seldon;* related to Old Norse *sjāldan,* Old High German *seltan*

select (sɪˈlɛkt) VERB [1] to choose (someone or something) in preference to another or others. ◆ ADJECTIVE *also* **selected.** [2] chosen in preference to another or others. [3] of particular quality or excellence. [4] limited as to membership or entry: *a select gathering.* [5] careful in making a choice.
▷**HISTORY** C16: from Latin *sēligere* to sort, from *sē-* apart + *legere* to choose
▸**seˈlectly** ADVERB ▸**seˈlectness** NOUN

selecta (sɪˈlɛktə) NOUN *Slang* a disc jockey.
▷**HISTORY** C20: phonetic rendering of SELECTOR

select committee NOUN (in Britain) a small committee composed of members of parliament, set up by either House of Parliament to investigate and report back on a specified matter of interest.

selectee (sɪˌlɛkˈti:) NOUN *US* a person who is selected, esp for military service.

selection (sɪˈlɛkʃən) NOUN [1] the act or an instance of selecting or the state of being selected. [2] a thing or number of things that have been selected. [3] a range from which something may be selected: *this shop has a good selection of clothes.* [4] *Biology* the natural or artificial process by which certain organisms or characters are reproduced and perpetuated in the species in preference to others. See also **natural selection.** [5] a contestant in a race chosen as likely to win or come second or third. [6] *Austral* **a** the act of free-selecting. **b** a tract of land acquired by free-selection.

selective (sɪˈlɛktɪv) ADJECTIVE [1] of or characterized by selection. [2] tending to choose carefully or characterized by careful choice. [3] *Electronics* occurring at, operating at, or capable of separating out a particular frequency or band of frequencies.
▸**seˈlectively** ADVERB ▸**seˈlectiveness** NOUN

selective attention NOUN *Psychol* the process by which a person can selectively pick out one message from a mixture of messages occurring simultaneously.

selective service NOUN *US* (formerly) compulsory military service under which men were conscripted selectively.

selective synchronization NOUN a sound-recording process that facilitates overdubs by feeding the recorded track to the performer straight from the recording head. Often shortened to: **sel-sync.**

selectivity (sɪˌlɛkˈtɪvɪtɪ) NOUN [1] the state or quality of being selective. [2] the degree to which a radio receiver or other circuit can respond to and separate the frequency of a desired signal from other frequencies by tuning. [3] the principle that welfare services should go only to those whose need is greatest, as revealed by needs tests, means tests, etc.

selectman (sɪˈlɛktmən) NOUN, *plural* **-men.** any of the members of the local boards of most New England towns.

selector (sɪˈlɛktə) NOUN [1] a person or thing that selects. [2] a device used in automatic telephone switching that connects one circuit with any one of a number of other circuits. [3] *Brit* a person who chooses the members of a sports team. [4] *Austral* the holder of a tract of land acquired by free-selection.

selectorate (sɪˈlɛktərɪt) NOUN a body of people responsible for making a selection, esp members of a political party who select candidates for an election.
▷**HISTORY** C20: from SELECT + (ELECT)ORATE

selenate (ˈsɛlɪˌneɪt) NOUN any salt or ester formed by replacing one or both of the hydrogens of selenic acid with metal ions or organic groups.
▷**HISTORY** C19: from SELENIUM + -ATE[1]

Selene (sɪˈli:nɪ) NOUN the Greek goddess of the moon. Roman counterpart: **Luna.**

selenic (sɪˈli:nɪk) ADJECTIVE of or containing selenium, esp in the hexavalent state.

selenic acid NOUN a colourless crystalline soluble strong dibasic acid analogous to sulphuric acid. Formula: H_2SeO_4.

selenious (sɪˈli:nɪəs) *or* **selenous** (sɪˈli:nəs) ADJECTIVE of or containing selenium in the divalent or tetravalent state.

selenious acid NOUN a white soluble crystalline strong dibasic acid analogous to sulphurous acid. Formula: H_2SeO_3.

selenite (ˈsɛlɪˌnaɪt) NOUN a colourless glassy variety of gypsum.
▷**HISTORY** C17: via Latin from Greek *selēnītēs lithos* moonstone, from *selēnē* moon; so called because it was believed to wax and wane with the moon

selenium (sɪˈli:nɪəm) NOUN a nonmetallic element that exists in several allotropic forms. It occurs free in volcanic areas and in sulphide ores, esp pyrite. The common form is a grey crystalline solid that is photoconductive, photovoltaic, and semiconducting: used in photocells, solar cells, and in xerography. Symbol: Se; atomic no.: 34; atomic wt.: 78.96; valency: –2, 4, or 6; relative density: 4.79 (grey); melting pt.: 221°C (grey); boiling pt.: 685°C (grey).
▷**HISTORY** C19: from New Latin, from Greek *selēnē* moon; named by analogy to TELLURIUM (from Latin *tellus* earth)

selenium cell NOUN a photoelectric cell containing a strip of selenium between two metal electrodes.

seleno- *or before a vowel* **selen-** COMBINING FORM denoting the moon: *selenology.*
▷**HISTORY** from Greek *selēnē* moon

selenodont (sɪˈli:nəˌdɒnt) ADJECTIVE [1] (of the teeth of certain mammals) having crescent-shaped ridges on the crowns, as in deer. ◆ NOUN [2] a mammal with selenodont teeth.
▷**HISTORY** C19: from SELENO- (moon-shaped) + -ODONT

selenography (ˌsi:lɪˈnɒgrəfɪ) NOUN the branch of astronomy concerned with the description and mapping of the surface features of the moon.
▸**selenograph** (sɪˈli:nəʊˌgrɑ:f, -ˌgræf) NOUN
▸**ˌseleˈnographer** *or* **ˌselleˈnographist** NOUN
▸**selenographic** (sɪˌli:nəʊˈgræfɪk) *or* **seˌlenoˈgraphical** ADJECTIVE ▸**seˌlenoˈgraphically** ADVERB

selenology (ˌsi:lɪˈnɒlədʒɪ) NOUN the branch of astronomy concerned with the moon, its physical characteristics, nature, origin, etc.
▸**selenological** (sɪˌli:nəʊˈlɒdʒɪkᵊl) ADJECTIVE
▸**ˌseleˈnologist** NOUN

selenomorphology (sɪˌli:nəʊmɔ:ˈfɒlədʒɪ) NOUN the study of the lunar surface and landscape.

Seleucia (sɪˈlu:ʃɪə) NOUN [1] an ancient city in Mesopotamia, on the River Tigris: founded by Seleucus Nicator in 312 B.C.; became the chief city of the Seleucid empire; sacked by the Romans around 162 A.D. [2] an ancient city in SE Asia Minor, on the River Calycadnus (modern Goksu Nehri): captured by the Turks in the 13th century; site of present-day Silifke (Turkey). Official name: **Seleucia Tracheotis** (ˌtrækɪˈəʊtɪs) *or* **Trachea** (trəˈkɪə). [3] an ancient port in Syria, on the River Orontes: the port of Antioch, of military importance during the wars between the Ptolemies and Seleucids; largely destroyed by earthquake in 526; site of present-day Samandağ (Turkey). Official name: **Seleucia Pieria** (paɪˈi:rɪə).

self (sɛlf) NOUN, *plural* **selves** (sɛlvz). [1] the distinct individuality or identity of a person or thing. [2] a person's usual or typical bodily make-up or personal characteristics: *she looked her old self again.* [3] **good self** (*or* **selves**). *Rare* a polite way of referring to or addressing a person (or persons), used following *your, his, her,* or *their.* [4] one's own welfare or interests: *he only thinks of self.* [5] an individual's consciousness of his own identity or being. [6] *Philosophy* (usually preceded by *the*) that which is essential to an individual, esp the mind or soul in Cartesian metaphysics; the ego. [7] a bird, animal. etc., that is a single colour throughout, esp a self-coloured pigeon. ◆ PRONOUN [8] *Not standard* myself, yourself, etc.: *seats for self and wife.* ◆ ADJECTIVE [9] of the same colour or material: *a dress with a self belt.* See also **self-coloured.** [10] *Obsolete* the same.
▷**HISTORY** Old English *seolf;* related to Old Norse *sjālfr,* Gothic *silba,* Old High German *selb*

self- COMBINING FORM [1] of oneself or itself:

self-defence; self-rule. 2 by, to, in, due to, for, or from the self: *self-employed; self-inflicted; self-respect.* 3 automatic or automatically: *self-propelled.*

self-abnegation NOUN the denial of one's own interests in favour of the interests of others.
▸ ˌself-ˈabneˌgating ADJECTIVE

self-absorbed ADJECTIVE preoccupied with one's own thoughts, emotions, life, etc.

self-absorption NOUN 1 preoccupation with oneself to the exclusion of others or the outside world. 2 *Physics* the process in which some of the radiation emitted by a material is absorbed by the material itself.

self-abuse NOUN 1 disparagement or misuse of one's own abilities, etc. 2 a censorious term for **masturbation.**

self-acting ADJECTIVE not requiring an external influence or control to function; automatic.
▸ ˌself-ˈaction NOUN

self-actualization NOUN *Psychol* the process of establishing oneself as a whole person, able to develop one's abilities and to understand oneself.

self-addressed ADJECTIVE 1 addressed for return to the sender. 2 directed to oneself: *a self-addressed remark.*

self-adhesive ADJECTIVE (of a letter, label, etc.) coated with an adhesive substance, esp where no moistening is needed.

self-administered ADJECTIVE (of medicine, etc.) given by oneself.

self-advancement NOUN the act or process of improving one's position, education, etc.

self-advocacy NOUN *Social welfare* (esp in the US) 1 **a** the practice of having mentally handicapped people speak for themselves and control their own affairs, rather than having nonhandicapped people automatically assume responsibility for them. See also **normalization. b** (*as modifier*): *a self-advocacy group.* 2 the act or condition of representing oneself, either generally in society or in formal proceedings, such as a court.

self-aggrandizement NOUN the act of increasing one's own power, importance, etc., esp in an aggressive or ruthless manner.
▸ ˌself-agˈgranˌdizing ADJECTIVE

self-analysis NOUN the act or process of analysing oneself.

self-annealing ADJECTIVE *Metallurgy* denoting certain metals, such as lead, tin, and zinc, that recrystallize at air temperatures and so may be cold-worked without strain-hardening.

self-annihilation NOUN the surrender of the self in mystical contemplation, union with God, etc.

self-appointed ADJECTIVE having assumed authority without the agreement of others: *a self-appointed critic.*

self-assertion NOUN the act or an instance of putting forward one's own opinions, etc., esp in an aggressive or conceited manner.
▸ ˌself-asˈserting ADJECTIVE ▸ ˌself-asˈsertingly ADVERB
▸ ˌself-asˈsertive ADJECTIVE ▸ ˌself-asˈsertively ADVERB
▸ ˌself-asˈsertiveness NOUN

self-assessment NOUN 1 an evaluation of one's own abilities and failings. 2 *Finance* a system to enable taxpayers to assess their own tax liabilities.

self-assurance NOUN confidence in the validity, value, etc., of one's own ideas, opinions, etc.

self-assured ADJECTIVE confident of one's own worth.
▸ ˌself-asˈsuredly ADVERB ▸ ˌself-asˈsuredness NOUN

self-aware ADJECTIVE conscious of one's own feelings, character, etc.

self-catering ADJECTIVE denoting accommodation in which the tenant or visitor provides and prepares his own food.

self-censorship NOUN the regulation of a group's actions and statements by its own members rather than an external agency.

self-centred ADJECTIVE totally preoccupied with one's own concerns.
▸ ˌself-ˈcentredly ADVERB ▸ ˌself-ˈcentredness NOUN

self-certification NOUN (in Britain) a formal assertion by a worker to his employer that absence from work for up to seven days was due to sickness. From 1982 this replaced a doctor's certificate for the purposes of paying sickness benefit. See also **sick note.**

self-cleaning ADJECTIVE (of an oven, filter, etc.) having a mechanism to clean itself.

self-coloured ADJECTIVE 1 having only a single and uniform colour: *self-coloured flowers; a self-coloured dress.* 2 (of cloth, material, etc.) **a** having the natural or original colour. **b** retaining the colour of the thread before weaving.

self-command NOUN another term for **self-control.**

self-compatible ADJECTIVE (of a plant) capable of self-fertilization.
▸ ˌself-comˌpatiˈbility NOUN

self-concept NOUN *Psychol* the whole set of attitudes, opinions, and cognitions that a person has of himself.

self-confessed ADJECTIVE according to one's own testimony or admission: *a self-confessed liar.*

self-confidence NOUN confidence in one's own powers, judgment, etc.
▸ ˌself-ˈconfident ADJECTIVE ▸ ˌself-ˈconfidently ADVERB

self-congratulation NOUN the state or an instance of congratulating or being pleased with oneself.

self-conscious ADJECTIVE 1 unduly aware of oneself as the object of the attention of others; embarrassed. 2 conscious of one's existence.
▸ ˌself-ˈconsciously ADVERB ▸ ˌself-ˈconsciousness NOUN

self-contained ADJECTIVE 1 containing within itself all parts necessary for completeness. 2 (of a flat) having its own kitchen, bathroom, and lavatory not shared by others and usually having its own entrance. 3 able or tending to keep one's feelings, thoughts, etc., to oneself; reserved. 4 able to control one's feelings or emotions in the presence of others.
▸ ˌself-conˈtainedly ADVERB ▸ ˌself-conˈtainedness NOUN

self-control NOUN the ability to exercise restraint or control over one's feelings, emotions, reactions, etc.
▸ ˌself-conˈtrolled ADJECTIVE ▸ ˌself-conˈtrolling ADJECTIVE

self-correcting ADJECTIVE capable of correcting itself without external aid.

self-critical ADJECTIVE critical of oneself: *his self-critical attitude.*

self-criticism NOUN unfavourable or severe judgement of oneself, one's abilities, one's actions, etc.

self-deception *or* **self-deceit** NOUN the act or an instance of deceiving oneself, esp as to the true nature of one's feelings or motives.
▸ ˌself-deˈceptive ADJECTIVE

self-defeating ADJECTIVE (of a plan, action, etc.) unable to achieve the intended result.

self-defence NOUN 1 the act of defending oneself, one's actions, ideas, etc. 2 boxing as a means of defending the person (esp in the phrase **noble art of self-defence**). 3 *Law* the right to defend one's person, family, or property against attack or threat of attack by the use of no more force than is reasonable.
▸ ˌself-deˈfensive ADJECTIVE

self-delusion NOUN the act or state of deceiving or deluding oneself.

self-denial NOUN the denial or sacrifice of one's own desires.
▸ ˌself-deˈnying ADJECTIVE ▸ ˌself-deˈnyingly ADVERB

self-deprecating *or* **self-depreciating** ADJECTIVE having a tendency to disparage oneself.

self-destruct VERB 1 (*intr*) to explode or disintegrate automatically as a result of pre-programming: *the missile self-destructed.* 2 to destroy oneself, one's reputation, etc., through one's habits or actions: *I totally self-destructed with drugs.* ◆ NOUN 3 (*as modifier*): *hit the self-destruct button.*

self-destruction NOUN the act or an instance of self-destructing.

self-determination NOUN 1 the power or ability to make a decision for oneself without influence from outside. 2 the right of a nation or people to determine its own form of government without influence from outside.
▸ ˌself-deˈtermined ADJECTIVE ▸ ˌself-deˈtermining ADJECTIVE

self-development NOUN the state or process of improving or developing oneself.

self-directed ADJECTIVE (of study, learning, etc.) regulated or conducted by oneself.

self-discipline NOUN the act of disciplining or power to discipline one's own feelings, desires, etc., esp with the intention of improving oneself.
▸ ˌself-ˈdisciplined ADJECTIVE

self-dissociation NOUN *Chem* the splitting of the molecules of certain highly polar liquids, such as water and liquid ammonia, into ions.

self-doubt NOUN the act or state of doubting oneself.

self-drive ADJECTIVE denoting or relating to a hired car that is driven by the hirer.

self-educated ADJECTIVE 1 educated through one's own efforts without formal instruction. 2 educated at one's own expense, without financial aid.
▸ ˌself-ˌeduˈcation NOUN

self-effacement NOUN the act of making oneself, one's actions, etc., inconspicuous, esp because of humility or timidity.

self-effacing ADJECTIVE tending to make oneself, one's actions, etc., inconspicuous, esp because of humility or timidity; modest.
▸ ˌself-efˈfacingly ADVERB

self-elected ADJECTIVE having been elected or appointed to a post, position, etc., by onself.

self-employed ADJECTIVE earning one's living in one's own business or through freelance work, rather than as the employee of another.
▸ ˌself-emˈployment NOUN

self-esteem NOUN 1 respect for or a favourable opinion of oneself. 2 an unduly high opinion of oneself; vanity.

self-evident ADJECTIVE containing its own evidence or proof without need of further demonstration.
▸ ˌself-ˈevidence NOUN ▸ ˌself-ˈevidently ADVERB

self-examination NOUN scrutiny of one's own conduct, motives, desires, etc.
▸ ˌself-exˈamining ADJECTIVE

self-excited ADJECTIVE 1 (of an electrical machine) having the current for the magnetic field system generated by the machine itself or by an auxiliary machine coupled to it. 2 (of an oscillator) generating its own energy and depending on resonant circuits for frequency determination.

self-exculpatory ADJECTIVE intended to excuse oneself from blame or guilt.

self-executing ADJECTIVE (of a law, treaty, or clause in a deed or contract, etc.) coming into effect automatically at a specified time, no legislation or other action being needed for enforcement.

self-existent ADJECTIVE *Philosophy* existing independently of any other being or cause.
▸ ˌself-exˈistence NOUN

self-explanatory *or less commonly* **self-explaining** ADJECTIVE understandable without explanation; self-evident.

self-expression NOUN the expression of one's own personality, feelings, etc., as in painting, poetry, or other creative activity.
▸ ˌself-exˈpressive ADJECTIVE

self-feeder NOUN any machine or device capable of automatically supplying materials when and where they are needed, esp one for making measured quantities of food constantly available to farm livestock.

self-fertilization NOUN fertilization in a plant or animal by the fusion of male and female gametes produced by the same individual. Compare **cross-fertilization** (sense 1).
▸ ˌself-ˈfertiˌlized ADJECTIVE ▸ ˌself-ˈfertiˌlizing *or* ˌself-ˈfertile ADJECTIVE

self-financing ADJECTIVE (of a student, business, etc.) financing oneself or itself without external grants or aid.

self-forgetful ADJECTIVE forgetful of one's own interests.
▸ ˌself-forˈgetfully ADVERB ▸ ˌself-forˈgetfulness NOUN

self-fulfilling ADJECTIVE (of an opinion or prediction) borne out because it is expected to be true or to happen: *a self-fulfilling prophecy.*

self-fulfilment NOUN the fulfilment of one's hopes, dreams, goals, etc.

self-government NOUN [1] the government of a country, nation, etc., by its own people. [2] the state of being self-controlled. [3] an archaic term for **self-control.**
▸ ˌ**self-ˈgoverned** ADJECTIVE ▸ ˌ**self-ˈgoverning** ADJECTIVE

self-harm NOUN the practice of cutting or otherwise wounding oneself, usually considered as indicating psychological disturbance.
▸ ˌ**self-ˈharming** NOUN

self-hatred NOUN a feeling of intense dislike for oneself: *feelings of self-hatred.*

selfheal (ˈsɛlfˌhiːl) NOUN [1] a low-growing European herbaceous plant, *Prunella vulgaris,* with tightly clustered violet-blue flowers and reputedly having healing powers: family *Lamiaceae* (labiates). [2] any of several other plants thought to have healing powers. ◆ Also called: **allheal, heal-all.**

self-healing NOUN **a** the act or instance of healing onself. **b** (*as modifier*): *the self-healing process.*

self-help NOUN [1] the act or state of providing the means to help oneself without relying on the assistance of others. [2] **a** the practice of solving one's problems by joining or forming a group designed to help those suffering from a particular problem. **b** (*as modifier*): *a self-help group.*

selfhood (ˈsɛlfhʊd) NOUN [1] *Philosophy* **a** the state of having a distinct identity. **b** the individuality so possessed. [2] a person's character. [3] the quality of being egocentric.

self-hypnosis NOUN the state or act of hypnotizing oneself.

self-identity NOUN the conscious recognition of the self as having a unique identity.

self-image NOUN one's own idea of oneself or sense of one's worth.

self-immolation NOUN the act or an instance of setting fire to oneself.

self-important ADJECTIVE having or showing an unduly high opinion of one's own abilities, importance, etc.
▸ ˌ**self-imˈportantly** ADVERB ▸ ˌ**self-imˈportance** NOUN

self-imposed ADJECTIVE (of a task, role, or circumstance) having been imposed on oneself by oneself.

self-improvement NOUN the improvement of one's status, position, education, etc., by one's own efforts.

self-incompatible ADJECTIVE (of a plant) incapable of self-fertilization because its own pollen is prevented from germinating on the stigma or the pollen tube is blocked before it reaches the egg cell.
▸ ˌ**self-ˌincomˌpatiˈbility** NOUN

self-induced ADJECTIVE [1] induced or brought on by oneself or itself. [2] *Electronics* produced by self-induction.

self-inductance NOUN the inherent inductance of a circuit, given by the ratio of the electromotive force produced in the circuit by self-induction to the rate of change of current producing it. It is usually expressed in henries. Symbol: *L.* Also called: **coefficient of self-induction.**

self-induction NOUN the production of an electromotive force in a circuit when the magnetic flux linked with the circuit changes as a result of a change in current in the same circuit. See also **self-inductance.** Compare **mutual induction.**
▸ ˌ**self-inˈductive** ADJECTIVE

self-indulgent ADJECTIVE tending to indulge one's own desires, etc.
▸ ˌ**self-inˈdulgence** NOUN ▸ ˌ**self-inˈdulgently** ADVERB

self-inflicted ADJECTIVE (of an injury) having been inflicted on oneself by oneself.

self-insurance NOUN the practice of insuring oneself or one's property by accumulating a reserve out of one's income or funds rather than by purchase of an insurance policy.

self-interest NOUN [1] one's personal interest or advantage. [2] the act or an instance of pursuing one's own interest.
▸ ˌ**self-ˈinterested** ADJECTIVE ▸ ˌ**self-ˈinterestedness** NOUN

selfish (ˈsɛlfɪʃ) ADJECTIVE [1] chiefly concerned with one's own interest, advantage, etc., esp to the total exclusion of the interests of others. [2] relating to or characterized by self-interest.
▸ ˈ**selfishly** ADVERB ▸ ˈ**selfishness** NOUN

self-justification NOUN the act or an instance of justifying or providing excuses for one's own behaviour, etc.

self-justifying ADJECTIVE offering excuses for one's behaviour, often when they are not called for.

self-knowledge NOUN knowledge of one's own character, etc.

selfless (ˈsɛlflɪs) ADJECTIVE having little concern for one's own interests.
▸ ˈ**selflessly** ADVERB ▸ ˈ**selflessness** NOUN

self-liquidating ADJECTIVE [1] (of a loan, bill of exchange, etc.) used to finance transactions whose proceeds are expected to accrue before the date of redemption or repayment. [2] (of a business transaction, project, investment, etc.) yielding proceeds sufficient to cover the initial outlay or to finance any recurrent outlays.

self-loading ADJECTIVE (of a firearm) utilizing some of the force of the explosion to eject the empty shell and replace it with a new one. Also: **autoloading.** See also **automatic** (sense 5), **semiautomatic** (sense 2).
▸ ˌ**self-ˈloader** NOUN

self-love NOUN the instinct or tendency to seek one's own well-being or to further one's own interest.

self-made ADJECTIVE [1] having achieved wealth, status, etc., by one's own efforts. [2] made by oneself.

self-motivated ADJECTIVE motivitated or driven by oneself or one's own desires, without any external agency.

self-mutilation NOUN the act or an instance of mutilating oneself.

self-opinionated *or less commonly* **self-opinioned** ADJECTIVE [1] having an unduly high regard for oneself or one's own opinions. [2] clinging stubbornly to one's own opinions.

self-parody NOUN the act or an instance of mimicking oneself in a humorous or satirical way.

self-perpetuating ADJECTIVE (of machine, emotion, idea, etc.) continuing or prevailing without any external agency or intervention.

self-pity NOUN the act or state of pitying oneself, esp in an exaggerated or self-indulgent manner.
▸ ˌ**self-ˈpitying** ADJECTIVE ▸ ˌ**self-ˈpityingly** ADVERB

self-pollination NOUN the transfer of pollen from the anthers to the stigma of the same flower or of another flower on the same plant. Compare **cross-pollination.**
▸ ˌ**self-ˈpolliˌnated** ADJECTIVE

self-portrait NOUN a portrait one draws or paints of oneself.

self-possessed ADJECTIVE having control of one's emotions, etc.
▸ ˌ**self-posˈsessedly** ADVERB ▸ ˌ**self-posˈsession** NOUN

self-praise NOUN the act or an instance of expressing commendation for oneself.

self-preservation NOUN the preservation of oneself from danger or injury, esp as a basic instinct.

self-proclaimed ADJECTIVE proclaimed or described by oneself: *the self-proclaimed leader.*

self-professed ADJECTIVE avowed or acknowledged by oneself.

self-promotion NOUN the act or practice of promoting one's own interests, profile, etc.

self-pronouncing ADJECTIVE (in a phonetic transcription) of, relating to, or denoting a word that, except for additional diacritic marks of stress, may keep the letters of its ordinary orthography to represent its pronunciation.

self-propelled ADJECTIVE (of a vehicle) provided with its own source of tractive power rather than requiring an external means of propulsion.
▸ ˌ**self-proˈpelling** ADJECTIVE

self-protection NOUN the act or an instance of protecting or defending oneself.
▸ ˌ**self-proˈtective** ADJECTIVE

self-punishment NOUN the act or an instance of punishing oneself.

self-questioning ADJECTIVE doubting or questioning oneself or one's abilities.

self-raising ADJECTIVE (of flour) having a raising agent, such as baking powder, already added.

self-realization NOUN the realization or fulfilment of one's own potential or abilities.

self-regard NOUN [1] concern for one's own interest. [2] proper esteem for oneself.

self-regarding ADJECTIVE [1] self-centred; egotistical. [2] *Philosophy* (of an action) affecting the interests of no-one other than the agent, and hence, according to John Stuart Mill, immune from moral criticism.

self-regulating ADJECTIVE (of a business, society, etc.) enforcing or upholding its own rules and laws without external agency of intervention.

self-regulating organization NOUN one of several British organizations set up in 1986 under the auspices of the Securities and Investment Board to regulate the activities of London investment markets. Abbreviation: **SRO.**

self-reliance NOUN reliance on one's own abilities, decisions, etc.
▸ ˌ**self-reˈliant** ADJECTIVE ▸ ˌ**self-reˈliantly** ADVERB

self-renunciation NOUN the renunciation of one's own rights, claims, interest, etc., esp in favour of those of others.
▸ ˌ**self-reˈnunciatory** ADJECTIVE

self-reproach NOUN the act of finding fault with or blaming oneself.
▸ ˌ**self-reˈproachful** ADJECTIVE ▸ ˌ**self-reˈproachfully** ADVERB

self-respect NOUN a proper sense of one's own dignity and integrity.
▸ ˌ**self-reˈspectful** *or* ˌ**self-reˈspecting** ADJECTIVE

self-restraint NOUN restraint imposed by oneself on one's own feelings, desires, etc.

self-righteous ADJECTIVE having or showing an exaggerated awareness of one's own virtuousness or rights.
▸ ˌ**self-ˈrighteously** ADVERB ▸ ˌ**self-ˈrighteousness** NOUN

self-rule NOUN another term for **self-government** (sense 1).

self-sacrifice NOUN the sacrifice of one's own desires, interest, etc., for the sake of duty or for the well-being of others.
▸ ˌ**self-ˈsacriˌficing** ADJECTIVE ▸ ˌ**self-ˈsacriˌficingly** ADVERB

selfsame (ˈsɛlfˌseɪm) ADJECTIVE (*prenominal*) the very same.

self-satisfied ADJECTIVE having or showing a complacent satisfaction with oneself, one's own actions, behaviour, etc.
▸ ˌ**self-ˌsatisˈfaction** NOUN

self-sealing ADJECTIVE (esp of an envelope) designed to become sealed with the application of pressure only.

self-seeking NOUN [1] the act or an instance of seeking one's own profit or interest, esp exclusively. ◆ ADJECTIVE [2] having or showing an exclusive preoccupation with one's own profit or interest: *a self-seeking attitude.*
▸ ˌ**self-ˈseeker** NOUN

self-service ADJECTIVE [1] of or denoting a shop, restaurant, petrol station, etc., where the customer serves himself. ◆ NOUN [2] the practice of serving oneself, as in a shop, etc.

self-serving ADJECTIVE habitually seeking one's own advantage, esp at the expense of others.

self-sown ADJECTIVE (of plants) growing from seed dispersed by any means other than by the agency of man or animals. Also: **self-seeded.**

self-starter NOUN [1] the former name for a **starter** (sense 1). [2] a person who is strongly motivated and shows initiative, esp at work.

self-styled ADJECTIVE (*prenominal*) claiming to be of a specified nature, quality, profession, etc.: *a self-styled expert.*

self-sufficient *or* **self-sufficing** ADJECTIVE able to provide for or support oneself without the help of others.
▸ ˌ**self-sufˈficiency** NOUN ▸ ˌ**self-sufˈficiently** ADVERB

self-suggestion NOUN another term for **autosuggestion.**

self-supporting ADJECTIVE [1] able to support or maintain oneself without the help of others. [2] able to stand up or hold firm without support, props, attachments, etc.

self-tanning *or* **self-tan** NOUN **a** cosmetic

substance applied to the skin to simulate a suntan. **b** (*as modifier*): *self-tanning lotion.*

self-tapping ADJECTIVE (of a screw) cutting its own thread when screwed into a plain hole in a metal sheet.

self-taught ADJECTIVE having learnt oneself without any external or formal instruction.

self-tender NOUN an offer by a company to buy back some or all of its shares from its shareholders, esp as a protection against an unwelcome takeover bid.

self-treatment NOUN the act or an instance of applying (medical) treatment to oneself.

self-understanding NOUN the ability to understand one's own actions.

self-violence NOUN *Euphemistic* suicide.

self-will NOUN stubborn adherence to one's own will, desires, etc., esp at the expense of others.
▸ **ˌself-ˈwilled** ADJECTIVE

self-winding ADJECTIVE (of a wrist watch) having a mechanism, activated by the movements of the wearer, in which a rotating or oscillating weight rewinds the mainspring.

self-worth NOUN respect for or a favourable opinion of oneself.

Seljuk (sɛlˈdʒuːk) *or* **Seljukian** (sɛlˈdʒuːkɪən) NOUN [1] a member of any of the pre-Ottoman Turkish dynasties ruling over large parts of Asia in the 11th, 12th, and 13th centuries A.D. ◆ ADJECTIVE [2] of or relating to these dynasties or to their subjects.
▷HISTORY C19: from Turkish

selkie (ˈsɛlkɪ) NOUN *Scot* a variant of **silkie.**

Selkirk Mountains PLURAL NOUN a mountain range in SW Canada, in SE British Columbia. Highest peak: Mount Sir Sandford, 3533 m (11 590 ft.).

Selkirk Rex NOUN a breed of large curly-haired cat.

Selkirkshire (ˈsɛlkɜːkˌʃɪə, -ʃə) NOUN (until 1975) a county of SE Scotland, now part of Scottish Borders.

sell (sɛl) VERB **sells, selling, sold.** [1] to dispose of or transfer or be disposed of or transferred to a purchaser in exchange for money or other consideration; put or be on sale. [2] to deal in (objects, property, etc.): *he sells used cars for a living.* [3] (*tr*) to give up or surrender for a price or reward: *to sell one's honour.* [4] to promote or facilitate the sale of (objects, property, etc.): *publicity sells many products.* [5] to induce or gain acceptance of: *to sell an idea.* [6] (*intr*) to be in demand on the market: *these dresses sell well in the spring.* [7] (*tr*) *Informal* to deceive or cheat. [8] (*tr; foll by on*) to persuade to accept or approve (of): *to sell a buyer on a purchase.* [9] **sell down the river.** *Informal* to betray. [10] **sell oneself. a** to convince someone else of one's potential or worth. **b** to give up one's moral or spiritual standards, etc. [11] **sell short. a** *Informal* to disparage or belittle. **b** *Finance* to sell securities or goods without owning them in anticipation of buying them before delivery at a lower price. ◆ NOUN [12] the act or an instance of selling. Compare **hard sell, soft sell.** [13] *Informal* **a** a trick, hoax, or deception. **b** *Irish* a great disappointment: *the service in the hotel was a sell.* ◆ See also **sell in, sell off, sell out, sell up.**
▷HISTORY Old English *sellan* to lend, deliver; related to Old Norse *selja* to sell, Gothic *saljan* to offer sacrifice, Old High German *sellen* to sell, Latin *cōnsilium* advice
▸ **ˈsellable** ADJECTIVE

Sellafield (ˈsɛləˌfiːld) NOUN the site of an atomic power station and nuclear reprocessing plant in NW England, in W Cumbria. Former name: **Windscale.**

sell-by date NOUN [1] a date printed on the packaging of perishable goods, indicating the date after which the goods should not be offered for sale. [2] **past one's sell-by date.** *Informal* beyond one's prime.

seller (ˈsɛlə) NOUN [1] a person who sells. [2] an article to be sold: *this item is always a good seller.* [3] short for **selling race.**

sellers' market NOUN a market in which demand exceeds supply and sellers can influence prices.

Sellers screw thread NOUN a thread form in a system of standard sizes proposed by Sellers in 1884 and later accepted as standard in the USA., having a 60° flank angle with a flat top and foot.
▷HISTORY named after William *Sellers* (1824–1905), US engineer

sell in VERB (*adverb*) [1] (*tr*) to sell (new products) to a retail outlet to be sold to the public. [2] (*intr*) to use the established system to one's advantage, rather than attempting to fight against it.

selling-plater NOUN [1] a horse that competes, or is only good enough to compete, in a selling race. [2] a person or thing of limited ability or value.

selling race *or* **plate** NOUN a horse race in which the winner must be offered for sale at auction.

sell off VERB (*tr, adverb*) to sell (remaining or unprofitable items), esp at low prices.

Sellotape (ˈsɛləˌteɪp) NOUN [1] *Trademark* a type of transparent adhesive tape made of cellulose or a similar substance. ◆ VERB [2] (*tr*) to seal or stick using adhesive tape.

sell out VERB (*adverb*) [1] Also (chiefly Brit): **sell up.** to dispose of (supplies of something) completely by selling. [2] (*tr*) *Informal* to betray, esp through a secret agreement. [3] (*intr*) *Informal* to abandon one's principles, standards, etc. ◆ NOUN **sellout.** [4] *Informal* a performance for which all tickets are sold. [5] a commercial success. [6] *Informal* a betrayal. [7] *Informal* a person who betrays their principles, standards, friends, etc.

sell-through ADJECTIVE [1] (of prerecorded video cassettes) sold without first being available for hire only. ◆ NOUN [2] the sale of prerecorded video cassettes in this way.

sell up VERB (*adverb*) *Chiefly Brit* [1] (*tr*) to sell all (the possessions or assets) of (a bankrupt debtor) in order to discharge his debts as far as possible. [2] (*intr*) to sell a business.

selsyn (ˈsɛlsɪn) NOUN another name for **synchro.**
▷HISTORY from SEL(F-) + SYN(CHRONOUS)

sel-sync (ˈsɛlˌsɪŋk) NOUN short for **selective synchronization.**

Seltzer (ˈsɛltsə) NOUN [1] a natural effervescent water with a high content of minerals. [2] a similar synthetic water, used as a beverage. Also called: **Seltzer water.**
▷HISTORY C18: changed from German *Selterser Wasser* water from (*Nieder*) *Selters,* district where mineral springs are located, near Wiesbaden, Germany

selva (ˈsɛlvə) NOUN [1] dense equatorial forest, esp in the Amazon basin, characterized by tall broad-leaved evergreen trees, epiphytes, lianas, etc. [2] a tract of such forest.
▷HISTORY C19: from Spanish and Portuguese, from Latin *silva* forest

selvage *or* **selvedge** (ˈsɛlvɪdʒ) NOUN [1] the finished nonfraying edge of a length of woven fabric. [2] a similar strip of material allowed in fabricating a metal or plastic article, used esp for handling components during manufacture.
▷HISTORY C15: from SELF + EDGE; related to Dutch *selfegghe,* German *Selbende*
▸ **ˈselvaged** ADJECTIVE

selves (sɛlvz) NOUN **a** the plural of **self. b** (*in combination*): *ourselves; yourselves; themselves.*

semanteme (sɪˈmæntiːm) NOUN another word for **sememe** (sense 2).

semantic (sɪˈmæntɪk) ADJECTIVE [1] of or relating to meaning or arising from distinctions between the meanings of different words or symbols. [2] of or relating to semantics. [3] *Logic* concerned with the interpretation of a formal theory, as when truth tables are given as an account of the sentential connectives.
▷HISTORY C19: from Greek *sēmantikos* having significance, from *sēmainein* to signify, from *sēma* a sign
▸ **seˈmantically** ADVERB

semantics (sɪˈmæntɪks) NOUN (*functioning as singular*) [1] the branch of linguistics that deals with the study of meaning, changes in meaning, and the principles that govern the relationship between sentences or words and their meanings. [2] the study of the relationships between signs and symbols and what they represent. [3] *Logic* **a** the study of interpretations of a formal theory. **b** the study of the relationship between the structure of a theory and its subject matter. **c** (of a formal theory) the principles that determine the truth or falsehood of sentences within the theory, and the references of its terms.
▸ **seˈmanticist** NOUN

semantic tableau NOUN *Logic* [1] a method of demonstrating the consistency or otherwise of a set of statements by constructing a diagrammatic representation of all the circumstances that satisfy the set of statements. [2] the diagram so constructed.

semaphore (ˈsɛməˌfɔː) NOUN [1] an apparatus for conveying information by means of visual signals, as with movable arms or railway signals, flags, etc. [2] a system of signalling by holding a flag in each hand and moving the arms to designated positions to denote each letter of the alphabet. ◆ VERB [3] to signal (information) by means of semaphore.
▷HISTORY C19: via French, from Greek *sēma* a signal + -PHORE
▸ **semaphoric** (ˌsɛməˈfɒrɪk) *or* **ˌsemaˈphorical** ADJECTIVE
▸ **ˌsemaˈphorically** ADVERB

Semarang *or* **Samarang** (səˈmɑːrɑːŋ) NOUN a port in S Indonesia, in N Java on the Java Sea. Pop.: 1 365 500 (1995 est.).

semasiology (sɪˌmeɪsɪˈɒlədʒɪ) NOUN another name for **semantics.**
▷HISTORY C19: from Greek *sēmasia* meaning, from *sēmainein* to signify + -LOGY
▸ **semasiological** (sɪˌmeɪsɪəˈlɒdʒɪkᵊl) ADJECTIVE
▸ **seˌmasioˈlogically** ADVERB ▸ **seˌmasiˈologist** NOUN

sematic (sɪˈmætɪk) ADJECTIVE (of the conspicuous coloration of certain animals) acting as a warning, esp to potential predators.
▷HISTORY C19: from Greek *sēma* a sign

sematology (ˌsɛməˈtɒlədʒɪ) NOUN another name for **semantics.**
▷HISTORY C19: from Greek *sēmat-, sēma* sign + -LOGY

semblable (ˈsɛmbləbᵊl) *Archaic* ◆ ADJECTIVE [1] resembling or similar. [2] apparent rather than real. ◆ NOUN [3] something that resembles another thing. [4] a resemblance.
▷HISTORY C14: from Old French, from *sembler* to seem; see SEMBLANCE
▸ **ˈsemblably** ADVERB

semblance (ˈsɛmbləns) NOUN [1] outward appearance, esp without any inner substance or reality. [2] a resemblance or copy.
▷HISTORY C13: from Old French, from *sembler* to seem, from Latin *simulāre* to imitate, from *similis* like

semé *or* **semée** (ˈsɛmeɪ; *French* səme) ADJECTIVE (*postpositive;* usually foll by *of*) *Heraldry* dotted (with): *semé of fleurs-de-lys gules.*
▷HISTORY C16: from French, literally: sown, from *semer* to sow, from Latin *sēmināre,* from *sēmen* seed

semei- for words beginning thus, see the more common spelling in **semi-.**

Semele (ˈsɛmɪlɪ) NOUN *Greek myth* mother of Dionysus by Zeus.

semelparous (ˈsɛməlˌpærəs) ADJECTIVE [1] Also: **hapaxanthic, monocarpic.** (of a plant) producing flowers and fruit only once before dying. [2] (of an animal) producing offspring only once during its lifetime.
▸ **ˈsemelˌparity** NOUN

sememe (ˈsiːmiːm) NOUN *Linguistics* [1] the meaning of a morpheme. [2] Also called: **semanteme.** a minimum unit of meaning in terms of which it is sometimes proposed that meaning in general might be analysed.
▷HISTORY C20 (coined in 1933 by Leonard Bloomfield (1887–1949), US linguist): from Greek *sēma* a sign + -EME

semen (ˈsiːmɛn) NOUN [1] the thick whitish fluid containing spermatozoa that is ejaculated from the male genital tract. [2] another name for **sperm**¹.
▷HISTORY C14: from Latin: seed

Semeru *or* **Semeroe** (səˈmɛruː) NOUN a volcano in Indonesia: the highest peak in Java. Height: 3676 m (12 060 ft.).

semester (sɪˈmɛstə) NOUN [1] (in some universities) either of two divisions of the academic year, ranging from 15 to 18 weeks. [2] (in German universities) a session of six months.
▷HISTORY C19: via German from Latin *sēmestris* half-yearly, from *sex* six + *mensis* a month
▸ **seˈmestral** ADJECTIVE

semi (ˈsɛmɪ) NOUN, *plural* **semis.** [1] *Brit* short for **semidetached** (house). [2] short for **semifinal.** [3] *US, Canadian, Austral, and NZ* short for **semitrailer.**

semi- PREFIX [1] half: *semicircle.* Compare **demi-** (sense 1), **hemi-.** [2] partially, partly, not completely, or almost: *semiprofessional; semifinal.* [3] occurring twice in a specified period of time: *semiannual; semiweekly.*
▷HISTORY from Latin; compare Old English *sōm-, sām-* half, Greek *hēmi-*

semiannual (ˌsɛmɪˈænjʊəl) ADJECTIVE [1] occurring every half-year. [2] lasting for half a year.
▸ˌ**semiˈannually** ADVERB

semiaquatic (ˌsɛmɪəˈkwætɪk) ADJECTIVE (of organisms, esp plants) occurring close to the water and sometimes within it.

semiarid (ˌsɛmɪˈærɪd) ADJECTIVE characterized by scanty rainfall and scrubby vegetation, often occurring in continental interiors: *the semiarid regions of Australia.*
▸ˌ**semiaˈridity** NOUN

semiautomatic (ˌsɛmɪˌɔːtəˈmætɪk) ADJECTIVE [1] partly automatic. [2] (of a firearm) self-loading but firing only one shot at each pull of the trigger. Compare **automatic** (sense 5). ◆ NOUN [3] a semiautomatic firearm.
▸ˌ**semiˌautoˈmatically** ADVERB

Semi-Bantu NOUN [1] a group of languages of W Africa, mainly SE Nigeria and Cameroon, that were not traditionally classed as Bantu but that show certain essential Bantu characteristics. They are now classed with Bantu in the Benue-Congo branch of the Niger-Congo family. ◆ ADJECTIVE [2] relating to or belonging to this group of languages.

semibold (ˌsɛmɪˈbəʊld) *Printing* ◆ ADJECTIVE [1] denoting a weight of typeface between medium and bold face. [2] denoting matter printed in this. ◆ NOUN [3] semibold type.

semibreve (ˈsɛmɪˌbriːv) NOUN *Music* a note, now the longest in common use, having a time value that may be divided by any power of 2 to give all other notes. Usual US and Canadian name: **whole note.** See also **breve** (sense 2).

semicentennial (ˌsɛmɪsɛnˈtɛnɪəl) ADJECTIVE [1] (*prenominal*) of or relating to the 50th anniversary of some event. [2] occurring once every 50 years. ◆ NOUN [3] a 50th anniversary.

semicircle (ˈsɛmɪˌsɜːkᵊl) NOUN [1] **a** one half of a circle. **b** half the circumference of a circle. [2] anything having the shape or form of half a circle.
▸**semicircular** (ˌsɛmɪˈsɜːkjʊlə) ADJECTIVE
▸ˌ**semiˈcircularly** ADVERB

semicircular canal NOUN *Anatomy* any of the three looped fluid-filled membranous tubes, at right angles to one another, that comprise the labyrinth of the ear: concerned with the sense of orientation and equilibrium.

semicolon (ˌsɛmɪˈkəʊlən) NOUN the punctuation mark (;) used to indicate a pause intermediate in value or length between that of a comma and that of a full stop.

semiconductor (ˌsɛmɪkənˈdʌktə) NOUN [1] a substance, such as germanium or silicon, that has an electrical conductivity that increases with temperature and is intermediate between that of a metal and an insulator. The behaviour may be exhibited by the pure substance (**intrinsic semiconductor**) or as a result of impurities (**extrinsic semiconductor**). [2] **a** a device, such as a transistor or integrated circuit, that depends on the properties of such a substance. **b** (*as modifier*): *a semiconductor diode.*
▸ˌ**semiconˈduction** NOUN

semiconscious (ˌsɛmɪˈkɒnʃəs) ADJECTIVE not fully conscious.
▸ˌ**semiˈconsciously** ADVERB ▸ˌ**semiˈconsciousness** NOUN

semidetached (ˌsɛmɪdɪˈtætʃt) ADJECTIVE **a** (of a building) joined to another on one side by a common wall. **b** (*as noun*): *they live in a suburban semidetached.*

semidetached binary NOUN a pair of stars that are so close together that mass transfer occurs from one to the other.

semidiurnal (ˌsɛmɪdaɪˈɜːnᵊl) ADJECTIVE [1] of or continuing during half a day. [2] occurring every 12 hours.

semidome (ˈsɛmɪˌdəʊm) NOUN a half-dome, esp one used to cover a semicircular apse.

semielliptical (ˌsɛmɪɪˈlɪptɪkᵊl) ADJECTIVE shaped like one half of an ellipse, esp one divided along the major axis.

semifinal (ˌsɛmɪˈfaɪnᵊl) NOUN **a** the round before the final in a competition. **b** (*as modifier*): *the semifinal draw.*

semifinalist (ˌsɛmɪˈfaɪnᵊlɪst) NOUN a player or team taking part in a semifinal.

semifluid (ˌsɛmɪˈfluːɪd) ADJECTIVE *also (rarely)* **semifluidic** (ˌsɛmɪfluːˈɪdɪk). [1] having properties between those of a liquid and those of a solid. ◆ NOUN [2] a substance that has such properties because of high viscosity: *tar is a semifluid.* Also: **semiliquid.**
▸ˌ**semifluˈidity** NOUN

semifreddo (ˌsɛmɪˈfrɛdəʊ) NOUN, *plural* **-dos.** a partially frozen Italian dessert similar to ice cream.
▷HISTORY Italian, literally: half cold

semiliterate (ˌsɛmɪˈlɪtərɪt) ADJECTIVE [1] hardly able to read or write. [2] able to read but not to write.

Sémillon (ˈseɪmiːjɒn; *French* semijɔ̃) NOUN [1] a white grape grown in the Bordeaux area of France and in Australia, used for making wine. [2] any of various white wines made from this grape.
▷HISTORY French

semilunar (ˌsɛmɪˈluːnə) ADJECTIVE shaped like a crescent or half-moon.

semilunar valve NOUN *Anatomy* either of two crescent-shaped valves, one in the aorta and one in the pulmonary artery, that prevent regurgitation of blood into the heart.

seminal (ˈsɛmɪnəl) ADJECTIVE [1] potentially capable of development. [2] highly original, influential and important. [3] rudimentary or unformed. [4] of or relating to semen: *seminal fluid.* [5] *Biology* of or relating to seed.
▷HISTORY C14: from Late Latin *sēminālis* belonging to seed, from Latin *sēmen* seed
▸ˌ**semiˈnality** NOUN ▸ˈ**seminally** ADVERB

seminar (ˈsɛmɪˌnɑː) NOUN [1] a small group of students meeting regularly under the guidance of a tutor, professor, etc., to exchange information, discuss theories, etc. [2] one such meeting or the place in which it is held. [3] a higher course for postgraduates. [4] any group or meeting for holding discussions or exchanging information.
▷HISTORY C19: via German from Latin *sēminārium* SEMINARY

seminarian (ˌsɛmɪˈnɛərɪən) NOUN a student at a seminary.

seminary (ˈsɛmɪnərɪ) NOUN, *plural* **-naries.** [1] an academy for the training of priests, rabbis, etc. [2] *US* another word for **seminar** (sense 1). [3] a place where something is grown.
▷HISTORY C15: from Latin *sēminārium* a nursery garden, from *sēmen* seed
▸ˌ**semiˈnarial** ADJECTIVE

semination (ˌsɛmɪˈneɪʃən) NOUN *Rare* the production, dispersal, or sowing of seed.
▷HISTORY C16: from Late Latin *sēminātiō*, from Latin *sēmināre* to sow, from *sēmen* seed

seminiferous (ˌsɛmɪˈnɪfərəs) ADJECTIVE [1] containing, conveying, or producing semen: *the seminiferous tubules of the testes.* [2] (of plants) bearing or producing seeds.
▷HISTORY C17: from Latin *sēmin-, sēmen* seed + connecting vowel + -FEROUS

Seminole (ˈsɛmɪˌnəʊl) NOUN [1] (*plural* **-noles** *or* **-nole**) a member of a North American Indian people consisting of Creeks who moved into Florida in the 18th century. [2] the language of this people, belonging to the Muskhogean family.
▷HISTORY from Creek *simanó-li* fugitive, from American Spanish *cimarrón* runaway

seminoma (ˌsɛmɪˈnəʊmə) NOUN *Pathol* a malignant tumour of the testicle.
▷HISTORY C20: from French *séminome*, from Latin *sēmen* semen + -OMA

semiochemical (ˌsɛmɪəʊˈkɛmɪkᵊl) NOUN a chemical substance produced by an animal and used in communications, such as a pheromone.
▷HISTORY C20: *semio-* from Greek *sēmeion* a sign + CHEMICAL

semiology *or* **semeiology** (ˌsɛmɪˈɒlədʒɪ, ˌsiːmɪ-) NOUN another word for **semiotics.**
▷HISTORY C17 (in the sense "sign language"): from Greek *sēmeion* sign + -LOGY
▸**semiologic** (ˌsɛmɪəˈlɒdʒɪk, ˌsiːmɪ-) ▸ˌ**semioˈlogical** *or* ˌ**semeioˈlogic** *or* ˌ**semeioˈlogical** ADJECTIVE ▸ˌ**semiˈologist** *or* ˌ**semeiˈologist** NOUN

semiotic *or* **semeiotic** (ˌsɛmɪˈɒtɪk, ˌsiːmɪ-) ADJECTIVE [1] relating to signs and symbols, esp spoken or written signs. [2] relating to semiotics. [3] of, relating to, or resembling the symptoms of disease; symptomatic.
▷HISTORY C17: from Greek *sēmeiōtikos* taking note of signs, from *sēmeion* a sign

semiotician (ˌsɛmɪəˈtɪʃən) NOUN a person who studies semiotics.

semiotics *or* **semeiotics** (ˌsɛmɪˈɒtɪks, ˌsiːmɪ-) NOUN (*functioning as singular*) [1] the study of signs and symbols, esp the relations between written or spoken signs and their referents in the physical world or the world of ideas. See also **semantics, syntactics, pragmatics.** [2] the scientific study of the symptoms of disease; symptomatology. ◆ Also called: **semiology, semeiology.**

Semipalatinsk (*Russian* sɪmipaˈlatinsk) NOUN a city in NE Kazakhstan on the Irtysh River; an important communications centre. Pop.: 269 600 (1999).

semipalmate (ˌsɛmɪˈpæmɪt) *or* **semipalmated** ADJECTIVE (of the feet of some birds) having the front three toes partly webbed.

semiparasitic (ˌsɛmɪˌpærəˈsɪtɪk) ADJECTIVE [1] (of plants, such as mistletoe) obtaining some food from a host but undergoing photosynthesis at the same time. [2] (of bacteria or fungi) usually parasitic but capable of living as a saprotroph.
▸**semiparasite** (ˌsɛmɪˈpærəsaɪt) NOUN ▸**semiparasitism** (ˌsɛmɪˈpærəsɪˌtɪzəm) NOUN

semipermeable (ˌsɛmɪˈpɜːmɪəbᵊl) ADJECTIVE (esp of a cell membrane) selectively permeable.
▸ˌ**semiˌpermeaˈbility** NOUN

semipolar bond (ˌsɛmɪˈpəʊlə) NOUN *Chem* another name for **coordinate bond.**

semiporcelain (ˌsɛmɪˈpɔːslɪn) NOUN a durable porcellaneous stoneware; stone china.

semipostal (ˌsɛmɪˈpəʊstᵊl) ADJECTIVE *Philately chiefly US* denoting stamps where all or part of the receipts from sale are given to some charitable cause.

semiprecious (ˌsɛmɪˈprɛʃəs) ADJECTIVE (of certain stones) having commercial value, but less than a precious stone.

semipro (ˈsɛmɪˌprəʊ) ADJECTIVE, NOUN, *plural* **-pros.** short for **semiprofessional.**

semiprofessional (ˌsɛmɪprəˈfɛʃənᵊl) ADJECTIVE [1] (of a person) engaged in an activity or sport part-time but for pay. [2] (of an activity or sport) engaged in by semiprofessional people. [3] of or relating to a person whose activities are professional in some respects: *a semiprofessional pianist.* ◆ NOUN [4] a semiprofessional person.
▸ˌ**semiproˈfessionally** ADVERB

semiquaver (ˈsɛmɪˌkweɪvə) NOUN *Music* a note having the time value of one-sixteenth of a semibreve. Usual US and Canadian name: **sixteenth note.**

semirigid (ˌsɛmɪˈrɪdʒɪd) ADJECTIVE [1] partly but not wholly rigid. [2] (of an airship) maintaining shape by means of a main supporting keel and internal gas pressure.

semiskilled (ˌsɛmɪˈskɪld) ADJECTIVE partly skilled or trained but not sufficiently so to perform specialized work.

semisolid (ˌsɛmɪˈsɒlɪd) ADJECTIVE [1] **a** having a viscosity and rigidity intermediate between that of a solid and a liquid. **b** partly solid. ◆ NOUN [2] a substance in this state.

semisolus (ˌsɛmɪˈsəʊləs) NOUN an advertisement that appears on the same page as another advertisement but not adjacent to it.

semisubmersible rig NOUN (in the oil industry) a type of drilling platform that floats supported by underwater pontoons, with much of its structure below the water line for stability in high winds: usually used only for exploratory drilling for oil or gas. Sometimes shortened to: **semisubmersible.**

Semite (ˈsiːmaɪt) *or less commonly* **Shemite** NOUN

1 a member of the group of Caucasoid peoples who speak a Semitic language, including the Jews and Arabs as well as the ancient Babylonians, Assyrians, and Phoenicians. 2 another word for a **Jew**.
▷HISTORY C19: from New Latin *sēmīta* descendant of Shem, via Greek *Sēm*, from Hebrew SHEM

Semitic (sɪˈmɪtɪk) *or less commonly* **Shemitic** NOUN 1 a branch or subfamily of the Afro-Asiatic family of languages that includes Arabic, Hebrew, Aramaic, Amharic, and such ancient languages as Akkadian and Phoenician. ◆ ADJECTIVE 2 denoting, relating to, or belonging to this group of languages. 3 denoting, belonging to, or characteristic of any of the peoples speaking a Semitic language, esp the Jews or the Arabs. 4 another word for **Jewish**.

Semitics (sɪˈmɪtɪks) NOUN (*functioning as singular*) the study of Semitic languages and culture.
▸**Semitist** (ˈsɛmɪtɪst) NOUN

Semito-Hamitic (ˈsɛmɪtəʊhæˈmɪtɪk) NOUN 1 a former name for the **Afro-Asiatic** family of languages. ◆ ADJECTIVE 2 denoting or belonging to this family of languages.

semitone (ˈsɛmɪˌtəʊn) NOUN an interval corresponding to a frequency difference of 100 cents as measured in the system of equal temperament, and denoting the pitch difference between certain adjacent degrees of the diatonic scale (**diatonic semitone**) or between one note and its sharpened or flattened equivalent (**chromatic semitone**); minor second. Also called (US and Canadian): **half step**. Compare **whole tone**.
▸**semitonic** (ˌsɛmɪˈtɒnɪk) ADJECTIVE ▸**ˌsemiˈtonally** ADVERB

semitrailer (ˌsɛmɪˈtreɪlə) NOUN a type of trailer or articulated lorry that has wheels only at the rear, the front end being supported by the towing vehicle.

semitropical (ˌsɛmɪˈtrɒpɪkᵊl) ADJECTIVE 1 partly tropical. 2 another word for **subtropical**.
▸**ˌsemiˈtropics** PLURAL NOUN

semivitreous (ˌsɛmɪˈvɪtrɪəs) ADJECTIVE 1 partially vitreous. 2 *Ceramics* not wholly impervious to liquid.

semivocal (ˌsɛmɪˈvəʊkᵊl) *or* **semivocalic** (ˌsɛmɪvəʊˈkælɪk) ADJECTIVE of or relating to a semivowel.

semivowel (ˈsɛmɪˌvaʊəl) NOUN *Phonetics* 1 a vowel-like sound that acts like a consonant, in that it serves the same function in a syllable carrying the same amount of prominence as a consonant relative to a true vowel, the nucleus of the syllable. In English and many other languages the chief semivowels are (w) in *well* and (j), represented as *y*, in *yell*. 2 a frictionless continuant classified as one of the liquids; (l) or (r). ◆ Also called: **glide**.

semiyearly (ˌsɛmɪˈjɪəlɪ) ADJECTIVE another word for **semiannual**.

semmit (ˈsɪmɪt, ˈsɛm-) NOUN *Scot* a vest.
▷HISTORY C15: of unknown origin

semolina (ˌsɛməˈliːnə) NOUN the large hard grains of wheat left after flour has been bolted, used for puddings, soups, etc.
▷HISTORY C18: from Italian *semolino*, diminutive of *semola* bran, from Latin *simila* very fine wheat flour

Sempach (*German* ˈzɛmpax) NOUN a village in central Switzerland, in Lucerne canton on **Lake Sempach**: scene of the victory (1386) of the Swiss over the Hapsburgs.

semper fidelis *Latin* (ˈsɛmpə fɪˈdeɪlɪs) always faithful.

semper paratus *Latin* (ˈsɛmpə pəˈrɑːtəs) always prepared.

sempervivum (ˌsɛmpəˈvaɪvəm) NOUN See **houseleek**.
▷HISTORY New Latin, from Latin *sempervivus* ever-living, from *semper* always + *vivere* to live

sempiternal (ˌsɛmpɪˈtɜːnᵊl) ADJECTIVE *Literary* everlasting; eternal.
▷HISTORY C15: from Old French *sempiternel*, from Late Latin *sempiternālis*, from Latin *sempiternus*, from *semper* always + *aeternus* ETERNAL
▸**ˌsempiˈternally** ADVERB ▸**sempiternity** (ˌsɛmpɪˈtɜːnɪtɪ) NOUN

semplice (ˈsɛmplɪtʃɪ) ADJECTIVE, ADVERB *Music* to be performed in a simple manner.
▷HISTORY Italian: simple, from Latin *simplex*

sempre (ˈsɛmprɪ) ADVERB *Music* (preceding a tempo or dynamic marking) always; consistently. It is used to indicate that a specified volume, tempo, etc., is to be sustained throughout a piece or passage.
▷HISTORY Italian: always, from Latin *semper*

sempstress (ˈsɛmpstrɪs) NOUN a rare word for **seamstress**.

Semtex (ˈsɛmtɛks) NOUN a pliable plastic explosive originally produced in the Czech Republic.
▷HISTORY C20: originally a trade name

sen (sɛn) NOUN, *plural* **sen**. a monetary unit of Brunei, worth one hundredth of a dollar, Cambodia, worth one hundredth of a riel, Indonesia, worth one hundredth of a rupiah, Malaysia, worth one hundredth of a ringgit, and formerly of Japan (where it is still used as a unit of account).
▷HISTORY C19: ultimately from Chinese *ch'ien* coin

SEN (in Britain) ABBREVIATION FOR (formerly) State Enrolled Nurse.

Sen. *or* **sen.** 1 senator. 2 senior.

sena (ˈseɪnɑː) NOUN (in India) the army: used in the names of certain paramilitary political organizations.
▷HISTORY Hindi

senarmontite (ˌsɛnɑːˈmɒntaɪt) NOUN a white or grey mineral consisting of antimony trioxide in cubic crystalline form. Formula: Sb_2O_3.
▷HISTORY C19: named after Henri de *Sénarmont* (died 1862), French mineralogist

senary (ˈsiːnərɪ) ADJECTIVE of or relating to the number six; having six parts or units.
▷HISTORY C17: from Latin *sēnārius*, from *sēnī* six each, from *sex* SIX

senate (ˈsɛnɪt) NOUN 1 any legislative or governing body considered to resemble a Senate. 2 the main governing body at some colleges and universities.
▷HISTORY C13: from Latin *senātus* council of the elders, from *senex* an old man

Senate (ˈsɛnɪt) NOUN (*sometimes not capital*) 1 the upper chamber of the legislatures of the US, Canada, Australia, and many other countries. 2 the legislative council of ancient Rome. Originally the council of the kings, the Senate became the highest legislative, judicial, and religious authority in republican Rome. 3 the ruling body of certain free cities in medieval and modern Europe.

senator (ˈsɛnətə) NOUN 1 (*often capital*) a member of a Senate or senate. 2 any legislator or statesman.

senatorial (ˌsɛnəˈtɔːrɪəl) ADJECTIVE 1 of, relating to, befitting, or characteristic of a senator. 2 composed of senators. 3 *Chiefly US* electing or entitled to representation by a senator: *senatorial districts*.
▸**ˌsenaˈtorially** ADVERB

senatus consultum *Latin* (səˈnɑːtəs kənˈsʊltəm) NOUN, *plural* ***senatus consulta*** (kənˈsʊltə). a decree of the Senate of ancient Rome, taking the form of advice to a magistrate.

send[1] (sɛnd) VERB **sends, sending, sent**. 1 (*tr*) to cause or order (a person or thing) to be taken, directed, or transmitted to another place: *to send a letter; she sent the salesman away*. 2 (when *intr*, foll by *for*; when *tr*, *takes an infinitive*) to dispatch a request or command (for something or to do something): *he sent for a bottle of wine; he sent to his son to come home*. 3 (*tr*) to direct or cause to go to a place or point: *his blow sent the champion to the floor*. 4 (*tr*) to bring to a state or condition: *this noise will send me mad*. 5 (*tr*; often foll by *forth, out*, etc.) to cause to issue; emit: *his cooking sent forth a lovely smell from the kitchen*. 6 (*tr*) to cause to happen or come: *misery sent by fate*. 7 to transmit (a message) by radio, esp in the form of pulses. 8 (*tr*) *Slang* to move to excitement or rapture: *this music really sends me*. 9 **send (someone) about his** *or* **her business**. to dismiss or get rid of (someone). 10 **send (someone) packing**. to dismiss or get rid of (someone) peremptorily. ◆ NOUN 11 another word for **swash** (sense 4). ◆ See also **send down, sendoff, send up**.
▷HISTORY Old English *sendan*; related to Old Norse *senda*, Gothic *sandjan*, Old High German *senten*
▸**ˈsendable** ADJECTIVE ▸**ˈsender** NOUN

send[2] (sɛnd) VERB **sends, sending, sent**, NOUN a variant spelling of **scend**.

Sendai (sɛnˈdaɪ) NOUN a city in central Japan, on NE Honshu: university (1907). Pop.: 971 263 (1995).

sendal (ˈsɛndᵊl) NOUN 1 a fine silk fabric used, esp in the Middle Ages, for ceremonial clothing, etc. 2 a garment of such fabric.
▷HISTORY C13: from Old French *cendal*, from Medieval Latin *cendalum*; probably related to Greek *sindon* fine linen

send down VERB (*tr, adverb*) *Brit* 1 to expel from a university, esp permanently. 2 *Informal* to send to prison.

sendoff (ˈsɛndˌɒf) NOUN *Informal* 1 a demonstration of good wishes to a person about to set off on a journey, new career, etc. 2 a start, esp an auspicious one, to a venture. ◆ VERB **send off**. (*tr, adverb*) 3 to cause to depart; despatch. 4 *Sport* (of the referee) to dismiss (a player) from the field of play for some offence. 5 *Informal* to give a sendoff to.

send up VERB (*tr, adverb*) 1 *Slang* to send to prison. 2 *Brit informal* to make fun of, esp by doing an imitation or parody of: *he sent up the teacher marvellously*. ◆ NOUN **send-up**. 3 *Brit informal* a parody or imitation.

Seneca (ˈsɛnɪkə) NOUN 1 (*plural* **-cas** *or* **-ca**) a member of a North American Indian people formerly living south of Lake Ontario; one of the Iroquois peoples. 2 the language of this people, belonging to the Iroquoian family.
▷HISTORY C19: from Dutch *Sennecaas* (plural), probably of Algonquian origin

senecio (sɪˈniːʃɪəʊ) NOUN, *plural* **-cios**. any plant of the genus *Senecio*, including groundsels, ragworts, and cinerarias: family *Asteraceae* (composites).

senega (ˈsɛnɪɡə) NOUN 1 a milkwort plant, *Polygala senega*, of the eastern US, with small white flowers. 2 the root of this plant, used as an expectorant. ◆ Also called: **senega snakeroot, seneca snakeroot**.
▷HISTORY C18: variant of *Seneca* (the Indian tribe)

Senegal (ˌsɛnɪˈɡɔːl) NOUN a republic in West Africa, on the Atlantic: made part of French West Africa in 1895; became fully independent in 1960; mostly low-lying, with semidesert in the north and tropical forest in the southwest. Official language: French. Religion: Muslim majority. Currency: franc. Capital: Dakar. Pop.: 10 285 000 (2001 est.). Area: 197 160 sq. km (76 124 sq. miles).

Senegalese (ˌsɛnɪɡəˈliːz) ADJECTIVE 1 of or relating to Senegal or its inhabitants. ◆ NOUN 2 a native or inhabitant of Senegal.

Senegambia (ˌsɛnəˈɡæmbɪə) NOUN a region of W Africa, between the Senegal and Gambia Rivers: now mostly in Senegal.

Senegambia Confederation NOUN an economic and political union (1982–89) between Senegal and The Gambia.

senescent (sɪˈnɛsᵊnt) ADJECTIVE 1 growing old. 2 characteristic of old age.
▷HISTORY C17: from Latin *senēscere* to grow old, from *senex* old
▸**seˈnescence** NOUN

seneschal (ˈsɛnɪʃəl) NOUN 1 a steward of the household of a medieval prince or nobleman who took charge of domestic arrangements, etc. 2 *Brit* a cathedral official.
▷HISTORY C14: from Old French, from Medieval Latin *siniscalcus*, of Germanic origin; related to Old High German *senescalh* oldest servant, from *sene-* old + *scalh* a servant

senile (ˈsiːnaɪl) ADJECTIVE 1 of, relating to, or characteristic of old age. 2 mentally or physically weak or infirm on account of old age. 3 (of land forms or rivers) at an advanced stage in the cycle of erosion. See **old** (sense 18).
▷HISTORY C17: from Latin *senīlis*, from *senex* an old man
▸**ˈsenilely** ADVERB ▸**senility** (sɪˈnɪlɪtɪ) NOUN

senile dementia NOUN dementia starting in old age with no precipitating physical cause.

senior (ˈsiːnjə) ADJECTIVE 1 higher in rank or length of service. 2 older in years: *senior citizens*. 3 of or relating to adulthood, maturity, or old age: *senior privileges*. 4 *Education* **a** of, relating to, or designating more advanced or older pupils. **b** of or relating to a secondary school. 5 *US* of, relating to,

or designating students in the fourth and final year at college. ◆ NOUN [6] a senior person. [7] an elderly person. [8] **a** a senior pupil, student, etc. **b** a fellow of senior rank in an English university.
▷HISTORY C14: from Latin: older, from *senex* old

Senior ('siːnjə) ADJECTIVE *Chiefly US* being the older: used to distinguish the father from the son with the same first name or names: *Charles Parker, Senior.* Abbreviations: **Sr, Sen.**

senior aircraftman NOUN a rank in the Royal Air Force comparable to that of a private in the army, though not the lowest rank in the Royal Air Force.

senior citizen NOUN an old age pensioner.

senior common room NOUN (in British universities, colleges, etc.) a common room for the use of academic staff. Compare **junior common room.**

seniority (ˌsiːnɪ'ɒrɪtɪ) NOUN, *plural* **-ties.** [1] the state of being senior. [2] precedence in rank, etc., due to senior status.

senior management NOUN another term for **top management.**

senior moment NOUN *Jocular* a lapse of memory common in elderly people.

senior service NOUN *Brit* the Royal Navy.

Senlac ('sɛnlæk) NOUN a hill in Sussex: site of the Battle of Hastings in 1066.

senna ('sɛnə) NOUN [1] any of various tropical plants of the leguminous genus *Cassia*, esp *C. angustifolia* (**Arabian senna**) and *C. acutifolia* (**Alexandrian senna**), having typically yellow flowers and long pods. [2] **senna leaf.** the dried leaflets of any of these plants, used as a cathartic and laxative. ◆ See also **bladder senna.**
▷HISTORY C16: via New Latin from Arabic *sanā*

Sennar ('sɛnɑː, sɛ'nɑː) NOUN [1] a region of the E Sudan, between the White Nile and the Blue Nile: a kingdom from the 16th to 19th centuries. [2] a town in this region, on the Blue Nile: the nearby **Sennar Dam** (1925) supplies irrigation water to Gezira. Pop.: 8000 (latest est.).

sennet ('sɛnɪt) NOUN a fanfare: used as a stage direction in Elizabethan drama.
▷HISTORY C16: probably variant of SIGNET (meaning "a sign")

sennight *or* **se'nnight** ('sɛnaɪt) NOUN an archaic word for **week.**
▷HISTORY Old English *seofan nihte;* see SEVEN, NIGHT

sennit ('sɛnɪt) NOUN [1] a flat braided cordage used on ships. [2] plaited straw, grass, palm leaves, etc., as for making hats.
▷HISTORY C17: of unknown origin

señor (sɛ'njɔː; *Spanish* se'ɲor) NOUN, *plural* **-ñors** *or* **-ñores** (*Spanish* -'ɲores). a Spaniard or Spanish-speaking man: a title of address equivalent to *Mr* when placed before a name or *sir* when used alone.
▷HISTORY Spanish, from Latin *senior* an older man, SENIOR

señora (sɛ'njɔːrə; *Spanish* se'ɲora) NOUN, *plural* **-ras** (-rəz; *Spanish* -ras). a married Spanish or Spanish-speaking woman: a title of address equivalent to *Mrs* when placed before a name or *madam* when used alone.

señorita (ˌsɛnjɔː'riːtə; *Spanish* seɲo'rita) NOUN, *plural* **-tas** (-təz; *Spanish* -tas). an unmarried Spanish or Spanish-speaking woman: a title of address equivalent to *Miss* when placed before a name or *madam* or *miss* when used alone.

sensate ('sɛnseɪt) ADJECTIVE [1] perceived by the senses. [2] *Obsolete* having the power of sensation.
▷HISTORY C16: from Late Latin *sensātus* endowed with sense, from Latin *sensus* SENSE
▸'**sensately** ADVERB

sensation (sɛn'seɪʃən) NOUN [1] the power of perceiving through the senses. [2] a physical condition or experience resulting from the stimulation of one of the sense organs: *a sensation of warmth.* [3] a general feeling or awareness: *a sensation of fear.* [4] a state of widespread public excitement: *his announcement caused a sensation.* [5] anything that causes such a state: *your speech was a sensation.*
▷HISTORY C17: from Medieval Latin *sensātiō,* from Late Latin *sensātus* SENSATE
▸**sen'sationless** ADJECTIVE

sensational (sɛn'seɪʃənᵊl) ADJECTIVE [1] causing or intended to cause intense feelings, esp of curiosity, horror, etc.: *sensational disclosures in the press.* [2] *Informal* extremely good: *a sensational skater.* [3] of or relating to the faculty of sensation. [4] *Philosophy* of or relating to sensationalism.
▸**sen'sationally** ADVERB

sensationalism (sɛn'seɪʃənᵊˌlɪzəm) NOUN [1] the use of sensational language, etc., to arouse an intense emotional response. [2] such sensational matter itself. [3] *Philosophy* **a** the doctrine that knowledge cannot go beyond the analysis of experience. **b** *Ethics* the doctrine that the ability to gratify the senses is the only criterion of goodness. [4] *Psychol* the theory that all experience and mental life may be explained in terms of sensations and remembered images. [5] *Aesthetics* the theory of the beauty of sensuality in the arts. ◆ Also called (for senses 3, 4): **sensationism.**
▸**sen'sationalist** NOUN, ADJECTIVE ▸**senˌsational'istic** ADJECTIVE

sensationalize *or* **sensationalise** (sɛn'seɪʃənəˌlaɪz) VERB (*tr*) to cause (events, esp in newspaper reports) to seem more vivid, shocking, etc., than they really are.

sense (sɛns) NOUN [1] any of the faculties by which the mind receives information about the external world or about the state of the body. In addition to the five traditional faculties of sight, hearing, touch, taste, and smell, the term includes the means by which bodily position, temperature, pain, balance, etc., are perceived. [2] such faculties collectively; the ability to perceive. [3] a feeling perceived through one of the senses: *a sense of warmth.* [4] a mental perception or awareness: *a sense of happiness.* [5] moral discernment; understanding: *a sense of right and wrong.* [6] (*sometimes plural*) sound practical judgment or intelligence: *he is a man without any sense.* [7] reason or purpose: *what is the sense of going out in the rain?* [8] substance or gist; meaning: *what is the sense of this proverb?* [9] specific meaning; definition: *in what sense are you using the word?* [10] an opinion or consensus. [11] *Maths* one of two opposite directions measured on a directed line; the sign as contrasted with the magnitude of a vector. [12] **make sense.** to be reasonable or understandable. [13] *Logic, linguistics* **a** the import of an expression as contrasted with its referent. Thus *the morning star* and *the evening star* have the same reference, Venus, but different senses. **b** the property of an expression by virtue of which its referent is determined. **c** that which one grasps in understanding an expression. [14] take leave of one's senses. See **leave²** (sense 8). ◆ VERB (*tr*) [15] to perceive through one or more of the senses. [16] to apprehend or detect without or in advance of the evidence of the senses. [17] to understand. [18] *Computing* **a** to test or locate the position of (a part of computer hardware). **b** to read (data).
▷HISTORY C14: from Latin *sēnsus,* from *sentīre* to feel

sense datum NOUN *Philosophy* a sensation detached both from any information it may convey and from its putative source in the external world, such as the bare awareness of a red visual field. Sense data are held by some philosophers to be the immediate objects of experience providing certain knowledge from which knowledge of material objects is inferred. See also **representationalism** (sense 1), **apriorism.**

sensei *Japanese* ('sɛnseɪ) NOUN a teacher or instructor, esp of karate or judo.
▷HISTORY Japanese: teacher, leader

senseless ('sɛnslɪs) ADJECTIVE [1] lacking in sense; foolish: *a senseless plan.* [2] lacking in feeling; unconscious. [3] lacking in perception; stupid.
▸'**senselessly** ADVERB ▸'**senselessness** NOUN

sense organ NOUN a structure in animals that is specialized for receiving external or internal stimuli and transmitting them in the form of nervous impulses to the brain.

sensibilia (ˌsɛnsɪ'bɪlɪə) NOUN that which can be sensed.
▷HISTORY Latin, neuter plural of *sensibilis* SENSIBLE

sensibility (ˌsɛnsɪ'bɪlɪtɪ) NOUN, *plural* **-ties.** [1] the ability to perceive or feel. [2] (*often plural*) the capacity for responding to emotion, impression, etc. [3] (*often plural*) the capacity for responding to aesthetic stimuli. [4] mental responsiveness; discernment; awareness. [5] (*usually plural*) emotional or moral feelings: *cruelty offends most people's sensibilities.* [6] the condition of a plant of being susceptible to external influences, esp attack by parasites.

sensible ('sɛnsɪbᵊl) ADJECTIVE [1] having or showing good sense or judgment: *a sensible decision.* [2] (of clothing) serviceable; practical: *sensible shoes.* [3] having the capacity for sensation; sensitive. [4] capable of being apprehended by the senses. [5] perceptible to the mind. [6] (sometimes foll by *of*) having perception; aware: *sensible of your kindness.* [7] readily perceived; considerable: *a sensible difference.* ◆ NOUN [8] Also called: **sensible note.** a less common term for **leading note.**
▷HISTORY C14: from Old French, from Late Latin *sēnsibilis,* from Latin *sentīre* to sense
▸'**sensibleness** NOUN ▸'**sensibly** ADVERB

sensible horizon NOUN See **horizon** (sense 2a).

sensillum (sɛn'sɪləm) NOUN, *plural* **-la** (-lə). a sense organ in insects, typically consisting of a receptor organ in the integument connected to sensory neurons.
▷HISTORY New Latin, diminutive of Latin *sensus* sense (Middle Latin: sense organ)

sensitive ('sɛnsɪtɪv) ADJECTIVE [1] having the power of sensation. [2] responsive to or aware of feelings, moods, reactions, etc. [3] easily irritated; delicate: *sensitive skin.* [4] affected by external conditions or stimuli. [5] easily offended. [6] of or relating to the senses or the power of sensation. [7] capable of registering small differences or changes in amounts, quality, etc.: *a sensitive instrument.* [8] *Photog* having a high sensitivity: *a sensitive emulsion.* [9] connected with matters affecting national security, esp through access to classified information. [10] (of a stock market or prices) quickly responsive to external influences and thus fluctuating or tending to fluctuate.
▷HISTORY C14: from Medieval Latin *sēnsitīvus,* from Latin *sentīre* to feel
▸'**sensitively** ADVERB ▸'**sensitiveness** NOUN

sensitive plant NOUN [1] a tropical American mimosa plant, *Mimosa pudica,* the leaflets and stems of which fold if touched. [2] any similar plant, such as the leguminous plant *Cassia nictitans* of E North America. [3] *Informal* a person who is easily upset.

sensitivity (ˌsɛnsɪ'tɪvɪtɪ) NOUN, *plural* **-ties.** [1] the state or quality of being sensitive. [2] *Physiol* the state, condition, or quality of reacting or being sensitive to an external stimulus, drug, allergen, etc. [3] *Electronics* the magnitude or time of response of an instrument, circuit, etc., to an input signal, such as a current. [4] *Photog* the degree of response of an emulsion to light or other actinic radiation, esp to light of a particular colour, expressed in terms of its speed.

sensitize *or* **sensitise** ('sɛnsɪˌtaɪz) VERB [1] to make or become sensitive. [2] (*tr*) to render (an individual) sensitive to a drug, allergen, etc. [3] (*tr*) *Photog* to make (a material) sensitive to light or to other actinic radiation, esp to light of a particular colour, by coating it with a photographic emulsion often containing special chemicals, such as dyes.
▸ˌ**sensiti'zation** *or* ˌ**sensiti'sation** NOUN ▸'**sensiˌtizer** *or* '**sensiˌtiser** NOUN

sensitometer (ˌsɛnsɪ'tɒmɪtə) NOUN an instrument for measuring the sensitivity to light of a photographic material over a range of exposures.
▸ˌ**sensi'tometry** NOUN

sensor ('sɛnsə) NOUN anything, such as a photoelectric cell, that receives a signal or stimulus and responds to it.
▷HISTORY C19: from Latin *sēnsus* perceived, from *sentīre* to observe

sensorimotor (ˌsɛnsərɪ'məʊtə) *or* **sensomotor** (ˌsɛnsə'məʊtə) ADJECTIVE of or relating to both the sensory and motor functions of an organism or to the nerves controlling them.

sensorium (sɛn'sɔːrɪəm) NOUN, *plural* **-riums** *or* **-ria** (-rɪə). [1] the area of the brain considered responsible for receiving and integrating sensations from the outside world. [2] *Physiol* the entire sensory and intellectual apparatus of the body.
▷HISTORY C17: from Late Latin, from Latin *sēnsus* felt, from *sentīre* to perceive

sensory ('sɛnsərɪ) *or less commonly* **sensorial** (sɛn'sɔːrɪəl) ADJECTIVE [1] of or relating to the senses

or the power of sensation. 2 of or relating to those processes and structures within an organism that receive stimuli from the environment and convey them to the brain.
▷HISTORY C18: from Latin *sensōrius,* from *sentīre* to feel

sensory deprivation NOUN *Psychol* an experimental situation in which all stimulation is cut off from the sensory receptors.

sensual ('sɛnsjʊəl) ADJECTIVE 1 of or relating to any of the senses or sense organs; bodily. 2 strongly or unduly inclined to gratification of the senses. 3 tending to arouse the bodily appetites, esp the sexual appetite. 4 of or relating to sensualism.
▷HISTORY C15: from Late Latin *sensuālis,* from Latin *sēnsus* SENSE. Compare French *sensuel,* Italian *sensuale*
▸**'sensually** ADVERB ▸**'sensualness** NOUN

sensualism ('sɛnsjʊəˌlɪzəm) NOUN 1 the quality or state of being sensual. 2 another word for **sensationalism** (senses 3a, 3b).

sensuality (ˌsɛnsjʊ'ælɪtɪ) NOUN, *plural* **-ties.** 1 the quality or state of being sensual. 2 excessive indulgence in sensual pleasures.
▸**sensualist** ('sɛnsjʊəlɪst) NOUN

sensum ('sɛnsəm) NOUN, *plural* **-sa** (-sə). another word for **sense datum.**

sensuous ('sɛnsjʊəs) ADJECTIVE 1 aesthetically pleasing to the senses. 2 appreciative of or moved by qualities perceived by the senses. 3 of, relating to, or derived from the senses.
▷HISTORY C17: apparently coined by Milton to avoid the unwanted overtones of SENSUAL; not in common use until C19: from Latin *sēnsus* SENSE + -OUS
▸**'sensuously** ADVERB ▸**'sensuousness** NOUN

Sensurround ('sɛnsəˌraʊnd) NOUN *Trademark* a sound reproduction system used esp in cinemas, in which low-frequency output causes bodily sensations in the audience, resulting in a feeling of involvement in the film.

sent[1] (sɛnt) VERB the past tense and past participle of **send**[1] and **send**[2].

sent[2] (sɛnt) NOUN, *plural* **-ti.** a monetary unit of Estonia, worth one hundredth of a kroon.
▷HISTORY C19: ultimately from Chinese *ch'ien* coin

sentence ('sɛntəns) NOUN 1 a sequence of words capable of standing alone to make an assertion, ask a question, or give a command, usually consisting of a subject and a predicate containing a finite verb. 2 the judgment formally pronounced upon a person convicted in criminal proceedings, esp the decision as to what punishment is to be imposed. 3 an opinion, judgment, or decision. 4 *Music* another word for **period** (sense 11). 5 any short passage of scripture employed in liturgical use: *the funeral sentences.* 6 *Logic* a well-formed expression, without variables. 7 *Archaic* a proverb, maxim, or aphorism. ◆ VERB 8 (*tr*) to pronounce sentence on (a convicted person) in a court of law: *the judge sentenced the murderer to life imprisonment.*
▷HISTORY C13: via Old French from Latin *sententia* a way of thinking, from *sentīre* to feel
▸**sentential** (sɛn'tɛnʃəl) ADJECTIVE ▸**sen'tentially** ADVERB

sentence connector NOUN a word or phrase that introduces a clause or sentence and serves as a transition between it and a previous clause or sentence, as for example *also* in *I'm buying eggs and also I'm looking for a dessert for tonight.* It may be preceded by a coordinating conjunction such as *and* in the above example.

sentence stress NOUN the stress given to a word or words in a sentence, often conveying nuances of meaning or emphasis.

sentence substitute NOUN a word or phrase, esp one traditionally classified as an adverb, that is used in place of a finite sentence, such as *yes, no, certainly,* and *never.*

sentencing circle NOUN a method of dispensing justice amongst native Canadian peoples involving discussion between offenders, victims, and members of the community.

sentential calculus NOUN *Logic* the formal theory the intended interpretation of which concerns the logical relations between sentences treated only as a whole and without regard to their internal structure.

sentential function NOUN another name for **open sentence.**

sententious (sɛn'tɛnʃəs) ADJECTIVE 1 characterized by or full of aphorisms, terse pithy sayings, or axioms. 2 constantly using aphorisms, etc. 3 tending to indulge in pompous moralizing.
▷HISTORY C15: from Latin *sententiōsus* full of meaning, from *sententia;* see SENTENCE
▸**sen'tentiously** ADVERB ▸**sen'tentiousness** NOUN

sentience ('sɛnʃəns) *or* **sentiency** NOUN 1 the state or quality of being sentient; awareness. 2 sense perception not involving intelligence or mental perception; feeling.

sentient ('sɛntɪənt) ADJECTIVE 1 having the power of sense perception or sensation; conscious. ◆ NOUN 2 *Rare* a sentient person or thing.
▷HISTORY C17: from Latin *sentiēns* feeling, from *sentīre* to perceive
▸**'sentiently** ADVERB

sentiment ('sɛntɪmənt) NOUN 1 susceptibility to tender, delicate, or romantic emotion: *she has too much sentiment to be successful.* 2 (*often plural*) a thought, opinion, or attitude. 3 exaggerated, overindulged, or mawkish feeling or emotion. 4 an expression of response to deep feeling, esp in art or literature. 5 a feeling, emotion, or awareness: *a sentiment of pity.* 6 a mental attitude modified or determined by feeling: *there is a strong revolutionary sentiment in his country.* 7 a feeling conveyed, or intended to be conveyed, in words.
▷HISTORY C17: from Medieval Latin *sentīmentum,* from Latin *sentīre* to feel

sentimental (ˌsɛntɪ'mɛntᵊl) ADJECTIVE 1 tending to indulge the emotions excessively. 2 making a direct appeal to the emotions, esp to romantic feelings. 3 relating to or characterized by sentiment.
▸**ˌsenti'mentally** ADVERB

sentimentalism (ˌsɛntɪ'mɛntᵊˌlɪzəm) NOUN 1 the state or quality of being sentimental. 2 an act, statement, etc., that is sentimental.
▸**ˌsenti'mentalist** NOUN

sentimentality (ˌsɛntɪmɛn'tælɪtɪ) NOUN, *plural* **-ties.** 1 the state, quality, or an instance of being sentimental. 2 an act, statement, etc., that is sentimental.

sentimentalize *or* **sentimentalise** (ˌsɛntɪ'mɛntᵊˌlaɪz) VERB to make sentimental or behave sentimentally.
▸**ˌsentiˌmentali'zation** *or* **ˌsentiˌmentali'sation** NOUN

sentimental value NOUN the value of an article in terms of its sentimental associations for a particular person.

sentinel ('sɛntɪnᵊl) NOUN 1 a person, such as a sentry, assigned to keep guard. 2 *Computing* a character used to indicate the beginning or end of a particular block of information. ◆ VERB **-nels, -nelling, -nelled.** (*tr*) 3 to guard as a sentinel. 4 to post as a sentinel. 5 to provide with a sentinel.
▷HISTORY C16: from Old French *sentinelle,* from Old Italian *sentinella,* from *sentina* watchfulness, from *sentire* to notice, from Latin

sentry ('sɛntrɪ) NOUN, *plural* **-tries.** 1 a soldier who guards or prevents unauthorized access to a place, keeps watch for danger, etc. 2 the watch kept by a sentry.
▷HISTORY C17: perhaps shortened from obsolete *centrinel,* C16 variant of SENTINEL

sentry box NOUN a small shelter with an open front in which a sentry may stand to be sheltered from the weather.

Senussi *or* **Senusi** (sɛ'nuːsɪ) NOUN, *plural* **-sis.** a member of a zealous and aggressive Muslim sect of North Africa and Arabia, founded in 1837 by **Sidi Mohammed ibn Ali al Senussi** (?1787–1859).
▸**Se'nussian** *or* **Se'nusian** ADJECTIVE

senza ('sɛntsɑː) PREPOSITION *Music* without; omitting.
▷HISTORY Italian

Seoul (səʊl) NOUN the capital of South Korea, in the west on the Han River: capital of Korea from 1392 to 1910, then seat of the Japanese administration until 1945; became capital of South Korea in 1948; cultural and educational centre. Pop.: 10 229 262 (1995).

SEPA ABBREVIATION FOR Scottish Environment Protection Agency.

sepal ('sɛpᵊl) NOUN any of the separate parts of the calyx of a flower.
▷HISTORY C19: from New Latin *sepalum: sep-,* from Greek *skepē* a covering + *-alum,* from New Latin *petalum* PETAL
▸**'sepalled** *or* **sepalous** ('sɛpələs) ADJECTIVE

sepaloid ('siːpəˌlɔɪd) *or* **sepaline** ADJECTIVE (esp of petals) resembling a sepal in structure and function.

-sepalous ADJECTIVE COMBINING FORM having sepals of a specified type or number: *polysepalous.*
▸**-sepaly** NOUN COMBINING FORM

separable ('sɛpərəbᵊl, 'sɛprəbᵊl) ADJECTIVE able to be separated, divided, or parted.
▸**ˌsepara'bility** *or* **'separableness** NOUN ▸**'separably** ADVERB

separate VERB ('sɛpəˌreɪt) 1 (*tr*) to act as a barrier between: *a range of mountains separates the two countries.* 2 to put or force or be put or forced apart. 3 to part or be parted from a mass or group. 4 (*tr*) to discriminate between: *to separate the men from the boys.* 5 to divide or be divided into component parts; sort or be sorted. 6 to sever or be severed. 7 (*intr*) (of a married couple) to cease living together by mutual agreement or after obtaining a decree of judicial separation. ◆ ADJECTIVE ('sɛprɪt, 'sɛpərɪt) 8 existing or considered independently: *a separate problem.* 9 disunited or apart. 10 set apart from the main body or mass. 11 distinct, individual, or particular. 12 solitary or withdrawn. 13 (*sometimes capital*) designating or relating to a Church or similar institution that has ceased to have associations with an original parent organization.
▷HISTORY C15: from Latin *sēparāre,* from *sē-* apart + *parāre* to obtain
▸**'separately** ADVERB ▸**'separateness** NOUN

separates ('sɛprɪts, 'sɛpərɪts) PLURAL NOUN women's outer garments that only cover part of the body and so are worn in combination with others, usually unmatching; skirts, blouses, jackets, trousers, etc. Compare **coordinates.**

separate school NOUN (in Canada) a school for a large religious minority financed by its rates and administered by its own school board but under the authority of the provincial department of education.

separating funnel NOUN *Chem* a large funnel having a tap in its output tube, used to separate immiscible liquids.

separation (ˌsɛpə'reɪʃən) NOUN 1 the act of separating or state of being separated. 2 the place or line where a separation is made. 3 a gap that separates. 4 *Family law* the cessation of cohabitation between a man and wife, either by mutual agreement or under a decree of a court. See **judicial separation.** Compare **divorce.** 5 **a** the act of jettisoning a burnt-out stage of a multistage rocket. **b** the instant at which such a stage is jettisoned.

separatist ('sɛpərətɪst, 'sɛprə-) *or* **separationist** NOUN **a** a person who advocates or practises secession from an organization or group. **b** (*as modifier*): *a separatist movement.*
▸**'separaˌtism** NOUN ▸**ˌsepara'tistic** ADJECTIVE

Separatist ('sɛpərətɪst, 'sɛprə-) NOUN (*sometimes not capital*) a person who advocates the secession of a province, esp Quebec, from Canada.
▸**'Separaˌtism** NOUN

separative ('sɛpərətɪv, 'sɛprə-) ADJECTIVE tending to separate or causing separation.
▸**'separatively** ADVERB ▸**'separativeness** NOUN

separator ('sɛpəˌreɪtə) NOUN 1 a person or thing that separates. 2 a device for separating things into constituent parts, as milk into cream, etc.
▸**'separatory** ADJECTIVE

separatrix ('sɛpəˌreɪtrɪks) NOUN, *plural* **separatrices** (ˌsɛpə'reɪtrɪˌsiːz). another name for **solidus** (sense 1).
▷HISTORY via New Latin from Late Latin, feminine of *sēparātor* one that separates

Sephardi (sɪ'fɑːdiː) NOUN, *plural* **-dim** (-dɪm). *Judaism* 1 **a** a Jew of Spanish, Portuguese, or North African descent. **b** (loosely) any Oriental Jew. 2 the pronunciation of Hebrew used by these Jews, and of Modern Hebrew as spoken in Israel. 3 (*modifier*) of or pertaining to the Sephardim, esp to their liturgy and ritual. 4 (*modifier*) of or pertaining to the liturgy adopted by certain European, esp Chassidic, communities who believe it to be more

authentic but nonetheless differing from the genuine Oriental liturgy. ◆ Compare **Ashkenazi.**
▷**HISTORY** C19: from Late Hebrew, from Hebrew *sepharad* a region mentioned in Obadiah 20, thought to have been Spain
▸**Se'phardic** ADJECTIVE

sepia ('si:pɪə) NOUN [1] a dark reddish-brown pigment obtained from the inky secretion of the cuttlefish. [2] any cuttlefish of the genus *Sepia*. [3] a brownish tone imparted to a photograph, esp an early one such as a calotype. It can be produced by first bleaching a print (after fixing) and then immersing it for a short time in a solution of sodium sulphide or of alkaline thiourea. [4] a brownish-grey to dark yellowish-brown colour. [5] a drawing or photograph in sepia. ◆ ADJECTIVE [6] of the colour sepia or done in sepia: *a sepia print.*
▷**HISTORY** C16: from Latin: a cuttlefish, from Greek; related to Greek *sēpein* to make rotten

sepiolite ('si:pɪəˌlaɪt) NOUN another name for **meerschaum** (sense 1).
▷**HISTORY** C19: from German *Sepiolith,* from Greek *sēpion* bone of a cuttlefish; see SEPIA, -LITE

sepmag ('sɛpˌmæg) ADJECTIVE designating a film or television programme for which the sound is recorded on separate magnetic material and run in synchronism with the picture.
▷**HISTORY** C20: from SEP(ARATE) + MAG(NETIC)

sepoy ('si:pɔɪ) NOUN (formerly) an Indian soldier in the service of the British.
▷**HISTORY** C18: from Portuguese *sipaio,* from Urdu *sipāhī,* from Persian: horseman, from *sipāh* army

Sepoy Rebellion *or* **Mutiny** NOUN the Indian Mutiny of 1857–58.

seppuku (sɛ'pu:ku:) NOUN another word for **hara-kiri.**
▷**HISTORY** from Japanese, from Chinese *ch'ieh* to cut + *fu* bowels

sepsis ('sɛpsɪs) NOUN the presence of pus-forming bacteria in the body.
▷**HISTORY** C19: via New Latin from Greek *sēpsis* a rotting; related to Greek *sēpein* to cause to decay

sept (sɛpt) NOUN [1] *Anthropol* a clan or group that believes itself to be descended from a common ancestor. [2] a branch of a tribe or nation, esp in medieval Ireland or Scotland.
▷**HISTORY** C16: perhaps variant of SECT

Sept. ABBREVIATION FOR: [1] September. [2] Septuagint.

septa ('sɛptə) NOUN the plural of **septum.**

septal ('sɛptəl) ADJECTIVE of or relating to a septum.

septarium (sɛp'tɛərɪəm) NOUN, *plural* **-ia** (-ɪə). a mass of mineral substance having cracks filled with another mineral, esp calcite.
▷**HISTORY** C18: from New Latin, from Latin SEPTUM
▸**sep'tarian** ADJECTIVE

septate ('sɛpteɪt) ADJECTIVE divided by septa: *a septate plant ovary.*
▷**HISTORY** C19: from New Latin *septātus* having a SEPTUM

septavalent (ˌsɛptə'veɪlənt) ADJECTIVE *Chem* another word for **heptavalent.**
▷**HISTORY** C19: from SEPT(IVALENT) + (HEPT)AVALENT

September (sɛp'tɛmbə) NOUN the ninth month of the year, consisting of 30 days.
▷**HISTORY** Old English, from Latin: the seventh (month) according to the original calendar of ancient Rome, from *septem* seven

September Massacre NOUN (during the French Revolution) the massacre of royalist prisoners and others in Paris between Sept. 2 and 6, 1792.

Septembrist (sɛp'tɛmbrɪst) NOUN *French history* a person who took part in the September Massacre.

septenary ('sɛptɪnərɪ) ADJECTIVE [1] of or relating to the number seven. [2] forming a group of seven. [3] another word for **septennial.** ◆ NOUN, *plural* **-naries.** [4] the number seven. [5] a group of seven things. [6] a period of seven years. [7] *Prosody* a line of seven metrical feet.
▷**HISTORY** C16: from Latin *septēnārius,* from *septēnī* seven each, from *septem* seven

septennial (sɛp'tɛnɪəl) ADJECTIVE [1] occurring every seven years. [2] relating to or lasting seven years.
▷**HISTORY** C17: from Latin *septennis,* from *septem* seven + *annus* a year
▸**sep'tennially** ADVERB

septennium (sɛp'tɛnɪəm) NOUN, *plural* **-niums, -nia** (-nɪə). a period or cycle of seven years.
▷**HISTORY** C19: from Latin, from *septem* seven + *-ennium,* from *annus* year

septentrion (sɛp'tɛntrɪˌɒn) NOUN *Archaic* the northern regions or the north.
▷**HISTORY** C14: from Latin *septentriōnēs,* literally: the seven ploughing oxen (the constellation of the Great Bear), from *septem* seven + *triōnēs* ploughing oxen
▸**sep'tentrional** ADJECTIVE

septet *or* **septette** (sɛp'tɛt) NOUN [1] *Music* a group of seven singers or instrumentalists or a piece of music composed for such a group. [2] a group of seven people or things.
▷**HISTORY** C19: from German, from Latin *septem* seven

septi-[1] *or before a vowel* **sept-** COMBINING FORM seven: *septivalent.*
▷**HISTORY** from Latin *septem*

septi-[2] COMBINING FORM septum: *septicidal.*

septic ('sɛptɪk) ADJECTIVE [1] of, relating to, or caused by sepsis. [2] of, relating to, or caused by putrefaction. ◆ NOUN [3] *Austral and NZ informal* short for **septic tank.**
▷**HISTORY** C17: from Latin *sēpticus,* from Greek *sēptikos,* from *sēptos* decayed, from *sēpein* to make rotten
▸**'septically** ADVERB ▸**septicity** (sɛp'tɪsɪtɪ) NOUN

septicaemia *or US* **septicemia** (ˌsɛptɪ'si:mɪə) NOUN a condition caused by pus-forming microorganisms in the blood. Nontechnical name: **blood poisoning.** See also **bacteraemia, pyaemia.**
▷**HISTORY** C19: from New Latin, from Greek *sēptik(os)* SEPTIC + -AEMIA
▸**ˌsepti'caemic** *or US* **ˌsepti'cemic** ADJECTIVE

septicidal (ˌsɛptɪ'saɪdᵊl) ADJECTIVE *Botany* (of a dehiscence) characterized by splitting along the partitions of the seed capsule.
▷**HISTORY** C19: from SEPTI-[2] + -CIDAL
▸**ˌsepti'cidally** ADVERB

septic tank NOUN a tank, usually below ground, for containing sewage to be decomposed by anaerobic bacteria.

septifragal (sɛp'tɪfrəgᵊl) ADJECTIVE (of a dehiscence) characterized by breaking apart from a natural line of division in the fruit.
▷**HISTORY** C19: from SEPTI-[2] + *-fragal,* from Latin *frangere* to break

septilateral (ˌsɛptɪ'lætərəl) ADJECTIVE having seven sides.

septillion (sɛp'tɪljən) NOUN, *plural* **-lions** *or* **-lion.** [1] (in Britain, France, and Germany) the number represented as one followed by 42 zeros (10^{42}). [2] (in the US and Canada) the number represented as one followed by 24 zeros (10^{24}). Brit word: **quadrillion.**
▷**HISTORY** C17: from French, from *sept* seven + *-illion,* on the model of *million*
▸**sep'tillionth** ADJECTIVE, NOUN

septime ('sɛpti:m) NOUN the seventh of eight basic positions from which a parry or attack can be made in fencing.
▷**HISTORY** C19: from Latin *septimus* seventh, from *septem* seven

septivalent (ˌsɛptɪ'veɪlənt) *or* **septavalent** (ˌsɛptə'veɪlənt) ADJECTIVE *Chem* another word for **heptavalent.**

septuagenarian (ˌsɛptjuədʒɪ'nɛərɪən) NOUN [1] a person who is from 70 to 79 years old. ◆ ADJECTIVE [2] being between 70 and 79 years old. [3] of or relating to a septuagenarian.
▷**HISTORY** C18: from Latin *septuāgēnārius,* from *septuāgēnī* seventy each, from *septuāgintā* seventy

Septuagesima (ˌsɛptjuə'dʒɛsɪmə) NOUN the third Sunday before Lent.
▷**HISTORY** C14: from Church Latin *septuāgēsima (diēs)* the seventieth (day); compare QUINQUAGESIMA

Septuagint ('sɛptjuəˌdʒɪnt) NOUN the principal Greek version of the Old Testament, including the Apocrypha, believed to have been translated by 70 or 72 scholars.
▷**HISTORY** C16: from Latin *septuāgintā* seventy

septum ('sɛptəm) NOUN, *plural* **-ta** (-tə). [1] *Biology, anatomy* a dividing partition between two tissues or cavities. [2] a dividing partition or membrane between two cavities in a mechanical device.

▷**HISTORY** C18: from Latin *saeptum* wall, from *saepīre* to enclose; related to Latin *saepēs* a fence

septuple ('sɛptjupᵊl) ADJECTIVE [1] seven times as much or many; sevenfold. [2] consisting of seven parts or members. ◆ VERB [3] (*tr*) to multiply by seven.
▷**HISTORY** C17: from Late Latin *septuplus,* from *septem* seven; compare QUADRUPLE

septuplet (sɛp'tju:plɪt, 'sɛptjuplɪt) NOUN [1] *Music* a group of seven notes played in a time value of six, eight, etc. [2] one of seven offspring produced at one birth. [3] a group of seven things.

septuplicate (sɛp'tju:plɪkət) NOUN [1] a group or set of seven things. ◆ ADJECTIVE [2] having or being in seven parts; sevenfold.

sepulchral (sɪ'pʌlkrəl) ADJECTIVE [1] suggestive of a tomb; gloomy. [2] of or relating to a sepulchre.
▸**se'pulchrally** ADVERB

sepulchre *or US* **sepulcher** ('sɛpəlkə) NOUN [1] a burial vault, tomb, or grave. [2] Also called: **Easter sepulchre.** a separate alcove in some medieval churches in which the Eucharistic elements were kept from Good Friday until the Easter ceremonies. ◆ VERB [3] (*tr*) to bury in a sepulchre.
▷**HISTORY** C12: from Old French *sépulcre,* from Latin *sepulcrum,* from *sepelīre* to bury

sepulture ('sɛpəltʃə) NOUN [1] the act of placing in a sepulchre. [2] an archaic word for **sepulchre.**
▷**HISTORY** C13: via Old French from Latin *sepultūra,* from *sepultus* buried, from *sepelīre* to bury

seq. ABBREVIATION FOR: [1] sequel. [2] sequens [Latin: the following (one)]

seqq. ABBREVIATION FOR sequentia [Latin: the following (ones)]

sequacious (sɪ'kweɪʃəs) ADJECTIVE [1] logically following in regular sequence. [2] ready to follow any leader; pliant.
▷**HISTORY** C17: from Latin *sequāx* pursuing, from *sequī* to follow
▸**se'quaciously** ADVERB ▸**sequacity** (sɪ'kwæsɪtɪ) NOUN

sequel ('si:kwəl) NOUN [1] anything that follows from something else; development. [2] a consequence or result. [3] a novel, play, etc., that continues a previously related story.
▷**HISTORY** C15: from Late Latin *sequēla,* from Latin *sequī* to follow

sequela (sɪ'kwi:lə) NOUN, *plural* **-lae** (-li:). (*often plural*) *Med* [1] any abnormal bodily condition or disease related to or arising from a pre-existing disease. [2] any complication of a disease.
▷**HISTORY** C18: from Latin: SEQUEL

sequence ('si:kwəns) NOUN [1] an arrangement of two or more things in a successive order. [2] the successive order of two or more things: *chronological sequence.* [3] a sequentially ordered set of related things or ideas. [4] an action or event that follows another or others. [5] **a** *Cards* a set of three or more consecutive cards, usually of the same suit. **b** *Bridge* a set of two or more consecutive cards. [6] *Music* an arrangement of notes or chords repeated several times at different pitches. [7] *Maths* **a** an ordered set of numbers or other mathematical entities in one-to-one correspondence with the integers 1 to *n*. **b** an ordered infinite set of mathematical entities in one-to-one correspondence with the natural numbers. [8] a section of a film constituting a single continuous uninterrupted episode. [9] *Biochem* the unique order of amino acids in the polypeptide chain of a protein or of nucleotides in the polynucleotide chain of DNA or RNA. [10] *RC Church* another word for **prose** (sense 4). ◆ VERB (*tr*) [11] to arrange in a sequence. [12] *Biochem* to determine the order of the units comprising (a protein, nucleic acid, genome, etc.).
▷**HISTORY** C14: from Medieval Latin *sequentia* that which follows, from Latin *sequī* to follow

sequence of tenses NOUN *Grammar* the sequence according to which the tense of a subordinate verb in a sentence is determined by the tense of the principal verb, as in *I believe he is lying, I believed he was lying,* etc.

sequencer ('si:kwənsə) NOUN [1] an electronic device that determines the order in which a number of operations occur. [2] an electronic device that sorts information into the required order for data processing. [3] a unit connected to a synthesizer, which is capable of memorizing sequences of notes.

sequencing ('si:kwənsɪŋ) NOUN *Biochem* [1] the procedure of determining the order of amino acids in the polypeptide chain of a protein (**protein sequencing**) or of nucleotides in a DNA section comprising a gene (**gene sequencing**). [2] Also called: **priority sequencing.** *Commerce* specifying the order in which jobs are to be processed, based on the allocation of priorities.

sequent ('si:kwənt) ADJECTIVE [1] following in order or succession. [2] following as a result; consequent. ◆ NOUN [3] something that follows; consequence. [4] *Logic* a formal representation of an argument. The inference of *A* from *A* & *B* is written *A* & *B* ⊢ *A*. The sequent ⊢ *A* represents the derivation of *A* from no assumptions and thus indicates that *A* is a theorem.
▷**HISTORY** C16: from Latin *sequēns,* from *sequī* to follow
▸**'sequently** ADVERB

sequential (sɪ'kwɛnʃəl) ADJECTIVE [1] characterized by or having a regular sequence. [2] another word for **sequent.**
▸**sequentiality** (sɪˌkwɛnʃɪ'ælɪtɪ) NOUN ▸**se'quentially** ADVERB

sequential access NOUN a method of reaching and reading data from a computer file by reading through the file from the beginning. Compare **direct access.**

sequential scanning NOUN a system of scanning a television picture along the lines in numerical sequence. Compare **interlaced scanning.**

sequester (sɪ'kwɛstə) VERB (*tr*) [1] to remove or separate. [2] (*usually passive*) to retire into seclusion. [3] *Law* to take (property) temporarily out of the possession of its owner, esp until the claims of creditors are satisfied or a court order is complied with. [4] *International law* to requisition or appropriate (enemy property).
▷**HISTORY** C14: from Late Latin *sequestrāre* to surrender for safekeeping, from Latin *sequester* a trustee
▸**se'questrable** ADJECTIVE

sequestrant (sɪ'kwɛstrənt) NOUN *Chem* any substance used to bring about sequestration, often by chelation. They are used in horticulture to counteract lime in the soil.

sequestrate (sɪ'kwɛstreɪt) VERB (*tr*) [1] *Law* a variant of **sequester** (sense 3). [2] *Chiefly Scots law* **a** to place (the property of a bankrupt) in the hands of a trustee for the benefit of his creditors. **b** to render (a person) bankrupt. [3] *Archaic* to seclude or separate.
▷**HISTORY** C16: from Late Latin *sequestrāre* to SEQUESTER
▸**sequestrator** ('si:kwɛsˌtreɪtə, sɪ'kwɛsˌtreɪtə) NOUN

sequestration (ˌsi:kwɛ'streɪʃən) NOUN [1] the act of sequestering or state of being sequestered. [2] *Law* the sequestering of property. [3] *Chem* the effective removal of ions from a solution by coordination with another type of ion or molecule to form complexes that do not have the same chemical behaviour as the original ions. See also **sequestrant.**

sequestrum (sɪ'kwɛstrəm) NOUN, *plural* **-tra** (-trə). *Pathol* a detached piece of necrotic bone that often migrates to a wound, abscess, etc. See **sequester.**
▷**HISTORY** C19: from New Latin, from Latin: something deposited
▸**se'questral** ADJECTIVE

sequin ('si:kwɪn) NOUN [1] a small piece of shiny often coloured metal foil or plastic, usually round, used to decorate garments, etc. [2] Also called: **zecchino.** any of various gold coins formerly minted in Italy, Turkey, and Malta.
▷**HISTORY** C17: via French from Italian *zecchino,* from *zecca* mint, from Arabic *sikkah* die for striking coins
▸**'sequined** ADJECTIVE

sequoia (sɪ'kwɔɪə) NOUN either of two giant Californian coniferous trees, *Sequoia sempervirens* (**redwood**) or *Sequoiadendron giganteum* (formerly *Sequoia gigantea*) (**big tree** or **giant sequoia**): family *Taxodiaceae.*
▷**HISTORY** C19: New Latin, named after *Sequoya,* known also as George Guess, (?1770–1843), American Indian scholar and leader

Sequoia National Park NOUN a national park in central California, in the Sierra Nevada Mountains: established in 1890 to protect groves of giant sequoias, some of which are about 4000 years old. Area: 1556 sq. km (601 sq. miles).

ser *or* **seer** (sɪə) NOUN a unit of weight used in India, usually taken as one fortieth of a maund.
▷**HISTORY** from Hindi

sera ('sɪərə) NOUN a plural of **serum.**

sérac ('sɛræk) NOUN a pinnacle of ice among crevasses on a glacier, usually on a steep slope.
▷**HISTORY** C19: from Swiss French: a variety of white cheese (hence the ice that it resembles), from Medieval Latin *serācium,* from Latin *serum* whey

seraglio (sɛ'rɑ:lɪˌəʊ) *or* **serail** (sə'raɪ, -'raɪl, -'reɪl) NOUN, *plural* **-raglios** *or* **-rails.** [1] the harem of a Muslim house or palace. [2] a sultan's palace, esp in the former Turkish empire. [3] the wives and concubines of a Muslim.
▷**HISTORY** C16: from Italian *serraglio* animal cage, from Medieval Latin *serrāculum* bolt, from Latin *sera* a door bar; associated also with Turkish *seray* palace

serai (sɛ'raɪ) NOUN (in the East) a caravanserai or inn.
▷**HISTORY** C17: from Turkish *saray* palace, from Persian *sarāī* palace; see CARAVANSERAI

Serajevo (*Serbo-Croat* 'sɛrajɛvɔ) NOUN a variant of **Sarajevo.**

Seram *or* **Ceram** (sɪ'ræm) NOUN an island in Indonesia, in the Moluccas, separated from New Guinea by the **Ceram Sea:** mountainous and densely forested. Area: 17 150 sq. km (6622 sq. miles). Also called: **Serang** (sə'ræŋ).

serape (sə'rɑ:pɪ) NOUN [1] a blanket-like shawl often of brightly-coloured wool worn by men in Latin America. [2] a large shawl worn around the shoulders by women as a fashion garment.

seraph ('sɛrəf) NOUN, *plural* **-aphs** *or* **-aphim** (-əfɪm). [1] *Theol* a member of the highest order of angels in the celestial hierarchies, often depicted as the winged head of a child. [2] *Old Testament* one of the fiery six-winged beings attendant upon Jehovah in Isaiah's vision (Isaiah 6).
▷**HISTORY** C17: back formation from plural *seraphim,* via Late Latin from Hebrew

seraphic (sɪ'ræfɪk) *or* **seraphical** ADJECTIVE [1] of or resembling a seraph. [2] blissfully serene; rapt.
▸**se'raphically** ADVERB

Serapis ('sɛrəpɪs) NOUN a Graeco-Egyptian god combining attributes of Apis and Osiris.

Serb (sɜ:b) NOUN, ADJECTIVE another word for **Serbian.**
▷**HISTORY** C19: from Serbian *Srb*

Serbia ('sɜ:bɪə) NOUN a constituent republic of the Union of Serbia and Montenegro: declared a kingdom in 1882; precipitated World War I by the conflict with Austria; became part of the Kingdom of the Serbs, Croats, and Slovenes (later called Yugoslavia) in 1918; with Montenegro formed the Federal Republic of Yugoslavia when the other constituent republics became independent in 1991–92; a new Union of Serbia and Montenegro formed in 2002; the autonomous region of Kosovo has been administered by the UN since the conflict of 1999. Capital: Belgrade. Pop.: 5 762 954 (1997 est.). Area: 88 361 sq. km (34 109 sq. miles). Former name: **Servia.** Serbian name: **Srbija.**

Serbia and Montenegro, Union of NOUN a country in SE Europe, consisting of the republics of Serbia and Montenegro; replaced the Federal Republic of Yugoslavia in 2002; chiefly mountainous, with the Danube plains in the N. Official language: Serbo-Croatian. Religion: Serbian Orthodox majority, with Roman Catholic and Muslim minorities. Currencies: new dinar and euro (in Montenegro and Kosovo). Capital: Belgrade. Pop.: 10 677 000 (2001 est.). Area: 102 173 sq. km (39 449 sq. miles).

Serbian ('sɜ:bɪən) *or* **Serb** ADJECTIVE [1] of, relating to, or characteristic of Serbia, its people, or their dialect of Serbo-Croat. ◆ NOUN [2] the dialect of Serbo-Croat spoken in Serbia. [3] **a** a native or inhabitant of Serbia. **b** a speaker of the Serbian dialect.

Serbo-Croat *or* **Serbo-Croatian** NOUN [1] the language of the Serbs and the Croats, belonging to the South Slavonic branch of the Indo-European family. The Serbian dialect is usually written in the Cyrillic alphabet, the Croatian in Roman. Also called: **Croato-Serb.** ◆ ADJECTIVE [2] of or relating to this language.

Sercq (sɛrk) NOUN the French name for **Sark.**

serdab ('sɜ:dæb, sə'dæb) NOUN a secret chamber in an ancient Egyptian tomb.
▷**HISTORY** C19 (earlier, in the sense: cellar): from Arabic: cellar, from Persian *sardāb* ice cellar, from *sard* cold + *āb* water

sere[1] *or* **sear** (sɪə) ADJECTIVE [1] *Archaic* dried up or withered. ◆ VERB, NOUN [2] a rare spelling of **sear** (sense 1).
▷**HISTORY** Old English *sēar;* see SEAR[1]

sere[2] (sɪə) NOUN the series of changes occurring in the ecological succession of a particular community.
▷**HISTORY** C20: from SERIES

serein (sə'reɪn) NOUN fine rain falling from a clear sky after sunset, esp in the tropics.
▷**HISTORY** C19: via French, from Old French *serain* dusk, from Latin *sērus* late

Seremban (sə'rɛmbən) NOUN a town in Peninsular Malaysia, capital of Negri Sembilan state. Pop.: 182 584 (1991).

serenade (ˌsɛrɪ'neɪd) NOUN [1] a piece of music appropriate to the evening, characteristically played outside the house of a woman. [2] a piece of music indicative or suggestive of this. [3] an extended composition in several movements similar to the modern suite or divertimento. ◆ VERB [4] (*tr*) to play a serenade for (someone). [5] (*intr*) to play a serenade. ◆ Compare **aubade.**
▷**HISTORY** C17: from French *sérénade,* from Italian *serenata,* from *sereno* peaceful, from Latin *serēnus* calm; also influenced in meaning by Italian *sera* evening, from Latin *sērus* late
▸**ˌsere'nader** NOUN

serenata (ˌsɛrɪ'nɑ:tə) NOUN [1] an 18th-century cantata, often dramatic in form. [2] another word for **serenade.**
▷**HISTORY** C18: from Italian; see SERENADE

serendipity (ˌsɛrən'dɪpɪtɪ) NOUN the faculty of making fortunate discoveries by accident.
▷**HISTORY** C18: coined by Horace Walpole, from the Persian fairytale *The Three Princes of Serendip,* in which the heroes possess this gift
▸**ˌseren'dipitous** ADJECTIVE

serene (sɪ'ri:n) ADJECTIVE [1] peaceful or tranquil; calm. [2] clear or bright: *a serene sky.* [3] (*often capital*) honoured: used as part of certain royal titles: *His Serene Highness.*
▷**HISTORY** C16: from Latin *serēnus*
▸**se'renely** ADVERB ▸**se'reneness** NOUN

serenity (sɪ'rɛnɪtɪ) NOUN, *plural* **-ties.** [1] the state or quality of being serene. [2] (*often capital*) a title of honour used of certain royal personages: preceded by *his, her,* etc.

serf (sɜ:f) NOUN (esp in medieval Europe) an unfree person, esp one bound to the land. If his lord sold the land, the serf was passed on to the new landlord.
▷**HISTORY** C15: from Old French, from Latin *servus* a slave; see SERVE
▸**'serfdom** *or* **'serfhood** NOUN ▸**'serfˌlike** ADJECTIVE

serge (sɜ:dʒ) NOUN [1] a twill-weave woollen or worsted fabric used for clothing. [2] a similar twilled cotton, silk, or rayon fabric.
▷**HISTORY** C14: from Old French *sarge,* from Vulgar Latin *sārica* (unattested), from Latin *sēricum,* from Greek *sērikon* silk, from *sērikos* silken, from *sēr* silkworm

sergeant ('sɑ:dʒənt) NOUN [1] a noncommissioned officer in certain armed forces, usually ranking above a corporal. [2] **a** (in Britain) a police officer ranking between constable and inspector. **b** (in the US) a police officer ranking below a captain. [3] See **sergeant at arms.** [4] a court or municipal officer who has ceremonial duties. [5] (formerly) a tenant by military service, not of knightly rank. [6] See **serjeant at law.** ◆ Also: **serjeant.**
▷**HISTORY** C12: from Old French *sergent,* from Latin *serviēns,* literally: serving, from *servīre* to SERVE
▸**sergeancy** ('sɑ:dʒənsɪ) *or* **'sergeantship** NOUN

sergeant at arms NOUN [1] an officer of a legislative or fraternal body responsible for maintaining internal order. [2] (formerly) an officer who served a monarch or noble, esp as an armed attendant. ◆ Also called: **sergeant, serjeant at arms, serjeant.**

sergeant at law NOUN a variant spelling of **serjeant at law.**

sergeant baker NOUN a large brightly-coloured fish of the genus *Latropiscis,* found in temperate reef waters of Australasia.
▷HISTORY named after *Sergeant (William) Baker,* a Norfolk Island colonist

sergeant major NOUN [1] a noncommissioned officer of the highest rank or having specific administrative tasks in branches of the armed forces of various countries. [2] a large damselfish, *Abudefduf saxatilis,* having a bluish-grey body marked with black stripes.

Sergipe (*Portuguese* ser'ʒipi) NOUN a state of NE Brazil: the smallest Brazilian state; a centre of resistance to Dutch conquest (17th century). Capital: Aracajú. Pop.: 1 779 522 (2000). Area: 13 672 sq. km (8492 sq. miles).

Sergt ABBREVIATION FOR Sergeant.

serial ('sɪərɪəl) NOUN [1] a novel, play, etc., presented in separate instalments at regular intervals. [2] a publication, usually regularly issued and consecutively numbered. ◆ ADJECTIVE [3] of, relating to, or resembling a series. [4] published or presented as a serial. [5] of or relating to such publication or presentation. [6] *Computing* of or operating on items of information, instructions, etc., in the order in which they occur. Compare **parallel** (sense 5). [7] of, relating to, or using the techniques of serialism. [8] *Logic, maths* (of a relation) connected, transitive, and asymmetric, thereby imposing an order on all the members of the domain, as *less than* on the natural numbers. See also **ordering.**
▷HISTORY C19: from New Latin *seriālis,* from Latin *seriēs* SERIES
▸'**serially** ADVERB

serial correlation NOUN *Statistics* another name for **autocorrelation.**

serialism ('sɪərɪəˌlɪzəm) NOUN (in 20th-century music) the use of a sequence of notes in a definite order as a thematic basis for a composition and a source from which the musical material is derived. See also **twelve-tone.**

serialize *or* **serialise** ('sɪərɪəˌlaɪz) VERB (*tr*) to publish or present in the form of a serial.
▸ˌ**seriali'zation** *or* ˌ**seriali'sation** NOUN

serial killer NOUN a person who carries out a series of murders.

serial monogamy NOUN the practice of having a number of long-term romantic or sexual partners in succession.

serial number NOUN any of the consecutive numbers assigned to machines, tools, books, etc.

seriate ('sɪərɪɪt) ADJECTIVE forming a series.
▸'**seriately** ADVERB

seriatim (ˌsɪərɪ'ætɪm, ˌsɛr-) ADVERB in a series; one after another in regular order.
▷HISTORY C17: from Medieval Latin, from Latin *seriēs* SERIES

sericeous (sɪ'rɪʃəs) ADJECTIVE *Botany* [1] covered with a layer of small silky hairs: *a sericeous leaf.* [2] silky.
▷HISTORY C18: from Late Latin *sēriceus* silken, from Latin *sēricus;* see SERGE

sericin ('sɛrɪsɪn) NOUN a gelatinous protein found on the fibres of raw silk.
▷HISTORY C19: from Latin *sēricum* silk + -IN

sericulture ('sɛrɪˌkʌltʃə) NOUN the rearing of silkworms for the production of raw silk.
▷HISTORY C19: via French; *seri-* from Latin *sēricum* silk, from Greek *sērikos* silken, from *sēr* a silkworm
▸ˌ**seri'cultural** ADJECTIVE ▸ˌ**seri'culturist** NOUN

seriema (ˌsɛrɪ'iːmə) NOUN either of two cranelike South American birds, *Cariama cristata* or *Chunga burmeisteri,* having a crest just above the bill, rounded wings, and a long tail: family *Cariamidae,* order *Gruiformes* (cranes, rails, etc.).
▷HISTORY C19: from New Latin, from Tupi *çariama* crested

series ('sɪəriːz, -rɪz) NOUN, *plural* **-ries.** [1] a group or connected succession of similar or related things, usually arranged in order. [2] a set of radio or television programmes having the same characters and setting but different stories. [3] a set of books having the same format, related content, etc., published by one firm. [4] a set of stamps, coins, etc., issued at a particular time. [5] *Maths* the sum of a finite or infinite sequence of numbers or quantities. See also **geometric series.** [6] *Electronics* **a** a configuration of two or more components connected in a circuit so that the same current flows in turn through each of them (esp in the phrase **in series**). **b** (*as modifier*): *a series circuit.* Compare **parallel** (sense 10). [7] *Rhetoric* a succession of coordinate elements in a sentence. [8] *Geology* a stratigraphical unit that is a subdivision of a system and represents the rocks formed during an epoch.
▷HISTORY C17: from Latin: a row, from *serere* to link

series resonance NOUN the resonance that results when circuit elements are connected with their inductance and capacitance in series, so that the impedance of the combination falls to a minimum at the resonant frequency. Compare **parallel resonance.**

series-wound ('sɪəriːzˌwaʊnd, -rɪz-) ADJECTIVE (of a motor or generator) having the field and armature circuits connected in series. Compare **shunt-wound.**

serif *or rarely* **seriph** ('sɛrɪf) NOUN *Printing* a small line at the extremities of a main stroke in a type character.
▷HISTORY C19: perhaps from Dutch *schreef* dash, probably of Germanic origin, compare Old High German *screvōn* to engrave

serigraph ('sɛrɪˌgræf, -ˌgrɑːf) NOUN a colour print made by an adaptation of the silk-screen process.
▷HISTORY C19: from *seri-,* from Latin *sēricum* silk + -GRAPH
▸**serigraphy** (sə'rɪgrəfɪ) NOUN

serin ('sɛrɪn) NOUN any of various small yellow-and-brown finches of the genus *Serinus,* esp *S. serinus,* of parts of Europe. See also **canary.**
▷HISTORY C16: from French, perhaps from Old Provençal *sirena* a bee-eater, from Latin *sīrēn,* a kind of bird, from SIREN

serine ('sɛriːn, 'sɪəriːn, -rɪn) NOUN a sweet-tasting amino acid that is synthesized in the body and is involved in the synthesis of cysteine; 2-amino-3-hydroxypropanoic acid. Formula: $CH_2(OH)CH(NH_2)COOH$.
▷HISTORY C19: from SERICIN + -INE^2

seringa (sə'rɪŋgə) NOUN [1] any of several euphorbiaceous trees of the Brazilian genus *Hevea,* that yield rubber. [2] a deciduous simaroubaceous tree, *Kirkia acuminata,* of southern Africa with a graceful shape.
▷HISTORY C18: from Portuguese, variant of SYRINGA

Seringapatam (səˌrɪŋgəpə'tæm) NOUN a small town in S India, in Karnataka on **Seringapatam Island** in the Cauvery River: capital of Mysore from 1610 to 1799, when it was besieged and captured by the British. Pop.: 21 902 (1991 est.).

seriocomic (ˌsɪərɪəʊ'kɒmɪk) *or less commonly* **seriocomical** ADJECTIVE mixing serious and comic elements.
▸ˌ**serio'comically** ADVERB

serious ('sɪərɪəs) ADJECTIVE [1] grave in nature or disposition; thoughtful: *a serious person.* [2] marked by deep feeling; in earnest; sincere: *is he serious or joking?* [3] concerned with important matters: *a serious conversation.* [4] requiring effort or concentration: *a serious book.* [5] giving rise to fear or anxiety; critical: *a serious illness.* [6] *Informal* worthy of regard because of substantial quantity or quality: *serious money; serious wine.* [7] *Informal* extreme or remarkable: *a serious haircut.*
▷HISTORY C15: from Late Latin *sēriōsus,* from Latin *sērius;* probably related to Old English *swǣr* gloomy, Gothic *swers* esteemed
▸'**seriousness** NOUN

seriously ('sɪərɪəslɪ) ADVERB [1] in a serious manner or to a serious degree. [2] *Informal* extremely or remarkably: *seriously tall.*

serjeant ('sɑːdʒənt) NOUN a variant spelling of **sergeant.**

serjeant at arms NOUN a variant spelling of **sergeant at arms.**

serjeant at law NOUN (formerly in England) a barrister of a special rank, to which he was raised by a writ under the Great Seal. Also called: **serjeant, sergeant at law, sergeant.**

sermon ('sɜːmən) NOUN [1] **a** an address of religious instruction or exhortation, often based on a passage from the Bible, esp one delivered during a church service. **b** a written version of such an address. [2] a serious speech, esp one administering reproof.
▷HISTORY C12: via Old French from Latin *sermō* discourse, probably from *serere* to join together
▸**sermonic** (sɜː'mɒnɪk) *or* **ser'monical** ADJECTIVE

sermonize *or* **sermonise** ('sɜːməˌnaɪz) VERB to talk to or address (a person or audience) as if delivering a sermon.
▸'**sermonˌizer** *or* '**sermonˌiser** NOUN

Sermon on the Mount NOUN *New Testament* a major discourse delivered by Christ, including the Beatitudes and the Lord's Prayer (Matthew 5–7).

sero- COMBINING FORM indicating a serum: *serotherapy.*

seroconvert (ˌsɪərəʊkən'vɜːt) VERB (*intr*) (of an individual) to produce antibodies specific to, and in response to the presence in the blood of, a particular antigen, such as a virus or vaccine.
▸ˌ**serocon'version** NOUN

serology (sɪ'rɒlədʒɪ) NOUN the science concerned with serums.
▸**serologic** (ˌsɪərə'lɒdʒɪk) *or* ˌ**sero'logical** ADJECTIVE
▸**se'rologist** NOUN

seronegative NOUN (ˌsɪərəʊ'nɛgətɪv), ADJECTIVE (of a person whose blood has been tested for a specific disease, such as AIDS) showing no serological reaction indicating the presence of the disease.

seropositive (ˌsɪərəʊ'pɒzɪtɪv) ADJECTIVE (of a person whose blood has been tested for a specific disease, such as AIDS) showing a serological reaction indicating the presence of the disease.

seropurulent (ˌsɪərəʊ'pjʊərələnt) ADJECTIVE *Pathol* composed of or containing both serum and pus.

serosa (sɪ'rəʊsə) NOUN [1] another name for **serous membrane.** [2] one of the thin membranes surrounding the embryo in an insect's egg.
▷HISTORY C19: from New Latin, from *serōsus* relating to SERUM

serotherapy (ˌsɪərəʊ'θɛrəpɪ) NOUN the treatment of disease by the injection of serum containing antibodies to the disease.

serotine ('sɛrəˌtaɪn) ADJECTIVE [1] Also: **serotinal** (sɪ'rɒtɪnᵊl), **serotinous.** *Biology* produced, flowering, or developing late in the season. ◆ NOUN [2] either of two insectivorous bats, *Eptesicus serotinus* or *Vespertilio serotinus:* family *Vespertilionidae.*
▷HISTORY C16: from Latin *sērōtinus* late, from *sērus* late; applied to the bats because they fly late in the evening

serotonin (ˌsɛrə'təʊnɪn) NOUN a compound that occurs in the brain, intestines, and blood platelets and acts as a neurotransmitter, as well as inducing vasoconstriction and contraction of smooth muscle; 5-hydroxytryptamine (5HT).
▷HISTORY from SERO- + TON(IC) + -IN

serotype ('sɪərəʊˌtaɪp) NOUN *Medicine* a category into which material, usually a bacterium, is placed based on its serological activity, esp in terms of the antigens it contains or the antibodies produced against it.

serous ('sɪərəs) ADJECTIVE of, resembling, producing, or containing serum.
▷HISTORY C16: from Latin *serōsus,* from SERUM
▸**serosity** (sɪ'rɒsɪtɪ) *or* '**serousness** NOUN

serous fluid NOUN a thin watery fluid found in many body cavities, esp those lined with serous membrane.

serous membrane NOUN any of the smooth moist delicate membranes, such as the pleura or peritoneum, that line the closed cavities of the body and secrete a watery exudate.

serow ('sɛrəʊ) NOUN either of two antelopes, *Capricornis sumatraensis* and *C. crispus,* of mountainous regions of S and SE Asia, having a dark coat and conical backward-pointing horns.
▷HISTORY C19: from Lepcha *să-ro* Tibetan goat

Seroxat ('sɛˌrɒksæt) NOUN *Trademark* a drug that prolongs the action of serotonin in the brain; used to treat depression and social anxiety.

Serpens ('sɜːpənz) NOUN, *Latin genitive* **Serpentis** (sə'pɛntɪs). a faint extensive constellation situated in the N and S equatorial regions and divided into two parts, **Serpens Caput** (the head) lying between Ophiuchus and Boötes and **Serpens Cauda** (the tail) between Ophiuchus and Aquila.
▷HISTORY Latin: SERPENT

serpent (ˈsɜːpənt) NOUN [1] a literary or dialect word for **snake.** [2] *Old Testament* a manifestation of Satan as a guileful tempter (Genesis 3:1–5). [3] a sly, deceitful, or unscrupulous person. [4] an obsolete wind instrument resembling a snake in shape, the bass form of the cornett. [5] a firework that moves about with a serpentine motion when ignited.
▷HISTORY C14: via Old French from Latin *serpēns* a creeping thing, from *serpere* to creep; related to Greek *herpein* to crawl

serpentine¹ (ˈsɜːpənˌtaɪn) ADJECTIVE [1] of, relating to, or resembling a serpent. [2] twisting; winding. ◆ NOUN [3] *Maths* a curve that is symmetric about the origin of and asymptotic to the *x*-axis.
▷HISTORY C14: from Late Latin *serpentīnus,* from *serpēns* SERPENT

serpentine² (ˈsɜːpənˌtaɪn) NOUN [1] a dark green or brown mineral with a greasy or silky lustre, found in igneous and metamorphic rocks. It is used as an ornamental stone; and one variety (chrysotile) is known as asbestos. Composition: hydrated magnesium silicate. Formula: $Mg_3Si_2O_5(OH)_4$ Crystal structure: monoclinic. [2] any of a group of minerals having the general formula $(Mg,Fe)_3Si_2O_5(OH)_4$.
▷HISTORY C15 *serpentyn,* from Medieval Latin *serpentīnum* SERPENTINE¹; referring to the snakelike patterns of these minerals

serpigo (sɜːˈpaɪɡəʊ) NOUN *Pathol* any progressive skin eruption, such as ringworm or herpes.
▷HISTORY C14: from Medieval Latin, from Latin *serpere* to creep
▸**serpiginous** (sɜːˈpɪdʒɪnəs) ADJECTIVE

SERPS *or* **Serps** (sɜːps) NOUN (in Britain) ACRONYM FOR state earnings-related pension scheme.

serpulid (ˈsɜːpjʊlɪd) NOUN a marine polychaete worm of the family *Serpulidae,* which constructs and lives in a calcareous tube attached to stones or seaweed and has a crown of ciliated tentacles.
▷HISTORY C19: Latin, from *serpula* a little serpent

serra (ˈsɛrə) NOUN, *plural* **-rae** (-riː). *Zoology* a sawlike part or organ.
▷HISTORY C19: from Latin: saw

serranid (səˈrænɪd, ˈsɛrə-) *or* **serranoid** (ˈsɛrəˌnɔɪd) NOUN [1] any of numerous mostly marine percoid fishes of the family *Serranidae:* includes the sea basses, sea perches, groupers, and jewfish. ◆ ADJECTIVE [2] of or belonging to the family *Serranidae.*
▷HISTORY C19: from New Latin *Serranidae,* from *serrānus* genus name from Latin *serra* sawfish

serrate ADJECTIVE (ˈsɛrɪt, -eɪt) [1] (of leaves) having a margin of forward pointing teeth. [2] having a notched or sawlike edge. ◆ VERB (səˈreɪt) [3] (*tr*) to make serrate.
▷HISTORY C17: from Latin *serrātus* saw-shaped, from *serra* a saw

serrated ADJECTIVE (səˈreɪtɪd) having a notched or sawlike edge.

serration (səˈreɪʃən) *or less commonly* **serrature** (ˈsɛrətʃə) NOUN [1] the state or condition of being serrated. [2] a row of notches or toothlike projections on an edge. [3] a single notch.

serried (ˈsɛrɪd) ADJECTIVE in close or compact formation: *serried ranks of troops.*
▷HISTORY C17: from Old French *serré* close-packed, from *serrer* to shut up; see SEAR²

serriform (ˈsɛrɪˌfɔːm) ADJECTIVE *Biology* resembling a notched or sawlike edge.
▷HISTORY *serri-,* from Latin *serra* saw

serrulate (ˈsɛrʊˌleɪt, -lɪt) *or* **serrulated** ADJECTIVE (esp of leaves) minutely serrate.
▷HISTORY C18: from New Latin *serrulātus,* from Latin *serrula* diminutive of *serra* a saw

serrulation (ˌsɛrʊˈleɪʃən) NOUN [1] any of the notches in a serrulate object. [2] the condition of being serrulate.

sertularian (ˌsɜːtjʊˈlɛərɪən) NOUN any of various hydroid coelenterates of the genus *Sertularia,* forming feathery colonies of long branched stems bearing stalkless paired polyps.
▷HISTORY C18: from New Latin *Sertulāria,* from Latin *sertula* diminutive of *serta* a garland

serum (ˈsɪərəm) NOUN, *plural* **-rums** *or* **-ra** (-rə). [1] See **blood serum.** [2] antitoxin obtained from the blood serum of immunized animals. [3] *Physiol, zoology* clear watery fluid, esp that exuded by serous membranes. [4] a less common word for **whey.**
▷HISTORY C17: from Latin: whey
▸ˈ**serumal** ADJECTIVE

serum albumin NOUN a form of albumin that is the most abundant protein constituent of blood plasma. See also **albumin.**

serum globulin NOUN the blood serum component consisting of proteins with a larger molecular weight than serum albumin. See also **immunoglobulin.**

serum hepatitis NOUN a former name for **hepatitis B.**

serum sickness NOUN an allergic reaction, such as vomiting, skin rash, etc., that sometimes follows 2-3 weeks after an injection of a foreign serum.

serval (ˈsɜːvᵊl) NOUN, *plural* **-vals** *or* **-val.** a slender feline mammal, *Felis serval,* of the African bush, having an orange-brown coat with black spots, large ears, and long legs.
▷HISTORY C18: via French from Late Latin *cervālis* staglike, from Latin *cervus* a stag

servant (ˈsɜːvᵊnt) NOUN [1] a person employed to work for another, esp one who performs household duties. [2] See **public servant.**
▷HISTORY C13: via Old French, from *servant* serving, from *servir* to SERVE
▸ˈ**servant-ˌlike** ADJECTIVE

serve (sɜːv) VERB [1] to be in the service of (a person). [2] to render or be of service to (a person, cause, etc.); help. [3] (in a shop) to give (customers) information about articles for sale and to hand over articles purchased. [4] (*tr*) to provide (guests, customers, etc.) with food, drink, etc.: *she served her guests with cocktails.* [5] to distribute or provide (food, drink, etc.) for guests, customers, etc.: *do you serve coffee?* [6] (*tr;* sometimes foll by *up*) to present (food, drink, etc.) in a specified manner: *cauliflower served with cheese sauce.* [7] (*tr*) to provide with a regular supply of. [8] (*tr*) to work actively for: *to serve the government.* [9] (*tr*) to pay homage to: *to serve God.* [10] to answer the requirements of; suit: *this will serve my purpose.* [11] (*intr; may take an infinitive*) to have a use; function: *this wood will serve to build a fire.* [12] to go through (a period of service, enlistment, imprisonment, etc.). [13] (*intr*) (of weather, conditions, etc.) to be favourable or suitable. [14] (*tr*) Also: **service.** (of a male animal) to copulate with (a female animal). [15] *Sport* to put (the ball) into play. [16] (*intr*) *RC Church* to act as server at Mass or other services. [17] (*tr*) to deliver (a legal document, esp a writ or summons) to (a person). [18] to provide (a machine, etc.) with an impulse or signal for control purposes or with a continuous supply of fuel, working material, etc. [19] (*tr*) *Nautical* to bind (a rope, spar, etc.) with wire or fine cord to protect it from chafing, etc. See also **seize** (sense 8). [20] **serve (a person) right.** *Informal* to pay (a person) back, esp for wrongful or foolish treatment or behaviour. ◆ NOUN [21] *Sport* short for **service** (sense 17). [22] *Austral* a portion or helping of food or drink.
▷HISTORY C13: from Old French *servir,* from Latin *servīre,* from *servus* a slave
▸ˈ**servable** *or* ˈ**serveable** ADJECTIVE

server (ˈsɜːvə) NOUN [1] a person who serves. [2] *Chiefly RC Church* a person who acts as acolyte or assists the priest at Mass. [3] something that is used in serving food and drink. [4] the player who serves in racket games. [5] *Computing* a computer or program that supplies data or resources to other machines on a network.

Servia (ˈsɜːvɪə) NOUN the former name of **Serbia.**

Servian (ˈsɜːvɪən) ADJECTIVE, NOUN a former word for **Serbian.**

service¹ (ˈsɜːvɪs) NOUN [1] an act of help or assistance. [2] an organized system of labour and material aids used to supply the needs of the public: *telephone service; bus service.* [3] the supply, installation, or maintenance of goods carried out by a dealer. [4] the state of availability for use by the public (esp in the phrases **into** *or* **out of service**). [5] a periodic overhaul made on a car, machine, etc. [6] the act or manner of serving guests, customers, etc., in a shop, hotel, restaurant, etc. [7] a department of public employment and its employees: *civil service.* [8] employment in or performance of work for another: *he has been in the service of our firm for ten years.* [9] the work of a public servant. [10] **a** one of the branches of the armed forces. **b** (*as modifier*): *service life.* [11] the state, position, or duties of a domestic servant (esp in the phrase **in service**). [12] the act or manner of serving food. [13] a complete set of dishes, cups, etc., for use at table. [14] public worship carried out according to certain prescribed forms: *divine service.* [15] the prescribed form according to which a specific kind of religious ceremony is to be carried out: *the burial service.* [16] a unified collection of musical settings of the canticles and other liturgical items prescribed by the Book of Common Prayer as used in the Church of England. [17] *Sport* **a** the act, manner, or right of serving a ball. **b** the game in which a particular player serves: *he has lost his service.* Often shortened to: **serve.** [18] (in feudal law) the duty owed by a tenant to his lord. [19] the serving of a writ, summons, etc., upon a person. [20] *Nautical* a length of tarred marline or small stuff used in serving. [21] (of male animals) the act of mating. [22] (*modifier*) of, relating to, or for the use of servants or employees. ◆ VERB (*tr*) [23] to make fit for use. [24] to supply with assistance. [25] to overhaul (a car, machine, etc.). [26] (of a male animal) to mate with (a female). [27] *Brit* to meet interest and capital payments on (debt). ◆ See also **services.**
▷HISTORY C12 *servise,* from Old French, from Latin *servitium* condition of a slave, from *servus* a slave

service² (ˈsɜːvɪs) NOUN See **service tree.**

serviceable (ˈsɜːvɪsəbᵊl) ADJECTIVE [1] capable of or ready for service; usable. [2] capable of giving good service; durable. [3] *Archaic* diligent in service.
▸ˌ**serviceaˈbility** *or* ˈ**serviceableness** NOUN ▸ˈ**serviceably** ADVERB

service area NOUN [1] a place on a motorway providing garage services, restaurants, toilet facilities, etc. [2] the area within which a satisfactory signal can be received from a given radio transmitter.

serviceberry (ˈsɜːvɪsˌbɛrɪ) NOUN, *plural* **-ries.** [1] Also called: **shadbush.** any of various North American rosaceous trees or shrubs of the genus *Amelanchier,* esp *A. canadensis,* which has white flowers and edible purplish berries. [2] the fruit of any of these plants. [3] the fruit of the service tree. ◆ Also called (for senses 1, 2): **shadberry, Juneberry.**

service ceiling NOUN the height above sea level, measured under standard conditions, at which the rate of climb of an aircraft has fallen to a specified amount. Compare **absolute ceiling.**

service charge NOUN a percentage of a bill, as at a restaurant or hotel, added to the total to pay for service.

service contract NOUN a contract between an employer and a senior employee, esp a director, executive, etc.

service flat NOUN *Brit* a flat in which domestic services are provided by the management. Also called (esp Austral): **serviced flat.**

service industry NOUN an industry that provides services, such as transport or entertainment, rather than goods.

service line NOUN (in certain racket games) [1] the line at the back of the court behind which the server must stand when serving. [2] a line indicating the boundary of a permissible service, as on the backwall of a squash court.

serviceman (ˈsɜːvɪsˌmæn, -mən) NOUN, *plural* **-men.** [1] Also called (feminine): **servicewoman.** a person who serves in the armed services of a country. [2] a man employed to service and maintain equipment.

service module NOUN a section of an Apollo spacecraft housing the rocket engine, radar, fuel cells, etc., and jettisoned on re-entry into the earth's atmosphere. See also **lunar module, command module.**

service road NOUN *Brit* a relatively narrow road running parallel to a main road and providing access to houses, shops, offices, factories, etc., situated along its length.

services (ˈsɜːvɪsɪz) PLURAL NOUN [1] work performed for remuneration. [2] (usually preceded by *the*) the armed forces. [3] (*sometimes singular*) *Economics* commodities, such as banking, that are mainly intangible and usually consumed concurrently with their production. Compare **goods**

(sense 2). [4] a system of providing the public with gas, water, etc.

service station NOUN [1] a place that supplies fuel, oil, etc., for motor vehicles and often carries out repairs, servicing, etc. [2] a place that repairs and sometimes supplies mechanical or electrical equipment.

service tree NOUN [1] Also called: **sorb.** a Eurasian rosaceous tree, *Sorbus domestica,* cultivated for its white flowers and brown edible apple-like fruits. [2] **wild service tree.** a similar and related Eurasian tree, *Sorbus torminalis.*
▷HISTORY *service,* from Old English *syrfe,* from Vulgar Latin *sorbea* (unattested), from Latin *sorbus* SORB

servient tenement ('sɜːvɪənt) NOUN *Property law* the land or tenement over which an easement or other encumbrance is exercised by the dominant tenement. Compare **dominant tenement.**

serviette (ˌsɜːvɪ'ɛt) NOUN *Chiefly Brit* a small square of cloth or paper used while eating to protect the clothes, wipe the mouth and hands, etc.
▷HISTORY C15: from Old French, from *servir* to SERVE; formed on the model of OUBLIETTE

servile ('sɜːvaɪl) ADJECTIVE [1] obsequious or fawning in attitude or behaviour; submissive. [2] of or suitable for a slave. [3] existing in or relating to a state of slavery. [4] (when *postpositive,* foll by *to*) submitting or obedient.
▷HISTORY C14: from Latin *servīlis,* from *servus* slave
▸**'servilely** ADVERB ▸**servility** (sɜː'vɪlɪtɪ) *or* **'servileness** NOUN

servile work NOUN *RC Church* work of a physical nature that is forbidden on Sundays and on certain holidays.

serving ('sɜːvɪŋ) NOUN a portion or helping of food or drink.

servitor ('sɜːvɪtə) NOUN *Archaic* a person who serves another.
▷HISTORY C14: from Old French *servitour,* from Late Latin *servītor,* from Latin *servīre* to SERVE

servitude ('sɜːvɪˌtjuːd) NOUN [1] the state or condition of a slave; bondage. [2] the state or condition of being subjected to or dominated by a person or thing: *servitude to drink.* [3] *Law* a burden attaching to an estate for the benefit of an adjoining estate or of some definite person. See also **easement.** [4] short for **penal servitude.**
▷HISTORY C15: via Old French from Latin *servitūdō,* from *servus* a slave

servo ('sɜːvəʊ) ADJECTIVE [1] (*prenominal*) of, relating to, forming part of, or activated by a servomechanism: *servo brakes.* ◆ NOUN, *plural* **-vos.** [2] *Informal* short for **servomechanism.**
▷HISTORY see SERVOMOTOR

servomechanism ('sɜːvəʊˌmɛkəˌnɪzəm, ˌsɜːvəʊ'mɛk-) NOUN a mechanical or electromechanical system for control of the position or speed of an output transducer. Negative feedback is incorporated to minimize discrepancies between the output state and the input control setting.
▸**servomechanical** (ˌsɜːvəʊmɪ'kænɪkᵊl) ADJECTIVE

servomotor ('sɜːvəʊˌməʊtə) NOUN any motor that supplies power to a servomechanism.
▷HISTORY C19: from French *servo-moteur,* from Latin *servus* slave + French *moteur* MOTOR

servqual ('sɜːvˌkwɒl) NOUN *Marketing* the provision of high-quality products by an organization backed by a high level of service for consumers.
▷HISTORY C20: from SERV(ICE)[1] + QUAL(ITY)

sesame ('sɛsəmɪ) NOUN [1] a tropical herbaceous plant, *Sesamum indicum,* of the East Indies, cultivated, esp in India, for its small oval seeds: family *Pedaliaceae.* [2] the seeds of this plant, used in flavouring bread and yielding an edible oil (**benne oil** or **gingili**). Also called: **benne, gingili, til.**
▷HISTORY C15: from Latin *sēsamum,* from Greek *sēsamon, sēsamē,* of Semitic origin; related to Arabic *simsim*

sesamoid ('sɛsəˌmɔɪd) ADJECTIVE *Anatomy* [1] of or relating to various small bones formed in tendons, such as the patella. [2] of or relating to any of various small cartilages, esp those of the nose.
▷HISTORY C17: from Latin *sēsamoīdēs* like sesame (seed), from Greek

sesh (sɛʃ) NOUN *Slang* short for **session.**

Sesotho (sɪ'suːtuː) NOUN the dialect of Sotho spoken by the Basotho: an official language of Lesotho. Also called: **Southern Sotho.** Former name: **Basuto.**

sesqui- PREFIX [1] indicating one and a half: *sesquicentennial.* [2] (in a chemical compound) indicating a ratio of two to three: *sesquioxide.*
▷HISTORY from Latin, contraction of SEMI- + *as* AS[2] + *-que* and

sesquialtera (ˌsɛskwɪ'æltərə) NOUN *Music* [1] a mixture stop on an organ. [2] another term for **hemiola.**
▷HISTORY C16: from Latin *sesqui-* half + *alter* second, other

sesquicarbonate (ˌsɛskwɪ'kɑːbəˌneɪt, -nɪt) NOUN a mixed salt consisting of a carbonate and a hydrogen carbonate, such as sodium sesquicarbonate, $Na_2CO_3.NaHCO_3.2H_2O$.

sesquicentennial (ˌsɛskwɪsɛn'tɛnɪəl) ADJECTIVE [1] of or relating to a period of 150 years. ◆ NOUN [2] a period or cycle of 150 years. [3] a 150th anniversary or its celebration.
▸**ˌsesquicen'tennially** ADVERB

sesquioxide (ˌsɛskwɪ'ɒksaɪd) NOUN any of certain oxides whose molecules contain three atoms of oxygen for every two atoms of the element: *chromium sesquioxide,* Cr_2O_3.

sesquipedalian (ˌsɛskwɪpɪ'deɪlɪən) *or less commonly* **sesquipedal** (sɛs'kwɪpədᵊl) ADJECTIVE [1] tending to use very long words. [2] (of words or expressions) long and ponderous; polysyllabic. ◆ NOUN [3] a polysyllabic word.
▷HISTORY C17: from Latin *sēsquipedālis* of a foot and a half (coined by Horace in *Ars Poetica*), from SESQUI- + *pedālis* of the foot, from *pēs* foot
▸**ˌsesquipe'dalianism** NOUN

sesquiterpene (ˌsɛskwɪ'tɜːpiːn) NOUN any of certain terpenes whose molecules contain one and a half times as many atoms as a normal terpene. Formula: $C_{15}H_{24}$.

sessile ('sɛsaɪl) ADJECTIVE [1] (of flowers or leaves) having no stalk; growing directly from the stem. [2] (of animals such as the barnacle) permanently attached to a substratum.
▷HISTORY C18: from Latin *sēssilis* concerning sitting, from *sedēre* to sit
▸**sessility** (sɛ'sɪlɪtɪ) NOUN

sessile oak NOUN another name for the **durmast** (sense 1).

session ('sɛʃən) NOUN [1] the meeting of a court, legislature, judicial body, etc., for the execution of its function or the transaction of business. [2] a single continuous meeting of such a body. [3] a series or period of such meetings. [4] *Education* **a** the time during which classes are held. **b** a school or university term or year. [5] *Presbyterian Church* the judicial and administrative body presiding over a local congregation and consisting of the minister and elders. [6] a meeting of a group of musicians to record in a studio. [7] a meeting of a group of people to pursue an activity. [8] any period devoted to an activity. [9] See **Court of Session.**
▷HISTORY C14: from Latin *sessiō* a sitting, from *sedēre* to sit
▸**'sessional** ADJECTIVE ▸**'sessionally** ADVERB

session musician NOUN a studio musician, esp one who works freelance.

sessions ('sɛʃənz) PLURAL NOUN the sittings or a sitting of justice in court. See **magistrates' court, quarter sessions.**

sesterce ('sɛstɜːs) *or* **sestertius** (sɛ'stɜːtɪəs) NOUN a silver or, later, bronze coin of ancient Rome worth a quarter of a denarius.
▷HISTORY C16: from Latin *sēstertius* a coin worth two and a half asses, from *sēmis* half + *tertius* a third

sestertium (sɛ'stɜːtɪəm) NOUN, *plural* **-tia** (-tɪə). an ancient Roman money of account equal to 1000 sesterces.
▷HISTORY C16: from Latin, from the phrase *mille sestertium* a thousand of sesterces; see SESTERCE

sestet (sɛ'stɛt) NOUN [1] *Prosody* the last six lines of a Petrarchan sonnet. [2] *Prosody* any six-line stanza. [3] another word for **sextet** (sense 1).
▷HISTORY C19: from Italian *sestetto,* from *sesto* sixth, from Latin *sextus,* from *sex* six

sestina (sɛ'stiːnə) NOUN an elaborate verse form of Italian origin, normally unrhymed, consisting of six stanzas of six lines each and a concluding tercet. The six final words of the lines in the first stanza are repeated in a different order in each of the remaining five stanzas and also in the concluding tercet. Also called: **sextain.**
▷HISTORY C19: from Italian, from *sesto* sixth, from Latin *sextus*

Sestos ('sɛstɒs) NOUN a ruined town in NW Turkey, at the narrowest point of the Dardanelles: N terminus of the bridge of boats built by Xerxes in 481 B.C. for the crossing of his armies of invasion.

set[1] (sɛt) VERB **sets, setting, set.** (*mainly tr*) [1] to put or place in position or into a specified state or condition: *to set a book on the table; to set someone free.* [2] (*also intr;* foll by *to* or *on*) to put or be put (to); apply or be applied: *he set fire to the house; they set the dogs on the scent.* [3] to put into order or readiness for use; prepare: *to set a trap; to set the table for dinner.* [4] (*also intr*) to put, form, or be formed into a jelled, firm, fixed, or rigid state: *the jelly set in three hours.* [5] (*also intr*) to put or be put into a position that will restore a normal state: *to set a broken bone.* [6] to adjust (a clock or other instrument) to a position. [7] to determine or establish: *we have set the date for our wedding.* [8] to prescribe or allot (an undertaking, course of study, etc.): *the examiners have set "Paradise Lost".* [9] to arrange in a particular fashion, esp an attractive one: *she set her hair; the jeweller set the diamonds in silver.* [10] (of clothes) to hang or fit (well or badly) when worn. [11] Also: **set to music.** to provide music for (a poem or other text to be sung). [12] Also: **set up.** *Printing* to arrange or produce (type, film, etc.) from (text or copy); compose. [13] to arrange (a stage, television studio, etc.) with scenery and props. [14] to describe or present (a scene or the background to a literary work, story, etc.) in words: *his novel is set in Russia.* [15] to present as a model of good or bad behaviour (esp in the phrases **set an example, set a good example, set a bad example**). [16] (foll by *on* or *by*) to value (something) at a specified price or estimation of worth: *he set a high price on his services.* [17] (foll by *at*) to price (the value of something) at a specified sum: *he set his services at £300.* [18] (*also intr*) to give or be given a particular direction: *his course was set to the East.* [19] (*also intr*) to rig (a sail) or (of a sail) to be rigged so as to catch the wind. [20] (*intr*) (of the sun, moon, etc.) to disappear beneath the horizon. [21] to leave (dough, etc.) in one place so that it may prove. [22] to sharpen (a cutting blade) by grinding or honing the angle adjacent to the cutting edge. [23] to displace alternate teeth of (a saw) to opposite sides of the blade in order to increase the cutting efficiency. [24] to sink (the head of a nail) below the surface surrounding it by using a nail set. [25] *Computing* to give (a binary circuit) the value 1. [26] (of plants) to produce (fruits, seeds, etc.) after pollination or (of fruits or seeds) to develop after pollination. [27] to plant (seeds, seedlings, etc.). [28] to place (a hen) on (eggs) for the purpose of incubation. [29] (*intr*) (of a gun dog) to turn in the direction of game, indicating its presence. [30] *Scot and Irish* to let or lease: *to set a house.* [31] *Bridge* to defeat (one's opponents) in their attempt to make a contract. [32] a dialect word for **sit.** [33] **set eyes on.** to see. ◆ NOUN [34] the act of setting or the state of being set. [35] a condition of firmness or hardness. [36] bearing, carriage, or posture: *the set of a gun dog when pointing.* [37] the fit or hang of a garment, esp when worn. [38] the scenery and other props used in and identifying the location of a stage or television production, film, etc. [39] Also called: **set width.** *Printing* **a** the width of the body of a piece of type. **b** the width of the lines of type in a page or column. [40] *Nautical* **a** the cut of the sails or the arrangement of the sails, spars, rigging, etc., of a vessel. **b** the direction from which a wind is blowing or towards which a tide or current is moving. [41] *Psychol* a temporary bias disposing an organism to react to a stimulus in one way rather than in others. [42] a seedling, cutting, or similar part that is ready for planting: *onion sets.* [43] a blacksmith's tool with a short head similar to a cold chisel set transversely onto a handle and used, when struck with a hammer, for cutting off lengths of iron bars. [44] See **nail set.** [45] the direction of flow of water. [46] a mechanical distortion of shape or alignment, such as a bend in a piece of metal. [47] the penetration of a driven pile for each blow

of the drop hammer. 48 a variant spelling of **sett.** ◆ ADJECTIVE 49 fixed or established by authority or agreement: *set hours of work.* 50 (*usually postpositive*) rigid or inflexible: *she is set in her ways.* 51 conventional, artificial, or stereotyped, rather than spontaneous: *she made her apology in set phrases.* 52 (*postpositive;* foll by *on* or *upon*) resolute in intention: *he is set upon marrying.* 53 (of a book, etc.) prescribed for students' preparation for an examination. ◆ See also **set about, set against, set aside, set back, set down, set forth, set in, set off, set on, set out, set to, set up, set upon.**
▷HISTORY Old English *settan,* causative of *sittan* to SIT; related to Old Frisian *setta,* Old High German *sezzan*

set² (sɛt) NOUN 1 a number of objects or people grouped or belonging together, often forming a unit or having certain features or characteristics in common: *a set of coins; John is in the top set for maths.* 2 a group of people who associate together, esp a clique: *he's part of the jet set.* 3 *Maths, logic* **a** Also called: **class.** a collection of numbers, objects, etc., that is treated as an entity: 3, the moon is the set the two members of which are the number 3 and the moon. **b** (in some formulations) a class that can itself be a member of other classes. 4 any apparatus that receives or transmits television or radio signals. 5 *Tennis, squash, badminton* one of the units of a match, in tennis one in which one player or pair of players must win at least six games: *Graf lost the first set.* 6 **a** the number of couples required for a formation dance. **b** a series of figures that make up a formation dance. 7 **a** a band's or performer's concert repertoire on a given occasion: *the set included no new numbers.* **b** a continuous performance: *the Who played two sets.* ◆ VERB **sets, setting, set.** 8 (*intr*) (in square dancing and country dancing) to perform a sequence of steps while facing towards another dancer: *set to your partners.* 9 (*usually tr*) to divide into sets: *in this school we set our older pupils for English.*
▷HISTORY C14 (in the obsolete sense: a religious sect): from Old French *sette,* from Latin *secta* SECT; later sense development influenced by the verb SET¹

seta ('siːtə) NOUN, *plural* **-tae** (-tiː). 1 (in invertebrates and some plants) any bristle or bristle-like appendage. 2 (in mosses) the stalk of the sporophyte that bears the capsule.
▷HISTORY C18: from Latin
▸**setaceous** (sɪ'teɪʃəs) ADJECTIVE ▸**se'taceously** ADVERB ▸**'setal** ADJECTIVE

set about VERB (*intr, preposition*) 1 to start or begin. 2 to attack physically or verbally.

set against VERB (*tr, preposition*) 1 to balance or compare: *to set a person's faults against his virtues.* 2 to cause to be hostile or unfriendly to.

set aside VERB (*tr, adverb*) 1 to reserve for a special purpose; put to one side. 2 to discard, dismiss, or quash.

set-aside NOUN **a** (in the European Union) a scheme in which a proportion of farmland is taken out of production in order to reduce surpluses or maintain or increase prices of a specific crop. **b** (*as modifier*): *set-aside land.*

set back VERB (*tr, adverb*) 1 to hinder; impede. 2 *Informal* to cost (a person) a specified amount. ◆ NOUN **setback.** 3 anything that serves to hinder or impede. 4 a recession in the upper part of a high building, esp one that increases the daylight at lower levels. 5 Also called: **offset, setoff.** a steplike shelf where a wall is reduced in thickness.

set chisel NOUN another name for **cold chisel.**

set down VERB (*tr, adverb*) 1 to write down or record. 2 to judge, consider, or regard: *he set him down as an idiot.* 3 (foll by *to*) to ascribe; attribute: *his attitude was set down to his illness.* 4 to reprove; rebuke. 5 to snub; dismiss. 6 *Brit* to allow (passengers) to alight from a bus, taxi, etc.

se tenant *French* (sə tənɑ̃) ADJECTIVE 1 denoting two postage stamps of different face values and sometimes of different designs in an unseparated pair. ◆ NOUN 2 such a pair of stamps.
▷HISTORY literally: holding together

set forth VERB (*adverb*) *Formal or archaic* 1 (*tr*) to state, express, or utter: *he set forth his objections.* 2 (*intr*) to start out on a journey: *the expedition set forth on the first of July.*

Seth (sɛθ) NOUN *Old Testament* Adam's third son, given by God in place of the murdered Abel (Genesis 4:25).

SETI ('sɛtɪ) NOUN ACRONYM FOR Search for Extraterrestrial Intelligence; the attempt to detect signals, esp radiowaves or light, from an intelligent extraterrestrial source.

setiferous (sɪ'tɪfərəs) *or* **setigerous** (sɪ'tɪdʒərəs) ADJECTIVE *Biology* bearing bristles.
▷HISTORY C19: see SETA, -FEROUS, -GEROUS

setiform ('siːtɪˌfɔːm) ADJECTIVE *Biology* shaped like a seta.

set in VERB (*intr, adverb*) 1 to become established: *the winter has set in.* 2 (of wind) to blow or (of current) to move towards shore. ◆ ADJECTIVE **set-in.** 3 (of a part) made separately and then added to a larger whole: *a set-in sleeve.*

setline ('sɛtˌlaɪn) NOUN any of various types of fishing line that consist of a long line suspended across a stream, between buoys, etc., and having shorter hooked and baited lines attached. See **trawl** (sense 2), **trotline.**

set off VERB (*adverb*) 1 (*intr*) to embark on a journey. 2 (*tr*) to cause (a person) to act or do something, such as laugh or tell stories. 3 (*tr*) to cause to explode. 4 (*tr*) to act as a foil or contrast to, esp so as to improve: *that brooch sets your dress off well.* 5 (*tr*) *Accounting* to cancel a credit on (one account) against a debit on another, both of which are in the name of the same person, enterprise, etc. 6 (*intr*) to bring a claim by way of setoff. ◆ NOUN **setoff.** 7 anything that serves as a counterbalance. 8 anything that serves to contrast with or enhance something else; foil. 9 another name for **setback** (sense 5). 10 a counterbalancing debt or claim offered by a debtor against a creditor. 11 a cross claim brought by a debtor that partly offsets the creditor's claim. ◆ See also **counterclaim.**

set-off NOUN *Printing* a fault in which ink is transferred from a heavily inked or undried printed sheet to the sheet next to it in a pile. Also called (esp Brit): **offset.**

set on VERB (*tr*) 1 (*preposition*) to cause to attack: *they set the dogs on him.* 2 (*adverb*) to instigate or incite; urge: *he set the child on to demand food.*

Seto Naikai ('sɛtəʊ 'naɪkaɪ) NOUN transliteration of the Japanese name for the **Inland Sea.**

setose ('siːtəʊs) ADJECTIVE *Biology* covered with setae; bristly.
▷HISTORY C17: from Latin *saetōsus,* from *saeta* a bristle

set out VERB (*adverb, mainly tr*) 1 to present, arrange, or display: *he set the flowers out in the vase.* 2 to give a full account of; explain exactly: *he set out the matter in full.* 3 to plan or lay out (a garden, etc.). 4 (*intr*) to begin or embark on an undertaking, esp a journey.

set piece NOUN 1 a work of literature, music, etc., often having a conventional or prescribed theme, intended to create an impressive effect. 2 a piece of scenery built to stand independently as part of a stage set. 3 a display of fireworks. 4 *Sport* a rehearsed team manoeuvre, usually attempted in continuous games at a restart of play, esp when the other side has been penalized for improper play.

set point NOUN *Tennis, squash, badminton* a point that would enable one side to win a set.

setscrew ('sɛtˌskruː) NOUN a screw that fits into the boss or hub of a wheel, coupling, cam, etc., and prevents motion of the part relative to the shaft on which it is mounted.

set square NOUN a thin flat piece of plastic, metal, etc., in the shape of a right-angled triangle, used in technical drawing.

sett *or* **set** (sɛt) NOUN 1 a small rectangular paving block made of stone, such as granite, used to provide a durable road surface. Compare **cobblestone.** 2 the burrow of a badger. 3 **a** a square in a pattern of tartan. **b** the pattern itself.
▷HISTORY C19: variant of SET¹ (noun)

settee (sɛ'tiː) NOUN a seat, for two or more people, with a back and usually with arms.
▷HISTORY C18: changed from SETTLE²

setter ('sɛtə) NOUN any of various breeds of large gun dog, having silky coats and plumed tails. See **English setter, Gordon setter, Irish setter.**
▷HISTORY C16: so called because they can be used to indicate where game is: see SET¹

set theory NOUN 1 *Maths* the branch of mathematics concerned with the properties and interrelationships of sets. 2 *Logic* a theory constructed within first-order logic that yields the mathematical theory of classes, esp one that distinguishes sets from proper classes as a means of avoiding certain paradoxes.

setting ('sɛtɪŋ) NOUN 1 the surroundings in which something is set; scene. 2 the scenery, properties, or background, used to create the location for a stage play, film, etc. 3 *Music* a composition consisting of a certain text and music provided or arranged for it. 4 the metal mounting and surround of a gem: *diamonds in an antique gold setting.* 5 the tableware, cutlery, etc., for a single place at table. 6 any of a series of points on a scale or dial that can be selected to control the level as of temperature, speed, etc., at which a machine functions. 7 a clutch of eggs in a bird's nest, esp a clutch of hen's eggs.

setting lotion NOUN a perfumed solution of gum or a synthetic resin in a solvent, used in hairdressing to make a set last longer.

setting rule NOUN *Printing* a metal strip used in the hand-setting of type in a composing stick to separate the line being set from the previous one.

settle¹ ('sɛtᵊl) VERB 1 (*tr*) to put in order; arrange in a desired state or condition: *he settled his affairs before he died.* 2 to arrange or be arranged in a fixed or comfortable position: *he settled himself by the fire.* 3 (*intr*) to come to rest or a halt: *a bird settled on the hedge.* 4 to take up or cause to take up residence: *the family settled in the country.* 5 to establish or become established in a way of life, job, residence, etc. 6 (*tr*) to migrate to and form a community; colonize. 7 to make or become quiet, calm, or stable. 8 (*intr*) to be cast or spread; come down: *fog settled over a wide area.* 9 to make (a liquid) clear or (of a liquid) to become clear; clarify. 10 to cause (sediment) to sink to the bottom, as in a liquid, or (of sediment) to sink thus. 11 to subside or cause to subside and become firm or compact: *the dust settled.* 12 (sometimes foll by *up*) to pay off or account for (a bill, debt, etc.). 13 (*tr*) to decide, conclude, or dispose of: *to settle an argument.* 14 (*intr;* often foll by *on* or *upon*) to agree or fix: *to settle upon a plan.* 15 (*tr;* usually foll by *on* or *upon*) to secure (title, property, etc.) to a person, as by making a deed of settlement, will, etc.: *he settled his property on his wife.* 16 to determine (a legal dispute, etc.) by agreement of the parties without resort to court action (esp in the phrase **settle out of court**). ◆ See also **settle down, settle for, settle in, settle with.**
▷HISTORY Old English *setlan;* related to Dutch *zetelen;* see SETTLE²
▸**'settleable** ADJECTIVE

settle² ('sɛtᵊl) NOUN a seat, for two or more people, usually made of wood with a high back and arms, and sometimes having a storage space in the boxlike seat.
▷HISTORY Old English *setl;* related to Old Saxon, Old High German *sezzal*

settle down VERB (*adverb, mainly intr*) 1 (*also tr*) to make or become quiet and orderly. 2 (often foll by *to*) to apply oneself diligently: *please settle down to work.* 3 to adopt an orderly and routine way of life, take up a permanent post, etc., esp after marriage.

settle for VERB (*intr, preposition*) to accept or agree to in spite of dispute or dissatisfaction.

settle in VERB (*adverb*) to become or help to become adapted to and at ease in a new home, environment, etc.

settlement ('sɛtᵊlmənt) NOUN 1 the act or state of settling or being settled. 2 the establishment of a new region; colonization. 3 a place newly settled; colony. 4 a collection of dwellings forming a community, esp on a frontier. 5 a community formed by members of a group, esp of a religious sect. 6 a public building used to provide educational and general welfare facilities for persons living in deprived areas. 7 a subsidence of all or part of a structure. 8 **a** the payment of an outstanding account, invoice, charge, etc. **b** (*as modifier*): *settlement day.* 9 an adjustment or agreement reached in matters of finance, business, etc. 10 *Law* **a** a conveyance, usually to trustees, of property to be enjoyed by several persons in succession. **b** the deed or other instrument conveying such property. **c** the determination of a dispute, etc., by mutual agreement without resorting to legal proceedings.

settler ('sɛtlə) NOUN a person who settles in a new country or a colony.

settler's clock NOUN *Austral* (formerly) an informal name for **kookaburra.**
▷HISTORY C19: so called because its laugh was heard at dawn and sunset

settle with VERB *(preposition)* 1 *(intr)* to pay a debt or bill to. 2 *(intr)* to make an agreement with. 3 to get one's revenge for (a wrong or injury) with (a person).

settlings ('sɛtlɪŋz) PLURAL NOUN any matter or substance that has settled at the bottom of a liquid; sediment; dregs.

settlor ('sɛtlə) NOUN *Law* a person who settles property on someone.

set to VERB *(intr, adverb)* 1 to begin working. 2 to start fighting. ◆ NOUN **set-to.** 3 *Informal* a brief disagreement or fight.

set-top box NOUN a device which converts the signals from a digital television broadcast into a form which can be viewed on a standard television set.

Setúbal *(Portuguese* sə'tuβal) NOUN a port in SW Portugal, on **Setúbal Bay** south of Lisbon: an earthquake in 1755 destroyed most of the old town. Pop.: 83 550 (1991).

set up VERB *(adverb, mainly tr)* 1 *(also intr)* to put into a position of power, etc. 2 *(also intr)* to begin or enable (someone) to begin (a new venture), as by acquiring or providing means, equipment, etc. 3 to build or construct: *to set up a shed.* 4 to raise, cause, or produce: *to set up a wail.* 5 to advance or propose: *to set up a theory.* 6 to restore the health of: *the sea air will set you up again.* 7 to establish (a record). 8 *Informal* to cause (a person) to be blamed, accused, etc. 9 *Informal* **a** to provide (drinks, etc.) for: *set 'em up, Joe!* **b** to pay for the drinks of: *I'll set up the next round.* 10 *Printing* another term for **set**[1] (sense 12). ◆ NOUN **setup.** 11 *Informal* the way in which anything is organized or arranged. 12 *Slang* an event the result of which is prearranged: *it's a setup.* 13 a prepared arrangement of materials, machines, etc., for a job or undertaking. 14 a station at which a surveying instrument, esp a theodolite, is set up. 15 *Films* the position of the camera, microphones, and performers at the beginning of a scene. ◆ ADJECTIVE **set-up.** 16 physically well-built.

set upon VERB *(intr, preposition)* to attack: *three thugs set upon him.*

set width NOUN another name for **set**[1] (sense 39).

Sevan (sɛ'vɑːn) NOUN **Lake.** a lake in Armenia at an altitude of 1914 m (6279 ft.). Area: 1417 sq. km (547 sq. miles).

Sevastopol *(Russian* sɪvas'tɔpəlj) NOUN a port, resort, and naval base in the S Ukraine, in the Crimea, on the Black Sea: captured and destroyed by British, French, and Turkish forces after a siege of 11 months (1854–55) during the Crimean War; taken by the Germans after a siege of 8 months (1942) during World War II. Pop.: 356 000 (1998 est.). English name: **Sebastopol.**

seven ('sɛvᵊn) NOUN 1 the cardinal number that is the sum of six and one and is a prime number. See also **number** (sense 1). 2 a numeral, 7, VII, etc., representing this number. 3 the amount or quantity that is one greater than six. 4 anything representing, represented by, or consisting of seven units, such as a playing card with seven symbols on it. 5 Also called: **seven o'clock.** seven hours after noon or midnight. ◆ DETERMINER 6 **a** amounting to seven: *seven swans a-swimming.* **b** *(as pronoun): you've eaten seven already.* ◆ Related prefixes: **hepta-, septi-.** ◆ See also **sevens.**
▷HISTORY Old English *seofon;* related to Gothic *sibun,* German *sieben,* Old Norse *sjau,* Latin *septem,* Greek *hepta,* Sanskrit *saptá*

Seven against Thebes PLURAL NOUN *Greek myth* the seven members of an expedition undertaken to regain for Polynices, a son of Oedipus, his share in the throne of Thebes from his usurping brother Eteocles. The seven are usually listed as Polynices, Adrastus, Amphiaraus, Capaneus, Hippomedon, Tydeus, and Parthenopaeus. The campaign failed and the warring brothers killed each other in single combat before the Theban walls. See also **Adrastus.**

seven deadly sins PLURAL NOUN a fuller name for the **deadly sins.**

sevenfold ('sɛvᵊn,fəʊld) ADJECTIVE 1 equal to or having seven times as many or as much. 2 composed of seven parts. ◆ ADVERB 3 by or up to seven times as many or as much.

Seven Hills of Rome PLURAL NOUN the hills on which the ancient city of Rome was built: the Palatine, Capitoline, Quirinal, Caelian, Aventine, Esquiline, and Viminal.

sevens ('sɛvᵊnz) NOUN *(functioning as singular)* a Rugby Union match or series of matches played with seven players on each side.

seven seas PLURAL NOUN the oceans of the world considered as the N and S Pacific, the N and S Atlantic, and the Arctic, Antarctic, and Indian Oceans.

seven-segment display NOUN an arrangement of seven bars forming a square figure of eight, used in electronic displays of alphanumeric characters: any letter or figure can be represented by illuminating selected bars.

Seven Sleepers PLURAL NOUN seven Christian youths from Ephesus who were walled up in a cave by the Emperor Decius in 250 A.D. and, according to legend, slept for 187 years.

seventeen ('sɛvᵊn'tiːn) NOUN 1 the cardinal number that is the sum of ten and seven and is a prime number. See also **number** (sense 1). 2 a numeral, 17, XVII, etc., representing this number. 3 the amount or quantity that is seven more than ten. 4 something represented by, representing, or consisting of 17 units. ◆ DETERMINER 5 **a** amounting to seventeen: *seventeen attempts.* **b** *(as pronoun): seventeen were sold.*
▷HISTORY Old English *seofontīene*

seventeenth ('sɛvᵊn'tiːnθ) ADJECTIVE 1 *(usually prenominal)* **a** coming after the sixteenth in numbering or counting order, position, time, etc.; being the ordinal number of *seventeen:* often written 17th. **b** *(as noun): the ship docks on the seventeenth.* ◆ NOUN 2 **a** one of 17 approximately equal parts of something. **b** *(as modifier): a seventeenth part.* 3 the fraction equal to one divided by 17 (1/17).

seventeen-year locust NOUN an E North American cicada, *Magicicada septendecim,* appearing in great numbers at infrequent intervals because its nymphs take 13 or 17 years to mature. Also called: **periodical cicada.**

seventh ('sɛvᵊnθ) ADJECTIVE 1 *(usually prenominal)* **a** coming after the sixth and before the eighth in numbering or counting order, position, time, etc.; being the ordinal number of *seven:* often written 7th. **b** *(as noun): she left on the seventh; he was the seventh to arrive.* ◆ NOUN 2 **a** one of seven equal or nearly equal parts of an object, quantity, measurement, etc. **b** *(as modifier): a seventh part.* 3 the fraction equal to one divided by seven (1/7). 4 *Music* **a** the interval between one note and another seven notes away from it counting inclusively along the diatonic scale. **b** one of two notes constituting such an interval in relation to the other. See also **major** (sense 14), **minor** (sense 4), **interval** (sense 5). **c** short for **seventh chord.** ◆ ADVERB 5 Also: **seventhly.** after the sixth person, position, event, etc. ◆ SENTENCE CONNECTOR 6 Also: **seventhly.** as the seventh point: linking what follows to the previous statements, as in a speech or argument.

seventh chord NOUN *Music* a chord consisting of a triad with a seventh added above the root. See **dominant seventh chord, diminished seventh chord, major seventh chord, minor seventh chord.**

Seventh-Day Adventist NOUN *Protestant theol* a member of that branch of the Adventists which constituted itself as a separate body after the expected Second Coming of Christ failed to be realized in 1844. They are strongly Protestant, believe that Christ's coming is imminent, and observe Saturday instead of Sunday as their Sabbath.

seventh heaven NOUN 1 the final state of eternal bliss, esp according to Talmudic and Muslim eschatology. 2 a state of supreme happiness.
▷HISTORY C19: so named from the belief that there are seven levels of heaven, the seventh and most exalted being the abode of God and the angels

seventieth ('sɛvᵊntɪɪθ) ADJECTIVE 1 *(usually prenominal)* **a** being the ordinal number of *seventy* in numbering or counting order, position, time, etc.: often written 70th. **b** *(as noun): the seventieth in line.* ◆ NOUN 2 **a** one of 70 approximately equal parts of something. **b** *(as modifier): a seventieth part.* 3 the fraction equal to one divided by 70 (1/70).

seventy ('sɛvᵊntɪ) NOUN, *plural* **-ties.** 1 the cardinal number that is the product of ten and seven. See also **number** (sense 1). 2 a numeral, 70, LXX, etc., representing this number. 3 *(plural)* the numbers 70–79, esp the 70th to the 79th year of a person's life or of a particular century. 4 the amount or quantity that is seven times as big as ten. 5 something represented by, representing, or consisting of 70 units. ◆ DETERMINER 6 **a** amounting to seventy: *the seventy varieties of fabric.* **b** *(as pronoun): to invite seventy to the wedding.*
▷HISTORY Old English *seofontig*

seven-up NOUN a card game in which the lead to each round determines the trump suit. Also called: **all fours, pitch.**

Seven Wonders of the World PLURAL NOUN the seven structures considered by ancient and medieval scholars to be the most wondrous of the ancient world. The list varies, but generally consists of the Pyramids of Egypt, the Hanging Gardens of Babylon, Phidias' statue of Zeus at Olympia, the temple of Artemis at Ephesus, the mausoleum of Halicarnassus, the Colossus of Rhodes, and the Pharos (or lighthouse) of Alexandria.

seven-year itch NOUN *Informal* a tendency towards infidelity, traditionally said to begin after about seven years of marriage.

Seven Years' War NOUN the war (1756–63) of Britain and Prussia, who emerged in the ascendant, against France and Austria, resulting from commercial and colonial rivalry between Britain and France and from the conflict in Germany between Prussia and Austria.

sever ('sɛvə) VERB 1 to put or be put apart; separate. 2 to divide or be divided into parts. 3 *(tr)* to break off or dissolve (a tie, relationship, etc.).
▷HISTORY C14 *severen,* from Old French *severer,* from Latin *sēparāre* to SEPARATE

severable ('sɛvərəbᵊl) ADJECTIVE 1 able to be severed. 2 *Law* capable of being separated, as a clause in an agreement: *a severable contract.*

several ('sɛvrəl) DETERMINER 1 **a** more than a few; an indefinite small number: *several people objected.* **b** *(as pronoun; functioning as plural): several of them know.* ◆ ADJECTIVE 2 *(prenominal)* various; separate: *the members with their several occupations.* 3 *(prenominal)* distinct; different: *three several times.* 4 *Law* capable of being dealt with separately; not shared. Compare **joint** (sense 15).
▷HISTORY C15: via Anglo-French from Medieval Latin *sēparālis,* from Latin *sēpār,* from *sēparāre* to SEPARATE

severally ('sɛvrəlɪ) ADVERB 1 separately, individually, or distinctly. 2 each in turn; respectively.

severalty ('sɛvrəltɪ) NOUN, *plural* **-ties.** 1 the state of being several or separate. 2 (usually preceded by *in) Property law* the tenure of property, esp land, in a person's own right and not jointly with another or others.

severance ('sɛvərəns) NOUN 1 the act of severing or state of being severed. 2 a separation. 3 *Law* the division into separate parts of a joint estate, contract, etc.

severance pay NOUN compensation paid by an organization to an employee who leaves because, through no fault of his own, the job to which he was appointed ceases to exist, as during rationalization, and no comparable job is available to him.

severe (sɪ'vɪə) ADJECTIVE 1 rigorous or harsh in the treatment of others; strict: *a severe parent.* 2 serious in appearance or manner; stern. 3 critical or dangerous: *a severe illness.* 4 causing misery or discomfort by its harshness: *severe weather.* 5 strictly restrained in appearance; austere: *a severe way of dressing.* 6 hard to endure, perform, or accomplish: *a severe test.* 7 rigidly precise or exact.
▷HISTORY C16: from Latin *sevērus*
▸**se'verely** ADVERB ▸**se'vereness** *or* **severity** (sɪ'vɛrɪtɪ) NOUN

Severn ('sɛvᵊn) NOUN 1 a river in E Wales and W

England, rising in Powys and flowing northeast and east into England, then south to the Bristol Channel. Length: about 290 km (180 miles). 2 a river in SE central Canada, in Ontario, flowing northeast to Hudson Bay. Length: about 676 km (420 miles).

Severnaya Zemlya (*Russian* 'sjevɪrnəjə zɪm'lja) NOUN an archipelago in the Arctic Ocean off the coast of N central Russia.

Seveso (sɛ'veɪsəʊ) NOUN a town in N Italy, near Milan: evacuated in 1976 after contamination by a poisonous cloud of dioxin gas released from a factory.

Seville (sə'vɪl) NOUN a port in SW Spain, on the Guadalquivir River: chief town of S Spain under the Vandals and Visigoths (5th–8th centuries); centre of Spanish colonial trade (16th–17th centuries); tourist centre. Pop.: 701 927 (1998 est.). Ancient name: **Hispalis.** Spanish name: **Sevilla** (se'βiʎa).

Seville orange NOUN 1 an orange tree, *Citrus aurantium,* of tropical and semitropical regions: grown for its bitter fruit, which is used to make marmalade. 2 the fruit of this tree. ◆ Also called: **bitter orange.**

Sèvres (*French* sɛvrə) NOUN porcelain ware manufactured at Sèvres, near Paris, from 1756, characterized by the use of clear colours and elaborate decorative detail.

sew (səʊ) VERB **sews, sewing, sewed; sewn** *or* **sewed.** 1 to join or decorate (pieces of fabric, etc.) by means of a thread repeatedly passed through with a needle or similar implement. 2 (*tr;* often foll by *on* or *up*) to attach, fasten, or close by sewing. 3 (*tr*) to make (a garment, etc.) by sewing. ◆ See also **sew up.**
▷HISTORY Old English *sēowan;* related to Old Norse *sȳja,* Gothic *siujan,* Old High German *siuwen,* Latin *suere* to sew, Sanskrit *sīvjati* he sews

sewage ('suːɪdʒ) NOUN waste matter from domestic or industrial establishments that is carried away in sewers or drains for dumping or conversion into a form that is not toxic.
▷HISTORY C19: back formation from SEWER[1]

sewage farm NOUN a place where sewage is treated, esp for use as manure.

sewage gas NOUN gas given off in the digestion of sewage consisting of approximately 66 per cent methane and 34 per cent carbon dioxide.

sewan ('siːwən) NOUN a variant spelling of **seawan.**

Seward Peninsula ('sjuːəd) NOUN a peninsula of W Alaska, on the Bering Strait. Length: about 290 km (180 miles).

sewellel (sɪ'wɛləl) NOUN another name for **mountain beaver** (see **beaver**[1] (sense 3)).
▷HISTORY C19: probably from Chinook

sewer[1] ('suːə) NOUN 1 a drain or pipe, esp one that is underground, used to carry away surface water or sewage. ◆ VERB 2 (*tr*) to provide with sewers.
▷HISTORY C15: from Old French *esseveur,* from *essever* to drain, from Vulgar Latin *exaquāre* (unattested), from Latin EX-[1] + *aqua* water

sewer[2] ('səʊə) NOUN a person or thing that sews.

sewer[3] ('suːə) NOUN (in medieval England) a servant of high rank in charge of the serving of meals and the seating of guests.
▷HISTORY C14: shortened from Anglo-French *asseour,* from Old French *asseoir* to cause to sit, from Latin *assidēre,* from *sedēre* to sit

sewerage ('suːərɪdʒ) NOUN 1 an arrangement of sewers. 2 the removal of surface water or sewage by means of sewers. 3 another word for **sewage.**

sewin *or* **sewen** ('sjʊən) NOUN (in Wales and Ireland) another name for the **sea trout.**
▷HISTORY C16: origin unknown

sewing ('səʊɪŋ) NOUN **a** a piece of cloth, etc., that is sewn or to be sewn. **b** (*as modifier*): *sewing basket.*

sewing machine NOUN any machine designed to sew material. It is now usually driven by electric motor but is sometimes operated by a foot treadle or by hand.

sewn (səʊn) VERB a past participle of **sew.**

sewn binding NOUN *Bookbinding* a style of binding where the backs of the gathered sections are sewn together before being inserted into a cover.

sew up VERB (*tr, adverb*) 1 to fasten or mend completely by sewing. 2 *US* to acquire sole use or control of. 3 *Informal* to complete or negotiate successfully: *to sew up a deal.*

sex (sɛks) NOUN 1 the sum of the characteristics that distinguish organisms on the basis of their reproductive function. 2 either of the two categories, male or female, into which organisms are placed on this basis. 3 short for **sexual intercourse.** 4 feelings or behaviour resulting from the urge to gratify the sexual instinct. 5 sexual matters in general. ◆ MODIFIER 6 of or concerning sexual matters: *sex education; sex hygiene.* 7 based on or arising from the difference between the sexes: *sex discrimination.* ◆ VERB 8 (*tr*) to ascertain the sex of.
▷HISTORY C14: from Latin *sexus;* compare *secāre* to divide

sex- COMBINING FORM six: *sexcentennial.*
▷HISTORY from Latin

sexagenarian (ˌsɛksədʒɪ'nɛərɪən) NOUN 1 a person from 60 to 69 years old. ◆ ADJECTIVE 2 being from 60 to 69 years old. 3 of or relating to a sexagenarian.
▷HISTORY C18: from Latin *sexāgēnārius,* from *sexāgēnī* sixty each, from *sexāgintā* sixty
▶**sexagenary** (sɛk'sædʒɪnərɪ) ADJECTIVE, NOUN

Sexagesima (ˌsɛksə'dʒɛsɪmə) NOUN the second Sunday before Lent.
▷HISTORY C16: from Latin: sixtieth, from *sexāgintā* sixty

sexagesimal (ˌsɛksə'dʒɛsɪməl) ADJECTIVE 1 relating to or based on the number 60: *sexagesimal measurement of angles.* ◆ NOUN 2 a fraction in which the denominator is some power of 60; a sixtieth.

sex-and-shopping ADJECTIVE (*prenominal*) (of a novel) belonging to a genre of novel in which the central character, a woman, has a number of sexual encounters, and the author mentions the name of many up-market products: *a sex-and-shopping blockbuster.*

sexangular (sɛks'æŋgjʊlə) ADJECTIVE another name for **hexagonal.**
▶**sex'angularly** ADVERB

sex appeal NOUN the quality or power of attracting the opposite sex.

sexcentenary (ˌsɛksɛn'tiːnərɪ) ADJECTIVE 1 of or relating to 600 or a period of 600 years. 2 of, relating to, or celebrating a 600th anniversary. ◆ NOUN, *plural* **-naries.** 3 a 600th anniversary or its celebration.
▷HISTORY C18: from Latin *sexcentēnī* six hundred each

sex change NOUN **a** a change in a person's physical sexual characteristics to those of the opposite sex, often achieved by surgery. **b** (*as modifier*): *a sex-change operation.*

sex chromosome NOUN either of the chromosomes determining the sex of animals. See also **X-chromosome, Y-chromosome.**

sexed (sɛkst) ADJECTIVE 1 (*in combination*) having a specified degree of sexuality: *undersexed.* 2 of, relating to, or having sexual differentiation.

sexennial (sɛk'sɛnɪəl) ADJECTIVE 1 occurring once every six years or over a period of six years. ◆ NOUN 2 a sixth anniversary.
▷HISTORY C17: from Latin *sexennis* of six years, from *sex* six + *annus* a year
▶**sex'ennially** ADVERB

sexercise ('sɛksəˌsaɪz) NOUN sexual activity, regarded as a way of keeping fit.

sex hormone NOUN an animal hormone affecting development and growth of reproductive organs and related parts.

sexism ('sɛksɪzəm) NOUN discrimination on the basis of sex, esp the oppression of women by men.
▷HISTORY C20: from SEX + -ISM, on the model of RACISM
▶**'sexist** NOUN, ADJECTIVE

sexivalent *or* **sexavalent** (ˌsɛksɪ'veɪlənt) ADJECTIVE *Chem* another word for **hexavalent.**

sexless ('sɛkslɪs) ADJECTIVE 1 having or showing no sexual differentiation. 2 having no sexual desires. 3 sexually unattractive.
▶**'sexlessly** ADVERB ▶**'sexlessness** NOUN

sex-limited ADJECTIVE *Genetics* of or designating a character or the gene producing it that appears in one sex only.

sex linkage NOUN *Genetics* the condition in which a particular gene is located on a sex chromosome, esp on the X-chromosome, so that the character controlled by the gene is associated with either of the sexes.
▶**'sexˌlinked** ADJECTIVE

sex object NOUN a person viewed or treated as a means of obtaining sexual gratification.

sexology (sɛk'sɒlədʒɪ) NOUN the study of sexual behaviour in human beings.
▶**sex'ologist** NOUN ▶**sexological** (ˌsɛksə'lɒdʒɪkᵊl) ADJECTIVE

sexpartite (sɛks'pɑːtaɪt) ADJECTIVE 1 (esp of vaults, arches, etc.) divided into or composed of six parts. 2 maintained by or involving six participants or groups of participants.

sexpert ('sɛkspɜːt) NOUN *Informal* a person who professes a knowledge of sexual matters.
▷HISTORY C20: a blend of SEX + EXPERT

sexploitation (ˌsɛksplɔɪ'teɪʃən) NOUN the commercial exploitation of sex in films and other media.
▷HISTORY C20: blend of SEX + EXPLOITATION

sexpot ('sɛksˌpɒt) NOUN *Slang* a person, esp a young woman, considered as being sexually very attractive.

sex shop NOUN **a** a shop selling aids purporting to increase the pleasurableness of sexual activity. **b** a shop selling erotica and pornographic material.

sex-starved ADJECTIVE deprived of sexual gratification.

sext (sɛkst) NOUN *Chiefly RC Church* the fourth of the seven canonical hours of the divine office or the prayers prescribed for it: originally the sixth hour of the day (noon).
▷HISTORY C15: from Church Latin *sexta hōra* the sixth hour

Sext (sɛkst) NOUN *RC Church* an official compilation of decretals issued by Boniface VIII in 1298 to supplement the five books of the Liber Extra. It forms part of the Corpus Juris Canonici. In full: **Liber Sextus.**

sextain ('sɛksteɪn) NOUN another word for **sestina.**
▷HISTORY C17: from obsolete French *sestine* SESTINA, but also influenced by obsolete *sixain* stanza of six lines

sextan ('sɛkstən) ADJECTIVE (of a fever) marked by paroxysms that recur after an interval of five days.
▷HISTORY C17: from Medieval Latin *sextana* (*febris*) (fever) of the sixth (day)

Sextans ('sɛkstənz) NOUN, *Latin genitive* **Sextantis** (sɛks'tæntɪs). a faint constellation lying on the celestial equator close to Leo and Hydra.
▷HISTORY New Latin: SEXTANT

sextant ('sɛkstənt) NOUN 1 an optical instrument used in navigation and consisting of a telescope through which a sighting of a heavenly body is taken, with protractors for determining its angular distance above the horizon or from another heavenly body. 2 a sixth part of a circle having an arc which subtends an angle of 60°.
▷HISTORY C17: from Latin *sextāns* one sixth of a unit

sextet *or* **sextette** (sɛks'tɛt) NOUN 1 *Music* a group of six singers or instrumentalists or a piece of music composed for such a group. 2 a group of six people or things.
▷HISTORY C19: variant of SESTET, with Latinization of *ses-*

sex-text VERB (*tr*) to send a text message of a sexual nature to (someone).

sex therapy NOUN treatment by counselling, behaviour modification, etc., for psychosexual and physical problems in sexual intercourse.
▶**sex therapist** NOUN

sextile ('sɛkstaɪl) NOUN 1 *Statistics* one of five actual or notional values of a variable dividing its distribution into six groups with equal frequencies. 2 *Astrology, astronomy* an aspect or position of 60° between two planets or other celestial bodies.
▷HISTORY C16: from Latin *sextīlis* one sixth (of a circle), from *sextus* sixth

sextillion (sɛks'tɪljən) NOUN, *plural* **-lions** *or* **-lion.** 1 (in Britain, France, and Germany) the number represented as one followed by 36 zeros (10^{36}). 2 (in the US and Canada) the number represented as one followed by 21 zeros (10^{21}).

▷HISTORY C17: from French, from SEX- + *-illion,* on the model of SEPTILLION
▸**sex'tillionth** ADJECTIVE, NOUN

sexto ('sɛkstəʊ) NOUN, *plural* **-tos**. another word for **sixmo.**
▷HISTORY C19: from Latin *sextus* sixth

sextodecimo (ˌsɛkstəʊ'dɛsɪˌməʊ) NOUN, *plural* **-mos**. *Bookbinding* another word for **sixteenmo.**
▷HISTORY C17: from Latin *sextusdecimus* sixteenth

sexton ('sɛkstən) NOUN 1 a person employed to act as caretaker of a church and its contents and graveyard, and often also as bell-ringer, gravedigger, etc. 2 another name for the **burying beetle.**
▷HISTORY C14: from Old French *secrestein,* from Medieval Latin *sacristānus* SACRISTAN

sex tourism NOUN tourism with the intention of exploiting permissive or poorly enforced local laws concerning sex, esp sex with children.

sextuple ('sɛkstjʊpᵊl) NOUN 1 a quantity or number six times as great as another. ◆ ADJECTIVE 2 six times as much or many; sixfold. 3 consisting of six parts or members. 4 (of musical time or rhythm) having six beats per bar.
▷HISTORY C17: Latin *sextus* sixth + *-uple,* as in QUADRUPLE

sextuplet ('sɛkstjʊplɪt) NOUN 1 one of six offspring born at one birth. 2 a group of six things. 3 *Music* a group of six notes played in a time value of four.

sextuplicate NOUN (sɛks'tu:pləkɪt, -ˌkeɪt, -'tju:-, -'tʌp-) 1 a group or set of six things, esp identical copies. ◆ ADJECTIVE (sɛks'tu:pləkɪt, -ˌkeɪt, -'tju:-, -'tʌp-) 2 six times as many, much, or often. 3 *Maths* raised to the sixth power. ◆ VERB (sɛks'tu:pləˌkeɪt, -'tju:-, -'tʌp-) 4 to multiply or become multiplied by six.
▷HISTORY C20: from SEXTU(PLE + DU)PLICATE

sex-typed ADJECTIVE characterized as appropriate for or of one sex rather than the other.
▸**'sex-ˌtyping** NOUN

sexual ('sɛksjʊəl) ADJECTIVE 1 of, relating to, or characterized by sex or sexuality. 2 (of reproduction) characterized by the union of male and female gametes. Compare **asexual** (sense 2).
▷HISTORY C17: from Late Latin *sexuālis;* see SEX
▸**'sexually** ADVERB

sexual dimorphism NOUN *Biology* differences in appearance between the males and females of a species.

sexual harassment NOUN the persistent unwelcome directing of sexual remarks and looks, and unnecessary physical contact at a person, usually a woman, esp in the workplace.

sexual intercourse NOUN the act carried out for procreation or for pleasure in which the insertion of the male's erect penis into the female's vagina is followed by rhythmic thrusting usually culminating in orgasm; copulation; coitus. Related adjective: **venereal.**

sexuality (ˌsɛksjʊ'ælɪtɪ) NOUN 1 the state or quality of being sexual. 2 preoccupation with or involvement in sexual matters. 3 the possession of sexual potency.

sexualize *or* **sexualise** ('sɛksjʊəˌlaɪz) VERB 1 to make or become sexual or sexually aware. 2 to give or acquire sexual associations.
▸**ˌsexuali'zation** *or* **ˌsexuali'sation** NOUN

sexual reproduction NOUN reproduction involving the fusion of a male and female haploid gamete.

sexual selection NOUN an evolutionary process in animals, in which selection by females of males with certain characters, such as large antlers or bright plumage, results in the preservation of these characters in the species.

sex up VERB (*tr, adverb*) *Informal* to make (something) more interesting or exciting: *the BBC decided to sex up the book's title.*

sex worker NOUN a prostitute.

sexy ('sɛksɪ) ADJECTIVE **sexier, sexiest.** *Informal* 1 provoking or intended to provoke sexual interest: *a sexy dress; a sexy book.* 2 feeling sexual interest; aroused. 3 interesting, exciting, or trendy: *a sexy project; a sexy new car.*
▸**'sexily** ADVERB ▸**'sexiness** NOUN

Seychelles (seɪ'ʃɛl, -'ʃɛlz) PLURAL NOUN a group of volcanic islands in the W Indian Ocean: taken by the British from the French in 1744: became an independent republic within the Commonwealth in 1976, incorporating the British Indian Ocean Territory islands of Aldabra, Farquhar and Desroches. Languages: Creole, English, and French. Religion: Roman Catholic majority. Currency: rupee. Capital: Victoria. Pop.: 80 600 (2001 est.). Area: 455 sq. km (176 sq. miles).

Seyfert galaxy ('saɪfət) NOUN any of a class of spiral galaxies having a very bright nucleus, possibly corresponding to an active period in the lives of all spiral galaxies.
▷HISTORY C20: named after Carl K. *Seyfert* (died 1960), US astronomer

Seyhan (seɪ'hɑ:n) NOUN another name for **Adana.**

sf, sf., sfz, *or* **sfz.** *Music* ABBREVIATION FOR sforzando.

SF *or* **sf** ABBREVIATION FOR science fiction.

SFA ABBREVIATION FOR: 1 Scottish Football Association. 2 Sweet Fanny Adams. See **fanny adams.**

Sfax (sfæks) NOUN a port in E Tunisia, on the Gulf of Gabès: the second largest town in Tunisia; commercial centre of a phosphate region. Pop.: 230 900 (1994).

sferics ('sfɛrɪks) NOUN the usual US spelling of **spherics**².

SFO ABBREVIATION FOR Serious Fraud Office: the department of the British government which investigates cases of serious financial fraud.

sforzando (sfɔ:'tsɑ:ndəʊ) *or* **sforzato** (sfɔ:'tsɑ:təʊ) *Music* ◆ ADJECTIVE, ADVERB 1 to be played with strong initial attack. Abbreviation: **sf.** ◆ NOUN 2 a symbol, mark, etc., such as >, written above a note, indicating this.
▷HISTORY C19: from Italian, from *sforzare* to force, from EX-¹ + *forzare,* from Vulgar Latin *fortiāre* (unattested) to FORCE¹

sfumato (sfu:'mɑ:təʊ) NOUN (in painting) a gradual transition between areas of different colour, avoiding sharp outlines.
▷HISTORY from Italian, from *sfumato* shaded off, from *sfumare* to shade off, from Latin EX-¹ + *fūmāre* to smoke

SFW (in South Africa) ABBREVIATION FOR Stellenbosch Farmers' Winery, South Africa's leading wine producer.

SFX *Films, television, etc.* 1 short for **sound effects.** 2 short for **special effects.**
▷HISTORY C20: S(OUND), S(PECIAL) + a phonetic respelling of EFFECTS

sg¹ ABBREVIATION FOR specific gravity.

sg² THE INTERNET DOMAIN NAME FOR Singapore.

SG ABBREVIATION FOR: 1 (in transformational grammar) singular. 2 solicitor general.

sgd ABBREVIATION FOR signed.

SGHWR ABBREVIATION FOR **steam-generating heavy-water reactor.**

sgian-dhu ('ski:ən'du:, 'ski:n-) NOUN *Scot* a dirk carried in the stocking by Highlanders.
▷HISTORY Gaelic *sgian* knife + *dhu* black

SGML ABBREVIATION FOR standard generalized mark-up language: an international standard used in publishing for defining the structure and formatting of documents.

SGP INTERNATIONAL CAR REGISTRATION FOR Singapore.

sgraffito (sgræ'fi:təʊ) NOUN, *plural* **-ti** (-tɪ). 1 a technique in mural or ceramic decoration in which the top layer of glaze, plaster, etc., is incised with a design to reveal parts of the ground. 2 such a decoration. 3 an object decorated in such a way.
▷HISTORY C18: from Italian, from *sgraffire* to scratch; see GRAFFITI

's Gravenhage (sxra:vən'ha:xə) NOUN the Dutch name for (The) **Hague.**

Sgt ABBREVIATION FOR Sergeant.

Sgt Maj. ABBREVIATION FOR Sergeant Major.

sh¹ (*spelling pron* ʃʃ) INTERJECTION an exclamation to request silence or quiet.

sh² THE INTERNET DOMAIN NAME FOR St. Helena.

SHA *Navigation* ABBREVIATION FOR sidereal hour angle.

Shaanxi ('ʃæn'ʃi:) *or* **Shensi** NOUN a province of NW China: one of the earliest centres of Chinese civilization; largely mountainous. Capital: Xi An. Pop.: 32 970 000 (2000 est.). Area: 195 800 sq. km (75 598 sq. miles).

Shaba ('ʃɑ:bə) NOUN a region of SE Democratic Republic of Congo (formerly Zaïre): site of a secessionist movement during the 1960s and again declared itself independent in 1993; important for hydroelectric power and rich mineral resources (copper and tin ore). Pop.: 4 125 000 (1998 est.). Area: 496 964 sq. km (191 878 sq. miles). Former name (until 1972): **Katanga.**

Shaban *or* **Shaaban** (ʃə'bɑ:n, ʃɑ:-) NOUN the eighth month of the Muslim year.
▷HISTORY from Arabic *sha'bān*

Shabbat (ʃɑ:'bɑ:t), **Shabbos,** *or* **Shabbes** ('ʃɑ:bəs) NOUN, *plural* **Shabbatot** (ˌʃɑ:bɑ:'tɒt), **Shabbosos** (ʃɑ:'bɒsəs) *or* **Shabbosim** (ʃɑ:bɒsəm). *Judaism* another word for the **Sabbath.**
▷HISTORY from Hebrew *shabbāth;* see SABBATH

shabby ('ʃæbɪ) ADJECTIVE **-bier, -biest.** 1 threadbare or dilapidated in appearance. 2 wearing worn and dirty clothes; seedy. 3 mean, despicable, or unworthy: *shabby treatment.* 4 dirty or squalid.
▷HISTORY C17: from Old English *sceabb* SCAB + -Y¹
▸**'shabbily** ADVERB ▸**'shabbiness** NOUN

shabby-genteel ADJECTIVE preserving or aspiring to the forms and manners of gentility despite appearing shabby.

Shabuoth (ʃə'vu:əs, -əʊs; *Hebrew* ʃavu:'ɔt) NOUN a variant spelling of **Shavuot.**

Shacharis *Hebrew* ('ʃɑxəˌrɑs) *or* ***Shaharith*** (ˌʃɑxɑ'rit) NOUN *Judaism* the morning service.

Shache ('ʃæ'tʃeɪ), **Soche,** *or* **So-ch'e** NOUN a town in W China, in the W Xinjiang Uygur AR: a centre of the caravan trade between China, India, and Transcaspian areas. Also called: **Yarkand.**

shack¹ (ʃæk) NOUN 1 a roughly built hut. 2 *South African* a building providing basic accommodation on a wilderness trail. ◆ VERB 3 See **shack up.**
▷HISTORY C19: perhaps from dialect *shackly* ramshackle, from dialect *shack* to shake

shack² (ʃæk) VERB *Midland English dialect* to evade (work or responsibility).

shackle ('ʃækᵊl) NOUN 1 (*often plural*) a metal ring or fastening, usually part of a pair used to secure a person's wrists or ankles; fetter. 2 (*often plural*) anything that confines or restricts freedom. 3 a rope, tether, or hobble for an animal. 4 a U-shaped bracket, the open end of which is closed by a bolt (**shackle pin**), used for securing ropes, chains, etc. ◆ VERB (*tr*) 5 to confine with or as if with shackles. 6 to fasten or connect with a shackle.
▷HISTORY Old English *sceacel;* related to Dutch *schakel,* Old Norse *skokull* wagon pole, Latin *cingere* to surround
▸**'shackler** NOUN

shacko ('ʃækəʊ) NOUN, *plural* **shackos** *or* **shackoes.** a variant spelling of **shako.**

shack up VERB (*intr, adverb;* usually foll by *with*) *Slang* to live or take up residence, esp with a mistress or lover.

shad (ʃæd) NOUN, *plural* **shad** *or* **shads.** 1 any of various herring-like food fishes of the genus *Alosa* and related genera, such as *A. alosa* (**allis shad**) of Europe, that migrate from the sea to freshwater to spawn: family *Clupeidae* (herrings). 2 any of various similar but unrelated fishes.
▷HISTORY Old English *sceadd;* related to Norwegian *skadd,* German *Schade* shad, Old Irish *scatān* herring, Latin *scatēre* to well up

shadberry ('ʃædbərɪ, -brɪ) NOUN, *plural* **-ries.** another name for **serviceberry** (senses 1, 2).
▷HISTORY C19: perhaps so called because they appear when SHAD fish are in the rivers to spawn

shadbush ('ʃædˌbʊʃ) NOUN another name for **serviceberry** (sense 1).

shadchan *Yiddish* ('ʃatxən; *Hebrew* ʃad'xɑn) NOUN, *plural* ***shadchanim*** (ʃat'xɔnɪm) *or* ***shadchans.*** a Jewish marriage broker.
▷HISTORY from Hebrew *shadhkhān,* from *shiddēkh* to arrange a marriage

shaddock ('ʃædək) NOUN another name for **pomelo.**
▷HISTORY C17: named after Captain *Shaddock,* who brought its seed from the East Indies to Jamaica in 1696

shade (ʃeɪd) NOUN 1 relative darkness produced

by the blocking out of light. [2] a place made relatively darker or cooler than other areas by the blocking of light, esp sunlight. [3] a position of relative obscurity. [4] something used to provide a shield or protection from a direct source of light, such as a lampshade. [5] a darker area indicated in a painting, drawing, etc., by shading. [6] a colour that varies slightly from a standard colour due to a difference in hue, saturation, or luminosity: *a darker shade of green.* [7] a slight amount: *a shade of difference.* [8] *Literary* a ghost. [9] an archaic word for **shadow.** [10] **put in the shade.** to appear better than (another); surpass. ◆ VERB *(mainly tr)* [11] to screen or protect from heat, light, view, etc. [12] to make darker or dimmer. [13] to represent (a darker area) in (a painting, drawing, etc.), by means of hatching, using a darker colour, etc. [14] *(also intr)* to change or cause to change slightly. [15] to lower (a price) slightly.
▷HISTORY Old English *sceadu;* related to Gothic *skadus,* Old High German *skato,* Old Irish *scāth* shadow, Greek *skotos* darkness, Swedish *skäddä* fog
▸ **'shadeless** ADJECTIVE

shades (ʃeɪdz) PLURAL NOUN [1] gathering darkness at nightfall. [2] a slang word for **sunglasses.** [3] *(often capital; preceded by the)* a literary term for **Hades.** [4] (foll by *of*) undertones or suggestions: *shades of my father!*

shading ('ʃeɪdɪŋ) NOUN the graded areas of tone, lines, dots, etc., indicating light and dark in a painting or drawing.

shadoof *or* **shaduf** (ʃə'du:f) NOUN a mechanism for raising water, consisting of a pivoted pole with a bucket at one end and a counterweight at the other, esp as used in Egypt and the Near East.
▷HISTORY C19: from Egyptian Arabic

shadow ('ʃædəʊ) NOUN [1] a dark image or shape cast on a surface by the interception of light rays by an opaque body. [2] an area of relative darkness. [3] the dark portions of a picture. [4] a hint, image, or faint semblance: *beyond a shadow of a doubt.* [5] a remnant or vestige: *a shadow of one's past self.* [6] a reflection. [7] a threatening influence; blight: *a shadow over one's happiness.* [8] a spectre. [9] an inseparable companion. [10] a person who trails another in secret, such as a detective. [11] *Med* a dark area on an X-ray film representing an opaque structure or part. [12] (in Jungian psychology) the archetype that represents man's animal ancestors. [13] *Archaic or rare* protection or shelter. [14] *(modifier) Brit* designating a member or members of the main opposition party in Parliament who would hold ministerial office if their party were in power: *shadow Chancellor; shadow cabinet.* ◆ VERB *(tr)* [15] to cast a shadow over. [16] to make dark or gloomy; blight. [17] to shade from light. [18] to follow or trail secretly. [19] (often foll by *forth*) to represent vaguely. [20] *Painting, drawing* another word for **shade** (sense 13).
▷HISTORY Old English *sceadwe,* oblique case of *sceadu* SHADE; related to Dutch *schaduw*
▸ **'shadower** NOUN ▸ **'shadowless** ADJECTIVE

shadow bands NOUN slow-moving waves of light and dark observed to move across light-coloured surfaces on the earth just before and after totality in a solar eclipse. They are thought to originate from the effects of irregular atmospheric refraction.

shadow-box VERB *(intr)* [1] *Boxing* to practise blows and footwork against an imaginary opponent. [2] to act or speak unconvincingly, without saying what one means, etc.: *he's just shadow-boxing.*
▸ **'shadow-ˌboxing** NOUN

shadowgraph ('ʃædəʊˌgrɑ:f, -ˌgræf) NOUN [1] a silhouette made by casting a shadow, usually of the hands, on a lighted surface. [2] another name for **radiograph.**

shadow mask NOUN *Television* a perforated metal sheet mounted close to the phosphor-dotted screen in some colour television tubes. The holes are positioned so that each of the three electron beams strikes the correct phosphor dot producing the required colour mixture in the image.

shadow play NOUN a theatrical entertainment using shadows thrown by puppets or actors onto a lighted screen.

shadow price NOUN *Economics* the calculated price of a good or service for which no market price exists.

shadow test NOUN *Med* another name for **retinoscopy.**

shadowy ('ʃædəʊɪ) ADJECTIVE [1] full of shadows; dark; shady. [2] resembling a shadow in faintness; vague. [3] illusory or imaginary. [4] mysterious or secretive: *a shadowy underworld figure.*
▸ **'shadowiness** NOUN

Shadrach ('ʃædræk, 'ʃeɪ-) NOUN *Old Testament* one of Daniel's three companions, who, together with Meshach and Abednego, was miraculously saved from destruction in Nebuchadnezzar's fiery furnace (Daniel 3:12–30).

shaduf (ʃə'du:f) NOUN a variant spelling of **shadoof.**

shady ('ʃeɪdɪ) ADJECTIVE **shadier, shadiest.** [1] full of shade; shaded. [2] affording or casting a shade. [3] dim, quiet, or concealed. [4] *Informal* dubious or questionable as to honesty or legality.
▸ **'shadily** ADVERB ▸ **'shadiness** NOUN

SHAEF (ʃeɪf) NOUN (in World War II) ACRONYM FOR Supreme Headquarters Allied Expeditionary Forces.

shaft (ʃɑ:ft) NOUN [1] the long narrow pole that forms the body of a spear, arrow, etc. [2] something directed at a person in the manner of a missile: *shafts of sarcasm.* [3] a ray, beam, or streak, esp of light. [4] a rod or pole forming the handle of a hammer, axe, golf club, etc. [5] a revolving rod that transmits motion or power: usually used of axial rotation. Compare **rod** (sense 9). [6] one of the two wooden poles by which an animal is harnessed to a vehicle. [7] *Anatomy* **a** the middle part (diaphysis) of a long bone. **b** the main portion of any elongated structure or part. [8] the middle part of a column or pier, between the base and the capital. [9] a column, obelisk, etc., esp one that forms a monument. [10] *Architect* a column that supports a vaulting rib, sometimes one of a set. [11] a vertical passageway through a building, as for a lift. [12] a vertical passageway into a mine. [13] *Ornithol* the central rib of a feather. [14] an archaic or literary word for **arrow.** [15] **get the shaft.** *US and Canadian slang* to be tricked or cheated. ◆ VERB [16] *Slang* to have sexual intercourse with (a woman). [17] *Slang* to trick or cheat.
▷HISTORY Old English *sceaft;* related to Old Norse *skapt,* German *Schaft,* Latin *scāpus* shaft, Greek *skeptron* SCEPTRE, Lettish *skeps* javelin

shaft feather NOUN *Archery* one of the two fletchings on an arrow. Compare **cock feather.**

shafting ('ʃɑ:ftɪŋ) NOUN [1] an assembly of rotating shafts for transmitting power. [2] the stock from which shafts are made. [3] *Architect* a set of shafts.

shag[1] (ʃæg) NOUN [1] a matted tangle, esp of hair, wool, etc. [2] a napped fabric, usually a rough wool. [3] shredded coarse tobacco. ◆ VERB **shags, shagging, shagged.** [4] *(tr)* to make shaggy.
▷HISTORY Old English *sceacga;* related to *sceaga* SHAW[1], Old Norse *skegg* beard, *skagi* tip, *skōgr* forest

shag[2] (ʃæg) NOUN [1] another name for the **green cormorant** (*Phalacrocorax aristotelis*). [2] **like a shag on a rock.** *Austral slang* abandoned and alone.
▷HISTORY C16: special use of SHAG[1], with reference to its crest

shag[3] (ʃæg) *Brit slang* ◆ VERB **shags, shagging, shagged.** [1] to have sexual intercourse with (a person). [2] *(tr; often foll by out; usually passive)* to exhaust; tire. ◆ NOUN [3] an act of sexual intercourse.
▷HISTORY C20: of unknown origin

> **Language note** Though still likely to cause offence to many older or more conservative people, this word has lost a lot of its shock value of late. It seems to have a jocular, relaxed connotation, which most of the other words in this field do not. No doubt its acceptability has been accelerated by its use in the title of an Austin Powers' film. Interestingly, though advertisements for the film caused a large number of complaints to the British Advertising Standards Authority, they were not upheld.

shagbark ('ʃægˌbɑ:k) *or* **shellbark** NOUN [1] a North American hickory tree, *Carya ovata,* having loose rough bark and edible nuts. [2] the wood of this tree, used for tool handles, fuel, etc. [3] the light-coloured hard-shelled nut of this tree.
▷HISTORY C18: so called because of the texture of its bark

shaggable ('ʃægəbᵊl) ADJECTIVE *Brit slang* sexually attractive.

shaggy ('ʃægɪ) ADJECTIVE **-gier, -giest.** [1] having or covered with rough unkempt fur, hair, wool, etc.: *a shaggy dog.* [2] rough or unkempt. [3] (in textiles) having a nap of long rough strands.
▸ **'shaggily** ADVERB ▸ **'shagginess** NOUN

shaggy cap NOUN an edible saprotrophic agaricaceous fungus, *Coprinus comatus,* having a white cap covered with shaggy scales.

shaggy dog story NOUN *Informal* a long rambling joke ending in a deliberate anticlimax, such as a pointless punch line.

shagreen (ʃæ'gri:n) NOUN [1] the rough skin of certain sharks and rays, used as an abrasive. [2] a rough leather made from certain animal hides.
▷HISTORY C17: from French *chagrin,* from Turkish *çagri* rump; also associated through folk etymology with SHAG[1], GREEN

shagroon (ʃæ'gru:n) NOUN *NZ history* a nineteenth-century Australian settler in Canterbury.
▷HISTORY perhaps from Irish *seachrān* wandering

shagtastic (ʃæg'tæstɪk) ADJECTIVE *Brit slang* [1] sexually attractive; sexy. [2] excellent; wonderful.
▷HISTORY C20: from SHAG[3] + (FAN)TASTIC

shah (ʃɑ:) NOUN a ruler of certain Middle Eastern countries, esp (formerly) Iran.
▷HISTORY C16: from Persian: king
▸ **'shahdom** NOUN

shahada (ʃə'hɑ:də) NOUN the Islamic declaration of faith, repeated daily by Muslims.
▷HISTORY from Arabic, literally: witnessing

Shahaptin (ʃə'hæptɪn), **Shahaptan** (ʃə'hæptən), *or* **Shahaptian** (ʃə'hæptɪən) NOUN variants of **Sahaptin.**

Shahjahanpur (ˌʃɑ:dʒəˌhɑ:n'pʊə) NOUN a city in N India, in central Uttar Pradesh: founded in 1647 in the reign of Shah Jahan. Pop.: 237 713 (1991).

shahtoosh (ˌʃɑ:'tu:ʃ) NOUN a soft wool that comes from the protected Tibetan antelope.

Shaitan (ʃaɪ'tɑ:n) NOUN (in Muslim countries) **a** Satan. **b** any evil spirit. **c** a vicious person or animal.
▷HISTORY C17: from Arabic *shaytān,* from Hebrew *śātān;* see SATAN

shake (ʃeɪk) VERB **shakes, shaking, shook, shaken** ('ʃeɪkᵊn). [1] to move or cause to move up and down or back and forth with short quick movements; vibrate. [2] to sway or totter or cause to sway or totter. [3] to clasp or grasp (the hand) of (a person) in greeting, agreement, etc.: *he shook John by the hand; he shook John's hand; they shook and were friends.* [4] **shake hands.** to clasp hands in greeting, agreement, etc. [5] **shake on it.** *Informal* to shake hands in agreement, reconciliation, etc. [6] to bring or come to a specified condition by or as if by shaking: *he shook free and ran.* [7] *(tr)* to wave or brandish: *he shook his sword.* [8] *(tr;* often foll by *up)* to rouse, stir, or agitate. [9] *(tr)* to shock, disturb, or upset: *he was shaken by the news of her death.* [10] *(tr)* to undermine or weaken: *the crisis shook his faith.* [11] to mix (dice) by rattling in a cup or the hand before throwing. [12] *(tr) Austral archaic slang* to steal. [13] *(tr) US and Canadian informal* to escape from: *can you shake that detective?* [14] *Music* to perform a trill on (a note). [15] *(tr) US informal* to fare or progress; happen as specified: *how's it shaking?* [16] **shake a leg.** *Informal* to hurry: usually used in the imperative. [17] **shake in one's shoes.** to tremble with fear or apprehension. [18] **shake one's head.** to indicate disagreement or disapproval by moving the head from side to side. [19] **shake the dust from one's feet.** to depart gladly or with the intention not to return. ◆ NOUN [20] the act or an instance of shaking. [21] a tremor or vibration. [22] **the shakes.** *Informal* a state of uncontrollable trembling or a condition that causes it, such as a fever. [23] *Informal* a very short period of time; jiffy: *in half a shake.* [24] a shingle or clapboard made from a short log by splitting it radially. [25] a fissure or crack in timber or rock. [26] an instance of shaking dice before casting. [27] *Music* another word for **trill**[1] (sense 1). [28] a dance, popular in the 1960s, in which the body is shaken

convulsively in time to the beat. [29] an informal name for **earthquake.** [30] short for **milk shake.** [31] **no great shakes.** *Informal* of no great merit or value; ordinary. ◆ See also **shake down, shake off, shake up.**
▷HISTORY Old English *sceacan;* related to Old Norse *skaka* to shake, Old High German *untscachōn* to be driven
▸ **'shakable** *or* **'shakeable** ADJECTIVE

shake down VERB *(adverb)* [1] to fall or settle or cause to fall or settle by shaking. [2] *(tr) US slang* to extort money from, esp by blackmail or threats of violence. [3] *(tr) US slang* to search thoroughly. [4] *(tr) Informal, chiefly US* to submit (a vessel, etc.) to a shakedown test. [5] *(intr)* to go to bed, esp to a makeshift bed. [6] *(intr)* (of a person, animal, etc.) to settle down. ◆ NOUN **shakedown.** [7] *US slang* a swindle or act of extortion. [8] *US slang* a thorough search. [9] a makeshift bed, esp of straw, blankets, etc. [10] *Informal, chiefly US* **a** a voyage to test the performance of a ship or aircraft or to familiarize the crew with their duties. **b** *(as modifier)*: *a shakedown run.*

shake off VERB *(adverb)* [1] to remove or be removed with or as if with a quick movement: *she shook off her depression.* [2] *(tr)* to escape from; elude: *they shook off the police.*

shake-out NOUN the process of reducing the number of people in a workforce in order to lower the costs of a company.

shaker ('ʃeɪkə) NOUN [1] a person or thing that shakes. [2] a container, often having a perforated top, from which something, such as a condiment, is shaken. [3] a container in which the ingredients of alcoholic drinks are shaken together.

Shakers ('ʃeɪkəz) PLURAL NOUN **the.** an American millenarian sect, founded in 1747 as an offshoot of the Quakers, given to ecstatic shaking, advocating celibacy for its members, and practising common ownership of property.

Shakespearean *or* **Shakespearian** (ʃeɪk'spɪərɪən) ADJECTIVE [1] of, relating to, or characteristic of William Shakespeare, the English dramatist and poet (1564–1616), or his works. ◆ NOUN [2] a student of or specialist in Shakespeare's works.

Shakespeareana ('ʃeɪk,spɪərɪ'ɑːnə, ʃeɪk,spɪər-) PLURAL NOUN collected writings or items relating to Shakespeare.

Shakespearean sonnet NOUN a sonnet form developed in 16th-century England and employed by Shakespeare, having the rhyme scheme a b a b c d c d e f e f g g. Also called: **Elizabethan sonnet, English sonnet.**

shake up VERB *(tr, adverb)* [1] to shake or agitate in order to mix. [2] to reorganize drastically. [3] to stir or rouse. [4] to restore the shape of (a pillow, cushion, etc.). [5] *Informal* to disturb or shock mentally or physically. ◆ NOUN **shake-up.** [6] *Informal* a radical or drastic reorganization.

Shakhty (*Russian* 'ʃaxtɪ) NOUN an industrial city in W Russia: the chief town of the E Donets Basin; a major coal-mining centre. Pop.: 224 400 (1999 est.).

shaking palsy NOUN another name for **Parkinson's disease.**

shako *or* **shacko** ('ʃækəʊ) NOUN, *plural* **shakos, shakoes** *or* **shackos, shackoes.** a tall usually cylindrical military headdress, having a plume and often a peak, popular esp in the 19th century.
▷HISTORY C19: via French from Hungarian *csákó,* from Middle High German *zacke* a sharp point

Shakta ('ʃʌktə) NOUN *Hinduism* a devotee of Sakti, the wife of Siva.
▷HISTORY from Sanskrit *śākta* concerning Sakti
▸ **'Shaktism** NOUN ▸ **'Shaktist** NOUN

Shakti ('ʃʌktɪ) NOUN a variant of **Sakti.**

shaky ('ʃeɪkɪ) ADJECTIVE **shakier, shakiest.** [1] tending to shake or tremble. [2] liable to prove defective; unreliable. [3] uncertain or questionable: *your arguments are very shaky.*
▸ **'shakily** ADVERB ▸ **'shakiness** NOUN

shale (ʃeɪl) NOUN a dark fine-grained laminated sedimentary rock formed by compression of successive layers of clay-rich sediment.
▷HISTORY Old English *scealu* SHELL; compare German *Schalstein* laminated limestone; see SCALE^1, SCALE^2
▸ **'shaly** ADJECTIVE

shale oil NOUN an oil distilled from shales and used as fuel.

shall (ʃæl; *unstressed* ʃəl) VERB, *past* **should.** (takes an infinitive without *to* or an implied infinitive) used as an auxiliary: [1] (esp with *I* or *we* as subject) to make the future tense: *we shall see you tomorrow.* Compare **will**^{1} (sense 1). [2] (with *you, he, she, it, they,* or a noun as subject) **a** to indicate determination on the part of the speaker, as in issuing a threat: *you shall pay for this!* **b** to indicate compulsion, now esp in official documents: *the Tenant shall return the keys to the Landlord.* **c** to indicate certainty or inevitability: *our day shall come.* [3] *(with any noun or pronoun as subject, esp in conditional clauses or clauses expressing doubt)* to indicate nonspecific futurity: *I don't think I shall ever see her again; he doubts whether he shall be in tomorrow.*
▷HISTORY Old English *sceal;* related to Old Norse *skal,* Old High German *scal,* Dutch *zal*

> **Language note** The usual rule given for the use of *shall* and *will* is that where the meaning is one of simple futurity, *shall* is used for the first person of the verb and *will* for the second and third: *I shall go tomorrow; they will be there now.* Where the meaning involves command, obligation, or determination, the positions are reversed: *it shall be done; I will definitely go.* However, *shall* has come to be largely neglected in favour of *will,* which has become the commonest form of the future in all three persons.

shalloon (ʃæ'luːn) NOUN a light twill-weave woollen fabric used chiefly for coat linings, etc.
▷HISTORY C17: from Old French *chalon,* from the name of *Châlons-sur-Marne,* France, where it originated

shallop ('ʃæləp) NOUN [1] a light boat used for rowing in shallow water. [2] (formerly) a two-masted gaff-rigged vessel.
▷HISTORY C16: from French *chaloupe,* from Dutch *sloep* SLOOP

shallot (ʃə'lɒt) NOUN [1] Also called: **scallion.** an alliaceous plant, *Allium ascalonicum,* cultivated for its edible bulb. [2] the bulb of this plant, which divides into small sections and is used in cooking for flavouring and as a vegetable.
▷HISTORY C17: from Old French *eschalotte,* from Old French *eschaloigne,* from Latin *Ascalōnia caepa* Ascalonian onion, from *Ascalon,* a Palestinian town

shallow ('ʃæləʊ) ADJECTIVE [1] having little depth. [2] lacking intellectual or mental depth or subtlety; superficial. ◆ NOUN [3] *(often plural)* a shallow place in a body of water; shoal. ◆ VERB [4] to make or become shallow.
▷HISTORY C15: related to Old English *sceald* shallow; see SHOAL^1
▸ **'shallowly** ADVERB ▸ **'shallowness** NOUN

shalom aleichem *Hebrew* (ʃa'lɔm a'lexem; *English* ʃə'lɒm ə'leɪxəm) INTERJECTION peace be to you: used by Jews as a greeting or farewell. Often shortened to: **shalom.**

shalt (ʃælt) VERB *Archaic or dialect* (used with the pronoun *thou* or its relative equivalent) a singular form of the present tense (indicative mood) of **shall.**

shalwar ('ʃælwɑː) NOUN a pair of loose-fitting trousers tapering to a narrow fit around the ankles, worn in the Indian subcontinent, often with a kameez.
▷HISTORY from Urdu and Persian *shalwār*

sham (ʃæm) NOUN [1] anything that is not what it purports or appears to be. [2] something false, fake, or fictitious that purports to be genuine. [3] a person who pretends to be something other than he is. ◆ ADJECTIVE [4] counterfeit or false; simulated. ◆ VERB **shams, shamming, shammed.** [5] to falsely assume the appearance of (something); counterfeit: *to sham illness.*
▷HISTORY C17: perhaps a Northern English dialect variant of SHAME
▸ **'shammer** NOUN

shaman ('ʃæmən) NOUN [1] a priest of shamanism. [2] a medicine man of a similar religion, esp among certain tribes of North American Indians.
▷HISTORY C17: from Russian *shaman,* from Tungusian *šaman,* from Pali *samana* Buddhist monk, ultimately from Sanskrit *śrama* religious exercise

▸ **shamanic** (ʃə'mænɪk) ADJECTIVE

shamanism ('ʃæmə,nɪzəm) NOUN [1] the religion of certain peoples of northern Asia, based on the belief that the world is pervaded by good and evil spirits who can be influenced or controlled only by the shamans. [2] any similar religion involving forms of spiritualism.
▸ **'shamanist** NOUN, ADJECTIVE ▸ **,shaman'istic** ADJECTIVE

Shamash ('ʃɑːmæʃ) NOUN the sun god of Assyria and Babylonia.
▷HISTORY from Akkadian: sun

shamateur ('ʃæmə,tɜː, -,tjʊə, -tə, -tʃə) NOUN a sportsperson who is officially an amateur but accepts payment.
▷HISTORY C20: from a blend of SHAM + AMATEUR

shamba ('ʃamba) NOUN (in E Africa) any field used for growing crops.
▷HISTORY Swahili

shamble ('ʃæmbᵊl) VERB [1] *(intr)* to walk or move along in an awkward or unsteady way. ◆ NOUN [2] an awkward or unsteady walk.
▷HISTORY C17: from *shamble* (adj) ungainly, perhaps from the phrase *shamble legs* legs resembling those of a meat vendor's table; see SHAMBLES
▸ **'shambling** ADJECTIVE, NOUN

shambles ('ʃæmbᵊlz) NOUN *(functioning as singular or plural)* [1] a place of great disorder: *the room was a shambles after the party.* [2] a place where animals are brought to be slaughtered. [3] any place of slaughter or carnage. [4] *Brit dialect* a row of covered stalls or shops where goods, originally meat, are sold.
▷HISTORY C14 *shamble* table used by meat vendors, from Old English *sceamel* stool, from Late Latin *scamellum* a small bench, from Latin *scamnum* stool

shambolic (ʃæm'bɒlɪk) ADJECTIVE *Informal* completely disorganized; chaotic.
▷HISTORY C20: irregularly formed from SHAMBLES

shame (ʃeɪm) NOUN [1] a painful emotion resulting from an awareness of having done something dishonourable, unworthy, degrading, etc. [2] capacity to feel such an emotion. [3] ignominy or disgrace. [4] a person or thing that causes this. [5] an occasion for regret, disappointment, etc.: *it's a shame you can't come with us.* [6] **put to shame. a** to disgrace. **b** to surpass totally. ◆ INTERJECTION [7] *South African informal* **a** an expression of sympathy. **b** an expression of pleasure or endearment. ◆ VERB *(tr)* [8] to cause to feel shame. [9] to bring shame on; disgrace. [10] (often foll by *into*) to compel through a sense of shame: *he shamed her into making an apology.* [11] **name and shame.** See **name** (sense 17).
▷HISTORY Old English *scamu;* related to Old Norse *skömm,* Old High German *skama*
▸ **'shamable** *or* **'shameable** ADJECTIVE

shamefaced ('ʃeɪm,feɪst) ADJECTIVE [1] bashful or modest. [2] showing a sense of shame.
▷HISTORY C16: alteration of earlier *shamefast,* from Old English *sceamfaest;* see SHAME, FAST^1
▸ **shamefacedly** (ʃeɪm'feɪsɪdlɪ, 'ʃeɪm,feɪstlɪ) ADVERB
▸ **shame'facedness** NOUN

shameful ('ʃeɪmfʊl) ADJECTIVE causing or deserving shame; scandalous.
▸ **'shamefully** ADVERB ▸ **'shamefulness** NOUN

shameless ('ʃeɪmlɪs) ADJECTIVE [1] having no sense of shame; brazen. [2] done without shame; without decency or modesty.
▸ **'shamelessly** ADVERB ▸ **'shamelessness** NOUN

shamina (,ʃæ'miːnə) NOUN a wool blend of pashm and shahtoosh.

shammes *or* **shammash** ('ʃɑːməs; *Hebrew* ʃa'maʃ) NOUN, *plural* **shammosim** *or* **shammashim** (*Hebrew* ʃa'mɔsɪm). *Judaism* [1] an official acting as the beadle, sexton, and caretaker of a synagogue. [2] the extra candle used on the Feast of Hanukkah to kindle the lamps or candles of the menorah.
▷HISTORY from Hebrew *shāmmāsh,* from Aramaic *shĕmāsh* to serve

shammy ('ʃæmɪ) NOUN, *plural* **-mies.** *Informal* another word for **chamois** (sense 3). Also called: **shammy leather.**
▷HISTORY C18: variant, influenced by the pronunciation, of CHAMOIS

Shamo ('ʃɑː'məʊ) NOUN transliteration of the Chinese name for the **Gobi.**

shampoo (ʃæm'puː) NOUN [1] a liquid or cream preparation of soap or detergent to wash the hair.

② a similar preparation for washing carpets, etc. ③ the process of shampooing. ◆ VERB **-poos, -pooing, -pooed.** ④ (*tr*) to wash (the hair, etc.) with such a preparation.
▷HISTORY C18: from Hindi *chāmpo,* from *chāmpnā* to knead
▸**sham'pooer** NOUN

shamrock ('ʃæmˌrɒk) NOUN a plant having leaves divided into three leaflets, variously identified as the wood sorrel, red clover, white clover, and black medick: the national emblem of Ireland.
▷HISTORY C16: from Irish Gaelic *seamrōg,* diminutive of *seamar* clover

shamus ('ʃɑːməs, 'ʃeɪ-) NOUN, *plural* **-muses.** *US slang* a police or private detective.
▷HISTORY probably from SHAMMES, influenced by Irish *Séamas* James

Shan (ʃɑːn) NOUN ① (*plural* **Shans** *or* **Shan**) a member of a Mongoloid people living in Myanmar, Thailand, and SW China. ② the language or group of dialects spoken by the Shan, belonging to the Sino-Tibetan family and closely related to Thai.

Shandong ('ʃæn'dʌŋ) *or* **Shantung** NOUN a province of NE China, on the Yellow Sea and the Gulf of Chihli: part of the earliest organized state of China (1520–1030 B.C.); consists chiefly of the fertile plain of the lower Yellow River, with mountains over 1500 m (5000 ft.) high in the centre. Capital: Jinan. Pop.: 90 790 000 (2000 est.). Area: 153 300 sq. km (59 189 sq. miles).

shandrydan ('ʃændrɪˌdæn) NOUN ① a two-wheeled cart or chaise, esp one with a hood. ② any decrepit old-fashioned conveyance.
▷HISTORY C19: of unknown origin

shandy ('ʃændɪ) *or US* **shandygaff** ('ʃændɪˌgæf) NOUN, *plural* **-dies** *or* **-gaffs.** an alcoholic drink made of beer and ginger beer or lemonade.
▷HISTORY C19: of unknown origin

Shangaan ('ʃaŋgɑːn) NOUN a member of any of the Tsonga-speaking Bantu peoples settled in Mozambique and NE Transvaal, esp one who works in a gold mine.

shanghai ('ʃæŋhaɪ, ʃæŋ'haɪ) *Slang* ◆ VERB **-hais, -haiing, -haied.** (*tr*) ① to kidnap (a man or seaman) for enforced service at sea, esp on a merchant ship. ② to force or trick (someone) into doing something, going somewhere, etc. ③ *Austral and NZ* to shoot with a catapult. ◆ NOUN ④ *Austral and NZ* a catapult.
▷HISTORY C19: from the city of SHANGHAI; from the forceful methods formerly used to collect crews for voyages to the Orient

Shanghai ('ʃæŋ'haɪ) NOUN a port in E China, in SE Jiangsu near the estuary of the Yangtze: the largest city in China and one of the largest ports in the world; a major cultural and industrial centre, with two universities. Pop.: 8 937 175 (1999 est.).

Shango ('ʃæŋgəʊ) NOUN **a** a W African religious cult surviving in some parts of the Caribbean. **b** (*as modifier*): *Shango ritual.*
▷HISTORY Yoruba

Shangri-la (ˌʃæŋgrɪ'lɑː) NOUN a remote or imaginary utopia.
▷HISTORY C20: from the name of an imaginary valley in the Himalayas, from *Lost Horizon* (1933), a novel by James Hilton

shank (ʃæŋk) NOUN ① *Anatomy* the shin. ② the corresponding part of the leg in vertebrates other than man. ③ a cut of meat from the top part of an animal's shank. ④ the main part of a tool, between the working part and the handle. ⑤ the part of a bolt between the thread and the head. ⑥ the cylindrical part of a bit by which it is held in the drill. ⑦ the ring or stem on the back of some buttons. ⑧ the stem or long narrow part of a key, anchor, hook, spoon handle, nail, pin, etc. ⑨ the band of a ring as distinguished from the setting. ⑩ **a** the part of a shoe connecting the wide part of the sole with the heel. **b** the metal or leather piece used for this. ⑪ *Printing* the body of a piece of type, between the shoulder and the foot. ⑫ *Engineering* a ladle used for molten metal. ⑬ *Music* another word for **crook** (sense 6). ◆ VERB ⑭ (*intr*) (of fruits, roots, etc.) to show disease symptoms, esp discoloration. ⑮ (*tr*) *Golf* to mishit (the ball) with the foot of the shaft rather than the face of the club.
▷HISTORY Old English *scanca;* related to Old Frisian *schanke,* Middle Low German *schenke,* Danish, Swedish *skank* leg

shanks's pony *or US and Canadian* **shanks's mare** ('ʃæŋksɪz) NOUN *Informal* one's own legs as a means of transportation.
▷HISTORY C18: from SHANK (in the sense: lower leg); probably with a pun on the surname *Shanks*

Shannon ('ʃænən) NOUN a river in the Republic of Ireland, rising in NW Co. Cavan and flowing south to the Atlantic by an estuary 113 km (70 miles) long: the longest river in the Republic of Ireland. Length: 260 km (161 miles).

shanny ('ʃænɪ) NOUN, *plural* **-nies.** a European blenny, *Blennius pholis,* of rocky coastal waters.
▷HISTORY C19: of obscure origin

Shansi ('ʃæn'siː) NOUN a variant transliteration of the Chinese name for **Shanxi.**

Shan State (ʃɑːn, ʃæn) NOUN an administrative division of E Myanmar: formed in 1947 from the joining of the Federation of Shan States with the Wa States; consists of the **Shan plateau** crossed by forested mountain ranges reaching over 2100 m (7000 ft.). Pop.: 4 416 000 (1994 est.). Area: 149 743 sq. km (57 816 sq. miles).

shan't (ʃɑːnt) CONTRACTION OF shall not.

Shantou *or* **Shantow** ('ʃæn'taʊ) NOUN a port in SE China, in E Guangdong near the mouth of the Han River: became a treaty port in 1869. Pop.: 831 949 (1999 est.). Also called: **Swatow.**

shantung (ˌʃæn'tʌŋ) NOUN ① a heavy silk fabric with a knobbly surface. ② a cotton or rayon imitation of this.
▷HISTORY C19: so called because it was first imported to Britain from SHANTUNG in China

Shantung ('ʃæn'tʌŋ) NOUN a variant transliteration of the Chinese name for **Shandong.**

shanty[1] ('ʃæntɪ) NOUN, *plural* **-ties.** ① a ramshackle hut; crude dwelling. ② *Austral and NZ* a public house, esp an unlicensed one. ③ (formerly, in Canada) **a** a log bunkhouse at a lumber camp. **b** the camp itself.
▷HISTORY C19: from Canadian French *chantier* cabin built in a lumber camp, from Old French *gantier* GANTRY

shanty[2], **shantey** ('ʃæntɪ), **chanty,** *or US* **chantey** ('ʃæntɪ, 'tʃæn-) NOUN, *plural* **-ties** *or* **-teys.** a song originally sung by sailors, esp a rhythmic one forming an accompaniment to work.
▷HISTORY C19: from French *chanter* to sing; see CHANT

shantytown ('ʃæntɪˌtaʊn) NOUN a town or section of a town or city inhabited by very poor people living in shanties.

Shanxi ('ʃæn'ʃiː) *or* **Shansi** NOUN a province of N China: China's richest coal reserves and much heavy industry. Capital: Taiyuan. Pop.: 32 970 000 (2000 est.). Area: 157 099 sq. km (60 656 sq. miles).

shape (ʃeɪp) NOUN ① the outward form of an object defined by outline. ② the figure or outline of the body of a person. ③ a phantom. ④ organized or definite form: *my plans are taking shape.* ⑤ the form that anything assumes; guise. ⑥ something used to provide or define form; pattern; mould. ⑦ condition or state of efficiency: *to be in good shape.* ⑧ **out of shape. a** in bad physical condition. **b** bent, twisted, or deformed. ⑨ **take shape.** to assume a definite form. ◆ VERB ⑩ (when *intr,* often foll by *into* or *up*) to receive or cause to receive shape or form. ⑪ (*tr*) to mould into a particular pattern or form; modify. ⑫ (*tr*) to plan, devise, or prepare: *to shape a plan of action.* ⑬ an obsolete word for **appoint.**
▷HISTORY Old English *gesceap,* literally: that which is created, from *sceippan* to create; related to *sceap* sexual organs, Old Norse *skap* destiny, Old High German *scaf* form
▸**'shapable** *or* **'shapeable** ADJECTIVE ▸**'shaper** NOUN

SHAPE (ʃeɪp) NOUN ACRONYM FOR Supreme Headquarters Allied Powers Europe.

-shaped (ʃeɪpt) ADJECTIVE COMBINING FORM having the shape of: *an L-shaped room; a pear-shaped figure.*

shapeless ('ʃeɪplɪs) ADJECTIVE ① having no definite shape or form: *a shapeless mass; a shapeless argument.* ② lacking a symmetrical or aesthetically pleasing shape: *a shapeless figure.*
▸**'shapelessly** ADVERB ▸**'shapelessness** NOUN

shapely ('ʃeɪplɪ) ADJECTIVE **-lier, -liest.** (esp of a woman's body or legs) pleasing or attractive in shape.
▸**'shapeliness** NOUN

shape up VERB (*intr, adverb*) ① *Informal* to proceed or develop satisfactorily. ② *Informal* to develop a definite or proper form. ◆ NOUN **shapeup.** ③ *US and Canadian* (formerly) a method of hiring dockers for a day or shift by having a union hiring boss select them from a gathering of applicants.

shard (ʃɑːd) *or* **sherd** NOUN ① a broken piece or fragment of a brittle substance, esp of pottery. ② *Zoology* a tough sheath, scale, or shell, esp the elytra of a beetle.
▷HISTORY Old English *sceard;* related to Old Norse *skarth* notch, Middle High German *scharte* notch

share[1] (ʃɛə) NOUN ① a part or portion of something owned, allotted to, or contributed by a person or group. ② (*often plural*) any of the equal parts, usually of low par value, into which the capital stock of a company is divided: ownership of shares carries the right to receive a proportion of the company's profits. See also **ordinary shares, preference shares.** ③ **go shares.** *Informal* to share (something) with another or others. ◆ VERB ④ (*tr;* often foll by *out*) to divide or apportion, esp equally. ⑤ (when *intr,* often foll by *in*) to receive or contribute a portion of: *we can share the cost of the petrol; six people shared in the inheritance.* ⑥ to join with another or others in the use of (something): *can I share your umbrella?*
▷HISTORY Old English *scearu;* related to Old Norse *skor* amount, Old High German *scara* crowd; see SHEAR
▸**'sharable** *or* **'shareable** ADJECTIVE ▸**'sharer** NOUN

share[2] (ʃɛə) NOUN short for **ploughshare.**
▷HISTORY Old English *scear;* related to Old Norse *skeri,* Old High German *scaro*

share certificate NOUN a document issued by a company certifying ownership of one or more of its shares. US equivalent: **stock certificate.**

sharecrop ('ʃɛəˌkrɒp) VERB **-crops, -cropping, -cropped.** *Chiefly US* to cultivate (farmland) as a sharecropper.

sharecropper ('ʃɛəˌkrɒpə) NOUN *Chiefly US* a farmer, esp a tenant farmer, who pays over a proportion of a crop or crops as rent.

shared care NOUN *Social welfare* an arrangement between a welfare agency and a family with a dependent handicapped member, whereby the agency takes the handicapped person into a home for respite care or in emergencies.

shared logic NOUN *Computing* the sharing of a central processing unit and associated software among several terminals.

shared ownership NOUN (in Britain) a form of house purchase whereby the purchaser buys a proportion of the dwelling, usually from a local authority or housing association, and rents the rest.

shared resources NOUN (*functioning as singular*) *Computing* the sharing of peripherals among several terminals.

sharefarmer ('ʃɛəˌfɑːmə) NOUN *Chiefly Austral* a farmer who pays a fee to another in return for use of land to raise crops, etc.

shareholder ('ʃɛəˌhəʊldə) NOUN the owner of one or more shares in a company.

share index NOUN an index showing the movement of share prices. See **Financial Times Industrial Ordinary Share Index, Financial Times Stock Exchange 100 Index.**

share market NOUN the usual NZ and Austral name for **stock exchange.**

share-milker NOUN (in New Zealand) a person who lives on a dairy farm milking the owner's herd for an agreed share of the profits and, usually, building his own herd simultaneously.

share of voice NOUN the proportion of the total audience or readership commanded by a media group across its full range of publishing and broadcasting activities.

share option NOUN a scheme giving employees an option to buy shares in the company for which they work at a favourable price or discount.

share premium NOUN *Brit* the excess of the amount actually subscribed for an issue of corporate capital over its par value. Also called (esp US): **capital surplus.**

share shop NOUN a stockbroker, bank, or other financial intermediary that handles the buying and selling of shares for members of the public, esp during a privatization issue.

shareware (ˈʃɛəˌwɛə) NOUN *Computing* software available to all users without the need for a licence and for which a token fee is requested.

Shari (ˈʃɑːrɪ) NOUN a variant spelling of **Chari** (the river).

sharia *or* **sheria** (ʃəˈriːə) NOUN the body of doctrines that regulate the lives of those who profess Islam.
▷HISTORY Arabic

sharif (ʃæˈriːf) NOUN a variant transliteration of **sherif.**

shark[1] (ʃɑːk) NOUN any of various usually ferocious selachian fishes, typically marine with a long body, two dorsal fins, rows of sharp teeth, and between five and seven gill slits on each side of the head.
▷HISTORY C16: of uncertain origin
▸ˈ**shark**ˌ**like** ADJECTIVE

shark[2] (ʃɑːk) NOUN 1 a person who preys on or victimizes others, esp by swindling or extortion. ◆ VERB 2 *Archaic* to obtain (something) by cheating or deception.
▷HISTORY C18: probably from German *Schurke* rogue; perhaps also influenced by SHARK[1]

shark bell NOUN *Chiefly Austral* a bell sounded to warn swimmers of the presence of sharks. Also: **shark alarm.**

shark net *or* **mesh** NOUN *Chiefly Austral* 1 a net for catching sharks. 2 a long piece of netting strung across a bay, inlet, etc., to exclude sharks.

shark patrol NOUN *Chiefly Austral* a watch for sharks kept by an aircraft flying over beaches used by swimmers.

shark repellents PLURAL NOUN *Finance* another name for **porcupine provisions.**

shark siren NOUN *Chiefly Austral* a siren sounded to warn swimmers of the presence of sharks.

sharkskin (ˈʃɑːkˌskɪn) NOUN a smooth glossy fabric of acetate rayon, used for sportswear, etc.

sharksucker (ˈʃɑːkˌsʌkə) NOUN an informal name for a **remora.**

shark watcher NOUN *Informal* a business consultant who assists companies in identifying and preventing unwelcome takeover bids.

Sharon (ˈʃærən) NOUN **Plain of.** a plain in W Israel, between the Mediterranean and the hills of Samaria, extending from Haifa to Tel Aviv.

sharon fruit (ˈʃærən) NOUN another name for **persimmon** (sense 2).

sharp (ʃɑːp) ADJECTIVE 1 having a keen edge suitable for cutting. 2 having an edge or point; not rounded or blunt. 3 involving a sudden change, esp in direction: *a sharp bend.* 4 moving, acting, or reacting quickly, efficiently, etc.: *sharp reflexes.* 5 clearly defined. 6 mentally acute; clever; astute. 7 sly or artful; clever in an underhand way: *sharp practice.* 8 bitter or harsh: *sharp words.* 9 shrill or penetrating: *a sharp cry.* 10 having an acrid taste. 11 keen; biting: *a sharp wind; sharp pain.* 12 *Music* **a** (*immediately postpositive*) denoting a note that has been raised in pitch by one chromatic semitone: *B sharp.* **b** (of an instrument, voice, etc.) out of tune by being or tending to be too high in pitch. Compare **flat**[1] (sense 23). 13 *Phonetics* a less common word for **fortis.** 14 *Informal* **a** stylish. **b** too smart. 15 **at the sharp end.** involved in the area of any activity where there is most difficulty, competition, danger, etc. ◆ ADVERB 16 in a sharp manner. 17 exactly: *six o'clock sharp.* 18 *Music* **a** higher than a standard pitch. **b** out of tune by being or tending to be too high in pitch: *she sings sharp.* Compare **flat**[1] (sense 29). ◆ NOUN 19 *Music* **a** an accidental that raises the pitch of the following note by one chromatic semitone. Usual symbol: ♯ **b** a note affected by this accidental. Compare **flat**[1] (sense 35). 20 a thin needle with a sharp point. 21 *Informal* a sharper. ◆ VERB 22 (*usually plural*) any medical instrument with sharp point or edge, esp a hypodermic needle. 23 (*tr*) *Music* the usual US and Canadian word for **sharpen.** ◆ INTERJECTION 23 *South African slang* an exclamation of full agreement or approval.
▷HISTORY Old English *scearp;* related to Old Norse *skarpr,* Old High German *scarpf,* Old Irish *cerb,* Lettish *skarbs*
▸ˈ**sharply** ADVERB ▸ˈ**sharpness** NOUN

sharpbender (ˈʃɑːpˌbɛndə) NOUN *Informal* an organization that has been underperforming its competitors but suddenly becomes more successful, often as a result of new management or changes in its business strategy.
▷HISTORY C20: from the sharp upward bend in its sales or profits

Shar Pei (ʃɑː ˈpeɪ) NOUN a compact squarely-built dog of a Chinese breed, with loose wrinkled skin and a harsh bristly coat.
▷HISTORY C20: from Chinese *shā pí,* literally: sand skin

sharpen (ˈʃɑːpᵊn) VERB 1 to make or become sharp or sharper. 2 *Music* to raise the pitch of (a note), esp by one chromatic semitone. Usual US and Canadian word: **sharp.**
▸ˈ**sharpener** NOUN

sharper (ˈʃɑːpə) NOUN a person who cheats or swindles; fraud.

Sharpeville (ˈʃɑːpvɪl) NOUN a town in E South Africa: scene of riots in 1960, when 69 demonstrators died, 1984, and 1985, when 19 died.

sharp-eyed ADJECTIVE 1 having very good eyesight. 2 observant or alert.

sharpie (ˈʃɑːpɪ) NOUN *Austral* a member of a teenage group having short hair and distinctive clothes. Compare **skinhead.**

sharpish (ˈʃɑːpɪʃ) ADJECTIVE 1 fairly sharp. ◆ ADVERB 2 *Informal* promptly; quickly.

sharp-set ADJECTIVE 1 set to give an acute cutting angle. 2 keenly hungry. 3 keen or eager.

sharpshooter (ˈʃɑːpˌʃuːtə) NOUN an expert marksman, esp with a rifle.
▸ˈ**sharp**ˌ**shooting** NOUN

sharp-sighted ADJECTIVE having keen vision; sharp-eyed.
▸ˌ**sharp-**ˈ**sightedly** ADVERB ▸ˌ**sharp-**ˈ**sightedness** NOUN

sharp-tongued ADJECTIVE bitter or critical in speech; sarcastic.

sharp-witted ADJECTIVE having or showing a keen intelligence; perceptive.
▸ˌ**sharp-**ˈ**wittedly** ADVERB ▸ˌ**sharp-**ˈ**wittedness** NOUN

shashlik *or* **shashlick** (ʃɑːˈʃlɪk, ˈʃɑːʃlɪk) NOUN a type of kebab.
▷HISTORY from Russian, of Turkic origin; compare *shish kebab*

Shasta daisy (ˈʃæstə) NOUN a Pyrenean plant, *Chrysanthemum maximum,* widely cultivated for its large white daisy-like flowers: family *Asteraceae* (composites).
▷HISTORY named after Mount *Shasta* in California

shastra (ˈʃɑːstrə), **shaster** (ˈʃɑːstə), *or* **sastra** NOUN any of the sacred writings of Hinduism.
▷HISTORY C17: from Sanskrit *śāstra,* from *śās* to teach

shat (ʃæt) VERB *Taboo* a past tense and past participle of **shit.**

Shatt-al-Arab (ˈʃætælˈærəb) NOUN a river in SE Iraq, formed by the confluence of the Tigris and Euphrates Rivers: flows southeast as part of the border between Iraq and Iran to the Persian Gulf. Length: 193 km (120 miles).

shatter (ˈʃætə) VERB 1 to break or be broken into many small pieces. 2 (*tr*) to impair or destroy: *his nerves were shattered by the torture.* 3 (*tr*) to dumbfound or thoroughly upset: *she was shattered by the news.* 4 (*tr*) *Informal* to cause to be tired out or exhausted. 5 an obsolete word for **scatter.** ◆ NOUN 6 (*usually plural*) *Obsolete or dialect* a fragment.
▷HISTORY C12: perhaps obscurely related to SCATTER
▸ˈ**shatterer** NOUN ▸ˈ**shattering** ADJECTIVE ▸ˈ**shatteringly** ADVERB

shattered (ˈʃætɪd) ADJECTIVE 1 broken into many small pieces. 2 impaired or destroyed. 3 dumbfounded or thoroughly upset. 4 *Informal* tired out or exhausted.

shatterproof (ˈʃætəˌpruːf) ADJECTIVE designed to resist shattering.

shave (ʃeɪv) VERB **shaves, shaving, shaved;** **shaved** *or* **shaven.** (*mainly tr*) 1 (*also intr*) to remove (the beard, hair, etc.) from (the face, head, or body) by scraping the skin with a razor. 2 to cut or trim very closely. 3 to reduce to shavings. 4 to remove thin slices from (wood, etc.) with a sharp cutting tool; plane or pare. 5 to touch or graze in passing. 6 *Informal* to reduce (a price) by a slight amount. 7 *US commerce* to purchase (a commercial paper) at a greater rate of discount than is customary or legal. ◆ NOUN 8 the act or an instance of shaving. 9 any tool for scraping. 10 a thin slice or shaving. 11 an instance of barely touching something. 12 **close shave.** *Informal* a narrow escape.
▷HISTORY Old English *sceafan;* related to Old Norse *skafa,* Gothic *skaban* to shave, Latin *scabere* to scrape
▸ˈ**shavable** *or* ˈ**shaveable** ADJECTIVE

shaveling (ˈʃeɪvlɪŋ) NOUN *Archaic* 1 *Derogatory* a priest or clergyman with a shaven head. 2 a young fellow; youth.

shaven (ˈʃeɪvᵊn) ADJECTIVE **a** closely shaved or tonsured. **b** (*in combination*): *clean-shaven.*

shaver (ˈʃeɪvə) NOUN 1 a person or thing that shaves. 2 Also called: **electric razor, electric shaver.** an electrically powered implement for shaving, having reciprocating or rotating blades behind a fine metal comb or pierced foil. 3 *Informal* a youngster, esp a young boy. 4 *Obsolete* a person who makes hard or extortionate bargains.

Shavian (ˈʃeɪvɪən) ADJECTIVE 1 of, relating to, or like George Bernard Shaw (1856–1950), the Irish dramatist and critic, his works, ideas, etc. ◆ NOUN 2 an admirer of Shaw or his works.
▸ˈ**Shavianism** NOUN

shaving (ˈʃeɪvɪŋ) NOUN 1 a thin paring or slice, esp of wood, that has been shaved from something. ◆ MODIFIER 2 used when shaving the face, etc.: *shaving cream.*

Shavuot *or* **Shabuoth** (ʃəˈvuːəs, -əʊs; *Hebrew* ʃavuːˈɔt) NOUN the Hebrew name for **Pentecost** (sense 2).
▷HISTORY from Hebrew *shābhūʿōth,* plural of *shābhūaʿ* week

shaw[1] (ʃɔː) NOUN *Archaic or dialect* a small wood; thicket; copse.
▷HISTORY Old English *sceaga;* related to Old Norse *skagi* tip, *skaga* to jut out, *skōgr* forest, *skegg* beard

shaw[2] (ʃɔː) *Scot* ◆ VERB 1 to show. ◆ NOUN 2 a show. 3 the part of a potato plant that is above ground.

shawl (ʃɔːl) NOUN a piece of fabric or knitted or crocheted material worn around the shoulders by women or wrapped around a baby.
▷HISTORY C17: from Persian *shāl*

shawl collar NOUN a collar rolled back in a continuous and tapering line along the surplice neckline of a garment.

shawlie (ˈʃɔːlɪ) NOUN *Irish* a disparaging term for a working-class woman who wears a shawl.

shawm (ʃɔːm) NOUN *Music* a medieval form of the oboe with a conical bore and flaring bell, blown through a double reed.
▷HISTORY C14 *shalmye,* from Old French *chalemie,* ultimately from Latin *calamus* a reed, from Greek *kalamos*

Shawnee (ʃɔːˈniː) NOUN 1 (*plural* **-nees** *or* **-nee**) a member of a North American Indian people formerly living along the Tennessee River. 2 the language of this people, belonging to the Algonquian family.
▷HISTORY C20: back formation from obsolete *Shawnese,* from Shawnee *Shaawanwaaki* people of the south, from *shaawanawa* south

Shawwal (ʃəˈwɑːl) NOUN the tenth month of the Muslim year.
▷HISTORY from Arabic

shay (ʃeɪ) NOUN a dialect word for **chaise.**
▷HISTORY C18: back formation from CHAISE, mistakenly thought to be plural

Shcheglovsk (*Russian* ʃtʃɪgˈlɔfsk) NOUN the former name (until 1932) of **Kemerovo.**

Shcherbakov (*Russian* ʃtʃɪrbaˈkɔf) NOUN a former name (from the Revolution until 1957) of **Rybinsk.**

she (ʃiː) PRONOUN (*subjective*) 1 refers to a female person or animal: *she is a doctor; she's a fine mare.* 2 refers to things personified as feminine, such as cars, ships, and nations. 3 *Austral and NZ* an informal word for **it** (esp in the phrases **she's apples, she'll be right,** etc.). ◆ NOUN 4 **a** a female person or animal. **b** (*in combination*): *she-cat.*

▷HISTORY Old English *sīe,* accusative of *sēo,* feminine demonstrative pronoun

> **Language note** See at **me**[1].

shea (ˈʃɪə) NOUN 1 a tropical African sapotaceous tree, *Butyrospermum parkii,* with oily seeds. 2 **shea butter.** the white butter-like fat obtained from the seeds of this plant and used as food, to make soaps, etc.
▷HISTORY C18: from Bambara *si*

sheading (ˈʃiːdɪŋ) NOUN any of the six subdivisions of the Isle of Man.
▷HISTORY variant of *shedding;* see SHED[2]

sheaf (ʃiːf) NOUN, *plural* **sheaves** (ʃiːvz). 1 a bundle of reaped but unthreshed corn tied with one or two bonds. 2 a bundle of objects tied together. 3 the arrows contained in a quiver. ◆ VERB 4 (*tr*) to bind or tie into a sheaf.
▷HISTORY Old English *sceaf,* related to Old High German *skoub* sheaf, Old Norse *skauf* tail, Gothic *skuft* tuft of hair

shear (ʃɪə) VERB **shears, shearing, sheared** *or Austral and NZ* **shore; sheared** *or* **shorn.** 1 (*tr*) to remove (the fleece or hair) of (sheep, etc.) by cutting or clipping. 2 to cut or cut through (something) with shears or a sharp instrument. 3 *Engineering* to cause (a part, member, shaft, etc.) to deform or fracture or (of a part, etc.) to deform or fracture as a result of excess torsion or transverse load. 4 (*tr;* often foll by *of*) to strip or divest: *to shear someone of his power.* 5 (when *intr,* foll by *through*) to move through (something) by or as if by cutting. 6 *Scot* to reap (corn, etc.) with a scythe or sickle. ◆ NOUN 7 the act, process, or an instance of shearing. 8 a shearing of a sheep or flock of sheep, esp when referred to as an indication of age: *a sheep of two shears.* 9 a form of deformation or fracture in which parallel planes in a body or assembly slide over one another. 10 *Physics* the deformation of a body, part, etc., expressed as the lateral displacement between two points in parallel planes divided by the distance between the planes. 11 either one of the blades of a pair of shears, scissors, etc. 12 a machine that cuts sheet material by passing a knife blade through it. 13 a device for lifting heavy loads consisting of a tackle supported by a framework held steady by guy ropes. ◆ See also **shears, shore.**
▷HISTORY Old English *sceran;* related to Old Norse *skera* to cut, Old Saxon, Old High German *skeran* to shear; see SHARE[2]
▸ˈ**shearer** NOUN

shearing gang NOUN *NZ* a group of itinerant workers who contract to shear, class, and bale a farmer's wool clip.

shearing shed NOUN *NZ* a farm building equipped with power machinery for sheepshearing and equipment for baling wool. Also called: **woolshed.**

shearlegs (ˈʃɪəˌlɛgz) NOUN a variant spelling of **sheerlegs.**

shearling (ˈʃɪəlɪŋ) NOUN 1 a young sheep after its first shearing. 2 the skin of such an animal.

shear pin NOUN an easily replaceable pin inserted in a machine at a critical point and designed to shear and stop the machine if the load becomes too great.

shears (ʃɪəz) PLURAL NOUN 1 **a** large scissors, as for cutting cloth, jointing poultry, etc. **b** a large scissor-like and usually hand-held cutting tool with flat blades, as for cutting hedges. 2 any of various analogous cutting or clipping implements or machines. 3 short for **sheerlegs.** 4 **off the shears.** *Austral informal* (of a sheep) newly shorn.

shear strength NOUN the degree to which a material or bond is able to resist shear.

shear stress NOUN the form of stress in a body, part, etc., that tends to produce cutting rather than stretching or bending.

shear stud NOUN a stud that transfers shear stress between metal and concrete in composite structural members in which the stud is welded to the metal component.

shearwater (ˈʃɪəˌwɔːtə) NOUN any of several oceanic birds of the genera *Puffinus,* such as *P. puffinus* (**Manx shearwater**), *Procellaria,* etc., specialized for an aerial or aquatic existence: family *Procellariidae,* order *Procellariiformes* (petrels).
▷HISTORY C17: so named because their wings seem to clip the waves when they are flying low

sheatfish (ˈʃiːtˌfɪʃ) NOUN, *plural* **-fish** *or* **-fishes.** another name for **European catfish** (see **silurid** (sense 1)).
▷HISTORY C16: variant of *sheathfish;* perhaps influenced by German *Schaid* sheatfish; see SHEATH, FISH

sheath (ʃiːθ) NOUN, *plural* **sheaths** (ʃiːðz). 1 a case or covering for the blade of a knife, sword, etc. 2 any similar close-fitting case. 3 *Biology* an enclosing or protective structure, such as a leaf base encasing the stem of a plant. 4 the protective covering on an electric cable. 5 a figure-hugging dress with a narrow tapering skirt. 6 another name for **condom.** ◆ VERB 7 (*tr*) another word for **sheathe.**
▷HISTORY Old English *scēath;* related to Old Norse *skeithir,* Old High German *sceida* a dividing; compare Old English *scādan* to divide

sheathbill (ˈʃiːθˌbɪl) NOUN either of two pigeon-like shore birds, *Chionis alba* or *C. minor,* of antarctic and subantarctic regions, constituting the family *Chionididae:* order *Charadriiformes.* They have a white plumage and a horny sheath at the base of the bill.

sheathe (ʃiːð) VERB (*tr*) 1 to insert (a knife, sword, etc.) into a sheath. 2 (esp of cats) to retract (the claws). 3 to surface with or encase in a sheath or sheathing.

sheathing (ˈʃiːðɪŋ) NOUN 1 any material used as an outer layer, as on a ship's hull. 2 boarding, etc., used to cover the wall studding or roof joists of a timber frame.

sheath knife NOUN a knife carried in or protected by a sheath.

sheave[1] (ʃiːv) VERB (*tr*) to gather or bind into sheaves.

sheave[2] (ʃiːv) NOUN a wheel with a grooved rim, esp one used as a pulley.
▷HISTORY C14: of Germanic origin; compare Old High German *scība* disc

sheaves (ʃiːvz) NOUN the plural of **sheaf.**

Sheba[1] (ˈʃiːbə) NOUN 1 Also called: **Saba.** the ancient kingdom of the Sabeans: a rich trading nation dealing in gold, spices, and precious stones (I Kings 10). 2 the region inhabited by this nation, located in the SW corner of the Arabian peninsula: modern Yemen.

Sheba[2] (ˈʃiːbə) NOUN **Queen of Sheba.** *Old Testament* a queen of the Sabeans, who visited Solomon (I Kings 10:1–13).

shebang (ʃɪˈbæŋ) NOUN *Slang* 1 a situation, matter, or affair (esp in the phrase **the whole shebang**). 2 a hut or shack.
▷HISTORY C19: of uncertain origin

Shebat (ʃɛˈvat) NOUN a variant spelling of **Shevat.**

shebeen *or* **shebean** (ʃɪˈbiːn) NOUN 1 *Irish, Scot, South African* a place where alcoholic drink is sold illegally. 2 (in Ireland) alcohol, esp home-distilled whiskey, sold without a licence. 3 (in South Africa) a place where Black African men engage in social drinking. 4 (in the US and Ireland) weak beer.
▷HISTORY C18: from Irish Gaelic *síbín* beer of poor quality

Shechem (ˈʃɛkəm, -ɛm) NOUN the ancient name of **Nablus.**

Shechina *or* **Shekinah** (ʃɛˈkaɪnə; *Hebrew* ʃəxiːˈna) NOUN *Judaism* 1 the radiance in which God's immanent presence in the midst of his people, esp in the Temple, is visibly manifested. 2 the divine presence itself as contrasted with the divine transcendence.
▷HISTORY C17: from Hebrew *shĕkhīnāh,* from *shākhan* to dwell

shechita *or* **shechitah** (ˈʃəxitɑ, ˈʃxitə) NOUN the Jewish method of killing animals for food.
▷HISTORY from Hebrew, literally: slaughter

shed[1] (ʃɛd) NOUN 1 a small building or lean-to of light construction, used for storage, shelter, etc. 2 a large roofed structure, esp one with open sides, used for storage, repairing locomotives, sheepshearing, etc. 3 a large retail outlet in the style of a warehouse. 4 *NZ* another name for **freezing works.** 5 *NZ* **in the shed.** at work. ◆ VERB **sheds, shedding, shedded.** 6 (*tr*) *NZ* to store (hay or wool) in a shed.
▷HISTORY Old English *sced;* probably variant of *scead* shelter, SHADE
▸ˈ**shedˌlike** ADJECTIVE

shed[2] (ʃɛd) VERB **sheds, shedding, shed.** (*mainly tr*) 1 to pour forth or cause to pour forth: *to shed tears; shed blood.* 2 **shed** (*or* **throw**) **light on** *or* **upon.** to clarify or supply additional information about. 3 to cast off or lose: *the snake shed its skin; trees shed their leaves.* 4 (of a lorry) to drop (its load) on the road by accident. 5 to repel: *this coat sheds water.* 6 (*also intr*) (in weaving) to form an opening between (the warp threads) in order to permit the passage of the shuttle. 7 (*tr*) *Dialect* to make a parting in (the hair). ◆ NOUN 8 (in weaving) the space made by shedding. 9 short for **watershed.** 10 *Chiefly Scot* a parting in the hair.
▷HISTORY Old English *sceadan;* related to Gothic *skaidan,* Old High German *skeidan* to separate; see SHEATH
▸ˈ**shedable** *or* ˈ**sheddable** ADJECTIVE

shed[3] (ʃɛd) VERB **sheds, shedding, shed.** 1 (*tr*) to separate or divide off (some farm animals) from the remainder of a group: *a good dog can shed his sheep in a matter of minutes.* ◆ NOUN 2 (of a dog) the action of separating farm animals.
▷HISTORY from SHED[2]
▸ˈ**shedding** NOUN

shed[4] (ʃɛd) NOUN *Physics* a former unit of nuclear cross section equal to 10^{-52} square metre.
▷HISTORY C20: from SHED[1]; so called by comparison to BARN[2] because of its smaller size

she'd (ʃiːd) CONTRACTION OF she had *or* she would.

shedder (ˈʃɛdə) NOUN 1 a person or thing that sheds. 2 an animal, such as a llama, snake, or lobster, that moults. 3 *NZ* a person who milks cows in a milking shed.

shed hand NOUN *Chiefly Austral and NZ* a worker in a sheepshearing shed.

shedload (ˈʃɛdˌləʊd) NOUN *Slang* a very large amount or number.

shed out VERB (*tr, adverb*) *NZ* to separate off (sheep that have lambed) and move them to better pasture.

shed up VERB (*tr, adverb*) *NZ* to store (hay) in a shed.

sheen (ʃiːn) NOUN 1 a gleaming or glistening brightness; lustre. 2 *Poetic* splendid clothing. ◆ ADJECTIVE 3 *Rare* shining and beautiful; radiant.
▷HISTORY Old English *sciene;* related to Old Norse *skjōni* white horse, Gothic *skauns* beautiful, Old High German *scōni* bright
▸ˈ**sheeny** ADJECTIVE

sheeny (ˈʃiːnɪ) NOUN, *plural* **sheenies.** *Slang* a derogatory word for a **Jew.**
▷HISTORY C19: of unknown origin

sheep (ʃiːp) NOUN, *plural* **sheep.** 1 any of various bovid mammals of the genus *Ovis* and related genera, esp *O. aries* (**domestic sheep**), having transversely ribbed horns and a narrow face. There are many breeds of domestic sheep, raised for their wool and for meat. Related adjective: **ovine.** 2 **Barbary sheep.** another name for **aoudad.** 3 a meek or timid person, esp one without initiative. 4 **separate the sheep from the goats.** to pick out the members of any group who are superior in some respects.
▷HISTORY Old English *sceap;* related to Old Frisian *skēp,* Old Saxon *scāp,* Old High German *scāf*
▸ˈ**sheepˌlike** ADJECTIVE

SHEEP ABBREVIATION FOR Sky High Earnings Expectations Possibly: applied to investments that appear to offer high returns but may be unreliable.

sheepcote (ˈʃiːpˌkəʊt) NOUN *Chiefly Brit* another word for **sheepfold.**

sheep-dip NOUN 1 any of several liquid disinfectants and insecticides in which sheep are immersed to kill vermin and germs in their fleece. 2 a deep trough containing such a liquid.

sheepdog (ˈʃiːpˌdɒg) NOUN 1 Also called: **shepherd dog.** a dog used for herding sheep. See **Border collie.** 2 any of various breeds of dog reared originally for herding sheep. See **Old English sheepdog, Shetland sheepdog.**

sheepdog trial NOUN (*often plural*) a competition in which sheepdogs are tested in their tasks.

sheepfold ('ʃiːpˌfəʊld) NOUN a pen or enclosure for sheep.

sheepish ('ʃiːpɪʃ) ADJECTIVE 1 abashed or embarrassed, esp through looking foolish or being in the wrong. 2 resembling a sheep in timidity or lack of initiative.
▸ **'sheepishly** ADVERB ▸ **'sheepishness** NOUN

sheep ked *or* **tick** NOUN a wingless dipterous fly, *Melophagus ovinus,* that is an external parasite of sheep: family *Hippoboscidae.*

sheep measles NOUN (*functioning as singular or plural*) a disease of sheep caused by infestation by the cysticerci of a dog tapeworm (*Taenia ovis*).

sheepo ('ʃiːpəʊ) NOUN, *plural* **sheepos**. *NZ* a person employed to bring sheep to the catching pen in a shearing shed.

sheep race NOUN *NZ* a single-file walkway for sheep at the entrance to a sheep-dip.

sheep's eyes PLURAL NOUN *Old-fashioned* amorous or inviting glances.

sheep's fescue NOUN a temperate perennial tufted grass, *Festuca ovina,* with narrow inwardly rolled leaves.
▹HISTORY C18: so called because it is often used for sheep pastures

sheepshank ('ʃiːpˌʃæŋk) NOUN a knot consisting of two hitches at the ends of a bight made in a rope to shorten it temporarily.

sheepshead ('ʃiːpsˌhɛd) NOUN, *plural* **-head** *or* **-heads**. any of several sparid fishes with strong crushing teeth, esp *Archosargus rhomboidalis,* of the American Atlantic, which is marked with dark bands.

sheepshearing ('ʃiːpˌʃɪərɪŋ) NOUN 1 the act or process of shearing sheep. 2 the season or an occasion of shearing sheep. 3 a feast held on such an occasion.
▸ **'sheepˌshearer** NOUN

sheepskin ('ʃiːpˌskɪn) NOUN **a** the skin of a sheep, esp when used for clothing, etc., or with the fleece removed and used for parchment. **b** (*as modifier*): *a sheepskin coat.*

sheep sorrel *or* **sheep's sorrel** NOUN a polygonaceous plant, *Rumex acetosella,* of the N hemisphere, having slightly bitter-tasting leaves and small reddish flowers.

sheep station *or* **run** NOUN *Austral and NZ* a large sheep farm. Also called: **run.**

sheep tick NOUN 1 a tick, *Ixodes ricinus,* that is parasitic on sheep, cattle, and man and transmits the disease louping ill in sheep. 2 another name for **sheep ked.**

sheepwalk ('ʃiːpˌwɔːk) NOUN *Chiefly Brit* a tract of land for grazing sheep.

sheer[1] (ʃɪə) ADJECTIVE 1 perpendicular; very steep: *a sheer cliff.* 2 (of textiles) so fine as to be transparent. 3 (*prenominal*) absolute; unmitigated: *sheer folly.* 4 *Obsolete* bright or shining. ◆ ADVERB 5 steeply or perpendicularly. 6 completely or absolutely. ◆ NOUN 7 any transparent fabric used for making garments.
▹HISTORY Old English *scīr;* related to Old Norse *skīrr* bright, Gothic *skeirs* clear, Middle High German *schīr*
▸ **'sheerly** ADVERB ▸ **'sheerness** NOUN

sheer[2] (ʃɪə) VERB (foll by *off* or *away* (*from*)) 1 to deviate or cause to deviate from a course. 2 (*intr*) to avoid an unpleasant person, thing, topic, etc. ◆ NOUN 3 the upward sweep of the deck or bulwarks of a vessel. 4 *Nautical* the position of a vessel relative to its mooring.
▹HISTORY C17: perhaps variant of SHEAR

sheerlegs *or* **shearlegs** ('ʃɪəˌlɛgz) NOUN (*functioning as singular*) a device for lifting heavy weights consisting of two or more spars lashed together at the upper ends from which a lifting tackle is suspended. Also called: **shears.**
▹HISTORY C19: variant of *shear legs*

Sheerness (ˌʃɪə'nɛs) NOUN a port and resort in SE England, in N Kent at the junction of the Medway estuary and the Thames: administratively part of Queenborough in Sheppey since 1968.

sheesh (ʃiːʃ) INTERJECTION *Informal* an exclamation of surprise or annoyance.

sheet[1] (ʃiːt) NOUN 1 a large rectangular piece of cotton, linen, etc., generally one of a pair used as inner bedclothes. 2 **a** a thin piece of a substance such as paper, glass, or metal, usually rectangular in form. **b** (*as modifier*): *sheet iron.* 3 a broad continuous surface; expanse or stretch: *a sheet of rain.* 4 a newspaper, esp a tabloid. 5 a piece of printed paper to be folded into a section for a book. 6 a page of stamps, usually of one denomination and already perforated. 7 any thin tabular mass of rock covering a large area. ◆ VERB 8 (*tr*) to provide with, cover, or wrap in a sheet. 9 (*intr*) (of rain, snow, etc.) to fall heavily.
▹HISTORY Old English *sciete;* related to *sceat* corner, lap, Old Norse *skaut,* Old High German *scōz* lap

sheet[2] (ʃiːt) NOUN *Nautical* a line or rope for controlling the position of a sail relative to the wind.
▹HISTORY Old English *scēata* corner of a sail; related to Middle Low German *schōte* rope attached to a sail; see SHEET[1]

sheet anchor NOUN 1 *Nautical* a large strong anchor for use in emergency. 2 a person or thing to be relied upon in an emergency.
▹HISTORY C17: from earlier *shute anker,* from *shoot* (obsolete) the sheet of a sail

sheet bend NOUN a knot used esp for joining ropes of different sizes. Also called: **becket bend, weaver's hitch.**

sheet down VERB (*intr, adverb*) (of rain) to fall heavily in sheets.

sheet-fed ADJECTIVE *Printing* involving or printing on separate sheets of paper. Compare **reel-fed.**

sheeting ('ʃiːtɪŋ) NOUN fabric from which sheets are made.

sheet lightning NOUN lightning that appears as a broad sheet, caused by the reflection of more distant lightning.

sheet metal NOUN metal in the form of a sheet, the thickness being intermediate between that of plate and that of foil.

sheet music NOUN 1 the printed or written copy of a short composition or piece, esp in the form of unbound leaves. 2 music in its written or printed form.

sheet pile NOUN *Civil engineering* one of a group of piles made of timber, steel, or prestressed concrete set close together to resist lateral pressure, as from earth or water. Compare **bearing pile.**

Sheffer's stroke NOUN *Logic* a function of two sentences, equivalent to the negation of their conjunction, and written *p*|*q* (*p* and *q* are both not true) where *p,q,* are the arguments: *p*|*q* is false only when *p,q* are both true. It is possible to construct all truth functions out of this one alone.
▹HISTORY named after H. M. *Sheffer* (1883–1964), US philosopher

Sheffield ('ʃɛfiːld) NOUN 1 a city in N England, in Sheffield unitary authority, South Yorkshire on the River Don: important centre of steel manufacture and of the cutlery industry; Sheffield university (1905) and Sheffield Hallam University (1992). Pop.: 431 607 (1991). 2 a unitary authority in N England, in South Yorkshire. Pop.: 513 234 (2001). Area: 368 sq. km (142 sq. miles).

Sheffield Shield NOUN (in Australia) the former name for the trophy of the annual interstate cricket competition.
▹HISTORY C19: named after Lord *Sheffield,* sponsor of a visiting English side in 1891–92, who inaugurated the Sheffield Shield competition in 1892

sheikh *or* **sheik** (ʃeɪk) NOUN (in Muslim countries) **a** the head of an Arab tribe, village, etc. **b** a venerable old man. **c** a high priest or religious leader, esp a Sufi master.
▹HISTORY C16: from Arabic *shaykh* old man

sheikhdom *or* **sheikdom** ('ʃeɪkdəm) NOUN the territory ruled by a sheikh.

sheila ('ʃiːlə) NOUN *Austral and NZ old-fashioned* an informal word for **girl** or **woman.**
▹HISTORY C19: from the girl's name *Sheila*

shekel *or* **sheqel** ('ʃɛkᵊl) NOUN 1 the standard monetary unit of modern Israel, divided into 100 agorot. 2 any of several former coins and units of weight of the Near East. 3 (*often plural*) *Informal* any coin or money.
▹HISTORY C16: from Hebrew *sheqel*

Shekinah (ʃɛ'kaɪnə; *Hebrew* ʃəxiː'na) NOUN *Judaism* a variant spelling of **Shechina.**

shelduck ('ʃɛlˌdʌk) *or masculine* **sheldrake** ('ʃɛlˌdreɪk) NOUN, *plural* **-ducks, -duck** *or* **-drakes, -drake**. any of various large usually brightly coloured gooselike ducks, such as *Tadorna tadorna* (**common shelduck**), of the Old World.
▹HISTORY C14 *shel,* probably from dialect *sheld* pied; related to Middle Dutch *schillede* variegated

shelf (ʃɛlf) NOUN, *plural* **shelves** (ʃɛlvz). 1 a thin flat plank of wood, metal, etc., fixed horizontally against a wall, etc., for the purpose of supporting objects. 2 something resembling this in shape or function. 3 the objects placed on a shelf, regarded collectively: *a shelf of books.* 4 a projecting layer of ice, rock, etc., on land or in the sea. See also **continental shelf.** 5 *Mining* a layer of bedrock hit when sinking a shaft. 6 *Archery* the part of the hand on which an arrow rests when the bow is grasped. 7 See **off the shelf.** 8 **on the shelf.** put aside or abandoned: used esp of unmarried women considered to be past the age of marriage. ◆ VERB 9 (*tr*) *Austral slang* to inform upon.
▹HISTORY Old English *scylfe* ship's deck; related to Middle Low German *schelf* shelf, Old English *scylf* crag
▸ **'shelfˌlike** ADJECTIVE

shelf ice NOUN a less common term for **ice shelf.**

shelf life NOUN the length of time a packaged food, chemical, etc., will last without deteriorating.

shelf-stacker NOUN a person whose job is to fill the shelves and displays in a supermarket or other shop with goods for sale.

shell (ʃɛl) NOUN 1 the protective calcareous or membranous outer layer of an egg, esp a bird's egg. 2 the hard outer covering of many molluscs that is secreted by the mantle. 3 any other hard outer layer, such as the exoskeleton of many arthropods. 4 the hard outer layer of some fruits, esp of nuts. 5 any hard outer case. 6 a hollow artillery projectile filled with explosive primed to explode either during flight, on impact, or after penetration. Compare **ball**[1] (sense 7a). 7 a small-arms cartridge comprising a hollow casing inside which is the primer, charge, and bullet. 8 a pyrotechnic cartridge designed to explode in the air. 9 *Rowing* a very light narrow racing boat. 10 the external structure of a building, esp one that is unfinished or one that has been gutted by fire. 11 the basic structural case of something, such as a machine, vehicle, etc. 12 *Physics* **a** a class of electron orbits in an atom in which the electrons have the same principal quantum number and orbital angular momentum quantum number and differences in their energy are small compared with differences in energy between shells. **b** an analogous energy state of nucleons in certain theories (**shell models**) of the structure of the atomic nucleus. 13 the pastry case of a pie, flan, etc. 14 a thin slab of concrete or a skeletal framework made of wood or metal that forms a shell-like roof. 15 *Brit* (in some schools) a class or form. 16 **come** (*or* **bring**) **out of one's shell.** to become (or help to become) less shy and reserved. ◆ VERB 17 to divest or be divested of a shell, husk, pod, etc. 18 to separate or be separated from an ear, husk, cob, etc. 19 (*tr*) to bombard with artillery shells. ◆ See also **shell out.**
▹HISTORY Old English *sciell;* related to Old Norse *skel* shell, Gothic *skalja* tile, Middle Low German *schelle* shell; see SCALE[1], SHALE
▸ **'shell-less** ADJECTIVE ▸ **'shell-ˌlike** ADJECTIVE ▸ **'shelly** ADJECTIVE

she'll (ʃiːl; *unstressed* ʃɪl) CONTRACTION OF she will *or* she shall.

shellac (ʃə'læk, 'ʃɛlæk) NOUN 1 a yellowish resin secreted by the lac insect, esp a commercial preparation of this used in varnishes, polishes, and leather dressings. 2 Also called: **shellac varnish.** a varnish made by dissolving shellac in ethanol or a similar solvent. 3 a gramophone record based on shellac. ◆ VERB **-lacs, -lacking, -lacked.** (*tr*) 4 to coat or treat (an article) with a shellac varnish. 5 *US slang* to defeat completely.
▹HISTORY C18: SHELL + LAC[1], translation of French *laque en écailles,* literally: lac in scales, that is, in thin plates
▸ **shel'lacker** NOUN

shellacking (ʃə'lækɪŋ, 'ʃɛlækɪŋ) NOUN *Slang, chiefly*

US and Canadian a complete defeat; a sound beating: *anyone who gives a shellacking to their bigger neighbours.*

shellback (ˈʃɛlˌbæk) NOUN [1] *Informal* a sailor who has crossed the equator. Compare **polliwog** (sense 2). [2] an experienced or old sailor.

shellbark (ˈʃɛlˌbɑːk) NOUN another name for **shagbark.**
▷HISTORY C19: so called from the texture of its bark

shell bean NOUN *US* any of various bean plants that are cultivated for their edible seeds rather than for their pods.

shell company NOUN *Business* [1] a near-defunct company, esp one with a stock-exchange listing, used as a vehicle for a thriving company. [2] a company that has ceased to trade but retains its registration and is sold for a small sum to enable its new owners to avoid the cost and trouble of registering a new company.

shellfire (ˈʃɛlˌfaɪə) NOUN the firing of artillery shells.

shellfish (ˈʃɛlˌfɪʃ) NOUN, *plural* **-fish** *or* **-fishes.** any aquatic invertebrate having a shell or shell-like carapace, esp such an animal used as human food. Examples are crustaceans such as crabs and lobsters and molluscs such as oysters.

shell game NOUN the US name for **thimblerig.**

shell gland NOUN *Zoology* a gland in certain invertebrates that secretes the components required for forming the shell of an egg.

shell jacket NOUN an army officer's waist-length mess jacket.

shell-like ADJECTIVE [1] resembling the empty shell of a mollusc. ◆ NOUN [2] *Slang* an ear (esp in the phrase **a word in your shell-like**).

shell out VERB *(adverb) Informal* to pay out or hand over (money).
▷HISTORY C19: from SHELL (in the sense: to remove from a pod or (figuratively) a purse)

shell program NOUN *Computing* a basic low-cost computer program that provides a framework within which the user can develop the program to suit his personal requirements.

shellproof (ˈʃɛlˌpruːf) ADJECTIVE designed, intended, or able to resist shellfire.

shell shock NOUN loss of sight, memory, etc., resulting from psychological strain during prolonged engagement in warfare. Also called: **combat neurosis.**

shell-shocked ADJECTIVE [1] suffering from shell shock. [2] in a state of stunned confusion or shock; dazed.

shell star NOUN *Astronomy* a type of star, usually of spectral type B to F, surrounded by a gaseous shell.

shell suit NOUN a lightweight tracksuit consisting of an inner cotton layer covered by a waterproof nylon layer.

Shelta (ˈʃɛltə) NOUN a secret language used by some itinerant tinkers in Ireland and parts of Britain, based on systematically altered Gaelic.
▷HISTORY C19: from earlier *sheldrū*, perhaps an arbitrary alteration of Old Irish *bēlre* speech

shelter (ˈʃɛltə) NOUN [1] something that provides cover or protection, as from weather or danger; place of refuge. [2] the protection afforded by such a cover; refuge. [3] the state of being sheltered. ◆ VERB [4] *(tr)* to provide with or protect by a shelter. [5] *(intr)* to take cover, as from rain; find refuge. [6] *(tr)* to act as a shelter for; take under one's protection.
▷HISTORY C16: of uncertain origin
▸ˈ**shelterer** NOUN ▸ˈ**shelterless** ADJECTIVE

shelter belt NOUN a row of trees planted to protect an area from the wind.

sheltered (ˈʃɛltəd) ADJECTIVE [1] protected from wind or weather: *a sheltered garden.* [2] protected from outside influences: *a sheltered upbringing.* [3] (of buildings) specially designed to provide a safe environment for the elderly, handicapped, or disabled: *sheltered workshops for the blind.* See also **sheltered housing.**

sheltered housing NOUN accommodation designed esp for the elderly or infirm consisting of a group of individual premises, often with some shared facilities and a caretaker. Also called: **sheltered accommodation, sheltered homes.**

shelter tent NOUN *US* a military tent for two men.

sheltie *or* **shelty** (ˈʃɛltɪ) NOUN, *plural* **-ties.** another name for **Shetland pony** or **Shetland sheepdog.**
▷HISTORY C17: probably from Orkney dialect *sjalti*, from Old Norse *Hjalti* Shetlander, from *Hjaltland* Shetland

shelve[1] (ʃɛlv) VERB *(tr)* [1] to place on a shelf. [2] to provide with shelves. [3] to put aside or postpone from consideration. [4] to dismiss or cause to retire.
▷HISTORY C16: from *shelves*, plural of SHELF
▸ˈ**shelver** NOUN

shelve[2] (ʃɛlv) VERB *(intr)* to slope away gradually; incline.
▷HISTORY C16: origin uncertain

shelves (ʃɛlvz) NOUN the plural of **shelf.**

shelving (ˈʃɛlvɪŋ) NOUN [1] material for making shelves. [2] a set of shelves; shelves collectively.

Shem (ʃɛm) NOUN *Old Testament* the eldest of Noah's three sons (Genesis 10:21). Douay spelling: **Sem** (sɛm).

Shema (ʃəˈmɑː) NOUN [1] the central statement of Jewish belief, the sentence "Hear, O Israel: the Lord is your God; the Lord is One" (Deuteronomy 6:4). [2] the section of the liturgy consisting of this and related biblical passages, Deuteronomy 6:4–9 and 11:13–21 and Numbers 15:37–41, recited in the morning and evening prayers and on retiring at night.
▷HISTORY Hebrew, literally: hear

Shembe (ˈʃɛmbɛ) NOUN (in South Africa) an African sect that combines Christianity with aspects of Bantu religion.

Shemini Atseres (ˈʃmini ɑˈtsɛrɛs) *or* **Shemini Atzereth** (ˈʃəmini ɑˈtsɛrɛt) NOUN *Judaism* the festival which follows upon Sukkoth on Tishri 22 (and 23 outside Israel), and includes Simchat Torah.

Shemite (ˈʃɛmaɪt) NOUN another word for **Semite.**

Shemitic (ʃəˈmɪtɪk) NOUN, ADJECTIVE another word for **Semitic.**

Shemona Esrei *Hebrew* (ʃəməˈna ɛsˈreɪ; *Yiddish* ˈʃmonə ˈɛsreɪ) NOUN *Judaism* another name for **Amidah.**
▷HISTORY literally: eighteen (blessings)

shemozzle (ʃɪˈmɒzᵊl) NOUN *Informal* a noisy confusion or dispute; uproar.
▷HISTORY C19: perhaps from Yiddish *shlimazl* misfortune

Shenandoah National Park (ˌʃɛnənˈdəʊə) NOUN a national park in N Virginia: established in 1935 to protect part of the Blue Ridge Mountains. Area: 782 sq. km (302 sq. miles).

shenanigan (ʃɪˈnænɪgən) NOUN *Informal* [1] *(usually plural)* roguishness; mischief. [2] an act of treachery; deception.
▷HISTORY C19: of unknown origin

shend (ʃɛnd) VERB **shends, shending, shent** (ʃɛnt). *(tr) Archaic* [1] to put to shame. [2] to chide or reproach. [3] to injure or destroy.
▷HISTORY Old English *gescendan*, from *scand* SHAME

Shensi (ˈʃɛnˈsiː) NOUN a variant transliteration of the Chinese name for **Shaanxi.**

Shenyang (ˈʃɛnˈjæŋ) NOUN a walled city in NE China in S Manchuria, capital of Liaoning province: capital of the Manchu dynasty from 1644–1912; seized by the Japanese in 1931. Pop.: 3 876 289 (1999 est.). Former name: **Mukden.**

she-oak NOUN any of various Australian trees of the genus *Casuarina*. See **casuarina.**
▷HISTORY C18 *she* (in the sense: inferior) + OAK

Sheol (ˈʃiːəʊl, -ɒl) NOUN *Old Testament* [1] the abode of the dead. [2] *(often not capital)* hell.
▷HISTORY C16: from Hebrew *shĕʼōl*

shepherd (ˈʃɛpəd) NOUN [1] a person employed to tend sheep. Female equivalent: **shepherdess.** Related adjectives: **bucolic, pastoral.** [2] a person, such as a clergyman, who watches over or guides a group of people. ◆ VERB *(tr)* [3] to guide or watch over in the manner of a shepherd. [4] *Australian Rules football* to prevent opponents from tackling (a member of one's own team) by blocking their path.
▷HISTORY from Old English *sceaphirde*. See SHEEP, HERD[2]

Shepherd NOUN *Astronomy* a small moon of (e.g.) Saturn orbiting close to the rings and partly responsible for ring stability.

shepherd dog NOUN another term for **sheepdog** (sense 1).

shepherd's needle NOUN a European umbelliferous plant, *Scandix pectenveneris*, with long needle-like fruits.

shepherd's pie NOUN *Chiefly Brit* a baked dish of minced meat covered with mashed potato. Also called: **cottage pie.**

shepherd's-purse NOUN a plant, *Capsella bursa-pastoris*, having small white flowers and flattened triangular seed pods: family *Brassicaceae* (crucifers).
▷HISTORY C15: compare Latin *bursa pastoris*, French *bourse-de-berger*, German *Hirtentasche*, Dutch *herdentasch*

shepherd's weatherglass NOUN *Brit* another name for the **scarlet pimpernel.**

Sheppey (ˈʃɛpɪ) NOUN **Isle of.** an island in SE England, off the N coast of Kent in the Thames estuary: separated from the mainland by **The Swale**, a narrow channel. Chief towns: Sheerness, Minster. Pop.: 31 854 (latest est.). Area: 80 sq. km (30 sq. miles).

sherang (ʃəˈræŋ) NOUN **head sherang.** *Austral and NZ* the boss; person in authority: *who is the head sherang around here?*

sherardize *or* **sherardise** (ˈʃɛrəˌdaɪz) VERB *Metallurgy* to coat (iron or steel) with zinc by heating in a container with zinc dust or (of iron or steel) to be coated in this way.
▷HISTORY C20: process named after *Sherard* Cowper-Coles (died 1936), English inventor
▸ˌ**sherardiˈzation** *or* ˌ**sherardiˈsation** NOUN

Sheraton (ˈʃɛrətən) ADJECTIVE denoting furniture made by or in the style of Thomas Sheraton, the English furniture maker (1751–1806), characterized by lightness, elegance, and the extensive use of inlay.

sherbet (ˈʃɜːbət) NOUN [1] a fruit-flavoured slightly effervescent powder, eaten as a sweet or used to make a drink: *lemon sherbet.* [2] another word (esp US and Canadian) for **sorbet** (sense 1). [3] *Austral slang* beer. [4] a cooling Oriental drink of sweetened fruit juice. [5] *South African informal* a euphemistic word for **shit.**
▷HISTORY C17: from Turkish *şerbet*, from Persian *sharbat*, from Arabic *sharbah* drink, from *shariba* to drink

Sherborne (ˈʃɛːbɔːn) NOUN a town in S England in Dorset: noted for its medieval abbey, ruined medieval castle, and Sherborne Castle a mansion built by Sir Walter Raleigh in 1594. Pop.: 7606 (1991).

Sherbrooke (ˈʃɜːˌbrʊk) NOUN a city in E Canada, in S Quebec: industrial and commercial centre. Pop.: 76 786 (1996).

sherd (ʃɜːd) NOUN a variant of **shard.**

sheria (ʃəˈriːə) NOUN a variant spelling of **sharia.**

sherif, shereef (ʃɛˈriːf), *or* **sharif** NOUN, *plural* **ashraf.** *Islam* [1] a descendant of Mohammed through his daughter Fatima. [2] (formerly) the governor of Mecca. [3] an honorific title accorded to any Muslim ruler.
▷HISTORY C16: from Arabic *sharīf* noble

sheriff (ˈʃɛrɪf) NOUN [1] (in the US) the chief law-enforcement officer in a county: popularly elected, except in Rhode Island. [2] (in England and Wales) the chief executive officer of the Crown in a county, having chiefly ceremonial duties. Related adjective: **shrieval.** [3] (in Scotland) a judge in any of the sheriff courts. [4] (in Australia) an administrative officer of the Supreme Court, who enforces judgments and the execution of writs, empanels juries, etc. [5] (in New Zealand) an officer of the High Court.
▷HISTORY Old English *scīrgerēfa*, from *scīr* SHIRE[1] + *gerēfa* REEVE[1]
▸ˈ**sheriffdom** NOUN

sheriff court NOUN (in Scotland) a court having jurisdiction to try summarily or on indictment all but the most serious crimes and to deal with most civil actions.

sherpa (ˈʃɜːpə) NOUN an official who makes preparations for or assists a government representative or important delegate at a summit meeting or conference.
▷HISTORY C20: from SHERPA, a member of a people

noted for providing assistance to mountaineers: from a pun on the different senses of SUMMIT

Sherpa ('ʃɜːpə) NOUN, *plural* **-pas** *or* **-pa**. a member of a people of Mongolian origin living on the southern slopes of the Himalayas in Nepal, noted as mountaineers.

sherry ('ʃɛrɪ) NOUN, *plural* **-ries**. a fortified wine, originally from the Jerez region in S Spain, usually drunk as an apéritif.
▷HISTORY C16: from earlier *sherris* (assumed to be plural), from Spanish *Xeres,* now *Jerez*

's Hertogenbosch (*Dutch* shɛrtoːxən'bɔs) NOUN a city in the S Netherlands, capital of North Brabant province: birthplace of Hieronymus Bosch. Pop.: 128 009 (1999 est.). Also called: **Den Bosch.** French name: **Bois-le-Duc.**

sherwani (ʃɛə'wɑːnɪ) NOUN, *plural* **-nis**. a long coat closed up to the neck, worn by men in India.
▷HISTORY Hindi

Sherwood Forest ('ʃɜːˌwʊd) NOUN an ancient forest in central England, in Nottinghamshire: formerly a royal hunting ground and much more extensive; famous as the home of Robin Hood.

she's (ʃiːz) CONTRACTION OF she is *or* she has.

Shetland ('ʃɛtlənd) NOUN *or* **Shetland Islands** PLURAL NOUN a group of about 100 islands (fewer than 20 inhabited), off the N coast of Scotland, which constitute an island authority of Scotland: a Norse dependency from the 8th century until 1472; noted for the breeding of Shetland ponies, knitwear manufacturing, and fishing; oil-related industries. Administrative centre: Lerwick. Pop.: 21 988 (2001). Area: 1426 sq. km (550 sq. miles). Official name (until 1974): **Zetland.**

Shetland pony NOUN a very small sturdy breed of pony with a long shaggy mane and tail. Also called: **sheltie.**

Shetland sheepdog NOUN a small dog similar in appearance to a rough collie. Also called: **sheltie.**

Shetland wool NOUN a fine loosely twisted wool yarn spun from the fleece of Shetland sheep and used esp for sweaters.

sheuch *or* **sheugh** (ʃuːx, ʃʌx) NOUN *Scot dialect* a ditch or trough.
▷HISTORY dialect variant of SOUGH[2]

Sheva Brachoth *or* **Sheva Brochos** (*Hebrew* 'ʃɛvɑ brɑ'xot; *Yiddish* 'ʃɛvə 'broxəs) PLURAL NOUN *Judaism* [1] the seven blessings said during the marriage service and repeated at the celebration thereafter. [2] any of the celebratory meals held on the seven days after a wedding.
▷HISTORY literally: seven blessings

Shevat *or* **Shebat** (ʃɛ'vat) NOUN (in the Jewish calendar) the eleventh month of the year according to biblical reckoning and the fifth month of the civil year.
▷HISTORY from Hebrew

shew (ʃəʊ) VERB **shews, shewing, shewed, shewn** (ʃəʊn) *or* **shewed**. an archaic spelling of **show**.
▸'**shewer** NOUN

shewbread *or* **showbread** ('ʃəʊˌbrɛd) NOUN *Old Testament* the loaves of bread placed every Sabbath on the table beside the altar of incense in the tabernacle or temple of ancient Israel (Exodus 25:30; Leviticus 24:5–9).
▷HISTORY on the model of German *Schaubrot,* a translation of the Greek *artoi enōpioi,* a translation of the Hebrew *lechem pānīm,* literally: bread of the presence

SHF *or* **shf** *Radio* ABBREVIATION FOR **superhigh frequency**.

Shiah *or* **Shia** ('ʃiːə) NOUN [1] one of the two main branches of Islam (the other being the Sunni), now mainly in Iran, which regards Mohammed's cousin Ali and his successors as the true imams. [2] another name for **Shiite.** ◆ ADJECTIVE [3] designating or characteristic of this sect or its beliefs and practices.
▷HISTORY C17: from Arabic *shī'ah* sect, from *shā'a* to follow

shiai ('ʃiːaɪ) NOUN a judo contest.
▷HISTORY Japanese

shiatsu (ˌʃiː'ætsuː) NOUN massage in which pressure is applied to the same points of the body as in acupuncture. Also called: **acupressure.**
▷HISTORY Japanese, from Chinese *chǐ* finger + *yā* pressure

shibboleth ('ʃɪbəˌlɛθ) NOUN [1] a belief, principle, or practice which is commonly adhered to but which is thought by some people to be inappropriate or out of date. [2] a custom, phrase, or use of language that acts as a test of belonging to, or as a stumbling block to becoming a member of, a particular social class, profession, etc.
▷HISTORY C14: from Hebrew, literally: ear of grain; the word is used in the Old Testament by the Gileadites as a test word for the Ephraimites, who could not pronounce the sound *sh*

shicker ('ʃɪkə) NOUN *Austral archaic slang* alcoholic drink; liquor.
▷HISTORY via Yiddish from Hebrew

shickered ('ʃɪkəd) ADJECTIVE *Austral and NZ slang* drunk; intoxicated.

shidduch *Yiddish* ('ʃɪdəx) NOUN, *plural* **shidduchim** (ʃɪ'duːxɪm). *Judaism* [1] **a** an arranged marriage. **b** the arrangement of a marriage. [2] any negotiated agreement.
▷HISTORY from Hebrew: see SHADCHAN

shied (ʃaɪd) VERB the past tense and past participle of **shy**[1] and **shy**[2].

shield (ʃiːld) NOUN [1] any protection used to intercept blows, missiles, etc., such as a tough piece of armour carried on the arm. [2] any similar protective device. [3] Also called: **scutcheon, escutcheon.** *Heraldry* a pointed stylized shield used for displaying armorial bearings. [4] anything that resembles a shield in shape, such as a prize in a sports competition. [5] the protective outer covering of an animal, such as the shell of a turtle. [6] *Physics* a structure of concrete, lead, etc., placed around a nuclear reactor or other source of radiation in order to prevent the escape of radiation. [7] a broad stable plateau of ancient Precambrian rocks forming the rigid nucleus of a particular continent. See **Baltic Shield, Canadian Shield.** [8] short for **dress shield.** [9] *Civil engineering* a hollow steel cylinder that protects men driving a circular tunnel through loose, soft, or water-bearing ground. [10] **the shield.** *Informal* **a** *Austral* short for the **Sheffield Shield. b** *NZ* short for the **Ranfurly Shield.** ◆ VERB [11] (*tr*) to protect, hide, or conceal (something) from danger or harm.
▷HISTORY Old English *scield;* related to Old Norse *skjöldr,* Gothic *skildus,* Old High German *scilt* shield, Old English *sciell* SHELL
▸'**shielder** NOUN ▸'**shield,like** ADJECTIVE

shield bug NOUN any shield-shaped herbivorous heteropterous insect of the superfamily *Pentamoidea,* esp any of the family *Pentatomidae.* Also called: **stink bug.**

shield cricket NOUN *Austral* the interstate cricket competition held for the Sheffield Shield.

shield fern NOUN any temperate woodland fern of the genus *Polystichum* having shield-shaped flaps covering the spore-producing bodies: family *Aspleniaceae.*

shield match NOUN **a** *Austral* a cricket match for the Sheffield Shield. **b** *NZ* a rugby match for the Ranfurly Shield.

Shield of David NOUN another term for the **Star of David.**

shield volcano NOUN a broad volcano built up from the repeated nonexplosive eruption of basalt to form a low dome or shield, usually having a large caldera at the summit.

shieling ('ʃiːlɪŋ) *or* **shiel** (ʃiːl) NOUN *Chiefly Scot* [1] a rough, sometimes temporary, hut or shelter used by people tending cattle on high or remote ground. [2] pasture land for the grazing of cattle in summer.
▷HISTORY C16: from Middle English *shale* hut, of unknown origin

shier[1] ('ʃaɪə) ADJECTIVE a comparative of **shy.**

shier[2] *or* **shyer** ('ʃaɪə) NOUN a horse that shies habitually.

shiest ('ʃaɪɪst) ADJECTIVE a superlative of **shy.**

shift (ʃɪft) VERB [1] to move or cause to move from one place or position to another. [2] (*tr*) to change for another or others. [3] to change (gear) in a motor vehicle. [4] (*intr*) (of a sound or set of sounds) to alter in a systematic way. [5] (*intr*) to provide for one's needs (esp in the phrase **shift for oneself**). [6] (*intr*) to proceed by indirect or evasive methods. [7] to remove or be removed, esp with difficulty: *no detergent can shift these stains.* [8] (*intr*) *Slang* to move quickly. [9] (*tr*) *Computing* to move (bits held in a store location) to the left or right. ◆ NOUN [10] the act or an instance of shifting. [11] a group of workers who work for a specific period. [12] the period of time worked by such a group. [13] an expedient, contrivance, or artifice. [14] the displacement of rocks, esp layers or seams in mining, at a geological fault. [15] an underskirt or dress with little shaping.
▷HISTORY Old English *sciftan;* related to Old Norse *skipta* to divide, Middle Low German *schiften,* to separate
▸'**shifter** NOUN

shifting cultivation NOUN a land-use system, esp in tropical Africa, in which a tract of land is cultivated until its fertility diminishes, when it is abandoned until this is restored naturally.

shifting spanner NOUN *Austral and NZ* an adjustable spanner. Also called: **shifter.**

shift key NOUN a key on a typewriter or computer keyboard used to type capital letters and certain numbers and symbols.

shiftless ('ʃɪftlɪs) ADJECTIVE lacking in ambition or initiative.
▸'**shiftlessly** ADVERB ▸'**shiftlessness** NOUN

shiftwork ('ʃɪftˌwɜːk) NOUN a system of employment where an individual's normal hours of work are, in part, outside the period of normal day working and may follow a different pattern in consecutive periods of weeks.

shifty ('ʃɪftɪ) ADJECTIVE **shiftier, shiftiest.** [1] given to evasions; artful. [2] furtive in character or appearance. [3] full of expedients; resourceful.
▸'**shiftily** ADVERB ▸'**shiftiness** NOUN

shigella (ʃɪ'gɛlə) NOUN any rod-shaped Gram-negative bacterium of the genus *Shigella;* some species cause dysentery.
▷HISTORY C20: named after K. *Shiga* (1870–1957), Japanese bacteriologist, who discovered it

shih-tzu ('ʃiː'tsuː) NOUN a small dog of a breed derived from crossing the Pekingese and the Tibetan apso. It has a long straight dense coat and carries its tail curled over its back.
▷HISTORY from Chinese, literally: lion

Shiism ('ʃiːɪzəm) NOUN *Islam* the beliefs and practices of Shiah.

shiitake (ˌʃɪɪ'tɑːkeɪ) *or* **shitake** NOUN, *plural* **-take.** a kind of mushroom widely used in Oriental cookery.
▷HISTORY C20: from Japanese *shii* tree + *take* mushroom

Shiite ('ʃiːaɪt) *or* **Shiah** *Islam* ◆ NOUN [1] an adherent of Shiah. ◆ ADJECTIVE [2] of or relating to Shiah.
▸**Shiitic** (ʃiː'ɪtɪk) ADJECTIVE

Shijiazhuang ('ʃiːdʒɑː'dʒwæŋ), **Shihchiachuang,** *or* **Shihkiachwang** (ˌʃiːtʃjɑː'tʃwæŋ) NOUN a city in NE China, capital of Hebei province: textile manufacturing. Pop.: 1 338 796 (1999 est.).

shikar (ʃɪ'kɑː) (in India) NOUN [1] hunting, esp big-game hunting. ◆ VERB **-kars, -karring, -karred.** [2] to hunt (game, esp big game).
▷HISTORY C17: via Urdu from Persian

shikari *or* **shikaree** (ʃɪ'kɑːrɪ) NOUN, *plural* **-ris** *or* **-rees.** (in India) a hunter.

Shikoku ('ʃiːkəʊˌkuː) NOUN the smallest of the four main islands of Japan, separated from Honshu by the Inland Sea: forested and mountainous. Pop.: 4 154 000 (2000 est.). Area: 17 759 sq. km (6857 sq. miles).

shiksa ('ʃɪksə) NOUN *Often derogatory* (used by Jews) [1] a non-Jewish girl. [2] a Jewish girl who fails to live up to traditional Jewish standards.
▷HISTORY Yiddish *shikse,* feminine of *sheygets* non-Jewish youth, from Hebrew *sheqeṣ* defect

shill (ʃɪl) NOUN *Slang* a confidence trickster's assistant, esp a person who poses as an ordinary customer, gambler, etc., in order to entice others to participate.
▷HISTORY C20: perhaps shortened from *shillaber* a circus barker, of unknown origin

shillelagh *or* **shillala** (ʃə'leɪlə, -lɪ; *Irish* ʃɪ'leːlə) NOUN (in Ireland) a stout club or cudgel, esp one made of oak or blackthorn.
▷HISTORY C18: from Irish Gaelic *sail* cudgel + *éille* leash, thong

shilling ('ʃɪlɪŋ) NOUN [1] a former British and

Australian silver or cupronickel coin worth one twentieth of a pound: not minted in Britain since 1970. Abbreviations: **s, sh.** 2 the standard monetary unit of Kenya, Somalia, Tanzania, and Uganda: divided into 100 cents. 3 an old monetary unit of the US varying in value in different states. 4 (*in combination*) *Scot* an indication of the strength and character of a beer, referring to the price after duty that was formerly paid per barrel: *sixty-shilling*. Symbol: **/-**.
▷HISTORY Old English *scilling;* related to Old Norse *skillingr,* Gothic *skilliggs,* Old High German *skilling*

shilling mark NOUN another name for **solidus** (sense 1).
▷HISTORY so named because it was used to separate shillings from pence when writing amounts less than one pound before the introduction of decimal currency in Britain. For example, *three shillings and eleven pence* was written *3/11*

Shillong (ʃɪˈlɒŋ) NOUN a city in NE India, capital of Meghalaya: situated on the **Shillong Plateau** at an altitude of 1520 m (4987 ft.); destroyed by earthquake in 1897 and rebuilt. Pop.: 131 719 (1991).

shillyshally (ˈʃɪlɪˌʃælɪ) *Informal* ◆ VERB **-lies, -lying, -lied.** 1 (*intr*) to be indecisive, esp over unimportant matters; hesitate. ◆ ADVERB 2 in an indecisive manner. ◆ ADJECTIVE 3 indecisive or hesitant. ◆ NOUN, *plural* **-lies.** 4 indecision or hesitation; vacillation.
▷HISTORY C18: from *shill I shall I,* by reduplication of *shall I*
▸ˈ**shilly,shallier** NOUN

Shiloh (ˈʃaɪləʊ) NOUN a town in central ancient Palestine, in Canaan on the E slope of Mount Ephraim: keeping place of the tabernacle and the ark; destroyed by the Philistines.

shilpit (ˈʃɪlpɪt) ADJECTIVE *Scot* puny; thin; weak-looking.
▷HISTORY C19: of unknown origin

shily (ˈʃaɪlɪ) ADVERB a less common spelling of **shyly.**

shim (ʃɪm) NOUN 1 a thin packing strip or washer often used with a number of similar washers or strips to adjust a clearance for gears, etc. 2 *Physics* a thin strip of magnetic material, such as soft iron, used to adjust a magnetic field. ◆ VERB **shims, shimming, shimmed.** 3 (*tr*) to modify a load, clearance, or magnetic field by the use of shims.

shimmer (ˈʃɪmə) VERB 1 (*intr*) to shine with a glistening or tremulous light. ◆ NOUN 2 a faint, glistening, or tremulous light.
▷HISTORY Old English *scimerian;* related to Middle Low German *schēmeren* to grow dark, Old Norse *skimi* brightness
▸ˈ**shimmering** ADJECTIVE ▸ˈ**shimmeringly** ADVERB

shimmery (ˈʃɪmərɪ) ADJECTIVE **-merier, -meriest.** 1 shining with a glistening or tremulous light. 2 glamorous; flashy.

shimmy (ˈʃɪmɪ) NOUN, *plural* **-mies.** 1 an American ragtime dance with much shaking of the hips and shoulders. 2 abnormal wobbling motion in a motor vehicle, esp in the front wheels or steering. 3 an informal word for **chemise.** ◆ VERB **-mies, -mying, -mied.** (*intr*) 4 to dance the shimmy. 5 to vibrate or wobble.
▷HISTORY C19: changed from CHEMISE, mistakenly assumed to be plural

Shimonoseki (ˌʃɪmənəʊˈsɛkɪ) NOUN a port in SW Japan, on SW Honshu: scene of the peace treaty (1895) ending the Sino-Japanese War; a heavy industrial centre. Pop.: 259 791 (1995).

shin[1] (ʃɪn) NOUN 1 the front part of the lower leg. 2 the front edge of the tibia. 3 *Chiefly Brit* a cut of beef, the lower foreleg. ◆ VERB **shins, shinning, shinned.** 4 (when *intr,* often foll by *up*) to climb (a pole, tree, etc.) by gripping with the hands or arms and the legs and hauling oneself up. 5 (*tr*) to kick (a person) in the shins.
▷HISTORY Old English *scinu;* related to Old High German *scina* needle, Norwegian dialect *skina* small disc

shin[2] (ʃɪn) NOUN the 22nd letter in the Hebrew alphabet (ש), transliterated as *sh.*
▷HISTORY from Hebrew *shīn,* literally: tooth

Shinar (ˈʃaɪnə) NOUN *Old Testament* the southern part of the valley of the Tigris and Euphrates, often identified with Sumer; Babylonia.

shinbone (ˈʃɪnˌbəʊn) NOUN the nontechnical name for **tibia** (sense 1).

shindig (ˈʃɪnˌdɪg) NOUN *Informal* 1 a noisy party, dance, etc. 2 another word for **shindy.**
▷HISTORY C19: variant of SHINDY

shindy (ˈʃɪndɪ) NOUN, *plural* **-dies.** *Informal* 1 a quarrel or commotion (esp in the phrase **kick up a shindy**). 2 another word for **shindig.**
▷HISTORY C19: variant of SHINTY

shine (ʃaɪn) VERB **shines, shining, shone.** 1 (*intr*) to emit light. 2 (*intr*) to glow or be bright with reflected light. 3 (*tr*) to direct the light of (a lamp, etc.): *he shone the torch in my eyes.* 4 (*tr; past tense and past participle* **shined**) to cause to gleam by polishing: *to shine shoes.* 5 (*intr*) to be conspicuously competent; excel: *she shines at tennis.* 6 (*intr*) to appear clearly; be conspicuous: *the truth shone out of his words.* ◆ NOUN 7 the state or quality of shining; sheen; lustre. 8 (**come**) **rain or shine. a** whatever the weather. **b** regardless of circumstances. 9 *Informal* short for **moonshine** (whisky). 10 *Informal* a liking or fancy (esp in the phrase **take a shine to**).
▷HISTORY Old English *scīnan;* related to Old Norse *skīna,* Gothic *skeinan,* Old High German *scīnan* to shine, Greek *skia* shadow

shiner (ˈʃaɪnə) NOUN 1 something that shines, such as a polishing device. 2 any of numerous small North American freshwater cyprinid fishes of the genus *Notropis* and related genera, such as *N. cornutus* (**common shiner**) and *Notemigonus crysoleucas* (**golden shiner**). 3 a popular name for the **mackerel.** 4 *Informal* a black eye. 5 *NZ old-fashioned informal* a vagrant or tramp.

shingle[1] (ˈʃɪŋgᵊl) NOUN 1 a thin rectangular tile, esp one made of wood, that is laid with others in overlapping rows to cover a roof or a wall. 2 a woman's short-cropped hairstyle. 3 *US and Canadian* a small signboard or nameplate fixed outside the office of a doctor, lawyer, etc. 4 **a shingle short.** *Austral informal* unintelligent or mentally subnormal. ◆ VERB (*tr*) 5 to cover (a roof or a wall) with shingles. 6 to cut (the hair) in a short-cropped style.
▷HISTORY C12 *scingle,* from Late Latin *scindula* a split piece of wood, from Latin *scindere* to split
▸ˈ**shingler** NOUN

shingle[2] (ˈʃɪŋgᵊl) NOUN 1 coarse gravel, esp the pebbles found on beaches. 2 a place or area strewn with shingle.
▷HISTORY C16: of Scandinavian origin; compare Norwegian *singl* pebbles, Frisian *singel* gravel
▸ˈ**shingly** ADJECTIVE

shingle[3] (ˈʃɪŋgᵊl) VERB (*tr*) *Metallurgy* to hammer or squeeze the slag out of (iron) after puddling in the production of wrought iron.
▷HISTORY C17: from Old French dialect *chingler* to whip, from *chingle* belt, from Latin *cingula* girdle; see CINGULUM

shingles (ˈʃɪŋgᵊlz) NOUN (*functioning as singular*) an acute viral disease affecting the ganglia of certain nerves, characterized by inflammation, pain, and skin eruptions along the course of the affected nerve. Technical names: **herpes zoster, zoster.**
▷HISTORY C14: from Medieval Latin *cingulum* girdle, rendering Greek *zōnē* ZONE

shinju (ˈʃɪndʒuː) NOUN (formerly, in Japan) a ritual double suicide of lovers.

shinkin (ˈʃɪŋkɪn) NOUN *South Wales dialect* a worthless person.
▷HISTORY Welsh, from the surname *Jenkin,* of Dutch origin

shinleaf (ˈʃɪnˌliːf) NOUN, *plural* **-leaves.** the usual US name for **wintergreen** (sense 3).

shinplaster (ˈʃɪnˌplɑːstə) NOUN *US, Canadian, and Austral* a promissory note on brittle paper, issued by an individual.
▷HISTORY C19: so called because of its resemblance to a sticking plaster

shin splints NOUN (*functioning as singular or plural*) a painful swelling of the front lower leg, associated with muscle or bone inflammation, and common among athletes and other sportspeople.

Shinto (ˈʃɪntəʊ) NOUN the indigenous religion of Japan, polytheistic in character and incorporating the worship of a number of ethnic divinities, from the chief of which the emperor is believed to be descended.
▷HISTORY C18: from Japanese: the way of the gods, from Chinese *shên* gods + *tao* way
▸ˈ**Shintoism** NOUN ▸ˈ**Shintoist** NOUN, ADJECTIVE

shinty (ˈʃɪntɪ) *or US and Canadian* **shinny** (ˈʃɪnɪ) NOUN, *plural* **-ties** *or* **-nies.** 1 a simple form of hockey of Scottish origin played with a ball and sticks curved at the lower end. 2 the stick used in this game. ◆ VERB **-ties, -tying, -tied** *or US and Canadian* **-nies, -nying, -nied.** (*intr*) 3 to play shinty.
▷HISTORY C17: possibly from Scottish Gaelic *sinteag* a pace, bound

shiny (ˈʃaɪnɪ) ADJECTIVE **shinier, shiniest.** 1 glossy or polished; bright. 2 (of clothes or material) worn to a smooth and glossy state, as by continual rubbing.
▸ˈ**shininess** NOUN

ship (ʃɪp) NOUN 1 a vessel propelled by engines or sails for navigating on the water, esp a large vessel that cannot be carried aboard another, as distinguished from a boat. 2 *Nautical* a large sailing vessel with three or more square-rigged masts. 3 the crew of a ship. 4 short for **airship** or **spaceship.** 5 *Informal* any vehicle or conveyance. 6 **when one's ship comes in.** when one has become successful or wealthy. ◆ VERB **ships, shipping, shipped.** 7 to place, transport, or travel on any conveyance, esp aboard a ship: *ship the microscopes by aeroplane; can we ship tomorrow?* 8 (*tr*) *Nautical* to take (water) over the side. 9 to bring or go aboard a vessel: *to ship oars.* 10 (*tr;* often foll by *off*) *Informal* to send away, often in order to be rid of: *they shipped the children off to boarding school.* 11 (*intr*) to engage to serve aboard a ship: *I shipped aboard a Liverpool liner.* 12 *Informal* (*tr*) to concede (a goal): *Celtic have shipped eight goals in three away matches.* ◆ See also **ship out.**
▷HISTORY Old English *scip;* related to Old Norse *skip,* Old High German *skif* ship, *scipfī* cup
▸ˈ**shippable** ADJECTIVE

-ship SUFFIX FORMING NOUNS 1 indicating state or condition: *fellowship.* 2 indicating rank, office, or position: *lordship.* 3 indicating craft or skill: *horsemanship; workmanship; scholarship.*
▷HISTORY Old English *-scipe;* compare SHAPE

shipboard (ˈʃɪpˌbɔːd) NOUN 1 (*modifier*) taking place, used, or intended for use aboard a ship: *a shipboard encounter.* 2 **on shipboard.** on board a ship.

ship-broker NOUN a person who acts for a shipowner by getting cargo and passengers for his ships and also handling insurance and other matters.

shipbuilder (ˈʃɪpˌbɪldə) NOUN a person or business engaged in the building of ships.
▸ˈ**ship,building** NOUN

ship chandler NOUN a person or business dealing in supplies for ships.
▸**ship chandlery** NOUN

Shipka Pass (ˈʃɪpkə) NOUN a pass over the Balkan Mountains in central Bulgaria: scene of a bloody Turkish defeat in the Russo-Turkish War (1877–78). Height: 1334 m (4376 ft.).

shipload (ˈʃɪpˌləʊd) NOUN the quantity carried by a ship.

shipmaster (ˈʃɪpˌmɑːstə) *or* **shipman** (ˈʃɪpmən) NOUN, *plural* **-masters** *or* **-men.** the master or captain of a ship.

shipmate (ˈʃɪpˌmeɪt) NOUN a sailor who serves on the same ship as another.

shipment (ˈʃɪpmənt) NOUN 1 **a** goods shipped together as part of the same lot: *a shipment of grain.* **b** (*as modifier*): *a shipment schedule.* 2 the act of shipping cargo.

ship money NOUN *English history* a tax levied to finance the fitting out of warships: abolished 1640.

ship of the line NOUN *Nautical* (formerly) a warship large enough to fight in the first line of battle.

ship out VERB (*adverb*) to depart or cause to depart by ship: *we shipped out at dawn; they shipped out the new recruits.*

shipowner (ˈʃɪpˌəʊnə) NOUN a person who owns or has shares in a ship or ships.

shipper (ˈʃɪpə) NOUN a person or company in the business of shipping freight.

shippie (ˈʃɪpɪ) NOUN *NZ slang* a prostitute who solicits at a port.

shipping (ˈʃɪpɪŋ) NOUN 1 **a** the business of transporting freight, esp by ship. **b** (*as modifier*): *a shipping magnate; shipping line.* 2 **a** ships collectively: *there is a lot of shipping in the Channel.* **b** the tonnage of a number of ships: *shipping for this year exceeded that of last.*

shipping agent NOUN a person or company whose business is to prepare shipping documents, arrange shipping space and insurance, and deal with customs requirements.

shipping clerk NOUN a person employed by a company to arrange, receive, record, and send shipments of goods.

shipping ton NOUN the full name for **ton**[1] (sense 5).

ship-rigged ADJECTIVE rigged as a full-rigged ship.

ship's articles *or* **shipping articles** PLURAL NOUN a type of contract by which sailors agree to the conditions, payment, etc., for the ship in which they are going to work.

ship's biscuit NOUN another name for **hardtack.**

ship's boy NOUN a young man or boy employed to attend the needs of passengers or officers aboard ship.

shipshape ('ʃɪpˌʃeɪp) ADJECTIVE 1 neat; orderly. ◆ ADVERB 2 in a neat and orderly manner.

ship's papers PLURAL NOUN the documents that are required by law to be carried by a ship for the purpose of ascertaining details of her ownership, nationality, destination, and cargo or to prove her neutrality.

shipway ('ʃɪpˌweɪ) NOUN 1 the structure on which a vessel is built, then launched. 2 a canal used by ships.

shipworm ('ʃɪpˌwɜːm) NOUN any wormlike marine bivalve mollusc of the genus *Teredo* and related genera and family *Teredinidae*. They bore into wooden piers, ships, etc., by means of drill-like shell valves. See also **piddock.**

shipwreck ('ʃɪpˌrɛk) NOUN 1 the partial or total destruction of a ship at sea. 2 a wrecked ship or part of such a ship. 3 ruin or destruction: *the shipwreck of all my hopes.* ◆ VERB (*tr*) 4 to wreck or destroy (a ship). 5 to bring to ruin or destruction.
▷HISTORY Old English *scipwræc,* from SHIP + *wræc* something driven by the sea; see WRACK[2]

shipwright ('ʃɪpˌraɪt) NOUN an artisan skilled in one or more of the tasks required to build vessels.

shipyard ('ʃɪpˌjɑːd) NOUN a place or facility for the building, maintenance, and repair of ships.

shiralee (ˌʃɪrəˈliː) NOUN *Austral history, informal* a swag; swagman's bundle.
▷HISTORY C19: of unknown origin

Shiraz[1] (ʃɪəˈrɑːz) NOUN a city in SW Iran, at an altitude of 1585 m (5200 ft.): an important Muslim cultural centre in the 14th century; university (1948); noted for fine carpets. Pop.: 1 053 025 (1996).

Shiraz[2] (ʃɪəˈrɑːz) NOUN the name used in Australia for the Syrah grape and wines.
▷HISTORY from SHIRAZ[1], where the wine supposedly originated

shire[1] (ʃaɪə) NOUN 1 **a** one of the British counties. **b** (*in combination*): *Yorkshire.* 2 (in Australia) a rural district having its own local council. 3 See **shire horse.** 4 the Midland counties of England, esp Northamptonshire and Leicestershire, famous for hunting, etc.
▷HISTORY Old English *scīr* office; related to Old High German *scīra* business

shire[2] (ʃaɪə) VERB (*tr*) *Ulster dialect* to refresh or rest: *let me get my head shired.*
▷HISTORY from Old English *scīr* clear

Shiré ('ʃɪəreɪ) NOUN a river in E central Africa, flowing from Lake Malawi through Malawi and Mozambique to the Zambezi. Length: 596 km (370 miles).

Shiré Highlands PLURAL NOUN an upland area of S Malawi. Average height: 900 m (3000 ft.).

shire horse NOUN a large heavy breed of carthorse with long hair on the fetlocks. Often shortened to: **shire.**
▷HISTORY C19: so called because the breed was originally reared in *the Shires.* See SHIRE[1]

shirk[1] (ʃɜːk) VERB 1 to avoid discharging (work, a duty, etc.); evade. ◆ NOUN *also* **shirker.** 2 a person who shirks.
▷HISTORY C17: probably from German *Schurke* rogue; see SHARK[2]

shirk[2] (ʃɜːk) NOUN *Islam* **a** the fundamental sin of regarding anything as equal to Allah. **b** any belief that is considered to be in opposition to Allah and Islam.
▷HISTORY from Arabic: association

shirr (ʃɜː) VERB 1 to gather (fabric) into two or more parallel rows to decorate a dress, blouse, etc., often using elastic thread. 2 (*tr*) to bake (eggs) out of their shells. ◆ NOUN *also* **shirring.** 3 a series of gathered rows decorating a dress, blouse, etc.
▷HISTORY C19: of unknown origin

shirt (ʃɜːt) NOUN 1 a garment worn on the upper part of the body, esp by men, usually of light material and typically having a collar and sleeves and buttoning up the front. 2 short for **nightshirt** or **undershirt.** 3 **keep your shirt on.** *Informal* refrain from losing your temper (often used as an exhortation to another). 4 **put** *or* **lose one's shirt on.** *Informal* to bet or lose all one has on (a horse, etc.).
▷HISTORY Old English *scyrte;* related to Old English *sceort* SHORT, Old Norse *skyrta* skirt, Middle High German *schurz* apron

shirtdress ('ʃɜːtˌdrɛs) NOUN a dress that resembles a lengthened shirt, often worn with a belt.

shirting ('ʃɜːtɪŋ) NOUN fabric used in making men's shirts.

shirt-lifter NOUN *Derogatory slang* a homosexual.

shirtsleeve ('ʃɜːtˌsliːv) NOUN 1 the sleeve of a shirt. 2 **in one's shirtsleeves.** not wearing a jacket.

shirt-tail NOUN the part of a shirt that extends below the waist.

shirtwaister ('ʃɜːtˌweɪstə) *or US and Canadian* **shirtwaist** NOUN a woman's dress with a tailored bodice resembling a shirt.

shirty ('ʃɜːtɪ) ADJECTIVE **shirtier, shirtiest.** *Slang, chiefly Brit* bad-tempered or annoyed.
▷HISTORY C19: perhaps based on such phrases as *to get someone's shirt out* to annoy someone
▸ **'shirtily** ADVERB ▸ **'shirtiness** NOUN

shish kebab ('ʃiːʃ kəˈbæb) NOUN a dish consisting of small pieces of meat and vegetables threaded onto skewers and grilled.
▷HISTORY from Turkish *şiş kebab,* from *şiş* skewer; see KEBAB

shit (ʃɪt) *Taboo* ◆ VERB **shits, shitting; shitted, shit** *or* **shat.** 1 to defecate. 2 (usually foll by *on*) *Slang* to give the worst possible treatment (to). ◆ NOUN 3 faeces; excrement. 4 rubbish; nonsense. 5 an obnoxious or worthless person. 6 cannabis resin or heroin. 7 **in the shit.** in trouble. 8 **the shit hits the fan.** the real trouble begins. ◆ INTERJECTION 9 an exclamation expressing anger, disgust, etc. Also (esp dialect): **shite** (ʃaɪt).
▷HISTORY Old English *scite* (unattested) dung, *scītan* to defecate, of Germanic origin; related to Old English *scēadan* to separate, Old Norse *skīta* to defecate, Middle Dutch *schitte* excrement
▸ **'shitty** ADJECTIVE ▸ **'shittily** ADVERB ▸ **'shittiness** NOUN

shitake (ˌʃɪˈtɑːkeɪ) NOUN a variant of **shiitake.**

shithead ('ʃɪtˌhɛd) NOUN *Taboo slang* a fool; idiot: used as a term of abuse.

shit-stir VERB (*intr*) *Slang* to make trouble.
▸ **'shit-ˌstirrer** NOUN

shittah ('ʃɪtə) NOUN, *plural* **shittim** ('ʃɪtɪm) *or* **shittahs.** a tree mentioned in the Old Testament, thought to be either of two Asian acacias, *Acacia seyal* or *A. tortilis,* having close-grained yellow-brown wood.
▷HISTORY C17: from Hebrew *shittāh;* related to Egyptian *sout* acacia

Shittim ('ʃɪtɪm) NOUN *Old Testament* the site to the east of the Jordan and northeast of the Dead Sea where the Israelites encamped before crossing the Jordan (Numbers 25:1–9).

shittim wood ('ʃɪtɪm) NOUN *Old Testament* a kind of wood, probably acacia, from which the Ark of the Covenant and parts of the tabernacle were made.
▷HISTORY C14: from Hebrew *shittīm,* plural of SHITTAH

shiur ('ʃiʊr, ʃiˈʊːr) NOUN, *plural* **shiurim** (ʃiʊˈrim, ʃiˈʊːrim). a lesson, esp one in which a passage of the Talmud is studied together by a group of people.
▷HISTORY from Hebrew, literally: measurement

shiv (ʃɪv) NOUN a variant spelling of **chiv.**

Shiva ('ʃiːvə, 'ʃɪvə) NOUN a variant spelling of **Siva.**
▸ **'Shivaism** NOUN ▸ **'Shivaist** NOUN, ADJECTIVE

shivah ('ʃivɑ, 'ʃivə) NOUN *Judaism* 1 the period of formal mourning lasting seven days from the funeral during which the mourner stays indoors and sits on a low stool. 2 **sit shivah.** to mourn.
▷HISTORY from Hebrew, literally: seven (days)

shivaree (ˌʃɪvəˈriː) NOUN a variant (esp US and Canadian) of **charivari.**

shive (ʃaɪv) NOUN 1 a flat cork or bung for wide-mouthed bottles. 2 an archaic word for **slice.**
▷HISTORY C13: from Middle Dutch or Middle Low German *schīve;* see SHEAVE[1]

shiver[1] ('ʃɪvə) VERB (*intr*) 1 to shake or tremble, as from cold or fear. 2 **a** (of a sail) to luff; flap or shake. **b** (of a sailing vessel) to sail close enough to the wind to make the sails luff. ◆ NOUN 3 the act of shivering; a tremulous motion. 4 **the shivers.** an attack of shivering, esp through fear or illness.
▷HISTORY C13 *chiveren,* perhaps variant of *chevelen* to chatter (used of teeth), from Old English *ceafl* JOWL[1]
▸ **'shiverer** NOUN ▸ **'shivering** ADJECTIVE

shiver[2] ('ʃɪvə) VERB 1 to break or cause to break into fragments. ◆ NOUN 2 a splintered piece.
▷HISTORY C13: of Germanic origin; compare Old High German *scivaro,* Middle Dutch *scheveren* to shiver, Old Norse *skīfa* to split

shivery ('ʃɪvərɪ) ADJECTIVE 1 inclined to shiver or tremble. 2 causing shivering, esp through cold or fear.

Shizuoka (ˌʃiːzuːˈəʊkə) NOUN a city in central Japan, on S Honshu: a centre for green tea; university (1949). Pop.: 474 089 (1995).

Shkodër (*Albanian* 'ʃkodər) NOUN a market town in NW Albania, on **Lake Shkodër**: an Illyrian capital in the first millennium B.C. Pop.: 83 700 (1991 est.). Italian name: **Scutari.**

shloshim ('ʃləʃim, 'ʃləʊʃim) NOUN *Judaism* the period of thirty days' deep mourning following a death.
▷HISTORY from Hebrew, literally: thirty (days)

Shluh (ʃəˈluː, ʃluː) NOUN 1 (*plural* **Shluhs** *or* **Shluh**) a member of a Berber people inhabiting the Atlas Mountains in Morocco and Algeria. 2 the dialect of Berber spoken by this people.

SHM ABBREVIATION FOR **simple harmonic motion.**

shmatte *Yiddish* ('ʃmɑtə) NOUN 1 a rag. 2 anything shabby. 3 (*modifier*) clothes: a jocular use: *the shmatte trade.*

shmo (ʃməʊ) NOUN, *plural* **shmoes.** a variant form of **schmo.**

Shoah ('ʃɔɑː) NOUN (in secular Judaism) a Hebrew word for **holocaust** (sense 2). See also **Churban** (sense 2).
▷HISTORY literally: destruction

shoal[1] (ʃəʊl) NOUN 1 a stretch of shallow water. 2 a sandbank or rocky area in a stretch of water, esp one that is visible at low water. ◆ VERB 3 to make or become shallow. 4 (*intr*) *Nautical* to sail into shallower water. ◆ ADJECTIVE *also* **shoaly.** 5 a less common word for **shallow.** 6 *Nautical* (of the draught of a vessel) drawing little water.
▷HISTORY Old English *sceald* SHALLOW
▸ **'shoaliness** NOUN

shoal[2] (ʃəʊl) NOUN 1 a large group of certain aquatic animals, esp fish. 2 a large group of people or things. ◆ VERB 3 (*intr*) to collect together in such a group.
▷HISTORY Old English *scolu;* related to Middle Low German, Middle Dutch *schōle* SCHOOL[2]

shoat *or* **shote** (ʃəʊt) NOUN a piglet that has recently been weaned.
▷HISTORY C15: related to West Flemish *schote*

shochet ('ʃɒkɛt, 'ʃɒxɛt) NOUN, *plural* **shochets, shochetim.** (in Judaism) a person who has been specially trained and licensed to slaughter animals and birds in accordance with the laws of shechita.
▷HISTORY C19: from Hebrew, literally: slaughtering

shock[1] (ʃɒk) VERB 1 to experience or cause to experience extreme horror, disgust, surprise, etc.: *the atrocities shocked us; she shocks easily.* 2 to cause a state of shock in (a person). 3 to come or cause to come into violent contact; jar. ◆ NOUN 4 a sudden and violent jarring blow or impact. 5 something that causes a sudden and violent disturbance in the emotions: *the shock of her father's death made her ill.* 6 *Pathol* a state of bodily collapse or near collapse caused by circulatory failure or sudden lowering of

the blood pressure, as from severe bleeding, burns, fright, etc.
▷HISTORY C16: from Old French *choc,* from *choquier* to make violent contact with, of Germanic origin; related to Middle High German *schoc*
▸'**shockable** ADJECTIVE ▸ˌ**shocka'bility** NOUN

shock[2] (ʃɒk) NOUN 1 a number of sheaves set on end in a field to dry. 2 a pile or stack of unthreshed corn. ◆ VERB 3 (*tr*) to set up (sheaves) in shocks.
▷HISTORY C14: probably of Germanic origin; compare Middle Low German, Middle Dutch *schok* shock of corn, group of sixty

shock[3] (ʃɒk) NOUN 1 a thick bushy mass, esp of hair. ◆ ADJECTIVE 2 *Rare* bushy; shaggy.
▷HISTORY C19: perhaps from SHOCK[2]

shock absorber NOUN any device designed to absorb mechanical shock, esp one fitted to a motor vehicle to damp the recoil of the suspension springs.

shocker ('ʃɒkə) NOUN *Informal* 1 a person or thing that shocks or horrifies. 2 a sensational novel, film, or play.

shockheaded ('ʃɒkˌhɛdɪd) ADJECTIVE having a head of bushy or tousled hair.

shock-horror ADJECTIVE *Facetious* (esp of newspaper headlines) sensationalistic: *shock-horror stories about the British diet.*
▷HISTORY C20: SHOCK[1] + HORROR

shocking ('ʃɒkɪŋ) ADJECTIVE 1 causing shock, horror, or disgust. 2 **shocking pink.** a vivid or garish shade of pink. 3 *Informal* very bad or terrible: *shocking weather.*
▸'**shockingly** ADVERB ▸'**shockingness** NOUN

shock jock NOUN *Informal* a radio disc jockey who is deliberately controversial or provocative.

shockproof ('ʃɒkˌpruːf) ADJECTIVE capable of absorbing shock without damage: *a shockproof watch.*

shockstall ('ʃɒkˌstɔːl) NOUN the loss of lift and increase of drag experienced by transonic aircraft when strong shock waves on the wings cause the airflow to separate from the wing surfaces.

shock therapy *or* **treatment** NOUN the treatment of certain psychotic conditions by injecting drugs or by passing an electric current through the brain (**electroconvulsive therapy**) to produce convulsions or coma.

shock troops PLURAL NOUN soldiers specially trained and equipped to carry out an assault.

shock tube NOUN an apparatus in which a gas is heated to very high temperatures by means of a shock wave, usually for spectroscopic investigation of the natures and reactions of the resulting radicals and excited molecules.

shock wave NOUN 1 a region across which there is a rapid pressure, temperature, and density rise, usually caused by a body moving supersonically in a gas or by a detonation. Often shortened to: **shock.** See also **sonic boom, shock tube.** 2 a feeling of shock, horror, surprise, etc. that affects many people as it spreads through a community. 3 the effect created on a queue of moving cars in the lane of a motorway when one car brakes suddenly and the cars behind have to brake as well, causing cars to slow down, sometimes for miles behind the first braking car.

shod (ʃɒd) VERB the past participle of **shoe.**

shoddy ('ʃɒdɪ) ADJECTIVE **-dier, -diest.** 1 imitating something of better quality. 2 of poor quality; trashy. 3 made of shoddy material. ◆ NOUN, *plural* **-dies.** 4 a yarn or fabric made from wool waste or clippings. 5 anything of inferior quality that is designed to simulate superior quality.
▷HISTORY C19: of unknown origin
▸'**shoddily** ADVERB ▸'**shoddiness** NOUN

shoe (ʃuː) NOUN 1 **a** one of a matching pair of coverings shaped to fit the foot, esp one ending below the ankle, having an upper of leather, plastic, etc., on a sole and heel of heavier leather, rubber, or synthetic material. **b** (*as modifier*): *shoe cleaner.* 2 anything resembling a shoe in shape, function, position, etc., such as a horseshoe. 3 a band of metal or wood on the bottom of the runner of a sledge. 4 (in baccarat, etc.) a boxlike device for holding several packs of cards and allowing the cards to be dispensed singly. 5 a base for the supports of a superstructure of a bridge, roof, etc. 6 a metal collector attached to an electric train that slides along the third rail and picks up power for the motor. 7 *Engineering* a lining to protect from and withstand wear: see **brake shoe, pile shoe.** 8 **be in (a person's) shoes.** *Informal* to be in (another person's) situation. ◆ VERB **shoes, shoeing, shod.** (*tr*) 9 to furnish with shoes. 10 to fit (a horse) with horseshoes. 11 to furnish with a hard cover, such as a metal plate, for protection against friction or bruising.
▷HISTORY Old English *scōh;* related to Old Norse *skōr,* Gothic *skōhs,* Old High German *scuoh*

shoebill ('ʃuːˌbɪl) NOUN a large wading bird, *Balaeniceps rex,* of tropical E African swamps, having a dark plumage, a large head, and a large broad bill: family *Balaenicipitidae,* order *Ciconiiformes.*
▷HISTORY C19: so named because of the shape of its bill

shoeblack ('ʃuːˌblæk) NOUN (esp formerly) a person who shines boots and shoes.

shoehorn ('ʃuːˌhɔːn) NOUN 1 a smooth curved implement of horn, metal, plastic, etc., inserted at the heel of a shoe to ease the foot into it. ◆ VERB 2 (*tr*) to cram (people or things) into a very small space.

shoelace ('ʃuːˌleɪs) NOUN a cord or lace for fastening shoes.

shoe leather NOUN 1 leather used to make shoes. 2 **save shoe leather.** to avoid wearing out shoes, as by taking a bus rather than walking.

shoemaker ('ʃuːˌmeɪkə) NOUN a person who makes or repairs shoes or boots.
▸'**shoeˌmaking** NOUN

Shoemaker-Levy 9 ('ʃuːˌmeɪkə liːvaɪ) NOUN a comet that was captured into an orbit around Jupiter and later broke up, the fragments colliding with Jupiter in July 1995.
▷HISTORY C20: after *Carolyn Shoemaker* (born 1929), and *Eugene Shoemaker* (1928–97), and *David Levy* (born 1948), US astronomers, who discovered the orbiting fragments

shoer ('ʃuːə) NOUN *Rare* a person who shoes horses; farrier.

shoeshine ('ʃuːˌʃaɪn) NOUN 1 the act or an instance of polishing a pair of shoes. 2 the appearance or shiny surface of polished shoes.

shoestring ('ʃuːˌstrɪŋ) NOUN 1 another word for **shoelace.** 2 *Informal* **a** a very small or petty amount of money (esp in the phrase **on a shoestring**). **b** (*as modifier*): *a shoestring budget.*

shoetree ('ʃuːˌtriː) NOUN a wooden or metal form inserted into a shoe or boot to stretch it or preserve its shape.

shofar *or* **shophar** ('ʃəʊfɑː; *Hebrew* ʃɔ'far) NOUN, *plural* **-fars, -phars** *or* **-froth, -phroth** (*Hebrew* -'frɔt). *Judaism* a ram's horn sounded in the synagogue daily during the month of Elul and repeatedly on Rosh Hashanah, and by the ancient Israelites as a warning, summons, etc.
▷HISTORY from Hebrew *shōphār* ram's horn

shogun ('ʃəʊˌguːn) NOUN *Japanese history* 1 (from 794 A.D.) a chief military commander. 2 (from about 1192 to 1867) any of a line of hereditary military dictators who relegated the emperors to a position of purely theoretical supremacy.
▷HISTORY C17: from Japanese, from Chinese *chiang chün* general, from *chiang* to lead + *chün* army
▸'**shoˌgunal** ADJECTIVE

shogunate ('ʃəʊgʊnɪt, -ˌneɪt) NOUN *Japanese history* the office or rule of a shogun.

shogun bond NOUN a bond sold on the Japanese market by a foreign institution and denominated in a foreign currency. Compare **samurai bond.**

shoji ('ʃəʊʒiː, -dʒiː) NOUN, *plural* **-ji** *or* **-jis.** 1 a rice-paper screen in a sliding wooden frame, used in Japanese houses as a partition. 2 any similar screen.
▷HISTORY C19: from Japanese, from *shō* to separate + *ji* a piece

Sholapur ('ʃəʊləˌpʊə) NOUN a city in SW India, in S Maharashtra: major textile centre. Pop.: 604 215 (1991).

Shona ('ʃɒnə) NOUN 1 (*plural* **-na** *or* **-nas**) a member of a Sotho people of S central Africa, living chiefly in Zimbabwe and Mozambique. 2 the language of this people, belonging to the Bantu group of the Niger-Congo family.

shone (ʃɒn; *US* ʃəʊn) VERB the past tense and past participle of **shine.**

shoneen ('ʃoːniːn) NOUN *Irish* an Irishman who imitates English ways.
▷HISTORY C19: from Irish Gaelic *Seoinín,* diminutive of *Seon* John (taken as typical English name)

shonky ('ʃɒŋkɪ) ADJECTIVE **-kier.** *Austral and NZ informal* 1 of dubious integrity or legality. 2 unreliable; unsound.
▷HISTORY C19: perhaps from Yiddish *shonniker* or from SH(ODDY) + (W)ONKY

shoo (ʃuː) INTERJECTION 1 go away!: used to drive away unwanted or annoying people, animals, etc. ◆ VERB **shoos, shooing, shooed.** 2 (*tr*) to drive away by or as if by crying "shoo". 3 (*intr*) to cry "shoo".
▷HISTORY C15: imitative; related to Middle High German *schū,* French *shou,* Italian *scio*

shoofly pie ('ʃuːˌflaɪ) NOUN *US* a dessert similar to treacle tart.

shoogle ('ʃʊgᵊl) *Dialect, chiefly Scot* ◆ VERB 1 to shake, sway, or rock back and forth. ◆ NOUN 2 a rocking motion; shake.
▷HISTORY from dialectal *shog, shug;* apparently related to German *schaukeln* to shake
▸'**shoogly** ADJECTIVE

shoo-in NOUN 1 a person or thing that is certain to win or succeed. 2 a match or contest that is easy to win.

shook[1] (ʃʊk) NOUN 1 (in timber working) a set of parts ready for assembly, esp of a barrel. 2 a group of sheaves piled together on end; shock.
▷HISTORY C18: of unknown origin

shook[2] (ʃʊk) VERB 1 the past tense of **shake.** ◆ ADJECTIVE 2 *Austral and NZ informal* keen on; enthusiastic about.

shool (ʃuːl) NOUN a dialect word for **shovel.**

shoon (ʃuːn) NOUN *Dialect, chiefly Scot* a plural of **shoe.**

shoot (ʃuːt) VERB **shoots, shooting, shot.** 1 (*tr*) to hit, wound, damage, or kill with a missile discharged from a weapon. 2 to discharge (a missile or missiles) from a weapon. 3 to fire (a weapon) or (of a weapon) to be fired. 4 to send out or be sent out as if from a weapon: *he shot questions at her.* 5 (*intr*) to move very rapidly; dart. 6 (*tr*) to slide or push into or out of a fastening: *to shoot a bolt.* 7 to emit (a ray of light) or (of a ray of light) to be emitted. 8 (*tr*) to go or pass quickly over or through: *to shoot rapids.* 9 (*intr*) to hunt game with a gun for sport. 10 (*tr*) to pass over (an area) in hunting game. 11 to extend or cause to extend; project. 12 (*tr*) to discharge down or as if down a chute. 13 (*intr*) (of a plant) to produce (buds, branches, etc.). 14 (*intr*) (of a seed) to germinate. 15 to photograph or record (a sequence, subject, etc.). 16 (*tr; usually passive*) to variegate or streak, as with colour. 17 *Sport* to hit or propel (the ball, etc.) towards the goal. 18 (*tr*) *Sport chiefly US and Canadian* to score (points, strokes, etc.): *he shot 72 on the first round.* 19 (*tr*) to plane (a board) to produce a straight edge. 20 (*tr*) *Mining* to detonate. 21 (*tr*) to measure the altitude of (a celestial body). 22 (often foll by *up*) *Slang* to inject (someone, esp oneself) with (a drug, esp heroin). 23 **shoot a line.** See **line**[1] (sense 58). 24 **shoot from the hip.** to speak bluntly or impulsively without concern for the consequences. 25 **shoot one's bolt.** See **bolt**[1] (sense 13). 26 **shoot oneself in the foot.** *Informal* to damage one's own cause inadvertently. 27 **shoot one's mouth off.** *Slang* **a** to talk indiscreetly. **b** to boast or exaggerate. 28 **shoot the breeze.** See **breeze**[1] (sense 5). ◆ NOUN 29 the act of shooting. 30 the action or motion of something that is shot. 31 the first aerial part of a plant to develop from a germinating seed. 32 any new growth of a plant, such as a bud, young branch, etc. 33 *Chiefly Brit* a meeting or party organized for hunting game with guns. 34 an area or series of coverts and woods where game can be hunted with guns. 35 a steep descent in a stream; rapid. 36 *Informal* a photographic assignment. 37 *Geology, mining* a narrow workable vein of ore. 38 *Obsolete* the reach of a shot. 39 **the whole shoot.** *Slang* everything. ◆ INTERJECTION 40 *US and Canadian* an exclamation expressing disbelief, scepticism, disgust, disappointment, etc. ◆ See also **shoot down, shoot out, shoot through, shoot up.**

▷HISTORY Old English *sceōtan;* related to Old Norse *skjōta,* Old High German *skiozan* to shoot, Old Slavonic *iskydati* to throw out

shoot down VERB *(tr, adverb)* [1] to shoot callously. [2] to cause to fall to earth by hitting with a missile. [3] to defeat or disprove: *he shot down her argument.*

shoot-'em-up *or* **shoot-em-up** NOUN *Informal* [1] a type of computer game, the object of which is to shoot as many enemies, targets, etc., as possible. [2] a fast-moving film involving many gunfights, battles, etc.

shooter ('ʃuːtə) NOUN [1] a person or thing that shoots. [2] *Slang* a gun. [3] *Cricket* a ball that unexpectedly travels low on pitching.

shooting box NOUN a small country house providing accommodation for a shooting party during the shooting season. Also called: **shooting lodge.**

shooting brake NOUN *Brit* a former name for **estate car.**

shooting gallery NOUN [1] an area, often enclosed, designed for target practice, shooting, etc. [2] *Slang* a house where heroin addicts inject themselves.

shooting guard NOUN *Basketball* the player responsible for attempting long-range shots.

shooting iron NOUN *US slang* a firearm, esp a pistol.

shooting script NOUN *Films* written instructions indicating to the cameraman the order of shooting.

shooting star NOUN an informal name for **meteor.**

shooting stick NOUN a device that resembles a walking stick, having a spike at one end and a folding seat at the other.

shoot out VERB *(tr, adverb)* [1] to fight to the finish by shooting (esp in the phrase **shoot it out**). ◆ NOUN **shoot-out.** [2] a conclusive gunfight.

shoot through VERB *(intr, adverb) Informal, chiefly Austral* to leave; depart.

shoot up VERB *(adverb)* [1] *(intr)* to grow or become taller very fast. [2] *(tr)* to hit with a number of shots. [3] *(tr)* to spread terror throughout (a place) by lawless and wanton shooting. [4] *(tr) Slang* to inject (someone, esp oneself) with (a drug, esp heroin).

shop (ʃɒp) NOUN [1] a place, esp a small building, for the retail sale of goods and services. [2] an act or instance of shopping, esp household shopping: *the weekly shop.* [3] a place for the performance of a specified type of work; workshop. [4] **all over the shop.** *Informal* **a** in disarray: *his papers were all over the shop.* **b** in every direction: *I've searched for it all over the shop.* [5] **shut up shop.** to close business at the end of the day or permanently. [6] **talk shop.** to speak about one's work, esp when meeting socially, sometimes with the effect of excluding those not similarly employed. ◆ VERB **shops, shopping, shopped.** [7] *(intr; often foll by for)* to visit a shop or shops in search of (goods) with the intention of buying them. [8] *(tr) Slang, chiefly Brit* to inform on or betray, esp to the police.
▷HISTORY Old English *sceoppa* stall, booth; related to Old High German *scopf* shed, Middle Dutch *schoppe* stall

shopaholic (ˌʃɒpəˈhɒlɪk) NOUN *Informal* a compulsive shopper.
▷HISTORY C20: from SHOP + -HOLIC
▸ ˌ**shopa'holism** NOUN

shop around VERB *(intr, adverb) Informal* [1] to visit a number of shops or stores to compare goods and prices. [2] to consider a number of possibilities before making a choice.

shop assistant NOUN a person who serves in a shop.

shop floor NOUN [1] the part of a factory housing the machines and men directly involved in production. [2] **a** workers, esp factory workers organized in a union. **b** *(as modifier): shop-floor protest.*

shophar ('ʃəʊfɑː; *Hebrew* ʃɔ'far) NOUN, *plural* **-phars** *or* **-phroth** (*Hebrew* -'frɔt). a variant spelling of **shofar.**

shopkeeper ('ʃɒpˌkiːpə) NOUN a person who owns or manages a shop or small store.
▸ **'shop**ˌ**keeping** NOUN

shopli[...] goods from a shop [...] a person who steals

shoplifting ('ʃɒpˌlɪftɪŋ) NOUN the act of stealing goods from a shop during shopping hours.

shopper ('ʃɒpə) NOUN a person who buys goods in a shop.

shopping ('ʃɒpɪŋ) NOUN [1] a number or collection of articles purchased. [2] the act or an instance of making purchases.

shopping bag lady NOUN another name for **bag lady.**

shopping centre NOUN [1] a purpose-built complex of shops, restaurants, etc., for the use of pedestrians. [2] the area of a town where most of the shops are situated.

shopping mall NOUN a large enclosed shopping centre.

shopping precinct NOUN a pedestrian area containing shops, restaurants, etc., forming a single architectural unit and usually providing car-parking facilities.

shopsoiled ('ʃɒpˌsɔɪld) ADJECTIVE [1] worn, faded, tarnished, etc., from being displayed in a shop or store. US word: **shopworn.** [2] no longer new or fresh.

shop steward NOUN a coworker elected by trade union members to represent them in discussions and negotiations with the management.

shoptalk ('ʃɒpˌtɔːk) NOUN conversation concerning one's work, esp when carried on outside business hours.

shopwalker ('ʃɒpˌwɔːkə) NOUN *Brit* a person employed by a departmental store to supervise sales personnel, assist customers, etc. US equivalent: **floorwalker.**

shopworn ('ʃɒpˌwɔːn) ADJECTIVE the US word for **shopsoiled.**

shoran ('ʃɔːræn) NOUN a short-range radar system by which an aircraft, ship, etc., can accurately determine its position by the time taken for a signal to be sent to two radar beacons at known locations and be returned.
▷HISTORY C20: *sho(rt) ra(nge) n(avigation)*

shore[1] (ʃɔː) NOUN [1] the land along the edge of a sea, lake, or wide river. Related adjective: **littoral.** [2] **a** land, as opposed to water (esp in the phrase **on shore**). **b** *(as modifier): shore duty.* [3] *Law* the tract of coastland lying between the ordinary marks of high and low water. [4] *(often plural)* a country: *his native shores.* ◆ VERB [5] *(tr)* to move or drag (a boat) onto a shore.
▷HISTORY C14: probably from Middle Low German, Middle Dutch *schōre;* compare Old High German *scorra* cliff; see SHEAR

shore[2] (ʃɔː) NOUN [1] a prop, post, or beam used to support a wall, building, ship in dry dock, etc. ◆ VERB [2] *(tr; often foll by up)* to prop or make safe with or as if with a shore.
▷HISTORY C15: from Middle Dutch *schōre;* related to Old Norse *skortha* prop
▸ **'shoring** NOUN

shore[3] (ʃɔː) VERB *Austral and NZ* a past tense of **shear.**

shore bird NOUN any of various birds that live close to water, esp any bird of the families *Charadriidae* or *Scolopacidae* (plovers, sandpipers, etc.). Also called (Brit): **wader.**

shore leave NOUN *Naval* [1] permission to go ashore. Compare **liberty** (sense 5). [2] time spent ashore during leave.

shoreless ('ʃɔːlɪs) ADJECTIVE [1] without a shore suitable for landing. [2] *Poetic* boundless; vast: *the shoreless wastes.*

shoreline ('ʃɔːˌlaɪn) NOUN the edge of a body of water.

shore patrol NOUN *US* a naval unit serving the same function as the military police.

shoreward ('ʃɔːwəd) ADJECTIVE [1] near or facing the shore. ◆ ADVERB *also* **shorewards.** [2] towards the shore.

shoreweed ('ʃɔːˌwiːd) NOUN a tufty aquatic perennial, *Littorella uniflora,* of the plantain family, that forms underwater mats but usually flowers only on muddy margins.

shorn (ʃɔːn) VERB a past participle of **shear.**

short (ʃɔːt) ADJECTIVE [1] of little length; not long. [2] of little height; not tall. [3] of limited duration. [4] not meeting a requirement; deficient: *the number of places laid at the table was short by four.* [5] *(postpositive;* often foll by *of* or *on)* lacking (in) or needful (of): *I'm always short of money.* [6] concise; succinct. [7] lacking in the power of retentiveness: *a short memory.* [8] abrupt to the point of rudeness: *the salesgirl was very short with him.* [9] *Finance* **a** not possessing the securities or commodities that have been sold under contract and therefore obliged to make a purchase before the delivery date. **b** of or relating to such sales, which depend on falling prices for profit. [10] *Phonetics* **a** denoting a vowel of relatively brief temporal duration. **b** classified as short, as distinguished from other vowels. Thus in English (ɪ) in *bin,* though of longer duration than (iː) in *beat,* is nevertheless regarded as a short vowel. **c** (in popular usage) denoting the qualities of the five English vowels represented orthographically in the words *pat, pet, pit, pot, put,* and *putt.* [11] *Prosody* **a** denoting a vowel that is phonetically short or a syllable containing such a vowel. In classical verse short vowels are followed by one consonant only or sometimes one consonant plus a following *l* or *r.* **b** (of a vowel or syllable in verse that is not quantitative) not carrying emphasis or accent; unstressed. [12] (of pastry) crumbly in texture. See also **shortcrust pastry.** [13] (of a drink of spirits) undiluted; neat. [14] **have (someone) by the short and curlies.** *Informal* to have (someone) completely in one's power. [15] **in short supply.** scarce. [16] **short and sweet.** unexpectedly brief. [17] **short for.** an abbreviation for. ◆ ADVERB [18] abruptly: *to stop short.* [19] briefly or concisely. [20] rudely or curtly. [21] *Finance* without possessing the securities or commodities at the time of their contractual sale: *to sell short.* [22] **caught** *or* **taken short.** having a sudden need to urinate or defecate. [23] **fall short. a** to prove inadequate. **b** (often foll by *of)* to fail to reach or measure up to (a standard). [24] **go short.** not to have a sufficient amount, etc. [25] **short of.** except: *nothing short of a miracle can save him now.* ◆ NOUN [26] anything that is short. [27] a drink of spirits as opposed to a long drink such as beer. [28] *Phonetics, prosody* a short vowel or syllable. [29] *Finance* **a** a short contract or sale. **b** a short seller. [30] a short film, usually of a factual nature. [31] See **short circuit** (sense 1). [32] **for short.** *Informal* as an abbreviation: *he is called Jim for short.* [33] **in short. a** as a summary. **b** in a few words. ◆ VERB [34] See **short circuit** (sense 2). ◆ See also **shorts.**
▷HISTORY Old English *scort;* related to Old Norse *skortr* a lack, *skera* to cut, Old High German *scurz* short
▸ **'shortness** NOUN

short account NOUN [1] the aggregate of short sales on an open market, esp a stock market. [2] the account of a stock-market speculator who sells short.

short-acting ADJECTIVE (of a drug) quickly effective, but requiring regularly repeated doses for long-term treatment, being rapidly absorbed, distributed in the body, and excreted. Compare **intermediate-acting, long-acting.**

shortage ('ʃɔːtɪdʒ) NOUN a deficiency or lack in the amount needed, expected, or due; deficit.

short bill NOUN a bill of exchange that is payable at sight, on demand, or within less than ten days.

shortbread ('ʃɔːtˌbrɛd) NOUN a rich crumbly biscuit made from dough with a large proportion of butter.
▷HISTORY C19: from SHORT (in the sense: crumbly)

shortcake ('ʃɔːtˌkeɪk) NOUN [1] a kind of shortbread made from a rich biscuit dough. [2] a dessert made of layers of shortcake filled with fruit and cream.
▷HISTORY C16: from SHORT (in the sense: crumbly)

short-change VERB *(tr)* [1] to give less than correct change to. [2] *Slang* to treat unfairly or dishonestly, esp by giving less than is deserved or expected.
▸ ˌ**short-'changer** NOUN

short circuit NOUN [1] a faulty or accidental connection between two points of different potential in an electric circuit, bypassing the load and establishing a path of low resistance through which an excessive current can flow. It can cause damage to the components if the circuit is not protected by a fuse. ◆ VERB **short-circuit.** [2] to develop or cause to develop a short circuit. [3] *(tr)* to bypass (a procedure, regulation, etc.). [4] *(tr)* to hinder or frustrate (plans, etc.). ◆ Sometimes (for senses 1, 2) shortened to: **short**.

short column NOUN a column whose relative dimensions ensure that when it is overloaded it fails by crushing, rather than buckling.

shortcoming (ˈʃɔːtˌkʌmɪŋ) NOUN a failing, defect, or deficiency.

short corner NOUN *Hockey* another name for **penalty corner**.

short covering NOUN [1] the purchase of securities or commodities by a short seller to meet delivery requirements. [2] the securities or commodities purchased.

shortcrust pastry (ˈʃɔːtˌkrʌst) NOUN a basic type of pastry that is made with half the quantity of fat to flour, and has a crisp but crumbly texture. Also called: **short pastry**.

short cut NOUN [1] a route that is shorter than the usual one. [2] a means of saving time or effort. ◆ VERB **short-cut, -cuts, -cutting, -cut**. [3] (*intr*) to use a short cut.
▷HISTORY C16: from CUT (in the sense: a direct route)

short-dated ADJECTIVE (of a gilt-edged security) having less than five years to run before redemption. Compare **medium-dated, long-dated**.

short-day ADJECTIVE (of plants) able to flower only if exposed to short periods of daylight (less than 12 hours), each followed by a long dark period. Compare **long-day**.

short division NOUN the division of numbers, usually integers, that can be worked out mentally rather than on paper.

shorten (ˈʃɔːtᵊn) VERB [1] to make or become short or shorter. [2] (*tr*) *Nautical* to reduce the area of (sail). [3] (*tr*) to make (pastry, bread, etc.) short, by adding butter or another fat. [4] *Gambling* to cause (the odds) to lessen or (of odds) to become less.
▸ **ˈshortener** NOUN

shortening (ˈʃɔːtᵊnɪŋ) NOUN butter, lard, or other fat, used in a dough, cake mixture, etc., to make the mixture short.

Shorter Catechism NOUN *Chiefly Presbyterian Church* the more widely used and influential of two catechisms of religious instruction drawn up in 1647.

shortfall (ˈʃɔːtˌfɔːl) NOUN [1] failure to meet a goal or a requirement. [2] the amount of such a failure; deficiency.

short fuse NOUN *Informal* a quick temper.

shorthand (ˈʃɔːtˌhænd) NOUN **a** a system of rapid handwriting employing simple strokes and other symbols to represent words or phrases. **b** (*as modifier*): *a shorthand typist*.

short-handed ADJECTIVE [1] lacking the usual or necessary number of assistants, workers, etc. [2] *Sport US and Canadian* with less than the full complement of players.
▸ **ˌshort-ˈhandedness** NOUN

shorthand typist NOUN *Brit* a person skilled in the use of shorthand and in typing. US and Canadian name: **stenographer**.

short head NOUN *Horse racing* a distance shorter than the length of a horse's head.

shorthold tenancy (ˈʃɔːtˌhəʊld) NOUN (in Britain) the letting of a dwelling by a nonresident private landlord for a fixed term of between one and five years at a fair rent.

shorthorn (ˈʃɔːtˌhɔːn) NOUN a short-horned breed of cattle with several regional varieties. Also called: **Durham**.

short hundredweight NOUN the full name for **hundredweight** (sense 2).

shortie *or* **shorty** (ˈʃɔːtɪ) NOUN [1] *Informal* **a** *plural* **shorties** a person or thing that is extremely short. **b** (*as modifier*): *a shortie nightdress*. [2] a Scot name for **shortbread**.

short jenny NOUN *Billiards* an in-off into a middle pocket. Compare **long jenny**.
▷HISTORY from *Jenny*, pet form of *Janet*

short leg NOUN *Cricket* **a** a fielding position on the leg side near the batsman's wicket. **b** a fielder in this position.

short list *Chiefly Brit* ◆ NOUN [1] a list of suitable applicants for a job, post, etc., from which the successful candidate will be selected. ◆ VERB (*tr*) **short-list**. [2] to put (someone) on a short list.

short-lived ADJECTIVE living or lasting only for a short time.

shortly (ˈʃɔːtlɪ) ADVERB [1] in a short time; soon. [2] in a few words; briefly. [3] in a curt or rude manner.

short metre NOUN a stanza form, used esp for hymns, consisting of four lines, the third of which has eight syllables, while the rest have six.

Short money NOUN (in Britain) the annual payment made to Opposition parties in the House of Commons to help them pay for certain services necessary to the carrying out of their parliamentary duties; established in 1975. Compare **Cranborne money**.
▷HISTORY named after the Rt Hon. Edward Short MP, Leader of the House of Commons in 1975

short odds PLURAL NOUN (in betting) an almost even chance.

short order NOUN *Chiefly US and Canadian* **a** food that is easily and quickly prepared. **b** (*as modifier*): *short-order counter*.

short-range ADJECTIVE of small or limited extent in time or distance: *a short-range forecast; a short-range gun*.

shorts (ʃɔːts) PLURAL NOUN [1] trousers reaching the top of the thigh or partway to the knee, worn by both sexes for sport, relaxing in summer, etc. [2] *Chiefly US and Canadian* men's underpants that usually reach mid-thigh. Usual Brit word: **pants**. [3] short-dated gilt-edged securities. [4] short-term bonds. [5] securities or commodities that have been sold short. [6] timber cut shorter than standard lengths. [7] a livestock feed containing a large proportion of bran and wheat germ. [8] items needed to make up a deficiency.

short selling NOUN *Finance* the practice of selling commodities, securities, currencies, etc. that one does not have in the expectation that falling prices will enable one to buy them in at a profit before they have to be delivered.

short shrift NOUN [1] brief and unsympathetic treatment. [2] (formerly) a brief period allowed to a condemned prisoner to make confession. [3] **make short shrift of**. to dispose of quickly and unsympathetically.

short-sighted ADJECTIVE [1] relating to or suffering from myopia. [2] lacking foresight: *a short-sighted plan*.
▸ **ˌshort-ˈsightedly** ADVERB ▸ **ˌshort-ˈsightedness** NOUN

short-spoken ADJECTIVE tending to be abrupt in speech.

short-staffed ADJECTIVE lacking an adequate number of staff, assistants, etc.

shortstop (ˈʃɔːtˌstɒp) NOUN *Baseball* **a** the fielding position to the left of second base viewed from home plate. **b** the player at this position.

short story NOUN a prose narrative of shorter length than the novel, esp one that concentrates on a single theme.

short straw NOUN **draw the short straw**. be the person (as in drawing lots) to whom an unwelcome task or fate falls.

short subject NOUN *Chiefly US* a short film, esp one presented between screenings of a feature film.

short-tailed shearwater NOUN *Austral* a large Australian shearwater that migrates to the northern hemisphere in the southern winter.

short-tempered ADJECTIVE easily moved to anger; irascible.

short-term ADJECTIVE [1] of, for, or extending over a limited period. [2] *Finance* extending over, maturing within, or required within a short period of time, usually twelve months: *short-term credit; short-term capital*.

short-termism NOUN the tendency to focus attention on short-term gains, often at the expense of long-term success or stability.

short-term memory NOUN *Psychol* that section of the memory storage system of limited capacity (approximately seven items) that is capable of storing material for a brief period of time. Compare **long-term memory**.

short time *or* **short-time working** NOUN a system of working, usually for a temporary period, when employees are required to work and be paid for fewer than their normal hours per week due to a shortage of work.

short ton NOUN the full name for **ton[1]** (sense 2).

short-waisted ADJECTIVE unusually short from the shoulders to the waist.

short wave NOUN **a** a radio wave with a wavelength in the range 10–100 metres. **b** (*as modifier*): *a short-wave broadcast*.

short-winded ADJECTIVE [1] tending to run out of breath, esp after exertion. [2] (of speech or writing) terse or abrupt.

Shoshone *or* **Shoshoni** (ʃəʊˈʃəʊnɪ) NOUN [1] (**pl, -nes, -ne** *or* **-nis, -ni**) a member of a North American Indian people of the southwestern US, related to the Aztecs. [2] the language of this people, belonging to the Uto-Aztecan family.

Shoshonean *or* **Shoshonian** (ʃəʊˈʃəʊnɪən, ˌʃəʊʃəˈniːən) NOUN a subfamily of North American Indian languages belonging to the Uto-Aztecan family, spoken mainly in the southwestern US.

shot[1] (ʃɒt) NOUN [1] the act or an instance of discharging a projectile. [2] (*plural* **shot**) a solid missile, such as an iron ball or a lead pellet, discharged from a firearm. [3] **a** small round pellets of lead collectively, as used in cartridges. **b** metal in the form of coarse powder or small pellets. [4] the distance that a discharged projectile travels or is capable of travelling. [5] a person who shoots, esp with regard to his ability: *he is a good shot*. [6] *Informal* an attempt; effort. [7] *Informal* a guess or conjecture. [8] any act of throwing or hitting something, as in certain sports. [9] the launching of a rocket, missile, etc., esp to a specified destination: *a moon shot*. [10] **a** a single photograph: *I took 16 shots of the wedding*. **b** a series of frames on cine film concerned with a single event. **c** a length of film taken by a single camera without breaks, used with others to build up a full motion picture or television film. [11] *Informal* an injection, as of a vaccine or narcotic drug. [12] *Informal* a glass of alcoholic drink, esp spirits. [13] *Sport* a heavy metal ball used in the shot put. [14] an explosive charge used in blasting. [15] globules of metal occurring in the body of a casting that are harder than the rest of the casting. [16] a unit of chain length equal to 75 feet (Brit.) or 90 feet (US). [17] **call the shots**. *Slang* to have control over an organization, course of action, etc. [18] **have a shot at**. *Informal* **a** to attempt. **b** *Austral* to jibe at or vex. [19] **like a shot**. very quickly, esp willingly. [20] **shot in the arm**. *Informal* anything that regenerates, increases confidence or efficiency, etc.: *his arrival was a shot in the arm for the company*. [21] **shot in the dark**. a wild guess. [22] **that's the shot**. *Austral informal* that is the right thing to do. ◆ VERB **shots, shotting, shotted**. [23] (*tr*) to weight or load with shot.
▷HISTORY Old English *scot*; related to Old Norse *skot*, Old High German *scoz* missile; see SHOOT

shot[2] (ʃɒt) VERB [1] the past tense and past participle of **shoot**. ◆ ADJECTIVE [2] (of textiles) woven to give a changing colour effect: *shot silk*. [3] streaked with colour. [4] *Slang* exhausted. [5] **get shot** *or* **shut of**. *Slang* to get rid of.

shot-blasting NOUN the cleaning of metal, etc., by a stream of shot.

shote (ʃəʊt) NOUN a variant spelling of **shoat**.

shotgun (ˈʃɒtˌɡʌn) NOUN [1] **a** a shoulder firearm with unrifled bore designed for the discharge of small shot at short range and used mainly for hunting small game. **b** (*as modifier*): *shotgun fire*. [2] *American football* an offensive formation in which the quarterback lines up for a snap unusually far behind the line of scrimmage. ◆ ADJECTIVE [3] *Chiefly US* involving coercion or duress: *a shotgun merger*. [4] *Chiefly US* involving or relying on speculative suggestions, etc.: *a shotgun therapy*. ◆ VERB **-guns, -gunning, -gunned**. [5] (*tr*) *US* to shoot or threaten with or as if with a shotgun.

shotgun wedding NOUN *Informal* a wedding into which one or both partners are coerced, usually because the woman is pregnant.

shot hole NOUN a drilled hole into which explosive is put for blasting.

shot noise *or* **effect** NOUN the inherent electronic noise arising in an electric current because of the discontinuous nature of ... (ˈʃɒtkɪ).
by electrons. Al... ...c event in which
sh...

contestants hurl or put a heavy metal ball or shot as far as possible. 2 a single put of the shot.
▸ 'shot-ˌputter NOUN

shott *or* **chott** (ʃɒt) NOUN 1 a shallow temporary salt lake or marsh in the North African desert. 2 the hollow in which it lies.
▷HISTORY C19: via French *chott* from Arabic *shatt*

shotten ('ʃɒtᵊn) ADJECTIVE 1 (of fish, esp herring) having recently spawned. 2 *Archaic* worthless or undesirable.
▷HISTORY C15: from obsolete past participle of SHOOT

shot tower NOUN a building formerly used in the production of shot, in which molten lead was graded and dropped from a great height into water, thus cooling it and forming the shot.

should (ʃʊd) VERB the past tense of **shall**: used as an auxiliary verb to indicate that an action is considered by the speaker to be obligatory (*you should go*) or to form the subjunctive mood with *I* or *we* (*I should like to see you; if I should be late, go without me*).
▷HISTORY Old English *sceold;* see SHALL

Language note *Should* has, as its most common meaning in modern English, the sense *ought* as in *I should go to the graduation, but I don't see how I can.* However, the older sense of the subjunctive of *shall* is often used with *I* or *we* to indicate a more polite form than *would: I should like to go, but I can't.* In much speech and writing, *should* has been replaced by *would* in contexts of this kind, but it remains in formal English when a conditional subjunctive is used: *should he choose to remain, he would be granted asylum.*

shoulder ('ʃəʊldə) NOUN 1 the part of the vertebrate body where the arm or a corresponding forelimb joins the trunk: the pectoral girdle and associated structures. 2 the joint at the junction of the forelimb with the pectoral girdle. 3 a cut of meat including the upper part of the foreleg. 4 *Printing* the flat surface of a piece of type from which the face rises. 5 *Tanning* the portion of a hide covering the shoulders and neck of the animal, usually including the cheeks. 6 the part of a garment that covers the shoulder. 7 anything that resembles a shoulder in shape or position. 8 the strip of unpaved land that borders a road. 9 *Engineering* a substantial projection or abrupt change in shape or diameter designed to withstand thrust. 10 *Photog* the portion of the characteristic curve of a photographic material indicating the maximum density that can be produced on the material. 11 *Jewellery* the part of a ring where the shank joins the setting. 12 **a shoulder to cry on.** a person one turns to for sympathy with one's troubles. 13 **give (someone) the cold shoulder.** *Informal* **a** to treat (someone) in a cold manner; snub. **b** to ignore or shun (someone). 14 **put one's shoulder to the wheel.** *Informal* to work very hard. 15 **rub shoulders with.** See **rub** (sense 11). 16 **shoulder to shoulder. a** side by side or close together. **b** in a corporate effort. ◆ VERB 17 (*tr*) to bear or carry (a burden, responsibility, etc.) as if on one's shoulders. 18 to push (something) with or as if with the shoulder. 19 (*tr*) to lift or carry on the shoulders. 20 **shoulder arms.** *Military* to bring the rifle vertically close to the right side with the muzzle uppermost and held at the trigger guard.
▷HISTORY Old English *sculdor;* related to Old High German *sculterra*

shoulder blade NOUN the nontechnical name for **scapula.**

shoulder pad NOUN a small pad inserted to raise or give shape to the shoulder of a garment.

shoulder patch NOUN *US military* an emblem worn high on the arm as an insignia. Also called: **shoulder flash.**

shoulder strap NOUN a strap over one or both of the shoulders, as to hold up a garment or to support a bag, etc.

shoulder surfing NOUN *Informal* a form of credit-card fraud in which the perpetrator stands behind and looks over the shoulder of the victim as he or she withdraws money from an automated teller machine, memorizes the card details, and later steals the card.

shouldn't ('ʃʊdᵊnt) VERB CONTRACTION OF should not.

shouldst (ʃʊdst) *or* **shouldest** ('ʃʊdɪst) VERB *Archaic or dialect* (used with the pronoun *thou* or its relative equivalent) a form of the past tense of **shall.**

shouse (ʃaʊs) *Austral slang* ◆ NOUN 1 a toilet; lavatory. ◆ ADJECTIVE 2 unwell or in poor spirits.
▷HISTORY C20: shortening of *shithouse*

shout (ʃaʊt) NOUN 1 a loud cry, esp to convey emotion or a command. 2 *Informal, Brit, Austral, and NZ* **a** a round, esp of drinks. **b** one's turn to buy a round of drinks. 3 *Informal* an occasion on which the members of an emergency service are called out on duty. ◆ VERB 4 to utter (something) in a loud cry; yell. 5 (*intr*) to make a loud noise. 6 (*tr*) *Austral and NZ informal* to treat (someone) to (something), esp a drink.
▷HISTORY C14: probably from Old Norse *skūta* taunt; related to Old Norse *skjōta* to SHOOT
▸ 'shouter NOUN

shout down VERB (*tr, adverb*) to drown, overwhelm, or silence by shouting or talking loudly.

shouty ('ʃaʊtɪ) ADJECTIVE *Informal* characterized by or involving shouting: *a shouty youth; shouty conversation.*

shove (ʃʌv) VERB 1 to give a thrust or push to (a person or thing). 2 (*tr*) to give a violent push to; jostle. 3 (*intr*) to push one's way roughly. 4 (*tr*) *Informal* to put (something) somewhere, esp hurriedly or carelessly: *shove it in the bin.* ◆ NOUN 5 the act or an instance of shoving. ◆ See also **shove off.**
▷HISTORY Old English *scūfan;* related to Old Norse *skūfa* to push, Gothic *afskiuban* to push away, Old High German *skioban* to shove
▸ 'shover NOUN

shove-halfpenny NOUN *Brit* a game in which players try to propel old halfpennies or polished discs with the hand into lined sections of a wooden or slate board.

shovel ('ʃʌvᵊl) NOUN 1 an instrument for lifting or scooping loose material, such as earth, coal, etc., consisting of a curved blade or a scoop attached to a handle. 2 any machine or part resembling a shovel in action. 3 Also called: **shovelful.** the amount that can be contained in a shovel. 4 short for **shovel hat.** ◆ VERB **-els, -elling, -elled** *or US* **-els, -eling, -eled.** 5 to lift (earth, etc.) with a shovel. 6 (*tr*) to clear or dig (a path) with or as if with a shovel. 7 (*tr*) to gather, load, or unload in a hurried or careless way: *he shovelled the food into his mouth and rushed away.*
▷HISTORY Old English *scofl;* related to Old High German *scūfla* shovel, Dutch *schoffel* hoe; see SHOVE
▸ 'shoveller *or US* 'shoveler NOUN

shovel beak NOUN *Vet science* a deformity of the beak in intensively reared chicks. Also called: **mandibular disease.**

shoveler ('ʃʌvələ) NOUN a duck, *Anas* (or *Spatula*) *clypeata,* of ponds and marshes, having a spoon-shaped bill, a blue patch on each wing, and in the male a green head, white breast, and reddish-brown body.

shovel hat NOUN a black felt hat worn by some clergymen, with a brim rolled up to resemble a shovel in shape.

shovelhead ('ʃʌvᵊlˌhɛd) NOUN a common shark, *Sphyrna tiburo,* of the Atlantic and Pacific Oceans, having a shovel-shaped head: family *Sphyrnidae* (hammerheads).

shovelnose ('ʃʌvᵊlˌnəʊz) NOUN an American freshwater sturgeon, *Scaphirhynchus platorynchus,* having a broad shovel-like snout.

shove off VERB (*intr, adverb; often imperative*) 1 to move from the shore in a boat. 2 *Informal* to go away; depart.

show (ʃəʊ) VERB **shows, showing, showed; shown** *or* **showed.** 1 to make, be, or become visible or noticeable: *to show one's dislike.* 2 (*tr*) to present to view; exhibit: *he showed me a picture.* 3 (*tr*) to indicate or explain; prove: *to show that the earth moves round the sun.* 4 (*tr*) to exhibit or present (oneself or itself) in a specific character: *to show oneself to be trustworthy.* 5 (*tr; foll by how and an* infinitive) to instruct by demonstration: *show me how to swim.* 6 (*tr*) to indicate or register: *a barometer shows changes in the weather.* 7 (*tr*) to grant or bestow: *to show favour to someone.* 8 (*intr*) to appear: *to show to advantage.* 9 to exhibit, display, or offer (goods, etc.) for sale: *three artists were showing at the gallery.* 10 (*tr*) to allege, as in a legal document: *to show cause.* 11 to present (a play, film, etc.) or (of a play, etc.) to be presented, as at a theatre or cinema. 12 (*tr*) to guide or escort: *please show me to my room.* 13 **show in** *or* **out.** to conduct a person into or out of a room or building by opening the door for him. 14 (*intr*) to win a place in a horse race, etc. 15 to give a performance of riding and handling (a horse) to display its best points. 16 (*intr*) *Informal* to put in an appearance; arrive. ◆ NOUN 17 a display or exhibition. 18 a public spectacle. 19 an ostentatious or pretentious display. 20 a theatrical or other entertainment. 21 a trace or indication. 22 *Obstetrics* a discharge of blood at the onset of labour. 23 *US, Austral, and NZ informal* a chance; opportunity (esp in the phrases **give someone a show, he's got no show of winning,** etc.). 24 a sporting event consisting of contests in which riders perform different exercises to show their skill and their horses' ability and breeding. 25 *Slang, chiefly Brit* a thing or affair (esp in the phrases **good show, bad show,** etc.). 26 *Austral and NZ mining* a slight indication of the presence of gold. 27 a display of farm animals, with associated competitions. 28 **for show.** in order to attract attention. 29 **run the show.** *Informal* to take charge of or manage an affair, business, etc. 30 **steal the show.** to draw the most attention or admiration, esp unexpectedly. 31 **stop the show.** *Informal* **a** (of a stage act, etc.) to receive so much applause as to interrupt the performance. **b** to be received with great enthusiasm. ◆ See also **show off, show up.**
▷HISTORY Old English *scēawian;* related to Old High German *scouwōn* to look, Old Norse *örskār* careful, Greek *thuoskoos* seer

show bill NOUN a poster advertising a play or show. Also called: **show card.**

showboat ('ʃəʊˌbəʊt) NOUN 1 a paddle-wheel river steamer with a theatre and a repertory company. ◆ VERB 2 (*intr*) to perform or behave in a showy and flamboyant way.

showbread ('ʃəʊˌbrɛd) NOUN a variant spelling of **shewbread.**

show business NOUN the entertainment industry, including theatre, films, television, and radio. Informal term: **show biz.**

show card NOUN 1 *Commerce* a tradesman's advertisement mounted on card as a poster. 2 another term for **show bill.**

showcase ('ʃəʊˌkeɪs) NOUN 1 a glass case used to display objects in a museum or shop. 2 a setting in which anything may be displayed to best advantage. ◆ VERB 3 (*tr*) to exhibit or display. ◆ ADJECTIVE 4 displayed or meriting display as in a showcase.

show copy NOUN *Films* a positive print of a film for use at an important presentation such as a premiere.

showd (ʃaʊd) *Northeast Scot dialect* ◆ VERB 1 (*intr*) to rock or sway to and fro. 2 (*tr*) to rock (a baby in one's arms or in a pram). ◆ NOUN 3 a rocking motion.
▷HISTORY from Old English *scūdan* to shake

show day NOUN (in Australia) a public holiday in a state on the date of its annual agricultural and industrial show.

showdown ('ʃəʊˌdaʊn) NOUN 1 *Informal* an action that brings matters to a head or acts as a conclusion or point of decision. 2 *Poker* the exposing of the cards in the players' hands on the table at the end of the game.

shower[1] ('ʃaʊə) NOUN 1 a brief period of rain, hail, sleet, or snow. 2 a sudden abundant fall or downpour, as of tears, sparks, or light. 3 a rush; outpouring: *a shower of praise.* 4 **a** a kind of bath in which a person stands upright and is sprayed with water from a nozzle. **b** the room, booth, etc., containing such a bath. Full name: **shower bath.** 5 *Brit slang* a derogatory term applied to a person or group, esp to a group considered as being slack, untidy, etc. 6 *US, Canadian, Austral, and NZ* a party held to honour and present gifts to a person, as to a

prospective bride. 7 a large number of particles formed by the collision of a cosmic-ray particle with a particle in the atmosphere. 8 *NZ* a light fabric cover thrown over a tea table to protect the food from flies, dust, etc. ◆ VERB 9 (*tr*) to sprinkle or spray with or as if with a shower: *shower the powder into the milk.* 10 (often with *it* as subject) to fall or cause to fall in the form of a shower. 11 (*tr*) to give (gifts, etc.) in abundance or present (a person) with (gifts, etc.): *they showered gifts on him.* 12 (*intr*) to take a shower.
▷HISTORY Old English *scūr;* related to Old Norse *skūr,* Old High German *skūr* shower, Latin *caurus* northwest wind
▸ **'showery** ADJECTIVE

shower² ('ʃəʊə) NOUN a person or thing that shows.

showerproof ('ʃaʊəˌpruːf) ADJECTIVE (of a garment, etc.) resistant to or partly impervious to rain.
▸ **'showerˌproofing** NOUN

showgirl ('ʃəʊˌgɜːl) NOUN a girl who appears in variety shows, nightclub acts, etc., esp as a singer or dancer.

showground ('ʃəʊˌgraʊnd) NOUN an open-air setting for agricultural displays, competitions, etc. Also called (Austral and NZ): **showgrounds.**

show house NOUN a house on a new estate that is decorated and furnished for prospective buyers to view.

showing ('ʃəʊɪŋ) NOUN 1 a presentation, exhibition, or display. 2 manner of presentation; performance. 3 evidence.

showjumping ('ʃəʊˌdʒʌmpɪŋ) NOUN the riding of horses in competitions to demonstrate skill in jumping over or between various obstacles.
▸ **'show-ˌjumper** NOUN

showman ('ʃəʊmən) NOUN, *plural* **-men.** 1 a person who presents or produces a theatrical show, etc. 2 a person skilled at presenting anything in an effective manner.
▸ **'showmanship** NOUN

shown (ʃəʊn) VERB a past participle of **show.**

show off VERB (*adverb*) 1 (*tr*) to exhibit or display so as to invite admiration. 2 (*intr*) *Informal* to behave in such a manner as to make an impression. ◆ NOUN **show-off.** 3 *Informal* a person who makes a vain display of himself.

show of hands NOUN the raising of hands to indicate voting for or against a proposition.

showpiece ('ʃəʊˌpiːs) NOUN 1 anything displayed or exhibited. 2 anything prized as a very fine example of its type.

showplace ('ʃəʊˌpleɪs) NOUN a place exhibited or visited for its beauty, historic interest, etc.

show pony NOUN *Informal* a person who tries to be the centre of attention; show-off.

showroom ('ʃəʊˌruːm, -ˌrʊm) NOUN a room in which goods, such as cars, are on display.

show stopper NOUN *Informal* a stage act, etc., that receives so much applause as to interrupt the performance.

show trial NOUN a trial conducted primarily to make a particular impression on the public or on other nations, esp one that demonstrates the power of the state over the individual.

show up VERB (*adverb*) 1 to reveal or be revealed clearly. 2 (*tr*) to expose or reveal the faults or defects of by comparison. 3 (*tr*) *Informal* to put to shame; embarrass: *he showed me up in front of my friends.* 4 (*intr*) *Informal* to appear or arrive.

showy ('ʃəʊɪ) ADJECTIVE **showier, showiest.** 1 gaudy, flashy, or ostentatious. 2 making a brilliant or imposing display.
▸ **'showily** ADVERB ▸ **'showiness** NOUN

shoyu ('ʃəʊˌjuː) NOUN a Japanese variety of soy sauce.
▷HISTORY C18: Japanese

shpt ABBREVIATION FOR shipment.

shrank (ʃræŋk) VERB a past tense of **shrink.**

shrapnel ('ʃræpnᵊl) NOUN 1 **a** a projectile containing a number of small pellets or bullets exploded before impact. **b** such projectiles collectively. 2 fragments from this or any other type of shell.
▷HISTORY C19: named after H. *Shrapnel* (1761–1842), English army officer, who invented it

shred (ʃred) NOUN 1 a long narrow strip or fragment torn or cut off. 2 a very small piece or amount; scrap. ◆ VERB **shreds, shredding, shredded** *or* **shred.** 3 (*tr*) to tear or cut into shreds.
▷HISTORY Old English *scread;* related to Old Norse *skrjōthr* torn-up book, Old High German *scrōt* cut-off piece; see SCROLL, SHROUD, SCREED
▸ **'shredder** NOUN

Shreveport ('ʃriːvˌpɔːt) NOUN a city in NW Louisiana, on the Red River: centre of an oil and natural-gas region. Pop.: 200 145 (2000).

shrew (ʃruː) NOUN 1 Also called: **shrewmouse.** any small mouse-like long-snouted mammal, such as *Sorex araneus* (**common shrew**), of the family *Soricidae:* order *Insectivora* (insectivores). See also **water shrew.** Related adjective: **soricine.** 2 a bad-tempered or mean-spirited woman.
▷HISTORY Old English *scrēawa;* related to Old High German *scrawaz* dwarf, Icelandic *skröggr* old man, Norwegian *skrugg* dwarf

shrewd (ʃruːd) ADJECTIVE 1 astute and penetrating, often with regard to business. 2 artful and crafty: *a shrewd politician.* 3 *Obsolete* **a** piercing: *a shrewd wind.* **b** spiteful.
▷HISTORY C14: from *shrew* (obsolete vb) to curse, from SHREW
▸ **'shrewdly** ADVERB ▸ **'shrewdness** NOUN

shrewdie ('ʃruːdɪ) NOUN *Austral and NZ informal* a shrewd person.
▷HISTORY C20: from SHREWD + -IE

shrewish ('ʃruːɪʃ) ADJECTIVE (esp of a woman) bad-tempered and nagging.
▸ **'shrewishly** ADVERB ▸ **'shrewishness** NOUN

shrew mole NOUN any of several moles, such as *Uropsilus soricipes* of E Asia or *Neurotrichus gibbsi* of E North America, having a long snout and long tail.

shrewmouse ('ʃruːˌmaʊs) NOUN, *plural* **-mice.** another name for **shrew,** esp the common shrew

Shrewsbury ('ʃrəʊzbərɪ, -brɪ, 'ʃruːz-) NOUN a town in W central England, administrative centre of Shropshire, on the River Severn: strategically situated near the Welsh border; market town. Pop.: 90 900 (1991).

shriek (ʃriːk) NOUN 1 a shrill and piercing cry. ◆ VERB 2 to produce or utter (words, sounds, etc.) in a shrill piercing tone.
▷HISTORY C16: probably from Old Norse *skrækja* to SCREECH[1]
▸ **'shrieker** NOUN

shrieval ('ʃriːvᵊl) ADJECTIVE of or relating to a sheriff.

shrievalty ('ʃriːvəltɪ) NOUN, *plural* **-ties.** 1 the office or term of office of a sheriff. 2 the jurisdiction of a sheriff.
▷HISTORY C16: from SHRIEVE, on the model of *mayoralty*

shrieve (ʃriːv) NOUN an archaic word for **sheriff.**

shrift (ʃrɪft) NOUN *Archaic* the act or an instance of shriving or being shriven. See also **short shrift.**
▷HISTORY Old English *scrift,* from Latin *scriptum* SCRIPT

shrike (ʃraɪk) NOUN 1 Also called: **butcherbird.** any songbird of the chiefly Old World family *Laniidae,* having a heavy hooked bill and feeding on smaller animals which they sometimes impale on thorns, barbed wire, etc. See also **bush shrike** (sense 1). 2 any of various similar but unrelated birds, such as the cuckoo shrikes. 3 **shrike thrush** *or* **tit.** another name for **thickhead** (the bird).
▷HISTORY Old English *scrīc* thrush; related to Middle Dutch *schrīk* corncrake; see SCREECH[1], SHRIEK

shrill (ʃrɪl) ADJECTIVE 1 sharp and high-pitched in quality. 2 emitting a sharp high-pitched sound. ◆ VERB 3 to utter (words, sounds, etc.) in a shrill tone. 4 (*tr*) *Rare* to cause to produce a shrill sound.
▷HISTORY C14: probably from Old English *scralletan;* related to German *schrill* shrill, Dutch *schrallen* to shriek
▸ **'shrillness** NOUN ▸ **'shrilly** ADVERB

shrimp (ʃrɪmp) NOUN 1 any of various chiefly marine decapod crustaceans of the genus *Crangon* and related genera, having a slender flattened body with a long tail and a single pair of pincers. 2 any of various similar but unrelated crustaceans, such as the opossum shrimp and mantis shrimp. 3 Also called: **freshwater shrimp.** any of various freshwater shrimplike amphipod crustaceans of the genus *Gammarus,* esp *G. pulex.* 4 Also called: **sand shrimp.** any of various shrimplike amphipod crustaceans of the genus *Gammarus,* esp *G. locusta.* ◆ See also **opossum shrimp.** 5 *Informal* a diminutive person, esp a child. ◆ VERB 6 (*intr*) to fish for shrimps.
▷HISTORY C14: probably of Germanic origin; compare Middle Low German *schrempen* to shrink; see SCRIMP, CRIMP
▸ **'shrimper** NOUN

shrine (ʃraɪn) NOUN 1 a place of worship hallowed by association with a sacred person or object. 2 a container for sacred relics. 3 the tomb of a saint or other holy person. 4 a place or site venerated for its association with a famous person or event. 5 *RC Church* a building, alcove, or shelf arranged as a setting for a statue, picture, or other representation of Christ, the Virgin Mary, or a saint. ◆ VERB 6 short for **enshrine.**
▷HISTORY Old English *scrīn,* from Latin *scrīnium* bookcase; related to Old Norse *skrin,* Old High German *skrīni*
▸ **'shrineˌlike** ADJECTIVE

shrink (ʃrɪŋk) VERB **shrinks, shrinking; shrank** *or* **shrunk; shrunk** *or* **shrunken.** 1 to contract or cause to contract as from wetness, heat, cold, etc. 2 to become or cause to become smaller in size. 3 (*intr;* often foll by *from*) **a** to recoil or withdraw: *to shrink from the sight of blood.* **b** to feel great reluctance (at): *to shrink from killing an animal.* ◆ NOUN 4 the act or an instance of shrinking. 5 a slang word for **psychiatrist.**
▷HISTORY Old English *scrincan;* related to Old Norse *skrokkr* torso, Old Swedish *skrunkin* wrinkled, Old Norse *hrukka* a crease, Icelandic *skrukka* wrinkled woman
▸ **'shrinkable** ADJECTIVE ▸ **'shrinker** NOUN ▸ **'shrinking** ADJECTIVE ▸ **'shrinkingly** ADVERB

shrinkage ('ʃrɪŋkɪdʒ) NOUN 1 the act or fact of shrinking. 2 the amount by which anything decreases in size, value, weight, etc. 3 the loss in body weight during shipment and preparation of livestock for marketing as meat. 4 the loss of merchandise in a retail store through theft or damage.

shrink fit NOUN *Engineering* a tight fit of a collar or wheel boss on a shaft obtained by expanding the collar or boss by heating to enable it to be threaded onto the shaft and then allowing it to cool, or by freezing the shaft to reduce its diameter to enable it to be threaded into the collar or boss and then allowing the shaft temperature to rise.

shrinking violet NOUN *Informal* a shy person.

shrink-wrap VERB **-wraps, -wrapping, -wrapped.** (*tr*) to package (a product) in a flexible plastic wrapping designed to shrink about its contours to protect and seal it.

shrive (ʃraɪv) VERB **shrives, shriving; shrove** *or* **shrived; shriven** ('ʃrɪvᵊn) *or* **shrived.** *Chiefly RC Church* 1 to hear the confession of (a penitent). 2 (*tr*) to impose a penance upon (a penitent) and grant him sacramental absolution. 3 (*intr*) to confess one's sins to a priest in order to obtain sacramental forgiveness.
▷HISTORY Old English *scrīfan,* from Latin *scrībere* to write
▸ **'shriver** NOUN

shrivel ('ʃrɪvᵊl) VERB **-els, -elling, -elled** *or US* **-els, -eling, -eled.** 1 to make or become shrunken and withered. 2 to lose or cause to lose vitality.
▷HISTORY C16: probably of Scandinavian origin; compare Swedish dialect *skryvla* wrinkle

shroff (ʃrɒf) NOUN 1 (in China, Japan, etc., esp formerly) an expert employed to separate counterfeit money or base coin from the genuine. 2 (in India) a moneychanger or banker. ◆ VERB 3 (*tr*) to test (money) and separate out the counterfeit and base.
▷HISTORY C17: from Portuguese *xarrafo,* from Hindi *sarrāf* moneychanger, from Arabic

Shropshire ('ʃrɒpˌʃɪə, -ʃə) NOUN 1 a county of W central England: Telford and Wrekin became an independent unitary authority in 1998; mainly agricultural. Administrative centre: Shrewsbury. Pop. (excluding Telford and Wrekin): 283 240 (2001). Area (excluding Telford and Wrekin): 3201 sq. km (1236 sq. miles). 2 a breed of medium-sized sheep having a dense fleece, originating from Shropshire and Staffordshire, England.

shroud (ʃraʊd) NOUN 1 a garment or piece of cloth used to wrap a dead body. 2 anything that envelops like a garment: *a shroud of mist.* 3 a protective covering for a piece of equipment. 4 *Astronautics* a streamlined protective covering used to protect the payload during a rocket-powered launch. 5 *Nautical* one of a pattern of ropes or cables used to stay a mast. 6 any of a set of wire cables stretched between a smokestack or similar structure and the ground, to prevent side sway. 7 Also called: **shroud line.** any of a set of lines running from the canopy of a parachute to the harness. ◆ VERB 8 (*tr*) to wrap in a shroud. 9 (*tr*) to cover, envelop, or hide. 10 *Archaic* to seek or give shelter.
▷HISTORY Old English *scrūd* garment; related to Old Norse *skrūth* gear
▸'**shroudless** ADJECTIVE

shroud-laid ADJECTIVE (of a rope) made with four strands twisted to the right, usually around a core.

shrove (ʃrəʊv) VERB a past tense of **shrive.**

Shrovetide ('ʃrəʊvˌtaɪd) NOUN the Sunday, Monday, and Tuesday before Ash Wednesday, formerly a time when confessions were made in preparation for Lent.

Shrove Tuesday NOUN the last day of Shrovetide; Pancake Day.

shrub[1] (ʃrʌb) NOUN a woody perennial plant, smaller than a tree, with several major branches arising from near the base of the main stem.
▷HISTORY Old English *scrybb;* related to Middle Low German *schrubben* coarse, uneven, Old Swedish *skrubba* to SCRUB[1]
▸'**shrub,like** ADJECTIVE

shrub[2] (ʃrʌb) NOUN 1 a mixed drink of rum, fruit juice, sugar, and spice. 2 mixed fruit juice, sugar, and spice made commercially to be mixed with rum or other spirits.
▷HISTORY C18: from Arabic *sharāb,* variant of *shurb* drink; see SHERBET

shrubbery ('ʃrʌbərɪ) NOUN, *plural* **-beries.** 1 a place where a number of shrubs are planted. 2 shrubs collectively.

shrubby ('ʃrʌbɪ) ADJECTIVE **-bier, -biest.** 1 consisting of, planted with, or abounding in shrubs. 2 resembling a shrub.
▸'**shrubbiness** NOUN

shrub layer NOUN See **layer** (sense 2).

shrug (ʃrʌg) VERB **shrugs, shrugging, shrugged.** 1 to draw up and drop (the shoulders) abruptly in a gesture expressing indifference, contempt, ignorance, etc. ◆ NOUN 2 the gesture so made. 3 a woman's short jacket or close-fitting cardigan.
▷HISTORY C14: of uncertain origin

shrug off VERB (*tr, adverb*) 1 to minimize the importance of; dismiss. 2 to get rid of. 3 to wriggle out of or push off (clothing).

shrunk (ʃrʌŋk) VERB a past participle and past tense of **shrink.**

shrunken ('ʃrʌŋkᵊn) VERB 1 a past participle of **shrink.** ◆ ADJECTIVE 2 (*usually prenominal*) reduced in size.

shtetl ('ʃtetᵊl) NOUN, *plural* **shtetlach** ('ʃtetla:x) *or* **shtetls.** (formerly) a small Jewish community in Eastern Europe.
▷HISTORY Yiddish, little town

shtick (ʃtɪk) *or* **schtick** NOUN *Slang* a comedian's routine; act; piece.
▷HISTORY C20: from Yiddish *shtik* piece, from Middle High German *stücke*

shtoom (ʃtʊm) ADJECTIVE *Slang* silent; dumb (esp in the phrase **keep shtoom**).
▷HISTORY from Yiddish, from German *stumm* silent

shuck (ʃʌk) NOUN 1 the outer covering of something, such as the husk of a grain of maize, a pea pod, or an oyster shell. ◆ VERB (*tr*) 2 to remove the shucks from. 3 *Informal, chiefly US and Canadian* to throw off or remove (clothes, etc.).
▷HISTORY C17: American dialect, of unknown origin
▸'**shucker** NOUN

shucks (ʃʌks) *US and Canadian informal* ◆ PLURAL NOUN 1 something of little value (esp in the phrase **not worth shucks**). ◆ INTERJECTION 2 an exclamation of disappointment, annoyance, etc.

shudder ('ʃʌdə) VERB 1 (*intr*) to shake or tremble suddenly and violently, as from horror, fear, aversion, etc. ◆ NOUN 2 the act of shuddering; convulsive shiver.
▷HISTORY C18: from Middle Low German *schōderen;* related to Old Frisian *skedda* to shake, Old High German *skutten* to shake
▸'**shuddering** ADJECTIVE ▸'**shudderingly** ADVERB
▸'**shuddery** ADJECTIVE

shuffle ('ʃʌfᵊl) VERB 1 to walk or move (the feet) with a slow dragging motion. 2 to change the position of (something), esp quickly or in order to deceive others. 3 (*tr*) to mix together in a careless manner: *he shuffled the papers nervously.* 4 to mix up (cards in a pack) to change their order. 5 (*intr*) to behave in an awkward, evasive, or underhand manner; equivocate. 6 (when *intr,* often foll by *into* or *out of*) to move or cause to move clumsily: *he shuffled out of the door.* 7 (*intr*) to dance the shuffle. ◆ NOUN 8 the act or an instance of shuffling. 9 a dance or dance step with short dragging movements of the feet.
▷HISTORY C16: probably from Low German *schüffeln;* see SHOVE
▸'**shuffler** NOUN

shuffleboard ('ʃʌfᵊlˌbɔ:d) NOUN 1 a game in which players push wooden or plastic discs with a long cue towards numbered scoring sections marked on a floor, esp a ship's deck. 2 the marked area on which this game is played.

shuffle off VERB (*tr, adverb*) to thrust off or put aside: *shuffle off responsibility.*

shuffle play NOUN a facility on a compact disc player that randomly selects a track from one of a number of compact discs.

shufty *or* **shufti** ('ʃʊftɪ, 'ʃʌftɪ) NOUN, *plural* **-ties.** *Brit slang* a look; peep.
▷HISTORY C20: from Arabic

Shufu *or* **Sufu** ('ʃu:'fu:) NOUN transliteration of the Chinese name for **Kashi.**

shuggy ('ʃʌgɪ) NOUN, *plural* **-gies.** *Northeastern English dialect* a swing, as at a fairground.
▷HISTORY from *shog, shug* to shake; see SHOOGLE

shul *or* **schul** (ʃu:l) NOUN the Yiddish word for **synagogue.**
▷HISTORY Yiddish: synagogue, from Old High German *scuola* SCHOOL[1]

Shulamite ('ʃu:ləˌmaɪt) NOUN *Old Testament* an epithet of uncertain meaning applied to the bride in the Song of Solomon 6:13.

Shulchan Aruch (ʃʊl'xɑn ɑr'ʊx, 'ʃʊlxən 'ɑʊrəx) NOUN the main codification of Jewish law derived from the Talmud, compiled by the 16th-century rabbi, Joseph Caro.

shun (ʃʌn) VERB **shuns, shunning, shunned.** (*tr*) to avoid deliberately; keep away from.
▷HISTORY Old English *scunian,* of obscure origin
▸'**shunnable** ADJECTIVE ▸'**shunner** NOUN

'shun (ʃʌn) INTERJECTION *Military* a clipped form of **attention** (sense 7).

shunt (ʃʌnt) VERB 1 to turn or cause to turn to one side; move or be moved aside. 2 *Railways* to transfer (rolling stock) from track to track. 3 *Electronics* to divert or be diverted through a shunt. 4 (*tr*) to evade by putting off onto someone else. 5 (*tr*) *Motor racing, slang* to crash (a car). ◆ NOUN 6 the act or an instance of shunting. 7 a railway point. 8 *Electronics* a low-resistance conductor connected in parallel across a device, circuit, or part of a circuit to provide an alternative path for a known fraction of the current. 9 *Med* a channel that bypasses the normal circulation of the blood: a congenital abnormality or surgically induced. 10 *Brit informal* a collision which occurs when a vehicle runs into the back of the vehicle in front.
▷HISTORY C13: perhaps from *shunen* to SHUN

shunter ('ʃʌntə) NOUN a small railway locomotive used for manoeuvring coaches rather than for making journeys.

shunt-wound ('ʃʌntˌwaʊnd) ADJECTIVE *Electrical engineering* (of a motor or generator) having the field and armature circuits connected in parallel. Compare **series-wound.**

shura *or* **shoora** ('ʃʊərə) NOUN 1 *Islam* a consultative council or assembly. 2 *Islam* the process of decision-making by consultation and deliberation.
▷HISTORY from Arabic *shūrā,* literally: consultation

shush (ʃʊʃ) INTERJECTION 1 be quiet! hush! ◆ VERB 2 to silence or calm (someone) by or as if by saying "shush".
▷HISTORY C20: reduplication of SH, influenced by HUSH[1]

Shushan ('ʃu:ʃæn) NOUN the Biblical name for **Susa.**

shut (ʃʌt) VERB **shuts, shutting, shut.** 1 to move (something) so as to cover an aperture; close: *to shut a door.* 2 to close (something) by bringing together the parts: *to shut a book.* 3 (*tr;* often foll by *up*) to close or lock the doors of: *to shut up a house.* 4 (*tr;* foll by *in, out,* etc.) to confine, enclose, or exclude: *to shut a child in a room.* 5 (*tr*) to prevent (a business, etc.) from operating. 6 **shut one's eyes to.** to ignore deliberately. 7 **shut the door on. a** to refuse to think about. **b** to render impossible. ◆ ADJECTIVE 8 closed or fastened. ◆ NOUN 9 the act or time of shutting. 10 the line along which pieces of metal are welded. 11 **get shut** *or* **shot of.** *Slang* to get rid of. ◆ See also **shutdown, shut-off, shutout, shut up.**
▷HISTORY Old English *scyttan;* related to Old Frisian *sketta* to shut in, Middle Dutch *schutten* to obstruct

shutdown ('ʃʌtˌdaʊn) NOUN 1 **a** the closing of a factory, shop, etc. **b** (*as modifier*): *shutdown costs.* ◆ VERB **shut down.** (*adverb*) 2 to cease or cause to cease operation. 3 (*tr*) to close by lowering. 4 (*tr*) (of fog) to descend and envelop. 5 (*intr;* foll by *on* or *upon*) *Informal* to put a stop to; clamp down on. 6 (*tr*) to reduce the power level of (a nuclear reactor) to the lowest possible value.

shuteye ('ʃʌtˌaɪ) NOUN an informal term for **sleep.**

shut-in NOUN 1 *Chiefly US and Canadian* **a** a person confined indoors by illness. **b** (*as modifier*): *a shut-in patient.* 2 *Psychiatry* a condition in which the person is highly withdrawn and unable to express his own feelings. See also **schizoid.**

shut-off NOUN 1 a device that shuts something off, esp a machine control. 2 a stoppage or cessation. ◆ VERB **shut off.** (*tr, adverb*) 3 to stem the flow of. 4 to block off the passage through. 5 to isolate or separate.

shutout ('ʃʌtˌaʊt) NOUN 1 a less common word for a **lockout.** 2 *Sport* a game in which the opposing team does not score. ◆ VERB **shut out.** (*tr, adverb*) 3 to keep out or exclude. 4 to conceal from sight: *we planted trees to shut out the view of the road.* 5 to prevent (an opponent) from scoring.

shut-out bid NOUN *Bridge* a pre-emptive bid.

shutter ('ʃʌtə) NOUN 1 a hinged doorlike cover, often louvred and usually one of a pair, for closing off a window. 2 **put up the shutters.** to close business at the end of the day or permanently. 3 *Photog* an opaque shield in a camera that, when tripped, admits light to expose the film or plate for a predetermined period, usually a fraction of a second. It is either built into the lens system or lies in the focal plane of the lens (**focal-plane shutter**). 4 *Photog* a rotating device in a film projector that permits an image to be projected onto the screen only when the film is momentarily stationary. 5 *Music* one of the louvred covers over the mouths of organ pipes, operated by the swell pedal. 6 a person or thing that shuts. ◆ VERB (*tr*) 7 to close with or as if with a shutter or shutters. 8 to equip with a shutter or shutters.

shuttering ('ʃʌtərɪŋ) NOUN another word (esp Brit) for **formwork.**

shutter priority NOUN *Photog* an automatic exposure system in which the photographer selects the shutter speed and the camera then automatically sets the correct aperture. Compare **aperture priority.**

shuttle ('ʃʌtᵊl) NOUN 1 a bobbin-like device used in weaving for passing the weft thread between the warp threads. 2 a small bobbin-like device used to hold the thread in a sewing machine or in tatting, knitting, etc. 3 **a** a bus, train, aircraft, etc., that plies between two points, esp one that offers a frequent service over a short route. **b** short for **space shuttle.** 4 **a** the movement between various countries of a diplomat in order to negotiate with rulers who refuse to meet each other. **b** (*as modifier*): *shuttle diplomacy.* 5 *Badminton* short for **shuttlecock.** ◆ VERB 6 to move or cause to move by or as if by a shuttle.
▷HISTORY Old English *scytel* bolt; related to Middle

High German *schüzzel*, Swedish *skyttel*. See SHOOT, SHOT

shuttle armature NOUN a simple H-shaped armature used in small direct-current motors.

shuttlecock ('ʃʌtᵊl,kɒk) NOUN [1] a light cone consisting of a cork stub with feathered flights, struck to and fro in badminton and battledore. Often shortened to: **shuttle.** [2] anything moved to and fro, as in an argument. ♦ VERB [3] to move or cause to move to and fro, like a shuttlecock.
▷**HISTORY** C16: from SHUTTLE + COCK[1]

shut up VERB (*adverb*) [1] (*tr*) to prevent all access to. [2] (*tr*) to confine or imprison. [3] *Informal* to cease to talk or make a noise or cause to cease to talk or make a noise: often used in commands. [4] (*intr*) (of horses in a race) to cease through exhaustion from maintaining a racing pace.

shwa (ʃwɑː) NOUN a variant spelling of **schwa**.

shy[1] (ʃaɪ) ADJECTIVE **shyer, shyest** *or* **shier, shiest.** [1] not at ease in the company of others. [2] easily frightened; timid. [3] (often foll by *of*) watchful or wary. [4] *Poker* (of a player) without enough money to back his bet. [5] (of plants and animals) not breeding or producing offspring freely. [6] (foll by *of*) *Informal, chiefly US and Canadian* short (of). [7] (*in combination*) showing reluctance or disinclination: *workshy*. ♦ VERB **shies, shying, shied.** (*intr*) [8] to move suddenly, as from fear: *the horse shied at the snake in the road.* [9] (usually foll by *off* or *away*) to draw back; recoil. ♦ NOUN, *plural* **shies.** [10] a sudden movement, as from fear.
▷**HISTORY** Old English *sceoh;* related to Old High German *sciuhen* to frighten away, Dutch *schuw* shy, Swedish *skygg*
▸**'shyer** NOUN ▸**'shyly** ADVERB ▸**'shyness** NOUN

shy[2] (ʃaɪ) VERB **shies, shying, shied.** [1] to throw (something) with a sideways motion. ♦ NOUN, *plural* **shies.** [2] a quick throw. [3] *Informal* a gibe. [4] *Informal* an attempt; experiment. [5] short for **cockshy.**
▷**HISTORY** C18: of Germanic origin; compare Old High German *sciuhen* to make timid, Middle Dutch *schüchteren* to chase away
▸**'shyer** NOUN

Shylock ('ʃaɪ,lɒk) NOUN a heartless or demanding creditor.
▷**HISTORY** C19: after *Shylock,* the name of the heartless usurer in Shakespeare's *The Merchant of Venice* (1596)

shypoo (ʃaɪ'puː) NOUN *Austral informal* **a** a liquor of poor quality. **b** a place where this is sold. **c** (*as modifier*): *a shypoo shanty*.
▷**HISTORY** C20: of uncertain origin

shyster ('ʃaɪstə) NOUN *Informal, chiefly US* a person, esp a lawyer or politician, who uses discreditable or unethical methods.
▷**HISTORY** C19: probably based on *Scheuster,* name of a disreputable 19th-century New York lawyer

si[1] (siː) NOUN *Music* a variant of **te**.

si[2] THE INTERNET DOMAIN NAME FOR Slovenia.

Si[1] (ʃiː) *or* **Si Kiang** NOUN a variant transliteration of the Chinese name for the **Xi**.

Si[2] THE CHEMICAL SYMBOL FOR silicon.

SI [1] SYMBOL FOR Système International (d'Unités). See **SI unit.** [2] *NZ* ♦ ABBREVIATION FOR South Island.

sial ('saɪəl) NOUN the silicon-rich and aluminium-rich rocks of the earth's continental upper crust, the most abundant individual rock being granite.
▷**HISTORY** C20: *si(licon)* + *al(uminium)*
▸**sialic** (saɪ'ælɪk) ADJECTIVE

sialagogue *or* **sialogogue** ('saɪələ,gɒg, saɪ'ælə,gɒg) NOUN *Med* any drug or agent that can stimulate the flow of saliva.
▷**HISTORY** C18: from New Latin *sialagōgus,* from Greek *sialon* saliva + -AGOGUE
▸**sialagogic** *or* **sialogogic** (,saɪələ'gɒdʒɪk) ADJECTIVE

Sialkot (sɪ'ælkɒt) NOUN a city in NE Pakistan: shrine of Guru Nanak. Pop. (urban area): 417 597 (1988).

sialoid ('saɪə,lɔɪd) ADJECTIVE resembling saliva.
▷**HISTORY** from Greek *sialon* saliva + -OID

Siam (saɪ'æm, 'saɪæm) NOUN [1] the former name (until 1939 and 1945–49) of **Thailand.** [2] **Gulf of.** an arm of the South China Sea between the Malay Peninsula and Indochina.

siamang ('saɪə,mæŋ) NOUN a large black gibbon, *Hylobates* (or *Symphalangus*) *syndactylus,* of Sumatra and the Malay Peninsula, having a large reddish-brown vocal sac beneath the chin and the second and third toes united.
▷**HISTORY** C19: from Malay

Siamese (,saɪə'miːz) NOUN, *plural* **-mese.** [1] See **Siamese cat.** ♦ ADJECTIVE [2] characteristic of, relating to, or being a Siamese twin. ♦ ADJECTIVE, NOUN [3] another word for **Thai.**

Siamese cat NOUN a short-haired breed of cat with a tapering tail, blue eyes, and dark ears, mask, tail, and paws.
▷**HISTORY** so called because the breed is believed to have originated in SIAM

Siamese fighting fish NOUN a brightly coloured labyrinth fish, *Betta splendens,* of Thailand and Malaysia, having large sail-like fins: the males are very pugnacious.

Siamese twins PLURAL NOUN non-technical name for **conjoined twins.**
▷**HISTORY** C19: named after a famous pair of conjoined twins, Chang and Eng (1811–74), who were born in SIAM

Sian (ʃjɑːn) NOUN a variant transliteration of the Chinese name for **Xi An.**

Siang (ʃjɑːŋ) NOUN a variant transliteration of the Chinese name for the **Xiang.**

Siangtan ('ʃjɑːŋ'tɑːn) NOUN a variant transliteration of the Chinese name for **Xiangtan.**

sib (sɪb) NOUN [1] a blood relative. [2] a brother or sister; sibling. [3] kinsmen collectively; kindred. [4] any social unit that is bonded by kinship through one line of descent only.
▷**HISTORY** Old English *sibb;* related to Old Norse *sifjar* relatives, Old High German *sippa* kinship, Latin *suus* one's own; see GOSSIP

SIB (in Britain) ABBREVIATION FOR (the former) **Securities and Investments Board.**

Siberia (saɪ'bɪərɪə) NOUN a vast region of Russia and N Kazakhstan: extends from the Ural Mountains to the Pacific and from the Arctic Ocean to the borders with China and Mongolia; colonized after the building of the Trans-Siberian Railway. Area: 13 807 037 sq. km (5 330 896 sq. miles).

Siberian (saɪ'bɪərɪən) ADJECTIVE [1] of or relating to Siberia or its inhabitants. ♦ NOUN [2] a native or inhabitant of Siberia.

Siberian forest cat NOUN a breed of powerfully-built long-haired cat, typically tabby with a white ruff and white paws.

sibilant ('sɪbɪlənt) ADJECTIVE [1] *Phonetics* relating to or denoting the consonants (s, z, ʃ, ʒ), all pronounced with a characteristic hissing sound. [2] having a hissing sound: *the sibilant sound of wind among the leaves.* ♦ NOUN [3] a sibilant consonant.
▷**HISTORY** C17: from Latin *sībilāre* to hiss, of imitative origin; compare Greek *sizein* to hiss
▸**'sibilance** *or* **'sibilancy** NOUN ▸**'sibilantly** ADVERB

sibilate ('sɪbɪ,leɪt) VERB to pronounce or utter (words or speech) with a hissing sound.
▸**,sibi'lation** NOUN

Sibiu (*Romanian* si'biu) NOUN an industrial town in W central Romania: originally a Roman city, refounded by German colonists in the 12th century. Pop.: 168 949 (1997 est.). German name: **Hermannstadt.** Hungarian name: **Nagyszeben.**

sibling ('sɪblɪŋ) NOUN [1] **a** a person's brother or sister. **b** (*as modifier*): *sibling rivalry*. [2] any fellow member of a sib.
▷**HISTORY** C19: specialized modern use of Old English *sibling* relative, from SIB; see -LING[1]

sibship ('sɪbʃɪp) NOUN a group of children of the same parents.

sibyl ('sɪbɪl) NOUN [1] (in ancient Greece and Rome) any of a number of women believed to be oracles or prophetesses, one of the most famous being the sibyl of Cumae, who guided Aeneas through the underworld. [2] a witch, fortune-teller, or sorceress.
▷**HISTORY** C13: ultimately from Greek *Sibulla,* of obscure origin
▸**sibylline** ('sɪbɪ,laɪn, sɪ'bɪlaɪn) *or* **sibyllic** *or* **sibylic** (sɪ'bɪlɪk) ADJECTIVE

Sibylline Books PLURAL NOUN (in ancient Rome) a collection of prophetic sayings, supposedly bought from the Cumaean sibyl, bearing upon Roman policy and religion.

sic[1] (sɪk) ADVERB so or thus: inserted in brackets in a written or printed text to indicate that an odd or questionable reading is what was actually written or printed.
▷**HISTORY** Latin

sic[2] (sɪk) VERB **sics, sicking, sicked.** (*tr*) [1] to turn on or attack: used only in commands, as to a dog. [2] to urge (a dog) to attack.
▷**HISTORY** C19: dialect variant of SEEK

sic[3] (sɪk) DETERMINER, ADVERB a Scot word for **such.**

Sicanian (sɪ'keɪnɪən) ADJECTIVE another word for **Sicilian.**

siccar ('sɪkər) ADJECTIVE *Scot* sure; certain. Also: **sicker.**
▷**HISTORY** Middle English, from Latin *sēcūrus* SECURE

siccative ('sɪkətɪv) NOUN a substance added to a liquid to promote drying: used in paints and some medicines.
▷**HISTORY** C16: from Late Latin *siccātīvus,* from Latin *siccāre* to dry up, from *siccus* dry

sice (saɪs) NOUN a variant spelling of **syce.**

sicht (sɪxt) NOUN, VERB a Scot word for **sight.**

Sichuan ('sɪ'tʃwɑːn) *or* **Szechwan** NOUN a province of SW China: the most populous administrative division in the country, esp in the central Red Basin, where it is crossed by three main tributaries of the Yangtze. Capital: Chengdu. Pop.: 83 290 000 (2000 est.). Area: about 569 800 sq. km (220 000 sq. miles).

Sicilia (si'tʃiːlja) NOUN the Latin and Italian name for **Sicily.**

Sicilian (sɪ'sɪlɪən) ADJECTIVE [1] of or relating to Sicily or its inhabitants. ♦ NOUN [2] a native or inhabitant of Sicily.

siciliano (sɪ,sɪlɪ'ɑːnəʊ, ,sɪtʃɪ'ljɑːnəʊ) NOUN, *plural* **-ianos.** [1] an old dance in six-beat or twelve-beat time. [2] music composed for or in the rhythm of this dance.
▷**HISTORY** Italian: Sicilian

Sicilian Vespers NOUN (*functioning as singular*) a revolt in 1282 against French rule in Sicily, in which the ringing of the vesper bells on Easter Monday served as the signal to massacre and drive out the French.

Sicily ('sɪsɪlɪ) NOUN the largest island in the Mediterranean, separated from the tip of SW Italy by the Strait of Messina: administratively an autonomous region of Italy; settled by Phoenicians, Greeks, and Carthaginians before the Roman conquest of 241 B.C.; under Normans (12th–13th centuries); formed the **Kingdom of the Two Sicilies** with Naples in 1815; mountainous and volcanic. Capital: Palermo. Pop.: 5 087 794 (2000 est.). Area: 25 460 sq. km (9830 sq. miles). Latin names: **Sicilia, Trinacria.** Italian name: **Sicilia.**

sick[1] (sɪk) ADJECTIVE [1] inclined or likely to vomit. [2] **a** suffering from ill health. **b** (*as collective noun; preceded by the*): *the sick.* [3] **a** of, relating to, or used by people who are unwell: *sick benefits.* **b** (*in combination*): *sickbed.* [4] deeply affected with a mental or spiritual feeling akin to physical sickness: *sick at heart.* [5] mentally, psychologically, or spiritually disturbed. [6] *Informal* delighting in or catering for the macabre or sadistic; morbid: *sick humour.* [7] (often foll by *of*) *Informal* Also: **sick and tired.** disgusted or weary, esp because satiated: *I am sick of his everlasting laughter.* [8] (often foll by *for*) weary with longing; pining: *I am sick for my own country.* [9] pallid or sickly. [10] not in working order. [11] (of land) unfit for the adequate production of certain crops. [12] **look sick.** *Slang* to be outclassed. ♦ NOUN, VERB [13] an informal word for **vomit.** ♦ See also **sick-out.**
▷**HISTORY** Old English *sēoc;* related to Old Norse *skjūkr,* Gothic *siuks,* Old High German *sioh*
▸**'sickish** ADJECTIVE

sick[2] (sɪk) VERB a variant spelling of **sic**[2].

sickbay ('sɪk,beɪ) NOUN a room or area for the treatment of the sick or injured, as on board a ship or at a boarding school.

sick building syndrome NOUN a group of symptoms, such as headaches, eye irritation, and lethargy, that may be experienced by workers in offices with limited ventilation.

sick-dog NOUN *Austral slang* [1] a calm and unruffled person. ♦ ADJECTIVE [2] excellent.

sicken ('sɪkən) VERB [1] to make or become sick,

nauseated, or disgusted. 2 (*intr;* often foll by *for*) to show symptoms (of an illness).

sickener ('sɪkᵊnə) NOUN 1 something that induces sickness or nausea. 2 a bright red basidiomycetous fungus of either of two species of *Russula,* notably the poisonous *R. emetica.*

sickening ('sɪkənɪŋ) ADJECTIVE 1 causing sickness or revulsion. 2 *Informal* extremely annoying.
▸'**sickeningly** ADVERB

sick headache NOUN 1 a headache accompanied by nausea. 2 a nontechnical name for **migraine.**

sickie ('sɪkɪ) NOUN *Informal* a day of sick leave from work, whether for genuine sickness or not.
▷HISTORY C20: from SICK[1] + -IE

sickle ('sɪkᵊl) NOUN an implement for cutting grass, corn, etc., having a curved blade and a short handle.
▷HISTORY Old English *sicol,* from Latin *sēcula;* related to *secāre* to cut

sick leave NOUN leave of absence from work through illness.

sicklebill ('sɪkᵊlˌbɪl) NOUN any of various birds having a markedly curved bill, such as *Falculea palliata,* a Madagascan bird of the family *Vangidae, Hemignathus procerus,* a Hawaiian honey creeper, and certain hummingbirds and birds of paradise.

sickle-cell anaemia NOUN a hereditary haemolytic anaemia, occurring in Black populations, and caused by mutant haemoglobin. The red blood cells become sickle-shaped. It is characterized by fever, abdominal pain, jaundice, leg ulcers, etc.

sickle feather NOUN (*often plural*) any of the elongated tail feathers of certain birds, esp the domestic cock.
▷HISTORY C17: so called because of its shape

sickle medick NOUN a small Eurasian leguminous plant, *Medicago falcata,* having trifoliate leaves, yellow flowers, and sickle-shaped pods. Also called: **yellow medick.**

sick list NOUN a list of the sick, esp in the army or navy.

sickly ('sɪklɪ) ADJECTIVE **-lier, -liest.** 1 disposed to frequent ailments; not healthy; weak. 2 of, relating to, or caused by sickness. 3 (of a smell, taste, etc.) causing revulsion or nausea. 4 (of light or colour) faint or feeble. 5 mawkish; insipid: *sickly affectation.* ◆ ADVERB 6 in a sick or sickly manner.
▸'**sickliness** NOUN

sickness ('sɪknɪs) NOUN 1 an illness or disease. 2 nausea or queasiness. 3 the state or an instance of being sick.

sickness benefit NOUN 1 (formerly, in the British National Insurance scheme) a weekly payment made to a person who had been off work through illness for more than three days and less than six months; replaced by **incapacity benefit** in 1995. 2 (in New Zealand) a payment made by the Department of Social Welfare to a person unable to work owing to a medical condition.

sick note NOUN *Brit informal* a document given to an employer certifying that an employee's absence from work of more than four days was due to illness. If the absence is for more than seven days the note must be signed by a doctor. See also **self-certification.**

sicko ('sɪkəʊ) *Informal* ◆ NOUN, *plural* **sickos.** 1 a person who is mentally disturbed or perverted. ◆ ADJECTIVE 2 perverted or in bad taste: *sicko prurience.*
▷HISTORY C20: from SICK[1] (sense 5) + -O

sick-out *US and Caribbean* ◆ NOUN 1 a form of industrial action in which all workers in a factory, etc., report sick simultaneously. ◆ VERB **sick out.** 2 (*intr, adverb*) to take part in such action.

sick pay NOUN wages paid to an employee while he is on sick leave.

sickroom ('sɪkˌru:m, -ˌrʊm) NOUN 1 a room to which a person who is ill is confined. 2 a room set aside, as in a school, for people who are taken ill.

sic passim *Latin* ('sɪk 'pæsɪm) a phrase used in printed works to indicate that a word, spelling, etc., occurs in the same form throughout.
▷HISTORY literally: thus everywhere

sic transit gloria mundi *Latin* ('sɪk 'trænsɪt 'glɔ:rɪˌɑ: 'mʊndi:) thus passes the glory of the world.

Sicyon ('sɪsɪˌɒn, 'sɪsɪən) NOUN an ancient city in S Greece, in the NE Peloponnese near Corinth: declined after 146 B.C.

sidalcea (sɪ'dælsɪə) NOUN any plant of the mostly perennial N American genus *Sidalcea,* related to and resembling mallow, esp *S. malvaeflora,* grown for its spikes of lilac, pink, or red flowers: family *Malvaceae.* Also called: **Greek mallow.**
▷HISTORY New Latin, from Greek *sidē* a plant name + *alkea* a kind of mallow

Siddhartha (sɪ'dɑ:tə) NOUN the personal name of the **Buddha.**

siddur *Hebrew* (si:'du:r; *English* 'sɪdʊə) NOUN, *plural* ***-durim*** (-du:'ri:m) *or* ***-durs.*** *Judaism* the Jewish prayer book.
▷HISTORY literally: order

side (saɪd) NOUN 1 a line or surface that borders anything. 2 *Geometry* **a** any line segment forming part of the perimeter of a plane geometric figure. **b** another name for **face** (sense 13). 3 either of two parts into which an object, surface, area, etc., can be divided, esp by a line, median, space, etc.: *the right side and the left side.* Related adjective: **lateral.** 4 either of the two surfaces of a flat object: *the right and wrong side of the cloth.* 5 a surface or part of an object that extends vertically: *the side of a cliff.* 6 either half of a human or animal body, esp the area around the waist, as divided by the median plane: *I have a pain in my side.* 7 the area immediately next to a person or thing: *he stood at her side.* 8 a district, point, or direction within an area identified by reference to a central point: *the south side of the city.* 9 the area at the edge of a room, road, etc., as distinguished from the middle. 10 aspect or part: *look on the bright side; his cruel side.* 11 one of two or more contesting factions, teams, etc. 12 a page in an essay, book, etc. 13 a position, opinion, etc., held in opposition to another in a dispute. 14 line of descent: *he gets his brains from his mother's side.* 15 *Informal* a television channel. 16 *Billiards, snooker* spin imparted to a ball by striking it off-centre with the cue. US and Canadian equivalent: **English.** 17 *Brit slang* insolence, arrogance, or pretentiousness: *to put on side.* 18 **on one side.** set apart from the rest, as provision for emergencies, etc., or to avoid muddling. 19 **on the side. a** apart from or in addition to the main object. **b** as a sideline. **c** *US* as a side dish. **d bit on the side.** See **bit** (sense 11). 20 **side by side. a** close together. **b** (foll by *with*) beside or near to. 21 **take sides.** to support one group, opinion, etc., as against another. 22 **on the weak, heavy,** etc., **side.** tending to be too weak, heavy, etc. ◆ ADJECTIVE 23 being on one side; lateral. 24 from or viewed as if from one side. 25 directed towards one side. 26 not main; subordinate or incidental: *side door; side road.* ◆ VERB 27 (*intr;* usually foll by *with*) to support or associate oneself with a faction, interest, etc. 28 (*tr*) to provide with siding or sides. 29 (*tr;* often foll by *away* or *up*) *Northern English dialect* to tidy up or clear (dishes, a table, etc.).
▷HISTORY Old English *sīde;* related to *sīd* wide, Old Norse *sītha* side, Old High German *sīta*

side arms PLURAL NOUN weapons carried on the person, by sling, belt, or holster, such as a sword, pistol, etc.

sideband ('saɪdˌbænd) NOUN the frequency band either above (**upper sideband**) or below (**lower sideband**) the carrier frequency, within which fall the spectral components produced by modulation of a carrier wave. See also **single sideband transmission.**

sideboard ('saɪdˌbɔ:d) NOUN a piece of furniture intended to stand at the side of a dining room, with drawers, cupboards, and shelves to hold silver, china, linen, etc.

sideboards ('saɪdˌbɔ:dz) PLURAL NOUN another term for **sideburns.**

sideburns ('saɪdˌbɜ:nz) PLURAL NOUN a man's whiskers grown down either side of the face in front of the ears. Also called: **sideboards, side whiskers,** (Austral) **sidelevers.**
▷HISTORY C19: variant of BURNSIDES

sidecar ('saɪdˌkɑ:) NOUN 1 a small car attached on one side to a motorcycle, usually for one passenger, the other side being supported by a single wheel. 2 a cocktail containing brandy with equal parts of Cointreau and lemon juice.

side chain NOUN *Chem* a group of atoms bound to an atom, usually a carbon, that forms part of a larger chain or ring in a molecule.

-sided ADJECTIVE (*in combination*) having a side or sides as specified: *three-sided; many-sided.*

side deal NOUN a transaction between two people for their private benefit, which is subsidiary to a contract negotiated by them on behalf of the organizations they represent.

side dish NOUN a portion of food served in addition to the main dish.

side-dress VERB (*tr*) to place fertilizers on or in the soil near the roots of (growing plants).

side drum NOUN a small double-headed drum carried at the side with snares that produce a rattling effect.

side effect NOUN 1 any unwanted nontherapeutic effect caused by a drug. Compare **aftereffect** (sense 2). 2 any secondary effect, esp an undesirable one.

side-foot *Soccer* ◆ NOUN 1 a shot or pass played with the side of the foot. ◆ VERB 2 (*tr*) to strike (a ball) with the side of the foot.

sidekick ('saɪdˌkɪk) NOUN *Informal* a close friend or follower who accompanies another on adventures, etc.

sidelight ('saɪdˌlaɪt) NOUN 1 light coming from the side. 2 a side window. 3 either of the two navigational running lights used by vessels at night, a red light on the port and a green on the starboard. 4 *Brit* either of two small lights on the front of a motor vehicle, used to indicate the presence of the vehicle at night rather than to assist the driver. 5 additional or incidental information.

sideline ('saɪdˌlaɪn) NOUN 1 *Sport* a line that marks the side boundary of a playing area. 2 a subsidiary interest or source of income. 3 an auxiliary business activity or line of merchandise. ◆ VERB (*tr*) 4 to prevent (a player) from taking part in a game. 5 to prevent (a person) from pursuing a particular activity, operation, career, etc.

sidelines ('saɪdˌlaɪnz) PLURAL NOUN 1 *Sport* the area immediately outside the playing area, where substitute players sit. 2 the peripheral areas of any region, organization, etc.

sidelong ('saɪdˌlɒŋ) ADJECTIVE (*prenominal*) 1 directed or inclining to one side. 2 indirect or oblique. ◆ ADVERB 3 from the side; obliquely.

sideman ('saɪdmən) NOUN, *plural* **-men.** a member of a dance band or a jazz group other than the leader.

side meat NOUN *US informal* salt pork or bacon.
▷HISTORY C19: so called because it comes from the side of the pig

sidereal (saɪ'dɪərɪəl) ADJECTIVE 1 of, relating to, or involving the stars. 2 determined with reference to one or more stars: *the sidereal day.*
▷HISTORY C17: from Latin *sīdereus,* from *sīdus* a star, a constellation
▸**si'dereally** ADVERB

sidereal day NOUN See **day** (sense 5).

sidereal hour NOUN a 24th part of a sidereal day.

sidereal month NOUN See **month** (sense 5).

sidereal period NOUN *Astronomy* the period of revolution of a body about another with respect to one or more distant stars.

sidereal time NOUN time based upon the rotation of the earth with respect to the distant stars, the **sidereal day** being the unit of measurement.

sidereal year NOUN See **year** (sense 5).

siderite ('saɪdəˌraɪt) NOUN 1 Also called: **chalybite.** a pale yellow to brownish-black mineral consisting chiefly of iron carbonate in hexagonal crystalline form. It occurs mainly in ore veins and sedimentary rocks and is an important source of iron. Formula: $FeCO_3$. 2 a meteorite consisting principally of metallic iron.
▸**sideritic** (ˌsaɪdə'rɪtɪk) ADJECTIVE

sidero- *or before a vowel* **sider-** COMBINING FORM indicating iron: *siderolite.*
▷HISTORY from Greek *sidēros*

sideroad ('saɪdˌrəʊd) NOUN *Canadian* (esp in Ontario) a road, usually north-south, going at right angles to concession roads.

siderolite ('saɪdərəˌlaɪt) NOUN a meteorite

consisting of a mixture of iron, nickel, and such ferromagnesian minerals as olivine and pyroxene.

siderophilin (ˌsɪdəˈrɒfəlɪn) NOUN another name for **transferrin.**
▷HISTORY from SIDERO- + -PHIL(E) + -IN

siderosis (ˌsaɪdəˈrəʊsɪs) NOUN 1 a lung disease caused by breathing in fine particles of iron or other metallic dust. 2 an excessive amount of iron in the blood or tissues.
▸**siderotic** (ˌsɪdəˈrɒtɪk) ADJECTIVE

siderostat (ˈsaɪdərəʊˌstæt) NOUN an astronomical instrument consisting essentially of a plane mirror driven about two axes so that light from a celestial body, esp the sun, is reflected along a constant direction for a long period of time. See also **heliostat.** Compare **coelostat.**
▷HISTORY C19: from *sidero-*, from Latin *sidus* a star + -STAT, on the model of HELIOSTAT
▸ˌ**sideroˈstatic** ADJECTIVE

side-saddle NOUN 1 a riding saddle originally designed for women riders in skirts who sit with both legs on the near side of the horse. ◆ ADVERB 2 on or as if on a side-saddle: *to be riding side-saddle.*

sideshow (ˈsaɪdˌʃəʊ) NOUN 1 a small show or entertainment offered in conjunction with a larger attraction, as at a circus or fair. 2 a subordinate event or incident.

sideslip (ˈsaɪdˌslɪp) NOUN 1 a sideways skid, as of a motor vehicle. 2 a sideways and downward movement towards the inside of a turn by an aircraft in a sharp bank. ◆ VERB **-slips, -slipping, -slipped.** 3 another name for **slip**[1] (sense 12).

sidesman (ˈsaɪdzmən) NOUN, *plural* **-men.** *Church of England* a man elected to help the parish church warden.

side-splitting ADJECTIVE 1 producing great mirth. 2 (of laughter) uproarious or very hearty.

sidestep (ˈsaɪdˌstɛp) VERB **-steps, -stepping, -stepped.** 1 to step aside from or out of the way of (something). 2 (*tr*) to dodge or circumvent. ◆ NOUN **side step.** 3 a movement to one side, as in dancing, boxing, etc.
▸ˈ**sideˌstepper** NOUN

side street NOUN a minor or unimportant street, esp one leading off a main thoroughfare.

sidestroke (ˈsaɪdˌstrəʊk) NOUN a type of swimming stroke in which the swimmer lies sideways in the water paddling with his arms and making a scissors kick with his legs.

sideswipe (ˈsaɪdˌswaɪp) NOUN 1 a glancing blow or hit along or from the side. 2 an unexpected criticism of someone or something while discussing another subject. ◆ VERB 3 to strike (someone) with such a blow.
▸ˈ**sideˌswiper** NOUN

side tone NOUN sound diverted from a telephone microphone to the earpiece so that a speaker hears his own voice at the same level and position as that of the respondent.

sidetrack (ˈsaɪdˌtræk) VERB 1 to distract or be distracted from a main subject or topic. ◆ NOUN 2 *US and Canadian* a railway siding. 3 the act or an instance of sidetracking; digression.

side-valve engine NOUN a type of internal-combustion engine in which the inlet and exhaust valves are in the cylinder block at the side of the pistons. Compare **overhead-valve engine.**

sidewalk (ˈsaɪdˌwɔːk) NOUN the US and Canadian word for **pavement.**

sidewall (ˈsaɪdˌwɔːl) NOUN either of the sides of a pneumatic tyre between the tread and the rim.

sideward (ˈsaɪdwəd) ADJECTIVE 1 directed or moving towards one side. ◆ ADVERB *also* **sidewards.** 2 towards one side.

sideways (ˈsaɪdˌweɪz) ADVERB 1 moving, facing, or inclining towards one side. 2 from one side; obliquely. 3 with one side forward. ◆ ADJECTIVE (*prenominal*) 4 moving or directed to or from one side. 5 towards or from one side.

sidewheel (ˈsaɪdˌwiːl) NOUN one of the paddle wheels of a sidewheeler.

sidewheeler (ˈsaɪdˌwiːlə) NOUN a vessel, esp a river boat, propelled by two large paddle wheels, one on each side. Compare **stern-wheeler.**

side whiskers PLURAL NOUN another name for **sideburns.**

sidewinder (ˈsaɪdˌwaɪndə) NOUN 1 a North American rattlesnake, *Crotalus cerastes,* that moves forwards by a sideways looping motion. 2 *Boxing US* a heavy swinging blow from the side. 3 a US air-to-air missile using infrared homing aids in seeking its target.

sidhe (ʃiː, ˈʃiːdɪ) PLURAL NOUN **the.** the inhabitants of fairyland; fairies.
▷HISTORY C18: from Irish Gaelic *aos sídhe* people of the fairy mound; compare BANSHEE

Sidi-bel-Abbès (*French* sidibɛlabɛs) NOUN a city in NW Algeria: headquarters of the Foreign Legion until Algerian independence (1962). Pop.: 180 260 (1998).

siding (ˈsaɪdɪŋ) NOUN 1 a short stretch of railway track connected to a main line, used for storing rolling stock or to enable trains on the same line to pass. 2 a short railway line giving access to the main line for freight from a factory, mine, quarry, etc. 3 *US and Canadian* material attached to the outside of a building to make it weatherproof.

sidle (ˈsaɪdᵊl) VERB (*intr*) 1 to move in a furtive or stealthy manner; edge along. 2 to move along sideways. ◆ NOUN 3 a sideways movement.
▷HISTORY C17: back formation from obsolete *sideling* sideways
▸ˈ**sidler** NOUN

Sidon (ˈsaɪdᵊn) NOUN the chief city of ancient Phoenicia: founded in the third millennium B.C.; wealthy through trade and the making of glass and purple dyes; now the Lebanese city of Saïda.

Sidonian (saɪˈdəʊnɪən) ADJECTIVE 1 of or relating to the ancient Phoenician city of Sidon or its inhabitants. ◆ NOUN 2 a native or inhabitant of Sidon.

Sidra (ˈsɪdrə) NOUN **Gulf of.** a wide inlet of the Mediterranean on the N coast of Libya.

SIDS ABBREVIATION FOR sudden infant death syndrome. See **cot death.**

siècle *French* (sjɛklə) NOUN a century, period, or era.

siege (siːdʒ) NOUN 1 **a** the offensive operations carried out to capture a fortified place by surrounding it, severing its communications and supply lines, and deploying weapons against it. **b** (*as modifier*): *siege warfare.* 2 a persistent attempt to gain something. 3 a long tedious period, as of illness, etc. 4 *Obsolete* a seat or throne. 5 **lay siege to.** to besiege. ◆ VERB 6 (*tr*) to besiege or assail.
▷HISTORY C13: from Old French *sege* a seat, from Vulgar Latin *sēdicāre* (unattested) to sit down, from Latin *sedēre*

siege mentality NOUN a state of mind in which a person believes that he or she is being constantly oppressed or attacked.

Siegen (ˈsiːgən) NOUN a city in NW Germany, in North Rhine-Westphalia: manufacturing centre: birthplace of Rubens. Pop.: 110 847 (1999 est.).

Siege Perilous NOUN (in Arthurian legend) the seat at the Round Table that could be filled only by the knight destined to find the Holy Grail and that was fatal to anyone else.
▷HISTORY from SIEGE (in the archaic sense: a seat or throne)

Siegfried (ˈsiːgfriːd; *German* ˈziːkfriːt) NOUN *German myth* a German prince, the son of Sigmund and husband of Kriemhild, who, in the *Nibelungenlied,* assumes possession of the treasure of the Nibelungs by slaying the dragon that guards it, wins Brunhild for King Gunther, and is eventually killed by Hagen. Norse equivalent: **Sigurd.**

Siegfried line NOUN the line of fortifications built by the Germans prior to and during World War II opposite the Maginot line in France.

Sieg Heil *German* (ziːk hail) hail to victory: a Nazi salute, often accompanied by the raising of the right arm.

siemens (ˈsiːmənz) NOUN, *plural* **siemens.** the derived SI unit of electrical conductance equal to 1 reciprocal ohm. Symbol: S. Formerly called: **mho.**

Siena (sɪˈɛnə; *Italian* ˈsjeːna) NOUN a walled city in central Italy, in Tuscany: founded by the Etruscans; important artistic centre (13th–14th centuries); university (13th century). Pop.: 58 278 (1990).

sienna (sɪˈɛnə) NOUN 1 a natural earth containing ferric oxide used as a yellowish-brown pigment when untreated (**raw sienna**) or a reddish-brown pigment when roasted (**burnt sienna**). 2 the colour of this pigment. See also **burnt sienna.**
▷HISTORY C18: from Italian *terra di Siena* earth of SIENA

sierra (sɪˈɛərə) NOUN a range of mountains with jagged peaks, esp in Spain or America.
▷HISTORY C17: from Spanish, literally: saw, from Latin *serra;* see SERRATE
▸**siˈerran** ADJECTIVE

Sierra (sɪˈɛərə) NOUN *Communications* a code word for the letter *s.*

Sierra Leone (sɪˈɛərə lɪˈəʊnɪ, lɪˈəʊn) NOUN a republic in W Africa, on the Atlantic: became a British colony in 1808 and gained independence (within the Commonwealth) in 1961; declared a republic in 1971; became a one-party state in 1978; multiparty democracy restored in 1991 but military rule was imposed following a coup in 1992, which led to civil unrest; consists of coastal swamps rising to a plateau in the east. Official language: English. Religion: Muslim majority and animist. Currency: leone. Capital: Freetown. Pop.: 5 427 000 (2001 est.). Area: 71 740 sq. km (27 699 sq. miles).

Sierra Leonean (sɪˈɛərə lɪˈəʊnɪən) ADJECTIVE 1 of or relating to Sierra Leone or its inhabitants. ◆ NOUN 2 a native or inhabitant of Sierra Leone.

Sierra Madre (*Spanish* ˈsjɛrra ˈmaðre) NOUN (*functioning as singular*) the main mountain system of Mexico, extending for 2500 km (1500 miles) southeast from the N border: consists of the **Sierra Madre Oriental** in the east, the **Sierra Madre Occidental** in the west, and the **Sierra Madre del Sur** in the south. Highest peak: Citlaltépetl, 5699 m (18 698 ft.).

Sierra Morena (*Spanish* ˈsjɛrra moˈrena) NOUN (*functioning as singular*) a mountain range in SW Spain, between the Guadiana and Guadalquivir Rivers. Highest peak: Estrella, 1299 m (4262 ft.).

Sierra Nevada NOUN (*functioning as singular*) 1 (sɪˈɛərə nɪˈvɑːdə) a mountain range in E California, parallel to the Coast Ranges. Highest peak: Mount Whitney, 4418 m (14 495 ft.). 2 (*Spanish* ˈsjɛrra neˈβaða) a mountain range in SE Spain, mostly in Granada and Almería provinces. Highest peak: Cerro de Mulhacén, 3478 m (11 411 ft.).

sies (sɪs, siːs) INTERJECTION *South African informal* a variant of **sis**[2].

siesta (sɪˈɛstə) NOUN a rest or nap, usually taken in the early afternoon, as in hot countries.
▷HISTORY C17: from Spanish, from Latin *sexta hōra* the sixth hour, that is, noon

sieve (sɪv) NOUN 1 a device for separating lumps from powdered material, straining liquids, grading particles, etc., consisting of a container with a mesh or perforated bottom through which the material is shaken or poured. 2 *Rare* a person who gossips and spreads secrets. 3 **memory** *or* **head like a sieve.** a very poor memory. ◆ VERB 4 to pass or cause to pass through a sieve. 5 (*tr;* often foll by *out*) to separate or remove (lumps, materials, etc.) by use of a sieve.
▷HISTORY Old English *sife;* related to Old Norse *sef* reed with hollow stalk, Old High German *sib* sieve, Dutch *zeef*
▸ˈ**sieveˌlike** ADJECTIVE

sievert (ˈsiːvət) NOUN 1 the derived SI unit of dose equivalent, equal to 1 joule per kilogram. 1 sievert is equivalent to 100 rems. Symbol: Sv. 2 (formerly) a unit of gamma radiation dose approximately equal to 8.4×10^{-2} gray.
▷HISTORY C20: named after Rolf *Sievert* (1896–1966), Swedish physicist

sieve tube NOUN *Botany* an element of phloem tissue consisting of a longitudinal row of thin-walled elongated cells with perforations in their connecting walls through which food materials pass.

sifaka (sɪˈfɑːkə) NOUN either of two large rare arboreal lemuroid primates, *Propithecus diadema* or *P. verreauxi,* of Madagascar, having long strikingly patterned or coloured fur: family *Indriidae.*
▷HISTORY from Malagasy

sift (sɪft) VERB 1 (*tr*) to sieve (sand, flour, etc.) in order to remove the coarser particles. 2 to scatter (something) over a surface through a sieve. 3 (*tr*) to separate with or as if with a sieve; distinguish between. 4 (*tr*) to examine minutely: *to sift evidence.* 5 (*intr*) to move as if through a sieve.

▷HISTORY Old English *siftan;* related to Middle Low German *siften* to sift, Dutch *ziften;* see SIEVE
▸**'sifter** NOUN

siftings ('sɪftɪŋz) PLURAL NOUN material or particles separated out by or as if by a sieve.

sig. ABBREVIATION FOR signature.

Sig. ABBREVIATION FOR: 1 (in prescriptions) signā. [Latin: sign] 2 (in prescriptions) signature. 3 signor. 4 signore.

sigh (saɪ) VERB 1 *(intr)* to draw in and exhale audibly a deep breath as an expression of weariness, despair, relief, etc. 2 *(intr)* to make a sound resembling this: *trees sighing in the wind.* 3 *(intr; often foll by for)* to yearn, long, or pine. 4 *(tr)* to utter or express with sighing. ◆ NOUN 5 the act or sound of sighing.
▷HISTORY Old English *sīcan,* of obscure origin
▸**'sigher** NOUN

sight (saɪt) NOUN 1 the power or faculty of seeing; perception by the eyes; vision. Related adjectives: **optical, visual.** 2 the act or an instance of seeing. 3 the range of vision: *within sight of land.* 4 range of mental vision; point of view; judgment: *in his sight she could do nothing wrong.* 5 a glimpse or view (esp in the phrases **catch sight of, lose sight of**). 6 anything that is seen. 7 *(often plural)* anything worth seeing; spectacle: *the sights of London.* 8 *Informal* anything unpleasant or undesirable to see: *his room was a sight!* 9 any of various devices or instruments used to assist the eye in making alignments or directional observations, esp such a device used in aiming a gun. 10 an observation or alignment made with such a device. 11 an opportunity for observation. 12 *Obsolete* insight or skill. 13 **a sight.** *Informal* a great deal: *she's a sight too good for him.* 14 **a sight for sore eyes.** a person or thing that one is pleased or relieved to see. 15 **at** *or* **on sight. a** as soon as seen. **b** on presentation: *a bill payable at sight.* 16 **know by sight.** to be familiar with the appearance of without having personal acquaintance: *I know Mr Brown by sight but we have never spoken.* 17 **not by a long sight.** *Informal* on no account; not at all. 18 **out of sight.** *Slang* **a** extreme or very unusual. **b** *(as interj.)*: *that's marvellous!* 19 **set one's sights on.** to have (a specified goal) in mind; aim for. 20 **sight unseen.** without having seen the object at issue: *to buy a car sight unseen.* ◆ VERB 21 *(tr)* to see, view, or glimpse. 22 *(tr)* **a** to furnish with a sight or sights. **b** to adjust the sight of. 23 to aim (a firearm) using the sight.
▷HISTORY Old English *sihth;* related to Old High German *siht;* see SEE[1]
▸**'sightable** ADJECTIVE

sight bill *or* **draft** NOUN variants of **demand bill.**

sighted ('saɪtɪd) ADJECTIVE 1 not blind. 2 *(in combination)* having sight of a specified kind: *short-sighted.*

sighter ('saɪtə) NOUN *Shooting, archery* any of six practice shots allowed to each competitor in a tournament.

sightless ('saɪtlɪs) ADJECTIVE 1 blind. 2 invisible.
▸**'sightlessly** ADVERB ▸**'sightlessness** NOUN

sightline ('saɪtˌlaɪn) NOUN an uninterrupted line of vision, as in a theatre, etc., or from a vehicle joining a road.

sightly ('saɪtlɪ) ADJECTIVE **-lier, -liest.** 1 pleasing or attractive to see. 2 *US* providing a pleasant view.
▸**'sightliness** NOUN

sight-read ('saɪtˌriːd) VERB **-reads, -reading, -read** (-ˌrɛd). to sing or play (music in a printed or written form) without previous preparation.
▸**'sight-ˌreader** NOUN ▸**'sight-ˌreading** NOUN

sightscreen ('saɪtˌskriːn) NOUN *Cricket* a large white screen placed near the boundary behind the bowler to help the batsman see the ball.

sightsee ('saɪtˌsiː) VERB **-sees, -seeing, -saw, -seen.** *Informal* to visit the famous or interesting sights of (a place).
▸**'sightˌseer** NOUN

sightseeing ('saɪtˌsiːɪŋ) NOUN *Informal* **a** the activity of visiting the famous or interesting sights of a place. **b** *(as modifier)*: *sightseeing trip.*

sigil ('sɪdʒɪl) NOUN *Rare* 1 a seal or signet. 2 a sign or image supposedly having magical power.
▷HISTORY C17: from Latin *sigillum* a little sign, from *signum* a SIGN
▸**sigillary** ('sɪdʒɪlərɪ) ADJECTIVE

sigla ('sɪglə) NOUN the list of symbols used in a book, usually collected together as part of the preliminaries.
▷HISTORY Latin: plural of *siglum,* diminutive of *signum* sign

siglos ('sɪglɒs) NOUN, *plural* **-loi** (-lɔɪ). a silver coin of ancient Persia worth one twentieth of a daric.

sigma ('sɪgmə) NOUN 1 the 18th letter in the Greek alphabet (Σ, σ or, when final, ς), a consonant, transliterated as *S.* 2 *Maths* the symbol Σ, indicating summation of the numbers or quantities indicated.
▷HISTORY Greek, of Semitic origin; related to Hebrew SAMEKH

sigmate ('sɪgmɪt, -meɪt) ADJECTIVE shaped like the Greek letter sigma or the Roman *S.*
▸**sigmation** (sɪg'meɪʃən) NOUN

sigmoid ('sɪgmɔɪd) ADJECTIVE *also* **sigmoidal.** 1 shaped like the letter S. 2 of or relating to the sigmoid colon of the large intestine. ◆ NOUN 3 See **sigmoid colon.**
▷HISTORY C17: from Greek *sigmoeidēs* sigma-shaped

sigmoid colon NOUN the S-shaped bend in the final portion of the large intestine that leads to the rectum. Also called: **sigmoid flexure.**

sigmoid flexure NOUN 1 *Zoology* an S-shaped curve, as in the necks of certain birds. 2 another name for **sigmoid colon.**

sigmoidoscope (sɪg'mɔɪdəˌskəʊp) NOUN an instrument incorporating a light for the direct observation of the colon, rectum, and sigmoid flexure.
▸**sigmoidoscopic** (sɪgˌmɔɪdə'skɒpɪk) ADJECTIVE
▸**sigmoidoscopy** (ˌsɪgmɔɪd'ɒskəpɪ) NOUN

Sigmund ('sɪgmənd, 'siːgmʊnd; *German* 'ziːkmʊnt) NOUN 1 *Norse myth* the father of the hero Sigurd. 2 Also called: **Siegmund** (*German* 'ziːkmʊnt). *German myth* king of the Netherlands, father of Siegfried.

sign (saɪn) NOUN 1 something that indicates or acts as a token of a fact, condition, etc., that is not immediately or outwardly observable. 2 an action or gesture intended to convey information, a command, etc. 3 **a** a board, placard, etc., displayed in public and inscribed with words or designs intended to inform, warn, etc. **b** *(as modifier)*: *a sign painter.* 4 an arbitrary or conventional mark or device that stands for a word, phrase, etc. 5 *Maths, logic* **a** any symbol indicating an operation: *a plus sign; an implication sign.* **b** the positivity or negativity of a number, quantity, or expression: *subtraction from zero changes the sign of an expression.* 6 an indication or vestige: *the house showed no signs of being occupied.* 7 a portentous or significant event. 8 an indication, such as a scent or spoor, of the presence of an animal. 9 *Med* any objective evidence of the presence of a disease or disorder. Compare **symptom** (sense 1). 10 *Astrology* See **sign of the zodiac.** ◆ VERB 11 to write (one's name) as a signature to (a document, etc.) in attestation, confirmation, ratification, etc. 12 *(intr; often foll by to)* to make a sign; signal. 13 to engage or be engaged by written agreement, as a player for a team, etc. 14 *(tr)* to outline in gestures a sign over, esp the sign of the cross. 15 *(tr)* to indicate by or as if by a sign; betoken. 16 *(intr)* to use sign language. ◆ See also **sign away, sign in, sign off, sign on, sign out, sign up.**
▷HISTORY C13: from Old French *signe,* from Latin *signum* a sign
▸**'signable** ADJECTIVE

signage ('saɪnɪdʒ) NOUN signs collectively, esp street signs or signs giving directions.

signal ('sɪgnᵊl) NOUN 1 any sign, gesture, token, etc., that serves to communicate information. 2 anything that acts as an incitement to action: *the rise in prices was a signal for rebellion.* 3 **a** a variable parameter, such as a current or electromagnetic wave, by which information is conveyed through an electronic circuit, communications system, etc. **b** the information so conveyed. **c** *(as modifier)*: *signal strength; a signal generator.* ◆ ADJECTIVE 4 distinguished or conspicuous. 5 used to give or act as a signal. ◆ VERB **-nals, -nalling, -nalled** *or US* **-nals, -naling, -naled.** 6 to communicate (a message, etc.) to (a person).
▷HISTORY C16: from Old French *seignal,* from Medieval Latin *signāle,* from Latin *signum* SIGN
▸**'signaller** *or US* **'signaler** NOUN

signal box NOUN 1 a building containing manually operated signal levers for all the railway lines in its section. 2 a control point for a large area of a railway system, operated electrically and semiautomatically.

signal generator NOUN *Electrical engineering* an apparatus used to generate a signal consisting of a known oscillating voltage, usually between 1 microvolt and 1 volt, over a range of frequencies, to test electronic equipment.

signalize *or* **signalise** ('sɪgnəˌlaɪz) VERB *(tr)* 1 to make noteworthy or conspicuous. 2 to point out carefully.

signally ('sɪgnəlɪ) ADVERB conspicuously or especially.

signalman ('sɪgnᵊlmən) NOUN, *plural* **-men.** 1 a railway employee in charge of the signals and points within a section. 2 a man who sends and receives signals, esp in the navy.

signalment ('sɪgnᵊlmənt) NOUN *US* a detailed description of a person, for identification or use in police records.
▷HISTORY from French *signalement,* from *signaler* to distinguish

signal-to-noise ratio NOUN the ratio of one parameter, such as power of a wanted signal to the same parameter of the noise at a specified point in an electronic circuit, etc.

signatory ('sɪgnətərɪ, -trɪ) NOUN, *plural* **-ries.** 1 a person who has signed a document such as a treaty or contract or an organization, state, etc., on whose behalf such a document has been signed. ◆ ADJECTIVE 2 having signed a document, treaty, etc.
▷HISTORY C17: from Latin *signātōrius* concerning sealing, from *signāre* to seal, from *signum* a mark

signature ('sɪgnɪtʃə) NOUN 1 the name of a person or a mark or sign representing his name, marked by himself or by an authorized deputy. 2 the act of signing one's name. 3 **a** a distinctive mark, characteristic, etc., that identifies a person or thing. **b** *(as modifier)*: *a signature fragrance.* 4 *Music* See **key signature, time signature.** 5 *US* the part of a medical prescription that instructs a patient how frequently and in what amounts he should take a drug or agent. Abbreviations: **Sig, S.** 6 *Printing* **a** a sheet of paper printed with several pages that upon folding will become a section or sections of a book. **b** such a sheet so folded. **c** a mark, esp a letter, printed on the first page of a signature.
▷HISTORY C16: from Old French, from Medieval Latin *signātura,* from Latin *signāre* to sign

signature tune NOUN *Brit* a melody used to introduce or identify a television or radio programme, a dance band, a performer, etc. Also called (esp US and Canadian): **theme song.**

sign away VERB *(tr, adverb)* to dispose of or lose by or as if by signing a document: *he signed away all his rights.*

signboard ('saɪnˌbɔːd) NOUN a board carrying a sign or notice, esp one used to advertise a product, event, etc.

signed minor NOUN *Maths* another name for **cofactor.**

signed-ranks test NOUN *Statistics* See **Wilcoxon test.**

signer ('saɪnə) NOUN 1 a person who signs something. 2 a person who uses sign language to communicate with deaf people.

signet ('sɪgnɪt) NOUN 1 a small seal, esp one as part of a finger ring. 2 a seal used to stamp or authenticate documents. 3 the impression made by such a seal. ◆ VERB 4 *(tr)* to stamp or authenticate with a signet.
▷HISTORY C14: from Medieval Latin *signētum* a little seal, from Latin *signum* a SIGN

signet ring NOUN a finger ring bearing a signet.

significance (sɪg'nɪfɪkəns) NOUN 1 consequence or importance. 2 something signified, expressed, or intended. 3 the state or quality of being significant. 4 *Statistics* **a** a measure of the confidence that can be placed in a result, esp a substantive causal hypothesis, as not being merely a matter of chance. **b** *(as modifier)*: *a significance level.* Compare **confidence level.** See also **hypothesis testing.**

significance test NOUN *Statistics* (in hypothesis testing) a test of whether the alternative hypothesis achieves the predetermined significance level in order to be accepted in preference to the null hypothesis.

significant (sɪɡˈnɪfɪkənt) ADJECTIVE 1 having or expressing a meaning; indicative. 2 having a covert or implied meaning; suggestive. 3 important, notable, or momentous. 4 *Statistics* of or relating to a difference between a result derived from a hypothesis and its observed value that is too large to be attributed to chance and that therefore tends to refute the hypothesis.
▷HISTORY C16: from Latin *significāre* to SIGNIFY
▸**sigˈnificantly** ADVERB

significant figures *or esp US* **significant digits** PLURAL NOUN 1 the figures of a number that express a magnitude to a specified degree of accuracy, rounding up or down the final figure: *3.141 59 to four significant figures is 3.142.* 2 the number of such figures: *3.142 has four significant figures.* Compare **decimal place** (sense 2).

significant other NOUN *US informal* a spouse or lover.

signification (ˌsɪɡnɪfɪˈkeɪʃən) NOUN 1 something that is signified; meaning or sense. 2 the act of signifying.

significative (sɪɡˈnɪfɪkətɪv) ADJECTIVE 1 (of a sign, mark, etc.) symbolic. 2 another word for **significant.**
▸**sigˈnificatively** ADVERB ▸**sigˈnificativeness** NOUN

signify (ˈsɪɡnɪˌfaɪ) VERB **-fies, -fying, -fied.** (when *tr, may take a clause as object*) 1 (*tr*) to indicate, show, or suggest. 2 (*tr*) to imply or portend: *the clouds signified the coming storm.* 3 (*tr*) to stand as a symbol, sign, etc. (for). 4 (*intr*) *Informal* to be significant or important.
▷HISTORY C13: from Old French *signifier,* from Latin *significāre,* from *signum* a sign, mark + *facere* to make
▸**ˈsigniˌfiable** ADJECTIVE ▸**ˈsigniˌfier** NOUN

sign in VERB (*adverb*) 1 to sign or cause to sign a register, as at a hotel, club, etc. 2 to make or become a member, as of a club.

signing (ˈsaɪnɪŋ) NOUN a specific set of manual signs used to communicate with deaf people.

sign language NOUN 1 another word for **signing.** 2 any system of communication by manual signs or gestures.

sign manual NOUN *Law* a person's signature in his own hand, esp that of a sovereign on an official document.

sign off VERB (*adverb*) 1 (*intr*) to announce the end of a radio or television programme, esp at the end of a day. 2 (*intr*) *Bridge* to make a conventional bid indicating to one's partner that one wishes the bidding to stop. 3 (*tr*) to withdraw or retire from (an activity). 4 (*tr*) (of a doctor) to declare (someone) unfit for work, because of illness. 5 (*intr*) *Brit* to terminate one's claim to unemployment benefit.

sign of the cross NOUN *Chiefly RC Church* a gesture in which the right hand is moved from the forehead to the breast and from the left shoulder to the right to describe the form of a cross in order to invoke the grace of Christ.

sign of the zodiac NOUN any of the 12 equal areas, 30° wide, into which the zodiac can be divided, named after the 12 zodiacal constellations. In astrology, it is thought that a person's psychological type and attitudes to life can be correlated with the sign in which the sun lay at the moment of his birth, with the ascendant sign, and to a lesser extent with the signs in which other planets lay at this time. Also called: **sign, star sign, sun sign.** See also **planet** (sense 3), **house** (sense 9).

sign on VERB (*adverb*) 1 (*tr*) to hire or employ. 2 (*intr*) to commit oneself to a job, activity, etc. 3 (*intr*) *Brit* to register as unemployed with the Department of Social Security.

signor *or* **signior** (ˈsiːnjɔː; *Italian* siɲˈɲor) NOUN, *plural* **-gnors** *or* **-gnori** (*Italian* -ˈɲori). an Italian man: usually used before a name as a title equivalent to *Mr.*

signora (siːnˈjɔːrə; *Italian* siɲˈɲora) NOUN, *plural* **-ras** *or* **-re** (*Italian* -re). a married Italian woman: a title of address equivalent to *Mrs* when placed before a name or *madam* when used alone.
▷HISTORY Italian, feminine of SIGNORE

signore (siːnˈjɔːriː; *Italian* siɲˈɲore) NOUN, *plural* **-ri** (-rɪ; *Italian* -ri). an Italian man: a title of respect equivalent to *sir.*
▷HISTORY Italian, ultimately from Latin *senior* an elder, from *senex* an old man

signorina (ˌsiːnjɔːˈriːnə; *Italian* siɲɲoˈrina) NOUN, *plural* **-nas** *or* **-ne** (*Italian* -ne). an unmarried Italian woman: a title of address equivalent to *Miss* when placed before a name or *madam* or *miss* when used alone.
▷HISTORY Italian, diminutive of SIGNORA

signory (ˈsiːnjərɪ) NOUN, *plural* **-gnories.** a variant spelling of **seigniory.**

sign out VERB (*adverb*) to sign (one's name) to indicate that one is leaving a place: *he signed out for the evening.*

signpost (ˈsaɪnˌpəʊst) NOUN 1 a post bearing a sign that shows the way, as at a roadside. 2 something that serves as a clue or indication; sign. ◆ VERB (*tr; usually passive*) 3 to mark with signposts. 4 to indicate direction towards: *the camp site is signposted from the road.*

sign test NOUN a statistical test used to analyse the direction of differences of scores between the same or matched pairs of subjects under two experimental conditions.

sign up VERB (*adverb*) to enlist or cause to enlist, as for military service.

Sigurd (ˈsɪɡʊəd; *German* ˈziːɡurt) NOUN *Norse myth* a hero who killed the dragon Fafnir to gain the treasure of Andvari, won Brynhild for Gunnar by deception, and then was killed by her when she discovered the fraud. His wife was Gudrun. German counterpart: **Siegfried.**

sik (sɪk) ADJECTIVE *Austral slang* excellent.

sika (ˈsiːkə) NOUN a Japanese forest-dwelling deer, *Cervus nippon,* having a brown coat, spotted with white in summer, and a large white patch on the rump.
▷HISTORY from Japanese *shika*

Sikang (ˈʃiːˈkæŋ) NOUN a former province of W China: established in 1928 from part of W Sichuan and E Tibet; dissolved in 1955.

Sikh (siːk) NOUN 1 a member of an Indian religion that separated from Hinduism and was founded in the 16th century, that teaches monotheism and that has the Granth as its chief religious document, rejecting the authority of the Vedas. ◆ ADJECTIVE 2 of or relating to the Sikhs or their religious beliefs and customs.
▷HISTORY C18: from Hindi, literally: disciple, from Sanskrit *śiksati* he studies
▸**ˈSikhˌism** NOUN

Si Kiang (ˈʃiː ˈkjæŋ, kaɪˈæŋ) NOUN See **Xi.**

Siking (ˈsiːˈkɪŋ) NOUN a former name for **Xi An.**

Sikkim (ˈsɪkɪm) NOUN a state of NE India: under British control (1861–1947); became an Indian protectorate in 1950 and an Indian state in 1975; lies in the Himalayas, rising to 8600 m (28 216 ft.) at Kanchenjunga in the north. Capital: Gangtok. Pop.: 540 493 (2001). Area: 7096 sq. km (2740 sq. miles).

Sikkimese (ˌsɪkɪˈmiːz) ADJECTIVE 1 of or relating to Sikkim or its inhabitants. ◆ NOUN 2 a native or inhabitant of Sikkim.

silage (ˈsaɪlɪdʒ) NOUN any crop harvested while green for fodder and kept succulent by partial fermentation in a silo. Also called: **ensilage.**
▷HISTORY C19: alteration (influenced by SILO) of ENSILAGE

Silastic (sɪˈlæstɪk) NOUN *Trademark* a flexible inert silicone rubber, used esp in prosthetic medicine.

sild (sɪld) NOUN any of various small young herrings, esp when prepared and canned in Norway.
▷HISTORY Norwegian

sile (saɪl) VERB (*tr*) *Northern English dialect* to pour with rain.
▷HISTORY probably from Old Norse; compare Swedish and Norwegian dialect *sila* to pass through a strainer

silence (ˈsaɪləns) NOUN 1 the state or quality of being silent. 2 the absence of sound or noise; stillness. 3 refusal or failure to speak, communicate, etc., when expected: *his silence on the subject of their promotion was alarming.* 4 a period of time without noise. 5 oblivion or obscurity. ◆ VERB (*tr*) 6 to bring to silence. 7 to put a stop to; extinguish: *to silence all complaint.*
▷HISTORY C13: via Old French from Latin *silentium,* from *silēre* to be quiet. See SILENT

silenced (ˈsaɪlənst) ADJECTIVE (of a clergyman) forbidden to preach or perform his clerical functions: *a silenced priest.*

silencer (ˈsaɪlənsə) NOUN 1 any device designed to reduce noise, esp the tubular device containing baffle plates in the exhaust system of a motor vehicle. US and Canadian name: **muffler.** 2 a tubular device fitted to the muzzle of a firearm to deaden the report. 3 a person or thing that silences.

silene (saɪˈliːnɪ) NOUN any plant of the large perennial genus *Silene,* with mostly red or pink flowers; many, esp *S.* or *Agrostemma coeli-rosa,* are grown as garden plants: family *Carophyllaceae.* See also **campion.**
▷HISTORY New Latin from Latin *silenus* viscaria

silent (ˈsaɪlənt) ADJECTIVE 1 characterized by an absence or near absence of noise or sound: *a silent house.* 2 tending to speak very little or not at all. 3 unable to speak. 4 failing to speak, communicate, etc., when expected: *the witness chose to remain silent.* 5 not spoken or expressed: *silent assent.* 6 not active or in operation: *a silent volcano.* 7 (of a letter) used in the conventional orthography of a word but no longer pronounced in that word: *the "k" in "know" is silent.* 8 denoting a film that has no accompanying soundtrack, esp one made before 1927, when such soundtracks were developed. ◆ NOUN 9 a silent film.
▷HISTORY C16: from Latin *silēns,* from *silēre* to be quiet
▸**ˈsilently** ADVERB ▸**ˈsilentness** NOUN

silent cop NOUN *Austral informal* a small hemispherical traffic marker at an intersection.

silent majority NOUN a presumed moderate majority of the citizens who are too passive to make their views known.

silent partner NOUN another name (esp US and Canadian) for **sleeping partner.**

Silenus (saɪˈliːnəs) NOUN *Greek myth* 1 chief of the satyrs and foster father to Dionysus: often depicted riding drunkenly on a donkey. 2 (*often not capital*) one of a class of woodland deities, closely similar to the satyrs.

silesia (saɪˈliːʃɪə) NOUN a twill-weave fabric of cotton or other fibre, used esp for pockets, linings, etc.
▷HISTORY C17: Latinized form of German *Schlesien* SILESIA

Silesia (saɪˈliːʃɪə) NOUN a region of central Europe around the upper and middle Oder valley: mostly annexed by Prussia in 1742 but became almost wholly Polish in 1945; rich coal and iron-ore deposits. Polish name: **Śląsk.** Czech name: **Slezsko.** German name: **Schlesien.**

Silesian (saɪˈliːʃɪən) ADJECTIVE 1 of or relating to Silesia or its inhabitants. ◆ NOUN 2 a native or inhabitant of Silesia.

silex (ˈsaɪlɛks) NOUN a type of heat-resistant glass made from fused quartz.
▷HISTORY C16: from Latin: hard stone, flint

silhouette (ˌsɪluːˈɛt) NOUN 1 the outline of a solid figure as cast by its shadow. 2 an outline drawing filled in with black, often a profile portrait cut out of black paper and mounted on a light ground. ◆ VERB 3 (*tr*) to cause to appear in silhouette.
▷HISTORY C18: named after Étienne de *Silhouette* (1709–67), French politician, perhaps referring to silhouettes as partial portraits, with a satirical allusion to Silhouette's brief career as controller general (1759)

silica (ˈsɪlɪkə) NOUN 1 the dioxide of silicon, occurring naturally as quartz, cristobalite, and tridymite. It is a refractory insoluble material used in the manufacture of glass, ceramics, and abrasives. 2 short for **silica glass.**
▷HISTORY C19: New Latin, from Latin: SILEX

silica gel NOUN an amorphous form of silica capable of absorbing large quantities of water: used in drying gases and oils, as a carrier for catalysts and an anticaking agent for cosmetics.

silica glass NOUN another name for **quartz glass.**

silicate (ˈsɪlɪkɪt, -ˌkeɪt) NOUN a salt or ester of silicic acid, esp one of a large number of usually insoluble salts with polymeric negative ions having a structure formed of tetrahedrons of SiO_4 groups linked in rings, chains, sheets, or three dimensional frameworks. Silicates constitute a large proportion of the earth's minerals and are present in cement and glass.

siliceous *or* **silicious** (sɪˈlɪʃəs) ADJECTIVE 1 of, relating to, or containing abundant silica: *siliceous deposits; a siliceous clay.* 2 (of plants) growing in or needing soil rich in silica.

silici- *or before a vowel* **silic-** COMBINING FORM indicating silica or silicon: *silicify.*

silicic (sɪˈlɪsɪk) ADJECTIVE of, concerned with, or containing silicon or an acid obtained from silicon.

silicic acid NOUN a white gelatinous substance obtained by adding an acid to a solution of sodium silicate. It has an ill-defined composition and is best regarded as hydrated silica, $SiO_2.nH_2O$.

silicide (ˈsɪlɪˌsaɪd) NOUN any one of a class of binary compounds formed between silicon and certain metals.

siliciferous (ˌsɪlɪˈsɪfərəs) ADJECTIVE containing or yielding silicon or silica.

silicify (sɪˈlɪsɪˌfaɪ) VERB **-fies, -fying, -fied.** to convert or be converted into silica: *silicified wood.*
▸**siˌlicifiˈcation** NOUN

silicium (sɪˈlɪsɪəm) NOUN a rare name for **silicon.**

silicle (ˈsɪlɪkᵊl) NOUN a variant of **silicula.**

silicon (ˈsɪlɪkən) NOUN **a** a brittle metalloid element that exists in two allotropic forms; occurs principally in sand, quartz, granite, feldspar, and clay. It is usually a grey crystalline solid but is also found as a brown amorphous powder. It is used in transistors, rectifiers, solar cells, and alloys. Its compounds are widely used in glass manufacture, the building industry, and in the form of silicones. Symbol: Si; atomic no.: 14; atomic wt.: 28.0855; valency: 4; relative density: 2.33; melting pt.: 1414°C; boiling pt.: 3267°C. **b** (*modifier; sometimes capital*) denoting an area of a country that contains a density of high-technology industry.
▹HISTORY C19: from SILICA, on the model of *boron, carbon*

Silicon Alley NOUN an area of New York City in which industries associated with information technology are concentrated.

silicon carbide NOUN an extremely hard bluish-black insoluble crystalline substance produced by heating carbon with sand at a high temperature and used as an abrasive and refractory material. Silicon carbide whiskers have a high tensile strength and are used in composites; very pure crystals are used as semiconductors. Formula: SiC.

silicon chip NOUN another term for **chip** (sense 8).

silicon-controlled rectifier NOUN a semiconductor rectifier whose forward current between two electrodes, the anode and cathode, is initiated by means of a signal applied to a third electrode, the gate. The current subsequently becomes independent of the signal. It is a type of thyristor. Abbreviation: **SCR.**

silicone (ˈsɪlɪˌkəʊn) NOUN *Chem* **a** any of a large class of polymeric synthetic materials that usually have resistance to temperature, water, and chemicals, and good insulating and lubricating properties, making them suitable for wide use as oils, water-repellents, resins, etc. Chemically they have alternate silicon and oxygen atoms with the silicon atoms bound to organic groups. **b** (*as modifier*): *silicone rubber.* ◆ See also **siloxane.**

Silicon Fen NOUN an area of Cambridgeshire, esp around the city of Cambridge, in which industries associated with information technology are concentrated.

Silicon Glen NOUN a collective term for the industries in Scotland associated with information technology, esp those concentrated in the central conurbation between Glasgow and Edinburgh.

silicon rectifier NOUN *Electronics* a rectifier consisting of a semiconductor diode using crystalline silicon.

Silicon Valley NOUN 1 an industrial strip in W California, extending S of San Francisco, in which the US information technology industry is concentrated. 2 any area in which industries associated with information technology are concentrated.

silicosis (ˌsɪlɪˈkəʊsɪs) NOUN *Pathol* a form of pneumoconiosis caused by breathing in tiny particles of silica, quartz, or slate, and characterized by shortness of breath and fibrotic changes in the tissues of the lungs.

silicula, silicle (ˈsɪlɪkᵊl) *or* **silicule** NOUN, *plural* **-liculae** (-ˈlɪkjuliː), **silicles, -cules.** *Botany* a short broad siliqua, occurring in such cruciferous plants as honesty and shepherd's-purse.
▹HISTORY C18: from Latin *silicula* a small pod; see SILIQUA

siliculose (sɪˈlɪkjuˌləʊs, -ˌləʊz) ADJECTIVE (of certain cruciferous plants such as honesty) producing siliculae.
▹HISTORY C18: from New Latin *siliculōsus,* from *silicula* a SILICLE

siliqua (sɪˈliːkwə, ˈsɪlɪkwə) *or* **silique** (sɪˈliːk, ˈsɪlɪk) NOUN, *plural* **-liquae** (-ˈliːkwiː), **-liquas** *or* **-liques.** the long dry dehiscent fruit of cruciferous plants, such as the wallflower, consisting of two compartments separated by a central septum to which the seeds are attached.
▹HISTORY C18: via French from Latin *siliqua* a pod
▸**siliquaceous** (ˌsɪlɪˈkweɪʃəs) ADJECTIVE ▸**siliquose** (ˈsɪlɪˌkwəʊs) *or* **siliquous** (ˈsɪlɪkwəs) ADJECTIVE

silk (sɪlk) NOUN 1 the very fine soft lustrous fibre produced by a silkworm to make its cocoon. 2 **a** thread or fabric made from this fibre. **b** (*as modifier*): *a silk dress.* 3 a garment made of this. 4 a very fine fibre produced by a spider to build its web, nest, or cocoon. 5 the tuft of long fine styles on an ear of maize. 6 *Brit* **a** the gown worn by a Queen's (or King's) Counsel. **b** *Informal* a Queen's (or King's) Counsel. **c take silk.** to become a Queen's (or King's) Counsel. ◆ VERB 7 (*intr*) *US and Canadian* (of maize) to develop long hairlike styles.
▹HISTORY Old English *sioluc;* compare Old Norse *silki,* Greek *sērikon,* Korean *sir;* all ultimately from Chinese *ssŭ* silk
▸**ˈsilkˌlike** ADJECTIVE

silkaline *or* **silkalene** (ˌsɪlkəˈliːn) NOUN a fine smooth cotton fabric used for linings, etc.
▹HISTORY C20: from SILK + *-aline,* from *-oline* as in CRINOLINE

silk cotton NOUN another name for **kapok.**

silk-cotton tree NOUN any of several tropical bombacaceous trees of the genus *Ceiba,* esp *Ceiba pentandra,* having seeds covered with silky hairs from which kapok is obtained. Also called: **kapok tree.**

silken (ˈsɪlkən) ADJECTIVE 1 made of silk. 2 resembling silk in smoothness or gloss. 3 dressed in silk. 4 soft and delicate. 5 *Rare* luxurious or elegant.

silk hat NOUN a man's top hat covered with silk.

silkie (ˈsɪlkɪ) *or* **selkie** NOUN a Scot word for a **seal** (the animal).
▹HISTORY from earlier Scot *selich,* Old English *seolh*

silk-screen printing NOUN another name for **screen process.**

silkweed (ˈsɪlkˌwiːd) NOUN another name for **milkweed** (sense 1).
▹HISTORY C19: so called because the pods contain a silklike down

silkworm (ˈsɪlkˌwɜːm) NOUN 1 the larva of the Chinese moth *Bombyx mori,* that feeds on the leaves of the mulberry tree: widely cultivated as a source of silk. 2 any of various similar or related larvae. 3 **silkworm moth.** the moth of any of these larvae.

silky (ˈsɪlkɪ) ADJECTIVE **silkier, silkiest.** 1 resembling silk in texture; glossy. 2 made of silk. 3 (of a voice, manner, etc.) suave; smooth. 4 *Botany* covered with long fine soft hairs: *silky leaves.*
▸**ˈsilkily** ADVERB ▸**ˈsilkiness** NOUN

silky oak NOUN any of several trees of the Australian genus *Grevillea,* esp *G. robusta,* having divided leaves, smooth glossy wood, and showy clusters of orange, red, or white flowers: cultivated in the tropics as shade trees: family *Proteaceae.*

silky terrier NOUN another name for a **Sydney silky.**

sill (sɪl) NOUN 1 a shelf at the bottom of a window inside a room. 2 a horizontal piece along the outside lower member of a window, that throws water clear of the wall below. 3 the lower horizontal member of a window or door frame. 4 a continuous horizontal member placed on top of a foundation wall in order to carry a timber framework. 5 a flat usually horizontal mass of igneous rock, situated between two layers of older sedimentary rock, that was formed by an intrusion of magma.
▹HISTORY Old English *syll;* related to Old Norse *svill* sill, Icelandic *svoli* tree trunk, Old High German *swella* sill, Latin *solum* ground

sillabub (ˈsɪləˌbʌb) NOUN a variant spelling of **syllabub.**

siller (ˈsɪlər) *Scot* ◆ NOUN 1 silver. 2 money. ◆ ADJECTIVE 3 silver.
▹HISTORY a Scot variant of SILVER

sillimanite (ˈsɪlɪməˌnaɪt) NOUN a white, brown, or green fibrous mineral that consists of aluminium silicate in orthorhombic crystalline form and occurs in metamorphic rocks. Formula: Al_2SiO_5.
▹HISTORY C19: named after Benjamin *Silliman* (1779–1864), US chemist

silly (ˈsɪlɪ) ADJECTIVE **-lier, -liest.** 1 lacking in good sense; absurd. 2 frivolous, trivial, or superficial. 3 feeble-minded. 4 dazed, as from a blow. 5 *Obsolete* homely or humble. ◆ NOUN 6 (*modifier*) *Cricket* (of a fielding position) near the batsman's wicket: *silly mid-on.* 7 (*plural* **-lies**) Also called: **silly-billy.** *Informal* a foolish person.
▹HISTORY C15 (in the sense: pitiable, hence the later senses: foolish): from Old English *sǣlig* (unattested) happy, from *sǣl* happiness; related to Gothic *sēls* good
▸**ˈsilliness** NOUN

silly season NOUN *Brit* a period, usually during the hot summer months, when journalists fill space reporting on frivolous events and activities.

silo (ˈsaɪləʊ) NOUN, *plural* **-los.** 1 a pit, trench, horizontal container, or tower, often cylindrical in shape, in which silage is made and stored. 2 a strengthened underground position in which missile systems are sited for protection against attack.
▹HISTORY C19: from Spanish, perhaps from Celtic

Siloam (saɪˈləʊəm, sɪ-) NOUN *Bible* a pool in Jerusalem where Jesus cured a man of his blindness (John 9).

siloxane (sɪˈlɒkseɪn) NOUN any of a class of compounds containing alternate silicon and oxygen atoms with the silicon atoms bound to hydrogen atoms or organic groups. Many are highly complex polymers. See also **silicone.**
▹HISTORY C20: from SIL(ICON) + OX(YGEN) + (METH)ANE

silt (sɪlt) NOUN 1 a fine deposit of mud, clay, etc., esp one in a river or lake. ◆ VERB 2 (usually foll by *up*) to fill or become filled with silt; choke.
▹HISTORY C15: of Scandinavian origin; compare Norwegian, Danish *sylt* salt marsh; related to Old High German *sulza* salt marsh; see SALT
▸**silˈtation** NOUN ▸**ˈsilty** ADJECTIVE

siltstone (ˈsɪltˌstəʊn) NOUN a variety of fine sandstone formed from consolidated silt.

Silures (saɪˈlʊəriːz) PLURAL NOUN a powerful and warlike tribe of ancient Britain, living chiefly in SE Wales, who fiercely resisted Roman invaders in the 1st century A.D.

Silurian (saɪˈlʊərɪən) ADJECTIVE 1 of, denoting, or formed in the third period of the Palaeozoic era, between the Ordovician and Devonian periods, which lasted for 25 million years, during which fishes first appeared. 2 of or relating to the Silures. ◆ NOUN 3 **the.** the Silurian period or rock system.

silurid (saɪˈlʊərɪd) NOUN 1 any freshwater teleost fish of the Eurasian family *Siluridae,* including catfish, such as *Silurus glanis* (**European catfish**), that have an elongated body, naked skin, and a long anal fin. ◆ ADJECTIVE 2 of, relating to, or belonging to the family *Siluridae.*
▹HISTORY C19: from Latin *silūrus,* from Greek *silouros* a river fish

silva (ˈsɪlvə) NOUN a variant spelling of **sylva.**

silvan (ˈsɪlvən) ADJECTIVE a variant spelling of **sylvan.**

Silvanus *or* **Sylvanus** (sɪlˈveɪnəs) NOUN *Roman myth* the Roman god of woodlands, fields, and flocks. Greek counterpart: **Pan.**

▷HISTORY Latin: from *silva* woodland

silver ('sɪlvə) NOUN 1 **a** a very ductile malleable brilliant greyish-white element having the highest electrical and thermal conductivity of any metal. It occurs free and in argentite and other ores: used in jewellery, tableware, coinage, electrical contacts, and in electroplating. Its compounds are used in photography. Symbol: Ag; atomic no.: 47; atomic wt.: 107.8682; valency: 1 or 2; relative density: 10.50; melting pt.: 961.93°C; boiling pt.: 2163°C. **b** (*as modifier*): *a silver coin.* Related adjective: **argent.** 2 coin made of, or having the appearance of, this metal. 3 cutlery, whether made of silver or not. 4 any household articles made of silver. 5 *Photog* any of a number of silver compounds used either as photosensitive substances in emulsions or as sensitizers. 6 **a** a brilliant or light greyish-white colour. **b** (*as adjective*): *silver hair.* 7 short for **silver medal.** ◆ ADJECTIVE 8 well-articulated: *silver speech.* 9 (*prenominal*) denoting the 25th in a series, esp an annual series: *a silver wedding anniversary.* ◆ VERB 10 (*tr*) to coat with silver or a silvery substance: *to silver a spoon.* 11 to become or cause to become silvery in colour.

▷HISTORY Old English *siolfor; related to Old Norse silfr,* Gothic *silubr,* Old High German *silabar,* Old Slavonic *sirebro*

▸'**silverer** NOUN ▸'**silvering** NOUN

silver age NOUN 1 (in Greek and Roman mythology) the second of the world's major epochs, inferior to the preceding golden age and characterized by opulence and irreligion. 2 the postclassical period of Latin literature, occupying the early part of the Roman imperial era, characterized by an overindulgence in elegance for its own sake and empty scholarly rhetoric.

silverback ('sɪlvə,bæk) NOUN an older male gorilla with grey hair on its back.

silver beet NOUN a variety of beet, *Beta vulgaris cicla,* having large firm green leaves: staple cooked green vegetable in Australia and New Zealand.

silver bell NOUN any of various deciduous trees of the styracaceous genus *Halesia,* esp *H. carolina,* of North America and China, having white bell-shaped flowers. Also called: **snowdrop tree.**

silver belly NOUN *NZ* a freshwater eel.

silver birch NOUN a betulaceous tree, *Betula pendula,* of N temperate regions of the Old World, having silvery-white peeling bark. See also **birch** (sense 1).

silver bromide NOUN a yellowish insoluble powder that darkens when exposed to light: used in making photographic emulsions. Formula: AgBr.

silver certificate NOUN (formerly) a banknote issued by the US Treasury to the public and redeemable in silver.

silver chloride NOUN a white insoluble powder that darkens on exposure to light because of the production of metallic silver: used in making photographic emulsions and papers. Formula: AgCl.

silver disc NOUN (in Britain) an album certified to have sold 60 000 copies or a single certified to have sold 200 000 copies. Compare **gold disc, platinum disc.**

silver-eye NOUN *Austral and NZ* another name for **white-eye.**

silver fern NOUN *NZ* 1 another name for **ponga.** 2 a formalized spray of fern leaf, silver on a black background: the symbol of New Zealand sporting teams, esp the All Blacks.

Silver Ferns PLURAL NOUN **the.** the women's international netball team of New Zealand.

silver fir NOUN any of various fir trees the leaves of which have a silvery undersurface, esp *Abies alba,* an important timber tree of central and S Europe.

silverfish ('sɪlvə,fɪʃ) NOUN, *plural* **-fish** *or* **-fishes.** 1 a silver variety of the goldfish *Carassius auratus.* 2 any of various other silvery fishes, such as the moonfish *Monodactylus argenteus.* 3 any of various small primitive wingless insects of the genus *Lepisma,* esp *L. saccharina,* that have long antennae and tail appendages and occur in buildings, feeding on food scraps, bookbindings, etc.: order *Thysanura* (bristletails).

silver fox NOUN 1 an American red fox in a colour phase in which the fur is black with long silver-tipped hairs. 2 the valuable fur or pelt of this animal.

silver frost NOUN another name for **glaze ice.**

silver-gilt NOUN silver covered with a thin film of gold.

silverhorn ('sɪlvə,hɔːn) NOUN any of various usually darkish caddis flies of the family *Leptoceridae,* characterized by very long pale antennae. The larvae are a favourite food of trout.

silver iodide NOUN a yellow insoluble powder that darkens on exposure to light: used in photography and artificial rainmaking. Formula: AgI.

silver lining NOUN a comforting or hopeful aspect of an otherwise desperate or unhappy situation (esp in the phrase **every cloud has a silver lining**).

silver maple NOUN a North American maple tree, *Acer saccharinum,* having five-lobed leaves that are green above and silvery-white beneath.

silver medal NOUN a medal of silver awarded to a competitor who comes second in a contest or race. Compare **gold medal, bronze medal.**

silvern ('sɪlvən) ADJECTIVE *Archaic or poetic* silver.

silver nitrate NOUN a white crystalline soluble poisonous substance used in making photographic emulsions, other silver salts, and as a medical antiseptic and astringent. Formula: $AgNO_3$. See also **lunar caustic.**

silver plate NOUN 1 a thin layer of silver deposited on a base metal. 2 articles, esp tableware, made of silver plate. ◆ VERB **silver-plate.** 3 (*tr*) to coat (a metal, object, etc.) with silver, as by electroplating.

silverpoint ('sɪlvə,pɔɪnt) NOUN a drawing technique popular esp in the 15th and 16th centuries, using an instrument with a silver wire tip on specially prepared paper.

silver screen NOUN **the.** *Informal* 1 films collectively or the film industry. 2 the screen onto which films are projected.

silver service NOUN (in restaurants) a style of serving food using a spoon and fork in one hand like a pair of tongs.

silverside ('sɪlvə,saɪd) NOUN 1 *Brit and NZ* a coarse cut of beef below the aitchbone and above the leg. 2 Also called: **silversides.** any small marine or freshwater teleost fish of the family *Atherinidae,* related to the grey mullets: includes the jacksmelt.

silversmith ('sɪlvə,smɪθ) NOUN a craftsman who makes or repairs articles of silver.

▸'**silver,smithing** NOUN

silver-spooned ADJECTIVE *Informal* born into, of, or relating to a wealthy upper-class family.

▷HISTORY C20: from *born with a silver spoon in one's mouth*; see SPOON

silver standard NOUN a monetary system in which the legal unit of currency is defined with reference to silver of a specified fineness and weight and sometimes (esp formerly) freely redeemable for it.

silver surfer NOUN *Informal* an older, esp retired, person who uses the Internet.

silvertail ('sɪlvə,teɪl) NOUN *Austral informal* a rich and influential person.

silver thaw NOUN *Canadian* 1 a freezing rainstorm. 2 another name for **glitter** (sense 7).

silver-tongued ADJECTIVE persuasive; eloquent.

silverware ('sɪlvə,wɛə) NOUN articles, esp tableware, made of or plated with silver.

silverweed ('sɪlvə,wiːd) NOUN 1 a rosaceous perennial creeping plant, *Potentilla anserina,* with silvery pinnate leaves and yellow flowers. 2 any of various convolvulaceous shrubs of the genus *Argyreia,* of SE Asia and Australia, having silvery leaves and purple flowers.

silvery ('sɪlvərɪ) ADJECTIVE 1 of or having the appearance of silver: *the silvery moon.* 2 containing or covered with silver. 3 having a clear ringing sound.

▸'**silveriness** NOUN

silver-Y moth NOUN a brownish noctuid moth, *Plusia gamma,* having a light Y-shaped marking on each forewing; it migrates in large flocks. Often shortened to: **silver-Y.**

silviculture ('sɪlvɪ,kʌltʃə) NOUN the branch of forestry that is concerned with the cultivation of trees.

▷HISTORY C20: *silvi-,* from Latin *silva* woodland + CULTURE

▸,**silvi'cultural** ADJECTIVE ▸,**silvi'culturist** NOUN

s'il vous plaît *French* (sil vu plɛ) if you please; please.

sim (sɪm) NOUN a computer game which simulates an activity such as playing a sport or flying an aircraft.

sima ('saɪmə) NOUN 1 the silicon-rich and magnesium-rich rocks of the earth's oceanic crust, the most abundant individual rock being basalt. 2 the earth's continental lower crust, probably comprised of gabbro rather than basalt.

▷HISTORY C20: from SI(LICA) + MA(GNESIA)

▸**simatic** (saɪ'mætɪk) ADJECTIVE

simar (sɪ'mɑː) NOUN a variant spelling of **cymar.**

simarouba *or* **simaruba** (,sɪmə'ruːbə) NOUN 1 any tropical American tree of the genus *Simarouba,* esp *S. amara,* having divided leaves and fleshy fruits: family *Simaroubaceae.* 2 the medicinal bark of any of these trees.

▷HISTORY C18: from New Latin, from Carib *simaruba*

simaroubaceous *or* **simarubaceous** (,sɪməruː'beɪʃəs) ADJECTIVE of, relating to, or belonging to the *Simaroubaceae,* a mainly tropical family of trees and shrubs that includes ailanthus and quassia.

simba ('sɪmbə) NOUN an E African word for **lion.**

▷HISTORY Swahili

Simbirsk (*Russian* sim'birsk) NOUN a city in W central Russia on the River Volga: birthplace of Lenin (V. I. Ulyanov). Pop.: 671 700 (1999 est.). Former name (1924–91): **Ulyanovsk.**

sim card NOUN ACRONYM FOR subscriber identity module card; a small card used in a mobile phone to store information about the network, telephone number, etc.

Simchath Torah, Simhath Torah, *or* **Simchas Torah** (sim'xɑt tɔr'ɑː, 'simxɑs 'tɑʊrɔ) NOUN a Jewish festival celebrated immediately after Sukkoth on Tishri 23 (in Israel, Tishri 22) to mark the completion of the annual cycle of Torah readings and its immediate recommencement.

▷HISTORY from Hebrew *śimhath tōrāh,* literally: celebration of the Torah

Simeon ('sɪmɪən) NOUN 1 **a** *Old Testament* the second son of Jacob and Leah. **b** the tribe descended from him. **c** the territory once occupied by this tribe in the extreme south of the land of Canaan. 2 *New Testament* a devout Jew, who recognized the infant Jesus as the Messiah and uttered the canticle *Nunc Dimittis* over him in the Temple (Luke 2:25–35).

Simferopol (*Russian* simfɪ'rɔpəlj) NOUN a city in the S Ukraine on the S Crimean Peninsula: a Scythian town in the 1st century B.C.; seized by the Russians in 1736. Pop.: 341 000 (1998 est.).

simian ('sɪmɪən) ADJECTIVE 1 Also (rare): **simious** ('sɪmɪəs). of, relating to, or resembling a monkey or ape. ◆ NOUN 2 a monkey or ape.

▷HISTORY C17: from Latin *sīmia* an ape, probably from *sīmus* flat-nosed, from Greek *sīmos*

similar ('sɪmɪlə) ADJECTIVE 1 showing resemblance in qualities, characteristics, or appearance; alike but not identical. 2 *Geometry* (of two or more figures) having corresponding angles equal and all corresponding sides in the same ratio. Compare **congruent** (sense 2). 3 *Maths* (of two classes) equinumerous.

▷HISTORY C17: from Old French *similaire,* from Latin *similis*

▸**similarity** (,sɪmɪ'lærɪtɪ) NOUN ▸'**similarly** ADVERB

> **Language note** *As* should not be used after *similar: Wilson held a similar position to Jones* (not *a similar position as Jones*); *the system is similar to the one in France* (not *similar as in France*).

simile ('sɪmɪlɪ) NOUN a figure of speech that expresses the resemblance of one thing to another of a different category, usually introduced by *as* or *like.* Compare **metaphor.**

▷HISTORY C14: from Latin *simile* something similar, from *similis* like

similitude (sɪ'mɪlɪˌtju:d) NOUN [1] likeness; similarity. [2] a thing or sometimes a person that is like or the counterpart of another. [3] *Archaic* a simile, allegory, or parable.
▷HISTORY C14: from Latin *similitūdō*, from *similis* like

simitar ('sɪmɪtə) NOUN a rare spelling of **scimitar**.

Simla ('sɪmlə) NOUN a city in N India, capital of Himachal Pradesh state: summer capital of India (1865–1939); hill resort and health centre. Pop.: 109 860 (1991).

simmer ('sɪmə) VERB [1] to cook (food) gently at or just below the boiling point. [2] (*intr*) to be about to break out in rage or excitement. ◆ NOUN [3] the act, sound, or state of simmering.
▷HISTORY C17: perhaps of imitative origin; compare German *summen* to hum

simmer dim ('sɪmər, -mə) NOUN *Scot* the night-long twilight found in the Northern Isles around midsummer.
▷HISTORY Scottish form of SUMMER[1] + DIM

simmer down VERB (*adverb*) [1] (*intr*) *Informal* to grow calmer or quieter, as after intense rage or excitement. [2] (*tr*) to reduce the volume of (a liquid) by boiling slowly.

simnel cake ('sɪmnᵊl) NOUN *Brit* a fruit cake, often coloured with saffron and covered with a layer of marzipan, traditionally eaten in Lent or at Easter.
▷HISTORY C13 *simenel*, from Old French, from Latin *simila* fine flour, probably of Semitic origin; related to Greek *semidalis* fine flour

simoniac (sɪ'məʊnɪˌæk) NOUN a person who is guilty of practising simony.
▸**simoniacal** (ˌsaɪmə'naɪəkᵊl) ADJECTIVE ▸ˌ**simo'niacally** ADVERB

Simon Peter NOUN *New Testament* the full name of the apostle Peter, a combination of his original name and the name given him by Christ (Matthew 16:17–18).

simon-pure ADJECTIVE real; genuine; authentic.
▷HISTORY C19: from the phrase *the real Simon Pure*, name of a character in the play *A Bold Stroke for a Wife* (1717) by Susannah Centlivre (1669–1723) who is impersonated by another character in some scenes

simony ('saɪmənɪ) NOUN *Christianity* the practice, now usually regarded as a sin, of buying or selling spiritual or Church benefits such as pardons, relics, etc., or preferments.
▷HISTORY C13: from Old French *simonie*, from Late Latin *sīmōnia*, from the name of *Simon Magus*, a Samaritan sorceror of the 1st century A.D.
▸'**simonist** NOUN

Simon Zelotes (zɪ'ləʊti:z) NOUN **Saint**. one of the 12 apostles, who had probably belonged to the Zealot party before becoming a Christian (Luke 6:15). Owing to a misinterpretation of two similar Aramaic words he is also, but mistakenly, called *the Canaanite* (Matthew 10:4). Feast day: Oct. 28 or May 10.

simoom (sɪ'mu:m) *or* **simoon** (sɪ'mu:n) NOUN a strong suffocating sand-laden wind of the deserts of Arabia and North Africa. Also called: **samiel**.
▷HISTORY from Arabic *samūm* poisonous, from *sam* poison, from Aramaic *sammā* poison

simp (sɪmp) NOUN *US slang* short for **simpleton**.

simpatico (sɪm'pɑ:tɪˌkəʊ, -'pæt-) ADJECTIVE *Informal* [1] pleasant or congenial. [2] of similar mind or temperament; compatible.
▷HISTORY Italian: from *simpatia* SYMPATHY

simper ('sɪmpə) VERB [1] (*intr*) to smile coyly, affectedly, or in a silly self-conscious way. [2] (*tr*) to utter (something) in a simpering manner. ◆ NOUN [3] a simpering smile; smirk.
▷HISTORY C16: probably from Dutch *simper* affected
▸'**simperer** NOUN ▸'**simpering** ADJECTIVE, NOUN
▸'**simperingly** ADVERB

simple ('sɪmpᵊl) ADJECTIVE [1] not involved or complicated; easy to understand or do: *a simple problem*. [2] plain; unadorned: *a simple dress*. [3] consisting of one element or part only; not combined or complex: *a simple mechanism*. [4] unaffected or unpretentious: *although he became famous, he remained a simple and well-liked man*. [5] not guileful; sincere; frank: *her simple explanation was readily accepted*. [6] of humble condition or rank: *the peasant was of simple birth*. [7] weak in intelligence; feeble-minded. [8] (*prenominal*) without additions or modifications; mere: *the witness told the simple truth*. [9] (*prenomina*) ordinary or straightforward: *a simple case of mumps*. [10] *Chem* (of a substance or material) consisting of only one chemical compound rather than a mixture of compounds. [11] *Maths* **a** (of a fraction) containing only integers. **b** (of an equation) containing variables to the first power only; linear. **c** (of a root of an equation) occurring only once; not multiple. [12] *Biology* not divided into parts: *a simple leaf*; *a simple eye*. [13] *Music* relating to or denoting a time where the number of beats per bar may be two, three, or four. ◆ NOUN *Archaic* [14] a simpleton; fool. [15] a plant, esp a herbaceous plant, having medicinal properties.
▷HISTORY C13: via Old French from Latin *simplex* plain
▸'**simpleness** NOUN

simple fraction NOUN a fraction in which the numerator and denominator are both integers expressed as a ratio rather than a decimal. Also called: **common fraction, vulgar fraction**.

simple fracture NOUN a fracture in which the broken bone does not pierce the skin. Also called: **closed fracture**. Compare **compound fracture**.

simple fruit NOUN a fruit, such as a grape or cherry, that is formed from only one ovary.

simple harmonic motion NOUN a form of periodic motion of a particle, etc., in which the acceleration is always directed towards some equilibrium point and is proportional to the displacement from this point. Abbreviation: **SHM**.

simple-hearted ADJECTIVE free from deceit; open; frank; sincere.

simple interest NOUN interest calculated or paid on the principal alone. Compare **compound interest**.

simple machine NOUN a simple device for altering the magnitude or direction of a force. The six basic types are the lever, wheel and axle, pulley, screw, wedge, and inclined plane.

simple microscope NOUN a microscope having a single lens; magnifying glass. Compare **compound microscope**.

simple-minded ADJECTIVE [1] stupid; foolish; feeble-minded. [2] unsophisticated; artless.
▸ˌ**simple-'mindedly** ADVERB ▸ˌ**simple-'mindedness** NOUN

simple sentence NOUN a sentence consisting of a single clause. Compare **compound sentence, complex sentence**.

Simple Simon NOUN a foolish man or boy; simpleton.
▷HISTORY C20: after the name of a character in a nursery rhyme

simple tense NOUN *Grammar* a tense of verbs, in English and other languages, not involving the use of an auxiliary verb in addition to the main verb, as for example the past *He drowned* as opposed to the future *He will drown*.

simpleton ('sɪmpᵊltən) NOUN a foolish or ignorant person.

simplex ('sɪmplɛks) ADJECTIVE [1] permitting the transmission of signals in only one direction in a radio circuit, etc. Compare **duplex**. ◆ NOUN [2] *Linguistics* a simple not a compound word. [3] *Geometry* the most elementary geometric figure in Euclidean space of a given dimension; a line segment in one-dimensional space or a triangle in two-dimensional space.
▷HISTORY C16: from Latin: simple, literally: one-fold, from *sim-* one + *plex*, from *plicāre* to fold; compare DUPLEX

simplicidentate (ˌsɪmplɪsɪ'dɛnteɪt) ADJECTIVE [1] of, relating to, or belonging to the *Simplicidentata*, a former suborder including all the mammals now classified as rodents: used when lagomorphs were included in the order *Rodentia*. ◆ NOUN [2] any animal of this type.

simplicity (sɪm'plɪsɪtɪ) NOUN the quality or condition of being simple.

simplify ('sɪmplɪˌfaɪ) VERB **-fies, -fying, -fied**. (*tr*) [1] to make less complicated, clearer, or easier. [2] *Maths* to reduce (an equation, fraction, etc.) to a simpler form by cancellation of common factors, regrouping of terms in the same variable, etc.
▷HISTORY C17: via French from Medieval Latin *simplificāre*, from Latin *simplus* simple + *facere* to make
▸ˌ**simplifi'cation** NOUN ▸'**simplificative** ADJECTIVE
▸'**simpliˌfier** NOUN

simplistic (sɪm'plɪstɪk) ADJECTIVE [1] characterized by extreme simplicity; naive. [2] oversimplifying complex problems; making unrealistically simple judgments or analyses.
▸'**simplism** NOUN ▸**sim'plistically** ADVERB

> **Language note** Since *simplistic* already has *too* as part of its meaning, it is tautologous to talk about something being *too simplistic* or *over-simplistic*.

Simplon Pass ('sɪmplɒn) NOUN a pass over the Lepontine Alps in S Switzerland, between Brig (Switzerland) and Iselle (Italy). Height: 2009 m (6590 ft.).

simply ('sɪmplɪ) ADVERB [1] in a simple manner. [2] merely; only. [3] absolutely; altogether; really: *a simply wonderful holiday*. ◆ SENTENCE MODIFIER [4] frankly; candidly.

Simpson Desert ('sɪmpsən) NOUN an uninhabited arid region in central Australia, mainly in the Northern Territory. Area: about 145 000 sq. km (56 000 sq. miles).

simul ('sɪməl) NOUN a shortened form of **simultaneous** (sense 2).

simulacrum (ˌsɪmjʊ'leɪkrəm) NOUN, *plural* **-cra** (-krə). *Archaic* [1] any image or representation of something. [2] a slight, unreal, or vague semblance of something; superficial likeness.
▷HISTORY C16: from Latin: likeness, from *simulāre* to imitate, from *similis* like

simulant ('sɪmjʊlənt) ADJECTIVE [1] simulating. [2] (esp of plant parts) resembling another part in structure or function.

simular ('sɪmjʊlə) *Archaic* ◆ NOUN [1] a person or thing that simulates or imitates; sham. ◆ ADJECTIVE [2] fake; simulated.

simulate VERB ('sɪmjʊˌleɪt) (*tr*) [1] to make a pretence of; feign: *to simulate anxiety*. [2] to reproduce the conditions of (a situation, etc.), as in carrying out an experiment: *to simulate weightlessness*. [3] to assume or have the appearance of; imitate. ◆ ADJECTIVE ('sɪmjʊlɪt, -ˌleɪt) [4] *Archaic* assumed or simulated.
▷HISTORY C17: from Latin *simulāre* to copy, from *similis* like
▸'**simulative** ADJECTIVE ▸'**simulatively** ADVERB

simulated ('sɪmjʊˌleɪtɪd) ADJECTIVE [1] (of fur, leather, pearls, etc.) being an imitation of the genuine article, usually made from cheaper material. [2] (of actions, qualities, emotions, etc.) imitated; feigned.

simulation (ˌsɪmjʊ'leɪʃən) NOUN [1] the act or an instance of simulating. [2] the assumption of a false appearance or form. [3] a representation of a problem, situation, etc., in mathematical terms, esp. using a computer. [4] *Maths, statistics, computing* the construction of a mathematical model for some process, situation, etc., in order to estimate its characteristics or solve problems about it probabilistically in terms of the model. [5] *Psychiatry* the conscious process of feigning illness in order to gain some particular end; malingering.

simulator ('sɪmjʊˌleɪtə) NOUN [1] any device or system that simulates specific conditions or the characteristics of a real process or machine for the purposes of research or operator training: *space simulator*. [2] a person who simulates.

simulcast ('sɪməlˌkɑ:st) VERB [1] (*tr*) to broadcast (a programme, etc.) simultaneously on radio and television. ◆ NOUN [2] a programme, etc., so broadcast.
▷HISTORY C20: from SIMUL(TANEOUS) + (BROAD)CAST

simultaneous (ˌsɪməl'teɪnɪəs; *US* ˌsaɪməl'teɪnɪəs) ADJECTIVE [1] occurring, existing, or operating at the same time; concurrent. ◆ NOUN [2] *Chess* a display in which one player plays a number of opponents at once, walking from board to board. Sometimes shortened to: **simul**.
▷HISTORY C17: formed on the model of INSTANTANEOUS from Latin *simul* at the same time, together
▸ˌ**simul'taneously** ADVERB ▸ˌ**simul'taneousness** *or* **simultaneity** (ˌsɪməltə'ni:ɪtɪ; *US* ˌsaɪməltə'ni:ɪtɪ) NOUN

simultaneous equations PLURAL NOUN a set of equations that are all satisfied by the same values of the variables.

sin¹ (sɪn) NOUN [1] *Theol* **a** a transgression of God's known will or any principle or law regarded as embodying this. **b** the condition of estrangement from God arising from such transgression. See also **actual sin, mortal sin, original sin, venial sin.** [2] any serious offence, as against a religious or moral principle. [3] any offence against a principle or standard. [4] **live in sin.** *Informal* (of an unmarried couple) to live together. ♦ VERB (*intr*) **sins, sinning, sinned** [5] *Theol* to commit a sin. [6] (usually foll by *against*) to commit an offence (against a person, principle, etc.).
▷HISTORY Old English *synn;* related to Old Norse *synth,* Old High German *suntea* sin, Latin *sons* guilty
▸'**sinner** NOUN

sin² (sɪn) PREPOSITION, CONJUNCTION, ADVERB a Scot dialect word for **since.**

sin³ (siːn) NOUN the 21st letter in the Hebrew alphabet (ש), transliterated as *S.*

sin⁴ (saɪn) *Maths* ABBREVIATION FOR sine.

SIN *or* **S.I.N.** (in Canada) ABBREVIATION FOR social insurance number.

Sinai ('saɪnaɪ) NOUN [1] a mountainous peninsula of NE Egypt at the N end of the Red Sea, between the Gulf of Suez and the Gulf of Aqaba: occupied by Israel in 1967; fully restored by 1982. [2] **Mount.** the mountain where Moses received the Law from God (Exodus 19–20): often identified as Jebel Musa, sometimes as Jebel Serbal, both on the S Sinai Peninsula.

Sinaitic (ˌsaɪnɪ'ɪtɪk) *or* **Sinaic** (sɪ'neɪɪk) ADJECTIVE [1] of or relating to the Sinai Peninsula. [2] of or relating to Mount Sinai.

Sinaloa (ˌsiːnə'ləʊə, ˌsɪn-; *Spanish* sina'loa) NOUN a state of W Mexico. Capital: Culiacán. Pop.: 2 534 835 (2000). Area: 58 092 sq. km (22 425 sq. miles).

sinanthropus (sɪn'ænθrəpəs) NOUN a primitive apelike man of the genus *Sinanthropus,* now considered a subspecies of *Homo erectus.* See also **Java man, Peking man.**
▷HISTORY C20: from New Latin, from Late Latin *Sīnae* the Chinese + *-anthropus,* from Greek *anthrōpos* man

sinapism ('sɪnəˌpɪzəm) NOUN a technical name for **mustard plaster.**
▷HISTORY C17: from Late Latin *sināpismus,* from Greek *sinapismos* application of mustard plaster, from *sinapi* mustard, of Egyptian origin

Sinarquist ('sɪnɑːkɪst, -kwɪst) NOUN (in Mexico) a member of a fascist movement in the 1930s and 1940s having links with the Nazis and the Falangists: hostile towards the US, Communism, Jews, organized labour, etc.
▷HISTORY C20: Mexican Spanish *sinarquista,* from Spanish *sin* without + *anarquista* anarchist
▸'**Sinarquism** NOUN

sin bin NOUN [1] *Slang* (in ice hockey, etc.) an area off the field of play where a player who has committed a foul can be sent to sit for a specified period. [2] *Brit informal* a special unit on a separate site from a school that disruptive schoolchildren attend until they can be reintegrated into their normal classes.

since (sɪns) PREPOSITION [1] during or throughout the period of time after: *since May it has only rained once.* ♦ CONJUNCTION (*subordinating*) [2] (sometimes preceded by *ever*) continuously from or starting from the time when: *since we last met, important things have happened.* [3] seeing that; because: *since you have no money, you can't come.* ♦ ADVERB [4] since that time: *he left yesterday and I haven't seen him since.*
▷HISTORY Old English *siththan,* literally: after that; related to Old High German *sīd* since, Latin *sērus* late

> **Language note** See at **ago.**

sincere (sɪn'sɪə) ADJECTIVE [1] not hypocritical or deceitful; open; genuine: *a sincere person; sincere regret.* [2] *Archaic* pure; unadulterated; unmixed. [3] *Obsolete* sound; whole.
▷HISTORY C16: from Latin *sincērus*
▸**sin'cerely** ADVERB ▸**sincerity** (sɪn'sɛrɪtɪ) *or* **sin'cereness** NOUN

sinciput ('sɪnsɪˌpʌt) NOUN, *plural* **sinciputs** *or* **sincipita** (sɪn'sɪpɪtə). *Anatomy* the forward upper part of the skull.
▷HISTORY C16: from Latin: half a head, from SEMI- + *caput* head
▸**sin'cipital** ADJECTIVE

Sind (sɪnd) NOUN a province of SE Pakistan, mainly in the lower Indus valley: formerly a province of British India; became a province of Pakistan in 1947; divided in 1955 between Hyderabad and Khairpur; reunited as a province in 1970. Capital: Karachi. Pop.: 29 991 000 (1998 est.). Area: 140 914 sq. km (54 407 sq. miles).

Sindhi ('sɪndɪ) NOUN [1] (*plural* **-dhi** *or* **-dhis**) a former inhabitant of Sind. The Muslim majority now lives in Pakistan while the Hindu minority has mostly moved to India. [2] the language of this people, belonging to the Indic branch of the Indo-European family.

sine¹ (saɪn) NOUN (of an angle) **a** a trigonometric function that in a right-angled triangle is the ratio of the length of the opposite side to that of the hypotenuse. **b** a function that in a circle centred at the origin of a Cartesian coordinate system is the ratio of the ordinate of a point on the circumference to the radius of the circle. Abbreviation: **sin.**
▷HISTORY C16: from Latin *sinus* a bend; in New Latin, *sinus* was mistaken as a translation of Arabic *jiba* sine (from Sanskrit *jīva,* literally: bowstring) because of confusion with Arabic *jaib* curve

sine² ('saɪnɪ) PREPOSITION (esp in Latin phrases or legal terms) lacking; without.

sinecure ('saɪnɪˌkjʊə) NOUN [1] a paid office or post involving minimal duties. [2] a Church benefice to which no spiritual or pastoral charge is attached.
▷HISTORY C17: from Medieval Latin phrase (*beneficium*) *sine cūrā* (benefice) without cure (of souls), from Latin *sine* without + *cūra* cure, care
▸'**sineˌcurism** NOUN ▸'**sineˌcurist** NOUN

sine curve NOUN a curve of the equation $y = \sin x$. Also called: **sinusoid.**

sine die *Latin* ('saɪnɪ 'daɪɪ) ADVERB, ADJECTIVE without a day fixed: *an adjournment sine die.*
▷HISTORY literally: without a day

sine prole *Latin* ('saɪnɪ 'prəʊlɪ) ADJECTIVE, ADVERB *Law* without issue (esp in the phrase ***demisit sine prole*** (died without issue)).

sine qua non *Latin* ('saɪnɪ kweɪ 'nɒn) NOUN an essential condition or requirement.
▷HISTORY literally: without which not

sinew ('sɪnjuː) NOUN [1] *Anatomy* another name for **tendon.** [2] (*often plural*) **a** a source of strength or power. **b** a literary word for **muscle.**
▷HISTORY Old English *sionu;* related to Old Norse *sin,* Old Saxon *sinewa,* Old High German *senawa* sinew, Lettish *pasainis* string
▸'**sinewless** ADJECTIVE

sine wave NOUN any oscillation, such as a sound wave or alternating current, whose waveform is that of a sine curve.

sinewy ('sɪnjuɪ) ADJECTIVE [1] consisting of or resembling a tendon or tendons. [2] muscular; brawny. [3] (esp of language, style, etc.) vigorous; forceful. [4] (of meat, etc.) tough; stringy.
▸'**sinewiness** NOUN

sinfonia (ˌsɪnfə'nɪə) NOUN, *plural* **-nie** (-'niːeɪ). [1] another word for **symphony** (senses 2, 3). [2] (*capital when part of a name*) a symphony orchestra.
▷HISTORY Italian

sinfonietta (ˌsɪnfən'jɛtə, -fəʊn-) NOUN [1] a short or light symphony. [2] (*capital when part of name*) a small symphony orchestra.
▷HISTORY Italian: a little symphony, from SINFONIA

sinful ('sɪnfʊl) ADJECTIVE [1] having committed or tending to commit sin: *a sinful person.* [2] characterized by or being a sin: *a sinful act.*
▸'**sinfully** ADVERB ▸'**sinfulness** NOUN

sing (sɪŋ) VERB **sings, singing, sang, sung.** [1] to produce or articulate (sounds, words, a song, etc.) with definite and usually specific musical intonation. [2] (when *intr,* often foll by *to*) to perform (a song) to the accompaniment (of): *to sing to a guitar.* [3] (*intr;* foll by *of*) to tell a story or tale in song (about): *I sing of a maiden.* [4] (*intr;* foll by *to*) to address a song (to) or perform a song (for). [5] (*intr*) to perform songs for a living, as a professional singer. [6] (*intr*) (esp of certain birds and insects) to utter calls or sounds reminiscent of music. [7] (when *intr,* usually foll by *of*) to tell (something) or give praise (to someone), esp in verse: *the poet who sings of the Trojan dead.* [8] (*intr*) to make a whining, ringing, or whistling sound: *the kettle is singing; the arrow sang past his ear.* [9] (*intr*) (of the ears) to experience a continuous ringing or humming sound. [10] (*tr*) (esp in church services) to chant or intone (a prayer, psalm, etc.). [11] (*tr*) to bring to a given state by singing: *to sing a child to sleep.* [12] (*intr*) *Slang, chiefly US* to confess or act as an informer. [13] (*intr*) *Austral* (in Aboriginal witchcraft) to bring about a person's death by incantation. The same power can sometimes be used beneficently. ♦ NOUN [14] *Informal* an act or performance of singing. [15] a ringing or whizzing sound, as of bullets. ♦ See also **sing along, sing out.**
▷HISTORY Old English *singan;* related to Old Norse *syngja* to sing, Gothic *siggwan,* Old High German *singan*
▸'**singable** ADJECTIVE ▸'**singing** ADJECTIVE, NOUN

> **Language note** See at **ring².**

sing. ABBREVIATION FOR singular.

sing along VERB (*intr, adverb*) [1] to join in singing with a performer. ♦ NOUN **sing-along.** [2] such a singsong.

Singapore (ˌsɪŋə'pɔː, ˌsɪŋgə-) NOUN [1] a republic in SE Asia, occupying one main island and about 58 small islands at the S end of the Malay Peninsula: established as a British trading post in 1819 and became part of the Straits Settlements in 1826; occupied by the Japanese (1942–45); a British colony from 1946, becoming self-governing in 1959; part of the Federation of Malaysia from 1963 to 1965, when it became an independent republic (within the Commonwealth). Official languages: Chinese, Malay, English, and Tamil. Religion: Buddhist, Taoist, traditional beliefs, and Muslim. Currency: Singapore dollar. Capital: Singapore. Pop.: 3 322 000 (2001 est.). Area: 646 sq. km (250 sq. miles). [2] the capital of the republic of Singapore: a major international port; administratively not treated as a city.

Singaporean (ˌsɪŋə'pɔːrɪən, ˌsɪŋgə-) ADJECTIVE [1] of or relating to Singapore or its inhabitants. ♦ NOUN [2] a native or inhabitant of Singapore.

singe (sɪndʒ) VERB **singes, singeing, singed.** [1] to burn or be burnt superficially; scorch: *to singe one's clothes.* [2] (*tr*) to burn the ends of (hair, etc.). [3] (*tr*) to expose (a carcass) to flame to remove bristles or hair. ♦ NOUN [4] a superficial burn.
▷HISTORY Old English *sengan;* related to Middle High German *sengen* to singe, Dutch *sengel* spark, Norwegian *sengla* to smell of burning, Swedish *sjängla* to singe, Icelandic *sāngr*

singer ('sɪŋə) NOUN [1] a person who sings, esp one who earns a living by singing. [2] a singing bird. [3] an obsolete word for **poet.**

singer-songwriter NOUN a performer who writes his or her own songs.

Singh (sɪŋ) NOUN a title assumed by a Sikh when he becomes a full member of the community.
▷HISTORY from Hindi, from Sanskrit *sinhá* a lion

Singhalese (ˌsɪŋə'liːz) NOUN, *plural* **-leses** *or* **-lese,** ADJECTIVE a variant spelling of **Sinhalese.**

singing hinny NOUN a type of currant cake popular in NE England which, when cooked on a griddle, makes a singing noise.
▷HISTORY *hinny* Scottish and N English variant of HONEY

singing telegram NOUN a greetings service in which a person is employed to present greetings by singing to the person celebrating.

single ('sɪŋgᵊl) ADJECTIVE (*usually prenominal*) [1] existing alone; solitary: *upon the hill stood a single tower.* [2] distinct from other things; unique or individual. [3] composed of one part. [4] designed for one user: *a single room; a single bed.* [5] (*also postpositive*) unmarried. [6] connected with the condition of being unmarried: *he led a single life.* [7] (esp of combat) involving two individuals; one

against one. 8 sufficient for one person or thing only: *a single portion of food.* 9 even one: *there wasn't a single person on the beach.* 10 (of a flower) having only one set or whorl of petals. 11 determined; single-minded: *a single devotion to duty.* 12 (of the eye) seeing correctly: *to consider something with a single eye.* 13 *Rare* honest or sincere; genuine. 14 *Archaic* (of ale, beer, etc.) mild in strength. ◆ NOUN 15 something forming one individual unit. 16 an unmarried person. 17 a gramophone record, CD, or cassette with a short recording, usually of pop music, on it. 18 *Golf* a game between two players. 19 *Cricket* a hit from which one run is scored. 20 **a** *Brit* a pound note. **b** *US and Canadian* a dollar note. 21 See **single ticket.** ◆ VERB 22 (*tr; usually foll by out*) to select from a group of people or things; distinguish by separation: *he singled him out for special mention.* 23 (*tr*) to thin out (seedlings). 24 short for **single-foot.** ◆ See also **singles.**
▷HISTORY C14: from Old French *sengle,* from Latin *singulus* individual
▶ **'singleness** NOUN

single-acting ADJECTIVE (of a reciprocating engine or pump) having a piston or pistons that are pressurized on one side only. Compare **double-acting** (sense 1).

single-action NOUN (*modifier*) (of a firearm) requiring the hammer to be cocked by hand before firing.

single-blind ADJECTIVE of or relating to an experiment, esp one to discover people's reactions to certain commodities, drugs, etc., in which the experimenters but not the subjects know the particulars of the test items during the experiment. Compare **double-blind.**

single bond NOUN *Chem* a covalent bond formed between two atoms by the sharing of one pair of electrons.

single-breasted ADJECTIVE (of a garment) having the fronts overlapping only slightly and with one row of fastenings.

single-cell protein NOUN protein that is produced by micro-organisms fermenting in liquid or gaseous petroleum fractions or other organic substances: used as a food supplement. Abbreviation: **SCP.**

single cream NOUN cream having a low fat content that does not thicken with beating.

single-cross NOUN *Genetics* a hybrid of the first generation between two inbred lines.

single-cut file NOUN a file with teeth in one direction only: used for filing soft material.

single-decker NOUN *Brit informal* a bus with only one passenger deck.

single density NOUN *Computing* a disk with the normal capacity for storage.

singledom ('sɪŋgəldəm) NOUN *Informal* the state of being unmarried or not involved in a long-term relationship.

single-end NOUN *Scot dialect* accommodation consisting of a single room.

single-ended ADJECTIVE *Electronics* (of an amplifier) having one side of the input and one side of the output connected to earth: used for an unbalanced signal.

single entry NOUN **a** a simple book-keeping system in which transactions are entered in one account only. Compare **double entry. b** (*as modifier*): *a single-entry account.*

single file NOUN a line of persons, animals, or things ranged one behind the other, either stationary or moving.

single-foot NOUN 1 a rapid showy gait of a horse in which each foot strikes the ground separately, as in a walk. ◆ VERB 2 to move or cause to move at this gait.

single-handed ADJECTIVE, ADVERB 1 unaided or working alone: *a single-handed crossing of the Atlantic.* 2 having or operated by one hand or one person only.
▶ **ˌsingle-'handedly** ADVERB ▶ **ˌsingle-'handedness** NOUN

single-lens reflex NOUN See **reflex camera.**

single market NOUN a market consisting of a number of nations, esp those of the European Union, in which goods, capital, and currencies can move freely across borders without tariffs or restrictions.

single-minded ADJECTIVE having but one aim or purpose; dedicated.
▶ **ˌsingle-'mindedly** ADVERB ▶ **ˌsingle-'mindedness** NOUN

single parent NOUN **a** a person who has a dependent child or dependent children and who is widowed, divorced, or unmarried. **b** (*as modifier*): *a single-parent family.* Also called (NZ): **solo parent.**

single-phase ADJECTIVE (of a system, circuit, or device) having, generating, or using a single alternating voltage.

singles ('sɪŋgəlz) PLURAL NOUN *Tennis, badminton* a match played with one person on each side.

singles bar NOUN a bar or club that is a social meeting place for single people.

single-sex ADJECTIVE (of schools, etc.) admitting members of one sex only; not coeducational.

single sideband transmission NOUN a method of transmitting radio waves in which either the upper or the lower sideband is transmitted, the carrier being either wholly or partially suppressed. This reduces the required bandwidth and improves the signal-to-noise ratio. Abbreviation: **SSB.**

single-space VERB (*tr*) to type (copy) without leaving a space between the lines.

single-step VERB **-steps, -stepping, -stepped.** (*tr*) *Computing* to perform a single instruction on (a program), generally under the control of a debug program.

singlestick ('sɪŋgəlˌstɪk) NOUN 1 a wooden stick used instead of a sword for fencing. 2 fencing with such a stick. 3 any short heavy stick.

singlet ('sɪŋglɪt) NOUN 1 *Chiefly Brit* a man's sleeveless undergarment covering the body from the shoulders to the hips. 2 the Austral name for **vest** (senses 1, 2). 3 *Chiefly Brit* a garment worn with shorts by athletes, boxers, etc. 4 *NZ* a black woollen outer garment worn by bushmen. 5 *Physics* a multiplet that has only one member. 6 *Chem* a chemical bond consisting of one electron.
▷HISTORY C18: from SINGLE, on the model of *doublet*

single tax NOUN *US* 1 a taxation system in which a tax on one commodity, usually land, is the only source of revenue. 2 such a tax.

single thread NOUN *Computing* the execution of an entire task from beginning to end without interruption.

single ticket NOUN *Brit* a ticket entitling a passenger to travel only to his destination, without returning. US and Canadian equivalent: **one-way ticket.** Compare **return ticket.**

singleton ('sɪŋgəltən) NOUN 1 *Bridge* an original holding of one card only in a suit. 2 a single object, individual, etc., separated or distinguished from a pair or group. 3 *Maths* a set containing only one member. 4 a person who is neither married nor in a relationship.
▷HISTORY C19: from SINGLE, on the model of SIMPLETON

single-tongue VERB *Music* to play (any nonlegato passage) on a wind instrument by obstructing and uncovering the air passage through the lips with the tongue. Compare **double-tongue, triple-tongue.**
▶ **single tonguing** NOUN

single-track ADJECTIVE 1 (of a railway) having only a single pair of lines, so that trains can travel in only one direction at a time. 2 (of a road) only wide enough for one vehicle. 3 able to think about only one thing; one-track.

Single Transferable Vote NOUN (*modifier*) of or relating to a system of voting in which voters list the candidates in order of preference. Any candidate achieving a predetermined proportion of the votes in a constituency is elected. Votes exceeding this amount and those cast for the bottom candidate are redistributed according to the stated preferences. Redistribution continues until all the seats are filled. Abbreviation: **STV.** See **proportional representation.**

singletree ('sɪŋgəlˌtriː) NOUN a variant, esp US and Austral, of **swingletree.**

Singlish ('sɪŋglɪʃ) NOUN a variety of English spoken in Singapore, incorporating elements of Chinese and Malay.
▷HISTORY C20: from a blend of SINGAPOREAN + ENGLISH

singly ('sɪŋglɪ) ADVERB 1 one at a time; one by one. 2 apart from others; separately; alone.

sing out VERB (*tr, adverb*) to call out in a loud voice; shout.

Sing Sing NOUN a prison in New York State, in Ossining.
▷HISTORY variant of *Ossining*

singsong ('sɪŋˌsɒŋ) NOUN 1 an accent, metre, or intonation that is characterized by an alternately rising and falling rhythm, as in a person's voice, piece of verse, etc. 2 *Brit* an informal session of singing, esp of popular or traditional songs. ◆ ADJECTIVE 3 having a regular or monotonous rising and falling rhythm: *a singsong accent.*

Singspiel *German* ('zɪŋʃpiːl) NOUN a type of comic opera in German with spoken dialogue, popular during the late 18th and early 19th centuries.
▷HISTORY literally: singing play

singular ('sɪŋgjʊlə) ADJECTIVE 1 remarkable; exceptional; extraordinary: *a singular feat.* 2 unusual; odd: *a singular character.* 3 unique. 4 denoting a word or an inflected form of a word indicating that not more than one referent is being referred to or described. 5 *Logic* of or referring to a specific thing or person as opposed to something general. ◆ NOUN 6 *Grammar* **a** the singular number. **b** a singular form of a word.
▷HISTORY C14: from Latin *singulāris* SINGLE
▶ **'singularly** ADVERB ▶ **'singularness** NOUN

singularity (ˌsɪŋgjʊ'lærɪtɪ) NOUN, *plural* **-ties.** 1 the state, fact, or quality of being singular. 2 something distinguishing a person or thing from others. 3 something remarkable or unusual. 4 *Maths* **a** a point at which a function is not differentiable although it is differentiable in a neighbourhood of that point. See also **pole**[2] (sense 4). **b** another word for **discontinuity.** 5 *Astronomy* a hypothetical point in space-time at which matter is infinitely compressed to infinitesimal volume.

singularize *or* **singularise** ('sɪŋgjʊləˌraɪz) VERB (*tr*) 1 to make (a word, etc.) singular. 2 to make conspicuous.
▶ **ˌsingulari'zation** *or* **ˌsingulari'sation** NOUN

singulary ('sɪŋgjʊlərɪ) ADJECTIVE *Logic, maths* (of an operator) monadic.

singultus (sɪŋ'gʌltəs) NOUN a technical name for **hiccup.**
▷HISTORY C18: from Latin, literally: a sob

sinh (ʃaɪn, sɪnʃ) NOUN hyperbolic sine; a hyperbolic function, $\sinh z = \frac{1}{2}(e^z - e^{-z})$, related to sine by the expression $\sinh iz = i \sin z$, where $i = \sqrt{-1}$.
▷HISTORY C20: from SIN(E)[1] + H(YPERBOLIC)

Sinhailien ('ʃɪn'haɪ'ljɛn) NOUN a variant transliteration of the Chinese name for **Lianyungang.**

Sinhalese (ˌsɪnhə'liːz) *or* **Singhalese** NOUN 1 (**pl, -leses** *or* **-lese**) a member of a people living chiefly in Sri Lanka, where they constitute the majority of the population. 2 the language of this people, belonging to the Indic branch of the Indo-European family: the official language of Sri Lanka. It is written in a script of Indian origin. ◆ ADJECTIVE 3 of or relating to this people or their language.

Sinicism ('saɪnɪˌsɪzəm, 'sɪn-) NOUN *Rare* a Chinese custom or idiom.
▷HISTORY C19: from Medieval Latin *Sinicus* Chinese, from Late Latin *Sīnae* the Chinese, from Greek *Sinai,* from Arabic *Sīn* China

Sining ('ʃiː'nɪŋ) NOUN variant transliteration of the Chinese name for **Xining.**

sinister ('sɪnɪstə) ADJECTIVE 1 threatening or suggesting evil or harm; ominous: *a sinister glance.* 2 evil or treacherous, esp in a mysterious way. 3 (*usually postpositive*) *Heraldry* of, on, or starting from the left side from the bearer's point of view and therefore on the spectator's right. 4 *Archaic* located on the left side. 5 *Archaic* (of signs, omens, etc.) unfavourable. ◆ Compare **dexter**[1].
▷HISTORY C15: from Latin *sinister* on the left-hand side, considered by Roman augurs to be the unlucky one
▶ **'sinisterly** ADVERB ▶ **'sinisterness** NOUN

sinistral ('sɪnɪstrəl) ADJECTIVE 1 of, relating to, or located on the left side, esp the left side of the body. 2 a technical term for **left-handed.** 3 (of the shells of certain gastropod molluscs) coiling in a clockwise direction from the apex. ◆ Compare **dextral.**
▷HISTORY C15 (in the obsolete sense: adverse, evil);

C19 (in current senses): from Medieval Latin *sinistrālis*. See SINISTER
▸'**sinistrally** ADVERB

sinistrodextral (ˌsɪnɪstrəʊ'dɛkstrəl) ADJECTIVE going or directed from left to right: *a sinistrodextral script*.
▹HISTORY See SINISTER, DEXTER[1]

sinistrorse ('sɪnɪˌstrɔːs, ˌsɪnɪ'strɔːs) ADJECTIVE (of some climbing plants) growing upwards in a spiral from right to left, or clockwise. Compare **dextrorse.**
▹HISTORY C19: from Latin *sinistrōrsus* turned towards the left, from *sinister* on the left + *vertere* to turn
▸ˌ**sinis'trorsal** ADJECTIVE ▸'**sinisˌtrorsely** ADVERB

sinistrous ('sɪnɪstrəs) ADJECTIVE *Archaic* 1 sinister or ill-omened. 2 sinistral.
▸'**sinistrously** ADVERB

Sinitic (sɪ'nɪtɪk) NOUN 1 a branch of the Sino-Tibetan family of languages, consisting of the various languages or dialects of Chinese. Compare **Tibeto-Burman.** ◆ ADJECTIVE 2 belonging or relating to this group of languages.

sink (sɪŋk) VERB **sinks, sinking, sank; sunk** *or* **sunken.** 1 to descend or cause to descend, esp beneath the surface of a liquid or soft substance. 2 (*intr*) to appear to move down towards or descend below the horizon. 3 (*intr*) to slope downwards; dip. 4 (*intr; often foll by in or into*) to pass into or gradually enter a specified lower state or condition: *to sink into apathy*. 5 to make or become lower in volume, pitch, etc. 6 to make or become lower in value, price, etc. 7 (*intr*) to become weaker in health, strength, etc. 8 to decline or cause to decline in moral value, worth, etc. 9 (*intr*) to seep or penetrate. 10 (*tr*) to suppress or conceal: *he sank his worries in drink*. 11 (*tr*) to dig, cut, drill, bore, or excavate (a hole, shaft, etc.). 12 (*tr*) to drive into the ground: *to sink a stake*. 13 (*tr; usually foll by in or into*) **a** to invest (money). **b** to lose (money) in an unwise or unfortunate investment. 14 (*tr*) to pay (a debt). 15 (*intr*) to become hollow; cave in: *his cheeks had sunk during his illness*. 16 (*tr*) to hit, throw, or propel (a ball) into a hole, basket, pocket, etc.: *he sank a 15-foot putt*. 17 (*tr*) *Brit informal* to drink, esp quickly: *he sank three pints in half an hour*. 18 **sink or swim.** to take risks where the alternatives are loss and failure or security and success. ◆ NOUN 19 a fixed basin, esp in a kitchen, made of stone, earthenware, metal, etc., used for washing. 20 See **sinkhole.** 21 another word for **cesspool.** 22 a place of vice or corruption. 23 an area of ground below that of the surrounding land, where water collects. 24 *Physics* a device or part of a system at which energy is removed from the system: *a heat sink*. ◆ ADJECTIVE 25 *Informal* (of a housing estate or school) deprived or having low standards of achievement.
▹HISTORY Old English *sincan*; related to Old Norse *sökkva* to sink, Gothic *siggan*, Old High German *sincan*, Swedish *sjunka*
▸'**sinkable** ADJECTIVE

sinkage ('sɪŋkɪdʒ) NOUN *Rare* the act of sinking or degree to which something sinks or has sunk.

sinker ('sɪŋkə) NOUN 1 a weight attached to a fishing line, net, etc., to cause it to sink in water. 2 a person who sinks shafts, etc. 3 *US* an informal word for **doughnut.** 4 **hook, line, and sinker.** See **hook** (sense 18).

sinkhole ('sɪŋkˌhəʊl) NOUN 1 Also called (esp Brit): **swallow hole.** a depression in the ground surface, esp in limestone, where a surface stream disappears underground. 2 a place into which foul matter runs.

Sinkiang-Uighur Autonomous Region ('sɪn'kjæŋ 'wiːgʊə) NOUN a variant transliteration of the Chinese name for the **Xinjiang Uygur Autonomous Region.**

sink in VERB (*intr, adverb*) to enter or penetrate the mind: *eventually the news sank in*.

sinking ('sɪŋkɪŋ) NOUN **a** a feeling in the stomach caused by hunger or uneasiness. **b** (*as modifier*): *a sinking feeling*.

sinking fund NOUN a fund accumulated out of a business enterprise's earnings or a government's revenue and invested to repay a long-term debt or meet a depreciation charge.

sinless ('sɪnlɪs) ADJECTIVE free from sin or guilt; innocent; pure.
▸'**sinlessly** ADVERB ▸'**sinlessness** NOUN

Sinn Féin ('ʃɪn 'feːn) NOUN an Irish republican political movement founded about 1905 and linked to the revolutionary Irish Republican Army: divided into a Provisional and an Official movement since a similar split in the IRA in late 1969.
▹HISTORY C20: from Irish: we ourselves
▸**Sinn Féiner** NOUN ▸**Sinn Féinism** NOUN

Sino- COMBINING FORM Chinese: *Sino-Tibetan; Sinology*.
▹HISTORY from French, from Late Latin *Sīnae* the Chinese, from Late Greek *Sinai*, from Arabic *Sīn* China, probably from Chinese *Ch'in*

Sinology (saɪ'nɒlədʒɪ, sɪ-) NOUN the study of Chinese history, language, culture, etc.
▸**Sinological** (ˌsaɪnə'lɒdʒɪkəl, ˌsɪn-) ADJECTIVE
▸**Si'nologist** NOUN ▸**Sinologue** ('saɪnəˌlɒg) NOUN

Sinope (sə'nəʊpɪ) NOUN *Astronomy* a small outer satellite of the planet Jupiter.

Sino-Tibetan ('saɪnəʊ-) NOUN 1 a family of languages that includes most of the languages of China, as well as Tibetan, Burmese, and possibly Thai. Their most noticeable phonological characteristic is the phonemic use of tones. ◆ ADJECTIVE 2 belonging or relating to this family of languages.

sinsemilla (ˌsɪnsə'miːljə) NOUN 1 a type of marijuana with a very high narcotic content. 2 the plant from which it is obtained, a strain of *Cannabis sativa*.
▹HISTORY C20: from American Spanish, literally: without seed

sin tax NOUN *Informal* a tax levied on something that is considered morally or medically harmful, such as alcohol or tobacco.

sinter ('sɪntə) NOUN 1 a whitish porous incrustation, usually consisting of silica, that is deposited from hot springs. 2 the product of a sintering process. 3 another name for **cinder** (sense 3). ◆ VERB 4 (*tr*) to form large particles, lumps, or masses from (metal powders or powdery ores) by heating or pressure or both.
▹HISTORY C18: German: CINDER

Sint Maarten (sɪnt 'maːrtə) NOUN the Dutch name for **Saint Martin.**

Sintra ('sɪntrə) NOUN a town in central Portugal, near Lisbon, in the Sintra mountains: noted for its castles and palaces and the beauty of its setting: tourism. Former name: **Cintra.**

sinuate ('sɪnjʊɪt, -ˌeɪt) *or* **sinuated** ADJECTIVE 1 Also: **sinuous.** (of leaves) having a strongly waved margin. 2 another word for **sinuous.**
▹HISTORY C17: from Latin *sinuātus* curved; see SINUS, -ATE[1]
▸'**sinuately** ADVERB

Sinŭiju (sɪˌnuːɪ'dʒuː) NOUN a port in North Korea, on the Yalu River opposite Andong, China: developed by the Japanese during their occupation (1910–45); industrial centre. Pop.: 289 000 (latest est.).

sinuosity (ˌsɪnjʊ'ɒsɪtɪ) *or less commonly* **sinuation** NOUN, *plural* **-osities** *or* **-ations.** 1 the quality of being sinuous. 2 a turn, curve, or intricacy.

sinuous ('sɪnjʊəs) ADJECTIVE 1 full of turns or curves; intricate. 2 devious; not straightforward. 3 supple; lithe. ◆ Also: **sinuate.**
▹HISTORY C16: from Latin *sinuōsus* winding, from *sinus* a curve
▸'**sinuously** ADVERB ▸'**sinuousness** NOUN

sinus ('saɪnəs) NOUN, *plural* **-nuses.** 1 *Anatomy* **a** any bodily cavity or hollow space. **b** a large channel for venous blood, esp between the brain and the skull. **c** any of the air cavities in the cranial bones. 2 *Pathol* a passage leading to a cavity containing pus. 3 *Botany* a small rounded notch between two lobes of a leaf, petal, etc. 4 an irregularly shaped cavity.
▹HISTORY C16: from Latin: a curve, bay

sinusitis (ˌsaɪnə'saɪtɪs) NOUN inflammation of the membrane lining a sinus, esp a nasal sinus.

sinusoid ('saɪnəˌsɔɪd) NOUN 1 any of the irregular terminal blood vessels that replace capillaries in certain organs, such as the liver, heart, spleen, and pancreas. 2 another name for **sine curve.** ◆ ADJECTIVE 3 resembling a sinus.
▹HISTORY C19: from French *sinusoïde*. See SINUS, -OID

sinusoidal (ˌsaɪnə'sɔɪdəl) ADJECTIVE 1 *Maths* of or relating to a sine curve. 2 *Physics* having a magnitude that varies as a sine curve.
▸ˌ**sinus'oidally** ADVERB

sinusoidal projection NOUN an equal-area map projection on which all parallels are straight lines and all except the prime meridian are sine curves, often used to show tropical latitudes. Also called: **Sanson-Flamsteed projection.**

Sion NOUN 1 (*French* sjɔ̃) a town in SW Switzerland, capital of Valais canton, on the River Rhône. Pop.: 24 538 (1990). Latin name: **Sedunum.** 2 ('saɪən) a variant of **Zion.**

Siouan ('suːən) NOUN 1 a family of North American Indian languages including Sioux, probably related to Iroquoian. ◆ ADJECTIVE 2 of or relating to the Sioux peoples or languages.

Sioux (suː) NOUN 1 (*plural* **Sioux** (suː, suːz)) a member of a group of North American Indian peoples formerly ranging over a wide area of the Plains from Lake Michigan to the Rocky Mountains. 2 any of the Siouan languages.
▹HISTORY from French, shortened from *Nadowessioux*, from Chippewa *Nadoweisiw*

sip (sɪp) VERB **sips, sipping, sipped.** 1 to drink (a liquid) by taking small mouthfuls; drink gingerly or delicately. ◆ NOUN 2 a small quantity of a liquid taken into the mouth and swallowed. 3 an act of sipping.
▹HISTORY C14: probably from Low German *sippen*
▸'**sipper** NOUN

siphon *or* **syphon** ('saɪfən) NOUN 1 a tube placed with one end at a certain level in a vessel of liquid and the other end outside the vessel below this level, so that atmospheric pressure forces the liquid through the tube and out of the vessel. 2 See **soda siphon.** 3 *Zoology* any of various tubular organs in different aquatic animals, such as molluscs and elasmobranch fishes, through which a fluid, esp water, passes. ◆ VERB 4 (often foll by *off*) to pass or draw off through or as if through a siphon.
▹HISTORY C17: from Latin *sīphō*, from Greek *siphōn* siphon
▸'**siphonage** NOUN ▸'**siphonal** *or* **siphonic** (saɪ'fɒnɪk) ADJECTIVE

siphon bottle NOUN another name (esp US) for **soda siphon.**

siphonophore ('saɪfənəˌfɔː, saɪ'fɒnə-) NOUN any marine colonial hydrozoan of the order *Siphonophora*, including the Portuguese man-of-war.
▹HISTORY C19: from New Latin *siphonophora*, from Greek *siphōnophoros* tube-bearing
▸**siphonophorous** (ˌsaɪfə'nɒfərəs) ADJECTIVE

siphonostele ('saɪfənəˌstiːl) NOUN *Botany* the cylinder of conducting tissue surrounding a central core of pith in certain stems. See also **stele** (sense 3).
▹HISTORY C19: from SIPHON + STELE
▸**siphonostelic** (ˌsaɪfənə'stiːlɪk) ADJECTIVE

Siple ('saɪpəl) NOUN **Mount.** a mountain in Antarctica, on the coast of Byrd Land. Height: 3100 m (10 171 ft.).

sipper ('sɪpə) NOUN *US informal* a drinking straw.

sippet ('sɪpɪt) NOUN a small piece of something, esp a piece of toast or fried bread eaten with soup or gravy.
▹HISTORY C16: used as diminutive of SOP; see -ET

SIPS ABBREVIATION FOR side impact protection system: bars built into certain cars to strengthen the bodywork.

sir (sɜː) NOUN 1 a formal or polite term of address for a man. 2 *Archaic* a gentleman of high social status.
▹HISTORY C13: variant of SIRE

Sir (sɜː) NOUN 1 a title of honour placed before the name of a knight or baronet: *Sir Walter Raleigh*. 2 *Archaic* a title placed before the name of a figure from ancient history.

Siracusa (sira'kuːza) NOUN the Italian name for **Syracuse.**

sirdar ('sɜːdɑː) NOUN 1 a general or military leader in Pakistan and India. 2 (formerly) the title of the British commander in chief of the Egyptian Army. 3 a variant spelling of **sardar.**
▹HISTORY from Hindi *sardār*, from Persian, from *sar* head + *dār* possession

sire (saɪə) NOUN 1 a male parent, esp of a horse or other domestic animal. 2 a respectful term of address, now used only in addressing a male

monarch. 3 *Obsolete* a man of high rank. ◆ VERB 4 (*tr*) (esp of a domestic animal) to father; beget.
▷HISTORY C13: from Old French, from Latin *senior* an elder, from *senex* an old man

siren ('saɪərən) NOUN 1 a device for emitting a loud wailing sound, esp as a warning or signal, typically consisting of a rotating perforated metal drum through which air or steam is passed under pressure. 2 (*sometimes capital*) *Greek myth* one of several sea nymphs whose seductive singing was believed to lure sailors to destruction on the rocks the nymphs inhabited. 3 **a** a woman considered to be dangerously alluring or seductive. **b** (*as modifier*): *her siren charms.* 4 any aquatic eel-like salamander of the North American family *Sirenidae,* having external gills, no hind limbs, and reduced forelimbs.
▷HISTORY C14: from Old French *sereine,* from Latin *sīrēn,* from Greek *seirēn*

sirenian (saɪ'ri:nɪən) ADJECTIVE 1 of, relating to, or belonging to the *Sirenia,* an order of aquatic herbivorous placental mammals having forelimbs modified as paddles, no hind limbs, and a horizontally flattened tail: contains only the dugong and manatees. ◆ NOUN 2 any animal belonging to the order *Sirenia;* a sea cow.

Siret (sɪ'rɛt) NOUN a river in SE Europe, rising in the Ukraine and flowing southeast through E Romania to the Danube. Length: about 450 km (280 miles).

Sirius ('sɪrɪəs) NOUN the brightest star in the sky after the sun, lying in the constellation Canis Major. It is a binary star whose companion, **Sirius B,** is a very faint white dwarf. Distance: 8.6 light years. Also called: **the Dog Star, Canicula, Sothis.** Related adjectives: **canicular, cynic.**
▷HISTORY C14: via Latin from Greek *Seirios,* of obscure origin

sirloin ('sɜ:ˌlɔɪn) NOUN a prime cut of beef from the loin, esp the upper part.
▷HISTORY C16 *surloyn,* from Old French *surlonge,* from *sur* above + *longe,* from *loigne* LOIN

sirocco (sɪ'rɒkəʊ) NOUN, *plural* **-cos.** 1 a hot oppressive and often dusty wind usually occurring in spring, beginning in N Africa and reaching S Europe. 2 any hot southerly wind, esp one moving to a low pressure centre.
▷HISTORY C17: from Italian, from Arabic *sharq* east wind

sironize *or* **sironise** ('saɪrəˌnaɪz) VERB (*tr*) *Austral* to treat (a woollen fabric) chemically to prevent it wrinkling after being washed.
▷HISTORY C20: from (C)SIRO + *-n-* + -IZE

siroset ('saɪrəʊˌsɛt) ADJECTIVE *Austral* of or relating to the chemical treatment of woollen fabrics to give a permanent-press effect, or a garment so treated.

sirrah ('sɪrə) NOUN *Archaic* a contemptuous term used in addressing a man or boy.
▷HISTORY C16: probably variant of SIRE

sirree (sə'ri:) INTERJECTION (*sometimes capital*) *US informal* an emphatic exclamation used with *yes* or *no.*

sir-reverence INTERJECTION *Obsolete* an expression of apology used esp to introduce taboo or vulgar words or phrases.
▷HISTORY C16: short for *save your reverence*

Sir Roger de Coverley NOUN an English country dance performed to a traditional tune by two rows of dancers facing each other.
▷HISTORY C18: alteration of *Roger of Coverley* influenced by *Sir Roger de Coverley,* a fictitious character appearing in the *Spectator* essays by Addison and Steele

sirup ('sɪrəp) NOUN *US* a less common spelling of **syrup.**

sirvente (sə'vɛnt) NOUN a verse form employed by the troubadours of Provence to satirize moral or political themes.
▷HISTORY C19: via French from Provençal *sirventes* song of a servant (that is, of a lover serving his mistress), from *sirvent* a servant, from Latin *servīre* to SERVE

sis[1] (sɪs) NOUN *Informal* short for **sister.**

sis[2] *or* **sies** (sɪs, si:s) INTERJECTION *South African informal* an exclamation of disgust.
▷HISTORY Afrikaans, possibly from Khoi

SIS ABBREVIATION FOR: 1 (in Britain) Secret Intelligence Service. Also called: **MI6.** 2 (in New Zealand) Security Intelligence Service.

sisal ('saɪsᵊl) NOUN 1 a Mexican agave plant, *Agave sisalana,* cultivated for its large fleshy leaves, which yield a stiff fibre used for making rope. 2 the fibre of this plant. 3 any of the fibres of certain similar or related plants. ◆ Also called: **sisal hemp.**
▷HISTORY C19: from Mexican Spanish, named after *Sisal,* a port in Yucatán, Mexico

Sisera ('sɪsərə) NOUN a defeated leader of the Canaanites, who was assassinated by Jael (Judges 4:17–21).

siskin ('sɪskɪn) NOUN 1 a yellow-and-black Eurasian finch, *Carduelis spinus.* 2 **pine siskin.** a North American finch, *Spinus pinus,* having a streaked yellowish-brown plumage.
▷HISTORY C16: from Middle Dutch *sīseken,* from Middle Low German *sīsek;* related to Czech *čížek,* Russian *chizh*

Sissinghurst Castle ('sɪsɪŋhɜ:st) NOUN a restored Elizabethan mansion near Cranbrook in Kent: noted for the gardens laid out in the 1930s by Victoria Sackville-West and Harold Nicolson.

sissy *or* **cissy** ('sɪsɪ) NOUN, *plural* **-sies.** 1 an effeminate, weak, or cowardly boy or man. ◆ ADJECTIVE 2 Also (informal or dialect): **'sissiˌfied** *or* **'cissiˌfied.** effeminate, weak, or cowardly.

sister ('sɪstə) NOUN 1 a female person having the same parents as another person. 2 See **half-sister, stepsister.** 3 a female person who belongs to the same group, trade union, etc., as another or others. 4 *Informal* a form of address to a woman or girl, used esp by Blacks in the US. 5 a senior nurse. 6 *Chiefly RC Church* a nun or a title given to a nun. 7 a woman fellow member of a Church or religious body. 8 (*modifier*) belonging to the same class, fleet, etc., as another or others: *a sister ship.* 9 (*modifier*) *Biology* denoting any of the cells or cell components formed by division of a parent cell or cell component: *sister nuclei.*
▷HISTORY Old English *sweostor;* related to Old Norse *systir,* Old High German *swester,* Gothic *swistar*

sisterhood ('sɪstəˌhʊd) NOUN 1 the state of being related as a sister or sisters. 2 a religious body or society of sisters, esp a community, order, or congregation of nuns. 3 the bond between women who support the Women's Movement.

sister-in-law NOUN, *plural* **sisters-in-law.** 1 the sister of one's husband or wife. 2 the wife of one's brother.

sisterly ('sɪstəlɪ) ADJECTIVE of, resembling, or suitable to a sister, esp in showing kindness and affection.
▸**'sisterliness** NOUN

Sistine Chapel ('sɪstaɪn, -ti:n) NOUN the chapel of the pope in the Vatican at Rome, built for Sixtus IV and decorated with frescoes by Michelangelo and others.
▷HISTORY Sistine, from Italian *Sistino* relating to *Sisto* Sixtus (Pope Sixtus IV)

sistroid ('sɪstrɔɪd) ADJECTIVE contained between the convex sides of two intersecting curves. Compare **cissoid** (sense 2).
▷HISTORY C20: from SISTRUM + -OID

sistrum ('sɪstrəm) NOUN, *plural* **-tra** (-trə). a musical instrument of ancient Egypt consisting of a metal rattle.
▷HISTORY C14: via Latin from Greek *seistron,* from *seiein* to shake

Sisyphean (ˌsɪsɪ'fi:ən) ADJECTIVE 1 relating to Sisyphus. 2 actually or seemingly endless and futile.

Sisyphus ('sɪsɪfəs) NOUN *Greek myth* a king of Corinth, punished in Hades for his misdeeds by eternally having to roll a heavy stone up a hill: every time he approached the top, the stone escaped his grasp and rolled to the bottom.

sit (sɪt) VERB **sits, sitting, sat.** (*mainly intr*) 1 (*also tr;* when *intr,* often foll by *down, in,* or *on*) to adopt or rest in a posture in which the body is supported on the buttocks and thighs and the torso is more or less upright: *to sit on a chair; sit a horse.* 2 (*tr*) to cause to adopt such a posture. 3 (of an animal) to adopt or rest in a posture with the hindquarters lowered to the ground. 4 (of a bird) to perch or roost. 5 (of a hen or other bird) to cover eggs to hatch them; brood. 6 to be situated or located. 7 (of the wind) to blow from the direction specified. 8 to adopt and maintain a posture for one's portrait to be painted, etc. 9 to occupy or be entitled to a seat in some official capacity, as a judge, elected representative, etc. 10 (of a deliberative body) to be convened or in session. 11 to remain inactive or unused: *his car sat in the garage for a year.* 12 to rest or lie as specified: *the nut was sitting so awkwardly that he couldn't turn it.* 13 (of a garment) to fit or hang as specified: *that dress sits well on you.* 14 to weigh, rest, or lie as specified: *greatness sits easily on him.* 15 (*tr*) *Chiefly Brit* to take (an examination): *he's sitting his bar finals.* 16 (usually foll by *for*) *Chiefly Brit* to be a candidate (for a qualification): *he's sitting for a BA.* 17 (*intr; in combination*) to look after a specified person or thing for someone else: *granny-sit.* 18 (*tr*) to have seating capacity for. 19 **sitting pretty.** *Informal* well placed or established financially, socially, etc. 20 **sit tight. a** to wait patiently; bide one's time. **b** to maintain one's position, stand, or opinion firmly. ◆ See also **sit back, sit down, sit-in, sit on, sit out, sit over, sit under, sit up.**
▷HISTORY Old English *sittan;* related to Old Norse *sitja,* Gothic *sitan,* Old High German *sizzen,* Latin *sedēre* to sit, Sanskrit *sīdati* he sits

SIT *Text messaging* ABBREVIATION FOR stay in touch.

Sita ('si:ta:) NOUN *Hinduism* goddess consort of the god Vishnu in the incarnation of Rama.

sitar (sɪ'tɑ:, 'sɪtɑ:) NOUN a stringed musical instrument, esp of India, having a long neck, a rounded body, and movable frets. The main strings, three to seven in number, overlie other sympathetic strings, the tuning depending on the raga being performed.
▷HISTORY from Hindi *sitār,* literally: three-stringed
▸**si'tarist** NOUN

sitatunga (ˌsɪtə'tʊŋgə) NOUN another name for **marshbuck.**

sit back VERB (*intr, adverb*) to relax, as when action should be taken: *many people just sit back and ignore the problems of today.*

sitcom ('sɪtˌkɒm) NOUN an informal term for **situation comedy.**

sit down VERB (*adverb*) 1 to adopt or cause (oneself or another) to adopt a sitting posture. 2 (*intr;* foll by *under*) to suffer (insults, etc.) without protests or resistance. ◆ NOUN **sit-down.** 3 a form of civil disobedience in which demonstrators sit down in a public place as a protest or to draw attention to a cause. 4 See **sit-down strike.** ◆ ADJECTIVE **sit-down.** 5 (of a meal, etc.) eaten while sitting down at a table.

sit-down money NOUN *Austral informal* social security benefits.

sit-down strike NOUN a strike in which workers refuse to leave their place of employment until a settlement is reached.

site (saɪt) NOUN 1 **a** the piece of land where something was, is, or is intended to be located: *a building site; archaeological site.* **b** (*as modifier*): *site office.* 2 an Internet location where information relating to a specific subject or group of subjects can be accessed. ◆ VERB 3 (*tr*) to locate, place, or install (something) in a specific place.
▷HISTORY C14: from Latin *situs* situation, from *sinere* to be placed

sitella (sɪ'tɛlə) NOUN *Austral* any of various small generally black-and-white birds of the genus *Neositta,* having a straight sharp beak and strong claws used to run up trees in search of insects: family *Sittidae* (nuthatches). Also called: **tree-runner.**
▷HISTORY C19: from New Latin, the diminutive of *sitta,* from Greek *sittē* nuthatch

sitfast ('sɪtˌfɑ:st) NOUN a sore on a horse's back caused by rubbing of the saddle.
▷HISTORY C17: from SIT + FAST[1] (in the sense: secure, fixed)

sith (sɪθ) ADVERB, CONJUNCTION, PREPOSITION an archaic word for **since.**
▷HISTORY Old English *siththa,* short for *siththan* SINCE

sithee ('sɪðɪ) INTERJECTION *Northern English dialect* look here! listen!

sit-in NOUN 1 a form of civil disobedience in which demonstrators occupy seats in a public place and refuse to move as a protest. 2 another term for **sit-down strike.** ◆ VERB **sit in.** (*intr, adverb*) 3 (often foll by *for*) to deputize (for). 4 (foll by *on*) to take part (in) as a visitor or guest: *we sat in on Professor Johnson's seminar.* 5 to organize or take part in a sit-in.

Sitka ('sɪtkə) NOUN a town in SE Alaska, in the Alexander Archipelago on W Baranof Island: capital of Russian America (1804–67) and of Alaska (1867–1906). Pop.: 8588 (1990).

sitkamer ('sɪtˌkɑːmə) NOUN *South African* a sitting room; lounge.
▷HISTORY from Afrikaans *sit* sitting + *kamer* room

sitka spruce ('sɪtkə) NOUN a tall North American spruce tree, *Picea sitchensis,* having yellowish-green needle-like leaves: yields valuable timber.
▷HISTORY C19: from SITKA

sitology (saɪ'tɒlədʒɪ) NOUN the scientific study of food, diet, and nutrition.
▷HISTORY C19: from Greek *sitos* food, grain + -LOGY

sit on VERB (*intr, preposition*) [1] to be a member of (a committee, etc.). [2] *Informal* to suppress. [3] *Informal* to check or rebuke.

sitosterol (saɪ'tɒstəˌrɒl) NOUN a white powder or waxy white solid extracted from soya beans, consisting of a mixture of isomers of the formula $C_{29}H_{50}O$ with other sterols: used in cosmetics and medicine.
▷HISTORY C20: from Greek *sitos* food, grain + STEROL

sit out VERB (*adverb*) [1] (*tr*) to endure to the end: *I sat out the play although it was terrible.* [2] (*tr*) to remain seated throughout (a dance, etc.). [3] (*intr*) *Chiefly Brit* to lean backwards over the side of a light sailing boat in order to carry the centre of gravity as far to windward as possible to reduce heeling. US and Canadian term: **hike out.**

sit over VERB (*intr, preposition*) *Cards* to be seated in an advantageous position on the left of (the player).

Sitsang ('siː'tsæŋ) NOUN a Chinese name for **Tibet.**

sittella NOUN a variant spelling of **sitella.**

sitter ('sɪtə) NOUN [1] a person or animal that sits. [2] a person who is posing for his or her portrait to be painted, carved, etc. [3] a broody hen or other bird that is sitting on its eggs to hatch them. [4] (*in combination*) a person who looks after a specified person or thing for someone else: *flat-sitter.* [5] short for **baby-sitter.** [6] anyone, other than the medium, taking part in a seance. [7] anything that is extremely easy, such as an easy catch in cricket.

sitting ('sɪtɪŋ) NOUN [1] a continuous period of being seated: *I read his novel at one sitting.* [2] such a period in a restaurant, canteen, etc., where space and other facilities are limited: *dinner will be served in two sittings.* [3] the act or period of posing for one's portrait to be painted, carved, etc. [4] a meeting, esp of an official body, to conduct business. [5] the incubation period of a bird's eggs during which the mother sits on them to keep them warm. ◆ ADJECTIVE [6] in office: *a sitting Member of Parliament.* [7] (of a hen) brooding eggs. [8] seated: *in a sitting position.*

sitting room NOUN a room in a private house or flat used for relaxation and entertainment of guests.

sitting target NOUN a person or thing in a defenceless or vulnerable position. Also called (informal): **sitting duck.**

sitting tenant NOUN a tenant occupying a house, flat, etc.

sitting trot NOUN a horse's trot during which the rider sits still in the saddle. Compare **rising trot.**

situate ('sɪtjuˌeɪt) VERB [1] (*tr; often passive*) to allot a site to; place; locate. ◆ ADJECTIVE [2] (now used esp in legal contexts) situated; located.
▷HISTORY C16: from Late Latin *situāre* to position, from Latin *situs* a SITE

situation (ˌsɪtju'eɪʃən) NOUN [1] physical placement, esp with regard to the surroundings. [2] **a** state of affairs; combination of circumstances. **b** a complex or critical state of affairs in a novel, play, etc. [3] social or financial status, position, or circumstances. [4] a position of employment; post.
▸ˌ**situ'ational** ADJECTIVE

> **Language note** *Situation* is often used in contexts in which it is redundant or imprecise. Typical examples are: *the company is in a crisis situation* or *people in a job situation.* In the first example, *situation* does not add to the meaning and should be omitted. In the second example, it would be clearer and more concise to substitute a phrase such as *people at work.*

situation comedy NOUN (on television or radio) a comedy series involving the same characters in various day-to-day situations which are developed as separate stories for each episode. Also called: **sitcom.**

situla ('sɪtjʊlə) NOUN, *plural* **-lae** (-liː). [1] a bucket-shaped container, usually of metal or pottery and often richly decorated: typical of the N Italian Iron Age. ◆ ADJECTIVE [2] of or relating to the type of designs usually associated with these containers.
▷HISTORY from Latin

sit under VERB (*intr, preposition*) *Cards* to be seated on the right of (the player).

sit up VERB (*adverb*) [1] to raise (oneself or another) from a recumbent to an upright or alert sitting posture. [2] (*intr*) to remain out of bed and awake, esp until a late hour. [3] (*intr*) *Informal* to become suddenly interested or alert: *devaluation of the dollar made the money market sit up.* ◆ NOUN **sit-up.** [4] a physical exercise in which the body is brought into a sitting position from one lying on the back.

situs ('saɪtəs) NOUN, *plural* **-tus.** position or location, esp the usual or right position of an organ or part of the body.
▷HISTORY C18: from Latin: site, situation, position

sitz bath (sɪts, zɪts) NOUN a bath in which the buttocks and hips are immersed in hot water, esp for therapeutic effects, as after perineal or pelvic surgery.
▷HISTORY half translation of German *Sitzbad,* from *Sitz* SEAT + *Bad* BATH[1]

sitzkrieg ('sɪtsˌkriːg, 'zɪts-) NOUN a period during a war in which both sides change positions very slowly or not at all.
▷HISTORY C20: from German, from *sitzen* to sit + *Krieg* war

sitzmark ('sɪtsˌmɑːk, 'zɪts-) NOUN *Skiing* a depression in the snow where a skier has fallen.
▷HISTORY German, literally: seat mark

SI unit NOUN any of the units adopted for international use under the Système International d'Unités, now employed for all scientific and most technical purposes. There are seven fundamental units: the metre, kilogram, second, ampere, kelvin, candela, and mole; and two supplementary units: the radian and the steradian. All other units are derived by multiplication or division of these units without the use of numerical factors.

Siva ('siːvə, 'sɪvə) *or* **Shiva** NOUN *Hinduism* the destroyer, one of the three chief divinities of the later Hindu pantheon, the other two being Brahma and Vishnu. Siva is also the god presiding over personal destinies.
▷HISTORY from Sanskrit *Śiva,* literally: the auspicious (one)

Sivaism ('siːvəˌɪzəm, 'sɪvə-) NOUN the cult of Siva.
▸'**Sivaist** NOUN ▸ˌ**Siva'istic** ADJECTIVE

Sivan (siː'vɑːn) NOUN (in the Jewish calendar) the third month of the year according to biblical reckoning and the ninth month of the civil year, usually falling within May and June.
▷HISTORY from Hebrew

Sivananda yoga (ˌsɪvə'nændə) NOUN a gentle form of yoga which concentrates on breathing control, stretching, and silent meditation.

Sivas (*Turkish* 'sivɑs) NOUN a city in central Turkey, at an altitude of 1347 m (4420 ft.): one of the chief cities in Asia Minor in ancient times; scene of the national congress (1919) leading to the revolution that established modern Turkey. Pop.: 232 352 (1997).

siwash ('saɪwɒʃ) NOUN [1] another name for **Cowichan sweater.** ◆ VERB [2] (*intr*) (in the Pacific Northwest) to camp out with only natural shelter.
▷HISTORY see SIWASH

Siwash ('saɪwɒʃ) (*sometimes not capital*) *Slang, derogatory* (in the Pacific Northwest) NOUN [1] a North American Indian. ◆ ADJECTIVE [2] of, characteristic of, or relating to Indians. [3] worthless, stingy, or bad: *he's siwash.*
▷HISTORY C19: from Chinook Jargon, from French *sauvage* SAVAGE

six (sɪks) NOUN [1] the cardinal number that is the sum of five and one. See also **number** (sense 1). [2] a numeral, 6, VI, etc., representing this number. [3] something representing, represented by, or consisting of six units, such as a playing card with six symbols on it. [4] Also called: **six o'clock.** six hours after noon or midnight. [5] Also called: **sixer.** *Cricket* **a** a stroke in which the ball crosses the boundary without bouncing. **b** the six runs scored for such a stroke. [6] a division of a Brownie Guide or Cub Scout pack. [7] **at sixes and sevens. a** in disagreement. **b** in a state of confusion. [8] **knock (someone) for six.** *Informal* to upset or overwhelm (someone) completely; stun. [9] **six of one and half a dozen of the other.** Also: **six and two threes.** a situation in which the alternatives are considered equivalent. ◆ DETERMINER [10] **a** amounting to six: *six nations.* **b** (*as pronoun*): *set the table for six.* ◆ Related prefixes: **hexa-, sex-.**
▷HISTORY Old English *siex;* related to Old Norse *sex,* Gothic *saihs,* Old High German *sehs,* Latin *sex,* Greek *hex,* Sanskrit *sastha*

Six (*French* sis) NOUN **Les** (le). a group of six young composers in France, who from about 1916 formed a temporary association as a result of interest in neoclassicism and in the music of Satie and the poetry of Cocteau. Its members were Darius Milhaud, Arthur Honegger, Francis Poulenc, Georges Auric, Louis Durey, and Germaine Tailleferre.

sixain ('sɪkseɪn) NOUN a stanza or poem of six lines.
▷HISTORY from French

Six Counties PLURAL NOUN the historic counties of Northern Ireland, which no longer have a local government function.

Six Day War NOUN a war fought in the Middle East in June 1967, lasting six days. In it Israel defeated Egypt, Jordan, and Syria, occupying the Gaza Strip, the Sinai, Jerusalem, the West Bank of the Jordan, and the Golan Heights.

six-eight time NOUN *Music* a form of compound duple time in which there are six quaver beats to the bar, indicated by the time signature $\frac{6}{8}$. Often shortened to: **six-eight.**

sixer ('sɪksə) NOUN a leader of a Brownie Guide or Cub Scout six.

six-finger country NOUN *Austral slang* an isolated area considered as being inhabited by people who practise inbreeding.

sixfold ('sɪksˌfəʊld) ADJECTIVE [1] equal to or having six times as many or as much. [2] composed of six parts. ◆ ADVERB [3] by or up to six times as many or as much.

six-footer NOUN a person who is at least six feet tall.

six-gun NOUN *US informal* another word for **six-shooter.**

sixmo ('sɪksməʊ) NOUN, *plural* **-mos.** [1] Also called: **sexto.** a book size resulting from folding a sheet of paper into six leaves or twelve pages, each one sixth the size of the sheet. Often written: **6mo, 6°.** [2] a book of this size.

Six Nations PLURAL NOUN (in North America) the Indian confederacy of the Cayugas, Mohawks, Oneidas, Onondagas, Senecas, and Tuscaroras. Also called: **Iroquois.** See also **Five Nations.**

six o'clock swill NOUN *Austral and NZ informal* a period of heavy drinking, esp during the years when hotels had to close their bars at 6.00 p.m.

six-pack NOUN [1] *Informal* a package containing six units, esp six cans of beer. [2] a set of highly developed abdominal muscles in a man. [3] (*modifier*) *Austral* arranged in standard sets of six: *six-pack apartment blocks.*

sixpence ('sɪkspəns) NOUN a small British cupronickel coin with a face value of six pennies, worth 2½ (new) pence, not minted since 1970.

sixpenny ('sɪkspənɪ) ADJECTIVE (*prenominal*) (of a nail) two inches in length.

six-shooter NOUN *US informal* a revolver with six chambers. Also called: **six-gun.**

sixte (sɪkst) NOUN the sixth of eight basic positions from which a parry or attack can be made in fencing.
▷HISTORY from French: (the) sixth (parrying position), from Latin *sextus* sixth

sixteen ('sɪks'tiːn) NOUN [1] the cardinal number that is the sum of ten and six. See also **number** (sense 1). [2] a numeral, 16, XVI, etc., representing this number. [3] *Music* the numeral 16 used as the lower figure of a time signature to indicate that the beat is measured in semiquavers. 4 something represented by, representing, or consisting of 16 units. ◆ DETERMINER 5 **a** amounting to sixteen: *sixteen tons.* **b** (*as pronoun*): *sixteen are known to the police.*

sixteenmo ('sɪks'tiːnməʊ) NOUN, *plural* **-mos.** 1 Also called: **sextodecimo.** a book size resulting from folding a sheet of paper into 16 leaves or 32 pages, each one sixteenth the size of the sheet. Often written: **16mo, 16°.** 2 a book of this size.

sixteenth ('sɪks'tiːnθ) ADJECTIVE 1 (*usually prenominal*) **a** coming after the fifteenth in numbering or counting order, position, time, etc.; being the ordinal number of *sixteen:* often written 16th. **b** (*as noun*): *the sixteenth of the month.* ◆ NOUN 2 **a** one of 16 equal or nearly equal parts of something. **b** (*as modifier*): *a sixteenth part.* 3 the fraction that is equal to one divided by 16 (1/16).

sixteenth note NOUN the usual US and Canadian name for **semiquaver.**

sixth (sɪksθ) ADJECTIVE 1 (*usually prenominal*) **a** coming after the fifth and before the seventh in numbering or counting order, position, time, etc.; being the ordinal number of *six:* often written 6th. **b** (*as noun*): *the sixth to go.* ◆ NOUN 2 **a** one of six equal or nearly equal parts of an object, quantity, measurement, etc. **b** (*as modifier*): *a sixth part.* 3 the fraction equal to one divided by six (1/6). 4 *Music* **a** the interval between one note and another note six notes away from it counting inclusively along the diatonic scale. **b** one of two notes constituting such an interval in relation to the other. See also **major** (sense 14), **minor** (sense 4), **interval** (sense 5). **c** short for **sixth chord.** ◆ ADVERB 5 Also: **sixthly.** after the fifth person, position, etc. ◆ SENTENCE CONNECTOR 6 Also: **sixthly.** as the sixth point: linking what follows to the previous statements.

sixth chord NOUN (in classical harmony) the first inversion of the triad, in which the note next above the root appears in the bass. See also **added sixth.**

sixth form NOUN (in England and Wales) the most senior class in a secondary school to which pupils, usually above the legal leaving age, may proceed to take A levels, retake GCSEs, etc.
► **'sixth-ˌformer** NOUN

sixth-form college NOUN (in England and Wales) a college offering A-level and other courses to pupils over sixteen from local schools, esp from those that do not have sixth forms.

sixth sense NOUN any supposed sense or means of perception, such as intuition or clairvoyance, other than the five senses of sight, hearing, touch, taste, and smell.

sixth year NOUN (in Scotland) the most senior class in a secondary school to which pupils, usually above the legal leaving age, may proceed to take sixth-year studies, retake or take additional Highers, etc.

sixtieth ('sɪkstɪɪθ) ADJECTIVE 1 (*usually prenominal*) **a** being the ordinal number of *sixty* in numbering or counting order, position, time, etc.: often written 60th. **b** (*as noun*): *the sixtieth in a row.* ◆ NOUN 2 **a** one of 60 approximately equal parts of something. **b** (*as modifier*): *a sixtieth part.* 3 the fraction equal to one divided by 60 (1/60).

sixty ('sɪkstɪ) NOUN, *plural* **-ties.** 1 the cardinal number that is the product of ten and six. See also **number** (sense 1). 2 a numeral, 60, LX, etc., representing sixty. 3 something represented by, representing, or consisting of 60 units. ◆ DETERMINER 4 **a** amounting to sixty: *sixty soldiers.* **b** (*as pronoun*): *sixty are dead.*
▷HISTORY Old English *sixtig*

sixty-fourmo (ˌsɪkstɪ'fɔːməʊ) NOUN, *plural* **-mos.** 1 a book size resulting from folding a sheet of paper into 64 leaves or 128 pages, each one sixty-fourth the size of the sheet. Often written: **64mo, 64°.** 2 a book of this size.

sixty-fourth note NOUN the usual US and Canadian name for **hemidemisemiquaver.**

sixty-four thousand dollar question NOUN a crucial question or issue.
▷HISTORY C20: an elaboration of the earlier *sixty-four dollar question,* so called from the top prize on the US radio show *Take It or Leave It* (1941–48)

sixty-nine NOUN another term for **soixante-neuf.**

six-yard line NOUN *Soccer* the line marking the limits of the goal area.

sizable *or* **sizeable** ('saɪzəbᵊl) ADJECTIVE quite large.
► **'sizableness** *or* **'sizeableness** NOUN ► **'sizably** *or* **'sizeably** ADVERB

sizar ('saɪzə) NOUN *Brit* (at Peterhouse, Cambridge, and Trinity College, Dublin) an undergraduate receiving a maintenance grant from the college.
▷HISTORY C16: from earlier *sizer,* from SIZE[1] (meaning "an allowance of food, etc.")
► **'sizarˌship** NOUN

size[1] (saɪz) NOUN 1 the dimensions, proportions, amount, or extent of something. 2 large or great dimensions, etc. 3 one of a series of graduated measurements, as of clothing: *she takes size 4 shoes.* 4 *Informal* state of affairs as summarized: *he's bankrupt, that's the size of it.* ◆ VERB 5 to sort according to size. 6 (*tr*) to make or cut to a particular size or sizes.
▷HISTORY C13: from Old French *sise,* shortened from *assise* ASSIZE
► **'sizer** NOUN

> **Language note** The use of *-size* and *-sized* after *large* or *small* is redundant, except when describing something which is made in specific sizes: *a large* (not *large-size*) *organization.* Similarly, *in size* is redundant in the expressions *large in size* and *small in size.*

size[2] (saɪz) NOUN 1 Also called: **sizing.** a thin gelatinous mixture, made from glue, clay, or wax, that is used as a sealer or filler on paper, cloth, or plaster surfaces. ◆ VERB 2 (*tr*) to treat or coat (a surface) with size.
▷HISTORY C15: perhaps from Old French *sise;* see SIZE[1]
► **'sizy** ADJECTIVE

sized (saɪzd) ADJECTIVE of a specified size: *medium-sized.*

> **Language note** See at **size[1]**.

sizeism ('saɪzɪzəm) NOUN discrimination on the basis of a person's size, esp against people considered to be overweight.
▷HISTORY C20: from SIZE[1] + -ISM, on the model of RACISM

size up VERB (*adverb*) 1 (*tr*) to make an assessment of (a person, problem, etc.). 2 to conform to or make so as to conform to certain specifications of dimension.

size-weight illusion NOUN a standard sense illusion that a small object is heavier than a large object of the same weight.

sizzle ('sɪzᵊl) VERB (*intr*) 1 to make the hissing sound characteristic of frying fat. 2 *Informal* to be very hot. 3 *Informal* to be very angry. ◆ NOUN 4 a hissing sound.
▷HISTORY C17: of imitative origin. Compare *siss* (now dialect) to hiss, West Frisian *size, siizje.* See also FIZZ and FIZZLE

sizzler ('sɪzlə) NOUN 1 something that sizzles. 2 *Informal* a very hot day.

sizzling ('sɪzlɪŋ) ADJECTIVE 1 extremely hot. 2 very passionate or erotic: *a sizzling sex scene.*

sj THE INTERNET DOMAIN NAME FOR Svalbard and Jan Mayen Islands.

SJ ABBREVIATION FOR **Society of Jesus.**

SJA ABBREVIATION FOR Saint John's Ambulance (Brigade or Association).

Sjælland (*Danish* 'sjɛlan) NOUN the Danish name for **Zealand.**

sjambok ('ʃæmbʌk, -bɒk) (in South Africa) NOUN 1 a heavy whip of rhinoceros or hippopotamus hide. ◆ VERB **-boks, -bokking, -bokked.** 2 (*tr*) to strike or beat with such a whip.
▷HISTORY C19: from Afrikaans, from Malay *samboq, chamboq,* from Urdu *chābuk*

SJC (in the US) ABBREVIATION FOR Supreme Judicial Court.

SJD ABBREVIATION FOR Doctor of Juridical Science.
▷HISTORY from Latin *Scientiae Juridicae Doctor*

sk[1] ABBREVIATION FOR sack.

sk[2] THE INTERNET DOMAIN NAME FOR Slovak Republic.

SK 1 ABBREVIATION FOR (esp in postal addresses) Saskatchewan. ◆ 2 INTERNATIONAL CAR REGISTRATION FOR Slovakia.

SK8 *Text messaging* ABBREVIATION FOR skate.

ska (skɑː) NOUN a type of West Indian pop music of the 1960s, accented on the second and fourth beats of a four-beat bar.

skag (skæg) NOUN a variant spelling of **scag[1]**.

Skagen ('skɑːgən) NOUN **Cape.** another name for the **Skaw.**

Skagerrak ('skægəˌræk) NOUN an arm of the North Sea between Denmark and Norway, merging with the Kattegat in the southeast.

skald *or* **scald** (skɔːld) NOUN (in ancient Scandinavia) a bard or minstrel.
▷HISTORY from Old Norse, of unknown origin
► **'skaldic** *or* **'scaldic** ADJECTIVE

skank (skæŋk) NOUN 1 a fast dance to reggae music. 2 *Slang* a promiscuous female. ◆ VERB (*intr*) 3 to perform this dance.

skanky ('skæŋkɪ) ADJECTIVE **-kier, -kiest.** *Slang* 1 dirty, foul-smelling, or unattractive. 2 promiscuous.
► **'skankiness** NOUN

skanky-ho NOUN *NZ slang* a promiscuous woman.

Skara Brae ('skærə) NOUN a neolithic village in NE Scotland, in the Orkney Islands: one of Europe's most perfectly preserved Stone Age villages, buried by a sand dune until uncovered by a storm in 1850.

skat (skæt) NOUN a three-handed card game using 32 cards, popular in German-speaking communities.
▷HISTORY C19: from German, from Italian *scarto* played cards, from *scartare* to discard, from *s-* EX-[1] + *carta,* from Latin *charta* CARD[1]

skate[1] (skeɪt) NOUN 1 See **roller skate, ice skate.** 2 the steel blade or runner of an ice skate. 3 such a blade fitted with straps for fastening to a shoe. 4 a current collector on an electric railway train that collects its current from a third rail. Compare **bow collector.** 5 **get one's skates on.** to hurry. ◆ VERB (*intr*) 6 to glide swiftly on skates. 7 to slide smoothly over a surface. 8 **skate on on thin ice.** to place oneself in a dangerous or delicate situation.
▷HISTORY C17: via Dutch from Old French *éschasse* stilt, probably of Germanic origin

skate[2] (skeɪt) NOUN, *plural* **skate** *or* **skates.** any large ray of the family *Rajidae,* of temperate and tropical seas, having flat pectoral fins continuous with the head, two dorsal fins, a short spineless tail, and a long snout.
▷HISTORY C14: from Old Norse *skata*

skate[3] (skeɪt) NOUN *US slang* a person; fellow.
▷HISTORY from Scottish and northern English dialect *skate,* a derogatory term of uncertain origin

skateboard ('skeɪtˌbɔːd) NOUN 1 a narrow board mounted on roller-skate wheels, usually ridden while standing up. ◆ VERB 2 (*intr*) to ride on a skateboard.
► **'skateˌboarder** NOUN ► **'skateˌboarding** NOUN

skate over VERB (*intr, preposition*) 1 to cross on or as if on skates. 2 to avoid dealing with (a matter) fully.

skater ('skeɪtə) NOUN 1 a person who skates. 2 See **pond-skater.**

skatole ('skætəʊl) NOUN a white or brownish crystalline solid with a strong faecal odour, found in faeces, beetroot, and coal tar; B-methylindole. Formula: C_9H_9N.
▷HISTORY C19: from Greek *skat-,* stem of *skōr* excrement + -OLE[1]

Skaw (skɔː) NOUN **the.** a cape at the N tip of Denmark. Also called: (Cape) **Skagen.**

skean (skiːn) NOUN a kind of double-edged dagger formerly used in Ireland and Scotland.
▷HISTORY from Irish and Scottish Gaelic *scian*

skean-dhu ('skiːən'duː, 'skiːn-) NOUN *Scot* a variant of **sgian-dhu.**

skedaddle (skɪ'dædᵊl) *Informal* ◆ VERB 1 (*intr*) to run off hastily. ◆ NOUN 2 a hasty retreat.
▷HISTORY C19: of unknown origin

skeet (skiːt) NOUN a form of clay-pigeon shooting in which targets are hurled from two traps at varying speeds and angles. Also called: **skeet shooting.**

▷HISTORY C20: changed from Old Norse *skeyti* a thrown object, from *skjōta* to shoot

skeg (skɛg) NOUN *Nautical* [1] a reinforcing brace between the after end of a keel and the rudderpost. [2] a support at the bottom of a rudder. [3] a projection from the forefoot of a vessel for towing paravanes. [4] any short keel-like projection at the stern of a boat. [5] *Austral* a rear fin on the underside of a surfboard.
▷HISTORY C16: of Scandinavian origin; compare Icelandic *skegg* cutwater

skein (skeɪn) NOUN [1] a length of yarn, etc., wound in a long coil. [2] something resembling this, such as a lock of hair. [3] a flock of geese flying. Compare **gaggle** (sense 2).
▷HISTORY C15: from Old French *escaigne*, of unknown origin

skeleton (ˈskɛlɪtən) NOUN [1] a hard framework consisting of inorganic material that supports and protects the soft parts of an animal's body and provides attachment for muscles: may be internal, as in vertebrates (see **endoskeleton**), or external, as in arthropods (see **exoskeleton**). [2] *Informal* a very thin emaciated person or animal. [3] the essential framework of any structure, such as a building or leaf, that supports or determines the shape of the rest of the structure. [4] an outline consisting of bare essentials: *the skeleton of a novel.* [5] (*modifier*) reduced to a minimum: *a skeleton staff.* [6] **skeleton in the cupboard** *or* (*US and Canadian*) **closet**. a scandalous fact or event in the past that is kept secret.
▷HISTORY C16: via New Latin from Greek: something desiccated, from *skellein* to dry up
▸ˈ**skeletal** ADJECTIVE ▸ˈ**skeletally** ADVERB ▸ˈ**skeleton-**ˌ**like** ADJECTIVE

skeletonize *or* **skeletonise** (ˈskɛlɪtəˌnaɪz) VERB (*tr*) [1] to reduce to a minimum framework, number, or outline. [2] to create the essential framework of.

skeleton key NOUN a key with the serrated edge filed down so that it can open numerous locks. Also called: **passkey**.
▷HISTORY C19: so called because it has been reduced to its essential parts

skelf (skɛlf) NOUN *Scot and northern English dialect* [1] a splinter of wood, esp when embedded accidentally in the skin. [2] a thin or diminutive person.
▷HISTORY from Scottish; see SHELF

skellum (ˈskɛləm) NOUN *Archaic and dialect* a rogue.
▷HISTORY C17: via Dutch from Old High German *skelmo* devil

skelly^1 (ˈskɛlɪ) NOUN, *plural* **-lies**. a whitefish, *Coregonus stigmaticus*, of certain lakes in the Lake District.
▷HISTORY C18: perhaps from dialect *skell* a shell or scale, and so called because of its large scales

skelly^2 (ˈskɛlɪ) *Scot and northern English dialect* ◆ VERB **-lies, -lying, -lied**. (*intr*) [1] to look sideways or squint. ◆ NOUN, *plural* **-lies**. [2] a quick look; glance. ◆ ADJECTIVE [3] Also: **skelly-eyed**. cross-eyed.
▷HISTORY probably from Old Norse, from *skjalgr* wry; related to Old English *sceolh* a squint

skelm (ˈskɛlᵊm) NOUN *South African informal* a villain or crook.
▷HISTORY Afrikaans

Skelmersdale (ˈskɛlməzˌdeɪl) NOUN a town in NW England, in Lancashire: designated a new town in 1962. Pop.: 42 104 (1991).

skelp^1 (skɛlp) *Dialect* ◆ VERB [1] (*tr*) to slap. ◆ NOUN [2] a slap.
▷HISTORY C15: probably of imitative origin

skelp^2 (skɛlp) NOUN sheet or plate metal that has been curved and welded to form a tube.
▷HISTORY C19: perhaps from Scottish Gaelic *sgealb* thin strip of wood

sken (skɛn) VERB **skens, skenning, skenned**. (*intr*) *Northern English dialect* to squint or stare.
▷HISTORY of obscure origin

skep (skɛp) NOUN [1] a beehive, esp one constructed of straw. [2] *Now chiefly dialect* a large basket of wickerwork or straw.
▷HISTORY Old English *sceppe*, from Old Norse *skeppa* bushel; related to Old High German *sceffil* bushel

skeptic (ˈskɛptɪk) NOUN, ADJECTIVE an archaic, and the usual US, spelling of **sceptic**.
▸ˈ**skeptical** ADJECTIVE ▸ˈ**skeptically** ADVERB ▸ˈ**skepticalness** NOUN ▸ˈ**skepticism** NOUN

skerrick (ˈskɛrɪk) NOUN *US, Austral, and NZ* a small fragment or amount (esp in the phrase **not a skerrick**).
▷HISTORY C20: northern English dialect, probably of Scandinavian origin

skerry (ˈskɛrɪ) NOUN, *plural* **-ries**. *Chiefly Scot* [1] a small rocky island. [2] a reef.
▷HISTORY C17: Orkney dialect, from Old Norse *sker* SCAR^2

sket (skɛt) VERB **skets, sketting, sketted**. (*tr*) *South Wales dialect* [1] to splash (water). [2] to splash (someone with water).
▷HISTORY perhaps from Old Norse *skjóta* to shoot

sketch (skɛtʃ) NOUN [1] a rapid drawing or painting, often a study for subsequent elaboration. [2] a brief usually descriptive and informal essay or other literary composition. [3] a short play, often comic, forming part of a revue. [4] a short evocative piece of instrumental music, esp for piano. [5] any brief outline. ◆ VERB [6] to make a rough drawing (of). [7] (*tr; often foll by out*) to make a brief description of.
▷HISTORY C17: from Dutch *schets*, via Italian from Latin *schedius* hastily made, from Greek *skhedios* unprepared
▸ˈ**sketchable** ADJECTIVE ▸ˈ**sketcher** NOUN

sketchbook (ˈskɛtʃˌbʊk) NOUN [1] a book of plain paper containing sketches or for making sketches in. [2] a book of literary sketches.

sketchy (ˈskɛtʃɪ) ADJECTIVE **sketchier, sketchiest**. [1] characteristic of a sketch; existing only in outline. [2] superficial or slight.
▸ˈ**sketchily** ADVERB ▸ˈ**sketchiness** NOUN

skew (skjuː) ADJECTIVE [1] placed in or turning into an oblique position or course. [2] *Machinery* having a component that is at an angle to the main axis of an assembly or is in some other way asymmetrical: *a skew bevel gear.* [3] *Maths* **a** composed of or being elements that are neither parallel nor intersecting as, for example, two lines not lying in the same plane in a three-dimensional space. **b** (of a curve) not lying in a plane. [4] (of a statistical distribution) not having equal probabilities above and below the mean; non-normal. [5] distorted or biased. ◆ NOUN [6] an oblique, slanting, or indirect course or position. [7] *Psychol* the system of relationships in a family in which one parent is extremely dominating while the other parent tends to be meekly compliant. ◆ VERB [8] to take or cause to take an oblique course or direction. [9] (*intr*) to look sideways; squint. [10] (*tr*) to place at an angle. [11] (*tr*) to distort or bias.
▷HISTORY C14: from Old Norman French *escuer* to shun, of Germanic origin; compare Middle Dutch *schuwen* to avoid

skew arch NOUN an arch or vault, esp one used in a bridge or tunnel, that is set at an oblique angle to the span.

skewback (ˈskjuːˌbæk) NOUN [1] the sloping surface on both sides of a segmental arch that takes the thrust. [2] one or more stones that provide such a surface.
▸ˈ**skew**ˌ**backed** ADJECTIVE

skewbald (ˈskjuːˌbɔːld) ADJECTIVE [1] marked or spotted in white and any colour except black. ◆ NOUN [2] a horse with this marking.
▷HISTORY C17: see SKEW, PIEBALD

skewer (ˈskjʊə) NOUN [1] a long pin for holding meat in position while being cooked, etc. [2] a similar pin having some other function. [3] *Chess* a tactical manoeuvre in which an attacked man is made to move and expose another man to capture. ◆ VERB [4] (*tr*) to drive a skewer through or fasten with a skewer.
▷HISTORY C17: probably from dialect *skiver*

skewness (ˈskjuːnɪs) NOUN [1] the quality or condition of being skew. [2] *Statistics* a measure of the symmetry of a distribution around its mean, esp the statistic $B_1 = m_3/(m_2)^{3/2}$, where m_2 and m_3 are respectively the second and third moments of the distribution around the mean. In a normal distribution, $B_1 = 0$. Compare **kurtosis**.

skew symmetry NOUN symmetry of top left with bottom right, and top right with bottom left.

skewwhiff (ˈskjuːˈwɪf) ADJECTIVE (*postpositive*) *Brit informal* not straight; askew.
▷HISTORY C18: probably influenced by ASKEW

ski (skiː) NOUN, *plural* **skis** *or* **ski**. [1] **a** one of a pair of wood, metal, or plastic runners that are used for gliding over snow. Skis are commonly attached to shoes for sport, but may also be used as landing gear for aircraft, etc. **b** (*as modifier*): *a ski boot.* [2] a water-ski. ◆ VERB **skis, skiing; skied** *or* **ski'd**. [3] (*intr*) to travel on skis.
▷HISTORY C19: from Norwegian, from Old Norse *skíth* snowshoes; related to Old English *scīd* piece of split wood
▸ˈ**skiable** ADJECTIVE ▸ˈ**skier** NOUN ▸ˈ**skiing** NOUN

skiamachy (skaɪˈæməkɪ) NOUN, *plural* **-chies**. a variant of **sciamachy**.

skiascope (ˈskaɪəˌskəʊp) NOUN *Med* a medical instrument for examining the eye to detect errors of refraction. Also called: **retinoscope**. See also **retinoscopy**.
▷HISTORY C19: from Greek *skia* a shadow + -SCOPE

skiascopy (skaɪˈæskəpɪ) NOUN *Med* another name for **retinoscopy**.

skibob (ˈskiːbɒb) NOUN a vehicle made of two short skis, the forward one having a steering handle and the rear one supporting a low seat, for gliding down snow slopes.
▷HISTORY C20: from SKI + BOB^2. See BOBSLEIGH
▸ˈ**skibobber** NOUN ▸ˈ**skibobbing** NOUN

skid (skɪd) VERB **skids, skidding, skidded**. [1] to cause (a vehicle) to slide sideways or (of a vehicle) to slide sideways while in motion, esp out of control. [2] (*intr*) to slide without revolving, as the wheel of a moving vehicle after sudden braking. [3] (*tr*) *US and Canadian* to put or haul on a skid, esp along a special track. [4] to cause (an aircraft) to slide sideways away from the centre of a turn when insufficiently banked or (of an aircraft) to slide in this manner. ◆ NOUN [5] an instance of sliding, esp sideways. [6] *Chiefly US and Canadian* one of the logs forming a skidway. [7] a support on which heavy objects may be stored and moved short distances by sliding. [8] a shoe or drag used to apply pressure to the metal rim of a wheel to act as a brake. [9] **on the skids**. in decline or about to fail.
▷HISTORY C17: perhaps of Scandinavian origin; compare SKI
▸ˈ**skiddy** ADJECTIVE

skidlid (ˈskɪdˌlɪd) NOUN a slang word for **crash helmet**.

Skidoo (skɪˈduː) NOUN *Trademark, Canadian* another name for **snowmobile**.

skidpan (ˈskɪdˌpæn) NOUN *Chiefly Brit* an area made slippery so that vehicle drivers can practise controlling skids.

skidproof (ˈskɪdˌpruːf) ADJECTIVE (of a road surface, tyre, etc.) preventing or resistant to skidding.

skid road NOUN (in the US and Canada) [1] a track made of a set of logs laid transversely on which freshly cut timber can be hauled. [2] **a** (in the West) the part of a town frequented by loggers. **b** another term for **skid row**.

skid row (rəʊ) *or* **skid road** NOUN *Slang, chiefly US and Canadian* a dilapidated section of a city inhabited by vagrants, etc.

skidway (ˈskɪdˌweɪ) NOUN *Chiefly US and Canadian* [1] a platform on which logs ready for sawing are piled. [2] a track made of logs for rolling objects along.

skied^1 (skaɪd) VERB the past tense and past participle of **sky**.

skied^2 (skiːd) VERB a past tense and past participle of **ski**.

Skien (*Norwegian* ˈʃeːən) NOUN a port in S Norway, on the **Skien River**: one of the oldest towns in Norway; timber industry. Pop.: 47 870 (1990).

skiff (skɪf) NOUN any of various small boats propelled by oars, sail, or motor.
▷HISTORY C18: from French *esquif*, from Old Italian *schifo* a boat, of Germanic origin; related to Old High German *schif* SHIP

skiffle^1 (ˈskɪfᵊl) NOUN a style of popular music of the 1950s, played chiefly on guitars and improvised percussion instruments.
▷HISTORY C20: of unknown origin

skiffle^2 (ˈskɪfᵊl) NOUN *Ulster dialect* a drizzle: *a skiffle of rain.*
▷HISTORY from Scottish *skiff*, from *skiff* to move

lightly, probably changed from *skift,* from Old Norse *skipta* SHIFT

skijoring (skiːˈdʒɔːrɪŋ) NOUN a sport in which a skier is pulled over snow or ice, usually by a horse.
▷HISTORY Norwegian *skikjöring,* literally: ski-driving
▸**skiˈjorer** NOUN

ski jump NOUN [1] a high ramp overhanging a slope from which skiers compete to make the longest jump. ◆ VERB **ski-jump.** [2] *(intr)* to perform a ski jump.
▸**ski jumper** NOUN

Skikda (ˈskɪkdɑː) NOUN a port in NE Algeria, on an inlet of the Mediterranean: founded by the French in 1838 on the site of a Roman city. Pop.: 152 335 (1998). Former name: **Philippeville.**

skilful *or US* **skillful** (ˈskɪlfʊl) ADJECTIVE [1] possessing or displaying accomplishment or skill. [2] involving or requiring accomplishment or skill.
▸**ˈskilfully** *or US* **ˈskillfully** ADVERB ▸**ˈskilfulness** *or US* **ˈskillfulness** NOUN

ski lift NOUN any of various devices for carrying skiers up a slope, such as a chairlift.

skill (skɪl) NOUN [1] special ability in a task, sport, etc., esp ability acquired by training. [2] something, esp a trade or technique, requiring special training or manual proficiency. [3] *Obsolete* understanding.
▷HISTORY C12: from Old Norse *skil* distinction; related to Middle Low German *schēle,* Middle Dutch *geschil* difference
▸**ˈskill-less** *or* **ˈskilless** ADJECTIVE

Skillcentre (ˈskɪlˌsɛntə) NOUN *Brit* any of a number of agencies attached to the Manpower Services Commission and funded by the Government to provide vocational training or retraining for employed or unemployed people.

skilled (skɪld) ADJECTIVE [1] possessing or demonstrating accomplishment, skill, or special training. [2] *(prenominal)* involving skill or special training: *a skilled job.*

skillet (ˈskɪlɪt) NOUN [1] a small frying pan. [2] *Chiefly Brit* a saucepan.
▷HISTORY C15: probably from *skele* bucket, of Scandinavian origin; related to Old Norse *skjōla* bucket

skilling (ˈskɪlɪŋ) NOUN a former Scandinavian coin of low denomination.
▷HISTORY C18: from Danish and Swedish; see SHILLING

skillion (ˈskɪlɪən) NOUN *Austral* **a** a part of a building having a lower, esp sloping, roof; lean-to. **b** *(as modifier): a skillion roof.*
▷HISTORY C19: from English dialect *skilling* outhouse

skilly (ˈskɪlɪ) NOUN *Chiefly Brit* a thin soup or gruel.
▷HISTORY C19: shortened from *skilligallee,* probably a fanciful formation

Skil Saw (skɪl) NOUN *Trademark* a portable electric saw.

skim (skɪm) VERB **skims, skimming, skimmed.** [1] *(tr)* to remove floating material from the surface of (a liquid), as with a spoon: *to skim milk.* [2] to glide smoothly or lightly over (a surface). [3] *(tr)* to throw (something) in a path over a surface, so as to bounce or ricochet: *to skim stones over water.* [4] (when *intr,* usually foll by *through*) to read (a book) in a superficial or cursory manner. [5] to cover (a liquid) with a thin layer or (of liquid) to become coated in this way, as with ice, scum, etc. ◆ NOUN [6] the act or process of skimming. [7] material skimmed off a liquid, esp off milk. [8] the liquid left after skimming. [9] any thin layer covering a surface. ◆ See also **skim off.**
▷HISTORY C15 *skimmen,* probably from *scumen* to skim; see SCUM

skimble-scamble (ˈskɪmbᵊlˈskæmbᵊl) *Archaic* ◆ ADJECTIVE [1] rambling; confused. ◆ NOUN [2] meaningless discourse.
▷HISTORY C16: whimsical formation based on dialect *scamble* to struggle

skimboard (ˈskɪmbɔːd) NOUN [1] a type of surfboard, shorter than standard and rounded at both ends. ◆ VERB [2] *(intr)* to surf on a skimboard.
▸**ˈskimˌboard** NOUN ▸**ˈskimˌboarder** NOUN

skimmed milk NOUN milk from which the cream has been removed. Also called: **skim milk.** Compare **whole milk.**

skimmer (ˈskɪmə) NOUN [1] a person or thing that skims. [2] any of several mainly tropical coastal aquatic birds of the genus *Rhynchops,* having long narrow wings and a bill with an elongated lower mandible for skimming food from the surface of the water: family *Rynchopidae,* order *Charadriiformes.* [3] a flat perforated spoon used for skimming fat from liquids.

skimmia (ˈskɪmɪə) NOUN any rutaceous shrub of the S and SE Asian genus *Skimmia,* grown for their ornamental red berries and evergreen foliage.
▷HISTORY C18: New Latin from Japanese *(mijama-)shikimi,* a native name of the plant

skimmings (ˈskɪmɪŋz) PLURAL NOUN [1] material that is skimmed off a liquid. [2] the froth containing concentrated ore removed during a flotation process. [3] slag, scum, or impurities removed from molten metals.

skim off VERB *(tr, adverb)* to take the best part of: *the teacher skimmed off the able pupils for his class.*

skimp (skɪmp) VERB [1] to be extremely sparing or supply (someone) sparingly; stint. [2] to perform (work, etc.) carelessly, hastily, or with inadequate materials.
▷HISTORY C17: perhaps a combination of SCANT and SCRIMP

skimpy (ˈskɪmpɪ) ADJECTIVE **skimpier, skimpiest.** [1] (of clothes, etc.) made of too little material; scanty. [2] excessively thrifty; mean; stingy.
▸**ˈskimpily** ADVERB ▸**ˈskimpiness** NOUN

skim-read VERB to read quickly and superficially, to pick up the important or significant details.

skin (skɪn) NOUN [1] **a** the tissue forming the outer covering of the vertebrate body: it consists of two layers (see **dermis, epidermis**), the outermost of which may be covered with hair, scales, feathers, etc. It is mainly protective and sensory in function. **b** *(as modifier): a skin disease.* Related adjectives: **cutaneous, dermatoid.** [2] a person's complexion: *a fair skin.* [3] any similar covering in a plant or lower animal. [4] any coating or film, such as one that forms on the surface of a liquid. [5] unsplit leather made from the outer covering of various mammals, reptiles, etc. Compare **hide²** (sense 1). [6] the outer covering of a fur-bearing animal, dressed and finished with the hair on. [7] a container made from animal skin. [8] the outer covering surface of a vessel, rocket, etc. [9] a person's skin regarded as his life: *to save one's skin.* [10] *(often plural) Informal* (in jazz or pop use) a drum. [11] *Informal* short for **skinhead.** [12] *Slang* a cigarette paper used for rolling a cannabis cigarette. [13] *Anglo-Irish slang* a person; sort: *he's a good old skin.* [14] **by the skin of one's teeth.** by a narrow margin; only just. [15] **get under one's skin.** *Informal* to irritate one. [16] **jump out of one's skin.** to be very startled. [17] **no skin off one's nose.** *Informal* not a matter that affects one adversely. [18] **thick** *(or* **thin) skin.** an insensitive *(or* sensitive) nature. ◆ VERB **skins, skinning, skinned.** [19] *(tr)* to remove the outer covering from (fruit, etc.). [20] *(tr)* to scrape a small piece of skin from (a part of oneself) in falling, etc.: *he skinned his knee.* [21] (often foll by *over*) to cover (something) with skin or a skinlike substance or (of something) to become covered in this way. [22] *(tr) Slang* to strip of money; swindle. ◆ ADJECTIVE [23] relating to or for the skin: *skin cream.* [24] *Slang, chiefly US* involving or depicting nudity: *skin magazines.* ◆ See also **skin up.**
▷HISTORY Old English *scinn,* from Old Norse *skinn*
▸**ˈskinless** ADJECTIVE ▸**ˈskinˌlike** ADJECTIVE

skin-deep ADJECTIVE [1] superficial; shallow. ◆ ADVERB [2] superficially.

skin diving NOUN the sport or activity of diving and underwater swimming without wearing a diver's costume.
▸**ˈskin-ˌdiver** NOUN

skin effect NOUN the tendency of alternating current to concentrate in the surface layer of a conductor, esp at high frequencies, thus increasing its effective resistance.

skin flick NOUN *Slang* a film containing much nudity and explicit sex for sensational purposes.

skinflint (ˈskɪnˌflɪnt) NOUN an ungenerous or niggardly person; miser.
▷HISTORY C18: referring to a person so avaricious that he would skin (swindle) a flint
▸**ˈskinˌflinty** ADJECTIVE

skin food NOUN a cosmetic cream for keeping the skin in good condition.

skin friction NOUN the friction acting on a solid body when it is moving through a fluid.

skinful (ˈskɪnˌfʊl) NOUN, *plural* **-fuls.** *Slang* sufficient alcoholic drink to make one drunk (esp in the phrase **have a skinful**).

skin game NOUN *Slang* a swindling trick.

skin graft NOUN a piece of skin removed from one part of the body and surgically grafted at the site of a severe burn or similar injury.

skinhead (ˈskɪnˌhɛd) NOUN [1] a member of a group of White youths, noted for their closely cropped hair, aggressive behaviour, and overt racism. [2] a closely cropped hairstyle.

skink (skɪŋk) NOUN any lizard of the family *Scincidae,* commonest in tropical Africa and Asia, having reduced limbs and an elongated body covered with smooth scales. Related adjective: **scincoid.**
▷HISTORY C16: from Latin *scincus* a lizard, from Greek *skinkos*

skinned (skɪnd) ADJECTIVE [1] stripped of the skin. [2] **a** having a skin as specified. **b** *(in combination): thick-skinned.* [3] **keep one's eyes skinned** *(or* **peeled).** to watch carefully (for).

skinner (ˈskɪnə) NOUN a person who prepares or deals in animal skins.

Skinner box NOUN a device for studying the learning behaviour of animals, esp rats and pigeons, consisting of a box in which the animal can move a lever to obtain a reward, such as a food pellet, or a punishment, such as an electric shock.
▷HISTORY C20: named after Burrhus Frederic *Skinner* (1904–90), US behavioural psychologist

skinny (ˈskɪnɪ) ADJECTIVE **-nier, -niest.** [1] lacking in flesh; thin. [2] consisting of or resembling skin.
▸**ˈskinniness** NOUN

skinny-dip VERB **-dips, -dipping, -dipped.** *(intr)* to swim in the nude.
▸**skinny dipping** NOUN

skin-pop *Slang* ◆ NOUN [1] the subcutaneous or intramuscular injection of a narcotic. ◆ VERB **-pops, -popping, -popped.** [2] *(intr)* to take drugs in such a way.

skint (skɪnt) ADJECTIVE *(usually postpositive) Brit slang* without money.
▷HISTORY variant of *skinned,* past participle of SKIN

skin test NOUN *Med* any test to determine immunity to a disease or hypersensitivity by introducing a small amount of the test substance beneath the skin or rubbing it into a fresh scratch. See **scratch test.**

skintight (ˈskɪnˈtaɪt) ADJECTIVE (of garments) fitting tightly over the body; clinging.

skin up VERB *(adverb) Slang* to roll (a cannabis cigarette).

skip¹ (skɪp) VERB **skips, skipping, skipped.** [1] (when *intr,* often foll by *over, along, into,* etc.) to spring or move lightly, esp to move by hopping from one foot to the other. [2] *(intr)* to jump over a skipping-rope. [3] to cause (a stone, etc.) to bounce or skim over a surface or (of a stone) to move in this way. [4] to omit (intervening matter), as in passing from one part or subject to another: *he skipped a chapter of the book.* [5] *(intr;* foll by *through) Informal* to read or deal with quickly or superficially: *he skipped through the accounts before dinner.* [6] **skip it!** *Informal* it doesn't matter! [7] *(tr) Informal* to miss deliberately: *to skip school.* [8] *(tr) Informal, chiefly US and Canadian* to leave (a place) in haste or secrecy: *to skip town.* ◆ NOUN [9] a skipping movement or gait. [10] the act of passing over or omitting. [11] *Music, US and Canadian* another word for **leap** (sense 10). ◆ See also **skip off.**
▷HISTORY C13: probably of Scandinavian origin; related to Old Norse *skopa* to take a run, obsolete Swedish *skuppa* to skip

skip² (skɪp) NOUN, VERB **skips, skipping, skipped.** *Informal* short for **skipper¹.**

skip³ (skɪp) NOUN [1] a large open container for transporting building materials, etc. [2] a cage used as a lift in mines, etc.
▷HISTORY C19: variant of SKEP

skip⁴ (skɪp) NOUN a college servant, esp of Trinity College, Dublin.
▷HISTORY C17: probably shortened from archaic *skip-kennel* a footman or lackey (from SKIP¹ + KENNEL²)

ski pants PLURAL NOUN trousers usually of stretch

material and kept taut by a strap under the foot, worn for skiing or as a fashion garment.

skip distance NOUN the shortest distance between a transmitter and a receiver that will permit reception of radio waves of a specified frequency by one reflection from the ionosphere.

skipjack ('skɪpˌdʒæk) NOUN, *plural* **-jack** *or* **-jacks.** 1 Also called: **skipjack tuna.** an important food fish, *Katsuwonus pelamis,* that has a striped abdomen and occurs in all tropical seas: family *Scombridae* (mackerels and tunas). 2 **black skipjack.** a small spotted tuna, *Euthynnus yaito,* of Indo-Pacific seas. 3 any of several other unrelated fishes, such as the alewife and bonito. 4 *Nautical* an American sloop used for oystering and as a yacht. 5 another name for a **click beetle.**
▷HISTORY C18: from SKIP[1] + JACK[1]

skiplane ('skiːˌpleɪn) NOUN an aircraft fitted with skis to enable it to land on and take off from snow.

skip off VERB (*intr, adverb*) *Brit informal* to leave work, school, etc., early or without authorization.

skipper[1] ('skɪpə) NOUN 1 the captain of any vessel. 2 the captain of an aircraft. 3 a manager or leader, as of a sporting team. ◆ VERB 4 to act as skipper (of).
▷HISTORY C14: from Middle Low German, Middle Dutch *schipper* shipper

skipper[2] ('skɪpə) NOUN 1 a person or thing that skips. 2 any small butterfly of the family *Hesperiidae,* having a hairy mothlike body and erratic darting flight. 3 another name for the **saury** (a fish).

skippering ('skɪpərɪŋ) NOUN *Slang* the practice of sleeping rough.
▷HISTORY C20: of unknown origin

skippet ('skɪpɪt) NOUN a small round box for preserving a document or seal.
▷HISTORY C14: perhaps from *skeppe* SKEP

skipping ('skɪpɪŋ) NOUN the act of jumping over a rope that is held and swung either by the person jumping or by two other people, as a game or for exercise.

skipping-rope NOUN *Brit* a cord, usually having handles at each end, that is held in the hands and swung round and down so that the holder or others can jump over it.

Skipton ('skɪptən) NOUN a market town in N England, in North Yorkshire: 11th-century castle. Pop.: 13 583 (1991).

skip-tooth saw NOUN a saw with alternate teeth absent.

skip zone NOUN a region surrounding a broadcasting station that cannot receive transmissions either directly or by reflection off the ionosphere.

skirl (skɜːl; *Scot* skɪrl) VERB (*intr*) 1 *Scot and northern English dialect* (esp of bagpipes) to emit a shrill sound. 2 to play the bagpipes. ◆ NOUN 3 the sound of bagpipes. 4 a shrill sound.
▷HISTORY C14: probably of Scandinavian origin; see SHRILL

skirmish ('skɜːmɪʃ) NOUN 1 a minor short-lived military engagement. 2 any brisk clash or encounter, usually of a minor nature. ◆ VERB 3 (*intr;* often foll by *with*) to engage in a skirmish.
▷HISTORY C14: from Old French *eskirmir,* of Germanic origin; related to Old High German *skirmen* to defend
▸'**skirmisher** NOUN

Skíros ('skirɔs) NOUN transliteration of the Modern Greek name for **Skyros.**

skirr (skɜː) VERB 1 (*intr;* usually foll by *off, away,* etc.) to move, run, or fly rapidly. 2 (*tr*) *Archaic or literary* to move rapidly over (an area, etc.), esp in order to find or apprehend. ◆ NOUN 3 a whirring or grating sound, as of the wings of birds in flight.
▷HISTORY C16: variant of SCOUR[2]

skirret ('skɪrɪt) NOUN an umbelliferous Old World plant, *Sium sisarum,* cultivated in parts of Europe for its edible tuberous roots.
▷HISTORY C14 *skirwhite,* perhaps from obsolete *skir* bright (see SHEER[1]) + WHITE

skirt (skɜːt) NOUN 1 a garment hanging from the waist, worn chiefly by women and girls. 2 the part of a dress below the waist. 3 Also called: **apron.** a frieze or circular flap, as round the base of a hovercraft. 4 the flaps on a saddle that protect a rider's legs. 5 *Brit* a cut of beef from the flank. 6 (*often plural*) a margin or outlying area. 7 *NZ* the lower part of a sheep's fleece. 8 **bit of skirt.** *Slang* a girl or woman. ◆ VERB 9 (*tr*) to form the edge of. 10 (*tr*) to provide with a border. 11 (when *intr,* foll by *around, along,* etc.) to pass (by) or be situated (near) the outer edge of (an area, etc.). 12 (*tr*) to avoid (a difficulty, etc.): *he skirted the issue.* 13 *Chiefly Austral and NZ* to remove the trimmings or inferior wool from (a fleece).
▷HISTORY C13: from Old Norse *skyrta* SHIRT
▸'**skirted** ADJECTIVE

skirter ('skɜːtə) NOUN *Austral* a man who skirts fleeces. See **skirt** (sense 13).

skirting ('skɜːtɪŋ) NOUN 1 a border, esp of wood or tiles, fixed round the base of an interior wall to protect it from kicks, dirt, etc. 2 material used or suitable for skirts.

skirting board NOUN a skirting made of wood. US and Canadian name: **baseboard.** US name: **mopboard.**

skirtings ('skɜːtɪŋz) PLURAL NOUN ragged edges trimmed from the fleece of a sheep.

ski run NOUN a trail, slope, or course for skiing.

ski stick *or* **pole** NOUN a stick, usually with a metal point and a disc to prevent it from sinking into the snow, used by skiers to gain momentum and maintain balance.

skit (skɪt) NOUN 1 a brief satirical theatrical sketch. 2 a short satirical piece of writing. 3 a trick or hoax.
▷HISTORY C18: related to earlier verb *skit* to move rapidly, hence to score a satirical hit, probably of Scandinavian origin; related to Old Norse *skjóta* to shoot

skitch (skɪtʃ) VERB (*tr*) *NZ* (of a dog) to attack; catch.

skite[1] (skəɪt) *Scot* ◆ VERB 1 (*intr*) to slide or slip, as on ice. 2 (*tr*) to strike with a sharp or glancing blow. ◆ NOUN 3 an instance of sliding or slipping. 4 a sharp or glancing blow. 5 **on the** (*or* **a**) **skite.** *Scot, Irish* on a drinking spree.
▷HISTORY C18: of uncertain origin

skite[2] (skaɪt) *Austral and NZ informal* ◆ VERB (*intr*) 1 to boast. ◆ NOUN 2 boastful talk. 3 a person who boasts.
▷HISTORY C19: from Scottish and northern English dialect; see SKATE[3]

ski touring NOUN long-distance hiking on skis over open, mountainous country; noncompetitive cross-country skiing.

ski tow NOUN a device for pulling skiers uphill, usually a motor-driven rope grasped by the skier while riding on his skis.

skitter ('skɪtə) VERB 1 (*intr;* often foll by *off*) to move or run rapidly or lightly; scamper. 2 to skim or cause to skim lightly and rapidly, as across the surface of water. 3 (*intr*) *Angling* to draw a bait lightly over the surface of water.
▷HISTORY C19: probably from dialect *skite* to dash about; related to Old Norse *skjōta* to SHOOT

skittish ('skɪtɪʃ) ADJECTIVE 1 playful, lively, or frivolous. 2 difficult to handle or predict. 3 *Now rare* coy.
▷HISTORY C15: probably of Scandinavian origin; compare Old Norse *skjōta* to SHOOT; see -ISH
▸'**skittishly** ADVERB ▸'**skittishness** NOUN

skittle ('skɪtᵊl) NOUN 1 a wooden or plastic pin, typically widest just above the base. 2 (*plural; functioning as singular*) Also called (esp US): **ninepins.** a bowling game in which players knock over as many skittles as possible by rolling a wooden ball at them. 3 **beer and skittles.** (*often used with a negative*) *Informal* an easy time; amusement.
▷HISTORY C17: of obscure origin; perhaps related to Swedish, Danish *skyttel* shuttle

skittle out VERB (*tr, adverb*) *Cricket* to dismiss (batsmen) quickly.

skive[1] (skaɪv) VERB (*tr*) to shave or remove the surface of (leather).
▷HISTORY C19: from Old Norse *skifa;* related to English dialect *shive* a slice of bread

skive[2] (skaɪv) VERB (when *intr,* often foll by *off*) *Brit informal* to evade (work or responsibility).
▷HISTORY C20: of unknown origin

skiver[1] ('skaɪvə) NOUN 1 the tanned outer layer split from a skin. 2 a person, tool, or machine that skives.

skiver[2] ('skaɪvə) NOUN *Brit slang* a person who persistently avoids work or responsibility.

skivvy[1] ('skɪvɪ) NOUN, *plural* **-vies.** 1 *Chiefly Brit often contemptuous* a servant, esp a female, who does menial work of all kinds; drudge. ◆ VERB **-vies, -vying, -vied.** 2 (*intr*) *Brit* to work as a skivvy.
▷HISTORY C20: of unknown origin

skivvy[2] ('skɪvɪ) NOUN, *plural* **-vies.** 1 *Slang, chiefly US* a man's T-shirt or vest. 2 (*plural*) *Slang, chiefly US* men's underwear. 3 *Austral and NZ* a garment resembling a sweater with long sleeves and a polo neck, usually made of stretch cotton or cotton and polyester and worn by either sex.
▷HISTORY of unknown origin

skokiaan ('skɔːkɪˌɑːn) NOUN (in South Africa) a potent alcoholic beverage drunk by Black Africans in shebeens.
▷HISTORY C20: from Afrikaans, of unknown origin

skol (skɒl) *or* **skoal** (skəʊl) SENTENCE SUBSTITUTE good health! (a drinking toast).
▷HISTORY C16: from Danish *skaal* bowl, from Old Norse *skal;* see SCALE[2]

skolly *or* **skollie** ('skɒlɪ) NOUN, *plural* **-lies.** *South African* a Coloured hooligan, usually one of a gang.
▷HISTORY C20: of unknown origin

skookum ('skuːkəm) ADJECTIVE *Canadian* strong or brave.
▷HISTORY C19: from Chinook Jargon

skool (skuːl) NOUN an ironically illiterate or childish spelling of **school.**

Skopje ('skɔːpjɛ) NOUN the capital of (the Former Yugoslav Republic of) Macedonia, on the Vardar River: became capital of Serbia in 1346 and of Macedonia in 1945; suffered a severe earthquake in 1963; university (1949). Pop.: 541 280 (1994). Serbo-Croat name: **Skoplje** ('skɔpljɛ). Turkish name (1392–1913): **Üsküb.**

skrike (skraɪk) VERB (*intr*) *Northern English dialect* to cry.

Skt *or* **Skr.** ABBREVIATION FOR Sanskrit.

skua ('skjuːə) NOUN any predatory gull-like bird of the family *Stercorariidae,* such as the **great skua** or **bonxie** (*Stercorarius skua*) or **arctic skua** (*S. parasiticus*) both of which harass terns or gulls into dropping or disgorging fish they have caught.
▷HISTORY C17: from New Latin, from Faeroese *skūgvur,* from Old Norse *skūfr*

skulduggery *or US* **skullduggery** (skʌl'dʌgərɪ) NOUN *Informal* underhand dealing; trickery.
▷HISTORY C19: altered from earlier Scot *sculduddery;* of obscure origin

skulk (skʌlk) VERB (*intr*) 1 to move stealthily so as to avoid notice. 2 to lie in hiding; lurk. 3 to shirk duty or evade responsibilities; malinger. ◆ NOUN 4 a person who skulks. 5 *Obsolete* a pack of foxes or other animals that creep about stealthily.
▷HISTORY C13: of Scandinavian origin; compare Norwegian *skulka* to lurk, Swedish *skolka,* Danish *skulke* to shirk
▸'**skulker** NOUN

skull (skʌl) NOUN 1 the bony skeleton of the head of vertebrates. See **cranium.** Related adjective: **cranial.** 2 *Often derogatory* the head regarded as the mind or intelligence: *to have a dense skull.* 3 a picture of a skull used to represent death or danger.
▷HISTORY C13: of Scandinavian origin; compare Old Norse *skoltr,* Norwegian *skult,* Swedish dialect *skulle*

skull and crossbones NOUN a picture of the human skull above two crossed thighbones, formerly on the pirate flag, now used as a warning of danger or death.

skullcap ('skʌlˌkæp) NOUN 1 a rounded brimless hat fitting the crown of the head. 2 the nontechnical name for **calvaria.** 3 any of various perennial plants of the genus *Scutellaria,* esp *S. galericulata,* that typically have helmet-shaped flowers: family *Lamiaceae* (labiates).

skunk (skʌŋk) NOUN, *plural* **skunks** *or* **skunk.** 1 any of various American musteline mammals of the subfamily *Mephitinae,* esp *Mephitis mephitis* (**striped skunk**), typically having a black and white coat and bushy tail: they eject an unpleasant-smelling fluid from the anal gland when attacked. 2 *Informal* a despicable person. 3 *Slang* a strain of cannabis

smoked for its exceptionally powerful psychoactive properties. ◆ VERB 4 *(tr) US and Canadian slang* to defeat overwhelmingly in a game.
▷HISTORY C17: from Algonquian; compare Abnaki *segākw* skunk

skunk cabbage NOUN 1 a low-growing fetid aroid swamp plant, *Symplocarpus foetidus* of E North America, having broad leaves and minute flowers enclosed in a mottled greenish or purple spathe. 2 a similar aroid plant, *Lysichitum americanum,* of the W coast of North America and N Asia. ◆ Also called: **skunkweed.**

sky (skaɪ) NOUN, *plural* **skies.** 1 *(sometimes plural)* the apparently dome-shaped expanse extending upwards from the horizon that is characteristically blue or grey during the day, red in the evening, and black at night. Related adjectives: **celestial, empyrean.** 2 outer space, as seen from the earth. 3 *(often plural)* weather, as described by the appearance of the upper air: *sunny skies.* 4 the source of divine power; heaven. 5 *Informal* the highest level of attainment: *the sky's the limit.* 6 **to the skies.** highly; extravagantly. ◆ VERB **skies, skying, skied.** 7 *Rowing* to lift (the blade of an oar) too high before a stroke. 8 *(tr) Informal* to hit (a ball) high in the air.
▷HISTORY C13: from Old Norse *ský;* related to Old English *scio* cloud, Old Saxon *skio,* Old Norse *skjār* transparent skin
▸ **'sky,like** ADJECTIVE

sky blue NOUN **a** a light or pale blue colour. **b** *(as adjective): a sky-blue jumper.*

sky-blue pink NOUN, ADJECTIVE a jocular name for a nonexistent, unknown, or unimportant colour.

skybox ('skaɪ,bɒks) NOUN *US* a luxurious suite high up in the stand of a sports stadium, which is rented out to groups of spectators, corporations, etc.

skydive ('skaɪ,daɪv) VERB **-dives, -diving, -dived** *or US* **-dove; -dived.** *(intr)* to take part in skydiving.
▸ **'sky,diver** NOUN

skydiving ('skaɪ,daɪvɪŋ) NOUN the sport of parachute jumping, in which participants perform manoeuvres before opening the parachute and attempt to land accurately.

Skye (skaɪ) NOUN a mountainous island off the NW coast of Scotland, the largest island of the Inner Hebrides: tourist centre. Chief town: Portree. Pop.: 7500 (latest est.). Area: 1735 sq. km (670 sq. miles).

Skye terrier NOUN a short-legged long-bodied breed of terrier with long wiry hair and erect ears.

sky-high ADJECTIVE, ADVERB 1 at or to an unprecedented or excessive level: *prices rocketed sky-high.* ◆ ADVERB 2 high into the air. 3 **blow sky-high.** to destroy completely.

skyjack ('skaɪ,dʒæk) VERB *(tr)* to commandeer (an aircraft), usually at gunpoint during flight, forcing the pilot to fly somewhere other than to the scheduled destination.
▷HISTORY C20: from SKY + HIJACK
▸ **'sky,jacker** NOUN

Skylab ('skaɪ,læb) NOUN a US space station launched in May 1973 into an orbit inclined at 50° to the equatorial plane at a mean altitude of 430 kilometres (270 miles), the astronauts working there under conditions of zero gravity. It disintegrated, unmanned, in 1979, with some parts landing in the outback of Australia.
▷HISTORY C20: from SKY + LAB(ORATORY)

skylark ('skaɪ,lɑːk) NOUN 1 an Old World lark, *Alauda arvensis,* noted for singing while hovering at a great height. 2 any of various Australian larks. ◆ VERB 3 *(intr) Informal* to romp or play jokes.
▸ **'sky,larker** NOUN

skylight ('skaɪ,laɪt) NOUN a window placed in a roof or ceiling to admit daylight. Also called: **fanlight.**

skylight filter NOUN *Photog* a very slightly pink filter that absorbs ultraviolet light and reduces haze and excessive blueness.

skyline ('skaɪ,laɪn) NOUN 1 the line at which the earth and sky appear to meet; horizon. 2 the outline of buildings, mountains, trees, etc., seen against the sky.

sky marker NOUN a parachute flare dropped to mark a target area.

sky marshal NOUN an armed security guard on a commercial aircraft.

sky pilot NOUN *Slang* a chaplain in one of the military services.

skyrocket ('skaɪ,rɒkɪt) NOUN 1 another word for **rocket**[1] (sense 1). ◆ VERB 2 *(intr) Informal* to rise rapidly, as in price.

Skyros *or* **Scyros** ('skiːrɒs) NOUN a Greek island in the Aegean, the largest island in the N Sporades. Pop.: 3000 (latest est.). Area: 199 sq. km (77 sq. miles). Modern Greek name: **Skíros.**

skysail ('skaɪ,seɪl) NOUN *Nautical* 1 a square sail set above the royal on a square-rigger. 2 a triangular sail set between the trucks of a racing schooner.

skyscape ('skaɪ,skeɪp) NOUN a painting, drawing, photograph, etc., representing or depicting the sky.

skyscraper ('skaɪ,skreɪpə) NOUN a very tall multistorey building.

sky show NOUN *Austral* a fireworks display.

skyward ('skaɪwəd) ADJECTIVE 1 directed or moving towards the sky. ◆ ADVERB 2 Also: **skywards.** towards the sky.

sky wave NOUN a radio wave reflected back to the earth by the ionosphere (**ionospheric wave**), permitting transmission around the curved surface of the earth. Compare **ground wave.**

skywriting ('skaɪ,raɪtɪŋ) NOUN 1 the forming of words in the sky by the release of smoke or vapour from an aircraft. 2 the words so formed.
▸ **'sky,writer** NOUN

sl[1] *Bibliog* ABBREVIATION FOR sine loco.
▷HISTORY Latin: without place (of publication)

sl[2] THE INTERNET DOMAIN NAME FOR Sierra Leone.

SL ABBREVIATION FOR Solicitor at Law.

S/L (in Canada) ABBREVIATION FOR Squadron Leader.

slab (slæb) NOUN 1 a broad flat thick piece of wood, stone, or other material. 2 a thick slice of cake, etc. 3 any of the outside parts of a log that are sawn off while the log is being made into planks. 4 *Mountaineering* a flat sheet of rock lying at an angle of between 30° and 60° from the horizontal. 5 a printer's ink table. 6 *(modifier) Austral and NZ* made or constructed of coarse wooden planks: *a slab hut.* 7 *Informal, chiefly Brit* an operating or mortuary table. ◆ VERB **slabs, slabbing, slabbed.** *(tr)* 8 to cut or make into a slab or slabs. 9 to cover or lay with slabs. 10 to saw slabs from (a log).
▷HISTORY C13: of unknown origin

slabber ('slæbə) VERB, NOUN a dialect word for **slobber.**
▷HISTORY C16: variant of SLOBBER

slack[1] (slæk) ADJECTIVE 1 not tight, tense, or taut. 2 negligent or careless. 3 (esp of water, etc.) moving slowly. 4 (of trade, etc.) not busy. 5 *Phonetics* another term for **lax** (sense 4). ◆ ADVERB 6 in a slack manner. ◆ NOUN 7 a part of a rope, etc., that is slack: *take in the slack.* 8 a period of decreased activity. 9 **a** a patch of water without current. **b** a slackening of a current. 10 *Prosody* (in sprung rhythm) the unstressed syllable or syllables. ◆ VERB 11 to neglect (one's duty, etc.). 12 *(often foll by off)* to loosen; to make slack. 13 *Chem* a less common word for **slake** (sense 3). ◆ See also **slacks.**
▷HISTORY Old English *slæc, sleac;* related to Old High German *slah,* Old Norse *slākr* bad, Latin *laxus* LAX
▸ **'slackly** ADVERB ▸ **'slackness** NOUN

slack[2] (slæk) NOUN small pieces of coal with a high ash content.
▷HISTORY C15: probably from Middle Low German *slecke;* related to Dutch *slak,* German *Schlacke* dross

slacken ('slækən) VERB (often foll by *off*) 1 to make or become looser. 2 to make or become slower, less intense, etc.

slacker ('slækə) NOUN 1 a person who evades work or duty; shirker. 2 *Informal* **a** an educated young adult characterized by cynicism and apathy. **b** *(as modifier): slacker culture.*

slacks (slæks) PLURAL NOUN informal trousers worn by both sexes.

slack suit NOUN *US* casual male dress consisting of slacks and a matching shirt or jacket.

slack water NOUN the period of still water around the turn of the tide, esp at low tide.

slag (slæg) NOUN 1 Also called: **cinder.** the fused material formed during the smelting or refining of metals by combining the flux with gangue, impurities in the metal, etc. It usually consists of a mixture of silicates with calcium, phosphorus, sulphur, etc. See also **basic slag.** 2 a mass of rough fragments of pyroclastic rock and cinders derived from a volcanic eruption; scoria. 3 a mixture of shale, clay, coal dust, and other mineral waste produced during coal mining. 4 *Brit slang* a coarse or dissipated girl or woman. ◆ VERB **slags, slagging, slagged.** 5 *(intr) Austral slang* to spit.
▷HISTORY C16: from Middle Low German *slagge,* perhaps from *slagen* to SLAY
▸ **'slagging** NOUN ▸ **'slaggy** ADJECTIVE

slag down VERB *(tr, adverb) Prison slang* to give a verbal lashing to.

slag heap NOUN a hillock of waste matter from coal mining, etc.

slain (sleɪn) VERB the past participle of **slay.**

slàinte mhath (,slɑːndʒə 'va), *or Scot* **slàinte,** *Irish* **sláinte mhaith** (,slɑːntə 'va) INTERJECTION a drinking toast; cheers.
▷HISTORY Gaelic: good health

slake (sleɪk) VERB 1 *(tr) Literary* to satisfy (thirst, desire, etc.). 2 *(tr) Poetic* to cool or refresh. 3 Also: **slack.** to undergo or cause to undergo the process in which lime reacts with water or moist air to produce calcium hydroxide. 4 *Archaic* to make or become less active or intense.
▷HISTORY Old English *slacian,* from *slæc* SLACK[1]; related to Dutch *slaken* to diminish, Icelandic *slaka*
▸ **'slakable** *or* **'slakeable** ADJECTIVE ▸ **'slaker** NOUN

slaked lime NOUN another name for **calcium hydroxide,** esp when made by adding water to calcium oxide

slalom ('slɑːləm) NOUN 1 *Skiing* a race, esp one downhill, over a winding course marked by artificial obstacles. 2 a similar type of obstacle race in canoes. ◆ VERB 3 *(intr)* to take part in a slalom.
▷HISTORY Norwegian, from *slad* sloping + *lom* path

slam[1] (slæm) VERB **slams, slamming, slammed.** 1 to cause (a door or window) to close noisily and with force or (of a door, etc.) to close in this way. 2 *(tr)* to throw (something) down noisily and violently. 3 *(tr) Slang* to criticize harshly. 4 *(intr; usually foll by into or out of) Informal* to go (into or out of a room, etc.) in violent haste or anger. 5 *(tr)* to strike with violent force. 6 *(tr) Informal* to defeat easily. ◆ NOUN 7 the act or noise of slamming. 8 *Slang* harsh criticism or abuse.
▷HISTORY C17: of Scandinavian origin; compare Old Norse *slamra,* Norwegian *slemma,* Swedish dialect *slämma*

slam[2] (slæm) NOUN 1 **a** the winning of all (**grand slam**) or all but one (**little** or **small slam**) of the 13 tricks at bridge or whist. **b** the bid to do so in bridge. 2 an old card game.
▷HISTORY C17: of uncertain origin

slam[3] (slæm) NOUN a poetry contest in which entrants compete with each other by reciting their work and are awarded points by the audience.
▷HISTORY C20: origin unknown

slam-bang ADVERB 1 another word (esp US) for **slap-bang.** 2 *US informal* carelessly; recklessly.

slam dance VERB to hurl oneself repeatedly into or through a crowd at a rock-music concert.

slam dunk *Basketball* ◆ NOUN 1 a scoring shot in which a player jumps up and forces the ball down through the basket. ◆ VERB **slam-dunk.** 2 to jump up and force (a ball) through a basket.

slammer ('slæmə) NOUN **the.** *Slang* prison.

slander ('slɑːndə) NOUN 1 *Law* **a** defamation in some transient form, as by spoken words, gestures, etc. **b** a slanderous statement, etc. 2 any false or defamatory words spoken about a person; calumny. ◆ VERB 3 to utter or circulate slander (about).
▷HISTORY C13: via Anglo-French from Old French *escandle,* from Late Latin *scandalum* a cause of offence; see SCANDAL
▸ **'slanderer** NOUN ▸ **'slanderous** ADJECTIVE ▸ **'slanderously** ADVERB ▸ **'slanderousness** NOUN

slang (slæŋ) NOUN 1 **a** vocabulary, idiom, etc., that is not appropriate to the standard form of a language or to formal contexts, may be restricted as to social status or distribution, and is characteristically more metaphorical and transitory than standard language. **b** *(as modifier): a slang word.*

2 another word for **jargon.** ◆ VERB 3 to abuse (someone) with vituperative language; insult.
▷HISTORY C18: of unknown origin
▸ **ˈslangy** ADJECTIVE ▸ **ˈslangily** ADVERB ▸ **ˈslanginess** NOUN

slanging match NOUN *Brit* a dispute in which insults and accusations are made by each party against the other.

slant (slɑːnt) VERB 1 to incline or be inclined at an oblique or sloping angle. 2 *(tr)* to write or present (news, etc.) with a bias. 3 *(intr; foll by towards)* (of a person's opinions) to be biased. ◆ NOUN 4 an inclined or oblique line or direction; slope. 5 a way of looking at something. 6 a bias or opinion, as in an article. 7 a less technical name for **solidus.** 8 **on a** (*or* **the**) **slant.** sloping. ◆ ADJECTIVE 9 oblique, sloping.
▷HISTORY C17: short for ASLANT, probably of Scandinavian origin
▸ **ˈslanting** ADJECTIVE ▸ **ˈslantingly** *or* **ˈslantly** ADVERB

slanter (ˈslæntə) NOUN *Austral obsolete informal* a variant of **slinter.**

slant rhyme NOUN *Prosody* another term for **half-rhyme.**

slantwise (ˈslɑːntˌwaɪz) *or* **slantways** (ˈslɑːntˌweɪz) ADVERB, ADJECTIVE *(prenominal)* in a slanting or oblique direction.

slap (slæp) NOUN 1 a sharp blow or smack, as with the open hand, something flat, etc. 2 the sound made by or as if by such a blow. 3 a sharp rebuke; reprimand. 4 **(a bit of) slap and tickle.** *Brit informal* sexual play. 5 **a slap in the face.** an insult or rebuff. 6 **a slap on the back.** congratulation. 7 **a slap on the wrist.** a light punishment or reprimand. ◆ VERB **slaps, slapping, slapped.** 8 *(tr)* to strike (a person or thing) sharply, as with the open hand or something flat. 9 *(tr)* to bring down (the hand, something flat, etc.) sharply. 10 (when *intr,* usually foll by *against*) to strike (something) with or as if with a slap. 11 *(tr) Informal, chiefly Brit* to apply in large quantities, haphazardly, etc.: *she slapped butter on the bread.* 12 **slap on the back.** to congratulate. ◆ ADVERB *Informal* 13 exactly; directly: *slap on time.* 14 forcibly or abruptly: *to fall slap on the floor.*
▷HISTORY C17: from Low German *slapp,* German *Schlappe,* of imitative origin
▸ **ˈslapper** NOUN

slap-bang ADVERB *Informal, chiefly Brit* 1 in a violent, sudden, or noisy manner. US equivalent: **slam-bang.** 2 directly or immediately: *slap-bang in the middle.*

slap bass NOUN a rock or jazz style of playing the electric or double bass in which the strings are plucked and released so as to vibrate sharply against the fretboard or fingerboard.

slapdash (ˈslæpˌdæʃ) ADVERB 1 in a careless, hasty, or haphazard manner. ◆ ADJECTIVE 2 careless, hasty, or haphazard. ◆ NOUN 3 slapdash activity or work. 4 another name for **roughcast** (sense 1).
▷HISTORY C17: from SLAP + DASH[1]

slap down VERB *(tr, adverb) Informal* to rebuke sharply, as for impertinence.

slap-happy ADJECTIVE *Informal* 1 cheerfully irresponsible or careless. 2 dazed or giddy from or as if from repeated blows; punch-drunk.

slaphead (ˈslæpˌhɛd) NOUN *Derogatory slang* a bald person.
▷HISTORY C20: from SLAP + HEAD

slapjack (ˈslæpˌdʒæk) NOUN 1 a simple card game. 2 *US* another word for **pancake.**
▷HISTORY C19: from SLAP + JACK[1]

slapped-cheek disease NOUN another name for **fifth disease.**

slapper (ˈslæpə) NOUN *Brit slang* a promiscuous woman.

slapshot (ˈslæpˌʃɒt) NOUN *Ice hockey* a hard, fast, often wild, shot executed with a powerful downward swing, and with the blade of the stick brushing firmly against the ice prior to striking the puck.

slapstick (ˈslæpˌstɪk) NOUN 1 **a** comedy characterized by horseplay and physical action. **b** *(as modifier)*: *slapstick humour.* 2 a flexible pair of paddles bound together at one end, formerly used in pantomime to strike a blow to a person with a loud clapping sound but without injury.

slap-up ADJECTIVE *(prenominal) Brit informal* (esp of meals) lavish; excellent; first-class.

slart (slɑːt) VERB *(tr) Northern English dialect* to spill (something): *to slart the salt.*

slash (slæʃ) VERB *(tr)* 1 to cut or lay about (a person or thing) with sharp sweeping strokes, as with a sword, knife, etc. 2 to lash with a whip. 3 to make large gashes in: *to slash tyres.* 4 to reduce (prices, etc.) drastically. 5 *Chiefly US* to criticize harshly. 6 to slit (the outer fabric of a garment) so that the lining material is revealed. 7 to clear (scrub or undergrowth) by cutting. ◆ NOUN 8 a sharp, sweeping stroke, as with a sword or whip. 9 a cut or rent made by such a stroke. 10 a decorative slit in a garment revealing the lining material. 11 *US and Canadian* **a** littered wood chips and broken branches that remain after trees have been cut down. **b** an area so littered. 12 another name for **solidus.** 13 *Brit slang* the act of urinating (esp in the phrase **have a slash**). 14 a genre of erotic fiction written by women to appeal to women.
▷HISTORY C14 *slaschen,* perhaps from Old French *esclachier* to break

slash-and-burn ADJECTIVE denoting a short-term method of cultivation in which land is cleared by destroying and burning trees and other vegetation for temporary agricultural use.

slasher (ˈslæʃə) NOUN 1 a person or thing that slashes. 2 *Austral and NZ* a wooden-handled cutting tool or tractor-drawn machine used for cutting scrub or undergrowth in the bush.

slasher movie NOUN *Slang* a film in which victims, usually women, are slashed with knives, razors, etc.

slashing (ˈslæʃɪŋ) ADJECTIVE aggressively or harshly critical (esp in the phrase **slashing attack**).
▸ **ˈslashingly** ADVERB

slash pocket NOUN a pocket in which the opening is a slit in the seam of a garment.

Śląsk (ʃlɔ̃sk) NOUN the Polish name for **Silesia.**

slat[1] (slæt) NOUN 1 a narrow thin strip of wood or metal, as used in a Venetian blind, etc. 2 a movable or fixed auxiliary aerofoil attached to the leading edge of an aircraft wing to increase lift, esp during landing and takeoff. ◆ VERB **slats, slatting, slatted.** 3 *(tr)* to provide with slats.
▷HISTORY C14: from Old French *esclat* splinter, from *esclater* to shatter

slat[2] (slæt) *Dialect* ◆ VERB **slats, slatting, slatted.** 1 *(tr)* to throw violently; fling carelessly. 2 *(intr)* to flap violently. ◆ NOUN 3 a sudden blow.
▷HISTORY C13: of Scandinavian origin; related to Old Norse, Icelandic *sletta* to slap

slat[3] (slæt) NOUN *Irish* a spent salmon.
▷HISTORY C19: of uncertain origin

slate[1] (sleɪt) NOUN 1 **a** a compact fine-grained metamorphic rock formed by the effects of heat and pressure on shale. It can be split into thin layers along natural cleavage planes and is used as a roofing and paving material. **b** *(as modifier)*: *a slate tile.* 2 a roofing tile of slate. 3 (formerly) a writing tablet of slate. 4 a dark grey colour, often with a purplish or bluish tinge. 5 *Chiefly US and Canadian* a list of candidates in an election. 6 *Films* **a** the reference information written on a clapperboard. **b** *Informal* the clapperboard itself. 7 **clean slate.** a record without dishonour. 8 **have a slate loose.** *Brit and Irish informal* to be eccentric or crazy. 9 **on the slate.** *Brit informal* on credit. 10 **wipe the slate clean.** *Informal* to make a fresh start, esp by forgetting past differences. ◆ VERB *(tr)* 11 to cover (a roof) with slates. 12 *Chiefly US* to enter (a person's name) on a list, esp on a political slate. 13 **a** to choose or destine: *he was slated to go far.* **b** to plan or schedule: *the trial is slated to begin in three weeks.* ◆ ADJECTIVE 14 of the colour slate.
▷HISTORY C14: from Old French *esclate,* from *esclat* a fragment; see SLAT[1]

slate[2] (sleɪt) VERB *(tr) Informal, chiefly Brit* 1 to criticize harshly; censure. 2 to punish or defeat severely.
▷HISTORY C19: probably from SLATE[1]

slater (ˈsleɪtə) NOUN 1 a person trained in laying roof slates. 2 *Dialect, Austral, and NZ* a woodlouse. See also **sea slater.**

slatey (ˈsleɪtɪ) ADJECTIVE **slatier, slatiest.** *Irish informal* slightly mad; crazy.

slather (ˈslæðə) NOUN 1 *(usually plural) Informal* a large quantity. 2 **open slather.** *Austral and NZ slang* a situation in which there are no restrictions; free-for-all. ◆ VERB *(tr) US and Canadian slang* 3 to squander or waste. 4 to spread thickly or lavishly.
▷HISTORY C19: of unknown origin

slating[1] (ˈsleɪtɪŋ) NOUN 1 the act or process of laying slates. 2 slates collectively, or material for making slates.

slating[2] (ˈsleɪtɪŋ) NOUN *Informal, chiefly Brit* a severe reprimand or critical attack.

slattern (ˈslætən) NOUN a slovenly woman or girl; slut.
▷HISTORY C17: probably from *slattering,* from dialect *slatter* to slop; perhaps from Scandinavian; compare Old Norse *sletta* to slap
▸ **ˈslatternly** ADJECTIVE ▸ **ˈslatternliness** NOUN

slaty (ˈsleɪtɪ) ADJECTIVE **slatier, slatiest.** 1 consisting of or resembling slate. 2 having the colour of slate.
▸ **ˈslatiness** NOUN

slaughter (ˈslɔːtə) NOUN 1 the killing of animals, esp for food. 2 the savage killing of a person. 3 the indiscriminate or brutal killing of large numbers of people, as in war; massacre. 4 *Informal* a resounding defeat. ◆ VERB *(tr)* 5 to kill (animals), esp for food. 6 to kill in a brutal manner. 7 to kill indiscriminately or in large numbers. 8 *Informal* to defeat resoundingly.
▷HISTORY Old English *sleaht;* related to Old Norse *slātr* hammering, *slātr* butchered meat, Old High German *slahta,* Gothic *slauhts,* German *Schlacht* battle
▸ **ˈslaughterer** NOUN ▸ **ˈslaughterous** ADJECTIVE

slaughterhouse (ˈslɔːtəˌhaʊs) NOUN a place where animals are butchered for food; abattoir.

slaughterman (ˈslɔːtəˌmæn) NOUN, *plural* **-men.** a person employed to kill animals in a slaughterhouse.

Slav (slɑːv) NOUN a member of any of the peoples of E Europe or NW Asia who speak a Slavonic language.
▷HISTORY C14: from Medieval Latin *Sclāvus* a captive Slav; see SLAVE

slave (sleɪv) NOUN 1 a person legally owned by another and having no freedom of action or right to property. 2 a person who is forced to work for another against his will. 3 a person under the domination of another person or some habit or influence: *a slave to television.* 4 a person who works in harsh conditions for low pay. 5 **a** a device that is controlled by or that duplicates the action of another similar device (the master device). **b** *(as modifier)*: *slave cylinder.* ◆ VERB 6 *(intr; often foll by away)* to work like a slave. 7 *(tr)* an archaic word for **enslave.**
▷HISTORY C13: via Old French from Medieval Latin *Sclāvus* a Slav, one held in bondage (from the fact that the Slavonic races were frequently conquered in the Middle Ages), from Late Greek *Sklabos* a Slav

slave ant NOUN any of various ants, esp *Formica fusca,* captured and forced to do the work of a colony of ants of another species (**slave-making ants**). See also **amazon ant.**

Slave Coast NOUN the coast of W Africa between the Volta River and Mount Cameroon, chiefly along the Bight of Benin: the main source of African slaves (16th–19th centuries).

slave cylinder NOUN a small cylinder containing a piston that operates the brake shoes or pads in hydraulic brakes or the working part in any other hydraulically operated system. Compare **master cylinder.**

slave-driver NOUN 1 (esp formerly) a person forcing slaves to work. 2 an employer who demands excessively hard work from his employees.

slaveholder (ˈsleɪvˌhəʊldə) NOUN a person who owns slaves.
▸ **ˈslaveˌholding** NOUN

slaver[1] (ˈsleɪvə) NOUN 1 an owner of or dealer in slaves. 2 another name for **slave ship.**

slaver[2] (ˈslævə) VERB *(intr)* 1 to dribble saliva. 2 (often foll by *over*) **a** to fawn or drool (over someone). **b** to show great desire (for); lust (after). ◆ NOUN 3 saliva dribbling from the mouth. 4 *Informal* drivel.
▷HISTORY C14: probably of Low Dutch origin; related to SLOBBER
▸ **ˈslaverer** NOUN

Slave River NOUN a river in W Canada, in the

Northwest Territories and NE Alberta, flowing from Lake Athabaska northwest to Great Slave Lake. Length: about 420 km (260 miles). Also called: **Great Slave River.**

slavery (ˈsleɪvərɪ) NOUN 1 the state or condition of being a slave; a civil relationship whereby one person has absolute power over another and controls his life, liberty, and fortune. 2 the subjection of a person to another person, esp in being forced into work. 3 the condition of being subject to some influence or habit. 4 work done in harsh conditions for low pay.

slave ship NOUN a ship used to transport slaves, esp formerly from Africa to the New World.

Slave State NOUN *US history* any of the 15 Southern states in which slavery was legal until the Civil War.

slave trade NOUN the business of trading in slaves, esp the transportation of Black Africans to America from the 16th to 19th centuries.
▸ **ˈslave-ˌtrader** NOUN ▸ **ˈslave-ˌtrading** NOUN

slavey (ˈsleɪvɪ) NOUN *Brit informal* a female general servant.
▷HISTORY C19: from SLAVE + -Y[2]

Slavey (ˈsleɪvɪ) NOUN a member of a Dene Native Canadian people of northern Canada.
▷HISTORY from Athapascan

Slavic (ˈslɑːvɪk) NOUN, ADJECTIVE another word (esp US) for **Slavonic.**

slavish (ˈsleɪvɪʃ) ADJECTIVE 1 of or befitting a slave. 2 being or resembling a slave; servile. 3 unoriginal; imitative. 4 *Archaic* ignoble.
▸ **ˈslavishly** ADVERB ▸ **ˈslavishness** NOUN

Slavism (ˈslɑːvɪzəm) NOUN anything characteristic of, peculiar to, or associated with the Slavs or the Slavonic languages.

Slavkov (ˈslafkɔf) NOUN the Czech name for **Austerlitz.**

slavocracy (sleɪˈvɒkrəsɪ) NOUN, *plural* **-cies.** (esp in the US before the Civil War) 1 slaveholders as a dominant class. 2 domination by slaveholders.

Slavonia (sləˈvəʊnɪə) NOUN a region in Croatia, mainly between the Drava and Sava Rivers.

Slavonian (sləˈvəʊnɪən) ADJECTIVE 1 of or relating to Slavonia, a region in Croatia, or its inhabitants. ◆ NOUN 2 a native or inhabitant of Slavonia.

Slavonic (sləˈvɒnɪk) *or esp US* **Slavic** NOUN 1 a branch of the Indo-European family of languages, usually divided into three subbranches: **South Slavonic** (including Old Church Slavonic, Serbo-Croat, Bulgarian, etc.), **East Slavonic** (including Ukrainian, Russian, etc.), and **West Slavonic** (including Polish, Czech, Slovak, etc.). 2 the unrecorded ancient language from which all of these languages developed. ◆ ADJECTIVE 3 of, denoting, or relating to this group of languages. 4 of, denoting, or relating to the people who speak these languages.
▷HISTORY C17: from Medieval Latin *Slavonicus, Sclavonicus,* from SLAVONIA

Slavophile (ˈslɑːvəʊfɪl, -ˌfaɪl) *or* **Slavophil** NOUN 1 a person who admires the Slavs or their cultures. 2 (*sometimes not capital*) (in 19th-century Russia) a person who believed in the superiority and advocated the supremacy of the Slavs. ◆ ADJECTIVE 3 admiring the Slavs and Slavonic culture, etc. 4 (*sometimes not capital*) (in 19th-century Russia) of, characteristic of, or relating to the Slavophiles.
▸ **Slavophilism** (sləˈvɒfɪˌlɪzəm, ˈslɑːvəʊfɪˌlɪzəm) NOUN

slaw (slɔː) NOUN *Chiefly US and Canadian* short for **coleslaw.**
▷HISTORY C19: from Danish *sla,* short for *salade* SALAD

slay (sleɪ) VERB **slays, slaying, slew, slain.** (*tr*) 1 *Archaic or literary* to kill, esp violently. 2 *Slang* to impress (someone of the opposite sex). 3 *Obsolete* to strike.
▷HISTORY Old English *slēan;* related to Old Norse *slā,* Gothic, Old High German *slahan* to strike, Old Irish *slacaim* I beat
▸ **ˈslayer** NOUN

SLBM ABBREVIATION FOR submarine-launched ballistic missile.

SLCM ABBREVIATION FOR sea-launched cruise missile: a type of cruise missile that can be launched from either a submarine or a surface ship.

sld ABBREVIATION FOR: 1 sailed. 2 sealed.

SLD ABBREVIATION FOR Social and Liberal Democratic Party (now the Liberal Democrats).

sleave (sliːv) NOUN 1 a tangled thread. 2 a thin filament unravelled from a thicker thread. 3 *Chiefly poetic* anything matted or complicated. ◆ VERB 4 to disentangle (twisted thread, etc.).
▷HISTORY Old English *slǣfan* to divide; related to Middle Low German *slēf,* Norwegian *sleiv* big spoon

sleaze (sliːz) NOUN *Informal* 1 sleaziness. 2 dishonest, disreputable, or immoral behaviour, especially of public officials or employees: *political sleaze.*

sleazeball (ˈsliːzˌbɔːl) NOUN *Slang* an odious and contemptible person.

sleazy (ˈsliːzɪ) ADJECTIVE **-zier, -ziest.** 1 sordid; disreputable: *a sleazy nightclub.* 2 thin or flimsy, as cloth.
▷HISTORY C17: origin uncertain
▸ **ˈsleazily** ADVERB ▸ **ˈsleaziness** NOUN

sled dog NOUN any of various hardy thick-coated breeds of dog, such as the Eskimo dog, the husky, and the malamute, developed for hauling sledges in various parts of the highest northern latitudes.

sledge[1] (slɛdʒ) *or esp US and Canadian* **sled** (slɛd) NOUN 1 Also called: **sleigh.** a vehicle mounted on runners, drawn by horses or dogs, for transporting people or goods, esp over snow. 2 a light wooden frame used, esp by children, for sliding over snow; toboggan. 3 *NZ* a farm vehicle mounted on runners, for use on rough or muddy ground. ◆ VERB 4 to convey, travel, or go by sledge.
▷HISTORY C17: from Middle Dutch *sleedse;* C14 *sled,* from Middle Low German, from Old Norse *slethi,* related to SLIDE
▸ **ˈsledger** NOUN

sledge[2] (slɛdʒ) NOUN short for **sledgehammer.**

sledge[3] (slɛdʒ) VERB 1 (*tr*) to bait (an opponent, esp a batsman in cricket) in order to upset his concentration. ◆ NOUN 2 an insult aimed at another player during a game of cricket.
▷HISTORY of uncertain origin; perhaps from SLEDGEHAMMER

sledgehammer (ˈslɛdʒˌhæmə) NOUN 1 a large heavy hammer with a long handle used with both hands for heavy work such as forging iron, breaking rocks, etc. 2 (*modifier*) resembling the action of a sledgehammer in power, ruthlessness, etc.: *a sledgehammer blow.* ◆ VERB 3 (*tr*) to strike (something) with or as if with a sledgehammer.
▷HISTORY C15 *sledge,* from Old English *slecg* a large hammer; related to Old Norse *sleggja,* Middle Dutch *slegge*

sleek (sliːk) ADJECTIVE 1 smooth and shiny; polished. 2 polished in speech or behaviour; unctuous. 3 (of an animal or bird) having a shiny healthy coat or feathers. 4 (of a person) having a prosperous appearance. ◆ VERB (*tr*) 5 to make smooth and glossy, as by grooming, etc. 6 (usually foll by *over*) to cover (up), as by making more agreeable; gloss (over).
▷HISTORY C16: variant of SLICK
▸ **ˈsleekly** ADVERB ▸ **ˈsleekness** NOUN ▸ **ˈsleeky** ADJECTIVE

sleekit (ˈsliːkɪt) ADJECTIVE *Scot* 1 smooth; glossy. 2 unctuous. 3 deceitful; crafty; sly.
▷HISTORY Scottish, from past participle of SLEEK

sleep (sliːp) NOUN 1 a periodic state of physiological rest during which consciousness is suspended and metabolic rate is decreased. See also **paradoxical sleep.** 2 *Botany* the nontechnical name for **nyctitropism.** 3 a period spent sleeping. 4 a state of quiescence or dormancy. 5 a poetic or euphemistic word for **death.** 6 *Informal* the dried mucoid particles often found in the corners of the eyes after sleeping. ◆ VERB **sleeps, sleeping, slept.** 7 (*intr*) to be in or as in the state of sleep. 8 (*intr*) (of plants) to show nyctitropism. 9 (*intr*) to be inactive or quiescent. 10 (*tr*) to have sleeping accommodation for (a certain number): *the boat could sleep six.* 11 (*tr;* foll by *away*) to pass (time) sleeping. 12 (*intr*) to fail to pay attention. 13 (*intr*) *Poetic or euphemistic* to be dead. 14 **sleep on it.** to give (something) extended consideration, esp overnight. ◆ See also **sleep around, sleep in, sleep off, sleep out, sleep through, sleep with.**
▷HISTORY Old English *slǣpan;* related to Old Frisian *slēpa,* Old Saxon *slāpan,* Old High German *slāfan,* German *schlaff* limp

sleep apnoea NOUN the temporary cessation of breathing during sleep, which in some cases is due to obstruction of the upper airway by enlarged tonsils, uvula, etc., causing the sufferer to snore loudly and fight for breath.

sleep around VERB (*intr, adverb*) *Informal* to be sexually promiscuous.

sleeper (ˈsliːpə) NOUN 1 a person, animal, or thing that sleeps. 2 a railway sleeping car or compartment. 3 *Brit* one of the blocks supporting the rails on a railway track. US and Canadian equivalent: **tie.** 4 a heavy timber beam, esp one that is laid horizontally on the ground. 5 *Chiefly Brit* a small plain gold circle worn in a pierced ear lobe to prevent the hole from closing up. 6 a wrestling hold in which a wrestler presses the sides of his opponent's neck, causing him to pass out. 7 *US* an unbranded calf. 8 Also called: **sleeper goby.** any gobioid fish of the family *Eleotridae,* of brackish or fresh tropical waters, resembling the gobies but lacking a ventral sucker. 9 *Informal* a person or thing that achieves unexpected success after an initial period of obscurity. 10 a spy planted in advance for future use, but not currently active.

sleeper terrorist NOUN a terrorist who is not currently active but assumes a guise in order to be in position, unsuspected, for future terrorist activities.

sleep hygiene NOUN the habits conducive to getting the right amount and quality of sleep.

sleep in VERB (*intr, adverb*) 1 *Brit* to sleep longer than usual. 2 to sleep at the place of one's employment.

sleeping bag NOUN a large well-padded bag designed for sleeping in, esp outdoors.

sleeping car NOUN a railway car fitted with compartments containing bunks for people to sleep in.

sleeping draught NOUN any drink containing a drug or agent that induces sleep.

sleeping partner NOUN a partner in a business who does not play an active role, esp one who supplies capital.

sleeping pill NOUN a pill or tablet containing a sedative drug, such as a barbiturate, used to induce sleep.

sleeping policeman NOUN a bump built across roads, esp in housing estates, to deter motorists from speeding.

sleeping sickness NOUN 1 Also called: **African sleeping sickness.** an African disease caused by infection with protozoans of the genus *Trypanosoma,* characterized by fever, wasting, and sluggishness. 2 Also called (esp formerly): **sleepy sickness.** an epidemic viral form of encephalitis characterized by extreme drowsiness. Technical name: **encephalitis lethargica.**

sleepless (ˈsliːplɪs) ADJECTIVE 1 without sleep or rest: *a sleepless journey.* 2 unable to sleep. 3 always watchful or alert. 4 *Chiefly poetic* always active or moving: *the sleepless tides.*
▸ **ˈsleeplessly** ADVERB ▸ **ˈsleeplessness** NOUN

sleep movement NOUN the folding together of leaflets, petals, etc., that occurs at night in certain plants, such as the prayer plant (*Maranta leuconura*).

sleep off VERB (*tr, adverb*) *Informal* to lose by sleeping: *to sleep off a hangover.*

sleep out VERB (*intr, adverb*) 1 (esp of a tramp) to sleep in the open air. 2 to sleep away from the place of work. ◆ NOUN **sleep-out.** 3 *Austral and NZ* an area of a veranda that has been glassed in or partitioned off so that it may be used as a bedroom.

sleepover (ˈsliːpˌəʊvə) NOUN *Informal, chiefly US* an instance of spending the night at someone else's home.

sleep through VERB (*intr, adverb*) *Informal* (of a baby) to sleep all night without waking up.

sleepwalk (ˈsliːpˌwɔːk) VERB (*intr*) to walk while asleep. See also **somnambulism.**
▸ **ˈsleepˌwalker** NOUN ▸ **ˈsleepˌwalking** NOUN, ADJECTIVE

sleep with VERB (*intr, preposition*) to have sexual intercourse and (usually) spend the night with. Also: **sleep together.**

sleepy (ˈsliːpɪ) ADJECTIVE **sleepier, sleepiest.** 1 inclined to or needing sleep; drowsy. 2 characterized by or exhibiting drowsiness,

sluggishness, etc. 3 conducive to sleep; soporific. 4 without activity or bustle: *a sleepy town.*
▸ **'sleepily** ADVERB ▸ **'sleepiness** NOUN

sleepyhead ('sli:pɪˌhɛd) NOUN *Informal* a sleepy or lazy person.
▸ **'sleepyˌheaded** ADJECTIVE

sleet (sli:t) NOUN 1 partly melted falling snow or hail or (esp US) partly frozen rain. 2 *Chiefly US* the thin coat of ice that forms when sleet or rain freezes on cold surfaces. ♦ VERB 3 (*intr*) to fall as sleet.
▹ **HISTORY** C13: from Germanic; compare Middle Low German *slōten* hail, Middle High German *slōze,* German *Schlossen* hailstones
▸ **'sleety** ADJECTIVE

sleeve (sli:v) NOUN 1 the part of a garment covering the arm. 2 a tubular piece that is forced or shrunk into a cylindrical bore to reduce the diameter of the bore or to line it with a different material; liner. 3 a tube fitted externally over two cylindrical parts in order to join them; bush. 4 a flat cardboard or plastic container to protect a gramophone record. US name: **jacket.** 5 **(have a few tricks) up one's sleeve.** (to have options, etc.) secretly ready. 6 **roll up one's sleeves.** to prepare oneself for work, a fight, etc. ♦ VERB 7 (*tr*) to provide with a sleeve or sleeves.
▹ **HISTORY** Old English *slīf, slēf;* related to Dutch *sloof* apron
▸ **'sleeveless** ADJECTIVE ▸ **'sleeveˌlike** ADJECTIVE

sleeve board NOUN a small ironing board for pressing sleeves, fitted onto an ironing board or table.

sleeveen ('sli:vi:n) NOUN *Irish* a sly obsequious smooth-tongued person.
▹ **HISTORY** from Irish Gaelic *slíbhín*

sleeve notes PLURAL NOUN the printed information on a record sleeve. US equivalent: **liner notes.**

sleeve valve NOUN (in an internal-combustion engine) a valve in the form of a thin steel sleeve fitted between the cylinder and piston and having a reciprocating and rotary oscillation movement.

sleeving ('sli:vɪŋ) NOUN *Electronics, chiefly Brit* tubular flexible insulation into which bare wire can be inserted. US and Canadian name: **spaghetti.**

sleigh (sleɪ) NOUN 1 another name for **sledge**[1] (sense 1). ♦ VERB 2 (*intr*) to travel by sleigh.
▹ **HISTORY** C18: from Dutch *slee,* variant of *slede* SLEDGE[1]
▸ **'sleigher** NOUN

sleight (slaɪt) NOUN *Archaic* 1 skill; dexterity. See also **sleight of hand.** 2 a trick or stratagem. 3 cunning; trickery.
▹ **HISTORY** C14: from Old Norse *slægth,* from *slægr* SLY

sleight of hand NOUN 1 manual dexterity used in performing conjuring tricks. 2 the performance of such tricks.

slender ('slɛndə) ADJECTIVE 1 of small width relative to length or height. 2 (esp of a person's figure) slim and well-formed. 3 small or inadequate in amount, size, etc.: *slender resources.* 4 (of hopes, etc.) having little foundation; feeble. 5 very small: *a slender margin.* 6 (of a sound) lacking volume. 7 *Phonetics* (now only in Irish phonology) relating to or denoting a close front vowel, such as *i* or *e.*
▹ **HISTORY** C14 *slendre,* of unknown origin
▸ **'slenderly** ADVERB ▸ **'slenderness** NOUN

slenderize *or* **slenderise** ('slɛndəˌraɪz) VERB *Chiefly US and Canadian* to make or become slender.

slept (slɛpt) VERB the past tense and past participle of **sleep.**

Slesvig ('sle:svi) NOUN the Danish name for **Schleswig.**

sleuth (slu:θ) NOUN 1 an informal word for **detective.** 2 short for **sleuthhound** (sense 1). ♦ VERB 3 (*tr*) to track or follow.
▹ **HISTORY** C19: short for *sleuthhound,* from C12 *sleuth* trail, from Old Norse *sloth;* see SLOT[2]

sleuthhound ('slu:θˌhaʊnd) NOUN 1 a dog trained to track people, esp a bloodhound. 2 an informal word for **detective.**

S level NOUN *Brit* a public examination in a subject taken for the General Certificate of Education: usually taken at the same time as A2 levels as an additional qualification.

slew[1] (slu:) VERB the past tense of **slay.**

slew[2] *or esp US* **slue** (slu:) VERB 1 to twist or be twisted sideways, esp awkwardly: *he slewed around in his chair.* 2 *Nautical* to cause (a mast) to rotate in its step or (of a mast) to rotate in its step. ♦ NOUN 3 the act of slewing.
▹ **HISTORY** C18: of unknown origin

slew[3] (slu:) NOUN a variant spelling (esp US) of **slough**[1] (sense 2).

slew[4] *or* **slue** (slu:) NOUN *Informal, chiefly US and Canadian* a great number or amount; a lot.
▹ **HISTORY** C20: from Irish Gaelic *sluagh;* related to Old Irish *slōg* army

slewed (slu:d) ADJECTIVE (*postpositive*) *Brit slang* intoxicated; drunk.
▹ **HISTORY** C19: from SLEW[2]

slew rate NOUN *Electronics* the rate at which an electronic amplifier can respond to an abrupt change of input level.

Slezsko ('slɛskɔ) NOUN the Czech name for **Silesia.**

slice (slaɪs) NOUN 1 a thin flat piece cut from something having bulk: *a slice of pork.* 2 a share or portion: *a slice of the company's revenue.* 3 any of various utensils having a broad flat blade and resembling a spatula. 4 (in golf, tennis, etc.) **a** the flight of a ball that travels obliquely because it has been struck off centre. **b** the action of hitting such a shot. **c** the shot so hit. ♦ VERB 5 to divide or cut (something) into parts or slices. 6 (when *intr,* usually foll by *through*) to cut in a clean and effortless manner. 7 (when *intr,* foll by *through*) to move or go (through something) like a knife: *the ship sliced through the water.* 8 (usually foll by *off, from, away,* etc.) to cut or be cut (from) a larger piece. 9 (*tr*) to remove by use of a slicing implement. 10 to hit (a ball) with a slice. 11 (*tr*) *Rowing* to put the blade of the oar into (the water) slantwise.
▹ **HISTORY** C14: from Old French *esclice* a piece split off, from *esclicier* to splinter
▸ **'sliceable** ADJECTIVE ▸ **'slicer** NOUN

slice bar NOUN an iron bar used for raking out furnaces.

slicer ('slaɪsə) NOUN 1 a machine that slices bread, etc., usually with an electrically driven band knife or circular knife. 2 *Electronics* a limiter having two boundary values, the portion of the signal between these values being passed on.

slick (slɪk) ADJECTIVE 1 flattering and glib: *a slick salesman.* 2 adroitly devised or executed: *a slick show.* 3 *Informal, chiefly US and Canadian* shrewd; sly. 4 *Informal* superficially attractive: *a slick publication.* 5 *Chiefly US and Canadian* smooth and glossy; slippery. ♦ NOUN 6 a slippery area, esp a patch of oil floating on water. 7 a chisel or other tool used for smoothing or polishing a surface. 8 the tyre of a racing car that has worn treads. ♦ VERB (*tr*) 9 *Chiefly US and Canadian* to make smooth or sleek. 10 *US and Canadian informal* (usually foll by *up*) to smarten or tidy (oneself). 11 (often foll by *up*) to make smooth or glossy.
▹ **HISTORY** C14: probably of Scandinavian origin; compare Icelandic, Norwegian *slikja* to be or make smooth
▸ **'slickly** ADVERB ▸ **'slickness** NOUN

slickenside ('slɪkənˌsaɪd) NOUN a rock surface with a polished appearance and fine parallel scratches caused by abrasion during fault displacement.
▹ **HISTORY** C18: from dialect *slicken,* variant of SLICK + SIDE

slicker ('slɪkə) NOUN 1 *Informal* a sly or untrustworthy person (esp in the phrase **city slicker**). 2 *US and Canadian* a shiny raincoat, esp an oilskin. 3 a small trowel used for smoothing the surfaces of a mould.
▸ **'slickered** ADJECTIVE

slide (slaɪd) VERB **slides, sliding, slid** (slɪd); **slid** *or* **slidden** ('slɪdᵊn). 1 to move or cause to move smoothly along a surface in continual contact with it: *doors that slide open; children sliding on the ice.* 2 (*intr*) to lose grip or balance: *he slid on his back.* 3 (*intr;* usually foll by *into, out of, away from,* etc.) to pass or move gradually and unobtrusively: *she slid into the room.* 4 (*intr;* usually foll by *into*) to go (into a specified condition) by degrees, unnoticeably, etc.: *he slid into loose living.* 5 (foll by *in, into,* etc.) to move (an object) unobtrusively or (of an object) to move in this way: *he slid the gun into his pocket.* 6 (*intr*) *Music* to execute a portamento. 7 **let slide.** to allow to follow a natural course, esp one leading to deterioration: *to let things slide.* ♦ NOUN 8 the act or an instance of sliding. 9 a smooth surface, as of ice or mud, for sliding on. 10 a construction incorporating an inclined smooth slope for sliding down in playgrounds, etc. 11 *Rowing* a sliding seat in a boat or its runners. 12 a thin glass plate on which specimens are mounted for microscopic study. 13 Also called: **transparency.** a positive photograph on a transparent base, mounted in a cardboard or plastic frame or between glass plates, that can be viewed by means of a slide projector. 14 Also called: **hair slide.** *Chiefly Brit* an ornamental clip to hold hair in place. US and Canadian name: **barrette.** 15 *Machinery* **a** a sliding part or member. **b** the track, guide, or channel on or in which such a part slides. 16 *Music* **a** the sliding curved tube of a trombone that is moved in or out to allow the production of different harmonic series and a wider range of notes. **b** a portamento. 17 *Music* **a** a metal or glass tube placed over a finger held against the frets of a guitar to produce a portamento. **b** the style of guitar playing using a slide. See also **bottleneck** (sense 3). 18 *Geology* **a** the rapid downward movement of a large mass of earth, rocks, etc., caused by erosion, faulting, etc. **b** the mass of material involved in this descent. See also **landslide.**
▹ **HISTORY** Old English *slīdan;* related to *slidor* slippery, *sliderian* to SLITHER, Middle High German *slīten*
▸ **'slidable** ADJECTIVE ▸ **'slider** NOUN

slide-action ADJECTIVE (of a shoulder firearm) ejecting the empty case and reloading by means of a sliding lever.

slide fastener NOUN *Chiefly US and Canadian* another name for **zip** (sense 1).

slide guitar NOUN a technique of guitar playing derived from bottleneck, using a steel or glass tube on one finger across the frets.

slide over VERB (*intr, preposition*) 1 to cross by or as if by sliding. 2 to avoid dealing with (a matter) fully.

slide rest NOUN *Engineering* a stack of platforms that sits on a lathe saddle and carries a tool post, and is adjustable in rotation and at right angles by a lathe operator.

slide rule NOUN *Obsolete* a mechanical calculating device consisting of two strips, one sliding along a central groove in the other, each strip graduated in two or more logarithmic scales of numbers, trigonometric functions, etc. It employs the same principles as logarithm tables.

slide trombone NOUN See **trombone.**

slide valve NOUN 1 a valve that slides across an aperture to expose the port or opening. 2 (*modifier*) fitted with slide valves: *a slide-valve engine.*

sliding ('slaɪdɪŋ) ADJECTIVE 1 rising or falling in accordance with given specifications: *fees were charged as a sliding percentage of income.* 2 regulated or moved by sliding.

sliding fit NOUN *Engineering* a fit that enables one part to be inserted into another by sliding or pushing, rather than by hammering. Also called: **push fit.**

sliding friction NOUN *Engineering* frictional resistance to relative movement of surfaces on loaded contact. Compare **rolling friction.**

sliding scale NOUN a variable scale according to which specified wages, tariffs, prices, etc., fluctuate in response to changes in some other factor, standard, or conditions.

sliding seat NOUN *Rowing* a seat that slides forwards and backwards with the oarsman, lengthening his stroke.

slier ('slaɪə) ADJECTIVE a comparative of **sly.**

sliest ('slaɪɪst) ADJECTIVE a superlative of **sly.**

Slieve Donard (sli:v 'dɒnɑ:d) NOUN a mountain in SE Northern Ireland, in the Mourne Mountains: highest peak in Northern Ireland. Height: 853 m (2798 ft.).

slight (slaɪt) ADJECTIVE 1 small in quantity or extent. 2 of small importance; trifling. 3 slim and delicate. 4 lacking in strength or substance. 5 *Southwest English dialect* ill. ♦ VERB (*tr*) 6 to show indifference or disregard for (someone); snub. 7 to treat as unimportant or trifling. 8 *US* to devote

inadequate attention to (work, duties, etc.). ◆ NOUN [9] an act or omission indicating supercilious neglect or indifference.
▷HISTORY C13: from Old Norse *slēttr* smooth; related to Old High German *slehtr,* Gothic *slaihts,* Middle Dutch *slecht* simple
▸'**slightness** NOUN

slighting ('slaɪtɪŋ) ADJECTIVE characteristic of a slight; disparaging; disdainful: *in a slighting manner.*
▸'**slightingly** ADVERB

slightly ('slaɪtlɪ) ADVERB in small measure or degree.

Sligo ('slaɪgəʊ) NOUN [1] a county of NW Republic of Ireland, on the Atlantic: has a deeply indented low-lying coast; livestock and dairy farming. County town: Sligo. Pop.: 55 821 (1996). Area: 1795 sq. km (693 sq. miles). [2] a port in NW Republic of Ireland, county town of Co. Sligo on **Sligo Bay**. Pop.: 17 300 (1991).

slily ('slaɪlɪ) ADVERB a variant spelling of **slyly**.

slim (slɪm) ADJECTIVE **slimmer, slimmest.** [1] small in width relative to height or length. [2] small in amount or quality: *slim chances of success.* ◆ VERB **slims, slimming, slimmed.** [3] to make or become slim, esp by diets and exercise. [4] to reduce or decrease or cause to be reduced or decreased. ◆ See also **slim down.**
▷HISTORY C17: from Dutch: crafty, from Middle Dutch *slimp* slanting; compare Old High German *slimbi* obliquity
▸'**slimly** ADVERB ▸'**slimmer** NOUN ▸'**slimness** NOUN

Slim (slɪm) NOUN the E African name for **AIDS**.
▷HISTORY from its wasting effects

slim down VERB (*adverb*) [1] to make or become slim, esp intentionally. [2] to make (an organization) more efficient or (of an organization) to become more efficient, esp by cutting staff. ◆ NOUN **slimdown.** [3] an instance of an organization slimming down.

slime (slaɪm) NOUN [1] soft thin runny mud or filth. [2] any moist viscous fluid, esp when noxious or unpleasant. [3] a mucous substance produced by various organisms, such as fish, slugs, and fungi. ◆ VERB (*tr*) [4] to cover with slime. [5] to remove slime from (fish) before canning.
▷HISTORY Old English *slīm;* related to Old Norse *slīm,* Old High German *slīmen* to smooth, Russian *slimák* snail, Latin *līmax* snail

slimeball ('slaɪmˌbɔːl) NOUN *Slang* an odious and contemptible person.

slime mould NOUN any of various simple spore-producing organisms typically found as slimy masses on rotting vegetation, where they engulf food particles by amoeboid movements. Formerly regarded as fungi, they are now classified as protoctists of the phyla *Myxomycota* (true, or cellular slime moulds) or *Acrasiomycota* (plasmodial slime moulds).

slimline ('slɪmˌlaɪn) ADJECTIVE slim; giving the appearance of or conducive to slimness.

slimming ('slɪmɪŋ) NOUN **a** the process of or concern with becoming slim or slimmer as by losing weight. **b** (*as modifier*): *slimming aids.*

slimsy ('slɪmzɪ) ADJECTIVE **-sier, -siest.** *US informal* frail.
▷HISTORY C19: from SLIM + FLIMSY

slimy ('slaɪmɪ) ADJECTIVE **slimier, slimiest.** [1] characterized by, covered with, containing, secreting, or resembling slime. [2] offensive or repulsive. [3] *Chiefly Brit* characterized by servility.
▸'**slimily** ADVERB ▸'**sliminess** NOUN

sling[1] (slɪŋ) NOUN [1] a simple weapon consisting of a loop of leather, etc., in which a stone is whirled and then let fly. [2] a rope or strap by which something may be secured or lifted. [3] a rope net swung from a crane, used for loading and unloading cargo. [4] *Nautical* **a** a halyard for a yard. **b** (*often plural*) the part of a yard where the sling is attached. [5] *Med* a wide piece of cloth suspended from the neck for supporting an injured hand or arm across the front of the body. [6] a loop or band attached to an object for carrying. [7] *Mountaineering* a loop of rope or tape used for support in belays, abseils, etc. [8] the act of slinging. ◆ VERB **slings, slinging, slung.** [9] (*tr*) to hurl with or as if with a sling. [10] to attach a sling or slings to (a load, etc.). [11] (*tr*) to carry or hang loosely from or as if from a sling: *to sling washing from the line.* [12] *Informal* to throw. [13] (*intr*) *Austral informal* to pay a part of one's wages or profits as a bribe or tip.
▷HISTORY C13: perhaps of Scandinavian origin; compare Old Norse *slyngva* to hurl, Old High German *slingan*
▸'**slinger** NOUN

sling[2] (slɪŋ) NOUN a mixed drink with a spirit base, usually sweetened.
▷HISTORY C19: of uncertain origin

slingback ('slɪŋˌbæk) NOUN **a** a shoe with a strap instead of a full covering for the heel. **b** (*as modifier*): *slingback shoes.*

slinger ring NOUN a tubular ring around the hub of an aircraft propeller through which antifreeze solution is spread over the propeller blades by centrifugal force.

sling off VERB (*intr, adverb;* often foll by *at*) *Austral and NZ informal* to laugh or jeer (at).

slingshot ('slɪŋˌʃɒt) NOUN [1] the US and Canadian name for **catapult** (sense 1). [2] another name for **sling**[1] (sense 1).

slink (slɪŋk) VERB **slinks, slinking, slunk.** [1] (*intr*) to move or act in a furtive or cringing manner from or as if from fear, guilt, etc. [2] (*intr*) to move in a sinuous alluring manner. [3] (*tr*) (of animals, esp cows) to give birth to prematurely. ◆ NOUN [4] **a** an animal, esp a calf, born prematurely. **b** (*as modifier*): *slink veal.*
▷HISTORY Old English *slincan;* related to Middle Low German *slinken* to shrink, Old Swedish *slinka* to creep, Danish *slunken* limp

slinky ('slɪŋkɪ) ADJECTIVE **slinkier, slinkiest.** *Informal* [1] moving in a sinuously graceful or provocative way. [2] (of clothes) figure-hugging; clinging. [3] characterized by furtive movements.
▸'**slinkily** ADVERB ▸'**slinkiness** NOUN

slinter ('slɪntə) NOUN *Austral and NZ informal* a dodge, trick, or stratagem. Also (Austral obsolete): **slanter, slenter.**
▷HISTORY from Dutch *slenter,* perhaps via S African *schlenter*

sliotar ('ʃlɪtər) NOUN the ball used in hurling.
▷HISTORY Irish Gaelic

slip[1] (slɪp) VERB **slips, slipping, slipped.** [1] to move or cause to move smoothly and easily. [2] (*tr*) to place, insert, or convey quickly or stealthily. [3] (*tr*) to put on or take off easily or quickly: *to slip on a sweater.* [4] (*intr*) to lose balance and slide unexpectedly: *he slipped on the ice.* [5] to let loose or be let loose. [6] to be released from (something); escape. [7] (*tr*) to let go (mooring or anchor lines) over the side. [8] (when *intr,* often foll by *from* or *out of*) to pass out of (the mind or memory). [9] (*tr*) to overlook, neglect, or miss: *to slip an opportunity.* [10] (*intr*) to move or pass swiftly or unperceived: *to slip quietly out of the room.* [11] (*intr;* sometimes foll by *up*) to make a mistake. [12] Also: **sideslip.** to cause (an aircraft) to slide sideways or (of an aircraft) to slide sideways. [13] (*intr*) to decline in health, mental ability, etc. [14] (*intr*) (of an intervertebral disc) to become displaced from the normal position. [15] (*tr*) to dislocate (a bone). [16] (of animals) to give birth to (offspring) prematurely. [17] (*tr*) to pass (a stitch) from one needle to another without knitting it. [18] **a** (*tr*) to operate (the clutch of a motor vehicle) so that it partially disengages. **b** (*intr*) (of the clutch of a motor vehicle) to fail to engage, esp as a result of wear. [19] **let slip. a** to allow to escape. **b** to say unintentionally. [20] **slip one over on.** *Slang* to hoodwink or trick. ◆ NOUN [21] the act or an instance of slipping. [22] a mistake or oversight: *a slip of the pen.* [23] a moral lapse or failing. [24] a woman's sleeveless undergarment, worn as a lining for and to give support to a dress. [25] *US and Canadian* a narrow space between two piers in which vessels may dock. [26] See **slipway.** [27] a kind of dog lead that allows for the quick release of the dog. [28] a small block of hard steel of known thickness used for measurement, usually forming one of a set. [29] the ratio between output speed and input speed of a transmission device when subtracted from unity, esp of a drive belt or clutch that is not transmitting full power. [30] *Cricket* **a** the position of the fielder who stands a little way behind and to the offside of the wicketkeeper. **b** the fielder himself. [31] the relative movement of rocks along a fault plane. [32] a landslide, esp one blocking a road or railway line. [33] *Metallurgy, crystallog* the deformation of a metallic crystal caused when one part glides over another part along a plane. [34] the deviation of a propeller from its helical path through a fluid, expressed as the difference between its actual forward motion and its theoretical forward motion in one revolution. [35] another name for **sideslip** (sense 1). [36] **give someone the slip.** to elude or escape from someone. ◆ See also **slip up.**
▷HISTORY C13: from Middle Low German or Dutch *slippen*
▸'**slipless** ADJECTIVE

slip[2] (slɪp) NOUN [1] a narrow piece; strip. [2] a small piece of paper: *a receipt slip.* [3] a part of a plant that, when detached from the parent, will grow into a new plant; cutting; scion. [4] a young slender person: *a slip of a child.* [5] *Dialect* a young pig. [6] *Printing* **a** a long galley. **b** a less common name for a **galley proof.** [7] *Chiefly US* a pew or similar long narrow seat. [8] a small piece of abrasive material of tapering section used in honing. ◆ VERB **slips, slipping, slipped.** [9] (*tr*) to detach (portions of stem, etc.) from (a plant) for propagation.
▷HISTORY C15: probably from Middle Low German, Middle Dutch *slippe* to cut, strip

slip[3] (slɪp) NOUN clay mixed with water to a creamy consistency, used for decorating or patching a ceramic piece.
▷HISTORY Old English *slyppe* slime; related to Norwegian *slipa* slime on fish; see SLOP[1]

slipcase ('slɪpˌkeɪs) NOUN a protective case for a book or set of books that is open at one end so that only the spines of the books are visible.

slipcover ('slɪpˌkʌvə) NOUN [1] the US and Canadian word for a **loose cover.** [2] *US and Canadian* a book jacket; dust cover.

slipe (slaɪp) NOUN *NZ* **a** wool removed from the pelt of a slaughtered sheep by immersion in a chemical bath. **b** (*as modifier*): *slipe wool.*
▷HISTORY from English dialect

slip flow NOUN *Physics* gas flow occurring at hypersonic speeds in which molecular shearing occurs.

slip gauge NOUN a very accurately ground block of hardened steel used to measure a gap with close accuracy: used mainly in tool-making and inspection.

slipknot ('slɪpˌnɒt) NOUN [1] Also called: **running knot.** a nooselike knot tied so that it will slip along the rope round which it is made. [2] a knot that can be easily untied by pulling one free end.

slipnoose ('slɪpˌnuːs) NOUN a noose made with a slipknot, so that it tightens when pulled.

slip-on ADJECTIVE [1] (of a garment or shoe) made so as to be easily and quickly put on or off. ◆ NOUN [2] a slip-on garment or shoe.

slipover ('slɪpˌəʊvə) ADJECTIVE [1] of or denoting a garment that can be put on easily over the head. ◆ NOUN [2] such a garment, esp a sleeveless pullover.

slippage ('slɪpɪdʒ) NOUN [1] the act or an instance of slipping. [2] the amount of slipping or the extent to which slipping occurs. [3] **a** an instance of not reaching a norm, target, etc. **b** the extent of this. [4] the power lost in a mechanical device or system as a result of slipping.

slipped disc NOUN *Pathol* a herniated intervertebral disc, often resulting in pain because of pressure on the spinal nerves.

slipper ('slɪpə) NOUN [1] a light shoe of some soft material, for wearing around the house. [2] a woman's evening or dancing shoe. ◆ VERB [3] (*tr*) *Informal* to hit or beat with a slipper.
▸'**slippered** ADJECTIVE ▸'**slipper-ˌlike** ADJECTIVE

slipper bath NOUN [1] a bath in the shape of a slipper, with a covered end. [2] (*plural*) *History* an establishment where members of the public paid to have a bath.

slipper satin NOUN a fine satin fabric with a mat finish.

slipperwort ('slɪpəˌwɜːt) NOUN another name for **calceolaria.**
▷HISTORY C19: so called because of the slipper-like shape of the flower

slippery ('slɪpərɪ, -prɪ) ADJECTIVE [1] causing or tending to cause objects to slip: *a slippery road.* [2] liable to slip from the grasp, a position, etc. [3] not to be relied upon; cunning and untrustworthy: *a slippery character.* [4] (esp of a situation) liable to

change; unstable. 5 **slippery slope.** a course of action that will lead to disaster or failure.
▷HISTORY C16: probably coined by Coverdale to translate German *schlipfferig* in Luther's Bible (Psalm 35:6); related to Old English *slipor* slippery
▸'**slipperily** ADVERB ▸'**slipperiness** NOUN

slippery dip NOUN *Austral informal* a long slide at a playground or funfair.

slippery elm NOUN 1 a tree, *Ulmus fulva,* of E North America, having oblong serrated leaves, notched winged fruits, and a mucilaginous inner bark. 2 the bark of this tree, used medicinally as a demulcent. ◆ Also called: **red elm.**

slippy ('slɪpɪ) ADJECTIVE **-pier, -piest.** 1 *Informal or dialect* another word for **slippery** (senses 1, 2). 2 *Brit informal* alert; quick.
▸'**slippiness** NOUN

slip rail NOUN *Austral and NZ* a rail in a fence that can be slipped out of place to make an opening.

slip ring NOUN *Electrical engineering* a metal ring, mounted on but insulated from a rotating shaft of a motor or generator, by means of which current can be led through stationary brushes into or out of a winding on the shaft.

slip road NOUN *Brit* a short road connecting a motorway, etc., to another road.

slipsheet ('slɪpˌʃi:t) NOUN 1 a sheet of paper that is interleaved between freshly printed sheets to prevent set-off. ◆ VERB 2 to interleave (printed sheets) with slipsheets.

slipshod ('slɪpˌʃɒd) ADJECTIVE 1 (of an action) negligent; careless. 2 (of a person's appearance) slovenly; down-at-heel.
▷HISTORY C16: from SLIP[1] + SHOD
▸'**slipˌshoddiness** *or* '**slipˌshodness** NOUN

slipslop ('slɪpˌslɒp) NOUN 1 *Archaic* weak or unappetizing food or drink. 2 *Informal* maudlin or trivial talk or writing.

slip-slop NOUN *S African* a rubber-soled sandal attached to the foot by a thong between the big toe and the next toe.

slip step NOUN a dance step made by moving the left foot one step sideways and closing the right foot to the left foot: used when dancing in a circle during Scottish reels and jigs.

slip stitch NOUN 1 a sewing stitch for securing hems, etc., in which only two or three threads of the material are caught up by the needle each time, so that the stitches are nearly invisible from the right side. ◆ VERB 2 (*tr*) to join (two edges) using slip stitches.
▷HISTORY C19: from SLIP[1]

slipstream ('slɪpˌstri:m) NOUN 1 Also called: **airstream, race. a** the stream of air forced backwards by an aircraft propeller. **b** a stream of air behind any moving object. ◆ VERB 2 *Motor racing* to follow (another car, etc.) closely in order to take advantage of the decreased wind resistance immediately behind it.

slip up VERB (*intr, adverb*) 1 *Informal* to make a blunder or mistake; err. 2 to fall over: *he slipped up in the street.* ◆ NOUN **slip-up.** 3 *Informal* a mistake, blunder, or mishap.

slipware ('slɪpˌwɛə) NOUN pottery that has been decorated with slip.

slipway ('slɪpˌweɪ) NOUN 1 the sloping area in a shipyard, containing the ways. 2 Also called: **marine railway.** the ways on which a vessel is launched. 3 the ramp of a whaling factory ship. 4 a pillowcase; pillowslip.

slit (slɪt) VERB **slits, slitting, slit.** (*tr*) 1 to make a straight long incision in; split open. 2 to cut into strips lengthwise. 3 to sever. ◆ NOUN 4 a long narrow cut. 5 a long narrow opening.
▷HISTORY Old English *slītan* to slice; related to Old Norse *slíta,* Old High German *slīzen*
▸'**slitter** NOUN

slither ('slɪðə) VERB 1 to move or slide or cause to move or slide unsteadily, as on a slippery surface. 2 (*intr*) to travel with a sliding motion. ◆ NOUN 3 a slithering motion.
▷HISTORY Old English *slidrian,* from *slīdan* to SLIDE

slithery ('slɪðərɪ) ADJECTIVE **-ier, -iest.** 1 moving with a slithering motion. 2 suggestive of a slithering creature.

slit pocket NOUN a pocket on the underside of a garment, reached through a vertical opening.

slit trench NOUN *Military* a narrow trench dug for the protection of a small number of people.

sliver ('slɪvə) NOUN 1 a thin piece that is cut or broken off lengthwise; splinter. 2 a loose strand or fibre obtained by carding. ◆ VERB 3 to divide or be divided into splinters; split. 4 (*tr*) to form (wool, etc.) into slivers.
▷HISTORY C14: from *sliven* to split
▸'**sliver-ˌlike** ADJECTIVE

slivovitz ('slɪvəvɪts, 'sli:və-) NOUN a plum brandy from E Europe.
▷HISTORY from Serbo-Croat *šljivovica,* from *sljiva* plum

SLO INTERNATIONAL CAR REGISTRATION FOR Slovenia.

Sloane Ranger (sləʊn) NOUN (in Britain) *Informal* a young upper-class or upper-middle-class person, esp a woman, having a home in London and in the country, characterized typically as wearing expensive informal country clothes. Also called: **Sloane.**
▷HISTORY C20: coined by Peter York, punning on *Sloane* Square, London SW1, and *Lone Ranger,* television cowboy character

slob (slɒb) NOUN 1 *Informal* a slovenly, unattractive, and lazy person. 2 *Irish* mire.
▷HISTORY C19: from Irish *slab* mud; compare SLAB
▸'**slobbish** ADJECTIVE

slobber ('slɒbə) *or* **slabber** VERB 1 to dribble (saliva, food, etc.) from the mouth. 2 (*intr*) to speak or write mawkishly. 3 (*tr*) to smear with matter dribbling from the mouth. ◆ NOUN 4 liquid or saliva spilt from the mouth. 5 maudlin language or behaviour.
▷HISTORY C15: from Middle Low German, Middle Dutch *slubberen;* see SLAVER[2]
▸'**slobberer** *or* '**slabberer** NOUN ▸'**slobbery** *or* '**slabbery** ADJECTIVE

slob ice NOUN *Canadian* sludgy masses of floating ice.
▷HISTORY see SLOB

sloe (sləʊ) NOUN 1 the small sour blue-black fruit of the blackthorn. 2 another name for **blackthorn.**
▷HISTORY Old English *slāh;* related to Old High German *slēha,* Middle Dutch *sleeuwe*

sloe-eyed ADJECTIVE having dark slanted or almond-shaped eyes.

sloe gin NOUN gin flavoured with sloe juice.

slog (slɒg) VERB **slogs, slogging, slogged.** 1 to hit with heavy blows, as in boxing. 2 (*intr*) to work hard; toil. 3 (*intr;* foll by *down, up, along,* etc.) to move with difficulty; plod. 4 *Cricket* to score freely by taking large swipes at the ball. ◆ NOUN 5 a tiring hike or walk. 6 long exhausting work. 7 a heavy blow or swipe.
▷HISTORY C19: of unknown origin
▸'**slogger** NOUN

slogan ('sləʊgən) NOUN 1 a distinctive or topical phrase used in politics, advertising, etc. 2 *Scot history* a Highland battle cry.
▷HISTORY C16: from Gaelic *sluagh-ghairm* war cry, from *sluagh* army + *gairm* cry

sloganeer (ˌsləʊgə'nɪə) NOUN 1 a person who coins or employs slogans frequently. ◆ VERB 2 (*intr*) to coin or employ slogans so as to sway opinion.

slommock ('slɒmək) VERB (*intr*) *Midland English dialect* to walk assertively with a hip-rolling gait.

slo-mo ('sləʊˌməʊ) NOUN, ADJECTIVE *Informal* a variant spelling of **slow-mo**, see **slow motion**.

sloop (slu:p) NOUN a single-masted sailing vessel, rigged fore-and-aft, with the mast stepped about one third of the overall length aft of the bow. Compare **cutter** (sense 2).
▷HISTORY C17: from Dutch *sloep;* related to French *chaloupe* launch, Old English *slūpan* to glide

sloop of war NOUN (formerly) a small fast sailing warship mounting some 10 to 30 small calibre guns on one deck.

sloop-rigged ADJECTIVE *Nautical* rigged as a sloop, typically with a jib and a mainsail.

sloot (slu:t) NOUN *South African* a ditch for irrigation or drainage.
▷HISTORY from Afrikaans, from Dutch *sluit, sluis* SLUICE

slop[1] (slɒp) VERB **slops, slopping, slopped.** 1 (when *intr,* often foll by *about*) to cause (liquid) to splash or spill or (of liquid) to splash or spill. 2 (*tr*) to splash liquid upon. 3 (*intr;* foll by *along, through,* etc.) to tramp (through) mud or slush. 4 (*tr*) to feed slop or swill to: *to slop the pigs.* 5 (*tr*) to ladle or serve, esp clumsily. 6 (*intr;* foll by *over*) *Informal, chiefly US and Canadian* to be unpleasantly effusive. ◆ NOUN 7 a puddle of spilt liquid. 8 (*plural*) wet feed, esp for pigs, made from kitchen waste, etc. 9 (*plural*) waste food or liquid refuse. 10 (*plural*) the beer, cider, etc., spilt from a barrel while being drawn. 11 (*often plural*) the residue left after spirits have been distilled. 12 (*often plural*) *Informal* liquid or semiliquid food of low quality. 13 soft mud, snow, etc. 14 *Informal* gushing speech or writing.
▷HISTORY C14: probably from Old English *-sloppe* in *cūsloppe* COWSLIP; see SLIP[3]

slop[2] (slɒp) NOUN 1 (*plural*) sailors' clothing and bedding issued from a ship's stores. 2 any loose article of clothing, esp a smock. 3 (*plural*) men's wide knee breeches worn in the 16th century. 4 (*plural*) shoddy manufactured clothing.
▷HISTORY Old English *oferslop* surplice; related to Old Norse *slopps* gown, Middle Dutch *slop*

slop around VERB (*intr*) to move around in a casual and idle way: *he slops around the house in old slippers.* Also: **slop about.**

slop basin NOUN a bowl or basin into which the dregs from teacups are emptied at the table.

slop chest NOUN a stock of merchandise, such as clothing, tobacco, etc., maintained aboard merchant ships for sale to the crew. Compare **small stores.**

slope (sləʊp) VERB 1 to lie or cause to lie at a slanting or oblique angle. 2 (*intr*) (esp of natural features) to follow an inclined course: *many paths sloped down the hillside.* 3 (*intr;* foll by *off, away,* etc.) to go furtively. 4 (*tr*) *Military* (formerly) to hold (a rifle) in the slope position (esp in the command **slope arms**). ◆ NOUN 5 an inclined portion of ground. 6 (*plural*) hills or foothills. 7 any inclined surface or line. 8 the degree or amount of such inclination. 9 *Maths* **a** (of a line) the tangent of the angle between the line and another line parallel to the *x*-axis. **b** the first derivative of the equation of a curve at a given point. 10 (formerly) the position adopted for British military drill when the rifle is rested on the shoulder.
▷HISTORY C15: short for *aslope,* perhaps from the past participle of Old English *āslūpan* to slip away, from *slūpan* to slip
▸'**sloper** NOUN ▸'**sloping** ADJECTIVE ▸'**slopingly** ADVERB ▸'**slopingness** NOUN

slop out VERB (*intr, adverb*) (of prisoners) to empty chamber pots and collect water for washing.

sloppy ('slɒpɪ) ADJECTIVE **-pier, -piest.** 1 (esp of ground conditions, etc.) wet; slushy. 2 *Informal* careless; untidy. 3 *Informal* mawkishly sentimental. 4 (of food or drink) watery and unappetizing. 5 splashed with slops. 6 (of clothes) loose; baggy.
▸'**sloppily** ADVERB ▸'**sloppiness** NOUN

sloppy joe (dʒəʊ) NOUN *Informal* a long baggy thin sweater.

slopwork ('slɒpˌwɜ:k) NOUN 1 the manufacture of cheap shoddy clothing or the clothes so produced. 2 any work of low quality.
▸'**slopˌworker** NOUN

slorm (slɔ:m) VERB *Midland English dialect* to wipe carelessly.

slosh (slɒʃ) NOUN 1 watery mud, snow, etc. 2 *Brit slang* a heavy blow. 3 the sound of splashing liquid. 4 a popular dance with a traditional routine of steps, kicks, and turns performed in lines. ◆ VERB 5 (*tr;* foll by *around, on, in,* etc.) *Informal* to throw or pour (liquid). 6 (when *intr,* often foll by *about* or *around*) *Informal* **a** to shake or stir (something) in a liquid. **b** (of a person) to splash (around) in water, etc. 7 (*tr*) *Brit slang* to deal a heavy blow to. 8 (usually foll by *about* or *around*) *Informal* to shake (a container of liquid) or (of liquid within a container) to be shaken.
▷HISTORY C19: variant of SLUSH, influenced by SLOP[1]
▸'**sloshy** ADJECTIVE

sloshed (slɒʃt) ADJECTIVE *Chiefly Brit* a slang word for **drunk.**

slot[1] (slɒt) NOUN 1 an elongated aperture or groove, such as one in a vending machine for inserting a coin. 2 an air passage in an aerofoil to direct air from the lower to the upper surface, esp the gap formed behind a slat. 3 a vertical opening between the leech of a foresail and a mast or the

luff of another sail through which air spills from one against the other to impart forward motion. **4** *Informal* a place in a series or scheme. ◆ VERB **slots, slotting, slotted.** **5** (*tr*) to furnish with a slot or slots. **6** (usually foll by *in* or *into*) to fit or adjust in a slot. **7** *Informal* to situate or be situated in a series or scheme.
▷HISTORY C13: from Old French *esclot* the depression of the breastbone, of unknown origin
▸ **'slotter** NOUN

slot[2] (slɒt) NOUN the trail of an animal, esp a deer.
▷HISTORY C16: from Old French *esclot* horse's hoof-print, probably of Scandinavian origin; compare Old Norse *sloth* track; see SLEUTH

slot aerial *or* **antenna** NOUN *Radio* a transmitting aerial in which the radiating elements are open slots in a surrounding metal sheet.

sloth (sləʊθ) NOUN **1** any of several shaggy-coated arboreal edentate mammals of the family *Bradypodidae*, esp *Bradypus tridactylus* (**three-toed sloth** or **ai**) or *Choloepus didactylus* (**two-toed sloth** or **unau**), of Central and South America. They are slow-moving, hanging upside down by their long arms and feeding on vegetation. **2** reluctance to work or exert oneself.
▷HISTORY Old English *slǣwth;* from *slǣw,* variant of *slāw* SLOW

sloth bear NOUN a bear, *Melursus ursinus,* of forests of S India and Sri Lanka, having a shaggy coat and an elongated snout specialized for feeding on termites.

slothful ('sləʊθfʊl) ADJECTIVE indolent.
▸ **'slothfully** ADVERB ▸ **'slothfulness** NOUN

slot machine NOUN a machine, esp one for selling small articles or for gambling, activated by placing a coin or metal disc in a slot.

slouch (slaʊtʃ) VERB **1** (*intr*) to sit or stand with a drooping bearing. **2** (*intr*) to walk or move with an awkward slovenly gait. **3** (*tr*) to cause (the shoulders) to droop. ◆ NOUN **4** a drooping carriage. **5** (*usually used in negative constructions*) *Informal* an incompetent or slovenly person: *he's no slouch at football.*
▷HISTORY C16: of unknown origin
▸ **'sloucher** NOUN ▸ **'slouching** ADJECTIVE ▸ **'slouchingly** ADVERB

slouch hat NOUN any soft hat with a brim that can be pulled down over the ears, esp an Australian army hat with the left side of the brim turned up.

slouchy ('slaʊtʃɪ) ADJECTIVE **-ier, -iest.** **1** slouching; lazy. **2** (of clothes) casual, soft, and relatively unstructured.
▸ **'slouchily** ADVERB ▸ **'slouchiness** NOUN

slough[1] (slaʊ) NOUN **1** a hollow filled with mud; bog. **2** (sluː) *US and Canadian* **a** (in the prairies) a large hole where water collects or the water in such a hole. **b** (in the northwest) a sluggish side channel of a river. **c** (on the Pacific coast) a marshy saltwater inlet. **3** despair or degradation.
▷HISTORY Old English *slōh;* related to Middle High German *sluoche* ditch, Swedish *slaga* swamp
▸ **'sloughy** ADJECTIVE

slough[2] (slʌf) NOUN **1** any outer covering that is shed, such as the dead outer layer of the skin of a snake, the cellular debris in a wound, etc. **2** Also: **sluff.** *Bridge* a discarded card. ◆ VERB **3** (often foll by *off*) to shed (a skin, etc.) or (of a skin, etc.) to be shed. **4** Also: **sluff.** *Bridge* to discard (a card or cards).
▷HISTORY C13: of Germanic origin; compare Middle Low German *slū* husk, German *Schlauch* hose, Norwegian *slō* fleshy part of a horn
▸ **'sloughy** ADJECTIVE

Slough (slaʊ) NOUN **1** an industrial town in SE central England, in Slough unitary authority, Berkshire; food products, high-tech industries. Pop.: 118 008 (1998 est.). **2** a unitary authority in SE central England, in Berkshire. Pop.: 119 070 (2001). Area: 28 sq. km (11 sq. miles).

slough off (slʌf) VERB (*tr, adverb*) to cast off (cares, etc.).

Slovak ('sləʊvæk) ADJECTIVE **1** of, relating to, or characteristic of Slovakia, its people, or their language. ◆ NOUN **2** the official language of Slovakia, belonging to the West Slavonic branch of the Indo-European family. Slovak is closely related to Czech; they are mutually intelligible. **3** a native or inhabitant of Slovakia.

Slovakia (sləʊ'vækɪə) NOUN a country in central Europe: part of Hungary from the 11th century until 1918, when it united with Bohemia and Moravia to form Czechoslovakia; it became independent in 1993. Official language: Slovak. Religion: Roman Catholic majority. Currency: koruna. Capital: Bratislava. Pop.: 5 410 000 (2001 est.). Area: 49 036 sq. km (18 940 sq. miles).

Slovakian (sləʊ'vækɪən) ADJECTIVE **1** of, relating to, or characteristic of Slovakia, its people, or the Slovak language. ◆ ADJECTIVE **2** a native or inhabitant of Slovakia.

sloven ('slʌvᵊn) NOUN a person who is habitually negligent in appearance, hygiene, or work.
▷HISTORY C15: probably related to Flemish *sloef* dirty, Dutch *slof* negligent

Slovene (sləʊ'viːn) ADJECTIVE *also* **Slovenian.** **1** of, relating to, or characteristic of Slovenia, its people, or their language. ◆ NOUN **2** Also: **Slovenian.** a South Slavonic language spoken in Slovenia, closely related to Serbo-Croat. **3** **a** a native or inhabitant of Slovenia. **b** a speaker of Slovene.

Slovenia (sləʊ'viːnɪə) NOUN a republic in S central Europe: settled by the Slovenes in the 6th century; joined Yugoslavia in 1918 and became an autonomous republic in 1946; became fully independent in 1992; rises over 2800 m (9000 ft.) in the Julian Alps. Official language: Slovene. Religion: Roman Catholic majority. Currency: tolar. Capital: Ljubljana. Pop.: 1 991 000 (2001 est.). Area: 20 251 sq. km (7819 sq. miles).

slovenly ('slʌvənlɪ) ADJECTIVE **1** frequently or habitually unclean or untidy. **2** negligent and careless; slipshod: *slovenly manners.* ◆ ADVERB **3** in a negligent or slovenly manner.
▸ **'slovenliness** NOUN

slow (sləʊ) ADJECTIVE **1** performed or occurring during a comparatively long interval of time. **2** lasting a comparatively long time: *a slow journey.* **3** characterized by lack of speed: *a slow walker.* **4** (*prenominal*) adapted to or productive of slow movement: *the slow lane of a motorway.* **5** (of a clock, etc.) indicating a time earlier than the correct time. **6** given to or characterized by a leisurely or lazy existence: *a slow town.* **7** not readily responsive to stimulation; intellectually unreceptive: *a slow mind.* **8** dull or uninteresting: *the play was very slow.* **9** not easily aroused: *a slow temperament.* **10** lacking promptness or immediacy: *a slow answer.* **11** unwilling to perform an action or enter into a state: *slow to anger.* **12** behind the times. **13** (of trade, etc.) unproductive; slack. **14** (of a fire) burning weakly. **15** (of an oven) cool. **16** *Photog* requiring a relatively long time of exposure to produce a given density: *a slow lens.* **17** *Sport* (of a track, etc.) tending to reduce the speed of the ball or the competitors. **18** *Cricket* (of a bowler, etc.) delivering the ball slowly, usually with spin. ◆ ADVERB **19** in a manner characterized by lack of speed; slowly. ◆ VERB **20** (often foll by *up* or *down*) to decrease or cause to decrease in speed, efficiency, etc.
▷HISTORY Old English *slāw* sluggish; related to Old High German *slēo* dull, Old Norse *slǣr,* Dutch *sleeuw* slow
▸ **'slowly** ADVERB ▸ **'slowness** NOUN

slow burn NOUN a steadily penetrating show of anger or contempt.

slowcoach ('sləʊˌkəʊtʃ) NOUN *Brit informal* a person who moves, acts, or works slowly. US and Canadian equivalent: **slowpoke.**

slowdown ('sləʊˌdaʊn) NOUN **1** the usual US and Canadian word for **go-slow.** **2** any slackening of pace.

slow food NOUN food that has been prepared with care, using high-quality ingredients.
▷HISTORY C20: by analogy with FAST FOOD

slow handclap NOUN *Brit* slow rhythmic clapping, esp used by an audience to indicate dissatisfaction or impatience.

slow march NOUN *Military* a march in slow time.

slow match NOUN a match or fuse that burns slowly without flame, esp a wick impregnated with potassium nitrate.

slow-mo *or* **slo-mo** ('sləʊˌməʊ) NOUN, ADJECTIVE *Informal* short for **slow motion.**

slow motion NOUN **1** *Films, television* action that is made to appear slower than normal by passing the film through the taking camera at a faster rate than normal or by replaying a video tape recording more slowly. ◆ ADJECTIVE **slow-motion.** **2** *Films, television* of or relating to such action. **3** moving or functioning at less than usual speed.

slow neutron NOUN *Physics* a neutron having a kinetic energy of less than 100 electronvolts.

slowpoke ('sləʊˌpəʊk) NOUN *Informal* the usual US and Canadian word for **slowcoach.**

slow time NOUN *Military* a slow marching pace, usually 65 or 75 paces to the minute: used esp in funeral ceremonies.

slow virus NOUN any of a class of virus-like disease-causing agents known as prions that are present in the body for a long time before becoming active or infectious and are very resistant to radiation and similar factors: believed to be the cause of BSE and scrapie.

slow-witted ADJECTIVE slow in comprehension; unintelligent.

slowworm ('sləʊˌwɜːm) NOUN a Eurasian legless lizard, *Anguis fragilis,* with a brownish-grey snakelike body: family *Anguidae.* Also called: **blindworm.**

SLR ABBREVIATION FOR single-lens reflex. See **reflex camera.**

SLSC *Austral* ABBREVIATION FOR Surf Life Saving Club.

slub (slʌb) NOUN **1** a lump in yarn or fabric, often made intentionally to give a knobbly effect. **2** a loosely twisted roll of fibre prepared for spinning. ◆ VERB **slubs, slubbing, slubbed.** **3** (*tr*) to draw out and twist (a sliver of fibre) preparatory to spinning. ◆ ADJECTIVE **4** (of material) having an irregular appearance.
▷HISTORY C18: of unknown origin

slubberdegullion (ˌslʌbədɪ'gʌlɪən) NOUN *Archaic* a slovenly or worthless person.
▷HISTORY C17: from *slubber* (chiefly dialect variant of SLOBBER) + invented ending

sludge (slʌdʒ) NOUN **1** soft mud, snow, etc. **2** any deposit or sediment. **3** a surface layer of ice that has a slushy appearance. **4** (in sewage disposal) the solid constituents of sewage that precipitate during treatment and are removed for subsequent purification.
▷HISTORY C17: probably related to SLUSH

sludgy ('slʌdʒɪ) ADJECTIVE **-ier, -iest.** consisting of, containing, or like sludge.

slue[1] (sluː) NOUN, VERB a variant spelling (esp US) of **slew**[2].

slue[2] (sluː) NOUN a variant spelling of **slough**[1] (sense 2).

slue[3] (sluː) NOUN *US informal* a variant spelling of **slew**[4].

sluff (slʌf) NOUN, VERB *Bridge* a variant spelling of **slough**[2].

slug[1] (slʌg) NOUN **1** any of various terrestrial gastropod molluscs of the genera *Limax, Arion,* etc., in which the body is elongated and the shell is absent or very much reduced. Compare **sea slug.** Related adjective: **limacine.** **2** any of various other invertebrates having a soft slimy body, esp the larvae of certain sawflies. **3** *Informal, chiefly US and Canadian* a slow-moving or lazy person or animal.
▷HISTORY C15 (in the sense: a slow person or animal): probably of Scandinavian origin; compare Norwegian (dialect) *sluggje*

slug[2] (slʌg) NOUN **1** an fps unit of mass; the mass that will acquire an acceleration of 1 foot per second per second when acted upon by a force of 1 pound. 1 slug is approximately equal to 32.17 pounds. **2** *Metallurgy* a metal blank from which small forgings are worked. **3** a bullet or pellet larger than a pellet of buckshot. **4** *Chiefly US and Canadian* a metal token for use in slot machines, etc. **5** *Printing* **a** a thick strip of type metal that is less than type-high and is used for spacing. **b** a similar strip carrying a type-high letter, used as a temporary mark by compositors. **c** a metal strip containing a line of characters as produced by a linecaster. **6** a draught of a drink, esp an alcoholic one. **7** a magnetic core that is screwed into or out of an inductance coil to adjust the tuning of a radio frequency amplifier.
▷HISTORY C17 (bullet), C19 (printing): perhaps from SLUG[1], with allusion to the shape of the animal

slug^{3} (slʌg) VERB **slugs, slugging, slugged.** [1] to hit very hard and solidly, as in boxing. [2] *(intr) US and Canadian* to plod as if through snow. [3] *(tr) Austral and NZ informal* to charge (someone) an exorbitant price. [4] **slug it out.** *Informal* to fight, compete, or struggle with fortitude. ◆ NOUN [5] an act of slugging; heavy blow. [6] *Austral and NZ informal* an exorbitant charge or price.
▷HISTORY C19: perhaps from SLUG^{2} (bullet)

slugabed ('slʌgəˌbɛd) NOUN a person who remains in bed through laziness.
▷HISTORY C16: from SLUG(GARD) + ABED

sluggard ('slʌgəd) NOUN [1] a person who is habitually indolent. ◆ ADJECTIVE [2] lazy.
▷HISTORY C14 *slogarde;* related to SLUG^{1}
▸ **'sluggardly** ADJECTIVE ▸ **'sluggardliness** NOUN
▸ **'sluggardness** NOUN

slugger ('slʌgə) NOUN (esp in boxing, baseball, etc.) a person who strikes hard.

sluggish ('slʌgɪʃ) ADJECTIVE [1] lacking energy; inactive; slow-moving. [2] functioning at below normal rate or level. [3] exhibiting poor response to stimulation.
▸ **'sluggishly** ADVERB ▸ **'sluggishness** NOUN

sluice (slu:s) NOUN [1] Also called: **sluiceway.** a channel that carries a rapid current of water, esp one that has a sluicegate to control the flow. [2] the body of water controlled by a sluicegate. [3] See **sluicegate.** [4] *Mining* an inclined trough for washing ore, esp one having riffles on the bottom to trap particles. [5] an artificial channel through which logs can be floated. [6] *Informal* a brief wash in running water. ◆ VERB [7] *(tr)* to draw out or drain (water, etc.) from (a pond, etc.) by means of a sluice. [8] *(tr)* to wash or irrigate with a stream of water. [9] *(tr) Mining* to wash in a sluice. [10] *(tr)* to send (logs, etc.) down a sluice. [11] *(intr; often foll by away or out)* (of water, etc.) to run or flow from or as if from a sluice. [12] *(tr)* to provide with a sluice.
▷HISTORY C14: from Old French *escluse,* from Late Latin *exclūsa aqua* water shut out, from Latin *exclūdere* to shut out, EXCLUDE
▸ **'sluiceˌlike** ADJECTIVE

sluicegate ('slu:sˌgeɪt) NOUN a valve or gate fitted to a sluice to control the rate of flow of water. Sometimes shortened to: **sluice.** See also **floodgate** (sense 1).

slum (slʌm) NOUN [1] a squalid overcrowded house, etc. [2] *(often plural)* a squalid section of a city, characterized by inferior living conditions and usually by overcrowding. [3] *(modifier)* of, relating to, or characteristic of slums: *slum conditions.* ◆ VERB **slums, slumming, slummed.** *(intr)* [4] to visit slums, esp for curiosity. [5] Also: **slum it.** to suffer conditions below those to which one is accustomed.
▷HISTORY C19: originally slang, of obscure origin
▸ **'slummer** NOUN ▸ **'slummy** ADJECTIVE

slumber ('slʌmbə) VERB [1] *(intr)* to sleep, esp peacefully. [2] *(intr)* to be quiescent or dormant. [3] *(tr; foll by away)* to spend (time) sleeping. ◆ NOUN [4] *(sometimes plural)* sleep. [5] a dormant or quiescent state.
▷HISTORY Old English *slūma* sleep (n); related to Middle High German *slummeren,* Dutch *sluimeren*
▸ **'slumberer** NOUN ▸ **'slumberless** ADJECTIVE

slumberous ('slʌmbərəs, -brəs) ADJECTIVE *Chiefly poetic* [1] sleepy; drowsy. [2] inducing sleep. [3] characteristic of slumber.
▸ **'slumberously** ADVERB ▸ **'slumberousness** NOUN

slumber party NOUN *US and Canadian* a party attended by girls who dress in night clothes and pass the night eating and talking.

slumgullion (slʌm'gʌljən, 'slʌmˌgʌl-) NOUN *US and Canadian* [1] *Slang* an inexpensive stew. [2] offal, esp the refuse from whale blubber. [3] a reddish mud deposited in mine sluices.
▷HISTORY C19: from *slum* in US sense slime + *gullion,* perhaps variant of *cullion* testicles

slumlord ('slʌmˌlɔ:d) NOUN *Informal, chiefly US and Canadian* an absentee landlord of slum property, esp one who profiteers.

slump (slʌmp) VERB *(intr)* [1] to sink or fall heavily and suddenly. [2] to relax ungracefully. [3] (of business activity, etc.) to decline suddenly; collapse. [4] (of health, interest, etc.) to deteriorate or decline suddenly or markedly. [5] (of soil or rock) to slip down a slope, esp a cliff, usually with a rotational movement. ◆ NOUN [6] a sudden or marked decline or failure, as in progress or achievement; collapse. [7] a decline in commercial activity, prices, etc. [8] *Economics* another word for **depression.** [9] the act of slumping. [10] a slipping of earth or rock; landslide.
▷HISTORY C17: probably of Scandinavian origin; compare Low German *slump* bog, Norwegian *slumpa* to fall

Slump (slʌmp) NOUN **the.** another name for the **Depression.**

slumpflation (slʌmp'fleɪʃən) NOUN a situation in which economic depression is combined with increasing inflation.
▷HISTORY C20: blend of SLUMP + INFLATION

slump test NOUN *Brit* a test to determine the relative water content of concrete, depending on the loss in height (slump) of a sample obtained from a cone-shaped mould.

slung (slʌŋ) ADJECTIVE the past tense and past participle of **sling**^{1}.

slung shot NOUN a weight attached to the end of a cord and used as a weapon.

slunk (slʌŋk) VERB the past tense and past participle of **slink.**

slur (slɜ:) VERB **slurs, slurring, slurred.** *(mainly tr)* [1] (often foll by *over*) to treat superficially, hastily, or without due deliberation; gloss. [2] *(also intr)* to pronounce or utter (words, etc.) indistinctly. [3] to speak disparagingly of or cast aspersions on. [4] *Music* to execute (a melodic interval of two or more notes) smoothly, as in legato performance. [5] *(also intr)* to blur or smear. [6] *Archaic* to stain or smear; sully. ◆ NOUN [7] an indistinct sound or utterance. [8] a slighting remark; aspersion. [9] a stain or disgrace, as upon one's reputation; stigma. [10] *Music* **a** a performance or execution of a melodic interval of two or more notes in a part. **b** the curved line (⌒ or ‿) indicating this. [11] a blur or smear.
▷HISTORY C15: probably from Middle Low German; compare Middle Low German *slūren* to drag, trail, Middle Dutch *sloren,* Dutch *sleuren*

slurp (slɜ:p) *Informal* ◆ VERB [1] to eat or drink (something) noisily. ◆ NOUN [2] a sound produced in this way.
▷HISTORY C17: from Middle Dutch *slorpen* to sip; related to German *schlürfen*

slurry ('slʌrɪ) NOUN, *plural* **-ries.** a suspension of solid particles in a liquid, as in a mixture of cement, clay, coal dust, manure, meat, etc. with water.
▷HISTORY C15 *slory;* see SLUR

slush (slʌʃ) NOUN [1] any watery muddy substance, esp melting snow. [2] *Informal* sloppily sentimental language. [3] *Nautical* waste fat from the galley of a ship. ◆ VERB [4] *(intr; often foll by along)* to make one's way through or as if through slush. [5] *(intr)* to make a slushing sound.
▷HISTORY C17: related to Danish *slus* sleet, Norwegian *slusk* slops; see SLUDGE, SLOSH

slush fund NOUN [1] a fund for financing political or commercial corruption. [2] *US nautical* a fund accumulated from the sale of slush from the galley.

slushy ('slʌʃɪ) ADJECTIVE **slushier, slushiest.** [1] of, resembling, or consisting of slush. ◆ NOUN, *plural* **slushies.** [2] an unskilled kitchen assistant.
▸ **'slushiness** NOUN

slut (slʌt) NOUN [1] a dirty slatternly woman. [2] an immoral woman. [3] *Archaic* a female dog.
▷HISTORY C14: of unknown origin
▸ **'sluttish** ADJECTIVE ▸ **'sluttishly** ADVERB ▸ **'sluttishness** NOUN

slutch (slʌtʃ) NOUN *Northern English dialect* mud.
▸ **'slutchy** ADJECTIVE

sly (slaɪ) ADJECTIVE **slyer, slyest** *or* **slier, sliest.** [1] crafty; artful: *a sly dodge.* [2] insidious; furtive: *a sly manner.* [3] playfully mischievous; roguish: *sly humour.* ◆ NOUN [4] **on the sly.** in a secretive manner.
▷HISTORY C12: from Old Norse *slǣgr* clever, literally: able to strike, from *slā* to SLAY
▸ **'slyly** *or* **'slily** ADVERB ▸ **'slyness** NOUN

slyboots ('slaɪˌbu:ts) PLURAL NOUN *(functioning as singular)* a person who is sly.

sly grog NOUN *Austral and NZ old-fashioned* illicitly sold liquor.

slype (slaɪp) NOUN a covered passageway in a cathedral or church that connects the transept to the chapterhouse.
▷HISTORY C19: probably from Middle Flemish *slijpen* to slip

sm THE INTERNET DOMAIN NAME FOR San Marino.

Sm THE CHEMICAL SYMBOL FOR samarium.

SM ABBREVIATION FOR: [1] sergeant major. [2] sadomasochism.

smack^{1} (smæk) NOUN [1] a smell or flavour that is distinctive though faint. [2] a distinctive trace or touch: *the smack of corruption.* [3] a small quantity, esp a mouthful or taste. [4] a slang word for **heroin.** ◆ VERB *(intr; foll by of)* [5] to have the characteristic smell or flavour (of something): *to smack of the sea.* [6] to have an element suggestive (of something): *his speeches smacked of bigotry.*
▷HISTORY Old English *smæc;* related to Old High German *smoc,* Icelandic *smekkr* a taste, Dutch *smaak*

smack^{2} (smæk) VERB [1] *(tr)* to strike or slap smartly, with or as if with the open hand. [2] to strike or send forcibly or loudly or to be struck or sent forcibly or loudly. [3] to open and close (the lips) loudly, esp to show pleasure. [4] *(tr)* to kiss noisily. ◆ NOUN [5] a sharp resounding slap or blow with something flat, or the sound of such a blow. [6] a loud kiss. [7] a sharp sound made by the lips, as in enjoyment. [8] **have a smack at.** *Informal, chiefly Brit* to attempt. [9] **smack in the eye.** *Informal, chiefly Brit* a snub or setback. ◆ ADVERB *Informal* [10] directly; squarely. [11] with a smack; sharply and unexpectedly.
▷HISTORY C16: from Middle Low German or Middle Dutch *smacken,* probably of imitative origin

smack^{3} (smæk) NOUN [1] a sailing vessel, usually sloop-rigged, used in coasting and fishing along the British coast. [2] a fishing vessel equipped with a well for keeping the catch alive.
▷HISTORY C17: from Low German *smack* or Dutch *smak,* of unknown origin

smacker ('smækə) NOUN *Slang* [1] a loud kiss; smack. [2] a pound note or dollar bill.

smackhead ('smækˌhɛd) NOUN *Brit slang* a person who is addicted to heroin.

smacking ('smækɪŋ) ADJECTIVE brisk; lively: *a smacking breeze.*

small (smɔ:l) ADJECTIVE [1] comparatively little; limited in size, number, importance, etc. [2] of little importance or on a minor scale: *a small business.* [3] lacking in moral or mental breadth or depth: *a small mind.* [4] modest or humble: *small beginnings.* [5] of low or inferior status, esp socially. [6] (of a child or animal) young; not mature. [7] unimportant, trivial: *a small matter.* [8] not outstanding: *a small actor.* [9] of, relating to, or designating the ordinary modern minuscule letter used in printing and cursive writing. Compare **capital**^{1} (sense 13). See also **lower case.** [10] lacking great strength or force: *a small effort.* [11] in fine particles: *small gravel.* [12] *Obsolete* (of beer, etc.) of low alcoholic strength. ◆ ADVERB [13] into small pieces: *cut it small.* [14] in a small or soft manner. [15] **feel small.** to be humiliated or inferior. ◆ NOUN [16] (often preceded by *the*) an object, person, or group considered to be small: *the small or the large?* [17] a small slender part, esp of the back. [18] *(plural) Informal, chiefly Brit* items of personal laundry, such as underwear.
▷HISTORY Old English *smæl;* related to Old High German *smal,* Old Norse *smali* small cattle
▸ **'smallish** ADJECTIVE ▸ **'smallness** NOUN

small advertisement *or* **small ad** NOUN a short, simply designed advertisement in a newspaper or magazine, usually set entirely in a small size of type. See **display advertisement.**

smallage ('smɔ:lɪdʒ) NOUN an archaic name for **wild celery.**
▷HISTORY C13: from earlier *smalache,* from *smal* SMALL + *ache* wild celery, from Old French, from Latin *apium*

small arms PLURAL NOUN portable firearms of relatively small calibre.

small beer NOUN *Informal, chiefly Brit* people or things of no importance.

small-bore ADJECTIVE (of a firearm) having a small bore, especially one of less than .22 calibre.

smallboy ('smɔ:lˌbɔɪ) NOUN the steward's assistant or deputy steward in European households in W Africa.

small calorie NOUN another name for **calorie.**

small capital NOUN a letter having the form of an upper-case letter but the same height as a lower-case letter.

small change NOUN [1] coins, esp those of low value. [2] a person or thing that is not outstanding or important.

small chop PLURAL NOUN *W African* cocktail snacks.

small circle NOUN a circular section of a sphere that does not contain the centre of the sphere. Compare **great circle.**

small claims court NOUN *Brit and Canadian* a local court with jurisdiction to try civil actions involving small claims.

smallclothes (ˈsmɔːlˌkləʊz, -ˌkləʊðz) PLURAL NOUN men's close-fitting knee breeches of the 18th and 19th centuries.

small forward NOUN *Basketball* a versatile attacking player.

small fry PLURAL NOUN [1] people or things regarded as unimportant. [2] young children. [3] young or small fishes.

small game NOUN *Brit* small animals that are hunted for sport.

small goods PLURAL NOUN *Austral and NZ* meats bought from a delicatessen, such as sausages.

smallholding (ˈsmɔːlˌhəʊldɪŋ) NOUN a holding of agricultural land smaller than a small farm.
▸ **ˈsmallˌholder** NOUN

small hours PLURAL NOUN **the.** the early hours of the morning, after midnight and before dawn.

small intestine NOUN the longest part of the alimentary canal, consisting of the duodenum, jejunum, and ileum, in which digestion is completed. Compare **large intestine.**

small letter NOUN a lower-case letter.

small-minded ADJECTIVE narrow-minded; petty; intolerant; mean.
▸ **ˌsmall-ˈmindedly** ADVERB ▸ **ˌsmall-ˈmindedness** NOUN

smallmouth bass (ˈsmɔːlˌmaʊθ ˈbæs) NOUN a North American freshwater black bass, *Micropterus dolomieu,* that is a popular game fish.

small pica NOUN (formerly) a size of printer's type approximately equal to 11 point.

small potatoes NOUN (*functioning as singular or plural*) *Informal, chiefly US and Canadian* someone or something of little significance or value, esp a small amount of money.

smallpox (ˈsmɔːlˌpɒks) NOUN an acute highly contagious viral disease characterized by high fever, severe prostration, and a pinkish rash changing in form from papules to pustules, which dry up and form scabs that are cast off, leaving pitted depressions. Technical name: **variola.** Related adjective: **variolous.**
▹**HISTORY** C16: from SMALL + POX. So called to distinguish it from *the Great Pox,* an archaic name for syphilis

small print NOUN matter in a contract, etc., printed in small type, esp when considered to be a trap for the unwary.

small-scale ADJECTIVE [1] of limited size or scope. [2] (of a map, model, etc.) giving a relatively small representation of something, usually missing out details.

small screen NOUN an informal name for **television.**

small slam NOUN *Bridge* another name for **little slam.**

small stores PLURAL NOUN *Navy* personal items, such as clothing, sold aboard ship or at a naval base. Compare **slop chest.**

small stuff NOUN *Nautical* any light twine or yarn used aboard ship for serving lines, etc.

smallsword (ˈsmɔːlˌsɔːd) NOUN a light sword used in the 17th and 18th centuries: formerly a fencing weapon.

small talk NOUN light conversation for social occasions.

small-time ADJECTIVE *Informal* insignificant; minor: *a small-time criminal.*
▸ **ˈsmall-ˈtimer** NOUN

small white NOUN a small white butterfly, *Artogeia rapae,* with scanty black markings, the larvae of which feed on brassica leaves.

smalt (smɔːlt) NOUN [1] a type of silica glass coloured deep blue with cobalt oxide. [2] a pigment made by crushing this glass, used in colouring enamels. [3] the blue colour of this pigment.
▹**HISTORY** C16: via French from Italian SMALTO, of Germanic origin; related to SMELT[1]

smaltite (ˈsmɔːltaɪt) NOUN a silver-white to greyish mineral consisting chiefly of cobalt arsenide with nickel in cubic crystalline form. It occurs in veins associated with silver, nickel, and copper minerals, and is an important ore of cobalt and nickel. Formula: $(Co,Ni)As_{3-x}$.
▹**HISTORY** C19: from SMALT + -ITE[1]

smalto (ˈsmɑːltəʊ) NOUN, *plural* **-tos** *or* **-ti** (-tiː). coloured glass, etc., used in mosaics.
▹**HISTORY** C18: from Italian; see SMALT

smaragd (ˈsmærægd) NOUN *Archaic* any green gemstone, such as the emerald.
▹**HISTORY** C13: via Latin from Greek *smaragdos;* see EMERALD
▸ **smaragdine** (sməˈrægdɪn) ADJECTIVE

smaragdite (sməˈrægdaɪt) NOUN a green fibrous amphibole mineral.

smarm (smɑːm) *Brit informal* ◆ VERB [1] (*tr;* often foll by *down*) to flatten (the hair, etc.) with cream or grease. [2] (when *intr,* foll by *up to*) to ingratiate oneself (with). ◆ NOUN [3] obsequious flattery.
▹**HISTORY** C19: of unknown origin

smarmy (ˈsmɑːmɪ) ADJECTIVE **smarmier, smarmiest.** *Brit informal* obsequiously flattering or unpleasantly suave.
▸ **ˈsmarmily** ADVERB ▸ **ˈsmarminess** NOUN

smart (smɑːt) ADJECTIVE [1] astute, as in business; clever or bright. [2] quick, witty, and often impertinent in speech: *a smart talker.* [3] fashionable; chic: *a smart hotel.* [4] well-kept; neat. [5] causing a sharp stinging pain. [6] vigorous or brisk. [7] *Dialect* considerable or numerous: *a smart price.* [8] (of systems) operating as if by human intelligence by using automatic computer control. [9] (of a projectile or bomb) containing a device that allows it to be guided to its target. ◆ VERB (*mainly intr*) [10] to feel, cause, or be the source of a sharp stinging physical pain or keen mental distress: *a nettle sting smarts; he smarted under their abuse.* [11] (often foll by *for*) to suffer a harsh penalty. ◆ NOUN [12] a stinging pain or feeling. ◆ ADVERB [13] in a smart manner.
▹**HISTORY** Old English *smeortan;* related to Old High German *smerzan,* Latin *mordēre* to bite, Greek *smerdnos* terrible
▸ **ˈsmartish** ADJECTIVE ▸ **ˈsmartly** ADVERB ▸ **ˈsmartness** NOUN

smart aleck (ˈælɪk) NOUN, *plural* **smart alecks.** *Informal* an irritatingly oversmart person.
▹**HISTORY** C19: from *Aleck, Alec,* short for *Alexander*
▸ **ˈsmart-ˌaleck** *or* **ˈsmart-ˌalecky** ADJECTIVE

smartarse (ˈsmɑːtˌɑːs) NOUN *Derogatory slang* **a** a clever person, esp one who parades his knowledge offensively. **b** (*as modifier*): *smartarse guidebooks.*
▸ **ˈsmartˌarsed** ADJECTIVE

smart card NOUN a plastic card with integrated circuits used for storing and processing computer data. Also called: **laser card, intelligent card.**

smarten (ˈsmɑːtᵊn) VERB (usually foll by *up*) [1] (*intr*) to make oneself neater. [2] (*tr*) to make quicker or livelier.

smart money NOUN [1] **a** money bet or invested by experienced gamblers or investors, esp with inside information. **b** the gamblers or investors themselves. [2] money paid in order to extricate oneself from an unpleasant situation or agreement, esp from military service. [3] money paid by an employer to someone injured while working for him. [4] *US law* damages awarded to a plaintiff where the wrong was aggravated by fraud, malice, etc.

smartmouth (ˈsmɑːtˌmaʊθ) NOUN *Informal* [1] a witty or sarcastic person. [2] witty or sarcastic comments.

smarts (smɑːts) PLURAL NOUN *Slang, chiefly US* know-how, intelligence, or wits: *street smarts.*

smart sanction NOUN (*often plural*) a sanction intended to affect a particular area of a country's activities or economy.

smart set NOUN (*functioning as singular or plural*) fashionable sophisticated people considered as a group.

smarty *or* **smartie** (ˈsmɑːtɪ) NOUN *Informal* a would-be clever person.

smarty-pants (ˈsmɑːtɪˌpænts) *or* **smarty-boots** (ˈsmɑːtɪˌbuːts) NOUN (*functioning as singular*) *Informal* a would-be clever person.

smash (smæʃ) VERB [1] to break into pieces violently and usually noisily. [2] (when *intr,* foll by *against, through, into,* etc.) to throw or crash (against) vigorously, causing shattering: *he smashed the equipment; it smashed against the wall.* [3] (*tr*) to hit forcefully and suddenly. [4] (*tr*) *Tennis, squash, badminton* to hit (the ball) fast and powerfully, esp with an overhead stroke. [5] (*tr*) to defeat or wreck (persons, theories, etc.). [6] (*tr*) to make bankrupt. [7] (*intr*) to collide violently; crash. [8] (*intr;* often foll by *up*) to go bankrupt. [9] **smash someone's face in.** *Informal* to beat someone severely. ◆ NOUN [10] an act, instance, or sound of smashing or the state of being smashed. [11] a violent collision, esp of vehicles. [12] a total failure or collapse, as of a business. [13] *Tennis, squash, badminton* a fast and powerful overhead stroke. [14] *Informal* **a** something having popular success. **b** (*in combination*): *smash-hit.* [15] *Slang* loose change; coins. ◆ ADVERB [16] with a smash.
▹**HISTORY** C18: probably from SM(ACK[2] + M)ASH
▸ **ˈsmashable** ADJECTIVE

smash-and-grab ADJECTIVE *Informal* of or relating to a robbery in which a shop window is broken and the contents removed.

smashed (smæʃt) ADJECTIVE *Slang* [1] completely intoxicated with alcohol. [2] noticeably under the influence of a drug.

smasher (ˈsmæʃə) NOUN *Informal, chiefly Brit* a person or thing that is very attractive or outstanding.

smashing (ˈsmæʃɪŋ) ADJECTIVE *Informal, chiefly Brit* excellent or first-rate; wonderful: *we had a smashing time.*

smash-up *Informal* ◆ NOUN [1] a bad collision, esp of cars. ◆ VERB **smash up.** [2] (*tr, adverb*) to damage to the point of complete destruction: *they smashed the place up.*

smatch (smætʃ) NOUN a less common word for **smack[1].**

smatter (ˈsmætə) NOUN [1] a smattering. ◆ VERB [2] (*intr*) *Rare* to prattle. [3] (*tr*) *Archaic* to dabble in.
▹**HISTORY** C14 (in the sense: to prattle): of uncertain origin; compare Middle High German *smetern* to gossip
▸ **ˈsmatterer** NOUN

smattering (ˈsmætərɪŋ) NOUN [1] a slight or superficial knowledge. [2] a small amount.
▸ **ˈsmatteringly** ADVERB

SMATV ABBREVIATION FOR (originally) small master antenna television; now more commonly, satellite master antenna television: a system for relaying broadcast television signals, embodying a master receiving antenna with distribution by cable to a small group of dwellings, such as a block of flats.

smaze (smeɪz) NOUN *US* a smoky haze, less damp than fog.
▹**HISTORY** C20: from SM(OKE + H)AZE[1]

SMD *Electronics* ABBREVIATION FOR surface-mounted device: a device such as resistor, capacitor, or integrated circuit on a printed circuit board.

SME INTERNATIONAL CAR REGISTRATION FOR Suriname.

smear (smɪə) VERB (*mainly tr*) [1] to bedaub or cover with oil, grease, etc. [2] to rub over or apply thickly. [3] to rub so as to produce a smudge. [4] to slander. [5] *US slang* to defeat completely. [6] (*intr*) to be or become smeared or dirtied. ◆ NOUN [7] a dirty mark or smudge. [8] **a** a slanderous attack. **b** (*as modifier*): *smear tactics.* [9] a preparation of blood, secretions, etc., smeared onto a glass slide for examination under a microscope.
▹**HISTORY** Old English *smeoru* (n); related to Old Norse *smjör* fat, Old High German *smero,* Greek *muron* ointment
▸ **ˈsmearer** NOUN

smear test NOUN *Med* another name for **Pap test.**

smeary (ˈsmɪərɪ) ADJECTIVE **-rier, -riest.** smeared, dirty; blurred by smearing.
▸ **ˈsmearily** ADVERB ▸ **ˈsmeariness** NOUN

smectic (ˈsmɛktɪk) ADJECTIVE *Chem* (of a substance) existing in or having a mesomorphic state in which

the molecules are oriented in layers. Compare **nematic.** See also **liquid crystal.**
▷HISTORY C17: via Latin from Greek *smēktikos,* from *smēkhein* to wash; from the soaplike consistency of a smectic substance

smectite (ˈsmɛktaɪt) NOUN any of a group of clay minerals of which montmorillonite and saponite are members.

smeddum (ˈsmɛdəm) NOUN *Scot* [1] any fine powder. [2] spirit or mettle; vigour.
▷HISTORY Old English *smedema* fine flour

smeech (smiːtʃ) NOUN, VERB a Southwest English dialect form of **smoke.**

smegma (ˈsmɛɡmə) NOUN *Physiol* a whitish sebaceous secretion that accumulates beneath the prepuce.
▷HISTORY C19: via Latin from Greek *smēgma* detergent, from *smekhein* to wash

smell (smɛl) VERB **smells, smelling, smelt** *or* **smelled.** [1] (*tr*) to perceive the scent or odour of (a substance) by means of the olfactory nerves. [2] (*copula*) to have a specified smell; appear to the sense of smell to be: *the beaches smell of seaweed; some tobacco smells very sweet.* [3] (*intr;* often foll by *of*) to emit an odour (of): *the park smells of flowers.* [4] (*intr*) to emit an unpleasant odour; stink. [5] (*tr;* often foll by *out*) to detect through shrewdness or instinct. [6] (*intr*) to have or use the sense of smell; sniff. [7] (*intr;* foll by *of*) to give indications (of): *he smells of money.* [8] (*intr;* foll by *around, about,* etc.) to search, investigate, or pry. [9] (*copula*) to be or seem to be untrustworthy or corrupt. [10] **smell a rat.** to detect something suspicious. ◆ NOUN [11] that sense (olfaction) by which scents or odours are perceived. Related adjective: **olfactory.** [12] anything detected by the sense of smell; odour; scent. [13] a trace or indication. [14] the act or an instance of smelling.
▷HISTORY C12: of uncertain origin; compare Middle Dutch *smölen* to scorch
▸ˈ**smeller** NOUN

smellies (ˈsmɛlɪz) PLURAL NOUN *Informal* pleasant-smelling products such as perfumes, body lotions, bath salts, etc.

smelling salts PLURAL NOUN a pungent preparation containing crystals of ammonium carbonate that has a stimulant action when sniffed in cases of faintness, headache, etc.

smelly (ˈsmɛlɪ) ADJECTIVE **smellier, smelliest.** having a strong or nasty smell.
▸ˈ**smelliness** NOUN

smelt[1] (smɛlt) VERB (*tr*) to extract (a metal) from (an ore) by heating.
▷HISTORY C15: from Middle Low German, Middle Dutch *smelten;* related to Old High German *smelzan* to melt

smelt[2] (smɛlt) NOUN, *plural* **smelt** *or* **smelts.** any marine or freshwater salmonoid food fish of the family *Osmeridae,* such as *Osmerus eperlanus* of Europe, having a long silvery body and occurring in temperate and cold northern waters.
▷HISTORY Old English *smylt;* related to Dutch, Danish *smelt,* Norwegian *smelta,* German *Schmelz*

smelt[3] (smɛlt) VERB a past tense and past participle of **smell.**

smelter (ˈsmɛltə) NOUN [1] a person engaged in smelting. [2] Also called: **smeltery** (ˈsmɛltərɪ). an industrial plant in which smelting is carried out.

smew (smjuː) NOUN a merganser, *Mergus albellus,* of N Europe and Asia, having a male plumage of white with black markings.
▷HISTORY C17: of uncertain origin

smidge (smɪdʒ) NOUN *Informal* a very small amount or part.
▷HISTORY C20: from SMIDGEN

smidgen *or* **smidgin** (ˈsmɪdʒən) NOUN *Informal* a very small amount or part.
▷HISTORY C20: of obscure origin

smilacaceous (ˌsmaɪləˈkeɪʃəs) ADJECTIVE of, relating to, or belonging to the *Smilacaceae,* a temperate and tropical family of monocotyledonous flowering plants, most of which are climbing shrubs with prickly stems: includes smilax.
▷HISTORY C19: via New Latin from Latin SMILAX

smilax (ˈsmaɪlæks) NOUN [1] any typically climbing shrub of the smilacaceous genus *Smilax,* of warm and tropical regions, having slightly lobed leaves, small greenish or yellow flowers, and berry-like fruits: includes the sarsaparilla plant and greenbrier. [2] a fragile, much branched liliaceous vine, *Asparagus asparagoides,* of southern Africa: cultivated by florists for its glossy bright green foliage.
▷HISTORY C17: via Latin from Greek: bindweed

smile (smaɪl) NOUN [1] a facial expression characterized by an upturning of the corners of the mouth, usually showing amusement, friendliness, etc., but sometimes scorn, etc. [2] favour or blessing: *the smile of fortune.* [3] an agreeable appearance. ◆ VERB [4] (*intr*) to wear or assume a smile. [5] (*intr;* foll by *at*) **a** to look (at) with a kindly or amused expression. **b** to look derisively (at) instead of being annoyed. **c** to bear (troubles, etc.) patiently. [6] (*intr;* foll by *on* or *upon*) to show approval; bestow a blessing. [7] (*tr*) to express by means of a smile: *she smiled a welcome.* [8] (*tr;* often foll by *away*) to drive away or change by smiling: *smile away one's tears.* [9] **come up smiling.** to recover cheerfully from misfortune.
▷HISTORY C13: probably of Scandinavian origin; compare Swedish *smila,* Danish *smile;* related to Middle High German *smielen*
▸ˈ**smiler** NOUN ▸ˈ**smiling** ADJECTIVE ▸ˈ**smilingly** ADVERB ▸ˈ**smilingness** NOUN

smiley (ˈsmaɪlɪ) ADJECTIVE [1] given to smiling; cheerful. [2] depicting a smile: *a smiley badge.* ◆ NOUN [3] any of a group of symbols depicting a smile, or other facial expression, used in electronic mail.

smir, smirr (smɪr), *or* **smur** *Scot* ◆ NOUN [1] drizzly rain. ◆ VERB **smirs** *or* **smirrs, smirring, smirred.** (*intr*) [2] to drizzle lightly.
▷HISTORY C19: of uncertain origin; compare Dutch *smoor* mist

smirch (smɜːtʃ) VERB (*tr*) [1] to dirty; soil. ◆ NOUN [2] the act of smirching or state of being smirched. [3] a smear or stain.
▷HISTORY C15 *smorchen,* of unknown origin
▸ˈ**smircher** NOUN

smirk (smɜːk) NOUN [1] a smile expressing scorn, smugness, etc., rather than pleasure. ◆ VERB [2] (*intr*) to give such a smile. [3] (*tr*) to express with such a smile.
▷HISTORY Old English *smearcian;* related to *smer* derision, Old High German *bismer* contempt, *bismerōn* to scorn
▸ˈ**smirker** NOUN ▸ˈ**smirking** ADJECTIVE ▸ˈ**smirkingly** ADVERB

smit (smɪt) NOUN **the.** *Scot and northern English dialect* an infection: *he's got the smit.*
▷HISTORY Old English *smitte* a spot, and *smittian* to smear; related to Old High German *smiz,* whence Middle High German *smitz*

smite (smaɪt) VERB **smites, smiting, smote; smitten** *or* **smit.** (*mainly tr*) *Now archaic in most senses* [1] to strike with a heavy blow or blows. [2] to damage with or as if with blows. [3] to afflict or affect severely: *smitten with flu.* [4] to afflict in order to punish. [5] (*intr;* foll by *on*) to strike forcibly or abruptly: *the sun smote down on him.*
▷HISTORY Old English *smītan;* related to Old High German *smīzan* to smear, Gothic *bismeitan,* Old Swedish *smēta* to daub
▸ˈ**smiter** NOUN

smith (smɪθ) NOUN [1] **a** a person who works in metal, esp one who shapes metal by hammering. **b** (*in combination*): *a silversmith.* [2] See **blacksmith.**
▷HISTORY Old English; related to Old Norse *smithr,* Old High German *smid,* Middle Low German *smīde* jewellery, Greek *smilē* carving knife

smithereens (ˌsmɪðəˈriːnz) PLURAL NOUN little shattered pieces or fragments.
▷HISTORY C19: from Irish Gaelic *smidirín,* from *smiodar*

smithery (ˈsmɪθərɪ) NOUN, *plural* **-eries.** [1] the trade or craft of a blacksmith. [2] a rare word for **smithy.**

Smithsonian Institution (smɪθˈsəʊnɪən) NOUN a national museum and institution in Washington, D.C., founded in 1846 from a bequest by James Smithson, primarily concerned with ethnology, zoology, and astrophysics.

smithsonite (ˈsmɪθsəˌnaɪt) NOUN a white mineral consisting of zinc carbonate in hexagonal crystalline form: occurs chiefly in dry limestone regions and is a source of zinc. Formula: $ZnCO_3$. Also called (US): **calamine.**
▷HISTORY C19: named after James Smithson (1765–1829), English chemist and mineralogist

smithy (ˈsmɪðɪ) NOUN, *plural* **smithies.** a place in which metal, usually iron or steel, is worked by heating and hammering; forge.
▷HISTORY Old English *smiththe;* related to Old Norse *smithja,* Old High German *smidda,* Middle Dutch *smisse*

smitten (ˈsmɪtᵊn) VERB a past participle of **smite.**

smock (smɒk) NOUN [1] any loose protective garment, worn by artists, laboratory technicians, etc. [2] a woman's loose blouse-like garment, reaching to below the waist, worn over slacks, etc. [3] Also called: **smock frock.** a loose protective overgarment decorated with smocking, worn formerly esp by farm workers. [4] *Archaic* a woman's loose undergarment, worn from the 16th to the 18th centuries. ◆ VERB [5] to ornament (a garment) with smocking.
▷HISTORY Old English *smocc;* related to Old High German *smocco,* Old Norse *smokkr* blouse, Middle High German *gesmuc* decoration
▸ˈ**smockˌlike** ADJECTIVE

smocking (ˈsmɒkɪŋ) NOUN ornamental needlework used to gather and stitch material in a honeycomb pattern so that the part below the gathers hangs in even folds.

smock mill NOUN a type of windmill having a revolving top.

smog (smɒɡ) NOUN a mixture of smoke, fog, and chemical fumes.
▷HISTORY C20: from SM(OKE + F)OG[1]
▸ˈ**smoggy** ADJECTIVE

smoke (sməʊk) NOUN [1] the product of combustion, consisting of fine particles of carbon carried by hot gases and air. [2] any cloud of fine particles suspended in a gas. [3] **a** the act of smoking tobacco or other substances, esp in a pipe or as a cigarette or cigar. **b** the duration of smoking such substances. [4] *Informal* **a** a cigarette or cigar. **b** a substance for smoking, such as pipe tobacco or marijuana. [5] something with no concrete or lasting substance: *everything turned to smoke.* [6] a thing or condition that obscures. [7] any of various colours similar to that of smoke, esp a dark grey with a bluish, yellowish, or greenish tinge. [8] **go** *or* **end up in smoke. a** to come to nothing. **b** to burn up vigorously. **c** to flare up in anger. ◆ VERB [9] (*intr*) to emit smoke or the like, sometimes excessively or in the wrong place. [10] **a** to draw in on (a burning cigarette, etc.) and exhale the smoke. **b** to use tobacco for smoking. [11] (*intr*) *Slang* to use marijuana for smoking. [12] (*tr*) to bring (oneself) into a specified state by smoking. [13] (*tr*) to subject or expose to smoke. [14] (*tr*) to cure (meat, fish, cheese, etc.) by treating with smoke. [15] (*tr*) to fumigate or purify the air of (rooms, etc.). [16] (*tr*) to darken (glass, etc.) by exposure to smoke. [17] (*intr*) *Slang* to move, drive, ride, etc., very fast. [18] (*tr*) *Obsolete* to tease or mock. [19] (*tr*) *Archaic* to suspect or detect. ◆ See also **smoke out.**
▷HISTORY Old English *smoca* (n); related to Middle Dutch *smieken* to emit smoke
▸ˈ**smokable** *or* ˈ**smokeable** ADJECTIVE

Smoke (sməʊk) NOUN **the.** short for **Big Smoke.**

smoke and mirrors NOUN irrelevant or misleading information serving to obscure the truth of a situation.
▷HISTORY C20: reference to the use of smoke and mirrors in conjuring illusions

smoke bomb NOUN a device that emits large quantities of smoke when ignited.

smoke-dried ADJECTIVE (of fish, meat, etc.) cured in smoke.

smoked rubber NOUN a type of crude natural rubber in the form of brown sheets obtained by coagulating latex with an acid, rolling it into sheets, and drying over open wood fires. It is the main raw material for natural rubber products. Also called: **ribbed and smoked sheet.** Compare **crepe rubber.**

smokeho (ˈsməʊkəʊ) NOUN a variant spelling of **smoko.**

smokehouse (ˈsməʊkˌhaʊs) NOUN a building or special construction for curing meat, fish, etc., by smoking.

smokejack (ˈsməʊkˌdʒæk) NOUN a device formerly

used for turning a roasting spit, operated by the movement of ascending gases in a chimney.
▷HISTORY C17: from SMOKE + JACK[1]

smokeless ('sməʊklɪs) ADJECTIVE having or producing little or no smoke: *smokeless fuel.*

smokeless powder NOUN any one of a number of explosives that burn with relatively little smoke. They consist mainly of nitrocellulose and are used as propellants.

smokeless zone NOUN an area designated by the local authority where only smokeless fuels are permitted.

smoke out VERB (*tr, adverb*) [1] to subject to smoke in order to drive out of hiding. [2] to bring into the open; expose to the public: *they smoked out the plot.*

smoker ('sməʊkə) NOUN [1] a person who habitually smokes tobacco. [2] Also called: **smoking compartment.** a compartment of a train where smoking is permitted. [3] an informal social gathering, as at a club. [4] a vent on the ocean floor from which hot water and minerals erupt.

Smokerlyzer ('sməʊkə,laɪzə) NOUN *Trademark* a device for estimating the amount of carbon monoxide in the breath: used in testing whether or not people, esp schoolchildren, have been smoking.
▷HISTORY C20: from SMOKER + (ANA)LYZER

smoke screen NOUN [1] *Military* a cloud of smoke produced by artificial means to obscure movements or positions. [2] something said or done in order to hide the truth.

smokestack ('sməʊk,stæk) NOUN a tall chimney that conveys smoke into the air. Sometimes shortened to: **stack.**

smokestack industry NOUN *Informal* any of the traditional British industries, esp heavy engineering or manufacturing, as opposed to such modern industries as electronics.

smoke tree NOUN [1] an anacardiaceous shrub, *Cotinus coggygria,* of S Europe and Asia, having clusters of yellowish feathery flowers. [2] a related tree, *Cotinus americanus,* of the southern US.
▷HISTORY C19: so named because of the similarity between its flower clusters and a cloud of smoke

smoking gun NOUN *Chiefly US and Canadian* a piece of irrefutable incriminating evidence.

smoking jacket NOUN a man's comfortable jacket of velvet, etc., closed by a tie belt or fastenings, worn at home.
▷HISTORY so called because it was formerly worn for smoking

smoking room *or esp Brit* **smoke room** NOUN a room, esp in a hotel or club, for those who wish to smoke.

smoko *or* **smokeho** ('sməʊkəʊ) NOUN, *plural* **-kos** *or* **-hos.** *Austral and NZ informal* a short break from work for tea, a cigarette, etc.
▷HISTORY C19: from SMOKE + -O

smoky ('sməʊkɪ) ADJECTIVE **smokier, smokiest.** [1] emitting, containing, or resembling smoke. [2] emitting smoke excessively or in the wrong place: *a smoky fireplace.* [3] of or tinged with the colour smoke: *a smoky cat.* [4] having the flavour of having been cured by smoking. [5] made dark, dirty, or hazy by smoke.
▶'**smokily** ADVERB ▶'**smokiness** NOUN

Smoky Mountains PLURAL NOUN See **Great Smoky Mountains.**

smoky quartz NOUN another name for **cairngorm.**
▷HISTORY so named because of its colour

smolder ('sməʊldə) VERB, NOUN the US spelling of **smoulder.**

Smolensk (*Russian* sma'ljɛnsk; *English* 'smɒlɛnsk) NOUN a city in W Russia, on the Dnieper River: a major commercial centre in medieval times; scene of severe fighting (1941 and 1943) in World War II. Pop.: 355 700 (1999 est.).

smolt (sməʊlt) NOUN a young salmon at the stage when it migrates from fresh water to the sea.
▷HISTORY C14: Scottish, of uncertain origin; perhaps related to SMELT[2]

smooch (smu:tʃ) *Informal* ◆ VERB (*intr*) [1] Also (Austral and NZ): **smoodge, smooge.** (of two people) to kiss and cuddle. [2] *Brit* to dance very slowly and amorously with one's arms around another person, or (of two people) to dance together in such a way. ◆ NOUN [3] the act of smooching. [4] *Brit* a piece of music played for dancing to slowly and amorously.
▷HISTORY C20: variant of dialect *smouch,* of imitative origin

smoodge *or* **smooge** (smu:dʒ) VERB *Austral and NZ* variants of **smooch** (sense 1).

smooth (smu:ð) ADJECTIVE [1] resting in the same plane; without bends or irregularities. [2] silky to the touch: *smooth velvet.* [3] lacking roughness of surface; flat. [4] tranquil or unruffled: *smooth temper.* [5] lacking obstructions or difficulties. [6] **a** suave or persuasive, esp as suggestive of insincerity. **b** (*in combination*): *smooth-tongued.* [7] (of the skin) free from hair. [8] of uniform consistency: *smooth batter.* [9] not erratic; free from jolts: *smooth driving.* [10] not harsh or astringent: *a smooth wine.* [11] having all projections worn away: *smooth tyres.* [12] *Maths* (of a curve) differentiable at every point. [13] *Phonetics* without preliminary or simultaneous aspiration. [14] gentle to the ear; flowing. [15] *Physics* (of a plane, surface, etc.) regarded as being frictionless. ◆ ADVERB [16] in a calm or even manner; smoothly. ◆ VERB (*mainly tr*) [17] (*also intr; often foll by down*) to make or become flattened or without roughness or obstructions. [18] (often foll by *out* or *away*) to take or rub (away) in order to make smooth: *she smoothed out the creases in her dress.* [19] to make calm; soothe. [20] to make easier: *smooth his path.* [21] *Electrical engineering* to remove alternating current ripple from the output of a direct current power supply. [22] *Obsolete* to make more polished or refined. ◆ NOUN [23] the smooth part of something. [24] the act of smoothing. [25] *Tennis, squash, badminton* the side of a racket on which the binding strings form a continuous line. Compare **rough** (sense 27). ◆ See also **smooth over.**
▷HISTORY Old English *smōth;* related to Old Saxon *māthmundi* gentle-minded, *smōthi* smooth
▶'**smoothable** ADJECTIVE ▶'**smoother** NOUN ▶'**smoothly** ADVERB ▶'**smoothness** NOUN

smoothbore ('smu:ð,bɔ:) NOUN [1] (*modifier*) (of a firearm) having an unrifled bore: *a smoothbore musket.* [2] such a firearm.
▶'**smooth,bored** ADJECTIVE

smooth breathing NOUN (in Greek) the sign (') placed over an initial vowel, indicating that (in ancient Greek) it was not pronounced with an *h.* Compare **rough breathing.**

smoothen ('smu:ðən) VERB to make or become smooth.

smooth hound NOUN any of several small sharks of the genus *Mustelus,* esp *M. mustelus,* a species of North Atlantic coastal regions: family *Triakidae.* See also **dogfish** (sense 3).
▷HISTORY C17: from HOUND(FISH); so called because it has no dorsal spines

smoothie *or* **smoothy** ('smu:ðɪ) NOUN, *plural* **smoothies.** [1] *Slang, usually derogatory* a person, esp a man, who is suave or slick, esp in speech, dress, or manner. [2] a smooth, thick drink made with puréed fresh fruit and yogurt, ice cream, or milk.

smoothing circuit NOUN *Electrical engineering* a circuit used to remove ripple from the output of a direct current power supply.

smoothing iron NOUN a former name for **iron** (senses 2, 3).

smooth muscle NOUN muscle that is capable of slow rhythmic involuntary contractions: occurs in the walls of the blood vessels, alimentary canal, etc. Compare **striped muscle.**
▷HISTORY so called because there is no cross-banding on the muscle

smooth over VERB (*tr*) to ease or gloss over: *to smooth over a situation.*

smooth snake NOUN any of several slender nonvenomous colubrid snakes of the European genus *Coronella,* esp *C. austriaca,* having very smooth scales and a reddish-brown coloration.

smooth-spoken ADJECTIVE speaking or spoken in a gently persuasive or competent manner.

smooth-tongued ADJECTIVE suave or persuasive in speech.

smorgasbord ('smɔ:gəs,bɔ:d, 'smɜ:-) NOUN a variety of cold or hot savoury dishes, such as pâté, smoked salmon, etc., served in Scandinavia as hors d'oeuvres or as a buffet meal.
▷HISTORY Swedish, from *smörgås* sandwich + *bord* table

smørrebrød (*Danish* 'smœrə,brœð) NOUN small open savoury sandwiches, served esp in Denmark as hors d'oeuvres, etc.
▷HISTORY Danish, from *smør* butter + *brød* bread

smote (sməʊt) VERB the past tense of **smite.**

smother ('smʌðə) VERB [1] to suffocate or stifle by cutting off or being cut off from the air. [2] (*tr*) to surround (with) or envelop (in): *he smothered her with love.* [3] (*tr*) to extinguish (a fire) by covering so as to cut it off from the air. [4] to be or cause to be suppressed or stifled: *smother a giggle.* [5] (*tr*) to cook or serve (food) thickly covered with sauce, etc. ◆ NOUN [6] anything, such as a cloud of smoke, that stifles. [7] a profusion or turmoil. [8] *Archaic* a state of smouldering or a smouldering fire.
▷HISTORY Old English *smorian* to suffocate; related to Middle Low German *smōren*
▶'**smothery** ADJECTIVE

smothered mate NOUN *Chess* checkmate given by a knight when the king is prevented from moving by surrounding men.

smoulder *or US* **smolder** ('sməʊldə) VERB (*intr*) [1] to burn slowly without flame, usually emitting smoke. [2] (esp of anger, etc.) to exist in a suppressed or half-suppressed state. [3] to have strong repressed or half repressed feelings, esp anger. ◆ NOUN [4] dense smoke, as from a smouldering fire. [5] a smouldering fire.
▷HISTORY C14: from *smolder* (n), of obscure origin

smout *or* **smowt** (smaʊt) NOUN *Scot* [1] a variant of **smolt.** [2] a child or undersized person.
▷HISTORY C16: a variant of SMOLT

SMP ABBREVIATION FOR statutory maternity pay.

smriti ('smrɪtɪ) NOUN a class of Hindu sacred literature derived from the Vedas, containing social, domestic, and religious teaching.
▷HISTORY from Sanskrit *smṛti* what is remembered, from *samarati* he remembers

SMS ABBREVIATION FOR short message service: a system used for sending text messages to and from mobile phones.

smudge (smʌdʒ) VERB [1] to smear, blur, or soil or cause to do so. [2] (*tr*) *Chiefly US and Canadian* to fill (an area) with smoke in order to drive insects away or guard against frost. ◆ NOUN [3] a smear or dirty mark. [4] a blurred form or area: *that smudge in the distance is a quarry.* [5] *Chiefly US and Canadian* a smoky fire for driving insects away or protecting fruit trees or plants from frost.
▷HISTORY C15: of uncertain origin
▶'**smudgeless** ADJECTIVE ▶'**smudgily** *or* '**smudgedly** ADVERB

smudging ('smʌdʒɪŋ) NOUN a traditional Native American method of using smoke from burning herbs to purify a space.

smudgy (smʌdʒɪ) ADJECTIVE [1] smeared, blurred, or soiled, or likely to become so. [2] made deliberately indistinct or cloudy: *smudgy colours.*
▶'**smudginess** NOUN

smug (smʌg) ADJECTIVE **smugger, smuggest.** [1] excessively self-satisfied or complacent. [2] *Archaic* trim or neat.
▷HISTORY C16: of Germanic origin; compare Low German *smuck* neat
▶'**smugly** ADVERB ▶'**smugness** NOUN

smuggery ('smʌgərɪ) NOUN the condition or an instance of being smug; smugness.

smuggle ('smʌgᵊl) VERB [1] to import or export (prohibited or dutiable goods) secretly. [2] (*tr; often foll by into or out of*) to bring or take secretly, as against the law or rules. [3] (*tr; foll by away*) to conceal; hide.
▷HISTORY C17: from Low German *smukkelen* and Dutch *smokkelen,* perhaps from Old English *smūgen* to creep; related to Old Norse *smjūga*
▶'**smuggler** NOUN ▶'**smuggling** NOUN

smur (smʌr) NOUN, VERB *Scot* a variant of **smir.**

smut (smʌt) NOUN [1] a small dark smudge or stain, esp one caused by soot. [2] a speck of soot or dirt. [3] something obscene or indecent. [4] **a** any of various fungal diseases of flowering plants, esp cereals, in which black sooty masses of spores cover the affected parts. **b** any parasitic basidiomycetous fungus of the order *Ustilaginales* that causes such a disease. [5] *Angling* a minute midge or other insect relished by trout. ◆ VERB **smuts, smutting, smutted.** [6] to mark or become marked or smudged, as with soot. [7] to affect (grain) or (of grain) to be affected

with smut. 8 (*tr*) to remove smut from (grain). 9 (*tr*) to make obscene. 10 (*intr*) to emit soot or smut. 11 (*intr*) *Angling* (of trout) to feed voraciously on smuts.
▷HISTORY Old English *smitte;* related to Middle High German *smitze;* associated with SMUDGE, SMUTCH
▸'**smutty** ADJECTIVE ▸'**smuttily** ADVERB ▸'**smuttiness** NOUN

smutch (smʌtʃ) VERB 1 (*tr*) to smudge; mark. ◆ NOUN 2 a mark; smudge. 3 soot; dirt.
▷HISTORY C16: probably from Middle High German *smutzen* to soil; see SMUT
▸'**smutchy** ADJECTIVE

SMV (in Canada) ABBREVIATION FOR Star of Military Valour.

Smyrna ('smɜːnə) NOUN an ancient city on the W coast of Asia Minor: a major trading centre in the ancient world; a centre of early Christianity.

sn THE INTERNET DOMAIN NAME FOR Senegal.

Sn THE CHEMICAL SYMBOL FOR tin.
▷HISTORY from New Latin *stannum*

SN INTERNATIONAL CAR REGISTRATION FOR Senegal.

snack (snæk) NOUN 1 a light quick meal eaten between or in place of main meals. 2 a sip or bite. 3 *Rare* a share. 4 *Austral informal* a very easy task. ◆ VERB 5 (*intr*) to eat a snack.
▷HISTORY C15: probably from Middle Dutch *snacken,* variant of *snappen* to SNAP

snack bar NOUN a place where light meals or snacks can be obtained, often with a self-service system.

snackette ('snækɛt) NOUN a Caribbean name for **snack bar.**

snaffle ('snæfᵊl) NOUN 1 Also called: **snaffle bit.** a simple jointed bit for a horse. ◆ VERB (*tr*) 2 *Brit informal* to steal or take for oneself. 3 to equip or control with a snaffle.
▷HISTORY C16: of uncertain origin; compare Old Frisian *snavel* mouth, Old High German *snabul* beak

snafu (snæ'fuː) *Slang, chiefly military* ◆ NOUN 1 confusion or chaos regarded as the normal state. ◆ ADJECTIVE 2 (*postpositive*) confused or muddled up, as usual. ◆ VERB **-fues, -fuing, -fued.** 3 (*tr*) *US and Canadian* to throw into chaos.
▷HISTORY C20: from *s(ituation) n(ormal): a(ll) f(ucked) u(p)*

snag (snæg) NOUN 1 a difficulty or disadvantage: *the snag is that I have nothing suitable to wear.* 2 a sharp protuberance, such as a tree stump. 3 a small loop or hole in a fabric caused by a sharp object. 4 *Engineering* a projection that brings to a stop a sliding or rotating component. 5 *Chiefly US and Canadian* a tree stump in a riverbed that is dangerous to navigation. 6 *US and Canadian* a standing dead tree, esp one used as a perch by an eagle. 7 (*plural*) *Austral slang* sausages. ◆ VERB **snags, snagging, snagged.** 8 (*tr*) to hinder or impede. 9 (*tr*) to tear or catch (fabric). 10 (*intr*) to develop a snag. 11 (*intr*) *Chiefly US and Canadian* (of a boat) to strike or be damaged by a snag. 12 (*tr*) *Chiefly US and Canadian* to clear (a stretch of water) of snags. 13 (*tr*) *US* to seize (an opportunity, benefit, etc.).
▷HISTORY C16: of Scandinavian origin; compare Old Norse *snaghyrndr* sharp-pointed, Norwegian *snage* spike, Icelandic *snagi* peg
▸'**snag,like** ADJECTIVE

snaggletooth ('snægᵊl,tuːθ) NOUN, *plural* **-teeth.** a tooth that is broken or projecting.
▸'**snaggle,toothed** ADJECTIVE

snaggy (snægɪ) ADJECTIVE **-gier, -giest.** having sharp protuberances.

snail (sneɪl) NOUN 1 any of numerous terrestrial or freshwater gastropod molluscs with a spirally coiled shell, esp any of the family *Helicidae,* such as *Helix aspersa* (**garden snail**). 2 any other gastropod with a spirally coiled shell, such as a whelk. 3 a slow-moving or lazy person or animal.
▷HISTORY Old English *snægl;* related to Old Norse *snigill,* Old High German *snecko*
▸'**snail-,like** ADJECTIVE

snail cam NOUN *Mechanical engineering* a cam with spiral cross section used for progressive lifting of a lever as the cam revolves.

snailfish ('sneɪl,fɪʃ) NOUN, *plural* **-fish** *or* **-fishes.** another name for **sea snail.**

snail mail *Informal* ◆ NOUN 1 the conventional postal system, as opposed to electronic mail. ◆ VERB **snail-mail.** 2 (*tr*) to send by the conventional postal system, rather than by electronic mail.
▷HISTORY C20: so named because of the relative slowness of the conventional postal system

snail's pace NOUN a very slow or sluggish speed or rate.

snake (sneɪk) NOUN 1 any reptile of the suborder *Ophidia* (or *Serpentes*), typically having a scaly cylindrical limbless body, fused eyelids, and a jaw modified for swallowing large prey: includes venomous forms such as cobras and rattlesnakes, large nonvenomous constrictors (boas and pythons), and small harmless types such as the grass snake. Related adjectives: **colubrine, ophidian.** 2 Also called: **snake in the grass.** a deceitful or treacherous person. 3 anything resembling a snake in appearance or action. 4 (in the European Union) a former system of managing a group of currencies by allowing the exchange rate of each of them only to fluctuate within narrow limits. 5 a tool in the form of a long flexible wire for unblocking drains. ◆ VERB 6 (*intr*) to glide or move like a snake. 7 (*tr*) *US* to haul (a heavy object, esp a log) by fastening a rope around one end of it. 8 (*tr*) *US* (often foll by *out*) to pull jerkily. 9 (*tr*) to move in or follow (a sinuous course).
▷HISTORY Old English *snaca;* related to Old Norse *snākr* snake, Old High German *snahhan* to crawl, Norwegian *snōk* snail
▸'**snake,like** ADJECTIVE

snakebird ('sneɪk,bɜːd) NOUN another name for **darter** (the bird).

snakebite ('sneɪk,baɪt) NOUN 1 a bite inflicted by a snake, esp a venomous one. 2 a drink of cider and lager.

snake charmer NOUN an entertainer, esp in Asia, who charms or appears to charm snakes by playing music and by rhythmic body movements.

snake dance NOUN 1 a ceremonial dance, performed by the priests of the American Hopi Indians, in which live snakes are held in the mouth. 2 **a** the swaying movements of snakes responding to a snake charmer. **b** a Hindu dance in which performers imitate such snake movements.

snake fly NOUN any of various neuropterous insects of the family *Raphidiidae,* having an elongated thorax: order *Megaloptera.*

snakehead ('sneɪk,hed) NOUN a Chinese criminal involved in the illegal transport of Chinese citizens to other parts of the world.
▷HISTORY C20: origin uncertain

snake juice NOUN *Austral slang* any strong alcoholic drink, esp when home-made.
▷HISTORY C19: perhaps so called from its poisonous effects

snakemouth ('sneɪk,maʊθ) NOUN a terrestrial orchid, *Pogonia ophioglossoides,* of E North America, having solitary fragrant pinkish-purple flowers.
▷HISTORY so called because of the alleged similarity between the shape of the flower and a snake's mouth

Snake River NOUN a river in the northwestern US, rising in NW Wyoming and flowing west through Idaho, turning north as part of the border between Idaho and Oregon, and flowing west to the Columbia River near Pasco, Washington. Length: 1670 km (1038 miles).

snakeroot ('sneɪk,ruːt) NOUN 1 any of various North American plants, such as *Aristolochia serpentaria* (**Virginia snakeroot**) and *Eupatorium urticaefolium* (**white snakeroot**), the roots or rhizomes of which have been used as a remedy for snakebite. 2 the rhizome or root of any such plant. 3 another name for **bistort** (senses 1, 2). ◆ Also called: **snakeweed.**

snakes and ladders NOUN (*functioning as singular*) a board game in which players move counters along a series of squares according to throws of a dice. A ladder provides a short cut to a square nearer the finish and a snake obliges a player to return to a square nearer the start.

snake's head NOUN a European fritillary plant, *Fritillaria meleagris,* of damp meadows, having purple-and-white chequered flowers.
▷HISTORY C19: so called because its buds are claimed to resemble a snake's head

snakeskin ('sneɪk,skɪn) NOUN the skin of a snake, esp when made into a leather valued for handbags, shoes, etc.

snaky ('sneɪkɪ) ADJECTIVE **snakier, snakiest.** 1 of or like a snake; sinuous. 2 treacherous or insidious. 3 infested with snakes. 4 *Austral and NZ informal* angry or bad-tempered.
▸'**snakily** ADVERB ▸'**snakiness** NOUN

snap (snæp) VERB **snaps, snapping, snapped.** 1 to break or cause to break suddenly, esp with a sharp sound. 2 to make or cause to make a sudden sharp cracking sound. 3 (*intr*) to give way or collapse suddenly, esp from strain. 4 to move, close, etc., or cause to move, close, etc., with a sudden sharp sound. 5 to move or cause to move in a sudden or abrupt way. 6 (*intr;* often foll by *at* or *up*) to seize something suddenly or quickly. 7 (when *intr,* often foll by *at*) to bite at (something) bringing the jaws rapidly together. 8 to speak (words) sharply or abruptly. 9 (*intr*) (of eyes) to flash or sparkle. 10 to take a snapshot of (something). 11 (*intr*) *Hunting* to fire a quick shot without taking deliberate aim. 12 (*tr*) *American football* to put (the ball) into play by sending it back from the line of scrimmage to a teammate. 13 **snap one's fingers at.** *Informal* **a** to dismiss with contempt. **b** to defy. 14 **snap out of it.** *Informal* to recover quickly, esp from depression, anger, or illness. ◆ NOUN 15 the act of breaking suddenly or the sound produced by a sudden breakage. 16 a sudden sharp sound, esp of bursting, popping, or cracking. 17 a catch, clasp, or fastener that operates with a snapping sound. 18 a sudden grab or bite. 19 the sudden release of something such as elastic thread. 20 a brisk movement of the thumb against one or more fingers. 21 a thin crisp biscuit: *ginger snaps.* 22 *Informal* See **snapshot.** 23 *Informal* vigour, liveliness, or energy. 24 *Informal* a task or job that is easy or profitable to do. 25 a short spell or period, esp of cold weather. 26 *Brit dialect* food, esp a packed lunch taken to work. 27 *Brit* a card game in which the word *snap* is called when two cards of equal value are turned up on the separate piles dealt by each player. 28 *American football* the start of each play when the centre passes the ball back from the line of scrimmage to a teammate. 29 (*modifier*) done on the spur of the moment, without consideration: *a snap decision.* 30 (*modifier*) closed or fastened with a snap. ◆ ADVERB 31 with a snap. ◆ INTERJECTION 32 **a** *Cards* the word called while playing snap. **b** an exclamation used to draw attention to the similarity of two things. ◆ See also **snap up.**
▷HISTORY C15: from Middle Low German or Middle Dutch *snappen* to seize; related to Old Norse *snapa* to snuffle
▸'**snapless** ADJECTIVE ▸'**snappable** ADJECTIVE

snapback ('snæp,bæk) NOUN a sudden rebound or change in direction.

snap bean NOUN *US and Canadian* 1 any of various bean plants that are cultivated in the US for their crisp edible unripe pods. 2 the pod of such a plant. ◆ See also **string bean.**
▷HISTORY C19: so called because the pods are broken into pieces for eating

snapdragon ('snæp,drægən) NOUN any of several scrophulariaceous chiefly Old World plants of the genus *Antirrhinum,* esp *A. majus,* of the Mediterranean region, having spikes of showy white, yellow, pink, red, or purplish flowers. Also called: **antirrhinum.**
▷HISTORY C16: so named because the flowers, which are claimed to look like a dragon's head, have a "mouth" which snaps shut if squeezed open and then released

snap fastener NOUN another name for **press stud.**

snapper ('snæpə) NOUN, *plural* **-per** *or* **-pers.** 1 any large sharp-toothed percoid food fish of the family *Lutjanidae* of warm and tropical coastal regions. See also **red snapper.** 2 a sparid food fish, *Chrysophrys auratus,* of Australia and New Zealand, that has a pinkish body covered with blue spots. 3 another name for the **bluefish** or the **snapping turtle.** 4 a person or thing that snaps. 5 *Informal* a person who take snapshots; photographer. ◆ Also called (for senses 1, 2): **schnapper.**

snapper up NOUN a person who snaps up bargains, etc.

snapping beetle NOUN another name for the **click beetle.**

snapping turtle NOUN any large aggressive North American river turtle of the family *Chelydridae,* esp *Chelydra serpentina* (**common snapping turtle**), having powerful hooked jaws and a rough shell. Also called: **snapper.**

snappy ('snæpɪ) ADJECTIVE **-pier, -piest.** 1 Also: **snappish.** apt to speak sharply or irritably. 2 Also: **snappish.** apt to snap or bite. 3 crackling in sound: *a snappy fire.* 4 brisk, sharp, or chilly: *a snappy pace; snappy weather.* 5 smart and fashionable: *a snappy dresser.* 6 **make it snappy.** *Slang* be quick! hurry up!
▸ **'snappily** ADVERB ▸ **'snappiness** NOUN

snap ring NOUN *Mountaineering* another name for **karabiner.**

snap roll NOUN a manoeuvre in which an aircraft makes a fast roll.

snapshot ('snæp,ʃɒt) NOUN an informal photograph taken with a simple camera. Often shortened to: **snap.**

snap shot NOUN *Sport* a sudden, fast shot at goal.

snaptin ('snæptɪn) NOUN *Northern English dialect* a container for food.
▹ **HISTORY** from SNAP (sense 26) + TIN

snap up VERB (*tr, adverb*) 1 to avail oneself of eagerly and quickly: *she snapped up the bargains.* 2 to interrupt abruptly.

snare[1] (snɛə) NOUN 1 a device for trapping birds or small animals, esp a flexible loop that is drawn tight around the prey. 2 a surgical instrument for removing certain tumours, consisting of a wire loop that may be drawn tight around their base to sever or uproot them. 3 anything that traps or entangles someone or something unawares. ◆ VERB (*tr*) 4 to catch (birds or small animals) with a snare. 5 to catch or trap in or as if in a snare; capture by trickery.
▹ **HISTORY** Old English *sneare,* from Old Norse *snara;* related to Old High German *snaraha*
▸ **'snareless** ADJECTIVE ▸ **'snarer** NOUN

snare[2] (snɛə) NOUN *Music* a set of gut strings wound with wire fitted against the lower drumhead of a snare drum. They produce a rattling sound when the drum is beaten. See **snare drum.**
▹ **HISTORY** C17: from Middle Dutch *snaer* or Middle Low German *snare* string; related to Gothic *snōrjō* basket

snare drum NOUN *Music* a cylindrical drum with two drumheads, the upper of which is struck and the lower fitted with a snare. See **snare[2].**

snarf (snɑːf) VERB *Informal* to eat or drink greedily.

snarky ('snɒːkɪ) ADJECTIVE *Informal* unpleasant and scornful.
▹ **HISTORY** C20: from SARCASTIC + NASTY

snarl[1] (snɑːl) VERB 1 (*intr*) (of an animal) to growl viciously, baring the teeth. 2 to speak or express (something) viciously or angrily. ◆ NOUN 3 a vicious growl, utterance, or facial expression. 4 the act of snarling.
▹ **HISTORY** C16: of Germanic origin; compare Middle Low German *snarren,* Middle Dutch *snarren* to drone
▸ **'snarling** ADJECTIVE ▸ **'snarlingly** ADVERB ▸ **'snarly** ADJECTIVE

snarl[2] (snɑːl) NOUN 1 a tangled mass of thread, hair, etc. 2 a complicated or confused state or situation. 3 a knot in wood. ◆ VERB 4 (often foll by *up*) to be, become, or make tangled or complicated. 5 (*tr;* often foll by *up*) to confuse mentally. 6 (*tr*) to flute or emboss (metal) by hammering on a tool held against the under surface.
▹ **HISTORY** C14: of Scandinavian origin; compare Old Swedish *snarel* noose, Old Norse *snara* SNARE[1]
▸ **'snarler** NOUN ▸ **'snarly** ADJECTIVE

snarler ('snɑːlə) NOUN 1 an animal or a person that snarls. 2 *NZ informal* a sausage.

snarl-up NOUN *Informal, chiefly Brit* a confusion, obstruction, or tangle, esp a traffic jam.

snatch (snætʃ) VERB 1 (*tr*) to seize or grasp (something) suddenly or peremptorily: *he snatched the chocolate out of my hand.* 2 (*intr;* usually foll by *at*) to seize or attempt to seize suddenly. 3 (*tr*) to take hurriedly: *to snatch some sleep.* 4 (*tr*) to remove suddenly: *she snatched her hand away.* 5 (*tr*) to gain, win, or rescue, esp narrowly: *they snatched victory in the closing seconds.* 6 (*tr*) (in weightlifting) to lift (a weight) with a snatch. 7 **snatch one's time.** *Austral informal* to leave a job, taking whatever pay is due. ◆ NOUN 8 an act of snatching. 9 a fragment or small incomplete part: *snatches of conversation.* 10 a brief spell: *snatches of time off.* 11 *Weightlifting* a lift in which the weight is raised in one quick motion from the floor to an overhead position. 12 *Slang, chiefly US* an act of kidnapping. 13 *Brit slang* a robbery: *a diamond snatch.*
▹ **HISTORY** C13 *snacchen;* related to Middle Dutch *snakken* to gasp, Old Norse *snaka* to sniff around
▸ **'snatcher** NOUN

snatch block NOUN *Nautical* a block that can be opened so that a rope can be inserted from the side, without threading it through from the end.
▹ **HISTORY** C17: so called because the rope can be inserted quickly: figuratively, the block snatches it. See SNATCH

snatch squad NOUN *Brit* a squad of soldiers or police trained to deal with demonstrations by picking out and arresting the alleged ringleaders.

snatchy ('snætʃɪ) ADJECTIVE **snatchier, snatchiest.** disconnected or spasmodic.
▸ **'snatchily** ADVERB

snath (snæθ) *or* **snathe** (sneɪð) NOUN the handle of a scythe.
▹ **HISTORY** C16: variant of earlier *snead,* from Old English *snǣd,* of obscure origin

snazzy ('snæzɪ) ADJECTIVE **-zier, -ziest.** *Informal* (esp of clothes) stylishly and often flashily attractive.
▹ **HISTORY** C20: perhaps from SN(APPY + J)AZZY
▸ **'snazzily** ADVERB ▸ **'snazziness** NOUN

SNCC (snɪk) NOUN (in the US) ACRONYM FOR Student Nonviolent Coordinating Committee (1960–69) and Student National Coordinating Committee (from 1969); a civil-rights organization.

SNCF ABBREVIATION FOR Société Nationale des Chemins de Fer: the French national railway system.

sneak (sniːk) VERB 1 (*intr;* often foll by *along, off, in,* etc.) to move furtively. 2 (*intr*) to behave in a cowardly or underhand manner. 3 (*tr*) to bring, take, or put stealthily. 4 (*intr*) *Informal, chiefly Brit* to tell tales (esp in schools). 5 (*tr*) *Informal* to steal. 6 (*intr;* foll by *off, out, away,* etc.) *Informal* to leave unobtrusively. ◆ NOUN 7 a person who acts in an underhand or cowardly manner, esp as an informer. 8 **a** a stealthy act or movement. **b** (*as modifier*): *a sneak attack.* 9 *Brit informal* an unobtrusive departure.
▹ **HISTORY** Old English *snīcan* to creep; from Old Norse *snīkja* to hanker after
▸ **'sneaky** ADJECTIVE ▸ **'sneakily** ADVERB ▸ **'sneakiness** NOUN

sneakers ('sniːkəz) PLURAL NOUN *Chiefly US and Canadian* canvas shoes with rubber soles worn for sports or informally.

sneaking ('sniːkɪŋ) ADJECTIVE 1 acting in a furtive or cowardly way. 2 secret: *a sneaking desire to marry a millionaire.* 3 slight but nagging (esp in the phrase **a sneaking suspicion**).
▸ **'sneakingly** ADVERB ▸ **'sneakingness** NOUN

sneak preview NOUN a screening of a film at an unexpected time to test audience reaction before its release.

sneak thief NOUN a person who steals paltry articles from premises, which he enters through open doors, windows, etc.

sneck[1] (snɛk) NOUN 1 a small squared stone used in a rubble wall to fill spaces between stones of different height. 2 *Dialect, chiefly Scot and northern English* the latch or catch of a door or gate. ◆ VERB 3 *Dialect, chiefly Scot and northern English* to fasten (a latch).
▹ **HISTORY** C15 *snekk,* of uncertain origin

sneck[2] (snɛk) NOUN, VERB a Scot word for **snick.**

sneer (snɪə) NOUN 1 a facial expression of scorn or contempt, typically with the upper lip curled. 2 a scornful or contemptuous remark or utterance. ◆ VERB 3 (*intr*) to assume a facial expression of scorn or contempt. 4 to say or utter (something) in a scornful or contemptuous manner.
▹ **HISTORY** C16: perhaps from Low Dutch; compare North Frisian *sneere* contempt
▸ **'sneerer** NOUN ▸ **'sneerful** ADJECTIVE ▸ **'sneering** ADJECTIVE, NOUN ▸ **'sneeringly** ADVERB

sneery ('snɪərɪ) ADJECTIVE **sneerier, sneeriest.** contemptuous or scornful; inclined to be dismissive.

sneeze (sniːz) VERB 1 (*intr*) to expel air and nasal secretions from the nose involuntarily, esp as the result of irritation of the nasal mucous membrane. ◆ NOUN 2 the act or sound of sneezing.
▹ **HISTORY** Old English *fnēosan* (unattested); related to Old Norse *fnӯsa,* Middle High German *fnūsen,* Greek *pneuma* breath
▸ **'sneezeless** ADJECTIVE ▸ **'sneezer** NOUN ▸ **'sneezy** ADJECTIVE

sneeze at VERB (*intr, prep.;* usually with a negative) *Informal* to dismiss lightly: *his offer is not to be sneezed at.*

sneezewood ('sniːz,wʊd) NOUN 1 a tree, *Ptaeroxylon utile,* native to southern Africa: family *Ptaeroxylaceae.* 2 the tough wood of this tree, which has a peppery smell and is used for bridges, piers, fencing posts, etc.

sneezewort ('sniːz,wɜːt) NOUN a Eurasian plant, *Achillea ptarmica,* having daisy-like flowers and long grey-green leaves, which cause sneezing when powdered: family *Asteraceae* (composites). See also **yarrow.**

snell (snɛl) ADJECTIVE *Scot* biting; bitter; sharp.
▹ **HISTORY** Old English *snel* quick, active

Snell's law (snɛlz) NOUN *Physics* the principle that the ratio of the sine of the angle of incidence to the sine of the angle of refraction is constant when a light ray passes from one medium to another.
▹ **HISTORY** C17: named after Willebrord *Snell* (1591–1626), Dutch physicist

SNG ABBREVIATION FOR synthetic natural gas.

snib (snɪb) *Scot* ◆ NOUN 1 the bolt or fastening of a door, window, etc. ◆ VERB **snibs, snibbing, snibbed.** (*tr*) 2 to bolt or fasten (a door).
▹ **HISTORY** C19: of uncertain origin; perhaps from Low German *snibbe* beak

snick (snɪk) NOUN 1 a small cut; notch. 2 a knot in thread, etc. 3 *Cricket* **a** a glancing blow off the edge of the bat. **b** the ball so hit. ◆ VERB (*tr*) 4 to cut a small corner or notch in (material, etc.). 5 *Cricket* to hit (the ball) with a snick.
▹ **HISTORY** C18: probably of Scandinavian origin; compare Old Norse *snikka* to whittle, Swedish *snicka*

snicker ('snɪkə) NOUN, VERB 1 another word, esp US and Canadian, for **snigger.** ◆ VERB 2 (of a horse) to whinny.
▹ **HISTORY** C17: probably of imitative origin

snickersnee ('snɪkə,sniː) NOUN *Archaic* 1 a knife for cutting or thrusting. 2 a fight with knives.
▹ **HISTORY** C17 *stick or snee,* from Dutch *steken* to STICK[2] + *snijen* to cut

snicket ('snɪkɪt) NOUN *Northern English dialect* a passageway between walls or fences.
▹ **HISTORY** of obscure origin

Snickometer (snɪ'kɒmɪtə) NOUN *Trademark, Cricket* a device, which uses sound waves recorded by the stump microphone, employed by TV commentators to determine whether or not a batsman has made contact with the ball.
▹ **HISTORY** C20: from SNICK (sense 5) + -METER

snide[1] (snaɪd) ADJECTIVE 1 Also: **snidey** ('snaɪdɪ). (of a remark, etc.) maliciously derogatory; supercilious. 2 counterfeit; sham. ◆ NOUN 3 *Slang* sham jewellery.
▹ **HISTORY** C19: of unknown origin
▸ **'snidely** ADVERB ▸ **'snideness** NOUN

snide[2] (snaɪd) VERB (*tr; usually passive* and foll by *with*) *Northern English dialect* to fill or load.

sniff (snɪf) VERB 1 to inhale through the nose, usually in short rapid audible inspirations, as for the purpose of identifying a scent, for clearing a congested nasal passage, or for taking a drug or intoxicating fumes. 2 (when *intr,* often foll by *at*) to perceive or attempt to perceive (a smell) by inhaling through the nose. ◆ NOUN 3 the act or sound of sniffing. 4 a smell perceived by sniffing, esp a faint scent.
▹ **HISTORY** C14: probably related to *snivelen* to SNIVEL
▸ **'sniffing** NOUN, ADJECTIVE

sniff at VERB (*intr, preposition*) to express contempt or dislike for.

sniffer ('snɪfə) NOUN a device for detecting hidden substances such as drugs or explosives, esp by their odour.

sniffer dog NOUN a police dog trained to detect drugs or explosives by smell.

sniffle (ˈsnɪfᵊl) VERB 1 (*intr*) to breathe audibly through the nose, as when the nasal passages are congested. ◆ NOUN 2 the act, sound, or an instance of sniffling.
▸ˈ**sniffler** NOUN ▸ˈ**sniffly** ADJECTIVE

sniffles (ˈsnɪfᵊlz) *or* **snuffles** PLURAL NOUN *Informal* 1 **the.** a cold in the head. 2 the sniffling that sometimes accompanies weeping or prolonged crying.

sniff out VERB (*tr, adverb*) to detect through shrewdness or instinct.

sniffy (ˈsnɪfɪ) ADJECTIVE **-fier, -fiest.** *Informal* contemptuous or disdainful.
▸ˈ**sniffily** ADVERB ▸ˈ**sniffiness** NOUN

snifter (ˈsnɪftə) NOUN 1 a pear-shaped glass with a short stem and a bowl that narrows towards the top so that the aroma of brandy or a liqueur is retained. 2 *Informal* a small quantity of alcoholic drink.
▹HISTORY C19: perhaps from dialect *snifter* to sniff, perhaps of Scandinavian origin; compare Danish *snifta* (obsolete) to sniff

snig (snɪg) VERB (*tr*) **snigs, snigging, snigged** *Austral and NZ* to drag (a log) along the ground by a chain fastened at one end.
▹HISTORY from English dialect

snigger (ˈsnɪgə) *or US and Canadian* **snicker** (ˈsnɪkə) NOUN 1 a sly or disrespectful laugh, esp one partly stifled. ◆ VERB (*intr*) 2 to utter such a laugh.
▹HISTORY C18: variant of SNICKER

snigging chain NOUN *Austral and NZ* a chain attached to a log when being hauled out of the bush.

sniggle (ˈsnɪgᵊl) VERB 1 (*intr*) to fish for eels by dangling or thrusting a baited hook into cavities. 2 (*tr*) to catch (eels) by sniggling. ◆ NOUN 3 the baited hook used for sniggling eels.
▹HISTORY C17: from C15 *snig* young eel
▸ˈ**sniggler** NOUN

snip (snɪp) VERB **snips, snipping, snipped.** 1 to cut or clip with a small quick stroke or a succession of small quick strokes, esp with scissors or shears. ◆ NOUN 2 the act of snipping. 3 the sound of scissors or shears closing. 4 Also called: **snipping.** a small piece of anything, esp one that has been snipped off. 5 a small cut made by snipping. 6 *Chiefly Brit* an informal word for **bargain.** 7 *Informal* something easily done; cinch. 8 *US and Canadian informal* a small or insignificant person or thing, esp an irritating or insolent one. ◆ INTERJECTION 9 (*often reiterated*) a representation of the sound of scissors or shears closing. ◆ See also **snips.**
▹HISTORY C16: from Low German, Dutch *snippen;* related to Middle High German *snipfen* to snap the fingers

snipe (snaɪp) NOUN, *plural* **snipe** *or* **snipes.** 1 any of various birds of the genus *Gallinago* (or *Capella*) and related genera, such as *G. gallinago* (**common** or **Wilson's snipe**), of marshes and river banks, having a long straight bill: family *Scolopacidae* (sandpipers, etc.), order *Charadriiformes*. 2 any of various similar related birds, such as certain sandpipers and curlews. 3 a shot, esp a gunshot, fired from a place of concealment. ◆ VERB 4 (when *intr,* often foll by *at*) to attack (a person or persons) with a rifle from a place of concealment. 5 (*intr;* often foll by *at*) to criticize adversely a person or persons from a position of security. 6 (*intr*) to hunt or shoot snipe.
▹HISTORY C14: from Old Norse *snīpa;* related to Old High German *snepfa* Middle Dutch *snippe*
▸ˈ**snipe,like** ADJECTIVE

snipefish (ˈsnaɪp,fɪʃ) NOUN, *plural* **-fish** *or* **-fishes.** any teleost fish of the family *Macrorhamphosidae,* of tropical and temperate seas, having a deep body, long snout, and a single long dorsal fin: order *Solenichthyes* (sea horses, etc.). Also called: **bellows fish.**
▹HISTORY C17: so called because of the resemblance between its snout and a snipe's bill

snipe fly NOUN any of various predatory dipterous flies of the family *Leptidae* (or *Rhagionidae*), such as *Rhagio scolopacea* of Europe, having an elongated body and long legs.
▹HISTORY named after the snipe because its flight resembles that of the bird

sniper (ˈsnaɪpə) NOUN a rifleman who fires from a concealed place, esp a military marksman who fires from cover usually at long ranges at individual enemy soldiers.

sniperscope (ˈsnaɪpə,skəʊp) NOUN a telescope with crosshairs mounted on a sniper's rifle.

snippet (ˈsnɪpɪt) NOUN a small scrap or fragment.
▹HISTORY C17: from SNIP + -ET
▸ˈ**snippetiness** NOUN ▸ˈ**snippety** ADJECTIVE

snippy (ˈsnɪpɪ) ADJECTIVE **-pier, -piest.** 1 scrappy; fragmentary. 2 *Informal* fault-finding. 3 *Dialect* mean; stingy.
▸ˈ**snippily** ADVERB ▸ˈ**snippiness** NOUN

snips (snɪps) PLURAL NOUN a small pair of shears used for cutting sheet metal. Also called: **tin snips.**

snit (snɪt) NOUN *US and Austral* a fit of temper.
▹HISTORY C20: of unknown origin

snitch (snɪtʃ) *Slang* ◆ VERB 1 (*tr*) to steal; take, esp in an underhand way. 2 (*intr*) to act as an informer. ◆ NOUN 3 an informer; telltale. 4 the nose.
▹HISTORY C17: of unknown origin
▸ˈ**snitcher** NOUN

snitchy (ˈsnɪtʃɪ) ADJECTIVE **snitchier, snitchiest.** *NZ informal* bad-tempered or irritable.

snivel (ˈsnɪvᵊl) VERB **-els, -elling, -elled** *or US* **-els, -eling, -eled.** 1 (*intr*) to sniffle as a sign of distress, esp contemptibly. 2 to utter (something) tearfully; whine. 3 (*intr*) to have a runny nose. ◆ NOUN 4 an instance of snivelling.
▹HISTORY C14 *snivelen;* related to Old English *snyflung* mucus, Dutch *snuffelen* to smell out, Old Norse *snoppa* snout
▸ˈ**sniveller** NOUN ▸ˈ**snivelling** ADJECTIVE, NOUN ▸ˈ**snivelly** ADJECTIVE

snob (snɒb) NOUN 1 **a** a person who strives to associate with those of higher social status and who behaves condescendingly to others. Compare **inverted snob. b** (*as modifier*): *snob appeal.* 2 a person having similar pretensions with regard to his tastes, etc.: *an intellectual snob.*
▹HISTORY C18 (in the sense: shoemaker; hence, C19: a person who flatters those of higher station, etc.): of unknown origin
▸ˈ**snobbery** NOUN ▸ˈ**snobbish** ADJECTIVE ▸ˈ**snobbishly** ADVERB ▸ˈ**snobbishness** *or* ˈ**snobbism** NOUN ▸ˈ**snobby** ADJECTIVE

SNOBOL (ˈsnəʊbɒl) NOUN String Oriented Symbolic Language: a computer-programming language for handling strings of symbols.

Sno-Cat (ˈsnəʊ,kæt) NOUN *Trademark* a type of snowmobile.

snoek (snʊk) NOUN a South African edible marine fish, *Thyrsites atun.*
▹HISTORY Afrikaans, from Dutch *snoek* pike

snoep (snʊp) ADJECTIVE *South African informal* mean or tight-fisted.
▹HISTORY Afrikaans *snoep* greedy

snog (snɒg) *Brit slang* ◆ VERB **snogs, snogging, snogged.** 1 to kiss and cuddle (someone). ◆ NOUN 2 the act of kissing and cuddling.
▹HISTORY of obscure origin

snood (snu:d) NOUN 1 a pouchlike hat, often of net, loosely holding a woman's hair at the back. 2 a headband, esp one formerly worn by young unmarried women in Scotland. 3 *Vet science* a long fleshy appendage that hangs over the upper beak of turkeys. ◆ VERB 4 (*tr*) to hold (the hair) in a snood.
▹HISTORY Old English *snōd;* of obscure origin

snook[1] (snu:k) NOUN, *plural* **snook** *or* **snooks.** 1 any of several large game fishes of the genus *Centropomus,* esp *C. undecimalis* of tropical American marine and fresh waters: family *Centropomidae* (robalos). 2 *Austral* the sea pike *Australuzza novaehollandiae.*
▹HISTORY C17: from Dutch *snoek* pike

snook[2] (snu:k) NOUN *Brit* **cock a snook. a** to make a rude gesture by putting one thumb to the nose with the fingers of the hand outstretched. **b** to show contempt by being insulting or offensive.
▹HISTORY C19: of obscure origin

snooker (ˈsnu:kə) NOUN 1 a game played on a billiard table with 15 red balls, six balls of other colours, and a white cue ball. The object is to pot the balls in a certain order. 2 a shot in which the cue ball is left in a position such that another ball blocks the object ball. The opponent is then usually forced to play the cue ball off a cushion. ◆ VERB (*tr*) 3 to leave (an opponent) in an unfavourable position by playing a snooker. 4 to place (someone) in a difficult situation. 5 (*often passive*) to thwart; defeat.
▹HISTORY C19: of unknown origin

snoop (snu:p) *Informal* ◆ VERB 1 (*intr;* often foll by *about* or *around*) to pry into the private business of others. ◆ NOUN 2 a person who pries into the business of others. 3 an act or instance of snooping.
▹HISTORY C19: from Dutch *snoepen* to eat furtively
▸ˈ**snoopy** ADJECTIVE

snooper (ˈsnu:pə) NOUN 1 a person who snoops. 2 *Brit informal* a person employed by the DSS to spy on claimants to make sure that they are not infringing the conditions of their eligibility for benefit.

snooperscope (ˈsnu:pə,skəʊp) NOUN *Military, US* an instrument that enables the user to see objects in the dark by illuminating the object with infrared radiation and converting the reflected radiation to a visual image.

snoot (snu:t) NOUN 1 *Slang* the nose. 2 *Photog, films, television* a cone-shaped fitment on a studio light to control the scene area illuminated.
▹HISTORY C20: variant of SNOUT

snooty (ˈsnu:tɪ) ADJECTIVE **snootier, snootiest.** *Informal* 1 aloof or supercilious. 2 snobbish or exclusive: *a snooty restaurant.*
▸ˈ**snootily** ADVERB ▸ˈ**snootiness** NOUN

snooze (snu:z) *Informal* ◆ VERB 1 (*intr*) to take a brief light sleep. ◆ NOUN 2 a nap.
▹HISTORY C18: of unknown origin
▸ˈ**snoozer** NOUN ▸ˈ**snoozy** ADJECTIVE

snore (snɔ:) VERB 1 (*intr*) to breathe through the mouth and nose while asleep with snorting sounds caused by vibrations of the soft palate. ◆ NOUN 2 the act or sound of snoring.
▹HISTORY C14: of imitative origin; related to Middle Low German, Middle Dutch *snorken;* see SNORT
▸ˈ**snorer** NOUN

snorkel (ˈsnɔ:kᵊl) NOUN 1 a device allowing a swimmer to breathe while face down on the surface of the water, consisting of a bent tube fitting into the mouth and projecting above the surface. 2 (on a submarine) a retractable vertical device containing air-intake and exhaust pipes for the engines and general ventilation: its use permits extended periods of submergence at periscope depth. 3 *Military* a similar device on a tank, enabling it to cross shallow water obstacles. 4 a type of parka or anorak with a hood that projects beyond the face. ◆ VERB **-kels, -kelling, -kelled** *or US* **-kels, -keling, -keled.** 5 (*intr*) to swim with a snorkel.
▹HISTORY C20: from German *Schnorchel;* related to German *schnarchen* to SNORE

snort (snɔ:t) VERB 1 (*intr*) to exhale forcibly through the nostrils, making a characteristic noise. 2 (*intr*) (of a person) to express contempt or annoyance by such an exhalation. 3 (*tr*) to utter in a contemptuous or annoyed manner. 4 *Slang* to inhale (a powdered drug) through the nostrils. ◆ NOUN 5 a forcible exhalation of air through the nostrils, esp (of persons) as a noise of contempt or annoyance. 6 *Slang* an instance of snorting a drug. 7 Also called: **snorter.** *Slang* a short drink, esp an alcoholic one. 8 *Slang* the snorkel on a submarine.
▹HISTORY C14 *snorten;* probably related to *snoren* to SNORE
▸ˈ**snorting** NOUN, ADJECTIVE ▸ˈ**snortingly** ADVERB

snorter (ˈsnɔ:tə) NOUN 1 a person or animal that snorts. 2 *Brit slang* something outstandingly impressive or difficult. 3 *Brit slang* something or someone ridiculous.

snot (snɒt) NOUN (*usually considered vulgar*) 1 nasal mucus or discharge. 2 *Slang* a contemptible person.
▹HISTORY Old English *gesnot;* related to Old High German *snuzza,* Norwegian, Danish *snot,* German *schneuzen* to blow one's nose

snotter (ˈsnɒtər) *Scot* ◆ NOUN 1 (*often plural*) another word for **snot.** ◆ VERB (*intr*) 2 to breathe through obstructed nostrils. 3 to snivel or blubber.

snotty (ˈsnɒtɪ) (*considered vulgar*) ADJECTIVE **-tier, -tiest.** 1 dirty with nasal discharge. 2 *Slang* contemptible; nasty. 3 snobbish; conceited. ◆ NOUN, *plural* **-ties.** 4 a slang word for **midshipman.**
▸ˈ**snottily** ADVERB ▸ˈ**snottiness** NOUN

snout (snaʊt) NOUN [1] the part of the head of a vertebrate, esp a mammal, consisting of the nose, jaws, and surrounding region, esp when elongated. [2] the corresponding part of the head of such insects as weevils. [3] anything projecting like a snout, such as a nozzle or the lower end of a glacier. [4] *Slang* a person's nose. [5] Also called: **snout moth.** a brownish noctuid moth, *Hypena proboscidalis,* that frequents nettles: named from the palps that project prominently from the head at rest. [6] *Brit slang* a cigarette or tobacco. [7] *Slang* an informer.
▷HISTORY C13: of Germanic origin; compare Old Norse *snyta,* Middle Low German, Middle Dutch *snūte*
▸ˈ**snouted** ADJECTIVE ▸ˈ**snoutless** ADJECTIVE ▸ˈ**snout,like** ADJECTIVE

snout beetle NOUN another name for **weevil** (sense 1).
▷HISTORY C19: so named because of its long proboscis

snow (snəʊ) NOUN [1] precipitation from clouds in the form of flakes of ice crystals formed in the upper atmosphere. Related adjective: **niveous.** [2] a layer of snowflakes on the ground. [3] a fall of such precipitation. [4] anything resembling snow in whiteness, softness, etc. [5] the random pattern of white spots on a television or radar screen, produced by noise in the receiver and occurring when the signal is weak or absent. [6] *Slang* cocaine. [7] See **carbon dioxide snow.** ◆ VERB [8] (*intr;* with *it* as subject) to be the case that snow is falling. [9] (*tr;* usually passive, foll by *over, under, in,* or *up*) to cover or confine with a heavy fall of snow. [10] (often with *it* as subject) to fall or cause to fall as or like snow. [11] (*tr*) *US and Canadian slang* to deceive or overwhelm with elaborate often insincere talk. See **snow job.** [12] **be snowed under.** to be overwhelmed, esp with paperwork.
▷HISTORY Old English *snāw;* related to Old Norse *snjōr,* Gothic *snaiws,* Old High German *snēo,* Greek *nipha*
▸ˈ**snowless** ADJECTIVE ▸ˈ**snow,like** ADJECTIVE

snow apple NOUN a Canadian variety of eating apple.

snowball (ˈsnəʊˌbɔːl) NOUN [1] snow pressed into a ball for throwing, as in play. [2] a drink made of advocaat and lemonade. [3] *Slang* a mixture of heroin and cocaine. [4] a dance started by one couple who separate and choose different partners. The process continues until all present are dancing. ◆ VERB [5] (*intr*) to increase rapidly in size, importance, etc.: *their woes have snowballed since last year.* [6] (*tr*) to throw snowballs at.

snowball tree NOUN any of several caprifoliaceous shrubs of the genus *Viburnum,* esp *V. opulus* var. *roseum,* a sterile cultivated variety with spherical clusters of white or pinkish flowers.

snowberry (ˈsnəʊbərɪ, -brɪ) NOUN, *plural* **-ries.** [1] any of several caprifoliaceous shrubs of the genus *Symphoricarpos,* esp *S. albus,* cultivated for their small pink flowers and white berries. [2] Also called: **waxberry.** any of the berries of such a plant. [3] any of various other white-berried plants.

snowbird (ˈsnəʊˌbɜːd) NOUN [1] another name for the **snow bunting.** [2] *US slang* a person addicted to cocaine, or sometimes heroin.

snow-blind ADJECTIVE temporarily unable to see or having impaired vision because of the intense reflection of sunlight from snow.
▸**snow blindness** NOUN

snowblink (ˈsnəʊˌblɪŋk) NOUN a whitish glare in the sky reflected from snow. Compare **iceblink.**

snowblower (ˈsnəʊˌbləʊə) NOUN a snow-clearing machine that sucks in snow and blows it away to one side.

snowboard (ˈsnəʊˌbɔːd) NOUN a shaped board, resembling a skateboard without wheels, on which a person can stand to slide across snow.
▷HISTORY C20: on the model of SURFBOARD

snowboarding (ˈsnəʊˌbɔːdɪŋ) NOUN the sport of moving across snow on a snowboard.

snowbound (ˈsnəʊˌbaʊnd) ADJECTIVE confined to one place by heavy falls or drifts of snow; snowed-in.

snow bridge NOUN *Mountaineering* a mass of snow bridging a crevasse, sometimes affording a risky way across it.

snow bunting NOUN a bunting, *Plectrophenax nivalis,* of northern and arctic regions, having a white plumage with dark markings on the wings, back, and tail.

snowcap (ˈsnəʊˌkæp) NOUN a cap of snow, as on the top of a mountain.

snowcapped (ˈsnəʊˌkæpt) ADJECTIVE (of a mountain, hill, etc.) having a cap of snow on the top.

snow cave NOUN *Mountaineering* another name for **snow hole.**

snow day NOUN *US* a day on which heavy snow makes it impossible for children to attend school.

snow devil NOUN *Canadian* a whirling column of snow.

Snowdon (ˈsnəʊdən) NOUN a mountain in NW Wales, in Gwynedd: the highest peak in Wales. Height: 1085 m (3560 ft.).

Snowdonia (snəʊˈdəʊnɪə) NOUN [1] a massif in NW Wales, in Gwynedd, the highest peak being Snowdon. [2] a national park in NW Wales, in Gwynedd and Conwy: includes the Snowdonia massif in the north. Area: 2189 sq. km (845 sq. miles).

snowdrift (ˈsnəʊˌdrɪft) NOUN a bank of deep snow driven together by the wind.

snowdrop (ˈsnəʊˌdrɒp) NOUN any of several amaryllidaceous plants of the Eurasian genus *Galanthus,* esp *G. nivalis,* having drooping white bell-shaped flowers that bloom in early spring.

snowdrop tree NOUN another name for **silver bell.**

snowed (snəʊd) ADJECTIVE *Slang* under the influence of narcotic drugs.

snowfall (ˈsnəʊˌfɔːl) NOUN [1] a fall of snow. [2] *Meteorol* the amount of snow received in a specified place and time.

snow fence NOUN a portable wire-and-paling fence erected to prevent snow from drifting across a road, drive, ski run, etc.

snowfield (ˈsnəʊˌfiːld) NOUN a large area of permanent snow.

snowflake (ˈsnəʊˌfleɪk) NOUN [1] one of the mass of small thin delicate arrangements of ice crystals that fall as snow. [2] any of various European amaryllidaceous plants of the genus *Leucojum,* such as *L. vernum* (**spring snowflake**), that have white nodding bell-shaped flowers.

snow goose NOUN a North American goose, *Anser hyperboreus* (or *Chen hyperborea* or *A. caerulescens*), having a white plumage with black wing tips.

snow grass NOUN [1] *Austral* any of various grey-green grasses of the genus *Poa,* of SE Australian mountain regions. [2] *NZ* any of various hill and high-country grasses of the genus *Danthonia.*

snow gum NOUN any of various eucalyptus trees that grow at high altitudes, esp *Eucalyptus pauciflora.*
▷HISTORY so called because it grows at high altitude

snow hole NOUN *Mountaineering* a shelter dug in deep usually drifted snow. Also called: **snow cave.**

snow-in-summer NOUN another name for **dusty miller** (sense 1).
▷HISTORY C19: so called from the appearance of its flowers

snow job NOUN *Slang, chiefly US and Canadian* an instance of deceiving or overwhelming someone with elaborate often insincere talk.

snow leopard NOUN a large feline mammal, *Panthera uncia,* of mountainous regions of central Asia, closely related to the leopard but having a long pale brown coat marked with black rosettes. Also called: **ounce.**

snow line NOUN the altitudinal or latitudinal limit of permanent snow.

snowman (ˈsnəʊˌmæn) NOUN, *plural* **-men.** a figure resembling a man, made of packed snow.

snowmobile (ˈsnəʊməˌbiːl) NOUN **a** a small open motor vehicle for travelling on snow, steered by two skis at the front and driven by a caterpillar track underneath. **b** Also called: **bombardier.** a larger closed motor vehicle with two skis at the front and a track at each side.

snow-on-the-mountain NOUN a North American euphorbiaceous plant, *Euphorbia marginata,* having white-edged leaves and showy white bracts surrounding small flowers.

snow plant NOUN a saprophytic plant, *Sarcodes sanguinea,* of mountain pine forests of W North America, having a fleshy scaly reddish stalk, no leaves, and pendulous scarlet flowers that are often produced before the snow melts: family *Monotropaceae.*

snowplough (ˈsnəʊˌplaʊ) NOUN [1] an implement or vehicle for clearing away snow. [2] *Skiing* a technique of turning the points of the skis inwards to turn or stop.

snowshed (ˈsnəʊˌʃɛd) NOUN a shelter built over an exposed section of railway track to prevent its blockage by snow.

snowshoe (ˈsnəʊˌʃuː) NOUN [1] a device to facilitate walking on snow, esp a racket-shaped frame with a network of thongs stretched across it. ◆ VERB **-shoes, -shoeing, -shoed.** [2] (*intr*) to walk or go using snowshoes.
▸ˈ**snow,shoer** NOUN

snowshoe cat NOUN a breed of cat with soft short hair, blue eyes, an inverted V-shaped marking on the face, and white feet.

snowshoe hare *or* **rabbit** NOUN a N North American hare, *Lepus americanus,* having brown fur in summer, white fur in winter, and heavily furred feet.

snowstorm (ˈsnəʊˌstɔːm) NOUN a storm with heavy snow.

snowtubing (ˈsnəʊˌtjuːɪŋ) NOUN the sport of moving across snow on a large inflated inner tube.

snow tyre NOUN a motor vehicle tyre with deep treads and ridges to give improved grip on snow and ice.

snow-white ADJECTIVE [1] white as snow. [2] pure as white snow.

snowy (ˈsnəʊɪ) ADJECTIVE **snowier, snowiest.** [1] covered with or abounding in snow: *snowy hills.* [2] characterized by snow: *snowy weather.* [3] resembling snow in whiteness, purity, etc.
▸ˈ**snowily** ADVERB ▸ˈ**snowiness** NOUN

snowy egret NOUN a small American egret, *Egretta thula,* having a white plumage, yellow legs, and a black bill.

Snowy Mountain ADJECTIVE of or relating to the Snowy Mountains of Australia or their inhabitants.

Snowy Mountains PLURAL NOUN a mountain range in SE Australia, part of the Australian Alps: famous hydroelectric scheme. Also called (Austral informal): **the Snowy, the Snowies.**

snowy owl NOUN a large owl, *Nyctea scandiaca,* of tundra regions, having a white plumage flecked with brown.

Snowy River NOUN a river in SE Australia, rising in SE New South Wales: waters diverted through a system of dams and tunnels across the watershed into the Murray and Murrumbidgee Rivers for hydroelectric power and to provide water for irrigation. Length: 426 km (265 miles).

SNP ABBREVIATION FOR **Scottish National Party.**

Snr *or* **snr** ABBREVIATION FOR senior.

snub (snʌb) VERB **snubs, snubbing, snubbed.** (*tr*) [1] to insult (someone) deliberately. [2] to stop or check the motion of (a boat, horse, etc.) by taking turns of a rope or cable around a post or other fixed object. ◆ NOUN [3] a deliberately insulting act or remark. [4] *Nautical* **a** an elastic shock absorber attached to a mooring line. **b** (*as modifier*): *a snub rope.* ◆ ADJECTIVE [5] short and blunt. See also **snub-nosed.**
▷HISTORY C14: from Old Norse *snubba* to scold; related to Norwegian, Swedish dialect *snubba* to cut short, Danish *snubbe*
▸ˈ**snubber** NOUN ▸ˈ**snubby** ADJECTIVE

snub-nosed ADJECTIVE [1] having a short turned-up nose. [2] (of a pistol) having an extremely short barrel.

snuck (snʌk) VERB *Chiefly US and Canadian, not standard* a past tense and past participle of **sneak.**

snuff[1] (snʌf) VERB [1] (*tr*) to inhale through the nose. [2] (when *intr,* often foll by *at*) (esp of an animal) to examine by sniffing. ◆ NOUN [3] an act or the sound of snuffing.
▷HISTORY C16: probably from Middle Dutch *snuffen* to snuffle, ultimately of imitative origin
▸ˈ**snuffer** NOUN

snuff² (snʌf) NOUN [1] finely powdered tobacco for sniffing up the nostrils or less commonly for chewing. [2] a small amount of this. [3] any powdered substance, esp one for sniffing up the nostrils. [4] **up to snuff.** *Informal* **a** in good health or in good condition. **b** *Chiefly Brit* not easily deceived. ♦ VERB [5] *(intr)* to use or inhale snuff.
▷HISTORY C17: from Dutch *snuf,* shortened from *snuftabale,* literally: tobacco for snuffing; see SNUFF¹

snuff³ (snʌf) VERB *(tr)* [1] (often foll by *out*) to extinguish (a light from a naked flame, esp a candle). [2] to cut off the charred part of (the wick of a candle, etc.). [3] (usually foll by *out*) *Informal* to suppress; put an end to. [4] **snuff it.** *Brit informal* to die. ♦ NOUN [5] the burned portion of the wick of a candle.
▷HISTORY C14 *snoffe,* of obscure origin

snuffbox (ˈsnʌfˌbɒks) NOUN a container, often of elaborate ornamental design, for holding small quantities of snuff.

snuff-dipping NOUN the practice of absorbing nicotine by holding in one's mouth, between the cheek and the gum, a small amount of tobacco, either loose or enclosed in a sachet.

snuffer (ˈsnʌfə) NOUN [1] a cone-shaped implement for extinguishing candles. [2] *(plural)* an instrument resembling a pair of scissors for trimming the wick or extinguishing the flame of a candle. [3] *Rare* a person who takes snuff.

snuffle (ˈsnʌfᵊl) VERB [1] *(intr)* to breathe noisily or with difficulty. [2] to say or speak in a nasal tone. [3] *(intr)* to snivel. ♦ NOUN [4] an act or the sound of snuffling. [5] a nasal tone or voice. [6] **the snuffles.** a condition characterized by snuffling.
▷HISTORY C16: from Low German or Dutch *snuffelen;* see SNUFF¹, SNIVEL
▸ˈ**snuffler** NOUN ▸ˈ**snuffly** ADJECTIVE

snuff movie *or* **film** NOUN *Slang* a pornographic film in which an unsuspecting actress or actor is murdered as the climax of the film.

snuffy (ˈsnʌfɪ) ADJECTIVE **snuffier, snuffiest.** [1] of, relating to, or resembling snuff. [2] covered with or smelling of snuff. [3] unpleasant; disagreeable.
▸ˈ**snuffiness** NOUN

snug (snʌg) ADJECTIVE **snugger, snuggest.** [1] comfortably warm and well-protected; cosy: *the children were snug in bed during the blizzard.* [2] small but comfortable: *a snug cottage.* [3] well-ordered; compact: *a snug boat.* [4] sheltered and secure: *a snug anchorage.* [5] fitting closely and comfortably. [6] offering safe concealment. ♦ NOUN [7] (in Britain and Ireland) one of the bars in certain pubs, offering intimate seating for only a few persons. [8] *Engineering* a small peg under the head of a bolt engaging with a slot in the bolted component to prevent the bolt turning when the nut is tightened. ♦ VERB **snugs, snugging, snugged.** [9] to make or become comfortable and warm. [10] *(tr) Nautical* to make (a vessel) ready for a storm by lashing down gear.
▷HISTORY C16 (in the sense: prepared for storms (used of a ship)): related to Old Icelandic *snöggr* short-haired, Swedish *snygg* tidy, Low German *snögger* smart
▸ˈ**snugly** ADVERB ▸ˈ**snugness** NOUN

snuggery (ˈsnʌgərɪ) NOUN, *plural* **-geries.** [1] a cosy and comfortable place or room. [2] another name for **snug** (sense 7).

snuggle (ˈsnʌgᵊl) VERB [1] *(usually intr;* usually foll by *down, up,* or *together)* to nestle into or draw close to (somebody or something) for warmth or from affection. ♦ NOUN [2] the act of snuggling.
▷HISTORY C17: frequentative SNUG (vb)

snye (snaɪ) NOUN *Canadian* a side channel of a river.
▷HISTORY from Canadian French *chenail,* from French *chenal* CHANNEL¹

so¹ (səʊ) ADVERB [1] (foll by an adjective or adverb and a correlative clause often introduced by *that*) to such an extent: *the river is so dirty that it smells.* [2] *(used with a negative;* it replaces the first *as* in an equative comparison) to the same extent as: *she is not so old as you.* [3] (intensifier): *it's so lovely; I love you so.* [4] in the state or manner expressed or implied: *they're happy and will remain so.* [5] *(not used with a negative;* foll by an auxiliary verb or *do, have,* or *be* used as main verbs) also; likewise: *I can speak Spanish and so can you.* [6] *Informal* indeed: used to contradict a negative statement: *You didn't tell the truth. I did so!* [7] *Archaic* provided that. [8] **and so on** *or* **forth.** and continuing similarly. [9] **just so.** See **just** (sense 19). [10] **or so.** approximately: *fifty or so people came to see me.* [11] **quite so.** I agree; exactly. [12] **so be it.** used to express agreement or resignation. [13] **so much. a** a certain degree or amount (of). **b** a lot (of): *it's just so much nonsense.* [14] **so much for. a** no more can or need be said about. **b** used to express contempt for something that has failed: *so much for your bright idea.* ♦ CONJUNCTION (subordinating; often foll by *that)* [15] in order (that): *to die so that you might live.* [16] with the consequence (that): *he was late home, so that there was trouble.* [17] **so as.** *(takes an infinitive)* in order (to): *to slim so as to lose weight.* ♦ SENTENCE CONNECTOR [18] in consequence; hence: *she wasn't needed, so she left.* [19] used to introduce a sentence expressing resignation, amazement, or sarcasm: *so you're publishing a book!* [20] thereupon; and then: *and so we ended up in France.* [21] used to introduce a sentence or clause to add emphasis: *he's crazy, so he is.* [22] **so what!** *Informal* what importance does that have? ♦ PRONOUN [23] used to substitute for a clause or sentence, which may be understood: *you'll stop because I said so.* ♦ ADJECTIVE [24] (used with *is, was,* etc.) factual; true: *it can't be so.* ♦ INTERJECTION [25] an exclamation of agreement, surprise, etc.
▷HISTORY Old English *swā;* related to Old Norse *svā,* Old High German *sō,* Dutch *zoo*

> **Language note** In formal English, *so* is not used as a conjunction, to indicate either purpose (*he left by a back door so he could avoid photographers*) or result (*the project was abandoned so his services were no longer needed*). In the former case *to* or *in order to* should be used instead, and in the latter case *and so* or *and therefore* would be more acceptable. The expression *so therefore* should not be used.

so² (səʊ) NOUN *Music* a variant spelling of **soh.**

so³ THE INTERNET DOMAIN NAME FOR Somalia.

SO INTERNATIONAL CAR REGISTRATION FOR Somalia.

S.O. *Baseball* ABBREVIATION FOR strike out.

soak (səʊk) VERB [1] to make, become, or be thoroughly wet or saturated, esp by immersion in a liquid. [2] (when *intr,* usually foll by *in* or *into*) (of a liquid) to penetrate or permeate. [3] *(tr;* usually foll by *in* or *up*) (of a permeable solid) to take in (a liquid) by absorption: *the earth soaks up rainwater.* [4] *(tr;* foll by *out* or *out of*) to remove by immersion in a liquid: *she soaked the stains out of the dress.* [5] *(tr) Metallurgy* to heat (a metal) prior to working. [6] *Informal* to drink excessively or make or become drunk. [7] *(tr) US and Canadian slang* to overcharge. [8] *(tr) Brit slang* to put in pawn. ♦ NOUN [9] the act of immersing in a liquid or the period of immersion. [10] the liquid in which something may be soaked, esp a solution containing detergent. [11] another name for **soakage** (sense 3). [12] *Brit informal* a heavy rainfall. [13] *Slang* a person who drinks to excess.
▷HISTORY Old English *sōcian* to cook; see SUCK
▸ˈ**soaker** NOUN ▸ˈ**soaking** NOUN, ADJECTIVE

soakage (ˈsəʊkɪdʒ) NOUN [1] the process or a period in which a permeable substance is soaked in a liquid. [2] liquid that has been soaked up or has seeped out. [3] Also called: **soak.** *Austral* a small pool of water or swampy patch.

soakaway (ˈsəʊkəˌweɪ) NOUN a pit filled with rubble, etc., into which rain or waste water drains.

so-and-so NOUN, *plural* **so-and-sos.** *Informal* [1] a person whose name is forgotten or ignored: *so-and-so came to see me.* [2] *Euphemistic* a person or thing regarded as unpleasant or difficult: *which so-and-so broke my razor?*

soap (səʊp) NOUN [1] a cleaning or emulsifying agent made by reacting animal or vegetable fats or oils with potassium or sodium hydroxide. Soaps often contain colouring matter and perfume and act by emulsifying grease and lowering the surface tension of water, so that it more readily penetrates open materials such as textiles. See also **detergent.** Related adjective: **saponaceous.** [2] any metallic salt of a fatty acid, such as palmitic or stearic acid. See also **metallic soap.** [3] *Slang* flattery or persuasive talk (esp in the phrase **soft soap**). [4] *Informal* short for **soap opera.** [5] *US and Canadian slang* money, esp for bribery. [6] **no soap.** *US and Canadian slang* not possible or successful. ♦ VERB [7] *(tr)* to apply soap to. [8] *(tr;* often foll by *up) Slang* **a** to flatter or talk persuasively to. **b** *US and Canadian* to bribe.
▷HISTORY Old English *sāpe;* related to Old High German *seipfa,* Old French *savon,* Latin *sāpō*
▸ˈ**soapless** ADJECTIVE ▸ˈ**soapˌlike** ADJECTIVE

soapbark (ˈsəʊpˌbɑːk) NOUN [1] Also called: **quillai.** a W South American rosaceous tree, *Quillaja saponaria,* with undivided evergreen leaves and small white flowers. [2] Also called: **quillai bark.** the inner bark of this tree, formerly used as soap and as a source of saponin. [3] any of several trees or shrubs that have a bark similar to this.

soapberry (ˈsəʊpˌberɪ) NOUN, *plural* **-ries.** [1] any of various chiefly tropical American sapindaceous trees of the genus *Sapindus,* esp *S. saponaria* (or *S. marginatus*), having pulpy fruit containing saponin. [2] a related plant, *S. drummondii,* of the southwestern US. [3] the fruit of any of these trees. ♦ Also called: **chinaberry.**

soap boiler NOUN a manufacturer of soap.
▸**soap boiling** NOUN

soapbox (ˈsəʊpˌbɒks) NOUN [1] a box or crate for packing soap. [2] a crate used as a platform for speech-making. [3] a child's homemade racing cart consisting of a wooden box set on a wooden frame with wheels and a steerable front axle.

soap bubble NOUN [1] a bubble formed from soapy water. [2] something that is ephemeral but attractive.

soapie *or* **soapy** (ˈsəʊpɪ) NOUN *Austral* an informal word for **soap opera.**

soapolallie (ˈsəʊpəˌlælɪ) NOUN *Canadian* a drink made by crushing soapberries.
▷HISTORY from SOAP(BERRY) + *lallie* (compare *-lolly* as in LOBLOLLY)

soap opera NOUN a serialized drama, usually dealing with domestic themes and characterized by sentimentality, broadcast on radio or television.
▷HISTORY C20: so called because manufacturers of soap were typical sponsors

soapstone (ˈsəʊpˌstəʊn) NOUN a massive compact soft variety of talc, used for making tabletops, hearths, ornaments, etc. Also called: **steatite.**
▷HISTORY C17: so called because it has a greasy feel and was sometimes used as soap

soapsuds (ˈsəʊpˌsʌdz) PLURAL NOUN foam or lather made from soap.
▸ˈ**soapˌsudsy** ADJECTIVE

soapwort (ˈsəʊpˌwɜːt) NOUN a Eurasian caryophyllaceous plant, *Saponaria officinalis,* having rounded clusters of fragrant pink or white flowers and leaves that were formerly used as a soap substitute. Also called: **bouncing Bet.**

soapy (ˈsəʊpɪ) ADJECTIVE **soapier, soapiest.** [1] containing or covered with soap: *soapy water.* [2] resembling or characteristic of soap. [3] *Slang* flattering or persuasive. ♦ NOUN, *plural* **-pies.** [4] *Austral* a variant of **soapie.**
▸ˈ**soapily** ADVERB ▸ˈ**soapiness** NOUN

soar (sɔː) VERB *(intr)* [1] to rise or fly upwards into the air. [2] (of a bird, aircraft, etc.) to glide while maintaining altitude by the use of ascending air currents. [3] to rise or increase in volume, size, etc.: *soaring prices.* ♦ NOUN [4] the act of soaring. [5] the altitude attained by soaring.
▷HISTORY C14: from Old French *essorer,* from Vulgar Latin *exaurāre* (unattested) to expose to the breezes, from Latin EX-¹ + *aura* a breeze
▸ˈ**soarer** NOUN

soaraway (ˈsɔːrəˌweɪ) ADJECTIVE exceedingly successful.

Soave (ˈswɑːveɪ) NOUN a dry white wine from the Veneto region of NE Italy.
▷HISTORY C20: named after a town near Verona where it is produced

Soay (ˈsəʊeɪ) NOUN a breed of small horned sheep having long legs and dark brown wool that is plucked rather than shorn; found mainly on St Kilda where they were probably introduced by the Vikings.
▷HISTORY named after *Soay,* an island in the St Kilda group, where they were first found

sob (sɒb) VERB **sobs, sobbing, sobbed.** [1] *(intr)* to weep with convulsive gasps. [2] *(tr)* to utter with sobs. [3] to cause (oneself) to be in a specified state by sobbing: *to sob oneself to sleep.* ♦ NOUN [4] a convulsive gasp made in weeping.

▷**HISTORY** C12: probably from Low German; compare Dutch *sabben* to suck
▸ **'sobber** NOUN

s.o.b. *Slang, chiefly US and Canadian* ABBREVIATION FOR son of a bitch.

soba ('səʊbə) NOUN (in Japanese cookery) noodles made from buckwheat flour.
▷**HISTORY** Japanese

sobeit (səʊ'bi:ɪt) CONJUNCTION *Archaic* provided that.
▷**HISTORY** C16: from SO[1] + BE + IT: originally three words

sober ('səʊbə) ADJECTIVE 1 not drunk. 2 not given to excessive indulgence in drink or any other activity. 3 sedate and rational: *a sober attitude to a problem.* 4 (of colours) plain and dull or subdued. 5 free from exaggeration or speculation: *he told us the sober truth.* ◆ VERB 6 (usually foll by *up*) to make or become less intoxicated, reckless, etc.
▷**HISTORY** C14 *sobre,* from Old French, from Latin *sōbrius*
▸ **'sobering** ADJECTIVE ▸ **'soberingly** ADVERB ▸ **'soberly** ADVERB ▸ **'soberness** NOUN

sobersides ('səʊbəˌsaɪdz) NOUN (*functioning as singular*) a solemn and sedate person.
▸ **'soberˌsided** ADJECTIVE

sobole ('səʊbəʊl) NOUN, *plural* **soboles** (-li:z). a creeping underground stem that produces roots and buds; a sucker.
▷**HISTORY** back formation from *soboles* (originally a sing.), from Latin *soboles* a shoot, from *subolescere* to grow

Sobranje (səʊ'brɑ:njɪ) NOUN the legislature of Bulgaria.

sobriety (səʊ'braɪətɪ) NOUN 1 the state or quality of being sober. 2 the quality of refraining from excess. 3 the quality of being serious or sedate.

sobriety coach NOUN a person who helps someone who has been dependent on alcohol or drugs to maintain an abstinent lifestyle.

sobriquet *or* **soubriquet** ('səʊbrɪˌkeɪ) NOUN a humorous epithet, assumed name, or nickname.
▷**HISTORY** C17: from French *soubriquet,* of uncertain origin

sob sister NOUN a journalist, esp a woman, on a newspaper or magazine who writes articles of sentimental appeal.

sob story NOUN a tale of personal distress intended to arouse sympathy, esp one offered as an excuse or apology.

sob stuff NOUN material such as films, stories, etc., that play upon the emotions by the overuse of pathos and sentiment.

Soc. *or* **soc.** ABBREVIATION FOR: 1 socialist. 2 society.

soca ('səʊkə) NOUN a mixture of soul and calypso music typical of the E Caribbean.
▷**HISTORY** C20: a blend of *soul* and *calypso*

socage ('sɒkɪdʒ) NOUN 1 *English legal history* the tenure of land by certain services, esp of an agricultural nature. 2 *English law* the freehold tenure of land.
▷**HISTORY** C14: from Anglo-French, from *soc* SOKE
▸ **'socager** NOUN

so-called ADJECTIVE **a** (*prenominal*) designated or styled by the name or word mentioned, esp (in the speaker's opinion) incorrectly: *a so-called genius.* **b** (*also used parenthetically after a noun*): *these experts, so-called, are no help.*

soccer ('sɒkə) NOUN **a** a game in which two teams of eleven players try to kick or head a ball into their opponent's goal, only the goalkeeper on either side being allowed to touch the ball with his hands and arms except in the case of throw-ins. **b** (*as modifier*): *a soccer player.* ◆ Also called: **Association Football.**
▷**HISTORY** C19: from (*as*)*soc.* + *-er*

soccer mom NOUN *US* a woman who devotes much of her spare time to her children's activities, typically driving them to and from sports events in which they are involved.

Socceroos (ˌsɒkə'ru:z) PLURAL NOUN *Informal* the Australian national soccer team.
▷**HISTORY** from SOCCER + (KANGAR)OO

Soche *or* **So-ch'e** ('səʊ'tʃɛ) NOUN a variant transliteration of the Chinese name for **Shache.**

Sochi (*Russian* 'sɔtʃi) NOUN a city and resort in SW Russia, in the Krasnodar Territory on the Black Sea: hot mineral springs. Pop.: 359 300 (1995 est.).

sociable ('səʊʃəbᵊl) ADJECTIVE 1 friendly or companionable. 2 (of an occasion) providing the opportunity for friendliness and conviviality. ◆ NOUN 3 *Chiefly US* another name for **social** (sense 9). 4 a type of open carriage with two seats facing each other.
▷**HISTORY** C16: via French from Latin *sociābilis,* from *sociāre* to unite, from *socius* an associate
▸ **ˌsocia'bility** *or* **'sociableness** NOUN ▸ **'sociably** ADVERB

social ('səʊʃəl) ADJECTIVE 1 living or preferring to live in a community rather than alone. 2 denoting or relating to human society or any of its subdivisions. 3 of, relating to, or characteristic of the experience, behaviour, and interaction of persons forming groups. 4 relating to or having the purpose of promoting companionship, communal activities, etc.: *a social club.* 5 relating to or engaged in social services: *a social worker.* 6 relating to or considered appropriate to a certain class of society, esp one thought superior. 7 (esp of certain species of insects) living together in organized colonies: *social bees.* Compare **solitary** (sense 6). 8 (of plant species) growing in clumps, usually over a wide area. ◆ NOUN 9 an informal gathering, esp of an organized group, to promote companionship, communal activity, etc.
▷**HISTORY** C16: from Latin *sociālis* companionable, from *socius* a comrade
▸ **'socially** ADVERB ▸ **'socialness** NOUN

social accounting NOUN the analysis of the economy by sectors leading to the calculation and publication of economic statistics, such as gross national product and national income. Also called: **national accounting.**

Social and Liberal Democratic Party NOUN (in Britain) a centrist political party formed in 1988 by the merging of the Liberal Party and part of the Social Democratic Party. In 1989 it changed its name to the Liberal Democrats.

social anthropology NOUN the branch of anthropology that deals with cultural and social phenomena such as kinship systems or beliefs, esp of nonliterate peoples.

social assistance NOUN a former name for **social security.**

social capital NOUN the network of social connections that exist between people, and their shared values and norms of behaviour, which enable and encourage mutually advantageous social cooperation.

Social Chapter NOUN the section of the **Maastricht Treaty** concerning working conditions, consultation of workers, employment rights, and social security. The UK government negotiated an opt-out clause from this section of the treaty in 1993 but adopted it in 1997.

Social Charter NOUN a declaration of the rights, minimum wages, maximum hours, etc., of workers in the European Union, later adopted in the Social Chapter.

social climber NOUN a person who seeks advancement to a higher social class, esp by obsequious behaviour. Sometimes shortened to: **climber.**
▸ **social climbing** NOUN

social contract *or* **compact** NOUN (in the theories of Locke, Hobbes, Rousseau, and others) an agreement, entered into by individuals, that results in the formation of the state or of organized society, the prime motive being the desire for protection, which entails the surrender of some or all personal liberties.

Social Credit NOUN (esp in Canada) a right-wing Populist political party, movement, or doctrine based on the socioeconomic theories of Major C. H. Douglas.
▸ **Social Crediter** NOUN

social democracy NOUN (*sometimes capital*) the beliefs, principles, practices, or programme of a Social Democratic Party or of social democrats.
▸ **social democratic** ADJECTIVE

social democrat NOUN 1 any socialist who believes in the gradual transformation of capitalism into democratic socialism. 2 (*usually capital*) a member of a Social Democratic Party.

Social Democratic and Labour Party NOUN a Northern Irish political party, which advocates peaceful union with the Republic of Ireland.

Social Democratic Party NOUN 1 (in Britain 1981–90) a centre political party founded by ex-members of the Labour Party. It formed an alliance with the Liberal Party and continued in a reduced form after many members left to join the Social and Liberal Democratic Party in 1988. 2 one of the two major political parties in Germany (formerly in West Germany), favouring gradual reform. 3 any of the parties in many other countries similar to that of Germany.

social dumping NOUN the practice of allowing employers to lower wages and reduce employees' benefits in order to attract and retain employment and investment.

Social Education Centre NOUN a daycentre, run by a local authority, for mentally handicapped people and sometimes also for physically handicapped or mentally ill adults.

social engineering NOUN the manipulation of the social position and function of individuals in order to manage change in a society.

social evolution NOUN *Sociol* the process of social development from an early simple type of social organization to one that is complex and highly specialized.

social exclusion NOUN *Sociol* the failure of society to provide certain individuals and groups with those rights and benefits normally available to its members, such as employment, adequate housing, health care, education and training, etc.

social fund NOUN (in Britain) a social security fund from which loans or payments may be made to people in cases of extreme need.

social housing NOUN accommodation provided by the state for renting.

social inclusion NOUN *Sociol* the provision of certain rights to all individuals and groups in society, such as employment, adequate housing, health care, education and training, etc.

social inquiry report NOUN (in Britain) a report on a person and his or her circumstances, which may be required by a court before sentencing and is made by a probation officer or a social worker from a local authority social services department.

social insurance NOUN government insurance providing coverage for the unemployed, the injured, the old, etc.: usually financed by contributions from employers and employees, as well as general government revenue. See also **social security, national insurance, social assistance.**

Social Insurance Number NOUN *Canadian* a nine-digit number used by the federal government to identify a citizen.

socialism ('səʊʃəˌlɪzəm) NOUN 1 an economic theory or system in which the means of production, distribution, and exchange are owned by the community collectively, usually through the state. It is characterized by production for use rather than profit, by equality of individual wealth, by the absence of competitive economic activity, and, usually, by government determination of investment, prices, and production levels. Compare **capitalism.** 2 any of various social or political theories or movements in which the common welfare is to be achieved through the establishment of a socialist economic system. 3 (in Leninist theory) a transitional stage after the proletarian revolution in the development of a society from capitalism to communism: characterized by the distribution of income according to work rather than need.

socialist ('səʊʃəlɪst) NOUN 1 a supporter or advocate of socialism or any party promoting socialism (**socialist party**). ◆ ADJECTIVE 2 of, characteristic of, implementing, or relating to socialism. 3 (*sometimes capital*) of, characteristic of, or relating to socialists or a socialist party.

socialistic (ˌsəʊʃə'lɪstɪk) ADJECTIVE resembling or sympathizing with socialism.
▸ **ˌsocial'istically** ADVERB

Socialist International NOUN an international association of largely anti-Communist Social Democratic Parties founded in Frankfurt in 1951.

Socialist Labor Party NOUN (in the US) a minor Marxist party founded in 1876.

socialist realism NOUN (in Communist countries, esp formerly) the doctrine that art, literature, etc. should present an idealized portrayal of reality, which glorifies the achievements of the Communist Party.

socialite (ˈsəʊʃəˌlaɪt) NOUN a person who is or seeks to be prominent in fashionable society.

sociality (ˌsəʊʃɪˈælɪtɪ) NOUN, *plural* **-ties.** 1 the tendency of groups and persons to develop social links and live in communities. 2 the quality or state of being social.

socialization *or* **socialisation** (ˌsəʊʃəlaɪˈzeɪʃən) NOUN 1 *Psychol* the modification from infancy of an individual's behaviour to conform with the demands of social life. 2 the act of socializing or the state of being socialized.

socialize *or* **socialise** (ˈsəʊʃəˌlaɪz) VERB 1 (*intr*) to behave in a friendly or sociable manner. 2 (*tr*) to prepare for life in society. 3 (*tr*) *Chiefly US* to alter or create so as to be in accordance with socialist principles, as by nationalization.
▸**ˈsocialˌizable** *or* **ˈsocialˌisable** ADJECTIVE ▸**ˈsocialˌizer** *or* **ˈsocialˌiser** NOUN

socially excluded ADJECTIVE **a** suffering from social exclusion. **b** (*as noun*): *the socially excluded.*

socially included ADJECTIVE **a** benefiting from social inclusion. **b** (*as noun*): *the socially included.*

social market NOUN **a** an economic system in which industry and commerce are run by private enterprise within limits set by the government to ensure equality of opportunity and social and environmental responsibility. **b** (*as modifier*): *a social-market economy.*

social organization NOUN *Sociol* the formation of a stable structure of relations inside a group, which provides a basis for order and patterns relationships for new members.

social phobia NOUN *Psychol* a type of anxiety disorder characterized by shyness and heightened self-consciousness in particular social situations.

social psychology NOUN *Psychol* the area of psychology concerned with the interaction between individuals and groups and the effect of society on behaviour.

social realism NOUN 1 the use of realist art, literature, etc. as a medium for social or political comment. 2 another name for **socialist realism.**

social science NOUN 1 the study of society and of the relationship of individual members within society, including economics, history, political science, psychology, anthropology, and sociology. 2 any of these subjects studied individually.
▸**social scientist** NOUN

social secretary NOUN 1 a member of an organization who arranges its social events. 2 a personal secretary who deals with private correspondence, etc.

social security NOUN 1 public provision for the economic, and sometimes social, welfare of the aged, unemployed, etc., esp through pensions and other monetary assistance. 2 (*often capitals*) a government programme designed to provide such assistance.

social services PLURAL NOUN welfare activities organized by the state or a local authority and carried out by trained personnel.

social stratification NOUN *Sociol* the hierarchical structures of class and status in any society.

social studies NOUN (*functioning as singular*) the study of how people live and organize themselves in society, embracing geography, history, economics, and other subjects.

social welfare NOUN 1 the various social services provided by a state for the benefit of its citizens. 2 (*capitals*) (in New Zealand) a government department concerned with pensions and benefits for the elderly, the sick, etc.

social work NOUN any of various social services designed to alleviate the conditions of the poor and aged and to increase the welfare of children.
▸**social worker** NOUN

societal (səˈsaɪətəl) ADJECTIVE of or relating to society, esp human society or social relations.
▸**soˈcietally** ADVERB

societal marketing NOUN 1 marketing that takes into account society's long-term welfare. 2 the marketing of a social or charitable cause, such as an environmental campaign.

society (səˈsaɪətɪ) NOUN, *plural* **-ties.** 1 the totality of social relationships among organized groups of human beings or animals. 2 a system of human organizations generating distinctive cultural patterns and institutions and usually providing protection, security, continuity, and a national identity for its members. 3 such a system with reference to its mode of social and economic organization or its dominant class: *middle-class society.* 4 those with whom one has companionship. 5 an organized group of people associated for some specific purpose or on account of some common interest: *a learned society.* 6 **a** the privileged class of people in a community, esp as considered superior or fashionable. **b** (*as modifier*): *a society woman.* 7 the social life and intercourse of such people: *to enter society as a debutante.* 8 companionship; the fact or state of being together with someone else: *I enjoy her society.* 9 *Ecology* a small community of plants within a larger association.
▷HISTORY C16: via Old French *societé* from Latin *societās,* from *socius* a comrade

Society Islands PLURAL NOUN a group of islands in the S Pacific: administratively part of French Polynesia; consists of the Windward Islands and the Leeward Islands; became a French protectorate in 1843 and a colony in 1880. Pop.: 189 524 (1996). Area: 1595 sq. km (616 sq. miles).

Society of Jesus NOUN the religious order of the Jesuits, founded by Ignatius Loyola.

Socinian (səʊˈsɪnɪən) NOUN 1 a supporter of the beliefs of Faustus and Laelius Socinus, who rejected such traditional Christian doctrines as the divinity of Christ, the Trinity, and original sin, and held that those who follow Christ's virtues will be granted salvation. ◆ ADJECTIVE 2 of or relating to the Socinians or their beliefs.
▸**Soˈcinianˌism** NOUN

socio- COMBINING FORM denoting social or society: *socioeconomic; sociopolitical; sociology.*

sociobiology (ˌsəʊsɪəʊbaɪˈɒlədʒɪ) NOUN the study of social behaviour in animals and humans, esp in relation to its survival value and evolutionary origins.
▸**ˌsociobiˈologist** NOUN

socioeconomic (ˌsəʊsɪəʊˌiːkəˈnɒmɪk, -ˌɛkə-) ADJECTIVE of, relating to, or involving both economic and social factors.
▸**ˌsocioˌecoˈnomically** ADVERB

sociol. ABBREVIATION FOR sociology.

sociolinguistics (ˌsəʊsɪəʊlɪŋˈgwɪstɪks) NOUN (*functioning as singular*) the study of language in relation to its social context.
▸**ˌsocioˈlinguist** NOUN ▸**ˌsociolinˈguistic** ADJECTIVE

sociology (ˌsəʊsɪˈɒlədʒɪ) NOUN the study of the development, organization, functioning, and classification of human societies.
▸**sociological** (ˌsəʊsɪəˈlɒdʒɪkəl) ADJECTIVE
▸**ˌsocioˈlogically** ADVERB ▸**ˌsociˈologist** NOUN

sociometry (ˌsəʊsɪˈɒmɪtrɪ) NOUN the study of sociological relationships, esp of preferences, within social groups.
▸**sociometric** (ˌsəʊsɪəˈmɛtrɪk) ADJECTIVE ▸**ˌsociˈometrist** NOUN

sociopath (ˈsəʊsɪəˌpæθ) NOUN *Psychiatry* another name for **psychopath.**
▸**ˌsocioˈpathic** ADJECTIVE ▸**sociopathy** (ˌsəʊsɪˈɒpəθɪ) NOUN

sociopolitical (ˌsəʊsɪəʊpəˈlɪtɪkəl) ADJECTIVE of, relating to, or involving both political and social factors.

sock[1] (sɒk) NOUN 1 a cloth covering for the foot, reaching to between the ankle and knee and worn inside a shoe. 2 an insole put in a shoe, as to make it fit better. 3 a light shoe worn by actors in ancient Greek and Roman comedy, sometimes taken to allude to comic drama in general (as in the phrase **sock and buskin**). See **buskin.** 4 another name for **windsock.** 5 **pull one's socks up.** *Brit informal* to make a determined effort, esp in order to regain control of a situation. 6 **put a sock in it.** *Brit slang* be quiet! ◆ VERB 7 (*tr*) to provide with socks. 8 **socked in.** *US and Canadian slang* (of an airport) closed by adverse weather conditions.
▷HISTORY Old English *socc* a light shoe, from Latin *soccus,* from Greek *sukkhos*

sock[2] (sɒk) *Slang* ◆ VERB 1 (*usually tr*) to hit with force. 2 **sock it to.** to make a forceful impression on. ◆ NOUN 3 a forceful blow.
▷HISTORY C17: of obscure origin

sock away VERB (*tr*) *US, Canadian, and NZ informal* to save up.

sockdologer *or* **sockdolager** (sɒkˈdɒlədʒə) NOUN *Slang, chiefly US* 1 a decisive blow or remark. 2 an outstanding person or thing.
▷HISTORY C19: of uncertain origin; perhaps from SOCK[2] + DOXOLOGY (in the sense: the closing act of a church service) + -ER[1]

socket (ˈsɒkɪt) NOUN 1 a device into which an electric plug can be inserted in order to make a connection in a circuit. 2 *Chiefly Brit* such a device mounted on a wall and connected to the electricity supply. Informal Brit names: **point, plug.** US and Canadian name: **outlet.** 3 a part with an opening or hollow into which some other part, such as a pipe, probe, etc., can be fitted. 4 a spanner head having a recess suitable to be fitted over the head of a bolt and a keyway into which a wrench can be fitted. 5 *Anatomy* **a** a bony hollow into which a part or structure fits: *a tooth socket; an eye socket.* **b** the receptacle of a ball-and-socket joint. ◆ VERB 6 (*tr*) to furnish with or place into a socket.
▷HISTORY C13: from Anglo-Norman *soket* a little ploughshare, from *soc,* of Celtic origin; compare Cornish *soch* ploughshare

socket wrench NOUN a wrench having a handle onto which socketed heads of various sizes can be fitted.

sockeye (ˈsɒkˌaɪ) NOUN a Pacific salmon, *Oncorhynchus nerka,* having red flesh and valued as a food fish. Also called: **red salmon.**
▷HISTORY by folk etymology from Salishan *sukkegh*

socle (ˈsəʊkəl) NOUN another name for **plinth** (sense 1).
▷HISTORY C18: via French from Italian *zoccolo,* from Latin *socculus* a little shoe, from *soccus* a SOCK[1]

socman (ˈsɒkmən, ˈsəʊk-) *or* **sokeman** (ˈsəʊkmən) NOUN, *plural* **-men.** *English history* a tenant holding land by socage.
▷HISTORY C16: from Anglo-Latin *socmannus;* see SOKE

Socotra, Sokotra, *or* **Suqutra** (səˈkəʊtrə) NOUN an island in the Indian Ocean, about 240 km (150 miles) off Cape Guardafui, Somalia: administratively part of Yemen. Capital: Tamrida. Area: 3100 sq. km (1200 sq. miles).

Socratic (sɒˈkrætɪk) ADJECTIVE 1 of or relating to Socrates, the Athenian philosopher (?470–399 B.C.), his methods, etc. ◆ NOUN 2 a person who follows the teachings of Socrates.
▸**Soˈcratically** ADVERB ▸**Soˈcratiˌcism** NOUN ▸**Socratist** (ˈsɒkrətɪst) NOUN

Socratic irony NOUN *Philosophy* a means by which the pretended ignorance of a skilful questioner leads the person answering to expose his own ignorance.

Socratic method NOUN *Philosophy* the method of instruction by question and answer used by Socrates in order to elicit from his pupils truths he considered to be implicitly known by all rational beings. Compare **maieutic.**

Socred (ˈsəʊkrɛd) *Canadian* ◆ NOUN 1 a supporter or member of a Social Credit movement or party. ◆ ADJECTIVE 2 of or relating to Social Credit.

sod[1] (sɒd) NOUN 1 a piece of grass-covered surface soil held together by the roots of the grass; turf. 2 *Poetic* the ground. ◆ VERB **sods, sodding, sodded.** 3 (*tr*) to cover with sods.
▷HISTORY C15: from Low German; compare Middle Low German, Middle Dutch *sode;* related to Old Frisian *sātha*

sod[2] (sɒd) *Slang, chiefly Brit* ◆ NOUN 1 a person considered to be obnoxious. 2 a jocular word for a person: *the poor sod hasn't been out for weeks.* 3 **sod all.** *Slang* nothing. ◆ INTERJECTION 4 **sod it.** a strong exclamation of annoyance. ◆ See also **sod off.**
▷HISTORY C19: shortened from SODOMITE
▸**ˈsodding** ADJECTIVE

soda (ˈsəʊdə) NOUN 1 any of a number of simple

inorganic compounds of sodium, such as sodium carbonate (**washing soda**), sodium bicarbonate (**baking soda**), and sodium hydroxide (**caustic soda**). 2 See **soda water.** 3 *US and Canadian* a fizzy drink. 4 the top card of the pack in faro. 5 **a soda.** *Austral slang* something easily done; a pushover.
▷**HISTORY** C16: from Medieval Latin, from *sodanum* barilla, a plant that was burned to obtain a type of sodium carbonate, perhaps of Arabic origin

soda ash NOUN the anhydrous commercial form of sodium carbonate.

soda biscuit NOUN a biscuit leavened with sodium bicarbonate.

soda bread NOUN a type of bread leavened with sodium bicarbonate combined with milk and cream of tartar.

soda fountain NOUN *US and Canadian* 1 a counter that serves drinks, snacks, etc. 2 an apparatus dispensing soda water.

soda jerk NOUN *US slang* a person who serves at a soda fountain.

soda lake NOUN a salt lake that has a high content of sodium salts, esp chlorides and sulphates.

soda lime NOUN a solid mixture of sodium and calcium hydroxides used to absorb carbon dioxide and to dry gases.

sodalite ('səʊdəˌlaɪt) NOUN a blue, grey, yellow, or colourless mineral consisting of sodium aluminium silicate and sodium chloride in cubic crystalline form. It occurs in basic igneous rocks. Formula: $Na_4Al_3Si_3O_{12}Cl$.
▷**HISTORY** C19: from SODA + -LITE

sodality (səʊ'dælɪtɪ) NOUN, *plural* **-ties.** 1 *RC Church* a religious or charitable society. 2 fraternity; fellowship.
▷**HISTORY** C16: from Latin *sodālitās* fellowship, from *sodālis* a comrade

sodamide ('səʊdəˌmaɪd) NOUN a white crystalline compound used as a dehydrating agent, as a chemical reagent, and in making sodium cyanide. Formula: $NaNH_2$. Also called: **sodium amide.**
▷**HISTORY** C19: from SOD(IUM) + AMIDE

soda nitre NOUN another name for **Chile saltpetre.**

soda pop NOUN *US informal* a fizzy drink.

soda siphon NOUN a sealed bottle containing and dispensing soda water. The water is forced up a tube reaching to the bottom of the bottle by the pressure of gas above the water. Also called (esp US): **siphon bottle.**

soda water NOUN an effervescent beverage made by charging water with carbon dioxide under pressure. Sometimes shortened to: **soda.**

sodden ('sɒdᵊn) ADJECTIVE 1 completely saturated. 2 **a** dulled, esp by excessive drinking. **b** (*in combination*): *a drink-sodden mind.* 3 heavy or doughy, as bread is when improperly cooked. ◆ VERB 4 to make or become sodden.
▷**HISTORY** C13 *soden,* past participle of SEETHE
▸**'soddenly** ADVERB ▸**'soddenness** NOUN

sod disease NOUN *Vet science* a disease of poultry characterized by blisters and scabs on the feet and legs.
▷**HISTORY** from prairie sods that the birds walked on in the US when the disease was first reported in 1920

sodger ('sodʒər) NOUN, VERB a dialect variant of **soldier.**

sodium ('səʊdɪəm) NOUN **a** a very reactive soft silvery-white element of the alkali metal group occurring principally in common salt, Chile saltpetre, and cryolite. Sodium and potassium ions maintain the essential electrolytic balance in living cells. It is used in the production of chemicals, in metallurgy, and, alloyed with potassium, as a cooling medium in nuclear reactors. Symbol: Na; atomic no.: 11; atomic wt.: 22.989768; valency: 1; relative density: 0.971; melting pt.: 97.81±0.03°C; boiling pt.: 892.9°C. **b** (*as modifier*): *sodium light.*
▷**HISTORY** C19: New Latin, from SODA + -IUM

sodium amytal NOUN another name for **Amytal.**

sodium benzoate NOUN a white crystalline soluble compound used as an antibacterial and antifungal agent in preserving food (**E211**), as an antiseptic, and in making dyes and pharmaceuticals. Formula: $(C_6H_5COO)Na$. Also called: **benzoate of soda.**

sodium bicarbonate NOUN a white crystalline soluble compound usually obtained by the Solvay process and used in effervescent drinks, baking powders, fire extinguishers, and in medicine as an antacid; sodium hydrogen carbonate. Formula: $NaHCO_3$. Also called: **bicarbonate of soda, baking soda.**

sodium carbonate NOUN a colourless or white odourless soluble crystalline compound existing in several hydrated forms and used in the manufacture of glass, ceramics, soap, and paper and as an industrial and domestic cleansing agent. It is made by the Solvay process and commonly obtained as the decahydrate (**washing soda** or **sal soda**) or a white anhydrous powder (**soda ash**). Formula: Na_2CO_3.

sodium chlorate NOUN a colourless crystalline soluble compound used as a bleaching agent, weak antiseptic, and weedkiller. Formula: $NaClO_3$.

sodium chloride NOUN common table salt; a soluble colourless crystalline compound occurring naturally as halite and in sea water: widely used as a seasoning and preservative for food and in the manufacture of chemicals, glass, and soap. Formula: NaCl. Also called: **salt.**

sodium cyanide NOUN a white odourless crystalline soluble poisonous compound with an odour of hydrogen cyanide when damp. It is used for extracting gold and silver from their ores and for case-hardening steel. Formula: NaCN.

sodium dichromate NOUN a soluble crystalline solid compound, usually obtained as red or orange crystals and used as an oxidizing agent, corrosion inhibitor, and mordant. Formula $Na_2Cr_2O_7$. Also called (not in technical usage): **sodium bichromate.**

sodium fluoroacetate (ˌflʊərəʊ'æsɪˌteɪt) NOUN a white crystalline odourless poisonous compound, used as a rodenticide. Formula: $(CH_2FCOO)Na$.

sodium glutamate ('gluːtəˌmeɪt) NOUN another name for **monosodium glutamate.**

sodium hydroxide NOUN a white deliquescent strongly alkaline solid used in the manufacture of rayon, paper, aluminium, soap, and sodium compounds. Formula: NaOH. Also called: **caustic soda.** See also **lye.**

sodium hyposulphite NOUN another name (not in technical usage) for **sodium thiosulphate.**

sodium lamp NOUN another name for **sodium-vapour lamp.**

sodium nitrate NOUN a white crystalline soluble solid compound occurring naturally as Chile saltpetre and caliche and used in matches, explosives, and rocket propellants, as a fertilizer, and as a curing salt for preserving food such as bacon, ham, and cheese (**E251**). Formula: $NaNO_3$.

Sodium Pentothal NOUN *Trademark* another name for **thiopental sodium.**

sodium perborate NOUN a white odourless crystalline compound used as an antiseptic and deodorant. Formula: $NaBO_3.4H_2O$.

sodium peroxide NOUN a yellowish-white odourless soluble powder formed when sodium reacts with an excess of oxygen: used as an oxidizing agent in chemical preparations, a bleaching agent, an antiseptic, and in removing carbon dioxide from air in submarines, etc. Formula: Na_2O_2.

sodium phosphate NOUN any sodium salt of any phosphoric acid, esp one of three salts of orthophosphoric acid having formulas NaH_2PO_4 (**monosodium dihydrogen orthophosphate**), Na_2HPO_4 (**disodium monohydrogen orthophosphate**), and Na_3PO_4 (**trisodium orthophosphate**).

sodium propionate NOUN a transparent crystalline soluble substance used as a medical fungicide and to prevent the growth of moulds, esp to retard spoilage in packed foods. Formula: $Na(C_2H_5COO)$.

sodium silicate NOUN 1 Also called: **soluble glass.** a substance having the general formula, $Na_2O.xSiO_2$, where *x* varies between 3 and 5, existing as an amorphous powder or present in a usually viscous aqueous solution. See **water glass.** 2 any sodium salt of orthosilicic acid or metasilicic acid.

sodium sulphate NOUN a solid white substance that occurs naturally as thenardite and is usually used as the white anhydrous compound (**salt cake**) or the white crystalline decahydrate (**Glauber's salt**) in making glass, detergents, and pulp. Formula: Na_2SO_4.

sodium thiosulphate NOUN a white soluble substance used, in the pentahydrate form, in photography as a fixer to dissolve unchanged silver halides and also to remove excess chlorine from chlorinated water. Formula: $Na_2S_2O_3$. Also called (not in technical usage): **sodium hyposulphite, hypo.**

sodium-vapour lamp NOUN a type of electric lamp consisting of a glass tube containing neon and sodium vapour at low pressure through which an electric current is passed to give an orange light. They are used in street lighting.

sod off VERB (*intr, adverb; usually imperative*) *Slang, chiefly Brit* to go away; depart.

> **Language note** This phrase was formerly considered to be taboo, and it was labelled as such in previous editions of *Collins English Dictionary*. However, it has now become acceptable in speech, although some older or more conservative people may object to its use.

Sodom ('sɒdəm) NOUN 1 *Old Testament* a city destroyed by God for its wickedness that, with Gomorrah, traditionally typifies depravity (Genesis 19:24). 2 this city as representing homosexuality. 3 any place notorious for depravity.

sodomite ('sɒdəˌmaɪt) NOUN a person who practises sodomy.

sodomize *or* **sodomise** ('sɒdəˌmaɪz) VERB (*tr*) to be the active partner in anal intercourse.

sodomy ('sɒdəmɪ) NOUN anal intercourse committed by a man with another man or a woman. Compare **buggery.**
▷**HISTORY** C13: via Old French *sodomie* from Latin (Vulgate) *Sodoma* Sodom

Sod's law (sɒdz) NOUN *Informal* a humorous or facetious precept stating that if something can go wrong or turn out inconveniently it will. Also called: **Murphy's Law.**

SOE (in New Zealand) ABBREVIATION FOR State Owned Enterprise.

Soemba ('suːmbə) NOUN a variant spelling of **Sumba.**

Soembawa (suːm'bɑːwə) NOUN a variant spelling of **Sumbawa.**

Soenda Islands ('suːndə) PLURAL NOUN a variant spelling of **Sunda Islands.**

Soenda Strait NOUN a variant spelling of **Sunda Strait.**

Soerabaja (ˌsʊərə'baɪə) NOUN a variant spelling of **Surabaya.**

soever (səʊ'ɛvə) ADVERB in any way at all: used to emphasize or make less precise a word or phrase, usually in combination with *what, where, when, how,* etc., or else separated by intervening words. Compare **whatsoever.**

sofa ('səʊfə) NOUN an upholstered seat with back and arms for two or more people.
▷**HISTORY** C17 (in the sense: dais upholstered as a seat): from Arabic *suffah*

sofa bed NOUN a sofa that can be converted into a bed.

sofar ('səʊfɑː) NOUN a system for determining a position at sea, esp that of survivors of a disaster, by exploding a charge underwater at that point. The times taken for the shock waves to travel through the water to three widely separated shore stations are used to calculate their position.
▷**HISTORY** C20: from *so(und) f(ixing) a(nd) r(anging)*

soffit ('sɒfɪt) NOUN 1 the underside of a part of a building or a structural component, such as an arch, beam, stair, etc. 2 Also called: **crown, vertex.** the upper inner surface of a drain or sewer. Compare **invert** (sense 6).
▷**HISTORY** C17: via French from Italian *soffitto,* from Latin *suffixus* something fixed underneath, from *suffigere,* from *sub-* under + *figere* to fasten

Sofia ('səʊfɪə) NOUN the capital of Bulgaria, in the west: colonized by the Romans in 29 A.D.; became capital of Bulgaria in 1879; university (1880). Pop.: 1 122 302 (1999 est.). Ancient name: **Serdica.** Bulgarian name: **Sofiya** ('sɔfiˌja).

S. of Sol. *Bible* ABBREVIATION FOR Song of Solomon.

soft (sɒft) ADJECTIVE 1 easy to dent, work, or cut without shattering; malleable. 2 not hard; giving little or no resistance to pressure or weight. 3 fine, light, smooth, or fluffy to the touch. 4 gentle; tranquil. 5 (of music, sounds, etc.) low and pleasing. 6 (of light, colour, etc.) not excessively bright or harsh. 7 (of a breeze, climate, etc.) temperate, mild, or pleasant. 8 *Dialect* drizzly or rainy: *a soft day; the weather has turned soft.* 9 slightly blurred; not sharply outlined: *soft focus.* 10 (of a diet) consisting of easily digestible foods. 11 kind or lenient, often excessively so. 12 easy to influence or impose upon. 13 prepared to compromise; not doctrinaire: *the soft left.* 14 *Informal* feeble or silly; simple (often in the phrase **soft in the head**). 15 unable to endure hardship, esp through too much pampering. 16 physically out of condition; flabby: *soft muscles.* 17 loving; tender: *soft words.* 18 *Informal* requiring little exertion; easy: *a soft job.* 19 *Chem* (of water) relatively free of mineral salts and therefore easily able to make soap lather. 20 (of a drug such as cannabis) nonaddictive or only mildly addictive. Compare **hard** (sense 19). 21 (of news coverage) concentrating on trivial stories or those with human interest. 22 *Phonetics* **a** an older word for **lenis. b** (not in technical usage) denoting the consonants *c* and *g* in English when they are pronounced as palatal or alveolar fricatives or affricates (s, dʒ, ʃ, ʒ, tʃ) before *e* and *i*, rather than as velar stops (k, g). **c** (in the Slavonic languages) palatalized before a front vowel or a special character (**soft sign**) written as ƅ. 23 **a** unprotected against attack: *a soft target.* **b** *Military* unarmoured, esp as applied to a truck by comparison with a tank. 24 *Finance chiefly US* (of prices, a market, etc.) unstable and tending to decline. 25 (of a currency) in relatively little demand, esp because of a weak balance of payments situation. 26 (of radiation, such as X-rays and ultraviolet radiation) having low energy and not capable of deep penetration of materials. 27 *Physics* (of valves or tubes) only partially evacuated. 28 related to the performance of non-specific, undefinable tasks: *soft skills such as customer services and office support.* 29 **soft on** *or* **about. a** gentle, sympathetic, or lenient towards. **b** feeling affection or infatuation for. ◆ ADVERB 30 in a soft manner: *to speak soft.* ◆ NOUN 31 a soft object, part, or piece. 32 *Informal* See **softie.** ◆ INTERJECTION *Archaic* 33 quiet! 34 wait!
▷HISTORY Old English *sōfte;* related to Old Saxon *sāfti,* Old High German *semfti* gentle
▸ˈ**softly** ADVERB

softa (ˈsɒftə) NOUN a Muslim student of divinity and jurisprudence, esp in Turkey.
▷HISTORY C17: from Turkish, from Persian *sōkhtah* aflame (with love of learning)

softball (ˈsɒftˌbɔːl) NOUN 1 a variation of baseball using a larger softer ball, pitched underhand. 2 the ball used. 3 *Cookery* the stage in the boiling of a sugar syrup at which it may be rubbed into balls after dipping in cold water.

soft-boiled ADJECTIVE 1 (of an egg) boiled for a short time so that the yolk is still soft. 2 *Informal* softhearted.

soft-centred ADJECTIVE (of a chocolate or boiled sweet) having a centre consisting of cream, jelly, etc.

soft chancre NOUN *Pathol* a venereal ulcer caused by an infection with the bacillus *Haemophilus ducrey* that is not syphilitic. Also called: **chancroid.**

soft clam NOUN another name for the **soft-shell clam.**

soft coal NOUN another name for **bituminous coal.**

soft-coated wheaten terrier NOUN a strongly-built medium-sized variety of terrier with a soft, wavy or curly, wheat-coloured coat.

soft commodities PLURAL NOUN nonmetal commodities such as cocoa, sugar, and grains, bought and sold on a futures market. Also called: **softs.**

soft-core ADJECTIVE (of pornography) suggestive and titillating through not being totally explicit or detailed.

soft-cover ADJECTIVE a less common word for **paperback.**

soft drink NOUN a nonalcoholic drink, usually cold.

soften (ˈsɒfᵊn) VERB 1 to make or become soft or softer. 2 to make or become gentler. 3 (*intr*) *Commerce* **a** (of demand, a market, etc.) to weaken. **b** (of a price) to fall.

softener (ˈsɒfᵊnə) NOUN 1 a substance added to another substance to increase its softness, pliability, or plasticity. 2 a substance, such as a zeolite, for softening water.

softening of the brain NOUN an abnormal softening of the tissues of the cerebrum characterized by various degrees of mental impairment.

soften up VERB (*adverb*) 1 to make or become soft. 2 (*tr*) to weaken (an enemy's defences) by shelling, bombing, etc. 3 (*tr*) to weaken the resistance of (a person) by persuasive talk, advances, etc.

soft-finned ADJECTIVE (of certain teleost fishes) having fins that are supported by flexible cartilaginous rays. See also **malacopterygian.** Compare **spiny-finned.**

soft-focus lens NOUN *Photog* a lens designed to produce an image that is uniformly very slightly out of focus: typically used for portrait work.

soft fruit NOUN *Brit* any of various types of small edible stoneless fruit, such as strawberries, raspberries, and currants, borne mainly on low-growing plants or bushes.

soft furnishings PLURAL NOUN *Brit* curtains, hangings, rugs, etc.

soft goods PLURAL NOUN textile fabrics and related merchandise.

soft-headed ADJECTIVE *Informal* feeble-minded; stupid; simple.
▸ˌ**soft-ˈheadedness** NOUN

softhearted (ˌsɒftˈhɑːtɪd) ADJECTIVE easily moved to pity.
▸ˌ**softˈheartedly** ADVERB ▸ˌ**softˈheartedness** NOUN

soft hyphen NOUN a hyphen, used in word processing to divide a word, which prints only when it appears at the end of a line. Also called: **optional hyphen.**

softie *or* **softy** (ˈsɒftɪ) NOUN, *plural* **softies.** *Informal* a person who is sentimental, weakly foolish, or lacking in physical endurance.

soft iron NOUN **a** iron that has a low carbon content and is easily magnetized and demagnetized with a small hysteresis loss. **b** (*as modifier*): *a soft-iron core.*

soft landing NOUN 1 a landing by a spacecraft on the moon or a planet at a sufficiently low velocity for the equipment or occupants to remain unharmed. 2 a decrease in demand that does not result in a country's economy falling into recession. ◆ Compare **hard landing.**

soft lens NOUN a flexible hydrogel lens worn on the surface of the eye to correct defects of vision. Compare **hard lens, gas-permeable lens.**

soft line NOUN a moderate flexible attitude or policy.
▸ˌ**soft-ˈliner** NOUN

soft loan NOUN a loan on which interest is not charged, such as a loan made to an undeveloped country.

softly-softly ADJECTIVE gradual, cautious, and discreet.

soft money NOUN *Politics* (in the US) money that can be spent by a political party on grass-roots organization, recruitment, advertising, etc.; it must be deposited in a party's non-federal (state-level) bank accounts, and must not be used in connection with presidential or congressional elections. Compare **hard money.**

softness (ˈsɒftnɪs) NOUN 1 the quality or an instance of being soft. 2 *Metallurgy* the tendency of a metal to distort easily. Compare **brittleness** (sense 2), **toughness** (sense 2).

soft option NOUN in a number of choices, the one considered to be easy or the easiest to do, involving the least difficulty or exertion.

soft palate NOUN the posterior fleshy portion of the roof of the mouth. It forms a movable muscular flap that seals off the nasopharynx during swallowing and speech.

soft paste NOUN **a** artificial porcelain made from clay, bone ash, etc. **b** (*as modifier*): *softpaste porcelain.*
▷HISTORY C19: from PASTE¹ (in the sense: the mixture from which porcelain is made); so called because of its consistency

soft-pedal VERB **-als, -alling, -alled** *or US* **-als, -aling, -aled.** (*tr*) 1 to mute the tone of (a piano) by depressing the soft pedal. 2 *Informal* to make (something, esp something unpleasant) less obvious by deliberately failing to emphasize or allude to it. ◆ NOUN **soft pedal.** 3 a foot-operated lever on a piano, the left one of two, that either moves the whole action closer to the strings so that the hammers strike with less force or causes fewer of the strings to sound. Compare **sustaining pedal.** See **piano¹.**

soft porn NOUN *Informal* soft-core pornography.

soft release NOUN a means of gradually accustoming wild animals to a new environment before releasing them into it.

soft rot NOUN any of various bacterial or fungal plant diseases characterized by watery disintegration of fruits, roots, etc.

softs (sɒfts) PLURAL NOUN another name for **soft commodities.**

soft science NOUN a science, such as sociology or anthropology, that deals with humans as its principle subject matter, and is therefore not generally considered to be based on rigorous experimentation.

soft sell NOUN a method of selling based on indirect suggestion or inducement. Compare **hard sell.**

soft-shell clam NOUN any of several marine clams of the genus *Mya,* esp *M. arenaria,* an edible species of coastal regions of the US and Europe, having a thin brittle shell. Sometimes shortened to: **soft-shell.** Compare **quahog.**

soft-shell crab NOUN a crab, esp of the edible species *Cancer pagurus,* that has recently moulted and has not yet formed its new shell. Compare **hard-shell crab.**

soft-shelled turtle NOUN any freshwater turtle of the family *Trionychidae,* having a flattened soft shell consisting of bony plates covered by a leathery skin.

soft-shoe NOUN (*modifier*) relating to a type of tap dancing performed wearing soft-soled shoes: *the soft-shoe shuffle.*

soft shoulder *or* **verge** NOUN a soft edge along the side of a road that is unsuitable for vehicles to drive on.

soft skills PLURAL NOUN desirable qualities for certain forms of employment that do not depend on acquired knowledge: they include common sense, the ability to deal with people, and a positive flexible attitude.

soft soap NOUN 1 *Med* another name for **green soap.** 2 *Informal* flattering, persuasive, or cajoling talk. ◆ VERB **soft-soap.** 3 *Informal* to use such talk on (a person).

soft-spoken ADJECTIVE 1 speaking or said with a soft gentle voice. 2 able to persuade or impress by glibness of tongue.

soft spot NOUN a sentimental fondness (esp in the phrase **have a soft spot for**).

soft tissue NOUN the soft parts of the human body as distinct from bone and cartilage.

soft top NOUN a convertible car with a roof made of fabric rather than metal.

soft touch NOUN *Informal* a person easily persuaded or imposed on, esp to lend money.

software (ˈsɒftˌwɛə) NOUN 1 *Computing* the programs that can be used with a particular computer system. Compare **hardware** (sense 2). 2 video cassettes and discs for use with a particular video system.

software house NOUN a commercial organization that specializes in the production of computer software packages.

soft wheat NOUN a type of wheat with soft kernels and a high starch content.

softwood (ˈsɒftˌwʊd) NOUN 1 the open-grained wood of any of numerous coniferous trees, such as pine and cedar, as distinguished from that of a dicotyledonous tree. 2 any tree yielding this wood. ◆ Compare **hardwood.**

SOGAT ('səʊgæt) NOUN (formerly, in Britain) ACRONYM FOR Society of Graphical and Allied Trades.

Sogdian ('sɒgdɪən) NOUN 1 a member of the people who lived in Sogdiana. 2 the language of this people, now almost extinct, belonging to the East Iranian branch of the Indo-European family. ◆ ADJECTIVE 3 of or relating to Sogdiana, its people, or their language.

Sogdiana (ˌsɒgdɪ'ɑːnə) NOUN a region of ancient central Asia. Its chief city was Samarkand.

soggy ('sɒgɪ) ADJECTIVE **-gier, -giest.** 1 soaked with liquid. 2 (of bread, pastry, etc.) moist and heavy. 3 *Informal* lacking in spirit or positiveness.
▷ HISTORY C18: probably from dialect *sog* marsh, of obscure origin
► **'soggily** ADVERB ► **'sogginess** NOUN

soh *or* **so** (səʊ) NOUN *Music* (in tonic sol-fa) the name used for the fifth note or dominant of any scale.
▷ HISTORY C13: see GAMUT

SOHF *Text messaging* ABBREVIATION FOR sense of humour failure.

soho (səʊ'həʊ) INTERJECTION 1 *Hunting* an exclamation announcing the sighting of a hare. 2 an exclamation announcing the discovery of something unexpected.
▷ HISTORY an Anglo-French hunting call, probably of exclamatory origin

Soho ('səʊhəʊ) NOUN a district of central London, in the City of Westminster: a foreign quarter since the late 17th century, now chiefly known for restaurants, nightclubs, striptease clubs, etc.

soi-disant *French* (swadizɑ̃) ADJECTIVE so-called; self-styled.
▷ HISTORY literally: calling oneself

soigné *or feminine* **soignée** ('swɑːnjeɪ; *French* swaɲe) ADJECTIVE well-groomed; elegant.
▷ HISTORY French, from *soigner* to take good care of, of Germanic origin; compare Old Saxon *sunnea* care

soil^{1} (sɔɪl) NOUN 1 the top layer of the land surface of the earth that is composed of disintegrated rock particles, humus, water, and air. See **zonal soil, azonal soil, intrazonal soil, horizon** (senses 4, 5). Related adjective: **telluric.** 2 a type of this material having specific characteristics: *loamy soil.* 3 land, country, or region: *one's native soil.* 4 **the soil.** life and work on a farm; land: *he belonged to the soil, as his forefathers had.* 5 any place or thing encouraging growth or development.
▷ HISTORY C14: from Anglo-Norman, from Latin *solium* a seat, but confused with Latin *solum* the ground

soil^{2} (sɔɪl) VERB 1 to make or become dirty or stained. 2 (*tr*) to pollute with sin or disgrace; sully; defile: *he soiled the family honour by his cowardice.* ◆ NOUN 3 the state or result of soiling. 4 refuse, manure, or excrement.
▷ HISTORY C13: from Old French *soillier* to defile, from *soil* pigsty, probably from Latin *sūs* a swine

soil^{3} (sɔɪl) VERB (*tr*) to feed (livestock) freshly cut green fodder either to fatten or purge them.
▷ HISTORY C17: perhaps from obsolete verb (C16) *soil* to manure, from SOIL^{2} (noun)

soilage ('sɔɪlɪdʒ) NOUN green fodder, esp when freshly cut and fed to livestock in a confined area.

soil bank NOUN (in the US) a federal programme by which farmers are paid to divert land to soil-enriching crops.

soil conservation NOUN the preservation of soil against deterioration or erosion, and the maintenance of the fertilizing elements for crop production.

soil creep NOUN the gradual downhill movement, under the force of gravity, of soil and loose rock material on a slope.

soil mechanics NOUN (*functioning as singular*) the study of the physical properties of soil, esp those properties that affect its ability to bear weight, such as water content, density, strength, etc.

soil pipe NOUN a pipe that conveys sewage or waste water from a toilet, etc., to a soil drain or sewer.

soilure ('sɔɪljə) NOUN *Archaic* 1 the act of soiling or the state of being soiled. 2 a stain or blot.
▷ HISTORY C13: from Old French *soilleure,* from *soillier* to SOIL^{2}

soiree ('swɑːreɪ) NOUN an evening party or other gathering given usually at a private house, esp where guests are invited to listen to, play, or dance to music.
▷ HISTORY C19: from French, from Old French *soir* evening, from Latin *sērum* a late time, from *sērus* late

Soissons (*French* swasɔ̃) NOUN a city in N France, on the Aisne River: has Roman remains and an 11th-century abbey. Pop.: 32 144 (1990).

soixante-neuf *French* (swasɑ̃tnœf) NOUN a sexual activity in which two people simultaneously stimulate each other's genitalia with their mouths. Also called: **sixty-nine.**
▷ HISTORY literally: sixty-nine, from the position adopted by the participants

sojourn ('sɒdʒɜːn, 'sʌdʒ-) NOUN 1 a temporary stay. ◆ VERB 2 (*intr*) to stay or reside temporarily.
▷ HISTORY C13: from Old French *sojorner,* from Vulgar Latin *subdiurnāre* (unattested) to spend a day, from Latin *sub-* during + Late Latin *diurnum* day
► **'sojourner** NOUN

soke (səʊk) NOUN *English legal history* 1 the right to hold a local court. 2 the territory under the jurisdiction of a particular court.
▷ HISTORY C14: from Medieval Latin *sōca,* from Old English *sōcn* a seeking; see SEEK

sokeman ('səʊkmən) NOUN, *plural* **-men.** (in the Danelaw) a freeman enjoying extensive rights, esp over his land.

Sokoto ('səʊkəˌtəʊ) NOUN 1 a state of NW Nigeria. Capital: Sokoto. Pop.: 4 524 162 (1992 est.). Area: 65 735 sq. km (25 380 sq. miles). 2 a town in NW Nigeria, capital of Sokoto state: capital of the Fulah Empire in the 19th century; Muslim place of pilgrimage. Pop.: 204 900 (1997 est.).

Sokotra (sə'kəʊtrə) NOUN a variant spelling of **Socotra.**

sol^{1} (sɒl) NOUN *Music* another name for **soh.**
▷ HISTORY C14: see GAMUT

sol^{2} (səʊl) NOUN 1 short for **new sol.** 2 a former French copper or silver coin, usually worth 12 deniers.
▷ HISTORY C16: from Old French, from Late Latin: SOLIDUS

sol^{3} (sɒl) NOUN a colloid that has a continuous liquid phase, esp one in which a solid is suspended in a liquid.
▷ HISTORY C20: shortened from HYDROSOL

Sol (sɒl) NOUN 1 the Roman god personifying the sun. Greek counterpart: **Helios.** 2 a poetic word for the **sun.**

Sol. ABBREVIATION FOR: 1 Also: **Solr.** solicitor. 2 *Bible* Solomon.

sola *Latin* ('səʊlə) ADJECTIVE the feminine form of **solus.**

solace ('sɒlɪs) NOUN 1 comfort in misery, disappointment, etc. 2 something that gives comfort or consolation. ◆ VERB (*tr*) 3 to give comfort or cheer to (a person) in time of sorrow, distress, etc. 4 to alleviate (sorrow, misery, etc.).
▷ HISTORY C13: from Old French *solas,* from Latin *sōlātium* comfort, from *sōlārī* to console
► **'solacer** NOUN

solan *or* **solan goose** ('səʊlən) NOUN an archaic name for the **gannet.**
▷ HISTORY C15 *soland,* of Scandinavian origin; compare Old Norse *sūla* gannet, *ōnd* duck

solanaceous (ˌsɒlə'neɪʃəs) ADJECTIVE of, relating to, or belonging to the *Solanaceae,* a family of plants having typically tubular flowers with reflexed petals, protruding anthers, and often poisonous or narcotic properties: includes the potato, tobacco, henbane, mandrake, and several nightshades.
▷ HISTORY C19: from New Latin *Sōlānāceae,* from Latin *sōlānum* nightshade

solander (sə'lændə) NOUN a box for botanical specimens, maps, colour plates, etc., made in the form of a book, the front cover being the lid.
▷ HISTORY C18: named after D. D. *Solander* (1736–82), Swedish botanist

solanine ('səʊləˌnaɪn) NOUN a poisonous alkaloid found in various solanaceous plants, including potatoes which have gone green through exposure to light.
▷ HISTORY C19: from SOLAN(UM) + -INE^{2}

solanum (səʊ'leɪnəm) NOUN any tree, shrub, or herbaceous plant of the mainly tropical solanaceous genus *Solanum:* includes the potato, aubergine, and certain nightshades.
▷ HISTORY C16: from Latin: nightshade

solar ('səʊlə) ADJECTIVE 1 of or relating to the sun: *solar eclipse.* 2 operating by or utilizing the energy of the sun: *solar cell.* 3 *Astronomy* determined from the motion of the earth relative to the sun: *solar year.* 4 *Astrology* subject to the influence of the sun.
▷ HISTORY C15: from Latin *sōlāris,* from *sōl* the sun

solar apex NOUN another name for **apex** (sense 4).

solar cell NOUN a photovoltaic cell that produces electricity from the sun's rays, used esp in spacecraft.

solar constant NOUN the rate at which the sun's energy is received per unit area at the top of the earth's atmosphere when the sun is at its mean distance from the earth and atmospheric absorption has been corrected for. Its value is 1367 watts per square metre.

solar day NOUN See **day** (sense 6).

solar eclipse NOUN See **eclipse** (sense 1).

solar energy NOUN energy obtained from solar power.

solar flare NOUN a brief powerful eruption of particles and intense electromagnetic radiation from the sun's surface, associated with sunspots and causing disturbances to radio communication on earth. Sometimes shortened to: **flare.** See also **solar wind.**

solar furnace NOUN a furnace utilizing the sun as a heat source, sunlight being concentrated at the focus of a system of concave mirrors.

solar heating NOUN heat radiation from the sun collected by heat-absorbing panels through which water is circulated: used for domestic hot water, central heating, and heating swimming pools.

solarimeter (ˌsəʊlə'rɪmɪtə) NOUN any of various instruments for measuring solar radiation, as by use of a bolometer or thermopile. Also called: **pyranometer.**

solarism ('səʊləˌrɪzəm) NOUN the explanation of myths in terms of the movements and influence of the sun.
► **'solarist** NOUN

solarium (səʊ'lɛərɪəm) NOUN, *plural* **-lariums** *or* **-laria** (-'lɛərɪə). 1 a room built largely of glass to afford exposure to the sun. 2 a bed equipped with ultraviolet lights used for acquiring an artificial suntan. 3 an establishment offering such facilities.
▷ HISTORY C19: from Latin: a terrace, from *sōl* sun

solarize *or* **solarise** ('səʊləˌraɪz) VERB (*tr*) 1 to treat by exposure to the sun's rays. 2 *Photog* to reverse some of the tones of (a negative or print) and introduce pronounced outlines of highlights, by exposing it briefly to light after developing and washing, and then redeveloping. 3 to expose (a patient) to the therapeutic effects of solar or ultraviolet light.
► **ˌsolari'zation** *or* **ˌsolari'sation** NOUN

solar mass NOUN an astronomical unit of mass equal to the sun's mass, 1.981×10^{30} kilograms. Symbol: $M_{\odot}$.

solar month NOUN See **month** (sense 4).

solar myth NOUN a myth explaining or allegorizing the origin or movement of the sun.

solar panel NOUN a panel exposed to radiation from the sun, used to heat water or, when mounted with solar cells, to produce electricity direct, esp for powering instruments in satellites.

solar plexus NOUN 1 *Anatomy* the network of sympathetic nerves situated behind the stomach that supply the abdominal organs. Also called: **coeliac plexus.** 2 (*not in technical usage*) the part of the stomach beneath the diaphragm; pit of the stomach.
▷ HISTORY C18: referring to resemblance between the radial network of nerves and ganglia and the rays of the sun

solar power NOUN heat radiation from the sun converted into electrical power.

solar system NOUN the system containing the sun and the bodies held in its gravitational field, including the planets (Mercury, Venus, Earth, Mars,

Jupiter, Saturn, Uranus, Neptune, Pluto), the asteroids, and comets.

solar wind (wɪnd) NOUN the constant stream of charged particles, esp protons and electrons, emitted by the sun at high velocities, its density and speed varying during periods of solar activity. It interacts with the earth's magnetic field, some of the particles being trapped by the magnetic lines of force, and causes auroral displays. See also **Van Allen belt, magnetosphere.**

solar year NOUN See **year** (sense 4).

solation (səʊˈleɪʃən) NOUN *Chem* the liquefaction of a gel.

solatium (səʊˈleɪʃɪəm) NOUN, *plural* **-tia** (-ʃɪə). *Law chiefly US and Scot* compensation awarded to a party for injury to the feelings as distinct from physical suffering and pecuniary loss.
▷HISTORY C19: from Latin: see SOLACE

sold (səʊld) VERB 1 the past tense and past participle of **sell.** ◆ ADJECTIVE 2 **sold on.** *Slang* uncritically attached to or enthusiastic about.

soldan (ˈsəʊldən, ˈsɒl-) NOUN an archaic word for **sultan.**
▷HISTORY C13: via Old French from Arabic: SULTAN

solder (ˈsɒldə; *US* ˈsɒdər) NOUN 1 an alloy for joining two metal surfaces by melting the alloy so that it forms a thin layer between the surfaces. **Soft solders** are alloys of lead and tin; **brazing solders** are alloys of copper and zinc. 2 something that joins things together firmly; a bond. ◆ VERB 3 to join or mend or be joined or mended with or as if with solder.
▷HISTORY C14: via Old French from Latin *solidāre* to strengthen, from *solidus* SOLID
▸ˈ**solderable** ADJECTIVE ▸ˈ**solderer** NOUN

soldering iron NOUN a hand tool consisting of a handle fixed to a copper tip that is heated, electrically or in a flame, and used to melt and apply solder.

soldier (ˈsəʊldʒə) NOUN 1 **a** a person who serves or has served in an army. **b** Also called: **common soldier.** a noncommissioned member of an army as opposed to a commissioned officer. 2 a person who works diligently for a cause. 3 a low-ranking member of the Mafia or other organized crime ring. 4 *Zoology* **a** an individual in a colony of social insects, esp ants, that has powerful jaws adapted for defending the colony, crushing large food particles, etc. **b** (*as modifier*): *soldier ant.* 5 *Informal* a strip of bread or toast that is dipped into a soft-boiled egg. ◆ VERB (*intr*) 6 to serve as a soldier. 7 *Obsolete slang* to malinger or shirk.
▷HISTORY C13: from Old French *soudier,* from *soude* (army) pay, from Late Latin *solidus* a gold coin, from Latin: firm

soldier beetle NOUN a yellowish-red cantharid beetle, *Rhagonycha fulva,* having a somewhat elongated body.

soldier bird NOUN *Austral* another name for **noisy miner.**

soldier crab NOUN a small blue Australian estuarine crab of the *Mictyris* genus usually found in large numbers.

soldierly (ˈsəʊldʒəlɪ) ADJECTIVE of or befitting a good soldier.
▸ˈ**soldierliness** NOUN

soldier of fortune NOUN a man who seeks money or adventure as a soldier; mercenary.

soldier on VERB (*intr, adverb*) to persist in one's efforts in spite of difficulties, pressure, etc.

soldier orchid NOUN a European orchid, *Orchis militaris,* having pale purple flowers with a four-lobed lower lip. Also called: **military orchid.**
▷HISTORY from an imagined resemblance to a soldier

soldier settlement NOUN *Austral* the allocation of Crown land for farming to ex-servicemen.
▸**soldier settler** NOUN

soldiery (ˈsəʊldʒərɪ) NOUN, *plural* **-dieries.** 1 soldiers collectively. 2 a group of soldiers. 3 the profession of being a soldier.

soldo (ˈsɒldəʊ; *Italian* ˈsoldo) NOUN, *plural* **-di** (-diː; *Italian* -di). a former Italian copper coin worth one twentieth of a lira.
▷HISTORY C16: from Italian, from Late Latin *solidum* a gold coin; see SOLDIER

sole[1] (səʊl) ADJECTIVE 1 (*prenominal*) being the only one; only. 2 (*prenominal*) of or relating to one individual or group and no other: *sole rights on a patent.* 3 *Law* having no wife or husband. See also **feme sole.** 4 an archaic word for **solitary.**
▷HISTORY C14: from Old French *soule,* from Latin *sōlus* alone
▸ˈ**soleness** NOUN

sole[2] (səʊl) NOUN 1 the underside of the foot. Related adjectives: **plantar, volar.** 2 the underside of a shoe. 3 **a** the bottom of a furrow. **b** the bottom of a plough. 4 the underside of a golf-club head. 5 the bottom of an oven, furnace, etc. ◆ VERB (*tr*) 6 to provide (a shoe) with a sole. 7 *Golf* to rest (the club) on the ground, as when preparing to make a stroke.
▷HISTORY C14: via Old French from Latin *solea* sandal; probably related to *solum* the ground
▸ˈ**soleless** ADJECTIVE

sole[3] (səʊl) NOUN, *plural* **sole** *or* **soles.** 1 any tongue-shaped flatfish of the family *Soleidae,* esp *Solea solea* (**European sole**): most common in warm seas and highly valued as food fishes. 2 any of certain other similar fishes.
▷HISTORY C14: via Old French from Vulgar Latin *sola* (unattested), from Latin *solea* a sandal (from the fish's shape)

solecism (ˈsɒlɪˌsɪzəm) NOUN 1 **a** the nonstandard use of a grammatical construction. **b** any mistake, incongruity, or absurdity. 2 a violation of good manners.
▷HISTORY C16: from Latin *soloecismus,* from Greek *soloikismos,* from *soloikos* speaking incorrectly, from *Soloi* an Athenian colony of Cilicia where the inhabitants spoke a corrupt form of Greek
▸ˈ**solecist** NOUN ▸ˌ**soleˈcistic** *or* ˌ**soleˈcistical** ADJECTIVE ▸ˌ**soleˈcistically** ADVERB

solely (ˈsəʊllɪ) ADVERB 1 only; completely; entirely. 2 without another or others; singly; alone. 3 for one thing only.

solemn (ˈsɒləm) ADJECTIVE 1 characterized or marked by seriousness or sincerity: *a solemn vow.* 2 characterized by pomp, ceremony, or formality. 3 serious, glum, or pompous. 4 inspiring awe: *a solemn occasion.* 5 performed with religious ceremony. 6 gloomy or sombre: *solemn colours.*
▷HISTORY C14: from Old French *solempne,* from Latin *sōllemnis* appointed, perhaps from *sollus* whole
▸ˈ**solemnly** ADVERB ▸ˈ**solemnness** *or* ˈ**solemness** NOUN

solemnify (səˈlɛmnɪˌfaɪ) VERB **-fies, -fying, -fied.** (*tr*) to make serious or grave.
▸**soˌlemnifiˈcation** NOUN

solemnity (səˈlɛmnɪtɪ) NOUN, *plural* **-ties.** 1 the state or quality of being solemn. 2 (*often plural*) solemn ceremony, observance, celebration, etc. 3 *Law* a formality necessary to validate a deed, act, contract, etc.

solemnize *or* **solemnise** (ˈsɒləmˌnaɪz) VERB (*tr*) 1 to celebrate or observe with rites or formal ceremonies, as a religious occasion. 2 to celebrate or perform the ceremony of (marriage). 3 to make solemn or serious. 4 to perform or hold (ceremonies, etc.) in due manner.
▸ˌ**solemniˈzation** *or* ˌ**solemniˈsation** NOUN ▸ˈ**solemˌnizer** *or* ˈ**solemˌniser** NOUN

Solemn League and Covenant NOUN See **Covenant.**

solenette (ˈsəʊləˌnɛt, ˈsəʊlˌnɛt) NOUN a small European sole, *Buglossidium luteum,* up to 13 cm (5 in.) in length; not caught commercially.
▷HISTORY SOLE[3] + -ETTE

solenodon (səˈlɛnədən) NOUN either of two rare shrewlike nocturnal mammals of the Caribbean, *Atopogale cubana* (**Cuban solenodon**) or *Solenodon paradoxus* (**Haitian solenodon**), having a long hairless tail and an elongated snout: family *Solenodontidae,* order *Insectivora* (insectivores).
▷HISTORY C19: from New Latin, from Latin *sōlēn* sea mussel, razor-shell (from Greek: pipe) + Greek *odōn* tooth

solenoid (ˈsəʊlɪˌnɔɪd) NOUN 1 a coil of wire, usually cylindrical, in which a magnetic field is set up by passing a current through it. 2 a coil of wire, partially surrounding an iron core, that is made to move inside the coil by the magnetic field set up by a current: used to convert electrical to mechanical energy, as in the operation of a switch. 3 such a device used as a relay, as in a motor vehicle for connecting the battery directly to the starter motor when activated by the ignition switch.
▷HISTORY C19: from French *solénoïde,* from Greek *sōlēn* a pipe, tube
▸ˌ**soleˈnoidal** ADJECTIVE ▸ˌ**soleˈnoidally** ADVERB

Solent (ˈsəʊlənt) NOUN **the.** a strait of the English Channel between the coast of Hampshire, on the English mainland, and the Isle of Wight. Width: up to 6 km (4 miles).

solera (səˈlɛərə) NOUN **a** a system for aging sherry and other fortified wines, in which younger wines in upper rows of casks are used to top up casks of older wines stored below in order to produce a consistently aged blend. **b** a blend of sherry produced by this system.
▷HISTORY Spanish, literally: bottom

Soleure (sɔlœr) NOUN the French name for **Solothurn.**

sol-fa (ˈsɒlˈfɑː) NOUN 1 short for **tonic sol-fa.** ◆ VERB **-fas, -faing, -faed.** 2 *US* to use tonic sol-fa syllables in singing (a tune).
▷HISTORY C16: see GAMUT

solfatara (ˌsɒlfəˈtɑːrə) NOUN a volcanic vent emitting only sulphurous gases and water vapour or sometimes hot mud.
▷HISTORY C18: from Italian: a sulphurous volcano near Naples, from *solfo* SULPHUR
▸ˌ**solfaˈtaric** ADJECTIVE

solfeggio (sɒlˈfɛdʒɪəʊ) *or* **solfège** (sɒlˈfɛʒ) NOUN, *plural* **-feggi** (-ˈfɛdʒiː), **-feggios** *or* **-fèges.** *Music* 1 a voice exercise in which runs, scales, etc., are sung to the same syllable or syllables. 2 solmization, esp the French or Italian system, in which the names correspond to the notes of the scale of C major.
▷HISTORY C18: from Italian *solfeggiare* to use the syllables sol-fa; see GAMUT

solferino (ˌsɒlfəˈriːnəʊ) NOUN **a** a moderate purplish-red colour. **b** (*as adjective*): *a solferino suit.*
▷HISTORY C19: from a dye discovered in 1859, the year a battle was fought at *Solferino,* a town in Italy

soli (ˈsəʊlɪ) ADJECTIVE, ADVERB *Music* (of a piece or passage) to be performed by or with soloists. Compare **tutti.**
▷HISTORY plural of SOLO

solicit (səˈlɪsɪt) VERB **-its, -iting, -ited.** 1 (when *intr,* foll by *for*) to make a request, application, or entreaty to (a person for business, support, etc.). 2 to accost (a person) with an offer of sexual relations in return for money. 3 to provoke or incite (a person) to do something wrong or illegal.
▷HISTORY C15: from Old French *solliciter* to disturb, from Latin *sollicitāre* to harass, from *sollicitus* agitated, from *sollus* whole + *citus,* from *ciēre* to excite
▸**soˌliciˈtation** NOUN

solicitor (səˈlɪsɪtə) NOUN 1 (in Britain) a lawyer who advises clients on matters of law, draws up legal documents, prepares cases for barristers, etc., and who may represent clients in certain courts. Compare **barrister.** 2 (in the US) an officer responsible for the legal affairs of a town, city, etc. 3 a person who solicits.
▸**soˈlicitorship** NOUN

Solicitor General NOUN, *plural* **Solicitors General.** 1 (in Britain) the law officer of the Crown ranking next to the Attorney General (in Scotland to the Lord Advocate) and acting as his assistant. 2 (in New Zealand) the government's chief lawyer: head of the Crown Law Office and prosecutor for the Crown.

solicitous (səˈlɪsɪtəs) ADJECTIVE 1 showing consideration, concern, attention, etc. 2 keenly anxious or willing; eager.
▷HISTORY C16: from Latin *sollicitus* anxious; see SOLICIT
▸**soˈlicitously** ADVERB ▸**soˈlicitousness** NOUN

solicitude (səˈlɪsɪˌtjuːd) NOUN 1 the state or quality of being solicitous. 2 (*often plural*) something that causes anxiety or concern. 3 anxiety or concern.

solid (ˈsɒlɪd) ADJECTIVE 1 of, concerned with, or being a substance in a physical state in which it resists changes in size and shape. Compare **liquid** (sense 1), **gas** (sense 1). 2 consisting of matter all through. 3 of the same substance all through: *solid rock.* 4 sound; proved or provable: *solid facts.* 5 reliable or sensible; upstanding: *a solid citizen.* 6 firm, strong, compact, or substantial: *a solid table;*

solid ground. [7] (of a meal or food) substantial. [8] (*often postpositive*) without interruption or respite; continuous: *solid bombardment.* [9] financially sound or solvent: *a solid institution.* [10] strongly linked or consolidated: *a solid relationship.* [11] *Geometry* having or relating to three dimensions: *a solid figure; solid geometry.* [12] (of a word composed of two or more other words or elements) written or printed as a single word without a hyphen. [13] *Printing* with no space or leads between lines of type. [14] **solid for.** unanimously in favour of. [15] (of a writer, work, performance, etc.) adequate; sensible. [16] of or having a single uniform colour or tone. [17] *NZ informal* excessive; unreasonably expensive. ◆ NOUN [18] *Geometry* **a** a closed surface in three-dimensional space. **b** such a surface together with the volume enclosed by it. [19] a solid substance, such as wood, iron, or diamond.
▷HISTORY C14: from Old French *solide,* from Latin *solidus* firm; related to Latin *sollus* whole
▸**solidity** (sə'lɪdɪtɪ) NOUN ▸**'solidly** ADVERB ▸**'solidness** NOUN

solidago (ˌsɒlɪ'deɪɡəʊ) NOUN, *plural* **-gos.** any plant of the chiefly American genus *Solidago,* which includes the goldenrods: family *Asteraceae* (composites).
▷HISTORY C18: via New Latin from Medieval Latin *soldago* a plant reputed to have healing properties, from *soldāre* to strengthen, from Latin *solidāre,* from *solidus* SOLID

solid angle NOUN a geometric surface consisting of lines originating from a common point (the vertex) and passing through a closed curve or polygon: measured in steradians.

solidarity (ˌsɒlɪ'dærɪtɪ) NOUN, *plural* **-ties.** unity of interests, sympathies, etc., as among members of the same class.

Solidarity (ˌsɒlɪ'dærɪtɪ) NOUN the organization of free trade unions in Poland: recognized in 1980; outlawed in 1982; legalized and led the new noncommunist government in 1989.
▷HISTORY C20: from Polish *solidarność*: solidarity

solidary ('sɒlɪdərɪ, -drɪ) ADJECTIVE marked by unity of interests, responsibilities, etc.
▷HISTORY C19: from French *solidaire,* from *solide* SOLID

solid fuel NOUN [1] a domestic or industrial fuel, such as coal or coke, that is a solid rather than an oil or gas. [2] Also called: **solid propellant.** a rocket fuel that is a solid rather than a liquid or a gas.

solid geometry NOUN the branch of geometry concerned with the properties of three-dimensional geometric figures.

solidify (sə'lɪdɪˌfaɪ) VERB **-fies, -fying, -fied.** [1] to make or become solid or hard. [2] to make or become strong, united, determined, etc.
▸**so'lidiˌfiable** ADJECTIVE ▸**soˌlidifi'cation** NOUN
▸**so'lidiˌfier** NOUN

solid injection NOUN injection of fuel directly into the cylinder of an internal-combustion engine without the assistance of an air blast to atomize the fuel. Also called (in a petrol engine): **direct injection.** Compare **blast injection.**

solid solution NOUN *Chem* a crystalline material in which two or more elements or compounds share a common lattice.

solid-state NOUN [1] (*modifier*) (of an electronic device) activated by a semiconductor component in which current flow is through solid material rather than in a vacuum. [2] (*modifier*) of, concerned with, characteristic of, or consisting of solid matter.

solid-state physics NOUN (*functioning as singular*) the branch of physics concerned with experimental and theoretical investigations of the properties of solids, such as superconductivity, photoconductivity, and ferromagnetism.

solidus ('sɒlɪdəs) NOUN, *plural* **-di** (-ˌdaɪ). [1] Also called: **diagonal, separatrix, shilling mark, slash, stroke, virgule.** a short oblique stroke used in text to separate items of information, such as days, months, and years in dates (*18/7/80*), alternative words (*and/or*), numerator from denominator in fractions (*55/103*), etc. [2] a gold coin of the Byzantine empire.
▷HISTORY C14: from Late Latin *solidus* (*nummus*) a gold coin (from *solidus* solid); in Medieval Latin, *solidus* referred to a shilling and was indicated by a long *s,* which ultimately became the virgule

solifidian (ˌsɒlɪ'fɪdɪən) NOUN *Christianity* a person who maintains that man is justified by faith alone.
▷HISTORY C16: from New Latin *sōlifidius,* from Latin *sōlus* sole + *fides* faith
▸**ˌsoli'fidianˌism** NOUN

solifluction *or* **solifluxion** ('sɒlɪˌflʌkʃən, 'səʊlɪ-) NOUN slow downhill movement of soil, saturated with meltwater, over a permanently frozen subsoil in tundra regions.
▷HISTORY C20: from Latin *solum* soil + *fluctio* act of flowing

Solihull (ˌsəʊlɪ'hʌl) NOUN [1] a town in central England, in Solihull unitary authority in the S West Midlands near Birmingham: mainly residential. Pop.: 94 531 (1991). [2] a unitary authority in central England, in the West Midlands. Pop.: 199 521 (2001). Area: 180 sq. km (70 sq. miles).

soliloquize *or* **soliloquise** (sə'lɪləˌkwaɪz) VERB (*intr*) to utter a soliloquy.
▸**soliloquist** (sə'lɪləkwɪst) *or* **so'liloˌquizer** *or* **so'liloˌquiser** NOUN

soliloquy (sə'lɪləkwɪ) NOUN, *plural* **-quies.** [1] the act of speaking alone or to oneself, esp as a theatrical device. [2] a speech in a play that is spoken in soliloquy: *Hamlet's first soliloquy.*
▷HISTORY C17: via Late Latin *sōliloquium,* from Latin *sōlus* sole + *loquī* to speak

> **Language note** *Soliloquy* is sometimes wrongly used where *monologue* is meant. Both words refer to a long speech by one person, but a *monologue* can be addressed to other people, whereas in a *soliloquy* the speaker is always talking to himself or herself.

Solimões (suli'mõəʃ) NOUN **the.** the Brazilian name for the Amazon from the Peruvian border to the Rio Negro.

Solingen (*German* 'zo:lɪŋən) NOUN a city in W Germany, in North Rhine-Westphalia: a major European centre of the cutlery industry. Pop.: 165 400 (1999 est.).

solipsism ('sɒlɪpˌsɪzəm) NOUN *Philosophy* the extreme form of scepticism which denies the possibility of any knowledge other than of one's own existence.
▷HISTORY C19: from Latin *sōlus* alone + *ipse* self
▸**'solipsist** NOUN, ADJECTIVE ▸**ˌsolip'sistic** ADJECTIVE

solitaire ('sɒlɪˌtɛə, ˌsɒlɪ'tɛə) NOUN [1] Also called: **pegboard.** a game played by one person, esp one involving moving and taking pegs in a pegboard or marbles on an indented circular board with the object of being left with only one. [2] the US name for **patience** (the card game). [3] a gem, esp a diamond, set alone in a ring. [4] any of several extinct birds of the genus *Pezophaps,* related to the dodo. [5] any of several dull grey North American songbirds of the genus *Myadestes:* subfamily *Turdinae* (thrushes).
▷HISTORY C18: from Old French: SOLITARY

solitary ('sɒlɪtərɪ, -trɪ) ADJECTIVE [1] following or enjoying a life of solitude: *a solitary disposition.* [2] experienced or performed alone: *a solitary walk.* [3] (of a place) unfrequented. [4] (*prenominal*) single; sole: *a solitary speck in the sky.* [5] having few companions; lonely. [6] (of animals) not living in organized colonies or large groups: *solitary bees; a solitary elephant.* Compare **social** (sense 7), **gregarious** (sense 2). [7] (of flowers) growing singly. ◆ NOUN, *plural* **-taries.** [8] a person who lives in seclusion; hermit; recluse. [9] *Informal* short for **solitary confinement.**
▷HISTORY C14: from Latin *sōlitārius,* from *sōlus* SOLE[1]
▸**'solitarily** ADVERB ▸**'solitariness** NOUN

solitary confinement NOUN isolation imposed on a prisoner, as by confinement in a special cell.

soliton ('sɒlɪˌtɒn) NOUN *Physics* an isolated particle-like wave that is a solution of certain equations for propagation, occurring when two solitary waves do not change their form after collision and subsequently travelling for considerable distances.
▷HISTORY C20: from *solit(ary)* + -ON

solitude ('sɒlɪˌtju:d) NOUN [1] the state of being solitary or secluded. [2] *Poetic* a solitary place.
▷HISTORY C14: from Latin *sōlitūdō,* from *sōlus* alone, SOLE[1]

▸**ˌsoli'tudinous** ADJECTIVE

solleret (ˌsɒlə'rɛt) NOUN a protective covering for the foot consisting of riveted plates of armour.
▷HISTORY C19: from French, diminutive of Old French *soller* shoe, from Late Latin *subtēl* arch beneath the foot, from SUB- + *tālus* ankle

sollicker ('sɒlɪkə) NOUN *Austral slang* something very large.
▷HISTORY C19: from English dialect

solmization *or* **solmisation** (ˌsɒlmɪ'zeɪʃən) NOUN *Music* a system of naming the notes of a scale by syllables instead of letters derived from the 11th-century hexachord system of Guido d'Arezzo, which assigns the names *ut* (or *do*), *re, mi, fa, sol, la, si* (or *ti*) to the degrees of the major scale of C (**fixed system**) or (excluding the syllables *ut* and *si*) to the major scale in any key (**movable system**). See also **tonic sol-fa.**
▷HISTORY C18: from French *solmisation,* from *solmiser* to use the sol-fa syllables, from SOL[1] + MI

solo ('səʊləʊ) NOUN, *plural* **-los.** [1] (*plural* **-los** *or* **-li** (-li:)) a musical composition for one performer with or without accompaniment. [2] any of various card games in which each person plays on his own instead of in partnership with another, such as solo whist. [3] a flight in which an aircraft pilot is unaccompanied. [4] **a** any performance, mountain climb, or other undertaking carried out by an individual without assistance from others. **b** (*as modifier*): *a solo attempt.* ◆ ADJECTIVE [5] *Music* unaccompanied: *a sonata for cello solo.* ◆ ADVERB [6] by oneself; alone: *to fly solo.* ◆ VERB [7] to undertake a venture alone, esp to operate an aircraft alone or climb alone.
▷HISTORY C17: via Italian from Latin *sōlus* alone, SOLE[1]

soloist ('səʊləʊɪst) NOUN a person who performs a solo.

Solo man NOUN a type of early man, *Homo soloensis,* of late Pleistocene times, having a skull resembling that of Neanderthal man but with a smaller cranial capacity.
▷HISTORY C20: after *Solo,* site in central Java where remains were found

Solomon ('sɒləmən) NOUN 10th century B.C., king of Israel, son of David and Bathsheba, credited with great wisdom.
▸**Solomonic** (ˌsɒlə'mɒnɪk) *or* **Solomonian** (ˌsɒlə'məʊnɪən) ADJECTIVE

Solomon Gundy ('sɒləmən 'ɡʌndɪ) NOUN *Canadian* a dish of salted marinated herring in vinegar and spices.
▷HISTORY from SALMAGUNDI

Solomon Islands PLURAL NOUN an independent state in the SW Pacific comprising an archipelago extending for almost 1450 km (900 miles) in a northwest–southeast direction: the northernmost islands of the archipelago (Buka and Bougainville) form part of Papua New Guinea; the main islands are Guadalcanal, Malaita, San Cristobal, New Georgia, Santa Isabel, and Choiseul: a member of the Commonwealth. Official language: English. Religion: Christian majority. Currency: Solomon Islands dollar. Capital: Honiara. Pop.: 480 000 (2001 est.). Area: 29 785 sq. km (11 500 sq. miles).

Solomon Islands Pidgin NOUN the variety of Neo-Melanesian spoken in the Solomon Islands and neighbouring islands.

Solomon's seal NOUN [1] another name for **Star of David.** [2] any of several liliaceous plants of the genus *Polygonatum* of N temperate regions, having greenish or yellow paired flowers, long narrow waxy leaves, and a thick underground stem with prominent leaf scars.
▷HISTORY C16: translation of Medieval Latin *sigillum Solomonis,* perhaps referring to the resemblance of the leaf scars to seals

solo mother NOUN *NZ* a mother with a dependent child or dependent children and no husband.

solonchak (ˌsɒlən'tʃæk) NOUN a type of intrazonal soil of arid regions with a greyish surface crust: contains large quantities of soluble salts.
▷HISTORY Russian, literally: salt marsh

solonetz *or* **solonets** (ˌsɒlə'nets) NOUN a type of intrazonal soil with a high saline content characterized by leaching.

▷**HISTORY** Russian *solonets* salt not obtained through decoction

so long SENTENCE SUBSTITUTE *Informal* farewell; goodbye.

solo parent NOUN *NZ* the usual name for **single parent**.

solo stop NOUN any of various organ stops designed to imitate a solo performance on a particular musical instrument.

Solothurn (*German* 'zo:loturn) NOUN 1 a canton of NW Switzerland. Capital: Solothurn. Pop.: 243 900 (2000 est.). Area: 793 sq. km (306 sq. miles). 2 a town in NW Switzerland, capital of Solothurn canton, on the Aare River. Pop.: 15 480 (1990 est.). ◆ French name: **Soleure**.

solo whist NOUN a version of whist for four players acting independently, each of whom may bid to win or lose a fixed number of tricks before play starts, trumps having usually been decided by cutting.

solstice ('sɒlstɪs) NOUN 1 either the shortest day of the year (**winter solstice**) or the longest day of the year (**summer solstice**). 2 either of the two points on the ecliptic at which the sun is overhead at the tropic of Cancer or Capricorn at the summer and winter solstices.
▷**HISTORY** C13: via Old French from Latin *sōlstitium*, literally: the (apparent) standing still of the sun, from *sōl* sun + *sistere* to stand still
▸**solstitial** (sɒl'stɪʃəl) ADJECTIVE

solubility (ˌsɒlju'bɪlɪtɪ) NOUN, *plural* **-ties**. 1 the ability of a substance to dissolve; the quality of being soluble. 2 a measure of this ability for a particular substance in a particular solvent, equal to the quantity of substance dissolving in a fixed quantity of solvent to form a saturated solution under specified temperature and pressure. It is expressed in grams per cubic decametre, grams per hundred grams of solvent, moles per mole, etc.

solubilize *or* **solubilise** ('sɒljubɪˌlaɪz) VERB to make or become soluble, as in the addition of detergents to fats to make them dissolve in water.

soluble ('sɒljubᵊl) ADJECTIVE 1 (of a substance) capable of being dissolved, esp easily dissolved in some solvent, usually water. 2 capable of being solved or answered.
▷**HISTORY** C14: from Late Latin *solūbilis*, from Latin *solvere* to dissolve
▸'**solubleness** NOUN ▸'**solubly** ADVERB

soluble glass NOUN another name for **sodium silicate** (sense 1).

soluble RNA NOUN another name for **transfer RNA**.

solum ('səuləm) NOUN, *plural* **-lums** *or* **-la** (-lə). the upper layers of the soil profile, affected by climate and vegetation.
▷**HISTORY** C19: New Latin from Latin: the ground

solus ('səuləs) ADJECTIVE 1 alone; separate. 2 of or denoting the position of an advertising poster or press advertisement that is separated from competing advertisements: *a solus position*. 3 of or denoting a retail outlet, such as a petrol station, that sells the products of one company exclusively: *a solus site*. 4 (*feminine* **sola**) alone; by oneself (formerly used in stage directions).
▷**HISTORY** C17: from Latin *sōlus* alone

solute (sɒ'lju:t) NOUN 1 the component of a solution that changes its state in forming the solution or the component that is not present in excess; the substance that is dissolved in another substance. Compare **solvent**. ◆ ADJECTIVE 2 *Botany, now rare* loose or unattached; free.
▷**HISTORY** C16: from Latin *solūtus* free, unfettered, from *solvere* to release

solution (sə'lu:ʃən) NOUN 1 a homogeneous mixture of two or more substances in which the molecules or atoms of the substances are completely dispersed. The constituents can be solids, liquids, or gases. 2 the act or process of forming a solution. 3 the state of being dissolved (esp in the phrase **in solution**). 4 a mixture of two or more substances in which one or more components are present as small particles with colloidal dimension; colloid: *a colloidal solution*. 5 a specific answer to or way of answering a problem. 6 the act or process of solving a problem. 7 *Maths* **a** the unique set of values that yield a true statement when substituted for the variables in an equation. **b** a member of a set of assignments of values to variables under which a given statement is satisfied; a member of a solution set. 8 the stage of a disease, following a crisis, resulting in its termination. 9 *Law* the payment, discharge, or satisfaction of a claim, debt, etc.
▷**HISTORY** C14: from Latin *solūtiō* an unloosing, from *solūtus*; see SOLUTE

solution set NOUN another name for **truth set**.

Solutrean (sə'lu:trɪən) ADJECTIVE of or relating to an Upper Palaeolithic culture of Europe that was characterized by leaf-shaped flint blades.
▷**HISTORY** C19: named after *Solutré*, village in central France where traces of this culture were originally found

solvable ('sɒlvəbᵊl) ADJECTIVE another word for **soluble** (sense 2).
▸ˌ**solva'bility** *or* '**solvableness** NOUN

solvate ('sɒlveɪt) VERB *Chem* to undergo, cause to undergo, or partake in solvation.
▷**HISTORY** C20: from SOLVENT

solvation (sɒl'veɪʃən) NOUN the process in which there is some chemical association between the molecules of a solute and those of the solvent. An example is an aqueous solution of copper sulphate which contains complex ions of the type $[Cu(H_2O)_4]^{2+}$.

Solvay process ('sɒlveɪ) NOUN an industrial process for manufacturing sodium carbonate. Carbon dioxide is passed into a solution of sodium chloride saturated with ammonia. Sodium bicarbonate is precipitated and heated to form the carbonate.
▷**HISTORY** C19: named after Ernest *Solvay* (1838–1922), Belgian chemist who invented a process using salt, limestone, and ammonia

solve (sɒlv) VERB (*tr*) 1 to find the explanation for or solution to (a mystery, problem, etc.). 2 *Maths* **a** to work out the answer to (a problem). **b** to obtain the roots of (an equation).
▷**HISTORY** C15: from Latin *solvere* to loosen, release, free from debt
▸'**solver** NOUN

solvency ('sɒlvənsɪ) NOUN ability to pay all debts.

solvent ('sɒlvənt) ADJECTIVE 1 capable of meeting financial obligations. 2 (of a substance, esp a liquid) capable of dissolving another substance. ◆ NOUN 3 a liquid capable of dissolving another substance: *water is a solvent for salt*. 4 the component of a solution that does not change its state in forming the solution or the component that is present in excess. Compare **solute**. 5 something that solves.
▷**HISTORY** C17: from Latin *solvēns* releasing, from *solvere* to free, SOLVE
▸'**solvently** ADVERB

solvent abuse NOUN the deliberate inhaling of intoxicating fumes given off by certain solvents such as toluene. See also **glue-sniffing**.

solvolysis (sɒl'vɒlɪsɪs) NOUN a chemical reaction occurring between a dissolved substance and its solvent. See also **hydrolysis**.
▷**HISTORY** from SOLV(ENT) + -LYSIS

Solway Firth ('sɒlweɪ) NOUN an inlet of the Irish Sea between SW Scotland and NW England. Length: about 56 km (35 miles).

som (sɒm) NOUN, *plural* **somy** ('sɒmɪ). the standard monetary unit of Kyrgyzstan, divided into 100 tyiyn.

SOM1 *Text messaging* ABBREVIATION FOR someone.

Som. ABBREVIATION FOR Somerset.

soma[1] ('səumə) NOUN, *plural* **-mata** (-mətə) *or* **-mas**. the body of an organism, esp an animal, as distinct from the germ cells.
▷**HISTORY** C19: via New Latin from Greek *sōma* the body

soma[2] ('səumə) NOUN an intoxicating plant juice drink used in Vedic rituals.
▷**HISTORY** from Sanskrit

somaesthesia, *or US* **somesthesia** (ˌsɒmɪs'θi:zɪə), **somaesthesis**, *US* **somesthesis** (ˌsɒmɪs'θi:sɪs) NOUN sensory perception of bodily feelings like touch, pain, position of the limbs, etc.
▷**HISTORY** C20: from Greek *sōma* body + AESTHESIA
▸**somaesthetic** *or US* **somesthetic** (ˌsɒmɪs'θetɪk) ADJECTIVE

Somali (səu'mɑ:lɪ) NOUN 1 (*plural* **-lis** *or* **-li**) a member of a tall dark-skinned people inhabiting Somalia. 2 the language of this people, belonging to the Cushitic subfamily of the Afro-Asiatic family of languages. ◆ ADJECTIVE 3 of, relating to, or characteristic of Somalia, the Somalis, or their language.

Somalia (səu'mɑ:lɪə) NOUN a republic in NE Africa, on the Indian Ocean and the Gulf of Aden: the north became a British protectorate in 1884; the east and south were established as an Italian protectorate in 1889; gained independence and united as the Somali Republic in 1960. In 1991 the former British Somaliland region in the north unilaterally declared itself independent as the Republic of Somaliland but this has not been recognized officially. Official languages: Arabic and Somali. Official religion: (Sunni) Muslim. Currency: Somali shilling. Capital: Mogadishu. Pop.: 7 489 000 (2001 est.). Area: 637 541 sq. km (246 154 sq. miles).

Somalian (səu'mɑ:lɪən) ADJECTIVE 1 of or relating to Somalia or its inhabitants. ◆ NOUN 2 a native or inhabitant of Somalia.

Somali cat NOUN a breed of cat with medium-length silky hair, large ears, and a bushy tail.

Somaliland (səu'mɑ:lɪˌlænd) NOUN a former region of E Africa, between the equator and the Gulf of Aden: includes Somalia, Djibouti, and SE Ethiopia.

soman ('səumən) NOUN an organophosphorus compound developed as a nerve gas in Germany during World War II.
▷**HISTORY** C20: from German, of uncertain origin

somatic (səu'mætɪk) ADJECTIVE 1 of or relating to the soma: *somatic cells*. 2 of or relating to an animal body or body wall as distinct from the viscera, limbs, and head. 3 of or relating to the human body as distinct from the mind: *a somatic disease*.
▷**HISTORY** C18: from Greek *sōmatikos* concerning the body, from *sōma* the body
▸**so'matically** ADVERB

somatic cell NOUN any of the cells of a plant or animal except the reproductive cells. Compare **germ cell**.

somatic mutation NOUN a mutation occurring in a somatic cell, resulting in a change in the morphology or some other aspect of one part of an organism (usually a plant). It may be maintained by vegetative propagation but not by sexual reproduction.

somatic nervous system NOUN *Physiol* the section of the nervous system responsible for sensation and control of the skeletal muscles. Compare **autonomic nervous system**.

somato- *or before a vowel* **somat-** COMBINING FORM body: *somatoplasm*.
▷**HISTORY** from Greek *sōma, sōmat-* body

somatogenic (səˌmætəu'dʒenɪk) ADJECTIVE *Med* originating in the cells of the body: of organic, rather than mental, origin: *a somatogenic disorder*.

somatology (ˌsəumə'tɒlədʒɪ) NOUN 1 the branch of biology concerned with the structure and function of the body. 2 the branch of anthropology dealing with the physical characteristics of man.
▸**somatologic** (ˌsəumətə'lɒdʒɪk) *or* ˌ**somato'logical** ADJECTIVE ▸ˌ**somato'logically** ADVERB ▸ˌ**soma'tologist** NOUN

somatomedin (ˌsəumətə'mi:dɪn) NOUN a protein hormone that promotes tissue growth under the influence of growth hormone.
▷**HISTORY** C20: from SOMATO- + Latin *medius* middle + -IN

somatoplasm ('səumətəˌplæzəm) NOUN *Biology* **a** the protoplasm of a somatic cell. **b** the somatic cells collectively. Compare **germ plasm**.
▸ˌ**somato'plastic** ADJECTIVE

somatopleure ('səumətəˌpluə, -ˌplɜ:) NOUN a mass of tissue in embryo vertebrates that is formed by fusion of the ectoderm with the outer layer of mesoderm: develops into the amnion, chorion, and part of the body wall.
▷**HISTORY** C19: from New Latin *somatopleura*, from SOMATO- + Greek *pleura* a side
▸ˌ**somato'pleural** *or* ˌ**somato'pleuric** ADJECTIVE

somatostatin (ˌsəumətə'stætɪn) NOUN a peptide

hormone that prevents the release of growth hormone from the pituitary gland.
▷HISTORY C20: from SOMATO- + -STAT + -IN

somatotonia (ˌsəʊmətəʊˈtəʊnɪə) NOUN a personality type characterized by assertiveness and energy: said to be correlated with a mesomorph body type. Compare **cerebrotonia, viscerotonia.**

somatotrophin (ˌsəʊmətəʊˈtrəʊfɪn) *or* **somatotropin** (ˌsəʊmətəʊˈtrəʊpɪn) NOUN other names for **growth hormone.**
▸ˌ**somatoˈtrophic** *or* ˌ**somatoˈtropic** ADJECTIVE

somatotype (ˈsəʊmətəˌtaɪp) NOUN a type or classification of physique or body build. See **endomorph, mesomorph, ectomorph.**

sombre *or US* **somber** (ˈsɒmbə) ADJECTIVE 1 dismal; melancholy: *a sombre mood.* 2 dim, gloomy, or shadowy. 3 (of colour, clothes, etc.) sober, dull, or dark.
▷HISTORY C18: from French, from Vulgar Latin *subumbrāre* (unattested) to shade, from Latin *sub* beneath + *umbra* shade
▸ˈ**sombrely** *or US* ˈ**somberly** ADVERB ▸ˈ**sombreness** *or US* ˈ**somberness** NOUN ▸**sombrous** (ˈsɒmbrəs) ADJECTIVE

sombrero (sɒmˈbrɛərəʊ) NOUN, *plural* **-ros.** a felt or straw hat with a wide brim, as worn by men in Mexico.
▷HISTORY C16: from Spanish, from *sombrero de sol* shade from the sun

some (sʌm; *unstressed* səm) DETERMINER 1 **a** (a) certain unknown or unspecified: *some lunatic drove into my car; some people never learn.* **b** (*as pronoun; functioning as singular or plural*): *some can teach and others can't.* 2 **a** an unknown or unspecified quantity or amount of: *there's some rice on the table; he owns some horses.* **b** (*as pronoun; functioning as singular or plural*): *we'll buy some.* 3 **a** a considerable number or amount of: *he lived some years afterwards.* **b** a little: *show him some respect.* 4 (*usually stressed*) *Informal* an impressive or remarkable: *that was some game!* 5 a certain amount (more) (in the phrases **some more** and (informal) **and then some**). 6 about; approximately: *he owes me some thirty pounds.* ◆ ADVERB 7 *US, not standard* to a certain degree or extent: *I guess I like him some.*
▷HISTORY Old English *sum;* related to Old Norse *sumr,* Gothic *sums,* Old High German *sum* some, Sanskrit *samá* any, Greek *hamē* somehow

-some¹ SUFFIX FORMING ADJECTIVES characterized by; tending to: *awesome; tiresome.*
▷HISTORY Old English *-sum;* related to Gothic *-sama,* German *-sam*

-some² SUFFIX FORMING NOUNS indicating a group of a specified number of members: *threesome.*
▷HISTORY Old English *sum,* special use of SOME (determiner)

-some³ (-səʊm) NOUN COMBINING FORM a body: *chromosome.*
▷HISTORY from Greek *sōma* body

somebody (ˈsʌmbədɪ) PRONOUN 1 some person; someone. ◆ NOUN, *plural* **-bodies.** 2 a person of greater importance than others: *he is somebody in this town.*

> **Language note** See at **everyone.**

someday (ˈsʌmˌdeɪ) ADVERB at some unspecified time in the (distant) future.

somehow (ˈsʌmˌhaʊ) ADVERB 1 in some unspecified way. 2 Also: **somehow or other.** by any means that are necessary.

someone (ˈsʌmˌwʌn, -wən) PRONOUN some person; somebody.

> **Language note** See at **everyone.**

someplace (ˈsʌmˌpleɪs) ADVERB *US and Canadian informal* in, at, or to some unspecified place or region.

somersault *or* **summersault** (ˈsʌməˌsɔːlt) NOUN 1 **a** a forward roll in which the head is placed on the ground and the trunk and legs are turned over it. **b** a similar roll in a backward direction. 2 an acrobatic feat in which either of these rolls are performed in midair, as in diving or gymnastics. 3 a complete reversal of opinion, policy, etc. ◆ VERB 4 (*intr*) to perform a somersault.
▷HISTORY C16: from Old French *soubresault,* probably from Old Provençal *sobresaut,* from *sobre* over (from Latin *super*) + *saut* a jump, leap (from Latin *saltus*)

Somerset (ˈsʌməsɪt, -ˌsɛt) NOUN a county of SW England, on the Bristol Channel: the Mendip Hills lie in the north and Exmoor in the west: the geographical and ceremonial county includes the unitary authorities of North Somerset and Bath and North East Somerset (both part of Avon county from 1975 until 1996): mainly agricultural (esp dairying and fruit). Administrative centre: Taunton. Pop. (excluding unitary authorities): 498 093 (2001). Area (excluding unitary authorities): 3452 sq. km (1332 sq. miles).

Somerset House NOUN a building in London, in the Strand, built (1776–86) by Sir William Chambers; formerly housed the General Register Office of births, marriages, and deaths: contains (from 1990) the art collections of the Courtauld Institute.

something (ˈsʌmθɪŋ) PRONOUN 1 an unspecified or unknown thing; some thing: *he knows something you don't; take something warm with you.* 2 **something or other.** one unspecified thing or an alternative thing. 3 an unspecified or unknown amount; bit: *something less than a hundred.* 4 an impressive or important person, thing, or event: *isn't that something?* ◆ ADVERB 5 to some degree; a little; somewhat: *to look something like me.* 6 (*foll by an adjective*) *Informal* (intensifier): *it hurts something awful.*

-something NOUN COMBINING FORM **a** a person whose age can be approximately expressed by a specified decade. **b** (*as modifier*): *the thirtysomething market.*
▷HISTORY C20: from the US television series *thirtysomething*

sometime (ˈsʌmˌtaɪm) ADVERB 1 at some unspecified point of time. ◆ ADJECTIVE 2 (*prenominal*) having been at one time; former: *the sometime President.* 3 (*prenominal*) *US* occasional; infrequent.

> **Language note** The form *sometime* should not be used to refer to a fairly long period of time: *he has been away for some time* (not *for sometime*).

sometimes (ˈsʌmˌtaɪmz) ADVERB 1 now and then; from time to time; occasionally. 2 *Obsolete* formerly; sometime.

someway (ˈsʌmˌweɪ) ADVERB in some unspecified manner.

somewhat (ˈsʌmˌwɒt) ADVERB (*not used with a negative*) rather; a bit: *she found it somewhat less easy than he.*

somewhere (ˈsʌmˌwɛə) ADVERB 1 in, to, or at some unknown or unspecified place or point: *somewhere in England; somewhere between 3 and 4 o'clock.* 2 **get somewhere.** *Informal* to make progress.

somewise (ˈsʌmˌwaɪz) ADVERB in some way or to some degree; somehow (archaic, except in the phrase **in somewise**).
▷HISTORY C15: from SOME + -WISE

somite (ˈsəʊmaɪt) NOUN 1 *Embryol* any of a series of dorsal paired segments of mesoderm occurring along the notochord in vertebrate embryos. It develops into muscle and bone in the adult animal. 2 *Zoology* another name for **metamere.**
▷HISTORY C19: from Greek *sōma* a body
▸**somital** (ˈsəʊmɪtᵊl) *or* **somitic** (səʊˈmɪtɪk) ADJECTIVE

Somme (*French* sɔm) NOUN 1 a department of N France, in Picardy region. Capital: Amiens. Pop.: 555 551 (1999). Area: 6277 sq. km (2448 sq. miles). 2 a river in N France, rising in Aisne department and flowing west to Amiens, then northwest to the English Channel: scene of heavy fighting in World War I. Length: 245 km (152 miles).

sommelier (ˈsʌməlˌjeɪ) NOUN a wine steward in a restaurant or hotel.
▷HISTORY French: butler, via Old French from Old Provençal *saumalier* pack-animal driver, from Late Latin *sagma* a packsaddle, from Greek

somnambulate (sɒmˈnæmbjʊˌleɪt) VERB (*intr*) to walk while asleep.
▷HISTORY C19: from Latin *somnus* sleep + *ambulāre* to walk
▸**somˈnambulance** NOUN ▸**somˈnambulant** ADJECTIVE, NOUN ▸**somˌnambuˈlation** NOUN ▸**somˈnambuˌlator** NOUN

somnambulism (sɒmˈnæmbjʊˌlɪzəm) NOUN a condition that is characterized by walking while asleep or in a hypnotic trance. Also called: **noctambulism.**
▸**somˈnambulist** NOUN ▸**somˌnambuˈlistic** ADJECTIVE

somni- *or before a vowel* **somn-** COMBINING FORM sleep: *somniferous.*
▷HISTORY from Latin *somnus*

somniferous (sɒmˈnɪfərəs) *or* **somnific** ADJECTIVE *Rare* tending to induce sleep.
▷HISTORY C17: from Latin *somnifer* (from *somnus* sleep + *ferre* to do) + -OUS
▸**somˈniferously** ADVERB

somniloquy (sɒmˈnɪləkwɪ) NOUN, *plural* **-quies.** *Rare* the act of talking in one's sleep.
▷HISTORY C19: from Latin *somnus* sleep + *loqui* to speak; compare SOLILOQUY
▸**somˈniloquist** NOUN ▸**somˈniloquous** ADJECTIVE

somnolent (ˈsɒmnələnt) ADJECTIVE 1 drowsy; sleepy. 2 causing drowsiness.
▷HISTORY C15: from Latin *somnus* sleep
▸ˈ**somnolence** *or* ˈ**somnolency** NOUN ▸ˈ**somnolently** ADVERB

Somnus (ˈsɒmnəs) NOUN the Roman god of sleep. Greek counterpart: **Hypnos.**

somoni (ˈsɒmɒnɪ) NOUN the standard monetary unit of Tajikistan, consisting of 100 dirams.

somy (ˈsɒmɪ) NOUN the plural of **som.**

son (sʌn) NOUN 1 a male offspring; a boy or man in relation to his parents. 2 a male descendant. 3 (*often capital*) a familiar term of address for a boy or man. 4 a male from a certain country, place, etc., or one closely connected with a certain environment: *a son of the circus.* ◆ Related adjective: **filial.**
▷HISTORY Old English *sunu;* related to Old Norse *sunr,* Gothic *sunus,* Old High German *sunu,* Lithuanian *sūnus,* Sanskrit *sūnu*
▸ˈ**sonless** ADJECTIVE ▸ˈ**sonˌlike** ADJECTIVE

Son (sʌn) NOUN *Christianity* the second person of the Trinity, Jesus Christ.

sonant (ˈsəʊnənt) ADJECTIVE 1 *Phonetics* denoting a voiced sound capable of forming a syllable or syllable nucleus. 2 inherently possessing, exhibiting, or producing a sound. ◆ NOUN 3 *Phonetics* a voiced sound belonging to the class of frictionless continuants or nasals (l, r, m, n, ŋ) considered from the point of view of being a vowel and, in this capacity, able to form a syllable or syllable nucleus.
▷HISTORY C19: from Latin *sonāns* sounding, from *sonāre* to make a noise, resound
▸ˈ**sonance** NOUN ▸**sonantal** (səʊˈnæntᵊl) *or* **soˈnantic** ADJECTIVE

sonar (ˈsəʊnɑː) NOUN a communication and position-finding device used in underwater navigation and target detection using echolocation.
▷HISTORY C20: from *so(und) na(vigation and) r(anging)*

sonata (səˈnɑːtə) NOUN 1 an instrumental composition, usually in three or more movements, for piano alone (**piano sonata**) or for any other instrument with or without piano accompaniment (**violin sonata, cello sonata,** etc.). See also **sonata form, symphony** (sense 1), **concerto** (sense 1). 2 a one-movement keyboard composition of the baroque period.
▷HISTORY C17: from Italian, from *sonare* to sound, from Latin

sonata form NOUN a musical structure consisting of an expanded ternary form whose three sections (exposition, development, and recapitulation), followed by a coda, are characteristic of the first movement in a sonata, symphony, string quartet, concerto, etc.

sonatina (ˌsɒnəˈtiːnə) NOUN a short sonata.
▷HISTORY C19: from Italian

sondage (sɒnˈdɑːʒ) NOUN, *plural* **-dages** (-ˈdɑːʒɪz, -ˈdɑːʒ). *Archaeol* a deep trial trench for inspecting stratigraphy.
▷HISTORY C20: from French: a sounding, from *sonder* to sound

sonde (sɒnd) NOUN a rocket, balloon, or probe used for observing in the upper atmosphere.

▷HISTORY C20: from French: plummet, plumb line; see SOUND[3]

sone (səun) NOUN a subjective unit of loudness equal to that experienced by a normal person hearing a 1 kHz tone at 40 dB.
▷HISTORY C20: from Latin *sonus* a sound

son et lumière (ˈsɒn eɪ ˈluːmɪˌɛə; *French* sɔ̃n e lymjɛr) NOUN an entertainment staged at night at a famous building, historical site, etc., whereby the history of the location is presented by means of lighting effects, sound effects, and narration.
▷HISTORY French, literally: sound and light

song (sɒŋ) NOUN [1] **a** a piece of music, usually employing a verbal text, composed for the voice, esp one intended for performance by a soloist. **b** the whole repertory of such pieces. **c** (*as modifier*): *a song book.* [2] poetical composition; poetry. [3] the characteristic tuneful call or sound made by certain birds or insects. [4] the act or process of singing: *they raised their voices in song.* [5] **for a song.** at a bargain price. [6] **on song.** *Brit informal* performing at peak efficiency or ability.
▷HISTORY Old English *sang;* related to Gothic *saggws,* Old High German *sang;* see SING
▸ˈ**song,like** ADJECTIVE

song and dance NOUN *Informal* [1] *Brit* a fuss, esp one that is unnecessary. [2] *US and Canadian* a long or elaborate story or explanation, esp one that is evasive.

songbird (ˈsɒŋˌbɜːd) NOUN [1] any passerine bird of the suborder *Oscines,* having highly developed vocal organs and, in most, a musical call. Related adjective: **oscine.** [2] any bird having a musical call.

song cycle NOUN any of several groups of songs written by composers during and after the Romantic period, each series employing texts, usually by one poet, relating a story or grouped around a central motif.

song form NOUN another name for **ternary form.**

songful (ˈsɒŋfʊl) ADJECTIVE tuneful; melodious.
▸ˈ**songfully** ADVERB ▸ˈ**songfulness** NOUN

Songhai (sɒŋˈgaɪ) NOUN [1] (*plural* **-ghai** *or* **-ghais**) a member of a Nilotic people of W Africa, living chiefly in Mali and Niger in the central Niger valley. [2] the language or group of dialects spoken by this people, now generally regarded as forming a branch of the Nilo-Saharan family.

Songhua (ˈsʌŋˈwɑː) NOUN a river in NE China, rising in SE Jilin province and flowing north and northeast to the Amur River near Tongjiang: the chief river of Manchuria and largest tributary of the Amur; frozen from November to April. Length: over 1300 km (800 miles). Also called: **Sungari.**

Song Koi *or* **Song Coi** (ˈsɒŋ ˈkɔɪ) NOUN transliteration of the Vietnamese name for the **Red River** (sense 3).

songkok (ˈsɒŋkɒ) NOUN (in Malaysia and Indonesia) a kind of oval brimless hat, resembling a skull.
▷HISTORY from Malay

Song of Solomon NOUN **the.** a book of the Old Testament consisting of a collection of dramatic love poems traditionally ascribed to Solomon. Also called: **Song of Songs, Canticle of Canticles.**

songololo (ˌsɒŋgəˈləʊləʊ) NOUN, *plural* **-los.** a millipede, *Jurus terrestris,* having a hard shiny dark brown segmented exoskeleton.
▷HISTORY from Nguni *ukusonga* to roll up

songsmith (ˈsaɒŋˌsmɪθ) NOUN a person who writes songs.

song sparrow NOUN a common North American finch, *Melospiza melodia,* having brown-and-white plumage and a melodious song.

songster (ˈsɒŋstə) NOUN [1] a singer or poet. [2] a singing bird; songbird.
▸ˈ**songstress** FEMININE NOUN

song thrush NOUN a common Old World thrush, *Turdus philomelos,* that has a brown back and spotted breast and is noted for its song.

songwriter (ˈsɒŋˌraɪtə) NOUN a person who composes the words or music for songs in a popular idiom.

sonic (ˈsɒnɪk) ADJECTIVE [1] of, involving, or producing sound. [2] having a speed about equal to that of sound in air: 331 metres per second (741 miles per hour) at 0°C.
▷HISTORY C20: from Latin *sonus* sound

sonic barrier NOUN another name for **sound barrier.**

sonic boom NOUN a loud explosive sound caused by the shock wave of an aircraft, etc., travelling at supersonic speed.

sonic depth finder NOUN an instrument for detecting the depth of water or of a submerged object by means of sound waves; Fathometer. See also **sonar.**

sonics (ˈsɒnɪks) NOUN (*functioning as singular*) *Physics* the study of mechanical vibrations in matter.

soniferous (sɒˈnɪfərəs) ADJECTIVE carrying or producing sound.

son-in-law NOUN, *plural* **sons-in-law.** the husband of one's daughter.

sonnet (ˈsɒnɪt) *Prosody* ◆ NOUN [1] a verse form of Italian origin consisting of 14 lines in iambic pentameter with rhymes arranged according to a fixed scheme, usually divided either into octave and sestet or, in the English form, into three quatrains and a couplet. ◆ VERB [2] (*intr*) to compose sonnets. [3] (*tr*) to celebrate in a sonnet.
▷HISTORY C16: via Italian from Old Provençal *sonet* a little poem, from *son* song, from Latin *sonus* a sound

sonneteer (ˌsɒnɪˈtɪə) NOUN a writer of sonnets.

sonny (ˈsʌnɪ) NOUN, *plural* **-nies.** *Often patronizing* a familiar term of address to a boy or man.
▷HISTORY C19: from SON + -Y[2]

sonobuoy (ˈsəʊnəˌbɔɪ) NOUN a buoy equipped to detect underwater noises and transmit them by radio.
▷HISTORY from SONIC + BUOY

son of a bitch NOUN, *plural* **sons of bitches.** *Slang, chiefly US and Canadian* [1] a worthless or contemptible person: used as an insult. [2] a humorous or affectionate term for a person, esp a man: *a lucky son of a bitch.*

son of a gun NOUN, *plural* **sons of guns.** *Slang, chiefly US and Canadian* a rogue or rascal: used as a jocular form of address.

son of God NOUN *Bible* [1] an angelic being. [2] a Christian believer.

Son of Man NOUN *Bible* a title of Jesus Christ.

sonogram (ˈsəʊnəˌgræm) NOUN *Physics* a three-dimensional representation of a sound signal, using coordinates of frequency, time, and intensity.

sonoluminescence (ˌsəʊnəʊˌluːmɪˈnɛsəns) NOUN luminescence produced by ultrasound.

Sonora (*Spanish* soˈnora) NOUN a state of NW Mexico, on the Gulf of California: consists of a narrow coastal plain rising inland to the Sierra Madre Occidental; an important mining area in colonial times. Capital: Hermosillo. Pop.: 2 213 370 (2000). Area: 184 934 sq. km (71 403 sq. miles).

sonorant (ˈsɒnərŋt) NOUN *Phonetics* [1] one of the frictionless continuants or nasals (l, r, m, n, ŋ) having consonantal or vocalic functions depending on its situation within the syllable. [2] either of the two consonants represented in English orthography by *w* or *y* and regarded as either consonantal or vocalic articulations of the vowels (iː) and (uː).
▷HISTORY from Latin *sonor* a noise + -ANT

sonorous (səˈnɔːrəs, ˈsɒnərəs) ADJECTIVE [1] producing or capable of producing sound. [2] (of language, sound, etc.) deep or resonant. [3] (esp of speech) high-flown; grandiloquent.
▷HISTORY C17: from Latin *sonōrus* loud, from *sonor* a noise
▸**sonority** (səˈnɒrɪtɪ) NOUN ▸**soˈnorously** ADVERB
▸**soˈnorousness** NOUN

Sons of Freedom PLURAL NOUN a Doukhobor sect, located largely in British Columbia: notorious for its acts of terrorism in opposition to the government in the 1950s and 1960s. Also called: **Freedomites.**

sonsy *or* **sonsie** (ˈsɒnsɪ) ADJECTIVE **-sier, -siest.** *Scot, Irish, and English dialect* [1] plump; buxom; comely. [2] cheerful; good-natured. [3] lucky.
▷HISTORY C16: from Gaelic *sonas* good fortune

Soo Canals (suː) PLURAL NOUN **the.** the two ship canals linking Lakes Superior and Huron. There is a canal on the Canadian and on the US side of the rapids of the St Mary's River. See also **Sault Sainte Marie.**

Soochow (ˈsuːˈtʃaʊ) NOUN a variant transliteration of the Chinese name for **Suzhou.**

sook[1] (sʊk) NOUN [1] *Southwest English dialect* a baby. [2] *Derogatory* a coward. [3] *NZ informal* a calf.
▷HISTORY perhaps from Old English *sūcan* to suck, influenced by Welsh *swci swead* tame

sook[2] *or* **souk** (suːk) *Scot* ◆ VERB [1] to suck. ◆ NOUN [2] the act or an instance of sucking. [3] a sycophant; toady.
▷HISTORY Old English *sūcan*

sool (suːl) VERB (*tr*) to incite (a dog) to attack.
▷HISTORY C17: from English dialect *sowl* (esp of a dog) to pull or seize roughly

soon (suːn) ADVERB [1] in or after a short time; in a little while; before long: *the doctor will soon be here.* [2] **as soon as.** at the very moment that: *she burst into tears as soon as she saw him.* [3] **as soon…as.** used to indicate that the second alternative mentioned is not preferable to the first: *I'd just as soon go by train as drive.*
▷HISTORY Old English *sōna;* related to Old High German *sāno,* Gothic *suns*

sooner (ˈsuːnə) ADVERB [1] the comparative of **soon:** *he came sooner than I thought.* [2] rather; in preference: *I'd sooner die than give up.* [3] **no sooner…than.** immediately after or when: *no sooner had he got home than the rain stopped; no sooner said than done.* [4] **sooner or later.** eventually; inevitably.

> **Language note** *When* is sometimes used instead of *than* after *no sooner,* but this use is generally regarded as incorrect: *no sooner had he arrived than* (not *when*) *the telephone rang.*

soonest (ˈsuːnəst) ADVERB [1] the superlative of **soon.** [2] as soon as possible; urgently; without delay: *send money soonest.*

soot (sʊt) NOUN [1] finely divided carbon deposited from flames during the incomplete combustion of organic substances such as coal. ◆ VERB [2] (*tr*) to cover with soot.
▷HISTORY Old English *sōt;* related to Old Norse, Middle Low German *sōt,* Lithuanian *sódis,* Old Slavonic *sažda,* Old Irish *sūide*

sooth (suːθ) *Archaic or poetic* ◆ NOUN [1] truth or reality (esp in the phrase **in sooth**). ◆ ADJECTIVE [2] true or real. [3] smooth.
▷HISTORY Old English *sōth;* related to Old Norse *sathr* true, Old High German *sand,* Gothic *sunja* truth, Latin *sōns* guilty, *sonticus* critical
▸ˈ**soothly** ADVERB

soothe (suːð) VERB [1] (*tr*) to make calm or tranquil. [2] (*tr*) to relieve or assuage (pain, longing, etc.). [3] (*intr*) to bring tranquillity or relief.
▷HISTORY C16 (in the sense: to mollify): from Old English *sōthian* to prove; related to Old Norse *sanna* to assert; see SOOTH
▸ˈ**soother** NOUN

soothfast (ˈsuːθˌfɑːst) ADJECTIVE *Archaic* [1] truthful. [2] loyal; true.
▷HISTORY from Old English *sōthfæst;* see SOOTH, FAST[1]

soothing (ˈsuːðɪŋ) ADJECTIVE having a calming, assuaging, or relieving effect.
▸ˈ**soothingly** ADVERB ▸ˈ**soothingness** NOUN

soothsay (ˈsuːθˌseɪ) VERB **-says, -saying, -said.** (*intr*) to predict the future.
▸ˈ**sooth,saying** NOUN

soothsayer (ˈsuːθˌseɪə) NOUN a seer or prophet.

sooty (ˈsʊtɪ) ADJECTIVE **sootier, sootiest.** [1] covered with soot. [2] resembling or consisting of soot.
▸ˈ**sootily** ADVERB ▸ˈ**sootiness** NOUN

sooty mould NOUN [1] a fungal plant disease characterized by a blackish growth covering the surface of leaves, fruits, etc. [2] any of various fungi, such as species of *Meliola* or *Capnodium,* that cause this disease.

sop (sɒp) NOUN [1] (*often plural*) food soaked in a liquid before being eaten. [2] a concession, bribe, etc., given to placate or mollify: *a sop to one's feelings.* [3] *Informal* a stupid or weak person. ◆ VERB **sops, sopping, sopped.** [4] (*tr*) to dip or soak (food) in liquid. [5] (when *intr,* often foll by *in*) to soak or be soaked. ◆ See also **sop up.**
▷HISTORY Old English *sopp;* related to Old Norse *soppa* SOUP, Old High German *sopfa* milk with bread; see SUP[2]

SOP ABBREVIATION FOR standard operating procedure.

sop. ABBREVIATION FOR soprano.

sophism ('sɒfɪzəm) NOUN an instance of sophistry. Compare **paralogism.**
▷HISTORY C14: from Latin *sophisma,* from Greek: ingenious trick, from *sophizesthai* to use clever deceit, from *sophos* wise, clever

sophist ('sɒfɪst) NOUN [1] *(often capital)* one of the pre-Socratic philosophers who were itinerant professional teachers of oratory and argument and who were prepared to enter into debate on any matter however specious. [2] a person who uses clever or quibbling arguments that are fundamentally unsound.
▷HISTORY C16: from Latin *sophista,* from Greek *sophistēs* a wise man, from *sophizesthai* to act craftily

sophister ('sɒfɪstə) NOUN [1] (esp formerly) a second-year undergraduate at certain British universities. [2] *Rare* another word for **sophist.**

sophistic (sə'fɪstɪk) *or* **sophistical** ADJECTIVE [1] of or relating to sophists or sophistry. [2] consisting of sophisms or sophistry; specious.
▸**so'phistically** ADVERB

sophisticate VERB (sə'fɪstɪˌkeɪt) [1] *(tr)* to make (someone) less natural or innocent, as by education. [2] to pervert or corrupt (an argument, etc.) by sophistry. [3] *(tr)* to make more complex or refined. [4] *Rare* to falsify (a text, etc.) by alterations. ◆ NOUN (sə'fɪstɪˌkeɪt, -kɪt) [5] a sophisticated person.
▷HISTORY C14: from Medieval Latin *sophisticāre,* from Latin *sophisticus* sophistic
▸**soˌphisti'cation** NOUN ▸**so'phistiˌcator** NOUN

sophisticated (sə'fɪstɪˌkeɪtɪd) ADJECTIVE [1] having refined or cultured tastes and habits. [2] appealing to sophisticates: *a sophisticated restaurant.* [3] unduly refined or cultured. [4] pretentiously or superficially wise. [5] (of machines, methods, etc.) complex and refined.
▸**so'phistiˌcatedly** ADVERB

sophistry ('sɒfɪstrɪ) NOUN, *plural* **-ries.** [1] **a** a method of argument that is seemingly plausible though actually invalid and misleading. **b** the art of using such arguments. [2] subtle but unsound or fallacious reasoning. [3] an instance of this; sophism.

sophomore ('sɒfəˌmɔː) NOUN *Chiefly US and Canadian* a second-year student at a secondary (high) school or college.
▷HISTORY C17: perhaps from earlier *sophumer,* from *sophum,* variant of SOPHISM + -ER[1]

Sophy *or* **Sophi** ('səʊfɪ) NOUN, *plural* **-phies.** (formerly) a title of the Persian monarchs.
▷HISTORY C16: from Latin *sophī* wise men, from Greek *sophos* wise

-sophy NOUN COMBINING FORM indicating knowledge or an intellectual system: *philosophy; theosophy.*
▷HISTORY from Greek *-sophia,* from *sophia* wisdom, from *sophos* wise
▸**-sophic** *or* **-sophical** ADJECTIVE COMBINING FORM

sopor ('səʊpə) NOUN an abnormally deep sleep; stupor.
▷HISTORY C17: from Latin: a deep sleep, death; related to *somnus* sleep

soporific (ˌsɒpə'rɪfɪk) ADJECTIVE *also or archaic* **soporiferous.** [1] inducing sleep. [2] drowsy; sleepy. ◆ NOUN [3] a drug or other agent that induces sleep.
▸**ˌsopo'rifically** ADVERB

sopping ('sɒpɪŋ) ADJECTIVE completely soaked; wet through. Also: **sopping wet.**

soppy ('sɒpɪ) ADJECTIVE **-pier, -piest.** [1] wet or soggy. [2] *Brit informal* silly or sentimental.
▸**'soppily** ADVERB ▸**'soppiness** NOUN

sopranino (ˌsɒprə'niːnəʊ) NOUN, *plural* **-nos. a** the instrument with the highest possible pitch in a family of instruments. **b** *(as modifier)*: *a sopranino recorder.*
▷HISTORY Italian, diminutive of SOPRANO

soprano (sə'prɑːnəʊ) NOUN, *plural* **-pranos** *or* **-prani** (-'prɑːniː). [1] the highest adult female voice, having a range approximately from middle C to the A a thirteenth above it. [2] the voice of a young boy before puberty. [3] a singer with such a voice. [4] the highest part of a piece of harmony. [5] **a** the highest or second highest instrument in a family of instruments. **b** *(as modifier)*: *a soprano saxophone.* ◆ See also **treble.**
▷HISTORY C18: from Italian, from *sopra* above, from Latin *suprā*

soprano clef NOUN the clef that establishes middle C as being on the bottom line of the staff. See also **C clef.**

sop up VERB *(tr, adverb)* to mop or take up (spilt water, etc.) with or as if with a sponge.

sora ('sɔːrə) NOUN a North American rail, *Porzana carolina,* with a greyish-brown plumage and yellow bill.
▷HISTORY C18: of unknown origin

Sorata *(Spanish* so'rata) NOUN **Mount.** a mountain in W Bolivia, in the Andes: the highest mountain in the Cordillera Real, with two peaks, Ancohuma, 6550 m (21 490 ft.), and Illampu, 6485 m (21 276 ft.).

sorb (sɔːb) NOUN [1] another name for **service tree** (sense 1). [2] any of various related trees, esp the mountain ash. [3] Also called: **sorb apple.** the fruit of any of these trees.
▷HISTORY C16: from Latin *sorbus* the sorb, service tree
▸**'sorbic** ADJECTIVE

Sorb (sɔːb) NOUN a member of a Slavonic people living chiefly in the rural areas of E Germany between the upper reaches of the Oder and Elbe rivers (Lusatia). Also called: **Wend, Lusatian.**

sorbefacient (ˌsɔːbɪ'feɪʃənt) ADJECTIVE [1] inducing absorption. ◆ NOUN [2] a sorbefacient drug.
▷HISTORY C19: from Latin *sorbē(re)* to absorb + -FACIENT

sorbet ('sɔːbeɪ, -bɪt) NOUN [1] a water ice made from fruit juice, egg whites, milk, etc. [2] a US word for **sherbet** (sense 2).
▷HISTORY C16: from French, from Old Italian *sorbetto,* from Turkish *şerbet,* from Arabic *sharbah* a drink

Sorbian ('sɔːbɪən) NOUN [1] a West Slavonic language spoken in the rural areas of E Germany between the upper reaches of the Oder and Elbe rivers; modern Wendish. ◆ ADJECTIVE [2] of or relating to the Sorbs or their language.

sorbic acid NOUN a white crystalline unsaturated carboxylic acid found in berries of the mountain ash and used to inhibit the growth of moulds and as an additive for certain synthetic coatings, as of cheese (**E200**); 2,4-hexadienoic acid. It exists as *cis-* and *trans-* isomers, the latter being the one usually obtained. Formula: $CH_3CH{:}CHCH{:}CHCOOH$.
▷HISTORY C19: from SORB (the tree), from its discovery in the berries of the mountain ash

sorbitol ('sɔːbɪˌtɒl) NOUN a white water-soluble crystalline alcohol with a sweet taste, found in certain fruits and berries and manufactured by the catalytic hydrogenation of sucrose: used as a sweetener (**E420**) and in the manufacture of ascorbic acid and synthetic resins. Formula: $C_6H_8(OH)_6$.
▷HISTORY C19: from SORB + -ITOL

Sorbonne *(French* sɔrbɔn) NOUN **the.** a part of the University of Paris containing the faculties of science and literature: founded in 1253 by Robert de Sorbon as a theological college; given to the university in 1808.

sorbo rubber ('sɔːbəʊ) NOUN *Brit* a spongy form of rubber.
▷HISTORY C20: from ABSORB

sorbose ('sɔːbəʊs) NOUN *Biochem* a sweet-tasting hexose sugar derived from the berries of the mountain ash by bacterial action: used in the synthesis of ascorbic acid. Formula: $CH_2OH(CHOH)_3COCH_2OH$.
▷HISTORY C19: from SORB + -OSE[2]

sorcerer ('sɔːsərə) *or feminine* **sorceress** ('sɔːsərɪs) NOUN a person who seeks to control and use magic powers; a wizard or magician.
▷HISTORY C16: from Old French *sorcier,* from Vulgar Latin *sortiārius* (unattested) caster of lots, from Latin *sors* lot

sorcery ('sɔːsərɪ) NOUN, *plural* **-ceries.** the art, practices, or spells of magic, esp black magic, by which it is sought to harness occult forces or evil spirits in order to produce preternatural effects in the world.
▷HISTORY C13: from Old French *sorcerie,* from *sorcier* SORCERER
▸**'sorcerous** ADJECTIVE

sordes ('sɔːdiːz) PLURAL NOUN *Med* dark incrustations on the lips and teeth of patients with prolonged fever.
▷HISTORY C18: from Latin *sordēs* filth

sordid ('sɔːdɪd) ADJECTIVE [1] dirty, foul, or squalid. [2] degraded; vile; base: *a sordid affair.* [3] selfish and grasping: *sordid avarice.*
▷HISTORY C16: from Latin *sordidus,* from *sordēre* to be dirty
▸**'sordidly** ADVERB ▸**'sordidness** NOUN

sordino (sɔː'diːnəʊ) NOUN, *plural* **-ni** (-niː). [1] a mute for a stringed or brass musical instrument. [2] any of the dampers that arrest the vibrations of piano strings. [3] **con sordino** *or* **sordini.** a musical direction to play with a mute. [4] **senza sordino** *or* **sordini.** a musical direction to remove or play without the mute or (on the piano) with the sustaining pedal pressed down. ◆ See also **sourdine.**
▷HISTORY Italian: from *sordo* deaf, from Latin *surdus*

sore (sɔː) ADJECTIVE [1] (esp of a wound, injury, etc.) painfully sensitive; tender. [2] causing annoyance: *a sore point.* [3] resentful; irked: *he was sore that nobody believed him.* [4] urgent; pressing: *in sore need.* [5] *(postpositive)* grieved; distressed. [6] causing grief or sorrow. ◆ NOUN [7] a painful or sensitive wound, injury, etc. [8] any cause of distress or vexation. ◆ ADVERB [9] *Archaic* direly; sorely (now only in such phrases as **sore pressed, sore afraid**).
▷HISTORY Old English *sār;* related to Old Norse *sārr,* Old High German *sēr,* Gothic *sair* sore, Latin *saevus* angry
▸**'soreness** NOUN

soredium (sɔː'riːdɪəm) NOUN an organ of vegetative reproduction in lichens consisting of a cluster of algal cells enclosed in fungal hyphae: dispersed by wind, insects, or other means.
▷HISTORY C19: New Latin, from Greek *sōros* a heap

sorehead ('sɔːˌhɛd) NOUN *Informal, chiefly US and Canadian* a peevish or disgruntled person.
▸**ˌsore'headedly** ADVERB ▸**ˌsore'headedness** NOUN

sorely ('sɔːlɪ) ADVERB [1] painfully or grievously: *sorely wounded.* [2] pressingly or greatly: *to be sorely taxed.*

sorghum ('sɔːgəm) NOUN any grass of the Old World genus *Sorghum,* having solid stems, large flower heads, and glossy seeds: cultivated for grain, hay, and as a source of syrup. See also **kaffir corn, durra.**
▷HISTORY C16: from New Latin, from Italian *sorgo,* probably from Vulgar Latin *Syricum grānum* (unattested) Syrian grain

sorgo *or* **sorgho** ('sɔːgəʊ) NOUN, *plural* **-gos** *or* **-ghos.** any of several varieties of sorghum that have watery sweet juice and are grown for fodder, silage, or syrup.
▷HISTORY Italian

sori ('sɔːraɪ) NOUN the plural of **sorus.**

soricine ('sɒrɪˌsaɪn) ADJECTIVE of, relating to, or resembling the shrews or the family *(Soricidae)* to which they belong.
▷HISTORY C18: from Latin *sōricīnus,* from *sōrex* a shrew

sorites (sɒ'raɪtiːz) NOUN *Logic* **a** a polysyllogism in which the premises are arranged so that intermediate conclusions are omitted, being understood, and only the final conclusion is stated. **b** a paradox of the form: *these few grains of sand do not constitute a heap, and the addition of a single grain never makes what is not yet a heap into a heap: so no matter how many single grains one adds it never becomes a heap.*
▷HISTORY C16: via Latin from Greek *sōreitēs,* literally: heaped, from *sōros* a heap
▸**soritical** (sɒ'rɪtɪkᵊl) *or* **so'ritic** ADJECTIVE

sorn (sɔːn) VERB *(intr,* often foll by *on* or *upon) Scot* to obtain food, lodging, etc., from another person by presuming on his generosity.
▷HISTORY C16: from earlier *sorren* a feudal obligation requiring vassals to offer free hospitality to their lord and his men, from obsolete Irish *sorthan* free quarters

Sorocaba *(Portuguese* soro'kaba) NOUN a city in S Brazil, in São Paulo state: industrial centre. Pop.: 487 907 (2000).

Soroptimist (sə'rɒptɪmɪst) NOUN a member of an organization of clubs (**Soroptimist International**) for professional and executive businesswomen.
▷HISTORY C20: from Latin *soror* sister + OPTIMIST

sororate ('sɒrəˌreɪt) NOUN the custom in some

societies of a widower marrying his deceased wife's younger sister.
▷HISTORY C20: from Latin *soror* a sister

sororicide (səˈrɒrɪˌsaɪd) NOUN [1] the act of killing one's own sister. [2] a person who kills his or her sister.
▷HISTORY C17: from Latin *sorōricīda* one who murders his sister, from *soror* sister + *caedere* to slay
▸**soˌroriˈcidal** ADJECTIVE

sorority (səˈrɒrɪtɪ) NOUN, *plural* **-ties.** *Chiefly US* a social club or society for university women.
▷HISTORY C16: from Medieval Latin *sorōritās*, from Latin *soror* sister

sorosis (səˈrəʊsɪs) NOUN, *plural* **-ses** (-siːz). a fleshy multiple fruit, such as that of the pineapple and mulberry, formed from flowers that are crowded together on a fleshy stem.
▷HISTORY C19: from New Latin, from Greek *sōros* a heap

sorption (ˈsɔːpʃən) NOUN the process in which one substance takes up or holds another; adsorption or absorption.
▷HISTORY C20: back formation from ABSORPTION, ADSORPTION

sorrel¹ (ˈsɒrəl) NOUN [1] **a** a light brown to brownish-orange colour. **b** (*as adjective*): *a sorrel carpet.* [2] a horse of this colour.
▷HISTORY C15: from Old French *sorel*, from *sor* a reddish brown, of Germanic origin; related to Middle Dutch *soor* desiccated

sorrel² (ˈsɒrəl) NOUN [1] any of several polygonaceous plants of the genus *Rumex*, esp *R. acetosa*, of Eurasia and North America, having acid-tasting leaves used in salads and sauces. See also **dock⁴**, **sheep sorrel.** [2] short for **wood sorrel.**
▷HISTORY C14: from Old French *surele*, from *sur* sour, of Germanic origin; related to Old High German *sūr* SOUR

sorrel tree NOUN a deciduous ericaceous tree, *Oxydendrum arboreum*, of E North America, having deeply fissured bark, sour-tasting leaves, and small white flowers. Also called: **sourwood.**
▷HISTORY C17: so called because the bitter flavour of the leaves is reminiscent of sorrel

Sorrento (səˈrɛntəʊ; *Italian* sorˈrɛnto) NOUN a port in SW Italy, in Campania on a mountainous peninsula between the Bay of Naples and the Gulf of Salerno: a resort since Roman times. Pop.: 17 500 (1990).

sorrow (ˈsɒrəʊ) NOUN [1] the characteristic feeling of sadness, grief, or regret associated with loss, bereavement, sympathy for another's suffering, for an injury done, etc. [2] a particular cause or source of regret, grief, etc. [3] Also called: **sorrowing.** the outward expression of grief or sadness. ◆ VERB [4] (*intr*) to mourn or grieve.
▷HISTORY Old English *sorg*; related to Old Norse *sorg*, Gothic *saurga*, Old High German *sworga*
▸**ˈsorrower** NOUN ▸**ˈsorrowful** ADJECTIVE ▸**ˈsorrowfully** ADVERB ▸**ˈsorrowfulness** NOUN

sorry (ˈsɒrɪ) ADJECTIVE **-rier, -riest.** [1] (*usually postpositive*; often foll by *for*) feeling or expressing pity, sympathy, remorse, grief, or regret: *I feel sorry for him.* [2] pitiful, wretched, or deplorable: *a sorry sight.* [3] poor; paltry: *a sorry excuse.* [4] affected by sorrow; sad. [5] causing sorrow or sadness. ◆ INTERJECTION [6] an exclamation expressing apology, used esp at the time of the misdemeanour, offence, etc.
▷HISTORY Old English *sārig*; related to Old High German *sērag*; see SORE
▸**ˈsorrily** ADVERB ▸**ˈsorriness** NOUN

sort (sɔːt) NOUN [1] a class, group, kind, etc., as distinguished by some common quality or characteristic. [2] *Informal* type of character, nature, etc.: *he's a good sort.* [3] a more or less definable or adequate example: *it's a sort of review.* [4] (*often plural*) *Printing* any of the individual characters making up a fount of type. [5] *Archaic* manner; way: *in this sort we struggled home.* [6] **after a sort.** to some extent. [7] **of sorts** *or* **of a sort. a** of an inferior kind. **b** of an indefinite kind. [8] **out of sorts.** not in normal good health, temper, etc. [9] **sort of.** in some way or other; as it were; rather. ◆ VERB [10] (*tr*) to arrange according to class, type, etc. [11] (*tr*) to put (something) into working order. [12] (*tr*) to arrange (computer information) by machine in an order convenient to the computer user. [13] (*tr*; foll by *with*) *Informal* to supply, esp with drugs. [14] (*intr*; foll by *with, together*, etc.) *Archaic or dialect* to associate, as on friendly terms. [15] (*intr*) *Archaic* to agree; accord.
▷HISTORY C14: from Old French, from Medieval Latin *sors* kind, from Latin: fate
▸**ˈsortable** ADJECTIVE ▸**ˈsortably** ADVERB ▸**ˈsorter** NOUN

> **Language note** See at **kind²**.

sortal (ˈsɔːtəl) NOUN *Logic, linguistics* [1] a concept grasp of which includes knowledge of criteria of individuation and reidentification, such as *dog* or *concerto*, but not *flesh* or *music.* [2] a count noun representing such a concept.

sort code NOUN a sequence of numbers printed on a cheque or embossed on a bank or building-society card that identifies the branch holding the account.

sorted (ˈsɔːtɪd) *Slang* ◆ INTERJECTION [1] an exclamation of satisfaction, approval, etc. ◆ ADJECTIVE [2] possessing the desired recreational drugs.

sortie (ˈsɔːtɪ) NOUN [1] **a** (of troops, etc.) the act of emerging from a contained or besieged position. **b** the troops doing this. [2] an operational flight made by one aircraft. ◆ VERB **-ties, -tieing, -tied.** [3] (*intr*) to make a sortie.
▷HISTORY C17: from French: a going out, from *sortir* to go out

sortilege (ˈsɔːtɪlɪdʒ) NOUN [1] the act or practice of divination by drawing lots. [2] magic or sorcery.
▷HISTORY C14: via Old French from Medieval Latin *sortilegium*, from Latin *sortilegus* a soothsayer, from *sors* fate + *legere* to select

sortition (sɔːˈtɪʃən) NOUN the act of casting lots.
▷HISTORY C16: from Latin *sortitio*, from *sortiri* to cast lots

sort out VERB (*tr, adverb*) [1] to find a solution to (a problem, etc.), esp to make clear or tidy: *it took a long time to sort out the mess.* [2] to take or separate, as from a larger group: *he sorted out the most likely ones.* [3] to organize into an orderly and disciplined group. [4] *Informal* to beat or punish.

sorus (ˈsɔːrəs) NOUN, *plural* **-ri** (-raɪ). [1] a cluster of sporangia on the undersurface of certain fern leaves. [2] any of various similar spore-producing structures in some lichens and fungi.
▷HISTORY C19: via New Latin from Greek *sōros* a heap

SOS NOUN [1] an internationally recognized distress signal in which the letters SOS are repeatedly spelt out, as by radio-telegraphy: used esp by ships and aircraft. [2] a message broadcast in an emergency for people otherwise unobtainable. [3] *Informal* a call for help.
▷HISTORY C20: letters chosen as the simplest to transmit and receive in Morse code; by folk etymology taken to be abbrev. for *save our souls*

sosatie (səˈsɑːtɪ) NOUN *South African* a skewer of curried meat pieces.
▷HISTORY Afrikaans

Sosnowiec (*Polish* sɔsˈnɔvjɛts) NOUN an industrial town in S Poland. Pop.: 244 102 (1999 est.).

so-so *Informal* ◆ ADJECTIVE [1] (*postpositive*) neither good nor bad. ◆ ADVERB [2] in an average or indifferent manner.

Sososholoza (ˌsəʊsəʊˈʃɒləʊzə) NOUN *South African* a popular Zulu choral song.
▷HISTORY from Zulu, literally: move forward

sostenuto (ˌsɒstəˈnuːtəʊ) ADJECTIVE, ADVERB *Music* (preceded by a tempo marking) to be performed in a smooth sustained manner.
▷HISTORY C18: from Italian, from *sostenere* to sustain, from Latin *sustinēre* to uphold

sostenuto pedal NOUN another word for **sustaining pedal.**

sot¹ (sɒt) NOUN [1] a habitual or chronic drunkard. [2] a person stupefied by or as if by drink.
▷HISTORY Old English, from Medieval Latin *sottus*; compare French *sot* a fool
▸**ˈsottish** ADJECTIVE

sot² (sɒt) ADVERB *Scot* indeed: used to contradict a negative statement: *I am not! — You are sot!*
▷HISTORY a variant of SO¹, altered to rhyme with *not*

soteriology (sɒˌtɪərɪˈɒlədʒɪ) NOUN *Theol* the doctrine of salvation.
▷HISTORY C19: from Greek *sōtēria* deliverance (from *sōtēr* a saviour) + -LOGY
▸**soteriologic** (sɒˌtɪərɪəˈlɒdʒɪk) *or* **soˌterioˈlogical** ADJECTIVE

Sothic (ˈsəʊθɪk, ˈsɒθ-) ADJECTIVE relating to the star Sirius or to the rising of this star.
▷HISTORY C19: from Greek *Sōthis*, from Egyptian, name of Sirius

Sothic year NOUN the fixed year of the ancient Egyptians, 365 days 6 hours long, beginning with the appearance of the star Sirius on the eastern horizon at dawn, which heralded the yearly flooding of the Nile. A **Sothic cycle** contained 1460 such years.

Sothis (ˈsəʊθɪs) NOUN another name for **Sirius.**
▷HISTORY Greek; see SOTHIC

Sotho (ˈsuːtuː, ˈsəʊtəʊ) NOUN [1] (*plural* **-tho** *or* **-thos**) a member of a large grouping of Negroid peoples of southern Africa, living chiefly in Botswana, South Africa, and Lesotho. [2] the group of mutually intelligible languages of this people, including Lesotho, Tswana, and Pedi. It belongs to the Bantu group of the Niger-Congo family. [3] (*plural* **-tho** *or* **-thos**) *South African* a member of the Basotho people; a Mosotho. [4] *South African* the dialect of Sotho spoken by the Basotho; Sesotho. It is an official language of Lesotho along with English. ◆ Former name (for senses 3, 4): **Basuto.**

Soto (soto) NOUN a Zen Buddhist school of Japan, characterized by the practice of sitting meditation leading to gradual enlightenment.

sotto voce (ˈsɒtəʊ ˈvəʊtʃɪ) ADVERB in an undertone.
▷HISTORY C18: from Italian: under (one's) voice

sou (suː) NOUN [1] a former French coin of low denomination. [2] a very small amount of money: *I haven't a sou to my name.*
▷HISTORY C19: from French, from Old French *sol*, from Latin: SOLIDUS

soubise (suːˈbiːz) NOUN a purée of onions mixed into a thick white sauce and served over eggs, fish, etc. Also called: **soubise sauce.**
▷HISTORY C18: named after Charles de Rohan *Soubise* (1715–87), marshal of France

soubrette (suːˈbrɛt) NOUN [1] a minor female role in comedy, often that of a pert lady's maid. [2] any pert or flirtatious girl.
▷HISTORY C18: from French: maidservant, from Provençal *soubreto*, from *soubret* conceited, from *soubra* to exceed, from Latin *superāre* to surmount, from *super* above
▸**souˈbrettish** ADJECTIVE

soubriquet (ˈsəʊbrɪˌkeɪ) NOUN a variant spelling of **sobriquet.**

souchong (ˈsuːˈʃɒŋ, -ˈtʃɒŋ) NOUN a black tea with large leaves.
▷HISTORY C18: from Chinese *hsiao-chung* small kind

Soudan (sudɑ̃) NOUN the French name for the **Sudan.**

souffle (ˈsuːfᵊl) NOUN *Med* a blowing sound or murmur heard in auscultation.
▷HISTORY C19: from French, from *souffler* to blow

soufflé (ˈsuːfleɪ) NOUN [1] a very light fluffy dish made with egg yolks and stiffly beaten egg whites combined with cheese, fish, etc. [2] a similar sweet or savoury cold dish, set with gelatine. ◆ ADJECTIVE *also* **souffléed.** [3] made light and puffy, as by beating and cooking.
▷HISTORY C19: from French, from *souffler* to blow, from Latin *sufflāre*

Soufrière (*French* sufrjɛr) NOUN [1] a volcano in the Caribbean, on N St Vincent: erupted in 1902, killing about 2000 people. Height: 1234 m (4048 ft.). [2] a volcano in the Caribbean, on S Montserrat: the highest point on the island. Height: 915 m (3002 ft.). [3] a volcano in the Caribbean, on Guadeloupe. Height: 1484 m (4869 ft.).

sough¹ (saʊ) VERB [1] (*intr*) (esp of the wind) to make a characteristic sighing sound. ◆ NOUN [2] a soft continuous murmuring sound.
▷HISTORY Old English *swōgan* to resound; related to Gothic *gaswogjan* to groan, Lithuanian *svageti* to sound, Latin *vāgīre* to lament

sough² (sʌf) NOUN *Northern English dialect* a sewer or drain or an outlet channel.

▷**HISTORY** of obscure origin

sought (sɔːt) VERB the past tense and past participle of **seek.**

sought-after ADJECTIVE in demand; wanted.

souk¹ *or* **suq** (suːk) NOUN (in Muslim countries, esp North Africa and the Middle East) an open-air marketplace.
▷**HISTORY** C20: from Arabic *sūq*

souk² (suːk) VERB, NOUN *Scot* a variant spelling of **sook².**

soukous (ˈsuːkʊs) NOUN a style of African popular music that originated in Zaïre (now the Democratic Republic of Congo), characterized by syncopated rhythms and intricate contrasting guitar melodies.
▷**HISTORY** C20: perhaps from French *secouer* to shake

soul (səʊl) NOUN [1] the spirit or immaterial part of man, the seat of human personality, intellect, will, and emotions, regarded as an entity that survives the body after death. Related adjective: **pneumatic.** [2] *Christianity* the spiritual part of a person, capable of redemption from the power of sin through divine grace. [3] the essential part or fundamental nature of anything. [4] a person's feelings or moral nature as distinct from other faculties. [5] **a** Also called: **soul music.** a type of Black music resulting from the addition of jazz, gospel, and pop elements to the urban blues style. **b** (*as modifier*): *a soul singer.* [6] (*modifier*) of or relating to Black Americans and their culture: *soul brother; soul food.* [7] nobility of spirit or temperament: *a man of great soul and courage.* [8] an inspiring spirit or leading figure, as of a cause or movement. [9] **the life and soul.** See **life** (sense 28). [10] a person regarded as typifying some characteristic or quality: *the soul of discretion.* [11] a person; individual: *an honest soul.* [12] **upon my soul!** an exclamation of surprise.
▷**HISTORY** Old English *sāwol;* related to Old Frisian *sēle,* Old Saxon *sēola,* Old High German *sēula* soul
▸ˈ**soul-ˌlike** ADJECTIVE

Soul (səʊl) NOUN *Christian Science* another word for **God.**

soul-destroying ADJECTIVE (of an occupation, situation, etc.) unremittingly monotonous.

soul food NOUN *Informal* food, such as chitterlings or yams, traditionally eaten by Black people in the southern US.

soulful (ˈsəʊlfʊl) ADJECTIVE *Sometimes ironic* expressing profound thoughts or feelings: *soulful music.*
▸ˈ**soulfully** ADVERB ▸ˈ**soulfulness** NOUN

soulless (ˈsəʊllɪs) ADJECTIVE [1] lacking any humanizing qualities or influences; dead; mechanical: *soulless work.* [2] (of a person) lacking in sensitivity or nobility. [3] heartless; cruel.
▸ˈ**soullessly** ADVERB ▸ˈ**soullessness** NOUN

soul mate NOUN a person for whom one has a deep affinity, esp a lover, wife, husband, etc.

soul-searching NOUN [1] deep or critical examination of one's motives, actions, beliefs, etc. ◆ ADJECTIVE [2] displaying the characteristics of deep or painful self-analysis.

sou marqué (ˈsuː mɑːˈkeɪ; *French* su marke) NOUN, *plural* **sous marqués** (ˈsu mɑːˈkeɪz; *French* su marke). a French copper coin of the 18th century.
▷**HISTORY** French, literally: a marked sou

sound¹ (saʊnd) NOUN [1] **a** a periodic disturbance in the pressure or density of a fluid or in the elastic strain of a solid, produced by a vibrating object. It has a velocity in air at sea level at 0°C of 331 metres per second (741 miles per hour) and travels as longitudinal waves. **b** (*as modifier*): *a sound wave.* [2] (*modifier*) of or relating to radio as distinguished from television: *sound broadcasting; sound radio.* [3] the sensation produced by such a periodic disturbance in the organs of hearing. [4] anything that can be heard. [5] a particular instance, quality, or type of sound: *the sound of running water.* [6] volume or quality of sound: *a radio with poor sound.* [7] the area or distance over which something can be heard: *to be born within the sound of Big Ben.* [8] the impression or implication of something: *I don't like the sound of that.* [9] *Phonetics* the auditory effect produced by a specific articulation or set of related articulations. [10] (*often plural*) *Slang* music, esp rock, jazz, or pop. ◆ VERB [11] to cause (something, such as an instrument) to make a sound or (of an instrument, etc.) to emit a sound. [12] to announce or be announced by a sound: *to sound the alarm.* [13] (*intr*) (of a sound) to be heard. [14] (*intr*) to resonate with a certain quality or intensity: *to sound loud.* [15] (*copula*) to give the impression of being as specified when read, heard, etc.: *to sound reasonable.* [16] (*tr*) to pronounce distinctly or audibly: *to sound one's consonants.* [17] (*intr;* usually foll by *in*) *Law* to have the essential quality or nature (of): *an action sounding in damages.* ◆ See also **sound off.**
▷**HISTORY** C13: from Old French *soner* to make a sound, from Latin *sonāre,* from *sonus* a sound
▸ˈ**soundable** ADJECTIVE

sound² (saʊnd) ADJECTIVE [1] free from damage, injury, decay, etc. [2] firm; solid; substantial: *a sound basis.* [3] financially safe or stable: *a sound investment.* [4] showing good judgment or reasoning; sensible; wise: *sound advice.* [5] valid, logical, or justifiable: *a sound argument.* [6] holding approved beliefs; ethically correct; upright; honest. [7] (of sleep) deep; peaceful; unbroken. [8] thorough; complete: *a sound examination.* [9] *Brit informal* excellent. [10] *Law* (of a title, etc.) free from defect; legally valid. [11] constituting a valid and justifiable application of correct principles; orthodox: *sound theology.* [12] *Logic* **a** (of a deductive argument) valid. **b** (of an inductive argument) according with whatever principles ensure the high probability of the truth of the conclusion given the truth of the premises. **c** another word for **consistent** (sense 5b). ◆ ADVERB [13] soundly; deeply: now archaic except when applied to sleep.
▷**HISTORY** Old English *sund;* related to Old Saxon *gisund,* Old High German *gisunt*
▸ˈ**soundly** ADVERB ▸ˈ**soundness** NOUN

sound³ (saʊnd) VERB [1] to measure the depth of (a well, the sea, etc.) by lowering a plumb line, by sonar, etc. [2] to seek to discover (someone's views, etc.), as by questioning. [3] (*intr*) (of a whale, etc.) to dive downwards swiftly and deeply. [4] *Med* **a** to probe or explore (a bodily cavity or passage) by means of a sound. **b** to examine (a patient) by means of percussion and auscultation. ◆ NOUN [5] *Med* an instrument for insertion into a bodily cavity or passage to dilate strictures, dislodge foreign material, etc. ◆ See also **sound out.**
▷**HISTORY** C14: from Old French *sonder,* from *sonde* sounding line, probably of Germanic origin; related to Old English *sundgyrd* sounding pole, Old Norse *sund* strait, SOUND⁴; see SWIM

sound⁴ (saʊnd) NOUN [1] a relatively narrow channel between two larger areas of sea or between an island and the mainland. [2] an inlet or deep bay of the sea. [3] the air bladder of a fish.
▷**HISTORY** Old English *sund* swimming, narrow sea; related to Middle Low German *sunt* strait; see SOUND³

Sound (saʊnd) NOUN **the.** a strait between SW Sweden and Sjælland (Denmark), linking the Kattegat with the Baltic: busy shipping lane; spanned by a bridge in 2000. Length: 113 km (70 miles). Narrowest point: 5 km (3 miles). Danish name: **Øresund.** Swedish name: **Öresund.**

soundalike (ˈsaʊndəˌlaɪk) NOUN **a** a person or thing that sounds like another, often well known, person or thing. **b** (*as modifier*): *a soundalike band.*

sound barrier NOUN (*not in technical usage*) a hypothetical barrier to flight at or above the speed of sound, when a sudden large increase in drag occurs. Also called: **sonic barrier, transonic barrier.**

sound bite NOUN a short pithy sentence or phrase extracted from a longer speech for use on radio or television.

sound bow (bəʊ) NOUN the thick part of a bell against which the hammer strikes.

soundbox (ˈsaʊndˌbɒks) NOUN the resonating chamber of the hollow body of a violin, guitar, etc.

sound check NOUN an on-the-spot rehearsal by a band before a gig to enable the sound engineer to set up the mixer.

sound effect NOUN any sound artificially produced, reproduced from a recording, etc., to create a theatrical effect, such as the bringing together of two halves of a hollow coconut shell to simulate a horse's gallop; used in plays, films, etc.

sounder¹ (ˈsaʊndə) NOUN an electromagnetic device formerly used in telegraphy to convert electric signals sent over wires into audible sounds.

sounder² (ˈsaʊndə) NOUN a person or device that measures the depth of water, etc.

sound head NOUN the part of a film projector that reproduces the sound in a film.

sound hole NOUN any of variously shaped apertures in the sounding board of certain stringed instruments, such as the 'f' shaped holes of a violin.

sounding¹ (ˈsaʊndɪŋ) ADJECTIVE [1] resounding; resonant. [2] having an imposing sound and little content; pompous: *sounding phrases.*
▸ˈ**soundingly** ADVERB

sounding² (ˈsaʊndɪŋ) NOUN [1] (*sometimes plural*) the act or process of measuring depth of water or examining the bottom of a river, lake, etc., as with a sounding line. [2] an observation or measurement of atmospheric conditions, as made using a radiosonde or rocketsonde. [3] (*often plural*) measurements taken by sounding. [4] (*plural*) a place where a sounding line will reach the bottom, esp less than 100 fathoms in depth. [5] **on** (*or* **off**) **soundings.** in waters less than (or more than) 100 fathoms in depth.

sounding board NOUN [1] Also called: **soundboard.** a thin wooden board in a piano or comprising the upper surface of a resonating chamber in a violin, cello, etc., serving to amplify the vibrations produced by the strings passing across it. See also **belly** (sense 6). [2] Also called: **soundboard.** a thin screen suspended over a pulpit, stage, etc., to reflect sound towards an audience. [3] a person, group, experiment, etc., used to test a new idea, policy, etc., for acceptance or applicability.

sounding lead (lɛd) NOUN a lead weight, usually conical and having a depression in the base for a dab of grease so that, when dropped to the bottom on a sounding line, a sample of sand, gravel, etc., can be retrieved.

sounding line NOUN a line marked off to indicate its length and having a sounding lead at one end. It is dropped over the side of a vessel to determine the depth of the water.

soundless¹ (ˈsaʊndlɪs) ADJECTIVE extremely still or silent.
▸ˈ**soundlessly** ADVERB ▸ˈ**soundlessness** NOUN

soundless² (ˈsaʊndlɪs) ADJECTIVE *Chiefly poetic* extremely deep.

sound mixer NOUN *Films, radio, television* [1] the person who mixes various sound sources into a composite programme. [2] a piece of equipment designed for mixing sound.

sound off VERB (*intr, adverb*) [1] to proclaim loudly, as in venting one's opinions, grievances, etc. [2] to speak angrily.

sound out VERB (*tr, adverb*) to question (someone) in order to discover (opinions, facts, etc.).

soundpost (ˈsaʊndˌpəʊst) NOUN *Music* a small post, usually of pine, on guitars, violins, etc., that joins the front surface to the back, helps to support the bridge, and allows the whole body of the instrument to vibrate.

soundproof (ˈsaʊndˌpruːf) ADJECTIVE [1] not penetrable by sound. ◆ VERB [2] (*tr*) to render soundproof.

sound ranging NOUN the determination of the location of a source of sound waves by measuring the time lapse between their transmission and their reception at microphones situated at three or more known positions.

sound shift NOUN a gradual alteration or series of alterations in the pronunciation of a set of sounds, esp of vowels. See also **Great Vowel Shift.**

sound spectrograph NOUN an electronic instrument that produces a record (**sound spectrogram**) of the way in which the frequencies and intensities of the components of a sound, such as a spoken word, vary with time.

sound stage NOUN a soundproof room or building in which cinematic films are shot.

sound system NOUN [1] any system of sounds, as in the speech of a language. [2] integrated equipment for producing amplified sound, as in a hi-fi or a mobile disco, or as a public-address system on stage.

soundtrack (ˈsaʊndˌtræk) NOUN [1] the recorded sound accompaniment to a film. Compare **commentary** (sense 2). [2] a narrow strip along the side of a spool of film, which carries the sound accompaniment. ◆ VERB [3] (*tr*) to provide a continuous accompaniment of sounds, esp music.

sound truck NOUN the US and Canadian name for a **loudspeaker van.**

sound wave NOUN a wave that propagates sound.

soup (suːp) NOUN [1] a liquid food made by boiling or simmering meat, fish, vegetables, etc., usually served hot at the beginning of a meal. [2] *Informal* a photographic developer. [3] *Informal* anything resembling soup in appearance or consistency, esp thick fog. See also **peasouper.** [4] a slang name for **nitroglycerine.** [5] **in the soup.** *Informal* in trouble or difficulties.
▷HISTORY C17: from Old French *soupe,* from Late Latin *suppa,* of Germanic origin; compare Middle High German *suppe,* Old Norse *soppa* soup

soupçon *French* (supsɔ̃) NOUN a slight amount; dash.
▷HISTORY C18: from French, ultimately from Latin *suspicio* SUSPICION

soupfin *or* **soupfin shark** (ˈsuːpˌfɪn) NOUN a Pacific requiem shark, *Galeorhinus zyopterus,* valued for its fins, which are used to make soup.

soup kitchen NOUN [1] a place or mobile stall where food and drink, esp soup, is served to destitute people. [2] *Military* a mobile kitchen.

soup plate NOUN a deep plate with a wide rim, used esp for drinking soup.

soup up *Informal* ◆ VERB (*tr, adverb*) [1] to modify (a vehicle or vehicle engine) in order to increase its power. [2] to make (something) more exciting or interesting. Also: **hot up,** (esp US and Canadian) **hop up.** ◆ ADJECTIVE **souped-up.** [3] (of a vehicle or vehicle engine) modified so as to be more powerful: *a souped-up scooter.* [4] more exciting or interesting: *a souped-up version of their last single.*

soupy (ˈsuːpɪ) ADJECTIVE **soupier, soupiest.** [1] having the appearance or consistency of soup. [2] *Informal, chiefly US and Canadian* emotional or sentimental.

sour (ˈsaʊə) ADJECTIVE [1] having or denoting a sharp biting taste like that of lemon juice or vinegar. Compare **bitter** (sense 1). [2] made acid or bad, as in the case of milk or alcohol, by the action of microorganisms. [3] having a rancid or unwholesome smell. [4] (of a person's temperament) sullen, morose, or disagreeable. [5] (esp of the weather or climate) harsh and unpleasant. [6] disagreeable; distasteful: *a sour experience.* [7] (of land, etc.) lacking in fertility, esp due to excessive acidity. [8] (of oil, gas, or petrol) containing a relatively large amount of sulphur compounds. [9] **go** *or* **turn sour.** to become unfavourable or inharmonious: *his marriage went sour.* ◆ NOUN [10] something sour. [11] *Chiefly US* any of several iced drinks usually made with spirits, lemon juice, and ice: *a whiskey sour.* [12] an acid used in laundering and bleaching clothes or in curing animal skins. ◆ VERB [13] to make or become sour.
▷HISTORY Old English *sūr;* related to Old Norse *sūrr,* Lithuanian *suras* salty, Old Slavonic *syrŭ* wet, raw, *surovu* green, raw, Sanskrit *surā* brandy
▸ˈ**sourish** ADJECTIVE ▸ˈ**sourly** ADVERB ▸ˈ**sourness** NOUN

Sour (sʊə) NOUN a variant spelling of **Sur.**

source (sɔːs) NOUN [1] the point or place from which something originates. [2] **a** a spring that forms the starting point of a stream; headspring. **b** the area where the headwaters of a river rise: *the source of the Nile.* [3] a person, group, etc., that creates, issues, or originates something: *the source of a complaint.* [4] **a** any person, book, organization, etc., from which information, evidence, etc., is obtained. **b** (*as modifier*): *source material.* [5] anything, such as a story or work of art, that provides a model or inspiration for a later work. [6] *Electronics* the electrode region in a field-effect transistor from which majority carriers flow into the interelectrode conductivity channel. [7] **at source.** at the point of origin. ◆ VERB [8] (*tr;* foll by *from*) to originate from. [9] (*tr*) to establish an originator or source of (a product, piece of information, etc.).
▷HISTORY C14: from Old French *sors,* from *sourdre* to spring forth, from Latin *surgere* to rise

source document NOUN a document that has been or will be transcribed to a word processor or to the memory bank of a computer.

source program NOUN an original computer program written by a programmer that is converted into the equivalent object program, written in machine language, by the compiler or assembler.

sour cherry NOUN [1] a Eurasian rosaceous tree, *Prunus cerasus,* with white flowers: cultivated for its tart red fruits. [2] the fruit of this tree. Compare **sweet cherry.** See also **morello, amarelle.**

sour cream NOUN cream soured by lactic acid bacteria, used in making salads, dips, etc. Also called: **soured cream.**

sourdine (sʊəˈdiːn) NOUN *Music* [1] a soft stop on an organ or harmonium. [2] another word for **sordino.**
▷HISTORY C17 (meaning: a muted trumpet): from French: a mute, from Italian; see SORDINO

sourdough (ˈsaʊəˌdəʊ) ADJECTIVE [1] *Dialect* (of bread) made with fermented dough used as a leaven. ◆ NOUN [2] (in Western US, Canada, and Alaska) an old-time prospector or pioneer.

sour gourd NOUN [1] a large bombacaceous tree, *Adansonia gregorii,* of N Australia, having gourdlike fruit. [2] the acid-tasting fruit of this tree, which has a woody rind and large seeds. [3] the fruit of the baobab tree.

sour grapes NOUN (*functioning as singular*) the attitude of affecting to despise something because one cannot or does not have it oneself.
▷HISTORY from a fable by Aesop

sour gum NOUN a cornaceous tree, *Nyssa sylvatica,* of the eastern US, having glossy leaves, soft wood, and sour purplish fruits. Also called: **black gum, pepperidge.** See also **tupelo.** Compare **sweet gum.**

sour mash NOUN *US* [1] a grain mash for use in distilling certain whiskeys, consisting of a mixture of new and old mash. [2] any whiskey distilled from such a mash.

sourpuss (ˈsaʊəˌpʊs) NOUN *Informal* a person whose facial expression or nature is habitually gloomy or sullen.
▷HISTORY C20: from SOUR + PUSS[2]

soursop (ˈsaʊəˌsɒp) NOUN [1] a small West Indian tree, *Annona muricata,* having large spiny fruit: family *Annonaceae.* [2] the fruit of this tree, which has a tart edible pulp. Compare **sweetsop.**
▷HISTORY C19: so called because of the flavour and consistency of the pulp

sourwood (ˈsaʊəˌwʊd) NOUN another name for **sorrel tree.**

sousaphone (ˈsuːzəˌfəʊn) NOUN *Music* a large tuba that encircles the player's body and has a bell facing forwards.
▷HISTORY C20: named after John Philip *Sousa* (1854–1932), US bandmaster and composer of military marches
▸ˈ**sousaˌphonist** NOUN

souse[1] (saʊs) VERB [1] to plunge (something, oneself, etc.) into water or other liquid. [2] to drench or be drenched. [3] (*tr*) to pour or dash (liquid) over (a person or thing). [4] to steep or cook (food) in a marinade. [5] (*tr; usually passive*) *Slang* to make drunk. ◆ NOUN [6] the liquid or brine used in pickling. [7] the act or process of sousing. [8] *Slang* a habitual drunkard.
▷HISTORY C14: from Old French *sous,* of Germanic origin; related to Old High German *sulza* brine

souse[2] (saʊs) *Falconry* (of hawks or falcons) VERB (*intr*) [1] (often foll by *on* or *upon*) to swoop suddenly downwards (on a prey). ◆ NOUN [2] a sudden downward swoop.
▷HISTORY C16: perhaps a variant of obsolete vb sense of SOURCE

souslik (ˈsuːslɪk) NOUN a variant spelling of **suslik.**

sou-sou *or* **susu** (ˈsuːsuː) NOUN *Caribbean* an arrangement made among friends whereby each person makes regular contributions to a fund, the money being drawn out periodically by each individual in turn.
▷HISTORY probably of W African origin, influenced by French *sou* small coin, via Creole

Sousse (suːs), **Susa,** *or* **Susah** NOUN a port in E Tunisia, on the Mediterranean: founded by the Phoenicians in the 9th century B.C. Pop.: 125 000 (1994). Ancient name: **Hadrumetum** (ˌhædrəˈmiːtəm).

soutache (suːˈtæʃ) NOUN a narrow braid used as a decorative trimming.
▷HISTORY C19: from French, from Hungarian *sujtas*

soutane (suːˈtæn) NOUN *RC Church* a priest's cassock.
▷HISTORY C19: from French, from Old Italian *sottana,* from Medieval Latin *subtanus* (adj) (worn) beneath, from Latin *subtus* below

souter *or* **soutar** (ˈsuːtər) NOUN *Scot and northern English* a shoemaker or cobbler.
▷HISTORY Old English *sūtere,* from Latin *sutor,* from *suere* to sew

souterrain (ˈsuːtəˌreɪn) NOUN *Archaeol* an underground chamber or passage.
▷HISTORY C18: from French

south (saʊθ) NOUN [1] one of the four cardinal points of the compass, at 180° from north and 90° clockwise from east and anticlockwise from west. [2] the direction along a meridian towards the South Pole. [3] **the south.** (*often capital*) any area lying in or towards the south. Related adjectives: **meridional, austral.** [4] (*usually capital*) *Cards* the player or position at the table corresponding to south on the compass. ◆ ADJECTIVE [5] situated in, moving towards, or facing the south. [6] (esp of the wind) from the south. ◆ ADVERB [7] in, to, or towards the south. [8] *Archaic* (of the wind) from the south. ◆ Symbol: S.
▷HISTORY Old English *sūth;* related to Old Norse *suthr* southward, Old High German *sundan* from the south

South (saʊθ) NOUN **the.** [1] the southern part of England, generally regarded as lying to the south of an imaginary line between the Wash and the Severn. [2] (in the US) **a** the area approximately south of Pennsylvania and the Ohio River, esp those states south of the Mason-Dixon line that formed the Confederacy during the Civil War. **b** the Confederacy itself. [3] the countries of the world that are not economically and technically advanced. ◆ ADJECTIVE [4] **a** of or denoting the southern part of a specified country, area, etc. **b** (*capital as part of a name*): *the South Pacific.*

South Africa NOUN **Republic of.** a republic occupying the southernmost part of the African continent: the Dutch Cape Colony (1652) was acquired by Britain in 1806 and British victory in the Boer War resulted in the formation of the Union of South Africa in 1910, which became a republic in 1961; implementation of the apartheid system began in 1948 and was abolished, following an intense civil rights campaign, in 1993 with multiracial elections held in 1994; a member of the Commonwealth, it withdrew in 1961 but was re-admitted in 1994. Mainly plateau with mountains in the south and east. Mineral production includes gold, diamonds, coal, and copper. Official languages: Afrikaans; English; Ndebele; Pedi; South Sotho; Swazi; Tsonga; Tswana; Venda; Xhosa; Zulu. Religion: Christian majority. Currency: rand. Capitals: Cape Town (legislative), Pretoria (administrative), Bloemfontein (judicial). Pop.: 43 586 000 (2001 est.). Area: 1 221 044 sq. km (471 445 sq. miles). Former name (1910–61): **Union of South Africa.**

South African ADJECTIVE [1] of or relating to the Republic of South Africa, its inhabitants, or any of their languages. ◆ NOUN [2] a native or inhabitant of the Republic of South Africa.

South African Dutch NOUN (not used in South Africa) another name for **Afrikaans.**

South America NOUN the fourth largest of the continents, bordering on the Caribbean in the north, the Pacific in the west, and the Atlantic in the east and joined to Central America by the Isthmus of Panama. It is dominated by the Andes Mountains, which extend over 7250 km (4500 miles) and include many volcanoes; ranges from dense tropical jungle, desert, and temperate plains to the cold wet windswept region of Tierra del Fuego. It comprises chiefly developing countries undergoing great changes. Pop.: 317 846 000 (1996). Area: 17 816 600 sq. km (6 879 000 sq. miles).

South American ADJECTIVE [1] of or relating to the continent of South America or its inhabitants. ◆ NOUN [2] a native or inhabitant of South America.

South American trypanosomiasis NOUN *Pathol* another name for **Chagas' disease.**

Southampton (saʊθˈæmptən, -ˈhæmp-) NOUN [1] a port in S England, in Southampton unitary authority, Hampshire on **Southampton Water** (an inlet of the English Channel): chief English passenger port; university (1952); shipyards and oil refinery. Pop.: 210 138 (1991). [2] a unitary authority in S England, in Hampshire. Pop.: 217 478 (2001). Area: 49 sq. km (19 sq. miles).

Southampton Island NOUN an island in N Canada, in Nunavut at the entrance to Hudson Bay: inhabited chiefly by Inuit. Area: 49 470 sq. km (19 100 sq. miles).

South Arabia NOUN **Federation of.** the former name (1963–67) of **South Yemen** (excluding Aden).

South Arabian ADJECTIVE [1] of or relating to the former South Arabia (now South Yemen) or its inhabitants. ◆ NOUN [2] a native or inhabitant of South Arabia.

South Australia NOUN a state of S central Australia, on the Great Australian Bight: generally arid, with the Great Victoria Desert in the west central part, the Lake Eyre basin in the northeast, and the Flinders Ranges, Murray River basin, and salt lakes in the southeast. Capital: Adelaide. Pop.: 1 493 070 (1999 est.). Area: 984 395 sq. km 380 070 sq. miles).

South Australian ADJECTIVE [1] of or relating to the state of South Australia or its inhabitants. ◆ NOUN [2] a native or inhabitant of South Australia.

South Ayrshire ('ɛəʃɪə, -ʃə) NOUN a council area of SW Scotland, on the Firth of Clyde: comprises the S part of the historical county of Ayrshire; formerly part of Strathclyde Region (1975–96): chiefly agricultural, with fishing and tourism. Administrative centre: Ayr. Pop.: 112 097 (2001). Area: 1202 sq. km (464 sq. miles).

South Bend NOUN a city in the US, in N Indiana: university (1842). Pop.: 107 789 (2000).

southbound ('saʊθˌbaʊnd) ADJECTIVE going or leading towards the south.

south by east NOUN [1] one point on the compass east of south; 168° 45′ clockwise from north. ◆ ADJECTIVE, ADVERB [2] in, from, or towards this direction.

south by west NOUN [1] one point on the compass west of south; 191° 15′ clockwise from north. ◆ ADJECTIVE, ADVERB [2] in, from, or towards this direction.

South Carolina NOUN a state of the southeastern US, on the Atlantic: the first state to secede from the Union in 1860; consists largely of low-lying coastal plains, rising in the northwest to the Blue Ridge Mountains; the largest US textile producer. Capital: Columbia. Pop.: 4 012 012 (2000). Area: 78 282 sq. km (30 225 sq. miles). Abbreviation and zip code: **SC.**

South Carolinian (ˌkærə'lɪnɪən) ADJECTIVE [1] of or relating to South Carolina or its inhabitants. ◆ NOUN [2] a native or inhabitant of South Carolina.

South China Sea NOUN part of the Pacific surrounded by SE China, Vietnam, the Malay Peninsula, Borneo, and the Philippines.

South Dakota NOUN a state of the western US: lies mostly in the Great Plains; the chief US producer of gold and beryl. Capital: Pierre. Pop.: 754 844 (2000). Area: 196 723 sq. km (75 955 sq. miles). Abbreviations: **S. Dak,** (with zip code) **SD.**

South Dakotan ADJECTIVE [1] of or relating to South Dakota or its inhabitants. ◆ NOUN [2] a native or inhabitant of South Dakota.

South Devon NOUN a breed of large red cattle originally from South Devon.

Southdown ('saʊθˌdaʊn) NOUN an English breed of sheep with short wool and a greyish-brown face and legs.

▷**HISTORY** C18: so called because it was originally bred on the SOUTH DOWNS

South Downs PLURAL NOUN a range of low hills in S England, extending from E Hampshire to East Sussex.

southeast (ˌsaʊθ'iːst; *Nautical* ˌsaʊ'iːst) NOUN [1] the point of the compass or the direction midway between south and east, 135° clockwise from north. ◆ ADJECTIVE *also* **southeastern.** [2] (*sometimes capital*) of or denoting the southeastern part of a specified country, area, etc. [3] situated in, proceeding towards, or facing the southeast. [4] (esp of the wind) from the southeast. ◆ ADVERB [5] in, to, towards, or (esp of the wind) from the southeast. ◆ Symbol: SE.

▸ˌ**south'easternmost** ADJECTIVE

Southeast (ˌsaʊθ'iːst) NOUN (usually preceded by *the*) the southeastern part of Britain, esp the London area.

Southeast Asia NOUN a region including Brunei, Cambodia, Indonesia, Laos, Malaysia, Myanmar, the Philippines, Thailand, and Vietnam.

Southeast Asian ADJECTIVE [1] of or relating to Southeast Asia or its inhabitants. ◆ NOUN [2] a native or inhabitant of Southeast Asia.

Southeast Asia Treaty Organization NOUN the full name of **SEATO.**

southeast by east NOUN [1] one point on the compass north of southeast; 123° 45′ clockwise from north. ◆ ADJECTIVE, ADVERB [2] in, from, or towards this direction.

southeast by south NOUN [1] one point on the compass south of southeast; 146° 15′ clockwise from north. ◆ ADJECTIVE, ADVERB [2] in, from, or towards this direction.

southeaster (ˌsaʊθ'iːstə; *Nautical* ˌsaʊ'iːstə) NOUN a strong wind or storm from the southeast.

southeasterly (ˌsaʊθ'iːstəlɪ; *Nautical* ˌsaʊ'iːstəlɪ) ADJECTIVE, ADVERB [1] in, towards, or (esp of a wind) from the southeast. ◆ NOUN, *plural* **-lies.** [2] a strong wind or storm from the southeast.

southeastward (ˌsaʊθ'iːstwəd; *Nautical* ˌsaʊ'iːstwəd) ADJECTIVE [1] towards or (esp of a wind) from the southeast. ◆ NOUN [2] a direction towards or area in the southeast. ◆ ADVERB [3] a variant of **southeastwards.**

southeastwards (ˌsaʊθ'iːstwədz; *Nautical* ˌsaʊ'iːstwədz) *or* **southeastward** ADVERB to the southeast.

Southend-on-Sea (ˌsaʊθ'end-) NOUN [1] a town in SE England, in SE Essex on the Thames estuary: one of England's largest resorts, extending for about 11 km (7 miles) along the coast. Pop.: 158 517 (1991). [2] a unitary authority in SE England, in Essex. Pop.: 160 256 (2001). Area: 42 sq. km (16 sq. miles).

souther ('saʊðə) NOUN a strong wind or storm from the south.

southerly ('sʌðəlɪ) ADJECTIVE [1] of, relating to, or situated in the south. ◆ ADVERB, ADJECTIVE [2] towards or in the direction of the south. [3] from the south: *a southerly wind.* ◆ NOUN, *plural* **-lies.** [4] a wind from the south.

▸'**southerliness** NOUN

southerly buster NOUN (*sometimes capitals*) a sudden violent cold wind on the SE coast of Australia causing a rapid drop in temperature. Sometimes shortened to: **southerly.**

southern ('sʌðən) ADJECTIVE [1] situated in or towards the south. [2] (of a wind, etc.) coming from the south. [3] native to, inhabiting, or growing in the south. [4] (*sometimes capital*) *Astronomy* south of the celestial equator.

Southern ('sʌðən) ADJECTIVE of, relating to, or characteristic of the south of a particular region or country.

Southern Alps PLURAL NOUN a mountain range in New Zealand, on South Island: the highest range in Australasia. Highest peak: Mount Cook, 3764 m (12 349 ft.).

Southern British English NOUN the dialect of spoken English regarded as standard in England and considered as having high social status in comparison with other British English dialects. Historically, it is derived from the S East Midland dialect of Middle English. Abbreviation: **SBE.** See also **Received Pronunciation.**

Southern Cross NOUN [1] a small conspicuous constellation in the S hemisphere lying in the Milky Way near Centaurus. The four brightest stars form a cross the longer arm of which points to the south celestial pole. Formal names: **Crux, Crux Australis.** [2] *Austral* the flag flown at the Eureka Stockade.

Southerner ('sʌðənə) NOUN (*sometimes not capital*) a native or inhabitant of the south of any specified region, esp the South of England or the Southern states of the US.

southern hemisphere NOUN (*often capitals*) [1] that half of the earth lying south of the equator. [2] *Astronomy* that half of the celestial sphere lying south of the celestial equator. ◆ Abbreviation: **S hemisphere.**

Southern Ireland NOUN See **Ireland**[1] (sense 2).

southern lights PLURAL NOUN another name for **aurora australis.**

southernly ('sʌðənlɪ) ADJECTIVE, ADVERB a less common word for **southerly.**

southernmost ('sʌðənˌməʊst) ADJECTIVE situated or occurring farthest south.

Southern Ocean NOUN another name for the **Antarctic Ocean.**

Southern Rhodesia NOUN the former name (until 1964) of **Zimbabwe.**

Southern Rhodesian ADJECTIVE [1] of or relating to the former Southern Rhodesia (now Zimbabwe) or its inhabitants. ◆ NOUN [2] a native or inhabitant of Southern Rhodesia.

Southern Sotho NOUN another name for **Sesotho.**

Southern Uplands PLURAL NOUN a hilly region extending across S Scotland: includes the Lowther, Moorfoot, and Lammermuir hills.

southernwood ('sʌðənˌwʊd) NOUN an aromatic shrubby wormwood, *Artemisia abrotanum,* of S Europe, having finely dissected leaves and small drooping heads of yellowish flowers. Also called: **old man, lad's love.**

▷**HISTORY** Old English. See SOUTHERN, WOOD

South Georgia NOUN an island in the S Atlantic, about 1300 km (800 miles) southeast of the Falkland Islands, part of the UK Overseas Territory of **South Georgia and the South Sandwich Islands.** Area: 3755 sq. km (1450 sq. miles).

South Georgian ADJECTIVE [1] of or relating to South Georgia or its inhabitants. ◆ NOUN [2] a native or inhabitant of South Georgia.

South Glamorgan NOUN a former county of S Wales, formed in 1974 from parts of Glamorgan and Monmouthshire plus the county borough of Cardiff: replaced in 1996 by the county boroughs of Cardiff and Vale of Glamorgan.

South Gloucestershire NOUN a unitary authority of SW England, in Gloucestershire: formerly (1974–96) part of the county of Avon. Pop.: 245 644 (2001). Area: 510 sq. km (197 sq. miles).

South Holland NOUN a province of the SW Netherlands, on the North Sea: lying mostly below sea level, it has a coastal strip of dunes and is drained chiefly by distributaries of the Rhine, with large areas of reclaimed land; the most densely populated province in the country, intensively cultivated and industrialized. Capital: The Hague. Pop.: 3 397 700 (2000 est.). Area: 3196 sq. km (1234 sq. miles). Dutch name: **Zuidholland.**

southing ('saʊðɪŋ) NOUN [1] *Navigation* movement, deviation, or distance covered in a southerly direction. [2] *Astronomy* a south or negative declination.

South Island NOUN **the.** the largest island of New Zealand, separated from the North Island by Cook Strait. Pop.: 942 213 (2001). Area: 153 947 sq. km (59 439 sq. miles).

South Korea NOUN a republic in NE Asia: established as a republic in 1948; invaded by North Korea and Chinese Communists in 1950 but division remained unchanged at the end of the war (1953); includes over 3000 islands; rapid industrialization. Language: Korean. Religions: Buddhist, Confucianist, Shamanist, and Chondokyo. Currency: won. Capital: Seoul. Pop.: 47 676 000 (2001 est.). Area: 98 477 sq. km (38 022 sq. miles). Korean name: **Hanguk.**

South Korean ADJECTIVE [1] of or relating to South Korea or its inhabitants. ◆ NOUN [2] a native or inhabitant of South Korea.

South Lanarkshire ('lænəkˌʃɪə, -ʃə) NOUN a council area of S Scotland, comprising the S part of the historical county of Lanarkshire: included within Strathclyde Region from 1975 to 1996: has uplands in the S and part of the Glasgow conurbation in the N: mainly agricultural. Administrative centre: Hamilton. Pop.: 302 216 (2001). Area: 1771 sq. km (684 sq. miles).

South Orkney Islands PLURAL NOUN a group of islands in the S Atlantic, southeast of Cape Horn: formerly a dependency of the Falkland Islands; part of British Antarctic Territory since 1962. Area: 621 sq. km (240 sq. miles).

South Ossetia (əˈsiːʃə) NOUN a region in Georgia on the S slopes of the Caucasus Mountains; in 1990 it voted to join Russia, leading to armed conflict with Georgian forces; it became an autonomous region in 1997. Capital: Tskhinvali. Pop.: 99 800 (1990). Area: 3900 sq. km (1500 sq. miles). Georgian name: **Tskhinvali.** Also called: **South Ossetian Autonomous Region.**

southpaw (ˈsaʊθˌpɔː) *Informal* ◆ NOUN [1] a boxer who leads with his right hand and off his right foot as opposed to the orthodox style of leading with the left. [2] any left-handed person. ◆ ADJECTIVE [3] of or relating to a southpaw.
▷HISTORY C20: from PAW (in the sense: hand): originally a term applied to a left-handed baseball player: perhaps so called because baseball pitchers traditionally face west, so that a left-handed pitcher would throw with the hand on the south side of his body

South Pole NOUN [1] the southernmost point on the earth's axis, at the latitude of 90°S. [2] *Astronomy* the point of intersection, in the constellation Octans, of the earth's extended axis and the southern half of the celestial sphere. [3] *(usually not capitals)* the south-seeking pole of a freely suspended magnet.

Southport (ˈsaʊθˌpɔːt) NOUN a town and resort in NW England, in Sefton unitary authority, Merseyside on the Irish Sea. Pop.: 90 959 (1991).

Southron (ˈsʌðrən) NOUN [1] *Chiefly Scot* a Southerner, esp an Englishman. [2] *Scot* the English language as spoken in England. [3] *Dialect, chiefly southern US* an inhabitant of the South, esp at the time of the Civil War. ◆ ADJECTIVE [4] *Chiefly Scot* of or relating to the South or to England.
▷HISTORY C15: Scottish variant of SOUTHERN

South Saskatchewan NOUN a river in S central Canada, rising in S Alberta and flowing east and northeast to join the North Saskatchewan River, forming the Saskatchewan River. Length: 1392 km (865 miles).

South Sea Bubble NOUN *Brit history* the financial crash that occurred in 1720 after the **South Sea Company** had taken over the national debt in return for a monopoly of trade with the South Seas, causing feverish speculation in their stocks.
▷HISTORY so named because the rapid expansion and sudden collapse of investment resembled the blowing up and bursting of a bubble

South Sea Islands PLURAL NOUN the islands in the S Pacific that constitute Oceania.

South Seas PLURAL NOUN the seas south of the equator.

South Shetland Islands PLURAL NOUN a group of islands in the S Atlantic, north of the Antarctic Peninsula: formerly a dependency of the Falkland Islands; part of British Antarctic Territory since 1962. Area: 4662 sq. km (1800 sq. miles).

South Shields NOUN a port in NE England, in South Tyneside unitary authority, Tyne and Wear on the Tyne estuary opposite North Shields. Pop.: 83 704 (1991).

south-southeast NOUN [1] the point on the compass or the direction midway between southeast and south; 157° 30′ clockwise from north. ◆ ADJECTIVE, ADVERB [2] in, from, or towards this direction. ◆ Symbol: SSE.

south-southwest NOUN [1] the point on the compass or the direction midway between south and southwest; 202° 30′ clockwise from north. ◆ ADJECTIVE, ADVERB [2] in, from, or towards this direction. ◆ Symbol: SSW.

South Tyneside (ˈtaɪnˌsaɪd) NOUN a unitary authority of NE England, in Tyne and Wear. Pop.: 152 785 (2001). Area: 64 sq. km (25 sq. miles).

South Tyrol *or* **Tirol** NOUN a former part of the Austrian state of Tyrol: ceded to Italy in 1919, becoming the Bolzano and Trento provinces of the Trentino-Alto Adige Autonomous Region. Area: 14 037 sq. km (5420 sq. miles).

South Vietnam NOUN a former republic (1955–76) occupying the S of present-day Vietnam on the South China Sea and the Gulf of Siam.

South Vietnamese ADJECTIVE [1] of or relating to the former South Vietnam (now part of Vietnam) or its inhabitants. ◆ NOUN [2] a native or inhabitant of South Vietnam.

southward (ˈsaʊθwəd; *Nautical* ˈsʌðəd) ADJECTIVE [1] situated, directed, or moving towards the south. ◆ NOUN [2] the southward part, direction, etc.; the south. ◆ ADVERB [3] a variant of **southwards.**
▶ˈ**southwardly** ADJECTIVE, ADVERB

southwards (ˈsaʊθwədz; *Nautical* ˈsʌðədz) *or* **southward** ADVERB towards the south.

Southwark (ˈsʌðək) NOUN a borough of S central Greater London, on the River Thames: site of the Globe Theatre, now reconstructed; the former docks and warehouses have been redeveloped. Pop.: 244 867 (2001). Area: 29 sq. km (11 sq. miles).

southwest (ˌsaʊθˈwest; *Nautical* ˌsaʊˈwest) NOUN [1] the point of the compass or the direction midway between west and south, 225° clockwise from north. ◆ ADJECTIVE *also* **southwestern.** [2] *(sometimes capital)* of or denoting the southwestern part of a specified country, area, etc.: *southwest Italy.* [3] situated in or towards the southwest. [4] (esp of the wind) from the southwest. ◆ ADVERB [5] in, to, towards, or (esp of the wind) from the southwest. ◆ Symbol: SW.
▶ˌ**southˈwesternmost** ADJECTIVE

Southwest (ˌsaʊθˈwest) NOUN (usually preceded by *the*) the southwestern part of Britain, esp Cornwall, Devon, and Somerset.

South West Africa NOUN another name for **Namibia.**

southwest by south NOUN [1] one point on the compass south of southwest; 213° 45′ clockwise from north. ◆ ADJECTIVE, ADVERB [2] in, from, or towards this direction.

southwest by west NOUN [1] one point on the compass north of southwest, 236° 15′ clockwise from north. ◆ ADJECTIVE, ADVERB [2] in, from, or towards this direction.

southwester (ˌsaʊθˈwestə; *Nautical* ˌsaʊˈwestə) NOUN a strong wind or storm from the southwest.

southwesterly (ˌsaʊθˈwestəlɪ; *Nautical* ˌsaʊˈwestəlɪ) ADJECTIVE, ADVERB [1] in, towards, or (esp of a wind) from the southwest. ◆ NOUN, *plural* **-lies.** [2] a wind or storm from the southwest.

southwestward (ˌsaʊθˈwestwəd; *Nautical* ˌsaʊˈwestwəd) ADJECTIVE [1] from or towards the southwest. ◆ ADVERB [2] a variant of **southwestwards.** ◆ NOUN [3] a direction towards or area in the southwest.
▶ˌ**southˈwestwardly** ADJECTIVE, ADVERB

southwestwards (ˌsaʊθˈwestwədz; *Nautical* ˌsaʊˈwestwədz) *or* **southwestward** ADVERB to the southwest.

South Yemen NOUN a former republic in SW Arabia, on the Gulf of Aden; now a part of Yemen: became a republic in 1967; merged with North Yemen in 1990. Official name (1967–90): **People's Democratic Republic of Yemen.** Name from 1963 to 1967 (excluding Aden): (Federation of) **South Arabia.** See also **Yemen, North Yemen.**

South Yorkshire NOUN a metropolitan county of N England, administered since 1986 by the unitary authorities of Barnsley, Doncaster, Sheffield, and Rotherham. Area: 1560 sq. km (602 sq. miles).

souvenir (ˌsuːvəˈnɪə, ˈsuːvəˌnɪə) NOUN [1] an object that recalls a certain place, occasion, or person; memento. ◆ VERB *(tr)* [2] *Austral and NZ euphemistic slang* to steal or keep (something, esp a small article) for one's own use; purloin.
▷HISTORY C18: from French, from *(se) souvenir* to remember, from Latin *subvenīre* to come to mind, from *sub-* up to + *venīre* to come

souvlakia (suːˈvlækɪə) NOUN a Greek dish of kebabs, esp made with lamb.
▷HISTORY C20: from Modern Greek

sou'wester (saʊˈwestə) NOUN a waterproof hat having a very broad rim behind, worn esp by seamen.
▷HISTORY C19: a contraction of SOUTHWESTER

sovereign (ˈsɒvrɪn) NOUN [1] a person exercising supreme authority, esp a monarch. [2] a former British gold coin worth one pound sterling. ◆ ADJECTIVE [3] supreme in rank or authority: *a sovereign lord.* [4] excellent or outstanding: *a sovereign remedy.* [5] of, relating to, or characteristic of a sovereign. [6] independent of outside authority: *a sovereign state.*
▷HISTORY C13: from Old French *soverain,* from Vulgar Latin *superānus* (unattested), from Latin *super* above; also influenced by REIGN
▶ˈ**sovereignly** ADVERB

sovereigntist (ˈsɒvrəntɪst) NOUN (in Canada) a supporter of sovereignty association.

sovereignty (ˈsɒvrəntɪ) NOUN, *plural* **-ties.** [1] supreme and unrestricted power, as of a state. [2] the position, dominion, or authority of a sovereign. [3] an independent state.

sovereignty association NOUN (in Canada) a proposed arrangement by which Quebec would become independent but would maintain a formal association with Canada.

Sovetsk (*Russian* saˈvjetsk) NOUN a town in W Russia, in the Kaliningrad Region on the Neman River: scene of the signing of the treaty (1807) between Napoleon I and Tsar Alexander I; passed from East Prussia to the Soviet Union in 1945. Former name (until 1945): **Tilsit.**

soviet (ˈsəʊvɪət, ˈsɒv-) NOUN [1] (in the former Soviet Union) an elected government council at the local, regional, and national levels, which culminated in the Supreme Soviet. [2] (in prerevolutionary Russia) a local revolutionary council. ◆ ADJECTIVE [3] of or relating to a soviet.
▷HISTORY C20: from Russian *sovyet* council, from Old Russian *sŭvětŭ*

Soviet (ˈsəʊvɪət, ˈsɒv-) ADJECTIVE of, characteristic of, or relating to the former Soviet Union, its people, or its government.

Soviet Central Asia NOUN the region of the former Soviet Union now occupied by Kazakhstan, Kyrgyzstan, Tajikistan, Turkmenistan, and Uzbekistan. Also called: **Russian Turkestan, West Turkestan.**

sovietism (ˈsəʊvɪɪˌtɪzəm, ˈsɒv-) NOUN *(sometimes capital)* [1] the principle or practice of government through soviets, esp as practised in the former Soviet Union. [2] any characteristic deemed representative of Soviet ideology.
▶ˈ**sovietist** NOUN, ADJECTIVE ▶ˌ**sovietˈistic** ADJECTIVE

sovietize *or* **sovietise** (ˈsəʊvɪɪˌtaɪz, ˈsɒv-) VERB *(tr; often capital)* [1] to bring (a country, person, etc.) under Soviet control or influence. [2] to cause (a country) to conform to the Soviet model in its social, political, and economic structure.
▶ˌ**sovietiˈzation** *or* ˌ**sovietiˈsation** NOUN

Sovietologist (ˌsəʊvɪəˈtɒlədʒɪst, ˌsɒv-) NOUN a person who has studied the political policies and developments of the former Soviet government.

Soviet Russia NOUN (formerly) another name for the **Russian Soviet Federative Socialist Republic** or the **Soviet Union.**

Soviets (ˈsəʊvɪəts, ˈsɒv-) NOUN the people or government of the former Soviet Union.

Soviet Union NOUN a former federal republic in E Europe and central and N Asia: the revolution of 1917 achieved the overthrow of the Russian monarchy and the USSR was established in 1922 as a Communist state. It was the largest country in the world, occupying a seventh of the total land surface. The collapse of Communist rule in 1991 was followed by declarations of independence by many of the constituent republics and the break-up of the Soviet Union. Official name: **Union of Soviet Socialist Republics.** Also called: **Russia, Soviet Russia.** Abbreviation: **USSR.**

Soviet Zone NOUN that part of Germany occupied by Soviet forces in 1945–49: transformed into the German Democratic Republic in 1949–50. Also called: **Russian Zone.**

sovkhoz (sɒfˈkɒz; *Russian* safˈxɔs)NOUN **pl, sovkhozy** (sɒfˈkɒzɪ; *Russian* safˈxɔzi). (in the former Soviet Union) a large mechanized farm owned by the state.
▷HISTORY C20: Russian, from *sovetskoe khozyaistvo* soviet economy

sovran (ˈsɒvrən) NOUN, ADJECTIVE a literary word for **sovereign.**
▶ˈ**sovranly** ADVERB ▶ˈ**sovranty** NOUN

sow[1] (səʊ) VERB **sows, sowing, sowed; sown** *or* **sowed.**

1 to scatter or place (seed, a crop, etc.) in or on (a piece of ground, field, etc.) so that it may grow: *to sow wheat; to sow a strip of land.* 2 (*tr*) to implant or introduce: *to sow a doubt in someone's mind.*
▷**HISTORY** Old English *sāwan;* related to Old Norse *sā,* Old High German *sāen,* Old Slavonic *seja,* Latin *serere* to sow
▸ˈ**sowable** ADJECTIVE ▸ˈ**sower** NOUN

sow[2] (saʊ) NOUN 1 a female adult pig. 2 the female of certain other animals, such as the mink. 3 *Metallurgy* **a** the channels for leading molten metal to the moulds in casting pig iron. **b** iron that has solidified in these channels.
▷**HISTORY** Old English *sugu;* related to Old Norse *sȳr,* Old High German *sū,* Latin *sūs,* Norwegian *sugga,* Dutch *zeug:* see SWINE

sowback (ˈsaʊˌbæk) NOUN another name for **hogback** (sense 1).

sowbread (ˈsaʊˌbrɛd) NOUN a S European primulaceous plant, *Cyclamen hederifolium,* with heart-shaped leaves and pink nodding flowers. See also **cyclamen** (sense 1).
▷**HISTORY** C16: from SOW[2] + BREAD, based on Medieval Latin *panis porcinus;* the tuberous roots are eaten by swine

sow bug (saʊ) NOUN *US and Canadian* any of various woodlice, esp any of the genera *Oniscus* and *Porcellio.*
▷**HISTORY** C18: from its resemblance to a pig in shape

sowens (ˈsəʊənz, ˈsuː-) NOUN *Scot* a pudding made from oatmeal husks steeped and boiled.
▷**HISTORY** C16: from Scottish Gaelic *sùghan,* from *sùgh* sap; related to Old High German *sūgan* to SUCK

Soweto (səˈwɛtəʊ, -ˈweɪtəʊ) NOUN a contiguous group of Black African townships southwest of Johannesburg, South Africa: the largest purely Black African urban settlement in southern Africa: scene of riots (1976) following protests against the use of Afrikaans in schools for Black African children. Area: 62 sq. km (24 sq. miles). Pop.: 1 098 094 (1996).
▷**HISTORY** C20: from *so(uth) we(st) to(wnship)*

sown (səʊn) VERB a past participle of **sow**[1].

sow thistle (saʊ) NOUN any of various plants of the Old World genus *Sonchus,* esp *S. oleraceus,* having milky juice, prickly leaves, and heads of yellow flowers: family *Asteraceae* (composites). Also called: **milk thistle,** (NZ) **puha,** (NZ) **rauriki.**
▷**HISTORY** C13: from *sugethistel,* perhaps variant of Old English *thugethistel, thuthistel* thowthistle, a dialect name of the sow thistle. See SOW[2], THISTLE

soya bean (ˈsɔɪə) *or US and Canadian* **soybean** (ˈsɔɪˌbiːn) NOUN 1 an Asian bean plant, *Glycine max* (or *G. soja*), cultivated for its nutritious seeds, for forage, and to improve the soil. 2 the seed of this plant, used as food, forage, and as the source of an oil.
▷**HISTORY** C17 *soya,* via Dutch *soya* from Japanese *shōyu,* from Chinese *chiang yu,* from *chiang* paste + *yu* sauce

soy sauce (sɔɪ) NOUN a salty dark brown sauce made from fermented soya beans, used esp in Japanese and Chinese cookery. Also called: **soya sauce.**

Soyuz (sɔɪˈjʊz) NOUN any of a series of Russian spacecraft used to ferry crew to and from space stations.
▷**HISTORY** C20: Russian: union

sozzled (ˈsɒzəld) ADJECTIVE an informal word for **drunk.**
▷**HISTORY** C19: perhaps from obsolete *sozzle* stupor; related to SOUSE[1]

sp ABBREVIATION FOR without issue.
▷**HISTORY** from Latin *sine prole*

SP ABBREVIATION FOR: 1 standard play: the standard recording speed on a VCR. 2 **starting price.** ◆ NOUN 3 *Brit slang* latest information.

sp. ABBREVIATION FOR: 1 special. 2 (*plural* **spp**) species. 3 specific.

Sp. ABBREVIATION FOR: 1 Spain. 2 Spaniard. 3 Spanish.

spa (spɑː) NOUN a mineral spring or a place or resort where such a spring is found.
▷**HISTORY** C17: named after SPA, Belgium

Spa (spɑː) NOUN a town in E Belgium, in Liège province: a resort with medicinal mineral springs (discovered in the 14th century). Pop.: 10 140 (1991).

SpA ABBREVIATION FOR Società per Azioni.
▷**HISTORY** Italian: limited company

SPA ABBREVIATION FOR Special Protection Area: an area designated by the European Union in order to protect endangered species, esp of birds.

space (speɪs) NOUN 1 the unlimited three-dimensional expanse in which all material objects are located. Related adjective: **spatial.** 2 an interval of distance or time between two points, objects, or events. 3 a blank portion or area. 4 **a** unoccupied area or room: *there is no space for a table.* **b** (*in combination*): *space-saving.* Related adjective: **spacious.** 5 freedom to do what a person wishes to for his or her own personal development. 6 **a** the region beyond the earth's atmosphere containing the other planets of the solar system, stars, galaxies, etc.; universe. **b** (*as modifier*): *a space probe; space navigation.* 7 **a** the region beyond the earth's atmosphere occurring between the celestial bodies of the universe. The density is normally negligible although cosmic rays, meteorites, gas clouds, etc., can occur. It can be divided into **cislunar space** (between the earth and moon), **interplanetary space, interstellar space,** and **intergalactic space. b** (*as modifier*): *a space station; a space simulator.* 8 a seat or place, as on a train, aircraft, etc. 9 *Printing* **a** a piece of metal, less than type-high, used to separate letters or words in hot-metal printing. **b** any of the gaps used to separate letters, words or lines in photocomposition, desktop publishing, etc. 10 *Music* any of the gaps between the lines that make up the staff. 11 *Maths* a collection of unspecified points having properties that obey a specified set of axioms: *Euclidean space.* 12 Also called: **spacing.** *Telegraphy* the period of time that separates complete letters, digits, and other characters in Morse code. ◆ VERB (*tr*) 13 to place or arrange at intervals or with spaces between. 14 to divide into or by spaces: *to space one's time evenly.* 15 *Printing* to separate (letters, words, or lines) by the insertion of spaces.
▷**HISTORY** C13: from Old French *espace,* from Latin *spatium*

space age NOUN 1 the period in which the exploration of space has become possible. ◆ ADJECTIVE **space-age.** 2 (*usually prenominal*) futuristic or ultramodern, esp when suggestive of space technology.

spaceband (ˈspeɪsˌbænd) NOUN *Printing* a device on a linecaster for evening up the spaces between words.

space-bar NOUN a horizontal bar on a typewriter that is depressed in order to leave a space between words, letters, etc.

space blanket NOUN a plastic insulating body wrapping coated on one or both sides with aluminium foil which reflects back most of the body heat lost by radiation: carried by climbers, mountaineers, etc., for use in cases of exposure or exhaustion.
▷**HISTORY** C20: material originally developed as part of the US space programme

space cadet NOUN *Slang* a person who is eccentric or out of touch with reality, as if affected by drugs.

space capsule NOUN a vehicle, sometimes carrying people or animals, designed to obtain scientific information from space, planets, etc., and be recovered on returning to earth.

space character NOUN *Computing* a keyed space in text or data.

spacecraft (ˈspeɪsˌkrɑːft) NOUN a manned or unmanned vehicle designed to orbit the earth or travel to celestial objects for the purpose of research, exploration, etc.

spaced out ADJECTIVE *Slang* intoxicated through or as if through taking a drug. Often shortened to: **spaced.**

space-filler NOUN a short article of little or no importance written to fill space in a magazine or newspaper.

space heater NOUN a heater used to warm the air in an enclosed area, such as a room or office.

Space Invaders NOUN (*functioning as singular*) *Trademark* a video or computer game, the object of which is to destroy attacking alien spacecraft.

spacelab (ˈspeɪsˌlæb) NOUN a laboratory in space where scientific experiments are performed, esp one developed by the European Space Agency and carried on a space shuttle.

space lattice NOUN *Crystallog* the more formal name for **lattice** (sense 4).

spaceless (ˈspeɪslɪs) ADJECTIVE *Chiefly literary* 1 having no limits in space; infinite or boundless. 2 occupying no space.

spaceman (ˈspeɪsˌmæn) *or feminine* **spacewoman** NOUN, *plural* **-men** *or feminine* **-women.** a person who travels in outer space, esp one trained to participate in a space flight.

space medicine NOUN the branch of medicine concerned with the effects on man of flight outside the earth's atmosphere. Compare **aviation medicine.**

space opera NOUN a science fiction drama, such as a film or television programme, esp one dealing with interplanetary flight.

space platform NOUN another name for **space station.**

spaceport (ˈspeɪsˌpɔːt) NOUN a base equipped to launch, maintain, and test spacecraft.

space probe NOUN a vehicle, such as a satellite, equipped to obtain scientific information, normally transmitted back to earth by radio, about the atmosphere, surface, and temperature of a planet, conditions in space, etc.

spacer (ˈspeɪsə) NOUN 1 a piece of material used to create or maintain a space between two things. 2 *Computing* a keyed space in text or data; space character. 3 a person who travels in outer space.

spaceship (ˈspeɪsˌʃɪp) NOUN a manned spacecraft.

space shuttle NOUN any of a series of reusable US space vehicles (*Columbia* (exploded 2003), *Challenger* (exploded 1986), *Discovery, Atlantis, Endeavour*) that can be launched into earth orbit transporting astronauts and equipment for a period of observation, research, etc., before re-entry and an unpowered landing on a runway; the first operational flight occurred in 1982.

space sickness NOUN the nausea that people can experience in the gravity-free environment of space.

space station NOUN any large manned artificial satellite designed to orbit the earth during a long period of time thus providing a base for scientific and medical research in space and a construction site, launch pad, and docking arrangements for spacecraft. Also called: **space platform, space laboratory.**

spacesuit (ˈspeɪsˌsuːt, -ˌsjuːt) NOUN any of various types of sealed and pressurized suits worn by astronauts or cosmonauts that provide an artificial atmosphere, acceptable temperature, radiocommunication link, and protection from radiation for work outside a spacecraft.

space-time *or* **space-time continuum** NOUN *Physics* the four-dimensional continuum having three spatial coordinates and one time coordinate that together completely specify the location of a particle or an event.

spacewalk (ˈspeɪsˌwɔːk) NOUN 1 the act or an instance of floating and manoeuvring in space, outside but attached by a lifeline to a spacecraft. Technical name: **extravehicular activity.** ◆ VERB 2 (*intr*) to float and manoeuvre in space while outside but attached to a spacecraft.

space writer NOUN a writer paid by the area of his copy.

spacey (ˈspeɪsɪ) ADJECTIVE **spacier, spaciest.** *Slang* vague and dreamy, as if under the influence of drugs.
▷**HISTORY** C20: SPACE + -EY

spacial (ˈspeɪʃəl) ADJECTIVE a variant spelling of **spatial.**

spacing (ˈspeɪsɪŋ) NOUN 1 the arrangement of letters, words, etc., on a page in order to achieve legibility or aesthetic appeal. 2 the arrangement of objects in a space.

spacious (ˈspeɪʃəs) ADJECTIVE having a large capacity or area.
▷**HISTORY** C14: from Latin *spātiōsus,* from *spatium* SPACE
▸ˈ**spaciously** ADVERB ▸ˈ**spaciousness** NOUN

SPAD (spæd) NOUN ACRONYM FOR signal passed at

danger: an incident in which a train goes through a red light.

spade[1] (speɪd) NOUN 1 a tool for digging, typically consisting of a flat rectangular steel blade attached to a long wooden handle. 2 **a** an object or part resembling a spade in shape. **b** (*as modifier*): *a spade beard.* 3 a heavy metallic projection attached to the trail of a gun carriage that embeds itself into the ground and so reduces recoil. 4 a type of oar blade that is comparatively broad and short. Compare **spoon** (sense 7). 5 a cutting tool for stripping the blubber from a whale or skin from a carcass. 6 **call a spade a spade.** to speak plainly and frankly. ◆ VERB 7 (*tr*) to use a spade on.
▷HISTORY Old English *spadu;* related to Old Norse *spathi,* Old High German *spato,* Greek *spathē* blade
▸**'spader** NOUN

spade[2] (speɪd) NOUN 1 **a** the black symbol on a playing card resembling a heart-shaped leaf with a stem. **b** a card with one or more of these symbols or (*when pl.*) the suit of cards so marked, usually the highest ranking of the four. 2 a derogatory word for **Black.** 3 **in spades.** *Informal* in an extreme or emphatic way.
▷HISTORY C16: from Italian *spada* sword, used as an emblem on playing cards, from Latin *spatha,* from Greek *spathē* blade, broadsword

spadefish ('speɪd,fɪʃ) NOUN, *plural* **-fish** *or* **-fishes.** any spiny-finned food fish of the family *Ephippidae,* esp *Chaetodipterus faber* of American Atlantic coastal waters, having a deeply compressed body.

spade foot NOUN a spadelike projection at the end of a chair leg.

spade guinea NOUN *Brit history* a guinea decorated with a spade-shaped shield, coined during the reign of George III.

spadework ('speɪd,wɜːk) NOUN dull or routine preparatory work.

spadger ('spædʒə) NOUN *English dialect* a sparrow.

spadiceous (speɪ'dɪʃəs) ADJECTIVE 1 *Botany* producing or resembling a spadix. 2 of a bright brown colour.
▷HISTORY C17: from New Latin *spādīceus,* from Latin *spādix* palm branch; see SPADIX

spadille (spə'dɪl) NOUN *Cards* (in ombre and quadrille) the ace of spades.
▷HISTORY C18: from French, from Spanish *espadilla,* diminutive of *espada* sword; see SPADE[2]

spadix ('speɪdɪks) NOUN, *plural* **spadices** (speɪ'daɪsiːz). a racemose inflorescence having many small sessile flowers borne on a fleshy stem, the whole usually being surrounded by a spathe: typical of aroid plants.
▷HISTORY C18: from Latin: pulled-off branch of a palm, with its fruit, from Greek: torn-off frond; related to Greek *span* to pull off

spae (speɪ) VERB *Scot* to foretell (the future).
▷HISTORY C14: from Old Norse

spaewife ('spe,wəɪf) NOUN, *plural* **-wives.** a woman who can supposedly foretell the future.

spag[1] (spæg) VERB **spags, spagging, spagged.** (*tr*) *South Wales dialect* (of a cat) to scratch (a person) with the claws.
▷HISTORY of uncertain origin

spag[2] (spæg) NOUN *Austral offensive slang* an Italian.
▷HISTORY from SPAGHETTI

spaghetti (spə'gɛtɪ) NOUN pasta in the form of long strings.
▷HISTORY C19: from Italian: little cords, from *spago* a cord

spaghetti junction NOUN an interchange, usually between motorways, in which there are a large number of underpasses and overpasses and intersecting roads used by a large volume of high-speed traffic.
▷HISTORY C20: from the nickname of the Gravelly Hill Interchange, Birmingham, where the M6, A38M, A38, and A5127 intersect

spaghettini (,spægɛ'tiːnɪ) NOUN pasta in the form of long thin strings.
▷HISTORY Italian: small spaghetti

spaghetti western NOUN a cowboy film about the American West made, esp by an Italian director, in Europe.

spagyric (spə'dʒɪrɪk) *or* **spagyrical** ADJECTIVE *Rare* of or relating to alchemy.
▷HISTORY C16: from New Latin *spagiricus,* probably coined by Paracelsus, of obscure origin
▸**spa'gyrically** ADVERB

spahi *or* **spahee** ('spɑːhiː, 'spɑːiː) NOUN, *plural* **-his** *or* **-hees.** 1 (formerly) an irregular cavalryman in the Turkish armed forces. 2 a member of a body of native Algerian cavalrymen in the French armed forces: disbanded after Algerian independence.
▷HISTORY C16: from Old French, from Turkish *sipahi,* from Persian *sipāhī* soldier; see SEPOY

Spain (speɪn) NOUN a kingdom of SW Europe, occupying the Iberian peninsula between the Mediterranean and the Atlantic: a leading European power in the 16th century, with many overseas possessions, esp in the New World; became a republic in 1931; under the fascist dictatorship of Franco following the Civil War (1936–39) until his death in 1975; a member of the European Union. It consists chiefly of a central plateau (the Meseta), with the Pyrenees and the Cantabrian Mountains in the north and the Sierra Nevada in the south. Official language: Castilian Spanish, with Catalan, Galician, and Basque official regional languages. Religion: Roman Catholic majority. Currency: euro. Capital: Madrid. Pop.: 40 144 000 (2001). Area: 504 748 sq. km (194 883 sq. miles). Spanish name: **España.**

spake (speɪk) VERB *Archaic or dialect* a past tense of **speak.**

Spalato ('spaːlato) NOUN the Italian name for **Split.**

Spalding ('spɔːldɪŋ) NOUN a town in E England, in S Lincolnshire: noted for its bulbfields. Pop.: 18 731 (1991).

spall (spɔːl) NOUN 1 a splinter or chip of ore, rock, or stone. ◆ VERB 2 to split or cause to split into such fragments.
▷HISTORY C15: of unknown origin

spallation (spə'leɪʃən) NOUN *Physics* a type of nuclear reaction in which a photon or particle hits a nucleus and causes it to emit many other particles or photons.
▷HISTORY C20: from SPALL + -ATION

spalpeen ('spælpiːn) NOUN *Irish* 1 an itinerant seasonal labourer. 2 a rascal or layabout.
▷HISTORY C18: from Irish Gaelic *spailpín* itinerant labourer

spam (spæm) *Computing, slang* ◆ VERB **spams, spamming, spammed.** 1 to send unsolicited electronic mail simultaneously to a number of newsgroups on the Internet. ◆ NOUN 2 unsolicited electronic mail sent in this way.
▷HISTORY C20: from the repeated use of the word *Spam* in a popular sketch from the British television show *Monty Python's Flying Circus,* first broadcast in 1969
▸**'spammer** NOUN

Spam (spæm) NOUN *Trademark* a kind of tinned luncheon meat, made largely from pork.

spammie ('spæmɪ) NOUN *Northern English dialect* a love bite.

span[1] (spæn) NOUN 1 the interval, space, or distance between two points, such as the ends of a bridge or arch. 2 the complete duration or extent: *the span of his life.* 3 *Psychol* the amount of material that can be processed in a single mental act: *apprehension span; span of attention.* 4 short for **wingspan.** 5 a unit of length based on the width of an expanded hand, usually taken as nine inches. ◆ VERB **spans, spanning, spanned.** (*tr*) 6 to stretch or extend across, over, or around. 7 to provide with something that extends across or around: *to span a river with a bridge.* 8 to measure or cover, esp with the extended hand.
▷HISTORY Old English *spann;* related to Old Norse *sponn,* Old High German *spanna*

span[2] (spæn) NOUN a team of horses or oxen, esp two matched animals.
▷HISTORY C16 (in the sense: yoke): from Middle Dutch: something stretched, from *spannen* to stretch; see SPAN[1]

span[3] (spæn) VERB *Archaic or dialect* a past tense of **spin.**

Span. ABBREVIATION FOR Spanish.

spancel ('spænsᵊl) NOUN 1 a length of rope for hobbling an animal, esp a horse or cow. ◆ VERB **-cels, -celling, -celled** *or US* **-cels, -celing, -celed.** 2 (*tr*) to hobble (an animal) with a loose rope.
▷HISTORY C17: from Low German *spansel,* from *spannen* to stretch; see SPAN[2]

spandex ('spændɛks) NOUN a type of synthetic stretch fabric made from polyurethane fibre.
▷HISTORY C20: coined from an anagram of *expands*

spandrel *or* **spandril** ('spændrəl) NOUN *Architect* 1 an approximately triangular surface bounded by the outer curve of an arch and the adjacent wall. 2 the surface area between two adjacent arches and the horizontal cornice above them.
▷HISTORY C15 *spaundrell,* from Anglo-French *spaundre* spandrel, from Old French *spandre* to spread, EXPAND

spang (spæŋ) ADVERB *US and Canadian informal* exactly, firmly, or straight: *spang on target.*
▷HISTORY C19: of unknown origin

spangle ('spæŋgᵊl) NOUN 1 a small thin piece of metal or other shiny material used as a decoration, esp on clothes; sequin. 2 any glittering or shiny spot or object. ◆ VERB 3 (*intr*) to glitter or shine with or like spangles. 4 (*tr*) to decorate or cover with spangles.
▷HISTORY C15: diminutive of *spange,* perhaps from Middle Dutch: clasp; compare Old Norse *spöng*
▸**'spangly** ADJECTIVE

Spanglish ('spæŋglɪʃ) *chiefly US* NOUN a variety of English heavily influenced by Spanish, commonly spoken in US Hispanic communities.
▷HISTORY C20: from a blend of SPANISH + ENGLISH

Spaniard ('spænjəd) NOUN 1 a native or inhabitant of Spain. 2 *NZ* short for **wild Spaniard.**

spaniel ('spænjəl) NOUN 1 any of several breeds of gundog with long drooping ears, a silky coat, and formerly a docked tail. See **clumber spaniel, cocker spaniel, field spaniel, springer spaniel, Sussex spaniel, water spaniel.** 2 either of two toy breeds of spaniel: see **King Charles spaniel.** 3 an obsequiously devoted person.
▷HISTORY C14: from Old French *espaigneul* Spanish (dog), from Old Provençal *espanhol,* ultimately from Latin *Hispāniolus* Spanish

Spanish ('spænɪʃ) NOUN 1 the official language of Spain, Mexico, and most countries of South and Central America except Brazil: also spoken in Africa, the Far East, and elsewhere. It is the native language of approximately 200 million people throughout the world. Spanish is an Indo-European language belonging to the Romance group. 2 **the Spanish.** (*functioning as plural*) Spaniards collectively. ◆ ADJECTIVE 3 of or relating to the Spanish language or its speakers. 4 of or relating to Spain or Spaniards.

Spanish America NOUN the parts of America colonized by Spaniards from the 16th century onwards and now chiefly Spanish-speaking: includes all of South America (except Brazil, Guyana, French Guiana, and Surinam), Central America (except Belize), Mexico, Cuba, Puerto Rico, the Dominican Republic, and a number of small Caribbean islands.

Spanish-American ADJECTIVE 1 of or relating to any of the Spanish-speaking countries or peoples of the Americas. ◆ NOUN 2 a native or inhabitant of Spanish America. 3 a Spanish-speaking person in the US.

Spanish-American War NOUN the war between the US and Spain (1898) resulting in Spain's withdrawal from Cuba and its cession of Guam, the Philippines, and Puerto Rico.

Spanish Armada NOUN the great fleet sent by Philip II of Spain against England in 1588: defeated in the Channel by the English fleets and almost completely destroyed by storms off the Hebrides. Also called: **the Armada.**

Spanish bayonet NOUN any of several American liliaceous plants of the genus *Yucca,* esp *Y. aloifolia,* that have a tall woody stem, stiff pointed leaves, and large clusters of white flowers: cultivated for ornament. See also **Adam's-needle.**

Spanish cedar NOUN a tall meliaceous tree, *Cedrela odorata,* of tropical America, the East Indies, and Australia, having smooth bark, pinnate leaves, yellow flowers, and light-coloured aromatic wood.

Spanish Civil War NOUN the civil war in Spain from 1936 to 1939 in which insurgent nationalists, led by General Franco, succeeded in overthrowing the republican government. During the war Spain became an ideological battleground for fascists and socialists from all countries.

Spanish customs *or* **practices** PLURAL NOUN *Informal* irregular practices among a group of workers to gain increased financial allowances, reduced working hours, etc. Also called: **old Spanish customs** *or* **practices.**

Spanish fly NOUN 1 a European blister beetle, *Lytta vesicatoria* (family *Meloidae*), the dried bodies of which yield the pharmaceutical product cantharides. 2 another name for **cantharides.**

Spanish Guinea NOUN the former name (until 1964) of **Equatorial Guinea.**

Spanish guitar NOUN the classic form of the guitar; a six-stringed instrument with a waisted body and a central sound hole.

Spanish Inquisition NOUN the institution that guarded the orthodoxy of Catholicism in Spain, chiefly by the persecution of heretics, Jews, etc., esp from the 15th to 17th centuries. See also **Inquisition.**

Spanish mackerel NOUN 1 Also called: **kingfish.** any scombroid food fish of the genus *Scomberomorus,* esp *S. maculatus,* of American coastal regions of the Atlantic: family *Scombridae* (mackerels, tunnies, etc.). 2 a mackerel, *Scomber colias,* of European and E North American coasts that is similar to the common Atlantic mackerel. 3 any of various related marine food fishes, esp *Scomberomerus commerson*

Spanish Main NOUN 1 the mainland of Spanish America, esp the N coast of South America from the Isthmus of Panama to the mouth of the Orinoco River, Venezuela. 2 the Caribbean Sea, the S part of which in colonial times was the route of Spanish treasure galleons and the haunt of pirates.

Spanish Moroccan ADJECTIVE 1 of or relating to the former Spanish colony of Spanish Morocco (now part of Morocco) or its inhabitants. ◆ NOUN 2 a native or inhabitant of Spanish Morocco.

Spanish Morocco NOUN a former Spanish colony on the N coast of Morocco: part of the kingdom of Morocco since 1956.

Spanish moss NOUN 1 an epiphytic bromeliaceous plant, *Tillandsia usneoides,* growing in tropical and subtropical regions as long bluish-grey strands suspended from the branches of trees. 2 a tropical lichen, *Usnea longissima,* growing as long trailing green threads from the branches of trees. Also called: **long moss.**

Spanish omelette NOUN an omelette made by adding green peppers, onions, tomato, etc., to the eggs.

Spanish onion NOUN any of several varieties of large mild-flavoured onions.

Spanish paprika NOUN a mild seasoning made from a variety of red pepper grown in Spain.

Spanish rice NOUN rice cooked with tomatoes, onions, green peppers, etc., and often flavoured with saffron.

Spanish Sahara NOUN the former name (until 1975) of **Western Sahara.**

Spanish topaz NOUN an orange-brown form of quartz, used as a gemstone.

Spanish West Africa NOUN a former overseas territory of Spain in NW Africa: divided in 1958 into the overseas provinces of Ifni and Spanish Sahara.

Spanish West African ADJECTIVE 1 of or relating to the former Spanish overseas territory of Spanish West Africa (now the overseas provinces of Ifni and Spanish Sahara) or its inhabitants. ◆ NOUN 2 a native or inhabitant of Spanish West Africa.

Spanish windlass NOUN a stick used as a device for twisting and tightening a rope or cable.

spank[1] (spæŋk) VERB 1 (*tr*) to slap or smack with the open hand, esp on the buttocks. ◆ NOUN 2 a slap or series of slaps with the flat of the hand.
▷HISTORY C18: probably of imitative origin

spank[2] (spæŋk) VERB (*intr*) to go at a quick and lively pace.
▷HISTORY C19: back formation from SPANKING[2]

spanker ('spæŋkə) NOUN 1 *Nautical* a fore-and-aft sail or a mast that is aftermost in a sailing vessel. 2 *Informal* a person or animal that moves at a quick smart pace. 3 *Informal* something outstandingly fine or large.

spanking[1] ('spæŋkɪŋ) NOUN a series of spanks, esp on the buttocks, usually as a punishment for children.

spanking[2] ('spæŋkɪŋ) ADJECTIVE (*prenominal*) 1 *Informal* outstandingly fine, smart, large, etc. 2 quick and energetic; lively. 3 (esp of a breeze) fresh and brisk.
▷HISTORY C17: of uncertain origin. Compare Danish *spanke* to strut

spanner ('spænə) NOUN 1 a steel hand tool with a handle carrying jaws or a hole of particular shape designed to grip a nut or bolt head. 2 *Brit informal* a source of impediment or annoyance (esp in the phrase **throw a spanner in the works**).
▷HISTORY C17: from German, from *spannen* to stretch, SPAN[1]

span-new ADJECTIVE *Archaic or dialect* absolutely new.
▷HISTORY C14: from Old Norse *spānnÿr,* from *spānn* chip + *nÿr* NEW

span of apprehension NOUN *Psychol* the maximum number of objects that can be correctly assessed after a brief presentation.

span roof NOUN a roof consisting of two equal sloping sides.

span saw NOUN *Building trades* another name for **frame saw.**

spanspek ('spɑnˌspek) NOUN *South African* a sweet rough-skinned melon; a cantaloupe: family *Cucurbitaceae.*
▷HISTORY C19: possibly from Afrikaans: literally, Spanish bacon

spansule ('spænsju:l) NOUN a modified-release capsule of a drug.

spar[1] (spɑ:) NOUN 1 **a** any piece of nautical gear resembling a pole and used as a mast, boom, gaff, etc. **b** (*as modifier*): *a spar buoy.* 2 a principal supporting structural member of an aerofoil that runs from tip to tip or root to tip.
▷HISTORY C13: from Old Norse *sperra* beam; related to Old High German *sparro,* Old French *esparre*

spar[2] (spɑ:) VERB **spars, sparring, sparred.** (*intr*) 1 *Boxing, martial arts* to fight using light blows, as in training. 2 to dispute or argue. 3 (of gamecocks) to fight with the feet or spurs. ◆ NOUN 4 an unaggressive fight. 5 an argument or wrangle. 6 *Informal* a close friend.
▷HISTORY Old English, perhaps from SPUR

spar[3] (spɑ:) NOUN any of various minerals, such as feldspar or calcite, that are light-coloured, microcrystalline, transparent to translucent, and easily cleavable. Related adjective: **spathic.**
▷HISTORY C16: from Middle Low German *spar;* related to Old English *spærstān;* see FELDSPAR

sparable ('spærəbᵊl) NOUN a small nail with no head, used for fixing the soles and heels of shoes.
▷HISTORY C17: changed from *sparrow-bill,* referring to the nail's shape

sparaxis (spəˈræksɪs) NOUN any plant of the cormous S African genus *Sparaxis,* esp *S. grandiflora* and *S. tricolor,* grown for their dainty spikes of star-shaped purple, red, or orange flowers: family *Iridaceae.*
▷HISTORY New Latin, from Greek *sparassein* to tear (from the appearance of the spathes)

spar buoy NOUN *Nautical* a buoy resembling a vertical log.

spare (spɛə) VERB 1 (*tr*) to refrain from killing, punishing, harming, or injuring. 2 (*tr*) to release or relieve, as from pain, suffering, etc. 3 (*tr*) to refrain from using: *spare the rod, spoil the child.* 4 (*tr*) to be able to afford or give: *I can't spare the time.* 5 (*usually passive*) (esp of Providence) to allow to survive: *I'll see you again next year if we are spared.* 6 (*intr*) *Now rare* to act or live frugally. 7 (*intr*) *Rare* to show mercy. 8 **not spare oneself.** to exert oneself to the full. 9 **to spare.** more than is required: *two minutes to spare.* ◆ ADJECTIVE 10 (*often immediately postpositive*) in excess of what is needed; additional: *are there any seats spare?* 11 able to be used when needed: *a spare part.* 12 (of a person) thin and lean. 13 scanty or meagre. 14 (*postpositive*) *Brit slang* upset, angry, or distracted (esp in the phrase **go spare**). ◆ NOUN 15 a duplicate kept as a replacement in case of damage or loss. 16 a spare tyre. 17 *Tenpin bowling* **a** the act of knocking down all the pins with the two bowls of a single frame. **b** the score thus made. Compare **strike** (sense 40).
▷HISTORY Old English *sparian* to refrain from injuring; related to Old Norse *spara,* Old High German *sparōn*
▶'**sparely** ADVERB ▶'**spareness** NOUN ▶'**sparer** NOUN

spare part NOUN a duplicate or replacement component for a machine or other equipment.

spare-part surgery NOUN surgical replacement of defective or damaged organs by transplant or insertion of artificial devices.

sparerib (ˌspɛəˈrɪb) NOUN a cut of pork ribs with most of the meat trimmed off.

spare tyre NOUN 1 an additional tyre, usually mounted on a wheel, carried by a motor vehicle in case of puncture. 2 *Brit slang, jocular* a deposit of fat just above the waist.

sparge (spɑ:dʒ) VERB *Rare* to sprinkle or scatter (something).
▷HISTORY C16: from Latin *spargere* to sprinkle
▶'**sparger** NOUN

sparid ('spærɪd) *or* **sparoid** NOUN 1 any marine percoid fish of the chiefly tropical and subtropical family *Sparidae,* having a deep compressed body and well-developed teeth: includes the sea breams and porgies. ◆ ADJECTIVE 2 of, relating to, or belonging to the family *Sparidae.*
▷HISTORY C20: from New Latin *Sparidae,* from Latin *sparus* a sea bream, from Greek *sparos*

sparing ('spɛərɪŋ) ADJECTIVE 1 (sometimes foll by *with* or *of*) economical or frugal (with). 2 scanty; meagre. 3 merciful or lenient.
▶'**sparingly** ADVERB ▶'**sparingness** NOUN

spark[1] (spɑ:k) NOUN 1 a fiery particle thrown out or left by burning material or caused by the friction of two hard surfaces. 2 **a** a momentary flash of light accompanied by a sharp crackling noise, produced by a sudden electrical discharge through the air or some other insulating medium between two points. **b** the electrical discharge itself. **c** (*as modifier*): *a spark gap.* 3 anything that serves to animate, kindle, or excite. 4 a trace or hint: *she doesn't show a spark of interest.* 5 vivacity, enthusiasm, or humour. 6 a small piece of diamond, as used in the cutting of glass. ◆ VERB 7 (*intr*) to give off sparks. 8 (*intr*) (of the sparking plug or ignition system of an internal-combustion engine) to produce a spark. 9 (*tr; often foll by off*) to kindle, excite, or animate. ◆ See also **spark off, sparks.**
▷HISTORY Old English *spearca;* related to Middle Low German *sparke,* Middle Dutch *spranke,* Lettish *spirgsti* cinders, Latin *spargere* to strew

spark[2] (spɑ:k) *Rare* (*except for sense 2*) ◆ NOUN 1 a fashionable or gallant young man. 2 **bright spark.** *Brit, usually ironic* a person who appears clever or witty: *some bright spark left the papers next to the open window.* ◆ VERB 3 to woo (a person).
▷HISTORY C16 (in the sense: beautiful or witty woman): perhaps of Scandinavian origin; compare Old Norse *sparkr* vivacious
▶'**sparkish** ADJECTIVE

spark chamber NOUN *Physics* a device for detecting ionizing radiation, consisting of two oppositely charged metal plates in a chamber containing inert gas, so that a particle passing through the chamber ionizes the gas and causes a spark to jump between the electrodes.

spark coil NOUN an induction coil used to produce spark discharges.

spark erosion NOUN *Engineering* a method of machining using a shaped electrode which erodes the workpiece by an electric spark discharge between itself and the workpiece.

spark gap NOUN the space between two electrodes across which a spark can jump. Sometimes shortened to: **gap.**

sparking plug NOUN a device screwed into the cylinder head of an internal-combustion engine to ignite the explosive mixture by means of an electric spark which jumps across a gap between a point earthed to the body of the plug and the tip of a central insulated rod. Also called: **spark plug.**

sparkle ('spɑ:kᵊl) VERB 1 to issue or reflect or cause to issue or reflect bright points of light. 2 (*intr*) (of wine, mineral water, etc.) to effervesce. 3 (*intr*) to be vivacious or witty. ◆ NOUN 4 a point of light, spark, or gleam. 5 vivacity or wit.
▷HISTORY C12 *sparklen,* frequentative of *sparken* to SPARK[1]

sparkler (ˈspɑːklə) NOUN 1 a type of firework that throws out showers of sparks. 2 *Informal* a sparkling gem.

sparkling wine NOUN a wine made effervescent by carbon dioxide gas, introduced artificially or produced naturally by secondary fermentation.

spark off VERB (*tr, adverb*) to bring into being or action; activate or initiate: *to spark off an argument*.

spark plug NOUN another name for **sparking plug**.

sparks (spɑːks) NOUN (*functioning as singular*) *Informal* 1 an electrician. 2 a radio officer, esp on a ship.

spark transmitter NOUN an early type of radio transmitter in which power is generated by discharging a capacitor through an inductor in series with a spark gap.

sparky (ˈspɑːkɪ) ADJECTIVE **sparkier, sparkiest**. lively; vivacious; spirited.

sparling (ˈspɑːlɪŋ) NOUN, *plural* **-lings** *or* **-ling**. 1 another name for the **European smelt** (see **smelt** (the fish)). 2 a young herring.
▷HISTORY C14 *sperlynge*, from Old French *esperling*, from Middle Dutch *spierlinc*, from *spier* young shoot

sparoid (ˈspærɔɪd) ADJECTIVE, NOUN another word for **sparid**.
▷HISTORY C19: from New Latin *Sparoīdēs*; see SPARID

sparring partner (ˈspɑːrɪŋ) NOUN 1 a person who practises with a boxer during training. 2 a person with whom one has friendly arguments.

sparrow (ˈspærəʊ) NOUN 1 any weaverbird of the genus *Passer* and related genera, esp the house sparrow, having a brown or grey plumage and feeding on seeds or insects. 2 *US and Canadian* any of various North American finches, such as the chipping sparrow (*Spizella passerina*), that have a dullish streaked plumage. ◆ See also **hedge sparrow, tree sparrow, song sparrow**. ◆ Related adjective: **passerine**.
▷HISTORY Old English *spearwa*; related to Old Norse *spörr*, Old High German *sparo*
▸ˈ**sparrow-ˌlike** ADJECTIVE

sparrowfart (ˈspærəʊˌfɑːt) NOUN *Slang* the very early morning: *he woke up at sparrowfart*.

sparrowgrass (ˈspærəʊˌgrɑːs) NOUN a dialect or popular name for **asparagus**.
▷HISTORY C17: variant of ASPARAGUS, associated by folk etymology with SPARROW and GRASS

sparrowhawk (ˈspærəʊˌhɔːk) NOUN any of several small hawks, esp *Accipiter nisus*, of Eurasia and N Africa that prey on smaller birds.

sparrow hawk NOUN a very small North American falcon, *Falco sparverius*, that is closely related to the kestrels.

sparry (ˈspɑːrɪ) ADJECTIVE *Geology* containing, relating to, or resembling spar: *sparry coal*.

sparse (spɑːs) ADJECTIVE scattered or scanty; not dense.
▷HISTORY C18: from Latin *sparsus*, from *spargere* to scatter
▸ˈ**sparsely** ADVERB ▸ˈ**sparseness** *or* ˈ**sparsity** NOUN

Sparta (ˈspɑːtə) NOUN an ancient Greek city in the S Peloponnese, famous for the discipline and military prowess of its citizens and for their austere way of life.

Spartacist (ˈspɑːtəsɪst) NOUN a member of a group of German radical socialists formed in 1916 and in 1919 becoming the German Communist Party, led by Karl Liebknecht and Rosa Luxemburg.
▷HISTORY C20: from the pen name Spartacus (after the Thracian slave (died 71 B.C.) who led a revolt of gladiators against Rome) adopted by Karl Liebknecht (1871–1919)

Spartan (ˈspɑːtᵊn) ADJECTIVE 1 of or relating to Sparta or its citizens. 2 (*sometimes not capital*) very strict or austere: *a Spartan upbringing*. 3 (*sometimes not capital*) possessing courage and resolve. ◆ NOUN 4 a citizen of Sparta. 5 (*sometimes not capital*) a disciplined or brave person. 6 a Canadian variety of eating apple.
▸ˈ**Spartanism** NOUN

sparteine (ˈspɑːtɪˌiːn, -ɪn) NOUN a viscous oily alkaloid extracted from the broom plant and lupin seeds. It has been used in medicine to treat heart arrhythmias.
▷HISTORY C19: from New Latin *Spartium*, from Greek *spartos* broom

spasm (ˈspæzəm) NOUN 1 an involuntary muscular contraction, esp one resulting in cramp or convulsion. 2 a sudden burst of activity, emotion, etc.
▷HISTORY C14: from Latin *spasmus*, from Greek *spasmos* a cramp, from *span* to tear

spasmodic (spæzˈmɒdɪk) *or rarely* **spasmodical** ADJECTIVE 1 taking place in sudden brief spells. 2 of or characterized by spasms.
▷HISTORY C17: New Latin, from Greek *spasmos* SPASM
▸**spasˈmodically** ADVERB

spastic (ˈspæstɪk) NOUN 1 a person who is affected by spasms or convulsions, esp one who has cerebral palsy. 2 *Offensive slang* a clumsy, incapable, or incompetent person. ◆ ADJECTIVE 3 affected by or resembling spasms. 4 *Offensive slang* clumsy, incapable or incompetent.
▷HISTORY C18: from Latin *spasticus*, from Greek *spastikos*, from *spasmos* SPASM
▸ˈ**spastically** ADVERB ▸**spasˈticity** (spæsˈtɪsɪtɪ) NOUN

spat[1] (spæt) NOUN 1 *Now rare* a slap or smack. 2 a slight quarrel. ◆ VERB **spats, spatting, spatted**. 3 *Now rare* to slap (someone). 4 (*intr*) *US, Canadian, and* (*rarely*) *NZ* to have a slight quarrel.
▷HISTORY C19: probably imitative of the sound of quarrelling

spat[2] (spæt) VERB a past tense and past participle of **spit**[1].

spat[3] (spæt) NOUN another name for **gaiter** (sense 2).
▷HISTORY C19: short for SPATTERDASH

spat[4] (spæt) NOUN 1 a larval oyster or similar bivalve mollusc, esp when it settles to the sea bottom and starts to develop a shell. 2 such oysters or other molluscs collectively.
▷HISTORY C17: from Anglo-Norman *spat*; perhaps related to SPIT[1]

spatchcock (ˈspætʃˌkɒk) NOUN 1 a chicken or game bird split down the back and grilled. Compare **spitchcock**. ◆ VERB (*tr*) 2 to interpolate (words, a story, etc.) into a sentence, narrative, etc., esp inappropriately.
▷HISTORY C18: perhaps variant of *spitchcock* eel when prepared and cooked

spate (speɪt) NOUN 1 a fast flow, rush, or outpouring: *a spate of words*. 2 *Chiefly Brit* a sudden flood: *the rivers were in spate*. 3 *Chiefly Brit* a sudden heavy downpour.
▷HISTORY C15 (Northern and Scottish): of unknown origin

spathe (speɪð) NOUN a large bract, often coloured, that surrounds the inflorescence of aroid plants and palms.
▷HISTORY C18: from Latin *spatha*, from Greek *spathē* a blade
▸**spathaceous** (spəˈθeɪʃəs) ADJECTIVE ▸**spathed** ADJECTIVE

spathic (ˈspæθɪk) *or* **spathose** (ˈspæθəʊs) ADJECTIVE (of minerals) resembling spar, esp in having good cleavage.
▷HISTORY C18: from German *Spat, Spath* SPAR[3]; related to Old High German *spān* chip; see SPOON

spathulate (ˈspæθjʊlɪt) ADJECTIVE another word for **spatulate** (sense 2).

spatial *or* **spacial** (ˈspeɪʃəl) ADJECTIVE 1 of or relating to space. 2 existing or happening in space.
▸**spatiality** (ˌspeɪʃɪˈælɪtɪ) NOUN ▸ˈ**spatially** ADVERB

spatial frequency NOUN *Television* the measure of fine detail in an optical image in terms of cycles per millimetre.

spatiotemporal (ˌspeɪʃɪəʊˈtɛmpərəl, -ˈtɛmprəl) ADJECTIVE 1 of or existing in both space and time. 2 of or concerned with space-time.
▷HISTORY C20: from Latin *spatium* space + *temporālis*, from *tempus* time
▸ˌ**spatioˈtemporally** ADVERB

Spätlese ADVERB (ˈʃpɛtˌleɪsə), NOUN a wine, usually white, produced in Germany from grapes which have been allowed to ripen for longer than usual.
▷HISTORY C20: from German, from *spät* late + *Lese* harvest, vintage

spatter (ˈspætə) VERB 1 to scatter or splash (a substance, esp a liquid) or (of a substance) to splash (something) in scattered drops: *to spatter mud on the car; mud spattered in her face*. 2 (*tr*) to sprinkle, cover, or spot (with a liquid). 3 (*tr*) to slander or defame. 4 (*intr*) to shower or rain down: *bullets spattered around them*. ◆ NOUN 5 the sound of something spattering. 6 something spattered, such as a spot or splash. 7 the act or an instance of spattering.
▷HISTORY C16: of imitative origin; related to Low German, Dutch *spatten* to spout, Frisian *spatteren* to splash

spatterdash (ˈspætəˌdæʃ) NOUN 1 *US* another name for **roughcast**. 2 (*plural*) long leather leggings worn in the 18th century, as to protect from mud when riding.
▷HISTORY C17: see SPATTER, DASH[1]

spatula (ˈspætjʊlə) NOUN a utensil with a broad flat, often flexible blade, used for lifting, spreading, or stirring foods, etc.
▷HISTORY C16: from Latin: a broad piece, from *spatha* a flat wooden implement; see SPATHE
▸ˈ**spatular** ADJECTIVE

spatulate (ˈspætjʊlɪt) ADJECTIVE 1 shaped like a spatula. 2 Also: **spathulate**. *Botany* having a narrow base and a broad rounded apex: *a spatulate leaf*.

spavin (ˈspævɪn) NOUN *Vet science* enlargement of the hock of a horse by a bony growth (**bony spavin**) or fluid accumulation in the joint (**bog spavin**), usually caused by inflammation or injury, and often resulting in lameness.
▷HISTORY C15: from Old French *espavin*, of unknown origin

spavined (ˈspævɪnd) ADJECTIVE 1 *Vet science* affected with spavin; lame. 2 decrepit or worn out.

spawn (spɔːn) NOUN 1 the mass of eggs deposited by fish, amphibians, or molluscs. 2 *Often derogatory* offspring, product, or yield. 3 *Botany* the nontechnical name for **mycelium**. ◆ VERB 4 (of fish, amphibians, etc.) to produce or deposit (eggs). 5 *Often derogatory* (of people) to produce (offspring). 6 (*tr*) to produce or engender.
▷HISTORY C14: from Anglo-Norman *espaundre*, from Old French *spandre* to spread out, EXPAND
▸ˈ**spawner** NOUN

spay (speɪ) VERB (*tr*) to remove the ovaries, and usually the uterus, from (a female animal).
▷HISTORY C15: from Old French *espeer* to cut with the sword, from *espee* sword, from Latin *spatha*

spaza shop (ˈspɑːzə) NOUN *South African slang* a small informal shop in a township, often run from a private house.
▷HISTORY from slang, dummy, camouflaged

SPCK (in Britain) ABBREVIATION FOR Society for Promoting Christian Knowledge.

SPD ABBREVIATION FOR Sozialdemokratische Partei Deutschlands.
▷HISTORY German: Social Democratic Party of Germany

speak (spiːk) VERB **speaks, speaking, spoke, spoken**. 1 to make (verbal utterances); utter (words). 2 to communicate or express (something) in or as if in words: *I speak the truth*. 3 (*intr*) to deliver a speech, discourse, etc. 4 (*tr*) to know how to talk in (a language or dialect): *he does not speak German*. 5 (*intr*) to make a characteristic sound: *the clock spoke*. 6 (*intr*) (of dogs, esp hounds used in hunting) to give tongue; bark. 7 (*tr*) *Nautical* to hail and converse or communicate with (another vessel) at sea. 8 (*intr*) (of a musical instrument) to produce a sound. 9 (*intr*; *foll by for*) to be a representative or advocate (of): *he speaks for all the members*. 10 **on speaking terms**. on good terms; friendly. 11 **so to speak**. in a manner of speaking; as it were. 12 **speak one's mind**. to express one's opinions frankly and plainly. 13 **to speak of**. of a significant or worthwhile nature: *we have had no support to speak of*. ◆ See also **speak for, speak out, speak to, speak up**.
▷HISTORY Old English *specan*; related to Old High German *spehhan*, Middle High German *spechten* to gossip, Middle Dutch *speken*; see SPEECH
▸ˈ**speakable** ADJECTIVE

-speak SUFFIX FORMING NOUNS *Informal* the language or jargon of a specific group, organization, or field: *computerspeak*.
▷HISTORY C20: formed on the pattern of NEWSPEAK

speakeasy (ˈspiːkˌiːzɪ) NOUN, *plural* **-easies**. *US* a place where alcoholic drink was sold illicitly during Prohibition.
▷HISTORY C19: from SPEAK + EASY (in the sense: gently, quietly)

speaker (ˈspiːkə) NOUN 1 a person who speaks, esp at a formal occasion. 2 See **loudspeaker**.
▸ˈ**speakership** NOUN

Speaker ('spiːkə) NOUN the presiding officer in any of numerous legislative bodies, including the House of Commons in Britain and Canada and the House of Representatives in the US, Australia, and New Zealand.

speak for VERB (*intr, preposition*) [1] to speak as a representative of (other people). [2] **speak for itself.** to be so evident that no further comment is necessary. [3] **speak for yourself.** *Informal* (*used as an imperative*) do not presume that other people agree with you.

speaking ('spiːkɪŋ) ADJECTIVE [1] (*prenominal*) eloquent, impressive, or striking. [2] **a** able to speak. **b** (*in combination*) able to speak a particular language: *French-speaking.*

speaking clock NOUN *Brit* a telephone service that gives a precise verbal statement of the correct time.

speaking in tongues NOUN another term for **gift of tongues.**

speaking trumpet NOUN a trumpet-shaped instrument used to carry the voice a great distance or held to the ear by a deaf person to aid his hearing.

speaking tube NOUN a tube or pipe for conveying a person's voice from one room, area, or building to another.

speak out VERB (*intr, adverb*) [1] to state one's beliefs, objections, etc., bravely and firmly. [2] to speak more loudly and clearly.

speak to VERB (*intr, preposition*) [1] to address (a person). [2] to reprimand: *your father will speak to you later.* [3] *Formal* to give evidence of or comments on (a subject): *who will speak to this item?*

speak up VERB (*intr, adverb*) [1] to speak more loudly. [2] to state one's beliefs, objections, etc., bravely and firmly.

spear[1] (spɪə) NOUN [1] a weapon consisting of a long shaft with a sharp pointed end of metal, stone, or wood that may be thrown or thrust. [2] a similar implement used to catch fish. [3] another name for **spearman.** ◆ VERB [4] to pierce (something) with or as if with a spear.
▷HISTORY Old English *spere;* related to Old Norse *spjör* spears, Greek *sparos* gilthead
▸**'spearer** NOUN

spear[2] (spɪə) NOUN a shoot, slender stalk or blade, as of grass, asparagus, or broccoli.
▷HISTORY C16: probably variant of SPIRE[1], influenced by SPEAR[1]

spearfish ('spɪəˌfɪʃ) NOUN, *plural* **-fish** *or* **-fishes.** another name for **marlin.**
▷HISTORY so named because of its long pointed jaw

spear grass NOUN *NZ* [1] another name for **wild Spaniard.** [2] any of various native Australian grasses, esp of the genera *Stipa* or *Heteropogon*, with sharp-pointed seeds [3] any of various grasses with sharp stiff blades or seeds.

spear gun NOUN a device for shooting spears underwater.

spearhead ('spɪəˌhɛd) NOUN [1] the pointed head of a spear. [2] the leading force in a military attack. [3] any person or thing that leads or initiates an attack, a campaign, etc. ◆ VERB [4] (*tr*) to lead or initiate (an attack, a campaign, etc.).

spearman ('spɪəmən) NOUN, *plural* **-men.** a soldier armed with a spear.

Spearman's rank-order coefficient ('spɪəmənz) NOUN a statistic measuring the extent to which two sets of discrete data place the distinct items in the same order, given by $r_S = 1 - 6\Sigma d^2/n(n^2 - 1)$, where Σd^2 is the sum of the squares of the differences of ranks between the two orderings and *n* is the number of items in each. Also called: **Spearman's rank-order correlation coefficient.**
▷HISTORY named after Charles E. *Spearman* (1863–1945), English mathematician and statistician

spearmint ('spɪəmɪnt) NOUN a purple-flowered mint plant, *Mentha spicata,* of S and central Europe, cultivated for its leaves, which yield an oil used for flavouring.
▷HISTORY C16: so called because of its long narrow leaves

spear side NOUN the male side or branch of a family. Compare **distaff side.**

spearwort ('spɪəˌwɜːt) NOUN any of several Eurasian ranunculaceous plants of the genus *Ranunculus,* such as *R. flammula* (**lesser spearwort**) and *R. lingua* (**great spearwort**), which grow in wet places and have long narrow leaves and yellow flowers. See also **buttercup.**

spec (spɛk) *Informal* ◆ NOUN [1] **on spec.** as a speculation or gamble: *all the tickets were sold so I went to the theatre on spec.* ◆ ADJECTIVE [2] (*prenominal*) *Austral and NZ* speculative: *a spec developer.*
▷HISTORY C19: short for SPECULATION OR SPECULATIVE

spec. ABBREVIATION FOR: [1] specification. [2] speculation.

special ('spɛʃəl) ADJECTIVE [1] distinguished, set apart from, or excelling others of its kind. [2] (*prenominal*) designed or reserved for a particular purpose: *a special tool for working leather.* [3] not usual or commonplace. [4] (*prenominal*) particular or primary: *his special interest was music.* [5] denoting or relating to the education of physically or mentally handicapped children: *a special school.* ◆ NOUN [6] a special person or thing, such as an extra edition of a newspaper or a train reserved for a particular purpose. [7] a dish or meal given prominence, esp at a low price, in a café, etc. [8] *Austral history, slang* a convict given special treatment on account of his education, social class, etc. [9] short for **special constable.** [10] *Austral, NZ, US and Canadian informal* an item in a store that is advertised at a reduced price; a loss leader. ◆ VERB **-cials, -cialling, -cialled.** (*tr*) [11] *NZ informal* to advertise and sell (an item) at a reduced price: *we are specialling butter this week.*
▷HISTORY C13: from Old French *especial,* from Latin *speciālis* individual, special, from *speciēs* appearance, SPECIES
▸**'specially** ADVERB ▸**'specialness** NOUN

Language note See at **especial.**

Special Air Service NOUN a regiment in the British Army specializing in clandestine operations.

special assessment NOUN (in the US) a special charge levied on property owners by a county or municipality to help pay the costs of a civic improvement that increases the value of their property.

Special Boat Service NOUN a unit of the Royal Marines specializing in reconnaissance and sabotage.

Special Branch NOUN (in Britain) the department of the police force that is concerned with political security.

special case NOUN *Law* an agreed written statement of facts submitted by litigants to a court for a decision on a point of law.

special clearing NOUN *Banking* (in Britain) the clearing of a cheque through a bank in less than the usual three days, for an additional charge.

special constable NOUN a person recruited for temporary or occasional police duties, esp in time of emergency.

special delivery NOUN the delivery of a piece of mail outside the time of a scheduled delivery.

special drawing rights PLURAL NOUN (*sometimes capitals*) the reserve assets of the International Monetary Fund on which member nations may draw in proportion to their contribution to the Fund. Abbreviation: **SDRs.**

special educational needs PLURAL NOUN another term for **special needs.**

special effects PLURAL NOUN *Films* techniques used in the production of scenes that cannot be achieved by normal techniques.

specialism ('spɛʃəˌlɪzəm) NOUN the act or process of specializing in something, or the thing itself.

specialist ('spɛʃəlɪst) NOUN [1] **a** a person who specializes in or devotes himself to a particular area of activity, field of research, etc. **b** (*as modifier*): *specialist knowledge.* [2] an enlisted rank in the US Army denoting technical qualifications that entitle the holder to a noncommissioned officer's pay. [3] *Ecology* an organism that has special nutritional requirements and lives in a restricted habitat that provides these. Compare **generalist.**
▸**ˌspecial'istic** ADJECTIVE

specialist registrar NOUN a hospital doctor senior to a house officer but junior to a consultant, specializing in medicine (**medical specialist registrar**), surgery (**surgical specialist registrar**) or some subspeciality of either.

speciality (ˌspɛʃɪ'ælɪtɪ) *or chiefly US and Canadian* **specialty** NOUN, *plural* **-ties.** [1] a special interest or skill. [2] **a** a service or product specialized in, as at a restaurant: *roast beef was a speciality of the house.* **b** (*as modifier*): *a speciality dish.* [3] a special or distinguishing feature or characteristic.

specialize *or* **specialise** ('spɛʃəˌlaɪz) VERB [1] (*intr*) to train in or devote oneself to a particular area of study, occupation, or activity. [2] (*usually passive*) to cause (organisms or their parts) to develop in a way most suited to a particular environment or way of life or (of organisms, etc.) to develop in this way. [3] (*tr*) to modify or make suitable for a special use or purpose. [4] (*tr*) to mention specifically; specify. [5] (*tr*) to endorse (a commercial paper) to a specific payee.
▸**ˌspeciali'zation** *or* **ˌspeciali'sation** NOUN

special jury NOUN (formerly) a jury whose members were drawn from some profession or rank of society as well as possessing the usual qualifications for jury service.

Special K NOUN *Slang* an animal anaesthetic, *ketamine hydrochloride,* sold illegally as a hallucinogenic drug.
▷HISTORY C20: named after a well-known brand of breakfast cereal

special licence NOUN *Brit* a licence permitting a marriage to take place by dispensing with the usual legal conditions.

special needs *or* **special educational needs** PLURAL NOUN **a** the educational requirements of pupils or students suffering from any of a wide range of physical disabilities, medical conditions, intellectual difficulties, or emotional problems, including deafness, blindness, dyslexia, learning difficulties, and behavioural problems. **b** (*as modifier*): *special-needs teachers.*

special pleading NOUN *Law* [1] a pleading that alleges new facts that offset those put forward by the other side rather than directly admitting or denying those facts. [2] a pleading that emphasizes the favourable aspects of a case while omitting the unfavourable.

special privilege NOUN a legally endorsed privilege granted exclusively to some individual or group.

special school NOUN *Brit* a school for children who are unable to benefit from ordinary schooling because they have learning difficulties, physical or mental handicaps, etc.

special sort NOUN *Printing* a character, such as an accented letter, that is not a usual member of any fount. Also called: **peculiar, arbitrary.**

special team NOUN *American football* any of several predetermined permutations of the players within a team that play in situations, such as kickoffs and attempts at field goals, where the standard offensive and defensive formations are not appropriate.

special theory of relativity NOUN the theory proposed in 1905 by Einstein, which assumes that the laws of physics are equally valid in all nonaccelerated frames of reference and that the speed of electromagnetic radiation in free space has the same value for all inertial observers. It leads to the idea of a space-time continuum and the equivalence of mass and energy. In combination with quantum mechanics it forms the basis of the theory of elementary particles. Also called: **special relativity.** See also **general theory of relativity, Einstein's law** (sense 1).

specialty ('spɛʃəltɪ) NOUN, *plural* **-ties.** [1] *Law* a formal contract or obligation expressed in a deed. [2] another word, chiefly US and Canadian, for **speciality.**

speciate ('spiːsɪˌeɪt) VERB to form or develop into a new biological species.
▷HISTORY C20: back formation from SPECIATION

speciation (ˌspiːʃɪ'eɪʃən) NOUN the evolutionary development of a biological species, as by geographical isolation of a group of individuals from the main stock.
▷HISTORY C20: from SPECIES + -ATION

specie ('spiːʃiː) NOUN [1] coin money, as

distinguished from bullion or paper money. [2] **in specie. a** (of money) in coin. **b** in kind. **c** *Law* in the actual form specified.
▷**HISTORY** C16: from the Latin phrase *in speciē* in kind

specie point NOUN another name for **gold point.**

species ('spiːʃiːz; *Latin* 'spiːʃɪˌiːz) NOUN, *plural* **-cies.** [1] *Biology* **a** any of the taxonomic groups into which a genus is divided, the members of which are capable of interbreeding: often containing subspecies, varieties, or races. A species is designated in italics by the genus name followed by the specific name, for example *Felis domesticus* (the domestic cat). Abbreviation: **sp. b** the animals of such a group. **c** any group of related animals or plants not necessarily of this taxonomic rank. [2] (*modifier*) denoting a plant that is a natural member of a species rather than a hybrid or cultivar: *a species clematis.* [3] *Logic* a group of objects or individuals, all sharing at least one common attribute, that forms a subdivision of a genus. [4] a kind, sort, or variety: *a species of treachery.* [5] *Chiefly RC Church* the outward form of the bread and wine in the Eucharist. [6] *Obsolete* an outward appearance or form. [7] *Obsolete* specie.
▷**HISTORY** C16: from Latin: appearance, from *specere* to look

speciesism ('spiːʃiːzˌɪzəm) NOUN a belief of humans that all other species of animals are inferior and may therefore be used for human benefit without regard to the suffering inflicted.
▷**HISTORY** C20: from SPECIES + -ISM
▸**'speciesist** ADJECTIVE

specifiable ('spɛsɪˌfaɪəbᵊl) ADJECTIVE able to be specified.

specific (spɪ'sɪfɪk) ADJECTIVE [1] explicit, particular, or definite: *please be more specific.* [2] relating to a specified or particular thing: *a specific treatment for arthritis.* [3] of or relating to a biological species: *specific differences.* [4] (of a disease) caused by a particular pathogenic agent. [5] *Physics* **a** characteristic of a property of a particular substance, esp in relation to the same property of a standard reference substance: *specific gravity.* **b** characteristic of a property of a particular substance per unit mass, length, area, volume, etc.: *specific heat.* **c** (of an extensive physical quantity) divided by mass: *specific heat capacity; specific volume.* [6] Also (rare): **specifical.** *International trade* denoting a tariff levied at a fixed sum per unit of weight, quantity, volume, etc., irrespective of value. ◆ NOUN [7] (*sometimes plural*) a designated quality, thing, etc. [8] *Med* any drug used to treat a particular disease.
▷**HISTORY** C17: from Medieval Latin *specificus,* from Latin SPECIES
▸**spe'cifically** ADVERB ▸**specificity** (ˌspɛsɪ'fɪsɪtɪ) NOUN

specification (ˌspɛsɪfɪ'keɪʃən) NOUN [1] the act or an instance of specifying. [2] (in patent law) a written statement accompanying an application for a patent that describes the nature of an invention. [3] a detailed description of the criteria for the constituents, construction, appearance, performance, etc., of a material, apparatus, etc., or of the standard of workmanship required in its manufacture. [4] an item, detail, etc., specified.

specific charge NOUN *Physics* the charge-to-mass ratio of an elementary particle.

specific gravity NOUN the ratio of the density of a substance to that of water. See **relative density.**

specific heat capacity NOUN the heat required to raise unit mass of a substance by unit temperature interval under specified conditions, such as constant pressure: usually measured in joules per kelvin per kilogram. Symbol: c_p (for constant pressure). Also called: **specific heat.**

specific humidity NOUN the mass of water vapour in a sample of moist air divided by the mass of the sample.

specific impulse NOUN the ratio of the thrust produced by a rocket engine to the rate of fuel consumption: it has units of time and is the length of time that unit weight of propellant would last if used to produce one unit of thrust continuously.

specific performance NOUN *Law* a remedy awarded by a court requiring a person to fulfil obligations under a contract where damages are an insufficient remedy.

specific resistance NOUN the former name for **resistivity.**

specific viscosity NOUN *Physics* a measure of the resistance to flow of a fluid, expressed as the ratio of the absolute viscosity of the fluid to that of a reference fluid (usually water in the case of liquids).

specific volume NOUN *Physics* the volume of matter per unit mass; the reciprocal of the density. Symbol: v.

specify ('spɛsɪˌfaɪ) VERB **-fies, -fying, -fied.** (*tr; may take a clause as object*) [1] to refer to or state specifically. [2] to state as a condition. [3] to state or include in the specification of.
▷**HISTORY** C13: from Medieval Latin *specificāre* to describe
▸**specificative** ('spɛsɪfɪˌkeɪtɪv) ADJECTIVE ▸**'speciˌfier** NOUN

specimen ('spɛsɪmɪn) NOUN [1] **a** an individual, object, or part regarded as typical of the group or class to which it belongs. **b** (*as modifier*): *a specimen signature; a specimen page.* [2] *Med* a sample of tissue, blood, urine, etc., taken for diagnostic examination or evaluation. [3] the whole or a part of an organism, plant, rock, etc., collected and preserved as an example of its class, species, etc. [4] *Informal, often derogatory* a person.
▷**HISTORY** C17: from Latin: mark, evidence, proof, from *specere* to look at

speciosity (ˌspiːʃɪ'ɒsɪtɪ) NOUN, *plural* **-ties.** [1] a thing or person that is deceptively attractive or plausible. [2] the state of being specious. [3] *Obsolete* the state of being beautiful.

specious ('spiːʃəs) ADJECTIVE [1] apparently correct or true, but actually wrong or false. [2] deceptively attractive in appearance.
▷**HISTORY** C14 (originally: fair): from Latin *speciōsus* plausible, from *speciēs* outward appearance, from *specere* to look at
▸**'speciously** ADVERB ▸**'speciousness** NOUN

speck (spɛk) NOUN [1] a very small mark or spot. [2] a small or tiny piece of something. ◆ VERB [3] (*tr*) to mark with specks or spots.
▷**HISTORY** Old English *specca;* related to Middle Dutch *spekelen* to sprinkle

speckle ('spɛkᵊl) NOUN [1] a small or slight mark usually of a contrasting colour, as on the skin, a bird's plumage, or eggs. ◆ VERB [2] (*tr*) to mark with or as if with speckles.
▷**HISTORY** C15: from Middle Dutch *spekkel;* see SPECK
▸**'speckled** ADJECTIVE

speckled trout NOUN another name for **brook trout.**

speckled wood NOUN a common woodland brown satyrid butterfly, *Pararge aegeria,* marked with pale orange or yellowish-white spots.

speckle interferometry NOUN *Astronomy* a technique to increase the angular resolution of telescopes that are impaired by atmospheric turbulence, in which the information from a number of exposures of very short duration is combined.

specs (spɛks) PLURAL NOUN *Informal* [1] short for **spectacles.** [2] short for **specifications.**

spec sheet NOUN a list describing the specifications of a product or property that is for sale.

spectacle ('spɛktəkᵊl) NOUN [1] a public display or performance, esp a showy or ceremonial one. [2] a thing or person seen, esp an unusual or ridiculous one: *he makes a spectacle of himself.* [3] a strange or interesting object or phenomenon. ◆ See also **spectacles.**
▷**HISTORY** C14: via Old French from Latin *spectaculum* a show, from *spectāre* to watch, from *specere* to look at

spectacled ('spɛktəkᵊld) ADJECTIVE [1] wearing glasses. [2] (of an animal) having markings around the eyes resembling a pair of glasses.

spectacles ('spɛktəkᵊlz) PLURAL NOUN [1] a pair of glasses for correcting defective vision. Often (informal) shortened to: **specs.** [2] **pair of spectacles.** *Cricket* a score of 0 in each innings of a match.

spectacular (spɛk'tækjʊlə) ADJECTIVE [1] of or resembling a spectacle; impressive, grand, or dramatic. [2] unusually marked or great: *a spectacular increase in spending.* ◆ NOUN [3] a lavishly produced performance.
▸**spec'tacularly** ADVERB

spectate (spɛk'teɪt) VERB (*intr*) to be a spectator; watch.
▷**HISTORY** C20: back formation from SPECTATOR

spectator (spɛk'teɪtə) NOUN a person viewing anything; onlooker; observer.
▷**HISTORY** C16: from Latin, from *spectāre* to watch; see SPECTACLE

spectator sport NOUN a sport that attracts more people as spectators than as participants.

spectra ('spɛktrə) NOUN the plural of **spectrum.**

spectral ('spɛktrəl) ADJECTIVE [1] of or like a spectre. [2] of or relating to a spectrum: *spectral colours.* [3] *Physics* (of a physical quantity) relating to a single wavelength of radiation: *spectral luminous efficiency.*
▸**spectrality** (spɛk'trælɪtɪ) *or* **'spectralness** NOUN
▸**'spectrally** ADVERB

spectral luminous efficiency NOUN a measure of the efficiency of radiation of a given wavelength in producing a visual sensation. It is equal to the ratio of the radiant flux at a standard wavelength to that at the given wavelength when the standard wavelength is chosen so that the maximum value of this ratio is unity. Symbol: $V(\lambda)$ (for photopic vision) *or* $V'(\lambda)$ (for scotopic vision).

spectral type *or* **class** NOUN any of various groups into which stars are classified according to characteristic spectral lines and bands. The most important classification (**Harvard classification**) has a series of classes O, B, A, F, G, K, M, the series also being a scale of diminishing surface temperature.

spectre *or US* **specter** ('spɛktə) NOUN [1] a ghost; phantom; apparition. [2] a mental image of something unpleasant or menacing: *the spectre of redundancy.*
▷**HISTORY** C17: from Latin *spectrum,* from *specere* to look at

spectrin ('spɛktrɪn) NOUN any one of a class of fibrous proteins found in the membranes of red blood cells, the brain, the intestine, etc.
▷**HISTORY** C20: from SPECTR(E) + -IN, referring to the ghosts (isolated cell membranes) of red blood cells, the source of the first known member of the class

spectro- COMBINING FORM indicating a spectrum: *spectrogram.*

spectrobolometer (ˌspɛktrəʊbəʊ'lɒmɪtə) NOUN a combined spectroscope and bolometer for determining the wavelength distribution of radiant energy emitted by a source.
▸**spectrobolometric** (ˌspɛktrəˌbəʊlə'mɛtrɪk) ADJECTIVE

spectrofluorimeter (ˌspɛktrəʊflʊə'rɪmɪtə) *or* **spectrofluorometer** NOUN an instrument for recording fluorescence emission and absorption spectra.

spectrograph ('spɛktrəʊˌgrɑːf, -ˌgræf) NOUN a spectroscope or spectrometer that produces a photographic record (**spectrogram**) of a spectrum. See also **sound spectrograph.**
▸**ˌspectro'graphic** ADJECTIVE ▸**ˌspectro'graphically** ADVERB
▸**spec'trography** NOUN

spectroheliograph (ˌspɛktrəʊ'hiːlɪəˌgrɑːf, -ˌgræf) NOUN an instrument used to obtain an image of the sun in light of a particular wavelength, such as calcium or hydrogen, to show the distribution of the element over the surface and in the solar atmosphere. The image obtained is a **spectroheliogram.**
▷**HISTORY** C19: from SPECTRO- + HELIO- + -GRAPH
▸**ˌspectroˌhelio'graphic** ADJECTIVE

spectrohelioscope (ˌspɛktrəʊ'hiːlɪəʊˌskəʊp) NOUN an instrument, similar to the spectroheliograph, used for observing solar radiation at one particular wavelength.
▸**spectrohelioscopic** (ˌspɛktrəʊˌhiːlɪəʊ'skɒpɪk) ADJECTIVE

spectrometer (spɛk'trɒmɪtə) NOUN any instrument for producing a spectrum, esp one in which wavelength, energy, intensity, etc., can be measured. See also **mass spectrometer.**
▸**spectrometric** (ˌspɛktrəʊ'mɛtrɪk) ADJECTIVE
▸**spec'trometry** NOUN

spectrophotometer (ˌspɛktrəʊfəʊ'tɒmɪtə) NOUN an instrument for producing or recording a spectrum and measuring the photometric intensity

of each wavelength present, esp such an instrument used for infrared, visible, and ultraviolet radiation. See also **spectrometer.**
▷HISTORY C19: from SPECTRO- + PHOTO- + -METER
▸**spectrophotometric** (ˌspɛktrəʊˌfəʊtəˈmɛtrɪk) ADJECTIVE ▸**ˌspectrophoˈtometry** NOUN

spectroscope (ˈspɛktrəˌskəʊp) NOUN any of a number of instruments for dispersing electromagnetic radiation and thus forming or recording a spectrum. See also **spectrometer.**
▷HISTORY C19: from SPECTRO- + -SCOPE; from French, or on the model of German *Spektroskop*
▸**spectroscopic** (ˌspɛktrəˈskɒpɪk) *or* **ˌspectroˈscopical** ADJECTIVE ▸**ˌspectroˈscopically** ADVERB

spectroscopic analysis NOUN the use of spectroscopy in determining the chemical or physical constitution of substances.

spectroscopy (spɛkˈtrɒskəpɪ) NOUN the science and practice of using spectrometers and spectroscopes and of analysing spectra, the methods employed depending on the radiation being examined. The techniques are widely used in chemical analysis and in studies of the properties of atoms, molecules, ions, etc.
▸**specˈtroscopist** NOUN

spectrum (ˈspɛktrəm) NOUN, *plural* **-tra** (-trə). [1] the distribution of colours produced when white light is dispersed by a prism or diffraction grating. There is a continuous change in wavelength from red, the longest wavelength, to violet, the shortest. Seven colours are usually distinguished: violet, indigo, blue, green, yellow, orange, and red. [2] the whole range of electromagnetic radiation with respect to its wavelength or frequency. [3] any particular distribution of electromagnetic radiation often showing lines or bands characteristic of the substance emitting the radiation or absorbing it. See also **absorption spectrum, emission spectrum.** [4] any similar distribution or record of the energies, velocities, masses, etc., of atoms, ions, electrons, etc.: *a mass spectrum.* [5] any range or scale, as of capabilities, emotions, or moods. [6] another name for an **afterimage.**
▷HISTORY C17: from Latin: appearance, image, from *spectāre* to observe, from *specere* to look at

spectrum analyser NOUN an instrument that splits an input waveform into its frequency components, which are then displayed.

spectrum analysis NOUN the analysis of a spectrum to determine the properties of its source, such as the analysis of the emission spectrum of a substance to determine the electron distribution in its molecules.

specular (ˈspɛkjʊlə) ADJECTIVE [1] of, relating to, or having the properties of a mirror: *specular reflection.* [2] of or relating to a speculum.
▷HISTORY C16: from Latin *speculāris,* from *speculum* a mirror, from *specere* to look at
▸**ˈspecularly** ADVERB

speculate (ˈspɛkjʊˌleɪt) VERB [1] (*when tr, takes a clause as object*) to conjecture without knowing the complete facts. [2] (*intr*) to buy or sell securities, property, etc., in the hope of deriving capital gains. [3] (*intr*) to risk loss for the possibility of considerable gain. [4] (*intr*) *NZ rugby* to make an emergency forward kick of the ball without taking any particular aim.
▷HISTORY C16: from Latin *speculārī* to spy out, from *specula* a watchtower, from *specere* to look at

speculation (ˌspɛkjʊˈleɪʃən) NOUN [1] the act or an instance of speculating. [2] a supposition, theory, or opinion arrived at through speculating. [3] investment involving high risk but also the possibility of high profits.

speculative (ˈspɛkjʊlətɪv) ADJECTIVE relating to or characterized by speculation, esp financial speculation.
▸**ˈspeculatively** ADVERB ▸**ˈspeculativeness** NOUN

speculator (ˈspɛkjʊˌleɪtə) NOUN [1] a person who speculates. [2] *NZ rugby* an undirected kick of the ball.

speculum (ˈspɛkjʊləm) NOUN, *plural* **-la** (-lə) *or* **-lums.** [1] a mirror, esp one made of polished metal for use in a telescope, etc. [2] *Med* an instrument for dilating a bodily cavity or passage to permit examination of its interior. [3] a patch of distinctive colour on the wing of a bird, esp in certain ducks.
▷HISTORY C16: from Latin: mirror, from *specere* to look at

speculum metal NOUN a white hard brittle corrosion-resistant alloy of copper (55–70 per cent) and tin with smaller amounts of other metals. It takes a high polish and is used for mirrors, lamp reflectors, ornamental ware, etc.

sped (spɛd) VERB a past tense and past participle of **speed.**

speech (spiːtʃ) NOUN [1] **a** the act or faculty of speaking, esp as possessed by persons: *to have speech with somebody.* **b** (*as modifier*): *speech therapy.* [2] that which is spoken; utterance. [3] a talk or address delivered to an audience. [4] a person's characteristic manner of speaking. [5] a national or regional language or dialect. [6] *Linguistics* another word for **parole** (sense 5).
▷HISTORY Old English *spēc;* related to *specan* to SPEAK

speech act NOUN *Philosophy* [1] an utterance that constitutes some act in addition to the mere act of uttering. [2] an act or type of act capable of being so performed. ◆ See also **performative.**

speech community NOUN a community consisting of all the speakers of a particular language or dialect.

speech day NOUN *Brit* (in schools) an annual day on which prizes are presented, speeches are made by guest speakers, etc.

speech from the throne NOUN (in Britain and the dominions of the Commonwealth) the speech at the opening of each session of Parliament in which the Government outlines its legislative programme. It is read by the sovereign or his or her representative. Also called (esp Brit): **Queen's** (*or* **King's**) **speech.**

speechify (ˈspiːtʃɪˌfaɪ) VERB **-fies, -fying, -fied.** (*intr*) [1] to make a speech or speeches. [2] to talk pompously and boringly.
▸**ˌspeechifiˈcation** NOUN ▸**ˈspeechiˌfier** NOUN

speechless (ˈspiːtʃlɪs) ADJECTIVE [1] not able to speak. [2] temporarily deprived of speech. [3] not expressed or able to be expressed in words: *speechless fear.*
▸**ˈspeechlessly** ADVERB ▸**ˈspeechlessness** NOUN

speech-reading NOUN another name for **lip-reading.**

speech recognition NOUN the understanding of continuous speech by a computer.

speech therapy NOUN treatment to improve the speech of children who have difficulty in learning to speak, for example because of partial deafness or brain damage, or to help restore the power of speech to adults who have lost it or partly lost it through accident or illness.
▸**speech therapist** NOUN

speed (spiːd) NOUN [1] the act or quality of acting or moving fast; rapidity. [2] the rate at which something moves, is done, or acts. [3] *Physics* **a** a scalar measure of the rate of movement of a body expressed either as the distance travelled divided by the time taken (**average speed**) or the rate of change of position with respect to time at a particular point (**instantaneous speed**). It is measured in metres per second, miles per hour, etc. **b** (not in technical usage) another word for **velocity** (sense 3). [4] a rate of rotation, usually expressed in revolutions per unit time. [5] **a** a gear ratio in a motor vehicle, bicycle, etc. **b** (*in combination*): *a three-speed gear.* [6] *Photog* a numerical expression of the sensitivity to light of a particular type of film, paper, or plate. See also **ISO rating.** [7] *Photog* a measure of the ability of a lens to pass light from an object to the image position, determined by the aperture and also the transmitting power of the lens. It increases as the f-number is decreased and vice versa. [8] a slang word for **amphetamine.** [9] *Archaic* prosperity or success. [10] **at speed.** quickly. [11] **up to speed. a** operating at an acceptable or competitive level. **b** in possession of all the relevant or necessary information. ◆ VERB **speeds, speeding, sped** *or* **speeded.** [12] to move or go or cause to move or go quickly. [13] (*intr*) to drive (a motor vehicle) at a high speed, esp above legal limits. [14] (*tr*) to help further the success or completion of. [15] (*intr*) *Slang* to take or be under the influence of amphetamines. [16] (*intr*) to operate or run at a high speed. [17] *Archaic* **a** (*intr*) to prosper or succeed. **b** (*tr*) to wish success to. ◆ See also **speed up.**
▷HISTORY Old English *spēd* (originally in the sense: success); related to *spōwan* to succeed, Latin *spēs* hope, Old Slavonic *spěti* to be lucky
▸**ˈspeeder** NOUN

speedball (ˈspiːdˌbɔːl) NOUN *Slang* a mixture of heroin with amphetamine or cocaine.

speedboat (ˈspiːdˌbəʊt) NOUN a high-speed motorboat having either an inboard or outboard motor.

speed chess NOUN a form of chess in which each player's game is limited to a total stipulated time, usually half an hour; the first player to exceed the time limit loses.

speedfreak (ˈspiːdˌfriːk) NOUN *Slang* an amphetamine addict.

speed limit NOUN the maximum permitted speed at which a vehicle may travel on certain roads.

speedo (ˈspiːdəʊ) NOUN, *plural* **speedos.** an informal name for **speedometer** or (Austral) **odometer.**

speedometer (spɪˈdɒmɪtə) NOUN a device fitted to a vehicle to measure and display the speed of travel. See also **mileometer.**

speed skating NOUN a form of ice skating in which contestants race against each other or the clock over various distances.

speedster (ˈspiːdstə) NOUN a fast car, esp a sports model.

speed trap NOUN a section of road on which the police check the speed of vehicles, often using radar.

speed up VERB (*adverb*) [1] to increase or cause to increase in speed or rate; accelerate. ◆ NOUN **speed-up.** [2] an instance of this; acceleration.

> **Language note** The past tense and past participle of *speed up* is *speeded up,* not *sped up.*

speedway (ˈspiːdˌweɪ) NOUN [1] **a** the sport of racing on light powerful motorcycles round cinder tracks. **b** (*as modifier*): *a speedway track.* [2] the track or stadium where such races are held. [3] *US and Canadian* **a** a racetrack for cars. **b** a road on which fast driving is allowed.

speedwell (ˈspiːdˌwɛl) NOUN any of various temperate scrophulariaceous plants of the genus *Veronica,* such as *V. officinalis* (**heath speedwell**) and *V. chamaedrys* (**germander speedwell**), having small blue or pinkish white flowers.
▷HISTORY C16: from SPEED + WELL[1]

Speedwriting (ˈspiːdˌraɪtɪŋ) NOUN *Trademark* a form of shorthand in which alphabetic combinations are used to represent groups of sounds or short common words.

speedy (ˈspiːdɪ) ADJECTIVE **speedier, speediest.** [1] characterized by speed of motion. [2] done or decided without delay; quick.
▸**ˈspeedily** ADVERB ▸**ˈspeediness** NOUN

speel (spiːl) NOUN *Manchester dialect* a splinter of wood.
▷HISTORY probably from Old Norse; compare Norwegian *spela, spila,* Swedish *spjela, spjele* SPILL[2]

speir *or* **speer** (spiːr) VERB *Scot* to ask; inquire.
▷HISTORY Old English *spyrian* to seek after, search for

speiss (spaɪs) NOUN the arsenides and antimonides that form when ores containing arsenic or antimony are smelted.
▷HISTORY C18: from German *Speise* food

spek (spek) NOUN *South African* bacon, fat, or fatty pork used for larding venison or other game.
▷HISTORY Afrikaans

spelaean *or* **spelean** (spɪˈliːən) ADJECTIVE of, found in, or inhabiting caves: *spelaean animals.*
▷HISTORY C19: via New Latin, from Latin *spēlaeum* a cave, from Greek *spēlaion*

speleology *or* **spelaeology** (ˌspiːlɪˈɒlədʒɪ) NOUN [1] the scientific study of caves, esp in respect of their geological formation, flora and fauna, etc. [2] the sport or pastime of exploring caves.
▷HISTORY C19: from Latin *spēlaeum* cave
▸**speleological** *or* **spelaeological** (ˌspiːlɪəˈlɒdʒɪkᵊl) ADJECTIVE ▸**ˌspeleˈologist** *or* **ˌspelaeˈologist** NOUN

speleotherapy (ˌspiːlɪəˈθɛrəpɪ) NOUN a form of treatment for asthma sufferers that takes place in clinics in disused mines, in which the air is free of pollen, dust mites, and the other irritants that provoke an allergic reaction; used to reduce the risk of heart disease.

spelk (spɛlk) NOUN *Scot and northern English dialect* a splinter of wood.
▷HISTORY from Old English *spelc, spilc* surgical splint; related to Old Norse *spelkur* splints

spell[1] (spɛl) VERB **spells, spelling, spelt** *or* **spelled.** 1 to write or name in correct order the letters that comprise the conventionally accepted form of (a word or part of a word). 2 (*tr*) (of letters) to go to make up the conventionally established form of (a word) when arranged correctly: *d-o-g spells dog.* 3 (*tr*) to indicate or signify: *such actions spell disaster for our cause.* ◆ See also **spell out.**
▷HISTORY C13: from Old French *espeller,* of Germanic origin; related to Old Norse *spialla* to talk, Middle High German *spellen*
▸ **'spellable** ADJECTIVE

spell[2] (spɛl) NOUN 1 a verbal formula considered as having magical force. 2 any influence that can control the mind or character; fascination. 3 a state induced by or as if by the pronouncing of a spell; trance: *to break the spell.* 4 **under a spell.** held in or as if in a spell. ◆ VERB 5 (*tr*) *Rare* to place under a spell.
▷HISTORY Old English *spell* speech; related to Old Norse *spjall* tale, Gothic *spill,* Old High German *spel*

spell[3] (spɛl) NOUN 1 an indeterminate, usually short, period of time: *a spell of cold weather.* 2 a period or tour of duty after which one person or group relieves another. 3 *Scot, Austral, and NZ* a period or interval of rest. ◆ VERB 4 (*tr*) to take over from (a person) for an interval of time; relieve temporarily. 5 **spell a paddock.** *NZ* to give a field a rest period by letting it lie fallow.
▷HISTORY Old English *spelian* to take the place of, of obscure origin

spellbind ('spɛl,baɪnd) VERB **-binds, -binding, -bound.** (*tr*) to cause to be spellbound; entrance or enthral.

spellbinder ('spɛl,baɪndə) NOUN 1 a person capable of holding others spellbound, esp a political speaker. 2 a novel, play, etc., that holds one enthralled.

spellbound ('spɛl,baʊnd) ADJECTIVE having one's attention held as though one is bound by a spell: *a spellbound audience.*

spellchecker ('spɛl,tʃɛkə) NOUN *Computing* a program that highlights any word in a word-processed document that is not recognized as being correctly spelt.

speller ('spɛlə) NOUN 1 a person who spells words in the manner specified: *a bad speller.* 2 a book designed to teach or improve spelling.

spellican ('spɛlɪkən) NOUN a variant spelling of **spillikin.**

spelling ('spɛlɪŋ) NOUN 1 the act or process of writing words by using the letters conventionally accepted for their formation; orthography. 2 the art or study of orthography. 3 the actual way in which a word is spelt. 4 the ability of a person to spell: *John's spelling is good.*

spelling bee NOUN a contest in which players are required to spell words according to orthographic conventions.
▷HISTORY C19: from BEE[2]

spelling pronunciation NOUN a pronunciation of a word that is influenced by the word's orthography and often comes about as the modification of an earlier or original rendering, such as the pronunciation of the British name *Mainwaring,* usually ('mænərɪŋ), as ('meɪn,wɛərɪŋ).

spell out VERB (*tr, adverb*) 1 to make clear, distinct, or explicit; clarify in detail: *let me spell out the implications.* 2 to read laboriously or with difficulty, working out each word letter by letter. 3 to discern by study; puzzle out.

spelt[1] (spɛlt) VERB a past tense and past participle of **spell**[1].

spelt[2] (spɛlt) NOUN a species of wheat, *Triticum spelta,* that was formerly much cultivated and was used to develop present-day cultivated wheats.
▷HISTORY Old English; related to Old Saxon *spelta,* Old High German *spelza*

spelter ('spɛltə) NOUN impure zinc, usually containing about 3 per cent of lead and other impurities.
▷HISTORY C17: probably from Middle Dutch *speauter,* of obscure origin; compare Old French *peautre* pewter, Italian *peltro* PEWTER

spelunker (spɪ'lʌŋkə) NOUN a person whose hobby is the exploration and study of caves.
▷HISTORY C20: from Latin *spēlunca,* from Greek *spēlunx* a cave
▸ **spe'lunking** NOUN

spence (spɛns) NOUN *Dialect* **a** a larder or pantry. **b** any monetary allowance. **c** a parlour, esp in a cottage.
▷HISTORY C14: from Old French *despense,* from Latin *dispendere* to distribute; see DISPENSE

spencer[1] ('spɛnsə) NOUN 1 a short fitted coat or jacket. 2 a woman's knitted vest.
▷HISTORY C18: named after Earl *Spencer* (1758–1834)

spencer[2] ('spɛnsə) NOUN *Nautical* a large loose-footed gaffsail on a square-rigger or barque.
▷HISTORY C19: perhaps after the surname *Spencer*

Spencer Gulf NOUN an inlet of the Indian Ocean in S Australia, between the Eyre and Yorke Peninsulas. Length: about 320 km (200 miles). Greatest width: about 145 km (90 miles).

spend (spɛnd) VERB **spends, spending, spent.** 1 to pay out (money, wealth, etc.). 2 (*tr*) to concentrate (time, effort, thought, etc.) upon an object, activity, etc. 3 (*tr*) to pass (time) in a specific way, activity, place, etc. 4 (*tr*) to use up completely: *the hurricane spent its force.* 5 (*tr*) to give up (one's blood, life, etc.) in a cause. 6 (*intr*) *Obsolete* to be used up or exhausted. 7 **spend a penny.** *Brit informal* to urinate. ◆ NOUN 8 an amount of money spent, esp regularly, or allocated to be spent. ◆ See also **spends.**
▷HISTORY Old English *spendan,* from Latin *expendere;* influenced also by Old French *despendre* to spend, from Latin *dispendere;* see EXPEND, DISPENSE
▸ **'spendable** ADJECTIVE

spender ('spɛndə) NOUN a person who spends money in a manner specified: *a big spender.*

spending money NOUN an allowance for small personal expenses; pocket money.

spends (spɛndz) PLURAL NOUN *Lancashire dialect* a child's pocket money.

spendthrift ('spɛnd,θrɪft) NOUN 1 a person who spends money in an extravagant manner. ◆ ADJECTIVE 2 (*usually prenominal*) of or like a spendthrift: *spendthrift economies.*
▷HISTORY C17: from SPEND + THRIFT

Spenserian sonnet NOUN *Prosody* a sonnet form used by the poet Spenser having the rhyme scheme a b a b b c b c c d c d e e.

Spenserian stanza NOUN *Prosody* the stanza form used by the poet Spenser in his poem *The Faerie Queene,* consisting of eight lines in iambic pentameter and a concluding Alexandrine, rhyming a b a b b c b c c.

spent (spɛnt) VERB 1 the past tense and past participle of **spend.** ◆ ADJECTIVE 2 used up or exhausted; consumed. 3 (of a fish) exhausted by spawning.

spent gnat NOUN an angler's name for the spinner of various mayflies, esp *Ephemeris danica* and *E. vulgata,* particularly when lying spent on the water surface after mating and egg-laying.

speos ('spiːɒs) NOUN (esp in ancient Egypt) a temple or tomb cut into a rock face.
▷HISTORY C19: Greek, literally: a cave, grotto

sperm[1] (spɜːm) NOUN, *plural* **sperms** *or* **sperm.** 1 another name for **semen.** 2 a male reproductive cell; male gamete.
▷HISTORY C14: from Late Latin *sperma,* from Greek; related to Greek *speirein* to sow

sperm[2] (spɜːm) NOUN short for **sperm whale, spermaceti** or **sperm oil.**

-sperm NOUN COMBINING FORM (in botany) a seed: *gymnosperm.*
▸ **-spermous** *or* **-spermal** ADJECTIVE COMBINING FORM

spermaceti (,spɜːmə'sɛtɪ, -'siːtɪ) NOUN a white waxy substance obtained from oil from the head of the sperm whale: used in cosmetics, candles, ointments, etc.
▷HISTORY C15: from Medieval Latin *sperma cētī* whale's sperm, from *sperma* SPERM[1] + Latin *cētus* whale, from Greek *kētos*

spermary ('spɜːmərɪ) NOUN, *plural* **-maries.** any organ in which spermatozoa are produced, esp a testis.

spermatheca (,spɜːmə'θiːkə) NOUN a sac or cavity within the body of many female invertebrates, esp insects, used for storing spermatozoa before fertilization takes place.
▷HISTORY C19: see SPERM[1], THECA
▸ **,sperma'thecal** ADJECTIVE

spermatic (spɜː'mætɪk), **spermic** ('spɜːmɪk), *or* **spermous** ('spɜːməs) ADJECTIVE 1 of or relating to spermatozoa: *spermatic fluid.* 2 of or relating to the testis: *the spermatic artery.* 3 of or relating to a spermary.
▷HISTORY C16: from Late Latin *spermaticus,* from Greek *spermatikos* concerning seed, from *sperma* seed, SPERM[1]
▸ **sper'matically** ADVERB

spermatic cord NOUN a cord in many male mammals that passes from each testis to the abdominal cavity and contains the spermatic artery and vein, vas deferens, and lymphatics.

spermatic fluid NOUN another name for **semen.**

spermatid ('spɜːmətɪd) NOUN *Zoology* any of four immature male gametes that are formed from a spermatocyte, each of which develops into a spermatozoon.

spermatium (spɜː'meɪtɪəm) NOUN, *plural* **-tia** (-tɪə). a nonmotile male reproductive cell in red algae and some fungi.
▷HISTORY C19: New Latin, from Greek *spermation* a little seed; see SPERM[1]

spermato-, spermo-, *or before a vowel* **spermat-, sperm-** COMBINING FORM 1 indicating sperm: *spermatogenesis.* 2 indicating seed: *spermatophyte.*
▷HISTORY from Greek *sperma, spermat-,* seed; see SPERM[1]

spermatocide ('spɜːmətəʊ,saɪd) NOUN a less common word for **spermicide.**
▸ **,spermato'cidal** ADJECTIVE

spermatocyte ('spɜːmətəʊ,saɪt) NOUN 1 *Zoology* an immature male germ cell, developed from a spermatogonium, that gives rise, by meiosis, to four spermatids. 2 *Botany* a male germ cell that develops into an antherozoid.

spermatogenesis (,spɜːmətəʊ'dʒɛnɪsɪs) NOUN the formation and maturation of spermatozoa in the testis. See also **spermatocyte** (sense 1).
▸ **spermatogenetic** (,spɜːmətəʊdʒə'nɛtɪk) ADJECTIVE

spermatogonium (,spɜːmətə'gəʊnɪəm) NOUN, *plural* **-nia** (-nɪə). *Zoology* an immature male germ cell that divides to form many spermatocytes.
▷HISTORY C19: from SPERMATO- + -GONIUM
▸ **,spermato'gonial** ADJECTIVE

spermatophore ('spɜːmətəʊ,fɔː) NOUN a capsule of spermatozoa extruded by some molluscs, crustaceans, annelids, and amphibians.
▸ **spermatophoral** (,spɜːmə'tɒfərəl) ADJECTIVE

spermatophyte ('spɜːmətəʊ,faɪt) *or* **spermophyte** NOUN (in traditional classifications) any plant of the major division *Spermatophyta,* which includes all seed-bearing plants: an angiosperm or a gymnosperm. Former name: **phanerogam.**
▸ **spermatophytic** (,spɜːmətəʊ'fɪtɪk) ADJECTIVE

spermatorrhoea *or esp US* **spermatorrhea** (,spɜːmətəʊ'rɪə) NOUN involuntary emission of semen without orgasm.

spermatozoid (,spɜːmətəʊ'zəʊɪd) NOUN *Botany* another name for **antherozoid.**

spermatozoon (,spɜːmətəʊ'zəʊɒn) NOUN, *plural* **-zoa** (-'zəʊə). any of the male reproductive cells released in the semen during ejaculation, consisting of a flattened egg-shaped head, a long neck, and a whiplike tail by which it moves to fertilize the female ovum. Also called: **sperm, zoosperm.**
▸ **,spermato'zoal** *or* **,spermato'zoan** *or* **,spermato'zoic** ADJECTIVE

sperm bank NOUN a place in which semen is stored until it is required for artificial insemination.

spermic ('spɜːmɪk) ADJECTIVE another word for **spermatic.**

spermicide ('spɜːmɪ,saɪd) NOUN any drug or other agent that kills spermatozoa.
▸ **,spermi'cidal** ADJECTIVE

spermine ('spɜːmiːn, -mɪn) NOUN a white or colourless basic water-soluble amine that is found in semen, sputum, and animal tissues; diaminopropyltetramethylenediamine. Formula: $C_{10}H_{26}N_4$.

spermiogenesis (ˌspɜːmɪəʊˈdʒɛnɪsɪs) NOUN the stage in spermatogenesis in which spermatozoa are formed from spermatids.
▸**spermiogenetic** (ˌspɜːmɪəʊdʒəˈnɛtɪk) ADJECTIVE

spermogonium (ˌspɜːməˈɡəʊnɪəm) NOUN, *plural* **-nia** (-nɪə). a reproductive body in some fungi and lichens, in which spermatia are formed.

sperm oil NOUN an oil obtained from the head of the sperm whale, used as a lubricant.

spermophile (ˈspɜːməʊˌfaɪl) NOUN any of various North American ground squirrels of the genera *Citellus, Spermophilopsis,* etc., regarded as pests in many regions.
▹HISTORY C19: from SPERM(AT)O- + -PHILE, on the model of New Latin *spermophilus* a seed-lover

spermophyte (ˈspɜːməʊˌfaɪt) NOUN a variant spelling of **spermatophyte.**

spermous (ˈspɜːməs) ADJECTIVE 1 of or relating to the sperm whale or its products. 2 another word for **spermatic.**

sperm whale NOUN a large toothed whale, *Physeter catodon,* having a square-shaped head and hunted for sperm oil, spermaceti, and ambergris: family *Physeteridae.* Also called: **cachalot.**
▹HISTORY C19: short for SPERMACETI *whale*

Sperrin Mountains (ˈspɛrɪn) NOUN a mountain range in NW Northern Ireland.

sperrylite (ˈspɛrɪˌlaɪt) NOUN a white metallic mineral consisting of platinum arsenide in cubic crystalline form. Formula: $PtAs_2$.
▹HISTORY C19: named after F. L. *Sperry,* Canadian chemist

spessartite (ˈspɛsəˌtaɪt) *or* **spessartine** NOUN a brownish red garnet that consists of manganese aluminium silicate and is used as a gemstone. Formula: $Mn_3Al_2(SiO_4)_3$.
▹HISTORY C19: named after *Spessart,* mountain range in Germany

speug (spjʌɡ) NOUN *Scot* a sparrow.
▹HISTORY of unknown origin

spew (spjuː) VERB 1 to eject (the contents of the stomach) involuntarily through the mouth; vomit. 2 to spit (spittle, phlegm, etc.) out of the mouth. 3 (usually foll by *out*) to send or be sent out in a stream: *flames spewed out.* ♦ NOUN 4 something ejected from the mouth. ♦ Also (archaic): **spue.**
▹HISTORY Old English *spīwan;* related to Old Norse *spȳja,* Gothic *speiwan,* Old High German *spīwan,* Latin *spuere,* Lithuanian *spiauti*
▸ˈ**spewer** NOUN

Spey (speɪ) NOUN a river in E Scotland, flowing generally northeast through the Grampian Mountains to the Moray Firth: salmon fishing. Length: 172 km (107 miles).

Speyer (*German* ˈʃpaiər) NOUN a port in SW Germany, in Rhineland-Palatinate on the Rhine: the scene of 50 imperial diets. Pop.: 47 450 (1991). English name: **Spires.**

SPF ABBREVIATION FOR sun protection factor: an indicator of how effectively a lotion, cosmetic, etc., protects the skin from the harmful rays of the sun.

S.P.F. ABBREVIATION FOR *Vet science* specific pathogen free; denoting animals specially bred to ensure that they are free of specified diseases.

sp. gr. ABBREVIATION FOR specific gravity.

sphagnum (ˈsfæɡnəm) NOUN any moss of the genus *Sphagnum,* of temperate bogs, having leaves capable of holding much water: layers of these mosses decay to form peat. Also called: **peat moss, bog moss.**
▹HISTORY C18: from New Latin, from Greek *sphagnos* a variety of moss
▸ˈ**sphagnous** ADJECTIVE

sphairee (sfaɪˈriː) NOUN *Austral* a game resembling tennis played with wooden bats and a perforated plastic ball, devised by F. A. Beck in 1961.
▹HISTORY from Greek *sphaira* a ball

sphalerite (ˈsfæləˌraɪt, ˈsfeɪlə-) NOUN a yellow to brownish-black mineral consisting of zinc sulphide in cubic crystalline form with varying amounts of iron, manganese, cadmium, gallium, and indium: the chief source of zinc. Formula: ZnS. Also called: **zinc blende.**
▹HISTORY C19: from Greek *sphaleros* deceitful, from *sphallein* to cause to stumble

sphene (sfiːn) NOUN a brown, yellow, green, or grey lustrous mineral consisting of calcium titanium silicate in monoclinic crystalline form. It occurs in metamorphic and acid igneous rocks and is used as a gemstone. Formula: $CaTiSiO_5$. Also called: **titanite.**
▹HISTORY C19: from French *sphène,* from Greek *sphēn* a wedge, alluding to its crystals

sphenic (ˈsfiːnɪk) ADJECTIVE having the shape of a wedge.
▹HISTORY from Greek *sphēn* a wedge

spheno- *or before a vowel* **sphen-** COMBINING FORM having the shape of a wedge: *sphenogram.*
▹HISTORY from Greek *sphēn* wedge

sphenodon (ˈsfiːnəˌdɒn) NOUN the technical name for the **tuatara.**
▹HISTORY C19: from Greek *sphēn* a wedge + *odōn* a tooth

sphenogram (ˈsfiːnəˌɡræm) NOUN a character used in cuneiform script.

sphenoid (ˈsfiːnɔɪd) ADJECTIVE *also* **sphenoidal.** 1 wedge-shaped. 2 of or relating to the sphenoid bone. ♦ NOUN 3 See **sphenoid bone.**

sphenoid bone NOUN the large butterfly-shaped compound bone at the base of the skull, containing a protective depression for the pituitary gland.

spheral (ˈsfɪərəl) ADJECTIVE 1 of or shaped like a sphere; spherical. 2 perfectly rounded; symmetrical.

sphere (sfɪə) NOUN 1 *Maths* **a** a three-dimensional closed surface such that every point on the surface is equidistant from a given point, the centre. **b** the solid figure bounded by this surface or the space enclosed by it. Equation: $(x-a)^2 + (y-b)^2 + (z-c)^2 = r^2$, where r is the radius and (a, b, c) are the coordinates of the centre; surface area: $4\pi r^2$; volume: $4\pi r^3/3$. 2 any object having approximately this shape; globe. 3 the night sky considered as a vaulted roof; firmament. 4 any heavenly object such as a planet, natural satellite, or star. 5 (in the Ptolemaic or Copernican systems of astronomy) one of a series of revolving hollow globes, arranged concentrically, on whose transparent surfaces the sun (or in the Copernican system the earth), the moon, the planets, and fixed stars were thought to be set, revolving around the earth (or in the Copernican system the sun). 6 particular field of activity; environment: *that's out of my sphere.* 7 a social class or stratum of society. ♦ VERB (*tr*) *Chiefly poetic* 8 to surround or encircle. 9 to place aloft or in the heavens.
▹HISTORY C14: from Late Latin *sphēra,* from Latin *sphaera* globe, from Greek *sphaira*

-sphere NOUN COMBINING FORM 1 having the shape or form of a sphere: *bathysphere.* 2 indicating a spherelike enveloping mass: *atmosphere.*
▸**-spheric** ADJECTIVE COMBINING FORM

sphere of influence NOUN a region of the world in which one state is dominant.

spherical (ˈsfɛrɪkᵊl) *or* **spheric** ADJECTIVE 1 shaped like a sphere. 2 of or relating to a sphere: *spherical geometry.* 3 *Geometry* formed on the surface of or inside a sphere: *a spherical triangle.* 4 **a** of or relating to heavenly bodies. **b** of or relating to the spheres of the Ptolemaic or the Copernican system.
▸ˈ**spherically** ADVERB ▸ˈ**sphericalness** NOUN

spherical aberration NOUN *Physics* a defect of optical systems that arises when light striking a mirror or lens near its edge is focused at different points on the axis to the light striking near the centre. The effect occurs when the mirror or lens has spherical surfaces. See also **aberration** (sense 4).

spherical angle NOUN an angle formed at the intersection of two great circles of a sphere.

spherical coordinates PLURAL NOUN three coordinates that define the location of a point in three-dimensional space in terms of the length r of its radius vector, the angle, θ, which this vector makes with one axis, and the angle, ϕ made by a second axis, perpendicular to the first, with the plane containing the first axis and the point. Usually written (r, θ, ϕ).

spherical geometry NOUN the branch of geometry concerned with the properties of figures formed on the surface of a sphere.

spherical polygon NOUN a closed geometric figure formed on the surface of a sphere that is bounded by three or more arcs of great circles.

spherical triangle NOUN a closed geometric figure formed on the surface of a sphere that is bounded by arcs of three great circles.

spherical trigonometry NOUN the branch of trigonometry concerned with the measurement of the angles and sides of spherical triangles.

sphericity (sfɪˈrɪsɪtɪ) NOUN the state or form of being spherical.

spherics[1] (ˈsfɛrɪks) NOUN (*functioning as singular*) the geometry and trigonometry of figures on the surface of a sphere.

spherics[2] *or US* **sferics** (ˈsfɛrɪks, ˈsfɪər-) NOUN (*functioning as singular*) short for **atmospherics.**

spheroid (ˈsfɪərɔɪd) NOUN *Maths* another name for **ellipsoid of revolution.**

spheroidal (sfɪəˈrɔɪdᵊl) ADJECTIVE 1 shaped like an ellipsoid of revolution; approximately spherical. 2 of or relating to an ellipsoid of revolution.
▸**spheˈroidally** *or* **spheˈroidically** ADVERB

spheroidicity (ˌsfɪərɔɪˈdɪsɪtɪ) NOUN the state or form of being spheroidal.

spherometer (sfɪəˈrɒmɪtə) NOUN an instrument for measuring the curvature of a surface.

spherule (ˈsfɛruːl) NOUN a very small sphere or globule.
▹HISTORY C17: from Late Latin *sphaerula* a little SPHERE
▸ˈ**spherular** ADJECTIVE

spherulite (ˈsfɛrʊˌlaɪt) NOUN any of several spherical masses of radiating needle-like crystals of one or more minerals occurring in rocks such as obsidian.
▸**spherulitic** (ˌsfɛrʊˈlɪtɪk) ADJECTIVE

sphery (ˈsfɪərɪ) ADJECTIVE *Poetic* 1 resembling a sphere. 2 resembling a celestial body or bodies; starlike.

sphincter (ˈsfɪŋktə) NOUN *Anatomy* a ring of muscle surrounding the opening of a hollow organ or body and contracting to close it.
▹HISTORY C16: from Late Latin, from Greek *sphinktēr,* from *sphingein* to grip tightly
▸ˈ**sphincteral** ADJECTIVE

sphingomyelin (ˌsfɪŋɡəʊˈmaɪəlɪn) NOUN *Biochem* any of a group of phospholipids, derived from sphingosine, that occur in biological membranes, being especially abundant in the brain.
▹HISTORY from *sphingo-,* from Greek *sphingein* to bind + MYELIN

sphingosine (ˈsfɪŋɡəsɪn, -ˌsiːn) NOUN *Biochem* a long-chain compound occurring in sphingomyelins and cerebrosides, and from which it can be released by hydrolysis. Formula: $CH_3(CH_2)_{12}CH{:}CHCH(OH)CH(NH_2)CH_2OH$.
▹HISTORY from *sphingos-,* from Greek *sphingein* to hold fast + -INE[2]

sphinx (sfɪŋks) NOUN, *plural* **sphinxes** *or* **sphinges** (ˈsfɪndʒiːz). 1 any of a number of huge stone statues built by the ancient Egyptians, having the body of a lion and the head of a man. 2 an inscrutable person.

Sphinx (sfɪŋks) NOUN **the.** 1 *Greek myth* a monster with a woman's head and a lion's body. She lay outside Thebes, asking travellers a riddle and killing them when they failed to answer it. Oedipus answered the riddle and the Sphinx then killed herself. 2 the huge statue of a sphinx near the pyramids at El Gîza in Egypt, of which the head is a carved portrait of the fourth-dynasty Pharaoh, Chephrēn.
▹HISTORY C16: via Latin from Greek, apparently from *sphingein* to hold fast

sphinxlike (ˈsfɪŋksˌlaɪk) ADJECTIVE like the Sphinx; enigmatic or inscrutable.

sphinx moth NOUN *US and Canadian* another name for the **hawk moth.**

sphragistics (sfrəˈdʒɪstɪks) NOUN (*functioning as singular*) the study of seals and signet rings.
▹HISTORY C19: from Greek *sphragistikos,* from *sphragizein* to seal, from *sphragis* a seal
▸**sphraˈgistic** ADJECTIVE

sp. ht ABBREVIATION FOR specific heat.

sphygmic (ˈsfɪɡmɪk) ADJECTIVE *Physiol* of or relating to the pulse.

sphygmo- *or before a vowel* **sphygm-** COMBINING FORM indicating the pulse: *sphygmomanometer.*
▷HISTORY from Greek *sphugmos* pulsation, from *sphuzein* to throb

sphygmograph (ˈsfɪɡməʊˌɡrɑːf, -ˌɡræf) NOUN *Med* an instrument for making a recording (**sphygmogram**) of variations in blood pressure and pulse.
▸**sphygmographic** (ˌsfɪɡməʊˈɡræfɪk) ADJECTIVE
▸**sphygmography** (sfɪɡˈmɒɡrəfɪ) NOUN

sphygmoid (ˈsfɪɡmɔɪd) ADJECTIVE *Physiol* resembling the pulse.

sphygmomanometer (ˌsfɪɡməʊməˈnɒmɪtə) NOUN *Med* an instrument for measuring arterial blood pressure.
▷HISTORY C19: from SPHYGMO- + MANOMETER, on the model of French *sphygmomanomètre*

Sphynx (sfɪŋks) NOUN a breed of medium-sized hairless cat with large ears and a long whiplike tail.

spic, spick, *or* **spik** (spɪk) NOUN *US slang* a derogatory word for a person from a Spanish-speaking country in South or Central America or a Spanish-speaking community in the US.
▷HISTORY C20: perhaps alluding to a foreigner's mispronunciation of *speak*

spica (ˈspaɪkə) NOUN, *plural* **-cae** (-siː) *or* **-cas.** [1] *Med* a spiral bandage formed by a series of overlapping figure-of-eight turns. [2] *Botany* another word for **spike**^{2} (sense 1).
▷HISTORY C15: from Latin: ear of corn

Spica (ˈspiːkə) NOUN the brightest star in the constellation Virgo. Distance: 260 light years.

spicate (ˈspaɪkeɪt) ADJECTIVE *Botany* having, arranged in, or relating to spikes: *a spicate inflorescence.*
▷HISTORY C17: from Latin *spīcātus* having spikes, from *spīca* a point

spiccato (spɪˈkɑːtəʊ) *Music* ◆ NOUN [1] a style of playing a bowed stringed instrument in which the bow bounces lightly off the strings. ◆ ADJECTIVE, ADVERB [2] to be played in this manner.
▷HISTORY Italian: detached, from *spiccare* to make distinct

spice (spaɪs) NOUN [1] **a** any of a variety of aromatic vegetable substances, such as ginger, cinnamon, nutmeg, used as flavourings. **b** these substances collectively. [2] something that represents or introduces zest, charm, or gusto. [3] *Rare* a small amount. [4] *Yorkshire dialect* confectionery. ◆ VERB (*tr*) [5] to prepare or flavour (food) with spices. [6] to introduce charm or zest into.
▷HISTORY C13: from Old French *espice,* from Late Latin *speciēs* (pl) spices, from Latin *speciēs* (sing.) kind; also associated with Late Latin *spīcea* (unattested) fragrant herb, from Latin *spīceus* having spikes of foliage; see SPICA
▸ˈ**spicer** NOUN

spiceberry (ˈspaɪsbərɪ, -brɪ) NOUN, *plural* **-ries.** [1] a myrtaceous tree, *Eugenia rhombea,* of the Caribbean and Florida, with orange or black edible fruits. [2] the fruit of this tree. [3] any of various other aromatic plants or shrubs having spicy edible berries, such as wintergreen.

spicebush (ˈspaɪsˌbʊʃ) NOUN a North American lauraceous shrub, *Lindera benzoin,* having yellow flowers and aromatic leaves and bark.

Spice Islands PLURAL NOUN the former name of the **Moluccas.**

spicery (ˈspaɪsərɪ) NOUN, *plural* **-eries.** [1] spices collectively. [2] the piquant or fragrant quality associated with spices. [3] *Obsolete* a place to store spices.

spick-and-span *or* **spic-and-span** (ˈspɪkənˈspæn) ADJECTIVE [1] extremely neat and clean. [2] new and fresh.
▷HISTORY C17: shortened from *spick-and-span-new,* from obsolete *spick* spike, nail + SPAN-NEW

spicule (ˈspɪkjuːl) NOUN [1] Also called: **spiculum. a** small slender pointed structure or crystal, esp any of the calcareous or siliceous elements of the skeleton of sponges, corals, etc. [2] *Astronomy* a spiked ejection of hot gas occurring over 5000 kilometres above the sun's surface (in its atmosphere) and having a diameter of about 1000 kilometres.
▷HISTORY C18: from Latin: SPICULUM
▸**spiculate** (ˈspɪkjʊˌleɪt, -lɪt) ADJECTIVE

spiculum (ˈspɪkjʊləm) NOUN, *plural* **-la** (-lə). another word for **spicule** (sense 1).
▷HISTORY C18: from Latin: small sharp point, from SPICA

spicy (ˈspaɪsɪ) ADJECTIVE **spicier, spiciest.** [1] seasoned with or containing spice. [2] highly flavoured; pungent. [3] *Informal* suggestive of scandal or sensation. [4] producing or yielding spices.
▸ˈ**spicily** ADVERB ▸ˈ**spiciness** NOUN

spider (ˈspaɪdə) NOUN [1] any predatory silk-producing arachnid of the order *Araneae,* having four pairs of legs and a rounded unsegmented body consisting of abdomen and cephalothorax. See also **wolf spider, trap-door spider, tarantula, black widow.** [2] any of various similar or related arachnids. [3] a hub fitted with radiating spokes or arms that serve to transmit power or support a load. [4] *Agriculture* an instrument used with a cultivator to pulverize soil. [5] any implement or tool having the shape of a spider. [6] *Nautical* a metal frame fitted at the base of a mast to which halyards are tied when not in use. [7] any part of a machine having a number of radiating spokes, tines, or arms. [8] Also called: **octopus** (sense 3). *Brit* a cluster of elastic straps fastened at a central point and used to hold a load on a car rack, motorcycle, etc. [9] *Billiards, snooker* a rest having long legs, used to raise the cue above the level of the height of the ball. [10] *Angling* an artificial fly tied with a hackle and no wings, perhaps originally thought to imitate a spider. [11] *Computing* a computer program that is capable of performing sophisticated, recursive searches on the Internet. [12] short for **spider phaeton.**
▷HISTORY Old English *spīthra;* related to Danish *spinder,* German *Spinne;* see SPIN

spider crab NOUN any of various crabs of the genera *Macropodia, Libinia,* etc., having a small triangular body and very long legs.

spider hole NOUN *Military* a foxhole with a camouflaged lid or cover in which a sniper hides.

spider-hunting wasp NOUN any solitary wasp of the superfamily *Pompiloidea,* having a slender elongated body: the fast-running female hunts spiders as a food store for her larvae.

spiderman (ˈspaɪdəˌmæn) NOUN, *plural* **-men.** *Informal* [1] *Chiefly Brit* a person who erects the steel structure of a building. [2] another name for a **steeplejack.**

spider mite NOUN any of various plant-feeding mites of the family *Tetranychidae,* esp *Panonychus ulmi* (**red spider mite**), which is a serious orchard pest.

spider monkey NOUN [1] any of several arboreal New World monkeys of the genus *Ateles,* of Central and South America, having very long legs, a long prehensile tail, and a small head. [2] **woolly spider monkey.** a rare related monkey, *Brachyteles arachnoides,* of SE Brazil.
▷HISTORY C18: so called because its long limbs resemble the legs of a spider

spider orchid NOUN any of several European orchids of the genus *Ophrys,* esp *O. sphegodes,* having a flower with yellow, green, or pink sepals and a broad brown velvety lip.

spider phaeton NOUN (formerly) a light horse-drawn carriage with a high body and large slender wheels. Sometimes shortened to: **spider.**

spider plant NOUN any of various house plants, esp *Chlorophytum elatum:* see **chlorophytum.**

spiderwort (ˈspaɪdəˌwɜːt) NOUN [1] any of various plants of the American genus *Tradescantia,* esp *T. virginiana,* having blue, purplish, or pink flowers and widely grown as house plants: family *Commelinaceae.* See also **tradescantia.** [2] any of various similar or related plants.
▷HISTORY C17: so called because of the spidery shape of its stamens

spidery (ˈspaɪdərɪ) ADJECTIVE thin and angular like a spider's legs: *spidery handwriting.*

spiegeleisen (ˈspiːɡəlˌaɪzən) NOUN a type of pig iron that is rich in manganese and carbon.
▷HISTORY C19: German, from *Spiegel* mirror + *Eisen* IRON

spiel (ʃpiːl) NOUN [1] a glib plausible style of talk, associated esp with salesmen. ◆ VERB [2] (*intr*) to deliver a prepared spiel. [3] (*tr;* usually foll by *off*) to recite (a prepared oration).
▷HISTORY C19: from German *Spiel* play
▸ˈ**spieler** NOUN

spif (spɪf) NOUN *Informal, chiefly Brit* a postage stamp perforated with the initials of a firm to avoid theft by employees. Former name: **perfin.**
▷HISTORY C20: from *s(tamp) p(erforated with) i(nitials of) f(irm)*

spiffing (ˈspɪfɪŋ) ADJECTIVE *Brit slang old-fashioned* excellent; splendid.
▷HISTORY C19: probably from dialect *spiff* spruce, smartly dressed

spiffy (ˈspɪfɪ) ADJECTIVE **-fier, -fiest.** *US and Canadian slang* smart; stylish.
▷HISTORY C19: from dialect *spiff*
▸ˈ**spiffily** ADVERB ▸ˈ**spiffiness** NOUN

spiflicate *or* **spifflicate** (ˈspɪflɪˌkeɪt) VERB (*tr*) *Brit school slang* to destroy; annihilate.
▷HISTORY C18: a humorous coinage

spignel (ˈspɪɡnəl) NOUN a European umbelliferous plant, *Meum athamanticum,* of mountain regions, having white flowers and finely divided aromatic leaves. Also called: **baldmoney, meu.**
▷HISTORY C16: of uncertain origin

spigot (ˈspɪɡət) NOUN [1] a stopper for the vent hole of a cask. [2] a tap, usually of wood, fitted to a cask. [3] a US name for **tap**^{2} (sense 1). [4] a short cylindrical projection on one component designed to fit into a hole on another, esp the male part of a joint (**spigot and socket joint**) between two pipes.
▷HISTORY C14: probably from Old Provençal *espiga* a head of grain, from Latin *spīca* a point

spik (spɪk) NOUN a variant spelling of **spic.**

spike^{1} (spaɪk) NOUN [1] a sharp point. [2] any sharp-pointed object, esp one made of metal. [3] a long metal nail. [4] *Physics* **a** a transient variation in voltage or current in an electric circuit. **b** a graphical recording of this, such as one of the peaks on an electroencephalogram. [5] (*plural*) shoes with metal projections on the sole and heel for greater traction, as used by athletes. [6] the straight unbranched antler of a young deer. [7] *Brit slang* another word for **dosshouse.** ◆ VERB (*tr*) [8] to secure or supply with or as with spikes. [9] to render ineffective or block the intentions of; thwart. [10] to impale on a spike. [11] to add alcohol to (a drink). [12] *Journalism* to reject (a news story). [13] *Volleyball* to hit (a ball) sharply downwards with an overarm motion from the front of one's own court into the opposing court. [14] (formerly) to render (a cannon) ineffective by blocking its vent with a spike. [15] **spike (someone's) guns.** to thwart (someone's) purpose.
▷HISTORY C13 *spyk;* related to Old English *spīcing* nail, Old Norse *spīk* splinter, Middle Low German *spīker* spike, Norwegian *spīk* SPOKE^{2}, Latin *spīca* sharp point; see SPIKE^{2}

spike^{2} (spaɪk) NOUN *Botany* [1] an inflorescence consisting of a raceme of sessile flowers, as in the gladiolus and sedges. [2] an ear of wheat, barley, or any other grass that has sessile spikelets.
▷HISTORY C14: from Latin *spīca* ear of corn

spike heel NOUN a very high heel on a woman's shoe, tapering to a very narrow tip. Often shortened to: **spike.** Also called (esp Brit): **stiletto, stiletto heel.**

spike lavender NOUN a Mediterranean lavender plant, *Lavandula latifolia,* having pale purple flowers and yielding an oil used in paints.
▷HISTORY C17: from dialect *spick* lavender, via Old French and Old Provençal from Latin *spīca* SPIKE^{2}

spikelet (ˈspaɪklɪt) NOUN [1] *Botany* the unit of a grass inflorescence, typically consisting of two bracts (glumes) surrounding one or more florets, each of which is itself surrounded by two bracts. ◆ See **lemma, palea.** [2] the small inflorescence of plants of other families, esp the sedges.

spikenard (ˈspaɪknɑːd, ˈspaɪkəˌnɑːd) NOUN [1] an aromatic Indian valerianaceous plant, *Nardostachys jatamans,* having rose-purple flowers. [2] an aromatic ointment obtained from this plant. [3] any of various similar or related plants. [4] a North American araliaceous plant, *Aralia racemosa,* having small green flowers and an aromatic root. ◆ Also called (for senses 1, 2): **nard.**
▷HISTORY C14: from Medieval Latin *spīca nardī;* see SPIKE^{2}, NARD

spike-rush NOUN any perennial plant of the temperate cyperaceous genus *Eleocharis,* occurring esp by ponds, and having underground stems, narrow leaves, and small flowers.

spiky (ˈspaɪkɪ) ADJECTIVE **spikier, spikiest.** [1] resembling a spike. [2] having a spike or spikes. [3] *Brit informal* ill-tempered. [4] characterized by violent or aggressive methods: *spiky protestors.*
▸ **ˈspikily** ADVERB ▸ **ˈspikiness** NOUN

spile (spaɪl) NOUN [1] a heavy timber stake or pile. [2] *US and Canadian* a spout for tapping sap from the sugar maple tree. [3] a plug or spigot. ◆ VERB *(tr)* [4] to provide or support with a spile. [5] *US* to tap (a tree) with a spile. [6] *Northern English dialect* a splinter.
▷HISTORY C16: probably from Middle Dutch *spile* peg; related to Icelandic *spila* skewer, Latin *spīna* thorn

spill^{1} (spɪl) VERB **spills, spilling, spilt** *or* **spilled.** *(mainly tr)* [1] (when *intr,* usually foll by *from, out of,* etc.) to fall or cause to fall from or as from a container, esp unintentionally. [2] to disgorge (contents, occupants, etc.) or (of contents, occupants, etc.) to be disgorged: *the car spilt its passengers onto the road; the crowd spilt out of the theatre.* [3] to shed (blood). [4] Also: **spill the beans.** *Informal* to disclose something confidential. [5] *Nautical* to let (wind) escape from a sail or (of the wind) to escape from a sail. ◆ NOUN [6] *Informal* a fall or tumble. [7] short for **spillway.** [8] a spilling of liquid, etc., or the amount spilt. [9] *Austral* the declaring of several political jobs vacant when one higher up becomes so: *the Prime Minister's resignation could mean a Cabinet spill.*
▷HISTORY Old English *spillan* to destroy; related to *spildan,* Old High German *spaltan* to split; see SPOIL
▸ **ˈspiller** NOUN

spill^{2} (spɪl) NOUN [1] a splinter of wood or strip of twisted paper with which pipes, fires, etc., are lit. [2] a small peg or rod made of metal.
▷HISTORY C13: of Germanic origin; compare Old High German *spilla,* Middle Dutch *spile* stake

spillage (ˈspɪlɪdʒ) NOUN [1] an instance or the process of spilling. [2] something spilt or the amount spilt.

spillikin, spilikin (ˈspɪlɪkɪn), *or* **spellican** (ˈspɛlɪkən) NOUN a thin strip of wood, cardboard, or plastic, esp one used in spillikins.

spillikins (ˈspɪlɪkɪnz) NOUN *(functioning as singular) Brit* a game in which players try to pick each spillikin from a heap without moving any of the others. Also called: **jackstraws.**
▷HISTORY C18: from SPILL^{2} + diminutive ending. See -KIN

spill over VERB [1] *(intr, adverb)* to overflow or be forced out of an area, container, etc. ◆ NOUN **spillover.** [2] *Chiefly US and Canadian* the act of spilling over. [3] *Chiefly US and Canadian* the excess part of something. [4] *Economics* any indirect effect of public expenditure. [5] *Astronomy* the part of the noise associated with a radio telescope using a dish antenna caused by pick-up by a secondary antenna from directions that do not intercept the dish.

spillway (ˈspɪlˌweɪ) NOUN a channel that carries away surplus water, as from a dam. Also called: **wasteweir, spill.**

spilt (spɪlt) VERB a past tense and past participle of **spill**^{1}.

spin (spɪn) VERB **spins, spinning, spun.** [1] to rotate or cause to rotate rapidly, as on an axis. [2] **a** to draw out and twist (natural fibres, as of silk or cotton) into a long continuous thread. **b** to make such a thread or filament from (synthetic resins, etc.), usually by forcing through a nozzle. [3] (of spiders, silkworms, etc.) to form (webs, cocoons, etc.) from a silky fibre exuded from the body. [4] *(tr)* to shape (metal) into a rounded form on a lathe. [5] *(tr) Informal* to tell (a tale, story, etc.) by drawing it out at great length (esp in the phrase **spin a yarn**). [6] to bowl, pitch, hit, or kick (a ball) so that it rotates in the air and changes direction or speed on bouncing, or (of a ball) to be projected in this way. [7] *(intr)* (of wheels) to revolve rapidly without causing propulsion. [8] to cause (an aircraft) to dive in a spiral descent or (of an aircraft) to dive in a spiral descent. [9] *(intr; foll by along)* to drive or travel swiftly. [10] *(tr)* Also: **spin-dry.** to rotate (clothes) in a washing machine in order to extract surplus water. [11] *(intr)* to reel or grow dizzy, as from turning around: *my head is spinning.* [12] *(intr)* to fish by drawing a revolving lure through the water. [13] *(intr) Informal* to present news or information in a way that creates a favourable impression. ◆ NOUN [14] a swift rotating motion; instance of spinning. [15] *Physics* **a** the intrinsic angular momentum of an elementary particle or atomic nucleus, as distinguished from any angular momentum resulting from its motion. **b** a quantum number determining values of this angular momentum in units of the Dirac constant, having integral or half-integral values. Symbol: *S or s.* [16] a condition of loss of control of an aircraft or an intentional flight manoeuvre in which the aircraft performs a continuous spiral descent because the angle of maximum lift is less than the angle of incidence. [17] a spinning motion imparted to a ball, etc. [18] (in skating) any of various movements involving spinning rapidly on the spot. [19] *Informal* a short or fast drive, ride, etc., esp in a car, for pleasure. [20] **flat spin.** *Informal, chiefly Brit* a state of agitation or confusion. [21] *Austral and NZ informal* a period of time or an experience; chance or luck; fortune: *a bad spin.* [22] *Commerce, informal* a sudden downward trend in prices, values, etc. [23] *Informal* the practice of presenting news or information in a way that creates a favourable impression. [24] **on the spin.** *Informal* one after another: *they have lost two finals on the spin.* ◆ See also **spin off, spin out.**
▷HISTORY Old English *spinnan;* related to Old Norse *spinna,* Old High German *spinnan* to spin, Lithuanian *pinu* to braid

spina bifida (ˈspaɪnə ˈbɪfɪdə) NOUN a congenital condition in which the meninges of the spinal cord protrude through a gap in the backbone, sometimes causing enlargement of the skull (due to accumulation of cerebrospinal fluid) and paralysis.
▷HISTORY New Latin; see SPINE, BIFID

spinach (ˈspɪnɪdʒ, -ɪtʃ) NOUN [1] a chenopodiaceous annual plant, *Spinacia oleracea,* cultivated for its dark green edible leaves. [2] the leaves of this plant, eaten as a vegetable.
▷HISTORY C16: from Old French *espinache,* from Old Spanish *espinaca,* from Arabic *isfānākh,* from Persian

spinal (ˈspaɪn^{ə}l) ADJECTIVE [1] of or relating to the spine or the spinal cord. [2] denoting a laboratory animal in which the spinal cord has been severed: *a spinal rat.* ◆ NOUN [3] short for **spinal anaesthesia.**
▸ **ˈspinally** ADVERB

spinal anaesthesia NOUN [1] *Surgery* anaesthesia of the lower half of the body produced by injecting an anaesthetic beneath the arachnoid membrane surrounding the spinal cord. See also **epidural** (sense 2). [2] *Pathol* loss of sensation in some part of the body as the result of injury of the spinal cord.

spinal canal NOUN the natural passage through the centre of the spinal column that contains the spinal cord.

spinal column NOUN a series of contiguous or interconnecting bony or cartilaginous segments that surround and protect the spinal cord. Also called: **spine, vertebral column.** Nontechnical name: **backbone.**

spinal cord NOUN the thick cord of nerve tissue within the spinal canal, which in man gives rise to 31 pairs of spinal nerves, and together with the brain forms the central nervous system.

spin bowler NOUN *Cricket* a bowler who specializes in bowling balls with a spinning motion.

spindle (ˈspɪnd^{ə}l) NOUN [1] a rod or stick that has a notch in the top, used to draw out natural fibres for spinning into thread, and a long narrow body around which the thread is wound when spun. [2] one of the thin rods or pins bearing bobbins upon which spun thread is wound in a spinning wheel or machine. [3] any of various parts in the form of a rod, esp a rotating rod that acts as an axle, mandrel, or arbor. [4] a piece of wood that has been turned, such as a baluster or table leg. [5] a small square metal shaft that passes through the lock of a door and to which the door knobs or handles are fixed. [6] a measure of length of yarn equal to 18 hanks (15 120 yards) for cotton or 14 400 yards for linen. [7] *Biology* a spindle-shaped structure formed by microtubules during mitosis or meiosis which draws the duplicated chromosomes apart as the cell divides. [8] a less common name for a **hydrometer.** [9] a tall pole with a marker at the top, fixed to an underwater obstruction as an aid to navigation. [10] a device consisting of a sharp upright spike on a pedestal on which bills, order forms, etc., are impaled. ◆ NOUN [11] short for: **spindle tree.** ◆ VERB [12] *(tr)* to form into a spindle or equip with spindles. [13] *(intr) Rare* (of a plant, stem, shoot, etc.) to grow rapidly and become elongated and thin.
▷HISTORY Old English *spinel;* related to *spinnan* to SPIN, Old Saxon *spinnila* spindle, Old High German *spinnala*

spindle-legged *or* **spindle-shanked** ADJECTIVE having long thin legs.

spindlelegs (ˈspɪnd^{ə}lˌlɛgz) *or* **spindleshanks** PLURAL NOUN [1] long thin legs. [2] *(functioning as singular)* a person who has long thin legs.

spindle tree NOUN any of various shrubs or trees of the genus *Euonymus,* esp *E. europaeus,* of Europe and W Asia, typically having red fruits and yielding a hard wood formerly used in making spindles: family *Celastraceae.*

spindling (ˈspɪndlɪŋ) ADJECTIVE [1] long and slender, esp disproportionately so. [2] (of stalks, shoots, etc.) becoming long and slender. ◆ NOUN [3] a spindling person or thing.

spindly (ˈspɪndlɪ) ADJECTIVE **-dlier, -dliest.** tall, slender, and frail; attenuated.

spin doctor NOUN *Informal* a person who provides a favourable slant to an item of news, potentially unpopular policy, etc., esp on behalf of a political personality or party.
▷HISTORY C20: from the spin given to a ball in various sports to make it go in the desired direction

spindrift (ˈspɪnˌdrɪft) NOUN [1] spray blown up from the surface of the sea. [2] powdery snow blown off a mountain. ◆ Also called: **spoondrift.**
▷HISTORY C17: of Scottish origin, possibly from a variant of obsolete *spoon* to scud + DRIFT

spin-dry VERB **-dries, -drying, -dried.** *(tr)* to dry (clothes, linen, etc.) in a spin-dryer.

spin-dryer NOUN a device that extracts water from clothes, linen, etc., by spinning them in a perforated drum.

spine (spaɪn) NOUN [1] the spinal column. [2] the sharply pointed tip or outgrowth of a leaf, stem, etc. [3] *Zoology* a hard pointed process or structure, such as the ray of a fin, the quill of a porcupine, or the ridge on a bone. [4] the back of a book, record sleeve, etc. [5] a ridge, esp of a hill. [6] strength of endurance, will, etc. [7] anything resembling the spinal column in function or importance; main support or feature.
▷HISTORY C14: from Old French *espine* spine, from Latin *spīna* thorn, backbone
▸ **spined** ADJECTIVE

spine-bashing NOUN *Austral informal* loafing or resting.
▸ **ˈspine-ˌbasher** NOUN

spine-chiller NOUN a book, film, etc., that arouses terror.

spine-chilling ADJECTIVE (of a book, film, etc.) arousing terror.

spinel (spɪˈnɛl) NOUN [1] any of a group of hard glassy minerals of variable colour consisting of oxides of aluminium, magnesium, chromium, iron, zinc, or manganese and occurring in the form of octahedral crystals: used as gemstones. [2] a hard, glassy mineral composed of magnesium-aluminium oxide found in metamorphosed limestones and many basic and ultrabasic igneous rocks. Formula: $MgAl_2O_4$.
▷HISTORY C16: from French *spinelle,* from Italian *spinella,* diminutive of *spina* a thorn, from Latin; so called from the shape of the crystals

spineless (ˈspaɪnlɪs) ADJECTIVE [1] lacking a backbone; invertebrate. [2] having no spiny processes: *spineless stems.* [3] lacking strength of character, resolution, or courage.
▸ **ˈspinelessly** ADVERB ▸ **ˈspinelessness** NOUN

spinescent (spaɪˈnɛs^{ə}nt) ADJECTIVE *Biology* [1] having or resembling a spine or spines. [2] becoming spiny.
▷HISTORY C18: from Late Latin *spīnēscere* to become thorny, from Latin *spīna* a thorn
▸ **spiˈnescence** NOUN

spinet (spɪˈnɛt, ˈspɪnɪt) NOUN a small type of harpsichord having one manual.
▷HISTORY C17: from Italian *spinetta,* perhaps from

Giovanni *Spinetti,* 16th-century Italian maker of musical instruments and its supposed inventor

spine-tingling ADJECTIVE causing a sensation of fear or excitement.

spiniferous (spaɪˈnɪfərəs) *or* **spinigerous** (spaɪˈnɪdʒərəs) ADJECTIVE (esp of plants) bearing spines or thorns.
▷HISTORY C17: from Late Latin *spīnifer* having spines, from Latin *spīna* a thorn, spine + *ferre* to bear

spinifex (ˈspɪnɪˌfɛks) NOUN 1 Also called: **porcupine grass.** *Austral* any of various coarse spiny-leaved inland grasses of the genus *Triodia.* 2 any grass of the SE Asian genus *Spinifex,* having pointed leaves and spiny seed heads: often planted to bind loose sand.
▷HISTORY C19: from New Latin, from Latin *spīna* a thorn + *-fex* maker, from *facere* to make

spin machine NOUN an organization or group of people acting together to present news or information in a way that creates a particular desired impression.

spinnaker (ˈspɪnəkə; *Nautical* ˈspæŋkə) NOUN a large light triangular racing sail set from the foremast of a yacht when running or on a broad reach.
▷HISTORY C19: probably from SPIN + (MO)NIKER, but traditionally derived from *Sphinx,* the yacht that first adopted this type of sail

spinner (ˈspɪnə) NOUN 1 a person or thing that spins. 2 *Informal* a spin doctor. 3 *Cricket* **a** a ball that is bowled with a spinning motion. **b** a bowler who specializes in bowling such balls. 4 a streamlined fairing that fits over and revolves with the hub of an aircraft propeller. 5 a fishing lure with a fin or wing that revolves when drawn through the water. 6 an angler's name for the mature adult form (imago) of various flies, especially the mayflies. Compare **dun**[2] (sense 3).

spinneret (ˈspɪnəˌrɛt) NOUN 1 any of several organs in spiders and certain insects through which silk threads are exuded. 2 a finely perforated dispenser through which a viscous liquid is extruded in the production of synthetic fibres.
▷HISTORY C18: from SPINNER + -ET

spinney (ˈspɪnɪ) NOUN *Chiefly Brit* a small wood or copse.
▷HISTORY C16: from Old French *espinei,* from *espine* thorn, from Latin *spīna*

spinning (ˈspɪnɪŋ) NOUN 1 **a** the act or process of spinning. **b** (*as modifier*): *spinning yarn.* 2 the act or technique of casting and drawing a revolving lure through the water so as to imitate the movement of a live fish, etc.

spinning jenny NOUN an early type of spinning frame with several spindles, invented by James Hargreaves in 1764.
▷HISTORY C18: see JENNY; the reason for the adoption of the woman's name is unclear

spinning mule NOUN *Textiles* See **mule**[1] (sense 3).

spinning top NOUN another name for **top**[2] (the toy).

spinning wheel NOUN a wheel-like machine for spinning at home, having one hand- or foot-operated spindle.

spinode (ˈspaɪnəʊd) NOUN *Maths* another name for **cusp** (sense 4).
▷HISTORY C19: from Latin *spīna* spine + NODE

spin off VERB 1 (*tr, preposition*) to turn (a part of a business enterprise) into a separate company. ◆ NOUN **spin-off.** 2 any product or development derived incidentally from the application of existing knowledge or enterprise. 3 a book, film, or television series derived from a similar successful book, film, or television series.

spinose (ˈspaɪnəʊs, spaɪˈnəʊs) ADJECTIVE (esp of plants) bearing many spines.
▷HISTORY C17: from Latin *spīnōsus* prickly, from *spīna* a thorn
▸ˈ**spinosely** ADVERB ▸**spinosity** (spaɪˈnɒsɪtɪ) NOUN

spinous (ˈspaɪnəs) ADJECTIVE *Biology* 1 resembling a spine or thorn: *the spinous process of a bone.* 2 having spines or spiny projections. 3 another word for **spinose.**

spin out VERB (*tr, adverb*) 1 to extend or protract (a story, etc.) by including superfluous detail; prolong. 2 to spend or pass (time). 3 to contrive to cause (money, etc.) to last as long as possible. ◆ NOUN **spinout.** 4 a spinning skid in a car that causes it to run off the road.

Spinozism (spɪˈnəʊzɪzəm) NOUN the philosophical system of Baruch Spinoza, the Dutch philosopher (1632–77), esp the concept of God as the unique reality possessing an infinite number of attributes of which we can know at least thought and extension.
▸**Spiˈnozist** NOUN

spin stabilization NOUN a technique by which a bullet, rocket, etc., is made to spin around its longitudinal axis to assist it in maintaining a steady flight path.

spinster (ˈspɪnstə) NOUN 1 an unmarried woman regarded as being beyond the age of marriage. 2 *Law* (in legal documents) a woman who has never married. Compare **feme sole.** 3 (formerly) a woman who spins thread for her living.
▷HISTORY C14 (in the sense: a person, esp a woman, whose occupation is spinning; C17: a woman still unmarried): from SPIN + -STER
▸ˈ**spinsterˌhood** NOUN ▸ˈ**spinsterish** ADJECTIVE

spinthariscope (spɪnˈθærɪˌskəʊp) NOUN a device for observing ionizing radiation, consisting of a tube with a magnifying lens at one end and a phosphorescent screen at the other. A particle hitting the screen produces a scintillation.
▷HISTORY C20: from Greek *spintharis* a little spark + -SCOPE

spinule (ˈspaɪnjuːl) NOUN *Biology* a very small spine, thorn, or prickle.
▷HISTORY C18: from Late Latin *spīnula*
▸**spinulose** (ˈspaɪnjʊˌləʊs) ADJECTIVE

spiny (ˈspaɪnɪ) ADJECTIVE **spinier, spiniest.** 1 (of animals) having or covered with quills or spines. 2 (of plants) covered with spines; thorny. 3 troublesome to handle; puzzling. 4 shaped like a spine.
▸ˈ**spininess** NOUN

spiny anteater NOUN another name for **echidna.**

spiny-finned ADJECTIVE (of certain fishes) having fins that are supported by stiff bony spines. See also **acanthopterygian.** Compare **soft-finned.**

spiny lobster NOUN any of various large edible marine decapod crustaceans of the genus *Palinurus* and related genera, having a very tough spiny carapace. Also called: **rock lobster, crawfish, langouste.**

spiracle (ˈspaɪərəkᵊl, ˈspaɪrə-) NOUN 1 any of several paired apertures in the cuticle of an insect, by which air enters and leaves the trachea. 2 a small paired rudimentary gill slit just behind the head in skates, rays, and related fishes. 3 any similar respiratory aperture, such as the blowhole in whales. 4 *Geology* a protrusion of sediment into a lava flow, formed by the explosive transition of water into steam.
▷HISTORY C14 (originally: breath): from Latin *spīrāculum* vent, from *spīrāre* to breathe
▸**spiracular** (spɪˈrækjʊlə) ADJECTIVE ▸**spiˈraculate** ADJECTIVE

spiraea *or esp US* **spirea** (spaɪˈrɪə) NOUN any rosaceous plant of the genus *Spiraea,* having sprays of small white or pink flowers. See also **meadowsweet** (sense 2), **hardhack.**
▷HISTORY C17: via Latin from Greek *speiraia,* from *speira* SPIRE[2]

spiral (ˈspaɪərəl) NOUN 1 *Geometry* one of several plane curves formed by a point winding about a fixed point at an ever-increasing distance from it. Polar equation of **Archimedes spiral:** $r = a\theta$; of **logarithmic spiral:** $\log r = a\theta$; of **hyperbolic spiral:** $r\theta = a$, (where a is a constant). 2 another name for **helix** (sense 1). 3 something that pursues a winding, usually upward, course or that displays a twisting form or shape. 4 a flight manoeuvre in which an aircraft descends describing a helix of comparatively large radius with the angle of attack within the normal flight range. Compare **spin** (sense 16). 5 *Economics* a continuous upward or downward movement in economic activity or prices, caused by interaction between prices, wages, demand, and production. ◆ ADJECTIVE 6 having the shape of a spiral. ◆ VERB **-rals, -ralling, -ralled** *or US* **-rals, -raling, -raled.** 7 to assume or cause to assume a spiral course or shape. 8 (*intr*) to increase or decrease with steady acceleration: *wages and prices continue to spiral.*
▷HISTORY C16: via French from Medieval Latin *spīrālis,* from Latin *spīra* a coil; see SPIRE[2]
▸ˈ**spirally** ADVERB

spiral binding NOUN *Bookbinding* a method of securing the pages of a publication by passing a coil of wire through small holes punched at the back edge of the covers and individual pages.

spiral galaxy NOUN a galaxy consisting of an ellipsoidal nucleus of old stars from opposite sides of which arms, containing younger stars, spiral outwards around the nucleus. In a **barred spiral** the arms originate at the ends of a bar-shaped nucleus.

spiral of Archimedes NOUN *Maths* a spiral having the equation $r = a\theta$, where a is a constant. It is the locus of a point moving to or from the origin at a constant speed along a line rotating around that origin at a constant speed.

spiral staircase NOUN a staircase constructed around a central axis.

spirant (ˈspaɪrənt) ADJECTIVE 1 *Phonetics* another word for **fricative.** ◆ NOUN 2 a fricative consonant.
▷HISTORY C19: from Latin *spīrāns* breathing, from *spīrāre* to breathe

spire[1] (spaɪə) NOUN 1 Also called: **steeple.** a tall structure that tapers upwards to a point, esp one on a tower or roof or one that forms the upper part of a steeple. 2 a slender tapering shoot or stem, such as a blade of grass. 3 the apical part of any tapering formation; summit. ◆ VERB 4 (*intr*) to assume the shape of a spire; point up. 5 (*tr*) to furnish with a spire or spires.
▷HISTORY Old English *spīr* blade; related to Old Norse *spīra* stalk, Middle Low German *spīr* shoot, Latin *spīna* thorn
▸ˈ**spiry** ADJECTIVE

spire[2] (spaɪə) NOUN 1 any of the coils or turns in a spiral structure. 2 the apical part of a spiral shell.
▷HISTORY C16: from Latin *spīra* a coil, from Greek *speira*
▸**spiriferous** (spaɪəˈrɪfərəs) ADJECTIVE

spirelet (ˈspaɪəlɪt) NOUN another name for **flèche** (sense 1).

spireme (ˈspaɪriːm) NOUN *Cytology* the tangled mass of chromatin threads into which the nucleus of a cell is resolved at the start of mitosis.
▷HISTORY C19: from Greek *speirēma* a coil, from *speira* a coil, SPIRE[2]

Spires (spaɪəz) NOUN the English name for **Speyer.**

spirillum (spaɪˈrɪləm) NOUN, *plural* **-la** (-lə). 1 any bacterium having a curved or spirally twisted rodlike body. Compare **coccus** (sense 1), **bacillus** (sense 1). 2 any bacterium of the genus *Spirillum,* such as *S. minus,* which causes ratbite fever.
▷HISTORY C19: from New Latin, literally: a little coil, from *spīra* a coil
▸**spiˈrillar** ADJECTIVE

spirit[1] (ˈspɪrɪt) NOUN 1 the force or principle of life that animates the body of living things. 2 temperament or disposition: *truculent in spirit.* 3 liveliness; mettle: *they set to it with spirit.* 4 the fundamental, emotional, and activating principle of a person; will: *the experience broke his spirit.* 5 a sense of loyalty or dedication: *team spirit.* 6 the prevailing element; feeling: *a spirit of joy pervaded the atmosphere.* 7 state of mind or mood; attitude: *he did it in the wrong spirit.* 8 (*plural*) an emotional state, esp with regard to exaltation or dejection: *in high spirits.* 9 a person characterized by some activity, quality, or disposition: *a leading spirit of the movement.* 10 the deeper more significant meaning as opposed to a pedantic interpretation: *the spirit of the law.* 11 that which constitutes a person's intangible being as contrasted with his physical presence: *I shall be with you in spirit.* 12 **a** an incorporeal being, esp the soul of a dead person. **b** (*as modifier*): *spirit world.* ◆ VERB (*tr*) 13 (usually foll by *away* or *off*) to carry off mysteriously or secretly. 14 (often foll by *up*) to impart animation or determination to.
▷HISTORY C13: from Old French *esperit,* from Latin *spīritus* breath, spirit; related to *spīrāre* to breathe

spirit[2] (ˈspɪrɪt) NOUN 1 (*often plural*) any distilled alcoholic liquor such as brandy, rum, whisky, or gin. 2 *Chem* **a** an aqueous solution of ethanol, esp one obtained by distillation. **b** the active principle or essence of a substance, extracted as a liquid, esp by distillation. 3 *Pharmacol* **a** a solution of a volatile substance, esp a volatile oil, in alcohol. **b** (*as

modifier): *a spirit burner.* [4] *Alchemy* any of the four substances sulphur, mercury, sal ammoniac, or arsenic.
▷HISTORY C14: special use of SPIRIT[1], name applied to alchemical substances (as in sense 4), hence extended to distilled liquids

Spirit (ˈspɪrɪt) NOUN **the.** [1] **a** another name for the **Holy Ghost. b** God, esp when regarded as transcending material limitations. [2] the influence of God or divine things upon the soul. [3] *Christian Science* God or divine substance.

spirited (ˈspɪrɪtɪd) ADJECTIVE [1] displaying animation, vigour, or liveliness. [2] (*in combination*) characterized by mood, temper, or disposition as specified: *high-spirited; public-spirited.*
▸ˈ**spiritedly** ADVERB ▸ˈ**spiritedness** NOUN

spirit gum NOUN a glue made from gum dissolved in ether used to stick a false beard, etc., onto the face.

spiritism (ˈspɪrɪˌtɪzəm) NOUN a less common word for **spiritualism.**
▸ˈ**spiritist** NOUN ▸ˌ**spiritˈistic** ADJECTIVE

spirit lamp NOUN a lamp that burns methylated or other spirits instead of oil.

spiritless (ˈspɪrɪtlɪs) ADJECTIVE lacking courage or liveliness; melancholic.
▸ˈ**spiritlessly** ADVERB ▸ˈ**spiritlessness** NOUN

spirit level NOUN a device for setting horizontal surfaces, consisting of an accurate block of material in which a sealed slightly curved tube partially filled with liquid is set so that the air bubble rests between two marks on the tube when the block is horizontal.

spirit of enterprise NOUN the motivation to set up and succeed in business or commerce.

spiritoso (ˌspɪrɪˈtəʊsəʊ) ADJECTIVE, ADVERB *Music* (often preceded by a tempo marking) to be played in a spirited or animated manner: *allegro spiritoso.*
▷HISTORY Italian, from *spirito* spirit, from Latin *spīritus* breath; see SPIRIT[1]

spiritous (ˈspɪrɪtəs) ADJECTIVE [1] a variant spelling of **spirituous.** [2] *Archaic* high-spirited. [3] *Archaic* ethereal; pure.

spirits of ammonia NOUN (*functioning as singular or plural*) another name for **sal volatile** (sense 2).

spirits of hartshorn NOUN (*functioning as singular or plural*) another name for **aqueous ammonia.** See **ammonium hydroxide.**

spirits of salt NOUN (*functioning as singular or plural*) a solution of hydrochloric acid in water.

spirits of turpentine NOUN (*functioning as singular or plural*) another name for **turpentine** (sense 3).

spirits of wine NOUN (*functioning as singular or plural*) another name for **alcohol** (sense 1).

spiritual (ˈspɪrɪtjʊəl) ADJECTIVE [1] relating to the spirit or soul and not to physical nature or matter; intangible. [2] of, relating to, or characteristic of sacred things, the Church, religion, etc. [3] standing in a relationship based on communication between the souls or minds of the persons involved: *a spiritual father.* [4] having a mind or emotions of a high and delicately refined quality. ◆ NOUN [5] See **Negro spiritual.** [6] (*often plural*) the sphere of religious, spiritual, or ecclesiastical matters, or such matters in themselves. [7] **the.** the realm of spirits.
▸ˈ**spiritually** ADVERB ▸ˈ**spiritualness** NOUN

spiritual bouquet NOUN *RC Church* a collection of private devotional acts and prayers chosen and performed by one person for the benefit of another.

spiritual incest NOUN *RC Church* [1] marriage or a sexual relationship between persons related by spiritual affinity or with a person under a solemn vow of chastity. [2] the holding of two benefices by the same priest or bishop.

spiritualism (ˈspɪrɪtjʊəˌlɪzəm) NOUN [1] the belief that the disembodied spirits of the dead, surviving in another world, can communicate with the living in this world, esp through mediums. [2] the doctrines and practices associated with this belief. [3] *Philosophy* the belief that because reality is to some extent immaterial it is therefore spiritual. [4] any doctrine (in philosophy, religion, etc.) that prefers the spiritual to the material. [5] the condition or quality of being spiritual.
▸ˈ**spiritualist** NOUN ▸ˌ**spirituaˈlistic** ADJECTIVE

spirituality (ˌspɪrɪtjʊˈælɪtɪ) NOUN, *plural* **-ties.** [1] the state or quality of being dedicated to God, religion, or spiritual things or values, esp as contrasted with material or temporal ones. [2] the condition or quality of being spiritual. [3] a distinctive approach to religion or prayer: *the spirituality of the desert Fathers.* [4] (*often plural*) Church property or revenue or a Church benefice.

spiritualize *or* **spiritualise** (ˈspɪrɪtjʊəˌlaɪz) VERB (*tr*) to make spiritual or infuse with spiritual content.
▸ˌ**spiritualiˈzation** *or* ˌ**spiritualiˈsation** NOUN
▸ˈ**spiritualˌizer** *or* ˈ**spiritualˌiser** NOUN

spiritualty (ˈspɪrɪtjʊəltɪ) NOUN, *plural* **-ties.** *Archaic* [1] the clergy collectively. [2] another word for **spirituality.**

spirituel (ˌspɪrɪtjʊˈɛl) ADJECTIVE having a refined and lively mind or wit. Also (feminine): **spirituelle** (ˌspɪrɪtjʊˈɛl).
▷HISTORY C17: from French

spirituous (ˈspɪrɪtjʊəs) ADJECTIVE [1] characterized by or containing alcohol. [2] (of a drink) being a spirit.
▸**spirituosity** (ˌspɪrɪtjʊˈɒsɪtɪ) *or* ˈ**spirituousness** NOUN

spiritus asper (ˈspɪrɪtəs ˈæspə) NOUN another term for **rough breathing.**
▷HISTORY Latin: rough breath

spiritus lenis NOUN another term for **smooth breathing.**
▷HISTORY Latin: gentle breath

spirit varnish NOUN a varnish consisting of a gum or resin, such as shellac or copal, dissolved in alcohol.

spirketting (ˈspɜːkɪtɪŋ) NOUN *Nautical* [1] deck planking near the bulwarks. [2] the interior lining between ports and the overhead interior surface of the cabin.
▷HISTORY C18: from obsolete *spirket* space between floor timbers in a ship

spiro-[1] COMBINING FORM indicating breath or respiration: *spirograph.*
▷HISTORY from Latin *spīrāre* to breathe

spiro-[2] COMBINING FORM spiral; coil: *spirochaete.*
▷HISTORY from Latin *spīra,* from Greek *speira* a coil

spirochaete *or US* **spirochete** (ˈspaɪrəʊˌkiːt) NOUN any of a group of spirally coiled rodlike bacteria that includes the causative agent of syphilis. See **treponema.**
▷HISTORY C19: from New Latin *spīrochaeta;* see SPIRO-[2], CHAETA

spirochaetosis *or US* **spirochetosis** (ˌspaɪrəʊkɪˈtəʊsɪs) NOUN any disease caused by a spirochaete.

spirograph (ˈspaɪrəˌgrɑːf, -ˌgræf) NOUN *Med* an instrument for recording the movements of breathing.
▸ˌ**spiroˈgraphic** ADJECTIVE

spirogyra (ˌspaɪrəˈdʒaɪərə) NOUN any green freshwater multicellular alga of the genus *Spirogyra,* consisting of minute filaments containing spirally coiled chloroplasts.
▷HISTORY C20: from New Latin, from SPIRO-[2] + Greek *guros* a circle

spiroid (ˈspaɪrɔɪd) ADJECTIVE resembling a spiral or displaying a spiral form.
▷HISTORY C19: from New Latin *spīroīdēs,* from Greek *speiroeidēs,* from *speira* a coil

spirometer (spaɪˈrɒmɪtə) NOUN an instrument for measuring the air capacity of the lungs. Compare **pneumatometer.**
▸**spirometric** (ˌspaɪrəˈmɛtrɪk) ADJECTIVE ▸**spiˈrometry** NOUN

spironolactone (ˌspaɪrənəʊˈlæktəʊn) NOUN a diuretic that increases water loss from the kidneys and is much used to treat oedema in heart and kidney failure.
▷HISTORY C20: from SPIRO-[2] + linking syllable *-no-* + LACTONE

spirt (spɜːt) NOUN a variant spelling of **spurt.**

spirula (ˈspaɪrʊlə) NOUN a tropical cephalopod mollusc, *Spirula peronii,* having prominent eyes, short arms, and a small flattened spirally coiled internal shell: order *Decapoda* (cuttlefish and squids).
▷HISTORY C19: via New Latin from Late Latin: a small twisted cake, from Latin *spīra* a coil

spirulina (ˌspɪrʊˈlaɪnə) NOUN any filamentous cyanobacterium of the genus *Spirulina*: processed as a valuable source of proteins and other nutrients.
▷HISTORY from New Latin *spirula* small spiral

spiry (ˈspaɪərɪ) ADJECTIVE *Poetic* of spiral form; helical.

spit[1] (spɪt) VERB **spits, spitting, spat** *or* **spit.** [1] (*intr*) to expel saliva from the mouth; expectorate. [2] (*intr*) *Informal* to show disdain or hatred by spitting. [3] (of a fire, hot fat, etc.) to eject (fragments of coal, sparks, etc.) violently and with an explosive sound; splutter. [4] (*intr*) to rain very lightly. [5] (*tr; often foll by out*) to eject or discharge (something) from the mouth: *he spat the food out; to spit blood.* [6] (*tr; often foll by out*) to utter (short sharp words or syllables), esp in a violent manner. [7] **spit chips.** Also (NZ): **spit tacks.** *Austral slang* to be very angry. [8] **spit it out!** *Brit informal* a command given to someone that he should speak forthwith. ◆ NOUN [9] another name for **spittle.** [10] a light or brief fall of rain, snow, etc. [11] the act or an instance of spitting. [12] *Informal, chiefly Brit* another word for **spitting image.**
▷HISTORY Old English *spittan;* related to *spǣtan* to spit, German dialect *spitzen*
▸ˈ**spitter** NOUN

spit[2] (spɪt) NOUN [1] a pointed rod on which meat is skewered and roasted before or over an open fire. [2] Also called: **rotisserie, rotating spit.** a similar device rotated by electricity or clockwork, fitted onto a cooker. [3] an elongated often hooked strip of sand or shingle projecting from the shore, deposited by longshore drift, and usually above water. ◆ VERB **spits, spitting, spitted.** [4] (*tr*) to impale on or transfix with or as if with a spit.
▷HISTORY Old English *spitu;* related to Old High German *spiz* spit, Norwegian *spit* tip

spit[3] (spɪt) NOUN the depth of earth cut by a spade; a spade's depth.
▷HISTORY C16: from Middle Dutch and Middle Low German *spit*

spital (ˈspɪtᵊl) NOUN *Obsolete* [1] a hospital, esp for the needy sick. [2] a highway shelter.
▷HISTORY C13 *spitel,* changed from Medieval Latin *hospitāle* HOSPITAL

spit and polish NOUN *Informal* punctilious attention to neatness, discipline, etc., esp in the armed forces.

spitchcock (ˈspɪtʃˌkɒk) NOUN an eel split and grilled or fried. Compare **spatchcock.**
▷HISTORY C16: of unknown origin; see SPATCHCOCK

spit curl NOUN the US and Canadian name for **kiss curl.**
▷HISTORY perhaps so called because it is sometimes plastered down with spittle

spite (spaɪt) NOUN [1] maliciousness involving the desire to harm another; venomous ill will. [2] an instance of such malice; grudge. [3] *Archaic* something that induces vexation. [4] **in spite of.** (*preposition*) in defiance of; regardless of; notwithstanding. ◆ VERB (*tr*) [5] to annoy in order to vent spite. [6] *Archaic* to offend.
▷HISTORY C13: variant of DESPITE

spiteful (ˈspaɪtfʊl) ADJECTIVE full of or motivated by spite; vindictive.
▸ˈ**spitefully** ADVERB ▸ˈ**spitefulness** NOUN

spitfire (ˈspɪtˌfaɪə) NOUN a person given to outbursts of spiteful temper and anger, esp a woman or girl.

Spithead (ˌspɪtˈhɛd) NOUN an extensive anchorage between the mainland of England and the Isle of Wight, off Portsmouth.

Spitsbergen (ˈspɪtsˌbɜːgən) NOUN another name for **Svalbard.**

spitsticker (ˈspɪtˌstɪkə) NOUN a wood-engraving tool with a fine prow-shaped point for cutting curved lines.

spitting distance NOUN a short space or distance.

spitting image NOUN *Informal* a person who bears a strong physical resemblance to another, esp to a relative. Also called: **spit, spit and image.**
▷HISTORY C19: modification of *spit and image,* from SPIT[1] (as in the phrase *the very spit of,* the exact likeness of (someone))

spitting snake NOUN another name for the **rinkhals.**

spittle (ˈspɪtᵊl) NOUN [1] the fluid secreted in the

mouth; saliva or spit. [2] Also called: **cuckoo spit, frog spit.** the frothy substance secreted on plants by the larvae of certain froghoppers.
▷HISTORY Old English *spǣtl* saliva; see SPIT[1]

spittle insect *or* **spittlebug** (ˈspɪtᵊlˌbʌg) NOUN other names for the **froghopper.**

spittoon (spɪˈtuːn) NOUN a receptacle for spit, usually in a public place.
▷HISTORY C19: from SPIT[1] + *-oon:* see SALOON, BALLOON, etc.

spitz (spɪts) NOUN any of various breeds of dog characterized by very dense hair, a stocky build, a pointed muzzle, erect ears, and a tightly curled tail.
▷HISTORY C19: from German, from *spitz* pointed

spiv (spɪv) NOUN *Brit slang* a person who makes a living by underhand dealings or swindling; black marketeer.
▷HISTORY C20: back formation from dialect *spiving* smart; compare SPIFFY, SPIFFING
▸ˈ**spivvy** ADJECTIVE

splake (spleɪk) NOUN a type of hybrid trout bred by Canadian zoologists.
▷HISTORY from *sp(eckled)* + *lake (trout)*

splanchnic (ˈsplæŋknɪk) ADJECTIVE of or relating to the viscera; visceral: *a splanchnic nerve.*
▷HISTORY C17: from New Latin *splanchnicus,* from Greek *splankhnikos* concerning the entrails, from *splankhna* the entrails

splash (splæʃ) VERB [1] to scatter (liquid) about in blobs; spatter. [2] to descend or cause to descend upon in blobs: *he splashed his jacket.* [3] to make (one's way) by or as if by splashing: *he splashed through the puddle.* [4] *(tr)* to print (a story or photograph) prominently in a newspaper. ◆ NOUN [5] an instance or sound of splashing. [6] an amount splashed. [7] a patch created by or as if by splashing: *a splash of colour.* [8] *Informal* an extravagant display, usually for effect (esp in the phrase **make a splash**). [9] a small amount of soda water, water, etc., added to an alcoholic drink.
▷HISTORY C18: alteration of PLASH[1]

splashback (ˈsplæʃˌbæk) NOUN a sheet of glass, plastic, etc., attached to a wall above a basin to protect the wall against splashing.

splashboard (ˈsplæʃˌbɔːd) NOUN [1] a guard on a vehicle to protect people from splashing water, mud, etc. [2] *Nautical* another word for **washboard** (sense 4b).

splashdown (ˈsplæʃˌdaʊn) NOUN [1] the controlled landing of a spacecraft on water at the end of a space flight. [2] the time scheduled for this event. ◆ VERB **splash down.** [3] *(intr, adverb)* (of a spacecraft) to make a splashdown.

splasher (ˈsplæʃə) NOUN anything used for protection against splashes.

splash out VERB *(adverb; often foll by on) Informal, chiefly Brit* to spend (money) freely or extravagantly (on something).

splashy (ˈsplæʃɪ) ADJECTIVE **splashier, splashiest.** [1] having irregular marks. [2] *Informal* done to attract attention or make a sensation; showy. [3] making a splash or splashes.
▸ˈ**splashily** ADVERB ▸ˈ**splashiness** NOUN

splat[1] (splæt) NOUN a wet slapping sound.
▷HISTORY C19: of imitative origin

splat[2] (splæt) NOUN a wide flat piece of wood, esp one that is the upright central part of a chair back.
▷HISTORY C19: perhaps related to Old English *splātan* to SPLIT

splatter (ˈsplætə) VERB [1] to splash with small blobs; spatter. ◆ NOUN [2] a splash of liquid, mud, etc.

splatter movie NOUN *Slang* a film in which the main feature is the graphic and gory murder of numerous victims.

splatterpunk (ˈsplætəˌpʌŋk) NOUN a literary genre characterized by graphically described scenes of an extremely gory nature.
▷HISTORY C20: from SPLATTER + PUNK[1]

splay (spleɪ) ADJECTIVE [1] spread out; broad and flat. [2] turned outwards in an awkward manner. ◆ VERB [3] to spread out; turn out or expand. [4] *(tr) Vet science* to dislocate (a joint). ◆ NOUN [5] a surface of a wall that forms an oblique angle to the main flat surfaces, esp at a doorway or window opening. [6] enlargement.
▷HISTORY C14: short for DISPLAY

Splayd (spleɪd) NOUN *Trademark, Austral* an implement combining the functions of knife, fork, and spoon.
▷HISTORY from SP(OON) + (BL)ADE

splayfoot (ˈspleɪˌfʊt) NOUN, *plural* **-feet.** [1] *Pathol* another word for **flatfoot** (sense 1). [2] a foot of which the toes are spread out, as in certain breeds of dog used in hunting waterfowl.
▸ˈ**splayˌfooted** ADJECTIVE ▸ˈ**splayˌfootedly** ADVERB

spleen (spliːn) NOUN [1] a spongy highly vascular organ situated near the stomach in man. It forms lymphocytes, produces antibodies, aids in destroying worn-out red blood cells, and filters bacteria and foreign particles from the blood. Related adjectives: **lienal, splenetic, splenic.** [2] the corresponding organ in other animals. [3] spitefulness or ill humour; peevishness: *to vent one's spleen.* [4] *Archaic* the organ in the human body considered to be the seat of the emotions. [5] *Archaic* another word for **melancholy.** [6] *Obsolete* whim; mood.
▷HISTORY C13: from Old French *esplen,* from Latin *splēn,* from Greek; related to Latin *lien* spleen
▸ˈ**spleenish** *or* ˈ**spleeny** ADJECTIVE

spleenful (ˈspliːnfʊl) ADJECTIVE affected by spleen; bad-tempered or irritable.
▸ˈ**spleenfully** ADVERB

spleenwort (ˈspliːnˌwɜːt) NOUN any of various ferns of the genus *Asplenium,* esp *A. trichomanes,* that often grows on walls, having linear or oblong sori on the undersurface of the fronds. See also **asplenium.**

splendent (ˈsplɛndənt) ADJECTIVE *Archaic* [1] shining brightly; lustrous: *a splendent sun.* [2] famous; illustrious.
▷HISTORY C15: from Latin *splendēns* brilliant, from *splendēre* to shine

splendid (ˈsplɛndɪd) ADJECTIVE [1] brilliant or fine, esp in appearance. [2] characterized by magnificence; imposing. [3] glorious or illustrious: *a splendid reputation.* [4] brightly gleaming; radiant: *her splendid face; splendid colours.* [5] very good or satisfactory: *a splendid time.*
▷HISTORY C17: from Latin *splendidus,* from *splendēre* to shine
▸ˈ**splendidly** ADVERB ▸ˈ**splendidness** NOUN

splendiferous (splɛnˈdɪfərəs) ADJECTIVE *Facetious* grand; splendid: *a really splendiferous meal.*
▷HISTORY C15: from Medieval Latin *splendiferus,* from Latin *splendor* radiance + *ferre* to bring
▸splenˈ**diferously** ADVERB ▸splenˈ**diferousness** NOUN

splendour *or US* **splendor** (ˈsplɛndə) NOUN [1] the state or quality of being splendid. [2] **sun in splendour.** *Heraldry* a representation of the sun with rays and a human face.
▸ˈ**splendorous** *or* **splendrous** (ˈsplɛndrəs) ADJECTIVE

splenectomy (splɪˈnɛktəmɪ) NOUN, *plural* **-mies.** surgical removal of the spleen.

splenetic (splɪˈnɛtɪk) ADJECTIVE [1] of or relating to the spleen. [2] spiteful or irritable; peevish. [3] *Obsolete* full of melancholy. ◆ NOUN [4] a spiteful or irritable person.
▷HISTORY C16: from Late Latin *splēnēticus,* from Latin *splēn* SPLEEN
▸spleˈ**netically** ADVERB

splenic (ˈsplɛnɪk, ˈspliː-) ADJECTIVE [1] of, relating to, or in the spleen. [2] having a disease or disorder of the spleen.

splenitis (splɪˈnaɪtɪs) NOUN inflammation of the spleen.

splenius (ˈspliːnɪəs) NOUN, *plural* **-nii** (-nɪˌaɪ). *Anatomy* either of two flat muscles situated at the back of the neck that rotate, flex, and extend the head and neck.
▷HISTORY C18: via New Latin from Greek *splēnion* a plaster
▸ˈ**splenial** ADJECTIVE

splenomegaly (ˌspliːnəʊˈmɛgəlɪ) NOUN *Pathol* abnormal enlargement of the spleen.
▷HISTORY C20: from Greek *splēno-,* from *splēn* SPLEEN + *megalo-,* from *megas* large + -Y[3]

splice (splaɪs) VERB *(tr)* [1] to join (two ropes) by intertwining the strands. [2] to join up the trimmed ends of (two pieces of wire, film, magnetic tape, etc.) with solder or an adhesive material. [3] to join (timbers) by overlapping and binding or bolting the ends together. [4] *(passive) Informal* to enter into marriage: *the couple got spliced last Saturday.* [5] **splice the mainbrace.** *Nautical history* to issue and partake of an extra allocation of alcoholic spirits. ◆ NOUN [6] a join made by splicing. [7] the place where such a join occurs. [8] the wedge-shaped end of a cricket-bat handle or similar instrument that fits into the blade.
▷HISTORY C16: probably from Middle Dutch *splissen;* related to German *spleissen,* Swedish *splitsa;* see SPLIT
▸ˈ**splicer** NOUN

spliff (splɪf) NOUN *Slang* [1] cannabis, used as a drug. [2] a cannabis cigarette.

spline (splaɪn) NOUN [1] any one of a series of narrow keys (**external splines**) formed longitudinally around the circumference of a shaft that fit into corresponding grooves (**internal splines**) in a mating part: used to prevent movement between two parts, esp in transmitting torque. [2] a long narrow strip of wood, metal, etc.; slat. [3] a thin narrow strip made of wood, metal, or plastic fitted into a groove in the edge of a board, tile, etc., to connect it to another. ◆ VERB [4] *(tr)* to provide (a shaft, part, etc.) with splines.
▷HISTORY C18: East Anglian dialect; perhaps related to Old English *splin* spindle; see SPLINT

splint (splɪnt) NOUN [1] a rigid support for restricting movement of an injured part, esp a broken bone. [2] a thin sliver of wood, esp one that is used to light cigars, a fire, etc. [3] a thin strip of wood woven with others to form a chair seat, basket, etc. [4] *Vet science* inflammation of the small metatarsal or metacarpal bones along the side of the cannon bone of a horse. [5] one of the overlapping metal plates used in armour after about 1330. [6] another word for **splinter.** ◆ VERB [7] to apply a splint to (a broken arm, etc.).
▷HISTORY C13: from Middle Low German *splinte;* related to Middle Dutch *splinte* splint, Old High German *spaltan* to split
▸ˈ**splintˌlike** ADJECTIVE

splint bone NOUN one of the rudimentary metacarpal or metatarsal bones in horses and similar animals, occurring on each side of the cannon bone.

splinter (ˈsplɪntə) NOUN [1] a very small sharp piece of wood, glass, metal, etc., characteristically long and thin, broken off from a whole. [2] a metal fragment, from the container of a shell, bomb, etc., thrown out during an explosion. ◆ VERB [3] to reduce or be reduced to sharp fragments; shatter. [4] to break or be broken off in small sharp fragments.
▷HISTORY C14: from Middle Dutch *splinter;* see SPLINT

splinter group NOUN a number of members of an organization, political party, etc., who split from the main body and form an independent association, usually as the result of dissension.

splintery (ˈsplɪntərɪ) ADJECTIVE liable to produce or break into splinters.

split (splɪt) VERB **splits, splitting, split.** [1] to break or cause to break, esp forcibly, by cleaving into separate pieces, often into two roughly equal pieces: *to split a brick.* [2] to separate or be separated from a whole: *he split a piece of wood from the block.* [3] to separate or be separated into factions, usually through discord. [4] *(often foll by up)* to separate or cause to separate through a disagreement. [5] *(when tr, often foll by up)* to divide or be divided among two or more persons: *split up the pie among the three of us.* [6] *Slang* to depart; leave: *let's split; we split the scene.* [7] *(tr)* to separate (something) into its components by interposing something else: *to split a word with hyphens.* [8] *(intr; usually foll by on) Slang* to betray the trust, plans, etc. (of); inform: *he split on me to the cops.* [9] *(tr) US politics* to mark (a ballot, etc.) so as to vote for the candidates of more than one party: *he split the ticket.* [10] *(tr)* to separate (an animal hide or skin) into layers. [11] **split hairs.** to make a fine but needless distinction. [12] **split one's sides.** to laugh very heartily. [13] **split the difference.** **a** to settle a dispute by effecting a compromise in which both sides give way to the same extent. **b** to divide a remainder equally. ◆ NOUN [14] the act or process of splitting. [15] a gap or rift caused or a piece removed by the process of splitting. [16] a breach or schism in a group or the faction resulting from such a breach. [17] a dessert of sliced fruit and ice cream, covered with whipped cream, nuts, etc.: *banana split.* [18] See **Devonshire split.** [19] **a** a separated

layer of an animal hide or skin other than the outer layer. **b** leather made from such a layer. 20 *Tenpin bowling* a formation of the pins after the first bowl in which there is a large gap between two pins or groups of pins. 21 *Informal* an arrangement or process of dividing up loot or money. ◆ ADJECTIVE 22 having been split; divided: *split logs.* 23 having a split or splits: *hair with split ends.* ◆ See also **splits, split up.**
▷HISTORY C16: from Middle Dutch *splitten* to cleave; related to Middle High German *splīzen;* see SPLICE
▸ **'splitter** NOUN

Split (*Serbo-Croat* split) NOUN a port and resort in W Croatia on the Adriatic: remains of the palace of Diocletian (295–305). Pop.: 173 692 (2001). Italian name: **Spalato.**

split brain NOUN a brain in which the tracts connecting the two halves of the cerebral cortex have been surgically split or are missing from birth.

split cane NOUN *Angling* bamboo split into strips of triangular section, tapered, and glued to form a stiff but flexible hexagonal rod: used, esp formerly, for making fishing rods.

split decision NOUN *Boxing* the award of a fight on a majority verdict of the judges as opposed to a unanimous decision.

split infinitive NOUN (in English grammar) an infinitive used with another word between *to* (the infinitive marker) and the verb itself, as in *I want to really finish it this time.*

> **Language note** The traditional rule against placing an adverb between *to* and its verb is gradually disappearing. Although it is true that a split infinitive may result in a clumsy sentence (*he decided to firmly and definitively deal with the problem*), this is not enough to justify the absolute condemnation that this practice has attracted. Indeed, very often the most natural position of the adverb is between *to* and the verb (*he decided to really try next time*) and to change it would result in an artificial and awkward construction (*he decided really to try next time*). The current view is therefore that the split infinitive is not a grammatical error. Nevertheless, many writers prefer to avoid splitting infinitives in formal written English, since readers with a more traditional point of view are likely to interpret this type of construction as incorrect.

split keyboarding NOUN *Computing* the act or practice of editing data from one terminal on another terminal.

split-level ADJECTIVE (of a house, room, etc.) having the floor level of one part about half a storey above or below the floor level of an adjoining part.

split-new ADJECTIVE *Scot* brand-new.

split pea NOUN a pea dried and split and used in soups, pease pudding, or as a vegetable.

split personality NOUN 1 the tendency to change rapidly in mood or temperament. 2 a nontechnical term for **multiple personality.**

split pin NOUN a metal pin made by bending double a wire, often of hemispherical section, so that it can be passed through a hole in a nut, shaft, etc., to secure another part by bending back the ends of the wire.

split ring NOUN a steel ring having two helical turns, often used as a key ring.

split run NOUN *Canadian* a divided print run of a periodical in which a number of copies contain advertisements not included in the rest, esp a Canadian edition of a US magazine which contains Canadian advertisements but no Canadian editorial content.

splits (splɪts) NOUN (*functioning as singular*) (in gymnastics, etc.) the act of sinking to the floor to achieve a sitting position in which both legs are straight, pointing in opposite directions, and at right angles to the body.

split-screen technique NOUN a cinematic device by which two or more complete images are projected simultaneously onto separate parts of the screen. Also called: **split screen.**

split second NOUN 1 an extremely small period of time; instant. ◆ ADJECTIVE **split-second.** (*prenominal*) 2 made or arrived at in an infinitely short time: *a split-second decision.* 3 depending upon minute precision: *split-second timing.*

split shift NOUN a work period divided into two parts that are separated by an interval longer than a normal rest period.

split ticket NOUN See **split** (sense 9). See also **straight ticket.**

split tin NOUN *Brit* a long loaf of bread split on top, giving a greater crust area.

splitting ('splɪtɪŋ) ADJECTIVE 1 (of a headache) intolerably painful; acute. 2 (of the head) assailed by an overpowering unbearable pain. ◆ NOUN 3 *Psychoanal* the Freudian defence mechanism in which an object or idea (or, alternatively, the ego) is separated into two or more parts in order to remove its threatening meaning.

split up VERB (*adverb*) 1 (*tr*) to separate out into parts; divide. 2 (*intr*) to become separated or parted through disagreement: *they split up after years of marriage.* 3 to break down or be capable of being broken down into constituent parts: *I have split up the question into three parts.* ◆ NOUN **split-up.** 4 the act or an instance of separating.

split wings PLURAL NOUN *Angling* **a** wings (of an artificial fly) that are dressed cocked up and separated into a V shape. **b** (*as modifier*): *a split-wing pattern.*

splodge (splɒdʒ) NOUN 1 a large irregular spot or blot. ◆ VERB 2 (*tr*) to mark (something) with such a blot or blots.
▷HISTORY C19: alteration of earlier SPLOTCH
▸ **'splodgy** ADJECTIVE

sploosh (spluːʃ) VERB 1 to splash or cause to splash about uncontrollably. ◆ NOUN 2 an instance or sound of splooshing.

splore (splɔːr) NOUN *Scot* a revel; binge; escapade.
▷HISTORY C18: of obscure origin

splosh (splɒʃ) VERB 1 to scatter (liquid) vigorously about in blobs: *visitors can splosh in the world's largest man-made waterfall.* ◆ NOUN 2 an instance or sound of sploshing.

splotch (splɒtʃ) NOUN, VERB the usual US word for **splodge.**
▷HISTORY C17: perhaps a blend of SPOT + BLOTCH
▸ **'splotchy** ADJECTIVE

splurge (splɜːdʒ) NOUN 1 an ostentatious display, esp of wealth. 2 a bout of unrestrained extravagance. ◆ VERB 3 (often foll by *on*) to spend (money) unrestrainedly or extravagantly.
▷HISTORY C19: of uncertain origin

splutter ('splʌtə) VERB 1 to spit out (saliva, food particles, etc.) from the mouth in an explosive manner, as through choking or laughing. 2 to utter (words) with spitting sounds, as through rage or choking. 3 to eject or be ejected in an explosive manner: *sparks spluttered from the fire.* 4 (*tr*) to bespatter (a person) with tiny particles explosively ejected: *he spluttered the boy next to him with ink.* ◆ NOUN 5 the process or noise of spluttering. 6 spluttering incoherent speech, esp in argument. 7 anything ejected through spluttering.
▷HISTORY C17: variant of SPUTTER, influenced by SPLASH
▸ **'splutterer** NOUN

spode (spəʊd) NOUN (*sometimes capital*) china or porcelain manufactured by Josiah Spode, English potter (1754–1827), or his company.

spodumene ('spɒdjʊˌmiːn) NOUN a greyish-white, green, or lilac pyroxene mineral consisting of lithium aluminium silicate in monoclinic crystalline form. It is an important ore of lithium and is used in the manufacture of glass and ceramics and as a gemstone. Formula: $LiAlSi_2O_6$.
▷HISTORY C19: from French *spodumène,* from German *Spodumen,* from Greek *spodoumenos,* from *spodousthai* to be burnt to ashes, from *spodos* wood ash

spoil (spɔɪl) VERB **spoils, spoiling, spoilt** *or* **spoiled.** 1 (*tr*) to cause damage to (something), in regard to its value, beauty, usefulness, etc. 2 (*tr*) to weaken the character of (a child) by complying unrestrainedly with its desires. 3 (*intr*) (of perishable substances) to become unfit for consumption or use: *the fruit must be eaten before it spoils.* 4 (*intr*) *Sport* to disrupt the play or style of an opponent, as to prevent him from settling into a rhythm. 5 *Archaic* to strip (a person or place) of (property or goods) by force or violence. 6 **be spoiling for.** to have an aggressive desire for (a fight, etc). ◆ NOUN 7 waste material thrown up by an excavation. 8 any treasure accumulated by a person: *this gold ring was part of the spoil.* 9 *Obsolete* **a** the act of plundering. **b** a strategically placed building, city, etc., captured as plunder. ◆ See also **spoils.**
▷HISTORY C13: from Old French *espoillier,* from Latin *spoliāre* to strip, from *spolium* booty

spoilage ('spɔɪlɪdʒ) NOUN 1 the act or an instance of spoiling or the state or condition of being spoilt. 2 an amount of material that has been wasted by being spoilt: *the spoilage of corn was considerable.*

spoiled priest NOUN *Irish* a person who was a student for the priesthood but who has withdrawn or been dismissed.

spoiler ('spɔɪlə) NOUN 1 plunderer or robber. 2 a person or thing that causes spoilage or corruption. 3 a device fitted to an aircraft wing to increase drag and reduce lift. It is usually extended into the airflow to assist descent and banking. Compare **air brake** (sense 2). 4 a similar device fitted to a car. 5 *Sport* a competitor who adopts spoiling tactics, as in boxing. 6 a magazine, newspaper, etc. produced specifically to coincide with the production of a rival magazine, newspaper, etc. in order to divert public interest and reduce its sales.

spoilfive ('spɔɪlˌfaɪv) NOUN a card game for two or more players with five cards each.

spoils (spɔɪlz) PLURAL NOUN 1 (*sometimes singular*) valuables seized by violence, esp in war. 2 *Chiefly US* the rewards and benefits of public office regarded as plunder for the winning party or candidate. See also **spoils system.**

spoilsman ('spɔɪlzmən) NOUN, *plural* **-men.** *US politics* a person who shares in the spoils of office or advocates the spoils system.

spoilsport ('spɔɪlˌspɔːt) NOUN *Informal* a person who spoils the pleasure of other people by his actions or attitudes.

spoils system NOUN *Chiefly US* the practice of filling appointive public offices with friends and supporters of the ruling political party. Compare **merit system.**

spoilt (spɔɪlt) VERB a past tense and past participle of **spoil.**

Spokane (spəʊ'kæn) NOUN a city in E Washington: commercial centre of an agricultural region. Pop.: 195 629 (2000).

spoke[1] (spəʊk) VERB 1 the past tense of **speak.** 2 *Archaic or dialect* a past participle of **speak.**

spoke[2] (spəʊk) NOUN 1 a radial member of a wheel, joining the hub to the rim. 2 a radial projection from the rim of a wheel, as in a ship's wheel. 3 a rung of a ladder. 4 **put a spoke in someone's wheel.** *Brit* to thwart someone's plans. ◆ VERB 5 (*tr*) to equip with or as if with spokes.
▷HISTORY Old English *spāca*

spoken ('spəʊkən) VERB 1 the past participle of **speak.** ◆ ADJECTIVE 2 uttered through the medium of speech. Compare **written.** 3 (*in combination*) having speech as specified: *soft-spoken.* 4 **spoken for.** engaged, reserved, or allocated.

spokeshave ('spəʊkˌʃeɪv) NOUN a small plane with two handles, one on each side of its blade, used for shaping or smoothing cylindrical wooden surfaces, such as spokes.

spokesman ('spəʊksmən), **spokesperson** ('spəʊksˌpɜːsᵊn), *or feminine* **spokeswoman** ('spəʊksˌwʊmən) NOUN, *plural* **-men, -persons** *or* **-people,** *or* **-women.** a person authorized to speak on behalf of another person, group of people, or organization.

spoliate ('spəʊlɪˌeɪt) VERB a less common word for **despoil.**

spoliation (ˌspəʊlɪ'eɪʃən) NOUN 1 the act or an instance of despoiling or plundering. 2 the authorized seizure or plundering of neutral vessels on the seas by a belligerent state in time of war. 3 *Law* the material alteration of a document so as to render it invalid. 4 *English ecclesiastical law* the taking of the fruits of a benefice by a person not entitled to them.

▷HISTORY C14: from Latin *spoliātiō*, from *spoliāre* to SPOIL
▸'**spoliatory** ADJECTIVE

spondaic (spɒn'deɪɪk) ADJECTIVE *Prosody* of, relating to, or consisting of spondees.

spondee ('spɒndiː) NOUN *Prosody* a metrical foot consisting of two long syllables (– –).
▷HISTORY C14: from Old French *spondée*, from Latin *spondēus*, from Greek *spondeios*, from *spondē* a ritual libation; from the use of spondee in the music that characteristically accompanied such ceremonies

spondulix *or* **spondulicks** (spɒn'djuːlɪks) NOUN *Slang* money.
▷HISTORY C19: of obscure origin

spondylitis (ˌspɒndɪ'laɪtɪs) NOUN inflammation of the vertebrae.
▷HISTORY C19: from New Latin, from Greek *spondulos* vertebra; see -ITIS

sponge (spʌndʒ) NOUN [1] any multicellular typically marine animal of the phylum *Porifera*, usually occurring in complex sessile colonies in which the porous body is supported by a fibrous, calcareous, or siliceous skeletal framework. [2] a piece of the light porous highly absorbent elastic skeleton of certain sponges, used in bathing, cleaning, etc. See also **spongin**. [3] any of a number of light porous elastic materials resembling a sponge. [4] another word for **sponger** (sense 1). [5] *Informal* a person who indulges in heavy drinking. [6] leavened dough, esp before kneading. [7] See **sponge cake**. [8] Also called: **sponge pudding**. *Brit* a light steamed or baked pudding, spongy in texture, made with various flavourings or fruit. [9] porous metal produced by electrolysis or by reducing a metal compound without fusion or sintering and capable of absorbing large quantities of gas: *platinum sponge*. [10] a rub with a sponge. [11] **throw in the sponge**. See **throw in** (sense 4). ◆ VERB [12] (*tr*; often foll by *off* or *down*) to clean (something) by wiping or rubbing with a damp or wet sponge. [13] (*tr*; usually foll by *off*, *away*, *out*, etc.) to remove (marks, etc.) by rubbing with a damp or wet sponge or cloth. [14] (when *tr*, often foll by *up*) to absorb (liquids, esp when spilt) in the manner of a sponge. [15] (*tr*; often foll by *off*) to get (something) from (someone) by presuming on his generosity: *to sponge a meal off someone*. [16] (*intr*; often foll by *off* or *on*) to obtain one's subsistence, welfare, etc., unjustifiably (from): *he sponges off his friends*. [17] (*intr*) to go collecting sponges. ◆ See also **sponge down**.
▷HISTORY Old English, from Latin *spongia*, from Greek
▸'**sponge,like** ADJECTIVE

sponge bag NOUN a small bag made of plastic, etc., that holds toilet articles, used esp when travelling.

sponge bath NOUN a washing of the body with a wet sponge or cloth, but without immersion in water.

sponge cake NOUN a light porous cake, made of eggs, sugar, flour, and flavourings traditionally without any fat.

sponge cloth NOUN any of various porous fabrics, usually made in a loose honeycomb weave.

sponge down VERB (*tr, adverb*) [1] to wipe clean with a damp sponge or cloth. ◆ NOUN **sponge-down**. [2] the act or instance of sponging down.

sponger ('spʌndʒə) NOUN [1] *Informal* a person who lives off other people by continually taking advantage of their generosity; parasite or scrounger. [2] a person or ship employed in collecting sponges.

spongiform ('spʌndʒɪˌfɔːm) ADJECTIVE [1] resembling a sponge in appearance, esp in having many holes. [2] denoting diseases characterized by this appearance of affected tissues.

spongin ('spʌndʒɪn) NOUN a fibrous horny protein that forms the skeletal framework of the bath sponge and related sponges.
▷HISTORY C19: from German, from Latin *spongia* SPONGE + -IN

spongioblast ('spʌndʒɪəʊˌblɑːst) NOUN any of numerous columnar epithelial cells in the brain and spinal cord that develop into neuroglia.
▷HISTORY C20: from Greek *spongia* SPONGE + -BLAST
▸**spongioblastic** (ˌspʌndʒɪəʊ'blæstɪk) ADJECTIVE

spongy ('spʌndʒɪ) ADJECTIVE **-gier, -giest**. [1] of or resembling a sponge, esp in texture, porosity, elasticity, or compressibility: *spongy bread; spongy bone*. [2] of or like a sponge in respect of its capacity to absorb fluid and yield it when compressed.
▸'**spongily** ADVERB ▸'**sponginess** NOUN

sponsion ('spɒnʃən) NOUN [1] the act or process of becoming surety; sponsorship. [2] (*often plural*) *International law* an unauthorized agreement made by a public officer, esp an admiral or general in time of war, requiring ratification by the government of the state concerned. [3] any act or promise, esp one made on behalf of someone else.
▷HISTORY C17: from Latin *sponsiō*, from *spondēre* to pledge

sponson ('spɒnsən) NOUN [1] *Naval* an outboard support for a gun enabling it to fire fore and aft. [2] a semicircular gun turret on the side of a tank. [3] a float or flotation chamber along the gunwale of a boat or ship. [4] a structural projection from the side of a paddle steamer for supporting a paddle wheel. [5] a structural unit attached to a helicopter fuselage by fixed struts, housing the main landing gear and inflatable flotation bags.
▷HISTORY C19: perhaps from EXPANSION

sponsor ('spɒnsə) NOUN [1] a person or group that provides funds for an activity, esp **a** a commercial organization that pays all or part of the cost of putting on a concert, sporting event, etc. **b** a person who donates money to a charity when the person requesting the donation has performed a specified activity as part of an organized fund-raising effort. [2] *Chiefly US and Canadian* a person or business firm that pays the costs of a radio or television programme in return for advertising time. [3] a legislator who presents and supports a bill, motion, etc. [4] Also called: **godparent**. **a** an authorized witness who makes the required promises on behalf of a person to be baptized and thereafter assumes responsibility for his Christian upbringing. **b** a person who presents a candidate for confirmation. [5] *Chiefly US* a person who undertakes responsibility for the actions, statements, obligations, etc., of another, as during a period of apprenticeship; guarantor. ◆ VERB [6] (*tr*) to act as a sponsor for.
▷HISTORY C17: from Latin, from *spondēre* to promise solemnly
▸**sponsorial** (spɒn'sɔːrɪəl) ADJECTIVE ▸'**sponsor,ship** NOUN

sponsored ('spɒnsəd) ADJECTIVE denoting an activity organized to raise money for a charity in which sponsors agree to donate money on completion of the activity, or a specified period or amount of it, by participants: *a sponsored walk*.

spontaneity (ˌspɒntə'niːɪtɪ, -'neɪ-) NOUN, PLURAL **-ties**. [1] the state or quality of being spontaneous. [2] (*often plural*) the exhibiting of actions, impulses, or behaviour that are stimulated by internal processes.

spontaneous (spɒn'teɪnɪəs) ADJECTIVE [1] occurring, produced, or performed through natural processes without external influence: *spontaneous movement*. [2] arising from an unforced personal impulse; voluntary; unpremeditated: *a spontaneous comment*. [3] (of plants) growing naturally; indigenous.
▷HISTORY C17: from Late Latin *spontāneus*, from Latin *sponte* voluntarily
▸**spon'taneously** ADVERB ▸**spon'taneousness** NOUN

spontaneous combustion NOUN the ignition of a substance or body as a result of internal oxidation processes, without the application of an external source of heat, occurring in finely powdered ores, coal, straw, etc.

spontaneous generation NOUN a theory, widely held in the 19th century and earlier but now discredited, stating that living organisms could arise directly and rapidly from nonliving material. Also called: **abiogenesis**.

spontaneous recovery NOUN *Psychol* the reappearance of a response after its extinction has been followed by a period of rest.

spontoon (spɒn'tuːn) NOUN a form of halberd carried by some junior infantry officers in the 18th and 19th centuries.
▷HISTORY C18: from French *esponton*, from Italian *spuntone*, from *punto* POINT

spoof (spuːf) *Informal* ◆ NOUN [1] a mildly satirical mockery or parody; lampoon: *a spoof on party politics*. [2] a good-humoured deception or trick; prank. ◆ VERB [3] to indulge in a spoof of (a person or thing). [4] to communicate electronically under a false identity.
▷HISTORY C19: coined by A. Roberts (1852–1933), English comedian, to designate a game of his own invention
▸'**spoofer** NOUN

spoofing NOUN the act or an instance of impersonating another person on the Internet or via email.

spook (spuːk) *Informal* ◆ NOUN [1] a ghost or a person suggestive of this. [2] *US and Canadian* a spy. ◆ VERB (*tr*) *US and Canadian* [3] to frighten: *to spook horses; to spook a person*. [4] (of a ghost) to haunt.
▷HISTORY C19: Dutch *spook*, from Middle Low German *spōk* ghost
▸'**spookish** ADJECTIVE

spooky ('spuːkɪ) ADJECTIVE **spookier, spookiest**. *Informal* [1] ghostly or eerie: *a spooky house*. [2] resembling or appropriate to a ghost. [3] *US* easily frightened; highly strung.
▸'**spookily** ADVERB ▸'**spookiness** NOUN

spool (spuːl) NOUN [1] a device around which magnetic tape, film, cotton, etc., can be automatically wound, with plates at top and bottom to prevent it from slipping off. [2] anything round which other materials, esp thread, are wound. ◆ VERB [3] (sometimes foll by *up*) to wind or be wound onto a spool or reel.
▷HISTORY C14: of Germanic origin; compare Old High German *spuolo*, Middle Dutch *spoele*

spoon (spuːn) NOUN [1] a metal, wooden, or plastic utensil having a shallow concave part, usually elliptical in shape, attached to a handle, used in eating or serving food, stirring, etc. [2] Also called: **spoonbait**. an angling lure for spinning or trolling, consisting of a bright piece of metal which swivels on a trace to which are attached a hook or hooks. [3] *Golf* a former name for a No. 3 wood. [4] *Informal* a foolish or useless person. [5] **be born with a silver spoon in one's mouth**. to inherit wealth or social standing. [6] **wooden spoon**. *Brit* another name for **booby prize**. [7] *Rowing* a type of oar blade that is curved at the edges and tip to gain a firm grip on the water. Compare **spade**[1] (sense 4). ◆ VERB [8] (*tr*) to scoop up or transfer (food, liquid, etc.) from one container to another with or as if with a spoon. [9] (*intr*) *Slang, old-fashioned* to kiss and cuddle. [10] to hollow out (a cavity or spoon-shaped bowl) (in something). [11] *Sport* to hit (a ball) with a weak lifting motion, as in golf, cricket, etc.
▷HISTORY Old English *spōn* splinter; related to Old Norse *spōnn* spoon, chip, Old High German *spān*

spoonbill ('spuːnˌbɪl) NOUN any of several wading birds of warm regions, such as *Platalea leucorodia* (**common spoonbill**) and *Ajaia ajaja* (**roseate spoonbill**), having a long horizontally flattened bill: family *Threskiornithidae*, order *Ciconiiformes*.

spoondrift ('spuːnˌdrɪft) NOUN a less common spelling of **spindrift**.

spoonerism ('spuːnəˌrɪzəm) NOUN the transposition of the initial consonants or consonant clusters of a pair of words, often resulting in an amusing ambiguity of meaning, such as *hush my brat* for *brush my hat*.
▷HISTORY C20: named after W. A. Spooner (1844–1930), English clergyman renowned for slips of this kind

spoon-feed VERB **-feeds, -feeding, -fed**. (*tr*) [1] to feed with a spoon. [2] to overindulge or spoil. [3] to provide (a person) with ready-made opinions, judgments, etc., depriving him of original thought or action.

spoonful ('spuːnˌfʊl) NOUN, *plural* **-fuls**. [1] the amount that a spoon is able to hold. [2] a small quantity.

spoony *or* **spooney** ('spuːnɪ) *Slang, rare, old-fashioned* ◆ ADJECTIVE **spoonier, spooniest**. [1] foolishly or stupidly amorous. ◆ NOUN, *plural* **spoonies**. [2] a fool or silly person, esp one in love.

spoor (spʊə, spɔː) NOUN [1] the trail of an animal or person, esp as discernible to the human eye. ◆ VERB [2] to track (an animal) by following its trail.
▷HISTORY C19: from Afrikaans, from Middle Dutch *spor*; related to Old English *spor* track, Old High German *spor*; see SPUR
▸'**spoorer** NOUN

Sporades ('spɒrəˌdiːz) PLURAL NOUN two groups of Greek islands in the Aegean: the **Northern Sporades**, lying northeast of Euboea, and the **Southern Sporades**, which include the Dodecanese and lie off the SW coast of Turkey.

sporadic (spəˈrædɪk) ADJECTIVE [1] occurring at irregular points in time; intermittent: *sporadic firing.* [2] scattered; isolated: *a sporadic disease.*
▷HISTORY C17: from Medieval Latin *sporadicus,* from Greek *sporadikos,* from *sporas* scattered; related to Greek *speirein* to sow; see SPORE
▸**spoˈradically** ADVERB ▸**spoˈradicalness** NOUN

sporangium (spəˈrændʒɪəm) NOUN, *plural* **-gia** (-dʒɪə). any organ, esp in fungi, in which asexual spores are produced.
▷HISTORY C19: from New Latin, from SPORO- + Greek *angeion* receptacle
▸**spoˈrangial** ADJECTIVE

spore (spɔː) NOUN [1] a reproductive body, produced by bacteria, fungi, various plants and some protozoans, that develops into a new individual. A **sexual spore** is formed after the fusion of gametes and an **asexual spore** is the result of asexual reproduction. [2] a germ cell, seed, dormant bacterium, or similar body. ◆ VERB [3] (*intr*) to produce, carry, or release spores.
▷HISTORY C19: from New Latin *spora,* from Greek: a sowing; related to Greek *speirein* to sow

spore case NOUN the nontechnical name for **sporangium.**

spore print NOUN *Botany* the pattern produced by placing the cap of a mushroom on a piece of paper and allowing the spores to fall.

sporo- *or before a vowel* **spor-** COMBINING FORM (in botany) spore: *sporophyte.*
▷HISTORY from New Latin *spora*

sporocarp (ˈspɔːrəʊˌkɑːp, ˈspɒ-) NOUN [1] a specialized leaf branch in certain aquatic ferns that encloses the sori. [2] the spore-producing structure in certain algae, lichens, and fungi.

sporocyst (ˈspɔːrəʊˌsɪst, ˈspɒ-) NOUN [1] a thick-walled rounded structure produced by sporozoan protozoans, in which sporozoites are formed. [2] the saclike larva of a trematode worm that produces redia larvae by asexual reproduction. [3] any similar structure containing spores.

sporocyte (ˈspɔːrəʊˌsaɪt, ˈspɒ-) NOUN a diploid cell that divides by meiosis to produce four haploid spores.

sporogenesis (ˌspɔːrəʊˈdʒɛnɪsɪs, ˌspɒ-) NOUN the process of spore formation in plants and animals.
▸**sporogenous** (spɔːˈrɒdʒɪnəs, spɒ-) ADJECTIVE

sporogonium (ˌspɔːrəʊˈɡəʊnɪəm, ˌspɒ-) NOUN, *plural* **-nia** (-nɪə). the sporophyte of mosses and liverworts, consisting of a spore-bearing capsule on a short stalk that arises from the parent plant (the gametophyte).
▸**ˌsporoˈgonial** ADJECTIVE

sporogony (spɔːˈrɒɡənɪ, -ˈrɒdʒ-, spɒ-) NOUN the process in sporozoans by which sporozoites are formed from an encysted zygote by multiple fission.

sporophore (ˈspɔːrəʊˌfɔː, ˈspɒ-) NOUN an organ in fungi that produces or carries spores, esp the massive spore-bearing body of mushrooms, etc.

sporophyll *or* **sporophyl** (ˈspɔːrəʊfɪl, ˈspɒ-) NOUN a leaf in ferns and other spore-bearing plants that bears the sporangia. See also **megasporophyll, microsporophyll.**

sporophyte (ˈspɔːrəʊˌfaɪt, ˈspɒ-) NOUN the diploid form of plants that have alternation of generations. It develops from a zygote and produces asexual spores. Compare **gametophyte.**
▸**sporophytic** (ˌspɔːrəˈfɪtɪk, ˌspɒ-) ADJECTIVE

-sporous ADJECTIVE COMBINING FORM (in botany) having a specified type or number of spores: *homosporous.*

sporozoan (ˌspɔːrəˈzəʊən, ˌspɒ-) NOUN [1] any parasitic protozoan of the phylum *Apicomplexa* (or *Sporozoa*), characterized by a complex life cycle, part of which is passed in the cells of the host, and the production of asexual spores: includes the malaria parasite. See **plasmodium** (sense 2). ◆ ADJECTIVE [2] of or relating to sporozoans.

sporozoite (ˌspɔːrəˈzəʊaɪt, ˌspɒ-) NOUN any of numerous small mobile usually infective individuals produced in sporozoans by sporogony.

sporran (ˈspɒrən) NOUN a large pouch, usually of fur, worn hanging from a belt in front of the kilt in men's Scottish Highland dress.
▷HISTORY C19: from Scottish Gaelic *sporan* purse; compare Irish Gaelic *sparán* purse, Late Latin *bursa* bag

sport (spɔːt) NOUN [1] an individual or group activity pursued for exercise or pleasure, often involving the testing of physical capabilities and taking the form of a competitive game such as football, tennis, etc. [2] such activities considered collectively. [3] any particular pastime indulged in for pleasure. [4] the pleasure derived from a pastime, esp hunting, shooting, or fishing: *we had good sport today.* [5] playful or good-humoured joking: *to say a thing in sport.* [6] derisive mockery or the object of such mockery: *to make sport of someone.* [7] someone or something that is controlled by external influences: *the sport of fate.* [8] *Informal* (sometimes qualified by *good, bad,* etc.) a person who reacts cheerfully in the face of adversity, esp a good loser. [9] *Informal* a person noted for being scrupulously fair and abiding by the rules of a game. [10] *Informal* a person who leads a merry existence, esp a gambler: *he's a bit of a sport.* [11] *Austral and NZ informal* a form of address used esp between males. [12] *Biology* **a** an animal or plant that differs conspicuously in one or more aspects from other organisms of the same species, usually because of a mutation. **b** an anomalous characteristic of such an organism. ◆ VERB [13] (*tr*) *Informal* to wear or display in an ostentatious or proud manner: *she was sporting a new hat.* [14] (*intr*) to skip about or frolic happily. [15] to amuse (oneself), esp in outdoor physical recreation. [16] (*intr; often foll by with*) to dally or trifle (with). [17] (*tr; often foll by away*) *Rare* to squander (time or money): *sporting one's life away.* [18] (*intr; often foll by with*) *Archaic* to make fun (of). [19] (*intr*) *Biology* to produce or undergo a mutation. ◆ See also **sports.**
▷HISTORY C15 *sporten,* variant of *disporten* to DISPORT
▸**ˈsporter** NOUN ▸**ˈsportful** ADJECTIVE ▸**ˈsportfully** ADVERB
▸**ˈsportfulness** NOUN

sporting (ˈspɔːtɪŋ) ADJECTIVE [1] (*prenominal*) of, relating to, or used or engaged in a sport or sports: *several sporting interests.* [2] relating or conforming to sportsmanship; fair. [3] of, relating to, or characterized by an interest in gambling. [4] willing to take a risk.
▸**ˈsportingly** ADVERB

sporting house NOUN [1] *US rare* a euphemistic word for **brothel.** [2] *Archaic* a tavern or inn frequented by gamblers or other sportsmen.

sportive (ˈspɔːtɪv) ADJECTIVE [1] playful or joyous. [2] done in jest rather than seriously. [3] of, relating to, or interested in sports. [4] *Obsolete* wanton or amorous: *a sportive wench.*
▸**ˈsportively** ADVERB ▸**ˈsportiveness** NOUN

sports (spɔːts) NOUN [1] (*modifier*) relating to, concerned with, or used in sports: *sports equipment.* [2] (*modifier*) relating to or similar to a sports car: *sports seats.* [3] Also called: **sports day.** *Brit* a meeting held at a school or college for competitions in various athletic events.

sports car NOUN a production car designed for speed, high acceleration, and manoeuvrability, having a low body and usually adequate seating for only two persons.

sportscast (ˈspɔːtsˌkɑːst) NOUN a radio or television broadcast consisting of sports news.
▸**ˈsportsˌcaster** NOUN

sports coat NOUN *US, Austral, and NZ* another name for **sports jacket.**

sports jacket NOUN a man's informal jacket, made esp of tweed: worn with trousers of different material. Also called (US, Austral, and NZ): **sports coat.**

sportsman (ˈspɔːtsmən) NOUN, *plural* **-men.** [1] a man who takes part in sports, esp of the outdoor type. [2] a person who exhibits qualities highly regarded in sport, such as fairness, generosity, observance of the rules, and good humour when losing.
▸**ˈsportsman-ˌlike** *or* **ˈsportsmanly** ADJECTIVE
▸**ˈsportsmanˌship** NOUN

sports medicine NOUN the branch of medicine concerned with injuries sustained through sport.

sportsperson (ˈspɔːtsˌpɜːsən) NOUN a person who takes part in sports, esp of the outdoor type.

sports shirt NOUN a man's informal shirt, sometimes of knitted wool or cotton, which may be worn outside the trousers.

sportswear (ˈspɔːtsˌwɛə) NOUN clothes worn for sport or outdoor leisure wear.

sportswoman (ˈspɔːtsˌwʊmən) NOUN, *plural* **-women.** a woman who takes part in sports, esp of the outdoor type.

sport utility vehicle *or* **sports utility vehicle** NOUN *Chiefly US* a high-powered car with four-wheel drive, originally designed for off-road use. Sometimes shortened to: **sport utility, sports utility.** Abbreviation: **SUV.**

sporty (ˈspɔːtɪ) ADJECTIVE **sportier, sportiest.** [1] (of a person) fond of sport or outdoor activities. [2] (of clothes) having the appearance of sportswear. [3] (of a car) having the performance or appearance of a sports car.
▸**ˈsportily** ADVERB ▸**ˈsportiness** NOUN

sporulate (ˈspɒrjʊˌleɪt) VERB (*intr*) to produce spores, esp by multiple fission.
▸**ˌsporuˈlation** NOUN

sporule (ˈspɒruːl) NOUN a spore, esp a very small spore.
▷HISTORY C19: from New Latin *sporula* a little SPORE

spot (spɒt) NOUN [1] a small mark on a surface, such as a circular patch or stain, differing in colour or texture from its surroundings. [2] a geographical area that is restricted in extent: *a beauty spot.* [3] a location: *this is the exact spot on which he died.* [4] a blemish of the skin, esp a pimple or one occurring through some disease. [5] a blemish on the character of a person; moral flaw. [6] *Informal* a place of entertainment: *we hit all the night spots.* [7] *Informal, chiefly Brit* a small quantity or amount: *a spot of lunch.* [8] *Informal* an awkward situation: *that puts me in a bit of a spot.* [9] a short period between regular television or radio programmes that is used for advertising. [10] a position or length of time in a show assigned to a specific performer. [11] short for **spotlight.** [12] (in billiards) **a** Also called: **spot ball.** the white ball that is distinguished from the plain by a mark or spot. **b** the player using this ball. [13] *Billiards, snooker* one of several small black dots on a table that mark where a ball is to be placed. [14] (*modifier*) **a** denoting or relating to goods, currencies, or securities available for immediate delivery and payment: *spot goods.* See also **spot market, spot price. b** involving immediate cash payment: *spot sales.* [15] **change one's spots.** (*used mainly in negative constructions*) to reform one's character. [16] **high spot.** an outstanding event: *the high spot of the holiday was the visit to the winery.* [17] **knock spots off.** to outstrip or outdo with ease. [18] **on the spot. a** immediately. **b** at the place in question. **c** in the best possible position to deal with a situation. **d** in an awkward predicament. **e** without moving from the place of one's location, etc. **f** (*as modifier*): *our on-the-spot reporter.* [19] **soft spot.** a special sympathetic affection or weakness for a person or thing. [20] **tight spot.** a serious, difficult, or dangerous situation. [21] **weak spot. a** some aspect of a character or situation that is susceptible to criticism. **b** a flaw in a person's knowledge: *classics is my weak spot.* ◆ VERB **spots, spotting, spotted.** [22] (*tr*) to observe or perceive suddenly, esp under difficult circumstances; discern. [23] to put stains or spots upon (something). [24] (*intr*) (of some fabrics) to be susceptible to spotting by or as if by water: *silk spots easily.* [25] (*tr*) to place here and there: *they spotted observers along the border.* [26] to look out for and note (trains, talent, etc.). [27] (*intr*) to rain slightly; spit. [28] (*tr*) *Billiards* to place (a ball) on one of the spots. [29] *Military* to adjust fire in order to correct deviations from (the target) by observation. [30] (*tr*) *US informal* to yield (an advantage or concession) to (one's opponent): *to spot someone a piece in chess.*
▷HISTORY C12 (in the sense: moral blemish): of German origin; compare Middle Dutch *spotte,* Old Norse *spotti*
▸**ˈspottable** ADJECTIVE

spot check NOUN [1] a quick random examination. [2] a check made without prior warning. ◆ VERB **spot-check.** [3] (*tr*) to perform a spot check on.

spot height NOUN a mark on a map indicating the height of a hill, mountain, etc.

spotless ('spɒtlɪs) ADJECTIVE [1] free from stains; immaculate. [2] free from moral impurity; unsullied: *a spotless character.*
▸ **'spotlessly** ADVERB ▸ **'spotlessness** NOUN

spotlight ('spɒt,laɪt) NOUN [1] a powerful light focused so as to illuminate a small area, usually mounted so that it can be directed at will. [2] **the.** the focus of attention. ◆ VERB **-lights, -lighting, -lit** *or* **-lighted.** (*tr*) [3] to direct a spotlight on. [4] to focus attention on.

spot market NOUN *Commerce* a market in which commodities, currencies, or securities are traded for immediate delivery. Compare **forward market.**

spot-on ADJECTIVE *Informal* absolutely correct; very accurate.

spot price NOUN the price of goods, currencies, or securities that are offered for immediate delivery and payment.

spotted ('spɒtɪd) ADJECTIVE [1] characterized by spots or marks, esp in having a pattern of spots. [2] stained or blemished; soiled or bespattered.

spotted crake NOUN a Eurasian rail, *Porzana porzana,* of swamps and marshes, having a buff speckled plumage and dark brown wings.

spotted dick NOUN *Brit* a steamed or boiled suet pudding containing dried fruit.
▷HISTORY C19: perhaps from the man's name *Dick* (short for *Richard*), or from dialect *dick* pudding. The dried fruit gives it a speckled appearance

spotted dog NOUN [1] an informal name for a **Dalmatian.** [2] another name for **spotted dick.**

spotted fever NOUN any of various severe febrile diseases characterized by small irregular spots on the skin, as in Rocky Mountain spotted fever or tick fever.

spotted flycatcher NOUN a European woodland songbird, *Muscicapa striata,* with a greyish-brown streaked plumage: family *Muscicapidae* (Old World flycatchers).

spotted gum NOUN [1] an Australian eucalyptus tree, *Eucalyptus maculata.* [2] the wood of this tree, used for shipbuilding, sleepers, etc.

spotted mackerel NOUN a small mackerel, *Scomberomorus queenslandicus,* of northern Australian waters.

Spotted Mist NOUN the former name for **Australian Mist.**

spotted orchid NOUN [1] any of various common Eurasian orchids, esp the **heath** and **common spotted orchids** (*Dactylorhiza maculata* and *D. fuchsii*). The flowers are variable but usually have dark blotches. [2] a tall orchid, *Dipodium punctatum,* with white pink-spotted flowers, found in Australia.

spotted sandpiper NOUN a North American sandpiper, *Actitis macularia,* having a spotted breast in its breeding plumage. Also called (US): **peetweet.**

spotter ('spɒtə) NOUN [1] **a** a person or thing that watches or observes. **b** (*as modifier*): *a spotter plane.* [2] a person who makes a hobby of watching for and noting numbers or types of trains, buses, etc.: *a train spotter.* [3] *Military* a person who orders or advises adjustment of fire on a target by observations. [4] a person, esp one engaged in civil defence, who watches for enemy aircraft. [5] *US informal* an employee assigned to spy on his colleagues in order to check on their honesty. [6] *Films* **a** a person who checks against irregularities and inconsistencies. **b** a person who searches for new material, performers, etc.

spottie ('spɒtɪ) NOUN *NZ* a young deer of up to three months of age.

spotty ('spɒtɪ) ADJECTIVE **-tier, -tiest.** [1] abounding in or characterized by spots or marks, esp on the skin: *a spotty face.* [2] not consistent or uniform; irregular or uneven, often in quality.
▸ **'spottily** ADVERB ▸ **'spottiness** NOUN

spot-weld VERB [1] (*tr*) to join (two pieces of metal, esp in the form of wire or sheet) by one or more small circular welds by means of heat, usually electrically generated, and pressure. ◆ NOUN [2] a weld so formed.
▸ **'spot-,welder** NOUN

spousal ('spaʊzᵊl) NOUN [1] (*often plural*) **a** the marriage ceremony. **b** a wedding. ◆ ADJECTIVE [2] of or relating to marriage.
▸ **'spousally** ADVERB

spouse NOUN (spaʊs, spaʊz) [1] a person's partner in marriage. Related adjective: **spousal.** ◆ VERB (spaʊz, spaʊs) [2] (*tr*) *Obsolete* to marry.
▷HISTORY C12: from Old French *spus* (masculine), *spuse* (feminine), from Latin *sponsus, sponsa* betrothed man or woman, from *spondēre* to promise solemnly

spout (spaʊt) VERB [1] to discharge (a liquid) in a continuous jet or in spurts, esp through a narrow gap or under pressure, or (of a liquid) to gush thus. [2] (of a whale, etc.) to discharge air through the blowhole, so that it forms a spray at the surface of the water. [3] *Informal* to utter (a stream of words) on a subject, often at length. ◆ NOUN [4] a tube, pipe, chute, etc., allowing the passage or pouring of liquids, grain, etc. [5] a continuous stream or jet of liquid. [6] short for **waterspout.** [7] **up the spout.** *Slang* **a** ruined or lost: *any hope of rescue is right up the spout.* **b** pregnant.
▷HISTORY C14: perhaps from Middle Dutch *spouten,* from Old Norse *spyta* to spit
▸ **'spouter** NOUN

spouting ('spaʊtɪŋ) NOUN *NZ* **a** a rainwater downpipe on the exterior of a building. **b** such pipes collectively.

spp. ABBREVIATION FOR species (plural).

SPQR ABBREVIATION FOR Senatus Populusque Romanus.
▷HISTORY Latin: the Senate and People of Rome.

SPR ABBREVIATION FOR Society for Psychical Research.

sprag (spræg) NOUN [1] a chock or steel bar used to prevent a vehicle from running backwards on an incline. [2] a support or post used in mining. [3] *NZ mining* a steel bar inserted into the wheels of a box to act as a brake.
▷HISTORY C19: of uncertain origin

sprain (spreɪn) VERB [1] (*tr*) to injure (a joint) by a sudden twisting or wrenching of its ligaments. ◆ NOUN [2] the resulting injury to such a joint, characterized by swelling and temporary disability.
▷HISTORY C17: of uncertain origin

spraint (spreɪnt) NOUN (*often plural*) a piece of otter's dung.
▷HISTORY C15 *sprayntes* (pl), from Medieval French *espraintes* otter's dung, from *espreindre* to press out: compare EXPRESS

sprang (spræŋ) VERB the past tense of **spring.**

sprat (spræt) NOUN [1] a small marine food fish, *Clupea sprattus,* of the NE Atlantic Ocean and North Sea: family *Clupeidae* (herrings). See also **brisling.** [2] any of various small or young herrings.
▷HISTORY C16: variant of Old English *sprott;* related to Middle Low German *sprott,* Norwegian *sprot* small rod

sprawl (sprɔːl) VERB [1] (*intr*) to sit or lie in an ungainly manner with one's limbs spread out. [2] to fall down or knock down with the limbs spread out in an ungainly way. [3] to spread out or cause to spread out in a straggling fashion: *his handwriting sprawled all over the paper.* ◆ NOUN [4] the act or an instance of sprawling. [5] a sprawling posture or arrangement of items. [6] **a** the urban area formed by the expansion of a town or city into surrounding countryside: *the urban sprawl.* **b** the process by which this has happened.
▷HISTORY Old English *spreawlian;* related to Old English *spryttan* to sprout, SPURT, Greek *speirein* to scatter
▸ **'sprawler** NOUN ▸ **'sprawly** ADJECTIVE

spray¹ (spreɪ) NOUN [1] fine particles of a liquid. [2] **a** a liquid, such as perfume, paint, etc., designed to be discharged from an aerosol or atomizer: *hair spray.* **b** the aerosol or atomizer itself. [3] a quantity of small objects flying through the air: *a spray of bullets.* ◆ VERB [4] to scatter (liquid) in the form of fine particles. [5] to discharge (a liquid) from an aerosol or atomizer. [6] (*tr*) to treat or bombard with a spray: *to spray the lawn.*
▷HISTORY C17: from Middle Dutch *sprāien;* related to Middle High German *spræjen*
▸ **'sprayer** NOUN

spray² (spreɪ) NOUN [1] a single slender shoot, twig, or branch that bears buds, leaves, flowers, or berries, either growing on or detached from a plant. [2] a small decorative bouquet or corsage of flowers and foliage. [3] a piece of jewellery designed to resemble a spray of flowers, leaves, etc.
▷HISTORY C13: of Germanic origin; compare Old English *spræc* young shoot, Old Norse *sprek* brittle wood, Old High German *sprahhula* splinter

spray gun NOUN a device that sprays a fluid in a finely divided form by atomizing the fluid in an air jet.

spread (sprɛd) VERB **spreads, spreading, spread.** [1] to extend or unfold or be extended or unfolded to the fullest width: *she spread the map on the table.* [2] to extend or cause to extend over a larger expanse of space or time: *the milk spread all over the floor; the political unrest spread over several years.* [3] to apply or be applied in a coating: *butter does not spread very well when cold.* [4] to distribute or be distributed over an area or region. [5] to display or be displayed in its fullest extent: *the landscape spread before us.* [6] (*tr*) to prepare (a table) for a meal. [7] (*tr*) to lay out (a meal) on a table. [8] to send or be sent out in all directions; disseminate or be disseminated: *someone has been spreading rumours; the disease spread quickly.* [9] (of rails, wires, etc.) to force or be forced apart. [10] to increase the breadth of (a part), esp to flatten the head of a rivet by pressing, hammering, or forging. [11] (*tr*) *Agriculture* **a** to lay out (hay) in a relatively thin layer to dry. **b** to scatter (seed, manure, etc.) over a relatively wide area. [12] (*tr; often foll by around*) *Informal* to make (oneself) agreeable to a large number of people, often of the opposite sex. [13] *Phonetics* to narrow and lengthen the aperture of (the lips) as for the articulation of a front vowel, such as (iː) in English *see* (siː). ◆ NOUN [14] the act or process of spreading; diffusion, dispersal, expansion, etc.: *the spread of the Christian religion.* [15] *Informal* the wingspan of an aircraft. [16] an extent of space or time; stretch: *a spread of 50 years.* [17] *Informal, chiefly US and Canadian* a ranch or relatively large tract of land. [18] the limit of something fully extended: *the spread of a bird's wings.* [19] a covering for a table or bed. [20] *Informal* a large meal or feast, esp when it is laid out on a table. [21] a food which can be spread on bread, etc.: *salmon spread.* [22] two facing pages in a book or other publication. [23] a widening of the hips and waist: *middle-age spread.* [24] *Stock Exchange* **a** the difference between the bid and offer prices quoted by a market maker. **b** the excess of the price at which stock is offered for public sale over the price paid for the same stock by an underwriter. **c** *Chiefly US* a double option. Compare **straddle** (sense 9). [25] *Jewellery* the apparent size of a gemstone when viewed from above expressed in carats: *a diamond with a spread of four carats.* ◆ ADJECTIVE [26] extended or stretched out, esp to the fullest extent. [27] (of a gem) shallow and flat. [28] *Phonetics* **a** (of the lips) forming a long narrow aperture. **b** (of speech sounds) articulated with spread lips: *(iː) in English "feel" is a spread vowel.*
▷HISTORY Old English *sprǣdan;* related to Old High German *spreiten* to spread, Old Lithuanian *sprainas* stiff
▸ **,spreada'bility** NOUN ▸ **'spreadable** ADJECTIVE

spread betting NOUN a form of gambling in which stakes are placed not on the results of contests but on the number of points scored, etc. Winnings and losses are calculated according to the accuracy or inaccuracy of the prediction.

spread eagle NOUN [1] the representation of an eagle with outstretched wings, used as an emblem of the US. [2] an acrobatic skating figure.

spread-eagle ADJECTIVE *also* **spread-eagled.** [1] lying or standing with arms and legs outstretched. ◆ VERB [2] to assume or cause to assume the shape of a spread eagle. [3] (*intr*) *Skating* to execute a spread eagle.

spreader ('sprɛdə) NOUN [1] a machine or device used for scattering bulk materials, esp manure or fertilizer, over a relatively wide area. [2] a device for keeping apart or spacing parallel objects, such as electric wires.

spread sampling NOUN the selection of a corpus for statistical analysis by selecting a number of short passages at random throughout the work and considering their aggregation. Compare **block sampling.**

spreadsheet ('sprɛd,ʃiːt) NOUN a computer program that allows easy entry and manipulation of figures, equations, and text, used esp for financial planning and budgeting.

spreathed (spri:ðd) ADJECTIVE *Southwestern English and south Wales dialect* sore; chapped.
▷**HISTORY** from *spreathe* to make sore: of obscure origin

sprechgesang (*German* ˈʃprɛçgəzaŋ) NOUN *Music* a type of vocalization between singing and recitation in which the voice sings the beginning of each note and then falls rapidly from the notated pitch. It was originated by Arnold Schoenberg, who used it in *Pierrot Lunaire* (1912).
▷**HISTORY** C20: from German, literally: speaking-song

sprechstimme (*German* ˈʃprɛçʃtɪmə) NOUN *Music* a vocal part employing sprechgesang.
▷**HISTORY** C20: from German: speaking voice

spree (spri:) NOUN [1] a session of considerable overindulgence, esp in drinking, squandering money, etc. [2] a romp.
▷**HISTORY** C19: perhaps changed from Scottish *spreath* plundered cattle, ultimately from Latin *praeda* booty

sprekelia (sprəˈki:lɪə) NOUN a bulbous plant, *Sprekelia formosissima,* from Mexico and Guatemala, related to hippeastrum and grown for its striking crimson or white pendent flowers, in the form of a cross: family *Amaryllidaceae.*
▷**HISTORY** named after J. H. von Sprekelsen (died 1764), German botanist

sprig (sprɪg) NOUN [1] a shoot, twig, or sprout of a tree, shrub, etc.; spray. [2] an ornamental device resembling a spray of leaves or flowers. [3] a small wire nail without a head. [4] *Informal, rare* a youth. [5] *Informal, rare* a person considered as the descendant of an established family, social class, etc. [6] *NZ* another name for **stud**[1] (sense 7). ◆ VERB **sprigs, sprigging, sprigged.** (*tr*) [7] to fasten or secure with sprigs. [8] to ornament (fabric, wallpaper, etc.) with a design of sprigs. [9] to make sprays from (twigs and branches).
▷**HISTORY** C15: probably of Germanic origin; compare Low German *sprick,* Swedish *sprygg*
▶ˈ**sprigger** NOUN ▶ˈ**spriggy** ADJECTIVE

sprightly (ˈspraɪtlɪ) ADJECTIVE **-lier, -liest.** [1] full of vitality; lively. ◆ ADVERB [2] *Obsolete* in a lively manner.
▷**HISTORY** C16: from *spright,* variant of SPRITE + -LY[1]
▶ˈ**sprightliness** NOUN

spring (sprɪŋ) VERB **springs, springing; sprang** *or* **sprung; sprung.** [1] to move or cause to move suddenly upwards or forwards in a single motion. [2] to release or be released from a forced position by elastic force: *the bolt sprang back.* [3] (*tr*) to leap or jump over. [4] (*intr*) to come, issue, or arise suddenly. [5] (*intr*) (of a part of a mechanism, etc.) to jump out of place. [6] to make (wood, etc.) warped or split or (of wood, etc.) to become warped or split. [7] to happen or cause to happen unexpectedly: *to spring a surprise; the boat sprung a leak.* [8] (*intr*) to develop or originate: *the idea sprang from a chance meeting.* [9] (*intr;* usually foll by *from*) to be descended: *he sprang from peasant stock.* [10] (*intr;* often foll by *up*) to come into being or appear suddenly: *factories springing up.* [11] (*tr*) (of a gun dog) to rouse (game) from cover. [12] (*intr*) (of game or quarry) to start or rise suddenly from cover. [13] (*intr*) to appear to have a strong upward movement: *the beam springs away from the pillar.* [14] to explode (a mine) or (of a mine) to explode. [15] (*tr*) to provide with a spring or springs. [16] (*tr*) *Informal* to arrange the escape of (someone) from prison. [17] (*intr*) *Archaic or poetic* (of daylight or dawn) to begin to appear. ◆ NOUN [18] the act or an instance of springing. [19] a leap, jump, or bound. [20] **a** the quality of resilience; elasticity. **b** (*as modifier*): *spring steel.* [21] the act or an instance of moving rapidly back from a position of tension. [22] **a** a natural outflow of ground water, as forming the source of a stream. **b** (*as modifier*): *spring water.* [23] **a** a device, such as a coil or strip of steel, that stores potential energy when it is compressed, stretched, or bent and releases it when the restraining force is removed. **b** (*as modifier*): *a spring mattress.* [24] a structural defect such as a warp or bend. [25] **a** (*sometimes capital*) the season of the year between winter and summer, astronomically from the March equinox to the June solstice in the N hemisphere and from the September equinox to the December solstice in the S hemisphere. **b** (*as modifier*): *spring showers.* Related adjective: **vernal.** [26] the earliest or freshest time of something. [27] a source or origin. [28] one of a set of strips of rubber, steel, etc., running down the inside of the handle of a cricket bat, hockey stick, etc. [29] Also called: **spring line.** *Nautical* a mooring line, usually one of a pair that cross amidships. [30] a flock of teal. [31] *Architect* another name for **springing.**
▷**HISTORY** Old English *springan;* related to Old Norse *springa,* Old High German *springan,* Sanskrit *sprhayati* he desires, Old Slavonic *pragu* grasshopper
▶ˈ**springless** ADJECTIVE ▶ˈ**spring,like** ADJECTIVE

spring balance *or esp US* **spring scale** NOUN a device in which an object to be weighed is attached to the end of a helical spring, the extension of which indicates the weight of the object on a calibrated scale.

spring beauty NOUN a pale green annual plant (*Claytonia perfoliata*) of the purslane family, originally North American, having small white flowers above fused leaves that encircle the stem.

springboard (ˈsprɪŋˌbɔ:d) NOUN [1] a flexible board, usually projecting low over the water, used for diving. [2] a similar board used for gaining height or momentum in gymnastics. [3] *Austral and NZ* a board inserted into the trunk of a tree at some height above the ground on which a lumberjack stands to chop down the tree. [4] anything that serves as a point of departure or initiation.

springbok *or less commonly* **springbuck** (ˈsprɪŋˌbʌk) NOUN, *plural* **-bok, -boks** *or* **-buck, -bucks.** an antelope, *Antidorcas marsupialis,* of semidesert regions of southern Africa, which moves in leaps exposing a patch of white erectile hairs on the rump that are usually covered by a fold of skin.
▷**HISTORY** C18: from Afrikaans, from Dutch *springen* to SPRING + *bok* goat, BUCK[1]

Springbok (ˈsprɪŋˌbʌk, -ˌbɒk) NOUN a person who has represented South Africa in a national sports team.

spring chicken NOUN [1] Also called: **springer.** *Chiefly US and Canadian* a young chicken, tender for cooking, esp one from two to ten months old. [2] **he** *or* **she is no spring chicken.** *Informal* he or she is no longer young.

spring-clean VERB [1] to clean (a house) thoroughly: traditionally at the end of the winter. ◆ NOUN [2] an instance of spring-cleaning.
▶ˌ**spring-**ˈ**cleaning** NOUN

springe (sprɪndʒ) NOUN [1] a snare set to catch small wild animals or birds and consisting of a loop attached to a bent twig or branch under tension. ◆ VERB [2] (*intr*) to set such a snare. [3] (*tr*) to catch (small wild animals or birds) with such a snare.
▷**HISTORY** C13: related to Old English *springan* to SPRING

springer (ˈsprɪŋə) NOUN [1] short for **springer spaniel.** [2] Also called: **springing cow.** a cow about to give birth. [3] a person or thing that springs. [4] *Architect* **a** the first and lowest stone of an arch. **b** the impost of an arch.

springer spaniel NOUN either of two breeds of large quick-moving spaniels bred to spring game, having a slightly domed head and ears of medium length. The **English springer spaniel** is the larger and can be of various colours; the **Welsh springer spaniel** is always a rich red and white.

spring fever NOUN the feeling of restlessness experienced by many people at the onset of spring.

Springfield (ˈsprɪŋˌfi:ld) NOUN [1] a city in S Massachusetts, on the Connecticut River: the site of the US arsenal and armoury (1794–1968), which developed the Springfield and Garand rifles. Pop.: 152 082 (2000). [2] a city in SW Missouri. Pop.: 151 580 (2000). [3] a city in central Illinois, capital of the state: the home and burial place of Abraham Lincoln. Pop.: 111 454 (2000).

Springfield rifle NOUN a magazine-fed bolt-action breech-loading .30 calibre rifle formerly used by the US Army.
▷**HISTORY** from SPRINGFIELD, Massachusetts

springhaas (ˈsprɪŋˌhɑ:s) NOUN, *plural* **-haas** *or* **-hase** (-ˌhɑ:zə). a S and E African nocturnal rodent, *Pedetes capensis,* resembling a small kangaroo: family *Pedetidae.*
▷**HISTORY** from Afrikaans: spring hare

springhalt (ˈsprɪŋˌhɔ:lt) NOUN *Vet science* another name for **stringhalt.**
▷**HISTORY** C17: probably an alteration, influenced by SPRING, of STRINGHALT

springhead (ˈsprɪŋˌhɛd) NOUN the source of a stream; spring.

springhouse (ˈsprɪŋˌhaʊs) NOUN a storehouse built over a spring for keeping dairy products and meat cool and fresh.

springing (ˈsprɪŋɪŋ) NOUN the level where an arch or vault rises from a support. Also called: **spring, springing line, springing point.**

springlet (ˈsprɪŋlɪt) NOUN a small spring; brooklet or rill.

spring lock NOUN a type of lock having a spring-loaded bolt, a key being required only to unlock it.

spring mattress NOUN a mattress containing an arrangement of spiral springs.

spring onion NOUN an immature form of the onion (*Allium cepa*), widely cultivated for its tiny bulb and long green leaves which are eaten in salads, etc. Also called: **green onion, scallion.**

spring roll NOUN a Chinese dish consisting of a savoury mixture of vegetables and meat rolled up in a thin pancake and fried.

Springs (sprɪŋz) NOUN a city in E South Africa: developed around a coal mine established in 1885 and later became a major world gold-mining centre, now with uranium extraction. Pop. (urban area): 160 795 (1996).

springtail (ˈsprɪŋˌteɪl) NOUN any primitive wingless insect of the order *Collembola,* having a forked springing organ with which it projects itself forward.

spring tide NOUN [1] either of the two tides that occur at or just after new moon and full moon when the tide-generating force of the sun acts in the same direction as that of the moon, reinforcing it and causing the greatest rise and fall in tidal level. The highest spring tides (**equinoctial springs**) occur at the equinoxes. Compare **neap tide.** [2] any great rush or flood.

springtime (ˈsprɪŋˌtaɪm) NOUN [1] Also called: **springtide** (ˈsprɪŋˌtaɪd). the season of spring. [2] the earliest, usually the most attractive, period of the existence of something.

springwood (ˈsprɪŋˌwʊd) NOUN the wood that is produced by a plant in the spring and early summer and consists of large thin-walled xylem cells. Compare **summerwood.**

springy (ˈsprɪŋɪ) ADJECTIVE **springier, springiest.** [1] possessing or characterized by resilience or bounce. [2] (of a place) having many wells or springs of water.
▶ˈ**springily** ADVERB ▶ˈ**springiness** NOUN

sprinkle (ˈsprɪŋkᵊl) VERB [1] to scatter (liquid, powder, etc.) in tiny particles or droplets over (something). [2] (*tr*) to distribute over (something): *the field was sprinkled with flowers.* [3] (*intr*) to drizzle slightly. ◆ NOUN [4] the act or an instance of sprinkling or a quantity that is sprinkled. [5] a slight drizzle.
▷**HISTORY** C14: probably from Middle Dutch *sprenkelen;* related to Old English *spearca* SPARK[1]

sprinkler (ˈsprɪŋklə) NOUN [1] a device perforated with small holes that is attached to a garden hose or watering can and used to spray plants, lawns, etc., with water. [2] a person or thing that sprinkles. [3] See **sprinkler system.**

sprinkler system NOUN a fire-extinguishing system that releases water from overhead pipes through nozzles (sprinklers) opened automatically by a rise in temperature.

sprinkling (ˈsprɪŋklɪŋ) NOUN a small quantity or amount: *a sprinkling of commonsense.*

sprint (sprɪnt) NOUN [1] *Athletics* a short race run at top speed, such as the 100 metres. [2] a fast finishing speed at the end of a longer race, as in running or cycling, etc. [3] any quick run. ◆ VERB (*intr*) [4] to go at top speed, as in running, cycling, etc.
▷**HISTORY** C16: from Scandinavian; related to Old English *gesprintan* to emit, Old Norse *spretta* to jump up, Old High German *sprinzan* to jump up, Swedish *sprata* to kick
▶ˈ**sprinter** NOUN

sprit (sprɪt) NOUN *Nautical* a light spar pivoted at

the mast and crossing a fore-and-aft quadrilateral sail diagonally to the peak.
▷HISTORY Old English *spreot;* related to Old High German *spriuzen* to support, Dutch *spriet* sprit, Norwegian *sprӯta*

sprite (spraɪt) NOUN [1] (in folklore) a nimble elflike creature, esp one associated with water. [2] a small dainty person. [3] an icon in a computer game which can be manoeuvred around the screen by means of a joystick, etc.
▷HISTORY C13: from Old French *esprit,* from Latin *spīritus* SPIRIT[1]

spritsail ('sprɪtˌseɪl; *Nautical* 'sprɪtsəl) NOUN *Nautical* [1] a rectangular sail mounted on a sprit in some 19th-century small vessels. [2] (in medieval rigging) a square sail mounted on a yard on the bowsprit.

spritzer ('sprɪtsə) NOUN a drink, usually white wine, with soda water added.
▷HISTORY from German *spritzen* to splash

spritzig *German* ('ʃprɪtsɪç; *English* 'sprɪtsɪg) ADJECTIVE (of wine) sparkling.
▷HISTORY German, from *spritzen* to splash

sprocket ('sprɒkɪt) NOUN [1] Also called: **sprocket wheel.** a relatively thin wheel having teeth projecting radially from the rim, esp one that drives or is driven by a chain. [2] an individual tooth on such a wheel. [3] a cylindrical wheel with teeth on one or both rims for pulling film through a camera or projector. [4] a small wedge-shaped piece of wood used to extend a roof over the eaves.
▷HISTORY C16: of unknown origin

sprog (sprɒg) NOUN *Slang* [1] a child; baby. [2] (esp in RAF) a recruit.

sprout (spraʊt) VERB [1] (of a plant, seed, etc.) to produce (new leaves, shoots, etc.). [2] (*intr;* often foll by *up*) to begin to grow or develop: *new office blocks are sprouting up all over the city.* ◆ NOUN [3] a newly grown shoot or bud. [4] something that grows like a sprout. [5] See **Brussels sprout.**
▷HISTORY Old English *sprūtan;* related to Middle High German *sprūzen* to sprout, Lettish *sprausties* to jostle

spruce[1] (spruːs) NOUN [1] any coniferous tree of the N temperate genus *Picea,* cultivated for timber and for ornament: family *Pinaceae.* They grow in a pyramidal shape and have needle-like leaves and light-coloured wood. See also **Norway spruce, blue spruce, white spruce, black spruce.** [2] the wood of any of these trees.
▷HISTORY C17: short for *Spruce fir,* from C14 *Spruce* Prussia, changed from *Pruce,* via Old French from Latin *Prussia*

spruce[2] (spruːs) ADJECTIVE neat, smart, and trim.
▷HISTORY C16: perhaps from *Spruce leather* a fashionable leather imported from Prussia; see SPRUCE[1]
▸'**sprucely** ADVERB ▸'**spruceness** NOUN

spruce beer NOUN an alcoholic drink made of fermented molasses flavoured with spruce twigs and cones.

spruce grouse NOUN a game bird, *Dendragapus canadensis,* occurring in Canadian coniferous forests.

spruce pine NOUN [1] a large pine tree, *Pinus glabra,* of the southeastern US. [2] any of several similar plants, such as certain pines, hemlocks, and spruces.

spruce up VERB (*adverb*) to make (oneself, a person, or thing) smart and neat.

sprue[1] (spruː) NOUN [1] a vertical channel in a mould through which plastic or molten metal is introduced or out of which it flows when the mould is filled. [2] plastic or metal that solidifies in a sprue.
▷HISTORY C19: of unknown origin

sprue[2] (spruː) NOUN a chronic disease, esp of tropical climates, characterized by flatulence, diarrhoea, frothy foul-smelling stools, and emaciation.
▷HISTORY C19: from Dutch *spruw;* related to Middle Low German *sprüwe* tumour

sprue[3] (spruː) NOUN *London dialect* an inferior type of asparagus.
▷HISTORY C19: of unknown origin

spruik ('spruːɪk) VERB (*intr*) *Austral archaic slang* to speak in public (used esp of a showman or salesman).
▷HISTORY C20: of unknown origin
▸'**spruiker** NOUN

spruit (spreɪt) NOUN *South African* a small tributary stream or watercourse.
▷HISTORY Afrikaans *spruit* offshoot, tributary

sprung (sprʌŋ) VERB the past participle and a past tense of **spring.**

sprung rhythm NOUN *Prosody* a type of poetic rhythm characterized by metrical feet of irregular composition, each having one strongly stressed syllable, often the first, and an indefinite number of unstressed syllables.

spry (spraɪ) ADJECTIVE **spryer, spryest** *or* **sprier, spriest.** active and brisk; nimble.
▷HISTORY C18: perhaps of Scandinavian origin; compare Swedish dialect *spragg* SPRIG
▸'**spryly** ADVERB ▸'**spryness** NOUN

spt ABBREVIATION FOR seaport.

SPUC (spʌk) NOUN ACRONYM FOR Society for the Protection of the Unborn Child.

spud (spʌd) NOUN [1] an informal word for **potato** (sense 1). [2] a narrow-bladed spade for cutting roots, digging up weeds, etc. [3] Also called: **spudder.** a tool, resembling a chisel, for removing bark from trees. ◆ VERB **spuds, spudding, spudded.** [4] (*tr*) to remove (bark) or eradicate (weeds) with a spud. [5] (*intr*) to drill the first foot of an oil-well.
▷HISTORY C15 *spudde* short knife, of unknown origin; applied later to a digging tool, and hence to a potato

spud-bashing NOUN *Brit slang, chiefly military* the task of peeling potatoes, given as a punishment.

spuddle ('spʌdᵊl) NOUN *Southwest English dialect* a feeble movement.

Spud Island NOUN a slang name for **Prince Edward Island.**

spue (spjuː) VERB **spues, spuing, spued.** an archaic spelling of **spew.**
▸'**spuer** NOUN

spuggy ('spʊgɪ) *or* **spug** (spʊg) NOUN, *plural* **spuggies** *or* **spugs.** *Northeast English dialect* a house sparrow. Compare **speug.**
▷HISTORY variant of Scottish *sprug,* of obscure origin

spume (spjuːm) NOUN [1] foam or surf, esp on the sea; froth. ◆ VERB [2] (*intr*) to foam or froth.
▷HISTORY C14: from Old French *espume,* from Latin *spūma;* related to *spuere* to SPEW
▸'**spumous** *or* '**spumy** ADJECTIVE

spumescent (spjuː'mɛsᵊnt) ADJECTIVE producing or resembling foam or froth.
▸**spu'mescence** NOUN

spumone *or* **spumoni** (spuː'məʊnɪ; *Italian* spu'moːne) NOUN, *plural* **-ni** (-nɪ). a creamy Italian ice cream, made in sections of different colouring, usually containing candied fruit and nuts.
▷HISTORY Italian, from *spuma* foam, SPUME

spun (spʌn) VERB [1] the past tense and past participle of **spin.** ◆ ADJECTIVE [2] formed or manufactured by spinning: *spun gold; spun glass.*

spunk (spʌŋk) NOUN [1] *Informal* courage or spirit. [2] *Brit* a slang word for **semen.** [3] touchwood or tinder, esp originally made from various spongy types of fungus. [4] *Austral and NZ informal* a person, esp male, who is attractive to the opposite sex.
▷HISTORY C16 (in the sense: a spark): from Scottish Gaelic *spong* tinder, sponge, from Latin *spongia* sponge
▸'**spunky** ADJECTIVE ▸'**spunkily** ADVERB

> **Language note** The second sense of this word was formerly considered to be taboo, and it was labelled as such in previous editions of *Collins English Dictionary.* However, it has now become acceptable in speech, although some older or more conservative people may object to its use.

spun silk NOUN yarn or fabric made from silk waste.

spun sugar NOUN *US* another term for **candyfloss.**

spun yarn NOUN *Nautical* small stuff made from rope yarns twisted together.

spur (spɜː) NOUN [1] a pointed device or sharp spiked wheel fixed to the heel of a rider's boot to enable him to urge his horse on. [2] anything serving to urge or encourage: *the increase in salary was a spur to their production.* [3] a sharp horny projection from the leg just above the claws in male birds, such as the domestic cock. [4] a pointed process in any of various animals; calcar. [5] a tubular extension at the base of the corolla in flowers such as larkspur. [6] a short or stunted branch of a tree. [7] a ridge projecting laterally from a mountain or mountain range. [8] a wooden prop or a masonry reinforcing pier. [9] another name for **groyne.** [10] Also called: **spur track.** a railway branch line or siding. [11] a short side road leading off a main road: *a motorway spur.* [12] a sharp cutting instrument attached to the leg of a gamecock. [13] **on the spur of the moment.** on impulse. [14] **win one's spurs. a** *History* to earn knighthood. **b** to prove one's ability; gain distinction. ◆ VERB **spurs, spurring, spurred.** [15] (*tr*) to goad or urge with or as if with spurs. [16] (*intr*) to go or ride quickly; press on. [17] (*tr*) to injure or strike with a spur. [18] (*tr*) to provide with a spur or spurs.
▷HISTORY Old English *spura;* related to Old Norse *spori,* Old High German *sporo*

spurge (spɜːdʒ) NOUN any of various euphorbiaceous plants of the genus *Euphorbia* that have milky sap and small flowers typically surrounded by conspicuous bracts. Some species have purgative properties.
▷HISTORY C14: from Old French *espurge,* from *espurgier* to purge, from Latin *expurgāre* to cleanse, from EX-[1] + *purgāre* to PURGE

spur gear *or* **wheel** NOUN a gear having involuted teeth either straight or helically cut on a cylindrical surface. Two such gears are used to transmit power between parallel shafts.

spurge laurel NOUN See **laurel** (sense 4).

spurious ('spjʊərɪəs) ADJECTIVE [1] not genuine or real. [2] (of a plant part or organ) having the appearance of another part but differing from it in origin, development, or function; false: *a spurious fruit.* [3] (of radiation) produced at an undesired frequency by a transmitter, causing interference, etc. [4] *Rare* illegitimate.
▷HISTORY C17: from Latin *spurius* of illegitimate birth
▸'**spuriously** ADVERB ▸'**spuriousness** NOUN

spurn (spɜːn) VERB [1] to reject (a person or thing) with contempt. [2] (when *intr,* often foll by *against*) *Archaic* to kick (at). ◆ NOUN [3] an instance of spurning. [4] *Archaic* a kick or thrust.
▷HISTORY Old English *spurnan;* related to Old Norse *sporna,* Old High German *spurnan,* Latin *spernere* to despise, Lithuanian *spiriu* to kick
▸'**spurner** NOUN

spurrey *or* **spurry** ('spʌrɪ) NOUN, *plural* **-ries.** any of several low-growing caryophyllaceous plants of the European genus *Spergula,* esp *S. arvensis,* having whorled leaves and small white flowers.
▷HISTORY C16: from Dutch *spurrie,* perhaps from Medieval Latin *spergula;* related to German *Spergel*

spurrier ('spʌrɪə) NOUN a maker of spurs.

spurt *or* **spirt** (spɜːt) VERB [1] to gush or cause to gush forth in a sudden stream or jet. [2] to make a sudden effort. ◆ NOUN [3] a sudden forceful stream or jet. [4] a short burst of activity, speed, or energy.
▷HISTORY C16: perhaps related to Middle High German *sprützen* to squirt

spur veins NOUN *Vet science* the veins of a horse that can be damaged by a rider's spurs.

Sputnik ('spʊtnɪk, 'spʌt-) NOUN any of a series of unmanned Soviet satellites, **Sputnik 1** (launched in 1957) being the first man-made satellite to orbit the earth.
▷HISTORY C20: from Russian, literally: fellow traveller, from *s-* with + *put* path + *-nik* suffix indicating agent

sputter ('spʌtə) VERB [1] another word for **splutter** (senses 1–3). [2] *Physics* **a** to undergo or cause to undergo a process in which atoms of a solid are removed from its surface by the impact of high-energy ions, as in a discharge tube. **b** to coat (a film of a metal) onto (a solid surface) by using this process. ◆ NOUN [3] the process or noise of sputtering. [4] incoherent stammering speech. [5] something that is ejected while sputtering.

▷HISTORY C16: from Dutch *sputteren*, of imitative origin
▸ **'sputterer** NOUN

sputum ('spju:təm) NOUN, *plural* **-ta** (-tə). 1 a mass of salivary matter ejected from the mouth. 2 saliva ejected from the mouth mixed with mucus or pus exuded from the respiratory passages, as in bronchitis or bronchiectasis.
▷HISTORY C17: from Latin: spittle, from *spuere* to spit out

spy (spaɪ) NOUN, *plural* **spies.** 1 a person employed by a state or institution to obtain secret information from rival countries, organizations, companies, etc. 2 a person who keeps secret watch on others. 3 *Obsolete* a close view. ◆ VERB **spies, spying, spied.** 4 (*intr*; usually foll by *on*) to keep a secret or furtive watch (on). 5 (*intr*) to engage in espionage. 6 (*tr*) to catch sight of; descry.
▷HISTORY C13 *spien*, from Old French *espier*, of Germanic origin; related to Old High German *spehōn*, Middle Dutch *spien*

spyglass ('spaɪˌglɑ:s) NOUN a small telescope.

spyhole ('spaɪˌhəʊl) NOUN a small hole in a door, etc. through which one may watch secretly; peephole.

spy out VERB (*tr, adverb*) 1 to discover by careful observation: *to spy out a route.* 2 to make a close scrutiny of: *to spy out the land.*

Spy Wednesday NOUN (in Ireland) the Wednesday before Easter, named for Judas' becoming a spy for the Sanhedrin.

sq. ABBREVIATION FOR: 1 sequence. 2 square. 3 (*plural* **sqq**) the following one. [from Latin *sequens*]

Sq. ABBREVIATION FOR: 1 Squadron. 2 (in place names) Square.

SQA (in Britain) ABBREVIATION FOR Scottish Qualifications Agency.

SQL ABBREVIATION FOR structured query language: a computer programming language used for database management.

sqn ABBREVIATION FOR squadron.

Sqn Ldr ABBREVIATION FOR squadron leader.

sqq. ABBREVIATION FOR the following ones.
▷HISTORY from Latin *sequentia*

squab (skwɒb) NOUN, *plural* **squabs** *or* **squab.** 1 a young unfledged bird, esp a pigeon. 2 a short fat person. 3 **a** a well-stuffed bolster or cushion. **b** a sofa. ◆ ADJECTIVE 4 (of birds) recently hatched and still unfledged. 5 short and fat.
▷HISTORY C17: probably of Germanic origin; compare Swedish dialect *sqvabb* flabby skin, *sqvabba* fat woman, German *Quabbe* soft mass, Norwegian *kvabb* mud
▸ **'squabby** ADJECTIVE

squabble ('skwɒbᵊl) VERB 1 (*intr*) to quarrel over a small matter. ◆ NOUN 2 a petty quarrel.
▷HISTORY C17: probably of Scandinavian origin; related to Swedish dialect *sqvabbel* to quarrel
▸ **'squabbler** NOUN

squacco ('skwækəʊ) NOUN, *plural* **-cos.** a S European heron, *Ardeola ralloides*, with a short thick neck and a buff-coloured plumage with white wings.
▷HISTORY C17: Italian dialect

squad (skwɒd) NOUN 1 the smallest military formation, typically comprising a dozen soldiers, used esp as a drill formation. 2 any small group of people engaged in a common pursuit. 3 *Sport* a number of players from which a team is to be selected.
▷HISTORY C17: from Old French *esquade*, from Old Spanish *escuadra*, from *escuadrar* to SQUARE, from the square formations used

squaddie *or* **squaddy** ('skwɒdɪ) NOUN, *plural* **-dies.** *Brit slang* a private soldier. Compare **swaddy.**
▷HISTORY C20: from SQUAD

squadron ('skwɒdrən) NOUN 1 **a** a subdivision of a naval fleet detached for a particular task. **b** a number of naval units usually of similar type and consisting of two or more divisions. 2 a cavalry unit comprising two or more troops, headquarters, and supporting arms. 3 the basic tactical and administrative air force unit comprising two or more flights. ◆ Abbreviation: **sqn.**
▷HISTORY C16: from Italian *squadrone* soldiers drawn up in square formation, from *squadro* SQUARE

squadron leader NOUN an officer holding commissioned rank, between flight lieutenant and wing commander in the air forces of Britain and certain other countries.

squalene ('skweɪˌli:n) NOUN *Biochem* a terpene first found in the liver of sharks but also present in the livers of most higher animals: an important precursor of cholesterol.
▷HISTORY C20: from New Latin *squalus* genus name of the shark

squalid ('skwɒlɪd) ADJECTIVE 1 dirty and repulsive, esp as a result of neglect or poverty. 2 sordid.
▷HISTORY C16: from Latin *squālidus*, from *squālēre* to be stiff with dirt
▸ **squalidity** (skwɒ'lɪdɪtɪ) *or* **'squalidness** NOUN
▸ **'squalidly** ADVERB

squall¹ (skwɔ:l) NOUN 1 a sudden strong wind or brief turbulent storm. 2 any sudden commotion or show of temper. ◆ VERB 3 (*intr*) to blow in a squall.
▷HISTORY C18: perhaps a special use of SQUALL²
▸ **'squallish** ADJECTIVE ▸ **'squally** ADJECTIVE

squall² (skwɔ:l) VERB 1 (*intr*) to cry noisily; yell. ◆ NOUN 2 a shrill or noisy yell or howl.
▷HISTORY C17: probably of Scandinavian origin; compare Icelandic *skvala* to shout; see SQUEAL
▸ **'squaller** NOUN

squall line NOUN a narrow zone along a cold front along which squalls occur. See also **line squall.**

squalor ('skwɒlə) NOUN the condition or quality of being squalid; disgusting dirt and filth.
▷HISTORY C17: from Latin

squama ('skweɪmə) NOUN, *plural* **-mae** (-mi:). *Biology* a scale or scalelike structure.
▷HISTORY C18: from Latin
▸ **squamate** ('skweɪmeɪt) ADJECTIVE

squamation (skweɪ'meɪʃən) NOUN 1 the condition of having or forming scales or squamae. 2 the arrangement of scales in fishes or reptiles.

squamiform ('skweɪmɪˌfɔ:m) ADJECTIVE *Biology* resembling a scale: *squamiform cells.*

squamosal (skwə'məʊsᵊl) NOUN 1 a thin platelike paired bone in the skull of vertebrates: in mammals it forms part of the temporal bone. ◆ ADJECTIVE 2 of or relating to this bone. 3 a less common word for **squamous.**

squamous ('skweɪməs) *or* **squamose** ('skweɪməʊs) ADJECTIVE *Biology* 1 (of epithelium) consisting of one or more layers of flat platelike cells. 2 covered with, formed of, or resembling scales.
▷HISTORY C16: from Latin *squāmōsus*, from *squāma* a scale
▸ **'squamously** *or* **'squamosely** ADVERB ▸ **'squamousness** *or* **'squamoseness** NOUN

squamulose ('skwæmjʊˌləʊs, -ˌləʊz, 'skweɪ-) ADJECTIVE (esp of plants or their parts) covered with minute scales.
▷HISTORY C19: from Latin *squāmula* diminutive of *squāma* a scale

squander ('skwɒndə) VERB (*tr*) 1 to spend wastefully or extravagantly; dissipate. 2 an obsolete word for **scatter.** ◆ NOUN 3 *Rare* extravagance or dissipation.
▷HISTORY C16: of unknown origin
▸ **'squanderer** NOUN

square (skwɛə) NOUN 1 a plane geometric figure having four equal sides and four right angles. Compare **rectangle, rhombus.** 2 any object, part, or arrangement having this or a similar shape: *a square of carpet; a square on a chess board.* 3 (*capital when part of name*) an open area in a town, sometimes including the surrounding buildings, which may form a square. 4 *Maths* the product of two equal factors; the second power: *9 is the square of 3, written* 3^2. 5 an instrument having two strips of wood, metal, etc., set in the shape of a T or L, used for constructing or testing right angles. 6 *Cricket* the closely-cut area in the middle of a ground on which wickets are prepared. 7 a body of soldiers drawn up in the form of a square. 8 *Rowing* the position of the blade of an oar perpendicular to the surface of the water just before and during a stroke. 9 *Informal* a person who is old-fashioned in views, customs, appearance, etc. 10 *Astrology* an aspect of about 90° between two planets, etc. Compare **conjunction** (sense 5), **opposition** (sense 9), **trine** (sense 1). 11 *Obsolete* a standard, pattern, or rule. 12 **back to square one.** indicating a return to the starting-point of an investigation, experiment, etc., because of failure, lack of progress, etc. 13 **on the square. a** at right angles. **b** on equal terms. **c** *Informal* honestly and openly. **d** *Slang* a phrase identifying someone as a Freemason: *he is on the square.* 14 **out of square. a** not at right angles or not having a right angle. **b** not in order or agreement. ◆ ADJECTIVE 15 being a square in shape. 16 having or forming one or more right angles or being at right angles to something. 17 square or rectangular in section: *a square bar.* 18 **a** (*prenominal*) denoting a measure of area of any shape: *a circle of four square feet.* **b** (*immediately postpositive*) denoting a square having a specified length on each side: *a board four feet square contains 16 square feet.* 19 fair and honest (esp in the phrase **a square deal**). 20 straight, even, or level: *a square surface.* 21 *Cricket* at right angles to the wicket: *square leg.* 22 *Sport* in a straight line across the pitch: *a square pass.* 23 *Nautical* (of the sails of a square-rigger) set at right angles to the keel. 24 *Informal* old-fashioned in views, customs, appearance, etc. 25 stocky or sturdy: *square shoulders.* 26 (*postpositive*) having no remaining debts or accounts to be settled. 27 (of a horse's gait) sound, steady, or regular. 28 (*prenominal*) unequivocal or straightforward: *a square contradiction.* 29 (*postpositive*) neat and tidy. 30 *Maths* (of a matrix) having the same number of rows and columns. 31 **all square.** on equal terms; even in score. 32 **square peg (in a round hole).** *Informal* a person or thing that is a misfit, such as an employee in a job for which he is unsuited. ◆ VERB (*mainly tr*) 33 to make into a square or similar shape. 34 *Maths* to raise (a number or quantity) to the second power. 35 to test or adjust for deviation with respect to a right angle, plane surface, etc. 36 (sometimes foll by *off*) to divide into squares. 37 to position so as to be rectangular, straight, or level: *square the shoulders.* 38 (sometimes foll by *up*) to settle (debts, accounts, etc.). 39 to level (the score) in a game, etc. 40 (*also intr*; often foll by *with*) to agree or cause to agree: *your ideas don't square with mine.* 41 *Rowing* to turn (an oar) perpendicular to the surface of the water just before commencing a stroke. 42 (in canoeing) to turn (a paddle) perpendicular to the direction of the canoe at the commencement of a stroke. Compare **feather** (sense 15). 43 to arrange (something), esp by a corrupt method or come to an arrangement with (someone), as by bribery. 44 **square the circle.** to attempt the impossible (in reference to the insoluble problem of constructing a square having exactly the same area as a given circle). ◆ ADVERB 45 in order to be square. 46 at right angles. 47 *Sport* in a straight line across the pitch: *pass the ball square.* 48 *Informal* squarely. ◆ See also **square away, square off, square up.**
▷HISTORY C13: from Old French *esquare*, from Vulgar Latin *exquadra* (unattested), from Latin EX¹ + *quadrāre* to make square; see QUADRANT
▸ **'squareness** NOUN ▸ **'squarer** NOUN ▸ **'squarish** ADJECTIVE

square away VERB (*adverb*) 1 to set the sails of (a square-rigger) at right angles to the keel. 2 (*tr*) *US and Canadian* to make neat and tidy.

square-bashing NOUN *Brit military slang* drill on a barrack square.

square bracket NOUN 1 either of a pair of characters [ ], used to enclose a section of writing or printing to separate it from the main text. 2 Also called: **bracket.** either of these characters used as a sign of aggregation in mathematical or logical expressions indicating that the expression contained in the brackets is to be evaluated first and treated as a unit in the evaluation of the whole.

square dance NOUN 1 *Chiefly US and Canadian* any of various formation dances, such as a quadrille, in which the couples form squares. ◆ VERB **square-dance.** 2 (*intr*) to perform such a dance.
▸ **'square-ˌdancer** NOUN

square knot NOUN another name for **reef knot.**

square leg NOUN *Cricket* 1 a fielding position on the on side approximately at right angles to the batsman. 2 a person who fields in this position.

squarely ('skwɛəlɪ) ADVERB 1 in a direct way; straight: *he hit me squarely on the nose.* 2 in an honest, frank, and just manner. 3 at right angles.

square matrix NOUN *Maths* a matrix in which the number of rows is equal to the number of columns.

square meal NOUN a substantial meal consisting of enough food to satisfy.

square measure NOUN a unit or system of units for measuring areas.

square number NOUN an integer, such as 1, 4, 9, or 16, that is the square of an integer.

square off VERB (*intr, adverb*) to assume a posture of offence or defence, as in boxing.

square of opposition NOUN See **opposition** (sense 10b).

square piano NOUN *Music* an obsolete form of piano, horizontally strung and with an oblong frame.

square-rigged ADJECTIVE *Nautical* rigged with square sails.

square-rigger NOUN *Nautical* a square-rigged ship.

square root NOUN a number or quantity that when multiplied by itself gives a given number or quantity: *2 is a square root of 4, usually written* $\sqrt{4}$ *or* $4^{1/2}$.

square sail NOUN *Nautical* a rectangular or square sail set on a horizontal yard rigged more or less athwartships.

square shooter NOUN *Informal, chiefly US* an honest or frank person.
▸**square shooting** NOUN

square tin NOUN *Brit* a medium-sized loaf having a crusty top, baked in a tin with a square base.

square up VERB (*adverb*) [1] to pay or settle (bills, debts, etc.). [2] *Informal* to arrange or be arranged satisfactorily. [3] (*intr;* foll by *to*) to prepare to be confronted (with), esp courageously. [4] (*tr;* foll by *to*) to adopt a position of readiness to fight (an opponent). [5] (*tr*) to transfer (a drawing) by aid of a network of squares.

square wave NOUN an oscillation, for example in voltage pulse, that alternates between two fixed values with a negligible transition time between the two, giving a rectangular waveform.

squarrose ('skwærəʊz, 'skwɒ-) ADJECTIVE [1] *Biology* having a rough surface, caused by the presence of projecting hairs, scales, etc. [2] *Botany* having or relating to parts that are recurved: *squarrose bracts*.
▹HISTORY C18: from Latin *squarrōsus* scabby

squash[1] (skwɒʃ) VERB [1] to press or squeeze or be pressed or squeezed in or down so as to crush, distort, or pulp. [2] (*tr*) to suppress or overcome. [3] (*tr*) to humiliate or crush (a person), esp with a disconcerting retort. [4] (*intr*) to make a sucking, splashing, or squelching sound. [5] (often foll by *in* or *into*) to enter or insert in a confined space. ◆ NOUN [6] *Brit* a still drink made from fruit juice or fruit syrup diluted with water. [7] a crush, esp of people in a confined space. [8] something that is squashed. [9] the act or sound of squashing or the state of being squashed. [10] Also called: **squash rackets, squash racquets.** a game for two or four players played in an enclosed court with a small rubber ball and light long-handled rackets. The ball may be hit against any of the walls but must hit the facing wall at a point above a horizontal line. See also **rackets.** [11] Also called: **squash tennis.** a similar game played with larger rackets and a larger pneumatic ball.
▹HISTORY C16: from Old French *esquasser*, from Vulgar Latin *exquassāre* (unattested), from Latin EX-[1] + *quassāre* to shatter
▸'**squasher** NOUN

squash[2] (skwɒʃ) NOUN, *plural* **squashes** *or* **squash**. *US and Canadian* [1] any of various marrow-like cucurbitaceous plants of the genus *Cucurbita*, esp *C. pepo* and *C. moschata*, the fruits of which have a hard rind surrounding edible flesh. [2] the fruit of any of these plants, eaten as a vegetable.
▹HISTORY C17: from Narraganset *askutasquash*, literally: green vegetable eaten green

squashable ('skwɒʃəbᵊl) ADJECTIVE [1] easily squashed; soft. [2] easily subdued, disconcerted, or humiliated.

squash bug NOUN any of various heteropterous insects of the family *Coreidae*, esp a North American species, *Anasa tristis*, which is a pest of squash, pumpkin, and related plants.

squash ladder NOUN a list showing the relative order of merit of a set of squash players determined by the winning player in each match taking the higher of the two players' positions.

squashy ('skwɒʃɪ) ADJECTIVE **squashier, squashiest.** [1] easily squashed; pulpy: *a squashy peach.* [2] soft and wet; marshy: *squashy ground.* [3] having a squashed appearance: *a squashy face.*
▸'**squashily** ADVERB ▸'**squashiness** NOUN

squat (skwɒt) VERB **squats, squatting, squatted.** (*intr*) [1] to rest in a crouching position with the knees bent and the weight on the feet. [2] to crouch down, esp in order to hide. [3] *Law* to occupy land or property to which the occupant has no legal title. ◆ ADJECTIVE [4] Also: **squatty** ('skwɒtɪ). short and broad: *a squat chair.* ◆ NOUN [5] a squatting position. [6] a house occupied by squatters.
▹HISTORY C13: from Old French *esquater*, from *es-* EX-[1] + *catir* to press together, from Vulgar Latin *coactīre* (unattested), from Latin *cōgere* to compress, from CO- + *agere* to drive
▸'**squatly** ADVERB ▸'**squatness** NOUN

squatter ('skwɒtə) NOUN [1] a person who occupies property or land to which he has no legal title. [2] (in Australia) **a** (formerly) a person who occupied a tract of land, esp pastoral land, as tenant of the Crown. **b** a farmer of sheep or cattle on a large scale. [3] (in New Zealand) a 19th-century settler who took up large acreage on a Crown lease.

squatter sovereignty NOUN a contemptuous term for **popular sovereignty**, used by its critics.

squat thrust NOUN an exercise in which the hands are kept on the floor with the arms held straight while the legs are straightened out behind and quickly drawn in towards the body again.

squattocracy (skwɒ'tɒkrəsɪ) NOUN *Chiefly Austral* squatters collectively, regarded as rich and influential. See **squatter** (sense 2b).
▹HISTORY C19: from SQUATTER + -CRACY

squaw (skwɔː) NOUN [1] *Offensive* a North American Indian woman. [2] *Slang, usually facetious* a woman or wife.
▹HISTORY C17: of Algonquian origin; compare Natick *squa* female creature

squawk (skwɔːk) NOUN [1] a loud raucous cry; screech. [2] *Informal* a loud complaint or protest. ◆ VERB [3] to utter a squawk or with a squawk. [4] (*intr*) *Informal* to complain loudly.
▹HISTORY C19: of imitative origin
▸'**squawker** NOUN

squaw man NOUN *Derogatory* a White or other non-Indian married to a North American Indian woman.

squeak (skwiːk) NOUN [1] a short shrill cry or high-pitched sound. [2] *Informal* an escape (esp in the phrases **narrow squeak, near squeak**). ◆ VERB [3] to make or cause to make a squeak. [4] (*intr;* usually foll by *through* or *by*) to pass with only a narrow margin: *to squeak through an examination.* [5] (*intr*) *Informal* to confess information about oneself or another. [6] (*tr*) to utter with a squeak.
▹HISTORY C17: probably of Scandinavian origin; compare Swedish *skväka* to croak
▸'**squeaker** NOUN ▸'**squeaky** ADJECTIVE ▸'**squeakily** ADVERB ▸'**squeakiness** NOUN

squeaky-clean ADJECTIVE [1] (of hair) washed so clean that wet strands squeak when rubbed. [2] completely clean. [3] *Informal, derogatory* (of a person) cultivating a virtuous and wholesome image.

squeal (skwiːl) NOUN [1] a high shrill yelp, as of pain. [2] a screaming sound, as of tyres when a car brakes suddenly. ◆ VERB [3] to utter a squeal or with a squeal. [4] (*intr*) *Slang* to confess information about another. [5] (*intr*) *Informal, chiefly Brit* to complain or protest loudly.
▹HISTORY C13 *squelen*, of imitative origin
▸'**squealer** NOUN

squeamish ('skwiːmɪʃ) ADJECTIVE [1] easily sickened or nauseated, as by the sight of blood. [2] easily shocked; fastidious or prudish. [3] easily frightened: *squeamish about spiders.*
▹HISTORY C15: from Anglo-French *escoymous*, of unknown origin
▸'**squeamishly** ADVERB ▸'**squeamishness** NOUN

squeegee ('skwiːdʒiː) *or less commonly* **squilgee** NOUN [1] an implement with a rubber blade used for wiping away surplus water from a surface, such as a windowpane. [2] any of various similar devices used in photography for pressing the water out of wet prints or negatives or for squeezing prints onto a glazing surface. ◆ VERB **-gees, -geeing, -geed.** [3] to remove (water or other liquid) from (something) by use of a squeegee. [4] (*tr*) to press down (a photographic print, etc.) with a squeegee.
▹HISTORY C19: probably of imitative origin, influenced by SQUEEZE

squeeze (skwiːz) VERB (*mainly tr*) [1] to grip or press firmly, esp so as to crush or distort; compress. [2] to crush or press (something) so as to extract (a liquid): *to squeeze the juice from an orange; to squeeze an orange.* [3] to apply gentle pressure to, as in affection or reassurance: *he squeezed her hand.* [4] to push or force in a confined space: *to squeeze six lettuces into one box; to squeeze through a crowd.* [5] to hug closely. [6] to oppress with exacting demands, such as excessive taxes. [7] to exert pressure on (someone) in order to extort (something): *to squeeze money out of a victim by blackmail.* [8] (*intr*) to yield under pressure. [9] to make an impression of (a coin, etc.) in a soft substance. [10] *Bridge, whist* to lead a card that forces (opponents) to discard potentially winning cards. ◆ NOUN [11] the act or an instance of squeezing or of being squeezed. [12] a hug or handclasp. [13] a crush of people in a confined space. [14] *Chiefly Brit* a condition of restricted credit imposed by a government to counteract price inflation. [15] an impression, esp of a coin, etc., made in a soft substance. [16] an amount extracted by squeezing: *add a squeeze of lemon juice.* [17] *Commerce* any action taken by a trader or traders on a market that forces buyers to make purchases and prices to rise. [18] *Informal* pressure brought to bear in order to extort something (esp in the phrase **put the squeeze on**). [19] Also called: **squeeze play.** *Bridge, whist* a manoeuvre that forces opponents to discard potentially winning cards. [20] *Informal* a person with whom one is having a romantic relationship.
▹HISTORY C16: from Middle English *queysen* to press, from Old English *cwȳsan*
▸'**squeezable** ADJECTIVE ▸'**squeezer** NOUN

squeeze-box NOUN an informal name for **concertina, accordion.**

squelch (skwɛltʃ) VERB [1] (*intr*) to walk laboriously through soft wet material or with wet shoes, making a sucking noise. [2] (*intr*) to make such a noise. [3] (*tr*) to crush completely; squash. [4] (*tr*) *Informal* to silence, as by a crushing retort. ◆ NOUN [5] a squelching sound. [6] something that has been squelched. [7] *Electronics* a circuit that cuts off the audio-frequency amplifier of a radio receiver in the absence of an input signal, in order to suppress background noise. [8] *Informal* a crushing remark.
▹HISTORY C17: of imitative origin
▸'**squelcher** NOUN ▸'**squelching** ADJECTIVE ▸'**squelchy** ADJECTIVE

squeteague (skwɪ'tiːg) NOUN, *plural* **-teague** *or* **-teagues.** any of various sciaenid food fishes of the genus *Cynoscion*, esp *C. regalis*, of the North American coast of the Atlantic Ocean.
▹HISTORY C19: from Narraganset *pesukwiteag*, literally: they give glue; so called because glue is made from them

squib (skwɪb) NOUN [1] a firework, usually having a tube filled with gunpowder, that burns with a hissing noise and culminates in a small explosion. [2] a firework that does not explode because of a fault; dud. [3] a short witty attack; lampoon. [4] an electric device for firing a rocket engine. [5] *Obsolete* an insignificant person. [6] *Austral and NZ slang* a coward. [7] **damp squib.** something intended but failing to impress. ◆ VERB **squibs, squibbing, squibbed.** [8] (*intr*) to sound, move, or explode like a squib. [9] (*intr*) to let off or shoot a squib. [10] to write a squib against (someone). [11] (*intr*) to move in a quick irregular fashion. [12] (*intr*) *Austral slang* to behave in a cowardly fashion.
▹HISTORY C16: probably imitative of a quick light explosion

squid[1] (skwɪd) NOUN, *plural* **squid** *or* **squids.** [1] any of various fast-moving pelagic cephalopod molluscs of the genera *Loligo, Ommastrephes*, etc., of most seas, having a torpedo-shaped body ranging from about 10 centimetres to 16.5 metres long and a pair of triangular tail fins: order *Decapoda* (decapods). See also **cuttlefish.** ◆ VERB **squids, squidding, squidded.** [2] (*intr*) (of a parachute) to assume an elongated squidlike shape owing to excess air pressure.

▹HISTORY C17: of unknown origin

squid² (skwɪd) NOUN *Brit slang* a pound sterling.
▹HISTORY C20: rhyming slang for QUID

SQUID ABBREVIATION FOR superconducting quantum interference device.

squidgy ('skwɪdʒɪ) ADJECTIVE **squidgier, squidgiest.** soft, moist, and squashy.
▹HISTORY of imitative origin

squiffy ('skwɪfɪ) ADJECTIVE **-fier, -fiest.** *Brit informal* slightly drunk. Also: **squiffed.**
▹HISTORY C19: of unknown origin

squiggle ('skwɪgᵊl) NOUN 1 a mark or movement in the form of a wavy line; curlicue. 2 an illegible scrawl. ◆ VERB 3 *(intr)* to wriggle. 4 *(intr)* to form or draw squiggles. 5 *(tr)* to make into squiggles.
▹HISTORY C19: perhaps a blend of SQUIRM + WIGGLE
▸'**squiggler** NOUN ▸'**squiggly** ADJECTIVE

squilgee ('skwɪldʒiː) NOUN a variant of **squeegee.**
▹HISTORY C19: perhaps from SQUEEGEE, influenced by SQUELCH

squill (skwɪl) NOUN 1 See **sea squill.** 2 the bulb of the sea squill, formerly used medicinally as an expectorant after being sliced and dried. 3 any Old World liliaceous plant of the genus *Scilla*, such as *S. verna* (**spring squill**) of Europe, having small blue or purple flowers.
▹HISTORY C14: from Latin *squilla* sea onion, from Greek *skilla*, of obscure origin

squilla ('skwɪlə) NOUN, *plural* **-las** *or* **-lae** (-liː). any mantis shrimp of the genus *Squilla*.
▹HISTORY C16: from Latin *squilla* shrimp, of obscure origin

squillion ('skwɪljən) *Informal* ◆ NOUN, *plural* **-lions** *or* **-lion.** 1 *(often plural)* an extremely large but unspecified number, quantity, or amount. ◆ DETERMINER 2 **a** amounting to a squillion. **b** *(as pronoun)*: *there were squillions of them everywhere.*

squinch (skwɪntʃ) NOUN a small arch, corbelling, etc., across an internal corner of a tower, used to support a superstructure such as a spire. Also called: **squinch arch.**
▹HISTORY C15: from obsolete *scunch*, from Middle English *sconcheon*, from Old French *escoinson*, from *es-* EX-¹ + *coin* corner

squint (skwɪnt) VERB 1 *(usually intr)* to cross or partly close (the eyes). 2 *(intr)* to have a squint. 3 *(intr)* to look or glance sideways or askance. ◆ NOUN 4 the nontechnical name for **strabismus.** 5 the act or an instance of squinting; glimpse. 6 Also called: **hagioscope.** a narrow oblique opening in a wall or pillar of a church to permit a view of the main altar from a side aisle or transept. 7 *Informal* a quick look; glance. ◆ ADJECTIVE 8 having a squint. 9 *Informal* crooked; askew.
▹HISTORY C14: short for ASQUINT
▸'**squinter** NOUN ▸'**squinty** ADJECTIVE

squint-eyed *or* **squinty-eyed** ADJECTIVE 1 having a squint. 2 looking sidelong.

squire (skwaɪə) NOUN 1 a country gentleman in England, esp the main landowner in a rural community. 2 *Feudal history* a young man of noble birth, who attended upon a knight. 3 *Rare* a man who courts or escorts a woman. 4 *Informal, chiefly Brit* a term of address used by one man to another, esp, unless ironic, to a member of a higher social class. 5 *Austral* an immature snapper (see **snapper** (sense 2)). ◆ VERB 6 *(tr)* (of a man) to escort (a woman).
▹HISTORY C13: from Old French *esquier*; see ESQUIRE

squirearchy *or* **squirarchy** ('skwaɪəˌrɑːkɪ) NOUN, *plural* **-chies.** 1 government by squires. 2 squires collectively, esp as a political or social force.
▹HISTORY C19: from SQUIRE + -ARCHY, on the model of HIERARCHY, MONARCHY, etc.
▸**squire'archal** *or* **squir'archal** *or* **squire'archical** *or* **squir'archical** ADJECTIVE

squireen (skwaɪ'riːn) *or* **squireling** ('skwaɪəlɪŋ) NOUN *Rare* a petty squire.
▹HISTORY C19: from SQUIRE + *-een*, Anglo-Irish diminutive suffix, from Irish Gaelic *-ín*

squirm (skwɜːm) VERB *(intr)* 1 to move with a wriggling motion; writhe. 2 to feel deep mental discomfort, guilt, embarrassment, etc. ◆ NOUN 3 a squirming movement.
▹HISTORY C17: of imitative origin (perhaps influenced by WORM)
▸'**squirmer** NOUN ▸'**squirming** ADJECTIVE ▸'**squirmingly** ADVERB

squirmy ('skwɜːmɪ) ADJECTIVE 1 moving with a wriggling motion. 2 making one squirm.

squirrel ('skwɪrəl; *US* 'skwɜːrəl, 'skwʌr-) NOUN, *plural* **-rels** *or* **-rel.** 1 any arboreal sciurine rodent of the genus *Sciurus*, such as *S. vulgaris* (**red squirrel**) or *S. carolinensis* (**grey squirrel**), having a bushy tail and feeding on nuts, seeds, etc. Related adjective: **sciurine.** 2 any other rodent of the family *Sciuridae*, such as a ground squirrel or a marmot. 3 the fur of such an animal. 4 *Informal* a person who hoards things. ◆ VERB **-rels, -relling, -relled** *or esp US* **-rels, -reling, -reled.** 5 *(tr; usually foll by away) Informal* to store for future use; hoard.
▹HISTORY C14: from Old French *esquireul*, from Late Latin *sciūrus*, from Greek *skiouros*, from *skia* shadow + *oura* tail
▸'**squirrel-ˌlike** ADJECTIVE

squirrel cage NOUN 1 a cage consisting of a cylindrical framework that is made to rotate by a small animal running inside the framework. 2 a repetitive purposeless task, way of life, etc. 3 Also called: **squirrel-cage motor.** *Electrical engineering* the rotor of an induction motor with a cylindrical winding having copper bars around the periphery parallel to the axis. 4 an electric fan with many long narrow blades arranged in parallel so as to form a cylinder about an axis around which they spin.

squirrel corn NOUN a North American plant, *Dicentra canadensis*, having yellow flowers and tubers resembling grains of corn: family *Fumariaceae*. Also called: **colicweed.**

squirrelfish ('skwɪrəlˌfɪʃ) NOUN, *plural* **-fish** *or* **-fishes.** any tropical marine brightly coloured teleost fish of the family *Holocentridae*.
▹HISTORY C18: so called because it can make a squirrel-like noise

squirrel monkey NOUN 1 a small New World monkey, *Saimiri sciureus*, of N South American forests, having a yellowish-green coat and orange feet and limbs. 2 **red-backed squirrel monkey.** a related species, *Saimiri oerstedi*, of Central America, having a reddish coat and dark brown limbs.
▹HISTORY C18: so called because it is small and tree-dwelling

squirrel-tail grass NOUN an annual grass, *Hordeum marinum*, of salt marsh margins of Europe, having bushy awns.

squirt (skwɜːt) VERB 1 to force (a liquid) or (of a liquid) to be forced out of a narrow opening. 2 *(tr)* to cover or spatter with liquid so ejected. ◆ NOUN 3 a jet or amount of liquid so ejected. 4 the act or an instance of squirting. 5 an instrument used for squirting. 6 *Informal* **a** a person regarded as insignificant or contemptible. **b** a short person.
▹HISTORY C15: of imitative origin
▸'**squirter** NOUN

squirt gun NOUN *US and Canadian* another name for **water pistol.**

squirting cucumber NOUN a hairy cucurbitaceous plant, *Ecballium elaterium*, of the Mediterranean region, having a fruit that discharges its seeds explosively when ripe.

squish (skwɪʃ) VERB 1 *(tr)* to crush, esp so as to make a soft splashing noise. 2 *(intr)* (of mud, etc.) to make a splashing noise: *the ground squishes as you tread.* ◆ NOUN 3 a soft squashing sound: *the ripe peach fell with a squish.*
▹HISTORY C17: of imitative origin

squishy ('skwɪʃɪ) ADJECTIVE **-ier, -iest.** soft and yielding to the touch.

squit (skwɪt) NOUN *Brit slang* 1 an insignificant person. 2 nonsense; rubbish.
▹HISTORY C19: dialectal variant of SQUIRT

squiz (skwɪz) NOUN, *plural* **squizzes.** *Austral and NZ slang* a look or glance, esp an inquisitive one.
▹HISTORY C20: perhaps a blend of SQUINT and QUIZ

sr¹ SYMBOL FOR steradian.

sr² THE INTERNET DOMAIN NAME FOR Surinam.

Sr ABBREVIATION FOR: 1 (after a name) senior. 2 Señor. 3 Sir. 4 Sister (religious). ◆ 5 THE CHEMICAL SYMBOL FOR strontium.

Sra ABBREVIATION FOR Señora.

SRA (in Britain) ABBREVIATION FOR Strategic Rail Authority.

Srbija ('sᵊrbija) NOUN the Serbian name for **Serbia.**

S-R connection NOUN *Psychol* stimulus-response connection; the basic unit of learning according to behaviourist learning theory. See also **reflex arc.**

Sri (ʃriː) NOUN *Hinduism* 1 the consort of Vishnu. 2 a title of honour used when addressing a distinguished Hindu.
▹HISTORY literally: majesty, holiness

Sri Lanka (ˌsriː 'læŋkə) NOUN a republic in S Asia, occupying the island of Ceylon: settled by the Sinhalese from S India in about 550 B.C.; became a British colony 1802; gained independence in 1948, becoming a republic within the Commonwealth in 1972. Exports include tea, cocoa, cinnamon, and copra. Official languages: Sinhalese and Tamil; English is also widely spoken. Religion: Hinayana Buddhist majority. Currency: Sri Lanka rupee. Capital: Colombo (administrative), Sri Jayewardenepura Kotte (legislative). Pop.: 19 399 000 (2001 est.). Area: 65 610 sq. km (25 332 sq. miles). Official name (since 1978): **Democratic Socialist Republic of Sri Lanka.** Former name (until 1972): **Ceylon.**

Sri Lankan (ˌsriː 'læŋkən) ADJECTIVE 1 of or relating to Sri Lanka or its inhabitants. ◆ NOUN 2 a native or inhabitant of Sri Lanka.

Srinagar (sriː'nʌgə) NOUN a city in N India, the summer capital of the state of Jammu and Kashmir, at an altitude of 1600 m (5250 ft.) on the Jhelum River: seat of the University of Jammu and Kashmir (1948). Pop.: 586 038 (1991).

SRN (formerly, in Britain) ABBREVIATION FOR State Registered Nurse.

SRO ABBREVIATION FOR: 1 standing room only. 2 *Brit* Statutory Rules and Orders. 3 self-regulatory organization.

Srta ABBREVIATION FOR Señorita.

SS ABBREVIATION FOR: 1 a paramilitary organization within the Nazi party that provided Hitler's bodyguard, security forces including the Gestapo, concentration camp guards, and a corp of combat troops (the Waffen-SS) in World War II. [German *Schutzstaffel* protection squad] 2 steamship. 3 Sunday school.

SS. ABBREVIATION FOR Saints.

SSB ABBREVIATION FOR single sideband (transmission).

SSC ABBREVIATION FOR: 1 (in India) Secondary School Certificate. 2 (in Scotland) solicitor to the Supreme Court.

SSD (in Britain) ABBREVIATION FOR Social Services Department.

SSE SYMBOL FOR south-southeast.

SSHA ABBREVIATION FOR Scottish Special Housing Association.

SSM ABBREVIATION FOR surface-to-surface missile.

SSN ABBREVIATION FOR severely subnormal; used of a person of very limited intelligence who needs special schooling.

SSP (in Britain) ABBREVIATION FOR statutory sick pay.

ssp. *plural* **sspp.** *Biology* ABBREVIATION FOR subspecies.

SSR ABBREVIATION FOR (formerly) Soviet Socialist Republic.

SSRI ABBREVIATION FOR selective serotonin reuptake inhibitor; any of a class of drugs, including fluvoxamine, paroxetine, fluoxetine (Prozac), and Lustral, that increase concentrations of serotonin in the brain: used in the treatment of depression.

SSSI (in Britain) ABBREVIATION FOR site of special scientific interest: an area identified by the Nature Conservancy Council or its successors as having flora, fauna, or geological features of special interest.

SST ABBREVIATION FOR supersonic transport.

SSTA ABBREVIATION FOR Scottish Secondary Teachers' Association.

SSW SYMBOL FOR south-southwest.

st¹ ABBREVIATION FOR short ton.

st² THE INTERNET DOMAIN NAME FOR São Tomé and Principe.

St ABBREVIATION FOR Saint (all entries that are usually preceded by *St* are in this dictionary listed alphabetically under **Saint**).

st. ABBREVIATION FOR: 1 stanza. 2 statute. 3 *Cricket* stumped by.

St. ABBREVIATION FOR: [1] statute. [2] Strait. [3] Street.

-st SUFFIX a variant of **-est**².

Sta (in the names of places or churches) ABBREVIATION FOR Saint (female).
▷HISTORY Italian *Santa*

stab (stæb) VERB **stabs, stabbing, stabbed.** [1] *(tr)* to pierce or injure with a sharp pointed instrument. [2] *(tr)* (of a sharp pointed instrument) to pierce or wound: *the knife stabbed her hand.* [3] (when *intr*, often foll by *at*) to make a thrust (at); jab: *he stabbed at the doorway.* [4] *(tr)* to inflict with a sharp pain. [5] **stab in the back. a** *(verb)* to do damage to the reputation of (a person, esp a friend) in a surreptitious way. **b** *(noun)* a treacherous action or remark that causes the downfall of or injury to a person. ◆ NOUN [6] the act or an instance of stabbing. [7] an injury or rift made by stabbing. [8] a sudden sensation, esp an unpleasant one: *a stab of pity.* [9] *Informal* an attempt (esp in the phrase **make a stab at**).
▷HISTORY C14: from *stabbe* stab wound; probably related to Middle English *stob* stick
▸'**stabber** NOUN

Stabat Mater ('stɑːbæt 'mɑːtə) NOUN [1] *RC Church* a Latin hymn, probably of the 13th century, commemorating the sorrows of the Virgin Mary at the crucifixion and used in the Mass and various other services. [2] a musical setting of this hymn.
▷HISTORY from the opening words, literally: the mother was standing

stabile ('steɪbaɪl) NOUN [1] *Arts* a stationary abstract construction, usually of wire, metal, wood, etc. Compare **mobile** (sense 6a). ◆ ADJECTIVE [2] fixed; stable. [3] resistant to chemical change.
▷HISTORY C18: from Latin *stabilis*

stability (stə'bɪlɪtɪ) NOUN, *plural* **-ties.** [1] the quality of being stable. [2] the ability of an aircraft to resume its original flight path after inadvertent displacement. [3] *Meteorol* **a** the condition of an air or water mass characterized by no upward movement. **b** the degree of susceptibility of an air mass to disturbance by convection currents. [4] *Ecology* the ability of an ecosystem to resist change. [5] *Electrical engineering* the ability of an electrical circuit to cope with changes in the operational conditions. [6] a vow taken by every Benedictine monk attaching him perpetually to the monastery where he is professed.

stability pact *or* **stability and growth pact** NOUN an agreement between the member states of the EU which have joined the single currency, the aim of which is to secure the currency's stability by imposing fines on member states whose budget deficits exceed 3 per cent of their gross domestic product.

stabilize *or* **stabilise** ('steɪbɪˌlaɪz) VERB [1] to make or become stable or more stable. [2] to keep or be kept stable. [3] to put or keep (an aircraft, vessel, etc.) in equilibrium by one or more special devices, or (of an aircraft, vessel, etc.) to become stable.
▸ˌ**stabiliˈzation** *or* ˌ**stabiliˈsation** NOUN

stabilizer *or* **stabiliser** ('steɪbɪˌlaɪzə) NOUN [1] any device for stabilizing an aircraft. See also **horizontal stabilizer, vertical stabilizer.** [2] a substance added to something to maintain it in a stable or unchanging state, such as an additive to food to preserve its texture during distribution and storage. [3] *Nautical* **a** a system of one or more pairs of fins projecting from the hull of a ship and controllable to counteract roll. **b** See **gyrostabilizer.** [4] either of a pair of brackets supporting a small wheel that can be fitted to the back wheel of a bicycle to help an inexperienced cyclist to maintain balance. [5] an electronic device for producing a direct current supply of constant voltage. [6] *Economics* a measure, such as progressive taxation, interest-rate control, or unemployment benefit, used to restrict swings in prices, employment, production, etc., in a free economy. [7] a person or thing that stabilizes.

stab kick NOUN *Australian Rules football* a rapid kick of the ball from one player to another member of his team. Also called: **stab pass.**

stable¹ ('steɪbᵊl) NOUN [1] a building, usually consisting of stalls, for the lodging of horses or other livestock. [2] the animals lodged in such a building, collectively. [3] **a** the racehorses belonging to a particular establishment or owner. **b** the establishment itself. **c** *(as modifier)*: *stable companion.* [4] *Informal* a source of training, such as a school, theatre, etc.: *the two athletes were out of the same stable.* [5] a number of people considered as a source of a particular talent: *a stable of writers.* [6] *(modifier)* of, relating to, or suitable for a stable: *stable manners.* ◆ VERB [7] to put, keep, or be kept in a stable.
▷HISTORY C13: from Old French *estable* cowshed, from Latin *stabulum* shed, from *stāre* to stand

stable² ('steɪbᵊl) ADJECTIVE [1] steady in position or balance; firm. [2] lasting or permanent: *a stable relationship.* [3] steadfast or firm of purpose. [4] (of an elementary particle, atomic nucleus, etc.) not undergoing decay; not radioactive: *a stable nuclide.* [5] (of a chemical compound) not readily partaking in a chemical change. [6] (of electronic equipment) with no tendency to self-oscillation.
▷HISTORY C13: from Old French *estable*, from Latin *stabilis* steady, from *stāre* to stand
▸'**stableness** NOUN ▸'**stably** ADVERB

stableboy ('steɪbᵊlˌbɔɪ) *or* **stableman** ('steɪbᵊlˌmæn, -mən) NOUN, *plural* **-boys** *or* **-men.** a boy or man who works in a stable.

stable door NOUN a door with an upper and lower leaf that may be opened separately. US and Canadian equivalent: **Dutch door.**

stable fly NOUN a blood-sucking muscid fly, *Stomoxys calcitrans*, that attacks man and domestic animals.

Stableford ('steɪbᵊlfəd) NOUN *Golf* **a** a scoring system in which points are awarded according to the number of strokes taken at each hole, whereby a hole completed in one stroke over par counts as one point, a hole completed in level par counts as two points, etc. **b** *(as modifier)*: *a Stableford competition.* Compare **match play, stroke play.**
▷HISTORY C20: named after its inventor, Dr Frank *Stableford* (1870–1959), English amateur golfer

stable lad NOUN a person who looks after the horses in a racing stable.

stabling ('steɪblɪŋ) NOUN stable buildings or accommodation.

stablish ('stæblɪʃ) VERB an archaic variant of **establish.**

Stabroek (*Dutch* 'staːbruːk) NOUN the former name (until 1812) of **Georgetown** (sense 1).

stacc. *Music* ABBREVIATION FOR staccato.

staccato (stə'kɑːtəʊ) ADJECTIVE [1] *Music* (of notes) short, clipped, and separate. [2] characterized by short abrupt sounds, as in speech: *a staccato command.* ◆ ADVERB [3] (esp used as a musical direction) in a staccato manner.
▷HISTORY C18: from Italian, from *staccare* to detach, shortened from *distaccare*

stachys ('steɪkɪs) NOUN any plant of the genus *Stachys*, esp *S. lanata* (lamb's ears) and *S. officinalis* (betony).
▷HISTORY New Latin, from Greek *stachys* ear of corn, used as a plant name

stack (stæk) NOUN [1] an ordered pile or heap. [2] a large orderly pile of hay, straw, etc., for storage in the open air. [3] *(often plural) Library science* compactly spaced bookshelves, used to house collections of books in an area usually prohibited to library users. [4] a number of aircraft circling an airport at different altitudes, awaiting their signal to land. [5] a large amount: *a stack of work.* [6] *Military* a pile of rifles or muskets in the shape of a cone. [7] *Brit* a measure of coal or wood equal to 108 cubic feet. [8] See **chimney stack, smokestack.** [9] a vertical pipe, such as the funnel of a ship or the soil pipe attached to the side of a building. [10] a high column of rock, esp one isolated from the mainland by the erosive action of the sea. [11] an area in a computer memory for temporary storage. ◆ VERB *(tr)* [12] to place in a stack; pile: *to stack bricks on a lorry.* [13] to load or fill up with piles of something: *to stack a lorry with bricks.* [14] to control (a number of aircraft waiting to land at an airport) so that each flies at a different altitude. [15] **stack the cards.** to prearrange the order of a pack of cards secretly so that the deal will benefit someone.
▷HISTORY C13: from Old Norse *stakkr* haystack, of Germanic origin; related to Russian *stog*
▸'**stackable** ADJECTIVE ▸'**stacker** NOUN

stacked (stækt) ADJECTIVE *Slang* a variant of **well-stacked.**

stacking ('stækɪŋ) NOUN the arrangement of aircraft traffic in busy flight lanes, esp while waiting to land at an airport, with a minimum vertical separation for safety of 1000 feet below 29 000 feet and 2000 feet above 29 000 feet.

stacking truck NOUN another name for **pallet truck.**

stacte ('stæktiː) NOUN *Old Testament* one of several sweet-smelling spices used in incense (Exodus 30:34).
▷HISTORY C14: via Latin from Greek *staktē* oil of myrrh, from *staktos* distilling a drop at a time, from *stazein* to flow, drip

staddle ('stædᵊl) NOUN [1] a support or prop, esp a low flat-topped stone structure for supporting hay or corn stacks about two feet above ground level. [2] a supporting frame for such a stack. [3] the lower part of a hay or corn stack.
▷HISTORY Old English *stathol* base; related to Old Norse *stothull* cow pen, Old High German *stadal* barn

staddlestone ('stædᵊlˌstəʊn) NOUN (formerly) one of several supports for a hayrick, consisting of a truncated conical stone surmounted by a flat circular stone.

stadholder *or* **stadtholder** ('stædˌhəʊldə) NOUN [1] the chief magistrate of the former Dutch republic or of any of its provinces (from about 1580 to 1802). [2] a viceroy or governor of a province.
▷HISTORY C16: partial translation of Dutch *stad houder*, from *stad* city (see STEAD) + *houder* holder
▸'**stadˌholderˌate** *or* '**stadˌholdership** *or* '**stadtˌholderˌate** *or* '**stadtˌholdership** NOUN

stadia¹ ('steɪdɪə) NOUN [1] **a** tacheometry that makes use of a telescopic surveying instrument and a graduated staff calibrated to correspond with the distance from the observer. **b** *(as modifier)*: *stadia surveying.* [2] the two parallel cross hairs or **stadia hairs** in the eyepiece of the instrument used. [3] the staff used.
▷HISTORY C19: probably from STADIA²

stadia² ('steɪdɪə) NOUN a plural of **stadium.**

stadiometer (ˌsteɪdɪ'ɒmɪtə) NOUN an instrument that measures the length of curves, dashes, etc., by running a toothed wheel along them.
▷HISTORY C19: from *stadio-*, from STADIUM + -METER

stadium ('steɪdɪəm) NOUN, *plural* **-diums** *or* **-dia** (-dɪə). [1] a sports arena with tiered seats for spectators. [2] (in ancient Greece) a course for races, usually located between two hills providing natural slopes for tiers of seats. [3] an ancient Greek measure of length equivalent to about 607 feet or 184 metres. [4] (in many arthropods) the interval between two consecutive moultings. [5] *Obsolete* a particular period or stage in the development of a disease.
▷HISTORY C16: via Latin from Greek *stadion*, changed from *spadion* a racecourse, from *spān* to pull; also influenced by Greek *stadios* steady

staff¹ (stɑːf) NOUN, *plural* **staffs** *for senses 1, 3, 4 or* **staffs** *or* **staves** (steɪvz) *for senses 5–9* [1] a group of people employed by a company, individual, etc., for executive, clerical, sales work, etc. [2] *(modifier)* attached to or provided for the staff of an establishment: *a staff doctor.* [3] the body of teachers or lecturers of an educational institution, as distinct from the students. [4] the officers appointed to assist a commander, service, or central headquarters organization in establishing policy, plans, etc. [5] a stick with some special use, such as a walking stick or an emblem of authority. [6] something that sustains or supports: *bread is the staff of life.* [7] a pole on which a flag is hung. [8] *Chiefly Brit* a graduated rod used in surveying, esp for sighting to with a levelling instrument. Usual US name: **rod.** [9] Also called: **stave.** *Music* **a** the system of horizontal lines grouped into sets of five (four in the case of plainsong) upon which music is written. The spaces between them are also used, being employed in conjunction with a clef in order to give a graphic indication of pitch. **b** any set of five lines in this system together with its clef: *the treble staff.* ◆ VERB [10] *(tr)* to provide with a staff.
▷HISTORY Old English *stæf*; related to Old Frisian *stef*, Old Saxon *staf*, German *Stab*, Old Norse *stafr*, Gothic *Stafs*; see STAVE

staff² (stɑːf) NOUN *US* a mixture of plaster and hair used to cover the external surface of temporary structures and for decoration.

▷HISTORY C19: of unknown origin

Staffa (ˈstæfə) NOUN an island in W Scotland, in the Inner Hebrides west of Mull: site of Fingal's Cave.

staff association NOUN an association of employees that performs some of the functions of a trade union, such as representing its members in discussions with the management, and may also have other social and professional purposes.

staff college NOUN a training centre for executive military personnel.

staff corporal NOUN a noncommissioned rank in the British Army above that of staff sergeant and below that of warrant officer.

staffer (ˈstɑːfə) NOUN *Informal* a member of staff, esp, in journalism, of editorial staff.

staffman (ˈstɑːfˌmæn) NOUN, *plural* **-men**. *Brit* a person who holds the levelling staff when a survey is being made.

staff nurse NOUN (formerly, in Britain) a qualified nurse ranking immediately below a sister.

staff of Aesculapius NOUN an emblem consisting of a staff with a serpent entwined around it, used by the Royal Medical Corps and the American Medical Association. Compare **caduceus** (sense 2).

staff officer NOUN a commissioned officer serving on the staff of a commander, service, or central headquarters.

Stafford (ˈstæfəd) NOUN a market town in central England, administrative centre of Staffordshire. Pop.: 61 885 (1991).

Staffordshire (ˈstæfədˌʃɪə, -ʃə) NOUN a county of central England: lowlands in the east and south rise to the Pennine uplands in the north; important in the history of industry, coal and iron having been worked at least as early as the 13th century. In 1974 the industrial area in the S passed to the new county of West Midlands; Stoke-on-Trent became an independent unitary authority in 1997. Administrative centre: Stafford. Pop. (excluding Stoke-on-Trent): 806 737 (2001). Area (excluding Stoke-on-Trent): 2624 sq. km (1013 sq. miles).

Staffordshire bull terrier NOUN a breed of smooth-coated terrier with a stocky frame and generally a pied or brindled coat. See also **bull terrier**.

Staffs (stæfs) ABBREVIATION FOR Staffordshire.

staff sergeant NOUN *Military* [1] *Brit* a noncommissioned officer holding a rank between sergeant and warrant officer and employed on administrative duties. [2] *US* a noncommissioned officer who ranks. **a** (in the Army) above sergeant and below sergeant first class. **b** (in the Air Force) above airman first class and below technical sergeant. **c** (in the Marine Corps) above sergeant and below gunnery sergeant.

stag (stæg) NOUN [1] the adult male of a deer, esp a red deer. [2] a man unaccompanied by a woman at a social gathering. [3] *Stock Exchange, Brit* **a** a speculator who applies for shares in a new issue in anticipation of a rise in price when trading commences in order to make a quick profit on resale. **b** (*as modifier*): *stag operations*. [4] (*modifier*) (of a social gathering) attended by men only. [5] (*modifier*) pornographic in content: *a stag show*. ◆ ADVERB [6] without a female escort. ◆ VERB (*tr*) [7] *Stock Exchange* to apply for (shares in a new issue) with the intention of selling them for a quick profit when trading commences.

▷HISTORY Old English *stagga* (unattested); related to Old Norse *steggr* male bird

stag beetle NOUN any lamellicorn beetle of the family *Lucanidae*, the males of which have large branched mandibles.

stage (steɪdʒ) NOUN [1] a distinct step or period of development, growth, or progress: *a child at the toddling stage*. [2] a raised area or platform. [3] the platform in a theatre where actors perform. [4] **the**. the theatre as a profession. [5] any scene regarded as a setting for an event or action. [6] a portion of a journey or a stopping place after such a portion. [7] short for **stagecoach**. [8] *Brit* a division of a bus route for which there is a fixed fare. [9] one of the separate propulsion units of a rocket that can be jettisoned when it has burnt out. See also **multistage** (sense 1). [10] any of the various distinct periods of growth or development in the life of an organism, esp an insect: *a larval stage; pupal stage*. [11] the organism itself at such a period of growth. [12] a small stratigraphical unit; a subdivision of a rock series or system. [13] the platform on a microscope on which the specimen is mounted for examination. [14] *Electronics* a part of a complex circuit, esp one of a number of transistors with the associated elements required to amplify a signal in an amplifier. [15] a university subject studied for one academic year: *Stage II French*. [16] **by** *or* **in easy stages**. not hurriedly: *he learned French by easy stages*. ◆ VERB [17] (*tr*) to perform (a play), esp on a stage: *we are going to stage "Hamlet"*. [18] (*tr*) to set the action of (a play) in a particular time or place. [19] (*tr*) to plan, organize, and carry out (an event). [20] (*intr*) *Obsolete* to travel by stagecoach.

▷HISTORY C13: from Old French *estage* position, from Vulgar Latin *staticum* (unattested), from Latin *stāre* to stand

stagecoach (ˈsteɪdʒˌkəʊtʃ) NOUN a large four-wheeled horse-drawn vehicle formerly used to carry passengers, mail, etc., on a regular route between towns and cities.

stagecraft (ˈsteɪdʒˌkrɑːft) NOUN skill in or the art of writing or staging plays.

stage direction NOUN *Theatre* an instruction to an actor or director, written into the script of a play.

stage-dive VERB (*intr*) to jump off the stage at a concert onto the crowd below.

▸ **ˈstage-ˌdiver** NOUN

stage door NOUN a door at a theatre leading backstage.

stage effect NOUN a special effect created on the stage by lighting, sound, etc.

stage fright NOUN nervousness or panic that may beset a person about to appear in front of an audience.

stagehand (ˈsteɪdʒˌhænd) NOUN a person who sets the stage, moves props, etc., in a theatrical production.

stage left NOUN the part of the stage to the left of a performer facing the audience.

stage-manage VERB [1] to work as stage manager for (a play, etc.). [2] (*tr*) to arrange, present, or supervise from behind the scenes: *to stage-manage a campaign*.

stage manager NOUN a person who supervises the stage arrangements of a theatrical production.

stager (ˈsteɪdʒə) NOUN [1] a person of experience; veteran (esp in the phrase **old stager**). [2] an archaic word for **actor**.

stage right NOUN the part of the stage to the right of a performer facing the audience.

stage-struck ADJECTIVE infatuated with the glamour of theatrical life, esp with the desire to act.

stage whisper NOUN [1] a loud whisper from one actor to another onstage intended to be heard by the audience. [2] any loud whisper that is intended to be overheard.

stagey (ˈsteɪdʒɪ) ADJECTIVE **stagier, stagiest**. a variant spelling (in the US) of **stagy**.

▸ **ˈstagily** ADVERB ▸ **ˈstaginess** NOUN

stagflation (stægˈfleɪʃən) NOUN a situation in which inflation is combined with stagnant or falling output and employment.

▷HISTORY C20: blend of STAGNATION + INFLATION

staggard (ˈstægəd) NOUN a male red deer in the fourth year of life.

▷HISTORY C15: see STAG, -ARD

stagger (ˈstægə) VERB [1] (*usually intr*) to walk or cause to walk unsteadily as if about to fall. [2] (*tr*) to astound or overwhelm, as with shock: *I am staggered by his ruthlessness*. [3] (*tr*) to place or arrange in alternating or overlapping positions or time periods to prevent confusion or congestion: *a staggered junction; to stagger holidays*. [4] (*intr*) to falter or hesitate: *his courage staggered in the face of the battle*. [5] (*tr*) to set (the wings of a biplane) so that the leading edge of one extends beyond that of the other. ◆ NOUN [6] the act or an instance of staggering. [7] a staggered arrangement on a biplane, etc. ◆ See also **staggers**.

▷HISTORY C13 dialect *stacker*, from Old Norse *staka* to push

▸ **ˈstaggerer** NOUN

staggerbush (ˈstægəˌbʊʃ) NOUN an ericaceous deciduous shrub, *Lyonia mariana*, of E North America, having white or pinkish flowers: it is poisonous to livestock.

▷HISTORY C19: so named because it was believed to cause STAGGERS in sheep

staggered directorships PLURAL NOUN *Business* a defence against unwelcome takeover bids in which a company resolves that its directors should serve staggered terms of office and that no director can be removed from office without just cause, thus preventing a bidder from controlling the board for some years.

staggered hours PLURAL NOUN a system of working in which the employees of an organization do not all arrive and leave at the same time, but have large periods of overlap.

staggering (ˈstægərɪŋ) ADJECTIVE astounding or overwhelming; shocking: *a staggering increase in demand*.

▸ **ˈstaggeringly** ADVERB

staggers (ˈstægəz) NOUN (*functioning as singular or plural*) [1] a form of vertigo associated with decompression sickness. [2] Also called: **blind staggers**. a disease of horses and some other domestic animals characterized by a swaying unsteady gait, caused by infection, toxins, or lesions of the central nervous system.

staghorn fern (ˈstægˌhɔːn) NOUN any of various tropical and subtropical ferns of the genus *Platycerium* with fronds resembling antlers.

staghound (ˈstægˌhaʊnd) NOUN a breed of hound similar in appearance to the foxhound but larger. It is bred for stag hunting.

staging (ˈsteɪdʒɪŋ) NOUN any temporary structure used in the process of building, esp the horizontal platforms supported by scaffolding.

▷HISTORY C14: from STAGE + -ING[1]

staging area NOUN a general locality used as a checkpoint or regrouping area for military formations in transit.

staging post NOUN a place where a journey is usually broken, esp a stopover on a flight.

Stagira (stəˈdʒaɪrə) NOUN an ancient city on the coast of Chalcidice in Macedonia: the birthplace of Aristotle.

Stagirite (ˈstædʒɪˌraɪt) NOUN [1] an inhabitant or native of Stagira. [2] an epithet of Aristotle.

stagnant (ˈstægnənt) ADJECTIVE [1] (of water, etc.) standing still; without flow or current. [2] brackish and foul from standing still. [3] stale, sluggish, or dull from inaction. [4] not growing or developing; static.

▷HISTORY C17: from Latin *stagnāns*, from *stagnāre* to be stagnant, from *stagnum* a pool

▸ **ˈstagnancy** *or* **ˈstagnance** NOUN ▸ **ˈstagnantly** ADVERB

stagnate (stægˈneɪt, ˈstægˌneɪt) VERB (*intr*) to be or to become stagnant.

▸ **stagˈnation** NOUN

stag night *or* **party** NOUN a party for men only, esp one held for a man before he is married. Compare **hen night, hen party**.

stag's horn *or* **staghorn** (ˈstægˌhɔːn) NOUN [1] the antlers of a stag used as a material for carved implements. [2] a creeping variety of club moss, *Lycopodium clavatum*, growing on moors and mountains, having silvery hair points on its leaves.

stagy *or US* **stagey** (ˈsteɪdʒɪ) ADJECTIVE **stagier, stagiest**. excessively theatrical or dramatic.

▸ **ˈstagily** ADVERB ▸ **ˈstaginess** NOUN

staid (steɪd) ADJECTIVE [1] of a settled, sedate, and steady character. [2] *Now rare* permanent.

▷HISTORY C16: obsolete past participle of STAY[1]

▸ **ˈstaidly** ADVERB ▸ **ˈstaidness** NOUN

stain (steɪn) VERB (*mainly tr*) [1] to mark or discolour with patches of something that dirties: *the dress was stained with coffee*. [2] to dye with a penetrating dyestuff or pigment. [3] to bring disgrace or shame on: *to stain someone's honour*. [4] to colour (specimens) for microscopic study by treatment with a dye or similar reagent. [5] (*intr*) to produce indelible marks or discoloration: *does ink stain?* ◆ NOUN [6] a spot, mark, or discoloration. [7] a moral taint; blemish or slur. [8] a dye or similar reagent, used to colour specimens for microscopic study. [9] a solution or liquid used to penetrate the surface of a material, esp wood, and impart a rich colour without covering up the surface or grain. [10]

any dye that is made into a solution and used to colour textiles and hides.
▷HISTORY C14 *steynen* (vb), shortened from *disteynen* to remove colour from, from Old French *desteindre* to discolour, from *des-* DIS-[1] + *teindre*, from Latin *tingere* to TINGE
▸'**stainable** ADJECTIVE ▸,**staina'bility** NOUN ▸'**stainer** NOUN

stained glass NOUN **a** a glass that has been coloured in any of various ways, as by fusing with a film of metallic oxide or burning pigment into the surface, used esp for church windows. **b** (*as modifier*): *a stained-glass window*.

stained glass ceiling NOUN a situation in a church organization in which promotion for a female member of the clergy appears to be possible, but discrimination prevents it.

Staines (steɪnz) NOUN a town in SE England, in N Surrey on the River Thames. Pop.: 51 167 (1991).

stainless ('steɪnlɪs) ADJECTIVE [1] resistant to discoloration, esp discoloration resulting from corrosion; rust-resistant: *stainless steel*. [2] having no blemish: *a stainless reputation*. ◆ NOUN [3] stainless steel.
▸'**stainlessly** ADVERB

stainless steel NOUN **a** a type of steel resistant to corrosion as a result of the presence of large amounts of chromium (12–15 per cent). The carbon content depends on the application, being 0.2–0.4 per cent for steel used in cutlery, etc., and about 1 per cent for use in scalpels and razor blades. **b** (*as modifier*): *stainless-steel cutlery*.

stair (stɛə) NOUN [1] one of a flight of stairs. [2] a series of steps: *a narrow stair*. ◆ See also **stairs**.
▷HISTORY Old English *stæger*; related to *stīg* narrow path, *stīgan* to ascend, descend, Old Norse *steigurligr* upright, Middle Dutch *steiger* ladder

staircase ('stɛə,keɪs) NOUN a flight of stairs, its supporting framework, and, usually, a handrail or banisters.

stairhead ('stɛə,hɛd) NOUN the top of a flight of stairs.

stair rod NOUN any of a series of rods placed in the angles between the steps of a carpeted staircase, used to hold the carpet in position.

stairs (stɛəz) PLURAL NOUN [1] a flight of steps leading from one storey or level to another, esp indoors. [2] **below stairs.** *Brit* in the servants' quarters; in domestic service.

stairway ('stɛə,weɪ) NOUN a means of access consisting of stairs; staircase or flight of steps.

stairwell ('stɛə,wɛl) NOUN a vertical shaft or opening that contains a staircase.

stake[1] (steɪk) NOUN [1] a stick or metal bar driven into the ground as a marker, part of a fence, support for a plant, etc. [2] one of a number of vertical posts that fit into sockets around a flat truck or railway wagon to hold the load in place. [3] a method or the practice of executing a person by binding him to a stake in the centre of a pile of wood that is then set on fire. [4] *Mormon Church* an administrative district consisting of a group of wards under the jurisdiction of a president. [5] **pull up stakes.** to leave one's home or temporary resting place and move on. ◆ VERB (*tr*) [6] to tie, fasten, or tether with or to a stake. [7] (often foll by *out* or *off*) to fence or surround with stakes. [8] (often foll by *out*) to lay (a claim) to land, rights, etc. [9] to support with a stake.
▷HISTORY Old English *staca* pin; related to Old Frisian *staka*, Old High German *stehho*, Old Norse *stjaki*; see STICK[1]

stake[2] (steɪk) NOUN [1] the money or valuables that a player must hazard in order to buy into a gambling game or make a bet. [2] an interest, often financial, held in something: *a stake in the company's future*. [3] (*often plural*) the money that a player has available for gambling. [4] (*often plural*) a prize in a race, etc., esp one made up of contributions from contestants or owners. [5] (*plural*) *Horse racing* a race in which all owners of competing horses contribute to the prize money. [6] *US and Canadian informal* short for **grubstake** (sense 1). [7] **at stake.** at risk: *two lives are at stake*. [8] **raise the stakes. a** to increase the amount of money or valuables hazarded in a gambling game. **b** to increase the costs, risks, or considerations involved in taking an action or reaching a conclusion: *the Libyan allegations raised the stakes in the propaganda war between Libya and the United States*. ◆ VERB (*tr*) [9] to hazard (money, etc.) on a result. [10] to invest in or support by supplying with money, etc.: *to stake a business enterprise*.
▷HISTORY C16: of uncertain origin

Staked Plain NOUN another name for the **Llano Estacado.**

stakeholder ('steɪk,həʊldə) NOUN [1] a person or group owning a significant percentage of a company's shares. [2] a person or group not owning shares in an enterprise but affected by or having an interest in its operations, such as the employees, customers, local community, etc. ◆ ADJECTIVE [3] of or relating to policies intended to allow people to participate in and benefit from decisions made by enterprises in which they have a stake: *a stakeholder economy*.

stakeholder pension NOUN (in Britain) a flexible pension scheme with low chargees, in which contributors can stop and restart payments and switch funds to another scheme without paying a penalty.

stakeout ('steɪkaʊt) *Slang, chiefly US and Canadian* ◆ NOUN [1] a police surveillance of an area, house, or criminal suspect. [2] an area or house kept under such surveillance. ◆ VERB **stake out.** [3] (*tr, adverb*) to keep under surveillance.

Stakhanovism (stæ'kænə,vɪzəm) NOUN (in the former Soviet Union) a system designed to raise production by offering incentives to efficient workers.
▷HISTORY C20: named after A. G. *Stakhanov* (1906–77), Soviet coal miner, the worker first awarded benefits under the system in 1935
▸**Sta'khanov,ite** NOUN

stalactite ('stæləkˌtaɪt) NOUN a cylindrical mass of calcium carbonate hanging from the roof of a limestone cave: formed by precipitation from continually dripping water. Compare **stalagmite.**
▷HISTORY C17: from New Latin *stalactites*, from Greek *stalaktos* dripping, from *stalassein* to drip
▸**stalactiform** (stə'læktɪ,fɔːm) ADJECTIVE ▸**stalactitic** (,stælək'tɪtɪk) *or* ,**stalac'titical** ADJECTIVE

stalag ('stælæg; *German* 'ʃtalak) NOUN a German prisoner-of-war camp in World War II, esp for noncommissioned officers and other ranks.
▷HISTORY short for *Stammlager* base camp, from *Stamm* base (related to STEM[1]) + *Lager* camp

stalagmite ('stæləg,maɪt) NOUN a cylindrical mass of calcium carbonate projecting upwards from the floor of a limestone cave: formed by precipitation from continually dripping water. Compare **stalactite.**
▷HISTORY C17: from New Latin *stalagmites*, from Greek *stalagmos* dripping; related to Greek *stalassein* to drip; compare STALACTITE
▸**stalagmitic** (,stæləg'mɪtɪk) *or* ,**stalag'mitical** ADJECTIVE

stale[1] (steɪl) ADJECTIVE [1] (esp of food) hard, musty, or dry from being kept too long. [2] (of beer, etc.) flat and tasteless from being kept open too long. [3] (of air) stagnant; foul. [4] uninteresting from overuse; hackneyed: *stale clichés*. [5] no longer new: *stale news*. [6] lacking in energy or ideas through overwork or lack of variety. [7] *Banking* (of a cheque) not negotiable by a bank as a result of not having been presented within six months of being written. [8] *Law* (of a claim, etc.) having lost its effectiveness or force, as by failure to act or by the lapse of time. ◆ VERB [9] to make or become stale.
▷HISTORY C13 (originally applied to liquor in the sense: well matured): probably via Norman French from Old French *estale* (unattested) motionless, of Frankish origin; related to STALL[1], INSTALL
▸'**stalely** ADVERB ▸'**staleness** NOUN

stale[2] (steɪl) VERB [1] (*intr*) (of livestock) to urinate. ◆ NOUN [2] the urine of horses or cattle.
▷HISTORY C15: perhaps from Old French *estaler* to stand in one position; see STALL[1]; compare Middle Low German *stallen* to urinate, Greek *stalassein* to drip

stale bull NOUN *Business* a dealer or speculator who holds unsold commodities after a rise in market prices but who cannot trade because there are no buyers at the new levels and because his financial commitments prevent him from making further purchases.

stalemate ('steɪl,meɪt) NOUN [1] a chess position in which any of a player's possible moves would place his king in check: in this position the game ends in a draw. [2] a situation in which two opposing forces find that further action is impossible or futile; deadlock. ◆ VERB [3] (*tr*) to subject to a stalemate.
▷HISTORY C18: from obsolete *stale*, from Old French *estal* STALL[1] + MATE[2]

Stalin ('stɑːlɪn) NOUN [1] Also called: **Stalino.** a former name (from after the Revolution until 1961) of **Donetsk.** [2] the former name (1950–61) of **Braşov.** [3] the former name (1949–56) of **Varna.**

Stalinabad (*Russian* stəlina'bat) NOUN the former name (1929–61) of **Dushanbe.**

Stalingrad ('stɑːlɪn,græd; *Russian* stəlin'grat) NOUN the former name (1925–61) of **Volgograd.**

Stalinism ('stɑːlɪ,nɪzəm) NOUN the theory and form of government associated with the Soviet leader Joseph Stalin (original name *Iosif Vissarionovich Dzhugashvili*; 1879–1953): a variant of Marxism-Leninism characterized by totalitarianism, rigid bureaucracy, and loyalty to the state.
▸'**Stalinist** NOUN, ADJECTIVE

Stalinogrod (*Polish* stali'nɔgrɔt) NOUN the former name (1953–56) for **Katowice.**

Stalin Peak NOUN a former name for **Kommunizma Peak.**

Stalinsk (*Russian* 'stalinsk) NOUN the former name (1932–61) of **Novokuznetsk.**

stalk[1] (stɔːk) NOUN [1] the main stem of a herbaceous plant. [2] any of various subsidiary plant stems, such as a leafstalk (petiole) or flower stalk (peduncle). [3] a slender supporting structure in animals such as crinoids and certain protozoans, coelenterates, and barnacles. [4] any long slender supporting shaft or column.
▷HISTORY C14: probably a diminutive formed from Old English *stalu* upright piece of wood; related to Old Frisian *staal* handle
▸**stalked** ADJECTIVE ▸'**stalkless** ADJECTIVE ▸'**stalk,like** ADJECTIVE

stalk[2] (stɔːk) VERB [1] to follow or approach (game, prey, etc.) stealthily and quietly. [2] to pursue persistently and, sometimes, attack (a person with whom one is obsessed, often a celebrity). [3] to spread over (a place) in a menacing or grim manner: *fever stalked the camp*. [4] (*intr*) to walk in a haughty, stiff, or threatening way: *he stalked out in disgust*. [5] to search or draw (a piece of land) for prey. ◆ NOUN [6] the act of stalking. [7] a stiff or threatening stride.
▷HISTORY Old English *bestealcian* to walk stealthily; related to Middle Low German *stolkeren*, Danish *stalke*
▸'**stalker** NOUN

stalking-horse NOUN [1] a horse or an imitation one used by a hunter to hide behind while stalking his quarry. [2] something serving as a means of concealing plans; pretext. [3] a candidate put forward by one group to divide the opposition or mask the candidacy of another person for whom the stalking-horse would then withdraw.

stalky ('stɔːkɪ) ADJECTIVE **stalkier, stalkiest.** [1] like a stalk; slender and tall. [2] having or abounding in stalks.
▸'**stalkily** ADVERB ▸'**stalkiness** NOUN

stall[1] (stɔːl) NOUN [1] **a** a compartment in a stable or shed for confining or feeding a single animal. **b** another name for **stable[1]** (sense 1). [2] a small often temporary stand or booth for the display and sale of goods. [3] (in a church) **a** one of a row of seats, usually divided from the others by armrests or a small screen, for the use of the choir or clergy. **b** a pen. [4] an instance of an engine stalling. [5] a condition of an aircraft in flight in which a reduction in speed or an increase in the aircraft's angle of attack causes a sudden loss of lift resulting in a downward plunge. [6] any small room or compartment. [7] *Brit* **a** a seat in a theatre or cinema that resembles a chair, usually fixed to the floor. **b** (*plural*) the area of seats on the ground floor of a theatre or cinema nearest to the stage or screen. [8] a tubelike covering for a finger, as in a glove. [9] (*plural*) short for **starting stalls.** [10] **set out one's stall.** *Brit* to make the necessary arrangements for the achievement of something and show that one is determined to achieve it. ◆ VERB [11] to cause (a motor vehicle or its engine) to stop, usually by

incorrect use of the clutch or incorrect adjustment of the fuel mixture, or (of an engine or motor vehicle) to stop, usually for these reasons. 12 to cause (an aircraft) to go into a stall or (of an aircraft) to go into a stall. 13 to stick or cause to stick fast, as in mud or snow. 14 (*tr*) to confine (an animal) in a stall.
▷HISTORY Old English *steall* a place for standing; related to Old High German *stall*, and *stellen* to set

stall[2] (stɔːl) VERB 1 to employ delaying tactics towards (someone); be evasive. 2 (*intr*) *Sport, chiefly US* to play or fight below one's best in order to deceive. ◆ NOUN 3 an evasive move; pretext.
▷HISTORY C16: from Anglo-French *estale* bird used as a decoy, influenced by STALL[1]

stall-feed VERB **-feeds, -feeding, -fed.** (*tr*) to keep and feed (an animal) in a stall, esp as an intensive method of fattening it for slaughter.

stallholder (ˈstɔːlˌhəʊldə) NOUN a person who sells goods at a market stall.

stalling angle NOUN the angle between the chord line of an aerofoil and the undisturbed relative airflow at which stalling occurs. Also called: **stall angle, critical angle.**

stallion (ˈstæljən) NOUN an uncastrated male horse, esp one used for breeding.
▷HISTORY C14: *staloun*, from Old French *estalon* of Germanic origin; related to Old High German *stal* STALL[1]

stalwart (ˈstɔːlwət) ADJECTIVE 1 strong and sturdy; robust. 2 solid, dependable, and courageous: *stalwart citizens.* 3 resolute and firm. ◆ NOUN 4 a stalwart person, esp a supporter.
▷HISTORY Old English *stælwirthe* serviceable, from *stǣl*, shortened from *stathol* support + *wierthe* WORTH[1]
▸ˈ**stalwartly** ADVERB ▸ˈ**stalwartness** NOUN

Stambul *or* **Stamboul** (stæmˈbuːl) NOUN the old part of Istanbul, Turkey, south of the Golden Horn: the site of ancient Byzantium; sometimes used as a name for the whole city.

stamen (ˈsteɪmɛn) NOUN, *plural* **stamens** *or* **stamina** (ˈstæmɪnə). the male reproductive organ of a flower, consisting of a stalk (filament) bearing an anther in which pollen is produced.
▷HISTORY C17: from Latin: the warp in an upright loom, from *stāre* to stand
▸**staminal** (ˈstæmɪnᵊl) ADJECTIVE ▸**staminiferous** (ˌstæmɪˈnɪfərəs) ADJECTIVE

Stamford (ˈstæmfəd) NOUN a city in SW Connecticut, on Long Island Sound: major chemical research laboratories. Pop.: 117 083 (2000).

Stamford Bridge NOUN a village in N England, east of York: site of a battle (1066) in which King Harold of England defeated his brother Tostig and King Harald Hardrada of Norway, three weeks before the Battle of Hastings.

stamina[1] (ˈstæmɪnə) NOUN enduring energy, strength, and resilience.
▷HISTORY C19: identical with STAMINA[2] from Latin *stāmen* thread, hence the threads of life spun out by the Fates, hence energy, etc.
▸ˈ**staminal** ADJECTIVE

stamina[2] (ˈstæmɪnə) NOUN a plural of **stamen.**

staminate (ˈstæmɪnɪt, -ˌneɪt) ADJECTIVE (of plants) having stamens, esp having stamens but no carpels; male.
▷HISTORY C19: from Latin *stāminātus* consisting of threads. See STAMEN, -ATE[1]

staminode (ˈstæmɪˌnəʊd) *or* **staminodium** (ˌstæmɪˈnəʊdɪəm) NOUN, *plural* **-nodes** *or* **-nodia** (-ˈnəʊdɪə). a stamen that produces no pollen.
▷HISTORY C19: from STAMEN + -ODE[1]

staminody (ˈstæmɪˌnəʊdɪ) NOUN the development of any of various plant organs, such as petals or sepals, into stamens.

stammel (ˈstæməl) NOUN 1 a coarse woollen cloth in former use for undergarments, etc., and usually dyed red. 2 the bright red colour of this cloth.
▷HISTORY C16: from Old French *estamin*, from Latin *stāmineus* made of threads, from *stāmen* a thread; see STAMEN

stammer (ˈstæmə) VERB 1 to speak or say (something) in a hesitant way, esp as a result of a speech disorder or through fear, stress, etc. ◆ NOUN 2 a speech disorder characterized by involuntary repetitions and hesitations.
▷HISTORY Old English *stamerian*; related to Old Saxon *stamarōn*, Old High German *stamm*
▸ˈ**stammerer** NOUN ▸ˈ**stammering** NOUN, ADJECTIVE
▸ˈ**stammeringly** ADVERB

stamp (stæmp) VERB 1 (when *intr*, often foll by *on*) to bring (the foot) down heavily (on the ground, etc.). 2 (*intr*) to walk with heavy or noisy footsteps. 3 (*intr*; foll by *on*) to repress, extinguish, or eradicate: *he stamped on any criticism.* 4 (*tr*) to impress or mark (a particular device or sign) on (something). 5 to mark (something) with an official impress, seal, or device: *to stamp a passport.* 6 (*tr*) to fix or impress permanently: *the date was stamped on her memory.* 7 (*tr*) to affix a postage stamp to. 8 (*tr*) to distinguish or reveal: *that behaviour stamps him as a cheat.* 9 to pound or crush (ores, etc.). ◆ NOUN 10 the act or an instance of stamping. 11 **a** See **postage stamp. b** a mark applied to postage stamps for cancellation purposes. 12 a similar piece of gummed paper used for commercial or trading purposes. 13 a block, die, etc., used for imprinting a design or device. 14 a design, device, or mark that has been stamped. 15 a characteristic feature or trait; hallmark: *the story had the stamp of authenticity.* 16 a piece of gummed paper or other mark applied to official documents to indicate payment of a fee, validity, ownership, etc. 17 *Brit informal* a national insurance contribution, formerly recorded by means of a stamp on an official card. 18 type or class: *we want to employ men of his stamp.* 19 an instrument or machine for crushing or pounding ores, etc., or the pestle in such a device. ◆ See also **stamp out.**
▷HISTORY Old English *stampe*; related to Old High German *stampfōn* to stamp, Old Norse *stappa*
▸ˈ**stamper** NOUN

Stamp Act NOUN a law passed by the British Parliament requiring all publications and legal and commercial documents in the American colonies to bear a tax stamp (1765): a cause of unrest in the colonies.

stamp collecting NOUN another name for **philately.**
▸**stamp collector** NOUN

stamp duty *or* **tax** NOUN a tax on legal documents, publications, etc., the payment of which is certified by the attaching or impressing of official stamps.

stampede (stæmˈpiːd) NOUN 1 an impulsive headlong rush of startled cattle or horses. 2 headlong rush of a crowd: *a stampede of shoppers.* 3 any sudden large-scale movement or other action, such as a rush of people to support a candidate. 4 *Western US and Canadian* a rodeo event featuring fairground and social elements. ◆ VERB 5 to run away or cause to run away in a stampede.
▷HISTORY C19: from American Spanish *estampida*, from Spanish: a din, from *estampar* to stamp, of Germanic origin; see STAMP
▸**stamˈpeder** NOUN

stamping ground NOUN a habitual or favourite meeting or gathering place.

stamp mill NOUN *Metallurgy* a machine for crushing ore.

stamp out VERB (*tr, adverb*) 1 to put out or extinguish by stamping: *to stamp out a fire.* 2 to crush or suppress by force: *to stamp out a rebellion.*

stance (stæns, stɑːns) NOUN 1 the manner and position in which a person or animal stands. 2 *Sport* the posture assumed when about to play the ball, as in golf, cricket, etc. 3 general emotional or intellectual attitude: *a leftist stance.* 4 *Scot* a place where buses or taxis wait. 5 *Mountaineering* a place at the top of a pitch where a climber can stand and belay.
▷HISTORY C16: via French from Italian *stanza* place for standing, from Latin *stāns*, from *stāre* to stand

stanch (stɑːntʃ) *or* **staunch** (stɔːntʃ) VERB 1 to stem the flow of (a liquid, esp blood) or (of a liquid) to stop flowing. 2 to prevent the flow of a liquid, esp blood, from (a hole, wound, etc.). 3 an archaic word for **assuage.** ◆ NOUN 4 a primitive form of lock in which boats are carried over shallow parts of a river in a rush of water released by the lock.
▷HISTORY C14: from Old French *estanchier*, from Vulgar Latin *stanticāre* (unattested) to cause to stand, from Latin *stāre* to stand, halt
▸ˈ**stanchable** *or* ˈ**staunchable** ADJECTIVE ▸ˈ**stancher** *or* ˈ**stauncher** NOUN

stanchion (ˈstɑːnʃən) NOUN 1 any vertical pole, rod, etc., used as a support. ◆ VERB 2 (*tr*) to provide or support with a stanchion or stanchions.
▷HISTORY C14: from Old French *estanchon*, from *estance*, from Vulgar Latin *stantia* (unattested) a standing, from Latin *stāre* to stand

stand (stænd) VERB **stands, standing, stood.** (*mainly intr*) 1 (*also tr*) to be or cause to be in an erect or upright position. 2 to rise to, assume, or maintain an upright position. 3 (*copula*) to have a specified height when standing: *to stand six feet.* 4 to be situated or located: *the house stands in the square.* 5 to be or exist in a specified state or condition: *to stand in awe of someone.* 6 to adopt or remain in a resolute position or attitude. 7 (*may take an infinitive*) to be in a specified position: *I stand to lose money in this venture; he stands high in the president's favour.* 8 to remain in force or continue in effect: *whatever the difficulties, my orders stand.* 9 to come to a stop or halt, esp temporarily. 10 (of water, etc.) to collect and remain without flowing. 11 (often foll by *at*) (of a score, account, etc.) to indicate the specified position of the parties involved: *the score stands at 20 to 1.* 12 (*also tr*; when *intr*, foll by *for*) to tolerate or bear: *I won't stand for your nonsense any longer; I can't stand spiders.* 13 (*tr*) to resist; survive: *to stand the test of time.* 14 (*tr*) to submit to: *to stand trial.* 15 (often foll by *for*) *Chiefly Brit* to be or become a candidate: *will he stand for Parliament?* 16 to navigate in a specified direction: *we were standing for Madeira when the storm broke.* 17 (of a gun dog) to point at game. 18 to halt, esp to give action, repel attack, or disrupt an enemy advance when retreating. 19 (of a male domestic animal, esp a stallion) to be available as a stud. 20 (*also tr*) *Printing* to keep (type that has been set) or (of such type) to be kept, for possible use in future printings. 21 (*tr*) *Informal* to bear the cost of; pay for: *to stand someone a drink.* 22 **stand a chance.** to have a hope or likelihood of winning, succeeding, etc. 23 **stand fast.** to maintain one's position firmly. 24 **stand one's ground.** to maintain a stance or position in the face of opposition. 25 **stand still. a** to remain motionless. **b** (foll by *for*) *US* to tolerate: *I won't stand still for your threats.* 26 **stand to (someone).** *Irish informal* to be useful to (someone): *your knowledge of English will stand to you.* ◆ NOUN 27 the act or an instance of standing. 28 an opinion, esp a resolutely held one: *he took a stand on capital punishment.* 29 a halt or standstill. 30 a place where a person or thing stands. 31 *Austral and NZ* **a** a position on the floor of a shearing shed allocated to one shearer. **b** the shearing equipment belonging to such a position. 32 a structure, usually of wood, on which people can sit or stand. 33 a frame or rack on which such articles as coats and hats may be hung. 34 a small table or piece of furniture where articles may be placed or stored: *a music stand.* 35 a supporting framework, esp for a tool or instrument. 36 a stall, booth, or counter from which goods may be sold. 37 an exhibition area in a trade fair. 38 a halt to give action, etc., esp one taken during a retreat and having some duration or some success. 39 *Cricket* an extended period at the wicket by two batsmen. 40 a growth of plants in a particular area, esp trees in a forest or a crop in a field. 41 a stop made by a touring theatrical company, pop group, etc., to give a performance (esp in the phrase **one-night stand**). 42 *South African* a plot or site earmarked for the erection of a building. 43 (of a gun dog) the act of pointing at game. 44 a complete set, esp of arms or armour for one man. 45 *Military* the flags of a regiment. ◆ See also **stand by, stand down, stand for, stand in, standoff, stand on, stand out, stand over, stand pat, stand to, stand up.**
▷HISTORY Old English *standan*; related to Old Norse *standa*, Old High German *stantan*, Latin *stāre* to stand; see STEAD
▸ˈ**stander** NOUN

stand-alone ADJECTIVE *Computing* (of a device or system) capable of operating independently of any other device or system.

standard (ˈstændəd) NOUN 1 an accepted or approved example of something against which others are judged or measured. 2 (*often plural*) a principle of propriety, honesty, and integrity: *she has no standards.* 3 a level of excellence or quality: *a low standard of living.* 4 any distinctive flag,

device, etc., as of a nation, sovereign, or special cause. 5 **a** any of a variety of naval or military flags. **b** the colours of a cavalry regiment. 6 a flag or emblem formerly used to show the central or rallying point of an army in battle. 7 a large tapering flag ending in two points, originally borne by a sovereign or high-ranking noble. 8 the commodity or commodities in which is stated the value of a basic monetary unit: *the gold standard*. 9 an authorized model of a unit of measure or weight. 10 a unit of board measure equal to 1980 board feet. 11 (in coinage) the prescribed proportion by weight of precious metal and base metal that each coin must contain. 12 an upright pole or beam, esp one used as a support. 13 **a** a piece of furniture consisting of an upright pole or beam on a base or support. **b** (*as modifier*): *a standard lamp*. 14 **a** a plant, esp a fruit tree, that is trained so that it has an upright stem free of branches. **b** (*as modifier*): *a standard cherry*. 15 a song or piece of music that has remained popular for many years. 16 the largest petal of a leguminous flower, such as a sweetpea. 17 (in New Zealand and, formerly, in England and Wales) a class or level of attainment in an elementary school. ◆ ADJECTIVE 18 of the usual, regularized, medium, or accepted kind: *a standard size*. 19 of recognized authority, competence, or excellence: *the standard work on Greece*. 20 denoting or characterized by idiom, vocabulary, etc., that is regarded as correct and acceptable by educated native speakers. Compare **nonstandard, informal.** 21 *Brit* (formerly) (of eggs) of a size that is smaller than *large* and larger than *medium*.
▷HISTORY C12: from Old French *estandart* gathering place, flag to mark such a place, probably of Germanic origin; compare Old High German *stantan* to stand, Old High German *ort* place

standard amenities PLURAL NOUN (in Britain) *Social welfare* the sanitary facilities recommended for all dwellings by the housing law: a fixed bath or shower, wash-hand basin, and sink, all supplied with hot and cold water, and a flush toilet.

standard assessment tasks, *or* **standard assessment tests,** *or* **standard attainment tests** PLURAL NOUN *Brit education* the former name for **National Tests.** Abbreviation: **SATS** (ˈsæts).

standard-bearer NOUN 1 an officer or man who carries a standard. 2 a leader of a cause or party.

standard-bred NOUN a US and Canadian breed of trotting and pacing horse, used esp for harness-racing.
▷HISTORY C19: so called because they are bred to attain a prescribed standard of speed

standard candle NOUN another name for **candela**: not in scientific usage because of possible confusion with the former **international candle**.

standard cell NOUN a voltaic cell producing a constant and accurately known electromotive force that can be used to calibrate voltage-measuring instruments.

standard cost NOUN *Accounting* the predetermined budgeted cost of a regular manufacturing process against which actual costs are compared.

standard deviation NOUN *Statistics* a measure of dispersion obtained by extracting the square root of the mean of the squared deviations of the observed values from their mean in a frequency distribution.

standard error NOUN *Statistics* the estimated standard deviation of a parameter, the value of which is not known exactly.

standard function NOUN *Computing* a subprogram provided by a translator that carries out a task, for example the computation of a mathematical function, such as sine, square root, etc.

standard gauge NOUN 1 a railway track with a distance of 4 ft. 8½ in. (1.435 m) between the lines; used on most railways. See also **narrow gauge, broad gauge.** ◆ ADJECTIVE **standard-gauge, standard-gauged.** 2 of, relating to, or denoting a railway with a standard gauge.

standard generalized mark-up language NOUN See **SGML.**

Standard Grade NOUN (in Scotland) a type of examination designed to test skills and the application of knowledge; replaced O grade.

standard housing benefit NOUN (in Britain) *Social welfare* a rebate of a proportion of a person's eligible housing costs paid by a local authority and calculated on the basis of level of income and family size.

standardize *or* **standardise** (ˈstændəˌdaɪz) VERB 1 to make or become standard. 2 (*tr*) to test by or compare with a standard.
▸ˌstandardiˈzation *or* ˌstandardiˈsation NOUN
▸ˈstandardˌizer *or* ˈstandardˌiser NOUN

standard model NOUN *Physics* a theory of fundamental interactions in which the electromagnetic, weak, and strong interactions are described in terms of the exchange of virtual particles.

standard normal distribution NOUN *Statistics* a normal distribution with mean zero and variance 1, with probability density function $[\exp(-\frac{1}{2}x^2)]/\sqrt{2\pi}$.

standard of living NOUN a level of subsistence or material welfare of a community, class, or person.

standard scratch score NOUN *Golf* the number of strokes a scratch player would need to go round a particular course, based on the length of each hole to the green and allowing 36 putts for the round.

standard time NOUN the official local time of a region or country determined by the distance from Greenwich of a line of longitude passing through the area.

stand by VERB 1 (*intr, adverb*) to be available and ready to act if needed or called upon. 2 (*intr, adverb*) to be present as an onlooker or without taking any action: *he stood by at the accident*. 3 (*intr, preposition*) to be faithful to: *to stand by one's principles*. 4 (*tr, adverb*) *English law* (of the Crown) to challenge (a juror) without needing to show cause. ◆ NOUN **stand-by.** 5 **a** a person or thing that is ready for use or can be relied on in an emergency. **b** (*as modifier*): *stand-by provisions*. 6 **on stand-by.** in a state of readiness for action or use. ◆ ADJECTIVE 7 (of an airline passenger, fare, or seat) not booked in advance but awaiting or subject to availability.

stand down VERB (*adverb*) 1 (*intr*) to resign or withdraw, esp in favour of another. 2 (*intr*) to leave the witness box in a court of law after giving evidence. 3 *Chiefly Brit* to go or be taken off duty.

standee (stænˈdiː) NOUN a person who stands, esp when there are no vacant seats.

standfirst (ˈstændˌfɜːst) NOUN *Journalism* an introductory paragraph in an article, printed in larger or bolder type or in capitals, which summarizes the article.

stand for VERB (*intr, preposition*) 1 to represent or mean. 2 *Chiefly Brit* to be or become a candidate for. 3 to support or recommend. 4 *Informal* to tolerate or bear: *he won't stand for any disobedience*.

stand in VERB 1 (*intr, adverb*; usually foll by *for*) to act as a substitute. 2 **stand (someone) in good stead.** to be of benefit or advantage to (someone). ◆ NOUN **stand-in.** 3 **a** a person or thing that serves as a substitute. **b** (*as modifier*): *a stand-in teacher*. 4 a person who substitutes for an actor during intervals of waiting or in dangerous stunts.

standing (ˈstændɪŋ) NOUN 1 social or financial position, status, or reputation: *a man of some standing*. 2 length of existence, experience, etc. 3 (*modifier*) used to stand in or on: *standing room*. ◆ ADJECTIVE 4 *Athletics* **a** (of the start of a race) begun from a standing position without the use of starting blocks. **b** (of a jump, leap, etc.) performed from a stationary position without a run-up. 5 (*prenominal*) permanent, fixed, or lasting. 6 (*prenominal*) still or stagnant: *a standing pond*. 7 *Printing* (of type) set and stored for future use. Compare **dead** (sense 17).

standing army NOUN a permanent army of paid soldiers maintained by a nation.

standing chop NOUN *NZ* (in an axemen's competition) a chop with the log standing upright. Compare **underhand chop.**

standing committee NOUN a permanent committee appointed to deal with a specified subject.

standing order NOUN 1 Also called: **banker's order.** an instruction to a bank by a depositor to pay a stated sum at regular intervals. Compare **direct debit.** 2 a rule or order governing the procedure, conduct, etc., of a legislative body. 3 *Military* one of a number of orders which have or are likely to have long-term validity.

standing rigging NOUN the stays, shrouds, and other more or less fixed, though adjustable, wires and ropes that support the masts of a sailing vessel. Compare **running rigging.**

standing wave NOUN *Physics* the periodic disturbance in a medium resulting from the combination of two waves of equal frequency and intensity travelling in opposite directions. There are generally two kinds of displacement, and the maximum value of the amplitude of one of these occurs at the same points as the minimum value of the amplitude of the other. Thus in the case of electromagnetic radiation the amplitude of the oscillations of the electric field has its greatest value at the points at which the magnetic oscillation is zero, and vice versa. Also called: **stationary wave.** Compare **node, antinode.**

standish (ˈstændɪʃ) NOUN a stand, usually of metal, for pens, ink bottles, etc.
▷HISTORY C15: of unknown origin

standoff (ˈstændˌɒf) NOUN 1 *US and Canadian* the act or an instance of standing off or apart. 2 a deadlock or stalemate. 3 any situation or disposition of forces that counterbalances or neutralizes. 4 *Rugby* short for **stand-off half.** ◆ VERB **stand off.** (*adverb*) 5 (*intr*) to navigate a vessel so as to avoid the shore, an obstruction, etc. 6 (*tr*) to keep or cause to keep at a distance. 7 (*intr*) to reach a deadlock or stalemate. 8 (*tr*) to dismiss (workers), esp temporarily.

stand-off half NOUN *Rugby* 1 a player who acts as a link between his scrum half and three-quarter backs. 2 this position in a team. ◆ Also called: **fly half.**

standoffish (ˌstændˈɒfɪʃ) ADJECTIVE reserved, haughty, or aloof.
▸ˌstandˈoffishly ADVERB ▸ˌstandˈoffishness NOUN

standoff missile NOUN a missile capable of striking a distant target after launch by an aircraft outside the range of missile defences.

stand oil NOUN a thick drying oil made by heating linseed, tung, or soya to over 300°C: used in oil enamel paints.

stand on VERB (*intr*) 1 (*adverb*) to continue to navigate a vessel on the same heading. 2 (*preposition*) to insist on: *to stand on ceremony*. 3 **stand on one's own (two) feet.** *Informal* to be independent or self-reliant.

stand out VERB (*intr, adverb*) 1 to be distinctive or conspicuous. 2 to refuse to agree, consent, or comply: *they stood out for a better price*. 3 to protrude or project. 4 to navigate a vessel away from a port, harbour, anchorage, etc. ◆ NOUN **standout.** 5 *Informal* **a** a person or thing that is distinctive or outstanding. **b** (*as modifier*): *the standout track from the album*. 6 a person who refuses to agree or consent.

stand over VERB 1 (*intr, preposition*) to watch closely; keep tight control over. 2 (*adverb*) to postpone or be postponed. 3 (*intr, preposition*) *Austral and NZ informal* to threaten or intimidate (a person). ◆ NOUN **standover.** 4 *Austral and NZ informal* a threatening or intimidating act.

standover man (ˈstændˌəʊvə) NOUN *Austral informal* a person who extorts money by intimidation.

stand pat VERB (*intr*) 1 *Poker* to refuse the right to change any of one's cards; keep one's hand unchanged. 2 to resist change or remain unchanged.
▸ˈstandˈpatter NOUN

standpipe (ˈstændˌpaɪp) NOUN 1 a vertical pipe, open at the upper end, attached to a pipeline or tank serving to limit the pressure head to that of the height of the pipe. 2 a temporary freshwater outlet installed in a street during a period when household water supplies are cut off.

standpoint (ˈstændˌpɔɪnt) NOUN a physical or mental position from which things are viewed.

standstill (ˈstændˌstɪl) NOUN a complete cessation of movement; stop; halt: *the car came to a standstill*.

standstill agreement NOUN an agreement that

preserves the status quo, esp one between two countries when one country cannot pay its debts to the other that a certain fixed extension of time will be given to repay the debts.

stand to VERB [1] *(adverb) Military* to assume positions or cause to assume positions to resist a possible attack. [2] **stand to reason.** to conform with the dictates of reason: *it stands to reason that pigs can't fly.*

stand up VERB *(adverb)* [1] *(intr)* to rise to the feet. [2] *(intr)* to resist or withstand wear, criticism, etc. [3] *(tr) Informal* to fail to keep an appointment with, esp intentionally. [4] **stand up for. a** to support, side with, or defend. **b** *US* to serve as best man for (the groom) at a wedding. [5] **stand up to. a** to confront or resist courageously. **b** to withstand or endure (wear, criticism, etc.). ◆ ADJECTIVE **stand-up.** *(prenominal)* [6] having or being in an erect position: *a stand-up collar.* [7] done, performed, taken, etc., while standing: *a stand-up meal.* [8] (of comedy or a comedian) performed or performing solo. [9] *Informal* (of a boxer) having an aggressive style without much leg movement: *a stand-up fighter.* ◆ NOUN **stand-up.** [10] a stand-up comedian. [11] stand-up comedy.

stane (steɪn) NOUN a Scot word for **stone.**

Stanford-Binet test (ˈstænfədbɪˈneɪ) NOUN *Psychol* a revision, esp for US use, of the Binet-Simon scale designed to measure mental ability by comparing the performance of an individual with the average performance for his age group. See also **Binet-Simon scale, intelligence test.**
▷HISTORY C20: named after *Stanford University*, California, and Alfred *Binet* (1857–1911), French psychologist

stang (stæŋ) VERB *Archaic or dialect* a past tense of **sting.**

stanhope (ˈstænəp) NOUN a light one-seater carriage with two or four wheels.
▷HISTORY C18: named after Fitzroy *Stanhope* (1787–1864), English clergyman for whom it was first built

stank[1] (stæŋk) VERB a past tense of **stink.**

stank[2] (stæŋk) NOUN [1] a small cofferdam, esp one of timber made watertight with clay. [2] *Scot and northern English dialect* a pond or pool. ◆ VERB [3] *(tr)* to make (a stream, cofferdam, etc.) watertight, esp with clay.
▷HISTORY C13: from Old French *estanc*, probably from *estancher* to stanch

stank[3] (stæŋk) NOUN *Dialect* [1] a drain, as in a roadway. [2] a draining board adjacent to a sink unit.
▷HISTORY special use of STANK[2] (in the sense: pool, pond)

Stanley (ˈstænlɪ) NOUN [1] the capital of the Falkland Islands, in NE East Falkland Island: scene of fighting in the Falklands War of 1982. Pop.: 1557 (1991). [2] a town in NE England, in N Durham. Pop.: 18 905 (1991). [3] **Mount.** a mountain in central Africa, between Uganda and the Democratic Republic of Congo (formerly Zaïre): the highest peak of the Ruwenzori range. Height: 5109 m (16 763 ft.). Congolese name: **Ngaliema Mountain.**

Stanley Falls PLURAL NOUN the former name of **Boyoma Falls.**

Stanley knife NOUN *Trademark* a type of knife used for carpet fitting, etc., consisting of a thick hollow metal handle with a short, very sharp, replaceable blade inserted at one end.
▷HISTORY C19: named after F.T. *Stanley*, US businessman and founder of the Stanley Rule and Level Company

Stanley Pool NOUN a lake between the Democratic Republic of Congo (formerly Zaïre) and Congo-Brazzaville, formed by a widening of the River Congo. Area: 829 sq. km (320 sq. miles). Congolese name: **Pool Malebo.**

Stanleyville (ˈstænlɪˌvɪl) NOUN the former name (until 1966) of **Kisangani.**

stann- COMBINING FORM denoting tin: *stannite.*
▷HISTORY from Late Latin *stannum* tin

Stannaries (ˈstænərɪz) NOUN **the.** a tin-mining district of Devon and Cornwall, formerly under the jurisdiction of special courts.

stannary (ˈstænərɪ) NOUN, *plural* **-ries.** a place or region where tin is mined or worked.
▷HISTORY C15: from Medieval Latin *stannāria*, from Late Latin: STANNUM, TIN

stannic (ˈstænɪk) ADJECTIVE of or containing tin, esp in the tetravalent state.
▷HISTORY C18: from Late Latin *stannum* tin

stannic sulphide NOUN an insoluble solid compound of tin usually existing as golden crystals or as a yellowish-brown powder: used as a pigment. Formula: SnS_2. See also **mosaic gold.**

stanniferous (stəˈnɪfərəs) ADJECTIVE containing tin; tin-bearing.
▷HISTORY C18: from Late Latin *stannum* tin + -FEROUS

stannite (ˈstænaɪt) NOUN a grey metallic mineral that consists of a sulphide of tin, copper, and iron and is a source of tin. Formula: Cu_2FeSnS_4.
▷HISTORY C19: from STANNUM + -ITE[1]

stannous (ˈstænəs) ADJECTIVE of or containing tin, esp in the divalent state.

stannum (ˈstænəm) NOUN an obsolete name for **tin** (the metal).
▷HISTORY C18: from Late Latin: tin, from Latin: alloy of silver and lead, perhaps of Celtic origin; compare Welsh *ystaen* tin

Stanovoi Range *or* **Stanovoy Range** (*Russian* stənaˈvɔj) NOUN a mountain range in SE Russia; forms part of the watershed between rivers flowing to the Arctic and the Pacific. Highest peak: Mount Skalisty, 2482 m (8143 ft.).

Stans (*German* ʃtans) NOUN a town in central Switzerland, capital of Nidwalden demicanton, 11 km (7 miles) southeast of Lucerne: tourist centre. Pop.: 5700 (latest est.).

stanza (ˈstænzə) NOUN [1] *Prosody* a fixed number of verse lines arranged in a definite metrical pattern, forming a unit of a poem. [2] *US and Austral* a half or a quarter in a football match.
▷HISTORY C16: from Italian: halting place, from Vulgar Latin *stantia* (unattested) station, from Latin *stāre* to stand
▸**ˈstanzaed** ADJECTIVE ▸**stanzaic** (stænˈzeɪɪk) ADJECTIVE

stapelia (stəˈpiːlɪə) NOUN any fleshy cactus-like leafless African plant of the asclepiadaceous genus *Stapelia*, having thick four-angled stems and large typically fetid mottled flowers.
▷HISTORY C18: from New Latin, named after J. B. van *Stapel*, (died 1636), Dutch botanist

stapes (ˈsteɪpiːz) NOUN, *plural* **stapes** *or* **stapedes** (stæˈpiːdiːz). the stirrup-shaped bone that is the innermost of three small bones in the middle ear of mammals. Nontechnical name: **stirrup bone.** Compare **incus, malleus.**
▷HISTORY C17: via New Latin from Medieval Latin, perhaps a variant of *staffa, stapeda* stirrup, influenced in form by Latin *stāre* to stand + *pēs* a foot
▸**stapedial** (stæˈpiːdɪəl) ADJECTIVE

staphylo- COMBINING FORM [1] uvula: *staphyloplasty.* [2] resembling a bunch of grapes: *staphylococcus.*
▷HISTORY from Greek *staphulē* bunch of grapes, uvula

staphylococcus (ˌstæfɪləʊˈkɒkəs) NOUN, *plural* **-cocci** (-ˈkɒkaɪ; *US* -ˈkɒksaɪ). any spherical Gram-positive bacterium of the genus *Staphylococcus*, typically occurring in clusters and including many pathogenic species, causing boils, infection in wounds, and septicaemia: family *Micrococcaceae*. Often shortened to: **staph.**
▷HISTORY C19: from STAPHYLO- (in the sense: like a bunch of grapes) + COCCUS so called because of their shape
▸**staphylococcal** (ˌstæfɪləʊˈkɒkᵊl) *or* **staphylococcic** (ˌstæfɪləʊˈkɒkɪk; *US* -ˈkɒksɪk) ADJECTIVE

staphyloplasty (ˈstæfɪləʊˌplæstɪ) NOUN plastic surgery or surgical repair involving the soft palate or the uvula.
▷HISTORY C19: from STAPHYLO- + -PLASTY
▸**ˌstaphyloˈplastic** ADJECTIVE

staphylorrhaphy (ˌstæfɪˈlɒrəfɪ) NOUN repair of a cleft palate by means of staphyloplasty and suturing.
▷HISTORY C19: from STAPHYLO- (in the sense: uvula) + Greek *raphē* a sewing or suture
▸**staphylorrhaphic** (ˌstæfɪlɒˈræfɪk) ADJECTIVE

staple[1] (ˈsteɪpᵊl) NOUN [1] a short length of thin wire bent into a square U-shape, used to fasten papers, cloth, etc. [2] a short length of stiff wire formed into a U-shape with pointed ends, used for holding a hasp to a post, securing electric cables, etc. ◆ VERB [3] *(tr)* to secure (papers, wire, etc.) with a staple or staples.
▷HISTORY Old English *stapol* prop, of Germanic origin; related to Middle Dutch *stapel* step, Old High German *staffal*

staple[2] (ˈsteɪpᵊl) ADJECTIVE [1] of prime importance; principal: *staple foods.* [2] (of a commodity) forming a predominant element in the product, consumption, or trade of a nation, region, etc. ◆ NOUN [3] a staple commodity. [4] a main constituent; integral part. [5] *Chiefly US and Canadian* a principal raw material produced or grown in a region. [6] the fibre of wool, cotton, etc., graded as to length and fineness. [7] (in medieval Europe) a town appointed to be the exclusive market for one or more major exports of the land. ◆ VERB [8] *(tr)* to arrange or sort (wool, cotton, etc.) according to length and fineness.
▷HISTORY C15: from Middle Dutch *stapel* warehouse; see STAPLE[1]

staple gun NOUN a mechanism that fixes staples to a surface.

stapler (ˈsteɪplə) NOUN a machine that inserts staples into sheets of paper, etc., to hold them together.

star (stɑː) NOUN [1] any of a vast number of celestial objects that are visible in the clear night sky as points of light. [2] **a** a hot gaseous mass, such as the sun, that radiates energy, esp as light and infrared radiation, usually derived from thermonuclear reactions in the interior, and in some cases as ultraviolet, radio waves, and X-rays. The surface temperature can range from about 2100 to 40 000°C. See also **Hertzsprung-Russell diagram, giant star, white dwarf, neutron star, black hole. b** *(as modifier)*: *a star catalogue.* Related adjectives: **astral, sidereal, stellar.** [3] *Astrology* **a** a celestial body, esp a planet, supposed to influence events, personalities, etc. **b** *(plural)* another name for **horoscope** (sense 1). [4] an emblem shaped like a conventionalized star, usually with five or more points, often used as a symbol of rank, an award, etc. [5] a small white blaze on the forehead of an animal, esp a horse. [6] Also called: **star facet.** any of the eight triangular facets cut in the crown of a brilliant. [7] **a** a distinguished or glamorous celebrity, often from the entertainment world. **b** *(as modifier)*: *star quality.* [8] another word for **asterisk.** [9] *Prison slang* a convict serving his first prison sentence. [10] **see stars.** to see or seem to see bright moving pinpoints of light, as from a blow on the head, increased blood pressure, etc. ◆ VERB **stars, starring, starred.** [11] *(tr)* to mark or decorate with a star or stars. [12] to feature or be featured as a star: *"Greed" starred Erich von Stroheim; Olivier starred in "Hamlet".*
▷HISTORY Old English *steorra*; related to Old Frisian *stēra*, Old Norse *stjarna*, German *Stern*, Latin *stella*
▸**ˈstarless** ADJECTIVE ▸**ˈstarˌlike** ADJECTIVE

star-apple NOUN [1] a West Indian sapotaceous tree, *Chrysophyllum cainito*, with smooth-skinned edible greenish-purple fruit. [2] the fruit of this tree which, when cut across, reveals a star-shaped arrangement of seeds.

Stara Zagora (*Bulgarian* ˈstara zaˈgɔra) NOUN a city in central Bulgaria: ceded to Bulgaria by Turkey in 1877. Pop.: 147 939 (1999 est.).

starboard (ˈstɑːbəd, -ˌbɔːd) NOUN [1] the right side of an aeroplane or vessel when facing the nose or bow. Compare **port**[2]. ◆ ADJECTIVE [2] relating to or on the starboard. ◆ VERB [3] to turn or be turned towards the starboard.
▷HISTORY Old English *stēorbord*, literally: steering side, from *stēor* steering paddle + *bord* side; see STEER[1], board; from the fact that boats were formerly steered by a paddle held over the right-hand side

starburst (ˈstɑːˌbɜːst) NOUN [1] a pattern of rays or lines radiating from a light source. [2] *Photog* a lens attachment which produces a starburst effect.

starch (stɑːtʃ) NOUN [1] a polysaccharide composed of glucose units that occurs widely in plant tissues in the form of storage granules, consisting of amylose and amylopectin. Related adjective: **amylaceous.** [2] Also called: **amylum.** a starch obtained from potatoes and some grain: it is fine white powder that forms a translucent viscous solution on boiling with water and is used to stiffen fabric and in many industrial processes. [3] any food

containing a large amount of starch, such as rice and potatoes. [4] stiff or pompous formality of manner or conduct. ◆ VERB [5] *(tr)* to stiffen with or soak in starch. ◆ ADJECTIVE [6] (of a person) formal; stiff.
▷HISTORY Old English *stercan* (unattested except by the past participle *sterced*) to stiffen; related to Old Saxon *sterkian*, Old High German *sterken* to strengthen, Dutch *sterken*; see STARK
▸ **'starcher** NOUN ▸ **'starch,like** ADJECTIVE

Star Chamber NOUN [1] *English history* the Privy Council sitting as a court of equity, esp powerful under the Tudor monarchs; abolished 1641. [2] *(sometimes not capitals)* any arbitrary tribunal dispensing summary justice. [3] *(sometimes not capitals)* (in Britain, in a Conservative government) a group of senior ministers who make the final decision on the public spending of each government department.

starch-reduced ADJECTIVE (of food, esp bread) having the starch content reduced, as in proprietary slimming products.

starchy ('stɑːtʃɪ) ADJECTIVE **starchier, starchiest.** [1] of, relating to, or containing starch: *starchy foods.* [2] extremely formal, stiff, or conventional: *a starchy manner.* [3] stiffened with starch.
▸ **'starchily** ADVERB ▸ **'starchiness** NOUN

star connection NOUN a connection used in a polyphase electrical device or system of devices in which the windings each have one end connected to a common junction, the **star point**, and the other end to a separate terminal. See also **Y connection.** Compare **delta connection.**

star-crossed ADJECTIVE dogged by ill luck; destined to misfortune.
▷HISTORY C16: from CROSS (in the sense: thwart): so called because of the astrological belief that the stars affect people's destinies

stardom ('stɑːdəm) NOUN [1] the fame and prestige of being a star in films, sport, etc. [2] the world of celebrities.

stardust ('stɑːˌdʌst) NOUN [1] dusty material found between the stars. [2] a large number of distant stars appearing to the observer as a cloud of dust. [2] a dreamy romantic or sentimental quality or feeling.

stare[1] (stɛə) VERB [1] *(intr; often foll by at)* to look or gaze fixedly, often with hostility or rudeness. [2] *(intr)* (of an animal's fur, bird's feathers, etc.) to stand on end because of fear, ill health, etc. [3] *(intr)* to stand out as obvious; glare. [4] **stare one in the face.** to be glaringly obvious or imminent. ◆ NOUN [5] the act or an instance of staring.
▷HISTORY Old English *starian*; related to Old Norse *stara*, Old High German *starēn* to stare, Greek *stereos* stiff, Latin *consternāre* to confuse
▸ **'starer** NOUN

stare[2] (stɛə) NOUN *Dialect* a starling.
▷HISTORY Old English *stær*

stare out *or* **down** VERB *(tr, adverb)* to look at (a person or animal) fixedly until his gaze is turned away.

starfish ('stɑːˌfɪʃ) NOUN, *plural* **-fish** *or* **-fishes.** any echinoderm of the class *Asteroidea*, such as *Asterias rubens*, typically having a flattened body covered with a flexible test and five arms radiating from a central disc.

starfished ('stɑːˌfɪʃd) ADJECTIVE *Informal* lying with arms and legs outstretched; spread-eagled.

starflower ('stɑːˌflaʊə) NOUN any of several plants with starlike flowers, esp the star-of-Bethlehem.

star fruit NOUN another name for **carambola.**

starfucker ('stɑːˌfʌkə) *Offensive taboo slang* NOUN [1] a person who seeks to have sexual relations with celebrities; groupie. [2] a person who seeks to associate with famous or powerful people.
▸ **'star,fucking** NOUN

stargaze ('stɑːˌgeɪz) VERB *(intr)* [1] to observe the stars. [2] to daydream.
▸ **'star,gazer** NOUN ▸ **'star,gazing** NOUN, ADJECTIVE

star grass NOUN any of various temperate and tropical plants of the amaryllidaceous genus *Hypoxis*, having long grasslike leaves and yellow star-shaped flowers.

stark (stɑːk) ADJECTIVE [1] *(usually prenominal)* devoid of any elaboration; blunt: *the stark facts.* [2] grim; desolate: *a stark landscape.* [3] *(usually prenominal)* utter; absolute: *stark folly.* [4] *Archaic* severe; violent. [5] *Archaic or poetic* rigid, as in death (esp in the phrases **stiff and stark, stark dead**). [6] short for **stark-naked.** ◆ ADVERB [7] completely: *stark mad.*
▷HISTORY Old English *stearc* stiff; related to Old Norse *sterkr*, Gothic *gastaurknan* to stiffen
▸ **'starkly** ADVERB ▸ **'starkness** NOUN

Stark effect (*German* ʃtark) NOUN the splitting of the lines of a spectrum when the source of light is subjected to a strong electrostatic field, discovered by Johannes Stark (1874–1957) in 1913.

stark-naked ADJECTIVE completely naked. Informal word: *(postpositive)* **starkers** ('stɑːkəz).
▷HISTORY C13 *stert naket*, literally: tail naked; *stert*, from Old English *steort* tail; related to Old Norse *stertr* tail + NAKED

starlet ('stɑːlɪt) NOUN [1] a young and inexperienced actress who is projected as a potential star. [2] a small star.

starlight ('stɑːˌlaɪt) NOUN [1] the light emanating from the stars. ◆ ADJECTIVE *also* **starlighted.** [2] of or like starlight. [3] Also: **starlit** ('stɑːˌlɪt). illuminated by starlight.

starling[1] ('stɑːlɪŋ) NOUN any gregarious passerine songbird of the Old World family *Sturnidae*, esp *Sturnus vulgaris*, which has a blackish plumage and a short tail.
▷HISTORY Old English *stærlinc*, from *stær* starling (related to Icelandic *stari*) + *-line* -LING[1]

starling[2] ('stɑːlɪŋ) NOUN an arrangement of piles that surround a pier of a bridge to protect it from debris, etc.
▷HISTORY C17: probably changed from *staddling*, from STADDLE

star-nosed mole NOUN an E North American amphibious mole, *Condylura cristata*, having a ring of pink fleshy tentacles around the nose.

star-of-Bethlehem NOUN [1] Also called: **starflower.** a Eurasian liliaceous plant, *Ornithogalum umbellatum*, naturalized in the eastern US, having narrow leaves and starlike white flowers. [2] any of several similar and related plants.

Star of Bethlehem NOUN the star that is supposed to have appeared above Bethlehem at the birth of Christ.

Star of Courage NOUN a Canadian award for bravery.

Star of David NOUN an emblem symbolizing Judaism and consisting of a six-pointed star formed by superimposing one inverted equilateral triangle upon another of equal size. Also called: **Magen David.**

starred (stɑːd) ADJECTIVE **a** having luck or fortune as specified. **b** *(in combination)*: *ill-starred.*

star ruby NOUN a ruby that resembles a starlike figure in reflected light because of its crystalline structure.

starry ('stɑːrɪ) ADJECTIVE **-rier, -riest.** [1] filled, covered with, or illuminated by stars. [2] of, like, or relating to a star or stars.
▸ **'starrily** ADVERB ▸ **'starriness** NOUN

starry-eyed ADJECTIVE given to naive wishes, judgments, etc.; full of unsophisticated optimism; gullible.

Stars and Bars NOUN *(functioning as singular)* **the.** the flag of the Confederate States of America.

Stars and Stripes NOUN *(functioning as singular)* **the.** the national flag of the United States of America, consisting of 50 white stars representing the present states on a blue field and seven red and six white horizontal stripes representing the original states. Also called: **the Star-Spangled Banner.**

star sapphire NOUN a sapphire showing a starlike figure in reflected light because of its crystalline structure.

star shell NOUN an artillery shell containing a flare or other illuminant: often containing a parachute to prolong the descent of the illuminating material.

star-spangled ADJECTIVE marked or decorated with stars.

Star-Spangled Banner NOUN **the.** [1] the national anthem of the United States of America. [2] another term for the **Stars and Stripes.**

star stream NOUN one of two main streams of stars that, because of the rotation of the Milky Way, appear to move in opposite directions, one towards Orion, the other towards Ara.

starstruck ('stɑːstrʌk) ADJECTIVE completely overawed by someone's celebrity status.

star-studded ADJECTIVE featuring a large proportion of well-known actors or other performers: *a star-studded cast.*

star system NOUN [1] *Astronomy* a group of celestial bodies that are associated as a result of natural laws. [2] the practice of casting one or two famous actors or actresses in a film, play, etc., so that their popularity ensures its success. [3] a design for laying cables for cable television in which each house is fed by an individual cable from a local central distribution point.

start (stɑːt) VERB [1] to begin or cause to begin (something or to do something); come or cause to come into being, operation, etc.: *he started a quarrel; they started to work.* [2] (when *intr*, sometimes foll by *on*) to make or cause to make a beginning of (a process, series of actions, etc.): *they started on the project.* [3] (sometimes foll by *up*) to set or be set in motion: *he started up the machine.* [4] *(intr)* to make a sudden involuntary movement of one's body, from or as if from fright; jump. [5] *(intr; sometimes foll by up, away, etc)* to spring or jump suddenly from a position or place. [6] to establish or be established; set up: *to start a business.* [7] *(tr)* to support (someone) in the first part of a venture, career, etc. [8] to work or cause to work loose. [9] to enter or be entered in a race. [10] *(intr)* to flow violently from a source: *wine started from a hole in the cask.* [11] *(tr)* to rouse (game) from a hiding place, lair, etc. [12] *(intr)* (esp of eyes) to bulge; pop. [13] an archaic word for **startle.** [14] *(intr) Brit informal* to commence quarrelling or causing a disturbance. [15] **to start with.** in the first place. ◆ NOUN [16] the first or first part of a series of actions or operations, a journey, etc. [17] the place or time of starting, as of a race or performance. [18] a signal to proceed, as in a race. [19] a lead or advantage, either in time or distance and usually of specified extent, in a competitive activity: *he had an hour's start on me.* [20] a slight involuntary movement of the body, as through fright, surprise, etc.: *she gave a start as I entered.* [21] an opportunity to enter a career, undertake a project, etc. [22] *Informal* a surprising incident. [23] a part that has come loose or been disengaged. [24] **by fits and starts.** spasmodically; without concerted effort. [25] **for a start.** in the first place. ◆ See also **start in, start off, start on, start out, start up.**
▷HISTORY Old English *styrtan*; related to Old Norse *sterta* to crease, Old High German *sturzen* to rush

START (stɑːt) NOUN ACRONYM FOR Strategic Arms Reduction Talks.

starter ('stɑːtə) NOUN [1] a device for starting an internal-combustion engine, usually consisting of a powerful electric motor that engages with the flywheel; formerly called: **self-starter.** [2] *US* a person who organizes the timely departure of buses, trains, etc. [3] a person who supervises and signals the start of a race. [4] a competitor who starts in a race or contest. [5] *Informal, chiefly Austral and NZ* an acceptable or practicable proposition, plan, idea, etc. [6] *Austral and NZ informal* a person who is willing to engage in a particular activity. [7] a culture of bacteria used to start fermentation, as in making cheese or yogurt. [8] *Chiefly Brit* the first course of a meal. [9] *(modifier)* designed to be used by a novice: *a starter kit.* [10] **for starters.** *Slang* in the first place. [11] **under starter's orders. a** (of horses in a race) awaiting the start signal. **b** (of a person) eager or ready to begin.

starter home NOUN a compact flat or house marketed by price and size specifications to suit the requirements of first-time home buyers.

star thistle NOUN any of several plants of the genus *Centaurea*, esp *C. calcitrapa*, of Eurasia, which has spiny purplish flower heads: family *Asteraceae* (composites). See also **centaury** (sense 2).
▷HISTORY C16: so called because it has a thistle-shaped flower surrounded by radiating spines

start in VERB *(adverb)* to undertake (something or doing something); commence or begin.

starting block NOUN one of a pair of adjustable devices with pads or blocks against which a sprinter braces his feet in crouch starts.

starting gate NOUN [1] a movable barrier so placed on the starting line of a racecourse that the raising of it releases all the contestants simultaneously. [2] the US name for **starting stalls.**

starting grid NOUN *Motor racing* a marked section of the track at the start where the cars line up according to their times in practice, the fastest occupying the front position.

starting price NOUN (esp in horse racing) the latest odds offered by bookmakers at the start of a race.

starting rate NOUN (in Britain) a rate of income tax below the basic rate.

starting stalls PLURAL NOUN *Brit* a line of stalls in which horses are enclosed at the start of a race and from which they are released by the simultaneous springing open of retaining barriers at the front of each stall.

startle ('stɑːtᵊl) VERB to be or cause to be surprised or frightened, esp so as to start involuntarily.
▷HISTORY Old English *steartlian* to stumble; related to Middle High German *starzen* to strut, Norwegian *sterta* to strain oneself
▸ **'startler** NOUN

startle colour NOUN *Zoology* a bright region of an animal's coloration, normally hidden from view and often part of a design resembling birds' eyes, etc., exposed when the animal is disturbed by a predator.

startling ('stɑːtlɪŋ) ADJECTIVE causing surprise or fear; striking; astonishing.
▸ **'startlingly** ADVERB

start off VERB (*adverb*) [1] (*intr*) to set out on a journey. [2] to be or make the first step in an activity; initiate: *he started the show off with a lively song*. [3] (*tr*) to cause (a person) to act or do something, such as to laugh, to tell stories, etc.

start on VERB (*intr, preposition*) *Brit informal* to pick a quarrel with (someone).

start out VERB (*intr, adverb*) [1] to set out on a journey. [2] to take the first steps, as in life, one's career, etc.: *he started out as a salesman*. [3] to take the first actions in an activity in a particular way or specified aim: *they started out wanting a house, but eventually bought a flat*.

start up VERB (*adverb*) [1] to come or cause to come into being for the first time; originate. [2] (*intr*) to spring or jump suddenly from a position or place. [3] to set in or go into motion, activity, etc.: *he started up the engine; the orchestra started up*. ◆ ADJECTIVE **start-up.** [4] of or relating to input, usually financial, made to establish a new project or business: *a start-up mortgage*. ◆ NOUN **start-up.** [5] a business enterprise that has been launched recently.

starvation (stɑː'veɪʃən) NOUN **a** the act or an instance of starving or state of being starved. **b** (*as modifier*): *a starvation diet; starvation wages*.

starve (stɑːv) VERB [1] to die or cause to die from lack of food. [2] to deprive (a person or animal) or (of a person, etc.) to be deprived of food. [3] (*intr*) *Informal* to be very hungry. [4] (foll by *of* or *for*) to deprive or be deprived (of something necessary), esp so as to cause suffering or malfunctioning: *the engine was starved of fuel*. [5] (*tr*; foll by *into*) to bring (to) a specified condition by starving: *to starve someone into submission*. [6] *Archaic* to be or cause to be extremely cold.
▷HISTORY Old English *steorfan* to die; related to Old Frisian *sterva* to die, Old High German *sterban* to die
▸ **'starver** NOUN

starveling ('stɑːvlɪŋ) *Archaic* ◆ NOUN [1] **a** a starving or poorly fed person, animal, etc. **b** (*as modifier*): *a starveling child*. ◆ ADJECTIVE [2] insufficient; meagre; scant.
▷HISTORY C16: from STARVE + -LING[1]

Star Wars NOUN (*functioning as singular*) [1] (in the US) a proposed system of artificial satellites armed with lasers to destroy enemy missiles in space. Formal name: **Strategic Defense Initiative.** Abbreviation: **SDI.** [2] (*modifier; sometimes not capitals*) of, relating to, or denoting this system: *Star Wars defence; star wars policy*.
▷HISTORY C20: popularly named after the science fiction film *Star Wars* (1977) by George Lucas

starwort ('stɑːˌwɜːt) NOUN [1] any of several plants with star-shaped flowers, esp the stitchwort. [2] **water starwort.** any of several aquatic plants of the genus *Callitriche*, having a star-shaped rosette of floating leaves: family *Callitrichaceae*.

stash (stæʃ) VERB [1] (*tr*; often foll by *away*) *Informal* to put or store (money, valuables, etc) in a secret place, as for safekeeping. ◆ NOUN [2] *Informal* a secret store or the place where this is hidden. [3] *Slang* drugs kept for personal consumption.
▷HISTORY C20: origin unknown

stashie ('stæʃɪ) NOUN *Scot* a variant of **stushie.**

Stasi ('stɑːzɪ) NOUN formerly, the secret police in East Germany.
▷HISTORY from German *Sta(ats)si(cherheitsdienst)*, literally: state security service

stasis ('steɪsɪs) NOUN [1] *Pathol* a stagnation in the normal flow of bodily fluids, such as the blood or urine. [2] *Literature* a state or condition in which there is no action or progress; static situation: *dramatic stasis*.
▷HISTORY C18: via New Latin from Greek: a standing, from *histanai* to cause to stand; related to Latin *stāre* to stand

stat. ABBREVIATION FOR: [1] (in prescriptions) immediately. [from Latin *statim*] [2] stationary. [3] statute.

-stat NOUN COMBINING FORM indicating a device that causes something to remain stationary or constant: *thermostat*.
▷HISTORY from Greek *-statēs*, from *histanai* to cause to stand

statant ('steɪtᵊnt) ADJECTIVE *Heraldry* (of an animal) in profile with all four feet on the ground.
▷HISTORY C15: from Latin, apparently from irregularly formed present participle of *stāre* to stand

state (steɪt) NOUN [1] the condition of a person, thing, etc., with regard to main attributes. [2] the structure, form, or constitution of something: *a solid state*. [3] any mode of existence. [4] position in life or society; estate. [5] ceremonious style, as befitting wealth or dignity: *to live in state*. [6] a sovereign political power or community. [7] the territory occupied by such a community. [8] the sphere of power in such a community: *affairs of state*. [9] (*often capital*) one of a number of areas or communities having their own governments and forming a federation under a sovereign government, as in the US. [10] (*often capital*) the body politic of a particular sovereign power, esp as contrasted with a rival authority such as the Church. [11] *Obsolete* a class or order; estate. [12] *Informal* a nervous, upset, or excited condition (esp in the phrase **in a state**). [13] **lie in state.** (of a body) to be placed on public view before burial. [14] **state of affairs.** a situation; present circumstances or condition. [15] **state of play.** the current situation. ◆ MODIFIER [16] controlled or financed by a state: *state university*. [17] of, relating to, or concerning the State: *State trial*. [18] involving ceremony or concerned with a ceremonious occasion: *state visit*. ◆ VERB (*tr; may take a clause as object*) [19] to articulate in words; utter. [20] to declare formally or publicly: *to state one's innocence*. [21] to resolve.
▷HISTORY C13: from Old French *estat*, from Latin *status* a standing, from *stāre* to stand
▸ **'statable** *or* **'stateable** ADJECTIVE ▸ **'statehood** NOUN

state bank NOUN (in the US) a commercial bank incorporated under a State charter and not required to be a member of the Federal Reserve System. Compare **national bank.**

state capitalism NOUN a form of capitalism in which the state owns or controls most of the means of production and other capital: often very similar to state socialism.

statecraft ('steɪtˌkrɑːft) NOUN the art of conducting public affairs; statesmanship.

stated ('steɪtɪd) ADJECTIVE [1] (esp of a sum) determined by agreement; fixed. [2] explicitly formulated or narrated: *a stated argument*.

stated case NOUN another term for **case stated.**

State Department NOUN the US government department in charge of foreign affairs.

state duma NOUN another name for **duma** (sense 3).

State Enrolled Nurse NOUN (formerly, in Britain) a nurse with training and examinations enabling him or her to perform many nursing services. Abbreviation: **SEN.**

state function NOUN *Physics* a thermodynamic quantity that has definite values for given states of a system, such as entropy, enthalpy, free energy, etc.

state house NOUN *NZ* a house built by the government for renting.

Statehouse ('steɪtˌhaʊs) NOUN [1] (in the US) the building which houses a state legislature; State capitol. [2] a building in which public affairs or state ceremonies are conducted.

stateless ('steɪtlɪs) ADJECTIVE [1] without nationality: *stateless persons*. [2] without a state or states. [3] *Chiefly Brit* without ceremonial dignity.
▸ **'statelessness** NOUN

statelet ('steɪtlɪt) NOUN a small state: *the Gaza Strip statelet*.

stately ('steɪtlɪ) ADJECTIVE **-lier, -liest.** [1] characterized by a graceful, dignified, and imposing appearance or manner. ◆ ADVERB [2] in a stately manner.
▸ **'stateliness** NOUN

stately home NOUN *Brit* a large mansion, esp one open to the public.

statement ('steɪtmənt) NOUN [1] the act of stating. [2] something that is stated, esp a formal prepared announcement or reply. [3] *Law* a declaration of matters of fact, esp in a pleading. [4] an account containing a summary of bills or invoices and displaying the total amount due. [5] an account prepared by a bank for each of its clients, usually at regular intervals, to show all credits and debits since the last account and the balance at the end of the period. [6] *Music* the presentation of a musical theme or idea, such as the subject of a fugue or sonata. [7] a computer instruction written in a source language, such as FORTRAN, which is converted into one or more machine code instructions by a compiler. [8] *Logic* the content of a sentence that affirms or denies something and may be true or false; what is thereby affirmed or denied abstracted from the act of uttering it. Thus *I am warm* said by me and *you are warm* said to me make the same statement. Compare **proposition** (sense 2b). [9] *Brit education* a legally binding account of the needs of a pupil with special educational needs and the provisions that will be made to meet them. ◆ VERB (*tr; usually passive*) [10] to assess (a pupil) with regard to his or her special educational needs.

statement of claim NOUN *Law* (in England) the first pleading made by the claimant in a civil court action showing the facts upon which he or she relies in support of the claim and the relief asked for.

statements of case PLURAL NOUN *Law* the formal written statements presented alternately by the plaintiff and defendant in a lawsuit setting out the respective matters relied upon. Former name: **pleadings.**

Staten Island ('stætᵊn) NOUN an island in SE New York State, in New York Harbor: a borough of New York city; heavy industry. Pop.: 378 977 (1990). Area: 155 sq. km (60 sq. miles).

state of the art NOUN [1] the level of knowledge and development achieved in a technique, science, etc., esp at present. ◆ ADJECTIVE (*prenominal*) **state-of-the-art.** [2] the most recent and therefore considered the best; up-to-the-minute: *a state-of-the-art amplifier*.

state of war NOUN [1] a period of armed conflict between states, regardless of whether or not war has been officially declared. [2] a legal condition begun by a declaration of war and ended formally, during which the rules of international law applicable to warfare may be invoked.

state prayers PLURAL NOUN *Church of England* prayers for the Sovereign, the royal family, the clergy, and Parliament said at matins and evensong.

State prison NOUN (in the US) a prison where persons convicted of serious crimes are confined.

stater ('steɪtə) NOUN any of various usually silver coins of ancient Greece.
▷HISTORY C14: via Late Latin from Greek *statēr* a standard of weight, from *histanai* to stand

State Registered Nurse NOUN (formerly in Britain) a nurse who had extensive training and passed examinations enabling him or her to perform all nursing services. Abbreviation: **SRN**. See **Registered General Nurse.**

stateroom ('steɪt,ruːm, -,rʊm) NOUN 1 a private cabin or room on a ship, train, etc. 2 *Chiefly Brit* a large room in a palace or other building for use on state occasions.

States (steɪts) NOUN (*functioning as singular or plural*) **the**. an informal name for the **United States of America.**

state school NOUN any school maintained by the state, in which education is free.

state services PLURAL NOUN *Church of England* services appointed to commemorate days of national celebration or deliverance such as the accession of a sovereign.

State Services Commission NOUN (in New Zealand) a government-appointed body in charge of the public service.

state's evidence NOUN (in the US) 1 the evidence for the prosecution given on behalf of a state in a criminal prosecution. 2 evidence given for the state by an accomplice against his former associates in crime (esp in the phrase **turn state's evidence**). Brit equivalent: **queen's** (or **king's**) **evidence.**

States General PLURAL NOUN 1 the bicameral legislature of the Netherlands. 2 *History* **a** an assembly of the estates of an entire country in contrast to those of a single province. **b** Also called: **Estates General.** the assembly of the estates of all France, last meeting in 1789. **c** the sovereign body of the Dutch republic from the 16th to 18th century.

stateside ('steɪt,saɪd) ADJECTIVE, ADVERB *US* of, in, to, or towards the US.

statesman ('steɪtsmən) NOUN, *plural* **-men.** 1 a political leader whose wisdom, integrity, etc., win great respect. 2 a person active and influential in the formulation of high government policy, such as a cabinet member. 3 a politician.
▸ **'statesman-,like** *or* **'statesmanly** ADJECTIVE
▸ **'statesmanship** NOUN ▸ **'states,woman** FEMININE NOUN

state socialism NOUN a variant of socialism in which the power of the state is employed for the purpose of creating an egalitarian society by means of public control of major industries, banks, etc., coupled with economic planning and a social security system.
▸ **state socialist** NOUN

States of the Church PLURAL NOUN another name for the **Papal States.**

states' rights PLURAL NOUN (*often capitals*) (in the US) 1 the rights and powers generally conceded to the states, or all those powers claimed for the states under some interpretations of the Constitution. 2 a doctrine advocating the severe curtailment of Federal powers by such an interpretation of the Constitution.
▸ **states' righter** NOUN

state trooper NOUN *US* a state policeman.

static ('stætɪk) ADJECTIVE *also* **statical.** 1 not active or moving; stationary. 2 (of a weight, force, or pressure) acting but causing no movement. 3 of or concerned with forces that do not produce movement. Compare **dynamic** (sense 1). 4 relating to or causing stationary electric charges; electrostatic. 5 of or relating to interference in the reception of radio or television transmissions. 6 of or concerned with statics. 7 *Sociol* characteristic of or relating to a society that has reached a state of equilibrium so that no changes are taking place. 8 *Computing* (of a memory) not needing its contents refreshed periodically. Compare **dynamic** (sense 5). ◆ NOUN 9 random hissing or crackling or a speckled picture caused by the interference of electrical disturbances in the reception of radio or television transmissions. 10 electric sparks or crackling produced by friction. ◆ See also **statics.**
▷ HISTORY C16: from New Latin *staticus*, from Greek *statikos* causing to stand, from *histanai* to stand, put on the scales
▸ **'statically** ADVERB

statice ('stætɪsɪ) NOUN a plant name formerly held to include both *Armeria* (see **thrift**) and *Limonium* (see **sea lavender**). The gardener's statice comprises various species of the latter, esp those whose flowers can be dried and kept: family *Plumbaginaceae.*
▷ HISTORY Latin: thrift, from Greek *statikē*, from *statikos* astringent (from a medicinal use of thrift)

static line NOUN a line attaching the pack of a parachute to an aircraft, so that the parachute is opened when it has fallen clear of the aircraft.

statics ('stætɪks) NOUN (*functioning as singular*) the branch of mechanics concerned with the forces that produce a state of equilibrium in a system of bodies. Compare **dynamics** (sense 1).

static tube NOUN an open-ended tube used to measure the static pressure at a point in a moving fluid and positioned in such a way that it is unaffected by the fluid's motion.

statin ('stætɪn) NOUN any of a class of drugs, including atorvastatin and simvastatin, that lower the levels of low-density lipoproteins in the blood by inhibiting the activity of an enzyme involved in the production of cholesterol in the liver.

station ('steɪʃən) NOUN 1 the place or position at which a thing or person stands or is supposed to stand. 2 **a** a place along a route or line at which a bus, train, etc., stops for fuel or to pick up or let off passengers or goods, esp one with ancillary buildings and services: *railway station.* **b** (*as modifier*): *a station buffet.* 3 **a** the headquarters or local offices of an official organization such as the police or fire services. **b** (*as modifier*): *a station sergeant.* See **police station, fire station.** 4 a building, depot, etc., with special equipment for some particular purpose: *power station; petrol station; television station.* 5 *Military* a place of duty: *an action station.* 6 *Navy* **a** a location to which a ship or fleet is assigned for duty. **b** an assigned location for a member of a ship's crew. 7 a radio or television channel. 8 a position or standing, as in a particular society or organization. 9 the type of one's occupation; calling. 10 (in British India) a place where the British district officials or garrison officers resided. 11 *Biology* the type of habitat occupied by a particular animal or plant. 12 *Austral and NZ* a large sheep or cattle farm. 13 *Surveying* a point at which a reading is made or which is used as a point of reference. 14 (*often capital*) *RC Church* **a** one of the Stations of the Cross. **b** any of the churches (**station churches**) in Rome that have been used from ancient times as points of assembly for religious processions and ceremonies on particular days (**station days**). 15 (*plural*) (in rural Ireland) mass, preceded by confessions, held annually in a parishioner's dwelling and attended by other parishioners. ◆ VERB 16 (*tr*) to place in or assign to a station.
▷ HISTORY C14: via Old French from Latin *statiō* a standing still, from *stāre* to stand

stationary ('steɪʃənərɪ) ADJECTIVE 1 not moving; standing still. 2 not able to be moved. 3 showing no change: *the doctors said his condition was stationary.* 4 tending to remain in one place.
▷ HISTORY C15: from Latin *statiōnārius*, from *statiō* STATION
▸ **'stationarily** ADVERB ▸ **'stationariness** NOUN

> **Language note** Avoid confusion with **stationery.**

stationary engine NOUN an engine that remains in a fixed position, esp one in a building that drives generators or other machinery.
▸ **stationary engineer** NOUN

stationary orbit NOUN *Astronautics* an orbit lying in, or approximately in, the plane of the equator for which the orbital period is equal to the spin period of the central body.

stationary point NOUN 1 a point on a curve at which the tangent is either horizontal or vertical, such as a maximum, a minimum, or a point of inflection. 2 *Astronomy* a point in the apparent path of a planet when it reverses direction.

stationary wave NOUN another name for **standing wave.**

stationer ('steɪʃənə) NOUN 1 a person who sells stationery or a shop where stationery is sold. 2 *Obsolete* a publisher or bookseller.
▷ HISTORY C14: from Medieval Latin *stationarius* a person having a regular station, hence a shopkeeper (esp a bookseller) as distinguished from an itinerant tradesman; see STATION

Stationers' Company NOUN a guild, established by Royal Charter from Queen Mary in 1557, composed of booksellers, printers, etc.

stationery ('steɪʃənərɪ) NOUN any writing materials, such as paper, envelopes, pens, ink, rulers, etc.

> **Language note** Avoid confusion with **stationary.**

Stationery Office NOUN **the.** (in the UK) the company that supplies the civil service with all its office supplies, machinery, printing and binding, etc.

station house NOUN *Chiefly US* a house that is situated by or serves as a station, esp as a police or fire station.

stationmaster ('steɪʃən,mɑːstə) *or* **station manager** NOUN the senior official in charge of a railway station.

Stations of the Cross PLURAL NOUN *RC Church* 1 a series of 14 crosses, often accompanied by 14 pictures or carvings, arranged in order around the walls of a church, to commemorate 14 supposed stages in Christ's journey to Calvary. 2 a devotion consisting of 14 prayers relating to each of these stages.

station wagon NOUN a US, Canadian, Austral, and NZ name for **estate car.**

statism ('steɪtɪzəm) NOUN the theory or practice of concentrating economic and political power in the state, resulting in a weak position for the individual or community with respect to the government.

statist ('steɪtɪst) NOUN 1 an advocate of statism. 2 a less common name for a **statistician.** 3 *Archaic* a politician or statesman. ◆ ADJECTIVE 4 of, characteristic of, advocating, or relating to statism.

statistic (stə'tɪstɪk) NOUN any function of a number of random variables, usually identically distributed, that may be used to estimate a population parameter. See also **sampling statistic, estimator** (sense 2), **parameter** (sense 3).

statistical (stə'tɪstɪkᵊl) ADJECTIVE of or relating to statistics.

statistical dependence NOUN a condition in which two random variables are not independent. *X* and *Y* are **positively dependent** if the conditional probability, $P(X|Y)$, of *X* given *Y* is greater than the probability, $P(X)$, of *X*, or equivalently if $P(X\&Y) > P(X).P(Y)$. They are **negatively dependent** if the inequalities are reversed.

statistical inference NOUN the theory, methods, and practice of forming judgments about the parameters of a population, usually on the basis of random sampling. Also called: **inferential statistics.** Compare **hypothesis testing.**

statistically (stə'tɪstɪkəlɪ, -klɪ) ADVERB in terms of or according to statistics.

statistical mechanics NOUN (*functioning as singular*) the study of the properties of physical systems as predicted by the statistical behaviour of their constituent particles.

statistical tables PLURAL NOUN tables showing the values of the cumulative distribution functions, probability functions, or probability density functions of certain common distributions for different values of their parameters, and used esp to determine whether or not a particular statistical result exceeds the required significance level. See **hypothesis testing.**

statistician (,stætɪ'stɪʃən) NOUN 1 a person who specializes in or is skilled at statistics. 2 a person who compiles statistics.

statistics (stə'tɪstɪks) NOUN 1 (*functioning as plural*) quantitative data on any subject, esp data comparing the distribution of some quantity for different subclasses of the population: *statistics for earnings by different age groups.* 2 (*functioning as singular*) **a** the classification and interpretation of such data in accordance with probability theory and the application of methods such as hypothesis testing to them. **b** the mathematical study of the theoretical nature of such distributions and tests. See also **descriptive statistics, statistical inference.**
▷ HISTORY C18 (originally "science dealing with facts of a state"): via German *Statistik*, from New Latin *statisticus* concerning state affairs, from Latin *status* STATE

stative ('steɪtɪv) *Grammar* ◆ ADJECTIVE [1] denoting a verb describing a state rather than an activity, act, or event, such as *know* and *want* as opposed to *leave* and *throw*. Compare **nonstative.** ◆ NOUN [2] a stative verb.
▷HISTORY C19: from New Latin *stativus*, from Latin *stāre* to stand

stato- COMBINING FORM static; standing; fixed: *statolith*.
▷HISTORY from Greek *statos* standing, set

statoblast ('stætəʊˌblɑːst) NOUN *Zoology* an encapsulated bud produced asexually by certain bryozoans that can survive adverse conditions and that gives rise to a new colony.

statocyst ('stætəʊsɪst) NOUN an organ of balance in some invertebrates, such as crustaceans, that consists of a sensory vesicle containing small granules (see **statolith**).

statolatry (steɪ'tɒlətrɪ) NOUN *Rare* the act or practice of idolizing the state.
▷HISTORY C19: from STATE + -LATRY

statolith ('stætəʊlɪθ) NOUN [1] Also called: **otolith.** any of the granules of calcium carbonate occurring in a statocyst: movement of statoliths, caused by a change in position of the animal, stimulates hair cells, which convey the information to the brain by nerve fibres. [2] any of various movable inclusions, such as starch grains, that occur in plant cells and are thought to function in geotropic responses.
▸ **ˌstato'lithic** ADJECTIVE

stator ('steɪtə) NOUN [1] the stationary part of a rotary machine or device, esp of a motor or generator. [2] a system of nonrotating radially arranged parts within a rotating assembly, esp the fixed blades of an axial flow compressor in a gas turbine. ◆ Compare **rotor** (sense 1).
▷HISTORY C20: from Latin: one who stands (by), from *stāre* to stand

statoscope ('stætəˌskəʊp) NOUN a very sensitive form of aneroid barometer used to detect and measure small variations in atmospheric pressure, such as one used in an aircraft to indicate small changes in altitude.

statuary ('stætjʊərɪ) NOUN [1] statues collectively. [2] the art of making statues. ◆ ADJECTIVE [3] of, relating to, or suitable for statues.
▷HISTORY C16: from Latin *statuārius*

statue ('stætjuː) NOUN a wooden, stone, metal, plaster, or other kind of sculpture of a human or animal figure, usually life-size or larger.
▷HISTORY C14: via Old French from Latin *statua*, from *statuere* to set up; compare STATUTE

statued ('stætjuːd) ADJECTIVE decorated with or portrayed in a statue or statues.

Statue of Liberty NOUN a monumental statue personifying liberty, in New York Harbor, on Liberty Island: a gift from France, erected in 1885. Official name: **Liberty Enlightening the World.**

statuesque (ˌstætjʊ'ɛsk) ADJECTIVE like a statue, esp in possessing great formal beauty or dignity.
▷HISTORY C19: from STATUE + -ESQUE, on the model of PICTURESQUE
▸ **ˌstatu'esquely** ADVERB ▸ **ˌstatu'esqueness** NOUN

statuette (ˌstætjʊ'ɛt) NOUN a small statue.

stature ('stætʃə) NOUN [1] the height of something, esp a person or animal when standing. [2] the degree of development of a person: *the stature of a champion*. [3] intellectual or moral greatness: *a man of stature*.
▷HISTORY C13: via Old French from Latin *statūra*, from *stāre* to stand

status ('steɪtəs) NOUN, *plural* **-tuses.** [1] a social or professional position, condition, or standing to which varying degrees of responsibility, privilege, and esteem are attached. [2] the relative position or standing of a person or thing. [3] a high position or standing; prestige: *he has acquired a new status since he has been in that job*. [4] the legal standing or condition of a person. [5] a state of affairs.
▷HISTORY C17: from Latin: posture, from *stāre* to stand

status asthmaticus (æs'mætɪkəs) NOUN a severe attack of asthma in which the patient may die from respiratory failure if not treated with inhaled oxygen or other appropriate measures.

status epilepticus (ˌɛpɪ'lɛptɪkəs) NOUN a condition in which repeated epileptic seizures occur without the patient gaining consciousness between them. If untreated for a prolonged period it can lead to long-term disability or death.

status Indian *Canadian* a member of a native Canadian people who is registered as an Indian under the federal Indian Act.

status quo (kwəʊ) NOUN (usually preceded by *the*) the existing state of affairs.
▷HISTORY literally: the state in which

status symbol NOUN a possession which is regarded as proof of the owner's social position, wealth, prestige, etc.

status zero NOUN the condition of young people who are out of school but not in further education or training, permanently or regularly out of work, and dropping out of the mainstream of society.

statutable ('stætjʊtəbᵊl) ADJECTIVE a variant of **statutory** (senses 2, 3).
▸ **'statutably** ADVERB

statute ('stætjuːt) NOUN [1] **a** an enactment of a legislative body expressed in a formal document. **b** this document. [2] a permanent rule made by a body or institution for the government of its internal affairs.
▷HISTORY C13: from Old French *estatut*, from Late Latin *statūtum*, from Latin *statuere* to set up, decree, ultimately from *stāre* to stand

statute book NOUN *Chiefly Brit* a register of enactments passed by the legislative body of a state, usually made up of a series of volumes that form a complete official record: *not on the statute book*.

statute law NOUN [1] a law enacted by a legislative body. [2] a particular example of this. ◆ Compare **common law, equity.**

statute mile NOUN a legal or formal name for **mile** (sense 1).

statute of limitations NOUN a legislative enactment prescribing the period of time within which proceedings must be instituted to enforce a right or bring an action at law. See also **laches.**

Statute of Westminster NOUN the act of Parliament (1931) that formally recognized the independence of the dominions within the Empire.

statutory ('stætjʊtərɪ, -trɪ) ADJECTIVE [1] of, relating to, or having the nature of a statute. [2] prescribed or authorized by statute. [3] (of an offence) **a** recognized by statute. **b** subject to a punishment or penalty prescribed by statute.
▸ **'statutorily** ADVERB

statutory declaration NOUN *Law* a declaration made under statutory authority before a justice of the peace or commissioner for oaths which may in certain cases be substituted for a statement on oath.

statutory order NOUN a statute that applies further legislation to an existing act.

statutory rape NOUN (in the US) the criminal offence of having sexual intercourse with a girl who has not reached the age of consent.

staun (stɔːn) VERB, NOUN a Scot word for **stand.**

staunch¹ (stɔːntʃ) ADJECTIVE [1] loyal, firm, and dependable: *a staunch supporter*. [2] solid or substantial in construction. [3] *Rare* (of a ship, etc.) watertight; seaworthy.
▷HISTORY C15: (originally: watertight): from Old French *estanche*, from *estanchier* to STANCH
▸ **'staunchly** ADVERB ▸ **'staunchness** NOUN

staunch² (stɔːntʃ) VERB, NOUN a variant spelling of **stanch.**

staurolite ('stɔːrəˌlaɪt) NOUN a brown glassy mineral consisting of iron aluminium silicate in the form of prismatic crystals: used as a gemstone. Formula: $Fe_2Al_9Si_4O_{11}(OH)_2$.
▷HISTORY C19: from Greek *stauros* a cross + -LITE
▸ **staurolitic** (ˌstɔːrə'lɪtɪk) ADJECTIVE

stauroscope ('stɔːrəˌskəʊp) NOUN *Obsolete* an optical instrument for studying the crystal structure of minerals under polarized light.
▷HISTORY C19: from Greek *stauros* a cross + -SCOPE
▸ **stauroscopic** (ˌstɔːrə'skɒpɪk) ADJECTIVE
▸ **ˌstauro'scopically** ADVERB

Stavanger (*Norwegian* sta'vaŋər) NOUN a port in SW Norway: canning and shipbuilding industries. Pop.: 108 818 (2000 est.).

stave (steɪv) NOUN [1] any one of a number of long strips of wood joined together to form a barrel, bucket, boat hull, etc. [2] any of various bars, slats, or rods, usually of wood, such as a rung of a ladder or a crosspiece bracing the legs of a chair. [3] any stick, staff, etc. [4] a stanza or verse of a poem. [5] *Music* **a** *Brit* an individual group of five lines and four spaces used in staff notation. **b** another word for **staff¹** (sense 9). ◆ VERB **staves, staving, staved** *or* **stove.** [6] (often foll by *in*) to break or crush (the staves of a boat, barrel, etc.) or (of the staves of a boat) to be broken or crushed. [7] (*tr*; usually foll by *in*) to burst or force (a hole in something). [8] (*tr*) to provide (a ladder, chair, etc.) with a stave or staves. [9] (*tr*) *Scot* to sprain (a finger, toe, etc.).
▷HISTORY C14: back formation from *staves*, plural of STAFF¹

stave off VERB (*tr, adverb*) to avert or hold off (something undesirable or harmful), esp temporarily: *to stave off hunger*.

staves (steɪvz) NOUN a plural of **staff¹** or **stave.**

stavesacre ('steɪvzˌeɪkə) NOUN [1] a Eurasian ranunculaceous plant, *Delphinium staphisagria*, having purple flowers and poisonous seeds. [2] the seeds of this plant, which have strong emetic and cathartic properties.
▷HISTORY C14 *staphisagre*, from Latin *staphis agria*, from Greek, from *staphis* raisin + *agria* wild

Stavropol (*Russian* 'stavrəpəlj) NOUN [1] a city in SW Russia: founded as a fortress in 1777. Pop.: 345 100 (1999 est.). Former name (1940–44): **Voroshilovsk.** [2] the former name (until 1964) of **Togliatti.**

stay¹ (steɪ) VERB [1] (*intr*) to continue or remain in a certain place, position, etc.: *to stay outside*. [2] (*copula*) to continue to be; remain: *to stay awake*. [3] (*intr*; often foll by *at*) to reside temporarily, esp as a guest: *to stay at a hotel*. [4] (*tr*) to remain for a specified period: *to stay the weekend*. [5] (*intr*) *Scot and South African* to reside permanently or habitually; live. [6] *Archaic* to stop or cause to stop. [7] (*intr*) to wait, pause, or tarry. [8] (*tr*) to delay or hinder. [9] (*tr*) **a** to discontinue or suspend (a judicial proceeding). **b** to hold in abeyance or restrain from enforcing (an order, decree, etc.). [10] to endure (something testing or difficult, such as a race): *a horse that stays the course*. [11] (*intr*; usually foll by *with*) to keep pace (with a competitor in a race, etc.). [12] (*intr*) *Poker* to raise one's stakes enough to stay in a round. [13] (*tr*) to hold back or restrain: *to stay one's anger*. [14] (*tr*) to satisfy or appease (an appetite, etc.) temporarily. [15] (*tr*) *Archaic* to quell or suppress. [16] (*intr*) *Archaic* to stand firm. [17] **stay put.** See **put** (sense 18). ◆ NOUN [18] the act of staying or sojourning in a place or the period during which one stays. [19] the act of stopping or restraining or state of being stopped, etc. [20] the suspension of a judicial proceeding, etc.: *stay of execution*. ◆ See also **stay out.**
▷HISTORY C15 *staien*, from Anglo-French *estaier*, to stay, from Old French *ester* to stay, from Latin *stāre* to stand

stay² (steɪ) NOUN [1] anything that supports or steadies, such as a prop or buttress. [2] a thin strip of metal, plastic, bone, etc., used to stiffen corsets, etc. ◆ VERB (*tr*) *Archaic* [3] (often foll by *up*) to prop or hold. [4] (often foll by *up*) to comfort or sustain. [5] (foll by *on* or *upon*) to cause to rely or depend. ◆ See also **stays** (sense 1).
▷HISTORY C16: from Old French *estaye*, of Germanic origin; compare STAY³

stay³ (steɪ) NOUN a rope, cable, or chain, usually one of a set, used for bracing uprights, such as masts, funnels, flagpoles, chimneys, etc.; guy. ◆ See also **stays** (senses 2, 3).
▷HISTORY Old English *stæg*; related to Old Norse *stag*, Middle Low German *stach*, Norwegian *stagle* wooden post

stay-at-home ADJECTIVE [1] (of a person) enjoying a quiet, settled, and unadventurous use of leisure. ◆ NOUN [2] a stay-at-home person. [3] a person who does not bother to vote in a political election.

stayer ('steɪə) NOUN [1] a person or thing that stays. [2] *Informal* **a** a persistent or tenacious person. **b** *Horse racing* a persistent horse.

staying power NOUN endurance; stamina.

Stayman ('steɪmən) NOUN (in contract bridge) a conventional response in clubs to a partner's opening no-trump bid, as a request for the partner to show any four-card major.

▷HISTORY C20: named after Samuel M. *Stayman* (1909–94), US bridge expert

stay out VERB *(adverb)* [1] *(intr)* to remain away from home: *the cat stayed out all night.* [2] *(tr)* to remain beyond the end of: *to stay out a welcome.* [3] *(tr)* to remain throughout: *to stay the night out.*

stays (steɪz) PLURAL NOUN [1] *Now rare* corsets with bones in them. [2] a position of a sailing vessel relative to the wind so that the sails are luffing or aback. Compare **irons** (sense 2). [3] **miss stays.** Also: **refuse stays.** (of a sailing vessel) to fail to come about.

staysail ('steɪˌseɪl) *Nautical* ('steɪsᵊl) NOUN an auxiliary sail, often triangular, set to catch the wind, as between the masts of a yawl (**mizzen staysail**), aft of a spinnaker (**spinnaker staysail**), etc.

stay stitching NOUN a line of stitches made in the seam allowance to prevent the edges from stretching.

stbd ABBREVIATION FOR starboard.

STC (in India) ABBREVIATION FOR State Trading Corporation.

std ABBREVIATION FOR standard.

STD ABBREVIATION FOR: [1] **subscriber trunk dialling.** [2] *NZ* subscriber toll dialling. [3] sexually transmitted disease. [4] Doctor of Sacred Theology.

STD code NOUN *Brit* a code of four or more digits, other than those comprising a subscriber's local telephone number, that determines the routing of a call.
▷HISTORY C20: *s(ubscriber) t(runk) d(ialling)*

Ste ABBREVIATION FOR Saint (female).
▷HISTORY French *Sainte*

stead (stɛd) NOUN [1] (preceded by *in*) *Rare* the place, function, or position that should be taken by another: *to come in someone's stead.* [2] **stand (someone) in good stead.** to be useful or of good service to (someone). ♦ VERB [3] *(tr) Archaic* to help or benefit.
▷HISTORY Old English *stede*; related to Old Norse *stathr* place, Old High German *stat* place, Latin *statiō* a standing, *statim* immediately

steadfast *or* **stedfast** ('stɛdfəst, -ˌfɑːst) ADJECTIVE [1] (esp of a person's gaze) fixed in intensity or direction; steady. [2] unwavering or determined in purpose, loyalty, etc.: *steadfast resolve.*
▸ **'steadfastly** *or* **'stedfastly** ADVERB ▸ **'steadfastness** *or* **'stedfastness** NOUN

Steadicam NOUN ('stɛdɪˌkæm), NOUN *Trademark* a mechanism for steadying a hand-held camera, consisting of a shock-absorbing arm to which the camera is attached and a harness worn by the camera operator.

steading ('stɛdɪŋ) NOUN *Brit* [1] a farmstead. [2] the outbuildings of a farm.
▷HISTORY C15: from STEAD + -ING[1]

steady ('stɛdɪ) ADJECTIVE **steadier, steadiest.** [1] not able to be moved or disturbed easily; stable. [2] free from fluctuation: *the level stayed steady.* [3] not easily excited; imperturbable. [4] staid; sober. [5] regular; habitual: *a steady drinker.* [6] continuous: *a steady flow.* [7] *Nautical* (of a vessel) keeping upright, as in heavy seas. ♦ VERB **steadies, steadying, steadied.** [8] to make or become steady. ♦ ADVERB [9] in a steady manner. [10] **go steady.** *Informal* to date one person regularly. ♦ NOUN, *plural* **steadies.** [11] *Informal* one's regular boyfriend or girlfriend. ♦ INTERJECTION [12] *Nautical* an order to the helmsman to stay on a steady course. [13] a warning to keep calm, be careful, etc. [14] *Brit* a command to get set to start, as in a race: *ready, steady, go!*
▷HISTORY C16: from STEAD + -Y[1]; related to Old High German *stātīg*, Middle Dutch *stēdig*
▸ **'steadier** NOUN ▸ **'steadily** ADVERB ▸ **'steadiness** NOUN

steady state NOUN *Physics* the condition of a system when some or all of the quantities describing it are independent of time but not necessarily in thermodynamic or chemical equilibrium. See also **equilibrium** (sense 6).

steady-state theory NOUN a cosmological theory postulating that the universe exists throughout time in a steady state such that the average density of matter does not vary with distance or time. Matter is continuously created in the space left by the receding stars and galaxies of the expanding universe. Compare **big-bang theory.**

steak (steɪk) NOUN [1] See **beefsteak.** [2] any of various cuts of beef of varying quality, used for braising, stewing, etc. [3] a thick slice of pork, veal, etc., or of a large fish, esp cod or salmon. [4] minced meat prepared in the same way as steak: *hamburger steak.*
▷HISTORY C15: from Old Norse *steik* roast; related to *steikja* to roast on a spit; see STICK[1]

steakhouse ('steɪkˌhaʊs) NOUN a restaurant that has steaks as its speciality.

steak tartare *or* **tartar** NOUN raw minced steak, mixed with onion, seasonings, and raw egg. Also called: **tartare steak, tartar steak.**

steal (stiːl) VERB **steals, stealing, stole, stolen.** [1] to take (something) from someone, etc. without permission or unlawfully, esp in a secret manner. [2] *(tr)* to obtain surreptitiously. [3] *(tr)* to appropriate (ideas, etc.) without acknowledgment, as in plagiarism. [4] to move or convey stealthily: *they stole along the corridor.* [5] *(intr)* to pass unnoticed: *the hours stole by.* [6] *(tr)* to win or gain by strategy or luck, as in various sports: *to steal a few yards.* [7] **steal a march on.** to obtain an advantage over, esp by a secret or underhand measure. [8] **steal someone's thunder.** to detract from the attention due to another by forestalling him. [9] **steal the show.** to be looked upon as the most interesting, popular, etc., esp unexpectedly. ♦ NOUN *Informal* [10] the act of stealing. [11] something stolen or acquired easily or at little cost.
▷HISTORY Old English *stelan*; related to Old Frisian, Old Norse *stela* Gothic *stilan*, German *stehlen*

stealer ('stiːlə) NOUN **a** a person who steals something. **b** *(in combination)*: *scene-stealer.*

stealth (stɛlθ) NOUN [1] the act or characteristic of moving with extreme care and quietness, esp so as to avoid detection: *the stealth of a cat.* [2] cunning or underhand procedure or dealing. [3] *Archaic* the act of stealing.
▷HISTORY C13 *stelthe*; see STEAL, -TH[1]
▸ **'stealthful** ADJECTIVE

Stealth (stɛlθ) NOUN *(modifier) Informal* denoting or referring to technology that aims to reduce the radar, thermal, and acoustic recognizability of aircraft and missiles.

Stealth bomber *or* **plane** NOUN a type of US military aircraft using advanced technology to render it virtually undetectable to sight, radar, or infrared sensors. Also called: **B-2.**

stealth tax NOUN *Brit informal* an indirect tax, such as that on fuel or pension funds, esp one of which people are unaware or that is felt to be unfair.

stealthy ('stɛlθɪ) ADJECTIVE **stealthier, stealthiest.** characterized by great caution, secrecy, etc.; furtive.
▸ **'stealthily** ADVERB ▸ **'stealthiness** NOUN

steam (stiːm) NOUN [1] the gas or vapour into which water is changed when boiled. [2] the mist formed when such gas or vapour condenses in the atmosphere. [3] any vaporous exhalation. [4] *Informal* power, energy, or speed. [5] **get up steam. a** (of a ship, etc.) to work up a sufficient head of steam in a boiler to drive an engine. **b** *Informal* to go quickly. [6] **let off steam.** *Informal* to release pent-up energy or emotions. [7] **under one's own steam.** without the assistance of others. [8] *Austral slang* cheap wine. [9] *(modifier)* driven, operated, heated, powered, etc., by steam: *a steam radiator.* [10] *(modifier)* treated by steam: *steam ironed; steam cleaning.* [11] *(modifier) Humorous* old-fashioned; outmoded: *steam radio.* ♦ VERB [12] to emit or be emitted as steam. [13] *(intr)* to generate steam, as a boiler, etc. [14] *(intr)* to move or travel by steam power, as a ship, etc. [15] *(intr) Informal* to proceed quickly and sometimes forcefully. [16] to cook or be cooked in steam. [17] *(tr)* to treat with steam or apply steam to, as in cleaning, pressing clothes, etc. ♦ See also **steam up.**
▷HISTORY Old English; related to Dutch *stoom* steam, perhaps to Old High German *stioban* to raise dust, Gothic *stubjus* dust

steam bath NOUN [1] a room or enclosure that can be filled with steam in which people bathe to induce sweating and refresh or cleanse themselves. [2] an act of taking such a bath. [3] an enclosure through which steam can be passed continuously, used in laboratories for sterilizing equipment, maintaining a constant temperature, etc.

steamboat ('stiːmˌbəʊt) NOUN a boat powered by a steam engine.

steam-boiler NOUN a vessel in which water is boiled to generate steam. An industrial boiler usually consists of a system of parallel tubes through which water passes, suspended above a furnace.

steam-chest NOUN a chamber that encloses the slide valve of a steam engine and forms a manifold for the steam supply to the valve.

steam coal NOUN coal suitable for use in producing steam, as in a steam-boiler.

steam-engine NOUN an engine that uses the thermal energy of steam to produce mechanical work, esp one in which steam from a boiler is expanded in a cylinder to drive a reciprocating piston.

steamer ('stiːmə) NOUN [1] a boat or ship driven by steam engines. [2] Also called: **steam box.** an apparatus for steaming wooden beams and planks to make them pliable for shipbuilding. [3] a vessel used to cook food by steam. [4] *Austral slang* a clash of sporting teams characterized by rough play.

steam-generating heavy-water reactor NOUN a nuclear reactor using heavy water as the moderator, light water (H_2O) as the coolant, and uranium oxide cased in zirconium alloy as the fuel. Abbreviation: **SGHWR.**

steamie ('stiːmɪ) NOUN *Scot urban dialect* a public wash house.

steaming ('stiːmɪŋ) ADJECTIVE [1] very hot. [2] *Informal* angry. [3] *Slang* drunk. ♦ NOUN [4] *Informal* robbery, esp of passengers in a railway carriage or bus, by a large gang of armed youths.

steam iron NOUN an electric iron that emits steam from channels in the iron face to facilitate the pressing and ironing of clothes, etc., the steam being produced from water contained within the iron.

steam jacket NOUN *Engineering* a jacket containing steam that surrounds and heats a cylinder.

steam organ NOUN a type of organ powered by steam, once common at fairgrounds, in which the pipes are sounded either by a keyboard or in a sequence determined by a moving punched card. US name: **calliope.**

steam point NOUN the temperature at which the maximum vapour pressure of water is equal to one atmosphere (1.01325×10^5 N/m^2). It has the value of 100° on the Celsius scale. Compare **ice point.**

steam reforming NOUN *Chem* a process in which methane from natural gas is heated, with steam, usually with a catalyst, to produce a mixture of carbon monoxide and hydrogen used in organic synthesis and as a fuel.

steam roller ('stiːmˌrəʊlə) NOUN [1] **a** a steam-powered vehicle with heavy rollers at the front and rear used for compressing road surfaces during road-making. **b** another word for **roadroller.** [2] **a** an overpowering force or a person with such force that overcomes all opposition. **b** *(as modifier)*: *steamroller tactics.* ♦ VERB [3] *(tr)* to crush (opposition, etc.) by overpowering force.

steam room NOUN a room that can be filled with steam for use as a steam bath.

steamship ('stiːmˌʃɪp) NOUN a ship powered by one or more steam engines.

steam-shovel NOUN a steam-driven mechanical excavator, esp one having a large bucket or grab on a beam slung from a revolving jib.

steamtight ('stiːmˌtaɪt) ADJECTIVE (of joints, cylinders, etc.) being sealed in such a way that steam cannot leak out.
▸ **'steamˌtightness** NOUN

steam trap NOUN a device in a steam pipe that collects and discharges condensed water.

steam turbine NOUN a turbine driven by steam.

steam up VERB *(adverb)* [1] to cover (windows, etc.) or (of windows, etc.) to become covered with a film of condensed steam. [2] *(tr; usually passive) Slang* to excite or make angry: *he's all steamed up about the delay.*

steam whistle NOUN a type of whistle sounded by a blast of steam, as used formerly in factories, on locomotives, etc.

steamy (ˈstiːmɪ) ADJECTIVE **steamier, steamiest.** [1] of, resembling, full of, or covered with steam. [2] *Informal* lustful or erotic: *steamy nightlife.*
▸ˈ**steamily** ADVERB ▸ˈ**steaminess** NOUN

steapsin (stɪˈæpsɪn) NOUN *Biochem* a pancreatic lipase.
▷**HISTORY** C19: from Greek *stear* fat + PEPSIN

stearate (ˈstɪəˌreɪt) NOUN any salt or ester of stearic acid.

stearic (stɪˈærɪk) ADJECTIVE [1] of or relating to suet or fat. [2] of, consisting of, containing, or derived from stearic acid.
▷**HISTORY** C19: from French *stéarique*, from Greek *stear* fat, tallow

stearic acid NOUN a colourless odourless insoluble waxy carboxylic acid used for making candles and suppositories; octadecanoic acid. Formula: $CH_3(CH_2)_{16}COOH$. See also **stearin** (sense 2).

stearin *or* **stearine** (ˈstɪərɪn) NOUN [1] Also called: **tristearin.** a colourless crystalline ester of glycerol and stearic acid, present in fats and used in soap and candles; glycerol tristearate; glycerol trioctadecanoate. Formula: $(C_{17}H_{35}COO)_3C_3H_5$. [2] another name for **stearic acid**, esp a commercial grade containing other fatty acids [3] fat in its solid form.
▷**HISTORY** C19: from French *stéarine*, from Greek *stear* fat, tallow + -IN

stearoptene (ˌstɪəˈrɒptiːn) NOUN the part of an essential oil that separates out as a solid on cooling or standing.
▷**HISTORY** C19: from New Latin *stearoptenum*, from Greek *stear* fat + *-ptenum*, from *ptēnos* winged (volatile)

steatite (ˈstɪəˌtaɪt) NOUN another name for **soapstone.**
▷**HISTORY** C18: from Latin *steatitēs*, from Greek *stear* fat + -ITE[1]
▸**steatitic** (ˌstɪəˈtɪtɪk) ADJECTIVE

steato- COMBINING FORM denoting fat.
▷**HISTORY** from Greek *stear, steat-* fat, tallow

steatolysis (ˌstɪəˈtɒlɪsɪs) NOUN *Physiol* [1] the digestive process whereby fats are emulsified and then hydrolysed to fatty acids and glycerine. [2] the breaking down of fat.

steatopygia (ˌstɪətəʊˈpɪdʒɪə, -ˈpaɪ-) *or* **steatopyga** (ˌstɪətəʊˈpaɪgə) NOUN excessive fatness of the buttocks.
▷**HISTORY** C19: from New Latin, from STEATO- + Greek *pugē* the buttocks
▸**steatopygic** (ˌstɪətəʊˈpɪdʒɪk) *or* **steatopygous** (ˌstɪəˈtɒpɪgəs) ADJECTIVE

steatorrhoea *or esp US* **steatorrhea** (ˌstɪətəˈrɪə) NOUN *Pathol* a condition in which the stools are abnormally fatty.

Stębark (ˈstɛmbark) NOUN the Polish name for **Tannenberg.**

stedfast (ˈstɛdfəst, -ˌfɑːst) ADJECTIVE a less common spelling of **steadfast.**

steed (stiːd) NOUN *Archaic or literary* a horse, esp one that is spirited or swift.
▷**HISTORY** Old English *stēda* stallion; related to German *Stute* female horse; see STUD[2]

steel (stiːl) NOUN [1] **a** any of various alloys based on iron containing carbon (usually 0.1–1.7 per cent) and often small quantities of other elements such as phosphorus, sulphur, manganese, chromium, and nickel. Steels exhibit a variety of properties, such as strength, machinability, malleability, etc., depending on their composition and the way they have been treated. **b** (*as modifier*): *steel girders*. See also **stainless steel.** [2] something that is made of steel. [3] a steel stiffener in a corset, etc. [4] a ridged steel rod with a handle used for sharpening knives. [5] the quality of hardness, esp with regard to a person's character or attitudes. [6] *Stock Exchange* the quotation for steel shares. See also **steels.** [7] (*modifier*) resembling steel: *steel determination.* ◆ VERB (*tr*) [8] to fit, plate, edge, or point with steel. [9] to make hard and unfeeling: *he steeled his heart against her sorrow; he steeled himself for the blow.*
▷**HISTORY** Old English *stēli*; related to Old High German *stehli*, Middle Dutch *stael*
▸ˈ**steely** ADJECTIVE ▸ˈ**steeliness** NOUN

steel band NOUN *Music* a type of instrumental band, popular in the Caribbean Islands, consisting mainly of tuned percussion instruments made chiefly from the heads of oil drums, hammered or embossed to obtain different notes.

steel blue NOUN **a** a dark bluish-grey colour. **b** (*as adjective*): *steel-blue eyes.*

steel engraving NOUN **a** a method or art of engraving (letters, etc.) on a steel plate. **b** a print made from such a plate.

steel grey NOUN **a** a dark grey colour, usually slightly purple. **b** (*as adjective*): *a steel-grey suit.*

steel guitar NOUN See **Hawaiian guitar, pedal steel guitar.**

steelhead (ˈstiːlˌhɛd) NOUN, *plural* **-heads** *or* **-head.** a silvery North Pacific variety of the rainbow trout (*Salmo gairdneri*).

steels (stiːlz) PLURAL NOUN *Stock Exchange* shares and bonds of steel companies.

steel wool NOUN a tangled or woven mass of fine steel fibres, used for cleaning or polishing.

steelwork (ˈstiːlˌwɜːk) NOUN a frame, foundation, building, or article made of steel: *the steelwork of a skyscraper.*
▸ˈ**steelˌworking** NOUN

steelworks (ˈstiːlˌwɜːks) NOUN (*functioning as singular or plural*) a plant in which steel is made from iron ore and rolled or forged into blooms, billets, bars, or sheets.
▸ˈ**steelˌworker** NOUN

steelyard (ˈstiːlˌjɑːd) NOUN a portable balance consisting of a pivoted bar with two unequal arms. The load is suspended from the shorter one and the bar is returned to the horizontal by adding weights to the longer one.
▷**HISTORY** C17: from STEEL + YARD[1] (in the archaic sense: a rod or pole)

steen (stɪən) NOUN *South African* [1] (in South Africa) the white grape variety known elsewhere as Chenin Blanc. [2] any of the white wines made from this grape.
▷**HISTORY** Afrikaans

steenbok (ˈstiːnˌbɒk) NOUN, *plural* **-boks** *or* **-bok.** a small antelope, *Raphicerus campestris*, of central and southern Africa, having a reddish-brown coat and straight smooth horns. Also called: **steinbok.**
▷**HISTORY** C18: from Afrikaans, from Dutch *steen* stone + *bok* BUCK[1]; Compare STEINBOCK

steenbras (ˈstiːnˌbræs) NOUN *South African* a variety of sea bream, *Lithognathos lithognathos*, valued as a food fish in South Africa.
▷**HISTORY** C17: from Afrikaans, from Dutch *steen* stone + *brasen* bream

steep[1] (stiːp) ADJECTIVE [1] **a** having or being a slope or gradient approaching the perpendicular. **b** (*as noun*): *the steep.* [2] *Informal* (of a fee, price, demand, etc.) unduly high; unreasonable (esp in the phrase **that's a bit steep**). [3] *Informal* excessively demanding or ambitious: *a steep task.* [4] *Brit informal* (of a statement) extreme or far-fetched. [5] *Obsolete* elevated.
▷**HISTORY** Old English *steap*; related to Old Frisian *stāp*, Old High German *stouf* cliff, Old Norse *staup*
▸ˈ**steeply** ADVERB ▸ˈ**steepness** NOUN

steep[2] (stiːp) VERB [1] to soak or be soaked in a liquid in order to soften, cleanse, extract an element, etc. [2] (*tr; usually passive*) to saturate; imbue: *steeped in ideology.* ◆ NOUN [3] an instance or the process of steeping or the condition of being steeped. [4] a liquid or solution used for the purpose of steeping something.
▷**HISTORY** Old English *stēpan*; related to *steap* vessel, cup, Old High German *stouf*, Old Norse *staup*, Middle Dutch *stōp*
▸ˈ**steeper** NOUN

steepen (ˈstiːpᵊn) VERB to become or cause to become steep or steeper.

steeple (ˈstiːpᵊl) NOUN [1] a tall ornamental tower that forms the superstructure of a church, temple, etc. [2] such a tower with the spire above it. [3] any spire or pointed structure.
▷**HISTORY** Old English *stēpel*; see STEEP[1]
▸ˈ**steepled** ADJECTIVE

steeplebush (ˈstiːpᵊlˌbʊʃ) NOUN another name for **hardhack.**
▷**HISTORY** C19: so called because of the shape of its flower clusters

steeplechase (ˈstiːpᵊlˌtʃeɪs) NOUN [1] a horse race over a course equipped with obstacles to be jumped, esp artificial hedges, ditches, water jumps, etc. [2] a track race, usually of 3000 metres, in which the runners have to leap hurdles, a water jump, etc. [3] *Archaic* **a** a horse race across a stretch of open countryside including obstacles to be jumped. **b** a rare word for **point-to-point.** ◆ VERB [4] (*intr*) to take part in a steeplechase.
▷**HISTORY** C19: so called because it originally took place cross-country, with a church tower serving as a landmark to guide the riders
▸ˈ**steepleˌchasing** NOUN

steeplechaser (ˈstiːpᵊlˌtʃeɪsə) NOUN a horse or an athlete that takes part in steeplechases.

steeplejack (ˈstiːpᵊlˌdʒæk) NOUN a person trained and skilled in the construction and repair of steeples, chimneys, etc.
▷**HISTORY** C19: from STEEPLE + JACK[1] (in the sense: a man or fellow)

steer[1] (stɪə) VERB [1] to direct the course of (a vehicle or vessel) with a steering wheel, rudder, etc. [2] (*tr*) to guide with tuition: *his teachers steered him through his exams.* [3] (*tr*) to direct the movements or course of (a person, conversation, etc.). [4] to pursue (a specified course). [5] (*intr*) (of a vessel, vehicle, etc.) to admit of being guided in a specified fashion: *this boat does not steer properly.* [6] **steer clear of.** to keep away from; shun. ◆ NOUN [7] *Chiefly US* information; guidance (esp in the phrase **a bum steer**).
▷**HISTORY** Old English *stieran*; related to Old Frisian *stiūra*, Old Norse *stýra*, German *stevern*; see STARBOARD, STERN[2]
▸ˈ**steerable** ADJECTIVE ▸ˈ**steerer** NOUN

steer[2] (stɪə) NOUN a castrated male ox or bull; bullock.
▷**HISTORY** Old English *stēor*; related to Old Norse *stjōrr*, Gothic *stiur*, Old High German *stior*, Middle Dutch *stēr*

steerage (ˈstɪərɪdʒ) NOUN [1] the cheapest accommodation on a passenger ship, originally the compartments containing the steering apparatus. [2] an instance or the practice of steering and the effect of this on a vessel or vehicle.

steerageway (ˈstɪərɪdʒˌweɪ) NOUN *Nautical* enough forward movement to allow a vessel to be steered.

steering column NOUN (in a motor vehicle) the shaft on which a steering wheel is mounted and by which it is connected with the steering gear.

steering committee NOUN a committee set up to prepare and arrange topics to be discussed, the order of business, etc., for a legislative assembly or other body.

steering gear NOUN any mechanism used for steering a vehicle, ship, aircraft, etc.

steering wheel NOUN a wheel turned by the driver of a motor vehicle, ship, etc., when he wishes to change direction. It is connected to the front wheels, rudder, etc.

steersman (ˈstɪəzmən) NOUN, *plural* **-men.** the helmsman of a vessel.

steeve[1] (stiːv) NOUN [1] a spar having a pulley block at one end, used for stowing cargo on a ship. ◆ VERB [2] (*tr*) to stow (cargo) securely in the hold of a ship.
▷**HISTORY** C15 *steven*, probably from Spanish *estibar* to pack tightly, from Latin *stīpāre* to cram full

steeve[2] (stiːv) *Nautical* ◆ VERB [1] to incline (a bowsprit or other spar) upwards or (of a bowsprit) to incline upwards at an angle from the horizontal. ◆ NOUN [2] such an angle.
▷**HISTORY** C17: of uncertain origin

Stefan's law (ˈstɛfənz) NOUN the principle that the energy radiated per second by unit area of a black body at thermodynamic temperature T is directly proportional to T^4. The constant of proportionality is the **Stefan constant**, equal to 5.670400×10^{-8} Wm^{-2} K^{-4}. Also called: **Stefan-Boltzmann law.**
▷**HISTORY** C19: named after Josef *Stefan* (1835–93), Austrian physicist

stegodon (ˈstɛgəˌdɒn) *or* **stegodont** (ˈstɛgəˌdɒnt) NOUN any proboscidean mammal of the genus *Stegodon*, of Pliocene to Pleistocene times, similar to the mastodons.
▷**HISTORY** C19: New Latin (literally: ridge-toothed),

from Greek *stegos* roof, from *stegein* to cover + *odōn* tooth

stegomyia (ˌstɛgəˈmaɪə) NOUN a former name for **aedes.**
▷HISTORY C19: from Greek *stegos* roof + *-myia,* from *muia* a fly

stegosaur (ˈstɛgəˌsɔː) *or* **stegosaurus** (ˌstɛgəˈsɔːrəs) NOUN any quadrupedal herbivorous ornithischian dinosaur of the suborder *Stegosauria,* esp any of the genus *Stegosaurus,* of Jurassic and early Cretaceous times, having an armour of bony plates.
▷HISTORY C19: from Greek *stegos* roof + -SAUR

Steier (*German* ˈʃtaiər) NOUN a variant spelling of **Steyr.**

Steiermark (ˈʃtaiərˌmark) NOUN the German name for **Styria.**

stein (staɪn) NOUN [1] an earthenware beer mug, esp of a German design. [2] the quantity contained in such a mug.
▷HISTORY German, literally: STONE

steinbock (ˈstaɪnˌbɒk) NOUN another name for **ibex.**
▷HISTORY C17: from German *Steinbock;* compare STEENBOK

steinbok (ˈstaɪnˌbɒk) NOUN, *plural* **-boks** *or* **-bok.** a variant spelling of **steenbok.**

stele (ˈstiːlɪ, stiːl) NOUN, *plural* **stelae** (ˈstiːliː) *or* **steles** (ˈstiːlɪz, stiːlz). [1] an upright stone slab or column decorated with figures or inscriptions, common in prehistoric times. [2] a prepared vertical surface that has a commemorative inscription or design, esp one on the face of a building. [3] the conducting tissue of the stems and roots of plants, which is in the form of a cylinder, principally containing xylem, phloem, and pericycle. See also **protostele, siphonostele.** ◆ Also called (for senses 1, 2): **stela** (ˈstiːlə).
▷HISTORY C19: from Greek *stēlē;* related to Greek *histanai* to stand, Latin *stāre*
▸**stelar** (ˈstiːlə) ADJECTIVE

stell (stɛl) NOUN a shelter for cattle or sheep built on moorland or hillsides.
▷HISTORY C19

stellar (ˈstɛlə) ADJECTIVE [1] of, relating to, involving, or resembling a star or stars. [2] of or relating to star entertainers. [3] *Informal* outstanding or immense: *companies are registering stellar profits.*
▷HISTORY C17: from Late Latin *stellāris,* from Latin *stella* star

stellarator (ˈstɛləˌreɪtə) NOUN *Physics* an apparatus used in research into thermonuclear reactions, consisting of a toroidal vessel designed so that a plasma may be contained within it by a helical magnetic field. The magnetic field is produced by current carrying coils.
▷HISTORY C20: from STELLAR + (GENER)ATOR

stellar evolution NOUN *Astronomy* the sequence of changes that occurs in a star as it ages.

stellate (ˈstɛlɪt, -eɪt) *or* **stellated** ADJECTIVE resembling a star in shape; radiating from the centre: *a stellate arrangement of petals.*
▷HISTORY C16: from Latin *stellātus* starry, from *stellāre* to stud with stars, from *stella* a star
▸ˈ**stellately** ADVERB

stelliferous (stɛˈlɪfərəs) ADJECTIVE full of stars.
▷HISTORY C16: from Latin *stellifer* star-bearing, from *stella* star; see -FEROUS

stelliform (ˈstɛlɪˌfɔːm) ADJECTIVE star-shaped.
▷HISTORY C18: from New Latin *stelliformis,* from Latin *stella* star + *forma* shape

stellify (ˈstɛlɪˌfaɪ) VERB **-fies, -fying, -fied.** to change or be changed into a star.
▷HISTORY C14: from Latin *stella* a star

Stellite (ˈstɛlaɪt) NOUN *Trademark* any of various alloys containing cobalt, chromium, carbon, tungsten, and molybdenum: characteristically very hard and wear-resistant, they are used as castings or hard surface-coatings.

stellular (ˈstɛljʊlə) ADJECTIVE [1] displaying or abounding in small stars: *a stellular pattern.* [2] resembling a little star or little stars.
▷HISTORY C18: from Late Latin *stellula,* diminutive of Latin *stella* star
▸ˈ**stellularly** ADVERB

stem[1] (stɛm) NOUN [1] the main axis of a plant, which bears the leaves, axillary buds, and flowers and contains a hollow cylinder of vascular tissue. [2] any similar subsidiary structure in such plants that bears a flower, fruit, or leaf. [3] a corresponding structure in algae and fungi. [4] any long slender part, such as the hollow part of a tobacco pipe that lies between the bit and the bowl, or the support between the base and the bowl of a wineglass, goblet, etc. [5] a banana stalk with several bunches attached. [6] the main line of descent or branch of a family. [7] a round pin in some locks on which a socket in the end of a key fits and about which it rotates. [8] any projecting feature of a component: a shank or cylindrical pin or rod, such as the pin that carries the winding knob on a watch. [9] *Linguistics* the form of a word that remains after removal of all inflectional affixes; the root of a word, esp as occurring together with a thematic element. Compare **root**[1] (sense 9). [10] the main, usually vertical, stroke of a letter or of a musical note such as a minim. [11] *Electronics* the tubular glass section projecting from the base of a light bulb or electronic valve, on which the filament or electrodes are mounted. [12] **a** the main upright timber or structure at the bow of a vessel. **b** the very forward end of a vessel (esp in the phrase **from stem to stern**). ◆ VERB **stems, stemming, stemmed.** [13] (*intr;* usually foll by *from*) to be derived; originate. [14] (*tr*) to make headway against (a tide, wind, etc.). [15] (*tr*) to remove or disengage the stem or stems from. [16] (*tr*) to supply (something) with a stem or stems.
▷HISTORY Old English *stemn;* related to Old Norse *stafn* stem of a ship, German *Stamm* tribe, Gothic *stōma* basis, Latin *stāmen* thread
▸ˈ**stemˌlike** ADJECTIVE ▸ˈ**stemmer** NOUN

stem[2] (stɛm) VERB **stems, stemming, stemmed.** [1] (*tr*) to restrain or stop (the flow of something) by or as if by damming up. [2] (*tr*) to pack tightly or stop up. [3] *Skiing* to manoeuvre (a ski or skis), as in performing a stem. ◆ NOUN [4] *Skiing* a technique in which the heel of one ski or both skis is forced outwards from the direction of movement in order to slow down or turn.
▷HISTORY C15 *stemmen,* from Old Norse *stemma;* related to Old Norse *stamr* blocked, stammering, German *stemmen* to prop; see STAMMER
▸ˈ**stemmer** NOUN

Stem (stɛm) NOUN **die.** (di) the South African national anthem until 1991, when it was joined by "Nkosi Sikelel' iAfrica".
▷HISTORY C19: from Afrikaans, the call

stem-and-leaf diagram NOUN *Statistics* a histogram in which the data points falling within each class interval are listed in order.

stem cell NOUN *Histology* an undifferentiated cell that gives rise to specialized cells, such as blood cells.

stem ginger NOUN the choice pieces of the underground stem of the ginger plant, which are crystallized or preserved in syrup and eaten as a sweetmeat.

stemhead (ˈstɛmˌhɛd) NOUN *Nautical* the head of the stem of a vessel.

stemma (ˈstɛmə) NOUN a family tree; pedigree.
▷HISTORY C19: via Latin from Greek *stemma* garland, wreath, from *stephein* to crown, wreathe

stemmed (stɛmd) ADJECTIVE [1] **a** having a stem. **b** (*in combination*): *a thin-stemmed plant; a long-stemmed glass.* [2] having had the stem or stems removed.

stemson (ˈstɛmsən) NOUN *Nautical* a curved timber scarfed into or bolted to the stem and keelson at the bow of a wooden vessel. Compare **sternson.**
▷HISTORY C18: from STEM[1] + (KEEL)SON

stem turn NOUN *Skiing* a turn in which the heel of one ski is stemmed and the other ski is brought parallel. Also called: **stem.**

stemware (ˈstɛmˌwɛə) NOUN a collective term for glasses, goblets, etc., with stems.

stem-winder NOUN a watch wound by an expanded crown on the bar projecting outside the case, as opposed to one wound by a separate key. Also called: **stem-winding watch.**

stench (stɛntʃ) NOUN a strong and extremely offensive odour; stink.
▷HISTORY Old English *stenc;* related to Old Saxon, Old High German *stank;* see STINK

stench trap NOUN a trap in a sewer that by means of a water seal prevents the upward passage of foul-smelling gases. Also called: **stink trap.**

stencil (ˈstɛnsᵊl) NOUN [1] a device for applying a design, characters, etc., to a surface, consisting of a thin sheet of plastic, metal, cardboard, etc. in which the design or characters have been cut so that ink or paint can be applied through the incisions onto the surface. [2] a decoration, design, or characters produced in this way. ◆ VERB **-cils, -cilling, -cilled** *or US* **-cils, -ciling, -ciled.** (*tr*) [3] to mark (a surface) with a stencil. [4] to produce (characters or a design) with a stencil.
▷HISTORY C14 *stanselen* to decorate with bright colours, from Old French *estenceler,* from *estencele* a spark, from Latin *scintilla*
▸ˈ**stenciller** NOUN

stengah (ˈstɛŋgə) NOUN another name for **stinger** (sense 3).
▷HISTORY from Malay *sa tengah* one half

Sten gun (stɛn) NOUN a light 9 mm sub-machine-gun formerly used in the British Army and Commonwealth forces, developed during World War II.
▷HISTORY C20: from *s* and *t* (initials of Shepherd and Turpin, the inventors) + *-en,* as in BREN GUN

steno (ˈstɛnəʊ) NOUN, *plural* **stenos.** *US and Canadian informal* short for **stenographer.**

steno- *or before a vowel* **sten-** COMBINING FORM indicating narrowness or contraction: *stenography; stenosis.*
▷HISTORY from Greek *stenos* narrow

stenograph (ˈstɛnəˌgræf, -ˌgrɑːf) NOUN [1] any of various keyboard machines for writing in shorthand. [2] any character used in shorthand. ◆ VERB [3] (*tr*) to record (speeches, minutes, letters, etc.) in shorthand.

stenographer (stəˈnɒgrəfə) NOUN the US and Canadian name for **shorthand typist.**

stenography (stəˈnɒgrəfɪ) NOUN [1] the act or process of writing in shorthand by hand or machine. [2] matter written in shorthand.
▸**stenographic** (ˌstɛnəˈgræfɪk) *or* ˌ**stenoˈgraphical** ADJECTIVE ▸ˌ**stenoˈgraphically** ADVERB

stenohaline (ˌstɛnəʊˈheɪliːn, -laɪn) ADJECTIVE (of certain aquatic animals) able to exist only within a narrow range of salinity. Compare **euryhaline.**
▷HISTORY C20: from STENO- + *haline,* from Greek *hals* salt + -INE[1]

stenopetalous (ˌstɛnəʊˈpɛtᵊləs) ADJECTIVE (of flowers) having narrow petals.

stenophagous (stəˈnɒfəgəs) ADJECTIVE (of animals) feeding on a single type or limited variety of food.
▷HISTORY C17: from STENO- + *-phagous* (via Latin from Greek *phagos* eating)

stenophyllous (ˌstɛnəʊˈfɪləs) ADJECTIVE (of plants) having narrow leaves.

stenosis (stɪˈnəʊsɪs) NOUN, *plural* **-ses** (-siːz). *Pathol* an abnormal narrowing of a bodily canal or passage.
▷HISTORY C19: via New Latin from Greek *stenōsis,* from *stenoun* to constrict, from *stenos* narrow
▸**stenotic** (stɪˈnɒtɪk) ADJECTIVE

stenothermal (ˌstɛnəˈθɜːməl) ADJECTIVE (of animals or plants) able to exist only within a narrow range of temperature. Compare **eurythermal.**

stenotopic (ˌstɛnəʊˈtɒpɪk) ADJECTIVE *Ecology* (of a species, group, etc.) able to tolerate only a narrow range of environmental changes. Also (sometimes (influenced by -TROPIC)): **stenotropic.** Compare **eurytopic.**
▷HISTORY from STENO- + *top* from Greek *topos* place + -IC

Stenotype (ˈstɛnəˌtaɪp) NOUN [1] *Trademark* a machine with a keyboard for recording speeches, etc., in a phonetic shorthand. [2] any machine resembling this. [3] the phonetic symbol typed in one stroke of such a machine.

stenotypy (ˈstɛnəˌtaɪpɪ) NOUN a form of shorthand in which alphabetic combinations are used to represent groups of sounds or short common words.
▷HISTORY C19: from STENO- + TYPE + -Y[3], on the model of STENOGRAPHY
▸**stenotypic** (ˌstɛnəˈtɪpɪk) ADJECTIVE ▸ˈ**stenoˌtypist** NOUN

stent (stɛnt) NOUN *Medicine* a tube of plastic or sprung metal mesh placed inside a hollow tube to reopen it or keep it open; uses in surgery include preventing a blood vessel from closing, esp after angioplasty, and assisting healing after an anastomosis.

stentor (ˈstɛntɔː) NOUN [1] a person with an unusually loud voice. [2] any trumpet-shaped protozoan of the genus *Stentor*, having a ciliated spiral feeding funnel at the wider end: phylum *Ciliophora* (ciliates).
▷HISTORY C19: after STENTOR

Stentor (ˈstɛntɔː) NOUN *Greek myth* a Greek herald with a powerful voice who died after he lost a shouting contest with Hermes, herald of the gods.

stentorian (stɛnˈtɔːrɪən) ADJECTIVE (of the voice, etc.) uncommonly loud: *stentorian tones*.

step (stɛp) NOUN [1] the act of motion brought about by raising the foot and setting it down again in coordination with the transference of the weight of the body. [2] the distance or space covered by such a motion. [3] the sound made by such a movement. [4] the impression made by such movement of the foot; footprint. [5] the manner of walking or moving the feet; gait: *he received his prize with a proud step*. [6] a sequence of foot movements that make up a particular dance or part of a dance: *I have mastered the steps of the waltz*. [7] any of several paces or rhythmic movements in marching, dancing, etc.: *the goose step*. [8] (*plural*) a course followed by a person in walking or as walking: *they followed in their leader's steps*. [9] one of a sequence of separate consecutive stages in the progression towards some goal: *another step towards socialism*. [10] a rank or grade in a series or scale: *he was always a step behind*. [11] an object or device that offers support for the foot when ascending or descending. [12] (*plural*) a flight of stairs, esp out of doors. [13] (*plural*) another name for **stepladder**. [14] a very short easily walked distance: *it is only a step to my place*. [15] *Music* a melodic interval of a second. See **whole tone, half-step**. [16] an offset or change in the level of a surface similar to the step of a stair. [17] a strong block or frame bolted onto the keel of a vessel and fitted to receive the base of a mast. [18] a ledge cut in mining or quarrying excavations. [19] **break step**. to cease to march in step. [20] **keep step**. to remain walking, marching, dancing, etc., in unison or in a specified rhythm. [21] **in step**. **a** marching, dancing, etc., in conformity with a specified pace or moving in unison with others. **b** *Informal* in agreement or harmony. [22] **out of step**. **a** not moving in conformity with a specified pace or in accordance with others. **b** *Informal* not in agreement; out of harmony. [23] **step by step**. with care and deliberation; gradually. [24] **take steps**. to undertake measures (to do something) with a view to the attainment of some end. [25] **watch one's step**. **a** *Informal* to conduct oneself with caution and good behaviour. **b** to walk or move carefully. ◆ VERB **steps, stepping, stepped**. [26] (*intr*) to move by raising the foot and then setting it down in a different position, transferring the weight of the body to this foot and repeating the process with the other foot. [27] (*intr;* often foll by *in, out,* etc.) to move or go on foot, esp for a short distance: *step this way, ladies*. [28] (*intr*) *Informal, chiefly US* to move, often in an attractive graceful manner, as in dancing: *he can really step around*. [29] (*intr;* usually foll by *on* or *upon*) to place or press the foot; tread: *to step on the accelerator*. [30] (*intr;* usually foll by *into*) to enter (into a situation) apparently with ease: *she stepped into a life of luxury*. [31] (*tr*) to walk or take (a number of paces, etc.): *to step ten paces*. [32] (*tr*) to perform the steps of: *they step the tango well*. [33] (*tr*) to set or place (the foot). [34] (*tr;* usually foll by *off* or *out*) to measure (some distance of ground) by stepping. [35] (*tr*) to arrange in or supply with a series of steps so as to avoid coincidence or symmetry. [36] (*tr*) to raise (a mast) and fit it into its step. ◆ See also **step down, step in, step on, step out, step up**.
▷HISTORY Old English *stepe, stæpe;* related to Old Frisian *stap, stepe,* Old High German *stapfo* (German *Stapfe* footprint), Old Norse *stapi* high rock
▸ˈ**step,like** ADJECTIVE

Step (stɛp) NOUN **a** a set of aerobic exercises designed to improve the cardiovascular system, which consists of stepping on and off a special box of adjustable height. **b** (*as modifier*): *Step aerobics*.

STEP (stɛp) NOUN ACRONYM FOR Special Temporary Employment Programme.

step- COMBINING FORM indicating relationship through the previous marriage of a spouse or parent rather than by blood: *stepson; stepfather*.
▷HISTORY Old English *stēop-;* compare *āstȳpan* to bereave

stepbrother (ˈstɛpˌbrʌðə) NOUN a son of one's stepmother or stepfather by a union with someone other than one's father or mother respectively.

step change NOUN a significant change, esp an improvement.

stepchild (ˈstɛpˌtʃaɪld) NOUN, *plural* **-children**. a stepson or stepdaughter.

stepdame (ˈstɛpˌdeɪm) NOUN an archaic word for **stepmother**.
▷HISTORY C14: from STEP- + DAME (in the archaic sense: mother; see DAM[2])

step dance NOUN a dance in which a display of steps is more important than gesture or posture, esp a solo dance.

stepdaughter (ˈstɛpˌdɔːtə) NOUN a daughter of one's husband or wife by a former union.

step down VERB (*adverb*) [1] (*tr*) to reduce gradually. [2] (*intr*) *Informal* to resign or abdicate (from a position). [3] (*intr*) *Informal* to assume an inferior or less senior position. ◆ ADJECTIVE **step-down**. (*prenominal*) [4] (of a transformer) reducing a high voltage applied to the primary winding to a lower voltage on the secondary winding. Compare **step-up** (sense 3). [5] decreasing or falling by stages. ◆ NOUN **step-down**. [6] *Informal* a decrease in quantity or size.

stepfather (ˈstɛpˌfɑːðə) NOUN a man who has married one's mother after the death or divorce of one's father.

step function NOUN an electrical waveform that rises or falls instantly from one level to another.

stephanotis (ˌstɛfəˈnəʊtɪs) NOUN any climbing asclepiadaceous shrub of the genus *Stephanotis,* esp *S. floribunda,* of Madagascar and Malaya: cultivated for their fragrant white waxy flowers.
▷HISTORY C19: via New Latin from Greek: fit for a crown, from *stephanos* a crown

step in VERB [1] (*intr, adverb*) *Informal* to intervene or involve oneself, esp dramatically or at a senior level. ◆ ADJECTIVE **step-in**. [2] (*prenominal*) (of garments, etc.) put on by being stepped into; without fastenings. [3] (of a ski binding) engaging automatically when the boot is positioned on the ski. ◆ NOUN **step-in**. [4] (*often plural*) a step-in garment, esp underwear.

stepladder (ˈstɛpˌlædə) NOUN a folding portable ladder that is made of broad flat steps fixed to a supporting frame hinged at the top to another supporting frame.

stepmother (ˈstɛpˌmʌðə) NOUN a woman who has married one's father after the death or divorce of one's mother.

step on VERB (*intr, preposition*) [1] to place or press the foot on. [2] *Informal* to behave harshly or contemptuously towards. [3] *Slang* to adulterate drugs. [4] **step on it**. *Informal* to go more quickly, hurry up.

step out VERB (*intr, adverb*) [1] to go outside or leave a room, building, etc., esp briefly. [2] to begin to walk more quickly and take longer strides. [3] *US and Canadian informal* to withdraw from involvement; bow out.

step-parent (ˈstɛpˌpɛərənt) NOUN a stepfather or stepmother.
▸ˈ**step-ˌparenting** NOUN

steppe (stɛp) NOUN (*often plural*) an extensive grassy plain usually without trees. Compare **prairie, pampas**.
▷HISTORY C17: from Old Russian *step* lowland

stepper (ˈstɛpə) NOUN a person who or animal that steps, esp a horse or a dancer.

Steppes (stɛps) PLURAL NOUN **the**. [1] the huge grasslands of Eurasia, chiefly in the Ukraine and Russia. [2] another name for **Kyrgyz Steppe**.

stepping stone NOUN [1] one of a series of stones acting as footrests for crossing streams, marshes, etc. [2] a circumstance that assists progress towards some goal.

stepsister (ˈstɛpˌsɪstə) NOUN a daughter of one's stepmother or stepfather by a union with someone other than one's father or mother respectively.

stepson (ˈstɛpˌsʌn) NOUN a son of one's husband or wife by a former union.

step up VERB (*adverb*) *Informal* [1] (*tr*) to increase or raise by stages; accelerate. [2] (*intr*) to make progress or effect an advancement; be promoted. ◆ ADJECTIVE **step-up**. (*prenominal*) [3] (of a transformer) increasing a low voltage applied to the primary winding to a higher voltage on the secondary winding. Compare **step-down** (sense 4). [4] *Informal* involving a rise by stages. ◆ NOUN **step-up**. [5] *Informal* an increment in quantity, size, etc.

stepwise (ˈstɛpˌwaɪz) ADJECTIVE [1] arranged in the manner of or resembling steps. [2] *Music, US* proceeding by melodic intervals of a second. ◆ ADVERB [3] with the form or appearance of steps; step by step. [4] *Music, US* in a stepwise motion.

-ster SUFFIX FORMING NOUNS [1] indicating a person who is engaged in a certain activity: *prankster; songster*. Compare **-stress**. [2] indicating a person associated with or being something specified: *mobster; youngster*.
▷HISTORY Old English *-estre*

steradian (stəˈreɪdɪən) NOUN an SI unit of solid angle; the angle that, having its vertex in the centre of a sphere, cuts off an area of the surface of the sphere equal to the square of the length of the radius. Symbol: sr.
▷HISTORY C19: from STEREO- + RADIAN

stercoraceous (ˌstɜːkəˈreɪʃəs) ADJECTIVE of, relating to, or consisting of dung or excrement.
▷HISTORY C18: from Latin *stercus* dung + -ACEOUS

stercoricolous (ˌstɜːkəˈrɪkələs) ADJECTIVE (of organisms) living in dung.
▷HISTORY C19: from Latin *stercus* dung + *colere* to live

sterculia (stɜːˈkjuːlɪə) NOUN a dietary fibre used as a food stabilizer and denture adhesive. It is the dried gum tapped from the trunk and stems of the tree *Sterculia urens,* native to Central India and Pakistan.

sterculiaceous (stɜːˌkjuːlɪˈeɪʃəs) ADJECTIVE of, relating to, or belonging to the *Sterculiaceae,* a chiefly tropical family of plants that includes cacao and cola.
▷HISTORY C18: via New Latin from Latin *Sterculius* god of manuring, from *stercus* dung, alluding to the odour of some species

stere (stɪə) NOUN a unit used to measure volumes of stacked timber equal to one cubic metre (35.315 cubic feet).
▷HISTORY C18: from French *stère,* from Greek *stereos* solid

stereo (ˈstɛrɪəʊ, ˈstɪər-) ADJECTIVE [1] short for **stereophonic** or **stereoscopic**. ◆ NOUN, *plural* **stereos**. [2] stereophonic sound: *to broadcast in stereo*. [3] a stereophonic record player, tape recorder, etc. [4] *Photog* **a** a stereoscopic photography. **b** a stereoscopic photograph. [5] *Printing* short for **stereotype**.
▷HISTORY C20: shortened form

stereo- *or sometimes before a vowel* **stere-** COMBINING FORM indicating three-dimensional quality or solidity: *stereoscope*.
▷HISTORY from Greek *stereos* solid

stereobate (ˈstɛrɪəʊˌbeɪt, ˈstɪər-) NOUN [1] another name for **stylobate**. [2] a foundation of a building in the form of a platform of masonry.
▷HISTORY C19: via Latin, from Greek *stereobatēs* from *stereos* solid + *-batēs* base, from *bainein* to walk

stereochemistry (ˌstɛrɪəʊˈkɛmɪstrɪ, ˌstɪər-) NOUN the study of the spatial arrangement of atoms in molecules and the effect of spatial arrangement on chemical properties.

stereochrome (ˈstɛrɪəʊˌkrəʊm, ˈstɪər-) NOUN [1] a picture made by stereochromy. ◆ VERB [2] (*tr*) to produce (a picture) by the process of stereochromy.

stereochromy (ˈstɛrɪəˌkrəʊmɪ, ˈstɪər-) NOUN a method of wall painting in which water glass is used either as a painting medium or as a final fixative coat.
▷HISTORY C19: via German *Stereochromie,* from STEREO- + Greek *khrōma* colour

stereognosis (ˌstɛrɪɒgˈnəʊsɪs, ˌstɪər-) NOUN the perception of depth or three-dimensionality through any of the senses.
▷HISTORY C20: STEREO- + GNOSIS

stereogram (ˈstɛrɪəˌgræm, ˈstɪər-) NOUN [1] *Brit* a stereo radiogram. [2] another name for **stereograph**.

stereograph (ˈstɛrɪəˌgræf, -ˌgrɑːf, ˈstɪər-) NOUN two almost identical pictures, or one special picture, that when viewed through special glasses or a stereoscope form a single three-dimensional image. Also called: **stereogram.**

stereography (ˌstɛrɪˈɒɡrəfɪ, ˌstɪər-) NOUN [1] the study and construction of geometrical solids. [2] the art of drawing a solid figure on a flat surface.
▸**stereographic** (ˌstɛrɪəˈɡræfɪk, ˌstɪər-) *or* ˌ**stereoˈgraphical** ADJECTIVE ▸ˌ**stereoˈgraphically** ADVERB

stereoisomer (ˌstɛrɪəʊˈaɪsəmə, ˌstɪər-) NOUN *Chem* one of the isomers of a compound that exhibits stereoisomerism.

stereoisomerism (ˌstɛrɪəʊaɪˈsɒməˌrɪzəm, ˌstɪər-) NOUN *Chem* isomerism caused by differences in the spatial arrangement of atoms in molecules.
▸**stereoisometric** (ˌstɛrɪəʊˌaɪsəˈmɛtrɪk, ˌstɪər-) ADJECTIVE

stereome (ˈstɛrɪˌəʊm) NOUN *Botany, now rare* the tissue of a plant that provides mechanical support.

stereometry (ˌstɛrɪˈɒmɪtrɪ, ˌstɪər-) NOUN the measurement of volume.
▸**stereometric** (ˌstɛrɪəʊˈmɛtrɪk, ˌstɪər-) *or* ˌ**stereoˈmetrical** ADJECTIVE

stereophonic (ˌstɛrɪəˈfɒnɪk, ˌstɪər-) ADJECTIVE (of a system for recording, reproducing, or broadcasting sound) using two or more separate microphones to feed two or more loudspeakers through separate channels in order to give a spatial effect to the sound. Often shortened to: **stereo.** Compare **monophonic, quadraphonics.**
▸ˌ**stereoˈphonically** ADVERB ▸**stereophony** (ˌstɛrɪˈɒfənɪ, ˌstɪər-) NOUN

stereopsis (ˌstɛrɪˈɒpsɪs, ˌstɪər-) NOUN stereoscopic vision.
▷HISTORY from STEREO- + Greek *opsis* vision

stereopticon (ˌstɛrɪˈɒptɪkᵊn, ˌstɪər-) NOUN a type of projector with two complete units arranged so that one picture dissolves as the next is forming.
▷HISTORY C19: from STEREO- + Greek *optikon,* neuter form of *optikos* OPTIC

stereoscope (ˈstɛrɪəˌskəʊp, ˈstɪər-) NOUN an optical instrument for viewing two-dimensional pictures and giving them an illusion of depth and relief. It has a binocular eyepiece through which two slightly different pictures of the same object are viewed, one with each eye.

stereoscopic (ˌstɛrɪəˈskɒpɪk, ˌstɪər-) ADJECTIVE [1] of, concerned with, or relating to seeing space three-dimensionally as a result of binocular disparity: *stereoscopic vision.* [2] of, relating to, or formed by a stereoscope.
▸ˌ**stereoˈscopically** ADVERB

stereoscopy (ˌstɛrɪˈɒskəpɪ, ˌstɪər-) NOUN [1] the viewing or appearance of objects in or as if in three dimensions. [2] the study and use of the stereoscope.
▸ˌ**stereˈoscopist** NOUN

stereospecific (ˌstɛrɪəʊspɪˈsɪfɪk, ˌstɪər-) ADJECTIVE *Chem* relating to or having fixed position in space, as in the spatial arrangements of atoms in certain polymers.

stereospecific catalyst NOUN *Chem* a catalyst for stereospecific chemical reactions. See also **Ziegler catalyst.**

stereospecific polymer NOUN an organic polymer in which the steric arrangements of groups on assymetric carbon atoms occur in a regular sequence. Many natural and synthetic rubbers are stereospecific polymers.

stereotactic (ˌstɛrɪəˈtæktɪk, ˌstɪər-) ADJECTIVE [1] of or relating to stereotaxis. [2] *Med* of or relating to precise localization of a tissue, esp in the brain: *stereotactic surgery.*
▸ˌ**stereoˈtactically** ADVERB

stereotaxis (ˌstɛrɪəˈtæksɪs, ˌstɪər-) NOUN the movement of an organism in response to the stimulus of contact with a solid object.
▷HISTORY C20: from STEREO- + -TAXIS

stereotomy (ˌstɛrɪˈɒtəmɪ, ˌstɪər-) NOUN the art of cutting three-dimensional solids into particular shapes.
▷HISTORY C18: from French *stéréotomie.* See STEREO-, -TOMY

stereotropism (ˌstɛrɪˈɒtrəˌpɪzəm, ˌstɪər-) NOUN another name for **thigmotropism.**
▸**stereotropic** (ˌstɛrɪəˈtrɒpɪk, ˌstɪər-) ADJECTIVE

stereotype (ˈstɛrɪəˌtaɪp, ˈstɪər-) NOUN [1] **a** a method of producing cast-metal printing plates from a mould made from a forme of type matter in papier-mâché or some other material. **b** the plate so made. [2] another word for **stereotypy.** [3] an idea, trait, convention, etc., that has grown stale through fixed usage. [4] *Sociol* a set of inaccurate, simplistic generalizations about a group that allows others to categorize them and treat them accordingly. ◆ VERB (*tr*) [5] **a** to make a stereotype of. **b** to print from a stereotype. [6] to impart a fixed usage or convention to.
▸ˈ**stereoˌtyper** *or* ˈ**stereoˌtypist** NOUN ▸**stereotypic** (ˌstɛrɪəˈtɪpɪk, ˌstɪər-) *or* ˌ**stereoˈtypical** ADJECTIVE

stereotyped (ˈstɛrɪəˌtaɪpt, ˈstɪər-) ADJECTIVE [1] lacking originality or individuality; conventional; trite. [2] reproduced from or on a stereotype printing plate.

stereotypy (ˈstɛrɪəˌtaɪpɪ, ˈstɪər-) NOUN [1] the act or process of making stereotype printing plates. [2] a tendency to think or act in rigid, repetitive, and often meaningless patterns.

stereovision (ˈstɛrɪəʊˌvɪʒən, ˈstɪər-) NOUN the perception or exhibition of three-dimensional objects in three dimensions.

steric (ˈstɛrɪk, ˈstɪər-) *or* **sterical** ADJECTIVE *Chem* of, concerned with, or caused by the spatial arrangement of atoms in a molecule.
▷HISTORY C19: from STEREO- + -IC
▸ˈ**sterically** ADVERB

sterigma (stəˈrɪɡmə) NOUN *Biology* a minute stalk bearing a spore or chain of spores in certain fungi.
▷HISTORY C19: New Latin from Greek *stērigma* support, from *stērizein* to sustain

sterilant (ˈstɛrɪlənt) NOUN any substance or agent used in sterilization.

sterile (ˈstɛraɪl) ADJECTIVE [1] unable to produce offspring; infertile. [2] free from living, esp pathogenic, microorganisms; aseptic. [3] (of plants or their parts) not producing or bearing seeds, fruit, spores, stamens, or pistils. [4] lacking inspiration or vitality; fruitless. [5] *Economics, US* (of gold) not being used to support credit creation or an increased money supply.
▷HISTORY C16: from Latin *sterilis*
▸ˈ**sterilely** ADVERB ▸**sterility** (stɛˈrɪlɪtɪ) NOUN

sterilization *or* **sterilisation** (ˌstɛrɪlaɪˈzeɪʃən) NOUN [1] the act or procedure of sterilizing or making sterile. [2] the state of being sterile; sterilized condition.

sterilize *or* **sterilise** (ˈstɛrɪˌlaɪz) VERB (*tr*) to render sterile; make infertile or barren.
▸ˈ**steriˌlizable** *or* ˈ**steriˌlisable** ADJECTIVE

sterilizer *or* **steriliser** (ˈstɛrɪˌlaɪzə) NOUN a person, substance, or device that sterilizes.

sterlet (ˈstɜːlɪt) NOUN a small sturgeon, *Acipenser ruthenus,* of seas and rivers in N Asia and E Europe: used as a food fish and a source of caviar.
▷HISTORY C16: from Russian *sterlyad,* of Germanic origin; compare Old High German *sturio* sturgeon

sterling (ˈstɜːlɪŋ) NOUN [1] **a** British money: *pound sterling.* **b** (*as modifier*): *sterling reserves.* [2] the official standard of fineness of British coins: for gold 0.91666 and for silver 0.925. [3] **a** short for **sterling silver. b** (*as modifier*): *a sterling bracelet.* [4] an article or articles manufactured from sterling silver. [5] a former British silver penny. ◆ ADJECTIVE [6] (*prenominal*) genuine and reliable; first-class: *sterling quality.*
▷HISTORY C13: probably from Old English *steorra* STAR + -LING[1]; referring to a small star on early Norman pennies; related to Old French *esterlin*

sterling area NOUN a group of countries that use sterling as a medium of international payments and sometimes informally as a currency against which to peg their own currencies. For these purposes they deposit sterling balances and hold gold and dollar reserves in the Bank of England. Also called: **sterling bloc, scheduled territories.**

sterling silver NOUN [1] an alloy containing not less than 92.5 per cent of silver, the remainder usually being copper. [2] sterling-silver articles collectively.

Sterlitamak (*Russian* stjerlitaˈmak) NOUN an industrial city in W Russia, in the Bashkir Republic. Pop.: 263 600 (1999 est.).

stern[1] (stɜːn) ADJECTIVE [1] showing uncompromising or inflexible resolve; firm, strict, or authoritarian. [2] lacking leniency or clemency; harsh or severe. [3] relentless; unyielding: *the stern demands of parenthood.* [4] having an austere or forbidding appearance or nature.
▷HISTORY Old English *styrne;* related to Old High German *stornēn* to alarm, Latin *sternāx* stubborn, Greek *stereos* hard
▸ˈ**sternly** ADVERB ▸ˈ**sternness** NOUN

stern[2] (stɜːn) NOUN [1] the rear or after part of a vessel, opposite the bow or stem. [2] the rear part of any object. [3] the tail of certain breeds of dog, such as the foxhound or beagle. ◆ ADJECTIVE [4] relating to or located at the stern.
▷HISTORY C13: from Old Norse *stjórn* steering; see STEER[1]

stern-chaser NOUN a gun mounted at the stern of a vessel for firing aft at a pursuing vessel.

sternforemost (ˈstɜːnˈfɔːməʊst) ADVERB *Nautical* backwards.

sternmost (ˈstɜːnˌməʊst) ADJECTIVE *Nautical* [1] farthest to the stern; aftmost. [2] nearest the stern.

sternpost (ˈstɜːnˌpəʊst) NOUN *Nautical* the main upright timber or structure at the stern of a vessel.

stern sheets PLURAL NOUN *Nautical* the part of an open boat near the stern.

sternson (ˈstɜːnsᵊn) NOUN *Nautical* a timber scarfed into or bolted to the sternpost and keelson at the stern of a wooden vessel. Compare **stemson.**
▷HISTORY C19: from STERN[2] + *-son,* on the model of KEELSON

sternum (ˈstɜːnəm) NOUN, *plural* **-na** (-nə) *or* **-nums.** [1] (in man) a long flat vertical bone, situated in front of the thorax, to which are attached the collarbone and the first seven pairs of ribs. Nontechnical name: **breastbone.** [2] the corresponding part in many other vertebrates. [3] a cuticular plate covering the ventral surface of a body segment of an arthropod. Compare **tergum.**
▷HISTORY C17: via New Latin from Greek *sternon* breastbone
▸ˈ**sternal** ADJECTIVE

sternutation (ˌstɜːnjʊˈteɪʃən) NOUN a sneeze or the act of sneezing.
▷HISTORY C16: from Late Latin *sternūtāre* to sneeze, from *sternuere* to sputter (of a light)

sternutator (ˈstɜːnjʊˌteɪtə) NOUN a substance that causes sneezing, coughing, and tears; used in chemical warfare.

sternutatory (stɜːˈnjuːtətərɪ, -trɪ) ADJECTIVE *also* **sternutative.** [1] causing or having the effect of sneezing. ◆ NOUN, *plural* **-tories.** [2] an agent or substance that causes sneezing.

sternwards (ˈstɜːnwədz) *or* **sternward** ADVERB *Nautical* towards the stern; astern.

sternway (ˈstɜːnˌweɪ) NOUN *Nautical* movement of a vessel sternforemost.

stern-wheeler NOUN a vessel, esp a riverboat, propelled by a large paddle wheel at the stern. Compare **sidewheeler.**

steroid (ˈstɪərɔɪd, ˈstɛr-) NOUN *Biochem* any of a large group of fat-soluble organic compounds containing a characteristic chemical ring system. The majority, including the sterols, bile acids, many hormones, and the D vitamins, have important physiological action.
▷HISTORY C20: from STEROL + -OID
▸**steˈroidal** ADJECTIVE

sterol (ˈstɛrɒl) NOUN *Biochem* any of a group of natural steroid alcohols, such as cholesterol and ergosterol, that are waxy insoluble substances.
▷HISTORY C20: shortened from CHOLESTEROL, ERGOSTEROL, etc.

stertor (ˈstɜːtə) NOUN laborious or noisy breathing caused by obstructed air passages.
▷HISTORY C17: from New Latin, from Latin *stertere* to snore

stertorous (ˈstɜːtərəs) ADJECTIVE [1] marked or accompanied by heavy snoring. [2] breathing in this way.
▸ˈ**stertorously** ADVERB ▸ˈ**stertorousness** NOUN

stet (stɛt) NOUN [1] a word or mark indicating that certain deleted typeset or written matter is to be retained. Compare **dele.** ◆ VERB **stets, stetting, stetted.** [2] (*tr*) to mark (matter to be retained) with a stet.
▷HISTORY Latin, literally: let it stand

stethoscope (ˈstɛθəˌskəʊp) NOUN [1] *Med* an instrument for listening to the sounds made within the body, typically consisting of a hollow disc that transmits the sound through hollow tubes to

earpieces. [2] a narrow cylinder expanded at both ends to recieve and transmit fetal sounds. Also called: **obstetric stethoscope.**
▷HISTORY C19: from French, from Greek *stēthos* breast + -SCOPE
▸**stethoscopic** (ˌstɛθəˈskɒpɪk) ADJECTIVE ▸**stethoscopy** (stɛˈθɒskəpɪ) NOUN

Stetson (ˈstetsᵊn) NOUN *Trademark* a type of felt hat with a broad brim and high crown, worn mainly by cowboys.
▷HISTORY C20: named after John *Stetson* (1830–1906), American hatmaker who designed it

Stettin (ʃtɛˈtiːn) NOUN the German name for **Szczecin.**

stevedore (ˈstiːvɪˌdɔː) NOUN [1] a person employed to load or unload ships. ◆ VERB [2] to load or unload (a ship, ship's cargo, etc.).
▷HISTORY C18: from Spanish *estibador* a packer, from *estibar* to load (a ship), from Latin *stīpāre* to pack full

stevedore's knot NOUN a knot forming a lump in a line, used by stevedores to secure ropes passing through holes.

Stevenage (ˈstiːvənɪdʒ) NOUN a town in SE England, in N Hertfordshire on the Great North Road: developed chiefly as the first of the new towns (1946). Pop.: 76 064 (1991).

Stevengraph (ˈstiːvᵊnˌgrɑːf) *or* **Stevensgraph** NOUN a picture, usually small, woven in silk.
▷HISTORY named after Thomas *Stevens* (1828–88), English weaver

stew[1] (stjuː) NOUN [1] **a** a dish of meat, fish, or other food, cooked by stewing. **b** (*as modifier*): *stew pot.* [2] *Informal* a difficult or worrying situation or a troubled state (esp in the phrase **in a stew**). [3] a heterogeneous mixture: *a stew of people of every race.* [4] (*usually plural*) *Archaic* a brothel. [5] *Obsolete* a public room for hot steam baths. ◆ VERB [6] to cook or cause to cook by long slow simmering. [7] (*intr*) *Informal* to be troubled or agitated. [8] (*intr*) *Informal* to be oppressed with heat or crowding. [9] to cause (tea) to become bitter or (of tea) to become bitter through infusing for too long. [10] **stew in one's own juice.** to suffer unaided the consequences of one's actions.
▷HISTORY C14 *stuen* to take a very hot bath, from Old French *estuver,* from Vulgar Latin *extūfāre* (unattested), from EX-[1] + (unattested) *tūfus* vapour, from Greek *tuphos*

stew[2] (stjuː) NOUN *Brit* [1] a fishpond or fishtank. [2] an artificial oyster bed.
▷HISTORY C14: from Old French *estui,* from *estoier* to shut up, confine, ultimately from Latin *studium* STUDY

steward (ˈstjuəd) NOUN [1] a person who administers the property, house, finances, etc., of another. [2] a person who manages the eating arrangements, staff, or service at a club, hotel, etc. [3] a waiter on a ship or aircraft. [4] a mess attendant in a naval mess afloat or ashore. [5] a person who helps to supervise some event or proceedings in an official capacity. [6] short for **shop steward.** ◆ VERB [7] to act or serve as a steward (of something).
▷HISTORY Old English *stigweard,* from *stig* hall (see STY) + *weard* WARD
▸**ˈsteward,ship** NOUN

stewardess (ˈstjuədɪs, ˌstjuəˈdɛs) NOUN a woman who performs a steward's job on an aircraft or ship.

Stewart Island NOUN the third largest island of New Zealand, in the SW Pacific off the S tip of South Island. Pop.: 450 (latest est.). Area: 1735 sq. km (670 sq. miles).

stewed (stjuːd) ADJECTIVE [1] (of meat, fruit, etc.) cooked by stewing. [2] *Brit* (of tea) having a bitter taste through having been left to infuse for too long. [3] a slang word for **drunk** (sense 1).

Steyr *or* **Steier** (*German* ˈʃtaiər) NOUN an industrial city in N central Austria, in Upper Austria. Pop.: 39 542 (1991).

stg ABBREVIATION FOR sterling.

stge ABBREVIATION FOR storage.

Sth ABBREVIATION FOR South.

sthenic (ˈsθɛnɪk) ADJECTIVE abounding in energy or bodily strength; active or strong.
▷HISTORY C18: from New Latin *sthenicus,* from Greek *sthenos* force, on the model of *asthenic*

Stheno (ˈsθiːnəʊ, ˈsθɛnəʊ) NOUN *Greek myth* one of the three Gorgons.

stibine (ˈstɪbaɪn) NOUN [1] a colourless slightly soluble poisonous gas with an offensive odour: made by the action of hydrochloric acid on an alloy of antimony and zinc. Formula: SbH_3. [2] any one of a class of stibine derivatives in which one or more hydrogen atoms have been replaced by organic groups.
▷HISTORY C19: from Latin STIBIUM + -INE[2]

stibium (ˈstɪbɪəm) NOUN an obsolete name for **antimony.**
▷HISTORY C14: from Latin: antimony (used as a cosmetic in ancient Rome), via Greek from Egyptian *stm*
▸**ˈstibial** ADJECTIVE

stibnite (ˈstɪbnaɪt) NOUN a soft greyish mineral consisting of antimony sulphide in orthorhombic crystalline form. It occurs in quartz veins and is the chief ore of antimony. Formula: Sb_2S_3.
▷HISTORY C19: from obsolete *stibine* stibnite + -ITE[1]

stich (stɪk) NOUN a line of poetry; verse.
▷HISTORY C18: from Greek *stikhos* row, verse; related to *steikhein* to walk
▸**ˈstichic** ADJECTIVE ▸**ˈstichically** ADVERB

stichometry (stɪˈkɒmɪtrɪ) NOUN *Prosody* the practice of writing out a prose text in lines that correspond to the sense units and indicate the phrasal rhythms.
▷HISTORY C18: from Late Greek *stikhometria.* See STICH, -METRY
▸**stichometric** (ˌstɪkəʊˈmɛtrɪk) *or* **ˌstichoˈmetrical** ADJECTIVE

stichomythia (ˌstɪkəʊˈmɪθɪə) *or* **stichomythy** (stɪˈkɒmɪθɪ) NOUN a form of dialogue originating in Greek drama in which single lines are uttered by alternate speakers.
▷HISTORY C19: from Greek *stikhomuthein* to speak alternate lines, from *stikhos* line + *muthos* speech; see MYTH
▸**ˌstichoˈmythic** ADJECTIVE

-stichous ADJECTIVE COMBINING FORM having a certain number of rows: *distichous.*
▷HISTORY from Late Latin *-stichus,* from Greek *-stikhos,* from *stikhos* line, row; see STICH

stick[1] (stɪk) NOUN [1] a small thin branch of a tree. [2] **a** any long thin piece of wood. **b** such a piece of wood having a characteristic shape for a special purpose: *a walking stick; a hockey stick.* **c** a baton, wand, staff, or rod. [3] an object or piece shaped like a stick: *a stick of celery; a stick of dynamite.* [4] See **control stick.** [5] *Informal* the lever used to change gear in a motor vehicle. [6] *Nautical* a mast or yard. [7] *Printing* See **composing stick.** [8] **a** a group of bombs arranged to fall at intervals across a target. **b** a number of paratroops jumping in sequence. [9] *Slang* **a** verbal abuse, criticism: *I got some stick for that blunder.* **b** physical power, force (esp in the phrase **give it some stick**). [10] (*usually plural*) a piece of furniture: *these few sticks are all I have.* [11] (*plural*) *Informal* a rural area considered remote or backward (esp in the phrase **in the sticks**). [12] (*plural*) *W and NW Canadian informal* the wooded interior part of the country. [13] (*plural*) *Hockey* a declaration made by the umpire if a player's stick is above the shoulders. [14] (*plural*) goalposts. [15] *US obsolete* a cannabis cigarette. [16] a means of coercion. [17] *Informal* a dull boring person. [18] (usually preceded by *old*) *Informal* a familiar name for a person: *not a bad old stick.* [19] **in a cleft stick.** in a difficult position. [20] **wrong end of the stick.** a complete misunderstanding of a situation, explanation, etc. ◆ VERB **sticks, sticking, sticked.** [21] to support (a plant) with sticks; stake.
▷HISTORY Old English *sticca;* related to Old Norse *stikka,* Old High German *stecca*

stick[2] (stɪk) VERB **sticks, sticking, stuck.** [1] (*tr*) to pierce or stab with or as if with something pointed. [2] to thrust or push (a sharp or pointed object) or (of a sharp or pointed object) to be pushed into or through another object. [3] (*tr*) to fasten in position by pushing or forcing a point into something: *to stick a peg in a hole.* [4] (*tr*) to fasten in position by or as if by pins, nails, etc.: *to stick a picture on the wall.* [5] (*tr*) to transfix or impale on a pointed object. [6] (*tr*) to cover with objects piercing or set in the surface. [7] (when *intr,* foll by *out, up, through,* etc.) to put forward or be put forward; protrude or cause to protrude: *to stick one's head out of the window.* [8] (*tr*) *Informal* to place or put in a specified position: *stick your coat on this chair.* [9] to fasten or be fastened by or as if by an adhesive substance: *stick the pages together; they won't stick.* [10] (*tr*) *Informal* to cause to become sticky. [11] (when *tr, usually passive*) to come or cause to come to a standstill: *we were stuck for hours in a traffic jam; the wheels stuck.* [12] (*intr*) to remain for a long time: *the memory sticks in my mind.* [13] (*tr*) *Slang, chiefly Brit* to tolerate; abide: *I can't stick that man.* [14] (*intr*) to be reluctant. [15] (*tr; usually passive*) *Informal* to cause to be at a loss; baffle, puzzle, or confuse: *I was totally stuck for an answer.* [16] (*tr*) *Slang* to force or impose something unpleasant on: *they stuck me with the bill for lunch.* [17] (*tr*) to kill by piercing or stabbing. [18] **stick in one's throat** (*or* **craw**). *Informal* to be difficult, or against one's conscience, for one to accept, utter, or believe. [19] **stick one's nose into.** See **nose** (sense 17). [20] **stick to the ribs.** *Informal* (of food) to be hearty and satisfying. ◆ NOUN [21] the state or condition of adhering. [22] *Informal* a substance causing adhesion. [23] *Obsolete* something that causes delay or stoppage. ◆ See also **stick around, stick at, stick by, stick down, stick out, stick to, stick together, stick-up, stick with, stuck.**
▷HISTORY Old English *stician;* related to Old High German *stehhan* to sting, Old Norse *steikja* to roast on a spit

stick around *or* **about** VERB (*intr, adverb*) *Informal* to remain in a place, esp awaiting something.

stick at VERB (*intr, preposition*) [1] to continue constantly at: *to stick at one's work.* [2] **stick at nothing.** to be prepared to do anything; be unscrupulous or ruthless.

stick by VERB (*intr, preposition*) to remain faithful to; adhere to.

stick down VERB (*tr, adverb*) *Informal* to write: *stick your name down here.*

sticker (ˈstɪkə) NOUN [1] an adhesive label, poster, or paper. [2] a person or thing that sticks. [3] a persevering or industrious person. [4] something prickly, such as a thorn, that clings to one's clothing, etc. [5] *Informal* something that perplexes. [6] *Informal* a knife used for stabbing or piercing.

stick float NOUN *Angling* a float attached at the top and bottom to the line.

stickhandle (ˈstɪkˌhændᵊl) VERB *Ice hockey* to manoeuvre (the puck) deftly.
▸**ˈstickˌhandler** NOUN

sticking plaster NOUN a thin cloth with an adhesive substance on one side, used for covering slight or superficial wounds. Usual US term: **adhesive tape.**

sticking point NOUN a problem or point on which agreement cannot be reached, preventing progress from being made.

stick insect NOUN any of various mostly tropical insects of the family *Phasmidae* that have an elongated cylindrical body and long legs and resemble twigs: order *Phasmida.* Also called (US and Canadian): **walking stick.** See also **leaf insect.**

stick-in-the-mud NOUN *Informal* a staid or predictably conservative person who lacks initiative or imagination.

stickle (ˈstɪkᵊl) VERB (*intr*) [1] to dispute stubbornly, esp about minor points. [2] to refuse to agree or concur, esp by making petty stipulations.
▷HISTORY C16 *stightle* (in the sense: to arbitrate): frequentative of Old English *stihtan* to arrange; related to Old Norse *stētta* to support

stickleback (ˈstɪkᵊlˌbæk) NOUN any small teleost fish of the family *Gasterosteidae,* such as *Gasterosteus aculeatus* (**three-spined stickleback**) of rivers and coastal regions and *G. pungitius* (**ten-spined stickleback**) confined to rivers. They have a series of spines along the back and occur in cold and temperate northern regions.
▷HISTORY C15: from Old English *sticel* prick, sting + BACK[1]

stickler (ˈstɪklə) NOUN [1] (usually foll by *for*) a person who makes insistent demands: *a stickler for accuracy.* [2] a problem or puzzle: *the investigation proved to be a stickler.*

stick-on (ˈstɪkɒn) NOUN *Informal* an event with a certain outcome.

stick out VERB (*adverb*) [1] to project or cause to

project. 2 (*tr*) *Informal* to endure (something disagreeable) (esp in the phrase **stick it out**). 3 **stick out a mile** *or* **like a sore thumb.** *Informal* to be extremely obvious. 4 **stick out for.** (*intr*) to insist on (a demand), refusing to yield until it is met: *the unions stuck out for a ten per cent wage rise.*

stick pin NOUN the US name for **tiepin.**

stickseed ('stɪk,siːd) NOUN any of various Eurasian and North American plants of the boraginaceous genus *Lappula,* having red-and-blue flowers and small prickly fruits. Also called: **beggar's-lice.**
▷HISTORY C19: from STICK²; so called because its seeds have adhesive hooks on them

stick shift NOUN *US and Canadian* 1 **a** a manually operated transmission system in a motor vehicle. **b** a motor vehicle having manual transmission. 2 a gear lever.

sticktight ('stɪk,taɪt) NOUN any of various plants, esp the bur marigold, that have barbed clinging fruits.

stick to VERB (*preposition, mainly intr*) 1 (*also tr*) to adhere or cause to adhere to. 2 to continue constantly at. 3 to remain faithful to. 4 not to move or digress from: *the speaker stuck closely to his subject.* 5 **stick to someone's fingers.** *Informal* to be stolen by someone.

stick together VERB (*intr, adverb*) *Informal* to remain loyal or friendly to one another.

stick-up NOUN 1 *Slang, chiefly US* a robbery at gunpoint; hold-up. ◆ VERB **stick up.** (*adverb*) 2 (*tr*) *Slang, chiefly US* to rob, esp at gunpoint. 3 (*intr; foll by for*) *Informal* to support or defend: *stick up for oneself.*

stickweed ('stɪk,wiːd) NOUN any of several plants that have clinging fruits or seeds, esp the ragweed.

stick with VERB (*intr, preposition*) *Informal* to persevere with; remain faithful to.

sticky ('stɪkɪ) ADJECTIVE **stickier, stickiest.** 1 covered or daubed with an adhesive or viscous substance: *sticky fingers.* 2 having the property of sticking to a surface. 3 (of weather or atmosphere) warm and humid; muggy. 4 (of prices) tending not to fall in deflationary conditions. 5 *Informal* difficult, awkward, or painful: *a sticky business.* 6 *US informal* sentimental. 7 (of a website) encouraging users to visit repeatedly. ◆ VERB **stickies, stickying, stickied.** 8 (*tr*) *Informal* to make sticky. ◆ NOUN, *plural* **stickies.** *Austral informal* 9 short for **stickybeak.** 10 an inquisitive look or stare (esp in the phrase **have a sticky at**).
▸ **'stickily** ADVERB ▸ **'stickiness** NOUN

stickybeak ('stɪkɪ,biːk) *Austral and NZ informal* ◆ NOUN 1 an inquisitive person. ◆ VERB 2 (*intr*) to pry.
▷HISTORY from STICKY + BEAK¹ (in the slang sense: a human nose)

sticky end NOUN *Informal* an unpleasant finish or death (esp in the phrase **come to** *or* **meet a sticky end**).

sticky-fingered ADJECTIVE *Informal* given to thieving.

sticky wicket NOUN 1 a cricket pitch that is rapidly being dried by the sun after rain and is particularly conducive to spin. 2 *Informal* a difficult or awkward situation (esp in the phrase **on a sticky wicket**).

sticky willie NOUN another name for **cleavers.**

stiction ('stɪkʃən) NOUN the frictional force to be overcome to set one object in motion when it is in contact with another.
▷HISTORY C20: blend of STATIC + FRICTION

stiff (stɪf) ADJECTIVE 1 not easily bent; rigid; inflexible. 2 not working or moving easily or smoothly: *a stiff handle.* 3 difficult to accept in its severity or harshness: *a stiff punishment.* 4 moving with pain or difficulty; not supple: *a stiff neck.* 5 difficult; arduous: *a stiff climb.* 6 unrelaxed or awkward; formal. 7 firmer than liquid in consistency; thick or viscous. 8 powerful; strong: *a stiff breeze; a stiff drink.* 9 excessively high: *a stiff price.* 10 *Nautical* (of a sailing vessel) relatively resistant to heeling or rolling. Compare **tender¹** (sense 11). 11 lacking grace or attractiveness. 12 stubborn or stubbornly maintained: *a stiff fight.* 13 *Obsolete* tightly stretched; taut. 14 *Slang, chiefly Austral* unlucky. 15 *Slang* intoxicated. 16 **stiff upper lip.** See **lip** (sense 9). 17 **stiff with.** *Informal* amply provided with. ◆ NOUN 18 *Slang* a corpse. 19 *Slang* anything thought to be a loser or a failure; flop. ◆ ADVERB 20 completely or utterly: *bored stiff; frozen stiff.* ◆ VERB 21 (*intr*) *Slang* to fail: *the film stiffed.* 22 (*tr*) *Slang, chiefly US* to cheat or swindle. 23 (*tr*) *Slang* to kill.
▷HISTORY Old English *stīf;* related to Old Norse *stīfla* to dam up, Middle Low German *stīf* stiff, Latin *stīpēs* wooden post, *stīpāre* to press
▸ **'stiffish** ADJECTIVE ▸ **'stiffly** ADVERB ▸ **'stiffness** NOUN

stiffen ('stɪfᵊn) VERB 1 to make or become stiff or stiffer. 2 (*intr*) to become suddenly tense or unyielding.
▸ **'stiffener** NOUN

stiff-necked ADJECTIVE haughtily stubborn or obstinate.

stiffy ('stɪfɪ) NOUN, *plural* **-fies.** *Slang* an erection of the penis.

stifle¹ ('staɪfᵊl) VERB 1 (*tr*) to smother or suppress: *stifle a cough.* 2 to feel or cause to feel discomfort and difficulty in breathing. 3 to prevent or be prevented from breathing so as to cause death. 4 (*tr*) to crush or stamp out.
▷HISTORY C14: variant of *stuflen,* probably from Old French *estouffer* to smother
▸ **'stifler** NOUN

stifle² ('staɪfᵊl) NOUN the joint in the hind leg of a horse, dog, etc., between the femur and tibia.
▷HISTORY C14: of unknown origin

stifling ('staɪflɪŋ) ADJECTIVE oppressively hot or stuffy: *a stifling atmosphere.*
▸ **'stiflingly** ADVERB

stigma ('stɪgmə) NOUN, *plural* **stigmas** *or for sense 7* **stigmata** ('stɪgmətə, stɪg'mɑːtə). 1 a distinguishing mark of social disgrace: *the stigma of having been in prison.* 2 a small scar or mark such as a birthmark. 3 *Pathol* **a** any mark on the skin, such as one characteristic of a specific disease. **b** any sign of a mental deficiency or emotional upset. 4 *Botany* the receptive surface of a carpel, where deposited pollen germinates. 5 *Zoology* **a** a pigmented eyespot in some protozoans and other invertebrates. **b** the spiracle of an insect. 6 *Archaic* a mark branded on the skin. 7 (*plural*) *Christianity* marks resembling the wounds of the crucified Christ, believed to appear on the bodies of certain individuals.
▷HISTORY C16: via Latin from Greek: brand, from *stizein* to tattoo

stigmasterol (stɪg'mæstə,rɒl) NOUN *Biochem* a sterol obtained from Calabar beans and soya beans and used in the manufacture of progesterone. Formula: $C_{29}H_{47}OH$.
▷HISTORY C20: from New Latin (*physo*)*stigma* genus name of the Calabar bean + STEROL; see PHYSOSTIGMINE

stigmatic (stɪg'mætɪk) ADJECTIVE 1 relating to or having a stigma or stigmata. 2 another word for **anastigmatic.** ◆ NOUN *also* **stigmatist** ('stɪgmətɪst). 3 *Chiefly RC Church* a person marked with the stigmata.

stigmatism ('stɪgmə,tɪzəm) NOUN 1 *Physics* the state or condition of being anastigmatic. 2 *Pathol* the condition resulting from or characterized by stigmata.

stigmatize *or* **stigmatise** ('stɪgmə,taɪz) VERB (*tr*) 1 to mark out or describe (as something bad). 2 to mark with a stigma or stigmata.
▸ **,stigmati'zation** *or* **,stigmati'sation** NOUN ▸ **'stigma,tizer** *or* **'stigma,tiser** NOUN

Stijl (staɪl) NOUN **De.** See **De Stijl.**

stilb (stɪlb) NOUN *Physics* a unit of luminance equal to 1 candela per square centimetre. Symbol: sb.
▷HISTORY C20: from Greek *stilbē* lamp

stilbene ('stɪlbiːn) NOUN a colourless or slightly yellow crystalline water-insoluble unsaturated hydrocarbon used in the manufacture of dyes; *trans*-1,2-diphenylethene. Formula: $C_6H_5CH{:}CHC_6H_5$.
▷HISTORY C19: from Greek *stilbos* glittering + -ENE

stilbestrol *or* **stilboestrol** (stɪl'biːstrəl) NOUN another name for **diethylstilbestrol.**
▷HISTORY C20: from STILBENE + OESTRUS + -OL¹

stilbite ('stɪlbaɪt) NOUN a white or yellow zeolite mineral consisting of hydrated calcium sodium aluminium silicate, often in the form of sheaves of monoclinic crystals. Formula: $(Na_2Ca)Al_2Si_7O_{18}.7H_2O$.
▷HISTORY C19: from Greek *stilbos* glittering (from *stilbein* to shine) + -ITE¹

stile¹ (staɪl) NOUN 1 a set of steps or rungs in a wall or fence to allow people, but not animals, to pass over. 2 short for **turnstile.**
▷HISTORY Old English *stigel;* related to *stīgan* to climb, Old High German *stigilla;* see STAIR

stile² (staɪl) NOUN a vertical framing member in a door, window frame, or piece of panelling. Compare **rail¹** (sense 3).
▷HISTORY C17: probably from Dutch *stijl* pillar, ultimately from Latin *stilus* writing instrument; see STYLE

stiletto (stɪ'lɛtəʊ) NOUN, *plural* **-tos.** 1 a small dagger with a slender tapered blade. 2 a sharply pointed tool used to make holes in leather, cloth, etc. 3 Also called: **spike heel, stiletto heel.** a very high heel on a woman's shoe, tapering to a very narrow tip. ◆ VERB **-toes, -toeing, -toed.** 4 (*tr*) to stab with a stiletto.
▷HISTORY C17: from Italian, from *stilo* a dagger, from Latin *stilus* a stake, pen; see STYLUS

still¹ (stɪl) ADJECTIVE 1 (*usually predicative*) motionless; stationary. 2 undisturbed or tranquil; silent and calm. 3 not sparkling or effervescent: *a still wine.* 4 gentle or quiet; subdued. 5 *Obsolete* (of a child) dead at birth. ◆ ADVERB 6 continuing now or in the future as in the past: *do you still love me?* 7 up to this or that time; yet: *I still don't know your name.* 8 (*often used with a comparative*) even or yet: *still more insults.* 9 quiet or without movement: *sit still.* 10 *Poetic and dialect* always. ◆ NOUN 11 *Poetic* silence or tranquillity: *the still of the night.* 12 **a** a still photograph, esp of a scene from a motion-picture film. **b** (*as modifier*): *a still camera.* ◆ VERB 13 to make or become still, quiet, or calm. 14 (*tr*) to allay or relieve: *her fears were stilled.* ◆ SENTENCE CONNECTOR 15 even then; nevertheless: *the child has some new toys and still cries.*
▷HISTORY Old English *stille;* related to Old Saxon, Old High German *stilli,* Dutch *stollen* to curdle, Sanskrit *sthānús* immobile
▸ **'stillness** NOUN

still² (stɪl) NOUN 1 an apparatus for carrying out distillation, consisting of a vessel in which a mixture is heated, a condenser to turn the vapour back to liquid, and a receiver to hold the distilled liquid, used esp in the manufacture of spirits. 2 a place where spirits are made; distillery.
▷HISTORY C16: from Old French *stiller* to drip, from Latin *stillāre,* from *stilla* a drip; see DISTIL

stillage ('stɪlɪdʒ) NOUN 1 a frame or stand for keeping things off the ground, such as casks in a brewery. 2 a container in which goods, machinery, etc., are transported.
▷HISTORY C16: probably from Dutch *stillagie* frame, scaffold, from *stellen* to stand; see -AGE

stillbirth ('stɪl,bɜːθ) NOUN 1 birth of a dead fetus or baby. 2 a stillborn fetus or baby.

stillborn ('stɪl,bɔːn) ADJECTIVE 1 (of a fetus) dead at birth. 2 (of an idea, plan, etc.) fruitless; abortive; unsuccessful. ◆ NOUN 3 a stillborn fetus or baby.

still frame NOUN continuous display of a single frame of a film or of a single picture from a television signal.

still hunt NOUN 1 the hunting of game by stalking or ambushing. ◆ VERB **still-hunt.** 2 to hunt (quarry) in this way.

stillicide ('stɪlɪ,saɪd) NOUN *Law* a right or duty relating to the drainage of water from the eaves of a roof onto adjacent land.
▷HISTORY C17: from Latin *stillicidium,* from *stilla* drop + *-cidium,* from *cadere* to fall

stilliform ('stɪlɪ,fɔːm) ADJECTIVE *Rare* having the shape of a drop or globule.
▷HISTORY C20: from Latin *stilla* a drop + -FORM

still life NOUN, *plural* **still lifes.** 1 **a** a painting or drawing of inanimate objects, such as fruit, flowers, etc. **b** (*as modifier*): *a still-life painting.* 2 the genre of such paintings.

still room NOUN *Brit* 1 a room in which distilling is carried out. 2 a pantry or storeroom, as in a large house.

Stillson wrench ('stɪlsᵊn) NOUN *Trademark* a large wrench having adjustable jaws that tighten as the pressure on the handle is increased.

stilly ADVERB ('stɪllɪ) 1 *Archaic or literary* quietly or calmly. ◆ ADJECTIVE ('stɪlɪ) 2 *Poetic* still, quiet, or calm.

stilt (stɪlt) NOUN 1 either of a pair of two long poles with footrests on which a person stands and walks, as used by circus clowns. 2 a long post or column that is used with others to support a building above ground level. 3 any of several shore birds of the genera *Himantopus* and *Cladorhynchus,* similar to the avocets but having a straight bill. ◆ VERB 4 (*tr*) to raise or place on or as if on stilts.
▷HISTORY C14 (in the sense: crutch, handle of a plough): related to Low German *stilte* pole, Norwegian *stilta*

stilted ('stɪltɪd) ADJECTIVE 1 (of speech, writing, etc.) formal, pompous, or bombastic. 2 not flowing continuously or naturally: *stilted conversation.* 3 *Architect* (of an arch) having vertical piers between the impost and the springing.
▸ **'stiltedly** ADVERB ▸ **'stiltedness** NOUN

Stilton ('stɪltən) NOUN *Trademark* either of two rich cheeses made from whole milk, blue-veined (**blue Stilton**) or white (**white Stilton**), both very strong in flavour.
▷HISTORY C18: named after *Stilton,* Cambridgeshire, where it was originally sold

stilt root NOUN a large prop root.

stim (stɪm) NOUN *Irish* (*used with a negative*) a very small amount: *I couldn't see a stim; she hasn't a stim of sense.*
▷HISTORY of uncertain origin

stimulant ('stɪmjʊlənt) NOUN 1 a drug or similar substance that increases physiological activity, esp of a particular organ. 2 any stimulating agent or thing. ◆ ADJECTIVE 3 increasing physiological activity; stimulating.
▷HISTORY C18: from Latin *stimulāns* goading, from *stimulāre* to urge on; see STIMULUS

stimulate ('stɪmjʊˌleɪt) VERB 1 (*tr; usually passive*) to fill (a person) with ideas or enthusiasm: *he was stimulated by the challenge.* 2 (*tr*) *Physiol* to excite (a nerve, organ, etc.) with a stimulus. 3 to encourage (something) to start or progress further: *a cut in interest rates should help stimulate economic recovery.*
▷HISTORY C16: from Latin *stimulāre;* see STIMULANT
▸ **'stimulable** ADJECTIVE ▸ **ˌstimu'lation** NOUN ▸ **'stimulative** ADJECTIVE, NOUN ▸ **'stimuˌlator** *or* **'stimuˌlater** NOUN

stimulating ('stɪmjʊˌleɪtɪŋ) ADJECTIVE 1 inspiring new ideas or enthusiasm. 2 (of a physical activity) making one feel refreshed and energetic.
▸ **'stimuˌlatingly** ADVERB

stimulus ('stɪmjʊləs) NOUN, *plural* **-li** (-ˌlaɪ, -ˌliː). 1 something that stimulates or acts as an incentive. 2 any drug, agent, electrical impulse, or other factor able to cause a response in an organism. 3 an object or event that is apprehended by the senses. 4 *Med* a former name for **stimulant.**
▷HISTORY C17: from Latin: a cattle goad

sting (stɪŋ) VERB **stings, stinging, stung.** 1 (of certain animals and plants) to inflict a wound on (an organism) by the injection of poison. 2 to feel or cause to feel a sharp mental or physical pain. 3 (*tr*) to goad or incite (esp in the phrase **sting into action**). 4 (*tr*) *Informal* to cheat, esp by overcharging. ◆ NOUN 5 a skin wound caused by the poison injected by certain insects or plants. 6 pain caused by or as if by the sting of a plant or animal. 7 a mental pain or pang: *a sting of conscience.* 8 a sharp pointed organ, such as the ovipositor of a wasp, by which poison can be injected into the prey. 9 the ability to sting: *a sharp sting in his criticism.* 10 something as painful or swift of action as a sting: *the sting of death.* 11 a sharp stimulus or incitement. 12 *Botany* another name for **stinging hair.** 13 *Slang* a swindle or fraud. 14 *Slang* a trap set up by the police to entice a person to commit a crime and thereby produce evidence. 15 **sting in the tail.** an unexpected and unpleasant ending.
▷HISTORY Old English *stingan;* related to Old Norse *stinga* to pierce, Gothic *usstangan* to pluck out, Greek *stakhus* ear of corn
▸ **'stinging** ADJECTIVE ▸ **'stingingly** ADVERB ▸ **'stingingness** NOUN

stingaree ('stɪŋəˌriː, ˌstɪŋə'riː) NOUN *US, Canadian, and Austral* a popular name for the **stingray.**
▷HISTORY C19: variant of STINGRAY

stinger ('stɪŋə) NOUN 1 a person, plant, animal, etc., that stings or hurts. 2 *Austral* any marine creature that stings its victims, esp the box jellyfish. 3 Also called: **stengah.** a whisky and soda with crushed ice.

Stinger ('stɪŋə) NOUN *Trademark* a device, consisting of a long track of raised spikes, laid across a road by police to puncture the tyres of escaping vehicles.

stinging hair NOUN a multicellular hair in plants, such as the stinging nettle, that injects an irritant fluid when in contact with an animal.

stinging nettle NOUN See **nettle** (sense 1).

stinging tree NOUN any of various Australian trees and shrubs of the genus *Dendrocnide* with rigid stinging hairs.

stingray ('stɪŋˌreɪ) NOUN any ray of the family *Dasyatidae,* having a whiplike tail bearing a serrated venomous spine capable of inflicting painful weals on man.

stingy¹ ('stɪndʒɪ) ADJECTIVE **-gier, -giest.** 1 unwilling to spend or give. 2 insufficient or scanty.
▷HISTORY C17 (perhaps in the sense: ill-tempered): perhaps from *stinge,* dialect variant of STING
▸ **'stingily** ADVERB ▸ **'stinginess** NOUN

stingy² ('stɪŋɪ) ADJECTIVE **stingier, stingiest.** 1 *Informal* stinging or capable of stinging. ◆ NOUN, *plural* **stingies.** 2 *South Wales dialect* a stinging nettle: *I put my hand on a stingy.*

stink (stɪŋk) NOUN 1 a strong foul smell; stench. 2 *Slang* a great deal of trouble (esp in the phrase **to make** *or* **raise a stink**). 3 **like stink.** intensely; furiously. ◆ VERB **stinks, stinking, stank** *or* **stunk; stunk.** (*mainly intr*) 4 to emit a foul smell. 5 *Slang* to be thoroughly bad or abhorrent: *this town stinks.* 6 *Informal* to have a very bad reputation: *his name stinks.* 7 to be of poor quality. 8 (foll by *of* or *with*) *Slang* to have or appear to have an excessive amount (of money). 9 (*tr;* usually foll by *up*) *Informal* to cause to stink. ◆ See also **stink out.**
▷HISTORY Old English *stincan;* related to Old Saxon *stinkan,* German *stinken,* Old Norse *stökkva* to burst; see STENCH

stink ball NOUN another name for **stinkpot** (sense 4).

stink bomb NOUN a small glass globe, used by practical jokers: it releases a liquid with an offensive smell when broken.

stinker ('stɪŋkə) NOUN 1 a person or thing that stinks. 2 *Slang* a difficult or very unpleasant person or thing. 3 *Slang* something of very poor quality. 4 *Informal* any of several fulmars or related birds that feed on carrion.

stinkhorn ('stɪŋkˌhɔːn) NOUN any of various basidiomycetous saprotrophic fungi of the genus *Phallus,* such as *P. impudicus,* having an offensive odour.

stinking ('stɪŋkɪŋ) ADJECTIVE 1 having a foul smell. 2 *Informal* unpleasant or disgusting. 3 (*postpositive*) *Slang* very drunk. ◆ ADVERB 4 *Informal* (intensifier, expressing contempt for the person referred to): *stinking rich.*
▸ **'stinkingly** ADVERB ▸ **'stinkingness** NOUN

stinking badger NOUN another name for **teledu.**

stinking iris NOUN an iris plant, *Iris foetidissima,* of W Europe and N Africa, having purplish flowers and a strong unpleasant smell when bruised. Also called: **gladdon.**

stinking smut NOUN a smut that affects wheat and is caused by the fungus *Tilletia caries.* Also called: **bunt.**

stinko ('stɪŋkəʊ) ADJECTIVE (*postpositive*) a slang word for **drunk.**

stink out VERB (*tr, adverb*) 1 to drive out or away by a foul smell. 2 *Brit* to cause to stink: *the smell of orange peel stinks out the room.*

stinkpot ('stɪŋkˌpɒt) NOUN 1 *Slang* a person or thing that stinks. 2 *Slang* a person considered to be unpleasant. 3 another name for **musk turtle.** 4 Also called: **stink ball.** *Military* (formerly) a container filled with material that gives off noxious or suffocating vapours.

stinkstone ('stɪŋkˌstəʊn) NOUN any of various rocks producing a fetid odour when struck, esp certain limestones.

stink trap NOUN another name for **stench trap.**

stinkweed ('stɪŋkˌwiːd) NOUN 1 Also called: **wall mustard.** a plant, *Diplotaxis muralis,* naturalized in Britain and S and central Europe, having pale yellow flowers, cylindrical seed pods, and a disagreeable smell when bruised: family *Brassicaceae* (crucifers). 2 any of various other ill-smelling plants, such as mayweed.

stinkwood ('stɪŋkˌwʊd) NOUN 1 any of various trees having offensive-smelling wood, esp *Ocotea bullata,* a southern African lauraceous tree yielding a hard wood used for furniture. 2 the heavy durable wood of any of these trees.

stinky ('stɪŋkɪ) ADJECTIVE **-ier, -iest.** 1 having a foul smell. 2 *Informal* unpleasant or disgusting. 3 *Informal* of poor quality; contemptible.

stint¹ (stɪnt) VERB 1 to be frugal or miserly towards (someone) with (something). 2 *Archaic* to stop or check (something). ◆ NOUN 3 an allotted or fixed amount of work. 4 a limitation or check. 5 *Obsolete* a pause or stoppage.
▷HISTORY Old English *styntan* to blunt; related to Old Norse *stytta* to cut short; see STUNT¹
▸ **'stinter** NOUN

stint² (stɪnt) NOUN any of various small sandpipers of the chiefly northern genus *Calidris* (or *Erolia*), such as *C. minuta* (**little stint**).
▷HISTORY Old English; related to Middle High German *stinz* small salmon, Swedish dialect *stinta* teenager; see STUNT¹

stipe (staɪp) NOUN 1 a stalk in plants that bears reproductive structures, esp the stalk bearing the cap of a mushroom. 2 the stalk that bears the leaflets of a fern or the thallus of a seaweed. 3 *Zoology* any stalklike part; stipes.
▷HISTORY C18: via French from Latin *stīpes* tree trunk; related to Latin *stīpāre* to pack closely; see STIFF

stipel ('staɪpᵊl) NOUN a small paired leaflike structure at the base of certain leaflets; secondary stipule.
▷HISTORY C19: via New Latin from Latin *stipula,* diminutive of *stīpes* a log
▸ **stipellate** (staɪ'pɛlɪt, -eɪt) ADJECTIVE

stipend ('staɪpɛnd) NOUN a fixed or regular amount of money paid as a salary or allowance, as to a clergyman.
▷HISTORY C15: from Old French *stipende,* from Latin *stīpendium* tax, from *stips* a contribution + *pendere* to pay out

stipendiary (staɪ'pɛndɪərɪ) ADJECTIVE 1 receiving or working for regular pay: *a stipendiary magistrate.* 2 paid for by a stipend. ◆ NOUN, *plural* **-aries.** 3 a person who receives regular payment.
▷HISTORY C16: from Latin *stīpendiārius* concerning tribute, from *stīpendium* STIPEND

stipes ('staɪpiːz) NOUN, *plural* **stipites** ('stɪpɪˌtiːz). *Zoology* 1 the second maxillary segment in insects and crustaceans. 2 the eyestalk of a crab or similar crustacean. 3 any similar stemlike structure.
▷HISTORY C18: from Latin; see STIPE
▸ **stipiform** ('staɪpɪˌfɔːm) *or* **stipitiform** ('stɪpɪtɪˌfɔːm) ADJECTIVE

stipitate ('stɪpɪˌteɪt) ADJECTIVE *Botany* possessing or borne on the end of a stipe.
▷HISTORY C18: from New Latin *stīpitātus* having a stalk, from Latin *stīpes;* see STIPE

stipple ('stɪpᵊl) VERB (*tr*) 1 to draw, engrave, or paint using dots or flecks. 2 to apply paint, powder, etc., to (something) with many light dabs. 3 to give (wet paint, cement, etc.) a granular effect. ◆ NOUN *also* **stippling.** 4 the technique of stippling or a picture produced by or using stippling.
▷HISTORY C18: from Dutch *stippelen,* from *stippen* to prick, from *stip* point
▸ **'stippler** NOUN

stipulate¹ ('stɪpjʊˌleɪt) VERB 1 (*tr; may take a clause as object*) to specify, often as a condition of an agreement. 2 (*intr;* foll by *for*) to insist (on) as a term of an agreement. 3 *Roman law* to make (an oral contract) in the form of question and answer necessary to render it legally valid. 4 (*tr; may take a clause as object*) to guarantee or promise.
▷HISTORY C17: from Latin *stipulārī,* probably from Old Latin *stipulus* firm, but perhaps from *stipula* a stalk, from the convention of breaking a straw to ratify a promise
▸ **stipulable** ('stɪpjʊləbᵊl) ADJECTIVE ▸ **ˌstipu'lation** NOUN

▸ˈstipuˌlator NOUN ▸**stipulatory** (ˈstɪpjulətərɪ, -trɪ) ADJECTIVE

stipulate² (ˈstɪpjulɪt, -ˌleɪt) ADJECTIVE (of a plant) having stipules.

stipule (ˈstɪpjuːl) NOUN a small paired usually leaflike outgrowth occurring at the base of a leaf or its stalk.
▷HISTORY C18: from Latin; see STIPE, STIPES
▸**stipular** (ˈstɪpjulə) ADJECTIVE

stir¹ (stɜː) VERB **stirs, stirring, stirred.** [1] to move an implement such as a spoon around in (a liquid) so as to mix up the constituents: *she stirred the porridge.* [2] to change or cause to change position; disturb or be disturbed: *he stirred in his sleep.* [3] (*intr; often foll by from*) to venture or depart (from one's usual or preferred place): *he won't stir from the fireside.* [4] (*intr*) to be active after a rest; be up and about. [5] (*tr*) to excite or stimulate, esp emotionally. [6] to move (oneself) briskly or vigorously; exert (oneself). [7] (*tr*) to rouse or awaken: *to stir someone from sleep; to stir memories.* [8] *Informal* (when *tr*, foll by *up*) to cause or incite others to cause (trouble, arguments, etc.). [9] **stir one's stumps.** *Informal* to move or become active. ◆ NOUN [10] the act or an instance of stirring or the state of being stirred. [11] a strong reaction, esp of excitement: *his publication caused a stir.* [12] a slight movement. [13] *NZ informal* a noisy party. ◆ See also **stir up.**
▷HISTORY Old English *styrian;* related to Middle High German *stürn* to poke, stir, Norwegian *styrja* to cause a commotion; see STORM, STURGEON
▸ˈ**stirrable** ADJECTIVE

stir² (stɜː) NOUN a slang word for **prison**: *in stir.*
▷HISTORY C19: perhaps from Romany *stariben* prison

Stir. ABBREVIATION FOR Stirlingshire.

stirabout (ˈstɜːrəˌbaut) NOUN [1] a kind of porridge orginally made in Ireland. [2] a bustling person.

stir-crazy ADJECTIVE *Slang* mentally disturbed as a result of being in prison or otherwise confined.

stir-fry (ˈstɜːˈfraɪ) VERB **-fries, -frying, -fried.** [1] to cook (small pieces of meat, vegetables, etc.) rapidly by stirring them in a wok or frying pan over a high heat: used esp for Chinese food. ◆ NOUN, *plural* **-fries.** [2] a dish cooked in this way.

stirk (stɜːk) NOUN [1] a heifer of 6 to 12 months old. [2] a yearling heifer or bullock.
▷HISTORY Old English *stierc;* related to Middle Low German *sterke,* Old High German *stero* ram, Latin *sterilis* sterile, Greek *steira;* see STEER²

Stirling (ˈstɜːlɪŋ) NOUN [1] a city in central Scotland, in Stirling council area on the River Forth: its castle was a regular residence of many Scottish monarchs between the 12th century and 1603. Pop.: 30 515 (1991). [2] a council area of central Scotland, created from part of Central Region in 1996; includes most of the historical county of Stirlingshire: the Forth valley rises to the Grampian Mountains in the N. Administrative centre: Stirling. Pop.: 86 212 (2001). Area: 2173 sq. km (839 sq. miles).

Stirling engine NOUN an external-combustion engine that uses air or an inert gas as the working fluid operating on a highly efficient thermodynamic cycle (the **Stirling cycle**).
▷HISTORY named after Robert *Stirling* (1790–1878), Scottish minister who invented it

Stirling's formula NOUN a formula giving the approximate value of the factorial of a large number *n*, as $n! \cong (n/e)^n\sqrt{(2\pi n)}$.
▷HISTORY named after James *Stirling* (1692–1770), Scottish mathematician

Stirlingshire (ˈstɜːlɪŋˌʃɪə, -ʃə) NOUN a former county of central Scotland: mostly became part of Central Region in 1975: now covered by the council areas of Stirling, Falkirk, and East Dunbartonshire.

stirps (stɜːps) NOUN, *plural* **stirpes** (ˈstɜːpiːz). [1] *Genealogy* a line of descendants from an ancestor; stock or strain. [2] *Botany* a race or variety, esp one in which the characters are maintained by cultivation.
▷HISTORY C17: from Latin: root, family origin

stirrer (ˈstɜːrə) NOUN [1] a person or thing that stirs. [2] *Informal* a person who deliberately causes trouble. [3] *Austral and NZ informal* a political activist or agitator.

stirring (ˈstɜːrɪŋ) ADJECTIVE [1] exciting the emotions; stimulating. [2] active, lively, or busy.
▸ˈ**stirringly** ADVERB

stirrup (ˈstɪrəp) NOUN [1] Also called: **stirrup iron.** either of two metal loops on a riding saddle, with a flat footpiece through which a rider puts his foot for support. They are attached to the saddle by **stirrup leathers.** [2] a U-shaped support or clamp made of metal, wood, leather, etc. [3] *Nautical* one of a set of ropes fastened to a yard at one end and having a thimble at the other through which a footrope is rove for support. [4] the usual US name for **étrier.**
▷HISTORY Old English *stigrāp,* from *stīg* path, step (related to Old High German *stīgan* to move up) + *rāp* ROPE; related to Old Norse *stigreip,* Old High German *stegareif*

stirrup bone NOUN the nontechnical name for **stapes.**
▷HISTORY C17: so called because of its stirrup-like shape

stirrup cup NOUN a cup containing an alcoholic drink offered to a horseman ready to ride away.

stirrup pump NOUN a hand-operated vertical reciprocating pump, such as one used in fire-fighting, etc., in which the base of the cylinder is placed in a bucket of water.

stir up VERB (*tr, adverb*) to set in motion; instigate: *he stirred up trouble.*

stishie (ˈstɪʃɪ) NOUN *Scot* a variant of **stushie.**

stitch (stɪtʃ) NOUN [1] a link made by drawing a thread through material by means of a needle. [2] a loop of yarn formed around an implement used in knitting, crocheting, etc. [3] a particular method of stitching or shape of stitch. [4] a sharp spasmodic pain in the side resulting from running or exercising. [5] (*usually used with a negative*) *Informal* the least fragment of clothing: *he wasn't wearing a stitch.* [6] *Agriculture* the ridge between two furrows. [7] **in stitches.** *Informal* laughing uncontrollably. [8] **drop a stitch.** to allow a loop of wool to fall off a knitting needle accidentally while knitting. ◆ VERB [9] (*tr*) to sew, fasten, etc., with stitches. [10] (*intr*) to be engaged in sewing. [11] (*tr*) to bind together (the leaves of a book, pamphlet, etc.) with wire staples or thread. ◆ NOUN, VERB [12] an informal word for **suture** (senses 1b, 6). ◆ See also **stitch up.**
▷HISTORY Old English *stice* sting; related to Old Frisian *steke,* Old High German *stih,* Gothic *stiks,* Old Norse *tikta* sharp
▸ˈ**stitcher** NOUN

stitchery (ˈstɪtʃərɪ) NOUN needlework, esp modern embroidery.

stitch up VERB (*tr, adverb*) [1] to join or mend by means of stitches or sutures. [2] *Slang* **a** to incriminate (someone) on a false charge by manufacturing evidence. **b** to betray, cheat, or defraud. [3] *Slang* to prearrange (something) in a clandestine manner. ◆ NOUN **stitch-up.** [4] *Slang* a matter that has been prearranged clandestinely.

stitch wheel NOUN a notched wheel used by a harness maker to mark out the spacing for stitching.

stitchwort (ˈstɪtʃˌwɜːt) NOUN any of several low-growing N temperate herbaceous plants of the caryophyllaceous genus *Stellaria,* having small white star-shaped flowers.
▷HISTORY C13: so named because it was once thought to be a remedy for stitches in the side

stithy (ˈstɪðɪ) NOUN, *plural* **stithies.** [1] *Archaic or dialect* a forge or anvil. ◆ VERB **stithies, stithying, stithied.** [2] (*tr*) *Obsolete* to forge on an anvil.
▷HISTORY C13: from Old Norse *stedhi*

stiver (ˈstaɪvə) NOUN [1] a former Dutch coin worth one twentieth of a guilder. [2] a small amount, esp of money.
▷HISTORY C16: from Dutch *stuiver;* related to Middle Low German *stüver,* Danish *styver*

stk ABBREVIATION FOR stock.

stoa (ˈstəuə) NOUN, *plural* **stoae** (ˈstəuiː) *or* **stoas.** a covered walk that has a colonnade on one or both sides, esp as used in ancient Greece.
▷HISTORY C17: from Greek

stoat (stəut) NOUN a small Eurasian musteline mammal, *Mustela erminea,* closely related to the weasels, having a brown coat and a black-tipped tail: in the northern parts of its range it has a white winter coat and is then known as an ermine.
▷HISTORY C15: of unknown origin

stob (stɒb) NOUN *Scot, northern English, and US dialect* a post or stump.
▷HISTORY C14: variant of STUB

stochastic (stɒˈkæstɪk) ADJECTIVE [1] *Statistics* **a** (of a random variable) having a probability distribution, usually with finite variance. **b** (of a process) involving a random variable the successive values of which are not independent. **c** (of a matrix) square with non-negative elements that add to unity in each row. [2] *Rare* involving conjecture.
▷HISTORY C17: from Greek *stokhastikos* capable of guessing, from *stokhazesthai* to aim at, conjecture, from *stokhos* a target
▸**stoˈchastically** ADVERB

stock (stɒk) NOUN [1] **a** (*sometimes plural*) the total goods or raw material kept on the premises of a shop or business. **b** (*as modifier*): *a stock clerk; stock book.* [2] a supply of something stored for future use: *he keeps a good stock of whisky.* [3] *Finance* **a** the capital raised by a company through the issue and subscription of shares entitling their holders to dividends, partial ownership, and usually voting rights. **b** the proportion of such capital held by an individual shareholder. **c** the shares of a specified company or industry. **d** (formerly) the part of an account or tally given to a creditor. **e** the debt represented by this. [4] standing or status. [5] **a** farm animals, such as cattle and sheep, bred and kept for their meat, skins, etc. **b** (*as modifier*): *stock farming.* [6] the trunk or main stem of a tree or other plant. [7] *Horticulture* **a** a rooted plant into which a scion is inserted during grafting. **b** a plant or stem from which cuttings are taken. See also **rootstock.** [8] the original type from which a particular race, family, group, etc., is derived. [9] a race, breed, or variety of animals or plants. [10] (*often plural*) a small pen in which a single animal can be confined. [11] a line of descent. [12] any of the major subdivisions of the human species; race or ethnic group. [13] the part of a rifle, sub-machine-gun, etc., into which the barrel and firing mechanism is set: held by the firer against the shoulder. [14] the handle of something, such as a whip or fishing rod. [15] the main body of a tool, such as the block of a plane. [16] short for **diestock, gunstock** or **rolling stock.** [17] (formerly) the part of a plough to which the irons and handles were attached. [18] the main upright part of a supporting structure. [19] a liquid or broth in which meat, fish, bones, or vegetables have been simmered for a long time. [20] film material before exposure and processing. [21] *Metallurgy* **a** a portion of metal cut from a bar upon which a specific process, such as forging, is to be carried out. **b** the material that is smelted in a blast furnace. [22] Also called: **gillyflower.** any of several plants of the genus *Matthiola,* such as *M. incana* and *M. bicornis* (**evening** or **night-scented stock**), of the Mediterranean region, cultivated for their brightly coloured flowers: *Brassicaceae* (crucifers). [23] **Virginian stock.** a similar and related North American plant, *Malcolmia maritima.* [24] a long usually white neckcloth wrapped around the neck, worn in the 18th century and as part of modern riding dress. [25] *Cards* a pile of cards left after the deal in certain games, from which players draw. [26] **a** the repertoire of plays available to a repertory company. **b** (*as modifier*): *a stock play.* [27] (on some types of anchors) a crosspiece at the top of the shank under the ring. [28] the centre of a wheel. [29] an exposed igneous intrusion that is smaller in area than a batholith. [30] a log or block of wood. [31] See **laughing stock.** [32] an archaic word for **stocking.** [33] **in stock. a** stored on the premises or available for sale or use. **b** supplied with goods of a specified kind. [34] **out of stock. a** not immediately available for sale or use. **b** not having goods of a specified kind immediately available. [35] **take stock. a** to make an inventory. **b** to make a general appraisal, esp of prospects, resources, etc. [36] **take stock in.** to attach importance to. [37] **lock, stock, and barrel.** See **lock¹** (sense 7). ◆ ADJECTIVE [38] staple, standard: *stock sizes in clothes.* [39] (*prenominal*) being a cliché; hackneyed: *a stock phrase.* ◆ VERB [40] (*tr*) to keep (goods) for sale. [41] (*intr; usually foll by up or up on*) to obtain a store of (something) for future use or sale: *to stock up on beer.* [42] (*tr*) to supply with live animals, fish, etc.: *to stock a farm.* [43] (*intr*) (of a

plant) to put forth new shoots. 44 (*tr*) *Obsolete* to punish by putting in the stocks. ♦ See also **stocks.**
▷HISTORY Old English *stocc* trunk (of a tree), stem, stick (the various senses developed from these meanings, as trunk of a tree, hence line of descent; structures made of timber; a store of timber or other goods for future use, hence an aggregate of goods, animals, etc.); related to Old Saxon, Old High German *stock* stick, stump
▸ **'stocker** NOUN

stockade (stɒ'keɪd) NOUN 1 an enclosure or barrier of stakes and timbers. 2 *US* a military prison or detention area. ♦ VERB 3 (*tr*) to surround with a stockade.
▷HISTORY C17: from Spanish *estacada,* from *estaca* a stake, post, of Germanic origin; see STAKE[1]

stock and station agent NOUN *Austral and NZ* a firm dealing in and financing farm activities.

stockbreeder ('stɒk,briːdə) NOUN a person who breeds or rears livestock as an occupation.
▸ **'stock,breeding** NOUN

stockbroker ('stɒk,brəʊkə) NOUN a person who buys and sells securities on a commission basis for customers. Often shortened to: **broker.**
▸ **stockbrokerage** ('stɒk,brəʊkərɪdʒ) *or* **'stock,broking** NOUN

stockbroker belt NOUN *Brit informal* the area outside a city, esp London, in which rich commuters live. Compare **exurbia.**

stock car NOUN 1 **a** a car, usually a production saloon, strengthened and modified for a form of racing in which the cars often collide. **b** (*as modifier*): *stock-car racing.* 2 the US and Canadian term for **cattle truck.**

stock certificate NOUN the US equivalent of **share certificate.**

stock company NOUN 1 *US* a business enterprise the capital of which is divided into transferable shares. 2 a US term for **repertory company.**

stock dove NOUN a European dove, *Columba oenas,* smaller than the wood pigeon and having a uniformly grey plumage.
▷HISTORY C14: so called because it lives in tree trunks. See STOCK

stock exchange NOUN (*often capitals*) 1 Also called: **stock market. a** a highly organized market facilitating the purchase and sale of securities and operated by professional stockbrokers and market makers according to fixed rules. **b** a place where securities are regularly traded. **c** (*as modifier*): *a stock-exchange operator; stock-exchange prices.* 2 the prices or trading activity of a stock exchange: *the stock exchange fell heavily today.*

stock farm NOUN a farm on which livestock is bred.
▸ **stock farmer** NOUN ▸ **stock farming** NOUN

stockfish ('stɒk,fɪʃ) NOUN, *plural* **-fish** *or* **-fishes.** fish, such as cod or haddock, cured by splitting and drying in the air.
▷HISTORY C13: of uncertain origin. Perhaps from STOCK (in the sense: stem, tree trunk) because it was dried on wooden racks. Compare Middle Dutch *stocvisch*

stockholder ('stɒk,həʊldə) NOUN 1 an owner of corporate capital stock. 2 *Austral* a person who keeps livestock.
▸ **'stock,holding** NOUN

Stockholm ('stɒkhəʊm; *Swedish* 'stɔkhɔlm) NOUN the capital of Sweden, a port in the E central part at the outflow of Lake Mälar into the Baltic: situated partly on the mainland and partly on islands; traditionally founded about 1250; university (1877). Pop.: 743 703 (2000 est.).

Stockholm syndrome NOUN a psychological condition in which hostages or kidnap victims become sympathetic towards their captors.
▷HISTORY C20: after a group of hostages in Stockholm in 1973

stockhorse ('stɒk,hɔːs) NOUN *Austral* a horse trained in the handling of stock.

stockinet (,stɒkɪ'nɛt) NOUN a machine-knitted elastic fabric used, esp formerly, for stockings, undergarments, etc.
▷HISTORY C19: perhaps changed from earlier *stocking-net*

stocking ('stɒkɪŋ) NOUN 1 one of a pair of close-fitting garments made of knitted yarn to cover the foot and part or all of the leg. 2 something resembling this in position, function, appearance, etc. 3 **in (one's) stocking** *or* **stockinged feet.** wearing stockings or socks but no shoes.
▷HISTORY C16: from dialect *stock* stocking + -ING[1]

stocking cap NOUN a conical knitted cap, often with a tassel.

stockinged ('stɒkɪŋd) ADJECTIVE wearing stockings or socks.

stockinger ('stɒkɪŋə) NOUN a person who knits on a stocking frame.

stocking filler NOUN *Brit* a present, esp a toy, of a size suitable for inclusion in a child's Christmas stocking.

stocking frame NOUN a type of knitting machine. Also called: **stocking loom, stocking machine.**

stocking mask NOUN a nylon stocking worn over the face by a criminal to disguise the features.

stocking stitch NOUN a pattern of stitches in knitting consisting of alternate rows of plain and purl stitch.
▷HISTORY C19: so named because of its use in hosiery

stock in trade NOUN 1 goods in stock necessary for carrying on a business. 2 anything constantly used by someone as a part of his profession, occupation, or trade: *friendliness is the salesman's stock in trade.*

stockish ('stɒkɪʃ) ADJECTIVE stupid or dull.
▸ **'stockishly** ADVERB ▸ **'stockishness** NOUN

stockist ('stɒkɪst) NOUN *Commerce Brit* a dealer who undertakes to maintain stocks of a specified product at or above a certain minimum in return for favourable buying terms granted by the manufacturer of the product.

stockjobber ('stɒk,dʒɒbə) NOUN 1 *Brit* (formerly) a wholesale dealer on a stock exchange who sold securities to brokers without transacting directly with the public. Often shortened to: **jobber.** See also **market maker.** 2 *US disparaging* a stockbroker, esp one dealing in worthless securities.
▸ **'stock,jobbery** *or* **'stock,jobbing** NOUN

stock lock NOUN a lock that is enclosed in a wooden case.

stockman ('stɒkmən, -,mæn) NOUN, *plural* **-men.** 1 **a** a man engaged in the rearing or care of farm livestock, esp cattle. **b** an owner of cattle or other livestock. 2 *US and Canadian* a man employed in a warehouse or stockroom.

stock market NOUN 1 another name for **stock exchange** (sense 1). 2 the usual US name for **stock exchange** (sense 2).

stockpile ('stɒk,paɪl) VERB 1 to acquire and store a large quantity of (something). ♦ NOUN 2 a large store or supply accumulated for future use.
▸ **'stock,piler** NOUN

Stockport ('stɒk,pɔːt) NOUN 1 a town in NW England, in Stockport unitary authority, Greater Manchester: an early textile centre and scene of several labour disturbances in the early 19th century; engineering, electronics. Pop.: 132 813 (1991). 2 a unitary authority in NW England, in Greater Manchester. Pop.: 84 544 (2001). Area: 126 sq. km (49 sq. miles).

stockpot ('stɒk,pɒt) NOUN *Chiefly Brit* a pot in which stock for soup, etc., is made or kept.

stockroom ('stɒk,ruːm, -,rʊm) NOUN a room in which a stock of goods is kept, as in a shop or factory.

stockroute ('stɒk,ruːt) NOUN *Austral and NZ* a route designated for droving sheep or cattle.

stocks (stɒks) PLURAL NOUN 1 *History* an instrument of punishment consisting of a heavy wooden frame with holes in which the feet, hands, or head of an offender were locked. 2 a frame in which an animal is held while receiving veterinary attention or while being shod. 3 a frame used to support a boat while under construction. 4 *Nautical* a vertical post or shaft at the forward edge of a rudder, extended upwards for attachment to the steering controls. 5 **on the stocks.** in preparation or under construction.

stock saddle NOUN *Chiefly US* a cowboy's saddle, esp an ornamental one.

stock-still ADVERB absolutely still; motionless.

stocktaking ('stɒk,teɪkɪŋ) NOUN 1 the examination, counting, and valuing of goods on hand in a shop or business. 2 a reassessment of one's current situation, progress, prospects, etc.

Stockton ('stɒktən) NOUN an inland port in central California, on the San Joaquin River: seat of the University of the Pacific (1851). Pop.: 243 771 (2000).

Stockton-on-Tees NOUN 1 a former port and industrial centre in NE England, in Stockton-on-Tees unitary authority, Co. Durham, on the River Tees: famous for the **Stockton-Darlington Railway** (1825), the first passenger-carrying railway in the world; now mainly residential. Pop.: 83 576 (1991). 2 a unitary authority in NE England, in Co. Durham and North Yorkshire: created in 1996 from part of Cleveland county. Pop.: 178 405 (2001). Area: 195 sq. km (75 sq. miles).

stock unit NOUN *NZ* **a** the tax basis for evaluating farmers' stock. Cattle, sheep, and deer are each given differing stock-unit values, the basic measure being the ewe equivalent. **b** (*as modifier*): *stock-unit values.*

stock watering NOUN *Business* the creation of more new shares in a company than is justified by its assets.

stock whip NOUN a whip with a long lash and a short handle, as used to herd cattle.

stocky ('stɒkɪ) ADJECTIVE **stockier, stockiest.** (usually of a person) thickset; sturdy.
▸ **'stockily** ADVERB ▸ **'stockiness** NOUN

stockyard ('stɒk,jɑːd) NOUN a large yard with pens or covered buildings where farm animals are assembled, sold, etc.

stodge (stɒdʒ) *Informal* ♦ NOUN 1 heavy filling starchy food. 2 *Dialect, chiefly southern English* baked or steamed pudding. 3 a dull person or subject. ♦ VERB 4 to stuff (oneself or another) with food.
▷HISTORY C17: perhaps a blend of STUFF + PODGE

stodgy ('stɒdʒɪ) ADJECTIVE **stodgier, stodgiest.** 1 (of food) heavy or uninteresting. 2 excessively formal and conventional.
▷HISTORY C19: from STODGE
▸ **'stodgily** ADVERB ▸ **'stodginess** NOUN

stoep (stup) NOUN *South African* a veranda.
▷HISTORY Afrikaans from Dutch

stogy *or* **stogey** ('stəʊgɪ) NOUN, *plural* **-gies.** *US* any long cylindrical inexpensive cigar.
▷HISTORY C19: from *stoga,* short for *Conestoga,* a town in Pennsylvania

stoic ('stəʊɪk) NOUN 1 a person who maintains stoical qualities. ♦ ADJECTIVE 2 a variant of **stoical.**

Stoic ('stəʊɪk) NOUN 1 a member of the ancient Greek school of philosophy founded by Zeno of Citium, the Greek philosopher (?336–?264 B.C.), holding that virtue and happiness can be attained only by submission to destiny and the natural law. ♦ ADJECTIVE 2 of or relating to the doctrines of the Stoics.
▷HISTORY C16: via Latin from Greek *stōikos,* from *stoa* the porch in Athens where Zeno taught

stoical ('stəʊɪkᵊl) ADJECTIVE characterized by impassivity or resignation.
▸ **'stoically** ADVERB ▸ **'stoicalness** NOUN

stoichiology, stoicheiology, *or* **stoechiology** (,stɔɪkɪ'ɒlədʒɪ) NOUN the branch of biology concerned with the study of the cellular components of animal tissues.
▷HISTORY C19: from Greek *stoikheion* element + -LOGY
▸ **stoichiological** *or* **stoicheiological** *or* **stoechiological** (,stɔɪkɪə'lɒdʒɪkᵊl) ADJECTIVE

stoichiometric, stoicheiometric, *or* **stoechiometric** (,stɔɪkɪə'mɛtrɪk) ADJECTIVE *Chem* 1 concerned with, involving, or having the exact proportions for a particular chemical reaction: *a stoichiometric mixture.* 2 (of a compound) having its component elements present in the exact proportions indicated by its formula. 3 of or concerned with stoichiometry.
▷HISTORY C19: see STOICHIOMETRY

stoichiometry, stoicheiometry, *or* **stoechiometry** (,stɔɪkɪ'ɒmɪtrɪ) NOUN the branch of chemistry concerned with the proportions in which elements are combined in compounds and

the quantitative relationships between reactants and products in chemical reactions.
▷HISTORY C19: from Greek *stoikheion* element + -METRY

stoicism ('stəʊɪˌsɪzəm) NOUN [1] indifference to pleasure and pain. [2] (*capital*) the philosophy of the Stoics.

stoke (stəʊk) VERB [1] to feed, stir, and tend (a fire, furnace, etc.). [2] (*tr*) to tend the furnace of; act as a stoker for. ◆ See also **stoke up**.
▷HISTORY C17: back formation from STOKER

stoked (stəʊkt) ADJECTIVE *NZ informal* very pleased; elated: *really stoked to have got the job.*

stokehold ('stəʊkˌhəʊld) NOUN *Nautical* [1] a coal bunker for a ship's furnace. [2] the hold for a ship's boilers; fire room.

stokehole ('stəʊkˌhəʊl) NOUN [1] another word for **stokehold**. [2] a hole in a furnace through which it is stoked.

Stoke-on-Trent NOUN [1] a city in central England, in Stoke-on-Trent unitary authority, Staffordshire on the River Trent: a centre of the pottery industry; university (1992). Pop.: 266 543 (1991). [2] a unitary authority in central England, in N Staffordshire. Pop.: 240 643 (2001). Area: 93 sq. km (36 sq. miles).

stoker ('stəʊkə) NOUN a person employed to tend a furnace, as on a steamship.
▷HISTORY C17: from Dutch, from *stoken* to STOKE

stokes (stəʊks) *or* **stoke** NOUN the cgs unit of kinematic viscosity, equal to the viscosity of a fluid in poise divided by its density in grams per cubic centimetre. 1 stokes is equivalent to 10^{-4} square metre per second. Symbol: St.
▷HISTORY C20: named after Sir George *Stokes* (1819–1903), British physicist

Stokesay Castle ('stəʊksɪ) NOUN a fortified manor house near Craven Arms in Shropshire: built in the 12th century, with a 16th-century gatehouse.

stoke up VERB (*adverb*) [1] to feed and tend (a fire, etc.) with fuel. [2] (*intr*) to fill oneself with food.

stokvel ('stɒkˌfel) NOUN *South African* a savings pool or syndicate, usually among Black people, in which funds are combined for mutual support or entertainment.
▷HISTORY C20: of uncertain origin

STOL (stɒl) NOUN [1] a system in which an aircraft can take off and land in a short distance. [2] an aircraft using this system. Compare **VTOL**.
▷HISTORY C20: *s(hort) t(ake) o(ff and) l(anding)*

stole[1] (stəʊl) VERB the past tense of **steal**.

stole[2] (stəʊl) NOUN [1] a long scarf or shawl, worn by women. [2] a long narrow scarf worn by various officiating clergymen.
▷HISTORY Old English *stole,* from Latin *stola,* Greek *stolē* clothing; related to *stellein* to array

stolen ('stəʊlən) VERB the past participle of **steal**.

stolid ('stɒlɪd) ADJECTIVE showing little or no emotion or interest.
▷HISTORY C17: from Latin *stolidus* dull; compare Latin *stultus* stupid; see STILL[1]
▸**stolidity** (stɒ'lɪdɪtɪ) *or* **'stolidness** NOUN ▸**'stolidly** ADVERB

stollen ('stəʊlən; *German* 'ʃtɔlən) NOUN a rich sweet bread containing nuts, raisins, etc.
▷HISTORY German, from *Stollen* wooden post, prop; so called from its shape; see STALL[1]

stolon ('stəʊlən) NOUN [1] a long horizontal stem, as of the currants, that grows along the surface of the soil and propagates by producing roots and shoots at the nodes or tip. [2] a branching structure in lower animals, esp the anchoring rootlike part of colonial organisms, such as hydroids, on which the polyps are borne.
▷HISTORY C17: from Latin *stolō* shoot
▸**stoloniferous** (ˌstəʊlə'nɪfərəs) ADJECTIVE

stoma ('stəʊmə) NOUN, *plural* **stomata** ('stəʊmətə, 'stɒm-, stəʊ'mɑːtə). [1] *Botany* an epidermal pore, present in large numbers in plant leaves, that controls the passage of gases into and out of a plant. [2] *Zoology, anatomy* a mouth or mouthlike part. [3] *Surgery* an artificial opening made in a tubular organ, esp the colon or ileum. See **colostomy, ileostomy**.
▷HISTORY C17: via New Latin from Greek: mouth

stomach ('stʌmək) NOUN [1] (in vertebrates) the enlarged muscular saclike part of the alimentary canal in which food is stored until it has been partially digested and rendered into chyme. Related adjective: **gastric**. [2] the corresponding digestive organ in invertebrates. [3] the abdominal region. [4] desire, appetite, or inclination: *I have no stomach for arguments.* [5] an archaic word for **temper**. [6] an obsolete word for **pride**. ◆ VERB (*tr; used mainly in negative constructions*) [7] to tolerate; bear: *I can't stomach his bragging.* [8] to eat or digest: *he cannot stomach oysters.*
▷HISTORY C14: from Old French *stomaque,* from Latin *stomachus* (believed to be the seat of the emotions), from Greek *stomakhos,* from *stoma* mouth

stomachache ('stʌməkˌeɪk) NOUN pain in the stomach or abdominal region, as from acute indigestion. Technical name: **gastralgia**. Also called: **stomach upset, upset stomach**.

stomacher ('stʌməkə) NOUN a decorative V-shaped panel of stiff material worn over the chest and stomach by men and women in the 16th century, later only by women.

stomachic (stə'mækɪk) ADJECTIVE *also* **stomachical**. [1] stimulating gastric activity. [2] of or relating to the stomach. ◆ NOUN [3] a stomachic medicine.

stomach pump NOUN *Med* a suction device for removing stomach contents by a tube inserted through the mouth.

stomach worm NOUN any of various nematode worms that are parasitic in the stomach of mammals, esp *Haemonchus contortus,* which infests sheep: family *Trichostrongylidae.*

stomachy ('stʌməkɪ) ADJECTIVE [1] having a large belly; paunchy. [2] *Dialect* easily angered; irritable.

stomack ('stʌmək) NOUN **have a stomack**. *E African informal* to be pregnant.

stomata ('stəʊmətə, 'stɒm-, stəʊ'mɑːtə) NOUN the plural of **stoma**.

stomatal ('stəʊmətᵊl, 'stɒm-) *or* **stomatous** ('stɒmətəs, 'stəʊ-) ADJECTIVE of, relating to, or possessing stomata or a stoma.

stomatic (stəʊ'mætɪk) ADJECTIVE of or relating to a mouth or mouthlike part.

stomatitis (ˌstəʊmə'taɪtɪs, ˌstɒm-) NOUN inflammation of the mouth.
▸**stomatitic** (ˌstəʊmə'tɪtɪk, ˌstɒm-) ADJECTIVE

stomato- *or before a vowel* **stomat-** COMBINING FORM indicating the mouth or a mouthlike part: *stomatology.*
▷HISTORY from Greek *stoma, stomat-*

stomatology (ˌstəʊmə'tɒlədʒɪ) NOUN the branch of medicine or dentistry concerned with the structures, functions, and diseases of the mouth.
▸**stomatological** (ˌstəʊmətə'lɒdʒɪkᵊl) ADJECTIVE

stomatoplasty ('stɒmətəˌplæstɪ, 'stəʊ-) NOUN plastic surgery or surgical repair involving the mouth.

stomatopod ('stɒmətəˌpɒd, 'stəʊ-) NOUN any marine crustacean of the order *Stomatopoda,* having abdominal gills: subclass *Malacostraca.* The group includes the mantis shrimp.
▷HISTORY C19: via New Latin from Greek *stoma* mouth + *-podos, pous* foot

-stome NOUN COMBINING FORM indicating a mouth or opening resembling a mouth: *peristome.*
▷HISTORY from Greek *stoma* mouth, and *stomion* little mouth

stomium ('stəʊmɪəm) NOUN the part of the sporangium of ferns that ruptures to release the spores.
▷HISTORY C20: via New Latin from Greek *stomion,* diminutive of *stoma* mouth

stomodaeum *or* **stomodeum** (ˌstəʊmə'diːəm, ˌstɒm-) NOUN, *plural* **-daea** *or* **-dea** (-'diːə). the oral cavity of a vertebrate embryo, which is formed from an invagination of the ectoderm and develops into the part of the alimentary canal between the mouth and stomach.
▷HISTORY C19: from New Latin, from Greek *stoma* mouth + *hodaios* on the way, from *hodos* way
▸**ˌstomo'daeal** *or* **ˌstomo'deal** ADJECTIVE

-stomous ADJECTIVE COMBINING FORM having a specified type of mouth: *monostomous.*

stomp (stɒmp) VERB (*intr*) [1] *Informal* to tread or stamp heavily. ◆ NOUN [2] a rhythmic stamping jazz dance.
▷HISTORY variant of STAMP

stomper (stɒmpə) NOUN [1] a rock or jazz song with a particularly strong and danceable beat. [2] a person or animal that stomps.

stompie ('stɒmpɪ) NOUN *South African slang* [1] a cigarette butt. [2] a short man.
▷HISTORY from Afrikaans *stomp* stump

-stomy NOUN COMBINING FORM indicating a surgical operation performed to make an artificial opening into or for a specified part: *cytostomy.*
▷HISTORY from Greek *-stomia,* from *stoma* mouth

stone (stəʊn) NOUN [1] the hard compact nonmetallic material of which rocks are made. Related adjective: **lithic**. [2] a small lump of rock; pebble. [3] *Jewellery* short for **gemstone**. [4] **a** a piece of rock designed or shaped for some particular purpose. **b** (*in combination*): *gravestone; millstone.* [5] **a** something that resembles a stone. **b** (*in combination*): *hailstone.* [6] the woody central part of such fruits as the peach and plum, that contains the seed; endocarp. [7] any similar hard part of a fruit, such as the stony seed of a date. [8] (*plural* **stone**) *Brit* a unit of weight, used esp to express human body weight, equal to 14 pounds or 6.350 kilograms. [9] Also called: **granite**. the rounded heavy mass of granite or iron used in the game of curling. [10] *Pathol* a nontechnical name for **calculus**. [11] *Printing* a table with a very flat iron or stone surface upon which hot-metal pages are composed into formes; imposition table. [12] *Rare* (in certain games) a piece or man. [13] **a** any of various dull grey colours. **b** (*as adjective*): *stone paint.* [14] (*modifier*) relating to or made of stone: *a stone house.* [15] (*modifier*) made of stoneware: *a stone jar.* [16] **cast a stone (at)**. cast aspersions (upon). [17] **heart of stone**. an obdurate or unemotional nature. [18] **leave no stone unturned**. to do everything possible to achieve an end. ◆ ADVERB [19] (*in combination*) completely: *stone-cold; stone-deaf.* ◆ VERB (*tr*) [20] to throw stones at, esp to kill. [21] to remove the stones from. [22] to furnish or provide with stones. [23] **stone the crows**. *Brit and Austral slang* an expression of surprise, dismay, etc.
▷HISTORY Old English *stān;* related to Old Saxon *stēn,* German *Stein,* Old Norse *steinn,* Gothic *stains,* Greek *stion* pebble
▸**'stonable** *or* **'stoneable** ADJECTIVE ▸**'stoneless** ADJECTIVE ▸**'stonelessness** NOUN ▸**'stoneˌlike** ADJECTIVE

Stone Age NOUN [1] a period in human culture identified by the use of stone implements and usually divided into the Palaeolithic, Mesolithic, and Neolithic stages. ◆ MODIFIER **Stone-Age**. [2] (*sometimes not capitals*) of or relating to this period: *stone-age man.*

stone axe NOUN [1] a primitive axe made of chipped stone. [2] a blunt axe used for cutting stone.

stone bass (bæs) NOUN a large sea perch, *Polyprion americanus,* of the Atlantic and Mediterranean. Also called: **wreckfish**.

stone-blind ADJECTIVE completely blind. Compare **sand-blind**.

stoneboat ('stəʊnˌbəʊt) NOUN *US and Canadian* a type of sleigh used for moving rocks from fields, for hauling milk cans, etc.

stone boiling NOUN a primitive method of boiling liquid with heated stones.

stone bramble NOUN a herbaceous Eurasian rosaceous plant, *Rubus saxatilis,* of stony places, having white flowers and berry-like scarlet fruits (drupelets). See also **bramble** (sense 1).
▷HISTORY C18: so called because it grows in stony places

stonecast ('stəʊnˌkɑːst) NOUN a less common name for **stone's throw**.

stonechat ('stəʊnˌtʃæt) NOUN an Old World songbird, *Saxicola torquata,* having a black plumage with a reddish-brown breast: subfamily *Turdinae* (thrushes).
▷HISTORY C18: so called from its cry, which sounds like clattering pebbles

stone-cold ADJECTIVE [1] completely cold. ◆ ADVERB [2] (intensifier): *stone-cold sober.*

stonecrop ('stəʊnˌkrɒp) NOUN [1] any of various N temperate crassulaceous plants of the genus *Sedum,* having fleshy leaves and typically red, yellow, or white flowers. [2] any of various similar or related plants.

▷HISTORY Old English: so named because it grows on rocks and walls

stone curlew NOUN any of several brownish shore birds of the family *Burhinidae,* esp *Burhinus oedicnemus,* having a large head and eyes: order *Charadriiformes*. Also called: **thick-knee.**
▷HISTORY C17: so called because it is found in stony habitats and resembles a curlew

stonecutter (ˈstəʊnˌkʌtə) NOUN [1] a person who is skilled in cutting and carving stone. [2] a machine used to dress stone.
▸ˈ**stone,cutting** NOUN

stoned (stəʊnd) ADJECTIVE *Slang* under the influence of drugs or alcohol.

stone-dead ADJECTIVE completely lifeless.

stone-deaf ADJECTIVE completely deaf.

stonefish (ˈstəʊnˌfɪʃ) NOUN, *plural* **-fish** *or* **-fishes.** a venomous tropical marine scorpaenid fish, *Synanceja verrucosa,* that resembles a piece of rock on the seabed.

stonefly (ˈstəʊnˌflaɪ) NOUN, *plural* **-flies.** any insect of the order *Plecoptera,* in which the larvae are aquatic, living beneath stones, and the adults have long antennae and two pairs of large wings and occur near water.
▷HISTORY C15: so called because its larvae live under stones in rivers

stone fruit NOUN the nontechnical name for **drupe.**

stoneground (ˈstəʊnˌgraʊnd) ADJECTIVE (of flour) ground with millstones.

Stonehenge (ˌstəʊnˈhɛndʒ) NOUN a prehistoric ruin in S England, in Wiltshire on Salisbury Plain: constructed over the period of roughly 3000–1600 B.C.; one of the most important megalithic monuments in Europe; believed to have had religious and astronomical purposes.

stone-lily NOUN the fossil of any of several species of sea lily or crinoid.

stone marten NOUN [1] a marten, *Martes foina,* of Eurasian woods and forests, having a brown coat with a pale underfur. [2] the highly valued fur of this animal.

stonemason (ˈstəʊnˌmeɪsᵊn) NOUN a person who is skilled in preparing stone for building.
▸ˈ**stone,masonry** NOUN

stone massage NOUN a form of massage using heated smooth stones.

stone parsley NOUN a roadside umbelliferous plant, *Sison amomum,* of W Europe and the Mediterranean region, having clusters of small white flowers and aromatic seeds.

stone pine NOUN a Mediterranean pine tree, *Pinus pinea,* having a short bole and radiating branches forming an umbrella shape. Also called: **umbrella pine.**

stone pit NOUN a less common name for **quarry**[1].

stoner (ˈstəʊnə) NOUN [1] a device for removing stones from fruit. [2] *Slang* a person who is habitually under the influence of drugs or alcohol.

stone roller NOUN a small silvery freshwater cyprinid fish, *Campostoma anomalum,* of the eastern US, having a narrow black stripe on the dorsal and anal fins.
▷HISTORY C19: so called because it pushes stones about in building its nest

stone saw NOUN an untoothed iron saw used to cut stone.

Stone sheep *or* **Stone's sheep** NOUN a wild sheep found in the Yukon and the northern Rocky Mountains.
▷HISTORY C19: after the US naturalist Andrew Jackson *Stone,* who first discovered the breed in 1896

stone shoot NOUN *Mountaineering* a long steeply sloping line of loose boulder-strewn scree.

stone's throw NOUN a short distance. Also called: **stonecast.**

stonewall (ˌstəʊnˈwɔːl) VERB [1] (*intr*) *Cricket* (of a batsman) to play defensively. [2] to obstruct or hinder (parliamentary business).
▸ˌ**stone**ˈ**waller** NOUN

stoneware (ˈstəʊnˌwɛə) NOUN [1] a hard opaque pottery, fired at a very high temperature. ◆ ADJECTIVE [2] made of stoneware.

stonewashed (ˈstəʊnˌwɒʃt) ADJECTIVE (of new clothes or fabric, esp denim jeans) given a worn faded look by being subjected to the abrasive action of many small pieces of pumice.

stonework (ˈstəʊnˌwɜːk) NOUN [1] any structure or part of a building made of stone. [2] the process of dressing or setting stones.
▸ˈ**stone,worker** NOUN

stonewort (ˈstəʊnˌwɜːt) NOUN any of various green algae of the genus *Chara,* which grow in brackish or fresh water and have jointed fronds encrusted with lime.

Stoney (ˈstəʊnɪ) NOUN a member of a Native Canadian people of Alberta.
▷HISTORY from Siouan

stonk (stɒŋk) VERB (*tr*) [1] to bombard (soldiers, buildings, etc.) with artillery. ◆ NOUN [2] a concentrated bombardment by artillery.
▷HISTORY C20: from *st(andard) (linear) (c)onc(entration)*

stonkered (ˈstɒŋkəd) ADJECTIVE *Slang* completely exhausted or beaten; whacked.
▷HISTORY C20: from *stonker* to beat, of unknown origin

stony *or* **stoney** (ˈstəʊnɪ) ADJECTIVE **stonier, stoniest.** [1] of or resembling stone. [2] abounding in stone or stones. [3] unfeeling, heartless, or obdurate. [4] short for **stony-broke.**
▸ˈ**stonily** ADVERB ▸ˈ**stoniness** NOUN

stony-broke ADJECTIVE *Brit slang* completely without money; penniless. US and Canadian term: **stone-broke.**

stony coral NOUN any coral of the order *Madreporaria,* having a calcareous skeleton, aggregations of which form reefs and islands.

stony-hearted ADJECTIVE unfeeling; hardhearted.
▸ˌ**stony**ˈ**heartedness** NOUN

stony meteorite NOUN a meteorite composed mainly of silicates.

stood (stʊd) VERB the past tense and past participle of **stand.**

stooge (stuːdʒ) NOUN [1] an actor who feeds lines to a comedian or acts as his foil or butt. [2] *Slang* someone who is taken advantage of by another. ◆ VERB (*intr*) [3] *Slang* to act as a stooge. [4] (foll by *about* or *around*) *Slang* (esp in the RAF) to fly or move about aimlessly.
▷HISTORY C20: of unknown origin

stook (stuːk) NOUN [1] a number of sheaves set upright in a field to dry with their heads together. ◆ VERB [2] (*tr*) to set up (sheaves) in stooks.
▷HISTORY C15: variant of *stouk,* of Germanic origin; compare Middle Low German *stūke,* Old High German *stūhha* sleeve
▸ˈ**stooker** NOUN

stookie (ˈstʊkɪ) NOUN *Scot* [1] stucco. [2] plaster; plaster of Paris. [3] a statue: *he stood there like a stookie.*

stool (stuːl) NOUN [1] a backless seat or footrest consisting of a small flat piece of wood, etc., resting on three or four legs, a pedestal, etc. [2] a rootstock or base of a plant, usually a woody plant, from which shoots, etc., are produced. [3] a cluster of shoots growing from such a base. [4] *Chiefly US* a decoy used in hunting. [5] waste matter evacuated from the bowels. [6] a lavatory seat. [7] (in W Africa, esp Ghana) a chief's throne. [8] **fall between two stools. a** to fail through vacillation between two alternatives. **b** to be in an unsatisfactory situation through not belonging to either of two categories or groups. ◆ VERB (*intr*) [9] (of a plant) to send up shoots from the base of the stem, rootstock, etc. [10] to lure wildfowl with a decoy.
▷HISTORY Old English *stōl;* related to Old Norse *stōll,* Gothic *stōls,* Old High German *stuol* chair, Greek *stulos* pillar

stool ball NOUN a game resembling cricket, still played by girls and women in Sussex, England.

stool pigeon NOUN [1] a living or dummy pigeon used to decoy others. [2] an informer for the police; nark. [3] *US slang* a person acting as a decoy.

stoop[1] (stuːp) VERB (*mainly intr*) [1] (*also tr*) to bend (the body or the top half of the body) forward and downward. [2] to carry oneself with head and shoulders habitually bent forward. [3] (often foll by *to*) to abase or degrade oneself. [4] (often foll by *to*) to condescend; deign. [5] (of a bird of prey) to swoop down. [6] *Archaic* to give in. ◆ NOUN [7] the act, position, or characteristic of stooping. [8] a lowering from a position of dignity or superiority. [9] a downward swoop, esp of a bird of prey.
▷HISTORY Old English *stūpan;* related to Middle Dutch *stupen* to bow, Old Norse *stūpa,* Norwegian *stupa* to fall; see STEEP[1]
▸ˈ**stooper** NOUN ▸ˈ**stooping** ADJECTIVE ▸ˈ**stoopingly** ADVERB

stoop[2] (stuːp) NOUN *US and Canadian* a small platform with steps up to it at the entrance to a building.
▷HISTORY C18: from Dutch *stoep,* of Germanic origin; compare Old High German *stuofa* stair, Old English *stōpel* footprint; see STEP

stoop[3] (stuːp) NOUN *Archaic* a pillar or post.
▷HISTORY C15: variant of dialect *stulpe,* probably from Old Norse *stolpe;* see STELE

stoop[4] (stuːp) NOUN a less common spelling of **stoup.**

stoor (stuːr) NOUN *Scot* a variant of **stour.**

stop (stɒp) VERB **stops, stopping, stopped.** [1] to cease from doing or being (something); discontinue: *stop talking.* [2] to cause (something moving) to halt or (of something moving) to come to a halt: *to stop a car; the car stopped.* [3] (*tr*) to prevent the continuance or completion of: *to stop a show.* [4] (*tr;* often foll by *from*) to prevent or restrain: *to stop George from fighting.* [5] (*tr*) to keep back: *to stop supplies to the navy.* [6] (*tr*) to intercept or hinder in transit: *to stop a letter.* [7] (*tr;* often foll by *up*) to block or plug, esp so as to close: *to stop up a pipe.* [8] (*tr;* often foll by *up*) to fill a hole or opening in: *to stop up a wall.* [9] (*tr*) to staunch or stem: *to stop a wound.* [10] (*tr*) to instruct a bank not to honour (a cheque). [11] (*tr*) to deduct (money) from pay. [12] (*tr*) *Brit* to provide with punctuation. [13] (*tr*) *Boxing* to beat (an opponent) either by a knockout or a technical knockout. [14] (*tr*) *Informal* to receive (a blow, hit, etc.). [15] (*intr*) to stay or rest: *we stopped at the Robinsons' for three nights.* [16] (*tr*) *Rare* to defeat, beat, or kill. [17] (*tr*) *Music* **a** to alter the vibrating length of (a string on a violin, guitar, etc.) by pressing down on it at some point with the finger. **b** to alter the vibrating length of an air column in a wind instrument by closing (a finger hole, etc.). **c** to produce (a note) in this manner. [18] (*tr*) to place a hand inside (the bell of a French horn) to alter the tone colour and pitch or play (a note) on a French horn in such a manner. [19] *Bridge* to have a protecting card or winner in (a suit in which one's opponents are strong). [20] **stop at nothing.** to be prepared to do anything; be unscrupulous or ruthless. ◆ NOUN [21] an arrest of movement or progress. [22] the act of stopping or the state of being stopped. [23] a place where something halts or pauses: *a bus stop.* [24] a stay in or as if in the course of a journey. [25] the act or an instance of blocking or obstructing. [26] a plug or stopper. [27] a block, screw, or other device or object that prevents, limits, or terminates the motion of a mechanism or moving part. [28] *Brit* a punctuation mark, esp a full stop. [29] Also called: **stop thrust.** *Fencing* a counterthrust made without a parry in the hope that one's blade will touch before one's opponent's blade. [30] short for **stop payment** or **stop order.** [31] *Music* **a** the act of stopping the string, finger hole, etc., of an instrument. **b** a set of organ pipes or harpsichord strings that may be allowed to sound as a group by muffling or silencing all other such sets. **c** a knob, lever, or handle on an organ, etc., that is operated to allow sets of pipes to sound. **d** an analogous device on a harpsichord or other instrument with variable registers, such as an electrophonic instrument. [32] **pull out all the stops. a** to play at full volume. **b** to spare no effort. [33] *Austral* a stud on a football boot. [34] the angle between the forehead and muzzle of a dog or cat, regarded as a point in breeding. [35] *Nautical* a short length of line or small stuff used as a tie, esp for a furled sail. [36] Also called: **stop consonant.** *Phonetics* any of a class of consonants articulated by first making a complete closure at some point of the vocal tract and then releasing it abruptly with audible plosion. Stops include the labials (p, b), the alveolars or dentals (t, d), the velars (k, g). Compare **continuant.** [37] Also called: **f-stop.** *Photog* **a** a setting of the aperture of a camera lens, calibrated to the corresponding f-number. **b** another name for **diaphragm** (sense 4). [38] a block or carving used to

complete the end of a moulding. 39 Also called: **stopper.** *Bridge* a protecting card or winner in a suit in which one's opponents are strong. ◆ See also **stop down, stop off, stop out, stopover, stops.**
▷HISTORY C14: from Old English *stoppian* (unattested), as in *forstoppian* to plug the ear, ultimately from Late Latin *stuppāre* to stop with a tow, from Latin *stuppa* tow, from Greek *stuppē*
▸ **'stoppable** ADJECTIVE

stopbank ('stɒpˌbæŋk) NOUN *NZ* an embankment to prevent flooding.

stop bath NOUN a weakly acidic solution used in photographic processing to stop the action of a developer on a film, plate, or paper before the material is immersed in fixer.

stop chorus NOUN *Jazz* a solo during which the rhythm section plays only the first beat of each phrase of music.

stopcock ('stɒpˌkɒk) NOUN a valve used to control or stop the flow of a fluid in a pipe.

stop down VERB (*adverb*) to reduce the size of the aperture of (a camera lens).

stope (stəʊp) NOUN 1 a steplike excavation made in a mine to extract ore. ◆ VERB 2 to mine (ore, etc.) by cutting stopes.
▷HISTORY C18: probably from Low German *stope;* see STOOP[2]

stop-frame ADJECTIVE *Films* of or relating to animated films involving models, puppets, etc., in which each frame is photographed individually: *stop-frame photography.*

stopgap ('stɒpˌgæp) NOUN **a** a temporary substitute for something else. **b** (*as modifier*): *a stopgap programme.*

stop-go ADJECTIVE *Brit* (of economic policy) characterized by deliberate alternate expansion and contraction of aggregate demand in an effort to curb inflation and eliminate balance of payments deficits, and yet maintain full employment.

stoping ('stəʊpɪŋ) NOUN *Geology* the process by which country rock is broken up and engulfed by the upward movement of magma. Also called: **magmatic stoping.** See also **stope.**

stoplight ('stɒpˌlaɪt) NOUN 1 a red light on a traffic signal indicating that vehicles or pedestrians coming towards it should stop. 2 another word for **brake light.**

stop-loss ADJECTIVE *Business* of or relating to an order to a broker in a commodity or security market to close an open position at a specified price in order to limit any loss.

stop-motion NOUN **a** a technique used in animation and photography in which a subject is filmed then adjusted a frame at a time. **b** (*as modifier*): *stop-motion animation.*

stop off, stop in, *or esp US* **stop by** VERB 1 (*intr, adverb;* often foll by *at*) to halt and call somewhere, as on a visit or errand, esp en route to another place. ◆ NOUN **stopoff.** 2 **a** a break in a journey. **b** (*as modifier*): *stopoff point.*

stop order NOUN *Stock Exchange* an instruction to a broker to sell one or more shares when the price offered for them falls below a stipulated level. Also called: **stop-loss order.**

stop out VERB (*tr, adverb*) to cover (part of the area) of a piece of cloth, printing plate, etc., to prevent it from being dyed, etched, etc.

stopover ('stɒpˌəʊvə) NOUN 1 a stopping place on a journey. ◆ VERB **stop over.** 2 (*intr, adverb*) to make a stopover.

stoppage ('stɒpɪdʒ) NOUN 1 the act of stopping or the state of being stopped. 2 something that stops or blocks. 3 a deduction of money, as from pay. 4 an organized cessation of work, as during a strike.

stoppage time NOUN *Sport* another name for **injury time.**

stop payment NOUN an instruction to a bank by the drawer of a cheque to refuse payment on it.

stopped (stɒpt) ADJECTIVE (of a pipe or tube, esp an organ pipe) closed at one end and thus sounding an octave lower than an open pipe of the same length.

stopper ('stɒpə) NOUN 1 Also called: **stopple** ('stɒp[ə]l). a plug or bung for closing a bottle, pipe, duct, etc. 2 a person or thing that stops or puts an end to something. 3 *Bridge* another name for **stop** (sense 39). ◆ VERB 4 (*tr*) Also: **stopple.** to close or fit with a stopper.

stopping ('stɒpɪŋ) NOUN 1 *Brit informal* a dental filling. 2 a solid barrier in a mine tunnel to seal off harmful gases, fire, fresh air from used air, etc. ◆ ADJECTIVE 3 *Chiefly Brit* making many stops in a journey: *a stopping train.*

stopping power NOUN *Physics* a measure of the effect a substance has on the kinetic energy of a particle passing through it.

stop press NOUN *Brit* 1 news items inserted into a newspaper after the printing has been started. 2 the space regularly left blank for this.

stops (stɒps) NOUN (*functioning as singular*) any one of several card games in which players must play their cards in certain sequences.

stop thrust NOUN *Fencing* another name for **stop** (sense 29).

stop time NOUN *Jazz* a passage where the beat stops temporarily.

stopwatch ('stɒpˌwɒtʃ) NOUN a type of watch used for timing events, such as sporting events, accurately, having a device for stopping the hand or hands instantly.

storage ('stɔːrɪdʒ) NOUN 1 the act of storing or the state of being stored. 2 space or area reserved for storing. 3 a charge made for storing. 4 *Computing* **a** the act or process of storing information in a computer memory or on a magnetic tape, disk, etc. **b** (*as modifier*): *a storage device; storage capacity.*

storage battery NOUN another name (esp US) for **accumulator** (sense 1).

storage capacity NOUN the maximum number of bits, bytes, words, or items that can be held in a memory system such as that of a computer or of the brain.

storage device NOUN a piece of computer equipment, such as a magnetic tape, disk, etc., in or on which data and instructions can be stored, usually in binary form.

storage heater NOUN an electric device capable of accumulating and radiating heat generated by off-peak electricity.

storage tube NOUN *Electronics* an electron tube in which information is stored as charges for a predetermined time.

storax ('stɔːræks) NOUN 1 any of numerous styracaceous trees or shrubs of the genus *Styrax,* of tropical and subtropical regions, having drooping showy white flowers. 2 a vanilla-scented solid resin obtained from one of these trees, *Styrax officinalis* of the Mediterranean region and SW Asia, formerly used as incense and in perfumery and medicine. 3 a liquid aromatic balsam obtained from liquidambar trees, esp *Liquidambar orientalis* of SW Asia, and used in perfumery and medicine.
▷HISTORY C14: via Late Latin from Greek, variant of STYRAX

store (stɔː) VERB 1 (*tr*) to keep, set aside, or accumulate for future use. 2 (*tr*) to place in a warehouse, depository, etc., for safekeeping. 3 (*tr*) to supply, provide, or stock. 4 (*intr*) to be put into storage. 5 *Computing* to enter or retain (information) in a storage device. ◆ NOUN 6 **a** an establishment for the retail sale of goods and services. **b** (*in combination*): *storefront.* 7 **a** a large supply or stock kept for future use. **b** (*as modifier*): *store ship.* 8 short for **department store.** 9 **a** a storage place such as a warehouse or depository. **b** (*in combination*): *storeman.* 10 the state of being stored (esp in the phrase **in store**). 11 a large amount or quantity. 12 *Computing, chiefly Brit* another name for **memory** (sense 7). 13 Also called: **store pig.** a pig that has not yet been weaned and weighs less than 40 kg. 14 **a** an animal bought lean to be fattened up for market. **b** (*as modifier*): *store cattle.* 15 **in store.** forthcoming or imminent. 16 **lay, put,** *or* **set store by.** to value or reckon as important. ◆ See also **stores.**
▷HISTORY C13: from Old French *estor,* from *estorer* to restore, from Latin *instaurāre* to refresh; related to Greek *stauros* stake
▸ **'storable** ADJECTIVE

store and forward VERB to store (information) in a computer for later forward transmission through a telecommunication network.

Store Bælt ('sdoːrə 'bɛld) NOUN the Danish name for the **Great Belt.**

store card NOUN another name for **charge card.**

storehouse ('stɔːˌhaʊs) NOUN a place where things are stored.

storekeeper ('stɔːˌkiːpə) NOUN a manager, owner, or keeper of a store.
▸ **'storeˌkeeping** NOUN

store of value NOUN *Economics* the function of money that enables goods and services to be paid for a considerable time after they have been acquired.

storeroom ('stɔːˌruːm, -ˌrʊm) NOUN 1 a room in which things are stored. 2 room for storing.

stores (stɔːz) PLURAL NOUN 1 a supply or stock of something, esp essentials, for a specific purpose: *the ship's stores.* 2 specifically, munitions slung externally on a military aircraft airframe.

storey *or US* **story** ('stɔːrɪ) NOUN, *plural* **-reys** *or* **-ries.** 1 a floor or level of a building. 2 a set of rooms on one level.
▷HISTORY C14: from Anglo-Latin *historia,* picture, from Latin: narrative, probably arising from the pictures on medieval windows

storeyed *or US* **storied** ('stɔːrɪd) ADJECTIVE **a** having a storey or storeys. **b** (*in combination*): *a two-storeyed house.*

storey house NOUN (in W Africa) a house having more than one storey.

storiated ('stɔːrɪˌeɪtɪd) ADJECTIVE another word for **historiated** or **storied** (sense 2).

storied ('stɔːrɪd) ADJECTIVE 1 recorded in history or in a story; fabled. 2 decorated with narrative scenes or pictures.

stork (stɔːk) NOUN 1 any large wading bird of the family *Ciconiidae,* chiefly of warm regions of the Old World, having very long legs and a long stout pointed bill, and typically having a white-and-black plumage: order *Ciconiiformes.* 2 (*sometimes capital*) a variety of domestic fancy pigeon resembling the fairy swallow.
▷HISTORY Old English *storc;* related to Old High German *storah,* Old Norse *storkr,* Old English *stearc* stiff; from the stiff appearance of its legs; see STARK

storksbill ('stɔːksˌbɪl) NOUN any of various geraniaceous plants of the genus *Erodium,* esp *E. cicutarium* (**common storksbill**), having pink or reddish-purple flowers and fruits with a beaklike process.

storm (stɔːm) NOUN 1 **a** a violent weather condition of strong winds, rain, hail, thunder, lightning, blowing sand, snow, etc. **b** (*as modifier*): *storm signal; storm sail.* **c** (*in combination*): *stormproof.* 2 *Meteorol* a violent gale of force 10 on the Beaufort scale reaching speeds of 55 to 63 mph. 3 a strong or violent reaction: *a storm of protest.* 4 a direct assault on a stronghold. 5 a heavy discharge or rain, as of bullets or missiles. 6 short for **storm window** (sense 1). 7 **storm in a teacup.** *Brit* a violent fuss or disturbance over a trivial matter. US equivalent: **tempest in a teapot.** 8 **take by storm. a** to capture or overrun by a violent assault. **b** to overwhelm and enthral. ◆ VERB 9 to attack or capture (something) suddenly and violently. 10 (*intr*) to be vociferously angry. 11 (*intr*) to move or rush violently or angrily. 12 (*intr;* with *it* as subject) to rain, hail, or snow hard and be very windy, often with thunder or lightning.
▷HISTORY Old English, related to Old Norse *stormr,* German *Sturm;* see STIR[1]
▸ **'stormˌlike** ADJECTIVE

storm belt NOUN an area of the earth's surface in which storms are frequent.

stormbound ('stɔːmˌbaʊnd) ADJECTIVE detained or harassed by storms.

storm centre NOUN 1 the centre of a cyclonic storm, etc., where pressure is lowest. 2 the centre of any disturbance or trouble.

storm cloud NOUN 1 a heavy dark cloud presaging rain or a storm. 2 a herald of disturbance, anger, or violence: *the storm clouds of war.*

storm-cock NOUN another name for **missel thrush.**
▷HISTORY C18: so called because it was believed to give forewarning of bad weather

storm collar NOUN a high collar on a coat.

storm cone NOUN *Brit* a canvas cone hoisted as a warning of high winds.

storm door NOUN an extra outer door for protection in bad weather.

stormer ('stɔːmə) NOUN *Informal* an outstanding example of its kind: *that film was a real stormer.*

storm glass NOUN a sealed tube containing a solution supposed to change in appearance according to the weather.

storming ('stɔːmɪŋ) ADJECTIVE *Informal* characterized by or displaying dynamism, speed, and energy: *a storming performance.*

storm lantern NOUN another name for **hurricane lamp.**

Stormont ('stɔːmənt) NOUN a suburb of Belfast: site of Parliament House (1928–30), formerly the seat of the parliament of Northern Ireland (1922–72) and since 1998 of the Northern Ireland assembly, and Stormont Castle, formerly the residence of the prime minister of Northern Ireland and since 1998 the office of the province's first minister.

storm petrel NOUN any small petrel, such as the northern *Hydrobates pelagicus,* of the family *Hydrobatidae,* typically having a dark plumage with paler underparts. Also called: **Mother Carey's chicken, stormy petrel.**
▷**HISTORY** C19: so named because it was thought to be a harbinger of rough weather

stormproof ('stɔːmˌpruːf) ADJECTIVE withstanding or giving protection against storms.

storm trooper NOUN [1] a member of the Nazi SA. [2] a member of a force of shock troops.

storm warning NOUN [1] a pattern of lights, flags, etc., displayed at certain ports as a warning to shipping of an approaching storm. [2] an announcement on radio or television of an approaching storm. [3] any warning of approaching danger or trouble.

storm window NOUN [1] an additional window fitted to the outside of an ordinary window to provide insulation against wind, cold, rain, etc. [2] a type of dormer window.

stormy ('stɔːmɪ) ADJECTIVE **stormier, stormiest.** [1] characterized by storms. [2] subject to, involving, or characterized by violent disturbance or emotional outburst.
▸**'stormily** ADVERB ▸**'storminess** NOUN

stormy petrel NOUN [1] another name for **storm petrel.** [2] a person who brings or portends trouble.

Stornoway ('stɔːnəˌweɪ) NOUN a port in NW Scotland, on the E coast of Lewis in the Outer Hebrides, administrative centre of the Western Isles. Pop.: 5975 (1991).

Storting *or* **Storthing** ('stɔːtɪŋ) NOUN the parliament of Norway. See also **Lagting, Odelsting.**
▷**HISTORY** C19: Norwegian, from *stor* great + *thing* assembly

story[1] ('stɔːrɪ) NOUN, *plural* **-ries.** [1] a narration of a chain of events told or written in prose or verse. [2] Also called: **short story.** a piece of fiction, briefer and usually less detailed than a novel. [3] Also called: **story line.** the plot of a book, film, etc. [4] an event that could be the subject of a narrative. [5] a report or statement on a matter or event. [6] the event or material for such a report. [7] *Informal* a lie, fib, or untruth. [8] **cut** (*or* **make**) **a long story short.** to leave out details in a narration. [9] *Informal* **the same old story.** the familiar or regular course of events. [10] **the story goes.** it is commonly said or believed. ◆ VERB **-ries, -rying, -ried.** (*tr*) [11] to decorate (a pot, wall, etc.) with scenes from history or legends.
▷**HISTORY** C13: from Anglo-French *estorie,* from Latin *historia;* see HISTORY

story[2] ('stɔːrɪ) NOUN, *plural* **-ries.** another spelling (esp US) of **storey.**

storyboard ('stɔːrɪˌbɔːd) NOUN (in films, television, advertising, etc.) a series of sketches or photographs showing the sequence of shots or images planned for a film.

storybook ('stɔːrɪˌbʊk) NOUN [1] a book containing stories, esp for children. ◆ ADJECTIVE [2] unreal or fantastic: *a storybook world.*

story line NOUN the plot of a book, film, play, etc.

storyteller ('stɔːrɪˌtɛlə) NOUN [1] a person who tells stories. [2] *Informal* a liar.
▸**'storyˌtelling** NOUN, ADJECTIVE

stoss (stɒs; *German* ʃtoːs) ADJECTIVE (of the side of a hill, crag, etc.) facing the onward flow of a glacier or the direction in which a former glacier flowed.
▷**HISTORY** German, from *stossen* to thrust

stot[1] (stɒt) NOUN *Dialect* [1] a bullock. [2] a castrated male ox.
▷**HISTORY** Old English

stot[2] (stɒt, stot) VERB **stots, stotting, stotted.** *Scot and northern English dialect* [1] to bounce or cause to bounce. [2] (*intr*) Also: **stotter.** to stagger.
▷**HISTORY** of obscure origin

stotin (stɒ'tiːn) NOUN, *plural* **stotin.** a monetary unit of Slovenia, worth one hundredth of a tolar.

stotinka (stɒ'tɪŋkə) NOUN, *plural* **-ki** (-kɪ). a monetary unit of Bulgaria, worth one hundredth of a lev.
▷**HISTORY** from Bulgarian; related to *suto* hundred

stotious ('staʊʃəs) ADJECTIVE *Now chiefly Irish dialect* drunk; inebriated.
▷**HISTORY** of obscure origin; perhaps from STOT[2]

stotter ('stɒtə; *Scot* 'stotər) *Scot dialect, chiefly Glasgow* ◆ VERB (*intr*) [1] to stagger. ◆ NOUN [2] anything outstanding, esp a good-looking person.
▷**HISTORY** from STOT[2]

stottie ('stɒtɪ) NOUN *Northeast English dialect* a wedge of bread cut from a flat round loaf (**stottie cake**) that has been split and filled with meat, cheese, etc.
▷**HISTORY** origin unknown

stound (staʊnd) NOUN *Brit dialect* [1] a short while; instant. [2] a pang or pain.
▷**HISTORY** Old English *stund;* related to Old High German *stunta* period of time, hour

stoup *or* **stoop** (stuːp) NOUN [1] a small basin for holy water. [2] *Scot and northern English dialect* Also: **stowp.** a bucket or drinking vessel.
▷**HISTORY** C14 (in the sense: bucket): of Scandinavian origin; compare Old Norse *staup* beaker, Old English *stēap* flagon; see STEEP[1]

stour (staʊə) *or Scot* **stoor** (stuːr) NOUN *Scot and northern English dialect* [1] turmoil or conflict. [2] dust; a cloud of dust.
▷**HISTORY** C14: from Old French *estour* armed combat, of Germanic origin; related to Old High German *sturm* STORM

Stour (staʊə) NOUN [1] Also called: **Great Stour.** a river in S England, in Kent, rising in the Weald and flowing N to the North Sea: separates the Isle of Thanet from the mainland. [2] any of several smaller rivers in England.

Stourbridge ('staʊəˌbrɪdʒ) NOUN an industrial town in W central England, in Dudley unitary authority, West Midlands. Pop.: 55 624 (1991).

Stourhead ('staʊəˌhɛd) NOUN a Palladian mansion near Mere in Wiltshire: built (1722) for Henry Hoare; famous for its landscaped gardens laid out (1741) by Flitcroft.

stoush (staʊʃ) *Austral and NZ slang* ◆ VERB [1] (*tr*) to hit or punch. ◆ NOUN [2] fighting, violence, or a fight.
▷**HISTORY** C19: of uncertain origin

stout (staʊt) ADJECTIVE [1] solidly built or corpulent. [2] (*prenominal*) resolute or valiant: *stout fellow.* [3] strong, substantial, and robust. [4] **a stout heart.** courage; resolution. ◆ NOUN [5] strong porter highly flavoured with malt.
▷**HISTORY** C14: from Old French *estout* bold, of Germanic origin; related to Middle High German *stolz* proud, Middle Dutch *stolt* brave
▸**'stoutish** ADJECTIVE ▸**'stoutly** ADVERB ▸**'stoutness** NOUN

stouthearted (ˌstaʊt'hɑːtɪd) ADJECTIVE valiant; brave.
▸**ˌstout'heartedly** ADVERB ▸**ˌstout'heartedness** NOUN

stove[1] (stəʊv) NOUN [1] another word for **cooker** (sense 1). [2] any heating apparatus, such as a kiln. ◆ VERB (*tr*) [3] to process (ceramics, metalwork, etc.) by heating in a stove. [4] *Scot* to stew (meat, vegetables, etc.).
▷**HISTORY** Old English *stofa* bathroom; related to Old High German *stuba* steam room, Greek *tuphos* smoke

stove[2] (stəʊv) VERB a past tense and past participle of **stave.**

stove enamel NOUN a type of enamel made heatproof by treatment in a stove.

stovepipe ('stəʊvˌpaɪp) NOUN [1] a pipe that serves as a flue to a stove. [2] Also called: **stovepipe hat.** a man's tall silk hat.

stovepipes ('stəʊvˌpaɪps) PLURAL NOUN *Informal* tight trousers with narrow legs.

stover ('stəʊvə) NOUN [1] *Chiefly Brit* fodder. [2] *US* cornstalks used as fodder.
▷**HISTORY** C14: shortened from ESTOVERS

stovetop ('stəʊvˌtɒp) NOUN the US word for **hob**[1] (sense 1).

stovies ('stovɪz, 'stəʊ-) PLURAL NOUN *Scot* potatoes stewed with onions.
▷**HISTORY** from STOVE[1]

stow (stəʊ) VERB (*tr*) [1] (often foll by *away*) to pack or store. [2] to fill by packing. [3] *Nautical* to pack or put away (cargo, sails and other gear, etc.). [4] to have enough room for. [5] (*usually imperative*) *Brit slang* to cease from: *stow your noise!; stow it!*
▷**HISTORY** Old English *stōwian* to keep, hold back, from *stōw* a place; related to Old High German *stouwen* to accuse, Gothic *stōjan* to judge, Old Slavonic *staviti* to place

stowage ('stəʊɪdʒ) NOUN [1] space, room, or a charge for stowing goods. [2] the act or an instance of stowing or the state of being stowed. [3] something that is stowed.

stowaway ('stəʊəˌweɪ) NOUN [1] a person who hides aboard a vehicle, ship, or aircraft in order to gain free passage. ◆ VERB **stow away.** [2] (*intr, adverb*) to travel in such a way.

Stowe (stəʊ) NOUN a mansion near Buckingham in N Buckinghamshire: built and decorated in the 17th and 18th centuries by Vanbrugh, Robert Adam, Grinling Gibbons, and William Kent; formerly the seat of the Dukes of Buckingham; fine landscaped gardens: now occupied by a public school.

stowp (staʊp) NOUN *Scot* a variant of **stoup** (sense 2).

STP ABBREVIATION FOR: [1] *Trademark* scientifically treated petroleum: an oil substitute promising renewed power for an internal-combustion engine. [2] Also: **NTP.** standard temperature and pressure: standard conditions of 0°C temperature and 101.325 kPa (760 mmHg) pressure. [3] Professor of Sacred Theology. [from Latin: *Sanctae Theologiae Professor*] ◆ NOUN [4] a synthetic hallucinogenic drug related to mescaline.
▷**HISTORY** Sense 4 from humorous reference to the extra power resulting from scientifically treated petroleum

str ABBREVIATION FOR steamer.

Strabane (strə'bæn) NOUN a district of W Northern Ireland, in Co. Tyrone. Pop.: 38 248 (2001). Area: 862 sq. km (333 sq. miles).

strabismus (strə'bɪzməs) NOUN abnormal alignment of one or both eyes, characterized by a turning inwards or outwards from the nose thus preventing parallel vision: caused by paralysis of an eye muscle, etc. Also called: **squint.**
▷**HISTORY** C17: via New Latin from Greek *strabismos,* from *strabizein* to squint, from *strabos* cross-eyed
▸**stra'bismal** *or* **stra'bismic** *or* **stra'bismical** ADJECTIVE

strabotomy (strə'bɒtəmɪ) NOUN, *plural* **-mies.** a former method of treating strabismus by surgical division of one or more muscles of the eye.
▷**HISTORY** C19: from French *strabotomie,* from Greek *strabos* squinting + -TOMY

straddle ('strædᵊl) VERB [1] (*tr*) to have one leg, part, or support on each side of. [2] (*tr*) *US and Canadian informal* to be in favour of both sides of (something). [3] (*intr*) to stand, walk, or sit with the legs apart. [4] (*tr*) to spread (the legs) apart. [5] *Military* to fire a number of shots slightly beyond and slightly short of (a target) to determine the correct range. [6] (*intr*) (in poker, of the second player after the dealer) to double the ante before looking at one's cards. ◆ NOUN [7] the act or position of straddling. [8] a noncommittal attitude or stand. [9] *Business* a contract or option permitting its purchaser to either sell or buy securities or commodities within a specified period of time at specified prices. It is a combination of a put and a call option. Compare **spread** (sense 24c). [10] *Athletics* a high-jumping technique in which the body is parallel with the bar and the legs straddle it at the highest point of the jump. [11] (in poker) the

stake put up after the ante in poker by the second player after the dealer. 12 *Irish* a wooden frame placed on a horse's back to which panniers are attached.
▷HISTORY C16: frequentative formed from obsolete *strad-* (Old English *strode*), past stem of STRIDE
▸ **'straddler** NOUN

Stradivarius (ˌstrædɪˈvɛərɪəs) NOUN any of a number of violins manufactured by Antonio Stradivari (?1644–1737) Italian violin, viola, and cello maker, or his family. Often (informal) shortened to: **Strad.**

strafe (streɪf, strɑːf) VERB (*tr*) 1 to machine-gun (troops, etc.) from the air. 2 *Slang* to punish harshly. ◆ NOUN 3 an act or instance of strafing.
▷HISTORY C20: from German *strafen* to punish
▸ **'strafer** NOUN

straggle (ˈstræɡᵊl) VERB (*intr*) 1 to go, come, or spread in a rambling or irregular way; stray. 2 to linger behind or wander from a main line or part.
▷HISTORY C14: of uncertain origin; perhaps related to STRAKE and STRETCH
▸ **'straggler** NOUN ▸ **'straggling** ADJECTIVE ▸ **'stragglingly** ADVERB ▸ **'straggly** ADJECTIVE

straight (streɪt) ADJECTIVE 1 not curved or crooked; continuing in the same direction without deviating. 2 straightforward, outright, or candid: *a straight rejection.* 3 even, level, or upright in shape or position. 4 in keeping with the facts; accurate. 5 honest, respectable, or reliable. 6 accurate or logical: *straight reasoning.* 7 continuous; uninterrupted. 8 (esp of an alcoholic drink) undiluted; neat. 9 not crisp, kinked, or curly: *straight hair.* 10 correctly arranged; orderly. 11 (of a play, acting style, etc.) straightforward or serious. 12 *Journalism* (of a story, article, etc.) giving the facts without unnecessary embellishment. 13 *US* sold at a fixed unit price irrespective of the quantity sold. 14 *Boxing* (of a blow) delivered with an unbent arm: *a straight left.* 15 (of the cylinders of an internal-combustion engine) in line, rather than in a V-formation or in some other arrangement: *a straight eight.* 16 a slang word for **heterosexual.** 17 *Informal* no longer owing or being owed something: *if you buy the next round we'll be straight.* 18 *Slang* conventional in views, customs, appearance, etc. 19 *Slang* not using narcotics; not addicted. ◆ ADVERB 20 in a straight line or direct course. 21 immediately; at once: *he came straight back.* 22 in an even, level, or upright position. 23 without cheating, lying, or unreliability: *tell it to me straight.* 24 continuously; uninterruptedly. 25 *US* without discount regardless of the quantity sold. 26 (often foll by *out*) frankly; candidly: *he told me straight out.* 27 **go straight.** *Informal* to reform after having been dishonest or a criminal. ◆ NOUN 28 the state of being straight. 29 a straight line, form, part, or position. 30 *Brit* a straight part of a racetrack. US name: **straightaway.** 31 *Poker* **a** five cards that are in sequence irrespective of suit. **b** a hand containing such a sequence. **c** (*as modifier*): *a straight flush.* 32 *Slang* a conventional person. 33 *Slang* a heterosexual person. 34 *Slang* a cigarette containing only tobacco, without marijuana, etc.
▷HISTORY C14: from the past participle of Old English *streccan* to STRETCH
▸ **'straightly** ADVERB ▸ **'straightness** NOUN

straight and narrow NOUN *Informal* the proper, honest, and moral path of behaviour.
▷HISTORY perhaps an alteration of *strait and narrow,* an allusion to Matthew 7:14: "strait is the gate, and narrow is the way, which leadeth unto life"

straight angle NOUN an angle of 180°.

straight-arm ADJECTIVE 1 *Rugby* (of a tackle) performed with the arm fully extended. ◆ VERB 2 (*tr*) to ward off (an opponent) with the arm outstretched.

straight arm lift NOUN a wrestling attack, in which a wrestler twists his opponent's arm against the joint and lifts him by it, often using his shoulder as a fulcrum.

straight arrow NOUN *Informal, chiefly US* **a** a clean-living and honest person. **b** (*as modifier*): *a straight-arrow cop.*

straightaway (ˌstreɪtəˈweɪ) ADVERB *also* **straight away.** 1 at once. ◆ NOUN 2 the US word for **straight** (sense 30).

straight bat NOUN 1 *Cricket* a bat held vertically. 2 *Brit informal* honest or honourable behaviour.

straight chain NOUN **a** an open chain of atoms in a molecule with no attached side chains. **b** (*as modifier*): *a straight-chain hydrocarbon.* ◆ Compare **branched chain.**

straight chair NOUN a straight-backed side chair.

straightedge (ˈstreɪtˌɛdʒ) NOUN a stiff strip of wood or metal that has one edge straight and true and is used for ruling and testing straight lines.
▸ **'straightˌedged** ADJECTIVE

straight-edge ADJECTIVE *Informal* not indulging in any kind of drug-taking or sexual activities.

straighten (ˈstreɪtᵊn) VERB (sometimes foll by *up* or *out*) 1 to make or become straight. 2 (*tr*) to make neat or tidy: *straighten your desk.*
▸ **'straightener** NOUN

straighten out VERB (*adverb*) 1 to make or become less complicated or confused: *the situation will straighten out.* 2 *US and Canadian* to reform or become reformed.

straighten up VERB (*adverb*) 1 to become or cause to become erect. 2 *Chiefly US* to reform or become reformed.

straight face NOUN a serious facial expression, esp one that conceals the impulse to laugh.
▸ **'straight-'faced** ADJECTIVE

straight fight NOUN a contest between two candidates only.

straight flush NOUN (in poker) five consecutive cards of the same suit.

straightforward (ˌstreɪtˈfɔːwəd) ADJECTIVE 1 (of a person) honest, frank, or simple. 2 *Chiefly Brit* (of a task, etc.) simple; easy. ◆ ADVERB, ADJECTIVE 3 in a straight course.
▸ **ˌstraight'forwardly** ADVERB ▸ **ˌstraight'forwardness** NOUN

straightjacket (ˈstreɪtˌdʒækɪt) NOUN a less common spelling of **straitjacket.**

straight joint NOUN a vertical joint in brickwork that is directly above a vertical joint in the course below.

straight-laced ADJECTIVE a variant spelling of **strait-laced.**

straight-line NOUN (*modifier*) 1 (of a machine) having components that are arranged in a row or that move in a straight line when in operation. 2 of or relating to a method of depreciation whereby equal charges are made against gross profit for each year of an asset's expected life.

straight man NOUN a subsidiary actor who acts as stooge to a comedian.

straight off ADVERB *Informal* without deliberation or hesitation: *tell me the answer straight off.*

straight-out ADJECTIVE *Informal* 1 complete; thoroughgoing. 2 frank or honest.

straight razor NOUN another name for **cut-throat** (sense 2).

straight ticket NOUN *US* a ballot for all the candidates of one and only one political party. Compare **split ticket.**

straight up SENTENCE SUBSTITUTE *Brit slang* honestly; truly; exactly.

straightway (ˈstreɪtˌweɪ) ADVERB *Archaic* at once.

strain[1] (streɪn) VERB 1 to draw or be drawn taut; stretch tight. 2 to exert, tax, or use (resources) to the utmost extent. 3 to injure or damage or be injured or damaged by overexertion: *he strained himself.* 4 to deform or be deformed as a result of a stress. 5 (*intr*) to make intense or violent efforts; strive. 6 to subject or be subjected to mental tension or stress. 7 to pour or pass (a substance) or (of a substance) to be poured or passed through a sieve, filter, or strainer. 8 (*tr*) to draw off or remove (one part of a substance or mixture from another) by or as if by filtering. 9 (*tr*) to clasp tightly; hug. 10 (*tr*) *Obsolete* to force or constrain. 11 (*intr;* foll by *at*) **a** to push, pull, or work with violent exertion (upon). **b** to strive (for). **c** to balk or scruple (from). ◆ NOUN 12 the act or an instance of straining. 13 the damage resulting from excessive exertion. 14 an intense physical or mental effort. 15 *Music* (*often plural*) a theme, melody, or tune. 16 a great demand on the emotions, resources, etc. 17 a feeling of tension and tiredness resulting from overwork, worry, etc.; stress. 18 a particular style or recurring theme in speech or writing. 19 *Physics* the change in dimension of a body under load expressed as the ratio of the total deflection or change in dimension to the original unloaded dimension. It may be a ratio of lengths, areas, or volumes.
▷HISTORY C13: from Old French *estreindre* to press together, from Latin *stringere* to bind tightly

strain[2] (streɪn) NOUN 1 the main body of descendants from one ancestor. 2 a group of organisms within a species or variety, distinguished by one or more minor characteristics. 3 a variety of bacterium or fungus, esp one used for a culture. 4 a streak; trace. 5 *Archaic* a kind, type, or sort.
▷HISTORY Old English *strēon;* related to Old High German *gistriuni* gain, Latin *struere* to CONSTRUCT

strained (streɪnd) ADJECTIVE 1 (of an action, performance, etc.) not natural or spontaneous. 2 (of an atmosphere, relationship, etc.) not relaxed; tense.

strainer (ˈstreɪnə) NOUN 1 a sieve used for straining sauces, vegetables, tea, etc. 2 a gauze or simple filter used to strain liquids. 3 *Austral and NZ* a self-locking device or a tool for tightening fencing wire. 4 *Austral and NZ* the main post in a wire fence, often diagonally braced.

strain gauge NOUN a device for measuring strain in a machine or other structure, usually consisting of a metal filament that is attached to it and receives the same strain. The strain can be measured by the change in the electrical properties of the filament.

strain hardening NOUN a process in which a metal is permanently deformed in order to increase its resistance to further deformation.

straining piece *or* **beam** NOUN a horizontal tie beam that connects the top of two queen posts of a roof truss.

strait (streɪt) NOUN 1 (*often plural*) **a** a narrow channel of the sea linking two larger areas of sea. **b** (*capital as part of a name*): *the Strait of Gibraltar.* 2 (*often plural*) a position of acute difficulty (often in the phrase **in dire** *or* **desperate straits**). 3 *Archaic* a narrow place or passage. ◆ ADJECTIVE *Archaic* 4 (of spaces, etc.) affording little room. 5 (of circumstances, etc.) limiting or difficult. 6 severe, strict, or scrupulous.
▷HISTORY C13: from Old French *estreit* narrow, from Latin *strictus* constricted, from *stringere* to bind tightly
▸ **'straitly** ADVERB ▸ **'straitness** NOUN

straiten (ˈstreɪtᵊn) VERB 1 (*tr; usually passive*) to embarrass or distress, esp financially. 2 (*tr*) to limit, confine, or restrict. 3 *Archaic* to make or become narrow.

straitjacket (ˈstreɪtˌdʒækɪt) NOUN 1 Also called: **straightjacket.** a jacket made of strong canvas material with long sleeves for binding the arms of violent prisoners or mental patients. 2 a severe restriction or limitation. ◆ VERB 3 (*tr*) to confine in or as if in a straitjacket.

strait-laced *or* **straight-laced** ADJECTIVE prudish or puritanical.

Straits Settlements (streɪts) NOUN (formerly) a British crown colony of SE Asia that included Singapore, Penang, Malacca, Labuan, and some smaller islands.

strake (streɪk) NOUN 1 **a** a curved metal plate forming part of the metal rim on a wooden wheel. **b** any metal plate let into a rubber tyre. 2 Also called: **streak.** *Nautical* one of a continuous range of planks or plates forming the side of a vessel. 3 a profiled piece of wood carried on an arm that rotates round a fixed post: used to sweep the internal shape of a mould, as for a bell or a ship's propeller blade, in sand or loam.
▷HISTORY C14: related to Old English *streccan* to STRETCH

Stralsund (*German* ˈʃtraːlzʊnt) NOUN a port in NE Germany, in Mecklenburg-West Pomerania on a strait of the Baltic: one of the leading towns of the Hanseatic League. Pop.: 71 620 (1991).

stramash (strəˈmæʃ) *Scot* ◆ NOUN 1 an uproar; tumult; brawl. ◆ VERB (*tr*) 2 to destroy; smash.
▷HISTORY C18: perhaps expanded from SMASH

stramonium (strəˈməʊnɪəm) NOUN 1 a preparation of the dried leaves and flowers of the thorn apple, containing hyoscyamine and formerly

used as a drug to treat asthma. [2] another name for **thorn apple** (sense 1).
▷HISTORY C17: from New Latin, of uncertain origin

strand¹ (strænd) VERB [1] to leave or drive (ships, fish, etc.) aground or ashore or (of ships, fish, etc.) to be left or driven ashore. [2] *(tr; usually passive)* to leave helpless, as without transport or money, etc. ◆ NOUN *Chiefly poetic* [3] a shore or beach. [4] a foreign country.
▷HISTORY Old English; related to Old Norse *strönd* side, Middle High German *strant* beach, Latin *sternere* to spread

strand² (strænd) NOUN [1] a set of or one of the individual fibres or threads of string, wire, etc., that form a rope, cable, etc. [2] a single length of string, hair, wool, wire, etc. [3] a string of pearls or beads. [4] a constituent element in a complex whole: *one strand of her argument.* ◆ VERB [5] *(tr)* to form (a rope, cable, etc.) by winding strands together.
▷HISTORY C15: of uncertain origin

Strand (strænd) NOUN **the.** a street in W central London, parallel to the Thames: famous for its hotels and theatres.

Strandloper (ˈstrantˌlʊəpə) NOUN a member of an extinct tribe of Khoikhoi or Bushmen who lived on sea food gathered on the beaches of southern Africa.
▷HISTORY C17: from Afrikaans *strand* beach + *loper* walker

strandwolf (ˈstrændˌwʊlf; *Afrikaans* ˈstrantˌvɔlf) NOUN, *plural* **-wolves.** a species of hyena (*Hyaena brunnea*) that scavenges on shores of southern Africa. Also called: **brown hyena.**
▷HISTORY C19: Afrikaans, from Dutch *strand* beach + Afrikaans *wolf* hyena

strange (streɪndʒ) ADJECTIVE [1] odd, unusual, or extraordinary in appearance, effect, manner, etc.; peculiar. [2] not known, seen, or experienced before; unfamiliar: *a strange land.* [3] not easily explained: *a strange phenomenon.* [4] (usually foll by *to*) inexperienced (in) or unaccustomed (to): *strange to a task.* [5] not of one's own kind, locality, etc.; alien; foreign. [6] shy; distant; reserved. [7] **strange to say.** it is unusual or surprising that. [8] *Physics* **a** denoting a particular flavour of quark. **b** denoting or relating to a hypothetical form of matter composed of such quarks: *strange matter; a strange star.* ◆ ADVERB [9] *Not standard* in a strange manner.
▷HISTORY C13: from Old French *estrange,* from Latin *extrāneus* foreign; see EXTRANEOUS
▸ˈ**strangely** ADVERB

strange attractor NOUN *Maths* a type of chaotic dynamical system.

strangeness (ˈstreɪndʒnɪs) NOUN [1] the state or quality of being strange. [2] *Physics* a property of certain elementary particles, characterized by a quantum number (**strangeness number**) conserved in strong and electromagnetic but not in weak interactions. It is associated with the presence of strange quarks.

stranger (ˈstreɪndʒə) NOUN [1] any person whom one does not know. [2] a person who is new to a particular locality, from another region, town, etc. [3] a guest or visitor. [4] (foll by *to*) a person who is unfamiliar (with) or new (to) something: *he is no stranger to computers.* [5] *Law* a person who is neither party nor privy to a transaction.

stranger's gallery NOUN another name for **public gallery.**

strangle (ˈstræŋɡᵊl) VERB [1] *(tr)* to kill by compressing the windpipe; throttle. [2] *(tr)* to prevent or inhibit the growth or development of: *to strangle originality.* [3] *(tr)* to suppress (an utterance) by or as if by swallowing suddenly: *to strangle a cry.* ◆ See also **strangles.**
▷HISTORY C13: via Old French, ultimately from Greek *strangalē* a halter

stranglehold (ˈstræŋɡᵊlˌhəʊld) NOUN [1] a wrestling hold in which a wrestler's arms are pressed against his opponent's windpipe. See also **Japanese stranglehold.** [2] complete power or control over a person or situation.

strangler (ˈstræŋɡlə) NOUN [1] a person or thing that strangles. [2] a plant, esp a fig in tropical rain forests, that starts as an epiphyte but sends roots to the ground and eventually forms a tree with many aerial roots, usually killing the host.

strangles (ˈstræŋɡᵊlz) NOUN *(functioning as singular)* an acute bacterial disease of horses caused by infection with *Streptococcus equi,* characterized by inflammation of the mucous membranes of the respiratory tract, resulting in abscesses and a nasal discharge. Also called: **equine distemper.**
▷HISTORY C18: from STRANGLE

strangulate (ˈstræŋɡjʊˌleɪt) VERB *(tr)* [1] to constrict (a hollow organ, vessel, etc.) so as to stop the natural flow of air, blood, etc., through it. [2] another word for **strangle.**
▷HISTORY C18: from Latin *strangulāt-,* past participle stem of *strangulāre* to STRANGLE
▸ˌ**stranguˈlation** NOUN

strangury (ˈstræŋɡjʊrɪ) NOUN *Pathol* painful excretion of urine, drop by drop, caused by muscular spasms of the urinary tract.
▷HISTORY C14: from Latin *strangūria,* from Greek, from *stranx* a drop squeezed out + *ouron* urine

Stranraer (strænˈrɑː) NOUN a market town in SW Scotland, in W Dumfries and Galloway: fishing port with a ferry service to Northern Ireland. Pop.: 11 348 (1991).

strap (stræp) NOUN [1] a long strip of leather or similar material, for binding trunks, baggage, or other objects. [2] a strip of leather or similar material used for carrying, lifting, or holding. [3] a loop of leather, rubber, etc., suspended from the roof in a bus or train for standing passengers to hold on to. [4] a razor strop. [5] *Business* a triple option on a security or commodity consisting of one put option and two call options at the same price and for the same period. Compare **strip²** (sense 5). [6] *Irish derogatory slang* a shameless or promiscuous woman. [7] **the strap.** a beating with a strap as a punishment. [8] short for **shoulder strap.** ◆ VERB **straps, strapping, strapped.** *(tr)* [9] to tie or bind with a strap. [10] to beat with a strap. [11] to sharpen with a strap or strop.
▷HISTORY C16: variant of STROP

straphanger (ˈstræpˌhæŋə) NOUN *Informal* a passenger in a bus, train, etc., who has to travel standing, esp by holding on to a strap.
▸ˈ**strapˌhanging** NOUN

strap hinge NOUN a hinge with a long leaf or flap attached to the face of a door, gate, etc.

strapless (ˈstræplɪs) ADJECTIVE (of a woman's formal dress, brassiere, etc.) without straps over the shoulders.

strapline (ˈstræpˌlaɪn) NOUN a subheading in a newspaper or magazine article or in any advertisement.

strap-oil NOUN *Slang* a beating.

strappado (strəˈpeɪdəʊ, -ˈpɑː-) NOUN, *plural* **-does.** a system of torture in which a victim was hoisted by a rope tied to his wrists and then allowed to drop until his fall was suddenly checked by the rope.
▷HISTORY C16: from French *strapade,* from Italian *strappare* to tug sharply, probably of Germanic origin; related to German (dialect) *strapfen* to make taut

strapped (stræpt) ADJECTIVE *(postpositive;* often foll by *for) Slang* badly in need (of money, manpower, etc.); short of.

strapper (ˈstræpə) NOUN *Informal* a strapping person.

strapping (ˈstræpɪŋ) ADJECTIVE *(prenominal)* tall and sturdy.
▷HISTORY C17: from STRAP (in the archaic sense: to work vigorously)

strap work NOUN *Architect* decorative work resembling interlacing straps.

Strasbourg (*French* strasbur; *English* ˈstræzbɜːɡ) NOUN a city in NE France, on the Rhine: the chief French inland port; under German rule (1870–1918); university (1567); seat of the Council of Europe and of the European Parliament. Pop.: 263 940 (1999). German name: **Strassburg** (ˈʃtraːsbʊrk).

strass (stræs) NOUN *Jewellery* another word for **paste¹** (sense 6).
▷HISTORY C19: German, named after J. *Strasser,* 18th-century German jeweller who invented it

strata (ˈstrɑːtə) NOUN a plural of **stratum.**

> **Language note** *Strata* is sometimes wrongly used as a singular noun: *this stratum* (not *strata*) *of society is often disregarded.*

stratagem (ˈstrætɪdʒəm) NOUN a plan or trick, esp one to deceive an enemy.
▷HISTORY C15: ultimately from Greek *stratēgos* a general, from *stratos* an army + *agein* to lead

strata title NOUN *Austral* a system of registered ownership of space in multistorey buildings, to be equivalent to the ownership of the land of a single-storey building. NZ equivalent: **stratum title.**

strategic (strəˈtiːdʒɪk) *or* **strategical** ADJECTIVE [1] of, relating to, or characteristic of strategy. [2] important to a strategy or to strategy in general. [3] (of weapons, attacks, etc.) directed against an enemy's homeland rather than used on a battlefield: *a strategic missile; strategic bombing.*
▸**straˈtegically** ADVERB

strategics (strəˈtiːdʒɪks) NOUN *(functioning as singular)* strategy, esp in a military sense.

strategist (ˈstrætɪdʒɪst) NOUN a specialist or expert in strategy.

strategy (ˈstrætɪdʒɪ) NOUN, *plural* **-gies.** [1] the art or science of the planning and conduct of a war; generalship. [2] a particular long-term plan for success, esp in business or politics. Compare **tactics** (sense 2). [3] a plan or stratagem.
▷HISTORY C17: from French *stratégie,* from Greek *stratēgia* function of a general; see STRATAGEM

Stratford-on-Avon *or* **Stratford-upon-Avon** (ˈstrætfəd) NOUN a market town in central England, in SW Warwickshire on the River Avon: the birthplace and burial place of William Shakespeare and home of the Royal Shakespeare Company; tourist centre. Pop.: 22 231 (1991).

strath (stræθ) NOUN *Scot* a broad flat river valley.
▷HISTORY C16: from Scot and Irish Gaelic *srath,* Welsh *ystrad*

Strathclyde Region (ˌstræθˈklaɪd) NOUN a former local government region in W Scotland: formed in 1975 from Glasgow, Renfrewshire, Lanarkshire, Buteshire, Dunbartonshire, and parts of Argyllshire, Ayrshire, and Stirlingshire; replaced in 1996 by the council areas of Glasgow, Renfrewshire, East Renfrewshire, Inverclyde, North Lanarkshire, South Lanarkshire, Argyll and Bute, East Dunbartonshire, West Dunbartonshire, North Ayrshire, South Ayrshire, and East Ayrshire.

strathspey (ˌstræθˈspeɪ) NOUN [1] a Scottish dance with gliding steps, slower than a reel. [2] a piece of music in four-four time composed for this dance.

strati- COMBINING FORM indicating stratum or strata: *stratiform; stratigraphy.*

straticulate (strəˈtɪkjʊlɪt, -ˌleɪt) ADJECTIVE (of a rock formation) composed of very thin even strata.
▷HISTORY C19: from New Latin *strāticulum* (unattested), diminutive of Latin *strātum* something strewn; see STRATUS
▸**straˌticuˈlation** NOUN

stratification (ˌstrætɪfɪˈkeɪʃən) NOUN [1] the arrangement of sedimentary rocks in distinct layers (strata), each layer representing the sediment deposited over a specific period. [2] the act of stratifying or state of being stratified. [3] *Sociol* See **social stratification.**
▷HISTORY C17 (in the obsolete sense: the act of depositing in layers) and C18 (in the current senses): from New Latin *strātificātiōnem,* from *stratificāre* to STRATIFY
▸ˌ**stratifiˈcational** ADJECTIVE

stratificational grammar NOUN *Linguistics* a theory of grammar analysing language in terms of several structural strata or layers with different syntactic rules.

stratified sample NOUN *Statistics* a sample that is not drawn at random from the whole population, but separately from a number of disjoint strata of the population in order to ensure a more representative sample. See also **frame** (sense 13).

stratiform (ˈstrætɪˌfɔːm) ADJECTIVE [1] (of rocks) occurring as or arranged in strata. [2] *Meteorol* resembling a stratus cloud.

stratify (ˈstrætɪˌfaɪ) VERB **-fies, -fying, -fied.** [1] to form or be formed in layers or strata. [2] *(tr)* to preserve or render fertile (seeds) by storing between layers of sand or earth. [3] *Sociol* to divide (a society) into horizontal status groups or (of a society) to develop such groups.
▷HISTORY C17: from French *stratifier,* from New Latin *stratificāre,* from Latin STRATUM

stratigraphy (strəˈtɪgrəfɪ) NOUN [1] the study of the composition, relative positions, etc., of rock strata in order to determine their geological history. Abbreviation: **stratig.** [2] *Archaeol* a vertical section through the earth showing the relative positions of the human artefacts and therefore the chronology of successive levels of occupation.
▸**stratigrapher** (strəˈtɪgrəfə) *or* **stratigraphist** (strəˈtɪgrəfɪst) NOUN ▸**stratigraphic** (ˌstrætɪˈgræfɪk) *or* **ˌstratiˈgraphical** ADJECTIVE

strato- COMBINING FORM [1] denoting stratus: *stratocumulus.* [2] denoting the stratosphere: *stratopause.*

stratocracy (strəˈtɒkrəsɪ) NOUN, *plural* **-cies.** military rule.
▷HISTORY C17: from Greek *stratos* an army + -CRACY
▸**stratocrat** (ˈstrætəˌkræt) NOUN ▸**stratocratic** (ˌstrætəˈkrætɪk) ADJECTIVE

stratocumulus (ˌstrætəʊˈkjuːmjʊləs, ˌstreɪtəʊ-) NOUN, *plural* **-li** (-ˌlaɪ). *Meteorol* a uniform stretch of cloud containing dark grey globular masses.

stratopause (ˈstrætəˌpɔːz) NOUN *Meteorol* the transitional zone of maximum temperature between the stratosphere and the mesosphere.

stratosphere (ˈstrætəˌsfɪə) NOUN the atmospheric layer lying between the troposphere and the mesosphere, in which temperature generally increases with height.
▸**stratospheric** (ˌstrætəˈsfɛrɪk) *or* **ˌstratoˈspherical** ADJECTIVE

stratum (ˈstrɑːtəm) NOUN, *plural* **-ta** (-tə) *or* **-tums.** [1] (*usually plural*) any of the distinct layers into which sedimentary rocks are divided. [2] *Biology* a single layer of tissue or cells. [3] a layer of any material, esp one of several parallel layers. [4] a layer of ocean or atmosphere either naturally or arbitrarily demarcated. [5] a level of a social hierarchy that is distinguished according to such criteria as educational achievement or caste status.
▷HISTORY C16: via New Latin from Latin: something strewn, from *sternere* to scatter
▸ˈ**stratal** ADJECTIVE

stratum title NOUN the NZ name for **strata title.**

stratus (ˈstreɪtəs) NOUN, *plural* **-ti** (-taɪ). a grey layer cloud. Compare **cirrus** (sense 1), **cumulus.**
▷HISTORY C19: via New Latin from Latin: strewn, from *sternere* to extend

stravaig (strəˈveɪg) VERB (*intr*) *Scot and northern English dialect* to wander aimlessly.
▷HISTORY C19: perhaps a variant of obsolete *extravage,* from Medieval Latin *extrāvagārī,* from *vagārī* to wander

straw¹ (strɔː) NOUN [1] **a** stalks of threshed grain, esp of wheat, rye, oats, or barley, used in plaiting hats, baskets, etc., or as fodder. **b** (*as modifier*): *a straw hat.* [2] a single dry or ripened stalk, esp of a grass. [3] a long thin hollow paper or plastic tube or stem of a plant, used for sucking up liquids into the mouth. [4] (*usually used with a negative*) anything of little value or importance: *I wouldn't give a straw for our chances.* [5] a measure or remedy that one turns to in desperation (esp in the phrases **clutch** *or* **grasp at a straw** *or* **straws**). [6] **a** a pale yellow colour. **b** (*as adjective*): *straw hair.* [7] **the last straw.** a small incident, setback, etc. that, coming after others, proves intolerable. [8] **straw in the wind.** a hint or indication. ◆ ADJECTIVE [9] *Chiefly US* having little value or substance. ◆ See also **man of straw.**
▷HISTORY Old English *streaw;* related to Old Norse *strā,* Old Frisian *strē,* Old High German *strō;* see STREW
▸ˈ**strawˌlike** ADJECTIVE

straw² (strɔː) VERB *Archaic* another word for **strew.**

strawberry (ˈstrɔːbərɪ, -brɪ) NOUN, *plural* **-ries.** [1] **a** any of various low-growing rosaceous plants of the genus *Fragaria,* such as *F. vesca* (**wild strawberry**) and *F. ananassa* (**garden strawberry**), which have white flowers and red edible fruits and spread by runners. **b** (*as modifier*): *a strawberry patch.* [2] **a** the fruit of any of these plants, consisting of a sweet fleshy receptacle bearing small seedlike parts (the true fruits). **b** (*as modifier*): *strawberry ice cream.* [3] **barren strawberry.** a related Eurasian plant, *Potentilla sterilis,* that does not produce edible fruit. [4] **a** a purplish-red colour. **b** (*as adjective*): *strawberry shoes.* [5] another name for **strawberry mark.**
▷HISTORY Old English *streawberige;* perhaps from the strawlike appearance of the runners

strawberry blonde ADJECTIVE [1] (of hair) reddish blonde. ◆ NOUN [2] a woman with such hair.

strawberry bush NOUN [1] an E North American shrub or small tree, *Euonymus americanus,* having pendulous capsules that split when ripe to reveal scarlet seeds: family *Celastraceae.* [2] any of various similar or related plants.

strawberry mark NOUN a soft vascular red birthmark. Technical name: **haemangioma simplex.** Also called: **strawberry.**

strawberry tomato NOUN [1] a tropical solanaceous annual plant, *Physalis peruviana,* having bell-shaped whitish-yellow flowers and small edible round yellow berries. [2] a similar and related plant, *Physalis pubescens.* [3] the fruit of either of these plants, eaten fresh or made into preserves and pickles. ◆ Also called: **Cape gooseberry.**

strawberry tree NOUN a S European evergreen tree, *Arbutus unedo,* having white or pink flowers and red strawberry-like berries. See also **arbutus.**

strawboard (ˈstrɔːˌbɔːd) NOUN a board made of compressed straw and adhesive, used esp in book covers.

strawflower (ˈstrɔːˌflaʊə) NOUN an Australian plant, *Helichrysum bracteatum,* in which the coloured bracts retain their colour when the plant is dried: family *Asteraceae* (composites). See also **immortelle.**

straw man NOUN *Chiefly US* [1] a figure of a man made from straw. [2] another term for **man of straw.**

straw poll *or chiefly US, Canadian, and NZ* **vote** NOUN an unofficial poll or vote taken to determine the opinion of a group or the public on some issue.

strawweight (ˈstrɔːˌweɪt) NOUN **a** a professional boxer weighing not more than 47.6 kg (105 pounds). **b** (*as modifier*): *the strawweight title.* ◆ Also called: **mini-flyweight.**

straw wine NOUN any of several wines made from grapes dried on straw mats to increase their sugar strength.

strawworm (ˈstrɔːˌwɜːm) NOUN another name for a **caddis worm.**

strawy (ˈstrɔːɪ) ADJECTIVE **strawier, strawiest.** containing straw, or like straw in colour or texture.

stray (streɪ) VERB (*intr*) [1] to wander away, as from the correct path or from a given area. [2] to wander haphazardly. [3] to digress from the point, lose concentration, etc. [4] to deviate from certain moral standards. ◆ NOUN [5] **a** a domestic animal, fowl, etc., that has wandered away from its place of keeping and is lost. **b** (*as modifier*): *stray dogs.* [6] a lost or homeless person, esp a child: *waifs and strays.* [7] an isolated or random occurrence, specimen, etc., that is out of place or outside the usual pattern. ◆ ADJECTIVE [8] scattered, random, or haphazard: *a stray bullet grazed his thigh.*
▷HISTORY C14: from Old French *estraier,* from Vulgar Latin *estragāre* (unattested), from Latin *extrā-* outside + *vagārī* to roam; see ASTRAY, EXTRAVAGANT, STRAVAIG
▸ˈ**strayer** NOUN

strays (streɪz) PLURAL NOUN [1] Also called: **stray capacitance.** *Electronics* undesired capacitance in equipment, occurring between the wiring, between the wiring and the chassis, or between components and the chassis. [2] *Telecomm* another word for **static** (sense 9).

strayve (streɪv) VERB (*intr*) **strayves, strayving, strayved** *Midland English dialect* to wander aimlessly.

streak¹ (striːk) NOUN [1] a long thin mark, stripe, or trace of some contrasting colour. [2] **a** (of lightning) a sudden flash. **b** (*as modifier*): *streak lightning.* [3] an element or trace, as of some quality or characteristic. [4] a strip, vein, or layer: *fatty streaks.* [5] a short stretch or run, esp of good or bad luck. [6] *Mineralogy* the powdery mark made by a mineral when rubbed on a hard or rough surface: its colour is an important distinguishing characteristic. [7] *Bacteriol* the inoculation of a solid culture medium by drawing a wire contaminated with the microorganisms across it. [8] *Informal* an act or the practice of running naked through a public place. ◆ VERB [9] (*tr*) to mark or daub with a streak or streaks. [10] (*intr*) to form streaks or become streaked. [11] (*intr*) to move rapidly in a straight line. [12] (*intr*) *Informal* to run naked through a crowd of people in a public place in order to shock or amuse them.
▷HISTORY Old English *strica,* related to Old Frisian *strike,* Old High German *strih,* Norwegian, Swedish *strika*
▸**streaked** ADJECTIVE ▸ˈ**streaker** NOUN ▸ˈ**streakˌlike** ADJECTIVE

streak² (striːk) NOUN a variant spelling of **strake** (sense 2).

streaking (ˈstriːkɪŋ) NOUN [1] an act or instance of running naked through a public place. [2] *Television* light or dark streaks to the right of a bright object in a television picture, caused by distortion in the transmission chain.

streaky (ˈstriːkɪ) ADJECTIVE **streakier, streakiest.** [1] marked with streaks. [2] occurring in streaks. [3] (of bacon) having alternate layers of meat and fat. [4] of varying or uneven quality.
▸ˈ**streakily** ADVERB ▸ˈ**streakiness** NOUN

stream (striːm) NOUN [1] a small river; brook. [2] any steady flow of water or other fluid. [3] something that resembles a stream in moving continuously in a line or particular direction. [4] a rapid or unbroken flow of speech, etc.: *a stream of abuse.* [5] *Brit* any of several parallel classes of schoolchildren, or divisions of children within a class, grouped together because of similar ability. [6] **go** (*or* **drift**) **with the stream.** to conform to the accepted standards. [7] **off stream.** (of an industrial plant, manufacturing process, etc.) shut down or not in production. [8] **on stream. a** (of an industrial plant, manufacturing process, etc.) in or about to go into operation or production. **b** available or in existence. ◆ VERB [9] to emit or be emitted in a continuous flow: *his nose streamed blood.* [10] (*intr*) to move in unbroken succession, as a crowd of people, vehicles, etc. [11] (*intr*) to float freely or with a waving motion: *bunting streamed in the wind.* [12] (*tr*) to unfurl (a flag, etc.). [13] (*intr*) to move causing a trail of light, condensed gas, etc., as a jet aircraft. [14] (when *intr,* often foll by *for*) *Mining* to wash (earth, gravel, etc.) in running water in prospecting (for gold, etc.), to expose the particles of ore or metal. [15] *Brit education* to group or divide (children) in streams.
▷HISTORY Old English; related to Old Frisian *strām,* Old Norse *straumr,* Old High German *stroum,* Greek *rheuma*
▸ˈ**streamlet** NOUN ▸ˈ**streamˌlike** ADJECTIVE

streamer (ˈstriːmə) NOUN [1] a long narrow flag or part of a flag. [2] a long narrow coiled ribbon of coloured paper that becomes unrolled when tossed. [3] a stream of light, esp one appearing in some forms of the aurora. [4] *Journalism* a large heavy headline printed across the width of a page of a newspaper. [5] *Computing* another word for **tape streamer.**

streamline (ˈstriːmˌlaɪn) NOUN [1] a contour on a body that offers the minimum resistance to a gas or liquid flowing around it. [2] an imaginary line in a fluid such that the tangent at any point indicates the direction of the velocity of a particle of the fluid at that point. ◆ VERB (*tr*) [3] to make streamlined.

streamlined (ˈstriːmˌlaɪnd) ADJECTIVE [1] offering or designed to offer the minimum resistance to the flow of a gas or liquid. [2] made more efficient, esp by simplifying.

streamline flow NOUN flow of a fluid in which its velocity at any point is constant or varies in a regular manner. It can be represented by streamlines. Also called: **viscous flow.** Compare **turbulent flow.** See also **laminar flow.**

stream of consciousness NOUN [1] *Psychol* the continuous flow of ideas, thoughts, and feelings forming the content of an individual's consciousness. The term was originated by William James. [2] **a** a literary technique that reveals the flow of thoughts and feelings of characters through long passages of soliloquy. **b** (*as modifier*): *a stream-of-consciousness novel.*

streamy (ˈstriːmɪ) ADJECTIVE **streamier, streamiest.** *Chiefly poetic* [1] (of an area, land, etc.) having many streams. [2] flowing or streaming.
▸ˈ**streaminess** NOUN

streel (striːl) NOUN *Irish* a slovenly woman.
▷HISTORY from Irish Gaelic *straoill*

street (striːt) NOUN [1] **a** (*capital when part of a name*) a public road that is usually lined with buildings, esp in a town: *Oxford Street.* **b** (*as modifier*): *a street*

directory. 2 the buildings lining a street. 3 the part of the road between the pavements, used by vehicles. 4 the people living, working, etc., in a particular street. 5 (*modifier*) of or relating to the urban counterculture: *street style; street drug.* 6 **man in the street.** an ordinary or average citizen. 7 **on the streets. a** earning a living as a prostitute. **b** homeless. 8 **(right) up one's street.** *Informal* (just) what one knows or likes best. 9 **streets ahead of.** *Informal* superior to, more advanced than, etc. 10 **streets apart.** *Informal* markedly different. ◆ VERB (*tr*) 11 *Austral* to outdistance.
▷HISTORY Old English *strǣt,* from Latin *via strāta* paved way (*strāta,* from *strātus,* past participle of *sternere* to stretch out); compare Old Frisian *strēte,* Old High German *strāza;* see STRATUS

street Arab NOUN *Literary and old-fashioned* a homeless child, esp one who survives by begging and stealing; urchin.

streetcar ('stri:tˌkɑ:) NOUN the usual US and Canadian name for **tram**[1] (sense 1).

street credibility NOUN a convincing command or display of the style, fashions, knowledge, etc., associated with urban counterculture. Often shortened to: **street cred.**
▸ˌ**street-ˈcredible** ADJECTIVE

street cry NOUN (*often plural*) the cry of a street hawker.

street door NOUN the door of a house that opens onto the street.

street furniture NOUN pieces of equipment, such as streetlights and pillar boxes, placed in the street for the benefit of the public.

street justice NOUN the punishment given by members of the public to people regarded as criminals or wrongdoers.

streetlight ('stri:tˌlaɪt) *or* **streetlamp** NOUN a light, esp one carried on a lamppost, that illuminates a road, etc.

street luge NOUN the sport of descending a steep road or track on a large type of skateboard on which riders lie on their backs, descending feet first.

street piano NOUN another name for **barrel organ.**

street theatre NOUN dramatic entertainments performed esp in shopping precincts.

street value NOUN the monetary worth of a commodity, usually an illicit commodity such as a drug, considered as the price it would fetch when sold to the ultimate user.

streetwalker ('stri:tˌwɔ:kə) NOUN a prostitute who solicits on the streets.
▸ˈ**streetˌwalking** NOUN, ADJECTIVE

streetwear ('stri:tˌwɛə) NOUN fashionable casual clothes.

streetwise ('stri:tˌwaɪz) ADJECTIVE attuned to and adept at surviving in an urban, poor and often criminal environment. Also: **street-smart.**
▸**street wisdom** NOUN

strelitzia (strɛˈlɪtsɪə) NOUN any southern African perennial herbaceous plant of the genus *Strelitzia,* cultivated for its showy flowers: includes the bird-of-paradise flower: family *Strelitziaceae.*
▷HISTORY C18: named after Charlotte of Mecklenburg-*Strelitz* (1744–1818), queen of Great Britain and Ireland

strength (strɛŋθ) NOUN 1 the state or quality of being physically or mentally strong. 2 the ability to withstand or exert great force, stress, or pressure. 3 something that is regarded as being beneficial or a source of power: *their chief strength is technology.* 4 potency, as of a drink, drug, etc. 5 power to convince; cogency: *the strength of an argument.* 6 degree of intensity or concentration of colour, light, sound, flavour, etc. 7 the full or part of the full complement as specified: *at full strength; below strength.* 8 *Finance* firmness of or a rising tendency in prices, esp security prices. 9 *Archaic or poetic* a stronghold or fortress. 10 *Austral and NZ informal* the general idea, the main purpose: *to get the strength of something.* 11 **from strength to strength.** with ever-increasing success. 12 **in strength.** in large numbers. 13 **on the strength of.** on the basis of or relying upon.
▷HISTORY Old English *strengthu;* related to Old High German *strengida;* see STRONG

strengthen ('strɛŋθən) VERB to make or become stronger.
▸ˈ**strengthener** NOUN

strenuous ('strɛnjuəs) ADJECTIVE 1 requiring or involving the use of great energy or effort. 2 characterized by great activity, effort, or endeavour.
▷HISTORY C16: from Latin *strēnuus* brisk, vigorous
▸**strenuosity** (ˌstrɛnjuˈɒsɪtɪ) *or* ˈ**strenuousness** NOUN
▸ˈ**strenuously** ADVERB

strep (strɛp) NOUN *Informal* short for **streptococcus.**

strepitoso (ˈstrɛpɪˈtəusəu) ADJECTIVE, ADVERB *Music* (to be performed) boisterously.
▷HISTORY Italian, literally; noisily

strepitous ('strɛpɪtəs) *or* **strepitant** ADJECTIVE *Rare* noisy; boisterous.
▷HISTORY C17: from Latin *strepitus* a din

strepto- COMBINING FORM 1 indicating a shape resembling a twisted chain: *streptococcus.* 2 indicating streptococcus: *streptolysin.*
▷HISTORY from Greek *streptos* twisted, from *strephein* to twist

streptocarpus (ˌstrɛptəˈkɑ:pəs) NOUN any plant of the typically stemless subtropical perennial genus *Streptocarpus,* some species of which are grown as greenhouse plants for their tubular flowers in a range of bright colours: family *Gesneriaceae.*
▷HISTORY New Latin, from Greek *streptos* twisted + *karpos* fruit (from the shape of the capsule)

streptococcus (ˌstrɛptəuˈkɒkəs) NOUN, *plural* **-cocci** (-ˈkɒkaɪ; *US* -ˈkɒksaɪ). any Gram-positive spherical bacterium of the genus *Streptococcus,* typically occurring in chains and including many pathogenic species, such as *S. pyogenes,* which causes scarlet fever, sore throat, etc.: family *Lactobacillaceae.* Often shortened to: **strep.**
▸**streptococcal** (ˌstrɛptəuˈkɒkᵊl) *or* (*less commonly*) **streptococcic** (ˌstrɛptəuˈkɒkɪk; *US* -ˈkɒksɪk) ADJECTIVE

streptokinase (ˌstrɛptəuˈkaɪneɪs) NOUN an enzyme produced by streptococci that causes the fibrin of certain animal species to undergo lysis.

streptomycin (ˌstrɛptəuˈmaɪsɪn) NOUN an antibiotic obtained from the bacterium *Streptomyces griseus:* used in the treatment of tuberculosis and Gram-negative bacterial infections. Formula: $C_{21}H_{39}N_7O_{12}$.
▷HISTORY from *Streptomyces,* genus name of bacteria (from STREPTO- + Greek *mukēs* fungus + -IN)

streptothricin (ˌstrɛptəuˈθraɪsɪn) NOUN an antibiotic active against bacteria and some fungi, produced by the bacterium *Streptomyces lavendulae.*
▷HISTORY from *Streptothrix,* genus name of bacteria (from STREPTO- + Greek *thrix* hair + -IN)

stress (strɛs) NOUN 1 special emphasis or significance attached to something. 2 mental, emotional, or physical strain or tension. 3 emphasis placed upon a syllable by pronouncing it more loudly than those that surround it. 4 such emphasis as part of a regular rhythmic beat in music or poetry. 5 a syllable so emphasized. 6 *Physics* **a** force or a system of forces producing deformation or strain. **b** the force acting per unit area. ◆ VERB 7 (*tr*) to give emphasis or prominence to. 8 (*tr*) to pronounce (a word or syllable) more loudly than those that surround it. 9 (*tr*) to subject to stress or strain. 10 *Informal* (*intr*) to become stressed or anxious.
▷HISTORY C14: *stresse,* shortened from DISTRESS
▸ˈ**stressful** ADJECTIVE ▸ˈ**stressfully** ADVERB ▸ˈ**stressfulness** NOUN

-stress SUFFIX FORMING NOUNS indicating a woman who performs or is engaged in a certain activity: *songstress; seamstress.* Compare **-ster** (sense 1).
▷HISTORY from -ST(E)R + -ESS

stress ball NOUN a small rubber ball squeezed in the hand as a means of relieving stress.

stressbuster ('strɛsˌbʌstə) NOUN a product, practice, system, etc. that is designed to alleviate stress.
▸ˈ**stressˌbusting** ADJECTIVE

stressor ('strɛsə) NOUN an event, experience, etc., that causes stress.

stretch (strɛtʃ) VERB 1 to draw out or extend or be drawn out or extended in length, area, etc. 2 to extend or be extended to an undue degree, esp so as to distort or lengthen permanently. 3 to extend (the limbs, body, etc.). 4 (*tr*) to reach or suspend (a rope, etc.) from one place to another. 5 (*tr*) to draw tight; tighten. 6 (often foll by *out, forward,* etc.) to reach or hold (out); extend. 7 (*intr;* usually foll by *over*) to extend in time: *the course stretched over three months.* 8 (*intr;* foll by *for, over,* etc.) (of a region, etc.) to extend in length or area. 9 (*intr*) (esp of a garment) to be capable of expanding, as to a larger size: *socks that will stretch.* 10 (*tr*) to put a great strain upon or extend to the limit. 11 to injure (a muscle, tendon, ligament, etc.) by means of a strain or sprain. 12 (*tr;* often foll by *out*) to make do with (limited resources): *to stretch one's budget.* 13 (*tr*) *Informal* to expand or elaborate (a story, etc.) beyond what is credible or acceptable: *that's stretching it a bit.* 14 (*tr; often passive*) to extend, as to the limit of one's abilities or talents. 15 *Archaic or slang* to hang or be hanged by the neck. 16 **stretch a point. a** to make a concession or exception not usually made. **b** to exaggerate. 17 **stretch one's legs.** to take a walk, esp after a period of inactivity. ◆ NOUN 18 the act of stretching or state of being stretched. 19 a large or continuous expanse or distance: *a stretch of water.* 20 extent in time, length, area, etc. 21 **a** capacity for being stretched, as in some garments. **b** (*as modifier*): *stretch pants.* 22 *Horse racing* the section or sections of a racecourse that are straight, esp the final straight section leading to the finishing line. 23 *Slang* a term of imprisonment. 24 **at a stretch.** *Chiefly Brit* **a** with some difficulty; by making a special effort. **b** if really necessary or in extreme circumstances.
▷HISTORY Old English *streccan;* related to Old Frisian *strekka,* Old High German *strecken;* see STRAIGHT, STRAKE
▸ˈ**stretchable** ADJECTIVE ▸ˌ**stretchaˈbility** NOUN

stretcher ('strɛtʃə) NOUN 1 a device for transporting the ill, wounded, or dead, consisting of a frame covered by canvas or other material. 2 a strengthening often decorative member joining the legs of a chair, table, etc. 3 the wooden frame on which canvas is stretched and fixed for oil painting. 4 a tie beam or brace used in a structural framework. 5 a brick or stone laid horizontally with its length parallel to the length of a wall. Compare **header** (sense 4). 6 *Rowing* a fixed board across a boat on which an oarsman braces his feet. 7 *Austral and NZ* a camp bed. 8 *Slang* an exaggeration or lie. ◆ VERB (*tr*) 9 to transport (a sick or injured person) on a stretcher.

stretcher-bearer NOUN a person who helps to carry a stretcher, esp in wartime.

stretch limo NOUN *Informal* a limousine that has been lengthened to provide extra seating accommodation and more legroom. In full: **stretch limousine.**

stretchmarks ('strɛtʃˌmɑ:ks) PLURAL NOUN marks that remain visible on the abdomen after its distension, esp in pregnancy.

stretchy ('strɛtʃɪ) ADJECTIVE **stretchier, stretchiest.** characterized by elasticity.
▸ˈ**stretchiness** NOUN

Stretford ('strɛtfəd) NOUN an industrial town in NW England, in Trafford unitary authority, Greater Manchester. Pop.: 43 953 (1991).

stretto ('strɛtəu) NOUN, *plural* **-tos** *or* **-ti** (-ti:). 1 (in a fugue) the close overlapping of two parts or voices, the second one entering before the first has completed its statement of the subject. 2 Also called: **stretta** ('strɛtə). a concluding passage in a composition, played at a faster speed than the earlier material.
▷HISTORY C17: from Italian, from Latin *strictus* tightly bound; see STRICT

streusel ('stru:sᵊl, 'strɔɪ-; *German* 'ʃtrɔyzəl) NOUN *Chiefly US* a crumbly topping for rich pastries.
▷HISTORY German, from *streuen* to STREW

strew (stru:) VERB **strews, strewing, strewed, strewn** *or* **strewed.** to spread or scatter or be spread or scattered, as over a surface or area.
▷HISTORY Old English *streowian;* related to Old Norse *strā,* Old High German *streuwen,* Latin *struere* to spread
▸ˈ**strewer** NOUN

strewth (stru:θ) INTERJECTION an expression of surprise or dismay.
▷HISTORY C19: alteration of *God's truth*

stria ('straɪə) NOUN, *plural* **striae** ('straɪi:). (*often*

plural) [1] Also called: **striation.** *Geology* any of the parallel scratches or grooves on the surface of a rock caused by abrasion resulting from the passage of a glacier, motion on a fault surface, etc. [2] fine ridges and grooves on the surface of a crystal caused by irregular growth. [3] *Biology, anatomy* a narrow band of colour or a ridge, groove, or similar linear mark, usually occurring in a parallel series. [4] *Architect* a narrow channel, such as a flute on the shaft of a column.
▷HISTORY C16: from Latin: a groove

striate ADJECTIVE ('straɪɪt) *also* **striated.** [1] marked with striae; striped. ◆ VERB ('straɪeɪt) [2] *(tr)* to mark with striae.
▷HISTORY C17: from Latin *striāre* to make grooves, from STRIA

striation (straɪ'eɪʃən) NOUN [1] an arrangement or pattern of striae. [2] the condition of being striate. [3] another word for **stria** (sense 1).

strick (strɪk) NOUN *Textiles* any bast fibres preparatory to being made into slivers.
▷HISTORY C15 *stric,* perhaps of Low German origin; compare Middle Dutch *stric,* Middle Low German *strik* rope

stricken ('strɪkən) ADJECTIVE [1] laid low, as by disease or sickness. [2] deeply affected, as by grief, love, etc. [3] *Archaic* wounded or injured.
▷HISTORY C14: past participle of STRIKE
▸'**strickenly** ADVERB

strickle ('strɪkᵊl) NOUN [1] Also called: **strike.** a board used for sweeping off excess material in a container. [2] a template used for shaping a mould. [3] a bar of abrasive material for sharpening a scythe. ◆ VERB [4] *(tr)* to level, form, or sharpen with a strickle.
▷HISTORY Old English *stricel;* related to Latin *strigilis* scraper, German *Striegel;* see STRIKE

strict (strɪkt) ADJECTIVE [1] adhering closely to specified rules, ordinances, etc.: *a strict faith.* [2] complied with or enforced stringently; rigorous: *a strict code of conduct.* [3] severely correct in attention to rules of conduct or morality: *a strict teacher.* [4] (of a punishment, etc.) harsh; severe. [5] *(prenominal)* complete; absolute: *in strict secrecy.* [6] *Logic, maths* (of a relation) **a** applying more narrowly than some other relation often given the same name, as *strict inclusion,* which holds only between pairs of sets that are distinct, while *simple inclusion* permits the case in which they are identical. See also **proper** (sense 9), **ordering. b** distinguished from a relation of the same name that is not the subject of formal study. [7] *Botany, rare* very straight, narrow, and upright: *strict panicles.*
▷HISTORY C16: from Latin *strictus,* from *stringere* to draw tight
▸'**strictly** ADVERB ▸'**strictness** NOUN

stricture ('strɪktʃə) NOUN [1] a severe criticism; censure. [2] *Pathol* an abnormal constriction of a tubular organ, structure, or part. [3] *Obsolete* severity.
▷HISTORY C14: from Latin *strictūra* contraction; see STRICT
▸'**strictured** ADJECTIVE

stride (straɪd) NOUN [1] a long step or pace. [2] the space measured by such a step. [3] a striding gait. [4] an act of forward movement by an animal, completed when the legs have returned to their initial relative positions. [5] progress or development (esp in the phrase **make rapid strides**). [6] a regular pace or rate of progress: *to get into one's stride; to be put off one's stride.* [7] *Rowing* the distance covered between strokes. [8] Also called: **stride piano.** *Jazz* a piano style characterized by single bass notes on the first and third beats and chords on the second and fourth. [9] *(plural) Informal, chiefly Austral* men's trousers. [10] **take (something) in one's stride.** to do (something) without difficulty or effort. ◆ VERB **strides, striding, strode, stridden.** [11] *(intr)* to walk with long regular or measured paces, as in haste, etc. [12] *(tr)* to cover or traverse by striding: *he strode thirty miles.* [13] (often foll by *over, across,* etc.) to cross (over a space, obstacle, etc.) with a stride. [14] *(intr) Rowing* to achieve the desired rhythm in a racing shell.
▷HISTORY Old English *strīdan;* related to Old High German *strītan* to quarrel; see STRADDLE
▸'**strider** NOUN

strident ('straɪdᵊnt) ADJECTIVE [1] (of a shout, voice, etc.) having or making a loud or harsh sound. [2] urgent, clamorous, or vociferous: *strident demands.*
▷HISTORY C17: from Latin *strīdēns,* from *strīdēre* to make a grating sound
▸'**stridence** *or* '**stridency** NOUN ▸'**stridently** ADVERB

stridor ('straɪdɔː) NOUN [1] *Pathol* a high-pitched whistling sound made during respiration, caused by obstruction of the air passages. [2] *Chiefly literary* a harsh or shrill sound.
▷HISTORY C17: from Latin; see STRIDENT

stridulate ('strɪdjʊˌleɪt) VERB *(intr)* (of insects such as the cricket) to produce sounds by rubbing one part of the body against another.
▷HISTORY C19: back formation from *stridulation,* from Latin *strīdulus* creaking, hissing, from *strīdēre* to make a harsh noise
▸ˌ**stridu'lation** NOUN ▸'**striduˌlator** NOUN ▸**stridulatory** ('strɪdjʊˌleɪtərɪ) ADJECTIVE

stridulous ('strɪdjʊləs) *or* **stridulant** ADJECTIVE [1] making a harsh, shrill, or grating noise. [2] *Pathol* of, relating to, or characterized by stridor.
▷HISTORY C17: from Latin *strīdulus,* from *strīdēre* to make a harsh noise. See STRIDENT
▸'**stridulously** *or* '**stridulantly** ADVERB ▸'**stridulousness** *or* '**stridulance** NOUN

strife (straɪf) NOUN [1] angry or violent struggle; conflict. [2] rivalry or contention, esp of a bitter kind. [3] *Austral and NZ* trouble or discord of any kind: *to get into strife.* [4] *Archaic* striving.
▷HISTORY C13: from Old French *estrif,* probably from *estriver* to STRIVE

strigiform ('strɪdʒɪˌfɔːm) ADJECTIVE of, relating to, or belonging to the *Strigiformes,* an order of birds comprising the owls.
▷HISTORY via New Latin from Latin *strix* a screech owl

strigil ('strɪdʒɪl) NOUN [1] a curved blade used by the ancient Romans and Greeks to scrape the body after bathing. [2] *Architect* a decorative fluting, esp one in the shape of the letter *S* as used in Roman architecture.
▷HISTORY C16: from Latin *strigilis,* from *stringere* to graze

strigose ('straɪgəʊs) ADJECTIVE [1] *Botany* bearing stiff hairs or bristles: *strigose leaves.* [2] *Zoology* marked with fine closely set grooves or ridges.
▷HISTORY C18: via New Latin *strigōsus,* from *striga* a bristle, from Latin: grain cut down

strike (straɪk) VERB **strikes, striking, struck.** [1] to deliver (a blow or stroke) to (a person). [2] to come or cause to come into sudden or violent contact (with). [3] *(tr)* to make an attack on. [4] to produce (fire, sparks, etc.) or (of fire, sparks, etc.) to be produced by ignition. [5] to cause (a match) to light by friction or (of a match) to be lighted. [6] to press (the key of a piano, organ, etc.) or to sound (a specific note) in this or a similar way. [7] to indicate (a specific time) by the sound of a hammer striking a bell or by any other percussive sound. [8] (of a venomous snake) to cause injury by biting. [9] *(tr)* to affect or cause to affect deeply, suddenly, or radically, as if by dealing a blow: *her appearance struck him as strange; I was struck on his art.* [10] *(past participle* **struck** *or* **stricken***) (tr; passive;* usually foll by *with)* to render incapable or nearly so: *she was stricken with grief.* [11] *(tr)* to enter the mind of: *it struck me that he had become very quiet.* [12] *(past participle* **struck** *or* **stricken***)* to render: *I was struck dumb.* [13] *(tr)* to be perceived by; catch: *the glint of metal struck his eye.* [14] to arrive at or come upon (something), esp suddenly or unexpectedly: *to strike the path for home; to strike upon a solution.* [15] *(intr;* sometimes foll by *out)* to set (out) or proceed, esp upon a new course: *to strike for the coast.* [16] *(tr; usually passive)* to afflict with a disease, esp unexpectedly: *he was struck with polio when he was six.* [17] *(tr)* to discover or come upon a source of (ore, petroleum, etc.). [18] *(tr)* (of a plant) to produce or send down (a root or roots). [19] *(tr)* to take apart or pack up; break (esp in the phrase **strike camp**). [20] *(tr)* to take down or dismantle (a stage set, formwork, etc.). [21] *(tr) Nautical* **a** to lower or remove (a specified piece of gear). **b** to haul down or dip (a flag, sail, etc.) in salute or in surrender. **c** to lower (cargo, etc.) into the hold of a ship. [22] to attack (an objective) with the intention of causing damage to, seizing, or destroying it. [23] to impale the hook in the mouth of (a fish) by suddenly tightening or jerking the line after the bait or fly has been taken. [24] *(tr)* to form or impress (a coin, metal, etc.) by or as if by stamping. [25] to level (a surface) by use of a flat board. [26] *(tr)* to assume or take up (an attitude, posture, etc.). [27] *(intr)* (of workers in a factory, etc.) to cease work collectively as a protest against working conditions, low pay, etc. [28] *(tr)* to reach by agreement: *to strike a bargain.* [29] *(tr)* to form (a jury, esp. a special jury) by cancelling certain names among those nominated for jury service until only the requisite number remains. See also **special jury.** [30] *(tr) Rowing* to make (a certain number of strokes) per minute: *Oxford were striking 38.* [31] to make a stroke or kick in swimming. [32] *(tr)* (in Malaysia) to win (a lottery or raffle). [33] **strike home. a** to deliver an effective blow. **b** to achieve the intended effect. [34] **strike (it) lucky.** to have some good luck. [35] **strike it rich.** *Informal* **a** to discover an extensive deposit of a mineral, petroleum, etc. **b** to have an unexpected financial success. ◆ NOUN [36] an act or instance of striking. [37] a cessation of work by workers in a factory, industry, etc., as a protest against working conditions or low pay: *the workers are on strike again.* [38] a military attack, esp. an air attack on a surface target: *air strike.* [39] *Baseball* a pitched ball judged good but missed or not swung at, three of which cause a batter to be out. [40] Also called: **ten-strike.** *Tenpin bowling* **a** the act or an instance of knocking down all the pins with the first bowl of a single frame. **b** the score thus made. Compare **spare** (sense 17). [41] a sound made by striking. [42] the mechanism that makes a clock strike. [43] the discovery of a source of ore, petroleum, etc. [44] the horizontal direction of a fault, rock stratum, etc., which is perpendicular to the direction of the dip. [45] *Angling* the act or an instance of striking. [46] the number of coins or medals made at one time. [47] another name for **strickle** (sense 1). [48] *Informal* an unexpected or complete success, esp. one that brings financial gain. [49] **take strike.** *Cricket* (of a batsman) to prepare to play a ball delivered by the bowler. ◆ See also **strike down, strike off, strike out, strike through, strike up.**
▷HISTORY Old English *strīcan;* related to Old Frisian *strīka* to stroke, Old High German *strīhhan* to smooth, Latin *stria* furrow
▸'**strikeless** ADJECTIVE

strikebound ('straɪkˌbaʊnd) ADJECTIVE (of a factory, etc.) closed or made inoperative by a strike.

strikebreaker ('straɪkˌbreɪkə) NOUN a person who tries to make a strike ineffectual by working or by taking the place of those on strike.
▸'**strikeˌbreaking** NOUN, ADJECTIVE

strike down VERB *(tr, adverb)* to cause to die, esp suddenly: *he was struck down in his prime.*

strike fault NOUN a fault that runs parallel to the strike of the affected rocks.

strike note *or esp US* **strike tone** NOUN the note produced by a bell when struck, defining its musical pitch.

strike off VERB *(tr)* [1] to remove or erase from (a list, record, etc.) by or as if by a stroke of the pen. [2] *(adverb)* to cut off or separate by or as if by a blow: *she was struck off from the inheritance.*

strike out VERB *(adverb)* [1] *(tr)* to remove or erase. [2] *(intr)* to start out or begin: *to strike out on one's own.* [3] *Baseball* to put out or be put out on strikes. [4] *(intr) US and Canadian informal* to fail utterly.

strike pay NOUN money paid to strikers from the funds of a trade union.

striker ('straɪkə) NOUN [1] a person who is on strike. [2] the hammer in a timepiece that rings a bell or alarm. [3] any part in a mechanical device that strikes something, such as the firing pin of a gun. [4] *Soccer, informal* an attacking player, esp one who generally positions himself near his opponent's goal in the hope of scoring. [5] *Cricket* the batsman who is about to play a ball. [6] **a** a person who harpoons whales or fish. **b** the harpoon itself.

strike-slip fault NOUN a geological fault on which the movement is along the strike of the fault.

strike through VERB *(tr)* to draw (a line) through (something) to delete it.

strike up VERB *(adverb)* [1] (of a band, orchestra, etc.) to begin to play or sing. [2] *(tr)* to bring about;

cause to begin: *to strike up a friendship.* [3] (*tr*) to emboss (patterns, etc.) on (metal).

striking ('straɪkɪŋ) ADJECTIVE [1] attracting attention; fine; impressive: *a striking beauty.* [2] conspicuous; noticeable: *a striking difference.* ▸**'strikingly** ADVERB ▸**'strikingness** NOUN

striking circle NOUN *Hockey* the semicircular area in front of each goal, which an attacking player must have entered before scoring a goal.

Strimmer ('strɪmə) NOUN *Trademark* an electrical tool for trimming the edges of lawns.

Strimon ('strimɔn) NOUN a transliteration of the Greek name for the **Struma.**

Strine (straɪn) NOUN a humorous transliteration of Australian pronunciation, as in *Gloria Soame* for *glorious home.*
▹**HISTORY** C20: a jocular rendering, coined by Alastair Morrison, of the Australian pronunciation of *Australian*

string (strɪŋ) NOUN [1] a thin length of cord, twine, fibre, or similar material used for tying, hanging, binding, etc. [2] a group of objects threaded on a single strand: *a string of beads.* [3] a series or succession of things, events, acts, utterances, etc.: *a string of oaths.* [4] a number, chain, or group of similar things, animals, etc., owned by or associated with one person or body: *a string of girlfriends.* [5] a tough fibre or cord in a plant: *the string of an orange; the string of a bean.* [6] *Music* a tightly stretched wire, cord, etc., found on stringed instruments, such as the violin, guitar, and piano. [7] short for **bowstring.** [8] *Architect* short for **string course** or **stringer** (sense 1). [9] *Maths, linguistics* a sequence of symbols or words. [10] *Linguistics* a linear sequence, such as a sentence as it is spoken. [11] *Physics* a one-dimensional entity postulated to be a fundamental component of matter in some theories of particle physics. See also **cosmic string.** [12] *Billiards* another word for **lag**[1] (sense 6). [13] a group of characters that can be treated as a unit by a computer program. [14] (*plural;* usually preceded by *the*) **a** violins, violas, cellos, and double basses collectively. **b** the section of a symphony orchestra constituted by such instruments. [15] (*plural*) complications or conditions (esp in the phrase **no strings attached**). [16] (*modifier*) composed of stringlike strands woven in a large mesh: *a string bag; string vest.* [17] **first (second,** etc.) **string.** a person or thing regarded as a primary (secondary, etc.) source of strength. [18] **keep on a string.** to have control or a hold over (a person), esp emotionally. [19] **pull strings.** *Informal* to exert personal influence, esp secretly or unofficially. [20] **pull the strings.** to have real or ultimate control of something. ◆ VERB **strings, stringing, strung** (strʌŋ). [21] (*tr*) to provide with a string or strings. [22] (*tr*) to suspend or stretch from one point to another. [23] (*tr*) to thread on a string. [24] (*tr*) to form or extend in a line or series. [25] (foll by *out*) to space or spread out at intervals. [26] (*tr;* usually foll by *up*) *Informal* to kill (a person) by hanging. [27] (*tr*) to remove the stringy parts from (vegetables, esp beans). [28] (*intr*) (esp of viscous liquids) to become stringy or ropey. [29] (*tr;* often foll by *up*) to cause to be tense or nervous. [30] *Billiards* another word for **lag**[1] (sense 3).
▹**HISTORY** Old English *streng;* related to Old High German *strang,* Old Norse *strengr;* see STRONG
▸**'string,like** ADJECTIVE

string along VERB (*adverb*) *Informal* [1] (*intr;* often foll by *with*) to agree or appear to be in agreement (with). [2] (*tr*) Also: **string on.** to deceive, fool, or hoax, esp in order to gain time.

string band NOUN [1] a band consisting of stringed instruments. [2] an informal name for **string orchestra.**

string bass (beɪs) NOUN another name for **double bass.**

string bean NOUN [1] any of several bean plants, such as the scarlet runner, cultivated for their edible unripe pods. See also **green bean, wax bean.** [2] *Informal* a tall thin person.

stringboard ('strɪŋ,bɔ:d) NOUN a skirting that covers the ends of the steps in a staircase. Also called: **stringer.**

string course NOUN another name for **cordon** (sense 4).

stringed (strɪŋd) ADJECTIVE (of musical instruments) having or provided with strings.

stringed instrument NOUN any musical instrument in which sound is produced by the vibration of a string across a soundboard or soundbox. Also called: **chordophone.**

stringendo (strɪn'dʒɛndəʊ) ADJECTIVE, ADVERB *Music* to be performed with increasing speed.
▹**HISTORY** Italian, from *stringere* to compress, from Latin: to draw tight; see STRINGENT

stringent ('strɪndʒənt) ADJECTIVE [1] requiring strict attention to rules, procedure, detail, etc. [2] *Finance* characterized by or causing a shortage of credit, loan capital, etc.
▹**HISTORY** C17: from Latin *stringere* to bind
▸**'stringency** NOUN ▸**'stringently** ADVERB

stringer ('strɪŋə) NOUN [1] *Architect* **a** a long horizontal beam that is used for structural purposes. **b** another name for **stringboard.** [2] *Nautical* a longitudinal structural brace for strengthening the hull of a vessel. [3] a journalist retained by a newspaper or news service on a part-time basis to cover a particular town or area.

stringhalt ('strɪŋ,hɔ:lt) NOUN *Vet science* a sudden spasmodic lifting of the hind leg of a horse, resulting from abnormal contraction of the flexor muscles of the hock. Also called: **springhalt.**
▹**HISTORY** C16: probably STRING + HALT[2]

string line NOUN *Billiards* another name for **baulk line** (sense 1).

string orchestra NOUN an orchestra consisting only of violins, violas, cellos, and double basses.

stringpiece ('strɪŋ,pi:s) NOUN a long horizontal timber beam used to strengthen or support a framework.

string quartet NOUN *Music* [1] an instrumental ensemble consisting of two violins, one viola, and one cello. [2] a piece of music written for such a group, usually having the form and commonest features of a sonata.

string tie NOUN a very narrow tie, usually tied in a bow.

string variable NOUN *Computing* data on which arithmetical operations will not be performed.

stringy ('strɪŋɪ) ADJECTIVE **stringier, stringiest.** [1] made of strings or resembling strings. [2] (of meat, etc.) fibrous. [3] (of a person's build) wiry; sinewy. [4] (of liquids) forming in strings.
▸**'stringily** ADVERB ▸**'stringiness** NOUN

stringy-bark NOUN *Austral* any of several eucalyptus trees having a fibrous bark.

strip[1] (strɪp) VERB **strips, stripping, stripped.** [1] to take or pull (the covering, clothes, etc.) off (oneself, another person, or thing): *to strip a wall; to strip a bed.* [2] (*intr*) **a** to remove all one's clothes. **b** to perform a striptease. [3] (*tr*) to denude or empty completely. [4] (*tr*) to deprive: *he was stripped of his pride.* [5] (*tr*) to rob or plunder. [6] (*tr*) to remove (paint, varnish, etc.) from (a surface, furniture, etc.) by sanding, with a solvent, etc.: *stripped pine.* [7] (*tr*) Also: **pluck.** to pull out the old coat of hair from (dogs of certain long- and wire-haired breeds). [8] **a** to remove the leaves from the stalks of (tobacco, etc.). **b** to separate the two sides of a leaf from the stem of (tobacco, etc.). [9] (*tr*) *Agriculture* to draw the last milk from each of the teats of (a cow). [10] to dismantle (an engine, mechanism, etc.). [11] to tear off or break (the thread) from (a screw, bolt, etc.) or (the teeth) from (a gear). [12] (often foll by *down*) to remove the accessories from (a motor vehicle): *his car was stripped down.* [13] to remove (the most volatile constituent) from (a mixture of liquids) by boiling, evaporation, or distillation. [14] *Printing* (usually foll by *in*) to combine (pieces of film or paper) to form a composite sheet from which a plate can be made. [15] (*tr*) (in freight transport) to unpack (a container). See also **stuffing and stripping.** ◆ NOUN [16] the act or an instance of undressing or of performing a striptease. ◆ See also **strip out.**
▹**HISTORY** Old English *bestriepan* to plunder; related to Old High German *stroufen* to plunder, strip

strip[2] (strɪp) NOUN [1] a relatively long, flat, narrow piece of something. [2] short for **airstrip.** [3] *Philately* a horizontal or vertical row of three or more unseparated postage stamps. [4] the clothes worn by the members of a team, esp a football team. [5] *Business* a triple option on a security or commodity consisting of one call option and two put options at the same price and for the same period. Compare **strap** (sense 5). [6] *NZ* short for **dosing strip.** [7] **tear (someone) off a strip.** *Informal* to rebuke (someone) angrily. ◆ VERB **strips, stripping, stripped.** [8] to cut or divide into strips.
▹**HISTORY** C15: from Middle Dutch *strīpe* STRIPE[1]

strip cartoon NOUN another term for **comic strip.**

strip club NOUN a small club in which striptease performances take place.

strip cropping NOUN a method of growing crops in strips or bands arranged to serve as barriers against erosion.

stripe[1] (straɪp) NOUN [1] a relatively long band of distinctive colour or texture that differs from the surrounding material or background. [2] a fabric having such bands. [3] a strip, band, or chevron of fabric worn on a military uniform, etc., esp one that indicates rank. [4] *Chiefly US and Canadian* kind; sort; type: *a man of a certain stripe.* ◆ VERB [5] (*tr*) to mark with a stripe or stripes.
▹**HISTORY** C17: probably from Middle Dutch *strīpe;* related to Middle High German *strīfe,* of obscure origin

stripe[2] (straɪp) NOUN a stroke from a whip, rod, cane, etc.
▹**HISTORY** C15: perhaps from Middle Low German *strippe;* related to STRIPE[1]

striped (straɪpt) ADJECTIVE marked or decorated with stripes.

striped muscle *or* **striated muscle** NOUN a type of contractile tissue that is marked by transverse striations; it is concerned with moving skeletal parts to which it is usually attached. Also called: **skeletal muscle.** Compare **smooth muscle.**

striper ('straɪpə) NOUN *Military, slang* an officer who has a stripe or stripes on his uniform, esp in the navy: *a two-striper* (lieutenant).

strip lighting NOUN electric lighting by means of long glass tubes that are fluorescent lamps or that contain long filaments.

stripling ('strɪplɪŋ) NOUN a lad.
▹**HISTORY** C13: from STRIP[2] + -LING[1]

strip mill NOUN a mill in which steel slabs are rolled into strips.

strip mining NOUN another term (esp US) for **opencast mining.**

strip out VERB [1] (*tr*) to remove the working parts of (a machine). [2] to remove (a chemical or component) from a mixture.

stripped-down ADJECTIVE reduced to the bare essentials; spare.

stripper ('strɪpə) NOUN [1] a striptease artist. [2] a person or thing that strips. [3] a device or substance for removing paint, varnish, etc.

strip poker NOUN a card game in which a player's losses are paid by removing an article of clothing.

strip-search VERB [1] (*tr*) (of police, customs officials, etc.) to strip (a prisoner or suspect) naked to search him or her for contraband, narcotics, etc. ◆ NOUN [2] a search that involves stripping a person naked.
▸**'strip-,searching** NOUN

striptease ('strɪp,ti:z) NOUN **a** a form of erotic entertainment in which a person gradually undresses to music. **b** (*as modifier*): *a striptease club.*
▹**HISTORY** from STRIP[1] + TEASE
▸**'strip,teaser** NOUN

stripy *or* **stripey** ('straɪpɪ) ADJECTIVE **stripier, stripiest.** marked by or with stripes; striped.

strive (straɪv) VERB **strives, striving, strove, striven** ('strɪvᵊn). [1] (*may take a clause as object or an infinitive*) to make a great and tenacious effort: *to strive to get promotion.* [2] (*intr*) to fight; contend.
▹**HISTORY** C13: from Old French *estriver,* of Germanic origin; related to Middle High German *streben* to strive, Old Norse *strītha* to fight
▸**'striver** NOUN

strobe (strəʊb) NOUN [1] short for **strobe lighting** or **stroboscope.** ◆ VERB [2] to give the appearance of arrested or slow motion by using intermittent illumination.

strobe lighting NOUN [1] a high-intensity flashing beam of light produced by rapid electrical discharges in a tube or by a perforated disc rotating in front of an intense light source: used in discotheques, etc. [2] the use of or the apparatus for producing such light. Sometimes shortened to: **strobe.**

strobe tuner NOUN an electronic instrument tuner that uses stroboscopic light.

strobic ('strəʊbɪk) ADJECTIVE spinning or appearing to spin.
▷HISTORY C19: from Greek *strobos* act of spinning

strobila ('strəʊbɪlə) NOUN, *plural* **-bilae** (-bɪliː). [1] the body of a tapeworm, consisting of a string of similar segments (proglottides). [2] a less common name for **scyphistoma.**
▷HISTORY C19: from New Latin, from Greek *strobilē* plug of lint twisted into a cone shape, from *strobilos* a fir cone

strobilaceous (ˌstrəʊbɪ'leɪʃəs) ADJECTIVE *Botany* relating to or resembling a cone or cones.

strobilation (ˌstrəʊbɪ'leɪʃən) NOUN asexual reproduction by division into segments, as in tapeworms and jellyfishes.

strobilus ('strəʊbɪləs) *or* **strobile** ('strəʊbaɪl) NOUN, *plural* **-biluses, -bili** (-bɪlaɪ) *or* **-biles.** *Botany* the technical name for **cone** (sense 3).
▷HISTORY C18: via Late Latin from Greek *strobilos* a fir cone; see STROBILA

stroboscope ('strəʊbəˌskəʊp) NOUN [1] an instrument producing a flashing light, the frequency of which can be synchronized with some multiple of the frequency of rotation, vibration, or operation of an object, etc., making it appear stationary. It is used to determine speeds of rotation or vibration, or to adjust objects or parts. Sometimes shortened to: **strobe.** [2] a similar device synchronized with the opening of the shutter of a camera so that a series of still photographs can be taken of a moving object.
▷HISTORY C19: from *strobo-*, from Greek *strobos* a twisting, whirling + -SCOPE
▸**stroboscopic** (ˌstrəʊbə'skɒpɪk) *or* ˌ**strobo'scopical** ADJECTIVE ▸ˌ**strobo'scopically** ADVERB

strode (strəʊd) VERB the past tense of **stride.**

stroganoff ('strɒgəˌnɒf) NOUN short for **beef stroganoff.**

stroke (strəʊk) NOUN [1] the act or an instance of striking; a blow, knock, or hit. [2] a sudden action, movement, or occurrence: *a stroke of luck.* [3] a brilliant or inspired act or feat: *a stroke of genius.* [4] *Pathol* apoplexy; rupture of a blood vessel in the brain resulting in loss of consciousness, often followed by paralysis, or embolism or thrombosis affecting a cerebral vessel. [5] **a** the striking of a clock. **b** the hour registered by the striking of a clock: *on the stroke of three.* [6] a mark, flourish, or line made by a writing implement. [7] another name for **solidus,** used esp when dictating or reading aloud [8] a light touch or caress, as with the fingers. [9] a pulsation, esp of the heart. [10] a single complete movement or one of a series of complete movements. [11] *Sport* the act or manner of striking the ball with a racket, club, bat, etc. [12] any one of the repeated movements used by a swimmer to propel himself through the water. [13] a manner of swimming, esp one of several named styles such as the crawl or butterfly. [14] **a** any one of a series of linear movements of a reciprocating part, such as a piston. **b** the distance travelled by such a part from one end of its movement to the other. [15] a single pull on an oar or oars in rowing. [16] manner or style of rowing. [17] the oarsman who sits nearest the stern of a shell, facing the cox, and sets the rate of striking for the rest of the crew. [18] *US informal* a compliment or comment that enhances a persons self-esteem. [19] *(modifier) Slang, chiefly US* pornographic; masturbatory: *stroke magazines.* [20] **a stroke (of work).** *(usually used with a negative)* a small amount of work. [21] **off one's stroke.** performing or working less well than usual. [22] **on the stroke (of).** punctually (at). ◆ VERB [23] *(tr)* to touch, brush, or caress lightly or gently. [24] *(tr)* to mark a line or a stroke on or through. [25] to act as the stroke of (a racing shell). [26] *(tr) Sport* to strike (a ball) with a smooth swinging blow. [27] *(tr) US and Canadian informal* to handle or influence (someone) with care, using persuasion, flattery, etc.
▷HISTORY Old English *strācian;* related to Middle Low German *strēken;* see STRIKE

stroke play NOUN *Golf* **a** scoring by counting the number of strokes taken. **b** *(as modifier)*: *a strokeplay tournament.* ◆ Also called: **medal play.** Compare **match play, Stableford.**

stroll (strəʊl) VERB [1] to walk about in a leisurely manner. [2] *(intr)* to wander from place to place. ◆ NOUN [3] a leisurely walk.
▷HISTORY C17: probably from dialect German *strollen,* of obscure origin; compare German *Strolch* tramp

stroller ('strəʊlə) NOUN the usual US, Canadian, and Austral word for **pushchair.**

stroma ('strəʊmə) NOUN, *plural* **-mata** (-mətə). *Biology* [1] the gel-like matrix of chloroplasts and certain cells. [2] the fibrous connective tissue forming the matrix of the mammalian ovary and testis. [3] a dense mass of hyphae that is produced by certain fungi and gives rise to spore-producing bodies.
▷HISTORY C19: via New Latin from Late Latin: a mattress, from Greek; related to Latin *sternere* to strew
▸**stromatic** (strəʊ'mætɪk) *or* '**stromatous** ADJECTIVE

stromatolite (strəʊ'mætəˌlaɪt) NOUN a rocky mass consisting of layers of calcareous material and sediment formed by the prolific growth of cyanobacteria: such structures date back to Precambrian times.
▷HISTORY C20: from Greek, from *strōma* covering + -LITE
▸**stromatolitic** (strəʊˌmætə'lɪtɪk) ADJECTIVE

Stromboli ('strɒmbəlɪ) NOUN an island in the Tyrrhenian Sea, in the Lipari Islands off the N coast of Sicily: famous for its active volcano, 927 m (3040 ft.) high.

Strombolian (strɒm'bəʊlɪən) ADJECTIVE relating to or denoting a type of volcanic eruption characterized by repeated fountaining or jetting of fluid lava into the air.

strong (strɒŋ) ADJECTIVE **stronger** ('strɒŋgə), **strongest** ('strɒŋgɪst). [1] involving or possessing physical or mental strength. [2] solid or robust in construction; not easily broken or injured. [3] having a resolute will or morally firm and incorruptible character. [4] intense in quality; not faint or feeble: *a strong voice; a strong smell.* [5] easily defensible; incontestable or formidable. [6] concentrated; not weak or diluted. [7] **a** *(postpositive)* containing or having a specified number: *a navy 40 000 strong.* **b** *(in combination)*: *a 40 000-strong navy.* [8] having an unpleasantly powerful taste or smell. [9] having an extreme or drastic effect: *strong discipline.* [10] emphatic or immoderate: *strong language.* [11] convincing, effective, or cogent. [12] (of a colour) having a high degree of saturation or purity; being less saturated than a vivid colour but more so than a moderate colour; produced by a concentrated quantity of colouring agent. [13] *Grammar* **a** denoting or belonging to a class of verbs, in certain languages including the Germanic languages, whose conjugation shows vowel gradation, as *sing, sang, sung.* **b** belonging to any part-of-speech class, in any of various languages, whose inflections follow the less regular of two possible patterns. Compare **weak** (sense 10). [14] (of a wind, current, etc.) moving fast. [15] (of a syllable) accented or stressed. [16] (of an industry, market, currency, securities, etc.) firm in price or characterized by firm or increasing prices. [17] (of certain acids and bases) producing high concentrations of hydrogen or hydroxide ions in aqueous solution. [18] *Irish* prosperous; well-to-do (esp in the phrase **a strong farmer**). [19] **have a strong stomach.** not to be prone to nausea. ◆ ADVERB [20] *Informal* in a strong way; effectively: *going strong.* [21] **come on strong.** to make a forceful or exaggerated impression.
▷HISTORY Old English *strang;* related to Old Norse *strangr,* Middle High German *strange,* Lettish *strans* courageous
▸'**strongish** ADJECTIVE ▸'**strongly** ADVERB ▸'**strongness** NOUN

strong-arm *Informal* ◆ NOUN [1] *(modifier)* relating to or involving physical force or violence: *strong-arm tactics.* ◆ VERB [2] *(tr)* to show violence towards.

strongbox ('strɒŋˌbɒks) NOUN a specially designed box or safe in which valuables are locked for safety.

strong breeze NOUN *Meteorol* a considerable wind of force six on the Beaufort scale, reaching speeds of 25–31 mph.

strong drink NOUN alcoholic drink.

strong-eye dog NOUN *NZ* a dog trained to control sheep by its gaze.

strong gale NOUN *Meteorol* a strong wind of force nine on the Beaufort scale, reaching speeds of 47–54 mph: capable of causing minor structural damage to buildings.

stronghold ('strɒŋˌhəʊld) NOUN [1] a defensible place; fortress. [2] a major centre or area of predominance.
▷HISTORY C15: from STRONG + HOLD[1] (in the archaic sense: a fortified place)

strong interaction *or* **force** NOUN *Physics* an interaction between elementary particles responsible for the forces between nucleons in the nucleus. It operates at distances less than about 10^{-15} metre, and is about a hundred times more powerful than the electromagnetic interaction. Also called: **strong nuclear interaction** *or* **force.** See **interaction** (sense 2).

strongman ('strɒŋˌmæn) NOUN, PLURAL **-men.** [1] a performer, esp one in a circus, who performs feats of strength. [2] any person regarded as a source of power, capability, initiative, etc.

strong meat NOUN anything arousing fear, anger, repulsion, etc., except among a tolerant or receptive minority: *some scenes in the film were strong meat.*

strong-minded ADJECTIVE having strength of mind; firm, resolute, and determined.
▸ˌ**strong-'mindedly** ADVERB ▸ˌ**strong-'mindedness** NOUN

strong point NOUN something at which one excels; forte: *tactfulness was never his strong point.*

strongpoint ('strɒŋˌpɔɪnt) NOUN *Military* [1] a location that is by its site and nature easily defended. [2] a spot in a defensive position that is heavily defended.

strongroom ('strɒŋˌruːm, -ˌrʊm) NOUN a specially designed room in which valuables are locked for safety.

strong waters PLURAL NOUN an archaic name for alcoholic drink.

strong-willed ADJECTIVE having strength of will.

strongyle ('strɒndʒɪl) *or* **strongyl** ('strɒndʒəl) NOUN any parasitic nematode worm of the family *Strongylidae,* chiefly occurring in the intestines of horses.
▷HISTORY C19: via New Latin *Strongylus,* from Greek *strongulos* round

strongyloidiasis (ˌstrɒndʒɪlɔɪ'daɪəsɪs) *or* **strongyloidosis** (-'dəʊsɪs) NOUN an intestinal disease caused by infection with the nematode worm *Strongyloides stercoralis.*

strontia ('strɒntɪə) NOUN another name for **strontium monoxide.**
▷HISTORY C19: changed from STRONTIAN

strontian ('strɒntɪən) NOUN [1] another name for **strontianite.** [2] another name for **strontium** or **strontium monoxide.**
▷HISTORY C18: named after a parish in Argyll, where it was discovered

strontianite ('strɒntɪəˌnaɪt) NOUN a white, lightly coloured, or colourless mineral consisting of strontium carbonate in orthorhombic crystalline form: it is a source of strontium compounds. Formula: $SrCO_3$.

strontium ('strɒntɪəm) NOUN a soft silvery-white element of the alkaline earth group of metals, occurring chiefly in celestite and strontianite. Its compounds burn with a crimson flame and are used in fireworks. The radioisotope **strontium-90,** with a half-life of 28.1 years, is used in nuclear power sources and is a hazardous nuclear fall-out product. Symbol: Sr; atomic no.: 38; atomic wt.: 87.62; valency: 2; relative density: 2.54; melting pt.: 769°C; boiling pt.: 1384°C.
▷HISTORY C19: from New Latin, from STRONTIAN

strontium monoxide NOUN a white insoluble solid substance used in making strontium salts and purifying sugar. Formula: SrO. Also called: **strontium oxide, strontia.**

strontium unit NOUN a unit expressing the concentration of strontium-90 in an organic medium, such as soil, milk, bone, etc., relative to the concentration of calcium in the same medium. Abbreviation: **SU.**

strop (strɒp) NOUN [1] a leather strap or an abrasive strip for sharpening razors. [2] a rope or metal band around a block or deadeye for support. [3] *Informal* a temper tantrum: *he threw a strop and stormed off.* ◆

VERB **strops, stropping, stropped.** 4 (*tr*) to sharpen (a razor, etc.) on a strop.
▷HISTORY C14 (in nautical use: a strip of rope): via Middle Low German or Middle Dutch *strop,* ultimately from Latin *stroppus,* from Greek *strophos* cord; see STROPHE

strophanthin (strəʊˈfænθɪn) NOUN a toxic glycoside or mixture of glycosides obtained from the ripe seeds of certain species of strophanthus: used as a cardiac stimulant.

strophanthus (strəʊˈfænθəs) NOUN 1 any small tree or shrub of the apocynaceous genus *Strophanthus,* of tropical Africa and Asia, having strap-shaped twisted petals. The seeds of certain species yield the drug strophanthin. 2 the seeds of any of these plants.
▷HISTORY C19: New Latin, from Greek *strophos* twisted cord + *anthos* flower

strophe (ˈstrəʊfɪ) NOUN *Prosody* 1 (in ancient Greek drama) **a** the first of two movements made by a chorus during the performance of a choral ode. **b** the first part of a choral ode sung during this movement. 2 (in classical verse) the first division of the threefold structure of a Pindaric ode. 3 the first of two metrical systems used alternately within a poem. ◆ See also **antistrophe, epode.**
▷HISTORY C17: from Greek: a verse, literally: a turning, from *strephein* to twist

strophic (ˈstrɒfɪk, ˈstrəʊ-) *or less commonly* **strophical** ADJECTIVE 1 of, relating to, or employing a strophe or strophes. 2 (of a song) having identical or related music in each verse. Compare **through-composed.**

stroppy (ˈstrɒpɪ) ADJECTIVE **-pier, -piest.** *Brit informal* angry or awkward.
▷HISTORY C20: changed and shortened from OBSTREPEROUS
▸ **ˈstroppily** ADVERB ▸ **ˈstroppiness** NOUN

stroud (straʊd) NOUN a coarse woollen fabric.
▷HISTORY C17: perhaps named after *Stroud,* textile centre in Gloucestershire

strove (strəʊv) VERB the past tense of **strive.**

strow (strəʊ) VERB **strows, strowing, strowed; strown** *or* **strowed.** an archaic variant of **strew.**

stroy (strɔɪ) VERB an archaic variant of **destroy.**
▸ **ˈstroyer** NOUN

struck (strʌk) VERB 1 the past tense and past participle of **strike.** ◆ ADJECTIVE 2 *Chiefly US and Canadian* (of an industry, factory, etc.) shut down or otherwise affected by a labour strike.

struck measure NOUN a measure of grain, etc., in which the contents are made level with the top of the container rather than being heaped.

structural (ˈstrʌktʃərəl) ADJECTIVE 1 of, relating to, or having structure or a structure. 2 of, relating to, or forming part of the structure of a building. 3 of or relating to the structure and deformation of rocks and other features of the earth's crust. 4 of or relating to the structure of organisms; morphological. 5 *Chem* of, concerned with, caused by, or involving the arrangement of atoms in molecules.
▸ **ˈstructurally** ADVERB

structural formula NOUN a chemical formula showing the composition and structure of a molecule. The atoms are represented by symbols and the structure is indicated by showing the relative positions of the atoms in space and the bonds between them: *H–C≡C–H is the structural formula of acetylene.* See also **empirical formula, molecular formula.**

structuralism (ˈstrʌktʃərəˌlɪzəm) NOUN 1 an approach to anthropology and other social sciences and to literature that interprets and analyses its material in terms of oppositions, contrasts, and hierarchical structures, esp as they might reflect universal mental characteristics or organizing principles. Compare **functionalism.** 2 an approach to linguistics that analyses and describes the structure of language, as distinguished from its comparative and historical aspects.
▸ **ˈstructuralist** NOUN, ADJECTIVE

structural linguistics NOUN (*functioning as singular*) a descriptive approach to a synchronic or diachronic analysis of language on the basis of its structure as reflected by irreducible units of phonological, morphological, and semantic features.

structural psychology NOUN (formerly) a school of psychology using introspection to analyse experience into basic units.

structural steel NOUN a strong mild steel used in construction work.

structural unemployment NOUN *Economics* unemployment resulting from changes in the structure of an industry as a result of changes in either technology or taste.

structure (ˈstrʌktʃə) NOUN 1 a complex construction or entity. 2 the arrangement and interrelationship of parts in a construction, such as a building. 3 the manner of construction or organization: *the structure of society.* 4 *Biology* morphology; form. 5 *Chem* the arrangement of atoms in a molecule of a chemical compound: *the structure of benzene.* 6 *Geology* the way in which a mineral, rock, rock mass or stratum, etc., is made up of its component parts. 7 *Now rare* the act of constructing. ◆ VERB 8 (*tr*) to impart a structure to.
▷HISTORY C15: from Latin *structūra,* from *struere* to build

structured (ˈstrʌktʃəd) ADJECTIVE 1 having a distinct physical shape or form, often provided by an internal structure. 2 planned in broad outline; organized: *structured play for preschoolers.* 3 having a definite predetermined pattern; rigid: *structured hierarchy.*

strudel (ˈstruːdᵊl; *German* ˈʃtruːdəl) NOUN a thin sheet of filled dough rolled up and baked: *apple strudel.*
▷HISTORY German, from Middle High German *strodel* eddy, whirlpool, so called from the way the pastry is rolled

struggle (ˈstrʌgᵊl) VERB 1 (*intr; usually foll by for or against; may take an infinitive*) to exert strength, energy, and force; work or strive: *to struggle to obtain freedom.* 2 (*intr*) to move about strenuously so as to escape from something confining. 3 (*intr*) to contend, battle, or fight. 4 (*intr*) to go or progress with difficulty. ◆ NOUN 5 a laboured or strenuous exertion or effort. 6 a fight or battle. 7 the act of struggling. 8 **the struggle.** *S African* the concerted opposition to the state during the apartheid era.
▷HISTORY C14: of obscure origin
▸ **ˈstruggler** NOUN ▸ **ˈstruggling** ADJECTIVE ▸ **ˈstrugglingly** ADVERB

struggle for existence NOUN (*not in technical usage*) competition between organisms of a population, esp as a factor in the evolution of plants and animals. See also **natural selection.**

strum (strʌm) VERB **strums, strumming, strummed.** 1 to sound (the strings of a guitar, banjo, etc.) with a downward or upward sweep of the thumb or of a plectrum. 2 to play (chords, a tune, etc.) in this way.
▷HISTORY C18: probably of imitative origin; see THRUM[1]
▸ **ˈstrummer** NOUN

struma (ˈstruːmə) NOUN, *plural* **-mae** (-miː). 1 *Pathol* an abnormal enlargement of the thyroid gland; goitre. 2 *Botany* a swelling, esp one at the base of a moss capsule. 3 another word for **scrofula.**
▷HISTORY C16: from Latin: a scrofulous tumour, from *struere* to heap up
▸ **strumatic** (struːˈmætɪk) *or* **strumous** (ˈstruːməs) *or* **strumose** (ˈstruːməʊs) ADJECTIVE

Struma (ˈstruːmə) NOUN a river in S Europe, rising in SW Bulgaria near Sofia and flowing generally southeast through Greece to the Aegean. Length: 362 km (225 miles). Greek names: **Strimon, Strymon.**

strumpet (ˈstrʌmpɪt) NOUN *Archaic* a prostitute or promiscuous woman.
▷HISTORY C14: of unknown origin

strung (strʌŋ) VERB 1 a past tense and past participle of **string.** ◆ ADJECTIVE 2 **a** (of a piano, etc.) provided with strings, esp of a specified kind or in a specified manner. **b** (*in combination*): *gut-strung.* 3 **highly strung.** very nervous or volatile in character. Usual US and Canadian phrase: **high-strung.**

strung out ADJECTIVE *Slang* 1 addicted to a drug. 2 (of a drug addict) suffering or distressed because of the lack of a drug.

strung up ADJECTIVE (*postpositive*) *Informal* tense or nervous.

strut (strʌt) VERB **struts, strutting, strutted.** 1 (*intr*) to walk in a pompous manner; swagger. 2 (*tr*) to support or provide with struts. 3 **strut one's stuff.** *Informal* to behave or perform in a proud and confident manner; show off. ◆ NOUN 4 a structural member used mainly in compression, esp as part of a framework. 5 an affected, proud, or stiff walk.
▷HISTORY C14 *strouten* (in the sense: swell, stand out; C16: to walk stiffly), from Old English *strūtian* to stand stiffly; related to Low German *strutt* stiff
▸ **ˈstrutter** NOUN ▸ **ˈstrutting** ADJECTIVE ▸ **ˈstruttingly** ADVERB

struthious (ˈstruːθɪəs) ADJECTIVE 1 (of birds) related to or resembling the ostrich. 2 of, relating to, or designating all flightless (ratite) birds.
▷HISTORY C18: from Late Latin *strūthiō,* from Greek *strouthiōn,* from *strouthos* an ostrich

strychnic (ˈstrɪknɪk) ADJECTIVE of, relating to, or derived from strychnine.

strychnine (ˈstrɪkniːn) NOUN a white crystalline very poisonous alkaloid, obtained from the plant nux vomica: formerly used in small quantities as a stimulant of the central nervous system and the appetite. Formula: $C_{21}H_{22}O_2N_2$.
▷HISTORY C19: via French from New Latin *Strychnos,* from Greek *strukhnos* nightshade

strychninism (ˈstrɪknɪˌnɪzəm) NOUN *Pathol* poisoning caused by the excessive or prolonged use of strychnine.

Strymon (ˈstraɪmən) NOUN transliteration of the Greek name for the **Struma.**

stub (stʌb) NOUN 1 a short piece remaining after something has been cut, removed, etc.: *a cigar stub.* 2 the residual piece or section of a receipt, ticket, cheque, etc. 3 the usual US and Canadian word for **counterfoil.** 4 any short projection or blunted end. 5 the stump of a tree or plant. ◆ VERB **stubs, stubbing, stubbed.** (*tr*) 6 to strike (one's toe, foot, etc.) painfully against a hard surface. 7 (usually foll by *out*) to put (out a cigarette or cigar) by pressing the end against a surface. 8 to clear (land) of stubs. 9 to dig up (the roots) of (a tree or bush).
▷HISTORY Old English *stubb;* related to Old Norse *stubbi,* Middle Dutch *stubbe,* Greek *stupos* stem, stump

stub axle NOUN a short axle that carries one of the front steered wheels of a motor vehicle and is capable of limited angular movement about a kingpin.

Stubbies (ˈstʌbɪz) PLURAL NOUN *Trademark, Austral* a type of shorts.

stubble (ˈstʌbᵊl) NOUN 1 **a** the stubs of stalks left in a field where a crop has been cut and harvested. **b** (*as modifier*): *a stubble field.* 2 any bristly growth or surface.
▷HISTORY C13: from Old French *estuble,* from Latin *stupula,* variant of *stipula* stalk, stem, stubble *or* **ˈstubbly** ◆ ADJECTIVE

stubbled (ˈstʌbᵊld) ADJECTIVE 1 **a** having the stubs of stalks left after a crop has been cut and harvested. 2 having a bristly growth or surface.

stubble-jumper NOUN *Canadian slang* a prairie grain farmer.

stubborn (ˈstʌbᵊn) ADJECTIVE 1 refusing to comply, agree, or give in; obstinate. 2 difficult to handle, treat, or overcome. 3 persistent and dogged: *a stubborn crusade.*
▷HISTORY C14 *stoborne,* of obscure origin
▸ **ˈstubbornly** ADVERB ▸ **ˈstubbornness** NOUN

stubby (ˈstʌbɪ) ADJECTIVE **-bier, -biest.** 1 short and broad; stumpy or thickset. 2 bristling and stiff. ◆ NOUN 3 Also called: **stubbie.** *Austral slang* a small bottle of beer.
▸ **ˈstubbily** ADVERB ▸ **ˈstubbiness** NOUN

stub nail NOUN 1 a short thick nail. 2 a worn nail in a horseshoe.

STUC ABBREVIATION FOR Scottish Trades Union Congress.

stucco (ˈstʌkəʊ) NOUN, *plural* **-coes** *or* **-cos.** 1 a weather-resistant mixture of dehydrated lime, powdered marble, and glue, used in decorative mouldings on buildings. 2 any of various types of cement or plaster used for coating outside walls. 3 Also called: **stuccowork.** decorative work moulded in stucco. ◆ VERB **-coes** *or* **-cos, -coing, -coed.** 4 (*tr*) to apply stucco to.
▷HISTORY C16: from Italian, of Germanic origin; compare Old High German *stukki* a fragment, crust, Old English *stycce*
▸ **ˈstuccoer** NOUN

stuck (stʌk) VERB 1 the past tense and past participle of **stick**[2]. ◆ ADJECTIVE 2 *Informal* baffled or nonplussed. 3 (foll by *on*) *Slang* keen (on) or infatuated (with). 4 **get stuck in** *or* **into.** *Informal* **a** to perform (a task) with determination. **b** to attack (a person) verbally or physically.

stuck-up ADJECTIVE *Informal* conceited, arrogant, or snobbish.
▸ **'stuck-'upness** NOUN

stud[1] (stʌd) NOUN 1 a large-headed nail or other projection protruding from a surface, usually as decoration. 2 a type of fastener consisting of two discs at either end of a short shank, used to fasten shirtfronts, collars, etc. 3 *Building trades* a vertical member made of timber, steel, etc., that is used with others to construct the framework of a wall. 4 a headless bolt that is threaded at both ends, the centre portion being unthreaded. 5 any short projection on a machine, such as the metal cylinder that forms a journal for the gears on a screw-cutting lathe. 6 the crossbar in the centre of a link of a heavy chain. 7 one of a number of rounded projections on the sole of a boot or shoe to give better grip, as on a football boot. ◆ VERB **studs, studding, studded.** (*tr*) 8 to provide, ornament, or make with studs. 9 to dot or cover (with): *the park was studded with daisies.* 10 *Building trades* to provide or support (a wall, partition, etc.) with studs.
▹ **HISTORY** Old English *studu;* related to Old Norse *stoth* post, Middle High German *stud* post

stud[2] (stʌd) NOUN 1 a group of pedigree animals, esp horses, kept for breeding purposes. 2 any male animal kept principally for breeding purposes, esp a stallion. 3 a farm or stable where a stud is kept. 4 the state or condition of being kept for breeding purposes: *at stud; put to stud.* 5 (*modifier*) of or relating to such animals or the place where they are kept: *a stud farm; a stud horse.* 6 *Slang* a virile or sexually active man. 7 short for **stud poker.**
▹ **HISTORY** Old English *stōd;* related to Old Norse *stōth,* Old High German *stuot*

studbook ('stʌd,bʊk) NOUN a written record of the pedigree of a purebred stock, esp of racehorses.

studding ('stʌdɪŋ) NOUN 1 building studs collectively, esp as used to form a wall or partition. See also **stud**[1] (sense 3). 2 material that is used to form studs or serve as studs.

studdingsail ('stʌdɪŋ,seɪl; *Nautical* 'stʌns^{ə}l) NOUN *Nautical* a light auxiliary sail set outboard on spars on either side of a square sail. Also called: **stunsail, stuns'l.**
▹ **HISTORY** C16: *studding,* perhaps from Middle Low German, Middle Dutch *stōtinge,* from *stōten* to thrust; related to German *stossen*

student ('stju:d^{ə}nt) NOUN 1 **a** a person following a course of study, as in a school, college, university, etc. **b** (*as modifier*): *student teacher.* 2 a person who makes a thorough study of a subject.
▹ **HISTORY** C15: from Latin *studēns* diligent, from *studēre* to be zealous; see STUDY

student adviser NOUN another word for **counsellor** (sense 6).

studentification (stju:,dɛntɪfɪ'keɪʃən) NOUN the renting of particular accommodation exclusively to students.

studentship ('stju:d^{ə}ntʃɪp) NOUN 1 the role or position of a student. 2 another word for **scholarship** (sense 3).

Student's t NOUN a statistic often used to test the hypothesis that a random sample of normally distributed observations has a given mean, μ; given by $t = (\bar{x} - \mu)\sqrt{n/s}$ where $\bar{x}$ is the mean of the sample, *s* is its standard deviation, and *n* is the size of the sample.
▹ **HISTORY** after *Student,* the pen name of W. S. Gosset (1876–1937), English statistician and research scientist

student teacher NOUN a person who is teaching in a school for a limited period under supervision as part of a course to qualify as a teacher.

studenty ('stju:dəntɪ) ADJECTIVE *Informal, sometimes derogatory* denoting or exhibiting the characteristics believed typical of an undergraduate student.

studhorse ('stʌd,hɔ:s) NOUN another word for **stallion.**

studied ('stʌdɪd) ADJECTIVE 1 carefully practised, designed, or premeditated: *a studied reply.* 2 an archaic word for **learned.**
▸ **'studiedly** ADVERB ▸ **'studiedness** NOUN

studio ('stju:dɪ,əʊ) NOUN, *plural* **-dios.** 1 a room in which an artist, photographer, or musician works. 2 a room used to record television or radio programmes, make films, etc. 3 (*plural*) the premises of a radio, television, or film company.
▹ **HISTORY** C19: from Italian, literally: study, from Latin *studium* diligence

studio couch NOUN an upholstered couch, usually backless, convertible into a double bed.

studio flat NOUN a flat with one main room.

studious ('stju:dɪəs) ADJECTIVE 1 given to study. 2 of a serious, thoughtful, and hard-working character. 3 showing deliberation, care, or precision.
▹ **HISTORY** C14: from Latin *studiōsus* devoted to, from *studium* assiduity
▸ **'studiously** ADVERB ▸ **'studiousness** NOUN

stud poker NOUN a variety of poker in which the first card is dealt face down before each player and the next four are dealt face up (**five-card stud**) or in which the first two cards and the last card are dealt face down and the intervening four cards are dealt face up (**seven-card stud**), with bets made after each round. Often shortened to: **stud.**
▹ **HISTORY** C19: from STUD[2] + POKER[2]

stud welding NOUN the semiautomatic welding of a stud or similar piece of metal to a flat part, usually by means of an electric arc.

studwork ('stʌd,wɜ:k) NOUN 1 work decorated with studs. 2 the supporting framework of a wall or partition.

study ('stʌdɪ) VERB **studies, studying, studied.** 1 to apply the mind to the learning or understanding of (a subject), esp by reading: *to study languages; to study all night.* 2 (*tr*) to investigate or examine, as by observation, research, etc.: *to study the effects of heat on metal.* 3 (*tr*) to look at minutely; scrutinize. 4 (*tr*) to give much careful or critical thought to. 5 to take a course in (a subject), as at a college. 6 (*tr*) to try to memorize: *to study a part for a play.* 7 (*intr*) to meditate or contemplate; reflect. ◆ NOUN, *plural* **studies.** 8 **a** the act or process of studying. **b** (*as modifier*): *study group.* 9 a room used for studying, reading, writing, etc. 10 (*often plural*) work relating to a particular discipline: *environmental studies.* 11 an investigation and analysis of a subject, situation, etc.: *a study of transport provision in rural districts.* 12 a product of studying, such as a written paper or book. 13 a drawing, sculpture, etc., executed for practice or in preparation for another work. 14 a musical composition intended to develop one aspect of performing technique: *a study in spiccato bowing.* 15 *Theatre* a person who memorizes a part in the manner specified: *a quick study.* 16 **in a brown study.** in a reverie or daydream.
▹ **HISTORY** C13: from Old French *estudie,* from Latin *studium* zeal, inclination, from *studēre* to be diligent

stuff (stʌf) VERB (*mainly tr*) 1 to pack or fill completely; cram. 2 (*intr*) to eat large quantities. 3 to force, shove, or squeeze: *to stuff money into a pocket.* 4 to fill (food such as poultry or tomatoes) with a stuffing. 5 to fill (an animal's skin) with material so as to restore the shape of the live animal. 6 *Slang* to have sexual intercourse with (a woman). 7 *Tanning* to treat (an animal skin or hide) with grease. 8 *US and Canadian* to fill (a ballot box) with a large number of fraudulent votes. 9 (in marine transport) to pack (a container). See also **stuffing and stripping.** 10 *Slang* to ruin, frustrate, or defeat. ◆ NOUN 11 the raw material or fabric of something. 12 woollen cloth or fabric. 13 any general or unspecified substance or accumulation of objects. 14 stupid or worthless actions, speech, ideas, etc. 15 subject matter, skill, etc.: *he knows his stuff.* 16 a slang word for **money.** 17 *Slang* a drug, esp cannabis. 18 *Informal* **do one's stuff.** to do what is expected of one. 19 **that's the stuff.** that is what is needed. 20 *Brit slang* a girl or woman considered sexually (esp in the phrase **bit of stuff**).
▹ **HISTORY** C14: from Old French *estoffe,* from *estoffer* to furnish, provide, of Germanic origin; related to Middle High German *stopfen* to cram full
▸ **'stuffer** NOUN

> **Language note** Sense 6 of this word was formerly considered to be taboo, and it was labelled as such in previous editions of *Collins English Dictionary.* However, it has now become acceptable in speech, although some older or more conservative people may object to its use.

stuffed (stʌft) ADJECTIVE 1 filled with something, esp (of poultry and other food) filled with stuffing. 2 (foll by *up*) (of the nasal passages) blocked with mucus. 3 **get stuffed!** *Brit slang* an exclamation of contemptuous anger or annoyance, esp against another person.

stuffed shirt NOUN *Informal* a pompous or formal person.

stuff gown NOUN *Brit* a woollen gown worn by a barrister who has not taken silk.

stuffing ('stʌfɪŋ) NOUN 1 the material with which something is stuffed. 2 a mixture of chopped and seasoned ingredients with which poultry, meat, etc., is stuffed before cooking. 3 **knock the stuffing out of (someone).** to upset or dishearten (someone) completely.

stuffing and stripping NOUN (in marine transport) the packing and unpacking of containers.

stuffing box NOUN a small chamber in which an annular packing is compressed around a reciprocating or rotating rod or shaft to form a seal. Also called: **packing box.**

stuffing nut NOUN a large nut that is tightened to compress the packing in a stuffing box.

stuffy ('stʌfɪ) ADJECTIVE **stuffier, stuffiest.** 1 lacking fresh air. 2 excessively dull, staid, or conventional. 3 (of the nasal passages) blocked with mucus.
▸ **'stuffily** ADVERB ▸ **'stuffiness** NOUN

stull (stʌl) NOUN *Mining* a timber prop or platform in a stope.
▹ **HISTORY** C18: perhaps from German *Stollen,* from Old High German *stollo*

stultify ('stʌltɪ,faɪ) VERB **-fies, -fying, -fied.** (*tr*) 1 to make useless, futile, or ineffectual, esp by routine. 2 to cause to appear absurd or inconsistent. 3 to prove (someone) to be of unsound mind and thus not legally responsible.
▹ **HISTORY** C18: from Latin *stultus* stupid + *facere* to make
▸ **,stultifi'cation** NOUN ▸ **'stulti,fier** NOUN

stum (stʌm) (in wine-making) NOUN 1 a less common word for **must**[2]. 2 partly fermented wine added to fermented wine as a preservative. ◆ VERB **stums, stumming, stummed.** 3 to preserve (wine) by adding stum.
▹ **HISTORY** C17: from Dutch *stom* dumb; related to German *stumm*

stumble ('stʌmb^{ə}l) VERB (*intr*) 1 to trip or fall while walking or running. 2 to walk in an awkward, unsteady, or unsure way. 3 to make mistakes or hesitate in speech or actions. 4 (foll by *across* or *upon*) to come (across) by accident. 5 to commit a grave mistake or sin. ◆ NOUN 6 a false step, trip, or blunder. 7 the act of stumbling.
▹ **HISTORY** C14: related to Norwegian *stumla,* Danish dialect *stumle;* see STAMMER
▸ **'stumbler** NOUN ▸ **'stumbling** ADJECTIVE ▸ **'stumblingly** ADVERB

stumbling block NOUN any impediment or obstacle.

stumer ('stju:mə) NOUN 1 *Slang* a forgery or cheat. 2 *Irish dialect* a poor bargain. 3 *Scot* a stupid person. 4 **come a stumer.** *Austral slang* to crash financially.
▹ **HISTORY** of unknown origin

stump (stʌmp) NOUN 1 the base part of a tree trunk left standing after the tree has been felled or has fallen. 2 the part of something, such as a tooth, limb, or blade, that remains after a larger part has been removed. 3 *Informal, facetious* **a** (*often plural*) a leg. **b stir one's stumps.** to move or become active. 4 *Cricket* any of three upright wooden sticks that, with two bails laid across them, form a wicket (the **stumps**). 5 Also called: **tortillon.** a short sharply-pointed stick of cork or rolled paper or leather, used in drawing and shading. 6 a heavy tread or the sound of heavy footsteps. 7 a platform used by an orator when addressing a meeting. 8 **on**

the stump. *Chiefly US and Canadian* engaged in campaigning, esp by political speech-making. [9] *(often plural) Austral* a pile used to support a house. ◆ VERB [10] *(tr)* to stop, confuse, or puzzle. [11] *(intr)* to plod or trudge heavily. [12] *(tr) Cricket* (of a fielder, esp a wicketkeeper) to dismiss (a batsman) by breaking his wicket with the ball or with the ball in the hand while he is out of his crease. [13] *Chiefly US and Canadian* to campaign or canvass (an area), esp by political speech-making. [14] *(tr)* to reduce to a stump; lop. [15] *(tr)* to clear (land) of stumps.
▷HISTORY C14: from Middle Low German *stump;* related to Dutch *stomp,* German *Stumpf;* see STAMP
▸**'stumper** NOUN

stumpage ('stʌmpɪdʒ) NOUN [1] *US and Canadian* standing timber or its value. [2] *US and Canadian* the right to fell timber on another person's land. [3] *Canadian* a tax or royalty payable on each tree felled, esp on crown land.

stump-jump plough NOUN *Austral* a plough designed for use on land not cleared of stumps.

stump ranch *or* **farm** NOUN *Canadian informal* (in British Columbia) an undeveloped ranch in the bush where animals graze among the stumps of felled trees.

stump up VERB *(adverb) Brit informal* to give (the money required).

stumpwork ('stʌmp,wɜːk) NOUN a type of embroidery of the 15th to 17th centuries featuring raised or embossed figures, padded with cotton wool or hair.

stumpy ('stʌmpɪ) ADJECTIVE **stumpier, stumpiest.** [1] short and thickset like a stump; stubby. [2] abounding in or full of stumps.
▸**'stumpiness** NOUN

stun (stʌn) VERB **stuns, stunning, stunned.** *(tr)* [1] to render unconscious, as by a heavy blow or fall. [2] to shock or overwhelm. [3] to surprise or astound. ◆ NOUN [4] the state or effect of being stunned.
▷HISTORY C13 *stunen,* from Old French *estoner* to daze, stupefy, from Vulgar Latin *extonāre* (unattested), from Latin EX-[1] + *tonāre* to thunder

stung (stʌŋ) VERB [1] the past tense and past participle of **sting.** ◆ ADJECTIVE [2] *Austral slang* drunk; intoxicated.

stun gun NOUN a device designed to immobilize an animal or person temporarily without inflicting serious injury.

stunk (stʌŋk) VERB a past tense and past participle of **stink.**

stunner ('stʌnə) NOUN *Informal* a person or thing of great beauty, quality, size, etc.

stunning ('stʌnɪŋ) ADJECTIVE *Informal* very attractive, impressive, astonishing, etc.
▸**'stunningly** ADVERB

stunsail *or* **stuns'l** ('stʌnsᵊl) NOUN another word for **studdingsail.**

stunt[1] (stʌnt) VERB [1] *(tr)* to prevent or impede (the growth or development) of (a plant, animal, etc.). ◆ NOUN [2] the act or an instance of stunting. [3] a person, animal, or plant that has been stunted.
▷HISTORY C17 (as vb: to check the growth of): perhaps from C15 *stont* of short duration, from Old English *stunt* simple, foolish; sense probably influenced by Old Norse *stuttr* short in stature, dwarfed
▸**'stunted** ADJECTIVE ▸**'stuntedness** NOUN

stunt[2] (stʌnt) NOUN [1] an acrobatic or dangerous piece of action in a film, television programme, etc. [2] anything spectacular or unusual done to gain publicity. ◆ VERB [3] *(intr)* to perform a stunt or stunts.
▷HISTORY C19: US student slang, of unknown origin

stuntman ('stʌntmən) *or feminine* **stuntwoman** NOUN, *plural* **-men** *or* **-women.** a person who performs dangerous acts in a film, television programme, etc. in place of an actor.

stupa ('stuːpə) NOUN a domed edifice housing Buddhist or Jain relics. Also called: **tope.**
▷HISTORY C19: from Sanskrit: dome

stupe[1] (stjuːp) NOUN *Med* a hot damp cloth, usually sprinkled with an irritant, applied to the body to relieve pain by counterirritation.
▷HISTORY C14: from Latin *stuppa* flax, from Greek *stuppē*

stupe[2] (stjuːp) NOUN *US slang* a stupid person; clot.

stupefacient (,stjuːpɪ'feɪʃɪənt) NOUN [1] a drug that causes stupor. ◆ ADJECTIVE [2] of, relating to, or designating this type of drug.
▷HISTORY C17: from Latin *stupefacere* to make senseless, from *stupēre* to be stunned + *facere* to make

stupefaction (,stjuːpɪ'fækʃən) NOUN [1] astonishment. [2] the act of stupefying or the state of being stupefied.

stupefy ('stjuːpɪ,faɪ) VERB **-fies, -fying, -fied.** *(tr)* [1] to render insensitive or lethargic. [2] to confuse or astound.
▷HISTORY C16: from Old French *stupefier,* from Latin *stupefacere;* see STUPEFACIENT
▸**'stupe,fier** NOUN ▸**'stupe,fying** ADJECTIVE ▸**'stupe,fyingly** ADVERB

stupendous (stjuː'pɛndəs) ADJECTIVE astounding, wonderful, huge, etc.
▷HISTORY C17: from Latin *stupēre* to be amazed
▸**stu'pendously** ADVERB ▸**stu'pendousness** NOUN

stupid ('stjuːpɪd) ADJECTIVE [1] lacking in common sense, perception, or normal intelligence. [2] *(usually postpositive)* stunned, dazed, or stupefied: *stupid from lack of sleep.* [3] having dull mental responses; slow-witted. [4] trivial, silly, or frivolous. ◆ NOUN [5] *Informal* a stupid person.
▷HISTORY C16: from French *stupide,* from Latin *stupidus* silly, from *stupēre* to be amazed
▸**'stupidly** ADVERB ▸**'stupidness** NOUN

stupidity (stjuː'pɪdɪtɪ) NOUN, *plural* **-ties.** [1] the quality or state of being stupid. [2] a stupid act, remark, etc.

stupor ('stjuːpə) NOUN [1] a state of unconsciousness. [2] mental dullness; torpor.
▷HISTORY C17: from Latin, from *stupēre* to be aghast
▸**'stuporous** ADJECTIVE

sturdy[1] ('stɜːdɪ) ADJECTIVE **-dier, -diest.** [1] healthy, strong, and vigorous. [2] strongly built; stalwart.
▷HISTORY C13 (in the sense: rash, harsh): from Old French *estordi* dazed, from *estordir* to stun, perhaps ultimately related to Latin *turdus* a thrush (taken as representing drunkenness)
▸**'sturdily** ADVERB ▸**'sturdiness** NOUN

sturdy[2] ('stɜːdɪ) NOUN *Vet science* another name for **staggers** (sense 2) or **gid** (in sheep).
▷HISTORY C17: from STURDY[1] (in the obsolete sense: giddy)
▸**'sturdied** ADJECTIVE

sturgeon ('stɜːdʒən) NOUN any primitive bony fish of the family *Acipenseridae,* of temperate waters of the N hemisphere, having an elongated snout and rows of spines along the body: valued as a source of caviar and isinglass.
▷HISTORY C13: from Old French *estourgeon,* of Germanic origin; related to Old English *styria,* Old High German *sturio*

Sturmabteilung *German* ('ʃturm'aptailuŋ) NOUN the full name of the Nazi **SA.**
▷HISTORY literally: storm division

Sturmer ('stɜːmə) NOUN a variety of eating apple having a pale green skin and crisp tart flesh.
▷HISTORY C19: named after *Sturmer,* Suffolk

Sturm und Drang *German* ('ʃturm unt 'draŋ) NOUN a German literary movement of the latter half of the 18th century, characterized by a reaction against rationalism.
▷HISTORY literally: storm and stress, from the title of a play by F. M. von Klinger (1752–1831), German dramatist

Sturt's desert pea NOUN *Austral* the desert pea.
▷HISTORY named after Charles *Sturt* (1795–1869), English explorer of the Australian interior

stushie ('stʊʃɪ), **stishie,** *or* **stashie** NOUN *Scot* [1] a commotion, rumpus, or row. [2] a state of excitement or anxiety; a tizzy. ◆ Also called: **stooshie, stoushie.**
▷HISTORY C19: perhaps shortened from *ecstasy*

stutter ('stʌtə) VERB [1] to speak (a word, phrase, etc.) with recurring repetition of consonants, esp initial ones. [2] to make (an abrupt sound) repeatedly: *the gun stuttered.* ◆ NOUN [3] the act or habit of stuttering. [4] a stuttering sound.
▷HISTORY C16: related to Middle Low German *stötern,* Old High German *stōzan* to push against, Latin *tundere* to beat
▸**'stutterer** NOUN ▸**'stuttering** NOUN, ADJECTIVE ▸**'stutteringly** ADVERB

Stuttgart (*German* 'ʃtʊtgart) NOUN an industrial city in W Germany, capital of Baden-Württemberg state, on the River Neckar: developed around a stud farm (*Stuotgarten*) of the Counts of Württemberg. Pop.: 581 200 (2000).

STV ABBREVIATION FOR: [1] Scottish Television. [2] **Single Transferable Vote.**

sty (staɪ) NOUN, *plural* **sties.** [1] a pen in which pigs are housed and fed. [2] any filthy or corrupt place. ◆ VERB **sties, stying, stied.** [3] to enclose or be enclosed in a sty.
▷HISTORY Old English *stig;* related to Old Norse *stīa* pen, fold, Old High German *stīga,* Middle Dutch *stije*

stye *or* **sty** (staɪ) NOUN, *plural* **styes** *or* **sties.** inflammation of a sebaceous gland of the eyelid, usually caused by bacteria.
▷HISTORY C15 *styanye* (mistakenly taken as *sty on eye*), from Old English *stīgend* rising, hence swelling, stye + *ye* eye

Stygian ('stɪdʒɪən) ADJECTIVE [1] of or relating to the river Styx. [2] *Chiefly literary* **a** dark, gloomy, or hellish. **b** completely inviolable, as a vow sworn by the river Styx.
▷HISTORY C16: from Latin *Stygius,* from Greek *Stugios,* from *Stux* STYX; related to *stugein* to hate

style (staɪl) NOUN [1] a form of appearance, design, or production; type or make: *a new style of house.* [2] the way in which something is done: *good or bad style.* [3] the manner in which something is expressed or performed, considered as separate from its intrinsic content, meaning, etc. [4] a distinctive, formal, or characteristic manner of expression in words, music, painting, etc. [5] elegance or refinement of manners, dress, etc. [6] prevailing fashion in dress, looks, etc. [7] a fashionable or ostentatious mode of existence: *to live in style.* [8] the particular mode of orthography, punctuation, design, etc., followed in a book, journal, etc., or in a printing or publishing house. [9] *Chiefly Brit* the distinguishing title or form of address of a person or firm. [10] *Botany* the stalk of a carpel, bearing the stigma. [11] *Zoology* a slender pointed structure, such as the piercing mouthparts of certain insects. [12] a method of expressing or calculating dates. See **Old Style, New Style.** [13] another word for **stylus** (sense 1). [14] the arm of a sundial. ◆ VERB *(mainly tr)* [15] to design, shape, or tailor: *to style hair.* [16] to adapt or make suitable (for). [17] to make consistent or correct according to a printing or publishing style. [18] to name or call; designate: *to style a man a fool.* [19] *(intr)* to decorate objects using a style or stylus.
▷HISTORY C13: from Latin *stylus, stilus* writing implement, hence characteristics of the writing, style
▸**'stylar** ADJECTIVE ▸**'styler** NOUN

stylebook ('staɪl,bʊk) NOUN a book containing rules and examples of punctuation, typography, etc., for the use of writers, editors, and printers.

stylet ('staɪlɪt) NOUN [1] *Surgery* **a** a wire for insertion into a flexible cannula or catheter to maintain its rigidity or patency during passage. **b** a slender probe. [2] *Zoology* any small pointed bristle-like part.
▷HISTORY C17: from French *stilet,* from Old Italian STILETTO; influenced in spelling by Latin *stylus* STYLE

stylie ('staɪlɪ) ADJECTIVE *NZ informal* fashion-conscious.

styliform ('staɪlɪ,fɔːm) ADJECTIVE *Zoology* shaped like a stylus or bristle: *a styliform antenna.*
▷HISTORY C16: from New Latin *stiliformis,* from Latin STYLUS

styling mousse NOUN *Hairdressing* a light foamy substance applied to the hair before styling in order to retain the shape of the style.

stylish ('staɪlɪʃ) ADJECTIVE having style; smart; fashionable.
▸**'stylishly** ADVERB ▸**'stylishness** NOUN

stylist ('staɪlɪst) NOUN [1] a person who performs, writes, or acts with attention to style. [2] a designer of clothes, décor, etc. [3] a hairdresser who styles hair. [4] a designer whose job is to coordinate the style of products, advertising material, etc.

stylistic (staɪ'lɪstɪk) ADJECTIVE of or relating to style, esp artistic or literary style.
▸**sty'listically** ADVERB

stylistics (staɪ'lɪstɪks) NOUN *(functioning as singular* or plural) a branch of linguistics concerned with the study of characteristic choices in use of language, esp literary language, as regards sound, form, or vocabulary, made by different individuals or social groups in different situations of use.

stylite ('staɪlaɪt) NOUN *Christianity* one of a class of recluses who in ancient times lived on the top of high pillars.
▷HISTORY C17: from Late Greek *stulitēs,* from Greek *stulos* a pillar
▸**stylitic** (staɪ'lɪtɪk) ADJECTIVE

stylize *or* **stylise** ('staɪlaɪz) VERB (*tr*) to give a conventional or established stylistic form to.
▸**ˌstyli'zation** *or* **ˌstyli'sation** NOUN ▸**'stylizer** *or* **'styliser** NOUN

stylo- *or before a vowel* **styl-** COMBINING FORM [1] (in biology) a style: *stylopodium.* [2] indicating a column or point: *stylobate; stylograph.*
▷HISTORY from Greek *stulos* column

stylobate ('staɪləˌbeɪt) NOUN a continuous horizontal course of masonry that supports a colonnade.
▷HISTORY C17: from Latin *stylobatēs,* from Greek *stulos* pillar + *-batēs,* from *bainein* to tread, walk

stylograph ('staɪləˌgræf, -ˌgrɑːf) NOUN a fountain pen having a fine hollow tube as the writing point instead of a nib.
▷HISTORY C19: from STYL(US) + -GRAPH

stylographic (ˌstaɪlə'græfɪk) *or* **stylographical** ADJECTIVE of or relating to a stylograph or stylography.
▸**ˌstylo'graphically** ADVERB

stylography (staɪ'lɒgrəfɪ) NOUN the art or method of writing, drawing, or engraving with a stylus or style.

styloid ('staɪlɔɪd) ADJECTIVE [1] resembling a stylus. [2] *Anatomy* of or relating to a projecting process of the temporal bone.
▷HISTORY C18: from New Latin *styloides,* from Greek *stuloeidēs* like a STYLUS; influenced also by Greek *stulos* pillar

stylolite ('staɪləˌlaɪt) NOUN any of the small striated columnar or irregular structures within the strata of some limestones.
▷HISTORY C19: from Greek *stulos* pillar + -LITE
▸**stylolitic** (ˌstaɪlə'lɪtɪk) ADJECTIVE

stylophone ('staɪləˌfəʊn) NOUN a type of battery-powered electronic instrument played with a steel-tipped penlike stylus.
▷HISTORY C20: from STYL(US) + -PHONE

stylopize *or* **stylopise** ('staɪləˌpaɪz) VERB (*tr*) (of a stylops) to parasitize (a host): *the bee was stylopized.*

stylopodium (ˌstaɪlə'pəʊdɪəm) NOUN, *plural* **-dia** (-dɪə). *Botany* a swelling at the base of the style in umbelliferous plants.
▷HISTORY C19: New Latin, from Greek *stulos* pillar + -PODIUM

stylops ('staɪlɒps) NOUN, *plural* **-lopes** (-ləˌpiːz). any insect of the order *Strepsiptera,* including the genus *Stylops,* living as a parasite in other insects, esp bees and wasps: the females remain in the body of the host but the males move between hosts.
▷HISTORY C19: New Latin, from Greek, from *stulos* a pillar + *ōps* an eye, from the fact that the male insect has stalked compound eyes

stylostixis (ˌstaɪləʊ'stɪksɪs) NOUN *Med* another name for **acupuncture.**
▷HISTORY C20: New Latin, from Greek *stulos* style (pointed instrument) + *stixis* mark, spot

stylus ('staɪləs) NOUN, *plural* **-li** (-laɪ) *or* **-luses.** [1] Also called: **style.** a pointed instrument for engraving, drawing, or writing. [2] a tool used in ancient times for writing on wax tablets, which was pointed at one end and blunt at the other for erasing mistakes. [3] a device attached to the cartridge in the pick-up arm of a record player that rests in the groove in the record, transmitting the vibrations to the sensing device in the cartridge. It consists of or is tipped with a hard material, such as diamond or sapphire.
▷HISTORY C18: from Latin, variant of *stilus* writing implement; see STYLE
▸**'stylar** ADJECTIVE

stymie *or* **stymy** ('staɪmɪ) VERB **-mies, -mieing, -mied** *or* **-mies, -mying, -mied.** (*tr; often passive*) [1] to hinder or thwart. [2] *Golf* to impede with a stymie. ◆ NOUN, *plural* **-mies.** [3] *Golf* (formerly) a situation on the green in which an opponent's ball is blocking the line between the hole and the ball about to be played: an obstructing ball may now be lifted and replaced by a marker. [4] a situation of obstruction.
▷HISTORY C19: of uncertain origin

stypsis ('stɪpsɪs) NOUN the action, application, or use of a styptic.
▷HISTORY C19: via New Latin from Late Latin: astringency, from Greek *stupsis,* from *stuphein* to contract

styptic ('stɪptɪk) ADJECTIVE [1] contracting the blood vessels or tissues. ◆ NOUN [2] a styptic drug.
▷HISTORY C14: via Late Latin, from Greek *stuptikos* capable of contracting; see STYPSIS
▸**stypticity** (stɪp'tɪsɪtɪ) NOUN

styptic pencil NOUN a styptic agent in the form of a small stick, for application to razor nicks, etc.

styracaceous (ˌstaɪrə'keɪʃəs) ADJECTIVE of, relating to, or belonging to the *Styracaceae,* a family of Asian and American trees and shrubs having leathery leaves: includes storax and silver bell.
▷HISTORY C19: *styrac-,* from STYRAX

styrax ('staɪræks) NOUN any tropical or subtropical tree of the genus *Styrax,* which includes the storaxes.
▷HISTORY C16: via Latin from Greek *sturax*

styrene ('staɪriːn) NOUN a colourless oily volatile flammable water-insoluble liquid made from ethylene and benzene. It is an unsaturated compound and readily polymerizes: used in making synthetic plastics and rubbers. Formula: $C_6H_5CH{:}CH_2$. See also **polystyrene.**
▷HISTORY C20: from STYR(AX) + -ENE

Styria ('stɪərɪə) NOUN a mountainous state of SE Austria: rich mineral resources. Capital: Graz. Pop.: 1 185 911 (2000). Area: 16 384 sq. km (6326 sq. miles). German name: **Steiermark.**

styrofoam ('staɪrəˌfəʊm) NOUN *Trademark* (*sometimes not capital*) a light, expanded polystyrene plastic.
▷HISTORY C20: from POLYSTYRENE + FOAM

Styx (stɪks) NOUN *Greek myth* a river in Hades across which Charon ferried the souls of the dead.
▷HISTORY from Greek *Stux;* related to *stugein* to hate

SU ABBREVIATION FOR: [1] **strontium unit.** ◆ [2] INTERNATIONAL CAR REGISTRATION FOR Belarus. [from *Soviet Union*]

suable ('sjuːəbᵊl) ADJECTIVE liable to be sued in a court.
▷HISTORY C17: from SUE + -ABLE
▸**ˌsua'bility** NOUN

Suakin ('suːɑːkɪn) NOUN a port in the NE Sudan, on the Red Sea: formerly the chief port of the African Red Sea; now obstructed by a coral reef. Pop.: 5511 (latest est.).

suasion ('sweɪʒən) NOUN a rare word for **persuasion.**
▷HISTORY C14: from Latin *suāsiō,* from *suādēre* to PERSUADE
▸**'suasive** ADJECTIVE

suave (swɑːv) ADJECTIVE (esp of a man) displaying smoothness and sophistication in manner or attitude; urbane.
▷HISTORY C16: from Latin *suāvis* sweet
▸**'suavely** ADVERB ▸**suavity** ('swɑːvɪtɪ) *or* **'suaveness** NOUN

sub (sʌb) NOUN [1] short for several words beginning with *sub-,* such as **subaltern, subeditor, submarine, subordinate, subscription, substandard, substitute,** and **substratum** (in photography). [2] *Brit informal* an advance payment of wages or salary. Formal term: **subsistence allowance.** ◆ VERB **subs, subbing, subbed.** [3] (*intr*) to serve as a substitute. [4] (*intr*) *Informal* to act as a substitute (for). [5] *Brit informal* to grant or receive (an advance payment of wages or salary). [6] (*tr*) *Informal* short for **subedit.** [7] (*tr*) *Photog* to apply a substratum to (a film or plate base).

sub. ABBREVIATION FOR: [1] subeditor. [2] subito (in music). [3] subscription. [4] substitute.

sub- PREFIX [1] situated under or beneath: *subterranean.* [2] secondary in rank; subordinate: *subeditor.* [3] falling short of; less than or imperfectly: *subarctic; subhuman.* [4] forming a subdivision or subordinate part of a whole: *subcommittee.* [5] (in chemistry) **a** indicating that a compound contains a relatively small proportion of a specified element: *suboxide.* **b** indicating that a salt is basic salt: *subacetate.*
▷HISTORY from Latin *sub*

subacetate (sʌb'æsɪˌteɪt) NOUN any one of certain crystalline basic acetates containing hydroxide ions in addition to acetate ions. For example, the subacetate of aluminium is probably $Al_3(OH)_2(CH_3COO)$.

subacid (sʌb'æsɪd) ADJECTIVE (esp of some fruits) moderately acid or sour.
▸**subacidity** (ˌsʌbə'sɪdɪtɪ) *or* **sub'acidness** NOUN
▸**sub'acidly** ADVERB

subacute (ˌsʌbə'kjuːt) ADJECTIVE intermediate between acute and chronic.

subadar *or* **subahdar** ('suːbəˌdɑː) NOUN (formerly) the chief native officer of a company of Indian soldiers in the British service. Also called: **subah.**
▷HISTORY C17: via Urdu from Persian, from *sūba* province + *-dār* holding

subah ('suːbɑː) NOUN (in India) [1] a province in the Mogul empire. [2] another word for **subadar.**
▷HISTORY C18: via Urdu and Persian from Arabic *sūba* province

subalpine (sʌb'ælpaɪn) ADJECTIVE [1] situated in or relating to the regions at the foot of mountains. [2] (of plants) growing below the treeline in mountainous regions.

subaltern ('sʌbᵊltən) NOUN [1] a commissioned officer below the rank of captain in certain armies, esp the British. [2] a person of inferior rank or position. [3] *Logic* **a** the relation of one proposition to another when the first is implied by the second, esp the relation of a particular to a universal proposition. **b** (*as modifier*): *a subaltern relation.* ◆ ADJECTIVE [4] of inferior position or rank.
▷HISTORY C16: from Late Latin *subalternus,* from Latin SUB- + *alternus* alternate, from *alter* the other

subalternate (sʌb'ɔːltənɪt) ADJECTIVE [1] (of leaves) having an arrangement intermediate between alternate and opposite. [2] following in turn. [3] of lesser quality or status.
▸**subalternation** (sʌbˌɔːltə'neɪʃən) NOUN

subantarctic (ˌsʌbænt'ɑːktɪk) ADJECTIVE of or relating to latitudes immediately north of the Antarctic Circle.

subapostolic (ˌsʌbæpə'stɒlɪk) ADJECTIVE *Christianity* of or relating to the era after that of the Apostles.

subaqua (ˌsʌb'ækwə) ADJECTIVE of or relating to underwater sport: *subaqua swimming; a subaqua club.*
▷HISTORY from SUB- + Latin *aqua* water

subaquatic (ˌsʌbə'kwætɪk, -'kwɒt-) ADJECTIVE [1] living or growing partly in water and partly on land. [2] of or relating to conditions, existence, or activities under water.

subaqueous (sʌb'eɪkwɪəs, -'ækwɪ-) ADJECTIVE occurring, appearing, formed, or used under water.

subarctic (sʌb'ɑːktɪk) ADJECTIVE of or relating to latitudes immediately south of the Arctic Circle.

subarid (sʌb'ærɪd) ADJECTIVE receiving slightly more rainfall than arid regions; moderately dry.

subassembly (ˌsʌbə'semblɪ) NOUN, *plural* **-blies.** a number of machine components integrated into a unit forming part of a larger assembly.

subastral (sʌb'æstrəl) ADJECTIVE a rare word for **terrestrial.**

subatomic (ˌsʌbə'tɒmɪk) ADJECTIVE [1] of, relating to, or being a particle making up an atom or a process occurring within atoms: *the electron is a subatomic particle.* [2] having dimensions smaller than atomic dimensions.

subaudition (ˌsʌbɔː'dɪʃən) NOUN [1] something that is not directly stated but implied. [2] the ability or act of understanding that which is only implied.
▷HISTORY C18: from Late Latin *subaudīre,* from SUB- + Latin *audīre* to hear

subauricular (ˌsʌbɔː'rɪkjulə) ADJECTIVE *Anatomy* situated below the auricle of the ear.

subaxillary (ˌsʌb'æksɪlərɪ) ADJECTIVE [1] situated or growing beneath the axil of a plant: *subaxillary bracts.* [2] situated beneath the armpit.

subbase ('sʌbˌbeɪs) NOUN the lowest part of a pedestal, base, or skirting. Compare **surbase.**

subbasement ('sʌbˌbeɪsmənt) NOUN an

underground storey of a building beneath the main basement.

subbass *or* **subbase** ('sʌbˌbeɪs) NOUN another name for **bourdon.**

Subbuteo (sə'bju:tɪəʊ) NOUN *Trademark* a football game played on a table, with toy players affixed to rounded bases which are flicked with the fingers.
▷HISTORY C20: arbitrarily named, from Latin *subbuteo,* the specific name of the hobby hawk *Falco subbuteo*

subcalibre *or US* **subcaliber** (sʌb'kælɪbə) ADJECTIVE [1] (of a projectile) having a calibre less than that of the firearm from which it is discharged and therefore either fitted with a disc or fired through a tube inserted into the barrel. [2] of, relating to, or firing subcalibre projectiles.

subcarrier ('sʌbˌkærɪə) NOUN a subsidiary carrier wave that is modulated with information and applied as modulation to a main carrier wave that is already modulated with other information.

subcartilaginous (sʌbˌkɑ:tɪ'lædʒɪnəs) ADJECTIVE [1] composed partly of cartilage: *a subcartilaginous skeleton.* [2] situated beneath a cartilage or a cartilaginous structure.

subcelestial (ˌsʌbsɪ'lɛstɪəl) ADJECTIVE [1] beneath the heavens; terrestrial. ◆ NOUN [2] a subcelestial object.

subception (səb'sɛpʃən) NOUN *Psychol* another word for **subliminal perception.**

subchloride (sʌb'klɔ:raɪd) NOUN a chloride of an element that contains less chlorine than its common chloride.

subclass ('sʌbˌklɑ:s) NOUN [1] a principal subdivision of a class. [2] *Biology* a taxonomic group that is a subdivision of a class. [3] *Maths* another name for **subset** (sense 1). ◆ VERB [4] *(tr)* to assign to a subclass.

sub-clause NOUN a subordinate section of a larger clause in a document, contract, etc.

subclavian (sʌb'kleɪvɪən) ADJECTIVE *Anatomy* (of an artery, vein, area, etc.) situated below the clavicle.
▷HISTORY C17: from New Latin *subclāvius,* from Latin SUB- + *clavis* key

subclimax (sʌb'klaɪmæks) NOUN *Ecology* a community in which development has been arrested before climax has been attained.
▸**subclimactic** (ˌsʌbklaɪ'mæktɪk) ADJECTIVE

subclinical (sʌb'klɪnɪkᵊl) ADJECTIVE *Med* of or relating to the stage in the course of a disease before the symptoms are first noted.
▸**sub'clinically** ADVERB

subcommission ('sʌbkəˌmɪʃən) NOUN a committee of people answering to a larger commission: *the doping subcommission reported to the medical commission.*

subcommittee ('sʌbkəˌmɪtɪ) NOUN a distinct and often subordinate division of a committee.

subconscious (sʌb'kɒnʃəs) ADJECTIVE [1] acting or existing without one's awareness: *subconscious motive.* ◆ NOUN [2] *Psychoanal* that part of the mind which is on the fringe of consciousness and contains material of which it is possible to become aware by redirecting attention. Compare **preconscious** (sense 2), **unconscious** (sense 5).
▸**sub'consciously** ADVERB ▸**sub'consciousness** NOUN

subcontinent (sʌb'kɒntɪnənt) NOUN a large land mass that is a distinct part of a continent, such as India is of Asia.
▸**subcontinental** (ˌsʌbkɒntɪ'nɛntᵊl) ADJECTIVE

subcontract NOUN (sʌb'kɒntrækt) [1] a subordinate contract under which the supply of materials, services, or labour is let out to someone other than a party to the main contract. ◆ VERB (ˌsʌbkən'trækt) [2] *(intr; often foll by for)* to enter into or make a subcontract. [3] *(tr)* to let out (work) on a subcontract.

subcontractor (ˌsʌbkən'træktə) NOUN a person, company, etc., that enters into a subcontract, esp a firm that undertakes to complete part of another's contract.

subcontrary (sʌb'kɒntrərɪ) *Logic* ◆ ADJECTIVE [1] (of a pair of propositions) related such that they cannot both be false at once, although they may be true together. Compare **contrary** (sense 5), **contradictory** (sense 3). ◆ NOUN, *plural* **-ries.** [2] a statement that cannot be false when a given statement is false.

subcortex (sʌb'kɔ:tɛks) NOUN, *plural* **-tices** (-tɪˌsi:z). *Anatomy* the matter of the brain situated beneath the cerebral cortex.
▸**subcortical** (sʌb'kɔ:tɪkᵊl) ADJECTIVE

subcritical (sʌb'krɪtɪkᵊl) ADJECTIVE *Physics* (of a nuclear reaction, power station, etc.) having or involving a chain reaction that is not self-sustaining; not yet critical.

subculture NOUN ('sʌbˌkʌltʃə) [1] a subdivision of a national culture or an enclave within it with a distinct integrated network of behaviour, beliefs, and attitudes. [2] a culture of microorganisms derived from another culture. ◆ VERB (sʌb'kʌltʃə) [3] *(tr)* to inoculate (bacteria from one culture medium) onto another medium.
▸**sub'cultural** ADJECTIVE

subcutaneous (ˌsʌbkju:'teɪnɪəs) ADJECTIVE *Med* situated, used, or introduced beneath the skin: *a subcutaneous injection.*
▷HISTORY C17: from Late Latin *subcutāneus,* from SUB- + Latin *cutis* skin + -EOUS
▸**ˌsubcu'taneously** ADVERB

subdeacon (ˌsʌb'di:kən) NOUN *Chiefly RC Church* [1] a cleric who assists at High Mass. [2] (formerly) a person ordained to the lowest of the major orders.
▸**subdeaconate** (sʌb'di:kənɪt) NOUN

subdelirium (ˌsʌbdə'lɪrɪəm) NOUN, *plural* **-liriums** *or* **-liria** (-'lɪrɪə). mild or intermittent delirium.

subdiaconate (ˌsʌbdaɪ'ækənɪt, -ˌneɪt) NOUN the rank or office of a subdeacon.
▷HISTORY C18: from Medieval Latin *subdiaconus* subdeacon + -ATE[2]; see DEACON
▸**ˌsubdi'aconal** ADJECTIVE

subdistrict ('sʌbˌdɪstrɪkt) NOUN **a** a smaller part of a larger area marked off for administrative or other purposes. **b** *(as modifier)*: *subdistrict regional police.*

subdivide (ˌsʌbdɪ'vaɪd, 'sʌbdɪˌvaɪd) VERB [1] to divide (something) resulting from an earlier division. [2] *(tr) US and Canadian* to divide (land) into lots for sale.
▸**ˌsubdi'vider** NOUN

subdivision ('sʌbdɪˌvɪʒən) NOUN [1] the process, instance, or state of being divided again following upon an earlier division. [2] a portion that is the result of subdividing. [3] *US and Canadian* a tract of land for building resulting from subdividing land. [4] *Canadian* a housing development built on such a tract.
▸**ˌsubdi'visional** ADJECTIVE

subdominant (sʌb'dɒmɪnənt) *Music* ◆ NOUN [1] the fourth degree of a major or minor scale. [2] a key or chord based on this. ◆ ADJECTIVE [3] of or relating to the subdominant.

subduct (səb'dʌkt) VERB *(tr)* [1] *Physiol* to draw or turn (the eye, etc.) downwards. [2] *Rare* to take away; deduct.
▷HISTORY C17: from Latin *subdūcere,* from SUB- + *dūcere* to lead, bring

subduction (səb'dʌkʃən) NOUN [1] the act of subducting, esp of turning the eye downwards. [2] *Geology* the process of one tectonic plate sliding under another, resulting in tensions and faulting in the earth's crust, with earthquakes and volcanic eruptions.

subduction zone NOUN *Geology* a long narrow, often arcuate, zone along which subduction takes place.

subdue (səb'dju:) VERB **-dues, -duing, -dued.** *(tr)* [1] to establish ascendancy over by force. [2] to overcome and bring under control, as by intimidation or persuasion. [3] to hold in check or repress (feelings, emotions, etc.). [4] to render less intense or less conspicuous.
▷HISTORY C14 *sobdue,* from Old French *soduire* to mislead, from Latin *subdūcere* to remove; English sense influenced by Latin *subdere* to subject
▸**sub'duable** ADJECTIVE ▸**sub'duably** ADVERB ▸**sub'dual** NOUN

subdued (səb'dju:d) ADJECTIVE [1] cowed, passive, or shy. [2] gentle or quiet: *a subdued whisper.* [3] (of colours, etc.) not harsh or bright: *subdued lighting.*
▸**sub'duedly** ADVERB ▸**sub'duedness** NOUN

subdural (sʌb'djʊərəl) ADJECTIVE *Anatomy* between the dura mater and the arachnoid: *subdural haematoma.*

subedit (sʌb'ɛdɪt) VERB to edit and correct (written or printed material).

subeditor (sʌb'ɛdɪtə) NOUN a person who checks and edits copy, esp on a newspaper.

subequatorial (sʌbˌɛkwə'tɔ:rɪəl) ADJECTIVE situated in or characteristic of regions immediately north or south of equatorial regions.

suberic acid (sju:'bɛrɪk) NOUN another name for **octanedioic acid.**
▷HISTORY C18: from French *subérique,* from Latin *sūber* cork (from which the acid is obtained)

suberin ('sju:bərɪn) NOUN a fatty or waxy substance that is present in the walls of cork cells, making them impermeable to water and resistant to decay.
▷HISTORY C19: from Latin *sūber* cork + -IN

suberize *or* **suberise** ('sju:bəˌraɪz) VERB *(tr) Botany* to impregnate (cell walls) with suberin during the formation of corky tissue.
▸**ˌsuberi'zation** *or* **ˌsuberi'sation** NOUN

suberose ('sju:bəˌrəʊs), **subereous** (sju:'bɛrɪəs), *or* **suberic** (sju:'bɛrɪk) ADJECTIVE *Botany* relating to, resembling, or consisting of cork; corky.

subfamily ('sʌbˌfæmɪlɪ) NOUN, *plural* **-lies.** [1] *Biology* a taxonomic group that is a subdivision of a family. [2] any analogous subdivision, as of a family of languages.

subfloor ('sʌbˌflɔ:) NOUN a rough floor that forms a base for a finished floor.

subfusc ('sʌbfʌsk) ADJECTIVE [1] devoid of brightness or appeal; drab, dull, or dark. ◆ NOUN [2] (at Oxford University) formal academic dress.
▷HISTORY C18: from Latin *subfuscus* dusky, from *fuscus* dark

subgenus (sʌb'dʒi:nəs, -'dʒɛn-, 'sʌbˌdʒi:nəs, -ˌdʒɛn-) NOUN, *plural* **-genera** (-'dʒɛnərə) *or* **-genuses.** *Biology* a taxonomic group that is a subdivision of a genus but of higher rank than a species.
▸**subgeneric** (ˌsʌbdʒə'nɛrɪk) ADJECTIVE

subglacial (sʌb'gleɪsɪəl) ADJECTIVE formed or occurring at the bottom of a glacier.
▸**sub'glacially** ADVERB

subgrade ('sʌbˌgreɪd) NOUN the ground beneath a roadway or pavement.

subgroup ('sʌbˌgru:p) NOUN [1] a distinct and often subordinate division of a group. [2] a mathematical group whose members are members of another group, both groups being subject to the same rule of combination.

subha ('su:ba:) NOUN *Islam* a string of beads used in praying and meditating.
▷HISTORY from Arabic

subharmonic (ˌsʌbhɑ:'mɒnɪk) NOUN a fraction of a frequency.

subheading ('sʌbˌhɛdɪŋ) *or* **subhead** NOUN [1] the heading or title of a subdivision or subsection of a printed work. [2] a division subordinate to a main heading or title.

subhuman (sʌb'hju:mən) ADJECTIVE [1] of, relating to, or designating animals that are below man (*Homo sapiens*) in evolutionary development. [2] less than human.

subimago (ˌsʌbɪ'meɪgəʊ) NOUN, *plural* **-imagoes** *or* **-imagines** (-ɪ'mædʒəˌni:z). the first winged stage of the mayfly, with dull opaque wings, known to anglers as a **dun**, before it metamorphoses into the shiny gauzy imago or **spinner.**

subindex (sʌb'ɪndɛks) NOUN, *plural* **-dices** (-dɪˌsi:z) *or* **-dexes.** [1] another word for **subscript** (sense 2). [2] *US* an index to a subcategory.

subinfeudate (ˌsʌbɪn'fju:deɪt) VERB to grant (lands) by subinfeudation.

subinfeudation (ˌsʌbɪnfjʊ'deɪʃən) NOUN [1] (in feudal society) the granting of land by a vassal to another man who became his vassal. [2] the tenure or relationship so established.

subinfeudatory (ˌsʌbɪn'fju:dətərɪ, -trɪ) (in feudal society) NOUN, *plural* **-ries.** [1] a man who held his fief by a subinfeudation. ◆ ADJECTIVE [2] of or relating to subinfeudation.

subirrigate (sʌb'ɪrɪˌgeɪt) VERB to irrigate (land) by means of an underground system of pipe lines or by natural moisture in the subsoil.
▸**ˌsubirri'gation** NOUN

subitize *or* **subitise** ('sʌbɪˌtaɪz) VERB *Psychol* to perceive the number of (a group of items) at a

glance and without counting: *the maximum number of items that can be subitized is about five.*
▷HISTORY C20: from Latin *subitus* sudden + -IZE

subito ('su:bɪˌtəʊ) ADVERB *Music* (preceding or following a dynamic marking, etc.) suddenly; immediately. Abbreviation: **sub.**
▷HISTORY C18: via Italian from Latin: suddenly, from *subitus* sudden, from *subīre* to approach, from SUB- (indicating stealth) + *īre* to go

subj. ABBREVIATION FOR: 1 subject. 2 subjective(ly). 3 subjunctive.

subjacent (sʌb'dʒeɪsᵊnt) ADJECTIVE 1 forming a foundation; underlying. 2 lower than though not directly below: *tall peaks and their subjacent valley.*
▷HISTORY C16: from Latin *subjacēre* to lie close, adjoin, be under, from SUB- + *jacēre* to lie
▸**sub'jacency** NOUN ▸**sub'jacently** ADVERB

subject NOUN ('sʌbdʒɪkt) 1 **a** the predominant theme or topic, as of a book, discussion, etc. **b** (*in combination*): *subject-heading.* 2 any branch of learning considered as a course of study. 3 *Grammar, logic* a word, phrase, or formal expression about which something is predicated or stated in a sentence; for example, *the cat* in the sentence *The cat catches mice.* 4 a person or thing that undergoes experiment, analysis, treatment, etc. 5 a person who lives under the rule of a monarch, government, etc. 6 an object, figure, scene, etc., as selected by an artist or photographer for representation. 7 *Philosophy* **a** that which thinks or feels as opposed to the object of thinking and feeling; the self or the mind. **b** a substance as opposed to its attributes. 8 Also called: **theme.** *Music* a melodic or thematic phrase used as the principal motif of a fugue, the basis from which the musical material is derived in a sonata-form movement, or the recurrent figure in a rondo. 9 *Logic* **a** the term of a categorial statement of which something is predicated. **b** the reference or denotation of the subject term of a statement. The subject of *John is tall* is not the name *John,* but John himself. 10 an originating motive. 11 **change the subject.** to select a new topic of conversation. ◆ ADJECTIVE ('sʌbdʒɪkt) (*usually postpositive* and foll by *to*) 12 being under the power or sovereignty of a ruler, government, etc.: *subject peoples.* 13 showing a tendency (towards): *a child subject to indiscipline.* 14 exposed or vulnerable: *subject to ribaldry.* 15 conditional upon: *the results are subject to correction.* ◆ ADVERB 16 **subject to.** (*preposition*) under the condition that: *we accept, subject to her agreement.* ◆ VERB (səb'dʒɛkt) (*tr*) 17 (foll by *to*) to cause to undergo the application (of): *they subjected him to torture.* 18 (*often passive;* foll by *to*) to expose or render vulnerable or liable (to some experience): *he was subjected to great danger.* 19 (foll by *to*) to bring under the control or authority (of): *to subject a soldier to discipline.* 20 *Now rare* to subdue or subjugate. 21 *Rare* to present for consideration; submit. 22 *Obsolete* to place below. ◆ Abbreviation: **subj.**
▷HISTORY C14: from Latin *subjectus* brought under, from *subicere* to place under, from SUB- + *jacere* to throw
▸**sub'jectable** ADJECTIVE ▸**subˌjecta'bility** NOUN ▸**'subjectless** ADJECTIVE ▸**'subject-ˌlike** ADJECTIVE

subject catalogue NOUN *Library science* a catalogue with entries arranged by subject in a classified sequence.

subjectify (səb'dʒɛktɪˌfaɪ) VERB **-fies, -fying, -fied.** (*tr*) to make subjective or interpret subjectively.
▸**subˌjectifi'cation** NOUN

subjection (səb'dʒɛkʃən) NOUN the act or process of subjecting or the state of being subjected.

subjective (səb'dʒɛktɪv) ADJECTIVE 1 belonging to, proceeding from, or relating to the mind of the thinking subject and not the nature of the object being considered. 2 of, relating to, or emanating from a person's emotions, prejudices, etc.: *subjective views.* 3 relating to the inherent nature of a person or thing; essential. 4 existing only as perceived and not as a thing in itself. 5 *Med* (of a symptom, condition, etc.) experienced only by the patient and incapable of being recognized or studied by anyone else. 6 *Grammar* denoting a case of nouns and pronouns, esp in languages having only two cases, that identifies the subject of a finite verb and (in formal use in English) is selected for predicate complements, as in *It is I.* See also **nominative** (sense 1). ◆ NOUN 7 *Grammar* **a** the subjective case. **b** a subjective word or speech element. ◆ Abbreviation: **subj.** Compare **objective.**
▸**sub'jectively** ADVERB ▸**ˌsubjec'tivity** *or* **sub'jectiveness** NOUN

subjective idealism NOUN *Philosophy* the theory that all experience is of ideas in the mind.

subjective intension NOUN *Logic* the associations that an expression has for an individual; the intension he believes it to have.

subjectivism (səb'dʒɛktɪˌvɪzəm) NOUN 1 the meta-ethical doctrine that there are no absolute moral values but that these are variable in the same way as taste is. 2 any similar philosophical theory, for example, about truth or perception. 3 any theological theory that attaches primary importance to religious experience. 4 the quality or condition of being subjective.
▸**sub'jectivist** NOUN ▸**subˌjecti'vistic** ADJECTIVE ▸**subˌjecti'vistically** ADVERB

subject matter NOUN the substance or main theme of a book, discussion, debate, etc.

subject-raising NOUN *Transformational grammar* a rule that moves the subject of a complement clause into the clause in which it is embedded, as in the derivation of *He is likely to be late* from *It is likely that he will be late.*

subjoin (sʌb'dʒɔɪn) VERB (*tr*) to add or attach at the end of something spoken, written, etc.
▷HISTORY C16: from French *subjoindre,* from Latin *subjungere* to add to, from *sub-* in addition + *jungere* to JOIN
▸**sub'joinder** NOUN ▸**subjunction** (sʌb'dʒʌŋkʃən) NOUN

sub judice ('dʒu:dɪsɪ) ADJECTIVE (*usually postpositive*) before a court of law or a judge; under judicial consideration.
▷HISTORY Latin

subjugate ('sʌbdʒʊˌgeɪt) VERB (*tr*) 1 to bring into subjection. 2 to make subservient or submissive.
▷HISTORY C15: from Late Latin *subjugāre* to subdue, from Latin SUB- + *jugum* yoke
▸**subjugable** ('sʌbdʒəgəbᵊl) ADJECTIVE ▸**ˌsubju'gation** NOUN ▸**'subjuˌgator** NOUN

subjunctive (səb'dʒʌŋktɪv) ADJECTIVE 1 *Grammar* denoting a mood of verbs used when the content of the clause is being doubted, supposed, feared true, etc., rather than being asserted. The rules for its use and the range of meanings it may possess vary considerably from language to language. In the following sentence, *were* is in the subjunctive: *I'd think very seriously about that if I were you.* Compare **indicative.** ◆ NOUN 2 *Grammar* **a** the subjunctive mood. **b** a verb in this mood. ◆ Abbreviation: **subj.**
▷HISTORY C16: via Late Latin *subjunctīvus,* from Latin *subjungere* to SUBJOIN
▸**sub'junctively** ADVERB

subkingdom (sʌb'kɪŋdəm) NOUN *Biology* a taxonomic group that is a subdivision of a kingdom.

sublapsarianism (ˌsʌblæp'sɛərɪəˌnɪzəm) NOUN another word for **infralapsarianism.**
▷HISTORY C17 *sublapsarian,* via New Latin, from Latin SUB- + *lāpsus* a fall
▸**ˌsublap'sarian** NOUN, ADJECTIVE

sublease NOUN ('sʌbˌli:s) 1 a lease of property made by a person who is himself a lessee or tenant of that property. ◆ VERB (sʌb'li:s) 2 to grant a sublease of (property); sublet. 3 (*tr*) to take, obtain, or hold by sublease.
▸**sublessee** (ˌsʌblɛ'si:) NOUN ▸**sublessor** (ˌsʌblɛ'sɔ:) NOUN

sublet VERB (sʌb'lɛt) **-lets, -letting, -let.** 1 to grant a sublease of (property). 2 to let out (work, etc.) under a subcontract. ◆ NOUN ('sʌbˌlɛt) 3 *Informal, chiefly US* a sublease.

sublieutenant (ˌsʌblə'tɛnənt) NOUN the most junior commissioned officer in the Royal Navy and certain other navies.
▸**ˌsublieu'tenancy** NOUN

sublimate ('sʌblɪˌmeɪt) VERB 1 *Psychol* to direct the energy of (a primitive impulse, esp a sexual one) into activities that are considered to be socially more acceptable. 2 (*tr*) to make purer; refine. ◆ NOUN 3 *Chem* the material obtained when a substance is sublimed. ◆ ADJECTIVE 4 exalted or purified.
▷HISTORY C16: from Latin *sublīmāre* to elevate, from *sublīmis* lofty; see SUBLIME
▸**sublimable** ('sʌbləməbᵊl) ADJECTIVE

sublimation (ˌsʌblɪ'meɪʃən) NOUN 1 (in Freudian psychology) the diversion of psychic energy derived from sexual impulses into nonsexual activity, esp of a creative nature. 2 the process or an instance of sublimating. 3 something sublimated. 4 *Chem* the process or instance or subliming.

sublime (sə'blaɪm) ADJECTIVE 1 of high moral, aesthetic, intellectual, or spiritual value; noble; exalted. 2 inspiring deep veneration, awe, or uplifting emotion because of its beauty, nobility, grandeur, or immensity. 3 unparalleled; supreme: *a sublime compliment.* 4 *Poetic* of proud bearing or aspect. 5 *Archaic* raised up. ◆ NOUN **the sublime.** 6 something that is sublime. 7 the ultimate degree or perfect example: *the sublime of folly.* ◆ VERB 8 (*tr*) to make higher or purer. 9 to change or cause to change directly from a solid to a vapour or gas without first melting: *to sublime iodine; many mercury salts sublime when heated.* 10 to undergo or cause to undergo this process followed by a reverse change directly from a vapour to a solid: *to sublime iodine onto glass.*
▷HISTORY C14: from Latin *sublīmis* lofty, perhaps from *sub-* up to + *līmen* lintel
▸**sub'limely** ADVERB ▸**sublimity** (sə'blɪmɪtɪ) NOUN

Sublime Porte NOUN the full name of the **Porte.**

subliminal (sʌb'lɪmɪnᵊl) ADJECTIVE 1 resulting from processes of which the individual is not aware. 2 (of stimuli) less than the minimum intensity or duration required to elicit a response.
▷HISTORY C19: from Latin SUB- below + *līmen* threshold
▸**sub'liminally** ADVERB

subliminal advertising NOUN a form of advertising on film or television that employs subliminal images to influence the viewer unconsciously.

subliminal perception NOUN *Psychol* perception of or reaction to a stimulus that occurs without awareness or consciousness. Also called: **subception.**

sublingual (sʌb'lɪŋgwəl) ADJECTIVE *Anatomy* situated beneath the tongue.

sublittoral (sʌb'lɪtərəl) ADJECTIVE 1 (of marine organisms) growing, living, or situated close to the seashore: *a sublittoral plant.* 2 of or relating to the zone between the low tide mark and 100 m depth.

sublunary (sʌb'lu:nərɪ) ADJECTIVE 1 situated between the moon and the earth. 2 of or relating to the earth or world.
▷HISTORY C16: via Late Latin, from Latin SUB- + *lūna* moon

subluxate (sʌb'lʌkseɪt) VERB (*tr*) *Pathol* to partially dislocate.
▸**ˌsublux'ation** NOUN

sub-machine-gun NOUN a portable automatic or semiautomatic light gun with a short barrel, firing pistol ammunition: designed to be fired from the hip or shoulder.

submarginal (sʌb'mɑ:dʒɪnᵊl) ADJECTIVE 1 below the minimum requirements. 2 situated close to the margin of an organ or part. 3 (of land) infertile and unprofitable for cultivation.
▸**sub'marginally** ADVERB

submarine ('sʌbməˌri:n, ˌsʌbmə'ri:n) NOUN 1 a vessel, esp one designed for warfare, capable of operating for protracted periods below the surface of the sea. Often shortened to: **sub.** 2 (*modifier*) **a** of or relating to a submarine: *a submarine captain.* **b** occurring or situated below the surface of the sea: *a submarine cable.*

submariner (sʌb'mærɪnə) NOUN a crewman in a submarine.

submaxillary (ˌsʌbmæk'sɪlərɪ) ADJECTIVE of, relating to, or situated close to the lower jaw.

submaxillary gland NOUN (in mammals) either of a pair of salivary glands situated on each side behind the lower jaw.

submediant (sʌb'mi:dɪənt) *Music* ◆ NOUN 1 the sixth degree of a major or minor scale. 2 a key or chord based on this. ◆ ADJECTIVE 3 of or relating to the submediant. ◆ Also (US and Canadian): **superdominant.**

submental (sʌb'mɛntᵊl) ADJECTIVE *Anatomy* situated beneath the chin.
▷HISTORY from SUB- + Latin *mentum* chin

submerge (səb'mɜ:dʒ) *or* **submerse** (səb'mɜ:s)

VERB [1] to plunge, sink, or dive or cause to plunge, sink, or dive below the surface of water, etc. [2] (*tr*) to cover with water or some other liquid. [3] (*tr*) to hide; suppress. [4] (*tr*) to overwhelm, as with work, difficulties, etc.
▷HISTORY C17: from Latin *submergere*, from SUB- + *mergere* to immerse
▸**sub'mergence** *or* **submersion** (səb'mɜːʃən) NOUN

submerged (səb'mɜːdʒd) *or* **submersed** (səb'mɜːst) ADJECTIVE [1] (of plants or plant parts) growing beneath the surface of the water. [2] hidden; obscured. [3] overwhelmed or overburdened.

submerged arc welding NOUN a type of heavy electric-arc welding using mechanically fed bare wire with the arc submerged in powdered flux to keep out oxygen.

submersible (səb'mɜːsəbəl) *or* **submergible** (səb'mɜːdʒɪbəl) ADJECTIVE [1] able to be submerged. [2] capable of operating under water, etc. ◆ NOUN [3] a vessel designed to operate under water for short periods. [4] a submarine taking one or more men that is designed and equipped to carry out work in deep water below the levels at which divers can work.
▸**sub,mersi'bility** *or* **sub,mergi'bility** NOUN

submicroscopic (,sʌbmaɪkrə'skɒpɪk) ADJECTIVE too small to be seen through an optical microscope.
▸**,submicro'scopically** ADVERB

subminiature (sʌb'mɪnɪətʃə) ADJECTIVE smaller than miniature.

subminiature camera NOUN a pocket-sized camera, usually using 16 millimetre film with a very fine grain so that negatives can produce considerably enlarged prints.

subminiaturize *or* **subminiaturise** (sʌb'mɪnɪətʃə,raɪz) VERB (*tr*) to make subminiature, as in the manufacture of electronic equipment, etc.
▸**sub,miniaturi'zation** *or* **sub,miniaturi'sation** NOUN

submiss (səb'mɪs) ADJECTIVE *Archaic or poetic* [1] docile; submissive. [2] soft in tone.
▷HISTORY C16: from Latin *submissus* lowered, gentle, from *submittere* to reduce, from SUB- + *mittere* to send

submission (səb'mɪʃən) NOUN [1] an act or instance of submitting. [2] something submitted; a proposal, argument, etc. [3] the quality or condition of being submissive to another. [4] the act of referring a document, etc., for the consideration of someone else. [5] *Law* **a** an agreement by the parties to a dispute to refer the matter to arbitration. **b** the instrument referring a disputed matter to arbitration. [6] (in wrestling) the act of causing such pain to one's opponent that he submits. Compare **fall** (sense 48). [7] *Archaic* a confession of error.

submissive (səb'mɪsɪv) ADJECTIVE of, tending towards, or indicating submission, humility, or servility.
▸**sub'missively** ADVERB ▸**sub'missiveness** NOUN

submit (səb'mɪt) VERB **-mits, -mitting, -mitted.** [1] (often foll by *to*) to yield (oneself), as to the will of another person, a superior force, etc. [2] (foll by *to*) to subject or be voluntarily subjected (to analysis, treatment, etc.). [3] (*tr;* often foll by *to*) to refer (something to someone) for judgment or consideration: *to submit a claim.* [4] (*tr; may take a clause as object*) to state, contend, or propose deferentially. [5] (*intr;* often foll by *to*) to defer or accede (to the decision, opinion, etc., of another).
▷HISTORY C14: from Latin *submittere* to place under, from SUB- + *mittere* to send
▸**sub'mittable** *or* **sub'missible** ADJECTIVE ▸**sub'mittal** NOUN
▸**sub'mitter** NOUN

submontane (sʌb'mɒnteɪn) ADJECTIVE [1] situated on or characteristic of the lower slopes of a mountain. [2] beneath a mountain or mountain range.
▷HISTORY C19: from Latin SUB- + *mōns* mountain
▸**sub'montanely** ADVERB

submucosa (,sʌbmjuː'kəʊsə) NOUN, *plural* **-cosae** (-'kəʊsiː). *Anatomy* the connective tissue beneath a mucous membrane.

submultiple (sʌb'mʌltɪpəl) NOUN [1] a number that can be divided into another number an integral number of times without a remainder. ◆ ADJECTIVE [2] being a submultiple of a quantity or number.

subnormal (sʌb'nɔːməl) ADJECTIVE [1] less than the normal. [2] having a low intelligence, esp having an IQ of less than 70. ◆ NOUN [3] a subnormal person.
▸**subnormality** (,sʌbnɔː'mælɪtɪ) NOUN ▸**sub'normally** ADVERB

subnuclear (sʌb'njuːklɪə) ADJECTIVE [1] of or relating to particles within the nucleus of an atom. [2] of a lesser level of organization than the nucleus of an atom.

suboceanic (sʌb,əʊʃɪ'ænɪk) ADJECTIVE formed or situated beneath the ocean or ocean floor.

subofficer (sʌb'ɒfɪsə) NOUN a subordinate officer.

suborbital (sʌb'ɔːbɪtəl) ADJECTIVE [1] (of a rocket, missile, etc.) having a flight path that is less than one complete orbit of the earth or other celestial body. [2] *Anatomy* situated beneath the orbit of the eye.

suborder ('sʌb,ɔːdə) NOUN *Biology* a taxonomic group that is a subdivision of an order.
▸**sub'ordinal** ADJECTIVE

subordinary (sʌb'ɔːdɪnərɪ, -dɪnrɪ) NOUN, *plural* **-naries.** any of several heraldic bearings of secondary importance to the ordinary, such as the lozenge, the orle, and the fret.

subordinate ADJECTIVE (sə'bɔːdɪnɪt) [1] of lesser order or importance. [2] under the authority or control of another: *a subordinate functionary.* ◆ NOUN (sə'bɔːdɪnɪt) [3] a person or thing that is subordinate. ◆ VERB (sə'bɔːdɪ,neɪt) (*tr; usually foll by to*) [4] to put in a lower rank or position (than). [5] to make subservient: *to subordinate mind to heart.*
▷HISTORY C15: from Medieval Latin *subordināre*, from Latin SUB- + *ordō* rank
▸**sub'ordinately** ADVERB ▸**sub,ordi'nation** *or* **sub'ordinateness** NOUN ▸**sub'ordinative** ADJECTIVE

subordinate clause NOUN *Grammar* a clause with an adjectival, adverbial, or nominal function, rather than one that functions as a separate sentence in its own right. Compare **coordinate clause, main clause.**

subordinated debt NOUN *Commerce* a debt that an unsecured creditor can only claim, in the event of a liquidation, after the claims of secured creditors have been paid.

subordinating conjunction NOUN a conjunction that introduces subordinate clauses, such as *if, because, although,* and *until.* Compare **coordinating conjunction.**

subordinationism (sə,bɔːdɪ'neɪʃə,nɪzəm) NOUN either of two interpretations of the doctrine of the Trinity, often regarded as heretical, according to which the Son is subordinate to the Father or the Holy Ghost is subordinate to both.
▸**sub,ordi'nationist** NOUN

suborn (sə'bɔːn) VERB (*tr*) [1] to bribe, incite, or instigate (a person) to commit a wrongful act. [2] *Criminal law* to induce (a witness) to commit perjury.
▷HISTORY C16: from Latin *subornāre*, from *sub-* secretly + *ornāre* to furnish
▸**subornation** (,sʌbɔː'neɪʃən) NOUN ▸**subornative** (sʌ'bɔːnətɪv) ADJECTIVE ▸**sub'orner** NOUN

Subotica (*Serbo-Croat* 'subɔtitsa) NOUN a town in NE Serbia and Montenegro, in Serbia near the border with Hungary: agricultural and industrial centre. Pop.: 100 386 (1991). Hungarian name: **Szabadka.**

suboxide (sʌb'ɒksaɪd) NOUN an oxide of an element containing less oxygen than the common oxide formed by the element: *carbon suboxide,* C_2O_3.

subphylum (sʌb'faɪləm) NOUN, *plural* **-la** (-lə). *Biology* a taxonomic group that is a subdivision of a phylum.
▸**sub'phylar** ADJECTIVE

subplot ('sʌb,plɒt) NOUN a subordinate or auxiliary plot in a novel, play, film, etc.

subpoena (səb'piːnə) NOUN [1] a writ issued by a court of justice requiring a person to appear before the court at a specified time. ◆ VERB **-nas, -naing, -naed.** [2] (*tr*) to serve with a subpoena.
▷HISTORY C15: from Latin: under penalty

subpopulation (,sʌbpɒpju'leɪʃən) NOUN *Statistics* a subgroup of a statistical population.

sub-post office NOUN (in Britain) a post office run by a **sub-postmaster** or **sub-postmistress** as a self-employed agent for the Post Office.

subprincipal (sʌb'prɪnsɪpəl) NOUN a vice-principal in a college, etc.

subprogram ('sʌb,prəʊgræm) NOUN *Computing* a part of a program that can be designed and tested independently.

subregion (sʌb'riːdʒən) NOUN a subdivision of a region, esp a zoogeographical or ecological region.
▸**sub'regional** ADJECTIVE

subreption (səb'rɛpʃən) NOUN [1] *Now rare* the concealment of facts in order to obtain a benefit, esp an ecclesiastical benefit or, in Scots Law, a grant from the Crown. Compare **obreption.** [2] any deceitful misrepresentation or concealment of facts.
▷HISTORY C17: from Latin *subreptiō* theft, from *subripere,* from *sub-* secretly + *rapere* to seize
▸**subreptitious** (,sʌbrɛp'tɪʃəs) ADJECTIVE

subrogate ('sʌbrə,geɪt) VERB (*tr*) *Law* to put (one person or thing) in the place of another in respect of a right or claim.
▷HISTORY C16: from Latin *subrogāre,* from *sub-* in place of + *rogāre* to ask

subrogation (,sʌbrə'geɪʃən) NOUN *Law* the substitution of one person or thing for another, esp the placing of a surety who has paid the debt in the place of the creditor, entitling him to payment from the original debtor.

sub rosa ('rəʊzə) ADVERB in secret.
▷HISTORY Latin, literally: under the rose; from the rose that, in ancient times, was hung over the council table, as a token of secrecy

subroutine ('sʌbruː,tiːn) NOUN a section of a computer program that is stored only once but can be used when required at several different points in the program, thus saving space. Also called: **procedure.**

sub-Saharan ADJECTIVE in, of, or relating to Africa south of the Sahara desert.

subscapular (sʌb'skæpjʊlə) ADJECTIVE [1] (of a muscle or artery) situated beneath the scapula. ◆ NOUN [2] any subscapular muscle or artery.

subscribe (səb'skraɪb) VERB [1] (usually foll by *to*) to pay or promise to pay (a sum of money) as a contribution (to a fund or charity, for a magazine, etc.), esp at regular intervals. [2] to inscribe or sign (one's name, etc.) at the end of a contract, will, or other document. [3] (*intr;* foll by *to*) to give support or approval: *to subscribe to the theory of transubstantiation.*
▷HISTORY C15: from Latin *subscrībere* to write underneath, from SUB- + *scrībere* to write
▸**sub'scriber** NOUN

subscriber trunk dialling NOUN *Brit* a service by which telephone subscribers can obtain trunk calls by dialling direct without the aid of an operator. Abbreviation: **STD.** US and Canadian equivalent: **direct distance dialing.**

subscript ('sʌbskrɪpt) ADJECTIVE [1] *Printing* (of a character) written or printed below the line. Compare **superscript.** ◆ NOUN [2] Also called: **subindex.** a subscript character.

subscription (səb'skrɪpʃən) NOUN [1] a payment or promise of payment for consecutive issues of a magazine, newspaper, book, etc., over a specified period of time. [2] **a** the advance purchase of tickets for a series of concerts, operas, etc. **b** (*as modifier*): *a subscription concert.* [3] an amount of money paid or promised, as to a charity, or the fund raised in this way. [4] an offer to buy shares or bonds issued by a company. [5] the act of signing one's name to a document, etc. [6] a signature or other appendage attached to the bottom of a document, etc. [7] agreement, consent, or acceptance expressed by or as if by signing one's name. [8] a signed document, statement, etc. [9] *Chiefly Brit* the membership dues or fees paid to a society or club. [10] acceptance of a fixed body of articles of faith, doctrines, or principles laid down as universally binding upon all the members of a Church. [11] *Med* that part of a written prescription directing the pharmacist how to mix and prepare the ingredients: rarely seen today as modern drugs are mostly prepackaged by the manufacturers. [12] an advance order for a new product. [13] **a** the sale of books, etc., prior to printing. **b** (*as modifier*): *a subscription edition.* [14] *Archaic* allegiance; submission. ◆ Abbreviation: **sub.**
▸**sub'scriptive** ADJECTIVE

subscription library NOUN a commercial lending library.

subscription television NOUN another name for **pay television.**

subsection (sʌbˈsɛkʃən) NOUN a section of a section; subdivision.

subsellium (sʌbˈsɛlɪəm) NOUN a rare word for **misericord** (sense 1).
▷HISTORY C19: from Latin, from SUB- + *sella* seat

subsequence (ˈsʌbsɪkwəns) NOUN [1] the fact or state of being subsequent. [2] a subsequent incident or occurrence. [3] (ˌsʌbˈsiːkwəns) *Maths* a sequence derived from a given sequence by selecting certain of its terms and retaining their order. Thus, <a_2, a_3> is a subsequence of <a_1, a_2, a_3>, while <a_3, a_2> is not.

subsequent (ˈsʌbsɪkwənt) ADJECTIVE occurring after; succeeding.
▷HISTORY C15: from Latin *subsequēns* following on, from *subsequī*, from *sub-* near + *sequī* to follow
▸ **ˈsubsequently** ADVERB ▸ **ˈsubsequentness** NOUN

subsere (ˈsʌbˌsɪə) NOUN a secondary sere arising when the progress of a sere towards its climax has been interrupted.
▷HISTORY C20: SUB- + SERE[2]

subserve (səbˈsɜːv) VERB (*tr*) [1] to be helpful or useful to. [2] *Obsolete* to be subordinate to.
▷HISTORY C17: from Latin *subservīre* to be subject to, from SUB- + *servīre* to serve

subservient (səbˈsɜːvɪənt) ADJECTIVE [1] obsequious in behaviour or attitude. [2] serving as a means to an end. [3] a less common word for **subordinate** (sense 2).
▷HISTORY C17: from Latin *subserviēns* complying with, from *subservīre* to SUBSERVE
▸ **subˈserviently** ADVERB ▸ **subˈservience** *or* **subˈserviency** NOUN

subset (ˈsʌbˌsɛt) NOUN [1] *Maths* **a** a set the members of which are all members of some given class: *A is a subset of B* is usually written $A \subseteq B$. **b proper subset.** one that is strictly contained within a larger class and excludes some of its members. Symbol: $A \subset B$. [2] a set within a larger set.

subshrub (ˈsʌbˌʃrʌb) NOUN a small bushy plant that is woody except for the tips of the branches.
▸ **ˈsubˌshrubby** ADJECTIVE

subside (səbˈsaɪd) VERB (*intr*) [1] to become less loud, excited, violent, etc.; abate. [2] to sink or fall to a lower level. [3] (of the surface of the earth, etc.) to cave in; collapse. [4] (of sediment, etc.) to sink or descend to the bottom; settle.
▷HISTORY C17: from Latin *subsīdere* to settle down, from *sub-* down + *sīdere* to settle
▸ **subˈsider** NOUN

subsidence (səbˈsaɪdᵊns, ˈsʌbsɪdᵊns) NOUN [1] the act or process of subsiding or the condition of having subsided. [2] *Geology* the gradual sinking of landforms to a lower level as a result of earth movements, mining operations, etc.

subsidiarity (səbˌsɪdɪˈærɪtɪ) NOUN [1] (in the Roman Catholic Church) a principle of social doctrine that all social bodies exist for the sake of the individual so that what individuals are able to do, society should not take over, and what small societies can do, larger societies should not take over. [2] (in political systems) the principle of devolving decisions to the lowest practical level.

subsidiary (səbˈsɪdɪərɪ) ADJECTIVE [1] serving to aid or supplement; auxiliary. [2] of lesser importance; subordinate in function. ◆ NOUN, *plural* **-aries**. [3] a person who or thing that is subsidiary. [4] short for **subsidiary company.**
▷HISTORY C16: from Latin *subsidiārius* supporting, from *subsidium* SUBSIDY
▸ **subˈsidiarily** ADVERB ▸ **subˈsidiariness** NOUN

subsidiary coin NOUN a coin of denomination smaller than that of the standard monetary unit.

subsidiary company NOUN a company with at least half of its capital stock owned by another company.

subsidize *or* **subsidise** (ˈsʌbsɪˌdaɪz) VERB (*tr*) [1] to aid or support with a subsidy. [2] to obtain the aid of by means of a subsidy.
▸ **ˌsubsiˈdizable** *or* **ˌsubsiˈdisable** ADJECTIVE
▸ **ˌsubsidiˈzation** *or* **ˌsubsidiˈsation** NOUN ▸ **ˈsubsiˌdizer** *or* **ˈsubsiˌdiser** NOUN

subsidy (ˈsʌbsɪdɪ) NOUN, *plural* **-dies**. [1] a financial aid supplied by a government, as to industry, for reasons of public welfare, the balance of payments, etc. [2] *English history* a financial grant made originally for special purposes by Parliament to the Crown. [3] any monetary contribution, grant, or aid.
▷HISTORY C14: from Anglo-Norman *subsidie*, from Latin *subsidium* assistance, from *subsidēre* to remain, from *sub-* down + *sedēre* to sit

subsist (səbˈsɪst) VERB (*mainly intr*) [1] (often foll by *on*) to be sustained; manage to live: *to subsist on milk*. [2] to continue in existence. [3] (foll by *in*) to lie or reside by virtue (of); consist. [4] *Philosophy* **a** to exist as a concept or relation rather than a fact. **b** to be conceivable. [5] (*tr*) *Obsolete* to provide with support.
▷HISTORY C16: from Latin *subsistere* to stand firm, from *sub-* up + *sistere* to make a stand
▸ **subˈsistent** ADJECTIVE ▸ **subˈsister** NOUN

subsistence (səbˈsɪstəns) NOUN [1] the means by which one maintains life. [2] the act or condition of subsisting. [3] a thing that has real existence. [4] the state of being inherent. [5] *Philosophy* an inferior mode of being ascribed to the references of general terms which do not in fact exist. See also **nonbeing.**

subsistence allowance NOUN *Chiefly Brit* [1] an advance paid to an employee before his pay begins. [2] a payment to an employee to reimburse expenses, as while on assignments.

subsistence farming NOUN a type of farming in which most of the produce (**subsistence crop**) is consumed by the farmer and his family, leaving little or nothing to be marketed.

subsistence level NOUN a standard of living barely adequate to support life.

subsistence wage NOUN the lowest wage upon which a worker and his family can survive.

subsocial (sʌbˈsəʊʃəl) ADJECTIVE lacking a complex or definite social structure.
▸ **subˈsocially** ADVERB

subsoil (ˈsʌbˌsɔɪl) NOUN [1] **a** Also called: **undersoil.** the layer of soil beneath the surface soil and overlying the bedrock. **b** (*as modifier*): *a subsoil plough*. ◆ VERB [2] (*tr*) to plough (land) to a depth below the normal ploughing level and so break up the subsoil.
▸ **ˈsubˌsoiler** NOUN

subsolar (sʌbˈsəʊlə) ADJECTIVE [1] (of a point on the earth) directly below the sun. [2] situated between the tropics; equatorial.

subsong (ˈsʌbˌsɒŋ) NOUN a subdued form of birdsong modified from the full territorial song and used by some birds esp in courtship.

subsonic (sʌbˈsɒnɪk) ADJECTIVE being, having, or travelling at a velocity below that of sound: *a subsonic aircraft*.

subspecies (ˈsʌbˌspiːʃiːz) NOUN, *plural* **-cies**. *Biology* a taxonomic group that is a subdivision of a species: usually occurs because of isolation within a species. Abbreviation: **ssp.**
▸ **subspecific** (ˌsʌbspɪˈsɪfɪk) ADJECTIVE ▸ **ˌsubspeˈcifically** ADVERB

subspontaneous (ˌsʌbspɒnˈteɪnɪəs) ADJECTIVE (of a plant species, such as rhododendron) spreading naturally after having originally been introduced.

subst. ABBREVIATION FOR: [1] substantive. [2] substitute.

substage (ˈsʌbˌsteɪdʒ) NOUN the part of a microscope below the stage, usually consisting of an adjustable assembly holding a condenser lens for illuminating the specimen.

substance (ˈsʌbstəns) NOUN [1] the tangible matter of which a thing consists. [2] a specific type of matter, esp a homogeneous material with a definite composition. [3] the essence, meaning, etc., of a written or spoken thought. [4] solid or meaningful quality. [5] material density: *a vacuum has no substance*. [6] material possessions or wealth: *a man of substance*. [7] *Philosophy* **a** the supposed immaterial substratum that can receive modifications and in which attributes and accidents inhere. **b** a thing considered as a continuing whole that survives the changeability of its properties. [8] *Christian Science* that which is eternal. [9] a euphemistic term for any illegal drug. [10] **in substance.** with regard to the salient points.
▷HISTORY C13: via Old French from Latin *substantia*, from *substāre*, from SUB- + *stāre* to stand
▸ **ˈsubstanceless** ADJECTIVE

substandard (sʌbˈstændəd) ADJECTIVE [1] below an established or required standard. [2] another word for **nonstandard.**

substantial (səbˈstænʃəl) ADJECTIVE [1] of a considerable size or value: *substantial funds*. [2] worthwhile; important: *a substantial reform*. [3] having wealth or importance. [4] (of food or a meal) sufficient and nourishing. [5] solid or strong in construction, quality, or character: *a substantial door*. [6] real; actual; true: *the evidence is substantial*. [7] of or relating to the basic or fundamental substance or aspects of a thing. [8] *Philosophy* of or relating to substance rather than to attributes, accidents, or modifications.
▸ **substantiality** (səbˌstænʃɪˈælɪtɪ) *or* **subˈstantialness** NOUN ▸ **subˈstantially** ADVERB

substantialism (səbˈstænʃəˌlɪzəm) NOUN *Philosophy* [1] the doctrine that a substantial reality underlies phenomena. [2] the doctrine that matter is a real substance.
▸ **subˈstantialist** NOUN

substantialize *or* **substantialise** (səbˈstænʃəˌlaɪz) VERB to make or become substantial or actual.

substantiate (səbˈstænʃɪˌeɪt) VERB (*tr*) [1] to establish as valid or genuine. [2] to give form or real existence to.
▷HISTORY C17: from New Latin *substantiāre*, from Latin *substantia* SUBSTANCE
▸ **subˌstantiˈation** NOUN ▸ **subˈstantiative** ADJECTIVE
▸ **subˈstantiˌator** NOUN

substantive (ˈsʌbstəntɪv) NOUN [1] *Grammar* a noun or pronoun used in place of a noun. ◆ ADJECTIVE [2] of, relating to, containing, or being the essential element of a thing. [3] having independent function, resources, or existence. [4] of substantial quantity. [5] solid in foundation or basis. [6] *Grammar* denoting, relating to, or standing in place of a noun. [7] (səbˈstæntɪv) relating to the essential legal principles administered by the courts, as opposed to practice and procedure. Compare **adjective** (sense 3). [8] (səbˈstæntɪv) (of a dye or colour) staining the material directly without use of a mordant. ◆ Abbreviations: **s, sb, subst.**
▷HISTORY C15: from Late Latin *substantīvus*, from Latin *substāre* to stand beneath; see SUBSTANCE
▸ **substantival** (ˌsʌbstənˈtaɪvᵊl) ADJECTIVE
▸ **ˌsubstanˈtivally** ADVERB ▸ **ˈsubstantively** ADVERB
▸ **ˈsubstantiveness** NOUN

substantive agreements (səbˈstæntɪv) PLURAL NOUN collective agreements that regulate jobs, pay, and conditions.

substantive rank (səbˈstæntɪv) NOUN a permanent rank in the armed services obtained by length of service, selection, etc.

substantivize *or* **substantivise** (ˈsʌbstəntɪˌvaɪz) VERB (*tr*) to make (a word other than a noun) play the grammatical role of a noun in a sentence.
▸ **ˌsubstantiviˈzation** *or* **ˌsubstantiviˈsation** NOUN

substation (ˈsʌbˌsteɪʃən) NOUN [1] a subsidiary station. [2] an installation at which electricity is received from one or more power stations for conversion from alternating to direct current, reducing the voltage, or switching before distribution by a low-tension network.

substituent (sʌbˈstɪtjʊənt) NOUN [1] *Chem* an atom or group that replaces another atom or group in a molecule or can be regarded as replacing an atom in a parent compound. ◆ ADJECTIVE [2] substituted or substitutable.
▷HISTORY C19: from Latin *substituere* to SUBSTITUTE

substitute (ˈsʌbstɪˌtjuːt) VERB [1] (often foll by *for*) to serve or cause to serve in place of another person or thing. [2] *Chem* to replace (an atom or group in a molecule) with (another atom or group). [3] *Logic, maths* to replace (one expression) by (another) in the context of a third, as replacing $x + y$ for x in $3x = k$ gives $3x + 3y = k$. ◆ NOUN [4] **a** a person or thing that serves in place of another, such as a player in a game who takes the place of an injured colleague. **b** (*as modifier*): *a substitute goalkeeper*. Often shortened to: **sub.** [5] *Grammar* another name for **pro-form.** [6] *Canadian* another name for **supply teacher.** [7] *Nautical* another word for **repeater** (sense 5). [8] (formerly) a person paid to replace another due for military service.

▷**HISTORY** C16: from Latin *substituere,* from *sub-* in place of + *statuere* to set up
▸ **ˌsubstiˈtutable** ADJECTIVE ▸ **ˌsubstiˌtutaˈbility** NOUN

> **Language note** *Substitute* is sometimes wrongly used where *replace* is meant: *he replaced* (not *substituted*) *the worn tyre with a new one.*

substitution (ˌsʌbstɪˈtjuːʃən) NOUN [1] the act of substituting or state of being substituted. [2] something or someone substituted. [3] *Maths* the replacement of a term of an equation by another that is known to have the same value in order to simplify the equation. [4] *Maths, logic* **a** the uniform replacement of one expression by another. **b** **substitution instance.** an expression so derived from another.

substitutive (ˈsʌbstɪˌtjuːtɪv) ADJECTIVE [1] acting or able to act as a substitute. [2] of or involving substitution.
▸ **ˈsubstiˌtutively** ADVERB

substitutivity (ˌsʌbstɪtjuːˈtɪvɪtɪ) NOUN *Logic, philosophy* the principle that expressions with the same reference can be substituted for one another without affecting the truth-value of any context in which they occur. See also **transparent context, opaque context.**

substrate (ˈsʌbstreɪt) NOUN [1] *Biochem* the substance upon which an enzyme acts. [2] another word for **substratum.** [3] *Electronics* the semiconductor base on which other material is deposited, esp in the construction of integrated circuits.

substratum (sʌbˈstrɑːtəm, -ˈstreɪ-) NOUN, *plural* **-strata** (-ˈstrɑːtə, -ˈstreɪtə). [1] any layer or stratum lying underneath another. [2] a basis or foundation; groundwork. [3] the nonliving material on which an animal or plant grows or lives. [4] *Geology* **a** the solid rock underlying soils, gravels, etc.; bedrock. **b** the surface to which a fixed organism is attached. [5] *Sociol* any of several subdivisions or grades within a stratum. [6] *Photog* a binding layer by which an emulsion is made to adhere to a glass or film base. Sometimes shortened to: **sub.** [7] *Philosophy* substance considered as that in which attributes and accidents inhere. [8] *Linguistics* the language of an indigenous population when replaced by the language of a conquering or colonizing population, esp as it influences the form of the dominant language or of any mixed languages arising from their contact. Compare **superstratum** (sense 2).
▷**HISTORY** C17: from New Latin, from Latin *substrātus* strewn beneath, from *substernere* to spread under, from SUB- + *sternere* to spread
▸ **subˈstrative** *or* **subˈstratal** ADJECTIVE

substructure (ˈsʌbˌstrʌktʃə) NOUN [1] a structure, pattern, etc., that forms the basis of anything. [2] a structure forming a foundation or framework for a building or other construction.
▸ **subˈstructural** ADJECTIVE

subsume (səbˈsjuːm) VERB (*tr*) [1] to incorporate (an idea, proposition, case, etc.) under a comprehensive or inclusive classification or heading. [2] to consider (an instance of something) as part of a general rule or principle.
▷**HISTORY** C16: from New Latin *subsumere,* from Latin SUB- + *sumere* to take
▸ **subˈsumable** ADJECTIVE

subsumption (səbˈsʌmpʃən) NOUN the act of subsuming or the state of being subsumed.
▸ **subˈsumptive** ADJECTIVE

sub-surface NOUN the layer just below the surface of water, the earth, etc.

subtangent (sʌbˈtændʒənt) NOUN *Geometry* a segment of the *x*-axis lying between the *x*-coordinate of the point at which a tangent is drawn to a curve and the intercept of the tangent with the axis.

subteen (ˌsʌbˈtiːn) NOUN *US and Canadian rare* a young person who has not yet become a teenager.

subtemperate (sʌbˈtɛmpərɪt) ADJECTIVE of or relating to the colder temperate regions.

subtenant (sʌbˈtɛnənt) NOUN a person who rents or leases property from a tenant.
▸ **subˈtenancy** NOUN

subtend (səbˈtɛnd) VERB (*tr*) [1] *Geometry* to be opposite to and delimit (an angle or side). [2] (of a bract, stem, etc.) to have (a bud or similar part) growing in its axil. [3] to mark off. [4] to underlie; be inherent in.
▷**HISTORY** C16: from Latin *subtendere* to extend beneath, from SUB- + *tendere* to stretch out

subterfuge (ˈsʌbtəˌfjuːdʒ) NOUN a stratagem employed to conceal something, evade an argument, etc.
▷**HISTORY** C16: from Late Latin *subterfugium,* from Latin *subterfugere* to escape by stealth, from *subter* secretly + *fugere* to flee

subterminal (sʌbˈtɜːmɪnᵊl) ADJECTIVE almost at an end.

subternatural (ˌsʌbtəˈnætʃərəl, -ˈnætʃrəl) ADJECTIVE *Rare* falling below what is accepted as natural; less than natural.
▷**HISTORY** C19: from Latin *subter-* below + NATURAL

subterranean (ˌsʌbtəˈreɪnɪən) ADJECTIVE [1] Also: **subterraneous, subterrestrial.** situated, living, or operating below the surface of the earth. [2] existing or operating in concealment.
▷**HISTORY** C17: from Latin *subterrāneus,* from SUB- + *terra* earth
▸ **ˌsubterˈraneanly** *or* **ˌsubterˈraneously** ADVERB

subtext (ˈsʌbˌtɛkst) NOUN [1] an underlying theme in a piece of writing. [2] a message which is not stated directly but can be inferred.

subtile (ˈsʌtᵊl) ADJECTIVE a rare spelling of **subtle.**
▸ **ˈsubtilely** ADVERB ▸ **subtility** (sʌbˈtɪlɪtɪ) *or* **ˈsubtileness** NOUN ▸ **ˈsubtilty** NOUN

subtilize *or* **subtilise** (ˈsʌtɪˌlaɪz) VERB [1] (*tr*) to bring to a purer state; refine. [2] to debate subtly. [3] (*tr*) to make (the mind, etc.) keener.
▸ **ˌsubtiliˈzation** *or* **ˌsubtiliˈsation** NOUN ▸ **ˈsubtilˌizer** *or* **ˈsubtilˌiser** NOUN

subtitle (ˈsʌbˌtaɪtᵊl) NOUN [1] an additional subordinate title given to a literary or other work. [2] (*often plural*) Also called: **caption.** *Films* **a** a written translation superimposed on a film that has foreign dialogue. **b** explanatory text on a silent film. ◆ VERB [3] (*tr; usually passive*) to provide a subtitle for.
▸ **subtitular** (sʌbˈtɪtjʊlə, -ˈtɪtʃə-) ADJECTIVE

subtle (ˈsʌtᵊl) ADJECTIVE [1] not immediately obvious or comprehensible. [2] difficult to detect or analyse, often through being delicate or highly refined: *a subtle scent.* [3] showing or making or capable of showing or making fine distinctions of meaning. [4] marked by or requiring mental acuteness or ingenuity; discriminating. [5] delicate or faint: *a subtle shade.* [6] cunning or wily: *a subtle rogue.* [7] operating or executed in secret: *a subtle intrigue.*
▷**HISTORY** C14: from Old French *soutil,* from Latin *subtīlis* finely woven
▸ **ˈsubtleness** NOUN ▸ **ˈsubtly** ADVERB

subtlety (ˈsʌtᵊltɪ) NOUN, *plural* **-ties.** [1] the state or quality of being subtle; delicacy. [2] a fine distinction or the ability to make such a distinction. [3] something subtle.

subtonic (sʌbˈtɒnɪk) NOUN *Music* the seventh degree of a major or minor scale. Also called: **leading note.**

subtopia (sʌbˈtəʊpɪə) NOUN *Brit* suburban development that encroaches on rural areas yet appears to offer the attractions of country life to suburban dwellers.
▷**HISTORY** C20: blend of SUBURB + UTOPIA
▸ **subˈtopian** ADJECTIVE

subtorrid (sʌbˈtɒrɪd) ADJECTIVE an obsolete word for **subtropical.**

subtotal (sʌbˈtəʊtᵊl, ˈsʌbˌtəʊtᵊl) NOUN [1] the total made up by a column of figures, etc., forming part of the total made up by a larger column or group. ◆ VERB **-tals, -talling, -talled** *or US* **-tals, -taling, -taled.** [2] to establish or work out a subtotal for (a column, group, etc.).

subtract (səbˈtrækt) VERB [1] to calculate the difference between (two numbers or quantities) by subtraction. [2] to remove (a part of a thing, quantity, etc.) from the whole.
▷**HISTORY** C16: from Latin *subtractus* withdrawn, from *subtrahere* to draw away from beneath, from SUB- + *trahere* to draw
▸ **subˈtracter** NOUN

subtraction (səbˈtrækʃən) NOUN [1] the act or process of subtracting. [2] a mathematical operation in which the difference between two numbers or quantities is calculated. Usually indicated by the symbol (–).

subtractive (səbˈtræktɪv) ADJECTIVE [1] able or tending to remove or subtract. [2] indicating or requiring subtraction; having a minus sign: *–x is a subtractive quantity.*

subtractive process NOUN a photographic process in which all but the desired colours are removed by passing the illuminating light through subtractive filters. Compare **additive process.**

subtrahend (ˈsʌbtrəˌhɛnd) NOUN the number to be subtracted from another number (the **minuend**).
▷**HISTORY** C17: from Latin *subtrahendus,* from *subtrahere* to SUBTRACT

subtreasury (sʌbˈtrɛʒərɪ) NOUN, *plural* **-uries.** *US* a branch treasury.
▸ **subˈtreasurer** NOUN ▸ **subˈtreasurership** NOUN

subtropical (sʌbˈtrɒpɪkᵊl) ADJECTIVE situated in, used in, characteristic of, or relating to the subtropics.

subtropics (sʌbˈtrɒpɪks) PLURAL NOUN the region lying between the tropics and temperate lands.

subtype (ˈsʌbˌtaɪp) NOUN a secondary or subordinate type or genre, esp a specific one considered as falling under a general classification.
▸ **subtypical** (sʌbˈtɪpɪkᵊl) ADJECTIVE

subulate (ˈsuːbjəlɪt, -ˌleɪt) ADJECTIVE (esp of plant parts) tapering to a point; awl-shaped.
▷**HISTORY** C18: from New Latin *subulatus* like an awl, from Latin *sūbula* awl

subunit (sʌbˈjunɪt) NOUN a distinct part or component of something larger.

suburb (ˈsʌbɜːb) NOUN a residential district situated on the outskirts of a city or town.
▷**HISTORY** C14: from Latin *suburbium,* from *sub-* close to + *urbs* a city
▸ **ˈsuburbed** ADJECTIVE

suburban (səˈbɜːbᵊn) ADJECTIVE [1] of, relating to, situated in, or inhabiting a suburb or the suburbs. [2] characteristic of or typifying a suburb or the suburbs. [3] *Mildly derogatory* narrow or unadventurous in outlook. ◆ NOUN [4] another word for **suburbanite.**

suburbanite (səˈbɜːbəˌnaɪt) NOUN a person who lives in a suburb.

suburbanize *or* **suburbanise** (sʌˈbɜːbəˌnaɪz) VERB (*tr*) to make suburban.

suburbia (səˈbɜːbɪə) NOUN [1] suburbs or the people living in them considered as an identifiable community or class in society. [2] the life, customs, etc., of suburbanites.

suburbicarian (səˌbɜːbɪˈkɛərɪən) ADJECTIVE *RC Church* situated near the city of Rome: used esp of the dioceses surrounding Rome.
▷**HISTORY** C17: from Late Latin *suburbicārius,* from *suburbium* SUBURB

subvene (səbˈviːn) VERB (*intr*) *Rare* to happen in such a way as to be of assistance, esp in preventing something.
▷**HISTORY** C18: from Latin *subvenīre,* from *venīre* to come

subvention (səbˈvɛnʃən) NOUN [1] a grant, aid, or subsidy, as from a government to an educational institution. [2] the act or process of providing aid or help of any sort. [3] *Sport* a fee paid indirectly to a supposedly amateur athlete for appearing at a meeting.
▷**HISTORY** C15: from Late Latin *subventiō* assistance, from Latin *subvenīre* to SUBVENE
▸ **subˈventionary** ADJECTIVE

subversion (səbˈvɜːʃən) NOUN [1] the act or an instance of subverting or overthrowing a legally constituted government, institution, etc. [2] the state of being subverted; destruction or ruin. [3] something that brings about an overthrow.
▷**HISTORY** C14: from Late Latin *subversiō* destruction, from Latin *subvertere* to SUBVERT

subversive (səbˈvɜːsɪv) ADJECTIVE [1] liable to subvert or overthrow a government, legally constituted institution, etc. ◆ NOUN [2] a person engaged in subversive activities, etc.
▸ **subˈversively** ADVERB ▸ **subˈversiveness** NOUN

subvert (səbˈvɜːt) VERB (*tr*) [1] to bring about the complete downfall or ruin of (something existing or established by a system of law, etc.). [2] to undermine the moral principles of (a person, etc.); corrupt.

▷HISTORY C14: from Latin *subvertere* to overturn, from *sub-* from below + *vertere* to turn
▸**sub'verter** NOUN

subviral (sʌb'vaɪrəl) ADJECTIVE of, caused by, or denoting a part of the structure of a virus.

subway ('sʌb,weɪ) NOUN 1 *Brit* an underground passage or tunnel enabling pedestrians to cross a road, railway, etc. 2 an underground passage or tunnel for traffic, electric power supplies, etc. 3 *Chiefly US and Canadian* an underground railway.

subzero (sʌb'zɪərəʊ) ADJECTIVE (esp of temperature) lower or less than zero.

succah (su'kɑ, 'sukɔ, 'sukə) NOUN *Judaism* a variant spelling of **sukkah**.

succedaneum (,sʌksɪ'deɪnɪəm) NOUN, *plural* **-nea** (-nɪə). *Obsolete* something that is used as a substitute, esp any medical drug or agent that may be taken or prescribed in place of another.
▷HISTORY C17: from Latin *succēdāneus* following after, from *succēdere* to SUCCEED
▸**,succe'daneous** ADJECTIVE

succeed (sək'si:d) VERB 1 *(intr)* to accomplish an aim, esp in the manner desired: *he succeeded in winning.* 2 *(intr)* to happen in the manner desired: *the plan succeeded.* 3 *(intr)* to acquit oneself satisfactorily or do well, as in a specified field: *to succeed in publishing.* 4 (when *intr,* often foll by *to*) to come next in order (after someone or something). 5 (when *intr,* often foll by *to*) to take over an office, post, etc. (from a person): *he succeeded to the vice presidency.* 6 *(intr;* usually foll by *to)* to come into possession (of property, etc.); inherit. 7 *(intr)* to have a result according to a specified manner: *the plan succeeded badly.* 8 *(intr)* to devolve upon: *the estate succeeded to his son.*
▷HISTORY C15: from Latin *succēdere* to follow after, from *sub-* after + *cēdere* to go
▸**suc'ceedable** ADJECTIVE ▸**suc'ceeder** NOUN
▸**suc'ceeding** ADJECTIVE ▸**suc'ceedingly** ADVERB

succentor (sək'sɛntə) NOUN the deputy of the precentor of a cathedral that has retained its statutes from pre-Reformation days.
▷HISTORY C17: from Late Latin: one who accompanies singing, from *succinere* to accompany, from Latin *canere* to sing
▸**suc'centorship** NOUN

succès de scandale *French* (syksɛ də skɑ̃dal) NOUN, *plural* ***succès de scandale***. success of a play, book, etc., because of notoriety or its scandalous character.
▷HISTORY literally: success of scandal

succès d'estime *French* (syksɛ dɛstim) NOUN, *plural* ***succès d'estime***. success, as of a book, play, etc., based on the appreciation of the critics rather than popular acclaim.
▷HISTORY literally: success of esteem

succès fou *French* (syksɛ fu) NOUN, *plural* ***succès fous*** (syksɛ fu). a fantastic success.
▷HISTORY literally: mad success

success (sək'sɛs) NOUN 1 the favourable outcome of something attempted. 2 the attainment of wealth, fame, etc. 3 an action, performance, etc., that is characterized by success. 4 a person or thing that is successful. 5 *Obsolete* any outcome.
▷HISTORY C16: from Latin *successus* an outcome, from *succēdere* to SUCCEED
▸**suc'cessless** ADJECTIVE

successful (sək'sɛsfʊl) ADJECTIVE 1 having succeeded in one's endeavours. 2 marked by a favourable outcome. 3 having obtained fame, wealth, etc.
▸**suc'cessfully** ADVERB ▸**suc'cessfulness** NOUN

succession (sək'sɛʃən) NOUN 1 the act or an instance of one person or thing following another. 2 a number of people or things following one another in order. 3 the act, process, or right by which one person succeeds to the office, etc., of another. 4 the order that determines how one person or thing follows another. 5 a line of descent to a title, etc. 6 *Ecology* the sum of the changes in the composition of a community that occur during its development towards a stable climax community. 7 **in succession.** in a manner such that one thing is followed uninterruptedly by another.
▷HISTORY C14: from Latin *successio,* from *succēdere* to SUCCEED
▸**suc'cessional** ADJECTIVE ▸**suc'cessionally** ADVERB

succession state NOUN any of a number of usually new states that are established in or expand over the territory formerly ruled by one large state: *Czechoslovakia was a succession state of the Austro-Hungarian monarchy.*

successive (sək'sɛsɪv) ADJECTIVE 1 following another without interruption. 2 of or involving succession: *a successive process.*
▸**suc'cessively** ADVERB ▸**suc'cessiveness** NOUN

successor (sək'sɛsə) NOUN 1 a person or thing that follows, esp a person who succeeds another in an office. 2 *Logic* the element related to a given element by a serial ordering, esp the natural number next larger to a given one. The successor of n is $n + 1$, usually written Sn or n'.
▸**suc'cessoral** ADJECTIVE

succinate ('sʌksɪ,neɪt) NOUN any salt or ester of succinic acid.
▷HISTORY C18: from SUCCIN(IC) + -ATE[2]

succinct (sək'sɪŋkt) ADJECTIVE 1 marked by brevity and clarity; concise. 2 compressed into a small area. 3 *Archaic* **a** encircled by or as if by a girdle. **b** drawn up tightly; closely fitting.
▷HISTORY C15: from Latin *succinctus* girt about, from *succingere* to gird from below, from *sub-* from below + *cingere* to gird
▸**suc'cinctly** ADVERB ▸**suc'cinctness** NOUN

succinic (sʌk'sɪnɪk) ADJECTIVE 1 of, relating to, or obtained from amber. 2 of, consisting of, containing, or derived from succinic acid.
▷HISTORY C18: from French *succinique,* from Latin *succinum* amber

succinic acid NOUN a colourless odourless water-soluble dicarboxylic acid found in plant and animal tissues: used in making lacquers, dyes, perfumes, etc.; 1,4-butanedioic acid. Formula: $HOOCCH_2:CH_2COOH$.

succise (sək'saɪz) ADJECTIVE *Botany* ending abruptly, as if cut off: *succise roots.*
▷HISTORY from Latin *succīsus* cut below

succory ('sʌkərɪ) NOUN, *plural* **-cories**. another name for **chicory.**
▷HISTORY C16: variant of *cicoree* CHICORY; related to Middle Low German *suckerie,* Dutch *suikerei*

succotash ('sʌkə,tæʃ) NOUN *US and Canadian* a mixture of cooked sweet corn kernels and lima beans, served as a vegetable.
▷HISTORY C18: from Narraganset *msiquatash,* literally: broken pieces

Succoth ('sʊkəʊt, -kəʊθ; *Hebrew* su:'kɔt) NOUN a variant spelling of **Sukkoth.**

succour *or US* **succor** ('sʌkə) NOUN 1 help or assistance, esp in time of difficulty. 2 a person or thing that provides help. ◆ VERB 3 *(tr)* to give aid to.
▷HISTORY C13: from Old French *sucurir,* from Latin *succurrere* to hurry to help, from *sub-* under + *currere* to run
▸**'succourable** *or US* **'succorable** ADJECTIVE ▸**'succourer** *or US* **'succorer** NOUN ▸**'succourless** *or US* **'succorless** ADJECTIVE

succubous ('sʌkjʊbəs) ADJECTIVE (of a liverwort) having the leaves arranged so that the upper margin of each leaf is covered by the lower margin of the next leaf along. ◆ Compare **incubous.**
▷HISTORY C19: from Late Latin *succubare:* see SUCCUBUS

succubus ('sʌkjʊbəs) NOUN, *plural* **-bi** (-,baɪ). 1 Also called: **succuba.** a female demon fabled to have sexual intercourse with sleeping men. Compare **incubus.** 2 any evil demon.
▷HISTORY C16: from Medieval Latin, from Late Latin *succuba* harlot, from Latin *succubāre* to lie beneath, from SUB- + *cubāre* to lie

succulent ('sʌkjʊlənt) ADJECTIVE 1 abundant in juices; juicy. 2 (of plants) having thick fleshy leaves or stems. 3 *Informal* stimulating interest, desire, etc. ◆ NOUN 4 a plant that is able to exist in arid or salty conditions by using water stored in its fleshy tissues.
▷HISTORY C17: from Latin *succulentus,* from *sūcus* juice
▸**'succulence** *or* **'succulency** NOUN ▸**'succulently** ADVERB

succumb (sə'kʌm) VERB *(intr;* often foll by *to)* 1 to give way in face of the overwhelming force (of) or desire (for). 2 to be fatally overwhelmed (by disease, old age, etc.); die (of).
▷HISTORY C15: from Latin *succumbere* to be overcome, from SUB- + *-cumbere* from *cubāre* to lie down
▸**suc'cumber** NOUN

succursal (sʌ'kɜːsᵊl) ADJECTIVE 1 (esp of a religious establishment) subsidiary. ◆ NOUN 2 a subsidiary establishment.
▷HISTORY C19: from French, from Medieval Latin *succursus,* from Latin *succurrere* to SUCCOUR

succuss (sʌ'kʌs) VERB 1 *Med* to shake (a patient) to detect the sound of fluid in the thoracic or another bodily cavity. 2 *Rare* to shake, esp with sudden force.
▷HISTORY C17: from Latin *succussus* flung aloft, from *succutere* to toss up, from *sub-* from below + *quatere* to shake
▸**succussion** (sʌ'kʌʃən) NOUN ▸**suc'cussive** ADJECTIVE

such (sʌtʃ) (often foll by a corresponding subordinate clause introduced by *that* or *as*) DETERMINER 1 **a** of the sort specified or understood: *such books shouldn't be sold here.* **b** *(as pronoun): such is life; robbers, rapists, and such.* 2 so great; so much: *such a help; I've never seen such weeping.* 3 **as such. a** in the capacity previously specified or understood: *a judge as such hasn't so much power.* **b** in itself or themselves: *intelligence as such can't guarantee success.* 4 **such and such.** specific, but not known or named: *at such and such a time.* 5 **such as. a** for example: *animals, such as elephants and tigers.* **b** of a similar kind as; like: *people such as your friend John make me angry.* **c** of the (usually small) amount, etc.: *the food, such as there was, was excellent.* 6 **such that.** so that: used to express purpose or result: *power such that it was effortless.* ◆ ADVERB 7 (intensifier): *such nice people; such a nice person that I gave him a present.*
▷HISTORY Old English *swilc;* related to Old Frisian *sālik,* Old Norse *slīkr,* Gothic *swaleiks,* Old High German *sulih*

suchlike ('sʌtʃ,laɪk) ADJECTIVE 1 *(prenominal)* of such a kind; similar: *John, Ken, and other suchlike idiots.* ◆ NOUN 2 such or similar persons or things: *hyenas, jackals, and suchlike.*

Su-chou ('su:'tʃaʊ) NOUN a variant transliteration of the Chinese name for **Suzhou.**

Süchow ('ʃu:'tʃaʊ) NOUN a variant transliteration of the Chinese name for **Xuzhou.**

suck (sʌk) VERB 1 to draw (a liquid or other substance) into the mouth by creating a partial vacuum in the mouth. 2 to draw in (fluid, etc.) by or as if by a similar action: *plants suck moisture from the soil.* 3 to drink milk from (a mother's breast); suckle. 4 *(tr)* to extract fluid content from (a solid food): *to suck a lemon.* 5 *(tr)* to take into the mouth and moisten, dissolve, or roll around with the tongue: *to suck one's thumb.* 6 *(tr;* often foll by *down, in,* etc.) to draw by using irresistible force: *the whirlpool sucked him down.* 7 *(intr)* (of a pump) to draw in air because of a low supply level or leaking valves, pipes, etc. 8 *(tr)* to assimilate or acquire (knowledge, comfort, etc.). 9 *(intr) Slang* to be contemptible or disgusting. ◆ NOUN 10 the act or an instance of sucking. 11 something that is sucked, esp milk from the mother's breast. 12 **give suck to.** to give (a baby or young animal) milk from the breast or udder. 13 an attracting or sucking force: *the suck of the whirlpool was very strong.* 14 a sound caused by sucking. 15 **suck it and see.** *Informal* to try something to find out what it is, what it is like, or how it works. ◆ See also **suck in, suck off, sucks, suck up to.**
▷HISTORY Old English *sūcan;* related to Old Norse *súga,* Middle Dutch *sūgen,* Latin *sūgere* to suck, exhaust; see SOAK
▸**'suckless** ADJECTIVE

sucker ('sʌkə) NOUN 1 a person or thing that sucks. 2 *Slang* a person who is easily deceived or swindled. 3 *Slang* a person who cannot resist the attractions of a particular type of person or thing: *he's a sucker for blondes.* 4 a young animal that is not yet weaned, esp a suckling pig. 5 *Zoology* an organ that is specialized for sucking or adhering. 6 a cup-shaped device, generally made of rubber, that may be attached to articles allowing them to adhere to a surface by suction. 7 *Botany* **a** a strong shoot that arises in a mature plant from a root, rhizome, or the base of the main stem. **b** a short branch of a parasitic plant that absorbs nutrients from the host. 8 a pipe or tube through which a fluid is drawn by suction. 9 any small mainly North American cyprinoid fish of the family *Catostomidae,* having toothless jaws and a large sucking mouth. [10] any of certain fishes that have sucking discs, esp the clingfish or sea snail. [11] a piston in a suction pump or the valve in such a piston. ◆ VERB [12] *(tr)* to strip off the suckers from (a plant). [13] *(intr)* (of a plant) to produce suckers.

suckerfish ('sʌkəˌfɪʃ) *or* **suckfish** NOUN, *plural* **-fish** *or* **-fishes**. other names for **remora**.
▷**HISTORY** C18: so called because of the suction disc on its head

sucker punch NOUN [1] a sudden surprise punch, esp from behind. [2] a sudden unexpected defeat or setback.

suck in VERB *(adverb)* [1] *(tr)* to attract by using an inexorable force, inducement, etc.: *the current sucked him in.* [2] to draw in (one's breath) sharply. [3] *(tr) Slang* to deceive or defraud.

sucking ('sʌkɪŋ) ADJECTIVE [1] not yet weaned: *sucking pig.* [2] not yet fledged: *sucking dove.*

sucking louse NOUN any insect of the order *Anoplura*. See **louse** (sense 1).
▷**HISTORY** so named because it has a mouth adapted for sucking the body fluids of its host

suckle ('sʌk^{ə}l) VERB [1] to give (a baby or young animal) milk from the breast or (of a baby, etc.) to suck milk from the breast. [2] *(tr)* to bring up; nurture.
▷**HISTORY** C15: probably back formation from SUCKLING
▸'**suckler** NOUN

suckling ('sʌklɪŋ) NOUN [1] an infant or young animal that is still taking milk from the mother. [2] a very young child.
▷**HISTORY** C15: see SUCK, -LING[1]; related to Middle Dutch *sūgeling,* Middle High German *sōgelinc*

suck off VERB *(tr, adverb) Slang* to perform the act of fellatio or cunnilingus on.

sucks (sʌks) INTERJECTION *Slang* [1] an expression of disappointment. [2] an exclamation of defiance or derision (esp in the phrase **yah boo sucks to you**).

suck up to VERB *(intr, adverb + preposition) Informal* to flatter for one's own profit; toady.

sucrase ('sju:kreɪz) NOUN another name for **invertase**.
▷**HISTORY** C19: from French *sucre* sugar + -ASE

sucre *(Spanish* 'sukre) NOUN the standard monetary unit of Ecuador, divided into 100 centavos.
▷**HISTORY** C19: after Antonio José de Sucre (1795–1830), South American liberator

Sucre *(Spanish* 'sukre) NOUN the legal capital of Bolivia, in the south central part of the country in the E Andes: university (1624). Pop.: 192 238 (2000 est.). Former name (until 1839): **Chuquisaca**.

sucrose ('sju:krəʊz, -krəʊs) NOUN the technical name for **sugar** (sense 1).
▷**HISTORY** C19: from French *sucre* sugar + -OSE[2]

suction ('sʌkʃən) NOUN [1] the act or process of sucking. [2] the force or condition produced by a pressure difference, as the force holding a suction cap onto a surface. [3] the act or process of producing such a force or condition.
▷**HISTORY** C17: from Late Latin *suctiō* a sucking, from Latin *sūgere* to suck
▸'**suctional** ADJECTIVE

suction pump NOUN a pump for raising water or other fluid by suction. It usually consists of a cylinder containing a piston fitted with a flap valve.

suction stop NOUN *Phonetics* another word for **click** (sense 3).

suction valve NOUN a nonreturn valve in a pump suction to prevent the pump draining or depriming when not in service. Also called: **foot valve.**

suctorial (sʌk'tɔ:rɪəl) ADJECTIVE [1] specialized for sucking or adhering: *the suctorial mouthparts of certain insects.* [2] relating to or possessing suckers or suction.
▷**HISTORY** C19: from New Latin *suctōrius,* from Latin *sūgere* to suck

SUD INTERNATIONAL CAR REGISTRATION FOR Sudan.

Sudan (su:'dɑ:n, -'dæn) NOUN [1] a republic in NE Africa, on the Red Sea: the largest country in Africa; conquered by Mehemet Ali of Egypt (1820–22) and made an Anglo-Egyptian condominium in 1899 after joint forces defeated the Mahdist revolt; became a republic in 1956; civil war has been waged between separatists, in the mainly Christian south, and the government since independence, apart from a period of peace (1972–83). It consists mainly of a plateau, with the Nubian Desert in the north. Official language: Arabic. Official religion: Muslim; there are large Christian and animist minorities. Currency: Sudanese dinar. Capital: Khartoum. Pop.: 36 080 000 (2001 est.). Area: 2 505 805 sq. km (967 491 sq. miles). Former name (1899–1956): **Anglo-Egyptian Sudan.** French name: **Soudan.** [2] **the.** a region stretching across Africa south of the Sahara and north of the tropical zone: inhabited chiefly by Negroid tribes rather than Arabs.

Sudanese (ˌsu:d^{ə}'ni:z) ADJECTIVE [1] of or relating to the republic of Sudan or its inhabitants. ◆ ADJECTIVE [2] of or relating to the African region of the Sudan or its inhabitants. ◆ NOUN [3] a native or inhabitant of the republic of Sudan. [4] a native or inhabitant of the African region of the Sudan.

Sudanic (su:'dænɪk) NOUN [1] a group of languages spoken in scattered areas of the Sudan, most of which are now generally assigned to the Chari-Nile branch of the Nilo-Saharan family. ◆ ADJECTIVE [2] relating to or belonging to this group of languages. [3] of or relating to the Sudan.

sudarium (sju'dɛərɪəm) NOUN, *plural* **-daria** (-'dɛərɪə). another word for **sudatorium** or **veronica**[2].
▷**HISTORY** C17: from Latin, from *sūdāre* to sweat

sudatorium (ˌsju:də'tɔ:rɪəm) *or* **sudatory** NOUN, *plural* **-toria** (-'tɔ:rɪə) *or* **-tories**. a room, esp in a Roman bathhouse, where sweating is induced by heat.
▷**HISTORY** C18: from Latin, from *sūdāre* to sweat

sudatory ('sju:dətərɪ, -trɪ) ADJECTIVE [1] relating to or producing sweating; sudorific. ◆ NOUN, *plural* **-ries**. [2] *Med* a sudatory agent. [3] another word for **sudatorium.**

Sudbury ('sʌdbərɪ, -brɪ) NOUN a city in central Canada, in Ontario: a major nickel-mining centre. Pop.: 92 059 (1996).

sudd (sʌd) NOUN floating masses of reeds and weeds that occur on the White Nile and obstruct navigation.
▷**HISTORY** C19: from Arabic, literally: obstruction

sudden ('sʌd^{ə}n) ADJECTIVE [1] occurring or performed quickly and without warning. [2] marked by haste; abrupt. [3] *Rare* rash; precipitate. ◆ NOUN [4] *Archaic* an abrupt occurrence or the occasion of such an occurrence (in the phrase **on a sudden**). [5] **all of a sudden.** without warning; unexpectedly. ◆ ADVERB [6] *Chiefly poetic* without warning; suddenly.
▷**HISTORY** C13: via French from Late Latin *subitāneus,* from Latin *subitus* unexpected, from *subīre* to happen unexpectedly, from *sub-* secretly + *īre* to go
▸'**suddenness** NOUN

sudden adult death syndrome NOUN the unexpected death of a young adult, usually due to undetected inherited heart disease. Also called: **sudden death syndrome, sudden cardiac death.** Abbrevs: **SADS, SDS, SCD.**

sudden death NOUN [1] (in sports, etc.) an extra game or contest to decide the winner of a tied competition. [2] an unexpected or quick death.

sudden infant death syndrome NOUN a technical term for **cot death.** Abbreviation: **SIDS.**

suddenly ('sʌd^{ə}nlɪ) ADVERB *(sentence modifier)* quickly and without warning; unexpectedly.

Sudetenland (su:'deɪt^{ə}nˌlænd) NOUN a mountainous region of the N Czech Republic: part of Czechoslovakia (1919–38; 1945–93); occupied by Germany (1938–45). Also called: **the Sudeten.**

Sudetes (su:'di:ti:z) *or* **Sudeten Mountains** PLURAL NOUN a mountain range in E central Europe, along the N border of the Czech Republic, extending into Germany and Poland: rich in minerals, esp coal. Highest peak: Schneekoppe, 1603 m (5259 ft.).

sudor ('sju:dɔ:) NOUN a technical name for **sweat.**
▷**HISTORY** Latin
▸**sudoral** ('sju:dərəl) ADJECTIVE

sudoriferous (ˌsju:də'rɪfərəs) ADJECTIVE producing or conveying sweat. Also: **sudoriparous** (ˌsju:də'rɪpərəs).
▷**HISTORY** C16: via New Latin from SUDOR + Latin *ferre* to bear
▸ˌ**sudor'iferousness** NOUN

sudorific (ˌsju:də'rɪfɪk) ADJECTIVE [1] producing or causing sweating; sudatory. ◆ NOUN [2] a sudorific agent.
▷**HISTORY** C17: from New Latin *sūdōrificus,* from SUDOR + Latin *facere* to make

Sudra ('sju:drə) NOUN the lowest of the four main Hindu castes, the workers.
▷**HISTORY** C17: from Sanskrit

suds (sʌdz) PLURAL NOUN [1] the bubbles on the surface of water in which soap, detergents, etc., have been dissolved; lather. [2] soapy water. [3] *Slang, chiefly US and Canadian* beer or the bubbles floating on it.
▷**HISTORY** C16: probably from Middle Dutch *sudse* marsh; related to Middle Low German *sudde* swamp; see SEETHE
▸'**sudsy** ADJECTIVE

sue (sju:, su:) VERB **sues, suing, sued.** [1] to institute legal proceedings (against). [2] to make suppliant requests of (someone for something). [3] *Archaic* to pay court (to).
▷**HISTORY** C13: via Anglo-Norman from Old French *sivre,* from Latin *sequī* to follow
▸'**suer** NOUN

suede (sweɪd) NOUN **a** a leather finished with a fine velvet-like nap, usually on the flesh side of the skin or hide, produced by abrasive action. **b** *(as modifier): a suede coat.*
▷**HISTORY** C19: from French *gants de Suède,* literally: gloves from Sweden

suent ('sju:ənt) ADJECTIVE *Southwest English dialect* smooth.

suet ('su:ɪt, 'sju:ɪt) NOUN a hard waxy fat around the kidneys and loins in sheep, cattle, etc., used in cooking and making tallow.
▷**HISTORY** C14: from Old French *seu,* from Latin *sēbum*
▸'**suety** ADJECTIVE

suet pudding NOUN *Brit* any of a variety of sweet or savoury puddings made with suet and steamed or boiled.

Suez ('su:ɪz) NOUN [1] a port in NE Egypt, at the head of the Gulf of Suez at the S end of the Suez Canal: an ancient trading site and a major naval station under the Ottoman Empire; port of departure for pilgrims to Mecca; oil-refining centre. It suffered severely in the Arab-Israeli conflicts of 1967 and 1973. Pop.: 417 610 (1996). [2] **Isthmus of.** a strip of land in NE Egypt, between the Mediterranean and the Red Sea: links Africa and Asia and is crossed by the Suez Canal. [3] **Gulf of.** the NW arm of the Red Sea: linked with the Mediterranean by the Suez Canal.

Suez Canal NOUN a sea-level canal in NE Egypt, crossing the Isthmus of Suez and linking the Mediterranean with the Red Sea: built (1854–69) by de Lesseps with French and Egyptian capital; nationalized in 1956 by the Egyptians. Length: 163 km (101 miles).

suf. ABBREVIATION FOR suffix.

Suff. ABBREVIATION FOR: [1] Suffolk. [2] Suffragan.

suffer ('sʌfə) VERB [1] to undergo or be subjected to (pain, punishment, etc.). [2] *(tr)* to undergo or experience (anything): *to suffer a change of management.* [3] *(intr)* to be set at a disadvantage: *this author suffers in translation.* [4] to be prepared to endure (pain, death, etc.): *he suffers for the cause of freedom.* [5] *(tr) Archaic* to permit (someone to do something): *suffer the little children to come unto me.* [6] **suffer from. a** to be ill with, esp recurrently. **b** to be given to: *he suffers from a tendency to exaggerate.*
▷**HISTORY** C13: from Old French *soffrir,* from Latin *sufferre,* from SUB- + *ferre* to bear
▸'**sufferer** NOUN

sufferable ('sʌfərəb^{ə}l, 'sʌfrə-) ADJECTIVE able to be tolerated or suffered; endurable.
▸'**sufferably** ADVERB

sufferance ('sʌfərəns, 'sʌfrəns) NOUN [1] tolerance arising from failure to prohibit; tacit permission. [2] capacity to endure pain, injury, etc. [3] the state or condition of suffering. [4] *Archaic* patient endurance. [5] **on sufferance.** with reluctance.
▷**HISTORY** C13: via Old French from Late Latin *sufferentia* endurance, from Latin *sufferre* to SUFFER

suffering (ˈsʌfərɪŋ, ˈsʌfrɪŋ) NOUN [1] the pain, misery, or loss experienced by a person who suffers. [2] the state or an instance of enduring pain, etc.
▸ˈ**sufferingly** ADVERB

suffice (səˈfaɪs) VERB [1] to be adequate or satisfactory for (something). [2] **suffice it to say that.** (*takes a clause as object*) let us say no more than that; I shall just say that.
▷HISTORY C14: from Old French *suffire,* from Latin *sufficere* from *sub-* below + *facere* to make
▸**sufˈficer** NOUN

sufficiency (səˈfɪʃənsɪ) NOUN, *plural* **-cies.** [1] the quality or condition of being sufficient. [2] an adequate amount or quantity, as of income. [3] *Archaic* efficiency.

sufficient (səˈfɪʃənt) ADJECTIVE [1] enough to meet a need or purpose; adequate. [2] *Logic* (of a condition) assuring the truth of a statement; requiring but not necessarily required by some other state of affairs. Compare **necessary** (sense 3e). [3] *Archaic* competent; capable. ◆ NOUN [4] a sufficient quantity.
▷HISTORY C14: from Latin *sufficiens* supplying the needs of, from *sufficere* to SUFFICE
▸**sufˈficiently** ADVERB

sufficient reason NOUN *Philosophy* [1] the principle that nothing happens by pure chance, but that an explanation must always be available. [2] the view that such an explanation is a reason for God to have chosen one alternative rather than another.

suffix NOUN (ˈsʌfɪks) [1] *Grammar* an affix that follows the stem to which it is attached, as for example *-s* and *-ness* in *dogs* and *softness*. Compare **prefix** (sense 1). [2] anything that is added at the end of something else. ◆ VERB (ˈsʌfɪks, səˈfɪks) [3] (*tr*) *Grammar* to add (a morpheme) as a suffix to the end of a word. [4] (*tr*) to add (something) at the end of a sentence, comment, or piece of writing.
▷HISTORY C18: from New Latin *suffixum,* from Latin *suffixus* fastened below, from *suffigere,* from SUB- + *figere* to fasten
▸**suffixal** (ˈsʌfɪksəl) ADJECTIVE ▸**suffixion** (sʌˈfɪkʃən) NOUN

sufflate (sʌˈfleɪt) VERB an archaic word for **inflate.**
▷HISTORY C17: from Latin *sufflāre* from SUB- + *flāre* blow
▸**sufˈflation** NOUN

suffocate (ˈsʌfəˌkeɪt) VERB [1] to kill or be killed by the deprivation of oxygen, as by obstruction of the air passage or inhalation of noxious gases. [2] to block the air passages or have the air passages blocked. [3] to feel or cause to feel discomfort from heat and lack of air.
▷HISTORY C16: from Latin *suffōcāre,* from SUB- + *faucēs* throat
▸ˈ**suffoˌcating** ADJECTIVE ▸ˈ**suffoˌcatingly** ADVERB
▸ˌ**suffoˈcation** NOUN ▸ˈ**suffoˌcative** ADJECTIVE

Suffolk[1] (ˈsʌfək) NOUN a county of SE England, on the North Sea: its coast is flat and marshy, indented by broad tidal estuaries. Administrative centre: Ipswich. Pop.: 668 548 (2001). Area: 3800 sq. km (1467 sq. miles).

Suffolk[2] (ˈsʌfək) NOUN a black-faced breed of sheep.

Suffolk punch NOUN a breed of draught horse with a chestnut coat and short legs.
▷HISTORY C18: from dialect *punch* squat, short and thick

Suffr. ABBREVIATION FOR Suffragan.

suffragan (ˈsʌfrəgən) ADJECTIVE [1] **a** (of any bishop of a diocese) subordinate to and assisting his superior archbishop or metropolitan. **b** (of any assistant bishop) having the duty of assisting the bishop of the diocese to which he is appointed but having no ordinary jurisdiction in that diocese. ◆ NOUN [2] a suffragan bishop.
▷HISTORY C14: from Medieval Latin *suffrāgāneus,* from *suffrāgium* assistance, from Latin: SUFFRAGE
▸ˈ**suffraganship** NOUN

suffrage (ˈsʌfrɪdʒ) NOUN [1] the right to vote, esp in public elections; franchise. [2] the exercise of such a right; casting a vote. [3] a supporting vote. [4] a prayer, esp a short intercessory prayer.
▷HISTORY C14: from Latin *suffrāgium*

suffragette (ˌsʌfrəˈdʒɛt) NOUN a female advocate of the extension of the franchise to women, esp a militant one, as in Britain at the beginning of the 20th century.
▷HISTORY C20: from SUFFRAG(E) + -ETTE
▸ˌ**suffraˈgettism** NOUN

suffragist (ˈsʌfrədʒɪst) NOUN an advocate of the extension of the franchise, esp to women.
▸ˈ**suffragism** NOUN

suffruticose (səˈfruːtɪˌkəʊz) ADJECTIVE (of a plant) having a permanent woody base and herbaceous branches.
▷HISTORY C18: from New Latin *suffruticōsus,* from Latin SUB- + *frutex* a shrub

suffumigate (səˈfjuːmɪˌgeɪt) VERB (*tr*) to fumigate from or as if from beneath.
▷HISTORY C16: from Latin *suffūmigāre,* from SUB- + *fūmigāre* to FUMIGATE
▸**sufˌfumiˈgation** NOUN

suffuse (səˈfjuːz) VERB (*tr; usually passive*) to spread or flood through or over (something): *the evening sky was suffused with red.*
▷HISTORY C16: from Latin *suffūsus* overspread with, from *suffundere,* from SUB- + *fundere* to pour
▸**suffusion** (səˈfjuːʒən) NOUN ▸**sufˈfusive** ADJECTIVE

Sufi (ˈsuːfɪ) NOUN, *plural* **-fis.** an adherent of any of various Muslim mystical orders or teachings, which emphasize the direct personal experience of God.
▷HISTORY C17: from Arabic *ṣūfīy,* literally: (man) of wool, from *ṣūf* wool; probably from the ascetic's woollen garments
▸ˈ**Sufic** ADJECTIVE

Sufism (ˈsuːfɪzəm) NOUN the mystical doctrines of the Sufis.
▸**Sufistic** (suːˈfɪstɪk) ADJECTIVE

Sufu (ˈʃuːˈfuː) NOUN a variant spelling of **Shufu.**

súgán (ˈsuːgɑːn) NOUN *Irish* [1] a straw rope. [2] **súgán chair.** a chair with a seat made from woven súgáns.
▷HISTORY Irish Gaelic

sugar (ˈʃʊgə) NOUN [1] Also called: **sucrose, saccharose.** a white crystalline sweet carbohydrate, a disaccharide, found in many plants and extracted from sugar cane and sugar beet: it is used esp as a sweetening agent in food and drinks. Formula: $C_{12}H_{22}O_{11}$. Related adjective: **saccharine.** [2] any of a class of simple water-soluble carbohydrates, such as sucrose, lactose, and fructose. [3] *Informal, chiefly US and Canadian* a term of affection, esp for one's sweetheart. [4] *Rare* a slang word for **money.** [5] a slang name for **LSD.** ◆ VERB [6] (*tr*) to add sugar to; make sweet. [7] (*tr*) to cover or sprinkle with sugar. [8] (*intr*) to produce sugar. [9] **sugar the pill** *or* **medicine.** to make something unpleasant more agreeable by adding something pleasant: *the government stopped wage increases but sugared the pill by reducing taxes.*
▷HISTORY C13 *suker,* from Old French *çucre,* from Medieval Latin *zuccārum,* from Italian *zucchero,* from Arabic *sukkar,* from Persian *shakar,* from Sanskrit *śarkarā*
▸ˈ**sugarless** ADJECTIVE ▸ˈ**sugar-ˌlike** ADJECTIVE

sugarallie (ˈʃʊgərˈælɪ) NOUN *Scot* liquorice.
▷HISTORY C19: from earlier *sugar alicreesh*

sugar apple NOUN another name for **sweetsop.**

sugar bag NOUN *Austral and NZ* a small hessian bag occasionally still used, esp in rural areas, as a rough-and-ready measure for dry goods.

sugar beet NOUN a variety of the plant *Beta vulgaris* that is cultivated for its white roots from which sugar is obtained. Compare **sugar cane.**

sugar bird NOUN a South African nectar-eating bird, *Promerops cafer,* with a long curved bill and long tail: family *Meliphagidae* (honey-eaters).

sugar bush NOUN an anacardiaceous evergreen shrub, *Rhus ovata,* of S California and Arizona, having pale oval leaves, spikes of yellow-tinged red flowers, and deep red fruits.

sugar candy NOUN [1] Also called: **rock candy.** large crystals of sugar formed by suspending strings in a strong sugar solution that hardens on the strings, used chiefly for sweetening coffee. [2] *Chiefly US* confectionery; sweets.

sugar cane NOUN a coarse perennial grass, *Saccharum officinarum,* of Old World tropical regions, having tall stout canes that yield sugar: widely cultivated in tropical regions. Compare **sugar beet.**

sugar-coat VERB (*tr*) [1] to coat or cover with sugar. [2] to cause to appear more attractive; make agreeable.

sugar corn NOUN another name for **sweet corn** (sense 1).

sugar daddy NOUN *Slang* a rich usually middle-aged or old man who bestows expensive gifts on a young person in return for companionship or sexual favours.

sugar diabetes NOUN an informal name for **diabetes mellitus.**

sugared (ˈʃʊgəd) ADJECTIVE made sweeter or more appealing with or as with sugar.

sugar glider NOUN a common Australian phalanger, *Petaurus breviceps,* that glides from tree to tree feeding on insects and nectar.

sugar gum NOUN *Austral* a small eucalyptus tree, *Eucalyptus cladocalyx,* having smooth bark and barrel-shaped fruits and grown for timber and ornament. It has sweet-tasting leaves which are often eaten by livestock.

sugaring (ˈʃʊgərɪŋ) NOUN a method of removing unwanted body hair, whereby a thick viscous paste of sugar and water is applied to the hair, allowed to thicken, and then removed sharply, pulling the hairs out by their roots.

sugar loaf NOUN [1] a large conical mass of hard refined sugar. See also **loaf sugar.** [2] something resembling this in shape.

Sugar Loaf Mountain NOUN a mountain in SE Brazil, in Rio de Janeiro on Guanabara Bay. Height: 390 m (1280 ft.). Portuguese name: **Pão de Açúcar.**

sugar maple NOUN a North American maple tree, *Acer saccharum,* that is grown as a source of sugar, which is extracted from the sap, and for its hard wood.

sugar of lead (lɛd) NOUN another name for **lead acetate.**

sugar of milk NOUN another name for **lactose.**

sugar pea NOUN another name for **mangetout.**

sugar pie NOUN *Canadian* an open pie with a brown sugar filling.

sugar pine NOUN a pine tree, *Pinus lambertiana,* of California and Oregon, having spreading pendulous branches, light brown cones, and sugary resin.

sugarplum (ˈʃʊgəˌplʌm) NOUN a crystallized plum.

sugar soap NOUN an alkaline compound used for cleaning or stripping paint.

sugary (ˈʃʊgərɪ) ADJECTIVE [1] of, like, or containing sugar. [2] containing too much sugar; excessively sweet. [3] deceptively pleasant; insincere.
▸ˈ**sugariness** NOUN

suggest (səˈdʒɛst; *US* səgˈdʒɛst) VERB (*tr; may take a clause as object*) [1] to put forward (a plan, idea, etc.) for consideration: *I suggest Smith for the post; a plan suggested itself.* [2] to evoke (a person, thing, etc.) in the mind of someone by the association of ideas: *that painting suggests home to me.* [3] to give an indirect or vague hint of: *his face always suggests his peace of mind.*
▷HISTORY C16: from Latin *suggerere* to bring up, from SUB- + *gerere* to bring
▸**sugˈgester** NOUN

suggestibility (səˌdʒɛstɪˈbɪlɪtɪ) NOUN *Psychol* a state, esp under hypnosis, in which a person will accept the suggestions of another person and act accordingly.

suggestible (səˈdʒɛstɪbᵊl) ADJECTIVE [1] easily influenced by ideas provided by other persons. [2] characteristic of something that can be suggested.
▸**sugˈgestibleness** NOUN ▸**sugˈgestibly** ADVERB

suggestion (səˈdʒɛstʃən) NOUN [1] something that is suggested. [2] a hint or indication: *a suggestion of the odour of violets.* [3] *Psychol* the process whereby the mere presentation of an idea to a receptive individual leads to the acceptance of that idea. See also **autosuggestion.**

suggestive (səˈdʒɛstɪv) ADJECTIVE [1] (*postpositive; foll by* of) conveying a hint (of something): *this painting is suggestive of a hot summer day.* [2] tending to suggest something improper or indecent. [3] able or liable to suggest an idea, plan, etc.
▸**sugˈgestively** ADVERB ▸**sugˈgestiveness** NOUN

suicidal (ˌsuːɪˈsaɪdᵊl, ˌsjuː-) ADJECTIVE [1] involving, indicating, or tending towards suicide. [2] liable to result in suicide: *a suicidal attempt.* [3] liable to

destroy or spoil one's own interests or prospects; dangerously rash.
▸ ˌ**suiˈcidally** ADVERB

suicide (ˈsuːɪˌsaɪd, ˈsjuː-) NOUN [1] the act or an instance of killing oneself intentionally. [2] the self-inflicted ruin of one's own prospects or interests: *a merger would be financial suicide.* [3] a person who kills himself intentionally. [4] (*modifier*) reckless; extremely dangerous: *a suicide mission.* [5] (*modifier*) (of an action) undertaken or (of a person) undertaking an action in the knowledge that it will result in the death of the person performing it in order that maximum damage may be inflicted on an enemy: *a suicide attack; suicide bomber.*
▷HISTORY C17: from New Latin *suīcīdium,* from Latin *suī* of oneself + *-cīdium,* from *caedere* to kill

sui generis (ˌsuːaɪ ˈdʒɛnərɪs) ADJECTIVE unique.
▷HISTORY Latin, literally: of its own kind

sui juris (ˈsuːaɪ ˈdʒʊərɪs) ADJECTIVE (*usually postpositive*) *Law* of full age and not under disability; legally competent to manage one's own affairs; independent.
▷HISTORY C17: from Latin, literally: of one's own right

suint (ˈsuːɪnt, swɪnt) NOUN a water-soluble substance found in the fleece of sheep, consisting of peptides, organic acids, metal ions, and inorganic cations and formed from dried perspiration.
▷HISTORY C18: from French *suer* to sweat, from Latin *sūdāre*

Suisse (sɥis) NOUN the French name for **Switzerland.**

suit (suːt, sjuːt) NOUN [1] any set of clothes of the same or similar material designed to be worn together, now usually (for men) a jacket with matching trousers or (for women) a jacket with matching or contrasting skirt or trousers. [2] (*in combination*) any outfit worn for a specific purpose: *a spacesuit.* [3] any set of items, such as the full complement of sails of a vessel or parts of personal armour. [4] any of the four sets of 13 cards in a pack of playing cards, being spades, hearts, diamonds, and clubs. The cards in each suit are two to ten, jack, queen, and king in the usual order of ascending value, with ace counting as either the highest or lowest according to the game. [5] a civil proceeding; lawsuit. [6] the act or process of suing in a court of law. [7] a petition or appeal made to a person of superior rank or status or the act of making such a petition. [8] *Slang* a business executive or white-collar manager. [9] a man's courting of a woman. [10] **follow suit. a** to play a card of the same suit as the card played immediately before it. **b** to act in the same way as someone else. [11] **strong** *or* **strongest suit.** something that one excels in. ◆ VERB [12] to make or be fit or appropriate for: *that dress suits you.* [13] to meet the requirements or standards (of). [14] to be agreeable or acceptable to (someone). [15] **suit oneself.** to pursue one's own intentions without reference to others.
▷HISTORY C13: from Old French *sieute* set of things, from *sivre* to follow; compare SUE
▸ ˈ**suitˌlike** ADJECTIVE

suitable (ˈsuːtəbᵊl, ˈsjuːt-) ADJECTIVE appropriate; proper; fit.
▸ ˌ**suitaˈbility** *or* ˈ**suitableness** NOUN ▸ ˈ**suitably** ADVERB

suitcase (ˈsuːtˌkeɪs, ˈsjuːt-) NOUN a portable rectangular travelling case, usually stiffened, for carrying clothing, etc.

suite (swiːt) NOUN [1] a series of items intended to be used together; set. [2] a number of connected rooms in a hotel forming one living unit: *the presidential suite.* [3] a matching set of furniture, esp of two armchairs and a settee. [4] a number of attendants or followers. [5] *Music* **a** an instrumental composition consisting of several movements in the same key based on or derived from dance rhythms, esp in the baroque period. **b** an instrumental composition in several movements less closely connected than a sonata. **c** a piece of music containing movements based on or extracted from music already used in an opera, ballet, play, etc.
▷HISTORY C17: from French, from Old French *sieute;* see SUIT

suiter (ˈsuːtə, ˈsjuːtə) NOUN a piece of luggage for carrying suits and dresses.

suiting (ˈsuːtɪŋ, ˈsjuːt-) NOUN a fabric used for suits.

suitor (ˈsuːtə, ˈsjuːt-) NOUN [1] a man who courts a woman; wooer. [2] *Law* a person who brings a suit in a court of law; plaintiff. [3] *Rare* a person who makes a request or appeal for anything.
▷HISTORY C13: from Anglo-Norman *suter,* from Latin *secūtor* follower, from *sequī* to follow

Sukarnapura (sʊˌkɑːnəˈpʊərə) NOUN a former name of **Jayapura.**

Sukarno Peak NOUN a former name of (Mount) **Jaya.**

Sukhumi (*Russian* suˈxumi) NOUN a port and resort in W Georgia, on the Black Sea: site of an ancient Greek colony. Pop.: 112 000 (1993).

sukiyaki (ˌsuːkɪˈjɑːkɪ) NOUN a Japanese dish consisting of very thinly sliced beef or other meat, vegetables, and seasonings cooked together quickly, usually at the table.
▷HISTORY from Japanese

sukkah *or* **succah** (sʊˈkɑ, ˈsʊkɔ, ˈsʊkə) NOUN a temporary structure with a roof of branches in which orthodox Jews eat and, if possible, sleep during the festival of Sukkoth. Also called: **tabernacle.**
▷HISTORY from Hebrew, literally: tabernacle

Sukkoth *or* **Succoth** (ˈsʊkəʊt, -kəʊθ; *Hebrew* suːˈkɔt) NOUN an eight-day Jewish harvest festival beginning on Tishri 15, which commemorates the period when the Israelites lived in the wilderness. Also called: **Feast of Tabernacles.**
▷HISTORY from Hebrew, literally: tabernacles

Sulawesi (ˌsuːləˈweɪsɪ) NOUN an island in E Indonesia: mountainous and forested, with volcanoes and hot springs. Pop.: 14 768 400 (1999 est.). Area (including adjacent islands): 229 108 sq. km (88 440 sq. miles). Also called: **Celebes.**

sulcate (ˈsʌlkeɪt) ADJECTIVE *Biology* marked with longitudinal parallel grooves: *sulcate stems.*
▷HISTORY C18: via Latin *sulcātus* from *sulcāre* to plough, from *sulcus* a furrow
▸ **sulˈcation** NOUN

sulcus (ˈsʌlkəs) NOUN, *plural* **-ci** (-saɪ). [1] a linear groove, furrow, or slight depression. [2] any of the narrow grooves on the surface of the brain that mark the cerebral convolutions. Compare **fissure.**
▷HISTORY C17: from Latin

sulf- COMBINING FORM a US variant of **sulph-.**

> **Language note** See at **sulph-.**

sulfadiazine (ˌsʌlfəˈdaɪəˌziːn) NOUN an important sulfa drug used chiefly in combination with an antibiotic. Formula: $C_{10}H_{10}N_4O_2S$.

sulfadimidine (ˌsʌlfəˈdaɪmɪˌdiːn) NOUN an antibacterial sulfa drug used in human and veterinary medicine. It is effective against chlamydia, toxoplasma, and cocidia. US name: **sulfamethazine.**

sulfa drug (ˈsʌlfə) NOUN any of a group of sulfonamide compounds that inhibit the activity of bacteria and are used in medicine to treat bacterial infections.

sulfamethazine (ˌsʌlfəˈmɛθəˌziːn) NOUN US name for **sulfadimidine.**

sulfathiazole (ˌsʌlfəˈθaɪəˌzəʊl) NOUN an antimicrobial sulfa drug used in veterinary medicine and formerly in clinical medicine. Formula: $C_9H_9N_3O_2S_2$.

sulfur (ˈsʌlfə) NOUN the US preferred spelling of **sulphur.**

sulk (sʌlk) VERB [1] (*intr*) to be silent and resentful because of a wrong done to one, esp in order to gain sympathy; brood sullenly: *the child sulked in a corner after being slapped.* ◆ NOUN [2] (*often plural*) a state or mood of feeling resentful or sullen: *he's in a sulk because he lost the game; he's got the sulks.* [3] Also: **sulker.** a person who sulks.
▷HISTORY C18: perhaps a back formation from SULKY[1]

sulky[1] (ˈsʌlkɪ) ADJECTIVE **sulkier, sulkiest.** [1] sullen, withdrawn, or moody, through or as if through resentment. [2] dull or dismal: *sulky weather.*
▷HISTORY C18: perhaps from obsolete *sulke* sluggish, probably related to Old English *āseolcan* to be lazy
▸ ˈ**sulkily** ADVERB ▸ ˈ**sulkiness** NOUN

sulky[2] (ˈsʌlkɪ) NOUN, *plural* **sulkies.** a light two-wheeled vehicle for one person, usually drawn by one horse.
▷HISTORY C18: from SULKY[1], because it can carry only one person

sullage (ˈsʌlɪdʒ) NOUN [1] filth or waste, esp sewage. [2] sediment deposited by running water.
▷HISTORY C16: perhaps from French *souiller* to sully; compare Old English *sol* mud

sullen (ˈsʌlən) ADJECTIVE [1] unwilling to talk or be sociable; sulky; morose. [2] sombre; gloomy: *a sullen day.* [3] *Literary* sluggish; slow: *a sullen stream.* [4] *Obsolete* threatening. ◆ NOUN [5] (*plural*) *Archaic* a sullen mood.
▷HISTORY C16: perhaps from Anglo-French *solain* (unattested), ultimately related to Latin *sōlus* alone
▸ ˈ**sullenly** ADVERB ▸ ˈ**sullenness** NOUN

Sullom Voe (ˈsʌləm vəʊ) NOUN a deep coastal inlet in the Shetland Islands, on the N coast of Mainland. It is used for the storage and transshipment of oil.

sully (ˈsʌlɪ) VERB **-lies, -lying, -lied.** [1] to stain or tarnish (a reputation, etc.) or (of a reputation) to become stained or tarnished. ◆ NOUN, *plural* **-lies.** [2] a stain. [3] the act of sullying.
▷HISTORY C16: probably from French *souiller* to soil
▸ ˈ**sulliable** ADJECTIVE

sulph- *or US* **sulf-** COMBINING FORM containing sulphur: *sulphate; sulphonic acid.*

> **Language note** The "ph" spelling of *sulphur* and related words is used in British English. In the US the spelling is *sulfur.* However, the recommended spelling in chemistry is *sulfur* and this is found in technical writing. Also the *sulf-* spelling is used in the names of generic drugs.

sulphanilamide (ˌsʌlfəˈnɪləˌmaɪd) NOUN a white odourless crystalline compound formerly used in medicine in the treatment of bacterial infections. Formula: $NH_2C_6H_4SO_2NH_2$. See also **sulfa drug.**

sulphate (ˈsʌlfeɪt) NOUN [1] any salt or ester of sulphuric acid, such as sodium sulphate, Na_2SO_4, sodium hydrogen sulphate, or diethyl sulphate, $(C_2H_5)_2SO_4$. [2] *Slang* amphetamine sulphate. Often shortened to: **sulph.** ◆ VERB [3] (*tr*) to treat with a sulphate or convert into a sulphate. [4] to undergo or cause to undergo the formation of a layer of lead sulphate on the plates of an accumulator.
▷HISTORY C18: from New Latin *sulfātum;* see SULPHUR
▸ **sulˈphation** NOUN

sulphate-resisting cement NOUN a type of Portland cement that resists normal concentrations of sulphates: used in concrete for flues and underwater work.

sulphide (ˈsʌlfaɪd) NOUN [1] a compound of sulphur with a more electropositive element. [2] another name for **thio-ether.**

sulphinyl (ˈsʌlfənɪl) NOUN (*modifier*) another term (no longer in technical usage) for **thionyl.**
▷HISTORY C20: from SULF- + -IN + -YL

sulphite (ˈsʌlfaɪt) NOUN any salt or ester of sulphurous acid, containing the ions SO_3^{2-} or HSO_3^- (**hydrogen sulphite**) or the groups $-SO_3$ or $-HSO_3$. The salts are usually soluble crystalline compounds.
▸ **sulphitic** (sʌlˈfɪtɪk) ADJECTIVE

sulphonamide (sʌlˈfɒnəˌmaɪd) NOUN any of a class of organic compounds that are amides of sulphonic acids containing the group $-SO_2NH_2$ or a group derived from this. An important class of sulphonamides are the sulfa drugs.

sulphonate (ˈsʌlfəˌneɪt) *Chem* ◆ NOUN [1] a salt or ester of any sulphonic acid containing the ion RSO_2O^- or the group RSO_2O-, R being an organic group. ◆ VERB [2] (*tr*) to introduce a sulphonic acid group, $-SO_2OH$, into (a molecule).

sulphone (ˈsʌlfəʊn) NOUN any of a class of organic compounds containing the divalent group $-SO_2$ linked to two other organic groups. Certain sulphones are used in the treatment of leprosy and tuberculosis.

sulphonic acid (sʌlˈfɒnɪk) NOUN any of a large group of strong organic acids that contain the group $-SO_2OH$ and are used in the manufacture of dyes and drugs.

sulphonium compound *or* **salt** (sʌl'fəʊnɪəm) NOUN any one of a class of salts derived by the addition of a proton to the sulphur atom of a thiol or thio-ether thus producing a positive ion (**sulphonium ion**).

sulphonmethane (ˌsʌlfɒn'mi:θeɪn) NOUN a colourless crystalline compound used medicinally as a hypnotic. Formula: $C_7H_{16}O_4S_2$.

sulphonyl ('sʌlfənɪl) NOUN (*modifier*) another term for **sulphuryl**.

sulphur *or US* **sulfur** ('sʌlfə) NOUN **a** an allotropic nonmetallic element, occurring free in volcanic regions and in combined state in gypsum, pyrite, and galena. The stable yellow rhombic form converts on heating to monoclinic needles. It is used in the production of sulphuric acid, in the vulcanization of rubber, and in fungicides. Symbol: S; atomic no.: 16; atomic wt.: 32.066; valency: 2, 4, or 6; relative density: 2.07 (rhombic), 1.957 (monoclinic); melting pt.: 115.22°C (rhombic), 119.0°C (monoclinic); boiling pt.: 444.674°C. Related adjective: **thionic**. **b** (*as modifier*): *sulphur springs*.
▷HISTORY C14 *soufre*, from Old French, from Latin *sulfur*
▸**sulphuric** *or US* **sulfuric** (sʌl'fjʊərɪk) ADJECTIVE

sulphurate ('sʌlfjʊˌreɪt) VERB (*tr*) to combine or treat with sulphur or a sulphur compound.
▸ˌ**sulphu'ration** NOUN

sulphur-bottom NOUN another name for **blue whale**.

sulphur-crested cockatoo NOUN a large Australian white parrot, *Kakatoe galerita*, with a yellow erectile crest. Also called: **white cockatoo**.

sulphur dioxide NOUN a colourless soluble pungent gas produced by burning sulphur. It is both an oxidizing and a reducing agent and is used in the manufacture of sulphuric acid, the preservation of a wide range of foodstuffs (**E220**), bleaching, and disinfecting. Formula: SO_2. Systematic name: **sulphur(IV) oxide**.

sulphureous (sʌl'fjʊərɪəs) ADJECTIVE [1] another word for **sulphurous** (sense 1). [2] of the yellow colour of sulphur.
▸**sul'phureously** ADVERB ▸**sul'phureousness** NOUN

sulphuret ('sʌlfjʊˌrɛt) VERB **-rets, -retting, -retted** *or US* **-rets, -reting, -reted**. (*tr*) to treat or combine with sulphur.

sulphuretted hydrogen NOUN another name for **hydrogen sulphide**.

sulphuric acid NOUN a colourless dense oily corrosive liquid produced by the reaction of sulphur trioxide with water and used in accumulators and in the manufacture of fertilizers, dyes, and explosives. Formula: H_2SO_4. Systematic name: **sulphuric(VI) acid**.

sulphurize *or* **sulphurise** ('sʌlfjʊˌraɪz) VERB (*tr*) to combine or treat with sulphur or a sulphur compound.
▸ˌ**sulphuri'zation** *or* ˌ**sulfuri'sation** NOUN

sulphurous ('sʌlfərəs) ADJECTIVE [1] Also: **sulphureous**. of, relating to, or resembling sulphur: *a sulphurous colour*. [2] of or containing sulphur with an oxidation state of 4: *sulphurous acid*. [3] of or relating to hellfire. [4] hot-tempered.
▸**'sulphurously** ADVERB ▸**'sulphurousness** NOUN

sulphurous acid NOUN an unstable acid produced when sulphur dioxide dissolves in water: used as a preservative for food and a bleaching agent. Formula: H_2SO_3. Systematic name: **sulphuric(IV) acid**.

sulphur trioxide NOUN a white corrosive substance existing in three crystalline forms of which the stable (*alpha-*) form is usually obtained as silky needles. It is produced by the oxidation of sulphur dioxide, and is used in the sulphonation of organic compounds. Formula: SO_3. Systematic name: **sulphur(VI) oxide**.

sulphur tuft NOUN a poisonous basidiomycetous fungus, *Hypholoma fasciculare*, having a sulphurous yellow cap and found in clumps on and around broad-leaved trees.

sulphuryl ('sʌlfjʊrɪl, -fərɪl) NOUN (*modifier*) of, consisting of, or containing the divalent group, $=SO_2$: *sulphuryl chloride*. Also: **sulphonyl** ('sʌlfəˌnɪl).

sultan ('sʌltən) NOUN [1] the sovereign of a Muslim country, esp of the former Ottoman Empire. [2] an arbitrary ruler; despot. [3] a small domestic fowl with a white crest and heavily feathered legs and feet: originated in Turkey.
▷HISTORY C16: from Medieval Latin *sultānus*, from Arabic *sultān* rule, from Aramaic *salita* to rule
▸**sultanic** (sʌl'tænɪk) ADJECTIVE ▸**'sultan-ˌlike** ADJECTIVE
▸**'sultanship** NOUN

sultana (sʌl'tɑ:nə) NOUN [1] **a** the dried fruit of a small white seedless grape, originally produced in SW Asia: used in cakes, curries, etc.; seedless raisin. **b** the grape itself. [2] Also called: **sultaness**. a wife, concubine, or female relative of a sultan. [3] a mistress; concubine.
▷HISTORY C16: from Italian, feminine of *sultano* SULTAN

sultanate ('sʌltəˌneɪt) NOUN [1] the territory or a country ruled by a sultan. [2] the office, rank, or jurisdiction of a sultan.

sultry ('sʌltrɪ) ADJECTIVE **-trier, -triest**. [1] (of weather or climate) oppressively hot and humid. [2] characterized by or emitting oppressive heat. [3] displaying or suggesting passion; sensual: *sultry eyes*.
▷HISTORY C16: from obsolete *sulter* to SWELTER + -Y[1]
▸**'sultrily** ADVERB ▸**'sultriness** NOUN

Sulu Archipelago ('su:lu:) NOUN a chain of over 500 islands in the SW Philippines, separating the Sulu Sea from the Celebes Sea: formerly a sultanate, ceded to the Philippines in 1940. Capital: Jolo. Pop.: 555 240 (latest est.). Area: 2686 sq. km (1037 sq. miles).

Sulu Sea NOUN part of the W Pacific between Borneo and the central Philippines.

sum[1] (sʌm) NOUN [1] **a** the result of the addition of numbers, quantities, objects, etc. **b** the cardinality of the union of disjoint sets whose cardinalities are the given numbers. [2] one or more columns or rows of numbers to be added, subtracted, multiplied, or divided. [3] *Maths* the limit of a series of sums of the first *n* terms of a converging infinite series as *n* tends to infinity. [4] (*plural*) another name for **number work**. [5] a quantity, esp of money: *he borrows enormous sums*. [6] the essence or gist of a matter (esp in the phrases **in sum, in sum and substance**). [7] a less common word for **summary**. [8] *Archaic* the summit or maximum. [9] (*modifier*) complete or final (esp in the phrase **sum total**). ◆ VERB **sums, summing, summed**. [10] (often foll by *up*) to add or form a total of (something). [11] (*tr*) to calculate the sum of (the terms in a sequence). ◆ See also **sum up**.
▷HISTORY C13 *summe*, from Old French, from Latin *summa* the top, sum, from *summus* highest, from *superus* in a higher position; see SUPER

sum[2] (sum) NOUN, *plural* **sumy** (sumɪ). the standard monetary unit of Uzbekistan, divided into 100 tiyin.

sumach *or US* **sumac** ('su:mæk, 'ʃu:-) NOUN [1] any temperate or subtropical shrub or small tree of the anacardiaceous genus *Rhus*, having compound leaves, clusters of green flowers, and red hairy fruits. See also **poison sumach**. [2] a preparation of powdered leaves of certain species of *Rhus*, esp *R. coriaria*, used in dyeing and tanning. [3] the wood of any of these plants.
▷HISTORY C14: via Old French from Arabic *summāq*

Sumatra (sʊ'mɑ:trə) NOUN a mountainous island in W Indonesia, in the Greater Sunda Islands, separated from the Malay Peninsula by the Strait of Malacca: Dutch control began in the 16th century; joined Indonesia in 1945. Pop.: 24 284 400 (1999 est.). Area: 473 606 sq. km (182 821 sq. miles).

Sumatran (sʊ'mɑ:trən) ADJECTIVE [1] of or relating to Sumatra or its inhabitants. ◆ NOUN [2] a native or inhabitant of Sumatra.

Sumba *or* **Soemba** ('su:mbə) NOUN an island in Indonesia, in the Lesser Sunda Islands, separated from Flores by the **Sumba Strait**: formerly important for sandalwood exports. Pop.: 355 073 (1990). Area: 11 153 sq. km (4306 sq. miles). Former name: **Sandalwood Island**.

Sumbawa *or* **Soembawa** (su:m'bɑ:wə) NOUN a mountainous island in Indonesia, in the Lesser Sunda Islands, between Lombok and Flores Islands. Pop.: 373 000 (1990 est.). Area: 14 750 sq. km (5695 sq. miles).

Sumer ('su:mə) NOUN the S region of Babylonia; seat of a civilization of city-states that reached its height in the 3rd millennium B.C.

Sumerian (su:'mɪərɪən, -'mɛər-) NOUN [1] a member of a people who established a civilization in Sumer during the 4th millennium B.C. [2] the extinct language of this people, of no known relationship to any other language. ◆ ADJECTIVE [3] of or relating to ancient Sumer, its inhabitants, or their language or civilization.

summa ('sʊmɑ:) NOUN, *plural* **-mae** (-mi:). [1] *Medieval Christianity, theol* a compendium of theology, philosophy, or canon law, or sometimes of all three together. The **Summa Theologica** of St Thomas Aquinas, written between 1265 and 1274, was the most famous of all such compendia. [2] *Rare* a comprehensive work or survey.
▷HISTORY C15: from Latin: SUM[1]

summa cum laude ('sʊmɑ: kʊm 'laʊdeɪ) ADVERB, ADJECTIVE *Chiefly US* with the utmost praise: the highest of three designations for above-average achievement in examinations. In Britain it is sometimes used to designate a first-class honours degree. Compare **cum laude, magna cum laude**.
▷HISTORY from Latin

summand ('sʌmænd, sʌ'mænd) NOUN a number or quantity forming part of a sum.
▷HISTORY C19: from Medieval Latin *summandus*, from Latin *summa* SUM[1]

summarize *or* **summarise** ('sʌməˌraɪz) VERB (*tr*) to make or be a summary of; express concisely.
▸**'summaˌrizable** *or* **'summaˌrisable** ADJECTIVE
▸ˌ**summari'zation** *or* ˌ**summari'sation** NOUN ▸**'summaˌrizer** *or* **'summaˌriser** *or* **'summarist** NOUN

summary ('sʌmərɪ) NOUN, *plural* **-maries**. [1] a brief account giving the main points of something. ◆ ADJECTIVE (*usually prenominal*) [2] performed arbitrarily and quickly, without formality: *a summary execution*. [3] (of legal proceedings) short and free from the complexities and delays of a full trial. [4] **summary jurisdiction**. the right a court has to adjudicate immediately upon some matter arising during its proceedings. [5] giving the gist or essence.
▷HISTORY C15: from Latin *summārium*, from *summa* SUM[1]
▸**'summarily** ADVERB ▸**'summariness** NOUN

summary offence NOUN an offence that is triable in a magistrates' court.

summat ('sʌmət) PRONOUN *Brit not standard* something: *you gonna do summat about it or what?*

summation (sʌ'meɪʃən) NOUN [1] the act or process of determining a sum; addition. [2] the result of such an act or process. [3] a summary. [4] *US law* the concluding statements made by opposing counsel in a case before a court.
▷HISTORY C18: from Medieval Latin *summātiō*, from *summāre* to total, from Latin *summa* SUM[1]
▸**sum'mational** ADJECTIVE ▸**'summative** ADJECTIVE

summative assessment ('sʌmətɪv) NOUN *Brit education* general assessment of a pupil's achievements over a range of subjects by means of a combined appraisal of formative assessments.

summer[1] ('sʌmə) NOUN [1] (*sometimes capital*) **a** the warmest season of the year, between spring and autumn, astronomically from the June solstice to the September equinox in the N hemisphere and at the opposite time of year in the S hemisphere. **b** (*as modifier*): *summer flowers; a summer dress*. Related adjective: **aestival**. [2] the period of hot weather associated with the summer. [3] a time of blossoming, greatest happiness, etc. [4] *Chiefly poetic* a year represented by this season: *a child of nine summers*. ◆ VERB [5] (*intr*) to spend the summer (at a place). [6] (*tr*) to keep or feed (farm animals) during the summer: *they summered their cattle on the mountain slopes*.
▷HISTORY Old English *sumor*; related to Old Frisian *sumur*, Old Norse *sumar*, Old High German *sumar*, Sanskrit *samā* season
▸**'summerless** ADJECTIVE ▸**'summer-ˌlike** ADJECTIVE
▸**'summerly** ADJECTIVE, ADVERB ▸**'summery** ADJECTIVE
▸**'summeriness** NOUN

summer[2] ('sʌmə) NOUN [1] Also called: **summer tree**. a large horizontal beam or girder, esp one that supports floor joists. [2] another name for **lintel**. [3] a stone on the top of a column, pier, or wall that supports an arch or lintel.
▷HISTORY C14: from Anglo-Norman *somer*, from Old French *somier* beam, packhorse, from Late Latin

sagmārius (*equus*) pack(horse), from *sagma* a packsaddle, from Greek

summer cypress NOUN another name for **kochia.**

summerhouse (ˈsʌməˌhaʊs) NOUN a small building in a garden or park, used for shade or recreation in the summer.

summer pudding NOUN *Brit* a pudding made by filling a bread-lined basin with a purée of fruit, leaving it to soak, and then turning it out.

summersault (ˈsʌməˌsɔːlt) NOUN, VERB a variant spelling of **somersault.**

summer school NOUN a school, academic course, etc., held during the summer.

summer solstice NOUN [1] the time at which the sun is at its northernmost point in the sky (southernmost point in the S hemisphere), appearing at noon at its highest altitude above the horizon. It occurs about June 21 (December 22 in the S hemisphere). [2] *Astronomy* the point on the celestial sphere, opposite the **winter solstice**, at which the ecliptic is furthest north from the celestial equator. Right ascension: 6 hours; declination: 23.5°.

summer sores NOUN *Vet science* a condition of horses in which itchy lesions are caused by infestation of wounds with *Habronema larvae* from flies.

summertime (ˈsʌməˌtaɪm) NOUN the period or season of summer.

summer time NOUN *Brit* any daylight-saving time, esp British Summer Time.

summerweight (ˈsʌməˌweɪt) ADJECTIVE (of clothes) suitable in weight for wear in the summer; relatively light.

summerwood (ˈsʌməˌwʊd) NOUN the wood that is produced by a plant near the end of the growing season: consists of small thick-walled xylem cells. Compare **springwood.**

summing-up NOUN [1] a review or summary of the main points of an argument, speech, etc. [2] a direction regarding the law and a summary of the evidence, given by a judge in his address to the jury before they retire to consider their verdict.

summit (ˈsʌmɪt) NOUN [1] the highest point or part, esp of a mountain or line of communication; top. [2] the highest possible degree or state; peak or climax: *the summit of ambition.* [3] the highest level, importance, or rank: *a meeting at the summit.* [4] **a** a meeting of chiefs of governments or other high officials. **b** (*as modifier*): *a summit conference.*
▷HISTORY C15: from Old French *somet,* diminutive of *som,* from Latin *summum;* see SUM¹
▸ˈ**summital** ADJECTIVE ▸ˈ**summitless** ADJECTIVE

summiteer (ˌsʌmɪˈtɪə) NOUN a person who participates in a summit conference.

summitry (ˈsʌmɪtrɪ) NOUN *Chiefly US* the practice of conducting international negotiations by summit conferences.

summon (ˈsʌmən) VERB (*tr*) [1] to order to come; send for, esp to attend court, by issuing a summons. [2] to order or instruct (to do something) or call (to something): *the bell summoned them to their work.* [3] to call upon to meet or convene. [4] (often foll by *up*) to muster or gather (one's strength, courage, etc.).
▷HISTORY C13: from Latin *summonēre* to give a discreet reminder, from *monēre* to advise
▸ˈ**summonable** ADJECTIVE

summons (ˈsʌmənz) NOUN, *plural* **-monses.** [1] a call, signal, or order to do something, esp to appear in person or attend at a specified place or time. [2] **a** an official order requiring a person to attend court, either to answer a charge or to give evidence. **b** the writ making such an order. Compare **warrant.** [3] a call or command given to the members of an assembly to convene a meeting. ♦ VERB [4] to take out a summons against (a person).
▷HISTORY C13: from Old French *somonse,* from *somondre* to SUMMON

summum bonum *Latin* (ˈsʊmʊm ˈbɒnʊm) NOUN the principle of goodness in which all moral values are included or from which they are derived; highest or supreme good.

sumo (ˈsuːməʊ) NOUN the national style of wrestling of Japan, the object of which is to force one's opponent to touch the ground with any part of his body except the soles of his feet or to step out of the ring.
▷HISTORY from Japanese *sumō*

sump (sʌmp) NOUN [1] a receptacle, such as the lower part of the crankcase of an internal-combustion engine, into which liquids, esp lubricants, can drain to form a reservoir. [2] another name for **cesspool.** [3] *Mining* **a** a depression at the bottom of a shaft where water collects before it is pumped away. **b** the front portion of a shaft or tunnel, ahead of the main bore. [4] *Brit dialect* a muddy pool or swamp.
▷HISTORY C17: from Middle Dutch *somp* marsh; see SWAMP

sumph (sʌmf) NOUN *Scot* a stupid person; simpleton.
▷HISTORY C18: of uncertain origin

sumpter (ˈsʌmptə) NOUN *Archaic* a packhorse, mule, or other beast of burden.
▷HISTORY C14: from Old French *sometier* driver of a baggage horse, from Vulgar Latin *sagmatārius* (unattested), from Late Latin *sagma* packsaddle

sumptuary (ˈsʌmptjʊərɪ) ADJECTIVE relating to or controlling expenditure or extravagance.
▷HISTORY C17: from Latin *sumptuārius* concerning expense, from *sumptus* expense, from *sūmere* to spend

sumptuary law NOUN (formerly) a law imposing restraint on luxury, esp by limiting personal expenditure or by regulating personal conduct in religious and moral spheres.

sumptuous (ˈsʌmptjʊəs) ADJECTIVE [1] expensive or extravagant: *sumptuous costumes.* [2] magnificent; splendid: *a sumptuous scene.*
▷HISTORY C16: from Old French *somptueux,* from Latin *sumptuōsus* costly, from *sumptus;* see SUMPTUARY
▸ˈ**sumptuously** ADVERB ▸ˈ**sumptuousness** *or* **sumptuosity** (ˌsʌmptjʊˈɒsɪtɪ) NOUN

sum up VERB (*adverb*) [1] to summarize (feelings, the main points of an argument, etc.): *the judge began to sum up.* [2] (*tr*) to form a quick opinion of: *I summed him up in five minutes.*

Sumy (*Russian* ˈsumi) NOUN a city in the Ukraine, on the River Pysol: site of early Slav settlements. Pop.: 299 800 (1998 est.).

sun (sʌn) NOUN [1] the star at the centre of our solar system. It is a gaseous body having a highly compressed core, in which energy is generated by thermonuclear reactions (at about 15 million kelvins), surrounded by less dense radiative and convective zones serving to transport the energy to the surface (the **photosphere**). The atmospheric layers (the **chromosphere** and **corona**) are normally invisible except during a total eclipse. Mass and diameter: 333 000 and 109 times that of earth respectively; mean distance from earth: 149.6 million km (1 astronomical unit). Related adjective: **solar.** [2] any star around which a planetary system revolves. [3] the sun as it appears at a particular time or place: *the winter sun.* [4] the radiant energy, esp heat and light, received from the sun; sunshine. [5] a person or thing considered as a source of radiant warmth, glory, etc. [6] a pictorial representation of the sun, often depicted with a human face. [7] *Poetic* a year or a day. [8] *Poetic* a climate. [9] *Archaic* sunrise or sunset (esp in the phrase **from sun to sun**). [10] **catch the sun.** to become slightly sunburnt. [11] **place in the sun.** a prominent or favourable position. [12] **take** *or* **shoot the sun.** *Nautical* to measure the altitude of the sun in order to determine latitude. [13] **touch of the sun.** slight sunstroke. [14] **under** *or* **beneath the sun.** on earth; at all: *nobody under the sun eats more than you do.* ♦ VERB **suns, sunning, sunned.** [15] to expose (oneself) to the sunshine. [16] (*tr*) to expose to the sunshine in order to warm, tan, etc.
▷HISTORY Old English *sunne;* related to Old High German *sunna,* Old Frisian *senne,* Gothic *sunno*
▸ˈ**sunˌlike** ADJECTIVE

Sun. ABBREVIATION FOR Sunday.

sunbake (ˈsʌnˌbeɪk) *Austral informal* ♦ VERB (*intr*) [1] to sunbathe, esp in order to become tanned. ♦ NOUN [2] a period of sunbaking.

sunbaked (ˈsʌnˌbeɪkt) ADJECTIVE [1] (esp of roads, etc.) dried or cracked by the sun's heat. [2] baked hard by the heat of the sun: *sunbaked bricks.*

sun bath NOUN the exposure of the body to the rays of the sun or a sun lamp, esp in order to get a suntan.

sunbathe (ˈsʌnˌbeɪð) VERB (*intr*) to bask in the sunshine, esp in order to get a suntan.
▸ˈ**sunˌbather** NOUN

sunbeam (ˈsʌnˌbiːm) NOUN [1] a beam, ray, or stream of sunlight. [2] *Austral slang* a piece of crockery or cutlery laid for a meal but remaining unused.
▸ˈ**sunˌbeamed** *or* ˈ**sunˌbeamy** ADJECTIVE

sun bear NOUN a small bear, *Helarctos malayanus,* of tropical forests in S and SE Asia, having a black coat and a yellowish snout and feeding mostly on honey and insects. Also called: **honey bear.**

sunbird (ˈsʌnˌbɜːd) NOUN any small songbird of the family *Nectariniidae,* of tropical regions of the Old World, esp Africa, having a long slender curved bill and a bright plumage in the males.

sun bittern NOUN a cranelike bird, *Eurypyga helias,* of tropical American forests, having a greyish plumage with orange and brown wings: family *Eurypygidae,* order *Gruiformes* (cranes, rails, etc.).

sun blind NOUN *Chiefly Brit* a blind, such as a Venetian blind, that shades a room from the sun's glare.

sun block NOUN a chemical, usually in the form of a cream, applied to exposed skin to block out all or almost all of the ultraviolet rays of the sun.

sunbonnet (ˈsʌnˌbɒnɪt) NOUN a hat that shades the face and neck from the sun, esp one made of cotton with a projecting brim now worn esp by babies.
▸ˈ**sunˌbonneted** ADJECTIVE

sunbow (ˈsʌnˌbəʊ) NOUN a bow of prismatic colours similar to a rainbow, produced when sunlight shines through spray.

sunburn (ˈsʌnˌbɜːn) NOUN [1] inflammation of the skin caused by overexposure to the sun. Technical name: **erythema solare.** [2] another word for **suntan.**
▸ˈ**sunˌburnt** *or* ˈ**sunˌburned** ADJECTIVE

sunburst (ˈsʌnˌbɜːst) NOUN [1] a burst of sunshine, as through a break in the clouds. [2] a pattern or design resembling that of the sun. [3] a jewelled brooch with this pattern.

sunburst pleats PLURAL NOUN the US term for **sunray pleats.**

Sunbury-on-Thames (ˈsʌnbərɪ, -brɪ) NOUN a town in SE England, in N Surrey. Pop.: 27 392 (1991).

sun-cured ADJECTIVE cured or preserved by exposure to the sun.

sundae (ˈsʌndɪ, -deɪ) NOUN ice cream topped with a sweet sauce, nuts, whipped cream, etc.
▷HISTORY C20: of uncertain origin

Sunda Islands (ˈsʌndə) *or* **Soenda Islands** PLURAL NOUN a chain of islands in the Malay Archipelago, consisting of the **Greater Sunda Islands** (chiefly Sumatra, Java, Borneo, and Sulawesi) and **Nusa Tenggara** (formerly the Lesser Sunda Islands).

sun dance NOUN a North American Indian ceremony associated with the sun, performed at the summer solstice.

Sunda Strait *or* **Soenda Strait** NOUN a strait between Sumatra and Java, linking the Java Sea with the Indian Ocean. Narrowest point: about 26 km (16 miles).

Sunday (ˈsʌndɪ) NOUN the first day of the week and the Christian day of worship.
▷HISTORY Old English *sunnandæg,* translation of Latin *diēs sōlis* day of the sun, translation of Greek *hēmera hēliou;* related to Old Norse *sunnu dagr,* German *Sonntag*

Sunday best NOUN one's best clothes, esp regarded as those most suitable for churchgoing.

Sunday driver NOUN *Informal* a person who drives slowly, timorously, or unskilfully, as if used to driving only on Sundays when the roads are relatively quiet.

Sunday painter NOUN a person who paints pictures as a hobby.

Sunday punch NOUN *Informal, chiefly US* [1] *Boxing* a heavy blow intended to knock out one's opponent. [2] any manoeuvre or action intended to crush an opponent.

Sunday school NOUN [1] **a** a school for the religious instruction of children on Sundays, usually held in a church hall and formerly also providing secular education. **b** (*as modifier*): *a Sunday-school outing.* [2] the members of such a school.

sun deck NOUN [1] an upper open deck on a passenger ship. [2] *US, Austral, and NZ* a balcony or deck attached to a house, originally used for sunbathing.

sunder ('sʌndə) *Archaic or literary* ◆ VERB [1] to break or cause to break apart or in pieces. ◆ NOUN [2] **in sunder.** into pieces; apart.
▷HISTORY Old English *sundrian;* related to Old Norse *sundr* asunder, Gothic *sundrō* apart, Old High German *suntar,* Latin *sine* without
▸**'sunderable** ADJECTIVE ▸**'sunderance** NOUN ▸**'sunderer** NOUN

Sunderland ('sʌndələnd) NOUN [1] a city and port in NE England, in Sunderland unitary authority, Tyne and Wear at the mouth of the River Wear: formerly known for shipbuilding; now has car manufacturing, chemicals; university (1992). Pop.: 183 310 (1991). [2] a unitary authority in NE England, in Tyne and Wear. Pop.: 280 807 (2001). Area: 138 sq. km (53 sq. miles).

sundew ('sʌn,dju:) NOUN any of several bog plants of the genus *Drosera,* having leaves covered with sticky hairs that trap and digest insects: family *Droseraceae.*
▷HISTORY C16: translation of Latin *ros solis*

sundial ('sʌn,daɪəl) NOUN a device indicating the time during the hours of sunlight by means of a stationary arm (the **gnomon**) that casts a shadow onto a plate or surface marked in hours at right angles to the gnomon.

sun disc NOUN a disc symbolizing the sun, esp one flanked by two serpents and the extended wings of a vulture, used as a religious figure in ancient Egypt.

sundog ('sʌn,dɒg) NOUN [1] another word for **parhelion.** [2] a small rainbow or halo near the horizon.

sundown ('sʌn,daʊn) NOUN another name for **sunset.**

sundowner ('sʌn,daʊnə) NOUN [1] *Austral and NZ obsolete slang* a tramp, esp one who seeks food and lodging at sundown when it is too late to work. [2] *Nautical* a strict ship's officer. [3] *Informal, chiefly Brit* an alcoholic drink taken at sunset. [4] *NZ slang* a lazy sheepdog.

sundress ('sʌn,drɛs) NOUN a dress for hot weather that exposes the shoulders, arms, and back, esp one with straps over the shoulders.

sun-dried ADJECTIVE dried or preserved by exposure to the sun.

sundry ('sʌndrɪ) DETERMINER [1] several or various; miscellaneous. ◆ PRONOUN [2] **all and sundry.** all the various people, individually and collectively. ◆ NOUN, *plural* **-dries.** [3] (*plural*) miscellaneous unspecified items. [4] an Austral name for **extra** (sense 6).
▷HISTORY Old English *syndrig* separate; related to Old High German *suntarīg;* see SUNDER, -Y[1]

sundry shop NOUN (in Malaysia) a shop, similar to a delicatessen, that sells predominantly Chinese foodstuffs.

sunfast ('sʌn,fɑ:st) ADJECTIVE *Chiefly US and Canadian* not fading in sunlight.

sunfish ('sʌn,fɪʃ) NOUN, *plural* **-fish** *or* **-fishes.** [1] any large plectognath fish of the family *Molidae,* of temperate and tropical seas, esp *Mola mola,* which has a large rounded compressed body, long pointed dorsal and anal fins, and a fringelike tail fin. [2] any of various small predatory North American freshwater percoid fishes of the family *Centrarchidae,* typically having a compressed brightly coloured body.

sunflower ('sʌn,flaʊə) NOUN [1] any of several American plants of the genus *Helianthus,* esp *H. annuus,* having very tall thick stems, large flower heads with yellow rays, and seeds used as food, esp for poultry: family *Asteraceae* (composites). See also **Jerusalem artichoke.** [2] **sunflower seed oil.** the oil extracted from sunflower seeds, used as a salad oil, in the manufacture of margarine, etc.

sung (sʌŋ) VERB [1] the past participle of **sing.** ◆ ADJECTIVE [2] produced by singing: *a sung syllable.*

> **Language note** See at **ring**[2].

sunglass ('sʌn,glɑ:s) NOUN a convex lens used to focus the sun's rays and thus produce heat or ignition; burning glass.

sunglasses ('sʌn,glɑ:sɪz) PLURAL NOUN glasses with darkened or polarizing lenses that protect the eyes from the sun's glare.

sunglow ('sʌn,gləʊ) NOUN a pinkish glow often seen in the sky before sunrise or after sunset. It is caused by scattering or diffraction of sunlight by particles in the atmosphere.

sun-god NOUN [1] the sun considered as a personal deity. [2] a deity associated with the sun or controlling its movements.

sungrebe ('sʌn,gri:b) NOUN another name for **finfoot.**

sunhat ('sʌn,hæt) NOUN a hat that shades the face and neck from the sun.

sunk (sʌŋk) VERB [1] a past participle of **sink.** ◆ ADJECTIVE [2] *Informal* with all hopes dashed; ruined: *if the police come while we're opening the safe, we'll be sunk.*

sunken ('sʌŋkən) VERB [1] a past participle of **sink.** ◆ ADJECTIVE [2] unhealthily hollow: *sunken cheeks.* [3] situated at a lower level than the surrounding or usual one. [4] situated under water; submerged. [5] depressed; low: *sunken spirits.*

sunk fence NOUN a ditch, one side of which is made into a retaining wall so as to enclose an area of land while remaining hidden in the total landscape. Also called: **ha-ha.**

sun lamp NOUN [1] a lamp that generates ultraviolet rays, used for obtaining an artificial suntan, for muscular therapy, etc. [2] a lamp used in film studios, etc., to give an intense beam of light by means of parabolic mirrors.

sunless ('sʌnlɪs) ADJECTIVE [1] without sun or sunshine. [2] gloomy; depressing.
▸**'sunlessly** ADVERB ▸**'sunlessness** NOUN

sunlight ('sʌnlaɪt) NOUN [1] the light emanating from the sun. [2] an area or the time characterized by sunshine.
▸**'sunlit** ADJECTIVE

sun lounge *or US* **sun parlor** NOUN a room with large windows positioned to receive as much sunlight as possible.

sunn (sʌn) NOUN [1] a leguminous plant, *Crotalaria juncea,* of the East Indies, having yellow flowers. [2] the hemplike fibre obtained from the inner bark of this plant, used in making rope, sacking, etc.
▷HISTORY C18: from Hindi *san,* from Sanskrit *śāṇá* hempen

Sunna ('sʌnə) NOUN the body of traditional Islamic law accepted by most orthodox Muslims as based on the words and acts of Mohammed.
▷HISTORY C18: from Arabic *sunnah* rule

Sunni ('sʌnɪ) NOUN [1] one of the two main branches of orthodox Islam (the other being the Shiah), consisting of those who acknowledge the authority of the Sunna. [2] (*plural* **-nis** *or* **-ni**) another term for **Sunnite.**

sunnies ('sʌnɪz) PLURAL NOUN *NZ informal* a pair of sunglasses.

Sunnite ('sʌnaɪt) NOUN *Islam* an adherent of the Sunni.

sunny ('sʌnɪ) ADJECTIVE **-nier, -niest.** [1] full of or exposed to sunlight. [2] radiating good humour. [3] of or resembling the sun.
▸**'sunnily** ADVERB ▸**'sunniness** NOUN

sunny side NOUN [1] the cheerful aspect or point of view: *look on the sunny side of things.* [2] **on the sunny side of.** *Informal* younger than (a specified age).

sunny-side up ADJECTIVE (of eggs) fried on one side only.

sunray pleats ('sʌn,reɪ) PLURAL NOUN *Brit* bias-cut knife pleats that are narrower at the top than at the bottom, producing a flared effect, used esp for skirts. US term: **sunburst pleats.**

sunrise ('sʌn,raɪz) NOUN [1] the daily appearance of the sun above the horizon. [2] the atmospheric phenomena accompanying this appearance. [3] Also called (esp US): **sunup.** the time at which the sun rises at a particular locality. [4] (*modifier*) of or relating to sunrise industry: *sunrise technology; sunrise sector.*

sunrise industry NOUN any of the high-technology industries, such as electronics, that hold promise of future development.

sunroof ('sʌn,ru:f) *or* **sunshine roof** NOUN a panel, often translucent, that may be opened in the roof of a car.

sunroom ('sʌn,ru:m, 'sʌn,rʊm) NOUN a room or glass-enclosed porch designed to display beautiful views, to admit and retain the sun's heat in cool countries, and reflect it away in warm countries.

sunscreen ('sʌn,skri:n) NOUN a cream or lotion applied to exposed skin to protect it from the ultraviolet rays of the sun.

sunset ('sʌn,sɛt) NOUN [1] the daily disappearance of the sun below the horizon. [2] the atmospheric phenomena accompanying this disappearance. [3] Also called: **sundown.** the time at which the sun sets at a particular locality. [4] the final stage or closing period, as of a person's life.

sunshade ('sʌn,ʃeɪd) NOUN a device, esp a parasol or awning, serving to shade from the sun.

sunshine ('sʌn,ʃaɪn) NOUN [1] the light received directly from the sun. [2] the warmth from the sun. [3] a sunny area. [4] a light-hearted or ironic term of address.
▸**'sun,shiny** ADJECTIVE

sunspot ('sʌn,spɒt) NOUN [1] any of the dark cool patches, with a diameter of up to several thousand kilometres, that appear on the surface of the sun and last about a week. They occur in approximately 11-year cycles and possess a strong magnetic field. [2] *Informal* a sunny holiday resort. [3] *Austral* a small cancerous spot produced by overexposure to the sun.
▸**'sun,spotted** ADJECTIVE

sunstar ('sʌn,stɑ:) NOUN any starfish of the genus *Solaster,* having up to 13 arms radiating from a central disc.

sunstone ('sʌn,stəʊn) NOUN another name for **aventurine** (sense 2).
▷HISTORY C17: so called because it contains red and gold flecks which reflect the light

sunstroke ('sʌn,strəʊk) NOUN heatstroke caused by prolonged exposure to intensely hot sunlight.

sunsuit ('sʌn,su:t, -,sju:t) NOUN a child's outfit consisting of a brief top and shorts or a short skirt.

suntan ('sʌn,tæn) NOUN **a** a brownish colouring of the skin caused by the formation of the pigment melanin within the skin on exposure to the ultraviolet rays of the sun or a sunlamp. Often shortened to: **tan. b** (*as modifier*): *suntan oil.*
▸**'sun,tanned** ADJECTIVE

suntrap ('sʌn,træp) NOUN a very sunny sheltered place.

sunup ('sʌn,ʌp) NOUN another name (esp US) for **sunrise** (sense 3).

sunward ('sʌnwəd) ADJECTIVE [1] directed or moving towards the sun. ◆ ADVERB [2] a variant of **sunwards.**

sunwards ('sʌnwədz) *or* **sunward** ADVERB towards the sun.

sunwise ('sʌn,waɪz) ADVERB moving in the same direction as the sun; clockwise.

suo jure ('su:əʊ 'dʒʊərɪ) ADVERB *Chiefly law* in one's own right.
▷HISTORY Latin

suo loco ('su:əʊ 'lɒkəʊ) ADVERB *Chiefly law* in a person or thing's own or rightful place.
▷HISTORY Latin

Suomi ('suɔmi) NOUN the Finnish name for **Finland.**

sup[1] (sʌp) VERB **sups, supping, supped.** [1] (*intr*) *Archaic* to have supper. [2] (*tr*) *Obsolete* to provide with supper.
▷HISTORY C13: from Old French *soper;* see SUP[2]

sup[2] (sʌp) VERB **sups, supping, supped.** [1] to partake of (liquid) by swallowing a little at a time. [2] *Scot and northern English dialect* to drink. ◆ NOUN [3] a sip.
▷HISTORY Old English *sūpan;* related to Old High German *sūfan,* German *saufen;* see also SUP[1]

sup. ABBREVIATION FOR: [1] above. [from Latin *supra*] [2] superior. [3] *Grammar* superlative.

super ('su:pə) ADJECTIVE [1] *Informal* outstanding; exceptionally fine. ◆ NOUN [2] petrol with a high octane rating. [3] *Informal* a superintendent or supervisor. [4] *Austral and NZ informal* superannuation benefits. [5] *Austral and NZ informal* superphosphate. ◆ INTERJECTION [6] *Brit informal* an enthusiastic expression of approval or assent.
▷HISTORY from Latin: above

super- PREFIX [1] placed above or over: *superscript.*

2 of greater size, extent, quality, etc.: *supermarket.* 3 surpassing others; outstanding: *superstar.* 4 beyond a standard or norm; exceeding or exceedingly: *supersonic.* 5 indicating that a chemical compound contains a specified element in a higher proportion than usual: *superoxide.*
▷HISTORY from Latin *super* above

superable (ˈsuːpərəbᵊl, -prəbᵊl) ADJECTIVE able to be surmounted or overcome.
▷HISTORY C17: from Latin *superābilis,* from *superāre* to overcome
▸ **ˌsuperaˈbility** *or* **ˈsuperableness** NOUN ▸ **ˈsuperably** ADVERB

superabound (ˌsuːpərəˈbaʊnd) VERB 1 (*intr*) to abound abnormally; be in surplus. 2 *Rare* to be more abundant than (something else).
▸ **superabundance** (ˌsuːpərəˈbʌndəns) NOUN
▸ **ˌsuperaˈbundant** ADJECTIVE

superadd (ˌsuːpərˈæd) VERB (*tr*) to add (something) to something that has already been added; add as extra.
▸ **ˌsuperadˈdition** NOUN ▸ **ˌsuperadˈditional** ADJECTIVE

superaerodynamics (ˌsuːpəˌɛərəʊdaɪˈnæmɪks) NOUN (*functioning as singular*) the study of aerodynamics at very high altitudes, where the air density is very low.

superaltar (ˈsuːpərˌɔːltə) NOUN *Christianity* a consecrated portable stone slab for use on an unconsecrated altar.

superannuate (ˌsuːpərˈænjʊˌeɪt) VERB (*tr*) 1 to pension off. 2 to discard as obsolete or old-fashioned.

superannuated (ˌsuːpərˈænjʊˌeɪtɪd) ADJECTIVE 1 discharged, esp with a pension, owing to age or illness. 2 too old to serve usefully. 3 obsolete.
▷HISTORY C17: from Medieval Latin *superannātus* aged more than one year, from Latin SUPER- + *annus* a year

superannuation (ˌsuːpərˌænjʊˈeɪʃən) NOUN 1 **a** the amount deducted regularly from employees' incomes in a contributory pension scheme. **b** the pension finally paid to such employees. 2 the act or process of superannuating or the condition of being superannuated.

superb (sʊˈpɜːb, sjʊ-) ADJECTIVE 1 surpassingly good; excellent: *a superb actor.* 2 majestic or imposing: *a superb mansion.* 3 magnificently rich; luxurious: *the jubilee was celebrated with a superb banquet.*
▷HISTORY C16: from Old French *superbe,* from Latin *superbus* distinguished, from *super* above
▸ **suˈperbly** ADVERB ▸ **suˈperbness** NOUN

superbazaar *or* **superbazar** (ˈsuːpəbəˈzɑː) NOUN (in India) a large department store or supermarket, esp one set up as a cooperative store by the government.

superb blue wren NOUN a small Australian bird, *Malurus cyaneus,* the adult male of which has bright blue plumage.

superbike (ˈsuːpəˌbaɪk) NOUN a high-performance motorcycle.

Super Bowl NOUN *American football* the main championship game of the sport, held annually in January between the champions of the American Football Conference and the National Football Conference.

superbug (ˈsuːpəˌbʌg) NOUN *Informal* an infective microorganism that has become resistant to antibiotics.

supercalender (ˌsuːpəˈkæləndə) NOUN 1 a calender with a number of rollers that gives a high gloss to paper. ◆ VERB 2 (*tr*) to produce a glossy finish on (paper) by pressing in a supercalender.
▸ **ˌsuperˈcalendered** ADJECTIVE

supercar (ˈsuːpəˌkɑː) NOUN a very expensive fast or powerful car with a centrally located engine.

supercargo (ˌsuːpəˈkɑːgəʊ) NOUN, *plural* **-goes.** an officer on a merchant ship who supervises commercial matters and is in charge of the cargo.
▷HISTORY C17: changed from Spanish *sobrecargo,* from *sobre* over (from Latin SUPER) + *cargo* CARGO

supercharge (ˈsuːpəˌtʃɑːdʒ) VERB (*tr*) 1 to increase the air intake pressure of (an internal-combustion engine) with a supercharger; boost. 2 to charge (the atmosphere, a remark, etc.) with an excess amount of (tension, emotion, etc.). 3 to apply pressure to (a fluid); pressurize.

supercharger (ˈsuːpəˌtʃɑːdʒə) NOUN a device, usually a fan or compressor driven by the engine, that increases the mass of air drawn into an internal-combustion engine by raising the intake pressure. Also called: **blower, booster.**

superciliary (ˌsuːpəˈsɪlɪərɪ) ADJECTIVE relating to or situated over the eyebrow or a corresponding region in lower animals.
▷HISTORY C18: from New Latin *superciliaris,* from Latin *supercilium,* from SUPER- + *cilium* eyelid

supercilious (ˌsuːpəˈsɪlɪəs) ADJECTIVE displaying arrogant pride, scorn, or indifference.
▷HISTORY C16: from Latin *superciliōsus,* from *supercilium* eyebrow; see SUPERCILIARY
▸ **ˌsuperˈciliously** ADVERB ▸ **ˌsuperˈciliousness** NOUN

superclass (ˈsuːpəˌklɑːs) NOUN a taxonomic group that is a subdivision of a subphylum.

supercolumnar (ˌsuːpəkəˈlʌmnə) ADJECTIVE *Architect* 1 having one colonnade above another. 2 placed above a colonnade or a column.
▸ **ˌsupercolˌumniˈation** NOUN

supercomputer (ˌsuːpəkəmˈpjuːtə) NOUN a powerful computer that can process large quantities of data of a similar type very quickly.

superconductivity (ˌsuːpəˌkɒndʌkˈtɪvɪtɪ) NOUN *Physics* the property of certain substances that have no electrical resistance. In metals it occurs at very low temperatures, but higher temperature superconductivity occurs in some ceramic materials.
▸ **superconduction** (ˌsuːpəkənˈdʌkʃən) NOUN
▸ **ˌsuperconˈductive** *or* **ˌsuperconˈducting** ADJECTIVE
▸ **ˌsuperconˈductor** NOUN

supercontinent (ˈsuːpəˌkɒntɪnənt) NOUN a great landmass thought to have existed in the geological past and to have split into smaller landmasses, which drifted and formed the present continents.

supercool (ˌsuːpəˈkuːl) VERB *Chem* to cool or be cooled without freezing or crystallization to a temperature below that at which freezing or crystallization should occur. Supercooled liquids are not in equilibrium.

supercritical (ˌsuːpəˈkrɪtɪkᵊl) ADJECTIVE 1 *Physics* (of a fluid) brought to a temperature and pressure higher than its critical temperature and pressure, so that its physical and chemical properties change. 2 *Nuclear physics* of or containing more than the critical mass.

superdense theory (ˌsuːpəˈdɛns) NOUN *Astronomy* a former name for the **big-bang theory.**

superdominant (ˌsuːpəˈdɒmɪnənt) NOUN *US and Canadian* another word for **submediant.**

super-duper (ˈsuːpəˈduːpə) ADJECTIVE *Informal* extremely pleasing, impressive, etc.: often used as an exclamation.

superego (ˌsuːpərˈiːgəʊ, -ˈɛgəʊ) NOUN, *plural* **-gos.** *Psychoanal* that part of the unconscious mind that acts as a conscience for the ego, developing mainly from the relationship between a child and his parents. See also **id, ego.**

superelastic (ˌsuːpərɪˈlæstɪk) ADJECTIVE *Physics* (of collisions) involving an overall increase in translational kinetic energy.

superelevation (ˌsuːpərˌɛlɪˈveɪʃən) NOUN 1 another name for **bank**² (sense 7). 2 the difference between the heights of the sides of a road or railway track on a bend.

supereminent (ˌsuːpərˈɛmɪnənt) ADJECTIVE of distinction, dignity, or rank superior to that of others; pre-eminent.
▸ **ˌsuperˈeminence** NOUN

supererogate (ˌsuːpərˈɛrəˌgeɪt) VERB (*intr*) *Obsolete* to do or perform more than is required.
▷HISTORY C16: from Late Latin *superērogāre* to spend over and above, from Latin SUPER- + *ērogāre* to pay out
▸ **ˌsuperˈeroˌgator** NOUN

supererogation (ˌsuːpərˌɛrəˈgeɪʃən) NOUN 1 the performance of work in excess of that required. 2 *RC Church* supererogatory prayers, devotions, etc.

supererogatory (ˌsuːpərɛˈrɒgətərɪ, -trɪ) ADJECTIVE 1 performed to an extent exceeding that required or expected. 2 exceeding what is needed; superfluous. 3 *RC Church* of, characterizing, or relating to prayers, good works, etc., performed over and above those prescribed as obligatory.
▷HISTORY C16: from Medieval Latin *superērogātōrius;* see SUPEREROGATE
▸ **ˌsupereˈrogatorily** ADVERB

superette (ˌsuːpəˈrɛt) NOUN *NZ informal* a small store or dairy laid out along the lines of a supermarket.

superfamily (ˈsuːpəˌfæmɪlɪ) NOUN, *plural* **-lies.** 1 *Biology* a taxonomic group that is a subdivision of a suborder. 2 any analogous group, such as a group of related languages.

superfecundation (ˌsuːpəˌfiːkənˈdeɪʃən) NOUN *Physiol* the fertilization of two or more ova, produced during the same menstrual cycle, by sperm ejaculated during two or more acts of sexual intercourse.

superfemale (ˈsuːpəˌfiːmeɪl) NOUN a former name for **metafemale.**

superfetation (ˌsuːpəfiːˈteɪʃən) NOUN *Physiol* the presence in the uterus of two fetuses developing from ova fertilized at different times.
▷HISTORY C17 *superfetate,* from Latin *superfētāre* to fertilize when already pregnant, from SUPER- + *fētāre* to impregnate, from *fētus* offspring
▸ **superfetate** (ˌsuːpəˈfiːteɪt) ADJECTIVE

superficial (ˌsuːpəˈfɪʃəl) ADJECTIVE 1 of, relating to, being near, or forming the surface: *superficial bruising.* 2 displaying a lack of thoroughness or care: *a superficial inspection.* 3 only outwardly apparent rather than genuine or actual: *the similarity was merely superficial.* 4 of little substance or significance; trivial: *superficial differences.* 5 lacking originality or profundity: *the film's plot was quite superficial.* 6 (of measurements) involving only the surface area.
▷HISTORY C14: from Late Latin *superficiālis* of the surface, from Latin SUPERFICIES
▸ **superficiality** (ˌsuːpəˌfɪʃɪˈælɪtɪ) *or* (*less commonly*) **ˌsuperˈficialness** NOUN ▸ **ˌsuperˈficially** ADVERB

superficies (ˌsuːpəˈfɪʃiːz) NOUN, *plural* **-cies.** *Rare* 1 a surface or outer face. 2 the outward form of a thing.
▷HISTORY C16: from Latin: upper side, from SUPER- + *faciēs* face

superfine (ˌsuːpəˈfaɪn) ADJECTIVE 1 of exceptional fineness or quality. 2 excessively refined.
▸ **ˌsuperˈfineness** NOUN

superfix (ˈsuːpəˌfɪks) NOUN *Linguistics* a suprasegmental feature distinguishing the meaning or grammatical function of one word or phrase from that of another, as stress does for example between the noun *conduct* and the verb *conduct.*
▷HISTORY from SUPER- + *-fix,* on the model of PREFIX, SUFFIX

superfluid (ˌsuːpəˈfluːɪd) NOUN 1 *Physics* a fluid in a state characterized by a very low viscosity, high thermal conductivity, high capillarity, etc. The only known example is that of liquid helium at temperatures close to absolute zero. ◆ ADJECTIVE 2 being or relating to a superfluid.

superfluidity (ˌsuːpəfluːˈɪdɪtɪ) NOUN *Physics* the state of being or property of becoming a superfluid.

superfluity (ˌsuːpəˈfluːɪtɪ) NOUN 1 the condition of being superfluous. 2 a quantity or thing that is in excess of what is needed. 3 a thing that is not needed.
▷HISTORY C14: from Old French *superfluité,* via Late Latin from Latin *superfluus* SUPERFLUOUS

superfluous (suːˈpɜːflʊəs) ADJECTIVE 1 exceeding what is sufficient or required. 2 not necessary or relevant; uncalled-for. 3 *Obsolete* extravagant in expenditure or oversupplied with possessions.
▷HISTORY C15: from Latin *superfluus* overflowing, from SUPER- + *fluere* to flow
▸ **suˈperfluously** ADVERB ▸ **suˈperfluousness** NOUN

superfuse (ˌsuːpəˈfjuːz) VERB *Obsolete* to pour or be poured so as to cover something.
▷HISTORY C17: from Latin *superfūsus* poured over, from *superfundere,* from SUPER- + *fundere* to pour
▸ **ˌsuperˈfusion** NOUN

Super-G NOUN *Skiing* a type of slalom in which the course is shorter than in a standard slalom and the obstacles are farther apart than in a giant slalom.
▷HISTORY C20: from SUPER- + G(IANT)

supergiant (ˈsuːpəˌdʒaɪənt) NOUN any of a class of extremely large and luminous stars, such as Betelgeuse, which have expanded to a large diameter and are eventually likely to explode as supernovae. Compare **giant star, white dwarf.**

superglacial (ˌsuːpəˈgleɪsɪəl) ADJECTIVE on or originating from the surface of a glacier.

superglue (ˈsuːpəˌgluː) NOUN any of various impact adhesives that quickly make an exceptionally strong bond.

supergrass (ˈsuːpəˌgrɑːs) NOUN an informer whose information implicates a large number of people in terrorist activities or other major crimes.

supergravity (ˌsuːpəˈgrævɪtɪ) NOUN *Physics* any of various theories in which supersymmetry is applied to the theory of gravitation.

supergroup (ˈsuːpəˌgruːp) NOUN a rock band whose members are individually famous from previous groups.

superheat (ˌsuːpəˈhiːt) VERB (*tr*) 1 to heat (a vapour, esp steam) to a temperature above its saturation point for a given pressure. 2 to heat (a liquid) to a temperature above its boiling point without boiling occurring. 3 to heat excessively; overheat.
▸**ˌsuperˈheater** NOUN

superheavy (ˌsuːpəˈhɛvɪ) NOUN *Physics* denoting or relating to elements of high atomic number (above 109) postulated to exist with special stability as a consequence of the shell model of the nucleus.

superheavyweight (ˌsuːpəˈhɛvɪweɪt) NOUN **a** an amateur boxer weighing more than 91 kg. **b** (*as modifier*): *a superheavyweight bout.*

superhero (ˈsuːpəˌhɪərəʊ) NOUN, *plural* **-roes.** any of various comic-strip characters with superhuman abilities or magical powers, wearing a distinctive costume, and fighting against evil.

super-heroine NOUN a fictional woman character with superhuman abilities or magical powers, wearing a distinctive costume, and fighting against evil.

superhet (ˈsuːpəˌhɛt) NOUN See **superheterodyne receiver.**

superheterodyne receiver (ˌsuːpəˈhɛtərəˌdaɪn) NOUN a radio receiver that combines two radio-frequency signals by heterodyne action, to produce a signal above the audible frequency limit. This signal is amplified and demodulated to give the desired audio-frequency signal. Sometimes shortened to: **superhet.**
▷HISTORY C20: from SUPER(SONIC) + HETERODYNE

superhigh frequency (ˈsuːpəˌhaɪ) NOUN a radio-frequency band or radio frequency lying between 30 000 and 3000 megahertz. Abbreviation: **SHF.**

superhighway (ˈsuːpəˌhaɪweɪ) NOUN *Chiefly US* a fast dual-carriageway road.

superhuman (ˌsuːpəˈhjuːmən) ADJECTIVE 1 having powers above and beyond those of mankind. 2 exceeding normal human ability or experience.
▸**ˌsuperhuˈmanity** *or* **ˌsuperˈhumanness** NOUN
▸**ˌsuperˈhumanly** ADVERB

superhumeral (ˌsuːpəˈhjuːmərəl) NOUN an ecclesiastical vestment worn over the shoulders.
▷HISTORY C17: from Late Latin *superhumerāle;* see SUPER-, HUMERAL

superimpose (ˌsuːpərɪmˈpəʊz) VERB (*tr*) 1 to set or place on or over something else. 2 (usually foll by *on* or *upon*) to add (to).
▸**ˌsuperˌimpoˈsition** NOUN

superincumbent (ˌsuːpərɪnˈkʌmbənt) ADJECTIVE 1 lying or being on top of something else. 2 situated or suspended above; overhanging.
▸**ˌsuperinˈcumbence** *or* **ˌsuperinˈcumbency** NOUN
▸**ˌsuperinˈcumbently** ADVERB

superinduce (ˌsuːpərɪnˈdjuːs) VERB (*tr*) to introduce as an additional feature, factor, etc.
▸**ˌsuperinˈducement** NOUN ▸**superinduction** (ˌsuːpərɪnˈdʌkʃən) NOUN

superintend (ˌsuːpərɪnˈtɛnd, ˌsuːprɪn-) VERB to undertake the direction or supervision (of); manage.
▷HISTORY C17: from Church Latin *superintendere,* from Latin SUPER- + *intendere* to give attention to
▸**ˌsuperinˈtendence** NOUN

superintendency (ˌsuːpərɪnˈtɛndənsɪ, ˌsuːprɪn-) NOUN, *plural* **-cies.** 1 the office or jurisdiction of a superintendent. 2 a district under the jurisdiction of a superintendent.

superintendent (ˌsuːpərɪnˈtɛndənt, ˌsuːprɪn-) NOUN 1 a person who directs and manages an organization, office, etc. 2 (in Britain) a senior police officer higher in rank than an inspector but lower than a chief superintendent. 3 (in the US) the head of a police department. 4 *Chiefly US and Canadian* a caretaker, esp of a block of apartments. ◆ ADJECTIVE 5 of or relating to supervision; superintending.
▷HISTORY C16: from Church Latin *superintendens* overseeing

superior (suːˈpɪərɪə) ADJECTIVE 1 greater in quality, quantity, etc. 2 of high or extraordinary worth, merit, etc. 3 higher in rank or status: *a superior tribunal.* 4 displaying a conscious sense of being above or better than others; supercilious. 5 (*often postpositive*; foll by *to*) not susceptible (to) or influenced (by). 6 placed higher up; situated further from the base. 7 *Astronomy* **a** (of a planet) having an orbit further from the sun than the orbit of the earth. **b** (of a conjunction) occurring when the sun lies between the earth and an inferior planet. 8 (of a plant ovary) situated above the calyx and other floral parts. 9 *Anatomy* (of one part in relation to another) situated above or higher. 10 *Printing* (of a character) written or printed above the line; superscript. ◆ NOUN 11 a person or thing of greater rank or quality. 12 *Printing* a character set in a superior position. 13 (*often capital*) the head of a community in a religious order.
▷HISTORY C14: from Latin, from *superus* placed above, from *super* above
▸**suˈperioress** FEMININE NOUN ▸**superiority** (suːˌpɪərɪˈɒrɪtɪ) NOUN ▸**suˈperiorly** ADVERB

> **Language note** *Superior* should not be used with *than: he is a better* (not *a superior*) *poet than his brother; his poetry is superior to* (not *superior than*) *his brother's.*

Superior (suːˈpɪərɪə, sjuː-) NOUN **Lake.** a lake in the N central US and S Canada: one of the largest freshwater lakes in the world and westernmost of the Great Lakes. Area: 82 362 sq. km (31 800 sq. miles).

superior court NOUN 1 (in England) a higher court not subject to control by any other court except by way of appeal. See also **Supreme Court of Judicature.** 2 *US* (in several states) a court of general jurisdiction ranking above the inferior courts and below courts of last resort.

superiority complex NOUN *Informal* an inflated estimate of one's own merit, usually manifested in arrogance.

superior planet NOUN any of the six planets (Mars, Jupiter, Saturn, Uranus, Neptune, and Pluto) whose orbit lies outside that of the earth.

superjacent (ˌsuːpəˈdʒeɪs^{ə}nt) ADJECTIVE lying immediately above or upon.
▷HISTORY C17: from Late Latin *superjacēre,* from Latin SUPER- + *jacēre* to lie

superkingdom (ˈsuːpəˌkɪŋdəm) NOUN another name for **domain** (sense 12).

superlative (suːˈpɜːlətɪv) ADJECTIVE 1 of outstanding quality, degree, etc.; supreme. 2 *Grammar* denoting the form of an adjective or adverb that expresses the highest or a very high degree of quality. In English the superlative degree is usually marked by the suffix *-est* or the word *most,* as in *loudest* or *most loudly.* Compare **positive** (sense 10), **comparative** (sense 3). 3 (of language or style) excessive; exaggerated. ◆ NOUN 4 a thing that excels all others or is of the highest quality. 5 *Grammar* the superlative form of an adjective. 6 the highest degree; peak.
▷HISTORY C14: from Old French *superlatif,* via Late Latin from Latin *superlātus* extravagant, from *superferre* to carry beyond, from SUPER- + *ferre* to bear
▸**suˈperlatively** ADVERB ▸**suˈperlativeness** NOUN

superload (ˈsuːpəˌləʊd) NOUN another name for **live load.**

superloo (ˈsuːpəˌluː) NOUN *Informal* an automated public toilet.

superluminal (ˌsuːpəˈluːmɪnəl) ADJECTIVE *Physics* of or relating to a speed or velocity exceeding the speed of light.

superlunar (ˌsuːpəˈluːnə) ADJECTIVE situated beyond the moon; celestial.
▸**ˌsuperˈlunary** ADJECTIVE

supermale (ˈsuːpəˌmeɪl) NOUN a former name for **metamale.**

superman (ˈsuːpəˌmæn) NOUN, *plural* **-men.** 1 (in the philosophy of Nietzsche) an ideal man who through integrity and creativity would rise above good and evil and who represents the goal of human evolution. 2 any man of apparently superhuman powers.

supermarket (ˈsuːpəˌmɑːkɪt) NOUN a large self-service store retailing food and household supplies.

supermax (ˈsuːpəˌmæks) NOUN (*modifier*) having or relating to the very highest levels of security: *a supermax jail.*

supermembrane (ˌsuːpəˈmɛmbreɪn) NOUN *Physics* a type of two-dimensional entity postulated in certain theories of elementary particles that involve supersymmetry.

supermini (ˈsuːpəˌmɪnɪ) NOUN a small car, usually a hatchback, that is economical to run but has a high level of performance.

supermodel (ˈsuːpəˌmɒd^{ə}l) NOUN a very successful and well-known photographic or catwalk model.

supermundane (ˌsuːpəˈmʌndeɪn) ADJECTIVE of or relating to what is elevated above earthly things.

supernal (suːˈpɜːn^{ə}l, sjuː-) ADJECTIVE *Literary* 1 of or from the world of the divine; celestial. 2 of or emanating from above or from the sky.
▷HISTORY C15: from Medieval Latin *supernālis,* from Latin *supernus* that is on high, from *super* above
▸**suˈpernally** ADVERB

supernatant (ˌsuːpəˈneɪt^{ə}nt) ADJECTIVE 1 floating on the surface or over something. 2 *Chem* (of a liquid) lying above a sediment or settled precipitate.
▷HISTORY C17: from Latin *supernatāre* to float, from SUPER- + *natāre* to swim
▸**ˌsupernaˈtation** NOUN

supernational (ˌsuːpəˈnæʃn^{ə}l) ADJECTIVE a less common word for **supranational.**
▸**ˌsuperˈnationalism** NOUN ▸**ˌsuperˈnationalist** NOUN
▸**ˌsuperˈnationally** ADVERB

supernatural (ˌsuːpəˈnætʃrəl, -ˈnætʃərəl) ADJECTIVE 1 of or relating to things that cannot be explained according to natural laws. 2 characteristic of or caused by or as if by a god; miraculous. 3 of, involving, or ascribed to occult beings. 4 exceeding the ordinary; abnormal. ◆ NOUN 5 **the.** supernatural forces, occurrences, and beings collectively or their realm.
▸**ˌsuperˈnaturally** ADVERB ▸**ˌsuperˈnaturalness** NOUN

supernaturalism (ˌsuːpəˈnætʃrəlɪzəm, -ˈnætʃərə-) NOUN 1 the quality or condition of being supernatural. 2 a supernatural agency, the effects of which are felt to be apparent in this world. 3 belief in supernatural forces or agencies as producing effects in this world.
▸**ˌsuperˈnaturalist** NOUN, ADJECTIVE ▸**ˌsuperˌnaturalˈistic** ADJECTIVE

supernormal (ˌsuːpəˈnɔːməl) ADJECTIVE greatly exceeding the normal.
▸**supernormality** (ˌsuːpənɔːˈmælɪtɪ) NOUN
▸**ˌsuperˈnormally** ADVERB

supernova (ˌsuːpəˈnəʊvə) NOUN, *plural* **-vae** (-viː) *or* **-vas.** a star that explodes catastrophically owing to either instabilities following the exhaustion of its nuclear fuel or gravitational collapse following the accretion of matter from an orbiting companion star, becoming for a few days up to one hundred million times brighter than the sun. The expanding shell of debris (the **supernova remnant**) creates a nebula that radiates radio waves, X-rays, and light, for hundreds or thousands of years. Compare **nova.**

supernumerary (ˌsuːpəˈnjuːmərərɪ, -ˈnjuːmrərɪ) ADJECTIVE 1 exceeding a regular or proper number; extra. 2 functioning as a substitute or assistant with regard to a regular body or staff. ◆ NOUN, *plural* **-aries.** 3 a person or thing that exceeds the normal, required, or regular number. 4 a person who functions as a substitute or assistant. 5 an actor who has no lines, esp a nonprofessional one.

▷HISTORY C17: from Late Latin *supernumerārius,* from Latin SUPER- + *numerus* number

supernurse ('su:pəˌnɜ:s) NOUN (in Britain) an experienced senior nurse on an elevated salary who is responsible for running clinics and managing nursing teams.

superorder ('su:pərˌɔ:də) NOUN *Biology* a taxonomic group that is a subdivision of a subclass.

superordinate ADJECTIVE (ˌsu:pər'ɔ:dɪnɪt) 1 of higher status or condition. ◆ NOUN (ˌsu:pər'ɔ:dɪnɪt) 2 a person or thing that is superordinate. 3 a word the meaning of which includes the meaning of another word or words: *"red" is a superordinate of "scarlet", "vermilion", and "crimson".* Compare **hyponym, synonym, antonym.** ◆ VERB (ˌsu:pər'ɔ:dɪˌneɪt) 4 (*tr*) *Rare* to make superordinate.

superorganic (ˌsu:pərɔ:'gænɪk) ADJECTIVE *Sociol* (no longer widely used) relating to those aspects of a culture that are conceived as being superior to the individual members of the society.
▸ˌ**superor'ganicism** NOUN ▸ˌ**superor'ganicist** NOUN

superoxide (ˌsu:pər'ɒksaɪd) NOUN any of certain metal oxides that contain the O_2^- ion: *potassium superoxide,* KO_2.

superphosphate (ˌsu:pə'fɒsfeɪt) NOUN 1 a mixture of the diacid calcium salt of orthophosphoric acid $Ca(H_2PO_4)_2$ with calcium sulphate and small quantities of other phosphates: used as a fertilizer. 2 a salt of phosphoric acid formed by incompletely replacing its acidic hydrogen atoms; acid phosphate; hydrogen phosphate.

superphysical (ˌsu:pə'fɪzɪkᵊl) ADJECTIVE not explained by the known physical laws and phenomena; supernatural.

superplastic (ˌsu:pə'plæstɪk) ADJECTIVE 1 (of a metal, alloy, etc.) very easily moulded at high temperatures without fracturing. ◆ NOUN 2 such a metal, alloy, etc.
▸ˌ**superplas'ticity** NOUN

superpose (ˌsu:pə'pəʊz) VERB (*tr*) 1 *Geometry* to transpose (the coordinates of one geometric figure) to coincide with those of another. 2 a rare word for **superimpose** (sense 1).
▷HISTORY C19: from French *superposer,* from Latin *superpōnere,* from SUPER- + *pōnere* to place
▸ˌ**super'posable** ADJECTIVE

superposition (ˌsu:pəpə'zɪʃən) NOUN 1 the act of superposing or state of being superposed. 2 *Geology* the principle that in any sequence of sedimentary rocks which has not been disturbed, the oldest strata lie at the bottom and the youngest at the top.

superpower ('su:pəˌpaʊə) NOUN 1 an extremely powerful state, such as the US. 2 extremely high power, esp electrical or mechanical.
▸'**superˌpowered** ADJECTIVE

superrealism (ˌsu:pə'rɪəˌlɪzəm) NOUN another name for **surrealism.**
▸ˌ**super'realist** NOUN, ADJECTIVE

supersaturated (ˌsu:pə'sætʃəˌreɪtɪd) ADJECTIVE 1 (of a solution) containing more solute than a saturated solution and therefore not in equilibrium. 2 (of a vapour) containing more material than a saturated vapour and therefore not in equilibrium.
▸ˌ**superˌsatu'ration** NOUN

superscribe (ˌsu:pə'skraɪb) VERB (*tr*) to write (an inscription, name, etc.) above, on top of, or outside.
▷HISTORY C16: from Latin *superscrībere,* from SUPER- + *scrībere* to write

superscript ('su:pəˌskrɪpt) ADJECTIVE 1 *Printing* (of a character) written or printed above the line; superior. Compare **subscript.** ◆ NOUN 2 a superscript or superior character. 3 *Obsolete* a superscription on a document, letter, etc.
▷HISTORY C16: from Latin *superscriptus;* see SUPERSCRIBE

superscription (ˌsu:pə'skrɪpʃən) NOUN 1 the act of superscribing. 2 a superscribed title, address, etc. 3 the symbol (R) at the head of a medical prescription, which stands for the Latin word *recipe* (take).

supersede (ˌsu:pə'si:d) VERB (*tr*) 1 to take the place of (something old-fashioned or less appropriate); supplant. 2 to replace in function, office, etc.; succeed. 3 to discard or set aside or cause to be set aside as obsolete or inferior.
▷HISTORY C15: via Old French from Latin *supersedēre* to sit above, from SUPER- + *sedēre* to sit
▸ˌ**super'sedable** ADJECTIVE ▸ˌ**super'sedence** NOUN ▸ˌ**super'seder** NOUN ▸**supersedure** (ˌsu:pə'si:dʒə) NOUN ▸**supersession** (ˌsu:pə'sɛʃən) NOUN

supersensible (ˌsu:pə'sɛnsɪbᵊl) *or* **supersensory** (ˌsu:pə'sɛnsərɪ) ADJECTIVE imperceptible to or beyond reach of the senses.
▸ˌ**super'sensibly** ADVERB

supersex ('su:pəˌsɛks) NOUN *Genetics* a sterile organism in which the ratio between the sex chromosomes is disturbed. See **metafemale, metamale.**

super-slick ADJECTIVE very well-executed or presented.

supersonic (ˌsu:pə'sɒnɪk) ADJECTIVE being, having, or capable of reaching a speed in excess of the speed of sound: *supersonic aircraft.*
▸ˌ**super'sonically** ADVERB

supersonics (ˌsu:pə'sɒnɪks) NOUN (*functioning as singular*) 1 the study of supersonic motion. 2 a less common name for **ultrasonics.**

superstar ('su:pəˌstɑ:) NOUN a popular singer, film star, etc., who is idolized by fans and elevated to a position of importance in the entertainment industry.
▸'**superˌstardom** NOUN

superstate ('su:pəˌsteɪt) NOUN a large state, esp created from a federation of states.

superstition (ˌsu:pə'stɪʃən) NOUN 1 irrational belief usually founded on ignorance or fear and characterized by obsessive reverence for omens, charms, etc. 2 a notion, act or ritual that derives from such belief. 3 any irrational belief, esp with regard to the unknown.
▷HISTORY C15: from Latin *superstitiō* dread of the supernatural, from *superstāre* to stand still by something (as in amazement)

superstitious (ˌsu:pə'stɪʃəs) ADJECTIVE 1 disposed to believe in superstition. 2 of or relating to superstition.
▸ˌ**super'stitiously** ADVERB ▸ˌ**super'stitiousness** NOUN

superstore ('su:pəˌstɔ:) NOUN a very large supermarket, often selling household goods, clothes, etc., as well as food.

superstratum (ˌsu:pə'strɑ:təm, -'streɪ-) NOUN, *plural* **-ta** (-tə) *or* **-tums.** 1 *Geology* a layer or stratum overlying another layer or similar structure. 2 *Linguistics* the language of a conquering or colonizing population as it supplants that of an indigenous population, as for example French and English in the Caribbean. Compare **substratum** (sense 8).

superstring ('su:pəˌstrɪŋ) NOUN *Physics* a type of one-dimensional entity postulated in certain theories of elementary particles that involve supersymmetry.

superstruct (ˌsu:pə'strʌkt) VERB (*tr*) to erect upon a foundation or on top of another building or part.

superstructure ('su:pəˌstrʌktʃə) NOUN 1 the part of a building above its foundation. 2 any structure or concept erected on something else. 3 *Nautical* any structure above the main deck of a ship with sides flush with the sides of the hull. 4 the part of a bridge supported by the piers and abutments. 5 (in Marxist theory) an edifice of interdependent agencies of the state, including legal and political institutions and ideologies, each possessing some autonomy but remaining products of the dominant mode of economic production.
▸'**superˌstructural** ADJECTIVE

supersymmetry (ˌsu:pə'sɪmɪtrɪ) NOUN *Physics* a symmetry of elementary particles having a higher order than that in the standard model, postulated to encompass the behaviour of both bosons and fermions.

supertanker ('su:pəˌtæŋkə) NOUN a large fast tanker of more than 275 000 tons capacity.

supertax ('su:pəˌtæks) NOUN a tax levied in addition to the basic tax, esp a graduated surtax on incomes above a certain level.

superteacher ('su:pəˌti:tʃə) NOUN *Brit education* an informal name for an **advanced skills teacher.**

supertitles ('su:pəˌtaɪtᵊlz) PLURAL NOUN another word for **surtitles.**

supertonic (ˌsu:pə'tɒnɪk) NOUN *Music* 1 the second degree of a major or minor scale. 2 a key or chord based on this.

Super Tuesday NOUN *US politics* the Tuesday, typically in March, on which party members in over 20 states vote in primary elections to select their party's presidential candidate.

Super Twelve NOUN an annual international southern hemisphere Rugby Union tournament between teams from South Africa, Australia, and New Zealand.

supervene (ˌsu:pə'vi:n) VERB (*intr*) 1 to follow closely; ensue. 2 to occur as an unexpected or extraneous development.
▷HISTORY C17: from Latin *supervenīre* to come upon, from SUPER- + *venīre* to come
▸ˌ**super'venience** *or* **supervention** (ˌsu:pə'vɛnʃən) NOUN

supervenient (ˌsu:pə'vi:nɪənt) ADJECTIVE 1 supervening. 2 *Philosophy* (of a property) inseparable from the other properties of something. Two objects may be identical except that one is red and the other not, but they cannot be identical except that one is beautiful and the other not; beauty is thus a supervenient property.

supervise ('su:pəˌvaɪz) VERB (*tr*) 1 to direct or oversee the performance or operation of. 2 to watch over so as to maintain order, etc.
▷HISTORY C16: from Medieval Latin *supervidēre,* from Latin SUPER- + *vidēre* to see
▸**supervision** (ˌsu:pə'vɪʒən) NOUN

supervision order NOUN (in Britain) *Social welfare* an order by a juvenile court requiring a named probation officer or local-authority social worker to advise, assist, and befriend a child or young person who is the subject of care proceedings, over a period of up to three years.

supervisor ('su:pəˌvaɪzə) NOUN 1 a person who manages or supervises. 2 a foreman or forewoman. 3 (in some British universities) a tutor supervising the work, esp research work, of a student. 4 (in some US schools) an administrator running a department of teachers. 5 (in some US states) the elected chief official of a township or other subdivision of a county. 6 *Obsolete* a spectator.
▸'**superˌvisorship** NOUN

supervisory ('su:pəˌvaɪzərɪ) ADJECTIVE of, involving, or limited to supervision: *a supervisory capacity.*

supervisory board NOUN a board of management of which nonmanagerial workers are members, having supervisory powers over some aspects of management decision-making.

superwaif ('su:pəˌweɪf) NOUN *Informal* a very young and very thin supermodel.

superweed ('su:pəˌwi:d) NOUN a hybrid plant that contains genes for herbicide resistance: produced by accidental crossing of genetically engineered crop plants with wild plants.

superwoman ('su:pəˌwʊmən) NOUN, *plural* **-women.** a woman who fulfils her many roles with apparently superhuman efficiency.

supinate ('su:pɪˌneɪt, 'sju:-) VERB to turn (the hand and forearm) so that the palm faces up or forwards.
▷HISTORY C19: from Latin *supīnāre* to lay on the back, from *supīnus* SUPINE
▸ˌ**supi'nation** NOUN

supinator ('su:pɪˌneɪtə, 'sju:-) NOUN *Anatomy* the muscle of the forearm that can produce the motion of supination.

supine ADJECTIVE (su:'paɪn, sju:-, 'su:paɪn, 'sju:-) 1 lying or resting on the back with the face, palm, etc., upwards. 2 displaying no interest or animation; lethargic. ◆ NOUN ('su:paɪn, 'sju:-) 3 *Grammar* a noun form derived from a verb in Latin, often used to express purpose with verbs of motion. Abbreviation: **sup.**
▷HISTORY C15: from Latin *supīnus* related to *sub* under, up; (in grammatical sense) from Latin *verbum supīnum* supine word (the reason for this use is unknown)
▸**su'pinely** ADVERB ▸**su'pineness** NOUN

suplex ('su:plɛks) NOUN a wrestling hold in which a wrestler grasps his opponent round the waist from behind and carries him backwards.
▷HISTORY C20: of uncertain origin

supper ('sʌpə) NOUN 1 an evening meal, esp a light one. 2 an evening social event featuring a supper. 3 **sing for one's supper.** to obtain something by performing a service. ◆ VERB 4 (*tr*) *Rare* to give supper to. 5 (*intr*) *Rare* to eat supper.

▷HISTORY C13: from Old French *soper;* see SUP[1]
▸'**supperless** ADJECTIVE

supper club NOUN *US and Canadian* (formerly) a small expensive nightclub.

supplant (sə'plɑːnt) VERB *(tr)* to take the place of, often by trickery or force: *he easily supplanted his rival.*
▷HISTORY C13: via Old French from Latin *supplantāre* to trip up, from *sub-* from below + *planta* sole of the foot
▸**supplantation** (ˌsʌplɑːn'teɪʃən) NOUN ▸**sup'planter** NOUN

supple ('sʌpᵊl) ADJECTIVE [1] bending easily without damage. [2] capable of or showing easy or graceful movement; lithe. [3] mentally flexible; responding readily. [4] disposed to agree, sometimes to the point of servility. ◆ VERB [5] *Rare* to make or become supple.
▷HISTORY C13: from Old French *souple,* from Latin *supplex* bowed
▸'**suppleness** NOUN

supplejack ('sʌpᵊlˌdʒæk) NOUN [1] a North American twining rhamnaceous woody vine, *Berchemia scandens,* that has greenish-white flowers and purple fruits. [2] a liliaceous plant of New Zealand, *Ripogonum scandens,* having tough climbing vines. [3] a tropical American woody sapindaceous vine, *Paullinia curassavica,* having strong supple wood. [4] any of various other vines with strong supple stems. [5] *US* a walking stick made from the wood of *Paullinia curassavica.*
▷HISTORY C18: from SUPPLE + JACK[1]

supplement NOUN ('sʌplɪmənt) [1] an addition designed to complete, make up for a deficiency, etc. [2] a section appended to a publication to supply further information, correct errors, etc. [3] a magazine or section inserted into a newspaper or periodical, such as one with colour photographs issued every week. [4] *Geometry* **a** either of a pair of angles whose sum is 180°. **b** an arc of a circle that when added to another arc forms a semicircle. ◆ Abbreviations: **sup., supp.** ◆ VERB ('sʌplɪˌmɛnt) [5] *(tr)* to provide a supplement to, esp in order to remedy a deficiency.
▷HISTORY C14: from Latin *supplēmentum,* from *supplēre* to SUPPLY[1]
▸ˌ**supplemen'tation** NOUN ▸'**suppleˌmenter** NOUN

supplementary (ˌsʌplɪ'mɛntərɪ, -trɪ) ADJECTIVE [1] Also (less commonly): **supplemental** (ˌsʌplɪ'mɛntᵊl). forming or acting as a supplement. ◆ NOUN, *plural* **-ries.** [2] a person or thing that is a supplement.
▸ˌ**supple'mentarily** *or (less commonly)* ˌ**supple'mentally** ADVERB

supplementary angle NOUN either of two angles whose sum is 180°. Compare **complementary angle.**

suppletion (sə'pliːʃən) NOUN the use of an unrelated word to complete the otherwise defective paradigm of a given word, as for example the use of *went* for the past tense of *go.*
▷HISTORY C14: from Medieval Latin *supplētiō* a completing, from Latin *supplēre* to SUPPLY[1]
▸**sup'pletive** NOUN, ADJECTIVE

suppletory ('sʌplɪtərɪ, -trɪ) ADJECTIVE *Archaic* remedying deficiencies; supplementary.
▸'**suppletorily** ADVERB

Supplex ('sʌplɛks) NOUN *Trademark* a type of synthetic fabric which is breathable, stretchable, and fast-drying, used esp for sportswear.

suppliant ('sʌplɪənt) ADJECTIVE [1] expressing entreaty or supplication. ◆ NOUN, ADJECTIVE [2] another word for **supplicant.**
▷HISTORY C15: from French *supplier* to beseech, from Latin *supplicāre* to kneel in entreaty; see SUPPLE
▸'**suppliantly** ADVERB ▸'**suppliance** NOUN

supplicant ('sʌplɪkənt) *or* **suppliant** NOUN [1] a person who supplicates. ◆ ADJECTIVE [2] entreating humbly; supplicating.
▷HISTORY C16: from Latin *supplicāns* beseeching; see SUPPLE

supplicate ('sʌplɪˌkeɪt) VERB [1] to make a humble request to (someone); plead. [2] *(tr)* to ask for or seek humbly.
▷HISTORY C15: from Latin *supplicāre* to beg on one's knees; see SUPPLE
▸'**suppliˌcatory** ADJECTIVE

supplication (ˌsʌplɪ'keɪʃən) NOUN [1] the act of supplicating. [2] a humble entreaty or petition; prayer.

supply[1] (sə'plaɪ) VERB **-plies, -plying, -plied.** [1] *(tr; often foll by with)* to furnish with something that is required: *to supply the community with good government.* [2] *(tr; often foll by to or for)* to make available or provide (something that is desired or lacking): *to supply books to the library.* [3] *(tr)* to provide for adequately; make good; satisfy: *who will supply their needs?* [4] to serve as a substitute, usually temporary, in (another's position, etc.): *there are no clergymen to supply the pulpit.* [5] *(tr) Brit* to fill (a vacancy, position, etc.). ◆ NOUN, *plural* **-plies.** [6] **a** the act of providing or something that is provided. **b** *(as modifier): a supply dump.* [7] *(often plural)* an amount available for use; stock. [8] *(plural)* food, equipment, etc., needed for a campaign or trip. [9] *Economics* **a** willingness and ability to offer goods and services for sale. **b** the amount of a commodity that producers are willing and able to offer for sale at a specified price. Compare **demand** (sense 9). [10] *Military* **a** the management and disposal of food and equipment. **b** *(as modifier): supply routes.* [11] *(often plural)* a grant of money voted by a legislature for government expenses, esp those not covered by other revenues. [12] (in Parliament and similar legislatures) the money voted annually for the expenses of the civil service and armed forces. [13] **a** a person who acts as a temporary substitute. **b** *(as modifier): a supply vicar.* [14] a source of electrical energy, gas, etc. [15] *Obsolete* aid or assistance.
▷HISTORY C14: from Old French *soupleier,* from Latin *supplēre* to complete, from *sub-* up + *plēre* to fill
▸**sup'pliable** ADJECTIVE ▸**sup'plier** NOUN

supply[2] ('sʌplɪ) *or* **supplely** ('sʌpᵊlɪ) ADVERB in a supple manner.

supply chain NOUN *Marketing* a channel of distribution beginning with the supplier of materials or components, extending through a manufacturing process to the distributor and retailer, and ultimately to the consumer.

supply-side economics NOUN *(functioning as singular)* a school of economic thought that emphasizes the importance to a strong economy of policies that remove impediments to supply.

supply teacher NOUN a teacher employed to replace other teachers when they are absent.

support (sə'pɔːt) VERB *(tr)* [1] to carry the weight of. [2] to bear or withstand (pressure, weight, etc.). [3] to provide the necessities of life for (a family, person, etc.). [4] to tend to establish (a theory, statement, etc.) by providing new facts; substantiate. [5] to speak in favour of (a motion). [6] to give aid or courage to. [7] to give approval to (a cause, principle, etc.); subscribe to: *to support a political candidature.* [8] to endure with forbearance: *I will no longer support bad behaviour.* [9] to give strength to; maintain: *to support a business.* [10] *(tr)* (in a concert) to perform earlier than (the main attraction). [11] *Films, theatre* **a** to play a subordinate role to. **b** to accompany (the feature) in a film programme. [12] to act or perform (a role or character). ◆ NOUN [13] the act of supporting or the condition of being supported. [14] a thing that bears the weight or part of the weight of a construction. [15] a person who or thing that furnishes aid. [16] the means of maintenance of a family, person, etc. [17] a band or entertainer not topping the bill. [18] (often preceded by *the*) an actor or group of actors playing subordinate roles. [19] *Med* an appliance worn to ease the strain on an injured bodily structure or part. [20] the solid material on which a painting is executed, such as canvas. [21] See **athletic support.**
▷HISTORY C14: from Old French *supporter,* from Latin *supportāre* to bring, from *sub-* up + *portāre* to carry
▸**sup'portless** ADJECTIVE

supportable (sə'pɔːtəbᵊl) ADJECTIVE able to be supported or endured; bearable.
▸**supˌporta'bility** *or* **sup'portableness** NOUN ▸**sup'portably** ADVERB

support area NOUN *Military* an area containing concentrations of personnel and materiel ready to support a force in the field.

supporter (sə'pɔːtə) NOUN [1] a person who or thing that acts as a support. [2] a person who backs a sports team, politician, etc. [3] a garment or device worn to ease the strain on or restrict the movement of a bodily structure or part. [4] *Heraldry* a figure or beast in a coat of arms depicted as holding up the shield.

supporting (sə'pɔːtɪŋ) ADJECTIVE [1] (of a role) being a fairly important but not leading part, esp in a play or film. [2] (of an actor or actress) playing a supporting role.

supportive (sə'pɔːtɪv) ADJECTIVE providing support, esp moral or emotional support.
▸**sup'portively** ADVERB ▸**sup'portiveness** NOUN

supportive therapy NOUN [1] *Med* any treatment, such as the intravenous administration of certain fluids, designed to reinforce or sustain the physiological well-being of a patient. [2] *Psychol* a form of therapy for mental disturbances employing guidance and encouragement to develop the patient's own resources.

suppose (sə'pəuz) VERB *(tr; may take a clause as object)* [1] to presume (something) to be true without certain knowledge: *I suppose he meant to kill her.* [2] to consider as a possible suggestion for the sake of discussion, elucidation, etc.; postulate: *suppose that he wins the election.* [3] (of theories, propositions, etc.) to imply the inference or assumption (of): *your policy supposes full employment.*
▷HISTORY C14: from Old French *supposer,* from Medieval Latin *suppōnere,* from Latin: to substitute, from SUB- + *pōnere* to put
▸**sup'posable** ADJECTIVE ▸**sup'poser** NOUN

supposed (sə'pəuzd, -'pəuzɪd) ADJECTIVE [1] *(prenominal)* presumed to be true without certain knowledge: *his supposed date of birth.* [2] *(prenominal)* believed to be true on slight grounds; highly doubtful: *the supposed existence of ghosts.* [3] (sə'pəuzd) *(postpositive; foll by to)* expected or obliged (to): *I'm supposed to be there at nine.* [4] *(postpositive; used in negative;* foll by *to)* expected or obliged not (to): *you're not supposed to walk on the grass.*
▸**supposedly** (sə'pəuzɪdlɪ) ADVERB

supposition (ˌsʌpə'zɪʃən) NOUN [1] the act of supposing. [2] a fact, theory, etc., that is supposed.
▸ˌ**suppo'sitional** ADJECTIVE ▸ˌ**suppo'sitionally** ADVERB ▸ˌ**suppo'sitionless** ADJECTIVE

suppositious (ˌsʌpə'zɪʃəs) ADJECTIVE deduced from supposition; hypothetical.
▸ˌ**suppo'sitiously** ADVERB ▸ˌ**suppo'sitiousness** NOUN

supposititious (səˌpɒzɪ'tɪʃəs) ADJECTIVE substituted with intent to mislead or deceive.
▸**supˌposi'titiously** ADVERB ▸**supˌposi'titiousness** NOUN

suppositive (sə'pɒzɪtɪv) ADJECTIVE [1] of, involving, or arising out of supposition. [2] *Grammar* denoting a conjunction introducing a clause expressing a supposition, as for example *if, supposing,* or *provided that.* ◆ NOUN [3] *Grammar* a suppositive conjunction.
▸**sup'positively** ADVERB

suppository (sə'pɒzɪtərɪ, -trɪ) NOUN, *plural* **-ries.** *Med* an encapsulated or solid medication for insertion into the vagina, rectum, or urethra, where it melts and releases the active substance.
▷HISTORY C14: from Medieval Latin *suppositōrium,* from Latin *suppositus* placed beneath, from *suppōnere;* see SUPPOSE

suppress (sə'prɛs) VERB *(tr)* [1] to put an end to; prohibit. [2] to hold in check; restrain: *I was obliged to suppress a smile.* [3] to withhold from circulation or publication: *to suppress seditious pamphlets.* [4] to stop the activities of; crush: *to suppress a rebellion.* [5] *Electronics* **a** to reduce or eliminate (unwanted oscillations) in a circuit. **b** to eliminate (a particular frequency or group of frequencies) in a signal. [6] *Psychiatry* **a** to resist consciously (an idea or a desire entering one's mind). **b** to exercise self-control by preventing the expression of (certain desires). Compare **repress** (sense 3).
▷HISTORY C14: from Latin *suppressus* held down, from *supprimere* to restrain, from *sub-* down + *premere* to press
▸**sup'presser** NOUN ▸**sup'pressible** ADJECTIVE

suppressant (sə'prɛsənt) ADJECTIVE [1] tending to suppress or restrain an action or condition. ◆ NOUN [2] a suppressant drug or agent: *a cough suppressant.*

suppressed carrier modulation NOUN *Radio* an amplitude-modulated wave in which only the sidebands are transmitted, the carrier being removed.

suppression (sə'prɛʃən) NOUN [1] the act or process of suppressing or the condition of being suppressed. [2] *Psychoanal* the conscious avoidance of unpleasant thoughts. Compare **repression** (sense 2). [3] *Electronics* the act or process of suppressing a frequency, oscillation, etc. [4] *Biology* the failure of an organ or part to develop. [5] *Med* the cessation of any physiological process.

suppressive (sə'prɛsɪv) ADJECTIVE [1] tending or acting to suppress; involving suppression. [2] *Psychiatry* tending to prevent the expression of certain of one's desires or to resist the emergence of mental symptoms.

suppressor (sə'prɛsə) NOUN [1] a person or thing that suppresses. [2] a device fitted to an electrical appliance to suppress unwanted electrical interference to audiovisual signals.

suppressor grid NOUN an electrode placed between the screen grid and anode of a valve. Its negative potential, relative to both screen and anode, prevents secondary electrons from the anode reaching the screen.

suppurate ('sʌpjʊˌreɪt) VERB (*intr*) *Pathol* (of a wound, sore, etc.) to discharge pus; fester.
▷HISTORY C16: from Latin *suppūrāre*, from SUB- + *pūs* PUS

suppuration (ˌsʌpjʊ'reɪʃən) NOUN [1] the discharging of pus from a wound, sore, etc. [2] the discharge itself.

suppurative ('sʌpjʊrətɪv) ADJECTIVE [1] causing suppuration. ♦ NOUN [2] any suppurative drug.

supra ('su:prə) ADVERB above, esp referring to earlier parts of a book etc.
▷HISTORY C15: from Latin; related to SUPER-

supra- PREFIX over, above, beyond, or greater than: *supranational*; *supramolecular*.
▷HISTORY from Latin *suprā* above

supraglottal (ˌsu:prə'glɒtᵊl, ˌsju:-) ADJECTIVE *Anatomy* situated above the glottis: *supraglottal obstruction*.

supralapsarian (ˌsu:prəlæp'sɛərɪən, ˌsju:-) NOUN *Christian theol, chiefly Calvinist* a person who believes that God decreed the election or nonelection of individuals to salvation even before the Fall. Compare **infralapsarian.**
▷HISTORY C17: from New Latin *suprālapsārius*, from Latin SUPRA- + *lapsus* a fall
▸ˌ**supralap'sarianism** NOUN

supraliminal (ˌsu:prə'lɪmɪnᵊl, ˌsju:-) ADJECTIVE of or relating to any stimulus that is above the threshold of sensory awareness. Compare **subliminal.**
▸ˌ**supra'liminally** ADVERB

supramaxillary (ˌsu:prəmæk'sɪlərɪ) ADJECTIVE of or relating to the upper jaw.

supramolecular (ˌsu:prəmə'lɛkjʊlə, ˌsju:-) ADJECTIVE [1] more complex than a molecule. [2] consisting of more than one molecule.

supranational (ˌsu:prə'næʃnᵊl, ˌsju:-) ADJECTIVE beyond the authority or jurisdiction of one national government: *the supranational institutions of the EU*.
▸ˌ**supra'nationalism** NOUN ▸ˌ**supra'nationally** ADVERB

supraorbital (ˌsu:prə'ɔ:bɪtᵊl, ˌsju:-) ADJECTIVE *Anatomy* situated above the orbit.

suprarenal (ˌsu:prə'ri:nᵊl, ˌsju:-) ADJECTIVE *Anatomy* situated above a kidney.
▷HISTORY C19: from New Latin *suprārēnālis*. See SUPRA-, RENAL

suprarenal gland NOUN another name for **adrenal gland.**

suprasegmental (ˌsu:prəsɛg'mɛntᵊl, ˌsju:-) ADJECTIVE *Linguistics* denoting those features of a sound or sequence of sounds that accompany rather than form part of the consecutive segments of a word or sentence, as for example stress and pitch in English.
▸ˌ**supraseg'mentally** ADVERB

supremacist (sʊ'prɛməsɪst, sjʊ-) NOUN [1] a person who promotes or advocates the supremacy of any particular group. ♦ ADJECTIVE [2] characterized by belief in the supremacy of any particular group.
▸**su'premacism** *or* **su'prematism** NOUN

supremacy (sʊ'prɛməsɪ, sjʊ-) NOUN [1] supreme power; authority. [2] the quality or condition of being supreme.

Suprematism (sʊ'prɛməˌtɪzəm, sjʊ-) NOUN a form of pure cubist art, launched in Russia in 1913, and based on the principle that paintings should be composed only of rectangles, circles, triangles, or crosses.
▷HISTORY C20: from *suprematist* a supporter of this theory, from French *suprémacie* SUPREMACY
▸**Su'prematist** NOUN, ADJECTIVE

supreme (sʊ'pri:m, sjʊ-) ADJECTIVE [1] of highest status or power: *a supreme tribunal*. [2] (*usually prenominal*) of highest quality, importance, etc.: *supreme endeavour*. [3] greatest in degree; extreme: *supreme folly*. [4] (*prenominal*) final or last, esp being last in one's life or progress; ultimate: *the supreme judgment*.
▷HISTORY C16: from Latin *suprēmus* highest, from *superus* that is above, from *super* above
▸**su'premely** ADVERB ▸**su'premeness** NOUN

suprême (sʊ'pri:m, -'prɛm, sjʊ-) NOUN [1] Also called: **suprême sauce.** a rich velouté sauce made with a base of veal or chicken stock, with cream or egg yolks added. [2] the best or most delicate part of meat, esp the breast and wing of chicken, cooked in suprême sauce.
▷HISTORY French: SUPREME

Supreme Being NOUN the most exalted being; God.

supreme commander NOUN the military officer in overall command of all forces in one theatre of operations.

Supreme Court NOUN (in the US) [1] the highest Federal court, possessing final appellate jurisdiction and exercising supervisory jurisdiction over the lower courts. [2] (in many states) the highest state court.

Supreme Court of Judicature NOUN (in England) a court formed in 1873 by the amalgamation of several superior courts into two divisions, the High Court of Justice and the Court of Appeal.

supreme sacrifice NOUN **the.** the sacrifice of one's life.

Supreme Soviet NOUN (in the former Soviet Union) [1] the bicameral legislature, comprising the **Soviet of the Union** and the **Soviet of the Nationalities;** officially the highest organ of state power. [2] a similar legislature in each former Soviet republic.

Supreme Truth Cult NOUN another name for **Aum Shinrikyo.**

supremo (sʊ'pri:məʊ, sjʊ-) NOUN, *plural* **-mos.** *Brit informal* a person in overall authority.
▷HISTORY C20: from SUPREME

Supt *or* **supt** ABBREVIATION FOR superintendent.

suq (su:k) NOUN a variant spelling of **souk**[1].

Suqutra (sə'kəʊtrə) NOUN a variant spelling of **Socotra.**

Sur *or* **Sour** (sʊə) NOUN transliteration of the Arabic name for **Tyre.**

sur-[1] PREFIX over; above; beyond: *surcharge*; *surrealism*. Compare **super-.**
▷HISTORY from Old French, from Latin SUPER-

sur-[2] PREFIX a variant of **sub-** before *r*: *surrogate*.

sura ('sʊərə) NOUN any of the 114 chapters of the Koran.
▷HISTORY C17: from Arabic *sūrah* section

surah ('sʊərə) NOUN a twill-weave fabric of silk or rayon, used for dresses, blouses, etc.
▷HISTORY C19: from the French pronunciation of SURAT

sural ('sjʊərəl) ADJECTIVE *Anatomy* of or relating to the calf of the leg.
▷HISTORY C17: via New Latin from Latin *sūra* calf

surat (sjʊ'ræt) NOUN (formerly) a cotton fabric from the Surat area of India.

surbase ('sɜ:ˌbeɪs) NOUN the uppermost part, such as a moulding, of a pedestal, base, or skirting. Compare **subbase.**
▸**sur'basement** NOUN

surbased ('sɜ:ˌbeɪst) ADJECTIVE *Architect* [1] having a surbase. [2] (of an arch) having a rise of less than half the span.
▷HISTORY C18: from French *surbaisser* to depress, from *sur-* (intensive) + *baisser* to lower, from *bas* low; see BASE[1]

surcease (sɜ:'si:s) *Archaic* ♦ NOUN [1] cessation or intermission. ♦ VERB [2] to desist from (some action). [3] to cease or cause to cease.
▷HISTORY C16: from earlier *sursesen*, from Old French *surseoir*, from Latin *supersedēre*; see SUPERSEDE

surcharge NOUN ('sɜ:ˌtʃɑ:dʒ) [1] a charge in addition to the usual payment, tax, etc. [2] an excessive sum charged, esp when unlawful. [3] an extra and usually excessive burden or supply. [4] *Law* the act or an instance of surcharging. [5] an overprint that alters the face value of a postage stamp. ♦ VERB (sɜ:'tʃɑ:dʒ, 'sɜ:ˌtʃɑ:dʒ) (*tr*) [6] to charge an additional sum, tax, etc. [7] to overcharge (a person) for something. [8] to put an extra physical burden upon; overload. [9] to fill to excess; overwhelm. [10] *Law* to insert credits that have been omitted in (an account). [11] to overprint a surcharge on (a stamp).
▸**sur'charger** NOUN

surcingle ('sɜ:ˌsɪŋgᵊl) NOUN [1] a girth for a horse which goes around the body, used esp with a racing saddle. [2] the belt worn with a cassock. ♦ VERB [3] to put a surcingle on or over (a horse).
▷HISTORY C14: from Old French *surcengle*, from *sur-* over + *cengle* a belt, from Latin *cingulum*

surcoat ('sɜ:ˌkəʊt) NOUN [1] a tunic, often embroidered with heraldic arms, worn by a knight over his armour during the Middle Ages. [2] an outer coat or other garment.

surculose ('sɜ:kjʊˌləʊs) ADJECTIVE (of a plant) bearing suckers.
▷HISTORY C19: from Latin *surculōsus* woody, from *surculus* twig, from *sūrus* a branch

surd (sɜ:d) NOUN [1] *Maths* an expression containing one or more irrational roots of numbers, such as $2\sqrt{3} + 3\sqrt{2} + 6$. [2] *Phonetics* a voiceless consonant, such as (t). ♦ ADJECTIVE [3] of or relating to a surd.
▷HISTORY C16: from Latin *surdus* muffled

sure (ʃʊə, ʃɔ:) ADJECTIVE [1] (sometimes foll by *of*) free from hesitancy or uncertainty (with regard to a belief, conviction, etc.): *we are sure of the accuracy of the data; I am sure that he is lying*. [2] (foll by *of*) having no doubt, as of the occurrence of a future state or event: *sure of success*. [3] always effective; unfailing: *a sure remedy*. [4] reliable in indication or accuracy: *a sure criterion*. [5] (of persons) worthy of trust or confidence: *a sure friend*. [6] not open to doubt: *sure proof*. [7] admitting of no vacillation or doubt: *he is very sure in his beliefs*. [8] bound to be or occur; inevitable: *victory is sure*. [9] (*postpositive*) bound inevitably (to be or do something); certain: *she is sure to be there tonight*. [10] physically secure or dependable: *a sure footing*. [11] *Obsolete* free from exposure to harm or danger. [12] **be sure.** (*usually imperative or dependent imperative; takes a clause as object or an infinitive*, sometimes with *to* replaced by *and*) to be careful or certain: *be sure and shut the door; I told him to be sure to shut the door*. [13] **for sure.** without a doubt; surely. [14] **make sure. a** (*takes a clause as object*) to make certain; ensure. **b** (foll by *of*) to establish or confirm power or possession (over). [15] **sure enough.** *Informal* as might have been confidently expected; definitely: often used as a sentence substitute. [16] **to be sure. a** without doubt; certainly. **b** it has to be acknowledged; admittedly. ♦ ADVERB [17] (*sentence substitute*) *Informal* willingly; yes. [18] (*sentence modifier*) *Informal, chiefly US and Canadian* without question; certainly.
▷HISTORY C14: from Old French *seur*, from Latin *sēcūrus* SECURE
▸'**sureness** NOUN

sure-fire ADJECTIVE (*usually prenominal*) *Informal* certain to succeed or meet expectations; assured.

sure-footed ADJECTIVE [1] unlikely to fall, slip, or stumble. [2] not likely to err or fail, as in judgment.
▸ˌ**sure-'footedly** ADVERB ▸ˌ**sure-'footedness** NOUN

surely ('ʃʊəlɪ, 'ʃɔ:-) ADVERB [1] without doubt; assuredly: *things could surely not have been worse*. [2] without fail; inexorably (esp in the phrase **slowly but surely**). [3] (*sentence modifier*) am I not right in thinking that?; I am sure that: *surely you don't mean it?* [4] *Rare* in a sure manner. [5] *Archaic* safely; securely. [6] (*sentence substitute*) *Chiefly US and Canadian* willingly; of course; yes.

sure thing *Informal* ♦ ADVERB [1] (*sentence substitute*) *Chiefly US* all right! yes indeed! used to express enthusiastic assent. ♦ NOUN [2] something guaranteed to be successful.

surety ('ʃʊətɪ, 'ʃʊərɪtɪ) NOUN, *plural* **-ties.** [1] a person who assumes legal responsibility for the fulfilment

of another's debt or obligation and himself becomes liable if the other defaults. [2] security given against loss or damage or as a guarantee that an obligation will be met. [3] *Obsolete* the quality or condition of being sure. [4] *Obsolete* a means of assurance or safety. [5] **stand surety.** to act as a surety.
▷HISTORY C14: from Old French *seurte,* from Latin *sēcūritās* SECURITY
▶ **ˈsuretyˌship** NOUN

surf (sɜːf) NOUN [1] waves breaking on the shore or on a reef. [2] foam caused by the breaking of waves. ◆ VERB [3] (*intr*) to take part in surfing. [4] **a** to move rapidly and easily through a particular medium: *surfing the Internet.* **b** (*in combination*): *channelsurfing.* [5] **a** *Informal* to be carried on top of something: *that guy's surfing the audience.* **b** (*in combination*): *trainsurfing.*
▷HISTORY C17: probably variant of SOUGH[1]
▶ **ˈsurfable** ADJECTIVE ▶ **ˈsurfˌlike** ADJECTIVE

surface (ˈsɜːfɪs) NOUN [1] **a** the exterior face of an object or one such face. **b** (*as modifier*): *surface gloss.* [2] **a** the area or size of such a face. **b** (*as modifier*): *surface measurements.* [3] material resembling such a face, with length and width but without depth. [4] **a** the superficial appearance as opposed to the real nature. **b** (*as modifier*): *a surface resemblance.* [5] *Geometry* **a** the complete boundary of a solid figure. **b** a continuous two-dimensional configuration. [6] **a** the uppermost level of the land or sea. **b** (*as modifier*): *surface transportation.* [7] **come to the surface.** to emerge; become apparent. [8] **on the surface.** to all appearances. ◆ VERB [9] to rise or cause to rise to or as if to the surface (of water, etc.). [10] (*tr*) to treat the surface of, as by polishing, smoothing, etc. [11] (*tr*) to furnish with a surface. [12] (*intr*) *Mining* **a** to work at or near the ground surface. **b** to wash surface ore deposits. [13] (*intr*) to become apparent; emerge. [14] (*intr*) *Informal* **a** to wake up. **b** to get up.
▷HISTORY C17: from French, from *sur* on + *face* FACE, probably on the model of Latin SUPERFICIES
▶ **ˈsurfaceless** ADJECTIVE ▶ **ˈsurfacer** NOUN

surface acoustic wave NOUN an acoustic wave generated on the surface of a piezoelectric substrate: used as a filter in electronic circuits.

surface-active ADJECTIVE (of a substance, esp a detergent) capable of lowering the surface tension of a liquid, usually water. See also **surfactant.**

surface condenser NOUN a steam condenser usually associated with a steam turbine in which the steam is condensed on the surface of tubes through which water is passed. Compare **jet condenser.**

surface friction drag NOUN the part of the drag on a body moving through a fluid that is dependent on the nature of the surface of the body. Also called: **skin friction.**

surface mail NOUN mail transported by land or sea. Compare **airmail.**

surface noise NOUN noise produced by the friction of the needle or stylus of a record player with the rotating record, caused by a static charge, dust, or irregularities on the surface of a record.

surface plate NOUN another name for **faceplate** (sense 2).

surface structure NOUN *Generative grammar* a representation of a string of words or morphemes as they occur in a sentence, together with labels and brackets that represent syntactic structure. Compare **deep structure.**

surface tension NOUN [1] a property of liquids caused by intermolecular forces near the surface leading to the apparent presence of a surface film and to capillarity, etc. [2] a measure of this property expressed as the force acting normal to one side of a line of unit length on the surface: measured in newtons per metre. Symbol: T, γ *or* σ.

surface-to-air ADJECTIVE of or relating to a missile launched from the surface of the earth against airborne targets.

surface-to-surface ADJECTIVE of or relating to a missile launched from the surface of the earth against surface targets.

surfactant (sɜːˈfæktənt) NOUN [1] Also called: **surface-active agent.** a substance, such as a detergent, that can reduce the surface tension of a liquid and thus allow it to foam or penetrate solids; a wetting agent. ◆ ADJECTIVE [2] having the properties of a surfactant.
▷HISTORY C20: *surf(ace)-act(ive) a(ge)nt*

surfbird (ˈsɜːfˌbɜːd) NOUN an American shore bird, *Aphriza virgata,* having a spotted plumage, with a black and white tail: family *Scolopacidae* (sandpipers, etc.), order *Charadriiformes.*

surfboard (ˈsɜːfˌbɔːd) NOUN a long narrow board used in surfing.

surfboat (ˈsɜːfˌbəʊt) NOUN a boat with a high bow and stern and flotation chambers, equipped for use in rough surf.

surfcasting (ˈsɜːfˌkɑːstɪŋ) NOUN fishing from the shore by casting into the surf.
▶ **ˈsurfˌcaster** NOUN

surfeit (ˈsɜːfɪt) NOUN [1] (usually foll by *of*) an excessive or immoderate amount. [2] overindulgence, esp in eating or drinking. [3] disgust, nausea, etc., caused by such overindulgence. ◆ VERB [4] (*tr*) to supply or feed excessively; satiate. [5] (*intr*) *Archaic* to eat, drink, or be supplied to excess. [6] (*intr*) *Obsolete* to feel uncomfortable as a consequence of overindulgence.
▷HISTORY C13: from French *sourfait,* from *sourfaire* to overdo, from SUR-[1] + *faire,* from Latin *facere* to do
▶ **ˈsurfeiter** NOUN

surfie (ˈsɜːfɪ) NOUN *Austral and NZ slang* a young person whose main interest is in surfing, esp when considered as a cult figure.

surfing (ˈsɜːfɪŋ) NOUN the sport of riding towards shore on the crest of a wave by standing or lying on a surfboard.
▶ **ˈsurfer** *or* **ˈsurfˌrider** NOUN

surf mat NOUN *Austral informal* a small inflatable rubber mattress used to ride on waves.

surf music NOUN a US West Coast style of pop music of the early 1960s, characterized by high harmony vocals and strong trebly guitar riffs.

surf 'n' turf NOUN a dish consisting of meat served with seafood.

surfperch (ˈsɜːfˌpɜːtʃ) NOUN any viviparous marine percoid fish of the family *Embiotocidae,* of North American Pacific coastal waters. Also called: **sea perch.**

surf scoter *or* **duck** NOUN a North American scoter, *Melanitta perspicillata,* having white patches on the head.

surg. ABBREVIATION FOR: [1] surgeon. [2] surgery. [3] surgical.

surge (sɜːdʒ) NOUN [1] a strong rush or sweep; sudden increase: *a surge of anger.* [2] the rolling swell of the sea, esp after the passage of a large wave. [3] a heavy rolling motion or sound: *the surge of the trumpets.* [4] an undulating rolling surface, as of hills. [5] a billowing cloud or volume. [6] *Nautical* a temporary release or slackening of a rope or cable. [7] a large momentary increase in the voltage or current in an electric circuit. [8] an upward instability or unevenness in the power output of an engine. [9] *Astronomy* a short-lived disturbance, occurring during the eruption of a solar flare. ◆ VERB [10] (*intr*) (of waves, the sea, etc.) to rise or roll with a heavy swelling motion. [11] (*intr*) to move like a heavy sea. [12] *Nautical* to slacken or temporarily release (a rope or cable) from a capstan or (of a rope, etc.) to be slackened or released and slip back. [13] (*intr*) (of an electric current or voltage) to undergo a large momentary increase. [14] (*tr*) *Rare* to cause to move in or as if in a wave or waves.
▷HISTORY C15: from Latin *surgere* to rise, from *sub-* up + *regere* to lead
▶ **ˈsurgeless** ADJECTIVE ▶ **ˈsurger** NOUN

surgeon (ˈsɜːdʒən) NOUN [1] a medical practioner who specializes in surgery. [2] a medical officer in the Royal Navy.
▷HISTORY C14: from Anglo-Norman *surgien,* from Old French *cirurgien;* see SURGERY

surgeoncy (ˈsɜːdʒənsɪ) NOUN, *plural* **-cies.** *Chiefly Brit* the office, duties, or position of a surgeon, esp in the army or navy.

surgeonfish (ˈsɜːdʒənˌfɪʃ) NOUN, *plural* **-fish** *or* **-fishes.** any tropical marine spiny-finned fish of the family *Acanthuridae,* having a compressed brightly coloured body with one or more knifelike spines at the base of the tail.

surgeon general NOUN, *plural* **surgeons general.** [1] (in the British, US, and certain other armies and navies) the senior officer of the medical service. [2] the head of the public health service in the US.

surgeon's knot NOUN a knot used by surgeons in tying ligatures, etc.

surgery (ˈsɜːdʒərɪ) NOUN, *plural* **-geries.** [1] the branch of medicine concerned with treating disease, injuries, etc., by means of manual or operative procedures, esp by incision into the body. [2] the performance of such procedures by a surgeon. [3] *Brit* a place where a doctor, dentist, etc., can be consulted. [4] *Brit* an occasion when an MP, lawyer, etc., is available for consultation. [5] *US and Canadian* an operating theatre where surgical operations are performed.
▷HISTORY C14: via Old French from Latin *chirurgia,* from Greek *kheirurgia,* from *kheir* hand + *ergon* work

surge tank NOUN *Engineering* a tank used to absorb surges in flow.

surge tide NOUN a powerful and often destructive tide that may occur when an abnormally high tide (e.g. at the autumn equinox) coincides with high wind and low atmospheric pressure.

surgical (ˈsɜːdʒɪkᵊl) ADJECTIVE of, relating to, involving, or used in surgery.
▶ **ˈsurgically** ADVERB

surgical boot NOUN a specially designed boot or shoe that compensates for deformities of the foot or leg.

surgical spirit NOUN methylated spirit containing small amounts of oil of wintergreen and castor oil: used medically for sterilizing.

Suribachi (ˌsʊərɪˈbɑːtʃɪ) NOUN **Mount.** a volcanic hill in the Volcano Islands, on Iwo Jima: site of a US victory (1945) over the Japanese in World War II.

suricate (ˈsjʊərɪˌkeɪt) NOUN another name for **slender-tailed meerkat** (see **meerkat**).
▷HISTORY C18: from French *surikate,* probably from a native South African word

surimi (ˌsuːˈriːmɪ) NOUN a blended seafood product made from precooked fish, restructured into stick shapes.

Surinam (ˌsʊərɪˈnæm) NOUN a republic in NE South America, on the Atlantic: became a self-governing part of the Netherlands in 1954 and fully independent in 1975. Official languages: Dutch; English is also widely spoken. Religion: Hindu, Christian, and Muslim. Currency: guilder. Capital: Paramaribo. Pop.: 434 000 (2001 est.). Area: 163 820 sq. km (63 251 sq. miles). Former names: **Dutch Guiana, Netherlands Guiana.**

Surinam toad NOUN another name for **pipa.**

surjection (sɜːˈdʒɛkʃən) NOUN a mathematical function or mapping for which every element of the image space is a value for some members of the domain. See also **injection** (sense 5), **bijection.**
▷HISTORY C20: from SUR-[1] + *-jection,* on the model of PROJECTION
▶ **surˈjective** ADJECTIVE

surly (ˈsɜːlɪ) ADJECTIVE **-lier, -liest.** [1] sullenly ill-tempered or rude. [2] (of an animal) ill-tempered or refractory. [3] dismal. [4] *Obsolete* arrogant.
▷HISTORY C16: from obsolete *sirly* haughty; see SIR
▶ **ˈsurlily** ADVERB ▶ **ˈsurliness** NOUN

surmise VERB (sɜːˈmaɪz) [1] (when *tr, may take a clause as object*) to infer (something) from incomplete or uncertain evidence. ◆ NOUN (sɜːˈmaɪz, ˈsɜːmaɪz) [2] an idea inferred from inconclusive evidence.
▷HISTORY C15: from Old French, from *surmettre* to accuse, from Latin *supermittere* to throw over, from SUPER- + *mittere* to send
▶ **surˈmisable** ADJECTIVE ▶ **surˈmiser** NOUN

surmount (sɜːˈmaʊnt) VERB (*tr*) [1] to prevail over; overcome: *to surmount tremendous difficulties.* [2] to ascend and cross to the opposite side of. [3] to lie on top of or rise above. [4] to put something on top of or above. [5] *Obsolete* to surpass or exceed.
▷HISTORY C14: from Old French *surmonter,* from SUR-[1] + *monter* to MOUNT[1]
▶ **surˈmountable** ADJECTIVE ▶ **surˈmountableness** NOUN
▶ **surˈmounter** NOUN

surmullet (sɜːˈmʌlɪt) NOUN a US name for the **red mullet.**
▷HISTORY C17: from French *sormulet,* from *sor* brown + MULLET

surname (ˈsɜːˌneɪm) NOUN [1] Also called: **last**

name, second name. a family name as opposed to a first or Christian name. 2 (formerly) a descriptive epithet attached to a person's name to denote a personal characteristic, profession, etc.; nickname. ◆ VERB 3 (*tr*) to furnish with or call by a surname.
▷HISTORY C14: via Anglo-French from Old French *surnom.* See SUR-[1], NAME
▸ **'sur,namer** NOUN

surpass (sɜːˈpɑːs) VERB (*tr*) 1 to be greater than in degree, extent, etc. 2 to be superior to in achievement or excellence. 3 to overstep the limit or range of: *the theory surpasses my comprehension.*
▷HISTORY C16: from French *surpasser,* from SUR-[1] + *passer* to PASS
▸ **sur'passable** ADJECTIVE

surpassing (sɜːˈpɑːsɪŋ) ADJECTIVE 1 exceptional; extraordinary. ◆ ADVERB 2 *Obsolete or poetic* (intensifier): *surpassing fair.*
▸ **sur'passingly** ADVERB

surplice (ˈsɜːplɪs) NOUN a loose wide-sleeved liturgical vestment of linen, reaching to the knees, worn over the cassock by clergymen, choristers, and acolytes.
▷HISTORY C13: via Anglo-French from Old French *sourpelis,* from Medieval Latin *superpellīcium,* from SUPER- + *pellīcium* coat made of skins, from Latin *pellis* a skin
▸ **'surpliced** ADJECTIVE

surplus (ˈsɜːpləs) NOUN, *plural* **-pluses.** 1 a quantity or amount in excess of what is required. 2 *Accounting* **a** an excess of total assets over total liabilities. **b** an excess of actual net assets over the nominal value of capital stock. **c** an excess of revenues over expenditures during a certain period of time. 3 *Economics* **a** an excess of government revenues over expenditures during a certain financial year. **b** an excess of receipts over payments on the balance of payments. ◆ ADJECTIVE 4 being in excess; extra.
▷HISTORY C14: from Old French, from Medieval Latin *superplūs,* from Latin SUPER- + *plūs* more

surplusage (ˈsɜːpləsɪdʒ) NOUN 1 *Law* (in pleading, etc.) irrelevant matter, such as a superfluous allegation. 2 an excess of words. 3 a less common word for **surplus.**

surprint (ˈsɜːˌprɪnt) VERB 1 (*tr*) to print (additional matter) over something already printed; overprint. ◆ NOUN 2 marks, printed matter, etc., that have been surprinted.

surprise (səˈpraɪz) VERB (*tr*) 1 to cause to feel amazement or wonder. 2 to encounter or discover unexpectedly or suddenly. 3 to capture or assault suddenly and without warning. 4 to present with something unexpected, such as a gift. 5 (foll by *into*) to provoke (someone) to unintended action by a trick, etc.: *to surprise a person into an indiscretion.* 6 (often foll by *from*) to elicit by unexpected behaviour or by a trick: *to surprise information from a prisoner.* ◆ NOUN 7 the act or an instance of surprising; the act of taking unawares. 8 a sudden or unexpected event, gift, etc. 9 the feeling or condition of being surprised; astonishment. 10 (*modifier*) causing, characterized by, or relying upon surprise: *a surprise move.* 11 **take by surprise. a** to come upon suddenly and without warning. **b** to capture unexpectedly or catch unprepared. **c** to astonish; amaze.
▷HISTORY C15: from Old French, from *surprendre* to overtake, from SUR-[1] + *prendre* from Latin *prehendere* to grasp; see PREHENSILE
▸ **sur'prisal** NOUN ▸ **sur'prised** ADJECTIVE ▸ **surprisedly** (səˈpraɪzɪdlɪ) ADVERB ▸ **sur'priser** NOUN

surprising (səˈpraɪzɪŋ) ADJECTIVE causing surprise; unexpected or amazing.
▸ **sur'prisingly** ADVERB ▸ **sur'prisingness** NOUN

surra (ˈsʊərə) NOUN a tropical febrile disease of cattle, horses, camels, and dogs, characterized by severe emaciation: caused by the protozoan *Trypanosoma evansi* and transmitted by fleas.
▷HISTORY from Marathi

surreal (səˈrɪəl) ADJECTIVE 1 suggestive of surrealism; dreamlike. ◆ NOUN 2 **the.** the atmosphere or qualities evoked by surrealism.

surrealism (səˈrɪəˌlɪzəm) NOUN (*sometimes capital*) a movement in art and literature in the 1920s, which developed esp from dada, characterized by the evocative juxtaposition of incongruous images in order to include unconscious and dream elements.
▷HISTORY C20: from French *surréalisme,* from SUR-[1] + *réalisme* REALISM
▸ **sur'realist** NOUN, ADJECTIVE ▸ **sur,real'istic** ADJECTIVE
▸ **sur,real'istically** ADVERB

surrebuttal (ˌsɜːrɪˈbʌtᵊl) NOUN *Law* (in pleading) the giving of evidence in support of a surrebutter.

surrebutter (ˌsɜːrɪˈbʌtə) NOUN *Law* (in pleading) the claimant's reply to the defendant's rebutter.

surrejoinder (ˌsɜːrɪˈdʒɔɪndə) NOUN *Law* (in pleading) the claimant's reply to the defendant's rejoinder.

surrender (səˈrɛndə) VERB 1 (*tr*) to relinquish to the control or possession of another under duress or on demand: *to surrender a city.* 2 (*tr*) to relinquish or forego (an office, position, etc.), esp as a voluntary concession to another: *he surrendered his place to a lady.* 3 to give (oneself) up physically, as or as if to an enemy. 4 to allow (oneself) to yield, as to a temptation, influence, etc. 5 (*tr*) to give up (hope, etc.). 6 (*tr*) *Law* to give up or restore (an estate), esp to give up a lease before expiration of the term. 7 (*tr*) *Obsolete* to return or render (thanks, etc.). 8 **surrender to bail.** to present oneself at court at the appointed time after having been on bail. ◆ NOUN 9 the act or instance of surrendering. 10 *Insurance* the voluntary discontinuation of a life policy by its holder in return for a consideration (the **surrender value**). 11 *Law* **a** the yielding up or restoring of an estate, esp the giving up of a lease before its term has expired. **b** the giving up to the appropriate authority of a fugitive from justice. **c** the act of surrendering or being surrendered to bail. **d** the deed by which a legal surrender is effected.
▷HISTORY C15: from Old French *surrendre* to yield, from SUR-[1] + *rendre* to RENDER
▸ **sur'renderer** NOUN

surreptitious (ˌsʌrəpˈtɪʃəs) ADJECTIVE 1 done, acquired, etc., in secret or by improper means. 2 operating by stealth. 3 characterized by fraud or misrepresentation of the truth.
▷HISTORY C15: from Latin *surreptīcius* furtive, from *surripere* to steal, from *sub-* secretly + *rapere* to snatch
▸ **,surrep'titiously** ADVERB ▸ **,surrep'titiousness** NOUN

surrey (ˈsʌrɪ) NOUN a light four-wheeled horse-drawn carriage having two or four seats.
▷HISTORY C19: shortened from *Surrey cart,* after SURREY, where it was originally made

Surrey (ˈsʌrɪ) NOUN a county of SE England, on the River Thames: urban in the northeast; crossed from east to west by the North Downs and drained by tributaries of the Thames. Administrative centre: Kingston upon Thames. Pop.: 1 059 015 (2001). Area: 1679 sq. km (648 sq. miles).

surrogate NOUN (ˈsʌrəgɪt) 1 a person or thing acting as a substitute. 2 *Chiefly Brit* a deputy, such as a clergyman appointed to deputize for a bishop in granting marriage licences. 3 *Psychiatry* a person who is a substitute for someone else, esp in childhood when different persons, such as a brother or teacher, can act as substitutes for the parents. 4 (in some US states) a judge with jurisdiction over the probate of wills, etc. 5 (*modifier*) of, relating to, or acting as a surrogate: *a surrogate pleasure.* ◆ VERB (ˈsʌrəˌgeɪt) (*tr*) 6 to put in another's position as a deputy, substitute, etc. 7 to appoint as a successor to oneself.
▷HISTORY C17: from Latin *surrogāre* to substitute; see SUBROGATE
▸ **'surrogateship** NOUN ▸ **,surro'gation** NOUN

surrogate mother NOUN a woman who bears a child on behalf of a couple unable to have a child, either by artificial insemination from the man or implantation of an embryo from the woman.
▸ **surrogacy** (ˈsʌrəgəsɪ) NOUN

surround (səˈraʊnd) VERB (*tr*) 1 to encircle or enclose or cause to be encircled or enclosed. 2 to deploy forces on all sides of (a place or military formation), so preventing access or retreat. 3 to exist around: *I dislike the people who surround her.* ◆ NOUN 4 *Chiefly Brit* a border, esp the area of uncovered floor between the walls of a room and the carpet or around an opening or panel. 5 *Chiefly US* **a** a method of capturing wild beasts by encircling the area in which they are believed to be. **b** the area so encircled.
▷HISTORY C15 *surrounden* to overflow, from Old French *suronder,* from Late Latin *superundāre,* from Latin SUPER- + *undāre* to abound, from *unda* a wave
▸ **sur'rounding** ADJECTIVE

surroundings (səˈraʊndɪŋz) PLURAL NOUN the conditions, scenery, etc., around a person, place, or thing; environment.

surround sound NOUN a system of sound recording and reproduction that uses three or more independent recording channels and loudspeakers in order to give the impression that the listener is surrounded by the sound sources. Compare **quadraphonics.** See also **ambisonics.**

sursum corda (ˈsɜːsəm ˈkɔːdə) NOUN 1 *RC Church* a Latin versicle meaning *Lift up your hearts,* said by the priest at Mass. 2 a cry of exhortation, hope, etc.
▷HISTORY C16: Latin, literally: up hearts

surtax (ˈsɜːˌtæks) NOUN 1 a tax, usually highly progressive, levied on the amount by which a person's income exceeds a specific level. 2 an additional tax on something that has already been taxed. ◆ VERB 3 (*tr*) to assess for liability to surtax; charge with an extra tax.

surtitles (ˈsɜːˌtaɪtᵊlz) PLURAL NOUN brief translations of the text of an opera or play that is being sung or spoken in a foreign language, projected above the stage.

surtout (ˈsɜːtuː; *French* syrtu) NOUN a man's overcoat resembling a frock coat, popular in the late 19th century.
▷HISTORY C17: from French, from *sur* over + *tout* all

surv. ABBREVIATION FOR: 1 Also: **survey.** surveying. 2 surveyor.

surveillance (sɜːˈveɪləns) NOUN close observation or supervision maintained over a person, group, etc., esp one in custody or under suspicion.
▷HISTORY C19: from French, from *surveiller* to watch over, from SUR-[1] + *veiller* to keep watch (from Latin *vigilāre;* see VIGIL)
▸ **sur'veillant** ADJECTIVE, NOUN

survey VERB (sɜːˈveɪ, ˈsɜːveɪ) 1 (*tr*) to view or consider in a comprehensive or general way: *to survey the situation.* 2 (*tr*) to examine carefully, as or as if to appraise value: *to survey oneself in a mirror.* 3 to plot a detailed map of (an area of land) by measuring or calculating distances and height. 4 *Brit* to inspect a building to determine its condition and value. 5 to examine a vessel thoroughly in order to determine its seaworthiness. 6 (*tr*) to run a statistical survey on (incomes, opinions, etc.). ◆ NOUN (ˈsɜːveɪ) 7 a comprehensive or general view: *a survey of English literature.* 8 a critical, detailed, and formal inspection: *a survey of the nation's hospitals.* 9 *Brit* an inspection of a building to determine its condition and value. 10 a report incorporating the results of such an inspection. 11 **a** a body of surveyors. **b** an area surveyed. 12 *Statistics* a random sample.
▷HISTORY C15: from French *surveoir,* from SUR-[1] + *veoir* to see, from Latin *vidēre*
▸ **sur'veyable** ADJECTIVE

surveying (sɜːˈveɪɪŋ) NOUN 1 the study or practice of measuring altitudes, angles, and distances on the land surface so that they can be accurately plotted on a map. 2 the setting out on the ground of the positions of proposed construction or engineering works.

surveyor (sɜːˈveɪə) NOUN 1 a person whose occupation is to survey land or buildings. See also **quantity surveyor.** 2 *Chiefly Brit* a person concerned with the official inspection of something for purposes of measurement and valuation. 3 a person who carries out surveys, esp of ships (**marine surveyor**) to determine seaworthiness, etc. 4 a customs official. 5 *Archaic* a supervisor.
▸ **sur'veyor,ship** NOUN

surveyor's chain NOUN a measuring chain 22 yards in length; Gunter's chain. See **chain** (sense 7).

surveyor's level NOUN another term for **level** (sense 19).

surveyor's measure NOUN the system of measurement based on the chain (66 feet) as a unit.

survival (səˈvaɪvᵊl) NOUN 1 a person or thing that survives, such as a custom. 2 **a** the act or fact of surviving or condition of having survived. **b** (*as modifier*): *survival kit.*

survival bag NOUN a large plastic bag carried by

climbers for use in an emergency as protection against exposure.

survivalist (sə'vaɪvəlɪst) NOUN *US* **a** a person who believes in ensuring his personal survival of a catastrophic event by arming himself and often by living in the wild. **b** (*as modifier*): *survivalist weapons.*
▸**sur'vival,ism** NOUN

survival of the fittest NOUN a popular term for **natural selection.**

survive (sə'vaɪv) VERB [1] (*tr*) to live after the death of (another): *he survived his wife by 12 years.* [2] to continue in existence or use after (a passage of time, an adversity, etc.). [3] *Informal* to endure (something): *I don't know how I survive such an awful job.*
▷HISTORY C15: from Old French *sourvivre,* from Latin *supervīvere,* from SUPER- + *vīvere* to live
▸**sur'vivable** ADJECTIVE ▸**sur,viva'bility** NOUN

survivor (sə'vaɪvə) NOUN [1] a person or thing that survives. [2] *Property law* one of two or more specified persons having joint interests in property who lives longer than the other or others and thereby becomes entitled to the whole property.
▸**sur'vivor,ship** NOUN

sus (sʌs) *Brit slang* ◆ NOUN [1] suspicion. [2] a suspect. ◆ ADJECTIVE [3] suspicious. ◆ VERB [4] a variant spelling of **suss** (sense 2). ◆ See also **sus laws.**
▷HISTORY C20: shortened from SUSPICION

Susa ('suːsə) NOUN an ancient city north of the Persian Gulf: capital of Elam and of the Persian Empire; flourished as a Greek polis under the Seleucids and Parthians. Biblical name: **Shushan.**

Susanna (suː'zænə) NOUN the book of the Apocrypha containing the story of Susanna, who was condemned to death for adultery because of a false accusation but saved by Daniel's sagacity.

susceptance (sə'sɛptəns) NOUN *Physics* the imaginary component of the admittance.
▷HISTORY C19: from SUSCEPT(IBILITY) + -ANCE

susceptibility (sə,sɛptə'bɪlɪtɪ) NOUN, *plural* **-ties.** [1] the quality or condition of being susceptible. [2] the ability or tendency to be impressed by emotional feelings; sensitivity. [3] (*plural*) emotional sensibilities; feelings. [4] *Physics* **a** Also called: **electric susceptibility.** (of a dielectric) the amount by which the relative permittivity differs from unity. Symbol: Χ. **b** Also called: **magnetic susceptibility.** (of a magnetic medium) the amount by which the relative permeability differs from unity. Symbol: K.

susceptible (sə'sɛptəbᵊl) ADJECTIVE [1] (*postpositive; foll by* of *or* to) yielding readily (to); capable (of): *hypotheses susceptible of refutation; susceptible to control.* [2] (*postpositive; foll by* to) liable to be afflicted (by): *susceptible to colds.* [3] easily impressed emotionally.
▷HISTORY C17: from Late Latin *susceptibilis,* from Latin *suscipere* to take up, from SUB- + *capere* to take
▸**sus'ceptibleness** NOUN ▸**sus'ceptibly** ADVERB

susceptive (sə'sɛptɪv) ADJECTIVE [1] another word for **receptive.** [2] a variant of **susceptible.**
▸**susceptivity** (,sʌsɛp'tɪvɪtɪ) *or* **sus'ceptiveness** NOUN

sushi ('suːʃɪ) NOUN a Japanese dish consisting of small cakes of cold rice with a topping esp of raw fish.
▷HISTORY from Japanese

Susian ('suːzɪən) NOUN, ADJECTIVE another word for **Elamite.**
▷HISTORY C16: from *Susiana,* a province of the ancient Persian Empire with its capital at SUSA

sus laws *or* **suss laws** PLURAL NOUN *Brit slang* laws authorizing the arrest and punishment of suspected persons frequenting, or loitering in, public places with criminal intent. In England, the sus law formed part of the Vagrancy Act of 1824, repealed in 1981.

suslik ('sʌslɪk) *or* **souslik** NOUN a central Eurasian ground squirrel, *Citellus citellus,* of dry open areas, having large eyes and small ears.
▷HISTORY from Russian

suspect VERB (sə'spɛkt) [1] (*tr*) to believe guilty of a specified offence without proof. [2] (*tr*) to think false, questionable, etc.: *she suspected his sincerity.* [3] (*tr; may take a clause as object*) to surmise to be the case; think probable: *to suspect fraud.* [4] (*intr*) to have suspicion. ◆ NOUN ('sʌspɛkt) [5] a person who is under suspicion. ◆ ADJECTIVE ('sʌspɛkt) [6] causing or open to suspicion.
▷HISTORY C14: from Latin *suspicere* to mistrust, from SUB- + *specere* to look
▸**sus'pecter** NOUN ▸**'suspectless** ADJECTIVE

suspend (sə'spɛnd) VERB [1] (*tr*) to hang from above so as to permit free movement. [2] (*tr; passive*) to cause to remain floating or hanging: *a cloud of smoke was suspended over the town.* [3] (*tr*) to render inoperative or cause to cease, esp temporarily: *to suspend interest payments.* [4] (*tr*) to hold in abeyance; postpone action on: *to suspend a decision.* [5] (*tr*) to debar temporarily from privilege, office, etc., as a punishment. [6] (*tr*) *Chem* to cause (particles) to be held in suspension in a fluid. [7] (*tr*) *Music* to continue (a note) until the next chord is sounded, with which it usually forms a dissonance. See **suspension** (sense 11). [8] (*intr*) to cease payment, as from incapacity to meet financial obligations. [9] (*tr*) *Obsolete* to put or keep in a state of anxiety or wonder. [10] (*intr*) *Obsolete* to be attached from above.
▷HISTORY C13: from Latin *suspendere* from SUB- + *pendere* to hang
▸**sus'pendible** *or* **sus'pensible** ADJECTIVE ▸**sus,pendi'bility** NOUN

suspended animation NOUN a temporary cessation of the vital functions, as by freezing an organism.

suspended sentence NOUN a sentence of imprisonment that is not served by an offender unless he commits a further offence during its currency. Compare **deferred sentence.**

suspender (sə'spɛndə) NOUN [1] (*often plural*) *Brit* **a** an elastic strap attached to a belt or corset having a fastener at the end, for holding up women's stockings. **b** a similar fastener attached to a garter worn by men in order to support socks. US and Canadian equivalent: **garter.** [2] (*plural*) the US and Canadian name for **braces.** [3] a person or thing that suspends, such as one of the vertical cables that carries the deck in a suspension bridge.

suspender belt NOUN a belt with suspenders hanging from it to hold up women's stockings. US and Canadian name: **garter belt.**

suspense (sə'spɛns) NOUN [1] the condition of being insecure or uncertain: *the matter of the succession remained in suspense for many years.* [2] mental uncertainty; anxiety: *their father's illness kept them in a state of suspense.* [3] excitement felt at the approach of the climax: *a play of terrifying suspense.* [4] the condition of being suspended.
▷HISTORY C15: from Medieval Latin *suspensum* delay, from Latin *suspendere* to hang up; see SUSPEND
▸**sus'penseful** ADJECTIVE

suspense account NOUN *Book-keeping* an account in which entries are made until determination of their proper disposition.

suspenser (sə'spɛnsə) NOUN a film that creates a feeling of suspense.

suspension (sə'spɛnʃən) NOUN [1] an interruption or temporary revocation: *the suspension of a law.* [2] a temporary debarment, as from position, privilege, etc. [3] a deferment, esp of a decision, judgment, etc. [4] *Law* **a** a postponement of execution of a sentence or the deferring of a judgment, etc. **b** a temporary extinguishment of a right or title. [5] cessation of payment of business debts, esp as a result of insolvency. [6] the act of suspending or the state of being suspended. [7] a system of springs, shock absorbers, etc., that supports the body of a wheeled or tracked vehicle and insulates it and its occupants from shocks transmitted by the wheels. See also **hydraulic suspension.** [8] a device or structure, usually a wire or spring, that serves to suspend or support something, such as the pendulum of a clock. [9] *Chem* a dispersion of fine solid or liquid particles in a fluid, the particles being supported by buoyancy. See also **colloid.** [10] the process by which eroded particles of rock are transported in a river. [11] *Music* one or more notes of a chord that are prolonged until a subsequent chord is sounded, usually to form a dissonance.

suspension bridge NOUN a bridge that has a deck suspended by cables or rods from other cables or chains that hang between two towers and are anchored at both ends.

suspension point NOUN *Chiefly US* one of a group of dots, usually three, used in written material to indicate the omission of a word or words. Compare **ellipsis** (sense 2).

suspensive (sə'spɛnsɪv) ADJECTIVE [1] having the power of deferment; effecting suspension. [2] causing, characterized by, or relating to suspense. [3] inclined to defer judgment; undecided.
▸**sus'pensively** ADVERB ▸**sus'pensiveness** NOUN

suspensoid (sə'spɛnsɔɪd) NOUN *Chem* a system consisting of a suspension of solid particles in a liquid.

suspensor (sə'spɛnsə) NOUN [1] another name for **suspensory** (sense 1). [2] *Botany* (in a seed) a row of cells attached to the embryo plant, by means of which it is pushed into the endosperm.

suspensory (sə'spɛnsərɪ) NOUN, *plural* **-ries.** [1] Also called: **suspensor.** *Anatomy* a ligament or muscle that holds a structure or part in position. [2] *Med* a bandage, sling, etc., for supporting a dependent part. [3] another name (esp US) for **athletic support.** ◆ ADJECTIVE [4] suspending or supporting. [5] *Anatomy* (of a ligament or muscle) supporting or holding a structure or part in position.

suspicion (sə'spɪʃən) NOUN [1] the act or an instance of suspecting; belief without sure proof, esp that something is wrong. [2] the feeling of mistrust of a person who suspects. [3] the state of being suspected: *to be shielded from suspicion.* [4] a slight trace. [5] **above suspicion.** in such a position that no guilt may be thought or implied, esp through having an unblemished reputation. [6] **on suspicion.** as a suspect. [7] **under suspicion.** regarded with distrust.
▷HISTORY C14: from Old French *sospeçon,* from Latin *suspīciō* distrust, from *suspicere* to mistrust; see SUSPECT
▸**sus'picional** ADJECTIVE ▸**sus'picionless** ADJECTIVE

suspicious (sə'spɪʃəs) ADJECTIVE [1] exciting or liable to excite suspicion; questionable. [2] disposed to suspect something wrong. [3] indicative or expressive of suspicion.
▸**sus'piciously** ADVERB ▸**sus'piciousness** NOUN

suspire (sə'spaɪə) VERB *Archaic or poetic* [1] to sigh or utter with a sigh; yearn. [2] (*intr*) to breathe; respire.
▷HISTORY C15: from Latin *suspīrāre* to take a deep breath, from SUB- + *spīrāre* to breathe
▸**suspiration** (,sʌspɪ'reɪʃən) NOUN

suss (sʌs) VERB (*tr*) *Slang* [1] (often foll by *out*) to attempt to work out (a situation, person's character, etc.), esp using one's intuition. [2] Also: **sus.** to become aware of; suspect (esp in the phrase **suss it**). ◆ NOUN [3] sharpness of mind; social astuteness. ◆ See also **sus laws.**
▷HISTORY C20: shortened from SUSPECT

sussed (sʌst) ADJECTIVE *Brit informal* well-informed; aware.

Sussex ('sʌsɪks) NOUN [1] (until 1974) a county of SE England, now divided into the separate counties of East Sussex and West Sussex. [2] (in Anglo-Saxon England) the kingdom of the South Saxons, which became a shire of the kingdom of Wessex in the early 9th century A.D. [3] a breed of red beef cattle originally from Sussex. [4] a heavy and long-established breed of domestic fowl used principally as a table bird.

Sussex spaniel NOUN a short-legged breed of spaniel with a golden-liver coloured coat.
▷HISTORY so named because it was bred in Sussex, in the late 18th century

sustain (sə'steɪn) VERB (*tr*) [1] to hold up under; withstand: *to sustain great provocation.* [2] to undergo (an injury, loss, etc.); suffer: *to sustain a broken arm.* [3] to maintain or prolong: *to sustain a discussion.* [4] to support physically from below. [5] to provide for or give support to, esp by supplying necessities: *to sustain one's family; to sustain a charity.* [6] to keep up the vitality or courage of. [7] to uphold or affirm the justice or validity of: *to sustain a decision.* [8] to establish the truth of; confirm. ◆ NOUN [9] *Music* the prolongation of a note, by playing technique or electronics.
▷HISTORY C13: via Old French from Latin *sustinēre* to hold up, from SUB- + *tenēre* to hold
▸**sus'tained** ADJECTIVE ▸**sustainedly** (sə'steɪnɪdlɪ) ADVERB
▸**sus'taining** ADJECTIVE ▸**sus'tainingly** ADVERB
▸**sus'tainment** NOUN

sustainable (sə'steɪnəbᵊl) ADJECTIVE [1] capable of being sustained. [2] (of economic development, energy sources, etc.) capable of being maintained at a steady level without exhausting natural resources or causing severe ecological damage: *sustainable development.* [3] (of economic growth) non-inflationary.

sustainer (səˈsteɪnə) NOUN a rocket engine that maintains the velocity of a space vehicle after the booster has been jettisoned.

sustaining pedal NOUN *Music* a foot-operated lever on a piano, usually the right one of two, that keeps the dampers raised from the strings when keys are released, allowing them to continue to vibrate. Compare **soft pedal.**

sustaining program NOUN *US and Canadian* a television or radio programme promoted by the broadcasting network or station itself and not by a commercial sponsor.

sustenance (ˈsʌstənəns) NOUN [1] means of sustaining health or life; nourishment. [2] means of maintenance; livelihood. [3] Also: **sustention** (səˈstenʃən). the act or process of sustaining or the quality of being sustained.
▷HISTORY C13: from Old French *sostenance,* from *sustenir* to SUSTAIN

sustentacular (ˌsʌstenˈtækjulə) ADJECTIVE *Anatomy* (of fibres, cells, etc.) supporting or forming a support.
▷HISTORY C19: from Latin *sustentāculum* a stay, from *sustentāre* to support, from *sustinēre* to SUSTAIN

sustentation (ˌsʌstenˈteɪʃən) NOUN a less common word for **sustenance.**
▷HISTORY C14: from Latin *sustentātio,* from *sustentāre,* frequentative of *sustinēre* to SUSTAIN

sustentation fund NOUN a fund, esp in the Church of Scotland, to augment the support of ministers.

susu (ˈsuːsuː) NOUN a variant form of **sou-sou.**

Susu (ˈsuːsuː) NOUN [1] (*plural* **-su** *or* **-sus**) a member of a Negroid people of W Africa, living chiefly in Guinea, the Sudan, and Sierra Leone. [2] the language of this people, belonging to the Mande branch of the Niger-Congo family.

susurrate (ˈsjuːsəˌreɪt) VERB (*intr*) *Literary* to make a soft rustling sound; whisper; murmur.
▷HISTORY C17: from Latin *susurrāre* to whisper
▸**susurrant** (sjuːˈsʌrənt) ADJECTIVE ▸**ˌsusurˈration** *or* **ˈsusurrus** NOUN

Suth. ABBREVIATION FOR Sutherland.

Sutherland (ˈsʌðələnd) NOUN (until 1975) a county of N Scotland, now part of Highland.

Sutherland Falls NOUN a waterfall in New Zealand, on SW South Island. Height: 580 m (1904 ft.).

sutler (ˈsʌtlə) NOUN (formerly) a merchant who accompanied an army in order to sell provisions to the soldiers.
▷HISTORY C16: from obsolete Dutch *soeteler,* from Middle Low German *suteler,* from Middle High German *sudelen* to do dirty work; related to SOOT, SEETHE
▸**ˈsutlerˌship** NOUN

sutra (ˈsuːtrə) NOUN [1] *Hinduism* Sanskrit sayings or collections of sayings on Vedic doctrine dating from about 200 A.D. onwards. [2] (*modifier*) *Hinduism* **a** of or relating to the last of the Vedic literary periods, from about 500 to 100 B.C.: *the sutra period.* **b** of or relating to the sutras or compilations of sutras of about 200 A.D. onwards. [3] *Buddhism* collections of dialogues and discourses of classic Mahayana Buddhism dating from the 2nd to the 6th centuries A.D.
▷HISTORY C19: from Sanskrit: list of rules

suttee (sʌˈtiː, ˈsʌtiː) NOUN [1] the former Hindu custom whereby a widow burnt herself to death on her husband's funeral pyre. [2] a Hindu widow who immolated herself in this way.
▷HISTORY C18: from Sanskrit *satī* virtuous woman, from *sat* good
▸**sutˈteeism** NOUN

Sutton (ˈsʌtᵊn) NOUN a borough of S Greater London. Pop.: 179 667 (2001). Area: 43 sq. km (17 sq. miles).

Sutton Coldfield (-ˈkəʊldˌfiːld) NOUN a town in central England, in Birmingham unitary authority, West Midlands; a residential suburb of Birmingham. Pop.: 106 001 (1991).

Sutton Hoo (huː) NOUN a 7th-century site in Suffolk where a Saxon long boat containing rich grave goods, probably for an East Anglian king, was found in 1939.

Sutton-in-Ashfield (-ˈæʃˌfiːld) NOUN a market town in N central England, in W Nottinghamshire. Pop.: 37 890 (1991).

suture (ˈsuːtʃə) NOUN [1] *Surgery* **a** catgut, silk thread, or wire used to stitch together two bodily surfaces. **b** the surgical seam formed after joining two surfaces. [2] *Anatomy* a type of immovable joint, esp between the bones of the skull (**cranial suture**). [3] a seam or joining, as in sewing. [4] *Zoology* a line of junction in a mollusc shell, esp the line between adjacent chambers of a nautiloid shell. [5] *Botany* a line marking the point of dehiscence in a seed pod or capsule. ◆ VERB [6] (*tr*) *Surgery* to join (the edges of a wound, etc.) by means of sutures.
▷HISTORY C16: from Latin *sūtūra,* from *suere* to SEW
▸**ˈsutural** ADJECTIVE ▸**ˈsuturally** ADVERB

SUV ABBREVIATION FOR **sport** *or* **sports utility vehicle.**

Suva (ˈsuːvə) NOUN the capital and chief port of Fiji, on the SE coast of Viti Levu; popular tourist resort; University of the South Pacific (1968). Pop.: 167 421 (1996).

Suwannee (suˈwɒnɪ) *or* **Swanee** NOUN a river in the southeastern US, rising in SE Georgia and flowing across Florida to the Gulf of Mexico at **Suwannee Sound.** Length: about 400 km (250 miles).

suzerain (ˈsuːzəˌreɪn) NOUN [1] **a** a state or sovereign exercising some degree of dominion over a dependent state, usually controlling its foreign affairs. **b** (*as modifier*): *a suzerain power.* [2] **a** a feudal overlord. **b** (*as modifier*): *suzerain lord.*
▷HISTORY C19: from French, from *sus* above (from Latin *sursum* turned upwards, from *sub-* up + *vertere* to turn) + *-erain,* as in *souverain* SOVEREIGN

suzerainty (ˈsuːzərəntɪ) NOUN, *plural* **-ties.** [1] the position, power, or dignity of a suzerain. [2] the relationship between suzerain and subject.

sv[1] ABBREVIATION FOR: [1] sailing vessel. [2] side valve. [3] sub verbo *or* voce.
▷HISTORY sense 3 from Latin: under the word *or* voice

sv[2] THE INTERNET DOMAIN NAME FOR El Salvador.

SV ABBREVIATION FOR: [1] Sancta Virgo. [Latin: Holy Virgin] [2] Sanctitas Vestra. [Latin: Your Holiness]

Svalbard (*Norwegian* ˈsvaːlbar) NOUN a Norwegian archipelago in the Arctic Ocean, about 650 km (400 miles) north of Norway: consists of the main group (Spitsbergen, North East Land, Edge Island, Barents Island, and Prince Charles Foreland) and a number of outlying islands; sovereignty long disputed but granted to Norway in 1920; coal mining. Administrative centre: Longyearbyen. Area: 62 050 sq. km (23 958 sq. miles). Also called: **Spitsbergen.**

svelte (svɛlt, sfɛlt) ADJECTIVE [1] attractively or gracefully slim; slender. [2] urbane or sophisticated.
▷HISTORY C19: from French, from Italian *svelto,* from *svellere* to pull out, from Latin *ēvellere,* from EX-[1] + *vellere* to pull

Svengali (svɛnˈgɑːlɪ) NOUN a person who controls another's mind, usually with sinister intentions.
▷HISTORY after a character in George Du Maurier's novel *Trilby* (1894)

Sverige (ˈsværjə) NOUN the Swedish name for **Sweden.**

SVGA ABBREVIATION FOR super video graphics array. See **VGA.**

Svizzera (ˈzvittsera) NOUN the Italian name for **Switzerland.**

SVQ ABBREVIATION FOR Scottish Vocational Qualification.

SW [1] SYMBOL FOR southwest(ern). ◆ [2] ABBREVIATION FOR **short wave.**

Sw. ABBREVIATION FOR: [1] Sweden. [2] Swedish.

swab (swɒb) NOUN [1] *Med* **a** a small piece of cotton, gauze, etc., for use in applying medication, cleansing a wound, or obtaining a specimen of a secretion, etc. **b** the specimen so obtained. [2] a mop for cleaning floors, decks, etc. [3] a brush used to clean a firearm's bore. [4] *Slang* an uncouth or worthless fellow. ◆ VERB **swabs, swabbing, swabbed.** [5] (*tr*) to clean or medicate with or as if with a swab. [6] (*tr; foll by up*) to take up with a swab.
▷HISTORY C16: probably from Middle Dutch *swabbe* mop; related to Norwegian *svabba* to splash, Dutch *zwabberen* to mop, German *schwappen* to slop over

swabber (ˈswɒbə) NOUN [1] a person who uses a swab. [2] a device designed for swabbing. [3] *Slang* an uncouth fellow.

Swabia (ˈsweɪbɪə) NOUN a region and former duchy (from the 10th century to 1313) of S Germany, now part of Baden-Württemberg and Bavaria: part of West Germany until 1990. German name: **Schwaben** (ˈʃvaːbᵊn).

Swabian (ˈsweɪbɪən) ADJECTIVE [1] of or relating to the German region of Swabia or its inhabitants. ◆ NOUN [2] a native or inhabitant of Swabia.

swacked (swækt) ADJECTIVE *Slang* in a state of intoxication, stupor, or euphoria induced by drugs or alcohol.
▷HISTORY C20: perhaps from Scottish *swack* a heavy blow, of imitative origin

swaddle (ˈswɒdᵊl) VERB (*tr*) [1] to wind a bandage round. [2] to wrap (a baby) in swaddling clothes. [3] to restrain as if by wrapping with bandages; smother. ◆ NOUN [4] *Chiefly US* swaddling clothes.
▷HISTORY C15: from Old English *swæthel* swaddling clothes; related to *swathian* to SWATHE

swaddling clothes PLURAL NOUN [1] long strips of linen or other cloth formerly wrapped round a newly born baby. [2] restrictions or supervision imposed on the immature.

swaddy *or* **swaddie** (ˈswɒdɪ) NOUN, *plural* **-dies.** *Brit slang* a private soldier. Compare **squaddie.**
▷HISTORY C19: from dialect *swad* a country bumpkin

Swadeshi (swəˈdeɪʃɪ) ADJECTIVE [1] (in present-day India) produced within the country; not imported. ◆ NOUN [2] (in British India) the encouragement of domestic production and boycott of foreign goods as part of the campaign for independence.
▷HISTORY C20: from Bengali *svadesī,* from Sanskrit *svadeśin,* from *sva* one's own + *deśa* country

swag (swæg) NOUN [1] *Slang* property obtained by theft or other illicit means. [2] *Slang* goods; valuables. [3] an ornamental festoon of fruit, flowers, or drapery or a representation of this. [4] a swaying movement; lurch. [5] *Midland English dialect* a depression filled with water, resulting from mining subsidence. [6] *Austral and NZ informal* (formerly) a swagman's pack containing personal belongings. [7] **go on the swag.** *Austral and NZ informal* to become a tramp. [8] **swags of.** *Austral and NZ informal* lots of. ◆ VERB **swags, swagging, swagged.** [9] *Chiefly Brit* to lurch or sag or cause to lurch or sag. [10] (*tr*) to adorn or arrange with swags. [11] (*intr*) *Austral informal* to tramp about carrying a pack of personal belongings.
▷HISTORY C17: perhaps of Scandinavian origin; compare Norwegian *svagga* to SWAY

swage (sweɪdʒ) NOUN [1] a shaped tool or die used in forming cold metal by hammering, pressing, etc. [2] a decorative moulding. ◆ VERB [3] (*tr*) to form (metal) with a swage.
▷HISTORY C19: from French *souage,* of unknown origin
▸**ˈswager** NOUN

swage block NOUN an iron block cut with holes, recesses, and grooves to assist in the cold-working of metal.

swagger[1] (ˈswægə) VERB [1] (*intr*) to walk or behave in an arrogant manner. [2] (*intr; often foll by about*) to brag loudly. [3] (*tr*) *Rare* to force, influence, etc., by blustering. ◆ NOUN [4] arrogant gait, conduct, or manner. ◆ ADJECTIVE [5] *Brit informal, rare* elegantly fashionable.
▷HISTORY C16: probably from SWAG
▸**ˈswaggerer** NOUN ▸**ˈswaggering** ADJECTIVE ▸**ˈswaggeringly** ADVERB

swagger[2] (ˈswægə) *or* **swaggie** (ˈswægɪ) NOUN other names for **swagman.**

swagger stick *or esp Brit* **swagger cane** NOUN a short cane or stick carried on occasion mainly by army officers.

swaggie (ˈswægɪ) NOUN *Austral and NZ slang* short for **swagman.**

swagman (ˈswægˌmæn, -mən) NOUN, *plural* **-men.** *Austral and NZ informal* a labourer who carries his personal possessions in a pack or swag while travelling about in search of work; vagrant worker. Also called: **swagger, swaggie.**

Swahili (swɑːˈhiːlɪ) NOUN [1] Also called: **Kiswahili.** a language of E Africa that is an official language of

Kenya and Tanzania and is widely used as a lingua franca throughout E and central Africa. It is a member of the Bantu group of the Niger-Congo family, originally spoken in Zanzibar, and has a large number of loan words taken from Arabic and other languages. [2] (*plural* **-lis** *or* **-li**) Also called: **Mswahili** *plural* **Waswahili.** a member of a people speaking this language, living chiefly in Zanzibar. ◆ ADJECTIVE [3] of or relating to the Swahilis or their language.
▷HISTORY C19: from Arabic *sawāhil* coasts
▸**Swaˈhilian** ADJECTIVE

swain (sweɪn) NOUN *Archaic or poetic* [1] a male lover or admirer. [2] a country youth.
▷HISTORY Old English *swān* swineherd; related to Old High German *swein,* Old Norse *sveinn* boy; see SWINE
▸ˈ**swainish** ADJECTIVE

swale (sweɪl) NOUN *Chiefly US* **a** a moist depression in a tract of land, usually with rank vegetation. **b** (*as modifier*): *swell and swale topography.*
▷HISTORY C16: probably of Scandinavian origin; compare Old Norse *svala* to chill

Swaledale (ˈsweɪlˌdeɪl) NOUN a breed of small hardy sheep kept esp in northern England for its coarse wool which is used for making tweeds and carpets.
▷HISTORY from *Swaledale,* Yorkshire

SWALK (swɔːlk) ACRONYM FOR sealed with a loving kiss: sometimes written on the back of envelopes.

swallow¹ (ˈswɒləʊ) VERB (*mainly tr*) [1] to pass (food, drink, etc.) through the mouth to the stomach by means of the muscular action of the oesophagus. [2] (often foll by *up*) to engulf or destroy as if by ingestion: *Nazi Germany swallowed up several small countries.* [3] *Informal* to believe gullibly: *he will never swallow such an excuse.* [4] to refrain from uttering or manifesting: *to swallow one's disappointment.* [5] to endure without retaliation. [6] to enunciate (words, etc.) indistinctly; mutter. [7] (often foll by *down*) to eat or drink reluctantly. [8] (*intr*) to perform or simulate the act of swallowing, as in gulping. [9] **swallow one's words.** to retract a statement, argument, etc., often in humiliating circumstances. ◆ NOUN [10] the act of swallowing. [11] the amount swallowed at any single time; mouthful. [12] Also called: **crown, throat.** *Nautical* the opening between the shell and the groove of the sheave of a block, through which the rope is passed. [13] *Rare* another word for **throat** or **gullet.** [14] *Rare* a capacity for swallowing; appetite.
▷HISTORY Old English *swelgan;* related to Old Norse *svelga,* Old High German *swelgan* to swallow, Swedish *svalg* gullet
▸ˈ**swallowable** ADJECTIVE ▸ˈ**swallower** NOUN

swallow² (ˈswɒləʊ) NOUN [1] any passerine songbird of the family *Hirundinidae,* esp *Hirundo rustica* (**common** or **barn swallow**), having long pointed wings, a forked tail, short legs, and a rapid flight. Related adjective: **hirundine.** [2] See **fairy swallow.**
▷HISTORY Old English *swealwe;* related to Old Frisian *swale,* Old Norse *svala,* Old High German *swalwa*
▸ˈ**swallow-ˌlike** ADJECTIVE

swallow dive NOUN a type of dive in which the diver arches back while in the air, keeping his legs straight and together and his arms outstretched, finally entering the water headfirst. US and Canadian equivalent: **swan dive.**

swallow hole NOUN *Chiefly Brit* another word for **sinkhole** (sense 1).

swallowtail (ˈswɒləʊˌteɪl) NOUN [1] any of various butterflies of the genus *Papilio* and related genera, esp *P. machaon* of Europe, having a tail-like extension of each hind wing: family *Papilionidae.* [2] the forked tail of a swallow or similar bird. [3] short for **swallow-tailed coat.**

swallow-tailed ADJECTIVE [1] (of a bird) having a deeply forked tail. [2] having a part resembling a swallow's tail.

swallow-tailed coat NOUN another name for **tail coat.**

swallowwort (ˈswɒləʊˌwɜːt) NOUN [1] any of several Eurasian vines of the genus *Cynanchum,* esp *C. nigrum,* having small brownish-purple flowers: family *Asclepiadaceae.* [2] a related European herbaceous plant, *Vincetoxicum officinale* (or *Cynanchum vincetoxicum*), having an emetic root. [3] another name for **greater celandine.**
▷HISTORY C16: so called because the shape of its pod is reminiscent of a flying swallow

swam (swæm) VERB the past tense of **swim.**

swami (ˈswɑːmɪ) NOUN, *plural* **-mies** *or* **-mis.** (in India) a title of respect for a Hindu saint or religious teacher.
▷HISTORY C18: from Hindi *svāmī,* from Sanskrit *svāmin* master, from *sva* one's own

swamp (swɒmp) NOUN [1] **a** permanently waterlogged ground that is usually overgrown and sometimes partly forested. Compare **marsh. b** (*as modifier*): *swamp fever.* ◆ VERB [2] to drench or submerge or be drenched or submerged. [3] *Nautical* to cause (a boat) to sink or fill with water or (of a boat) to sink or fill with water. [4] to overburden or overwhelm or be overburdened or overwhelmed, as by excess work or great numbers: *we have been swamped with applications.* [5] to sink or stick or cause to sink or stick in or as if in a swamp. [6] (*tr*) to render helpless.
▷HISTORY C17: probably from Middle Dutch *somp;* compare Middle High German *sumpf,* Old Norse *svöppr* sponge, Greek *somphos* spongy
▸ˈ**swampish** ADJECTIVE ▸ˈ**swampless** ADJECTIVE ▸ˈ**swampy** ADJECTIVE

swamp boat NOUN a shallow-draught boat powered by an æroplane engine mounted on a raised structure for use in swamps. Also called: **airboat.**

swamp buggy NOUN (esp in the US and Canada) a light aerofoil conveyance for use in regions with swamps, lakes, etc.

swamp cypress NOUN a North American deciduous coniferous tree, *Taxodium distichum,* that grows in swamps and sends up aerial roots from its base. Also called: **bald cypress.**

swamper (ˈswɒmpə) NOUN *US* **a** a person who lives or works in a swampy region, esp in the southern US. **b** a person who clears a swamp of trees and undergrowth or who clears a path in a forest for transporting logs.

swamp fever NOUN [1] Also called: **equine infectious anaemia.** a viral disease of horses characterized by recurring fever, staggering gait, and general debility. [2] *US* another name for **malaria.**

swampland (ˈswɒmpˌlænd) NOUN a permanently waterlogged area; marshland.

swan (swɒn) NOUN [1] any large aquatic bird of the genera *Cygnus* and *Coscoroba,* having a long neck and usually a white plumage: family *Anatidae,* order *Anseriformes.* [2] *Rare, literary* **a** a poet. **b** (*capital when part of a title or epithet*): *the Swan of Avon* (Shakespeare). ◆ VERB **swans, swanning, swanned.** [3] (*intr; usually foll by around* or *about*) *Informal* to wander idly.
▷HISTORY Old English; related to Old Norse *svanr,* Middle Low German *swōn*
▸ˈ**swanˌlike** ADJECTIVE

Swan (swɒn) NOUN a river in SW Western Australia, rising as the Avon northeast of Narrogin and flowing northwest and west to the Indian Ocean below Perth. Length: about 240 km (150 miles).

swan dive NOUN the US and Canadian name for **swallow dive.**

Swanee (ˈswɒnɪ) NOUN a variant spelling of **Suwannee.**

swanherd (ˈswɒnˌhɜːd) NOUN a person who herds swans.

swank (swæŋk) *Informal* ◆ VERB [1] (*intr*) to show off or swagger. ◆ NOUN [2] Also called: **swankpot.** *Brit* a swaggering or conceited person. [3] *Chiefly US* elegance or style, esp of a showy kind. [4] swagger; ostentation. ◆ ADJECTIVE [5] another word (esp US) for **swanky.**
▷HISTORY C19: perhaps from Middle High German *swanken* to sway; see SWAG

swanky (ˈswæŋkɪ) ADJECTIVE **swankier, swankiest.** *Informal* [1] expensive and showy; stylish: *a swanky hotel.* [2] boastful or conceited.
▸ˈ**swankily** ADVERB ▸ˈ**swankiness** NOUN

swan maiden NOUN any of a group of maidens in folklore who by magic are transformed into swans.

Swanndri *or* **Swandri** (ˈswɒnˌdraɪ) NOUN, *plural* **-dris.** *Trademark, NZ* an all-weather heavy woollen shirt. Also called: **swannie** (ˈswɒnɪ).

swan neck NOUN a tube, rail, etc., curved like a swan's neck.

swannery (ˈswɒnərɪ) NOUN, *plural* **-neries.** a place where swans are kept and bred.

swan's-down NOUN [1] the fine soft down feathers of a swan, used to trim powder puffs, clothes, etc. [2] a thick soft fabric of wool with silk, cotton, or rayon, used for infants' clothing, etc. [3] a cotton fabric with a heavy nap.

Swansea (ˈswɒnzɪ) NOUN [1] a port in S Wales, in Swansea county on an inlet of the Bristol Channel (**Swansea Bay**); a metallurgical and oil-refining centre; university (1920). Pop.: 171 038 (1991). [2] a county of S Wales on the Bristol Channel, created in 1996 from part of West Glamorgan: includes the Swansea conurbation and the Gower peninsula. Administrative centre: Swansea. Pop.: 223 293 (2001). Area: 378 sq. km (146 sq. miles).

swanskin (ˈswɒnˌskɪn) NOUN [1] the skin of a swan with the feathers attached. [2] a fine twill-weave flannel fabric.

swan song NOUN [1] the last act, appearance, publication, or utterance of a person before retirement or death. [2] the song that a dying swan is said to sing.

swan-upping NOUN *Brit* [1] the practice or action of marking nicks in swans' beaks as a sign of ownership. [2] the annual swan-upping of royal cygnets on the River Thames.
▷HISTORY C16: from UP (in the archaic sense: to catch and mark a swan)

Swanz (swɒnz) PLURAL NOUN **the.** the women's international soccer team of New Zealand.

swap *or* **swop** (swɒp) VERB **swaps, swapping, swapped** *or* **swops, swopping, swopped.** [1] to trade or exchange (something or someone) for another. ◆ NOUN [2] an exchange. [3] something that is exchanged. [4] *Finance* Also called: **swap option, swaption.** a contract in which the parties to it exchange liabilities on outstanding debts, often exchanging fixed interest-rate for floating-rate debts (**debt swap**), either as a means of managing debt or in trading (**swap trading**).
▷HISTORY C14 (in the sense: to shake hands on a bargain, strike): probably of imitative origin
▸ˈ**swapper** *or* ˈ**swopper** NOUN

SWAPO *or* **Swapo** (ˈswɑːpəʊ) NOUN ACRONYM FOR South-West Africa People's Organization.

swap shop NOUN a place or occasion at which articles no longer wanted may be exchanged for other articles.

swaption (ˈswɒpʃən) NOUN another name for **swap** (sense 4).

swaraj (swəˈrɑːdʒ) NOUN (in British India) self-government; independence.
▷HISTORY C20: from Sanskrit *svarāj,* from *sva* self + *rājya* rule
▸**swaˈrajism** NOUN ▸**swaˈrajist** NOUN, ADJECTIVE

sward (swɔːd) NOUN [1] turf or grass or a stretch of turf or grass. ◆ VERB [2] to cover or become covered with grass.
▷HISTORY Old English *sweard* skin; related to Old Frisian *swarde* scalp, Middle High German *swart* hide

swarf (swɔːf, swɑːf) NOUN [1] material removed by cutting or grinding tools in the machining of metals, stone, etc. [2] radioactive metal waste from a nuclear power station. [3] small fragments of disintegrating spacecraft, orbiting the earth.
▷HISTORY C16: of Scandinavian origin; related to Old Norse *svarf* metallic dust

swarm¹ (swɔːm) NOUN [1] a group of social insects, esp bees led by a queen, that has left the parent hive in order to start a new colony. [2] a large mass of small animals, esp insects. [3] a throng or mass, esp when moving or in turmoil. ◆ VERB [4] (*intr*) (of small animals, esp bees) to move in or form a swarm. [5] (*intr*) to congregate, move about or proceed in large numbers. [6] (when *intr,* often foll by *with*) to overrun or be overrun (with): *the house swarmed with rats.* [7] (*tr*) to cause to swarm.
▷HISTORY Old English *swearm;* related to Old Norse *svarmr* uproar, Old High German *swaram* swarm

swarm² (swɔːm) VERB (when *intr,* usually foll by

up) to climb (a ladder, etc.) by gripping with the hands and feet: *the boys swarmed up the rigging.*
▷**HISTORY** C16: of unknown origin

swarm cell *or* **spore** NOUN another name for **zoospore.**

swart (swɔːt) *or* **swarth** (swɔːθ) ADJECTIVE *Archaic or dialect* swarthy.
▷**HISTORY** Old English *sweart;* related to Old Frisian *swart,* Old Norse *svartr,* Old High German *swarz* black, Latin *sordēs* dirt; see SORDID
▸ **'swartness** *or* **'swarthness** NOUN

swarthy ('swɔːðɪ) ADJECTIVE **swarthier, swarthiest.** dark-hued or dark-complexioned.
▷**HISTORY** C16: from obsolete *swarty,* from SWART + -Y[1]
▸ **'swarthily** ADVERB ▸ **'swarthiness** NOUN

swash (swɒʃ) VERB [1] (*intr*) (esp of water or things in water) to wash or move with noisy splashing. [2] (*tr*) to dash (a liquid, esp water) against or upon. [3] (*intr*) *Archaic* to swagger or bluster. ◆ NOUN [4] Also called: **send.** the dashing movement or sound of water, such as that of waves on a beach. Compare **backwash.** [5] any other swashing movement or sound. [6] a sandbar washed by the waves. [7] Also called: **swash channel.** a channel of moving water cutting through or running behind a sandbank. [8] *Archaic* **a** swagger or bluster. **b** a swashbuckler.
▷**HISTORY** C16: probably of imitative origin

swashbuckler ('swɒʃˌbʌklə) NOUN a swaggering or flamboyant adventurer.
▷**HISTORY** C16: from SWASH (in the archaic sense: to make the noise of a sword striking a shield) + BUCKLER

swashbuckling ('swɒʃˌbʌklɪŋ) ADJECTIVE (*usually prenominal*) [1] of or characteristic of a swashbuckler. [2] (esp of films in period costume) full of adventure and excitement.

swash letter NOUN *Printing* a decorative letter, esp an ornamental italic capital.
▷**HISTORY** C17 *swash* (n, in the sense: the decorative flourish of an ornamental letter) from *aswash* aslant

swash plate NOUN *Engineering* a collar or face plate on a shaft that is inclined at an oblique angle to the axis of rotation and either imparts reciprocating motion to push rods parallel to the shaft axis as in a **swash plate pump** or, conversely, converts reciprocating motion to rotation as in a **swash plate motor.** Also called: **wobble plate.**
▷**HISTORY** from *swash* (obsolete n) an oblique figure or ornament, from *aswash:* see SWASH LETTER

swastika ('swɒstɪkə) NOUN [1] a primitive religious symbol or ornament in the shape of a Greek cross, usually having the ends of the arms bent at right angles in either a clockwise or anticlockwise direction. [2] this symbol with clockwise arms, officially adopted in 1935 as the emblem of Nazi Germany.
▷**HISTORY** C19: from Sanskrit *svastika,* from *svasti* prosperity; from the belief that it brings good luck

swat[1] (swɒt) VERB **swats, swatting, swatted.** (*tr*) [1] to strike or hit sharply: *to swat a fly.* ◆ NOUN [2] another word (esp Brit) for **swatter** (sense 1). [3] a sharp or violent blow. ◆ Also: **swot.**
▷**HISTORY** C17: northern English dialect and US variant of SQUAT

swat[2] (swɒt) VERB **swats, swatting, swatted,** NOUN a variant of **swot**[1].

Swat (swɒt) NOUN [1] a former princely state of NW India: passed to Pakistan in 1947. [2] a river in Pakistan, rising in the north and flowing south to the Kabul River north of Peshawar. Length: about 640 km (400 miles).

SWAT (swɒt) NOUN ACRONYM FOR Special Weapons and Tactics: a military-like unit within the US police force, trained to deal with specially dangerous situations, such as hostage-taking and riots.

swatch (swɒtʃ) NOUN [1] a sample of cloth. [2] a number of such samples, usually fastened together in book form. [3] *Printing* **a** a small sample of colour supplied to the printer for matching during printing. **b** a sample of ink spread on paper by a printer to check the accuracy of a required colour.
▷**HISTORY** C16: Scottish and northern English, of uncertain origin

swath (swɔːθ) *or* **swathe** (sweɪð) NOUN, *plural* **swaths** (swɔːðz) *or* **swathes.** [1] the width of one sweep of a scythe or of the blade of a mowing machine. [2] the strip cut by either of these in one course. [3] the quantity of cut grass, hay, or similar crop left in one course of such mowing. [4] a long narrow strip or belt.
▷**HISTORY** Old English *swæth;* related to Old Norse *svath* smooth patch

swathe (sweɪð) VERB (*tr*) [1] to bandage (a wound, limb, etc.), esp completely. [2] to wrap a band, garment, etc., around, esp so as to cover completely; swaddle. [3] to envelop. ◆ NOUN [4] a bandage or wrapping. [5] a variant spelling of **swath.**
▷**HISTORY** Old English *swathian;* related to *swæthel* swaddling clothes, Old High German *swedil,* Dutch *zwadel;* see SWADDLE
▸ **'swathable** *or* **'swatheable** ADJECTIVE

swatter ('swɒtə) NOUN [1] a device for killing insects, esp a meshed flat attached to a handle. [2] a person who swats.

sway (sweɪ) VERB [1] (*usually intr*) to swing or cause to swing to and fro. [2] (*usually intr*) to lean or incline or cause to lean or incline to one side or in different directions in turn. [3] (*usually intr*) to vacillate or cause to vacillate between two or more opinions. [4] to be influenced or swerve or influence or cause to swerve to or from a purpose or opinion. [5] (*tr*) *Nautical* to hoist (a yard, mast, or other spar). [6] *Archaic or poetic* to rule or wield power (over). [7] (*tr*) *Archaic* to wield (a weapon). ◆ NOUN [8] control; power. [9] a swinging or leaning movement. [10] *Archaic* dominion; governing authority. [11] **hold sway.** to be master; reign.
▷**HISTORY** C16: probably from Old Norse *sveigja* to bend; related to Dutch *zwaaien,* Low German *swājen*
▸ **'swayable** ADJECTIVE ▸ **'swayer** NOUN ▸ **'swayful** ADJECTIVE

sway-back NOUN [1] *Vet science* an abnormal sagging or concavity of the spine in older horses. [2] a paralytic disease of new-born and young lambs caused by demyelination of the central nervous system due to copper deficiency.
▸ **'sway-ˌbacked** ADJECTIVE

Swazi ('swɑːzɪ) NOUN [1] (*plural* **-zis** *or* **-zi**) a member of a racially mixed people of southern Africa living chiefly in Swaziland, who first formed into a strong political group in the late 19th century. [2] the language of this people: an official language of Swaziland along with English. It belongs to the Niger-Congo family and is closely related to Xhosa and Zulu.

Swaziland ('swɑːzɪˌlænd) NOUN a kingdom in southern Africa: made a protectorate of the Transvaal by Britain in 1894; gained independence in 1968; a member of the Commonwealth. Official languages: Swazi and English. Religion: Christian majority, traditional beliefs. Currency: lilangeni (plural emalangeni). Capital: Mbabane (administrative), Lobamba (legislative). Pop.: 1 104 000 (2001 est.). Area: 17 363 sq. km (6704 sq. miles).

swazzle *or* **swozzle** ('swɒzəl) NOUN a small metal instrument held in the mouth of a Punch and Judy puppeteer, used to produce the characteristic shrill voice of Mr Punch.
▷**HISTORY** C19: imitative of the sound produced

swear (swɛə) VERB **swears, swearing, swore, sworn.** [1] to declare or affirm (a statement) as true, esp by invoking a deity, etc., as witness. [2] (foll by *by*) **a** to invoke (a deity, etc.) by name as a witness or guarantee to an oath. **b** to trust implicitly; have complete confidence (in). [3] (*intr; often foll by at*) to curse, blaspheme, or use swearwords. [4] (*when tr, may take a clause as object or an infinitive*) to promise solemnly on oath; vow. [5] (*tr*) to assert or affirm with great emphasis or earnestness. [6] (*intr*) to give evidence or make any statement or solemn declaration on oath. [7] to take an oath in order to add force or solemnity to (a statement or declaration). [8] **swear blind.** *Informal* to assert emphatically. ◆ NOUN [9] a period of swearing.
▷**HISTORY** Old English *swerian;* related to Old Norse *sverja,* Gothic *swaran,* Old Frisian *swera,* German *schwören*
▸ **'swearer** NOUN

swear in VERB (*tr, adverb*) to administer an oath to (a person) on his assuming office, entering the witness box to give evidence, etc.

swear off VERB (*intr, preposition*) to promise to abstain from something: *to swear off drink.*

swear out VERB (*tr, adverb*) *US* to secure the issue of (a warrant for an arrest) by making a charge under oath.

swearword ('swɛəˌwɜːd) NOUN a socially taboo word or phrase of a profane, obscene, or insulting character.

sweat (swɛt) NOUN [1] the secretion from the sweat glands, esp when profuse and visible, as during strenuous activity, from excessive heat, etc.; commonly also called perspiration. Related adjectives: **sudatory, sudorific.** [2] the act or process of secreting this fluid. [3] the act of inducing the exudation of moisture. [4] drops of moisture given forth or gathered on the surface of something. [5] *Informal* a state or condition of worry or eagerness (esp in the phrase **in a sweat**). [6] *Slang* drudgery or hard labour: *mowing lawns is a real sweat!* [7] *Chiefly US* an exercise gallop given to a horse, esp on the day of a race. [8] *Slang, chiefly Brit* a soldier, esp one who is old and experienced. [9] **no sweat!** (*interjection*) *Slang* an expression suggesting that something can be done without problems or difficulty. ◆ VERB **sweats, sweating, sweat** *or* **sweated.** [10] to secrete (sweat) through the pores of the skin, esp profusely. [11] (*tr*) to make wet or stain with sweat. [12] to give forth or cause to give forth (moisture) in droplets: *a sweating cheese; the maple sweats sap.* [13] (*intr*) to collect and condense moisture on an outer surface: *a glass of beer sweating in the sun.* [14] (*intr*) (of a liquid) to pass through a porous surface in droplets. [15] (of tobacco leaves, cut and dried hay, etc.) to exude moisture and, sometimes, begin to ferment or to cause (tobacco leaves, etc.) to exude moisture. [16] (*tr*) to heat (food, esp vegetables) slowly in butter in a tightly closed saucepan. [17] (*tr*) to join (pieces of metal) by pressing together and heating. [18] (*tr*) to heat (solder) until it melts. [19] (*tr*) to heat (a partially fused metal) to extract an easily fusible constituent. [20] to shake together (coins, esp gold coins) so as to remove particles for illegal use. [21] *Informal* to suffer anxiety, impatience, or distress. [22] *Informal* to overwork or be overworked. [23] (*tr*) *Informal* to employ at very low wages and under bad conditions. [24] (*tr*) *Informal* to extort, esp by torture: *to sweat information out of a captive.* [25] (*intr*) *Informal* to suffer punishment: *you'll sweat for this!* [26] **sweat blood.** *Informal* **a** to work very hard. **b** to be filled with anxiety or impatience. ◆ See also **sweat off, sweat out.**
▷**HISTORY** Old English *swætan* to sweat, from *swāt* sweat; related to Old Saxon *swēt,* Old Norse *sveiti,* Old High German *sweiz,* Latin *sūdor,* Sanskrit *svedas*
▸ **'sweatless** ADJECTIVE

sweatband ('swɛtˌbænd) NOUN [1] a band of material set in a hat or cap to protect it from sweat. [2] a piece of cloth tied around the forehead to keep sweat out of the eyes or around the wrist to keep the hands dry, as in sports.

sweatbox ('swɛtˌbɒks) NOUN [1] a device for causing tobacco leaves, fruit, or hides to sweat. [2] a very small pen or cubicle where a pig is fattened intensively. [3] *Informal, chiefly US* a narrow room or cell for a prisoner. [4] *Informal* any place where a person sweats on account of confinement, heat, etc.

sweated ('swɛtɪd) ADJECTIVE [1] made by exploited labour: *sweated goods.* [2] (of workers, etc.) forced to work in poor conditions for low pay.

sweater ('swɛtə) NOUN [1] **a** a garment made of knitted or crocheted material covering the upper part of the body, esp a heavy one worn for warmth. **b** (*as modifier*): *a sweater dress.* [2] a person or thing that sweats. [3] an employer who overworks and underpays his employees.

sweater girl NOUN *Slang, now rare* a young woman or girl with large breasts who wears tight sweaters.

sweat gland NOUN any of the coiled tubular subcutaneous glands that secrete sweat by means of a duct that opens on to the skin.

sweating sickness NOUN [1] the nontechnical name for **miliary fever.** [2] an acute infectious febrile disease that was widespread in Europe during the late 15th century, characterized by profuse sweating. [3] a disease of cattle, esp calves, prevalent in southern Africa. Transmitted by ticks, it is characterized by sweating, hair loss, and inflammation of the mouth and eyes.

sweat lodge NOUN (among native North American peoples) a structure in which water is poured onto hot stones to make the occupants sweat for religious or medicinal purposes.

sweat off *or* **away** VERB (*tr, adverb*) *Informal* to get rid of (weight) by strenuous exercise or sweating.

sweat out VERB (*tr, adverb*) 1 to cure or lessen the effects of (a cold, respiratory infection, etc.) by sweating. 2 *Informal* to endure (hardships) for a time (often in the phrase **sweat it out**). 3 **sweat one's guts out.** *Informal* to work extremely hard.

sweat pants PLURAL NOUN loose thick cotton trousers with elasticated cuffs and an elasticated or drawstring waist, worn esp by athletes warming up or training.

sweats (swɛts) PLURAL NOUN sweatshirts and sweat-suit trousers: *jeans and sweats.*

sweatshirt (ˈswɛtˌʃɜːt) NOUN a long-sleeved knitted cotton sweater worn by athletes, etc.

sweatshop (ˈswɛtˌʃɒp) NOUN a workshop where employees work long hours under bad conditions for low wages.

sweat suit NOUN a suit worn by athletes for training comprising knitted cotton trousers fitting closely at the ankle and a light cotton sweater.

sweaty (ˈswɛtɪ) ADJECTIVE **sweatier, sweatiest.** 1 covered with sweat; sweating. 2 smelling of or like sweat. 3 causing sweat.
▸ **ˈsweatily** ADVERB ▸ **ˈsweatiness** NOUN

swede (swiːd) NOUN 1 a Eurasian plant, *Brassica napus* (or *B. napobrassica*), cultivated for its bulbous edible root, which is used as a vegetable and as cattle fodder: family *Brassicaceae* (crucifers). 2 the root of this plant. 3 *NZ* a slang word for **head** (sense 1). ◆ Also called (for senses 1, 2): **Swedish turnip.** US and Canadian name: **rutabaga.**
▷HISTORY C19: so called after being introduced into Scotland from Sweden in the 18th century

Swede (swiːd) NOUN a native, citizen, or inhabitant of Sweden.

Sweden (ˈswiːdᵊn) NOUN a kingdom in NW Europe, occupying the E part of the Scandinavian Peninsula, on the Gulf of Bothnia and the Baltic: first united during the Viking period (8th–11th centuries); a member of the European Union. About 50 per cent of the total area is forest and 9 per cent lakes. Exports include timber, pulp, paper, iron ore, and steel. Official language: Swedish. Official religion: Church of Sweden (Lutheran). Currency: krona. Capital: Stockholm. Pop.: 8 888 000 (2001 est.). Area: 449 793 sq. km (173 665 sq. miles). Swedish name: **Sverige.**

Swedenborgianism (ˌswiːdᵊnˈbɔːdʒɪəˌnɪzəm, -gɪ-) *or* **Swedenborgism** (ˈswiːdᵊnˌbɔːdʒɪzəm, -gɪz-) NOUN the system of philosophical and religious doctrines of Emanuel Swedenborg, the Swedish scientist and theologian (1688–1772), emphasizing the spiritual structure of the universe, the possibility of direct contact with spirits, and the divinity of Christ. This provided the basis for the **New Jerusalem Church** (or **New Church**) founded by Swedenborg's followers.
▸ **ˌSwedenˈborgian** NOUN, ADJECTIVE

Swedish (ˈswiːdɪʃ) ADJECTIVE 1 of, relating to, or characteristic of Sweden, its people, or their language. ◆ NOUN 2 the official language of Sweden, belonging to the North Germanic branch of the Indo-European family: one of the two official languages of Finland. 3 **the Swedish.** (*functioning as plural*) the people of Sweden collectively.

Swedish massage NOUN massage combined with a system (**Swedish movements** or **gymnastics**) of passive and active exercising of muscles and joints.

Swedish mile NOUN a unit of length used in Sweden, equal to 10 kilometres.

Swedish vallhund (ˈvælˌhʊnd) NOUN a small sturdy dog of a Swedish breed with a long body and pricked pointed ears.
▷HISTORY from Swedish *vall* + *hund* dog

sweeny (ˈswiːnɪ) NOUN *Vet science* a wasting of the shoulder muscles of a horse, esp as the result of a nerve injury.
▷HISTORY C19: probably from German dialect *Schweine* emaciation, atrophy

sweep (swiːp) VERB **sweeps, sweeping, swept.** 1 to clean or clear (a space, chimney, etc.) with a brush, broom, etc. 2 (often foll by *up*) to remove or collect (dirt, rubbish, etc.) with a brush, broom, etc. 3 to move in a smooth or continuous manner, esp quickly or forcibly: *cars swept along the road.* 4 to move in a proud or dignified fashion: *she swept past.* 5 to spread or pass rapidly across, through, or along (a region, area, etc.): *the news swept through the town.* 6 (*tr*) to direct (the gaze, line of fire, etc.) over; survey. 7 (*tr; foll by away or off*) to overwhelm emotionally: *she was swept away by his charm.* 8 (*tr*) to brush or lightly touch (a surface, etc.): *the dress swept along the ground.* 9 (*tr; often foll by away*) to convey, clear, or abolish, esp with strong or continuous movements: *the sea swept the sandcastle away; secondary modern schools were swept away.* 10 (*intr*) to extend gracefully or majestically, esp in a wide circle: *the plains sweep down to the sea.* 11 to search (a body of water) for mines, etc., by dragging. 12 to search (a room, area, etc.) electronically to detect spying devices. 13 (*tr*) to win overwhelmingly, esp in an election: *Labour swept the country.* 14 *Cricket* to play (a ball) with a sweep. 15 (*tr*) to propel (a boat) with sweeps. 16 **sweep the board. a** (in gambling) to win all the cards or money. **b** to win every event or prize in a contest. 17 **sweep (something) under the carpet.** to conceal (something, esp a problem) in the hope that it will be overlooked by others. ◆ NOUN 18 the act or an instance of sweeping; removal by or as if by a brush or broom. 19 a swift or steady movement, esp in an arc: *with a sweep of his arms.* 20 the distance, arc, etc., through which something, such as a pendulum, moves. 21 a wide expanse or scope: *the sweep of the plains.* 22 any curving line or contour. 23 *Cards* **a** the winning of every trick in a hand of whist. **b** the taking, by pairing, of all exposed cards in cassino. 24 short for **sweepstake.** 25 *Cricket* a shot in which the ball is hit more or less square on the leg side from a half-kneeling position with the bat held nearly horizontal. 26 **a** a long oar used on an open boat. **b** *Austral* a person steering a surf boat with such an oar. 27 any of the sails of a windmill. 28 *Electronics* a steady horizontal or circular movement of an electron beam across or around the fluorescent screen of a cathode-ray tube. 29 *Agriculture* **a** a rakelike attachment for the front of a motor vehicle for pushing hay into piles. **b** a triangular blade on a cultivator used to cut through roots below the surface of the soil. 30 a curving driveway. 31 *Chiefly Brit* See **chimney sweep.** 32 another name for **swipe** (sense 6). 33 **clean sweep. a** an overwhelming victory or success. **b** a complete change; purge: *to make a clean sweep.*
▷HISTORY C13 *swepen;* related to Old English *swāpan,* Old Norse *sveipa;* see SWIPE, SWOOP
▸ **ˈsweepy** ADJECTIVE

sweepback (ˈswiːpˌbæk) NOUN the rearward inclination of a component or surface, such as an aircraft wing, fin, etc.

sweeper (ˈswiːpə) NOUN 1 a person employed to sweep, such as a roadsweeper. 2 any device for sweeping: *a carpet sweeper.* 3 *Informal, Soccer* a player who supports the main defenders, as by intercepting loose balls, etc.

sweep hand NOUN *Horology* a long hand that registers seconds or fractions of seconds on the perimeter of the dial.

sweeping (ˈswiːpɪŋ) ADJECTIVE 1 comprehensive and wide-ranging: *sweeping reforms.* 2 indiscriminate or without reservations: *sweeping statements.* 3 decisive or overwhelming: *a sweeping victory.* 4 taking in a wide area: *a sweeping glance.* 5 driving steadily onwards, esp over a large area: *a sweeping attack.*
▸ **ˈsweepingly** ADVERB ▸ **ˈsweepingness** NOUN

sweepings (ˈswiːpɪŋz) PLURAL NOUN debris, litter, or refuse.

sweep-saw NOUN a saw with a thin blade that can be used for cutting curved shapes.

sweepstake (ˈswiːpˌsteɪk) *or esp US* **sweepstakes** NOUN 1 **a** a lottery in which the stakes of the participants constitute the prize. **b** the prize itself. 2 any event involving a lottery, esp a horse race in which the prize is the competitors' stakes. ◆ Often shortened to: **sweep.**
▷HISTORY C15: originally referring to someone who *sweeps* or takes all the stakes in a game

sweer (swiːr) VERB *Scot* a variant spelling of **sweir**[1] and **sweir**[2].

sweet (swiːt) ADJECTIVE 1 having or denoting a pleasant taste like that of sugar. 2 agreeable to the senses or the mind: *sweet music.* 3 having pleasant manners; gentle: *a sweet child.* 4 (of wine, etc.) having a relatively high sugar content; not dry. 5 (of foods) not decaying or rancid: *sweet milk.* 6 not salty: *sweet water.* 7 free from unpleasant odours: *sweet air.* 8 containing no corrosive substances: *sweet soil.* 9 (of petrol) containing no sulphur compounds. 10 sentimental or unrealistic. 11 individual; particular: *the electorate went its own sweet way.* 12 *Jazz* performed with a regular beat, with the emphasis on clearly outlined melody and little improvisation. 13 *Austral slang* satisfactory or in order; all right. 14 *Archaic* respected; dear (used in polite forms of address): *sweet sir.* 15 smooth and precise; perfectly executed: *a sweet shot.* 16 **sweet on.** fond of or infatuated with. 17 **keep (someone) sweet.** to ingratiate oneself in order to ensure cooperation. ◆ ADVERB 18 *Informal* in a sweet manner. ◆ NOUN 19 a sweet taste or smell; sweetness in general. 20 (*often plural*) *Brit* any of numerous kinds of confectionery consisting wholly or partly of sugar, esp of sugar boiled and crystallized (**boiled sweets**). 21 *Brit* a pudding, fruit, or any sweet dish served as a dessert. 22 dear; sweetheart (used as a form of address). 23 anything that is sweet. 24 (*often plural*) a pleasurable experience, state, etc.: *the sweets of success.* 25 *US* See **sweet potato.**
▷HISTORY Old English *swēte;* related to Old Saxon *swōti,* Old High German *suozi,* Old Norse *sœtr,* Latin *suādus* persuasive, *suāvis* sweet, Greek *hēdus,* Sanskrit *svādu;* see PERSUADE, SUAVE
▸ **ˈsweetish** ADJECTIVE ▸ **ˈsweetly** ADVERB ▸ **ˈsweetness** NOUN

sweet alyssum NOUN a Mediterranean plant, *Lobularia maritima,* having clusters of small fragrant white or violet flowers, that is widely grown in gardens: family *Brassicaceae* (crucifers). See also **alyssum.**

sweet-and-sour ADJECTIVE (of food) cooked in a sauce made from sugar and vinegar and other ingredients.

sweet basil NOUN See **basil** (sense 1).

sweet bay NOUN a small tree, *Magnolia virginiana,* of SE North America, having large fragrant white flowers: family *Magnoliaceae* (magnolias). Sometimes shortened to: **bay.**

sweetbread (ˈswiːtˌbrɛd) NOUN the pancreas (**stomach sweetbread**) or the thymus gland (**neck** or **throat sweetbread**) of an animal, used for food.
▷HISTORY C16: SWEET + BREAD, perhaps from Old English *brǣd* meat; related to Old Saxon *brādo* ham, Old High German *brāt,* Old Norse *brāth*

sweetbrier (ˈswiːtˌbraɪə) NOUN a Eurasian rose, *Rosa rubiginosa,* having a tall bristly stem, fragrant leaves, and single pink flowers. Also called: **eglantine.**

sweet cherry NOUN 1 either of two types of cherry tree that are cultivated for their red edible sweet fruit, the gean having tender-fleshed fruit, the bigarreau having firm-fleshed fruit. 2 the fruit of any of these trees. See also **heart cherry.** ◆ Also called: **dessert cherry.** Compare **sour cherry.**

sweet chestnut NOUN See **chestnut** (sense 1).

sweet cicely NOUN 1 Also called: **myrrh.** an aromatic umbelliferous European plant, *Myrrhis odorata,* having compound leaves and clusters of small white flowers. 2 the leaves of this plant, formerly used in cookery for their flavour of aniseed. 3 any of various plants of the umbelliferous genus *Osmorhiza,* of Asia and America, having aromatic roots and clusters of small white flowers.

sweet cider NOUN 1 *Brit* cider having a high sugar content. 2 *US and Canadian* unfermented apple juice. Compare **hard cider.**

sweet clover NOUN another name for **melilot.**

sweet corn NOUN 1 Also called: **sugar corn, green corn.** a variety of maize, *Zea mays saccharata,* whose kernels are rich in sugar and eaten as a vegetable when young. 2 the unripe ears of maize, esp the sweet kernels removed from the cob, cooked as a vegetable.

sweeten (ˈswiːtᵊn) VERB (*mainly tr*) 1 (*also intr*) to make or become sweet or sweeter. 2 to mollify or soften (a person). 3 to make more agreeable. 4 (*also intr*) *Chem* to free or be freed from unpleasant odours, acidic or corrosive substances, or the like. 5 *Finance, chiefly US* to raise the value of (loan collateral) by adding more securities. 6 *Informal poker* to enlarge (the pot) by adding chips.

sweetener ('swi:tᵊnə) NOUN 1 a sweetening agent, esp one that does not contain sugar. 2 *Informal* a bribe. 3 *Informal* a financial inducement.

sweetening ('swi:tᵊnɪŋ) NOUN something that sweetens.

sweet fern NOUN a North American shrub, *Comptonia* (or *Myrica*) *asplenifolia,* having scented fernlike leaves and heads of brownish flowers: family *Myricaceae*.

sweet flag NOUN an aroid marsh plant, *Acorus calamus,* having swordlike leaves, small greenish flowers, and aromatic roots. Also called: **calamus.**
▷HISTORY C18: see FLAG²

sweet gale NOUN a shrub, *Myrica gale,* of northern swamp regions, having yellow catkin-like flowers and aromatic leaves: family *Myricaceae*. Also called: **bog myrtle.** Often shortened to: **gale.**
▷HISTORY C17: see GALE²

sweet gum NOUN 1 a North American liquidambar tree, *Liquidambar styraciflua,* having prickly spherical fruit clusters and fragrant sap: the wood (called **satin walnut**) is used to make furniture. Compare **sour gum.** 2 the sap of this tree. ◆ Also called: **red gum.**

sweetheart ('swi:tˌhɑ:t) NOUN 1 a person loved by another. 2 *Informal* a lovable, generous, or obliging person. 3 a term of endearment for a beloved or lovable person. ◆ ADJECTIVE 4 of or relating to a garment with a sweetheart neckline: *sweetheart cardigan.*

sweetheart agreement NOUN 1 an industrial agreement made at a local level between an employer and employees, often with clauses advantageous to the employer, such as no strikes, but without the recognition of the national union representing the employees. 2 *Austral* an industrial agreement negotiated directly between employers and employees, without resort to arbitration.

sweetheart neckline NOUN a neckline on a woman's dress that is low at the front and shaped like the top of a heart.

sweetie ('swi:tɪ) NOUN *Informal* 1 sweetheart; darling: used as a term of endearment. 2 *Brit* another word for **sweet** (sense 20). 3 *Chiefly Brit* an endearing person. 4 a large seedless variety of grapefruit which has a green to yellow rind and juicy sweet pulp.

sweetiewife ('swi:tɪˌwaɪf) NOUN, *plural* **-wives**. *Scot dialect* 1 a garrulous person. 2 (formerly) a woman selling sweets.

sweeting ('swi:tɪŋ) NOUN 1 a variety of sweet apple. 2 an archaic word for **sweetheart.**

sweetman ('swi:tˌmæn) NOUN, *plural* **-men**. (in the Caribbean) a man kept by a woman.

sweet marjoram NOUN another name for **marjoram** (sense 1).

sweet marten NOUN a name for the pine marten, referring to the fact that its scent glands produce a less offensive scent marker than that of the polecat (the foul marten or foumart).

sweetmeal ('swi:tˌmi:l) ADJECTIVE (of biscuits) sweet and wholemeal.

sweetmeat ('swi:tˌmi:t) NOUN a sweetened delicacy, such as a preserve, sweet, or, formerly, a cake or pastry.

sweetness and light NOUN an apparently affable reasonableness.
▷HISTORY C19: adopted by Matthew Arnold from Swift's *Battle of the Books* (1704)

sweet oil NOUN another name for **olive oil.**

sweet pea NOUN a climbing leguminous plant, *Lathyrus odoratus,* of S Europe, widely cultivated for its butterfly-shaped fragrant flowers of delicate pastel colours.

sweet pepper NOUN 1 a pepper plant, *Capsicum frutescens grossum,* with large bell-shaped fruits that are eaten unripe (**green pepper**) or ripe (**red pepper**). 2 the fruit of this plant.

sweet potato NOUN 1 a convolvulaceous twining plant, *Ipomoea batatas,* of tropical America, cultivated in the tropics for its edible fleshy yellow root. 2 the root of this plant. ◆ Also called (NZ): **kumara.**

sweet shop NOUN *Chiefly Brit* a shop solely or largely selling sweets, esp boiled sweets.

sweetsop ('swi:tˌsɒp) NOUN 1 a small West Indian tree, *Annona squamosa,* having yellowish-green fruit: family *Annonaceae*. 2 the fruit of this tree, which has a sweet edible pulp. ◆ Also called: **sugar apple, custard apple.** Compare **soursop.**
▷HISTORY C19: so called because of the flavour and consistency of its pulp

sweet spot NOUN *Sport* the centre area of a racquet, golf club, etc., from which the cleanest shots are made.

sweet-talk *Informal* ◆ VERB 1 to coax, flatter, or cajole (someone). ◆ NOUN **sweet talk.** 2 cajolery; coaxing.

sweet tooth NOUN a strong liking for sweet foods.

sweet william NOUN a widely cultivated Eurasian caryophyllaceous plant, *Dianthus barbatus,* with flat clusters of white, pink, red, or purple flowers.

sweet woodruff NOUN a Eurasian and North African rubiaceous plant, *Galium odoratum* (or *Asperula odorata*), having whorls of leaves and clusters of fragrant white flowers.

sweir¹ (swi:r) VERB, NOUN a Scot word for **swear.**

sweir² (swi:r) ADJECTIVE *Scot* 1 lazy. 2 loath; disinclined.
▷HISTORY Old English

swell (swɛl) VERB **swells, swelling, swelled, swollen** *or* **swelled.** 1 to grow or cause to grow in size, esp as a result of internal pressure. Compare **contract** (senses 1, 3). 2 to expand or cause to expand at a particular point or above the surrounding level; protrude. 3 to grow or cause to grow in size, amount, intensity, or degree: *the party is swelling with new recruits.* 4 to puff or be puffed up with pride or another emotion. 5 (*intr*) (of seas or lakes) to rise in waves. 6 (*intr*) to well up or overflow. 7 (*tr*) to make (a musical phrase) increase gradually in volume and then diminish. ◆ NOUN 8 **a** the undulating movement of the surface of the open sea. **b** a succession of waves or a single large wave. 9 a swelling or being swollen; expansion. 10 an increase in quantity or degree; inflation. 11 a bulge; protuberance. 12 a gentle hill. 13 *Informal* a person very fashionably dressed. 14 *Informal* a man of high social or political standing. 15 *Music* a crescendo followed by an immediate diminuendo. 16 Also called: **swell organ.** *Music* **a** a set of pipes on an organ housed in a box (**swell box**) fitted with a shutter operated by a pedal, which can be opened or closed to control the volume. **b** the manual on an organ controlling this. Compare **choir** (sense 4), **great** (sense 21). ◆ ADJECTIVE 17 *Informal* stylish or grand. 18 *Slang* excellent; first-class.
▷HISTORY Old English *swellan;* related to Old Norse *svella,* Old Frisian *swella,* German *schwellen*

swelled head *or* **swollen head** NOUN *Informal* an inflated view of one's own worth, often caused by sudden success.

swelled-headed, swell-headed, *or* **swollen-headed** ADJECTIVE *Informal* conceited.

swellfish ('swɛlˌfɪʃ) NOUN, *plural* **-fish** *or* **-fishes**. a popular name for **puffer** (sense 2).

swelling ('swɛlɪŋ) NOUN 1 the act of expansion or inflation. 2 the state of being or becoming swollen. 3 a swollen or inflated part or area. 4 an abnormal enlargement of a bodily structure or part, esp as the result of injury. Related adjective: **tumescent.**

swelter ('swɛltə) VERB 1 (*intr*) to suffer under oppressive heat, esp to sweat and feel faint. 2 (*tr*) *Archaic* to exude (venom). 3 (*tr*) *Rare* to cause to suffer under oppressive heat. ◆ NOUN 4 a sweltering condition (esp in the phrase **in a swelter**). 5 oppressive humid heat.
▷HISTORY C15 *swelten,* from Old English *sweltan* to die; related to Old Norse *svelta* to starve, Old High German *swelzan* to burn with passion; see SULTRY

sweltering ('swɛltərɪŋ) ADJECTIVE oppressively hot and humid: *a sweltering day.*
▶'**swelteringly** ADVERB

swept (swɛpt) VERB the past tense of **sweep.**

sweptback ('swɛptˌbæk) ADJECTIVE (of an aircraft wing) having leading edge and trailing edges inclined backwards towards the rear of the fuselage.

swept volume NOUN another term for **volumetric displacement.**

sweptwing ('swɛptˌwɪŋ) ADJECTIVE (of an aircraft, winged missile, etc.) having wings swept (usually) backwards.

swerve (swɜ:v) VERB 1 to turn or cause to turn aside, usually sharply or suddenly, from a course. 2 (*tr*) to avoid (a person or event). ◆ NOUN 3 the act, instance, or degree of swerving.
▷HISTORY Old English *sweorfan* to scour; related to Old High German *swerban* to wipe off, Gothic *afswairban* to wipe off, Old Norse *sverfa* to file
▶'**swervable** ADJECTIVE ▶'**swerver** NOUN

sweven ('swɛvᵊn) NOUN *Archaic* a vision or dream.
▷HISTORY Old English *swefn;* related to Old Norse *svefn* dream, sleep, Lithuanian *sāpnas,* Old Slavonic *sunu,* Latin *somnus*

SWFF *Austral* ABBREVIATION FOR saltwater fly-fishing.

SWG Standard Wire Gauge; a notation for the diameters of metal rods or thickness of metal sheet ranging from 16 mm to 0.02 mm or from 0.5 inch to 0.001 inch.

swidden ('swɪdən) NOUN **a** an area of land where slash-and-burn techniques have been used to prepare it for cultivation. **b** (*as modifier*): *small-scale swidden agriculture.*
▷HISTORY C18: Northern English dialect variant of *swithen* to burn

swift (swɪft) ADJECTIVE 1 moving or able to move quickly; fast. 2 occurring or performed quickly or suddenly; instant: *a swift response.* 3 (*postpositive;* foll by *to*) prompt to act or respond: *swift to take revenge.* ◆ ADVERB 4 **a** swiftly or quickly. **b** (*in combination*): *swift-moving.* ◆ NOUN 5 any bird of the families *Apodidae* and *Hemiprocnidae,* such as *Apus apus* (**common swift**) of the Old World: order *Apodiformes*. They have long narrow wings and spend most of the time on the wing. 6 (*sometimes capital*) a variety of domestic fancy pigeon originating in Egypt and Syria and having an appearance somewhat similar to a swift. 7 short for **swift moth.** 8 any of certain North American lizards of the genera *Sceloporus* and *Uta* that can run very rapidly: family *Iguanidae* (iguanas). 9 the main cylinder in a carding machine. 10 an expanding circular frame used to hold skeins of silk, wool, etc.
▷HISTORY Old English, from *swīfan* to turn; related to Old Norse *svifa* to rove, Old Frisian *swīvia* to waver, Old High German *sweib* a reversal; see SWIVEL
▶'**swiftly** ADVERB ▶'**swiftness** NOUN

swifter ('swɪftə) NOUN *Nautical* a line run around the ends of capstan bars to prevent their falling out of their sockets.
▷HISTORY C17: related to the nautical term *swift* to fasten with tight-drawn ropes; probably Scandinavian in origin: compare Old Norse *svipta* to reef

swift fox NOUN a small fox, *Vulpes velox,* of the plains of W North America. Also called: **kit fox.**

Swiftian ('swɪftɪən) ADJECTIVE of, relating to, or reminiscent of Jonathan Swift, the Anglo-Irish satirist and churchman (1667–1745).

swiftie *or* **swifty** ('swɪftɪ) NOUN (*plural* **-ties**) *Slang, chiefly Austral* a trick, ruse, or deception.

swiftlet ('swɪftlɪt) NOUN any of various small swifts of the Asian genus *Collocalia* that often live in caves and use echolocation: the nests, which are made of hardened saliva, are used in oriental cookery to make birds' nest soup.

swift moth NOUN any of five species of fast-flying moths of the family *Hepialidae,* regarded as primitive in development, having forewings and hind wings similar in size and shape: the best known is the **ghost swift,** *Hepialus humili.* Often shortened to: **swift.**

swig (swɪg) *Informal* ◆ NOUN 1 a large swallow or deep drink, esp from a bottle. ◆ VERB **swigs, swigging, swigged.** 2 to drink (some liquid) deeply, esp from a bottle.
▷HISTORY C16: of unknown origin
▶'**swigger** NOUN

swiler (ˈswaɪlə) NOUN *Canadian* (in Newfoundland) a seal hunter.
▷HISTORY variant of SEALER[2]

swill (swɪl) VERB 1 to drink large quantities of (liquid, esp alcoholic drink); guzzle. 2 (*tr; often foll by out*) *Chiefly Brit* to drench or rinse in large amounts of water. 3 (*tr*) to feed swill to (pigs, etc.). ◆ NOUN 4 wet feed, esp for pigs, consisting of kitchen waste, skimmed milk, etc. 5 garbage or refuse, esp from a kitchen. 6 a deep draught of drink, esp beer. 7 any liquid mess. 8 the act of swilling.
▷HISTORY Old English *swilian* to wash out
▸ˈ**swiller** NOUN

swim (swɪm) VERB **swims, swimming, swam, swum.** 1 (*intr*) to move along in water, etc., by means of movements of the body or parts of the body, esp the arms and legs, or (in the case of fish) tail and fins. 2 (*tr*) to cover (a distance or stretch of water) in this way. 3 (*tr*) to compete in (a race) in this way. 4 (*intr*) to be supported by and on a liquid; float. 5 (*tr*) to use (a particular stroke) in swimming. 6 (*intr*) to move smoothly, usually through air or over a surface. 7 (*intr*) to reel or seem to reel: *my head swam; the room swam around me.* 8 (*intr; often foll by in or with*) to be covered or flooded with water or other liquid. 9 (*intr; often foll by in*) to be liberally supplied (with): *he's swimming in money.* 10 (*tr*) to cause to float or swim. 11 (*tr*) to provide (something) with water deep enough to float in. 12 **swim with** (*or* **against**) **the stream** *or* **tide.** to conform to (or resist) prevailing opinion. ◆ NOUN 13 the act, an instance, or period of swimming. 14 any graceful gliding motion. 15 a condition of dizziness; swoon. 16 a pool in a river good for fishing. 17 **in the swim.** *Informal* fashionable or active in social or political activities.
▷HISTORY Old English *swimman;* related to Old Norse *svima,* German *schwimmen,* Gothic *swumsl* pond, Norwegian *svamla* to paddle
▸ˈ**swimmable** ADJECTIVE ▸ˈ**swimmer** NOUN ▸ˈ**swimming** NOUN, ADJECTIVE

swim bladder NOUN *Ichthyol* another name for **air bladder** (sense 1).

swimfeeder (ˈswɪmˌfiːdə) NOUN *Angling* a device containing bait, attached to the line to ensure the gradual baiting of the swim from under the surface.

swimmeret (ˈswɪməˌrɛt) NOUN any of the small paired appendages on the abdomen of crustaceans, used chiefly in locomotion and reproduction. Also called: **pleopod.**
▷HISTORY C19: from SWIM + -ER[1] + -ET

swimmers (swɪməz) PLURAL NOUN *Austral* a swimming costume.

swimming bath NOUN (*often plural*) an indoor swimming pool.

swimming costume *or* **bathing costume** NOUN *Chiefly Brit* any apparel worn for swimming or sunbathing, such as a woman's one-piece garment covering most of the torso but not the limbs.

swimmingly (ˈswɪmɪŋlɪ) ADVERB successfully, effortlessly, or well (esp in the phrase **go swimmingly**).

swimming pool NOUN an artificial pool for swimming.

swimsuit (ˈswɪmˌsuːt, -ˌsjuːt) NOUN a woman's one-piece swimming garment that leaves the arms and legs bare.

swindle (ˈswɪndᵊl) VERB 1 to cheat (someone) of money, etc.; defraud. 2 (*tr*) to obtain (money, etc.) by fraud. ◆ NOUN 3 a fraudulent scheme or transaction.
▷HISTORY C18: back formation from German *Schwindler,* from *schwindeln,* from Old High German *swintilōn,* frequentative of *swintan* to disappear
▸ˈ**swindler** NOUN

swindle sheet NOUN a slang term for **expense account.**

Swindon (ˈswɪndən) NOUN 1 a town in S England, in NE Wiltshire: railway workshops, high technology. Pop.: 145 236 (1991). 2 a unitary authority in S England, in Wiltshire. Pop.: 80 061 (2001). Area: 230 sq. km (89 sq. miles).

swine (swaɪn) NOUN 1 (*plural* **swines**) a coarse or contemptible person. 2 (*plural* **swine**) another name for a **pig.**
▷HISTORY Old English *swīn;* related to Old Norse *svīn,* Gothic *swein,* Latin *suīnus* relating to swine
▸ˈ**swineˌlike** ADJECTIVE ▸ˈ**swinish** ADJECTIVE ▸ˈ**swinishly** ADVERB ▸ˈ**swinishness** NOUN

swine fever NOUN an infectious viral disease of pigs, characterized by fever, refusal to eat, weight loss, and diarrhoea. US term: **hog cholera.**

swineherd (ˈswaɪnˌhɜːd) NOUN *Archaic* a person who looks after pigs.

swinepox (ˈswaɪnˌpɒks) NOUN 1 Also called: **variola porcina** (pɔːˈsɑɪnə). an acute infectious viral disease of pigs characterized by skin eruptions. 2 a form of chickenpox in which the skin eruptions are not pitted.

swine's cress NOUN another name for **wart cress.**

swine vesicular disease NOUN a viral disease of swine characterized by vesicular lesions on the feet, legs, snout, and tongue.

swing (swɪŋ) VERB **swings, swinging, swung.** 1 to move or cause to move rhythmically to and fro, as a free-hanging object; sway. 2 (*intr*) to move, walk, etc., with a relaxed and swaying motion. 3 to pivot or cause to pivot, as on a hinge. 4 to move or cause to move in a curve: *the car swung around the bend.* 5 to move or cause to move by suspending or being suspended. 6 to hang or be hung so as to be able to turn freely. 7 (*intr*) *Slang* to be hanged: *he'll swing for it.* 8 to alter or cause to alter habits, a course, etc. 9 (*tr*) *Informal* to influence or manipulate successfully: *I hope he can swing the deal.* 10 (*tr; foll by up*) to raise or hoist, esp in a sweeping motion. 11 (*intr; often foll by at*) to hit out or strike (at), esp with a sweeping motion. 12 (*tr*) to wave (a weapon, etc.) in a sweeping motion; flourish. 13 to arrange or play (music) with the rhythmically flexible and compulsive quality associated with jazz. 14 (*intr*) (of popular music, esp jazz, or of the musicians who play it) to have this quality. 15 *Slang* to be lively and modern. 16 (*intr*) *Slang* to swap sexual partners in a group, esp habitually. 17 (*intr*) *Cricket* to bowl (a ball) with swing or (of a ball) to move with a swing. 18 to turn (a ship or aircraft) in order to test compass error. 19 **swing both ways.** *Slang* to enjoy sexual partners of both sexes. 20 **swing the lead.** *Informal* to malinger or make up excuses. ◆ NOUN 21 the act or manner of swinging or the distance covered while swinging: *a wide swing.* 22 a sweeping stroke or blow. 23 *Boxing* a wide punch from the side similar to but longer than a hook. 24 *Cricket* the lateral movement of a bowled ball through the air. 25 any free-swaying motion. 26 any curving movement; sweep. 27 something that swings or is swung, esp a suspended seat on which a person may sit and swing back and forth. 28 **a** a kind of popular dance music influenced by jazz, usually played by big bands and originating in the 1930s. **b** (*as modifier*): *swing music.* 29 See **swingbeat.** 30 *Prosody* a steady distinct rhythm or cadence in prose or verse. 31 *Informal* the normal round or pace: *get into the swing of things.* 32 **a** a fluctuation, as in some business activity, voting pattern etc. **b** (*as modifier*) able to bring about a swing in a voting pattern: *swing party.* 33 *US informal* free scope; freedom of activity. 34 *Chiefly US* a circular tour. 35 *Canadian* a tour of a particular area or region. 36 **go with a swing.** to go well; be successful. 37 **in full swing.** at the height of activity. 38 **swings and roundabouts.** equal advantages and disadvantages.
▷HISTORY Old English *swingan;* related to Old Frisian *swinga,* Old High German *swingan*

swingbeat (ˈswɪŋˌbiːt) NOUN a type of modern dance music that combines soul, rhythm and blues, and hip-hop.

swingboat (ˈswɪŋˌbəʊt) NOUN a piece of fairground equipment consisting of a boat-shaped carriage for swinging in.

swing bridge NOUN 1 Also called: **pivot bridge, turn bridge.** a low bridge that can be rotated about a vertical axis, esp to permit the passage of ships. Compare **drawbridge.** 2 *NZ* a pedestrian bridge over a river, suspended by heavy wire cables.

swing door *or* **swinging door** NOUN a door pivoted or hung on double-sided hinges so that it can open either way.

swinge (swɪndʒ) VERB **swinges, swingeing** *or* **swinging, swinged.** (*tr*) *Archaic* to beat, flog, or punish.
▷HISTORY Old English *swengan;* related to Old Frisian *swenga* to drench, Gothic *afswaggwjan* to cause to sway; see SWING

swingeing (ˈswɪndʒɪŋ) ADJECTIVE *Chiefly Brit* punishing; severe.

swinger (ˈswɪŋə) *Slang* NOUN 1 *Slang* a person regarded as being modern and lively. 2 a person who swaps sexual partners in a group, esp habitually.

swinging (ˈswɪŋɪŋ) ADJECTIVE 1 moving rhythmically to and fro. 2 *Slang* modern and lively.
▸ˈ**swinging** ADJECTIVE ▸ˈ**swingingly** ADVERB

swinging voter NOUN an Austral and NZ informal term for **floating voter.**

swingle (ˈswɪŋgᵊl) NOUN 1 a flat-bladed wooden instrument used for beating and scraping flax or hemp to remove coarse matter from it. ◆ VERB 2 (*tr*) to use a swingle on.
▷HISTORY Old English *swingel* stroke; related to Middle High German *swüngel,* Middle Dutch *swinghel*

swingletree (ˈswɪŋgᵊlˌtriː) NOUN a crossbar in a horse's harness to which the ends of the traces are attached. Also called: **whippletree,** (esp US) **whiffletree.**
▷HISTORY C15: from SWINGLE + TREE (in the sense: a post or bar)

swingometer (swɪŋˈɒmɪtə) NOUN a device used in television broadcasting during a general election to indicate the swing of votes from one political party to another.

swing shift NOUN the usual US and Canadian term for **backshift.**

swing-wing ADJECTIVE 1 of or relating to a variable-geometry aircraft. ◆ NOUN 2 **a** such an aircraft. **b** either wing of such an aircraft.

swink (swɪŋk) *Archaic* ◆ VERB 1 (*intr*) to toil or drudge. ◆ NOUN 2 toil or drudgery.
▷HISTORY Old English *swinc,* from *swincan*
▸ˈ**swinker** NOUN

swipe (swaɪp) VERB 1 (when *intr,* usually foll by *at*) *Informal* to hit hard with a sweeping blow. 2 (*tr*) *Slang* to steal. 3 (*tr*) to pass a machine-readable card, such as a credit card, debit card, etc., through a machine that electronically interprets the information encoded, usu. in a magnetic strip, on the card. ◆ NOUN 4 *Informal* a hard blow. 5 an unexpected criticism of someone or something while discussing another subject. 6 Also called: **sweep.** a type of lever for raising and lowering a weight, such as a bucket in a well.
▷HISTORY C19: perhaps related to SWEEP

swipes (swaɪps) PLURAL NOUN *Brit slang* beer, esp when poor or weak.
▷HISTORY C18: probably related to SWEEP

swipple *or* **swiple** (ˈswɪpᵊl) NOUN the part of a flail that strikes the grain.
▷HISTORY C15 *swipyl,* variant of *swepyl,* from *swep(en)* to SWEEP + *-yl,* suffix denoting an instrument

swirl (swɜːl) VERB 1 to turn or cause to turn in a twisting spinning fashion. 2 (*intr*) to be dizzy; swim: *my head was swirling.* ◆ NOUN 3 a whirling or spinning motion, esp in water. 4 a whorl; curl. 5 the act of swirling or stirring. 6 dizzy confusion.
▷HISTORY C15: probably from Dutch *zwirrelen;* related to Norwegian *svirla,* German *schwirren*
▸ˈ**swirling** ADJECTIVE ▸ˈ**swirlingly** ADVERB ▸ˈ**swirly** ADJECTIVE

swish (swɪʃ) VERB 1 to move with or make or cause to move with or make a whistling or hissing sound. 2 (*intr*) (esp of fabrics) to rustle. 3 (*tr*) *Slang, now rare* to whip; flog. 4 (*tr; foll by off*) to cut with a swishing blow. ◆ NOUN 5 a hissing or rustling sound or movement. 6 a rod for flogging or a blow from such a rod. 7 *US slang* an effeminate male homosexual. 8 a W African building material composed of mortar and mud or laterite, or more recently of cement and earth. ◆ ADJECTIVE 9 *Informal, chiefly Brit* fashionable; smart. 10 *US slang* effeminate and homosexual.
▷HISTORY C18: of imitative origin
▸ˈ**swisher** NOUN ▸ˈ**swishing** ADJECTIVE ▸ˈ**swishingly** ADVERB

swishy (ˈswɪʃɪ) ADJECTIVE **-shier, -shiest.** 1 moving with a swishing sound. 2 *US slang* effeminate and homosexual.

Swiss (swɪs) ADJECTIVE [1] of, relating to, or characteristic of Switzerland, its inhabitants, or their dialects of German, French, and Italian. ◆ NOUN [2] a native, inhabitant, or citizen of Switzerland.

Swiss chard NOUN another name for **chard.**

Swiss cheese NOUN a hard white or pale yellow cheese with holes, such as Gruyère or Emmenthal.

Swiss cheese plant NOUN See **monstera.**

Swiss Guard NOUN [1] the bodyguard of the pope, recruited from Swiss nationals. [2] a member of this bodyguard. [3] one of a group of Swiss mercenaries who acted as bodyguards to the French kings: destroyed in the Revolution.

swiss muslin NOUN a fine muslin dress fabric, usually having a raised or woven pattern of dolls or figures.
▷HISTORY C19: so called because it was formerly imported from Switzerland

swiss roll NOUN a sponge cake spread with jam, cream, or some other filling, and rolled up.

Swiss tournament NOUN (in certain games and sports) a tournament system in which players are paired in each round according to the scores they then have, playing a new opponent each time. More players can take part than in an all-play-all tournament of the same duration.
▷HISTORY named from a chess tournament held in Zürich in 1895

switch (swɪtʃ) NOUN [1] a mechanical, electrical, electronic, or optical device for opening or closing a circuit or for diverting energy from one part of a circuit to another. [2] a swift and usually sudden shift or change. [3] an exchange or swap. [4] a flexible rod or twig, used esp for punishment. [5] the sharp movement or blow of such an instrument. [6] a tress of false hair used to give added length or bulk to a woman's own hairstyle. [7] the tassel-like tip of the tail of cattle and certain other animals. [8] any of various card games in which the suit is changed during play. [9] *US and Canadian* a railway siding. [10] *US and Canadian* a railway point. [11] *Austral informal* See **switchboard.** ◆ VERB [12] to shift, change, turn aside, or change the direction of (something). [13] to exchange (places); replace (something by something else): *the battalions switched fronts.* [14] *Chiefly US and Canadian* to transfer (rolling stock) from one railway track to another. [15] *(tr)* to cause (an electric current) to start or stop flowing or to change its path by operating a switch. [16] to swing or cause to swing, esp back and forth. [17] *(tr)* to lash or whip with or as if with a switch. ◆ See also **switch off, switch on.**
▷HISTORY C16: perhaps from Middle Dutch *swijch* branch, twig
▸ˈ**switcher** NOUN ▸ˈ**switchˌlike** ADJECTIVE

switchback (ˈswɪtʃˌbæk) NOUN [1] a mountain road, railway, or track which rises and falls sharply many times or a sharp rise and fall on such a road, railway, or track. [2] another word (esp Brit) for **big dipper.**

switchblade *or* **switchblade knife** (ˈswɪtʃˌbleɪd) NOUN another name (esp US and Canadian) for **flick knife.**

switchboard (ˈswɪtʃˌbɔːd) NOUN [1] an installation in a telephone exchange, office, hotel, etc., at which the interconnection of telephone lines is manually controlled. [2] an assembly of switchgear for the control of power supplies in an installation or building.

switched-on ADJECTIVE *Informal* well-informed or aware of what is up to date.

switched-star ADJECTIVE denoting or relating to a cable television system in which only one or two programme channels are fed to each subscriber, who can select other channels by remote control of a central switching point: *a switched-star network.* Compare **tree-and-branch.**

switcheroo (ˌswɪtʃəˈruː) NOUN *US slang* a surprising or unexpected change or variation.
▷HISTORY C20: from SWITCH

switchgear (ˈswɪtʃˌgɪə) NOUN *Electrical engineering* any of several devices used for opening and closing electric circuits, esp those that pass high currents.

switchgirl (ˈswɪtʃˌgɜːl) NOUN *Informal, chiefly Austral* a woman who operates a telephone switchboard.

switch-hitter NOUN *US and Canadian* [1] *Baseball* a batsman who can hit either right- or left-handed. [2] *Slang* a bisexual person.

switchman (ˈswɪtʃmən) NOUN, *plural* **-men.** the US and Canadian name for **pointsman.**

switch off VERB *(adverb)* [1] to cause (a device) to stop operating by or as if by moving a switch, knob, or lever; turn off. [2] *Informal* to cease to interest or be interested; make or become bored, alienated, etc.

switch on VERB *(adverb)* [1] to cause (a device) to operate by or as if by moving a switch, knob, or lever; turn on. [2] *(tr) Informal* to produce (charm, tears, etc.) suddenly or automatically. [3] *(tr) Informal* (now slightly dated) to make up-to-date, esp regarding outlook, dress, etc. [4] *(tr) Slang* to arouse emotionally or sexually. [5] *(intr) Slang* to take or become intoxicated by drugs. [6] *(tr) Slang* to introduce (someone) to drugs.

switch selling NOUN a system of selling, now illegal in Britain, whereby potential customers are attracted by a special offer on some goods but the salesman's real aim is to sell other more expensive goods instead.

switch yard NOUN *US and Canadian* an area in a railway system where rolling stock is shunted, as in forming trains.

swither (ˈswɪðər) *Scot* ◆ VERB *(intr)* [1] to hesitate; vacillate; be perplexed. ◆ NOUN [2] hesitation; perplexity; agitation.
▷HISTORY C16: of unknown origin

Switz. *or* **Swit.** ABBREVIATION FOR Switzerland.

Switzer (ˈswɪtsə) NOUN [1] a less common word for **Swiss.** [2] a member of the Swiss Guard.
▷HISTORY C16: from Middle High German, from *Swīz* Switzerland

Switzerland (ˈswɪtsələnd) NOUN a federal republic in W central Europe: the cantons of Schwyz, Uri, and Unterwalden formed a defensive league against the Hapsburgs in 1291, later joined by other cantons; gained independence in 1499; adopted a policy of permanent neutrality from 1516; a leading centre of the Reformation in the 16th century. It lies in the Jura Mountains and the Alps, with a plateau between the two ranges. Official languages: German, French, and Italian; Romansch minority. Religion: mostly Protestant and Roman Catholic. Currency: Swiss franc. Capital: Bern. Pop.: 7 222 000 (2001 est.). Area: 41 288 sq. km (15 941 sq. miles). German name: **Schweiz.** French name: **Suisse.** Italian name: **Svizzera.** Latin name: **Helvetia** (hɛlˈviːʃə).

swive (swaɪv) VERB *Archaic* to have sexual intercourse with (a person).
▷HISTORY Old English *swīfan* to revolve, SWIVEL

swivel (ˈswɪvᵊl) NOUN [1] a coupling device which allows an attached object to turn freely. [2] such a device made of two parts which turn independently, such as a compound link of a chain. [3] **a** a pivot on which is mounted a gun that may be swung from side to side in a horizontal plane. **b** Also called: **swivel gun.** the gun itself. ◆ VERB **-els, -elling, -elled** *or US* **-els, -eling, -eled.** [4] to turn or swing on or as if on a pivot. [5] *(tr)* to provide with, secure by, or support with a swivel.
▷HISTORY C14: from Old English *swīfan* to turn; see SWIFT
▸ˈ**swivel-ˌlike** ADJECTIVE

swivel chair NOUN a chair, the seat of which is joined to the legs by a swivel and which thus may be spun round.

swivel pin NOUN another name for **kingpin** (sense 3).

swiz *or* **swizz** (swɪz) NOUN *Brit informal* a swindle or disappointment; swizzle.

swizzle (ˈswɪzᵊl) NOUN [1] *US* an unshaken cocktail. [2] a Caribbean drink of milk and rum. [3] *Brit informal* a swiz. ◆ VERB [4] *(tr)* to stir a swizzle stick in (a drink). [5] *Brit informal* to swindle; cheat.
▷HISTORY C19: of unknown origin

swizzle stick NOUN a small rod used to agitate an effervescent drink to facilitate the escape of carbon dioxide.

swob (swɒb) NOUN, VERB **swobs, swobbing, swobbed.** a less common word for **swab.**

swoffing (ˈswɒfɪŋ) NOUN *Austral* the sport of saltwater fly-fishing.
▷HISTORY C20: formed from *s(alt)wa(ter) f(ly) f(ishing)*
▸ˈ**swoffer** NOUN

swollen (ˈswəʊlən) VERB [1] a past participle of **swell.** ◆ ADJECTIVE [2] tumid or enlarged by or as if by swelling. [3] turgid or bombastic.
▸ˈ**swollenly** ADVERB ▸ˈ**swollenness** NOUN

swollen head NOUN another term for **swelled head.**

swollen-headed ADJECTIVE *Informal* conceited.

swoon (swuːn) VERB *(intr)* [1] a literary word for **faint.** [2] to become ecstatic. ◆ NOUN [3] an instance of fainting. ◆ Also (archaic or dialect): **swound.**
▷HISTORY Old English *geswōgen* insensible, past participle of *swōgan* (unattested except in compounds) to suffocate
▸ˈ**swooning** ADJECTIVE ▸ˈ**swooningly** ADVERB

swoop (swuːp) VERB [1] *(intr; usually foll by down, on, or upon)* to sweep or pounce suddenly. [2] *(tr; often foll by up, away, or off)* to seize or scoop suddenly. ◆ NOUN [3] the act of swooping. [4] a swift descent.
▷HISTORY Old English *swāpan* to sweep; related to Old High German *sweifan* to swing around, Old Norse *sveipa* to throw

swoosh (swuʃ) VERB [1] to make or cause to make a rustling or swirling sound, esp when moving or pouring out. ◆ NOUN [2] a swirling or rustling sound or movement.
▷HISTORY C20: of imitative origin (probably influenced by SWISH and SWOOP)

swop (swɒp) NOUN, VERB **swops, swopping, swopped.** a variant spelling of **swap.**

sword (sɔːd) NOUN [1] a thrusting, striking, or cutting weapon with a long blade having one or two cutting edges, a hilt, and usually a crosspiece or guard. [2] such a weapon worn on ceremonial occasions as a symbol of authority. [3] something resembling a sword, such as the snout of a swordfish. [4] **cross swords.** to argue or fight. [5] **the sword. a** violence or power, esp military power. **b** death; destruction: *to put to the sword.*
▷HISTORY Old English *sweord;* related to Old Saxon *swerd,* Old Norse *sverth,* Old High German *swert*
▸ˈ**swordless** ADJECTIVE ▸ˈ**swordˌlike** ADJECTIVE

sword bayonet NOUN a bayonet with a swordlike blade and hilt, capable of use as a sword.

swordbearer (ˈsɔːdˌbɛərə) NOUN an official who carries a ceremonial sword.

sword belt NOUN a belt with a sling or strap for a sword.

swordbill (ˈsɔːdˌbɪl) NOUN a South American hummingbird, *Ensifera ensifera,* having a bill as long as its body.

sword cane NOUN another name for **swordstick.**

swordcraft (ˈsɔːdˌkrɑːft) NOUN the art of using a sword.

sword dance NOUN a dance in which the performers dance nimbly over swords on the ground or brandish them in the air.
▸**sword dancer** NOUN ▸**sword dancing** NOUN

sword fern NOUN any of numerous ferns having sword-shaped fronds.

swordfish (ˈsɔːdˌfɪʃ) NOUN, *plural* **-fish** *or* **-fishes.** a large scombroid fish, *Xiphias gladius,* with a very long upper jaw: valued as a food and game fish: family *Xiphiidae.*

sword grass NOUN any of various grasses and other plants having sword-shaped sharp leaves.

sword knot NOUN a loop on the hilt of a sword by which it was attached to the wrist, now purely decorative.

sword lily NOUN another name for **gladiolus** (sense 1).
▷HISTORY C18: so called because of its sword-shaped leaves

Sword of Damocles NOUN a closely impending disaster.
▷HISTORY see DAMOCLES

swordplay (ˈsɔːdˌpleɪ) NOUN [1] the action or art of fighting with a sword. [2] verbal sparring.
▸ˈ**swordˌplayer** NOUN

swordsman (ˈsɔːdzmən) NOUN, *plural* **-men.** one who uses or is skilled in the use of a sword.
▸ˈ**swordsmanˌship** NOUN

swordstick ('sɔːdˌstɪk) NOUN a hollow walking stick containing a short sword or dagger.

sword-swallower NOUN a performer who simulates the swallowing of swords.

swordtail ('sɔːdˌteɪl) NOUN any of several small freshwater cyprinodont fishes of the genus *Xiphophorus,* esp *X. helleri,* of Central America, having a long swordlike tail.

swore (swɔː) VERB the past tense of **swear.**

sworn (swɔːn) VERB 1 the past participle of **swear.** ◆ ADJECTIVE 2 bound, pledged, or made inveterate, by or as if by an oath: *a sworn statement; he was sworn to God.*

swot[1] (swɒt) *Brit informal* ◆ VERB **swots, swotting, swotted.** 1 (often foll by *up*) to study (a subject) intensively, as for an examination; cram. ◆ NOUN 2 Also called: **swotter** ('swɒtə). a person who works or studies hard. 3 hard work or grind. ◆ Also: **swat.**
▷HISTORY C19: dialect variant of SWEAT (n)

swot[2] (swɒt) VERB **swots, swotting, swotted,** NOUN a variant of **swat**[1].

SWOT ABBREVIATION FOR strengths, weaknesses, opportunities, and threats: an analysis of a product made before it is marketed.

swotty ('swɒtɪ) ADJECTIVE *Brit informal* given to studying hard, esp to the exclusion of other activities.

swound (swaʊnd) NOUN, VERB an archaic or dialect word for **swoon.**

swounds *or* **'swounds** (zwaʊndz, zaʊndz) INTERJECTION *Archaic* less common spellings of **zounds.**

swozzle ('swɒzəl) NOUN a variant spelling of **swazzle.**

swum (swʌm) VERB the past participle of **swim.**

swung (swʌŋ) VERB the past tense and past participle of **swing.**

swung dash NOUN a mark, ~, traditionally used in text to indicate the omission of a word or part of a word.

swy (swaɪ) NOUN *Austral* another name for **two-up.**
▷HISTORY C20: from German *zwei* two

sy THE INTERNET DOMAIN NAME FOR Syrian Arab Republic.

SY INTERNATIONAL CAR REGISTRATION FOR Seychelles.

Sybaris ('sɪbərɪs) NOUN a Greek colony in S Italy, on the Gulf of Taranto: notorious for its luxurious living, founded about 720 B.C. and sacked in 510 B.C.

sybarite ('sɪbəˌraɪt) NOUN 1 (*sometimes capital*) a devotee of luxury and the sensual vices. ◆ ADJECTIVE 2 luxurious; sensuous.
▷HISTORY C16: from Latin *Sybarīta,* from Greek *Subaritēs* inhabitant of SYBARIS
▸**sybaritic** (ˌsɪbəˈrɪtɪk) *or* (*less commonly*) **ˌsybaˈritical** ADJECTIVE ▸**ˌsybaˈritically** ADVERB ▸**ˈsybaritism** NOUN

Sybarite ('sɪbəˌraɪt) NOUN a native or inhabitant of the ancient Greek colony of Sybaris.

Sybaritic (ˌsɪbəˈrɪtɪk) ADJECTIVE of or relating to the ancient Greek colony of Sybaris or its inhabitants.

sybo, syboe, *or* **sybow** ('saɪbɪ, 'saɪ-, -bo) NOUN, *plural* **syboes** *or* **sybows.** *Scot* a spring onion.
▷HISTORY C16: from *cibol,* from French *ciboule,* from Latin *cepulla* onion bed, from *cepa* onion

sycamine ('sɪkəˌmaɪn) NOUN a mulberry tree mentioned in the Bible, thought to be the black mulberry, *Morus nigra.*
▷HISTORY C16: from Latin *sȳcamīnus,* from Greek *sukaminon,* from Hebrew *shiqmāh*

sycamore ('sɪkəˌmɔː) NOUN 1 a Eurasian maple tree, *Acer pseudoplatanus,* naturalized in Britain and North America, having five-lobed leaves, yellow flowers, and two-winged fruits. 2 *US and Canadian* an American plane tree, *Platanus occidentalis.* See **plane tree.** 3 Also: **sycomore.** a moraceous tree, *Ficus sycomorus,* of N Africa and W Asia, having an edible figlike fruit.
▷HISTORY C14: from Old French *sicamor,* from Latin *sȳcomorus,* from Greek *sukomoros,* from *sukon* fig + *moron* mulberry

syce, sice, *or* **saice** (saɪs) NOUN 1 (formerly, in India) a servant employed to look after horses, drive carriages, etc. 2 (in Malaysia) a driver or chauffeur.
▷HISTORY C17: from Urdu *sā'is,* from Arabic, from *sāsa* to administer

sycee *or* **sycee silver** (saɪ'siː) NOUN silver ingots formerly used as a medium of exchange in China.
▷HISTORY C18: from Chinese *saì sz* fine silk; so called because the silver can be made into threads as fine as silk

syconium (saɪ'kəʊnɪəm) NOUN, *plural* **-nia** (-nɪə). *Botany* the fleshy fruit of the fig, consisting of a greatly enlarged receptacle completely surrounding the inflorescence.
▷HISTORY C19: from New Latin, from Greek *sukon* fig

sycophant ('sɪkəfənt) NOUN a person who uses flattery to win favour from individuals wielding influence; toady.
▷HISTORY C16: from Latin *sȳcophanta,* from Greek *sukophantēs,* literally: the person showing a fig, apparently referring to the fig sign used in making an accusation, from *sukon* fig + *phainein* to show; sense probably developed from "accuser" to "informer, flatterer"
▸**ˈsycophancy** NOUN

sycophantic (ˌsɪkəˈfæntɪk) ADJECTIVE using flattery to win favour from individuals wielding influence; toadyish; obsequious.
▸**ˌsycoˈphantically** ADVERB

sycosis (saɪ'kəʊsɪs) NOUN chronic inflammation of the hair follicles, esp those of the beard, caused by a staphylococcal infection.
▷HISTORY C16: via New Latin from Greek *sukōsis,* from *sukon* fig

Sydenham's chorea ('sɪd^{ə}nəmz) NOUN a form of chorea affecting children, often associated with rheumatic fever. Nontechnical name: **Saint Vitus's dance.**
▷HISTORY named after T. *Sydenham* (1624–89), English physician

Sydney ('sɪdnɪ) NOUN 1 a port in SE Australia, capital of New South Wales, on an inlet of the S Pacific: the largest city in Australia and the first British settlement, established as a penal colony in 1788; developed rapidly after 1820 with the discovery of gold in its hinterland; large wool market; three universities. Pop. (urban area): 3 276 207 (1998 est.). 2 a port in SE Canada, in Nova Scotia on NE Cape Breton Island: capital of Cape Breton Island until 1820, when the island united administratively with Nova Scotia. Pop.: 26 063 (1991).

Sydneysider ('sɪdnɪˌsaɪdə) NOUN *Chiefly Austral* a resident of Sydney.

Sydney silky NOUN, *plural* **-kies** a small silky-coated breed of terrier, originally from Australia. Also called: **silky terrier.**

syenite ('saɪəˌnaɪt) NOUN a light-coloured coarse-grained plutonic igneous rock consisting of feldspars with hornblende or biotite.
▷HISTORY C18: from French *syénite,* from Latin *syēnītēs lapis* stone from *Syene* (Aswan), where it was originally quarried
▸**syenitic** (ˌsaɪəˈnɪtɪk) ADJECTIVE

SYHA ABBREVIATION FOR Scottish Youth Hostels Association.

Syktyvkar (*Russian* siktif'kar) NOUN a city in NW Russia, capital of the Komi Republic: timber industry. Pop.: 230 900 (1999 est.).

syllabary ('sɪləbərɪ) NOUN, *plural* **-baries.** 1 a table or list of syllables. 2 a set of symbols used in certain writing systems, such as one used for Japanese, in which each symbol represents a spoken syllable.
▷HISTORY C16: from New Latin *syllabārium,* from Latin *syllaba* SYLLABLE

syllabi ('sɪləˌbaɪ) NOUN a plural of **syllabus.**

syllabic (sɪ'læbɪk) ADJECTIVE 1 of or relating to syllables or the division of a word into syllables. 2 denoting a kind of verse line based on a specific number of syllables rather than being regulated by stresses or quantities. 3 (of a consonant) constituting a syllable. 4 (of plainsong and similar chanting) having each syllable sung to a different note. ◆ NOUN 5 a syllabic consonant.
▸**sylˈlabically** ADVERB

syllabify (sɪ'læbɪˌfaɪ) *or* **syllabicate** VERB **-fies, -fying, -fied** *or* **-cates, -cating, -cated.** (*tr*) to divide (a word) into its constituent syllables.
▸**sylˌlabifiˈcation** *or* **sylˌlabiˈcation** NOUN

syllabism ('sɪləˌbɪzəm) NOUN use of a writing system consisting of characters for syllables rather than for individual sounds or whole words. Also called: **syllabography.**

syllable ('sɪləb^{ə}l) NOUN 1 a combination or set of one or more units of sound in a language that must consist of a sonorous element (a sonant or vowel) and may or may not contain less sonorous elements (consonants or semivowels) flanking it on either or both sides: for example "paper" has two syllables. See also **open** (sense 34b), **closed** (sense 6a). 2 (in the writing systems of certain languages, esp ancient ones) a symbol or set of symbols standing for a syllable. 3 the least mention in speech or print: *don't breathe a syllable of it.* 4 **in words of one syllable.** simply; bluntly. ◆ VERB 5 to pronounce syllables of (a text); articulate. 6 (*tr*) to write down in syllables.
▷HISTORY C14: via Old French from Latin *syllaba,* from Greek *sullabē,* from *sullambanein* to collect together, from *sul-* SYN- + *lambanein* to take

syllabogram (sɪ'læbəʊˌgræm) NOUN a written symbol representing a single syllable.

syllabography (ˌsɪləˈbɒgrəfɪ) NOUN another word for **syllabism.** Compare **logography, phonography.**

syllabub *or* **sillabub** ('sɪləˌbʌb) NOUN 1 a spiced drink made of milk with rum, port, brandy, or wine, often hot. 2 *Brit* a cold dessert made from milk or cream beaten with sugar, wine, and lemon juice.
▷HISTORY C16: of unknown origin

syllabus ('sɪləbəs) NOUN, *plural* **-buses** *or* **-bi** (-ˌbaɪ). 1 an outline of a course of studies, text, etc. 2 *Brit* **a** the subjects studied for a particular course. **b** a document which lists these subjects and states how the course will be assessed.
▷HISTORY C17: from Late Latin, erroneously from Latin *sittybus* parchment strip giving title and author, from Greek *sittuba*

Syllabus ('sɪləbəs) NOUN *RC Church* 1 Also called: **Syllabus of Errors.** a list of 80 doctrinal theses condemned as erroneous by Pius IX in 1864. 2 a list of 65 Modernist propositions condemned as erroneous by Pius X in 1907.

syllepsis (sɪ'lɛpsɪs) NOUN, *plural* **-ses** (-siːz). 1 (in grammar or rhetoric) the use of a single sentence construction in which a verb, adjective, etc. is made to cover two syntactical functions, as the verb form *have* in *she and they have promised to come.* 2 another word for **zeugma.**
▷HISTORY C16: from Late Latin, from Greek *sullēpsis,* from *sul-* SYN- + *lēpsis* a taking, from *lambanein* to take
▸**sylˈleptic** ADJECTIVE ▸**sylˈleptically** ADVERB

syllogism ('sɪləˌdʒɪzəm) NOUN 1 a deductive inference consisting of two premises and a conclusion, all of which are categorial propositions. The subject of the conclusion is the **minor term** and its predicate the **major term;** the **middle term** occurs in both premises but not the conclusion. There are 256 such arguments but only 24 are valid. *Some men are mortal; some men are angelic; so some mortals are angelic* is invalid, while *some temples are in ruins; all ruins are fascinating; so some temples are fascinating* is valid. Here *fascinating, in ruins,* and *temples* are respectively major, middle, and minor terms. 2 a deductive inference of certain other forms with two premises, such as the **hypothetical syllogism,** *if P then Q; if Q then R; so if P then R.* 3 a piece of deductive reasoning from the general to the particular. 4 a subtle or deceptive piece of reasoning.
▷HISTORY C14: via Latin from Greek *sullogismos,* from *sullogizesthai* to reckon together, from *sul-* SYN- + *logizesthai* to calculate, from *logos* a discourse

syllogistic (ˌsɪləˈdʒɪstɪk) ADJECTIVE *also* **syllogistical.** 1 of, relating to or consisting of syllogisms. ◆ NOUN (*often plural*) 2 the branch of logic concerned with syllogisms. 3 reasoning by means of syllogisms.
▸**ˌsylloˈgistically** ADVERB

syllogize *or* **syllogise** ('sɪləˌdʒaɪz) VERB to reason or infer by using syllogisms.
▷HISTORY C15: via Old French from Late Latin *syllogizāre,* from Greek *sullogizesthai;* see SYLLOGISM
▸**ˌsyllogiˈzation** *or* **ˌsyllogiˈsation** NOUN ▸**ˈsylloˌgizer** *or* **ˈsylloˌgiser** NOUN

sylph (sɪlf) NOUN 1 a slender graceful girl or young woman. 2 any of a class of imaginary beings assumed to inhabit the air.

▷HISTORY C17: from New Latin *sylphus,* probably coined from Latin *silva* wood + Greek *numphē* NYMPH
▸ **'sylph,like** *or (less commonly)* **'sylphic** *or* **'sylphish** *or* **'sylphy** ADJECTIVE

sylva *or* **silva** ('sɪlvə) NOUN, *plural* **-vas** *or* **-vae** (-viː). the trees growing in a particular region.
▷HISTORY C17: Latin *silva* a wood

sylvan *or* **silvan** ('sɪlvən) *Chiefly poetic* ◆ ADJECTIVE [1] of, characteristic of, or consisting of woods or forests. [2] living or located in woods or forests. [3] idyllically rural or rustic. ◆ NOUN [4] an inhabitant of the woods, esp a spirit.
▷HISTORY C16: from Latin *silvānus,* from *silva* forest

sylvanite ('sɪlvə,naɪt) NOUN a silver-white mineral consisting of a telluride of gold and silver in the form of elongated striated crystals: a source of gold in Australia and North America. Formula: $(Au,Ag)Te_2$.
▷HISTORY C18: from (TRAN)SYLVAN(IA) + -ITE[1], with reference to the region where it was first found

Sylvanus (sɪl'veɪnəs) NOUN a variant spelling of **Silvanus.**

sylvatic (sɪl'vætɪk) ADJECTIVE growing, living, or occurring in a wood or beneath a tree. Also: **sylvestral** (sɪl'vɛstrəl).

sylviculture ('sɪlvɪ,kʌltʃə) NOUN a variant spelling of **silviculture.**

sylvite ('sɪlvaɪt) *or* **sylvine** ('sɪlviːn) NOUN a soluble colourless, white, or coloured mineral consisting of potassium chloride in cubic crystalline form with sodium impurities: it occurs chiefly in sedimentary beds and is an important ore of potassium. Formula: KCl.
▷HISTORY C19: *sylvite,* alteration of *sylvine,* from New Latin *sal digestiva Sylvii* digestive salt of Sylvius, after Franciscus *Sylvius* (died 1672), German anatomist. See -ITE[1], -INE[2]

sym- PREFIX a variant of **syn-** before *b, p,* and *m.*

symbiont ('sɪmbɪ,ɒnt) NOUN an organism living in a state of symbiosis.
▷HISTORY C19: from Greek *sumbioun* to live together, from *bioun* to live
▸ **,symbi'ontic** ADJECTIVE ▸ **,symbi'ontically** ADVERB

symbiosis (,sɪmbɪ'əʊsɪs, ,sɪmbaɪ'əʊsɪs) NOUN [1] a close and usually obligatory association of two organisms of different species that live together, often to their mutual benefit. [2] a similar relationship between interdependent persons or groups.
▷HISTORY C19: via New Latin from Greek: a living together; see SYMBIONT
▸ **,symbi'otic** *or (less commonly)* **,symbi'otical** ADJECTIVE

symbol ('sɪmb^{ə}l) NOUN [1] something that represents or stands for something else, usually by convention or association, esp a material object used to represent something abstract. [2] an object, person, idea, etc., used in a literary work, film, etc., to stand for or suggest something else with which it is associated either explicitly or in some more subtle way. [3] a letter, figure, or sign used in mathematics, science, music, etc. to represent a quantity, phenomenon, operation, function, etc. [4] *Psychoanal* the end product, in the form of an object or act, of a conflict in the unconscious between repression processes and the actions and thoughts being repressed: *the symbols of dreams.* [5] *Psychol* any mental process that represents some feature of external reality. ◆ VERB **-bols, -bolling, -bolled** *or US* **-bols, -boling, -boled.** [6] *(tr)* another word for **symbolize.**
▷HISTORY C15: from Church Latin *symbolum,* from Greek *sumbolon* sign, from *sumballein* to throw together, from SYN- + *ballein* to throw

symbolic (sɪm'bɒlɪk) *or* **symbolical** ADJECTIVE [1] of or relating to a symbol or symbols. [2] serving as a symbol. [3] characterized by the use of symbols or symbolism.
▸ **sym'bolically** ADVERB ▸ **sym'bolicalness** NOUN

symbolical books PLURAL NOUN *Christianity* the books containing the creeds, beliefs, or doctrine of religious groups that have emerged since the Reformation.

symbolic logic NOUN another term for **formal logic.**

symbolism ('sɪmbə,lɪzəm) NOUN [1] the representation of something in symbolic form or the attribution of symbolic meaning or character to something. [2] a system of symbols or symbolic representation. [3] a symbolic significance or quality. [4] *(often capital)* a late 19th-century movement in art that sought to express mystical or abstract ideas through the symbolic use of images. See also **synthetism.** [5] *Theol* any symbolist interpretation of the Eucharist.

symbolist ('sɪmbəlɪst) NOUN [1] a person who uses or can interpret symbols, esp as a means to revealing aspects of truth and reality. [2] an artist or writer who practises symbolism in his work. [3] *(usually capital)* a writer associated with the symbolist movement. [4] *(often capital)* an artist associated with the movement of symbolism. [5] *Christian theol* a person who rejects any interpretation of the Eucharist that suggests that Christ is really present in it, and who maintains that the bread and wine are only symbols of his body and blood. ◆ ADJECTIVE [6] of, relating to, or characterizing symbolism or symbolists.
▸ **,symbol'istic** ADJECTIVE ▸ **,symbol'istically** ADVERB

symbolist movement NOUN *(usually capital)* a movement beginning in French and Belgian poetry towards the end of the 19th century with the verse of Mallarmé, Valéry, Verlaine, Rimbaud, Maeterlinck, and others, and seeking to express states of mind rather than objective reality by making use of the power of words and images to suggest as well as denote.

symbolize *or* **symbolise** ('sɪmbə,laɪz) VERB [1] *(tr)* to serve as or be a symbol of. [2] *(tr; usually foll by by)* to represent by a symbol or symbols. [3] *(intr)* to use symbols. [4] *(tr)* to treat or regard as symbolic or figurative.
▸ **,symboli'zation** *or* **,symboli'sation** NOUN

symbology (sɪm'bɒlədʒɪ) NOUN the use, study, or interpretation of symbols.
▸ **symbological** (,sɪmbə'lɒdʒɪk^{ə}l) ADJECTIVE
▸ **sym'bologist** NOUN

symbol retailer NOUN any member of a voluntary group of independent retailers, often using a common name or symbol, formed to obtain better prices from wholesalers or manufacturers in competition with supermarket chains. Also called: **voluntary retailer.**

symmetallism *or US* **symmetalism** (sɪ'mɛtə,lɪzəm) NOUN [1] the use of an alloy of two or more metals in fixed relative value as the standard of value and currency. [2] the economic policies and doctrine supporting a symmetallic standard.
▷HISTORY C19: from SYM- + *-metallism,* on the model of BIMETALLISM
▸ **,symme'tallic** ADJECTIVE

symmetric (sɪ'mɛtrɪk) ADJECTIVE [1] *Logic, maths* (of a relation) holding between a pair of arguments *x* and *y* when and only when it holds between *y* and *x,* as *... is a sibling of ...* but not *... is a brother of ....* Compare **asymmetric** (sense 5), **antisymmetric, nonsymmetric.** [2] another word for **symmetrical** (sense 5).

symmetrical (sɪ'mɛtrɪk^{ə}l) ADJECTIVE [1] possessing or displaying symmetry. Compare **asymmetric.** [2] *Maths* **a** (of two points) capable of being joined by a line that is bisected by a given point or bisected perpendicularly by a given line or plane: *the points (x, y) and (–x, –y) are symmetrical about the origin.* **b** (of a configuration) having pairs of points that are symmetrical about a given point, line, or plane: *a circle is symmetrical about a diameter.* **c** (of an equation or function of two or more variables) remaining unchanged in form after an interchange of two variables: $x + y = z$ *is a symmetrical equation.* [3] *Chem* (of a compound) having a molecular structure in which substituents are symmetrical about the molecule. [4] *Botany* another word for **isomerous.** [5] Also: **symmetric.** (of a disease, infection, etc.) affecting both sides of the body or corresponding parts, such as both legs.
▸ **sym'metrically** ADVERB ▸ **sym'metricalness** NOUN

symmetric matrix NOUN *Maths* a square matrix that is equal to its transpose, being symmetrical about its main diagonal. A **skew symmetric matrix** is equal to the negation of its transpose. Compare **orthogonal matrix.**

symmetrize *or* **symmetrise** ('sɪmɪ,traɪz) VERB *(tr)* to render symmetrical or perfectly balanced.
▸ **,symmetri'zation** *or* **,symmetri'sation** NOUN

symmetry ('sɪmɪtrɪ) NOUN, *plural* **-tries.** [1] similarity, correspondence, or balance among systems or parts of a system. [2] *Maths* an exact correspondence in position or form about a given point, line, or plane. See **symmetrical** (sense 2). [3] beauty or harmony of form based on a proportionate arrangement of parts. [4] *Physics* the independence of a property with respect to direction; isotropy.
▷HISTORY C16: from Latin *symmetria,* from Greek *summetria* proportion, from SYN- + *metron* measure

sympathectomy (,sɪmpə'θɛktəmɪ) NOUN, *plural* **-mies.** the surgical excision or chemical destruction (**chemical sympathectomy**) of one or more parts of the sympathetic nervous system.
▷HISTORY C20: from SYMPATHETIC + -ECTOMY

sympathetic (,sɪmpə'θɛtɪk) ADJECTIVE [1] characterized by, feeling, or showing sympathy; understanding. [2] in accord with the subject's personality or mood; congenial: *a sympathetic atmosphere.* [3] (when *postpositive,* often foll by *to* or *towards*) showing agreement (with) or favour (towards): *sympathetic to the proposals.* [4] *Anatomy, physiol* of or relating to the division of the autonomic nervous system that acts in opposition to the parasympathetic system by accelerating the heartbeat, dilating the bronchi, inhibiting the smooth muscles of the digestive tract, etc. Compare **parasympathetic.** [5] relating to vibrations occurring as a result of similar vibrations in a neighbouring body: *sympathetic strings on a sitar.*
▸ **,sympa'thetically** ADVERB

sympathetic ink NOUN another term for **invisible ink.**

sympathetic magic NOUN a type of magic in which it is sought to produce a large-scale effect, often at a distance, by performing some small-scale ceremony resembling it, such as the pouring of water on an altar to induce rainfall.

sympathin ('sɪmpəθɪn) NOUN a substance released at certain sympathetic nerve endings: thought to be identical with adrenaline.
▷HISTORY C20: from SYMPATH(ETIC) + -IN

sympathize *or* **sympathise** ('sɪmpə,θaɪz) VERB *(intr; often foll by with)* [1] to feel or express compassion or sympathy (for); commiserate: *he sympathized with my troubles.* [2] to share or understand the sentiments or ideas (of); be in sympathy (with).
▸ **'sympa,thizer** *or* **'sympa,thiser** NOUN

sympatholytic (,sɪmpəθəʊ'lɪtɪk) *Med* ◆ ADJECTIVE [1] **a** inhibiting or antagonistic to nerve impulses of the sympathetic nervous system. **b** of or relating to such inhibition. ◆ NOUN [2] a sympatholytic drug. Compare **sympathomimetic.**
▷HISTORY C20: from SYMPATH(ETIC) + -LYTIC

sympathomimetic (,sɪmpəθəʊmɪ'mɛtɪk) *Med* ◆ ADJECTIVE [1] causing a physiological effect similar to that produced by stimulation of the sympathetic nervous system. ◆ NOUN [2] a sympathomimetic drug. Compare **sympatholytic.**
▷HISTORY C20: from SYMPATH(ETIC) + MIMETIC

sympathy ('sɪmpəθɪ) NOUN, *plural* **-thies.** [1] the sharing of another's emotions, esp of sorrow or anguish; pity; compassion. [2] an affinity or harmony, usually of feelings or interests, between persons or things: *to be in sympathy with someone.* [3] mutual affection or understanding arising from such a relationship; congeniality. [4] the condition of a physical system or body when its behaviour is similar or corresponds to that of a different system that influences it, such as the vibration of sympathetic strings. [5] *(sometimes plural)* a feeling of loyalty, support, or accord, as for an idea, cause, etc. [6] *Physiol* the mutual relationship between two organs or parts whereby a change in one has an effect on the other.
▷HISTORY C16: from Latin *sympathīa,* from Greek *sumpatheia,* from *sumpathēs,* from SYN- + *pathos* suffering

sympathy strike NOUN a strike organized in support of another section of workers or a cause and not because of direct grievances. Also called: **sympathetic strike.**

sympatric (sɪm'pætrɪk) ADJECTIVE (of biological speciation or species) taking place or existing in the same or overlapping geographical areas. Compare **allopatric.**
▷HISTORY C20: from SYN- + *-patric,* from Greek *patra* native land, from *patēr* father

▸**sym'patrically** ADVERB

sympetalous (sɪm'pɛtələs) ADJECTIVE *Botany* another word for **gamopetalous.**

symphile ('sɪmfaɪl) NOUN an insect or other organism that lives in the nests of social insects, esp ants and termites, and is fed and reared by the inmates. Compare **synoekete.**
▹**HISTORY** C20: from Greek *sumphilein* to love mutually; see SYN-, -PHILE

symphonic poem NOUN *Music* an extended orchestral composition, originated by Liszt, based on nonmusical material, such as a work of literature or folk tale. Also called: **tone poem.**

symphonious (sɪm'fəʊnɪəs) ADJECTIVE *Literary* harmonious or concordant.
▸**sym'phoniously** ADVERB

symphonist ('sɪmfənɪst) NOUN a person who composes symphonies.

symphony ('sɪmfənɪ) NOUN, *plural* **-nies.** [1] an extended large-scale orchestral composition, usually with several movements, at least one of which is in sonata form. The classical form of the symphony was fixed by Haydn and Mozart, but the innovations of subsequent composers have freed it entirely from classical constraints. It continues to be a vehicle for serious, large-scale orchestral music. [2] a piece of instrumental music in up to three very short movements, used as an overture to or interlude in a baroque opera. [3] any purely orchestral movement in a vocal work, such as a cantata or oratorio. [4] short for **symphony orchestra.** [5] (in musical theory, esp of classical Greece) **a** another word for **consonance** (sense 3). Compare **diaphony** (sense 2). **b** the interval of unison. [6] anything distinguished by a harmonious composition: *the picture was a symphony of green.* [7] *Archaic* harmony in general; concord.
▹**HISTORY** C13: from Old French *symphonie,* from Latin *symphōnia* concord, concert, from Greek *sumphōnia,* from SYN- + *phōnē* sound
▸**symphonic** (sɪm'fɒnɪk) ADJECTIVE ▸**sym'phonically** ADVERB

symphony orchestra NOUN *Music* an orchestra capable of performing symphonies, esp the large orchestra comprising strings, brass, woodwind, harp and percussion.

symphysis ('sɪmfɪsɪs) NOUN, *plural* **-ses** (-ˌsiːz). [1] *Anatomy, botany* a growing together of parts or structures, such as two bony surfaces joined by an intermediate layer of fibrous cartilage. [2] a line marking this growing together. [3] *Pathol* an abnormal adhesion of two or more parts or structures.
▹**HISTORY** C16: via New Latin from Greek *sumphusis,* from *sumphuein,* from SYN- + *phuein* to grow
▸**symphysial** *or* **symphyseal** (sɪm'fɪzɪəl) ADJECTIVE
▸**symphystic** (sɪm'fɪstɪk) *or* **sym'phytic** ADJECTIVE

symplast ('sɪmplæst) NOUN *Botany* the continuous system of protoplasts, linked by plasmodesmata and bounded by the cell wall.
▸**sym'plastic** ADJECTIVE

sympodium (sɪm'pəʊdɪəm) NOUN, *plural* **-dia** (-dɪə). the main axis of growth in the grapevine and similar plants: a lateral branch that arises from just behind the apex of the main stem, which ceases to grow, and continues growing in the same direction as the main stem. Compare **monopodium.**
▹**HISTORY** C19: from New Latin, from SYN- + Greek *podion* a little foot, from *pous* foot
▸**sym'podial** ADJECTIVE ▸**sym'podially** ADVERB

symposiac (sɪm'pəʊzɪˌæk) ADJECTIVE [1] of, suitable for, or occurring at a symposium. ◆ NOUN [2] an archaic word for **symposium.**
▹**HISTORY** C17: from Latin *symposiacus;* see SYMPOSIUM

symposiarch (sɪm'pəʊzɪˌɑːk) NOUN [1] the president of a symposium, esp in classical Greece. [2] a rare word for **toastmaster.**
▹**HISTORY** C17: from Greek; see SYMPOSIUM, -ARCH

symposiast (sɪm'pəʊzɪˌæst) NOUN a person who takes part in a symposium.

symposium (sɪm'pəʊzɪəm) NOUN, *plural* **-siums** *or* **-sia** (-zɪə). [1] a conference or meeting for the discussion of some subject, esp an academic topic or social problem. [2] a collection of scholarly contributions, usually published together, on a given subject. [3] (in classical Greece) a drinking party with intellectual conversation, music, etc.
▹**HISTORY** C16: via Latin from Greek *sumposion,* from *sumpinein* to drink together, from *sum-* SYN- + *pinein* to drink

symptom ('sɪmptəm) NOUN [1] *Med* any sensation or change in bodily function experienced by a patient that is associated with a particular disease. Compare **sign** (sense 9). [2] any phenomenon or circumstance accompanying something and regarded as evidence of its existence; indication.
▹**HISTORY** C16: from Late Latin *symptōma,* from Greek *sumptōma* chance, from *sumpiptein* to occur, from SYN- + *piptein* to fall
▸**'symptomless** ADJECTIVE

symptomatic (ˌsɪmptə'mætɪk) ADJECTIVE [1] (often foll by *of*) being a symptom; indicative: *symptomatic of insanity.* [2] of or relating to a symptom or symptoms. [3] according to symptoms: *a symptomatic analysis of a case.*
▸**ˌsympto'matically** ADVERB

symptomatology (ˌsɪmptəmə'tɒlədʒɪ) *or* **symptomology** NOUN the branch of medicine concerned with the study and classification of the symptoms of disease.

syn (saɪn, sɪn) ADVERB, PREPOSITION, CONJUNCTION a variant of **syne**[1].

syn. ABBREVIATION FOR synonym(ous).

syn- PREFIX [1] with or together: *synecology.* [2] fusion: *syngamy.*
▹**HISTORY** from Greek *sun* together, with

synaeresis (sɪ'nɪərɪsɪs) NOUN a variant spelling of **syneresis.**

synaesthesia *or US* **synesthesia** (ˌsɪniːs'θiːzɪə) NOUN [1] *Physiol* a sensation experienced in a part of the body other than the part stimulated. [2] *Psychol* the subjective sensation of a sense other than the one being stimulated. For example, a sound may evoke sensations of colour.
▹**HISTORY** from New Latin, from SYN- + *-esthesia,* from Greek *aisthēsis* sensation
▸**synaesthetic** *or US* **synesthetic** (ˌsɪniːs'θɛtɪk) ADJECTIVE

synagogue ('sɪnəˌgɒg) NOUN [1] **a** a building for Jewish religious services and usually also for religious instruction. **b** (*as modifier*): *synagogue services.* [2] a congregation of Jews who assemble for worship or religious study. [3] the religion of Judaism as organized in such congregations.
▹**HISTORY** C12: from Old French *sinagogue,* from Late Latin *synagōga,* from Greek *sunagōgē* a gathering, from *sunagein* to bring together, from SYN- + *agein* to lead
▸**synagogical** (ˌsɪnə'gɒdʒɪkᵊl) *or* **synagogal** ('sɪnəˌgɒgᵊl) ADJECTIVE

synalepha *or* **synaloepha** (ˌsɪnə'liːfə) NOUN *Linguistics* vowel elision, esp as it arises when one word ends in a vowel and the following word begins with one.
▹**HISTORY** C16: from Late Latin *synaloepha,* from Greek *sunaliphē,* from SYN- + *aleiphein* to melt, smear

synapse ('saɪnæps) NOUN the point at which a nerve impulse is relayed from the terminal portion of an axon to the dendrites of an adjacent neuron.

synapsis (sɪ'næpsɪs) NOUN, *plural* **-ses** (-siːz). [1] *Cytology* the association in pairs of homologous chromosomes at the start of meiosis. [2] another word for **synapse.**
▹**HISTORY** C19: from New Latin, from Greek *sunapsis* junction, from *sunaptein* to join together, from SYN- + *haptein* to connect

synaptic (sɪ'næptɪk) *or* **synaptical** ADJECTIVE of or relating to a synapse.
▸**syn'aptically** ADVERB

synarchy ('sɪnəkɪ) NOUN, *plural* **-chies.** joint rule.
▹**HISTORY** C18: from Greek *sunarchia,* from *sunarchein* to rule jointly

synarthrosis (ˌsɪnɑː'θrəʊsɪs) NOUN, *plural* **-ses** (-siːz). *Anatomy* any of various joints which lack a synovial cavity and are virtually immovable; a fixed joint.
▹**HISTORY** via New Latin from Greek *sunarthrōsis,* from *sunarthrousthai* to be connected by joints, from *sun-* SYN- + *arthron* a joint
▸**ˌsynar'throdial** ADJECTIVE ▸**ˌsynar'throdially** ADVERB

sync *or* **synch** (sɪŋk) *Films, television, computing* ◆ VERB [1] an informal word for **synchronize.** ◆ NOUN [2] an informal word for **synchronization** (esp in the phrases **in** *or* **out of sync**).

syncarp ('sɪnkɑːp) NOUN *Botany* a fleshy multiple fruit, formed from two or more carpels of one flower or the aggregated fruits of several flowers.
▹**HISTORY** C19: from New Latin *syncarpium,* from SYN- + Greek *karpos* fruit

syncarpous (sɪn'kɑːpəs) ADJECTIVE [1] (of the ovaries of certain flowering plants) consisting of united carpels. Compare **apocarpous.** [2] of or relating to a syncarp.
▸**syncarpy** ('sɪnkɑːpɪ) NOUN

syncategorematic (sɪnˌkætəˌgɔːrə'mætɪk) ADJECTIVE *Philosophy* applying to expressions that are not in any of Aristotle's categories, but form meaningful expressions together with them, such as conjunctions and adverbs.

synchro ('sɪŋkrəʊ) NOUN, *plural* **-chros.** [1] any of a number of electrical devices in which the angular position of a rotating part is transformed into a voltage, or vice versa. Also called: **selsyn.** [2] short for **synchronized swimming.**

synchro- COMBINING FORM indicating synchronization: *synchroflash.*

synchrocyclotron (ˌsɪŋkrəʊ'saɪkləˌtrɒn) NOUN a type of cyclotron in which the frequency of the electric field is modulated to allow for relativistic effects at high velocities and thus produce higher energies.

synchroflash ('sɪŋkrəʊˌflæʃ) NOUN a mechanism in a camera that enables the shutter to be fully open while the light from a flashbulb or electronic flash is at its brightest.

synchromesh ('sɪŋkrəʊˌmɛʃ) ADJECTIVE [1] (of a gearbox, etc.) having a system of clutches that synchronizes the speeds of the driving and driven members before engagement to avoid shock in gear changing and to reduce noise and wear. ◆ NOUN [2] a gear system having these features.
▹**HISTORY** C20: shortened from *synchronized mesh*

synchronic (sɪn'krɒnɪk) ADJECTIVE [1] concerned with the events or phenomena at a particular period without considering historical antecedents: *synchronic linguistics.* Compare **diachronic.** [2] synchronous.
▸**syn'chronically** ADVERB

synchronicity (ˌsɪnkrə'nɪsɪtɪ) NOUN an apparently meaningful coincidence in time of two or more similar or identical events that are causally unrelated.
▹**HISTORY** C20: coined by Carl Jung from SYNCHRONIC + -ITY

synchronism ('sɪŋkrəˌnɪzəm) NOUN [1] the quality or condition of being synchronous. [2] a chronological usually tabular list of historical persons and events, arranged to show parallel or synchronous occurrence. [3] the representation in a work of art of one or more incidents that occurred at separate times.
▹**HISTORY** C16: from Greek *sunkhronismos;* see SYNCHRONOUS, -ISM

synchronistic (ˌsɪŋkrə'nɪstɪk) ADJECTIVE of, relating to, or exhibiting synchronism.
▸**ˌsynchro'nistically** ADVERB

synchronize *or* **synchronise** ('sɪŋkrəˌnaɪz) VERB [1] (when *intr,* usually foll by *with*) to occur or recur or cause to occur or recur at the same time or in unison. [2] to indicate or cause to indicate the same time: *synchronize your watches.* [3] (*tr*) *Films* to establish (the picture and soundtrack records) in their correct relative position. [4] (*tr*) to designate (events) as simultaneous.
▸**ˌsynchroni'zation** *or* **ˌsynchroni'sation** NOUN
▸**'synchroˌnizer** *or* **'synchroˌniser** NOUN

synchronized swimming NOUN the art or sport of one or more swimmers moving in patterns in the water in time to music. Sometimes shortened to: **synchro** *or* **synchro swimming.**

synchronous ('sɪŋkrənəs) ADJECTIVE [1] occurring at the same time; contemporaneous. [2] *Physics* (of periodic phenomena, such as voltages) having the same frequency and phase. [3] occurring or recurring exactly together and at the same rate: *the synchronous flapping of a bird's wings.*
▹**HISTORY** C17: from Late Latin *synchronus,* from Greek *sunkhronos,* from SYN- + *khronos* time
▸**'synchronously** ADVERB ▸**'synchronousness** NOUN

synchronous converter NOUN a synchronous machine that converts alternating current to direct current, or vice versa.

synchronous machine NOUN an electrical machine, whose rotating speed is proportional to the frequency of the alternating-current supply and independent of the load.

synchronous motor NOUN an alternating-current motor that runs at a speed that is equal to or is a multiple of the frequency of the supply.

synchronous orbit NOUN *Astronautics* an orbit in which the orbital period of a satellite is identical to the spin period of the central body.

synchrony ('sɪŋkrənɪ) NOUN the state of being synchronous; simultaneity.

synchroscope ('sɪŋkrəˌskəʊp) *or* **synchronoscope** (sɪŋ'krɒnəˌskəʊp) NOUN an instrument used to indicate whether two periodic quantities or motions are synchronous.

synchrotron ('sɪŋkrəˌtrɒn) NOUN a type of particle accelerator similar to a betatron but having an electric field of fixed frequency with electrons but not with protons as well as a changing magnetic field. It is capable of producing very high energies in the GeV range.
▷HISTORY C20: from SYNCHRO- + (ELEC)TRON

synchrotron radiation NOUN electromagnetic radiation emitted in narrow beams tangential to the orbit of very high energy charged particles, such as electrons, spiralling along the lines of force in a strong magnetic field. It occurs in synchrotron accelerators and in many cosmic environments, such as radio galaxies and supernova remnants.

synclastic (sɪŋ'klæstɪk) ADJECTIVE *Maths* (of a surface) having a curvature at a given point and in a particular direction that is of the same sign as the curvature at that point in perpendicular direction. Compare **anticlastic.**
▷HISTORY C19: from SYN- (alike) + Greek *klastos* bent, from *klan* to bend

syncline ('sɪŋklaɪn) NOUN a downward fold of stratified rock in which the strata slope towards a vertical axis. Compare **anticline.**
▷HISTORY C19: from SYN- + Greek *klīnein* to lean
▸**syn'clinal** ADJECTIVE

synclinorium (ˌsɪŋklɪ'nɔːrɪəm) NOUN, *plural* **-ria** (-rɪə). a vast elongated syncline with its strata further folded into anticlines and synclines.
▷HISTORY C19: New Latin, from SYNCLINE + *-orium,* suffix indicating a place

Syncom ('sɪnˌkɒm) NOUN a communications satellite in stationary orbit.
▷HISTORY C20: from *syn(chronous) com(munication)*

syncopate ('sɪŋkəˌpeɪt) VERB (*tr*) [1] *Music* to modify or treat (a beat, rhythm, note, etc.) by syncopation. [2] to shorten (a word) by omitting sounds or letters from the middle.
▷HISTORY C17: from Medieval Latin *syncopāre* to omit a letter or syllable, from Late Latin *syncopa* SYNCOPE
▸**'syncoˌpator** NOUN

syncopation (ˌsɪŋkə'peɪʃən) NOUN [1] *Music* **a** the displacement of the usual rhythmic accent away from a strong beat onto a weak beat. **b** a note, beat, rhythm, etc., produced by syncopation. [2] another word for **syncope** (sense 2).

syncope ('sɪŋkəpɪ) NOUN [1] *Pathol* a technical word for a **faint.** [2] the omission of one or more sounds or letters from the middle of a word.
▷HISTORY C16: from Late Latin *syncopa,* from Greek *sunkopē* a cutting off, from SYN- + *koptein* to cut
▸**syncopic** (sɪŋ'kɒpɪk) *or* **'syncopal** ADJECTIVE

syncretism ('sɪŋkrɪˌtɪzəm) NOUN [1] the tendency to syncretize. [2] the historical tendency of languages to reduce their use of inflection, as in the development of Old English with all its case endings into Modern English.
▷HISTORY C17: from New Latin *syncrētismus,* from Greek *sunkrētismos* alliance of Cretans, from *sunkrētizein* to join forces (in the manner of the Cretan towns), from SYN- + *Krēs* a Cretan
▸**syncretic** (sɪŋ'kretɪk) *or* **ˌsyncre'tistic** ADJECTIVE
▸**'syncretist** NOUN

syncretize *or* **syncretise** ('sɪŋkrɪˌtaɪz) VERB to combine or attempt to combine the characteristic teachings, beliefs, or practices of (differing systems of religion or philosophy).
▸**ˌsyncreti'zation** *or* **ˌsyncreti'sation** NOUN

syncytium (sɪn'sɪtɪəm) NOUN, *plural* **-cytia** (-'sɪtɪə). *Zoology* a mass of cytoplasm containing many nuclei and enclosed in a cell membrane.
▷HISTORY C19: New Latin; see SYN-, CYTO-, -IUM
▸**syn'cytial** ADJECTIVE

synd (saɪnd) VERB, NOUN *Scot* a variant of **syne**[2].

syndactyl (sɪn'dæktɪl) ADJECTIVE [1] (of certain animals) having two or more digits growing fused together. ◆ NOUN [2] an animal with this arrangement of digits.
▸**syn'dactylism** NOUN

syndesis (sɪn'diːsɪs) NOUN *Grammar* [1] the use of syndetic constructions. [2] another name for **polysyndeton** (sense 2).
▷HISTORY C20: from Greek, from *sundein* to bind together, from SYN- + *dein* to bind

syndesmosis (ˌsɪndɛs'məʊsɪs) NOUN, *plural* **-ses** (-siːz). *Anatomy* a type of joint in which the articulating bones are held together by a ligament of connective tissue.
▷HISTORY New Latin, from Greek *sundein* to bind together; see SYNDESIS
▸**syndesmotic** (ˌsɪndɛs'mɒtɪk) ADJECTIVE

syndetic (sɪn'dɛtɪk) ADJECTIVE denoting a grammatical construction in which two clauses are connected by a conjunction. Compare **asyndetic** (sense 2).
▷HISTORY C17: from Greek *sundetikos,* from *sundetos* bound together; see SYNDESIS
▸**syn'detically** ADVERB

syndeton (sɪn'diːt^{ə}n) NOUN *Grammar* a syndetic construction. Compare **asyndeton** (sense 2).
▷HISTORY C20: from Greek *sundeton* a bond, from *sundein* to bind together; see SYNDESIS

syndic ('sɪndɪk) NOUN [1] *Brit* a business agent of some universities or other bodies. [2] (in several countries) a government administrator or magistrate with varying powers.
▷HISTORY C17: via Old French from Late Latin *syndicus,* from Greek *sundikos* defendant's advocate, from SYN- + *dikē* justice
▸**'syndicˌship** NOUN ▸**'syndical** ADJECTIVE

syndicalism ('sɪndɪkəˌlɪzəm) NOUN [1] a revolutionary movement and theory advocating the seizure of the means of production and distribution by syndicates of workers through direct action, esp a general strike. [2] an economic system resulting from such action.
▸**'syndical** ADJECTIVE ▸**'syndicalist** ADJECTIVE, NOUN
▸**ˌsyndical'istic** ADJECTIVE

syndicate NOUN ('sɪndɪkɪt) [1] an association of business enterprises or individuals organized to undertake a joint project requiring considerable capital. [2] a news agency that sells articles, photographs, etc., to a number of newspapers for simultaneous publication. [3] any association formed to carry out an enterprise or enterprises of common interest to its members. [4] a board of syndics or the office of syndic. [5] (in Italy under the Fascists) a local organization of employers or employees. ◆ VERB ('sɪndɪˌkeɪt) [6] (*tr*) to sell (articles, photographs, etc.) to several newspapers for simultaneous publication. [7] (*tr*) *US* to sell (a programme or programmes) to several local commercial television or radio stations. [8] to form a syndicate of (people).
▷HISTORY C17: from Old French *syndicat* office of a SYNDIC
▸**ˌsyndi'cation** NOUN

syndiotactic (ˌsɪndɪəʊ'tæktɪk) ADJECTIVE *Chem* (of a stereospecific polymer) having alternating stereochemical configurations of the groups on successive carbon atoms in the chain. Compare **isotactic.**
▷HISTORY C20: from *syndyo,* from Greek *sunduo* two together + -TACTIC

syndrome ('sɪndrəʊm) NOUN [1] *Med* any combination of signs and symptoms that are indicative of a particular disease or disorder. [2] a symptom, characteristic, or set of symptoms or characteristics indicating the existence of a condition, problem, etc.
▷HISTORY C16: via New Latin from Greek *sundromē,* literally: a running together, from SYN- + *dramein* to run
▸**syndromic** (sɪn'drɒmɪk) ADJECTIVE

syne[1] *or* **syn** (saɪn) ADVERB, PREPOSITION, CONJUNCTION a Scot word for **since.**
▷HISTORY C14: probably related to Old English *sīth* since

syne[2] (saɪn) *or* **synd** *Scot* ◆ VERB [1] (*tr*) to rinse; wash out. ◆ NOUN [2] a rinse.
▷HISTORY C14: of uncertain origin

synecdoche (sɪn'ɛkdəkɪ) NOUN a figure of speech in which a part is substituted for a whole or a whole for a part, as in *50 head of cattle* for *50 cows,* or *the army* for *a soldier.*
▷HISTORY C14: via Latin from Greek *sunekdokhē,* from SYN- + *ekdokhē* interpretation, from *dekhesthai* to accept
▸**synecdochic** (ˌsɪnɛk'dɒkɪk) *or* **ˌsynec'dochical** ADJECTIVE ▸**ˌsynec'dochically** ADVERB

synecious (sɪ'niːʃəs) ADJECTIVE a variant spelling of **synoecious.**

synecology (ˌsɪnɪ'kɒlədʒɪ) NOUN the ecological study of communities of plants and animals. Compare **autecology.**
▸**synecologic** (sɪnˌɛkə'lɒdʒɪk) *or* **synˌeco'logical** ADJECTIVE ▸**synˌeco'logically** ADVERB

synectics (sɪ'nɛktɪks) NOUN (*functioning as singular*) a method of identifying and solving problems that depends on creative thinking, the use of analogy, and informal conversation among a small group of individuals with diverse experience and expertise.
▷HISTORY C20: from SYN- + ECTO- + -ICS, in the sense: working together from outside

syneresis *or* **synaeresis** (sɪ'nɪərɪsɪs) NOUN [1] *Chem* the process in which a gel contracts on standing and exudes liquid, as in the separation of whey in cheese-making. [2] the contraction of two vowels into a diphthong. [3] another word for **synizesis.**
▷HISTORY C16: via Late Latin from Greek *sunairesis* a shortening, from *sunairein* to draw together, from SYN- + *hairein* to take

synergetic (ˌsɪnə'dʒɛtɪk) *or* **synergistic** ADJECTIVE another word for **synergistic.**
▷HISTORY C17: from Greek *sunergētikos,* from SYN- + *-ergētikos,* from *ergon* work; see ENERGY

synergism ('sɪnəˌdʒɪzəm, sɪ'nɜː-) NOUN [1] Also called: **synergy.** the working together of two or more drugs, muscles, etc., to produce an effect greater than the sum of their individual effects. [2] another name for **synergy** (sense 1). [3] *Christian theol* the doctrine or belief that the human will cooperates with the Holy Spirit and with divine grace, esp in the act of conversion or regeneration.
▷HISTORY C18: from New Latin *synergismus,* from Greek *sunergos,* from SYN- + *ergon* work

synergist ('sɪnədʒɪst, sɪ'nɜː-) NOUN [1] a drug, muscle, etc., that increases the action of another. [2] *Christian theol* an upholder of synergism. ◆ ADJECTIVE [3] of or relating to synergism.

synergistic (ˌsɪnə'dʒɪstɪk) *or* **synergetic** (ˌsɪnə'dʒɛtɪk) ADJECTIVE [1] acting together. [2] (of people, groups, or companies) working together in a creative, innovative, and productive manner.
▷HISTORY C17: from Greek *sunergētikos,* from SYN- + *-ergētikos,* from *ergon* work; see ENERGY
▸**ˌsyner'gistically** *or* **ˌsyner'getically** ADVERB

synergy ('sɪnədʒɪ) NOUN, *plural* **-gies.** [1] Also called: **synergism.** the potential ability of individual organizations or groups to be more successful or productive as a result of a merger. [2] another name for **synergism** (sense 1).
▷HISTORY C19: from New Latin *synergia,* from Greek *sunergos;* see SYNERGISM
▸**synergic** (sɪ'nɜːdʒɪk) ADJECTIVE

synesis ('sɪnɪsɪs) NOUN a grammatical construction in which the inflection or form of a word is conditioned by the meaning rather than the syntax, as for example the plural form *have* with the singular noun *group* in the sentence *the group have already assembled.*
▷HISTORY via New Latin from Greek *sunesis* union, from *sunienai* to bring together, from SYN- + *hienai* to send

synesthesia (ˌsɪniːs'θiːzɪə) NOUN the usual US spelling of **synaesthesia.**
▸**synesthetic** (ˌsɪniːs'θɛtɪk) ADJECTIVE

syngamy ('sɪŋgəmɪ) *or* **syngenesis** (sɪn'dʒɛnɪsɪs) NOUN other names for **sexual reproduction.**

▸**syngamic** (sɪŋˈgæmɪk) *or* **syngamous** (ˈsɪŋgəməs) ADJECTIVE

synizesis (ˌsɪnɪˈziːsɪs) NOUN 1 *Phonetics* the contraction of two vowels originally belonging to separate syllables into a single syllable, without diphthongization. Compare **syneresis.** 2 *Cytology* the contraction of chromatin towards one side of the nucleus during the prophase of meiosis.
▷HISTORY C19: via Late Latin from Greek *sunizēsis* a collapse, from *sunizanein* to sink down, from SYN- + *hizein* to sit

synkaryon (sɪnˈkærɪˌɒn) NOUN *Biology* the nucleus of a fertilized egg.
▷HISTORY C20: New Latin, from SYN- + Greek *karuon* a nut
▸**synˌkaryˈonic** ADJECTIVE

synod (ˈsɪnəd, ˈsɪnɒd) NOUN a local or special ecclesiastical council, esp of a diocese, formally convened to discuss ecclesiastical affairs.
▷HISTORY C14: from Late Latin *synodus,* from Greek *sunodos,* from SYN- + *hodos* a way
▸ˈ**synodal** *or (less commonly)* **synˈodical** ADJECTIVE

synodic (sɪˈnɒdɪk) ADJECTIVE relating to or involving a conjunction or two successive conjunctions of the same star, planet, or satellite: *the synodic month.*

synodic month NOUN See **month** (sense 6).

Synod of Whitby NOUN the synod held in 664 at Whitby at which the Roman date for Easter was accepted and the Church in England became aligned with Rome.

synoecious, synecious (sɪˈniːʃəs), *or* **synoicous** (sɪˈnɔɪkəs) ADJECTIVE (of a bryophyte) having male and female organs together on a branch, usually mixed at the tip.
▷HISTORY C19: SYN- + *-oecious,* from Greek *oikion* diminutive of *oikos* house

synoekete (sɪˈniːkiːt) *or* **synoecete** (sɪˈniːsiːt) NOUN an insect that lives in the nests of social insects, esp ants, without receiving any attentions from the inmates. Compare **symphile.**
▷HISTORY C20: from Greek *sunoiketēs* house-fellow, from *sunoikia* community

synonym (ˈsɪnənɪm) NOUN 1 a word that means the same or nearly the same as another word, such as *bucket* and *pail.* 2 a word or phrase used as another name for something, such as *Hellene* for a *Greek.* 3 *Biology* a taxonomic name that has been superseded or rejected.
▷HISTORY C16: via Late Latin from Greek *sunōnumon,* from SYN- + *onoma* name
▸ˌ**synoˈnymic** *or* ˌ**synoˈnymical** ADJECTIVE ▸ˌ**synoˈnymity** NOUN

synonymize *or* **synonymise** (sɪˈnɒnɪˌmaɪz) VERB *(tr)* to analyse the synonyms of or provide with synonyms.

synonymous (sɪˈnɒnɪməs) ADJECTIVE 1 (often foll by *with*) being a synonym (of). 2 *(postpositive;* foll by *with*) closely associated (with) or suggestive (of): *his name was synonymous with greed.*
▸**synˈonymously** ADVERB ▸**synˈonymousness** NOUN

synonymy (sɪˈnɒnɪmɪ) NOUN, *plural* **-mies.** 1 the study of synonyms. 2 the character of being synonymous; equivalence. 3 a list or collection of synonyms, esp one in which their meanings are discriminated. 4 *Biology* a collection of the synonyms of a species or group.

synop. ABBREVIATION FOR synopsis.

synopsis (sɪˈnɒpsɪs) NOUN, *plural* **-ses** (-siːz). a condensation or brief review of a subject; summary.
▷HISTORY C17: via Late Latin from Greek *sunopsis,* from SYN- + *opsis* view

synopsize *or* **synopsise** (sɪˈnɒpsaɪz) VERB *(tr)* 1 to make a synopsis of. 2 *US* variants of **epitomize.**

synoptic (sɪˈnɒptɪk) ADJECTIVE 1 of or relating to a synopsis. 2 *(often capital) Bible* **a** (of the Gospels of Matthew, Mark, and Luke) presenting the narrative of Christ's life, ministry, etc. from a point of view held in common by all three, and with close similarities in content, order, etc. **b** of, relating to, or characterizing these three Gospels. 3 *Meteorol* showing or concerned with the distribution of meteorological conditions over a wide area at a given time: *a synoptic chart.* ◆ NOUN 4 *(often capital) Bible* **a** any of the three synoptic Gospels. **b** any of the authors of these three Gospels.
▷HISTORY C18: from Greek *sunoptikos,* from SYNOPSIS
▸**synˈoptically** ADVERB ▸**synˈoptist** NOUN

synovia (saɪˈnəʊvɪə, sɪ-) NOUN a transparent viscid lubricating fluid, secreted by the membrane lining joints, tendon sheaths, etc.
▷HISTORY C17: from New Latin, probably from SYN- + Latin *ōvum* egg

synovial (saɪˈnəʊvɪəl, sɪ-) ADJECTIVE of or relating to the synovia; (of a joint) surrounded by a synovia-secreting membrane.
▸**synˈovially** ADVERB

synovitis (ˌsaɪnəʊˈvaɪtɪs, ˌsɪn-) NOUN inflammation of the membrane surrounding a joint.
▸**synovitic** (ˌsaɪnəʊˈvɪtɪk, ˌsɪn-) ADJECTIVE

synroc (ˈsɪnˌrɒk) NOUN a titanium-ceramic substance that can incorporate nuclear waste in its crystals.
▷HISTORY from *syn(thetic)* + *roc(k)*

synsepalous (sɪnˈsɛpələs) ADJECTIVE another word for **gamosepalous.**

syntactic (sɪnˈtæktɪk) ADJECTIVE 1 Also: **syntactical.** relating to or determined by syntax. 2 *Logic, linguistics* describable wholly with respect to the grammatical structure of an expression or the rules of well-formedness of a formal system.
▸**synˈtactically** ADVERB

syntactics (sɪnˈtæktɪks) NOUN *(functioning as singular)* the branch of semiotics that deals with the formal properties of symbol systems; proof theory.

syntagma (sɪnˈtægmə) *or* **syntagm** (ˈsɪnˌtæm) NOUN, *plural* **-tagmata** (-ˈtægmətə) *or* **-tagms.** 1 a syntactic unit or a word or phrase forming a syntactic unit. 2 a systematic collection of statements or propositions.
▷HISTORY C17: from Late Latin, from Greek, from *suntassein* to put in order; see SYNTAX

syntagmatic (ˌsɪntægˈmætɪk) ADJECTIVE 1 of or denoting a syntagma. 2 Also: **syntagmic** (sɪnˈtægmɪk). *Linguistics* denoting or concerning the relationship between a word and other members of a syntactic unit containing it.

syntax (ˈsɪntæks) NOUN 1 the branch of linguistics that deals with the grammatical arrangement of words and morphemes in the sentences of a language or of languages in general. 2 the totality of facts about the grammatical arrangement of words in a language. 3 a systematic statement of the rules governing the grammatical arrangement of words and morphemes in a language. 4 *Logic* a systematic statement of the rules governing the properly formed formulas of a logical system. 5 any orderly arrangement or system.
▷HISTORY C17: from Late Latin *syntaxis,* from Greek *suntaxis,* from *suntassein* to put in order, from SYN- + *tassein* to arrange

synth (sɪnθ) NOUN short for **synthesizer.**

synthesis (ˈsɪnθɪsɪs) NOUN, *plural* **-ses** (-ˌsiːz). 1 the process of combining objects or ideas into a complex whole. Compare **analysis.** 2 the combination or whole produced by such a process. 3 the process of producing a compound by a chemical reaction or series of reactions, usually from simpler or commonly available starting materials. 4 *Linguistics* the use of inflections rather than word order and function words to express the syntactic relations in a language. Compare **analysis** (sense 5). 5 *Philosophy, archaic* synthetic reasoning. 6 *Philosophy* **a** (in the writings of Kant) the unification of one concept with another not contained in it. Compare **analysis** (sense 7). **b** the final stage in the Hegelian dialectic, that resolves the contradiction between thesis and antithesis.
▷HISTORY C17: via Latin from Greek *sunthesis,* from *suntithenai* to put together, from SYN- + *tithenai* to place
▸ˈ**synthesist** NOUN

synthesis gas NOUN *Chem* 1 a mixture of carbon dioxide, carbon monoxide, and hydrogen formerly made by using water gas and reacting it with steam to enrich the proportion of hydrogen for use in the synthesis of ammonia. 2 a similar mixture of gases made by steam reforming natural gas, used for synthesizing organic chemicals and as a fuel.

synthesize (ˈsɪnθɪˌsaɪz), **synthetize, synthesise,** *or* **synthetise** VERB 1 to combine or cause to combine into a whole. 2 *(tr)* to produce by synthesis.
▸ˌ**synthesiˈzation** *or* ˌ**synthetiˈzation** *or* ˌ**synthesiˈsation** *or* ˌ**synthetiˈsation** NOUN

synthesizer (ˈsɪnθɪˌsaɪzə) NOUN 1 an electrophonic instrument, usually operated by means of a keyboard and pedals, in which sounds are produced by voltage-controlled oscillators, filters, and amplifiers, with an envelope generator module that controls attack, decay, sustain, and release. 2 a person or thing that synthesizes.

synthespian (ˌsɪnˈθɛspɪən) NOUN a computer-generated image of a film actor, esp used in place of the real actor when shooting special effects or stunts.
▷HISTORY C20: from SYN(THETIC) + THESPIAN

synthetic (sɪnˈθɛtɪk) ADJECTIVE *also* **synthetical.** 1 (of a substance or material) made artificially by chemical reaction. 2 not genuine; insincere: *synthetic compassion.* 3 denoting languages, such as Latin, whose morphology is characterized by synthesis. Compare **polysynthetic, agglutinative** (sense 2), **analytic** (sense 3). 4 *Philosophy* **a** (of a proposition) having a truth-value that is not determined solely by virtue of the meanings of the words, as in *all men are arrogant.* **b** contingent. Compare **a posteriori, empirical.** ◆ NOUN 5 a synthetic substance or material.
▷HISTORY C17: from New Latin *syntheticus,* from Greek *sunthetikos* expert in putting together, from *suntithenai* to put together; see SYNTHESIS
▸**synˈthetically** ADVERB

synthetic resin NOUN See **resin** (sense 2).

synthetic rubber NOUN any of various synthetic materials, similar to natural rubber, made by polymerizing unsaturated hydrocarbons, such as isoprene and butadiene.

synthetism (ˈsɪnθɪˌtɪzəm) NOUN *(often capital)* the symbolism of Paul Gauguin, the French postimpressionist painter (1848–1903) and the Nabis, a group of French painters much influenced by him, who reacted against the impressionists and realists by seeking to produce brightly coloured abstractions of their inner experience.
▷HISTORY C19: from Greek *sunthetos* composite; see SYNTHETIC
▸ˈ**synthetist** NOUN

synth-pop NOUN a type of pop music in which synthesizers are used to create the dominant sound.

syntonic (sɪnˈtɒnɪk) ADJECTIVE *Psychol* emotionally in harmony with one's environment.
▷HISTORY C20: from Greek *suntonos* in harmony with; see SYN-, TONE
▸**synˈtonically** ADVERB

Syon House (ˈsaɪən) NOUN a mansion near Brentford in London: originally a monastery, rebuilt in the 16th century, altered by Inigo Jones in the 17th century, and by Robert Adam in the 18th century; seat of the Dukes of Northumberland; gardens laid out by Capability Brown.

sypher (ˈsaɪfə) VERB *(tr)* to lap (a chamfered edge of one plank over that of another) in order to form a flush surface.
▷HISTORY C19: variant of CIPHER
▸ˈ**syphering** NOUN

syphilis (ˈsɪfɪlɪs) NOUN a venereal disease caused by infection with the microorganism *Treponema pallidum:* characterized by an ulcerating chancre, usually on the genitals and progressing through the lymphatic system to nearly all tissues of the body, producing serious clinical manifestations.
▷HISTORY C18: from New Latin *Syphilis (sive Morbus Gallicus)* "Syphilis (or the French disease)", title of a poem (1530) by G. Fracastoro, Italian physician and poet, in which a shepherd *Syphilus* is portrayed as the first victim of the disease
▸**syphilitic** (ˌsɪfɪˈlɪtɪk) ADJECTIVE ▸ˌ**syphiˈlitically** ADVERB ▸ˈ**syphiˌloid** ADJECTIVE

syphilology (ˌsɪfɪˈlɒlədʒɪ) NOUN the branch of medicine concerned with the study and treatment of syphilis.
▸ˌ**syphiˈlologist** NOUN

syphiloma (ˌsɪfɪˈləʊmə) NOUN, *plural* **-mas** *or* **-mata** (-mətə). *Pathol* a tumour or gumma caused by infection with syphilis.
▷HISTORY C19: from SYPHILIS + *-oma,* as in *sarcoma*

syphon ('saɪfᵊn) NOUN a variant spelling of **siphon.**

SYR INTERNATIONAL CAR REGISTRATION FOR Syria.

Syr. ABBREVIATION FOR: 1 Syria. 2 Syriac. 3 Syrian.

Syracuse NOUN 1 ('saɪrəˌkju:z) a port in SW Italy, in SE Sicily on the Ionian Sea: founded in 734 B.C. by Greeks from Corinth and taken by the Romans in 212 B.C., after a siege of three years. Pop.: 126 282 (2000 est.). Italian name: **Siracusa.** 2 ('sɪrəˌkju:s) a city in central New York State, on Lake Onondaga: site of the capital of the Iroquois Indian federation. Pop.: 147 306 (2000).

Syrah ('saɪrə) NOUN 1 a red grape grown in France and Australia, used, often in a blend, for making wine. 2 any of various wines made from this grape. Australian name: **Shiraz.**
▷HISTORY from SHIRAZ[1], the city in Iran where the wine supposedly originated

Syr Darya (*Russian* sir darʲ'ja) NOUN a river in central Asia, formed from two headstreams rising in the Tian Shan: flows generally west to the Aral Sea: the longest river in central Asia. Length: (from the source of the Naryn) 2900 km (1800 miles). Ancient name: **Jaxartes.**

Syria ('sɪrɪə) NOUN 1 a republic in W Asia, on the Mediterranean: ruled by the Ottoman Turks (1516–1918); made a French mandate in 1920; became independent in 1944; joined Egypt in the United Arab Republic (1958–61). Official language: Arabic. Religion: Muslim majority. Currency: Syrian pound. Capital: Damascus. Pop.: 16 729 000 (2001 est.). Area: 185 180 sq. km (71 498 sq. miles). 2 (formerly) the region between the Mediterranean, the Euphrates, the Taurus, and the Arabian Desert.

Syriac ('sɪrɪˌæk) NOUN a dialect of Aramaic spoken in Syria until about the 13th century A.D. and still in use as a liturgical language of certain Eastern churches.

Syrian ('sɪrɪən) ADJECTIVE 1 of, relating to, or characteristic of Syria, its people, or their dialect of Arabic. 2 *Eastern Church* of or relating to Christians who belong to churches with Syriac liturgies. ◆ NOUN 3 a native or inhabitant of Syria. 4 *Eastern Church* a Syrian Christian.

syringa (sɪ'rɪŋgə) NOUN another name for **mock orange** and **lilac** (sense 1).
▷HISTORY C17: from New Latin, from Greek *surinx* tube, alluding to the use of its hollow stems for pipes

syringe ('sɪrɪndʒ, sɪ'rɪndʒ) NOUN 1 *Med* an instrument, such as a hypodermic syringe or a rubber ball with a slender nozzle, for use in withdrawing or injecting fluids, cleaning wounds, etc. 2 any similar device for injecting, spraying, or extracting liquids by means of pressure or suction. ◆ VERB 3 (*tr*) to cleanse, inject, or spray with a syringe.
▷HISTORY C15: from Late Latin, from Latin: SYRINX

syringomyelia (səˌrɪŋgəumaɪ'i:lɪə) NOUN a chronic progressive disease of the spinal cord in which cavities form in the grey matter: characterized by loss of the sense of pain and temperature.
▷HISTORY C19: *syringo-*, from Greek: SYRINX + *-myelia* from Greek *muelos* marrow
▸**syringomyelic** (səˌrɪŋgəumaɪ'ɛlɪk) ADJECTIVE

syrinx ('sɪrɪŋks) NOUN, *plural* **syringes** (sɪ'rɪndʒi:z) *or* **syrinxes.** 1 the vocal organ of a bird, which is situated in the lower part of the trachea. 2 (in classical Greek music) a panpipe or set of panpipes. 3 *Anatomy* another name for the **Eustachian tube.**
▷HISTORY C17: via Latin from Greek *surinx* pipe
▸**syringeal** (sɪ'rɪndʒɪəl) ADJECTIVE

Syrinx ('sɪrɪŋks) NOUN *Greek myth* a nymph who was changed into a reed to save her from the amorous pursuit of Pan. From this reed Pan then fashioned his musical pipes.

Syro- ('saɪrəu-) COMBINING FORM 1 indicating Syrian and: *Syro-Lebanese.* 2 indicating Syriac and: *Syro-Aramaic.*
▷HISTORY from Greek *Suro-*, from *Suros* a Syrian

syrphid ('sɜ:fɪd) NOUN any dipterous fly of the family *Syrphidae,* typically having a coloration mimicking that of certain bees and wasps: includes the hover flies.
▷HISTORY C19: from Greek *surphos* gnat

Syrtis Major ('sɜ:tɪs) NOUN a conspicuous dark region visible in the N hemisphere of Mars.

syrup ('sɪrəp) NOUN 1 a solution of sugar dissolved in water and often flavoured with fruit juice: used for sweetening fruit, etc. 2 any of various thick sweet liquids prepared for cooking or table use from molasses, sugars, etc. 3 a liquid medicine containing a sugar solution for flavouring or preservation. 4 *Brit slang* a wig. ◆ VERB (*tr*) 5 to bring to the consistency of syrup. 6 to cover, fill, or sweeten with syrup. ◆ Also: **sirup.**
▷HISTORY C15: from Medieval Latin *syrupus,* from Arabic *sharāb* a drink, from *shariba* to drink: sense 4 from rhyming slang *syrup of fig*
▸**'syrup-ˌlike** ADJECTIVE

syrupy ('sɪrəpɪ) ADJECTIVE 1 (of a liquid) thick or sweet. 2 cloyingly sentimental: *a syrupy version of the Blue Danube.*

sysop *or* **SYSOP** ('sɪsˌɒp) NOUN *Computing* a person who runs a system or network.
▷HISTORY C20: SYS(TEM) + OP(ERATOR)

syssarcosis (ˌsɪsɑ:'kəusɪs) NOUN, *plural* **-ses** (-si:z). *Anatomy* the union or articulation of bones by muscle.
▷HISTORY C17: from New Latin, from Greek *sussarkōsis,* from *sussarkousthai,* from *sus-* SYN- + *sarkoun* to become fleshy, from *sarx* flesh
▸**syssarcotic** (ˌsɪsɑ:'kɒtɪk) ADJECTIVE

systaltic (sɪ'stæltɪk) ADJECTIVE (esp of the action of the heart) of, relating to, or characterized by alternate contractions and dilations; pulsating.
▷HISTORY C17: from Late Latin *systalticus,* from Greek *sustaltikos,* from *sustellein* to contract, from SYN- + *stellein* to place

system ('sɪstəm) NOUN 1 a group or combination of interrelated, interdependent, or interacting elements forming a collective entity; a methodical or coordinated assemblage of parts, facts, concepts, etc.: *a system of currency; the Copernican system.* 2 any scheme of classification or arrangement: *a chronological system.* 3 a network of communications, transportation, or distribution. 4 a method or complex of methods: *he has a perfect system at roulette.* 5 orderliness; an ordered manner. 6 **the system.** (*often capital*) society seen as an environment exploiting, restricting, and repressing individuals. 7 an organism considered as a functioning entity. 8 any of various bodily parts or structures that are anatomically or physiologically related: *the digestive system.* 9 one's physiological or psychological constitution: *get it out of your system.* 10 any assembly of electronic, electrical, or mechanical components with interdependent functions, usually forming a self-contained unit: *a brake system.* 11 a group of celestial bodies that are associated as a result of natural laws, esp gravitational attraction: *the solar system.* 12 *Chem* a sample of matter in which there are one or more substances in one or more phases. See also **phase rule.** 13 a point of view or doctrine used to interpret a branch of knowledge. 14 *Mineralogy* one of a group of divisions into which crystals may be placed on the basis of the lengths and inclinations of their axes. also called **crystal system.** 15 *Geology* a stratigraphical unit for the rock strata formed during a period of geological time. It can be subdivided into series.
▷HISTORY C17: from French *système,* from Late Latin *systēma,* from Greek *sustēma,* from SYN- + *histanai* to cause to stand
▸**'systemless** ADJECTIVE

systematic (ˌsɪstɪ'mætɪk) ADJECTIVE 1 characterized by the use of order and planning; methodical: *a systematic administrator.* 2 comprising or resembling a system: *systematic theology.* 3 Also: **systematical** (sɪstə'mætɪkᵊl). *Biology* of or relating to the taxonomic classification of organisms.
▸**ˌsystem'atically** ADVERB

systematic desensitization NOUN *Psychol* a treatment of phobias in which the patient while relaxed is exposed, often only in imagination, to progressively more frightening aspects of the phobia.

systematics (ˌsɪstɪ'mætɪks) NOUN (*functioning as singular*) the study of systems and the principles of classification and nomenclature.

systematism ('sɪstɪməˌtɪzəm) NOUN 1 the practice of classifying or systematizing. 2 adherence to a system. 3 a systematic classification; systematized arrangement.

systematist ('sɪstɪmətɪst) NOUN 1 a person who constructs systems. 2 an adherent of a system. 3 a taxonomist.

systematize ('sɪstɪməˌtaɪz), **systemize, systematise,** *or* **systemise** VERB (*tr*) to arrange in a system.
▸**ˌsystemati'zation** *or* **ˌsystemati'sation** *or* **ˌsystemi'zation** *or* **ˌsystemi'sation** NOUN ▸**'systemaˌtizer** *or* **'systemaˌtiser** *or* **'systemˌizer** *or* **'systemˌiser** NOUN

systematology (ˌsɪstɪmə'tɒlədʒɪ) NOUN the study of the nature and formation of systems.

system building NOUN a method of building in which prefabricated components are used to speed the construction of buildings.
▸**system built** ADJECTIVE

Système International d'Unités (*French* sistɛm ɛ̃tɛrnasjɔnal dynite) NOUN the International System of units. See **SI unit.**

systemic (sɪ'stɛmɪk, -'sti:-) ADJECTIVE 1 another word for **systematic** (senses 1, 2). 2 *Physiol* (of a poison, disease, etc.) affecting the entire body. 3 (of a pesticide, fungicide, etc.) spreading through all the parts of a plant and making it toxic to pests or parasites without destroying it. ◆ NOUN 4 a systemic pesticide, fungicide, etc.
▸**sys'temically** ADVERB

systemic availability NOUN another name for **bioavailability.**

systemic grammar NOUN a grammar in which description is founded on the relationships among the various units at different ranks of a language, and in which language is viewed as a system of meaning-creating choices. Compare **transformational grammar, case grammar.**

systems analysis NOUN the analysis of the requirements of a task and the expression of those requirements in a form that permits the assembly of computer hardware and software to perform the task.
▸**systems analyst** NOUN

systems disk NOUN a disk used to store computer programs, esp the basic operating programs of a computer.

systems engineering NOUN the branch of engineering, based on systems analysis and information theory, concerned with the design of integrated systems.

systems theory NOUN an approach to industrial relations which likens the enterprise to an organism with interdependent parts, each with its own specific function and interrelated responsibilities.

systole ('sɪstəlɪ) NOUN contraction of the heart, during which blood is pumped into the aorta and the arteries that lead to the lungs. Compare **diastole.**
▷HISTORY C16: via Late Latin from Greek *sustolē,* from *sustellein* to contract; see SYSTALTIC
▸**systolic** (sɪ'stɒlɪk) ADJECTIVE

syver *or* **siver** ('saɪvər) NOUN *Scot* 1 a street drain or the grating over it. 2 a street gutter.
▷HISTORY C17: of uncertain origin

syzygy ('sɪzɪdʒɪ) NOUN, *plural* **-gies.** 1 either of the two positions (conjunction or opposition) of a celestial body when sun, earth, and the body lie in a straight line: *the moon is at syzygy when full.* 2 (in classical prosody) a metrical unit of two feet. 3 *Rare* any pair, usually of opposites. 4 *Biology* the aggregation in a mass of certain protozoans, esp when occurring before sexual reproduction.
▷HISTORY C17: from Late Latin *syzygia,* from Greek *suzugia,* from *suzugos* yoked together, from SYN- + *zugon* a yoke
▸**syzygial** (sɪ'zɪdʒɪəl) *or* **syzygetic** (ˌsɪzɪ'dʒɛtɪk) *or* **syzygal** ('sɪzɪgᵊl) ADJECTIVE ▸**ˌsyzy'getically** ADVERB

SZ THE INTERNET DOMAIN NAME FOR Swaziland.

Szabadka ('sɔbɔtkɔ) NOUN the Hungarian name for **Subotica.**

Szczecin (*Polish* 'ʃtʃɛtʃin) NOUN a port in NW Poland, on the River Oder: the busiest Polish port and leading coal exporter; shipbuilding. Pop.: 416 988 (1999 est.). German name: **Stettin.**

Szechwan ('seɪ'tʃwɑ:n) NOUN a variant transliteration of the Chinese name for **Sichuan.**

Tt

t *or* **T** (tiː) NOUN, *plural* **t's, T's** *or* **Ts.** [1] the 20th letter and 16th consonant of the modern English alphabet. [2] a speech sound represented by this letter, usually a voiceless alveolar stop, as in *tame.* [3] **a** something shaped like a T. **b** (*in combination*): *a T-junction.* [4] **to a T.** in every detail; perfectly: *the work suited her to a T.*

t SYMBOL FOR: [1] tonne(s). [2] troy (weight). [3] *Statistics* distribution. [4] *Statistics* See **Student's t.**

T SYMBOL FOR: [1] absolute temperature. [2] tera-. [3] *Chem* tritium. [4] *Biochem* thymine. [5] tesla. [6] surface tension. ◆ [7] INTERNATIONAL CAR REGISTRATION FOR Thailand.

t. ABBREVIATION FOR: [1] *Commerce* tare. [2] teaspoon(ful). [3] temperature. [4] *Music* tempo. [5] tenor. [6] *Grammar* tense. [7] ton(s). [8] transitive.

't CONTRACTION OF it.

T- ABBREVIATION FOR trainer (aircraft): *T-37.*

ta (tɑː) INTERJECTION *Brit informal* thank you.
▷HISTORY C18: imitative of baby talk

Ta THE CHEMICAL SYMBOL FOR tantalum.

TA (in Britain) ABBREVIATION FOR Territorial Army (now superseded by **TAVR**).

taal (tɑːl) NOUN **the.** *South African* language: usually, by implication, Afrikaans.
▷HISTORY Afrikaans from Dutch

Taal (tɑːˈɑːl) NOUN an active volcano in the Philippines, on S Luzon on an island in the centre of **Lake Taal**. Height: 300 m (984 ft.). Area of lake: 243 sq. km (94 sq. miles).

taata (ˈtata) NOUN *E African* a child's word for **father.**

tab^{1} (tæb) NOUN [1] a small flap of material, esp one on a garment for decoration or for fastening to a button. [2] any similar flap, such as a piece of paper attached to a file for identification. [3] a small auxiliary aerofoil on the trailing edge of a rudder, aileron, or elevator, etc., to assist in the control of the aircraft in flight. See also **trim tab.** [4] *Brit military* the insignia on the collar of a staff officer. [5] *Chiefly US and Canadian* a bill, esp one for a meal or drinks. [6] *Scot and northern English dialect* a cigarette. [7] **keep tabs on.** *Informal* to keep a watchful eye on. ◆ VERB **tabs, tabbing, tabbed.** [8] (*tr*) to supply (files, clothing, etc.) with a tab or tabs.
▷HISTORY C17: of unknown origin

tab^{2} (tæb) NOUN [1] short for **tabulator** or **tablet.** [2] *Slang* a portion of a drug, esp LSD or ecstasy.

TAB ABBREVIATION FOR: [1] typhoid-paratyphoid A and B (vaccine). [2] *Austral and NZ* Totalizator Agency Board.

tab. ABBREVIATION FOR table (list or chart).

tabanid (ˈtæbənɪd) NOUN any stout-bodied fly of the dipterous family *Tabanidae,* the females of which have mouthparts specialized for sucking blood: includes the horseflies.
▷HISTORY C19: from Latin *tabānus* horsefly

tabard (ˈtæbəd) NOUN a sleeveless or short-sleeved jacket, esp one worn by a herald, bearing a coat of arms, or by a knight over his armour.
▷HISTORY C13: from Old French *tabart,* of uncertain origin

tabaret (ˈtæbərɪt) NOUN a hard-wearing fabric of silk or similar cloth with stripes of satin or moire, used esp for upholstery.
▷HISTORY C19: perhaps from TABBY^{1}

Tabasco^{1} (təˈbæskəʊ) NOUN *Trademark* a very hot red sauce made from matured capsicums.

Tabasco^{2} (*Spanish* taˈβasko) NOUN a state in SE Mexico, on the Gulf of Campeche: mostly flat and marshy with extensive jungles; hot and humid climate. Capital: Villahermosa. Pop.: 1 889 367 (2000). Area: 24 661 sq. km (9520 sq. miles).

tabbouleh *or* **tabbouli** (təˈbuːlɪ) NOUN a kind of Middle Eastern salad made with cracked wheat, mint, parsley, and usually cucumber.
▷HISTORY C20: from Arabic *tabbūla*

tabby^{1} (ˈtæbɪ) NOUN a fabric with a watered pattern, esp silk or taffeta.
▷HISTORY C17: from Old French *tabis* silk cloth, from Arabic *al-'attabiya,* literally: the quarter of (Prince) 'Attab, the part of Baghdad where the fabric was first made

tabby^{2} (ˈtæbɪ) ADJECTIVE [1] (esp of cats) brindled with dark stripes or wavy markings on a lighter background. [2] having a wavy or striped pattern, particularly in colours of grey and brown. ◆ NOUN, *plural* **-bies.** [3] a tabby cat. [4] any female domestic cat. [5] *Brit informal* a gossiping old woman. [6] *Austral slang* any girl or woman.
▷HISTORY C17: from *Tabby,* pet form of the girl's name *Tabitha,* probably influenced by TABBY^{1}

tabernacle (ˈtæbəˌnækəl) NOUN [1] (*often capital*) *Old Testament* **a** the portable sanctuary in the form of a tent in which the ancient Israelites carried the Ark of the Covenant (Exodus 25–27). **b** the Jewish Temple regarded as the shrine of the divine presence. [2] *Judaism* an English word for **sukkah.** [3] a meeting place for worship used by Mormons or Nonconformists. [4] a small ornamented cupboard or box used for the reserved sacrament of the Eucharist. [5] the human body regarded as the temporary dwelling of the soul. [6] *Chiefly RC Church* a canopied niche or recess forming the shrine of a statue. [7] *Nautical* a strong framework for holding the foot of a mast stepped on deck, allowing it to be swung down horizontally to pass under low bridges, etc.
▷HISTORY C13: from Latin *tabernāculum* a tent, from *taberna* a hut; see TAVERN
▸ˌ**taber'nacular** ADJECTIVE

Tabernacles (ˈtæbəˌnækəlz) PLURAL NOUN *Judaism* an English name for **Sukkoth.**

tabes (ˈteɪbiːz) NOUN, *plural* **tabes.** [1] a wasting of a bodily organ or part. [2] short for **tabes dorsalis.**
▷HISTORY C17: from Latin: a wasting away
▸**tabetic** (təˈbɛtɪk) ADJECTIVE

tabescent (təˈbɛsənt) ADJECTIVE [1] progressively emaciating; wasting away. [2] of, relating to, or having tabes.
▷HISTORY C19: from Latin *tābēscere,* from TABES
▸**ta'bescence** NOUN

tabes dorsalis (dɔːˈsɑːlɪs) NOUN a form of late syphilis that attacks the spinal cord causing degeneration of the nerve fibres, pains in the legs, paralysis of the leg muscles, acute abdominal pain, etc. Also called: **locomotor ataxia.**
▷HISTORY New Latin, literally: tabes of the back; see TABES, DORSAL

tab-hang VERB *Midland English dialect* to eavesdrop.

tabla (ˈtʌblə, ˈtɑːblɑː) NOUN a musical instrument of India consisting of a pair of drums whose pitches can be varied.
▷HISTORY Hindu, from Arabic *tabla* drum

tablature (ˈtæblətʃə) NOUN [1] *Music* any of a number of forms of musical notation, esp for playing the lute, consisting of letters and signs indicating rhythm and fingering. [2] an engraved or painted tablet or other flat surface.
▷HISTORY C16: from French, ultimately from Latin *tabulātum* wooden floor, from *tabula* a plank

table (ˈteɪbəl) NOUN [1] a flat horizontal slab or board, usually supported by one or more legs, on which objects may be placed. Related adjective: **mensal.** [2] **a** such a slab or board on which food is served: *we were six at table.* **b** (*as modifier*): *table linen.* **c** (*in combination*): *a tablecloth.* [3] food as served in a particular household or restaurant: *a good table.* [4] such a piece of furniture specially designed for any of various purposes: *a backgammon table; bird table.* [5] **a** a company of persons assembled for a meal, game, etc. **b** (*as modifier*): *table talk.* [6] any flat or level area, such as a plateau. [7] a rectangular panel set below or above the face of a wall. [8] *Architect* another name for **cordon** (sense 4). [9] an upper horizontal facet of a cut gem. [10] *Music* the sounding board of a violin, guitar, or similar stringed instrument. [11] **a** an arrangement of words, numbers, or signs, usually in parallel columns, to display data or relations: *a table of contents.* **b** See **multiplication table.** [12] a tablet on which laws were inscribed by the ancient Romans, the Hebrews, etc. [13] *Palmistry* an area of the palm's surface bounded by four lines. [14] *Printing* a slab of smooth metal on which ink is rolled to its proper consistency. [15] **a** either of the two bony plates that form the inner and outer parts of the flat bones of the cranium. **b** any thin flat plate, esp of bone. [16] **on the table.** put forward for discussion and acceptance: *we currently have our final offer on the table.* [17] **turn the tables on (someone).** to cause a complete reversal of circumstances, esp to defeat or get the better of (someone) who was previously in a stronger position. ◆ VERB (*tr*) [18] to place on a table. [19] *Brit* to submit (a bill, etc.) for consideration by a legislative body. [20] *US* to suspend discussion of (a bill, etc.) indefinitely or for some time. [21] to enter in or form into a list; tabulate.
▷HISTORY C12: via Old French from Latin *tabula* a writing tablet
▸'**tableful** NOUN ▸'**tableless** ADJECTIVE

tableau (ˈtæbləʊ) NOUN, *plural* **-leaux** (-ləʊ, -ləʊz) *or* **-leaus.** [1] See ***tableau vivant.*** [2] a pause during or at the end of a scene on stage when all the performers briefly freeze in position. [3] any dramatic group or scene. [4] *Logic* short for **semantic tableau.**
▷HISTORY C17: from French, from Old French *tablel* a picture, diminutive of TABLE

tableau vivant *French* (tablo vivɑ̃) NOUN, *plural* ***tableaux vivants*** (tablo vivɑ̃). a representation of a scene, painting, sculpture, etc., by a person or group posed silent and motionless.
▷HISTORY C19: literally: living picture

Table Bay NOUN the large bay on which Cape Town is situated, on the SW coast of South Africa.

tablecloth (ˈteɪbəlˌklɒθ) NOUN a cloth for covering the top of a table, esp during meals.

table dancing NOUN a form of entertainment in which naked or scantily dressed women dance erotically at the tables of individual members of the audience, who must remain seated.
▸**table dancer** NOUN

table d'hôte (ˈtɑːbəl ˈdəʊt; *French* tablə dot) ADJECTIVE [1] (of a meal) consisting of a set number of courses with limited choice of dishes offered at a fixed price. Compare **à la carte, prix fixe.** ◆ NOUN, *plural* **tables d'hôte** (ˈtɑːbəlz ˈdəʊt; *French* tablə dot). [2] a table d'hôte meal or menu.
▷HISTORY C17: from French, literally: the host's table

tableland (ˈteɪbəlˌlænd) NOUN flat elevated land; a plateau.

table licence NOUN a licence authorizing the sale of alcoholic drinks with meals only.

table money NOUN an allowance for official entertaining of visitors, clients, etc., esp in the army.

Table Mountain NOUN a mountain in SW South Africa, overlooking Cape Town and Table Bay: flat-topped and steep-sided. Height: 1087 m (3567 ft.).

table napkin NOUN See **napkin** (sense 1).

table-rapping NOUN the sounds of knocking or tapping made without any apparent physical agency while a group of people sit round a table, and attributed by spiritualists to the spirit of a dead person using this as a means of communication with the living.

table salt NOUN salt that is used at table rather than for cooking.

tablespoon (ˈteɪbəlˌspuːn) NOUN [1] a spoon, larger than a dessertspoon, used for serving food, etc. [2] Also called: **tablespoonful.** the amount contained in such a spoon. [3] a unit of capacity used in cooking, medicine, etc., equal to half a fluid ounce or three teaspoons.

tablet ('tæblɪt) NOUN 1 a medicinal formulation made of a compressed powdered substance containing an active drug and excipients. 2 a flattish cake of some substance, such as soap. 3 *Scot* a sweet made of butter, sugar, and condensed milk, usually shaped in a flat oblong block. 4 a slab of stone, wood, etc., esp one formerly used for inscriptions. 5 **a** a thinner rigid sheet, as of bark, ivory, etc., used for similar purposes. **b** (*often plural*) a set or pair of these fastened together, as in a book. 6 a pad of writing paper. 7 *NZ* a token giving right of way to the driver of a train on a single line section.
▷HISTORY C14: from Old French *tablete* a little table, from Latin *tabula* a board

table talk NOUN informal conversation on a range of topics, as that at table during and after a meal.

table tennis NOUN a miniature form of tennis played on a table with small bats and a light hollow ball.

table-turning NOUN 1 the movement of a table attributed by spiritualists to the power of spirits working through a group of persons placing their hands or fingers on the table top. 2 *Often derogatory* spiritualism in general.

tableware ('teɪbəlˌwɛə) NOUN articles such as dishes, plates, knives, forks, etc., used at meals.

table wine NOUN a wine considered suitable for drinking with a meal.

tabloid ('tæblɔɪd) NOUN 1 a newspaper with pages about 30 cm (12 inches) by 40 cm (16 inches), usually characterized by an emphasis on photographs and a concise and often sensational style. Compare **broadsheet.** 2 (*modifier*) designed to appeal to a mass audience or readership; sensationalist: *the tabloid press; tabloid television.*
▷HISTORY C20: from earlier *Tabloid,* a trademark for a medicine in tablet form

taboo *or* **tabu** (tə'buː) ADJECTIVE 1 forbidden or disapproved of; placed under a social prohibition or ban: *taboo words.* 2 (in Polynesia and other islands of the South Pacific) marked off as simultaneously sacred and forbidden. ◆ NOUN, *plural* **-boos** *or* **-bus.** 3 any prohibition resulting from social or other conventions. 4 ritual restriction or prohibition, esp of something that is considered holy or unclean. ◆ VERB 5 (*tr*) to place under a taboo.
▷HISTORY C18: from Tongan *tapu*

tabor *or* **tabour** ('teɪbə) NOUN *Music* a small drum used esp in the Middle Ages, struck with one hand while the other held a three-holed pipe. See **pipe**[1] (sense 7).
▷HISTORY C13: from Old French *tabour,* perhaps from Persian *tabīr*
▸ **'taborer** *or* **'tabourer** NOUN

Tabor ('teɪbə) NOUN **Mount.** a mountain in N Israel, near Nazareth: traditionally regarded as the mountain where the Transfiguration took place. Height: 588 m (1929 ft.).

taboret *or* **tabouret** ('tæbərɪt) NOUN 1 a low stool, originally in the shape of a drum. 2 a frame, usually round, for stretching out cloth while it is being embroidered. 3 Also called: **taborin, tabourin** ('tæbərɪn). a small tabor.
▷HISTORY C17: from French *tabouret,* diminutive of TABOR

Tabriz (tæ'briːz) NOUN a city in NW Iran: an ancient city, situated in a volcanic region of hot springs; university (1947); carpet manufacturing. Pop.: 1 191 043 (1996). Ancient name: **Tauris** ('tɔːrɪs).

tabular ('tæbjʊlə) ADJECTIVE 1 arranged in systematic or table form. 2 calculated from or by means of a table. 3 like a table in form; flat.
▷HISTORY C17: from Latin *tabulāris* concerning boards, from *tabula* a board
▸ **'tabularly** ADVERB

tabula rasa ('tæbjʊlə 'rɑːsə) NOUN, *plural* **tabulae rasae** ('tæbjʊliː 'rɑːsiː). 1 (esp in the philosophy of Locke) the mind in its uninformed original state. 2 an opportunity for a fresh start; clean slate.
▷HISTORY Latin: a scraped tablet (one from which the writing has been erased)

tabulate VERB ('tæbjʊˌleɪt) (*tr*) 1 Also: **tabularize** ('tæbjʊləˌraɪz). to set out, arrange, or write in tabular form. 2 to form or cut with a flat surface. ◆ ADJECTIVE ('tæbjʊlɪt, -ˌleɪt) 3 having a flat surface. 4 (of certain corals) having transverse skeletal plates.
▷HISTORY C18: from Latin *tabula* a board
▸ **'tabulable** ADJECTIVE ▸ **ˌtabu'lation** NOUN

tabulator ('tæbjʊˌleɪtə) NOUN 1 a device for setting the automatic stops that locate the column margins on a typewriter. 2 *Computing* a machine that reads data from one medium, such as punched cards, producing lists, tabulations, or totals, usually on a continuous sheet of paper. 3 any machine that tabulates data.

tabun (tɑː'buːn) NOUN an organic compound used in chemical warfare as a lethal nerve gas. Formula: $C_2H_5OP(O)(CN)N(CH_3)_2$.
▷HISTORY C20: from German, of uncertain origin

TAC (in South Africa) ABBREVIATION FOR Treatment Action Campaign, a pressure group that campaigns for the medical rights of pregnant women with HIV or AIDS.

tacamahac ('tækəməˌhæk) *or* **tacmahack** NOUN 1 any of several strong-smelling resinous gums obtained from certain trees, used in making ointments, incense, etc. 2 any tree yielding this resin, esp the balsam poplar.
▷HISTORY C16: from Spanish *tacamahaca,* from Nahuatl *tecomahca* aromatic resin

Tacan ('tækən) NOUN an electronic ultrahigh-frequency navigation system for aircraft which gives a continuous indication of bearing and distance from a transmitting station.
▷HISTORY C20: *tac(tical) a(ir) n(avigation)*

tace (tæs, teɪs) NOUN a less common word for **tasset.**

tacet ('teɪsɛt, 'tæs-) VERB (*intr*) (on a musical score) a direction indicating that a particular instrument or singer does not take part in a movement or part of a movement.
▷HISTORY C18: from Latin: it is silent, from *tacēre* to be quiet

tache[1] (tæʃ, tɑːʃ) NOUN *Archaic* a buckle, clasp, or hook.
▷HISTORY C17: from Old French, of Germanic origin; compare TACK[1]

tache[2] (tæʃ) NOUN *Informal* short for **moustache.**

tacheo- COMBINING FORM a variant of **tachy-.**

tacheometer (ˌtækɪ'ɒmɪtə) *or* **tachymeter** NOUN *Surveying* a type of theodolite designed for the rapid measurement of distances, elevations, and directions.

tacheometry (ˌtækɪ'ɒmɪtrɪ) *or* **tachymetry** NOUN *Surveying* the measurement of distance, etc., using a tacheometer.
▸ **tacheometric** (ˌtækɪə'mɛtrɪk) *or* **ˌtacheo'metrical** *or* **ˌtachy'metric** *or* **ˌtachy'metrical** ADJECTIVE
▸ **ˌtacheo'metrically** *or* **ˌtachy'metrically** ADVERB

tachina fly ('tækɪnə) NOUN any bristly fly of the dipterous family *Tachinidae,* the larvae of which live parasitically in caterpillars, beetles, hymenopterans, and other insects.
▷HISTORY C19: via New Latin *Tachina,* from Greek *takhinos* swift, from *takhos* fleetness

tachisme ('tɑːʃɪzəm; *French* taʃism) NOUN a type of action painting evolved in France in which haphazard dabs and blots of colour are treated as a means of instinctive or unconscious expression.
▷HISTORY C20: French, from *tache* stain

tachistoscope (tə'kɪstəˌskəʊp) NOUN an instrument, used mainly in experiments on perception and memory, for displaying visual images for very brief intervals, usually a fraction of a second.
▷HISTORY C20: from Greek *takhistos* swiftest (see TACHY-) + -SCOPE
▸ **tachistoscopic** (təˌkɪstə'skɒpɪk) ADJECTIVE
▸ **taˌchisto'scopically** ADVERB

tacho- COMBINING FORM speed: *tachograph; tachometer.*
▷HISTORY from Greek *takhos*

tachograph ('tækəˌgrɑːf, -ˌgræf) NOUN a tachometer that produces a graphical record (**tachogram**) of its readings, esp a device for recording the speed of and distance covered by a heavy goods vehicle. Often shortened to: **tacho.**

tachometer (tæ'kɒmɪtə) NOUN any device for measuring speed, esp the rate of revolution of a shaft. Tachometers (rev counters) are often fitted to cars to indicate the number of revolutions per minute of the engine.
▸ **tachometric** (ˌtækə'mɛtrɪk) *or* **ˌtacho'metrical** ADJECTIVE
▸ **ˌtacho'metrically** ADVERB ▸ **ta'chometry** NOUN

tachy- *or* **tacheo-** COMBINING FORM swift or accelerated: *tachycardia; tachygraphy; tachylyte; tachyon; tachyphylaxis.*
▷HISTORY from Greek *takhus* swift

tachycardia (ˌtækɪ'kɑːdɪə) NOUN *Pathol* abnormally rapid beating of the heart, esp over 100 beats per minute. Compare **bradycardia.**
▸ **tachycardiac** (ˌtækɪ'kɑːdɪˌæk) ADJECTIVE

tachygraphy (tæ'kɪgrəfɪ) NOUN shorthand, esp as used in ancient Rome or Greece.
▸ **ta'chygrapher** *or* **ta'chygraphist** NOUN ▸ **tachygraphic** (ˌtækɪ'græfɪk) ADJECTIVE ▸ **ˌtachy'graphically** ADVERB

tachylyte *or* **tachylite** ('tækɪˌlaɪt) NOUN a black basaltic glass often found on the edges of intrusions of basalt.
▷HISTORY C19: from German *Tachylit,* from TACHY- + Greek *lutos* soluble, melting, from *luein* to release; so called because it fuses easily when heated. The form *tachylite* is influenced by -LITE stone
▸ **tachylytic** (ˌtækɪ'lɪtɪk) *or* **ˌtachy'litic** ADJECTIVE

tachymeter (tæ'kɪmɪtə) NOUN another name for **tacheometer.**

tachymetry (tæ'kɪmɪtrɪ) NOUN another name for **tacheometry.**

tachyon ('tækɪˌɒn) NOUN *Physics* a hypothetical elementary particle capable of travelling faster than the velocity of light.
▷HISTORY C20: from TACHY- + -ON

tachyphylaxis (ˌtækɪfɪ'læksɪs) NOUN very rapid development of tolerance or immunity to the effects of a drug.
▷HISTORY New Latin, from TACHY- + *phylaxis* on the model of *prophylaxis.* See PROPHYLACTIC

tachypnoea *or US* **tachypnea** (ˌtækɪp'nɪə) NOUN *Pathol* abnormally rapid breathing.

tacit ('tæsɪt) ADJECTIVE 1 implied or inferred without direct expression; understood: *a tacit agreement.* 2 created or having effect by operation of law, rather than by being directly expressed.
▷HISTORY C17: from Latin *tacitus,* past participle of *tacēre* to be silent
▸ **'tacitly** ADVERB ▸ **'tacitness** NOUN

taciturn ('tæsɪˌtɜːn) ADJECTIVE habitually silent, reserved, or uncommunicative; not inclined to conversation.
▷HISTORY C18: from Latin *taciturnus,* from *tacitus* silent, from *tacēre* to be silent
▸ **ˌtaci'turnity** NOUN ▸ **'taciˌturnly** ADVERB

tack[1] (tæk) NOUN 1 a short sharp-pointed nail, usually with a flat and comparatively large head. 2 *Brit* a long loose temporary stitch used in dressmaking, etc. 3 See **tailor's-tack.** 4 a temporary fastening. 5 stickiness, as of newly applied paint, varnish, etc. 6 *Nautical* the heading of a vessel sailing to windward, stated in terms of the side of the sail against which the wind is pressing. 7 *Nautical* **a** a course sailed by a sailing vessel with the wind blowing from forward of the beam. **b** one such course or a zigzag pattern of such courses. 8 *Nautical* **a** a sheet for controlling the weather clew of a course. **b** the weather clew itself. 9 *Nautical* the forward lower clew of a fore-and-aft sail. 10 a course of action differing from some previous course: *he went off on a fresh tack.* 11 **on the wrong tack.** under a false impression. ◆ VERB 12 (*tr*) to secure by a tack or series of tacks. 13 *Brit* to sew (something) with long loose temporary stitches. 14 (*tr*) to attach or append: *tack this letter onto the other papers.* 15 *Nautical* to change the heading of (a sailing vessel) to the opposite tack. 16 *Nautical* to steer (a sailing vessel) on alternate tacks. 17 (*intr*) *Nautical* (of a sailing vessel) to proceed on a different tack or to alternate tacks. 18 (*intr*) to follow a zigzag route; keep changing one's course of action.
▷HISTORY C14 *tak* fastening, nail; related to Middle Low German *tacke* pointed instrument
▸ **'tacker** NOUN ▸ **'tackless** ADJECTIVE

tack[2] (tæk) NOUN *Informal* food, esp when regarded as inferior or distasteful. See also **hardtack.**
▷HISTORY C19: of unknown origin

tack[3] (tæk) NOUN **a** riding harness for horses, such as saddles, bridles, etc. **b** (*as modifier*): *the tack room.*
▷HISTORY C20: shortened from TACKLE

tack[4] (tæk) NOUN *Scot* 1 a lease. 2 an area of land held on a lease.

▷HISTORY C15: from *tak* a Scots word for *take*

tacker ('tækə) NOUN *Austral slang* a young person; child.

tacket ('tækɪt) NOUN *Scot and northern English dialect* a nail, esp a hobnail.
▷HISTORY C14: from TACK[1]
▸'**tackety** ADJECTIVE

tack hammer NOUN a light hammer for driving tacks.

tackies *or* **takkies** ('tækɪz) PLURAL NOUN, *singular* **tacky**. *South African informal* tennis shoes or plimsolls.
▷HISTORY C20: probably from TACKY[1], with reference to their nonslip rubber soles

tackle ('tækəl; *Nautical often* 'teɪkəl) NOUN 1 any mechanical system for lifting or pulling, esp an arrangement of ropes and pulleys designed to lift heavy weights. 2 the equipment required for a particular occupation, etc.: *fishing tackle*. 3 *Nautical* the halyards and other running rigging aboard a vessel. 4 *Slang* a man's genitals. 5 *Sport* a physical challenge to an opponent, as to prevent his progress with the ball. 6 *American football* a defensive lineman. ◆ VERB 7 (*tr*) to undertake (a task, problem, etc.). 8 (*tr*) to confront (a person, esp an opponent) with a difficult proposition. 9 *Sport* (esp in football games) to challenge (an opponent) with a tackle.
▷HISTORY C13: related to Middle Low German *takel* ship's rigging, Middle Dutch *taken* to TAKE
▸'**tackler** NOUN

tack rag NOUN *Building trades* a cotton cloth impregnated with an oil, used to remove dust from a surface prior to painting.

tacksman ('tæksmən) NOUN, *plural* **-men**. a leaseholder, esp a tenant in the Highlands who sublets.
▷HISTORY C16: from TACK[4]

tack welding NOUN *Engineering* short intermittent welds made to hold components in place before full welding is begun.

tacky[1] *or* **tackey** ('tækɪ) ADJECTIVE **tackier, tackiest**. slightly sticky or adhesive: *the varnish was still tacky*.
▷HISTORY C18: from TACK[1] (in the sense: stickiness)
▸'**tackily** ADVERB ▸'**tackiness** NOUN

tacky[2] ('tækɪ) ADJECTIVE **tackier, tackiest**. *Informal* 1 shabby or shoddy. 2 ostentatious and vulgar. 3 *US* (of a person) dowdy; seedy.
▷HISTORY C19: from dialect *tacky* an inferior horse, of unknown origin
▸'**tackiness** NOUN

tacmahack ('tækməˌhæk) NOUN a variant of **tacamahac**.

Tacna-Arica (*Spanish* 'taknaa'rika) NOUN a coastal desert region of W South America, long disputed by Chile and Peru: divided in 1929 into the Peruvian department of Tacna and the Chilean department of Arica.

tacnode ('tækˌnəʊd) NOUN another name for **osculation** (sense 1).
▷HISTORY C19: from Latin *tactus* touch (from *tangere* to touch) + NODE

taco ('tɑːkəʊ) NOUN, *plural* **-cos**. *Mexican cookery* a tortilla folded into a roll with a filling and usually fried.
▷HISTORY from Mexican Spanish, from Spanish: literally, a snack, a bite to eat

Tacoma (tə'kəʊmə) NOUN a port in W Washington, on Puget Sound: industrial centre. Pop.: 193 556 (2000).

taconite ('tækəˌnaɪt) NOUN a fine-grained sedimentary rock containing magnetite, haematite, and silica, which occurs in the Lake Superior region: a low-grade iron ore.
▷HISTORY C20: named after the *Taconic* Mountains in New England

tact (tækt) NOUN 1 a sense of what is fitting and considerate in dealing with others, so as to avoid giving offence or to win good will; discretion. 2 skill or judgment in handling difficult or delicate situations; diplomacy.
▷HISTORY C17: from Latin *tactus* a touching, from *tangere* to touch
▸'**tactful** ADJECTIVE ▸'**tactfully** ADVERB ▸'**tactfulness** NOUN ▸'**tactless** ADJECTIVE ▸'**tactlessly** ADVERB ▸'**tactlessness** NOUN

tactic ('tæktɪk) NOUN a piece of tactics; tactical move. See also **tactics**.

-tactic ADJECTIVE COMBINING FORM having a specified kind of pattern or arrangement or having an orientation determined by a specified force: *syndiotactic; phototactic*.
▷HISTORY from Greek *taktikos* relating to order or arrangement; see TACTICS

tactical ('tæktɪkəl) ADJECTIVE 1 of, relating to, or employing tactics: *a tactical error*. 2 (of weapons, attacks, etc.) used in or supporting limited military operations: *a tactical missile; tactical bombing*. 3 skilful or diplomatic: *a tactical manoeuvre*.
▸'**tactically** ADVERB

tactical voting NOUN (in an election) the practice of casting one's vote not for the party of one's choice but for the second strongest contender in order to defeat the likeliest winner.

tactics ('tæktɪks) PLURAL NOUN 1 (*functioning as singular*) *Military* the art and science of the detailed direction and control of movement or manoeuvre of forces in battle to achieve an aim or task. 2 the manoeuvres used or plans followed to achieve a particular short-term aim.
▷HISTORY C17: from New Latin *tactica*, from Greek *ta taktika* the matters of arrangement, neuter plural of *taktikos* concerning arrangement or order, from *taktos* arranged (for battle), from *tassein* to arrange
▸**tac'tician** NOUN

tactile ('tæktaɪl) ADJECTIVE 1 of, relating to, affecting, or having a sense of touch: *a tactile organ; tactile stimuli*. 2 *Now rare* capable of being touched; tangible.
▷HISTORY C17: from Latin *tactilis*, from *tangere* to touch
▸**tactility** (tæk'tɪlɪtɪ) NOUN

taction ('tækʃən) NOUN *Obsolete* the act of touching; contact.
▷HISTORY C17: from Latin *tactiō* a touching, from *tangere* to touch

tactual ('tæktjʊəl) ADJECTIVE 1 caused by touch; causing a tactile sensation. 2 of or relating to the tactile sense or the organs of touch.
▷HISTORY C17: from Latin *tactus* a touching; see TACT
▸'**tactually** ADVERB

tad (tæd) NOUN *Informal* 1 *US and Canadian* a small boy; lad. 2 *US and Canadian* a small bit or piece. 3 **a tad**. a little; rather: *she may be a tad short but she got a top modelling job*.
▷HISTORY C20: short for TADPOLE

Tadmor ('tædmɔː) NOUN the biblical name for **Palmyra**.

tadpole ('tædˌpəʊl) NOUN the aquatic larva of frogs, toads, etc., which develops from a limbless tailed form with external gills into a form with internal gills, limbs, and a reduced tail.
▷HISTORY C15 *taddepol*, from *tadde* TOAD + *pol* head, POLL

Tadzhik *or* **Tadjik** ('tɑːdʒɪk, tɑː'dʒiːk) NOUN, *plural* **-dzhik** *or* **-djik**. variant spellings of **Tajik**.

Tadzhikistan *or* **Tadjikistan** (tɑːˌdʒɪkɪ'stɑːn, -stæn) NOUN variant spellings of **Tajikistan**.

tae[1] (te) PREPOSITION, ADVERB a Scot word for **to**.

tae[2] (te) ADVERB a Scot word for **too**.

tae[3] (te) NOUN a Scot word for **toe**.

Tae Bo ('taɪ 'bəʊ) NOUN a form of exercise based on martial arts movements.
▷HISTORY C20: from TAE (KWON DO) + BO(XING)

taedium vitae ('tiːdɪəm 'viːtaɪ, 'vaɪtiː) NOUN the feeling that life is boring and dull.
▷HISTORY Latin, literally: weariness of life

Taegu (tɛ'guː) NOUN a city in SE South Korea: textile and agricultural trading centre. Pop.: 2 449 139 (1995).

Taejon (tɛ'dʒɒn) NOUN a city in W South Korea: market centre of an agricultural region. Pop.: 1 272 143 (1995).

tae kwon do ('taɪ 'kwɒn 'dəʊ, 'teɪ) NOUN a Korean martial art that resembles karate.
▷HISTORY C20: Korean *tae* kick + *kwon* fist + *do* way, method

tael (teɪl) NOUN 1 a unit of weight, used in the Far East, having various values between one to two and a half ounces. 2 (formerly) a Chinese monetary unit equivalent in value to a tael weight of standard silver.
▷HISTORY C16: from Portuguese, from Malay *tahil* weight, perhaps from Hindi *tolā* weight of a new rupee, from Sanskrit *tulā* weight

ta'en (teɪn) VERB a poetic contraction of **taken**.

taenia *or US* **tenia** ('tiːnɪə) NOUN, *plural* **-niae** (-nɪˌiː). 1 (in ancient Greece) a narrow fillet or headband for the hair. 2 *Architect* the fillet between the architrave and frieze of a Doric entablature. 3 *Anatomy* any bandlike structure or part. 4 any tapeworm of the genus *Taenia*, such as *T. soleum*, a parasite of man that uses the pig as its intermediate host.
▷HISTORY C16: via Latin from Greek *tainia* narrow strip; related to Greek *teinein* to stretch

taeniacide *or US* **teniacide** ('tiːnɪəˌsaɪd) NOUN a substance, esp a drug, that kills tapeworms.

taeniafuge *or US* **teniafuge** ('tiːnɪəˌfjuːdʒ) NOUN a substance, esp a drug, that expels tapeworms from the body of their host.

taeniasis *or US* **teniasis** (tiː'naɪəsɪs) NOUN *Pathol* infestation with tapeworms of the genus *Taenia*.

TAFE ('tæfɪ) NOUN (in Australia) ◆ ACRONYM FOR Technical and Further Education.

Tafelwein ('tɑːfəlˌvaɪn) NOUN German table wine.
▷HISTORY C20: from German *Tafel* table + *Wein* wine

taffeta ('tæfɪtə) NOUN 1 **a** a crisp lustrous plain-weave silk, rayon, etc., used esp for women's clothes. **b** (*as modifier*): *a taffeta petticoat*. 2 any of various similar fabrics.
▷HISTORY C14: from Medieval Latin *taffata*, from Persian *tāftah* spun, from *tāftan* to spin

taffrail ('tæfˌreɪl) NOUN *Nautical* 1 a rail at the stern or above the transom of a vessel. 2 the upper part of the transom of a vessel, esp a sailing vessel, often ornately decorated.
▷HISTORY C19: changed (through influence of RAIL[1]) from earlier *tafferel*, from Dutch *taffereel* panel (hence applied to the part of a vessel decorated with carved panels), variant of *tafeleel* (unattested), from *tafel* TABLE

taffy ('tæfɪ) NOUN, *plural* **-fies**. 1 *US and Canadian* a chewy sweet made of brown sugar or molasses and butter, boiled and then pulled so that it becomes glossy. 2 *Chiefly US and Canadian* a less common term for **toffee**.
▷HISTORY C19: perhaps from TAFIA

Taffy ('tæfɪ) NOUN, *plural* **-fies**. a slang word or nickname for a Welshman.
▷HISTORY C17: from the supposed Welsh pronunciation of *Davy* (from *David*, Welsh *Dafydd*), a common Welsh Christian name

tafia *or* **taffia** ('tæfɪə) NOUN a type of rum, esp from Guyana or the Caribbean.
▷HISTORY C18: from French, from West Indian Creole, probably from RATAFIA

Tafilelt (tæ'fiːlɛlt) *or* **Tafilalet** (ˌtæfɪ'lɑːlɛt) NOUN an oasis in SE Morocco, the largest in the Sahara. Area: about 1300 sq. km (500 sq. miles).

tag[1] (tæg) NOUN 1 a piece or strip of paper, plastic, leather, etc., for attaching to something by one end as a mark or label: *a price tag*. 2 an electronic device worn, usually on the wrist or ankle, by an offender serving a noncustodial sentence, which monitors the offender's whereabouts by means of a link to a central computer through the telephone system. Also called: **electronic tag**. 3 a small piece of material hanging from or loosely attached to a part or piece. 4 a point of metal or other hard substance at the end of a cord, lace, etc., to prevent it from fraying and to facilitate threading. 5 an epithet or verbal appendage, the refrain of a song, the moral of a fable, etc. 6 a brief quotation, esp one in a foreign language: *his speech was interlarded with Horatian tags*. 7 *Grammar* **a** Also called: **tag question**. a clause added on to another clause to invite the hearer's agreement or conversational cooperation. Tags are usually in the form of a question with a pronoun as subject, the antecedent of which is the subject of the main clause; as *isn't it* in *the bread is on the table, isn't it?* **b** a linguistic item added on to a sentence but not forming part of it, as *John* in *are you there, John?* 8 an ornamental flourish as at the end of a signature. 9 the contrastingly coloured tip to an animal's tail. 10 a matted lock of wool or hair. 11

Angling a strand of tinsel, wire, etc., tied to the body of an artificial fly. 12 *Slang* a graffito consisting of a nickname or personal symbol. ◆ VERB **tags, tagging, tagged.** (*mainly tr*) 13 to mark with a tag. 14 to monitor the whereabouts of (an offender) by means of an electronic tag. 15 to add or append as a tag. 16 to supply (prose or blank verse) with rhymes. 17 (*intr; usually foll by on or along*) to trail (behind): *many small boys tagged on behind the procession.* 18 to name or call (someone something): *they tagged him Lanky.* 19 to cut the tags of wool or hair from (an animal). 20 *Slang* to paint one's tag on (a building, wall, etc.).
▷HISTORY C15: of uncertain origin; related to Swedish *tagg* point, perhaps also to TACK[1]

tag[2] (tæg) NOUN 1 Also called: **tig.** a children's game in which one player chases the others in an attempt to catch one of them who will then become the chaser. 2 the act of tagging one's partner in tag wrestling. 3 (*modifier*) denoting or relating to a wrestling contest between two teams of two wrestlers, in which only one from each team may be in the ring at one time. The contestant outside the ring may change places with his team-mate inside the ring after touching his hand. ◆ VERB **tags, tagging, tagged.** (*tr*) 4 to catch (another child) in the game of tag. 5 (in tag wrestling) to touch the hand of (one's partner).
▷HISTORY C18: perhaps from TAG[1]

Tagalog (tə'gɑːlɒg) NOUN 1 (*plural* **-logs** *or* **-log**) a member of a people of the Philippines, living chiefly in the region around Manila. 2 the language of this people, belonging to the Malayo-Polynesian family: the official language of the Philippines. ◆ ADJECTIVE 3 of or relating to this people or their language.

Taganrog (*Russian* təgan'rɔk) NOUN a port in SW Russia, on the **Gulf of Taganrog** (an inlet of the Sea of Azov): founded in 1698 as a naval base and fortress by Peter the Great: industrial centre. Pop.: 287 600 (1999 est.).

tagareen (təgɑː'riːn) NOUN *English dialect* a junk shop.

tag end NOUN 1 the last part of something: *the tag end of the day.* 2 a loose end of cloth, thread, etc.

tagetes (tæ'dʒiːtiːz) NOUN See **marigold** (sense 1).

taggers ('tægəz) PLURAL NOUN very thin iron or steel sheet coated with tin.
▷HISTORY C19: perhaps so called because it was used to make tags for laces

tagine *or* **tajine** (tæ'ʒiːn) NOUN 1 a large, heavy N African cooking pot with a conical lid. 2 a N African stew with vegetables, olives, lemon, garlic and spices, cooked in a tagine.
▷HISTORY from Moroccan Arabic *tažin*, from Arabic *tājin* frying pan

tagliatelle (ˌtæljə'tɛlɪ) NOUN a form of pasta made in narrow strips.
▷HISTORY Italian, from *tagliare* to cut

tag line NOUN 1 an amusing or memorable phrase designed to catch attention in an advertisement. 2 another name for **punch line.**

tagma ('tægmə) NOUN, *plural* **-mata** (-mətə). *Zoology* a distinct region of the body of an arthropod, such as the head, thorax, or abdomen of an insect.
▷HISTORY C19: from Greek: something arranged, from *tassein* to put in order

tagmeme ('tægmiːm) NOUN *Linguistics* a class of speech elements all of which may fulfil the same grammatical role in a sentence; the minimum unit of analysis in tagmemics.
▷HISTORY C20: from Greek *tagma* order, from *tassein* to put in order + -EME
▸**tag'memic** ADJECTIVE

tagmemics (tæg'miːmɪks) PLURAL NOUN (*functioning as singular*) *Linguistics* a type of grammatical analysis based on the concept of function in sentence slots and the determination of classes of words that can fill each slot.

taguan ('tægˌwæn) NOUN a large nocturnal flying squirrel, *Petaurista petaurista,* of high forests in the East Indies that uses its long tail as a rudder.
▷HISTORY C19: its Filipino name

Tagus ('teɪgəs) NOUN a river in SW Europe, rising in E central Spain and flowing west to the border with Portugal, then southwest to the Atlantic at Lisbon: the longest river of the Iberian Peninsula. Length: 1007 km (626 miles). Portuguese name: **Tejo.** Spanish name: **Tajo.**

taha Maori ('tɑːhə) NOUN *NZ* a Maori perspective or dimension of a subject.
▷HISTORY Maori

tahini (tə'hiːnɪ) *or* **tahina** (tə'hiːnə) NOUN a paste made from sesame seeds originating in the Middle East, often used as an ingredient of hummus and other dips.
▷HISTORY from Arabic

Tahiti (tə'hiːtɪ) NOUN an island in the S Pacific, in the Windward group of the Society Islands: the largest and most important island in French Polynesia; became a French protectorate in 1842 and a colony in 1880. Capital: Papeete. Pop.: 115 820 (latest est.). Area: 1005 sq. km (388 sq. miles).

Tahitian (tə'hiːtɪən, tə'hiːʃɪən) ADJECTIVE 1 of or relating to Tahiti or its inhabitants. ◆ NOUN 2 a native or inhabitant of Tahiti.

Tahltan ('tæltən) NOUN 1 a member of a North American Indian people inhabiting NW British Columbia. 2 the language of this people, belonging to the Athapascan group of the Na-Dene phylum.

Tahoe ('tɑːhəʊ, 'teɪ-) NOUN **Lake.** a lake between E California and W Nevada, in the Sierra Nevada Mountains at an altitude of 1899 m (6229 ft.). Area: about 520 sq. km (200 sq. miles).

tahr *or* **thar** (tɑː) NOUN any of several goatlike bovid mammals of the genus *Hemitragus,* such as *H. jemlahicus* (**Himalayan tahr**), of mountainous regions of S and SW Asia, having a shaggy coat and curved horns.
▷HISTORY from Nepali *thār*

tahsil (tə'siːl) NOUN an administrative division of a zila in certain states in India.
▷HISTORY Urdu, from Arabic: collection

tahsildar (tə'siːldɑː) NOUN the officer in charge of the collection of revenues, etc., in a tahsil.
▷HISTORY C18: via Hindi from Persian, from TAHSIL + Persian *-dār* having

Tai (taɪ) ADJECTIVE, NOUN a variant spelling of **Thai.**

TAI ABBREVIATION FOR **International Atomic Time.**

taiaha ('taɪəˌhɑː) NOUN *NZ* a carved weapon in the form of a staff, now used in Maori ceremonial oratory.
▷HISTORY Maori

t'ai chi ch'uan ('taɪ dʒiː 'tʃwɑːn) NOUN a Chinese system of callisthenics characterized by coordinated and rhythmic movements. Often shortened to: **t'ai chi** ('taɪ 'dʒiː).
▷HISTORY Chinese, literally: great art of boxing

Taichung *or* **T'ai-chung** ('taɪ'tʃʊŋ) NOUN a city in W Taiwan (Republic of China): commercial centre of an agricultural region. Pop.: 940 589 (2000 est.).

taig (teɪg) NOUN *Ulster dialect, often derogatory* a Roman Catholic.
▷HISTORY variant of the Irish name *Tadhg,* originally signifying any Irishman

taiga ('taɪgə) NOUN the coniferous forests extending across much of subarctic North America and Eurasia, bordered by tundra to the north and steppe to the south.
▷HISTORY from Russian, of Turkic origin; compare Turkish *dağ* mountain

taihoa ('taɪhəʊə) INTERJECTION *NZ* hold on! no hurry!
▷HISTORY Maori

taikonaut ('taɪkəʊˌnɔːt) NOUN an astronaut from the People's Republic of China.
▷HISTORY C20: from Cantonese *taikon(g)* cosmos + -NAUT

tail[1] (teɪl) NOUN 1 the region of the vertebrate body that is posterior to or above the anus and contains an elongation of the vertebral column, esp forming a flexible movable appendage. Related adjective: **caudal.** 2 anything resembling such an appendage in form or position; the bottom, lowest, or rear part: *the tail of a shirt.* 3 the last part or parts: *the tail of the storm.* 4 the rear part of an aircraft including the fin, tail plane, and control surfaces; empennage. 5 *Astronomy* the luminous stream of gas and dust particles, up to 200 million kilometres long, driven from the head of a comet, when close to the sun, under the effect of the solar wind and light pressure. 6 the rear portion of a bomb, rocket, missile, etc., usually fitted with guiding or stabilizing vanes. 7 a line of people or things. 8 a long braid or tress of hair: *a ponytail; a pigtail.* 9 *Angling* Also called: **tailfly.** the lowest fly on a wet-fly cast. 10 a final short line in a stanza. 11 *Informal* a person employed to follow and spy upon another or others. 12 an informal word for **buttocks.** 13 *Taboo slang* **a** the female genitals. **b** a woman considered sexually (esp in the phrases **piece of tail, bit of tail**). 14 *Printing* **a** the margin at the foot of a page. **b** the bottom edge of a book. 15 the lower end of a pool or part of a stream. 16 *Informal* the course or track of a fleeing person or animal: *the police are on my tail.* 17 (*modifier*) coming from or situated in the rear: *a tail wind.* 18 **turn tail.** to run away; escape. 19 **with one's tail between one's legs.** in a state of utter defeat or confusion. ◆ VERB 20 to form or cause to form the tail. 21 to remove the tail of (an animal); dock. 22 (*tr*) to remove the stalk of: *to top and tail the gooseberries.* 23 (*tr*) to connect (objects, ideas, etc.) together by or as if by the tail. 24 (*tr*) *Informal* to follow stealthily. 25 (*tr*) *Austral* to tend (cattle) on foot. 26 (*intr*) (of a vessel) to assume a specified position, as when at a mooring. 27 to build the end of (a brick, joist, etc.) into a wall or (of a brick, etc.) to have one end built into a wall. ◆ See also **tail off, tail out, tails.**
▷HISTORY Old English *tægel;* related to Old Norse *tagl* horse's tail, Gothic *tagl* hair, Old High German *zagal* tail
▸**'tailless** ADJECTIVE ▸**'taillessly** ADVERB ▸**'taillessness** NOUN ▸**'tail-ˌlike** ADJECTIVE

tail[2] (teɪl) *Property law* ◆ NOUN 1 the limitation of an estate or interest to a person and the heirs of his body. See also **entail.** ◆ ADJECTIVE 2 (*immediately postpositive*) (of an estate or interest) limited in this way.
▷HISTORY C15: from Old French *taille* a division; see TAILOR, TALLY
▸**'tailless** ADJECTIVE

tailback ('teɪlˌbæk) NOUN a queue of traffic stretching back from an obstruction.

tailboard ('teɪlˌbɔːd) NOUN a board at the rear of a lorry, wagon, etc., that can be removed or let down on a hinge.

tail coat NOUN 1 Also called: **tails.** a man's black coat having a horizontal cut over the hips and a tapering tail with a vertical slit up to the waist: worn as part of full evening dress. 2 Also called: **swallow-tailed coat.** another name for **morning coat.**

tail covert NOUN any of the covert feathers of a bird covering the bases of the tail feathers.

tail end NOUN the last, endmost, or final part.

tail fan NOUN the fanned structure at the hind end of a lobster or related crustacean, formed from the telson and uropods.

tailgate ('teɪlˌgeɪt) NOUN 1 another name for **tailboard.** 2 a door at the rear of a hatchback vehicle. ◆ VERB 3 to drive very close behind (a vehicle).
▸**'tailˌgater** NOUN

tail gate NOUN a gate that is used to control the flow of water at the lower end of a lock. Compare **head gate.**

tail-heavy ADJECTIVE (of an aircraft) having too much weight at the rear because of overloading or poor design.

tailing ('teɪlɪŋ) NOUN the part of a beam, rafter, projecting brick or stone, etc., embedded in a wall.

tailings ('teɪlɪŋz) PLURAL NOUN waste left over after certain processes, such as from an ore-crushing plant or in milling grain.

taille (taɪ; *French* tɑj) NOUN, *plural* **tailles** (taɪ, taɪz; *French* tɑj). (in France before 1789) a tax levied by a king or overlord on his subjects.
▷HISTORY C17: from French, from Old French *taillier* to shape; see TAILOR

tail-light *or* **tail lamp** NOUN other names for **rear light.**

tail off *or* **away** VERB (*adverb, usually intr*) to decrease or cause to decrease in quantity, degree, etc., esp gradually: *his interest in collecting stamps tailed off over the years.*

tailor ('teɪlə) NOUN 1 a person who makes, repairs, or alters outer garments, esp menswear. Related adjective: **sartorial.** 2 a voracious and active marine

food fish, *Pomatomus saltator,* of Australia with scissor-like teeth. ◆ VERB [3] to cut or style (material, clothes, etc.) to satisfy certain requirements. [4] (*tr*) to adapt so as to make suitable for something specific: *he tailored his speech to suit a younger audience.* [5] (*intr*) to follow the occupation of a tailor.
▷HISTORY C13: from Anglo-Norman *taillour,* from Old French *taillier* to cut, from Latin *tālea* a cutting; related to Greek *talis* girl of marriageable age

tailorbird ('teɪlə,bɜːd) NOUN any of several tropical Asian warblers of the genus *Orthotomus,* which build nests by sewing together large leaves using plant fibres.

tailor-made ADJECTIVE [1] made by a tailor to fit exactly: *a tailor-made suit.* [2] perfectly meeting a particular purpose: *a girl tailor-made for him.* ◆ NOUN [3] a tailor-made garment. [4] *Slang* a cigarette made in a factory rather than rolled by hand.

tailor's chalk NOUN pipeclay used by tailors and dressmakers to mark seams, darts, etc., on material.

tailor's-tack NOUN one of a series of loose looped stitches used to transfer markings for seams, darts, etc., from a paper pattern to material.

tail out VERB (*tr, adverb*) to guide (timber) as it emerges from a power saw.

tailpiece ('teɪl,piːs) NOUN [1] an extension or appendage that lengthens or completes something. [2] *Printing* a decorative design at the foot of a page or end of a chapter. [3] *Music* a piece of wood to which the strings of a violin, etc., are attached at their lower end. It is suspended between the taut strings and the bottom of the violin by a piece of gut or metal. [4] Also called: **tail beam.** *Architect* a short beam or rafter that has one end embedded in a wall.

tailpipe ('teɪl,paɪp) NOUN a pipe from which the exhaust gases from an internal-combustion engine are discharged, esp the terminal pipe of the exhaust system of a motor vehicle.

tailplane ('teɪl,pleɪn) NOUN a small horizontal wing at the tail of an aircraft to provide longitudinal stability. Also called (esp US): **horizontal stabilizer.**

tailrace ('teɪl,reɪs) NOUN [1] a channel that carries water away from a water wheel, turbine, etc. Compare **headrace.** [2] *Mining* the channel for removing tailings in water.

tail rotor NOUN a small propeller fitted to the rear of a helicopter to counteract the torque reaction of the main rotor and thus prevent the body of the helicopter from rotating in an opposite direction.

tails (teɪlz) PLURAL NOUN [1] an informal name for **tail coat.** ◆ INTERJECTION, ADVERB [2] with the reverse side of a coin uppermost: used as a call before tossing a coin. Compare **heads.**

tailskid ('teɪl,skɪd) NOUN [1] a runner under the tail of an aircraft. [2] a rear-wheel skid of a motor vehicle.

tailspin ('teɪl,spɪn) NOUN [1] *Aeronautics* another name for **spin** (sense 16). [2] *Informal* a state of confusion or panic.

tailstock ('teɪl,stɒk) NOUN a casting that slides on the bed of a lathe in alignment with the headstock and is locked in position to support the free end of a workpiece.

tail wheel NOUN a wheel fitted to the rear of a vehicle, esp the landing wheel under the tail of an aircraft.

tailwind ('teɪl,wɪnd) NOUN a wind blowing in the same direction as the course of an aircraft or ship. Compare **headwind.**

Taimyr Peninsula (*Russian* taj'mir) NOUN a large peninsula of N central Russia, between the Kara Sea and the Laptev Sea. Also called: **Taymyr Peninsula.**

tain (teɪn) NOUN tinfoil used in backing mirrors.
▷HISTORY from French, from *étain* tin, from Old French *estain,* from Latin *stagnum* alloy of silver and lead; see STANNUM

Tainan *or* **T'ai-nan** ('taɪ'næn) NOUN a city in the SW Republic of China (Taiwan): an early centre of Chinese emigration from the mainland; largest city and capital of the island (1638–1885); Chengkung University. Pop.: 728 060 (2000 est.).

Taínaron ('tɛnarɔn) NOUN transliteration of the Modern Greek name for (Cape) **Matapan.**

Taino ('taɪnəʊ) NOUN [1] (*plural* **-nos** *or* **-no**) a member of an American Indian people of the Greater Antilles and the Bahamas. [2] the language of this people, belonging to the Arawakan family.

taint (teɪnt) VERB [1] to affect or be affected by pollution or contamination: *oil has tainted the water.* [2] to tarnish (someone's reputation, etc.). ◆ NOUN [3] a defect or flaw: *a taint on someone's reputation.* [4] a trace of contamination or infection.
▷HISTORY C14: (influenced by *attaint* infected, from ATTAIN) from Old French *teindre* to dye, from Latin *tingere* to dye
▸ **'taintless** ADJECTIVE

taipan[1] ('taɪ,pæn) NOUN a large highly venomous elapid snake, *Oxyuranus scutellatus,* of NE Australia.
▷HISTORY C20: from a native Australian language

taipan[2] ('taɪ,pæn) NOUN the foreign head of a business in China.
▷HISTORY C19: from dialectal form of Chinese *tai* great + *ban* company, class

Taipei *or* **T'ai-pei** ('taɪ'peɪ) NOUN the capital of the Republic of China (Taiwan), at the N tip of the island: became capital in 1885; industrial centre; two universities. Pop.: 2 641 312 (2000 est.).

Taiping ('taɪ'pɪŋ) NOUN *History* a person who supported or took part in the movement of religious mysticism and agrarian unrest in China between 1850 and 1864 (**Taiping rebellion**), which weakened the Manchu dynasty but was eventually suppressed with foreign aid.
▷HISTORY C19: from Chinese, from *tai* great + *ping* peace

Taiwan ('taɪ'wɑːn) NOUN an island in SE Asia between the East China Sea and the South China Sea, off the SE coast of the People's Republic of China: the principal territory of the Republic of China. Pop.: 22 340 000 (2001 est.). Former name: **Formosa.**

Taiwanese (,taɪwɑː'niːz) ADJECTIVE [1] of or relating to Taiwan or its inhabitants. ◆ NOUN [2] a native or inhabitant of Taiwan.

Taiwan Strait NOUN another name for **Formosa Strait.**

Taiyuan *or* **T'ai-yüan** ('taɪjuː'ɑːn) NOUN a city in N China, capital of Shanxi: founded before 450 A.D.; an industrial centre, surrounded by China's largest reserves of high-grade bituminous coal. Pop.: 1 500 000 (1991 est.).

Ta'izz (tæ'ɪz, teɪ'iːz) NOUN a town in SW Yemen, formerly in North Yemen: agricultural trading centre. Pop.: 178 043 (1995 est.).

taj (tɑːdʒ) NOUN a tall conical cap worn as a mark of distinction by Muslims.
▷HISTORY via Arabic from Persian: crown, crest

Tajik ('tɑːdʒɪk, tɑː'dʒiːk) NOUN, *plural* **-jik.** a member of a Persian-speaking Muslim people inhabiting Tajikistan and parts of Sinkiang in W China.

Tajiki, Tadzhiki (tɑː'dʒiːkiː, -'dʒiː-), **Tajik,** *or* **Tadzhik** NOUN [1] the language of the Tajik, belonging to the West Iranian subbranch of the Indo-European family. ◆ ADJECTIVE [2] of or relating to the Tajik or their language.

Tajikistan, Tadzhikistan, *or* **Tadjikistan** (tɑː,dʒɪkɪ'stɑːn, -stæn) NOUN a republic in central Asia: under Uzbek rule from the 15th century until taken over by Russia in the 1860s, it became an autonomous Soviet republic in 1929 and gained full independence from the Soviet Union in 1991; it is mainly mountainous. Official language: Tajiki. Religion: believers are mainly Muslim. Currency: somoni. Capital: Dushanbe. Pop.: 6 252 000 (2001 est.). Area: 143 100 sq. km (55 240 sq. miles).

tajine (tæ'ʒiːn) NOUN a variant spelling of **tagine.**

Taj Mahal ('tɑːdʒ mə'hɑːl) NOUN a white marble mausoleum in central India, in Agra on the Jumna River: built (1632–43) by the emperor Shah Jahan in memory of his beloved wife, Mumtaz Mahal; regarded as the finest example of Mogul architecture.
▷HISTORY Urdu, literally: crown of buildings

Tajo ('taxo) NOUN the Spanish name for the **Tagus.**

taka ('tɑːkɑː) NOUN the standard monetary unit of Bangladesh, divided into 100 paise.
▷HISTORY from Bengali

takahe ('tɑːkə,hiː) NOUN a very rare flightless New Zealand rail, *Notornis mantelli.*
▷HISTORY from Maori, of imitative origin

Takamatsu (,tækə'mætsuː) NOUN a port in SW Japan, on NE Shikoku on the Inland Sea. Pop.: 330 997 (1995).

Takao (tæ'kaʊ) NOUN the Japanese name for **Kaohsiung.**

take[1] (teɪk) VERB **takes, taking, took, taken.** (*mainly tr*) [1] (*also intr*) to gain possession of (something) by force or effort. [2] to appropriate or steal: *to take other people's belongings.* [3] to receive or accept into a relationship with oneself: *to take a wife.* [4] to pay for or buy. [5] to rent or lease: *to take a flat in town.* [6] to receive or obtain by regular payment: *we take a newspaper every day.* [7] to obtain by competing for; win: *to take first prize.* [8] to obtain or derive from a source: *he took his good manners from his older brother.* [9] to assume the obligations of: *to take office.* [10] to endure, esp with fortitude: *to take punishment.* [11] to adopt as a symbol of duty, obligation, etc.: *to take the veil.* [12] to receive or react to in a specified way: *she took the news very well.* [13] to adopt as one's own: *to take someone's part in a quarrel.* [14] to receive and make use of: *to take advice.* [15] to receive into the body, as by eating, inhaling, etc.: *to take a breath.* [16] to eat, drink, etc., esp habitually: *to take sugar in one's tea.* [17] to have or be engaged in for one's benefit or use: *to take a rest.* [18] to work at or study: *to take economics at college.* [19] to make, do, or perform (an action): *to take a leap.* [20] to make use of: *to take an opportunity.* [21] to put into effect; adopt: *to take measures.* [22] (*also intr*) to make a photograph of or admit of being photographed. [23] to act or perform: *she takes the part of the Queen.* [24] to write down or copy: *to take notes.* [25] to experience or feel: *to take pride in one's appearance; to take offence.* [26] to consider, believe, or regard: *I take him to be honest.* [27] to consider or accept as valid: *I take your point.* [28] to hold or maintain in the mind: *his father took a dim view of his career.* [29] to deal or contend with: *the tennis champion took her opponent's best strokes without difficulty.* [30] to use as a particular case: *take hotels for example.* [31] (*intr; often foll by from*) to diminish or detract: *the actor's bad performance took from the effect of the play.* [32] to confront successfully: *the horse took the jump at the third attempt.* [33] (*intr*) to have or produce the intended effect; succeed: *her vaccination took; the glue is taking well.* [34] (*intr*) (of seeds, plants, etc.) to start growing successfully. [35] to aim or direct: *he took a swipe at his opponent.* [36] to deal a blow to in a specified place. [37] *Archaic* to have sexual intercourse with. [38] to carry off or remove from a place. [39] to carry along or have in one's possession: *don't forget to take your umbrella.* [40] to convey or transport: *the train will take us out of the city.* [41] to use as a means of transport: *I shall take the bus.* [42] to conduct or lead: *this road takes you to the station.* [43] to escort or accompany: *may I take you out tonight?* [44] to bring or deliver to a state, position, etc.: *his ability took him to the forefront in his field.* [45] to go to look for; seek: *to take cover.* [46] to ascertain or determine by measuring, computing, etc.: *to take a pulse; take a reading from a dial.* [47] (*intr*) (of a mechanism) to catch or engage (a part). [48] to put an end to; destroy: *she took her own life.* [49] to come upon unexpectedly; discover. [50] to contract: *he took a chill.* [51] to affect or attack: *the fever took him one night.* [52] (*copula*) to become suddenly or be rendered (ill): *he took sick; he was taken sick.* [53] (*also intr*) to absorb or become absorbed by something: *to take a polish.* [54] (*usually passive*) to charm or captivate: *she was very taken with the puppy.* [55] (*intr*) to be or become popular; win favour. [56] to require or need: *this job will take a lot of attention; that task will take all your time.* [57] to subtract or deduct: *to take six from ten leaves four.* [58] to hold or contain: *the suitcase won't take all your clothes.* [59] to quote or copy: *he has taken several paragraphs from the book for his essay.* [60] to proceed to occupy: *to take a seat.* [61] (often foll by *to*) to use or employ: *to take steps to ascertain the answer.* [62] to win or capture (a trick, counter, piece, etc.). [63] (*also intr*) to catch as prey or catch prey. [64] *Slang* to cheat, deceive, or victimize. [65] **take amiss.** to be annoyed or offended by. [66] **take at one's word.** See **word** (sense 17). [67] **take care.** to pay attention; be heedful. [68] **take care of.** to assume responsibility for; look after. [69] **take chances** *or* **a chance.** to behave in a risky manner. [70] **take five** (*or* **ten**). *Informal, chiefly US and Canadian* to take a break of five (or ten) minutes. [71] **take heart.** to become encouraged.

[72] **take it.** **a** to assume; believe: *I take it you'll be back later.* **b** *Informal* to stand up to or endure criticism, abuse, harsh treatment, etc. [73] **take one's time.** to use as much time as is needed; not rush. [74] **take place.** to happen or occur. [75] **take (someone's) name in vain.** **a** to use a name, esp of God, disrespectfully or irreverently. **b** *Jocular* to say (someone's) name. [76] **take (something) upon oneself.** to assume the right to do or responsibility for (something). ◆ NOUN [77] the act of taking. [78] the number of quarry killed or captured on one occasion. [79] *Informal, chiefly US* the amount of anything taken, esp money. [80] *Films, music* **a** one of a series of recordings from which the best will be selected for release. **b** the process of taking one such recording. **c** a scene or part of a scene photographed without interruption. [81] *Informal* **a** any objective indication of a successful vaccination, such as a local skin reaction. **b** a successful skin graft. [82] *Printing* a part of an article, story, etc., given to a compositor or keyboard operator for setting in type. [83] *Informal* a try or attempt. [84] *Informal, chiefly US* a version or interpretation: *Cronenberg's harsh take on the sci-fi story.* ◆ See also **take aback, take after, take against, take apart, take away, take back, take down, take for, take in, take off, take on, take out, take over, take to, take up.**
▷**HISTORY** Old English *tacan,* from Old Norse *taka;* related to Gothic *tekan* to touch
▸ **'takable** *or* **'takeable** ADJECTIVE

take[2] ('tɑːkɪ) NOUN *NZ* a topic or cause.
▷**HISTORY** Maori

take aback VERB (*tr, adverb*) to astonish or disconcert.

take after VERB (*intr, preposition*) [1] to resemble in appearance, character, behaviour, etc. [2] to follow as an example.

take against VERB (*intr, preposition*) to start to dislike, esp without good reason.

take apart VERB (*tr, adverb*) [1] to separate (something) into component parts. [2] to criticize or punish severely: *the reviewers took the new play apart.*

take away VERB (*tr, adverb*) [1] to deduct; subtract: *take away four from nine to leave five.* ◆ PREPOSITION [2] minus: *nine take away four is five.* ◆ ADJECTIVE **takeaway.** *Brit, Austral, and NZ.* [3] sold for consumption away from the premises on which it is prepared: *a takeaway meal.* [4] preparing and selling food for consumption away from the premises: *a takeaway Indian restaurant.* ◆ NOUN **takeaway.** *Brit, Austral, and NZ.* [5] a shop or restaurant that sells such food: *let's go to the Chinese takeaway.* [6] a meal bought at such a shop or restaurant: *we'll have a Chinese takeaway tonight to save cooking.* ◆ Scot word (for senses 3–6): **carry-out.** US and Canadian word (for senses 3–6): **takeout.**

take back VERB (*adverb, mainly tr*) [1] to retract or withdraw (something said, written, promised, etc.). [2] to regain possession of. [3] to return for exchange: *to take back a substandard garment.* [4] to accept (someone) back (into one's home, affections, etc.). [5] to remind one of the past; cause one to reminisce: *that tune really takes me back.* [6] (*also intr*) *Printing* to move (copy) to the previous line.

take down VERB (*tr, adverb*) [1] to record in writing. [2] to dismantle or tear down: *to take down an old shed.* [3] to lower or reduce in power, arrogance, etc. (esp in the phrase **to take down a peg**). ◆ ADJECTIVE **take-down.** [4] made or intended to be disassembled.

take for VERB (*tr, preposition*) *Informal* to consider or suppose to be, esp mistakenly: *the fake coins were taken for genuine; who do you take me for?*

take-home pay NOUN the remainder of one's pay after all income tax and other compulsory deductions have been made.

take in VERB (*tr, adverb*) [1] to comprehend or understand. [2] to include or comprise: *his thesis takes in that point.* [3] to receive into one's house in exchange for payment: *to take in washing; take in lodgers.* [4] to make (an article of clothing, etc.) smaller by altering seams. [5] to include: *the tour takes in the islands as well as the mainland.* [6] *Informal* to cheat or deceive. [7] to go to; visit: *let's take in a movie tonight.* ◆ NOUN **take-in.** [8] *Informal* the act or an instance of cheating or deceiving.

taken ('teɪkən) VERB [1] the past participle of **take.** ◆ ADJECTIVE [2] (*postpositive; foll by with*) enthusiastically impressed (by); infatuated (with).

take off VERB (*adverb*) [1] (*tr*) to remove or discard (a garment). [2] (*intr*) (of an aircraft) to become airborne. [3] *Informal* to set out or cause to set out on a journey: *they took off for Spain.* [4] (*tr*) (of a disease) to prove fatal to; kill. [5] (*tr*) *Informal* to mimic or imitate, esp in an amusing or satirical manner. [6] (*intr*) *Informal* to become successful or popular, esp suddenly. ◆ NOUN **takeoff.** [7] the act or process of making an aircraft airborne. [8] the stage of a country's economic development when rapid and sustained economic growth is first achieved. [9] *Informal* an act of mimicry; imitation.

take on VERB (*adverb, mainly tr*) [1] to employ or hire: *to take on new workmen.* [2] to assume or acquire: *his voice took on a plaintive note.* [3] to agree to do; undertake: *I'll take on that job for you.* [4] to compete against, oppose, or fight: *I will take him on at tennis; I'll take him on any time.* [5] (*intr*) *Informal* to exhibit great emotion, esp grief.

take out VERB (*tr, adverb*) [1] to extract or remove. [2] to obtain or secure (a licence, patent, etc.) from an authority. [3] to go out with; escort: *George is taking Susan out next week.* [4] *Bridge* to bid a different suit from (one's partner) in order to rescue him from a difficult contract. [5] *Slang* to kill or destroy. [6] *Austral informal* to win, esp in sport: *he took out the tennis championship.* [7] **take it** *or* **a lot out of.** *Informal* to sap the energy or vitality of. [8] **take out on.** *Informal* to vent (anger, frustration, etc.) on (esp an innocent person). [9] **take someone out of himself.** *Informal* to make someone forget his anxieties, problems, etc. ◆ ADJECTIVE **takeout.** [10] *Bridge* of or designating a conventional informatory bid, asking one's partner to bid another suit. ◆ ADJECTIVE, NOUN [11] an informal word (chiefly US and Canadian) for **takeaway** (senses 3–6).

take over VERB (*adverb*) [1] to assume the control or management of. [2] *Printing* to move (copy) to the next line. ◆ NOUN **takeover.** [3] **a** the act of seizing or assuming power, control, etc. **b** (*as modifier*): *takeover bid.* [4] *Sport* another word for **changeover** (sense 3).

taker ('teɪkə) NOUN a person who takes something, esp a bet, wager, or offer of purchase.

take to VERB (*intr, preposition*) [1] to make for; flee to: *to take to the hills.* [2] to form a liking for, esp after a short acquaintance: *I took to him straightaway.* [3] to have recourse to: *to take to the bottle.* [4] **take to heart.** to regard seriously.

take up VERB (*adverb, mainly tr*) [1] to adopt the study, practice, or activity of: *to take up gardening.* [2] *Austral and NZ* to occupy and break in (uncultivated land): *he took up some hundreds of acres in the back country.* [3] to shorten (a garment or part of a garment): *she took all her skirts up three inches.* [4] to pay off (a note, mortgage, etc.). [5] to agree to or accept (an invitation, etc.). [6] to pursue further or resume (something): *he took up French where he left off.* [7] to absorb (a liquid). [8] to adopt as a protégé; act as a patron to. [9] to occupy or fill (space or time). [10] to interrupt, esp in order to contradict or criticize. [11] **take up on.** **a** to argue or dispute with (someone): *can I take you up on two points in your talk?* **b** to accept what is offered by (someone): *let me take you up on your invitation.* [12] **take up with.** **a** to discuss with (someone); refer to: *to take up a fault with the manufacturers.* **b** (*intr*) to begin to keep company or associate with. ◆ NOUN **take-up.** [13] **a** the claiming or acceptance of something, esp a state benefit, that is due or available. **b** (*as modifier*): *take-up rate.* [14] *Machinery* the distance through which a part must move to absorb the free play in a system. [15] (*modifier*) denoting the part of a mechanism on which film, tape, or wire is wound up: *a take-up spool on a tape recorder.*

takin ('tɑːkiːn) NOUN a massive bovid mammal, *Budorcas taxicolor,* of mountainous regions of S Asia, having a shaggy coat, short legs, and horns that point backwards and upwards.
▷**HISTORY** C19: from Mishmi

taking ('teɪkɪŋ) ADJECTIVE [1] charming, fascinating, or intriguing. [2] *Informal* infectious; catching. ◆ NOUN [3] something taken. [4] (*plural*) receipts; earnings.
▸ **'takingly** ADVERB ▸ **'takingness** NOUN

takkies ('tækɪz) PLURAL NOUN *South African informal* a variant spelling of **tackies.**

Takoradi (ˌtɑːkə'rɑːdɪ) NOUN the chief port of Ghana, in the southwest on the Gulf of Guinea: modern harbour opened in 1928. Pop. (with Sekondi): 103 600 (1988 est.).

tala ('tɑːlə) NOUN the standard monetary unit of Samoa, divided into 100 sene.

Talaing (tɑː'laɪŋ) NOUN another name for **Mon.**

talapoin ('tæləˌpɔɪn) NOUN [1] the smallest of the guenon monkeys, *Cercopithecus talapoin,* of swampy central W African forests, having olive-green fur and slightly webbed digits. [2] (in Myanmar and Thailand) **a** a Buddhist monk. **b** a title of respect used in addressing such a monk.
▷**HISTORY** C16: from French, literally: Buddhist monk, from Portuguese *talapão,* from Mon *tala pōi* our lord; originally jocular, from the appearance of the monkey

talaria (tə'lɛərɪə) PLURAL NOUN *Greek myth* winged sandals, such as those worn by Hermes.
▷**HISTORY** C16: from Latin, from *tālāris* belonging to the ankle, from *tālus* ankle

Talavera de la Reina (*Spanish* tala'βera ðe la 'rɛina) NOUN a walled town in central Spain, on the Tagus River: scene of the defeat of the French by British and Spanish forces (1809) during the Peninsular War; agricultural processing centre. Pop.: 68 640 (1991).

talbot ('tɔːlbət) NOUN (formerly) an ancient breed of large hound, usually white or light-coloured, having pendulous ears and strong powers of scent.
▷**HISTORY** C16: supposed to have been brought to England by the *Talbot* family

talc (tælk) NOUN *also* **talcum.** [1] See **talcum powder.** [2] a white, grey, brown, or pale green mineral, found in metamorphic rocks. It is used in the manufacture of talcum powder and electrical insulators. Composition: hydrated magnesium silicate. Formula: $Mg_3Si_4O_{10}(OH)_2$. Crystal structure: monoclinic. ◆ VERB **talcs, talcking, talcked** *or* **talcs, talcing, talced.** [3] (*tr*) to apply talc to.
▷**HISTORY** C16: from Medieval Latin *talcum,* from Arabic *talq* mica, from Persian *talk*
▸ **'talcose** *or* **'talcous** ADJECTIVE

Talca (*Spanish* 'talka) NOUN a city in central Chile: scene of the declaration of Chilean independence (1818). Pop.: 174 858 (1999 est.).

Talcahuano (*Spanish* talka'wano) NOUN a port in S central Chile, near Concepción on an inlet of the Pacific: oil refinery. Pop.: 269 265 (1999 est.).

talcum powder ('tælkəm) NOUN a powder made of purified talc, usually scented, used for perfuming the body and for absorbing excess moisture. Often shortened to: **talc.**

tale (teɪl) NOUN [1] a report, narrative, or story. [2] one of a group of short stories connected by an overall narrative framework. [3] **a** a malicious or meddlesome rumour or piece of gossip: *to bear tales against someone.* **b** (*in combination*): *talebearer; taleteller.* [4] a fictitious or false statement. [5] **tell tales.** **a** to tell fanciful lies. **b** to report malicious stories, trivial complaints, etc., esp to someone in authority. [6] **tell a tale.** to reveal something important. [7] **tell its own tale.** to be self-evident. [8] *Archaic* **a** a number; amount. **b** computation or enumeration. [9] an obsolete word for **talk.**
▷**HISTORY** Old English *talu* list; related to Old Frisian *tele* talk, Old Saxon, Old Norse *tala* talk, number, Old High German *zala* number

Taleb ('tælɪb) NOUN (in Afghanistan) a member of the Taliban.

talent ('tælənt) NOUN [1] innate ability, aptitude, or faculty, esp when unspecified; above average ability: *a talent for cooking; a child with talent.* [2] a person or persons possessing such ability. [3] any of various ancient units of weight and money. [4] *Informal* members of the opposite sex collectively, esp those living in a particular place: *the local talent.* [5] an obsolete word for **inclination.**
▷**HISTORY** Old English *talente,* from Latin *talenta,* pl of *talentum* sum of money, from Greek *talanton* unit of money or weight; in Medieval Latin the sense was extended to ability through the influence of the parable of the talents (Matthew 25:14–30)
▸ **'talented** ADJECTIVE

talent scout NOUN a person whose occupation is the search for talented artists, sportsmen, performers, etc., for engagements as professionals.

taler (ˈtɑːlə) NOUN, *plural* **-ler** *or* **-lers**. a variant spelling of **thaler.**

tales (ˈteɪliːz) NOUN *Law* [1] (*functioning as plural*) a group of persons summoned from among those present in court or from bystanders to fill vacancies on a jury panel. [2] (*functioning as singular*) the writ summoning such jurors.
▷HISTORY C15: from Medieval Latin phrase *tālēs dē circumstantibus* such men from among the bystanders, from Latin *tālis* such
▸ˈ**talesman** NOUN

Taliban, Taleban, *or* **Talibaan** (ˈtælɪbæn) NOUN (in Afghanistan) a fundamentalist Islamic army: in 1996 it defeated the ruling mujaheddin factions and seized control of the country; overthrown in 2001 by US-led forces.
▷HISTORY C20: from Arabic *tāliban* seekers

taligrade (ˈtælɪˌgreɪd) ADJECTIVE (of mammals) walking on the outer side of the foot.
▷HISTORY C20: from New Latin, from Latin *tālus* ankle, heel + -GRADE

talion (ˈtælɪən) NOUN the system or legal principle of making the punishment correspond to the crime; retaliation.
▷HISTORY C15: via Old French from Latin *tāliō*, from *tālis* such

taliped (ˈtælɪˌpɛd) ADJECTIVE [1] *Pathol* having a club foot. ◆ NOUN [2] a club-footed person.
▷HISTORY C19: see TALIPES

talipes (ˈtælɪˌpiːz) NOUN [1] a congenital deformity of the foot by which it is twisted in any of various positions. [2] a technical name for **club foot.**
▷HISTORY C19: New Latin, from Latin *tālus* ankle + *pēs* foot

talipot *or* **talipot palm** (ˈtælɪˌpɒt) NOUN a palm tree, *Corypha umbraculifera,* of the East Indies, having large leaves that are used for fans, thatching houses, etc.
▷HISTORY C17: from Bengali: palm leaf, from Sanskrit *tālī* fan palm + *pattra* leaf

talisman (ˈtælɪzmən) NOUN, *plural* **-mans.** [1] a stone or other small object, usually inscribed or carved, believed to protect the wearer from evil influences. [2] anything thought to have magical or protective powers.
▷HISTORY C17: via French or Spanish from Arabic *tilsam,* from Medieval Greek *telesma* ritual, from Greek: consecration, from *telein* to perform a rite, complete, from *telos* end, result
▸**talismanic** (ˌtælɪzˈmænɪk) ADJECTIVE

talk (tɔːk) VERB [1] (*intr;* often foll by *to* or *with*) to express one's thoughts, feelings, or desires by means of words (to); speak (to). [2] (*intr*) to communicate or exchange thoughts by other means: *lovers talk with their eyes.* [3] (*intr;* usually foll by *about*) to exchange ideas, pleasantries, or opinions (about): *to talk about the weather.* [4] (*intr*) to articulate words; verbalize: *his baby can talk.* [5] (*tr*) to give voice to; utter: *to talk rubbish.* [6] (*tr*) to hold a conversation about; discuss: *to talk business.* [7] (*intr*) to reveal information: *the prisoner talked after torture.* [8] (*tr*) to know how to communicate in (a language or idiom): *he talks English.* [9] (*intr*) to spread rumours or gossip: *we don't want the neighbours to talk.* [10] (*intr*) to make sounds suggestive of talking. [11] (*intr*) to be effective or persuasive: *money talks.* [12] **now you're talking.** *Informal* at last you're saying something agreeable. [13] **talk big.** to boast or brag. [14] **talk shop.** to speak about one's work, esp when meeting socially, sometimes with the effect of excluding those not similarly employed. [15] **you can talk.** *Informal* you don't have to worry about doing a particular thing yourself. [16] **you can** *or* **can't talk.** *Informal* you yourself are guilty of offending in the very matter you are upholding or decrying. ◆ NOUN [17] a speech or lecture: *a talk on ancient Rome.* [18] an exchange of ideas or thoughts: *a business talk with a colleague.* [19] idle chatter, gossip, or rumour: *there has been a lot of talk about you two.* [20] a subject of conversation; theme: *our talk was of war.* [21] (*often plural*) a conference, discussion, or negotiation: *talks about a settlement.* [22] a specific manner of speaking: *children's talk.* ◆ See also **talk about, talk at, talk back, talk down, talk into, talk out, talk round, talk through, talk up.**
▷HISTORY C13 *talkien* to talk; related to Old English *talu* TALE, Frisian *talken* to talk
▸ˈ**talkable** ADJECTIVE ▸ˌ**talkaˈbility** NOUN ▸ˈ**talker** NOUN

talk about VERB (*intr, preposition*) [1] to discuss. [2] used informally and often ironically to add emphasis to a statement: *all his plays have such ridiculous plots — talk about good drama!* [3] **know what one is talking about.** to have thorough or specialized knowledge.

talk at VERB (*intr, preposition*) to speak to (a person) in a way that indicates a response is not really wanted: *I wish he'd talk to me rather than at me.*

talkative (ˈtɔːkətɪv) ADJECTIVE given to talking a great deal.
▸ˈ**talkatively** ADVERB ▸ˈ**talkativeness** NOUN

talk back VERB (*intr, adverb*) [1] to answer boldly or impudently. [2] *NZ* to conduct a telephone dialogue for immediate transmission over the air. ◆ NOUN **talkback.** [3] *Television, radio* a system of telephone links enabling spoken directions to be given during the production of a programme. [4] *NZ* **a** a broadcast telephone dialogue. **b** (*as modifier*): *a talkback show.*

talkbox (ˈtɔːkˌbɒks) NOUN another name for **voice box** (sense 2).

talk down VERB (*adverb*) [1] (*intr;* often foll by *to*) to behave (towards) in a superior or haughty manner. [2] (*tr*) to override (a person or argument) by continuous or loud talking. [3] (*tr*) to give instructions to (an aircraft) by radio to enable it to land.

talkie (ˈtɔːkɪ) NOUN *Informal* an early film with a soundtrack. Full name: **talking picture.**

Talking Book NOUN *Trademark* a recording of a book, designed to be used by blind people.

talking head NOUN (on television) a person, such as a newscaster, who is shown only from the shoulders up, and speaks without the use of any illustrative material.

talking shop NOUN *Informal* a group or committee that has discussions that never result in action.

talking-to NOUN *Informal* a session of criticism, as of the work or attitude of a subordinate by a person in authority.

talk into VERB (*tr, preposition*) to persuade to by talking: *I talked him into buying the house.*

talk out VERB (*adverb*) [1] (*tr*) to resolve or eliminate by talking: *they talked out their differences.* [2] (*tr*) *Brit* to block (a bill, etc.) in a legislative body by lengthy discussion. [3] **talk out of.** to dissuade from by talking: *she was talked out of marriage.*

talk round VERB [1] (*tr, adverb*) Also: **talk over.** to persuade to one's opinion: *I talked him round to buying a car.* [2] (*intr, preposition*) to discuss the arguments relating to (a subject), esp without coming to a conclusion: *to talk round the problem of the human condition.* [3] (*intr, preposition*) to discuss (a subject) vaguely without considering basic facts: *they talked round the idea of moving house quite forgetting they hadn't enough money.*

talk show NOUN [1] a television or radio show in which guests discuss controversial topics or personal issues. [2] US name for **chat show.**

talk through VERB (*tr*) [1] (*adverb*) to discuss (a problem or situation) in detail. [2] (*preposition*) to explain to (a person) all the stages of a process: *ask a friend to talk you through the exercise.*

talk up VERB (*tr, adverb*) to speak of or discuss favourably in order to arouse interest or support.

talky (ˈtɔːkɪ) ADJECTIVE **talkier, talkiest.** containing too much dialogue or inconsequential talk: *a talky novel.*

tall (tɔːl) ADJECTIVE [1] of more than average height. [2] **a** (*postpositive*) having a specified height: *a woman five feet tall.* **b** (*in combination*): *a twenty-foot-tall partition.* [3] *Informal* exaggerated or incredible: *a tall story.* [4] *Informal* difficult to accomplish: *a tall order.* [5] an archaic word for **excellent.**
▷HISTORY C14 (in the sense: big, comely, valiant); related to Old English *getæl* prompt, Old High German *gizal* quick, Gothic *untals* foolish
▸ˈ**tallness** NOUN

tallage (ˈtælɪdʒ) *English history* ◆ NOUN [1] **a** a tax levied by the Norman and early Angevin kings on their Crown lands and royal towns. **b** a toll levied by a lord upon his tenants or by a feudal lord upon his vassals. ◆ VERB [2] (*tr*) to levy a tax (upon); impose a tax (upon).
▷HISTORY C13: from Old French *taillage,* from *taillier* to cut; see TAILOR

Tallahassee (ˌtæləˈhæsɪ) NOUN a city in N Florida, capital of the state: two universities. Pop.: 150 624 (2000).

Tall Blacks PLURAL NOUN **the.** the international basketball team of New Zealand.

tallboy (ˈtɔːlˌbɔɪ) NOUN [1] a high chest of drawers made in two sections and placed one on top of the other; chest-on-chest. [2] a fitting on the top of a chimney to prevent downdraughts.
▷HISTORY C18: from TALL + BOY

tallet (ˈtælət) NOUN *Western English dialect* a loft.
▷HISTORY Welsh *taflod,* from Late Latin *tābulata* flooring

Tallinn *or* **Tallin** (ˈtælɪn) NOUN the capital of Estonia, on the Gulf of Finland: founded by the Danes in 1219; a port and naval base. Pop.: 404 000 (2000 est.). German name: **Reval.**

tallis (ˈtɑlɪs) *or* **tallith** (tɑˈlit) NOUN *Judaism* a fringed shawl worn by Jewish men during morning prayers.
▷HISTORY from Hebrew, literally: a cover

tallit (ˈtælɪθ; *Hebrew* taˈliːt) NOUN, *plural* **tallaisim** (tæˈleɪsɪm), **tallites** *or* **tallitot** (*Hebrew* -liːˈtɒt). [1] a white shawl with fringed corners worn over the head and shoulders by Jewish males during religious services. [2] a smaller form of this worn under the outer garment during waking hours by some Jewish males.
▷HISTORY C17: from Hebrew *tallīt*

tall oil NOUN any of various oily liquid mixtures obtained by acidifying the liquor resulting from the treatment of wood pulp with sodium hydroxide: it contains chiefly rosin acids and fatty acids and is used in making soaps and lubricants.
▷HISTORY C20: partial translation of German *Tallöl,* from Swedish *tallolja,* from *tall* pine + *olja* OIL

tallow (ˈtæləʊ) NOUN [1] a fatty substance consisting of a mixture of glycerides, including stearic, palmitic, and oleic acids and extracted chiefly from the suet of sheep and cattle: used for making soap, candles, food, etc. ◆ VERB [2] (*tr*) to cover or smear with tallow.
▷HISTORY Old English *tælg,* a dye; related to Middle Low German *talch* tallow, Dutch *talk,* Icelandic *tólg*
▸ˈ**tallowy** ADJECTIVE

tallow wood NOUN *Austral* a tall eucalyptus tree, *Eucalyptus microcorys,* of coastal regions, having soft fibrous bark and conical fruits and yielding a greasy timber.

tall poppy NOUN *Austral informal* a person who has a high salary or is otherwise prominent.
▷HISTORY perhaps from Tarquin's decapitation of the tallest poppies in his garden, to indicate the fate of the most prominent citizens of Gabii

tall poppy syndrome NOUN *Austral informal* a tendency to disparage any person who has achieved great prominence or wealth.

tall ship NOUN any square-rigged sailing ship.

tally (ˈtælɪ) VERB **-lies, -lying, -lied.** [1] (*intr*) to correspond one with the other: *the two stories don't tally.* [2] (*tr*) to supply with an identifying tag. [3] (*intr*) to keep score. [4] (*tr*) *Obsolete* to record or mark. ◆ NOUN, *plural* **-lies.** [5] any record of debit, credit, the score in a game, etc. [6] a ticket, label, or mark, used as a means of identification, classification, etc. [7] a counterpart or duplicate of something, such as the counterfoil of a cheque. [8] a stick used (esp formerly) as a record of the amount of a debt according to the notches cut in it. [9] a notch or mark cut in or made on such a stick. [10] a mark or number of marks used to represent a certain number in counting. [11] *Austral and NZ* the total number of sheep shorn by one shearer in a specified period of time.
▷HISTORY C15: from Medieval Latin *tālea,* from Latin: a stick; related to Latin *tālus* heel
▸ˈ**tallier** NOUN

tally clerk NOUN a person, esp on a wharf or dock or in an airport, who checks the count of goods being loaded or unloaded.

tally-ho (ˌtælɪˈhəʊ) INTERJECTION [1] the cry of a participant at a hunt to encourage the hounds when the quarry is sighted. ◆ NOUN, *plural* **-hos.** [2] an instance of crying tally-ho. [3] another name for

a **four-in-hand** (sense 1). ◆ VERB **-hos, -hoing, -hoed** *or* **-ho'd.** 4 (*intr*) to make the cry of tally-ho.
▷**HISTORY** C18: perhaps from French *taïaut* cry used in hunting

tallyman ('tælɪmən) NOUN, *plural* **-men.** 1 a scorekeeper or recorder. 2 *Dialect* a travelling salesman for a firm specializing in hire-purchase.
▸ **'tally,woman** FEMININE NOUN

tally-woman NOUN *Northern English dialect* a mistress.

Talmud ('tælmʊd) NOUN *Judaism* 1 the primary source of Jewish religious law, consisting of the Mishnah and the Gemara. 2 either of two recensions of this compilation, the Palestinian Talmud of about 375 A.D., or the longer and more important Babylonian Talmud of about 500 A.D.
▷**HISTORY** C16: from Hebrew *talmūdh,* literally: instruction, from *lāmadh* to learn
▸ **Tal'mudic** *or* **Tal'mudical** ADJECTIVE ▸ **'Talmudism** NOUN

Talmudist ('tælmʊdɪst) NOUN 1 a scholar specializing in the study of the Talmud. 2 any of the writers of or contributors to the Talmud.

talon ('tælən) NOUN 1 a sharply hooked claw, esp of a bird of prey. 2 anything resembling a bird's claw. 3 the part of a lock that the key presses on when it is turned. 4 *Cards* the pile of cards left after the deal. 5 *Architect* another name for **ogee.** 6 *Stock Exchange* a printed slip attached to some bearer bonds to enable the holder to apply for a new sheet of coupons.
▷**HISTORY** C14: from Old French: heel, from Latin *tālus* heel
▸ **'taloned** ADJECTIVE

Talos ('teɪlɒs) NOUN *Greek myth* the nephew and apprentice of Daedalus, who surpassed his uncle as an inventor and was killed by him out of jealousy.

taluk ('tɑːlʊk, tɑː'lʊk), **taluka,** *or* **talooka** (tɑː'luːkə) NOUN (in India) 1 a subdivision of a district; a group of several villages organized for revenue purposes. 2 a hereditary estate.
▷**HISTORY** C18: from Urdu *ta' alluk* estate, ultimately from Arabic

talus[1] ('teɪləs) NOUN, *plural* **-li** (-laɪ). the bone of the ankle that articulates with the leg bones to form the ankle joint. Nontechnical name: **anklebone.**
▷**HISTORY** C18: from Latin: ankle

talus[2] ('teɪləs) NOUN, *plural* **-luses.** 1 *Geology* another name for **scree.** 2 *Fortifications* the sloping side of a wall.
▷**HISTORY** C17: from French, from Latin *talūtium* slope, perhaps of Iberian origin

talweg ('tɑːlveg) NOUN a variant spelling of **thalweg.**

tam (tæm) NOUN short for **tam-o'-shanter.**

tamale (tə'mɑːlɪ) NOUN a Mexican dish made of minced meat mixed with crushed maize and seasonings, wrapped in maize husks and steamed.
▷**HISTORY** C19: erroneously for *tamal,* from Mexican Spanish, from Nahuatl *tamalli*

tamandua (ˌtæmən'dʊə) *or* **tamandu** ('tæmənˌduː) NOUN a small arboreal edentate mammal, *Tamandua tetradactyla,* of Central and South America, having a prehensile tail and tubular mouth specialized for feeding on termites: family *Myrmecophagidae.* Also called: **lesser anteater.**
▷**HISTORY** C17: via Portuguese from Tupi: ant trapper, from *taixi* ant + *mondé* to catch

tamarack ('tæməˌræk) NOUN 1 any of several North American larches, esp *Larix laricina,* which has reddish-brown bark, bluish-green needle-like leaves, and shiny oval cones. 2 the wood of any of these trees.
▷**HISTORY** C19: from Algonquian

tamarau *or* **tamarao** ('tæməˌraʊ) NOUN a small rare member of the cattle tribe, *Anoa mindorensis,* of lowland areas of Mindoro in the Philippines. Compare **anoa.**
▷**HISTORY** from Tagalog *tamaráw*

tamari (tə'mɒːrɪ) NOUN a Japanese variety of soy sauce.
▷**HISTORY** Japanese

tamarillo (ˌtæmə'rɪləʊ) NOUN, *plural* **-los.** another name for **tree tomato.**

tamarin ('tæmərɪn) NOUN any of numerous small monkeys of the genera *Saguinus* (or *Leontocebus*) and *Leontideus,* of South and Central American forests; similar to the marmosets: family *Callithricidae.*
▷**HISTORY** C18: via French from Galibi

tamarind ('tæmərɪnd) NOUN 1 a leguminous tropical evergreen tree, *Tamarindus indica,* having pale yellow red-streaked flowers and brown pulpy pods, each surrounded by a brittle shell. 2 the acid fruit of this tree, used as a food and to make beverages and medicines. 3 the wood of this tree.
▷**HISTORY** C16: from Medieval Latin *tamarindus,* ultimately from Arabic *tamr hindī* Indian date, from *tamr* date + *hindī* Indian, from *Hind* India

tamarisk ('tæmərɪsk) NOUN any of various ornamental trees and shrubs of the genus *Tamarix,* of the Mediterranean region and S and SE Asia, having scalelike leaves, slender branches, and feathery clusters of pink or whitish flowers: family *Tamaricaceae.*
▷**HISTORY** C15: from Late Latin *tamariscus,* from Latin *tamarix*

tamasha (tə'mɑːʃə) NOUN (in India) a show; entertainment.
▷**HISTORY** C17: via Urdu from Arabic: a stroll, saunter

Tamatave (*French* tamatav) NOUN the former name (until 1979) of **Toamasina.**

Tamaulipas (*Spanish* tamau'lipas) NOUN a state of NE Mexico, on the Gulf of Mexico. Capital: Ciudad Victoria. Pop.: 2 747 114 (2000). Area: 79 829 sq. km (30 822 sq. miles).

tambac ('tæmbæk) NOUN a variant spelling of **tombac.**

Tambora ('tæmbəˌrɑː) NOUN a volcano in Indonesia, on N Sumbawa: violent eruption of 1815 reduced its height from about 4000 m (13 000 ft.) to 2850 m (9400 ft.).

tambour ('tæmbʊə) NOUN 1 *Real Tennis* the sloping buttress on one side of the receiver's end of the court. 2 a small round embroidery frame, consisting of two concentric hoops over which the fabric is stretched while being worked. 3 embroidered work done on such a frame. 4 a sliding door on desks, cabinets, etc., made of thin strips of wood glued side by side onto a canvas backing. 5 *Architect* a wall that is circular in plan, esp one that supports a dome or one that is surrounded by a colonnade. 6 a drum. ◆ VERB 7 to embroider (fabric or a design) on a tambour.
▷**HISTORY** C15: from French, from *tabour* TABOR

tamboura (tæm'bʊərə) NOUN an instrument with a long neck, four strings, and no frets, used in Indian music to provide a drone.
▷**HISTORY** from Persian *tanbūr,* from Arabic *tunbūr*

tambourin ('tæmbʊrɪn) NOUN 1 an 18th-century Provençal folk dance. 2 a piece of music composed for or in the rhythm of this dance. 3 a small drum.
▷**HISTORY** C18: from French: a little drum, from TAMBOUR

tambourine (ˌtæmbə'riːn) NOUN *Music* a percussion instrument consisting of a single drumhead of skin stretched over a circular wooden frame hung with pairs of metal discs that jingle when it is struck or shaken.
▷**HISTORY** C16: from Middle Flemish *tamborijn* a little drum, from Old French: TAMBOURIN
▸ **ˌtambou'rinist** NOUN

Tambov (*Russian* tam'bɔf) NOUN an industrial city in W Russia: founded in 1636 as a Muscovite fort; a major engineering centre. Pop.: 315 100 (1999 est.).

tame (teɪm) ADJECTIVE 1 changed by man from a naturally wild state into a tractable, domesticated, or cultivated condition. 2 (of animals) not fearful of human contact. 3 lacking in spirit or initiative; meek or submissive: *a tame personality.* 4 flat, insipid, or uninspiring: *a tame ending to a book.* 5 slow-moving: *a tame current.* ◆ VERB (*tr*) 6 to make tame; domesticate. 7 to break the spirit of, subdue, or curb. 8 to tone down, soften, or mitigate.
▷**HISTORY** Old English *tam;* related to Old Norse *tamr,* Old High German *zam*
▸ **'tamable** *or* **'tameable** ADJECTIVE ▸ **ˌtama'bility** *or* **ˌtamea'bility** *or* **'tamableness** *or* **'tameableness** NOUN
▸ **'tameless** ADJECTIVE ▸ **'tamely** ADVERB ▸ **'tameness** NOUN
▸ **'tamer** NOUN

Tameside ('teɪmˌsaɪd) NOUN a unitary authority of NW England, in Greater Manchester. Pop.: 213 045 (2001). Area: 103 sq. km (40 sq. miles).

Tamil ('tæmɪl) NOUN 1 (*plural* **-ils** *or* **-il**) a member of a mixed Dravidian and Caucasoid people of S India and Sri Lanka. 2 the language of this people: the state language of Tamil Nadu, also spoken in Sri Lanka and elsewhere, belonging to the Dravidian family of languages. ◆ ADJECTIVE 3 of or relating to this people or their language.

Tamil Eelam ('tæmɪl 'iːlæm) NOUN the separate Tamil state that the **Tamil Tigers** have sought to establish in northern Sri Lanka.
▷**HISTORY** from Tamil *eelam* homeland

Tamil Nadu ('tæmɪl nɑː'duː) NOUN a state of SE India, on the Coromandel Coast: reorganized in 1956 and 1960 and made smaller; consists of a coastal plain backed by hills, including the Nilgiri Hills in the west. Capital: Madras. Pop.: 62 110 839 (2001). Area: 130 058 sq. km (50 216 sq. miles). Former name (until 1968): **Madras.**

Tamil Tigers PLURAL NOUN (usually preceded by *the*) a Sri Lankan Tamil separatist movement founded in the early 1970s that seeks to establish an independent Tamil homeland (Tamil Eelam) in northern Sri Lanka.

tamis ('tæmɪ, -ɪs) NOUN, *plural* **-ises** (-ɪz, -ɪsɪz). a less common word for **tammy**[3] (sense 1).

Tammany Hall ('tæmənɪ) NOUN *US politics* the central organization of the Democratic Party in New York county. Originally founded as a benevolent society (**Tammany Society**) in 1789, Tammany Hall was notorious for the corruption in city and state politics that it fostered in the 19th and early 20th centuries. Also called: **Tammany.**
▸ **'Tammanyism** NOUN ▸ **'Tammanyite** NOUN

tammar ('tæmə) NOUN a small scrub wallaby, *Macropus eugenii,* of Australia, having a thick dark-coloured coat.
▷**HISTORY** C19: from a native Australian language

Tammerfors (tamər'fɔrs) NOUN the Swedish name for **Tampere.**

Tammuz ('tæmuːz, -ʊz) NOUN (in the Jewish calendar) the fourth month of the year according to biblical reckoning and the tenth month of the civil year, usually falling within June and July.
▷**HISTORY** from Hebrew

tammy[1] ('tæmɪ) NOUN, *plural* **-mies.** a glazed woollen or mixed fabric, used for linings, undergarments, etc.
▷**HISTORY** C17: of unknown origin

tammy[2] ('tæmɪ) NOUN, *plural* **-mies.** another word for **tam-o'-shanter.**

tammy[3] ('tæmɪ) NOUN, *plural* **-mies.** 1 Also called: **tammy cloth, tamis.** (esp formerly) a rough-textured woollen cloth used for straining sauces, soups, etc. ◆ VERB **-mies, -mying, -mied.** 2 (*tr*) (esp formerly) to strain (sauce, soup, etc.) through a tammy.
▷**HISTORY** C18: changed (through influence of TAMMY[1]) from French *tamis,* perhaps of Celtic origin; compare Breton *tamouez* strainer

tam-o'-shanter (ˌtæmə'ʃæntə) NOUN a Scottish brimless wool cap with a bobble in the centre, usually worn pulled down at one side. Also called: **tam, tammy.**
▷**HISTORY** C19: named after the hero of Burns' poem *Tam o' Shanter* (1790)

tamoxifen (tə'mɒksɪfen) NOUN a drug that antagonizes the action of oestrogen and is used to treat breast cancer and some types of infertility in women.
▷**HISTORY** C20: altered from T(RANS-) + AM(INE) + OXY-[2] + PHEN(OL)

tamp[1] (tæmp) VERB (*tr*) 1 to force or pack down firmly by repeated blows. 2 to pack sand, earth, etc. into (a drill hole) over an explosive.
▷**HISTORY** C17: probably a back formation from *tampin* (obsolete variant of TAMPION), which was taken as being a present participle *tamping*

tamp[2] (tæmp) VERB *South Wales dialect* 1 (*tr*) to bounce (a ball). 2 (*intr;* usually foll by *down*) to pour with rain.
▷**HISTORY** probably special use of TAMP[1]

Tampa ('tæmpə) NOUN a port and resort in W Florida, on **Tampa Bay** (an arm of the Gulf of Mexico): two universities. Pop.: 303 447 (2000).

tamper[1] ('tæmpə) VERB (*intr*) 1 (usually foll by *with*) to interfere or meddle. 2 to use corrupt practices such as bribery or blackmail. 3 (usually foll by *with*) to attempt to influence or corrupt, esp by bribery: *to tamper with the jury.*
▷**HISTORY** C16: alteration of TEMPER (verb)
▸ **'tamperer** NOUN

tamper² ('tæmpə) NOUN [1] a person or thing that tamps, esp an instrument for packing down tobacco in a pipe. [2] a casing around the core of a nuclear weapon to increase its efficiency by reflecting neutrons and delaying the expansion.

Tampere (*Finnish* 'tampɛrɛ) NOUN a city in SW Finland: the second largest town in Finland; textile manufacturing. Pop.: 193 174 (2000 est.). Swedish name: **Tammerfors.**

Tampico (*Spanish* tam'piko) NOUN a port and resort in E Mexico, in Tamaulipas on the Pánuco River: oil refining. Pop.: 294 789 (2000 est.).

tamping *or* **tamping mad** ('tæmpɪŋ) ADJECTIVE *South Wales dialect* very angry.
▷HISTORY see TAMP¹

tampion ('tæmpɪən) *or* **tompion** NOUN a plug placed in a gun's muzzle when the gun is not in use to keep out moisture and dust.
▷HISTORY C15: from French: TAMPON

tampon ('tæmpɒn) NOUN [1] a plug of lint, cotton wool, cotton, etc., inserted into an open wound or body cavity to stop the flow of blood, absorb secretions, etc., esp one inserted into the vagina to absorb menstrual blood. ◆ VERB [2] (*tr*) to plug (a wound, etc.) with a tampon.
▷HISTORY C19: via French from Old French *tapon* a little plug, from *tape* a plug, of Germanic origin
▸**'tamponage** NOUN

tam-tam NOUN another name for **gong** (sense 1).
▷HISTORY from Hindi: see TOM-TOM

tamworth ('tæmwəθ) NOUN (*often capital*) any of a hardy rare breed of long-bodied reddish pigs.
▷HISTORY named after TAMWORTH, England, where it was developed

Tamworth ('tæmwəθ) NOUN [1] a market town in W central England, in SE Staffordshire. Pop.: 68 440 (1991). [2] a city in SE Australia, in E central New South Wales: industrial centre of an agricultural region. Pop.: 33 900 (latest est.).

tan¹ (tæn) NOUN [1] the brown colour produced by the skin after intensive exposure to ultraviolet rays, esp those of the sun. [2] a light or moderate yellowish-brown colour. [3] short for **tanbark.** ◆ VERB **tans, tanning, tanned.** [4] to go brown or cause to go brown after exposure to ultraviolet rays: *she tans easily.* [5] to convert (a skin or hide) into leather by treating it with a tanning agent, such as vegetable tannins, chromium salts, fish oils, or formaldehyde. [6] (*tr*) *Slang* to beat or flog. ◆ ADJECTIVE **tanner, tannest.** [7] of the colour tan: *tan gloves.* [8] used in or relating to tanning.
▷HISTORY Old English *tannian* (unattested as infinitive, attested as *getanned,* past participle), from Medieval Latin *tannāre,* from *tannum* tanbark, perhaps of Celtic origin; compare Irish *tana* thin
▸**'tannable** ADJECTIVE ▸**'tannish** ADJECTIVE

tan² (tæn) ABBREVIATION FOR tangent (sense 2).

tana ('tɑːnə) NOUN [1] a small Madagascan lemur, *Phaner furcifer.* [2] a large tree shrew, *Tupaia tana,* of Sumatra and Borneo.
▷HISTORY C19: from Malay *tūpai tana* ground squirrel

Tana ('tɑːnə) NOUN [1] **Lake.** Also called: (Lake) **Tsana.** a lake in NW Ethiopia, on a plateau 1800 m (6000 ft.) high: the largest lake of Ethiopia; source of the Blue Nile. Area: 3673 sq. km (1418 sq. miles). [2] a river in E Kenya, rising in the Aberdare Range and flowing in a wide curve east to the Indian Ocean: the longest river in Kenya. Length: 708 km (440 miles). [3] a river in NE Norway, flowing generally northeast as part of the border between Norway and Finland to the Arctic Ocean by Tana Fjord. Length: about 320 km (200 miles). Finnish name: **Teno.**

Tanach *Hebrew* (ta'nax) NOUN the Hebrew Bible as used by Jews, divided into the Torah, Prophets, and Hagiographa.
▷HISTORY from Hebrew, acronym formed from *tōrāh* (the Pentateuch), *nebī'im* (the prophets), and *ketūbim* (the Hagiographa)

tanager ('tænədʒə) NOUN any American songbird of the family *Thraupidae,* having a short thick bill and a brilliantly coloured male plumage.
▷HISTORY C19: from New Latin *tanagra,* based on Tupi *tangara*

Tanagra ('tænəgrə) NOUN a town in ancient Boeotia, famous for terracotta figurines of the same name, first discovered in its necropolis.

Tanana ('tænənɑː) NOUN a river in central Alaska, rising in the Wrangell Mountains and flowing northwest to the Yukon River. Length: about 765 km (475 miles).

Tananarive (*French* tananariv) NOUN the former name of **Antananarivo.**

tanbark ('tænˌbɑːk) NOUN the bark of certain trees, esp the oak and hemlock, used as a source of tannin. Often shortened to: **tan.**

tandem ('tændəm) NOUN [1] a bicycle with two sets of pedals and two saddles, arranged one behind the other for two riders. [2] a two-wheeled carriage drawn by two horses harnessed one behind the other. [3] a team of two horses so harnessed. [4] any arrangement of two things in which one is placed behind the other. [5] **in tandem.** together or in conjunction. ◆ ADJECTIVE [6] *Brit* used as, used in, or routed through an intermediate automatic telephone exchange: *a tandem exchange.* ◆ ADVERB [7] one behind the other: *to ride tandem.*
▷HISTORY C18: whimsical use of Latin *tandem* at length, to indicate a vehicle of elongated appearance

tandem roller NOUN a type of road roller in which the front and back wheels consist of rollers of about the same diameter.

T & G ABBREVIATION FOR Transport and General Workers' Union.

Tandjungpriok *or* **Tanjungpriok** (ˌtændʒʊŋ'priːɒk) NOUN a port in Indonesia, on the NW coast of Java adjoining the capital, Jakarta: a major shipping and distributing centre for the whole archipelago.

tandoori (tæn'dʊərɪ) NOUN **a** an Indian method of cooking meat or vegetables on a spit in a clay oven. **b** (*as modifier*): *tandoori chicken.*
▷HISTORY from Urdu, from *tandoor* an oven

tang (tæŋ) NOUN [1] a strong taste or flavour: *the tang of the sea.* [2] a pungent or characteristic smell: *the tang of peat fires.* [3] a trace, touch, or hint of something: *a tang of cloves in the apple pie.* [4] the pointed end of a tool, such as a chisel, file, knife, etc., which is fitted into a handle, shaft, or stock.
▷HISTORY C14: from Old Norse *tangi* point; related to Danish *tange* point, spit

Tang (tæŋ) NOUN the imperial dynasty of China from 618–907 A.D.

tanga ('tæŋgə) NOUN [1] a triangular loincloth worn by indigenous peoples in tropical America. [2] a type of very brief bikini.
▷HISTORY from Portuguese, ultimately of Banth origin

Tanga ('tæŋgə) NOUN a port in N Tanzania, on the Indian Ocean: Tanzania's second port. Pop.: 187 155 (latest est.).

Tanganyika (ˌtæŋgə'njiːkə) NOUN [1] a former state in E Africa: became part of German East Africa in 1884; ceded to Britain as a League of Nations mandate in 1919 and as a UN trust territory in 1946; gained independence in 1961 and united with Zanzibar in 1964 as the United Republic of Tanzania. [2] **Lake.** a lake in central Africa between Tanzania and the Democratic Republic of Congo (formerly Zaïre), bordering also on Burundi and Zambia, in the Great Rift Valley: the longest freshwater lake in the world. Area: 32 893 sq. km (12 700 sq. miles). Length: 676 km (420 miles).

Tanganyikan (ˌtæŋgə'njiːkən) ADJECTIVE [1] of or relating to the former state of Tanganyika (now part of Tanzania) or its inhabitants. ◆ NOUN [2] a native of inhabitant of Tanganyika.

tangata tiriti (ˌtʌŋɑːtə tɪ'riːtɪ) NOUN *NZ* a Maori term for non-Maori people.
▷HISTORY Maori, literally: people of the Treaty (of Waitangi)

tangata whenua (ˌtʌŋɑːtə fə'nuːə) NOUN *NZ* the indigenous Maori people of a particular area of New Zealand or of the country as a whole.
▷HISTORY Maori, literally: people of the land

tangelo ('tændʒəˌləʊ) NOUN, *plural* **-los.** [1] a hybrid produced by crossing a tangerine tree with a grapefruit tree. [2] the fruit of this hybrid, having orange acid-tasting flesh.
▷HISTORY C20: from TANG(ERINE) + (POM)ELO

tangent ('tændʒənt) NOUN [1] a geometric line, curve, plane, or curved surface that touches another curve or surface at one point but does not intersect it. [2] (of an angle) a trigonometric function that in a right-angled triangle is the ratio of the length of the opposite side to that of the adjacent side; the ratio of sine to cosine. Abbreviation: **tan.** [3] the straight part on a survey line between curves. [4] *Music* a part of the action of a clavichord consisting of a small piece of metal that strikes the string to produce a note. [5] **on** *or* **at a tangent.** on a completely different or divergent course, esp of thought: *to go off at a tangent.* ◆ ADJECTIVE [6] **a** of or involving a tangent. **b** touching at a single point. [7] touching. [8] almost irrelevant.
▷HISTORY C16: from Latin phrase *līnea tangēns* the touching line, from *tangere* to touch
▸**'tangency** NOUN

tangent galvanometer NOUN a type of galvanometer having a vertical coil of wire with a horizontal magnetic needle at its centre. The current to be measured is passed through the coil and produces a proportional magnetic field which deflects the needle.

tangential (tæn'dʒɛnʃəl) ADJECTIVE [1] of, being, relating to, or in the direction of a tangent. [2] Also: **transverse.** *Astronomy* (of velocity) in a direction perpendicular to the line of sight of a celestial object. Compare **radial** (sense 6). [3] of superficial relevance only; digressive.
▸**tanˌgenti'ality** NOUN ▸**tan'gentially** *or* **tan'gentally** ADVERB

tangerine (ˌtændʒə'riːn) NOUN [1] an Asian citrus tree, *Citrus reticulata,* cultivated for its small edible orange-like fruits. [2] the fruit of this tree, having a loose rind and sweet spicy flesh. [3] **a** a reddish-orange colour. **b** (*as adjective*): *a tangerine door.*
▷HISTORY C19: from TANGIER

Tangerine (ˌtændʒə'riːn) NOUN [1] a native of inhabitant of Tangier. ◆ ADJECTIVE [2] of or relating to Tangier or its inhabitants.

tangi ('tʌŋiː) NOUN, *plural* **-gis.** *NZ* [1] a Maori funeral ceremony. [2] *Informal* a lamentation.
▷HISTORY Maori

tangible ('tændʒəbᵊl) ADJECTIVE [1] capable of being touched or felt; having real substance: *a tangible object.* [2] capable of being clearly grasped by the mind; substantial rather than imaginary: *tangible evidence.* [3] having a physical existence; corporeal: *tangible assets.* ◆ NOUN [4] (*often plural*) a tangible thing or asset.
▷HISTORY C16: from Late Latin *tangibilis,* from Latin *tangere* to touch
▸**ˌtangi'bility** *or* **'tangibleness** NOUN ▸**'tangibly** ADVERB

Tangier (tæn'dʒɪə) NOUN a port in N Morocco, on the Strait of Gibraltar: a Phoenician trading post in the 15th century B.C.; a neutral international zone (1923–56); made the summer capital of Morocco and a free port in 1962; commercial and financial centre. Pop.: 521 735 (1994).

tangle¹ ('tæŋgᵊl) NOUN [1] a confused or complicated mass of hairs, lines, fibres, etc., knotted or coiled together. [2] a complicated problem, condition, or situation. ◆ VERB [3] to become or cause to become twisted together in a confused mass. [4] (*intr; often foll by with*) to come into conflict; contend: *to tangle with the police.* [5] (*tr*) to involve in matters which hinder or confuse: *to tangle someone in a shady deal.* [6] (*tr*) to ensnare or trap, as in a net.
▷HISTORY C14 *tangilen,* variant of *tagilen,* probably of Scandinavian origin; related to Swedish dialect *taggla* to entangle
▸**'tanglement** NOUN ▸**'tangler** NOUN ▸**'tangly** ADJECTIVE

tangle² *or* **tangle weed** ('tæŋgᵊl) NOUN alternative names (esp Scot) for **oarweed.**
▷HISTORY C16: of Scandinavian origin: compare Danish *tang* seaweed

tango ('tæŋgəʊ) NOUN, *plural* **-gos.** [1] a Latin American dance in duple time, characterized by long gliding steps and sudden pauses. [2] a piece of music composed for or in the rhythm of this dance. ◆ VERB **-goes, -going, -goed.** [3] (*intr*) to perform this dance.
▷HISTORY C20: from American Spanish, probably of Niger-Congo origin; compare Ibibio *tamgu* to dance
▸**'tangoist** NOUN

Tango ('tæŋgəʊ) NOUN *Communications* a code word for the letter *t.*

tangram ('tæŋgræm) NOUN a Chinese puzzle in

which a square, cut into a parallelogram, a square, and five triangles, is formed into figures.
▷HISTORY C19: perhaps from Chinese *t'ang* Chinese + -GRAM

Tangshan ('tæŋ'ʃæn) NOUN an industrial city in NE China, in Hebei province. Pop.: 1 210 842 (1999 est.).

tangy ('tæŋɪ) ADJECTIVE **tangier, tangiest**. having a pungent, fresh, or briny flavour or aroma: *a tangy sea breeze*.

tanh (θæn, tænʃ) NOUN hyperbolic tangent; a hyperbolic function that is the ratio of sinh to cosh.
▷HISTORY C20: from TAN(GENT) + H(YPERBOLIC)

Tanis ('teɪnɪs) NOUN an ancient city located in the E part of the Nile delta: abandoned after the 6th century B.C.; at one time the capital of Egypt. Biblical name: **Zoan.**

tanist ('tænɪst) NOUN *History* the heir apparent of a Celtic chieftain chosen by election during the chief's lifetime: usually the worthiest of his kin.
▷HISTORY C16: from Irish Gaelic *tánaiste,* literally: the second person
▸**'tanistry** NOUN

taniwha ('tʌni:fɑ:, 'tænəwɑ:) NOUN *NZ* a legendary Maori monster.
▷HISTORY Maori

Tanjore (tæn'dʒɔ:) NOUN the former name of **Thanjavur.**

Tanjungpriok (ˌtændʒʊŋ'pri:ɒk) NOUN a variant spelling of **Tandjungpriok.**

tank (tæŋk) NOUN [1] a large container or reservoir for the storage of liquids or gases: *tanks for storing oil.* [2] **a** an armoured combat vehicle moving on tracks and armed with guns, etc., originally developed in World War I. **b** (*as modifier*): *a tank commander; a tank brigade.* [3] *Brit and US dialect* a reservoir, lake, or pond. [4] *Photog* **a** a light-tight container inside which a film can be processed in daylight, the solutions and rinsing waters being poured in and out without light entering. **b** any large dish or container used for processing a number of strips or sheets of film. [5] *Slang, chiefly US* **a** a jail. **b** a jail cell. [6] Also called: **tankful.** the quantity contained in a tank. [7] *Austral* a dam formed by excavation. ◆ VERB [8] (*tr*) to put or keep in a tank. [9] (*intr*) to move like a tank, esp heavily and rapidly. [10] *Slang* to defeat heavily. [11] (*intr*) *Informal* to fail, esp commercially. ◆ See also **tank up.**
▷HISTORY C17: from Gujarati *tānkh* artificial lake, but influenced also by Portuguese *tanque,* from *estanque* pond, from *estancar* to dam up, from Vulgar Latin *stanticāre* (unattested) to block, STANCH
▸**'tankless** ADJECTIVE ▸**'tank,like** ADJECTIVE

tanka ('tɑ:ŋkə) NOUN, *plural* **-kas** *or* **-ka.** a Japanese verse form consisting of five lines, the first and third having five syllables, the others seven.
▷HISTORY C19: from Japanese, from *tan* short + *ka* verse

tankage ('tæŋkɪdʒ) NOUN [1] the capacity or contents of a tank or tanks. [2] the act of storing in a tank or tanks, or a fee charged for such storage. [3] *Agriculture* **a** fertilizer consisting of the dried and ground residues of animal carcasses. **b** a protein supplement feed for livestock.

tankard ('tæŋkəd) NOUN **a** a large one-handled drinking vessel, commonly made of silver, pewter, or glass, sometimes fitted with a hinged lid. **b** the quantity contained in a tankard.
▷HISTORY C14: related to Middle Dutch *tankaert,* French *tanquart*

tank engine *or* **locomotive** NOUN a steam locomotive that carries its water supply in tanks mounted around its boiler.

tanker ('tæŋkə) NOUN a ship, lorry, or aeroplane designed to carry liquid in bulk, such as oil.

tank farming NOUN another name for **hydroponics.**
▸**tank farmer** NOUN

tankini (ˌtæŋ'ki:nɪ) NOUN a woman's two-piece swimming costume consisting of a vest or camisole top and bikini briefs.
▷HISTORY C20: a blend of TANK (TOP) and (BIK)INI

tank top NOUN a sleeveless upper garment with wide shoulder straps and a low neck, usually worn over a shirt, blouse, or jumper.
▷HISTORY C20: named after *tank suits,* one-piece bathing costumes of the 1920s worn in tanks or swimming pools

tank trap NOUN any obstacle, such as a number of concrete stumps set in the ground, designed to stop a military tank.

tank up VERB (*adverb*) *Chiefly Brit* [1] to fill the tank of (a vehicle) with petrol. [2] *Slang* to imbibe or cause to imbibe a large quantity of alcoholic drink.

tank wagon *or esp US and Canadian* **tank car** NOUN a form of railway wagon carrying a tank for the transport of liquids.

tannage ('tænɪdʒ) NOUN [1] the act or process of tanning. [2] a skin or hide that has been tanned.

tannate ('tæneɪt) NOUN any salt or ester of tannic acid.

Tannenberg (*German* 'tanənbɛrk) NOUN a village in N Poland, formerly in East Prussia: site of a decisive defeat of the Teutonic Knights by the Poles in 1410 and of a decisive German victory over the Russians in 1914. Polish name: **Stębark.**

tanner[1] ('tænə) NOUN a person who tans skins and hides.

tanner[2] ('tænə) NOUN *Brit* (formerly) an informal word for **sixpence.**
▷HISTORY C19: of unknown origin

tannery ('tænərɪ) NOUN, *plural* **-neries.** a place or building where skins and hides are tanned.

tannic ('tænɪk) ADJECTIVE of, relating to, containing, or produced from tan, tannin, or tannic acid.

tannie ('tʌnɪ) NOUN *South African* a title of respect used to refer to an elderly woman.
▷HISTORY Afrikaans; literally: aunt

tannin ('tænɪn) NOUN any of a class of yellowish or brownish solid compounds found in many plants and used as tanning agents, mordants, medical astringents, etc. Tannins are derivatives of gallic acid with the approximate formula $C_{76}H_{52}O_{46}$. Also called: **tannic acid.**
▷HISTORY C19: from French *tanin,* from TAN[1]

Tannoy ('tænɔɪ) NOUN *Trademark* a sound-amplifying apparatus used as a public-address system esp in a large building, such as a university.

Tans (tænz) PLURAL NOUN **the.** *Irish informal* short for the **Black and Tans.**

tansy ('tænzɪ) NOUN, *plural* **-sies.** [1] any of numerous plants of the genus *Tanacetum,* esp *T. vulgare,* having yellow flowers in flat-topped clusters and formerly used in medicine and for seasoning: family *Asteraceae* (composites). [2] any of various similar plants.
▷HISTORY C15: from Old French *tanesie,* from Medieval Latin *athanasia* tansy (with reference to its alleged power to prolong life), from Greek: immortality

Tanta ('tæntə) NOUN a city in N Egypt, on the Nile delta: noted for its Muslim festivals. Pop.: 371 010 (1996).

tantalate ('tæntəˌleɪt) NOUN any of various salts of tantalic acid formed when the pentoxide of tantalum dissolves in an alkali.

tantalic (tæn'tælɪk) ADJECTIVE of or containing tantalum, esp in the pentavalent state.

tantalic acid NOUN a white gelatinous substance produced by hydrolysis of tantalic halides. It dissolves in strong bases to give tantalates.

tantalite ('tæntəˌlaɪt) NOUN a heavy brownish mineral consisting of a tantalum oxide of iron and manganese in orthorhombic crystalline form: it occurs in coarse granite, often with columbite, and is an ore of tantalum. Formula: $(Fe,Mn)(Ta,Nb)_2O_6$.
▷HISTORY C19: from TANTALUM + -ITE[1]

tantalize *or* **tantalise** ('tæntəˌlaɪz) VERB (*tr*) to tease or make frustrated, as by tormenting with the sight of something greatly desired but inaccessible.
▷HISTORY C16: from the punishment of TANTALUS
▸ˌ**tantali'zation** *or* ˌ**tantali'sation** NOUN ▸**'tantaˌlizer** *or* **'tantaˌliser** NOUN ▸**'tantaˌlizing** *or* **'tantaˌlising** ADJECTIVE ▸**'tantaˌlizingly** *or* **'tantaˌlisingly** ADVERB

tantalous ('tæntələs) ADJECTIVE of or containing tantalum in the trivalent state.
▷HISTORY C19: from TANTAL(UM) + -OUS

tantalum ('tæntələm) NOUN a hard greyish-white metallic element that occurs with niobium in tantalite and columbite: used in electrical capacitors in most circuit boards and in alloys to increase hardness and chemical resistance, esp in surgical instruments. Symbol: Ta; atomic no.: 73; atomic wt.: 180.9479; valency: 2, 3, 4, or 5; relative density: 16.654; melting pt.: 3020°C; boiling pt.: 5458±100°C.
▷HISTORY C19: named after TANTALUS, with reference to the metal's incapacity to absorb acids

tantalus ('tæntələs) NOUN *Brit* a case in which bottles may be locked with their contents tantalizingly visible.

Tantalus ('tæntələs) NOUN *Greek myth* a king, the father of Pelops, punished in Hades for his misdeeds by having to stand in water that recedes when he tries to drink it and under fruit that moves away as he reaches for it.

tantamount ('tæntəˌmaʊnt) ADJECTIVE (*postpositive; foll by to*) as good (as); equivalent in effect (to): *his statement was tantamount to an admission of guilt.*
▷HISTORY C17: basically from Anglo-French *tant amunter* to amount to as much, from *tant* so much + *amunter* to AMOUNT

tantara ('tæntərə, tæn'tɑ:rə) NOUN a blast, as on a trumpet or horn.
▷HISTORY C16: from Latin *taratantara,* imitative of the sound of the tuba

tantivy (tæn'tɪvɪ) ADVERB [1] at full speed; rapidly. ◆ NOUN, *plural* **-tivies,** INTERJECTION [2] a hunting cry, esp at full gallop.
▷HISTORY C17: perhaps imitative of galloping hooves

tant mieux *French* (tɑ̃ mjø) so much the better.

tanto ('tæntəʊ; *Italian* 'tanto) ADVERB too much: *allegro ma non tanto.* See **non troppo.**
▷HISTORY C19: from Italian, from Latin *tantum* so much

tant pis *French* (tɑ̃ pi) so much the worse.

Tantra ('tæntrə, 'tʌn-) NOUN *Hinduism, Buddhism* the sacred books of Tantrism, written between the 7th and 17th centuries A.D., mainly in the form of a dialogue between Siva and his wife.
▷HISTORY C18: from Sanskrit: warp, hence underlying principle, from *tanoti* he weaves

Tantric ('tæntrɪk) ADJECTIVE *Hinduism, Buddhism* of or relating to Tantrism.

Tantrism ('tæntrɪzəm) NOUN [1] a movement within Hinduism combining magical and mystical elements and with sacred writings of its own. [2] a similar movement within Buddhism.
▷HISTORY C18: from Sanskrit *tantra,* literally: warp, hence, doctrine
▸**'Tantrist** NOUN

tantrum ('tæntrəm) NOUN (*often plural*) a childish fit of rage; outburst of bad temper.
▷HISTORY C18: of unknown origin

Tan-tung ('tæn'tʊŋ) NOUN a variant transliteration of the Chinese name for **Andong.**

Tanzania (ˌtænzə'nɪə) NOUN a republic in E Africa, on the Indian Ocean: formed by the union of the independent states of Tanganyika and Zanzibar in 1964; a member of the Commonwealth. Exports include coffee, tea, sisal, and cotton. Official languages: Swahili and English. Religions: Christian, Muslim, and animist. Currency: Tanzanian shilling. Capital: Dodoma. Pop.: 36 232 000 (2001 est.). Area: 945 203 sq. km (364 943 sq. miles).

Tanzanian (ˌtænzə'nɪən) ADJECTIVE [1] of or relating to Tanzania or its inhabitants. ◆ NOUN [2] a native or inhabitant of Tanzania.

Tanzim ('tænˌzɪm) NOUN a Palestinian militia belonging to a militant faction of Al Fatah.

Tao (taʊ) NOUN (in the philosophy of Taoism) [1] that in virtue of which all things happen or exist. [2] the rational basis of human conduct. [3] the course of life and its relation to eternal truth.
▷HISTORY Chinese, literally: path, way

Taoiseach ('ti:ʃæx) NOUN the prime minister of the Republic of Ireland.
▷HISTORY from Irish Gaelic, literally: leader

Taoism ('taʊɪzəm) NOUN [1] the philosophy of Lao Zi, the Chinese philosopher (?604–?531 B.C.), that advocates a simple honest life and noninterference with the course of natural events. [2] a popular Chinese system of religion and philosophy claiming to be teachings of Lao Zi but also incorporating pantheism and sorcery.
▸**'Taoist** NOUN, ADJECTIVE ▸**Tao'istic** ADJECTIVE

taonga (tɑˈɔŋgə) NOUN *NZ* treasure; anything highly prized.
▷HISTORY Maori

tap¹ (tæp) VERB **taps, tapping, tapped.** 1 to strike (something) lightly and usually repeatedly: *to tap the table; to tap on the table.* 2 (*tr*) to produce by striking in this way: *to tap a rhythm.* 3 (*tr*) to strike lightly with (something): *to tap one's finger on the desk.* 4 (*intr*) to walk with a tapping sound: *she tapped across the floor.* 5 (*tr*) to attach metal or leather reinforcing pieces to (the toe or heel of a shoe). ◆ NOUN 6 a light blow or knock, or the sound made by it. 7 the metal piece attached to the toe or heel of a shoe used for tap-dancing. 8 short for **tap-dancing.** 9 *Phonetics* the contact made between the tip of the tongue and the alveolar ridge as the tongue is flicked upwards in the execution of a flap or vibrates rapidly in the execution of a trill or roll. ◆ See also **taps.**
▷HISTORY C13 *tappen,* probably from Old French *taper,* of Germanic origin; related to Middle Low German *tappen* to pluck, Swedish dialect *täpa* to tap
▸ˈ**tappable** ADJECTIVE

tap² (tæp) NOUN 1 a valve by which a fluid flow from a pipe can be controlled by opening and closing an orifice. US name: **faucet.** 2 a stopper to plug a cask or barrel and enable the contents to be drawn out in a controlled flow. 3 a particular quality of alcoholic drink, esp when contained in casks: *an excellent tap.* 4 *Brit* short for **taproom.** 5 the surgical withdrawal of fluid from a bodily cavity: *a spinal tap.* 6 Also called: **screw tap.** a tool for cutting female screw threads, consisting of a threaded steel cylinder with longitudinal grooves forming cutting edges. Compare **die²** (sense 2). 7 *Electronics, chiefly US and Canadian* a connection made at some point between the end terminals of an inductor, resistor, or some other component. Usual Brit name: **tapping.** 8 *Stock Exchange* **a** an issue of a government security released slowly onto the market when its market price reaches a predetermined level. **b** (*as modifier*): *tap stock; tap issue.* 9 a concealed listening or recording device connected to a telephone or telegraph wire for the purpose of obtaining information secretly. 10 **on tap. a** *Informal* ready for immediate use. **b** (of drinks) on draught. ◆ VERB **taps, tapping, tapped.** (*tr*) 11 to furnish with a tap. 12 to draw off with or as if with a tap. 13 to cut into (a tree) and draw off sap from it. 14 *Brit informal* to ask or beg (someone) for money: *he tapped me for a fiver.* 15 **a** to connect a tap to (a telephone or telegraph wire). **b** to listen in secret to (a telephone message, etc.) by means of a tap. 16 to make a connection to (a pipe, drain, etc.). 17 to cut a female screw thread in (an object or material) by use of a tap. 18 to withdraw (fluid) from (a bodily cavity). 19 *Informal* (of a sports team or an employer) to make an illicit attempt to recruit (a player or employee bound by an existing contract).
▷HISTORY Old English *tæppa;* related to Old Norse *tappi* tap, Old High German *zapfo*
▸ˈ**tappable** ADJECTIVE

tap³ (tæp) NOUN, VERB a Scot word for **top¹.**

tapa (ˈtɑːpə) NOUN 1 the inner bark of the paper mulberry. 2 a paper-like cloth made from this in the Pacific islands.
▷HISTORY C19: from Marquesan and Tahitian

tapadera (ˌtæpəˈdɛərə) NOUN the leather covering for the stirrup on an American saddle.
▷HISTORY via American Spanish from Spanish: cover, from *tapar* to cover, of Germanic origin; compare TAMPON, TAP²

Tapajós (*Portuguese* tapaˈʒɔs) NOUN a river in N Brazil, rising in N central Mato Grosso and flowing northeast to the Amazon. Length: about 800 km (500 miles).

tapas (ˈtæpəs) PLURAL NOUN **a** light snacks or appetizers, usually eaten with drinks. **b** (*as modifier*): *a tapas bar.*
▷HISTORY from Spanish *tapa* cover, lid

tap dance NOUN 1 a step dance in which the performer wears shoes equipped with taps that make a rhythmic sound on the stage as he dances. ◆ VERB **tap-dance.** (*intr*) 2 to perform a tap dance.
▸ˈ**tap-ˌdancer** NOUN ▸ˈ**tap-ˌdancing** NOUN

tape (teɪp) NOUN 1 a long thin strip, made of cotton, linen, etc., used for binding, fastening, etc. 2 any long narrow strip of cellulose, paper, metal, etc., having similar uses. 3 a string stretched across the track at the end of a race course. 4 *Military slang, chiefly Brit* another word for **stripe¹** (sense 3). 5 See **magnetic tape, ticker tape, paper tape, tape recording.** ◆ VERB (*mainly tr*) 6 (*also intr*) Also: **tape-record.** to record (speech, music, etc.). 7 to furnish with tapes. 8 to bind, measure, secure, or wrap with tape. 9 (*usually passive*) *Brit informal* to take stock of (a person or situation); sum up: *he's got the job taped.*
▷HISTORY Old English *tæppe;* related to Old Frisian *tapia* to pull, Middle Dutch *tapen* to tear
▸ˈ**tapeˌlike** ADJECTIVE ▸ˈ**taper** NOUN

tape deck NOUN 1 a tape recording unit in a hi-fi system. 2 the platform supporting the spools, cassettes, or cartridges of a tape recorder, incorporating the motor or motors that drive them and the playback, recording, and erasing heads. ◆ Sometimes shortened to: **deck.**

tape echo NOUN a means of delaying the repeat of a sound by adjusting the time lapse between the recording and playback heads of a tape recorder. Also called: **tape slap.**

tape grass NOUN any of several submerged freshwater plants of the genus *Vallisneria,* esp *V. spiralis,* of warm temperate regions, having ribbon-like leaves: family *Hydrocharitaceae.*

tape machine NOUN 1 another word for **tape recorder.** 2 a telegraphic receiving device that records messages electronically or on ticker tape. US equivalent: **ticker.**

tape measure NOUN a tape or length of metal marked off in inches, centimetres, etc., used principally for measuring and fitting garments. Also called (esp US): **tapeline.**

tapenade (ˈtæpənɑːd) NOUN a savoury paste made from capers, olives, and anchovies, with olive oil and lemon juice.
▷HISTORY C20: French, from Provençal *tapéo* capers

taper (ˈteɪpə) VERB 1 to become or cause to become narrower towards one end: *the spire tapers to a point.* 2 (often foll by *off*) to become or cause to become smaller or less significant. ◆ NOUN 3 a thin candle. 4 a thin wooden or waxed strip for transferring a flame; spill. 5 a narrowing. 6 *Engineering* (in conical parts) the amount of variation in the diameter per unit of length. 7 any feeble source of light.
▷HISTORY Old English *tapor,* probably from Latin *papȳrus* PAPYRUS (from its use as a wick)
▸ˈ**taperer** NOUN ▸ˈ**tapering** ADJECTIVE ▸ˈ**taperingly** ADVERB

tape-record VERB to make a tape recording (of).

tape recorder NOUN an electrical device used for recording sounds on magnetic tape and usually also for reproducing them, consisting of a tape deck and one or more amplifiers and loudspeakers.

tape recording NOUN 1 the act or process of recording on magnetic tape. 2 the speech, music, etc., so recorded.

tapered roller bearing NOUN *Engineering* a rolling bearing that uses tapered rollers running in coned races and is able to accept axial thrust as well as providing shaft location. Compare **thrust bearing.**

taper pin NOUN a short round metal rod having a small amount of taper so that when driven into a hole it tightens on the taper so that it can act as a stop or wedge.

taper relief NOUN (in Britain) a system of relief from capital gains tax under which the percentage of a chargeable gain considered taxable is reduced for each whole year (from April 1998) that the asset was held by the vendor.

tape slap NOUN another term for **tape echo.**

tape streamer NOUN *Computing* an electromechanical device that enables data to be copied byte by byte from a hard disk onto magnetic tape for security or storage.

tapestry (ˈtæpɪstrɪ) NOUN, *plural* **-tries.** 1 a heavy ornamental fabric, often in the form of a picture, used for wall hangings, furnishings, etc., and made by weaving coloured threads into a fixed warp. 2 another word for **needlepoint.** 3 a colourful and complicated situation: *the rich tapestry of London life.*
▷HISTORY C15: from Old French *tapisserie* carpeting, from Old French *tapiz* carpet; see TAPIS
▸ˈ**tapestried** ADJECTIVE ▸ˈ**tapestry-ˌlike** ADJECTIVE

tapestry moth NOUN one of the larger tineid moths, *Trichophaga tapetzella,* the larvae of which devour animal fibres. It is brown, with white-tipped forewings, and prefers damp environments.

tape transport NOUN the motorized mechanism that moves tape evenly across the recording and playback heads of a tape recorder or cassette player.

tapetum (təˈpiːtəm) NOUN, *plural* **-ta** (-tə). 1 a layer of nutritive cells in the sporangia of ferns and anthers of flowering plants that surrounds developing spore cells. 2 **a** a membranous reflecting layer of cells in the choroid of the eye of nocturnal vertebrates. **b** a similar structure in the eyes of certain nocturnal insects. 3 *Anatomy* a covering layer of cells behind the retina of the eye.
▷HISTORY C18: from New Latin, from Medieval Latin: covering, from Latin *tapēte* carpet, from Greek *tapēs* carpet
▸taˈ**petal** ADJECTIVE

tapeworm (ˈteɪpˌwɜːm) NOUN any parasitic ribbon-like flatworm of the class *Cestoda,* having a body divided into many egg-producing segments and lacking a mouth and gut. The adults inhabit the intestines of vertebrates. See also **echinococcus, taenia.**

taphephobia (ˌtæfɪˈfəʊbɪə) NOUN *Med* a pathological fear of being buried alive.
▷HISTORY from Greek *taphos* grave + -PHOBIA
▸ˌ**tapheˈphobic** ADJECTIVE

taphole (ˈtæpˌhəʊl) NOUN a hole in a furnace for running off molten metal or slag.

taphonomy (təˈfɒnəmɪ) NOUN the study of the processes affecting an organism after death that result in its fossilization.
▷HISTORY C20: from Greek *taphos* grave + -NOMY
▸**taphonomic** (ˌtæfəˈnɒmɪk) *or* ˌ**taphoˈnomical** ADJECTIVE

taphouse (ˈtæpˌhaʊs) NOUN *Now rare* an inn or bar.

taphrogenesis (ˌtæfrəʊˈdʒɛnɪsɪs) NOUN *Geology* the process of forming rifts, resulting in regional faulting and subsidence.
▷HISTORY C20: from German *Tafrogenese,* from Greek *taphros* pit + -GENESIS

tap-in NOUN *Soccer* a goal scored without great effort by simply knocking the ball into the goal from close range.

tapioca (ˌtæpɪˈəʊkə) NOUN a beadlike starch obtained from cassava root, used in cooking as a thickening agent, esp in puddings.
▷HISTORY C18: via Portuguese from Tupi *tipioca* pressed-out juice, from *tipi* residue + *ok* to squeeze out

tapir (ˈteɪpə) NOUN, *plural* **-pirs** *or* **-pir.** any perissodactyl mammal of the genus *Tapirus,* such as *T. indicus* (**Malayan tapir**), of South and Central America and SE Asia, having an elongated snout, three-toed hind legs, and four-toed forelegs: family *Tapiridae.*
▷HISTORY C18: from Tupi *tapiira*

tapis (ˈtæpiː, ˈtæpɪ; *French* tapi) NOUN, *plural* **tapis.** tapestry or carpeting, esp as formerly used to cover a table in a council chamber.
▷HISTORY C17: from French, from Old French *tapiz,* from Greek *tapētion* rug, from *tapēs* carpet

tapper (ˈtæpə) NOUN 1 a person who taps. 2 a tool or instrument that taps. 3 *Northern English dialect* an unstable and violent person.

tappet (ˈtæpɪt) NOUN a mechanical part that reciprocates to receive or transmit intermittent motion, esp the part of an internal-combustion engine that transmits motion from the camshaft to the push rods or valves.
▷HISTORY C18: from TAP¹ + -ET

tappit-hen (ˈtæpɪtˈhɛn) NOUN *Scot* 1 a hen with a crest. 2 a pewter tankard, usually with a distinctive knob on the lid.
▷HISTORY C18: from Scottish *tappit* topped, crested + HEN

taproom (ˈtæpˌruːm, -ˌrʊm) NOUN a bar, as in a hotel or pub.

taproot (ˈtæpˌruːt) NOUN the large single root of plants such as the dandelion, which grows vertically downwards and bears smaller lateral roots.
▷HISTORY C17: from TAP² + ROOT¹
▸ˈ**tapˌrooted** ADJECTIVE

taps (tæps) NOUN (*functioning as singular*) 1 *Chiefly US* **a** (in army camps, etc.) a signal given on a bugle,

drum, etc., indicating that lights are to be put out. **b** any similar signal, as at a military funeral. [2] (in the Guide movement) a closing song sung at an evening camp fire or at the end of a meeting.
▷HISTORY C19: from TAP[1]

tapsalteerie ('tæpsəl'ti:rɪ) ADJECTIVE, ADVERB, NOUN *Scot* topsy-turvy.
▷HISTORY C17: of uncertain origin

tapster ('tæpstə) NOUN [1] *Rare* a barman. [2] (in W Africa) a man who taps palm trees to collect and sell palm wine.
▷HISTORY Old English *tæppestre,* feminine of *tæppere,* from *tappian* to TAP[2]
▸'**tapstress** FEMININE NOUN

tapu ('tɑ:pu:) ADJECTIVE *NZ* sacred; forbidden.
▷HISTORY Maori, from Tongan

tap water NOUN water drawn off through taps from pipes in a house, as distinguished from distilled water, mineral water, etc.

tar¹ (tɑ:) NOUN [1] any of various dark viscid substances obtained by the destructive distillation of organic matter such as coal, wood, or peat. [2] another name for **coal tar.** ◆ VERB **tars, tarring, tarred.** (*tr*) [3] to coat with tar. [4] **tar and feather.** to punish by smearing tar and feathers over (someone). [5] **tarred with the same brush.** regarded as having the same faults.
▷HISTORY Old English *teoru;* related to Old Frisian *tera,* Old Norse *tjara,* Middle Low German *tere* tar, Gothic *triu* tree
▸'**tarry** ADJECTIVE ▸'**tarriness** NOUN

tar² (tɑ:) NOUN an informal word for **seaman.**
▷HISTORY C17: short for TARPAULIN

ta-ra (tæ'rɑ:) SENTENCE SUBSTITUTE *Informal, chiefly Northern English* goodbye; farewell.
▷HISTORY C20: variant of TA-TA

Tara ('tærə, 'tɑ:rə) NOUN a village in Co. Meath near Dublin, by the **Hill of Tara**, the historic seat of the ancient Irish kings.

Tarabulus el Gharb (tə'rɑ:bələs ɛl 'gɑ:b) NOUN transliteration of the Arabic name for **Tripoli** (Libya).

Tarabulus esh Sham (tə'rɑ:bələs ɛʃ 'ʃæm) NOUN transliteration of the Arabic name for **Tripoli** (Lebanon).

taradiddle ('tærə,dɪdəl) NOUN another spelling of **tarradiddle.**

tarakihi ('tærə,ki:hi:) *or* **terakihi** NOUN, *plural* **-kihis.** a common edible sea fish of New Zealand waters.

taramasalata (,tærəməsə'lɑ:tə) NOUN a creamy pale pink pâté, made from the roe of grey mullet or smoked cod and served as an hors d'oeuvre.
▷HISTORY C20: from Modern Greek, from *tarama* cod's roe

Taranaki gate (,tærə'næki:) NOUN *NZ* a rough-and-ready gate in a fence made from wire and battens.
▷HISTORY first used on dairy farms in *Taranaki,* province of NZ

Taranaki wind NOUN *NZ informal* natural gas from Taranaki.

tarantass (,tɑ:rən'tæs) NOUN a large horse-drawn four-wheeled Russian carriage without springs.
▷HISTORY C19: from Russian *tarantas,* from Kazan Tatar *taryntas*

tarantella (,tærən'tɛlə) NOUN [1] a peasant dance from S Italy. [2] a piece of music composed for or in the rhythm of this dance, in fast six-eight time.
▷HISTORY C18: from Italian, from *Taranto* TARANTO; associated with TARANTISM

tarantism ('tærən,tɪzəm) NOUN a nervous disorder marked by uncontrollable bodily movement, widespread in S Italy during the 15th to 17th centuries: popularly thought to be caused by the bite of a tarantula.
▷HISTORY C17: from New Latin *tarantismus,* from TARANTO; see TARANTULA

Taranto (tə'ræntəʊ; *Italian* 'ta:ranto) NOUN a port in SE Italy, in Apulia on the **Gulf of Taranto** (an inlet of the Ionian Sea): the chief city of Magna Graecia; taken by the Romans in 272 B.C. Pop.: 208 214 (2000 est.). Latin name: **Tarentum.**

tarantula (tə'ræntjʊlə) NOUN, *plural* **-las** *or* **-lae** (-,li:). [1] any of various large hairy mostly tropical spiders of the American family *Theraphosidae.* [2] a large hairy spider, *Lycosa tarentula* of S Europe, the bite of which was formerly thought to cause tarantism.
▷HISTORY C16: from Medieval Latin, from Old Italian *tarantola,* from TARANTO

Tarantula nebula NOUN a huge bright emission nebula located in the S hemisphere in the Large Magellanic Cloud.

Tararua biscuit ('tɑ:rɑ:,ru:ə) NOUN *NZ informal* a tramper's home-made biscuit with a high calorie content.

Tarawa (tə'rɑ:wə) NOUN an atoll in Kiribati, occupying a chain of islets surrounding a lagoon in the W central Pacific: the capital of Kiribati, Bairiki, is on this atoll. Pop.: 32 354 (1995).

taraxacum (tə'ræksəkəm) NOUN [1] any perennial plant of the genus *Taraxacum,* such as the dandelion, having dense heads of small yellow flowers and seeds with a feathery attachment: family *Asteraceae* (composites). [2] the dried root of the dandelion, used as a laxative, diuretic, and tonic.
▷HISTORY C18: from Medieval Latin, from Arabic *tarakhshaqūn* wild chicory, perhaps of Persian origin

Tarbes (*French* tarb) NOUN a town in SW France: noted for the breeding of Anglo-Arab horses. Pop.: 50 228 (1990).

tarboosh, tarbush, *or* **tarbouche** (tɑ:'bu:ʃ) NOUN a felt or cloth brimless cap resembling the fez, usually red and often with a silk tassel, worn alone or as part of a turban by Muslim men.
▷HISTORY C18: from Arabic *tarbūsh*

tar boy NOUN *Austral and NZ informal* a boy who applies tar to the skin of sheep cut during shearing.

Tardenoisian (,tɑ:də'nɔɪzɪən) ADJECTIVE of or referring to a Mesolithic culture characterized by small flint instruments.
▷HISTORY C20: after *Tardenois,* France, where implements were found

tardigrade ('tɑ:dɪ,greɪd) NOUN [1] any minute aquatic segmented eight-legged invertebrate of the phylum *Tardigrada,* related to the arthropods, occurring in soil, ditches, etc. Popular name: **water bear.** ◆ ADJECTIVE [2] of, relating to, or belonging to the *Tardigrada.*
▷HISTORY C17: via Latin *tardigradus,* from *tardus* sluggish + *gradī* to walk

tardy ('tɑ:dɪ) ADJECTIVE **-dier, -diest.** [1] occurring later than expected: *tardy retribution.* [2] slow in progress, growth, etc.: *a tardy reader.*
▷HISTORY C15: from Old French *tardif,* from Latin *tardus* slow
▸'**tardily** ADVERB ▸'**tardiness** NOUN

tare¹ (tɛə) NOUN [1] any of various vetch plants, such as *Vicia hirsuta* (**hairy tare**) of Eurasia and N Africa. [2] the seed of any of these plants. [3] *Bible* a troublesome weed, thought to be the darnel.
▷HISTORY C14: of unknown origin

tare² (tɛə) NOUN [1] the weight of the wrapping or container in which goods are packed. [2] a deduction from gross weight to compensate for this. [3] the weight of a vehicle without its cargo, passengers, etc. [4] an empty container used as a counterbalance in determining net weight. ◆ VERB [5] (*tr*) to weigh (a package, etc.) in order to calculate the amount of tare.
▷HISTORY C15: from Old French: waste, from Medieval Latin *tara,* from Arabic *tarhah* something discarded, from *taraha* to reject

Tarentum (tə'rɛntəm) NOUN the Latin name of **Taranto.**

targe (tɑ:dʒ) NOUN an archaic word for **shield.**
▷HISTORY C13: from Old French, of Germanic origin; related to Old High German *zarga* rim, frame, Old Norse *targa* shield

target ('tɑ:gɪt) NOUN [1] **a** an object or area at which an archer or marksman aims, usually a round flat surface marked with concentric rings. **b** (*as modifier*): *target practice.* [2] **a** any point or area aimed at; the object of an attack or a takeover bid. **b** (*as modifier*): *target area; target company.* [3] a fixed goal or objective: *the target for the appeal is £10 000.* [4] a person or thing at which an action or remark is directed or the object of a person's feelings: *a target for the teacher's sarcasm.* [5] a joint of lamb consisting of the breast and neck. [6] *Surveying* a marker on which sights are taken, such as the sliding marker on a levelling staff. [7] (formerly) a small round shield. [8] *Physics, electronics* **a** a substance, object, or system subjected to bombardment by electrons or other particles, or to irradiation. **b** an electrode in a television camera tube whose surface, on which image information is stored, is scanned by the electron beam. [9] *Electronics* an object to be detected by the reflection of a radar or sonar signal, etc. [10] **on target.** on the correct course to meet a target or objective. ◆ VERB **-gets, -geting, -geted.** (*tr*) [11] to make a target of. [12] to direct or aim: *to target benefits at those most in need.*
▷HISTORY C14: from Old French *targette* a little shield, from Old French TARGE
▸'**targetless** ADJECTIVE

targetitis (,tɑ:gɪt'aɪtɪs) NOUN *Jocular* the setting of more targets than is strictly necessary for the effective functioning of an organization, esp when it leads to an increase in bureaucracy.
▷HISTORY C20: TARGET + -ITIS (sense 2)

target language NOUN [1] the language into which a text, document, etc., is translated. [2] a language that is being or is to be learnt.

target man NOUN *Soccer* an attacking player to whom high crosses and centres are played, esp a tall forward.

Targum ('tɑ:gəm; *Hebrew* tar'gum) NOUN an Aramaic translation, usually in the form of an expanded paraphrase, of various books or sections of the Old Testament.
▷HISTORY C16: from Aramaic: interpretation
▸**Targumic** (tɑ:'gu:mɪk) *or* **Tar'gumical** ADJECTIVE
▸'**Targumist** NOUN

tariff ('tærɪf) NOUN [1] **a** a tax levied by a government on imports or occasionally exports for purposes of protection, support of the balance of payments, or the raising of revenue. **b** a system or list of such taxes. [2] any schedule of prices, fees, fares, etc. [3] *Chiefly Brit* **a** a method of charging for the supply of services, esp public services, such as gas and electricity: *block tariff.* **b** a schedule of such charges. [4] *Chiefly Brit* a bill of fare with prices listed; menu. ◆ VERB (*tr*) [5] *Brit* the level of punishment imposed for a criminal offence. [6] to set a tariff on. [7] to set a price on according to a schedule of tariffs.
▷HISTORY C16: from Italian *tariffa,* from Arabic *ta'rīfa* to inform
▸'**tariffless** ADJECTIVE

tariff office NOUN *Insurance* a company whose premiums are based on a tariff agreed with other insurance companies.

Tarim ('tɑ:'ri:m) NOUN a river in NW China, in Xinjiang Uygur AR: flows east along the N edge of the Taklimakan Shama desert, dividing repeatedly and forming lakes among the dunes, finally disappearing in the Lop Nor depression; the chief river of Xinjiang Uygur AR; drains the great **Tarim Basin** between the Tian Shan and Kunlun mountain systems of central Asia, an area of about 906 500 sq. km (350 000 sq. miles). Length: 2190 km (1360 miles).

tarlatan ('tɑ:lətən) NOUN an open-weave cotton fabric, used for stiffening garments.
▷HISTORY C18: from French *tarlatane,* variant of *tarnatane* type of muslin, perhaps of Indian origin

Tarmac ('tɑ:mæk) NOUN [1] *Trademark* (*often not capital*) a paving material that consists of crushed stone rolled and bound with a mixture of tar and bitumen, esp as used for a road, airport runway, etc. Full name: **Tarmacadam** (,tɑ:mə'kædəm). See also **macadam.** ◆ VERB **-macs, -macking, -macked.** (*tr*) [2] (*usually not capital*) to apply Tarmac to.

tarn (tɑ:n) NOUN a small mountain lake or pool.
▷HISTORY C14: of Scandinavian origin; related to Old Norse *tjörn* pool

Tarn (*French* tarn) NOUN [1] a department of S France, in Midi-Pyrénées region. Capital: Albi. Pop.: 343 402 (1999). Area: 5780 sq. km (2254 sq. miles). [2] a river in SW France, rising in the Massif Central and flowing generally west to the Garonne River. Length: 375 km (233 miles).

tarnal ('tɑ:nəl) *US dialect* ◆ ADJECTIVE [1] (*prenominal*) damned. ◆ ADVERB [2] (intensifier): *tarnal lucky!*
▷HISTORY C18: aphetic dialect pronunciation of ETERNAL
▸'**tarnally** ADVERB

tarnation (tɑ:'neɪʃən) NOUN a euphemism for **damnation.**

Tarn-et-Garonne (*French* tarnegarɔn) NOUN a department of SW France, in Midi-Pyrénées region. Capital: Montauban. Pop.: 206 034 (1999). Area: 3731 sq. km (1455 sq. miles).

tarnish (ˈtɑːnɪʃ) VERB 1 to lose or cause to lose the shine, esp by exposure to air or moisture resulting in surface oxidation; discolour: *silver tarnishes quickly*. 2 to stain or become stained; taint or spoil: *a fraud that tarnished his reputation*. ◆ NOUN 3 a tarnished condition, surface, or film.
▷HISTORY C16: from Old French *ternir* to make dull, from *terne* lustreless, of Germanic origin; related to Old High German *tarnen* to conceal, Old English *dierne* hidden
▸ˈ**tarnishable** ADJECTIVE ▸ˈ**tarnisher** NOUN

Tarnopol (tarˈnɔpɔl) NOUN the Polish name for **Ternopol**.

Tarnów (*Polish* ˈtarnuf) NOUN an industrial city in SE Poland. Pop.: 121 494 (1999 est.).

taro (ˈtɑːrəʊ) NOUN, *plural* **-ros**. 1 an aroid plant, *Colocasia esculenta*, cultivated in the tropics for its large edible rootstock. 2 the rootstock of this plant. ◆ Also called: **elephant's-ear, dasheen, eddo, Chinese eddo.**
▷HISTORY C18: from Tahitian and Maori

tarot (ˈtærəʊ) NOUN 1 one of a special pack of cards, now used mainly for fortune-telling, consisting of 78 cards (4 suits of 14 cards each (the minor arcana), and 22 other cards (the major arcana)). 2 a card in a tarot pack with distinctive symbolic design, such as the Wheel of Fortune. ◆ ADJECTIVE 3 relating to tarot cards.
▷HISTORY C16: from French, from Old Italian *tarocco*, of unknown origin

tarp (tɑːp) NOUN *US, Austral, and NZ* an informal word for **tarpaulin**.

tarpan (ˈtɑːpæn) NOUN a European wild horse, *Equus caballus gomelini*, common in prehistoric times but now extinct.
▷HISTORY from Kirghiz Tatar

tarpaulin (tɑːˈpɔːlɪn) NOUN 1 a heavy hard-wearing waterproof fabric made of canvas or similar material coated with tar, wax, or paint, for outdoor use as a protective covering against moisture. 2 a sheet of this fabric. 3 a hat of or covered with this fabric, esp a sailor's hat. 4 a rare word for **seaman**.
▷HISTORY C17: probably from TAR[1] + PALL[1] + -ING[1]

Tarpeia (tɑːˈpiːə) NOUN (in Roman legend) a vestal virgin, who betrayed Rome to the Sabines and was killed by them when she requested a reward.

Tarpeian Rock (tɑːˈpiːən) NOUN (in ancient Rome) a cliff on the Capitoline hill from which traitors were hurled.

tarpon (ˈtɑːpən) NOUN, *plural* **-pons** *or* **-pon**. 1 a large silvery clupeoid game fish, *Tarpon atlanticus*, of warm Atlantic waters, having a compressed body covered with large scales: family *Elopidae*. 2 *Austral* another name for **ox-eye herring**. 3 any similar related fish.
▷HISTORY C17: perhaps from Dutch *tarpoen*, of unknown origin

Tarquin (ˈtɑːkwɪn) NOUN 1 Latin name *Lucius Tarquinius Priscus*. fifth legendary king of Rome (616–578 B.C.). 2 Latin name *Lucius Tarquinius Superbus*. seventh and last legendary king of Rome (534–510 B.C.).

tarradiddle (ˈtærəˌdɪdᵊl) NOUN 1 a trifling lie. 2 nonsense; twaddle.
▷HISTORY of unknown origin

tarragon (ˈtærəgən) NOUN 1 an aromatic perennial plant, *Artemisia dracunculus*, of the Old World, having whitish flowers and small toothed leaves, which are used as seasoning: family *Asteraceae* (composites). 2 the leaves of this plant. ◆ Also called: **estragon**.
▷HISTORY C16: from Old French *targon*, from Medieval Latin *tarcon*, from Arabic *tarkhūn*, perhaps from Greek *drakontion* adderwort

Tarragona (*Spanish* tarraˈɣona) NOUN a port in NE Spain, on the Mediterranean: one of the richest seaports of the Roman Empire; destroyed by the Moors (714). Pop.: 112 795 (1998 est.). Latin name: **Tarraco** (təˈrɑːkəʊ).

Tarrasa (*Spanish* taˈrrasa) NOUN a city in NE Spain: textile centre. Pop.: 165 654 (1998 est.).

tarriance (ˈtærɪəns) NOUN an archaic word for **delay**.

tarry (ˈtærɪ) VERB **-ries, -rying, -ried**. 1 (*intr*) to delay in coming or going; linger. 2 (*intr*) to remain temporarily or briefly. 3 (*intr*) to wait or stay. 4 (*tr*) *Archaic or poetic* to await. ◆ NOUN, *plural* **-ries**. 5 *Rare* a stay.
▷HISTORY C14 *tarien*, of uncertain origin
▸ˈ**tarrier** NOUN

tarsal (ˈtɑːsᵊl) ADJECTIVE 1 of, relating to, or constituting the tarsus or tarsi. ◆ NOUN 2 a tarsal bone.

tar sand NOUN a sandstone in which hydrocarbons have been trapped; the lighter compounds evaporate, leaving a residue of asphalt in the rock pores.

tarseal (ˈtɑːˌsiːl) NOUN *NZ* 1 the bitumen surface of a road. 2 **the**. the main highway.

Tarshish (ˈtɑːʃɪʃ) NOUN *Old Testament* an ancient port, mentioned in I Kings 10:22, situated in Spain or in one of the Phoenician colonies in Sardinia.

tarsia (ˈtɑːsɪə) NOUN another term for **intarsia**.
▷HISTORY C17: from Italian, from Arabic *tarsi'*; see INTARSIA

tarsier (ˈtɑːsɪə) NOUN any of several nocturnal arboreal prosimian primates of the genus *Tarsius*, of Indonesia and the Philippines, having huge eyes, long hind legs, and digits ending in pads to facilitate climbing: family *Tarsiidae*.
▷HISTORY C18: from French, from *tarse* the flat of the foot; see TARSUS

tarsometatarsus (ˌtɑːsəʊˌmɛtəˈtɑːsəs) NOUN, *plural* **-si** (-saɪ). a bone in the lower part of a bird's leg consisting of the metatarsal bones and some of the tarsal bones fused together.
▷HISTORY C19: *tarso-*, from TARSUS + METATARSUS
▸ˌ**tarsoˌmetaˈtarsal** ADJECTIVE

tarsus (ˈtɑːsəs) NOUN, *plural* **-si** (-saɪ). 1 the bones of the ankle and heel, collectively. 2 **a** the corresponding part in other mammals and in amphibians and reptiles. **b** another name for **tarsometatarsus**. 3 the dense connective tissue supporting the free edge of each eyelid. 4 the part of an insect's leg that lies distal to the tibia.
▷HISTORY C17: from New Latin, from Greek *tarsos* flat surface, instep

Tarsus (ˈtɑːsəs) NOUN 1 a city in SE Turkey, on the Tarsus River: site of ruins of ancient Tarsus, capital of Cilicia, and birthplace of St. Paul. Pop.: 190 184 (1997). 2 a river in SE Turkey, in Cilicia, rising in the Taurus Mountains and flowing south past Tarsus to the Mediterranean. Length: 153 km (95 miles). Ancient name: **Cydnus**.

tart[1] (tɑːt) NOUN a pastry case often having no top crust, with a sweet filling of fruit, jam, custard, etc.
▷HISTORY C14: from Old French *tarte*, of uncertain origin; compare Medieval Latin *tarte*

tart[2] (tɑːt) ADJECTIVE 1 (of a flavour, food, etc.) sour, acid, or astringent. 2 cutting, sharp, or caustic: *a tart remark*.
▷HISTORY Old English *teart* rough; related to Dutch *tarten* to defy, Middle High German *traz* defiance
▸ˈ**tartish** ADJECTIVE ▸ˈ**tartishly** ADVERB ▸ˈ**tartly** ADVERB
▸ˈ**tartness** NOUN

tart[3] (tɑːt) NOUN *Informal* a promiscuous woman, esp a prostitute: often a term of abuse. See also **tart up**.
▷HISTORY C19: shortened from SWEETHEART
▸ˈ**tarty** ADJECTIVE

tartan[1] (ˈtɑːtᵊn) NOUN 1 **a** a design of straight lines, crossing at right angles to give a chequered appearance, esp the distinctive design or designs associated with each Scottish clan: *the Buchanan tartan*. **b** (*as modifier*): *a tartan kilt*. 2 a woollen fabric or garment with this design. 3 **the tartan**. Highland dress.
▷HISTORY C16: perhaps from Old French *tertaine* linsey-woolsey, from Old Spanish *tiritaña* a fine silk fabric, from *tiritar* to rustle
▸ˈ**tartaned** ADJECTIVE

tartan[2] (ˈtɑːtᵊn) NOUN a single-masted vessel used in the Mediterranean, usually with a lateen sail.
▷HISTORY C17: from French, perhaps from Provençal *tartana* falcon, buzzard, since a ship was frequently given the name of a bird

tartanry (ˈtɑːtᵊnrɪ) NOUN *Derogatory* the excessive use of tartan and other Scottish imagery to produce a distorted sentimental view of Scotland and its history.
▷HISTORY C20: TARTAN[1] + -RY

tartar[1] (ˈtɑːtə) NOUN 1 *Dentistry* a hard crusty deposit on the teeth, consisting of food, cellular debris, and mineral salts. 2 Also called: **argol**. a brownish-red substance consisting mainly of potassium hydrogen tartrate, present in grape juice and deposited during the fermentation of wine.
▷HISTORY C14: from Medieval Latin *tartarum*, from Medieval Greek *tartaron*

tartar[2] (ˈtɑːtə) NOUN (*sometimes capital*) a fearsome or formidable person.
▷HISTORY C16: special use of TARTAR

Tartar (ˈtɑːtə) NOUN, ADJECTIVE a variant spelling of **Tatar**.

tartare *or* **tartar sauce** NOUN a mayonnaise sauce mixed with hard-boiled egg yolks, chopped herbs, capers, and gherkins.
▷HISTORY from French *sauce tartare*, from TARTAR

Tartarean (tɑːˈtɛərɪən, -ˈtɑːrɪ-) ADJECTIVE *Literary* of or relating to Tartarus; infernal.

tartar emetic NOUN another name for **antimony potassium tartrate**.

Tartarian (tɑːˈtɛərɪən) ADJECTIVE a variant spelling of **Tatarian**.

tartaric (tɑːˈtærɪk) ADJECTIVE of, concerned with, containing, or derived from tartar or tartaric acid. Systematic name: **2,3-dihydroxybutanedioic acid**.

Tartaric (tɑːˈtærɪk) ADJECTIVE a variant spelling of **Tataric**.

tartaric acid NOUN a colourless or white odourless crystalline water-soluble dicarboxylic acid existing in four stereoisomeric forms, the commonest being the dextrorotatory (*d*-) compound which is found in many fruits: used as a food additive (**E334**) in soft drinks, confectionery, and baking powders and in tanning and photography. Formula: HOOCCH(OH)CH(OH)COOH.

tartarize *or* **tartarise** (ˈtɑːtəˌraɪz) VERB (*tr*) to impregnate or treat with tartar or tartar emetic.
▸ˌ**tartariˈzation** *or* ˌ**tartariˈsation** NOUN

tartarous (ˈtɑːtərəs) ADJECTIVE consisting of, containing, or resembling tartar.

tartar steak NOUN a variant term for **steak tartare**.

Tartarus (ˈtɑːtərəs) NOUN *Greek myth* 1 an abyss under Hades where the Titans were imprisoned. 2 a part of Hades reserved for evildoers. 3 the underworld; Hades. 4 a primordial god who became the father of the monster Typhon.
▷HISTORY C16: from Latin, from Greek *Tartaros*, of obscure origin

Tartary (ˈtɑːtərɪ) NOUN a variant spelling of **Tatary**.

tartlet (ˈtɑːtlɪt) NOUN *Brit* an individual pastry case with a filling of fruit or other sweet or savoury mixture.

tartrate (ˈtɑːtreɪt) NOUN any salt or ester of tartaric acid.

tartrated (ˈtɑːtreɪtɪd) ADJECTIVE being in the form of a tartrate.

tartrazine (ˈtɑːtrəˌziːn, -zɪn) NOUN an azo dye that produces a yellow colour: widely used as a food additive (**E102**) in convenience foods, soft drinks, sweets, etc., and in drugs, and also to dye textiles.

Tartu (*Russian* ˈtartu) NOUN a city in SE Estonia: became Russian in 1704 after successive Russian, Polish, and Swedish rule; became part of independent Estonia in 1991; university (1632). Pop.: 101 000 (2000 est.). Former name (11th century until 1918): **Yurev**. German name: **Dorpat**.

Tartuffe *or* **Tartufe** (tɑːˈtʊf, -ˈtuːf) NOUN a person who hypocritically pretends to be deeply pious.
▷HISTORY from the character in the comedy *Tartuffe* (1664) by the French dramatist Molière (1622–73)
▸**Tarˈtuffian** *or* **Tarˈtufian** ADJECTIVE

tart up VERB (*tr, adverb*) *Brit informal* 1 to dress and make (oneself) up in a provocative way. 2 to decorate or improve the appearance of: *to tart up a bar*.

tarwhine (ˈtɑːˌwaɪn) NOUN a bream, *Rhabdosargus sarba*, of E Australia, silver in colour with gold streaks.
▷HISTORY from a native Australian language

Tarzan (ˈtɑːzən) NOUN (*sometimes not capital*)

Informal often ironic a man with great physical strength, agility, and virility.
▷**HISTORY** C20: after the hero of a series of stories by Edgar Rice Burroughs (1875–1950), US novelist

Taser (ˈteɪzə) (*sometimes not capital*) NOUN 1 *Trademark* a weapon that fires electrical probes that give an electric shock, causing temporary paralysis. ◆ VERB 2 (*tr*) to stun (someone) with a taser.

Tashi Lama (ˈtɑːʃɪ ˈlɑːmə) NOUN another name for the **Panchen Lama**.
▷**HISTORY** from *Tashi* (*Lumpo*), the name of the Tibetan monastery over which this Lama presides

Tashkent (*Russian* taʃˈkjɛnt) NOUN the capital of Uzbekistan: one of the oldest and largest cities in central Asia; cotton textile manufacturing. Pop.: 2 124 000 (1998 est.).

tasimeter (təˈsɪmɪtə) NOUN a device for measuring small temperature changes. It depends on the changes of pressure resulting from expanding or contracting solids.
▷**HISTORY** C19 *tasi-*, from Greek *tasis* tension + -METER
▸**tasimetric** (ˌtæsɪˈmɛtrɪk) ADJECTIVE ▸**taˈsimetry** NOUN

task (tɑːsk) NOUN 1 a specific piece of work required to be done as a duty or chore. 2 an unpleasant or difficult job or duty. 3 any piece of work. 4 **take to task.** to criticize or reprove. ◆ VERB (*tr*) 5 to assign a task to. 6 to subject to severe strain; tax.
▷**HISTORY** C13: from Old French *tasche*, from Medieval Latin *tasca*, from *taxa* tax, from Latin *taxāre* to TAX
▸**ˈtasker** NOUN ▸**ˈtaskless** ADJECTIVE

task force NOUN 1 a temporary grouping of military units formed to undertake a specific mission. 2 any semipermanent organization set up to carry out a continuing task.

taskmaster (ˈtɑːskˌmɑːstə) NOUN a person, discipline, etc., that enforces work, esp hard or continuous work: *his teacher is a hard taskmaster.*
▸**ˈtaskˌmistress** FEMININE NOUN

task-oriented ADJECTIVE focusing on the completion of particular tasks as a measure of success.

taskwork (ˈtɑːskˌwɜːk) NOUN 1 hard or unpleasant work. 2 a rare word for **piecework.**

Tasmania (tæzˈmeɪnɪə) NOUN an island in the S Pacific, south of mainland Australia: forms, with offshore islands, the smallest state of Australia; discovered by the Dutch explorer Tasman in 1642; used as a penal colony by the British (1803–53); mostly forested and mountainous. Capital: Hobart. Pop.: 470 260 (1999 est.). Area: 68 332 sq. km (26 383 sq. miles). Former name (1642–1855): **Van Diemen's Land.**

Tasmanian (tæzˈmeɪnɪən) ADJECTIVE 1 of or relating to Tasmania or its inhabitants. ◆ NOUN 2 a native or inhabitant of Tasmania.

Tasmanian devil NOUN a small ferocious carnivorous marsupial, *Sarcophilus harrisi*, of Tasmania, having black fur with pale markings, strong jaws, and short legs: family *Dasyuridae*. Also called: **ursine dasyure.**

Tasmanian wolf *or* **tiger** NOUN other names for **thylacine.**

Tasman Sea NOUN the part of the Pacific between SE Australia and NW New Zealand.

tass (tæs) *or* **tassie** (ˈtæsɪ) NOUN *Scot and northern English dialect* 1 a cup, goblet, or glass. 2 the contents of such a vessel.
▷**HISTORY** C15: from Old French *tasse* cup, from Arabic *tassah* basin, from Persian *tast*

Tass (tæs) NOUN (formerly) the principal news agency of the Soviet Union: replaced in 1992 by **Itar Tass.**
▷**HISTORY** *T*(*elegrafnoye*) *A*(*genstvo*) *S*(*ovetskovo*) *S*(*oyuza*) Telegraphic Agency of the Soviet Union

tassel (ˈtæsᵊl) NOUN 1 a tuft of loose threads secured by a knot or ornamental knob, used to decorate soft furnishings, clothes, etc. 2 anything resembling this tuft, esp the tuft of stamens at the tip of a maize inflorescence. ◆ VERB **-sels, -selling, -selled** *or US* **-sels, -seling, -seled.** 3 (*tr*) to adorn with a tassel or tassels. 4 (*intr*) (of maize) to produce stamens in a tuft. 5 (*tr*) to remove the tassels from.
▷**HISTORY** C13: from Old French, from Vulgar Latin *tassellus* (unattested), changed from Latin *taxillus* a small die, from *tālus* gaming die
▸**ˈtasselly** ADJECTIVE

tasset (ˈtæsɪt), **tasse** (tæs), *or less commonly* **tace** NOUN a piece of armour consisting of one or more plates fastened on to the bottom of a cuirass to protect the thigh.
▷**HISTORY** C19: from French *tassette* small pouch, from Old French *tasse* purse

Tassie *or* **Tassy** (ˈtæzɪ) NOUN, *plural* **-sies.** *Austral informal* 1 Tasmania. 2 a native or inhabitant of Tasmania.

taste (teɪst) NOUN 1 the sense by which the qualities and flavour of a substance are distinguished by the taste buds. 2 the sensation experienced by means of the taste buds. 3 the act of tasting. 4 a small amount eaten, drunk, or tried on the tongue. 5 a brief experience of something: *a taste of the whip.* 6 a preference or liking for something; inclination: *to have a taste for danger.* 7 the ability to make discerning judgments about aesthetic, artistic, and intellectual matters; discrimination: *to have taste.* 8 judgment of aesthetic or social matters according to a generally accepted standard: *bad taste.* 9 discretion; delicacy: *that remark lacks taste.* 10 *Obsolete* the act of testing. ◆ VERB 11 to distinguish the taste of (a substance) by means of the taste buds. 12 (*usually tr*) to take a small amount of (a food, liquid, etc.) into the mouth, esp in order to test the quality: *to taste the wine.* 13 (often foll by *of*) to have a specific flavour or taste: *the tea tastes of soap; this apple tastes sour.* 14 (when *intr*, usually foll by *of*) to have an experience of (something): *to taste success.* 15 (*tr*) an archaic word for **enjoy.** 16 (*tr*) *Obsolete* to test by touching.
▷**HISTORY** C13: from Old French *taster*, ultimately from Latin *taxāre* to appraise
▸**ˈtastable** ADJECTIVE

taste bud NOUN any of the elevated oval-shaped sensory end organs on the surface of the tongue, by means of which the sensation of taste is experienced.

tasteful (ˈteɪstfʊl) ADJECTIVE 1 indicating good taste: *a tasteful design.* 2 a rare word for **tasty.**
▸**ˈtastefully** ADVERB ▸**ˈtastefulness** NOUN

tasteless (ˈteɪstlɪs) ADJECTIVE 1 lacking in flavour; insipid. 2 lacking social or aesthetic taste. 3 *Rare* unable to taste.
▸**ˈtastelessly** ADVERB ▸**ˈtastelessness** NOUN

tastemaker (ˈteɪstˌmeɪkə) NOUN a person or group that sets a new fashion.

taster (ˈteɪstə) NOUN 1 a person who samples food or drink for quality. 2 any device used in tasting or sampling. 3 a person employed, esp formerly, to taste food and drink prepared for a king, etc., to test for poison. 4 a sample or preview of a product, experience, etc., intended to stimulate interest in the product, experience, etc., itself: *the single serves as a taster for the band's new album.*

-tastic ADJECTIVE COMBINING FORM *Jocular* denoting excellence in a specified area: *the fun-tastic theme park; their poptastic new single.*
▷**HISTORY** C20: from (FAN)TASTIC

tasty (ˈteɪstɪ) ADJECTIVE **tastier, tastiest.** 1 having a pleasant flavour. 2 *Brit informal* attractive: used chiefly by men when talking of women. 3 *Brit informal* skilful or impressive: *she was a bit tasty with a cutlass.* 4 *NZ* (of cheddar cheese) having a strong flavour.
▸**ˈtastily** ADVERB ▸**ˈtastiness** NOUN

tat[1] (tæt) VERB **tats, tatting, tatted.** to make (something) by tatting.
▷**HISTORY** C19: of unknown origin

tat[2] (tæt) NOUN 1 tatty articles or a tatty condition. 2 tasteless articles. 3 a tangled mass.
▷**HISTORY** C20: back formation from TATTY

tat[3] (tæt) NOUN short for **tattoo**[2] (sense 2).

tat[4] (tæt) NOUN See **tit for tat.**

ta-ta (tæˈtɑː) SENTENCE SUBSTITUTE *Brit informal* goodbye; farewell.
▷**HISTORY** C19: of unknown origin

tatahash (ˈteɪtəhæʃ) NOUN *Northern English dialect* a stew containing potatoes and cheap cuts of meat.

tatami (təˈtɑːmɪ, tæˈtæmɪ) NOUN, *plural* **-mi** *or* **-mis.** a thick rectangular mat of woven straw, used as a standard to measure a Japanese room.
▷**HISTORY** Japanese

Tatar *or* **Tartar** (ˈtɑːtə) NOUN 1 **a** a member of a Mongoloid people who under Genghis Khan established a vast and powerful state in central Asia from the 13th century until conquered by Russia in 1552. **b** a descendant of this people, now scattered throughout Russia but living chiefly in the Tatar Republic. 2 any of the languages spoken by the present-day Tatars, belonging to various branches of the Turkic family of languages, esp Kazan Tatar. ◆ ADJECTIVE 3 of, relating to, or characteristic of the Tatars.
▷**HISTORY** C14: from Old French *Tartare*, from Medieval Latin *Tartarus* (associated with Latin *Tartarus* the underworld), from Persian *Tātār*
▸**Tatarian** (tɑːˈtɛərɪən) *or* **Tarˈtarian** *or* **Tataric** (tɑːˈtærɪk) *or* **Tarˈtaric** ADJECTIVE

Tatar Republic NOUN a constituent republic of W Russia, around the confluence of the Volga and Kama Rivers. Capital: Kazan. Pop.: 3 779 000 (2000 est.) Area: 68 000 sq. km (26 250 sq. miles).

Tatar Strait NOUN an arm of the Pacific between the mainland of SE Russia and Sakhalin Island, linking the Sea of Japan with the Sea of Okhotsk. Length: about 560 km (350 miles). Also called: **Gulf of Tatary.**

Tatary *or* **Tartary** (ˈtɑːtərɪ) NOUN 1 a historical region (with indefinite boundaries) in E Europe and Asia, inhabited by Bulgars until overrun by the Tatars in the mid-13th century: extended as far east as the Pacific under Genghis Khan. 2 **Gulf of.** another name for the **Tatar Strait.**

Tate Galleries PLURAL NOUN two art galleries in London, the original Tate Gallery (1897), now **Tate Britain**, and **Tate Modern**, created in the former Bankside power station in 2000.

tater (ˈteɪtə) NOUN a dialect word for **potato.**

tatouay (ˈtætʊˌeɪ, ˌtɑːtʊˈaɪ) NOUN a large armadillo, *Cabassous tatouay*, of South America.
▷**HISTORY** C16: from Spanish *tatuay*, from Guarani *tatu ai*, from *tatu* armadillo + *ai* worthless (because inedible)

Tatra Mountains (ˈtɑːtrə, ˈtæt-) PLURAL NOUN a mountain range along the border between Slovakia and Poland, extending for about 64 km (40 miles): the highest range of the central Carpathians. Highest peak: Gerlachovka, 2663 m (8737 ft.). Also called: **High Tatra.**

TATT ABBREVIATION FOR tired all the time: a term used to describe a set of symptoms often related to doctors by patients.

tatter (ˈtætə) VERB 1 to make or become ragged or worn to shreds. ◆ NOUN 2 (*plural*) torn or ragged pieces, esp of material. 3 **in tatters. a** torn to pieces; in shreds. **b** destroyed or ruined.
▷**HISTORY** C14: of Scandinavian origin; compare Icelandic *töturr* rag, Old English *tættec*, Old High German *zæter* rag

tatterdemalion (ˌtætədɪˈmeɪljən, -ˈmæl-) NOUN *Rare* **a** a person dressed in ragged clothes. **b** (*as modifier*): *a tatterdemalion dress.*
▷**HISTORY** C17: from TATTER + *-demalion*, of uncertain origin

tattered (ˈtætəd) ADJECTIVE 1 ragged or worn: *a tattered old book.* 2 wearing ragged or torn clothing: *tattered refugees.* 3 damaged, defeated, or in disarray: *he believes he can bring the tattered party together.*

tattersall (ˈtætəˌsɔːl) NOUN **a** a fabric, sometimes brightly coloured, having stripes or bars in a checked or squared pattern. **b** (*as modifier*): *a tattersall coat.*
▷**HISTORY** C19: after TATTERSALL'S; the horse blankets at the market originally had this pattern

Tattersall's (ˈtætəˌsɔːlz) NOUN 1 a large horse market in London founded in the eighteenth century. 2 *Austral* a large-scale lottery based in Melbourne. Also (informal): **Tatt's.** 3 a name used for sportsmen's clubs in Australia.
▷**HISTORY** named after Richard *Tattersall* (died 1795), English horseman, who founded the market

tattie *or* **tatty** (ˈtætɪ) NOUN, *plural* **-ties.** a Scot or dialect word for **potato.**

tattie-bogle (ˌtætɪˈbogᵊl) NOUN *Scot* a scarecrow.
▷**HISTORY** TATTIE + BOGLE[1]

tattie-peelin (ˈtætɪˈpiːlɪn) ADJECTIVE *Central Scot dialect* (esp of speech) highfalutin, affected, or pretentious.

▷**HISTORY** from *potato-peeling;* sense development obscure

tatting ('tætɪŋ) NOUN [1] an intricate type of lace made by looping a thread of cotton or linen by means of a hand shuttle. [2] the act or work of producing this.
▷**HISTORY** C19: of unknown origin

tattle ('tætᵊl) VERB [1] (*intr*) to gossip about another's personal matters or secrets. [2] (*tr*) to reveal by gossiping: *to tattle a person's secrets.* [3] (*intr*) to talk idly; chat. ◆ NOUN [4] the act or an instance of tattling. [5] a scandalmonger or gossip.
▷**HISTORY** C15 (in the sense: to stammer, hesitate): from Middle Dutch *tatelen* to prate, of imitative origin

tattler ('tætlə) NOUN [1] a person who tattles; gossip. [2] any of several sandpipers of the genus *Heteroscelus,* such as *H. incanus* (**Polynesian tattler**), of Pacific coastal regions.

tattletale ('tætᵊl,teɪl) *Chiefly US and Canadian* ◆ NOUN [1] a scandalmonger or gossip. [2] another word for **telltale** (sense 1).

tattoo[1] (tæ'tu:) NOUN, *plural* **-toos.** [1] (formerly) a signal by drum or bugle ordering the military to return to their quarters. [2] a military display or pageant, usually at night. [3] any similar beating on a drum, etc.
▷**HISTORY** C17: from Dutch *taptoe,* from the command *tap toe!* turn off the taps! from *tap* tap of a barrel + *toe* to shut

tattoo[2] (tæ'tu:) VERB **-toos, -tooing, -tooed.** [1] to make (pictures or designs) on (the skin) by pricking and staining with indelible colours. ◆ NOUN, *plural* **-toos.** [2] a design made by this process. [3] the practice of tattooing.
▷**HISTORY** C18: from Tahitian *tatau*
▸**tat'tooer** *or* **tat'tooist** NOUN

tatty ('tætɪ) ADJECTIVE **-tier, -tiest.** *Chiefly Brit* worn out, shabby, tawdry, or unkempt.
▷**HISTORY** C16: of Scottish origin, probably related to Old English *tættec* a tatter
▸**'tattily** ADVERB ▸**'tattiness** NOUN

tau (tɔ:, taʊ) NOUN the 19th letter in the Greek alphabet (Τ or τ), a consonant, transliterated as *t.*
▷**HISTORY** C13: via Latin from Greek, of Semitic origin; see TAV

tau cross NOUN a cross shaped like the Greek letter tau. Also called: **Saint Anthony's cross.**

taught (tɔ:t) VERB the past tense and past participle of **teach.**

tauiwi (taʊ'i:wɪ) NOUN *NZ* a Maori term for the non-Maori people of New Zealand.
▷**HISTORY** Maori, literally: foreign race

tau neutrino NOUN *Physics* a type of neutrino associated with tau particles.

taunt[1] (tɔ:nt) VERB (*tr*) [1] to provoke or deride with mockery, contempt, or criticism. [2] to tease; tantalize. ◆ NOUN [3] a jeering remark. [4] *Archaic* the object of mockery.
▷**HISTORY** C16: from French phrase *tant pour tant* like for like, rejoinder
▸**'taunter** NOUN ▸**'taunting** ADJECTIVE ▸**'tauntingly** ADVERB

taunt[2] (tɔ:nt) ADJECTIVE *Nautical* (of the mast or masts of a sailing vessel) unusually tall.
▷**HISTORY** C15: of uncertain origin

Taunton ('tɔ:ntən) NOUN a market town in SW England, administrative centre of Somerset: scene of Judge Jeffreys' "Bloody Assize" (1685) after the Battle of Sedgemoor. Pop.: 55 855 (1991).

tauon ('taʊɒn) NOUN *Physics* a negatively charged elementary particle of mass 3477.48 × electron mass classed as a lepton, with an associated antiparticle and neutrino.
▷**HISTORY** C20: from Greek letter TAU + -ON

tau particle NOUN *Physics* another name for **tauon.**

taupe (təʊp) NOUN **a** a brownish-grey colour. **b** (*as adjective*): *a taupe coat.*
▷**HISTORY** C20: from French, literally: mole, from Latin *talpa*

Taupo ('taʊpəʊ) NOUN **Lake.** a lake in New Zealand, on central North Island: the largest lake of New Zealand. Area: 616 sq. km (238 sq. miles).

Tauranga (taʊ'ræŋə) NOUN a port in New Zealand, on NE North Island on the Bay of Plenty: exports dairy produce, meat, and timber. Pop.: 76 100 (1994).

taurine[1] ('tɔ:raɪn) ADJECTIVE of, relating to, or resembling a bull.
▷**HISTORY** C17: from Latin *taurīnus,* from *taurus* a bull

taurine[2] ('tɔ:ri:n, -rɪn) NOUN a derivative of the amino acid, cysteine, obtained from the bile of animals; 2-aminoethanesulphonic acid. Formula: $NH_2CH_2CH_2SO_3H$.
▷**HISTORY** C19: from TAURO- (as in *taurocholic* acid, so called because discovered in ox bile) + -INE[2]

tauro- *or before a vowel* **taur-** COMBINING FORM denoting a bull: *tauromachy.*
▷**HISTORY** from Latin *taurus* bull, Greek *tauros*

tauromachy (tɔ:'rɒməkɪ) NOUN the art or act of bullfighting.
▷**HISTORY** C19: Greek *tauromakhia,* from TAURO- + *makhē* fight
▸**tauromachian** (,tɔ:rə'meɪkɪən) ADJECTIVE

Taurus ('tɔ:rəs) NOUN, *Latin genitive* **Tauri** ('tɔ:raɪ). [1] *Astronomy* a zodiacal constellation in the N hemisphere lying close to Orion and between Aries and Gemini. It contains the star Aldebaran, the star clusters Hyades and Pleiades, and the Crab Nebula. [2] *Astrology* **a** Also called: **the Bull.** the second sign of the zodiac, symbol ♉, having a fixed earth classification and ruled by the planet Venus. The sun is in this sign between about April 20 and May 20. **b** a person born when the sun is in this sign. ◆ ADJECTIVE [3] born under or characteristic of Taurus. ◆ Also (for senses 2b, 3): **Taurean** ('tɔ:rɪən, tɔ:'rɪən).
▷**HISTORY** C14: from Latin: bull

Taurus Mountains PLURAL NOUN a mountain range in S Turkey, parallel to the Mediterranean coast: crossed by the Cilician Gates; continued in the northeast by the Anti-Taurus range. Highest peak: Kaldi Dağ, 3734 m (12 251 ft.).

taut (tɔ:t) ADJECTIVE [1] tightly stretched; tense. [2] showing nervous strain; stressed. [3] *Chiefly nautical* in good order; neat.
▷**HISTORY** C14 *tought;* probably related to Old English *togian* to TOW[1]
▸**'tautly** ADVERB ▸**'tautness** NOUN

tauten ('tɔ:tᵊn) VERB to make or become taut or tense.

tauto- *or before a vowel* **taut-** COMBINING FORM identical or same: *tautology; tautonym.*
▷**HISTORY** from Greek *tauto,* from *to auto*

tautog (tɔ:'tɒg) NOUN a large dark-coloured wrasse, *Tautoga onitis,* of the North American coast of the Atlantic Ocean: used as a food fish. Also called: **blackfish.**
▷**HISTORY** C17: from Narraganset *tautauog,* plural of *tautau* sheepshead

tautologize *or* **tautologise** (tɔ:'tɒlə,dʒaɪz) VERB (*intr*) to express oneself tautologically.
▸**tau'tologist** NOUN

tautology (tɔ:'tɒlədʒɪ) NOUN, *plural* **-gies.** [1] the use of words that merely repeat elements of the meaning already conveyed, as in the sentence *Will these supplies be adequate enough?* in place of *Will these supplies be adequate?* [2] *Logic* a statement that is always true, esp a truth-functional expression that takes the value true for all combinations of values of its components, as in *either the sun is out or the sun is not out.* Compare **inconsistency** (sense 3), **contingency** (sense 5).
▷**HISTORY** C16: from Late Latin *tautologia,* from Greek, from *tautologos*
▸**tautological** (,tɔ:tᵊ'lɒdʒɪkᵊl) *or* **,tauto'logic** *or* **tau'tologous** ADJECTIVE ▸**,tauto'logically** *or* **tau'tologously** ADVERB

tautomer ('tɔ:təmə) NOUN either of the two forms of a chemical compound that exhibits tautomerism.

tautomerism (tɔ:'tɒmə,rɪzəm) NOUN the ability of certain chemical compounds to exist as a mixture of two interconvertible isomers in equilibrium. See also **keto-enol tautomerism.**
▷**HISTORY** C19: from TAUTO- + ISOMERISM
▸**tautomeric** (,tɔ:tə'mɛrɪk) ADJECTIVE

tautonym ('tɔ:tənɪm) NOUN *Biology* a taxonomic name in which the generic and specific components are the same, as in *Rattus rattus* (black rat).
▷**HISTORY** C20: from Greek *tautonymos.* See TAUTO-, -ONYM
▸**,tauto'nymic** *or* **tautonymous** (tɔ:'tɒnɪməs) ADJECTIVE
▸**tau'tonymy** NOUN

tav *or* **taw** (tɑ:v, tɑ:f; *Hebrew* tav, taf) NOUN the 23rd and last letter in the Hebrew alphabet (ת), transliterated as *t* or when final *th.*
▷**HISTORY** from Hebrew: cross, mark

Tavel (tɑ:'vɛl) NOUN a fine rosé wine produced in the Rhône valley near the small town of Tavel in S France.

tavern ('tævən) NOUN [1] a less common word for **pub.** [2] *US, Eastern Canadian, and NZ* a place licensed for the sale and consumption of alcoholic drink.
▷**HISTORY** C13: from Old French *taverne,* from Latin *taberna* hut

taverna (tə'vɜ:nə) NOUN [1] (in Greece) a guesthouse that has its own bar. [2] a Greek restaurant.
▷**HISTORY** C20: Modern Greek, from Latin *taberna*

taverner ('tævənə) NOUN [1] *Archaic* a keeper of a tavern. [2] *Obsolete* a constant frequenter of taverns.

TAVR ABBREVIATION FOR Territorial and Army Volunteer Reserve.

taw[1] (tɔ:) NOUN [1] the line from which the players shoot in marbles. [2] **back to taws.** *Austral informal* back to the beginning. [3] a large marble used for shooting. [4] a game of marbles.
▷**HISTORY** C18: of unknown origin

taw[2] (tɔ:) VERB (*tr*) [1] to convert (skins) into white leather by treatment with mineral salts, such as alum and salt, rather than by normal tanning processes. [2] *Archaic or dialect* to flog; beat.
▷**HISTORY** Old English *tawian;* compare Old High German *zouwen* to prepare, Gothic *taujan* to make
▸**'tawer** NOUN

tawa ('tɑ:wə) NOUN a tall timber tree, *Beilschmiedia tawa,* of New Zealand, having edible purple berries.
▷**HISTORY** Maori

tawai ('tɑ:,waɪ) *or* **tawhai** ('tɑ:,hwaɪ) NOUN any of various species of beech of the genus *Nothofagus* of New Zealand, originally called "birches" by the settlers.
▷**HISTORY** Maori

tawdry ('tɔ:drɪ) ADJECTIVE **-drier, -driest.** cheap, showy, and of poor quality: *tawdry jewellery.*
▷**HISTORY** C16 *tawdry lace,* shortened and altered from *Seynt Audries lace,* finery sold at the fair of St *Audrey* (Etheldrida), 7th-century queen of Northumbria and patron saint of Ely, Cambridgeshire
▸**'tawdrily** ADVERB ▸**'tawdriness** NOUN

tawny *or* **tawney** ('tɔ:nɪ) NOUN **a** a light brown to brownish-orange colour. **b** (*as adjective*): *tawny port.*
▷**HISTORY** C14: from Old French *tané,* from *taner* to TAN[1]
▸**'tawniness** NOUN

tawny owl NOUN a European owl, *Strix aluco,* having a reddish-brown or grey plumage, black eyes, and a round head. Also called: **brown owl, wood owl.**

Tawny Owl NOUN a name (no longer in official use) for an assistant Brownie Guider.

tawny pipit NOUN a small sandy-brown European bird, *Anthus campestris,* of the wagtail family; an irregular migrant to some parts of Britain.

tawse *or* **taws** (tɔ:z) *Chiefly Scot* ◆ NOUN [1] a leather strap having one end cut into thongs, formerly used as an instrument of punishment by a schoolteacher. ◆ VERB [2] to punish (someone) with or as if with a tawse; whip.
▷**HISTORY** C16: probably plural of obsolete *taw* strip of leather; see TAW[2]

tax (tæks) NOUN [1] a compulsory financial contribution imposed by a government to raise revenue, levied on the income or property of persons or organizations, on the production costs or sales prices of goods and services, etc. [2] a heavy demand on something; strain: *a tax on our resources.* ◆ VERB (*tr*) [3] to levy a tax on (persons, companies, etc., or their incomes, etc.). [4] to make heavy demands on; strain: *to tax one's intellect.* [5] to accuse, charge, or blame: *he was taxed with the crime.* [6] to determine (the amount legally chargeable or allowable to a party to a legal action), as by examining the solicitor's bill of costs: *to tax costs.* [7] *Brit informal* to steal.
▷**HISTORY** C13: from Old French *taxer,* from Latin *taxāre* to appraise, from *tangere* to touch
▸**'taxer** NOUN ▸**'taxless** ADJECTIVE

taxable ('tæksəbᵊl) ADJECTIVE [1] capable of being

taxed; able to bear tax. 2 subject to tax. ◆ NOUN 3 (*often plural*) *US* a person, income, property, etc., that is subject to tax.
▸ ˌtaxa'bility *or* 'taxableness NOUN ▸ 'taxably ADVERB

taxaceous (tæk'seɪʃəs) ADJECTIVE of, relating to, or belonging to the *Taxaceae,* a family of coniferous trees that includes the yews.
▷ HISTORY C19: from New Latin *taxāceus,* from Latin *taxus* a yew

taxation (tæk'seɪʃən) NOUN 1 the act or principle of levying taxes or the condition of being taxed. 2 **a** an amount assessed as tax. **b** a tax rate. 3 revenue from taxes.
▸ tax'ational ADJECTIVE

tax avoidance NOUN reduction or minimization of tax liability by lawful methods. Compare **tax evasion.**

tax credit NOUN (in Britain) a social security benefit paid in the form of an additional income tax allowance.

tax-deductible ADJECTIVE (of an expense, loss, etc.) legally deductible from income or wealth before tax assessment.

tax disc NOUN a paper disc displayed on the windscreen of a motor vehicle showing that the tax due on it has been paid.

taxeme ('tæksiːm) NOUN *Linguistics* any element of speech that may differentiate one utterance from another with a different meaning, such as the occurrence of a particular phoneme, the presence of a certain intonation, or a distinctive word order.
▷ HISTORY C20: from Greek *taxis* order, arrangement + -EME
▸ tax'emic ADJECTIVE

tax evasion NOUN reduction or minimization of tax liability by illegal methods. Compare **tax avoidance.**

tax-exempt ADJECTIVE 1 (of an income or property) exempt from taxation. 2 (of an asset) earning income that is not subject to taxation.

tax exile NOUN a person having a high income who chooses to live abroad so as to avoid paying high taxes.

tax-free ADJECTIVE not needing to have tax paid on it: *tax-free savings schemes.*

tax haven NOUN a country or state having a lower rate of taxation than elsewhere.

tax holiday NOUN a period during which tax concessions are made for some reason; examples include an export incentive or an incentive to start a new business given by some governments, in which a company is excused all or part of its tax liability.

taxi ('tæksɪ) NOUN, *plural* **taxis** *or* **taxies.** 1 Also called: **cab, taxicab.** a car, usually fitted with a taximeter, that may be hired, along with its driver, to carry passengers to any specified destination. ◆ VERB **taxies, taxiing** *or* **taxying, taxied.** 2 to cause (an aircraft) to move along the ground under its own power, esp before takeoff and after landing, or (of an aircraft) to move along the ground in this way. 3 (*intr*) to travel in a taxi.
▷ HISTORY C20: shortened from *taximeter cab*

taxi dancing NOUN a system, as in a dance hall or hotel, whereby a person pays a partner (**taxi dancer**) for a dance, payment being required for each individual dance during an evening.

taxidermy ('tæksɪˌdɜːmɪ) NOUN the art or process of preparing, stuffing, and mounting animal skins so that they have a lifelike appearance.
▷ HISTORY C19: from Greek *taxis* arrangement + *-dermy,* from Greek *derma* skin
▸ ˌtaxi'dermal *or* ˌtaxi'dermic ADJECTIVE ▸ 'taxiˌdermist NOUN

taximeter ('tæksɪˌmiːtə) NOUN a meter fitted to a taxi to register the fare, based on the length of the journey.
▷ HISTORY C19: from French *taximètre;* see TAX, -METER

taxing ('tæksɪŋ) ADJECTIVE demanding, onerous, and wearing.
▸ 'taxingly ADVERB

taxiplane ('tæksɪˌpleɪn) NOUN *US* an aircraft that is available for hire.

taxi rank NOUN a place where taxis wait to be hired.

taxis ('tæksɪs) NOUN 1 the movement of a cell or organism in a particular direction in response to an external stimulus. 2 *Surgery* the repositioning of a displaced organ or part by manual manipulation only.
▷ HISTORY C18: via New Latin from Greek: arrangement, from *tassein* to place in order

-taxis *or* **-taxy** NOUN COMBINING FORM 1 indicating movement towards or away from a specified stimulus: *thermotaxis.* 2 order or arrangement: *phyllotaxis.*
▷ HISTORY from New Latin, from Greek *taxis* order
▸ **-tactic** *or* **-taxic** ADJECTIVE COMBINING FORM

taxi truck NOUN *Austral* a truck with a driver that can be hired.

taxiway ('tæksɪˌweɪ) NOUN a marked path along which aircraft taxi to or from a runway, parking area, etc. Also called: **taxi strip, peritrack.**

tax loss NOUN a loss sustained by a company that can be set against future profits for tax purposes.

taxman ('tæksˌmæn) NOUN, *plural* **-men.** 1 a collector of taxes. 2 *Informal* a tax-collecting body personified: *he was convicted of conspiring to cheat the taxman of five million pounds.*

taxon ('tæksɒn) NOUN, *plural* **taxa** ('tæksə). *Biology* any taxonomic group or rank.
▷ HISTORY C20: back formation from TAXONOMY

taxonomy (tæk'sɒnəmɪ) NOUN 1 **a** the branch of biology concerned with the classification of organisms into groups based on similarities of structure, origin, etc. **b** the practice of arranging organisms in this way. 2 the science or practice of classification.
▷ HISTORY C19: from French *taxonomie,* from Greek *taxis* order + -NOMY
▸ **taxonomic** (ˌtæksə'nɒmɪk) *or* ˌtaxo'nomical ADJECTIVE
▸ ˌtaxo'nomically ADVERB ▸ tax'onomist *or* tax'onomer NOUN

taxpayer ('tæksˌpeɪə) NOUN a person or organization that pays taxes or is liable to taxation.
▸ 'taxˌpaying ADJECTIVE

tax rate NOUN the percentage of income, wealth, etc., assessed as payable in taxation.

tax relief NOUN a reduction in the amount of tax a person or company has to pay.

tax return NOUN a declaration of personal income made annually to the tax authorities and used as a basis for assessing an individual's liability for taxation.

tax shelter NOUN *Commerce* a form into which business or financial activities may be organized to minimize taxation.

-taxy NOUN COMBINING FORM a variant of **-taxis.**

tax year NOUN a period of twelve months used by a government as a basis for calculating taxes.

tay (teɪ) NOUN an Irish dialect word for **tea.**

Tay (teɪ) NOUN 1 **Firth of.** the estuary of the River Tay on the North Sea coast of Scotland. Length: 40 km (25 miles). 2 a river in central Scotland, flowing northeast through Loch Tay, then southeast to the Firth of Tay: the longest river in Scotland; noted for salmon fishing. Length: 193 km (120 miles). 3 **Loch.** a lake in central Scotland, in Stirling council area. Length: 23 km (14 miles).

tayberry ('teɪbərɪ) NOUN, *plural* **-ries.** 1 a hybrid shrub produced by crossing a blackberry, raspberry, and loganberry. 2 the large sweet red fruit of this plant.
▷ HISTORY C20: so named because first grown at Blairgowrie on *Tayside,* Scotland

Taylor's Gold NOUN a variety of pear from New Zealand.

Taylor's series NOUN *Maths* an infinite sum giving the value of a function f(*z*) in the neighbourhood of a point *a* in terms of the derivatives of the function evaluated at *a*. Under certain conditions, the series has the form $f(z) = f(a) + [f'(a)(z-a)]/1! + [f''(a)(z-a)^2]/2! + \ldots$ See also **Maclaurin's series.**
▷ HISTORY C18: named after Brook *Taylor* (1685–1731), English mathematician

Taymyr Peninsula (taɪ'mɪə) NOUN a variant spelling of **Taimyr Peninsula.**

tayra ('taɪrə) NOUN a large arboreal musteline mammal, *Eira barbara,* of Central and South America, having a dark brown body and paler head.
▷ HISTORY C19: from Tupi *taira*

Tay-Sachs disease (ˌteɪ'sæks) NOUN an inherited disorder, caused by a faulty recessive gene, in which lipids accumulate in the brain, leading to mental retardation and blindness. It occurs mostly in Ashkenazi Jews.
▷ HISTORY C20: named after W. *Tay* (1843–1927), British physician, and B. *Sachs* (1858–1944), US neurologist

Tayside Region ('teɪˌsaɪd) NOUN a former local government region in E Scotland: formed in 1975 from Angus, Kinross-shire, and most of Perthshire; replaced in 1996 by the council areas of Angus, City of Dundee, and Perth and Kinross.

tazza ('tætsə) NOUN a wine cup with a shallow bowl and a circular foot.
▷ HISTORY C19: from Italian, probably from Arabic *tassah* bowl

tb ABBREVIATION FOR: 1 trial balance. 2 Also: **TB.** tuberculosis.

Tb THE CHEMICAL SYMBOL FOR terbium.

TB ABBREVIATION FOR: 1 torpedo boat. 2 Also: **tb.** tuberculosis.

T-bar NOUN 1 a T-shaped wrench for use with a socket. 2 a metal bar having a T-shaped cross section. 3 a T-shaped bar on a ski tow which skiers hold on to while being pulled up slopes. 4 (*modifier*) another term for **T-strap.**

tbc *or* **TBC** ABBREVIATION FOR to be confirmed.

Tbilisi (dbɪ'liːsɪ) NOUN the capital of Georgia, on the Kura River: founded in 458; taken by the Russians in 1801; university (1918); a major industrial centre. Pop.: 1 398 968 (1997 est.). Russian name: **Tiflis.**

T-bone steak NOUN a large choice steak cut from the sirloin of beef, containing a T-shaped bone.

tbs. *or* **tbsp.** ABBREVIATION FOR tablespoon(ful).

TBT ABBREVIATION FOR tri-*n*-butyl tin: a biocide used in marine paints to prevent fouling.

tc THE INTERNET DOMAIN NAME FOR Turks and Caicos Islands.

Tc THE CHEMICAL SYMBOL FOR technetium.

TC (on cars, etc.) ABBREVIATION FOR twin carburettors.

TCA cycle ABBREVIATION FOR tricarboxylic acid cycle: another name for **Krebs cycle.**

TCAS ABBREVIATION FOR traffic collision avoidance system: a safety system in aircraft that is designed to prevent mid-air collisions.

T-cell NOUN another name for **T-lymphocyte.**

TCH *or* **TD** INTERNATIONAL CAR REGISTRATION FOR Chad.
▷ HISTORY from TCHAD

Tchad (tʃad) NOUN the French name for **Chad.**

Tchebychev's inequality (ˌtʃebɪ'ʃɒfs) NOUN See **Chebyshev's inequality.**

TCM ABBREVIATION FOR traditional Chinese medicine: Chinese-based alternative therapies, including acupuncture, certain forms of massage, and some herbal remedies.

TCP NOUN *Trademark* a mild disinfectant used for cleansing minor wounds, gargling, etc.
▷ HISTORY abbrev. for *t(ri)c(hloro)p(henylmethyliodisalicyl)*

td THE INTERNET DOMAIN NAME FOR Chad.

TD ABBREVIATION FOR: 1 (in Ireland) Teachta Dála. [Irish Gaelic: member of the Dáil.] 2 technical drawing. 3 (in Britain) Territorial Decoration. 4 Also: **td.** touchdown.

t.d.c. ABBREVIATION FOR top dead-centre.

t distribution NOUN See **Student's t.**

tdm ABBREVIATION FOR time-division multiplex. See **multiplex** (sense 1).

te *or* **ti** (tiː) NOUN *Music* (in tonic sol-fa) the syllable used for the seventh note or subtonic of any scale.
▷ HISTORY see GAMUT

Te THE CHEMICAL SYMBOL FOR tellurium.

tea (tiː) NOUN 1 an evergreen shrub or small tree, *Camellia sinensis,* of tropical and subtropical Asia, having toothed leathery leaves and white fragrant flowers: family *Theaceae.* 2 **a** the dried shredded leaves of this shrub, used to make a beverage by infusion in boiling water. **b** such a beverage, served hot or iced. **c** (*as modifier*): *tea caddy; tea urn.* 3 **a**

any of various plants that are similar to *Camellia sinensis* or are used to make a tealike beverage. **b** any such beverage. [4] *Chiefly Brit* **a** Also called: **afternoon tea.** a light meal eaten in mid-afternoon, usually consisting of tea and cakes, biscuits, or sandwiches. **b** (*as modifier*): *a tea party.* **c** Also called: **high tea.** afternoon tea that also includes a light cooked dish. [5] *Brit, Austral, and NZ* the main evening meal. [6] *US and Canadian dated slang* marijuana. [7] **tea and sympathy.** *Informal* a caring attitude, esp to someone in trouble.
▷HISTORY C17: from Chinese (Amoy) *t'e,* from Ancient Chinese *d'a*

tea bag NOUN a small bag of paper or cloth containing tea leaves, infused in boiling water to make tea.

tea ball NOUN *Chiefly US* a perforated metal ball filled with tea leaves and put in boiling water to make tea.

teaberry ('tiːbərɪ, -brɪ) NOUN, *plural* **-ries.** [1] the berry of the wintergreen (*Gaultheria procumbens*). [2] another name for **wintergreen** (sense 1).
▷HISTORY C19: so called because its dried leaves have been used as a substitute for tea

tea biscuit NOUN *Brit* any of various semisweet biscuits.

teabread ('tiːˌbrɛd) NOUN [1] a loaf-shaped cake that contains dried fruit which has been steeped in cold tea before baking: served sliced and buttered. [2] any of a variety of loaf-shaped, usually light, cakes: *banana teabread.*

tea break NOUN *Brit* a short rest period during working hours during which tea, coffee, etc. is drunk.

TEAC ('tiːæk) (in New Zealand) NOUN ACRONYM FOR Tertiary Education Advisory Committee.

teacake ('tiːˌkeɪk) NOUN *Brit* a flat cake made from a yeast dough with raisins in it, usually eaten toasted and buttered.

teacart ('tiːˌkɑːt) NOUN a US and Canadian word for **tea trolley.**

teach (tiːtʃ) VERB **teaches, teaching, taught.** [1] (*tr; may take a clause as object or an infinitive;* often foll by *how*) to help to learn; tell or show (how): *to teach someone to paint; to teach someone how to paint.* [2] to give instruction or lessons in (a subject) to (a person or animal): *to teach French; to teach children; she teaches.* [3] (*tr; may take a clause as object or an infinitive*) to cause to learn or understand: *experience taught him that he could not be a journalist.* [4] Also: **teach (someone) a lesson.** *Informal* to cause (someone) to suffer the unpleasant consequences of some action or behaviour.
▷HISTORY Old English *tǣcan;* related to *tācen* TOKEN, Old Frisian *tēken,* Old Saxon *tēkan,* Old High German *zeihhan,* Old Norse *teikn* sign
▸ **'teachable** ADJECTIVE

teacher ('tiːtʃə) NOUN [1] a person whose occupation is teaching others, esp children. [2] a personified concept that teaches: *nature is a good teacher.*
▸ **'teacherless** ADJECTIVE

teachers' centre NOUN (in Britain) a place that provides a central store of educational aids, such as films and display material, and also in-service training, and is available for use to all the teachers within a particular area.

teach-in NOUN an informal conference, esp on a topical subject, usually held at a university or college and involving a panel of visiting speakers, lecturers, students, etc.

teaching ('tiːtʃɪŋ) NOUN [1] the art or profession of a teacher. [2] (*sometimes plural*) something taught; precept. [3] (*modifier*) denoting a person or institution that teaches: *a teaching hospital.* [4] (*modifier*) used in teaching: *teaching aids.*

teaching aid NOUN any device, object, or machine used by a teacher to clarify or enliven a subject.

teaching assistant NOUN another name for: **classroom assistant.**

teaching fellow NOUN a postgraduate student who is given tuition, accommodation, expenses, etc., in return for some teaching duties.
▸ **teaching fellowship** NOUN

teaching hospital NOUN a hospital that is affiliated to a medical school and provides the students with teaching and supervised practical experience.

teaching machine NOUN a machine that presents information and questions to the user, registers the answers, and indicates whether these are correct or acceptable.

teaching practice NOUN a temporary period of teaching in a school undertaken under supervision by a person who is training to become a teacher.

tea cloth NOUN another name for **tea towel.**

tea cosy NOUN a covering for a teapot to keep the contents hot, often having holes for the handle and spout.

teacup ('tiːˌkʌp) NOUN [1] a cup out of which tea may be drunk, larger than a coffee cup. [2] Also called: **teacupful.** the amount a teacup will hold, about four fluid ounces.

tea dance NOUN a dance held in the afternoon at which tea is served.

tea garden NOUN [1] an open-air restaurant that serves tea and light refreshments. [2] a tea plantation.

tea gown NOUN (formerly) a long loose decorative dress worn esp when entertaining guests to afternoon tea.

teahouse ('tiːˌhaʊs) NOUN a restaurant, esp in Japan or China, where tea and light refreshments are served.

teak (tiːk) NOUN [1] a large verbenaceous tree, *Tectona grandis,* of the East Indies, having white flowers and yielding a valuable dense wood. [2] the hard resinous yellowish-brown wood of this tree, used for furniture making, etc. [3] any of various similar trees or their wood. [4] a brown or yellowish-brown colour.
▷HISTORY C17: from Portuguese *teca,* from Malayalam *tēkka*

teakettle ('tiːˌkɛtᵊl) NOUN a kettle for boiling water to make tea.

teal (tiːl) NOUN, *plural* **teals** *or* **teal.** [1] any of various small ducks, such as the Eurasian *Anas crecca* (**common teal**) that are related to the mallard and frequent ponds, lakes, and marshes. [2] a greenish-blue colour.
▷HISTORY C14: related to Middle Low German *tēlink,* Middle Dutch *tēling*

tea lady NOUN a woman employed in a factory, office, etc. to make tea during a tea break.

tea leaf NOUN [1] the dried leaf of the tea shrub, used to make tea. [2] (*usually plural*) shredded parts of these leaves, esp after infusion. [3] *Brit and Austral slang* a thief.
▷HISTORY sense 3 rhyming slang

tea light NOUN a small round candle in a disposable metal container.

team (tiːm) NOUN (*sometimes functioning as plural*) [1] a group of players organized to work together. [2] a group of players forming one of the sides in a sporting contest. [3] two or more animals working together to pull a vehicle or agricultural implement. [4] such animals and the vehicle: *the coachman riding his team.* [5] *Dialect* a flock, herd, or brood. [6] *Obsolete* ancestry. ◆ VERB [7] (when *intr,* often foll by *up*) to make or cause to make a team: *he teamed George with Robert.* [8] (*tr*) *US and Canadian* to drag or transport in or by a team. [9] (*intr*) *US and Canadian* to drive a team.
▷HISTORY Old English *team* offspring; related to Old Frisian *tām* bridle, Old Norse *taumr* chain yoking animals together, Old High German *zoum* bridle

tea-maker NOUN a device with perforations used to infuse tea in a cup of boiling water. Also called (esp Brit): **infuser, tea egg.**

team-mate NOUN a fellow member of a team.

team spirit NOUN willingness to cooperate as part of a team.

teamster ('tiːmstə) NOUN [1] a driver of a team of horses used for haulage. [2] *US and Canadian* the driver of a lorry.

team teaching NOUN a system whereby two or more teachers pool their skills, knowledge, etc., to teach combined classes.

teamwork ('tiːmˌwɜːk) NOUN [1] the cooperative work done by a team. [2] the ability to work efficiently as a team.

tea party NOUN a social gathering in the afternoon at which tea is served.

teapot ('tiːˌpɒt) NOUN a container with a lid, spout, and handle, in which tea is made and from which it is served.

teapoy ('tiːpɔɪ) NOUN [1] a small table or stand with a tripod base. [2] a tea caddy on such a table or stand.
▷HISTORY C19: from Hindi *tipāī,* from Sanskrit *tri* three + *pāda* foot; compare Persian *sīpae* three-legged stand

tear[1] (tɪə) NOUN [1] a drop of the secretion of the lacrimal glands. See **tears.** [2] something shaped like a hanging drop: *a tear of amber.* ◆ Also called: **teardrop.**
▷HISTORY Old English *tēar,* related to Old Frisian, Old Norse *tār,* Old High German *zahar,* Greek *dakri*
▸ **'tearless** ADJECTIVE

tear[2] (tɛə) VERB **tears, tearing, tore, torn.** [1] to cause (material, paper, etc.) to come apart or (of material, etc.) to come apart; rip. [2] (*tr*) to make (a hole or split) in (something): *to tear a hole in a dress.* [3] (*intr;* often foll by *along*) to hurry or rush: *to tear along the street.* [4] (*tr;* usually foll by *away* or *from*) to remove or take by force. [5] (when *intr,* often foll by *at*) to cause pain, distress, or anguish (to): *it tore at my heartstrings to see the starving child.* [6] **tear one's hair.** *Informal* to be angry, frustrated, very worried, etc. ◆ NOUN [7] a hole, cut, or split. [8] the act of tearing. [9] a great hurry; rush. [10] **on a tear.** *Slang* showing a sudden burst of energy. ◆ See also **tear away, tear down, tear into, tear off, torn.**
▷HISTORY Old English *teran;* related to Old Saxon *terian,* Gothic *gatairan* to destroy, Old High German *zeran* to destroy
▸ **'tearable** ADJECTIVE ▸ **'tearer** NOUN

tear away (tɛə) VERB [1] (*tr, adverb*) to persuade (oneself or someone else) to leave: *I couldn't tear myself away from the television.* ◆ NOUN **tearaway.** [2] *Brit* **a** a reckless impetuous unruly person. **b** (*as modifier*): *a tearaway young man.*

tear down (tɛə) VERB (*tr, adverb*) to destroy or demolish: *to tear a wall down; to tear down an argument.*

tear duct (tɪə) NOUN the nontechnical name for **lacrimal duct.**

tearful ('tɪəfʊl) ADJECTIVE [1] about to cry. [2] accompanying or indicative of weeping: *a tearful expression.* [3] tending to produce tears; sad.
▸ **'tearfully** ADVERB ▸ **'tearfulness** NOUN

tear gas (tɪə) NOUN any one of a number of gases or vapours that make the eyes smart and water, causing temporary blindness; usually dispersed from grenades and used in warfare and to control riots. Also called: **lacrimator.**

tearing ('tɛərɪŋ) ADJECTIVE violent or furious (esp in the phrase **tearing hurry** *or* **rush**).

tear into (tɛə) VERB (*intr, preposition*) *Informal* to attack vigorously and damagingly.

tear-jerker ('tɪəˌdʒɜːkə) NOUN *Informal* an excessively sentimental film, play, book, etc.

tear off (tɛə) VERB [1] (*tr*) to separate by tearing. [2] (*intr, adverb*) to rush away; hurry. [3] (*tr, adverb*) to produce in a hurry; do quickly and carelessly: *to tear off a letter.* [4] **tear (someone) off a strip.** *Brit informal* to reprimand or rebuke (someone) forcibly. ◆ ADJECTIVE **tear-off.** [5] (of paper, etc.) produced in a roll or block and marked with perforations so that one section at a time can be torn off.

tearoom ('tiːˌruːm, -ˌrʊm) NOUN [1] another name for **teashop.** [2] *NZ* a room in a school or university where hot drinks are served.

tea rose NOUN [1] any of several varieties of hybrid rose that are derived from *Rosa odorata* and have pink or yellow flowers with a scent resembling that of tea. [2] **a** a yellowish-pink colour. **b** (*as adjective*): *tea-rose walls.*

tears (tɪəz) PLURAL NOUN [1] the clear salty solution secreted by the lacrimal glands that lubricates and cleanses the surface of the eyeball and inner surface of the eyelids. Related adjective: **lachrymal.** [2] a state of intense frustration (esp in the phrase **bored to tears**). [3] **in tears.** weeping. [4] **without tears.** presented so as to be easily assimilated: *reading without tears.*

tear sheet (tɛə) NOUN a page in a newspaper or periodical that is cut or perforated so that it can be easily torn out.

teary ('tɪərɪ) ADJECTIVE **tearier, teariest.** [1] covered with, characterized by, or secreting tears. [2] given to weeping; tearful.
▸ **'tearily** ADVERB ▸ **'teariness** NOUN

tease (ti:z) VERB [1] to annoy (someone) by deliberately offering something with the intention of delaying or withdrawing the offer. [2] to arouse sexual desire in (someone) with no intention of satisfying it. [3] to vex (someone) maliciously or playfully, esp by ridicule. [4] (*tr*) to separate the fibres of; comb; card. [5] (*tr*) to raise the nap of (a fabric) with a teasel. [6] another word (esp US and Canadian) for **backcomb.** [7] (*tr*) to loosen or pull apart (biological tissues, etc.) by delicate agitation or prodding with an instrument. ◆ NOUN [8] a person or thing that teases. [9] the act of teasing. ◆ See also **tease out.**
▷HISTORY Old English *tǣsan;* related to Old High German *zeisan* to pick
▸ **'teasing** ADJECTIVE ▸ **'teasingly** ADVERB

teasel, teazel, *or* **teazle** ('ti:zəl) NOUN [1] any of various stout biennial plants of the genus *Dipsacus,* of Eurasia and N Africa, having prickly leaves and prickly heads of yellow or purple flowers: family *Dipsacaceae.* See also **fuller's teasel.** [2] **a** the prickly dried flower head of the fuller's teasel, used for teasing. **b** any manufactured implement used for the same purpose. ◆ VERB **-sels, -selling, -selled** *or US* **-sels, -seling, -seled.** [3] (*tr*) to tease (a fabric).
▷HISTORY Old English *tǣsel;* related to Old High German *zeisala* teasel, Norwegian *tīsl* undergrowth, *tīsla* to tear to bits; see TEASE
▸ **'teaseller** NOUN

tease out VERB (*tr, adverb*) to extract (information) with difficulty.

teaser ('ti:zə) NOUN [1] a person who teases. [2] a preliminary advertisement in a campaign that attracts attention by making people curious to know what product is being advertised. [3] a difficult question. [4] *Vet science* a vasectomized male animal, such as an ox, used to detect oestrus in females.

tea service *or* **set** NOUN the china or pottery articles used in serving tea, including a teapot, cups, saucers, etc.

teashop ('ti:ˌʃɒp) NOUN *Brit* a restaurant where tea and light refreshments are served. Also called: **tearoom.**

teaspoon ('ti:ˌspu:n) NOUN [1] a small spoon used for stirring tea, eating certain desserts, etc. [2] Also called: **teaspoonful** ('ti:ˌspu:nfʊl). the amount contained in such a spoon. [3] a unit of capacity used in cooking, medicine, etc., equal to about one fluid dram.

teat (ti:t) NOUN [1] **a** the nipple of a mammary gland. **b** (in cows, etc.) any of the projections from the udder through which milk is discharged. See **nipple.** [2] something resembling a teat in shape or function, such as the rubber mouthpiece of a feeding bottle.
▷HISTORY C13: from Old French *tete,* of Germanic origin; compare Old English *titt,* Middle High German *zitze*

tea towel *or* **cloth** NOUN a towel for drying dishes and kitchen utensils. US name: **dishtowel.**

tea tree NOUN any of various myrtaceous trees of the genus *Leptospermum,* of Australia and New Zealand, that yield an oil used as an antiseptic.

tea trolley NOUN *Brit* a trolley from which tea is served.

tea wagon NOUN a US and Canadian name for **tea trolley.**

Tebet (te'vet) NOUN a variant spelling of **Tevet.**

tebi- ('tɛbɪ) PREFIX *Computing* denoting 2^{40}: *tebibyte.* Symbol: Ti.
▷HISTORY C20: from TE(RA-) + BI(NARY)

tec *or* **'tec** (tɛk) NOUN *Informal* short for **detective.**

TEC (tɛk) (in Britain) NOUN ACRONYM FOR Training and Enterprise Council. See **Training Agency.**

tech (tɛk) NOUN *Informal* short for **technical college.**

tech. ABBREVIATION FOR: [1] technical. [2] technology.

techie *or* **techy** ('tɛkɪ) *Informal* ◆ NOUN, *plural* **techies.** [1] a person who is skilled in the use of technological devices, such as computers. ◆ ADJECTIVE [2] of, relating to, or skilled in the use of technological devices, such as computers.

technetium (tɛk'ni:ʃɪəm) NOUN a silvery-grey metallic element, artificially produced by bombardment of molybdenum by deuterons: used to inhibit corrosion in steel. The radioisotope **technetium-99m,** with a half-life of six hours, is used in radiotherapy. Symbol: Tc; atomic no.: 43; half-life of most stable isotope, ^{97}Tc: 2.6×10^6 years; valency: 0, 2, 4, 5, 6, or 7; relative density: 11.50 (calculated); melting pt.: 2204°C; boiling pt.: 4265°C.
▷HISTORY C20: New Latin, from Greek *tekhnētos* manmade, from *tekhnasthai* to devise artificially, from *tekhnē* skill

technic NOUN [1] (tɛk'ni:k) another word for **technique.** [2] ('tɛknɪk) another word for **technics.**
▷HISTORY C17: from Latin *technicus,* from Greek *tekhnikos,* from *tekhnē* art, skill

technical ('tɛknɪkᵊl) ADJECTIVE [1] of, relating to, or specializing in industrial, practical, or mechanical arts and applied sciences: *a technical institute.* [2] skilled in practical and mechanical arts rather than theoretical or abstract thinking. [3] relating to or characteristic of a particular field of activity: *the technical jargon of linguistics.* [4] existing by virtue of a strict application of the rules or a strict interpretation of the wording: *a technical loophole in the law; a technical victory.* [5] of, derived from, or showing technique: *technical brilliance.* [6] (of a financial market) having prices determined by internal speculative or manipulative factors rather than by general or economic conditions: *a technical rally.*
▸ **'technically** ADVERB ▸ **'technicalness** NOUN

technical area NOUN *Soccer* the area at the side of the pitch to which managers, trainers, coaches, etc. are restricted during play.

technical college NOUN *Brit* an institution for further education that provides courses in technology, art, secretarial skills, agriculture, etc. Sometimes (informal) shortened to: **tech.**

technical drawing NOUN the study and practice, esp as a subject taught in school, of the basic techniques of draughtsmanship, as employed in mechanical drawing, architecture, etc. Abbreviation: **TD.**

technical institute NOUN *NZ* a higher-education institution. Sometimes (informal) shortened to: **tech.**

technicality (ˌtɛknɪ'kælɪtɪ) NOUN, *plural* **-ties.** [1] a petty formal point arising from a strict interpretation of rules, etc.: *the case was dismissed on a technicality.* [2] the state or quality of being technical. [3] technical methods and vocabulary.

technical knockout NOUN *Boxing* a judgment of a knockout given when a boxer is in the referee's opinion too badly beaten to continue without risk of serious injury.

technical sergeant NOUN a noncommissioned officer in the US Marine Corps or Air Force ranking immediately subordinate to a master sergeant.

technician (tɛk'nɪʃən) NOUN [1] a person skilled in mechanical or industrial techniques or in a particular technical field. [2] a person employed in a laboratory, technical college, or scientific establishment to do practical work. [3] a person having specific artistic or mechanical skill, esp if lacking original flair or genius.

Technicolor ('tɛknɪˌkʌlə) NOUN *Trademark* the process of producing colour film by means of superimposing synchronized films of the same scene, each of which has a different colour filter, to obtain the desired mix of colour.

technicolour ('tɛknɪˌkʌlə) *or* **technicoloured** ('tɛknɪˌkʌləd) ADJECTIVE brightly, showily, or garishly coloured; vividly noticeable.

technics ('tɛknɪks) NOUN (*functioning as singular*) the study or theory of industry and industrial arts; technology.

technikon ('tɛknɪ'kɒn) NOUN *South African* a technical college.

technique *or* **technic** (tɛk'ni:k) NOUN [1] a practical method, skill, or art applied to a particular task. [2] proficiency in a practical or mechanical skill. [3] special facility; knack: *he had the technique of turning everything to his advantage.*
▷HISTORY C19: from French, from *technique* (adj) TECHNIC

techno ('tɛknəʊ) NOUN a type of very fast dance music, using electronic sounds and fast heavy beats.

techno- COMBINING FORM [1] craft or art: *technology; technography.* [2] technological or technical: *technocracy.* [3] relating to or using technology: *technophobia.*
▷HISTORY from Greek *tekhnē* skill

technocracy (tɛk'nɒkrəsɪ) NOUN, *plural* **-cies.** [1] a theory or system of society according to which government is controlled by scientists, engineers, and other experts. [2] a body of such experts. [3] a state considered to be governed or organized according to these principles.
▸ **technocrat** ('tɛknəˌkræt) NOUN ▸ **ˌtechno'cratic** ADJECTIVE

technofear ('tɛknəˌfɪə) NOUN fear of using technological devices, such as computers; technophobia.

technography (tɛk'nɒgrəfɪ) NOUN the study and description of the historical development of the arts and sciences in the context of their ethnic and geographical background.

technol. ABBREVIATION FOR: [1] technological. [2] technology.

technology (tɛk'nɒlədʒɪ) NOUN, *plural* **-gies.** [1] the application of practical sciences to industry or commerce. [2] the methods, theory, and practices governing such application: *a highly developed technology.* [3] the total knowledge and skills available to any human society for industry, art, science, etc.
▷HISTORY C17: from Greek *tekhnologia* systematic treatment, from *tekhnē* art, skill
▸ **technological** (ˌtɛknə'lɒdʒɪkᵊl) ADJECTIVE ▸ **ˌtechno'logically** ADVERB ▸ **tech'nologist** NOUN

technology agreement NOUN a framework designed by trade unions for negotiating changes in employment caused by the introduction of new technology.

technophile ('tɛknəʊˌfaɪl) NOUN [1] a person who is enthusiastic about technology. ◆ ADJECTIVE [2] enthusiastic about technology.

technophobe ('tɛknəʊˌfəʊb) NOUN [1] someone who fears the effects of technological development on society and the environment. [2] someone who is afraid of using technological devices, such as computers.

technophobia (ˌtɛknəʊ'fəʊbɪə) NOUN [1] fear of the effects of technological developments on society or the environment. [2] fear of using technological devices, such as computers.

technostructure ('tɛknəʊˌstrʌktʃə) NOUN the people who control the technology of a society, such as professional administrators, experts in business management, etc.

techy[1] ('tɛkɪ) NOUN, *plural* **techies,** ADJECTIVE *Informal* a variant spelling of **techie.**

techy[2] ('tɛtʃɪ) ADJECTIVE **techier, techiest.** a variant spelling of **tetchy.**
▸ **'techily** ADVERB ▸ **'techiness** NOUN

tectibranch ('tɛktɪˌbræŋk) NOUN a mollusc of the suborder *Tectibranchia* (or *Tectibranchiata*) (order: *Opisthobranchia*) which includes the sea slugs and sea hares.
▷HISTORY C19: New Latin, from *tectus* covered, from *tegere* to cover + *branchia:* see -BRANCH

tectonic (tɛk'tɒnɪk) ADJECTIVE [1] denoting or relating to construction or building. [2] *Geology* **a** (of landforms, rock masses, etc.) resulting from distortion of the earth's crust due to forces within it. **b** (of processes, movements, etc.) occurring within the earth's crust and causing structural deformation.
▷HISTORY C17: from Late Latin *tectonicus,* from Greek *tektonikos* belonging to carpentry, from *tektōn* a builder
▸ **tec'tonically** ADVERB

tectonics (tɛk'tɒnɪks) NOUN (*functioning as singular*) [1] the art and science of construction or building. [2] the study of the processes by which the earth's crust has attained its present structure. See also **plate tectonics.**

tectorial membrane (tɛk'tɔ:rɪəl) NOUN the membrane in the inner ear that covers the organ of Corti.
▷HISTORY C19: *tectorial,* from Latin *tectōrium* a covering, from *tegere* to cover

tectrix ('tɛktrɪks) NOUN, *plural* **tectrices** ('tɛktrɪˌsiːz, tɛk'traɪsiːz). (*usually plural*) *Ornithol* another name for **covert** (sense 6).
▷HISTORY C19: New Latin, from Latin *tector* plasterer, from *tegere* to cover
▸**tectricial** (tɛk'trɪʃəl) ADJECTIVE

ted[1] (tɛd) VERB **teds, tedding, tedded.** to shake out and loosen (hay), so as to dry it.
▷HISTORY C15: from Old Norse *tethja;* related to *tad* dung, Old High German *zetten* to spread

ted[2] (tɛd) NOUN *Informal* short for **teddy boy.**

tedder ('tɛdə) NOUN **1** a machine equipped with a series of small rotating forks for tedding hay. **2** a person who teds.

teddy ('tɛdɪ) NOUN, *plural* **-dies.** a woman's one-piece undergarment, incorporating a chemise top and panties.

teddy bear NOUN a stuffed toy bear made from soft or fluffy material. Often shortened to: **teddy.**
▷HISTORY C20: from *Teddy,* from *Theodore,* after Theodore Roosevelt (1858–1919), 26th president of the US (1901–09), who was well known as a hunter of bears

teddy boy NOUN **1** (in Britain, esp in the mid-1950s) one of a cult of youths who wore mock Edwardian fashions, such as tight narrow trousers, pointed shoes, and long sideboards. Often shortened to: **ted. 2** any tough or delinquent youth.
▷HISTORY C20: from *Teddy,* from *Edward,* referring to the Edwardian dress

teddy girl NOUN a girl companion to a teddy boy.

Te Deum (ˌtiː 'diːəm) NOUN **1** an ancient Latin hymn in rhythmic prose, sung or recited at matins in the Roman Catholic Church and in English translation at morning prayer in the Church of England and used by both Churches as an expression of thanksgiving on special occasions. **2** a musical setting of this hymn. **3** a service of thanksgiving in which the recital of this hymn forms a central part.
▷HISTORY from the Latin canticle beginning *Tē Deum laudāmus,* literally: Thee, God, we praise

tedious ('tiːdɪəs) ADJECTIVE **1** causing fatigue or tedium; monotonous. **2** *Obsolete* progressing very slowly.
▸**'tediously** ADVERB ▸**'tediousness** NOUN

tedium ('tiːdɪəm) NOUN the state of being bored or the quality of being boring; monotony.
▷HISTORY C17: from Latin *taedium,* from *taedēre* to weary

tee[1] (tiː) NOUN **1** a pipe fitting in the form of a letter T, used to join three pipes. **2** a metal section with a cross section in the form of a letter T, such as a rolled-steel joist. **3** any part or component shaped like a T.

tee[2] (tiː) *Golf* ◆ NOUN **1** Also called: **teeing ground.** an area, often slightly elevated, from which the first stroke of a hole is made. **2** a support for a golf ball, usually a small wooden or plastic peg, used when teeing off or in long grass, etc. ◆ VERB **tees, teeing, teed. 3** (when *intr,* often foll by *up*) to position (the ball) ready for striking, on or as if on a tee. ◆ See also **tee off.**
▷HISTORY C17 *teaz,* of unknown origin

tee[3] (tiː) NOUN a mark used as a target in certain games such as curling and quoits.
▷HISTORY C18: perhaps from T-shaped marks, which may have originally been used in curling

tee-hee *or* **te-hee** ('tiː'hiː) INTERJECTION **1** an exclamation of laughter, esp when mocking. ◆ NOUN **2** a chuckle. ◆ VERB **-hees, -heeing, -heed. 3** (*intr*) to snigger or laugh, esp derisively.
▷HISTORY C14: of imitative origin

tee-joint NOUN a variant spelling of **T-joint.**

teem[1] (tiːm) VERB **1** (*intr;* usually foll by *with*) to be prolific or abundant (in); abound (in). **2** *Obsolete* to bring forth (young).
▷HISTORY Old English *tēman* to produce offspring; related to West Saxon *tīeman;* see TEAM

teem[2] (tiːm) VERB **1** (*intr;* often foll by *down* or *with rain*) to pour in torrents: *it's teeming down.* **2** (*tr*) to pour or empty out.
▷HISTORY C15 *temen* to empty, from Old Norse *tœma;* related to Old English *tōm,* Old High German *zuomīg* empty
▸**'teemer** NOUN

teen[1] (tiːn) ADJECTIVE *Informal* another word for **teenage.**

teen[2] (tiːn) NOUN *Obsolete* affliction or woe.
▷HISTORY Old English *tēona;* related to Old Saxon *tiono,* Old Frisian *tiona* injury

-teen NOUN COMBINING FORM ten: added to modified forms of the numbers 3 to 9 to form the numbers 13 to 19.
▷HISTORY Old English *-tēne, -tȳne*
▸**-teenth** ADJECTIVE COMBINING FORM

teenage ('tiːnˌeɪdʒ) ADJECTIVE *also* **teenaged. 1** (*prenominal*) of or relating to the time in a person's life between the ages of 13 and 19 inclusive. ◆ NOUN **2** this period of time.

teenager ('tiːnˌeɪdʒə) NOUN a person between the ages of 13 and 19 inclusive.

teens (tiːnz) PLURAL NOUN **1** the years of a person's life between the ages of 13 and 19 inclusive. **2** all the numbers that end in *-teen.*

teeny ('tiːnɪ) ADJECTIVE **-nier, -niest.** *Informal* extremely small; tiny. Also: **teeny-weeny** ('tiːnɪ'wiːnɪ) *or* **teensy-weensy** ('tiːnzɪ'wiːnzɪ).
▷HISTORY C19: variant of TINY

teenybopper ('tiːnɪˌbɒpə) NOUN *Slang* a young teenager, usually a girl, who avidly follows fashions in clothes and pop music.
▷HISTORY C20: *teeny,* from TEENAGE + *-bopper* see BOP[1]
▸**'teenyˌbop** ADJECTIVE

tee off VERB (*adverb*) **1** *Golf* to strike (the ball) from a tee, as when starting a hole. **2** *Informal* to begin; start.

teepee ('tiːpiː) NOUN a variant spelling of **tepee.**

tee-piece NOUN a variant spelling of **T-piece.**

tee-plate NOUN a variant spelling of **T-plate.**

Tees (tiːz) NOUN a river in N England, rising in the N Pennines and flowing southeast and east to the North Sea at Middlesbrough. Length: 113 km (70 miles).

tee shirt NOUN a variant of **T-shirt.**

tee-square NOUN a variant spelling of **T-square.**

Teesside ('tiːzˌsaɪd) NOUN the industrial region around the lower Tees valley and estuary: a county borough, containing Middlesbrough, from 1968 to 1974.

teeter ('tiːtə) VERB **1** to move or cause to move unsteadily; wobble. ◆ NOUN, VERB **2** another word for **seesaw.**
▷HISTORY C19: from Middle English *titeren,* related to Old Norse *titra* to tremble, Old High German *zittarōn* to shiver

teeth (tiːθ) NOUN **1** the plural of **tooth. 2** the most violent part: *the teeth of the gale.* **3** the power to produce a desired effect: *that law has no teeth.* **4 by the skin of one's teeth.** See **skin** (sense 14). **5 get one's teeth into.** to become engrossed in. **6 in the teeth of.** in direct opposition to; against: *in the teeth of violent criticism he went ahead with his plan.* **7 to the teeth.** to the greatest possible degree: *armed to the teeth.* **8 show one's teeth.** to threaten, esp in a defensive manner.

teethe (tiːð) VERB (*intr*) to cut one's baby (deciduous) teeth.

teething ring NOUN a plastic, hard rubber, or bone ring on which babies may bite while teething.

teething troubles PLURAL NOUN the difficulties or problems that arise during the initial stages of a project, enterprise, etc.

teetotal (tiː'təʊtᵊl) ADJECTIVE **1** of, relating to, or practising abstinence from alcoholic drink. **2** *Dialect* complete.
▷HISTORY C19: allegedly coined in 1833 by Richard Turner, English advocate of total abstinence from alcoholic liquors; probably from TOTAL, with emphatic reduplication
▸**tee'totaller** NOUN ▸**tee'totally** ADVERB ▸**tee'totalism** NOUN

teetotum (tiː'təʊtəm) NOUN *Archaic* **1** a spinning top bearing letters of the alphabet on its four sides. **2** such a top used as a die in gambling games.
▷HISTORY C18: from *T totum,* from *T* initial inscribed on one of the faces + *totum* the name of the toy, from Latin *tōtum* the whole

tef *or* **teff** (tɛf) NOUN an annual grass, *Eragrostis abyssinica,* of NE Africa, grown for its grain.
▷HISTORY C18: from Amharic *ṭēf*

tefillah *or* **tephillah** (tə'filə) NOUN, *plural* **-lin** (-lin). *Judaism* another name for **phylactery** (sense 1).
▷HISTORY from Hebrew

TEFL ('tɛfᵊl) ACRONYM FOR Teaching (of) English as a Foreign Language.

Teflon ('tɛflɒn) NOUN **1** a trademark for **polytetrafluoroethylene** when used in nonstick cooking vessels. ◆ ADJECTIVE **2** *Facetious* denoting the ability to evade blame: *the Teflon president.*

teg (tɛg) NOUN **1** a two-year-old sheep. **2** the fleece of a two-year-old sheep.
▷HISTORY C16: of unknown origin

tegmen ('tɛgmən) NOUN, *plural* **-mina** (-mɪnə). either of the leathery forewings of the cockroach and related insects. **3** any similar covering or layer.
▷HISTORY C19: from Latin: a cover, variant of *tegimen,* from *tegere* to cover
▸**'tegminal** ADJECTIVE

Tegucigalpa (*Spanish* teɣuθi'ɣalpa) NOUN the capital of Honduras, in the south on the Choluteca River: founded about 1579; university (1847). Pop.: 988 400 (1999 est.).

tegular ('tɛgjʊlə) ADJECTIVE **1** of, relating to, or resembling a tile or tiles. **2** *Biology* overlapping like a series of tiles: *tegular scales.*
▷HISTORY C18: from Latin *tēgula* a tile, from *tegere* to cover
▸**'tegularly** ADVERB

tegument ('tɛgjʊmənt) NOUN a less common word for **integument.**
▷HISTORY C15: from Latin *tegumentum* a covering, from *tegere* to cover
▸**tegumental** (ˌtɛgjʊ'mɛntᵊl) *or* ˌ**tegu'mentary** ADJECTIVE

te-hee ('tiː'hiː) INTERJECTION, NOUN, VERB a variant spelling of **tee-hee.**

Tehran *or* **Teheran** (tɛə'rɑːn, -'ræn) NOUN the capital of Iran, at the foot of the Elburz Mountains: built on the site of the ancient capital Ray, destroyed by Mongols in 1220; became capital in the 1790s; three universities. Pop.: 16 758 845 (1996).

Tehuantepec (tə'wɑːntəˌpɛk) NOUN **Isthmus of.** the narrowest part of S Mexico, with the Bay of Campeche on the north coast and the **Gulf of Tehuantepec** (an inlet of the Pacific) on the south coast.

Teide *or* **Teyde** (*Spanish* 'teiðe) NOUN **Pico de** ('piko de). a volcanic mountain in the Canary Islands, on Tenerife. Height: 3718 m (12 198 ft.).

te igitur *Latin* (teɪ 'ɪgɪˌtʊə; *English* teɪ 'ɪdʒɪˌtʊə) NOUN *RC Church* the first prayer of the canon of the Mass, which begins *Te igitur clementissime Pater* (*Thee, therefore, most merciful Father*).

teind (tiːnd) NOUN, VERB a Scot and northern English word for **tithe.**

Tejo ('təʒu) NOUN the Portuguese name for the **Tagus.**

tektite ('tɛktaɪt) NOUN a small dark glassy object found in several areas around the world, thought to be a product of meteorite impact. See also **moldavite.**
▷HISTORY C20: from Greek *tēktos* molten

tel- COMBINING FORM a variant of **tele-** and **telo-** before a vowel.

tela ('tiːlə) NOUN, *plural* **-lae** (-liː). *Anatomy* any delicate tissue or weblike structure.
▷HISTORY from New Latin, from Latin: a web

telaesthesia *or US* **telesthesia** (ˌtɛlɪs'θiːzɪə) NOUN the alleged perception of events that are beyond the normal range of perceptual processes. Compare **telegnosis, clairvoyance.**
▸**telaesthetic** *or* (*US*) **telesthetic** (ˌtɛlɪs'θɛtɪk) ADJECTIVE

telamon ('tɛləmən) NOUN, *plural* **telamones** (ˌtɛlə'məʊniːz) *or* **-mons.** a column in the form of a male figure, used to support an entablature. Also called: **atlas.** Compare **caryatid.**
▷HISTORY C18: via Latin from Greek, from *tlēnai* to bear

Telamon ('tɛləmən, -ˌmɒn) NOUN *Greek myth* a king of Salamis; brother of Peleus and father of Teucer and Ajax.

Telanaipura (ˌtɛlənaɪ'pʊərə) NOUN another name for **Jambi.**

telangiectasis (tɪˌlændʒɪ'ɛktəsɪs) *or* **telangiectasia** (tɪˌlændʒɪɛk'teɪzɪə) NOUN, *plural* **-ses** (-ˌsiːz). *Pathol* an abnormal dilation of the

capillaries or terminal arteries producing blotched red spots, esp on the face or thighs.
▷HISTORY C19: New Latin, from Greek *telos* end + *angeion* vessel + *ektasis* dilation
▸**telangiectatic** (tɪˌlændʒɪɛkˈtætɪk) ADJECTIVE

Telautograph (tɛlˈɔːtəˌɡræf, -ˌɡrɑːf) NOUN *Trademark* a telegraphic device for reproducing handwriting, drawings, etc., the movements of an electromagnetically controlled pen at one end being transmitted along a line to a similar pen at the receiving end.
▸**telˌautoˈgraphic** ADJECTIVE ▸**telautography** (ˌtɛlɔːˈtɒɡrəfɪ) NOUN

Tel Aviv (ˈtɛl əˈviːv) NOUN a city in W Israel, on the Mediterranean: the largest city and chief financial centre in Israel; incorporated the city of Jaffa in 1950; university (1953): the capital of Israel according to the UN and international law. Pop.: 348 100 (1999 est.). Official name: **Tel Aviv-Jaffa** (ˈtɛl əˈviːvˈdʒæfə).

telco (ˈtɛlˌkəʊ) NOUN a telecommunications company.
▷HISTORY C20: from TEL(ECOMMUNICATIONS) + CO(MPANY)

Telcom (ˈtɛlˌkɒm) NOUN the official telephone service in South Africa.

tele- *or before a vowel* **tel-** COMBINING FORM 1 at or over a distance; distant: *telescope; telegony; telekinesis; telemeter.* 2 television: *telecast.* 3 by means of or via telephone or television.
▷HISTORY from Greek *tele* far

telecast (ˈtɛlɪˌkɑːst) VERB **-casts, -casting, -cast** *or* **-casted.** 1 to broadcast (a programme) by television. ◆ NOUN 2 a television broadcast.
▸**ˈteleˌcaster** NOUN

telecine (ˈtɛlɪˌsɪnɪ) NOUN apparatus for producing a television signal from cinematograph film.

telecom (ˈtɛlɪˌkɒm) *or* **telecoms** (ˈtɛlɪˌkɒmz) NOUN (*functioning as singular*) short for **telecommunications.**

telecommunication (ˌtɛlɪkəˌmjuːnɪˈkeɪʃən) NOUN the telegraphic or telephonic communication of audio, video, or digital information over a distance by means of radio waves, optical signals, etc., or along a transmission line.

telecommunications (ˌtɛlɪkəˌmjuːnɪˈkeɪʃənz) NOUN (*functioning as singular*) the science and technology of communications by telephony, radio, television, etc.

telecommuting (ˈtɛlɪkəˌmjuːtɪŋ) NOUN another name for **teleworking.**
▸**ˈtelecomˌmuter** NOUN

teleconference (ˈtɛlɪˌkɒnfərəns) NOUN a conference in which the participants communicate from different places via a telephone or video network.

teleconnection (ˈtɛlɪkəˌnɛkʃən) NOUN 1 connection via telephone or television. 2 long-distance relationship between weather patterns, as when evaporation from the Amazon basin falls as rain in S Africa, etc.

telecottage (ˈtɛlɪˌkɒtɪdʒ) NOUN a communal workplace, situated in a rural area, which contains computers and other facilities linked into a communications network, thereby enabling people to work from remote locations.

teledu (ˈtɛlɪˌduː) NOUN a badger, *Mydaus javanensis,* of SE Asia and Indonesia, having dark brown hair with a white stripe along the back and producing a fetid secretion from the anal glands when attacked.
▷HISTORY C19: from Malay

téléférique (teɪleɪferˈiːk) NOUN a variant spelling of **téléphérique.**

telega (tɛˈleɪɡə) NOUN a rough four-wheeled cart used in Russia.
▷HISTORY C16: from Russian

telegenic (ˌtɛlɪˈdʒɛnɪk) ADJECTIVE having or showing a pleasant television image.
▷HISTORY C20: from TELE(VISION) + (PHOTO)GENIC
▸**ˌteleˈgenically** ADVERB

telegnosis (ˌtɛləˈnəʊsɪs, ˌtɛləɡ-) NOUN knowledge about distant events alleged to have been obtained without the use of any normal sensory mechanism. Compare **clairvoyance.**
▷HISTORY C20: from TELE- + *-gnosis,* from Greek *gnōsis* knowledge
▸**telegnostic** (ˌtɛləˈnɒstɪk, ˌtɛləɡ-) ADJECTIVE

Telegonus (tɪˈlɛɡənəs) NOUN *Greek myth* a son of Odysseus and Circe, who sought his father and mistakenly killed him, later marrying Odysseus' widow Penelope.

telegony (tɪˈlɛɡənɪ) NOUN *Genetics* the supposed influence of a previous sire on offspring borne by a female to other sires.
▷HISTORY C19: from TELE- + -GONY. Compare Greek *tēlegonos* "born far from one's homeland"
▸**telegonic** (ˌtɛlɪˈɡɒnɪk) *or* **teˈlegonous** ADJECTIVE

telegram (ˈtɛlɪˌɡræm) NOUN a communication transmitted by telegraph. See also **cable** (sense 5), **Telemessage.**
▸**telegrammatic** (ˌtɛlɪɡrəˈmætɪk) *or* **ˌteleˈgrammic** ADJECTIVE

telegraph (ˈtɛlɪˌɡræf, -ˌɡrɑːf) NOUN 1 **a** a device, system, or process by which information can be transmitted over a distance, esp using radio signals or coded electrical signals sent along a transmission line connected to a transmitting and a receiving instrument. **b** (*as modifier*): *telegraph pole.* 2 a message transmitted by such a device, system, or process; telegram. ◆ VERB 3 to send a telegram to (a person or place); wire. 4 (*tr*) to transmit or send by telegraph. 5 (*tr*) *Boxing, informal* to prepare to deliver (a punch) so obviously that one's opponent has ample time to avoid it. 6 (*tr*) to give advance notice of (anything), esp unintentionally. 7 (*tr*) *Canadian informal* to cast (votes) illegally by impersonating registered voters.
▸**telegraphist** (tɪˈlɛɡrəfɪst) *or* **teˈlegrapher** NOUN

telegraphic (ˌtɛlɪˈɡræfɪk) ADJECTIVE 1 used in or transmitted by telegraphy. 2 of or relating to a telegraph. 3 having a concise style; clipped: *telegraphic speech.*
▸**ˌteleˈgraphically** ADVERB

telegraph plant NOUN a small tropical Asian leguminous shrub, *Desmodium gyrans,* having small leaflets that turn in various directions during the day and droop at night.

telegraphy (tɪˈlɛɡrəfɪ) NOUN 1 a system of telecommunications involving any process providing reproduction at a distance of written, printed, or pictorial matter. See also **facsimile** (sense 2). 2 the skill or process of operating a telegraph.

Telegu (ˈtɛləˌɡuː) NOUN, ADJECTIVE a variant spelling of **Telugu.**

telekinesis (ˌtɛlɪkɪˈniːsɪs, -kaɪ-) NOUN 1 the movement of a body caused by thought or willpower without the application of a physical force. 2 the ability to cause such movement.
▸**telekinetic** (ˌtɛlɪkɪˈnɛtɪk, -kaɪ-) ADJECTIVE

Telemachus (tɪˈlɛməkəs) NOUN *Greek myth* the son of Odysseus and Penelope, who helped his father slay his mother's suitors.

telemark (ˈtɛlɪˌmɑːk) NOUN 1 *Skiing* a turn in which one ski is placed far forward of the other and turned gradually inwards. 2 a step in ballroom dancing involving a heel pivot.
▷HISTORY C20: named after *Telemark,* county in Norway

telemarketing (ˈtɛlɪˌmɑːkɪtɪŋ) NOUN another name for **telesales.**
▷HISTORY C20: short for TELE(PHONE) MARKETING
▸**ˈteleˌmarketer** NOUN

telematics (ˌtɛlɪˈmætɪks) NOUN (*functioning as singular*) the branch of science concerned with the use of technological devices to transmit information over long distances.
▷HISTORY C20: from TELE- + (INFOR)MATICS
▸**ˌteleˈmatic** ADJECTIVE

telemedicine (ˈtɛlɪˌmɛdɪsɪn, -ˌmɛdsɪn) NOUN the treatment of disease or injury by consultation with a specialist in a distant place, esp by means of a computer or satellite link.

Telemessage (ˈtɛlɪˌmɛsɪdʒ) NOUN *Trademark* a message sent by telephone or telex and delivered in printed form; in Britain, it has replaced the telegram.

telemeter (tɪˈlɛmɪtə) NOUN 1 any device for recording or measuring a distant event and transmitting the data to a receiver or observer. 2 any device or apparatus used to measure a distance without directly comparing it with a measuring rod, etc., esp one that depends on the measurement of angles. ◆ VERB 3 (*tr*) to obtain and transmit (data) from a distant source, esp from a spacecraft.
▸**telemetric** (ˌtɛlɪˈmɛtrɪk) *or* **ˌteleˈmetrical** ADJECTIVE
▸**ˌteleˈmetrically** ADVERB

telemetry (tɪˈlɛmɪtrɪ) NOUN 1 the use of radio waves, telephone lines, etc., to transmit the readings of measuring instruments to a device on which the readings can be indicated or recorded. See also **radiotelemetry.** 2 the measurement of linear distance using a tellurometer.

telencephalon (ˌtɛlɛnˈsɛfəˌlɒn) NOUN the cerebrum together with related parts of the hypothalamus and the third ventricle.
▸**telencephalic** (ˌtɛlɛnsɪˈfælɪk) ADJECTIVE

teleological argument NOUN *Philosophy* the argument purporting to prove the existence of God from empirical facts, the premise being that the universe shows evidence of order and hence design. Also called: **argument from design.** Compare **ontological argument, cosmological argument.**

teleology (ˌtɛlɪˈɒlədʒɪ, ˌtiːlɪ-) NOUN 1 *Philosophy* **a** the doctrine that there is evidence of purpose or design in the universe, and esp that this provides proof of the existence of a Designer. **b** the belief that certain phenomena are best explained in terms of purpose rather than cause. **c** the systematic study of such phenomena. ◆ See also **final cause.** 2 *Biology* the belief that natural phenomena have a predetermined purpose and are not determined by mechanical laws.
▷HISTORY C18: from New Latin *teleologia,* from Greek *telos* end + -LOGY
▸**teleological** (ˌtɛlɪəˈlɒdʒɪkᵊl, ˌtiːlɪ-) *or* **ˌteleoˈlogic** ADJECTIVE ▸**ˌteleoˈlogically** ADVERB ▸**ˌteleˈologism** NOUN
▸**ˌteleˈologist** NOUN

teleost (ˈtɛlɪˌɒst, ˈtiːlɪ-) NOUN 1 any bony fish of the subclass *Teleostei,* having rayed fins and a swim bladder: the group contains most of the bony fishes, including the herrings, carps, eels, cod, perches, etc. ◆ ADJECTIVE 2 of, relating to, or belonging to the *Teleostei.*
▷HISTORY C19: from New Latin *teleosteī* (pl) creatures having complete skeletons, from Greek *teleos* complete + *osteon* bone

telepath (ˈtɛlɪˌpæθ) NOUN 1 a person who is telepathic. ◆ VERB (*intr*) 2 to practise telepathy.

telepathize *or* **telepathise** (tɪˈlɛpəˌθaɪz) VERB (*intr*) to practise telepathy.

telepathy (tɪˈlɛpəθɪ) NOUN *Psychol* the communication between people of thoughts, feelings, desires, etc., involving mechanisms that cannot be understood in terms of known scientific laws. Also called: **thought transference.** Compare **telegnosis, clairvoyance.**
▷HISTORY C19: from TELE- + Greek *patheia* feeling, perception: see -PATHY
▸**telepathic** (ˌtɛlɪˈpæθɪk) ADJECTIVE ▸**ˌteleˈpathically** ADVERB ▸**teˈlepathist** NOUN

téléphérique *or* **téléférique** (teɪleɪferˈiːk) NOUN 1 a mountain cable car. 2 a cableway.
▷HISTORY C20: from French

telephone (ˈtɛlɪˌfəʊn) NOUN 1 **a** Also called: **telephone set.** an electrical device for transmitting speech, consisting of a microphone and receiver mounted on a handset. **b** (*as modifier*): *a telephone receiver.* 2 **a** a worldwide system of communications using telephones. The microphone in one telephone converts sound waves into electrical signals that are transmitted along a telephone wire or by radio to one or more distant sets, the receivers of which reconvert the incoming signal into the original sound. **b** (*as modifier*): *a telephone exchange; a telephone call.* 3 See **telephone box.** ◆ VERB 4 to call or talk to (a person) by telephone. 5 to transmit (a recorded message, radio or television programme, or other information) by telephone, using special transmitting and receiving equipment. ◆ Often shortened to: **phone.**
▸**ˈteleˌphoner** NOUN ▸**telephonic** (ˌtɛlɪˈfɒnɪk) ADJECTIVE
▸**ˌteleˈphonically** ADVERB

telephone answering machine NOUN the full name for **answering machine.**

telephone banking NOUN a facility enabling customers to make use of banking services, such as oral payment instructions, account movements, raising loans, etc., over the telephone rather than by personal visit.

telephone box NOUN an enclosure from which a paid telephone call can be made. Also called: **telephone kiosk, telephone booth.**

telephone directory NOUN a book listing the names, addresses, and telephone numbers of subscribers in a particular area.

telephone number NOUN 1 a set of figures identifying the telephone of a particular subscriber, and used in making connections to that telephone. 2 (*plural*) extremely large numbers, esp in reference to salaries or prices.

telephone selling NOUN another name for **telesales.**

telephonist (tɪˈlɛfənɪst) NOUN *Brit* a person who operates a telephone switchboard. Also called (esp US): **telephone operator.**

telephony (tɪˈlɛfənɪ) NOUN a system of telecommunications for the transmission of speech or other sounds.

telephotography (ˌtɛlɪfəˈtɒgrəfɪ) NOUN the process or technique of photographing distant objects using a telephoto lens.
▸**telephotographic** (ˌtɛlɪˌfəʊtəˈgræfɪk) ADJECTIVE

telephoto lens (ˈtɛlɪˌfəʊtəʊ) NOUN a compound camera lens in which the focal length is greater than that of a simple lens of the same dimensions and thus produces a magnified image of a distant object. See also **zoom lens.**

telepoint (ˈtɛlɪˌpɔɪnt) NOUN **a** a system providing a place where a cordless telephone can be connected to a telephone network. **b** a place where a cordless telephone can be connected to a telephone network.

teleport (ˈtɛlɪˌpɔːt) VERB (*tr*) to move by means of telekinesis.
▷HISTORY C20: from TELE- + PORT[5]

telepresence (ˈtɛlɪˌprɛzəns) NOUN the use of virtual reality technology to operate machinery by remote control or to create the effect of being at a different or imaginary location.

teleprinter (ˈtɛlɪˌprɪntə) NOUN 1 a telegraph apparatus consisting of a keyboard transmitter, which converts a typed message into coded pulses for transmission along a wire or cable, and a printing receiver, which converts incoming signals and prints out the message. US name: **teletypewriter.** See also **telex, radioteletype.** 2 a network of such devices, formerly used for communicating information, etc. 3 a similar device used for direct input/output of data into a computer at a distant location.

teleprocessing (ˌtɛlɪˈprəʊsɛsɪŋ) NOUN the use of remote computer terminals connected to a central computer to process data.

Teleprompter (ˈtɛlɪˌprɒmptə) NOUN *Trademark* the US and Canadian name for **Autocue.**

Teleran (ˈtɛləˌræn) NOUN *Trademark* an electronic navigational aid in which the image of a ground-based radar system is televised to aircraft in flight so that a pilot can see the position of his aircraft in relation to others.
▷HISTORY C20: from *Tele(vision) R(adar) A(ir) N(avigation)*

telerecording (ˌtɛlɪrɪˈkɔːdɪŋ) NOUN the recording of television signals on tape or, more usually, on film.

telesales (ˈtɛlɪˌseɪlz) NOUN (*functioning as singular*) the selling or attempted selling of a particular commodity or service by a salesman who makes his initial approach by telephone. Also called: **telemarketing, telephone selling.**

telescience (ˈtɛlɪˌsaɪəns) NOUN *Astronautics* the investigation of remotely controlled scientific experiments.

telescope (ˈtɛlɪˌskəʊp) NOUN 1 an optical instrument for making distant objects appear larger and brighter by use of a combination of lenses (**refracting telescope**) or lenses and curved mirrors (**reflecting telescope**). See also **terrestrial telescope, astronomical telescope, Cassegrain telescope, Galilean telescope, Newtonian telescope.** 2 any instrument, such as a radio telescope, for collecting, focusing, and detecting electromagnetic radiation from space. ◆ VERB 3 to crush together or be crushed together, as in a collision: *the front of the car was telescoped by the impact.* 4 to fit together like a set of cylinders that slide into one another, thus allowing extension and shortening. 5 to make or become smaller or shorter: *the novel was telescoped into a short play.*
▷HISTORY C17: from Italian *telescopio* or New Latin *telescopium,* literally: far-seeing instrument; see TELE-, -SCOPE

telescopic (ˌtɛlɪˈskɒpɪk) ADJECTIVE 1 of or relating to a telescope. 2 seen through or obtained by means of a telescope. 3 visible only with the aid of a telescope. 4 able to see far. 5 having or consisting of parts that telescope: *a telescopic umbrella.*
▸ˌ**teleˈscopically** ADVERB

telescopic sight NOUN a telescope mounted on a rifle, etc., used for sighting.

Telescopium (ˌtɛlɪˈskəʊpɪəm) NOUN, *Latin genitive* **Telescopii** (ˌtɛlɪˈskəʊpɪˌaɪ). an inconspicuous constellation in the S hemisphere, close to Sagittarius and Ara.
▷HISTORY New Latin; see TELESCOPE

telescopy (tɪˈlɛskəpɪ) NOUN the branch of astronomy concerned with the use and design of telescopes.

teleshopping (ˈtɛlɪˌʃɒpɪŋ) NOUN the purchase of goods by telephone or via the Internet.

telesis (ˈtɛlɪsɪs) NOUN the purposeful use of natural and social processes to obtain specific social goals.
▷HISTORY C19: from Greek: event, from *telein* to fulfil, from *telos* end

telesoftware (ˌtɛlɪˈsɒftwɛə) NOUN the transmission of computer programs on a teletext system.

telespectroscope (ˌtɛlɪˈspɛktrəˌskəʊp) NOUN a combination of a telescope and a spectroscope, used for spectroscopic analysis of radiation from stars and other celestial bodies.

telestereoscope (ˌtɛlɪˈstɪərɪəˌskəʊp, -ˈstɛrɪə-) NOUN an optical instrument for obtaining stereoscopic images of distant objects.

telesthesia (ˌtɛlɪsˈθiːzɪə) NOUN the usual US spelling of **telaesthesia.**
▸**telesthetic** (ˌtɛlɪsˈθɛtɪk) ADJECTIVE

telestich (tɪˈlɛstɪk, ˈtɛlɪˌstɪk) NOUN a short poem in which the last letters of each successive line form a word.
▷HISTORY C17: from Greek *telos* end + STICH

teletex (ˈtɛlɪˌtɛks) NOUN an international means of communicating text between a variety of terminals.

Teletext (ˈtɛlɪˌtɛkst) NOUN *Trademark* a form of Videotex in which information is broadcast by a television station and received on an adapted television set. **Ceefax** is provided by the BBC and **Oracle** by ITV.

telethon (ˈtɛləˌθɒn) NOUN a lengthy television programme to raise charity funds, etc.
▷HISTORY C20: from TELE- + MARATHON

Teletype (ˈtɛlɪˌtaɪp) NOUN 1 *Trademark* a type of teleprinter. 2 (*sometimes not capital*) a network of such devices, used for communicating messages, information, etc. ◆ VERB 3 (*sometimes not capital*) to transmit (a message) by Teletype.

Teletypesetter (ˌtɛlɪˈtaɪpˌsɛtə, ˈtɛlɪˌtaɪp-) NOUN *Trademark Printing* a keyboard device whose output can either be punched tape, which can be used directly to operate a line-casting machine, or be transmitted by cable or wire to operate such a machine indirectly.
▸ˌ**teleˈtypeˌsetting** NOUN

teletypewriter (ˌtɛlɪˈtaɪpˌraɪtə, ˈtɛlɪˌtaɪp-) NOUN a US name for **teleprinter.**

teleutospore (tɪˈluːtəˌspɔː) NOUN another name for **teliospore.**
▷HISTORY C19: from Greek *teleutē,* from *telos* end + SPORE
▸**teˌleutoˈsporic** ADJECTIVE

televangelist (ˌtɛlɪˈvændʒəlɪst) NOUN *US* an evangelical preacher who appears regularly on television, preaching the gospel and appealing for donations from viewers.
▷HISTORY C20: from TELE(VISION + E)VANGELIST

televise (ˈtɛlɪˌvaɪz) VERB 1 to put (a programme) on television. 2 (*tr*) to transmit (a programme, signal, etc.) by television.

television (ˈtɛlɪˌvɪʒən) NOUN 1 the system or process of producing on a distant screen a series of transient visible images, usually with an accompanying sound signal. Electrical signals, converted from optical images by a camera tube, are transmitted by UHF or VHF radio waves or by cable and reconverted into optical images by means of a television tube inside a television set. 2 Also called: **television set.** a device designed to receive and convert incoming electrical signals into a series of visible images on a screen together with accompanying sound. 3 the content, etc., of television programmes. 4 the occupation or profession concerned with any aspect of the broadcasting of television programmes: *he's in television.* 5 (*modifier*) of, relating to, or used in the transmission or reception of video and audio UHF or VHF radio signals: *a television transmitter.* ◆ Abbreviation: **TV.**
▷HISTORY C20: from TELE- + VISION
▸ˌ**teleˈvisional** ADJECTIVE ▸ˌ**teleˈvisionally** ADVERB
▸ˌ**teleˈvisionary** ADJECTIVE

television tube NOUN a cathode-ray tube designed for the reproduction of television pictures. Sometimes shortened to: **tube.** Also called: **picture tube.**

televisual (ˌtɛlɪˈvɪʒʊəl, -zjʊ-) ADJECTIVE relating to, shown on, or suitable for production on television.
▸ˌ**teleˈvisually** ADVERB

teleworking (ˈtɛlɪˌwɜːkɪŋ) NOUN the use of home computers, telephones, etc., to enable a person to work from home while maintaining contact with colleagues, customers, or a central office. Also called: **telecommuting.**
▸ˈ**teleˌworker** NOUN

telewriter (ˈtɛlɪˌraɪtə) NOUN a telegraphic device for reproducing handwriting by converting the manually controlled movements of a pen into signals that, after transmission, control the movements of a similar pen.

telex (ˈtɛlɛks) NOUN 1 an international telegraph service in which teleprinters are rented out to subscribers for the purpose of direct communication. 2 a teleprinter used in such a service. 3 a message transmitted or received by telex. ◆ VERB 4 to transmit (a message) to (a person, office, etc.) by telex.
▷HISTORY C20: from *tel(eprinter) ex(change)*

telfer (ˈtɛlfə) NOUN a variant spelling of **telpher.**

telferage (ˈtɛlfərɪdʒ) NOUN a variant spelling of **telpherage.**

Telford (ˈtɛlfəd) NOUN a town in W central England, in Telford and Wrekin unitary authority, Shropshire: designated a new town in 1963. Pop.: 119 340 (1991).

Telford and Wrekin NOUN a unitary authority in W Central England, in Shropshire. Pop.: 158 285 (2001). Area: 289 sq. km (112 sq. miles).

telic (ˈtɛlɪk) ADJECTIVE 1 directed or moving towards some goal; purposeful. 2 (of a clause or phrase) expressing purpose.
▷HISTORY C19: from Greek *telikos* final, from *telos* end

Telidon (ˈtɛlɪˌdɒn) NOUN *Trademark* a Canadian interactive viewdata service.

teliospore (ˈtiːlɪəˌspɔː) NOUN any of the dark noninfective spores that are produced in each telium of the rust fungi and remain dormant during the winter. Also called: **teleutospore.**
▷HISTORY C20: from TELIUM + SPORE

telium (ˈtiːlɪəm, ˈtɛl-) NOUN, *plural* **telia** (ˈtiːlɪə, ˈtɛlɪə). the spore-producing body of some rust fungi in which the teliospores are formed.
▷HISTORY C20: New Latin, from Greek *teleion,* from *teleios* complete, from *telos* end
▸ˈ**telial** ADJECTIVE

tell[1] (tɛl) VERB **tells, telling, told.** 1 (when *tr, may take a clause as object*) to let know or notify: *he told me that he would go.* 2 (*tr*) to order or instruct (someone to do something): *I told her to send the letter airmail.* 3 (when *intr,* usually foll by *of*) to give an account or narration (of something): *she told me her troubles.* 4 (*tr*) to communicate by words; utter: *to tell the truth.* 5 (*tr*) to make known; disclose: *to tell fortunes.* 6 (*intr;* often foll by *of*) to serve as an indication: *her blush told of her embarrassment.* 7 (*tr;* used with *can,* etc.; *may take a clause as object*) to comprehend, discover, or discern: *I can tell what is wrong.* 8 (*tr;* used with *can,* etc.) to distinguish or discriminate: *he couldn't tell chalk from cheese.* 9 (*intr*) to have or produce an impact, effect, or strain: *every step told on his bruised feet.* 10 (*intr;* sometimes foll by *on*) *Informal* to reveal secrets or gossip (about): *don't tell!; she told on him.* 11 (*tr*) to assure: *I*

tell you, I've had enough! [12] (*tr*) to count (votes). [13] (*intr*) *Dialect* to talk or chatter. [14] *Informal, chiefly US* to tell the truth no matter how unpleasant it is. [15] **tell the time.** to read the time from a clock. [16] **you're telling me.** *Slang* I know that very well. ◆ See also **tell apart, tell off.**
▷HISTORY Old English *tellan;* related to Old Saxon *tellian,* Old High German *zellen* to tell, count, Old Norse *telja*
▸ **'tellable** ADJECTIVE

tell[2] (tɛl) NOUN a large mound resulting from the accumulation of rubbish on a long-settled site, esp one with mudbrick buildings, particularly in the Middle East.
▷HISTORY C19: from Arabic *tall*

tell apart VERB (*tr, adverb*) to distinguish between; discern: *can you tell the twins apart?*

Tell el Amarna ('tɛl ɛl ə'mɑːnə) NOUN a group of ruins and rock tombs in Upper Egypt, on the Nile below Asyut: site of the capital of Amenhotep IV, built about 1375 B.C.; excavated from 1891 onwards.

teller ('tɛlə) NOUN [1] another name for **cashier**[1] (sense 2). [2] a person appointed to count votes in a legislative body, assembly, etc. [3] a person who tells; narrator.
▸ **'teller,ship** NOUN

tellin ('tɛlɪn) NOUN any of various slim marine bivalve molluscs of the genus *Tellina* (or *Macoma*) that live in intertidal sand, esp the smooth oval delicately tinted *T. tenuis.*
▷HISTORY from New Latin *tellina,* from Greek *tellinē* a shellfish

telling ('tɛlɪŋ) ADJECTIVE [1] having a marked effect or impact: *a telling blow.* [2] revealing: *a telling smile.*
▸ **'tellingly** ADVERB

tell off VERB (*tr, adverb*) [1] *Informal* to reprimand; scold: *they told me off for stealing apples.* [2] to count and dismiss: *he told off four more soldiers.*
▸ **telling off** *or* **telling-off** NOUN

telltale ('tɛl,teɪl) NOUN [1] a person who tells tales about others. [2] **a** an outward indication of something concealed. **b** (*as modifier*): *a telltale paw mark.* [3] any of various indicators or recording devices used to monitor a process, machine, etc. [4] *Nautical* **a** another word for **dogvane. b** one of a pair of light vanes mounted on the main shrouds of a sailing boat to indicate the apparent direction of the wind.

tellurate ('tɛlju,reɪt) NOUN any salt or ester of telluric acid.

tellurian (tɛ'lʊərɪən) ADJECTIVE [1] of or relating to the earth. ◆ NOUN [2] (esp in science fiction) an inhabitant of the earth.
▷HISTORY C19: from Latin *tellūs* the earth

telluric[1] (tɛ'lʊərɪk) ADJECTIVE [1] of, relating to, or originating on or in the earth or soil; terrestrial, esp in reference to natural electrical or magnetic fields. [2] *Astronomy* (of spectral lines or bands) observed in the spectra of celestial objects and caused by oxygen, water vapour, and carbon dioxide in the earth's atmosphere.
▷HISTORY C19: from Latin *tellūs* the earth

telluric[2] (tɛ'lʊərɪk) ADJECTIVE of or containing tellurium, esp in a high valence state.
▷HISTORY C20: from TELLUR(IUM) + -IC

telluric acid NOUN a white crystalline dibasic acid produced by the oxidation of tellurium by hydrogen peroxide. Formula: H_6TeO_6.

telluride ('tɛlju,raɪd) NOUN any compound of tellurium, esp one formed between tellurium and a more electropositive element or group.

tellurion *or* **tellurian** (tɛ'lʊərɪən) NOUN an instrument that shows how day and night and the seasons result from the tilt of the earth, its rotation on its axis, and its revolution around the sun.
▷HISTORY C19: from Latin *tellūs* the earth

tellurite ('tɛlju,raɪt) NOUN any salt or ester of tellurous acid.

tellurium (tɛ'lʊərɪəm) NOUN a brittle silvery-white nonmetallic element occurring both uncombined and in combination with metals: used in alloys of lead and copper and as a semiconductor. Symbol: Te; atomic no.: 52; atomic wt.: 127.60; valency: 2, 4, or 6; relative density: 6.24; melting pt.: 449.57±0.3°C; boiling pt.: 988°C.
▷HISTORY C19: New Latin, from Latin *tellūs* the earth, formed by analogy with URANIUM

tellurize *or* **tellurise** ('tɛlju,raɪz) VERB (*tr*) to mix or combine with tellurium.

tellurometer (,tɛlju'rɒmɪtə) NOUN *Surveying* an electronic instrument for measuring distances of up to about 30 miles that consists of two units, one at each end of the distance to be measured, between which radio waves are transmitted.
▷HISTORY C20: from Latin *tellūs* the earth + -METER

tellurous ('tɛljurəs, tɛ'lʊərəs) ADJECTIVE of or containing tellurium, esp in a low valence state.

Tellus ('tɛləs) NOUN the Roman goddess of the earth; protectress of marriage, fertility, and the dead.

telly ('tɛlɪ) NOUN, *plural* **-lies.** *Informal, chiefly Brit* short for **television.**

telo- *or before a vowel* **tel-** COMBINING FORM [1] complete; final; perfect: *telophase.* [2] end; at the end: *telencephalon.*
▷HISTORY from Greek *telos* end

telocentric (,tɛlə'sɛntrɪk) ADJECTIVE *Genetics* (of a chromosome) having the centromere at or close to the end.

telomerization *or* **telomerisation** (tɛ,lɒməraɪ'zeɪʃən) NOUN *Chem* polymerization in the presence of a chain transfer agent to yield a series of products of low molecular weight.
▷HISTORY C20: from TELO- + -MER

telophase ('tɛlə,feɪz) NOUN [1] the final stage of mitosis, during which a set of chromosomes is present at each end of the cell and a nuclear membrane forms around each, producing two new nuclei. See also **prophase, metaphase, anaphase.** [2] the corresponding stage of the first division of meiosis.
▸ **,telo'phasic** ADJECTIVE

telpher *or* **telfer** ('tɛlfə) NOUN [1] a load-carrying car in a telpherage. [2] **a** another word for **telpherage. b** (*as modifier*): *a telpher line; a telpher system.* ◆ VERB [3] (*tr*) to transport (a load) by means of a telpherage.
▷HISTORY C19: changed from *telephore,* from TELE- + -PHORE
▸ **'telpheric** *or* **'telferic** ADJECTIVE

telpherage *or* **telferage** ('tɛlfərɪdʒ) NOUN an overhead transport system in which an electrically driven truck runs along a single rail or cable, the load being suspended in a separate car beneath. Also called: **telpher line, telpher.**

telson ('tɛlsən) NOUN the last segment or an appendage on the last segment of the body of crustaceans and arachnids.
▷HISTORY C19: from Greek: a boundary; probably related to *telos* end
▸ **telsonic** (tɛl'sɒnɪk) ADJECTIVE

Telstar ('tɛl,stɑː) NOUN either of two low-altitude active communications satellites launched in 1962 and 1963 by the US and used in the transmission of television programmes, telephone messages, etc.

Telugu *or* **Telegu** ('tɛlə,guː) NOUN [1] a language of SE India, belonging to the Dravidian family of languages: the state language of Andhra Pradesh. [2] (*plural* **-gus** *or* **-gu**) a member of the people who speak this language. ◆ ADJECTIVE [3] of or relating to this people or their language.

Telukbetung *or* **Teloekbetoeng** (tə,lukbə'tuŋ) NOUN a port in Indonesia, in S Sumatra on the Sunda Strait. Pop.: 284 275 (latest est.).

Tema ('tiːmə) NOUN a port in SE Ghana on the Atlantic: new harbour opened in 1962; oil-refining. Pop. (urban area): 300 000 (1998 est.).

temazepam (tə'mæzə,pæm) NOUN a benzodiazepine sedative; the gel-like capsule formulation is properly taken orally but has also been melted and injected by drug users.

Témbi ('tɛmbiː) NOUN transliteration of the Modern Greek name for **Tempe.**

temblor ('tɛmblə, -blɔː) NOUN, *plural* **temblors** or **temblores** (tɛm'blɔːreɪz). *Chiefly US* an earthquake or earth tremor.
▷HISTORY C19: American Spanish, from Spanish *temblar* to shake, tremble

temerity (tɪ'mɛrɪtɪ) NOUN rashness or boldness.
▷HISTORY C15: from Latin *temeritās* accident, from *temere* at random
▸ **temerarious** (,tɛmə'rɛərɪəs) ADJECTIVE

Temesvár ('tɛmɛʃvaːr) NOUN the Hungarian name for **Timişoara.**

Temne ('tɛmnɪ, 'tɪm-) NOUN [1] (*plural* **-nes** *or* **-ne**) a member of a Negroid people of N Sierra Leone. [2] the language of this people, closely related to Bantu.

temp (tɛmp) *Informal* ◆ NOUN [1] a person, esp a typist or other office worker, employed on a temporary basis. ◆ VERB (*intr*) [2] to work as a temp.

temp. ABBREVIATION FOR: [1] temperate. [2] temperature. [3] temporary. [4] tempore.
▷HISTORY (for sense 4) Latin: in the time of

Tempe ('tɛmpɪ) NOUN **Vale of.** a wooded valley in E Greece, in Thessaly between the mountains Olympus and Ossa. Modern Greek name: **Témbi.**

tempeh ('tɛmpeɪ) NOUN fermented soya beans.
▷HISTORY C20: from Indonesian *tempe*

temper ('tɛmpə) NOUN [1] a frame of mind; mood or humour: *a good temper.* [2] a sudden outburst of anger; tantrum. [3] a tendency to exhibit uncontrolled anger; irritability. [4] a mental condition of moderation and calm (esp in the phrases **keep one's temper, lose one's temper, out of temper**). [5] the degree of hardness, elasticity, or a similar property of a metal or metal object. ◆ VERB (*tr*) [6] to make more temperate, acceptable, or suitable by adding something else; moderate: *he tempered his criticism with kindly sympathy.* [7] to strengthen or toughen (a metal or metal article) by heat treatment, as by heating and quenching. [8] *Music* **a** to adjust the frequency differences between the notes of a scale on (a keyboard instrument) in order to allow modulation into other keys. **b** to make such an adjustment to the pitches of notes in (a scale). [9] a rare word for **adapt.** [10] an archaic word for **mix.**
▷HISTORY Old English *temprian* to mingle, (influenced by Old French *temprer*), from Latin *temperāre* to mix, probably from *tempus* time
▸ **'temperable** ADJECTIVE ▸ **,tempera'bility** NOUN ▸ **'temperer** NOUN

tempera ('tɛmpərə) NOUN [1] a painting medium for powdered pigments, consisting usually of egg yolk and water. [2] **a** any emulsion used as a painting medium, with casein, glue, wax, etc., as a base. **b** the paint made from mixing this with pigment. [3] the technique of painting with tempera.
▷HISTORY C19: from Italian phrase *pingere a tempera* painting in tempera, from *temperare* to mingle; see TEMPER

temperament ('tɛmpərəmənt, -prəmənt) NOUN [1] an individual's character, disposition, and tendencies as revealed in his reactions. [2] excitability, moodiness, or anger, esp when displayed openly: *an actress with temperament.* [3] the characteristic way an individual behaves, esp towards other people. See also **character, personality.** [4] **a** an adjustment made to the frequency differences between notes on a keyboard instrument to allow modulation to other keys. **b** any of several systems of such adjustment, such as **just temperament,** a system not practically possible on keyboard instruments (see **just intonation**), **mean-tone temperament,** a system giving an approximation to natural tuning, and **equal temperament,** the system commonly used in keyboard instruments, giving a scale based on an octave divided into twelve exactly equal semitones. [5] *Obsolete* the characteristic way an individual behaves, viewed as the result of the influence of the four humours (blood, phlegm, yellow bile, and black bile). [6] *Archaic* compromise or adjustment. [7] an obsolete word for **temperature.**
▷HISTORY C15: from Latin *temperāmentum* a mixing in proportion, from *temperāre* to TEMPER

temperamental (,tɛmpərə'mɛntᵊl, -prə'mɛntᵊl) ADJECTIVE [1] easily upset or irritated; excitable; volatile. [2] of, relating to, or caused by temperament. [3] *Informal* working erratically and inconsistently; unreliable: *a temperamental sewing machine.*
▸ **,tempera'mentally** ADVERB

temperance ('tɛmpərəns) NOUN [1] restraint or moderation, esp in yielding to one's appetites or desires. [2] abstinence from alcoholic drink.
▷HISTORY C14: from Latin *temperantia,* from *temperāre* to regulate

temperate ('tɛmpərɪt, 'tɛmprɪt) ADJECTIVE 1 having a climate intermediate between tropical and polar; moderate or mild in temperature. 2 mild in quality or character; exhibiting temperance.
▷HISTORY C14: from Latin *temperātus*
▸'**temperately** ADVERB ▸'**temperateness** NOUN

Temperate Zone NOUN those parts of the earth's surface lying between the Arctic Circle and the tropic of Cancer and between the Antarctic Circle and the tropic of Capricorn.

temperature ('tɛmprɪtʃə) NOUN 1 the degree of hotness of a body, substance, or medium; a physical property related to the average kinetic energy of the atoms or molecules of a substance. 2 a measure of this degree of hotness, indicated on a scale that has one or more fixed reference points. 3 *Informal* a body temperature in excess of the normal. 4 *Archaic* **a** compromise. **b** temperament. **c** temperance.
▷HISTORY C16 (originally: a mingling): from Latin *temperātūra* proportion, from *temperāre* to TEMPER

temperature gradient NOUN the rate of change in temperature in a given direction, esp in altitude.

temperature-humidity index NOUN an index of the effect on human comfort of temperature and humidity levels, 65 being the highest comfortable level.

temperature inversion NOUN *Meteorol* an abnormal increase in temperature with height in the troposphere.

tempered ('tɛmpəd) ADJECTIVE 1 *Music* **a** (of a scale) having the frequency differences between notes adjusted in accordance with the system of equal temperament. See **temperament. b** (of an interval) expanded or contracted from the state of being pure. 2 (*in combination*) having a temper or temperament as specified: *ill-tempered.*

tempest ('tɛmpɪst) NOUN 1 *Chiefly literary* a violent wind or storm. 2 a violent commotion, uproar, or disturbance. ♦ VERB 3 (*tr*) *Poetic* to agitate or disturb violently.
▷HISTORY C13: from Old French *tempeste,* from Latin *tempestās* storm, from *tempus* time

tempestuous (tɛm'pɛstjʊəs) ADJECTIVE 1 of or relating to a tempest. 2 violent or stormy: *a tempestuous love affair.*
▸**tem'pestuously** ADVERB ▸**tem'pestuousness** NOUN

tempi ('tɛmpi:) NOUN (in musical senses) the plural of **tempo.**

Templar ('tɛmplə) NOUN 1 a member of a military religious order (**Knights of the Temple of Solomon**) founded by Crusaders in Jerusalem around 1118 to defend the Holy Sepulchre and Christian pilgrims; suppressed in 1312. 2 (*sometimes not capital*) *Brit* a lawyer, esp a barrister, who lives or has chambers in the Inner or Middle Temple in London.
▷HISTORY C13: from Medieval Latin *templārius* of the temple, from Latin *templum* TEMPLE[1]; first applied to the knightly order because their house was near the site of the Temple of Solomon

template *or* **templet** ('tɛmplɪt) NOUN 1 a gauge or pattern, cut out in wood or metal, used in woodwork, etc., to help shape something accurately. 2 a pattern cut out in card or plastic, used in various crafts to reproduce shapes. 3 a short beam, made of metal, wood, or stone, that is used to spread a load, as over a doorway. 4 *Biochem* the molecular structure of a compound that serves as a pattern for the production of the molecular structure of another specific compound in a reaction.
▷HISTORY C17 *templet* (later spelling influenced by PLATE), probably from French, diminutive of TEMPLE[3]

temple[1] ('tɛmpᵊl) NOUN 1 a building or place dedicated to the worship of a deity or deities. 2 a Mormon church. 3 *US* another name for a **synagogue.** 4 any Christian church, esp a large or imposing one. 5 any place or object regarded as a shrine where God makes himself present, esp the body of a person who has been sanctified or saved by grace. 6 a building regarded as the focus of an activity, interest, or practice: *a temple of the arts.*
▷HISTORY Old English *tempel,* from Latin *templum;* probably related to Latin *tempus* TIME, Greek *temenos* sacred enclosure, literally: a place cut off, from *temnein* to cut
▸'**templed** ADJECTIVE ▸'**temple-,like** ADJECTIVE

temple[2] ('tɛmpᵊl) NOUN the region on each side of the head in front of the ear and above the cheek bone. Related adjective: **temporal.**
▷HISTORY C14: from Old French *temple,* from Latin *tempora* the temples, from *tempus* temple of the head

temple[3] ('tɛmpᵊl) NOUN the part of a loom that keeps the cloth being woven stretched to the correct width.
▷HISTORY C15: from French, from Latin *templum* a small timber

Temple ('tɛmpᵊl) NOUN 1 either of two buildings in London and Paris that belonged to the Templars. The one in London now houses two of the chief law societies. 2 any of three buildings or groups of buildings erected by the Jews in ancient Jerusalem for the worship of Jehovah.

Temple of Artemis NOUN the large temple at Ephesus, on the W coast of Asia Minor: one of the Seven Wonders of the World.

tempo ('tɛmpəʊ) NOUN, *plural* **-pos** *or* **-pi** (-pi:). 1 the speed at which a piece or passage of music is meant to be played, usually indicated by a musical direction (**tempo marking**) or metronome marking. 2 rate or pace.
▷HISTORY C18: from Italian, from Latin *tempus* time

tempolabile (,tɛmpəʊ'leɪbaɪl) ADJECTIVE *Chem* changing irregularly with time.

temporal[1] ('tɛmpərəl, 'tɛmprəl) ADJECTIVE 1 of or relating to time. 2 of or relating to secular as opposed to spiritual or religious affairs: *the lords spiritual and temporal.* 3 lasting for a relatively short time. 4 *Grammar* of or relating to tense or the linguistic expression of time in general: *a temporal adverb.*
▷HISTORY C14: from Latin *temporālis,* from *tempus* time
▸'**temporally** ADVERB ▸'**temporalness** NOUN

temporal[2] ('tɛmpərəl, 'tɛmprəl) ADJECTIVE *Anatomy* of, relating to, or near the temple or temples.
▷HISTORY C16: from Late Latin *temporālis* belonging to the temples; see TEMPLE[2]

temporal bone NOUN either of two compound bones forming part of the sides and base of the skull: they surround the organs of hearing.

temporality (,tɛmpə'rælɪtɪ) NOUN, *plural* **-ties.** 1 the state or quality of being temporal. 2 something temporal. 3 (*often plural*) a secular possession or revenue belonging to a Church, a group within the Church, or the clergy.

temporal lobe NOUN the laterally protruding portion of each cerebral hemisphere, situated below the parietal lobe and associated with sound perception and interpretation: it is thought to be the centre for memory recall.

temporary ('tɛmpərərɪ, 'tɛmprərɪ) ADJECTIVE 1 not permanent; provisional: *temporary accommodation.* 2 lasting only a short time; transitory: *temporary relief from pain.* ♦ NOUN, *plural* **-raries.** 3 a person, esp a secretary or other office worker, employed on a temporary basis. Often shortened to: **temp.**
▷HISTORY C16: from Latin *temporārius,* from *tempus* time
▸'**temporarily** ADVERB ▸'**temporariness** NOUN

temporary hardness NOUN *Chem* hardness of water due to the presence of magnesium and calcium hydrogencarbonates, which can be precipitated as carbonates by boiling.

temporize *or* **temporise** ('tɛmpə,raɪz) VERB (*intr*) 1 to delay, act evasively, or protract a discussion, negotiation, etc., esp in order to gain time or effect a compromise. 2 to adapt oneself to the circumstances or occasion, as by temporary or apparent agreement.
▷HISTORY C16: from French *temporiser,* from Medieval Latin *temporizāre,* from Latin *tempus* time
▸,**tempori'zation** *or* ,**tempori'sation** NOUN ▸'**tempo,rizer** *or* '**tempo,riser** NOUN

tempt (tɛmpt) VERB (*tr*) 1 to attempt to persuade or entice to do something, esp something morally wrong or unwise. 2 to allure, invite, or attract. 3 to give rise to a desire in (someone) to do something; dispose: *their unfriendliness tempted me to leave the party.* 4 to risk provoking (esp in the phrase **tempt fate**).
▷HISTORY C13: from Old French *tempter,* from Latin *temptāre* to test
▸'**temptable** ADJECTIVE ▸'**tempter** NOUN

temptation (tɛmp'teɪʃən) NOUN 1 the act of tempting or the state of being tempted. 2 a person or thing that tempts.

Tempter ('tɛmptə) NOUN **the.** Satan regarded as trying to lead men into sin.

tempting ('tɛmptɪŋ) ADJECTIVE attractive or inviting: *a tempting meal.*
▸'**temptingly** ADVERB ▸'**temptingness** NOUN

temptress ('tɛmptrɪs) NOUN a woman who sets out to allure or seduce a man or men; seductress.

tempura ('tɛmpərə) NOUN a Japanese dish of seafood or vegetables dipped in batter and deep-fried, often at the table.
▷HISTORY from Japanese: fried food

tempus fugit *Latin* ('tɛmpəs 'fju:dʒɪt, -gɪt) time flies.

Temuco (*Spanish* te'muko) NOUN a city in S Chile: agricultural trading centre. Pop.: 253 451 (1999 est.).

ten (tɛn) NOUN 1 the cardinal number that is the sum of nine and one. It is the base of the decimal number system and the base of the common logarithm. See also **number** (sense 1). 2 a numeral, 10, X, etc., representing this number. 3 something representing, represented by, or consisting of ten units, such as a playing card with ten symbols on it. 4 Also called: **ten o'clock.** ten hours after noon or midnight. ♦ DETERMINER 5 **a** amounting to ten: *ten tigers.* **b** (*as pronoun*): *to sell only ten.* ♦ Related adjective: **decimal.** Related prefixes: **deca-, deci-.**
▷HISTORY Old English *tēn;* related to Old Saxon *tehan,* Old High German *zehan,* Gothic *taihun,* Latin *decem,* Greek *deka,* Sanskrit *dasa*

ten- COMBINING FORM a variant of **teno-** before a vowel.

tenable ('tɛnəbᵊl) ADJECTIVE able to be upheld, believed, maintained, or defended.
▷HISTORY C16: from Old French, from *tenir* to hold, from Latin *tenēre*
▸,**tena'bility** *or* '**tenableness** NOUN ▸'**tenably** ADVERB

tenace ('tɛneɪs) NOUN *Bridge, whist* a holding of two nonconsecutive high cards of a suit, such as the ace and queen.
▷HISTORY C17: from French, from Spanish *tenaza* forceps, ultimately from Latin *tenāx* holding fast, from *tenēre* to hold

tenacious (tɪ'neɪʃəs) ADJECTIVE 1 holding or grasping firmly; forceful: *a tenacious grip.* 2 retentive: *a tenacious memory.* 3 stubborn or persistent: *a tenacious character.* 4 holding together firmly; tough or cohesive: *tenacious cement.* 5 tending to stick or adhere: *tenacious mud.*
▷HISTORY C16: from Latin *tenāx,* from *tenēre* to hold
▸**te'naciously** ADVERB ▸**te'naciousness** *or* **tenacity** (tɪ'næsɪtɪ) NOUN

ten-acre block NOUN *NZ* a block of subdivided farming land, usually within commuting distance of a city, that provides a semirural way of life.

tenaculum (tɪ'nækjʊləm) NOUN, *plural* **-la** (-lə). a surgical or dissecting instrument for grasping and holding parts, consisting of a slender hook mounted in a handle.
▷HISTORY C17: from Late Latin, from Latin *tenēre* to hold

tenaille (tɛ'neɪl) NOUN *Fortifications* a low outwork in the main ditch between two bastions.
▷HISTORY C16: from French, literally: tongs, from Late Latin *tenācula,* pl of TENACULUM

tena koe (tə'nɑ: 'kwɔɪ) INTERJECTION *NZ* a Maori greeting to one person.

tenancy ('tɛnənsɪ) NOUN, *plural* **-cies.** 1 the temporary possession or holding by a tenant of lands or property owned by another. 2 the period of holding or occupying such property. 3 the period of holding office, a position, etc. 4 property held or occupied by a tenant.

tenant ('tɛnənt) NOUN 1 a person who holds, occupies, or possesses land or property by any kind of right or title, esp from a landlord under a lease. 2 a person who has the use of a house, flat, etc., subject to the payment of rent. 3 any holder or occupant. ♦ VERB 4 (*tr*) to hold (land or property) as a tenant. 5 (*intr;* foll by *in*) *Rare* to dwell.
▷HISTORY C14: from Old French, literally: (one who is) holding, from *tenir* to hold, from Latin *tenēre*

▸ˈ**tenantable** ADJECTIVE ▸ˈ**tenantless** ADJECTIVE ▸ˈ**tenant-ˌlike** ADJECTIVE

tenant farmer NOUN a person who farms land rented from another, the rent usually taking the form of part of the crops grown or livestock reared.

tenant-in-chief NOUN (in feudal society) a tenant who held some or all of his lands directly from the king.

tenantry (ˈtɛnəntrɪ) NOUN **1** tenants collectively, esp those with the same landlord. **2** the status or condition of being a tenant.

tenants association NOUN an organization of tenants, usually with a written constitution and charitable status, whose aim is to improve the housing conditions, amenities, community life, and contractual positions of its members. See also **community association, residents association.**

tenants' charter NOUN (in Britain) a package of legal rights to which tenants of local authorities, new towns, and housing associations are entitled, including security of tenure, and the rights to buy the dwelling cheaply, to take in lodgers, and to sublet.

Tencel (ˈtɛnˌsɛl) NOUN *Trademark* a fabric made from wood pulp cellulose, having a silky texture.

tench (tɛntʃ) NOUN a European freshwater cyprinid game fish, *Tinca tinca,* having a thickset dark greenish body with a barbel at each side of the mouth.
▷HISTORY C14: from Old French *tenche,* from Late Latin *tinca*

Ten Commandments PLURAL NOUN **the.** *Old Testament* the commandments summarizing the basic obligations of man towards God and his fellow men, delivered to Moses on Mount Sinai engraved on two tables of stone (Exodus 20:1–17). Also called: **the Decalogue.**

tend¹ (tɛnd) VERB (when *intr,* usually foll by *to* or *towards*) **1** (when *tr, takes an infinitive*) to have a general disposition (to do something); be inclined: *children tend to prefer sweets to meat.* **2** (*intr*) to have or be an influence (towards a specific result); be conducive: *the party atmosphere tends to hilarity.* **3** (*intr*) to go or move (in a particular direction): *to tend to the south.*
▷HISTORY C14: from Old French *tendre,* from Latin *tendere* to stretch

tend² (tɛnd) VERB **1** (*tr*) to care for: *to tend wounded soldiers.* **2** (when *intr,* often foll by *to*) to attend (to): *to tend to someone's needs.* **3** (*tr*) to handle or control: *to tend a fire.* **4** (*intr;* often foll by *to*) *Informal, chiefly US and Canadian* to pay attention.
▷HISTORY C14: variant of ATTEND

tendance (ˈtɛndəns) NOUN **1** *Rare* care and attention; ministration. **2** *Obsolete* attendants collectively.

tendency (ˈtɛndənsɪ) NOUN, *plural* **-cies. 1** (often foll by *to*) an inclination, predisposition, propensity, or leaning: *she has a tendency to be frivolous; a tendency to frivolity.* **2** the general course, purport, or drift of something, esp a written work. **3** a faction, esp one within a political party: *the militant tendency.*
▷HISTORY C17: from Medieval Latin *tendentia,* from Latin *tendere* to TEND¹

tendentious *or* **tendencious** (tɛnˈdɛnʃəs) ADJECTIVE having or showing an intentional tendency or bias, esp a controversial one.
▷HISTORY C20: from TENDENCY
▸**tenˈdentiously** *or* **tenˈdenciously** *or* **tenˈdentially** *or* **tenˈdencially** ADVERB ▸**tenˈdentiousness** *or* **tenˈdenciousness** NOUN

tender¹ (ˈtɛndə) ADJECTIVE **1** easily broken, cut, or crushed; soft; not tough: *a tender steak.* **2** easily damaged; vulnerable or sensitive: *a tender youth; at a tender age.* **3** having or expressing warm and affectionate feelings: *a tender smile.* **4** kind, merciful, or sympathetic: *a tender heart.* **5** arousing warm feelings; touching: *a tender memory.* **6** gentle and delicate: *a tender breeze.* **7** requiring care in handling; ticklish: *a tender question.* **8** painful or sore: *a tender wound.* **9** sensitive to moral or spiritual feelings: *a tender conscience.* **10** (*postpositive;* foll by *of*) careful or protective: *tender of one's emotions.* **11** (of a sailing vessel) easily keeled over by a wind; crank. Compare **stiff** (sense 10). ◆ VERB **12** (*tr*) *Rare* **a** to make tender. **b** to treat tenderly.
▷HISTORY C13: from Old French *tendre,* from Latin *tener* delicate
▸ˈ**tenderly** ADVERB ▸ˈ**tenderness** NOUN

tender² (ˈtɛndə) VERB **1** (*tr*) to give, present, or offer: *to tender one's resignation; tender a bid.* **2** (*intr;* foll by *for*) to make a formal offer or estimate for (a job or contract). **3** (*tr*) *Law* to offer (money or goods) in settlement of a debt or claim. ◆ NOUN **4** the act or an instance of tendering; offer. **5** *Commerce* a formal offer to supply specified goods or services at a stated cost or rate. **6** something, esp money, used as an official medium of payment: *legal tender.*
▷HISTORY C16: from Anglo-French *tendre,* from Latin *tendere* to extend; see TEND¹
▸ˈ**tenderable** ADJECTIVE ▸ˈ**tenderer** NOUN

tender³ (ˈtɛndə) NOUN **1** a small boat, such as a dinghy, towed or carried by a yacht or ship. **2** a vehicle drawn behind a steam locomotive to carry the fuel and water. **3** an ancillary vehicle used to carry supplies, spare parts, etc., for a mobile operation, such as an outside broadcast. **4** a person who tends.
▷HISTORY C15: variant of *attender*

tenderfoot (ˈtɛndəˌfʊt) NOUN, *plural* **-foots** *or* **-feet. 1** a newcomer, esp to the mines or ranches of the southwestern US. **2** (formerly) a beginner in the Scouts or Guides.

tenderhearted (ˌtɛndəˈhɑːtɪd) ADJECTIVE having a compassionate, kindly, or sensitive disposition.
▸ˌ**tenderˈheartedly** ADVERB ▸ˌ**tenderˈheartedness** NOUN

tenderize *or* **tenderise** (ˈtɛndəˌraɪz) VERB (*tr*) to make (meat) tender by pounding it to break down the fibres, by steeping it in a marinade, or by treating it with a tenderizer.
▸ˌ**tenderiˈzation** *or* ˌ**tenderiˈsation** NOUN

tenderizer *or* **tenderiser** (ˈtɛndəˌraɪzə) NOUN a substance, such as the plant enzyme papain, rubbed onto meat to soften the fibres and make it more tender.

tenderloin (ˈtɛndəˌlɔɪn) NOUN **1** a tender cut of pork or other meat from between the sirloin and ribs. **2** *US* a district of a city that is particularly noted for vice and corruption.
▷HISTORY sense 2 from *Tenderloin,* former district of New York City, regarded as an easy source of bribes for a corrupt policeman

tendinous (ˈtɛndɪnəs) ADJECTIVE of, relating to, possessing, or resembling tendons; sinewy.
▷HISTORY C17: from New Latin *tendinōsus,* from Medieval Latin *tendō* TENDON

tendon (ˈtɛndən) NOUN a cord or band of white inelastic collagenous tissue that attaches a muscle to a bone or some other part; sinew.
▷HISTORY C16: from Medieval Latin *tendō,* from Latin *tendere* to stretch; related to Greek *tenōn* sinew

tendril (ˈtɛndrɪl) NOUN **1** a specialized threadlike part of a leaf or stem that attaches climbing plants to a support by twining or adhering. **2** something resembling a tendril, such as a wisp of hair.
▷HISTORY C16: perhaps from Old French *tendron* tendril (confused with Old French *tendron* bud), from Medieval Latin *tendō* TENDON
▸ˈ**tendrillar** *or* ˈ**tendrilous** ADJECTIVE

Tenebrae (ˈtɛnəˌbreɪ) NOUN (*functioning as singular or plural*) *RC Church* (formerly) the matins and lauds for Thursday, Friday, and Saturday of Holy Week, usually sung in the evenings or at night.
▷HISTORY C17: from Latin: darkness

tenebrism (ˈtɛnəˌbrɪzəm) NOUN (*sometimes capital*) a school, style, or method of painting, adopted chiefly by 17th-century Spanish and Neapolitan painters, esp Caravaggio, characterized by large areas of dark colours, usually relieved with a shaft of light.
▸ˈ**tenebrist** NOUN, ADJECTIVE

tenebrous (ˈtɛnəbrəs) *or* **tenebrious** (təˈnɛbrɪəs) ADJECTIVE gloomy, shadowy, or dark.
▷HISTORY C15: from Latin *tenebrōsus* from *tenebrae* darkness
▸**tenebrosity** (ˌtɛnəˈbrɒsɪtɪ) *or* ˈ**tenebrousness** *or* **teˈnebriousness** NOUN

Tenedos (ˈtɛnɪˌdɒs) NOUN an island in the NE Aegean, near the entrance to the Dardanelles: in Greek legend the base of the Greek fleet during the siege of Troy. Modern Turkish name: **Bozcaada.**

tenement (ˈtɛnəmənt) NOUN **1** Also called: **tenement building.** (now esp in Scotland) a large building divided into separate flats. **2** a dwelling place or residence, esp one intended for rent. **3** *Chiefly Brit* a room or flat for rent. **4** *Property law* any form of permanent property, such as land, dwellings, offices, etc.
▷HISTORY C14: from Medieval Latin *tenementum,* from Latin *tenēre* to hold
▸**tenemental** (ˌtɛnəˈmɛntᵊl) *or* ˌ**teneˈmentary** ADJECTIVE ▸ˈ**teneˌmented** ADJECTIVE

Tenerife (ˌtɛnəˈriːf; *Spanish* teneˈrife) NOUN a Spanish island in the Atlantic, off the NW coast of Africa: the largest of the Canary Islands; volcanic and mountainous; tourism and agriculture. Capital: Santa Cruz. Pop.: 560 000 (latest est.). Area: 2058 sq. km (795 sq. miles).

tenesmus (tɪˈnɛzməs, -ˈnɛs-) NOUN *Pathol* an ineffective painful straining to empty the bowels in response to the sensation of a desire to defecate, without producing a significant quantity of faeces.
▷HISTORY C16: from Medieval Latin, from Latin *tēnesmos,* from Greek *teinesmos,* from *teinein* to strain
▸**teˈnesmic** ADJECTIVE

tenet (ˈtɛnɪt, ˈtiːnɪt) NOUN a belief, opinion, or dogma.
▷HISTORY C17: from Latin, literally: he (it) holds, from *tenēre* to hold

tenfold (ˈtɛnˌfəʊld) ADJECTIVE **1** equal to or having 10 times as many or as much: *a tenfold increase in population.* **2** composed of 10 parts. ◆ ADVERB **3** by or up to 10 times as many or as much: *the population increased tenfold.*

ten-gallon hat NOUN (in the US and Canada) a cowboy's broad-brimmed felt hat with a very high crown.
▷HISTORY C20: so called because of its large size

tenge (tɛŋˈgeɪ) NOUN the standard monetary unit of Kazakhstan, divided into 100 tiyn.

Tengri Khan (ˈtɛŋgrɪ ˈkɑːn) NOUN a mountain in central Asia, on the border between Kyrgyzstan and the Xinjiang Uygur Autonomous Region of W China. Height: 6995 m (22 951 ft.).

Tengri Nor (ˈtɛŋgrɪ ˈnɔː) NOUN another name for **Nam Co.**

Ten Gurus PLURAL NOUN the ten leaders of the Sikh religion from the founder of Sikhism Guru Nanak (1469–1538) to Guru Govind Singh (1666–1708), who ended the line of gurus by calling on Sikhs to rely on the holy text of the Granth to guide them.

tenia (ˈtiːnɪə) NOUN, *plural* **-niae** (-nɪˌiː). the US spelling of **taenia.**

teniacide (ˈtiːnɪəˌsaɪd) NOUN the US spelling of **taeniacide.**

teniafuge (ˈtiːnɪəˌfjuːdʒ) NOUN the US spelling of **taeniafuge.**

teniasis (tiːˈnaɪəsɪs) NOUN the US spelling of **taeniasis.**

Tenn. ABBREVIATION FOR Tennessee.

tenner (ˈtɛnə) NOUN *Informal* **1** *Brit* **a** a ten-pound note. **b** the sum of ten pounds. **2** *US* a ten-dollar bill.

Tennessean (ˌtɛnɪˈsiːən) NOUN **1** a native or inhabitant of Tennessee. ◆ ADJECTIVE **2** of or relating to Tennessee or its inhabitants.

Tennessee (ˌtɛnɪˈsiː) NOUN **1** a state of the E central US: consists of a plain in the west, rising to the Appalachians and the Cumberland Plateau in the east. Capital: Nashville. Pop.: 5 689 283 (2000). Area: 109 412 sq. km (42 244 sq. miles). Abbreviations: **Tenn,** (with zip code) **TN. 2** a river in the E central US, flowing southwest from E Tennessee into N Alabama, then west and north to the Ohio River at Paducah: the longest tributary of the Ohio; includes a series of dams and reservoirs under the Tennessee Valley Authority. Length: 1049 km (652 miles).

Tennessee Walking Horse NOUN an American breed of horse, marked by its stamina and trained to move at a fast running walk. Often shortened to: **Walking Horse.**

tennis (ˈtɛnɪs) NOUN **a** a racket game played between two players or pairs of players who hit a ball to and fro over a net on a rectangular court of grass, asphalt, clay, etc. See also **lawn tennis, real tennis, court tennis, table tennis. b** (*as modifier*): *tennis court; tennis racket.*
▷HISTORY C14: probably from Anglo-French *tenetz*

hold (imperative), from Old French *tenir* to hold, from Latin *tenēre*

tennis ball NOUN a hollow rubber ball covered with felt, used in tennis.

tennis elbow NOUN a painful inflammation of the elbow caused by exertion in playing tennis and similar games.

tennis shoe NOUN a rubber-soled canvas shoe tied with laces.

tenno (ˈtɛnəʊ) NOUN, *plural* **-no** *or* **-nos**. the formal title of the Japanese emperor, esp when regarded as a divine religious leader.
▷HISTORY from Japanese *tennō*

Tennysonian (ˌtɛnɪˈsəʊnɪən) ADJECTIVE 1 of, relating to, or reminiscent of Alfred, Lord Tennyson, the English poet (1809–92). ◆ NOUN 2 a follower or admirer of Tennyson.

Teno (ˈtɛnɔ) NOUN the Finnish name for **Tana** (sense 3).

teno- *or before a vowel* **ten-** COMBINING FORM tendon: *tenosynovitis*.
▷HISTORY from Greek *tenōn*

Tenochtitlán (tɛˌnɔːtʃtiːˈtlɑːn) NOUN an ancient city and capital of the Aztec empire on the present site of Mexico City; razed by Cortés in 1521.

tenon (ˈtɛnən) NOUN 1 the projecting end of a piece of wood formed to fit into a corresponding mortise in another piece. ◆ VERB (*tr*) 2 to form a tenon on (a piece of wood). 3 to join with a tenon and mortise.
▷HISTORY C15: from Old French, from *tenir* to hold, from Latin *tenēre*
▸ˈ**tenoner** NOUN

tenon saw NOUN a small fine-toothed saw with a strong back, used esp for cutting tenons.

tenor (ˈtɛnə) NOUN 1 *Music* **a** the male voice intermediate between alto and baritone, having a range approximately from the B a ninth below middle C to the G a fifth above it. **b** a singer with such a voice. **c** a saxophone, horn, recorder, etc., intermediate in compass and size between the alto and baritone or bass. **d** (*as modifier*): *a tenor sax*. 2 general drift of thought; purpose: *to follow the tenor of an argument*. 3 **a** (in early polyphonic music) the part singing the melody or the cantus firmus. **b** (in four-part harmony) the second lowest part lying directly above the bass. 4 *Bell-ringing* **a** the heaviest and lowest-pitched bell in a ring. **b** (*as modifier*): *a tenor bell*. 5 a settled course of progress. 6 *Archaic* general tendency. 7 *Finance* the time required for a bill of exchange or promissory note to become due for payment. 8 *Law* **a** the exact words of a deed, etc., as distinct from their effect. **b** an exact copy or transcript.
▷HISTORY C13 (originally: general meaning or sense): from Old French *tenour*, from Latin *tenor* a continuous holding to a course, from *tenēre* to hold; musical sense via Italian *tenore*, referring to the voice part that was continuous, that is, to which the melody was assigned
▸ˈ**tenorless** ADJECTIVE

tenor clef NOUN the clef that establishes middle C as being on the fourth line of the staff, used for the writing of music for the bassoon, cello, or tenor trombone. See also **C clef**.

tenorite (ˈtɛnəˌraɪt) NOUN a black mineral found in copper deposits and consisting of copper oxide in the form of either metallic scales or earthy masses. Formula: CuO.
▷HISTORY C19: named after G. *Tenore* (died 1861), Italian botanist

tenorrhaphy (tɪˈnɒrəfɪ) NOUN, *plural* **-phies**. *Surgery* the union of torn or divided tendons by means of sutures.
▷HISTORY C19: from TENO- + Greek *raphē* a sewing or suture

tenosynovitis (ˈtɛnəʊˌsaɪnəʊˈvaɪtɪs) NOUN painful swelling and inflammation of tendons, usually of the wrist, often the result of repetitive movements such as typing.

tenotomy (təˈnɒtəmɪ) NOUN, *plural* **-mies**. surgical division of a tendon.
▸**teˈnotomist** NOUN

tenpenny (ˈtɛnpənɪ) ADJECTIVE (*prenominal*) *US and Canadian* (of a nail) three inches in length.

tenpin (ˈtɛnˌpɪn) NOUN one of the pins used in tenpin bowling. See also **tenpins**.

tenpin bowling NOUN a bowling game in which heavy bowls are rolled down a long lane to knock over the ten target pins at the other end. Also called (esp US and Canadian): **tenpins**.

tenpins (ˈtɛnˌpɪnz) NOUN (*functioning as singular*) the US and Canadian name for **tenpin bowling**.

tenrec (ˈtɛnrɛk) NOUN any small mammal, such as *Tenrec ecaudatus* (**tailless tenrec**), of the Madagascan family *Tenrecidae*, resembling hedgehogs or shrews: order *Insectivora* (insectivores).
▷HISTORY C18: via French from Malagasy *tràndraka*

TENS (tɛnz) NOUN ACRONYM FOR transcutaneous electrical nerve stimulation: the application of low-voltage electric impulses to the skin to relieve rheumatic pain and provide some pain relief in labour. The pulses are said to stimulate the release of pain-killing endorphins.

tense[1] (tɛns) ADJECTIVE 1 stretched or stressed tightly; taut or rigid. 2 under mental or emotional strain. 3 producing mental or emotional strain: *a tense day*. 4 (of a speech sound) pronounced with considerable muscular effort and having relatively precise accuracy of articulation and considerable duration: *in English the vowel* (iː) *in "beam" is tense*. Compare **lax** (sense 4). ◆ VERB 5 (often foll by *up*) to make or become tense.
▷HISTORY C17: from Latin *tensus* taut, from *tendere* to stretch
▸ˈ**tensely** ADVERB ▸ˈ**tenseness** NOUN

tense[2] (tɛns) NOUN *Grammar* a category of the verb or verbal inflections, such as present, past, and future, that expresses the temporal relations between what is reported in a sentence and the time of its utterance.
▷HISTORY C14: from Old French *tens* time, from Latin *tempus*
▸ˈ**tenseless** ADJECTIVE

tense logic NOUN *Logic* the study of the logical properties of tense operators, and of the logical relations between sentences having tense, by means of consideration of appropriate formal systems.

tensible (ˈtɛnsəbᵊl) ADJECTIVE capable of being stretched; tensile.
▸ˌ**tensiˈbility** *or* ˈ**tensibleness** NOUN ▸ˈ**tensibly** ADVERB

tensile (ˈtɛnsaɪl) ADJECTIVE 1 of or relating to tension. 2 sufficiently ductile to be stretched or drawn out.
▷HISTORY C17: from New Latin *tensilis*, from Latin *tendere* to stretch
▸ˈ**tensilely** ADVERB ▸**tensility** (tɛnˈsɪlɪtɪ) *or* ˈ**tensileness** NOUN

tensile strength NOUN a measure of the ability of a material to withstand a longitudinal stress, expressed as the greatest stress that the material can stand without breaking.

tensimeter (tɛnˈsɪmɪtə) NOUN an instrument used to compare the vapour pressures of two liquids, usually consisting of two sealed bulbs containing the liquids, each being connected to one limb of a manometer.
▷HISTORY C20: from TENSI(ON) + -METER

tensiometer (ˌtɛnsɪˈɒmɪtə) NOUN 1 an instrument for measuring the tensile strength of a wire, beam, etc. 2 a device that measures differences in vapour pressures. It is used to determine transition points by observing changes of vapour pressure with temperature. 3 an instrument for measuring the surface tension of a liquid, usually consisting of a sensitive balance for measuring the force needed to pull a wire ring from the surface of the liquid. 4 an instrument for measuring the moisture content of soil.

tension (ˈtɛnʃən) NOUN 1 the act of stretching or the state or degree of being stretched. 2 mental or emotional strain; stress. 3 a situation or condition of hostility, suspense, or uneasiness. 4 *Physics* a force that tends to produce an elongation of a body or structure. 5 *Physics* **a** voltage, electromotive force, or potential difference. **b** (*in combination*): *high-tension; low-tension*. 6 a device for regulating the tension in a part, string, thread, etc., as in a sewing machine. 7 *Knitting* the degree of tightness or looseness with which a person knits.
▷HISTORY C16: from Latin *tensiō*, from *tendere* to strain
▸ˈ**tensional** ADJECTIVE ▸ˈ**tensionless** ADJECTIVE

tensity (ˈtɛnsɪtɪ) NOUN a rare word for **tension** (senses 1–3).

tensive (ˈtɛnsɪv) ADJECTIVE of or causing tension or strain.

tensor (ˈtɛnsə, -sɔː) NOUN 1 *Anatomy* any muscle that can cause a part to become firm or tense. 2 *Maths* a set of components, functions of the coordinates of any point in space, that transform linearly between coordinate systems. For three-dimensional space there are 3^r components, where *r* is the rank. A tensor of zero rank is a scalar, of rank one, a vector.
▷HISTORY C18: from New Latin, literally: a stretcher
▸**tensorial** (tɛnˈsɔːrɪəl) ADJECTIVE

ten-strike NOUN *Tenpin bowling* another word for **strike** (sense 40).

tent[1] (tɛnt) NOUN 1 **a** a portable shelter of canvas, plastic, or other waterproof material supported on poles and fastened to the ground by pegs and ropes. **b** (*as modifier*): *tent peg*. 2 something resembling this in function or shape. ◆ VERB 3 (*intr*) to camp in a tent. 4 (*tr*) to cover with or as if with a tent or tents. 5 (*tr*) to provide with a tent as shelter.
▷HISTORY C13: from Old French *tente*, from Latin *tentōrium* something stretched out, from *tendere* to stretch
▸ˈ**tented** ADJECTIVE ▸ˈ**tentless** ADJECTIVE ▸ˈ**tentˌlike** ADJECTIVE

tent[2] (tɛnt) *Med* ◆ NOUN 1 a plug of soft material for insertion into a bodily canal, etc., to dilate it or maintain its patency. ◆ VERB 2 (*tr*) to insert such a plug into (a bodily canal, etc.).
▷HISTORY C14 (in the sense: a probe): from Old French *tente* (noun), ultimately from Latin *temptāre* to try; see TEMPT

tent[3] (tɛnt) NOUN *Obsolete* a red table wine from Alicante, Spain.
▷HISTORY C16: from Spanish *tinto* dark-coloured; see TINT

tent[4] (tɛnt) *Scot* ◆ NOUN 1 heed; attention. ◆ VERB (*tr*) 2 to pay attention to; take notice of. 3 to attend to.
▷HISTORY C14: from *attent* ATTEND and INTENT
▸ˈ**tenter** NOUN

tentacle (ˈtɛntəkᵊl) NOUN 1 any of various elongated flexible organs that occur near the mouth in many invertebrates and are used for feeding, grasping, etc. 2 any of the hairs on the leaf of an insectivorous plant that are used to capture prey. 3 something resembling a tentacle, esp in its ability to reach out or grasp.
▷HISTORY C18: from New Latin *tentāculum*, from Latin *tentāre*, variant of *temptāre* to feel
▸ˈ**tentacled** ADJECTIVE ▸ˈ**tentacle-ˌlike** *or* **tentaculoid** (tɛnˈtækjʊˌlɔɪd) ADJECTIVE ▸**tentacular** (tɛnˈtækjʊlə) ADJECTIVE

tentage (ˈtɛntɪdʒ) NOUN 1 tents collectively. 2 a supply of tents or tenting equipment.

tentation (tɛnˈteɪʃən) NOUN a method of achieving the correct adjustment of a mechanical device by a series of trials.
▷HISTORY C14: from Latin *tentātiō*, variant of *temptātiō* TEMPTATION

tentative (ˈtɛntətɪv) ADJECTIVE 1 provisional or experimental; conjectural. 2 hesitant, uncertain, or cautious.
▷HISTORY C16: from Medieval Latin *tentātīvus*, from Latin *tentāre* to test
▸ˈ**tentatively** ADVERB ▸ˈ**tentativeness** NOUN

tent caterpillar NOUN the larva of various moths of the family *Lasiocampidae*, esp *Malacosoma americana* of North America, which build communal webs in trees.

tent dress NOUN a very full tent-shaped dress, having no darts, waistline, etc.

tenter (ˈtɛntə) NOUN 1 a frame on which cloth is stretched during the manufacturing process in order that it may retain its shape while drying. 2 a person who stretches cloth on a tenter. ◆ VERB 3 (*tr*) to stretch (cloth) on a tenter.
▷HISTORY C14: from Medieval Latin *tentōrium*, from Latin *tentus* stretched, from *tendere* to stretch

tenterhook (ˈtɛntəˌhʊk) NOUN 1 one of a series of hooks or bent nails used to hold cloth stretched on a tenter. 2 **on tenterhooks**. in a state of tension or suspense.

tenth (tɛnθ) ADJECTIVE 1 (*usually prenominal*) **a** coming after the ninth in numbering or counting order, position, time, etc.; being the ordinal number of *ten*: often written 10th. **b** (*as noun*): *see*

you on the tenth; tenth in line. ◆ NOUN 2 **a** one of 10 approximately equal parts of something. **b** (*as modifier*): *a tenth part.* 3 one of 10 equal divisions of a particular measurement, etc. Related prefix: **deci-**: *decibel.* 4 the fraction equal to one divided by ten (1/10). 5 *Music* **a** an interval of one octave plus a third. **b** one of two notes constituting such an interval in relation to the other. ◆ ADVERB 6 Also: **tenthly.** after the ninth person, position, event, etc. ◆ SENTENCE CONNECTOR 7 Also: **tenthly.** as the 10th point: linking what follows with the previous statements, as in a speech or argument.
▷**HISTORY** C12 *tenthe,* from Old English *tēotha;* see TEN, -TH[2]

tent stitch NOUN another term for **petit point** (sense 1).
▷**HISTORY** C17: of uncertain origin

tenuis (ˈtɛnjʊɪs) NOUN, *plural* **tenues** (ˈtɛnjʊˌiːz). (in the grammar of classical Greek) any of the voiceless stops as represented by kappa, pi, or tau (k, p, t).
▷**HISTORY** C17: from Latin: thin

tenuous (ˈtɛnjʊəs) ADJECTIVE 1 insignificant or flimsy: *a tenuous argument.* 2 slim, fine, or delicate: *a tenuous thread.* 3 diluted or rarefied in consistency or density: *a tenuous fluid.*
▷**HISTORY** C16: from Latin *tenuis*
▸**tenuity** (tɛˈnjuːɪtɪ) *or* **ˈtenuousness** NOUN ▸**ˈtenuously** ADVERB

tenure (ˈtɛnjʊə, ˈtɛnjə) NOUN 1 the possession or holding of an office or position. 2 the length of time an office, position, etc., lasts; term. 3 *Chiefly US and Canadian* the improved security status of a person after having been in the employ of the same company or institution for a specified period. 4 the right to permanent employment until retirement, esp for teachers, lecturers, etc. 5 *Property law* **a** the holding or occupying of property, esp realty, in return for services rendered, etc. **b** the duration of such holding or occupation.
▷**HISTORY** C15: from Old French, from Medieval Latin *tenitūra,* ultimately from Latin *tenēre* to hold
▸**tenˈurial** ADJECTIVE ▸**tenˈurially** ADVERB

tenured (ˈtɛnjʊəd, ˈtɛnjəd) ADJECTIVE *Chiefly US and Canadian* **a** having tenure of office: *a tenured professor.* **b** guaranteeing tenure of office: *a tenured post.*

tenuto (tɪˈnjuːtəʊ) ADJECTIVE, ADVERB *Music* (of a note) to be held for or beyond its full time value. Symbol: ˉ (written above a note).
▷**HISTORY** from Italian, literally: held, from *tenere* to hold, from Latin *tenēre*

ten-yard rule NOUN *Rugby* the rule allowing a referee, when a player disputes the award of a penalty or free kick, to penalize the offending side further by moving the place from which the kick is to be taken ten yards further forward.

teocalli (ˌtiːəʊˈkælɪ) NOUN, *plural* **-lis.** any of various truncated pyramids built by the Aztecs as bases for their temples.
▷**HISTORY** C17: from Nahuatl, from *teotl* god + *calli* house

teosinte (ˌtiːəʊˈsɪntɪ) NOUN a tall Central American annual grass, *Euchlaena mexicana,* related to maize and grown for forage in the southern US.
▷**HISTORY** C19: from Nahuatl *teocentli,* from *teotl* god + *centli* dry ear of corn

tepal (ˈtiːpᵊl, ˈtɛpᵊl) NOUN any of the subdivisions of a perianth that is not clearly differentiated into calyx and corolla.
▷**HISTORY** C20: from French *tépale* changed (on analogy with *sépale* sepal) from *pétale* PETAL

tepee *or* **teepee** (ˈtiːpiː) NOUN a cone-shaped tent of animal skins used by certain North American Indians.
▷**HISTORY** C19: from Siouan *tīpī,* from *ti* to dwell + *pi* used for

tepefy (ˈtɛpɪˌfaɪ) VERB **-fies, -fying, -fied.** to make or become tepid.
▷**HISTORY** C17: from Latin *tepēre*
▸**tepefaction** (ˌtɛpɪˈfækʃən) NOUN

tephra (ˈtɛfrə) NOUN *Chiefly US* solid matter ejected during a volcanic eruption.
▷**HISTORY** C20: Greek, literally: ashes

tephrite (ˈtɛfraɪt) NOUN a variety of basalt containing plagioclase, augite, and a feldspathoid, commonly nepheline, or leucite.
▷**HISTORY** C17: from Greek *tephros,* from *tephra* ashes; see -ITE[1]
▸**tephritic** (tɪˈfrɪtɪk) ADJECTIVE

Tepic (*Spanish* teˈpik) NOUN a city in W central Mexico, capital of Nayarit state: agricultural, trading and processing centre. Pop.: 265 681 (2000 est.).

tepid (ˈtɛpɪd) ADJECTIVE 1 slightly warm; lukewarm. 2 relatively unenthusiastic or apathetic: *the play had a tepid reception.*
▷**HISTORY** C14: from Latin *tepidus,* from *tepēre* to be lukewarm
▸**teˈpidity** *or* **ˈtepidness** NOUN ▸**ˈtepidly** ADVERB

tequila (tɪˈkiːlə) NOUN 1 a spirit that is distilled in Mexico from an agave plant and forms the basis of many mixed drinks. 2 the plant, *Agave tequilana,* from which this drink is made.
▷**HISTORY** C19: from Mexican Spanish, from *Tequila,* region of Mexico

ter- COMBINING FORM three, third, or three times: *tercentenary.*
▷**HISTORY** from Latin *ter* thrice; related to *trēs* THREE

tera- PREFIX denoting 10^{12}: *terameter.* Symbol: T.
▷**HISTORY** from Greek *teras* monster

teraflop (ˈtɛrəˌflɒp) NOUN *Computing* a measure of processing speed, consisting of a thousand billion floating-point operations a second.
▷**HISTORY** C20: from TERA- + *flo(ating) p(oint)*

teraglin (təˈræglən) NOUN an edible marine fish, *Zeluco atelodus,* of Australia which has fine scales and is blue in colour.
▷**HISTORY** from a native Australian language

Terai (təˈraɪ) NOUN 1 (in India) a belt of marshy land at the foot of mountains, esp at the foot of the Himalayas in N India. 2 a felt hat with a wide brim worn in subtropical regions.

terakihi (ˌtɛrəˈkiːhiː) NOUN, *plural* **-kihis.** See **tarakihi.**

teraph (ˈtɛrəf) NOUN, *plural* **-aphim** (-əfɪm). *Old Testament* any of various small household gods or images venerated by ancient Semitic peoples. (Genesis 31:19–21; I Samuel 19:13–16).
▷**HISTORY** C14: from Hebrew, of uncertain origin

terat- *or* **terato-** COMBINING FORM indicating a monster or something abnormal: *teratism; teratoid.*
▷**HISTORY** from Greek *terat-, teras* monster, prodigy

teratism (ˈtɛrəˌtɪzəm) NOUN a malformed animal or human, esp in the fetal stage; monster.

teratogen (ˈtɛrətədʒən, tɪˈrætə-) NOUN any substance, organism, or process that causes malformations in a fetus. Teratogens include certain drugs (such as thalidomide), infections (such as German measles), and ionizing radiation.
▸**ˌteratoˈgenic** ADJECTIVE ▸**ˌteratoˈgenicist** NOUN
▸**ˌteratogeˈnicity** NOUN

teratoid (ˈtɛrəˌtɔɪd) ADJECTIVE *Biology* resembling a monster.

teratology (ˌtɛrəˈtɒlədʒɪ) NOUN 1 the branch of medical science concerned with the development of physical abnormalities during the fetal or early embryonic stage. 2 the branch of biology that is concerned with the structure, development, etc., of monsters. 3 a collection of tales about mythical or fantastic creatures, monsters, etc.
▸**teratologic** (ˌtɛrətəˈlɒdʒɪk) *or* **ˌteratoˈlogical** ADJECTIVE
▸**ˌteraˈtologist** NOUN

teratoma (ˌtɛrəˈtəʊmə) NOUN, *plural* **-mata** (-mətə) *or* **-mas.** a tumour or group of tumours composed of tissue foreign to the site of growth.

teratophobia (ˌtɛrətəʊˈfəʊbɪə) NOUN *Psychiatry* fear of giving birth to a monster.

terbia (ˈtɜːbɪə) NOUN another name (not in technical usage) for **terbium oxide.**

terbium (ˈtɜːbɪəm) NOUN a soft malleable silvery-grey element of the lanthanide series of metals, occurring in gadolinite and monazite and used in lasers and for doping solid-state devices. Symbol: Tb; atomic no.: 65; atomic wt.: 158.92534; valency: 3 or 4; relative density: 8.230; melting pt.: 1356°C; boiling pt.: 3230°C.
▷**HISTORY** C19: from New Latin, named after *Ytterby,* Sweden, village where it was discovered
▸**ˈterbic** ADJECTIVE

terbium metal NOUN *Chem* any of a group of related lanthanides, including terbium, europium, and gadolinium.

terbium oxide NOUN an amorphous white insoluble powder. Formula: Tb_2O_3. Also called: **terbia.**

terce (tɜːs) *or* **tierce** NOUN *Chiefly RC Church* the third of the seven canonical hours of the divine office, originally fixed at the third hour of the day, about 9 a.m.
▷**HISTORY** a variant of TIERCE

Terceira (*Portuguese* tərˈsəirə) NOUN an island in the N Atlantic, in the Azores: NATO military air base. Pop.: 60 000 (latest est.). Area: 397 sq. km (153 sq. miles).

tercel (ˈtɜːsᵊl) *or* **tiercel** NOUN a male falcon or hawk, esp as used in falconry.
▷**HISTORY** C14: from Old French, from Vulgar Latin *tertiolus* (unattested), from Latin *tertius* third, referring to the tradition that only one egg in three hatched a male chick

tercentenary (ˌtɜːsɛnˈtiːnərɪ) *or* **tercentennial** ADJECTIVE 1 of or relating to a period of 300 years. 2 of or relating to a 300th anniversary or its celebration. ◆ NOUN, *plural* **-tenaries** *or* **-tennials.** 3 an anniversary of 300 years or its celebration. ◆ Also: **tricentennial.**

tercet (ˈtɜːsɪt, tɜːˈsɛt) NOUN a group of three lines of verse that rhyme together or are connected by rhyme with adjacent groups of three lines.
▷**HISTORY** C16: from French, from Italian *terzetto,* diminutive of *terzo* third, from Latin *tertius*

terebene (ˈtɛrəˌbiːn) NOUN a mixture of hydrocarbons prepared from oil of turpentine and sulphuric acid, used to make paints and varnishes and medicinally as an expectorant and antiseptic.
▷**HISTORY** C19: from TEREB(INTH) + -ENE

terebic acid (təˈrɛbɪk) NOUN a white crystalline carboxylic acid produced by the action of nitric acid on turpentine. Formula: $C_7H_{10}O_4$.
▷**HISTORY** C19: from TEREB(INTH) + -IC

terebinth (ˈtɛrɪbɪnθ) NOUN a small anacardiaceous tree, *Pistacia terebinthus,* of the Mediterranean region, having winged leafstalks and clusters of small flowers, and yielding a turpentine.
▷**HISTORY** C14: from Latin *terebinthus,* from Greek *terebinthos* turpentine tree

terebinthine (ˌtɛrɪˈbɪnθaɪn) ADJECTIVE 1 of or relating to terebinth or related plants. 2 of, consisting of, or resembling turpentine.

terebrate (ˈtɛrɪˌbreɪt) ADJECTIVE (of animals, esp insects) having a boring or penetrating organ, such as a sting.
▷**HISTORY** C20: from Latin *terebra* borer + -ATE[1]

teredo (təˈriːdəʊ) NOUN, *plural* **-dos** *or* **-dines** (-dɪˌniːz). any marine bivalve mollusc of the genus *Teredo.* See **shipworm.**
▷**HISTORY** C17: via Latin from Greek *terēdōn* wood-boring worm; related to Greek *tetrainein* to pierce

Terengganu (tərɛŋˈgɑːnuː) NOUN a variant spelling of **Trengganu.**

te reo (teɪ ˈreɪəʊ) NOUN *NZ* the Maori language.
▷**HISTORY** Maori, literally: the language

terephthalic acid (ˌtɛrɛfˈθælɪk) NOUN a white crystalline water-insoluble carboxylic acid used in making polyester resins such as Terylene; 1,4-benzenedicarboxylic acid. Formula: $C_6H_4(COOH)_2$.
▷**HISTORY** C20: from TEREBENE + PHTHALIC ACID

Teresina (*Portuguese* tereˈzina) NOUN an inland port in NE Brazil, capital of Piauí state, on the Parnaíba River: chief commercial centre of the Parnaíba valley. Pop.: 676 596 (1991). Former name: **Therezina.**

terete (ˈtɛriːt) ADJECTIVE (esp of plant parts) smooth and usually cylindrical and tapering.
▷**HISTORY** C17: from Latin *teres* smooth, from *terere* to rub

Tereus (ˈtɪərɪəs) NOUN *Greek myth* a prince of Thrace, who raped Philomela, sister of his wife Procne, and was punished by being turned into a hoopoe.

tergiversate (ˈtɜːdʒɪvəˌseɪt) VERB (*intr*) 1 to change sides or loyalties; apostatize. 2 to be evasive or ambiguous; equivocate.
▷**HISTORY** C17: from Latin *tergiversārī* to turn one's back, from *tergum* back + *vertere* to turn
▸**ˌtergiverˈsation** NOUN ▸**ˈtergiverˌsator** *or* **tergiversant** (ˈtɜːdʒɪˌvɜːsᵊnt) NOUN ▸**ˌtergiˈversatory** ADJECTIVE

tergum (ˈtɜːgəm) NOUN, *plural* **-ga** (-gə). a cuticular

plate covering the dorsal surface of a body segment of an arthropod. Compare **sternum** (sense 3).
▷HISTORY C19: from Latin: the back
▸ **'tergal** ADJECTIVE

teriyaki (ˌtɛrɪ'jækɪ) ADJECTIVE [1] *Japanese cookery* basted with soy sauce and rice wine and broiled over an open fire. ◆ NOUN [2] a dish prepared in this way.
▷HISTORY from Japanese, from *teri* glaze + *yaki* to broil

term (tɜːm) NOUN [1] a name, expression, or word used for some particular thing, esp in a specialized field of knowledge: *a medical term.* [2] any word or expression. [3] a limited period of time: *his second term of office; a prison term.* [4] any of the divisions of the academic year during which a school, college, etc., is in session. [5] a point in time determined for an event or for the end of a period. [6] Also called: **full term.** the period at which childbirth is imminent. [7] *Law* **a** an estate or interest in land limited to run for a specified period: *a term of years.* **b** the duration of an estate, etc. **c** (formerly) a period of time during which sessions of courts of law were held. **d** time allowed to a debtor to settle. [8] *Maths* either of the expressions the ratio of which is a fraction or proportion, any of the separate elements of a sequence, or any of the individual addends of a polynomial or series. [9] *Logic* **a** the word or phrase that forms either the subject or predicate of a proposition. **b** a name or variable, as opposed to a predicate. **c** one of the relata of a relation. **d** any of the three subjects or predicates occurring in a syllogism. [10] Also called: **terminal, terminus, terminal figure.** *Architect* a sculptured post, esp one in the form of an armless bust or an animal on the top of a square pillar. [11] *Australian Rules football* the usual word for **quarter** (sense 10). [12] *Archaic* a boundary or limit. ◆ VERB [13] *(tr)* to designate; call: *he was termed a thief.* ◆ See also **terms.**
▷HISTORY C13: from Old French *terme,* from Latin *terminus* end
▸ **'termly** ADVERB

termagant ('tɜːməgənt) NOUN **a** a shrewish woman; scold. **b** *(as modifier)*: *a termagant woman.*
▷HISTORY C13: from earlier *Tervagaunt,* from Old French *Tervagan,* from Italian *Trivigante;* after an arrogant character in medieval mystery plays who was supposed to be a Muslim deity
▸ **'termagancy** NOUN ▸ **'termagantly** ADVERB

termer ('tɜːmə) NOUN a variant spelling of **termor.**

-termer NOUN *(in combination)* a person serving a specified length of time in prison: *a short-termer.*

terminable ('tɜːmɪnəb^{ə}l, 'tɜːmnəb^{ə}l) ADJECTIVE [1] able to be terminated. [2] terminating after a specific period or event: *a terminable annuity.*
▸ **ˌtermina'bility** *or* **'terminableness** NOUN ▸ **'terminably** ADVERB

terminal ('tɜːmɪn^{ə}l) ADJECTIVE [1] of, being, or situated at an end, terminus, or boundary: *a terminal station; terminal buds.* [2] of, relating to, or occurring after or in a term: *terminal leave.* [3] (of a disease) terminating in death: *terminal cancer.* [4] *Informal* extreme: *terminal boredom.* [5] of or relating to the storage or delivery of freight at a warehouse: *a terminal service.* ◆ NOUN [6] a terminating point, part, or place. [7] **a** a point at which current enters or leaves an electrical device, such as a battery or a circuit. **b** a conductor by which current enters or leaves at such a point. [8] *Computing* a device having input/output links with a computer but situated at a distance from the computer. [9] *Architect* **a** an ornamental carving at the end of a structure. **b** another name for **term** (sense 10). [10] **a** a point or station usually at the end of the line of a railway, serving as an important access point for passengers or freight. **b** a less common name for **terminus.** [11] a purpose-built reception and departure structure at the terminus of a bus, sea, or air transport route. [12] a site where raw material is unloaded, stored, in some cases reprocessed, and reloaded for further transportation, esp an onshore installation designed to receive offshore oil or gas from tankers or a pipeline. [13] *Physiol* **a** the smallest arteriole before its division into capillaries. **b** either of two veins that collect blood from the thalamus and surrounding structures and empty it into the internal cerebral vein. **c** the portion of a bronchiole just before it subdivides into the air sacs of the lungs.
▷HISTORY C15: from Latin *terminālis,* from *terminus* end
▸ **'terminally** ADVERB

terminal market NOUN a commodity market in a trading centre rather than at a producing centre.

terminal platform NOUN (in the oil industry) an offshore platform from which oil or gas is pumped ashore through a pipeline.

terminal velocity NOUN [1] the constant maximum velocity reached by a body falling under gravity through a fluid, esp the atmosphere. [2] the velocity of a missile or projectile when it reaches its target. [3] the maximum velocity attained by a rocket, missile, or shell flying in a parabolic flight path. [4] the maximum velocity that an aircraft can attain, as determined by its total drag.

terminate ('tɜːmɪˌneɪt) VERB [1] (when *intr,* often foll by *in* or *with*) to form, be, or put an end (to); conclude: *to terminate a pregnancy; their relationship terminated amicably.* [2] *(tr)* to connect (suitable circuitry) to the end of an electrical transmission line to absorb the energy and avoid reflections. [3] *(intr) Maths* (of a decimal expansion) to have only a finite number of digits.
▷HISTORY C16: from Latin *terminātus* limited, from *termināre* to set boundaries, from *terminus* end
▸ **'terminative** ADJECTIVE ▸ **'terminatory** ADJECTIVE

termination (ˌtɜːmɪ'neɪʃən) NOUN [1] the act of terminating or the state of being terminated. [2] something that terminates. [3] a final result.
▸ **ˌtermi'national** ADJECTIVE

terminator ('tɜːmɪˌneɪtə) NOUN the line dividing the illuminated and dark part of the moon or a planet.

terminator seed NOUN a seed that produces sterile plants, used in some genetically modified crops so that a new supply of seeds has to be bought every year.

terminology (ˌtɜːmɪ'nɒlədʒɪ) NOUN, *plural* **-gies.** [1] the body of specialized words relating to a particular subject. [2] the study of terms.
▷HISTORY C19: from Medieval Latin *terminus* term, from Latin: end
▸ **terminological** (ˌtɜːmɪnə'lɒdʒɪk^{ə}l) ADJECTIVE
▸ **ˌtermino'logically** ADVERB ▸ **ˌtermi'nologist** NOUN

term insurance NOUN life assurance, usually low in cost and offering no cash value, that provides for the payment of a specified sum of money only if the insured dies within a stipulated period of time.

terminus ('tɜːmɪnəs) NOUN, *plural* **-ni** (-naɪ) *or* **-nuses.** [1] the last or final part or point. [2] either end of a railway, bus route, etc., or a station or town at such a point. [3] a goal aimed for. [4] a boundary or boundary marker. [5] *Architect* another name for **term** (sense 10).
▷HISTORY C16: from Latin: end; related to Greek *termōn* boundary

Terminus ('tɜːmɪnəs) NOUN the Roman god of boundaries.

terminus ad quem *Latin* ('tɜːmɪˌnʊs æd 'kwɛm) NOUN the aim or terminal point.
▷HISTORY literally: the end to which

terminus a quo *Latin* ('tɜːmɪˌnʊs ɑː 'kwəʊ) NOUN the starting point; beginning.
▷HISTORY literally: the end from which

termitarium (ˌtɜːmɪ'tɛərɪəm) NOUN, *plural* **-ia** (-ɪə). the nest of a termite colony.
▷HISTORY C20: from TERMITE + -ARIUM

termite ('tɜːmaɪt) NOUN any whitish ant-like social insect of the order *Isoptera,* of warm and tropical regions. Some species feed on wood, causing damage to furniture, buildings, trees, etc. Also called: **white ant.**
▷HISTORY C18: from New Latin *termitēs* white ants, pl of *termes,* from Latin: a woodworm; related to Greek *tetrainein* to bore through
▸ **termitic** (tɜː'mɪtɪk) ADJECTIVE

termless ('tɜːmlɪs) ADJECTIVE [1] without limit or boundary. [2] unconditional. [3] an archaic word for **indescribable.**

termor *or* **termer** ('tɜːmə) NOUN *Property law* a person who holds an estate for a term of years or until he dies.
▷HISTORY C14: from Anglo-French *termer,* from *terme* TERM

terms (tɜːmz) PLURAL NOUN [1] (usually specified prenominally) the actual language or mode of presentation used: *he described the project in loose terms.* [2] conditions of an agreement: *you work here on our terms.* [3] a sum of money paid for a service or credit; charges. [4] (usually preceded by *on*) mutual relationship or standing: *they are on affectionate terms.* [5] **in terms of.** as expressed by; regarding: *in terms of money he was no better off.* [6] **come to terms.** to reach acceptance or agreement: *to come to terms with one's failings.*

terms of trade PLURAL NOUN *Economics, Brit* the ratio of export prices to import prices. It measures a nation's trading position, which improves when export prices rise faster or fall slower than import prices.

tern[1] (tɜːn) NOUN any aquatic bird of the subfamily *Sterninae,* having a forked tail, long narrow wings, a pointed bill, and a typically black-and-white plumage: family *Laridae* (gulls, etc.), order *Charadriiformes.*
▷HISTORY C18: from Old Norse *therna;* related to Norwegian *terna,* Swedish *tärna*

tern[2] (tɜːn) NOUN [1] a three-masted schooner. [2] *Rare* a group of three.
▷HISTORY C14: from Old French *terne,* from Italian *terno,* from Latin *ternī* three each; related to Latin *ter* thrice, *trēs* three

ternary ('tɜːnərɪ) ADJECTIVE [1] consisting of three or groups of three. [2] *Maths* **a** (of a number system) to the base three. **b** involving or containing three variables. [3] (of an alloy, mixture, or chemical compound) having three different components or composed of three different elements. ◆ NOUN, *plural* **-ries.** [4] a group of three.
▷HISTORY C14: from Latin *ternārius,* from *ternī* three each

ternary form NOUN a musical structure consisting of two contrasting sections followed by a repetition of the first; the form *aba.* Also called: **song form.**

ternate ('tɜːnɪt, -neɪt) ADJECTIVE [1] (esp of a leaf) consisting of three leaflets or other parts. [2] (esp of plants) having groups of three members.
▷HISTORY C18: from New Latin *ternātus,* from Medieval Latin *ternāre* to increase threefold
▸ **'ternately** ADVERB

terne (tɜːn) NOUN [1] Also called: **terne metal.** an alloy of lead containing tin (10–20 per cent) and antimony (1.5–2 per cent). [2] Also called: **terne plate.** steel plate coated with this alloy.
▷HISTORY C16: perhaps from French *terne* dull, from Old French *ternir* to TARNISH

Terni (*Italian* 'tɛrni) NOUN an industrial city in central Italy, in Umbria: site of waterfalls created in Roman times. Pop.: 107 770 (2000 est.).

ternion ('tɜːnɪən) NOUN *Rare* a group of three.
▷HISTORY C16: from Latin *terniō* triad, from *ternī* three each; related to *ter* thrice

Ternopol (*Russian* tɪr'nɔpəlj) NOUN a town in the W Ukraine, on the River Seret: formerly under Polish rule. Pop.: 235 100 (1998 est.). Polish name: **Tarnopol.**

terotechnology (ˌtɪərəʊtɛk'nɒlədʒɪ, ˌtɛr-) NOUN a branch of technology that utilizes management, financial, and engineering expertise in the installation and efficient operation and maintenance of equipment and machinery.
▷HISTORY C20: from Greek *tērein* to care for + TECHNOLOGY

terpene ('tɜːpiːn) NOUN any one of a class of unsaturated hydrocarbons, such as the carotenes, that are found in the essential oils of many plants. Their molecules contain isoprene units and have the general formula $(C_5H_8)_n$.
▷HISTORY C19: *terp-* from obsolete *terpentine* TURPENTINE + -ENE
▸ **ter'penic** ADJECTIVE

terpineol (tɜː'pɪnɪˌɒl) NOUN a terpene alcohol with an odour of lilac, present in several essential oils. It is used as a solvent and in flavourings and perfumes. Formula: $C_{10}H_{17}OH$.
▷HISTORY C20: from TERPENE + -INE[2] + -OL[1]

Terpsichore (tɜːp'sɪkərɪ) NOUN the Muse of the dance and of choral song.
▷HISTORY C18: via Latin from Greek, from *terpsikhoros* delighting in the dance, from *terpein* to delight + *khoros* dance; see CHORUS

Terpsichorean (ˌtɜːpsɪkə'riːən, -'kɔːrɪən) *Often used facetiously* ◆ ADJECTIVE *also* **Terpsichoreal.** [1] of or relating to dancing or the art of dancing. ◆ NOUN 2 a dancer.

terr. ABBREVIATION FOR: 1 terrace. 2 territory.

terra ('tɛrə) NOUN (in legal contexts) earth or land.
▷HISTORY from Latin

terra alba ('ælbə) NOUN 1 a white finely powdered form of gypsum, used to make paints, paper, etc. 2 any of various other white earthy substances, such as kaolin, pipeclay, and magnesia.
▷HISTORY from Latin, literally: white earth

terrace ('tɛrəs) NOUN 1 a horizontal flat area of ground, often one of a series in a slope. 2 **a** a row of houses, usually identical and having common dividing walls, or the street onto which they face. **b** (*cap when part of a street name*): *Grosvenor Terrace.* 3 a paved area alongside a building, serving partly as a garden. 4 a balcony or patio. 5 the flat roof of a house built in a Spanish or Oriental style. 6 a flat area bounded by a short steep slope formed by the down-cutting of a river or by erosion. 7 (*usually plural*) **a** unroofed tiers around a football pitch on which the spectators stand. **b** the spectators themselves. ◆ VERB 8 (*tr*) to make into or provide with a terrace or terraces.
▷HISTORY C16: from Old French *terrasse,* from Old Provençal *terrassa* pile of earth, from *terra* earth, from Latin
► **'terraceless** ADJECTIVE

terraced house NOUN *Brit* a house that is part of a terrace. US and Canadian names: **row house, town house.**
► **terraced housing** NOUN

terracing ('tɛrəsɪŋ) NOUN 1 a series of terraces, esp one dividing a slope into a steplike system of flat narrow fields. 2 the act of making a terrace or terraces. 3 another name for **terrace** (sense 7a).

terracotta (ˌtɛrə'kɒtə) NOUN 1 a hard unglazed brownish-red earthenware, or the clay from which it is made. 2 something made of terracotta, such as a sculpture. 3 a strong reddish-brown to brownish-orange colour. ◆ ADJECTIVE 4 made of terracotta: *a terracotta urn.* 5 of the colour terracotta: *a terracotta carpet.*
▷HISTORY C18: from Italian, literally: baked earth

terra firma ('fɜːmə) NOUN the solid earth; firm ground.
▷HISTORY C17: from Latin

terrain (tə'reɪn, 'tɛreɪn) NOUN 1 ground or a piece of ground, esp with reference to its physical character or military potential: *radio reception can be difficult in mountainous terrain; a rocky terrain.* 2 a variant spelling of **terrane.**
▷HISTORY C18: from French, ultimately from Latin *terrēnum* ground, from *terra* earth

terra incognita *Latin* ('tɛrə ɪn'kɒgnɪtə) NOUN an unexplored or unknown land, region, or area for study.

Terramycin (ˌtɛrə'maɪsɪn) NOUN *Trademark* a broad-spectrum antibiotic, oxytetracycline, used in treating various infections.

terrane *or* **terrain** ('tɛreɪn) NOUN 1 a series of rock formations, esp one having a prevalent type of rock. 2 an allocthonous, fault-bounded section of the earth's crust.
▷HISTORY C19: see TERRAIN

terrapin ('tɛrəpɪn) NOUN any of various web-footed chelonian reptiles that live on land and in fresh water and feed on small aquatic animals: family *Emydidae.* Also called: **water tortoise.**
▷HISTORY C17: of Algonquian origin; compare Delaware *torope* turtle

terrarium (tɛ'rɛərɪəm) NOUN, *plural* **-rariums** *or* **-raria** (-'rɛərɪə). 1 an enclosure for keeping small land animals. 2 a glass container, often a globe, in which plants are grown.
▷HISTORY C19: New Latin, from Latin *terra* earth

terra sigillata ('tɛrə ˌsɪdʒɪ'lɑːtə) NOUN 1 *Rare* a reddish-brown clayey earth found on the Aegean island of Lemnos: formerly used as an astringent and in the making of earthenware pottery. 2 any similar earth resembling this. 3 earthenware pottery made from this or a similar earth, esp Samian ware.
▷HISTORY from Latin: sealed earth

terrazzo (tɛ'rætsəʊ) NOUN a floor or wall finish made by setting marble or other stone chips into a layer of mortar and polishing the surface.
▷HISTORY C20: from Italian: TERRACE

Terre Adélie (*French* tɛr adeli) NOUN the French name for **Adélie Land.**

terrene (tɛ'riːn) ADJECTIVE 1 of or relating to the earth; worldly; mundane. 2 *Rare* of earth; earthy. ◆ NOUN 3 a land. 4 a rare word for **earth.**
▷HISTORY C14: from Anglo-Norman, from Latin *terrēnus,* from *terra* earth
► **ter'renely** ADVERB

terreplein ('tɛəˌpleɪn) NOUN 1 the top of a rampart where guns are placed behind the parapet. 2 an embankment with a level top surface.
▷HISTORY C16: from French, from Medieval Latin phrase *terrā plēnus* filled with earth

terrestrial (tə'rɛstrɪəl) ADJECTIVE 1 of or relating to the earth. 2 of or belonging to the land as opposed to the sea or air. 3 (of animals and plants) living or growing on the land. 4 earthly, worldly, or mundane. 5 (of television signals) sent over the earth's surface from a transmitter on land, rather than by satellite. ◆ NOUN 6 an inhabitant of the earth.
▷HISTORY C15: from Latin *terrestris,* from *terra* earth
► **ter'restrially** ADVERB ► **ter'restrialness** NOUN

terrestrial guidance NOUN a method of missile or rocket guidance in which the flight path is controlled by reference to the strength and direction of the earth's gravitational or magnetic field. Compare **inertial guidance.**

terrestrial telescope NOUN a telescope for use on earth rather than for making astronomical observations. Such telescopes contain an additional lens or prism system to produce an erect image. Compare **astronomical telescope.**

terret ('tɛrɪt) NOUN 1 either of the two metal rings on a harness saddle through which the reins are passed. 2 the ring on a dog's collar for attaching the lead.
▷HISTORY C15: variant of *toret,* from Old French, diminutive of *tor* loop; see TOUR

terre-verte ('tɛəˌvɜːt) NOUN 1 a greyish-green pigment used in paints, consisting of powdered glauconite. ◆ ADJECTIVE 2 of a greyish-green colour.
▷HISTORY C17: from French, literally: green earth

terrible ('tɛrəbᵊl) ADJECTIVE 1 very serious or extreme: *a terrible cough.* 2 *Informal* of poor quality; unpleasant or bad: *a terrible meal; a terrible play.* 3 causing terror. 4 causing awe: *the terrible nature of God.*
▷HISTORY C15: from Latin *terribilis,* from *terrēre* to terrify
► **'terribleness** NOUN

terribly ('tɛrəblɪ) ADVERB 1 in a terrible manner. 2 (intensifier): *you're terribly kind.*

terricolous (tɛ'rɪkələs) ADJECTIVE living on or in the soil.
▷HISTORY C19: from Latin *terricola,* from *terra* earth + *colere* to inhabit

terrier[1] ('tɛrɪə) NOUN any of several usually small, active, and short-bodied breeds of dog, originally trained to hunt animals living underground.
▷HISTORY C15: from Old French *chien terrier* earth dog, from Medieval Latin *terrārius* belonging to the earth, from Latin *terra* earth

terrier[2] ('tɛrɪə) NOUN *English legal history* a register or survey of land.
▷HISTORY C15: from Old French, from Medieval Latin *terrārius* of the land, from Latin *terra* land

Terrier ('tɛrɪə) NOUN *Informal* a member of the British Army's Territorial and Volunteer Reserve.

terrific (tə'rɪfɪk) ADJECTIVE 1 very great or intense: *a terrific noise.* 2 *Informal* very good; excellent: *a terrific singer.* 3 very frightening.
▷HISTORY C17: from Latin *terrificus,* from *terrēre* to frighten; see -FIC
► **ter'rifically** ADVERB

terrify ('tɛrɪˌfaɪ) VERB **-fies, -fying, -fied.** (*tr*) to inspire fear or dread in; frighten greatly.
▷HISTORY C16: from Latin *terrificāre,* from *terrēre* to alarm + *facere* to cause
► **'terriˌfier** NOUN

terrifying ('tɛrɪˌfaɪɪŋ) ADJECTIVE causing great fear or dread; extremely frightening.
► **'terriˌfyingly** ADVERB

terrigenous (tɛ'rɪdʒɪnəs) ADJECTIVE 1 of or produced by the earth. 2 (of geological deposits) formed in the sea from material derived from the land by erosion.
▷HISTORY C17: from Latin *terrigenus,* from *terra* earth + *gignere* to beget

terrine (tɛ'riːn) NOUN 1 an oval earthenware cooking dish with a tightly fitting lid used for pâtés, etc. 2 the food cooked or served in such a dish, esp pâté. 3 another word for **tureen.**
▷HISTORY C18: earlier form of TUREEN

territorial (ˌtɛrɪ'tɔːrɪəl) ADJECTIVE 1 of or relating to a territory or territories. 2 restricted to or owned by a particular territory: *the Indian territorial waters.* 3 local or regional. 4 pertaining to a territorial army, providing a reserve of trained men for use in emergency.
► **ˌterri'torially** ADVERB

Territorial (ˌtɛrɪ'tɔːrɪəl) NOUN a member of a territorial army, esp the British Army's Territorial and Volunteer Reserve.

Territorial Army NOUN (in Britain) a standing reserve army originally organized between 1907 and 1908. Full name: **Territorial and Volunteer Reserve.**

territorialism (ˌtɛrɪ'tɔːrɪəlɪzəm) NOUN 1 a social system under which the predominant force in the state is the landed class. 2 a former Protestant theory that the civil government has the right to determine the religious beliefs of the subjects of a state.
► **ˌterri'torialist** NOUN

territoriality (ˌtɛrɪˌtɔːrɪ'ælɪtɪ) NOUN 1 the state or rank of being a territory. 2 the behaviour shown by an animal when establishing and defending its territory.

territorialize *or* **territorialise** (ˌtɛrɪ'tɔːrɪəˌlaɪz) VERB (*tr*) 1 to make a territory of. 2 to place on a territorial basis: *the militia was territorialized.* 3 to enlarge (a country) by acquiring more territory. 4 to make territorial.
► **ˌterriˌtoriali'zation** *or* **ˌterriˌtoriali'sation** NOUN

territorial waters PLURAL NOUN the waters over which a nation exercises jurisdiction and control.

Territorian (ˌtɛrɪ'tɔːrɪən) NOUN *Austral* an inhabitant of the Northern Territory.

territory ('tɛrɪtərɪ, -trɪ) NOUN, *plural* **-ries.** 1 any tract of land; district. 2 the geographical domain under the jurisdiction of a political unit, esp of a sovereign state. 3 the district for which an agent, etc., is responsible: *a salesman's territory.* 4 an area inhabited and defended by an individual animal or a breeding group of animals. 5 an area of knowledge: *science isn't my territory.* 6 (in football, hockey, etc.) the area defended by a team. 7 (*often capital*) a region of a country, esp of a federal state, that enjoys less autonomy and a lower status than most constituent parts of the state. 8 (*often capital*) a protectorate or other dependency of a country.
▷HISTORY C15: from Latin *territōrium* land surrounding a town, from *terra* land

Territory ('tɛrɪtərɪ, -trɪ) NOUN **the.** *Austral* See **Northern Territory.**

terroir *French* (tɛrwar) NOUN *Winemaking* the combination of factors, including soil, climate, and environment, that gives a wine its distinctive character.
▷HISTORY literally: soil

terror ('tɛrə) NOUN 1 great fear, panic, or dread. 2 a person or thing that inspires great dread. 3 *Informal* a troublesome person or thing, esp a child. 4 terrorism.
▷HISTORY C14: from Old French *terreur,* from Latin *terror,* from *terrēre* to frighten; related to Greek *trein* to run away in terror
► **'terrorful** ADJECTIVE ► **'terrorless** ADJECTIVE

terrorism ('tɛrəˌrɪzəm) NOUN 1 systematic use of violence and intimidation to achieve some goal. 2 the act of terrorizing. 3 the state of being terrorized.

terrorist ('tɛrərɪst) NOUN **a** a person who employs terror or terrorism, esp as a political weapon. **b** (*as modifier*): *terrorist tactics.*
► **ˌterror'istic** ADJECTIVE

terrorize *or* **terrorise** ('tɛrəˌraɪz) VERB (*tr*) 1 to coerce or control by violence, fear, threats, etc. 2 to inspire with dread; terrify.
► **ˌterrori'zation** *or* **ˌterrori'sation** NOUN ► **'terrorˌizer** *or* **'terrorˌiser** NOUN

terror-stricken *or* **terror-struck** ADJECTIVE in a state of terror.

terry ('tɛrɪ) NOUN, *plural* **-ries.** [1] an uncut loop in the pile of towelling or a similar fabric. [2] **a** a fabric with such a pile on both sides. **b** (*as modifier*): *a terry towel.*
▷HISTORY C18: perhaps variant of TERRET

terse (tɜːs) ADJECTIVE [1] neatly brief and concise. [2] curt; abrupt.
▷HISTORY C17: from Latin *tersus* precise, from *tergēre* to polish
▸'**tersely** ADVERB ▸'**terseness** NOUN

tertial ('tɜːʃəl) ADJECTIVE, NOUN another word for **tertiary** (senses 5, 6).
▷HISTORY C19: from Latin *tertius* third, from *ter* thrice, from *trēs* three

tertian ('tɜːʃən) ADJECTIVE [1] (of a fever or the symptoms of a disease, esp malaria) occurring every other day. ◆ NOUN [2] a tertian fever or symptoms.
▷HISTORY C14: from Latin *febris tertiāna* fever occurring every third day, reckoned inclusively, from *tertius* third

tertiary ('tɜːʃərɪ) ADJECTIVE [1] third in degree, order, etc. [2] (of education) taking place after secondary school, such as at university, college, etc. [3] (of an industry) involving services as opposed to extraction or manufacture, such as transport, finance, etc. Compare **primary** (sense 8b), **secondary** (sense 7). [4] *RC Church* of or relating to a Third Order. [5] *Chem* **a** (of an organic compound) having a functional group attached to a carbon atom that is attached to three other groups. **b** (of an amine) having three organic groups attached to a nitrogen atom. **c** (of a salt) derived from a tribasic acid by replacement of all its acidic hydrogen atoms with metal atoms or electropositive groups. [6] Also: **tertial.** *Ornithol, rare* of, relating to, or designating any of the small flight feathers attached to the part of the humerus nearest to the body. ◆ NOUN, *plural* **-tiaries.** [7] Also called: **tertial.** *Ornithol, rare* any of the tertiary feathers. [8] *RC Church* a member of a Third Order.
▷HISTORY C16: from Latin *tertiārius* containing one third, from *tertius* third

Tertiary ('tɜːʃərɪ) ADJECTIVE [1] of, denoting, or formed in the first period of the Cenozoic era, which lasted for 63 million years, during which mammals became dominant. ◆ NOUN [2] **the.** the Tertiary period or rock system, divided into Palaeocene, Eocene, Oligocene, Miocene, and Pliocene epochs or series.

tertiary bursary NOUN *NZ* a noncompetitive award granted to all pupils who have passed a university entrance examination.

tertiary college NOUN *Brit* a college system incorporating the secondary school sixth form and vocational courses.

tertiary colour NOUN a colour formed by mixing two secondary colours.

tertium quid ('tɜːtɪəm 'kwɪd) NOUN an unknown or indefinite thing related in some way to two known or definite things, but distinct from both: *there is either right or wrong, with no tertium quid.*
▷HISTORY C18: from Late Latin, rendering Greek *triton ti* some third thing

Teruel (*Spanish* te'rwel) NOUN a city in E central Spain: 15th-century cathedral; scene of fierce fighting during the Spanish Civil War. Pop.: 31 000 (1991).

tervalent (tɜː'veɪlənt) ADJECTIVE *Chem* another word for **trivalent.**
▸**ter'valency** NOUN

Terylene ('tɛrɪˌliːn) NOUN *Trademark* a synthetic polyester fibre or fabric based on terephthalic acid, characterized by lightness and crease resistance and used for clothing, sheets, ropes, sails, etc. US name (trademark): **Dacron.**

terza rima ('tɛətsə 'riːmə) NOUN, *plural* **terze rime** ('tɛətseɪ 'riːmeɪ). a verse form of Italian origin consisting of a series of tercets in which the middle line of one tercet rhymes with the first and third lines of the next.
▷HISTORY C19: from Italian, literally: third rhyme

terzetto (tɜː'tsɛtəʊ) NOUN, *plural* **-tos** *or* **-ti** (-tɪ). *Music* a trio, esp a vocal one.
▷HISTORY C18: Italian: trio; see TERCET

TES ABBREVIATION FOR Times Educational Supplement.

TE score (in Australia) ABBREVIATION FOR Tertiary Entrance score: a score based on a pupil's performance in secondary school that determines his or her prospects of gaining entrance to tertiary educational institutions.

TESL ('tɛsᵊl) ACRONYM FOR Teaching (of) English as a Second Language.

tesla ('tɛslə) NOUN the derived SI unit of magnetic flux density equal to a flux of 1 weber in an area of 1 square metre. Symbol: T.
▷HISTORY C20: named after Nikola *Tesla* (1857–1943), Croatian-born US electrical engineer and inventor

tesla coil NOUN a step-up transformer with an air core, used for producing high voltages at high frequencies. The secondary circuit is tuned to resonate with the primary winding.
▷HISTORY C20: named after Nikola *Tesla* (1857–1943), Croatian-born US electrical engineer and inventor

TESSA ('tɛsə) NOUN (in Britain) ◆ ACRONYM FOR Tax Exempt Special Savings Account; a former (available 1991–99) tax-free savings scheme.

tessellate ('tɛsɪˌleɪt) VERB [1] (*tr*) to construct, pave, or inlay with a mosaic of small tiles. [2] (*intr*) (of identical shapes) to fit together exactly: *triangles will tessellate but octagons will not.*
▷HISTORY C18: from Latin *tessellātus* checked, from *tessella* small stone cube, from TESSERA

tessellation (ˌtɛsɪ'leɪʃən) NOUN [1] the act of tessellating. [2] the form or a specimen of tessellated work.

tessera ('tɛsərə) NOUN, *plural* **-serae** (-səˌriː). [1] a small square tile of stone, glass, etc., used in mosaics. [2] a die, tally, etc., used in classical times, made of bone or wood.
▷HISTORY C17: from Latin, from Ionic Greek *tesseres* four
▸'**tesseral** ADJECTIVE

Tessin (tɛ'siːn) NOUN the German name for **Ticino.**

tessitura (ˌtɛsɪ'tʊərə) NOUN *Music* [1] the general pitch level of a piece of vocal music: *an uncomfortably high tessitura.* [2] the compass or range of a voice.
▷HISTORY Italian: texture, from Latin *textura;* see TEXTURE

test¹ (tɛst) VERB [1] to ascertain (the worth, capability, or endurance) of (a person or thing) by subjection to certain examinations; try. [2] (often foll by *for*) to carry out an examination on (a substance, material, or system) by applying some chemical or physical procedure designed to indicate the presence of a substance or the possession of a property: *to test food for arsenic; to test for magnetization.* [3] (*intr*) to achieve a specified result in a test: *a quarter of the patients at the clinic tested positive for the AIDS virus.* [4] (*tr*) to put under severe strain: *the long delay tested my patience.* [5] **test the water.** to make an exploratory or initial approach; sound out. ◆ NOUN [6] a method, practice, or examination designed to test a person or thing. [7] a series of questions or problems designed to test a specific skill or knowledge: *an intelligence test.* [8] a standard of judgment; criterion. [9] **a** a chemical reaction or physical procedure for testing a substance, material, etc. **b** a chemical reagent used in such a procedure: *litmus is a test for acids.* **c** the result of the procedure or the evidence gained from it: *the test for alcohol was positive.* [10] *Sport* See **test match.** [11] *Archaic* a declaration or confirmation of truth, loyalty, etc.; oath. [12] (*modifier*) performed as a test: *test drive; test flight.*
▷HISTORY C14 (in the sense: vessel used in treating metals): from Latin *testum* earthen vessel
▸'**testable** ADJECTIVE ▸ˌ**testa'bility** NOUN ▸'**testing** ADJECTIVE

test² (tɛst) NOUN [1] the hard or tough outer covering of certain invertebrates and tunicates. [2] a variant of **testa.**
▷HISTORY C19: from Latin *testa* shell

testa ('tɛstə) NOUN, *plural* **-tae** (-tiː). a hard protective outer layer of the seeds of flowering plants; seed coat.
▷HISTORY C18: from Latin: shell; see TEST²

testaceous (tɛ'steɪʃəs) ADJECTIVE *Biology* [1] of, relating to, or possessing a test or testa. [2] of the reddish-brown colour of terra cotta.
▷HISTORY C17: from Latin *testācens,* from TESTA

Test Act NOUN a law passed in 1673 in England to exclude Catholics from public life by requiring all persons holding offices under the Crown, such as army officers, to take the Anglican Communion and perform other acts forbidden to a Catholic: repealed in 1828.

testament ('tɛstəmənt) NOUN [1] *Law* a will setting out the disposition of personal property (esp in the phrase **last will and testament**). [2] a proof, attestation, or tribute: *his success was a testament to his skills.* [3] **a** a covenant instituted between God and man, esp the covenant of Moses or that instituted by Christ. **b** a copy of either the Old or the New Testament, or of the complete Bible.
▷HISTORY C14: from Latin: a will, from *testārī* to bear witness, from *testis* a witness
▸ˌ**testa'mental** ADJECTIVE

Testament ('tɛstəmənt) NOUN [1] either of the two main parts of the Bible; the Old Testament or the New Testament. [2] the New Testament as distinct from the Old.

testamentary (ˌtɛstə'mɛntərɪ) ADJECTIVE [1] of or relating to a will or testament. [2] derived from, bequeathed, or appointed by a will. [3] contained or set forth in a will.

testate ('tɛsteɪt, 'tɛstɪt) ADJECTIVE [1] having left a legally valid will at death. ◆ NOUN [2] a person who dies testate. ◆ Compare **intestate.**
▷HISTORY C15: from Latin *testārī* to make a will; see TESTAMENT
▸**testacy** ('tɛstəsɪ) NOUN

testator (tɛ'steɪtə) *or feminine* **testatrix** (tɛ'steɪtrɪks) NOUN a person who makes a will, esp one who dies testate.
▷HISTORY C15: from Anglo-French *testatour,* from Late Latin *testātor,* from Latin *testārī* to make a will; see TESTAMENT

test ban NOUN an agreement among nations to forgo tests of some or all types of nuclear weapons.

test-bed NOUN *Engineering* an area equipped with instruments, etc., used for testing machinery, engines, etc., under working conditions.

test card *or* **pattern** NOUN a complex pattern used to test the characteristics of a television transmission system.

test case NOUN a legal action that serves as a precedent in deciding similar succeeding cases.

test-drive VERB (*tr*) **-drives, -driving, -drove, -driven** to drive (a car or other motor vehicle) for a limited period in order to assess its capabilities and limitations.

tester¹ ('tɛstə) NOUN a person or thing that tests or is used for testing.

tester² ('tɛstə) NOUN (in furniture) a canopy, esp the canopy over a four-poster bed.
▷HISTORY C14: from Medieval Latin *testerium,* from Late Latin *testa* a skull, from Latin: shell

tester³ ('tɛstə) NOUN another name for **teston** (sense 2).

testes ('tɛstiːz) NOUN the plural of **testis.**

testicle ('tɛstɪkᵊl) NOUN either of the two male reproductive glands, in most mammals enclosed within the scrotum, that produce spermatozoa and the hormone testosterone. Also called: **testis.**
▷HISTORY C15: from Latin *testiculus,* diminutive of *testis* testicle
▸**testicular** (tɛ'stɪkjʊlə) ADJECTIVE

testiculate (tɛ'stɪkjʊlɪt) ADJECTIVE *Botany* shaped like testicles: *the testiculate tubers of certain orchids.*
▷HISTORY C18: from Late Latin *testiculātus;* see TESTICLE

testify ('tɛstɪˌfaɪ) VERB **-fies, -fying, -fied.** [1] (when *tr, may take a clause as object*) to state (something) formally as a declaration of fact: *I testify that I know nothing about him.* [2] *Law* to declare or give (evidence) under oath, esp in court. [3] (when *intr,* often foll by *to*) to be evidence (of); serve as witness (to): *the money testified to his good faith.* [4] (*tr*) to declare or acknowledge openly.
▷HISTORY C14: from Latin *testificārī,* from *testis* witness
▸ˌ**testifi'cation** NOUN ▸'**testiˌfier** NOUN

testimonial (ˌtɛstɪ'məʊnɪəl) NOUN [1] **a** a recommendation of the character, ability, etc., of a person or of the quality of a consumer product or service, esp by a person whose opinion is valued. **b** (*as modifier*): *testimonial advertising*. 2 a formal statement of truth or fact. 3 a tribute given for services or achievements. 4 a sports match to raise money for a particular player. ◆ ADJECTIVE 5 of or relating to a testimony or testimonial.

> **Language note** *Testimonial* is sometimes wrongly used where *testimony* is meant: *his re-election is a testimony* (not *a testimonial*) *to his popularity with his constituents.*

testimony ('tɛstɪmənɪ) NOUN, *plural* **-nies**. 1 a declaration of truth or fact. 2 *Law* evidence given by a witness, esp orally in court under oath or affirmation. 3 evidence testifying to something: *her success was a testimony to her good luck.* 4 *Old Testament* **a** the Ten Commandments, as inscribed on the two stone tables. **b** the Ark of the Covenant as the receptacle of these (Exodus 25:16; 16:34).
▷ **HISTORY** C15: from Latin *testimōnium*, from *testis* witness

testing station NOUN *NZ* an establishment licensed to issue warrants of fitness for motor vehicles.

testis ('tɛstɪs) NOUN, *plural* **-tes** (-tiːz). another word for **testicle.**
▷ **HISTORY** C17: from Latin, literally: witness (to masculinity)

test marketing NOUN the use of a representative segment of a total market for experimental purposes, as to test a new product about to be launched or a price change.

test match NOUN (in various sports, esp cricket) an international match, esp one of a series.

teston ('tɛstən) *or* **testoon** (tɛ'stuːn) NOUN 1 a French silver coin of the 16th century. 2 Also called: **tester.** an English silver coin of the 16th century, originally worth one shilling, bearing the head of Henry VIII.
▷ **HISTORY** C16: from Italian *testone*, from *testa* head, from Late Latin: skull, from Latin: shell

testosterone (tɛ'stɒstəˌrəʊn) NOUN a potent steroid hormone secreted mainly by the testes. It can be extracted from the testes of animals or synthesized and used to treat androgen deficiency or promote anabolism. Formula: $C_{19}H_{28}O_2$.
▷ **HISTORY** C20: from TESTIS + STEROL + -ONE

test paper NOUN 1 *Chem* paper impregnated with an indicator for use in chemical tests. See also **litmus.** 2 *Brit education* **a** the question sheet of a test. **b** the paper completed by a test candidate.

test pilot NOUN a pilot who flies aircraft of new design to test their performance in the air.

test tube NOUN 1 a cylindrical round-bottomed glass tube open at one end: used in scientific experiments. 2 (*modifier*) made synthetically in, or as if in, a test tube: *a test-tube product.*

test-tube baby NOUN 1 a fetus that has developed from an ovum fertilized in an artificial womb. 2 a baby conceived by artificial insemination.

testudinal (tɛ'stjuːdɪnᵊl) *or* **testudinary** ADJECTIVE of, relating to, or resembling a tortoise or turtle or the shell of either of these animals.
▷ **HISTORY** C19: from Latin TESTUDO

testudo (tɛ'stjuːdəʊ) NOUN, *plural* **-dines** (-dɪˌniːz). a form of shelter used by the ancient Roman Army for protection against attack from above, consisting either of a mobile arched structure or of overlapping shields held by the soldiers over their heads.
▷ **HISTORY** C17: from Latin: a tortoise, from *testa* a shell

testy ('tɛstɪ) ADJECTIVE **-tier, -tiest**. irritable or touchy.
▷ **HISTORY** C14: from Anglo-Norman *testif* headstrong, from Old French *teste* head, from Late Latin *testa* skull, from Latin: shell
▸ **'testily** ADVERB ▸ **'testiness** NOUN

Tet (tɛt) NOUN the New Year as celebrated in Vietnam during the first seven days of the first lunar month of the year.
▷ **HISTORY** Vietnamese

tetanic (tə'tænɪk) ADJECTIVE 1 of, relating to, or producing tetanus or the spasms of tetanus. ◆ NOUN 2 a tetanic drug or agent.
▸ **te'tanically** ADVERB

tetanize *or* **tetanise** ('tɛtəˌnaɪz) VERB (*tr*) to induce tetanus in (a muscle); affect (a muscle) with tetanic spasms.
▸ **ˌtetani'zation** *or* **ˌtetani'sation** NOUN

tetanus ('tɛtənəs) NOUN 1 Also called: **lockjaw.** an acute infectious disease in which sustained muscular spasm, contraction, and convulsion are caused by the release of exotoxins from the bacterium, *Clostridium tetani*: infection usually occurs through a contaminated wound. 2 *Physiol* any tense contraction of a muscle, esp when produced by electric shocks.
▷ **HISTORY** C16: via Latin from Greek *tetanos*, from *tetanos* taut, from *teinein* to stretch
▸ **'tetanal** ADJECTIVE ▸ **'tetaˌnoid** ADJECTIVE

tetany ('tɛtənɪ) NOUN *Pathol* an abnormal increase in the excitability of nerves and muscles resulting in spasms of the arms and legs, caused by a deficiency of parathyroid secretion.
▷ **HISTORY** C19: from French *tétanie*. See TETANUS

tetartohedral (tɪˌtɑːtəʊ'hiːdrəl) ADJECTIVE (of a crystal) having one quarter of the number of faces necessary for the full symmetry of its crystal system.
▷ **HISTORY** C19: from Greek *tetartos* one fourth + -HEDRAL
▸ **teˌtarto'hedrally** ADVERB ▸ **teˌtarto'hedralism** *or* **teˌtarto'hedrism** NOUN

tetchy ('tɛtʃɪ) ADJECTIVE **tetchier, tetchiest**. being or inclined to be cross, irritable, or touchy.
▷ **HISTORY** C16: probably from obsolete *tetch* defect, from Old French *tache* spot, of Germanic origin
▸ **'tetchily** ADVERB ▸ **'tetchiness** NOUN

tête-à-tête (ˌteɪtə'teɪt) NOUN, *plural* **-têtes** *or* **-tête**. 1 **a** a private conversation between two people. **b** (*as modifier*): *a tête-à-tête conversation.* 2 a small sofa for two people, esp one that is S-shaped in plan so that the sitters are almost face to face. ◆ ADVERB 3 intimately; in private.
▷ **HISTORY** C17: from French, literally: head to head

tête-bêche (tɛt'bɛʃ) ADJECTIVE *Philately* (of an unseparated pair of stamps) printed so that one is inverted in relation to the other.
▷ **HISTORY** C19: from French, from *tête* head + *bêche*, from obsolete *béchevet* double-headed (originally of a bed)

teth (tɛs; *Hebrew* tet) NOUN the ninth letter of the Hebrew alphabet (ט) transliterated as *t* and pronounced more or less like English *t* with pharyngeal articulation.

tether ('tɛðə) NOUN 1 a restricting rope, chain, etc., by which an animal is tied to a particular spot. 2 the range of one's endurance, etc. 3 **at the end of one's tether.** distressed or exasperated to the limit of one's endurance. ◆ VERB (*tr*) 4 to tie or limit with or as if with a tether.
▷ **HISTORY** C14: from Old Norse *tjothr*; related to Middle Dutch *tūder* tether, Old High German *zeotar* pole of a wagon

Tethys¹ ('tiːθɪs, 'tɛθ-) NOUN *Greek myth* a Titaness and sea goddess, wife of Oceanus.

Tethys² ('tiːθɪs, 'tɛθ-) NOUN a large satellite of the planet Saturn.

Tethys³ ('tiːθɪs, 'tɛθ-) NOUN the sea that lay between Laurasia and Gondwanaland, the two supercontinents formed by the first split of the larger supercontinent Pangaea. The Tethys Sea can be regarded as the predecessor of today's smaller Mediterranean. See also **Pangaea.**

Teton Range ('tiːtᵊn) NOUN a mountain range in the N central US, mainly in NW Wyoming. Highest peak: Grand Teton, 4196 m (13 766 ft.).

tetra ('tɛtrə) NOUN, *plural* **-ra** *or* **-ras.** any of various brightly coloured tropical freshwater fishes of the genus *Hemigrammus* and related genera: family *Characidae* (characins).
▷ **HISTORY** C20: short for New Latin *tetragonopterus* (former genus name), from TETRAGON + -O- + *-pterous*, from Greek *pteron* wing

tetra- *or before a vowel* **tetr-** COMBINING FORM four: *tetrameter.*
▷ **HISTORY** from Greek

tetrabasic (ˌtɛtrə'beɪsɪk) ADJECTIVE (of an acid) containing four replaceable hydrogen atoms.
▸ **tetrabasicity** (ˌtɛtrəbeɪ'sɪsɪtɪ) NOUN

tetrabrach ('tɛtrəˌbræk) NOUN (in classical prosody) a word or metrical foot composed of four short syllables (⏑⏑⏑⏑).
▷ **HISTORY** C19: from Greek *tetrabrakhus*, from TETRA- + *brakhus* short

tetrabranchiate ADJECTIVE (ˌtɛtrə'bræŋkɪɪt, -ˌeɪt) 1 of, relating to, or belonging to the *Tetrabranchiata*, a former order of cephalopod molluscs having four gills and including the pearly nautilus. ◆ NOUN (ˌtɛtrə'bræŋkɪˌeɪt) 2 any mollusc belonging to the *Tetrabranchiata.*

tetrachloride (ˌtɛtrə'klɔːraɪd) NOUN any compound that contains four chlorine atoms per molecule: *carbon tetrachloride*, CCl_4.

tetrachloromethane ('tɛtrəklɔːrəʊˌmiːθeɪn) NOUN the systematic name for **carbon tetrachloride.**

tetrachord ('tɛtrəˌkɔːd) NOUN (in musical theory, esp of classical Greece) any of several groups of four notes in descending order, in which the first and last notes form a perfect fourth.
▷ **HISTORY** C17: from Greek *tetrakhordos* four-stringed, from TETRA- + *khordē* a string
▸ **ˌtetra'chordal** ADJECTIVE

tetracid (tɛ'træsɪd) ADJECTIVE (of a base) capable of reacting with four molecules of a monobasic acid.

tetracyclic (ˌtɛtrə'saɪklɪk) ADJECTIVE *Chem* (of a compound) containing four rings in its molecular structure.

tetracycline (ˌtɛtrə'saɪklaɪn, -klɪn) NOUN an antibiotic synthesized from chlortetracycline or derived from the bacterium *Streptomyces viridifaciens:* used in treating rickettsial infections and various bacterial infections. Formula: $C_{22}H_{24}N_2O_8$.
▷ **HISTORY** C20: from TETRA- + CYCL(IC) + -INE²

tetrad ('tɛtræd) NOUN 1 a group or series of four. 2 the number four. 3 *Botany* a group of four cells formed by meiosis from one diploid cell. 4 *Genetics* a four-stranded structure, formed during the pachytene stage of meiosis, consisting of paired homologous chromosomes that have each divided into two chromatids. 5 *Chem* an element, atom, group, or ion with a valency of four. 6 *Ecology* a square of 2 × 2 km used in distribution mapping.
▷ **HISTORY** C17: from Greek *tetras*, from *tettares* four

tetradactyl (ˌtɛtrə'dæktɪl) NOUN 1 a four-toed animal. ◆ ADJECTIVE *also* **ˌtetra'dactylous.** 2 having four toes or fingers.
▷ **HISTORY** C19: from Greek *tetradaktulos*, from TETRA- + *dactulos* finger

tetradymite (tɛ'trædɪˌmaɪt) NOUN a grey metallic mineral consisting of a telluride and sulphide of bismuth. Formula: Bi_2Te_2S.
▷ **HISTORY** C19: from Late Greek *tetradumos* fourfold, from Greek TETRA- + *didumos* double

tetradynamous (ˌtɛtrə'daɪnəməs, -'dɪn-) ADJECTIVE (of plants) having six stamens, two of which are shorter than the others.
▷ **HISTORY** C19: from TETRA- + Greek *dunamis* power

tetraethyl lead (ˌtɛtrə'iːθaɪl lɛd) NOUN a colourless oily insoluble liquid used in petrol to prevent knocking. Formula: $Pb(C_2H_5)_4$. Systematic name: **lead tetraethyl.**

tetrafluoroethene ('tɛtrəˌfluərəʊ'ɛθiːn) NOUN *Chem* a dense colourless gas that is polymerized to make polytetrafluorethene (PTFE). Formula: $F_2C{:}CF_2$. Also called: **tetrafluoroethylene.**
▷ **HISTORY** C20: from TETRA- + FLUORO- + ETHENE

tetragon ('tɛtrəˌgɒn) NOUN a less common name for **quadrilateral** (sense 2).
▷ **HISTORY** C17: from Greek *tetragōnon*; see TETRA-, -GON

tetragonal (tɛ'trægənᵊl) ADJECTIVE 1 Also: **dimetric.** *Crystallog* relating or belonging to the crystal system characterized by three mutually perpendicular axes of which only two are equal. 2 of, relating to, or shaped like a quadrilateral.
▸ **te'tragonally** ADVERB ▸ **te'tragonalness** NOUN

tetragram ('tɛtrəˌgræm) NOUN any word of four letters.

Tetragrammaton (ˌtɛtrə'græmətᵊn) NOUN *Bible* the Hebrew name for God revealed to Moses on Mount Sinai (Exodus 3), consisting of the four consonants Y H V H (or Y H W H) and regarded by Jews as too sacred to be pronounced. It is usually transliterated as *Jehovah* or *Yahweh*. Sometimes shortened to: **Tetragram.**

▷HISTORY C14: from Greek, from *tetragrammatos* having four letters, from TETRA- + *gramma* letter

tetrahedrite (ˌtɛtrəˈhiːdraɪt) NOUN a grey metallic mineral consisting of a sulphide of copper, iron, and antimony, often in the form of tetrahedral crystals: it is a source of copper. Formula: $(Cu,Fe)_{12}Sb_4S_{13}$.

tetrahedron (ˌtɛtrəˈhiːdrən) NOUN, *plural* **-drons** *or* **-dra** (-drə). [1] a solid figure having four plane faces. A **regular tetrahedron** has faces that are equilateral triangles. See also **polyhedron.** [2] any object shaped like a tetrahedron.
▷HISTORY C16: from New Latin, from Late Greek *tetraedron;* see TETRA-, -HEDRON
▸ˌ**tetraˈhedral** ADJECTIVE ▸ˌ**tetraˈhedrally** ADVERB

tetrahydrocannabidinol (ˈtɛtrəˈhaɪdrəʊˌkænəˈbɪdɪnɒl) NOUN the full name for **THC**.

tetralogy (tɛˈtrælədʒɪ) NOUN, *plural* **-gies.** [1] a series of four related works, as in drama or opera. [2] (in ancient Greece) a group of four dramas, the first three tragic and the last satiric. [3] *Pathol* a group of four symptoms present in one disorder, esp Fallot's tetralogy.
▷HISTORY C17: from Greek *tetralogia;* see TETRA-, -LOGY

tetramerous (tɛˈtræmərəs) ADJECTIVE [1] (esp of animals or plants) having or consisting of four parts. [2] (of certain flowers) having parts arranged in whorls of four members.
▷HISTORY C19: from New Latin *tetramerus,* from Greek *tetramerēs*
▸**teˈtramerism** NOUN

tetrameter (tɛˈtræmɪtə) NOUN *Prosody* [1] a line of verse consisting of four metrical feet. [2] a verse composed of such lines. [3] (in classical prosody) a line of verse composed of four dipodies.

tetramethyldiarsine (ˌtɛtrəˌmiːθaɪldaɪˈɑːsiːn) NOUN an oily slightly water-soluble poisonous liquid with garlic-like odour. Its derivatives are used as accelerators for rubber. Also called (not in technical usage): **cacodyl, dicacodyl.**

tetraplegia (ˌtɛtrəˈpliːdʒɪə) NOUN another name for **quadriplegia.**
▷HISTORY from TETRA- + Greek *plegē* a blow, from *plēssein* to strike
▸ˌ**tetraˈplegic** ADJECTIVE

tetraploid (ˈtɛtrəˌplɔɪd) *Genetics* ◆ ADJECTIVE [1] having four times the haploid number of chromosomes in the nucleus. ◆ NOUN [2] a tetraploid organism, nucleus, or cell.

tetrapod (ˈtɛtrəˌpɒd) NOUN [1] any vertebrate that has four limbs. [2] Also called: **caltrop.** a device consisting of four arms radiating from a central point, each at about 109° to the others, so that regardless of its position on a surface, three arms form a supporting tripod and the fourth is vertical. [3] *Engineering* a very large cast concrete structure of a similar shape piled in large numbers round breakwaters and sea defence systems to dissipate the energy of the waves.

tetrapody (tɛˈtræpədɪ) NOUN, *plural* **-dies.** *Prosody* a metrical unit consisting of four feet.
▸**tetrapodic** (ˌtɛtrəˈpɒdɪk) ADJECTIVE

tetrapterous (tɛˈtræptərəs) ADJECTIVE [1] (of certain insects) having four wings. [2] *Biology* having four winglike extensions or parts.
▷HISTORY C19: from New Latin *tetrapterus,* from Greek *tetrapteros,* from TETRA- + *pteron* wing

tetrarch (ˈtɛtrɑːk) NOUN [1] the ruler of one fourth of a country. [2] a subordinate ruler, esp of Syria under the Roman Empire. [3] the commander of one of the smaller subdivisions of a Macedonian phalanx. [4] any of four joint rulers.
▷HISTORY C14: from Greek *tetrarkhēs;* see TETRA-, -ARCH
▸**tetrarchate** (tɛˈtrɑːˌkeɪt, -kɪt) NOUN ▸**teˈtrarchic** *or* **teˈtrarchical** ADJECTIVE ▸**ˈtetrarchy** NOUN

tetraspore (ˈtɛtrəˌspɔː) NOUN any of the asexual spores that are produced in groups of four in the sporangium (**tetrasporangium**) of any of the red algae.
▸**tetrasporic** (ˌtɛtrəˈspɒrɪk) *or* **tetrasporous** (ˌtɛtrəˈspɔːrəs, tɪˈtræspərəs) ADJECTIVE

tetrastich (ˈtɛtrəˌstɪk) NOUN a poem, stanza, or strophe that consists of four lines.
▷HISTORY C16: via Latin from Greek *tetrastikhon,* from TETRA- + *stikhos* row
▸**tetrastichic** (ˌtɛtrəˈstɪkɪk) *or* **tetrastichal** (tɛˈtræstɪkᵊl) ADJECTIVE

tetrastichous (tɛˈtræstɪkəs) ADJECTIVE (of flowers or leaves on a stalk) arranged in four vertical rows.

tetrasyllable (ˌtɛtrəˈsɪləbᵊl) NOUN a word of four syllables.
▸**tetrasyllabic** (ˌtɛtrəsɪˈlæbɪk) *or* ˌ**tetrasylˈlabical** ADJECTIVE

tetratomic (ˌtɛtrəˈtɒmɪk) ADJECTIVE composed of four atoms or having four atoms per molecule: *phosgene has tetratomic molecules.*

tetravalent (ˌtɛtrəˈveɪlənt) ADJECTIVE *Chem* [1] having a valency of four. [2] Also: **quadrivalent.** having four valencies.
▸ˌ**tetraˈvalency** NOUN

tetrode (ˈtɛtrəʊd) NOUN [1] an electronic valve having four electrodes, namely a cathode, control grid, screen grid, and anode. [2] (*modifier*) (of a transistor) having two terminals on the base or gate to improve the performance at high frequencies.

tetroxide (tɛˈtrɒksaɪd) *or* **tetroxid** (tɛˈtrɒksɪd) NOUN any oxide that contains four oxygen atoms per molecule: *osmium tetroxide,* OsO_4.

tetryl (ˈtɛtrɪl) NOUN a yellow crystalline explosive solid used in detonators; trinitrophenylmethylnitramine. Formula: $(NO_2)_3C_6H_2N(NO_2)CH_3$. Also called: **nitramine.**

tetter (ˈtɛtə) NOUN [1] a blister or pimple. [2] *Informal* any of various skin eruptions, such as eczema.
▷HISTORY Old English *teter;* related to Old High German *zitaroh,* Sanskrit *dadru,* Late Latin *derbita*

Tetuán (tɛˈtwɑːn) NOUN a city in N Morocco: capital of Spanish Morocco (1912–56). Pop.: 277 516 (1994 est.).

Teucer (ˈtjuːsə) NOUN *Greek myth* [1] a Cretan leader, who founded Troy. [2] a son of Telamon and Hesione, who distinguished himself by his archery on the side of the Greeks in the Trojan War.

teuchter (ˈtjuːxtər) NOUN *Scot* (*sometimes capital*) **a** a derogatory word used by Lowlanders for a Highlander. **b** (*as modifier*): *teuchter music.*
▷HISTORY C20: of uncertain origin

Teucrian (ˈtjuːkrɪən) NOUN, ADJECTIVE another word for **Trojan.**

Teutoburger Wald (*German* ˈtɔytoburgər valt) NOUN a low wooded mountain range in N Germany: possible site of the annihilation of three Roman legions by Germans under Arminius in 9 A.D.

Teuton (ˈtjuːtən) NOUN [1] a member of an ancient Germanic people from Jutland who migrated to S Gaul in the 2nd century B.C.: annihilated by a Roman army in 102 B.C. [2] a member of any people speaking a Germanic language, esp a German. ◆ ADJECTIVE [3] Teutonic.
▷HISTORY C18: from Latin *Teutonī* the Teutons, of Germanic origin

Teutonic (tjuːˈtɒnɪk) ADJECTIVE [1] characteristic of or relating to the German people: *Teutonic thoroughness.* [2] of or relating to the ancient Teutons. [3] (not used in linguistics) of or relating to the Germanic languages. ◆ NOUN [4] an obsolete name for **Germanic.**
▸**Teuˈtonically** ADVERB

Teutonic order NOUN a military and religious order of German knights, priests, and serving brothers founded about 1190 during the Third Crusade, later conquering large parts of the Baltic provinces and Russia. Also called: **Teutonic Knights.**

Teutonism (ˈtjuːtəˌnɪzəm) NOUN [1] a German idiom, custom, or characteristic. [2] German society or civilization.

Teutonize *or* **Teutonise** (ˈtjuːtəˌnaɪz) VERB to make or become German or Germanic; Germanize.
▸ˌ**Teutoniˈzation** *or* ˌ**Teutoniˈsation** NOUN

Tevere (ˈteːvere) NOUN the Italian name for the **Tiber.**

Tevet *or* **Tebet** (teˈvet) NOUN (in the Jewish calendar) the tenth month of the year according to biblical reckoning and the fourth month of the civil year, usually falling within December and January.
▷HISTORY from Hebrew

Tewkesbury (ˈtjuːksbərɪ, -brɪ) NOUN a town in W England, in N Gloucestershire at the confluence of the Rivers Severn and Avon: scene of a decisive battle (1471) of the Wars of the Roses in which the Yorkists defeated the Lancastrians; 12th-century abbey. Pop.: 9488 (1991).

tex NOUN a unit of weight used to measure the density of yarns. It is equal to 1 gram per 1000 metres.
▷HISTORY C20: from French, from *textile* TEXTILE

Tex. ABBREVIATION FOR: [1] Texan. [2] Texas.

Texan (ˈtɛksən) NOUN [1] a native or inhabitant of Texas. ◆ ADJECTIVE [2] of or relating to Texas or its inhabitants.

Texas (ˈtɛksəs) NOUN a state of the southwestern US, on the Gulf of Mexico: the second largest state; part of Mexico from 1821 to 1836, when it was declared an independent republic; joined the US in 1845; consists chiefly of a plain, with a wide flat coastal belt rising up to the semiarid Sacramento and Davis Mountains of the southwest; a major producer of cotton, rice, and livestock; the chief US producer of oil and gas; a leading world supplier of sulphur. Capital: Austin. Pop.: 20 851 820 (2000). Area: 678 927 sq. km (262 134 sq. miles). Abbreviations: **Tex,** (with zip code) **TX.**

Texas fever NOUN *Vet science* another name for **blackwater fever.**

Texas hedge NOUN *Finance* the opposite of a normal hedging operation, in which risk is increased by buying more than one financial instrument of the same kind.

Texas Rangers PLURAL NOUN the state police of Texas, originally formed in the 19th century to defend outlying regions against Indians and Mexicans and to fight lawlessness.

Texel (ˈtɛksᵊl) NOUN a breed of sheep originating from the Netherlands having a heavy white fleece: kept for the production of lean lambs.
▷HISTORY C20: named after *Texel,* one of the West Frisian Islands off the Netherlands

Tex-Mex (ˈtɛksˌmɛks) ADJECTIVE of, relating to, or denoting the Texan version of something Mexican, such as music, food, or language.

text (tɛkst) NOUN [1] the main body of a printed or written work as distinct from commentary, notes, illustrations, etc. [2] the words of something printed or written. [3] (*often plural*) a book prescribed as part of a course of study. [4] *Computing* the words printed, written, or displayed on a visual display unit. [5] the original exact wording of a work, esp the Bible, as distinct from a revision or translation. [6] a short passage of the Bible used as a starting point for a sermon or adduced as proof of a doctrine. [7] the topic or subject of a discussion or work. [8] *Printing* any one of several styles of letters or types. [9] short for **textbook.** ◆ VERB [10] to send a text message from a mobile phone.
▷HISTORY C14: from Medieval Latin *textus* version, from Latin *textus* texture, from *texere* to compose
▸**ˈtextless** ADJECTIVE

textbook (ˈtɛkstˌbʊk) NOUN **a** a book used as a standard source of information on a particular subject. **b** (*as modifier*): *a textbook example.*
▸**ˈtextˌbookish** ADJECTIVE

texter (ˈtɛkstə) NOUN a person who communicates by text messaging.

textile (ˈtɛkstaɪl) NOUN [1] any fabric or cloth, esp woven. [2] raw material suitable to be made into cloth; fibre or yarn. [3] a non-nudist, as described by nudists; one who wears clothes. ◆ ADJECTIVE [4] of or relating to fabrics or the making of fabrics.
▷HISTORY C17: from Latin *textilis* woven, from *texere* to weave

text message NOUN a message sent by means of a mobile phone.

text messaging NOUN communication by means of text messages sent from mobile phones.

text processing NOUN the handling of alphabetic characters by a computer.

textual (ˈtɛkstjʊəl) ADJECTIVE [1] of or relating to a text or texts. [2] based on or conforming to a text.
▸**ˈtextually** ADVERB

textual criticism NOUN [1] the scholarly study of manuscripts, esp of the Bible, in an effort to establish the original text. [2] literary criticism emphasizing a close analysis of the text.
▸**textual critic** NOUN

textualism (ˈtɛkstjʊəˌlɪzəm) NOUN [1] doctrinaire adherence to a text, esp of the Bible. [2] textual criticism, esp of the Bible.
▸**ˈtextualist** NOUN, ADJECTIVE

textuary ('tɛkstjʊərɪ) ADJECTIVE 1 of, relating to, or contained in a text. ◆ NOUN, *plural* **-aries**. 2 a textual critic.

texture ('tɛkstʃə) NOUN 1 the surface of a material, esp as perceived by the sense of touch: *a wall with a rough texture*. 2 the structure, appearance, and feel of a woven fabric. 3 the general structure and disposition of the constituent parts of something: *the texture of a cake*. 4 the distinctive character or quality of something: *the texture of life in America*. 5 the nature of a surface other than smooth: *woollen cloth has plenty of texture*. 6 *Art* the representation of the nature of a surface: *the painter caught the grainy texture of the sand*. 7 **a** music considered as the interrelationship between the horizontally presented aspects of melody and rhythm and the vertically represented aspect of harmony: *a contrapuntal texture*. **b** the nature and quality of the instrumentation of a passage, piece, etc. ◆ VERB 8 (*tr*) to give a distinctive usually rough or grainy texture to.
▷HISTORY C15: from Latin *textūra* web, from *texere* to weave
▸**'textural** ADJECTIVE ▸**'texturally** ADVERB ▸**'textureless** ADJECTIVE

Teyde (*Spanish* 'tɛiðe) NOUN a variant spelling of **Teide**.

tf THE INTERNET DOMAIN NAME FOR French Southern Territories.

tg[1] *Biology* ABBREVIATION FOR type genus.

tg[2] THE INTERNET DOMAIN NAME FOR Togo.

TG 1 ABBREVIATION FOR **transformational grammar**. ◆ 2 INTERNATIONAL CAR REGISTRATION FOR Togo.

T-group NOUN *Psychol* a group that meets for educational or therapeutic purposes to study its own communication.
▷HISTORY C20: from (*Sensitivity*) *T*(*raining*) *Group*

TGV (*French* teʒeve) (in France) ABBREVIATION FOR train à grande vitesse: a high-speed passenger train.

TGWU (in Britain) ABBREVIATION FOR Transport and General Workers' Union.

th THE INTERNET DOMAIN NAME FOR Thailand.

Th THE CHEMICAL SYMBOL FOR thorium.

-th[1] SUFFIX FORMING NOUNS 1 (*from verbs*) indicating an action or its consequence: *growth*. 2 (*from adjectives*) indicating a quality: *width*.
▷HISTORY from Old English *-thu, -tho*

-th[2] *or* **-eth** SUFFIX forming ordinal numbers: *fourth; thousandth*.
▷HISTORY from Old English *-(o)tha, -(o)the*

Thabana-Ntlenyana (tɑː'bɑːnəᵊn'tleɪnjənə) NOUN a mountain in Lesotho: the highest peak of the Drakensberg Mountains. Height: 3482 m (11 425 ft.). Also called: **Thadentsonyane, Thabantshonyana.**

Thaddeus *or* **Thadeus** ('θædɪəs) NOUN *New Testament* one of the 12 apostles (Matthew 10:3; Mark 3:18), traditionally identified with Jude.

Thadentsonyane (ˌtɑːdən'tsɒnjənə) NOUN another name for **Thabana-Ntlenyana.**

Thai (taɪ) ADJECTIVE 1 of, relating to, or characteristic of Thailand, its people, or their language. ◆ NOUN 2 (*plural* **Thais** *or* **Thai**) a native or inhabitant of Thailand. 3 the language of Thailand, sometimes classified as belonging to the Sino-Tibetan family. ◆ Also called: **Siamese.**

Thailand ('taɪˌlænd) NOUN a kingdom in SE Asia, on the Andaman Sea and the Gulf of Siam: united as a kingdom in 1350 and became a major SE Asian power; consists chiefly of a central plain around the Chao Phraya river system, mountains rising over 2400 m (8000 ft.) in the northwest, and rainforest the length of the S peninsula. Official language: Thai. Official religion: (Hinayana) Buddhist. Currency: baht. Capital: Bangkok. Pop.: 61 251 000 (2001 est.). Area: 513 998 sq. km (198 455 sq. miles). Former name (until 1939 and 1945–49): **Siam.**

thalamencephalon (ˌθæləmɛn'sɛfəˌlɒn) NOUN, *plural* **-lons** *or* **-la** (-lə). *Anatomy* 1 the part of the diencephalon of the brain that includes the thalamus, pineal gland, and adjacent structures. 2 another name for **diencephalon.**
▸**thalamencephalic** (ˌθæləˌmɛnsə'fælɪk) ADJECTIVE

thalamus ('θæləməs) NOUN, *plural* **-mi** (-ˌmaɪ). 1 either of the two contiguous egg-shaped masses of grey matter at the base of the brain. 2 both of these masses considered as a functional unit. 3 the receptacle or torus of a flower.
▷HISTORY C18: from Latin, Greek *thalamos* inner room; probably related to Greek *tholos* vault
▸**thalamic** (θə'læmɪk) ADJECTIVE ▸**tha'lamically** ADVERB

thalassaemia *or US* **thalassemia** (ˌθælə'siːmɪə) NOUN a hereditary disease, common in many parts of the world, resulting from defects in the synthesis of the red blood pigment haemoglobin. Also called: **Cooley's anaemia** ('kuːlɪz).
▷HISTORY New Latin, from Greek *thalassa* sea + -AEMIA, from it being esp prevalent round the eastern Mediterranean Sea

thalassic (θə'læsɪk) ADJECTIVE 1 of or relating to the sea. 2 of or relating to small or inland seas, as opposed to open waters. 3 inhabiting or growing in the sea; marine: *thalassic fauna*.
▷HISTORY C19: from French *thalassique*, from Greek *thalassa* sea

thalassocracy (ˌθælə'sɒkrəsɪ) *or* **thalattocracy** NOUN the government of a nation having dominion over large expanses of the seas.
▷HISTORY C19: from Attic Greek *thalassocratia*, from *thalassa* sea + -CRACY

thalassotherapy (ˌθæləsəʊ'θɛrəpɪ) NOUN the use of sea water and marine products as a therapeutic treatment.
▷HISTORY C20: from Greek *thalassa* sea + THERAPY

thaler *or* **taler** ('tɑːlə) NOUN, *plural* **-ler** *or* **-lers**. a former German, Austrian, or Swiss silver coin.
▷HISTORY from German; see DOLLAR

thali ('tɑːlɪ) NOUN *Indian cookery* a meal consisting of several small meat or vegetable dishes accompanied by rice, bread, etc., and sometimes by a starter or a sweet.
▷HISTORY C20: from Hindi *thālī* a plate or tray on which food is served

Thalia (θə'laɪə) NOUN *Greek myth* 1 the Muse of comedy and pastoral poetry. 2 one of the three Graces.
▷HISTORY C17: via Latin from Greek, from *thaleia* blooming

thalidomide (θə'lɪdəˌmaɪd) NOUN **a** a synthetic drug formerly used as a sedative and hypnotic but withdrawn from the market when found to cause abnormalities in developing fetuses. Formula: $C_{13}H_{10}N_2O_4$. **b** (*as modifier*): *a thalidomide baby*.
▷HISTORY C20: from THALLIC + *-id-* (from IMIDE) + IMIDE

thallic ('θælɪk) ADJECTIVE of or containing thallium, esp in the trivalent state.

thallium ('θælɪəm) NOUN a soft malleable highly toxic white metallic element used as a rodent and insect poison and in low-melting glass. Its compounds are used as infrared detectors and in photoelectric cells. Symbol: Tl; atomic no.: 81; atomic wt.: 204.3833; valency: 1 or 3; relative density: 11.85; melting pt.: 304°C; boiling pt.: 1473±10°C.
▷HISTORY C19: from New Latin, from Greek *thallos* a green shoot; referring to the green line in its spectrum

thallophyte ('θæləˌfaɪt) NOUN *Obsolete* any organism of the former division *Thallophyta*, lacking true stems, leaves, and roots: includes the algae, fungi, lichens, and bacteria, all now regarded as separate phyla.
▷HISTORY C19: from New Latin *thallophyta*, from Greek *thallos* a young shoot + *phuton* a plant
▸**thallophytic** (ˌθælə'fɪtɪk) ADJECTIVE

thallous ('θæləs) ADJECTIVE of or containing thallium, esp in the monovalent state.

thallus ('θæləs) NOUN, *plural* **thalli** ('θælaɪ) *or* **thalluses**. the undifferentiated vegetative body of algae, fungi, and lichens.
▷HISTORY C19: from Latin, from Greek *thallos* green shoot, from *thallein* to bloom
▸**'thalloid** ADJECTIVE

thalweg *or* **talweg** ('tɑːlvɛg) NOUN *Geography, rare* 1 the longitudinal outline of a riverbed from source to mouth. 2 the line of steepest descent from any point on the land surface.
▷HISTORY C19: from German, from *Thal* valley + *Weg* way, path

Thames NOUN 1 (tɛmz) a river in S England, rising in the Cotswolds in several headstreams and flowing generally east through London to the North Sea by a large estuary. Length: 346 km (215 miles). Ancient name: **Tamesis** ('tæməsɪs). 2 (teɪmz, θeɪmz) a river in SE Canada, in Ontario, flowing south to London, then southwest to Lake St Clair. Length: 217 km (135 miles).

Thammuz ('tæmuːz, -ʊz) NOUN a variant spelling of **Tammuz.**

than (ðæn; *unstressed* ðən) CONJUNCTION (*coordinating*), PREPOSITION 1 used to introduce the second element of a comparison, the first element of which expresses difference: *shorter than you; couldn't do otherwise than love him; he swims faster than I run*. 2 used after adverbs such as *rather* or *sooner* to introduce a rejected alternative in an expression of preference: *rather than be imprisoned, I shall die*. 3 **other than.** besides; in addition to.
▷HISTORY Old English *thanne*; related to Old Saxon, Old High German *thanna*; see THEN

> **Language note** In formal English, *than* is usually regarded as a conjunction governing an unexpressed verb: *he does it far better than I (do)*. The case of any pronoun therefore depends on whether it is the subject or object of the unexpressed verb: *she likes him more than I (like him); she likes him more than (she likes) me*. However in ordinary speech and writing *than* is usually treated as a preposition and is followed by the object form of a pronoun: *my brother is younger than me*.

thanatology (ˌθænə'tɒlədʒɪ) NOUN the scientific study of death and the phenomena and practices relating to it.
▷HISTORY C19: from Greek *thanatos* death + -LOGY

thanatopsis (ˌθænə'tɒpsɪs) NOUN a meditation on death, as in a poem.
▷HISTORY C19: from Greek *thanatos* death + *opsis* a view

Thanatos ('θænəˌtɒs) NOUN the Greek personification of death: son of Nyx, goddess of night. Roman counterpart: **Mors.** Thanatos was the name chosen by Freud to represent a universal death instinct. Compare **Eros**[1].
▸**Thanatotic** (ˌθænə'tɒtɪk) ADJECTIVE

thane *or commonly* **thegn** (θeɪn) NOUN 1 (in Anglo-Saxon England) a member of an aristocratic class, ranking below an ealdorman, whose status was hereditary and who held land from the king or from another nobleman in return for certain services. 2 (in medieval Scotland) **a** a person of rank, often the chief of a clan, holding land from the king. **b** a lesser noble who was a Crown official holding authority over an area of land.
▷HISTORY Old English *thegn*; related to Old Saxon, Old High German *thegan* thane
▸**thanage** ('θeɪnɪdʒ) NOUN

Thanet ('θænɪt) NOUN **Isle of.** an island in SE England, in NE Kent, separated from the mainland by two branches of the River Stour: scene of many Norse invasions. Area: 109 sq. km (42 sq. miles).

thangka ('θæŋkə) NOUN (in Tibetan Buddhism) a religious painting on a scroll.
▷HISTORY from Tibetan

Thanjavur (ˌtʌndʒə'vʊə) NOUN a city in SE India, in E Tamil Nadu: headquarters of the earliest Protestant missions in India. Pop.: 202 013 (1991). Former name: **Tanjore.**

thank (θæŋk) VERB (*tr*) 1 to convey feelings of gratitude to. 2 to hold responsible: *he has his creditors to thank for his bankruptcy*. 3 used in exclamations of relief: *thank goodness; thank God*. 4 **I'll thank you to.** used ironically to intensify a command, request, etc.: *I'll thank you to mind your own business*.
▷HISTORY Old English *thancian*; related to Old Frisian *thankia*, Old Norse *thakka*, Old Saxon, Old High German *thancōn*

thankful ('θæŋkfʊl) ADJECTIVE grateful and appreciative.
▸**'thankfulness** NOUN

thankfully ('θæŋkfʊlɪ) ADVERB 1 showing

gratitude or appreciation. [2] *Informal* fortunately: *thankfully she was not injured.*

> **Language note** The use of *thankfully* to mean *fortunately* was formerly considered incorrect by many people, but has now become acceptable in informal contexts.

thankless (ˈθæŋklɪs) ADJECTIVE [1] receiving no thanks or appreciation: *a thankless job.* [2] ungrateful: *a thankless pupil.*
▸ **ˈthanklessly** ADVERB ▸ **ˈthanklessness** NOUN

thanks (θæŋks) PLURAL NOUN [1] an expression of appreciation or gratitude or an acknowledgment of services or favours given. [2] **thanks to.** because of: *thanks to him we lost the match.* ◆ INTERJECTION [3] *Informal* an exclamation expressing acknowledgment, gratitude, or appreciation.

thanksgiving (ˈθæŋksˌɡɪvɪŋ; *US* θæŋksˈɡɪvɪŋ) NOUN [1] the act of giving thanks. [2] **a** an expression of thanks to God. **b** a public act of religious observance or a celebration in acknowledgment of divine favours.

Thanksgiving Day NOUN an annual day of holiday celebrated in thanksgiving to God on the fourth Thursday of November in the United States, and on the second Monday of October in Canada. Often shortened to: **Thanksgiving.**

thank you INTERJECTION, NOUN a conventional expression of gratitude.

Thapsus (ˈθæpsəs) NOUN an ancient town near Carthage in North Africa: site of Caesar's victory over Pompey in 46 B.C.

thar (tɑː) NOUN a variant spelling of **tahr.**

Thar Desert (tɑː) NOUN a desert in NW India, mainly in NW Rajasthan state and extending into Pakistan. Area: over 260 000 sq. km (100 000 sq. miles). Also called: **Indian Desert, Great Indian Desert.**

Thásos (ˈθæsɒs) NOUN a Greek island in the N Aegean: colonized by Greeks from Paros in the 7th century B.C. as a gold-mining centre; under Turkish rule (1455–1912). Pop.: 13 110 (latest est.). Area: 379 sq. km (146 sq. miles).

that (ðæt; *unstressed* ðət) DETERMINER (*used before a singular noun*) [1] **a** used preceding a noun that has been mentioned at some time or is understood: *that idea of yours.* **b** (*as pronoun*): *don't eat that; that's what I mean.* [2] **a** used preceding a noun that denotes something more remote or removed: *that dress is cheaper than this one; that building over there is for sale.* **b** (*as pronoun*): *that is John and this is his wife; give me that.* Compare **this.** [3] used to refer to something that is familiar: *that old chap from across the street.* [4] **and (all) that.** *Informal* everything connected with the subject mentioned: *he knows a lot about building and that.* [5] **at that.** (*completive-intensive*) additionally, all things considered, or nevertheless: *he's a pleasant fellow at that; I might decide to go at that.* [6] **like that. a** with ease; effortlessly: *he gave me the answer just like that.* **b** of such a nature, character, etc.: *he paid for all our tickets — he's like that.* [7] **that is. a** to be precise. **b** in other words. **c** for example. [8] **that's more like it.** that is better, an improvement, etc. [9] **that's that.** there is no more to be done, discussed, etc. [10] **with** (*or* **at**) **that.** thereupon; having said or done that. ◆ CONJUNCTION (*subordinating*) [11] used to introduce a noun clause: *I believe that you'll come.* [12] Also: **so that, in order that.** used to introduce a clause of purpose: *they fought that others might have peace.* [13] used to introduce a clause of result: *he laughed so hard that he cried.* [14] used to introduce a clause after an understood sentence expressing desire, indignation, or amazement: *oh, that I had never lived!* ◆ ADVERB [15] used with adjectives or adverbs to reinforce the specification of a precise degree already mentioned: *go just that fast and you should be safe.* [16] Also: **all that.** (*usually used with a negative*) *Informal* (intensifier): *he wasn't that upset at the news.* [17] *Dialect* (intensifier): *the cat was that weak after the fight.* ◆ PRONOUN [18] used to introduce a restrictive relative clause: *the book that we want.* [19] used to introduce a clause with the verb *to be* to emphasize the extent to which the preceding noun is applicable: *genius that she is, she outwitted the computer.*
▷ HISTORY Old English *thæt;* related to Old Frisian *thet,* Old Norse, Old Saxon *that,* Old High German *daz,* Greek *to,* Latin *istud,* Sanskrit *tad*

> **Language note** Precise stylists maintain a distinction between *that* and *which*: *that* is used as a relative pronoun in restrictive clauses and *which* in nonrestrictive clauses. In *the book that is on the table is mine,* the clause *that is on the table* is used to distinguish one particular book (the one on the table) from another or others (which may be anywhere, but not on the table). In *the book, which is on the table, is mine,* the *which* clause is merely descriptive or incidental. The more formal the level of language, the more important it is to preserve the distinction between the two relative pronouns; but in informal or colloquial usage, the words are often used interchangeably.

thatch (θætʃ) NOUN [1] **a** Also called: **thatching.** a roofing material that consists of straw, reed, etc. **b** a roof made of such a material. [2] anything resembling this, such as the hair of the head. [3] Also called: **thatch palm.** any of various palms with leaves suitable for thatching. ◆ VERB [4] to cover (a roof) with thatch.
▷ HISTORY Old English *theccan* to cover; related to *thæc* roof, Old Saxon *thekkian* to thatch, Old High German *decchen,* Old Norse *thekja*
▸ **ˈthatcher** NOUN ▸ **ˈthatchless** ADJECTIVE ▸ **ˈthatchy** ADJECTIVE

Thatcherism (ˈθætʃəˌrɪzəm) NOUN the policies of monetarism, privatization, and self-help promoted by the British Conservative stateswoman and prime minister (1979–90) Margaret, Baroness Thatcher (born Margaret Hilda Roberts, 1925).
▸ **Thatcherite** (ˈθætʃəˌraɪt) NOUN, ADJECTIVE

thaumato- *or before a vowel* **thaumat-** COMBINING FORM miracle; marvel: *thaumaturge.*
▷ HISTORY from Greek *thauma, thaumat-* a marvel

thaumatology (ˌθɔːməˈtɒlədʒɪ) NOUN the study of or a treatise on miracles.

thaumatrope (ˈθɔːməˌtrəʊp) NOUN a toy in which partial pictures on the two sides of a card appear to merge when the card is twirled rapidly.
▷ HISTORY C19: from THAUMATO- + -TROPE
▸ **thaumatropical** (ˌθɔːməˈtrɒpɪkᵊl) ADJECTIVE

thaumaturge (ˈθɔːməˌtɜːdʒ) NOUN *Rare* a performer of miracles; magician.
▷ HISTORY C18: from Medieval Latin *thaumaturgus,* from Greek *thaumatourgos* miracle-working, from THAUMATO- + *-ourgos* working, from *ergon* work
▸ **ˈthaumaˌturgy** NOUN ▸ **ˌthaumaˈturgic** ADJECTIVE

thaw (θɔː) VERB [1] to melt or cause to melt from a solid frozen state: *the snow thawed.* [2] to become or cause to become unfrozen; defrost. [3] (*intr*) to be the case that the ice or snow is melting: *it's thawing fast.* [4] (*intr*) to become more sociable, relaxed, or friendly. ◆ NOUN [5] the act or process of thawing. [6] a spell of relatively warm weather, causing snow or ice to melt. [7] an increase in relaxation or friendliness.
▷ HISTORY Old English *thawian;* related to Old High German *douwen* to thaw, Old Norse *theyja* to thaw, Latin *tabēre* to waste away
▸ **ˈthawer** NOUN ▸ **ˈthawless** ADJECTIVE

ThB ABBREVIATION FOR Bachelor of Theology.

ThD ABBREVIATION FOR Doctor of Theology.

the[1] (*stressed or emphatic* ðiː; *unstressed before a consonant* ðə; *unstressed before a vowel* ðɪ) DETERMINER (*article*) [1] used preceding a noun that has been previously specified: *the pain should disappear soon; the man then opened the door.* Compare **a[1]**. [2] used with a qualifying word or phrase to indicate a particular person, object, etc., as distinct from others: *ask the man standing outside; give me the blue one.* Compare **a[1]**. [3] used preceding certain nouns associated with one's culture, society, or community: *to go to the doctor; listen to the news; watch the television.* [4] used preceding present participles and adjectives when they function as nouns: *the singing is awful; the dead salute you.* [5] used preceding titles and certain uniquely specific or proper nouns, such as place names: *the United States; the Honourable Edward Brown; the Chairman; the moon.* [6] used preceding a qualifying adjective or noun in certain names or titles: *William the Conqueror; Edward the First.* [7] used preceding a noun to make it refer to its class generically: *the white seal is hunted for its fur; this is good for the throat; to play the piano.* [8] used instead of *my, your, her,* etc., with parts of the body: *take me by the hand.* [9] (*usually stressed*) the best, only, or most remarkable: *Harry's is the club in this town.* [10] used with proper nouns when qualified: *written by the young Hardy.* [11] another word for **per,** esp with nouns or noun phrases of cost *fifty pence the pound.* [12] *Often facetious or derogatory* my; our: *the wife goes out on Thursdays.* [13] used preceding a unit of time in phrases or titles indicating an outstanding person, event, etc.: *match of the day; housewife of the year.*
▷ HISTORY Middle English, from Old English *thē,* a demonstrative adjective that later superseded *sē* (masculine singular) and *sēo, sio* (feminine singular); related to Old Frisian *thi, thiu,* Old High German *der, diu*

the[2] (ðə, ðɪ) ADVERB [1] (often foll by *for*) used before comparative adjectives or adverbs for emphasis: *she looks the happier for her trip.* [2] used correlatively before each of two comparative adjectives or adverbs to indicate equality: *the sooner you come, the better; the more I see you, the more I love you.*
▷ HISTORY Old English *thī, thȳ,* instrumental case of THE[1] and THAT; related to Old Norse *thī,* Gothic *thei*

the- COMBINING FORM a variant of **theo-** before a vowel.

theaceous (θiːˈeɪʃəs) ADJECTIVE of, relating to, or belonging to the *Theaceae,* a family of evergreen trees and shrubs of tropical and warm regions: includes the tea plant.

theanthropism (θiːˈænθrəˌpɪzəm) NOUN [1] the ascription of human traits or characteristics to a god or gods. [2] *Christian theol* the doctrine of the hypostatic union of the divine and human natures in the single person of Christ.
▷ HISTORY C19: from Ecclesiastical Greek *theanthrōpos* (from *theos* god + *anthrōpos* man) + -ISM
▸ **ˌtheanˈthropic** ADJECTIVE ▸ **theˈanthropist** NOUN

thearchy (ˈθiːɑːkɪ) NOUN, *plural* **-chies.** rule or government by God or gods; theocracy.
▷ HISTORY C17: from Church Greek *thearkhia;* see THEO-, -ARCHY
▸ **theˈarchic** ADJECTIVE

theatre *or US* **theater** (ˈθɪətə) NOUN [1] **a** a building designed for the performance of plays, operas, etc. **b** (*as modifier*): *a theatre ticket.* **c** (*in combination*): *a theatregoer.* [2] a large room or hall, usually with a raised platform and tiered seats for an audience, used for lectures, film shows, etc. [3] Also called: **operating theatre.** a room in a hospital or other medical centre equipped for surgical operations. [4] plays regarded collectively as a form of art. [5] **the theatre.** the world of actors, theatrical companies, etc.: *the glamour of the theatre.* [6] a setting for dramatic or important events. [7] writing that is suitable for dramatic presentation: *a good piece of theatre.* [8] *US, Austral, NZ* the usual word for **cinema** (sense 1). [9] a major area of military activity: *the theatre of operations.* [10] a circular or semicircular open-air building with tiers of seats.
▷ HISTORY C14: from Latin *theātrum,* from Greek *theatron* place for viewing, from *theasthai* to look at; related to Greek *thauma* miracle

theatre-in-the-round NOUN, *plural* **theatres-in-the-round.** [1] a theatre with seats arranged around a central acting area. [2] drama written or designed for performance in such a theatre. ◆ Also called: **arena theatre.**

theatre of cruelty NOUN a type of theatre advocated by Antonin Artaud in *Le Théâtre et son double* that seeks to communicate to its audience a sense of pain, suffering, and evil, using gesture, movement, sound, and symbolism rather than language.

theatre of the absurd NOUN drama in which normal conventions and dramatic structure are ignored or modified in order to present life as irrational or meaningless.

theatrical (θɪˈætrɪkᵊl) ADJECTIVE [1] of or relating to the theatre or dramatic performances. [2] exaggerated and affected in manner or behaviour; histrionic.
▸ **theˌatriˈcality** *or* **theˈatricalness** NOUN ▸ **theˈatrically** ADVERB

theatricals (θɪˈætrɪkᵊlz) PLURAL NOUN dramatic performances and entertainments, esp as given by amateurs.

theatrics (θɪˈætrɪks) NOUN (*functioning as singular*)

[1] the art of staging plays. [2] exaggerated mannerisms or displays of emotions.

Thebaic (θɪˈbeɪɪk) ADJECTIVE [1] of or relating to the ancient Greek city of Thebes or its inhabitants. [2] of or relating to the ancient Egyptian city of Thebes or its inhabitants.

Thebaid (ˈθiːbeɪɪd, -bɪ-) NOUN the territory around ancient Thebes in Egypt, or sometimes around Thebes in Greece.

thebaine (ˈθiːbəˌiːn, θɪˈbeiːn, -aɪn) NOUN a poisonous white crystalline alkaloid, found in opium but without opioid actions. Formula: $C_{19}H_{21}NO_3$. Also called: **paramorphine**.
▷HISTORY C19: from New Latin *thebaia* opium of Thebes (with reference to Egypt as a chief source of opium) + -INE[2]

Theban (ˈθiːbən) ADJECTIVE [1] of or relating to the ancient Greek city of Thebes or its inhabitants. [2] of or relating to the ancient Egyptian city of Thebes or its inhabitants. ◆ NOUN [3] a native or inhabitant of Thebes.

Thebe (ˈθiːbɪ) NOUN *Astronomy* an inner satellite of Jupiter discovered in 1979.
▷HISTORY C20: named after *Thebe*, mythical queen of THEBES

Thebes (θiːbz) NOUN [1] (in ancient Greece) the chief city of Boeotia, destroyed by Alexander the Great (336 B.C.). [2] (in ancient Egypt) a city on the Nile: at various times capital of Upper Egypt or of the entire country.

theca (ˈθiːkə) NOUN, *plural* **-cae** (-siː). [1] *Botany* an enclosing organ, cell, or spore case, esp the capsule of a moss. [2] *Zoology* a hard outer covering, such as the cup-shaped container of a coral polyp.
▷HISTORY C17: from Latin *thēca*, from Greek *thēkē* case; related to Greek *tithenai* to place
▸ˈ**thecal** *or* ˈ**thecate** ADJECTIVE

thecodont (ˈθiːkəˌdɒnt) ADJECTIVE [1] (of mammals and certain reptiles) having teeth that grow in sockets. [2] of or relating to teeth of this type. ◆ NOUN [3] any extinct reptile of the order *Thecodontia*, of Triassic times, having teeth set in sockets: they gave rise to the dinosaurs, crocodiles, pterodactyls, and birds.
▷HISTORY C20: New Latin *Thecondontia*, from Greek *thēkē* case + -ODONT

thé dansant *French* (te dɑ̃sɑ̃) NOUN, *plural* ***thés dansant*** (te dɑ̃sɑ̃). a dance held while afternoon tea is served, popular in the 1920s and 1930s.
▷HISTORY literally: dancing tea

thee (ðiː) PRONOUN [1] the objective form of **thou**[1]. [2] (*subjective*) *Rare* refers to the person addressed: used mainly by members of the Society of Friends.
▷HISTORY Old English *thē*; see THOU[1]

theft (θɛft) NOUN [1] *Criminal law* the dishonest taking of property belonging to another person with the intention of depriving the owner permanently of its possession. [2] *Rare* something stolen.
▷HISTORY Old English *thēofth*; related to Old Norse *thȳfth*, Old Frisian *thiūvethe*, Middle Dutch *düfte*; see THIEF
▸ˈ**theftless** ADJECTIVE

thegn (θeɪn) NOUN a variant spelling of **thane**.

theine (ˈθiːiːn, -ɪn) NOUN another name for **caffeine**, esp when present in tea
▷HISTORY C19: from New Latin *thea* tea + -INE[2]

their (ðɛə) DETERMINER [1] of, belonging to, or associated in some way with them: *their finest hour; their own clothes; she tried to combat their mocking her.* [2] belonging to or associated in some way with people in general not including the speaker or people addressed: *in many countries they wash their clothes in the river.* [3] belonging to or associated in some way with an indefinite antecedent such as *one, whoever*, or *anybody*: *everyone should bring their own lunch.*
▷HISTORY C12: from Old Norse *theira* (genitive plural); see THEY, THEM

Language note See at **they**.

theirs (ðɛəz) PRONOUN [1] something or someone belonging to or associated in some way with them: *theirs is difficult.* [2] *Not standard* something or someone belonging to or associated in some way with an indefinite antecedent such as *one, whoever*, or *anybody*: *everyone thinks theirs is best.* [3] **of theirs.** belonging to or associated with them.

theism (ˈθiːɪzəm) NOUN [1] the form of the belief in one God as the transcendent creator and ruler of the universe that does not necessarily entail further belief in divine revelation. Compare **deism.** [2] the belief in the existence of a God or gods. Compare **atheism.**
▷HISTORY C17: from Greek *theos* god + -ISM
▸ˈ**theist** NOUN, ADJECTIVE ▸**theˈistic** *or* **theˈistical** ADJECTIVE ▸**theˈistically** ADVERB

them (ðɛm; *unstressed* ðəm) PRONOUN [1] (*objective*) refers to things or people other than the speaker or people addressed: *I'll kill them; what happened to them?* [2] *Chiefly US* a dialect word for **themselves** when used as an indirect object: *they got them a new vice president.* ◆ DETERMINER [3] a nonstandard word for **those**: *three of them oranges.*
▷HISTORY Old English *thǣm*, influenced by Old Norse *theim*; related to Old Frisian *thām*, Old Saxon, Old High German *thēm*, Old Norse *theimr*, Gothic *thaim*

Language note See at **me**[1], **they**.

thematic (θɪˈmætɪk) ADJECTIVE [1] of, relating to, or consisting of a theme or themes. [2] *Linguistics* denoting a word that is the theme of a sentence. [3] *Grammar* **a** denoting a vowel or other sound or sequence of sounds that occurs between the root of a word and any inflectional or derivational suffixes. **b** of or relating to the stem or root of a word. ◆ NOUN [4] *Grammar* a thematic vowel: *"-o-" is a thematic in the combining form "psycho-".*
▸**theˈmatically** ADVERB

thematic apperception test NOUN *Psychol* a projective test in which drawings of interacting people are shown and the person being tested is asked to make up a story about them.

thematization *or* **thematisation** (ˌθiːmətaɪˈzeɪʃən) NOUN *Linguistics* the mental act or process of selecting particular topics as themes in discourse or words as themes in sentences.

theme (θiːm) NOUN [1] an idea or topic expanded in a discourse, discussion, etc. [2] (in literature, music, art, etc.) a unifying idea, image, or motif, repeated or developed throughout a work. [3] *Music* a group of notes forming a recognizable melodic unit, often used as the basis of the musical material in a composition. [4] a short essay, esp one set as an exercise for a student. [5] *Linguistics* the first major constituent of a sentence, usually but not necessarily the subject. In the sentence *history I do like*, "history" is the theme of the sentence, even though it is the object of the verb. [6] *Grammar* another word for **root**[1] (sense 9) or **stem**[1] (sense 9). [7] (in the Byzantine Empire) a territorial unit consisting of several provinces under a military commander. [8] (*modifier*) planned or designed round one unifying subject, image, etc.: *a theme holiday.* ◆ VERB (*tr*) [9] to design, decorate, arrange, etc., in accordance with a theme.
▷HISTORY C13: from Latin *thema*, from Greek: deposit, from *tithenai* to lay down
▸ˈ**themeless** ADJECTIVE

theme park NOUN an area planned as a leisure attraction, in which all the displays, buildings, activities, etc., are based on or relate to one particular subject.

theme song NOUN [1] a melody used, esp in a film score, to set a mood, introduce a character, etc. [2] another term for **signature tune.**

Themis (ˈθiːmɪs) NOUN *Greek myth* a goddess of order and justice.

themselves (ðəmˈsɛlvz) PRONOUN [1] **a** the reflexive form of *they* or *them*. **b** (intensifier): *the team themselves voted on it.* [2] (*preceded by a copula*) their normal or usual selves: *they don't seem themselves any more.* [3] Also: **themself.** *Not standard* a reflexive form of an indefinite antecedent such as *one, whoever*, or *anybody*: *everyone has to look after themselves.*

then (ðɛn) ADVERB [1] at that time; over that period of time. [2] (*sentence modifier*) in that case; that being so: *then why don't you ask her?; if he comes, then you'll have to leave; go on then, take it.* [3] **then and there.** a variant of **there and then**: see **there** (sense 6). ◆ SENTENCE CONNECTOR [4] after that; with that: *then John left the room and didn't return.* ◆ NOUN [5] that time: *before then; from then on.* ◆ ADJECTIVE [6] (*prenominal*) existing, functioning, etc., at that time: *the then prime minister.*
▷HISTORY Old English *thenne*; related to Old Saxon, Old High German *thanna*; see THAN

thenar (ˈθiːnɑː) *Anatomy* ◆ NOUN [1] the palm of the hand. [2] the fleshy area of the palm at the base of the thumb. ◆ ADJECTIVE [3] of or relating to the palm or the region at the base of the thumb.
▷HISTORY C17: via New Latin from Greek; related to Old High German *tenar* palm of the hand

thenardite (θɪˈnɑːdaɪt, tɪ-) NOUN a whitish vitreous mineral that consists of anhydrous sodium sulphate and occurs in saline residues. Formula: Na_2SO_4.
▷HISTORY C19: named after Baron L. J. *Thénard* (1777–1857), French chemist; see -ITE[1]

Thénard's blue (ˈteɪnɑːz, -nɑːdz) NOUN another name for **cobalt blue.**
▷HISTORY C19: named after Baron L. J. *Thénard*; see THENARDITE

thence (ðɛns) ADVERB [1] from that place. [2] Also: **thenceforth** (ˈðɛnsˈfɔːθ). from that time or event; thereafter. [3] therefore.
▷HISTORY C13: *thannes*, from *thanne*, from Old English *thanon*; related to Gothic *thanana*, Old Norse *thanan*

thenceforward (ˈðɛnsˈfɔːwəd) *or* **thenceforwards** ADVERB from that time or place on; thence.

theo- *or before a vowel* **the-** COMBINING FORM indicating God or gods: *theology.*
▷HISTORY from Greek *theos* god

theobromine (ˌθiːəʊˈbrəʊmiːn, -mɪn) NOUN a white crystalline slightly water-soluble alkaloid that occurs in many plants, such as tea and cacao: formerly used to treat asthma. Formula: $C_7H_8N_4O_2$. See also **xanthine** (sense 2).
▷HISTORY C18: from New Latin *theobroma* genus of trees, literally: food of the gods, from THEO- + Greek *brōma* food + -INE[2]

theocentric (ˌθɪəˈsɛntrɪk) ADJECTIVE *Theol* having God as the focal point of attention.
▸ˌ**theocenˈtricity** NOUN ▸ˌ**theoˈcentrism** *or* **theocentricism** (ˌθiːəʊˈsɛntrɪˌsɪzəm) NOUN

theocracy (θɪˈɒkrəsɪ) NOUN, *plural* **-cies.** [1] government by a deity or by a priesthood. [2] a community or political unit under such government.
▸ˈ**theoˌcrat** NOUN ▸ˌ**theoˈcratic** *or* ˌ**theoˈcratical** ADJECTIVE ▸ˌ**theoˈcratically** ADVERB

theocrasy (θɪˈɒkrəsɪ) NOUN [1] a mingling into one of deities or divine attributes previously regarded as distinct. [2] the union of the soul with God in mysticism.
▷HISTORY C19: from Greek *theokrasia*, from THEO- + *-krasia* from *krasis* a blending

theodicy (θɪˈɒdɪsɪ) NOUN, *plural* **-cies.** the branch of theology concerned with defending the attributes of God against objections resulting from physical and moral evil.
▷HISTORY C18: coined by Leibnitz in French as *théodicée*, from THEO- + Greek *dikē* justice
▸**theˌodiˈcean** ADJECTIVE

theodolite (θɪˈɒdəˌlaɪt) NOUN a surveying instrument for measuring horizontal and vertical angles, consisting of a small tripod-mounted telescope that is free to move in both the horizontal and vertical planes. Also called (in the US and Canada): **transit.**
▷HISTORY C16: from New Latin *theodolitus*, of uncertain origin
▸**theodolitic** (θɪˌɒdəˈlɪtɪk) ADJECTIVE

theogony (θɪˈɒgənɪ) NOUN, *plural* **-nies.** [1] the origin and descent of the gods. [2] an account of this, often recited in epic poetry.
▷HISTORY C17: from Greek *theogonia*; see THEO-, -GONY
▸**theogonic** (ˌθɪəˈgɒnɪk) ADJECTIVE ▸**theˈogonist** NOUN

theol. ABBREVIATION FOR: [1] theologian. [2] theological. [3] theology.

theologian (ˌθɪəˈləʊdʒɪən) NOUN a person versed in or engaged in the study of theology, esp Christian theology.

theological (ˌθɪəˈlɒdʒɪkᵊl) ADJECTIVE [1] of, relating

to, or based on theology. 2 based on God's revelation to man of his nature, his designs, and his will.
▸ˌtheoˈlogically ADVERB

theological virtues PLURAL NOUN (esp among the scholastics) those virtues that are infused into man by a special grace of God, specifically faith, hope, and charity. Compare **natural virtues.**

theologize *or* **theologise** (θɪˈɒləˌdʒaɪz) VERB 1 (*intr*) to speculate upon theological subjects, engage in theological study or discussion, or formulate theological arguments. 2 (*tr*) to render theological or treat from a theological point of view.
▸**theˌologiˈzation** *or* **theˌologiˈsation** NOUN ▸**theˈoloˌgizer** *or* **theˈoloˌgiser** NOUN

theology (θɪˈɒlədʒɪ) NOUN, *plural* **-gies.** 1 the systematic study of the existence and nature of the divine and its relationship to and influence upon other beings. 2 a specific branch of this study, undertaken from the perspective of a particular group: *feminist theology.* 3 the systematic study of Christian revelation concerning God's nature and purpose, esp through the teaching of the Church. 4 a specific system, form, or branch of this study, esp for those preparing for the ministry or priesthood.
▷HISTORY C14: from Late Latin *theologia,* from Latin; see THEO-, -LOGY
▸**theˈologist** NOUN

theomachy (θɪˈɒməkɪ) NOUN, *plural* **-chies.** a battle among the gods or against them.
▷HISTORY C16: from Greek *theomakhia,* from THEO- + *makhē* battle

theomancy (ˈθiːəʊmænsɪ) NOUN divination or prophecy by an oracle or by people directly inspired by a god.
▷HISTORY C17: from THEO- + -MANCY

theomania (ˌθɪəˈmeɪnɪə) NOUN religious madness, esp when it takes the form of believing oneself to be a god.
▸ˌ**theoˈmaniˌac** NOUN

theomorphic (ˌθɪəˈmɔːfɪk) ADJECTIVE of or relating to the conception or representation of man as having the form of God or a deity.
▷HISTORY C19: from Greek *theomorphos,* from THEO- + *morphē* form
▸ˌ**theoˈmorphism** NOUN

theonomy (θɪˈɒnəmɪ) NOUN the state of being governed by God.

theopathy (θɪˈɒpəθɪ) NOUN religious emotion engendered by the contemplation of or meditation upon God.
▷HISTORY C18: from THEO- + *-pathy,* from SYMPATHY
▸**theopathetic** (ˌθɪəpəˈθɛtɪk) *or* **theopathic** (ˌθɪəˈpæθɪk) ADJECTIVE

theophagy (θɪˈɒfədʒɪ) NOUN, *plural* **-gies.** the sacramental eating of a god.

theophany (θɪˈɒfənɪ) NOUN, *plural* **-nies.** *Theol* a manifestation of a deity to man in a form that, though visible, is not necessarily material.
▷HISTORY C17: from Late Latin *theophania,* from Late Greek *theophaneia,* from THEO- + *phainein* to show
▸**theophanic** (θɪəˈfænɪk) *or* **theˈophanous** ADJECTIVE

Theophilus (θɪˈɒfɪləs) NOUN a conspicuous crater in the SE quadrant of the moon, 100 kilometres in diameter.
▷HISTORY after *Theophilus* (died 842 A.D.), Byzantine emperor and patron of learning
▸ˌ**theoˈphobiˌac** NOUN

theophylline (ˌθɪəˈfɪliːn, -ɪn, θɪˈɒfɪlɪn) NOUN a white crystalline slightly water-soluble alkaloid that is an isomer of theobromine: it occurs in plants, such as tea, and is used to treat asthma. Formula: $C_7H_8N_4O_2$. See also **xanthine** (sense 2).
▷HISTORY C19: from THEO(BROMINE) + PHYLLO- + -INE[2]

theorbo (θɪˈɔːbəʊ) NOUN, *plural* **-bos.** *Music* an obsolete form of the lute, having two necks, one above the other, the second neck carrying a set of unstopped sympathetic bass strings.
▷HISTORY C17: from Italian *teorba,* probably from Venetian, variant of *tuorba* travelling bag, ultimately from Turkish *torba* bag
▸**theˈorbist** NOUN

theorem (ˈθɪərəm) NOUN *Maths, logic* a statement or formula that can be deduced from the axioms of a formal system by means of its rules of inference.
▷HISTORY C16: from Late Latin *theōrēma,* from Greek: something to be viewed, from *theōrein* to view
▸**theorematic** (ˌθɪərəˈmætɪk) *or* **theoremic** (ˌθɪəˈrɛmɪk) ADJECTIVE ▸ˌ**theoreˈmatically** ADVERB

theoretic (ˌθɪəˈrɛtɪk) ADJECTIVE 1 another word for **theoretical.** ◆ NOUN 2 another word for **theoretics.**

theoretical (ˌθɪəˈrɛtɪkᵊl) *or* **theoretic** ADJECTIVE 1 of or based on theory. 2 lacking practical application or actual existence; hypothetical. 3 using or dealing in theory; impractical.
▸ˌ**theoˈretically** ADVERB

theoretician (ˌθɪərɪˈtɪʃən) NOUN a student or user of the theory rather than the practical aspects of a subject.

theoretics (ˌθɪəˈrɛtɪks) NOUN (*functioning as singular or plural*) the theory of a particular subject. Also called (less commonly): **theoretic.**

theorist (ˈθɪərɪst) NOUN the originator of a theory; a person who is concerned with theory; a theoretician.

theorize *or* **theorise** (ˈθɪəˌraɪz) VERB (*intr*) to produce or use theories; speculate.
▸ˌ**theoriˈzation** *or* ˌ**theoriˈsation** NOUN ▸ˈ**theoˌrizer** *or* ˈ**theoˌriser** NOUN

theory (ˈθɪərɪ) NOUN, *plural* **-ries.** 1 a system of rules, procedures, and assumptions used to produce a result. 2 abstract knowledge or reasoning. 3 a speculative or conjectural view or idea: *I have a theory about that.* 4 an ideal or hypothetical situation (esp in the phrase **in theory**). 5 a set of hypotheses related by logical or mathematical arguments to explain and predict a wide variety of connected phenomena in general terms: *the theory of relativity.* 6 a nontechnical name for **hypothesis** (sense 1).
▷HISTORY C16: from Late Latin *theōria,* from Greek: a sight, from *theōrein* to gaze upon

theory-laden ADJECTIVE (of an expression) capable of being understood only within the context of a specific theory, as for example *superego,* which requires the apparatus of Freudian theory in explanation.

theory of games NOUN another name for **game theory.**

theos. ABBREVIATION FOR: 1 theosophical. 2 theosophy.

theosophy (θɪˈɒsəfɪ) NOUN 1 any of various religious or philosophical systems claiming to be based on or to express an intuitive insight into the divine nature. 2 the system of beliefs of the Theosophical Society founded in 1875, claiming to be derived from the sacred writings of Brahmanism and Buddhism, but denying the existence of any personal God.
▷HISTORY C17: from Medieval Latin *theosophia,* from Late Greek; see THEO-, -SOPHY
▸**theosophical** (ˌθɪəˈsɒfɪkᵊl) ADJECTIVE ▸ˌ**theoˈsophically** ADVERB ▸**theˈosophism** NOUN ▸**theˈosophist** NOUN

Thera (ˈθɪərə) NOUN a Greek island in the Aegean Sea, in the Cyclades: site of a Minoan settlement and of the volcano that ended Minoan civilization on Crete. Pop.: 7000 (latest est.). Also called: **Santoríni.** Modern Greek name: **Thíra.**

therapeutic (ˌθɛrəˈpjuːtɪk) ADJECTIVE 1 of or relating to the treatment of disease; curative. 2 serving or performed to maintain health: *therapeutic abortion.*
▷HISTORY C17: from New Latin *therapeuticus,* from Greek *therapeutikos,* from *therapeuein* to minister to, from *theraps* an attendant
▸ˌ**theraˈpeutically** ADVERB

therapeutic cloning NOUN the permitted creation of cloned human tissues for surgical transplant.

therapeutics (ˌθɛrəˈpjuːtɪks) NOUN (*functioning as singular*) the branch of medicine concerned with the treatment of disease.

therapist (ˈθɛrəpɪst) NOUN a person skilled in a particular type of therapy: *a physical therapist.*

therapsid (θəˈræpsɪd) NOUN any extinct reptile of the order *Therapsida,* of Permian to Triassic times: considered to be the ancestors of mammals.
▷HISTORY C20: from New Latin *Therapsida,* from Greek *theraps* attendant

therapy (ˈθɛrəpɪ) NOUN, *plural* **-pies. a** the treatment of physical, mental, or social disorders or disease. **b** (*in combination*): *physiotherapy; electrotherapy.*
▷HISTORY C19: from New Latin *therapia,* from Greek *therapeia* attendance; see THERAPEUTIC

Theravada (ˌθɛrəˈvɑːdə) NOUN the southern school of Buddhism, the name preferred by Hinayana Buddhists for their doctrines.
▷HISTORY from Pali: doctrine of the elders

there (ðɛə) ADVERB 1 in, at, or to that place, point, case, or respect: *we never go there; I'm afraid I disagree with you there.* ◆ PRONOUN 2 used as a grammatical subject with some verbs, esp *be,* when the true subject is an indefinite or mass noun phrase following the verb as complement: *there is a girl in that office; there doesn't seem to be any water left.* ◆ ADJECTIVE 3 (*postpositive*) who or which is in that place or position: *that boy there did it.* 4 **all there.** (*predicative*) having his wits about him; of normal intelligence. 5 **so there.** an exclamation that usually follows a declaration of refusal or defiance: *you can't have any more, so there!* 6 **there and then.** on the spot; immediately; instantly. 7 **there it is.** that is the state of affairs. 8 **there you are. a** an expression used when handing a person something requested or desired. **b** an exclamation of triumph: *there you are, I knew that would happen!* ◆ NOUN 9 that place: *near there; from there.* ◆ INTERJECTION 10 an expression of sympathy, as in consoling a child.
▷HISTORY Old English *thǣr;* related to Old Frisian *thēr,* Old Saxon, Old High German *thār,* Old Norse, Gothic *thar*

> **Language note** In correct usage, the verb should agree with the number of the subject in such constructions as *there is a man waiting* and *there are several people waiting.* However, where the subject is compound, it is common in speech to use the singular as in *there's a police car and an ambulance outside.*

thereabouts (ˈðɛərəˌbaʊts) *or US* **thereabout** ADVERB near that place, time, amount, etc.: *fifty or thereabouts.*

thereafter (ˌðɛərˈɑːftə) ADVERB from that time on or after that time: *thereafter, he ceased to pay attention.*

thereat (ˌðɛərˈæt) ADVERB *Rare* 1 at that point or time. 2 for that reason.

thereby (ˌðɛəˈbaɪ, ˈðɛəˌbaɪ) ADVERB 1 by that means; because of that. 2 *Archaic* by or near that place; thereabouts.

therefor (ˌðɛəˈfɔː) ADVERB *Archaic* for this, that, or it: *he will be richer therefor.*

therefore (ˈðɛəˌfɔː) SENTENCE CONNECTOR 1 thus; hence: used to mark an inference on the speaker's part: *those people have their umbrellas up: therefore, it must be raining.* 2 consequently; as a result: *they heard the warning on the radio and therefore took another route.*

therefrom (ˌðɛəˈfrɒm) ADVERB *Archaic* from that or there: *the roads that lead therefrom.*

therein (ˌðɛərˈɪn) ADVERB *Formal* in or into that place, thing, etc.

thereinafter (ˌðɛərɪnˈɑːftə) ADVERB *Formal* from this point on in that document, statement, etc.

thereinto (ˌðɛərˈɪntuː) ADVERB *Formal* into that place, circumstance, etc.

theremin (ˈθɛrəmɪn) NOUN an electronic musical instrument, played by moving the hands through electromagnetic fields created by two metal rods.
▷HISTORY C20: named after Leon *Theremin* (1896-1993), Russian scientist who invented it

thereof (ˌðɛərˈɒv) ADVERB *Formal* 1 of or concerning that or it. 2 from or because of that.

thereon (ˌðɛərˈɒn) ADVERB an archaic word for **thereupon.**

thereto (ˌðɛəˈtuː) ADVERB 1 *Formal* to that or it: *the form attached thereto.* 2 *Obsolete* in addition to that.

theretofore (ˌðɛətuˈfɔː) ADVERB *Formal* before that time; previous to that.

thereunder (ˌðɛərˈʌndə) ADVERB *Formal* 1 (in documents, etc.) below that or it; subsequently in that; thereafter. 2 under the terms or authority of that.

thereupon (ˌðɛərəˈpɒn) ADVERB 1 immediately after that; at that point: *thereupon, the whole class applauded.* 2 *Formal* upon that thing, point, subject, etc.

therewith (ˌðɛəˈwɪθ, -ˈwɪð) *or* **therewithal**

ADVERB [1] *Formal* with or in addition to that. [2] a less common word for **thereupon** (sense 1). [3] *Archaic* by means of or on account of that.

Therezina (*Portuguese* tere'zina) NOUN the former name of **Teresina.**

theriac ('θɪərɪæk) NOUN *Archaic* an ointment or potion of varying composition, used as an antidote to a poison.
▷HISTORY C14: from Latin *thēriaca* antidote to poison

therianthropic (ˌθɪərɪən'θrɒpɪk) ADJECTIVE [1] (of certain mythical creatures or deities) having a partly animal, partly human form. [2] of or relating to such creatures or deities.
▷HISTORY C19: from Greek *thērion* wild animal + *anthrōpos* man
▸**therianthropism** (ˌθɪərɪ'ænθrəˌpɪzəm) NOUN

theriomorphic (ˌθɪərɪəʊ'mɔːfɪk) *or* **theriomorphous** ADJECTIVE (esp of a deity) possessing or depicted in the form of a beast.
▷HISTORY C19: from Greek *thēriomorphos,* from *thērion* wild animal + *morphē* shape
▸**'therioˌmorph** NOUN

therm (θɜːm) NOUN *Brit* a unit of heat equal to 100 000 British thermal units. One therm is equal to $1.055\,056 \times 10^8$ joules.
▷HISTORY C19: from Greek *thermē* heat

thermae ('θɜːmiː) PLURAL NOUN public baths or hot springs, esp in ancient Greece or Rome.
▷HISTORY C17: from Latin, from Greek *thermai,* pl of *thermē* heat

thermaesthesia *or US* **thermesthesia** (ˌθɜːmɪs'θiːzɪə) NOUN sensitivity to various degrees of heat and cold.
▷HISTORY C19: from New Latin, from THERM- + Greek *aisthēsis* feeling

thermal ('θɜːməl) ADJECTIVE [1] Also: **thermic** ('θɜːmɪk). of, relating to, caused by, or generating heat or increased temperature. [2] hot or warm: *thermal baths; thermal spring.* [3] (of garments or fabrics) specially designed so as to have exceptional heat-retaining properties. ◆ NOUN [4] *Meteorol* a column of rising air caused by local unequal heating of the land surface, and used by gliders and birds to gain height. [5] (*plural*) thermal garments, esp underclothes.
▸**'thermally** ADVERB

thermal barrier NOUN an obstacle to flight at very high speeds as a result of the heating effect of air friction. Also called: **heat barrier.**

thermal conductivity NOUN a measure of the ability of a substance to conduct heat, determined by the rate of heat flow normally through an area in the substance divided by the area and by minus the component of the temperature gradient in the direction of flow: measured in watts per metre per kelvin. Symbol: λ or *k*. Sometimes shortened to: **conductivity.**

thermal efficiency NOUN the ratio of the work done by a heat engine to the energy supplied to it. Compare **efficiency.**

thermal equator NOUN an imaginary line round the earth running through the point on each meridian with the highest average temperature. It lies mainly to the north because of the larger landmasses and therefore greater summer heating.

thermal imaging NOUN the use of heat-sensitive equipment to detect or provide images of people or things.

thermalize *or* **thermalise** ('θɜːməˌlaɪz) VERB *Physics* to undergo or cause to undergo a process in which neutrons lose energy in a moderator and become thermal neutrons.
▸ˌ**thermali'zation** *or* ˌ**thermali'sation** NOUN

thermal neutrons PLURAL NOUN slow neutrons that are approximately in thermal equilibrium with a moderator. They have a distribution of speeds similar to that of the molecules of a gas at the temperature of the moderator. Data concerning nuclear interactions are often given for standard thermal neutrons of speed 2200 metres per second, which is approximately the most probable speed at normal laboratory temperatures.

thermal noise NOUN electrical noise caused by thermal agitation of conducting electrons.

thermal printer NOUN *Computing* another name for **electrothermal printer.**

thermal reactor NOUN a nuclear reactor in which most of the fission is caused by thermal neutrons.

thermal shock NOUN a fluctuation in temperature causing stress in a material. It often results in fracture, esp in brittle materials such as ceramics.

thermette (θɜː'mɛt) NOUN *NZ* a device, used outdoors, for boiling water rapidly.

Thermidor *French* (tɛrmidɔr) NOUN the month of heat: the eleventh month of the French revolutionary calendar, extending from July 20 to Aug. 18. Also called: **Fervidor.**
▷HISTORY C19: from French, from Greek *thermē* heat + *dōron* gift

thermion ('θɜːmɪən) NOUN *Physics* an electron or ion emitted by a body at high temperature.

thermionic (ˌθɜːmɪ'ɒnɪk) ADJECTIVE of, relating to, or operated by electrons emitted from materials at high temperatures: *a thermionic valve.*

thermionic current NOUN an electric current produced between two electrodes as a result of electrons emitted by thermionic emission.

thermionic emission NOUN the emission of electrons from very hot solids or liquids: used for producing electrons in valves, electron microscopes, X-ray tubes, etc.

thermionics (ˌθɜːmɪ'ɒnɪks) NOUN (*functioning as singular*) the branch of electronics concerned with the emission of electrons by hot bodies and with devices based on this effect, esp the study and design of thermionic valves.

thermionic valve *or esp US and Canadian* **tube** NOUN an electronic valve in which electrons are emitted from a heated rather than a cold cathode.

thermistor (θɜː'mɪstə) NOUN a semiconductor device having a resistance that decreases rapidly with an increase in temperature. It is used for temperature measurement, to compensate for temperature variations in a circuit, etc.
▷HISTORY C20: from THERMO- + (RES)ISTOR

Thermit ('θɜːmɪt) *or* **Thermite** ('θɜːmaɪt) NOUN *Trademark* a mixture of aluminium powder and a metal oxide, such as iron oxide, which when ignited reacts with the evolution of heat to yield aluminium oxide and molten metal: used for welding and in some types of incendiary bombs.

thermite process NOUN another name for **aluminothermy.**

thermo- *or before a vowel* **therm-** COMBINING FORM related to, caused by, or measuring heat: *thermodynamics; thermophile.*
▷HISTORY from Greek *thermos* hot, *thermē* heat

thermobarograph (ˌθɜːməʊ'bærəˌgrɑːf, -ˌgræf) NOUN a device that simultaneously records the temperature and pressure of the atmosphere.

thermobarometer (ˌθɜːməʊbə'rɒmɪtə) NOUN an apparatus that provides an accurate measurement of pressure by observation of the change in the boiling point of a fluid.

thermochemistry (ˌθɜːməʊ'kɛmɪstrɪ) NOUN the branch of chemistry concerned with the study and measurement of the heat evolved or absorbed during chemical reactions.
▸ˌ**thermo'chemical** ADJECTIVE ▸ˌ**thermo'chemically** ADVERB ▸ˌ**thermo'chemist** NOUN

thermochromism (ˌθɜːməʊ'krəʊmɪzəm) NOUN a phenomenon in which certain dyes made from liquid crystals change colour reversibly when their temperature is changed.
▸**'thermochromy** NOUN ▸ˌ**thermo'chromic** ADJECTIVE

thermocline ('θɜːməʊˌklaɪn) NOUN a temperature gradient in a thermally stratified body of water, such as a lake.

thermocouple ('θɜːməʊˌkʌpᵊl) NOUN [1] a device for measuring temperature consisting of a pair of wires of different metals or semiconductors joined at both ends. One junction is at the temperature to be measured, the second at a fixed temperature. The electromotive force generated depends upon the temperature difference. [2] a similar device with only one junction between two dissimilar metals or semiconductors.
▷HISTORY C19: from THERMO- + COUPLE

thermodynamic (ˌθɜːməʊdaɪ'næmɪk) *or* **thermodynamical** ADJECTIVE [1] of or concerned with thermodynamics. [2] determined by or obeying the laws of thermodynamics.
▸ˌ**thermody'namically** ADVERB

thermodynamic equilibrium NOUN the condition of an isolated system in which the quantities that specify its properties, such as pressure, temperature, etc., all remain unchanged. Sometimes shortened to: **equilibrium.**

thermodynamics (ˌθɜːməʊdaɪ'næmɪks) NOUN (*functioning as singular*) the branch of physical science concerned with the interrelationship and interconversion of different forms of energy and the behaviour of macroscopic systems in terms of certain basic quantities, such as pressure, temperature, etc. See also **law of thermodynamics.**

thermodynamic temperature NOUN temperature defined in terms of the laws of thermodynamics and not in terms of the properties of any real material. It is usually expressed on the Kelvin scale. Also called: **absolute temperature.**

thermoelectric (ˌθɜːməʊɪ'lɛktrɪk) *or* **thermoelectrical** ADJECTIVE [1] of, relating to, used in, or operated by the generation of an electromotive force by the Seebeck effect or the Thomson effect: *a thermoelectric thermometer.* [2] of, relating to, used in, or operated by the production or absorption of heat by the Peltier effect: *a thermoelectric cooler.*
▸ˌ**thermoe'lectrically** ADVERB

thermoelectric effect NOUN another name for the **Seebeck effect** or **Peltier effect.**

thermoelectricity (ˌθɜːməʊɪlɛk'trɪsɪtɪ) NOUN [1] electricity generated by a thermocouple. [2] the study of the relationship between heat and electrical energy. See also **Seebeck effect, Peltier effect.**

thermoelectron (ˌθɜːməʊɪ'lɛktrɒn) NOUN an electron emitted at high temperature, such as one produced in a thermionic valve.

thermogenesis (ˌθɜːməʊ'dʒɛnɪsɪs) NOUN the production of heat by metabolic processes.
▸**thermogenous** (θɜː'mɒdʒɪnəs) *or* **thermogenetic** (ˌθɜːməʊdʒɪ'nɛtɪk) *or* ˌ**thermo'genic** ADJECTIVE

thermogram ('θɜːməʊˌgræm) NOUN [1] *Med* a picture produced by thermography, using photographic film sensitive to infrared radiation. [2] the record produced by a thermograph.

thermograph ('θɜːməʊˌgrɑːf, -ˌgræf) NOUN a type of thermometer that produces a continuous record of a fluctuating temperature.

thermography (θɜː'mɒgrəfɪ) NOUN [1] any writing, printing, or recording process involving the use of heat. [2] a printing process which produces raised characters by heating special powder or ink placed on the paper. [3] *Med* the measurement and recording of heat produced by a part of the body: used in the diagnosis of tumours, esp of the breast (**mammothermography**), which have an increased blood supply and therefore generate more heat than normal tissue. See also **thermogram.**
▸**ther'mographer** NOUN ▸**thermographic** (ˌθɜːməʊ'græfɪk) ADJECTIVE

thermojunction (ˌθɜːməʊ'dʒʌŋkʃən) NOUN a point of electrical contact between two dissimilar metals across which a voltage appears, the magnitude of which depends on the temperature of the contact and the nature of the metals. See also **Seebeck effect.**

thermolabile (ˌθɜːməʊ'leɪbɪl) ADJECTIVE (of certain biochemical and chemical compounds) easily decomposed or subject to a loss of characteristic properties by the action of heat: *a thermolabile enzyme.* Compare **thermostable** (sense 1).
▷HISTORY C20: from THERMO- + LABILE

thermoluminescence (ˌθɜːməʊˌluːmɪ'nɛsəns) NOUN phosphorescence of certain materials or objects as a result of heating. It is caused by pre-irradiation of the material inducing defects which are removed by the heat, the energy released appearing as light: used in archaeological dating.
▸ˌ**thermoˌlumi'nescent** ADJECTIVE

thermolysis (θɜː'mɒlɪsɪs) NOUN [1] *Physiol* loss of heat from the body. [2] the dissociation of a substance as a result of heating.
▸**thermolytic** (ˌθɜːməʊ'lɪtɪk) ADJECTIVE

thermomagnetic (ˌθɜːməʊmæg'nɛtɪk) ADJECTIVE of or concerned with the relationship between heat and magnetism, esp the change in temperature of a body when it is magnetized or demagnetized. Former term: **pyromagnetic.**

thermometer (θəˈmɒmɪtə) NOUN an instrument used to measure temperature, esp one in which a thin column of liquid, such as mercury, expands and contracts within a graduated sealed tube. See also **clinical thermometer, gas thermometer, resistance thermometer, thermocouple, pyrometer.**

thermometry (θəˈmɒmɪtrɪ) NOUN the branch of physics concerned with the measurement of temperature and the design and use of thermometers and pyrometers.
▸**thermometric** (ˌθɜːməˈmɛtrɪk) *or* ˌ**thermoˈmetrical** ADJECTIVE ▸ˌ**thermoˈmetrically** ADVERB

thermomotor (ˌθɜːməʊˈməʊtə) NOUN an engine that produces force from the expansion of a heated fluid.

thermonasty (ˈθɜːməʊˌnæstɪ) NOUN *Botany* a nastic movement in response to a temperature change, as occurs in the opening of certain flowers.

thermonuclear (ˌθɜːməʊˈnjuːklɪə) ADJECTIVE [1] involving nuclear fusion: *a thermonuclear reaction; thermonuclear energy*. [2] involving thermonuclear weapons: *a thermonuclear war.*

thermonuclear bomb NOUN another name for **fusion bomb.**

thermonuclear reaction NOUN a nuclear fusion reaction occurring at a very high temperature: responsible for the energy produced in the sun, nuclear weapons, and fusion reactors. See **nuclear fusion, hydrogen bomb.**

thermoperiodism (ˌθɜːməʊˈpɪərɪədɪzəm) *or* **thermoperiodicity** (ˌθɜːməʊˌpɪərɪəˈdɪsɪtɪ) NOUN *Botany* the response of a plant to cycles of temperature fluctuation.
▸ˌ**thermoˌperiˈodic** ADJECTIVE

thermophile (ˈθɜːməʊˌfaɪl) *or* **thermophil** (ˈθɜːməʊˌfɪl) NOUN [1] an organism, esp a bacterium or plant, that thrives under warm conditions. ◆ ADJECTIVE [2] thriving under warm conditions.
▸ˌ**thermoˈphilic** *or* **thermophilous** (θɜːˈmɒfɪləs) ADJECTIVE

thermopile (ˈθɜːməʊˌpaɪl) NOUN an instrument for detecting and measuring heat radiation or for generating a thermoelectric current. It consists of a number of thermocouple junctions, usually joined together in series.
▷**HISTORY** C19: from THERMO- + PILE[1] (in the sense: voltaic pile)

thermoplastic (ˌθɜːməʊˈplæstɪk) ADJECTIVE [1] (of a material, esp a synthetic plastic or resin) becoming soft when heated and rehardening on cooling without appreciable change of properties. Compare **thermosetting.** ◆ NOUN [2] a synthetic plastic or resin, such as polystyrene, with these properties.
▸**thermoplasticity** (ˌθɜːməʊplæˈstɪsɪtɪ) NOUN

Thermopylae (θəˈmɒpəˌliː) NOUN (in ancient Greece) a narrow pass between the mountains and the sea linking Locris and Thessaly: a defensible position on a traditional invasion route from N Greece; scene of a famous battle (480 B.C.) in which a greatly outnumbered Greek army under Leonidas fought to the death to delay the advance of the Persians during their attempted conquest of Greece.

Thermos *or* **Thermos flask** (ˈθɜːməs) NOUN *Trademark* a type of stoppered vacuum flask used to preserve the temperature of its contents. See also **Dewar flask.**

thermoscope (ˈθɜːməˌskəʊp) NOUN a device that indicates a change in temperature, esp one that does not measure the actual temperature.
▸**thermoscopic** (ˌθɜːməˈskɒpɪk) *or* ˌ**thermoˈscopical** ADJECTIVE ▸ˌ**thermoˈscopically** ADVERB

thermosetting (ˌθɜːməʊˈsɛtɪŋ) ADJECTIVE (of a material, esp a synthetic plastic or resin) hardening permanently after one application of heat and pressure. Thermosetting plastics, such as phenol-formaldehyde, cannot be remoulded. Compare **thermoplastic.**

thermosiphon (ˌθɜːməʊˈsaɪfən) NOUN a system in which a coolant is circulated by convection caused by a difference in density between the hot and cold portions of the liquid.

thermosphere (ˈθɜːməˌsfɪə) NOUN an atmospheric layer lying between the mesosphere and the exosphere, reaching an altitude of about 400 kilometres where the temperature is over 1000°C.

thermostable (ˌθɜːməʊˈsteɪbᵊl) ADJECTIVE [1] (of certain chemical and biochemical compounds) capable of withstanding moderate heat without loss of characteristic properties: *a thermostable plastic.* Compare **thermolabile.** [2] not affected by high temperatures.
▸**thermostability** (ˌθɜːməʊstəˈbɪlɪtɪ) NOUN

thermostat (ˈθɜːməˌstæt) NOUN [1] a device that maintains a system at a constant temperature. It often consists of a bimetallic strip that bends as it expands and contracts with temperature, thus breaking and making contact with an electrical power supply. [2] a similar device that actuates equipment, such as a sprinkler, when a certain temperature is reached.
▸ˌ**thermoˈstatic** ADJECTIVE ▸ˌ**thermoˈstatically** ADVERB

thermostatics (ˌθɜːməˈstætɪks) NOUN (*functioning as singular*) the branch of science concerned with thermal equilibrium.

thermotaxis (ˌθɜːməʊˈtæksɪs) NOUN the directional movement of an organism in response to the stimulus of a source of heat.
▸ˌ**thermoˈtaxic** ADJECTIVE

thermotensile (ˌθɜːməʊˈtɛnsaɪl) ADJECTIVE of or relating to tensile strength in so far as it is affected by temperature.

thermotherapy (ˌθɜːməʊˈθɛrəpɪ) NOUN *Med* treatment of a bodily structure or part by the application of heat.

thermotolerant (ˌθɜːməʊˈtɒlərənt) ADJECTIVE (of plants) able to tolerate, but not thriving in, high temperatures.

thermotropism (ˌθɜːməʊˈtrəʊpɪzəm) NOUN the directional growth of a plant in response to the stimulus of heat.
▸ˌ**thermoˈtropic** ADJECTIVE

-thermy NOUN COMBINING FORM indicating heat: *diathermy.*
▷**HISTORY** from New Latin *-thermia,* from Greek *thermē*
▸**-thermic** *or* **-thermal** ADJECTIVE COMBINING FORM

theroid (ˈθɪərɔɪd) ADJECTIVE of, relating to, or resembling a beast.
▷**HISTORY** C19: from Greek *thēroeidēs,* from *thēr* wild animal; see -OID

therophyte (ˈθɪərəˌfaɪt) NOUN a plant that overwinters as a seed.
▷**HISTORY** from Greek *theros* summer + -PHYTE

theropod (ˈθɪərəpɒd) NOUN any bipedal carnivorous saurischian dinosaur of the suborder *Theropoda,* having strong hind legs and grasping hands. They lived in Triassic to Cretaceous times and included tyrannosaurs and megalosaurs.
▷**HISTORY** C19: from New Latin *theropoda,* from Greek *thēr* beast + *pous* foot
▸**theropodan** (θɪˈrɒpədᵊn) NOUN, ADJECTIVE

Thersites (θəˈsaɪtiːz) NOUN the ugliest and most evil-tongued fighter on the Greek side in the Trojan War, killed by Achilles when he mocked him.

thersitical (θəˈsɪtɪkᵊl) ADJECTIVE *Rare* abusive and loud.
▷**HISTORY** C17: from THERSITES

thesaurus (θɪˈsɔːrəs) NOUN, *plural* **-ruses** *or* **-ri** (-raɪ). [1] a book containing systematized lists of synonyms and related words. [2] a dictionary of selected words or topics. [3] *Rare* a treasury.
▷**HISTORY** C18: from Latin, Greek: TREASURE

these (ðiːz) DETERMINER **a** the form of **this** used before a plural noun: *these men.* **b** (*as pronoun*): *I don't much care for these.*

Theseus (ˈθiːsɪəs) NOUN *Greek myth* a hero of Attica, noted for his many great deeds, among them the slaying of the Minotaur, the conquest of the Amazons, whose queen he married, and participation in the Calydonian hunt.
▸**Thesean** (θɪˈsiːən) ADJECTIVE

thesis (ˈθiːsɪs) NOUN, *plural* **-ses** (-siːz). [1] a dissertation resulting from original research, esp when submitted by a candidate for a degree or diploma. [2] a doctrine maintained or promoted in argument. [3] a subject for a discussion or essay. [4] an unproved statement, esp one put forward as a premise in an argument. [5] *Music* the downbeat of a bar, as indicated in conducting. [6] (in classical prosody) the syllable or part of a metrical foot not receiving the ictus. Compare **arsis.** [7] *Philosophy* the first stage in the Hegelian dialectic, that is challenged by the antithesis.
▷**HISTORY** C16: via Late Latin from Greek: a placing, from *tithenai* to place

thespian (ˈθɛspɪən) ADJECTIVE [1] of or relating to drama and the theatre; dramatic. ◆ NOUN [2] *Often facetious* an actor or actress.
▷**HISTORY** C19: from Thespis, the 6th century B.C. Greek poet, regarded as the founder of tragic drama

Thess. *Bible* ABBREVIATION FOR Thessalonians.

Thessalian (θɛˈseɪlɪən) ADJECTIVE [1] of or relating to the Greek region of Thessaly or its inhabitants. ◆ NOUN [2] a native or inhabitant of Thessaly.

Thessalonian (ˌθɛsəˈləʊnɪən) ADJECTIVE [1] of or relating to ancient Thessalonica (modern Salonika). ◆ NOUN [2] an inhabitant of ancient Thessalonica.

Thessalonians (ˌθɛsəˈləʊnɪənz) NOUN (*functioning as singular*) either of two books of the New Testament (in full **The First and Second Epistles of Paul the Apostle to the Thessalonians**).

Thessaloníki (*Greek* θεsaloˈniki) NOUN a port in NE Greece, in central Macedonia at the head of the **Gulf of Salonika** (an inlet of the Aegean): capital of the Roman province of Macedonia; university (1926). Pop.: 377 951 (1991). Latin name: **Thessalonica** (ˌθɛsəˈlɒnɪkə). English name: **Salonika** *or* **Salonica.**

Thessaly (ˈθɛsəlɪ) NOUN a region of E Central Greece, on the Aegean: an extensive fertile plain, edged with mountains. Pop.: 754 893 (2001). Area: 14 037 sq. km (5418 sq. miles). Modern Greek name: **Thessalía** (ˌθɛsaˈljia).

theta (ˈθiːtə) NOUN [1] the eighth letter of the Greek alphabet (Θ, θ), a consonant, transliterated as *th.* [2] the lower-case form of this letter used in phonetic transcription to represent the voiceless dental fricative *th* as in *thick, both.* Compare **edh.**
▷**HISTORY** C17: from Greek, of Semitic origin; compare Hebrew *tēth*

Thetford Mines (ˈθɛtfəd) NOUN a city in SE Canada, in S Quebec: asbestos industry. Pop.: 17 273 (1991).

thetic (ˈθɛtɪk) ADJECTIVE [1] (in classical prosody) of, bearing, or relating to a metrical stress. [2] positive and arbitrary; prescriptive.
▷**HISTORY** C17: from Greek *thetikos,* from *thetos* laid down, from *tithenai* to place
▸ˈ**thetically** ADVERB

Thetis (ˈθiːtɪs) NOUN one of the Nereids and mother of Achilles by Peleus.

theurgy (ˈθiːˌɜːdʒɪ) NOUN, *plural* **-gies.** [1] **a** the intervention of a divine or supernatural agency in the affairs of man. **b** the working of miracles by such intervention. [2] beneficent magic as taught and performed by Egyptian Neoplatonists and others.
▷**HISTORY** C16: from Late Latin *theūrgia,* from Late Greek *theourgia* the practice of magic, from *theo-* THEO- + *-urgia,* from *ergon* work
▸**theˈurgic** *or* **theˈurgical** ADJECTIVE ▸**theˈurgically** ADVERB
▸ˈ**theurgist** NOUN

thew (θjuː) NOUN [1] muscle, esp if strong or well-developed. [2] (*plural*) muscular strength.
▷**HISTORY** Old English *thēaw;* related to Old Saxon, Old High German *thau* discipline, Latin *tuērī* to observe, *tūtus* secure
▸ˈ**thewy** ADJECTIVE ▸ˈ**thewless** ADJECTIVE

they (ðeɪ) PRONOUN (*subjective*) [1] refers to people or things other than the speaker or people addressed: *they fight among themselves.* [2] refers to unspecified people or people in general not including the speaker or people addressed: *in Australia they have Christmas in the summer.* [3] *Not standard* refers to an indefinite antecedent such as *one, whoever,* or *anybody*: *if anyone objects, they can go.* [4] an archaic word for **those:** *blessed are they that mourn.*
▷**HISTORY** C12: *thei* from Old Norse *their,* masculine nominative plural, equivalent to Old English *thā*

Language note It was formerly considered correct to use *he, him,* or *his* after pronouns such as *everyone, no-one, anyone,* or *someone* as in *everyone did his best,* but it is now more common to use *they, them,* or *their,* and this use has become acceptable in all but the most formal contexts: *everyone did their best.*

they'd (ðeɪd) CONTRACTION OF they would *or* they had.

they'll (ðeɪl) CONTRACTION OF they will *or* they shall.

they're (ðɛə, ˈðeɪə) CONTRACTION OF they are.

they've (ðeɪv) CONTRACTION OF they have.

THI ABBREVIATION FOR **temperature-humidity index.**

thi- COMBINING FORM a variant of **thio-.**

thiamine (ˈθaɪəˌmiːn, -mɪn) *or* **thiamin** (ˈθaɪəmɪn) NOUN *Biochem* a soluble white crystalline vitamin that occurs in the outer coat of rice and other grains. It forms part of the vitamin B complex and is essential for carbohydrate metabolism: deficiency leads to nervous disorders and to the disease beriberi. Formula: $C_{12}H_{17}ON_4SCl.H_2O$. Also called: **vitamin B$_1$, aneurin.**
▷**HISTORY** C20: THIO- + (VIT)AMIN

thiazine (ˈθaɪəˌziːn, -ˌzaɪn) NOUN any of a group of organic compounds containing a ring system composed of four carbon atoms, a sulphur atom, and a nitrogen atom.

thiazole (ˈθaɪəˌzəʊl) *or* **thiazol** (ˈθaɪəˌzɒl) NOUN [1] a colourless liquid with a pungent smell that contains a ring system composed of three carbon atoms, a sulphur atom, and a nitrogen atom. It is used in dyes and fungicides. Formula: C_3H_3NS. [2] any of a group of compounds derived from this substance that are used in dyes.

thick (θɪk) ADJECTIVE [1] of relatively great extent from one surface to the other; fat, broad, or deep: *a thick slice of bread.* [2] **a** (*postpositive*) of specific fatness: *ten centimetres thick.* **b** (*in combination*): *a six-inch-thick wall.* [3] having a relatively dense consistency; not transparent: *thick soup.* [4] abundantly covered or filled: *a piano thick with dust.* [5] impenetrable; dense: *a thick fog.* [6] stupid, slow, or insensitive: *a thick person.* [7] throaty or badly articulated: *a voice thick with emotion.* [8] (of accents, etc.) pronounced. [9] *Informal* very friendly (esp in the phrase **thick as thieves**). [10] **a bit thick.** *Brit* unfair or excessive. [11] **a thick ear.** *Informal* a blow on the ear delivered as punishment, in anger, etc. ◆ ADVERB [12] in order to produce something thick: *to slice bread thick.* [13] profusely; in quick succession (esp in the phrase **thick and fast**). [14] **lay it on thick.** *Informal* **a** to exaggerate a story, statement, etc. **b** to flatter excessively. ◆ NOUN [15] a thick piece or part. [16] **the thick.** the busiest or most intense part. [17] **through thick and thin.** in good times and bad.
▷**HISTORY** Old English *thicce;* related to Old Saxon, Old High German *thikki,* Old Norse *thykkr*
▸ **ˈthickish** ADJECTIVE ▸ **ˈthickly** ADVERB

thick client NOUN *Computing* a computer having its own hard drive, as opposed to one on a network where most functions are carried out on a central server. See **thin client.**

thicken (ˈθɪkən) VERB [1] to make or become thick or thicker: *thicken the soup by adding flour.* [2] (*intr*) to become more involved: *the plot thickened.*
▸ **ˈthickener** NOUN

thickening (ˈθɪkənɪŋ) NOUN [1] something added to a liquid to thicken it. [2] a thickened part or piece.

thicket (ˈθɪkɪt) NOUN a dense growth of small trees, shrubs, and similar plants.
▷**HISTORY** Old English *thiccet;* see THICK

thickhead (ˈθɪkˌhɛd) NOUN [1] a stupid or ignorant person; fool. [2] Also called: **whistler.** any of various Australian and SE Asian songbirds of the family *Muscicapidae* (flycatchers, etc.).
▸ **ˌthickˈheaded** ADJECTIVE ▸ **ˌthickˈheadedness** NOUN

thickie *or* **thicky** (ˈθɪkɪ) NOUN, *plural* **-ies.** *Brit slang* a variant of **thicko.**

thick-knee NOUN another name for **stone curlew.**
▷**HISTORY** C19: so called because it has thick knee joints

thickleaf (ˈθɪkˌliːf) NOUN, *plural* **-leaves.** any of various succulent plants of the crassulaceous genus *Crassula,* having sessile or short-stalked fleshy leaves.

thickness (ˈθɪknɪs) NOUN [1] the state or quality of being thick. [2] the dimension through an object, as opposed to length or width. [3] a layer of something. [4] a thick part.

thicko (ˈθɪkəʊ) NOUN, *plural* **thickos** *or* **thickoes.** *Brit slang* a slow-witted unintelligent person. Also: **thickie, thicky.**

thickset (ˌθɪkˈsɛt) ADJECTIVE [1] stocky in build; sturdy. [2] densely planted or placed. ◆ NOUN [3] a rare word for **thicket.**

thick-skinned ADJECTIVE insensitive to criticism or hints; not easily upset or affected.

thick-witted *or* **thick-skulled** ADJECTIVE stupid, dull, foolish, or slow to learn.
▸ **ˌthick-ˈwittedly** ADVERB ▸ **ˌthick-ˈwittedness** NOUN

thief (θiːf) NOUN, *plural* **thieves** (θiːvz). [1] a person who steals something from another. [2] *Criminal law* a person who commits theft.
▷**HISTORY** Old English *thēof;* related to Old Frisian *thiāf,* Old Saxon *thiof,* Old High German *diob,* Old Norse *thjōfr,* Gothic *thiufs*
▸ **ˈthievish** ADJECTIVE ▸ **ˈthievishly** ADVERB ▸ **ˈthievishness** NOUN

thieve (θiːv) VERB to steal (someone's possessions).
▷**HISTORY** Old English *thēofian,* from *thēof* THIEF
▸ **ˈthievery** NOUN

thieving (ˈθiːvɪŋ) ADJECTIVE given to stealing other people's possessions.

thigh (θaɪ) NOUN [1] the part of the leg between the hip and the knee in man. [2] the corresponding part in other vertebrates and insects. ◆ Related adjectives: **crural, femoral.**
▷**HISTORY** Old English *thēh;* related to Old Frisian *thiāch,* Old High German *dioh* thigh, Old Norse *thjō* buttock, Old Slavonic *tyku* fat

thighbone (ˈθaɪˌbəʊn) NOUN a nontechnical name for the **femur.**

thigmotaxis (ˌθɪgməˈtæksɪs) NOUN another name for **stereotaxis.**
▷**HISTORY** C19: from Greek *thigma* touch + -TAXIS
▸ **ˌthigmoˈtactic** ADJECTIVE ▸ **ˌthigmoˈtactically** ADVERB

thigmotropism (ˌθɪgməʊˈtrəʊpɪzəm) NOUN the directional growth of a plant, in response to the stimulus of direct contact. Also called: **haptotropism, stereotropism.**
▷**HISTORY** C19: from Greek *thigma* touch + -TROPISM
▸ **ˌthigmoˈtropic** ADJECTIVE

thill (θɪl) NOUN *Archaic* another word for **shaft** (sense 6).
▷**HISTORY** C14: perhaps related to Old English *thille* board, planking, Old High German *dilla* plank, Old Norse *thili*

thimble (ˈθɪmbᵊl) NOUN [1] a cap of metal, plastic, etc., used to protect the end of the finger when sewing. [2] any small metal cap resembling this. [3] *Nautical* a loop of metal having a groove at its outer edge for a rope or cable, for lining the inside of an eye. [4] short for **thimbleful.**
▷**HISTORY** Old English *thȳmel* thumbstall, from *thūma* THUMB

thimbleful (ˈθɪmbᵊlˌfʊl) NOUN a very small amount, esp of a liquid.

thimblerig (ˈθɪmbᵊlˌrɪg) NOUN [1] a game in which the operator rapidly moves about three inverted thimbles, often with sleight of hand, one of which conceals a token, the other player betting on which thimble the token is under. ◆ VERB **-rigs, -rigging, -rigged.** (*tr*) [2] to cheat or swindle, as in this game.
▷**HISTORY** C19: from THIMBLE + *rig* (in obsolete sense: a trick, scheme)
▸ **ˈthimbleˌrigger** NOUN

thimbleweed (ˈθɪmbᵊlˌwiːd) NOUN *US* any of various plants having a thimble-shaped fruit, esp an American anemone, *Anemone virginiana,* and a rudbeckia, *Rudbeckia laciniata.*

thimblewit (ˈθɪmbᵊlˌwɪt) NOUN *Chiefly US* a silly or dimwitted person; dunce.
▸ **ˈthimbleˌwitted** ADJECTIVE

Thimbu (ˈθɪmbuː) *or* **Thimphu** (ˈθɪmfuː) NOUN the capital of Bhutan, in the west in the foothills of the E Himalayas: became the official capital in 1962. Pop.: 30 340 (1993 est.).

thimerosal (θaɪˈmɛrəˌsæl) NOUN a creamy white crystalline compound of mercury, used in solution as an antiseptic. Formula: $C_9H_9HgNaO_2S$.
▷**HISTORY** C20: from THIO- + MER(CURY) + SAL(ICYLATE)

thin (θɪn) ADJECTIVE **thinner, thinnest.** [1] of relatively small extent from one side or surface to the other; fine or narrow. [2] slim or lean. [3] sparsely placed; meagre: *thin hair.* [4] of relatively low density or viscosity: *a thin liquid.* [5] weak; poor; insufficient: *a thin disguise.* [6] (of a photographic negative) having low density, usually insufficient to produce a satisfactory positive. [7] *Mountaineering* a climb or pitch on which the holds are few and small. [8] **thin on the ground.** few in number; scarce. ◆ ADVERB [9] in order to produce something thin: *to cut bread thin.* ◆ VERB **thins, thinning, thinned.** [10] to make or become thin or sparse.
▷**HISTORY** Old English *thynne;* related to Old Frisian *thenne,* Old Saxon, Old High German *thunni,* Old Norse *thunnr,* Latin *tenuis* thin, Greek *teinein* to stretch
▸ **ˈthinly** ADVERB ▸ **ˈthinness** NOUN

thin client NOUN *Computing* a computer on a network where most functions are carried out on a central server. See **thick client.**

thine (ðaɪn) DETERMINER *Archaic* **a** (*preceding a vowel*) of, belonging to, or associated in some way with you (thou): *thine eyes.* **b** (*as pronoun*): *thine is the greatest burden.* ◆ Compare **thy.**
▷**HISTORY** Old English *thīn;* related to Old High German *dīn,* Gothic *theina*

thin-film ADJECTIVE (of an electronic component, device, or circuit) composed of one or more extremely thin layers of metal, semiconductor, etc., deposited on a ceramic or glass substrate: *thin-film capacitor.*

thing[1] (θɪŋ) NOUN [1] an object, fact, affair, circumstance, or concept considered as being a separate entity. [2] any inanimate object. [3] an object or entity that cannot or need not be precisely named. [4] *Informal* a person or animal regarded as the object of pity, contempt, etc.: *you poor thing.* [5] an event or act. [6] a thought or statement. [7] *Law* any object or right that may be the subject of property (as distinguished from a person). [8] a device, means, or instrument. [9] (*often plural*) a possession, article of clothing, etc. [10] *Informal* the normal pattern of behaviour in a particular context: *not interested in the marriage thing.* [11] *Informal* a mental attitude, preoccupation or obsession (esp in the phrase **have a thing about**). [12] an activity or mode of behaviour satisfying to one's personality (esp in the phrase **do one's (own) thing**). [13] **the done thing.** acceptable or normal behaviour. [14] **the thing.** the latest fashion. [15] **be on to a good thing.** to be in a profitable situation or position. [16] **make a thing of.** to make a fuss about; exaggerate the importance of.
▷**HISTORY** Old English *thing* assembly; related to Old Norse *thing* assembly, Old High German *ding* assembly

thing[2] (θɪŋ, tɪŋ) NOUN (*often capital*) a law court or public assembly in the Scandinavian countries. Also: **ting.**
▷**HISTORY** C19: from Old Norse *thing* assembly (the same word as THING[1])

thing-in-itself NOUN (in the philosophy of Kant) an element of the noumenal rather than the phenomenal world, of which the senses give no knowledge but whose bare existence can be inferred from the nature of experience.

thingumabob *or* **thingamabob** (ˈθɪŋəməˌbɒb) NOUN *Informal* a person or thing the name of which is unknown, temporarily forgotten, or deliberately overlooked. Also: **thingumajig, thingamajig** (ˈθɪŋəməˌdʒɪg) *or* **thingummy** (ˈθɪŋəmɪ).
▷**HISTORY** C18: from THING[1], with humorous suffix

think (θɪŋk) VERB **thinks, thinking, thought.** [1] (*tr; may take a clause as object*) to consider, judge, or believe: *he thinks my ideas impractical.* [2] (*intr;* often foll by *about*) to exercise the mind as in order to make a decision; ponder. [3] (*intr*) to be capable of conscious thought: *man is the only animal that thinks.* [4] to remember; recollect: *I can't think what his name is.* [5] (*intr;* foll by *of*) to make the mental choice (of): *think of a number.* [6] (*may take a clause as object or an infinitive*) **a** to expect; suppose: *I didn't think to see you here.* **b** to be considerate or aware enough (to do something): *he did not think to thank them.* [7] (*intr;* foll by *of*) to consider; regard: *she thinks of herself as a poet.* [8] (*intr*) to focus the attention on being: *think thin; think big.* [9] (*tr*) to bring into or out of a specified condition by thinking: *to think away one's fears.* [10] **I don't think.** *Slang* a phrase added to an ironical statement: *you're the paragon of virtue, I don't think.* [11] **think again.** to reconsider one's decision, opinion, etc. [12] **think better of. a** to change one's mind about (a course of action, decision, etc.). **b** to have a more favourable opinion of (a person). [13] **think much of.** (*usually negative*) to have a high opinion of. [14] **think nothing of. a** to regard as routine, easy, or natural. **b** to have no compunction

or hesitation about. **c** to have a very low opinion of. 15 **think twice.** to consider carefully before deciding (about something). ◆ NOUN 16 *Informal* a careful, open-minded assessment: *let's have a fresh think about this problem.* 17 (*modifier*) *Informal* characterized by or involving thinkers, thinking, or thought: *a think session.* 18 **you've** (**he's, she's,** etc.) **got another think coming.** *Slang* you (etc.) are mistaken and will soon have to alter your opinion. ◆ See also **think out, think over, think up.**
▷HISTORY Old English *thencan;* related to Old Frisian *thenza,* Old Saxon *thenkian,* Old High German *denken,* Old Norse *thekkja,* Gothic *thagkjan*
▸ **'thinker** NOUN

thinkable ('θɪŋkəbᵊl) ADJECTIVE able to be conceived or considered; possible; feasible.

thinking ('θɪŋkɪŋ) NOUN 1 opinion or judgment. 2 the process of thought. ◆ ADJECTIVE 3 (*prenominal*) using or capable of using intelligent thought: *thinking people.* 4 **put on one's thinking cap.** to ponder a matter or problem.

think out *or* **through** VERB (*tr, adverb*) to consider carefully and rationally in order to reach a conclusion.

think over VERB (*tr, adverb*) to ponder or consider: *to think over a problem.*

thinkpiece ('θɪŋk,piːs) NOUN a newspaper or magazine article expressing the writer's thoughts or opinions about a particular matter.

think-tank NOUN *Informal* a group of specialists organized by a business enterprise, governmental body, etc., and commissioned to undertake intensive study and research into specified problems.

think up VERB (*tr, adverb*) to invent or devise: *to think up a plan.*

thin-layer chromatography NOUN a form of chromatography in which components of a liquid mixture are separated by means of a thin layer of adsorbent material coated on a glass, plastic, or foil sheet. Abbreviation: **TLC.**

thinner ('θɪnə) NOUN (*often plural, functioning as singular*) a solvent, such as turpentine, added to paint or varnish to dilute it, reduce its opacity or viscosity, or increase its penetration into the ground.

thin-skinned ADJECTIVE sensitive to criticism or hints; easily upset or affected.

thio- *or before a vowel* **thi-** COMBINING FORM indicating that a chemical compound contains sulphur, esp denoting that a compound is derived from a specified compound by the replacement of an oxygen atom with a sulphur atom: *thiol; thiosulphate.*
▷HISTORY from Greek *theion* sulphur

thioalcohol (ˌθaɪəʊ'ælkəˌhɒl) NOUN another name for a **thiol.**

thiocarbamide (ˌθaɪəʊ'kɑːbəˌmaɪd) NOUN another name for **thiourea.**

thiocyanate (ˌθaɪəʊ'saɪəˌneɪt) NOUN any salt or ester of thiocyanic acid.

thiocyanic acid (ˌθaɪəʊsaɪ'ænɪk) NOUN an unstable acid known in the form of thiocyanate salts. Formula: HSCN.

thio-ether (ˌθaɪəʊ'iːθə) NOUN any of a class of organic compounds in which a sulphur atom is bound to two hydrocarbon groups.

thiofuran (ˌθaɪəʊ'fjʊəræn) NOUN another name for **thiophen.**
▷HISTORY C20: from THIO- + FURAN

thiol ('θaɪɒl) NOUN any of a class of sulphur-containing organic compounds with the formula RSH, where R is an organic group. Also called (not in technical usage): **mercaptan.**

thionate ('θaɪəˌneɪt) NOUN any salt or ester of thionic acid.

thionic (θaɪ'ɒnɪk) ADJECTIVE of, relating to, or containing sulphur.

thionine ('θaɪəʊˌniːn, -ˌnaɪn) *or* **thionin** ('θaɪənɪn) NOUN 1 a crystalline derivative of thiazine used as a violet dye to stain microscope specimens. 2 any of a class of related dyes.
▷HISTORY C19: by shortening, from *ergothioneine,* a crystalline betaine found in ergot and blood

thionyl ('θaɪənɪl) NOUN (*modifier*) of, consisting of, or containing the divalent group SO: *a thionyl group or radical; thionyl chloride.* Also: **sulphinyl.**
▷HISTORY C19 *thion-,* from Greek *theion* sulphur + -YL

thiopental sodium (ˌθaɪəʊ'pentæl) NOUN a barbiturate drug used in medicine as an intravenous general anaesthetic. Formula: $C_{11}H_{17}NaN_2O_2S$. Also called: **Sodium Pentothal.** See also **truth drug.**

thiophen ('θaɪəʊˌfen) *or* **thiophene** ('θaɪəʊˌfiːn) NOUN a colourless liquid heterocyclic compound found in the benzene fraction of coal tar and manufactured from butane and sulphur. It has an odour resembling that of benzene and is used as a solvent and in the manufacture of dyes, pharmaceuticals, and resins. Formula: C_4H_4S. Also called: **thiofuran.**

thiosinamine (ˌθaɪəʊ'sɪnəˌmiːn, -sɪ'næmɪn) NOUN a white crystalline bitter-tasting compound with a slight garlic-like odour, occurring in mustard oil and used in organic synthesis; 1-allyl-2-thiourea. Formula: $CH_2{:}CHCH_2NHCSNH_2$.
▷HISTORY C19: from THIO- + *sin-* (from Latin *sināpis* mustard) + AMINE

thiosulphate (ˌθaɪəʊ'sʌlfeɪt) NOUN any salt of thiosulphuric acid.

thiosulphuric acid (ˌθaɪəʊsʌl'fjʊərɪk) NOUN an unstable acid known only in solutions and in the form of its salts. Formula: $H_2S_2O_3$.

thiouracil (ˌθaɪəʊ'jʊərəsɪl) NOUN a white crystalline water-insoluble substance with an intensely bitter taste, used in medicine to treat hyperthyroidism; 2-thio-4-oxypyrimidine. Formula: $C_4H_4N_2OS$.
▷HISTORY from THIO- + *uracil* (URO-[1] + AC(ETIC) + *-il* -ILE)

thiourea (ˌθaɪəʊ'jʊərɪə) NOUN a white water-soluble crystalline substance with a bitter taste that forms addition compounds with metal ions and is used in photographic fixing, rubber vulcanization, and the manufacture of synthetic resins. Formula: H_2NCSNH_2.

third (θɜːd) ADJECTIVE (*usually prenominal*) 1 **a** coming after the second and preceding the fourth in numbering or counting order, position, time, etc.; being the ordinal number of *three:* often written 3rd. **b** (*as noun*): *he arrives on the third; the third got a prize.* 2 rated, graded, or ranked below the second level. 3 denoting the third from lowest forward ratio of a gearbox in a motor vehicle. ◆ NOUN 4 **a** one of three equal or nearly equal parts of an object, quantity, etc. **b** (*as modifier*): *a third part.* 5 the fraction equal to one divided by three (1/3). 6 the forward ratio above second of a gearbox in a motor vehicle. In some vehicles it is the top gear. 7 **a** the interval between one note and another three notes away from it counting inclusively along the diatonic scale. **b** one of two notes constituting such an interval in relation to the other. See also **interval** (sense 5), **major** (sense 14a), **minor** (sense 4d). 8 *Brit* an honours degree of the third and usually the lowest class. Full term: **third class honours degree.** 9 (*plural*) goods of a standard lower than that of seconds. ◆ ADVERB 10 Also: **thirdly.** in the third place. ◆ SENTENCE CONNECTOR 11 Also: **thirdly.** as the third point: linking what follows with the previous statements as in a speech or argument.
▷HISTORY Old English *thirda,* variant of *thridda;* related to Old Frisian *thredda,* Old Saxon *thriddio,* Old High German *drittio,* Old Norse *thrithi,* Latin *tertius*
▸ **'thirdly** ADVERB

Third Age NOUN **the.** old age, esp when viewed as an opportunity for travel, further education, etc.

third class NOUN 1 the class or grade next in value, quality, etc., to the second. ◆ ADJECTIVE (**third-class** when prenominal) 2 of the class or grade next in value, quality, etc., to the second. 3 of or denoting the class of accommodation in a hotel, on a ship, etc., next in quality and price to the second: usually the cheapest. 4 (in the US and Canada) of or relating to a class of mail consisting largely of unsealed printed matter. 5 *Brit* See **third** (sense 8). ◆ ADVERB 6 by third-class mail, transport, etc.

third degree NOUN *Informal* torture or bullying, esp used to extort confessions or information.

third-degree burn NOUN *Pathol* See **burn**[1] (sense 22).

third dimension NOUN the additional dimension by which a solid object may be distinguished from a two-dimensional drawing or picture of it or from any planar object.

third estate NOUN the third order or class in a country or society divided into estates, esp for representation in a parliament; the commons, townsmen, or middle class.

third eye NOUN the pineal gland, believed by some people to be the source of spiritual insight.

third eyelid NOUN another name for **nictitating membrane.**

third house NOUN *US* a political lobby for a special interest.

Third International NOUN another name for **Comintern.**

third man NOUN *Cricket* **a** a fielding position on the off side near the boundary behind the batsman's wicket. **b** a fielder in this position.

third man argument NOUN (in the philosophy of Aristotle) the argument against the existence of Platonic Forms that since the Form of Man is itself a perfect man, a further form (the "third" man) would be required to explain this, and so ad infinitum.

Third Market NOUN a market established by the London Stock Exchange in 1987 to trade in shares in companies required to provide less detailed information than that required by the main market or the unlisted securities market.

Third Order NOUN *RC Church* a religious society of laymen affiliated to one of the religious orders and following a mitigated form of religious rule.

third party NOUN 1 a person who is involved by chance or only incidentally in a legal proceeding, agreement, or other transaction, esp one against whom a defendant claims indemnity. ◆ ADJECTIVE 2 *Insurance* providing protection against liability caused by accidental injury or death of other persons or damage to their property.

third person NOUN a grammatical category of pronouns and verbs used when referring to objects or individuals other than the speaker or his addressee(s).

third rail NOUN an extra rail from which an electric train picks up current by means of a sliding collector to feed power to its motors.

third-rate ADJECTIVE not of high quality; mediocre or inferior.
▸ **'third-'rater** NOUN

third reading NOUN (in a legislative assembly) 1 *Brit* the process of discussing the committee's report on a bill. 2 *US* the final consideration of a bill.

Third Reich NOUN See **Reich**[1] (sense 4).

Third Republic NOUN in France. 1 the governmental system established after the fall of Napoleon III in the Franco-Prussian War and lasting until the German occupation of 1940. 2 the period during which this governmental system functioned (1870–1940).

third space NOUN *Informal* the coffee shop considered as an alternative to a bar or restaurant as a place to socialize outside the home.

thirdstream ('θɜːdˌstriːm) ADJECTIVE 1 (of music) combining jazz and classical elements. ◆ NOUN 2 such music.

Third Way NOUN **a** a political ideology that seeks to combine egalitarian and individualist policies, and elements of socialism and capitalism. **b** (*as modifier*): *Third Way government.*

Third World NOUN the less economically advanced countries of Africa, Asia, and Latin America collectively, esp when viewed as underdeveloped and as neutral in the East-West alignment. Also called: **developing world.**

thirl[1] (θɜːl) VERB (*tr*) *Dialect* **a** to bore or drill. **b** to thrill.
▷HISTORY Old English *thyrelian,* from *thyrel* hole; see NOSTRIL

thirl[2] (θɪrl, θɜːl) VERB (*tr*) *Chiefly Scot* to enslave; bind.
▷HISTORY C16: variant of earlier *thrill* THRALL

thirlage ('θɜːlɪdʒ) NOUN *Scots law* (formerly) 1 an obligation imposed upon tenants of certain lands

requiring them to have their grain ground at a specified mill. 2 the fee paid for grinding the grain.
▷**HISTORY** C16: variant of earlier *thrillage*, from *thrill*, Scottish variant of THRALL

Thirlmere ('θɜːlmɪə) NOUN a lake in NW England, in Cumbria in the Lake District: provides part of Manchester's water supply. Length: 6 km (4 miles).

thirst (θɜːst) NOUN 1 a craving to drink, accompanied by a feeling of dryness in the mouth and throat. 2 an eager longing, craving, or yearning: *a thirst for knowledge*. ◆ VERB (*intr*) 3 to feel a thirst: *to thirst for a drink; to thirst after righteousness*.
▷**HISTORY** Old English *thyrstan*, from *thurst* thirst; related to Old Norse *thyrsta* to thirst, Old High German *dursten* to thirst, Latin *torrēre* to parch

thirsty ('θɜːstɪ) ADJECTIVE **thirstier, thirstiest.** 1 feeling a desire to drink. 2 dry; arid: *the thirsty soil*. 3 (foll by *for*) feeling an eager desire: *thirsty for information*. 4 causing thirst: *thirsty work*.
▸ **'thirstily** ADVERB ▸ **'thirstiness** NOUN

thirteen ('θɜː'tiːn) NOUN 1 the cardinal number that is the sum of ten and three and is a prime number. See also **number** (sense 1). 2 a numeral, 13, XIII, etc., representing this number. 3 the amount or quantity that is three more than ten; baker's dozen. 4 something represented by, representing, or consisting of 13 units. ◆ DETERMINER 5 **a** amounting to thirteen: *thirteen buses*. **b** (*as pronoun*): *thirteen of them fell*.
▷**HISTORY** Old English *threotēne;* see THREE, -TEEN

thirteenth ('θɜː'tiːnθ) ADJECTIVE 1 (*usually prenominal*) **a** coming after the twelfth in numbering or counting order, position, time, etc.; being the ordinal number of *thirteen:* often written 13th. **b** (*as noun*): *Friday the thirteenth*. ◆ NOUN 2 **a** one of 13 equal or nearly equal parts of something. **b** (*as modifier*): *a thirteenth part*. 3 the fraction equal to one divided by 13 (1/13). 4 *Music* **a** an interval of one octave plus a sixth. See also **interval** (sense 5). **b** short for **thirteenth chord.**

thirteenth chord NOUN a chord much used in jazz and pop, consisting of a major or minor triad upon which are superimposed the seventh, ninth, eleventh, and thirteenth above the root. Often shortened to: **thirteenth.**

thirtieth ('θɜːtɪɪθ) ADJECTIVE 1 (*usually prenominal*) **a** being the ordinal number of *thirty* in counting order, position, time, etc.: often written 30th. **b** (*as noun*): *the thirtieth of the month*. ◆ NOUN 2 **a** one of 30 approximately equal parts of something. **b** (*as modifier*): *a thirtieth part*. 3 the fraction equal to one divided by 30 (1/30).

thirty ('θɜːtɪ) NOUN, *plural* **-ties.** 1 the cardinal number that is the product of ten and three. See also **number** (sense 1). 2 a numeral, 30, XXX, etc., representing this number. 3 (*plural*) the numbers 30–39, esp the 30th to the 39th year of a person's life or of a century. 4 the amount or quantity that is three times as big as ten. 5 something representing, represented by, or consisting of 30 units. ◆ DETERMINER 6 **a** amounting to thirty: *thirty trees*. **b** (*as pronoun*): *thirty are broken*.
▷**HISTORY** Old English *thrītig;* see THREE, -TY[1]

Thirty-nine Articles PLURAL NOUN a set of formulas defining the doctrinal position of the Church of England, drawn up in the 16th century, to which the clergy are required to give general consent.

thirty-second note NOUN the usual US and Canadian name for **demisemiquaver.**

thirty-three NOUN a former name for **LP**[1].
▷**HISTORY** C20: so called because it is played at thirty-three and a third revolutions per minute

thirty-twomo (ˌθɜːtɪ'tuːməʊ) NOUN, *plural* **-mos.** a book size resulting from folding a sheet of paper into 32 leaves or 64 pages. Often written: **32mo, 32°.**

Thirty Years' War NOUN a major conflict involving principally Austria, Denmark, France, Holland, the German states, Spain, and Sweden, that devastated central Europe, esp large areas of Germany (1618–48). It began as a war between Protestants and Catholics but was gradually transformed into a struggle to determine whether the German emperor could assert more than nominal authority over his princely vassals. The Peace of Westphalia gave the German states their sovereignty and the right of religious toleration and confirmed French ascendancy.

Thiruvananthapuram (ˌθɪruːvə'næntaˌpuːrɑːm) NOUN the official name of **Trivandrum.**

this (ðɪs) DETERMINER (*used before a singular noun*) 1 **a** used preceding a noun referring to something or someone that is closer: distinct from **that**: *this dress is cheaper than that one; look at this picture*. **b** (*as pronoun*): *this is Mary and that is her boyfriend; take this*. 2 **a** used preceding a noun that has just been mentioned or is understood: *this plan of yours won't work*. **b** (*as pronoun*): *I first saw this on Sunday*. 3 **a** used to refer to something about to be said, read, etc.: *consider this argument*. **b** (*as pronoun*): *listen to this*. 4 **a** the present or immediate: *this time you'll know better*. **b** (*as pronoun*): *before this, I was mistaken*. 5 *Informal* an emphatic form of **a**[1] or **the**[1]: used esp on relating a story: *I saw this big brown bear*. 6 **this and that.** various unspecified and trivial actions, matters, objects, etc. 7 **this here.** *US not standard* an emphatic form of **this** (senses 1–3). 8 **with** (*or* **at**) **this.** after this; thereupon. ◆ ADVERB 9 used with adjectives and adverbs to specify a precise degree that is about to be mentioned: *go just this fast and you'll be safe*.
▷**HISTORY** Old English *thēs, thēos, this* (masculine, feminine, neuter singular); related to Old Saxon *thit,* Old High German *diz,* Old Norse *thessi*

Thisbe ('θɪzbɪ) NOUN See **Pyramus and Thisbe.**

thistle ('θɪsᵊl) NOUN 1 any of numerous plants of the genera *Cirsium, Carduus,* and related genera, having prickly-edged leaves, pink, purple, yellow, or white dense flower heads, and feathery hairs on the seeds: family *Asteraceae* (composites). 2 a thistle, or a representation of one, as the national emblem of Scotland.
▷**HISTORY** Old English *thīstel,* related to Old Saxon, Old High German *thīstil,* Old Norse *thīstill*
▸ **'thistly** ADJECTIVE

Thistle ('θɪsᵊl) NOUN **the.** 1 See **Order of the Thistle.** 2 (*sometimes not capital*) **a** the emblem of this Order. **b** membership of this Order.

thistledown ('θɪsᵊlˌdaʊn) NOUN 1 the mass of feathery plumed seeds produced by a thistle. 2 anything resembling this.

thither ('ðɪðə) *or* **thitherward** ADVERB *Obsolete or formal* to or towards that place; in that direction: *the flowers and music which attract people thither*.
▷**HISTORY** Old English *thider,* variant of *thæder,* influenced by *hider* HITHER; related to Old Norse *thathra* there

thitherto (ˌðɪðə'tuː, 'ðɪðəˌtuː) ADVERB *Obsolete or formal* until that time.

thixotropic (ˌθɪksə'trɒpɪk) ADJECTIVE (of fluids and gels) having a viscosity that decreases when a stress is applied, as when stirred: *thixotropic paints*.
▷**HISTORY** C20: from Greek *thixis* the act of touching + -TROPIC
▸**thixotropy** (θɪk'sɒtrəpɪ) NOUN ▸**thixotrope** ('θɪksəˌtrəʊp) NOUN

tho' *or* **tho** (ðəʊ) CONJUNCTION, ADVERB *Informal* a variant spelling of **though.**

thole[1] (θəʊl) *or* **tholepin** ('θəʊlˌpɪn) NOUN a wooden pin or one of a pair, set upright in the gunwales of a rowing boat to serve as a fulcrum in rowing.
▷**HISTORY** Old English *tholl,* related to Middle Low German *dolle,* Norwegian *toll,* Icelandic *thollr*

thole[2] (θəʊl) VERB 1 (*tr*) *Scot and northern English dialect* to put up with; bear. 2 an archaic word for **suffer.**
▷**HISTORY** Old English *tholian;* related to Old Saxon, Old High German *tholōn,* Old Norse *thola* to endure: compare Latin *tollere* to bear up

tholos ('θəʊlɒs) NOUN, *plural* **-loi** (-lɔɪ). a dry-stone beehive-shaped tomb associated with the Mycenaean culture of Greece in the 16th to the 12th century B.C.
▷**HISTORY** C17: from Greek

Thomism ('təʊmɪzəm) NOUN the comprehensive system of philosophy and theology developed by the Italian theologian, scholastic philosopher, and Dominican friar Saint Thomas Aquinas (1225–74), and since taught and maintained by his followers, esp in the Dominican order.
▸ **'Thomist** NOUN, ADJECTIVE ▸**Tho'mistic** *or* **Tho'mistical** ADJECTIVE

Thompson sub-machine-gun NOUN *Trademark* a .45 calibre sub-machine-gun. Also called: **Tommy gun.**
▷**HISTORY** C20: after John T. *Thompson* (1860–1940), US Army officer, its coinventor

Thomson effect NOUN *Physics* the phenomenon in which a temperature gradient along a metallic (or semiconductor) wire or strip causes an electric potential gradient to form along its length.
▷**HISTORY** named after Sir William *Thomson,* 1st Baron Kelvin (1824–1907), British physicist

thon (ðɒn) DETERMINER a Scot word for **yon.**
▷**HISTORY** C19: of uncertain origin

-thon SUFFIX FORMING NOUNS indicating a large-scale event or operation of a specified kind: *telethon*.
▷**HISTORY** C20: on the pattern of MARATHON

Thonburi (ˌtɒnbʊ'riː) NOUN a city in central Thailand, part of Bankok Metropolis on the Chao Phraya River; the national capital (1767–82).

thonder ('ðɒndər) ADVERB, DETERMINER a Scot word for **yonder.**
▷**HISTORY** C19: of uncertain origin

thong (θɒŋ) NOUN 1 a thin strip of leather or other material, such as one used for lashing things together. 2 a whip or whiplash, esp one made of leather. 3 *US, Canadian, Austral, and NZ* the usual name for **flip-flop** (sense 5). 4 **a** a skimpy article of beachwear, worn by men or women, consisting of thin strips of leather or cloth attached to a piece of material that covers the genitals while leaving the buttocks bare. **b** a similar item of underwear.
▷**HISTORY** Old English *thwang;* related to Old High German *dwang* reins, Old Norse *thvengr* strap

Thor (θɔː) NOUN *Norse myth* the god of thunder, depicted as wielding a hammer, emblematic of the thunderbolt.
▷**HISTORY** Old English *Thōr,* from Old Norse *thōrr* THUNDER

thoracentesis (ˌθɔːrəsɛn'tiːsɪs) *or* **thoracocentesis** (ˌθɔːrəkəʊsɛn'tiːsɪs) NOUN *Med* the surgical puncture of the pleural cavity using a hollow needle, in order to withdraw fluid, drain blood, etc. Also called: **pleurocentesis.**

thoracic (θɔː'ræsɪk) ADJECTIVE of, near, or relating to the thorax.

thoracic duct NOUN the major duct of the lymphatic system, beginning below the diaphragm and ascending in front of the spinal column to the base of the neck.

thoraco- *or before a vowel* **thorac-** COMBINING FORM thorax: *thoracotomy*.

thoracoplasty ('θɔːrəkəʊˌplæstɪ) NOUN, *plural* **-ties.** 1 plastic surgery of the thorax. 2 surgical removal of several ribs or a part of them to permit the collapse of a diseased lung, used in cases of pulmonary tuberculosis and bronchiectasis.

thoracoscope ('θɔːrəkəʊˌskəʊp) NOUN *Med* an instrument used for examining the pleural cavity.

thoracotomy (ˌθɔːrə'kɒtəmɪ) NOUN, *plural* **-mies.** surgical incision into the chest wall.

thorax ('θɔːræks) NOUN, *plural* **thoraxes** *or* **thoraces** ('θɔːrəˌsiːz, θɔː'reɪsiːz). 1 the part of the human body enclosed by the ribs. 2 the corresponding part in other vertebrates. 3 the part of an insect's body between the head and abdomen, which bears the wings and legs.
▷**HISTORY** C16: via Latin from Greek *thōrax* breastplate, chest

thoria ('θɔːrɪə) NOUN another name for **thorium dioxide.**
▷**HISTORY** C19: THORIUM + *-a,* on the model of *magnesia*

thorianite ('θɔːrɪəˌnaɪt) NOUN a rare black mineral consisting of thorium and uranium oxides. Formula: $ThO_2.U_3O_8$.

thorite ('θɔːraɪt) NOUN a yellow, brownish, or black radioactive mineral consisting of tetragonal thorium silicate. It occurs in coarse granite and is a source of thorium. Formula: $ThSiO_4$.

thorium ('θɔːrɪəm) NOUN a soft ductile silvery-white metallic element. It is radioactive and occurs in thorite and monazite: used in gas mantles, magnesium alloys, electronic equipment, and as a nuclear power source. Symbol: Th; atomic no.: 90; atomic wt.: 232.0381; half-life of most stable isotope, ^{232}Th: 1.41×10^{10} years; valency: 4;

relative density: 11.72; melting pt.: 1755°C; boiling pt.: 4788°C.
▷HISTORY C19: New Latin, from THOR + -IUM
▸ˈthoric ADJECTIVE

thorium dioxide NOUN a heavy insoluble white powder used in incandescent mantles. Formula: ThO_2. Also called: **thoria.**

thorium series NOUN a radioactive series that starts with thorium-232 and ends with lead-208.

thorn (θɔːn) NOUN [1] a sharp pointed woody extension of a stem or leaf. Compare **prickle** (sense 1). [2] **a** any of various trees or shrubs having thorns, esp the hawthorn. **b** the wood of any of these plants. [3] short for **thorn moth.** [4] a Germanic character of runic origin (Þ) used in Old and Modern Icelandic to represent the voiceless dental fricative sound of *th,* as in *thin, bath.* Its use in phonetics for the same purpose is now obsolete. See **theta.** [5] this same character as used in Old and Middle English as an alternative to *edh,* but indistinguishable from it in function or sound. Compare **edh.** [6] *Zoology* any of various sharp spiny parts. [7] a source of irritation (esp in the phrases **a thorn in one's side** *or* **flesh**).
▷HISTORY Old English; related to Old High German *dorn,* Old Norse *thorn*
▸ˈthornless ADJECTIVE

Thorn (toːrn) NOUN the German name for **Toruń.**

thorn apple NOUN [1] a poisonous solanaceous plant, *Datura stramonium,* of the N hemisphere, having white funnel-shaped flowers and spiny capsule fruits. US name: **jimson weed.** See also **stramonium.** [2] any other plant of the genus *Datura.* [3] the fruit of certain types of hawthorn.

thornback (ˈθɔːnˌbæk) NOUN [1] a European ray, *Raja clavata,* having a row of spines along the back and tail. [2] a similar fish, *Platyrhinoidis triseriata,* of the Pacific Ocean.

thornbill (ˈθɔːnˌbɪl) NOUN [1] any of various South American hummingbirds of the genera *Chalcostigma, Ramphomicron,* etc., having a thornlike bill. [2] Also called: **thornbill warbler.** any of various Australasian wrens of the genus *Acanthiza* and related genera: family *Muscicapidae.* [3] any of various other birds with thornlike bills.

Thorndike's law *or* **Thorndike's law of effect** (ˈθɔːnˌdaɪk) NOUN the principle that all learnt behaviour is regulated by rewards and punishments, proposed by Edward Lee Thorndike (1874–1949), US psychologist.

thorn moth NOUN any of various woodland geometrid moths, typified by the **large thorn** (*Ennomos autumnaria*), having wings set somewhat at an angle and held up when at rest. Often shortened to: **thorn.**

thorny (ˈθɔːnɪ) ADJECTIVE **thornier, thorniest.** [1] bearing or covered with thorns. [2] difficult or unpleasant: *a thorny problem.* [3] sharp.
▸ˈthornily ADVERB ▸ˈthorniness NOUN

thoron (ˈθɔːrɒn) NOUN a radioisotope of radon that is a decay product of thorium. Symbol: Tn or ^{220}Rn; atomic no.: 86; half-life: 54.5s.
▷HISTORY C20: from THORIUM + -ON

thorough (ˈθʌrə) ADJECTIVE [1] carried out completely and carefully: *a thorough search.* [2] (*prenominal*) utter: *a thorough bore.* [3] painstakingly careful: *my work is thorough.*
▷HISTORY Old English *thurh;* related to Old Frisian *thruch,* Old Saxon *thuru,* Old High German *duruh;* see THROUGH
▸ˈthoroughly ADVERB ▸ˈthoroughness NOUN

Thorough (ˈθʌrə) NOUN thoroughgoing policy, as adopted in England by Strafford and Laud during the reign of Charles I.

thorough bass (beɪs) NOUN **a** Also called: **basso continuo. continuo.** (esp during the baroque period) a bass part underlying a piece of concerted music. It is played on a keyboard instrument, usually supported by a cello, viola da gamba, etc. See also **figured bass. b** (*as modifier*): *a thorough-bass part.*

thorough brace NOUN *Chiefly US* either of two strong leather straps upon which the body of certain types of carriage is supported.
▸ˈthorough-ˌbraced ADJECTIVE

thoroughbred (ˈθʌrəˌbrɛd) ADJECTIVE [1] purebred. ◆ NOUN [2] a pedigree animal; purebred. [3] a person regarded as being of good breeding.

Thoroughbred (ˈθʌrəˌbrɛd) NOUN a British breed of horse the ancestry of which can be traced to English mares and Arab sires; most often used as a racehorse.

thoroughfare (ˈθʌrəˌfɛə) NOUN [1] a road from one place to another, esp a main road. [2] way through or access: *no thoroughfare.*

thoroughgoing (ˈθʌrəˌɡəʊɪŋ) ADJECTIVE [1] extremely thorough. [2] (*usually prenominal*) absolute; complete: *thoroughgoing incompetence.*
▸ˈthoroughˌgoingly ADVERB ▸ˈthoroughˌgoingness NOUN

thoroughpaced (ˈθʌrəˌpeɪst) ADJECTIVE [1] (of a horse) showing performing ability in all paces. [2] thoroughgoing.

thoroughpin (ˈθʌrəˌpɪn) NOUN an inflammation and swelling on both sides of the hock joint of a horse affecting the sheath of the deep flexor tendon.
▷HISTORY C18: so called because it makes the leg look as if it has a pin stuck through it

thorp *or* **thorpe** (θɔːp) NOUN *Obsolete except in place names* a small village.
▷HISTORY Old English; related to Old Norse *thorp* village, Old High German *dorf,* Gothic *thaurp*

Thorshavn (*Danish* ˈtɔːrshaun) NOUN the capital of the Faeroe Islands, a port on the northernmost island. Pop.: 16 474 (2000 est.).

those (ðəʊz) DETERMINER the form of **that** used before a plural noun.
▷HISTORY Old English *thās,* plural of THIS

Thoth (θəʊθ, taʊt) NOUN (in Egyptian mythology) a moon deity, scribe of the gods and protector of learning and the arts.

thou[1] (ðaʊ) PRONOUN (*subjective*) [1] *Archaic dialect* refers to the person addressed: used mainly in familiar address or to a younger person or inferior. [2] (*usually capital*) refers to God when addressed in prayer, etc.
▷HISTORY Old English *thū;* related to Old Saxon *thū,* Old High German *du,* Old Norse *thū,* Latin *tū,* Doric Greek *tu*

thou[2] (θaʊ) NOUN, *plural* **thous** *or* **thou.** [1] one thousandth of an inch. 1 thou is equal to 0.0254 millimetre. [2] *Informal* short for **thousand.**

though (ðəʊ) CONJUNCTION (*subordinating*) [1] (sometimes preceded by *even*) despite the fact that: *though he tries hard, he always fails; poor though she is, her life is happy.* [2] **as though.** as if: *he looked as though he'd seen a ghost.* ◆ ADVERB [3] nevertheless; however: *he can't dance: he sings well, though.*
▷HISTORY Old English *theah;* related to Old Frisian *thāch,* Old Saxon, Old High German *thōh,* Old Norse *thō*

thought (θɔːt) VERB [1] the past tense and past participle of **think.** ◆ NOUN [2] the act or process of thinking; deliberation, meditation, or reflection. [3] a concept, opinion, or idea. [4] philosophical or intellectual ideas typical of a particular time or place: *German thought in the 19th century.* [5] application of mental attention; consideration: *he gave the matter some thought.* [6] purpose or intention: *I have no thought of giving up.* [7] expectation: *no thought of reward.* [8] a small amount; trifle: *you could be a thought more enthusiastic.* [9] kindness or regard: *he has no thought for his widowed mother.*
▷HISTORY Old English *thōht;* related to Old Frisian *thochta,* Old Saxon, Old High German *githācht*

thought disorder NOUN *Psychiatry* a cognitive disorder in which the patient's thoughts or conversations are characterized by irrationality or sudden changes of subject.

thoughtful (ˈθɔːtfʊl) ADJECTIVE [1] considerate in the treatment of other people. [2] showing careful thought. [3] pensive; reflective.
▸ˈthoughtfully ADVERB ▸ˈthoughtfulness NOUN

thoughtless (ˈθɔːtlɪs) ADJECTIVE [1] inconsiderate: *a thoughtless remark.* [2] having or showing lack of thought: *a thoughtless essay.* [3] unable to think; not having the power of thought.
▸ˈthoughtlessly ADVERB ▸ˈthoughtlessness NOUN

thought-out ADJECTIVE conceived and developed by careful thought: *a well thought-out scheme.*

thought police NOUN a group of people with totalitarian views on a given subject, who constantly monitor others for any deviation from prescribed thinking.
▷HISTORY C20: from the *Thought Police* described by George Orwell in his novel *Nineteen Eighty-Four* (1949)

thought transference NOUN *Psychol* another name for **telepathy.**

thousand (ˈθaʊzənd) NOUN [1] the cardinal number that is the product of 10 and 100. See also **number** (sense 1). [2] a numeral, 1000, 10^3, M, etc., representing this number. [3] (*often plural*) a very large but unspecified number, amount, or quantity: *they are thousands of miles away.* [4] (*plural*) the numbers 2000–9999: *the price of the picture was in the thousands.* [5] the amount or quantity that is one hundred times greater than ten. [6] something represented by, representing, or consisting of 1000 units. [7] *Maths* the position containing a digit representing that number followed by three zeros: *in 4760, 4 is in the thousand's place.* ◆ DETERMINER [8] **a** amounting to a thousand: *a thousand ships.* **b** (*as pronoun*): *a thousand is hardly enough.* [9] amounting to 1000 times a particular scientific unit. Related prefix: **kilo-.** ◆ Related adjective: **millenary.**
▷HISTORY Old English *thūsend;* related to Old Saxon *thūsind,* Old High German *thūsunt,* Old Norse *thūsund*

Thousand and One Nights NOUN See **Arabian Nights' Entertainments.**

Thousand Guineas NOUN **the** (*functioning as singular*) *usually written* **1000 Guineas.** an annual horse race, restricted to fillies, run at Newmarket since 1814. Also called: **the One Thousand Guineas.**

Thousand Island ADJECTIVE of or relating to the Thousand Islands or their inhabitants.

Thousand Island dressing NOUN a salad dressing made from mayonnaise with ketchup, chopped gherkins, etc.
▷HISTORY probably from the THOUSAND ISLANDS

Thousand Islands PLURAL NOUN a group of about 1500 islands between the US and Canada, in the upper St Lawrence River: administratively divided between the US and Canada.

thousandth (ˈθaʊzənθ) ADJECTIVE [1] (*usually prenominal*) **a** being the ordinal number of 1000 in numbering or counting order, position, time, etc. **b** (*as noun*): *the thousandth in succession.* ◆ NOUN [2] **a** one of 1000 approximately equal parts of something. **b** (*as modifier*): *a thousandth part.* [3] one of 1000 equal divisions of a particular scientific quantity. Related prefix: **milli-:** *millivolt.* [4] the fraction equal to one divided by 1000 (1/1000).

Thrace (θreɪs) NOUN [1] an ancient country in the E Balkan Peninsula: successively under the Persians, Macedonians, and Romans. [2] a region of SE Europe, corresponding to the S part of the ancient country: divided by the Maritsa River into **Western Thrace** (Greece) and **Eastern Thrace** (Turkey).

Thracian (ˈθreɪʃɪən) NOUN [1] a member of an ancient Indo-European people who lived in the SE corner of the Balkan Peninsula. [2] the ancient language spoken by this people, belonging to the Thraco-Phrygian branch of the Indo-European family: extinct by the early Middle Ages. ◆ ADJECTIVE [3] of or relating to Thrace, its inhabitants, or the extinct Thracian language.

Thraco-Phrygian (ˌθreɪkəʊˈfrɪdʒɪən) NOUN [1] a branch of the Indo-European family of languages, all members of which are extinct except for Armenian. ◆ ADJECTIVE [2] relating to or belonging to this group of languages.
▷HISTORY from *Thraco-,* from Greek *Thraikē* Thrace; see PHRYGIAN

thraiping (ˈθreɪpɪŋ) NOUN [1] *Northern English dialect* a thrashing. [2] an utter defeat in a game or contest: *we gave their team a good thraiping.*

thrall (θrɔːl) NOUN [1] Also called: **thraldom,** (US) **thralldom** (ˈθrɔːldəm). the state or condition of being in the power of another person. [2] a person who is in such a state. [3] a person totally subject to some need, desire, appetite, etc. ◆ VERB [4] (*tr*) to enslave or dominate.
▷HISTORY Old English *thrǣl* slave, from Old Norse *thrǣll*

thrang (θræŋ) *Scot* ◆ NOUN [1] a throng; crowd. ◆ VERB [2] to throng; crowd. ◆ ADJECTIVE [3] crowded; busy. [4] engaged or occupied; busy.
▷HISTORY Scot variant of THRONG

thrapple (ˈθræpᵊl) *Scot* ◆ NOUN [1] the throat or windpipe. ◆ VERB [2] to throttle.

▷HISTORY C18: a variant of earlier *thropple,* of uncertain origin

thrash (θræʃ) VERB 1 *(tr)* to beat soundly, as with a whip or stick. 2 *(tr)* to defeat totally; overwhelm. 3 *(intr)* to beat or plunge about in a wild manner. 4 *(intr)* to move the legs up and down in the water, as in certain swimming strokes. 5 to sail (a boat) against the wind or tide or (of a boat) to sail in this way. 6 another word for **thresh.** ◆ NOUN 7 the act of thrashing; blow; beating. 8 *Informal* a party or similar social gathering. ◆ See also **thrash out.**
▷HISTORY Old English *threscan;* related to Old High German *dreskan,* Old Norse *thriskja*

thrasher[1] (ˈθræʃə) NOUN another name for **thresher** (the shark).

thrasher[2] (ˈθræʃə) NOUN any of various brown thrushlike American songbirds of the genus *Toxostoma* and related genera, having a long downward-curving bill and long tail: family *Mimidae* (mockingbirds).
▷HISTORY C19: perhaps from English dialect *thresher, thrusher* a thrush

thrashing (ˈθræʃɪŋ) NOUN a physical assault; flogging.

thrash metal NOUN a type of very fast, very loud rock music that combines elements of heavy metal and punk rock. Often shortened to: **thrash.**

thrash out VERB *(tr, adverb)* to discuss fully or vehemently, esp in order to come to a solution or agreement.

thrasonical (θrəˈsɒnɪkəl) ADJECTIVE *Rare* bragging; boastful.
▷HISTORY C16: from Latin *Thrasō* name of boastful soldier in *Eunuchus,* a play by Terence, from Greek *Thrasōn,* from *thrasus* forceful
▸**thraˈsonically** ADVERB

thrave (θreɪv) NOUN *Scot and northern English dialect* twenty-four sheaves of corn.
▷HISTORY Old English *threfe,* of Scandinavian origin

thrawn (θrɔːn) ADJECTIVE *Scot and northern English dialect* 1 crooked or twisted. 2 stubborn; perverse.
▷HISTORY Northern English dialect, variant of THROWN, from Old English *thrāwan* to twist about, THROW

thread (θrɛd) NOUN 1 a fine strand, filament or fibre of some material. 2 a fine cord of twisted filaments, esp of cotton, used in sewing, weaving, etc. 3 any of the filaments of which a spider's web is made. 4 any fine line, stream, mark, or piece: *from the air, the path was a thread of white.* 5 a helical groove in a cylindrical hole (**female thread**), formed by a tap or lathe tool, or a helical ridge on a cylindrical bar, rod, shank, etc. (**male thread**), formed by a die or lathe tool. 6 a very thin seam of coal or vein of ore. 7 something acting as the continuous link or theme of a whole: *the thread of the story.* 8 the course of an individual's life believed in Greek mythology to be spun, measured, and cut by the Fates. ◆ VERB 9 *(tr)* to pass (thread, film, magnetic tape, etc.) through (something): *to thread a needle; to thread cotton through a needle.* 10 *(tr)* to string on a thread: *she threaded the beads.* 11 to make (one's way) through or over (something). 12 *(tr)* to produce a screw thread by cutting, rolling, tapping, or grinding. 13 *(tr)* to pervade: *hysteria threaded his account.* 14 *(intr)* (of boiling syrup) to form a fine thread when poured from a spoon. ◆ See also **threads.**
▷HISTORY Old English *thrǣd;* related to Old Frisian *thrēd,* Old High German *drāt,* Old Norse *thrāthr* thread
▸**ˈthreader** NOUN ▸**ˈthreadless** ADJECTIVE ▸**ˈthreadˌlike** ADJECTIVE

threadbare (ˈθrɛdˌbɛə) ADJECTIVE 1 (of cloth, clothing, etc.) having the nap worn off so that the threads are exposed. 2 meagre or poor: *a threadbare existence.* 3 hackneyed: *a threadbare argument.* 4 wearing threadbare clothes; shabby.
▸**ˈthreadˌbareness** NOUN

threadfin (ˈθrɛdˌfɪn) NOUN, *plural* **-fin** *or* **-fins.** any spiny-finned tropical marine fish of the family *Polynemidae,* having pectoral fins consisting partly of long threadlike rays.

thread mark NOUN a mark put into paper money to prevent counterfeiting, consisting of a pattern of silk fibres.

Threadneedle Street (ˌθrɛdˈniːdəl, ˈθrɛdˌniːdəl) NOUN a street in the City of London famous for its banks, including the Bank of England, known as **The Old Lady of Threadneedle Street.**

thread rolling NOUN *Engineering* the production of a screw thread by a rolling swaging process using hardened profiled rollers. Rolled threads are stronger than threads machined by a cutting tool.

threads (θrɛdz) PLURAL NOUN a slang word for **clothes.**

thread vein NOUN a small red or purple capillary near to the surface of the skin.

threadworm (ˈθrɛdˌwɜːm) NOUN any of various nematodes, esp the pinworm.

thready (ˈθrɛdɪ) ADJECTIVE **threadier, threadiest.** 1 of, relating to, or resembling a thread or threads. 2 *Med* (of the pulse) barely perceptible; weak; fine. 3 sounding thin, weak, or reedy: *a thready tenor.*
▸**ˈthreadiness** NOUN

threap *or* **threep** (θriːp) VERB *(tr) Scot and northern English dialect* 1 to scold. 2 to contradict.
▷HISTORY Old English *thrēapian* to blame; related to Old Frisian *thrūwa,* Old High German *threwen,* Old Norse *threa*
▸**ˈthreaper** *or* **ˈthreeper** NOUN

threat (θrɛt) NOUN 1 a declaration of the intention to inflict harm, pain, or misery. 2 an indication of imminent harm, danger, or pain. 3 a person or thing that is regarded as dangerous or likely to inflict pain or misery. ◆ VERB 4 an archaic word for **threaten.**
▷HISTORY Old English; related to Old Norse *thraut,* Middle Low German *drōt*

threaten (ˈθrɛtən) VERB 1 *(tr)* to be a threat to. 2 to be a menacing indication of (something); portend: *dark clouds threatened rain.* 3 (when *tr, may take a clause as object*) to express a threat to (a person or people).
▸**ˈthreatener** NOUN ▸**ˈthreatening** ADJECTIVE
▸**ˈthreateningly** ADVERB

three (θriː) NOUN 1 the cardinal number that is the sum of two and one and is a prime number. See also **number** (sense 1). 2 a numeral, 3, III, (iii), representing this number. 3 the amount or quantity that is one greater than two. 4 something representing, represented by, or consisting of three units such as a playing card with three symbols on it. 5 Also called: **three o'clock.** three hours after noon or midnight. ◆ DETERMINER 6 **a** amounting to three: *three ships.* **b** *(as pronoun): three were killed.* ◆ Related adjectives: **ternary, tertiary, treble, triple.** ◆ Related prefixes **tri-, ter-.**
▷HISTORY Old English *thrēo;* related to Old Norse *thrīr,* Old High German *drī,* Latin *trēs,* Greek *treis*

three-card trick NOUN a game in which players bet on which of three inverted playing cards is the queen.

three-colour ADJECTIVE of, relating to, or comprising a colour print or a photomechanical process in which a picture is reproduced by superimposing three prints from half-tone plates in inks corresponding to the three primary colours.

three-D *or* **3-D** NOUN a three-dimensional effect.

three-day event NOUN See **eventing.**

three-day measles NOUN *Pathol* an informal name for **rubella.**

three-decker NOUN 1 **a** anything having three levels or layers. **b** *(as modifier): a three-decker sandwich.* 2 a warship with guns on three decks.

three-dimensional, three-D, *or* **3-D** ADJECTIVE 1 of, having, or relating to three dimensions: *three-dimensional space.* 2 (of a film, transparency, etc.) simulating the effect of depth by presenting slightly different views of a scene to each eye. 3 having volume. 4 lifelike or real.

threefold (ˈθriːˌfəʊld) ADJECTIVE 1 equal to or having three times as many or as much; triple: *a threefold decrease.* 2 composed of three parts: *a threefold purpose.* ◆ ADVERB 3 by or up to three times as many or as much.

three-four time NOUN *Music* a form of simple triple time in which there are three crotchet beats to the bar, indicated by the time signature $\frac{3}{4}$. Often shortened to: **three-four.** Also called (esp US and Canadian): **three-quarter time.**

three-gaited ADJECTIVE *Chiefly US* (of a horse) having the three usual paces, the walk, trot, and canter.

three-legged race NOUN a race in which pairs of competitors run with their adjacent legs tied together.

three-line whip NOUN See **whip** (sense 20c).

three-mile limit NOUN *International law* the range of a nation's territorial waters, extending to three nautical miles from shore.

threep (θriːp) VERB a variant spelling of **threap.**

threepenny bit *or* **thrupenny bit** (ˈθrʌpnɪ, -ənɪ, ˈθrɛp-) NOUN a twelve-sided British coin of nickel-brass, valued at three old pence, obsolete since 1971.

three-phase ADJECTIVE (of an electrical system, circuit, or device) having, generating, or using three alternating voltages of the same frequency, displaced in phase by 120°.

three-piece ADJECTIVE 1 having three pieces, esp (of a suit, suite, etc.) consisting of three matching parts. ◆ NOUN 2 a three-piece suite, suit, etc.

three-ply ADJECTIVE 1 having three layers or thicknesses. 2 **a** (of knitting wool, etc.) three-stranded. **b** *(as noun): the sweater was knitted in three-ply.*

three-point landing NOUN 1 an aircraft landing in which the two main wheels and the nose or tail wheel all touch the ground simultaneously. 2 a successful conclusion.

three-point turn NOUN a turn reversing the direction of motion of a motor vehicle using forward and reverse gears alternately, and completed after only three movements.

three-quarter ADJECTIVE 1 being three quarters of something: *a three-quarter turn.* 2 being of three quarters the normal length. ◆ NOUN 3 *Rugby* **a** any of the four players between the fullback and the halfbacks. **b** this position. **c** *(as modifier): three-quarter play.*

three-quarter binding NOUN a bookbinding style in which the spine and much of the sides are in a different material (esp leather) from the rest of the covers.

three-ring circus NOUN *US and Canadian* 1 a circus with three rings in which separate performances are carried on simultaneously. 2 a situation of confusion, characterized by a bewildering variety of events or activities.

Three Rivers NOUN the English name for **Trois Rivières.**

three Rs PLURAL NOUN **the.** the three skills regarded as the fundamentals of education; reading, writing, and arithmetic.
▷HISTORY from the humorous spelling *reading, 'riting,* and *'rithmetic*

threescore (ˈθriːˈskɔː) DETERMINER an archaic word for **sixty.**

threesome (ˈθriːsəm) NOUN 1 a group of three. 2 *Golf* a match in which a single player playing his own ball competes against two others playing alternate strokes on the same ball. 3 any game, etc., for three people. 4 *(modifier)* performed by three: *a threesome game.*

three-square ADJECTIVE having a cross section that is an equilateral triangle: *a three-square file.*

three-way ADJECTIVE 1 providing connections to three routes from a central point. 2 involving three things or people.

three-wheeler NOUN a light car that has three wheels.

thremmatology (ˌθrɛməˈtɒlədʒɪ) NOUN the science of breeding domesticated animals and plants.
▷HISTORY C19: from Greek *thremma* nursling + -LOGY

threnody (ˈθrɛnədɪ, ˈθriː-) *or* **threnode** (ˈθriːnəʊd, ˈθrɛn-) NOUN, *plural* **threnodies** *or* **threnodes.** an ode, song, or speech of lamentation, esp for the dead.
▷HISTORY C17: from Greek *thrēnōidia,* from *thrēnos* dirge + *ōidē* song
▸**threnodial** (θrɪˈnəʊdɪəl) *or* **threnodic** (θrɪˈnɒdɪk) ADJECTIVE ▸**threnodist** (ˈθrɛnədɪst, ˈθriː-) NOUN

threonine (ˈθriːəˌniːn, -nɪn) NOUN an essential amino acid that occurs in certain proteins.
▷HISTORY C20 *threon-,* probably from Greek *eruthron,* from *eruthros* red (see ERYTHRO-) + -INE[2]

thresh (θrɛʃ) VERB 1 to beat or rub stalks of ripe

corn or a similar crop either with a hand implement or a machine to separate the grain from the husks and straw. 2 (*tr*) to beat or strike. 3 (*intr; often foll by about*) to toss and turn; thrash. ◆ NOUN 4 the act of threshing.
▷HISTORY Old English *threscan;* related to Gothic *thriskan,* Old Norse *thriskja;* see THRASH

thresher (ˈθrɛʃə) NOUN 1 a person who threshes. 2 short for **threshing machine.** 3 Also called: **thrasher, thresher shark.** any of various large sharks of the genus *Alopias,* esp *A. vulpinus,* occurring in tropical and temperate seas: family *Alopiidae.* They have a very long whiplike tail with which they are thought to round up the small fish on which they feed.

threshing machine NOUN a machine for threshing crops.

threshold (ˈθrɛʃəʊld, ˈθrɛʃˌhəʊld) NOUN 1 Also called: **doorsill.** a sill, esp one made of stone or hardwood, placed at a doorway. 2 any doorway or entrance. 3 the starting point of an experience, event, or venture: *on the threshold of manhood.* 4 *Psychol* the strength at which a stimulus is just perceived: *the threshold of consciousness.* Compare **absolute threshold, difference threshold.** 5 **a** a level or point at which something would happen, would cease to happen, or would take effect, become true, etc. **b** (*as modifier*): *threshold price; threshold effect.* 6 **a** the minimum intensity or value of a signal, etc., that will produce a response or specified effect: *a frequency threshold.* **b** (*as modifier*): *a threshold current.* 7 (*modifier*) designating or relating to a pay agreement, clause, etc., that raises wages to compensate for increases in the cost of living. ◆ Related adjective: **liminal.**
▷HISTORY Old English *therscold;* related to Old Norse *threskoldr,* Old High German *driscubli,* Old Swedish *thriskuldi*

threshold agreement NOUN an agreement between an employer and employees or their union to increase wages by a specified sum if inflation exceeds a specified level in a specified time.

thresh out VERB another term for **thrash out.**

threw (θruː) VERB the past tense of **throw.**

thrice (θraɪs) ADVERB 1 three times. 2 in threefold degree. 3 *Archaic* greatly.
▷HISTORY Old English *thrīwa, thrīga;* see THREE

thrift (θrɪft) NOUN 1 wisdom and caution in the management of money. 2 Also called: **sea pink.** any of numerous perennial plumbaginaceous low-growing plants of the genus *Armeria,* esp *A. maritima,* of Europe, W Asia, and North America, having narrow leaves and round heads of pink or white flowers. 3 *Rare* vigorous thriving or growth, as of a plant. 4 *US* a building society, savings bank, or credit union. 5 an obsolete word for **prosperity.**
▷HISTORY C13: from Old Norse: success; see THRIVE
▸ˈ**thriftless** ADJECTIVE ▸ˈ**thriftlessly** ADVERB
▸ˈ**thriftlessness** NOUN

thrifty (ˈθrɪftɪ) ADJECTIVE **thriftier, thriftiest.** 1 showing thrift; economical or frugal. 2 *Rare* thriving or prospering.
▸ˈ**thriftily** ADVERB ▸ˈ**thriftiness** NOUN

thrill (θrɪl) NOUN 1 a sudden sensation of excitement and pleasure: *seeing his book for sale gave him a thrill.* 2 a situation producing such a sensation: *it was a thrill to see Rome for the first time.* 3 a trembling sensation caused by fear or emotional shock. 4 *Pathol* an abnormal slight tremor associated with a heart or vascular murmur, felt on palpation. ◆ VERB 5 to feel or cause to feel a thrill. 6 to tremble or cause to tremble; vibrate or quiver.
▷HISTORY Old English *thyrlian* to pierce, from *thyrel* hole; see NOSTRIL, THROUGH

thriller (ˈθrɪlə) NOUN 1 a book, film, play, etc., depicting crime, mystery, or espionage in an atmosphere of excitement and suspense. 2 a person or thing that thrills.

thrilling (ˈθrɪlɪŋ) ADJECTIVE 1 very exciting or stimulating. 2 vibrating or trembling.
▸ˈ**thrillingly** ADVERB

thrill-seeker NOUN a person who enjoys taking part in extreme sports and other activities involving physical risk.

thrips (θrɪps) NOUN, *plural* **thrips.** any of various small slender-bodied insects of the order *Thysanoptera,* typically having piercing mouthparts and narrow feathery wings and feeding on plant sap. Some species are serious plant pests.
▷HISTORY C18: via New Latin from Greek: woodworm

thrive (θraɪv) VERB **thrives, thriving; thrived** *or* **throve; thrived** *or* **thriven** (ˈθrɪvᵊn). (*intr*) 1 to grow strongly and vigorously. 2 to do well; prosper.
▷HISTORY C13: from Old Norse *thrīfask* to grasp for oneself, reflexive of *thrīfa* to grasp, of obscure origin
▸ˈ**thriver** NOUN ▸ˈ**thriving** ADJECTIVE ▸ˈ**thrivingly** ADVERB

thro' *or* **thro** (θruː) PREPOSITION, ADVERB *Informal or poetic* variant spellings of **through.**

throat (θrəʊt) NOUN 1 **a** that part of the alimentary and respiratory tracts extending from the back of the mouth (nasopharynx) to just below the larynx. **b** the front part of the neck. 2 something resembling a throat, esp in shape or function: *the throat of a chimney.* 3 *Botany* the gaping part of a tubular corolla or perianth. 4 *Informal* a sore throat. 5 **cut one's (own) throat.** to bring about one's own ruin. 6 **have by the throat.** to have compete control over (a person or thing). 7 **jump down someone's throat.** See **jump** (sense 24). 8 **ram or force (something) down someone's throat.** to insist that someone listen to or accept (something): *he rammed his own opinions down my throat.* 9 **stick in one's throat** (*or* **craw**). *Informal* to be difficult, or against one's conscience, for one to accept, utter, or believe. ◆ Related adjectives: **gular, guttural, jugular, laryngeal.**
▷HISTORY Old English *throtu;* related to Old High German *drozza* throat, Old Norse *throti* swelling

throatlash (ˈθrəʊtˌlæʃ) *or* **throatlatch** NOUN the strap that holds a bridle in place, fastening under the horse's jaw.

throat microphone NOUN a type of microphone that is held against the throat to pick up voice vibrations. Also called: **throat mike.**

throaty (ˈθrəʊtɪ) ADJECTIVE **throatier, throatiest.** 1 indicating a sore throat; hoarse: *a throaty cough.* 2 of, relating to, or produced in or by the throat. 3 deep, husky, or guttural.
▸ˈ**throatily** ADVERB ▸ˈ**throatiness** NOUN

throb (θrɒb) VERB **throbs, throbbing, throbbed.** (*intr*) 1 to pulsate or beat repeatedly, esp with increased force: *to throb with pain.* 2 (of engines, drums, etc.) to have a strong rhythmic vibration or beat. ◆ NOUN 3 the act or an instance of throbbing, esp a rapid pulsation as of the heart: *a throb of pleasure.*
▷HISTORY C14: perhaps of imitative origin
▸ˈ**throbbing** ADJECTIVE ▸ˈ**throbbingly** ADVERB

throe (θrəʊ) NOUN *Rare* a pang or pain.
▷HISTORY Old English *thrāwu* threat; related to Old High German *drawa* threat, Old Norse *thrā* desire, *thrauka* to endure

throes (θrəʊz) PLURAL NOUN 1 a condition of violent pangs, pain, or convulsions: *death throes.* 2 struggling with great effort with: *a country in the throes of revolution.*

thrombin (ˈθrɒmbɪn) NOUN *Biochem* an enzyme that acts on fibrinogen in blood causing it to clot.

thrombo- *or sometimes before a vowel* **thromb-** COMBINING FORM indicating a blood clot: *thromboembolism.*
▷HISTORY from Greek *thrombos* lump, clot

thrombocyte (ˈθrɒmbəˌsaɪt) NOUN another name for **platelet.**
▸**thrombocytic** (ˌθrɒmbəˈsɪtɪk) ADJECTIVE

thrombocytopenia (ˌθrɒmbəʊˌsaɪtəʊˈpiːnɪə) NOUN *Pathol* an abnormal decrease in the number of platelets in the blood.
▷HISTORY C20: from German *thrombocytopenie* from THROMBOCYTE + Greek *penia* poverty

thromboembolism (ˌθrɒmbəʊˈɛmbəˌlɪzəm) NOUN *Pathol* the obstruction of a blood vessel by a thrombus that has become detached from its original site.

thrombogen (ˈθrɒmbəˌdʒɛn) NOUN a protein present in blood that is essential for the formation of thrombin.

thrombokinase (ˌθrɒmbəʊˈkaɪneɪs) NOUN another name for **thromboplastin.**

thrombolytic (ˌθrɒmbəˈlɪtɪk) ADJECTIVE 1 causing the break-up of a blood clot. ◆ NOUN 2 a thrombolytic drug.

thrombophlebitis (ˌθrɒmbəʊflɪˈbaɪtɪs) NOUN inflammation of a vein associated with the formation of a thrombus.

thromboplastic (ˌθrɒmbəʊˈplæstɪk) ADJECTIVE causing or enhancing the formation of a blood clot.

thromboplastin (ˌθrɒmbəʊˈplæstɪn) NOUN any of a group of substances that are liberated from damaged blood platelets and other tissues and convert prothrombin to thrombin. Also called: **thrombokinase.**

thrombose (ˈθrɒmbəʊz) VERB to become or affect with a thrombus.
▷HISTORY C19: back formation from THROMBOSIS

thrombosis (θrɒmˈbəʊsɪs) NOUN, *plural* **-ses** (siːz). 1 the formation or presence of a thrombus. 2 *Informal* short for **coronary thrombosis.**
▷HISTORY C18: from New Latin, from Greek: curdling, from *thrombousthai* to clot, from *thrombos* THROMBUS
▸**thrombotic** (θrɒmˈbɒtɪk) ADJECTIVE

thrombus (ˈθrɒmbəs) NOUN, *plural* **-bi** (-baɪ). a clot of coagulated blood that forms within a blood vessel or inside the heart and remains at the site of its formation, often impeding the flow of blood. Compare **embolus.**
▷HISTORY C17: from New Latin, from Greek *thrombos* lump, of obscure origin

throne (θrəʊn) NOUN 1 the ceremonial seat occupied by a monarch, bishop, etc. on occasions of state. 2 the power, duties, or rank ascribed to a royal person. 3 a person holding royal rank. 4 (*plural; often capital*) the third of the nine orders into which the angels are traditionally divided in medieval angelology. ◆ VERB 5 to place or be placed on a throne.
▷HISTORY C13: from Old French *trone,* from Latin *thronus,* from Greek *thronos* throne
▸ˈ**throneless** ADJECTIVE

throng (θrɒŋ) NOUN 1 a great number of people or things crowded together. ◆ VERB 2 to gather in or fill (a place) in large numbers; crowd. 3 (*tr*) to hem in (a person); jostle. ◆ ADJECTIVE 4 *Yorkshire dialect* (*postpositive*) busy.
▷HISTORY Old English *gethrang;* related to Old Norse *throng,* Old High German *drangōd*

thronner (ˈθrɒnə) NOUN *Northern English dialect* a person who is good at doing odd jobs.

throstle (ˈθrɒsᵊl) NOUN 1 a poetic name for **thrush**[1], esp the song thrush 2 a spinning machine for wool or cotton in which the fibres are twisted and wound continuously.
▷HISTORY Old English; related to Old Saxon *throsla,* Old Norse *thröstr,* Middle High German *drostel*

throttle (ˈθrɒtᵊl) NOUN 1 Also called: **throttle valve.** any device that controls the quantity of fuel or fuel and air mixture entering an engine. 2 an informal or dialect word for **throat.** ◆ VERB (*tr*) 3 to kill or injure by squeezing the throat. 4 to suppress: *to throttle the press.* 5 to control or restrict (a flow of fluid) by means of a throttle valve.
▷HISTORY C14: *throtelen,* from *throte* THROAT
▸ˈ**throttler** NOUN

through (θruː) PREPOSITION 1 going in or starting at one side and coming out or stopping at the other side of: *a path through the wood.* 2 occupying or visiting several points scattered around in (an area). 3 as a result of; by means of: *the thieves were captured through his vigilance.* 4 *Chiefly US* up to and including: *Monday through Friday.* 5 during: *through the night.* 6 at the end of; having (esp successfully) completed. 7 **through with.** having finished with (esp when dissatisfied with). ◆ ADJECTIVE 8 (*postpositive*) having successfully completed some specified activity. 9 (on a telephone line) connected. 10 (*postpositive*) no longer able to function successfully in some specified capacity: *as a journalist, you're through.* 11 (*prenominal*) (of a route, journey, etc.) continuous or unbroken: *a through train.* ◆ ADVERB 12 through some specified thing, place, or period of time. 13 thoroughly; completely. ◆ Also: (informal or poetic) **thro',** (informal or poetic) **thro,** (chiefly US) **thru.**
▷HISTORY Old English *thurh;* related to Old Frisian *thruch,* Old Saxon *thuru,* Old High German *duruh*

through bridge NOUN *Civil engineering* a bridge in which the track is carried by the lower horizontal members.

through-composed ADJECTIVE *Music* of or relating to a song in stanzaic form, in which different music is provided for each stanza. Compare **strophic** (sense 2).

throughly ('θruːlɪ) ADVERB *Archaic* thoroughly; completely.

through-other ADJECTIVE *Scot* [1] untidy or dishevelled. [2] mixed up; in disorder.

throughout (θruː'aʊt) PREPOSITION [1] right through; through the whole of (a place or a period of time): *throughout the day.* ◆ ADVERB [2] through the whole of some specified period or area.

throughput ('θruːˌpʊt) NOUN the quantity of raw material or information processed or communicated in a given period, esp by a computer.

throughway ('θruːˌweɪ) NOUN *US* a thoroughfare, esp a motorway.

throve (θrəʊv) VERB a past tense of **thrive.**

throw (θrəʊ) VERB **throws, throwing, threw, thrown.** (*mainly tr*) [1] (*also intr*) to project or cast (something) through the air, esp with a rapid motion of the arm and wrist. [2] (foll by *in, on, onto,* etc.) to put or move suddenly, carelessly, or violently: *she threw her clothes onto the bed.* [3] to bring to or cause to be in a specified state or condition, esp suddenly or unexpectedly: *the news threw the family into a panic.* [4] to direct or cast (a shadow, light, etc.). [5] to project (the voice) so as to make it appear to come from other than its source. [6] to give or hold (a party). [7] to cause to fall or be upset; dislodge: *the horse soon threw his rider.* [8] **a** to tip (dice) out onto a flat surface. **b** to obtain (a specified number) in this way. [9] to shape (clay) on a potter's wheel. [10] to move (a switch or lever) to engage or disengage a mechanism. [11] to be subjected to (a fit). [12] to turn (wood, etc.) on a lathe. [13] *Informal* to baffle or astonish; confuse: *the last question on the test paper threw me.* [14] *Boxing* to deliver (a punch). [15] *Wrestling* to hurl (an opponent) to the ground. [16] *Informal* to lose (a contest, fight, etc.) deliberately, esp in boxing. [17] **a** to play (a card). **b** to discard (a card). [18] (of a female animal, esp a cow) to give birth to (young). [19] to twist or spin (filaments) into thread. [20] **throw cold water on (something).** *Informal* to be unenthusiastic about or discourage (something). [21] **throw oneself at.** to strive actively to attract the attention or affection of. [22] **throw oneself into.** to involve oneself enthusiastically in. [23] **throw oneself on.** to rely entirely upon: *he threw himself on the mercy of the police.* ◆ NOUN [24] the act or an instance of throwing. [25] the distance or extent over which anything may be thrown: *a stone's throw.* [26] *Informal* a chance, venture, or try. [27] an act or result of throwing dice. [28] **a** the eccentricity of a cam. **b** the radial distance between the central axis of a crankshaft and the axis of a crankpin forming part of the shaft. [29] a decorative light blanket or cover, as thrown over a chair. [30] a sheet of fabric used for draping over an easel or unfinished painting, etc., to keep the dust off. [31] *Geology* the vertical displacement of rock strata at a fault. [32] *Physics* the deflection of a measuring instrument as a result of a sudden fluctuation. ◆ See also **throw about, throwaway, throwback, throw in, throw off, throw out, throw over, throw together, throw up.**
▷HISTORY Old English *thrāwan* to turn, torment; related to Old High German *drāen* to twist, Latin *terere* to rub
▸ **'thrower** NOUN

throw about VERB (*tr, adverb*) [1] to spend (one's money) in a reckless and flaunting manner. [2] **throw one's weight about.** *Informal* to act in an authoritarian or aggressive manner.

throwaway ('θrəʊəˌweɪ) ADJECTIVE (*prenominal*) [1] said or done incidentally, esp for rhetorical effect; casual: *a throwaway remark.* [2] **a** anything designed to be discarded after use rather than reused, refilled, etc.; disposable. **b** (*as modifier*): *a throwaway carton.* ◆ NOUN [3] *Chiefly US and Canadian* a handbill or advertisement distributed in a public place. ◆ VERB **throw away.** (*tr, adverb*) [4] to get rid of; discard. [5] to fail to make good use of; waste: *to throw away all one's money on horses.*

throwback ('θrəʊˌbæk) NOUN [1] **a** a person, animal, or plant that has the characteristics of an earlier or more primitive type. **b** a reversion to such an organism. ◆ VERB **throw back.** (*adverb*) [2] (*intr*) to revert to an earlier or more primitive type. [3] (*tr;* foll by *on*) to force to depend (on): *the crisis threw her back on her faith in God.*

throw in VERB (*tr, adverb*) [1] to add (something extra) at no additional cost. [2] to contribute or interpose (a remark, argument, etc.), esp in a discussion. [3] **throw in one's hand. a** (in cards) to concede defeat by putting one's cards down. **b** to give in and accept defeat; discontinue a venture. [4] **throw in the towel** (*or* **sponge**). **a** (in boxing) to concede defeat by the throwing of a towel (or sponge) into the ring by a second. **b** to give in and accept defeat; discontinue a venture. ◆ NOUN **throw-in.** [5] *Soccer* the method of putting the ball into play after it has gone into touch by throwing it two-handed from behind the head to a teammate, both feet being kept on the ground.

throwing stick NOUN a primitive device for hurling a spear with greater leverage, consisting of a rod with a groove in it and a hook or projection at the back end to hold the weapon until its release.

thrown (θrəʊn) VERB the past participle of **throw.**

throw off VERB (*mainly tr, adverb*) [1] to free oneself of; discard. [2] to produce or utter in a casual manner: *to throw off a witty remark.* [3] to escape from or elude: *the fox rapidly threw off his pursuers.* [4] to confuse or disconcert: *the interruption threw the young pianist off.* [5] (*intr,* often foll by *at*) *Austral and NZ informal* to deride or ridicule.

throw out VERB (*tr, adverb*) [1] to discard or reject. [2] to expel or dismiss, esp forcibly. [3] to construct (something projecting or prominent, such as a wing of a building). [4] to put forward or offer: *the chairman threw out a new proposal.* [5] to utter in a casual or indirect manner: *to throw out a hint.* [6] to confuse or disconcert: *the noise threw his concentration out.* [7] to give off or emit. [8] *Cricket* (of a fielder) to put (the batsman) out by throwing the ball to hit the wicket. [9] *Baseball* to make a throw to a teammate who in turn puts out (a base runner).

throw over VERB (*tr, adverb*) to forsake or abandon; jilt.

throwster ('θrəʊstə) NOUN a person who twists silk or other fibres into yarn.
▷HISTORY C15 *throwestre,* from THROW + -STER

throw together VERB (*tr, adverb*) [1] to assemble hurriedly. [2] to cause to become casually acquainted.

throw up VERB (*adverb, mainly tr*) [1] to give up; abandon, relinquish. [2] to build or construct hastily. [3] to reveal; produce: *every generation throws up its own leaders.* [4] (*also intr*) *Informal* to vomit.

throw weight NOUN the maximum weight of supplementary mechanisms that can be lifted by the boost stages of a particular missile.

thru (θruː) PREPOSITION (*adverb, adjective*) *Chiefly US* a variant spelling of **through.**

thrum¹ (θrʌm) VERB **thrums, thrumming, thrummed.** [1] to strum rhythmically but without expression on (a musical instrument). [2] (*intr*) to drum incessantly: *rain thrummed on the roof.* [3] to repeat (something) monotonously. ◆ NOUN [4] a repetitive strumming or recitation.
▷HISTORY C16: of imitative origin
▸ **'thrummer** NOUN

thrum² (θrʌm) *Textiles* ◆ NOUN [1] **a** any of the unwoven ends of warp thread remaining on the loom when the web has been removed. **b** such ends of thread collectively. [2] a fringe or tassel of short unwoven threads. ◆ VERB **thrums, thrumming, thrummed.** [3] (*tr*) to trim with thrums.
▷HISTORY C14: from Old English; related to Old High German *drum* remnant, Dutch *dreum*

thrum-eyed ADJECTIVE (of flowers, esp primulas) having the stigma on a short style below the anthers, which lie in the mouth of the corolla on big stamens. Compare **pin-eyed.**
▷HISTORY C19: from THRUM², because of the ring of anthers visible at the neck of the corolla

thrupenny bit ('θrʌpnɪ, -ənɪ, 'θrɛp-) NOUN a variant spelling of **threepenny bit.**

thrush¹ (θrʌʃ) NOUN any songbird of the subfamily *Turdinae,* esp those having a brown plumage with a spotted breast, such as the mistle thrush and song thrush: family *Muscicapidae.* Compare **water thrush.** Related adjective: **turdine.**
▷HISTORY Old English *thrȳsce;* related to Old High German *drōsca;* see THROSTLE, THROAT

thrush² (θrʌʃ) NOUN [1] **a** a fungal disease of the mouth, esp of infants, and the genitals, characterized by the formation of whitish spots and caused by infection with the fungus *Candida albicans.* **b** another word for **sprue.** [2] a softening of the frog of a horse's hoof characterized by degeneration and a thick foul discharge.
▷HISTORY C17: related to Old Danish *törsk,* Danish *troske*

thrust (θrʌst) VERB **thrusts, thrusting, thrust.** [1] (*tr*) to push (someone or something) with force or sudden strength: *she thrust him away; she thrust it into the fire.* [2] (*tr*) to force or impose upon (someone) or into (some condition or situation): *they thrust extra responsibilities upon her; she was thrust into the limelight.* [3] (*tr;* foll by *through*) to pierce; stab. [4] (*intr;* usually foll by *through* or *into*) to force a passage or entrance. [5] (*intr*) to push forwards, upwards, or outwards. [6] (*intr;* foll by *at*) to make a stab or lunge at (a person or thing). ◆ NOUN [7] a forceful drive, push, stab, or lunge. [8] a force, esp one that produces motion. [9] **a** a propulsive force produced by the fluid pressure or the change of momentum of the fluid in a jet engine, rocket engine, etc. **b** a similar force produced by a propeller. [10] a pressure that is exerted continuously by one part of an object, structure, etc., against another, esp the axial force by or on a shaft. [11] *Geology* **a** the compressive force in the earth's crust that produces recumbent folds and thrust or reverse faults. **b** See **thrust fault.** [12] *Civil engineering* a force exerted in a downwards and outwards direction, as by an arch or rafter, or the horizontal force exerted by retained earth. [13] force, impetus, or drive: *a man with thrust and energy.* [14] the essential or most forceful part: *the thrust of the argument.*
▷HISTORY C12: from Old Norse *thrysta;* related to Latin *trūdere;* see INTRUDE

thrust bearing NOUN *Engineering* a low-friction bearing on a rotating shaft that resists axial thrust in the shaft. Usually it consists of a collar which bears against a ring of well lubricated stationary and sometimes tilting pads. Compare **tapered roller bearing.**

thruster ('θrʌstə) NOUN [1] a person or thing that thrusts. [2] Also called: **vernier rocket.** a small rocket engine, esp one used to correct the altitude or course of a spacecraft. [3] an auxiliary propeller on a ship, capable of acting athwartships.

thrust fault NOUN a fault in which the rocks on the upper side of an inclined fault plane have been displaced upwards, usually by compression; a reverse fault.

thrusting ('θrʌstɪŋ) ADJECTIVE ambitious and having great drive: *a thrusting young executive.*

thrutch (θrʌtʃ) NOUN *Northern English dialect* a narrow, fast-moving stream.

thud (θʌd) NOUN [1] a dull heavy sound: *the book fell to the ground with a thud.* [2] a blow or fall that causes such a sound. ◆ VERB **thuds, thudding, thudded.** [3] to make or cause to make such a sound.
▷HISTORY Old English *thyddan* to strike; related to *thoddettan* to beat, perhaps of imitative origin

thug (θʌg) NOUN [1] a tough and violent man, esp a criminal. [2] (*sometimes capital*) (formerly) a member of an organization of robbers and assassins in India who typically strangled their victims.
▷HISTORY C19: from Hindi *thag* thief, from Sanskrit *sthaga* scoundrel, from *sthagati* to conceal
▸ **'thuggery** NOUN ▸ **'thuggish** ADJECTIVE

thuggee (θʌ'giː) NOUN *History* the methods and practices of the thugs of India.
▷HISTORY C19: from Hindi *thagī;* see THUG

thuja *or* **thuya** ('θuːjə) NOUN any of various coniferous trees of the genus *Thuja,* of North America and East Asia, having scalelike leaves, small cones, and an aromatic wood: family *Cupressaceae.* See also **arbor vitae.**
▷HISTORY C18: from New Latin, from Medieval Latin *thuia,* ultimately from Greek *thua* name of an African tree

Thule ('θjuːlɪ) NOUN [1] Also called: **ultima Thule.** a region believed by ancient geographers to be the northernmost land in the inhabited world: sometimes thought to have been Iceland, Norway, or one of the Shetland Islands. 2 an Eskimo settlement in NW Greenland: a Danish trading post, founded in 1910, and US air force base.

thulium ('θju:lɪəm) NOUN a malleable ductile silvery-grey element occurring principally in monazite. The radioisotope **thulium-170** is used as an electron source in portable X-ray units. Symbol: Tm; atomic no.: 69; atomic wt.: 168.93421; valency: 3; relative density: 9.321; melting pt.: 1545°C; boiling pt.: 1950°C.
▷HISTORY C19: New Latin, from THULE + -IUM

thumb (θʌm) NOUN 1 the first and usually shortest and thickest of the digits of the hand, composed of two short bones. Technical name: **pollex.** Related adjective: **pollical.** 2 the corresponding digit in other vertebrates. 3 the part of a glove shaped to fit the thumb. 4 *Architect* another name for **ovolo.** 5 **all thumbs.** clumsy. 6 **thumbs down.** an indication of refusal, disapproval, or negation: *he gave the thumbs down on our proposal.* 7 **thumbs up.** an indication of encouragement, approval, or acceptance. 8 **under someone's thumb.** at someone's mercy or command. ◆ VERB 9 (*tr*) to touch, mark, or move with the thumb. 10 to attempt to obtain (a lift or ride) by signalling with the thumb. 11 (when *intr,* often foll by *through*) to flip the pages of (a book, magazine, etc.) perfunctorily in order to glance at the contents. 12 **thumb one's nose at.** to deride or mock, esp by placing the thumb on the nose with fingers extended.
▷HISTORY Old English *thūma;* related to Old Saxon *thūma,* Old High German *thūmo,* Old Norse *thumall* thumb of a glove, Latin *tumēre* to swell
▸ **'thumbless** ADJECTIVE ▸ **'thumb,like** ADJECTIVE

thumb index NOUN 1 a series of indentations cut into the fore edge of a book to facilitate quick reference. ◆ VERB **thumb-index.** 2 (*tr*) to furnish with a thumb index.

thumb knot NOUN another name for **overhand knot.**

thumbnail ('θʌm,neɪl) NOUN 1 the nail of the thumb. 2 (*modifier*) concise and brief: *a thumbnail sketch.* 3 *Computing* a small image which can be expanded.

thumbnut ('θʌm,nʌt) NOUN a nut with projections enabling it to be turned by the thumb and forefinger; wing nut.

thumb piano NOUN another name for **mbira.**

thumbprint ('θʌm,prɪnt) NOUN an impression of the upper part of the thumb, used esp for identification purposes. See **fingerprint.**

thumbscrew ('θʌm,skru:) NOUN 1 an instrument of torture that pinches or crushes the thumbs. 2 a screw with projections on its head enabling it to be turned by the thumb and forefinger.

thumbstall ('θʌm,stɔ:l) NOUN a protective sheathlike cover for the thumb.

thumbtack ('θʌm,tæk) NOUN the US and Canadian name for **drawing pin.**

Thummim ('θʌmɪm) NOUN *Old Testament* See **Urim and Thummim.**

thump (θʌmp) NOUN 1 the sound of a heavy solid body hitting or pounding a comparatively soft surface. 2 a heavy blow with the hand: *he gave me a thump on the back.* ◆ VERB 3 (*tr*) to strike or beat heavily; pound. 4 (*intr*) to throb, beat, or pound violently: *his heart thumped with excitement.*
▷HISTORY C16: related to Icelandic, Swedish dialect *dumpa* to thump; see THUD, BUMP
▸ **'thumper** NOUN

thumping ('θʌmpɪŋ) ADJECTIVE (*prenominal*) *Slang* huge or excessive: *a thumping loss.*
▸ **'thumpingly** ADVERB

Thun (*German* tu:n) NOUN 1 a town in central Switzerland, in Bern canton on Lake Thun. Pop.: 36 700 (1990 est.). 2 a lake in central Switzerland, formed by a widening of the Aar River. Length: about 17 km (11 miles). Width: 3 km (2 miles). German name: **Thuner See.**

thunbergia (θʊn'bɜ:dʒɪə) NOUN any plant of the typically climbing tropical genus *Thunbergia* such as black-eyed Susan: family *Acanthaceae.*
▷HISTORY named after K. P. *Thunberg* (1743–1822), Swedish traveller and botanist

thunder ('θʌndə) NOUN 1 a loud cracking or deep rumbling noise caused by the rapid expansion of atmospheric gases which are suddenly heated by lightning. 2 any loud booming sound. 3 *Rare* a violent threat or denunciation. 4 **steal someone's thunder.** to detract from the attention due to another by forestalling him. ◆ VERB 5 to make (a loud sound) or utter (words) in a manner suggesting thunder. 6 (*intr; with it as subject*) to be the case that thunder is being heard. 7 (*intr*) to move fast and heavily: *the bus thundered downhill.* 8 (*intr*) to utter vehement threats or denunciation; rail.
▷HISTORY Old English *thunor;* related to Old Saxon *thunar,* Old High German *donar,* Old Norse *thōrr;* see THOR, THURSDAY
▸ **'thunderer** NOUN ▸ **'thundery** ADJECTIVE

Thunder Bay NOUN a port in central Canada, in Ontario on Lake Superior: formed in 1970 by the amalgamation of Fort William and Port Arthur; the head of the St Lawrence Seaway for Canada. Pop.: 113 662 (1996).

thunderbird ('θʌndə,bɜ:d) NOUN a legendary bird that produces thunder, lightning, and rain according to the folk belief of several North American Indian peoples.

thunderbolt ('θʌndə,bəʊlt) NOUN 1 a flash of lightning accompanying thunder. 2 the imagined agency of destruction produced by a flash of lightning. 3 (in mythology) the destructive weapon wielded by several gods, esp the Greek god Zeus. See also **Thor.** 4 something very startling.

thunderbox ('θʌndə,bɒks) NOUN *Slang* 1 a portable boxlike lavatory seat that can be placed over a hole in the ground. 2 any portable lavatory.

thunderclap ('θʌndə,klæp) NOUN 1 a loud outburst of thunder. 2 something as violent or unexpected as a clap of thunder.

thundercloud ('θʌndə,klaʊd) NOUN 1 a towering electrically charged cumulonimbus cloud associated with thunderstorms. 2 anything that is threatening.

thunderhead ('θʌndə,hɛd) NOUN *Chiefly US and Canadian* the anvil-shaped top of a cumulonimbus cloud.

thundering ('θʌndərɪŋ) ADJECTIVE (*prenominal*) *Slang* very great or excessive: *a thundering idiot.*
▸ **'thunderingly** ADVERB

thunderous ('θʌndərəs) ADJECTIVE 1 resembling thunder, esp in loudness: *thunderous clapping.* 2 threatening and extremely angry: *she gave him a thunderous look.*
▸ **'thunderously** ADVERB

thunder sheet NOUN a large sheet of metal that can be shaken to produce a noise resembling thunder as a sound effect for a theatrical production.

thundershower ('θʌndə,ʃaʊə) NOUN a heavy shower during a thunderstorm.

thunderstone ('θʌndə,stəʊn) NOUN 1 a long tapering stone, fossil, or similar object, formerly thought to be a thunderbolt. 2 an archaic word for **thunderbolt.**

thunderstorm ('θʌndə,stɔ:m) NOUN a storm caused by strong rising air currents and characterized by thunder and lightning and usually heavy rain or hail.

thunderstruck ('θʌndə,strʌk) *or* **thunderstricken** ('θʌndə,strɪkən) ADJECTIVE 1 completely taken aback; amazed or shocked. 2 *Rare* struck by lightning.

thunk (θʌŋk) NOUN, VERB *Informal* another word for **thud.**

Thurgau (*German* 'tu:rgau) NOUN a canton of NE Switzerland, on Lake Constance: annexed by the confederated Swiss states in 1460. Capital: Frauenfeld. Pop.: 227 300 (2000 est.). Area: 1007 sq. km (389 sq. miles). French name: **Thurgovie** (tyrgɔvi).

thurible ('θjʊərɪbᵊl) NOUN another word for **censer.**
▷HISTORY C15: from Latin *tūribulum* censer, from *tūs* incense

thurifer ('θjʊərɪfə) NOUN a person appointed to carry the censer at religious ceremonies.
▷HISTORY C19: from Latin, from *tūs* incense + *ferre* to carry

Thuringia (θjʊ'rɪndʒɪə) NOUN a state of central Germany, formerly in East Germany. Pop.: 2 449 100 (2001 est.). German name: **Thüringen** ('ty:rɪŋən).

Thuringian (θjʊ'rɪndʒɪən) ADJECTIVE 1 of or relating to the German state of Thuringia or its inhabitants. ◆ NOUN 2 a native or inhabitant of Thuringia.

Thuringian Forest NOUN a forested mountainous region in E central Germany, rising over 900 m (3000 ft.). German name: **Thüringer Wald** ('ty:rɪŋər 'valt).

Thurrock ('θʌrək) NOUN a unitary authority in SE England, in Essex. Pop.: 143 042 (2001). Area: 163 sq. km (63 sq. miles).

Thurs. ABBREVIATION FOR Thursday.

Thursday ('θɜ:zdɪ) NOUN the fifth day of the week; fourth day of the working week.
▷HISTORY Old English *Thursdæg,* literally: Thor's day; related to Old High German *Donares tag;* see THOR, THUNDER, DAY

Thursday Island NOUN an island in Torres Strait, between NE Australia and New Guinea: administratively part of Queensland, Australia. Area: 4 sq. km (1.5 sq. miles).

thus (ðʌs) ADVERB 1 in this manner: *do it thus.* 2 to such a degree: *thus far and no further.* ◆ SENTENCE CONNECTOR 3 therefore: *We have failed. Thus we have to take the consequences.*
▷HISTORY Old English; related to Old Frisian, Old Saxon *thus*

thuya ('θu:jə) NOUN a variant spelling of **thuja.**

thwack (θwæk) VERB 1 to beat, hit, or flog, esp with something flat. ◆ NOUN 2 **a** a blow with something flat. **b** the sound made by it. ◆ INTERJECTION 3 an exclamation imitative of this sound.
▷HISTORY C16: of imitative origin
▸ **'thwacker** NOUN

thwaite (θweɪt) NOUN *Obsolete except in place names* a piece of land cleared from forest or reclaimed from wasteland.
▷HISTORY from Old Norse *thveit* paddock

thwart (θwɔ:t) VERB 1 to oppose successfully or prevent; frustrate: *they thwarted the plan.* 2 *Obsolete* to be or move across. ◆ NOUN 3 *Nautical* **a** a seat lying across a boat and occupied by an oarsman. **b** ◆ ADJECTIVE 4 passing or being situated across. 5 *Archaic* perverse or stubborn. ◆ PREPOSITION, ADVERB 6 *Obsolete* across.
▷HISTORY C13: from Old Norse *thvert,* from *thverr* transverse; related to Old English *thweorh* crooked, Old High German *twerh* transverse
▸ **'thwartedly** ADVERB ▸ **'thwarter** NOUN

THX *Text messaging* ABBREVIATION FOR thanks.

thy (ðaɪ) DETERMINER (*usually preceding a consonant*) *Archaic* belonging to or associated in some way with you (thou): *thy goodness and mercy.* Compare **thine.**
▷HISTORY C12: variant of THINE

Thyestes (θaɪ'ɛsti:z) NOUN *Greek myth* son of Pelops and brother of Atreus, with whose wife he committed adultery. In revenge, Atreus killed Thyestes' sons and served them to their father at a banquet.
▸ **Thyestean** *or* **Thyestian** (θaɪ'ɛstɪən, ,θaɪɛ'sti:ən) ADJECTIVE

thylacine ('θaɪlə,saɪn) NOUN an extinct or very rare doglike carnivorous marsupial, *Thylacinus cynocephalus,* of Tasmania, having greyish-brown fur with dark vertical stripes on the back: family *Dasyuridae.* Also called: **Tasmanian wolf.**
▷HISTORY C19: from New Latin *thӯlacīnus,* from Greek *thulakos* pouch, sack

thyme (taɪm) NOUN any of various small shrubs of the temperate genus *Thymus,* having a strong mintlike odour, small leaves, and white, pink, or red flowers: family *Lamiaceae* (labiates).
▷HISTORY C14: from Old French *thym,* from Latin *thymum,* from Greek *thumon,* from *thuein* to make a burnt offering
▸ **'thymy** ADJECTIVE

thymectomy (θaɪ'mɛktəmɪ) NOUN, *plural* **-mies.** surgical removal of the thymus.

thymelaeaceous (,θɪmɪlɪ'eɪʃəs) ADJECTIVE of, relating to, or belonging to the *Thymelaeaceae,* a family of trees and shrubs having tough acrid bark and simple leaves: includes spurge laurel, leatherwood, and mezereon.
▷HISTORY C19: via New Latin, from Greek *thumelaia,* from *thumon* THYME + *elaia* olive

-thymia NOUN COMBINING FORM indicating a certain

emotional condition, mood, or state of mind: *cyclothymia*.
▷HISTORY New Latin, from Greek *thumos* temper

thymic ('θaɪmɪk) ADJECTIVE of or relating to the thymus.

thymidine ('θaɪmɪˌdiːn) NOUN the crystalline nucleoside of thymine, found in DNA. Formula: $C_{10}H_{14}N_2O_5$.
▷HISTORY C20: from THYM(INE) + -IDE + -INE²

thymidylic acid (ˌθaɪmɪ'dɪlɪk) NOUN a nucleotide consisting of thymine, deoxyribose, and a phosphate group. It is a constituent of DNA. Also called: **thymidine monophosphate.**

thymine ('θaɪmiːn) NOUN a white crystalline pyrimidine base found in DNA. Formula: $C_5H_6N_2O_2$.
▷HISTORY C19: from THYMIC (see THYMUS) + -INE²

thymocyte ('θaɪməsaɪt) NOUN a lymphocyte found in the thymus.

thymol ('θaɪmɒl) NOUN a white crystalline substance with an aromatic odour, obtained from the oil of thyme and used as a fungicide, antiseptic, and anthelmintic and in perfumery and embalming; 2-isopropylphenol. Formula: $(CH_3)_2CHC_6H_3(CH_3)OH$.
▷HISTORY C19: from THYME + -OL²

thymus ('θaɪməs) NOUN, *plural* **-muses** *or* **-mi** (-maɪ). a glandular organ of vertebrates, consisting in man of two lobes situated below the thyroid. In early life it produces lymphocytes and is thought to influence certain immunological responses. It atrophies with age and is almost nonexistent in the adult.
▷HISTORY C17: from New Latin, from Greek *thumos* sweetbread

thyratron ('θaɪrəˌtrɒn) NOUN *Electronics* a gas-filled tube that has three electrodes and can be switched between an 'off' state and an 'on' state. It has been superseded, except for application involving high-power switching, by the thyristor.
▷HISTORY C20: originally a trademark, from Greek *thura* door, valve + -TRON

thyristor (θaɪ'rɪstə) NOUN any of a group of semiconductor devices, such as the silicon-controlled rectifier, that can be switched between two states.
▷HISTORY C20: from THYR(ATRON) + (TRANS)ISTOR

thyro- *or before a vowel* **thyr-** COMBINING FORM thyroid: *thyrotoxicosis; thyrotropin.*

thyrocalcitonin (ˌθaɪrəʊˌkælsɪ'təʊnɪn) NOUN another name for **calcitonin.**
▷HISTORY C20: from THYRO- + CALCITONIN

thyroid ('θaɪrɔɪd) ADJECTIVE [1] of or relating to the thyroid gland. [2] of or relating to the largest cartilage of the larynx. ◆ NOUN [3] See **thyroid gland.** [4] Also: **thyroid extract.** the powdered preparation made from the thyroid gland of certain animals, used to treat hypothyroidism.
▷HISTORY C18: from New Latin *thyroidēs*, from Greek *thureoeidēs*, from *thureos* oblong (literally: door-shaped) shield, from *thura* door

thyroidectomy (ˌθaɪrɔɪ'dɛktəmɪ) NOUN, *plural* **-mies.** surgical removal of all or part of the thyroid gland.

thyroid gland NOUN an endocrine gland of vertebrates, consisting in man of two lobes near the base of the neck. It secretes hormones that control metabolism and body growth.

thyroiditis (ˌθaɪrɔɪ'daɪtɪs) NOUN inflammation of the thyroid gland.

thyroid-stimulating hormone NOUN another name for **thyrotropin.** Abbreviation: **TSH.**

thyrotoxicosis (ˌθaɪrəʊˌtɒksɪ'kəʊsɪs) NOUN another name for **hyperthyroidism.**

thyrotropin (ˌθaɪrəʊ'trəʊpɪn) *or* **thyrotrophin** NOUN a glycoprotein hormone secreted by the anterior lobe of the pituitary gland: it stimulates the activity of the thyroid gland. Also called: **thyroid-stimulating hormone.**
▷HISTORY C20: from THYRO- + -TROPE + -IN

thyroxine (θaɪ'rɒksiːn, -sɪn) *or* **thyroxin** (θaɪ'rɒksɪn) NOUN the principal hormone produced by the thyroid gland: it increases the metabolic rate of tissues and also controls growth, as in amphibian metamorphosis. It can be synthesized or extracted from the thyroid glands of animals and used to treat hypothyroidism. Chemical name: tetra-iodothyronine; formula: $C_{15}H_{11}I_4NO_4$.
▷HISTORY C19: from THYRO- + OXY-² + -INE²

thyrse (θɜːs) *or* **thyrsus** ('θɜːsəs) NOUN, *plural* **thyrses** *or* **thyrsi** ('θɜːsaɪ). *Botany* a type of inflorescence, occurring in the lilac and grape, in which the main branch is racemose and the lateral branches cymose.
▷HISTORY C17: from French: THYRSUS
▸'**thyrsoid** ADJECTIVE

thyrsus ('θɜːsəs) NOUN, *plural* **-si** (-saɪ). [1] *Greek myth* a staff, usually one tipped with a pine cone, borne by Dionysus (Bacchus) and his followers. [2] a variant spelling of **thyrse.**
▷HISTORY C18: from Latin, from Greek *thursos* stalk

thysanuran (ˌθɪsə'njʊərən) NOUN [1] any primitive wingless insect of the order *Thysanura*, which comprises the bristletails. ◆ ADJECTIVE [2] of, relating to, or belonging to the order *Thysanura.*
▷HISTORY C19: from New Latin, from Greek *thusanos* fringe + *oura* tail
▸ˌ**thysa'nurous** ADJECTIVE

thyself (ðaɪ'sɛlf) PRONOUN *Archaic* **a** the reflexive form of **thou** or **thee. b** (intensifier): *thou, thyself, wouldst know.*

ti¹ (tiː) NOUN *Music* a variant spelling of **te.**

ti² (tiː) NOUN, *plural* **tis.** [1] a woody palmlike agave plant, *Cordyline terminalis,* of the East Indies, having white, mauve, or reddish flowers. The sword-shaped leaves are used for garments, fodder, thatch, etc., and the root for food and liquor. [2] a similar and related plant, *Cordyline australis,* of New Zealand.
▷HISTORY of Polynesian origin

Ti THE CHEMICAL SYMBOL FOR titanium.

TIA *Med* ABBREVIATION FOR transient ischaemic attack; a stroke causing minor and temporary symptoms.

Tia Juana ('tɪə 'wɑːnə; *Spanish* 'tia 'xwana) NOUN a variant spelling of **Tijuana.**

Tia Maria ('tɪə mə'rɪə) NOUN *Trademark* a coffee-flavoured liqueur from the Caribbean.

Tianjin ('tjɛn'dʒɪn), **Tientsin,** *or* **T'ien-ching** NOUN an industrial city in NE China, in Hebei province, on the Grand Canal, 51 km (32 miles) from the Yellow Sea: the third largest city in China; seat of Nankai University (1919). Pop.: 4 835 327 (1999 est.).

Tian Shan *or* **Tien Shan** ('tjɛn'ʃɑːn) NOUN a great mountain system of central Asia, in Kyrgyzstan and the Xinjiang Uygur Autonomous Region of W China, extending for about 2500 km (1500 miles). Highest peak: Pobeda Peak, 7439 m (24 406 ft.). Russian name: **Tyan-Shan.**

tiara (tɪ'ɑːrə) NOUN [1] a woman's semicircular jewelled headdress for formal occasions. [2] a high headdress worn by Persian kings in ancient times. [3] *RC Church* **a** a headdress worn by the pope, consisting of a beehive-shaped diadem surrounded by three coronets. **b** the office or rank of pope.
▷HISTORY C16: via Latin from Greek, of Oriental origin
▸**ti'araed** ADJECTIVE

Tiber ('taɪbə) NOUN a river in central Italy, rising in the Tuscan Apennines and flowing south through Rome to the Tyrrhenian Sea. Length: 405 km (252 miles). Ancient name: **Tiberis** ('tiːbərɪs). Italian name: **Tevere.**

Tiberias (taɪ'bɪərɪˌæs) NOUN [1] a resort in N Israel, on the Sea of Galilee: an important Jewish centre after the destruction of Jerusalem by the Romans. Pop.: 35 400 (latest est.). [2] **Lake.** another name for the (Sea of) **Galilee.**

Tibesti *or* **Tibesti Massif** (tɪ'bɛstɪ) NOUN a mountain range of volcanic origin in NW Chad, in the central Sahara extending for about 480 km (300 miles). Highest peak: Emi Koussi, 3415 m (11 204 ft.).

Tibet (tɪ'bɛt) NOUN an autonomous region of SW China: Europeans strictly excluded in the 19th century; invaded by China in 1950; rebellion (1959) against Chinese rule suppressed and the Dalai Lama fled to India; military rule imposed (1989–90) after continued demands for independence; consists largely of a vast high plateau between the Himalayas and Kunlun Mountains; formerly a theocracy and the centre of Lamaism. Capital: Lhasa. Pop.: 2 620 000 (2000 est.). Area: 1 221 601 sq. km (471 660 sq. miles). Chinese names: **Xizang Autonomous Region, Sitsang.**

Tibetan (tɪ'bɛtᵊn) ADJECTIVE [1] of, relating to, or characteristic of Tibet, its people, or their language. ◆ NOUN [2] a native or inhabitant of Tibet. [3] the language of Tibet, belonging to the Sino-Tibetan family.

Tibetan mastiff NOUN a heavy well-built dog of a Tibetan breed with a long thick coat and a bushy tail carried curled over its back, often used as a guard dog.

Tibetan spaniel NOUN a small long-bodied variety of spaniel with a long silky coat and a well-feathered tail carried curled over its back.

Tibetan terrier NOUN a breed of dog with a long dense shaggy coat: it resembles a small Old English sheepdog.

Tibeto-Burman (tɪ'bɛtəʊ'bɜːmən) NOUN [1] a branch of the Sino-Tibetan family of languages, sometimes regarded as a family in its own right. Compare **Sinitic.** ◆ ADJECTIVE [2] belonging or relating to this group of languages.

tibia ('tɪbɪə) NOUN, *plural* **tibiae** ('tɪbɪˌiː) *or* **tibias.** [1] Also called: **shinbone.** the inner and thicker of the two bones of the human leg between the knee and ankle. Compare **fibula.** [2] the corresponding bone in other vertebrates. [3] the fourth segment of an insect's leg, lying between the femur and the tarsus.
▷HISTORY C16: from Latin: leg, pipe
▸'**tibial** ADJECTIVE

tibiotarsus (ˌtɪbɪəʊ'tɑːsəs) NOUN the bone in the leg of a bird formed by fusion of the tibia and some of the tarsal bones.
▷HISTORY C19: from *tibio-* (combining form of TIBIA) + TARSUS

Tibur ('taɪbə) NOUN the ancient name for **Tivoli.**

tic (tɪk) NOUN *Pathol* [1] spasmodic twitching of a particular group of muscles. [2] See **tic douloureux.**
▷HISTORY C19: from French, of uncertain origin; compare Italian *ticche*

tical (tɪ'kɑːl, -'kɔːl, 'tiːkᵊl) NOUN, *plural* **-cals** *or* **-cal.** [1] the former standard monetary unit of Thailand, replaced by the baht in 1928. [2] a unit of weight, formerly used in Thailand, equal to about half an ounce or 14 grams.
▷HISTORY C17: via Siamese and Portuguese from Malay *tikal* monetary unit

tic douloureux ('tɪk ˌduːlə'ruː) NOUN a condition of momentary stabbing pain along the trigeminal nerve. Also called: **trigeminal neuralgia.**
▷HISTORY C19: from French, literally: painful tic

tichy ('tɪtʃɪ) ADJECTIVE **tichier, tichiest.** a variant spelling of **titchy.**

Ticino (*Italian* ti'tʃiːno) NOUN [1] a canton in S Switzerland: predominantly Italian-speaking and Roman Catholic; mountainous. Capital: Bellinzona. Pop.: 308 500 (2000 est.). Area: 2810 sq. km (1085 sq. miles). German name: **Tessin.** [2] a river in S central Europe, rising in S central Switzerland and flowing southeast and west to Lake Maggiore, then southeast to the River Po. Length: 248 km (154 miles).

tick¹ (tɪk) NOUN [1] a recurrent metallic tapping or clicking sound, such as that made by a clock or watch. [2] *Brit informal* a moment or instant. [3] a mark (✓) or dash used to check off or indicate the correctness of something. [4] *Commerce* the smallest increment of a price fluctuation in a commodity exchange. Tick size is usually 0.01% of the nominal value of the trading unit. ◆ VERB [5] to produce a recurrent tapping sound or indicate by such a sound: *the clock ticked the minutes away.* [6] (when *tr,* often foll by *off*) to mark or check (something, such as a list) with a tick. [7] **what makes someone tick.** *Informal* the basic drive or motivation of a person. ◆ See also **tick off, tick over.**
▷HISTORY C13: from Low German *tikk* touch; related to Old High German *zekōn* to pluck, Norwegian *tikke* to touch

tick² (tɪk) NOUN [1] any of various small parasitic arachnids of the families *Ixodidae* (**hard ticks**) and *Argasidae,* (**soft ticks**), typically living on the skin of warm-blooded animals and feeding on the blood and tissues of their hosts: order *Acarina* (mites and ticks). See also **sheep tick** (sense 1). Related adjective: **acaroid.** [2] any of certain other arachnids of the order *Acarina.* [3] any of certain insects of the

dipterous family *Hippoboscidae* that are ectoparasitic on horses, cattle, sheep, etc., esp the sheep ked.
▷HISTORY Old English *ticca;* related to Middle High German *zeche* tick, Middle Irish *dega* stag beetle

tick³ (tɪk) NOUN 1 the strong covering of a pillow, mattress, etc. 2 *Informal* short for **ticking**.
▷HISTORY C15: probably from Middle Dutch *tīke;* related to Old High German *ziecha* pillow cover, Latin *tēca* case, Greek *thēkē*

tick⁴ (tɪk) NOUN *Brit informal* account or credit (esp in the phrase **on tick**).
▷HISTORY C17: shortened from TICKET

tick-bird NOUN another name for **oxpecker**.
▷HISTORY C19: so called because it eats insects off animals' backs

tick-borne typhus NOUN another name for **Rocky Mountain spotted fever**.

ticker ('tɪkə) NOUN 1 *Slang* **a** the heart. **b** a watch. 2 a person or thing that ticks. 3 *Stock Exchange* the US word for **tape machine** (sense 2).

ticker tape NOUN 1 *Stock Exchange* a continuous paper ribbon on which a tape machine automatically prints current stock quotations. 2 **ticker-tape reception** (*or* **parade**). (mainly in New York) the showering of the motorcade of a distinguished politician, visiting head of state, etc., with ticker tape as a sign of welcome.

ticket ('tɪkɪt) NOUN 1 **a** a piece of paper, cardboard, etc., showing that the holder is entitled to certain rights, such as travel on a train or bus, entry to a place of public entertainment, etc. **b** (*modifier*) concerned with or relating to the issue, sale, or checking of tickets: *a ticket office; ticket collector.* 2 a piece of card, cloth, etc., attached to an article showing information such as its price, size, or washing instructions. 3 a summons served for a parking offence or violation of traffic regulations. 4 *Informal* the certificate of competence issued to a ship's captain or an aircraft pilot. 5 *Chiefly US and NZ* the group of candidates nominated by one party in an election; slate. 6 *Chiefly US* the declared policy of a political party at an election. 7 *Brit informal* a certificate of discharge from the armed forces. 8 *Informal* the right or appropriate thing: *that's the ticket.* 9 **have (got) tickets on oneself**. *Austral informal* to be conceited. ♦ VERB **-ets, -eting, -eted**. (*tr*) 10 to issue or attach a ticket or tickets to. 11 *Informal* to earmark for a particular purpose.
▷HISTORY C17: from Old French *etiquet,* from *estiquier* to stick on, from Middle Dutch *steken* to STICK²
▸'**ticketing** NOUN

ticket day NOUN (on the London Stock Exchange) the day on which selling brokers receive from buying brokers the names of investors who have made purchases during the previous account. Also called: **name day**. Compare **account day**.

ticket of leave NOUN (formerly in Britain) a permit allowing a convict (**ticket-of-leave man**) to leave prison, after serving only part of his sentence, with certain restrictions placed on him.

tickets ('tɪkɪts) PLURAL NOUN *South African informal* the end; that was it.
▷HISTORY of unknown origin

ticket tout NOUN See **tout** (sense 6).

tickety-boo (ˌtɪkɪtɪ'buː) ADJECTIVE *Brit old-fashioned informal* as it should be; correct; satisfactory.
▷HISTORY C20: of obscure origin

tickey ('tɪkɪ) NOUN a South African threepenny piece, which was replaced by the five-cent coin in 1961.
▷HISTORY of uncertain origin

tick fever NOUN 1 any acute infectious febrile disease caused by the bite of an infected tick. 2 another name for **Rocky Mountain spotted fever**.

ticking ('tɪkɪŋ) NOUN a strong cotton fabric, often striped, used esp for mattress and pillow covers.
▷HISTORY C17: from TICK³

ticklace ('tɪkəˌlæs) NOUN *Canadian* (in Newfoundland) a kittiwake.
▷HISTORY imitative of the bird's cry

tickle ('tɪkᵊl) VERB 1 to touch, stroke, or poke (a person, part of the body, etc.) so as to produce pleasure, laughter, or a twitching sensation. 2 (*tr*) to excite pleasurably; gratify. 3 (*tr*) to delight or entertain (often in the phrase **tickle one's fancy**). 4 (*intr*) to itch or tingle. 5 (*tr*) to catch (a fish, esp a trout) by grasping it with the hands and gently moving the fingers into its gills. 6 **tickle pink** *or* **to death**. *Informal* to please greatly: *he was tickled pink to be elected president.* ♦ NOUN 7 a sensation of light stroking or itching. 8 the act of tickling.
▷HISTORY C14: related to Old English *tinclian,* Old High German *kizziton,* Old Norse *kitla,* Latin *titillāre* to TITILLATE
▸'**tickly** ADJECTIVE

tickler ('tɪklə) NOUN 1 *Informal, chiefly Brit* a difficult or delicate problem. 2 Also called: **tickler file**. *US* a memorandum book or file. 3 *Accounting US* a single-entry business journal. 4 a person or thing that tickles.

tickler coil NOUN a small inductance coil connected in series in the anode circuit of a valve and magnetically coupled to a coil in the grid circuit to provide feedback.

ticklish ('tɪklɪʃ) ADJECTIVE 1 susceptible and sensitive to being tickled. 2 delicate or difficult: *a ticklish situation.* 3 easily upset or offended.
▸'**ticklishly** ADVERB ▸'**ticklishness** NOUN

tick off VERB (*tr, adverb*) 1 to mark with a tick. 2 *Informal, chiefly Brit* to scold; reprimand.
▸**ticking off** *or* **ticking-off** NOUN

tick over VERB (*intr, adverb*) 1 Also: **idle**. *Brit* (of an engine) to run at low speed with the throttle control closed and the transmission disengaged. 2 to run smoothly without any major changes: *keep the firm ticking over until I get back.* ♦ NOUN **tick-over**. 3 *Brit* **a** the speed of an engine when it is ticking over. **b** (*as modifier*): *tick-over speed.*

ticktack ('tɪkˌtæk) NOUN 1 *Brit* a system of sign language, mainly using the hands, by which bookmakers transmit their odds to each other at racecourses. 2 *US* a ticking sound, as made by a clock.
▷HISTORY from TICK¹

tick-tack-toe (ˌtɪktæk'təʊ) *or* **tick-tack-too** (ˌtɪktæk'tuː) NOUN the usual US and Canadian term for **noughts and crosses**.
▷HISTORY C19: from TICKTACK (meaning: an obsolete variety of backgammon)

ticktock ('tɪkˌtɒk) NOUN 1 a ticking sound as made by a clock. ♦ VERB 2 (*intr*) to make a ticking sound.

tick trefoil NOUN any of various tropical and subtropical leguminous plants of the genus *Desmodium,* having trifoliate leaves, clusters of small purplish or white flowers, and sticky jointed seed pods, which separate into segments that cling to animals. Also called: **beggar-ticks**.

Ticonderoga (ˌtaɪkɒndə'rəʊgə) NOUN a village in NE New York State, on Lake George: site of Fort Ticonderoga, scene of battles between the British and French (1758–59) and a strategic point in the War of American Independence.

t.i.d. (in prescriptions) ABBREVIATION FOR ter in die.
▷HISTORY Latin: three times a day

tidal ('taɪdᵊl) ADJECTIVE 1 relating to, characterized by, or affected by tides: *a tidal estuary.* 2 dependent on the state of the tide: *a tidal ferry.* 3 (of a glacier) reaching the sea and discharging floes or icebergs.
▸'**tidally** ADVERB

tidal basin NOUN a basin for vessels that is filled at high tide.

tidal energy NOUN energy obtained by harnessing tidal power.

tidal power NOUN the use of the rise and fall of tides involving very large volumes of water at low heads to generate electric power.

tidal volume NOUN 1 the volume of water associated with a rising tide. 2 *Physiol* the amount of air passing into and out of the lungs during normal breathing.

tidal wave NOUN 1 a name (not accepted in technical usage) for **tsunami**. 2 an unusually large incoming wave, often caused by high winds and spring tides. 3 a forceful and widespread movement in public opinion, action, etc.

tidbit ('tɪdˌbɪt) NOUN the usual US spelling of **titbit**.

tiddler ('tɪdlə) NOUN *Brit informal* 1 a very small fish or aquatic creature, esp a stickleback, minnow, or tadpole. 2 a small child, esp one undersized for its age.
▷HISTORY C19: from dialectal *tittlebat,* childish variant of STICKLEBACK, influenced by TIDDLY¹

tiddly¹ ('tɪdlɪ) ADJECTIVE **-dlier, -dliest**. *Brit* small; tiny.
▷HISTORY C19: childish variant of LITTLE

tiddly² ('tɪdlɪ) ADJECTIVE **-dlier, -dliest**. *Slang, chiefly Brit* slightly drunk.
▷HISTORY C19 (meaning: a drink): of unknown origin

tiddlywink ('tɪdlɪˌwɪŋk) NOUN any of the discs used in the game of tiddlywinks.

tiddlywinks ('tɪdlɪˌwɪŋks) NOUN (*functioning as singular*) a game in which players try to flick discs of plastic into a cup by pressing them sharply on the side with other larger discs.
▷HISTORY C19: probably from TIDDLY¹ + dialect *wink,* variant of WINCH¹

tide¹ (taɪd) NOUN 1 the cyclic rise and fall of sea level caused by the gravitational pull of the sun and moon. There are usually two high tides and two low tides in each lunar day. See also **tide-generating force, neap tide, spring tide**. 2 the current, ebb, or flow of water at a specified place resulting from these changes in level: *the tide is coming in.* 3 See **ebb** (sense 3) and **flood** (sense 3). 4 a widespread tendency or movement: *the tide of resentment against the government.* 5 a critical point in time; turning point: *the tide of his fortunes.* 6 *Northern English dialect* a fair or holiday. 7 *Archaic except in combination* a season or time: *Christmastide.* 8 *Rare* any body of mobile water, such as a stream. 9 *Archaic* a favourable opportunity. ♦ VERB 10 to carry or be carried with or as if with the tide. 11 (*intr*) to ebb and flow like the tide.
▷HISTORY Old English *tīd* time; related to Old High German *zīt,* Old Norse *tīthr* time
▸'**tideless** ADJECTIVE ▸'**tideˌlike** ADJECTIVE

tide² (taɪd) VERB (*intr*) *Archaic* to happen.
▷HISTORY Old English *tīdan;* related to Old Frisian *tīdia* to proceed to, Middle Low German *tīden* to hurry, Old Norse *tītha* to desire

tide-gauge NOUN a gauge used to measure extremes or the present level of tidal movement.

tide-generating force NOUN the difference between the force of gravity exerted by the moon or the sun on a particle of water in the ocean and that exerted on an equal mass of matter at the centre of the earth. The lunar tide-generating forces are about 2.2 times greater than are the solar ones. See also **neap tide, spring tide, tide¹**.

tideland ('taɪdˌlænd) NOUN *US* land between high-water and low-water marks.

tidemark ('taɪdˌmɑːk) NOUN 1 a mark left by the highest or lowest point of a tide. 2 a marker indicating the highest or lowest point reached by a tide. 3 *Chiefly Brit* a mark showing a level reached by a liquid: *a tidemark on the bath.* 4 *Informal, chiefly Brit* a dirty mark on the skin, indicating the extent to which someone has washed.

tide over VERB (*tr*) to help to get through (a period of difficulty, distress, etc.): *the money tided him over until he got a job.*

tide race NOUN a fast-running tidal current.

tide-rip NOUN another word for **riptide** (sense 1).

tide table NOUN a table showing the height of the tide at different times of day over a period at a particular place.

tidewaiter ('taɪdˌweɪtə) NOUN (formerly) a customs officer who boarded and inspected incoming ships.

tidewater ('taɪdˌwɔːtə) NOUN 1 water that advances and recedes with the tide. 2 water that covers land that is dry at low tide. 3 *US* **a** coastal land drained by tidal streams. **b** (*as modifier*): *tidewater regions.*

tideway ('taɪdˌweɪ) NOUN a strong tidal current or its channel, esp the tidal part of a river.

tidings ('taɪdɪŋz) PLURAL NOUN information or news.
▷HISTORY Old English *tīdung;* related to Middle Low German *tīdinge* information, Old Norse *tidhendi* events; see TIDE²

tidy ('taɪdɪ) ADJECTIVE **-dier, -diest**. 1 characterized by or indicating neatness and order. 2 *Informal* considerable: *a tidy sum of money.* ♦ VERB **-dies, -dying, -died**. 3 (when *intr,* usually foll by *up*) to put (things) in order; neaten. ♦ NOUN, *plural* **-dies**. 4 **a** a

small container in which odds and ends are kept. **b** **sink tidy.** a container with holes in the bottom, kept in the sink to retain rubbish that might clog the plug hole. [5] *Chiefly US and Canadian* an ornamental protective covering for the back or arms of a chair.
▷HISTORY C13 (in the sense: timely, seasonable, excellent): from TIDE[1] + -Y[1]; related to Dutch *tijdig* timely
▸ **'tidily** ADVERB ▸ **'tidiness** NOUN

tie (taɪ) VERB **ties, tying, tied.** [1] (when *tr*, often foll by *up*) to fasten or be fastened with string, thread, etc. [2] to make (a knot or bow) in (something): *to tie a knot; tie a ribbon.* [3] (*tr*) to restrict or secure. [4] to equal the score of a competitor or fellow candidate. [5] (*tr*) *Informal* to unite in marriage. [6] *Music* **a** to execute (two successive notes of the same pitch) as though they formed one note of composite time value. **b** to connect (two printed notes) with a tie. [7] **fit to be tied.** *Slang* very angry or upset. ◆ NOUN [8] a bond, link, or fastening. [9] a restriction or restraint. [10] a string, wire, ribbon, etc., with which something is tied. [11] a long narrow piece of material worn, esp by men, under the collar of a shirt, tied in a knot close to the throat with the ends hanging down the front. US name: **necktie.** [12] **a** an equality in score, attainment, etc., in a contest. **b** the match or competition in which such a result is attained. [13] a structural member carrying tension, such as a tie beam or tie rod. [14] *Sport, Brit* a match or game in an eliminating competition: *a cup tie.* [15] (*usually plural*) a shoe fastened by means of laces. [16] the US and Canadian name for **sleeper** (on a railway track). [17] *Music* a slur connecting two notes of the same pitch indicating that the sound is to be prolonged for their joint time value. [18] *Surveying* one of two measurements running from two points on a survey line to a point of detail to fix its position. [19] *Lacemaking* another name for **bride**[2]. ◆ See also **tie in, tie up.**
▷HISTORY Old English *tīgan* to tie; related to Old Norse *teygja* to draw, stretch out, Old English *tēon* to pull; see TUG, TOW[1], TIGHT

tieback ('taɪˌbæk) NOUN **a** a length of cord, ribbon, or other fabric used for tying a curtain to one side. **b** a curtain having such a device.

tie beam NOUN a horizontal beam that serves to prevent two other structural members from separating, esp one that connects two corresponding rafters in a roof or roof truss.

tie-break *or* **tie-breaker** ('taɪˌbreɪkə) NOUN [1] *Tennis* a method of deciding quickly the result of a set drawn at six-all, usually involving the playing of one deciding game for the best of twelve points in which the service changes after every two points. [2] any contest or game played to decide a winner when contestants have tied scores.

tie clasp NOUN a clip, often ornamental, which holds a tie in place against a shirt. Also called: **tie clip.**

tied (taɪd) ADJECTIVE *Brit* [1] (of a public house, retail shop, etc.) obliged to sell only the beer, products, etc. of a particular producer: *a tied house; tied outlet.* [2] (of a house or cottage) rented out to the tenant for as long as he is employed by the owner. [3] (of a loan) made by one nation to another on condition that the money is spent on goods or services provided by the lending nation.

tie-dyed ADJECTIVE (of textiles) given a pattern by tie-dyeing.

tie-dyeing NOUN a method of dyeing textiles to produce patterns by tying sections of the cloth together so that they will not absorb the dye. Also called: **tie-and-dye.**

tie in VERB (*adverb*) [1] to come or bring into a certain relationship; coordinate. ◆ NOUN **tie-in.** [2] a link, relationship, or coordination. [3] publicity material, a book, tape, etc., linked to a film or broadcast programme or series. [4] *US* **a** a sale or advertisement offering products of which a purchaser must buy one or more in addition to his purchase. **b** an item sold or advertised in this way, esp the extra item. **c** (*as modifier*): *a tie-in sale.*

tie line NOUN a telephone line between two private branch exchanges or private exchanges that may or may not pass through a main exchange.

tiemannite ('tiːməˌnaɪt) NOUN a grey mineral consisting of mercury selenide. Formula: HgSe.
▷HISTORY C19: named after J. C. W. F. *Tiemann* (1848–99), German scientist

Tien Shan ('tjɛn'ʃɑːn) NOUN a variant transliteration of the Chinese name for the **Tian Shan.**

Tientsin ('tjɛn'tsɪn) NOUN a variant transliteration of the Chinese name for **Tianjin.**

tiepin ('taɪˌpɪn) NOUN an ornamental pin of various shapes used to pin the two ends of a tie to a shirt.

tier[1] (tɪə) NOUN [1] one of a set of rows placed one above and behind the other, such as theatre seats. [2] **a** a layer or level. **b** (*in combination*): *a three-tier cake.* [3] a rank, order, or row. ◆ VERB [4] to be or arrange in tiers.
▷HISTORY C16: from Old French *tire* rank, of Germanic origin; compare Old English *tīr* embellishment

tier[2] ('taɪə) NOUN a person or thing that ties.

tierce (tɪəs) NOUN [1] a variant of **terce.** [2] the third of eight basic positions from which a parry or attack can be made in fencing. [3] (tɜːs) *Cards* a sequence of three cards in the same suit. [4] an obsolete measure of capacity equal to 42 wine gallons.
▷HISTORY C15: from Old French, feminine of *tiers* third, from Latin *tertius*

tierce de Picardie (*French* tjɛrs də pikardi) NOUN another term for **Picardy third.**

tiercel ('tɪəsᵊl) NOUN a variant of **tercel.**

tie rod NOUN any rod- or bar-shaped structural member designed to prevent the separation of two parts, as in a vehicle.

Tierra del Fuego (*Spanish* 'tjɛrra ðɛl 'fweɣo) NOUN an archipelago at the S extremity of South America, separated from the mainland by the Strait of Magellan: the west and south belong to Chile, the east to Argentina, and several islands are disputed. Area: 73 643 sq. km (28 434 sq. miles).

tie up VERB (*adverb*) [1] (*tr*) to attach or bind securely with or as if with string, rope, etc. [2] to moor (a vessel). [3] (*tr; often passive*) to engage the attentions of: *he's tied up at the moment and can't see you.* [4] (*tr; often passive*) to conclude (the organization of something): *the plans for the trip were tied up well in advance.* [5] to come or bring to a complete standstill. [6] (*tr*) to invest or commit (funds, etc.) and so make unavailable for other uses. [7] (*tr*) to subject (property) to conditions that prevent sale, alienation, or other action. ◆ NOUN **tie-up.** [8] a link or connection. [9] *Chiefly US and Canadian* a standstill. [10] *Chiefly US and Canadian* an informal term for **traffic jam.**

tiff[1] (tɪf) NOUN [1] a petty quarrel. [2] a fit of ill humour. ◆ VERB [3] (*intr*) to have or be in a tiff.
▷HISTORY C18: of unknown origin

tiff[2] (tɪf) NOUN *Archaic* a small draught of alcoholic drink; dram.
▷HISTORY C18: see TIFFIN

Tiffanie ('tɪfənɪ) NOUN a breed of cat with semi-long hair, having a white undercoat with the ends coloured. Also called: **Australian Tiffanie, Asian semi-longhair.**

tiffany ('tɪfənɪ) NOUN, *plural* **-nies.** a sheer fine gauzy fabric.
▷HISTORY C17: (in the sense: a fine dress worn on Twelfth Night): from Old French *tifanie,* from ecclesiastical Latin *theophania* Epiphany; see THEOPHANY

Tiffany NOUN, *plural* **-nies.** another name for **Chantilly** (sense 2).

Tiffany glass NOUN another term for **Favrile glass.**

tiffin ('tɪfɪn) NOUN (in India) a light meal, esp one taken at midday.
▷HISTORY C18: probably from obsolete *tiffing,* from *tiff* to sip

Tiflis (tɪf'liːs) NOUN transliteration of the Russian name for **Tbilisi.**

tig (tɪg) NOUN, VERB **tigs, tigging, tigged.** another name for **tag**[1] (senses 1, 4).

tiger ('taɪgə) NOUN [1] a large feline mammal, *Panthera tigris,* of forests in most of Asia, having a tawny yellow coat with black stripes. [2] (*not in technical use*) any of various other animals, such as the jaguar, leopard, and thylacine. [3] a dynamic, forceful, or cruel person. [4] **a** a country, esp in E Asia, that is achieving rapid economic growth. **b** (*as modifier*): *a tiger economy.* [5] *Archaic* a servant in livery, esp a page or groom. [6] short for **tiger moth.** [7] *Informal* to find oneself in a situation that has turned out to be much more difficult to control than one had expected.
▷HISTORY C13: from Old French *tigre,* from Latin *tigris,* from Greek, of Iranian origin
▸ **'tigerish** *or* **'tigrish** ADJECTIVE ▸ **'tigerishly** ADVERB ▸ **'tigerishness** NOUN ▸ **'tiger-like** ADJECTIVE

Tiger ('taɪgə) NOUN See **TIGR.**

Tiger balm NOUN *Trademark* a mentholated ointment widely used as a panacea.

tiger beetle NOUN any active predatory beetle of the family *Cicindelidae,* chiefly of warm dry regions, having powerful mandibles and long legs.
▷HISTORY C19: so called because it has patterned, sometimes striped, wing covers

tiger cat NOUN [1] a medium-sized feline mammal, *Felis tigrina,* of Central and South America, having a dark-striped coat. [2] any similar feline with tiger-like markings, such as the margay.

tiger lily NOUN [1] a lily plant, *Lilium tigrinum,* of China and Japan, cultivated for its flowers, which have black-spotted orange reflexed petals. [2] any of various similar lilies.

tiger market NOUN *Informal* any of the four most important markets on the Pacific rim after Japan: Hong Kong, South Korea, Singapore, and Taiwan. Compare **dragon market.**

tiger moth NOUN any of a group of arctiid moths, mostly boldly marked, often in black, orange, and yellow, of the genera *Arctia, Parasemia, Euplagia,* etc., producing woolly bear larvae and typified by the **garden tiger** (*Arctia caja*). Often shortened to: **tiger.**

tiger prawn NOUN a large edible prawn of the genus *Penaeus* with dark bands across the body, fished commercially in the Indian and Pacific oceans.

tiger's-eye ('taɪgəzˌaɪ) *or* **tigereye** ('taɪgərˌaɪ) NOUN [1] a golden brown silicified variety of crocidolite, used as an ornamental stone. [2] a glaze resembling this, used on pottery.

tiger shark NOUN [1] a voracious omnivorous requiem shark, *Galeocerdo cuvieri,* chiefly of tropical waters, having a striped or spotted body. [2] any of certain other spotted sharks, such as *Stegostoma tigrinum,* of the Indian Ocean.

tiger snake NOUN a highly venomous brown-and-yellow elapid snake, *Notechis scutatus,* of Australia.

Tiggerish ('tɪgərɪʃ) ADJECTIVE irrepressibly bouncy and cheerful.
▷HISTORY C20: after *Tigger,* a character in the Winnie the Pooh children's stories by the English writer A. A. Milne (1882–1956)

tight (taɪt) ADJECTIVE [1] stretched or drawn so as not to be loose; taut: *a tight cord.* [2] fitting or covering in a close manner: *a tight dress.* [3] held, made, fixed, or closed firmly and securely: *a tight knot.* [4] **a** of close and compact construction or organization, esp so as to be impervious to water, air, etc. **b** (*in combination*): *watertight; airtight.* [5] unyielding or stringent: *to keep a tight hold on resources.* [6] cramped or constricted: *a tight fit.* [7] mean or miserly. [8] difficult and problematic: *a tight situation.* [9] hardly profitable: *a tight bargain.* [10] *Economics* **a** (of a commodity) difficult to obtain; in excess demand. **b** (of funds, money, etc.) difficult and expensive to borrow because of high demand or restrictive monetary policy. **c** (of markets) characterized by excess demand or scarcity with prices tending to rise. Compare **easy** (sense 8). [11] (of a match or game) very close or even. [12] (of a team or group, esp of a pop group) playing well together, in a disciplined coordinated way. [13] *Informal* drunk. [14] *Informal* (of a person) showing tension. [15] *Archaic or dialect* neat. ◆ ADVERB [16] in a close, firm, or secure way: *pull it tight.* [17] **sit tight. a** to wait patiently; bide one's time. **b** to maintain one's position, stand, or opinion firmly. [18] **sleep tight.** to sleep soundly.
▷HISTORY C14: probably variant of *thight,* from Old Norse *thēttr* close; related to Middle High German *dīhte* thick
▸ **'tightly** ADVERB ▸ **'tightness** NOUN

tightass (ˈtaɪtˌæs) NOUN *Slang, chiefly US* an inhibited or excessively self-controlled person.
▸ **ˈtightˌassed** ADJECTIVE

tighten (ˈtaɪtᵊn) VERB [1] to make or become tight or tighter. [2] **tighten one's belt.** to economize.
▸ **ˈtightener** NOUN

tightfisted (ˌtaɪtˈfɪstɪd) ADJECTIVE mean; miserly.

tight head NOUN *Rugby* the prop on the hooker's right in the front row of a scrum. Compare **loose head.**

tightknit (ˌtaɪtˈnɪt) ADJECTIVE [1] closely integrated: *a tightknit community.* [2] organized carefully and concisely.

tight-lipped ADJECTIVE [1] reticent, secretive, or taciturn. [2] with the lips pressed tightly together, as through anger.

tightrope (ˈtaɪtˌrəʊp) NOUN [1] a rope or cable stretched taut above the ground on which acrobats walk or perform balancing feats. [2] to be in a difficult situation that demands careful and considered behaviour.

tightrope walker NOUN an acrobat who performs on a tightrope.
▸ **tightrope walking** NOUN

tights (taɪts) PLURAL NOUN [1] **a** Also called (US, Canadian, Austral, and NZ): **pantihose.** a one-piece clinging garment covering the body from the waist to the feet, worn by women in place of stockings. **b** *US and Canadian* Also called: **leotards.** a similar, tight-fitting garment worn instead of trousers by either sex. [2] a similar garment formerly worn by men, as in the 16th century with a doublet.

tightwad (ˈtaɪtˌwɒd) NOUN *Slang, chiefly US and Canadian* a stingy person; miser.

tiglic acid (ˈtɪɡlɪk) NOUN a syrupy liquid or crystalline colourless unsaturated carboxylic acid, with the *trans*-configuration, found in croton oil and used in perfumery; *trans*-2-methyl-2-butenoic acid. Formula: $CH_3CH{:}C(CH_3)COOH$.
▷ HISTORY C19 *tiglic,* from New Latin phrase *Croton tiglium* (name of the croton plant), of uncertain origin

Ti2GO *Text messaging* ABBREVIATION FOR time to go.

tigon (ˈtaɪɡən) *or* **tiglon** (ˈtɪɡlɒn) NOUN the hybrid offspring of a male tiger and a female lion.

TIGR ABBREVIATION FOR Treasury Investment Growth Receipts: a bond denominated in dollars and linked to US treasury bonds, the yield on which is taxed in the UK as income when it is cashed or redeemed. Also called: **Tiger.**

Tigré *or* **Tigray** (ˈtiːɡreɪ) NOUN [1] an autonomous region of N Ethiopia, bordering on Eritrea: formerly a separate kingdom. Capital: Mekele. Pop.: 3 136 267 (1994). Area: 53 498 sq. km (20 656 sq. miles). [2] a language of NE Ethiopia, belonging to the SE Semitic subfamily of the Afro-Asiatic family.

tigress (ˈtaɪɡrɪs) NOUN [1] a female tiger. [2] a fierce, cruel, or wildly passionate woman.

tigridia (taɪˈɡrɪdɪə) NOUN any plant of the bulbous genus *Tigridia,* native to subtropical and tropical America, esp *T. pavonia,* the tiger flower or peacock tiger flower, grown for its large strikingly marked red, white, or yellow concave flowers: family *Iridaceae.*
▷ HISTORY New Latin, from Greek *tigris, tigridis* tiger

Tigrinya (tɪˈɡriːnjə) NOUN a language of N Ethiopia, belonging to the SE Semitic subfamily of the Afro-Asiatic family.

Tigris (ˈtaɪɡrɪs) NOUN a river in SW Asia, rising in E Turkey and flowing southeast through Baghdad to the Euphrates in SE Iraq, forming the delta of the Shatt-al-Arab, which flows into the Persian Gulf: part of a canal and irrigation system as early as 2400 B.C., with many ancient cities (including Nineveh) on its banks. Length: 1900 km (1180 miles).

TIG welding (tɪɡ) NOUN tungsten-electrode inert gas welding: a method of welding in which the arc is maintained by a tungsten electrode and shielded from the access of air by an inert gas. Compare **MIG welding.**

Tihwa *or* **Tihua** (ˈtiːˈhwɑː) NOUN a former name for **Urumchi.**

Tijuana (tiːˈwɑːnə; *Spanish* tiˈxwana) *or* **Tia Juana** NOUN a city in NW Mexico, in Baja California. Pop. (urban area): 1 150 000 (2000 est.).

tika (ˈtiːkə) NOUN a variant of **tikka**[2].

tikanga (təˈkæŋə) NOUN *NZ* Maori ways or customs.
▷ HISTORY Maori

tike (taɪk) NOUN a variant spelling of **tyke.**

tiki (ˈtiːkɪ) NOUN [1] an amulet or figurine in the form of a carved representation of an ancestor, worn in some Maori cultures. ◆ VERB [2] (*intr*) *NZ* to take a scenic tour around an area.
▷ HISTORY from Maori

tiki tour NOUN *NZ* a scenic tour of an area.

tikka[1] (ˈtiːkə) ADJECTIVE (*immediately postpositive*) *Indian cookery* (of meat, esp chicken or lamb) marinated in spices then dry-roasted, usu. in a clay oven.

tikka[2] *or* **tika** (ˈtiːkə) NOUN [1] another word for **tilak.** [2] the act of marking a tikka on the forehead.
▷ HISTORY from Hindi *tika,* Punjabi *tikka* spot, mark

tikoloshe (ˌtɪkɒˈlɒʃ, -ˈlɒʃɪ) NOUN a variant of **tokoloshe.**

til (tɪl, tiːl) NOUN another name for **sesame,** esp a variety grown in India
▷ HISTORY C19: from Hindi, from Sanskrit *tilá* sesame

tilak (ˈtɪlək) NOUN, *plural* **-ak** *or* **-aks.** a coloured spot or mark worn by Hindus, esp on the forehead, often indicating membership of a religious sect, caste, etc., or (in the case of a woman) marital status.
▷ HISTORY from Sanskrit *tilaka*

tilapia (tɪˈlæpɪə, -ˈleɪ-) NOUN any mouthbrooding cichlid fish of the African freshwater genus *Tilapia:* used as food fishes.
▷ HISTORY C18: from New Latin

Tilburg (ˈtɪlbɜːɡ; *Dutch* ˈtɪlbyrx) NOUN a city in the S Netherlands, in North Brabant: textile industries. Pop.: 190 559 (1999 est.).

tilbury (ˈtɪlbərɪ, -brɪ) NOUN, *plural* **-buries.** a light two-wheeled horse-drawn open carriage, seating two people.
▷ HISTORY C19: probably named after the inventor

Tilbury (ˈtɪlbərɪ, -brɪ) NOUN an area in Essex, on the River Thames: extensive docks; principal container port of the Port of London.

tilde (ˈtɪldə) NOUN the diacritical mark (~) placed over a letter to indicate a palatal nasal consonant, as in Spanish *señor.* This symbol is also used in the International Phonetic Alphabet to represent any nasalized vowel.
▷ HISTORY C19: from Spanish, from Latin *titulus* title, superscription

tile (taɪl) NOUN [1] a flat thin slab of fired clay, rubber, linoleum, etc., usually square or rectangular and sometimes ornamental, used with others to cover a roof, floor, wall, etc. Related adjective: **tegular.** [2] a short pipe made of earthenware, concrete, or plastic, used with others to form a drain. [3] tiles collectively. [4] a rectangular block used as a playing piece in mah jong and other games. [5] *Brit old-fashioned slang* a hat. [6] **on the tiles.** *Informal* on a spree, esp of drinking or debauchery. ◆ VERB [7] (*tr*) to cover with tiles.
▷ HISTORY Old English *tīgele,* from Latin *tēgula;* related to German *Ziegel*
▸ **ˈtiler** NOUN

tilefish (ˈtaɪlˌfɪʃ) NOUN, *plural* **-fish** *or* **-fishes.** a large brightly coloured deep-sea percoid food fish, *Lopholatilus chamaeleonticeps,* of warm and tropical seas, esp the North American coast of the Atlantic: family *Branchiostegidae.*
▷ HISTORY C19: from New Latin *-tilus,* ending of genus name *Lopholatilus;* perhaps also from a resemblance between its colours and patterning and ornamental tiles

tiliaceous (ˌtɪlɪˈeɪʃəs) ADJECTIVE of, relating to, or belonging to the *Tiliaceae,* a family of flowering plants, mostly trees and shrubs of warm and tropical regions: includes linden and jute.
▷ HISTORY C19: from Late Latin *tiliāceus,* from Latin *tilia* linden

tiling (ˈtaɪlɪŋ) NOUN [1] tiles collectively. [2] something made of or surfaced with tiles.

till[1] (tɪl) CONJUNCTION, PREPOSITION [1] short for **until.** Also (not standard): 'til. [2] *Scot* to; towards. [3] *Dialect* in order that: *come here till I tell you.*
▷ HISTORY Old English *til;* related to Old Norse *til* to, Old High German *zil* goal, aim

> **Language note** *Till* is a variant of *until* that is acceptable at all levels of language. *Until* is, however, often preferred at the beginning of a sentence in formal writing: *until his behaviour improves, he cannot become a member.*

till[2] (tɪl) VERB (*tr*) [1] to cultivate and work (land) for the raising of crops. [2] another word for **plough.**
▷ HISTORY Old English *tilian* to try, obtain; related to Old Frisian *tilia* to obtain, Old Saxon *tilōn* to obtain, Old High German *zilōn* to hasten towards
▸ **ˈtillable** ADJECTIVE ▸ **ˈtiller** NOUN

till[3] (tɪl) NOUN a box, case, or drawer into which the money taken from customers is put, now usually part of a cash register.
▷ HISTORY C15 *tylle,* of obscure origin

till[4] (tɪl) NOUN an unstratified glacial deposit consisting of rock fragments of various sizes. The most common is boulder clay.
▷ HISTORY C17: of unknown origin

tillage (ˈtɪlɪdʒ) NOUN [1] the act, process, or art of tilling. [2] tilled land.

tillandsia (tɪˈlændzɪə) NOUN any bromeliaceous epiphytic plant of the genus *Tillandsia,* such as Spanish moss, of tropical and subtropical America.
▷ HISTORY C18: New Latin, named after Elias *Tillands* (died 1693), Finno-Swedish botanist

tiller[1] (ˈtɪlə) NOUN *Nautical* a handle fixed to the top of a rudderpost to serve as a lever in steering it.
▷ HISTORY C14: from Anglo-French *teiler* beam of a loom, from Medieval Latin *tēlārium,* from Latin *tēla* web
▸ **ˈtillerless** ADJECTIVE

tiller[2] (ˈtɪlə) NOUN [1] a shoot that arises from the base of the stem in grasses. [2] a less common name for **sapling.** ◆ VERB [3] (*intr*) (of a plant) to produce tillers.
▷ HISTORY Old English *telgor* twig; related to Icelandic *tjalga* branch

Till Eulenspiegel (ˈtɪl ˈɔɪlənˌʃpiːɡᵊl) NOUN ?14th century, legendary German peasant, whose pranks became the subject of many tales.

tillicum (ˈtɪlɪkəm) NOUN *US and Canadian informal* (in the Pacific Northwest) a friend.
▷ HISTORY from Chinook Jargon, from Chinook *tlxam* kin, esp as distinguished from chiefs

Tilsit (ˈtɪlzɪt) NOUN the former name (until 1945) of **Sovetsk.**

tilt[1] (tɪlt) VERB [1] to incline or cause to incline at an angle. [2] (*usually intr*) to attack or overthrow (a person or people) in a tilt or joust. [3] (when *intr,* often foll by *at*) to aim or thrust: *to tilt a lance.* [4] (*tr*) to work or forge with a tilt hammer. ◆ NOUN [5] a slope or angle: *at a tilt.* [6] the act of tilting. [7] (esp in medieval Europe) **a** a jousting contest. **b** a thrust with a lance or pole delivered during a tournament. [8] an attempt to win a contest. [9] See **tilt hammer.** [10] **(at) full tilt.** at full speed or force.
▷ HISTORY Old English *tealtian;* related to Dutch *touteren* to totter, Norwegian *tylta* to tiptoe, *tylten* unsteady
▸ **ˈtilter** NOUN

tilt[2] (tɪlt) NOUN [1] an awning or canopy, usually of canvas, for a boat, booth, etc. ◆ VERB [2] (*tr*) to cover or provide with a tilt.
▷ HISTORY Old English *teld;* related to Old High German *zelt* tent, Old Norse *tjald* tent

tilth (tɪlθ) NOUN [1] the act or process of tilling land. [2] the condition of soil or land that has been tilled, esp with respect to suitability for promoting plant growth.
▷ HISTORY Old English *tilthe;* see TILL[2]

tilt hammer NOUN a drop hammer consisting of a heavy head moving at the end of a pivoted arm; used in forging.

tiltyard (ˈtɪltˌjɑːd) NOUN (formerly) an enclosed area for tilting.

Tim. *Bible* ABBREVIATION FOR Timothy.

Timaru (ˈtɪməˌruː) NOUN a port and resort in S New Zealand, on E South Island. Pop.: 15 350 (1995 est.).

timbal *or* **tymbal** (ˈtɪmbᵊl) NOUN *Music* a type of kettledrum.
▷ HISTORY C17: from French *timbale,* from Old French *tamballe,* (associated also with *cymbale*

cymbal), from Old Spanish *atabal,* from Arabic *at-tabl* the drum

timbale (tæm'bɑ:l; *French* tɛ̃bal) NOUN [1] a mixture of meat, fish, etc., in a rich sauce, cooked in a mould lined with potato or pastry. [2] a plain straight-sided mould in which such a dish is prepared.
▷HISTORY C19: from French: kettledrum

timber ('tɪmbə) NOUN [1] **a** wood, esp when regarded as a construction material. Usual US and Canadian word: **lumber. b** (*as modifier*): *a timber cottage.* [2] **a** trees collectively. **b** *Chiefly US* woodland. [3] a piece of wood used in a structure. [4] *Nautical* a frame in a wooden vessel. [5] potential material, for a post, rank, etc.: *he is managerial timber.* ◆ VERB [6] (*tr*) to provide with timbers. ◆ INTERJECTION [7] a lumberjack's shouted warning when a tree is about to fall.
▷HISTORY Old English; related to Old High German *zimbar* wood, Old Norse *timbr* timber, Latin *domus* house

timbered ('tɪmbəd) ADJECTIVE [1] made of or containing timber or timbers. [2] covered with trees; wooded.

timberhead ('tɪmbə,hɛd) NOUN *Nautical* a timber, the top of which rises above deck level and is used as a bollard.

timber hitch NOUN a knot used for tying a rope round a spar, log, etc., for haulage.

timbering ('tɪmbərɪŋ) NOUN [1] timbers collectively. [2] work made of timber.

timberland ('tɪmbə,lænd) NOUN *US and Canadian* land covered with trees grown for their timber.

timber line NOUN the altitudinal or latitudinal limit of normal tree growth. See also **tree line.**

timberman ('tɪmbəmən) NOUN, *plural* **-men.** any of various longicorn beetles that have destructive wood-eating larvae. Also called: **timberman beetle.**

timber wolf NOUN a variety of the wolf, *Canis lupus,* having a grey brindled coat and occurring in forested northern regions, esp of North America. Also called: **grey wolf.**

timberwork ('tɪmbə,wɜ:k) NOUN a structure made of timber.

timberyard ('tɪmbə,jɑ:d) NOUN *Brit* an establishment where timber and sometimes other building materials are stored or sold. US and Canadian word: **lumberyard.**

timbre ('tɪmbə, 'tæmbə; *French* tɛ̃brə) NOUN [1] *Phonetics* the distinctive tone quality differentiating one vowel or sonant from another. [2] *Music* tone colour or quality of sound, esp a specific type of tone colour.
▷HISTORY C19: from French: note of a bell, from Old French: drum, from Medieval Greek *timbanon,* from Greek *tumpanon* drum

timbrel ('tɪmbrəl) NOUN *Chiefly biblical* another word for **tambourine.**
▷HISTORY C16: from Old French; see TIMBRE

Timbuktu (,tɪmbʌk'tu:) NOUN [1] a town in central Mali, on the River Niger: terminus of a trans-Saharan caravan route; a great Muslim centre (14th–16th centuries). Pop.: 31 925 (latest est.). French name: **Tombouctou.** [2] any distant or outlandish place: *from here to Timbuktu.*

time (taɪm) NOUN [1] **a** the continuous passage of existence in which events pass from a state of potentiality in the future, through the present, to a state of finality in the past. **b** (*as modifier*): *time travel.* Related adjective: **temporal.** [2] *Physics* a quantity measuring duration, usually with reference to a periodic process such as the rotation of the earth or the vibration of electromagnetic radiation emitted from certain atoms (see **caesium clock, second**[2] (sense 1)). In classical mechanics, time is absolute in the sense that the time of an event is independent of the observer. According to the theory of relativity it depends on the observer's frame of reference. Time is considered as a fourth coordinate required, along with three spatial coordinates, to specify an event. See **space-time continuum.** [3] a specific point on this continuum expressed in terms of hours and minutes: *the time is four o'clock.* [4] a system of reckoning for expressing time: *Greenwich mean time.* [5] **a** a definite and measurable portion of this continuum. **b** (*as modifier*): *time limit.* [6] **a** an accepted period such as a day, season, etc. **b** (*in combination*): *springtime.* [7] an unspecified interval; a while: *I was there for a time.* [8] (*often plural*) a period or point marked by specific attributes or events: *the Victorian times; time for breakfast.* [9] a sufficient interval or period: *have you got time to help me?* [10] an instance or occasion: *I called you three times.* [11] an occasion or period of specified quality: *have a good time; a miserable time.* [12] the duration of human existence. [13] the heyday of human life: *in her time she was a great star.* [14] a suitable period or moment: *it's time I told you.* [15] the expected interval in which something is done: *the flying time from New York to London was seven hours.* [16] a particularly important moment, esp childbirth or death: *her time had come.* [17] (*plural*) indicating a degree or amount calculated by multiplication with the number specified: *ten times three is thirty; he earns four times as much as me.* [18] (*often plural*) the fashions, thought, etc., of the present age (esp in the phrases **ahead of one's time, behind the times**). [19] *Brit* (in bars, pubs, etc.) short for **closing time.** [20] *Informal* a term in jail (esp in the phrase **do time**). [21] **a** a customary or full period of work. **b** the rate of pay for this period. [22] Also (esp US): **metre. a** the system of combining beats or pulses in music into successive groupings by which the rhythm of the music is established. **b** a specific system having a specific number of beats in each grouping or bar: *duple time.* [23] *Music* short for **time value.** [24] *Prosody* a unit of duration used in the measurement of poetic metre; mora. [25] **against time.** in an effort to complete something in a limited period. [26] **ahead of time.** before the deadline. [27] **all in good time.** in due course. [28] **all the time.** continuously. [29] **at one time. a** once; formerly. **b** simultaneously. [30] **at the same time. a** simultaneously. **b** nevertheless; however. [31] **at times.** sometimes. [32] **beat time.** (of a conductor, etc.) to indicate the tempo or pulse of a piece of music by waving a baton or a hand, tapping out the beats, etc. [33] **before one's time.** prematurely. [34] **for the time being.** for the moment; temporarily. [35] **from time to time.** at intervals; occasionally. [36] **gain time.** See **gain**[1] (sense 9). [37] **have no time for.** to have no patience with; not tolerate. [38] **in good time. a** early. **b** quickly. [39] **in no time.** very quickly; almost instantaneously. [40] **in one's own time. a** outside paid working hours. **b** at one's own rate. [41] **in time. a** early or at the appointed time. **b** eventually. **c** *Music* at a correct metrical or rhythmic pulse. [42] **keep time.** to observe correctly the accent or rhythmic pulse of a piece of music in relation to tempo. [43] **lose time.** (of a timepiece) to operate too slowly. [44] **lose no time.** to do something without delay. [45] **make time. a** to find an opportunity. **b** (often foll by *with*) *US informal* to succeed in seducing. [46] See **mark** (sense 35). [47] **in the nick of time.** at the last possible moment; at the critical moment. [48] **on time. a** at the expected or scheduled time. **b** *US* payable in instalments. [49] **pass the time of day.** to exchange casual greetings (with an acquaintance). [50] **time about.** *Scot* alternately; turn and turn about. [51] **time and again.** frequently. [52] **time off.** a period when one is absent from work for a holiday, through sickness, etc. [53] **time on.** the Austral equivalent of **extra time.** [54] **time out of mind.** from time immemorial. [55] **time of one's life.** a memorably enjoyable time. [56] (*modifier*) operating automatically at or for a set time, for security or convenience: *time lock; time switch.* ◆ VERB (*tr*) [57] to ascertain or calculate the duration or speed of. [58] to set a time for. [59] to adjust to keep accurate time. [60] to pick a suitable time for. [61] *Sport* to control the execution or speed of (an action, esp a shot or stroke) so that it has its full effect at the right moment. ◆ INTERJECTION [62] the word called out by a publican signalling that it is closing time.
▷HISTORY Old English *tīma;* related to Old English *tīd* time, Old Norse *tīmi,* Alemannic *zīme;* see TIDE[1]

time and a half NOUN the rate of pay equalling one and a half times the normal rate, often offered for overtime work.

time and motion study NOUN the analysis of industrial or work procedures to determine the most efficient methods of operation. Also: **time and motion, time study, motion study.**

time bomb NOUN a bomb containing a timing mechanism that determines the time at which it will detonate.

time capsule NOUN a container holding articles, documents, etc., representative of the current age, buried in the earth or in the foundations of a new building for discovery in the future.

timecard ('taɪm,kɑ:d) NOUN a card used with a time clock.

time charter NOUN the hire of a ship or aircraft for a specified period. Compare **voyage charter.**

time clock NOUN a clock which records, by punching or stamping cards inserted into it, the time of arrival or departure of people, such as employees in a factory.

time code NOUN (on video or audio tape) a separate track on which time references are continually recorded in digital form as an aid to editing.

time constant NOUN *Electronics* the time required for the current or voltage in a circuit to rise or fall exponentially through approximately 63 per cent of its amplitude.

time-consuming ADJECTIVE taking up or involving a great deal of time.

time deposit NOUN a bank deposit from which withdrawals may be made only after advance notice or at a specified future date. Compare **demand deposit.**

time dilation *or* **dilatation** NOUN the principle predicted by relativity that time intervals between events in a system have larger values measured by an observer moving with respect to the system than those measured by an observer at rest with respect to it.

time-division multiplex NOUN See **multiplex** (sense 1).

time exposure NOUN [1] an exposure of a photographic film for a relatively long period, usually a few seconds. [2] a photograph produced by such an exposure.

time-honoured ADJECTIVE having been observed for a long time and sanctioned by custom.

time immemorial NOUN [1] the distant past beyond memory or record. [2] *Law* time beyond legal memory, fixed by English statute as before the reign of Richard I (1189).

timekeeper ('taɪm,ki:pə) NOUN [1] a person or thing that keeps or records time. [2] an employee who maintains a record of the hours worked by the other employees. [3] a device for indicating time; timepiece. [4] an employee with respect to his record of punctuality: *a good timekeeper.*
▸ **'time,keeping** NOUN

time-lag NOUN an interval between two connected events.

time-lapse photography NOUN the technique of recording a very slow process, such as the withering of a flower, by taking a large number of photographs on a strip of film at regular intervals. The film is then projected at normal speed.

timeless ('taɪmlɪs) ADJECTIVE [1] unaffected or unchanged by time; ageless. [2] eternal. [3] an archaic word for **untimely.**
▸ **'timelessly** ADVERB ▸ **'timelessness** NOUN

timeline ('taɪm,laɪn) NOUN a graphic representation showing the passage of time as a line.

time loan NOUN a loan repayable before or at a specified future date. Compare **call loan.**

timely ('taɪmlɪ) ADJECTIVE **-lier, -liest,** ADVERB [1] at the right or an opportune or appropriate time. [2] an archaic word for **early.**
▸ **'timeliness** NOUN

time machine NOUN (in science fiction) a machine in which people or objects can be transported into the past or the future.

timeous ('taɪməs) ADJECTIVE *Scot* in good time; sufficiently early: *a timeous warning.*
▷HISTORY C15: Scottish; see TIME, -OUS
▸ **'timeously** ADVERB

time-out NOUN [1] *Sport* an interruption in play during which players rest, discuss tactics, or make substitutions. [2] a break taken during working hours. [3] *Computing* a condition occurring when the amount of time a computer has been instructed to wait for another device to perform a task has expired, usually indicated by an error message. ◆ VERB (*intr*) **time out.** [4] (of a computer) to stop operating because of a time-out.

timepiece (ˈtaɪmˌpiːs) NOUN [1] any of various devices, such as a clock, watch, or chronometer, which measure and indicate time. [2] a device which indicates the time but does not strike or otherwise audibly mark the hours.

time-poor ADJECTIVE [1] lacking spare time or leisure time. [2] under pressure to complete activities quickly.

timer (ˈtaɪmə) NOUN [1] a device for measuring, recording, or indicating time. [2] a switch or regulator that causes a mechanism to operate at a specific time or at predetermined intervals. [3] a person or thing that times.

time-saving (ˈtaɪmˌseɪvɪŋ) ADJECTIVE shortening the length of time required for an operation, activity, etc.
▸ **ˈtime-ˌsaver** NOUN

timescale (ˈtaɪmˌskeɪl) NOUN the span of time within which certain events occur or are scheduled to occur considered in relation to any broader period of time.

time-sensitive ADJECTIVE [1] physically changing as time passes. [2] only relevant or applicable for a short period of time.

time series NOUN *Statistics* a series of values of a variable taken in successive periods of time.

time-served ADJECTIVE (of a craftsman or tradesman) having completed an apprenticeship; fully trained and competent: *a time-served mechanic.*

timeserver (ˈtaɪmˌsɜːvə) NOUN a person who compromises and changes his opinions, way of life, etc., to suit the current fashions.
▸ **ˈtimeˌserving** ADJECTIVE, NOUN

time-share ADJECTIVE denoting, relating to, or forming part of time sharing of property: *time-share villas.*

time sharing NOUN [1] **a** a system of part ownership of a property, such as a flat or villa, for use as a holiday home, whereby each participant buys the right to use the property for the same fixed period annually. **b** (*as modifier*): *a time-sharing system.* [2] **a** a system by which users at different terminals of a computer can, because of its high speed, apparently communicate with it at the same time. Compare **batch processing. b** (*as modifier*): *a time-sharing computer.*

time sheet NOUN a card on which are recorded the hours spent working by an employee or employees.

time signal NOUN an announcement of the correct time, esp on radio or television.

time signature NOUN *Music* a sign usually consisting of two figures, one above the other, the upper figure representing the number of beats per bar and the lower one the time value of each beat. This sign is placed after the key signature at the outset of a piece or section of a piece.

time sovereignty NOUN control by an employee of the use of his or her time, involving flexibility of working hours.

Times Square NOUN a square formed by the intersection of Broadway and Seventh Avenue in New York City, extending from 42nd to 45th Street.

time-stamp VERB (*tr*) to assign an accurate time to (a message, transaction, etc.).

time study NOUN short for **time and motion study.**

time switch NOUN an electric switch that can be set to operate an appliance, such as a light or an oven, at a particular time.

timetable (ˈtaɪmˌteɪbəl) NOUN [1] a list or table of events arranged according to the time when they take place; schedule. ◆ VERB [2] (*tr*) to include in or arrange according to a timetable. [3] (*intr*) to draw up a timetable.

time trial NOUN (esp in cycling) a race in which the competitors compete against the clock over a specified course.
▸ **ˈtime-ˌtrialling** NOUN

time value NOUN *Music* the duration of a given printed note relative to other notes in a composition or section and considered in relation to the basic tempo. Often shortened to: **time.** Also called: **note value, time.**

time warp NOUN [1] any distortion of space-time. [2] a hypothetical distortion of time in which people and events from one age can be imagined to exist in another age. [3] *Informal* an illusion in which time appears to stand still: *he is living in a time warp.*

timework (ˈtaɪmˌwɜːk) NOUN work paid for by the length of time taken, esp by the hour or the day. Compare **piecework.**
▸ **ˈtimeˌworker** NOUN

timeworn (ˈtaɪmˌwɔːn) ADJECTIVE [1] showing the adverse effects of overlong use or of old age. [2] hackneyed; trite.

time zone NOUN a region throughout which the same standard time is used. There are 24 time zones in the world, demarcated approximately by meridians at 15° intervals, an hour apart. See also **zonetime.**

timid (ˈtɪmɪd) ADJECTIVE [1] easily frightened or upset, esp by human contact; shy. [2] indicating shyness or fear.
▷ **HISTORY** C16: from Latin *timidus,* from *timēre* to fear
▸ **tiˈmidity** *or* **ˈtimidness** NOUN ▸ **ˈtimidly** ADVERB

timing (ˈtaɪmɪŋ) NOUN the process or art of regulating actions or remarks in relation to others to produce the best effect, as in music, the theatre, sport, etc.

timing gear NOUN (in an internal-combustion engine) the drive between the crankshaft and the camshaft, usually giving a ratio of 2 : 1.

Timişoara (*Romanian* timiˈʃwara) NOUN a city in W Romania: formerly under Turkish and then Hapsburg rule, being allotted to Romania in 1920; scene of violence during the revolution of 1989. Pop.: 334 098 (1997 est.). Hungarian name: **Temesvár.**

timocracy (taɪˈmɒkrəsɪ) NOUN, *plural* **-cies.** [1] a political unit or system in which possession of property serves as the first requirement for participation in government. [2] a political unit or system in which love of honour is deemed the guiding principle of government.
▷ **HISTORY** C16: from Old French *tymocracie,* ultimately from Greek *timokratia,* from *timē* worth, honour, price + -CRACY
▸ **timocratic** (ˌtaɪməˈkrætɪk) *or* ˌ**timoˈcratical** ADJECTIVE

Timor (ˈtiːmɔː, ˈtaɪ-) NOUN an island in the Malay Archipelago, the largest and easternmost of the Lesser Sunda Islands: the west was a Dutch possession until 1949, when it became part of Indonesia: the east was held by Portugal until 1975, when it declared independence but was immediately invaded by Indonesia; East Timor finally became an independent state in 2002. Area: 30 775 sq. km (11 883 sq. miles).

timorous (ˈtɪmərəs) ADJECTIVE [1] fearful or timid. [2] indicating fear or timidity.
▷ **HISTORY** C15: from Old French *temoros,* from Medieval Latin *timōrōsus,* from Latin *timor* fear, from *timēre* to be afraid
▸ **ˈtimorously** ADVERB ▸ **ˈtimorousness** NOUN

Timor pony NOUN a small stocky breed of pony originally bred in Timor, used on Australian ranches.

Timor Sea NOUN an arm of the Indian Ocean between Australia and Timor. Width: about 480 km (300 miles).

timothy grass *or* **timothy** (ˈtɪməθɪ) NOUN a perennial grass, *Phleum pratense,* of temperate regions, having erect stiff stems and cylindrical flower spikes: grown for hay and pasture.
▷ **HISTORY** C18: apparently named after a *Timothy* Hanson, who brought it to colonial Carolina

timpani *or* **tympani** (ˈtɪmpənɪ) PLURAL NOUN (*sometimes functioning as singular*) a set of kettledrums, two or more in number. Often (informal) shortened to: **timps.**
▷ **HISTORY** from Italian, pl of *timpano* kettledrum, from Latin: TYMPANUM
▸ **ˈtimpanist** *or* **ˈtympanist** NOUN

tin (tɪn) NOUN [1] a metallic element, occurring in cassiterite, that has several allotropes; the ordinary malleable silvery-white metal slowly changes below 13.2°C to a grey powder. It is used extensively in alloys, esp bronze and pewter, and as a noncorroding coating for steel. Symbol: Sn; atomic no.: 50; atomic wt.: 118.710; valency: 2 or 4; relative density: 5.75 (grey), 7.31 (white); melting pt.: 231.9°C; boiling pt.: 2603°C. Related adjectives: **stannic, stannous.** [2] Also called (esp US and Canadian): **can.** an airtight sealed container of thin sheet metal coated with tin, used for preserving and storing food or drink. [3] any container made of metallic tin. [4] **fill her tins.** *NZ* to complete a home baking of cakes, biscuits, etc. [5] Also called: **tinful.** the contents of a tin or the amount a tin will hold. [6] *Brit, Austral, and NZ* corrugated or galvanized iron: *a tin roof.* [7] any metal regarded as cheap or flimsy. [8] *Brit* a loaf of bread with a rectangular shape, baked in a tin. [9] *Slang* money. ◆ VERB **tins, tinning, tinned.** (*tr*) [10] to put (food, etc.) into a tin or tins; preserve in a tin. [11] to plate or coat with tin. [12] to prepare (a metal) for soldering or brazing by applying a thin layer of solder to the surface.
▷ **HISTORY** Old English; related to Old Norse *tin,* Old High German *zin*
▸ **ˈtinˌlike** ADJECTIVE

tinamou (ˈtɪnəˌmuː) NOUN any bird of the order *Tinamiformes* of Central and South America, having small wings, a heavy body, and an inconspicuous plumage.
▷ **HISTORY** C18: via French from Carib (Galibi) *tinamu*

tincal (ˈtɪŋkəl) NOUN another name for **borax** (sense 1).
▷ **HISTORY** C17: from Malay *tingkal,* from Sanskrit *tankana*

tin can NOUN a metal food container, esp when empty.

tinct (tɪŋkt) NOUN, VERB [1] an obsolete word for **tint.** ◆ ADJECTIVE [2] *Poetic* tinted or coloured.
▷ **HISTORY** C15: from Latin *tinctus,* from *tingere* to colour

tinctorial (tɪŋkˈtɔːrɪəl) ADJECTIVE [1] of or relating to colouring, staining, or dyeing. [2] imbuing with colour.
▷ **HISTORY** C17: from Latin *tinctōrius,* from *tingere* to tinge
▸ **tincˈtorially** ADVERB

tincture (ˈtɪŋktʃə) NOUN [1] *Pharmacol* a medicinal extract in a solution of alcohol. [2] a tint, colour, or tinge. [3] a slight flavour, aroma, or trace. [4] any one of the colours or either of the metals used on heraldic arms. [5] *Obsolete* a dye or pigment. ◆ VERB [6] (*tr*) to give a tint or colour to.
▷ **HISTORY** C14: from Latin *tinctūra* a dyeing, from *tingere* to dye

tinder (ˈtɪndə) NOUN [1] dry wood or other easily combustible material used for lighting a fire. [2] anything inflammatory or dangerous: *his speech was tinder to the demonstrators' unrest.*
▷ **HISTORY** Old English *tynder;* related to Old Norse *tundr,* Old High German *zuntara*
▸ **ˈtindery** ADJECTIVE

tinderbox (ˈtɪndəˌbɒks) NOUN [1] a box used formerly for holding tinder, esp one fitted with a flint and steel. [2] a person or thing that is particularly touchy or explosive.

tine (taɪn) NOUN [1] a slender prong, esp of a fork. [2] any of the sharp terminal branches of a deer's antler.
▷ **HISTORY** Old English *tind;* related to Old Norse *tindr,* Old High German *zint*
▸ **tined** ADJECTIVE

tinea (ˈtɪnɪə) NOUN any fungal skin disease, esp ringworm.
▷ **HISTORY** C17: from Latin: worm
▸ **ˈtineal** ADJECTIVE

tineid (ˈtɪnɪɪd) NOUN [1] any moth of the family *Tineidae,* which includes the clothes moths. ◆ ADJECTIVE [2] of, relating to, or belonging to the family *Tineidae.*
▷ **HISTORY** C19: from New Latin *Tineidae,* from Latin: TINEA

tinfoil (ˈtɪnˌfɔɪl) NOUN [1] thin foil made of tin or an alloy of tin and lead. [2] thin foil made of aluminium; used for wrapping foodstuffs.

ting[1] (tɪŋ) NOUN [1] a high metallic sound such as that made by a small bell. ◆ VERB [2] to make or cause to make such a sound.
▷ **HISTORY** C15: of imitative origin

ting[2] (tɪŋ) NOUN (*often capital*) a variant spelling of **thing**[2].

ting-a-ling (ˈtɪŋəˈlɪŋ) NOUN the sound of a small bell.

tinge (tɪndʒ) NOUN [1] a slight tint or colouring: *her hair had a tinge of grey.* [2] any slight addition. ◆ VERB

tinges, tingeing *or* **tinging, tinged**. (*tr*) 3 to colour or tint faintly. 4 to impart a slight trace to: *her thoughts were tinged with nostalgia.*
▷HISTORY C15: from Latin *tingere* to colour

tingle ('tɪŋgᵊl) VERB 1 (*usually intr*) to feel or cause to feel a prickling, itching, or stinging sensation of the flesh, as from a cold plunge or electric shock. ◆ NOUN 2 a sensation of tingling.
▷HISTORY C14: perhaps a variant of TINKLE
▸'**tingler** NOUN ▸'**tingling** ADJECTIVE ▸'**tinglingly** ADVERB ▸'**tingly** ADJECTIVE

tin god NOUN 1 a self-important dictatorial person. 2 a person erroneously regarded as holy or venerable.

tin hat NOUN *Obsolete informal* a steel helmet worn by military personnel for protection against small metal fragments.

tinhorn ('tɪn,hɔːn) *US slang* ◆ NOUN 1 a cheap pretentious person, esp a gambler with extravagant claims. ◆ ADJECTIVE 2 cheap and showy.

tinker ('tɪŋkə) NOUN 1 (esp formerly) a travelling mender of pots and pans. 2 a clumsy worker. 3 the act of tinkering. 4 *Scot and Irish* another name for a **Gypsy**. 5 *Brit informal* a mischievous child. 6 any of several small mackerels that occur off the North American coast of the Atlantic. ◆ VERB 7 (*intr; foll by with*) to play, fiddle, or meddle (with machinery, etc.), esp while undertaking repairs. 8 to mend (pots and pans) as a tinker.
▷HISTORY C13 *tinkere*, perhaps from *tink* tinkle, of imitative origin
▸'**tinkerer** NOUN

tinker's damn *or* **cuss** NOUN *Slang* the slightest heed (esp in the phrase **not give a tinker's damn** *or* **cuss**).

tinkle ('tɪŋkᵊl) VERB 1 to ring or cause to ring with a series of high tinny sounds, like a small bell. 2 (*tr*) to announce or summon by such a ringing. 3 (*intr*) *Brit informal* to urinate. ◆ NOUN 4 a high clear ringing sound. 5 the act of tinkling. 6 *Brit informal* a telephone call.
▷HISTORY C14: of imitative origin
▸'**tinkling** ADJECTIVE, NOUN ▸'**tinkly** ADJECTIVE

tin lizzie ('lɪzɪ) NOUN *Informal* an old or decrepit car; jalopy.
▷HISTORY originally a nickname for the Model T Ford

tinned (tɪnd) ADJECTIVE 1 plated, coated, or treated with tin. 2 *Chiefly Brit* preserved or stored in airtight tins: *tinned soup.* 3 coated with a layer of solder.

tinner ('tɪnə) NOUN 1 a tin miner. 2 a worker in tin; tinsmith. 3 a person or organization that puts food, etc., into tins; canner.

tinnitus (tɪ'naɪtəs) NOUN *Pathol* a ringing, hissing, or booming sensation in one or both ears, caused by infection of the middle or inner ear, a side effect of certain drugs, etc.
▷HISTORY C19: from Latin, from *tinnīre* to ring

tinny ('tɪnɪ) ADJECTIVE **-nier, -niest**. 1 of, relating to, or resembling tin. 2 cheap, badly made, or shoddy. 3 (of a sound) high, thin, and metallic. 4 (of food or drink) flavoured with metal, as from a container. 5 *Austral informal* lucky. ◆ NOUN, *plural* **-nies**. 6 *Austral slang* a can of beer. 7 *Austral informal* Also: **tinnie**. a small fishing or pleasure boat with an aluminium hull.
▸'**tinnily** ADVERB ▸'**tinniness** NOUN

tin-opener NOUN a small tool for opening tins.

Tin Pan Alley NOUN 1 a district in a city concerned with the production of popular music, originally a small district in New York. 2 *Derogatory* the strictly commercial side of show business and pop music.

tin plate NOUN 1 thin steel sheet coated with a layer of tin that protects the steel from corrosion. ◆ VERB **tin-plate**. 2 (*tr*) to coat (a metal or object) with a layer of tin, usually either by electroplating or by dipping in a bath of molten tin.
▸'**tin-,plater** NOUN

tinpot ('tɪn,pɒt) ADJECTIVE (*prenominal*) *Brit informal* 1 inferior, cheap, or worthless. 2 paltry; unimportant.

tinsel ('tɪnsəl) NOUN 1 a decoration consisting of a piece of string with thin strips of metal foil attached along its length. 2 a yarn or fabric interwoven with strands of glittering thread. 3 anything cheap, showy, and gaudy. ◆ VERB **-sels, -selling, -selled** *or US* **-sels, -seling, -seled**. (*tr*) 4 to decorate with or as if with tinsel: *snow tinsels the trees*. 5 to give a gaudy appearance to. ◆ ADJECTIVE 6 made of or decorated with tinsel. 7 showily but cheaply attractive; gaudy.
▷HISTORY C16: from Old French *estincele* a spark, from Latin *scintilla;* compare STENCIL
▸'**tinsel-,like** ADJECTIVE ▸'**tinselly** ADJECTIVE

Tinseltown ('tɪnsəl,taʊn) NOUN an informal name for **Hollywood**.
▷HISTORY C20: from the insubstantial glitter of the film world

tinsmith ('tɪn,smɪθ) NOUN a person who works with tin or tin plate.

tin soldier NOUN 1 a miniature toy soldier, usually made of lead. 2 a person who enjoys playing at being a soldier.

tinstone ('tɪn,stəʊn) NOUN another name for **cassiterite**.

tint (tɪnt) NOUN 1 a shade of a colour, esp a pale one. 2 a colour that is softened or desaturated by the addition of white. 3 a tinge. 4 a semipermanent dye for the hair. 5 a trace or hint: *a tint of jealousy in his voice*. 6 *Engraving* uniform shading, produced esp by hatching. 7 *Printing* a panel of colour serving as a background to letters or other matter. ◆ VERB 8 (*tr*) to colour or tinge. 9 (*tr*) to change or influence slightly: *his answer was tinted by his prior knowledge*. 10 (*intr*) to acquire a tint.
▷HISTORY C18: from earlier TINCT
▸'**tinter** NOUN

Tintagel Head (tɪn'tædʒəl) NOUN a promontory in SW England, on the W coast of Cornwall: ruins of **Tintagel Castle**, legendary birthplace of King Arthur.

tintinnabulation (,tɪntɪ,næbjʊ'leɪʃən) NOUN the act or an instance of the ringing or pealing of bells.
▸**,tintin'nabular** *or* **,tintin'nabulary** *or* **,tintin'nabulous** ADJECTIVE

tintinnabulum (,tɪntɪ'næbjʊləm) NOUN, *plural* **-la** (-lə). a small high-pitched bell.
▷HISTORY C16: from Latin, from *tintinnāre* to tinkle, from *tinnīre* to ring; see TINNITUS

tintometer (tɪn'tɒmɪtə) NOUN another name for **colorimeter** (sense 1).

tint tool NOUN a kind of burin used in wood engraving for carving lines of even thickness, as in hatching.

tintype ('tɪn,taɪp) NOUN another name for **ferrotype** (senses 1, 2).

tinware ('tɪn,wɛə) NOUN objects made of tin plate.

tin whistle NOUN another name for **penny whistle**.

tinwork ('tɪn,wɜːk) NOUN objects made of tin.

tinworks ('tɪn,wɜːks) NOUN (*functioning as singular or plural*) a place where tin is mined, smelted, or rolled.

tiny ('taɪnɪ) ADJECTIVE **tinier, tiniest**. very small; minute.
▷HISTORY C16 *tine*, of uncertain origin
▸'**tinily** ADVERB ▸'**tininess** NOUN

-tion SUFFIX FORMING NOUNS indicating state, condition, action, process, or result: *election; prohibition*. Compare **-ation, -ion**.
▷HISTORY from Old French, from Latin *-tiō, -tiōn-*

tip¹ (tɪp) NOUN 1 the extreme end of something, esp a narrow or pointed end. 2 the top or summit. 3 a small piece forming an extremity or end: *a metal tip on a cane*. ◆ VERB **tips, tipping, tipped**. (*tr*) 4 to adorn or mark the tip of. 5 to cause to form a tip.
▷HISTORY C15: from Old Norse *typpa;* related to Middle Low German, Middle Dutch *tip*
▸'**tipless** ADJECTIVE

tip² (tɪp) VERB **tips, tipping, tipped**. 1 to tilt or cause to tilt. 2 (usually foll by *over* or *up*) to tilt or cause to tilt, so as to overturn or fall. 3 *Brit* to dump (rubbish, etc.). 4 **tip one's hat**. to take off, raise, or touch one's hat in salutation. ◆ NOUN 5 the act of tipping or the state of being tipped. 6 *Brit* a dump for refuse, etc.
▷HISTORY C14: of uncertain origin; related to TOP¹, TOPPLE
▸'**tippable** ADJECTIVE

tip³ (tɪp) NOUN 1 a payment given for services in excess of the standard charge; gratuity. 2 a helpful hint, warning, or other piece of information. 3 a piece of inside information, esp in betting or investing. ◆ VERB **tips, tipping, tipped**. 4 to give a tip to (a person).
▷HISTORY C18: perhaps from TIP⁴

tip⁴ (tɪp) VERB **tips, tipping, tipped**. (*tr*.) 1 to hit or strike lightly. 2 to hit (a ball) indirectly so that it glances off the bat in cricket. ◆ NOUN 3 a light blow. 4 a glancing hit in cricket.
▷HISTORY C13: perhaps from Low German *tippen*

tip and run NOUN 1 a form of cricket in which the batsman must run if his bat touches the ball. ◆ ADJECTIVE **tip-and-run**. 2 (*prenominal*) characterized by a rapid departure immediately after striking: *a tip-and-run raid*.

tipcat ('tɪp,kæt) NOUN a game in which a short sharp-ended piece of wood (the cat) is tipped in the air with a stick.

tipi ('tiːpɪ) NOUN, *plural* **-pis**. a variant spelling of **tepee**.

tip-off NOUN 1 a warning or hint, esp given confidentially and based on inside information. 2 *Basketball* the act or an instance of putting the ball in play by a jump ball. ◆ VERB **tip off**. 3 (*tr, adverb*) to give a hint or warning to.

tippee (tɪ'piː) NOUN a person who receives a tip, esp regarding share prices.

tipper ('tɪpə) NOUN 1 a person who gives or leaves a tip: *he is a generous tipper*. 2 short for **tipper truck**.

Tipperary (,tɪpə'rɛərɪ) NOUN a county of S Republic of Ireland, in Munster province; divided into the North Riding and South Riding: mountainous. County town: Clonmel. Pop.: 133 535 (1996). Area: 4255 sq. km (1643 sq. miles).

tipper truck *or* **lorry** NOUN a truck or lorry the rear platform of which can be raised at the front end to enable the load to be discharged by gravity. Also called: **tip truck**.

tippet ('tɪpɪt) NOUN 1 a woman's fur cape for the shoulders, often consisting of the whole fur of a fox, marten, etc. 2 the long stole of Anglican clergy worn during a service. 3 a long streamer-like part to a sleeve, hood, etc., esp in the 16th century. 4 the ruff of a bird. 5 a tippet feather or something similar used in dressing some artificial angling flies.
▷HISTORY C14: perhaps from TIP¹

tipple¹ ('tɪpᵊl) VERB 1 to make a habit of taking (alcoholic drink), esp in small quantities. ◆ NOUN 2 alcoholic drink.
▷HISTORY C15: back formation from obsolete *tippler* tapster, of unknown origin
▸'**tippler** NOUN

tipple² ('tɪpᵊl) NOUN 1 a device for overturning ore trucks, mine cars, etc., so that they discharge their load. 2 a place at which such trucks are tipped and unloaded. ◆ VERB 3 *Northern English dialect* to fall or cause to fall.
▷HISTORY C19: from *tipple* to overturn, from TIP²

tippler ('tɪplə) NOUN (*sometimes capital*) 1 a variety of domestic pigeon bred mainly for flying. Also called: **high-flying tippler**. 2 a domestic fancy pigeon of a smaller rounder type kept mainly for exhibition. Usual name: **show tippler**.
▷HISTORY C19: from TIPPLE² + -ER¹

tipstaff ('tɪp,stɑːf) NOUN 1 a court official having miscellaneous duties, mostly concerned with the maintenance of order in court. 2 a metal-tipped staff formerly used as a symbol of office.
▷HISTORY C16 *tipped staff;* see TIP¹, STAFF¹

tipster ('tɪpstə) NOUN a person who sells tips on horse racing, the stock market, etc.

tipsy ('tɪpsɪ) ADJECTIVE **-sier, -siest**. 1 slightly drunk. 2 slightly tilted or tipped; askew.
▷HISTORY C16: from TIP²
▸'**tipsily** ADVERB ▸'**tipsiness** NOUN

tipsy cake NOUN *Brit* a kind of trifle made from a sponge cake soaked with white wine or sherry and decorated with almonds and crystallized fruit.

tip-tilted ADJECTIVE (of a nose) slightly turned up.

tiptoe ('tɪp,təʊ) VERB **-toes, -toeing, -toed**. (*intr*) 1 to walk with the heels off the ground and the weight supported by the ball of the foot and the toes. 2 to walk silently or stealthily. ◆ NOUN 3 **on tiptoe**. **a** on the tips of the toes or on the ball of the foot and the toes. **b** eagerly anticipating something. **c** stealthily or silently. ◆ ADVERB 4 on tiptoe. ◆ ADJECTIVE 5 walking or standing on tiptoe. 6 stealthy or silent.

tiptop (ˌtɪpˈtɒp) ADJECTIVE, ADVERB [1] at the highest point of health, excellence, etc. [2] at the topmost point. ◆ NOUN [3] the best in quality. [4] the topmost point.

tip truck NOUN another name for **tipper truck**.

tipuna *or* **tupuna** (təˈpuːnə) NOUN *NZ* an ancestor.
▷HISTORY Maori

tip-up ADJECTIVE (*prenominal*) able to be turned upwards around a hinge or pivot: *a tip-up seat.*

TIR (on continental lorries) ABBREVIATION FOR Transports Internationaux Routiers.
▷HISTORY French: International Road Transport

tirade (taɪˈreɪd) NOUN [1] a long angry speech or denunciation. [2] *Prosody, rare* a speech or passage dealing with a single theme.
▷HISTORY C19: from French, literally: a pulling, from Italian *tirata,* from *tirare* to pull, of uncertain origin

tiramisu (ˌtiːrəmiːˈsuː) NOUN an Italian dessert made with sponge soaked in coffee and Marsala, topped with soft cheese and powdered chocolate.
▷HISTORY C20: from Italian *tira!* pull! + *mi* me + *su* up

Tiran (tɪˈrɑːn) NOUN **Strait of.** a strait between the Gulf of Aqaba and the Red Sea. Length: 16 km (10 miles). Width: 8 km (5 miles).

Tirana (tɪˈrɑːnə) *or* **Tiranë** (*Albanian* tiˈranə) NOUN the capital of Albania, in the central part 32 km (20 miles) from the Adriatic: founded in the early 17th century by Turks; became capital in 1920; the country's largest city and industrial centre. Pop.: 279 000 (1999 est.).

tire[1] (ˈtaɪə) VERB [1] (*tr*) to reduce the energy of, esp by exertion; weary. [2] (*tr; often passive*) to reduce the tolerance of; bore or irritate: *I'm tired of the children's chatter.* [3] (*intr*) to become wearied or bored; flag.
▷HISTORY Old English *tēorian,* of unknown origin
▸ˈ**tiring** ADJECTIVE

tire[2] (ˈtaɪə) NOUN, VERB the US spelling of **tyre**.

tire[3] (ˈtaɪə) VERB, NOUN an archaic word for **attire**.

tired (ˈtaɪəd) ADJECTIVE [1] weary; fatigued. [2] (foll by *of*) **a** having lost interest in; bored: *I'm tired of playing cards.* **b** having lost patience with; exasperated by: *I'm tired of his eternal excuses.* [3] hackneyed; stale: *the same tired old jokes.* [4] **tired and emotional.** a euphemism for slightly drunk.
▸ˈ**tiredly** ADVERB ▸ˈ**tiredness** NOUN

Tiree (taɪˈriː) NOUN an island off the W coast of Scotland, in the Inner Hebrides. Pop.: 1054 (latest est.). Area: 78 sq. km (30 sq. miles).

tireless (ˈtaɪəlɪs) ADJECTIVE unable to be tired; indefatigable.
▸ˈ**tirelessly** ADVERB ▸ˈ**tirelessness** NOUN

Tiresias (taɪˈriːsɪˌæs) NOUN *Greek myth* a blind soothsayer of Thebes, who revealed to Oedipus that the latter had murdered his father and married his mother.

tiresome (ˈtaɪəsəm) ADJECTIVE boring and irritating; irksome.
▸ˈ**tiresomely** ADVERB ▸ˈ**tiresomeness** NOUN

tirewoman (ˈtaɪəˌwʊmən) NOUN, *plural* **-women**. an obsolete term for **lady's maid**.
▷HISTORY C17: see TIRE[3]

Tîrgu Mureş (*Romanian* ˈtirgu ˈmureʃ) NOUN a city in central Romania: manufacturing and cultural centre. Pop.: 165 534 (1997 est.).

Tirich Mir (ˈtɪərɪtʃ ˈmɪə) NOUN a mountain in N Pakistan: highest peak of the Hindu Kush. Height: 7690 m (25 230 ft.).

tiring room NOUN *Archaic* a dressing room in a theatre.

tiro (ˈtaɪrəʊ) NOUN, *plural* **-ros**. a variant spelling of **tyro**.

Tirol (tɪˈrəʊl, ˈtɪrəʊl; *German* tiˈroːl) NOUN a variant spelling of **Tyrol**.

Tirolean (ˌtɪrəʊˈlɪən) ADJECTIVE, NOUN a variant spelling of **Tyrolean**.

Tirolese (ˌtɪrəˈliːz) ADJECTIVE, NOUN a variant spelling of **Tyrolese**.

Tiros (ˈtaɪrəʊs) NOUN one of a series of US weather satellites carrying infrared and television camera equipment for transmitting meteorological data to the earth.
▷HISTORY C20: from *T(elevision and) I(nfra-)R(ed) O(bservation) S(atellite)*

Tiruchirapalli (ˌtɪrətʃɪrəˈpʌlɪ, tɪˌruːtʃɪˈrɑːpəlɪ) *or* **Trichinopoly** NOUN an industrial city in S India, in central Tamil Nadu on the Cauvery River: dominated by a rock fortress 83 m (273 ft.) high. Pop.: 387 223 (1991).

Tirunelveli (ˌtɪruˈnɛlvɛlɪ) NOUN a city in S India, in Tamil Nadu: site of St Francis Xavier's first preaching in India; textile manufacturing. Pop.: 135 825 (1991).

'tis (tɪz) *Poetic or dialect* CONTRACTION OF it is.

Tisa (ˈtisa) NOUN the Slavonic and Romanian name for the **Tisza**.

tisane (tɪˈzæn) NOUN an infusion of dried or fresh leaves or flowers, as camomile.
▷HISTORY C19: from French, from Latin *ptisana* barley water; see PTISAN

Tishah b'Av (tiˈʃa bəˈav) NOUN *Judaism* the ninth day of the month of Av observed as a fast day in memory of the destruction of the First and Second Temples.

Tishri (tɪʃˈriː) NOUN (in the Jewish calendar) the seventh month of the year according to biblical reckoning and the first month of the civil year, usually falling within September and October.
▷HISTORY from Hebrew

Tisiphone (tɪˈsɪfənɪ) NOUN *Greek myth* one of the three Furies; the others are Alecto and Megaera.

tissue (ˈtɪsjuː, ˈtɪʃuː) NOUN [1] a part of an organism consisting of a large number of cells having a similar structure and function: *connective tissue; nerve tissue.* [2] a thin piece of soft absorbent paper, usually of two or more layers, used as a disposable handkerchief, towel, etc. [3] See **tissue paper**. [4] an interwoven series: *a tissue of lies.* [5] a woven cloth, esp of a light gauzy nature, originally interwoven with threads of gold or silver. ◆ VERB (*tr*) [6] *Rare* to weave into tissue. [7] to decorate or clothe with tissue or tissue paper.
▷HISTORY C14: from Old French *tissu* woven cloth, from *tistre* to weave, from Latin *texere*

tissue culture NOUN [1] the growth of small pieces of animal or plant tissue in a sterile controlled medium. [2] the tissue produced as a result of this process.

tissue paper NOUN very thin soft delicate paper used to wrap breakable goods, as decoration, etc.

tissue type NOUN the inherited chemical characteristics of the bodily tissue of an individual that are recognized and, when grafted, are accepted or rejected by the immune system of another individual. The tissue type is determined by the histocompatibility antigens.

Tisza (*Hungarian* ˈtisɔ) NOUN a river in S central Europe, rising in the W Ukraine and flowing west, forming part of the border between the Ukraine and Romania, then southwest across Hungary into Serbia to join the Danube north of Belgrade. Slavonic and Romanian name: **Tisa**.

tit[1] (tɪt) NOUN [1] any of numerous small active Old World songbirds of the family *Paridae* (titmice), esp those of the genus *Parus* (bluetit, great tit, etc.). They have a short bill and feed on insects and seeds. [2] any of various similar small birds. [3] *Archaic or dialect* a worthless or worn-out horse; nag.
▷HISTORY C16: perhaps of imitative origin, applied to small animate or inanimate objects; compare Icelandic *tittr* pin

tit[2] (tɪt) NOUN [1] *Slang* a female breast. [2] a teat or nipple. [3] *Derogatory* a girl or young woman. [4] *Slang* a despicable or unpleasant person: often used as a term of address.
▷HISTORY Old English *titt;* related to Middle Low German *titte,* Norwegian *titta*

Tit. *Bible* ABBREVIATION FOR Titus.

titan (ˈtaɪtᵊn) NOUN a person of great strength or size.
▷HISTORY C17: from TITAN[1]

Titan[1] (ˈtaɪtᵊn) *or feminine* **Titaness** NOUN *Greek myth* [1] any of a family of primordial gods, the sons and daughters of Uranus (sky) and Gaea (earth). [2] any of the offspring of the children of Uranus and Gaea.

Titan[2] (ˈtaɪtᵊn) NOUN the largest satellite of the planet Saturn, having a thick atmosphere consisting mainly of nitrogen. Diameter: 5150 km.

titanate (ˈtaɪtəˌneɪt) NOUN any salt or ester of titanic acid.

Titanesque (ˌtaɪtəˈnɛsk) ADJECTIVE resembling a Titan; gigantic.

titania (taɪˈteɪnɪə) NOUN another name for **titanium dioxide**.

Titania[1] (tɪˈtɑːnɪə) NOUN [1] (in medieval folklore) the queen of the fairies and wife of Oberon. [2] (in classical antiquity) a poetic epithet used variously to characterize Circe, Diana, Latona, or Pyrrha.

Titania[2] (tɪˈtɑːnɪə) NOUN the largest of the satellites of Uranus and the second furthest from the planet.

titanic[1] (taɪˈtænɪk) ADJECTIVE of or containing titanium, esp in the tetravalent state.

titanic[2] (taɪˈtænɪk) ADJECTIVE possessing or requiring colossal strength: *a titanic battle.*
▸**tiˈtanically** ADVERB

Titanic (taɪˈtænɪk) NOUN **the.** a luxury British liner that struck an iceberg near Newfoundland on its maiden voyage on the night of April 14–15, 1912, with the loss of 1513 lives.

titanic acid NOUN any of various white substances regarded as hydrated forms of titanium dioxide, typical formulas being H_4TiO_4 and H_2TiO_3.

titanic oxide NOUN another name for **titanium dioxide**.

titaniferous (ˌtaɪtəˈnɪfərəs) ADJECTIVE of or containing titanium; bearing titanium: *a titaniferous ore.*

Titanism (ˈtaɪtəˌnɪzəm) NOUN a spirit of defiance of and rebellion against authority, social convention, etc.

titanite (ˈtaɪtəˌnaɪt) NOUN another name for **sphene**.
▷HISTORY C19: from German *Titanit,* so named because it contained TITANIUM

titanium (taɪˈteɪnɪəm) NOUN a strong malleable white metallic element, which is very corrosion-resistant and occurs in rutile and ilmenite. It is used in the manufacture of strong lightweight alloys, esp aircraft parts. Symbol: Ti; atomic no.: 22; atomic wt.: 47.88; valency: 2, 3, or 4; relative density: 4.54; melting pt.: 1670±10°C; boiling pt.: 3289°C.
▷HISTORY C18: New Latin; see TITAN, -IUM

titanium dioxide NOUN a white insoluble powder occurring naturally as rutile and used chiefly as a pigment of high covering power and durability. Formula: TiO_2. Also called: **titanium oxide, titanic oxide, titania**.

Titanomachy (ˌtaɪtəˈnɒməkɪ) NOUN *Greek myth* the unsuccessful revolt of the family of the Titan Iapetus against Zeus.
▷HISTORY C19: from Greek *titanomakhia,* from TITAN[1] + *makhē* a battle

titanosaur (taɪˈtænəˌsɔː) NOUN any of various herbivorous quadrupedal dinosaurs of the family *Titanosauridae,* of Jurassic and Cretaceous times: suborder *Sauropoda* (sauropods).
▷HISTORY C19: from New Latin *Tītānosaurus,* from Greek TITAN + -SAUR

titanothere (taɪˈtænəˌθɪə) NOUN any of various very large horse-like perissodactyl mammals of the genera *Menodus, Brontotherium,* etc., that lived in Eocene and Oligocene times in North America. See also **chalicothere**.
▷HISTORY C19: from New Latin *Tītānotherium* giant animal, from Greek TITAN + *thēr* wild beast

titanous (taɪˈtænəs) ADJECTIVE of or containing titanium, esp in the trivalent state.

titarakura (ˈtiːtɑːrəˌkuːrə) NOUN *NZ* another name for **bully**[2].

titbit (ˈtɪtˌbɪt) *or esp US* **tidbit** NOUN [1] a tasty small piece of food; dainty. [2] a pleasing scrap of anything, such as scandal.
▷HISTORY C17: perhaps from dialect *tid* tender, of obscure origin

titchy *or* **tichy** (ˈtɪtʃɪ) ADJECTIVE **titchier, titchiest**. *Brit slang* very small; tiny.
▷HISTORY C20: from *tich* or *titch* a small person, from *Little Tich,* the stage name of Harry Relph (1867–1928), English actor noted for his small stature

titer (ˈtaɪtə, ˈtiː-) NOUN the usual US spelling of **titre**.

titfer ('tɪtfə) NOUN *Brit slang* a hat.
▷HISTORY from rhyming slang *tit for tat* hat

tit for tat NOUN an equivalent given in return or retaliation; blow for blow.
▷HISTORY C16: from earlier *tip for tap*

tithable ('taɪðəbəl) ADJECTIVE 1 (until 1936) liable to pay tithes. 2 (of property, etc.) subject to the payment of tithes.

tithe (taɪð) NOUN 1 (*often plural*) *Christianity* a tenth part of agricultural or other produce, personal income, or profits, contributed either voluntarily or as a tax for the support of the church or clergy or for charitable purposes. 2 any levy, esp of one tenth. 3 a tenth or very small part of anything. ♦ VERB 4 (*tr*) **a** to exact or demand a tithe or tithes from (an individual or group). **b** to levy a tithe upon (a crop or amount of produce, etc.). 5 (*intr*) to pay a tithe or tithes.
▷HISTORY Old English *teogoth;* related to Old Frisian *tegotha,* Old Saxon *tegotho,* Old High German *zehando,* Old Norse *tīundi,* Gothic *taihunda*
▸**'tither** NOUN

tithe barn NOUN a large barn where, formerly, the agricultural tithe of a parish was stored.

tithing ('taɪðɪŋ) NOUN *English history* 1 **a** a tithe; tenth. **b** the exacting or paying of tithes. 2 a company of ten householders in the system of frankpledge. 3 a rural division, originally regarded as a tenth of a hundred.

Tithonus (tɪ'θəʊnəs) NOUN *Greek myth* the son of Laomedon of Troy who was loved by the goddess Eos. She asked that he be made immortal but forgot to ask that he be made eternally young. When he aged she turned him into a grasshopper.

titi[1] ('tiːtiː) NOUN, *plural* **-tis**. any of several small omnivorous New World monkeys of the genus *Callicebus,* of South America, having long beautifully coloured fur and a long nonprehensile tail.
▷HISTORY via Spanish from Aymaran, literally: little cat

titi[2] ('tiːtiː) NOUN, *plural* **-tis**. any of various evergreen shrubs or small trees of the family *Cyrillaceae* of the southern US, esp the leatherwood and *Cliftonia monophylla,* which has white or pinkish fragrant flowers.
▷HISTORY C19: of American Indian origin

Titian ('tɪʃən) ADJECTIVE (*sometimes not capital*) reddish-gold, like the hair colour used in many of the works of Titian (original name *Tiziano Vecellio*), the Italian painter of the Venetian school (?1490–1576). Also called: **Titian red.**

Titicaca (*Spanish* titi'kaka) NOUN **Lake.** a lake between S Peru and W Bolivia, in the Andes: the highest large lake in the world; drained by the Desaguadero River flowing into Lake Poopó. Area: 8135 sq. km (3141 sq. miles). Altitude: 3809 m (12 497 ft.). Depth: 370 m (1214 ft.).

titillate ('tɪtɪˌleɪt) VERB (*tr*) 1 to arouse, tease, interest, or excite pleasurably and often superficially. 2 to cause a tickling or tingling sensation in, esp by touching.
▷HISTORY C17: from Latin *tītillāre*
▸**'titilˌlating** ADJECTIVE ▸**'titilˌlatingly** ADVERB ▸**ˌtitil'lation** NOUN ▸**'titilˌlative** ADJECTIVE

titivate *or* **tittivate** ('tɪtɪˌveɪt) VERB 1 to smarten up (oneself or another), as by making up, doing the hair, etc. 2 (*tr*) to smarten up (a thing): *to titivate a restaurant.*
▷HISTORY C19: earlier *tidivate,* perhaps based on TIDY and CULTIVATE
▸**ˌtiti'vation** *or* **ˌtitti'vation** NOUN ▸**'titiˌvator** *or* **'tittiˌvator** NOUN

titlark ('tɪtˌlɑːk) NOUN another name for **pipit**, esp the meadow pipit (*Anthus pratensis*)
▷HISTORY C17: from TIT[1] + LARK[1]

title ('taɪtəl) NOUN 1 the distinctive name of a work of art, musical or literary composition, etc. 2 a descriptive name, caption, or heading of a section of a book, speech, etc. 3 See **title page.** 4 a name or epithet signifying rank, office, or function. 5 a formal designation, such as *Mr, Mrs,* or *Miss.* 6 an appellation designating nobility. 7 *Films* **a** short for **subtitle** (sense 2). **b** written material giving credits in a film or television programme. 8 *Sport* a championship. 9 *Property law* **a** the legal right to possession of property, esp real property. **b** the basis of such right. **c** the documentary evidence of such right: *title deeds.* 10 *Law* **a** the heading or a division of a statute, book of law, etc. **b** the heading of a suit or action at law. 11 **a** any customary or established right. **b** a claim based on such a right. 12 a definite spiritual charge or office in the church, without appointment to which a candidate for holy orders cannot lawfully be ordained. 13 *RC Church* a titular church. ♦ VERB 14 (*tr*) to give a title to.
▷HISTORY C13: from Old French, from Latin *titulus*

titled ('taɪtəld) ADJECTIVE having a title: *the titled classes.*

title deed NOUN a deed or document evidencing a person's legal right or title to property, esp real property.

titleholder ('taɪtəlˌhəʊldə) NOUN a person who holds a title, esp a sporting championship.
▸**'titleˌholding** ADJECTIVE

title page NOUN the page in a book that bears the title, author's name, publisher's imprint, etc.

title role NOUN the role of the character after whom a play, etc., is named.

titman ('tɪtmən) NOUN, *plural* **-men**. (of pigs) the runt of a litter.
▷HISTORY *tit-* (as in TITMOUSE) + MAN

titmouse ('tɪtˌmaʊs) NOUN, *plural* **-mice**. (*usually plural*) any small active songbird of the family *Paridae,* esp those of the genus *Parus* (see **tit**[1]).
▷HISTORY C14 *titemous,* from *tite* (see TIT[1]) + MOUSE

Titograd (*Serbo-Croat* 'titɔgraːd) NOUN the former name (1946–92) of **Podgorica.**

Titoism ('tiːtəʊˌɪzəm) NOUN 1 the variant of Communism practised by the Yugoslav statesman Marshal Tito (original name *Josip Broz;* 1892–1980) in the former Yugoslavia, characterized by independence from the Soviet bloc and neutrality in East-West controversies, a considerable amount of decentralization, and a large degree of worker control of industries. 2 any variant of Communism resembling Titoism.
▸**'Titoist** NOUN, ADJECTIVE

titrant ('taɪtrənt) NOUN the solution in a titration that is added from a burette to a measured quantity of another solution.

titrate ('taɪtreɪt) VERB (*tr*) to measure the volume or concentration of (a solution) by titration.
▷HISTORY C19: from French *titrer;* see TITRE
▸**ti'tratable** ADJECTIVE

titration (taɪ'treɪʃən) NOUN an operation, used in volumetric analysis, in which a measured amount of one solution is added to a known quantity of another solution until the reaction between the two is complete. If the concentration of one solution is known, that of the other can be calculated.

titre *or US* **titer** ('taɪtə, 'tiː-) NOUN 1 **a** the concentration of a solution as determined by titration. **b** the minimum quantity of a solution required to complete a reaction in a titration. 2 the quantity of antibody present in an organism.
▷HISTORY C19: from French *titre* proportion of gold or silver in an alloy, from Old French *title* TITLE

titter ('tɪtə) VERB 1 (*intr*) to snigger, esp derisively or in a suppressed way. 2 (*tr*) to express by tittering. ♦ NOUN 3 a suppressed laugh, chuckle, or snigger.
▷HISTORY C17: of imitative origin
▸**'titterer** NOUN ▸**'tittering** ADJECTIVE ▸**'titteringly** ADVERB

tittivate ('tɪtɪˌveɪt) VERB a less common spelling of **titivate.**

tittle ('tɪtəl) NOUN 1 a small mark in printing or writing, esp a diacritic. 2 a jot; particle.
▷HISTORY C14: from Medieval Latin *titulus* label, from Latin: TITLE

tittle-tattle NOUN 1 idle chat or gossip. ♦ VERB 2 (*intr*) to chatter or gossip.
▸**'tittle-ˌtattler** NOUN

tittup ('tɪtəp) VERB **-tups, -tupping, -tupped** *or US* **-tups, -tuping, -tuped.** 1 (*intr*) to prance or frolic. ♦ NOUN 2 a caper. 3 the sound made by high-heeled shoes.
▷HISTORY C18 (in the sense: a horse's gallop): probably imitative

titubation (ˌtɪtjʊ'beɪʃən) NOUN *Pathol* 1 a disordered gait characterized by stumbling or staggering, often caused by a lesion of the cerebellum. 2 Also called: **lingual titubation.** stuttering or stammering.
▷HISTORY C17: from Latin *titubātiō,* from *titubāre* to reel

titular ('tɪtjʊlə) *or* **titulary** ('tɪtjʊlərɪ) ADJECTIVE 1 of, relating to, or of the nature of a title. 2 in name only. 3 bearing a title. 4 giving a title. 5 *RC Church* designating any of certain churches in Rome to whom cardinals or bishops are attached as their nominal incumbents. ♦ NOUN, *plural* **-lars** *or* **-laries.** 6 the bearer of a title. 7 the bearer of a nominal office.
▷HISTORY C18: from French *titulaire,* from Latin *titulus* TITLE
▸**'titularly** ADVERB

titulus ('tɪtjʊləs) NOUN, *plural* **-li** (-laɪ). (in crucifixion) a sign attached to the top of the cross on which were written the condemned man's name and crime.
▷HISTORY from Latin, literally: inscription, label, title

Titus ('taɪtəs) NOUN *New Testament* the epistle written by Saint Paul to Titus, his Greek disciple and helper (in full **The Epistle of Paul the Apostle to Titus**), containing advice on pastoral matters.

Tiu ('tiːuː) NOUN (in Anglo-Saxon mythology) the god of war and the sky. Norse counterpart: **Tyr.**

Tiv (tɪv) NOUN 1 (*plural* **Tivs** *or* **Tiv**) a member of a Negroid people of W Africa, living chiefly in the savanna of the Benue area of S Nigeria and noted by anthropologists for having no chiefs. 2 the language of this people, belonging to the Benue-Congo branch of the Niger-Congo family.

Tivoli ('tɪvəlɪ; *Italian* 'tiːvoli) NOUN a town in central Italy, east of Rome: a summer resort in Roman times; contains the Renaissance Villa d'Este and the remains of Hadrian's Villa. Pop.: 55 030 (1990). Ancient name: **Tibur.**

tix (tɪks) PLURAL NOUN *Informal* tickets.
▷HISTORY C20: from *tics,* shortened from *tickets*

tizzy ('tɪzɪ) NOUN, *plural* **-zies.** *Informal* a state of confusion, anxiety, or excitement. Also called: **tizz, tiz-woz** ('tɪzˌwɒz).
▷HISTORY C19: of unknown origin

tj THE INTERNET DOMAIN NAME FOR Tajikistan.

TJ INTERNATIONAL CAR REGISTRATION FOR Tajikistan.

Tjirebon *or* **Cheribon** ('tʃɪərəˌbɒn) NOUN a port in S central Indonesia, on N Java on the Java Sea: scene of the signing of the **Tjirebon Agreement** of Indonesian independence (1946) by the Netherlands. Pop.: 245 307 (1990).

T-joint NOUN a right-angled joint, esp one in wood, making the shape of the letter T.

T-junction NOUN a road junction in which one road joins another at right angles but does not cross it.

tk THE INTERNET DOMAIN NAME FOR Tokelau.

TKO *Boxing* ABBREVIATION FOR **technical knockout.**

Tl THE CHEMICAL SYMBOL FOR thallium.

TLA ABBREVIATION FOR: 1 three-letter abbreviation. 2 three-letter acronym.

Tlaxcala (*Spanish* tlas'kala) NOUN 1 a state of S central Mexico: the smallest Mexican state; formerly an Indian principality, the chief Indian ally of Cortés in the conquest of Mexico. Capital: Tlaxcala. Pop.: 961 912 (2000 est.). Area: 3914 sq. km (1511 sq. miles). 2 a city in E central Mexico, on the central plateau, capital of Tlaxcala state: the church of San Francisco (founded 1521 by Cortés) is the oldest in the Americas. Pop.: 25 000 (1990 est.). Official name: **Tlaxcala de Xicohténcatl.**

TLC *Informal* ♦ ABBREVIATION FOR: 1 tender loving care. 2 **thin-layer chromatography.**

Tlemcen (*French* tsɛn) NOUN a city in NW Algeria: capital of an Arab kingdom from the 12th to the late 14th century. Pop.: 155 162 (1998).

Tlingit ('tlɪŋgɪt) NOUN 1 (*plural* **-gits** *or* **-git**) a member of a seafaring group of North American Indian peoples inhabiting S Alaska and N British Columbia. 2 the language of these peoples, belonging to the Na-Dene phylum.

TLS ABBREVIATION FOR Times Literary Supplement.

T-lymphocyte NOUN a type of lymphocyte that matures in the thymus gland and has an important role in the immune response. There are several subclasses: **killer T-cells** are responsible for killing cells that are infected by a virus; **helper T-cells**

induce other cells (**B-lymphocytes**) to produce antibodies. Also called: **T-cell.**

tm THE INTERNET DOMAIN NAME FOR Turkmenistan.

Tm THE CHEMICAL SYMBOL FOR thulium.

TM 1 ABBREVIATION FOR **transcendental meditation.** ◆ 2 INTERNATIONAL CAR REGISTRATION FOR Turkmenistan.

T-man NOUN, *plural* **-men.** *US* a law-enforcement agent of the US Treasury.

tmesis (tə'mi:sɪs, 'mi:sɪs) NOUN interpolation of a word or group of words between the parts of a compound word.
▷HISTORY C16: via Latin from Greek, literally: a cutting, from *temnein* to cut

TMI ABBREVIATION FOR too much information: an expression of distaste or boredom at the information being offered.

TMT ABBREVIATION FOR telecommunications, media, and technology.

TMV ABBREVIATION FOR **tobacco mosaic virus.**

tn THE INTERNET DOMAIN NAME FOR Tunisia.

TN 1 ABBREVIATION FOR Tennessee. ◆ 2 INTERNATIONAL CAR REGISTRATION FOR Tunisia.

tng ABBREVIATION FOR training.

TNT NOUN 2,4,6-trinitrotoluene; a yellow solid: used chiefly as a high explosive and is also an intermediate in the manufacture of dyestuffs. Formula: $CH_3C_6H_2(NO_2)_3$.

T-number *or* **T number** NOUN *Photog* a function of the f-number of a camera lens that takes into account the amount of light actually transmitted by the lens.
▷HISTORY from *T(otal Light Transmission) Number*

to¹ (tu:; *unstressed before a vowel* tʊ; *unstressed before a consonant* tə) PREPOSITION 1 used to indicate the destination of the subject or object of an action: *he climbed to the top.* 2 used to mark the indirect object of a verb in a sentence: *telling stories to children.* 3 used to mark the infinitive of a verb: *he wanted to go.* 4 as far as; until: *working from Monday to Friday.* 5 used to indicate equality: *16 ounces to the pound.* 6 against; upon; onto: *put your ear to the wall.* 7 before the hour of: *five minutes to four.* 8 accompanied by: *dancing to loud music.* 9 as compared with, as against: *the score was eight to three.* 10 used to indicate a resulting condition: *he tore her dress to shreds; they starved to death.* 11 a dialect word for **at¹**. *he's to town; where's it to.* ◆ ADVERB 12 towards a fixed position, esp (of a door) closed.
▷HISTORY Old English *tō*; related to Old Frisian, Old Saxon *to,* Old High German *zuo,* Latin *do-* as in *dōnec* until

to² THE INTERNET DOMAIN NAME FOR Tonga.

toad (təʊd) NOUN 1 any anuran amphibian of the class *Bufonidae,* such as *Bufo bufo* (**common toad**) of Europe. They are similar to frogs but are more terrestrial, having a drier warty skin. Related adjective: **batrachian.** 2 any of various similar amphibians of different families. 3 a loathsome person.
▷HISTORY Old English *tādige,* of unknown origin; see TADPOLE
▸ **'toadish** *or* **'toad,like** ADJECTIVE

toadeater ('təʊd,i:tə) NOUN a rare word for **toady** (sense 1).
▷HISTORY C17: originally a mountebank's assistant who would pretend to eat toads (believed to be poisonous), hence a servile flatterer, toady

toadfish ('təʊd,fɪʃ) NOUN, *plural* **-fish** *or* **-fishes.** any spiny-finned bottom-dwelling marine fish of the family *Batrachoididae,* of tropical and temperate seas, having a flattened tapering body and a wide mouth.

toadflax ('təʊd,flæks) NOUN any of various scrophulariaceous plants of the genus *Linaria,* esp *L. vulgaris,* having narrow leaves and spurred two-lipped yellow-orange flowers. Also called: **butter-and-eggs.**

toad-in-the-hole NOUN *Brit and Austral* a dish made of sausages baked in a batter.

toad spit *or* **spittle** NOUN another name for **cuckoo spit.**

toadstone ('təʊd,stəʊn) NOUN *Rare* an amygdaloidal basalt occurring in the limestone regions of Derbyshire.
▷HISTORY C18: perhaps from a supposed resemblance to a toad's spotted skin

toadstool ('təʊd,stu:l) NOUN (*not in technical use*) any basidiomycetous fungus with a capped spore-producing body that is not edible. Compare **mushroom** (sense 1a).
▷HISTORY C14: from TOAD + STOOL

toady ('təʊdɪ) NOUN, *plural* **toadies.** 1 a person who flatters and ingratiates himself in a servile way; sycophant. ◆ VERB **toadies, toadying, toadied.** 2 to fawn on and flatter (someone).
▷HISTORY C19: shortened from TOADEATER
▸ **'toadyish** ADJECTIVE ▸ **'toadyism** NOUN

Toamasina (*Portuguese* tõʊma'sinə) NOUN a port in E Madagascar, on the Indian Ocean: the country's chief commercial centre. Pop.: 127 441 (1993). Former name (until 1979): **Tamatave.**

to and fro ADJECTIVE, ADVERB **to-and-fro.** 1 back and forth. 2 here and there.
▸ **toing and froing** NOUN

toast¹ (təʊst) NOUN 1 sliced bread browned by exposure to heat, usually under a grill, over a fire, or in a toaster. 2 **be toast.** *Informal* to face certain destruction or defeat. ◆ VERB 3 (*tr*) to brown under a grill or over a fire: *to toast cheese.* 4 to warm or be warmed in a similar manner: *to toast one's hands by the fire.*
▷HISTORY C14: from Old French *toster,* from Latin *tōstus* parched, baked from *torrēre* to dry with heat; see THIRST, TORRID
▸ **'toasty** ADJECTIVE

toast² (təʊst) NOUN 1 a tribute or proposal of health, success, etc., given to a person or thing by a company of people and marked by raising glasses and drinking together. 2 a person or thing honoured by such a tribute or proposal. 3 (esp formerly) an attractive woman to whom such tributes are frequently made: *she was the toast of the town.* ◆ VERB 4 to propose or drink a toast to (a person or thing). 5 (*intr*) to add vocal effects to a prerecorded track: a disc-jockey technique. See also **rap¹** (sense 6).
▷HISTORY C17 (in the sense: a lady to whom the company is asked to drink): from TOAST¹,from the idea that the name of the lady would flavour the drink like a piece of spiced toast
▸ **'toaster** NOUN

toaster ('təʊstə) NOUN a device for toasting bread, usually electric, and often equipped with an automatic timer.

toastmaster ('təʊst,mɑ:stə) NOUN a person who introduces after-dinner speakers, proposes or announces toasts, etc., at public or formal dinners.
▸ **'toast,mistress** FEMININE NOUN

toast rack NOUN a small stand consisting of a usually oblong base with a number of open-sided partitions between which pieces of toast may be stood upright.

toasty *or* **toastie** ('təʊstɪ) NOUN, *plural* **toasties.** a toasted sandwich.

Tob. ABBREVIATION FOR Tobit.

tobacco (tə'bækəʊ) NOUN, *plural* **-cos** *or* **-coes.** 1 any of numerous solanaceous plants of the genus *Nicotiana,* having mildly narcotic properties, tapering hairy leaves, and tubular or funnel-shaped fragrant flowers. The species *N. tabacum* is cultivated as the chief source of commercial tobacco. 2 the leaves of certain of these plants dried and prepared for snuff, chewing, or smoking.
▷HISTORY C16: from Spanish *tabaco,* perhaps from Taino: leaves rolled for smoking, assumed by the Spaniards to be the name of the plant
▸ **to'baccoless** ADJECTIVE

tobacco mosaic virus NOUN the virus that causes mosaic disease in tobacco and related plants: its discovery in 1892 provided the first evidence of the existence of viruses. Abbreviation: **TMV.**

tobacconist (tə'bækənɪst) NOUN *Chiefly Brit* a person or shop that sells tobacco, cigarettes, pipes, etc.

Tobago (tə'beɪgəʊ) NOUN an island in the SE Caribbean, northeast of Trinidad: ceded to Britain in 1814; joined with Trinidad in 1888 as a British colony; part of the independent republic of Trinidad and Tobago. Pop.: 46 400 (1990).

Tobagonian (,təʊbə'gəʊnɪən) ADJECTIVE 1 of or relating to Tobago or its inhabitants. ◆ NOUN 2 a native or inhabitant of Tobago.

-to-be ADJECTIVE (*in combination*) about to be; future: *a mother-to-be; the bride-to-be.*

Tobin tax ('təʊbɪn) NOUN a proposed tax on foreign-exchange transactions intended to discourage destabilizing speculation while also raising large revenues that could be channelled to the developing world.
▷HISTORY late C20: after James *Tobin* (1918–2002), US economist who proposed it

Tobit ('təʊbɪt) NOUN *Old Testament* 1 a pious Jew who was released from blindness through the help of the archangel Raphael. 2 a book of the Apocrypha relating this story.

toboggan (tə'bɒgən) NOUN 1 a light wooden frame on runners used for sliding over snow and ice. 2 a long narrow sledge made of a thin board curved upwards and backwards at the front. ◆ VERB **-gans, -ganing, -ganed.** (*intr*) 3 to ride on a toboggan.
▷HISTORY C19: from Canadian French, from Algonquian; related to Abnaki *udābāgan*
▸ **to'bogganer** *or* **to'bogganist** NOUN

Tobol (*Russian* ta'bɔl) NOUN a river in central Asia, rising in N Kazakhstan and flowing northeast into Russia to join the Irtysh River. Length: about 1300 km (800 miles).

Tobolsk (*Russian* ta'bɔljsk) NOUN a town in central Russia, at the confluence of the Irtysh and Tobol Rivers: the chief centre for the early Russian colonization of Siberia. Pop.: 100 000 (1989 est.).

Tobruk (tə'brʊk, təʊ-) NOUN a small port in NE Libya, in E Cyrenaica on the Mediterranean coast road: scene of severe fighting in World War II: taken from the Italians by the British in January 1941, from the British by the Germans in June 1942, and finally taken by the British in November 1942.

toby ('təʊbɪ) NOUN, *plural* **-bies.** a water stopcock at the boundary of a street and house section.

toby jug ('təʊbɪ) NOUN a beer mug or jug typically in the form of a stout seated man wearing a three-cornered hat and smoking a pipe. Also called: **toby.**
▷HISTORY C19: from the familiar form of the Christian name *Tobias*

TOC *or* **toc** (tɒk) NOUN ACRONYM FOR train operating company.

Tocantins (*Portuguese* tokã'tĩs) NOUN 1 a state of N Brazil, created from the northern part of Goiás state in 1988. Capital: Palmas. Pop.: 1 155 251 (2000). Area: 278 421 sq. km (107 499 sq. miles). 2 a river in E Brazil, rising in S central Goiás state and flowing generally north to the Pará River. Length: about 2700 km (1700 miles).

toccata (tə'kɑ:tə) NOUN a rapid keyboard composition for organ, harpsichord, etc., dating from the baroque period, usually in a rhythmically free style.
▷HISTORY C18: from Italian, literally: touched, from *toccare* to play (an instrument), TOUCH

Toc H ('tɒk 'eɪtʃ) NOUN a society formed in England after World War I to fight loneliness and hate and to encourage Christian comradeship.
▷HISTORY C20: from the obsolete telegraphic code for *T.H.,* initials of *Talbot House,* Poperinge, Belgium, the original headquarters of the society

Tocharian *or* **Tokharian** (tɒ'kɑ:rɪən) NOUN 1 a member of an Asian people with a complex material culture, sometimes thought to be of European origin, who lived in the Tarim Basin until overcome by the Uighurs around 800 A.D. 2 the language of this people, known from records in a N Indian script of the 7th and 8th centuries A.D. It belongs to the Indo-European family, is regarded as forming an independent branch, and shows closer affinities with the W or European group than with the E or Indo-Iranian group. The language is recorded in two dialects, known as **Tocharian A** and **Tocharian B.**
▷HISTORY C20: ultimately from Greek *Tokharoi,* name of uncertain origin

tocher ('tɒxər) *Scot* ◆ NOUN 1 a dowry. ◆ VERB (*tr*) 2 to give a dowry to.
▷HISTORY C15: from Scot Gaelic *tochradh*

tockley ('tɒklɪ) NOUN *Austral* a slang word for **penis.**

tocky ('tɒkɪ) ADJECTIVE **tockier, tockiest.** *Midland English dialect* muddy.

tocology *or* **tokology** (tɒ'kɒlədʒɪ) NOUN the branch of medicine concerned with childbirth; obstetrics.
▷HISTORY C19: from Greek *tokos* childbirth, from *tiktein* to bear

tocopherol (tɒ'kɒfəˌrɒl) NOUN *Biochem* any of a group of fat-soluble alcohols that occur in wheat-germ oil, watercress, lettuce, egg yolk, etc. They are thought to be necessary for healthy human reproduction. Also called: **vitamin E.**
▷HISTORY C20: from *toco-*, from Greek *tokos* offspring (see TOCOLOGY) + *-pher-*, from *pherein* to bear + -OL[1]

tocsin ('tɒksɪn) NOUN 1 an alarm or warning signal, esp one sounded on a bell. 2 an alarm bell.
▷HISTORY C16: from French, from Old French *toquassen*, from Old Provençal *tocasenh*, from *tocar* to TOUCH + *senh* bell, from Latin *signum*

tod[1] (tɒd) NOUN *Brit* a unit of weight, used for wool, etc., usually equal to 28 pounds.
▷HISTORY C15: probably related to Frisian *todde* rag, Old High German *zotta* tuft of hair

tod[2] (tɒd) NOUN **on one's tod.** *Brit slang* on one's own.
▷HISTORY C19: rhyming slang *Tod Sloan/alone*, after *Tod* Sloan, a jockey

tod[3] (tɒd) NOUN a Scot and northern English dialect word for a **fox.**
▷HISTORY C12: of unknown origin

today (tə'deɪ) NOUN 1 this day, as distinct from yesterday or tomorrow. 2 the present age: *children of today.* ◆ ADVERB 3 during or on this day. 4 nowadays.
▷HISTORY Old English *tō dæge*, literally: on this day, from TO[1] + *dæge*, dative of *dæg* DAY

toddle ('tɒdᵊl) VERB (*intr*) 1 to walk with short unsteady steps, as a child does when learning to walk. 2 (foll by *off*) *Jocular* to depart. 3 (foll by *round, over*, etc.) *Jocular* to stroll; amble. ◆ NOUN 4 the act or an instance of toddling.
▷HISTORY C16 (Scottish and northern English): of obscure origin

toddler ('tɒdlə) NOUN 1 a young child, usually one between the ages of one and two and a half. 2 (*modifier*) designed or suitable for a toddler: *toddler suits.*
▸'**toddler,hood** NOUN

toddy ('tɒdɪ) NOUN, *plural* **-dies.** 1 a drink made from spirits, esp whisky, with hot water, sugar, and usually lemon juice. 2 **a** the sap of various palm trees (**toddy** or **wine palms**), used as a beverage. **b** the liquor prepared from this sap. 3 (in Malaysia) a milky-white sour alcoholic drink made from fermented coconut milk, drunk chiefly by Indians.
▷HISTORY C17: from Hindi *tārī* juice of the palmyra palm, from *tār* palmyra palm, from Sanskrit *tāra*, probably of Dravidian origin

to-do (tə'du:) NOUN, *plural* **-dos.** a commotion, fuss, or quarrel.

tody ('təʊdɪ) NOUN, *plural* **-dies.** any small bird of the family *Todidae* of the Caribbean, having a red-and-green plumage and long straight bill: order *Coraciiformes* (kingfishers, etc.).
▷HISTORY C18: from French *todier*, from Latin *todus* small bird

toe (təʊ) NOUN 1 any one of the digits of the foot. 2 the corresponding part in other vertebrates. 3 the part of a shoe, sock, etc., covering the toes. 4 anything resembling a toe in shape or position. 5 the front part of the head of a golf club, hockey stick, etc. 6 the lower bearing of a vertical shaft assembly. 7 the tip of a cam follower that engages the cam profile. 8 **dip one's toe** (*or* **toes**) **in.** *Informal* to begin doing or try something new or unfamiliar. 9 **on one's toes.** alert. 10 **tread on someone's toes.** to offend or insult a person, esp by trespassing on his field of responsibility. 11 **turn up one's toes.** *Informal* to die. 12 *Austral slang* speed: *a player with plenty of toe.* ◆ VERB **toes, toeing, toed.** 13 (*tr*) to touch, kick, or mark with the toe. 14 (*tr*) *Golf* to strike (the ball) with the toe of the club. 15 (*tr*) to drive (a nail, spike, etc.) obliquely. 16 (*intr*) to walk with the toes pointing in a specified direction: *to toe inwards.* 17 to conform to expected standards, attitudes, etc.
▷HISTORY Old English *tā*; related to Old Frisian *tāne*, Old Norse *tā*, Old High German *zēha*, Latin *digitus* finger
▸'**toe,like** ADJECTIVE

toea ('təʊɑ:) NOUN, *plural* **toea.** a monetary unit of Papua New Guinea, worth one-hundredth of a kina.
▷HISTORY from a Papuan language

toe and heel NOUN a technique used by racing drivers while changing gear on sharp bends, in which the brake is operated by the toe (or heel) of the right foot while the heel (or toe) simultaneously operates the accelerator.

toecap ('təʊˌkæp) NOUN a reinforced covering for the toe of a boot or shoe.

toe crack NOUN *Vet science* a sand crack occurring on the forepart of the hind foot of a horse.

toe-curling ADJECTIVE *Informal* causing feelings of acute embarrassment.
▸'**toe-,curlingly** ADVERB

toed (təʊd) ADJECTIVE 1 having a part resembling a toe. 2 (of a vertical or oblique member of a timber frame) fixed by nails driven in at the foot. 3 (*in combination*) having a toe or toes as specified: *five-toed.*

toe dance NOUN 1 a dance performed on tiptoe. ◆ VERB **toe-dance.** 2 (*intr*) *Ballet* to dance on pointes.
▸**toe dancer** NOUN

toehold ('təʊˌhəʊld) NOUN 1 a small foothold to facilitate climbing. 2 any means of gaining access, support, etc.: *the socialist party gained a toehold in the local elections.* 3 a wrestling hold in which the opponent's toe is held and his leg twisted against the joints.

toe-in NOUN a slight forward convergence given to the wheels of motor vehicles to improve steering and equalize tyre wear.

toenail ('təʊˌneɪl) NOUN 1 a thin horny translucent plate covering part of the dorsal surface of the end joint of each toe. Related adjectives: **ungual, ungular.** 2 *Carpentry* a nail driven obliquely, as in joining one beam at right angles to another. 3 *Printing, slang* a parenthesis. ◆ VERB 4 (*tr*) *Carpentry* to join (beams) by driving nails obliquely.

toerag ('təʊˌræg) NOUN *Brit slang* a contemptible or despicable person.
▷HISTORY C20: originally, a beggar, tramp: from the pieces of rag they wrapped round their feet

toetoe ('tɔɪtɔɪ, 'təʊi:ˌtəʊi:, ˌtəʊi:'təʊi:) NOUN See **toitoi.**

toey ('təʊɪ) ADJECTIVE *Austral slang* 1 (of a person) nervous or anxious. 2 *Rare* (of a horse) eager to race. 3 **toey as a Roman sandal.** very anxious.

toff (tɒf) NOUN *Brit slang* a rich, well-dressed, or upper-class person, esp a man.
▷HISTORY C19: perhaps variant of TUFT, nickname for a titled student at Oxford University, wearing a cap with a gold tassel

toffee *or* **toffy** ('tɒfɪ) NOUN, *plural* **-fees** *or* **-fies.** 1 a sweet made from sugar or treacle boiled with butter, nuts, etc. 2 **for toffee.** (preceded by *can't*) *Informal* to be incompetent at a specified activity: *he can't sing for toffee.*
▷HISTORY C19: variant of earlier TAFFY

toffee-apple NOUN an apple fixed on a stick and coated with a thin layer of toffee.

toffee-nosed ADJECTIVE *Slang, chiefly Brit* pretentious or supercilious; used esp of snobbish people.
▷HISTORY C20: perhaps coined as a pun on *toffy* stylish, grand: see TOFF

toffish ('tɒfɪʃ) ADJECTIVE *Brit informal* belonging to or characteristic of the upper class.

toft (tɒft) NOUN *Brit history* 1 a homestead. 2 an entire holding, consisting of a homestead and the attached arable land.
▷HISTORY Old English, from Old Norse *topt*

tofu ('təʊˌfu:) NOUN unfermented soya-bean curd, a food with a soft cheeselike consistency made from soya-bean milk.
▷HISTORY from Japanese

tog[1] (tɒg) *Informal* ◆ VERB **togs, togging, togged.** 1 (often foll by *up* or *out*) to dress oneself, esp in smart clothes. ◆ NOUN 2 See **togs.**
▷HISTORY C18: probably short for obsolete cant *togemans* coat, from Latin *toga* TOGA + *-mans*, of uncertain origin

tog[2] (tɒg) NOUN **a** a unit of thermal resistance used to measure the power of insulation of a fabric, garment, quilt, etc. The tog-value of an article is equal to ten times the temperature difference between its two faces, in degrees Celsius, when the flow of heat across it is equal to one watt per m². **b** (*as modifier*): *tog-rating.*
▷HISTORY C20: arbitrary coinage from TOG[1] (noun)

toga ('təʊgə) NOUN 1 a garment worn by citizens of ancient Rome, consisting of a piece of cloth draped around the body. 2 the official vestment of certain offices.
▷HISTORY C16: from Latin, related to *tegere* to cover
▸**togaed** ('təʊgəd) ADJECTIVE

toga praetexta (pri:'tɛkstə) NOUN (in ancient Rome) a toga with a broad purple border worn by certain magistrates and priests and by boys until they assumed the toga virilis.
▷HISTORY Latin, literally: bordered toga

toga virilis (vɪ'raɪlɪs) NOUN (in ancient Rome) the toga assumed by a youth at the age of 14 as a symbol of manhood and citizenship.
▷HISTORY Latin, literally: manly (i.e., man's) toga

together (tə'gɛðə) ADVERB 1 with cooperation and interchange between constituent elements, members, etc.: *we worked together.* 2 in or into contact or union with each other: *to stick papers together.* 3 in or into one place or assembly; with each other: *the people are gathered together.* 4 at the same time: *we left school together.* 5 considered collectively or jointly: *all our wages put together couldn't buy that car.* 6 continuously: *working for eight hours together.* 7 closely, cohesively, or compactly united or held: *water will hold the dough together.* 8 mutually or reciprocally: *to multiply seven and eight together.* 9 *Informal* organized: *to get things together.* 10 **together with.** in addition to. ◆ ADJECTIVE 11 *Slang* self-possessed and well-organized; mentally and emotionally stable: *she's a very together lady.*
▷HISTORY Old English *tōgædre*; related to Old Frisian *togadera*, Middle High German *gater*; see GATHER

Language note See at **plus.**

togetherness (tə'gɛðənɪs) NOUN a feeling of closeness or affection from being united with other people.

togger ('tɒgə) VERB (*intr*) *Northern English dialect* to play football.

toggery ('tɒgərɪ) NOUN *Informal* clothes; togs.

toggle ('tɒgᵊl) NOUN 1 a wooden peg or metal rod fixed crosswise through an eye at the end of a rope, chain, or cable, for fastening temporarily by insertion through an eye in another rope, chain, etc. 2 a wooden or plastic bar-shaped button inserted through a loop for fastening. 3 a pin inserted into a nautical knot to keep it secure. 4 *Machinery* a toggle joint or a device having such a joint. ◆ VERB 5 (*tr*) to supply or fasten with a toggle or toggles. 6 *Computing* (*intr*, often foll by *between*) to switch to a different option, view, application, etc.
▷HISTORY C18: of unknown origin
▸'**toggler** NOUN

toggle iron NOUN a whaling harpoon with a pivoting barb near its head to prevent a harpooned whale pulling free. Also called: **toggle harpoon.**

toggle joint NOUN a device consisting of two arms pivoted at a common joint and at their outer ends and used to apply pressure by straightening the angle between the two arms.

toggle switch NOUN 1 an electric switch having a projecting lever that is manipulated in a particular way to open or close a circuit. 2 a computer device that is used to turn a feature on or off.

Togliatti (ˌtɒlɪ'ætɪ) NOUN a city in W central Russia, on the Volga River: automobile industry: renamed in honour of Palmiro Togliatti, an Italian communist. Pop.: 720 300 (1999 est.). Former name (until 1964): **Stavropol.** Russian name: **Tolyatti.**

Togo ('təʊgəʊ) NOUN a republic in West Africa, on the Gulf of Guinea: became French Togoland (a League of Nations mandate) after the division of German Togoland in 1922; independent since 1960. Official language: French. Religion: animist majority. Currency: franc. Capital: Lomé. Pop.: 5 153 000 (2001 est.). Area: 56 700 sq. km (20 900 sq. miles).

Togoland ('təʊgəʊˌlænd) NOUN a former German

protectorate in West Africa on the Gulf of Guinea: divided in 1922 into the League of Nations mandates of British Togoland (west) and French Togoland (east); the former joined Ghana in 1957; the latter became independent as Togo in 1960.

Togolander (ˈtəʊgəʊˌlændə) NOUN a native or inhabitant of the former British Togoland (now part of Ghana) or French Togoland (now Togo).

Togolese (ˌtəʊgəˈliːz) ADJECTIVE [1] of or relating to Togo or its inhabitants. ◆ NOUN [2] a native or inhabitant of Togo.

togs (tɒgz) PLURAL NOUN *Informal* [1] clothes. [2] *Austral, NZ, and Irish* a swimming costume.
▷HISTORY from TOG[1]

toheroa (ˌtəʊəˈrəʊə) NOUN [1] a bivalve mollusc, *Amphidesma* (or *Semele*) *ventricosum,* of New Zealand. [2] a greenish soup made of this.
▷HISTORY from Maori

tohunga (ˈtɒhʊŋə, tɒˈhʊŋə) NOUN *NZ* a Maori priest, the repository of traditional lore.

toil[1] (tɔɪl) NOUN [1] hard or exhausting work. [2] an obsolete word for **strife.** ◆ VERB [3] (*intr*) to labour. [4] (*intr*) to progress with slow painful movements: *to toil up a hill.* [5] (*tr*) *Archaic* to achieve by toil.
▷HISTORY C13: from Anglo-French *toiler* to struggle, from Old French *toeillier* to confuse, from Latin *tudiculāre* to stir, from *tudicula* machine for bruising olives, from *tudes* a hammer, from *tundere* to beat
▸ **ˈtoiler** NOUN

toil[2] (tɔɪl) NOUN [1] (*often plural*) a net or snare: *the toils of fortune had ensnared him.* [2] *Archaic* a trap for wild beasts.
▷HISTORY C16: from Old French *toile,* from Latin *tēla* loom

toile (twɑːl) NOUN [1] a transparent linen or cotton fabric. [2] a garment of exclusive design made up in cheap cloth so that alterations and experiments can be made.
▷HISTORY C19: from French, from Latin *tēla* a loom

toilet (ˈtɔɪlɪt) NOUN [1] another word for **lavatory.** [2] *Old-fashioned* the act of dressing and preparing oneself: *to make one's toilet.* [3] *Old-fashioned* a dressing table or the articles used when making one's toilet. [4] *Rare* costume. [5] the cleansing of a wound, etc., after an operation or childbirth.
▷HISTORY C16: from French *toilette* dress, from TOILE

toilet paper *or* **tissue** NOUN thin absorbent paper, often wound in a roll round a cardboard cylinder (**toilet roll**), used for cleaning oneself after defecation or urination.

toiletry (ˈtɔɪlɪtrɪ) NOUN, *plural* **-ries.** an object or cosmetic used in making up, dressing, etc.

toilet set NOUN a matching set consisting of a hairbrush, comb, mirror, and clothes brush.

toilet soap NOUN a mild soap, often coloured and scented, used for washing oneself.

toilette (twɑːˈlɛt; *French* twalɛt) NOUN *Usually literary or affected* another word for **toilet** (sense 2).
▷HISTORY C16: from French; see TOILET

toilet training NOUN the process of teaching young children to control the timing of bladder and bowel movements and to use the lavatory.

toilet water NOUN a form of liquid perfume lighter than cologne. Compare **cologne.** Also called: **eau de toilette.**

toilsome (ˈtɔɪlsəm) *or* **toilful** ADJECTIVE laborious.
▸ **ˈtoilsomely** ADVERB ▸ **ˈtoilsomeness** NOUN

toitoi[1] (ˈtɔɪtɔɪ) *or* **toetoe** NOUN, *plural* **-tois** *or* **-toes.** any of various tall grasses of the genus *Cortaderia* of New Zealand, with feathery fronds.
▷HISTORY Maori

toitoi[2] (ˈtɔɪtɔɪ) NOUN *NZ* another name for **bully[2].**

tokamak (ˈtɒkəˌmæk) NOUN *Physics* a toroidal reactor used in thermonuclear experiments, in which a strong helical magnetic field keeps the plasma from contacting the external walls. The magnetic field is produced partly by current-carrying coils and partly by a large inductively driven current through the plasma.
▷HISTORY C20: from Russian *to(roidál'naya) kám(era s) ak(siál'nym magnitnym pólem),* toroidal chamber with magnetic field

tokay (ˈtəʊkeɪ) NOUN a small gecko, *Gekko gecko,* of S and SE Asia, having a retractile claw at the tip of each digit.
▷HISTORY from Malay *toke,* of imitative origin

Tokay (təʊˈkeɪ) NOUN [1] a fine sweet wine made near Tokaj, Hungary. [2] a variety of large sweet grape used to make this wine. [3] a similar wine made elsewhere.

toke (təʊk) *Slang* ◆ NOUN [1] a draw on a cannabis cigarette. ◆ VERB (*intr*) [2] to take a draw on a cannabis cigarette.
▸ **ˈtoker** NOUN

Tokelau Islands (ˈtəʊkəˌlaʊ) PLURAL NOUN an island group in the South Pacific composed of three atolls, Nukunono, Atafu, and Fakaofo, which in 1948 was included within the territorial boundaries of New Zealand. Pop.: 1577 (1991). Area: about 11 sq. km (4 sq. miles).

token (ˈtəʊkən) NOUN [1] an indication, warning, or sign of something. [2] a symbol or visible representation of something. [3] something that indicates authority, proof, or authenticity. [4] a metal or plastic disc, such as a substitute for currency for use in slot machines. [5] a memento. [6] a gift voucher that can be used as payment for goods of a specified value. [7] (*modifier*) as a matter of form only; nominal: *a token increase in salary.* [8] *Linguistics* a symbol regarded as an individual concrete mark, not as a class of identical symbols. Compare **type** (sense 11). [9] *Philosophy* an individual instance: if the same sentence has different truth-values on different occasions of utterance the truth-value may be said to attach to the sentence-token. Compare **type** (sense 13). [10] **by the same token.** moreover and for the same or a similar reason. ◆ VERB [11] (*tr*) to act or serve as a warning or symbol of; betoken.
▷HISTORY Old English *tācen;* related to Old Frisian *tēken,* Old Saxon *tēkan,* Old High German *zeihhan,* Old Norse *teikn;* see TEACH

token economy NOUN a type of psychotherapy in which the inmates of an institution are rewarded for good behaviour with tokens that can be exchanged for privileges.

tokenism (ˈtəʊkəˌnɪzəm) NOUN the practice of making only a token effort or doing no more than the minimum, esp in order to comply with a law.
▸ **ˌtokenˈistic** ADJECTIVE

token money NOUN coins of the regular issue having greater face value than the value of their metal content.

token payment NOUN a small payment made in acknowledgment of the existence of debt.

token strike NOUN a brief strike intended to convey strength of feeling on a disputed issue.

token vote NOUN a Parliamentary vote of money in which the amount quoted to aid discussion is not intended to be binding.

Tokharian (tɒˈkɑːrɪən) NOUN a variant spelling of **Tocharian.**

tokology (tɒˈkɒlədʒɪ) NOUN a variant spelling of **tocology.**

tokoloshe (ˌtɒkɒˈlɒʃ, -ˈlɒʃɪ) NOUN (in Bantu folklore) a malevolent mythical manlike animal of short stature. Also called: **tikoloshe.**
▷HISTORY from Xhosa *uthikoloshe*

Tokyo (ˈtəʊkjəʊ, -kɪˌəʊ) NOUN the capital of Japan, a port on SE Honshu on **Tokyo Bay** (an inlet of the Pacific): part of the largest conurbation in the world (the Tokyo-Yukohama metropolitan area) of over 25 million people; major industrial centre and the chief cultural centre of Japan. Pop.: 7 966 195 (1995).

tola (ˈtəʊlə) NOUN a unit of weight, used in India, equal to 180 ser or 180 grains.
▷HISTORY C17: from Hindi *tolā,* from Sanskrit *tulā* scale, from *tul* to weigh

tolan (ˈtəʊlæn) *or* **tolane** (ˈtəʊleɪn) NOUN a white crystalline derivative of acetylene; diphenylacetylene; diphenylethyne. Formula: $C_6H_5C{:}CC_6H_5$.
▷HISTORY C19: from TOL(UENE) + *-an* (see -ANE)

tolar (ˈtɒlɑː) NOUN, *plural* **tolarji** (ˈtɒlɑːjɪ). the standard monetary unit of Slovenia, divided into 100 stotin.
▷HISTORY C20: Slovene, from German *Taler* DOLLAR

tolbooth (ˈtəʊlˌbuːθ, -ˌbuːð, ˈtɒl-) NOUN [1] *Chiefly Scot* a town hall. [2] a variant spelling of **tollbooth.**

tolbutamide (tɒlˈbjuːtəˌmaɪd) NOUN a synthetic crystalline compound administered orally in the treatment of diabetes to lower blood glucose concentrations. Formula: $C_{12}H_{18}N_2O_3S$.
▷HISTORY C20: from TOL(UYL) + BUT(YRIC ACID) + AMIDE

told (təʊld) VERB [1] the past tense and past participle of **tell[1].** ◆ ADJECTIVE [2] See **all told.**

tole (təʊl) NOUN enamelled or lacquered metal ware, usually gilded, popular in the 18th century.
▷HISTORY from French *tôle* sheet metal, from French (dialect): table, from Latin *tabula* table

Toledo NOUN [1] (tɒˈleɪdəʊ; *Spanish* toˈleðo) a city in central Spain, on the River Tagus: capital of Visigothic Spain, and of Castile from 1087 to 1560; famous for steel and swords since the first century. Pop.: 63 560 (1991). Ancient name: **Toletum** (təˈliːtəm). [2] (təˈliːdəʊ) an inland port in NW Ohio, on Lake Erie: one of the largest coal-shipping ports in the world; transportation and industrial centre; university (1872). Pop.: 313 619 (2000). [3] a fine-tapered sword or sword blade.

tolerable (ˈtɒlərəbᵊl) ADJECTIVE [1] able to be tolerated; endurable. [2] permissible. [3] *Informal* fairly good.
▸ **ˈtolerableness** *or* **ˌtoleraˈbility** NOUN ▸ **ˈtolerably** ADVERB

tolerance (ˈtɒlərəns) NOUN [1] the state or quality of being tolerant. [2] capacity to endure something, esp pain or hardship. [3] the permitted variation in some measurement or other characteristic of an object or workpiece. [4] *Physiol* the capacity of an organism to endure the effects of a poison or other substance, esp after it has been taken over a prolonged period.

tolerance zone NOUN an designated area where prostitutes can work without being arrested.

tolerant (ˈtɒlərənt) ADJECTIVE [1] able to tolerate the beliefs, actions, opinions, etc., of others. [2] permissive. [3] able to withstand extremes, as of heat and cold. [4] *Med* (of a patient) exhibiting tolerance to a drug.
▸ **ˈtolerantly** ADVERB

tolerate (ˈtɒləˌreɪt) VERB (*tr*) [1] to treat with indulgence, liberality, or forbearance. [2] to permit. [3] to be able to bear; put up with. [4] *Med* to have tolerance for (a drug, poison, etc.).
▷HISTORY C16: from Latin *tolerāre* sustain; related to THOLE[2]
▸ **ˈtolerative** ADJECTIVE ▸ **ˈtolerˌator** NOUN

toleration (ˌtɒləˈreɪʃən) NOUN [1] the act or practice of tolerating. [2] freedom to hold religious opinions that differ from the established or prescribed religion of a country.
▸ **ˌtolerˈationism** NOUN ▸ **ˌtolerˈationist** NOUN

tolidine (ˈtɒlɪˌdiːn) NOUN any of several isomeric compounds, esp the *ortho-* isomer, which is a white or reddish crystalline substance used in the manufacture of dyes and resins. Formula: $(C_6H_3NH_2CH_3)_2$.
▷HISTORY C19: from TOL(UENE) + -ID[3] + -INE[2]

Tolima (*Spanish* toˈlima) NOUN a volcano in W Colombia, in the Andes. Height: 5215 m (17 110 ft.).

toll[1] (təʊl) VERB [1] to ring or cause to ring slowly and recurrently. [2] (*tr*) to summon, warn, or announce by tolling. [3] *US and Canadian* to decoy (game, esp ducks). ◆ NOUN [4] the act or sound of tolling.
▷HISTORY C15: perhaps related to Old English *-tyllan,* as in *fortyllan* to attract

toll[2] (təʊl, tɒl) NOUN [1] **a** an amount of money levied, esp for the use of certain roads, bridges, etc., to cover the cost of maintenance. **b** (*as modifier*): *toll road; toll bridge.* [2] loss or damage incurred through an accident, disaster, etc.: *the war took its toll of the inhabitants.* [3] Also called: **tollage.** (formerly) the right to levy a toll. [4] Also called: **toll charge.** *NZ* a charge for a telephone call beyond a free-dialling area.
▷HISTORY Old English *toln;* related to Old Frisian *tolene,* Old High German *zol* toll, from Late Latin *telōnium* customs house, from Greek *telōnion,* ultimately from *telos* tax

tollbooth *or* **tolbooth** (ˈtəʊlˌbuːθ, -ˌbuːð, ˈtɒl-) NOUN a booth or kiosk at which a toll is collected.

toll call NOUN [1] *Brit obsolete* a short-distance trunk call. [2] *US* a long-distance telephone call at a rate higher than that for a local call. [3] *NZ* a telephone call beyond a free-dialling area for which a charge is made.

tollgate ('təʊl,geɪt, 'tɒl-) NOUN a gate across a toll road or bridge at which travellers must stop and pay.

tollhouse ('təʊl,haʊs, 'tɒl-) NOUN a small house at a tollgate occupied by a toll collector.

tolly *or* **tollie** ('tɒlɪ) NOUN, *plural* **-lies**. *South African* a castrated calf.
▷HISTORY C19: from Xhosa *ithole* calf on which the horns have begun to appear

Tolpuddle Martyrs ('tɒl,pʌdᵊl) NOUN six farm workers sentenced to transportation for seven years in 1834 for administering an unlawful oath to form a trade union in the village of Tolpuddle, Dorset.

Toltec ('tɒltɛk) NOUN, *plural* **-tecs** *or* **-tec**. [1] a member of a Central American Indian people who dominated the valley of Mexico from their capital Tula from about 950 to 1160 A.D., when the valley was overrun by the Aztecs. ◆ ADJECTIVE *also* **Toltecan**. [2] of or relating to this people.
▷HISTORY C19: from Spanish *tolteca*, of American Indian origin

tolu (tɒ'lu:) NOUN an aromatic balsam obtained from a South American tree, *Myroxylon balsamum*. See **balsam** (sense 1).
▷HISTORY C17: after *Santiago de Tolu*, Colombia, from which it was exported

toluate ('tɒljʊ,eɪt) NOUN any salt or ester of any of the three isomeric forms of toluic acid.
▷HISTORY C19: from TOLU(IC ACID) + -ATE[1]

Toluca (*Spanish* to'luka) NOUN [1] a city in S central Mexico, capital of Mexico state, at an altitude of 2640 m (8660 ft.). Pop.: 435 000 (2000 est.). Official name: **Toluca de Lerdo** (de'lɛrðo). [2] **Nevado de** (ne'βaðo de) a volcano in central Mexico, in Mexico state near Toluca: crater partly filled by a lake. Height: 4577 m (15 017 ft.).

toluene ('tɒljʊ,i:n) NOUN a colourless volatile flammable liquid with an odour resembling that of benzene, obtained from petroleum and coal tar and used as a solvent and in the manufacture of many organic chemicals. Formula: $C_6H_5CH_3$.
▷HISTORY C19: from TOLU + -ENE, since it was previously obtained from tolu

toluic acid (tɒ'lu:ɪk) NOUN a white crystalline derivative of toluene existing in three isomeric forms; methylbenzoic acid. The *ortho-* and *para-* isomers are used in synthetic resins and the *meta-* isomer is used as an insect repellent. Formula: $C_6H_4CH_3COOH$.
▷HISTORY C19: from TOLU(ENE) + -IC

toluidine (tɒ'lju:ɪ,di:n) NOUN an amine derived from toluene existing in three isomeric forms; aminotoluene. The *ortho-* and *meta-* isomers are liquids and the *para-* isomer is a crystalline solid. All three are used in making dyes. Formula: $C_6H_4CH_3NH_2$.
▷HISTORY C19: from TOLU(ENE) + -IDE + -INE[2]

toluol ('tɒljʊ,ɒl) NOUN another name for **toluene**.

toluyl ('tɒljʊɪl) NOUN (*modifier*) of, consisting of, or containing any of three isomeric groups $CH_3C_6H_4CO$-, derived from a toluic acid by removal of the hydroxyl group: *toluyl group or radical*.
▷HISTORY C19: from TOLU(ENE) + -YL

tolyl ('tɒlɪl) NOUN [1] (*modifier*) of, consisting of, or containing any of three isomeric groups, $CH_3C_6H_4$-, derived from toluene: *tolyl group or radical*. [2] (*modifier*) another word for **benzyl**. Also called: α-**tolyl**.
▷HISTORY C19: from TOLU (see TOLUENE) + -YL

tom[1] (tɒm) NOUN **a** the male of various animals, esp the cat. **b** (*as modifier*): *a tom turkey*. **c** (*in combination*): *a tomcat*.
▷HISTORY C16: special use of the shortened form of *Thomas*, applied to any male, often implying a common or ordinary type of person, etc.

tom[2] (tɒm) NOUN *Austral and NZ* a temporary supporting post.
▷HISTORY from a specialized use of TOM[1]

tomahawk ('tɒmə,hɔ:k) NOUN [1] a fighting axe, with a stone or later an iron head, used by the North American Indians. [2] *Chiefly Austral* the usual word for **hatchet**.
▷HISTORY C17: from Virginia Algonquian *tamahaac*

tomalley ('tɒmælɪ) NOUN fat from a lobster, called "liver", and eaten as a delicacy.
▷HISTORY C17: of Caribbean origin; compare Galibi *tumali* sauce of crab or lobster liver

toman (tə'mɑ:n) NOUN a gold coin formerly issued in Persia.
▷HISTORY C16: from Persian, of Mongolian origin

Tom and Jerry NOUN *US* a hot mixed drink containing rum, brandy, egg, nutmeg, and sometimes milk.

tomato (tə'mɑ:təʊ) NOUN, *plural* **-toes**. [1] a solanaceous plant, *Lycopersicon* (or *Lycopersicum*) *esculentum*, of South America, widely cultivated for its red fleshy many-seeded edible fruits. [2] the fruit of this plant, which has slightly acid-tasting flesh and is eaten in salads, as a vegetable, etc. [3] *US and Canadian slang* a girl or woman.
▷HISTORY C17 *tomate*, from Spanish, from Nahuatl *tomatl*

tomb (tu:m) NOUN [1] a place, esp a vault beneath the ground, for the burial of a corpse. [2] a stone or other monument to the dead. [3] **the tomb.** a poetic term for **death.** [4] anything serving as a burial place: *the sea was his tomb*. ◆ VERB [5] (*tr*) *Rare* to place in a tomb; entomb.
▷HISTORY C13: from Old French *tombe*, from Late Latin *tumba* burial mound, from Greek *tumbos*; related to Latin *tumēre* to swell, Middle Irish *tomm* hill
▸ **'tomb,like** ADJECTIVE

tombac ('tɒmbæk) *or* **tambac** ('tæmbæk) NOUN any of various brittle alloys containing copper and zinc and sometimes tin and arsenic: used for making cheap jewellery, etc.
▷HISTORY C17: from French, from Dutch *tombak*, from Malay *tambâga* copper, apparently from Sanskrit *tāmraka*, from *tāmra* dark coppery red

tombola (tɒm'bəʊlə) NOUN *Brit* a type of lottery, esp at a fête, in which tickets are drawn from a revolving drum.
▷HISTORY C19: from Italian, from *tombolare* to somersault; see TUMBLE

tombolo ('tɒmbə,ləʊ) NOUN, *plural* **-los**. a narrow sand or shingle bar linking a small island with another island or the mainland.
▷HISTORY C20: from Italian, from Latin *tumulus* mound; see TUMULUS

Tombouctou (tɔ̃buktu) NOUN the French name for **Timbuktu**.

tomboy ('tɒm,bɔɪ) NOUN a girl who acts or dresses in a boyish way, liking rough outdoor activities.
▸ **'tom,boyish** ADJECTIVE ▸ **'tom,boyishly** ADVERB
▸ **'tom,boyishness** NOUN

tombstone ('tu:m,stəʊn) NOUN another word for **gravestone**.

Tombstone ('tu:m,stəʊn) NOUN a town in the US, in Arizona: scene of the gunfight at the OK Corral in 1881. Pop.: 1220 (1990).

Tom Collins NOUN a long drink consisting of gin, lime or lemon juice, sugar or syrup, and soda water.

Tom, Dick, and (or) Harry NOUN an ordinary, undistinguished, or common person (esp in the phrases **every Tom, Dick, and Harry; any Tom, Dick, or Harry**).

tome (təʊm) NOUN [1] a large weighty book. [2] one of the several volumes of a work.
▷HISTORY C16: from French, from Latin *tomus* section of larger work, from Greek *tomos* a slice, from *temnein* to cut; related to Latin *tondēre* to shear

-tome NOUN COMBINING FORM indicating an instrument for cutting: *osteotome*.
▷HISTORY from Greek *tomē* a cutting, *tomos* a slice, from *temnein* to cut

tomentum (tə'mɛntəm) NOUN, *plural* **-ta** (-tə). [1] a feltlike covering of downy hairs on leaves and other plant parts. [2] a network of minute blood vessels occurring in the human brain between the pia mater and cerebral cortex.
▷HISTORY C17: New Latin, from Latin: stuffing for cushions; related to Latin *tumēre* to swell
▸ **tomentose** (tə'mɛntəʊs) ADJECTIVE

tomfool (,tɒm'fu:l) NOUN **a** a fool. **b** (*as modifier*): *tomfool ideas*.
▷HISTORY C14: from TOM[1] + FOOL[1]
▸ **,tom'foolish** ADJECTIVE ▸ **,tom'foolishness** NOUN

tomfoolery (,tɒm'fu:lərɪ) NOUN, *plural* **-eries**. [1] foolish behaviour. [2] utter nonsense; rubbish.

tommy ('tɒmɪ) NOUN, *plural* **-mies**. (*often capital*) *Brit informal* a private in the British Army. Also called: **Tommy Atkins** ('ætkɪnz).
▷HISTORY C19: originally *Thomas Atkins*, a name representing a typical private in specimen forms; compare TOM[1]

tommy bar NOUN a short bar used as a lever to provide torque for tightening a box spanner or key.

Tommy gun NOUN an informal name for **Thompson sub-machine-gun**.

tommyrot ('tɒmɪ,rɒt) NOUN utter nonsense; tomfoolery.

tommy rough NOUN *Austral* another name for **roughie[1]**.

tomography (tə'mɒgrəfɪ) NOUN any of a number of techniques used to obtain an X-ray photograph of a selected plane section of the human body or some other solid object.
▷HISTORY C20: from Greek *tomē* a cutting + -GRAPHY

tomorrow (tə'mɒrəʊ) NOUN [1] the day after today. [2] the future. ◆ ADVERB [3] on the day after today. [4] at some time in the future.
▷HISTORY Old English *tō morgenne*, from TO[1] (at, on) + *morgenne*, dative of *morgen* MORNING; see MORROW

tompion ('tɒmpɪən) NOUN a variant of **tampion**.

Tomsk (*Russian* tɔmsk) NOUN a city in central Russia: formerly an important gold-mining town and administrative centre for a large area of Siberia; university (1888); engineering industries. Pop.: 481 400 (1999 est.).

Tom Thumb NOUN a dwarf; midget.
▷HISTORY after *Tom Thumb*, the tiny hero of several English folk tales

tomtit ('tɒm,tɪt) NOUN *Brit* any of various tits, esp the bluetit.

tom-tom NOUN [1] a drum associated either with the American Indians or with Eastern cultures, usually beaten with the hands as a signalling instrument. [2] a standard cylindrical drum, normally with one drumhead. [3] a monotonous drumming or beating sound. ◆ VERB [4] (*tr*) *Informal* to pass (information, esp gossip) around a community very quickly.
▷HISTORY C17: from Hindi *tamtam*, of imitative origin

-tomy NOUN COMBINING FORM indicating a surgical cutting of a specified part or tissue: *lobotomy*.
▷HISTORY from Greek *-tomia*; see -TOME

ton[1] (tʌn) NOUN [1] Also called: **long ton.** *Brit* a unit of weight equal to 2240 pounds or 1016.046909 kilograms. [2] Also called: **short ton, net ton.** *US* a unit of weight equal to 2000 pounds or 907.184 kilograms. [3] Also called: **metric ton, tonne.** a unit of weight equal to 1000 kilograms. [4] Also called: **freight ton.** a unit of volume or weight used for charging or measuring freight in shipping. It depends on the type of material being shipped but is often taken as 40 cubic feet, 1 cubic metre, or 1000 kilograms: *freight is charged at £40 per ton of 1 cubic metre*. [5] Also called: **measurement ton, shipping ton.** a unit of volume used in shipping freight, equal to 40 cubic feet, irrespective of the commodity shipped. [6] Also called: **displacement ton.** a unit used for measuring the displacement of a ship, equal to 35 cubic feet of sea water or 2240 pounds. [7] Also called: **register ton.** a unit of internal capacity of ships equal to 100 cubic feet. ◆ See also **tons.**
▷HISTORY C14: variant of TUN

ton[2] *French* (tɔ̃) NOUN style, fashion, or distinction.
▷HISTORY C18: from French, from Latin *tonus* TONE

ton[3] (tʌn) NOUN *Slang, chiefly Brit* a score or achievement of a hundred, esp a hundred miles per hour, as on a motorcycle.
▷HISTORY C20: special use of TON[1] applied to quantities of one hundred

tonal ('təʊnᵊl) ADJECTIVE [1] of or relating to tone. [2] of, relating to, or utilizing the diatonic system; having an established key. Compare **atonal.** [3] **a** (of an answer in a fugue) not having the same melodic intervals as the subject, so as to remain in the original key. **b** denoting a fugue as having such an answer. Compare **real[1]** (sense 11).
▸ **'tonally** ADVERB

tonality (təʊ'nælɪtɪ) NOUN, *plural* **-ties.** [1] *Music* **a** the actual or implied presence of a musical key in a composition. **b** the system of major and minor keys prevalent in Western music since the decline of modes. Compare **atonality.** [2] the overall scheme of colours and tones in a painting.

to-name NOUN *Scot* a nickname used to distinguish one person from others of the same name.

Tonbridge ('tʌn,brɪdʒ) NOUN a market town in SE England, in SW Kent on the River Medway. Pop.: 34 260 (1991).

tondo ('tɒndəʊ) NOUN, *plural* **-di** (-diː). a circular easel painting or relief carving.
▷HISTORY C19: from Italian: a circle, shortened from *rotondo* round

tone (təʊn) NOUN [1] sound with reference to quality, pitch, or volume. [2] short for **tone colour.** [3] *US and Canadian* another word for **note** (sense 10). [4] (in acoustic analysis) a sound resulting from periodic or regular vibrations, composed either of a simple sinusoidal waveform (**pure tone**) or of several such waveforms superimposed upon one main one (**compound tone**). [5] an interval of a major second; whole tone. [6] Also called: **Gregorian tone.** any of several plainsong melodies or other chants used in the singing of psalms. [7] *Linguistics* any of the pitch levels or pitch contours at which a syllable may be pronounced, such as high tone, falling tone, etc. [8] the quality or character of a sound: *a nervous tone of voice.* [9] general aspect, quality, or style: *I didn't like the tone of his speech.* [10] high quality or style: *to lower the tone of a place.* [11] the quality of a given colour, as modified by mixture with white or black; shade; tint: *a tone of red.* [12] *Physiol* **a** the normal tension of a muscle at rest. **b** the natural firmness of the tissues and normal functioning of bodily organs in health. [13] the overall effect of the colour values and gradations of light and dark in a picture. [14] *Photog* a colour or shade of colour, including black or grey, of a particular area on a negative or positive that can be distinguished from surrounding lighter or darker areas. ◆ VERB [15] (*intr; often foll by with*) to be of a matching or similar tone (to): *the curtains tone with the carpet.* [16] (*tr*) to give a tone to or correct the tone of. [17] (*tr*) *Photog* to soften or change the colour of the tones of (a photographic image) by chemical means. [18] an archaic word for **intone.** ◆ See also **tone down, tone up.**
▷HISTORY C14: from Latin *tonus,* from Greek *tonos* tension, tone, from *teinein* to stretch

tone arm NOUN another name for **pick-up** (sense 1).

tone cluster NOUN *Music* a group of adjacent notes played simultaneously, either in an orchestral score or, on the piano, by depressing a whole set of adjacent keys.

tone colour NOUN the quality of a musical sound that is conditioned or distinguished by the upper partials or overtones present in it. Often shortened to: **tone.** See also **timbre** (sense 2).

tone control NOUN a device in a radio, etc., by which the relative intensities of high and low frequencies may be varied.

tone-deaf ADJECTIVE unable to distinguish subtle differences in musical pitch.
▸**tone deafness** NOUN

tone down VERB (*adverb*) to moderate or become moderated in tone: *to tone down an argument; to tone down a bright colour.*

tone language NOUN a language, such as Chinese or certain African languages, in which differences in tone may make differences in meaning.

toneless ('təʊnlɪs) ADJECTIVE [1] having no tone. [2] lacking colour or vitality.
▸**'tonelessly** ADVERB ▸**'tonelessness** NOUN

toneme ('təʊniːm) NOUN *Linguistics* a phoneme that is distinguished from another phoneme only by its tone.
▷HISTORY C20: from TONE + -EME
▸**to'nemic** ADJECTIVE

tone poem NOUN another term for **symphonic poem.**

toner ('təʊnə) NOUN [1] a person or thing that tones or produces tones, esp a concentrated pure organic pigment. [2] a cosmetic preparation that is applied to produce a required effect, such as one that softens or alters hair colour or one that reduces the oiliness of the skin. [3] *Photog* a chemical solution that softens or alters the colour of the tones of a photographic image. [4] a powdered chemical used in photocopying machines and laser printers, which is transferred onto paper to form the printed image.

tone row *or* **series** NOUN *Music* a group of notes having a characteristic pattern or order that forms the basis of the musical material in a serial composition, esp one consisting of the twelve notes of the chromatic scale. Also called: **note row.** See also **serialism, twelve-tone.**

tone-setter NOUN a person or thing that establishes the quality or character that is to be followed subsequently.

tonetic (təʊ'nɛtɪk) ADJECTIVE (of a language) distinguishing words semantically by distinction of tone as well as by other sounds. See **tone language.**
▷HISTORY C20: from TONE + *-etic,* as in PHONETIC
▸**to'netically** ADVERB

tone up VERB (*adverb*) to make or become more vigorous, healthy, etc.: *exercise tones up the muscles.*

tong[1] (tɒŋ) VERB (*tr*) [1] to gather or seize with tongs. [2] to curl or style (hair) with curling tongs.

tong[2] (tɒŋ) NOUN (formerly) a Chinese secret society or association, esp one popularly assumed to engage in criminal activities.
▷HISTORY C20: from Chinese (Cantonese) *t'ong* meeting place

tonga ('tɒŋgə) NOUN a light two-wheeled vehicle used in rural areas of India.
▷HISTORY C19: from Hindi *tāngā*

Tonga[1] ('tɒŋgə, 'tɒŋə) NOUN [1] (*plural* **-gas** *or* **-ga**) a member of a Negroid people of S central Africa, living chiefly in Zambia and Zimbabwe. [2] the language of this people, belonging to the Bantu group of the Niger-Congo family.

Tonga[2] ('tɒŋə, 'tɒŋgə) NOUN a kingdom occupying an archipelago of more than 150 volcanic and coral islands in the SW Pacific, east of Fiji: inhabited by Polynesians; became a British protectorate in 1900 and gained independence in 1970; a member of the Commonwealth. Official languages: Tongan and English. Religion: Christian majority. Currency: pa'anga. Capital: Nuku'alofa. Pop.: 101 000 (2001 est.). Area: 750 sq. km (290 sq. miles). Also called: **Friendly Islands.**

Tongan ('tɒŋən) ADJECTIVE [1] of or relating to the kingdom of Tonga, its inhabitants, or their language. ◆ NOUN [2] a member of the people that inhabits Tonga. [3] the language of this people, belonging to the Polynesian family.

tongs (tɒŋz) PLURAL NOUN a tool for grasping or lifting, consisting of a hinged, sprung, or pivoted pair of arms or levers, joined at one end. Also called: **pair of tongs.**
▷HISTORY plural of Old English *tange;* related to Old Saxon *tanga,* Old High German *zanga,* Old Norse *tong*

tongue (tʌŋ) NOUN [1] a movable mass of muscular tissue attached to the floor of the mouth in most vertebrates. It is the organ of taste and aids the mastication and swallowing of food. In man it plays an important part in the articulation of speech sounds. Related adjectives: **glottic, lingual.** [2] an analogous organ in invertebrates. [3] the tongue of certain animals used as food. [4] a language, dialect, or idiom: *the English tongue.* [5] the ability to speak: *to lose one's tongue.* [6] a manner of speaking: *a glib tongue.* [7] utterance or voice (esp in the phrase **give tongue**). [8] (*plural*) See **gift of tongues.** [9] anything which resembles a tongue in shape or function: *a tongue of flame; a tongue of the sea.* [10] a promontory or spit of land. [11] a flap of leather on a shoe, either for decoration or under the laces or buckles to protect the instep. [12] *Music* the reed of an oboe or similar instrument. [13] the clapper of a bell. [14] the harnessing pole of a horse-drawn vehicle. [15] a long and narrow projection on a machine or structural part that serves as a guide for assembly or as a securing device. [16] a projecting strip along an edge of a board that is made to fit a corresponding groove in the edge of another board. [17] **hold one's tongue.** to keep quiet. [18] **on the tip of one's tongue.** about to come to mind: *her name was on the tip of his tongue.* [19] **with (one's) tongue in (one's) cheek.** Also: **tongue in cheek.** with insincere or ironical intent. ◆ VERB **tongues, tonguing, tongued.** [20] to articulate (notes played on a wind instrument) by the process of tonguing. [21] (*tr*) to lick, feel, or touch with the tongue. [22] (*tr*) *Carpentry* to provide (a board) with a tongue. [23] (*intr*) (of a piece of land) to project into a body of water. [24] (*tr*) *Obsolete* to reproach; scold.
▷HISTORY Old English *tunge;* related to Old Saxon, Old Norse *tunga,* Old High German *zunga,* Latin *lingua*
▸**'tongueless** ADJECTIVE ▸**'tongue,like** ADJECTIVE

tongue-and-groove joint NOUN a joint made between two boards by means of a tongue along the edge of one board that fits into a groove along the edge of the other board.

tongued (tʌŋd) ADJECTIVE [1] **a** having a tongue or tongues. **b** (*in combination*): *long-tongued.* [2] (*in combination*) having a manner of speech as specified: *sharp-tongued.*

tongue-lash VERB (*tr*) to reprimand severely; scold.
▸**'tongue-,lashing** NOUN, ADJECTIVE

tongue-tie NOUN a congenital condition in which the tongue has restricted mobility as the result of an abnormally short frenulum.

tongue-tied ADJECTIVE [1] speechless, esp with embarrassment or shyness. [2] having a condition of tongue-tie.

tongue twister NOUN a sentence or phrase that is difficult to articulate clearly and quickly, such as *Peter Piper picked a peck of pickled pepper.*

tongue worm NOUN *Vet science* a parasitic worm, *Linguatula serrata,* found in the nose of dogs, so called because of the shape of the worm.

tonguing ('tʌŋɪŋ) NOUN a technique of articulating notes on a wind instrument. See **single-tongue, double-tongue, triple-tongue.**

tonic ('tɒnɪk) NOUN [1] a medicinal preparation intended to improve and strengthen the functioning of the body or increase the feeling of wellbeing. [2] anything that enlivens or strengthens: *his speech was a tonic to the audience.* [3] Also called: **tonic water.** a mineral water, usually carbonated and containing quinine and often mixed with gin or other alcoholic drinks. [4] *Music* **a** the first degree of a major or minor scale and the tonal centre of a piece composed in a particular key. **b** a key or chord based on this. [5] a stressed syllable in a word. ◆ ADJECTIVE [6] serving to enliven and invigorate: *a tonic wine.* [7] of or relating to a tone or tones. [8] *Music* of or relating to the first degree of a major or minor scale. [9] of or denoting the general effect of colour and light and shade in a picture. [10] *Physiol* of, relating to, characterized by, or affecting normal muscular or bodily tone: *a tonic spasm.* [11] of or relating to stress or the main stress in a word. [12] denoting a tone language.
▷HISTORY C17: from New Latin *tonicus,* from Greek *tonikos* concerning tone, from *tonos* TONE
▸**'tonically** ADVERB

tonic accent NOUN [1] emphasis imparted to a note by virtue of its having a higher pitch, rather than greater stress or long duration relative to other notes. [2] another term for **pitch accent.**

tonicity (təʊ'nɪsɪtɪ) NOUN [1] the state, condition, or quality of being tonic. [2] *Physiol* another name for **tonus.**

tonic sol-fa NOUN a method of teaching music, esp singing, used mainly in Britain, by which the syllables of a movable system of solmization are used as names for the notes of the major scale in any key. In this system *sol* is usually replaced by *so* as the name of the fifth degree. See **solmization.**

tonight (tə'naɪt) NOUN [1] the night or evening of this present day. ◆ ADVERB [2] in or during the night or evening of this day. [3] *Archaic* last night.
▷HISTORY Old English *tōniht,* from TO[1] (at) + NIGHT

2NITE *Text messaging* ABBREVIATION FOR tonight.

tonk[1] (tɒŋk) VERB *Informal* to strike with a heavy blow.
▷HISTORY C20: of imitative origin

tonk[2] (tɒŋk) NOUN *Austral slang* an effete or effeminate man.
▷HISTORY C20: origin unknown

tonka bean ('tɒŋkə) NOUN [1] a tall leguminous tree, *Coumarouna odorata,* of tropical America, having fragrant black almond-shaped seeds. [2] the seeds of this tree, used in the manufacture of perfumes, snuff, etc.
▷HISTORY C18: probably from Tupi *tonka*

Tonkin ('tɒn'kɪn) *or* **Tongking** ('tɒŋ'kɪŋ) NOUN [1]

a former state of N French Indochina (1883–1946), on the Gulf of Tonkin: forms the largest part of N Vietnam. [2] **Gulf of.** an arm of the South China Sea, bordered by N Vietnam, the Leizhou Peninsula of SW China, and Hainan Island. Length: about 500 km (300 miles).

Tonkinese (ˌtɒnkɪnˈiːz) *or* **Tongkingese** (ˌtɒŋkɪŋˈiːz) NOUN, *plural* **-ese.** a breed of medium-sized cat with almond-shaped aqua-coloured eyes and a soft silky coat.

Tonle Sap (ˈtɒnlɪ ˈsæp) NOUN a lake in W central Cambodia, linked with the Mekong River by the **Tonle Sap River**. Area: (dry season) about 2600 sq. km (1000 sq. miles); (rainy season) about 10 000 sq. km (3860 sq. miles).

tonnage *or* **tunnage** (ˈtʌnɪdʒ) NOUN [1] the capacity of a merchant ship expressed in tons, for which purpose a ton is considered as 40 cubic feet of freight or 100 cubic feet of bulk cargo, unless such an amount would weigh more than 2000 pounds in which case the actual weight is used. [2] the weight of the cargo of a merchant ship. [3] the total amount of shipping of a port or nation, estimated by the capacity of its ships. [4] a duty on ships based either on their capacity or their register tonnage.
▷HISTORY C15: from Old French, from *tonne* barrel

tonne (tʌn) NOUN a unit of mass equal to 1000 kg or 2204.6 pounds. Also called (not in technical use): **metric ton.**
▷HISTORY from French

tonneau (ˈtɒnəʊ) NOUN, *plural* **-neaus** *or* **-neaux** (-nəʊ, -nəʊz). [1] Also called: **tonneau cover. a** a detachable cover to protect the rear part of an open car when it is not carrying passengers. **b** a similar cover that fits over all the passenger seats, but not the driver's, in an open vehicle. [2] *Rare* the part of an open car in which the rear passengers sit.
▷HISTORY C20: from French: special type of vehicle body, from Old French *tonnel* cask, from *tonne* tun

tonometer (təʊˈnɒmɪtə) NOUN [1] an instrument for measuring the pitch of a sound, esp one consisting of a set of tuning forks. [2] any of various types of instrument for measuring pressure or tension, such as the blood pressure, vapour pressure, etc.
▷HISTORY C18: from Greek *tonos* TONE + -METER
▸**tonometric** (ˌtɒnəˈmɛtrɪk, ˌtəʊ-) ADJECTIVE ▸**toˈnometry** NOUN

tonoplast (ˈtəʊnəˌplæst) NOUN *Botany* the membrane enclosing a vacuole in a plant cell.
▷HISTORY C20: from Greek *tonos* tone + -PLAST

tons (tʌnz) *Informal* ◆ PLURAL NOUN [1] a large amount or number: *tons of money; I have tons of shoes.* ◆ ADVERB [2] (intensifier): *I looked and felt tons better.*

tonsil (ˈtɒnsəl) NOUN [1] Also called: **palatine tonsil.** either of two small masses of lymphatic tissue situated one on each side of the back of the mouth. Related adjective: **amygdaline.** [2] *Anatomy* any small rounded mass of tissue, esp lymphatic tissue.
▷HISTORY C17: from Latin *tōnsillae* (pl) tonsils, of uncertain origin
▸**ˈtonsillar** *or* **ˈtonsillary** ADJECTIVE

tonsillectomy (ˌtɒnsɪˈlɛktəmɪ) NOUN, *plural* **-mies.** surgical removal of the palatine tonsils.

tonsillitis (ˌtɒnsɪˈlaɪtɪs) NOUN inflammation of the palatine tonsils, causing enlargement, occasionally to the extent that they nearly touch one another.
▸**tonsillitic** (ˌtɒnsɪˈlɪtɪk) ADJECTIVE

tonsillotomy (ˌtɒnsɪˈlɒtəmɪ) NOUN, *plural* **-mies.** surgical incision into one or both of the palatine tonsils, usually followed by removal (tonsillectomy).

tonsorial (tɒnˈsɔːrɪəl) ADJECTIVE *Often facetious* of or relating to barbering or hairdressing.
▷HISTORY C19: from Latin *tōnsōrius* concerning shaving, from *tondēre* to shave

tonsure (ˈtɒnʃə) NOUN [1] (in certain religions and monastic orders) **a** the shaving of the head or the crown of the head only. **b** the part of the head left bare by shaving. **c** the state of being shaven thus. ◆ VERB [2] (*tr*) to shave the head of.
▷HISTORY C14: from Latin *tōnsūra* a clipping, from *tondēre* to shave
▸**ˈtonsured** ADJECTIVE

tontine (ˈtɒntiːn, tɒnˈtiːn) NOUN [1] **a** an annuity scheme by which several subscribers accumulate and invest a common fund out of which they receive an annuity that increases as subscribers die until the last survivor takes the whole. **b** the subscribers to such a scheme collectively. **c** the share of each subscriber. **d** the common fund accumulated. **e** (*as modifier*): *a tontine fund.* [2] a system of mutual life assurance by which benefits are received by those participants who survive and maintain their policies throughout a stipulated period (the **tontine period**).
▷HISTORY C18: from French, named after Lorenzo *Tonti,* Neapolitan banker who devised the scheme

ton-up *Brit informal* ◆ ADJECTIVE (*prenominal*) [1] (esp of a motorcycle) capable of speeds of a hundred miles per hour or more. [2] liking to travel at such speeds: *a ton-up boy.* ◆ NOUN [3] a person who habitually rides at such speeds.

tonus (ˈtəʊnəs) NOUN *Physiol* the normal tension of a muscle at rest; tone.
▷HISTORY C19: from Latin, from Greek *tonos* TONE

tony (ˈtəʊnɪ) ADJECTIVE **tonier, toniest.** *US and Canadian informal* stylish or distinctive; classy.
▷HISTORY C20: from TONE

Tony (ˈtəʊnɪ) NOUN, *plural* **Tonies** *or* **Tonys.** any of several medallions awarded annually in the United States by a professional school for the performing arts for outstanding achievement in the theatre.
▷HISTORY from *Tony,* the nickname of Antoinette Perry (died 1946), US actress and producer

too (tuː) ADVERB [1] as well; in addition; also: *can I come too?* [2] in or to an excessive degree; more than a fitting or desirable amount: *I have too many things to do.* [3] extremely: *you're too kind.* [4] *US and Canadian informal* indeed: used to reinforce a command: *you will too do it!* [5] **too right!** *Brit, Austral, and NZ* certainly; indeed.
▷HISTORY Old English *tō;* related to Old Frisian, Old Saxon *to,* Old High German *zou;* see TO[1]

> **Language note** See at **very**.

toodle-oo (ˌtuːdᵊlˈuː) *or* **toodle-pip** SENTENCE SUBSTITUTE *Brit informal, rare* goodbye.
▷HISTORY C20: perhaps imitative of the horn of a car

took (tʊk) VERB the past tense of **take.**

tool (tuːl) NOUN [1] **a** an implement, such as a hammer, saw, or spade, that is used by hand. **b** a power-driven instrument; machine tool. **c** (*in combination*): *a toolkit.* [2] the cutting part of such an instrument. [3] **a** any of the instruments used by a bookbinder to impress a design on a book cover. **b** a design so impressed. [4] anything used as a means of performing an operation or achieving an end: *he used his boss's absence as a tool for gaining influence.* [5] a person used to perform dishonourable or unpleasant tasks for another. [6] a necessary medium for or adjunct to one's profession: *numbers are the tools of the mathematician's trade.* [7] *Slang* another word for **penis.** [8] *Brit* an underworld slang word for **gun.** ◆ VERB [9] to work, cut, shape, or form (something) with a tool or tools. [10] (*tr*) to decorate (a book cover) with a bookbinder's tool. [11] (*tr;* often foll by *up*) to furnish with tools. [12] (when *intr,* often foll by *along*) to drive (a vehicle) or (of a vehicle) to be driven, esp in a leisurely or casual style.
▷HISTORY Old English *tōl;* related to Old Norse *tōl* weapon, Old English *tawian* to prepare; see TAW[2]
▸**ˈtooler** NOUN ▸**ˈtool-less** ADJECTIVE

tooled up ADJECTIVE *Slang* equipped with a weapon, esp a gun.

tooling (ˈtuːlɪŋ) NOUN [1] any decorative work done with a tool, esp a design stamped onto a book cover, piece of leatherwork, etc. [2] the selection, provision, and setting up of tools, esp for a machining operation.

toolkit (ˈtuːlˌkɪt) NOUN [1] a set of tools designed to be used together or for a particular purpose. [2] software designed to perform a specific function, esp to solve a problem: *your on-line printer toolkit.*

tool-maker (ˈtuːlˌmeɪkə) NOUN a person who specializes in the production or reconditioning of precision tools, cutters, etc.
▸**ˈtool-ˌmaking** NOUN

tool post NOUN the rigid holding device which holds the cutting tool on a lathe and some other machine tools.

tool pusher NOUN a foreman who supervises drilling operations on an oil rig.

toolroom (ˈtuːlruːm, -rʊm) NOUN a room, as in a machine shop, where tools are made or stored.

tool shed NOUN a small shed in the garden or yard of a house used for storing tools, esp those for gardening.

tool steel NOUN any of various steels whose hardness and ability to retain a cutting edge make them suitable for use in tools for cutting wood and metal.

toon[1] (tuːn) NOUN [1] a large meliaceous tree, *Cedrela toona,* of the East Indies and Australia, having clusters of flowers from which a dye is obtained. [2] the close-grained red wood of this tree, used for furniture, carvings, etc.
▷HISTORY from Hindi *tūn,* from Sanskrit *tunna*

toon[2] (tuːn) NOUN a cartoon character.

toonie *or* **twonie** (ˈtuːnɪ) NOUN *Canadian informal* a Canadian two-dollar coin.

toorie *or* **tourie** (ˈtʊrɪ) NOUN *Scot* [1] a tassel or bobble on a bonnet. [2] Also: **toorie bonnet.** a bonnet with a toorie.
▷HISTORY C19: from Scot *toor* tower

tooshie (ˈtʊʃɪ) ADJECTIVE *Austral slang* angry; upset.
▷HISTORY from TUSH buttocks, by analogy with ARSEY

toot[1] (tuːt) VERB [1] to give or cause to give (a short blast, hoot, or whistle): *to toot a horn; to toot a blast; the train tooted.* ◆ NOUN [2] the sound made by or as if by a horn, whistle, etc. [3] *Slang* any drug for snorting, esp cocaine. [4] *US and Canadian slang* a drinking spree. [5] (tʊt) *Austral slang* a lavatory.
▷HISTORY C16: from Middle Low German *tuten,* of imitative origin
▸**ˈtooter** NOUN

toot[2] (tuːt) NOUN *NZ* an informal name for **tutu**[2]**.**

tooth (tuːθ) NOUN, *plural* **teeth** (tiːθ). [1] any of various bonelike structures set in the jaws of most vertebrates and modified, according to the species, for biting, tearing, or chewing. Related adjective: **dental.** [2] any of various similar structures in invertebrates, occurring in the mouth or alimentary canal. [3] anything resembling a tooth in shape, prominence, or function: *the tooth of a comb.* [4] any of the various small indentations occurring on the margin of a leaf, petal, etc. [5] any one of a number of uniform projections on a gear, sprocket, rack, etc., by which drive is transmitted. [6] taste or appetite (esp in the phrase **sweet tooth**). [7] **long in the tooth.** old or ageing: used originally of horses, because their gums recede with age. [8] **tooth and nail.** with ferocity and force: *we fought tooth and nail.* ◆ VERB (tuːð, tuːθ) [9] (*tr*) to provide with a tooth or teeth. [10] (*intr*) (of two gearwheels) to engage.
▷HISTORY Old English *tōth;* related to Old Saxon *tand,* Old High German *zand,* Old Norse *tonn,* Gothic *tunthus,* Latin *dens*
▸**ˈtoothless** ADJECTIVE ▸**ˈtoothˌlike** ADJECTIVE

toothache (ˈtuːθˌeɪk) NOUN a pain in or about a tooth. Technical name: **odontalgia.**

toothache tree NOUN another name for **prickly ash.**

toothbrush (ˈtuːθˌbrʌʃ) NOUN a small brush, usually with a long handle, for cleaning the teeth.

toothed (tuːθt) ADJECTIVE **a** having a tooth or teeth. **b** (*in combination*): *sabre-toothed; six-toothed.*

toothed whale NOUN any whale belonging to the cetacean suborder *Odontoceti,* having a single blowhole and numerous simple teeth and feeding on fish, smaller mammals, molluscs, etc.: includes dolphins and porpoises. Compare **whalebone whale.**

toothpaste (ˈtuːθˌpeɪst) NOUN a paste used for cleaning the teeth, applied with a toothbrush.

toothpick (ˈtuːθˌpɪk) NOUN [1] a small sharp sliver of wood, plastic, etc., used for extracting pieces of food from between the teeth. [2] a slang word for **bowie knife.**

tooth powder NOUN a powder used for cleaning the teeth, applied with a toothbrush.

tooth shell NOUN another name for the **tusk shell.**

toothsome (ˈtuːθsəm) ADJECTIVE [1] of delicious or appetizing appearance, flavour, or smell. [2] attractive; alluring.
▸**ˈtoothsomely** ADVERB ▸**ˈtoothsomeness** NOUN

toothwort ('tu:θ,wɜ:t) NOUN [1] a parasitic European scrophulariaceous plant, *Lathraea squamaria*, having no green parts, scaly cream or pink stems, pinkish flowers, and a rhizome covered with toothlike scales. [2] any North American or Eurasian plant of the genus *Dentaria*, having creeping rhizomes covered with toothlike projections: family *Brassicaceae* (crucifers). See also **crinkleroot**.

toothy ('tu:θɪ) ADJECTIVE **toothier, toothiest**. having or showing numerous, large, or projecting teeth: *a toothy grin*.
▸ **'toothily** ADVERB ▸ **'toothiness** NOUN

tootle[1] ('tu:tᵊl) VERB [1] to toot or hoot softly or repeatedly: *the flute tootled quietly*. ◆ NOUN [2] a soft hoot or series of hoots.
▷HISTORY C19: from TOOT[1]
▸ **'tootler** NOUN

tootle[2] ('tu:tᵊl) *Brit informal* ◆ VERB [1] (*intr*) to go, esp by car. ◆ NOUN [2] a drive, esp a short pleasure trip.
▷HISTORY C19: from TOOTLE[1], imitative of the horn of a car

toots (tʊts) *or* **tootsy** NOUN, *plural* **tootses** *or* **tootsies**. *Informal, chiefly US* darling; sweetheart.
▷HISTORY C20: perhaps related to earlier dialect *toot* worthless person, of obscure origin

tootsy *or* **tootsie** ('tʊtsɪ) NOUN, *plural* **-sies**. a child's word for **toe**.

Toowoomba (tə'wʊmbə) NOUN a city in E Australia, in SE Queensland: agricultural and industrial centre. Pop.: 86 968 (1998 est.).

top[1] (tɒp) NOUN [1] the highest or uppermost part of anything: *the top of a hill*. [2] the most important or successful position: *to be at the top of the class; the top of the table*. [3] the part of a plant that is above ground: *carrot tops*. [4] a thing that forms or covers the uppermost part of anything, esp a lid or cap: *put the top on the saucepan*. [5] the highest degree or point: *at the top of his career*. [6] the most important person: *he's the top of this organization*. [7] the best or finest part of anything: *we've got the top of this year's graduates*. [8] the loudest or highest pitch (esp in the phrase **top of one's voice**). [9] short for **top gear**. [10] *Cards* the highest card of a suit in a player's hand. [11] *Sport* **a** a stroke that hits the ball above its centre. **b** short for **topspin**. [12] a platform around the head of a lower mast of a sailing vessel, the edges of which serve to extend the topmast shrouds. [13] *Chem* the part of a volatile liquid mixture that distils first. [14] a garment, esp for a woman, that extends from the shoulders to the waist or hips. [15] **a** the high-frequency content of an audio signal. **b** (*as modifier*): *this amplifier has a good top response*. [16] **blow one's top**. *Informal* to lose one's temper. [17] **on top of**. **a** in addition to: *on top of his accident, he caught pneumonia*. **b** *Informal* in complete control of (a difficult situation, job, etc.). [18] **off the top of one's head**. with no previous preparation; extempore. [19] **over the top**. **a** over the parapet or leading edge of a trench. **b** over the limit; excessive(ly); lacking restraint or a sense of proportion. [20] **the top of the morning**. a morning greeting regarded as characteristic of Irishmen. ◆ ADJECTIVE [21] of, relating to, serving as, or situated on the top: *the top book in a pile*. [22] *Brit informal* excellent: *a top night out*. ◆ VERB **tops, topping, topped**. (*mainly tr*) [23] to form a top on (something): *to top a cake with whipped cream*. [24] to remove the top of or from: *to top carrots*. [25] to reach or pass the top of: *we topped the mountain*. [26] to be at the top of: *he tops the team*. [27] to exceed or surpass. [28] *Slang* to kill, esp by hanging. [29] (*also intr*) *Sport* **a** to hit (a ball) above the centre. **b** to make (a stroke) by hitting the ball in this way. [30] *Chem* to distil off (the most volatile part) from a liquid mixture. [31] to add other colorants to (a dye) in order to modify the shade produced. [32] **top and tail**. **a** to trim off the ends of (fruit or vegetables) before cooking them. **b** to wash a baby's face and bottom without immersion in a bath. ◆ See also **top off, top out, tops, top up**.
▷HISTORY Old English *topp*; related to Old High German *zopf* plait, Old Norse *toppr* tuft

top[2] (tɒp) NOUN [1] a toy that is spun on its pointed base by a flick of the fingers, by pushing a handle at the top up and down, etc. [2] anything that spins or whirls around. [3] **sleep like a top**. to sleep very soundly.
▷HISTORY Old English, of unknown origin

top- COMBINING FORM a variant of **topo-** before a vowel.

topagnosia (,tɒpæg'nəʊzɪə) *or* **topagnosis** (,tɒpæg'nəʊsɪs) NOUN a symptom of disease of or damage to the brain in which a person cannot identify a part of the body that has been touched.

topalgia (tɒ'pældʒɪə) NOUN pain restricted to a particular spot: a neurotic or hysterical symptom.

toparch ('tɒpɑ:k) NOUN the ruler of a small state or realm.
▷HISTORY C17: from Greek *toparchēs*, from *topos* a place + -ARCH
▸ **'toparchy** NOUN

topaz ('təʊpæz) NOUN [1] a white or colourless mineral often tinted by impurities, found in cavities in igneous rocks and in quartz veins. It is used as a gemstone. Composition: hydrated aluminium silicate. Formula: $Al_2SiO_4(F,OH)_2$. Crystal structure: orthorhombic. [2] **oriental topaz**. a yellowish-brown variety of sapphire. [3] **false topaz**. another name for **citrine**. [4] **a** a yellowish-brown colour, as in some varieties of topaz. **b** (*as adjective*): *topaz eyes*. [5] either of two South American hummingbirds, *Topaza pyra* and *T. pella*.
▷HISTORY C13: from Old French *topaze*, from Latin *topazus*, from Greek *topazos*

topazolite (təʊ'pæzə,laɪt) NOUN a yellowish-green variety of andradite garnet.
▷HISTORY C19: from TOPAZ + -LITE; so called because it is the same colour as some topaz

top banana NOUN *Slang, chiefly US* [1] the leading comedian in vaudeville, burlesque, etc. [2] the leader; boss.

top boot NOUN a high boot, often with a decorative or contrasting upper section.

top brass NOUN (*functioning as plural*) *Informal* the most important or high-ranking officials or leaders, as in politics, industry, etc. See also **brass** (sense 5).

top cat NOUN *Informal* **a** the most powerful or important person. **b** (*as modifier*): *the top-cat jobs*.

topcoat ('tɒp,kəʊt) NOUN an outdoor coat worn over a suit, etc.

top dead-centre NOUN *Engineering* the position of the crank of a reciprocating engine or pump when the piston is at the top of its stroke. Abbreviation: **t.d.c.**

top dog NOUN *Informal* the leader or chief of a group.

top dollar NOUN *Informal* the highest level of payment.

top-down ADJECTIVE controlled, directed, or organized from the top.

top drawer NOUN people of the highest standing, esp socially (esp in the phrase **out of the top drawer**).

top-dress VERB (*tr*) to spread manure or fertilizer on the surface of (land) without working it into the soil.

top dressing NOUN [1] a surface application of manure or fertilizer to land. [2] a thin layer of loose gravel that covers the top of a road surface.

tope[1] (təʊp) VERB to consume (alcoholic drink) as a regular habit, usually in large quantities.
▷HISTORY C17: from French *toper* to keep an agreement, from Spanish *topar* to take a bet; probably because a wager was generally followed by a drink
▸ **'toper** NOUN

tope[2] (təʊp) NOUN [1] a small grey requiem shark, *Galeorhinus galeus*, of European coastal waters. [2] any of various other small sharks.
▷HISTORY C17: of uncertain origin; compare Norfolk dialect *toper* dogfish

tope[3] (təʊp) NOUN another name for a **stupa**.
▷HISTORY C19: from Hindi *tōp*; compare Sanskrit *stūpa* STUPA

topee *or* **topi** ('təʊpi:, -pɪ) NOUN, *plural* **-pees** *or* **-pis**. another name for **pith helmet**.
▷HISTORY C19: from Hindi *topī* hat

Topeka (tə'pi:kə) NOUN a city in E central Kansas, capital of the state, on the Kansas River: university (1865). Pop.: 122 377 (2000).

top end NOUN (in vertical engines) another name for **little end** (sense 1).

Top End NOUN **the**. *Austral* the northern part of the Northern Territory.

top-end ADJECTIVE of or relating to the best or most expensive products of their kind: *a range of top-end vehicles*.

top-flight ADJECTIVE of superior or excellent quality; outstanding.

topfull ('tɒp,fʊl) ADJECTIVE *Rare* full to the top.

topgallant (,tɒp'gælənt; *Nautical* tə'gælənt) NOUN [1] Also called: **topgallant mast**. a mast on a square-rigger above a topmast or an extension of a topmast. [2] Also called: **topgallant sail**. a sail set on a yard of a topgallant mast. [3] (*modifier*) of or relating to a topgallant.
▷HISTORY C16: from TOP[1] + GALLANT

top gear NOUN the highest gear in a motor vehicle, often shortened to **top**.

top hat NOUN a man's hat with a tall cylindrical crown and narrow brim, often made of silk, now worn for some formal occasions. Also called: **high hat**.

top-hat scheme NOUN *Informal* a pension scheme for the senior executives of an organization.

top-heavy ADJECTIVE [1] unstable or unbalanced through being overloaded at the top. [2] *Finance* (of an enterprise or its capital structure) characterized by or containing too much debt capital in relation to revenue or profit so that too little is left over for dividend distributions; overcapitalized. [3] (of a business enterprise) having too many executives.
▸ **,top-'heavily** ADVERB ▸ **,top-'heaviness** NOUN

Tophet *or* **Topheth** ('təʊfɛt) NOUN *Old Testament* a place in the valley immediately to the southwest of Jerusalem; the Shrine of Moloch, where human sacrifices were offered.
▷HISTORY from Hebrew *Tōpheth*

top-hole INTERJECTION, ADJECTIVE *Brit informal* excellent; splendid.

tophus ('təʊfəs) NOUN, *plural* **-phi** (-faɪ). *Pathol* a deposit of sodium urate in the helix of the ear or surrounding a joint: a diagnostic of advanced or chronic gout. Also called: **chalkstone**.
▷HISTORY C16: from Latin, variant of *tōfus* TUFA, TUFF
▸ **tophaceous** (təʊ'feɪʃəs) ADJECTIVE

topi[1] ('təʊpɪ) NOUN, *plural* **-pis**. [1] an antelope, *Damaliscus korrigum*, of grasslands and semideserts of Africa, having angular curved horns and an elongated muzzle.
▷HISTORY C19: from an African language

topi[2] ('təʊpi:, -pɪ) NOUN, *plural* **-pis**. [1] another name for **pith helmet**.
▷HISTORY C19: from Hindi: hat

topiary ('təʊpɪərɪ) ADJECTIVE [1] of, relating to, or characterized by the trimming or training of trees or bushes into artificial decorative animal, geometric, or other shapes. ◆ NOUN [2] (*plural* **-aries**) **a** topiary work. **b** a topiary garden. [3] the art of topiary.
▷HISTORY C16: from French *topiaire*, from Latin *topia* decorative garden work, from Greek *topion* little place, from *topos* place
▸ **topiarian** (,təʊpɪ'ɛərɪən) ADJECTIVE ▸ **'topiarist** NOUN

topic ('tɒpɪk) NOUN [1] a subject or theme of a speech, essay, book, etc. [2] a subject of conversation; item of discussion. [3] (in rhetoric, logic, etc.) a category or class of arguments or ideas which may be drawn on to furnish proofs.
▷HISTORY C16: from Latin *topica* translating Greek *ta topika*, literally: matters relating to commonplaces, title of a treatise by Aristotle, from *topoi*, pl of *topos* place, commonplace

topical ('tɒpɪkᵊl) ADJECTIVE [1] of, relating to, or constituting current affairs. [2] relating to a particular place; local. [3] of or relating to a topic or topics. [4] (of a drug, ointment, etc.) for application to the body surface; local.
▸ **topicality** (,tɒpɪ'kælɪtɪ) NOUN ▸ **'topically** ADVERB

topic sentence NOUN a sentence in a paragraph that expresses the main idea or point of the whole paragraph.

topknot ('tɒp,nɒt) NOUN [1] a crest, tuft, decorative bow, chignon, etc., on the top of the head. [2] any of several European flatfishes of the genus *Zeugopterus* and related genera, esp *Z. punctatus*, which has an oval dark brown body marked with darker blotches: family *Bothidae* (turbot, etc.).

topless ('tɒplɪs) ADJECTIVE [1] having no top. [2] **a**

denoting a costume which has no covering for the breasts. **b** wearing such a costume. 3 *Archaic* immeasurably high.
▸ **'toplessness** NOUN

top-level NOUN (*modifier*) of, involving, or by those on the highest level of influence or authority: *top-level talks*.

toplofty ('tɒpˌlɒftɪ) ADJECTIVE *Informal* haughty or pretentious.
▸ **'topˌloftily** ADVERB ▸ **'topˌloftiness** NOUN

top management *or* **senior management** NOUN the most senior staff of an organization or business, including the heads of various divisions or departments led by the chief executive. Compare **middle management.**

topmast ('tɒpˌmɑːst; *Nautical* 'tɒpməst) NOUN the mast next above a lower mast on a sailing vessel.

topminnow ('tɒpˌmɪnəʊ) NOUN, *plural* **-now** *or* **-nows.** any of various small American freshwater cyprinodont fishes that are either viviparous (genera *Heterandria, Gambusia,* etc.) or egg-laying (genus *Fundulus*).
▷ HISTORY from TOP[1] + MINNOW; so called because they are small and swim near the surface of the water

topmost ('tɒpˌməʊst) ADJECTIVE highest; at or nearest the top.

top-notch ('tɒp'nɒtʃ) ADJECTIVE *Informal* excellent; superb.
▸ **top-'notcher** NOUN

topo ('tɒpəʊ) NOUN, *plural* **topos.** *Mountaineering* a picture of a mountain with details of climbing routes superimposed on it.
▷ HISTORY C20: shortened from *topographical picture*

topo- *or before a vowel* **top-** COMBINING FORM indicating place or region: *topography; topology; toponym; topotype*.
▷ HISTORY from Greek *topos* a place, commonplace

topochemistry ('tɒpəˌkɛmɪstrɪ) NOUN *Chem* the study of reactions that only occur at specific regions in a system.

top off VERB (*tr, adverb*) to finish or complete, esp with some decisive action: *he topped off the affair by committing suicide*.

topog. ABBREVIATION FOR: 1 topographical. 2 topography.

topography (tə'pɒgrəfɪ) NOUN, *plural* **-phies.** 1 the study or detailed description of the surface features of a region. 2 the detailed mapping of the configuration of a region. 3 the land forms or surface configuration of a region. 4 the surveying of a region's surface features. 5 the study or description of the configuration of any object.
▸ **to'pographer** NOUN ▸ **topographic** (ˌtɒpə'græfɪk) *or* **ˌtopo'graphical** ADJECTIVE ▸ **ˌtopo'graphically** ADVERB

topological group NOUN *Maths* a group, such as the set of all real numbers, that constitutes a topological space and in which multiplication and inversion are continuous.

topological space NOUN *Maths* a set *S* with an associated family of subsets τ that is closed under set union and finite intersection. *S* and the empty set are members of τ.

topology (tə'pɒlədʒɪ) NOUN 1 the branch of mathematics concerned with generalization of the concepts of continuity, limit, etc. 2 a branch of geometry describing the properties of a figure that are unaffected by continuous distortion, such as stretching or knotting. Former name: **analysis situs.** 3 *Maths* a family of subsets of a given set *S*, such that *S* is a topological space. 4 the arrangement and interlinking of computers in a computer network. 5 the study of the topography of a given place, esp as far as it reflects its history. 6 the anatomy of any specific bodily area, structure, or part.
▸ **topologic** (ˌtɒpə'lɒdʒɪk) *or* **ˌtopo'logical** ADJECTIVE ▸ **ˌtopo'logically** ADVERB ▸ **to'pologist** NOUN

toponym ('tɒpənɪm) NOUN 1 the name of a place. 2 any name derived from a place name.

toponymy (tə'pɒnɪmɪ) NOUN 1 the study of place names. 2 *Rare* the anatomical nomenclature of bodily regions, as distinguished from that of specific organs or structures.
▸ **toponymic** (ˌtɒpə'nɪmɪk) *or* **ˌtopo'nymical** ADJECTIVE

topos ('tɒpɒs) NOUN, *plural* **-oi** (-ɔɪ). a basic theme or concept, esp a stock topic in rhetoric.
▷ HISTORY C20: Greek, literally: place

topotype ('tɒpəˌtaɪp) NOUN a specimen plant or animal taken from an area regarded as the typical habitat.

top out VERB (*adverb*) to place the highest stone on (a building) or perform a ceremony on this occasion.

topper ('tɒpə) NOUN 1 an informal name for **top hat.** 2 a person or thing that tops. 3 *Informal* a remark that caps the one before.

topping ('tɒpɪŋ) NOUN 1 something that tops something else, esp a sauce or garnish for food. 2 *Angling* part of a brightly-coloured feather, usually from a golden pheasant crest, used to top some artificial flies. ◆ ADJECTIVE 3 high or superior in rank, degree, etc. 4 *Brit slang* excellent; splendid.

topping lift NOUN *Nautical* a line or cable for raising the end of a boom that is away from the mast.

topple ('tɒp[ə]l) VERB 1 to tip over or cause to tip over, esp from a height. 2 (*intr*) to lean precariously or totter. 3 (*tr*) to overthrow; oust.
▷ HISTORY C16: frequentative of TOP[1] (verb)

tops (tɒps) *Slang* ◆ NOUN 1 a person or thing of top quality. ◆ ADJECTIVE 2 (*postpositive*) excellent; superb.

topsail ('tɒpˌseɪl; *Nautical* 'tɒps[ə]l) NOUN a square sail carried on a yard set on a topmast.

top-secret ADJECTIVE containing information whose disclosure would cause exceedingly grave damage to the nation and therefore classified as needing the highest level of secrecy and security.

top-shell NOUN any marine gastropod mollusc of the mainly tropical Old World family *Trochidae,* having a typically brightly coloured top-shaped or conical shell.

topside ('tɒpˌsaɪd) NOUN 1 the uppermost side of anything. 2 *Brit and NZ* a lean cut of beef from the thigh containing no bone. 3 (*often plural*) **a** the part of a ship's sides above the waterline. **b** the parts of a ship above decks.

top slicing NOUN the act or process of using a specific part of a sum of money for a special purpose, such as assessing a taxable gain.

topsoil ('tɒpˌsɔɪl) NOUN 1 the surface layer of soil. ◆ VERB 2 (*tr*) to spread topsoil on (land). 3 (*tr*) to remove the topsoil from (land).

topspin ('tɒpˌspɪn) NOUN *Sport* spin imparted to make a ball bounce or travel exceptionally far, high, or quickly, as by hitting it with a sharp forward and upward stroke. Compare **backspin.**

topsy-turvy ('tɒpsɪ'tɜːvɪ) ADJECTIVE 1 upside down. 2 in a state of confusion. ◆ ADVERB 3 in a topsy-turvy manner. ◆ NOUN 4 a topsy-turvy state.
▷ HISTORY C16: probably from *tops,* plural of TOP[1] + obsolete *tervy* to turn upside down; perhaps related to Old English *tearflian* to roll over

top up VERB (*tr, adverb*) *Brit* 1 to raise the level of (a liquid, powder, etc.) in (a container), usually bringing it to the brim of the container: *top up the sugar in those bowls*. 2 **a** to increase the benefits from (an insurance scheme), esp to increase a pension when a salary rise enables higher premiums to be paid. **b** to add money to (a loan, bank account, etc.) in order to keep it at a constant or acceptable level. ◆ NOUN **top-up.** 3 **a** an amount added to something in order to raise it to or maintain it at a desired level. **b** (*as modifier*): *a top-up loan; a top-up policy*.

toque (təʊk) NOUN 1 a woman's small round brimless hat, popular esp in Edwardian times. 2 a hat with a small brim and a pouched crown, popular in the 16th century. 3 *Canadian* same as **tuque** (sense 2). 4 a chef's tall white hat.
▷ HISTORY C16: from French, from Old Spanish *toca* headdress, probably from Basque *tauka* hat

tor (tɔː) NOUN 1 a high hill, esp a bare rocky one. 2 *Chiefly southwestern Brit* a prominent rock or heap of rocks, esp on a hill.
▷ HISTORY Old English *torr,* probably of Celtic origin; compare Scottish Gaelic *torr* pile, Welsh *twr*

Torah ('taʊrə; *Hebrew* tɔ'ra) NOUN 1 **a** the Pentateuch. **b** the scroll on which this is written, used in synagogue services. 2 the whole body of traditional Jewish teaching, including the Oral Law. 3 (*modifier*) promoting or according with traditional Jewish Law.
▷ HISTORY C16: from Hebrew: precept, from *yārāh* to instruct

Torbay (ˌtɔː'beɪ) NOUN 1 a unitary authority in SW England, in Devon, consisting of Torquay and two neighbouring coastal resorts. Pop.: 129 702 (2001). Area: 63 sq. km (24 sq. miles). 2 Also: **Tor Bay.** an inlet of the English Channel on the coast of SW England, near Torquay.

torbernite ('tɔːbəˌnaɪt) NOUN a green secondary mineral consisting of hydrated copper uranium phosphate in the form of square platelike crystals. Formula: $Cu(UO_2)_2(PO_4)_2.12H_2O$.
▷ HISTORY C19: named after *Torbern* O. Bergman (1735–84), Swedish chemist; see -ITE[1]

torc (tɔːk) NOUN another spelling of **torque** (sense 1).

torch (tɔːtʃ) NOUN 1 a small portable electric lamp powered by one or more dry batteries. US and Canadian word: **flashlight.** 2 a wooden or tow shaft dipped in wax or tallow and set alight. 3 anything regarded as a source of enlightenment, guidance, etc.: *the torch of evangelism*. 4 any apparatus that burns with a hot flame for welding, brazing, or soldering. 5 **carry a torch for.** to be in love with, esp unrequitedly. 6 **put to the torch.** to set fire to; burn down: *the looted monastery was put to the torch*. ◆ VERB 7 (*tr*) *Slang* to set fire to, esp deliberately as an act of arson.
▷ HISTORY C13: from Old French *torche* handful of twisted straw, from Vulgar Latin *torca* (unattested), from Latin *torquēre* to twist
▸ **'torchˌlike** ADJECTIVE

torchbearer ('tɔːtʃˌbɛərə) NOUN 1 a person or thing that carries a torch. 2 a person who leads or inspires.

torchère (tɔː'ʃɛə) NOUN a tall narrow stand for holding a candelabrum.
▷ HISTORY C20: from French, from *torche* TORCH

torchier *or* **torchiere** ('tɔːtʃɪə) NOUN a standing lamp with a bowl for casting light upwards and so giving all-round indirect illumination.
▷ HISTORY C20: from TORCHÈRE

torchon lace ('tɔːʃən; *French* tɔrʃɔ̃) NOUN a coarse linen or cotton lace with a simple openwork pattern.
▷ HISTORY C19 *torchon,* from French: a cleaning cloth, from *torcher* to wipe, from Old French *torche* bundle of straw; see TORCH

torch song NOUN a sentimental or romantic popular song, usually sung by a woman.
▷ HISTORY C20: from the phrase *to carry a torch for (someone)*
▸ **torch singer** NOUN

torchwood ('tɔːtʃˌwʊd) NOUN 1 any of various rutaceous trees or shrubs of the genus *Amyris,* esp *A. balsamifera,* of Florida and the Caribbean, having hard resinous wood used for torches. 2 any of various similar trees the wood of which is used for torches. 3 the wood of any of these trees.

tore[1] (tɔː) VERB the past tense of **tear.**

tore[2] (tɔː) NOUN *Architect* another name for **torus** (sense 1).
▷ HISTORY C17: from French, from Latin: TORUS

toreador ('tɒrɪəˌdɔː) NOUN a bullfighter.
▷ HISTORY C17: from Spanish, from *torear* to take part in bullfighting, from *toro* a bull, from Latin *taurus;* compare STEER[2]

toreador pants PLURAL NOUN tight-fitting women's trousers reaching to midcalf or above the ankle.

torero (tɒ'rɛərəʊ) NOUN, *plural* **-ros.** a bullfighter, esp one who fights on foot.
▷ HISTORY C18: from Spanish, from Late Latin *taurārius,* from Latin *taurus* a bull

toreutics (tə'ruːtɪks) NOUN (*functioning as singular or plural*) the art of making detailed ornamental reliefs, esp in metal, by embossing and chasing.
▷ HISTORY C19: from Greek *toreutikos* concerning work in relief, from *toreuein* to bore through, from *toreus* tool for boring
▸ **to'reutic** ADJECTIVE

Torfaen ('tɔːˌvæn) NOUN a county borough of SE Wales, created in 1996 from part of Gwent. Administrative centre: Pontypool. Pop.: 90 967 (2001). Area: 290 sq. km (112 sq. miles).

tori ('tɔːraɪ) NOUN the plural of **torus.**

toric ('tɒrɪk) ADJECTIVE of, relating to, or having the form of a torus.

toric lens NOUN a lens used to correct astigmatism, having one of its surfaces shaped like part of a torus so that its focal lengths are different in different meridians.

torii ('tɔːrɪˌiː) NOUN, *plural* **-rii**. a gateway, esp one at the entrance to a Japanese Shinto temple.
▷HISTORY C19: from Japanese, literally: a perch for birds

Torino (to'riːno) NOUN the Italian name for **Turin.**

torment VERB *(tr)* (tɔː'mɛnt) [1] to afflict with great pain, suffering, or anguish; torture. [2] to tease or pester in an annoying way: *stop tormenting the dog.* ◆ NOUN ('tɔːmɛnt) [3] physical or mental pain. [4] a source of pain, worry, annoyance, etc. [5] *Archaic* an instrument of torture. [6] *Archaic* the infliction of torture.
▷HISTORY C13: from Old French, from Latin *tormentum,* from *torquēre*
▸**tor'mented** ADJECTIVE ▸**tor'mentedly** ADVERB ▸**tor'menting** ADJECTIVE ▸**tor'mentingly** ADVERB

tormentil ('tɔːməntɪl) NOUN a rosaceous downy perennial plant, *Potentilla erecta,* of Europe and W Asia, having serrated leaves, four-petalled yellow flowers, and an astringent root used in medicine, tanning, and dyeing. Also called: **bloodroot.**
▷HISTORY C15: from Old French *tormentille,* from Medieval Latin *tormentilla,* from Latin *tormentum* agony; referring to its use in relieving pain; see TORMENT

tormentor *or* **tormenter** (tɔː'mɛntə) NOUN [1] a person or thing that torments. [2] a curtain or movable piece of stage scenery at either side of the proscenium arch, used to mask lights or exits and entrances. [3] *Films* a panel of sound-insulating material placed outside the field of the camera to control the acoustics on the sound stage.

torn (tɔːn) VERB [1] the past participle of **tear** (sense 2). [2] **that's torn it.** *Brit slang* an unexpected event or circumstance has upset one's plans. ◆ ADJECTIVE [3] split or cut. [4] divided or undecided, as in preference: *he was torn between staying and leaving.*

tornado (tɔː'neɪdəʊ) NOUN, *plural* **-does** *or* **-dos.** [1] Also called: **cyclone,** (US and Canadian informal) **twister.** a violent storm with winds whirling around a small area of extremely low pressure, usually characterized by a dark funnel-shaped cloud causing damage along its path. [2] a small but violent squall or whirlwind, such as those occurring on the West African coast. [3] any violently active or destructive person or thing.
▷HISTORY C16: probably alteration of Spanish *tronada* thunderstorm (from *tronar* to thunder, from Latin *tonāre*), through influence of *tornar* to turn, from Latin *tornāre* to turn in a lathe
▸**tornadic** (tɔː'nædɪk) ADJECTIVE ▸**tor'nado-ˌlike** ADJECTIVE

toroid ('tɔːrɔɪd) NOUN [1] *Geometry* a surface generated by rotating a closed plane curve about a coplanar line that does not intersect the curve. [2] the solid enclosed by such a surface. See also **torus.**
▸**to'roidal** ADJECTIVE

Toronto (tə'rɒntəʊ) NOUN a city in S central Canada, capital of Ontario, on Lake Ontario: the major industrial centre of Canada; two universities. Pop.: 653 734 (1996), with a metropolitan area of 4 338 400 (1995).

Toronto Blessing NOUN **the.** a variety of emotional reactions such as laughing, weeping, and fainting, experienced by participants in a form of charismatic Christian worship.
▷HISTORY C20: from TORONTO, where it originated

Torontonian (tɒrən'təʊnɪən) ADJECTIVE [1] of or relating to Toronto or its inhabitants. ◆ NOUN [2] a native or inhabitant of Toronto.

torose ('tɔːrəʊz, tɔː'rəʊz) *or* **torous** ('tɔːrəs) ADJECTIVE *Biology* (of a cylindrical part) having irregular swellings; knotted.
▷HISTORY C18: from Latin *torōsus* muscular, from *torus* a swelling
▸**torosity** (tɔː'rɒsɪtɪ) NOUN

torpedo (tɔː'piːdəʊ) NOUN, *plural* **-does.** [1] a cylindrical self-propelled weapon carrying explosives that is launched from aircraft, ships, or submarines and follows an underwater path to hit its target. [2] *Obsolete* a submarine mine. [3] *US and Canadian* a firework containing gravel and a percussion cap that explodes when dashed against a hard surface. [4] *US and Canadian* a detonator placed on a railway line as a danger signal. [5] any of various electric rays of the genus *Torpedo.* ◆ VERB **-does, -doing, -doed.** *(tr)* [6] to hit (a ship, etc.) with one or a number of torpedoes. [7] to render ineffective; destroy or wreck: *to torpedo the administration's plan.*
▷HISTORY C16: from Latin: crampfish (whose electric discharges can cause numbness), from *torpēre* to be inactive; see TORPID
▸**tor'pedo-ˌlike** ADJECTIVE

torpedo boat NOUN (formerly) a small high-speed warship designed to carry out torpedo attacks in coastal waters.

torpedo-boat destroyer NOUN (formerly) a large powerful high-speed torpedo boat designed to destroy enemy torpedo boats: a forerunner of the modern destroyer, from which the name is derived.

torpedo tube NOUN the tube from which a torpedo is discharged from submarines or surface ships.

torpid ('tɔːpɪd) ADJECTIVE [1] apathetic, sluggish, or lethargic. [2] (of a hibernating animal) dormant; having greatly reduced metabolic activity. [3] unable to move or feel.
▷HISTORY C17: from Latin *torpidus,* from *torpēre* to be numb, motionless
▸**tor'pidity** NOUN ▸**'torpidly** ADVERB

torpor ('tɔːpə) NOUN a state of torpidity.
▷HISTORY C17: from Latin: inactivity, from *torpēre* to be motionless
▸**ˌtorpor'ific** ADJECTIVE

Torquay (ˌtɔː'kiː) NOUN a town and resort in SW England, in Torbay unitary authority, S Devon. Pop.: 61 300 (est.).

torque (tɔːk) NOUN [1] Also: **torc.** a necklace or armband made of twisted metal, worn esp by the ancient Britons and Gauls. [2] any force or system of forces that causes or tends to cause rotation. [3] the ability of a shaft to cause rotation.
▷HISTORY C19: from Latin *torquēs* necklace, and *torquēre* to twist

torque converter NOUN a hydraulic device for the smooth transmission of power in which an engine-driven impeller transmits its momentum to a fluid held in a sealed container, which in turn drives a rotor. Also called: **hydraulic coupling.**

torque meter NOUN *Engineering* a device designed to determine the torque or torsion in a shaft, usually by measuring the twist in a calibrated length of shafting. Also called: **torsion meter.**

torques ('tɔːkwiːz) NOUN a distinctive band of hair, feathers, skin, or colour around the neck of an animal; a collar.
▷HISTORY C17: from Latin: necklace, from *torquēre* to twist
▸**torquate** ('tɔːkwɪt, -kweɪt) ADJECTIVE

torque spanner NOUN a spanner having a torque-limiting mechanism which can be set to a predetermined value.

torque wrench NOUN a type of wrench with a gauge attached to indicate the torque applied to the workpiece.

torr (tɔː) NOUN, *plural* **torr.** a unit of pressure equal to one millimetre of mercury (133.322 newtons per square metre).
▷HISTORY C20: named after Evangelista *Torricelli* (1608–47), Italian physicist and mathematician

Torrance ('tɒrəns) NOUN a city in SW California, southwest of Los Angeles: developed rapidly with the discovery of oil. Pop.: 137 946 (2000).

Torre del Greco (*Italian* 'torre del 'grɛːko) NOUN a city in SW Italy, in Campania near Vesuvius on the Bay of Naples: damaged several times by eruptions. Pop.: 100 688 (1992).

torrefy ('tɒrɪˌfaɪ) VERB **-fies, -fying, -fied.** *(tr)* to dry (drugs, ores, etc.) by subjection to intense heat; roast.
▷HISTORY C17: from French *torréfier,* from Latin *torrefacere,* from *torrēre* to parch + *facere* to make
▸**torrefaction** (ˌtɒrɪ'fækʃən) NOUN

Torrens ('tɒrənz) NOUN **Lake.** a shallow salt lake in E central South Australia, about 8 m (25 ft.) below sea level. Area: 5776 sq. km (2230 sq. miles).

Torrens title NOUN *Austral* legal title to land based on record of registration rather than on title deeds.
▷HISTORY from Sir Robert Richard *Torrens* (1814–84), who introduced the system as premier of South Australia in 1857

torrent ('tɒrənt) NOUN [1] a fast, voluminous, or violent stream of water or other liquid. [2] an overwhelming flow of thoughts, words, sound, etc. ◆ ADJECTIVE [3] *Rare* like or relating to a torrent.
▷HISTORY C17: from French, from Latin *torrēns* (noun), from *torrēns* (adjective) burning, from *torrēre* to burn

torrential (tɒ'rɛnʃəl, tə-) ADJECTIVE [1] of or relating to a torrent. [2] pouring or flowing fast, violently, or heavily: *torrential rain.* [3] abundant, overwhelming, or irrepressible: *torrential abuse.*
▸**tor'rentially** ADVERB

Torreón (*Spanish* tɔrrɛ'ɔn) NOUN an industrial city in N Mexico, in Coahuila state. Pop.: 505 000 (2000 est.).

Torres Strait ('tɔːrɪz, 'tɒr-) NOUN a strait between NE Australia and S New Guinea, linking the Arafura Sea with the Coral Sea. Width: about 145 km (90 miles).

Torricellian tube (ˌtɒrɪ'sɛlɪən) NOUN a vertical glass tube partly evacuated and partly filled with mercury, the height of which is used as a measure of atmospheric pressure.
▷HISTORY C17: named after Evangelista *Torricelli* (1608–47), Italian physicist and mathematician

Torricellian vacuum NOUN the vacuum at the top of a Torricellian tube.
▷HISTORY C17: named after Evangelista *Torricelli* (1608–47), Italian physicist and mathematician

torrid ('tɒrɪd) ADJECTIVE [1] so hot and dry as to parch or scorch. [2] arid or parched. [3] highly charged emotionally: *a torrid love scene.*
▷HISTORY C16: from Latin *torridus,* from *torrēre* to scorch
▸**tor'ridity** *or* **'torridness** NOUN ▸**'torridly** ADVERB

Torrid Zone NOUN *Rare* that part of the earth's surface lying between the tropics of Cancer and Capricorn.

torsade (tɔː'seɪd) NOUN an ornamental twist or twisted cord, as on hats.
▷HISTORY C19: from French, from obsolete *tors* twisted, from Late Latin *torsus,* from Latin *torquēre* to twist

torsi ('tɔːsɪ) NOUN *Rare* a plural of **torso.**

torsibility (ˌtɔːsə'bɪlɪtɪ) NOUN [1] the ability to be twisted. [2] the degree of resistance to or the capacity of recovering from being twisted.

torsion ('tɔːʃən) NOUN [1] **a** the twisting of a part by application of equal and opposite torques at either end. **b** the condition of twist and shear stress produced by a torque on a part or component. [2] the act of twisting or the state of being twisted.
▷HISTORY C15: from Old French, from medical Latin *torsiō* griping pains, from Latin *torquēre* to twist, torture
▸**'torsional** ADJECTIVE ▸**'torsionally** ADVERB

torsion balance NOUN an instrument used to measure small forces, esp electric or magnetic forces, by the torsion they produce in a thin wire, thread, or rod.

torsion bar NOUN a metal bar acting as a torsional spring, esp as used in the suspensions of some motor vehicles.

torsion meter NOUN another name for **torque meter.**

torsk (tɔːsk) NOUN, *plural* **torsks** *or* **torsk.** a gadoid food fish, *Brosmius brosme,* of northern coastal waters, having a single long dorsal fin. Usual US and Canadian name: **cusk.**
▷HISTORY C17: of Scandinavian origin; related to Old Norse *thorskr* codfish, Danish *torsk*

torso ('tɔːsəʊ) NOUN, *plural* **-sos** *or* **-si** (-sɪ). [1] the trunk of the human body. [2] a statue of a nude human trunk, esp without the head or limbs. [3] something regarded as incomplete or truncated.
▷HISTORY C18: from Italian: stalk, stump, from Latin: THYRSUS

tort (tɔːt) NOUN *Law* a civil wrong arising from an act or failure to act, independently of any contract, for which an action for personal injury or property damages may be brought.
▷HISTORY C14: from Old French, from Medieval

Latin *tortum,* literally: something twisted, from Latin *torquēre* to twist

torte (tɔːt; *German* 'tɔrtə) NOUN a rich cake, originating in Austria, usually decorated or filled with cream, fruit, nuts, and jam.
▷HISTORY C16: ultimately perhaps from Late Latin *tōrta* a round loaf, of uncertain origin

tortellini (ˌtɔːtəˈliːnɪ) NOUN pasta cut into small rounds, folded about a filling, and boiled.
▷HISTORY from Italian, diminutive of *tortelli* a type of pie, ultimately from Late Latin *tōrta* a round loaf or cake; see TORTE

tort-feasor (ˈtɔːtˈfiːzə) NOUN *Law* a person guilty of tort.
▷HISTORY C17: from Old French, literally: wrongdoer, from TORT + *faiseur,* from *faire* to do

torticollis (ˌtɔːtɪˈkɒlɪs) NOUN *Pathol* an abnormal position of the head, usually with the neck bent to one side, caused congenitally by contracture of muscles, muscular spasm, etc.
▷HISTORY C19: New Latin, from Latin *tortus* twisted (from *torquēre* to twist) + *collum* neck
▸ **ˌtorti'collar** ADJECTIVE

tortile (ˈtɔːtaɪl) ADJECTIVE *Rare* twisted or coiled.
▷HISTORY C17: from Latin *tortilis* winding, from *tortus* twisted, from *torquēre* to twist
▸ **tortility** (tɔːˈtɪlɪtɪ) NOUN

tortilla (tɔːˈtiːə) NOUN *Mexican cookery* a kind of thin pancake made from corn meal and cooked on a hot griddle until dry.
▷HISTORY C17: from Spanish: a little cake, from *torta* a round cake, from Late Latin; see TORTE

tortillon (ˌtɔːtiːˈɒn, -ˈəʊn; *French* tɔrtijɔ̃) NOUN another word for **stump** (sense 5).
▷HISTORY from French: something twisted, from Old French *tortiller* to twist

tortious (ˈtɔːʃəs) ADJECTIVE *Law* having the nature of or involving a tort; wrongful.
▷HISTORY C14: from Anglo-French *torcious,* from *torcion,* literally: a twisting, from Late Latin *tortiō* torment, from Latin *torquēre* to twist; influenced in meaning by TORT
▸ **'tortiously** ADVERB

tortoise (ˈtɔːtəs) NOUN [1] any herbivorous terrestrial chelonian reptile of the family *Testudinidae,* of most warm regions, having a heavy dome-shaped shell and clawed limbs. Related adjectives: **chelonian, testudinal.** [2] **water tortoise.** another name for **terrapin.** [3] a slow-moving person. [4] another word for **testudo.** ◆ See also **giant tortoise.**
▷HISTORY C15: probably from Old French *tortue* (influenced by Latin *tortus* twisted), from Medieval Latin *tortūca,* from Late Latin *tartarūcha* coming from Tartarus, from Greek *tartaroukhos;* referring to the belief that the tortoise originated in the underworld

tortoise beetle NOUN a metallic-coloured leaf beetle of the genus *Cassida,* in which the elytra and terga cover the body like a shell.

tortoiseshell (ˈtɔːtəsˌʃɛl) NOUN [1] a horny translucent yellow-and-brown mottled substance obtained from the outer layer of the shell of the hawksbill turtle: used for making ornaments, jewellery, etc. [2] a similar synthetic substance, esp plastic or celluloid, now more widely used than the natural product. [3] a breed of domestic cat, usually female, having black, cream, and brownish markings. [4] any of several nymphalid butterflies of the genus *Nymphalis,* and related genera, having orange-brown wings with black markings. [5] **tortoiseshell turtle.** another name for **hawksbill turtle.** [6] **a** a yellowish-brown mottled colour. **b** (*as adjective*): *a tortoiseshell décor.* [7] (*modifier*) made of tortoiseshell: *a tortoiseshell comb.*

Tortola (tɔːˈtəʊlə) NOUN an island in the NE Caribbean, in the Leeward Islands group: chief island of the British Virgin Islands. Pop.: 13 568 (1991). Area: 62 sq. km (24 sq. miles).

tortoni (tɔːˈtəʊnɪ) NOUN a rich ice cream often flavoured with sherry.
▷HISTORY from Italian: probably from the name of a 19th-century Italian caterer in Paris

tortricid (ˈtɔːtrɪsɪd) NOUN [1] any small moth of the chiefly temperate family *Tortricidae,* the larvae of which live concealed in leaves, which they roll or tie together, and are pests of fruit and forest trees: includes the codling moth. ◆ ADJECTIVE [2] of, relating to, or belonging to the family *Tortricidae.*
▷HISTORY C19: from New Latin *Tortrīcidae,* from *tortrix,* feminine of *tortor,* literally: twister, referring to the leaf-rolling of the larvae, from *torquēre* to twist

Tortuga (tɔːˈtuːgə) NOUN an island in the Caribbean, off the NW coast of Haiti: haunt of pirates in the 17th century. Area: 180 sq. km (70 sq. miles). French name: **La Tortue** (la tɔrty).

tortuosity (ˌtɔːtjʊˈɒsɪtɪ) NOUN, *plural* **-ties.** [1] the state or quality of being tortuous. [2] a twist, turn, or coil.

tortuous (ˈtɔːtjʊəs) ADJECTIVE [1] twisted or winding: *a tortuous road.* [2] devious or cunning: *a tortuous mind.* [3] intricate.
▸ **'tortuously** ADVERB ▸ **'tortuousness** NOUN

torture (ˈtɔːtʃə) VERB (*tr*) [1] to cause extreme physical pain to, esp in order to extract information, break resistance, etc.: *to torture prisoners.* [2] to give mental anguish to. [3] to twist into a grotesque form. ◆ NOUN [4] physical or mental anguish. [5] the practice of torturing a person. [6] a cause of mental agony or worry.
▷HISTORY C16: from Late Latin *tortūra* a twisting, from *torquēre* to twist
▸ **'tortured** ADJECTIVE ▸ **'torturedly** ADVERB ▸ **'torturer** NOUN ▸ **'torturesome** *or* **'torturous** ADJECTIVE ▸ **'torturing** ADJECTIVE ▸ **'torturingly** ADVERB ▸ **'torturously** ADVERB

> **Language note** The adjective *torturous* is sometimes confused with *tortuous.* One speaks of a *torturous* experience, i.e. one that involves pain or suffering, but of a *tortuous* road, i.e. one that winds or twists.

Toruń (*Polish* ˈtɔrunj) NOUN an industrial city in N Poland, on the River Vistula: developed around a castle that was founded by the Teutonic Knights in 1230; under Prussian rule (1793–1919). Pop.: 206 158 (1999 est.). German name: **Thorn.**

torus (ˈtɔːrəs) NOUN, *plural* **-ri** (-raɪ). [1] Also called: **tore.** a large convex moulding approximately semicircular in cross section, esp one used on the base of a classical column. [2] *Geometry* a ring-shaped surface generated by rotating a circle about a coplanar line that does not intersect the circle. Area: $4\pi^2Rr$; volume: $2\pi^2Rr^2$, where *r* is the radius of the circle and *R* is the distance from the line to the centre of the circle. [3] *Botany* another name for **receptacle** (sense 2). [4] *Anatomy* a ridge, fold, or similar linear elevation.
▷HISTORY C16: from Latin: a swelling, of obscure origin

Tory (ˈtɔːrɪ) NOUN, *plural* **-ries.** [1] a member or supporter of the Conservative Party in Great Britain or Canada. [2] a member of the English political party that opposed the exclusion of James, Duke of York from the royal succession (1679–80). Tory remained the label for subsequent major conservative interests until they gave birth to the Conservative Party in the 1830s. [3] an American supporter of the British cause; loyalist. Compare **Whig.** [4] (*sometimes not capital*) an ultraconservative or reactionary. [5] (in the 17th century) an Irish Roman Catholic, esp an outlaw who preyed upon English settlers. ◆ ADJECTIVE [6] of, characteristic of, or relating to Tories. [7] (*sometimes not capital*) ultraconservative or reactionary.
▷HISTORY C17: from Irish *tōraidhe* outlaw, from Middle Irish *tōir* pursuit
▸ **'Toryish** ADJECTIVE ▸ **'Toryism** NOUN

tosa (ˈtəʊsə) NOUN a large dog, usually red in colour, which is a cross between a mastiff and a Great Dane: originally developed for dog-fighting; it is not recognized as a breed by kennel clubs outside Japan.
▷HISTORY C20: from the name of a province of the island of Shikoku, Japan

Toscana (tosˈkaːna) NOUN the Italian name for **Tuscany.**

tosh (tɒʃ) NOUN *Slang, chiefly Brit* nonsense; rubbish.
▷HISTORY C19: of unknown origin

toss (tɒs) VERB [1] (*tr*) to throw lightly or with a flourish, esp with the palm of the hand upwards. [2] to fling or be flung about, esp constantly or regularly in an agitated or violent way: *a ship tosses in a storm.* [3] to discuss or put forward for discussion in an informal way. [4] (*tr*) (of an animal such as a horse) to throw (its rider). [5] (*tr*) (of an animal) to butt with the head or the horns and throw into the air: *the bull tossed the matador.* [6] (*tr*) to shake, agitate, or disturb. [7] to toss up a coin with (someone) in order to decide or allot something: *I'll toss you for it; let's toss for it.* [8] (*intr*) to move away angrily or impatiently: *she tossed out of the room.* ◆ NOUN [9] an abrupt movement. [10] a rolling or pitching motion. [11] the act or an instance of tossing. [12] the act of tossing up a coin. See **toss-up.** [13] **argue the toss.** to wrangle or dispute at length. [14] a fall from a horse or other animal. [15] **give a toss.** *Slang* to be concerned or interested (esp in the phrase **not give a toss**).
▷HISTORY C16: of Scandinavian origin; related to Norwegian, Swedish *tossa* to strew

tosser (ˈtɒsə) NOUN *Brit slang* a stupid or despicable person.
▷HISTORY C20: probably from TOSS OFF (to masturbate)

toss off VERB (*adverb*) [1] (*tr*) to perform, write, consume, etc., quickly and easily: *he tossed off a letter to Jim.* [2] (*tr*) to drink quickly at one draught. [3] (*intr*) *Brit slang* to masturbate.

tosspot (ˈtɒsˌpɒt) NOUN [1] *Archaic or literary* a habitual drinker. [2] *Brit slang* a stupid or contemptible person.

toss up VERB (*adverb*) [1] to spin (a coin) in the air in order to decide between alternatives by guessing which side will fall uppermost. [2] (*tr*) to prepare (food) quickly. ◆ NOUN **toss-up.** [3] an instance of tossing up a coin. [4] *Informal* an even chance or risk; gamble.

tostada (tɒˈstɑːdə) *or* **tostado** (tɒˈstɑːdəʊ) NOUN, *plural* **-das** *or* **-dos.** a crispy deep-fried tortilla topped with meat, cheese, and refried beans.
▷HISTORY Spanish, literally: toasted, past participle of *tostar*

tot[1] (tɒt) NOUN [1] a young child; toddler. [2] *Chiefly Brit* a small amount of anything. [3] a small measure of spirits.
▷HISTORY C18: perhaps short for *totterer;* see TOTTER

tot[2] (tɒt) VERB **tots, totting, totted.** (usually foll by *up*) *Chiefly Brit* to total; add.
▷HISTORY C17: shortened from TOTAL or from Latin *totum* all

total (ˈtəʊtᵊl) NOUN [1] the whole, esp regarded as the complete sum of a number of parts. ◆ ADJECTIVE [2] complete; absolute: *the evening was a total failure; a total eclipse.* [3] (*prenominal*) being or related to a total: *the total number of passengers.* ◆ VERB **-tals, -talling, -talled** *or US* **-tals, -taling, -taled.** [4] (when *intr,* sometimes foll by *to*) to amount: *to total six pounds.* [5] (*tr*) to add up: *to total a list of prices.* [6] (*tr*) *Slang* to kill or badly injure (someone). [7] (*tr*) *Chiefly US* to damage (a vehicle) beyond repair.
▷HISTORY C14: from Old French, from Medieval Latin *tōtālis,* from Latin *tōtus* all
▸ **'totally** ADVERB

total allergy syndrome NOUN a condition in which a person suffers from a large number of symptoms that are claimed to be caused by allergies to various substances used or encountered in modern life.

total depravity NOUN *Chiefly Calvinist theol* the doctrine that man's nature is totally corrupt as a result of the Fall.

total eclipse NOUN an eclipse as seen from a particular area of the earth's surface where the eclipsed body is completely hidden. Compare **annular eclipse, partial eclipse.**

total fighting NOUN a combat sport in which very few restrictions are placed on the type of blows or tactics that may be used.

total football NOUN an attacking style of play, popularized by the Dutch national team of the 1970s, in which there are no fixed positions and every outfield player can join in the attack.

total heat NOUN another term for **enthalpy.**

total internal reflection NOUN *Physics* the complete reflection of a light ray at the boundary of two media, when the ray is in the medium with greater refractive index.

totalitarian (təʊˌtælɪˈtɛərɪən) ADJECTIVE [1] of, denoting, relating to, or characteristic of a dictatorial one-party state that regulates every

realm of life. ◆ NOUN [2] a person who advocates or practises totalitarian policies.
▷HISTORY from TOTALITY + -ARIAN
▶**toˌtaliˈtarianism** NOUN

totality (təʊˈtælɪtɪ) NOUN, *plural* **-ties.** [1] the whole amount. [2] the state of being total. [3] the state or period of an eclipse when light from the eclipsed body is totally obscured.

totalizator (ˈtəʊtəlaɪˌzeɪtə), **totalizer, totalisator,** *or* **totaliser** NOUN [1] a system of betting on horse races in which the aggregate stake, less an administration charge and tax, is paid out to winners in proportion to their stake. [2] the machine that records bets in this system and works out odds, pays out winnings, etc. [3] an apparatus for registering totals, as of a particular function or measurement. ◆ US and Canadian term (for senses 1, 2): **pari-mutuel.**

totalize *or* **totalise** (ˈtəʊtəˌlaɪz) VERB to combine or make into a total.
▶ **ˌtotaliˈzation** *or* **ˌtotaliˈsation** NOUN

totalizer *or* **totaliser** (ˈtəʊtəˌlaɪzə) NOUN [1] a variant of **totalizator.** [2] *Chiefly US* an adding machine.

total quality management NOUN an approach to the management of an organization that integrates the needs of customers with a deep understanding of the technical details, costs, and human-resource relationships of the organization. Abbreviation: **TQM.**

total recall NOUN *Psychol* the faculty or an instance of complete and clear recall of every detail of something.

total serialism *or* **serialization** NOUN (in some music after 1945) the use of serial techniques applied to such elements as rhythm, dynamics, and tone colour, as found in the early works of Karlheinz Stockhausen, the German composer (born 1928), Pierre Boulez, the French composer and conductor (born 1925), etc.

totaquine (ˈtəʊtəˌkwiːn, -kwɪn) NOUN a mixture of quinine and other alkaloids derived from cinchona bark, used as a substitute for quinine in treating malaria.
▷HISTORY C20: from New Latin *tōtaquīna,* from TOTA(L) + Spanish *quina* cinchona bark; see QUININE

totara (ˈtəʊtərə) NOUN a tall coniferous forest tree, *Podocarpus totara,* of New Zealand, having a hard durable wood.
▷HISTORY Maori

tote[1] (təʊt) *Informal* ◆ VERB [1] (*tr*) to carry, convey, or drag. ◆ NOUN [2] the act of or an instance of toting. [3] something toted.
▷HISTORY C17: of obscure origin
▶ **ˈtoter** NOUN

tote[2] (təʊt) NOUN (usually preceded by *the*) *Informal* short for **totalizator** (senses 1, 2).

tote bag NOUN a large roomy handbag or shopping bag.

totem (ˈtəʊtəm) NOUN [1] (in some societies, esp among North American Indians) an object, species of animal or plant, or natural phenomenon symbolizing a clan, family, etc., often having ritual associations. [2] a representation of such an object.
▷HISTORY C18: from Ojibwa *nintōtēm* mark of my family
▶**totemic** (təʊˈtɛmɪk) ADJECTIVE ▶**toˈtemically** ADVERB

totemism (ˈtəʊtəˌmɪzəm) NOUN [1] the belief in kinship of groups or individuals having a common totem. [2] the rituals, taboos, and other practices associated with such a belief.
▶ **ˈtotemist** NOUN ▶ **ˌtotemˈistic** ADJECTIVE

totem pole NOUN a pole carved or painted with totemic figures set up by certain North American Indians, esp those of the NW Pacific coast, within a village as a tribal symbol or, sometimes, in memory of a dead person.

tother *or* **t'other** (ˈtʌðə) ADJECTIVE, NOUN *Archaic or dialect* the other.
▷HISTORY C13 *the tother,* by mistaken division from *thet other* (*thet,* from Old English *thæt,* neuter of THE[1])

totipalmate (ˌtəʊtɪˈpælmɪt, -ˌmeɪt) ADJECTIVE (of certain birds) having all four toes webbed.
▷HISTORY C19: from Latin *tōtus* entire + *palmate,* from Latin *palmātus* shaped like a hand, from *palma* PALM[1]
▶ **ˌtotipalˈmation** NOUN

totipotent (təʊˈtɪpətənt) ADJECTIVE (of an animal cell) capable of differentiation and so forming a new individual, tissue, organ, etc.
▷HISTORY C20: from Latin *tōtus* entire + POTENT[1]
▶**toˈtipotency** NOUN

totter (ˈtɒtə) VERB (*intr*) [1] to walk or move in an unsteady manner, as from old age. [2] to sway or shake as if about to fall. [3] to be failing, unstable, or precarious. ◆ NOUN [4] the act or an instance of tottering.
▷HISTORY C12: perhaps from Old English *tealtrian* to waver, and Middle Dutch *touteren* to stagger
▶ **ˈtotterer** NOUN ▶ **ˈtottering** ADJECTIVE ▶ **ˈtotteringly** ADVERB ▶ **ˈtottery** ADJECTIVE

tottie *or* **totty** (ˈtɒtɪ) ADJECTIVE *Chiefly Scot* very small; tiny.
▷HISTORY from TOT[1]

totting (ˈtɒtɪŋ) NOUN *Brit* the practice of searching through rubbish for usable or saleable items.
▷HISTORY C19: of unknown origin

totty (ˈtɒtɪ) NOUN *Brit informal* people, esp women, collectively considered as sexual objects.
▷HISTORY C19: diminutive of TOT[1]

toucan (ˈtuːkən) NOUN any tropical American arboreal fruit-eating bird of the family *Ramphastidae,* having a large brightly coloured bill with serrated edges and a bright plumage.
▷HISTORY C16: from French, from Portuguese *tucano,* from Tupi *tucana,* probably imitative of its cry

touch (tʌtʃ) NOUN [1] the sense by which the texture and other qualities of objects can be experienced when they come in contact with a part of the body surface, esp the tips of the fingers. Related adjectives: **haptic, tactile, tactual.** [2] the quality of an object as perceived by this sense; feel; feeling. [3] the act or an instance of something coming into contact with the body. [4] a gentle push, tap, or caress. [5] a small amount; hint: *a touch of sarcasm.* [6] a noticeable effect; influence: *the house needed a woman's touch.* [7] any slight stroke or mark: *with a touch of his brush he captured the scene.* [8] characteristic manner or style: *the artist had a distinctive touch.* [9] a detail of some work, esp a literary or artistic work: *she added a few finishing touches to the book.* [10] a slight attack, as of a disease: *a touch of bronchitis.* [11] a specific ability or facility: *the champion appeared to have lost his touch.* [12] the state of being aware of a situation or in contact with someone: *to get in touch with someone.* [13] the state of being in physical contact. [14] a trial or test (esp in the phrase **put to the touch**). [15] *Rugby, soccer* the area outside the touchlines, beyond which the ball is out of play (esp in the phrase **in touch**). [16] *Archaic* **a** an official stamp on metal indicating standard purity. **b** the die stamp used to apply this mark. Now usually called: **hallmark.** [17] a scoring hit in competitive fencing. [18] an estimate of the amount of gold in an alloy as obtained by use of a touchstone. [19] the technique of fingering a keyboard instrument. [20] the quality of the action of a keyboard instrument with regard to the relative ease with which the keys may be depressed: *this piano has a nice touch.* [21] *Bell-ringing* any series of changes where the permutations are fewer in number than for a peal. [22] *Slang* **a** the act of asking for money as a loan or gift, often by devious means. **b** the money received in this way. **c** a person asked for money in this way: *he was an easy touch.* ◆ VERB [23] (*tr*) to cause or permit a part of the body to come into contact with. [24] (*tr*) to tap, feel, or strike, esp with the hand: *don't touch the cake!* [25] to come or cause (something) to come into contact with (something else): *their hands touched briefly; he touched the match to the fuse.* [26] (*intr*) to be in contact. [27] (*tr; usually used with a negative*) to take hold of (a person or thing), esp in violence: *don't touch the baby!* [28] to be adjacent to (each other): *the two properties touch.* [29] (*tr*) to move or disturb by handling: *someone's touched my desk.* [30] (*tr*) to have an effect on: *the war scarcely touched our town.* [31] (*tr*) to produce an emotional response in: *his sad story touched her.* [32] (*tr*) to affect; concern. [33] (*tr; usually used with a negative*) to partake of, eat, or drink. [34] (*tr; usually used with a negative*) to handle or deal with: *I wouldn't touch that business.* [35] (when *intr,* often foll by *on*) to allude (to) briefly or in passing: *the speech touched on several subjects.* [36] (*tr*) to tinge or tint slightly: *brown hair touched with gold.* [37] (*tr*) to spoil or injure slightly: *blackfly touched the flowers.* [38] (*tr*) to mark, as with a brush or pen. [39] (*tr*) to compare to in quality or attainment; equal or match: *there's no-one to touch him.* [40] (*tr*) to reach or attain: *he touched the high point in his career.* [41] (*intr*) to dock or stop briefly: *the ship touches at Tenerife.* [42] (*tr*) *Slang* to ask for a loan or gift of money from. [43] *Rare* **a** to finger (the keys or strings of an instrument). **b** to play (a tune, piece of music, etc.) in this way. [44] **touch base.** See **base**[1] (sense 26). ◆ See also **touchdown, touch off, touch up.**
▷HISTORY C13: from Old French *tochier,* from Vulgar Latin *toccāre* (unattested) to strike, ring (a bell), probably imitative of a tapping sound
▶ **ˈtouchable** ADJECTIVE ▶ **ˈtouchableness** NOUN ▶ **ˈtoucher** NOUN ▶ **ˈtouchless** ADJECTIVE

touch and go ADJECTIVE (**touch-and-go** when prenominal) risky or critical: *a touch-and-go situation.*

touchback (ˈtʌtʃˌbæk) NOUN *American football* a play in which the ball is put down by a player behind his own goal line when the ball has been put across the goal line by an opponent. Compare **safety** (sense 4b).

touchdown (ˈtʌtʃˌdaʊn) NOUN [1] the moment at which a landing aircraft or spacecraft comes into contact with the landing surface. [2] *Rugby* the act of placing or touching the ball on the ground behind the goal line, as in scoring a try. [3] *American football* a scoring play worth six points, achieved by being in possession of the ball in the opposing team's end zone. Abbreviation: **TD.** See also **field goal.** ◆ VERB **touch down.** (*intr, adverb*) [4] (of a space vehicle, aircraft, etc.) to land. [5] *Rugby* to place the ball behind the goal line, as when scoring a try. [6] *Informal* to pause during a busy schedule in order to catch up, reorganize, or rest.

touché (tuːˈʃeɪ) INTERJECTION [1] an acknowledgment that a scoring hit has been made in a fencing competition. [2] an acknowledgment of the striking home of a remark or the capping of a witticism.
▷HISTORY from French, literally: touched

touched (tʌtʃt) ADJECTIVE (*postpositive*) [1] moved to sympathy or emotion; affected. [2] showing slight insanity.

touch football NOUN an informal version of American football chiefly characterized by players being touched rather than tackled.

touchhole (ˈtʌtʃˌhəʊl) NOUN a hole in the breech of early cannon and firearms through which the charge was ignited.

touching (ˈtʌtʃɪŋ) ADJECTIVE [1] evoking or eliciting tender feelings: *your sympathy is touching.* ◆ PREPOSITION [2] on the subject of; relating to.
▶ **ˈtouchingly** ADVERB ▶ **ˈtouchingness** NOUN

touch-in-goal NOUN *Rugby* the area at each end of a pitch between the goal line and the dead-ball line.

touch judge NOUN one of the two linesmen in rugby.

touchline (ˈtʌtʃˌlaɪn) NOUN either of the lines marking the side of the playing area in certain games, such as rugby.

touchmark (ˈtʌtʃˌmɑːk) NOUN a maker's mark stamped on pewter objects.

touch-me-not NOUN any of several balsaminaceous plants of the genus *Impatiens,* esp *I. noli-me-tangere,* having yellow spurred flowers and seed pods that burst open at a touch when ripe. Also called: **noli-me-tangere.**

touch off VERB (*tr, adverb*) [1] to cause to explode, as by touching with a match. [2] to cause (a disturbance, violence, etc.) to begin: *the marchers' action touched off riots.*

touchpaper (ˈtʌtʃˌpeɪpə) NOUN [1] paper soaked in saltpetre and used for firing gunpowder. [2] **light the (blue) touchpaper.** to do something that will cause much anger or excitement.

touch screen NOUN **a** a visual display unit screen that allows the user to give commands to the computer by touching parts of the screen instead of using the keyboard. **b** (*as modifier*): *a touch-screen computer.*

touchstone (ˈtʌtʃˌstəʊn) NOUN [1] a criterion or standard by which judgment is made. [2] a hard dark siliceous stone, such as basalt or jasper, that is used to test the quality of gold and silver from the colour of the streak they produce on it.

touch system NOUN a typing system in which the fingers are trained to find the correct keys, permitting the typist to read and type copy without looking at the keyboard.

touch-tone ADJECTIVE of or relating to a telephone dialling system in which each of the buttons pressed generates a tone of a different pitch, which is transmitted to the exchange.

touch-type VERB *(intr)* to type without having to look at the keys of the typewriter.
▸ **'touch-ˌtypist** NOUN

touch up VERB *(tr, adverb)* [1] to put extra or finishing touches to. [2] to enhance, renovate, or falsify by putting extra touches to: *to touch up a photograph.* [3] to stimulate or rouse as by a tap or light blow. [4] *Brit slang* to touch or caress (someone), esp to arouse sexual feelings. ◆ NOUN **touch-up.** [5] a renovation or retouching, as of a painting.

touchwood ('tʌtʃˌwʊd) NOUN something, esp dry wood or fungus material such as amadou, used as tinder.
▷HISTORY C16: TOUCH (in the sense: to kindle) + WOOD[1]

touchy ('tʌtʃɪ) ADJECTIVE **touchier, touchiest.** [1] easily upset or irritated; oversensitive. [2] extremely risky. [3] easily ignited.
▸ **'touchily** ADVERB ▸ **'touchiness** NOUN

touchy-feely NOUN ('tʌtʃɪ'fiːlɪ), ADJECTIVE *Informal, sometimes derogatory* openly displaying one's emotions and affections.
▸ **'touchy-'feeliness** NOUN

tough (tʌf) ADJECTIVE [1] strong or resilient; durable: *a tough material.* [2] not tender: *he could not eat the tough steak.* [3] having a great capacity for endurance; hardy and fit: *a tough mountaineer.* [4] rough or pugnacious: *a tough gangster.* [5] resolute or intractable: *a tough employer.* [6] difficult or troublesome to do or deal with: *a tough problem.* [7] *Informal* unfortunate or unlucky: *it's tough on him.* ◆ NOUN [8] a rough, vicious, or pugnacious person. ◆ ADVERB [9] *Informal* violently, aggressively, or intractably: *to treat someone tough.* [10] **hang tough.** *Informal* to be or appear to be strong or determined. ◆ VERB *(tr)* [11] *Slang* to stand firm, hold out against (a difficulty or difficult situation) (esp in **tough it out**).
▷HISTORY Old English *tōh;* related to Old High German *zāhi* tough, Old Norse *tā* trodden ground in front of a house
▸ **'toughish** ADJECTIVE ▸ **'toughly** ADVERB

toughen ('tʌfən) VERB to make or become tough or tougher.

tough love NOUN the practice of taking a stern attitude towards a relative or friend suffering from an addiction, etc., to help the addict overcome the problem.

tough-minded ADJECTIVE practical, unsentimental, stern or intractable.
▸ **ˌtough-'mindedly** ADVERB ▸ **ˌtough-'mindedness** NOUN

toughness ('tʌfnɪs) NOUN [1] the quality or an instance of being tough. [2] *Metallurgy* the ability of a metal to withstand repeated twisting and bending, measured by the energy in kilojoules needed to break it. Compare **brittleness** (sense 2), **softness** (sense 2).

Toul (tuːl) NOUN a town in NE France: a leading episcopal see in the Middle Ages. Pop.: 17 406 (1982).

Toulon *(French* tulɔ̃) NOUN a fortified port and naval base in SE France, on the Mediterranean: naval arsenal developed by Henry IV and Richelieu, later fortified by Vauban. Pop.: 159 389 (1990).

Toulouse (tuː'luːz) NOUN a city in S France, on the Garonne River: scene of severe religious strife in the early 13th and mid-16th centuries; university (1229). Pop.: 390 413 (1999). Ancient name: **Tolosa** (tə'ləʊsə).

toun (tuːn) NOUN *Scot* [1] a town. [2] a farmstead.

toupee ('tuːpeɪ) NOUN [1] a wig or hairpiece worn, esp by men, to cover a bald or balding place. [2] (formerly) a prominent lock on a periwig, esp in the 18th century.
▷HISTORY C18: apparently from French *toupet* forelock, from Old French *toup* top, of Germanic origin; see TOP[1]

tour (tʊə) NOUN [1] an extended journey, usually taken for pleasure, visiting places of interest along the route. [2] *Military* a period of service, esp in one place of duty. [3] a short trip, as for inspection. [4] a trip made by a theatre company, orchestra, etc., to perform in several different places: *a concert tour.* [5] an overseas trip made by a cricket or rugby team, etc., to play in several places. ◆ VERB [6] to make a tour of (a place). [7] to perform (a show) or promote (a product) in several different places.
▷HISTORY C14: from Old French: a turn, from Latin *tornus* a lathe, from Greek *tornos;* compare TURN

touraco *or* **turaco** ('tʊərəˌkəʊ) NOUN, *plural* **-cos.** any brightly coloured crested arboreal African bird of the family *Musophagidae:* order *Cuculiformes* (cuckoos, etc.).
▷HISTORY C18: of West African origin

Touraine *(French* turɛn) NOUN a former province of NW central France: at its height in the 16th century as an area of royal residences, esp along the Loire. Chief town: Tours.

Tourane (tuː'rɑːn) NOUN the former name of **Da Nang.**

tourbillion (tʊə'bɪljən) NOUN a rare word for **whirlwind.**
▷HISTORY C15: from French *tourbillon,* ultimately from Latin *turbō* something that spins, from *turbāre* to confuse

Tourcoing *(French* turkwɛ̃) NOUN a town in NE France: textile manufacturing. Pop.: 93 765 (1990).

tour de force *French* (tur də fɔrs; *English* 'tʊə də 'fɔːs) NOUN, *plural* ***tours de force*** (tur; *English* 'tʊə). a masterly or brilliant stroke, creation, effect, or accomplishment.
▷HISTORY literally: feat of skill or strength

tourer ('tʊərə) NOUN a large open car with a folding top, usually seating a driver and four passengers. Also called (esp US): **touring car.**

Tourette syndrome (tʊə'rɛt) NOUN a brain disorder characterized by involuntary outbursts of swearing, spitting, barking, etc., and sudden involuntary movements. Also called: **Gilles de la Tourette syndrome, Tourette's syndrome, Tourette's.**
▷HISTORY C20: named after Georges Gilles de la Tourette (1857–1904), French neurologist

tourie ('tʊrɪ) NOUN *Scot* a variant spelling of **toorie.**

tourism ('tʊərɪzəm) NOUN tourist travel and the services connected with it, esp when regarded as an industry.

tourist ('tʊərɪst) NOUN [1] **a** a person who travels for pleasure, usually sightseeing and staying in hotels. **b** *(as modifier): tourist attractions.* [2] a person on an excursion or sightseeing tour. [3] a person travelling abroad as a member of a sports team that is playing a series of usually international matches. [4] Also called: **tourist class.** the lowest class of accommodation on a passenger ship. ◆ ADJECTIVE [5] of or relating to tourist accommodation.
▸ **tour'istic** ADJECTIVE

touristy ('tʊərɪstɪ) ADJECTIVE *Informal, often derogatory* abounding in or designed for tourists.

tourmaline ('tʊəməˌliːn) NOUN any of a group of hard glassy minerals of variable colour consisting of complex borosilicates of aluminium with quantities of lithium, sodium, calcium, potassium, iron, and magnesium in hexagonal crystalline form: used in optical and electrical equipment and in jewellery.
▷HISTORY C18: from German *Turmalin,* from Sinhalese *toramalli* carnelian
▸ **tourmalinic** (ˌtʊəmə'lɪnɪk) ADJECTIVE

Tournai *(French* turnɛ) NOUN a city in W Belgium, in Hainaut province on the River Scheldt: under several different European rulers until 1814. Pop.: 68 086 (1995 est.). Flemish name: **Doornik.**

tournament ('tʊənəmənt, 'tɔː-, 'tɜː-) NOUN [1] a sporting competition in which contestants play a series of games to determine an overall winner. [2] a meeting for athletic or other sporting contestants: *an archery tournament.* [3] *Medieval history* **a** (originally) a martial sport or contest in which mounted combatants fought for a prize. **b** (later) a meeting for knightly sports and exercises.
▷HISTORY C13: from Old French *torneiement,* from *torneier* to fight on horseback, literally: to turn, from the constant wheeling round of the combatants; see TOURNEY

tournedos ('tʊənəˌdəʊ) NOUN, *plural* **-dos** (-ˌdəʊz). a thick round steak of beef cut from the fillet or undercut of sirloin.
▷HISTORY from French, from *tourner* to TURN + *dos* back

tourney ('tʊənɪ, 'tɔː-) *Medieval history* ◆ NOUN [1] a knightly tournament. ◆ VERB [2] *(intr)* to engage in a tourney.
▷HISTORY C13: from Old French *torneier,* from Vulgar Latin *tornidiāre* (unattested) to turn constantly, from Latin *tornāre* to TURN (in a lathe); see TOURNAMENT
▸ **'tourneyer** NOUN

tourniquet ('tʊənɪˌkeɪ, 'tɔː-) NOUN *Med* any instrument or device for temporarily constricting an artery of the arm or leg to control bleeding.
▷HISTORY C17: from French: device that operates by turning, from *tourner* to TURN

tour operator NOUN a person or company that provides package holidays.

Tours *(French* tur) NOUN a town in W central France, on the River Loire: nearby is the scene of the defeat of the Arabs in 732, which ended the advance of Islam in W Europe. Pop.: 132 820 (1999).

tourtière (ˌtuːrtɪ'ɛə; *French* turtjɛr) NOUN *Canadian* a type of meat pie.
▷HISTORY from French

tousle ('taʊzᵊl) VERB *(tr)* [1] to tangle, ruffle, or disarrange. [2] to treat roughly. ◆ NOUN [3] a disorderly, tangled, or rumpled state. [4] a dishevelled or disordered mass, esp of hair.
▷HISTORY C15: from Low German *tūsen* to shake; related to Old High German *zirzūsōn* to tear to pieces

tous-les-mois (ˌtuːleɪ'mwɑː) NOUN [1] a large widely cultivated plant, *Canna edulis,* of the Caribbean and South America, having purplish stems and leaves, bright red flowers and edible tubers: family *Cannaceae.* [2] Also called: **Queensland arrowroot.** the tuber of this plant, used as a source of starch.
▷HISTORY C19: from French, literally: all the months, probably an attempt to give phonetic reproduction of *tolomane,* from native West Indian name

tout (taʊt) VERB [1] to solicit (business, customers, etc.) or hawk (merchandise), esp in a brazen way. [2] *(intr)* **a** to spy on racehorses being trained in order to obtain information for betting purposes. **b** to sell, or attempt to sell, such information or to take bets, esp in public places. [3] *(tr) Informal* to recommend flatteringly or excessively. ◆ NOUN [4] **a** a person who spies on racehorses so as to obtain betting information to sell. **b** a person who sells information obtained by such spying. [5] a person who solicits business in a brazen way. [6] Also called: **ticket tout.** a person who sells tickets unofficially for a heavily booked sporting event, concert, etc., at greatly inflated prices. [7] *Northern Ireland* a police informer.
▷HISTORY C14 (in the sense: to peer, look out): related to Old English *tӯtan* to peep out
▸ **'touter** NOUN

tout à fait *French* (tut a fɛ) ADVERB completely; absolutely.

tout court *French* (tu kur) ADVERB simply; briefly.

tout de suite *French* (tud sɥit) ADVERB at once; immediately.

tout ensemble *French* (tut ɑ̃sɑ̃blə) ADVERB [1] everything considered; all in all. ◆ NOUN [2] the total impression or effect.

tout le monde *French* (tu lə mɔ̃d) NOUN all the world; everyone.

touzle ('taʊzᵊl) VERB, NOUN a rare spelling of **tousle.**

tovarisch, tovarich, *or* **tovarish** (tə'vɑːrɪʃ; *Russian* ta'varjiʃtʃ) NOUN comrade: a term of address.
▷HISTORY from Russian

tow[1] (təʊ) VERB [1] *(tr)* to pull or drag (a vehicle, boat, etc.), esp by means of a rope or cable. ◆ NOUN [2] the act or an instance of towing. [3] the state of being towed (esp in the phrases **in tow, under tow, on tow**). [4] something towed. [5] something used for towing. [6] **in tow.** in one's charge or under one's influence. [7] *Informal* (in motor racing, etc.) the act

of taking advantage of the slipstream of another car (esp in the phrase **get a tow**). [8] short for **ski tow**.
▷HISTORY Old English *togian;* related to Old Frisian *togia,* Old Norse *toga,* Old High German *zogōn*
▸ **'towable** ADJECTIVE

tow² (təʊ) NOUN [1] the fibres of hemp, flax, jute, etc., in the scutched state. [2] synthetic fibres preparatory to spinning. [3] the coarser fibres discarded after combing.
▷HISTORY Old English *tōw;* related to Old Saxon *tou,* Old Norse *tō* tuft of wool, Dutch *touwen* to spin
▸ **'towy** ADJECTIVE

towage ('təʊɪdʒ) NOUN [1] a charge made for towing. [2] the act of towing or the state of being towed.

toward ADJECTIVE ('təʊəd) [1] *Now rare* in progress; afoot. [2] *Obsolete* about to happen; imminent. [3] *Obsolete* promising or favourable. ◆ PREPOSITION (tə'wɔːd, tɔːd) [4] a variant of **towards**.
▷HISTORY Old English *tōweard;* see TO, -WARD

towardly ('təʊədlɪ) ADJECTIVE *Archaic* [1] compliant. [2] propitious or suitable.
▸ **'towardliness** *or* **'towardness** NOUN

towards (tə'wɔːdz, tɔːdz) PREPOSITION [1] in the direction or vicinity of: *towards London.* [2] with regard to: *her feelings towards me.* [3] as a contribution or help to: *money towards a new car.* [4] just before: *towards one o'clock.* [5] *Irish* in comparison with: *it's no work towards having to do it by hand.* ◆ Also: **toward.**

towbar ('təʊˌbɑː) NOUN a rigid metal bar or frame used for towing vehicles. Compare **towrope, towline.**

towboat ('təʊˌbəʊt) NOUN another word for **tug** (the boat).

tow-coloured ADJECTIVE pale yellow; flaxen.

towel ('taʊəl) NOUN [1] a square or rectangular piece of absorbent cloth or paper used for drying the body. [2] a similar piece of cloth used for drying plates, cutlery, etc. [3] **throw in the towel.** See **throw in** (sense 4). ◆ VERB **-els, -elling, -elled** *or US* **-els, -eling, -eled.** [4] *(tr)* to dry or wipe with a towel. [5] *(tr; often foll by up) Austral slang* to assault or beat (a person).
▷HISTORY C13: from Old French *toaille,* of Germanic origin; related to Old High German *dwahal* bath, Old Saxon *twahila* towel, Gothic *thwahan* to wash

towelling ('taʊəlɪŋ) NOUN an absorbent fabric, esp with a nap, used for making towels, bathrobes, etc.

towel rail NOUN a rail or frame in a bathroom, etc., for hanging towels on.

tower ('taʊə) NOUN [1] a tall, usually square or circular structure, sometimes part of a larger building and usually built for a specific purpose: *a church tower; a control tower.* [2] a place of defence or retreat. [3] a mobile structure used in medieval warfare to attack a castle, etc. [4] **tower of strength.** a person who gives support, comfort, etc. ◆ VERB [5] *(intr)* to be or rise like a tower; loom.
▷HISTORY C12: from Old French *tur,* from Latin *turris,* from Greek

tower crane NOUN a rotatable cantilever jib on top of a steelwork tower used on building sites where the operator needs to command a good view of the site.

towered ('taʊəd) ADJECTIVE **a** having a tower or towers. **b** *(in combination): four-towered; high-towered.*

Tower Hamlets NOUN a borough of E Greater London, on the River Thames: contains the main part of the East End. Pop.: 196 121 (2001). Area: 20 sq. km (8 sq. miles).

towering ('taʊərɪŋ) ADJECTIVE [1] very tall; lofty. [2] outstanding, as in importance or stature. [3] *(prenominal)* very intense: *a towering rage.*
▸ **'toweringly** ADVERB

Tower of London NOUN a fortress in the City of London, on the River Thames: begun 1078; later extended and used as a palace, the main state prison, and now as a museum containing the crown jewels.

tow-haired (ˌtəʊ'hɛəd) ADJECTIVE having blond and sometimes tousled hair.

towhead ('təʊˌhɛd) NOUN *Often disparaging* [1] a person with blond or yellowish hair. [2] a head of such hair.
▷HISTORY from TOW² (flax)

towheaded (ˌtəʊ'hɛdɪd) ADJECTIVE *Often disparaging* (of a person) having blond or yellowish hair.

towhee ('taʊhɪ, 'təʊ-) NOUN any of various North American brownish-coloured sparrows of the genera *Pipilo* and *Chlorura.*
▷HISTORY C18: imitative of its note

towie ('taʊɪ) NOUN *Austral informal* a truck used for towing.

towing path NOUN another name for **towpath.**

towkay (taʊ'keɪ) NOUN sir; master: used as a form of address.
▷HISTORY of Chinese origin

towline ('təʊˌlaɪn) NOUN another name for **towrope.**

town (taʊn) NOUN [1] **a** a densely populated urban area, typically smaller than a city and larger than a village, having some local powers of government and a fixed boundary. **b** *(as modifier): town life.* Related adjective: **urban.** [2] a city, borough, or other urban area. [3] (in the US) a territorial unit of local government that is smaller than a county; township. [4] the nearest town or commercial district. [5] London or the chief city of an area. [6] the inhabitants of a town. [7] the permanent residents of a university town as opposed to the university staff and students. Compare **gown** (sense 3). [8] **go to town. a** to make a supreme or unrestricted effort; go all out. **b** *Austral and NZ informal* to lose one's temper. [9] **on the town.** seeking out entertainments and amusements.
▷HISTORY Old English *tūn* village; related to Old Saxon, Old Norse *tūn,* Old High German *zūn* fence, Old Irish *dūn*
▸ **'townish** ADJECTIVE ▸ **'townless** ADJECTIVE

town clerk NOUN [1] (in Britain until 1974) the secretary and chief administrative officer of a town or city. [2] (in the US) the official who keeps the records of a town.

town crier NOUN (formerly) a person employed by a town to make public announcements in the streets.

town gas NOUN coal gas manufactured for domestic and industrial use.

town hall NOUN the chief building in which municipal business is transacted, often with a hall for public meetings.

townhall clock ('taʊnˌhɔːl) NOUN *Brit* another name for **moschatel.**

town house NOUN [1] a terraced house in an urban area, esp a fashionable one, often having the main living room on the first floor with an integral garage on the ground floor. [2] a person's town residence as distinct from his country residence. [3] another name (now chiefly Scot) for **town hall.** [4] a US and Canadian name for **terraced house.**

townie ('taʊnɪ) *or* **townee** (taʊ'niː) NOUN *Informal, often disparaging* a permanent resident in a town, esp as distinct from country dwellers or students.

townland ('taʊnlænd) NOUN *Irish* a division of land of various sizes.

town meeting NOUN *US* [1] an assembly of the inhabitants of a town. [2] (esp in New England) an assembly of the qualified voters of a town. Such a meeting may exercise all the powers of local government.

town milk NOUN *NZ* milk treated by pasteurization for direct consumption, as opposed to dairy factory milk for the production of butter, cheese, etc.

town planning NOUN the comprehensive planning of the physical and social development of a town, including the construction of facilities. US term: **city planning.**
▸ **town planner** NOUN

townscape ('taʊnskeɪp) NOUN a view of an urban scene.

township ('taʊnʃɪp) NOUN [1] a small town. [2] (in the Scottish Highlands and islands) a small crofting community. [3] (in the US and Canada) a territorial area, esp a subdivision of a county: often organized as a unit of local government. [4] (formerly, in South Africa) a planned urban settlement of Black Africans or Coloured people. Compare **location** (sense 4). [5] *English history* **a** any of the local districts of a large parish, each division containing a village or small town. **b** the particular manor or parish itself as a territorial division. **c** the inhabitants of a township collectively.

townsman ('taʊnzmən) NOUN, *plural* **-men.** [1] an inhabitant of a town. [2] a person from the same town as oneself.
▸ **'towns͵woman** FEMININE NOUN

townspeople ('taʊnzˌpiːpᵊl) *or* **townsfolk** NOUN the inhabitants of a town; citizens.

Townsville ('taʊnzvɪl) NOUN a port in E Australia, in NE Queensland on the Coral Sea: centre of a vast agricultural and mining hinterland. Pop.: 87 235 (1998 est.).

towpath ('təʊˌpɑːθ) NOUN a path beside a canal or river, used by people or animals towing boats. Also called: **towing path.**

towrope ('təʊˌrəʊp) NOUN a rope or cable used for towing a vehicle or vessel. Also called: **towline.**

tow truck NOUN a US and Canadian name for **breakdown van.**

tox. *or* **toxicol.** ABBREVIATION FOR toxicology.

tox-, toxic-, *or before a consonant* **toxo-, toxico-** *combining form.* indicating poison: *toxalbumin.*
▷HISTORY from Latin *toxicum*

toxaemia *or US* **toxemia** (tɒk'siːmɪə) NOUN [1] a condition characterized by the presence of bacterial toxins in the blood. [2] the condition in pregnancy of pre-eclampsia or eclampsia.
▷HISTORY C19: from TOX- + -AEMIA
▸ **tox'aemic** *or (US)* **tox'emic** ADJECTIVE

toxalbumin (ˌtɒksæl'bjuːmɪn) NOUN *Biochem* any of a group of toxic albumins that occur in certain plants, such as toadstools, and in snake venom.

toxaphene ('tɒksəˌfiːn) NOUN an amber waxy solid with a pleasant pine odour, consisting of chlorinated terpenes, esp chlorinated camphene: used as an insecticide.

toxic ('tɒksɪk) ADJECTIVE [1] of, relating to, or caused by a toxin or poison; poisonous. [2] harmful or deadly.
▷HISTORY C17: from medical Latin *toxicus,* from Latin *toxicum* poison, from Greek *toxikon (pharmakon)* (poison) used on arrows, from *toxon* arrow
▸ **'toxically** ADVERB

toxicant ('tɒksɪkənt) NOUN [1] a toxic substance; poison. [2] a rare word for **intoxicant.** ◆ ADJECTIVE [3] poisonous; toxic.
▷HISTORY C19: from Medieval Latin *toxicāre* to poison; see TOXIC

toxic effect NOUN an adverse effect of a drug produced by an exaggeration of the effect that produces the theraputic response.

toxicity (tɒk'sɪsɪtɪ) NOUN [1] the degree of strength of a poison. [2] the state or quality of being poisonous.

toxicogenic (ˌtɒksɪkəʊ'dʒɛnɪk) ADJECTIVE [1] producing toxic substances or effects. [2] caused or produced by a toxin.

toxicology (ˌtɒksɪ'kɒlədʒɪ) NOUN the branch of science concerned with poisons, their nature, effects, and antidotes.
▸ **toxicological** (ˌtɒksɪkə'lɒdʒɪkᵊl) *or* **ˌtoxico'logic** ADJECTIVE ▸ **ˌtoxico'logically** ADVERB ▸ **ˌtoxi'cologist** NOUN

toxicosis (ˌtɒksɪ'kəʊsɪs) NOUN any disease or condition caused by poisoning.
▷HISTORY C19: from New Latin, from TOXIC + -OSIS

toxic shock syndrome NOUN a potentially fatal condition in women, characterized by fever, stomachache, a painful rash, and a drop in blood pressure, that is caused by staphylococcal blood poisoning, most commonly from a retained tampon during menstruation.

toxin ('tɒksɪn) NOUN [1] any of various poisonous substances produced by microorganisms that stimulate the production of neutralizing substances (antitoxins) in the body. See also **endotoxin, exotoxin.** [2] any other poisonous substance of plant or animal origin.

toxin-antitoxin NOUN a mixture of a specific toxin and antitoxin. The diphtheria toxin-antitoxin was formerly used in the US for active immunization.

toxocariasis (ˌtɒksəkə'raɪəsɪs) NOUN the infection of humans with the larvae of a genus of roundworms, *Toxocara,* of dogs and cats. It can cause swelling of the liver and, sometimes, damage to the eyes.

toxoid ('tɒksɔɪd) NOUN a toxin that has been treated to reduce its toxicity and is used in immunization to stimulate production of antitoxins.

toxophilite (tɒk'sɒfɪˌlaɪt) *Formal* ◆ NOUN [1] an archer. ◆ ADJECTIVE [2] of or relating to archery.
▷HISTORY C18: from *Toxophilus,* the title of a book (1545) by Ascham, designed to mean: a lover of the bow, from Greek *toxon* bow + *philos* loving
▸**tox'ophily** NOUN

toxoplasmosis (ˌtɒksəʊplæz'məʊsɪs) NOUN a protozoal disease characterized by jaundice, enlarged liver and spleen, and convulsions, caused by infection with *Toxoplasma gondii.*
▸**ˌtoxo'plasmic** ADJECTIVE

toy (tɔɪ) NOUN [1] an object designed to be played with. [2] **a** something that is a nonfunctioning replica of something else, esp a miniature one. **b** (*as modifier*): *a toy guitar.* [3] any small thing of little value; trifle. [4] **a** something small or miniature, esp a miniature variety of a breed of dog. **b** (*as modifier*): *a toy poodle.* ◆ VERB [5] (*intr;* usually foll by *with*) to play, fiddle, or flirt.
▷HISTORY C16 (in the sense: amorous dalliance): of uncertain origin
▸**'toyer** NOUN ▸**'toyless** ADJECTIVE ▸**'toyˌlike** ADJECTIVE

Toyama ('təʊjɑːˌmɑː) NOUN a city in central Japan, on W Honshu on **Toyama Bay** (an inlet of the Sea of Japan): chemical and textile centre. Pop.: 325 303 (1995).

toy boy NOUN the much younger male lover of an older woman.

toytown ('tɔɪˌtaʊn) ADJECTIVE [1] having an unreal and picturesque appearance: *toytown chalets.* [2] not deserving to be taken seriously: *toytown revolutionaries.*
▷HISTORY C20: from *Toy Town,* the fictional setting of children's stories by Enid Blyton

toy-toy *or* **toyi-toyi** ('tɔɪ'tɔɪ) *South African* ◆ NOUN [1] a dance expressing defiance and protest. ◆ VERB [2] (*intr*) to dance in this way.
▷HISTORY of uncertain origin

tp THE INTERNET DOMAIN NAME FOR East Timor.

TPI ABBREVIATION FOR tax and price index: a measure of the increase in taxable income needed to compensate for an increase in retail prices.

T-piece NOUN a strut or part shaped like a T.

T-plate NOUN a metal plate shaped like a T used to strengthen or effect a right-angled joint between two beams, etc.

TPN NOUN *Biochem* triphosphopyridine nucleotide; a former name for **NADP**.

Tpr ABBREVIATION FOR Trooper.

TPWS ABBREVIATION FOR train protection warning system: a rail safety system fitted to track signals.

TQM ABBREVIATION FOR **total quality management**.

tr¹ ABBREVIATION FOR treasurer.

tr² THE INTERNET DOMAIN NAME FOR Turkey.

TR INTERNATIONAL CAR REGISTRATION FOR Turkey.

tr. ABBREVIATION FOR: [1] transitive. [2] translated. [3] *Music* trill.

trabeated ('treɪbɪˌeɪtɪd) *or* **trabeate** ('treɪbɪɪt, -ˌeɪt) ADJECTIVE *Architect* constructed with horizontal beams as opposed to arches. Compare **arcuate.**
▷HISTORY C19: back formation from *trabeation,* from Latin *trabs* a beam
▸**ˌtrabe'ation** NOUN

trabecula (trə'bɛkjʊlə) NOUN, *plural* **-lae** (-ˌliː). *Anatomy, botany* [1] any of various rod-shaped structures that divide organs into separate chambers. [2] any of various rod-shaped cells or structures that bridge a cavity, as within the capsule of a moss or across the lumen of a cell.
▷HISTORY C19: via New Latin from Latin: a little beam, from *trabs* a beam
▸**tra'becular** *or* **tra'beculate** ADJECTIVE

trabs (træbz) PLURAL NOUN *Northern English dialect* training shoes.

Trabzon ('trɑːbzɔːn) *or* **Trebizond** NOUN a port in NE Turkey, on the Black Sea: founded as a Greek colony in the 8th century B.C. at the terminus of an important trade route from central Europe to Asia. Pop.: 182 552 (1997).

tracasserie (trə'kæsərɪ) NOUN a turmoil; annoyance.
▷HISTORY from French, from *tracasser* to fuss about

trace¹ (treɪs) NOUN [1] a mark or other sign that something has been in a place; vestige. [2] a tiny or scarcely detectable amount or characteristic. [3] a footprint or other indication of the passage of an animal or person. [4] any line drawn by a recording instrument or a record consisting of a number of such lines. [5] something drawn, such as a tracing. [6] *Chiefly US* a beaten track or path. [7] the postulated alteration in the cells of the nervous system that occurs as the result of any experience or learning. See also **memory trace, engram.** [8] *Geometry* the intersection of a surface with a coordinate plane. [9] *Maths* the sum of the diagonal entries of a square matrix. [10] *Linguistics* a symbol inserted in the constituent structure of a sentence to mark the position from which a constituent has been moved in a generative process. [11] *Meteorol* an amount of precipitation that is too small to be measured. [12] *Archaic* a way taken; route. ◆ VERB [13] (*tr*) to follow, discover, or ascertain the course or development of (something): *to trace the history of China.* [14] (*tr*) to track down and find, as by following a trail. [15] to copy (a design, map, etc.) by drawing over the lines visible through a superimposed sheet of transparent paper or other material. [16] (*tr;* often foll by *out*) **a** to draw or delineate a plan or diagram of: *she spent hours tracing the models one at a time.* **b** to outline or sketch (an idea, policy, etc.): *he traced out his scheme for the robbery.* [17] (*tr*) to decorate with tracery. [18] (*tr*) to imprint (a design) on cloth, etc. [19] (usually foll by *back*) to follow or be followed to source; date back: *his ancestors trace back to the 16th century.* [20] *Archaic* to make one's way over, through, or along (something).
▷HISTORY C13: from French *tracier,* from Vulgar Latin *tractiāre* (unattested) to drag, from Latin *tractus,* from *trahere* to drag
▸**'traceable** ADJECTIVE ▸**ˌtracea'bility** *or* **'traceableness** NOUN ▸**'traceably** ADVERB ▸**'traceless** ADJECTIVE ▸**'tracelessly** ADVERB

trace² (treɪs) NOUN [1] either of the two side straps that connect a horse's harness to the swingletree. [2] *Angling* a length of nylon or, formerly, gut attaching a hook or fly to a line. [3] **kick over the traces.** to escape or defy control.
▷HISTORY C14 *trais,* from Old French *trait,* ultimately from Latin *trahere* to drag

trace element NOUN any of various chemical elements, such as iron, manganese, zinc, copper, and iodine, that occur in very small amounts in organisms and are essential for many physiological and biochemical processes.

trace fossil NOUN the fossilized remains of a track, trail, footprint, burrow, etc., of an organism.

tracer ('treɪsə) NOUN [1] a person or thing that traces. [2] **a** a projectile that can be observed when in flight by the burning of chemical substances in its base. **b** ammunition consisting of such projectiles. **c** (*as modifier*): *tracer fire.* [3] *Med* any radioactive isotope introduced into the body to study metabolic processes, absorption, etc., by following its progress through the body with a gamma camera or other detector. [4] an investigation to trace missing cargo, mail, etc.

tracer bullet NOUN a round of small arms ammunition containing a tracer.

tracery ('treɪsərɪ) NOUN, *plural* **-eries.** [1] a pattern of interlacing ribs, esp as used in the upper part of a Gothic window, etc. [2] any fine pattern resembling this.
▸**'traceried** ADJECTIVE

trachea (trə'kiːə) NOUN, *plural* **-cheae** (-'kiːiː). [1] *Anatomy, zoology* the membranous tube with cartilaginous rings that conveys inhaled air from the larynx to the bronchi. Nontechnical name: **windpipe.** [2] any of the tubes in insects and related animals that convey air from the spiracles to the tissues. [3] *Botany* another name for **vessel** (sense 5). or **tracheid.**
▷HISTORY C16: from Medieval Latin, from Greek *trakheia,* shortened from (*artēria*) *trakheia* rough (artery), from *trakhus* rough
▸**tra'cheal** *or* **tra'cheate** ADJECTIVE

tracheid ('treɪkɪɪd) *or* **tracheide** NOUN *Botany* an element of xylem tissue consisting of an elongated lignified cell with tapering ends and large pits.
▷HISTORY C19: from TRACHEA (in the sense: a vessel in a plant) + -ID²
▸**tracheidal** (trə'kiːɪdᵊl, ˌtreɪkɪ'aɪdᵊl) ADJECTIVE

tracheitis (ˌtreɪkɪ'aɪtɪs) NOUN inflammation of the trachea.

tracheo- *or before a vowel* **trache-** COMBINING FORM denoting the trachea: *tracheotomy.*

tracheophyte ('treɪkɪəʊˌfaɪt) NOUN any plant that has a conducting system of xylem and phloem elements; a vascular plant.

tracheostomy (ˌtrækɪ'ɒstəmɪ) NOUN, *plural* **-mies.** the surgical formation of a temporary or permanent opening into the trachea following tracheotomy.

tracheotomy (ˌtrækɪ'ɒtəmɪ) NOUN, *plural* **-mies.** surgical incision into the trachea, usually performed when the upper air passage has been blocked.

trachoma (trə'kəʊmə) NOUN a chronic contagious disease of the eye characterized by inflammation of the conjunctiva and cornea and the formation of scar tissue, caused by infection with the virus-like bacterium *Chlamydia trachomatis.*
▷HISTORY C17: from New Latin, from Greek *trakhōma* roughness, from *trakhus* rough
▸**trachomatous** (trə'kɒmətəs, -'kəʊ-) ADJECTIVE

trachyte ('treɪkaɪt, 'træ-) NOUN a light-coloured fine-grained volcanic rock of rough texture consisting of feldspars with small amounts of pyroxene or amphibole.
▷HISTORY C19: from French, from Greek *trakhutēs,* from *trakhus* rough
▸**trachytoid** ('trækɪˌtɔɪd, 'treɪ-) ADJECTIVE

trachytic (trə'kɪtɪk) ADJECTIVE (of the texture of certain igneous rocks) characterized by a parallel arrangement of crystals, which mark the flow of the lava when still molten.

tracing ('treɪsɪŋ) NOUN [1] a copy made by tracing. [2] the act of making a trace. [3] a record made by an instrument.

tracing paper NOUN strong transparent paper used for tracing.

track (træk) NOUN [1] the mark or trail left by something that has passed by: *the track of an animal.* [2] any road or path affording passage, esp a rough one. [3] a rail or pair of parallel rails on which a vehicle, such as a locomotive, runs, esp the rails together with the sleepers, ballast, etc., on a railway. [4] a course of action, thought, etc.: *don't start on that track again!* [5] a line of motion or travel, such as flight. [6] an endless jointed metal band driven by the wheels of a vehicle such as a tank or tractor to enable it to move across rough or muddy ground. [7] *Physics* the path of a particle of ionizing radiation as observed in a cloud chamber, bubble chamber, or photographic emulsion. [8] **a** a course for running or racing. **b** (*as modifier*): *track events.* [9] *US and Canadian* **a** sports performed on a track. **b** track and field events as a whole. [10] a path on a magnetic recording medium, esp magnetic tape, on which information, such as music or speech, from a single input channel is recorded. [11] any of a number of separate sections in the recording on a record, CD, or cassette. [12] a metal path that makes the interconnections on an integrated circuit. [13] the distance between the points of contact with the ground of a pair of wheels, such as the front wheels of a motor vehicle or the paired wheels of an aircraft undercarriage. [14] a hypothetical trace made on the surface of the earth by a point directly below an aircraft in flight. [15] **keep** (*or* **lose**) **track of.** to follow (or fail to follow) the passage, course, or progress of. [16] **off the beaten track.** See **beaten** (sense 4). [17] **off the track.** away from what is correct or true. [18] **on the track of.** on the scent or trail of; pursuing. [19] **the right** (*or* **wrong**) **track.** pursuing the correct (or incorrect) line of investigation, inquiry, etc. ◆ VERB [20] to follow the trail of (a person, animal, etc.). [21] to follow the flight path of (a satellite, spacecraft, etc.) by picking up radio or radar signals transmitted or reflected by it. [22] *US railways* **a** to provide with a track. **b** to run on a track of (a certain width). [23] (of a camera or camera operator) to follow (a moving object) in any direction while operating. [24] to move (a camera) towards the scene (**track in**) or away from the scene (**track out**). [25] to follow a track through (a place): *to*

track the jungles. [26] (*intr*) (of the pick-up, stylus, etc., of a record player) to follow the groove of a record: *the pick-up tracks badly.* ◆ See also **tracks.**
▷HISTORY C15: from Old French *trac*, probably of Germanic origin; related to Middle Dutch *tracken* to pull, Middle Low German *trecken*; compare Norwegian *trakke* to trample
▸ˈ**trackable** ADJECTIVE ▸ˈ**tracker** NOUN

trackball (ˈtræk,bɔːl) *or* **trackerball** (ˈtrækə,bɔːl) NOUN *Computing* a device consisting of a small ball, mounted in a cup, which can be rotated to move the cursor around the screen.

track down VERB (*tr, adverb*) to find by tracking or pursuing.

tracker dog NOUN a dog specially trained to hunt fugitives or to search for missing people.

tracker fund NOUN *Finance* an investment fund that is administered so that its value changes in line with the average value of shares in a market.

track event NOUN a competition in athletics, such as relay running or sprinting, that takes place on a running track.

tracking (ˈtrækɪŋ) NOUN [1] the act or process of following something or someone. [2] *Electrical engineering* a leakage of electric current between two points separated by an insulating material caused by dirt, carbon particles, moisture, etc.

tracking radar NOUN a radar system emitting a narrow beam which oscillates about the target, thus compensating for abrupt changes of direction.

tracking shot NOUN a camera shot in which the cameraman follows a specific person or event in the action.

tracking station NOUN a station that can use a radio or radar beam to determine and follow the path of an object, esp a spacecraft or satellite, in space or in the atmosphere.

tracklaying (ˈtræk,leɪɪŋ) ADJECTIVE (of a vehicle) having an endless jointed metal band around the wheels.

trackless (ˈtræklɪs) ADJECTIVE [1] having or leaving no trace or trail: *a trackless jungle.* [2] (of a vehicle) using or having no tracks.
▸ˈ**tracklessly** ADVERB ▸ˈ**tracklessness** NOUN

trackman (ˈtrækmən) NOUN, *plural* **-men.** the US and Canadian name for **platelayer.**

track meet NOUN *US and Canadian* an athletics meeting.

track record NOUN *Informal* the past record of the accomplishments and failures of a person, business, etc.

track rod NOUN the rod connecting the two front wheels of a motor vehicle ensuring that they turn at the same angle.

tracks (træks) PLURAL NOUN [1] (*sometimes singular*) marks, such as footprints, tyre impressions, etc., left by someone or something that has passed. [2] **in one's tracks.** on the very spot where one is standing (esp in the phrase **stop in one's tracks**). [3] **make tracks.** to leave or depart. [4] **make tracks for.** to go or head towards. [5] **the wrong side of the tracks.** the unfashionable or poor district or stratum of a community.

track shoe NOUN either of a pair of light running shoes fitted with steel spikes for better grip. Also called: **spike.**

tracksuit (ˈtræk,suːt, -,sjuːt) NOUN a warm suit worn by athletes, etc. usually over the clothes, esp during training.

tract[1] (trækt) NOUN [1] an extended area, as of land. [2] *Anatomy* a system of organs, glands, or other tissues that has a particular function: *the digestive tract.* [3] a bundle of nerve fibres having the same function, origin, and termination: *the optic tract.* [4] *Archaic* an extended period of time.
▷HISTORY C15: from Latin *tractus* a stretching out, from *trahere* to drag

tract[2] (trækt) NOUN a treatise or pamphlet, esp a religious or moralistic one.
▷HISTORY C15: from Latin *tractātus* TRACTATE

tract[3] (trækt) NOUN *RC Church* an anthem in some Masses.
▷HISTORY C14: from Medieval Latin *tractus cantus* extended song; see TRACT[1]

tractable (ˈtræktəbᵊl) ADJECTIVE [1] easily controlled or persuaded. [2] readily worked; malleable.
▷HISTORY C16: from Latin *tractābilis*, from *tractāre* to manage, from *trahere* to draw
▸,**tractaˈbility** *or* ˈ**tractableness** NOUN ▸ˈ**tractably** ADVERB

Tractarianism (trækˈtɛərɪə,nɪzəm) NOUN another name for the **Oxford Movement.**
▸**Tracˈtarian** NOUN, ADJECTIVE

tractate (ˈtrækteɪt) NOUN [1] a short tract; treatise. [2] *Judaism* one of the volumes of the Talmud.
▷HISTORY C15: from Latin *tractātus*, from *tractāre* to handle; see TRACTABLE

tractile (ˈtræktaɪl) ADJECTIVE capable of being drawn out; ductile.
▷HISTORY C17: from Latin *trahere* to drag
▸**tractility** (trækˈtɪlɪtɪ) NOUN

traction (ˈtrækʃən) NOUN [1] the act of drawing or pulling, esp by motive power. [2] the state of being drawn or pulled. [3] *Med* the application of a steady pull on a part during healing of a fractured or dislocated bone, using a system of weights and pulleys or splints. [4] the adhesive friction between a wheel and a surface, as between a driving wheel of a motor vehicle and the road.
▷HISTORY C17: from Medieval Latin *tractiō*, from Latin *tractus* dragged; see TRACTILE
▸ˈ**tractional** ADJECTIVE ▸**tractive** (ˈtræktɪv) ADJECTIVE

traction control NOUN (in motor racing cars) a method of preventing wheels from spinning when traction is applied by limiting the amount of power supplied to the wheel.

traction engine NOUN a steam-powered locomotive used, esp formerly, for drawing heavy loads along roads or over rough ground. It usually has two large rear wheels and a rope drum for haulage purposes.

traction load NOUN *Geology* the solid material that is carried along the bed of a river.

tractive force NOUN the force measured in the drawbar of a locomotive or tractor.

tractor (ˈtræktə) NOUN [1] a motor vehicle used to pull heavy loads, esp farm machinery such as a plough or harvester. It usually has two large rear wheels with deeply treaded tyres. [2] a short motor vehicle with a powerful engine and a driver's cab, used to pull a trailer, as in an articulated lorry. [3] an aircraft with its propeller or propellers mounted in front of the engine.
▷HISTORY C18: from Late Latin: one who pulls, from *trahere* to drag

tractorfeed (ˈtræktə,fiːd) NOUN *Computing* the automatic movement of a continuous roll of edge-perforated paper through the platen of the printer.

trad (træd) NOUN [1] *Chiefly Brit* traditional jazz, as revived in the 1950s. ◆ ADJECTIVE [2] short for **traditional.**

trade (treɪd) NOUN [1] the act or an instance of buying and selling goods and services either on the domestic (wholesale and retail) markets or on the international (import, export, and entrepôt) markets. Related adjective: **mercantile.** [2] a personal occupation, esp a craft requiring skill. [3] the people and practices of an industry, craft, or business. [4] exchange of one thing for something else. [5] the regular clientele of a firm or industry. [6] amount of custom or commercial dealings; business. [7] a specified market or business: *the tailoring trade.* [8] an occupation in commerce, as opposed to a profession. [9] commercial customers, as opposed to the general public: *trade only; trade advertising.* [10] *Homosexual slang* a sexual partner or sexual partners collectively. [11] *Archaic* a custom or habit. ◆ VERB [12] (*tr*) to buy and sell (commercial merchandise). [13] to exchange (one thing) for another. [14] (*intr*) to engage in trade. [15] (*intr*) to deal or do business (with): *we trade with them regularly.* ◆ ADJECTIVE [16] intended for or available only to people in industry or business: *trade prices.* ◆ See also **trade down, trade-in, trade on, trade up.**
▷HISTORY C14 (in the sense: track, hence, a regular business): related to Old Saxon *trada*, Old High German *trata* track; see TREAD
▸ˈ**tradable** *or* ˈ**tradeable** ADJECTIVE ▸ˈ**tradeless** ADJECTIVE

trade agreement NOUN a commercial treaty between two or more nations.

trade association NOUN an association of organizations in the same trade formed to further their collective interests, esp in negotiating with governments, trade unions, etc.

trade bill NOUN a bill of exchange drawn on and accepted (**trade acceptance**) by a trader in payment for goods.

trade book *or* **edition** NOUN an ordinary edition of a book sold in the normal way in shops, as opposed to a de luxe or mail-order edition.

trade cycle NOUN the recurrent fluctuation between boom and depression in the economic activity of a capitalist country. Also called (esp US and Canadian): **business cycle.**

trade discount NOUN a sum or percentage deducted from the list price of a commodity allowed by a manufacturer, distributor, or wholesaler to a retailer or by one enterprise to another in the same trade.

traded option NOUN *Stock Exchange* an option that can itself be bought and sold on a stock exchange. Compare **traditional option.**

trade down VERB (*intr, adverb*) to sell a large or relatively expensive house, car, etc., and replace it with a smaller or less expensive one.

trade gap NOUN the amount by which the value of a country's visible imports exceeds that of visible exports; an unfavourable balance of trade.

trade-in NOUN [1] **a** a used article given in part payment for the purchase of a new article. **b** a transaction involving such part payment. **c** the valuation put on the article traded in. **d** (*as modifier*): *a trade-in dealer.* ◆ VERB **trade in.** [2] (*tr, adverb*) to give (a used article) as part payment for the purchase of a new article.

trade journal NOUN a periodical containing new developments, discussions, etc., concerning a trade or profession.

trade-last NOUN *US informal* a compliment that one has heard about someone, which one offers to tell to that person in exchange for a compliment heard about oneself.

trademark (ˈtreɪd,mɑːk) NOUN [1] the name or other symbol used to identify the goods produced by a particular manufacturer or distributed by a particular dealer and to distinguish them from products associated with competing manufacturers or dealers. A trademark that has been officially registered and is therefore legally protected is known as a **Registered Trademark.** [2] any distinctive sign or mark of the presence of a person or animal. ◆ VERB (*tr*) [3] to label with a trademark. [4] to register as a trademark.

trade name NOUN [1] the name used by a trade to refer to a commodity, service, etc. [2] the name under which a commercial enterprise operates in business.

trade-off NOUN an exchange, esp as a compromise.

trade on VERB (*intr, preposition*) to exploit or take advantage of: *he traded on her endless patience.*

trade plate NOUN a numberplate attached temporarily to a vehicle by a dealer, etc., before the vehicle has been registered.

trader (ˈtreɪdə) NOUN [1] a person who engages in trade; dealer; merchant. [2] a vessel regularly employed in foreign or coastal trade. [3] *Stock Exchange US* a member who operates mainly on his own account rather than for customers' accounts.
▸ˈ**trader,ship** NOUN

trade reference NOUN a reference in which one trader gives his opinion as to the creditworthiness of another trader in the same trade, esp to a supplier.

tradescantia (,trædɛsˈkænʃɪə) NOUN any plant of the American genus *Tradescantia*, widely cultivated for their striped variegated leaves: family *Commelinaceae*. See also **wandering Jew, spiderwort.**
▷HISTORY C18: New Latin, named after John *Tradescant* (1570–1638), English botanist and gardener

trade school NOUN a school or teaching unit organized by an industry or large company to provide trade training, apprentice education, and similar courses.

Trades Council NOUN (in Britain) an association of the different trade unions in one town or area.

trade secret NOUN a secret formula, technique,

process, etc., known and used to advantage by only one manufacturer.

tradesman ('treɪdzmən) NOUN, *plural* **-men.** 1 a man engaged in trade, esp a retail dealer. 2 a skilled worker.
▸'**trades,woman** FEMININE NOUN

tradespeople ('treɪdz,pi:pᵊl) *or* **tradesfolk** ('treɪdz,fəʊk) PLURAL NOUN *Chiefly Brit* people engaged in trade, esp shopkeepers.

Trades Union Congress NOUN the major association of British trade unions, which includes all the larger unions. Abbreviation: **TUC.**

trade union *or* **trades union** NOUN an association of employees formed to improve their incomes and working conditions by collective bargaining with the employer or employer organizations.
▸**trade unionism** *or* **trades unionism** NOUN ▸**trade unionist** *or* **trades unionist** NOUN

trade up VERB (*intr, adverb*) to sell a small or relatively inexpensive house, car, etc., and replace it with a larger or more expensive one.

trade-weighted ADJECTIVE (of exchange rates) weighted according to the volume of trade between the various countries involved.

trade wind (wɪnd) NOUN a wind blowing obliquely towards the equator either from the northeast in the N hemisphere or the southeast in the S hemisphere, approximately between latitudes 30° N and S, forming part of the planetary wind system.
▷HISTORY C17: from *to blow trade* to blow steadily in one direction, from TRADE in the obsolete sense: a track

trading card NOUN any of a set of cards printed with images or information relating to a specific subject, intended to be traded between collectors seeking to acquire a full set.

trading estate NOUN *Chiefly Brit* a large area in which a number of commercial or industrial firms are situated. Also called: **industrial estate.**

trading post NOUN 1 a general store established by a trader in an unsettled or thinly populated region. 2 *Stock Exchange* a booth or location on an exchange floor at which a particular security is traded.

trading stamp NOUN (esp formerly) a stamp of stated value given by some retail organizations to customers, according to the value of their purchases and redeemable for articles offered on a premium list.

tradition (trə'dɪʃən) NOUN 1 the handing down from generation to generation of the same customs, beliefs, etc., esp by word of mouth. 2 the body of customs, thought, practices, etc., belonging to a particular country, people, family, or institution over a relatively long period. 3 a specific custom or practice of long standing. 4 *Christianity* a doctrine or body of doctrines regarded as having been established by Christ or the apostles though not contained in Scripture. 5 (*often capital*) *Judaism* a body of laws regarded as having been handed down from Moses orally and only committed to writing in the 2nd century A.D. 6 the beliefs and customs of Islam supplementing the Koran, esp as embodied in the Sunna. 7 *Law, chiefly Roman and Scots* the act of formally transferring ownership of movable property; delivery.
▷HISTORY C14: from Latin *trāditiō* a handing down, surrender, from *trādere* to give up, transmit, from TRANS- + *dāre* to give
▸**tra'ditionless** ADJECTIVE ▸**tra'ditionist** NOUN

traditional (trə'dɪʃənᵊl) ADJECTIVE 1 of, relating to, or being a tradition. 2 of or relating to the style of jazz originating in New Orleans, characterized by collective improvisation by a front line of trumpet, trombone, and clarinet accompanied by various rhythm instruments.
▸**traditionality** (trə,dɪʃə'nælɪtɪ) NOUN ▸**tra'ditionally** ADVERB

traditionalism (trə'dɪʃənᵊ,lɪzəm) NOUN 1 the doctrine that all knowledge originates in divine revelation and is perpetuated by tradition. 2 adherence to tradition, esp in religion.
▸**tra'ditionalist** NOUN, ADJECTIVE ▸**tra,ditional'istic** ADJECTIVE

traditional option NOUN *Stock Exchange* an option that once purchased cannot be resold. Compare **traded option.**

traditional policy NOUN a life assurance policy in which the policyholder's premiums are paid into a general fund and his investment benefits are calculated according to actuarial formulae. Compare **unit-linked policy.**

traditional weapon NOUN *South African* a weapon having ceremonial tribal significance, such as an assegai or knobkerrie.

traditor ('trædɪtə) NOUN, *plural* **traditores** (,trædɪ'tɔ:ri:z) *or* **traditors.** *Early Church* a Christian who betrayed his fellow Christians at the time of the Roman persecutions.
▷HISTORY C15: from Latin: traitor, from *trādere* to hand over

traduce (trə'dju:s) VERB (*tr*) to speak badly of.
▷HISTORY C16: from Latin *trādūcere* to lead over, transmit, disgrace, from TRANS- + *dūcere* to lead
▸**tra'ducement** NOUN ▸**tra'ducer** NOUN ▸**tra'ducible** ADJECTIVE

traducianism (trə'dju:ʃə,nɪzəm) NOUN the theory that the soul is transmitted to a child in the act of generation or concomitantly with its body. Compare **creationism.**
▷HISTORY C18: from Church Latin *trādūciānus*, from *trādux* transmission; see TRADUCE
▸**tra'ducianist** *or* **tra'ducian** NOUN, ADJECTIVE
▸**tra,ducian'istic** ADJECTIVE

Trafalgar (trə'fælgə; *Spanish* trafal'ɣar) NOUN **Cape.** a cape on the SW coast of Spain, south of Cádiz: scene of the decisive naval battle (1805) in which the French and Spanish fleets were defeated by the British under Nelson, who was mortally wounded.

traffic ('træfɪk) NOUN 1 **a** the vehicles coming and going in a street, town, etc. **b** (*as modifier*): *traffic lights.* 2 the movement of vehicles, people, etc., in a particular place or for a particular purpose: *sea traffic.* 3 **a** the business of commercial transportation by land, sea, or air. **b** the freight, passengers, etc., transported. 4 (usually foll by *with*) dealings or business: *have no traffic with that man.* 5 trade, esp of an illicit or improper kind: *drug traffic.* 6 the aggregate volume of messages transmitted through a communications system in a given period. 7 *Chiefly US* the number of customers patronizing a commercial establishment in a given time period. ◆ VERB **-fics, -ficking, -ficked.** (*intr*) 8 (often foll by *in*) to carry on trade or business, esp of an illicit kind. 9 (usually foll by *with*) to have dealings.
▷HISTORY C16: from Old French *trafique*, from Old Italian *traffico*, from *trafficare* to engage in trade
▸'**trafficker** NOUN ▸'**trafficless** ADJECTIVE

trafficator ('træfɪ,keɪtə) NOUN (formerly) an illuminated arm on a motor vehicle that was raised to indicate a left or right turn. Compare **indicator** (sense 5).

traffic calming NOUN the use of a series of devices, such as bends and humps in the road, to slow down traffic, esp in residential areas.

traffic circle NOUN the US and Canadian name for **roundabout** (sense 2).

traffic cop NOUN *Informal* a policeman who supervises road traffic.

traffic court NOUN *Law* a magistrates' court dealing with traffic offences.

traffic engineering NOUN a discipline which includes the design of highways and pedestrian ways, the study and application of traffic statistics, and the environmental aspects of the transportation of goods and people.

traffic island NOUN a raised area in the middle of a road, designed as a guide for traffic and to provide a stopping place for pedestrians.

traffic jam NOUN a number of vehicles so obstructed that they can scarcely move.
▸'**traffic-,jammed** ADJECTIVE

trafficky ('træfɪkɪ) ADJECTIVE *Informal* (of a street, area, town, etc.) busy with motor vehicles.

traffic light *or* **signal** NOUN one of a set of coloured lights placed at crossroads, junctions, etc., to control the flow of traffic. A red light indicates that traffic must stop and a green light that it may go: usually an amber warning light is added between the red and the green.

traffic pattern NOUN a pattern of permitted lanes in the air around an airport to which an aircraft is restricted.

traffic warden NOUN *Brit* a person who is appointed to supervise road traffic and report traffic offences.

Trafford ('træfəd) NOUN a unitary authority in NW England, in Greater Manchester. Pop.: 210 135 (2001). Area: 106 sq. km (41 sq. miles).

tragacanth ('trægə,kænθ) NOUN 1 any of various spiny leguminous plants of the genus *Astragalus*, esp *A. gummifer*, of Asia, having clusters of white, yellow, or purple flowers, and yielding a substance that is made into a gum. 2 the gum obtained from any of these plants, used in the manufacture of pills and lozenges, etc.
▷HISTORY C16: from French *tragacante*, from Latin *tragacantha* goat's thorn, from Greek *tragakantha*, from *tragos* goat + *akantha* thorn

tragedian (trə'dʒi:dɪən) *or feminine* **tragedienne** (trə,dʒi:dɪ'ɛn) NOUN 1 an actor who specializes in tragic roles. 2 a writer of tragedy.

tragedy ('trædʒɪdɪ) NOUN, *plural* **-dies.** 1 (esp in classical and Renaissance drama) a play in which the protagonist, usually a man of importance and outstanding personal qualities, falls to disaster through the combination of a personal failing and circumstances with which he cannot deal. 2 (in later drama, such as that of Ibsen) a play in which the protagonist is overcome by a combination of social and psychological circumstances. 3 any dramatic or literary composition dealing with serious or sombre themes and ending with disaster. 4 (in medieval literature) a literary work in which a great person falls from prosperity to disaster, often through no fault of his own. 5 the branch of drama dealing with such themes. 6 the unfortunate aspect of something. 7 a shocking or sad event; disaster. ◆ Compare **comedy.**
▷HISTORY C14: from Old French *tragédie*, from Latin *tragoedia*, from Greek *tragōidia*, from *tragos* goat + *ōidē* song; perhaps a reference to the goat-satyrs of Peloponnesian plays

tragic ('trædʒɪk) *or less commonly* **tragical** ADJECTIVE 1 of, relating to, or characteristic of tragedy. 2 mournful or pitiable: *a tragic face.*
▸'**tragically** ADVERB

tragic flaw NOUN a failing of character in the hero of a tragedy that brings about his downfall.

tragic irony NOUN the use of dramatic irony in a tragedy (originally, in Greek tragedy), so that the audience is aware that a character's words or actions will bring about a tragic or fatal result, while the character himself is not.

tragicomedy (,trædʒɪ'kɒmɪdɪ) NOUN, *plural* **-dies.** 1 **a** a drama in which aspects of both tragedy and comedy are found. **b** the dramatic genre of works of this kind. 2 an event or incident having both comic and tragic aspects.
▷HISTORY C16: from French, ultimately from Late Latin *tragicōmoedia*; see TRAGEDY, COMEDY
▸,**tragi'comic** *or* ,**tragi'comical** ADJECTIVE
▸,**tragi'comically** ADVERB

tragopan ('trægə,pæn) NOUN any pheasant of the genus *Tragopan*, of S and SE Asia, having a brilliant plumage and brightly coloured fleshy processes on the head.
▷HISTORY C19: via Latin from Greek, from *tragos* goat + PAN

tragus ('treɪgəs) NOUN, *plural* **-gi** (-dʒaɪ). 1 the cartilaginous fleshy projection that partially covers the entrance to the external ear. 2 any of the hairs that grow just inside this entrance.
▷HISTORY C17: from Late Latin, from Greek *tragos* hairy projection of the ear, literally: goat
▸'**tragal** ADJECTIVE

trail (treɪl) VERB 1 to drag or stream, or permit to drag or stream along a surface, esp the ground: *her skirt trailed; she trailed her skipping rope.* 2 to make (a track or path) through (a place): *to trail a way; to trail a jungle.* 3 to chase, follow, or hunt (an animal or person) by following marks or tracks. 4 (when *intr*, often foll by *behind*) to lag or linger behind (a person or thing). 5 (*intr*) to be falling behind in a race or competition: *the favourite is trailing at the last fence.* 6 (*tr*) to tow (a boat, caravan, etc.) behind a motor vehicle. 7 (*tr*) to carry (a rifle) at the full length of the right arm in a horizontal position, with the muzzle to the fore. 8 (*intr*) to move

wearily or slowly: *we trailed through the city.* 9 (*tr*) (on television or radio) to advertise (a future programme) with short extracts. 10 **trail one's coat.** to invite a quarrel by deliberately provocative behaviour. ◆ NOUN 11 a print, mark, or marks made by a person, animal, or object. 12 the act or an instance of trailing. 13 the scent left by a moving person or animal that is followed by a hunting animal. 14 a path, track, or road, esp one roughly blazed. 15 something that trails behind or trails in loops or strands. 16 the part of a towed gun carriage and limber that connects the two when in movement and rests on the ground as a partial support when unlimbered. 17 *Engineering* the distance between the point of contact of a steerable wheel and a line drawn from the swivel pin axis to the ground.
▷HISTORY C14: from Old French *trailler* to draw, tow, from Vulgar Latin *tragulāre* (unattested), from Latin *trāgula* dragnet, from *trahere* to drag; compare Middle Dutch *traghelen* to drag
▸ **'trail-less** ADJECTIVE

trail away *or* **off** VERB (*intr, adverb*) to become fainter, quieter, or weaker: *his voice trailed off.*

trail bike NOUN a motorcycle adapted for riding on rough tracks.

trailblazer ('treɪlˌbleɪzə) NOUN 1 a leader or pioneer in a particular field. 2 a person who blazes a trail.
▸ **'trail,blazing** ADJECTIVE, NOUN

trailer ('treɪlə) NOUN 1 a road vehicle, usually two-wheeled, towed by a motor vehicle: used for transporting boats, etc. 2 the part of an articulated lorry that is drawn by the cab. 3 a series of short extracts from a film, used to advertise it in a cinema or on television. 4 a person or thing that trails. 5 the US and Canadian name for **caravan** (sense 1).

trailer park NOUN *US* a mobile home site.

trailer trash NOUN *Disparaging* **a** poor people living in trailer parks in the US. **b** (*as modifier*): *trailer-trash culture.*

trailing ('treɪlɪŋ) ADJECTIVE (of a plant) having a long stem which spreads over the ground or hangs loosely: *trailing ivy.*

trailing arbutus NOUN a creeping evergreen ericaceous plant, *Epigaea repens*, of E North America, having clusters of fragrant pink or white flowers. Also called: **mayflower.**

trailing edge NOUN 1 the rear edge of a propeller blade or aerofoil. Compare **leading edge.** 2 *Physics* the edge of a pulse signal as its amplitude falls.

trailing vortex drag NOUN drag arising from vortices that occur behind a body moving through a gas or liquid. Often shortened to: **vortex drag.** Former name: **induced drag.**

trail rope NOUN 1 another name for **dragrope** (sense 2). 2 a long rope formerly used for various military purposes, esp to allow a vehicle, horses, or men to pull a gun carriage.

train (treɪn) VERB 1 (*tr*) to guide or teach (to do something), as by subjecting to various exercises or experiences: *to train a man to fight.* 2 (*tr*) to control or guide towards a specific goal: *to train a plant up a wall.* 3 (*intr*) to do exercises and prepare for a specific purpose: *the athlete trained for the Olympics.* 4 (*tr*) to improve or curb by subjecting to discipline: *to train the mind.* 5 (*tr*) to focus or bring to bear (on something): *to train a telescope on the moon.* ◆ NOUN 6 **a** a line of coaches or wagons coupled together and drawn by a railway locomotive. **b** (*as modifier*): *a train ferry.* 7 a sequence or series, as of events, thoughts, etc.: *a train of disasters.* 8 a procession of people, vehicles, etc., travelling together, such as one carrying supplies of ammunition or equipment in support of a military operation. 9 a series of interacting parts through which motion is transmitted: *a train of gears.* 10 a fuse or line of gunpowder to an explosive charge, etc. 11 something drawn along, such as the long back section of a dress that trails along the floor behind the wearer. 12 a retinue or suite. 13 proper order or course.
▷HISTORY C14: from Old French *trahiner*, from Vulgar Latin *tragīnāre* (unattested) to draw; related to Latin *trahere* to drag
▸ **'trainable** ADJECTIVE ▸ **'trainless** ADJECTIVE

trainband ('treɪnˌbænd) NOUN a company of English militia from the 16th to the 18th century.
▷HISTORY C17: altered from *trained band*

trainbearer ('treɪnˌbɛərə) NOUN an attendant in a procession who holds up the train of a dignitary's robe.

trainee (treɪ'niː) NOUN **a** a person undergoing training. **b** (*as modifier*): *a trainee journalist.*

trainer ('treɪnə) NOUN 1 a person who trains athletes in a sport. 2 a piece of equipment employed in training, such as a simulated aircraft cockpit. 3 *Horse racing* a person who schools racehorses and prepares them for racing. 4 (*plural*) an informal name for **training shoes.**

training ('treɪnɪŋ) NOUN 1 **a** the process of bringing a person, etc., to an agreed standard of proficiency, etc., by practice and instruction: *training for the priesthood; physical training.* **b** (*as modifier*): *training college.* 2 **in training. a** undergoing physical training. **b** physically fit. 3 **out of training.** physically unfit.

Training Agency NOUN (in Britain) an organization established in 1989 to replace the Training Commission, which itself replaced the Manpower Services Commission; it provides training and retraining for adult workers and operates the Youth Training Scheme, in England and Wales working through the local **Training and Enterprise Councils** (TECs) and in Scotland through the Local Enterprise Companies (LECs) set up in 1990.

training shoes PLURAL NOUN 1 running shoes for sports training, esp in contrast to studded or spiked shoes worn for the sport itself. 2 shoes in the style of those used for sports training. ◆ Also called: **trainers.**

train oil NOUN oil obtained from the blubber of various marine animals, esp the whale.
▷HISTORY C16: from earlier *train* or *trane*, from Middle Low German *trān* or Middle Dutch *traen* tear, exudation

train smash NOUN *South African informal* a disaster or serious setback (esp in the phrase **it's not a train smash**).

train spotter NOUN 1 a person who collects the numbers of railway locomotives. 2 *Informal* a person who is obsessed with trivial details, esp of a subject generally considered uninteresting.

trainspotterish ('treɪnˌspɒtərɪʃ) ADJECTIVE *Informal* obsessed with trivial details, esp of a subject generally considered uninteresting.

traipse *or* **trapes** (treɪps) *Informal* ◆ VERB 1 (*intr*) to walk heavily or tiredly. ◆ NOUN 2 a long or tiring walk; trudge.
▷HISTORY C16: of unknown origin

trait (treɪt, treɪ) NOUN 1 a characteristic feature or quality distinguishing a particular person or thing. 2 *Rare* a touch or stroke.
▷HISTORY C16: from French, from Old French: a pulling, from Latin *tractus*, from *trahere* to drag

traitor ('treɪtə) NOUN a person who is guilty of treason or treachery, in betraying friends, country, a cause or trust, etc.
▷HISTORY C13: from Old French *traitour*, from Latin *trāditor* TRADITOR
▸ **'traitorous** ADJECTIVE ▸ **'traitorously** ADVERB ▸ **'traitor,ship** NOUN ▸ **'traitress** FEMININE NOUN

traject (trə'dʒɛkt) VERB (*tr*) *Archaic* to transport or transmit.
▷HISTORY C17: from Latin *trājectus* cast over, from *trāicere* to throw across, from TRANS- + *iacere* to throw
▸ **tra'jection** NOUN

trajectory (trə'dʒɛktərɪ, -trɪ) NOUN, *plural* **-ries.** 1 the path described by an object moving in air or space under the influence of such forces as thrust, wind resistance, and gravity, esp the curved path of a projectile. 2 *Geometry* a curve that cuts a family of curves or surfaces at a constant angle.
▸ **trajectile** (trə'dʒɛktaɪl) ADJECTIVE

tra-la (ˌtrɑː'lɑː) *or* **tra-la-la** ('trɑːlɑːlɑː) NOUN a set of nonsensical syllables used in humming music, esp for a melody or refrain.

Tralee (trə'liː) NOUN a market town in SW Republic of Ireland, county town of Kerry, near **Tralee Bay** (an inlet of the Atlantic). Pop.: 17 200 (1991).

TRALI NOUN ABBREVIATION FOR transfusion-related acute lung injury: a potentially fatal condition that can affect a female blood donor who has been pregnant.

tram¹ (træm) NOUN 1 Also called: **tramcar.** an electrically driven public transport vehicle that runs on rails let into the surface of the road, power usually being taken from an overhead wire. US and Canadian names: **streetcar, trolley car.** 2 a small vehicle on rails for carrying loads in a mine; tub.
▷HISTORY C16 (in the sense: shaft of a cart): probably from Low German *traam* beam; compare Old Norse *thrömr*, Middle Dutch *traem* beam, tooth of a rake
▸ **'tramless** ADJECTIVE

tram² (træm) NOUN 1 *Machinery* a fine adjustment that ensures correct function or alignment. ◆ VERB **trams, tramming, trammed.** 2 (*tr*) to adjust (a mechanism) to a fine degree of accuracy.
▷HISTORY C19: short for TRAMMEL

tram³ (træm) NOUN (in weaving) a weft yarn of two or more twisted strands of silk.
▷HISTORY C17: from French *trame*, from Latin *trāma*; related to Latin *trāns* across, *trāmes* footpath

TRAM flap (træm) NOUN ACRONYM FOR transverse rectus abdominis myocutaneous flap: a piece of tissue, consisting of skin, muscle, and fat, taken from the abdomen of a woman and used in the reconstruction of her breast after mastectomy.

tramline ('træmˌlaɪn) NOUN 1 (*often plural*) Also called: **tramway.** the tracks on which a tram runs. 2 the route taken by a tram. 3 (*often plural*) the outer markings along the sides of a tennis or badminton court. 4 (*plural*) a set of guiding principles.

trammel ('træməl) NOUN 1 (*often plural*) a hindrance to free action or movement. 2 Also called: **trammel net.** a fishing net in three sections, the two outer nets having a large mesh and the middle one a fine mesh. 3 *Rare* a fowling net. 4 *US* a fetter or shackle, esp one used in teaching a horse to amble. 5 a device for drawing ellipses consisting of a flat sheet of metal, plastic, or wood having a cruciform slot in which run two pegs attached to a beam. The free end of the beam describes an ellipse. 6 (*sometimes plural*) another name for **beam compass.** 7 Also called: **tram.** a gauge for setting up machines correctly. 8 a device set in a fireplace to support cooking pots. ◆ VERB **-els, -elling, -elled** *or US* **-els, -eling, -eled.** (*tr*) 9 to hinder or restrain. 10 to catch or ensnare. 11 to produce an accurate setting of (a machine adjustment), as with a trammel.
▷HISTORY C14: from Old French *tramail* three-mesh net, from Late Latin *trēmaculum*, from Latin *trēs* three + *macula* hole, mesh in a net
▸ **'trammeller** *or* (*US*) **'trammeler** NOUN

trammie ('træmɪ) NOUN *Austral informal* the conductor or driver of a tram.

tramontane (trə'mɒnteɪn) ADJECTIVE *also* **transmontane.** 1 being or coming from the far side of the mountains, esp from the other side of the Alps as seen from Italy. 2 foreign or barbarous. 3 (of a wind) blowing down from the mountains. ◆ NOUN 4 an inhabitant of a tramontane country. 5 Also called: **tramontana.** a cold dry wind blowing south or southwest from the mountains in Italy and the W Mediterranean. 6 *Rare* a foreigner or barbarian.
▷HISTORY C16: from Italian *tramontano*, from Latin *trānsmontānus*, from TRANS- + *montānus*, from *mōns* mountain

tramp (træmp) VERB 1 (*intr*) to walk long and far; hike. 2 to walk heavily or firmly across or through (a place); march or trudge. 3 (*intr*) to wander about as a vagabond or tramp. 4 (*tr*) to make (a journey) or traverse (a place) on foot, esp laboriously or wearily: *to tramp the streets in search of work.* 5 (*tr*) to tread or trample. 6 (*intr*) *NZ* to walk for sport or recreation, esp in the bush. ◆ NOUN 7 a person who travels about on foot, usually with no permanent home, living by begging or doing casual work. 8 a long hard walk; hike. 9 a heavy or rhythmic step or tread. 10 the sound of heavy treading. 11 Also called: **tramp steamer.** a merchant ship that does not run between ports on a regular schedule but carries cargo wherever the shippers desire. 12 *Slang, chiefly US and Canadian* a prostitute or promiscuous girl or woman. 13 an iron plate on the sole of a boot.
▷HISTORY C14: probably from Middle Low German *trampen*; compare Gothic *ana-trimpan* to press heavily upon, German *trampen* to hitchhike

▸ˈ**tramping** NOUN ▸ˈ**trampish** ADJECTIVE

tramper (ˈtræmpə) NOUN 1 a person who tramps. 2 a person who walks long distances, often over rough terrain, for recreation.

tramping club NOUN *NZ* an organization of people who walk for recreation, esp in the bush.

tramping hut NOUN *NZ* a hut in the bush for the use of trampers.

trample (ˈtræmpᵊl) VERB (when *intr*, usually foll by *on, upon*, or *over*) 1 to stamp or walk roughly (on): *to trample the flowers*. 2 to encroach (upon) so as to violate or hurt: *to trample on someone's feelings*. ♦ NOUN 3 the action or sound of trampling.
▷HISTORY C14: frequentative of TRAMP; compare Middle High German *trampeln*
▸ˈ**trampler** NOUN

trampoline (ˈtræmpəlɪn, -ˌliːn) NOUN 1 a tough canvas sheet suspended by springs or elasticated cords from a frame, used by acrobats, gymnasts, etc. ♦ VERB 2 (*intr*) to exercise on a trampoline.
▷HISTORY C18: via Spanish from Italian *trampolino*, from *trampoli* stilts, of Germanic origin; compare TRAMPLE
▸ˈ**trampoliner** *or* ˈ**trampolinist** NOUN

tramway (ˈtræmˌweɪ) NOUN 1 another name for **tramline** (sense 1). 2 *Brit* **a** a public transportation system using trams. **b** the company owning or running such a system. 3 Also called (esp US): **tramroad.** a small or temporary railway for moving freight along tracks, as in a quarry.

trance (trɑːns) NOUN 1 a hypnotic state resembling sleep. 2 any mental state in which a person is unaware or apparently unaware of the environment, characterized by loss of voluntary movement, rigidity, and lack of sensitivity to external stimuli. 3 a dazed or stunned state. 4 a state of ecstasy or mystic absorption so intense as to cause a temporary loss of consciousness at the earthly level. 5 *Spiritualism* a state in which a medium, having temporarily lost consciousness, can supposedly be controlled by an intelligence from without as a means of communication with the dead. 6 a type of electronic dance music with repetitive rhythms, aiming at a hypnotic effect. ♦ VERB 6 (*tr*) to put into or as into a trance. ♦ See also **trance out.**
▷HISTORY C14: from Old French *transe*, from *transir* to faint, pass away, from Latin *trānsīre* to go over, from TRANS- + *īre* to go
▸ˈ**trance,like** ADJECTIVE

trance out VERB (*intr, adverb*) *Slang* to go into a trancelike or ecstatic state, esp through the effects of drugs or music.

tranche (trɑːnʃ) NOUN a portion or instalment, esp of a loan or share issue.
▷HISTORY from French, literally: a slice

trannie *or* **tranny** (ˈtrænɪ) NOUN, *plural* **-nies.** 1 a transistor radio. 2 a transvestite.

tranquil (ˈtræŋkwɪl) ADJECTIVE calm, peaceful or quiet.
▷HISTORY C17: from Latin *tranquillus*
▸ˈ**tranquilly** ADVERB ▸ˈ**tranquilness** NOUN

tranquillity *or sometimes US* **tranquility** (træŋˈkwɪlɪtɪ) NOUN a state of calm or quietude.

tranquillize, tranquillise, *or US* **tranquilize** (ˈtræŋkwɪˌlaɪz) VERB to make or become calm or calmer.
▸ˌ**tranquilliˈzation** *or* ˌ**tranquilliˈsation** *or* (*US*) ˌ**tranquiliˈzation** NOUN

tranquillizer, tranquilliser, *or US* **tranquilizer** (ˈtræŋkwɪˌlaɪzə) NOUN 1 a drug that calms a person without affecting clarity of consciousness. 2 anything that tranquillizes.

trans. ABBREVIATION FOR: 1 transaction. 2 transferred. 3 transitive. 4 translated. 5 translator.

trans- *or sometimes before s-* **tran-** PREFIX 1 across, beyond, crossing, on the other side: *transoceanic; trans-Siberian; transatlantic*. 2 changing thoroughly: *transliterate*. 3 transcending: *transubstantiation*. 4 transversely: *transect*. 5 (*often in italics*) indicating that a chemical compound has a molecular structure in which two groups or atoms are on opposite sides of a double bond: *trans-butadiene*. Compare **cis-** (sense 2).
▷HISTORY from Latin *trāns* across, through, beyond

transact (trænˈzækt) VERB to do, conduct, or negotiate (business, a deal, etc.).
▷HISTORY C16: from Latin *trānsactus*, from *trānsigere*, literally: to drive through, from TRANS- + *agere* to drive
▸**transˈactor** NOUN

transactinide (ˌtrænsˈæktɪˌnaɪd) NOUN any artificially produced element with an atomic number greater than 103.
▷HISTORY C20: from TRANS- + ACTINIDE

transaction (trænˈzækʃən) NOUN 1 something that is transacted, esp a business deal or negotiation. 2 the act of transacting or the state of being transacted. 3 (*plural*) the published records of the proceedings of a society, conference, etc. 4 (in business computing) the act of obtaining and paying for an item or service. 5 (in general computing) the transmission and processing of an item of data.
▸**transˈactional** ADJECTIVE ▸**transˈactionally** ADVERB

transactional analysis NOUN *Psychol* a form of psychotherapy that attributes neuroses to lack of balance in the personality between the conflicting ego-states of child, adult, and parent.

transalpine (trænzˈælpaɪn) ADJECTIVE (*prenominal*) 1 situated in or relating to places beyond the Alps, esp from Italy. 2 passing over the Alps. ♦ NOUN 3 a transalpine person.

Transalpine Gaul NOUN (in the ancient world) that part of Gaul northwest of the Alps.

transaminase (trænzˈæmɪˌneɪz, -ˌneɪs) NOUN *Biochem* an enzyme that catalyses the transfer of an amino group from one molecule, esp an amino acid, to another, esp a keto acid, in the process of transamination.

transatlantic (ˌtrænzətˈlæntɪk) ADJECTIVE 1 on or from the other side of the Atlantic. 2 crossing the Atlantic.

transcalent (trænsˈkeɪlənt) ADJECTIVE *Rare* permitting the passage of heat.
▷HISTORY C19: TRANS- + *-calent*, from Latin *calēre* to be hot
▸**transˈcalency** NOUN

Transcaucasia (ˌtrænskɔːˈkeɪzjə) NOUN a region in central Asia, south of the Caucasus Mountains between the Black and Caspian Seas in Georgia, Armenia, and Azerbaijan: a constituent republic of the Soviet Union from 1918 until 1936.

Transcaucasian (ˌtrænskɔːˈkeɪzjən) ADJECTIVE 1 of or relating to the central Asian region of Transcaucasia or its inhabitants. ♦ NOUN 2 a native or inhabitant of Transcaucasia.

transceiver (trænˈsiːvə) NOUN a device which transmits and receives radio or electronic signals.
▷HISTORY C20: from TRANS(MITTER) + (RE)CEIVER

transcend (trænˈsɛnd) VERB 1 to go above or beyond (a limit, expectation, etc.), as in degree or excellence. 2 (*tr*) to be superior to. 3 *Philosophy, theol* (esp of the Deity) to exist beyond (the material world).
▷HISTORY C14: from Latin *trānscendere* to climb over, from TRANS- + *scandere* to climb
▸**transˈcendingly** ADVERB

transcendent (trænˈsɛndənt) ADJECTIVE 1 exceeding or surpassing in degree or excellence. 2 **a** (in the philosophy of Kant) beyond or before experience; a priori. **b** (of a concept) falling outside a given set of categories. **c** beyond consciousness or direct apprehension. 3 *Theol* (of God) having continuous existence outside the created world. 4 free from the limitations inherent in matter. ♦ NOUN 5 *Philosophy* a transcendent thing.
▸**tranˈscendence** NOUN ▸**tranˈscendency** NOUN
▸**tranˈscendently** ADVERB ▸**tranˈscendentness** NOUN

transcendental (ˌtrænsɛnˈdɛntᵊl) ADJECTIVE 1 transcendent, superior, or surpassing. 2 (in the philosophy of Kant). **a** (of a judgment or logical deduction) being both synthetic and a priori. **b** of or relating to knowledge of the presuppositions of thought. 3 *Philosophy* beyond our experience of phenomena, although not beyond potential knowledge. 4 *Theol* surpassing the natural plane of reality or knowledge; supernatural or mystical.
▸ˌ**transcendenˈtality** NOUN ▸ˌ**transcenˈdentally** ADVERB

transcendental argument NOUN *Philosophy* an argument designed to make explicit the conditions under which a certain kind of knowledge is possible, esp those of Kant.

transcendental function NOUN *Maths* a function that is not capable of expression in terms of a finite number of arithmetical operations, such as sin *x*.

transcendental idealism NOUN *Philosophy* the Kantian doctrine that reality consists not of appearances, but of some other order of being whose existence can be inferred from the nature of human reason.

transcendentalism (ˌtrænsɛnˈdɛntəˌlɪzəm) NOUN 1 **a** any system of philosophy, esp that of Immanuel Kant, the German philosopher (1724–1804), holding that the key to knowledge of the nature of reality lies in the critical examination of the processes of reason on which depends the nature of experience. **b** any system of philosophy, esp that of Emerson, that emphasizes intuition as a means to knowledge or the importance of the search for the divine. 2 vague philosophical speculation. 3 the state of being transcendental. 4 something, such as thought or language, that is transcendental.
▸ˌ**transcenˈdentalist** NOUN, ADJECTIVE

Transcendental Meditation NOUN *Trademark in the US* a technique, based on Hindu traditions, for relaxing and refreshing the mind and body through the silent repetition of a mantra. Disseminated by an international organization founded by Maharishi Mahesh Yogi (born 1917), an Indian-born guru. Abbreviation: **TM.**

transcendental number NOUN *Maths* a number or quantity that is real but nonalgebraic, that is, one that is not a root of any polynomial with rational coefficients such as π or *e*.

transcontinental (ˌtrænzkɒntɪˈnɛntᵊl) ADJECTIVE 1 crossing a continent. 2 on or from the far side of a continent.
▸ˌ**transcontiˈnentally** ADVERB

transcribe (trænˈskraɪb) VERB (*tr*) 1 to write, type, or print out fully from speech, notes, etc. 2 to make a phonetic transcription of. 3 to transliterate or translate. 4 to make an electrical recording of (a programme or speech) for a later broadcast. 5 *Music* to rewrite (a piece of music) for an instrument or medium other than that originally intended; arrange. 6 *Computing* **a** to transfer (information) from one storage device, such as punched cards, to another, such as magnetic tape. **b** to transfer (information) from a computer to an external storage device. 7 (*usually passive*) *Biochem* to convert the genetic information in (a strand of DNA) into a strand of RNA, esp messenger RNA. See also **genetic code, translate** (sense 6).
▷HISTORY C16: from Latin *transcrībere*, from TRANS- + *scrībere* to write
▸**tranˈscribable** ADJECTIVE ▸**tranˈscriber** NOUN

transcript (ˈtrænskrɪpt) NOUN 1 a written, typed, or printed copy or manuscript made by transcribing. 2 *Education chiefly US and Canadian* an official record of a student's school progress and achievements. 3 any reproduction or copy.
▷HISTORY C13: from Latin *transcriptum*, from *transcrībere* to TRANSCRIBE

transcriptase (trænˈskrɪpteɪz) NOUN See **reverse transcriptase.**

transcription (trænˈskrɪpʃən) NOUN 1 the act or an instance of transcribing or the state of being transcribed. 2 something transcribed. 3 a representation in writing of the actual pronunciation of a speech sound, word, or piece of continuous text, using not a conventional orthography but a symbol or set of symbols specially designated as standing for corresponding phonetic values.
▸**tranˈscriptional** *or* **tranˈscriptive** ADJECTIVE
▸**tranˈscriptionally** *or* **tranˈscriptively** ADVERB

transculturation (ˌtrænzkʌltʃʊˈreɪʃən) NOUN the introduction of foreign elements into an established culture.

transcurrent (trænzˈkʌrənt) ADJECTIVE running across; transverse.

transdermal (trænzˈdɜːməl) ADJECTIVE (of a medicine) entering the bloodstream by absorption through the skin.
▷HISTORY C20: from TRANS- + DERMAL

Transdniestria (ˈtrænsdnɪˌɛstrɪə) NOUN a region of E Moldova: unilaterally declared itself independent and was the scene of fighting between government troops and separatists in 1992.

transducer (trænzˈdjuːsə) NOUN any device, such as a microphone or electric motor, that converts one form of energy into another.
▷HISTORY C20: from Latin *transducere* to lead across, from TRANS- + *ducere* to lead

transduction (trænzˈdʌkʃən) NOUN *Genetics* the transfer by a bacteriophage of genetic material from one bacterium to another.
▷HISTORY C17: from Latin *transductiō*, variant of *trāductiō* a leading along, from *trādūcere* to lead over; see TRADUCE

transect VERB (*tr*) (trænˈsɛkt) 1 to cut or divide crossways. ◆ NOUN (ˈtrænsɛkt) 2 a sample strip of land used to monitor plant distribution, animal populations, etc., within a given area.
▷HISTORY C17: from Latin TRANS- + *secāre* to cut
▸**tranˈsection** NOUN

transept (ˈtrænsept) NOUN either of the two wings of a cruciform church at right angles to the nave.
▷HISTORY C16: from Anglo-Latin *transeptum*, from Latin TRANS- + *saeptum* enclosure
▸**tranˈseptal** ADJECTIVE

transeunt (ˈtrænsɪənt) *or* **transient** ADJECTIVE *Philosophy* (of a mental act) causing effects outside the mind. Compare **immanent** (sense 2).
▷HISTORY C17: from Latin *transiēns* going over, from *transīre* to pass over; see TRANCE

trans-fatty acid NOUN a polyunsaturated fatty acid that has been converted from the cis-form by hydrogenation: used in the manufacture of margarine.

transfect (trænsˈfɛkt) VERB (*tr*) to bring about transfection in.
▷HISTORY from TRANS- + (IN)FECT

transfection (trænsˈfɛkʃən) NOUN the transfer into another cell of genetic material isolated from a cell or virus.

transfer VERB (trænsˈfɜː) **-fers, -ferring, -ferred.** 1 to change or go or cause to change or go from one thing, person, or point to another: *they transferred from the Park Hotel to the Imperial; she transferred her affections to her dog.* 2 to change (buses, trains, etc.). 3 *Law* to make over (property, etc.) to another; convey. 4 to displace (a drawing, design, etc.) from one surface to another. 5 (of a football player, esp a professional) to change clubs or (of a club, manager, etc.) to sell or release (a player) to another club. 6 to leave one school, college, etc., and enrol at another. 7 to change (the meaning of a word, etc.), esp by metaphorical extension. ◆ NOUN (ˈtrænsfɜː) 8 the act, process, or system of transferring, or the state of being transferred. 9 **a** a person or thing that transfers or is transferred. **b** (*as modifier*): *a transfer student.* 10 a design or drawing that is transferred from one surface to another, as by ironing a printed design onto cloth. 11 *Law* the passing of title to property or other right from one person to another by act of the parties or by operation of law; conveyance. 12 *Finance* **a** the act of transferring the title of ownership to shares or registered bonds in the books of the issuing enterprise. **b** (*as modifier*): *transfer deed; transfer form.* 13 any document or form effecting or regulating a transfer. 14 *Chiefly US and Canadian* a ticket that allows a passenger to change routes.
▷HISTORY C14: from Latin *transferre*, from TRANS- + *ferre* to carry
▸**transˈferable** *or* **transˈferrable** ADJECTIVE
▸**ˌtransferaˈbility** NOUN

transferable vote NOUN a vote that is transferred to a second candidate indicated by the voter if the first is eliminated from the ballot.

transferase (ˈtrænsfəˌreɪs) NOUN any enzyme that catalyses the transfer of a chemical group from one substance to another.

transfer characteristic NOUN *Electronics* the relationship between output and input of an electronic or electromechanical system, esp as depicted graphically.

transferee (ˌtrænsfəˈriː) NOUN 1 *Property law* a person to whom property is transferred. 2 a person who is transferred.

transference (ˈtrænsfərəns, -frəns) NOUN 1 the act or an instance of transferring or the state of being transferred. 2 *Psychoanal* the redirection of attitudes and emotions towards a substitute, such as towards the analyst during therapy.
▸**transferential** (ˌtrænsfəˈrɛnʃəl) ADJECTIVE

transfer fee NOUN a sum of money paid by one football club to another for a transferred player.

transfer list NOUN a list of football players available for transfer.

transferor *or* **transferrer** (trænsˈfɜːrə) NOUN *Property law* a person who makes a transfer, as of property.

transfer payment NOUN (*usually plural*) money received by an individual or family from the state or other body, often a pension or unemployment benefit. It is not reckoned when calculating the national income as it is money transferred rather than paid for merchandise or a service rendered.

transfer pricing NOUN the setting of a price for the transfer of raw materials, components, products, or services between the trading units of a large organization.

transferral *or* **transferal** (ˌtrænsˈfɛrəl) NOUN the act or an instance of transferring or being transferred.

transferrin (trænsˈfɜːrɪn) NOUN *Biochem* any of a group of blood glycoproteins that transport iron. Also called: **beta globulin, siderophilin.**
▷HISTORY C20: from TRANS- + FERRO- + -IN

transfer RNA NOUN *Biochem* any of several soluble forms of RNA of low molecular weight, each of which transports a specific amino acid to a ribosome during protein synthesis. Sometimes shortened to: **t-RNA.** Also called: **soluble RNA.** See also **messenger RNA, genetic code.**

transfiguration (ˌtrænsfɪgjʊˈreɪʃən) NOUN the act or an instance of transfiguring or the state of being transfigured.

Transfiguration (ˌtrænsfɪgjʊˈreɪʃən) NOUN 1 *New Testament* the change in the appearance of Christ that took place before three disciples (Matthew 17:1–9). 2 the Church festival held in commemoration of this on Aug. 6.

transfigure (trænsˈfɪgə) VERB (*usually tr*) 1 to change or cause to change in appearance. 2 to become or cause to become more exalted.
▷HISTORY C13: from Latin *transfigūrāre*, from TRANS- + *figūra* appearance
▸**transˈfigurement** NOUN

transfinite (trænsˈfaɪnaɪt) ADJECTIVE extending beyond the finite.

transfinite number NOUN a cardinal or ordinal number used in the comparison of infinite sets for which several types of infinity can be classified: *the set of integers and the set of real numbers have different transfinite numbers.*

transfix (trænsˈfɪks) VERB **-fixes, -fixing, -fixed** *or* **-fixt.** (*tr*) 1 to render motionless, esp with horror or shock. 2 to impale or fix with a sharp weapon or other device. 3 *Med* to cut through (a limb or other organ), as in amputation.
▷HISTORY C16: from Latin *transfīgere* to pierce through, from TRANS- + *fīgere* to thrust in
▸**transfixion** (trænsˈfɪkʃən) NOUN

transform VERB (trænsˈfɔːm) 1 to alter or be altered radically in form, function, etc. 2 (*tr*) to convert (one form of energy) to another form. 3 (*tr*) *Maths* to change the form of (an equation, expression, etc.) by a mathematical transformation. 4 (*tr*) to increase or decrease (an alternating current or voltage) using a transformer. ◆ NOUN (ˈtrænsˌfɔːm) 5 *Maths* the result of a mathematical transformation, esp (of a matrix or an element of a group) another related to the given one by $B=X^{-1}AX$ for some appropriate X.
▷HISTORY C14: from Latin *transformāre*, from TRANS- + *formāre* to FORM
▸**transˈformable** ADJECTIVE ▸**transˈformative** ADJECTIVE

transformation (ˌtrænsfəˈmeɪʃən) NOUN 1 a change or alteration, esp a radical one. 2 the act of transforming or the state of being transformed. 3 *Maths* **a** a change in position or direction of the reference axes in a coordinate system without an alteration in their relative angle. **b** an equivalent change in an expression or equation resulting from the substitution of one set of variables by another. 4 *Physics* a change in an atomic nucleus to a different nuclide as the result of the emission of either an alpha-particle or a beta-particle. Compare **transition** (sense 5). 5 *Linguistics* another word for **transformational rule.** 6 an apparently miraculous change in the appearance of a stage set.
▸**ˌtransforˈmational** ADJECTIVE

transformational grammar NOUN a grammatical description of a language making essential use of transformational rules. Such grammars are usually but not necessarily generative grammars. Compare **systemic grammar, case grammar.**

transformational rule NOUN 1 *Generative grammar* a rule that converts one phrase marker into another. Taken together, these rules, which form the **transformational component** of the grammar, convert the deep structures of sentences into their surface structures. 2 (*plural*) *Logic* a rule that specifies in purely syntactic terms a method by which theorems may be derived from the axioms of a formal system.

transformer (trænsˈfɔːmə) NOUN 1 a device that transfers an alternating current from one circuit to one or more other circuits, usually with an increase (**step-up transformer**) or decrease (**step-down transformer**) of voltage. The input current is fed to a primary winding, the output being taken from a secondary winding or windings inductively linked to the primary. 2 a person or thing that transforms.

transformism (trænsˈfɔːmɪzəm) NOUN a less common word for **evolution**, esp the theory of evolution
▸**transˈformist** NOUN

transfuse (trænsˈfjuːz) VERB (*tr*) 1 to permeate or infuse: *a blush transfused her face.* 2 **a** to inject (blood, etc.) into a blood vessel. **b** to give a transfusion to (a patient). 3 *Rare* to transfer from one vessel to another, esp by pouring.
▷HISTORY C15: from Latin *transfundere* to pour out, from TRANS- + *fundere* to pour
▸**transˈfuser** NOUN ▸**transˈfusible** *or* **transˈfusable** ADJECTIVE ▸**transˈfusive** ADJECTIVE

transfusion (trænsˈfjuːʒən) NOUN 1 the act or an instance of transfusing. 2 the injection of blood, blood plasma, etc., into the blood vessels of a patient.

transgender (ˌtrænzˈdʒɛndə) ADJECTIVE of or relating to a person who wants to belong to the opposite sex.
▸**ˌtransˈgendered** ADJECTIVE

transgene (ˈtrænzˌdʒiːn) NOUN a gene that is transferred from an organism of one species to an organism of another species by genetic engineering.

transgenic (trænzˈdʒɛnɪk) ADJECTIVE (of an animal or plant) containing genetic material artificially transferred from another species.

transgress (trænzˈgrɛs) VERB 1 to break (a law, rule, etc.). 2 to go beyond or overstep (a limit).
▷HISTORY C16: from Latin *transgredī*, from TRANS- + *gradī* to step
▸**transˈgressively** ADVERB ▸**transˈgressor** NOUN

transgression (trænzˈgrɛʃən) NOUN 1 a breach of a law, etc.; sin or crime. 2 the act or an instance of transgressing.

transgressive (ˌtrænzˈgrɛsɪv) ADJECTIVE going beyond accept boundaries of taste, convention, or the law: *transgressive art; transgressive pursuits.*

tranship (trænˈʃɪp) VERB **-ships, -shipping, -shipped.** a variant spelling of **transship.**
▸**tranˈshipment** NOUN

transhumance (trænsˈhjuːməns) NOUN the seasonal migration of livestock to suitable grazing grounds.
▷HISTORY C20: from French, from *transhumer* to change one's pastures, from Spanish *trashumar*, from Latin TRANS- + *humus* ground
▸**transˈhumant** ADJECTIVE

transient (ˈtrænzɪənt) ADJECTIVE 1 for a short time only; temporary or transitory. 2 *Philosophy* a variant of **transeunt.** ◆ NOUN 3 a transient person or thing. 4 *Physics* a brief change in the state of a system, such as a sudden short-lived oscillation in the current flowing through a circuit.
▷HISTORY C17: from Latin *transiēns* going over, from *transīre* to pass over, from TRANS- + *īre* to go
▸**ˈtransiently** ADVERB ▸**ˈtransience** *or* **ˈtransiency** NOUN

transilient (trænˈsɪlɪənt) ADJECTIVE passing quickly from one thing to another.

▷HISTORY C19: from Latin *transilīre* to jump over, from TRANS- + *salīre* to leap
▸**tran'silience** NOUN

transilluminate (ˌtrænzɪ'luːmɪˌneɪt) VERB (*tr*) *Med* to pass a light through the wall of (a bodily cavity, membrane, etc.) in order to detect fluid, lesions, etc.
▸**ˌtransilˌlumi'nation** NOUN ▸**ˌtransil'lumiˌnator** NOUN

transistor (træn'zɪstə) NOUN [1] a semiconductor device, having three or more terminals attached to electrode regions, in which current flowing between two electrodes is controlled by a voltage or current applied to one or more specified electrodes. The device is capable of amplification, etc., and has replaced the valve in most circuits since it is much smaller, more robust, and works at a much lower voltage. See also **junction transistor, field-effect transistor.** [2] *Informal* a transistor radio.
▷HISTORY C20: originally a trademark, from TRANSFER + RESISTOR, referring to the transfer of electric signals across a resistor

transistorize *or* **transistorise** (træn'zɪstəˌraɪz) VERB [1] to convert (a system, device, industry, etc.) to the use or manufacture of or operation by transistors and other solid-state components. [2] to equip (a device or circuit) with transistors and other solid-state components.

transit ('trænsɪt, 'trænz-) NOUN [1] **a** the passage or conveyance of goods or people. **b** (*as modifier*): *a transit visa.* [2] a change or transition. [3] a route. [4] *Astronomy* **a** the passage of a celestial body or satellite across the face of a relatively larger body as seen from the earth. **b** the apparent passage of a celestial body across the meridian, caused by the earth's diurnal rotation. [5] *Astrology* the passage of a planet across some special point on the zodiac. [6] **in transit.** while being conveyed; during passage. ◆ VERB [7] to make a transit through or over (something). [8] *Astronomy* to make a transit across (a celestial body or the meridian). [9] to cause (the telescope of a surveying instrument) to turn over or (of such a telescope) to be turned over in a vertical plane so that it points in the opposite direction.
▷HISTORY C15: from Latin *transitus* a going over, from *transīre* to pass over; see TRANSIENT
▸**'transitable** ADJECTIVE

transit camp NOUN a camp in which refugees, soldiers, etc., live temporarily before moving to another destination.

transit instrument NOUN an astronomical instrument, mounted on an E-W axis, in which the reticle of a telescope is always in the plane of the meridian. It is used to time the transit of a star, etc., across the meridian.

transition (træn'zɪʃən) NOUN [1] change or passage from one state or stage to another. [2] the period of time during which something changes from one state or stage to another. [3] *Music* **a** a movement from one key to another; modulation. **b** a linking passage between two divisions in a composition; bridge. [4] Also called: **transitional.** a style of architecture that was used in western Europe in the late 11th and early 12th century, characterized by late Romanesque forms combined with early Gothic details. [5] *Physics* **a** any change that results in a change of physical properties of a substance or system, such as a change of phase or molecular structure. **b** a change in the configuration of an atomic nucleus, involving either a change in energy level resulting from the emission of a gamma-ray photon or a transformation to another element or isotope. [6] a sentence, passage, etc., that connects a topic to one that follows or that links sections of a written work.
▷HISTORY C16: from Latin *transitio*; see TRANSIENT
▸**tran'sitional** *or* (*rarely*) **tran'sitionary** ADJECTIVE
▸**tran'sitionally** ADVERB

transition element *or* **metal** NOUN *Chem* any element belonging to one of three series of elements with atomic numbers between 21 and 30, 39 and 48, and 57 and 80. They have an incomplete penultimate electron shell and tend to exhibit more than one valency and to form complexes.

transition point NOUN [1] **a** the point at which a transition of physical properties takes place, such as the point at which laminar flow changes to turbulent flow. [2] See **transition temperature.**

transition temperature NOUN the temperature at which a sudden change of physical properties occurs, such as a change of phase or crystalline structure, or at which a substance becomes superconducting.

transitive ('trænsɪtɪv) ADJECTIVE [1] *Grammar* **a** denoting an occurrence of a verb when it requires a direct object or denoting a verb that customarily requires a direct object: *"to find" is a transitive verb.* **b** (*as noun*): *these verbs are transitives.* [2] *Grammar* denoting an adjective, such as *fond*, or a noun, such as *husband*, that requires a noun phrase and cannot be used without some implicit or explicit reference to such a noun phrase. [3] *Logic, maths* having the property that if one object bears a relationship to a second object that also bears the same relationship to a third object, then the first object bears this relationship to the third object: *mathematical equality is transitive, since if x = y and y = z then x = z.* ◆ Compare **intransitive.**
▷HISTORY C16: from Late Latin *transitīvus* from Latin *transitus* a going over; see TRANSIENT
▸**'transitively** ADVERB ▸**ˌtransi'tivity** *or* **'transitiveness** NOUN

transitory ('trænsɪtərɪ, -trɪ) ADJECTIVE of short duration; transient or ephemeral.
▷HISTORY C14: from Church Latin *transitōrius* passing, from Latin *transitus* a crossing over; see TRANSIENT
▸**'transitorily** ADVERB ▸**'transitoriness** NOUN

transitory action NOUN *Law* an action that can be brought in any country regardless of where it originated.

transit theodolite NOUN a theodolite the telescope of which can be rotated completely about its horizontal axis.

Trans-Jordan NOUN the former name (1922–49) of **Jordan.**

Trans-Jordanian ADJECTIVE [1] of or relating to the former Trans-Jordan (now Jordan) or its inhabitants. ◆ NOUN [2] a native or inhabitant of Trans-Jordan.

Transkei (træn'skaɪ) NOUN a former Bantu homeland in South Africa: the largest of South Africa's Bantu homelands and the first Bantu self-governing territory (1963); declared an independent state in 1976 but this status was not recognized outside South Africa; abolished in 1993 when South African citizenship was restored to its inhabitants. Capital: Umtata.

Transkeian (træns'kaɪən) ADJECTIVE [1] of or relating to the former Bantu homeland of Transkei (now part of South Africa) or its inhabitants. ◆ NOUN [2] a native or inhabitant of Transkei.

translate (træns'leɪt, trænz-) VERB [1] to express or be capable of being expressed in another language or dialect: *he translated Shakespeare into Afrikaans; his books translate well.* [2] (*intr*) to act as translator. [3] (*tr*) to express or explain in simple or less technical language. [4] (*tr*) to interpret or infer the significance of (gestures, symbols, etc.). [5] (*tr*) to transform or convert: *to translate hope into reality.* [6] (*tr; usually passive*) *Biochem* to transform the molecular structure of (messenger RNA) into a polypeptide chain by means of the information stored in the genetic code. See also **transcribe** (sense 7). [7] to move or carry from one place or position to another. [8] (*tr*) **a** to transfer (a cleric) from one ecclesiastical office to another. **b** to transfer (a see) from one place to another. [9] (*tr*) *RC Church* to transfer (the body or the relics of a saint) from one resting place to another. [10] (*tr*) *Theol* to transfer (a person) from one place or plane of existence to another, as from earth to heaven. [11] *Maths, physics* to move (a figure or body) laterally, without rotation, dilation, or angular displacement. [12] (*intr*) (of an aircraft, missile, etc.) to fly or move from one position to another. [13] (*tr*) *Archaic* to bring to a state of spiritual or emotional ecstasy.
▷HISTORY C13: from Latin *translātus* transferred, carried over, from *transferre* to TRANSFER
▸**trans'latable** ADJECTIVE ▸**ˌtranslata'bility** NOUN

translation (træns'leɪʃən, trænz-) NOUN [1] something that is or has been translated, esp a written text. [2] the act of translating or the state of being translated. [3] *Maths* a transformation in which the origin of a coordinate system is moved to another position so that each axis retains the same direction or, equivalently, a figure or curve is moved so that it retains the same orientation to the axes.
▸**trans'lational** ADJECTIVE

translator (træns'leɪtə, trænz-) NOUN [1] a person or machine that translates speech or writing. [2] *Radio* a relay transmitter that retransmits a signal on a carrier frequency different from that on which it was received. [3] *Computing* a computer program that converts a program from one language to another.
▸**ˌtransla'torial** ADJECTIVE

transliterate (trænz'lɪtəˌreɪt) VERB (*tr*) to transcribe (a word, etc., in one alphabet) into corresponding letters of another alphabet: *the Greek word λογοσ can be transliterated as "logos".*
▷HISTORY C19: TRANS- + *-literate*, from Latin *līttera* LETTER
▸**ˌtransliter'ation** NOUN ▸**trans'literˌator** NOUN

translocate (ˌtrænzləʊ'keɪt) VERB (*tr*) to move; displace.

translocation (ˌtrænzləʊ'keɪʃən) NOUN [1] *Genetics* the transfer of one part of a chromosome to another part of the same or a different chromosome, resulting in rearrangement of the genes. [2] *Botany* the transport of minerals, sugars, etc., in solution within a plant. [3] a movement from one position or place to another.

translucent (trænz'luːsᵊnt) ADJECTIVE allowing light to pass through partially or diffusely; semitransparent.
▷HISTORY C16: from Latin *translūcēre* to shine through, from TRANS- + *lūcēre* to shine
▸**trans'lucence** *or* **trans'lucency** NOUN ▸**trans'lucently** ADVERB

translunar (trænz'luːnə) *or* **translunary** (trænz'luːnərɪ) ADJECTIVE [1] lying beyond the moon. Compare **cislunar.** [2] unworldly or ethereal.

transmarine (ˌtrænzmə'riːn) ADJECTIVE a less common word for **overseas.**
▷HISTORY C16: from Latin *transmarīnus*, from TRANS- + *marīnus*, from *mare* sea

transmigrant (trænz'maɪgrənt, 'trænzmɪgrənt) NOUN [1] an emigrant on the way to the country of immigration. ◆ ADJECTIVE [2] passing through from one place or stage to another.

transmigrate (ˌtrænzmaɪ'greɪt) VERB (*intr*) [1] to move from one place, state, or stage to another. [2] (of souls) to pass from one body into another at death.
▸**ˌtransmi'gration** NOUN ▸**ˌtransmi'grational** ADJECTIVE
▸**trans'migrative** ADJECTIVE ▸**ˌtransmi'grator** NOUN
▸**trans'migratory** ADJECTIVE

transmissible spongiform encephalopathy NOUN the full name for **TSE.**

transmission (trænz'mɪʃən) NOUN [1] the act or process of transmitting. [2] something that is transmitted. [3] the extent to which a body or medium transmits light, sound, or some other form of energy. [4] the transference of motive force or power. [5] a system of shafts, gears, torque converters, etc., that transmits power, esp the arrangement of such parts that transmits the power of the engine to the driving wheels of a motor vehicle. [6] the act or process of sending a message, picture, or other information from one location to one or more other locations by means of radio waves, electrical signals, light signals, etc. [7] a radio or television broadcast.
▷HISTORY C17: from Latin *transmissiō* a sending across; see TRANSMIT
▸**trans'missible** ADJECTIVE ▸**transˌmissi'bility** NOUN
▸**trans'missive** ADJECTIVE ▸**trans'missively** ADVERB
▸**trans'missiveness** NOUN

transmission density NOUN *Physics* a measure of the extent to which a substance transmits light or other electromagnetic radiation, equal to the logarithm to base ten of the reciprocal of the transmittance. Symbol: τ. Former name: **optical density.**

transmission line NOUN a coaxial cable, waveguide, or other system of conductors that transfers electrical signals from one location to another. Sometimes shortened to: **line.**

transmissivity (ˌtrænzmɪ'sɪvɪtɪ) NOUN *Physics* a measure of the ability of a material to transmit radiation, equal to the internal transmittance of the material under conditions in which the path of the radiation has unit length.

transmit (trænz'mɪt) VERB **-mits, -mitting, -mitted.** [1] (*tr*) to pass or cause to go from one place or person to another; transfer. [2] (*tr*) to pass on or impart (a disease, infection, etc.). [3] (*tr*) to hand down to posterity. [4] (*tr; usually passive*) to pass (an inheritable characteristic) from parent to offspring. [5] to allow the passage of (particles, energy, etc.): *radio waves are transmitted through the atmosphere.* [6] **a** to send out (signals) by means of radio waves or along a transmission line. **b** to broadcast (a radio or television programme). [7] (*tr*) to transfer (a force, motion, power, etc.) from one part of a mechanical system to another.
▷HISTORY C14: from Latin *transmittere* to send across, from TRANS- + *mittere* to send
▸**trans'mittable** *or* **trans'mittible** ADJECTIVE ▸**trans'mittal** NOUN

transmittance (trænz'mɪtəns) NOUN [1] the act of transmitting. [2] Also called: **transmission factor.** *Physics* a measure of the ability of anything to transmit radiation, equal to the ratio of the transmitted flux to the incident flux; the reciprocal of the opacity. For a plate of material the ratio of the flux leaving the entry surface to that reaching the exit surface is the internal transmittance. Symbol: τ. Compare **reflectance, absorptance.**

transmittancy (trænz'mɪtənsɪ) NOUN *Physics* a measure of the extent to which a solution transmits radiation. It is equal to the ratio of the transmittance of the solution to the transmittance of a pure solvent of the same dimensions.

transmitter (trænz'mɪtə) NOUN [1] a person or thing that transmits. [2] the equipment used for generating and amplifying a radio-frequency carrier, modulating the carrier with information, and feeding it to an aerial for transmission. [3] the microphone in a telephone that converts sound waves into audio-frequency electrical signals. [4] a device that converts mechanical movements into coded electrical signals transmitted along a telegraph circuit. [5] *Physiol* short for **neurotransmitter.**

transmittivity (ˌtrænzmɪ'tɪvɪtɪ) NOUN *Physics* the transmittance of unit thickness of a substance, neglecting any scattering effects.

transmogrify (trænz'mɒgrɪˌfaɪ) VERB **-fies, -fying, -fied.** (*tr*) *Jocular* to change or transform into a different shape, esp a grotesque or bizarre one.
▷HISTORY C17: of unknown origin
▸**transˌmogrifi'cation** NOUN

transmontane (ˌtrænzmɒn'teɪn) ADJECTIVE, NOUN another word for **tramontane.**

transmundane (trænz'mʌndeɪn) ADJECTIVE beyond this world or worldly considerations.

transmutation (ˌtrænzmjuː'teɪʃən) NOUN [1] the act or an instance of transmuting. [2] the change of one chemical element into another by a nuclear reaction. [3] the attempted conversion, by alchemists, of base metals into gold or silver.
▸**ˌtransmu'tational** *or* **trans'mutative** ADJECTIVE
▸**ˌtransmu'tationist** NOUN, ADJECTIVE

transmute (trænz'mjuːt) VERB (*tr*) [1] to change the form, character, or substance of. [2] to alter (an element, metal, etc.) by alchemy.
▷HISTORY C15: via Old French from Latin *transmūtāre* to shift, from TRANS- + *mūtāre* to change
▸**transˌmuta'bility** NOUN ▸**trans'mutable** ADJECTIVE
▸**trans'mutably** ADVERB ▸**trans'muter** NOUN

transnational (trænz'næʃənəl) ADJECTIVE extending beyond the boundaries, interests, etc., of a single nation.

Transnet ('trænzˌnɛt) NOUN *South African* the official rail and transport service in South Africa.

Trans-New Guinea phylum NOUN the largest grouping of the non-Austronesian languages of Papua and New Guinea and the surrounding regions. Older term: **New Guinea Macrophylum.**

transoceanic ('trænzˌəʊʃɪ'ænɪk) ADJECTIVE [1] on or from the other side of an ocean. [2] crossing an ocean.

transom ('trænsəm) NOUN [1] Also called: **traverse.** a horizontal member across a window. Compare **mullion.** [2] a horizontal member that separates a door from a window over it. [3] the usual US name for **fanlight.** [4] *Nautical* **a** a surface forming the stern of a vessel, either vertical or canted either forwards (**reverse transom**) or aft at the upper side. **b** any of several transverse beams used for strengthening the stern of a vessel.
▷HISTORY C14: earlier *traversayn*, from Old French *traversin*, from TRAVERSE
▸**'transomed** ADJECTIVE

transonic (træn'sɒnɪk) ADJECTIVE of or relating to conditions when travelling at or near the speed of sound.

transonic barrier NOUN another name for **sound barrier.**

transpacific (ˌtrænzpə'sɪfɪk) ADJECTIVE [1] crossing the Pacific. [2] on or from the other side of the Pacific.

transpadane ('trænzpəˌdeɪn, træns'peɪdeɪn) ADJECTIVE (*prenominal*) on or from the far (or north) side of the River Po, as viewed from Rome. Compare **cispadane.**
▷HISTORY C17: from Latin *Transpadānus*, from TRANS- + *Padus* the River Po

transparency (træns'pærənsɪ, -'pɛər-) NOUN, *plural* **-cies.** [1] Also called: **transparence.** the state of being transparent. [2] Also called: **slide.** a positive photograph on a transparent base, usually mounted in a frame or between glass plates. It can be viewed by means of a slide projector.

transparent (træns'pærənt, -'pɛər-) ADJECTIVE [1] permitting the uninterrupted passage of light; clear: *a window is transparent.* [2] easy to see through, understand, or recognize; obvious. [3] (of a substance or object) permitting the free passage of electromagnetic radiation: *a substance that is transparent to X-rays.* [4] candid, open, or frank.
▷HISTORY C15: from Medieval Latin *transpārēre* to show through, from Latin TRANS- + *pārēre* to appear
▸**trans'parently** ADVERB ▸**trans'parentness** NOUN

transparent context NOUN *Philosophy, logic* an expression in which any term may be replaced by another with the same reference without changing its truth-value. Compare **opaque context.**

transpicuous (træn'spɪkjʊəs) ADJECTIVE a less common word for **transparent.**
▷HISTORY C17: from Medieval Latin *transpicuus*, from Latin *transpicere* to look through, from TRANS- + *specere* to look
▸**tran'spicuously** ADVERB

transpierce (træns'pɪəs) VERB (*tr*) to pierce through.

transpire (træn'spaɪə) VERB [1] (*intr*) to come to light; be known. [2] (*intr*) *Informal* to happen or occur. [3] *Physiol* to give off or exhale (water or vapour) through the skin, a mucous membrane, etc. [4] (of plants) to lose (water in the form of water vapour), esp through the stomata of the leaves.
▷HISTORY C16: from Medieval Latin *transpīrāre*, from Latin TRANS- + *spīrāre* to breathe
▸**tran'spirable** ADJECTIVE ▸**transpiration** (ˌtrænspə'reɪʃən) NOUN ▸**tran'spiratory** ADJECTIVE

> **Language note** It is often maintained that *transpire* should not be used to mean happen or occur, as in *the event transpired late in the evening*, and that the word is properly used to mean become known, as in *it transpired later that the thief had been caught.* The word is, however, widely used in the former sense, esp in spoken English.

transplant VERB (træns'plɑːnt) [1] (*tr*) to remove or transfer (esp a plant) from one place to another. [2] (*intr*) to be capable of being transplanted. [3] *Surgery* to transfer (an organ or tissue) from one part of the body to another or from one person or animal to another during a grafting or transplant operation. ◆ NOUN ('trænsˌplɑːnt) [4] *Surgery* **a** the procedure involved in such a transfer. **b** the organ or tissue transplanted.
▸**trans'plantable** ADJECTIVE ▸**ˌtransplan'tation** NOUN
▸**trans'planter** NOUN

transpolar (trænz'pəʊlə) ADJECTIVE crossing a polar region.

transponder *or* **transpondor** (træn'spɒndə) NOUN [1] a type of radio or radar transmitter-receiver that transmits signals automatically when it receives predetermined signals. [2] the receiver and transmitter in a communications or broadcast satellite, relaying received signals back to earth.
▷HISTORY C20: from TRANSMITTER + RESPONDER

transpontine (trænz'pɒntaɪn) ADJECTIVE [1] on or from the far side of a bridge. [2] *Archaic* on or from the south side of the Thames in London.
▷HISTORY C19: TRANS- + *-pontine*, from Latin *pōns* bridge

transport VERB (træns'pɔːt) (*tr*) [1] to carry or cause to go from one place to another, esp over some distance. [2] to deport or exile to a penal colony. [3] (*usually passive*) to have a strong emotional effect on. ◆ NOUN ('trænsˌpɔːt) [4] **a** the business or system of transporting goods or people. **b** (*as modifier*): *a modernized transport system.* [5] *Brit* freight vehicles generally. [6] **a** a vehicle used to transport goods or people, esp lorries or ships used to convey troops. **b** (*as modifier*): *a transport plane.* [7] the act of transporting or the state of being transported. [8] ecstasy, rapture, or any powerful emotion. [9] a convict sentenced to be transported.
▷HISTORY C14: from Latin *transportāre*, from TRANS- + *portāre* to carry
▸**trans'portable** ADJECTIVE ▸**ˌtransporta'bility** NOUN
▸**trans'porter** NOUN ▸**trans'portive** ADJECTIVE

transportation (ˌtrænspɔː'teɪʃən) NOUN [1] a means or system of transporting. [2] the act of transporting or the state of being transported. [3] (esp formerly) deportation to a penal colony. [4] *Chiefly US* a ticket or fare.

transport café NOUN *Brit* an inexpensive eating place on a main route, used mainly by long-distance lorry drivers.

transporter bridge NOUN a bridge consisting of a movable platform suspended from cables, for transporting vehicles, etc., across a body of water.

transpose (træns'pəʊz) VERB [1] (*tr*) to alter the positions of; interchange, as words in a sentence; put into a different order. [2] *Music* **a** to play (notes, music, etc.) in a different key from that originally intended. **b** to move (a note or series of notes) upwards or downwards in pitch. [3] (*tr*) *Maths* to move (a term) from one side of an equation to the other with a corresponding reversal in sign. ◆ NOUN [4] *Maths* the matrix resulting from interchanging the rows and columns of a given matrix.
▷HISTORY C14: from Old French *transposer*, from Latin *transpōnere* to remove, from TRANS- + *pōnere* to place
▸**trans'posable** ADJECTIVE ▸**transˌposa'bility** NOUN
▸**trans'posal** NOUN ▸**trans'poser** NOUN

transposing instrument NOUN a musical instrument, esp a horn or clarinet, pitched in a key other than C major, but whose music is written down as if its basic scale were C major. A piece of music in the key of F intended to be played on a horn pitched in F is therefore written down a fourth lower than an ordinary part in that key and has the same key signature as a part written in C.

transposition (ˌtrænspə'zɪʃən) NOUN [1] the act of transposing or the state of being transposed. [2] something transposed.
▸**ˌtranspo'sitional** *or* **transpositive** (træns'pɒzɪtɪv) ADJECTIVE

transposon (træns'pəʊzɒn) NOUN *Genetics* a genetic element that can move from one site in a chromosome to another site in the same or a different chromosome and thus alter the genetic constitution of the organism.
▷HISTORY C20: TRANSPOS(E) + -ON

transputer (trænz'pjuːtə) NOUN *Computing* a type of fast, powerful microchip that is the equivalent of a 32-bit microprocessor with its own RAM facility.
▷HISTORY C20: from TRANS(ISTOR) + (COM)PUTER

transsexual *or* **transexual** (trænz'sɛksjʊəl) NOUN [1] a person who permanently acts the part of and completely identifies with the opposite sex. [2] a person who has undergone medical and surgical procedures to alter external sexual characteristics to those of the opposite sex.

transsexualism *or* **transexualism** (trænz'sɛksjʊəˌlɪzəm) NOUN a strong desire to change sex.

transship (træns'ʃɪp) *or* **tranship** VERB **-ships, -shipping, -shipped.** to transfer or be transferred from one vessel or vehicle to another.
▸**trans'shipment** *or* **tran'shipment** NOUN

Trans-Siberian Railway NOUN a railway in S Russia, extending from Moscow to Vladivostok on the Pacific: constructed between 1891 and 1916, making possible the settlement and industrialization of sparsely inhabited regions. Length: 9335 km (5800 miles).

transubstantiate (ˌtrænsəbˈstænʃɪˌeɪt) VERB 1 (*intr*) *RC theol* (of the Eucharistic bread and wine) to undergo transubstantiation. 2 (*tr*) to change (one substance) into another; transmute.
▷HISTORY C16: from Medieval Latin *transsubstantiāre*, from Latin TRANS- + *substantia* SUBSTANCE
▸ˌtransubˈstantial ADJECTIVE ▸ˌtransubˈstantially ADVERB

transubstantiation (ˌtrænsəbˌstænʃɪˈeɪʃən) NOUN 1 (esp in Roman Catholic theology). **a** the doctrine that the whole substance of the bread and wine changes into the substance of the body and blood of Christ when consecrated in the Eucharist. **b** the mystical process by which this is believed to take place during consecration. Compare **consubstantiation.** 2 a substantial change; transmutation.
▸ˌtransubˌstantiˈationalist NOUN

transudate (ˈtrænsʊˌdeɪt) NOUN 1 *Physiol* any fluid without a high protein content that passes through a membrane, esp through the wall of a capillary. Compare **exudate** (sense 2). 2 anything that has been transuded.

transude (trænˈsjuːd) VERB (of a fluid) to ooze or pass through interstices, pores, or small holes.
▷HISTORY C17: from New Latin *transūdāre*, from Latin TRANS- + *sūdāre* to sweat
▸**transudation** (ˌtrænsjʊˈdeɪʃən) NOUN ▸tranˈsudatory ADJECTIVE

transuranic (ˌtrænzjʊˈrænɪk), **transuranian** (ˌtrænzjʊˈreɪnɪən), *or* **transuranium** ADJECTIVE 1 (of an element) having an atomic number greater than that of uranium. 2 of, relating to, or having the behaviour of transuranic elements.
▷HISTORY C20: from TRANS- + *uranic*, from URANIUM

Transvaal (ˈtrænzvɑːl) NOUN former province of NE South Africa: colonized by the Boers after the Great Trek (1836); became a British colony in 1902; joined South Africa in 1910; replaced in 1994. Capital: Pretoria.

Transvaalian (trænzˈvɑːlɪən) ADJECTIVE of or relating to the former South African province of Transvaal or its inhabitants.

transvalue (trænzˈvæljuː) VERB **-ues, -uing, -ued.** (*tr*) to evaluate by a principle that varies from the accepted standards.
▸transˌvaluˈation NOUN ▸transˈvaluer NOUN

transversal (trænzˈvɜːsᵊl) NOUN 1 *Geometry* a line intersecting two or more other lines. ◆ ADJECTIVE 2 a less common word for **transverse.**
▸transˈversally ADVERB

transverse (trænzˈvɜːs) ADJECTIVE 1 crossing from side to side; athwart; crossways. 2 *Geometry* denoting the axis that passes through the foci of a hyperbola. 3 (of a flute, etc.) held almost at right angles to the player's mouth, so that the breath passes over a hole in the side to create a vibrating air column within the tube of the instrument. 4 *Astronomy* another word for **tangential** (sense 2). ◆ NOUN 5 a transverse piece or object.
▷HISTORY C16: from Latin *transversus*, from *transvertere* to turn across, from TRANS- + *vertere* to turn
▸transˈversely ADVERB ▸transˈverseness NOUN

transverse colon NOUN *Anatomy* the part of the large intestine passing transversely in front of the liver and stomach.

transverse flute NOUN the normal orchestral flute, as opposed to the recorder (or **fipple flute**).

transverse process NOUN *Anatomy* either of the projections that arise from either side of a vertebra and provide articulation for the ribs.

transverse wave NOUN a wave, such as an electromagnetic wave, that is propagated in a direction perpendicular to the direction of displacement of the transmitting field or medium. Compare **longitudinal wave.**

transverter (trænzˈvɜːtə) NOUN a piece of equipment attached to a radio transceiver to enable it to transmit and receive on additional frequencies.

transvestite (trænzˈvestaɪt) NOUN a person who seeks sexual pleasure from wearing clothes that are normally associated with the opposite sex.
▷HISTORY C19: from German *Transvestit*, from TRANS- + Latin *vestītus* clothed, from *vestīre* to clothe
▸transˈvestism *or* transˈvestitism NOUN

Transylvania (ˌtrænsɪlˈveɪnɪə) NOUN a region of central and NW Romania: belonged to Hungary from the 11th century until 1918; restored to Romania in 1947.

Transylvanian Alps (ˌtrænsɪlˈveɪnɪən) PLURAL NOUN a mountain range in S Romania; a SW extension of the Carpathian Mountains. Highest peak: Mount Negoiu, 2548 m (8360 ft.).

trap[1] (træp) NOUN 1 a mechanical device or enclosed place or pit in which something, esp an animal, is caught or penned. 2 any device or plan for tricking a person or thing into being caught unawares. 3 anything resembling a trap or prison. 4 a fitting for a pipe in the form of a U-shaped or S-shaped bend that contains standing water to prevent the passage of gases. 5 any similar device. 6 a device that hurls clay pigeons into the air to be fired at by trapshooters. 7 any one of a line of boxlike stalls in which greyhounds are enclosed before the start of a race. 8 See **trap door.** 9 a light two-wheeled carriage. 10 a slang word for **mouth.** 11 *Golf* an obstacle or hazard, esp a bunker. 12 (*plural*) *Jazz, slang* percussion instruments. 13 (*usually plural*) *Austral obsolete slang* a policeman. ◆ VERB **traps, trapping, trapped.** 14 (*tr*) to catch, take, or pen in or as if in a trap; entrap. 15 (*tr*) to ensnare by trickery; trick. 16 (*tr*) to provide (a pipe) with a trap. 17 to set traps in (a place), esp for animals.
▷HISTORY Old English *træppe*; related to Middle Low German *trappe*, Medieval Latin *trappa*
▸ˈtrapˌlike ADJECTIVE

trap[2] (træp) NOUN 1 an obsolete word for **trappings** (sense 2). ◆ VERB **traps, trapping, trapped.** 2 (*tr; often foll by out*) to dress or adorn. See also **traps.**
▷HISTORY C11: probably from Old French *drap* cloth

trap[3] (træp) *or* **traprock** NOUN 1 any fine-grained often columnar dark igneous rock, esp basalt. 2 any rock in which oil or gas has accumulated.
▷HISTORY C18: from Swedish *trappa* stair (from its steplike formation); see TRAP[1]

trapan (trəˈpæn) VERB **-pans, -panning, -panned,** NOUN a variant spelling of **trepan** (sense 2).
▸traˈpanner NOUN

Trapani (*Italian* ˈtraːpani) NOUN a port in S Italy, in NW Sicily: Carthaginian naval base, ceded to the Romans after the First Punic War. Pop.: 72 840 (1990).

trap door NOUN 1 a door or flap flush with and covering an opening, esp in a ceiling. 2 the opening so covered.

trap-door spider NOUN any of various spiders of the family *Ctenizidae* that construct a silk-lined hole in the ground closed by a hinged door of earth and silk.

trapes (treɪps) VERB, NOUN a less common spelling of **traipse.**

trapeze (trəˈpiːz) NOUN 1 a free-swinging bar attached to two ropes, used by circus acrobats, etc. 2 a sling like a bosun's chair at one end of a line attached to the masthead of a light racing sailing boat, used in sitting out.
▷HISTORY C19: from French *trapèze*, from New Latin; see TRAPEZIUM

trapeziform (trəˈpiːzɪˌfɔːm) ADJECTIVE *Rare* shaped like a trapezium: *a trapeziform part.*

trapezium (trəˈpiːzɪəm) NOUN, *plural* **-ziums** *or* **-zia** (-zɪə). 1 *Chiefly Brit* a quadrilateral having two parallel sides of unequal length. Usual US and Canadian name: **trapezoid.** 2 *Now chiefly US and Canadian* a quadrilateral having neither pair of sides parallel. 3 a small bone of the wrist near the base of the thumb.
▷HISTORY C16: via Late Latin from Greek *trapezion*, from *trapeza* table
▸traˈpezial ADJECTIVE

trapezius (trəˈpiːzɪəs) NOUN, *plural* **-uses.** either of two flat triangular muscles, one covering each side of the back and shoulders, that rotate the shoulder blades.
▷HISTORY C18: from New Latin *trapezius* (*musculus*) trapezium-shaped (muscle)

trapezohedron (trəˌpiːzəʊˈhiːdrən) NOUN, *plural* **-drons** *or* **-dra** (-drə). *Crystallog* a crystal form in which all the crystal's faces are trapeziums.
▷HISTORY C19: from *trapezo-* combining form of TRAPEZIUM + -HEDRON, on the model of TETRAHEDRON
▸traˌpezoˈhedral ADJECTIVE

trapezoid (ˈtræpɪˌzɔɪd) NOUN 1 a quadrilateral having neither pair of sides parallel. 2 the usual US and Canadian name for **trapezium.** 3 a small bone of the wrist near the base of the index finger.
▷HISTORY C18: from New Latin *trapezoidēs*, from Late Greek *trapezoeidēs* trapezium-shaped, from *trapeza* table

trapezoid rule NOUN a rule for estimating the area of an irregular figure, by dividing it into parallel strips of equal width, each strip being a trapezium. It can also be adapted to obtaining an approximate value of a definite integral.

trappean (ˈtræpɪən, trəˈpiən) ADJECTIVE *Rare* of, relating to, or consisting of igneous rock, esp a basalt.
▷HISTORY C19: from TRAP[3]

trapper (ˈtræpə) NOUN a person who traps animals, esp for their furs or skins.

trappings (ˈtræpɪŋz) PLURAL NOUN 1 the accessories and adornments that characterize or symbolize a condition, office, etc.: *the visible trappings of success.* 2 ceremonial harness for a horse or other animal, including bridles, saddles, etc.
▷HISTORY C16: from TRAP[2]

Trappist (ˈtræpɪst) NOUN **a** a member of a branch of the Cistercian order of Christian monks, the Reformed Cistercians of the Strict Observance which originated at La Trappe in France in 1664. They are noted for their rule of silence. **b** (*as modifier*): *a Trappist monk.*

traprock (ˈtræpˌrɒk) NOUN another name for **trap**[3].

traps (træps) PLURAL NOUN belongings; luggage.
▷HISTORY C19: probably shortened from TRAPPINGS

trapshooting (ˈtræpˌʃuːtɪŋ) NOUN the sport of shooting at clay pigeons thrown up by a trap.
▸ˈtrapˌshooter NOUN

trapunto (trəˈpʊntəʊ) NOUN, *plural* **-tos.** a type of quilting that is only partly padded in a design.
▷HISTORY Italian, from *trapungere* to embroider, from *pungere* to prick (from Latin)

trash[1] (træʃ) NOUN 1 foolish ideas or talk; nonsense. 2 *Chiefly US and Canadian* useless or unwanted matter or objects. 3 a literary or artistic production of poor quality. 4 *Chiefly US and Canadian* a poor or worthless person or a group of such people. 5 bits that are broken or lopped off, esp the trimmings from trees or plants. 6 the dry remains of sugar cane after the juice has been extracted. ◆ VERB 7 to remove the outer leaves and branches from (growing plants, esp sugar cane). 8 *Slang* to attack or destroy (someone or something) wilfully or maliciously.
▷HISTORY C16: of obscure origin; perhaps related to Norwegian *trask*
▸ˈtrashery NOUN

trash[2] (træʃ) *Archaic* ◆ VERB 1 (*tr*) to restrain with or as if with a lead. ◆ NOUN 2 a lead for a dog.
▷HISTORY C17: perhaps from obsolete French *tracier* to track, TRACE[1]

trash can NOUN a US name for **dustbin.** Also called: **ash can, garbage can.**

trashed (træʃt) ADJECTIVE *Informal* drunk.

trash farming NOUN *US* cultivation by leaving stubble, etc., on the surface of the soil to serve as a mulch.

trashy (ˈtræʃɪ) ADJECTIVE **trashier, trashiest.** cheap, worthless, or badly made.
▸ˈtrashily ADVERB ▸ˈtrashiness NOUN

Trasimene (ˈtræzɪˌmiːn) NOUN **Lake.** a lake in central Italy, in Umbria: the largest lake in central Italy; scene of Hannibal's victory over the Romans in 217 B.C. Area: 128 sq. km (49 sq. miles). Italian name: **Trasimeno.** Also called: (Lake) **Perugia.**

trass (træs) NOUN a variety of the volcanic rock tuff, used to make a hydraulic cement.
▷HISTORY from Dutch *tras, tarasse*, from Italian *terrazza* worthless earth; see TERRACE

trattoria (ˌtrætəˈrɪə) NOUN an Italian restaurant.
▷HISTORY C19: from Italian, from *trattore* innkeeper, from French *traiteur*, from Old French *tretier* to TREAT

trauchle (ˈtrɒxᵊl) *Scot* ◆ NOUN 1 work or a task

that is tiring, monotonous, and lengthy. ◆ VERB (*intr*) 2 to walk or work slowly and wearily.
▷HISTORY C19: of uncertain origin

trauchled ('trɒxəld) *Scot* ADJECTIVE exhausted by long hard work or concern.

trauma ('trɔːmə) NOUN, *plural* **-mata** (-mətə) *or* **-mas.** 1 *Psychol* a powerful shock that may have long-lasting effects. 2 *Pathol* any bodily injury or wound.
▷HISTORY C18: from Greek: a wound
▸**traumatic** (trɔː'mætɪk) ADJECTIVE ▸**trau'matically** ADVERB

traumatism ('trɔːməˌtɪzəm) NOUN 1 any abnormal bodily condition caused by injury, wound, or shock. 2 (not in technical usage) another name for **trauma** (sense 2).

traumatize *or* **traumatise** ('trɔːməˌtaɪz) VERB 1 (*tr*) to wound or injure (the body). 2 to subject or be subjected to mental trauma.
▸ˌ**traumati'zation** *or* ˌ**traumati'sation** NOUN

travail ('træveɪl) *Literary* ◆ NOUN 1 painful or excessive labour or exertion. 2 the pangs of childbirth; labour. ◆ VERB 3 (*intr*) to suffer or labour painfully, esp in childbirth.
▷HISTORY C13: from Old French *travaillier*, from Vulgar Latin *tripaliāre* (unattested) to torture, from Late Latin *trepālium* instrument of torture, from Latin *tripālis* having three stakes, from *trēs* three + *pālus* stake

Travancore (ˌtrævən'kɔː) NOUN a former princely state of S India which joined with Cochin in 1949 to form **Travancore-Cochin**: part of Kerala state since 1956.

trave (treɪv) NOUN 1 a stout wooden cage in which difficult horses are shod. 2 another name for **crossbeam.** 3 a bay formed by crossbeams.
▷HISTORY C15: from Old French *trave* beam, from Latin *trabs*

travel ('trævəl) VERB **-els, -elling, -elled** *or US* **-els, -eling, -eled.** (*mainly intr*) 1 to go, move, or journey from one place to another: *he travels to improve his mind; she travelled across France.* 2 (*tr*) to go, move, or journey through or across (an area, region, etc.): *he travelled the country.* 3 to go, move, or cover a specified or unspecified distance. 4 to go from place to place as a salesman: *to travel in textiles.* 5 (esp of perishable goods) to withstand a journey. 6 (of light, sound, etc.) to be transmitted or move: *the sound travelled for miles.* 7 to progress or advance. 8 *Basketball* to take an excessive number of steps while holding the ball. 9 (of part of a mechanism) to move in a fixed predetermined path. 10 *Informal* to move rapidly: *that car certainly travels.* 11 (often foll by *with*) *Informal* to be in the company (of); associate. ◆ NOUN 12 **a** the act of travelling. **b** (*as modifier*): *a travel brochure.* Related adjective: **itinerant.** 13 (*usually plural*) a tour or journey. 14 the distance moved by a mechanical part, such as the stroke of a piston. 15 movement or passage.
▷HISTORY C14 *travaillen* to make a journey, from Old French *travaillier* to TRAVAIL

travel agency *or* **bureau** NOUN an agency that arranges and negotiates flights, holidays, etc., for travellers.
▸**travel agent** NOUN

travelator ('trævəˌleɪtə) NOUN a variant spelling of **travolator.**

travelled *or US* **traveled** ('trævəld) ADJECTIVE having experienced or undergone much travelling: *a travelled urbane epicure.*

traveller *or US* **traveler** ('trævələ, 'trævlə) NOUN 1 a person who travels, esp habitually. 2 See **travelling salesman.** 3 (*sometimes capital*) a member of the travelling people. 4 a part of a mechanism that moves in a fixed course. 5 *Nautical* **a** a thimble fitted to slide freely on a rope, spar, or rod. **b** the fixed rod on which such a thimble slides. 6 *Austral* a swagman.

traveller's cheque NOUN a cheque in any of various denominations sold for use abroad by a bank, etc., to the bearer, who signs it on purchase and can cash it by signing it again.

traveller's joy NOUN a ranunculaceous Old World climbing plant, *Clematis vitalba*, having white flowers and heads of feathery plumed fruits. Also called: **old man's beard.**

travelling people *or* **folk** PLURAL NOUN (*sometimes capitals*) *Brit* Gypsies or other itinerant people: a term used esp by such people of themselves.

travelling salesman NOUN a salesman who travels within an assigned territory in order to sell merchandise or to solicit orders for the commercial enterprise he represents by direct personal contact with customers and potential customers. Also called: **commercial traveller, traveller.**

travelling wave NOUN **a** a wave carrying energy away from its source. **b** (*as modifier*): *a travelling-wave aerial.*

travelling-wave tube NOUN an electronic tube in which an electron beam interacts with a distributed high-frequency magnetic field so that energy is transferred from the beam to the field.

travelogue *or sometimes US* **travelog** ('trævəˌlɒg) NOUN a film, lecture, or brochure on travels and travelling.
▷HISTORY C20: from TRAVEL + -LOGUE

travel-sick ADJECTIVE nauseated from riding in a moving vehicle.
▸'**travel-ˌsickness** NOUN

traverse ('trævɜːs, trə'vɜːs) VERB 1 to pass or go over or back and forth over (something); cross. 2 (*tr*) to go against; oppose; obstruct. 3 to move or cause to move sideways or crosswise. 4 (*tr*) to extend or reach across. 5 to turn (an artillery gun) laterally on its pivot or mount or (of an artillery gun) to turn laterally. 6 (*tr*) to look over or examine carefully. 7 (*tr*) *Law* to deny (an allegation of fact), as in pleading. 8 (*intr*) *Fencing* to slide one's blade towards an opponent's hilt while applying pressure against his blade. 9 *Mountaineering* to move across (a face) horizontally. 10 (*tr*) *Nautical* to brace (a yard) fore and aft. ◆ NOUN 11 something being or lying across, such as a transom. 12 a gallery or loft inside a building that crosses it. 13 *Maths* another name for **transversal** (sense 1). 14 an obstruction or hindrance. 15 *Fortifications* a protective bank or other barrier across a trench or rampart. 16 a railing, screen, or curtain. 17 the act or an instance of traversing or crossing. 18 a path or road across. 19 *Nautical* the zigzag course of a vessel tacking frequently. 20 *Law* the formal denial of a fact alleged in the opposite party's pleading. 21 *Surveying* a survey consisting of a series of straight lines, the length of each and the angle between them being measured. 22 *Mountaineering* a horizontal move across a face. ◆ ADJECTIVE 23 being or lying across; transverse. ◆ ADVERB 24 an archaic word for **across.**
▷HISTORY C14: from Old French *traverser*, from Late Latin *trānsversāre*, from Latin *trānsversus* TRANSVERSE
▸'**traversable** ADJECTIVE ▸**tra'versal** NOUN ▸'**traverser** NOUN

travertine *or* **travertin** ('trævətɪn) NOUN a porous rock consisting of calcium carbonate, used for building. Also called: **calc-sinter.**
▷HISTORY C18: from Italian *travertino* (influenced by *tra-* TRANS-), from Latin *lapis Tīburtīnus* Tiburtine stone, from *Tībur*s the district around Tibur (now Tivoli)

travesty ('trævɪstɪ) NOUN, *plural* **-ties.** 1 a farcical or grotesque imitation; mockery; parody. ◆ VERB **-ties, -tying, -tied.** (*tr*) 2 to make or be a travesty of.
▷HISTORY C17: from French *travesti* disguised, from *travestir* to disguise, from Italian *travestire*, from *tra-* TRANS- + *vestire* to clothe

travois (trə'vɔɪ) NOUN, *plural* **-vois** (-'vɔɪz). a sled formerly used by the Plains Indians of North America, consisting of two poles joined by a frame and dragged by an animal.
▷HISTORY from Canadian French, from French *travail* TRAVE

travolator *or* **travelator** ('trævəˌleɪtə) NOUN a moving pavement for transporting pedestrians, as in a shopping precinct or an airport.
▷HISTORY C20: coined on the model of ESCALATOR

trawl (trɔːl) NOUN *Sea fishing* 1 Also called: **trawl net.** a large net, usually in the shape of a sock or bag, drawn at deep levels behind special boats (trawlers). 2 Also called: **trawl line.** a long line to which numerous shorter hooked lines are attached, suspended between buoys. See also **setline, trotline.** 3 the act of trawling. ◆ VERB 4 *Sea fishing* to catch or try to catch (fish) with a trawl net or trawl line. 5 *Sea fishing* (*tr*) to drag (a trawl net) or suspend (a trawl line). 6 (*intr*; foll by *for*) to seek or gather (something, such as information, or someone, such as a likely appointee) from a wide variety of sources. ◆ NOUN, VERB 7 *Angling* another word for **troll**[1].
▷HISTORY C17: from Middle Dutch *traghelen* to drag, from Latin *trāgula* dragnet; see TRAIL

trawler ('trɔːlə) NOUN 1 a vessel used for trawling. 2 a person who trawls.

tray (treɪ) NOUN 1 a thin flat board or plate of metal, plastic, etc., usually with a raised edge, on which things can be carried. 2 a shallow receptacle for papers, etc., sometimes forming a drawer in a cabinet or box.
▷HISTORY Old English *trieg*; related to Old Swedish *trö* corn measure, Old Norse *treyja* carrier, Greek *driti* tub, German *Trog* TROUGH

traymobile ('treɪməˌbiːl) NOUN *Austral informal* a small table on casters used for conveying food, drink, etc.

TRC (in South Africa) ABBREVIATION FOR Truth and Reconciliation Commission, a body established in 1996 to investigate political crimes committed under the apartheid system.

treacherous ('tretʃərəs) ADJECTIVE 1 betraying or likely to betray faith or confidence. 2 unstable, unreliable, or dangerous: *treacherous weather; treacherous ground.*
▸'**treacherously** ADVERB ▸'**treacherousness** NOUN

treachery ('tretʃərɪ) NOUN, *plural* **-eries.** 1 the act or an instance of wilful betrayal. 2 the disposition to betray.
▷HISTORY C13: from Old French *trecherie*, from *trechier* to cheat; compare TRICK

treacle ('triːkəl) NOUN 1 Also called: **black treacle.** *Brit* a dark viscous syrup obtained during the refining of sugar. 2 *Brit* another name for **golden syrup.** 3 anything sweet and cloying. 4 *Obsolete* any of various preparations used as an antidote to poisoning.
▷HISTORY C14: from Old French *triacle*, from Latin *thēriaca* antidote to poison
▸'**treacly** ADJECTIVE ▸'**treacliness** NOUN

treacle mustard NOUN a N temperate cruciferous annual plant, *Erysimum cheiranthoides*, having small yellow flowers. It is a common weed in cultivated ground.
▷HISTORY C16: so called because of its alleged medicinal properties. See TREACLE

tread (tred) VERB **treads, treading, trod, trodden** *or* **trod.** 1 to walk or trample in, on, over, or across (something). 2 (when *intr*, foll by *on*) to crush or squash by or as if by treading: *to tread grapes; to tread on a spider.* 3 (*intr*; sometimes foll by *on*) to subdue or repress, as by doing injury (to): *to tread on one's inferiors.* 4 (*tr*) to do by walking or dancing: *to tread a measure.* 5 (*tr*) (of a male bird) to copulate with (a female bird). 6 **tread lightly.** to proceed with delicacy or tact. 7 **tread on (someone's) toes.** to offend or insult (someone), esp by infringing on his sphere of action, etc. 8 **tread water.** to stay afloat in an upright position by moving the legs in a walking motion. ◆ NOUN 9 a manner or style of walking, dancing, etc.: *a light tread.* 10 the act of treading. 11 the top surface of a step in a staircase. 12 the outer part of a tyre or wheel that makes contact with the road, esp the grooved surface of a pneumatic tyre. 13 the part of a rail that wheels touch. 14 the part of a shoe that is generally in contact with the ground. 15 *Vet science* an injury to a horse's foot caused by the opposite foot, or the foot of another horse. 16 a rare word for **footprint.**
▷HISTORY Old English *tredan*; related to Old Norse *trotha*, Old High German *tretan*, Swedish *träda*
▸'**treader** NOUN

treadle ('tredəl) NOUN 1 **a** a rocking lever operated by the foot to drive a machine. **b** (*as modifier*): *a treadle sewing machine.* ◆ VERB 2 to work (a machine) with a treadle.
▷HISTORY Old English *tredel*, from *trǣde* something firm, from *tredan* to TREAD
▸'**treadler** NOUN

treadmill ('tredˌmɪl) NOUN 1 Also called: **treadwheel.** (formerly) an apparatus used to produce rotation, in which the weight of men or animals climbing steps on or around the periphery of a cylinder or wheel caused it to turn. 2 a dreary round or routine. 3 an exercise machine that consists of a continuous moving belt on which to walk or jog.

treas. ABBREVIATION FOR: [1] treasurer. [2] treasury.

treason ('triːzᵊn) NOUN [1] violation or betrayal of the allegiance that a person owes his sovereign or his country, esp by attempting to overthrow the government; high treason. [2] any treachery or betrayal.
▷**HISTORY** C13: from Old French *traïson*, from Latin *trāditiō* a handing over; see TRADITION, TRADITOR
▸ **'treasonable** *or* **'treasonous** ADJECTIVE ▸ **'treasonableness** NOUN ▸ **'treasonably** ADVERB

treasure ('trɛʒə) NOUN [1] wealth and riches, usually hoarded, esp in the form of money, precious metals, or gems. [2] a thing or person that is highly prized or valued. ◆ VERB (*tr*) [3] to prize highly as valuable, rare, or costly. [4] to store up and save; hoard.
▷**HISTORY** C12: from Old French *tresor*, from Latin *thēsaurus* anything hoarded, from Greek *thēsauros*
▸ **'treasurable** ADJECTIVE ▸ **'treasureless** ADJECTIVE

treasure flower NOUN another name for **gazania.**

treasure hunt NOUN a game in which players act upon successive clues and are eventually directed to a prize.

treasurer ('trɛʒərə) NOUN a person appointed to look after the funds of a society, company, city, or other governing body.
▸ **'treasurership** NOUN

Treasurer ('trɛʒərə) NOUN (in the Commonwealth of Australia and each of the Australian states) the minister of finance.

treasure-trove NOUN (in Britain) [1] *Law* valuable articles, such as coins, bullion, etc., found hidden in the earth or elsewhere and of unknown ownership. Such articles become the property of the Crown, which compensates the finder if the treasure is declared. In 1996 treasure was defined as any item over 300 years old and containing more than 5% precious metal. [2] anything similarly discovered that is of value.
▷**HISTORY** C16: from Anglo-French *tresor trové* treasure found, from Old French *tresor* TREASURE + *trover* to find

treasury ('trɛʒərɪ) NOUN, *plural* **-uries.** [1] a storage place for treasure. [2] the revenues or funds of a government, private organization, or individual. [3] a place where funds are kept and disbursed. [4] Also: **treasure house.** a collection or source of valuable items: *a treasury of information.*
▷**HISTORY** C13: from Old French *tresorie*, from *tresor* TREASURE

Treasury ('trɛʒərɪ) NOUN (in various countries) the government department in charge of finance. In Britain the Treasury is also responsible for economic strategy.

Treasury Bench NOUN (in Britain) the front bench to the right of the Speaker in the House of Commons, traditionally reserved for members of the Government.

Treasury bill NOUN a short-term noninterest-bearing obligation issued by the Treasury, payable to bearer and maturing usually in three months, within which it is tradable on a discount basis on the open market.

treasury bond NOUN a long-term interest-bearing bond issued by the US Treasury.

treasury certificate NOUN a short-term obligation issued by the US Treasury, maturing in 12 months with interest payable by coupon redemption.

treasury note NOUN a note issued by a government treasury and generally receivable as legal tender for any debt, esp **a** a medium-term interest-bearing obligation issued by the US Treasury, maturing in from one to five years. **b** Also called: **currency note.** a note issued by the British Treasury in 1914 to the value of £1 or ten shillings: amalgamated with banknotes in 1928.

treasury tag NOUN a short piece of cord having metal ends one of which can be slotted inside the other: used for holding papers together or fastening them into a file.

treat (triːt) NOUN [1] a celebration, entertainment, gift, or feast given for or to someone and paid for by another. [2] any delightful surprise or specially pleasant occasion. [3] the act of treating. ◆ VERB [4] (*tr*) to deal with or regard in a certain manner: *she treats school as a joke.* [5] (*tr*) to apply treatment to: *to treat a patient for malaria.* [6] (*tr*) to subject to a process or to the application of a substance: *to treat photographic film with developer.* [7] (often foll by *to*) to provide (someone) (with) as a treat: *he treated the children to a trip to the zoo.* [8] (*intr*; usually foll by *of*) *Formal* to deal (with), as in writing or speaking. [9] (*intr*) *Formal* to discuss settlement; negotiate.
▷**HISTORY** C13: from Old French *tretier*, from Latin *tractāre* to manage, from *trahere* to drag
▸ **'treatable** ADJECTIVE ▸ **'treater** NOUN

treatise ('triːtɪz) NOUN [1] a formal work on a subject, esp one that deals systematically with its principles and conclusions. [2] an obsolete word for **narrative.**
▷**HISTORY** C14: from Anglo-French *tretiz*, from Old French *tretier* to TREAT

treatment ('triːtmənt) NOUN [1] the application of medicines, surgery, psychotherapy, etc., to a patient or to a disease or symptom. [2] the manner of handling or dealing with a person or thing, as in a literary or artistic work. [3] the act, practice, or manner of treating. [4] *Films* an expansion of a script into sequence form, indicating camera angles, dialogue, etc. [5] **the treatment.** *Slang* the usual manner of dealing with a particular type of person (esp in the phrase **give someone the (full) treatment**).

treaty ('triːtɪ) NOUN, *plural* **-ties.** [1] **a** a formal agreement or contract between two or more states, such as an alliance or trade arrangement. **b** the document in which such a contract is written. [2] any international agreement. [3] any pact or agreement. [4] an agreement between two parties concerning the purchase of property at a price privately agreed between them. [5] *Archaic* negotiation towards an agreement. [6] (in Canada) **a** any of the formal agreements between Indian bands and the federal government by which the Indians surrender their land rights in return for various forms of aid. **b** (*as modifier*): *treaty Indians; treaty money.* [7] an obsolete word for **entreaty.**
▷**HISTORY** C14: from Old French *traité*, from Medieval Latin *tractātus* treaty, from Latin: discussion, from *tractāre* to manage; see TREAT
▸ **'treatyless** ADJECTIVE

treaty port NOUN (in China, Japan, and Korea during the second half of the 19th and first half of the 20th century) a city, esp a port, in which foreigners, esp Westerners, were allowed by treaty to conduct trade.

Trebizond ('trɛbɪˌzɒnd) NOUN a variant of **Trabzon.**

treble ('trɛbᵊl) ADJECTIVE [1] threefold; triple. [2] of, relating to, or denoting a soprano voice or part or a high-pitched instrument. ◆ NOUN [3] treble the amount, size, etc. [4] a soprano voice or part or a high-pitched instrument. [5] the highest register of a musical instrument. [6] **a** the high-frequency response of an audio amplifier, esp in a record player or tape recorder. **b** a control knob on such an instrument by means of which the high-frequency gain can be increased or decreased. [7] *Bell-ringing* the lightest and highest bell in a ring. [8] **a** the narrow inner ring on a dartboard. **b** a hit on this ring. ◆ VERB [9] to make or become three times as much.
▷**HISTORY** C14: from Old French, from Latin *triplus* threefold, TRIPLE
▸ **'trebleness** NOUN ▸ **'trebly** ADVERB, ADJECTIVE

treble chance NOUN a method of betting in football pools in which the chances of winning are related to the number of draws and the number of home and away wins forecast by the competitor.

treble clef NOUN *Music* the clef that establishes G a fifth above middle C as being on the second line of the staff. Symbol: 𝄞.

Treblinka (trɛ'blɪŋkə) NOUN a Nazi concentration camp in central Poland, on the Bug River northeast of Warsaw: chiefly remembered as the place where the Jews of the Warsaw ghetto were put to death.

trebuchet ('trɛbjʊˌʃɛt) *or* **trebucket** ('triːbʌkɪt) NOUN a large medieval siege engine for hurling missiles consisting of a sling on a pivoted wooden arm set in motion by the fall of a weight.
▷**HISTORY** C13: from Old French, from *trebuchier* to stumble, from *tre-* TRANS- + *-buchier*, from *buc* trunk of the body, of Germanic origin; compare Old High German *būh* belly, Old English *buc*

trecento (treɪ'tʃɛntəʊ) NOUN the 14th century, esp with reference to Italian art and literature.
▷**HISTORY** C19: shortened from Italian *mille trecento* one thousand three hundred
▸ **tre'centist** NOUN

tree (triː) NOUN [1] any large woody perennial plant with a distinct trunk giving rise to branches or leaves at some distance from the ground. Related adjective: **arboreal.** [2] any plant that resembles this but has a trunk not made of wood, such as a palm tree. [3] a wooden post, bar, etc. [4] See **family tree, shoetree, saddletree.** [5] *Chem* a treelike crystal growth; dendrite. [6] **a** a branching diagrammatic representation of something, such as the grammatical structure of a sentence. **b** (*as modifier*): *a tree diagram.* [7] an archaic word for **gallows.** [8] *Archaic* the cross on which Christ was crucified. [9] **at the top of the tree.** in the highest position of a profession, etc. [10] **up a tree.** *US and Canadian informal* in a difficult situation; trapped or stumped. ◆ VERB **trees, treeing, treed.** (*tr*) [11] to drive or force up a tree. [12] to shape or stretch (a shoe) on a shoetree.
▷**HISTORY** Old English *trēo*; related to Old Frisian, Old Norse *trē*, Old Saxon *trio*, Gothic *triu*, Greek *doru* wood, *drus* tree
▸ **'treeless** ADJECTIVE ▸ **'treelessness** NOUN ▸ **'tree,like** ADJECTIVE

tree-and-branch ADJECTIVE denoting a cable television system in which all available programme channels are fed to each subscriber. Compare **switched-star.**

tree creeper NOUN any small songbird of the family *Certhiidae* of the N hemisphere, having a brown-and-white plumage and slender downward-curving bill. They creep up trees to feed on insects.

tree farm NOUN an area of forest in which the growth of the trees is managed on a commercial basis.

tree fern NOUN any of numerous large tropical ferns, mainly of the family *Cyatheaceae*, having a trunklike stem bearing fronds at the top.

tree frog NOUN [1] any arboreal frog of the family *Hylidae*, chiefly of SE Asia, Australia, and America. They are strong jumpers and have long toes ending in adhesive discs, which assist in climbing. [2] any of various other arboreal frogs of different families.

tree heath NOUN another name for **briar**[1] (sense 1).

treehopper ('triːˌhɒpə) NOUN any homopterous insect of the family *Membracidae*, which live among trees and other plants and typically have a large hoodlike thoracic process curving backwards over the body.

tree-hugger ('triːˌhʌgə) NOUN *Informal, derogatory* an environmental campaigner.
▷**HISTORY** C20: from the tactic of embracing trees to prevent their being felled

tree kangaroo NOUN any of several arboreal kangaroos of the genus *Dendrolagus*, of New Guinea and N Australia, having hind and forelegs of a similar length and a long tail.

tree layer NOUN See **layer** (sense 2).

tree line NOUN the zone, at high altitudes or high latitudes, beyond which no trees grow. Trees growing between the timber line and the tree line are typically stunted.

tree mallow NOUN a malvaceous treelike plant, *Lavatera arborea*, of rocky coastal areas of Europe and N Africa, having a woody stem, rounded leaves, and red-purple flowers.

treen ('triːən) ADJECTIVE [1] made of wood; wooden. ◆ NOUN [2] another name for **treenware.** [3] the art of making treenware.
▷**HISTORY** Old English *trēowen*, from *trēow* TREE

treenail, trenail ('triːneɪl, 'trɛnᵊl), *or* **trunnel** ('trʌnᵊl) NOUN a dowel used for pinning planks or timbers together.

treenware ('triːənˌwɛə) NOUN dishes and other household utensils made of wood, as by pioneers in North America.
▷**HISTORY** from TREEN + WARE[1]

tree of heaven NOUN another name for **ailanthus.**

tree of knowledge of good and evil NOUN *Old Testament* the tree in the Garden of Eden bearing the forbidden fruit that Adam and Eve ate, thus incurring loss of primal innocence (Genesis 2:9; 3:2–7).

tree of life NOUN 1 *Old Testament* a tree in the Garden of Eden, the fruit of which had the power of conferring eternal life (Genesis 2:9; 3:22). 2 *New Testament* a tree in the heavenly Jerusalem, for the healing of the nations (Revelation 22:2).

tree ring NOUN another name for **annual ring**.

tree runner NOUN *Austral* another name for **sitella**.

tree shrew NOUN any of numerous small arboreal mammals of the family *Tupaiidae* and order *Scandentia*, of SE Asia, having large eyes and resembling squirrels.

tree snake NOUN any of various slender arboreal colubrid snakes of the genera *Chlorophis* (**green tree snakes**), *Chrysopelea* (**golden tree snakes**), etc.

tree sparrow NOUN 1 a small European weaverbird, *Passer montanus*, similar to the house sparrow but having a brown head. 2 a small North American finch, *Spizella arborea*, having a reddish-brown head, grey underparts, and brown striped back and wings.

tree surgery NOUN the treatment of damaged trees by filling cavities, applying braces, etc.
▸**tree surgeon** NOUN

tree toad NOUN a less common name for **tree frog**.

tree tomato NOUN 1 an arborescent shrub, *Cyphomandra betacea* or *C. crassifolia*, native to South America but widely cultivated, bearing red egg-shaped edible fruit: family *Solanaceae*. 2 the fruit of this plant. Also called: **tamarillo**.

treeware ('tri:ˌwɛə) NOUN books, magazines, or other reading materials that are printed on paper made from wood pulp as opposed to texts in the form of computer software, CD-ROM, audio books, etc.

tref, treif (treɪf), *or* **treifa** ('treɪfə) ADJECTIVE *Judaism* ritually unfit to be eaten; not kosher.
▷HISTORY Yiddish, from Hebrew *terēphāh*, literally: torn (i.e., animal meat torn by beasts), from *tāraf* to tear

trefoil ('trɛfɔɪl) NOUN 1 any of numerous leguminous plants of the temperate genus *Trifolium*, having leaves divided into three leaflets and dense heads of small white, yellow, red, or purple flowers. 2 any of various related plants having leaves divided into three leaflets, such as bird's-foot trefoil. 3 a leaf having three leaflets. 4 *Architect* an ornament in the form of three arcs arranged in a circle.
▷HISTORY C14: from Anglo-French *trifoil*, from Latin *trifolium* three-leaved herb, from TRI- + *folium* leaf
▸'**trefoiled** ADJECTIVE

trehala (trɪ'hɑːlə) NOUN an edible sugary substance obtained from the pupal cocoon of an Asian weevil, *Larinus maculatus*.
▷HISTORY C19: from Turkish *tīgāla*, from Persian *tīghāl*

trehalose ('triːhəˌləʊs, -ˌləʊz) NOUN a white crystalline disaccharide that occurs in yeast and certain fungi. Formula: $C_{12}H_{22}O_{11}$.
▷HISTORY C19: from TREHALA

treillage ('treɪlɪdʒ) NOUN latticework; trellis.
▷HISTORY C17: from French, from Old French *treille* bower, from Latin *trichila*; see -AGE

trek (trɛk) NOUN 1 a long and often difficult journey. 2 *South African* a journey or stage of a journey, esp a migration by ox wagon. ◆ VERB **treks, trekking, trekked**. 3 (*intr*) to make a trek. 4 (*tr*) *South African* (of an ox, etc.) to draw (a load).
▷HISTORY C19: from Afrikaans, from Middle Dutch *trekken* to travel; related to Old Frisian *trekka*
▸'**trekker** NOUN

trellis ('trɛlɪs) NOUN 1 a structure or pattern of latticework, esp one used to support climbing plants. 2 an arch made of latticework. ◆ VERB (*tr*) 3 to interweave (strips of wood, etc.) to make a trellis. 4 to provide or support with a trellis.
▷HISTORY C14: from Old French *treliz* fabric of open texture, from Late Latin *trilīcius* woven with three threads, from Latin TRI- + *līcium* thread
▸'**trellis-ˌlike** ADJECTIVE

trelliswork ('trɛlɪsˌwɜːk) NOUN **a** work or patterns of trellis; latticework. **b** (*as modifier*): *a trelliswork fence*.

trematode ('trɛməˌtəʊd, 'triː-) NOUN any parasitic flatworm of the class *Trematoda*, which includes the flukes.
▷HISTORY C19: from New Latin *Trematoda*, from Greek *trēmatōdēs* full of holes, from *trēma* a hole

tremble ('trɛmbᵊl) VERB (*intr*) 1 to vibrate with short slight movements; quiver. 2 to shake involuntarily, as with cold or fear; shiver. 3 to experience fear or anxiety. ◆ NOUN 4 the act or an instance of trembling.
▷HISTORY C14: from Old French *trembler*, from Medieval Latin *tremulāre*, from Latin *tremulus* quivering, from *tremere* to quake
▸'**trembling** ADJECTIVE ▸'**tremblingly** ADVERB ▸'**trembly** ADJECTIVE

trembler ('trɛmblə) NOUN *Electrical engineering* a device that vibrates to make or break an electrical circuit.

trembles ('trɛmbᵊlz) NOUN (*functioning as singular*) 1 Also called: **milk sickness**. a disease of cattle and sheep characterized by muscular incoordination and tremor, caused by ingestion of white snakeroot or rayless goldenrod. 2 a nontechnical name for **Parkinson's disease**.

trembling poplar NOUN another name for **aspen**.

tremendous (trɪ'mɛndəs) ADJECTIVE 1 vast; huge. 2 *Informal* very exciting or unusual. 3 *Informal* (intensifier): *a tremendous help*. 4 *Archaic* terrible or dreadful.
▷HISTORY C17: from Latin *tremendus* terrible, literally: that is to be trembled at, from *tremere* to quake
▸**tre'mendously** ADVERB ▸**tre'mendousness** NOUN

tremie ('trɛmɪ) NOUN *Civil engineering* a large metal hopper and pipe used to distribute freshly mixed concrete over an underwater site. The foot of the pipe is kept below the concrete level, while the upper level of the concrete in the pipe is kept above the water level to prevent the water diluting the concrete.
▷HISTORY C20: from French, from Italian *tramoggia*, from Latin *trimodia* a three-peck measure

tremolite ('trɛməˌlaɪt) NOUN a white or pale green mineral of the amphibole group consisting of calcium magnesium silicate. When occurring in fibrous habit, it is used as a form of asbestos Formula: $Ca_2(Mg,Fe)_5Si_8O_{22}(OH)_2$.
▷HISTORY C18: from *Tremola*, name of Swiss valley where it was found + -ITE

tremolo ('trɛməˌləʊ) NOUN, *plural* **-los**. *Music* 1 **a** (in playing the violin, cello, etc.) the rapid repetition of a single note produced by a quick back-and-forth movement of the bow. **b** the rapid reiteration of two notes usually a third or greater interval apart (**fingered tremolo**). Compare **trill**[1] (sense 1). 2 (in singing) a fluctuation in pitch. Compare **vibrato**. 3 a vocal ornament of late renaissance music consisting of the increasingly rapid reiteration of a single note. 4 another word for **tremulant**.
▷HISTORY C19: from Italian: quavering, from Medieval Latin *tremulāre* to TREMBLE

tremolo arm NOUN a metal lever attached to the bridge of an electric guitar, used to vary the pitch of a played note.

tremor ('trɛmə) NOUN 1 an involuntary shudder or vibration, as from illness, fear, shock, etc. 2 any trembling or quivering movement. 3 a vibrating or trembling effect, as of sound or light. 4 Also called: **earth tremor**. a minor earthquake. ◆ VERB (*intr*) 5 to tremble.
▷HISTORY C14: from Latin: a shaking, from *tremere* to tremble, quake
▸'**tremorless** ADJECTIVE ▸'**tremorous** ADJECTIVE

tremulant ('trɛmjʊlənt) NOUN *Music* **a** a device on an organ by which the wind stream is made to fluctuate in intensity producing a tremolo effect. **b** a device on an electrophonic instrument designed to produce a similar effect.
▷HISTORY C19: from Medieval Latin *tremulāre* to TREMBLE

tremulous ('trɛmjʊləs) ADJECTIVE 1 vibrating slightly; quavering; trembling: *a tremulous voice*. 2 showing or characterized by fear, anxiety, excitement, etc.
▷HISTORY C17: from Latin *tremulus* quivering, from *tremere* to shake
▸'**tremulously** ADVERB ▸'**tremulousness** NOUN

trenail ('triːneɪl, 'trɛnᵊl) NOUN a variant spelling of **treenail**.

trench (trɛntʃ) NOUN 1 a deep ditch or furrow. 2 a ditch dug as a fortification, having a parapet of the excavated earth. ◆ VERB 3 to make a trench in (a place). 4 (*tr*) to fortify with a trench or trenches. 5 to slash or be slashed. 6 (*intr*; foll by *on* or *upon*) to encroach or verge. ◆ See also **trenches**.
▷HISTORY C14: from Old French *trenche* something cut, from *trenchier* to cut, from Latin *truncāre* to cut off

trenchant ('trɛntʃənt) ADJECTIVE 1 keen or incisive: *trenchant criticism*. 2 vigorous and effective: *a trenchant foreign policy*. 3 distinctly defined: *a trenchant outline*. 4 *Archaic or poetic* sharp: *a trenchant sword*.
▷HISTORY C14: from Old French *trenchant* cutting, from *trenchier* to cut; see TRENCH
▸'**trenchancy** NOUN ▸'**trenchantly** ADVERB

trench coat NOUN a belted double-breasted waterproof coat of gabardine, etc., resembling a military officer's coat.

trencher[1] ('trɛntʃə) NOUN 1 (esp formerly) a wooden board on which food was served or cut. 2 Also called: **trencher cap**. another name for **mortarboard** (sense 1).
▷HISTORY C14 *trenchour* knife, plate for carving on, from Old French *trencheoir*, from *trenchier* to cut; see TRENCH

trencher[2] ('trɛntʃə) NOUN a person or thing that digs trenches.

trencherman ('trɛntʃəmən) NOUN, *plural* **-men**. 1 a person who enjoys food; hearty eater. 2 *Archaic* a person who sponges on others; parasite.
▷HISTORY C16: from TRENCHER[1] + MAN

trenches ('trɛntʃɪz) PLURAL NOUN a system of excavations used for the protection of troops, esp those (**the Trenches**) used at the front line in World War I.

trench fever NOUN an acute infectious disease characterized by fever and muscular aches and pains, caused by the microorganism *Rickettsia quintana* and transmitted by the bite of a body louse.

trench foot NOUN a form of frostbite affecting the feet of persons standing for long periods in cold water.

trench knife NOUN a double-edged steel knife, often with a guard in the form of a knuckle-duster, designed for close combat.
▷HISTORY C20: so called because such knives were carried by patrols in the Trenches during World War I

trench mortar NOUN a portable mortar used in trench warfare to shoot projectiles at a high trajectory over a short range.

trench mouth NOUN a bacterial ulcerative disease characterized by inflammation of the tonsils, gums, etc.
▷HISTORY C20: so called because it was prevalent in soldiers in the Trenches during World War I

trench warfare NOUN a type of warfare in which opposing armies face each other in entrenched positions.

trend (trɛnd) NOUN 1 general tendency or direction. 2 fashion; mode. ◆ VERB 3 (*intr*) to take a certain trend.
▷HISTORY Old English *trendan* to turn; related to Middle Low German *trenden*

trendify ('trɛndɪˌfaɪ) VERB **-fies, -fying, -fied**. (*tr*) to render fashionable; remodel in line with current trends.

trendsetter ('trɛndˌsɛtə) NOUN a person or thing that creates, or may create, a new fashion.
▸'**trendˌsetting** ADJECTIVE

trendy ('trɛndɪ) *Brit informal, often derogatory* ◆ ADJECTIVE **trendier, trendiest**. 1 consciously fashionable. ◆ NOUN, *plural* **trendies**. 2 a trendy person.
▸'**trendily** ADVERB ▸'**trendiness** NOUN

Trengganu *or* **Terengganu** (trɛŋ'gɑːnuː, tɛrɛŋ-) NOUN a state of E Peninsular Malaysia, on the South China Sea: under Thai suzerainty until becoming a British protectorate in 1909; joined the Federation of Malaya in 1948; an isolated forested region; mainly agricultural. Capital: Kuala Trengganu. Pop.:

879 691 (2000). Area: 13 020 sq. km (5027 sq. miles).

Trent (trɛnt) NOUN [1] a river in central England, rising in Staffordshire and flowing generally northeast into the Humber: the chief river of the Midlands. Length: 270 km (170 miles). [2] Also: **Trient.** the German name for **Trento.**

trente et quarante (*French* trɑ̃t e karɑ̃t) NOUN another name for **rouge et noir.**
▷HISTORY C17: French, literally: thirty and forty; referring to the rule that forty is the maximum number that may be dealt and the winning colour is the one closest to thirty-one

Trentino-Alto Adige (trɛnˈtiːnəʊˈɑːltəʊ ˈɑːdɪˌdʒeɪ) NOUN a region of N Italy: consists of the part of the Tyrol south of the Brenner Pass, ceded by Austria after World War I. Pop.: 936 256 (2000 est.). Area: 13 613 sq. km (5256 sq. miles). Former name (until 1947): **Venezia Tridentina.**

Trento (*Italian* ˈtrɛnto) NOUN a city in N Italy, in Trentino-Alto Adige region on the Adige River: Roman military base; seat of the Council of Trent. Pop.: 104 906 (2000 est.). Latin name: **Tridentum.** German name: **Trent.**

Trenton (ˈtrɛntən) NOUN a city in W New Jersey, capital of the state, on the Delaware River: settled by English Quakers in 1679; scene of the defeat of the British by Washington (1776) during the War of American Independence. Pop.: 85 403 (2000).

trepan[1] (trɪˈpæn) NOUN [1] *Surgery* an instrument resembling a carpenter's brace and bit formerly used to remove circular sections of bone (esp from the skull). Compare **trephine.** [2] a tool for cutting out circular blanks or for making grooves around a fixed centre. [3] **a** the operation of cutting a hole with such a tool. **b** the hole so produced. ◆ VERB **-pans, -panning, -panned.** (*tr*) [4] to cut (a hole or groove) with a trepan. [5] *Surgery* another word for **trephine.**
▷HISTORY C14: from Medieval Latin *trepanum* rotary saw, from Greek *trupanon* auger, from *trupan* to bore, from *trupa* a hole
▸**trepanation** (ˌtrɛpəˈneɪʃən) NOUN ▸**treˈpanner** NOUN

trepan[2] (trɪˈpæn) *or* **trapan** (trəˈpæn) *Archaic* ◆ VERB **-pans, -panning, -panned.** (*tr*) [1] to entice, ensnare, or entrap. [2] to swindle or cheat. ◆ NOUN [3] a person or thing that traps.
▷HISTORY C17: of uncertain origin

trepang (trɪˈpæŋ) NOUN any of various large sea cucumbers of tropical Oriental seas, the body walls of which are used as food by the Japanese and Chinese. Also called: **bêche-de-mer.**
▷HISTORY C18: from Malay *tĕripang*

trephine (trɪˈfiːn) NOUN [1] a surgical sawlike instrument for removing circular sections of bone, esp from the skull. ◆ VERB [2] (*tr*) to remove a circular section of bone from (esp the skull). ◆ Also called: **trepan.**
▷HISTORY C17: from French *tréphine*, from obsolete English *trefine* TREPAN[1], allegedly from Latin *trēs fīnēs* literally: three ends; influenced also by English *trepane* TREPAN[1]
▸**trephination** (ˌtrɛfɪˈneɪʃən) NOUN

trepidation (ˌtrɛpɪˈdeɪʃən) NOUN [1] a state of fear or anxiety. [2] a condition of quaking or palpitation, esp one caused by anxiety.
▷HISTORY C17: from Latin *trepidātiō*, from *trepidāre* to be in a state of alarm; compare INTREPID

treponema (ˌtrɛpəˈniːmə) *or* **treponeme** (ˈtrɛpəniːm) NOUN, *plural* **-nemas, -nemata** (-ˈniːmətə) *or* **-nemes.** any anaerobic spirochaete bacterium of the genus *Treponema*, such as *T. pallidum* which causes syphilis.
▷HISTORY C19: from New Latin, from Greek *trepein* to turn + *nēma* thread
▸**treponematous** (ˌtrɛpəˈnɛmətəs) ADJECTIVE

trespass (ˈtrɛspəs) VERB (*intr*) [1] (often foll by *on* or *upon*) to go or intrude (on the property, privacy, or preserves of another) with no right or permission. [2] *Law* to commit trespass, esp to enter wrongfully upon land belonging to another. [3] *Archaic* (often foll by *against*) to sin or transgress. ◆ NOUN [4] *Law* **a** any unlawful act committed with force or violence, actual or implied, which causes injury to another person, his property, or his rights. **b** a wrongful entry upon another's land. **c** an action to recover damages for such injury or wrongful entry. [5] an intrusion on another's privacy or preserves. [6] a sin or offence.
▷HISTORY C13: from Old French *trespas* a passage, from *trespasser* to pass through, from *tres-* TRANS- + *passer*, ultimately from Latin *passus* a PACE[1]
▸**ˈtrespasser** NOUN

tress (trɛs) NOUN [1] (*often plural*) a lock of hair, esp a long lock of woman's hair. [2] a plait or braid of hair. ◆ VERB (*tr*) [3] to arrange in tresses.
▷HISTORY C13: from Old French *trece*, of uncertain origin
▸**ˈtressy** ADJECTIVE

tressed (trɛst) ADJECTIVE (*in combination*) having a tress or tresses as specified: *gold-tressed; long-tressed.*

tressure (ˈtrɛʃə, ˈtrɛsjʊə) NOUN *Heraldry* a narrow inner border on a shield, usually decorated with fleurs-de-lys.
▷HISTORY C14: from Old French *tressour*, from *trecier* to plait, from *trece* TRESS
▸**ˈtressured** ADJECTIVE

trestle (ˈtrɛsᵊl) NOUN [1] a framework in the form of a horizontal member supported at each end by a pair of splayed legs, used to carry scaffold boards, a table top, etc. [2] **a** a braced structural tower-like framework of timber, metal, or reinforced concrete that is used to support a bridge or ropeway. **b** a bridge constructed of such frameworks.
▷HISTORY C14: from Old French *trestel*, ultimately from Latin *trānstrum* TRANSOM

trestletree (ˈtrɛsᵊlˌtriː) NOUN *Nautical* either of a pair of fore-and-aft timbers fixed horizontally on opposite sides of a lower masthead to support an upper mast.

trestlework (ˈtrɛsᵊlˌwɜːk) NOUN an arrangement of trestles, esp one that supports or makes a bridge.

tret (trɛt) NOUN *Commerce* (formerly) an allowance according to weight granted to purchasers for waste due to transportation. It was calculated after deduction for tare.
▷HISTORY C15: from Old French *trait* pull, tilt of the scale; see TRAIT

trevally (trɪˈvælɪ) NOUN, *plural* **-lies.** any of various marine food and game fishes of the genus *Caranx*: family *Carangidae*.
▷HISTORY C19: probably alteration of *cavally*; see CAVALLA

Trèves (trɛv) NOUN the French name for **Trier.**

Treviso (*Italian* treˈviːzo) NOUN a city in N Italy, in Veneto region: agricultural market centre. Pop.: 84 066 (1990).

Trevor Nunn (ˌtrɛvə ˈnʌn) NOUN *Brit informal* a university degree graded 2:1 (second class upper bracket). Often shortened to: **Trevor.**
▷HISTORY C20: from rhyming slang, after *Trevor Nunn* (born 1940), British theatre director

trews (truːz) PLURAL NOUN *Chiefly Brit* close-fitting trousers, esp of tartan cloth and worn by certain Scottish soldiers.
▷HISTORY C16: from Scottish Gaelic *triubhas*, from Old French *trebus*; see TROUSERS

trey (treɪ) NOUN any card or dice throw with three spots.
▷HISTORY C14: from Old French *treis* three, from Latin *trēs*

TRH ABBREVIATION FOR Their Royal Highnesses.

tri- PREFIX [1] three or thrice: *triaxial; trigon; trisect.* [2] occurring every three: *trimonthly.*
▷HISTORY from Latin *trēs*, Greek *treis*

triable (ˈtraɪəbᵊl) ADJECTIVE [1] **a** liable to be tried judicially. **b** subject to examination or determination by a court of law. [2] *Rare* able to be tested.
▸**ˈtriableness** NOUN

triacid (traɪˈæsɪd) ADJECTIVE (of a base) capable of reacting with three molecules of a monobasic acid.

triad (ˈtraɪæd) NOUN [1] a group of three; trio. [2] *Chem* an atom, element, group, or ion that has a valency of three. [3] *Music* a three-note chord consisting of a note and the third and fifth above it. [4] an aphoristic literary form used in medieval Welsh and Irish literature. [5] the US strategic nuclear force, consisting of intercontinental ballistic missiles, submarine-launched ballistic missiles, and bombers.
▷HISTORY C16: from Late Latin *trias*, from Greek; related to Greek *treis* three
▸**triˈadic** ADJECTIVE ▸**ˈtriadism** NOUN

Triad (ˈtraɪæd) NOUN any of several Chinese secret societies, esp one involved in criminal activities, such as drug trafficking.

triage (ˈtraɪɪdʒ) NOUN [1] the principle or practice of sorting casualties in battle or disaster or other patients into categories of priority for treatment. [2] the principle or practice of allocating limited resources, as of food or foreign aid, on a basis of expediency rather than according to moral principles or the needs of the recipients.
▷HISTORY C18 (in the sense: sorting (goods) according to quality): from French; see TRY, -AGE

trial[1] (ˈtraɪəl, traɪl) NOUN [1] **a** the act or an instance of trying or proving; test or experiment. **b** (*as modifier*): *a trial run.* [2] *Law* **a** the judicial examination of the issues in a civil or criminal cause by a competent tribunal and the determination of these issues in accordance with the law of the land. **b** the determination of an accused person's guilt or innocence after hearing evidence for the prosecution and for the accused and the judicial examination of the issues involved. **c** (*as modifier*): *trial proceedings.* [3] an effort or attempt to do something: *we had three trials at the climb.* [4] trouble or grief. [5] an annoying or frustrating person or thing. [6] (*often plural*) a competition for individuals: *sheepdog trials.* [7] a motorcycling competition in which the skills of the riders are tested over rough ground. [8] *Ceramics* a piece of sample material used for testing the heat of a kiln and its effects. [9] **on trial. a** undergoing trial, esp before a court of law. **b** being tested, as before a commitment to purchase. ◆ VERB **trials, trialling, trialled.** (*tr*) [10] to test or make experimental use of (something): *the idea has been trialled in several schools.*
▷HISTORY C16: from Anglo-French, from *trier* to TRY
▸**ˈtrialling** NOUN

trial[2] (ˈtraɪəl) NOUN *Grammar* [1] a grammatical number occurring in some languages for words in contexts where exactly three of their referents are described or referred to. [2] (*modifier*) relating to or inflected for this number.
▷HISTORY C19: from TRI- + -AL[1]

trial and error NOUN a method of discovery, solving problems, etc., based on practical experiment and experience rather than on theory: *he learned to cook by trial and error.*

trial balance NOUN *Book-keeping* a statement of all the debit and credit balances in the ledger of a double-entry system, drawn up to test their equality.

trial balloon NOUN a tentative action or statement designed to test public opinion on a controversial matter. Compare **ballon d'essai.**

trial by battle *or* **trial by combat** NOUN *History* a method of trying an accused person or of settling a dispute by a personal fight between the two parties involved or, in some circumstances, their permitted champions, in the presence of a judge. It was introduced to England after the Norman Conquest and abolished in 1819.

trial court NOUN *Law* the first court before which the facts of a case are decided.

triallist *or* **trialist** (ˈtraɪəlɪst, ˈtraɪlɪst) NOUN [1] a person who takes part in a competition, esp a motorcycle trial. [2] *Sport* a person who takes part in a preliminary match or heat held to determine selection for an event, a team, etc.

trial run NOUN [1] a test drive in a vehicle to assess its performance. [2] a test or rehearsal of something new or untried to assess its effectiveness.

triangle (ˈtraɪˌæŋɡᵊl) NOUN [1] *Geometry* a three-sided polygon that can be classified by angle, as in an acute triangle, or by side, as in an equilateral triangle. Sum of interior angles: 180°; area: ½ base × height. [2] any object shaped like a triangle. [3] any situation involving three parties or points of view. See also **eternal triangle.** [4] *Music* a percussion instrument consisting of a sonorous metal bar bent into a triangular shape, beaten with a metal stick. [5] a group of three.
▷HISTORY C14: from Latin *triangulum* (noun), from *triangulus* (adjective), from TRI- + *angulus* corner
▸**ˈtriˌangled** ADJECTIVE

triangle of forces NOUN *Physics* a triangle whose sides represent the magnitudes and directions of three forces in equilibrium whose resultant is zero and which are therefore in equilibrium.

triangular (traɪˈæŋgjʊlə) ADJECTIVE [1] Also: **trigonal.** of, shaped like, or relating to a triangle; having three corners or sides. [2] of or involving three participants, pieces, or units. [3] *Maths* having a base shaped like a triangle.
▸**triangularity** (traɪˌæŋgjʊˈlærɪtɪ) NOUN ▸**triˈangularly** ADVERB

triangulate VERB (traɪˈæŋgjʊˌleɪt) *(tr)* [1] **a** to survey by the method of triangulation. **b** to calculate trigonometrically. [2] to divide into triangles. [3] to make triangular. ◆ ADJECTIVE (traɪˈæŋgjʊlɪt, -ˌleɪt) [4] marked with or composed of triangles.
▸**triˈangulately** ADVERB

triangulation (traɪˌæŋgjʊˈleɪʃən) NOUN [1] a method of surveying in which an area is divided into triangles, one side (the base line) and all angles of which are measured and the lengths of the other lines calculated trigonometrically. [2] the network of triangles so formed. [3] the fixing of an unknown point, as in navigation, by making it one vertex of a triangle, the other two being known. [4] *Chess* a key manoeuvre in the endgame in which the king moves thrice in a triangular path to leave the opposing king with the move and at a disadvantage.

triangulation station NOUN a point used in triangulation as a basis for making maps. Triangulation stations are marked in a number of ways, such as by a tapering stone pillar on a hilltop. Also called (informal): **trig point,** (Austral and NZ) **trig.**

Triangulum (traɪˈæŋgjʊləm) NOUN, *Latin genitive* **Trianguli** (traɪˈæŋgjʊˌlaɪ). a small triangular constellation in the N hemisphere, close to Perseus and Aries.

Triangulum Australe (ɒˈstreɪlɪ) NOUN, *Latin genitive* **Trianguli Australis** (ɒˈstreɪlɪs). a small bright triangular constellation in the S hemisphere, lying between Ara and the Southern Cross, that contains an open star cluster.
▹HISTORY New Latin: southern triangle

triarchy (ˈtraɪɑːkɪ) NOUN, *plural* **-chies.** [1] government by three people; a triumvirate. [2] a country ruled by three people. [3] an association of three territories each governed by its own ruler. [4] any of the three such territories.

Triassic (traɪˈæsɪk) ADJECTIVE ◆ [1] NOUN of, denoting, or formed in the first period of the Mesozoic era that lasted for 42 million years and during which reptiles flourished. [2] **the.** Also called: **Trias.** the Triassic period or rock system.
▹HISTORY C19: from Latin *trias* triad, with reference to the three subdivisions

triathlon (traɪˈæθlɒn) NOUN an athletic contest in which each athlete competes in three different events, swimming, cycling, and running.
▹HISTORY C20: from TRI- + Greek *athlon* contest
▸ˌ**triˈathlete** NOUN

triatomic (ˌtraɪəˈtɒmɪk) ADJECTIVE *Chem* having three atoms in the molecule.
▸ˌ**triaˈtomically** ADVERB

triaxial (traɪˈæksɪəl) ADJECTIVE having three axes.

triazine (ˈtraɪəˌziːn, -zɪn, traɪˈæziːn, -zɪn) *or* **triazin** (ˈtraɪəzɪn, traɪˈæzɪn) NOUN [1] any of three azines that contain three nitrogen atoms in their molecules. Formula: $C_3H_3N_3$. [2] any substituted derivative of any of these compounds.

triazole (ˈtraɪəˌzɒl, -ˌzəʊl, traɪˈæzɒl, -zəʊl) NOUN [1] any of four heterocyclic compounds having a five-membered ring with the formula $C_2H_3N_3$. [2] any substituted derivative of any of these compounds.
▹HISTORY C19: from TRI- + AZOLE
▸**triazolic** (ˌtraɪəˈzɒlɪk) ADJECTIVE

tribade (ˈtrɪbəd) NOUN a lesbian, esp one who practises tribadism.
▹HISTORY C17: from Latin *tribas*, from Greek *tribein* to rub
▸**tribadic** (trɪˈbædɪk) ADJECTIVE

tribadism (ˈtrɪbəˌdɪzəm) NOUN a lesbian practice in which one partner lies on top of the other and simulates the male role in heterosexual intercourse.

tribal (ˈtraɪbᵊl) ADJECTIVE [1] of or denoting a tribe or tribes: *tribal chiefs in northern Yemen.* [2] displaying loyalty to a tribe, group, or tribal values: *the tribal loyalties of Labour MPs.*
▸ˈ**tribally** ADVERB

tribalism (ˈtraɪbəˌlɪzəm) NOUN [1] the state of existing as a separate tribe or tribes. [2] the customs and beliefs of a tribal society. [3] loyalty to a tribe or tribal values.
▸ˈ**tribalist** NOUN, ADJECTIVE ▸ˌ**tribalˈistic** ADJECTIVE

tribasic (traɪˈbeɪsɪk) ADJECTIVE [1] (of an acid) containing three replaceable hydrogen atoms in the molecule. [2] (of a molecule) containing three monovalent basic atoms or groups in the molecule.

tribe (traɪb) NOUN [1] a social division of a people, esp of a preliterate people, defined in terms of common descent, territory, culture, etc. [2] an ethnic or ancestral division of ancient cultures, esp of one of the following. **a** any of the three divisions of the ancient Romans, the Latins, Sabines, and Etruscans. **b** one of the later political divisions of the Roman people. **c** any of the 12 divisions of ancient Israel, each of which was named after and believed to be descended from one of the 12 patriarchs. **d** a phyle of ancient Greece. [3] *Informal often jocular* **a** a large number of persons, animals, etc. **b** a specific class or group of persons. **c** a family, esp a large one. [4] *Biology* a taxonomic group that is a subdivision of a subfamily. [5] *Stockbreeding* a strain of animals descended from a common female ancestor through the female line.
▹HISTORY C13: from Latin *tribus;* probably related to Latin *trēs* three
▸ˈ**tribeless** ADJECTIVE

tribesman (ˈtraɪbzmən) NOUN, *plural* **-men.** a member of a tribe.

triblet (ˈtrɪblɪt) NOUN a spindle or mandrel used in making rings, tubes, etc.
▹HISTORY C17: from French *triboulet*, of unknown origin

tribo- COMBINING FORM indicating friction: *triboelectricity.*
▹HISTORY from Greek *tribein* to rub

triboelectricity (ˌtraɪbəʊɪlekˈtrɪsɪtɪ, -ˌiːlek-) NOUN static electricity generated by friction. Also called: **frictional electricity.**
▸ˌ**triboeˈlectric** ADJECTIVE

tribology (traɪˈbɒlədʒɪ) NOUN the study of friction, lubrication, and wear between moving surfaces.

triboluminescence (ˌtraɪbəʊˌluːmɪˈnesəns) NOUN luminescence produced by friction, such as the emission of light when certain crystals are crushed.
▸ˌ**triboˌlumiˈnescent** ADJECTIVE

tribrach[1] (ˈtraɪbræk, ˈtrɪb-) NOUN *Prosody* a metrical foot of three short syllables (⏑⏑⏑).
▹HISTORY C16: from Latin *tribrachys*, from Greek *tribrakhus*, from TRI- + *brakhus* short
▸**triˈbrachic** *or* **triˈbrachial** ADJECTIVE

tribrach[2] (ˈtrɪbræk) NOUN *Archaeol* a three-armed object, esp a flint implement.
▹HISTORY C19: from TRI- + Greek *brakhiōn* arm

tribromoethanol (traɪˌbrəʊməʊˈɛθəˌnɒl) NOUN a soluble white crystalline compound with a slight aromatic odour, used as a general anaesthetic; 2,2,2-tribromoethanol. Formula: CBr_3CH_2OH.

tribulation (ˌtrɪbjʊˈleɪʃən) NOUN [1] a cause of distress. [2] a state of suffering or distress.
▹HISTORY C13: from Old French, from Church Latin *trībulātiō*, from Latin *trībulāre* to afflict, from *trībulum* a threshing board, from *terere* to rub

tribunal (traɪˈbjuːnᵊl, trɪ-) NOUN [1] a court of justice or any place where justice is administered. [2] (in Britain) a special court, convened by the government to inquire into a specific matter. [3] a raised platform containing the seat of a judge or magistrate, originally that in a Roman basilica.
▹HISTORY C16: from Latin *tribūnus* TRIBUNE[1]

tribunate (ˈtrɪbjʊnɪt) *or* **tribuneship** NOUN the office or rank of a tribune.

tribune[1] (ˈtrɪbjuːn) NOUN [1] (in ancient Rome) **a** an officer elected by the plebs to protect their interests. Originally there were two of these officers but finally there were ten. **b** a senior military officer. [2] a person or institution that upholds public rights; champion.
▹HISTORY C14: from Latin *tribunus*, probably from *tribus* TRIBE
▸ˈ**tribunary** ADJECTIVE

tribune[2] (ˈtrɪbjuːn) NOUN [1] **a** the apse of a Christian basilica that contains the bishop's throne. **b** the throne itself. [2] a gallery or raised area in a church. [3] *Rare* a raised platform from which a speaker may address an audience; dais.
▹HISTORY C17: via French from Italian *tribuna*, from Medieval Latin *tribūna*, variant of Latin *tribūnal* TRIBUNAL

Tribune Group NOUN (in Britain) a group made up of left-wing Labour Members of Parliament: founded 1966.
▹HISTORY named after the *Tribune* newspaper, with which it is associated
▸ˈ**Tribunˌite** NOUN, ADJECTIVE

tributary (ˈtrɪbjʊtərɪ, -trɪ) NOUN, *plural* **-taries.** [1] a stream, river, or glacier that feeds another larger one. [2] a person, nation, or people that pays tribute. ◆ ADJECTIVE [3] (of a stream, etc.) feeding a larger stream. [4] given or owed as a tribute. [5] paying tribute.
▸ˈ**tributarily** ADVERB

tribute (ˈtrɪbjuːt) NOUN [1] a gift or statement made in acknowledgment, gratitude, or admiration. [2] **a** a payment by one ruler or state to another, usually as an acknowledgment of submission. **b** any tax levied for such a payment. [3] (in feudal society) homage or a payment rendered by a vassal to his lord. [4] the obligation to pay tribute.
▹HISTORY C14: from Latin *tribūtum*, from *tribuere* to grant (originally: to distribute among the tribes), from *tribus* TRIBE

tricarboxylic acid cycle (traɪˌkɑːbɒkˈsɪlɪk) NOUN *Biochem* another name for **Krebs cycle.** Abbreviation: **TCA cycle.**

trice[1] (traɪs) NOUN moment; instant (esp in the phrase **in a trice**).
▹HISTORY C15 (in the phrase *at* or *in a trice*, in the sense: at one tug): apparent substantive use of TRICE[2]

trice[2] (traɪs) VERB *(tr;* often foll by *up) Nautical* to haul up or secure.
▹HISTORY C15: from Middle Dutch *trīsen*, from *trīse* pulley

tricentenary (ˌtraɪsenˈtiːnərɪ) *or* **tricentennial** (ˌtraɪsenˈtenɪəl) ADJECTIVE [1] of or relating to a period of 300 years. [2] of or relating to a 300th anniversary or its celebration. ◆ NOUN [3] an anniversary of 300 years or its celebration. ◆ Also: **tercentenary, tercentennial.**

triceps (ˈtraɪseps) NOUN, *plural* **-cepses** (-sepsɪz) *or* **-ceps.** any muscle having three heads, esp the one *(triceps brachii)* that extends the forearm.
▹HISTORY C16: from Latin, from TRI- + *caput* head

triceratops (traɪˈserəˌtɒps) NOUN any rhinoceros-like herbivorous dinosaur of the ornithischian genus *Triceratops*, of Cretaceous times, having a heavily armoured neck and three horns on the skull.
▹HISTORY C19: from New Latin, from TRI- + Greek *kerat-, keras* horn + *ōps* eye

trich- COMBINING FORM a variant of **tricho-** before a vowel.

trichiasis (trɪˈkaɪəsɪs) NOUN *Pathol* [1] an abnormal position of the eyelashes that causes irritation when they rub against the eyeball. [2] the presence of hairlike filaments in the urine.
▹HISTORY C17: via Late Latin from Greek *trikhiasis*, from *thrix* a hair + -IASIS

trichina (trɪˈkaɪnə) NOUN, *plural* **-nae** (-niː). a parasitic nematode worm, *Trichinella spiralis*, occurring in the intestines of pigs, rats, and man and producing larvae that form cysts in skeletal muscle.
▹HISTORY C19: from New Latin, from Greek *trikhinos* relating to hair, from *thrix* a hair

trichinize *or* **trichinise** (ˈtrɪkɪˌnaɪz) VERB *(tr)* to infest (an organism) with trichinae.
▸ˌ**trichiniˈzation** *or* ˌ**trichiniˈsation** NOUN

Trichinopoly (ˌtrɪkɪˈnɒpəlɪ) NOUN another name for **Tiruchirapalli.**

trichinosis (ˌtrɪkɪˈnəʊsɪs) NOUN a disease characterized by nausea, fever, diarrhoea, and swelling of the muscles, caused by ingestion of pork infected with trichina larvae. Also called: **trichiniasis** (ˌtrɪkɪˈnaɪəsɪs).
▹HISTORY C19: from New Latin TRICHINA

trichinous (ˈtrɪkɪnəs) ADJECTIVE [1] of, relating to, or having trichinosis. [2] infested with trichinae.

trichite ('trɪkaɪt) NOUN 1 any of various needle-shaped crystals that occur in some glassy volcanic rocks. 2 *Biology* any of various hairlike structures.
▸**trichitic** (trɪ'kɪtɪk) ADJECTIVE

trichloride (traɪ'klɔːraɪd) NOUN any compound that contains three chlorine atoms per molecule.

trichloroacetic acid (traɪˌklɔːrəʊə'siːtɪk, -'sɛtɪk) NOUN a corrosive deliquescent crystalline acid with a characteristic odour, used as a veterinary astringent and antiseptic. Formula: CCl_3COOH.

trichloroethane (traɪˌklɔːrəʊ'iːθeɪn) NOUN a volatile nonflammable colourless liquid with low toxicity used for cleaning electrical apparatus and as a solvent; 1,2,3-trichloroethane. Formula: CH_3CCl_3. Also called: **methyl chloroform.**

trichloroethylene (traɪˌklɔːrəʊ'ɛθɪˌliːn) *or* **trichlorethylene** NOUN a volatile nonflammable mobile colourless liquid with an odour resembling that of chloroform. It is a good solvent for certain organic materials and is also an inhalation anaesthetic. Formula $CHCl{:}CCl_2$.

trichlorophenoxyacetic acid (traɪ'klɔːrəʊfəˌnɒksɪə'siːtɪk) NOUN an insoluble crystalline solid; 2,4,5-trichlorophenoxyacetic acid. It is a plant hormone and is used as a weedkiller. Formula: $C_8H_5Cl_3O_3$. Also called: **2,4,5-T.**

tricho- *or before a vowel* **trich-** COMBINING FORM indicating hair or a part resembling hair: *trichocyst*.
▷HISTORY from Greek *thrix* (genitive *trikhos*) hair

trichocyst ('trɪkəˌsɪst) NOUN any of various cavities on the surface of some ciliate protozoans, each containing a sensory thread that can be ejected.
▸ˌ**tricho'cystic** ADJECTIVE

trichogyne ('trɪkəˌdʒaɪn, -dʒɪn) NOUN a hairlike projection of the female reproductive organs of certain algae, fungi, and lichens, which receives the male gametes before fertilization takes place.
▷HISTORY C19: from TRICHO- + Greek *gunē* woman
▸ˌ**tricho'gynial** *or* ˌ**tricho'gynic** ADJECTIVE

trichoid ('trɪkɔɪd) ADJECTIVE *Zoology* resembling a hair; hairlike.

trichology (trɪ'kɒlədʒɪ) NOUN the branch of medicine concerned with the hair and its diseases.
▸**trichological** (ˌtrɪkə'lɒdʒɪkᵊl) ADJECTIVE ▸**tri'chologist** NOUN

trichome ('traɪkəʊm, 'trɪk-) NOUN 1 any hairlike outgrowth from the surface of a plant. 2 any of the threadlike structures that make up the filaments of blue-green algae.
▷HISTORY C19: from Greek *trikhōma*, from *trikhoun* to cover with hair, from *thrix* a hair
▸**trichomic** (trɪ'kɒmɪk) ADJECTIVE

trichomonad (ˌtrɪkəʊ'mɒnæd) NOUN any parasitic flagellate protozoan of the genus *Trichomonas*, occurring in the digestive and reproductive systems of man and animals.
▸**trichomonadal** (ˌtrɪkəʊ'mɒnədəl) *or* **trichomona** (ˌtrɪkə'mɒnᵊl, -'məʊ-, trɪ'kɒmənᵊl) ADJECTIVE

trichomoniasis (ˌtrɪkəʊmə'naɪəsɪs) NOUN 1 inflammation of the vagina characterized by a frothy discharge, caused by infection with parasitic protozoa (*Trichomonas vaginalis*). 2 any infection caused by parasitic protozoa of the genus *Trichomonas*.
▷HISTORY C19: New Latin; see TRICHOMONAD, -IASIS

trichopteran (traɪ'kɒptərən) NOUN 1 any insect of the order *Trichoptera*, which comprises the caddis flies. ◆ ADJECTIVE 2 Also: **trichopterous** (trɪ'kɒptərəs). of, relating to, or belonging to the order *Trichoptera*.
▷HISTORY C19: from New Latin *Trichoptera*, literally: having hairy wings, from Greek *thrix* a hair + *pteron* wing

trichosis (trɪ'kəʊsɪs) NOUN any abnormal condition or disease of the hair.
▷HISTORY C19: via New Latin from Greek *trikhōsis* growth of hair

trichotomy (traɪ'kɒtəmɪ) NOUN, *plural* **-mies.** 1 division into three categories. 2 *Theol* the division of man into body, spirit, and soul.
▷HISTORY C17: probably from New Latin *trichotomia*, from Greek *trikhotomein* to divide into three, from *trikha* triple + *temnein* to cut
▸**trichotomic** (ˌtrɪkə'tɒmɪk) *or* **tri'chotomous** ADJECTIVE
▸**tri'chotomously** ADVERB

trichroism ('traɪkrəʊˌɪzəm) NOUN a property of biaxial crystals as a result of which they show a perceptible difference in colour when viewed along three different axes. See **pleochroism.**
▷HISTORY C19: from Greek *trikhroos* three-coloured, from TRI- + *khrōma* colour
▸**tri'chroic** ADJECTIVE

trichromat ('traɪkrəʊˌmæt) NOUN any person with normal colour vision, who can therefore see the three primary colours.

trichromatic (ˌtraɪkrəʊ'mætɪk) *or* **trichromic** (traɪ'krəʊmɪk) ADJECTIVE 1 *Photog, printing* involving the combination of three primary colours in the production of any colour. 2 of, relating to, or having normal colour vision. 3 having or involving three colours.

trichromatism (traɪ'krəʊməˌtɪzəm) NOUN 1 the use or combination of three primary colours for colour reproduction in photography, printing, television, etc. 2 *Rare* the state of being trichromatic.

trichuriasis (ˌtrɪkjʊə'raɪəsɪs) NOUN infection of the large intestine with the whipworm *Trichuris trichiura*, resulting in anaemia, weakness, etc.

trick (trɪk) NOUN 1 a deceitful, cunning, or underhand action or plan. 2 **a** a mischievous, malicious, or humorous action or plan; joke: *the boys are up to their tricks again*. **b** (*as modifier*): *a trick spider*. 3 an illusory or magical feat or device. 4 a simple feat learned by an animal or person. 5 an adroit or ingenious device; knack: *a trick of the trade*. 6 a behavioural trait, habit, or mannerism. 7 a turn or round of duty or work. 8 *Cards* **a** a batch of cards containing one from each player, usually played in turn and won by the player or side that plays the card with the highest value. **b** a card that can potentially win a trick. 9 **can't take a trick.** *Austral slang* to be consistently unsuccessful or unlucky. 10 **do the trick.** *Informal* to produce the right or desired result. 11 **how's tricks?** *Slang* how are you? 12 **turn a trick.** *Slang* (of a prostitute) to gain a customer. ◆ VERB 13 to defraud, deceive, or cheat (someone), esp by means of a trick.
▷HISTORY C15: from Old Northern French *trique*, from *trikier* to deceive, from Old French *trichier*, ultimately from Latin *trīcārī* to play tricks
▸**'tricker** NOUN ▸**'trickless** ADJECTIVE

trick cyclist NOUN a slang term for **psychiatrist.**

trickery ('trɪkərɪ) NOUN, *plural* **-eries.** the practice or an instance of using tricks: *he obtained the money by trickery*.

trickle ('trɪkᵊl) VERB 1 to run or cause to run in thin or slow streams: *she trickled the sand through her fingers*. 2 (*intr*) to move, go, or pass gradually: *the crowd trickled away*. ◆ NOUN 3 a thin, irregular, or slow flow of something. 4 the act of trickling.
▷HISTORY C14: perhaps of imitative origin
▸**'trickling** ADJECTIVE ▸**'tricklingly** ADVERB ▸**'trickly** ADJECTIVE

trickle charger NOUN a small mains-operated battery charger, esp one that delivers less than 5 amperes and is used by car owners.

trickle-down ADJECTIVE of or concerning the theory that granting concessions such as tax cuts to the rich will benefit all levels of society by stimulating the economy.

trick or treat SENTENCE SUBSTITUTE *Chiefly US and Canadian* the cry by children at Halloween when they call at houses, indicating that they want a present or money or else they will play a trick on the householder.

trick out *or* **up** VERB (*tr, adverb*) to dress up; deck out: *tricked out in frilly dresses*.

trickster ('trɪkstə) NOUN a person who deceives or plays tricks.

tricksy ('trɪksɪ) ADJECTIVE **-sier, -siest.** 1 playing tricks habitually; mischievous. 2 crafty or difficult to deal with. 3 *Archaic* well-dressed; spruce; smart.
▸**'tricksiness** NOUN

tricktrack ('trɪkˌtræk) NOUN a variant spelling of **trictrac.**

tricky ('trɪkɪ) ADJECTIVE **trickier, trickiest.** 1 involving snags or difficulties: *a tricky job*. 2 needing careful and tactful handling: *a tricky situation*. 3 characterized by tricks; sly; wily: *a tricky dealer*.
▸**'trickily** ADVERB ▸**'trickiness** NOUN

triclinic (traɪ'klɪnɪk) ADJECTIVE relating to or belonging to the crystal system characterized by three unequal axes, no pair of which are perpendicular. Also: **anorthic.**

triclinium (traɪ'klɪnɪəm) NOUN, *plural* **-ia** (-ɪə). (in ancient Rome) 1 an arrangement of three couches around a table for reclining upon while dining. 2 a dining room, esp one containing such an arrangement of couches.
▷HISTORY C17: from Latin, from Greek *triklinion*, from TRI- + *klinē* a couch

tricolour *or US* **tricolor** ('trɪkələ, 'traɪˌkʌlə) ADJECTIVE *also* **tricoloured,** *or US* **tricolored** ('traɪˌkʌləd). 1 having or involving three colours. ◆ NOUN 2 (*often capital*) the French national flag, having three equal vertical stripes in blue, white, and red. 3 any flag, badge, ribbon, etc., with three colours.

tricorn ('traɪˌkɔːn) NOUN *also* **tricorne.** 1 a cocked hat with opposing brims turned back and caught in three places. 2 an imaginary animal having three horns. ◆ ADJECTIVE *also* **tricornered.** 3 having three horns or corners.
▷HISTORY C18: from Latin *tricornis*, from TRI- + *cornu* HORN

tricostate (traɪ'kɒsteɪt) ADJECTIVE *Biology* having three ribs or riblike parts: *tricostate leaves*.
▷HISTORY C19: from TRI- + COSTATE

tricot ('trɪkəʊ, 'triː-) NOUN 1 a thin rayon or nylon fabric knitted or resembling knitting, used for dresses, etc. 2 a type of ribbed dress fabric.
▷HISTORY C19: from French, from *tricoter* to knit, of unknown origin

tricotine (ˌtrɪkə'tiːn, ˌtriː-) NOUN a twill-weave woollen fabric resembling gabardine.
▷HISTORY C20: from French; see TRICOT

tricrotic (traɪ'krɒtɪk) ADJECTIVE *Physiol* (of the pulse) having a tracing characterized by three elevations with each beat.
▷HISTORY C19: from Greek *trikrotos* having three beats, from TRI- + *krotos* a beat
▸**tricrotism** ('traɪkrəˌtɪzəm, 'trɪk-) NOUN

trictrac *or* **tricktrack** ('trɪkˌtræk) NOUN a game similar to backgammon.
▷HISTORY C17: from French, imitative

tricuspid (traɪ'kʌspɪd) *Anatomy* ◆ ADJECTIVE *also* **tricuspidal.** 1 **a** having three points, cusps, or segments: *a tricuspid tooth; a tricuspid valve*. **b** ◆ NOUN 2 a tooth having three cusps.

tricycle ('traɪsɪkᵊl) NOUN 1 a three-wheeled cycle, esp one driven by pedals. 2 a three-wheeler for invalids. ◆ VERB 3 (*intr*) to ride a tricycle.
▸**'tricyclist** NOUN

tricyclic (traɪ'saɪklɪk) ADJECTIVE 1 (of a chemical compound) containing three rings in the molecular structure. ◆ NOUN 2 an antidepressant drug having a tricyclic molecular structure.

tridactyl (traɪ'dæktᵊl) *or* **tridactylous** ADJECTIVE having three digits on one hand or foot.

trident ('traɪdᵊnt) NOUN 1 a three-pronged spear, originally from the East. 2 (in Greek and Roman mythology) the three-pronged spear that the sea god Poseidon (Neptune) is represented as carrying. 3 a three-pronged instrument, weapon, or symbol. ◆ ADJECTIVE 4 having three prongs.
▷HISTORY C16: from Latin *tridēns* three-pronged, from TRI- + *dēns* tooth

Trident ('traɪdᵊnt) NOUN a type of US submarine-launched ballistic missile with independently targetable warheads.

tridentate (traɪ'dɛnteɪt) *or* **tridental** ADJECTIVE *Anatomy, botany* having three prongs, teeth, or points.

Tridentine (traɪ'dɛntaɪn) ADJECTIVE 1 *History* **a** of or relating to the Council of Trent. **b** in accord with Tridentine doctrine. ◆ NOUN 2 an orthodox Roman Catholic.
▷HISTORY C16: from Medieval Latin *Tridentīnus*, from *Tridentum* TRENT

Tridentum (traɪ'dɛntəm) NOUN the Latin name for **Trento.**

tridimensional (ˌtraɪdɪ'mɛnʃənᵊl, -daɪ-) ADJECTIVE a less common word for **three-dimensional.**
▸ˌ**tridiˌmension'ality** NOUN ▸ˌ**tridi'mensionally** ADVERB

triduum ('trɪdjʊəm, 'traɪ-) NOUN *RC Church* a period of three days for prayer before a feast.
▷HISTORY C19: Latin, perhaps from *triduum spatium* a space of three days

triecious (traɪ'iːʃəs) ADJECTIVE a variant spelling of **trioecious.**

tried (traɪd) VERB the past tense and past participle of **try.**

triella (traɪ'ɛlə) NOUN *Austral* three nominated horse races in which the punter bets on selecting the three winners.

triene ('traɪˌiːn) NOUN a chemical compound containing three double bonds.

triennial (traɪ'ɛnɪəl) ADJECTIVE ◆ [1] NOUN relating to, lasting for, or occurring every three years. [2] a third anniversary. [3] a triennial period, thing, or occurrence.
▷HISTORY C17: from Latin TRIENNIUM
▸**tri'ennially** ADVERB

triennium (traɪ'ɛnɪəm) NOUN, *plural* **-niums** *or* **-nia** (-nɪə). a period or cycle of three years.
▷HISTORY C19: from Latin, from TRI- + *annus* a year

Trient (tri'ɛnt) NOUN the German name for **Trento.** Also: **Trent.**

trier ('traɪə) NOUN a person or thing that tries.

Trier (*German* triːr) NOUN a city in W Germany, in the Rhineland-Palatinate on the Moselle River: one of the oldest towns of central Europe, ancient capital of a Celto-Germanic tribe (the **Treveri**); an early centre of Christianity, ruled by powerful archbishops until the 18th century; wine trade; important Roman remains. Pop.: 98 750 (1991). Latin name: **Augusta Treverorum** (aʊ'guːstə ˌtrɛvə'rəʊrəm). French name: **Trèves.**

trierarch ('traɪəˌrɑːk) NOUN *Greek history* [1] a citizen responsible for fitting out a state trireme, esp in Athens. [2] the captain of a trireme.
▷HISTORY C17: from Latin, from Greek *triērarkhos*, from *triērēs* equipped with three banks of oars + *arkhein* to command

trierarchy ('traɪəˌrɑːkɪ) NOUN, *plural* **-chies.** *Greek history* [1] the responsibility for fitting out a state trireme, esp in Athens. [2] the office of a trierarch. [3] trierarchs collectively.

Trieste (triː'ɛst; *Italian* tri'ɛste) NOUN [1] a port in NE Italy, capital of Friuli-Venezia Giulia region, on the **Gulf of Trieste** at the head of the Adriatic Sea: under Austrian rule (1382–1918); capital of the Free Territory of Trieste (1947–54); important transit port for central Europe. Pop.: 216 459 (2000 est.). Slovene and Serbo-Croat name: **Trst.** [2] **Free Territory of.** a former territory on the N Adriatic: established by the UN in 1947; most of the N part passed to Italy and the remainder to Yugoslavia in 1954.

trifacial (traɪ'feɪʃəl) ADJECTIVE another word for **trigeminal.**

trifecta (traɪ'fɛktə) NOUN a form of betting in which the punter selects the first three place-winners in a horse race in the correct order.
▷HISTORY from TRI- + *(per)fecta*, a US system of betting

triffid ('trɪfɪd) NOUN any of a species of fictional plants that supposedly grew to a gigantic size, were capable of moving about, and could kill humans.
▷HISTORY from the science fiction novel *The Day of the Triffids* (1951) by John Wyndham

trifid ('traɪfɪd) ADJECTIVE divided or split into three parts or lobes.
▷HISTORY C18: from Latin *trifidus* from TRI- + *findere* to split

trifle ('traɪfᵊl) NOUN [1] a thing of little or no value or significance. [2] a small amount; bit: *a trifle more enthusiasm.* [3] *Brit* a cold dessert made with sponge cake spread with jam or fruit, soaked in wine or sherry, covered with a custard sauce and cream, and decorated. [4] a type of pewter of medium hardness. [5] articles made from this pewter. ◆ VERB [6] *(intr;* usually foll by *with)* to deal (with) as if worthless; dally: *to trifle with a person's affections.* [7] to waste (time) frivolously.
▷HISTORY C13: from Old French *trufle* mockery, from *trufler* to cheat
▸**'trifler** NOUN

trifling ('traɪflɪŋ) ADJECTIVE [1] insignificant or petty. [2] frivolous or idle.
▸**'triflingly** ADVERB ▸**'triflingness** NOUN

trifocal ADJECTIVE (traɪ'fəʊkᵊl) [1] having three focuses. [2] having three focal lengths. ◆ NOUN (traɪ'fəʊkᵊl, 'traɪˌfəʊkᵊl) [3] *(plural)* glasses that have trifocal lenses.

trifold ('traɪˌfəʊld) ADJECTIVE a less common word for **triple.**

trifoliate (traɪ'fəʊlɪɪt, -ˌeɪt) *or* **trifoliated** ADJECTIVE having three leaves, leaflike parts, or (of a compound leaf) leaflets.

trifolium (traɪ'fəʊlɪəm) NOUN any leguminous plant of the temperate genus *Trifolium*, having leaves divided into three leaflets and dense heads of small white, yellow, red, or purple flowers: includes the clovers and trefoils.
▷HISTORY C17: from Latin, from TRI- + *folium* leaf

triforium (traɪ'fɔːrɪəm) NOUN, *plural* **-ria** (-rɪə). an arcade above the arches of the nave, choir, or transept of a church.
▷HISTORY C18: from Anglo-Latin, apparently from Latin TRI- + *foris* a doorway; referring to the fact that each bay characteristically had three openings
▸**tri'forial** ADJECTIVE

trifurcate ('traɪfɜːkɪt, -ˌkeɪt) *or* **trifurcated** ADJECTIVE having three branches or forks.
▷HISTORY from Latin *trifurcus*, from TRI- + *furca* a fork
▸ˌ**trifur'cation** NOUN

trig[1] (trɪg) *Archaic or dialect* ◆ ADJECTIVE [1] neat or spruce. ◆ VERB **trigs, trigging, trigged.** [2] to make or become trim or spruce.
▷HISTORY C12 (originally: trusty): of Scandinavian origin; related to Old Norse *tryggr* true
▸**'trigly** ADVERB ▸**'trigness** NOUN

trig[2] (trɪg) *Chiefly dialect* ◆ NOUN [1] a wedge or prop. ◆ VERB **trigs, trigging, trigged.** *(tr)* [2] to block or stop. [3] to prop or support.
▷HISTORY C16: probably of Scandinavian origin; compare Old Norse *tryggja* to make secure; see TRIG[1]

trig. ABBREVIATION FOR: [1] trigonometry. [2] trigonometrical.

trigeminal (traɪ'dʒɛmɪnᵊl) ADJECTIVE *Anatomy* of or relating to the trigeminal nerve.
▷HISTORY C19: from Latin *trigeminus* triplet, from TRI- + *geminus* twin

trigeminal nerve NOUN either one of the fifth pair of cranial nerves, which supply the muscles of the mandible and maxilla. Their ophthalmic branches supply the area around the orbit of the eye, the nasal cavity, and the forehead.

trigeminal neuralgia NOUN *Pathol* another name for **tic douloureux.**

trigger ('trɪgə) NOUN [1] a small projecting lever that activates the firing mechanism of a firearm. [2] *Machinery* a device that releases a spring-loaded mechanism or a similar arrangement. [3] any event that sets a course of action in motion. ◆ VERB *(tr)* [4] (usually foll by *off)* to give rise (to); set off. [5] to fire or set in motion by or as by pulling a trigger.
▷HISTORY C17 *tricker*, from Dutch *trekker*, from *trekken* to pull; see TREK
▸**'triggered** ADJECTIVE ▸**'triggerless** ADJECTIVE

triggerfish ('trɪgəˌfɪʃ) NOUN, *plural* **-fish** *or* **-fishes.** any plectognath fish of the family *Balistidae*, of tropical and temperate seas. They have a compressed body with erectile spines in the first dorsal fin.

trigger-happy ADJECTIVE *Informal* [1] tending to resort to the use of firearms or violence irresponsibly. [2] tending to act rashly or without due consideration.

triggerman ('trɪgəˌmæn) NOUN, *plural* **-men.** a person, esp a criminal, who shoots another person.

trigger plant NOUN *Austral* any of several small grasslike plants of the genus *Stylidium*, having sensitive stamens that are erected when disturbed: family *Stylidiaceae.*

trigger word NOUN a word that initiates a process or course of action.

triglyceride (traɪ'glɪsəˌraɪd) NOUN any ester of glycerol and one or more carboxylic acids, in which each glycerol molecule has combined with three carboxylic acid molecules. Most natural fats and oils are triglycerides.

triglyph ('traɪˌglɪf) NOUN *Architect* a stone block in a Doric frieze, having three vertical channels.
▷HISTORY C16: via Latin from Greek *trigluphos* three-grooved, from *tri-* TRI- + *gluphē* carving. See GLYPH
▸**tri'glyphic** ADJECTIVE

trigon ('traɪgɒn) NOUN [1] (in classical Greece or Rome) a triangular harp or lyre. [2] an archaic word for **triangle.**
▷HISTORY C17: via Latin from Greek *trigōnon* triangle. See TRI-, -GON

trigonal ('trɪgənᵊl) ADJECTIVE [1] another word for **triangular** (sense 1). [2] Also: **rhombohedral.** relating or belonging to the crystal system characterized by three equal axes that are equally inclined and not perpendicular to each other.

trigonometric function NOUN [1] Also called: **circular function.** any of a group of functions of an angle expressed as a ratio of two of the sides of a right-angled triangle containing the angle. The group includes sine, cosine, tangent, secant, cosecant, and cotangent. [2] any function containing only sines, cosines, etc., and constants.

trigonometry (ˌtrɪgə'nɒmɪtrɪ) NOUN the branch of mathematics concerned with the properties of trigonometric functions and their application to the determination of the angles and sides of triangles. Used in surveying, navigation, etc. Abbreviation: **trig.**
▷HISTORY C17: from New Latin *trigōnometria* from Greek *trigōnon* triangle
▸**trigonometric** (ˌtrɪgənə'mɛtrɪk) *or* ˌ**trigono'metrical** ADJECTIVE ▸ˌ**trigono'metrically** ADVERB

trigonous ('trɪgənəs) ADJECTIVE (of stems, seeds, and similar parts) having a triangular cross section.

trig point NOUN an informal name for **triangulation station.** Also called (Austral and NZ): **trig.**

trigraph ('traɪˌgrɑːf, -ˌgræf) NOUN a combination of three letters used to represent a single speech sound or phoneme, such as *eau* in French *beau.*
▸**trigraphic** (traɪ'græfɪk) ADJECTIVE

trihalomethane (traɪˌheɪləʊ'miːθeɪn) NOUN a type of chemical compound in which three of the hydrogen atoms in a methane molecule have been replaced by halogen atoms, esp by chlorine in drinking water. Trihalomethanes are thought to be carcinogenic.

trihedral (traɪ'hiːdrəl) ADJECTIVE [1] having or formed by three plane faces meeting at a point. ◆ NOUN [2] a figure formed by the intersection of three lines in different planes.
▷HISTORY C18: from TRI- + Greek *hedra* base, seat + -AL[1]

trihedron (traɪ'hiːdrən) NOUN, *plural* **-drons** *or* **-dra** (-drə). a figure determined by the intersection of three planes.

trihydrate (traɪ'haɪdreɪt) NOUN *Chem* a substance that contains three molecules of water.
▸**tri'hydrated** ADJECTIVE

trihydric (traɪ'haɪdrɪk) *or* **trihydroxy** (ˌtraɪhaɪ'drɒksɪ) ADJECTIVE (of an alcohol or similar compound) containing three hydroxyl groups.

triiodomethane (ˌtraɪaɪˌəʊdəʊ'miːθeɪn) NOUN another name for **iodoform.**

triiodothyronine (ˌtraɪaɪˌəʊdəʊ'θaɪrəˌniːn) NOUN an amino acid hormone that contains iodine and is secreted by the thyroid gland with thyroxine, to which it has a similar action. Formula: $C_{15}H_{12}I_3NO_4$.
▷HISTORY C20: from TRI- + IODO- + THYRO- + -INE2

trike (traɪk) NOUN [1] short for **tricycle.** [2] short for **trichloroethylene.**

trilateral (traɪ'lætərəl) ADJECTIVE having three sides.
▸**tri'laterally** ADVERB

trilateration (ˌtraɪlætə'reɪʃən) NOUN a method of surveying in which a whole area is divided into triangles, the sides of which are measured, usually by electromagnetic distance measuring for geodetic control or by chain survey for a detailed survey.

trilby ('trɪlbɪ) NOUN, *plural* **-bies.** [1] *Chiefly Brit* a man's soft felt hat with an indented crown. [2] *(plural) Slang* feet.
▷HISTORY C19: named after *Trilby*, the heroine of a dramatized novel (1893) of that title by George du Maurier

trilemma (traɪ'lɛmə) NOUN [1] a quandary posed by three alternative courses of action. [2] an argument one of the premises of which is the disjunction of three statements from each of which the same conclusion is derived.
▷HISTORY C17: formed on the model of DILEMMA, from TRI- + Greek *lēmma* assumption

trilinear (traɪˈlɪnɪə) ADJECTIVE consisting of, bounded by, or relating to three lines.

trilingual (traɪˈlɪŋgwəl) ADJECTIVE [1] able to speak three languages fluently. [2] expressed or written in three languages.
▸**triˈlingualism** NOUN ▸**triˈlingually** ADVERB

triliteral (traɪˈlɪtərəl) ADJECTIVE [1] having three letters. [2] (of a word root in Semitic languages) consisting of three consonants. ◆ NOUN [3] a word root of three consonants.

trilithon (traɪˈlɪθɒn, ˈtraɪlɪˌθɒn) *or* **trilith** (ˈtraɪlɪθ) NOUN a structure consisting of two upright stones with a third placed across the top, such as those of Stonehenge.
▷**HISTORY** C18: from Greek; see TRI-, -LITH
▸**trilithic** (traɪˈlɪθɪk) ADJECTIVE

trill[1] (trɪl) NOUN [1] *Music* a melodic ornament consisting of a rapid alternation between a principal note and the note a whole tone or semitone above it. Usual symbol: *tr.* or *tr* (written above a note). [2] a shrill warbling sound, esp as made by some birds. [3] *Phonetics* **a** the articulation of an (r) sound produced by holding the tip of the tongue close to the alveolar ridge, allowing the tongue to make a succession of taps against the ridge. **b** the production of a similar effect using the uvula against the back of the tongue. ◆ VERB [4] to sound, sing, or play (a trill or with a trill). [5] (*tr*) to pronounce (an (r) sound) by the production of a trill.
▷**HISTORY** C17: from Italian *trillo*, from *trillare*, apparently from Middle Dutch *trillen* to vibrate

trill[2] (trɪl) VERB, NOUN an archaic or poetic word for **trickle.**
▷**HISTORY** C14: probably of Scandinavian origin; related to Norwegian *trilla* to roll; see TRILL[1]

trillion (ˈtrɪljən) NOUN [1] the number represented as one followed by twelve zeros (10^{12}); a million million. [2] (formerly, in Britain) the number represented as one followed by eighteen zeros (10^{18}); a million million million. [3] (*often plural*) an exceptionally large but unspecified number. ◆ DETERMINER [4] (preceded by *a* or a numeral) **a** amounting to a trillion: *a trillion stars.* **b** (*as pronoun*): *there are three trillion.*
▷**HISTORY** C17: from French, on the model of *million*
▸**ˈtrillionth** NOUN, ADJECTIVE

trillionaire (ˌtrɪljəˈnɛə) NOUN a person whose assets are worth over a trillion of the monetary units of his or her country.

trillium (ˈtrɪljəm) NOUN any herbaceous plant of the genus *Trillium*, of Asia and North America, having a whorl of three leaves at the top of the stem with a single central white, pink, or purple three-petalled flower: family *Trilliaceae*.
▷**HISTORY** C18: from New Latin, modification by Linnaeus of Swedish *trilling* triplet

trilobate (traɪˈləʊbeɪt, ˈtraɪləˌbeɪt) ADJECTIVE (esp of a leaf) consisting of or having three lobes or parts.

trilobite (ˈtraɪləˌbaɪt) NOUN any extinct marine arthropod of the group *Trilobita*, abundant in Palaeozoic times, having a segmented exoskeleton divided into three parts.
▷**HISTORY** C19: from New Latin *Trilobītēs*, from Greek *trilobos* having three lobes; see TRI-, LOBE
▸**trilobitic** (ˌtraɪləˈbɪtɪk) ADJECTIVE

trilocular (traɪˈlɒkjʊlə) ADJECTIVE (esp of a plant ovary or anther) having or consisting of three chambers or cavities.
▷**HISTORY** C18: from TRI- + Latin *loculus* compartment (from *locus* place) + -AR

trilogy (ˈtrɪlədʒɪ) NOUN, *plural* **-gies.** [1] a series of three related works, esp in literature, etc. [2] (in ancient Greece) a series of three tragedies performed together at the Dionysian festivals.
▷**HISTORY** C19: from Greek *trilogia*; see TRI-, -LOGY

trim (trɪm) ADJECTIVE **trimmer, trimmest.** [1] neat and spruce in appearance. [2] slim; slender. [3] in good condition. ◆ VERB **trims, trimming, trimmed.** (*mainly tr*) [4] to put in good order, esp by cutting or pruning. [5] to shape and finish (timber). [6] to adorn or decorate. [7] (sometimes foll by *off* or *away*) to cut so as to remove: *to trim off a branch.* [8] to cut down to the desired size or shape: *to trim material to a pattern.* [9] *Dialect* to decorate: *to trim a Christmas tree.* [10] *Nautical* **a** (*also intr*) to adjust the balance of (a vessel) or (of a vessel) to maintain an even balance, by distribution of ballast, cargo, etc. **b** (*also intr*) to adjust (a vessel's sails) to take advantage of the wind. **c** to stow (cargo). [11] to balance (an aircraft) before flight by adjusting the position of the load or in flight by the use of trim tabs, fuel transfer, etc. [12] (*also intr*) to modify (one's opinions, etc.) to suit opposing factions or for expediency. [13] *Informal* to thrash or beat. [14] *Informal* to rebuke. [15] *Obsolete* to furnish or equip. ◆ NOUN [16] a decoration or adornment. [17] the upholstery and decorative facings, as on the door panels, of a car's interior. [18] proper order or fitness; good shape: *in trim.* [19] a haircut that neatens but does not alter the existing hairstyle. [20] *Nautical* **a** the general set and appearance of a vessel. **b** the difference between the draught of a vessel at the bow and at the stern. **c** the fitness of a vessel. **d** the position of a vessel's sails relative to the wind. **e** the relative buoyancy of a submarine. [21] dress or equipment. [22] *US* window-dressing. [23] the attitude of an aircraft in flight when the pilot allows the main control surfaces to take up their own positions. [24] *Films* a section of shot cut out during editing. [25] material that is trimmed off. [26] decorative mouldings, such as architraves, picture rails, etc.
▷**HISTORY** Old English *trymman* to strengthen; related to *trum* strong, Old Irish *druma* tree, Russian *drom* thicket
▸**ˈtrimly** ADVERB ▸**ˈtrimness** NOUN

Trim (trɪm) NOUN the county town of Meath, Republic of Ireland; 12th-century castle, medieval cathedral; textiles and machinery. Pop.: 18 120 (1991).

trimaran (ˈtraɪməˌræn) NOUN a vessel, usually of shallow draught, with two hulls flanking the main hull.
▷**HISTORY** C20: from TRI- + (CATA)MARAN

trimer (ˈtraɪmə) NOUN a polymer or a molecule of a polymer consisting of three identical monomers.
▸**trimeric** (traɪˈmɛrɪk) ADJECTIVE

trimerous (ˈtrɪmərəs) ADJECTIVE [1] (of plants) having parts arranged in groups of three. [2] consisting of or having three parts.

trimester (traɪˈmɛstə) NOUN [1] a period of three months. [2] (in some US and Canadian universities or schools) any of the three academic sessions.
▷**HISTORY** C19: from French *trimestre*, from Latin *trimēstris* of three months, from TRI- + *mēnsis* month
▸**triˈmestral** *or* **triˈmestrial** ADJECTIVE

trimeter (ˈtrɪmɪtə) *Prosody* ◆ NOUN [1] a verse line consisting of three metrical feet. ◆ ADJECTIVE [2] designating such a line.

trimethadione (ˌtraɪmɛθəˈdaɪəʊn) NOUN a crystalline compound with a bitter taste and camphor-like odour, used in the treatment of epilepsy. Formula: $C_6H_9NO_3$.
▷**HISTORY** from TRI- + METH(YL) + DI-[1] + -ONE

trimetric (traɪˈmɛtrɪk) *or* **trimetrical** ADJECTIVE [1] *Prosody* of, relating to, or consisting of a trimeter or trimeters. [2] *Crystallog* another word for **orthorhombic.**

trimetric projection NOUN a geometric projection, used in mechanical drawing, in which the three axes are at arbitrary angles, often using different linear scales.

trimetrogon (traɪˈmɛtrəˌgɒn) NOUN **a** a method of aerial photography for rapid topographic mapping, in which one vertical and two oblique photographs are taken simultaneously. **b** (*as modifier*): *trimetrogon photography.*
▷**HISTORY** from TRI- + *metro-*, from Greek *metron* measure + -GON

trimmer (ˈtrɪmə) NOUN [1] Also called: **trimmer joist.** a beam in a floor or roof structure attached to truncated joists in order to leave an opening for a staircase, chimney, etc. [2] a machine for trimming timber. [3] Also called: **trimming capacitor.** *Electronics* a variable capacitor of small capacitance used for making fine adjustments, etc. [4] a person who alters his opinions on the grounds of expediency. [5] a person who fits out motor vehicles.

trimming (ˈtrɪmɪŋ) NOUN [1] an extra piece used to decorate or complete. [2] (*plural*) usual or traditional accompaniments: *roast turkey with all the trimmings.* [3] (*plural*) parts that are cut off. [4] (*plural*) *Dialect* ornaments; decorations: *Christmas trimmings.* [5] *Informal* a reproof, beating, or defeat.

trimolecular (ˌtraɪməˈlɛkjʊlə) ADJECTIVE *Chem* of, concerned with, formed from, or involving three molecules.

trimonthly (traɪˈmʌnθlɪ) ADJECTIVE, ADVERB every three months.

trimorph (ˈtraɪmɔːf) NOUN [1] a substance, esp a mineral, that exists in three distinct forms. [2] any of the forms in which such a structure exists.

trimorphism (traɪˈmɔːfɪzəm) NOUN [1] *Biology* the property exhibited by certain species of having or occurring in three different forms. [2] the property of certain minerals of existing in three crystalline forms.
▷**HISTORY** C19: from Greek *trimorphos* (from TRI- + *morphē* form) + -ISM
▸**triˈmorphic** *or* **triˈmorphous** ADJECTIVE

trim size NOUN the size of a book or a page of a book after all excess material has been trimmed off.

trim tab NOUN a small control surface attached to the trailing edge of a main control surface to enable the pilot to trim an aircraft.

Trimurti (trɪˈmʊətɪ) NOUN the triad of the three chief gods of later Hinduism, consisting of Brahma the Creator, Vishnu the Sustainer, and Siva the Destroyer.
▷**HISTORY** from Sanskrit, from *tri* three + *mūrti* form

Trinacria (trɪˈneɪkrɪə, traɪ-) NOUN the Latin name for **Sicily.**
▸**Triˈnacrian** ADJECTIVE

Trinacrian (trɪˈneɪkrɪən, traɪ-) ADJECTIVE of or relating to Trinacria (the Latin name for Sicily) or its inhabitants.

trinary (ˈtraɪnərɪ) ADJECTIVE [1] made up of three parts; ternary. [2] going in threes.
▷**HISTORY** C15: from Late Latin *trīnārius* of three sorts, from Latin *trīnī* three each, from *trēs* three

Trincomalee (ˌtrɪŋkəʊməˈliː) NOUN a port in NE Sri Lanka, on the **Bay of Trincomalee** (an inlet of the Bay of Bengal); British naval base until 1957. Pop.: 51 000 (latest est.).

trine (traɪn) NOUN [1] *Astrology* an aspect of 120° between two planets, an orb of 8° being allowed. Compare **conjunction** (sense 5), **opposition** (sense 9), **square** (sense 10). [2] anything comprising three parts. ◆ ADJECTIVE [3] of or relating to a trine. [4] threefold; triple.
▷**HISTORY** C14: from Old French *trin*, from Latin *trīnus* triple, from *trēs* three
▸**ˈtrinal** ADJECTIVE

Trini (ˈtrɪnɪ) NOUN, *plural* **Trinis.** *Caribbean informal* a native or inhabitant of Trinidad; Trinidadian.
▷**HISTORY** C20: a shortened form of *Trinidadian*

Trinidad (ˈtrɪnɪˌdæd) NOUN an island in the West Indies, off the NE coast of Venezuela: colonized by the Spanish in the 17th century and ceded to Britain in 1802; joined with Tobago in 1888 as a British colony; now part of the independent republic of Trinidad and Tobago. Pop.: 1 184 106 (1990).

Trinidad and Tobago NOUN an independent republic in the Caribbean, occupying the two southernmost islands of the Lesser Antilles: became a British colony in 1888 and gained independence in 1962; became a republic in 1976; a member of the Commonwealth. Official language: English. Religion: Christian majority, with a large Hindu minority. Currency: Trinidad and Tobago dollar. Capital: Port of Spain. Pop.: 1 298 000 (2001 est.). Area: 5128 sq. km (1980 sq. miles).

Trinidadian (ˌtrɪnɪˈdædɪən) ADJECTIVE [1] of or relating to Trinidad or its inhabitants. ◆ NOUN [2] a native or inhabitant of Trinidad.

Trinil man (ˈtriːnɪl) NOUN another name for **Java man.**
▷**HISTORY** C20: named after the village in Java where remains were found

Trinitarian (ˌtrɪnɪˈtɛərɪən) NOUN [1] a person who believes in the doctrine of the Trinity. [2] a member of the Holy Trinity. See **Trinity** (sense 3). ◆ ADJECTIVE [3] of or relating to the doctrine of the Trinity or those who uphold it. [4] of or relating to the Holy Trinity.
▸**ˌTriniˈtarianˌism** NOUN

trinitrobenzene (traɪˌnaɪtrəʊˈbɛnziːn, -bɛnˈziːn) NOUN any of three explosive crystalline isomeric compounds with the formula $C_6H_3(NO_2)_3$. They are less sensitive to impact than TNT but more powerful in their explosive force.

trinitrocresol (traɪˌnaɪtrəʊ'kri:sɒl) NOUN a yellow crystalline highly explosive compound. Formula: $CH_3C_6H(OH)(NO_2)_3$.

trinitroglycerine (traɪˌnaɪtrəʊ'glɪsəˌri:n) NOUN the full name for **nitroglycerine.**

trinitrophenol (traɪˌnaɪtrəʊ'fi:nɒl) NOUN another name for **picric acid.**

trinitrotoluene (traɪˌnaɪtrəʊ'tɒljʊˌi:n) *or* **trinitrotoluol** (traɪˌnaɪtrəʊ'tɒljʊˌɒl) NOUN the full name for **TNT.**

trinity ('trɪnɪtɪ) NOUN, *plural* **-ties.** 1 a group of three. 2 the state of being threefold.
▷HISTORY C13: from Old French *trinite*, from Late Latin *trīnitās*, from Latin *trīnus* triple

Trinity ('trɪnɪtɪ) NOUN 1 Also called: **Holy Trinity, Blessed Trinity.** *Christian theol* the union of three persons, the Father, Son, and Holy Spirit, in one Godhead. 2 See **Trinity Sunday.** 3 **Holy Trinity.** a religious order founded in 1198.

Trinity Brethren PLURAL NOUN the members of Trinity House.

Trinity House NOUN an association that provides lighthouses, buoys, etc., around the British coast.

Trinity Sunday NOUN the Sunday after Whit Sunday.

Trinity term NOUN the summer term at the Inns of Court and some educational establishments.

trinket ('trɪŋkɪt) NOUN 1 a small or worthless ornament or piece of jewellery. 2 a trivial object; trifle.
▷HISTORY C16: perhaps from earlier *trenket* little knife, via Old Northern French, from Latin *truncāre* to lop
▸**'trinketry** NOUN

trinocular (traɪ'nɒkjʊlə) ADJECTIVE of or relating to a binocular microscope having a lens for photographic recording while direct visual observation is taking place.
▷HISTORY C20: from TRI- + (BI)NOCULAR

trinomial (traɪ'nəʊmɪəl) ADJECTIVE 1 *Maths* consisting of or relating to three terms. 2 *Biology* denoting or relating to the three-part name of an organism that incorporates its genus, species, and subspecies. ◆ NOUN 3 *Maths* a polynomial consisting of three terms, such as $ax^2 + bx + c$. 4 *Biology* the third word in the trinomial name of an organism, which distinguishes between subspecies.
▷HISTORY C18: TRI- + *-nomial* on the model of *binomial*
▸**tri'nomially** ADVERB

trio ('tri:əʊ) NOUN, *plural* **trios.** 1 a group of three people or things. 2 *Music* **a** a group of three singers or instrumentalists or a piece of music composed for such a group. **b** a subordinate section in a scherzo, minuet, etc., that is contrastive in style and often in a related key. 3 *Piquet* three cards of the same rank.
▷HISTORY C18: from Italian, ultimately from Latin *trēs* three; compare DUO

triode ('traɪəʊd) NOUN 1 an electronic valve having three electrodes, a cathode, an anode, and a grid, the potential of the grid controlling the flow of electrons between the cathode and anode. It has been replaced by the transistor. 2 any electronic device, such as a thyratron, having three electrodes.
▷HISTORY C20: TRI- + ELECTRODE

trioecious *or* **triecious** (traɪ'i:ʃəs) ADJECTIVE (of a plant species) having male, female, and hermaphrodite flowers in three different plants.
▷HISTORY C18: from New Latin *trioecia*, from Greek TRI- + *oikos* house

triol ('traɪɒl) NOUN any of a class of alcohols that have three hydroxyl groups per molecule. Also called: **trihydric alcohol.**
▷HISTORY from TRI- + -OL[1]

triolein (traɪ'əʊlɪɪn) NOUN a naturally occurring glyceride of oleic acid, found in fats and oils. Formula: $(C_{17}H_{33}COO)_3C_3H_5$. Also called: **olein.**

triolet ('tri:əʊˌlɛt) NOUN a verse form of eight lines, having the first line repeated as the fourth and seventh and the second line as the eighth, rhyming a b a a a b a b.
▷HISTORY C17: from French: a little TRIO

triose ('traɪəʊz, -əʊs) NOUN a simple monosaccharide produced by the oxidation of glycerol. Formula: $CH_2OHCHOHCHO$.

trio sonata NOUN 1 a type of baroque composition in several movements scored for two upper parts and a bass part. 2 a similar type of composition played on a keyboard instrument, esp an organ.

trioxide (traɪ'ɒksaɪd) NOUN any oxide that contains three oxygen atoms per molecule: *sulphur trioxide, SO_3.*

trip (trɪp) NOUN 1 an outward and return journey, often for a specific purpose. 2 any tour, journey, or voyage. 3 a false step; stumble. 4 any slip or blunder. 5 a light step or tread. 6 a manoeuvre or device to cause someone to trip. 7 Also called: **tripper. a** any catch on a mechanism that acts as a switch. **b** (*as modifier*): *trip button.* 8 a surge in the conditions of a chemical or other automatic process resulting in an instability. 9 *Informal* a hallucinogenic drug experience. 10 *Informal* any stimulating, profound, etc., experience. ◆ VERB **trips, tripping, tripped.** 11 (often foll by *up*, or when *intr*, by *on* or *over*) to stumble or cause to stumble. 12 to make or cause to make a mistake or blunder. 13 (*tr*; often foll by *up*) to trap or catch in a mistake. 14 (*intr*) to go on a short tour or journey. 15 (*intr*) to move or tread lightly. 16 (*intr*) *Informal* to experience the effects of LSD or any other hallucinogenic drug. 17 (*tr*) **a** to activate (a mechanical trip). **b trip a switch.** to switch electric power off by moving the switch armature to disconnect the supply. ◆ See also **trip out.**
▷HISTORY C14: from Old French *triper* to tread, of Germanic origin; related to Low German *trippen* to stamp, Middle Dutch *trippen* to walk trippingly, *trepelen* to trample
▸**'trippingly** ADVERB

tripalmitin (traɪ'pælmɪtɪn) NOUN another name for **palmitin.**

tripartite (traɪ'pɑ:taɪt) ADJECTIVE 1 divided into or composed of three parts. 2 involving three participants. 3 (esp of leaves) consisting of three parts formed by divisions extending almost to the base.
▸**tri'partitely** ADVERB

tripartition (ˌtraɪpɑ:'tɪʃən) NOUN division into or among three.

tripe (traɪp) NOUN 1 the stomach lining of an ox, cow, or other ruminant, prepared for cooking. 2 *Informal* something silly; rubbish. 3 (*plural*) *Archaic informal* intestines; belly.
▷HISTORY C13: from Old French, of unknown origin

tripersonal (traɪ'pɜ:sənᵊl) ADJECTIVE *Christian theol* (of God) existing as the Trinity. Compare **unipersonal.**
▸**ˌtriperson'ality** NOUN

triphammer ('trɪpˌhæmə) NOUN a power hammer that is raised or tilted by a cam and allowed to fall under gravity.

triphenylmethane (traɪˌfi:naɪl'mi:θeɪn, -ˌfɛn-) NOUN a colourless crystalline solid used for the preparation of many dyes. Formula: $(C_6H_5)_3CH$.

triphibious (traɪ'fɪbɪəs) ADJECTIVE (esp of military operations) occurring on land, at sea, and in the air.
▷HISTORY C20: from TRI- + (AM)PHIBIOUS

trip-hop ('trɪpˌhɒp) NOUN a type of British electronic dance music of the 1990s, influenced by drug culture.
▷HISTORY C20: TRIP (in the sense: drug experience) + HIP-HOP

triphthong ('trɪfθɒŋ, 'trɪp-) NOUN 1 a composite vowel sound during the articulation of which the vocal organs move from one position through a second, ending in a third. 2 a trigraph representing a composite vowel sound such as this.
▷HISTORY C16: via New Latin from Medieval Greek *triphthongos*, from TRI- + *phthongos* sound; compare DIPHTHONG
▸**triph'thongal** ADJECTIVE

triphylite ('trɪfɪˌlaɪt) NOUN a bluish-grey rare mineral that consists of lithium iron phosphate in orthorhombic crystalline form and occurs in pegmatites. Formula: $LiFePO_4$.
▷HISTORY C19: from TRI- + *phyl-*, from Greek *phulon* family + -ITE1, referring to its three bases

tripinnate (traɪ'pɪnɪt, -eɪt) ADJECTIVE (of a bipinnate leaf) having the pinnules themselves pinnate.
▸**tri'pinnately** ADVERB

Tripitaka (trɪ'pɪtəkə) NOUN *Buddhism* the three collections of books making up the Buddhist canon of scriptures.
▷HISTORY from Pali *tri* three + *pitaka* basket

triplane ('traɪˌpleɪn) NOUN an aeroplane having three wings arranged one above the other.

triple ('trɪpᵊl) ADJECTIVE 1 consisting of three parts; threefold. 2 (of musical time or rhythm) having three beats in each bar. 3 three times as great or as much. ◆ NOUN 4 a threefold amount. 5 a group of three. ◆ VERB 6 to increase or become increased threefold; treble.
▷HISTORY C16: from Latin *triplus*
▸**'triply** ADVERB

triple A NOUN *Military* anti-aircraft artillery: written as **AAA.**

Triple Alliance NOUN 1 the secret alliance between Germany, Austria-Hungary, and Italy formed in 1882 and lasting until 1914. 2 the alliance of France, the Netherlands, and Britain against Spain in 1717. 3 the alliance of England, Sweden, and the Netherlands against France in 1668.

triple bond NOUN a type of chemical bond consisting of three distinct covalent bonds linking two atoms in a molecule.

triple crown NOUN 1 *RC Church* the Pope's tiara. 2 *Horse racing* the winning of three important races in one season. 3 (*often capital*) *Rugby Union* a victory by Scotland, England, Wales, or Ireland in all three games against the others in the annual Six (formerly, Five) Nations Championship. Compare **grand slam** (sense 3).

Triple Entente NOUN the understanding between Britain, France, and Russia that developed between 1894 and 1907 and counterbalanced the Triple Alliance of 1882. The Entente became a formal alliance on the outbreak of World War I and was ended by the Russian Revolution in 1917.

triple expansion engine NOUN (formerly) a steam engine in which the steam is expanded in three stages in cylinders of increasing diameter to accommodate the increasing volume of the steam.

triple jump NOUN an athletic event in which the competitor has to perform successively a hop, a step, and a jump in continuous movement. Also called: **hop, step, and jump.**

triple-nerved ADJECTIVE (of a leaf) having three main veins.

triple point NOUN *Chem* the temperature and pressure at which the three phases of a substance are in equilibrium. The triple point of water, 273.16 K at a pressure of 611.2 Pa, is the basis of the definition of the kelvin.

triplet ('trɪplɪt) NOUN 1 a group or set of three similar things. 2 one of three offspring born at one birth. 3 *Music* a group of three notes played in a time value of two, four, etc. 4 *Chem* a state of a molecule or free radical in which there are two unpaired electrons.
▷HISTORY C17: from TRIPLE, on the model of *doublet*

tripletail ('trɪpᵊlˌteɪl) NOUN, *plural* **-tail** *or* **-tails.** any percoid fish of the family *Lobotidae*, esp *Lobotes surinamensis*, of brackish waters of SE Asia, having tail-like dorsal and anal fins.

triple time NOUN musical time with three beats in each bar.

triple-tongue VERB *Music* to play (very quick staccato passages of notes grouped in threes) on a wind instrument by a combination of single- and double-tonguing. Compare **single-tongue, double-tongue.**
▸**triple tonguing** NOUN

triplex ('trɪplɛks) ADJECTIVE a less common word for **triple.**
▷HISTORY C17: from Latin: threefold, from TRI- + *-plex* -FOLD

Triplex ('trɪplɛks) NOUN *Trademark, Brit* a laminated safety glass, as used in car windows.

triplicate ADJECTIVE ('trɪplɪkɪt) 1 triple. ◆ VERB ('trɪplɪˌkeɪt) 2 to multiply or be multiplied by three. ◆ NOUN ('trɪplɪkɪt) 3 **a** a group of three things. **b** one of such a group. 4 **in triplicate.** written out three times.

▷**HISTORY** C15: from Latin *triplicāre* to triple, from TRIPLEX
▸ˌ**tripliˈcation** NOUN

triplicity (trɪˈplɪsɪtɪ) NOUN, *plural* **-ties.** 1 a group of three things. 2 the state of being three. 3 *Astrology* any of four groups, earth, air, fire, and water, each consisting of three signs of the zodiac that are thought to have something in common in their nature.
▷**HISTORY** C14: from Late Latin *triplicitās*, from Latin *triplex* threefold; see TRIPLEX

triploblastic (ˌtrɪpləʊˈblæstɪk) ADJECTIVE (of all multicellular animals except coelenterates) having a body developed from all three germ layers. Compare **diploblastic.**
▷**HISTORY** C19: from *triplo-* threefold (from Greek *triploos*) + -BLAST

triploid (ˈtrɪplɔɪd) ADJECTIVE 1 having or relating to three times the haploid number of chromosomes: *a triploid organism.* ◆ NOUN 2 a triploid organism.
▷**HISTORY** C19: from Greek *tripl(oos)* triple + (HAPL)OID

tripod (ˈtraɪpɒd) NOUN 1 an adjustable and usually collapsible three-legged stand to which a camera, etc., can be attached to hold it steady. 2 a stand or table having three legs.
▷**HISTORY** C17: via Latin from Greek *tripod-, tripous* three-footed, from TRI- + *pous* foot
▸**tripodal** (ˈtrɪpədᵊl) ADJECTIVE

tripody (ˈtrɪpədɪ) NOUN, *plural* **-dies.** *Prosody* a metrical unit consisting of three feet.

tripoli (ˈtrɪpəlɪ) NOUN a lightweight porous siliceous rock derived by weathering and used in a powdered form as a polish, filter, etc.
▷**HISTORY** C17: named after TRIPOLI, in Libya or in Lebanon

Tripoli (ˈtrɪpəlɪ) NOUN 1 the capital and chief port of Libya, in the northwest on the Mediterranean: founded by Phoenicians in about the 7th century B.C.; the only city that has survived of the three (Oea, Leptis Magna, and Sabratha) that formed the African Tripolis ("three cities"); fishing and manufacturing centre. Pop. (urban area): 1 140 000 (1995 est.). Ancient name: **Oea** (ˈiːə). Arabic name: **Tarabulus el Gharb.** 2 a port in N Lebanon, on the Mediterranean: the second largest town in Lebanon; taken by the Crusaders in 1109 after a siege of five years; oil-refining and manufacturing centre. Pop.: 160 000 (1998 est.). Ancient name: **Tripolis.** Arabic name: **Tarabulus esh Sham.**

Tripolitania (ˌtrɪpəlɪˈteɪnɪə) NOUN the NW part of Libya: established as a Phoenician colony in the 7th century B.C.; taken by the Turks in 1551 and became one of the Barbary states; under Italian rule from 1912 until World War II.

Tripolitanian (ˌtrɪpəlɪˈteɪnɪən) ADJECTIVE 1 of or relating to Tripolitania (now part of Libya) or its inhabitants. ◆ NOUN 2 a native or inhabitant of Tripolitania.

tripos (ˈtraɪpɒs) NOUN *Brit* the final honours degree examinations in all subjects at Cambridge University.
▷**HISTORY** C16: from Latin *tripūs*, influenced by Greek noun ending *-os*

trip out VERB (*adverb*) (of an electrical circuit) to disconnect or be disconnected or (of a machine) to stop or be stopped by means of a trip switch or trip button.

tripper (ˈtrɪpə) NOUN 1 a person who goes on a trip. 2 *Chiefly Brit* a tourist; excursionist. 3 another word for **trip** (sense 7). 4 **a** any device that generates a signal causing a trip to operate. **b** the signal so generated.

trippet (ˈtrɪpɪt) NOUN any mechanism that strikes or is struck at regular intervals, as by a cam.
▷**HISTORY** C15 (in the sense: a piece of wood used in a game): from *trippen* to TRIP

trippy (ˈtrɪpɪ) ADJECTIVE **-pier, -piest.** *Informal* suggestive of or resembling the effect produced by a hallucinogenic drug.

trip switch NOUN an electric switch arranged to interrupt a circuit suddenly and disconnect power from a running machine so that the machine is stopped.

triptane (ˈtrɪpteɪn) NOUN a colourless highly flammable liquid alkane hydrocarbon, isomeric with heptane, used in aviation fuel; 2,2,3-trimethylbutane. Formula: $CH_3C(CH_3)_2CH(CH_3)CH_3$.
▷**HISTORY** C20: shortened and altered from *trimethylbutane*; see TRI-, METHYL, BUTANE

tripterous (ˈtrɪptərəs) ADJECTIVE (of fruits, seeds, etc.) having three winglike extensions or parts.
▷**HISTORY** C19: from TRI- + Greek *-pteros*, from *pteron* wing

Triptolemus (trɪpˈtɒlɪməs) NOUN *Greek myth* a favourite of Demeter, sent by her to teach mankind agriculture.

triptych (ˈtrɪptɪk) NOUN 1 a set of three pictures or panels, usually hinged so that the two wing panels fold over the larger central one: often used as an altarpiece. 2 a set of three hinged writing tablets.
▷**HISTORY** C18: from Greek *triptukhos*, from TRI- + *ptux* plate; compare DIPTYCH

triptyque (trɪpˈtiːk) NOUN a customs permit for the temporary importation of a motor vehicle.
▷**HISTORY** from French: TRIPTYCH (referring to its three sections)

Tripura (ˈtrɪpʊrə) NOUN a state of NE India: formerly a princely state, ruled by the Maharajahs for over 1300 years; became a union territory in 1956 and a state in 1972; extensive jungles. Capital: Agartala. Pop.: 3 191 168 (2001). Area: 10 486 sq. km (4051 sq. miles).

tripwire (ˈtrɪpˌwaɪə) NOUN a wire that activates a trap, mine, etc., when tripped over.

triquetrous (traɪˈkwiːtrəs, -ˈkwɛ-) ADJECTIVE triangular, esp in cross section: *a triquetrous stem.*
▷**HISTORY** C17: from Latin *triquetrus* having three corners

triradiate (traɪˈreɪdɪɪt, -ˌeɪt) ADJECTIVE *Biology* having or consisting of three rays or radiating branches.
▸**triˈradiately** ADVERB

trireme (ˈtraɪriːm) NOUN a galley, developed by the ancient Greeks as a warship, with three banks of oars on each side.
▷**HISTORY** C17: from Latin *trirēmis*, from TRI- + *rēmus* oar

trisaccharide (traɪˈsækəˌraɪd) NOUN an oligosaccharide whose molecules have three linked monosaccharide molecules.

trisect (traɪˈsɛkt) VERB (*tr*) to divide into three parts, esp three equal parts.
▷**HISTORY** C17: TRI- + *-sect* from Latin *secāre* to cut
▸**trisection** (traɪˈsɛkʃən) NOUN ▸**triˈsector** NOUN

triserial (traɪˈsɪərɪəl) ADJECTIVE arranged in three rows or series.

trishaw (ˈtraɪˌʃɔː) NOUN another name for **rickshaw** (sense 2).
▷**HISTORY** C20: from TRI- + RICKSHAW

triskaidekaphobia (ˌtrɪskaɪˌdɛkəˈfəʊbɪə) NOUN an abnormal fear of the number thirteen.
▷**HISTORY** C20: from Greek *triskaideka* thirteen + -PHOBIA
▸ˌ**triskaiˌdekaˈphobic** ADJECTIVE, NOUN

triskelion (trɪˈskɛlɪˌɒn, -ən) *or* **triskele** (ˈtrɪskiːl) NOUN, *plural* **triskelia** (trɪˈskɛlɪə) *or* **triskeles.** a symbol consisting of three bent limbs or lines radiating from a centre.
▷**HISTORY** C19: from Greek *triskelēs* three-legged, from TRI- + *skelos* leg

Trismegistus (ˌtrɪsmɪˈdʒɪstəs) NOUN See **Hermes Trismegistus.**

trismus (ˈtrɪzməs) NOUN *Pathol* the state or condition of being unable to open the mouth because of sustained contractions of the jaw muscles, caused by a form of tetanus. Nontechnical name: **lockjaw.**
▷**HISTORY** C17: from New Latin, from Greek *trismos* a grinding
▸ˈ**trismic** ADJECTIVE

trisoctahedron (trɪsˌɒktəˈhiːdrən) NOUN, *plural* **-drons** *or* **-dra** (-drə). a solid figure having 24 identical triangular faces, groups of three faces being formed on an underlying octahedron.
▷**HISTORY** C19: from Greek *tris* three times + OCTAHEDRON
▸**trisˌoctaˈhedral** ADJECTIVE

trisomy (ˈtraɪsəʊmɪ) NOUN the condition of having one chromosome of the set represented three times in an otherwise diploid organism, cell, etc. Trisomy of chromosome 21 results in Down's syndrome.
▷**HISTORY** C20: from TRI- + (CHROMO)SOM(E) + -Y[3]
▸**trisomic** (traɪˈsəʊmɪk) ADJECTIVE

Tristan (ˈtrɪstən) *or* **Tristram** (ˈtrɪstrəm) NOUN (in medieval romance) the nephew of King Mark of Cornwall who fell in love with his uncle's bride, Iseult, after they mistakenly drank a love potion.

Tristan da Cunha (ˈtrɪstən də ˈkuːnjə) NOUN a group of four small volcanic islands in the S Atlantic, about halfway between South Africa and South America: comprises the main island of Tristan and the uninhabited islands of Gough, Inaccessible, and Nightingale; discovered in 1506 by the Portuguese admiral Tristão da Cunha; annexed to Britain in 1816; whole population of Tristan evacuated for two years after the volcanic eruption of 1961. Pop.: 288 (1994 est.). Area: about 100 sq. km (40 sq. miles).

tristate (ˈtraɪˌsteɪt) ADJECTIVE (of a digital computer chip) having high, low, and floating output states.

triste (triːst) *or* **tristful** (ˈtrɪstfʊl) ADJECTIVE archaic words for **sad.**
▷**HISTORY** from French
▸ˈ**tristfully** ADVERB ▸ˈ**tristfulness** NOUN

tristearin (traɪˈstɪərɪn) NOUN another name for **stearin.**

tristich (ˈtrɪstɪk) NOUN *Prosody* a poem, stanza, or strophe that consists of three lines.
▷**HISTORY** C19: from Greek, from TRI- + *stikhos* STICH, on the model of DISTICH
▸**trisˈtichic** ADJECTIVE

tristichous (ˈtrɪstɪkəs) ADJECTIVE arranged in three rows, esp (of plants) having three vertical rows of leaves.

tristimulus values (traɪˈstɪmjʊləs) PLURAL NOUN three values that together are used to describe a colour and are the amounts of three reference colours that can be mixed to give the same visual sensation as the colour considered. Symbol: X, Y, Z. See also **chromaticity coordinates.**

trisulphide (traɪˈsʌlfaɪd) NOUN any sulphide containing three sulphur atoms per molecule.

trisyllable (traɪˈsɪləbᵊl) NOUN a word of three syllables.
▸**trisyllabic** (ˌtraɪsɪˈlæbɪk) ADJECTIVE ▸ˌ**trisylˈlabically** ADVERB

tritanopia (ˌtraɪtəˈnəʊpɪə, ˌtrɪt-) NOUN a form of colour blindness in which there is a tendency to confuse blues and greens and in which sensitivity to blue is reduced.
▷**HISTORY** C19/20: from New Latin, from Greek *tritos* third + New Latin *anopia* blindness; signifying that only two thirds of the spectrum can be distinguished
▸**tritanopic** (ˌtraɪtəˈnɒpɪk, ˌtrɪt-) ADJECTIVE

trite (traɪt) ADJECTIVE 1 hackneyed; dull: *a trite comment.* 2 *Archaic* frayed or worn out.
▷**HISTORY** C16: from Latin *trītus* worn down, from *terere* to rub
▸ˈ**tritely** ADVERB ▸ˈ**triteness** NOUN

tritheism (ˈtraɪθɪˌɪzəm) NOUN *Theol* belief in three gods, esp in the Trinity as consisting of three distinct gods.
▸ˈ**tritheist** NOUN, ADJECTIVE ▸ˌ**tritheˈistic** *or* ˌ**tritheˈistical** ADJECTIVE

tritiate (ˈtrɪtɪˌeɪt) VERB (*tr*) to replace normal hydrogen atoms in (a compound) by those of tritium.
▷**HISTORY** C20: from TRITI(UM) + -ATE[1]
▸ˌ**tritiˈation** NOUN

triticale (ˌtrɪtɪˈkɑːlɪ) NOUN a fertile hybrid cereal, a cross between wheat (*Triticum*) and rye (*Secale*), produced by polyploidy.
▷**HISTORY** C20: from *Tritic(um)* + (*Sec*)*ale*

triticum (ˈtrɪtɪkəm) NOUN any annual cereal grass of the genus *Triticum*, which includes the wheats.
▷**HISTORY** C19: Latin, literally: wheat, probably from *tritum*, supine of *terere* to grind

tritium (ˈtrɪtɪəm) NOUN a radioactive isotope of hydrogen, occurring in trace amounts in natural hydrogen and produced in a nuclear reactor. Tritiated compounds are used as tracers. Symbol: T or ^{3}H; half-life: 12.5 years.
▷**HISTORY** C20: New Latin, from Greek *tritos* third

triton[1] (ˈtraɪtᵊn) NOUN any of various chiefly tropical marine gastropod molluscs of the genera

Charonia, *Cymatium*, etc., having large beautifully-coloured spiral shells.
▷HISTORY C16: via Latin from Greek *tritōn*

triton[2] ('traɪtɒn) NOUN *Physics* a nucleus of an atom of tritium, containing two neutrons and one proton.
▷HISTORY C20: from TRIT(IUM) + -ON

Triton[1] ('traɪtᵊn) NOUN *Greek myth* [1] a sea god, son of Poseidon and Amphitrite, depicted as having the upper parts of a man with a fish's tail and holding a trumpet made from a conch shell. [2] one of a class of minor sea deities.

Triton[2] ('traɪtᵊn) NOUN the largest satellite of the planet Neptune. Diameter: 2700 km.

tritone ('traɪˌtəʊn) NOUN a musical interval consisting of three whole tones; augmented fourth.

tritonia (traɪ'təʊnɪə) NOUN any plant of the perennial cormous S. African genus *Tritonia*, with typically scarlet or orange flowers: family *Iridaceae*.
▷HISTORY New Latin, from Greek *Tritōn* TRITON[1]

triturate ('trɪtjʊˌreɪt) VERB [1] (*tr*) to grind or rub into a fine powder or pulp; masticate. ◆ NOUN [2] the powder or pulp resulting from this grinding.
▷HISTORY C17: from Late Latin *trītūrāre* to thresh, from Latin *trītūra* a threshing, from *terere* to grind
▸**'triturable** ADJECTIVE ▸**'trituˌrator** NOUN

trituration (ˌtrɪtjʊ'reɪʃən) NOUN [1] the act of triturating or the state of being triturated. [2] *Pharmacol* a mixture of one or more finely ground powdered drugs.

triumph ('traɪəmf) NOUN [1] the feeling of exultation and happiness derived from a victory or major achievement. [2] the act or condition of being victorious; victory. [3] (in ancient Rome) a ritual procession to the Capitoline Hill held in honour of a victorious general. [4] *Obsolete* a public display or celebration. [5] *Cards* an obsolete word for **trump**[1]. ◆ VERB (*intr*) [6] (often foll by *over*) to win a victory or control: *to triumph over one's weaknesses.* [7] to rejoice over a victory. [8] to celebrate a Roman triumph.
▷HISTORY C14: from Old French *triumphe*, from Latin *triumphus*, from Old Latin *triumpus*; probably related to Greek *thriambos* Bacchic hymn
▸**'triumpher** NOUN

triumphal (traɪ'ʌmfəl) ADJECTIVE [1] celebrating a triumph: *a triumphal procession.* [2] resembling triumph.

triumphal arch NOUN an arch built to commemorate a victory.

triumphalism (traɪ'ʌmfəlɪzəm) NOUN excessive celebration of the defeat of one's enemies or opponents.
▸**tri'umphalist** ADJECTIVE

triumphant (traɪ'ʌmfənt) ADJECTIVE [1] experiencing or displaying triumph. [2] exultant through triumph. [3] *Obsolete* **a** magnificent. **b** triumphal.
▸**tri'umphantly** ADVERB

triumvir (traɪ'ʌmvə) NOUN, *plural* **-virs** *or* **-viri** (-vɪˌriː). (esp in ancient Rome) a member of a triumvirate.
▷HISTORY C16: from Latin: one of three administrators, from *triumvirōrum* of three men, from *trēs* three + *vir* man
▸**tri'umviral** ADJECTIVE

triumvirate (traɪ'ʌmvɪrɪt) NOUN [1] (in ancient Rome) **a** a board of three officials jointly responsible for some task. **b** the political alliance of Caesar, Crassus, and Pompey, formed in 60 B.C. (**First Triumvirate**). **c** the coalition and joint rule of the Roman Empire by Antony, Lepidus, and Octavian, begun in 43 B.C. (**Second Triumvirate**). [2] any joint rule by three men. [3] any group of three men associated in some way. [4] the office of a triumvir.

triune ('traɪjuːn) ADJECTIVE [1] constituting three in one, esp the three persons in one God of the Trinity. ◆ NOUN [2] a group of three. [3] (*often capital*) another word for **Trinity**.
▷HISTORY C17: TRI- + *-une*, from Latin *ūnus* one
▸**tri'unity** NOUN

Triunitarian (traɪˌjuːnɪ'tɛərɪən) NOUN, ADJECTIVE a less common word for **Trinitarian.**

trivalent (traɪ'veɪlənt, 'trɪvələnt) ADJECTIVE *Chem* [1] having a valency of three. [2] having three valencies. Also: **tervalent.**
▸**tri'valency** NOUN

Trivandrum (trɪ'vændrəm) NOUN a city in S India, capital of Kerala, on the Malabar Coast: made capital of the kingdom of Travancore in 1745; University of Kerala (1937). Pop.: 524 006 (1991). Official name: **Thiruvananthapuram.**

trivet ('trɪvɪt) NOUN [1] a stand, usually three-legged and metal, on which cooking vessels are placed over a fire. [2] a short metal stand on which hot dishes are placed on a table. [3] **as right as a trivet.** *Old-fashioned* in perfect health.
▷HISTORY Old English *trefet* (influenced by Old English *thrifēte* having three feet), from Latin *tripēs* having three feet

trivia ('trɪvɪə) NOUN (*functioning as singular or plural*) petty details or considerations; trifles; trivialities.
▷HISTORY from New Latin, plural of Latin *trivium* junction of three roads; for meaning, see TRIVIAL

trivial ('trɪvɪəl) ADJECTIVE [1] of little importance; petty or frivolous: *trivial complaints.* [2] ordinary or commonplace; trite: *trivial conversation.* [3] *Maths* (of the solutions of a set of homogeneous equations) having zero values for all the variables. [4] *Biology* denoting the specific name of an organism in binomial nomenclature. [5] *Biology, chem* denoting the popular name of an organism or substance, as opposed to the scientific one. [6] of or relating to the trivium.
▷HISTORY C15: from Latin *triviālis* belonging to the public streets, common, from *trivium* crossroads, junction of three roads, from TRI- + *via* road
▸**'trivially** ADVERB ▸**'trivialness** NOUN

triviality (ˌtrɪvɪ'ælɪtɪ) NOUN, *plural* **-ties.** [1] the state or quality of being trivial. [2] something, such as a remark, that is trivial. ◆ Also called: **trivialism** ('trɪvɪəˌlɪzəm).

trivialize ('trɪvɪəˌlaɪz) *or* **trivialise** VERB (*tr*) to cause to seem trivial or more trivial; minimize: *he trivialized his injuries.*
▸**ˌtriviali'zation** *or* **ˌtriviali'sation** NOUN

trivium ('trɪvɪəm) NOUN, *plural* **-ia** (-ɪə). (in medieval learning) the lower division of the seven liberal arts, consisting of grammar, rhetoric, and logic. Compare **quadrivium.**
▷HISTORY C19: from Medieval Latin, from Latin: crossroads; see TRIVIAL

triweekly (traɪ'wiːklɪ) ADJECTIVE, ADVERB [1] every three weeks. [2] three times a week. ◆ NOUN, *plural* **-lies.** [3] a triweekly publication.

-trix SUFFIX FORMING NOUNS indicating a feminine agent, corresponding to nouns ending in *-tor*: *executrix.*
▷HISTORY from Latin

t-RNA ABBREVIATION FOR transfer RNA.

Troas ('trəʊæs) NOUN the region of NW Asia Minor surrounding the ancient city of Troy. Also called: **the Troad** ('trəʊæd).

troat (trəʊt) VERB (*intr*) (of a rutting buck) to call or bellow.
▷HISTORY C17: probably related to Old French *trout, trut*, a cry used by hunters to urge on the dogs

Trobriand Islander ('trəʊbrɪˌænd) NOUN a native or inhabitant of the Trobriand Islands of Papua New Guinea.

Trobriand Islands ('trəʊbrɪˌænd) PLURAL NOUN a group of coral islands in the Solomon Sea, north of the E part of New Guinea: part of Papua New Guinea. Area: about 440 sq. km (170 sq. miles).

trocar ('trəʊkɑː) NOUN a surgical instrument for removing fluid from bodily cavities, consisting of a puncturing device situated inside a tube.
▷HISTORY C18: from French *trocart* literally: with three sides, from *trois* three + *carre* side

trochaic (trəʊ'keɪɪk) *Prosody* ◆ ADJECTIVE [1] of, relating to, or consisting of trochees. ◆ NOUN [2] another word for **trochee.** [3] a verse composed of trochees.
▸**tro'chaically** ADVERB

trochal ('trəʊkᵊl) ADJECTIVE *Zoology* shaped like a wheel: *the trochal disc of a rotifer.*
▷HISTORY C19: from Greek *trokhos* wheel

trochanter (trəʊ'kæntə) NOUN [1] any of several processes on the upper part of the vertebrate femur, to which muscles are attached. [2] the third segment of an insect's leg.
▷HISTORY C17: via French from Greek *trokhantēr*, from *trekhein* to run

troche (trəʊʃ) NOUN *Med* another name for **lozenge** (sense 1).
▷HISTORY C16: from French *trochisque*, from Late Latin *trochiscus*, from Greek *trokhiskos* little wheel, from *trokhos* wheel

trochee ('trəʊkiː) NOUN *Prosody* a metrical foot of two syllables, the first long and the second short (–⏑). Compare **iamb.**
▷HISTORY C16: via Latin from Greek *trokhaios pous*, literally: a running foot, from *trekhein* to run

trochelminth ('trɒkᵊlˌmɪnθ) NOUN any invertebrate of the former taxonomic group *Trochelminthes*, which included the rotifers and gastrotrichs, now classed as separate phyla.
▷HISTORY C19: from New Latin *trochelminthes*, from Greek *trokhos* wheel, from *trekhein* to run + HELMINTH

trochilus ('trɒkɪləs) NOUN, *plural* **-li** (-ˌlaɪ). [1] another name for **hummingbird.** [2] any of several Old World warblers, esp *Phylloscopus trochilus* (willow warbler).
▷HISTORY C16: via Latin from Greek *trokhilos* name of a small Egyptian bird said by ancient writers to pick the teeth of crocodiles, from *trekhein* to run

trochlea ('trɒklɪə) NOUN, *plural* **-leae** (-lɪˌiː). any bony or cartilaginous part with a grooved surface over which a bone, tendon, etc., may slide or articulate.
▷HISTORY C17: from Latin, from Greek *trokhileia* a sheaf of pulleys; related to *trokhos* wheel, *trekhein* to run

trochlear nerve NOUN either one of the fourth pair of cranial nerves, which supply the superior oblique muscle of the eye.

trochoid ('trəʊkɔɪd) NOUN [1] the curve described by a fixed point on the radius or extended radius of a circle as the circle rolls along a straight line. ◆ ADJECTIVE *also* **trochoidal.** [2] rotating or capable of rotating about a central axis. [3] *Anatomy* (of a structure or part) resembling or functioning as a pivot or pulley.
▷HISTORY C18: from Greek *trokhoeidēs* circular, from *trokhos* wheel
▸**tro'choidally** ADVERB

trochophore ('trɒkəˌfɔː) *or* **trochosphere** ('trɒkəsˌfɪə) NOUN the ciliated planktonic larva of many invertebrates, including polychaete worms, molluscs, and rotifers.
▷HISTORY C19: from Greek *trokhos* wheel + -PHORE

trod (trɒd) VERB the past tense and a past participle of **tread.**

trodden ('trɒdᵊn) VERB a past participle of **tread.**

trode (trəʊd) VERB *Archaic* a past tense of **tread.**

trog (trɒg) VERB **trog, trogging, trogged.** (*intr*; often foll by *along*) *Brit informal* to walk, esp aimlessly or heavily; stroll.
▷HISTORY C20: perhaps a blend of TRUDGE and SLOG

troglodyte ('trɒgləˌdaɪt) NOUN [1] a cave dweller, esp one of the prehistoric peoples thought to have lived in caves. [2] *Informal* a person who lives alone and appears eccentric.
▷HISTORY C16: via Latin from Greek *trōglodutēs* one who enters caves, from *trōglē* hole + *duein* to enter
▸**troglodytic** (ˌtrɒglə'dɪtɪk) *or* **ˌtroglo'dytical** ADJECTIVE

trogon ('trəʊgɒn) NOUN any bird of the order *Trogoniformes* of tropical and subtropical regions of America, Africa, and Asia. They have a brilliant plumage, short hooked bill, and long tail. See also **quetzal.**
▷HISTORY C18: from New Latin, from Greek *trōgōn*, from *trōgein* to gnaw

troika ('trɔɪkə) NOUN [1] a Russian vehicle drawn by three horses abreast. [2] three horses harnessed abreast. [3] a triumvirate.
▷HISTORY C19: from Russian, from *troe* three

troilism ('trɔɪlɪzəm) NOUN sexual activity involving three people.
▷HISTORY C20: perhaps from French *trois* three (compare MÉNAGE À TROIS) + *-l-*, as in DUALISM
▸**'troilist** ADJECTIVE

Troilus ('trɔɪləs, 'trəʊɪləs) NOUN *Greek myth* the youngest son of King Priam and Queen Hecuba, slain at Troy. In medieval romance he is portrayed as the lover of Cressida.

Trois Rivières (*French* trwɑ rivjɛr) NOUN a port in central Canada, in Quebec on the St Lawrence River: one of the world's largest centres of newsprint production. Pop.: 49 426 (1991), with a metropolitan area of 136 300 (1991). English name: **Three Rivers.**

Trojan (ˈtrəʊdʒən) NOUN [1] a native or inhabitant of ancient Troy. [2] a person who is hard-working and determined. ◆ ADJECTIVE [3] of or relating to ancient Troy or its inhabitants.

Trojan asteroid NOUN one of a number of asteroids that have the same mean motion and orbit as Jupiter, preceding or following the planet by a longitude of 60°.

Trojan Horse NOUN [1] Also called: **the Wooden Horse.** *Greek myth* the huge wooden hollow figure of a horse left outside Troy by the Greeks when they feigned retreat and dragged inside by the Trojans. The men concealed inside it opened the city to the final Greek assault. [2] a trap intended to undermine an enemy. [3] *Computing* a bug inserted into a program or system designed to be activated after a certain time or a certain number of operations.

Trojan War NOUN *Greek myth* a war fought by the Greeks against the Trojans to avenge the abduction of Helen from her Greek husband Menelaus by Paris, son of the Trojan king. It lasted ten years and ended in the sack of Troy.

troll[1] (trəʊl) VERB [1] *Angling* **a** to draw (a baited line, etc.) through the water, often from a boat. **b** to fish (a stretch of water) by trolling. **c** to fish (for) by trolling. [2] to roll or cause to roll. [3] *Archaic* to sing (a refrain, chorus, etc.) or (of a refrain, etc.) to be sung in a loud hearty voice. [4] *(intr) Brit informal* to walk or stroll. [5] *(intr) Homosexual slang* to stroll around looking for sexual partners; cruise. ◆ NOUN [6] the act or an instance of trolling. [7] *Angling* a bait or lure used in trolling, such as a spinner.
▷HISTORY C14: from Old French *troller* to run about; related to Middle High German *trollen* to run with short steps
▸ˈ**troller** NOUN

troll[2] (trəʊl) NOUN (in Scandinavian folklore) one of a class of supernatural creatures that dwell in caves or mountains and are depicted either as dwarfs or as giants.
▷HISTORY C19: from Old Norse: demon; related to Danish *trold*

trolley (ˈtrɒlɪ) NOUN [1] *Brit* a small table on casters used for conveying food, drink, etc. [2] *Brit* a wheeled cart or stand pushed by hand and used for moving heavy items, such as shopping in a supermarket or luggage at a railway station. [3] *Brit* (in a hospital) a bed mounted on casters and used for moving patients who are unconscious, immobilized, etc. [4] *Brit* See **trolley-bus.** [5] *US and Canadian* See **trolley car.** [6] a device that collects the current from an overhead wire (**trolley wire**), third rail, etc., to drive the motor of an electric vehicle. [7] a pulley or truck that travels along an overhead wire in order to support a suspended load. [8] *Chiefly Brit* a low truck running on rails, used in factories, mines, etc., and on railways. [9] a truck, cage, or basket suspended from an overhead track or cable for carrying loads in a mine, quarry, etc. [10] **off one's trolley.** *Slang* **a** mentally confused or disorganized. **b** insane. ◆ VERB [11] *(tr)* to transport (a person or object) on a trolley. ◆ See also **trolleys.**
▷HISTORY C19: probably from TROLL[1]

trolleybus (ˈtrɒlɪˌbʌs) NOUN an electrically driven public-transport vehicle that does not run on rails but takes its power from an overhead wire through a trolley.

trolley car NOUN a US and Canadian name for **tram**[1] (sense 1).

trolley dolly NOUN *Informal* a female flight attendant.

trolleys (ˈtrɒlɪz) PLURAL NOUN *Slang* men's underpants.

trollius (ˈtrɒlɪəs) NOUN See **globeflower.**
▷HISTORY New Latin, from German *Trollblume* globeflower

trollop (ˈtrɒləp) NOUN [1] a promiscuous woman, esp a prostitute. [2] an untidy woman; slattern.
▷HISTORY C17: perhaps from German dialect *Trolle* prostitute; perhaps related to TRULL
▸**trollopy** ADJECTIVE

tromba marina (ˈtrɒmbə məˈriːnə) NOUN an obsolete viol with a long thin body and a single string. It resembled the natural trumpet in its range of notes (limited to harmonics) and its tone.
▷HISTORY from Italian, literally: marine trumpet

trombidiasis (ˌtrɒmbɪˈdaɪəsɪs) NOUN *Pathol* infestation with mites of the family *Trombiculidae.*
▷HISTORY C20: New Latin, from *Trombid(ium)* genus name + -IASIS

trombone (trɒmˈbəʊn) NOUN [1] a brass instrument, a low-pitched counterpart of the trumpet, consisting of a tube the effective length of which is varied by means of a U-shaped slide. The usual forms of this instrument are the **tenor trombone** (range: about two and a half octaves upwards from E) and the **bass trombone** (pitched a fourth lower). [2] a person who plays this instrument in an orchestra.
▷HISTORY C18: from Italian, from *tromba* a trumpet, from Old High German *trumba*
▸**tromˈbonist** NOUN

trommel (ˈtrɒməl) NOUN a revolving cylindrical sieve used to screen crushed ore.
▷HISTORY C19: from German: a drum

trompe (trɒmp) NOUN an apparatus for supplying the blast of air in a forge, consisting of a thin column down which water falls, drawing in air through side openings.
▷HISTORY C19: from French, literally: trumpet

trompe l'oeil (*French* trɔ̃p lœj) NOUN, *plural* **trompe l'oeils** (trɔ̃p lœj). [1] a painting or decoration giving a convincing illusion of reality. [2] an effect of this kind.
▷HISTORY from French, literally: deception of the eye

Tromsø (ˈtrɒmsəʊ; *Norwegian* ˈtrumsø) NOUN a port in N Norway, on a small island between Kvaløy and the mainland: fishing and sealing centre. Pop.: 51 218 (1990).

tron (trɒn) NOUN [1] a public weighing machine. [2] the place where a tron is set up; marketplace.
▷HISTORY C15: from Old French *trone,* from Latin *trutina,* from Greek *trutanē* balance, set of scales

-tron SUFFIX FORMING NOUNS [1] indicating a vacuum tube: *magnetron.* [2] indicating an instrument for accelerating atomic or subatomic particles: *synchrotron.*
▷HISTORY from Greek, suffix indicating instrument

trona (ˈtrəʊnə) NOUN a greyish mineral that consists of hydrated sodium carbonate and occurs in salt deposits. Formula: $Na_2CO_3NaHCO_3.2H_2O$.
▷HISTORY C18: from Swedish, probably from Arabic *natrūn* NATRON

tronc (trɒŋk) NOUN a pool into which waiters, waitresses, hotel workers, etc., pay their tips and into which some managements pay service charges for later distribution to staff by a **tronc master**, according to agreed percentages.
▷HISTORY C20: from French: collecting box

Trondheim (ˈtrɒndˌhaɪm; *Norwegian* ˈtrɔnhɛim) NOUN a port in central Norway, on **Trondheim Fjord** (an inlet of the Norwegian Sea): national capital until 1380; seat of the Technical University of Norway. Pop.: 148 859 (2000 est.). Former name (until the 16th century and from 1930 to 1931): **Nidaros.**

tronk (trɒŋk) NOUN *South African informal* jail.
▷HISTORY Afrikaans

troop (truːp) NOUN [1] a large group or assembly; flock: *a troop of children.* [2] a subdivision of a cavalry squadron or artillery battery of about platoon size. [3] *(plural)* armed forces; soldiers. [4] a large group of Scouts comprising several patrols. [5] an archaic spelling of **troupe.** ◆ VERB [6] *(intr)* to gather, move, or march in or as if in a crowd. [7] *(tr) Military, chiefly Brit* to parade (the colour or flag) ceremonially: *trooping the colour.* [8] *(tr) Brit military slang* (formerly) to report (a serviceman) for a breach of discipline. [9] *(intr)* an archaic word for **consort** (sense 1).
▷HISTORY C16: from French *troupe,* from *troupeau* flock, of Germanic origin

troop carrier NOUN a vehicle, aircraft, or ship designed for the carriage of troops.

trooper (ˈtruːpə) NOUN [1] a soldier in a cavalry regiment. [2] *US and Austral* a mounted policeman. [3] *US* a state policeman. [4] a cavalry horse. [5] *Informal, chiefly Brit* a troopship.

troopship (ˈtruːpˌʃɪp) NOUN a ship, usually a converted merchant ship, used to transport military personnel.

troostite (ˈtruːstaɪt) NOUN a reddish or greyish mineral that is a variety of willemite in which some of the zinc is replaced by manganese.
▷HISTORY C19: named after Gerard *Troost* (died 1850), US geologist

tropaeolin (trəʊˈpiːəlɪn) NOUN any of certain yellow and orange azo dyes of complex structure.
▷HISTORY C19: see TROPAEOLUM, -IN

tropaeolum (trəʊˈpiːələm) NOUN, *plural* **-lums** *or* **-la** (-lə). any garden plant of the genus *Tropaeolum* esp the nasturtium.
▷HISTORY C18: from New Latin, from Latin *tropaeum* TROPHY; referring to the shield-shaped leaves and helmet-shaped flowers

trope (trəʊp) NOUN [1] *Rhetoric* a word or expression used in a figurative sense. [2] an interpolation of words or music into the plainsong settings of the Roman Catholic liturgy.
▷HISTORY C16: from Latin *tropus* figurative use of a word, from Greek *tropos* style, turn; related to *trepein* to turn

-trope NOUN COMBINING FORM indicating a turning towards, development in the direction of, or affinity to: *heliotrope.*
▷HISTORY from Greek *tropos* a turn

trophallaxis (ˌtrɒfəˈlæksɪs) NOUN the exchange of regurgitated food that occurs between adults and larvae in colonies of social insects.
▷HISTORY C19/20: from New Latin, from TROPHO- + Greek *allaxis* exchange, from *allassein* to change, from *allos* other
▸ˌ**trophalˈlactic** ADJECTIVE

trophic (ˈtrɒfɪk) ADJECTIVE of or relating to nutrition: *the trophic levels of a food chain.*
▷HISTORY C19: from Greek *trophikos,* from *trophē* food, from *trephein* to feed
▸ˈ**trophically** ADVERB

tropho- *or before a vowel* **troph-** COMBINING FORM indicating nourishment or nutrition: *trophozoite.*
▷HISTORY from Greek *trophē* food, from *trephein* to feed

trophoblast (ˈtrɒfəˌblæst) NOUN the outer layer of cells of the embryo of placental mammals, which is attached to the uterus wall and absorbs nourishment from the uterine fluids.
▷HISTORY C19: from TROPHO- + -BLAST
▸ˌ**trophoˈblastic** ADJECTIVE

trophoplasm (ˈtrɒfəˌplæzəm) NOUN *Biology* the cytoplasm that is involved in the nutritive processes of a cell.

trophozoite (ˌtrɒfəˈzəʊaɪt) NOUN the form of a sporozoan protozoan in the feeding stage. In the malaria parasite this stage occurs in the human red blood cell. Compare **merozoite.**

trophy (ˈtrəʊfɪ) NOUN, *plural* **-phies.** [1] an object such as a silver or gold cup that is symbolic of victory in a contest, esp a sporting contest; prize. [2] a memento of success, esp one taken in war or hunting. [3] (in ancient Greece and Rome) **a** a memorial to a victory, usually consisting of captured arms raised on the battlefield or in a public place. **b** a representation of such a memorial. [4] an ornamental carving that represents a group of weapons, etc. [5] *(modifier) Informal* highly desirable and regarded as a symbol of wealth or success: *a trophy wife.*
▷HISTORY C16: from French *trophée,* from Latin *tropaeum,* from Greek *tropaion,* from *tropē* a turning, defeat of the enemy; related to Greek *trepein* to turn

-trophy NOUN COMBINING FORM indicating a certain type of nourishment or growth: *dystrophy.*
▷HISTORY from Greek *-trophia,* from *trophē* nourishment
▸**-trophic** ADJECTIVE COMBINING FORM

tropic (ˈtrɒpɪk) NOUN [1] *(sometimes capital)* either of the parallel lines of latitude at about 23½°N (**tropic of Cancer**) and 23½°S (**tropic of Capricorn**) of the equator. [2] **the tropics.** *(often capital)* that part of the earth's surface between the tropics of Cancer and Capricorn; the Torrid Zone. [3] *Astronomy* either of the two parallel circles on the celestial sphere having the same latitudes and names as the corresponding lines on the earth. ◆ ADJECTIVE [4] a less common word for **tropical.**
▷HISTORY C14: from Late Latin *tropicus* belonging to a turn, from Greek *tropikos,* from *tropos* a turn; from the ancient belief that the sun turned back at the solstices

-tropic ADJECTIVE COMBINING FORM turning or

developing in response to a certain stimulus: *heliotropic*.
▷HISTORY from Greek *tropos* a turn; see TROPE

tropical (ˈtrɒpɪkᵊl) ADJECTIVE 1 situated in, used in, characteristic of, or relating to the tropics. 2 (of weather) very hot, esp when humid. 3 *Rhetoric* of or relating to a trope.
▸ˌtropiˈcality NOUN ▸ˈtropically ADVERB

tropicalize (ˈtrɒpɪkᵊˌlaɪz) VERB (*tr*) to adapt to tropical use, temperatures, etc.
▸ˌtropicaliˈzation *or* ˌtropicaliˈsation NOUN

tropical year NOUN another name for **solar year**. See **year** (sense 4).

tropicbird (ˈtrɒpɪkˌbɜːd) NOUN any aquatic bird of the tropical family *Phaethontidae*, having long slender tail feathers and a white plumage with black markings: order *Pelecaniformes* (pelicans, cormorants, etc.).
▷HISTORY C17: so called because it is found in the tropical regions

tropine (ˈtrəʊpiːn, -pɪn) NOUN a white crystalline poisonous hygroscopic alkaloid obtained by heating atropine or hyoscyamine with barium hydroxide. Formula: $C_8H_{15}NO$.
▷HISTORY C19: shortened from ATROPINE

tropism (ˈtrəʊpɪzəm) NOUN the response of an organism, esp a plant, to an external stimulus by growth in a direction determined by the stimulus.
▷HISTORY from Greek *tropos* a turn
▸ˌtropisˈmatic ADJECTIVE ▸tropistic (trəʊˈpɪstɪk) ADJECTIVE

-tropism *or* **-tropy** NOUN COMBINING FORM indicating a tendency to turn or develop in response to a certain stimulus: *phototropism*.
▷HISTORY from Greek *tropos* a turn

tropo- COMBINING FORM indicating change or a turning: *tropophyte*.
▷HISTORY from Greek *tropos* a turn

tropology (trɒˈpɒlədʒɪ) NOUN, *plural* **-gies**. 1 *Rhetoric* the use of figurative language in speech or writing. 2 *Christian theol* the educing of moral or figurative meanings from the Scriptures. 3 a treatise on tropes or figures of speech.
▷HISTORY C16: via Late Latin from Greek *tropalogia*; see TROPE, -LOGY
▸ˌtropoˈlogic *or* ˌtropoˈlogical ADJECTIVE

tropopause (ˈtrɒpəˌpɔːz) NOUN *Meteorol* the plane of discontinuity between the troposphere and the stratosphere, characterized by a sharp change in the lapse rate and varying in altitude from about 18 km (11 miles) above the equator to 6 km (4 miles) at the Poles.

tropophyte (ˈtrɒpəˌfaɪt) NOUN a plant living in a seasonal climate that can become dormant in unfavourable conditions.
▸tropophytic (ˌtrɒpəˈfɪtɪk) ADJECTIVE

troposphere (ˈtrɒpəˌsfɪə) NOUN the lowest atmospheric layer, about 18 kilometres (11 miles) thick at the equator to about 6 km (4 miles) at the Poles, in which air temperature decreases normally with height at about 6.5°C per km.
▸ˌtropoˈspheric ADJECTIVE

-tropous ADJECTIVE COMBINING FORM indicating a turning away: *anatropous*.
▷HISTORY from Greek *-tropos* concerning a turn

troppo¹ (ˈtrɒpəʊ) ADVERB *Music* too much; excessively. See **non troppo**.
▷HISTORY Italian

troppo² (ˈtrɒpəʊ) ADJECTIVE *Austral slang* mentally affected by a tropical climate.

Trossachs (ˈtrɒsəks) NOUN (*functioning as plural or singular*) **the**. 1 a narrow wooded valley in central Scotland, between Loch Achray and Loch Katrine: made famous by Sir Walter Scott's descriptions. 2 (popularly) the area extending northwards from Loch Ard and Aberfoyle to Lochs Katrine, Achray, and Venachar.

trot (trɒt) VERB **trots, trotting, trotted**. 1 to move or cause to move at a trot. 2 *Angling* to fish (a fast-moving stream or river) by using a float and weighted line that carries the baited hook just above the bottom. ◆ NOUN 3 a gait of a horse or other quadruped, faster than a walk, in which diagonally opposite legs come down together. See also **jog trot, rising trot, sitting trot**. 4 a steady brisk pace. 5 (in harness racing) a race for horses that have been trained to trot fast. 6 *Angling* **a** one of the short lines attached to a trotline. **b** the trotline. 7 *Austral and NZ informal* a run of luck: *a good trot*. 8 *Chiefly Brit* a small child; tot. 9 *US slang* a student's crib. 10 **on the trot**. *Informal* **a** one after the other: *to read two books on the trot*. **b** busy, esp on one's feet. 11 **the trots**. *Informal* **a** diarrhoea. **b** *NZ* trotting races.
▷HISTORY C13: from Old French *trot*, from *troter* to trot, of Germanic origin; related to Middle High German *trotten* to run

Trot (trɒt) NOUN *Informal* a follower of Trotsky; Trotskyist.

troth (trəʊθ) NOUN *Archaic* 1 a pledge or oath of fidelity, esp a betrothal. 2 truth (esp in the phrase **in troth**). 3 loyalty; fidelity.
▷HISTORY Old English *trēowth*; related to Old High German *gitriuwida* loyalty; see TRUTH

trothplight (ˈtrəʊθˌplaɪt) *Archaic* ◆ NOUN 1 a betrothal. ◆ VERB 2 (*tr*) to betroth. ◆ ADJECTIVE 3 betrothed; engaged.
▷HISTORY C14: from TROTH + PLIGHT²

trotline (ˈtrɒtˌlaɪn) NOUN *Angling* a long line suspended across a stream, river, etc., to which shorter hooked and baited lines are attached. Compare **trawl** (sense 2). See also **setline**.

trot out VERB (*tr, adverb*) *Informal* to bring forward, as for approbation or admiration, esp repeatedly: *he trots out the same excuses every time*.

Trotskyism (ˈtrɒtskɪˌɪzəm) NOUN the theory of Communism developed by the Russian revolutionary Leon Trotsky (original name *Lev Davidovich Bronstein*; 1879–1940), in which he called for immediate worldwide revolution by the proletariat.
▸ˈTrotskyist *or* ˈTrotskyite NOUN, ADJECTIVE

Trotskyist International NOUN any of several international Trotskyist organizations that have developed from the international federation of anti-Stalinist Communists founded by Trotsky in 1936.

trotter (ˈtrɒtə) NOUN 1 a person or animal that trots, esp a horse that is specially trained to trot fast. 2 (*usually plural*) the foot of certain animals, esp of pigs.

trotting race NOUN the NZ term for **harness race**.

trotyl (ˈtrəʊtɪl, -tiːl) NOUN another name for **TNT**.
▷HISTORY C20: from (TRINI)TROT(OLUENE) + -YL

troubadour (ˈtruːbəˌdʊə) NOUN 1 any of a class of lyric poets who flourished principally in Provence and N Italy from the 11th to the 13th centuries, writing chiefly on courtly love in complex metric form. 2 a singer.
▷HISTORY C18: from French, from Old Provençal *trobador*, from *trobar* to write verses, perhaps ultimately from Latin *tropus* TROPE

trouble (ˈtrʌbᵊl) NOUN 1 a state or condition of mental distress or anxiety. 2 a state or condition of disorder or unrest: *industrial trouble*. 3 a condition of disease, pain, or malfunctioning: *she has liver trouble*. 4 a cause of distress, disturbance, or pain; problem: *what is the trouble?* 5 effort or exertion taken to do something: *he took a lot of trouble over this design*. 6 liability to suffer punishment or misfortune (esp in the phrase **be in trouble**): *he's in trouble with the police*. 7 a personal quality that is regarded as a weakness, handicap, or cause of annoyance: *his trouble is that he's too soft*. 8 (*plural*) **a** political unrest or public disturbances. **b** **the Troubles**. political violence in Ireland during the 1920s or in Northern Ireland since the late 1960s. 9 the condition of an unmarried girl who becomes pregnant (esp in the phrase **in trouble**). ◆ VERB 10 (*tr*) to cause trouble to; upset, pain, or worry. 11 (*intr; usually with a negative and foll by about*) to put oneself to inconvenience; be concerned: *don't trouble about me*. 12 (*intr*; usually with a negative) to take pains; exert oneself: *please don't trouble to write everything down*. 13 (*tr*) to cause inconvenience or discomfort to: *does this noise trouble you?* 14 (*tr; usually passive*) to agitate or make rough: *the seas were troubled*. 15 (*tr*) *Caribbean* to interfere with: *he wouldn't like anyone to trouble his new bicycle*.
▷HISTORY C13: from Old French *troubler*, from Vulgar Latin *turbulāre* (unattested), from Late Latin *turbidāre*, from *turbidus* confused, from *turba* commotion
▸ˈtroubled ADJECTIVE ▸ˈtroubler NOUN

troublemaker (ˈtrʌbᵊlˌmeɪkə) NOUN a person who makes trouble, esp between people.
▸ˈtroubleˌmaking ADJECTIVE, NOUN

troubleshooter (ˈtrʌbᵊlˌʃuːtə) NOUN a person who locates the cause of trouble and removes or treats it.
▸ˈtroubleˌshooting NOUN, ADJECTIVE

troublesome (ˈtrʌbᵊlsəm) ADJECTIVE 1 causing a great deal of trouble; worrying, upsetting, or annoying. 2 characterized by violence; turbulent.
▸ˈtroublesomely ADVERB ▸ˈtroublesomeness NOUN

trouble spot NOUN a place of recurring trouble, esp of political unrest.

troublous (ˈtrʌbləs) ADJECTIVE *Archaic or literary* unsettled; agitated.
▸ˈtroublously ADVERB ▸ˈtroublousness NOUN

trouch (traʊtʃ) NOUN *Southwestern English dialect* rubbish; junk.

trough (trɒf) NOUN 1 a narrow open container, esp one in which food or water for animals is put. 2 a narrow channel, gutter, or gulley. 3 a narrow depression either in the land surface, ocean bed, or between two successive waves. 4 *Meteorol* an elongated area of low pressure, esp an extension of a depression. Compare **ridge** (sense 6). 5 a single or temporary low point; depression. 6 *Physics* the portion of a wave, such as a light wave, in which the amplitude lies below its average value. 7 *Economics* the lowest point or most depressed stage of the trade cycle. ◆ VERB 8 (*intr*) *Informal* to eat, consume, or take greedily.
▷HISTORY Old English *trōh*; related to Old Saxon, Old Norse *trog* trough, Dutch *trügge* ladle
▸ˈtroughˌlike ADJECTIVE

trounce (traʊns) VERB (*tr*) to beat or defeat utterly; thrash.
▷HISTORY C16: of unknown origin

troupe (truːp) NOUN 1 a company of actors or other performers, esp one that travels. ◆ VERB 2 (*intr*) (esp of actors) to move or travel in a group.
▷HISTORY C19: from French; see TROOP

trouper (ˈtruːpə) NOUN 1 a member of a troupe. 2 an experienced or dependable worker or associate.

troupial (ˈtruːpɪəl) NOUN any of various American orioles of the genus *Icterus*, esp *I. icterus*, a bright orange-and-black South American bird.
▷HISTORY C19: from French *troupiale*, from *troupe* flock; referring to its gregarious habits

trous-de-loup (ˌtruːdᵊˈluː) NOUN, *plural* **trous-de-loup** (ˌtruːdᵊˈluː). *Military* any of a series of conical-shaped pits with a stake fixed in the centre, formerly used as protection against enemy cavalry.
▷HISTORY C18: from French, literally: wolf's holes

trouse (traʊz) PLURAL NOUN *Brit* close-fitting breeches worn in Ireland.
▷HISTORY from Irish and Scot Gaelic *triubhas*: compare TREWS

trouser (ˈtraʊzə) NOUN 1 (*modifier*) of or relating to trousers: *trouser buttons*. ◆ VERB 2 (*tr*) *Slang* to take (something, esp money), often surreptitiously or unlawfully.

trousers (ˈtraʊzəz) PLURAL NOUN 1 a garment shaped to cover the body from the waist to the ankles or knees with separate tube-shaped sections for both legs. 2 **wear the trousers**. *Brit informal* to have control, esp in a marriage. US equivalent: **wear the pants**.
▷HISTORY C17: from earlier *trouse*, a variant of TREWS, influenced by DRAWERS
▸ˈtrousered ADJECTIVE ▸ˈtrouserless ADJECTIVE

trouser suit NOUN *Chiefly Brit* a woman's suit of a jacket or top and trousers. Also called (esp US and Canadian): **pant suit**.

trousseau (ˈtruːsəʊ) NOUN, *plural* **-seaux** *or* **-seaus** (-səʊz). the clothes, linen, etc., collected by a bride for her marriage.
▷HISTORY C19: from Old French, literally: a little bundle, from *trusse* a bundle; see TRUSS

trout (traʊt) NOUN, *plural* **trout** *or* **trouts**. 1 any of various game fishes, esp *Salmo trutta* and related species, mostly of fresh water in northern regions: family *Salmonidae* (salmon). They resemble salmon but are smaller and spotted. 2 any of various similar or related fishes, such as a sea trout. 3 *Austral* any of various fishes of the *Salmo* or *Oncorhynchus* genera smaller than the salmon, esp European and American varieties naturalized in

Australia. [4] *Brit informal* an irritating or grumpy person, esp a woman.
▷HISTORY Old English *trūht*, from Late Latin *tructa*, from Greek *troktēs* sharp-toothed fish

trouvère (tru:ˈvɛə; *French* truvɛr) *or* **trouveur** (*French* truvœr) NOUN any of a group of poets of N France during the 12th and 13th centuries who composed chiefly narrative works.
▷HISTORY C19: from French, from Old French *troveor*, from *trover* to compose; related to TROUBADOUR

trove (trəuv) NOUN See **treasure-trove.**

trover (ˈtrəuvə) NOUN *Law* (formerly) the act of wrongfully assuming proprietary rights over personal goods or property belonging to another.
▷HISTORY C16: from Old French, from *trover* to find; see TROUVÈRE, TROUBADOUR

trow (trəu) VERB *Archaic* to think, believe, or trust.
▷HISTORY Old English *treow*; related to Old Frisian *triūwe*, Old Saxon *treuwa*, Old High German *triuwa*; see TROTH, TRUE

Trowbridge (ˈtrəuˌbrɪdʒ) NOUN a market town in SW England, administrative centre of Wiltshire: woollen manufacturing. Pop.: 29 334 (1991).

trowel (ˈtrauəl) NOUN [1] any of various small hand tools having a flat metal blade attached to a handle, used for scooping or spreading plaster or similar materials. [2] a similar tool with a curved blade used by gardeners for lifting plants, etc. ◆ VERB **-els, -elling, -elled** *or US* **-els, -eling, -eled.** [3] (*tr*) to use a trowel on (plaster, soil, etc.).
▷HISTORY C14: from Old French *truele*, from Latin *trulla* a scoop, from *trua* a stirring spoon
▸ **ˈtroweller** *or* (*US*) **ˈtroweler** NOUN

Troy (trɔɪ) NOUN any of nine ancient cities in NW Asia Minor, each of which was built on the ruins of its predecessor. The seventh was the site of the Trojan War (mid-13th century B.C.). Greek name: **Ilion.** Latin name: **Ilium.** Related adjective: **Trojan.**

Troyes (*French* trwa) NOUN an industrial city in NE France: became prosperous through its great fairs in the early Middle Ages. Pop.: 59 271 (1990).

troy weight *or* **troy** (trɔɪ) NOUN a system of weights used for precious metals and gemstones, based on the grain, which is identical to the avoirdupois grain. 24 grains = 1 pennyweight; 20 pennyweights = 1 (troy) ounce; 12 ounces = 1 (troy) pound.
▷HISTORY C14: named after the city of *Troyes*, France, where it was first used

trs *Printing* ABBREVIATION FOR transpose.

Trst (trst) NOUN the Slovene and Serbo-Croat name for **Trieste.**

truant (ˈtru:ənt) NOUN [1] a person who is absent without leave, esp from school. ◆ ADJECTIVE [2] being or relating to a truant. ◆ VERB [3] (*intr*) to play truant.
▷HISTORY C13: from Old French: vagabond, probably of Celtic origin; compare Welsh *truan* miserable, Old Irish *trōg* wretched
▸ **ˈtruancy** NOUN

truce (tru:s) NOUN [1] an agreement to stop fighting, esp temporarily. [2] temporary cessation of something unpleasant.
▷HISTORY C13: from the plural of Old English *treow* TROW; see TRUE, TRUST

Trucial States (ˈtru:ʃəl) PLURAL NOUN a former name (until 1971) of the **United Arab Emirates.** Also called: **Trucial Sheikdoms, Trucial Oman, Trucial Coast.**

truck[1] (trʌk) NOUN [1] *Brit* a vehicle for carrying freight on a railway; wagon. [2] another name (esp US, Canadian, and Austral) for **lorry** (sense 1). [3] a frame carrying two or more pairs of wheels and usually springs and brakes, attached under an end of a railway coach, etc. [4] *Nautical* **a** a disc-shaped block fixed to the head of a mast having sheave holes for receiving signal halyards. **b** the head of a mast itself. [5] any wheeled vehicle used to move goods. ◆ VERB [6] to convey (goods) in a truck. [7] (*intr*) *Chiefly US and Canadian* to drive a truck.
▷HISTORY C17: perhaps shortened from TRUCKLE[2]

truck[2] (trʌk) NOUN [1] commercial goods. [2] dealings (esp in the phrase **have no truck with**). [3] commercial exchange. [4] *Archaic* payment of wages in kind. [5] miscellaneous articles. [6] *Informal* rubbish. [7] *US and Canadian* vegetables grown for market. ◆ VERB [8] *Archaic* to exchange (goods); barter. [9] (*intr*) to traffic or negotiate.
▷HISTORY C13: from Old French *troquer* (unattested) to barter, equivalent to Medieval Latin *trocare*, of unknown origin

truckage (ˈtrʌkɪdʒ) NOUN *US* [1] conveyance of cargo by truck. [2] the charge for this.

trucker[1] (ˈtrʌkə) NOUN *Chiefly US and Canadian* [1] a lorry driver. [2] a person who arranges for the transport of goods by lorry.

trucker[2] (ˈtrʌkə) NOUN *US and Canadian* [1] a market gardener. [2] another word for **hawker.**

truck farm NOUN *US and Canadian* a market garden.
▸ **truck farmer** NOUN ▸ **truck farming** NOUN

truckie (ˈtrʌkɪ) NOUN *Austral informal* a truck driver.

trucking[1] (ˈtrʌkɪŋ) NOUN *Chiefly US and Canadian* the transportation of goods by lorry.

trucking[2] (ˈtrʌkɪŋ) NOUN [1] the usual US and Canadian term for **market gardening.** [2] commercial exchange; barter.

truckle[1] (ˈtrʌkᵊl) VERB (*intr*; usually foll by *to*) to yield weakly; give in.
▷HISTORY C17: from obsolete *truckle* to sleep in a truckle bed; see TRUCKLE[2]
▸ **ˈtruckler** NOUN

truckle[2] (ˈtrʌkᵊl) NOUN [1] a small wheel; caster. [2] a small barrel-shaped cheese. ◆ VERB [3] (*intr*) to roll on truckles. [4] (*tr*) to push (a piece of furniture) along on truckles.
▷HISTORY C15 *trokel*, from Anglo-Norman *trocle*, from Latin *trochlea* sheaf of a pulley; see TROCHLEA

truckle bed NOUN a low bed on wheels, stored under a larger bed, used esp formerly by a servant.

truckload (ˈtrʌkˌləud) NOUN the amount carried by a truck.

truck system NOUN a system during the early years of the Industrial Revolution of forcing workers to accept payment of wages in kind, usually to the employer's advantage.
▷HISTORY C19: from TRUCK[2]

truculent (ˈtrʌkjulənt) ADJECTIVE [1] defiantly aggressive, sullen, or obstreperous. [2] *Archaic* savage, fierce, or harsh.
▷HISTORY C16: from Latin *truculentus*, from *trux* fierce
▸ **ˈtruculence** *or* **ˈtruculency** NOUN ▸ **ˈtruculently** ADVERB

trudge (trʌdʒ) VERB [1] (*intr*) to walk or plod heavily or wearily. [2] (*tr*) to pass through or over by trudging. ◆ NOUN [3] a long tiring walk.
▷HISTORY C16: of obscure origin
▸ **ˈtrudger** NOUN

trudgen (ˈtrʌdʒən) NOUN a type of swimming stroke that uses overarm action, as in the crawl, and a scissors kick.
▷HISTORY C19: named after John *Trudgen*, English swimmer, who introduced it

true (tru:) ADJECTIVE **truer, truest.** [1] not false, fictional, or illusory; factual or factually accurate; conforming with reality. [2] (*prenominal*) being of real or natural origin; genuine; not synthetic: *true leather.* [3] **a** unswervingly faithful and loyal to friends, a cause, etc.: *a true follower.* **b** (*as collective noun*; preceded by *the*): *the loyal and the true.* [4] faithful to a particular concept of truth, esp of religious truth: *a true believer.* [5] conforming to a required standard, law, or pattern: *a true aim; a true fit.* [6] exactly in tune: *a true note.* [7] (of a compass bearing) according to the earth's geographical rather than magnetic poles: *true north.* [8] *Biology* conforming to the typical structure of a designated type: *sphagnum moss is a true moss, Spanish moss is not.* [9] *Physics* not apparent or relative; taking into account all complicating factors: *the true expansion of a liquid takes into account the expansion of the container.* Compare **apparent** (sense 3). [10] **not true.** *Informal* unbelievable; remarkable: *she's got so much money it's not true.* [11] **true to life.** exactly comparable with reality. ◆ NOUN [12] correct alignment (esp in the phrases **in true, out of true**). ◆ ADVERB [13] truthfully; rightly. [14] precisely or unswervingly: *he shot true.* [15] *Biology* without variation from the ancestral type: *to breed true.* ◆ VERB **trues, truing, trued.** [16] (*tr*) to adjust so as to make true.
▷HISTORY Old English *triewe*; related to Old Frisian *triūwe*, Old Saxon, Old High German *triuwi* loyal, Old Norse *tryggr*; see TROW, TRUST
▸ **ˈtrueness** NOUN

true bill NOUN *Criminal law* (formerly in Britain; now only US) the endorsement made on a bill of indictment by a grand jury certifying it to be supported by sufficient evidence to warrant committing the accused to trial.

true-blue ADJECTIVE [1] unwaveringly or staunchly loyal, esp to a person, a cause, etc. ◆ NOUN **true blue.** [2] *Chiefly Brit* a staunch royalist or Conservative.

true-born ADJECTIVE being such by birth: *a true-born Japanese.*

true level NOUN a hypothetical surface that is perpendicular at every point to the plumb line, such as the mean sea level or geoid: *a still liquid surface is at true level.*

true-life ADJECTIVE directly comparable to reality: *a true-life romance.*

truelove (ˈtru:ˌlʌv) NOUN [1] someone truly loved; sweetheart. [2] another name for **herb Paris.**

truelove knot *or* **true-lovers' knot** NOUN a complicated bowknot that is hard to untie, symbolizing ties of love.

true north NOUN the direction from any point along a meridian towards the North Pole. Also called: **geographic north.** Compare **magnetic north.**

true rib NOUN any of the upper seven pairs of ribs in man.

true time NOUN the time shown by a sundial; solar time. When the sun is at the highest point in its daily path, the true time is exactly noon. Compare **mean time.**

truffle (ˈtrʌfᵊl) NOUN [1] Also called: **earthnut.** any of various edible saprotrophic ascomycetous subterranean fungi of the European genus *Tuber*. They have a tuberous appearance and are regarded as a delicacy. [2] Also called: **rum truffle.** *Chiefly Brit* a sweet resembling this fungus in shape, flavoured with chocolate or rum.
▷HISTORY C16: from French *truffe*, from Old Provençal *trufa*, ultimately from Latin *tūber*

trug (trʌg) NOUN *Brit* a long shallow basket made of curved strips of wood and used for carrying flowers, fruit, etc.
▷HISTORY C16: perhaps dialect variant of TROUGH

trugo (ˈtru:gəu) NOUN *Austral* a game similar to croquet, originally improvised in Victoria from the rubber discs used as buffers on railway carriages.
▷HISTORY from *true go*, when the wheel is hit between the goalposts

truism (ˈtru:ɪzəm) NOUN an obvious truth; platitude.
▷HISTORY C18: from TRUE + -ISM
▸ **truˈistic** ADJECTIVE

Trujillo (*Spanish* truˈxijo) NOUN a city in NW Peru: founded 1535; university (1824); centre of a district producing rice and sugar cane. Pop.: 603 657 (1998 est.).

Truk Islands (trʌk) PLURAL NOUN a group of islands in the W Pacific, in the E Caroline Islands: administratively part of the US Trust Territory of the Pacific Islands from 1947; became self-governing in 1979 as part of the Federated States of Micronesia; consists of 11 chief islands; a major Japanese naval base during World War II. Pop.: 52 870 (1994). Area: 130 sq. km (50 sq. miles).

trull (trʌl) NOUN *Archaic* a prostitute; harlot.
▷HISTORY C16: from German *Trulle*; see TROLLOP

truly (ˈtru:lɪ) ADVERB [1] in a true, just, or faithful manner. [2] (intensifier): *a truly great man.* [3] indeed; really. ◆ See also **yours truly.**

trumeau (truˈməu) NOUN, *plural* **-meaux** (-məuz). *Architect* a section of a wall or pillar between two openings.
▷HISTORY from French

trump[1] (trʌmp) NOUN [1] Also called: **trump card. a** any card from the suit chosen as trumps. **b** this suit itself; trumps. [2] Also called: **trump card.** a decisive or advantageous move, resource, action, etc. [3] *Informal* a fine or reliable person. ◆ VERB [4] to play a trump card on (a suit, or a particular card of a suit, that is not trumps). [5] (*tr*) to outdo or surpass. ◆ See also **trumps, trump up.**
▷HISTORY C16: variant of TRIUMPH
▸ **ˈtrumpless** ADJECTIVE

trump² (trʌmp) *Archaic or literary* ◆ NOUN [1] a trumpet or the sound produced by one. [2] **the last trump.** the final trumpet call that according to the belief of some will awaken and raise the dead on the Day of Judgment. ◆ VERB [3] (*intr*) to produce a sound upon or as if upon the trumpet. [4] (*tr*) to proclaim or announce with or as if with a fanfare.
▷HISTORY C13: from Old French *trompe*, from Old High German *trumpa* trumpet; compare TROMBONE

trumpery (ˈtrʌmpərɪ) NOUN, *plural* **-eries.** [1] foolish talk or actions. [2] a useless or worthless article; trinket. ◆ ADJECTIVE [3] useless or worthless.
▷HISTORY C15: from Old French *tromperie* deceit, from *tromper* to cheat

trumpet (ˈtrʌmpɪt) NOUN [1] a valved brass instrument of brilliant tone consisting of a narrow tube of cylindrical bore ending in a flared bell, normally pitched in B flat. Range: two and a half octaves upwards from F sharp on the fourth line of the bass staff. [2] any instrument consisting of a valveless tube ending in a bell, esp a straight instrument used for fanfares, signals, etc. [3] a person who plays a trumpet in an orchestra. [4] a loud sound such as that of a trumpet, esp when made by an animal: *the trumpet of the elephants.* [5] an eight-foot reed stop on an organ. [6] something resembling a trumpet in shape, esp in having a flared bell. [7] short for **ear trumpet.** [8] **blow one's own trumpet.** to boast about oneself; brag. ◆ VERB **-pets, -peting, -peted.** [9] to proclaim or sound loudly.
▷HISTORY C13: from Old French *trompette* a little TRUMP²
▸ˈ**trumpet-ˌlike** ADJECTIVE

trumpeter (ˈtrʌmpɪtə) NOUN [1] a person who plays the trumpet, esp one whose duty it is to play fanfares, signals, etc. [2] any of three birds of the genus *Psophia* of the forests of South America, having a rounded body, long legs, and a glossy blackish plumage: family *Psophiidae*, order *Gruiformes* (cranes, rails, etc.). [3] (*sometimes capital*) a breed of domestic fancy pigeon with a long ruff.

trumpeter swan NOUN a large swan, *Cygnus buccinator*, of W North America, having a white plumage and black bill.

trumpet flower NOUN [1] any of various plants having trumpet-shaped flowers. [2] the flower of any of these plants.

trumpet honeysuckle NOUN a North American honeysuckle shrub, *Lonicera sempervirens*, having orange, scarlet, or yellow trumpet-shaped flowers.

trumpet vine NOUN either of two bignoniaceous vines, *Campsis radicans* of the eastern US or *C. grandiflora* of E Asia, with clumps of trumpet-shaped flowers: grown as ornamentals. Also called: **trumpet climber, trumpet flower.**

trumpetweed (ˈtrʌmpɪtˌwiːd) NOUN *US* any of various eupatorium plants, esp joe-pye weed.
▷HISTORY C19: so called because it has a hollow stem which children sometimes use as imitation trumpets

trumps (trʌmps) PLURAL NOUN [1] (*sometimes singular*) *Cards* any one of the four suits, decided by cutting or bidding, that outranks all the other suits for the duration of a deal or game. [2] **turn up trumps.** (of a person) to bring about a happy or successful conclusion (to an event, problem, etc.), esp unexpectedly.

trump up VERB (*tr, adverb*) to concoct or invent (a charge, accusation, etc.) so as to deceive or implicate someone.

truncate VERB (trʌŋˈkeɪt, ˈtrʌŋkeɪt) [1] (*tr*) to shorten by cutting off a part, end, or top. ◆ ADJECTIVE (ˈtrʌŋkeɪt) [2] cut short; truncated. [3] *Biology* having a blunt end, as though cut off at the tip: *a truncate leaf.*
▷HISTORY C15: from Latin *truncāre* to lop
▸ˈ**truncately** ADVERB ▸**trunˈcation** NOUN

truncated (trʌŋˈkeɪtɪd) ADJECTIVE [1] *Maths* (of a cone, pyramid, prism, etc.) having an apex or end removed by a plane intersection that is usually nonparallel to the base. [2] (of a crystal) having edges or corners cut off. [3] shortened by or as if by cutting off; truncate.

truncheon (ˈtrʌntʃən) NOUN [1] *Chiefly Brit* a short thick club or cudgel carried by a policeman. [2] a baton of office: *a marshal's truncheon.* [3] *Archaic* a short club or cudgel. [4] the shaft of a spear. ◆ VERB [5] (*tr*) to beat with a truncheon.
▷HISTORY C16: from Old French *tronchon* stump, from Latin *truncus* trunk; see TRUNCATE

trundle (ˈtrʌndᵊl) VERB [1] to move heavily on or as if on wheels: *the bus trundled by.* [2] (*tr*) *Archaic* to rotate or spin. ◆ NOUN [3] the act or an instance of trundling. [4] a small wheel or roller. [5] **a** the pinion of a lantern. **b** any of the bars in a lantern pinion. [6] a small truck with low wheels.
▷HISTORY Old English *tryndel*; related to Middle High German *trendel* disc

trundle bed NOUN a less common word for **truckle bed.**

trundler (ˈtrʌndlə) NOUN *NZ* [1] a golf bag or shopping trolley. [2] a child's pushchair.

trunk (trʌŋk) NOUN [1] the main stem of a tree, usually thick and upright, covered with bark and having branches at some distance from the ground. [2] a large strong case or box used to contain clothes and other personal effects when travelling and for storage. [3] *Anatomy* the body excluding the head, neck, and limbs; torso. [4] the elongated prehensile nasal part of an elephant; proboscis. [5] the US and Canadian name for **boot¹** (sense 2). [6] *Anatomy* the main stem of a nerve, blood vessel, etc. [7] *Nautical* a watertight boxlike cover within a vessel with its top above the waterline, such as one used to enclose a centreboard. [8] an enclosed duct or passageway for ventilation, etc. [9] (*modifier*) of or relating to a main road, railway, etc., in a network: *a trunk line.* ◆ See also **trunks.**
▷HISTORY C15: from Old French *tronc*, from Latin *truncus*, from *truncus* (adj) lopped
▸ˈ**trunkˌful** NOUN ▸ˈ**trunkless** ADJECTIVE

trunk cabin NOUN *Nautical* a long relatively low cabin above the deck of a yacht.

trunk call NOUN *Chiefly Brit* a long-distance telephone call.

trunk curl NOUN another name for **sit-up.**

trunkfish (ˈtrʌŋkˌfɪʃ) NOUN, *plural* **-fish** *or* **-fishes.** any tropical plectognath fish of the family *Ostraciidae*, having the body encased in bony plates with openings for the fins, eyes, mouth, etc. Also called: **boxfish, cowfish.**

trunk hose NOUN a man's puffed-out breeches reaching to the thighs and worn with tights in the 16th century.
▷HISTORY C17: of uncertain origin; perhaps from the obsolete *trunk* to truncate

trunking (ˈtrʌŋkɪŋ) NOUN [1] *Telecomm* the cables that take a common route through an exchange building linking ranks of selectors. [2] plastic housing used to conceal wires, etc.; casing. [3] the delivery of goods over long distances, esp by road vehicles to local distribution centres, from which deliveries and collections are made.

trunk line NOUN [1] a direct link between two telephone exchanges or switchboards that are a considerable distance apart. [2] the main route or routes on a railway.

trunk road NOUN *Brit* a main road, esp one that is suitable for heavy vehicles.

trunks (trʌŋks) PLURAL NOUN [1] Also called: **swimming trunks.** a man's garment worn for swimming, either fairly loose and extending from the waist to the thigh or briefer and close-fitting. [2] shorts worn for some sports. [3] *Chiefly Brit* men's underpants with legs that reach midthigh.

trunnel (ˈtrʌnᵊl) NOUN a variant spelling of **treenail.**

trunnion (ˈtrʌnjən) NOUN [1] one of a pair of coaxial projections attached to opposite sides of a container, cannon, etc., to provide a support about which it can turn in a vertical. [2] the structure supporting such a projection.
▷HISTORY C17: from Old French *trognon* trunk
▸ˈ**trunnioned** ADJECTIVE

Truro (ˈtrʊərəʊ) NOUN a market town in SW England, administrative centre of Cornwall. Pop.: 18 966 (1991).

truss (trʌs) VERB tr. [1] (sometimes foll by *up*) to tie, bind, or bundle: *to truss up a prisoner.* [2] to fasten or bind the wings and legs of (a fowl) before cooking to keep them in place. [3] to support or stiffen (a roof, bridge, etc.) with structural members. [4] *Informal* to confine (the body or a part of it) in tight clothes. [5] *Falconry* (of falcons) to hold (the quarry) in the stoop without letting go. [6] *Med* to supply or support with a truss. ◆ NOUN [7] a structural framework of wood or metal, esp one arranged in triangles, used to support a roof, bridge, etc. [8] *Med* a device for holding a hernia in place, typically consisting of a pad held in position by a belt. [9] *Horticulture* a cluster of flowers or fruit growing at the end of a single stalk. [10] *Nautical* a metal fitting fixed to a yard at its centre for holding it to a mast while allowing movement. [11] *Architect* another name for **corbel.** [12] a bundle or pack. [13] *Chiefly Brit* a bundle of hay or straw, esp one having a fixed weight of 36, 56, or 60 pounds.
▷HISTORY C13: from Old French *trousse*, from *trousser*, apparently from Vulgar Latin *torciāre* (unattested), from *torca* (unattested) a bundle, TORCH
▸ˈ**trusser** NOUN

truss bridge NOUN a bridge that is constructed of trusses.

trussing (ˈtrʌsɪŋ) NOUN *Engineering* [1] a system of trusses, esp for strengthening or reinforcing a structure. [2] the parts or members that form a truss.

trust (trʌst) NOUN [1] reliance on and confidence in the truth, worth, reliability, etc., of a person or thing; faith. Related adjective: **fiducial.** [2] a group of commercial enterprises combined to monopolize and control the market for any commodity: illegal in the US. [3] the obligation of someone in a responsible position: *a position of trust.* [4] custody, charge, or care: *a child placed in my trust.* [5] a person or thing in which confidence or faith is placed. [6] commercial credit. [7] **a** an arrangement whereby a person to whom the legal title to property is conveyed (the trustee) holds such property for the benefit of those entitled to the beneficial interest. **b** property that is the subject of such an arrangement. **c** the confidence put in the trustee. Related adjective: **fiduciary.** [8] (in the British National Health Service) a self-governing hospital, group of hospitals, or other body providing health-care services, which operates as an independent commercial unit within the NHS. [9] See **trust company, trust account** (sense 2). [10] (*modifier*) of or relating to a trust or trusts: *trust property.* ◆ VERB [11] (*tr; may take a clause as object*) to expect, hope, or suppose: *I trust that you are well.* [12] (when *tr, may take an infinitive;* when *intr,* often foll by *in* or *to*) to place confidence in (someone to do something); have faith (in); rely (upon): *I trust him to tell her.* [13] (*tr*) to consign for care: *the child was trusted to my care.* [14] (*tr*) to allow (someone to do something) with confidence in his or her good sense or honesty: *I trust my daughter to go.* [15] (*tr*) to extend business credit to.
▷HISTORY C13: from Old Norse *traust*; related to Old High German *trost* solace
▸ˈ**trustable** ADJECTIVE ▸ˌ**trustaˈbility** NOUN ▸ˈ**truster** NOUN

trust account NOUN [1] Also called: **trustee account.** a savings account deposited in the name of a trustee who controls it during his lifetime, after which the balance is payable to a prenominated beneficiary. [2] property under the control of a trustee or trustees.

trustafarian (ˌtrʌstəˈfɛərɪən) NOUN (*sometimes capital*) *Brit informal* a young person from a wealthy background whose trust fund enables him or her to eschew conventional attitudes to work, dress, drug taking, etc.
▷HISTORY C20: from TRUST (FUND) + (RAST)AFARIAN

trustbuster (ˈtrʌstˌbʌstə) NOUN *US informal* a person who seeks the dissolution of corporate trusts, esp a federal official who prosecutes trusts under the antitrust laws.
▸ˈ**trustˌbusting** NOUN

trust company NOUN a commercial bank or other enterprise organized to perform trustee functions. Also called: **trust corporation.**

trust deed NOUN a document that transfers the legal title to property to a trustee.

trustee (trʌˈstiː) NOUN [1] a person to whom the legal title to property is entrusted to hold or use for another's benefit. [2] a member of a board that manages the affairs and administers the funds of an institution or organization.

trustee in bankruptcy NOUN a person entrusted with the administration of a bankrupt's affairs and with realizing his assets for the benefit of the creditors.

trustee investment NOUN *Stock Exchange* an investment in which trustees are authorized to invest money belonging to a trust fund.

trusteeship (trʌ'sti:ʃɪp) NOUN [1] the office or function of a trustee. [2] **a** the administration or government of a territory by a foreign country under the supervision of the **Trusteeship Council** of the United Nations. **b** (*often capital*) any such dependent territory; trust territory.

trustful ('trʌstfʊl) *or* **trusting** ADJECTIVE characterized by a tendency or readiness to trust others.
▸ **'trustfully** *or* **'trustingly** ADVERB ▸ **'trustfulness** *or* **'trustingness** NOUN

trust fund NOUN money, securities, etc., held in trust.

trust hotel *or* **tavern** NOUN *NZ* a licensed hotel or a bar owned by a publicly elected committee as trustees, the profits of which go to public amenities.

trustless ('trʌstlɪs) ADJECTIVE *Archaic or literary* [1] untrustworthy; deceitful. [2] distrusting; suspicious; wary.
▸ **'trustlessly** ADVERB ▸ **'trustlessness** NOUN

trust territory NOUN (*sometimes capital*) another name for a **trusteeship** (sense 2).

trustworthy ('trʌstˌwɜːðɪ) ADJECTIVE worthy of being trusted; honest, reliable, or dependable.
▸ **'trustˌworthily** ADVERB ▸ **'trustˌworthiness** NOUN

trusty ('trʌstɪ) ADJECTIVE **trustier, trustiest.** [1] faithful or reliable. [2] *Archaic* trusting. ◆ NOUN, *plural* **trusties.** [3] someone who is trusted, esp a convict to whom special privileges are granted.
▸ **'trustily** ADVERB ▸ **'trustiness** NOUN

truth (truːθ) NOUN [1] the quality of being true, genuine, actual, or factual: *the truth of his statement was attested.* [2] something that is true as opposed to false: *you did not tell me the truth.* [3] a proven or verified principle or statement; fact: *the truths of astronomy.* [4] (*usually plural*) a system of concepts purporting to represent some aspect of the world: *the truths of ancient religions.* [5] fidelity to a required standard or law. [6] faithful reproduction or portrayal: *the truth of a portrait.* [7] an obvious fact; truism; platitude. [8] honesty, reliability, or veracity: *the truth of her nature.* [9] accuracy, as in the setting, adjustment, or position of something, such as a mechanical instrument. [10] the state or quality of being faithful; allegiance. ◆ Related adjectives: **veritable, veracious.**
▷ **HISTORY** Old English *triewth*; related to Old High German *gitriuwida* fidelity, Old Norse *tryggr* true
▸ **'truthless** ADJECTIVE

truth-condition NOUN *Logic, philosophy* [1] the circumstances under which a statement is true. [2] a statement of these circumstances: sometimes identified with the meaning of the statement.

truth drug *or* **serum** NOUN *Informal* any of various drugs supposed to have the property of making people tell the truth, as by relaxing them.

truthful ('truːθfʊl) ADJECTIVE [1] telling or expressing the truth; honest or candid. [2] realistic: *a truthful portrayal of the king.*
▸ **'truthfully** ADVERB ▸ **'truthfulness** NOUN

truth-function NOUN *Logic* [1] a function that determines the truth-value of a complex sentence solely in terms of the truth-values of the component sentences without reference to their meaning. [2] a complex sentence whose truth-value is so determined, such as a negation or conjunction.

truth set NOUN [1] *Logic, maths* Also called: **solution set.** the set of values that satisfy an open sentence, equation, inequality, etc., having no unique solution. [2] *Logic* the set of possible worlds in which a statement is true.

truth table NOUN [1] a table, used in logic, indicating the truth-value of a compound statement for every truth-value of its component propositions. [2] a similar table, used in transistor technology, to indicate the value of the output signal of a logic circuit for every value of input signal.

truth-value NOUN *Logic* **a** either of the values, true or false, that may be taken by a statement. **b** by analogy, any of the values that a semantic theory may accord to a statement.

truth-value gap NOUN *Logic* the possibility in certain semantic systems of a statement being neither true nor false while also not being determinately of any third truth-value, as *all my children are asleep* uttered by a childless person.

try (traɪ) VERB **tries, trying, tried.** [1] (when *tr, may take an infinitive,* sometimes with *to* replaced by *and*) to make an effort or attempt: *he tried to climb a cliff.* [2] (*tr;* often foll by *out*) to sample, test, or give experimental use to (something) in order to determine its quality, worth, etc.: *try her cheese flan.* [3] (*tr*) to put strain or stress on: *he tries my patience.* [4] (*tr; often passive*) to give pain, affliction, or vexation to: *I have been sorely tried by those children.* [5] **a** to examine and determine the issues involved in (a cause) in a court of law. **b** to hear evidence in order to determine the guilt or innocence of (an accused). **c** to sit as judge at the trial of (an issue or person). [6] (*tr*) to melt (fat, lard, etc.) in order to separate out impurities. [7] (*tr;* usually foll by *out*) *Obsolete* to extract (a material) from an ore, mixture, etc., usually by heat; refine. ◆ NOUN, *plural* **tries.** [8] an experiment or trial. [9] an attempt or effort. [10] *Rugby* the act of an attacking player touching the ball down behind the opposing team's goal line, scoring five or, in Rugby League, four points. [11] Also called: **try for a point.** *American football* an attempt made after a touchdown to score an extra point by kicking a goal or, for two extra points, by running the ball or completing a pass across the opponents' goal line.
▷ **HISTORY** C13: from Old French *trier* to sort, sift, of uncertain origin

> **Language note** The use of *and* instead of *to* after *try* is very common, but should be avoided in formal writing: *we must try to prevent* (not *try and prevent*) *this happening.*

trying ('traɪɪŋ) ADJECTIVE upsetting, difficult, or annoying: *a trying day at the office.*
▸ **'tryingly** ADVERB ▸ **'tryingness** NOUN

trying plane NOUN a plane with a long body for planing the edges of long boards.

tryma ('traɪmə) NOUN, *plural* **-mata** (-mətə). *Botany* a drupe produced by the walnut and similar plants, in which the endocarp is a hard shell and the epicarp is dehiscent.
▷ **HISTORY** C19: from New Latin, from Greek *truma* a hole (referring to the hollow drupe), from *truein* to wear away

try on VERB (*tr, adverb*) [1] to put on (an article of clothing) to find out whether it fits or is suitable. [2] **try it on.** *Informal* to attempt to deceive or fool someone. ◆ NOUN **try-on.** [3] *Brit informal* an action or statement made to test out a person's gullibility, tolerance, etc.

try out VERB (*adverb*) [1] (*tr*) to test or put to experimental use: *I'm going to try the new car out.* [2] (when *intr,* usually foll by *for*) *US and Canadian* (of an athlete, actor, etc.) to undergo a test or to submit (an athlete, actor, etc.) to a test to determine suitability for a place in a team, an acting role, etc. ◆ NOUN **tryout.** [3] *Chiefly US and Canadian* a trial or test, as of an athlete or actor.

trypan blue ('trɪpən, 'trɪpæn, trɪ'pæn) NOUN a dye obtained from tolidine that is absorbed by the macrophages of the reticuloendothelial system and is therefore used for staining cells in biological research.
▷ **HISTORY** so called because it is *trypano-cidal*: see TRYPANOSOME, -CIDE

trypanosome ('trɪpənəˌsəʊm) NOUN any parasitic flagellate protozoan of the genus *Trypanosoma,* which lives in the blood of vertebrates, is transmitted by certain insects, and causes sleeping sickness and certain other diseases.
▷ **HISTORY** C19: from New Latin *Trypanosoma,* from Greek *trupanon* borer + *sōma* body
▸ **ˌtrypano'somal** *or* **trypanosomic** (ˌtrɪpənə'sɒmɪk) ADJECTIVE

trypanosomiasis (ˌtrɪpənəsə'maɪəsɪs) NOUN any infection of an animal or human with a trypanosome. See also **sleeping sickness, Chagas' disease.**

tryparsamide (trɪ'pɑːsəmɪd) NOUN a synthetic crystalline compound of arsenic used in the treatment of trypanosomal and other protozoan infections. Formula: $C_8H_{10}AsN_2O_4Na.\ \frac{1}{2}H_2O$.
▷ **HISTORY** C20: from a trademark

trypsin ('trɪpsɪn) NOUN an enzyme occurring in pancreatic juice: it catalyses the hydrolysis of proteins to peptides and is secreted from the pancreas in the form of trypsinogen. See also **chymotrypsin.**
▷ **HISTORY** C19 *tryp-,* from Greek *tripsis* a rubbing, from *tribein* to rub + -IN; referring to the fact that it was originally produced by rubbing the pancreas with glycerine
▸ **tryptic** ('trɪptɪk) ADJECTIVE

trypsinogen (trɪp'sɪnədʒən) NOUN the inactive precursor of trypsin that is converted to trypsin by the enzyme enterokinase.

tryptophan ('trɪptəˌfæn) NOUN an essential amino acid; a component of proteins necessary for growth.
▷ **HISTORY** C20: from TRYPT(IC) + -O + *-phan* variant of -PHANE

trysail ('traɪˌseɪl; *Nautical* 'traɪsᵊl) NOUN a small fore-and-aft sail, triangular or square, set on the mainmast of a sailing vessel in foul weather to help keep her head to the wind. Also called: **storm trysail.**

try square NOUN a device for testing or laying out right angles, usually consisting of a metal blade fixed at right angles to a wooden handle.

tryst (trɪst, traɪst) *Archaic or literary* ◆ NOUN [1] an appointment to meet, esp secretly. [2] the place of such a meeting or the meeting itself. ◆ VERB [3] (*intr*) to meet at or arrange a tryst.
▷ **HISTORY** C14: from Old French *triste* lookout post, apparently of Scandinavian origin; compare Old Norse *traust* trust
▸ **'tryster** NOUN

tsade ('tsɑːdiː, 'sɑː-; *Hebrew* 'tsadi) NOUN a variant spelling of **sadhe.**

Tsana ('tsɑːnə) NOUN **Lake.** another name for (Lake) **Tana.**

tsantsa ('tsæntsə) NOUN (among the Shuar subgroup of the Jivaro people of Ecuador) the shrunken head of an enemy kept as a trophy.
▷ **HISTORY** from Shuar

tsar *or* **czar** (zɑː, tsɑː) NOUN [1] (until 1917) the emperor of Russia. [2] a tyrant; autocrat. [3] *Informal* a public official charged with responsibility for dealing with a certain problem or issue: *a drugs tsar.* [4] *Informal* a person in authority; leader. [5] (formerly) any of several S Slavonic rulers, such as any of the princes of Serbia in the 14th century. Also (less commonly): **tzar.**
▷ **HISTORY** from Russian *tsar,* via Gothic *kaisar* from Latin: from *Caesar* emperor, from the cognomen of Gaius Julius Caesar (100–44 B.C.), Roman general, statesman, and historian
▸ **'tsardom** *or* **'czardom** NOUN

tsarevitch *or* **czarevitch** ('zɑːrəvɪtʃ) NOUN a son of a Russian tsar, esp the eldest son.
▷ **HISTORY** from Russian *tsarevich,* from TSAR + *-evich,* masculine patronymic suffix

tsarevna *or* **czarevna** (zɑː'rɛvnə) NOUN [1] a daughter of a Russian tsar. [2] the wife of a Russian tsarevitch.
▷ **HISTORY** from Russian, from TSAR + *-evna,* feminine patronymic suffix

tsarina, czarina (zɑː'riːnə), **tsaritsa,** *or* **czaritza** (zɑː'rɪtsə) NOUN the wife of a Russian tsar; Russian empress.
▷ **HISTORY** from Italian, Spanish *czarina,* from German *Czarin*

tsarism *or* **czarism** ('zɑːrɪzəm) NOUN [1] a system of government by a tsar, esp in Russia until 1917. [2] absolute rule; dictatorship.
▸ **'tsarist** *or* **'czarist** NOUN, ADJECTIVE

Tsaritsyn (*Russian* tsa'ritsin) NOUN a former name (until 1925) of **Volgograd.**

TSB ABBREVIATION FOR (the former) Trustee Savings Bank, now incorporated in Lloyds TSB.

TSE ABBREVIATION FOR: [1] transmissible spongiform encephalopathy: any of a group of degenerative brain diseases, including BSE in cattle, that can be transmitted from one individual or species to another. [2] Toronto Stock Exchange.

Tselinograd (*Russian* tsəlɪna'grat) NOUN a former name (1961–94) for **Akmola.**

tsetse fly *or* **tzetze fly** ('tsɛtsɪ) NOUN any of various bloodsucking African dipterous flies of the

genus *Glossina*, which transmit the pathogens of various diseases: family *Muscidae*.
▷HISTORY C19: via Afrikaans from Tswana

TSH ABBREVIATION FOR thyroid-stimulating hormone; another name for **thyrotropin**.

Tshiluba (tʃɪˈluːbə) NOUN the language of the Luba people, used as a trade language in the Democratic Republic of Congo (formerly Zaïre). See **Luba**.

T-shirt *or* **tee shirt** NOUN a lightweight simple garment for the upper body, usually short-sleeved.
▷HISTORY so called because of its shape

Tsimshian (ˈtʃɪmʃɪən) NOUN [1] a member of a Native Canadian people of northern British Columbia. [2] the Penutian language of this people.
▷HISTORY C19: from Tsimshian, inside the Skeena River

Tsinan (ˈtsiːˈnæn) NOUN a variant transliteration of the Chinese name for **Jinan**.

Tsinghai (ˈtsɪŋˈhaɪ) NOUN [1] a variant transliteration of the Chinese name for **Qinghai**. [2] a variant transliteration of the Chinese name for **Koko Nor**.

Tsingtao (ˈtsɪŋˈtaʊ) NOUN a variant transliteration of the Chinese name for **Qingdao**.

Tsingyuan (ˈtsɪŋˈjwɑːn) *or* **Ch'ing-yüan** NOUN the former name of **Baoding**.

Tsitsihar (ˈtsɪtsɪˌhɑː) NOUN a variant transliteration of the Chinese name for **Qiqihar**.

tsitsith (ˈtsɪtsɪs, tsiːˈtsiːt) NOUN (*functioning as singular or plural*) *Judaism* the tassels or fringes of thread attached to the four corners of the tallith.
▷HISTORY from Hebrew *sīsīth*

Tskhinvali (ˈtskɪnˌvɑːlɪ) NOUN the Georgian name for **South Ossetia**.

TSO ABBREVIATION FOR The Stationery Office, formerly His (or Her) Majesty's Stationery Office.

Tsonga (ˈtsɒŋgə) NOUN [1] (*plural* **-ga** *or* **-gas**) a member of a Negroid people of S Mozambique, Swaziland, and South Africa. [2] the language of this people, belonging to the Bantu group of the Niger-Congo family.

tsotsi (ˈtsɒtsɪ, ˈtsɔː-) NOUN, *plural* **-tsis**. a Black street thug or gang member; wide boy.
▷HISTORY C20: perhaps from Nguni *tsotsa* to dress flashily

tsotsitaal (ˈtsɔːtsɪˌtɑːl) NOUN *South African* a type of street slang used by tsotsis.
▷HISTORY C20: from Nguni *tsotsi* thug + Afrikaans *taal* language

tsp. ABBREVIATION FOR teaspoon.

T-square NOUN a T-shaped ruler used in mechanical drawing, consisting of a short crosspiece, which slides along the edge of the drawing board, and a long horizontal piece: used for drawing horizontal lines and to support set squares when drawing vertical and inclined lines.

T-stop NOUN a setting of the lens aperture on a camera calibrated photometrically and assigned a T-number.

T-strap NOUN (*modifier*) denoting a type of woman's shoe fastened with a T-shaped strap having one part passing across the ankle and the other attached to it in the middle and lying along the length of the foot. Also called: **T-bar**.

Tsugaru Strait (ˈtsugɑˌru) NOUN a channel between N Honshu and S Hokkaido islands, Japan. Width: about 30 km (20 miles).

tsunami (tsʊˈnæmɪ) NOUN, *plural* **-mis** *or* **-mi**. [1] a large, often destructive, sea wave produced by a submarine earthquake, subsidence, or volcanic eruption. Sometimes incorrectly called a tidal wave. [2] a sudden increase in or overwhelming number or volume of: *the tsunami of Olympic visitors*.
▷HISTORY from Japanese, from *tsu* port + *nami* wave

Tsushima (ˈtsuːʃiːˌmɑː) NOUN a group of five rocky islands between Japan and South Korea, in the Korea Strait: administratively part of Japan; scene of a naval defeat for the Russians (1905) during the Russo-Japanese war. Pop.: 50 810 (latest est.). Area: 698 sq. km (269 sq. miles).

tsutsugamushi disease (ˌtsʊtsʊgəˈmʊʃɪ) NOUN [1] one of the five major groups of acute infectious rickettsial diseases affecting man, common in Asia and including scrub typhus. It is caused by the microorganism *Rickettsia tsutsugamushi*, transmitted by the bite of mites. [2] another name for **scrub typhus**.
▷HISTORY from Japanese, from *tsutsuga* disease + *mushi* insect

Tswana (ˈtswɑːnə) NOUN [1] (*plural* **-na**, **-nas**) a member of a mixed Negroid and Bushman people of the Sotho group of southern Africa, living chiefly in Botswana. [2] the language of this people, belonging to the Bantu group of the Niger-Congo family: the principal language of Botswana.

tt THE INTERNET DOMAIN NAME FOR Trinidad and Tobago.

TT ABBREVIATION FOR: [1] teetotal. [2] teetotaller. [3] telegraphic transfer: a method of sending money abroad by cabled transfer between banks. [4] Tourist Trophy (annual motorcycle races held in the Isle of Man). [5] tuberculin-tested. ◆ [6] INTERNATIONAL CAR REGISTRATION FOR Trinidad and Tobago.

TTA (in Britain) ABBREVIATION FOR Teacher Training Agency.

TTFN ABBREVIATION FOR ta-ta for now.

TTL ABBREVIATION FOR: [1] transistor transistor logic: a method of constructing electronic logic circuits. [2] through-the-lens: denoting a system of light metering in cameras.

TTYL *Text messaging* ABBREVIATION FOR talk to you later.

TU ABBREVIATION FOR trade union.

Tuamotu Archipelago (ˌtuːəˈməʊtuː) NOUN a group of about 80 coral islands in the S Pacific, in French Polynesia. Pop.: 15 370 (1996). Area: 860 sq. km (332 sq. miles). Also called: **Low Archipelago, Paumotu Archipelago**.

tuan[1] (ˈtuːɑːn) NOUN (in Malay-speaking countries) sir; lord: a form of address used as a mark of respect.
▷HISTORY Malay

tuan[2] (ˈtuːən, ˈtjuː-) NOUN a flying phalanger, *Phascogale tapoatafa*, of Australia. It is about the size of a rat, bluish grey in colour, brush-tailed, arboreal, and nocturnal. Also called: **wambenger, brush-tailed phascogale, phascogale**.
▷HISTORY C19: from a native Australian language

Tuareg (ˈtwɑːrɛg) NOUN [1] (*plural*) **-reg** *or* **-regs** a member of a nomadic Berber people of the Sahara. [2] the dialect of Berber spoken by this people.

tuart (ˈtuːɑːt) NOUN a eucalyptus tree, *Eucalyptus gomphocephala*, of Australia, yielding a very durable light-coloured timber.
▷HISTORY from a native Australian language

tuatara (ˌtuːəˈtɑːrə) NOUN a greenish-grey lizard-like rhynchocephalian reptile, *Sphenodon punctatus*, occurring only on certain small islands near New Zealand: it is the sole surviving member of a group common in Mesozoic times.
▷HISTORY C19: from Maori, from *tua* back + *tara* spine

tub (tʌb) NOUN [1] a low wide open container, typically round, originally one made of wood and used esp for washing: now made of wood, plastic, metal, etc., and used in a variety of domestic and industrial situations. [2] a small plastic or cardboard container of similar shape for ice cream, margarine, etc. [3] Also called: **bathtub**. another word (esp US and Canadian) for **bath**[1] (sense 1). [4] Also called: **tubful**. the amount a tub will hold. [5] a clumsy slow boat or ship. [6] *Informal* (in rowing) a heavy wide boat used for training novice oarsmen. [7] Also called: **tram, hutch**. **a** a small vehicle on rails for carrying loads in a mine. **b** a container for lifting coal or ore up a mine shaft; skip. ◆ VERB **tubs, tubbing, tubbed**. [8] *Brit informal* to wash (oneself or another) in a tub. [9] (*tr*) to keep or put in a tub.
▷HISTORY C14: from Middle Dutch *tubbe*
▸ˈ**tubbable** ADJECTIVE ▸ˈ**tubber** NOUN

tuba (ˈtjuːbə) NOUN, *plural* **-bas** *or* **-bae** (-biː). [1] a valved brass instrument of bass pitch, in which the bell points upwards and the mouthpiece projects at right angles. The tube is of conical bore and the mouthpiece cup-shaped. [2] any other bass brass instrument such as the euphonium, helicon, etc. [3] a powerful reed stop on an organ. [4] a form of trumpet of ancient Rome.
▷HISTORY Latin

tubal (ˈtjuːbᵊl) ADJECTIVE [1] of or relating to a tube. [2] of, relating to, or developing in a Fallopian tube: *a tubal pregnancy*.

Tubal-cain (ˈtjuːbᵊlˌkeɪn) NOUN *Old Testament* a son of Lamech, said in Genesis 4:22 to be the first artificer of metals.

tubal ligation NOUN the tying of the Fallopian tubes as a method of sterilization.

tubate (ˈtjuːbeɪt) ADJECTIVE a less common word for **tubular**.

tubby (ˈtʌbɪ) ADJECTIVE **-bier, -biest**. [1] plump. [2] shaped like a tub. [3] *Rare* having little resonance.
▸ˈ**tubbiness** NOUN

tube (tjuːb) NOUN [1] a long hollow and typically cylindrical object, used for the passage of fluids or as a container. [2] a collapsible cylindrical container of soft metal or plastic closed with a cap, used to hold viscous liquids or pastes. [3] *Anatomy* **a** short for **Eustachian tube** or **Fallopian tube**. **b** any hollow cylindrical structure. [4] *Botany* **a** the lower part of a gamopetalous corolla or gamosepalous calyx, below the lobes. **b** any other hollow structure in a plant. [5] *Brit* **the tube**. **a** Also called: **the underground**. an underground railway system. US and Canadian equivalent: **subway**. **b** the tunnels through which the railway runs. **c** the train itself. **d** (*capital*) *Trademark* the London underground railway system. [6] *Electronics* **a** another name for **valve** (sense 3). **b** See **electron tube, cathode-ray tube, television tube**. [7] (preceded by *the*) *Slang* a television set. [8] *Austral slang* a bottle or can of beer. [9] *Surfing* the cylindrical passage formed when a wave breaks and the crest tips forward. [10] an archaic word for **telescope**. ◆ VERB (*tr*) [11] to fit or supply with a tube or tubes. [12] to carry or convey in a tube. [13] to shape like a tube.
▷HISTORY C17: from Latin *tubus*
▸ˈ**tube-like** ADJECTIVE

tube fly NOUN *Angling* an artificial fly with the body tied on a hollow tube that can slide up the leader when a fish takes.

tube foot NOUN any of numerous tubular outgrowths of the body wall of most echinoderms that are used as organs of locomotion and respiration and to aid ingestion of food.

tubeless tyre NOUN a pneumatic tyre in which the outer casing makes an airtight seal with the rim of the wheel so that an inner tube is unnecessary.

tuber (ˈtjuːbə) NOUN [1] a fleshy underground stem (as in the potato) or root (as in the dahlia) that is an organ of vegetative reproduction and food storage. [2] *Anatomy* a raised area; swelling.
▷HISTORY C17: from Latin *tūber* hump

tubercle (ˈtjuːbəkᵊl) NOUN [1] any small rounded nodule or elevation, esp on the skin, on a bone, or on a plant. [2] any small rounded pathological lesion of the tissues, esp one characteristic of tuberculosis.
▷HISTORY C16: from Latin *tūberculum* a little swelling, diminutive of TUBER

tubercle bacillus NOUN a rodlike Gram-positive bacterium, *Mycobacterium tuberculosis*, that causes tuberculosis: family *Mycobacteriaceae*.

tubercular (tjʊˈbɜːkjʊlə) ADJECTIVE [1] of, relating to, or symptomatic of tuberculosis. [2] of or relating to a tubercle or tubercles. [3] characterized by the presence of tubercles. ◆ NOUN [4] a person with tuberculosis.
▸**tuˈbercularly** ADVERB

tuberculate (tjʊˈbɜːkjʊlɪt) ADJECTIVE covered with tubercles.
▸**tuˈberculately** ADVERB ▸**tuˌbercuˈlation** NOUN

tuberculin (tjʊˈbɜːkjʊlɪn) NOUN a sterile liquid prepared from cultures of attenuated tubercle bacillus and used in the diagnosis of tuberculosis.

tuberculin-tested ADJECTIVE (of milk) produced by cows that have been certified as free of tuberculosis.

tuberculosis (tjʊˌbɜːkjʊˈləʊsɪs) NOUN a communicable disease caused by infection with the tubercle bacillus, most frequently affecting the lungs (**pulmonary tuberculosis**). Also called: **consumption, phthisis**. Abbreviation: **TB**.
▷HISTORY C19: from New Latin; see TUBERCLE, -OSIS

tuberculous (tjʊˈbɜːkjʊləs) ADJECTIVE of or relating to tuberculosis or tubercles; tubercular.
▸**tuˈberculously** ADVERB

tuberose NOUN (ˈtjuːbəˌrəʊz) [1] a perennial Mexican agave plant, *Polianthes tuberosa*, having a tuberous root and spikes of white fragrant lily-like

flowers. ◆ ADJECTIVE ('tju:bəˌrəʊs) [2] a variant of **tuberous.**
▷HISTORY C17: from Latin *tūberōsus* full of lumps; referring to its root

tuberosity (ˌtju:bə'rɒsɪtɪ) NOUN, *plural* **-ties.** any protuberance on a bone, esp for the attachment of a muscle or ligament.

tuberous ('tju:bərəs) *or* **tuberose** ('tju:bəˌrəʊs) ADJECTIVE [1] (of plants or their parts) forming, bearing, or resembling a tuber or tubers: *a tuberous root.* [2] *Anatomy* of, relating to, or having warty protuberances or tubers.
▷HISTORY C17: from Latin *tūberōsus* full of knobs; see TUBER

tube worm NOUN any of various polychaete worms that construct and live in a tube made of sand, lime, etc.

tubicolous (tju:'bɪkələs) ADJECTIVE (of certain invertebrate animals) living in a self-constructed tube.

tubifex ('tju:bɪˌfɛks) NOUN, *plural* **-fex** *or* **-fexes.** any small reddish freshwater oligochaete worm of the genus *Tubifex;* it characteristically lives in a tube in sand and is used as food for aquarium fish.
▷HISTORY C19: from New Latin, from Latin *tubus* tube + *facere* to make, do

tubing ('tju:bɪŋ) NOUN [1] tubes collectively. [2] a length of tube. [3] a system of tubes. [4] fabric in the form of a tube, used for pillowcases and some cushions; piping.

Tübingen ('tju:bɪŋən) NOUN a town in SW Germany, in Baden-Württemberg: university (1477). Pop.: 76 040 (latest est.).

tub-thumper NOUN a noisy, violent, or ranting public speaker.

tub-thumping ADJECTIVE [1] (of a speech or speaker) noisy, violent, or ranting. ◆ NOUN [2] noisy, violent, or ranting public speaking.

Tubuai Islands (ˌtu:bu:'aɪ) PLURAL NOUN a chain of small islands extending about 1400 km (850 miles) in the S Pacific, in French Polynesia; discovered by Captain Cook in 1777; annexed by France in 1880. Pop.: 6510 (latest est.). Area: 173 sq. km (67 sq. miles). Also called: **Austral Islands.**

tubular ('tju:bjʊlə) ADJECTIVE [1] Also: **tubiform** ('tju:bɪˌfɔ:m). having the form of a tube or tubes. [2] of or relating to a tube or tubing.
▸ ˌ**tubu'larity** NOUN ▸ '**tubularly** ADVERB

tubular bells PLURAL NOUN *Music* an orchestral percussion instrument of 18 chromatically tuned metal tubes suspended vertically and struck near the top.

tubulate VERB *(tr)* ('tju:bjʊˌleɪt) [1] to form or shape into a tube. [2] to fit or furnish with a tube. ◆ ADJECTIVE ('tju:bjʊlɪt, -ˌleɪt) [3] a less common word for **tubular.**
▷HISTORY C18: from Latin *tubulātus,* from *tubulus* a little pipe, from *tubus* pipe
▸ ˌ**tubu'lation** NOUN ▸ '**tubuˌlator** NOUN

tubule ('tju:bju:l) NOUN any small tubular structure, esp one in an animal, as in the kidney, testis, etc.
▷HISTORY C17: from Latin *tubulus* a little TUBE

tubuliflorous (ˌtju:bjʊlɪ'flɔ:rəs) ADJECTIVE (of plants) having flowers or florets with tubular corollas.
▷HISTORY C19: from TUBULE + -FLOROUS

tubulous ('tju:bjʊləs) ADJECTIVE [1] tube-shaped; tubular. [2] characterized by or consisting of small tubes.
▷HISTORY C17: from New Latin *tubulōsus*
▸ '**tubulously** ADVERB

TUC (in Britain) ABBREVIATION FOR **Trades Union Congress.**

Tucana (tu:'kɑ:nə) NOUN, *Latin genitive* **Tucanae** (tu:'kɑ:ni:). a faint extensive constellation in the S hemisphere close to Hydrus and Eridanus, containing most of the Small Magellanic Cloud.
▷HISTORY probably from Tupi: toucan

tuchun (tu:'tʃu:n) NOUN (formerly) a Chinese military governor or warlord.
▷HISTORY from Chinese, from *tu* to superintend + *chün* troops

tuck[1] (tʌk) VERB [1] *(tr)* to push or fold into a small confined space or concealed place or between two surfaces: *to tuck a letter into an envelope.* [2] *(tr)* to thrust the loose ends or sides of (something) into a confining space, so as to make neat and secure: *to tuck the sheets under the mattress.* [3] to make a tuck or tucks in (a garment). [4] *(usually tr)* to draw together, contract, or pucker. ◆ NOUN [5] a tucked object or part. [6] a pleat or fold in a part of a garment, usually stitched down so as to make it a better fit or as decoration. [7] the part of a vessel where the after ends of the planking or plating meet at the sternpost. [8] *Brit* **a** an informal or schoolchild's word for **food,** esp cakes and sweets **b** *(as modifier): a tuck box.* [9] a position of the body in certain dives in which the legs are bent with the knees drawn up against the chest and tightly clasped. ◆ See also **tuck away, tuck in.**
▷HISTORY C14: from Old English *tūcian* to torment; related to Middle Dutch *tucken* to tug, Old High German *zucchen* to twitch

tuck[2] (tʌk) NOUN *Archaic* a rapier.
▷HISTORY C16: from French *estoc* sword, from Old French: tree trunk, sword, of Germanic origin

tuck[3] (tʌk) *Dialect* ◆ NOUN [1] a touch, blow, or stroke. ◆ VERB [2] *(tr)* to touch or strike. [3] *(intr)* to throb or bump.
▷HISTORY C16: from Middle English *tukken* to beat a drum, from Old Northern French *toquer* to TOUCH; compare TUCKET

Tuck (tʌk) NOUN **Friar.** See **Friar Tuck.**

tuck away VERB *(tr, adverb) Informal* [1] to eat (a large amount of food). [2] to store, esp in a place difficult to find.

tucker[1] ('tʌkə) NOUN [1] a person or thing that tucks. [2] a detachable yoke of lace, linen, etc., often white, worn over the breast, as of a low-cut dress. [3] an attachment on a sewing machine used for making tucks at regular intervals. [4] *Austral and NZ old-fashioned* an informal word for **food.**

tucker[2] ('tʌkə) VERB *(tr; often passive;* usually foll by *out) Informal, chiefly US and Canadian* to weary or tire completely.

tucker-bag *or* **tuckerbox** ('tʌkəˌbɒks) NOUN *Austral informal old-fashioned* a bag or box used for carrying food.

tucket ('tʌkɪt) NOUN *Archaic* a flourish on a trumpet.
▷HISTORY C16: from Old Northern French *toquer* to sound (on a drum)

tuck in VERB *(adverb)* [1] *(tr)* Also: **tuck into.** to put to bed and make snug. [2] *(tr)* to thrust the loose ends or sides of (something) into a confining space: *tuck the blankets in.* [3] *(intr)* Also: **tuck into.** *Informal* to eat, esp heartily. ◆ NOUN **tuck-in.** [4] *Brit informal* a meal, esp a large one.

tuck shop NOUN *Chiefly Brit* a shop, esp one in or near a school, where food such as cakes and sweets are sold.

tucotuco (ˌtu:kəʊ'tu:kəʊ) *or* **tucutucu** (ˌtu:ku:'tu:ku:) NOUN any of various colonial burrowing South American hystricomorph rodents of the genus *Ctenomys,* having long-clawed feet and a stocky body: family *Ctenomyidae.*
▷HISTORY C19: of South American Indian origin

Tucson ('tu:sɒn) NOUN a city in SE Arizona, at an altitude of 700m (2400 ft.): resort and seat of the University of Arizona (1891). Pop.: 486 699 (2000).

Tucumán *(Spanish* tuku'man) NOUN a city in NW Argentina: scene of the declaration (1816) of Argentinian independence from Spain; university (1914). Pop.: 519 252 (1999 est.).

'tude (tju:d, tu:d) NOUN *Slang* a hostile or defiant manner.
▷HISTORY C20: from ATTITUDE

-tude SUFFIX FORMING NOUNS indicating state or condition: *plenitude.*
▷HISTORY from Latin *-tūdō*

Tudor ('tju:də) ADJECTIVE denoting a style of architecture of the late perpendicular period and characterized by half-timbered houses.
▷HISTORY from the Tudor royal house of England, ruling from 1485 to 1603

Tudorbethan (ˌtju:də'bi:θən) ADJECTIVE *Disparaging* (of a contemporary building) imitative of Tudor and Elizabethan architecture.

Tues. ABBREVIATION FOR Tuesday.

Tuesday ('tju:zdɪ) NOUN the third day of the week; second day of the working week.
▷HISTORY Old English *tīwesdæg,* literally: day of Tiw, representing Latin *diēs Martis* day of Mars; compare Old Norse *týsdagr,* Old High German *zīostag;* see TIU, DAY

TUF (in New Zealand) ABBREVIATION FOR Trade Union Federation.

tufa ('tju:fə) NOUN a soft porous rock consisting of calcium carbonate deposited from springs rich in lime. Also called: **calc-tufa.**
▷HISTORY C18: from Italian *tufo,* from Late Latin *tōfus*
▸ **tufaceous** (tju:'feɪʃəs) ADJECTIVE

tuff (tʌf) NOUN a rock formed by the fusing together on the ground of small rock fragments (less than 2 mm across) ejected from a volcano.
▷HISTORY C16: from Old French *tuf,* from Italian *tufo;* see TUFA
▸ **tuffaceous** (tʌ'feɪʃəs) ADJECTIVE

tuffet ('tʌfɪt) NOUN a small mound or low seat.
▷HISTORY C16: alteration of TUFT

tuft (tʌft) NOUN [1] a bunch of feathers, grass, hair, etc., held together at the base. [2] a cluster of threads drawn tightly through upholstery, a mattress, a quilt, etc., to secure and strengthen the padding. [3] a small clump of trees or bushes. [4] (formerly) a gold tassel on the cap worn by titled undergraduates at English universities. [5] a person entitled to wear such a tassel. ◆ VERB [6] *(tr)* to provide or decorate with a tuft or tufts. [7] to form or be formed into tufts. [8] to secure and strengthen (a mattress, quilt, etc.) with tufts.
▷HISTORY C14: perhaps from Old French *tufe,* of Germanic origin; compare TOP[1]
▸ '**tufter** NOUN ▸ '**tufty** ADJECTIVE

tufted ('tʌftɪd) ADJECTIVE [1] having a tuft or tufts. [2] (of plants or plant parts) having or consisting of one or more groups of short branches all arising at the same level.

tufted duck NOUN a European lake-dwelling duck, *Aythya fuligula,* the male of which has a black plumage with white underparts and a long black drooping crest.

tug (tʌg) VERB **tugs, tugging, tugged.** [1] (when *intr,* sometimes foll by *at)* to pull or drag with sharp or powerful movements: *the boy tugged at the door handle.* [2] *(tr)* to tow (a vessel) by means of a tug. [3] *(intr)* to work; toil. ◆ NOUN [4] a strong pull or jerk: *he gave the rope a tug.* [5] Also called: **tugboat.** a boat with a powerful engine, used for towing barges, ships, etc. [6] a hard struggle or fight. [7] a less common word for **trace**[2] (sense 1).
▷HISTORY C13: related to Old English *tēon* to TOW[1]
▸ '**tugger** NOUN

Tugela (tu:'geɪlə) NOUN a river in E South Africa, rising in the Drakensberg where it forms the **Tugela Falls,** 856 m (2810 ft.) high, before flowing east to the Indian Ocean: scene of battles during the Zulu War (1879) and the Boer War (1899–1902). Length: about 500 km (312 miles).

tug-of-love NOUN a conflict over custody of a child between divorced parents or between natural parents and foster or adoptive parents.

tug-of-war NOUN [1] a contest in which two people or teams pull opposite ends of a rope in an attempt to drag the opposition over a central line. [2] any hard struggle, esp between two equally matched factions.

tugrik *or* **tughrik** ('tu:ˌgri:k) NOUN the standard monetary unit of Mongolia, divided into 100 möngös.
▷HISTORY from Mongolian

tui ('tu:ɪ) NOUN, *plural* **tuis.** a New Zealand honeyeater, *Prosthemadera novaeseelandiae,* having a glossy bluish-green plumage with white feathers at the throat: it mimics human speech and the songs of other birds.
▷HISTORY from Maori

Tuileries ('twi:lərɪ; *French* tɥilri) NOUN a former royal residence in Paris: begun in 1564 by Catherine de' Medici and burned in 1871 by the Commune; site of the **Tuileries Gardens** (a park near the Louvre).

tuition (tju:'ɪʃən) NOUN [1] instruction, esp that received in a small group or individually. [2] the payment for instruction, esp in colleges or universities.
▷HISTORY C15: from Old French *tuicion,* from Latin *tuitiō* a guarding, from *tuērī* to watch over
▸ **tu'itional** ADJECTIVE

Tukkie ('tʌkɪ) NOUN *South African informal* a student at the University of Pretoria, esp one representing the University in a sport.
▷HISTORY from the initials of *Transvaalse Universiteits Kollege*

tuktu *or* **tuktoo** ('tʌkˌtu:) NOUN (in Canada) another name for **caribou**.
▷HISTORY from Eskimo

Tula (*Russian* 'tulə) NOUN an industrial city in W central Russia. Pop.: 513 100 (1999 est.).

tularaemia *or US* **tularemia** (ˌtu:lə'ri:mɪə) NOUN an acute infectious bacterial disease of rodents, transmitted to man by infected ticks or flies or by handling contaminated flesh. It is characterized by fever, chills, and inflammation of the lymph glands. Also called: **rabbit fever**.
▷HISTORY C19/20: from New Latin, from *Tulare*, county in California where it was first observed; see -AEMIA
▸ **ˌtula'raemic** *or* **ˌtula'remic** ADJECTIVE

tulip ('tju:lɪp) NOUN 1 any spring-blooming liliaceous plant of the temperate Eurasian genus *Tulipa*, having tapering bulbs, long broad pointed leaves, and single showy bell-shaped flowers. 2 the flower or bulb of any of these plants.
▷HISTORY C17: from New Latin *tulipa*, from Turkish *tülbend* turban, which the opened bloom was thought to resemble
▸ **'tulip-ˌlike** ADJECTIVE

tulip tree NOUN 1 Also called: **tulip poplar, yellow poplar**. a North American magnoliaceous forest tree, *Liriodendron tulipifera*, having tulip-shaped greenish-yellow flowers and long conelike fruits. 2 a similar and related Chinese tree, *L. chinense*. 3 any of various other trees with tulip-shaped flowers, such as the magnolia.

tulipwood ('tju:lɪpˌwʊd) NOUN 1 Also called: **white poplar, yellow poplar**. the light soft wood of the tulip tree, used in making furniture and veneer. 2 any of several woods having stripes or streaks of colour, esp that of *Dalbergia variabilis*, a tree of tropical South America.

Tullamore (tʌlə'mɔ:) NOUN the county town of Offaly, Republic of Ireland; food processing and brewing. Pop.: 8485 (latest est.).

tulle (tju:l) NOUN a fine net fabric of silk, rayon, etc., used for evening dresses, as a trimming for hats, etc.
▷HISTORY C19: from French, from *Tulle*, city in S central France, where it was first manufactured

tullibee ('tʌlɪbi:) NOUN a cisco of the Great Lakes of Canada, *Coregonus artedii tullibee*.
▷HISTORY C19: from French *toulibi*, from Ojibwa

Tulsa ('tʌlsə) NOUN a city in NE Oklahoma, on the Arkansas River: a major oil centre; two universities. Pop.: 393 049 (2000).

tum (tʌm) NOUN an informal or childish word for **stomach**.

tumble ('tʌmbᵊl) VERB 1 to fall or cause to fall, esp awkwardly, precipitately, or violently. 2 (*intr*; usually foll by *about*) to roll or twist, esp in playing: *the kittens tumbled about on the floor*. 3 (*intr*) to perform leaps, somersaults, etc. 4 to go or move in a heedless or hasty way. 5 (*tr*) to polish (gemstones) in a tumbler. 6 (*tr*) to disturb, rumple, or toss around: *to tumble the bedclothes*. ◆ NOUN 7 the act or an instance of tumbling. 8 a fall or toss. 9 an acrobatic feat, esp a somersault. 10 a state of confusion. 11 a confused heap or pile: *a tumble of clothes*. ◆ See also **tumble to**.
▷HISTORY Old English *tumbian*, from Old French *tomber*; related to Old High German *tūmōn* to turn

tumbledown ('tʌmbᵊlˌdaʊn) ADJECTIVE falling to pieces; dilapidated; crumbling.

tumble-dry VERB **-dries, -drying, -dried**. (*tr*) to dry (laundry) in a tumble dryer.

tumble dryer *or* **tumble drier** NOUN a machine that dries wet laundry by rotating it in warmed air inside a metal drum. Also called: **tumbler dryer, tumbler**.

tumblehome ('tʌmbᵊlˌhəʊm) NOUN the inward curvature of the upper parts of the sides of a vessel at or near the stern.

tumbler ('tʌmblə) NOUN 1 **a** a flat-bottomed drinking glass with no handle or stem. Originally, a tumbler had a round or pointed base and so could not stand upright. **b** Also called: **tumblerful**. the contents or quantity such a glass holds. 2 a person, esp a professional entertainer, who performs somersaults and other acrobatic feats. 3 another name for **tumble dryer**. 4 Also called: **tumbling box**. a pivoted box or drum rotated so that the contents (usually inferior gemstones) tumble about and become smooth and polished. 5 the part of a lock that retains or releases the bolt and is moved by the action of a key. 6 a lever in a gunlock that receives the action of the mainspring when the trigger is pressed and thus forces the hammer forwards. 7 **a** a part that moves a gear in a train of gears into and out of engagement. **b** a single cog or cam that transmits motion to the part with which it engages. 8 a toy, often a doll, that is so weighted that it rocks when touched. 9 (*often capital*) a breed of domestic pigeon kept for exhibition or flying. The performing varieties execute backward somersaults in flight.

tumbler gear NOUN a train of gears in which the gear-selection mechanism is operated by tumblers.

tumbler switch NOUN a switch that is turned over to connect or disconnect an electric current.

tumble to VERB (*intr, preposition*) *Informal* to understand; become aware of: *she tumbled to his plan quickly*.

tumbleweed ('tʌmbᵊlˌwi:d) NOUN any densely branched plant that breaks off near the ground on withering and is rolled about by the wind, esp one of several amaranths of the western US and Australia.

tumbrel *or* **tumbril** ('tʌmbrəl) NOUN 1 a farm cart for carrying dung, esp one that tilts backwards to deposit its load. A cart of this type was used to take condemned prisoners to the guillotine during the French Revolution. 2 (formerly) a covered cart that accompanied artillery in order to carry ammunition, tools, etc. 3 an obsolete word for a **ducking stool**.
▷HISTORY C14 *tumberell* ducking stool, from Medieval Latin *tumbrellum* from Old French *tumberel* dump cart, from *tomber* to tumble, of Germanic origin

tumefacient (ˌtju:mɪ'feɪʃɪənt) ADJECTIVE producing or capable of producing swelling: *a tumefacient drug*.
▷HISTORY C16: from Latin *tumefacere* to cause to swell, from *tumēre* to swell + *facere* to cause

tumefaction (ˌtju:mɪ'fækʃən) NOUN 1 the act or process of swelling. 2 a puffy or swollen structure or part.

tumefy ('tju:mɪˌfaɪ) VERB **-fies, -fying, -fied**. to make or become tumid; swell or puff up.
▷HISTORY C16: from French *tuméfier*, from Latin *tumefacere*; see TUMEFACIENT

tumescent (tju:'mɛsənt) ADJECTIVE swollen or becoming swollen.
▷HISTORY C19: from Latin *tumescere* to begin to swell, from *tumēre*
▸ **tu'mescence** NOUN

tumid ('tju:mɪd) ADJECTIVE 1 (of an organ or part) enlarged or swollen. 2 bulging or protuberant. 3 pompous or fulsome in style: *tumid prose*.
▷HISTORY C16: from Latin *tumidus*, from *tumēre* to swell
▸ **tu'midity** *or* **'tumidness** NOUN ▸ **'tumidly** ADVERB

tummler ('tʌmlə) NOUN a comedian or other entertainer employed to encourage audience participation or to encourage guests at a resort to take part in communal activities.
▷HISTORY C20: Yiddish, from *tumlen* to stir, bustle

tummy ('tʌmɪ) NOUN, *plural* **-mies**. an informal or childish word for **stomach**.

tummy tuck NOUN *Informal* the surgical removal of abdominal fat and skin for cosmetic purposes.

tumour *or US* **tumor** ('tju:mə) NOUN 1 *Pathol* **a** any abnormal swelling. **b** a mass of tissue formed by a new growth of cells, normally independent of the surrounding structures. 2 *Obsolete* pompous style or language.
▷HISTORY C16: from Latin, from *tumēre* to swell
▸ **'tumorous** *or* **'tumoral** ADJECTIVE

tump (tʌmp) NOUN *Western English dialect* a small mound or clump.
▷HISTORY C16: of unknown origin

tumpline ('tʌmpˌlaɪn) NOUN (in the US and Canada, esp formerly) a leather or cloth band strung across the forehead or chest and attached to a pack or load in order to support it. Also called: **tump**.
▷HISTORY C19: from *tump*, of Algonquian origin + LINE[1]; compare Abnaki *mădŭmbi* pack strap

tumular ('tju:mjʊlə) ADJECTIVE of, relating to, or like a mound.

tumulose ('tju:mjʊləʊs) *or* **tumulous** ('tju:mjʊləs) ADJECTIVE 1 abounding in small hills or mounds. 2 being or resembling a mound.
▷HISTORY C18: from Latin *tumulōsus*, from *tumulus* a hillock
▸ **tumulosity** (ˌtju:mjʊ'lɒsɪtɪ) NOUN

tumult ('tju:mʌlt) NOUN 1 a loud confused noise, as of a crowd; commotion. 2 violent agitation or disturbance. 3 great emotional or mental agitation.
▷HISTORY C15: from Latin *tumultus*, from *tumēre* to swell up

tumultuous (tju:'mʌltjʊəs) ADJECTIVE 1 uproarious, riotous, or turbulent: *a tumultuous welcome*. 2 greatly agitated, confused, or disturbed: *a tumultuous dream*. 3 making a loud or unruly disturbance: *tumultuous insurgents*.
▸ **tu'multuously** ADVERB ▸ **tu'multuousness** NOUN

tumulus ('tju:mjʊləs) NOUN, *plural* **-li** (-li:). *Archaeol* (no longer in technical usage) another word for **barrow**[2].
▷HISTORY C17: from Latin: a hillock, from *tumēre* to swell up

tun (tʌn) NOUN 1 a large beer cask. 2 a measure of capacity, usually equal to 252 wine gallons. 3 a cask used during the manufacture of beer. ◆ VERB **tuns, tunning, tunned**. 4 (*tr*) to put into or keep in tuns.
▷HISTORY Old English *tunne*; related to Old High German, Old Norse *tunna*, Medieval Latin *tunna*

tuna[1] ('tju:nə) NOUN, *plural* **-na** *or* **-nas**. another name for **tunny** (sense 1).
▷HISTORY C20: from American Spanish, from Spanish *atún*, from Arabic *tūn*, from Latin *thunnus* tunny, from Greek

tuna[2] ('tju:nə) NOUN 1 any of various tropical American prickly pear cacti, esp *Opuntia tuna*, that are cultivated for their sweet edible fruits. 2 the fruit of any of these cacti.
▷HISTORY C16: via Spanish from Taino

tunable *or* **tuneable** ('tju:nəbᵊl) ADJECTIVE 1 able to be tuned. 2 *Archaic or poetic* melodious or tuneful.

Tunbridge Wells ('tʌnˌbrɪdʒ) NOUN a town and resort in SE England, in SW Kent: chalybeate spring discovered in 1606; an important social centre in the 17th and 18th centuries. Pop.: 60 272 (1991). Official name: **Royal Tunbridge Wells**.

tundra ('tʌndrə) NOUN **a** a vast treeless zone lying between the ice cap and the timber line of North America and Eurasia and having a permanently frozen subsoil. **b** (*as modifier*): *tundra vegetation*.
▷HISTORY C19: from Russian, from Lapp *tundar* hill; related to Finnish *tunturi* treeless hill

tune (tju:n) NOUN 1 a melody, esp one for which harmony is not essential. 2 the most important part in a musical texture: *the cello has the tune at that point*. 3 the condition of producing accurately pitched notes, intervals, etc. (esp in the phrases **in tune, out of tune**): *he can't sing in tune*. 4 accurate correspondence of pitch and intonation between instruments (esp in the phrases **in tune, out of tune**): *the violin is not in tune with the piano*. 5 the correct adjustment of a radio, television, or some other electronic circuit with respect to the required frequency (esp in the phrases **in tune, out of tune**). 6 a frame of mind; disposition or mood. 7 *Obsolete* a musical sound; note. 8 **call the tune**. to be in control of the proceedings. 9 **change one's tune** *or* **sing another** (*or* **a different**) **tune**. to alter one's attitude or tone of speech. 10 **to the tune of**. *Informal* to the amount or extent of: *costs to the tune of a hundred pounds*. ◆ VERB 11 to adjust (a musical instrument or a changeable part of one) to a certain pitch. 12 to adjust (a note, etc.) so as to bring it into harmony or concord. 13 (*tr*) to adapt or adjust (oneself); attune: *to tune oneself to a slower life*. 14 (*tr*; often foll by *up*) to make fine adjustments to (an engine, machine, etc.) to obtain optimum performance. 15 *Electronics* to adjust (one or more circuits) for resonance at a desired frequency. 16

Obsolete to utter (something) musically or in the form of a melody; sing. ◆ See also **tune in, tune out, tune up.**
▷HISTORY C14: variant of TONE

tuneful ('tju:nfʊl) ADJECTIVE [1] having a pleasant or catchy tune; melodious. [2] producing a melody or music: *a tuneful blackbird.*
▸ **'tunefully** ADVERB ▸ **'tunefulness** NOUN

tune in VERB *(adverb;* often foll by *to)* [1] to adjust (a radio or television) to receive (a station or programme). [2] *Slang* to make or become more aware, knowledgeable, etc. (about).

tuneless ('tju:nlɪs) ADJECTIVE [1] having no melody or tune. [2] *Chiefly poetic* not producing or able to produce music; silent.
▸ **'tunelessly** ADVERB ▸ **'tunelessness** NOUN

tune out VERB *(intr, adverb;* often foll by *of) Informal* to cease to take an interest (in) or pay attention (to): *many people had tuned out of politics.*

tuner ('tju:nə) NOUN [1] a person who tunes instruments, esp pianos. [2] the part of a radio or television receiver for selecting only those signals having a particular frequency.

tunesmith ('tju:nˌsmɪθ) NOUN *Informal* a composer of light or popular music and songs.

tune up VERB *(adverb)* [1] to adjust (a musical instrument) to a particular pitch, esp a standard one. [2] (esp of an orchestra or other instrumental ensemble) to tune (instruments) to a common pitch. [3] *(tr)* to adjust (an engine) in (a car, etc.) to improve performance. ◆ NOUN **tune-up.** [4] adjustments made to an engine to improve its performance.

tung oil (tʌŋ) NOUN a fast-drying oil obtained from the seeds of a central Asian euphorbiaceous tree, *Aleurites fordii*, used in paints, varnishes, etc., as a drying agent and to give a water-resistant finish. Also called: **Chinese wood oil.**
▷HISTORY partial translation of Chinese *yu t'ung* tung tree oil, from *yu* oil + *t'ung* tung tree

tungstate ('tʌŋsteɪt) NOUN a salt of tungstic acid.
▷HISTORY C20: from TUNGST(EN) + -ATE[1]

tungsten ('tʌŋstən) NOUN a hard malleable ductile greyish-white element. It occurs principally in wolframite and scheelite and is used in lamp filaments, electrical contact points, X-ray targets, and, alloyed with steel, in high-speed cutting tools. Symbol: W; atomic no.: 74; atomic wt.: 183.85; valency: 2–6; relative density: 19.3; melting pt.: 3422±20°C; boiling pt.: 5555°C. Also called: **wolfram.**
▷HISTORY C18: from Swedish *tung* heavy + *sten* STONE

tungsten carbide NOUN a fine very hard crystalline grey powder produced by heating tungsten and carbon to a very high temperature: used in the manufacture of drill bits, dies, etc. Symbol: WC; melting pt.: 2870°C.

tungsten lamp NOUN a lamp in which light is produced by a tungsten filament heated to incandescence by an electric current. The glass bulb enclosing the filament contains a low pressure of inert gas, usually argon. Sometimes small amounts of a halogen, such as iodine, are added to improve the intensity **(tungsten-halogen lamp).**

tungsten steel NOUN any of various hard steels containing tungsten (1–20 per cent) and traces of carbon. They are resistant to wear at high temperatures and are used in tools.

tungstic ('tʌŋstɪk) ADJECTIVE of or containing tungsten, esp in a high valence state.
▷HISTORY C18: from TUNGST(EN) + -IC

tungstic acid NOUN any of various oxyacids of tungsten obtained by neutralizing alkaline solutions of tungstates. They are often polymeric substances, typical examples being H_2WO_4 **(orthotungstic acid)**, $H_2W_4O_{13}$ **(metatungstic acid)**, and $H_{10}W_{12}O_{14}$ **(paratungstic acid).**

tungstite ('tʌŋstaɪt) NOUN a yellow earthy rare secondary mineral that consists of tungsten oxide and occurs with tungsten ores. Formula: WO_3.
▷HISTORY C20: from TUNGST(EN) + -ITE[1]

tungstous ('tʌŋstəs) ADJECTIVE of or containing tungsten in a low valence state.

Tungting *or* **Tung-t'ing** (ˌtʊŋ'tɪŋ) NOUN a variant transliteration of the Chinese name for the **Dongting.**

Tungus ('tʊŋgʊs) NOUN [1] *(plural* **-guses** *or* **-gus)** a member of a formerly nomadic Mongoloid people of E Siberia. [2] Also called: **Evenki.** the language of this people, belonging to the Tungusic branch of the Altaic family.

Tungusic (tʊŋ'gʊsɪk) NOUN [1] a branch or subfamily of the Altaic family of languages, including Tungus and Manchu. ◆ ADJECTIVE *also* **Tungusian.** [2] of or relating to these languages or their speakers.

Tunguska *(Russian* tun'guskə) NOUN any of three rivers in Russia, in central Siberia, all tributaries of the Yenisei: the **Lower** (Nizhnyaya) **Tunguska** 2690 km (1670 miles) long; the **Stony** (Podkamennaya) **Tunguska** 1550 km (960 miles) long; the **Upper** (Verkhnyaya) **Tunguska** which is the lower course of the Angara.

tunic ('tju:nɪk) NOUN [1] any of various hip-length or knee-length garments, such as the loose sleeveless garb worn in ancient Greece or Rome, the jacket of some soldiers, or a woman's hip-length garment, worn with a skirt or trousers. [2] *Anatomy, botany, zoology* a covering, lining, or enveloping membrane of an organ or part. ◆ See also **tunica.** [3] *Chiefly RC Church* another word for **tunicle.**
▷HISTORY Old English *tunice* (unattested except in the accusative case), from Latin *tunica*

tunica ('tju:nɪkə) NOUN [1] *Anatomy* tissue forming a layer or covering of an organ or part, such as any of the tissue layers of a blood vessel wall. [2] *Botany* the outer layer or layers of cells of the meristem at a shoot tip, which produces the epidermis and cells beneath it. ◆ Compare **corpus** (sense 4).
▷HISTORY C17: from Latin *tunica* TUNIC

tunicate ('tju:nɪkɪt, -ˌkeɪt) NOUN [1] any minute primitive marine chordate animal of the subphylum *Tunicata* (or *Urochordata, Urochorda*). The adults have a saclike unsegmented body enclosed in a cellulose-like outer covering (tunic) and only the larval forms have a notochord: includes the sea squirts. See also **ascidian.** ◆ ADJECTIVE *also* **tunicated.** [2] of, relating to, or belonging to the subphylum *Tunicata.* [3] (esp of a bulb) having or consisting of concentric layers of tissue.
▷HISTORY C18: from Latin *tunicātus* clad in a TUNIC

tunicle ('tju:nɪkᵊl) NOUN *Chiefly RC Church* the liturgical vestment worn by the subdeacon and bishops at High Mass and other religious ceremonies.
▷HISTORY C14: from Latin *tunicula* a little TUNIC

tuning ('tju:nɪŋ) NOUN *Music* [1] a set of pitches to which the open strings of a guitar, violin, etc., are tuned: *the normal tuning on a violin is G, D, A, E.* [2] the accurate pitching of notes and intervals by a choir, orchestra, etc.; intonation.

tuning fork NOUN a two-pronged metal fork that when struck produces a pure note of constant specified pitch. It is used to tune musical instruments and in acoustics.

tuning key NOUN a device that may be placed over a wrest pin on a piano, etc., and turned to alter the tension and pitch of a string.

Tunis ('tju:nɪs) NOUN the capital and chief port of Tunisia, in the northeast on the **Gulf of Tunis** (an inlet of the Mediterranean): dates from Carthaginian times, the ruins of ancient Carthage lying to the northeast; university (1960). Pop.: 674 100 (1994).

Tunisia (tju:'nɪzɪə, -'nɪsɪə) NOUN a republic in N Africa, on the Mediterranean: settled by the Phoenicians in the 12th century B.C.; made a French protectorate in 1881 and gained independence in 1955. It consists chiefly of the Sahara in the south, a central plateau, and the Atlas Mountains in the north. Exports include textiles, petroleum, and phosphates. Official language: Arabic; French is also widely spoken. Official religion: Muslim. Currency: dinar. Capital: Tunis. Pop.: 9 828 000 (1998 est.). Area: 164 150 sq. km (63 380 sq. miles).

Tunisian (tju:'nɪzɪən, -'nɪsɪən) ADJECTIVE [1] of or relating to Tunisia or its inhabitants. ◆ NOUN [2] a native or inhabitant of Tunisia.

tunnage ('tʌnɪdʒ) NOUN a variant spelling of **tonnage.**

tunnel ('tʌnᵊl) NOUN [1] an underground passageway, esp one for trains or cars that passes under a mountain, river, or a congested urban area. [2] any passage or channel through or under something. [3] a dialect word for **funnel.** [4] *Obsolete* the flue of a chimney. ◆ VERB **-nels, -nelling, -nelled** *or US* **-nels, -neling, -neled.** [5] *(tr)* to make or force (a way) through or under (something): *to tunnel a hole in the wall; to tunnel the cliff.* [6] *(intr;* foll by *through, under,* etc) to make or force a way (through or under something): *he tunnelled through the bracken.*
▷HISTORY C15: from Old French *tonel* cask, from *tonne* tun, from Medieval Latin *tonna* barrel, of Celtic origin
▸ **'tunneller** *or (US)* **'tunneler** NOUN

tunnel diode NOUN an extremely stable semiconductor diode, having a very narrow highly doped p-n junction, in which electrons travel across the junction by means of the tunnel effect. Also called: **Esaki diode.**

tunnel disease NOUN another name (esp formerly) for **decompression sickness.**
▷HISTORY so called because it used to be common among people who were digging tunnels

tunnel effect NOUN *Physics* the phenomenon in which an object, usually an elementary particle, tunnels through a potential barrier even though it does not have sufficient energy to surmount the barrier. It is explained by wave mechanics and is the cause of alpha decay, field emission, and certain conduction processes in semiconductors.

tunnel vault NOUN another name for **barrel vault.**

tunnel vision NOUN [1] a condition in which peripheral vision is greatly restricted. [2] narrowness of viewpoint resulting from concentration on a single idea, opinion, etc., to the exclusion of others.

tunny ('tʌnɪ) NOUN, *plural* **-nies** *or* **-ny.** [1] Also called: **tuna.** any of various large marine spiny-finned fishes of the genus *Thunnus*, esp *T. thynnus*, chiefly of warm waters: family *Scombridae.* They have a spindle-shaped body and widely forked tail, and are important food fishes. [2] any of various similar and related fishes.
▷HISTORY C16: from Old French *thon*, from Old Provençal *ton*, from Latin *thunnus*, from Greek

tup (tʌp) NOUN [1] *Chiefly Brit* an uncastrated male sheep; ram. [2] the head of a pile-driver or steam hammer. ◆ VERB **tups, tupping, tupped.** *(tr)* [3] to cause (a ram) to mate with a ewe, or (of a ram) to mate with (a ewe). [4] *Lancashire dialect* to butt (someone), as in a fight.
▷HISTORY C14: of unknown origin

Tupamaro (ˌtu:pə'mɑ:rəʊ) NOUN, *plural* **-ros.** any of a group of Marxist urban guerrillas in Uruguay.
▷HISTORY C20: after *Tupac Amaru*, 18th-century Peruvian Indian who led a rebellion against the Spaniards

tupelo ('tju:pɪˌləʊ) NOUN, *plural* **-los.** [1] any of several cornaceous trees of the genus *Nyssa*, esp *N. aquatica*, a large tree of deep swamps and rivers of the southern US. [2] the light strong wood of any of these trees.
▷HISTORY C18: from Creek *ito opilwa*, from *ito* tree + *opilwa* swamp

Tupi (tu:'pi:) NOUN [1] *(plural* **-pis** *or* **-pi)** a member of a South American Indian people of Brazil and Paraguay. [2] the language of this people, belonging to the Tupi-Guarani family.
▸ **Tu'pian** ADJECTIVE

Tupi-Guarani NOUN a family of South American Indian languages spoken in Brazil, Paraguay, and certain adjacent regions: possibly distantly related to Quechua.
▸ **'Tupiˌ-Guara'nian** ADJECTIVE

tupik *or* **tupek** ('tu:pək) NOUN *Canadian* (esp in the Arctic) a tent of animal skins, a traditional type of Inuit summer dwelling.
▷HISTORY from Eskimo *tupiq*

-tuple NOUN AND ADJECTIVE COMBINING FORM indicating a set of the number specified.

tuppence ('tʌpəns) NOUN *Brit* a variant spelling of **twopence.**

tuppenny ('tʌpənɪ) ADJECTIVE a variant spelling of **twopenny.**

Tupperware ('tʌpəweə) NOUN *Trademark* a range of plastic containers used for storing food.
▷HISTORY C20: *Tupper*, US manufacturing company + WARE[1]

tupuna (tə'pu:nə) NOUN a variant spelling of **tipuna.**

Tupungato *(Spanish* tupuŋ'gato) NOUN a mountain on the border between Argentina and Chile, in the Andes. Height: 6550 m (21 484 ft.).

tuque (tu:k) NOUN *Canadian* 1 a knitted cap with a long tapering end. 2 Also called: **toque.** a close-fitting knitted hat often with a tassel or pompom.
▷HISTORY C19: from Canadian French, from French: TOQUE

tu quoque *Latin* (tju: 'kwəʊkwɪ) INTERJECTION you likewise: a retort made by a person accused of a crime implying that the accuser is also guilty of the same crime.

turaco ('tʊərəˌkəʊ) NOUN, *plural* **-cos.** a variant spelling of **touraco.**

turangawaewae (təˌrʌŋgəˈweɪweɪ) NOUN *NZ* the area that is a person's home.
▷HISTORY Maori, literally: standing on one's feet

Turanian (tjʊ'reɪnɪən) NOUN 1 a member of any of the peoples inhabiting ancient Turkestan, or their descendants. 2 another name for **Ural-Altaic.** ◆ ADJECTIVE 3 of or relating to the Ural-Altaic languages or any of the peoples who speak them. 4 of or relating to Turkestan or its people.

turban ('tɜ:bᵊn) NOUN 1 a man's headdress, worn esp by Muslims, Hindus, and Sikhs, made by swathing a length of linen, silk, etc., around the head or around a caplike base. 2 a woman's brimless hat resembling this. 3 any headdress resembling this.
▷HISTORY C16: from Turkish *tülbend*, from Persian *dulband*
▸'**turbaned** ADJECTIVE ▸'**turban-ˌlike** ADJECTIVE

turbary ('tɜ:bərɪ) NOUN, *plural* **-ries.** 1 land where peat or turf is cut or has been cut. 2 Also called: **common of turbary.** (in England) the legal right to cut peat for fuel on a common.
▷HISTORY C14: from Old French *turbarie*, from Medieval Latin *turbāria*, from *turba* peat, TURF

turbellarian (ˌtɜ:bɪ'lɛərɪən) NOUN 1 any typically aquatic free-living flatworm of the class *Turbellaria*, having a ciliated epidermis and a simple life cycle: includes the planarians. ◆ ADJECTIVE 2 of, relating to, or belonging to the class *Turbellaria*.
▷HISTORY C19: from New Latin *Turbellāria*, from Latin *turbellae* (pl) bustle, from *turba* brawl, referring to the swirling motion created in the water

turbid ('tɜ:bɪd) ADJECTIVE 1 muddy or opaque, as a liquid clouded with a suspension of particles. 2 dense, thick, or cloudy: *turbid fog.* 3 in turmoil or confusion.
▷HISTORY C17: from Latin *turbidus*, from *turbāre* to agitate, from *turba* crowd
▸**tur'bidity** *or* '**turbidness** NOUN ▸'**turbidly** ADVERB

turbidimeter (ˌtɜ:bɪ'dɪmɪtə) NOUN a device that measures the turbidity of a liquid.

turbidite ('tɜ:bɪˌdaɪt) NOUN a sediment deposited by a turbidity current.
▷HISTORY C20: from TURBID + -ITE[1]

turbidity current NOUN a swirling mass of water and suspended material stirred up by a tsunami, a storm, a river in flood, etc.

turbinate ('tɜ:bɪnɪt, -ˌneɪt) *or* **turbinal** ('tɜ:bɪnᵊl) ADJECTIVE *also* **turbinated.** 1 *Anatomy* of or relating to any of the thin scroll-shaped bones situated on the walls of the nasal passages. 2 shaped like a spiral or scroll. 3 (esp of the shells of certain molluscs) shaped like an inverted cone. ◆ NOUN 4 Also called: **nasal concha.** a turbinate bone. 5 a turbinate shell.
▷HISTORY C17: from Latin *turbō* spinning top
▸ˌ**turbi'nation** NOUN

turbine ('tɜ:bɪn, -baɪn) NOUN any of various types of machine in which the kinetic energy of a moving fluid is converted into mechanical energy by causing a bladed rotor to rotate. The moving fluid may be water, steam, air, or combustion products of a fuel. See also **reaction turbine, impulse turbine, gas turbine.**
▷HISTORY C19: from French, from Latin *turbō* whirlwind, from *turbāre* to throw into confusion

turbine blade NOUN any of a number of bladelike vanes assembled around the periphery of a turbine rotor to guide the steam or gas flow.

turbit ('tɜ:bɪt) NOUN a crested breed of domestic pigeon.
▷HISTORY C17: from Latin *turbō* spinning top, with reference to the bird's shape; compare TURBOT

turbo- COMBINING FORM of, relating to, or driven by a turbine: *turbofan.*

turbocar ('tɜ:bəʊˌkɑ:) NOUN a car driven by a gas turbine.

turbo-charge VERB (*tr*) 1 to supply (an internal-combustion engine or a motor vehicle) with a turbocharger. 2 to inject extra force and energy into (an activity, undertaking, etc.): *a turbo-charged version of the show.*

turbocharger ('tɜ:bəʊˌtʃɑ:dʒə) NOUN a centrifugal compressor which boosts the intake pressure of an internal-combustion engine, driven by an exhaust-gas turbine fitted to the engine's exhaust manifold.

turbo-electric (ˌtɜ:bəʊɪ'lɛktrɪk) ADJECTIVE of, relating to, or using an electric generator driven by a turbine: *turbo-electric propulsion.*

turbofan (ˌtɜ:bəʊ'fæn) NOUN 1 Also called: **high bypass ratio engine.** a type of by-pass engine in which a large fan driven by a turbine and housed in a short duct forces air rearwards around the exhaust gases in order to increase the propulsive thrust. 2 an aircraft driven by one or more turbofans. 3 the ducted fan in such an engine. Also called (for senses 1, 2): **fanjet.**

turbogenerator (ˌtɜ:bəʊ'dʒɛnəˌreɪtə) NOUN a large electrical generator driven by a steam turbine.

turbojet (ˌtɜ:bəʊ'dʒɛt) NOUN 1 short for **turbojet engine.** 2 an aircraft powered by one or more turbojet engines.

turbojet engine NOUN a gas turbine in which the exhaust gases provide the propulsive thrust to drive an aircraft.

turboprop (ˌtɜ:bəʊ'prɒp) NOUN 1 an aircraft propulsion unit where a propeller is driven by a gas turbine. 2 an aircraft powered by turboprops.

turbosupercharger (ˌtɜ:bəʊ'su:pəˌtʃɑ:dʒə) NOUN *Obsolete* a supercharging device for an internal-combustion engine, consisting of a turbine driven by the exhaust gases.

turbot ('tɜ:bət) NOUN, *plural* **-bot** *or* **-bots.** 1 a European flatfish, *Scophthalmus maximus*, having a pale brown speckled scaleless body covered with tubercles: family *Bothidae*. It is highly valued as a food fish. 2 any of various similar or related fishes.
▷HISTORY C13: from Old French *tourbot*, from Medieval Latin *turbō*, from Latin: spinning top, from a fancied similarity in shape; see TURBIT, TURBINE

turbulence ('tɜ:bjʊləns) *or rarely* **turbulency** NOUN 1 a state or condition of confusion, movement, or agitation; disorder. 2 *Meteorol* local instability in the atmosphere, oceans, or rivers. 3 turbulent flow in a liquid or gas.

turbulent ('tɜ:bjʊlənt) ADJECTIVE 1 being in a state of turbulence. 2 wild or insubordinate; unruly.
▷HISTORY C16: from Latin *turbulentus*, from *turba* confusion
▸'**turbulently** ADVERB

turbulent flow NOUN flow of a fluid in which its velocity at any point varies rapidly in an irregular manner. Compare **laminar flow.** See also **streamline flow.**

Turco ('tɜ:kəʊ) NOUN, *plural* **-cos.** (formerly) an Algerian serving in the light infantry of the French army.
▷HISTORY C19: via French from Italian: a Turk

Turco- *or* **Turko-** COMBINING FORM indicating Turkey or Turkish: *Turco-Greek.*

turd (tɜ:d) NOUN *Slang* 1 a lump of dung; piece of excrement. 2 an unpleasant or contemptible person or thing.
▷HISTORY Old English *tord*; related to Old Norse *tordy fill* dung beetle, Dutch *tort* dung

> **Language note** This word was formerly considered to be taboo, and it was labelled as such in previous editions of *Collins English Dictionary*. However, it has now become acceptable in speech, although some older or more conservative people may object to its use.

turdine ('tɜ:daɪn, -dɪn) ADJECTIVE of, relating to, or characteristic of thrushes.
▷HISTORY C19: from Latin *turdus* thrush

tureen (tə'ri:n) NOUN a large deep usually rounded dish with a cover, used for serving soups, stews, etc.
▷HISTORY C18: from French *terrine* earthenware vessel, from *terrin* made of earthenware, from Vulgar Latin *terrīnus* (unattested) earthen, from Latin *terra* earth

turf (tɜ:f) NOUN, *plural* **turfs** *or* **turves** (tɜ:vz). 1 the surface layer of fields and pastures, consisting of earth containing a dense growth of grasses with their roots; sod. 2 a piece cut from this layer, used to form lawns, verges, etc. 3 **a** a track, usually of grass or dirt, where horse races are run. **b** horse racing as a sport or industry. 4 *US slang* the territory or area of activity over which a person or group claims exclusive rights. 5 an area of knowledge or influence: *he's on home turf when it comes to music.* 6 another term for **peat.** 7 **go with the turf.** *Informal* to be an unavoidable part of a particular situation or process. ◆ VERB 8 (*tr*) to cover with pieces of turf.
▷HISTORY Old English; related to Old Norse *torfa*, Old High German *zurba*, Sanskrit *darbha* tuft of grass

turf accountant NOUN *Brit* a formal name for a **bookmaker.**

turfman ('tɜ:fmən) NOUN, *plural* **-men.** *Chiefly US* a person devoted to horse racing. Also called: **turfite** ('tɜ:faɪt).

turf out VERB (*tr, adverb*) *Brit informal* to throw out or dismiss; eject: *we were turfed out of the club.*

turf war NOUN *Informal* 1 a dispute between criminals or gangs over the right to operate within a particular area. 2 any dispute in which one party seeks to obtain increased rights or influence.

turfy ('tɜ:fɪ) ADJECTIVE **turfier, turfiest.** 1 of, covered with, or resembling turf. 2 relating to or characteristic of horse racing or persons connected with it.
▸'**turfiness** NOUN

turgent ('tɜ:dʒənt) ADJECTIVE an obsolete word for **turgid.**
▷HISTORY C15: from Latin *turgēre* to swell
▸'**turgently** ADVERB

turgescent (tɜ:'dʒɛsᵊnt) ADJECTIVE becoming or being swollen; inflated; tumid.
▸**tur'gescence** *or* **tur'gescency** NOUN

turgid ('tɜ:dʒɪd) ADJECTIVE 1 swollen and distended; congested. 2 (of style or language) pompous and high-flown; bombastic.
▷HISTORY C17: from Latin *turgidus*, from *turgēre* to swell
▸**tur'gidity** *or* '**turgidness** NOUN ▸'**turgidly** ADVERB

turgite ('tɜ:dʒaɪt) NOUN a red or black mineral consisting of hydrated ferric oxide. Formula: $Fe_2O_3.nH_2O$.

turgor ('tɜ:gə) NOUN the normal rigid state of a cell, caused by pressure of the cell contents against the cell wall or membrane. ◆ See also **turgor pressure.**
▷HISTORY C19: from Late Latin: a swelling, from Latin *turgēre* to swell

turgor pressure NOUN the pressure exerted on a plant cell wall by water passing into the cell by osmosis. Also called: **hydrostatic pressure.**

Turin (tjʊə'rɪn) NOUN a city in NW Italy, capital of Piedmont region, on the River Po: became capital of the Kingdom of Sardinia in 1720; first capital (1861–65) of united Italy; university (1405); a major industrial centre, producing most of Italy's cars. Pop.: 903 703 (2000 est.). Italian name: **Torino.**

Turing machine NOUN a hypothetical universal computing machine able to modify its original instructions by reading, erasing, or writing a new symbol on a moving tape of fixed length that acts as its program. The concept was instrumental in the early development of computer systems.
▷HISTORY C20: after Alan *Turing* (1912–54), English mathematician

Turing test NOUN a proposed test of a computer's ability to think, requiring that the covert substitution of the computer for one of the participants in a keyboard and screen dialogue should be undetectable by the remaining human participant.
▷HISTORY C20: after Alan *Turing* (1912–54), English mathematician

turion ('tʊərɪən) NOUN a perennating bud produced by many aquatic plants: it detaches from the parent plant and remains dormant until the following spring.

▷**HISTORY** C17: from French *turion*, from Latin *turio* shoot

Turk (tɜːk) NOUN [1] a native, inhabitant, or citizen of Turkey. [2] a native speaker of any Turkic language, such as an inhabitant of Turkmenistan or Kyrgyzstan. [3] *Obsolete, derogatory* a violent, brutal, or domineering person.

Turk. ABBREVIATION FOR: [1] Turkey. [2] Turkish.

Turkana (tɜːˈkɑːnə) NOUN **Lake.** a long narrow lake in E Africa, in the Great Rift Valley. Area: 7104 sq. km (2743 sq. miles). Former name: (Lake) **Rudolf.**

Turkestan *or* **Turkistan** (ˌtɜːkɪˈstɑːn) NOUN an extensive region of central Asia between Siberia in the north and Tibet, India, Afghanistan, and Iran in the south: formerly divided into **West (Russian) Turkestan** (also called Soviet Central Asia), comprising present-day Turkmenistan, Uzbekistan, Tajikistan, and Kyrgyzstan and the S part of Kazakhstan, and **East (Chinese) Turkestan** consisting of the Xinjiang Uygur Autonomous Region.

Turkestani (ˌtɜːkɪˈstɑːnɪ) ADJECTIVE [1] of or relating to the central Asian region of Turkestan or its inhabitants. ◆ NOUN [2] a native or inhabitant of Turkestan.

turkey (ˈtɜːkɪ) NOUN, *plural* **-keys** *or* **-key.** [1] a large gallinaceous bird, *Meleagris gallopavo*, of North America, having a bare wattled head and neck and a brownish iridescent plumage. The male is brighter and has a fan-shaped tail. A domestic variety is widely bred for its flesh. [2] the flesh of the turkey used as food. [3] a similar and related bird, *Agriocharis ocellata* (**ocellated turkey**), of Central and N South America. [4] any of various Australian birds considered to resemble the turkey, such as the bush turkey. [5] *Slang, chiefly US and Canadian* **a** a dramatic production that fails; flop. **b** a thing or person that fails; dud. [6] *Slang, chiefly US and Canadian* a stupid, incompetent, or unappealing person. [7] *Slang* (in tenpin bowling) three strikes in a row. [8] See **cold turkey.** [9] **talk turkey.** *Informal, chiefly US and Canadian* to discuss frankly and practically.

▷**HISTORY** C16: shortened from *Turkey cock* (*hen*), used at first to designate the African guinea fowl (apparently because the bird was brought through Turkish territory), later applied by mistake to the American bird

Turkey (ˈtɜːkɪ) NOUN a republic in W Asia and SE Europe, between the Black Sea, the Mediterranean, and the Aegean: one of the oldest inhabited regions of the world; the centre of the Ottoman Empire; became a republic in 1923. The major Asian part, consisting mainly of an arid plateau, is separated from European Turkey by the Bosporus, Sea of Marmara, and Dardanelles. Official languages: Turkish; Kurdish and Arabic minority languages. Religion: Muslim majority. Currency: lira. Capital: Ankara. Pop.: 66 229 000 (2001 est.). Area: 780 576 sq. km (301 380 sq. miles).

turkey brown NOUN an angler's name for a species of mayfly, *Paraleptophlebia submarginata*.

turkey buzzard *or* **vulture** NOUN a New World vulture, *Cathartes aura*, having a dark plumage and naked red head.

Turkey carpet NOUN a wool carpet made in one piece and having a deep velvety pile and rich glowing colours.

turkey cock NOUN [1] a male turkey. [2] an arrogant person.

turkey nest NOUN *Austral* a small earth dam adjacent to, and higher than, a larger earth dam, to feed water by gravity to a cattle trough, etc.

Turkey oak NOUN an oak tree, *Quercus cerris*, of W and S Europe, with deeply lobed hairy leaves.

▷**HISTORY** C18: so called because its acorns are often eaten by turkeys

Turkey red NOUN [1] **a** a moderate or bright red colour. **b** (*as adjective*): *a Turkey-red fabric.* [2] a cotton fabric of a bright red colour.

turkey trot NOUN an early ragtime one-step, popular in the period of World War I.

Turki (ˈtɜːkɪ) ADJECTIVE [1] of or relating to the Turkic languages, esp those of central Asia. [2] of or relating to speakers of these languages. ◆ NOUN [3] these languages collectively; esp Eastern Turkic.

Turkic (ˈtɜːkɪk) NOUN a branch or subfamily of the Altaic family of languages, including Turkish, Turkmen, Kirghiz, Tatar, etc., members of which are found from Turkey to NE China, esp in central Asia.

Turkish (ˈtɜːkɪʃ) ADJECTIVE [1] of, relating to, or characteristic of Turkey, its people, or their language. ◆ NOUN [2] the official language of Turkey, belonging to the Turkic branch of the Altaic family. See also **Osmanli.**

▸ **ˈTurkishness** NOUN

Turkish Angora (æŋˈɡɔːrə) NOUN a long-haired breed of cat, similar to the Persian.

Turkish bath NOUN [1] a type of bath in which the bather sweats freely in hot dry air, is then washed, often massaged, and has a cold plunge or shower. [2] (*sometimes plural*) an establishment where such a bath is obtainable.

Turkish coffee NOUN very strong black coffee made with finely ground coffee beans.

Turkish delight NOUN a jelly-like sweet flavoured with flower essences, usually cut into cubes and covered in icing sugar.

Turkish Empire NOUN another name for the **Ottoman Empire.**

Turkish tobacco NOUN a fragrant dark tobacco cultivated in E Europe, esp Turkey and Greece.

Turkish towel NOUN a rough loose-piled towel; terry towel.

Turkish Van NOUN a breed of cat with soft white semi-long hair and coloured markings on the head and tail.

▷**HISTORY** C20: named after *Van*, town in Turkey

Turkism (ˈtɜːkɪzəm) NOUN *Rare* [1] the culture, beliefs, and customs of the Turks. [2] a Turkish word, fashion, etc.

Turkmen (ˈtɜːkmɛn) NOUN the language of the Turkomans, belonging to the Turkic branch of the Altaic family.

Turkmenistan (ˌtɜːkmɛnɪˈstɑːn) NOUN a republic in central Asia; the area has been occupied by a succession of empires; a Turkmen state was established in the 15th century but suffered almost continual civil strife and was gradually conquered by Russia; in 1918 it became a Soviet republic and gained independence from the Soviet Union in 1991: deserts including the **Kara Kum** cover most of the region; agricultural communities are concentrated around oases; there are rich mineral deposits. Official language: Turkmen. Religion: believers are mainly Muslim. Currency: manat. Capital: Ashkhabad. Pop.: 5 462 000 (2001 est.). Area: 488 100 sq. km (186 400 sq. miles).

Turko- COMBINING FORM a variant spelling of **Turco-.**

Turkoman (ˈtɜːkəmən) *or* **Turkman** NOUN [1] (*plural* **-mans** *or* **-men**) a member of a formerly nomadic people of central Asia, now living chiefly in Turkmenistan and in NE Iran. [2] the Turkmen language. ◆ ADJECTIVE [3] of or relating to this people or their language.

▷**HISTORY** C16: from Medieval Latin *Turcomannus*, from Persian *turkumān* resembling a Turk, from *turk* Turk + *māndan* to be like

Turks and Caicos Islands PLURAL NOUN a UK Overseas Territory in the Caribbean, southeast of the Bahamas: consists of the eight **Turks Islands**, separated by the Turks Island Passage from the Caicos group, which has six main islands. Capital: Grand Turk. Pop.: 23 000 (1999 est.). Area: 430 sq. km (166 sq. miles).

Turk's-cap lily NOUN any of several cultivated lilies, such as *Lilium martagon* and *L. superbum*, that have brightly coloured flowers with reflexed petals. See also **martagon.**

▷**HISTORY** C17: so called because of a resemblance between its flowers and a turban

Turk's-head NOUN an ornamental turban-like knot made by weaving small cord around a larger rope.

Turku (*Finnish* ˈturku) NOUN a city and port in SW Finland, on the Gulf of Bothnia: capital of Finland until 1812. Pop.: 166 929 (1997 est.). Swedish name: **Åbo.**

turlough (ˈtɜːlɒx) NOUN a seasonal lake or pond: a low-lying area on limestone, esp in Ireland, that becomes flooded in wet weather by the upsurge of underlying ground water.

▷**HISTORY** C17: from Irish *tur* dry + LOUGH

turmeric (ˈtɜːmərɪk) NOUN [1] a tropical Asian zingiberaceous plant, *Curcuma longa*, having yellow flowers and an aromatic underground stem. [2] the powdered stem of this plant, used as a condiment and as a yellow dye. [3] any of several other plants with similar roots.

▷**HISTORY** C16: from Old French *terre merite*, from Medieval Latin *terra merita*, literally: meritorious earth, name applied for obscure reasons to curcuma

turmeric paper NOUN *Chem* paper impregnated with turmeric used as a test for alkalis, which turn it brown, and for boric acid, which turns it reddish brown.

turmoil (ˈtɜːmɔɪl) NOUN [1] violent or confused movement; agitation; tumult. ◆ VERB [2] *Archaic* to make or become turbulent.

▷**HISTORY** C16: perhaps from TURN + MOIL

turn (tɜːn) VERB [1] to move or cause to move around an axis: *a wheel turning; to turn a knob.* [2] (sometimes foll by *round*) to change or cause to change positions by moving through an arc of a circle: *he turned the chair to face the light.* [3] to change or cause to change in course, direction, etc.: *he turned left at the main road.* [4] (of soldiers, ships, etc.) to alter the direction of advance by changing direction simultaneously or (of a commander) to cause the direction of advance to be altered simultaneously. [5] to go or pass to the other side of (a corner, etc.). [6] to assume or cause to assume a rounded, curved, or folded form: *the road turns here.* [7] to reverse or cause to reverse position. [8] (*tr*) to pass round (an enemy or enemy position) so as to attack it from the flank or rear: *the Germans turned the Maginot line.* [9] (*tr*) to perform or do by a rotating movement: *to turn a somersault.* [10] (*tr*) to shape or cut a thread in (a workpiece, esp one of metal, wood, or plastic) by rotating it on a lathe against a fixed cutting tool. [11] (when *intr*, foll by *into* or *to*) to change or convert or be changed or converted: *the alchemists tried to turn base metals into gold.* [12] (foll by *into*) to change or cause to change in nature, character, etc.: *the frog turned into a prince.* [13] (*copula*) to change so as to become: *he turned nasty when he heard the price.* [14] to cause (foliage, etc.) to change colour or (of foliage, etc.) to change colour: *frost turned the trees a vivid orange.* [15] to cause (milk, etc.) to become rancid or sour or (of milk, etc.) to become rancid or sour. [16] to change or cause to change in subject, trend, etc.: *the conversation turned to fishing.* [17] to direct or apply or be directed or applied: *he turned his attention to the problem.* [18] (*intr*; usually foll by *to*) to appeal or apply (to) for help, advice, etc.: *she was very frightened and didn't know where to turn.* [19] to reach, pass, or progress beyond in age, time, etc.: *she has just turned twenty.* [20] (*tr*) to cause or allow to go: *to turn an animal loose.* [21] to affect or be affected with nausea: *the sight of the dead body turned his stomach.* [22] to affect or be affected with giddiness: *my head is turning.* [23] (*tr*) to affect the mental or emotional stability of (esp in the phrase **turn (someone's) head**). [24] (*tr*) to release from a container: *she turned the fruit into a basin.* [25] (*tr*) to render into another language. [26] (usually foll by *against* or *from*) to transfer or reverse or cause to transfer or reverse (one's loyalties, affections, etc.). [27] (*tr*) to cause (an enemy agent) to become a double agent working for one's own side: *the bureau turned some of the spies it had caught.* [28] (*tr*) to bring (soil) from lower layers to the surface. [29] to blunt (an edge) or (of an edge) to become blunted. [30] (*tr*) to give a graceful form to: *to turn a compliment.* [31] (*tr*) to reverse (a cuff, collar, etc.) in order to hide the outer worn side. [32] (*intr*) *US* to be merchandised as specified: *shirts are turning well this week.* [33] *Cricket* to spin (the ball) or (of the ball) to spin. [34] **turn one's hand to.** to undertake (something, esp something practical). [35] **turn tail.** to run away; flee. [36] **turn the tables (on someone).** See **table** (sense 17). [37] **turn the tide.** to reverse the general course of events. ◆ NOUN [38] an act or instance of turning or the state of being turned or the material turned: *a turn of a rope around a bollard.* [39] a movement of complete or partial rotation. [40] a change or reversal of direction or position. [41] direction or drift: *his thoughts took a new turn.* [42] a deviation or departure from a course or tendency. [43] the place, point, or time at which a deviation or change occurs. [44] another word for **turning** (sense 1). [45] the right or opportunity to do something in an agreed order or succession: *we'll take turns to play;*

now it's George's turn; you must not play out of turn. [46] a change in nature, condition, etc.: *his illness took a turn for the worse.* [47] a period of action, work, etc. [48] a short walk, ride, or excursion: *to take a turn in the park.* [49] natural inclination: *he is of a speculative turn of mind; she has a turn for needlework.* [50] distinctive form or style: *a neat turn of phrase.* [51] requirement, need, or advantage: *to serve someone's turn.* [52] a deed performed that helps or hinders someone: *to do an old lady a good turn.* [53] a twist, bend, or distortion in shape. [54] *Music* a melodic ornament that makes a turn around a note, beginning with the note above, in a variety of sequences. [55] *Theatre, chiefly Brit* a short theatrical act, esp in music hall, cabaret, etc. [56] *Stock Exchange* **a** *Brit* the difference between a market maker's bid and offer prices, representing the market maker's profit. **b** a transaction including both a purchase and a sale. [57] a military manoeuvre in which men or ships alter their direction of advance together. [58] *Austral slang* a party. [59] *Informal* a shock or surprise: *the bad news gave her quite a turn.* [60] **at every turn.** on all sides or occasions. [61] **by turns.** one after another; alternately. [62] **on the turn.** *Informal* **a** at the point of change. **b** about to go rancid. [63] **out of turn. a** not in the correct or agreed order of succession. **b** improperly, inappropriately, or inopportunely. [64] **turn and turn about.** one after another; alternately. [65] **to a turn.** to the proper amount; perfectly: *cooked to a turn.* ◆ See also **turn against, turn away, turn down, turn in, turn off, turn on, turn out, turn over, turn to, turn up.**
▷HISTORY Old English *tyrnian*, from Old French *torner*, from Latin *tornāre* to turn in a lathe, from *tornus* lathe, from Greek *tornos* dividers
▸ **'turnable** ADJECTIVE

turnabout ('tɜːnəˌbaʊt) NOUN [1] the act of turning so as to face a different direction. [2] a change or reversal of opinion, attitude, etc.

turn against VERB (*preposition*) to change or cause to change one's attitude so as to become hostile or to retaliate.

turnaround ('tɜːnəˌraʊnd) NOUN [1] **a** the act or process in which a ship, aircraft, etc., unloads passengers and freight at the end of a trip and reloads for the next trip. **b** the time taken for this. [2] the total time taken by a ship, aircraft, or other vehicle in a round trip. [3] a complete reversal of a situation or set of circumstances. Also called: **turnround.**

turnaround time NOUN *Computing* the total time taken between the submission of a program for execution and the return of the complete output to the customer.

turn away VERB (*adverb*) [1] to move or cause to move in a different direction so as not to face something: *one of the children turned away while the others hid.* [2] (*tr*) to refuse admittance or assistance to: *dozens of people were turned away from the hostel.*

turn bridge NOUN another name for **swing bridge.**

turnbuckle ('tɜːnˌbʌkᵊl) NOUN an open mechanical sleeve usually having a swivel at one end and a thread at the other to enable a threaded wire or rope to be tightened.
▷HISTORY C19: from TURN + BUCKLE

turncoat ('tɜːnˌkəʊt) NOUN a person who deserts one cause or party for the opposite faction; renegade.

turncock ('tɜːnˌkɒk) NOUN (formerly) an official employed to turn on the water for the mains supply.

turn down VERB (*tr, adverb*) [1] to reduce (the volume or brightness) of (something): *turn the radio down.* [2] to reject or refuse. [3] to fold down (a collar, sheets on a bed, etc.). ◆ ADJECTIVE **turndown.** [4] (*prenominal*) capable of being or designed to be folded or doubled down.

turner ('tɜːnə) NOUN [1] a person or thing that turns, esp a person who operates a lathe. [2] (*US*) a member of a society of gymnasts.

turnery ('tɜːnərɪ) NOUN, *plural* **-eries.** [1] objects made on a lathe. [2] Also called: **turning.** the process or skill of turning objects on a lathe. [3] the workshop of a lathe operator.

turn in VERB (*adverb*) *Informal* [1] (*intr*) to go to bed for the night. [2] (*tr*) to hand in; deliver: *to turn in an essay.* [3] (*tr*) to deliver (someone accused of a crime) into police custody. [4] to give up or conclude (something): *we turned in the game when it began to rain.* [5] (*tr*) to record (a score, etc.). [6] **turn in on oneself.** to withdraw or cause to withdraw from contact with others and become preoccupied with one's own problems.

turning ('tɜːnɪŋ) NOUN [1] Also called: **turn.** a road, river, or path that turns off the main way: *the fourth turning on the right.* [2] the point where such a way turns off. [3] a bend in a straight course. [4] an object made on a lathe. [5] another name for **turnery** (sense 2). [6] (*plural*) the waste produced in turning on a lathe.

turning circle NOUN the smallest circle in which a vehicle can turn.

turning point NOUN [1] a moment when the course of events is changed: *the turning point of his career.* [2] a point at which there is a change in direction or motion. [3] *Maths* a stationary point at which the first derivative of a function changes sign, so that typically its graph does not cross a horizontal tangent. [4] *Surveying* a point to which a foresight and a backsight are taken in levelling; change point.

turnip ('tɜːnɪp) NOUN [1] a widely cultivated plant, *Brassica rapa*, of the Mediterranean region, with a large yellow or white edible root: family *Brassicaceae* (crucifers). [2] the root of this plant, which is eaten as a vegetable. [3] any of several similar or related plants. [4] another name for **kohlrabi.** ◆ Also called (for senses 1, 2): **navew.**
▷HISTORY C16: from earlier *turnepe*, perhaps from TURN (indicating its rounded shape) + *nepe*, from Latin *nāpus* turnip; see NEEP

turnip moth NOUN a common noctuid moth, *Agrotis segetum*, drab grey-brown in colour, the larvae of which feed on root crops and brassica stems.

turnkey ('tɜːnˌkiː) NOUN [1] *Archaic* a keeper of the keys, esp in a prison; warder or jailer. ◆ ADJECTIVE [2] denoting a project, as in civil engineering, in which a single contractor has responsibility for the complete job from the start to the time of installation or occupancy.

turnkey project NOUN *Engineering* a complete project usually including many major units of plant completed under one overall contract, such as a chemical works or power station complex.
▷HISTORY C20: from use of *turnkey* in the construction industry to describe the day a job will be completed and the owner able to turn the key in the door

turnkey system NOUN a computer or computer system supplied to a customer in such a complete form that it can be put to immediate use.

turn off VERB [1] to leave (a road, pathway, etc.). [2] (of a road, pathway, etc.) to deviate from (another road, etc.). [3] (*tr, adverb*) to cause (something) to cease operating by turning a knob, pushing a button, etc.: *to turn off the radio.* [4] (*tr*) *Informal* to cause (a person, etc.) to feel dislike or distaste for (something): *this music turns me off.* [5] (*tr, adverb*) *Brit informal* to dismiss from employment. ◆ NOUN **turn-off.** [6] a road or other way branching off from the main thoroughfare. [7] *Informal* a person or thing that elicits dislike or distaste.

turn on VERB [1] (*tr, adverb*) to cause (something) to operate by turning a knob, etc.: *to turn on the light.* [2] (*intr, preposition*) to depend or hinge on: *the success of the party turns on you.* [3] (*preposition*) to change or cause to change one's attitude so as to become hostile or to retaliate: *the dog turned on the children.* [4] (*tr, adverb*) *Informal* to produce (charm, tears, etc.) suddenly or automatically. [5] (*tr, preposition, foll by to*) *Informal* to interest (someone) in something: *how to turn kids on to drama.* [6] (*tr, adverb*) *Slang* to arouse emotionally or sexually. [7] (*intr, adverb*) *Slang* to take or become intoxicated by drugs. [8] (*tr, adverb*) *Slang* to introduce (someone) to drugs. ◆ NOUN **turn-on.** [9] *Slang* a person or thing that causes emotional or sexual arousal.

turn out VERB (*adverb*) [1] (*tr*) to cause (something, esp a light) to cease operating by or as if by turning a knob, etc. [2] (*tr*) to produce by an effort or process: *she turned out 50 units per hour.* [3] (*tr*) to dismiss, discharge, or expel: *the family had been turned out of their home.* [4] (*tr*) to empty the contents of, esp in order to clean, tidy, or rearrange: *to turn out one's pockets.* [5] (*copula*) **a** to prove to be: *her work turned out to be badly done.* **b** to end up; result: *it all turned out well.* [6] (*tr*) to fit as with clothes: *that woman turns her children out well.* [7] (*intr*) to assemble or gather: *a crowd turned out for the fair.* [8] (of a soldier) to parade or to call (a soldier) to parade. [9] (*intr*) *Informal* to get out of bed. [10] (*intr; foll by for*) *Informal* to make an appearance, esp in a sporting competition: *he was asked to turn out for Liverpool.* ◆ NOUN **turnout.** [11] the body of people appearing together at a gathering. [12] the quantity or amount produced. [13] an array of clothing or equipment. [14] the manner in which a person or thing is arrayed or equipped.

turn over VERB (*adverb*) [1] to change or cause to change position, esp so as to reverse top and bottom. [2] to start (an engine), esp with a starting handle, or (of an engine) to start or function correctly. [3] to shift or cause to shift position, as by rolling from side to side. [4] (*tr*) to deliver; transfer. [5] (*tr*) to consider carefully: *he turned over the problem for hours.* [6] (*tr*) **a** to sell and replenish (stock in trade). **b** to transact business and so generate gross revenue of (a specified sum). [7] (*tr*) to invest and recover (capital). [8] (*tr*) *Slang* to rob. [9] (*tr*) *Slang* to defeat utterly. [10] **turn over a new leaf.** to reform; resolve to improve one's behaviour. ◆ NOUN **turnover.** [11] **a** the amount of business, usually expressed in terms of gross revenue, transacted during a specified period. **b** (*as modifier*): *a turnover tax.* [12] the rate at which stock in trade is sold and replenished. [13] a change or reversal of position. [14] a small semicircular or triangular pastry case filled with fruit, jam, etc. [15] **a** the number of workers employed by a firm in a given period to replace those who have left. **b** the ratio between this number and the average number of employees during the same period. [16] *Banking* the amount of capital funds loaned on call during a specified period. ◆ ADJECTIVE [17] (*prenominal*) able or designed to be turned or folded over: *a turnover collar.*

turnpike ('tɜːnˌpaɪk) NOUN [1] (between the mid-16th and late 19th centuries). **a** gates or some other barrier set across a road to prevent passage until a toll had been paid. **b** a road on which a turnpike was operated. [2] an obsolete word for **turnstile** (sense 1). [3] *US* a motorway for use of which a toll is charged.
▷HISTORY C15: from TURN + PIKE[2]

turnround ('tɜːnˌraʊnd) NOUN another word for **turnaround.**

turnsole ('tɜːnˌsəʊl) NOUN [1] any of various plants having flowers that are said to turn towards the sun. [2] a euphorbiaceous plant, *Croton tinctoria*, of the Mediterranean region that yields a purple dye. [3] the dye extracted from this plant.
▷HISTORY C14: from Old French *tournesole*, from Old Italian *tornasole*, from *tornare* to TURN + *sole* sun, from Latin *sōl* sun

turnspit ('tɜːnˌspɪt) NOUN [1] (formerly) a servant or small dog whose job was to turn the spit on which meat, poultry, etc., was roasting. [2] a spit that can be so turned.

turnstile ('tɜːnˌstaɪl) NOUN [1] a mechanical gate or barrier with metal arms that are turned to admit one person at a time, usually in one direction only. [2] any similar device that admits foot passengers but no large animals or vehicles. [3] *Logic* Also called: **gatepost.** a symbol of the form ⊢, ⊨, or ⊩, used to represent logical consequence when inserted between expressions to form a sequent, or when prefixed to a single expression to indicate its status as a theorem.

turnstone ('tɜːnˌstəʊn) NOUN either of two shore birds of the genus *Arenaria*, esp *A. interpres* (**ruddy turnstone**). They are related and similar to plovers and sandpipers.
▷HISTORY C17: so called because it turns over stones in search of food

turntable ('tɜːnˌteɪbᵊl) NOUN [1] the circular horizontal platform that rotates a gramophone record while it is being played. [2] a flat circular platform that can be rotated about its centre, used for turning locomotives and cars. [3] the revolvable platform on a microscope on which specimens are examined.

turntable ladder NOUN *Brit* a power-operated extending ladder mounted on a fire engine. US and Canadian name: **aerial ladder.**

turn to VERB (*intr, adverb*) to set about a task: *we must turn to and finish our work.*

turn up VERB (*adverb*) [1] (*intr*) to arrive or appear: *he turned up late at the party.* [2] to find or be found, esp by accident: *his book turned up in the cupboard.* [3] (*tr*) to increase the flow, volume, etc., of: *to turn up the radio.* [4] (*tr*) *Informal* to cause to vomit. ◆ NOUN **turn-up.** [5] (*often plural*) *Brit* the turned-up fold at the bottom of some trouser legs. US and Canadian name: **cuff.** [6] *Informal* an unexpected or chance occurrence.

turpentine ('tɜ:pᵊnˌtaɪn) NOUN [1] Also called: **gum turpentine.** any of various viscous oleoresins obtained from various coniferous trees, esp from the longleaf pine, and used as the main source of commercial turpentine. [2] a brownish-yellow sticky viscous oleoresin that exudes from the terebinth tree. [3] Also called: **oil of turpentine, spirits of turpentine.** a colourless flammable volatile liquid with a pungent odour, distilled from turpentine oleoresin. It is an essential oil containing a mixture of terpenes and is used as a solvent for paints and in medicine as a rubefacient and expectorant. Sometimes (esp Brit) shortened to: **turps.** [4] Also called: **turpentine substitute, white spirit.** (*not in technical usage*) any one of a number of thinners for paints and varnishes, consisting of fractions of petroleum. Related adjective: **terebinthine.** ◆ VERB (*tr*) [5] to treat or saturate with turpentine. [6] to extract crude turpentine from (trees).
▷HISTORY C14 *terebentyne*, from Medieval Latin *terbentīna*, from Latin *terebinthīna* turpentine, from *terebinthus* the turpentine tree, TEREBINTH

turpentine tree NOUN [1] a tropical African leguminous tree, *Copaifera mopane*, yielding a hard dark wood and a useful resin. [2] either of two Australian evergreen myrtaceous trees, *Syncarpia laurifolia* or *S. glomulifera*, that have durable wood and are sometimes planted as shade trees.

turpeth ('tɜ:pɪθ) NOUN [1] a convolvulaceous plant, *Operculina turpethum*, of the East Indies, having roots with purgative properties. [2] the root of this plant or the drug obtained from it.
▷HISTORY C14: from Medieval Latin *turbithum*, ultimately from Arabic *turbid*

turpitude ('tɜ:pɪˌtju:d) NOUN base character or action; depravity.
▷HISTORY C15: from Latin *turpitūdō* ugliness, from *turpis* base

turps (tɜ:ps) NOUN (*functioning as singular*) [1] *Brit* short for **turpentine** (sense 3). [2] *Austral and NZ slang* alcoholic drink, esp beer (esp in the phrase **on the turps**).

turquoise ('tɜ:kwɔɪz, -kwɑ:z) NOUN [1] a greenish-blue fine-grained secondary mineral consisting of hydrated copper aluminium phosphate. It occurs in igneous rocks rich in aluminium and is used as a gemstone. Formula: $CuAl_6(PO_4)_4(OH)_8.4H_2O$. [2] **a** the colour of turquoise. **b** (*as adjective*): *a turquoise dress.*
▷HISTORY C14: from Old French *turqueise* Turkish (stone)

turret ('tʌrɪt) NOUN [1] a small tower that projects from the wall of a building, esp a medieval castle. [2] **a** a self-contained structure, capable of rotation, in which weapons are mounted, esp in tanks and warships. **b** a similar structure on an aircraft that houses one or more guns and sometimes a gunner. [3] a tall wooden tower on wheels used formerly by besiegers to scale the walls of a fortress. [4] (on a machine tool) a turret-like steel structure with tools projecting radially that can be indexed round to select or to bring each tool to bear on the work.
▷HISTORY C14: from Old French *torete*, from *tor* tower, from Latin *turris*

turreted ('tʌrɪtɪd), **turriculate** (tʌ'rɪkjʊlɪt, -ˌleɪt), *or* **turriculated** ADJECTIVE [1] having or resembling a turret or turrets. [2] (of a gastropod shell) having the shape of a long spiral.

turret lathe NOUN another name for **capstan lathe.**

turtle¹ ('tɜ:tᵊl) NOUN [1] any of various aquatic chelonian reptiles, esp those of the marine family *Chelonidae*, having a flattened shell enclosing the body and flipper-like limbs adapted for swimming. Related adjectives: **chelonian, testudinal.** [2] *US and Canadian* any of the chelonian reptiles, including the tortoises and terrapins. [3] *Nautical* a zip bag made as part of a spinnaker for holding the sail so that it can be set rapidly. [4] **turn turtle.** to capsize. ◆ VERB [5] (*intr*) to catch or hunt turtles.
▷HISTORY C17: from French *tortue* TORTOISE (influenced by TURTLE²)
▸'**turtler** NOUN

turtle² ('tɜ:tᵊl) NOUN an archaic name for **turtledove.**
▷HISTORY Old English *turtla*, from Latin *turtur*, of imitative origin; related to German *Turteltaube*

turtleback ('tɜ:tᵊlˌbæk) NOUN [1] an arched projection over the upper deck of a ship at the bow and sometimes at the stern for protection in heavy seas. [2] (*now obsolete in archaeological usage*) a crude convex stone axe.

turtledove ('tɜ:tᵊlˌdʌv) NOUN [1] any of several Old World doves of the genus *Streptopelia*, having a brown plumage with speckled wings and a long dark tail. [2] a gentle or loving person.
▷HISTORY see TURTLE²

turtleneck ('tɜ:tᵊlˌnɛk) NOUN **a** a round high close-fitting neck on a sweater or the sweater itself. **b** (*as modifier*): *a turtleneck sweater.*

turves (tɜ:vz) NOUN a plural of **turf.**

Tuscan ('tʌskən) ADJECTIVE [1] of or relating to Tuscany, its inhabitants, or their dialect of Italian. [2] of, denoting, or relating to one of the five classical orders of architecture: characterized by a column with an unfluted shaft and a capital and base with mouldings but no decoration. See also **Ionic, Composite, Doric, Corinthian.** ◆ NOUN [3] a native or inhabitant of Tuscany. [4] any of the dialects of Italian spoken in Tuscany, esp the dialect of Florence: the standard form of Italian.

Tuscany ('tʌskənɪ) NOUN a region of central Italy, on the Ligurian and Tyrrhenian Seas: corresponds roughly to ancient Etruria; a region of numerous small states in medieval times; united in the 15th and 16th centuries under Florence; united with the rest of Italy in 1861. Capital: Florence. Pop.: 3 536 392 (2000 est.). Area: 22 990 sq. km (8876 sq. miles). Italian name: **Toscana.**

Tuscarora (ˌtʌskə'rɔ:rə) NOUN [1] (*plural* **-ras** *or* **-ra**) a member of a North American Indian people formerly living in North Carolina, who later moved to New York State and joined the Iroquois. [2] the language of this people, belonging to the Iroquoian family.

tusche (tʊʃ) NOUN a substance used in lithography for drawing the design and as a resist in silk-screen printing and lithography.
▷HISTORY from German, from *tuschen* to touch up with colour or ink, from French *toucher* to TOUCH

Tusculan ('tʌskjʊlən) ADJECTIVE of or relating to the ancient Italian city of Tusculum or its inhabitants.

tush¹ (tʌʃ) INTERJECTION *Archaic* an exclamation of disapproval or contempt.
▷HISTORY C15: Middle English, of imitative origin

tush² (tʌʃ) NOUN *Rare* a small tusk.
▷HISTORY Old English *tūsc*; see TUSK

tush³ (tʊʃ) NOUN *US slang* the buttocks.
▷HISTORY C20: from Yiddish *tokhes*, from Hebrew *tahath* beneath

tushery ('tʌʃərɪ) NOUN *Literary* the use of affectedly archaic language in novels, etc.
▷HISTORY coined by Robert Louis Stevenson (1850–94), Scottish writer, from TUSH¹ + -ERY

tusk (tʌsk) NOUN [1] a pointed elongated usually paired tooth in the elephant, walrus, and certain other mammals that is often used for fighting. [2] the canine tooth of certain animals, esp horses. [3] a sharp pointed projection. [4] Also called: **tusk tenon.** *Building trades* a tenon shaped with an additional oblique shoulder to make a stronger joint. ◆ VERB [5] to stab, tear, or gore with the tusks.
▷HISTORY Old English *tūsc*; related to Old Frisian *tosk*; see TOOTH
▸**tusked** ADJECTIVE ▸'**tuskˌlike** ADJECTIVE

tusker ('tʌskə) NOUN any animal with prominent tusks, esp a wild boar or elephant.

tusk shell NOUN any of various burrowing seashore molluscs of the genus *Dentalium* and related genera that have a long narrow tubular shell open at both ends: class *Scaphopoda*. Also called: **tooth shell.**

tussis ('tʌsɪs) NOUN the technical name for a **cough.** See **pertussis.**
▷HISTORY Latin: cough
▸'**tussal** ADJECTIVE ▸'**tussive** ADJECTIVE

tussle ('tʌsᵊl) VERB [1] (*intr*) to fight or wrestle in a vigorous way; struggle. ◆ NOUN [2] a vigorous fight; scuffle; struggle.
▷HISTORY C15: related to Old High German *zūsen*; see TOUSLE

tussock ('tʌsək) NOUN [1] a dense tuft of vegetation, esp of grass. [2] *Austral and NZ* **a** short for **tussock grass. b the.** country where tussock grass grows.
▷HISTORY C16: perhaps related to TUSK
▸'**tussocky** ADJECTIVE

tussock grass NOUN *Austral and NZ* any of several pasture grasses of the genus *Poa*.

tussock moth NOUN any of various pale or dull-coloured moths of the family *Lymantriidae* (or *Laparidae*), the hairy caterpillars of which are pests of many trees. See also **gipsy moth, brown-tail moth, goldtail moth.**
▷HISTORY C19: so named because of the tufts of hair on the caterpillars

tussore (tʊ'sɔ:, 'tʌsə), **tusser** ('tʌsə), *or chiefly US* **tussah** ('tʌsə) NOUN [1] a strong coarse brownish Indian silk obtained from the cocoons of an Oriental saturniid silkworm, *Antheraea paphia.* [2] a fabric woven from this silk. [3] the silkworm producing this silk.
▷HISTORY C17: from Hindi *tasar* shuttle, from Sanskrit *tasara* a wild silkworm

tut INTERJECTION (*pronounced as an alveolar click* (*spelling pron.* tʌt)) ◆ NOUN, VERB **tuts, tutting, tutted.** short for **tut-tut.**

tutee (tju:'ti:) NOUN one who is tutored, esp in a university.

tutelage ('tju:tɪlɪdʒ) NOUN [1] the act or office of a guardian or tutor. [2] instruction or guidance, esp by a tutor. [3] the condition of being under the supervision of a guardian or tutor.
▷HISTORY C17: from Latin *tūtēla* a caring for, from *tuērī* to watch over; compare TUITION

tutelary ('tju:tɪlərɪ) *or* **tutelar** ('tju:tɪlə) ADJECTIVE [1] invested with the role of guardian or protector. [2] of or relating to a guardian or guardianship. ◆ NOUN, *plural* **-laries** *or* **-lars.** [3] a tutelary person, deity, or saint.

tutiorism ('tju:tɪəˌrɪzəm) NOUN (in Roman Catholic moral theology) the doctrine that in cases of moral doubt it is best to follow the safer course or that in agreement with the law.
▷HISTORY C19: from Latin *tutior* safer, comparative of *tutus* safe
▸'**tutiorist** NOUN

tutor ('tju:tə) NOUN [1] a teacher, usually instructing individual pupils and often engaged privately. [2] (at universities, colleges, etc.) a member of staff responsible for the teaching and supervision of a certain number of students. [3] *Scots law* the guardian of a pupil. See **pupil¹** (sense 2). ◆ VERB [4] to act as a tutor to (someone); instruct. [5] (*tr*) to act as guardian to; have care of. [6] (*intr*) *Chiefly US* to study under a tutor. [7] (*tr*) *Rare* to admonish, discipline, or reprimand.
▷HISTORY C14: from Latin: a watcher, from *tuērī* to watch over
▸'**tutorage** *or* '**tutorˌship** NOUN

tutorial (tju:'tɔ:rɪəl) NOUN [1] a period of intensive tuition given by a tutor to an individual student or to a small group of students. ◆ ADJECTIVE [2] of or relating to a tutor.

tutorial system NOUN a system, mainly in universities, in which students receive guidance in academic or personal matters from tutors.

tutsan ('tʌtsən) NOUN a woodland shrub, *Hypericum androsaemum*, of Europe and W Asia, having yellow flowers and reddish-purple fruits: family *Hypericaceae*. See also **Saint John's wort.**
▷HISTORY C15: from Old French *toute-saine* (unattested), literally: all healthy

Tutsi ('tu:tsɪ) NOUN, *plural* **-si** *or* **-sis.** a member of a people of Rwanda and Burundi, probably a Nilotic people.

tutti ('tʊtɪ) ADJECTIVE, ADVERB *Music* to be performed by the whole orchestra, choir, etc. Compare **soli.**
▷HISTORY C18: from Italian, pl of *tutto* all, from Latin *tōtus*

tutti-frutti ('tu:tɪ'fru:tɪ) NOUN [1] (*plural* **-fruttis**) an ice cream or a confection containing small pieces of

candied or fresh fruits. [2] a preserve of chopped mixed fruits, often with brandy syrup. [3] a flavour like that of many fruits combined. ◆ ADJECTIVE [4] having such a flavour.
▷HISTORY from Italian, literally: all the fruits

tut-tut INTERJECTION *(pronounced as alveolar clicks (spelling pron.* ˈtʌtˈtʌt)) [1] an exclamation of mild reprimand, disapproval, or surprise. ◆ VERB **-tuts, -tutting, -tutted.** [2] *(intr)* to express disapproval by the exclamation of "tut-tut.". ◆ NOUN [3] the act of tut-tutting. ◆ Often shortened to: **tut.**

tutty (ˈtʌtɪ) NOUN finely powdered impure zinc oxide obtained from the flues of zinc-smelting furnaces and used as a polishing powder.
▷HISTORY C14: from Old French *tutie,* from Arabic *tūtiyā,* probably from Persian, from Sanskrit *tuttha*

tutu[1] (ˈtuːtuː) NOUN a very short skirt worn by ballerinas, made of projecting layers of stiffened sheer material.
▷HISTORY from French, changed from the nursery word *cucu* backside, from *cul,* from Latin *cūlus* the buttocks

tutu[2] (ˈtuːtuː) NOUN a shrub, *Coriaria arborea,* of New Zealand, having seeds that are poisonous to farm animals.
▷HISTORY Maori

Tutuila (ˌtuːtuːˈiːlə) NOUN the largest island of American Samoa, in the SW Pacific. Chief town and port: Pago Pago. Pop.: 54 108 (2000). Area: 135 sq. km (52 sq. miles).

Tuvalu (ˌtuːvəˈluː) NOUN a country in the SW Pacific, comprising a group of nine coral islands: established as a British protectorate in 1892. From 1915 until 1975 the islands formed part of the British colony of the Gilbert and Ellice Islands; achieved full independence in 1978; a special member of the Commonwealth (not represented at meetings of Commonwealth heads of state). Languages: English and Tuvaluan. Religion: Christian majority. Currency: Australian dollar; Tuvalu dollars are also used. Capital: Funafuti. Pop.: 11 000 (2001 est.). Area: 26 sq. km (10 sq. miles). Former names: **Lagoon Islands, Ellice Islands.**

Tuvaluan (ˌtuːvəˈluːən) ADJECTIVE [1] relating to, denoting, or characteristic of Tuvalu, its inhabitants, or their language. ◆ NOUN [2] a native or inhabitant of Tuvalu. [3] the Austronesian language of Tuvalu.

Tuva Republic (ˈtuːvə) NOUN a constituent republic of S Russia: mountainous. Capital: Kizyl. Pop.: 311 000 (2000 est.). Area: 170 500 sq. km (65 800 sq. miles). Also called: **Tuvinian Autonomous Republic.**

tu-whit tu-whoo (təˈwɪt təˈwuː) INTERJECTION an imitation or representation of the sound made by an owl.

tuxedo (tʌkˈsiːdəʊ) NOUN, *plural* **-dos.** the usual US and Canadian name for **dinner jacket,** often shortened to **tux.**
▷HISTORY C19: named after a country club in *Tuxedo Park,* New York

Tuxtla Gutiérrez (*Spanish* ˈtustla guˈtjɛrrɛθ) NOUN a city in SE Mexico, capital of Chiapas state: agricultural centre. Pop.: 425 000 (2000 est.).

tuyère (ˈtwiːɛə, ˈtwaɪə; *French* tyjɛr) *or* **twyer** (ˈtwaɪə) NOUN a water-cooled nozzle through which air is blown into a cupola, blast furnace, or forge.
▷HISTORY C18: from French, from *tuyau* pipe, from Old French *tuel,* probably of Germanic origin

tv THE INTERNET DOMAIN NAME FOR Tuvalu.

TV ABBREVIATION FOR: [1] television. [2] transvestite.

TVEI (in Britain) ABBREVIATION FOR technical and vocational educational initiative: a national educational scheme in which pupils gain practical experience in technology and industry often through work placement.

Tver (*Russian* tvjerj) NOUN a city in central Russia, at the confluence of the Volga and Tversta Rivers: chief port of the upper Volga, linked by canal with Moscow. Pop.: 457 100 (1999 est.). Former name (1932–91): **Kalinin.**

TVM ABBREVIATION FOR television movie: a film made specifically for television, and not intended for release in cinemas.

TVNZ ABBREVIATION FOR Television New Zealand.

TVP ABBREVIATION FOR textured vegetable protein: a protein obtained from soya beans or other vegetables that have been spun into fibres and flavoured: used esp as a substitute for meat.

TVR ABBREVIATION FOR television rating: a measurement of the popularity of a television programme based on a survey.

TVRO ABBREVIATION FOR television receive only: an antenna and associated apparatus for reception from a broadcasting satellite.

tw THE INTERNET DOMAIN NAME FOR Taiwan.

twa (twɔː) *or* **twae** (twe) NOUN, DETERMINER a Scot word for **two.**

twaddle (ˈtwɒdᵊl) NOUN [1] silly, trivial, or pretentious talk or writing; nonsense. ◆ VERB [2] to talk or write (something) in a silly or pretentious way.
▷HISTORY C16 *twattle,* variant of *twittle* or *tittle;* see TITTLE-TATTLE
▸ˈ**twaddler** NOUN

twain (tweɪn) DETERMINER, NOUN an archaic word for **two.**
▷HISTORY Old English *twēgen;* related to Old Saxon *twēne,* Old High German *zwēne,* Old Norse *tveir,* Gothic *twai*

twang (twæŋ) NOUN [1] a sharp ringing sound produced by or as if by the plucking of a taut string: *the twang of a guitar.* [2] the act of plucking a string to produce such a sound. [3] a strongly nasal quality in a person's speech, esp in certain dialects. ◆ VERB [4] to make or cause to make a twang: *to twang a guitar.* [5] to strum (music, a tune, etc.): *to twang on a guitar.* [6] to speak or utter with a sharp nasal voice. [7] *(intr)* to be released or move with a twang: *the arrow twanged away.*
▷HISTORY C16: of imitative origin
▸ˈ**twangy** ADJECTIVE

'twas (twɒz; *unstressed* twəz) *Poetic or dialect* CONTRACTION OF it was.

twat (twæt, twɒt) NOUN *Taboo slang* [1] the female genitals. [2] a girl or woman considered sexually. [3] a foolish or despicable person.
▷HISTORY of unknown origin

twattle (ˈtwɒtᵊl) NOUN a rare word for **twaddle.**

twayblade (ˈtweɪˌbleɪd) NOUN [1] any terrestrial orchid of the genus *Listera,* having a basal pair of oval unstalked leaves arranged opposite each other. [2] any of various other orchids with paired basal leaves.
▷HISTORY C16: translation of Medieval Latin *bifolium* having two leaves, from obsolete *tway* TWO + BLADE

tweak (twiːk) VERB *(tr)* [1] to twist, jerk, or pinch with a sharp or sudden movement: *to tweak someone's nose.* [2] *Motor racing slang* to tune (a car or engine) for peak performance. [3] *Informal* to make a minor alteration. ◆ NOUN [4] an instance of tweaking. [5] *Informal* a minor alteration.
▷HISTORY Old English *twiccian;* related to Old High German *zwecchōn;* see TWITCH
▸ˈ**tweaky** ADJECTIVE

tweaker (ˈtwiːkə) NOUN *Slang* an engineer's small screwdriver, used for fine adjustments.

twee (twiː) ADJECTIVE *Brit* excessively sentimental, sweet, or pretty.
▷HISTORY C19: from *tweet,* mincing or affected pronunciation of SWEET
▸ˈ**tweely** ADVERB ▸ˈ**tweeness** NOUN

tweed (twiːd) NOUN [1] **a** a thick woollen often knobbly cloth produced originally in Scotland. **b** *(as modifier): a tweed coat.* [2] *(plural)* clothes made of this cloth, esp a man's or woman's suit. [3] *(plural) Austral informal* trousers.
▷HISTORY C19: probably from *tweel,* a Scottish variant of TWILL, influenced by TWEED

Tweed (twiːd) NOUN a river in SE Scotland and NE England, flowing east and forming part of the border between Scotland and England, then crossing into England to enter the North Sea at Berwick. Length: 156 km (97 miles).

Tweeddale (ˈtwiːdˌdeɪl) NOUN another name for **Peeblesshire.**

Tweedledum and Tweedledee (ˌtwiːdᵊlˈdʌm, ˌtwiːdᵊlˈdiː) NOUN any two persons or things that differ only slightly from each other; two of a kind.
▷HISTORY C19: from the proverbial names of George Frederick Handel (1685–1759), German composer, and the musician Buononcini, who were supported by rival factions though it was thought by some that there was nothing to choose between them. The names were popularized by Lewis Carroll's use of them in *Through the Looking Glass* (1872)

tweedy (ˈtwiːdɪ) ADJECTIVE **tweedier, tweediest.** [1] of, made of, or resembling tweed. [2] showing a fondness for a hearty outdoor life, usually associated with wearers of tweeds.
▸ˈ**tweediness** NOUN

'tween (twiːn) *Poetic or dialect* CONTRACTION OF between.

tweenager (ˈtwiːnˌeɪdʒə) NOUN *Informal* a child of approximately eight to fourteen years of age.
▷HISTORY from (BE)TWEEN + (TEEN)AGER

'tween deck *or* **decks** NOUN *Nautical* a space between two continuous decks of a vessel.

tweeny (ˈtwiːnɪ) NOUN, *plural* **tweenies.** [1] *Brit informal obsolete* a maid who assists both cook and housemaid. [2] Also: **tweenie.** *Informal* **a** a child of approximately eight to fourteen years of age. **b** *(as modifier): tweeny magazines.*
▷HISTORY C19: shortened from BETWEEN (for sense 1, that is, a maid between cook and housemaid)

tweet (twiːt) INTERJECTION [1] *(often reiterated)* an imitation or representation of the thin chirping sound made by small or young birds. ◆ VERB [2] *(intr)* to make this sound.
▷HISTORY C19: of imitative origin

tweeter (ˈtwiːtə) NOUN a loudspeaker used in high-fidelity systems for the reproduction of high audio frequencies. It is usually employed in conjunction with a woofer and a crossover network.
▷HISTORY C20: from TWEET

tweeze (twiːz) VERB *Chiefly US* to take hold of or pluck (hair, small objects, etc.) with or as if with tweezers.
▷HISTORY C17: back formation from TWEEZERS

tweezers (ˈtwiːzəz) PLURAL NOUN a small pincer-like instrument for handling small objects, plucking out hairs, etc. Also called: **pair of tweezers,** (esp US) **tweezer.**
▷HISTORY C17: plural of *tweezer* (on the model of *scissors,* etc.), from *tweeze* case of instruments, from French *étuis* cases (of instruments), from Old French *estuier* to preserve, from Vulgar Latin *studiāre* (unattested) to keep, from Latin *studēre* to care about

twelfth (twɛlfθ) ADJECTIVE [1] *(usually prenominal)* **a** coming after the eleventh in number or counting order, position, time, etc.; being the ordinal number of *twelve:* often written 12th. **b** *(as noun): the twelfth of the month.* ◆ NOUN [2] **a** one of 12 equal or nearly equal parts of an object, quantity, measurement, etc. **b** *(as modifier): a twelfth part.* [3] the fraction equal to one divided by 12 (1/12). [4] *Music* **a** an interval of one octave plus a fifth. **b** one of two notes constituting such an interval in relation to the other. **c** an organ stop sounding a note one octave and a fifth higher than that normally produced by the key depressed.
▷HISTORY from Old English *twelfta*

Twelfth Day NOUN **a** Jan. 6, the twelfth day after Christmas and the feast of the Epiphany, formerly observed as the final day of the Christmas celebrations. **b** *(as modifier): Twelfth-Day celebrations.*

twelfth man NOUN a reserve player in a cricket team.

Twelfth Night NOUN **a** the evening of Jan. 5, the eve of Twelfth Day, formerly observed with various festal celebrations. **b** the evening of Twelfth Day itself. **c** *(as modifier): Twelfth-Night customs.*

Twelfthtide (ˈtwɛlfθˌtaɪd) NOUN **a** the season of Epiphany. **b** *(as modifier): the Twelfthtide celebrations.*

twelve (twɛlv) NOUN [1] the cardinal number that is the sum of ten and two. See also **number** (sense 1). [2] a numeral, 12, XII, etc., representing this number. [3] something represented by, representing, or consisting of 12 units. [4] Also called: **twelve o'clock.** noon or midnight. ◆ DETERMINER [5] **a** amounting to twelve: *twelve loaves.* **b** *(as pronoun): twelve have arrived.* ◆ Related adjective: **duodecimal.** Related prefix: **dodeca-.** See also **dozen.**
▷HISTORY Old English *twelf;* related to Old Frisian *twelif,* Old High German *zwelif,* Old Norse *tolf,* Gothic *twalif*

twelve-inch NOUN a gramophone record 12 inches in diameter and played at 45 revolutions per minute, usually containing an extended remix of a single.

twelve-mile limit NOUN the offshore boundary 12 miles from the coast claimed by some states as marking the extent of their territorial jurisdiction.

twelvemo ('twɛlvməʊ) NOUN, *plural* **-mos.** *Bookbinding* another word for **duodecimo.**

twelvemonth ('twɛlvˌmʌnθ) NOUN *Chiefly Brit* an archaic or dialect word for a **year.**

twelve pitch NOUN another name for **elite** (sense 2).

twelve-step ADJECTIVE *Chiefly US* of or relating to a method of treatment for addiction which consists of twelve stages and stresses the need for patients to acknowledge their problem and to take personal responsibility for it.

Twelve Tables PLURAL NOUN **the.** the earliest code of Roman civil, criminal, and religious law, promulgated in 451–450 B.C.

twelve-tone ADJECTIVE of, relating to, or denoting the type of serial music invented and developed by Arnold Schoenberg, which uses as musical material a tone row formed by the 12 semitones of the chromatic scale, together with its inverted and retrograde versions. The technique has been applied in various ways by different composers and usually results in music in which there are few, if any, tonal centres. See **serialism.**

twentieth ('twɛntɪɪθ) ADJECTIVE 1 (*usually prenominal*) **a** coming after the nineteenth in numbering or counting order, position, time, etc.; being the ordinal number of *twenty:* often written 20th. **b** (*as noun*): *he left on the twentieth.* ◆ NOUN 2 **a** one of 20 approximately equal parts of something. **b** (*as modifier*): *a twentieth part.* 3 the fraction that is equal to one divided by 20 (1/20).
▷HISTORY from Old English *twentigotha*

twenty ('twɛntɪ) NOUN, *plural* **-ties.** 1 the cardinal number that is the product of ten and two; a score. See also **number** (sense 1). 2 a numeral, 20, XX, etc., representing this number. 3 something representing, represented by, or consisting of 20 units. ◆ DETERMINER 4 **a** amounting to twenty: *twenty questions.* **b** (*as pronoun*): *to order twenty.* ◆ Related adjectives: **vicenary, vigesimal.** Related prefix: **icosa-.**
▷HISTORY Old English *twēntig;* related to Old High German *zweinzug,* German *zwanzig*

twenty-four-seven *or* **24/7** ADVERB *Informal* twenty-four hours a day, seven days a week; constantly; all the time: *consultants would no longer be available 24/7.*

twenty-one NOUN another name (esp US) for **pontoon**[2] (sense 1).

twenty-six counties PLURAL NOUN the counties of the Republic of Ireland.

twenty-sixer NOUN *Canadian informal* a liquor bottle of around 26 ounces (0.750 litre) capacity.

twenty-twenty ADJECTIVE *Med* (of vision) being of normal acuity: usually written 20/20.

'twere (twɜː; *unstressed* twə) *Poetic or dialect* CONTRACTION OF it were.

twerp *or* **twirp** (twɜːp) NOUN *Informal* a silly, weak-minded, or contemptible person.
▷HISTORY C20: of unknown origin
▸ **'twerpy** *or* **'twirpy** ADJECTIVE

Twi (twiː) NOUN 1 a language of S Ghana: one of the two chief dialects of Akan. Formerly called: **Ashanti.** Compare **Fanti.** 2 (*plural* **Twi** *or* **Twis**) a member of the Negroid people who speak this language.

twibill *or* **twibil** ('twaɪˌbɪl) NOUN 1 a mattock with a blade shaped like an adze at one end and like an axe at the other. 2 *Archaic* a double-bladed battle-axe.
▷HISTORY Old English, from *twi-* two, double + *bill* sword, BILL[3]

twice (twaɪs) ADVERB 1 two times; on two occasions or in two cases: *he coughed twice.* 2 double in degree or quantity: *twice as long.*
▷HISTORY Old English *twiwa;* related to Old Norse *tvisvar,* Middle Low German *twiges*

twice-laid ADJECTIVE 1 made from strands of used rope. 2 made from old or used material or retwisted yarn.
▷HISTORY C16: from LAY[1] (in the sense: to twist together)

twice-told ADJECTIVE hackneyed through repeated use.

Twickenham ('twɪkənəm) NOUN a former town in SE England, on the River Thames: part of the Greater London borough of Richmond-upon-Thames since 1965; contains the English Rugby Football Union ground.

twiddle ('twɪdᵊl) VERB 1 (when *intr,* often foll by *with*) to twirl or fiddle (with), often in an idle way. 2 to do nothing; be unoccupied. 3 (*intr*) to turn, twirl, or rotate. 4 (*intr*) *Rare* to be occupied with trifles. ◆ NOUN 5 an act or instance of twiddling.
▷HISTORY C16: probably a blend of TWIRL + FIDDLE
▸ **'twiddler** NOUN

twig[1] (twɪg) NOUN 1 any small branch or shoot of a tree or other woody plant. 2 something resembling this, esp a minute branch of a blood vessel.
▷HISTORY Old English *twigge;* related to Old Norse *dvika* consisting of two, Old High German *zwīg* twig, Old Danish *tvige* fork
▸ **'twigˌlike** ADJECTIVE

twig[2] (twɪg) VERB **twigs, twigging, twigged.** *Brit informal* 1 to understand (something). 2 to find out or suddenly comprehend (something): *he hasn't twigged yet.* 3 (*tr*) *Rare* to perceive (something).
▷HISTORY C18: perhaps from Scottish Gaelic *tuig* I understand

twiggy ('twɪgɪ) ADJECTIVE **-gier, -giest.** 1 of or relating to a twig or twigs. 2 covered with twigs. 3 slender or fragile.

twilight ('twaɪˌlaɪt) NOUN 1 the soft diffused light occurring when the sun is just below the horizon, esp following sunset. Related adjective: **crepuscular.** 2 the period in which this light occurs. 3 the period of time during which the sun is a specified angular distance below the horizon (6°, 12°, and 18° for **civil twilight, nautical twilight,** and **astronomical twilight,** respectively). 4 any faint light. 5 a period in which strength, importance, etc., are waning: *the twilight of his life.* 6 (*modifier*) **a** of or relating to the period towards the end of the day: *the twilight shift.* **b** of or relating to the final phase of a particular era: *the twilight days of the Bush presidency.* **c** denoting irregularity and obscurity: *a twilight existence.*
▷HISTORY C15: literally: half-light (between day and night), from Old English *twi-* half + LIGHT[1]
▸ **twilit** ('twaɪˌlɪt) ADJECTIVE

Twilight of the Gods NOUN another term for **Götterdämmerung** or **Ragnarök.**

twilight sleep NOUN *Med* a state of partial anaesthesia in which the patient retains a slight degree of consciousness.

twilight zone NOUN 1 any indefinite or transitional condition or area. 2 an area of a city or town, usually surrounding the central business district, where houses have become dilapidated. 3 the lowest level of the ocean to which light can penetrate.

twill (twɪl) ADJECTIVE 1 (in textiles) of or designating a weave in which the weft yarns are worked around two or more warp yarns to produce an effect of parallel diagonal lines or ribs. ◆ NOUN 2 any fabric so woven. ◆ VERB 3 (*tr*) to weave in this fashion.
▷HISTORY Old English *twilic* having a double thread; related to Old High German *zwilīth* twill, Latin *bilīx* two-threaded

'twill (twɪl) *Poetic or dialect* CONTRACTION OF it will.

twin (twɪn) NOUN 1 **a** either of two persons or animals conceived at the same time. **b** (*as modifier*): *a twin brother.* See also **identical** (sense 3), **fraternal** (sense 3). 2 **a** either of two persons or things that are identical or very similar; counterpart. **b** (*as modifier*): *twin carburettors.* 3 Also called: **macle.** a crystal consisting of two parts each of which has a definite orientation to the other. ◆ VERB **twins, twinning, twinned.** 4 to pair or be paired together; couple. 5 (*intr*) to bear twins. 6 (*intr*) (of a crystal) to form into a twin. 7 (*intr*) *Archaic* to be born as a twin. 8 (*tr*) **a** to create a reciprocal relation between (two towns in different countries); pair (a town) with another in a different country. **b** (*intr*) (of a town) to be paired with a town in a different country.
▷HISTORY Old English *twinn;* related to Old High German *zwiniling* twin, Old Norse *tvinnr* double
▸ **'twinning** NOUN

twin bed NOUN one of a pair of matching single beds.

twinberry ('twɪnbərɪ, -brɪ) NOUN, *plural* **-ries.** another name for **partridgeberry** (sense 1).

twin bill NOUN *US* an informal name for **double feature** or **double-header** (sense 2).

twine (twaɪn) NOUN 1 string made by twisting together fibres of hemp, cotton, etc. 2 the act or an instance of twining. 3 something produced or characterized by twining. 4 a twist, coil, or convolution. 5 a knot, tangle, or snarl. ◆ VERB 6 (*tr*) to twist together; interweave: *she twined the wicker to make a basket.* 7 (*tr*) to form by or as if by twining: *to twine a garland.* 8 (when *intr,* often foll by *around*) to wind or cause to wind, esp in spirals: *the creeper twines around the tree.*
▷HISTORY Old English *twīn;* related to Old Frisian *twīne,* Dutch *twijn* twine, Lithuanian *dvynu* twins; see TWIN
▸ **'twiner** NOUN

twinflower ('twɪnˌflaʊə) NOUN an evergreen caprifoliaceous trailing shrub, *Linnaea borealis,* of circumpolar distribution, having round leaves, white or pink fragrant bell-shaped flowers arranged in pairs, and yellow fruits.

twinge (twɪndʒ) NOUN 1 a sudden brief darting or stabbing pain. 2 a sharp emotional pang: *a twinge of conscience.* ◆ VERB 3 to have or cause to have a twinge. 4 (*tr*) *Obsolete* to pinch; tweak.
▷HISTORY Old English *twengan* to pinch; related to Old High German *zwengen*

twink (twɪŋk) NOUN *NZ* white correction fluid for deleting written text.

twinkle ('twɪŋkᵊl) VERB (*mainly intr*) 1 to emit or reflect light in a flickering manner; shine brightly and intermittently; sparkle: *twinkling stars.* 2 (of the eyes) to sparkle, esp with amusement or delight. 3 *Rare* to move about quickly. 4 (*also tr*) *Rare* to wink (the eyes); blink. ◆ NOUN 5 an intermittent gleam of light; flickering brightness; sparkle or glimmer. 6 an instant. 7 a rare word for **wink**[1].
▷HISTORY Old English *twinclian;* related to Middle High German *zwinken* to blink
▸ **'twinkler** NOUN

twinkling ('twɪŋklɪŋ) *or* **twink** (twɪŋk) NOUN a very short time; instant; moment. Also called: **twinkling of an eye.**

twink out VERB (*tr, adverb*) *NZ* to delete (written text) with white correction fluid.

twin-lens reflex NOUN See **reflex camera.**

twin paradox NOUN a phenomenon predicted by relativity. One of a pair of identical twins is supposed to live normally in an inertial system whilst the other is accelerated to a high speed in a spaceship, travels for a long time, and finally returns to rest beside his twin. The travelled twin will be found to be younger than his brother.

Twins (twɪnz) PLURAL NOUN **the.** the constellation Gemini, the third sign of the zodiac.

twin-screw ADJECTIVE (of a vessel) having two propellers.

twinset ('twɪnˌsɛt) NOUN *Brit* a matching jumper and cardigan.

twin town NOUN *Brit* a town that has civic associations, such as reciprocal visits and cultural exchanges, with a foreign town, usually of similar size and sometimes with other similarities, as in commercial activities.

twin-tub NOUN a type of washing machine that has two revolving drums, one for washing and the other for spin-drying.

twirl (twɜːl) VERB 1 to move or cause to move around rapidly and repeatedly in a circle. 2 (*tr*) to twist, wind, or twiddle, often idly: *she twirled her hair around her finger.* 3 (*intr;* often foll by *around* or *about*) to turn suddenly to face another way: *she twirled around angrily to face him.* ◆ NOUN 4 an act of rotating or being rotated; whirl or twist. 5 something wound around or twirled; coil. 6 a written flourish or squiggle.
▷HISTORY C16: perhaps a blend of TWIST + WHIRL
▸ **'twirler** NOUN

twirp (twɜːp) NOUN a variant spelling of **twerp.**

twist (twɪst) VERB 1 to cause (one end or part) to turn or (of one end or part) to turn in the opposite direction from another; coil or spin. 2 to distort or be distorted; change in shape. 3 to wind or cause to wind; twine, coil, or intertwine: *to twist flowers into a wreath.* 4 to force or be forced out of the natural form or position: *to twist one's ankle.* 5 (*usually passive*) to change or cause to change for the worse in character, meaning, etc.; pervert: *his ideas are twisted; she twisted the statement.* 6 to revolve or cause to revolve; rotate. 7 (*tr*) to wrench with a turning action: *to twist something from someone's grasp.* 8 (*intr*) to follow a winding course. 9 (*intr*) to squirm, as with pain. 10 (*intr*) to dance the twist. 11 (*tr*) *Brit informal* to cheat; swindle. 12 **twist someone's arm.** to persuade or coerce someone. ◆ NOUN 13 the act or an instance of twisting. 14 something formed by or as if by twisting: *a twist of hair.* 15 a decisive change of direction, aim, meaning, or character. 16 (in a novel, play, etc.) an unexpected event, revelation, or other development. 17 a bend: *a twist in the road.* 18 a distortion of the original or natural shape or form. 19 a jerky pull, wrench, or turn. 20 a strange personal characteristic, esp a bad one. 21 a confused mess, tangle, or knot made by twisting. 22 a twisted thread used in sewing where extra strength is needed. 23 (in weaving) a specified direction of twisting the yarn. 24 **the twist.** a modern dance popular in the 1960s, in which couples vigorously twist the hips in time to rhythmic music. 25 a bread loaf or roll made of one or more pieces of twisted dough. 26 a thin sliver of peel from a lemon, lime, etc., twisted and added to a drink. 27 **a** a cigar made by twisting three cigars around one another. **b** chewing tobacco made in the form of a roll by twisting the leaves together. 28 *Physics* torsional deformation or shear stress or strain. 29 *Sport chiefly US and Canadian* spin given to a ball in various games, esp. baseball. 30 the extent to which the grooves in the bore of a rifled firearm are spiralled. 31 **round the twist.** *Brit slang* mad; eccentric.
▷HISTORY Old English; related to German dialect *Zwist* a quarrel, Dutch *twisten* to quarrel
▸ **'twistable** ADJECTIVE ▸ **ˌtwista'bility** NOUN ▸ **'twisted** ADJECTIVE ▸ **'twisting** ADJECTIVE ▸ **'twisty** ADJECTIVE

twist drill NOUN a drill bit having two helical grooves running from the point along the shank to clear swarf and cuttings.

twister ('twɪstə) NOUN 1 *Brit* a swindling or dishonest person. 2 a person or thing that twists, such as a device used in making ropes. 3 *US and Canadian* an informal name for **tornado.** 4 a ball moving with a twisting motion.

twist grip NOUN a handlebar control in the form of a ratchet-controlled rotating grip, used on some bicycles and motorcycles as a gear-change control and on motorcycles as an accelerator.

twit¹ (twɪt) VERB **twits, twitting, twitted.** 1 (*tr*) to tease, taunt, or reproach, often in jest. ◆ NOUN 2 *US and Canadian informal* a nervous or excitable state. 3 *Rare* a reproach; taunt.
▷HISTORY Old English *ætwītan,* from *æt* against + *wītan* to accuse; related to Old High German *wīzan* to punish

twit² (twɪt) NOUN *Informal, chiefly Brit* a foolish or stupid person; idiot.
▷HISTORY C19: from TWIT¹ (originally in the sense: a person given to twitting)

twitch (twɪtʃ) VERB 1 to move or cause to move in a jerky spasmodic way. 2 (*tr*) to pull or draw (something) with a quick jerky movement. 3 (*intr*) to hurt with a sharp spasmodic pain. 4 (*tr*) *Rare* to nip. ◆ NOUN 5 a sharp jerking movement. 6 a mental or physical twinge. 7 a sudden muscular spasm, esp one caused by a nervous condition. Compare **tic.** 8 a loop of cord used to control a horse by drawing it tight about its upper lip.
▷HISTORY Old English *twiccian* to pluck; related to Old High German *zwecchōn* to pinch, Dutch *twicken*
▸ **twitching** ADJECTIVE, NOUN

twitcher ('twɪtʃə) NOUN 1 a person or thing that twitches. 2 *Informal* a bird-watcher who tries to spot as many rare varieties as possible.

twitch grass NOUN another name for **couch grass.** Sometimes shortened to: **twitch.**
▷HISTORY C16: a variant of QUITCH GRASS

twitchy ('twɪtʃɪ) ADJECTIVE nervous, worried, and ill-at-ease: *he was twitchy with anticipation.*

twite (twaɪt) NOUN a N European finch, *Acanthis flavirostris,* with a brown streaked plumage.
▷HISTORY C16: imitative of its cry

twitten ('twɪtᵊn) NOUN *Southeast English dialect* a narrow alleyway.

twitter ('twɪtə) VERB 1 (*intr*) (esp of a bird) to utter a succession of chirping sounds. 2 (*intr*) to talk or move rapidly and tremulously. 3 (*intr*) to giggle: *her schoolmates twittered behind their desks.* 4 (*tr*) to utter in a chirping way. ◆ NOUN 5 a twittering sound, esp of a bird. 6 the act of twittering. 7 a state of nervous excitement (esp in the phrase **in a twitter**).
▷HISTORY C14: of imitative origin
▸ **'twitterer** NOUN ▸ **'twittery** ADJECTIVE

'twixt *or* **twixt** (twɪkst) *Poetic* CONTRACTION OF betwixt.

two (tuː) NOUN 1 the cardinal number that is the sum of one and one. It is a prime number. See also **number** (sense 1). 2 a numeral, 2, II, (ii), etc., representing this number. 3 *Music* the numeral 2 used as the lower figure in a time signature, indicating that the beat is measured in minims. 4 something representing, represented by, or consisting of two units, such as a playing card with two symbols on it. 5 Also called: **two o'clock.** two hours after noon or midnight. 6 **in two.** in or into two parts: *break the bread in two.* 7 **put two and two together.** to make an inference from available evidence, esp an obvious inference. 8 **that makes two of us.** the same applies to me. ◆ DETERMINER 9 **a** amounting to two: *two nails.* **b** (*as pronoun*): *he bought two.* ◆ Related adjectives: **binary, double, dual.** Related prefixes: **di-, bi-.**
▷HISTORY Old English *twā* (feminine); related to Old High German *zwā,* Old Norse *tvau,* Latin, Greek *duo*

Two-and-a-half International NOUN another name for the **Vienna Union.**

two-bit ADJECTIVE (*prenominal*) *Slang, chiefly US and Canadian* worth next to nothing; cheap.
▷HISTORY C20: from the phrase *two bits* a small sum

two-by-four NOUN 1 a length of untrimmed timber with a cross section that measures 2 inches by 4 inches. 2 a trimmed timber joist with a cross section that measures 1½ inches by 3½ inches.

twoccing *or* **twocking** ('twɒkɪŋ) NOUN *Brit slang* the act of breaking into a motor vehicle and driving it away.
▷HISTORY C20: from *T(aking) W(ithout) O(wner's) C(onsent),* the legal offence with which car thieves may be charged
▸ **'twoccer** *or* **'twocker** NOUN

two-cycle ADJECTIVE the US and Canadian word for **two-stroke.**

two-dimensional ADJECTIVE 1 of, having, or relating to two dimensions, usually describable in terms of length and breadth or length and height. 2 lying on a plane; having an area but not enclosing any volume. 3 lacking in depth, as characters in a literary work. 4 (of painting or drawing) lacking the characteristics of form or depth.
▸ **'two-diˌmension'ality** NOUN ▸ **'two-di'mensionally** ADVERB

two-edged ADJECTIVE 1 having two cutting edges. 2 (esp of a remark) having two interpretations, such as *she looks nice when she smiles.*

two-faced ADJECTIVE deceitful; insincere; hypocritical.
▸ **two-facedly** ('tuː'feɪsɪdlɪ, -'feɪst-) ADVERB
▸ **'two-'facedness** NOUN

two-fisted ADJECTIVE *US* strong, tough, and vigorous: *a hard-drinking two-fisted hunter.*

twofold ('tuːˌfəʊld) ADJECTIVE 1 equal to twice as many or twice as much; double: *a twofold increase.* 2 composed of two parts; dual: *a twofold reason.* ◆ ADVERB 3 doubly.

two-four NOUN *Canadian informal* a box containing 24 bottles of beer.

two-four time NOUN *Music* a form of simple duple time in which there are two crotchet beats in each bar.

two-handed ADJECTIVE 1 requiring the use of both hands. 2 ambidextrous. 3 requiring the participation or cooperation of two people.
▸ **'two-'handedly** ADVERB

two-hander (ˌtuː'hændə) NOUN a play for two actors.

two-line NOUN (*modifier*) (formerly) denoting double the normal size of printer's type: *two-line pica (24 point).*

two-name paper NOUN *US finance* a commercial paper signed by two persons both of whom accept full liability.

twonie ('tuːnɪ) NOUN variant spelling of **toonie.**

Two Oceans NOUN (*functioning as singular*) an annual road marathon run in Cape Town, South Africa.

two-pack ADJECTIVE (of a paint, filler, etc.) supplied as two separate components, for example a base and a catalyst, that are mixed together immediately before use.

two-party system NOUN a condition or system in which two major parties dominate a political unit.

twopence *or* **tuppence** ('tʌpəns) NOUN *Brit* 1 the sum of two pennies. 2 (*used with a negative*) something of little value (in the phrase **not care** *or* **give twopence**). 3 a former British silver coin, now only coined as Maundy money.

twopenny *or* **tuppenny** ('tʌpənɪ) ADJECTIVE *Chiefly Brit* 1 Also: **twopenny-halfpenny.** cheap or tawdry. 2 (intensifier): *a twopenny damn.* 3 worth two pence.

two-phase ADJECTIVE (of an electrical circuit, device, etc.) generating or using two alternating voltages of the same frequency, displaced in phase by 90°. Also: **quarter-phase.**

two-piece ADJECTIVE 1 consisting of two separate parts, usually matching, as of a garment. ◆ NOUN 2 such an outfit.

two-ply ADJECTIVE 1 made of two thicknesses, layers, or strands. ◆ NOUN, *plural* **-plies.** 2 a two-ply wood, knitting yarn, etc.

two-pot screamer NOUN *Austral slang* a person easily influenced by alcohol.

two-seater NOUN a vehicle providing seats for two people.

Two Sicilies PLURAL NOUN **the.** a former kingdom of S Italy, consisting of the kingdoms of Sicily and Naples (1061–1860).

two-sided ADJECTIVE 1 having two sides or aspects. 2 controversial; debatable: *a two-sided argument.*

twosome ('tuːsəm) NOUN 1 two together, esp two people. 2 a match between two people. 3 (*modifier*) consisting of or played by two: *a twosome performance.*

two-spot NOUN a card with two pips; two; deuce.

two-step NOUN 1 an old-time dance in duple time. 2 a piece of music composed for or in the rhythm of such a dance.

two-stroke ADJECTIVE relating to or designating an internal-combustion engine whose piston makes two strokes for every explosion. US and Canadian word: **two-cycle.** Compare **four-stroke.**

two-tailed ADJECTIVE *Statistics* (of a significance test) concerned with the hypothesis that an observed value of a sampling statistic differs significantly from a given value, where an error in either direction is relevant: for instance, in testing the fairness of scales, an inspector will seek to exclude both overweight and underweight goods. Compare **one-tailed.**

two-tailed pasha NOUN a distinctive vanessid butterfly of S Europe, *Charaxes jasius,* having mottled brown wings with a yellow-orange margin and frilled hind edges.

Two Thousand Guineas NOUN (*functioning as singular*) *usually written* **2000 Guineas** an annual horse race run at Newmarket since 1809.

two-tier ADJECTIVE involving or comprising two levels of structure, policy, etc.

two-time VERB *Informal* to deceive (someone, esp a lover) by carrying on a relationship with another.
▸ **ˌtwo-'timer** NOUN

two-tone ADJECTIVE 1 of two colours or two

shades of the same colour. [2] (esp of sirens, car horns, etc.) producing or consisting of two notes.

two-tooth NOUN, *plural* **-tooths**. *Austral and NZ* a sheep between one and two years old with two permanent incisor teeth.

'twould (twʊd) *Poetic or dialect* CONTRACTION OF it would.

two-up NOUN *Chiefly Austral* a gambling game in which two coins are tossed or spun. Bets are made on both coins landing with the same face uppermost.

two-way ADJECTIVE [1] moving, permitting movement, or operating in either of two opposite directions: *two-way traffic; a two-way valve.* [2] involving two participants: *a two-way agreement.* [3] involving reciprocal obligation or mutual action: *a two-way process.* [4] (of a radio, telephone, etc.) allowing communications in two directions using both transmitting and receiving equipment.

two-way mirror NOUN a half-silvered sheet of glass that functions as a mirror when viewed from one side but is translucent from the other.

two-way street NOUN an arrangement or a situation involving reciprocal obligation or mutual action.

twp (tʊp) ADJECTIVE (*predicative*) *South Wales dialect* stupid; daft.
▷HISTORY Welsh

twyer ('twaɪə) NOUN a variant of **tuyère.**

TX *Text messaging* ◆ ABBREVIATION FOR: [1] Texas. [2] thanks.

TXT *Text messaging* ABBREVIATION FOR text.

-ty[1] SUFFIX OF NUMERALS denoting a multiple of ten: *sixty; seventy.*
▷HISTORY from Old English *-tig* TEN

-ty[2] SUFFIX FORMING NOUNS indicating state, condition, or quality: *cruelty.*
▷HISTORY from Old French *-te, -tet,* from Latin *-tās, -tāt-;* related to Greek *-tēs*

Tyan-Shan ('tjan'ʃan) NOUN transliteration of the Russian name for the **Tian Shan.**

Tyburn ('taɪbɜːn) NOUN (formerly) a place of execution in London, on the **River Tyburn** (a tributary of the Thames, now entirely below ground).

Tyche ('taɪkɪ) NOUN *Greek myth* the goddess of fortune. Roman counterpart: **Fortuna.**

ychism ('taɪkɪzəm) NOUN *Philosophy* the theory hat chance is an objective reality at work in the niverse, esp in evolutionary adaptations.
HISTORY from Greek *tukhē* chance

'ycho ('taɪkəʊ) NOUN a relatively young crater in he SW quadrant of the moon, 4 km deep and 84 m in diameter, with a central peak. It is the centre f a conspicuous system of rays.
HISTORY named after *Tycho* Brahe (1546–1601), anish astronomer

ycoon (taɪ'kuːn) NOUN [1] a business man of great ealth and power. [2] an archaic name for a **shogun.**
HISTORY C19: from Japanese *taikun,* from Chinese great + *chün* ruler

yke *or* **tike** (taɪk) NOUN [1] a dog, esp a mongrel. *Informal* a small or cheeky child: used esp in fectionate reproof. [3] *Brit dialect* a rough -mannered person. [4] Also called: **Yorkshire tyke.** *it slang often offensive* a person from Yorkshire. [5] *ustral slang offensive* a Roman Catholic.
HISTORY C14: from Old Norse *tīk* bitch

'lopod ('taɪləʊˌpɒd) NOUN any artiodactyl ammal of the suborder *Tylopoda,* having padded, ther than hoofed, digits: includes the camels and mas.
HISTORY C19: from New Latin, from Greek *tulos* ob or *tulē* cushion + -POD

losis (taɪ'ləʊsɪs) NOUN *Botany* a bladder-like tgrowth from certain cells in woody tissue that tends into and blocks adjacent conducting xylem lls.
ISTORY C19: from Greek *tulōsis,* from *tulos* knob *tulē* callus + -OSIS

mbal ('tɪmbᵊl) NOUN a variant spelling of **timbal.**

mpan ('tɪmpən) NOUN [1] a membrane stretched er a frame or resonating cylinder, bowl, etc. [2] *nting* packing interposed on a hand-operated text ween the platen and the paper to be printed in order to provide an even impression. [3] *Architect* another name for **tympanum** (sense 3).
▷HISTORY Old English *timpana,* from Latin; see TYMPANUM

tympani ('tɪmpənɪ) PLURAL NOUN a variant spelling of **timpani.**

tympanic (tɪm'pænɪk) ADJECTIVE [1] *Anatomy, architect* of, relating to, or having a tympanum. [2] of, relating to, or resembling a drumhead.

tympanic bone NOUN the part of the temporal bone in the mammalian skull that surrounds the auditory canal.

tympanic membrane NOUN the thin translucent oval membrane separating the external ear from the middle ear. It transmits vibrations produced by sound waves, via the ossicles, to the cochlea. Also called: **tympanum.** Nontechnical name: **eardrum.**

tympanist ('tɪmpənɪst) NOUN a person who plays a drum, now specifically the kettledrum.

tympanites (ˌtɪmpə'naɪtiːz) NOUN distension of the abdomen caused by an abnormal accumulation of gas in the intestinal or peritoneal cavity, as in peritonitis. Also called: **meteorism, tympany.**
▷HISTORY C14: from Late Latin, from Greek *tumpanitēs* concerning a drum, from *tumpanon* drum
▸**tympanitic** (ˌtɪmpə'nɪtɪk) ADJECTIVE

tympanitis (ˌtɪmpə'naɪtɪs) NOUN inflammation of the eardrum. Also called: **otitis media.**

tympanum ('tɪmpənəm) NOUN, *plural* **-nums** *or* **-na** (-nə). [1] **a** the cavity of the middle ear. **b** another name for **tympanic membrane.** [2] any diaphragm resembling that in the middle ear in function. [3] Also called: **tympan.** *Architect* **a** the recessed space bounded by the cornices of a pediment, esp one that is triangular in shape and ornamented. **b** the recessed space bounded by an arch and the lintel of a doorway or window below it. [4] *Music* a tympan or drum. [5] a scoop wheel for raising water.
▷HISTORY C17: from Latin, from Greek *tumpanon* drum; related to Greek *tuptein* to beat

tympany ('tɪmpənɪ) NOUN, *plural* **-nies.** [1] another name for **tympanites.** [2] *Obsolete* excessive pride or arrogance.

Tyndall effect NOUN the phenomenon in which light is scattered by particles of matter in its path. It enables a beam of light to become visible by illuminating dust particles, etc.
▷HISTORY C19: named after John *Tyndall* (1820–93), Irish physicist

tyndallimetry (ˌtɪndᵊl'ɪmɪtrɪ) NOUN *Chem* the determination of the concentration of suspended material in a liquid by measuring the amount of light scattered.
▷HISTORY C20: from TYNDALL EFFECT + -METRY

Tyndareus (tɪn'dærɪəs) NOUN *Greek myth* a Spartan king; the husband of Leda.

Tyne (taɪn) NOUN a river in N England, flowing east to the North Sea. Length: 48 km (30 miles).

Tyne and Wear NOUN a metropolitan county of NE England, administered since 1986 by the unitary authorities of Newcastle upon Tyne, North Tyneside, Gateshead, South Tyneside, and Sunderland. Area: 540 sq. km (208 sq. miles).

Tynemouth ('taɪnˌmaʊθ) NOUN a port in NE England, in North Tyneside unitary authority, Tyne and Wear, at the mouth of the River Tyne: includes the port and industrial centre of North Shields; fishing, ship-repairing, and marine engineering. Pop.: 20 716 (1991).

Tyneside ('taɪnˌsaɪd) NOUN the conurbation on the banks of the Tyne from Newcastle to the coast. Related word: **Geordie.**

Tynwald ('tɪnwəld, 'taɪn-) NOUN **the.** the Parliament of the Isle of Man, consisting of the crown, lieutenant governor, House of Keys, and legislative council. Full name: **Tynwald Court.**
▷HISTORY C15: from Old Norse *thingvollr,* from *thing* assembly + *vollr* field

typ., typo., *or* **typog.** ABBREVIATION FOR: [1] typographer. [2] typographic(al). [3] typography.

typal ('taɪpᵊl) ADJECTIVE a rare word for **typical.**

type (taɪp) NOUN [1] a kind, class, or category, the constituents of which share similar characteristics. [2] a subdivision of a particular class of things or people; sort: *what type of shampoo do you use?* [3] the general form, plan, or design distinguishing a particular group. [4] *Informal* a person w… particular quality: *he's the administrative t…* *Informal* a person, esp of a specified kind: *he's … strange type.* [6] **a** a small block of metal or more rarely wood bearing a letter or character in relief for use in printing. **b** such pieces collectively. [7] characters printed from type; print. [8] *Biology* **a** the taxonomic group the characteristics of which are used for defining the next highest group, for example *Rattus norvegicus* (brown rat) is the type species of the rat genus *Rattus.* **b** (*as modifier*): *a type genus; a type species.* [9] See **type specimen.** [10] the characteristic device on a coin. [11] *Linguistics* a symbol regarded as standing for the class of all symbols identical to it. Compare **token** (sense 8). [12] *Logic* a class of expressions or of the entities they represent that can all enter into the same syntactic relations. The **theory of types** was advanced by Bertrand Russell to avoid the liar paradox, Russell's paradox, etc. [13] *Philosophy* a universal. If a sentence always has the same meaning whenever it is used, the meaning is said to be a property of the sentence-type. Compare **token** (sense 9). [14] *Chiefly Christian theol* a figure, episode, or symbolic factor resembling some future reality in such a way as to foreshadow or prefigure it. [15] *Rare* a distinctive sign or mark. ◆ VERB [16] to write (copy) on a typewriter. [17] (*tr*) to be a symbol of; typify. [18] (*tr*) to decide the type of; clarify into a type. [19] (*tr*) *Med* to determine the blood group of (a blood sample). [20] (*tr*) *Chiefly Christian theol* to foreshadow or serve as a symbol of (some future reality).
▷HISTORY C15: from Latin *typus* figure, from Greek *tupos* image, from *tuptein* to strike

-type NOUN, COMBINING FORM [1] type or form: *archetype.* [2] printing type or photographic process: *collotype.*
▷HISTORY from Latin *-typus,* from Greek *-typos,* from *tupos* TYPE

typebar ('taɪpˌbɑː) NOUN one of the bars in a typewriter that carry the type and are operated by keys.

typecase ('taɪpˌkeɪs) NOUN a compartmental tray for storing printer's type.

typecast ('taɪpˌkɑːst) VERB **-casts, -casting, -cast.** (*tr*) to cast (an actor) in the same kind of role continually, esp because of his physical appearance or previous success in such roles.
▸**'typeˌcaster** NOUN

typeface ('taɪpˌfeɪs) NOUN another name for **face** (sense 17).

type founder NOUN a person who casts metallic printer's type.
▸**type founding** NOUN ▸**type foundry** NOUN

type-high ADJECTIVE having the height of a piece of type, standardized as 0.918 inches.

type metal NOUN *Printing* an alloy of tin, lead, and antimony, from which type is cast.

type I error NOUN *Statistics* the error of rejecting the null hypothesis when it is true, the probability of which is the significance level of a result.

typescript ('taɪpˌskrɪpt) NOUN [1] a typed copy of a document, literary script, etc. [2] any typewritten material.

typeset ('taɪpˌsɛt) VERB **-sets, -setting, -set.** (*tr*) *Printing* to set (textual matter) in type.

typesetter ('taɪpˌsɛtə) NOUN [1] a person who sets type; compositor. [2] a typesetting machine.

type specimen NOUN *Biology* the original specimen from which a description of a new species is made. Also called: **holotype.**

type II error NOUN *Statistics* the error of not rejecting the null hypothesis when it is false. The probability of avoiding such an error is the power of the test and is a function of the alternative hypothesis.

typewrite ('taɪpˌraɪt) VERB **-writes, -writing, -wrote, -written.** to write by means of a typewriter; type.

typewriter ('taɪpˌraɪtə) NOUN [1] a keyboard machine for writing mechanically in characters resembling print. It may be operated entirely by hand (**manual typewriter**) or be powered by electricity (**electric typewriter**). [2] *Printing* a style of type resembling typescript.

typewriting ('taɪpˌraɪtɪŋ) NOUN [1] the act or skill of using a typewriter. [2] copy produced by a typewriter; typescript.

typhlitis (tɪf'laɪtɪs) NOUN [1] inflammation of the caecum. [2] an obsolete name for **appendicitis.**
▷HISTORY C19: from New Latin, from Greek *tuphlon* the caecum, from *tuphlos* blind
▸**typhlitic** (tɪf'lɪtɪk) ADJECTIVE

typhlology (tɪf'lɒlədʒɪ) NOUN the branch of science concerned with blindness and the care of the blind.
▷HISTORY C19: from Greek *tuphlos* blind

Typhoeus (taɪ'fiːəs) NOUN *Greek myth* the son of Gaea and Tartarus who had a hundred dragon heads, which spurted fire, and a bellowing many-tongued voice. He created the whirlwinds and fought with Zeus before the god hurled him beneath Mount Etna.
▸**Ty'phoean** ADJECTIVE

typhogenic (ˌtaɪfəʊ'dʒɛnɪk) ADJECTIVE causing typhus or typhoid fever.

typhoid ('taɪfɔɪd) *Pathol* ◆ ADJECTIVE *also* **typhoidal.** [1] resembling typhus. ◆ NOUN [2] short for **typhoid fever.**

typhoid fever NOUN an acute infectious disease characterized by high fever, rose-coloured spots on the chest or abdomen, abdominal pain, and occasionally intestinal bleeding. It is caused by the bacillus *Salmonella typhosa* ingested with food or water. Also called: **enteric fever.**
▷HISTORY C19: from TYPHUS + -OID; so called because the symptoms resemble those of typhus

typhoidin (taɪ'fɔɪdɪn) NOUN *Med* a culture of dead typhoid bacillus for injection into the skin to test for typhoid fever.

Typhon ('taɪfɒn) NOUN *Greek myth* a monster and one of the whirlwinds: later confused with his father Typhoeus.

typhoon (taɪ'fuːn) NOUN [1] a violent tropical storm or cyclone, esp in the China seas and W Pacific. [2] a violent storm of India.
▷HISTORY C16: from Chinese *tai fung* great wind, from *tai* great + *fung* wind; influenced by Greek *tuphōn* whirlwind
▸**typhonic** (taɪ'fɒnɪk) ADJECTIVE

typhus ('taɪfəs) NOUN any one of a group of acute infectious rickettsial diseases characterized by high fever, skin rash, and severe headache. Also called: **typhus fever.**
▷HISTORY C18: from New Latin *tȳphus,* from Greek *tuphos* fever; related to *tuphein* to smoke
▸**'typhous** ADJECTIVE

typical ('tɪpɪkəl) ADJECTIVE [1] being or serving as a representative example of a particular type; characteristic: *the painting is a typical Rembrandt.* [2] considered to be an example of some undesirable trait: *that is typical of you!* [3] of or relating to a representative specimen or type. [4] conforming to a type. [5] *Biology* having most of the characteristics of a particular taxonomic group: *a typical species of a genus.* ◆ Also (poetic): **typic.**
▷HISTORY C17: from Medieval Latin *typicālis,* from Late Latin *typicus* figurative, from Greek *tupikos,* from *tupos* TYPE
▸**'typically** ADVERB ▸**'typicalness** *or* ˌ**typicality** NOUN

typify ('tɪpɪˌfaɪ) VERB **-fies, -fying, -fied.** (*tr*) [1] to be typical of; characterize. [2] to symbolize or represent completely, by or as if by a type.
▷HISTORY C17: from Latin *typus* TYPE + -IFY
▸ˌ**typifi'cation** NOUN ▸**'typiˌfier** NOUN

typing ('taɪpɪŋ) NOUN [1] the work or activity of using a typewriter or word processor. [2] the skill of using a typewriter quickly and accurately.

typist ('taɪpɪst) NOUN a person who types, esp for a living.

typo ('taɪpəʊ) NOUN, *plural* **-pos.** *Informal* a typographical error. Also called (Brit): **literal.**

typo. *or* **typog.** ABBREV variants of **typ.**

typographer (taɪ'pɒgrəfə) NOUN [1] a person skilled in typography. [2] another name for **compositor.**

typography (taɪ'pɒgrəfɪ) NOUN [1] the art, craft, or process of composing type and printing from it. [2] the selection and planning of type for printed publications.
▸**typographical** (ˌtaɪpə'græfɪkəl) *or* ˌ**typo'graphic** ADJECTIVE ▸ˌ**typo'graphically** ADVERB

typology (taɪ'pɒlədʒɪ) NOUN *Chiefly Christian theol* the doctrine or study of types or of the correspondence between them and the realities which they typify.
▸**typological** (ˌtaɪpə'lɒdʒɪkəl) *or* ˌ**typo'logic** ADJECTIVE ▸ˌ**typo'logically** ADVERB ▸**ty'pologist** NOUN

typothetae (taɪ'pɒθɪˌtiː, ˌtaɪpə'θiːtiː) PLURAL NOUN *US* printers collectively; used in the names of organized associations, as of master printers.
▷HISTORY C19: New Latin: typesetters, from Greek *tupos* TYPE + *thetēs* one who places, from *tithenai* to place

Tyr *or* **Tyrr** (tjʊə, tɪə) NOUN *Norse myth* the god of war, son of Odin. Anglo-Saxon counterpart: **Tiu.**

tyramine ('taɪrəˌmiːn, 'tɪ-) NOUN a colourless crystalline amine derived from phenol and found in ripe cheese, ergot, decayed animal tissue, and mistletoe and used for its sympathomimetic action; 4-hydroxyphenethylamine. Formula: $(C_2H_4NH_2)C_6H_4OH$.
▷HISTORY C20: from TYR(OSINE) + AMINE

tyrannical (tɪ'rænɪkəl) *or* **tyrannic** ADJECTIVE characteristic of or relating to a tyrant or to tyranny; oppressive.
▸**ty'rannically** ADVERB ▸**ty'rannicalness** NOUN

tyrannicide (tɪ'rænɪˌsaɪd) NOUN [1] the killing of a tyrant. [2] a person who kills a tyrant.
▸**tyrˌranni'cidal** ADJECTIVE

tyrannize *or* **tyrannise** ('tɪrəˌnaɪz) VERB (when *intr,* often foll by *over*) to rule or exercise power (over) in a cruel or oppressive manner.
▸**'tyranˌnizer** *or* **'tyranˌniser** NOUN

tyrannosaurus (tɪˌrænə'sɔːrəs) *or* **tyrannosaur** (tɪ'rænəˌsɔː) NOUN any large carnivorous bipedal dinosaur of the genus *Tyrannosaurus,* common in North America in upper Jurassic and Cretaceous times: suborder *Theropoda* (theropods).
▷HISTORY C19: from New Latin, from Greek *turannos* TYRANT + *sauros* lizard

tyranny ('tɪrənɪ) NOUN, *plural* **-nies.** [1] **a** government by a tyrant or tyrants; despotism. **b** similarly oppressive and unjust government by more than one person. [2] arbitrary, unreasonable, or despotic behaviour or use of authority: *the teacher's tyranny.* [3] any harsh discipline or oppression: *the tyranny of the clock.* [4] a political unit ruled by a tyrant. [5] (esp in ancient Greece) government by a usurper. [6] a tyrannical act.
▷HISTORY C14: from Old French *tyrannie,* from Medieval Latin *tyrannia,* from Latin *tyrannus* TYRANT
▸**'tyrannous** ADJECTIVE ▸**'tyrannously** ADVERB
▸**'tyrannousness** NOUN

tyrant ('taɪrənt) NOUN [1] a person who governs oppressively, unjustly, and arbitrarily; despot. [2] any person who exercises authority in a tyrannical manner. [3] anything that exercises tyrannical influence. [4] (esp in ancient Greece) a ruler whose authority lacked the sanction of law or custom; usurper.
▷HISTORY C13: from Old French *tyrant,* from Latin *tyrannus,* from Greek *turannos*

tyrant flycatcher NOUN any passerine bird of the American family *Tyrannidae.* Often shortened to: **flycatcher.**

tyre *or US* **tire** ('taɪə) NOUN [1] a rubber ring placed over the rim of a wheel of a road vehicle to provide traction and reduce road shocks, esp a hollow inflated ring (**pneumatic tyre**) consisting of a reinforced outer casing enclosing an inner tube. See also **tubeless tyre, cross-ply, radial-ply.** [2] a ring of wear-resisting steel shrunk thermally onto a cast-iron railway wheel. [3] a metal band or hoop attached to the rim of a wooden cartwheel. ◆ VERB [4] (*tr*) to fit a tyre or tyres to (a wheel, vehicle, etc.).
▷HISTORY C18: variant of C15 *tire,* probably from TIRE[3]

Tyre *or* **Tyr** ('taɪə) NOUN a port in S Lebanon, on the Mediterranean: founded about the 15th century B.C.; for centuries a major Phoenician seaport, famous for silks and its Tyrian-purple dye; now a small market town. Pop.: 70 000 (1991 est.). Arabic name: **Sur.**

Tyrian ('tɪrɪən) NOUN [1] a native or inhabitant of ancient Tyre. [2] short for **Tyrian purple** (sense 2). ◆ ADJECTIVE [3] of or relating to ancient Tyre.

Tyrian purple NOUN [1] a deep purple dye obtained from molluscs of the genus *Murex* and highly prized in antiquity. [2] **a** a vivid purplish-red colour. **b** (*as adjective*): *a Tyrian-purple robe.* Sometimes shortened to: **Tyrian.**

tyro *or* **tiro** ('taɪrəʊ) NOUN, *plural* **-ros.** a novice or beginner.
▷HISTORY C17: from Latin *tīrō* recruit
▸**tyronic** *or* **tironic** (taɪ'rɒnɪk) ADJECTIVE

tyrocidine (ˌtaɪrəʊ'saɪdiːn) NOUN an antibiotic that is the main constituent of tyrothricin.
▷HISTORY C20: from TYRO(SINE) + -CID(E) + -INE[1]

Tyrol *or* **Tirol** (tɪ'rəʊl, 'tɪrəʊl; *German* ti'roːl) NOUN a mountainous state of W Austria: passed to the Hapsburgs in 1363; S part transferred to Italy in 1919. Capital: Innsbruck. Pop.: 675 063 (2001). Area: 12 648 sq. km (4883 sq. miles).

Tyrolese (ˌtɪrə'liːz) *or* **Tyrolean** (ˌtɪrəʊ'lɪən) ADJECTIVE [1] of or relating to the Austrian state of Tyrol or its inhabitants. ◆ NOUN [2] a native or inhabitant of Tyrol.

Tyrolienne (tɪˌrəʊlɪ'ɛn) NOUN [1] a lively peasant dance from the Tyrol. [2] a song composed for or in the style of this dance, characterized by the yodel.
▷HISTORY French: of the TYROL

Tyrone (tɪ'rəʊn) NOUN a historical county of W Northern Ireland, occupying almost a quarter of the total area of Northern Ireland; in 1973 its administrative functions were devolved to several district councils.

tyropitta (tɪ'rɒpɪtə) NOUN a Greek cheese pie.
▷HISTORY C20: from Modern Greek

tyrosinase (ˌtaɪrəʊsɪ'neɪz, ˌtɪrəʊ-) NOUN an enzyme occurring in many organisms that is a catalyst in the conversion of tyrosine to the pigment melanin; inactivity of this enzyme results in albinism.

tyrosine ('taɪrəˌsiːn, -sɪn, 'tɪrə-) NOUN an aromatic nonessential amino acid; a component of proteins. It is a metabolic precursor of thyroxine, the pigment melanin, and other biologically important compounds.
▷HISTORY C19: from Greek *turos* cheese + -INE[2]

tyrothricin (ˌtaɪrəʊ'θraɪsɪn) NOUN an antibiotic, obtained from the soil bacterium *Bacillus brevis,* consisting of tyrocidine and gramicidin and active against Gram-positive bacteria such as staphylococci and streptococci: applied locally for the treatment of ulcers and abscesses.
▷HISTORY C20: from New Latin *Tyrothrix* (genus name), from Greek *turos* cheese + *thrix* hair

Tyrr (tjʊə, tɪə) NOUN a variant spelling of **Tyr.**

Tyrrhenian Sea (tɪ'riːnɪən) NOUN an arm of the Mediterranean between Italy and the islands of Corsica, Sardinia, and Sicily.

Tyumen (*Russian* tju'mjenj) NOUN a port in S central Russia, on the Tura River: one of the oldest Russian towns in Siberia; industrial centre with nearby oil and natural gas reserves. Pop.: 503 800 (1999 est.).

tz THE INTERNET DOMAIN NAME FOR Tanzania.

tzar (zɑː) NOUN a less common spelling of **tsar.**
▸**'tzarism** NOUN

tzatziki (tsæt'sɪkɪ) NOUN a Greek dip made from yogurt, chopped cucumber, and mint.
▷HISTORY C20: from Modern Greek

Tzekung ('tsɛ'kʊŋ) *or* **Tzu-kung** ('tsuː'kʊŋ) NOUN a variant transliteration of the Chinese name for **Zigong.**

tzetze fly ('tsɛtsɪ) NOUN a variant spelling of **tsetse fly.**

Tzigane (tsɪ'gɑːn, sɪ-) NOUN **a** a Gypsy, esp a Hungarian one. **b** (*as modifier*): *Tzigane music.*
▷HISTORY C19: via French from Hungarian *czigány* Gypsy, of uncertain origin

tzitzit ('tsɪtzɪt; *Hebrew* tsit'siːt) PLURAL NOUN the fringes or tassels on the corners of the tallit.
▷HISTORY from Hebrew, literally: tassel

Tzu-po ('tsuː'pəʊ) *or* **Tzepo** ('tsɛ'pəʊ) NOUN a variant transliteration of the Chinese name for **Zibo.**

Uu

u *or* **U** (juː) NOUN, *plural* **u's, U's** *or* **Us.** 1 the 21st letter and fifth vowel of the modern English alphabet. 2 any of several speech sounds represented by this letter, in English as in *mute, cut, hurt, sure, pull,* or *minus.* 3 **a** something shaped like a U. **b** (*in combination*): *a U-bolt; a U-turn.*

U¹ SYMBOL FOR: 1 united. 2 unionist. 3 university. 4 (in Britain) **a** universal (used to describe a category of film certified as suitable for viewing by anyone). **b** (*as modifier*): *a U film.* 5 *Chem* uranium. 6 *Biochem* uracil. *Text messaging* ◆ ABBREVIATION FOR: 7 you. ◆ ADJECTIVE 8 *Brit dated informal* (esp of language habits) characteristic of or appropriate to the upper class. Compare **non-U.**

U² (uː) NOUN a Burmese title of respect for men, equivalent to *Mr.*

U. ABBREVIATION FOR: 1 *Maths* union. 2 unit. 3 united. 4 university. 5 upper.

U2 *Text messaging* ABBREVIATION FOR you too.

ua THE INTERNET DOMAIN NAME FOR Ukraine.

UA 1 ABBREVIATION FOR (in Britain) **unitary authority.** ◆ 2 INTERNATIONAL CAR REGISTRATION FOR Ukraine.

UAE ABBREVIATION FOR United Arab Emirates.

UAM ABBREVIATION FOR underwater-to-air missile.

UAR ABBREVIATION FOR United Arab Republic.

UART (ˈjuːˌɑːt) NOUN *Electronics* ◆ ACRONYM FOR Universal Asynchronous Receiver Transmitter.

UAV ABBREVIATION FOR unmanned aerial vehicle.

UB40 NOUN (in Britain) 1 a registration card issued by the Department of Employment to a person registering as unemployed. 2 *Informal* a person registered as unemployed.

Ubangi (juːˈbæŋgɪ) NOUN a river in central Africa, flowing west and south, forming the border between the Democratic Republic of Congo (formerly Zaïre) and the Central African Republic and Congo-Brazzaville, into the River Congo. Length (with the Uele): 2250 km (1400 miles). French name: **Oubangui.**

Ubangi-Shari NOUN a former name (until 1958) of the **Central African Republic.**

U-bend NOUN a U-shaped bend in a pipe or drain that traps water in the lower part of the U and prevents the escape of noxious fumes or vapours; trap.

uber- *or* **über-** (ˈuːbə) COMBINING FORM indicating the highest, greatest, or most extreme example of something: *America's ubernerd, Bill Gates; the uber-hip young Bohemians.*
▷HISTORY C20: from German *über* over, above

Übermensch *German* (ˈyːbərˌmɛnʃ) NOUN, *plural* **-menschen** (-mɛnʃən). (esp in the writings of Nietzsche) the German word for **superman.**
▷HISTORY literally: over-man

uberrima fides (ˈjuːbəˌriːmə ˈfaɪdiːz, juːˈbɛrɪmə) NOUN another name for **utmost good faith.**
▷HISTORY Latin: utmost good faith

ubiety (juːˈbaɪɪtɪ) NOUN the condition of being in a particular place.
▷HISTORY C17: from Latin *ubī* where + *-ety,* on the model of *society*

ubiquinone (juːˈbɪkwɪˌnəʊn) NOUN another name for **coenzyme Q.**

ubiquitarian (juːˌbɪkwɪˈtɛərɪən) NOUN 1 a member of the Lutheran church who holds that Christ is no more present in the elements of the Eucharist than elsewhere, as he is present in all places at all times. ◆ ADJECTIVE 2 denoting, relating to, or holding this belief.
▷HISTORY C17: from Latin *ubīque* everywhere; see UBIQUITOUS
▸**uˌbiquiˈtarianˌism** NOUN

ubiquitous (juːˈbɪkwɪtəs) ADJECTIVE having or seeming to have the ability to be everywhere at once; omnipresent.
▷HISTORY C14: from Latin *ubīque* everywhere, from *ubī* where
▸**uˈbiquitously** ADVERB ▸**uˈbiquity** *or* **uˈbiquitousness** NOUN

ubi supra *Latin* (ˈuːbɪ ˈsuːprɑː) where (mentioned or cited) above.

U-boat NOUN a German submarine, esp in World Wars I and II.
▷HISTORY from German *U-Boot,* abbreviation for *Unterseeboot,* literally: undersea boat

U bolt NOUN a metal bar bent into the shape of a *U* and threaded at both ends to receive securing nuts: used to secure leaf springs, ring bolts, shackles, etc.

UBR ABBREVIATION FOR **Uniform Business Rate.**

Ubuntu (ʊˈbuːntʊ) NOUN *South African* humanity or fellow feeling; kindness.
▷HISTORY Nguni

UC ABBREVIATION FOR University College.

u.c. *Printing* ABBREVIATION FOR upper case.

UCAS (ˈjuːkæs) NOUN (in Britain) ◆ ACRONYM FOR Universities and Colleges Admissions Service.

UCATT (ˈʌkət) NOUN ACRONYM FOR Union of Construction, Allied Trades and Technicians.

Ucayali (*Spanish* ukaˈjali) NOUN a river in E Peru, flowing north into the Marañón above Iquitos. Length: 1600 km (1000 miles).

UCCA (ˈʌkə) NOUN (formerly, in Britain) ◆ ACRONYM FOR Universities Central Council on Admissions.

UCL ABBREVIATION FOR University College London.

UCT ABBREVIATION FOR University of Cape Town.

UDA ABBREVIATION FOR **Ulster Defence Association.**

Udaipur (uːˈdaɪpʊə, ˈuːdaɪˌpʊə) NOUN 1 Also called: **Mewar.** a former state of NW India: became part of Rajasthan in 1947. 2 a city in NW India, in S Rajasthan. Pop.: 308 571 (1991).

udal (ˈjuːdᵊl) NOUN *Law* a form of freehold possession of land existing in northern Europe before the introduction of the feudal system and still used in Orkney and Shetland.
▷HISTORY C16: Orkney and Shetland dialect, from Old Norse *othal;* related to Old English *ēthel, ōethel,* Old High German *wodal*

UDC (formerly, in Britain) ABBREVIATION FOR Urban District Council.

udder (ˈʌdə) NOUN the large baglike mammary gland of cows, sheep, etc., having two or more teats.
▷HISTORY Old English *ūder;* related to Old High German *ūtar,* Old Norse *jūr,* Latin *über,* Sanskrit *ūdhar*

UDI ABBREVIATION FOR **Unilateral Declaration of Independence.**

Udine (*Italian* ˈuːdine) NOUN a city in NE Italy, in Friuli-Venezia Giulia region: partially damaged in an earthquake in 1976. Pop.: 98 872 (1990).

Udmurt Republic (ˈʊdmʊət) NOUN a constituent republic of W central Russia, in the basin of the middle Kama. Capital: Izhevsk. Pop.: 1 639 000 (1999 est.). Area: 42 100 sq. km (16 250 sq. miles).

udo (ˈuːdəʊ) NOUN, *plural* **udos.** a stout araliaceous perennial plant, *Aralia cordata,* of Japan and China, having berry-like black fruits and young shoots that are edible when blanched.
▷HISTORY from Japanese

udometer (juːˈdɒmɪtə) NOUN an archaic term for **rain gauge.**
▷HISTORY C19: from French, from Latin *ūdus* damp

udon (ˈuːdɒn) NOUN (in Japanese cookery) large noodles made of wheat flour.
▷HISTORY Japanese

UDR ABBREVIATION FOR Ulster Defence Regiment.

U4E *Text messaging* ABBREVIATION FOR yours for ever.

UEFA (juːˈeɪfə) NOUN ACRONYM FOR Union of European Football Associations.

Uele (ˈweɪlə) NOUN a river in central Africa, rising near the border between the Democratic Republic of Congo (formerly Zaïre) and Uganda and flowing west to join the Bomu River and form the Ubangi River. Length: about 1100 km (700 miles).

Ufa (*Russian* uˈfa) NOUN a city in W central Russia, capital of the Bashkir Republic: university (1957). Pop.: 1 088 900 (1999 est.).

Uffizi (juːˈfɪtsɪ) NOUN an art gallery in Florence; built by Giorgio Vasari in the 16th century and opened as a museum in 1765: contains chiefly Italian Renaissance paintings.

UFO (*sometimes* ˈjuːfəʊ) ABBREVIATION FOR unidentified flying object.

ufology (ˌjuːˈfɒlədʒɪ) NOUN the study of UFOs.
▸**uˈfologist** NOUN

ug THE INTERNET DOMAIN NAME FOR Uganda.

ugali (uːˈgaliː) NOUN *E African* a type of stiff porridge made by mixing corn meal with boiling water: the basic starch constituent of a meal.
▷HISTORY from Swahili

Uganda (juːˈgændə) NOUN a republic in E Africa: British protectorate established in 1894–96; gained independence in 1962 and became a republic in 1963; a member of the Commonwealth. It consists mostly of a savanna plateau with part of Lake Victoria in the southeast and mountains in the southwest, reaching 5109 m (16 763 ft.) in the Ruwenzori Range. Official language: English; Swahili, Luganda, and Luo are also widely spoken. Religion: Christian majority. Currency: Ugandan shilling. Capital: Kampala. Pop.: 23 986 000 (2001 est.). Area: 235 886 sq. km (91 076 sq. miles).

Ugandan (juːˈgændən) ADJECTIVE 1 of or relating to Uganda or its inhabitants. ◆ NOUN 2 a native or inhabitant of Uganda.

Ugaritic (ˌuːgəˈrɪtɪk) NOUN 1 an extinct Semitic language of N Syria. ◆ ADJECTIVE 2 of or relating to this language.
▷HISTORY C19: after *Ugarit* (modern name: Ras Shamra), an ancient Syrian city-state

UGC (in Britain) ABBREVIATION FOR University Grants Committee.

ugh (ʊx, ʊh, ʌh) INTERJECTION an exclamation of disgust, annoyance, or dislike.

UGLI (ˈʌglɪ) NOUN, *plural* **UGLIS** *or* **UGLIES.** *Trademark* a large juicy yellow-skinned citrus fruit of the Caribbean: a cross between a tangerine, grapefruit, and orange. Also called: **UGLI fruit.**
▷HISTORY C20: probably an alteration of UGLY, referring to its wrinkled skin

uglify (ˈʌglɪˌfaɪ) VERB **-fies, -fying, -fied.** to make or become ugly or more ugly.
▸**ˌuglifiˈcation** NOUN ▸**ˈugliˌfier** NOUN

ugly (ˈʌglɪ) ADJECTIVE **-lier, -liest.** 1 of unpleasant or unsightly appearance. 2 repulsive, objectionable, or displeasing in any way: *war is ugly.* 3 ominous or menacing: *an ugly situation.* 4 bad-tempered, angry, or sullen: *an ugly mood.*
▷HISTORY C13: from Old Norse *uggligr* dreadful, from *ugga* fear
▸**ˈuglily** ADVERB ▸**ˈugliness** NOUN

ugly duckling NOUN a person or thing, initially ugly or unpromising, that changes into something beautiful or admirable.
▷HISTORY an allusion to *The Ugly Duckling,* a story by Hans Christian Andersen

Ugrian (ˈuːgrɪən, ˈjuː-) ADJECTIVE 1 of or relating to a light-haired subdivision of the Turanian people, who include the Samoyeds, Voguls, Ostyaks, and Magyars. ◆ NOUN 2 a member of this group of peoples. 3 another word for **Ugric.**
▷HISTORY C19: from Old Russian *Ugre* Hungarians

Ugric (ˈuːgrɪk, ˈjuː-) NOUN 1 one of the two branches of the Finno-Ugric family of languages, including Hungarian and some languages of NW Siberia. Compare **Finnic.** ◆ ADJECTIVE 2 of or relating to this group of languages or their speakers.

UHF *Radio* ABBREVIATION FOR **ultrahigh frequency.**

uh-huh (ə'hə) SENTENCE SUBSTITUTE *Informal* a less emphatic variant of **yes.**

uhlan *or* **ulan** ('u:lɑ:n, 'ju:lən) NOUN *History* a member of a body of lancers first employed in the Polish army and later in W European armies.
▷HISTORY C18: via German from Polish *ulan,* from Turkish *ōlan* young man

UHT ABBREVIATION FOR ultra heat treated.

uh-uh ('ʌ'ʌ) SENTENCE SUBSTITUTE *Informal, chiefly US* a less emphatic variant of **no**[1].

uhuru (u:'hu:ru:) NOUN (esp in E Africa) [1] national independence. [2] freedom.
▷HISTORY C20: from Swahili

Uigur *or* **Uighur** ('wi:guə) NOUN [1] (*plural* **-gur** *or* **-gurs**) a member of a Mongoloid people of NW China, Uzbekistan, Kyrgyzstan, and Kazakhstan. [2] the language of this people, belonging to the Turkic branch of the Altaic family.
▸**Ui'gurian** *or* **Ui'ghurian** ▸**Ui'guric** *or* **Ui'ghuric** ADJECTIVE

uillean pipes ('u:lɪən) PLURAL NOUN bagpipes developed in Ireland and operated by squeezing bellows under the arm. Also called: **Irish pipes, union pipes.**
▷HISTORY C19: Irish *píob uilleann,* from *píob* pipe + *uilleann* genitive sing. of *uille* elbow

Uinta Mountains (jʊ'ɪntə) PLURAL NOUN a mountain range in NE Utah: part of the Rocky Mountains. Highest peak: Kings Peak, 4123 m (13 528 ft.).

uintathere (ju:'ɪntə,θɪə) NOUN any of various extinct Tertiary rhinoceros-like mammals of North America, having six horny processes on the head. Also called: **dinoceras.**
▷HISTORY from *Uinta,* a county in Wyoming + Greek *thērion* wild animal

uitlander ('eɪt,landə, -,læn-, 'ɔɪt-) NOUN (*sometimes capital*) *South African* a foreigner; alien.
▷HISTORY C19: Afrikaans: outlander

ujamaa village (u:dʒa'ma) NOUN (*sometimes capitals*) a communally organized village in Tanzania.
▷HISTORY C20: *ujamaa* socialism, from Swahili: brotherhood

Ujiji (u:'dʒi:dʒɪ) NOUN a town in W Tanzania, on Lake Tanganyika: a former slave and ivory centre; the place where Stanley found Livingstone in 1871. It merged with the neighbouring town of Kigoma to form Kigoma-Ujiji in the 1960s.

Ujjain (u:'dʒeɪn) NOUN a city in W central India, in Madhya Pradesh: one of the seven sacred cities of the Hindus; a major agricultural trade centre. Pop.: 362 266 (1991).

Ujung Pandang ('u:dʒʊŋ pæn'dæŋ) NOUN a port in central Indonesia, on SW Sulawesi: an important native port before Portuguese (16th century) and Dutch (17th century) control; capital of Dutch East Indonesia (1946–49); a major Indonesian distribution and transshipment port. Pop.: 1 091 800 (1995 est.). Also called: **Makasar, Makassar, Macassar.**

uk THE INTERNET DOMAIN NAME FOR United Kingdom.

UK ABBREVIATION FOR United Kingdom.

UKAEA ABBREVIATION FOR United Kingdom Atomic Energy Authority.

ukase (ju:'keɪz) NOUN [1] (in imperial Russia) an edict of the tsar. [2] a rare word for **edict.**
▷HISTORY C18: from Russian *ukaz,* from *ukazat* to command

UKCC ABBREVIATION FOR United Kingdom Central Council for Nursing, Midwifery, and Health Visiting.

ukiyo-e (,u:ki:jəʊ'jeɪ) NOUN a school of Japanese painting depicting subjects from everyday life.
▷HISTORY Japanese: pictures of the floating world

UK Overseas Territory NOUN any of the territories that are governed by the UK but lie outside the British Isles; many were formerly British **crown colonies**: includes Bermuda, Falkland Islands, and Montserrat.

Ukr. ABBREVIATION FOR Ukraine.

Ukraine (ju:'kreɪn) NOUN **the.** a republic in SE Europe, on the Black Sea and the Sea of Azov: ruled by the Khazars (7th–9th centuries), by Ruik princes with the Mongol conquest in the 13th century, then by Lithuania, by Poland, and by Russia; one of the four original republics that formed the Soviet Union in 1922; unilaterally declared independence in 1990, which was recognized in 1991: consists chiefly of lowlands; economy based on rich agriculture and mineral resources and on the major heavy industries of the Donets Basin. Official language: Ukrainian. Religion: believers are mainly Christian. Currency: hryvna. Capital: Kiev. Pop.: 48 767 000 (2001 est). Area: 603 700 sq. km (231 990 sq. miles).

Ukrainian (ju:'kreɪnɪən) ADJECTIVE [1] of or relating to the Ukraine, its people, or their language. ◆ NOUN [2] the official language of the Ukraine: an East Slavonic language closely related to Russian. [3] a native or inhabitant of the Ukraine. ◆ Formerly called: **Little Russian.**

ukulele *or* **ukelele** (,ju:kə'leɪlɪ) NOUN a small four-stringed guitar, esp of Hawaii.
▷HISTORY C19: from Hawaiian, literally: jumping flea, from *'uku* flea + *lele* jumping

ulan ('u:lɑ:n, 'ju:lən) NOUN a less common variant of **uhlan.**

Ulan Bator (ʊ'lɑ:n 'bɑ:tɔ:) NOUN the capital of Mongolia, in the N central part: developed in the mid-17th century around the Da Khure monastery, residence until 1924 of successive "living Buddhas" (third in rank of Buddhist-Lamaist leaders), and main junction of caravan routes across Mongolia; university (1942); industrial and commercial centre. Pop.: 691 000 (2000 est.). Former name (until 1924): **Urga.** Chinese name: **Kulun.**

Ulan-Ude (ʊ'lɑ:nʊ'dɛ) NOUN an industrial city in SE Russia, capital of the Buryat Republic: an important rail junction. Pop.: 371 400 (1999 est.). Former name (until 1934): **Verkhne-Udinsk.**

ULCC ABBREVIATION FOR **ultralarge crude carrier.**

ulcer ('ʌlsə) NOUN [1] a disintegration of the surface of the skin or a mucous membrane resulting in an open sore that heals very slowly. See also **peptic ulcer.** [2] a source or element of corruption or evil.
▷HISTORY C14: from Latin *ulcus;* related to Greek *helkos* a sore

ulcerate ('ʌlsə,reɪt) VERB to make or become ulcerous.

ulceration (,ʌlsə'reɪʃən) NOUN [1] the development or formation of an ulcer. [2] an ulcer or an ulcerous condition.

ulcerative ('ʌlsərətɪv) ADJECTIVE of, relating to, or characterized by ulceration: *ulcerative colitis.*

ulcerous ('ʌlsərəs) ADJECTIVE [1] relating to, characteristic of, or characterized by an ulcer or ulcers. [2] being or having a corrupting influence.
▸**'ulcerously** ADVERB ▸**'ulcerousness** NOUN

-ule SUFFIX FORMING NOUNS indicating smallness: *globule.*
▷HISTORY from Latin *-ulus,* diminutive suffix

Uleåborg ('u:lio,bɔrjə) NOUN the Swedish name for **Oulu.**

ulema ('u:lɪmə) NOUN [1] a body of Muslim scholars or religious leaders. [2] a member of this body.
▷HISTORY C17: from Arabic *'ulamā* scholars, from *'alama* to know

-ulent SUFFIX FORMING ADJECTIVES abundant or full of: *fraudulent.*
▷HISTORY from Latin *-ulentus*

ullage ('ʌlɪdʒ) NOUN [1] the volume by which a liquid container falls short of being full. [2] **a** the quantity of liquid lost from a container due to leakage or evaporation. **b** (in customs terminology) the amount of liquid remaining in a container after such loss. ◆ VERB (*tr*) [3] to create ullage in. [4] to determine the amount of ullage in. [5] to fill up ullage in.
▷HISTORY C15: from Old French *ouillage* filling of a cask, from *ouiller* to fill a cask, from *ouil* eye, from Latin *oculus* eye
▸**'ullaged** ADJECTIVE

ullage rocket NOUN a small hydrogen peroxide rocket engine that produces sufficient acceleration to keep propellants in their places when the main rocket is shut off.

Ullswater ('ʌlz,wɔ:tə) NOUN a lake in NW England, in Cumbria in the Lake District. Length: 12 km (7.5 miles).

Ulm (*German* ʊlm) NOUN an industrial city in S Germany, in Baden-Württemberg on the Danube: a free imperial city (1155–1802). Pop.: 116 000 (1999 est.).

ulmaceous (ʌl'meɪʃəs) ADJECTIVE of, relating to, or belonging to the *Ulmaceae,* a temperate and tropical family of deciduous trees and shrubs having scaly buds, simple serrated leaves, and typically winged fruits: includes the elms.
▷HISTORY C19: via New Latin *Ulmāceae,* from Latin *ulmus* elm tree

ulna ('ʌlnə) NOUN, *plural* **-nae** (-ni:) *or* **-nas.** [1] the inner and longer of the two bones of the human forearm. [2] the corresponding bone in other vertebrates.
▷HISTORY C16: from Latin: elbow, ELL[1]
▸**'ulnar** ADJECTIVE

ulnar nerve NOUN a nerve situated along the inner side of the arm and passing close to the surface of the skin near the elbow. See **funny bone.**

ulotrichous (ju:'lɒtrɪkəs) ADJECTIVE having woolly or curly hair.
▷HISTORY C19: from New Latin *Ulotrichī* (classification applied to humans having this type of hair), from Greek *oulothrix,* from *oulos* curly + *thrix* hair
▸**u'lotrichy** NOUN

ulster ('ʌlstə) NOUN a man's heavy double-breasted overcoat with a belt or half-belt at the back.
▷HISTORY C19: so called because it was first produced in Northern Ireland

Ulster ('ʌlstə) NOUN [1] a province and former kingdom of N Ireland: passed to the English Crown in 1461; confiscated land given to English and Scottish Protestant settlers in the 17th century, giving rise to serious long-term conflict; partitioned in 1921, six counties forming Northern Ireland and three counties joining the Republic of Ireland. Pop. (three Ulster counties of the Republic of Ireland): 234 251 (1996); (six Ulster counties of Northern Ireland): 1 691 800 (1999 est.). Area (Republic of Ireland): 8013 sq. km (3094 sq. miles); (Northern Ireland): 14 121 sq. km (5452 sq. miles). [2] an informal name for **Northern Ireland.**

Ulster Defence Association NOUN (in Northern Ireland) a Loyalist paramilitary organization. Abbreviation: **UDA.**

Ulster Democratic Unionist Party NOUN a Northern Irish political party advocating the maintenance of union with the UK.

Ulsterman ('ʌlstəmən) NOUN, *plural* **-men.** a native or inhabitant of Ulster.
▸**'Ulster,woman** FEMININE NOUN

Ulster Unionist Council NOUN a Northern Irish political party advocating the maintenance of union with the UK.

ult. ABBREVIATION FOR: [1] ultimate(ly). [2] Also: **ulto.** ultimo.

ulterior (ʌl'tɪərɪə) ADJECTIVE [1] lying beneath or beyond what is revealed, evident, or supposed: *ulterior motives.* [2] succeeding, subsequent, or later. [3] lying beyond a certain line or point.
▷HISTORY C17: from Latin: further, from *ulter* beyond
▸**ul'teriorly** ADVERB

ultima ('ʌltɪmə) NOUN the final syllable of a word.
▷HISTORY from Latin: the last, feminine of *ultimus* last; see ULTIMATE

ultimate ('ʌltɪmɪt) ADJECTIVE [1] conclusive in a series or process; last; final: *an ultimate question.* [2] the highest or most significant: *the ultimate goal.* [3] elemental, fundamental, basic, or essential. [4] most extreme: *genocide is the ultimate abuse of human rights.* [5] final or total: *an ultimate cost of twenty million pounds.* ◆ NOUN [6] the most significant, highest, furthest, or greatest thing.
▷HISTORY C17: from Late Latin *ultimāre* to come to an end, from Latin *ultimus* last, from *ulter* distant
▸**'ultimateness** NOUN

ultimate constituent NOUN a constituent of something, such as a linguistic construction, that cannot be further subdivided in the terms of the analysis being undertaken. Compare **immediate constituent.**

ultimately ('ʌltɪmɪtlɪ) ADVERB in the end; at last; finally.

ultimate strength NOUN the maximum tensile stress that a material can withstand before rupture.

ultima Thule ('θju:lɪ) NOUN [1] another name for

Thule. [2] any distant or unknown region. [3] a remote goal or aim.
▷HISTORY Latin: the most distant Thule

ultimatum (ˌʌltɪˈmeɪtəm) NOUN, *plural* **-tums** *or* **-ta** (-tə). [1] a final communication by a party, esp a government, setting forth conditions on which it insists, as during negotiations on some topic. [2] any final or peremptory demand, offer, or proposal.
▷HISTORY C18: from New Latin, neuter of *ultimatus* ULTIMATE

ultimo (ˈʌltɪˌməʊ) ADVERB *Now rare except when abbreviated in formal correspondence* in or during the previous month: *a letter of the 7th ultimo.* Abbreviation: **ult.** Compare **instant, proximo.**
▷HISTORY C16: from Latin *ultimō* on the last

ultimogeniture (ˌʌltɪməʊˈdʒɛnɪtʃə) NOUN *Law* [1] a principle of inheritance whereby the youngest son succeeds to the estate of his ancestor. Compare **primogeniture.** [2] another name for **borough-English.**
▷HISTORY C19: *ultimo-* from Latin *ultimus* last + Late Latin *genitura* a birth; compare PRIMOGENITURE

ultra (ˈʌltrə) ADJECTIVE [1] extreme or immoderate, esp in beliefs or opinions. ◆ NOUN [2] an extremist.
▷HISTORY C19: from Latin: beyond, from *ulter* distant

ultra- PREFIX [1] beyond or surpassing a specified extent, range, or limit: *ultramicroscopic.* [2] extreme or extremely: *ultramodern.*
▷HISTORY from Latin *ultrā* beyond; see ULTRA

ultrabasic (ˌʌltrəˈbeɪsɪk) ADJECTIVE (of such igneous rocks as peridotite) containing less than 45 per cent silica.

ultracentrifuge (ˌʌltrəˈsɛntrɪˌfjuːdʒ) *Chem* ◆ NOUN [1] a high-speed centrifuge used to separate colloidal solutions. ◆ VERB [2] (*tr*) to subject to the action of an ultracentrifuge.
▸**ultracentrifugal** (ˌʌltrəsɛnˈtrɪfjʊgᵊl, -ˌsɛntrɪˈfjuːgᵊl) ADJECTIVE ▸**ˌultracenˈtrifugally** ADVERB
▸**ultracentrifugation** (ˌʌltrəˌsɛntrɪfjʊˈgeɪʃən) NOUN

ultraconservative (ˌʌltrəkənˈsɜːvətɪv) ADJECTIVE [1] highly reactionary. ◆ NOUN [2] a reactionary person.

ultra-distance NOUN (*modifier*) *Athletics* covering a distance in excess of 30 miles, often as part of a longer race or competition: *an ultra-distance runner.*

ultrafiche (ˈʌltrəˌfiːʃ) NOUN a sheet of film, usually the size of a filing card, that is similar to a microfiche but has a much larger number of microcopies.
▷HISTORY C20: from ULTRA- + French *fiche* small card. See MICROFICHE

ultrafilter (ˌʌltrəˈfɪltə) NOUN a filter with small pores used to separate very small particles from a suspension or colloidal solution.
▸**ultrafiltration** (ˌʌltrəfɪlˈtreɪʃən) NOUN

ultra filtration NOUN *Engineering* filtration that removes particles less than 10 microns (10^{-6}m) in diameter.

ultrahigh frequency (ˈʌltrəˌhaɪ) NOUN a radio-frequency band or radio frequency lying between 3000 and 300 megahertz. Abbreviation: **UHF.**

ultraism (ˈʌltrəˌɪzəm) NOUN extreme philosophy, belief, or action.
▸**ˈultraist** NOUN, ADJECTIVE ▸**ˌultraˈistic** ADJECTIVE

ultralarge crude carrier (ˌʌltrəˈlɑːdʒ) NOUN an oil tanker with a capacity of over 400 000 tons.

ultramarine (ˌʌltrəməˈriːn) NOUN [1] a blue pigment consisting of sodium and aluminium silicates and some sodium sulphide, obtained by powdering natural lapis lazuli or made synthetically: used in paints, printing ink, plastics, etc. [2] a vivid blue colour. ◆ ADJECTIVE [3] of the colour ultramarine. [4] from across the seas.
▷HISTORY C17: from Medieval Latin *ultramarinus,* from *ultrā* beyond (see ULTRA-) + *mare* sea; so called because the lapis lazuli from which the pigment was made was imported from Asia

ultramicrometer (ˌʌltrəmaɪˈkrɒmɪtə) NOUN a micrometer for measuring extremely small distances.

ultramicroscope (ˌʌltrəˈmaɪkrəˌskəʊp) NOUN a microscope used for studying colloids, in which the sample is strongly illuminated from the side and colloidal particles are seen as bright points on a dark background. Also called: **dark-field microscope.**

ultramicroscopic (ˌʌltrəˌmaɪkrəˈskɒpɪk) ADJECTIVE [1] too small to be seen with an optical microscope. [2] of or relating to an ultramicroscope.
▸**ultramicroscopy** (ˌʌltrəmaɪˈkrɒskəpɪ) NOUN

ultramodern (ˌʌltrəˈmɒdən) ADJECTIVE extremely modern.
▸**ˌultraˈmodernism** NOUN ▸**ˌultraˈmodernist** NOUN
▸**ˌultraˌmodernˈistic** ADJECTIVE

ultramontane (ˌʌltrəmɒnˈteɪn) ADJECTIVE [1] on the other side of the mountains, esp the Alps, from the speaker or writer. Compare **cismontane.** [2] of or relating to a movement in the Roman Catholic Church which favours the centralized authority and influence of the pope as opposed to local independence. Compare **cisalpine** (sense 2). ◆ NOUN [3] a resident or native from beyond the mountains, esp the Alps. [4] a member of the ultramontane party of the Roman Catholic Church.

ultramontanism (ˌʌltrəˈmɒntɪˌnɪzəm) NOUN *RC Church* the doctrine of central papal supremacy. Compare **Gallicanism.**
▸**ˌultraˈmontanist** NOUN

ultramundane (ˌʌltrəˈmʌndeɪn) ADJECTIVE extending beyond the world, this life, or the universe.

ultranationalism (ˌʌltrəˈnæʃnəˌlɪzəm) NOUN extreme devotion to one's own nation.
▸**ˌultraˈnational** ADJECTIVE ▸**ˌultraˈnationalist** ADJECTIVE, NOUN ▸**ˌultraˌnationalˈistic** ADJECTIVE

ultrared (ˌʌltrəˈrɛd) ADJECTIVE an obsolete word for **infrared.**

ultrashort (ˌʌltrəˈʃɔːt) ADJECTIVE (of a radio wave) having a wavelength shorter than 10 metres.

ultrasonic (ˌʌltrəˈsɒnɪk) ADJECTIVE of, concerned with, or producing waves with the same nature as sound waves but frequencies above audio frequencies. See also **ultrasound.**
▸**ˌultraˈsonically** ADVERB

ultrasonic cleaning NOUN the use of ultrasound to vibrate a piece to be cleaned while the piece is immersed in a cleaning fluid. The process produces a very high degree of cleanliness, and is used for jewellery and ornately shaped items.

ultrasonics (ˌʌltrəˈsɒnɪks) NOUN (*functioning as singular*) the branch of physics concerned with ultrasonic waves. Also called: **supersonics.**

ultrasonic testing NOUN *Engineering* the scanning of material with an ultrasonic beam, during which reflections from faults in the material can be detected: a powerful nondestructive test method.

ultrasonic welding NOUN the use of high-energy vibration of ultrasonic frequency to produce a weld between two components which are held in close contact.

ultrasonography (ˌʌltrəsəˈnɒgrəfɪ) NOUN the technique of using ultrasound to produce pictures of structures within the body, as for example of a fetus.

ultrasound (ˈʌltrəˌsaʊnd) NOUN ultrasonic waves at frequencies above the audible range (above about 20 kHz), used in cleaning metallic parts, echo sounding, medical diagnosis and therapy, etc.

ultrasound scanner NOUN a device used to examine an internal bodily structure by the use of ultrasonic waves, esp for the diagnosis of abnormality in a fetus.

ultrastructure (ˈʌltrəˌstrʌktʃə) NOUN the minute structure of a tissue or cell, as revealed by microscopy, esp electron microscopy.
▸**ˌultraˈstructural** ADJECTIVE

ultraviolet (ˌʌltrəˈvaɪəlɪt) NOUN [1] the part of the electromagnetic spectrum with wavelengths shorter than light but longer than X-rays; in the range 0.4×10^{-6} and 1×10^{-8} metres. ◆ ADJECTIVE [2] of, relating to, or consisting of radiation lying in the ultraviolet: *ultraviolet radiation.* Abbreviation: **UV.**

ultraviolet astronomy NOUN the study of radiation from celestial sources in the wavelength range 91.2 to 320 nanometres, 12 to 91.2 nanometres being the extreme ultraviolet range.

ultra vires (ˈvaɪriːz) ADVERB, ADJECTIVE (*predicative*) *Law* beyond the legal power or authority of a person, corporation, agent, etc.
▷HISTORY Latin, literally: beyond strength

ultravirus (ˌʌltrəˈvaɪrəs) NOUN a virus small enough to pass through the finest filter.

ululate (ˈjuːljʊˌleɪt) VERB (*intr*) to howl or wail, as with grief.
▷HISTORY C17: from Latin *ululāre* to howl, from *ulula* screech owl
▸**ˈululant** ADJECTIVE ▸**ˌuluˈlation** NOUN

Uluru (ˌuːləˈruː) NOUN the world's largest monolith, in the Northern Territory of Australia: sacred to local Aboriginal people. Height: 330m (1100 ft.). Base circumference: 9 km (5.6 miles). Former name: **Ayers Rock.**

Ulyanovsk (*Russian* uljˈjanəfsk) NOUN the former name (1924–91) of **Simbirsk.**

Ulysses (ˈjuːlɪˌsiːz, juːˈlɪsiːz) NOUN the Latin name of **Odysseus.**

um¹ (ʌm, ᵊm) INTERJECTION a representation of a common sound made when hesitating in speech.

um² THE INTERNET DOMAIN NAME FOR US Minor Outlying Islands.

umbel (ˈʌmbᵊl) NOUN an inflorescence, characteristic of umbelliferous plants, in which the flowers arise from the same point in the main stem and have stalks of the same length, to give a cluster with the youngest flowers at the centre.
▷HISTORY C16: from Latin *umbella* a sunshade, from *umbra* shade
▸**umbellate** (ˈʌmbɪlɪt, -ˌleɪt) *or* **umbellar** (ʌmˈbɛlə) *or* **ˈumbelˌlated** ADJECTIVE ▸**ˈumbellately** ADVERB

umbelliferous (ˌʌmbɪˈlɪfərəs) ADJECTIVE [1] of, relating to, or belonging to the *Umbelliferae,* a family of herbaceous plants and shrubs, typically having hollow stems, divided or compound leaves, and flowers in umbels: includes fennel, dill, parsley, carrot, celery, and parsnip. [2] designating any other plant bearing umbels.
▷HISTORY C17: from New Latin *umbellifer,* from Latin *umbella* sunshade + *ferre* to bear
▸**umˈbellifer** NOUN

umbellule (ʌmˈbɛljuːl, ˈʌmbɪˌljuːl) NOUN any of the small secondary umbels that make up a compound umbel.
▷HISTORY C18: from New Latin *umbellula,* diminutive of Latin *umbella;* see UMBEL
▸**umbellulate** (ʌmˈbɛljʊlɪt, -ˌleɪt) ADJECTIVE

umber (ˈʌmbə) NOUN [1] any of various natural brown earths containing ferric oxide together with lime and oxides of aluminium, manganese, and silicon. See also **burnt umber.** [2] any of the dark brown to greenish-brown colours produced by this pigment. [3] short for **umber moth.** [4] *Obsolete* **a** shade or shadow. **b** any dark, dusky, or indefinite colour. ◆ ADJECTIVE [5] of, relating to, or stained with umber.
▷HISTORY C16: from French (*terre d'*)*ombre* or Italian (*terra di*) *ombra* shadow (earth), from Latin *umbra* shade

umber moth NOUN any of various brownish geometrid moths, esp the **waved umber** (*Menophra abruptaria*) and **small waved umber** (*Horisme vitalbata*), that are cryptically marked to merge with tree bark, and the **mottled umber** (*Erannis defoliaria*) whose looper larvae can strip branches and even trees. Often shortened to: **umber.**

umbilical (ʌmˈbɪlɪkᵊl, ˌʌmbɪˈlaɪkᵊl) ADJECTIVE [1] of, relating to, or resembling the umbilicus or the umbilical cord. [2] in the region of the umbilicus: *an umbilical hernia.* ◆ NOUN [3] short for **umbilical cord.**
▸**umˈbilically** ADVERB

umbilical cord NOUN [1] the long flexible tubelike structure connecting a fetus with the placenta: it provides a means of metabolic interchange with the mother. [2] any flexible cord, tube, or cable used to transfer information, power, oxygen, etc., as between an astronaut walking in space and his spacecraft or a deep-sea diver and his craft.

umbilicate (ʌmˈbɪlɪkɪt, -ˌkeɪt) ADJECTIVE [1] having an umbilicus or navel. [2] having a central depression: *an umbilicate leaf.* [3] shaped like a navel, as some bacterial colonies.

umbilication (ʌmˌbɪlɪˈkeɪʃən) NOUN [1] *Biology, anatomy* a navel-like notch or depression, as in the centre of a vesicle. [2] the condition of being umbilicated.

umbilicus (ʌmˈbɪlɪkəs, ˌʌmbɪˈlaɪkəs) NOUN, *plural* **-bilici** (-ˈbɪlɪˌsaɪ, -bɪˈlaɪsaɪ). [1] *Biology* a hollow or navel-like structure, such as the cavity at the base of a gastropod shell. [2] *Anatomy* a technical name for the **navel.**

▷HISTORY C18: from Latin: navel, centre; compare Latin *umbō* shield boss, Greek *omphalos* navel
▸**umbiliform** (ʌmˈbɪlɪˌfɔːm) ADJECTIVE

umble pie (ˈʌmbᵊl) NOUN See **humble pie** (sense 1).

umbles (ˈʌmbᵊlz) PLURAL NOUN another term for **numbles**.

umbo (ˈʌmbəʊ) NOUN, *plural* **umbones** (ʌmˈbəʊniːz) *or* **umbos**. [1] a small hump projecting from the centre of the cap in certain mushrooms. [2] a hooked prominence occurring at the apex of each half of the shell of a bivalve mollusc. [3] *Anatomy* the slightly convex area at the centre of the outer surface of the eardrum, where the malleus is attached on the internal surface. [4] a large projecting central boss on a shield, esp on a Saxon shield.
▷HISTORY C18: from Latin: boss of a shield, projecting piece
▸**umbonate** (ˈʌmbənɪt, -ˌneɪt) *or* **umbonal** (ˈʌmbənᵊl) *or* **umbonic** (ʌmˈbɒnɪk) ADJECTIVE

umbra (ˈʌmbrə) NOUN, *plural* **-brae** (-briː) *or* **-bras**. [1] a region of complete shadow resulting from the total obstruction of light by an opaque object, esp the shadow cast by the moon onto the earth during a solar eclipse. [2] the darker inner region of a sunspot. ◆ Compare **penumbra**.
▷HISTORY C16: from Latin: shade, shadow
▸ˈ**umbral** ADJECTIVE

umbrage (ˈʌmbrɪdʒ) NOUN [1] displeasure or resentment; offence (in the phrase **give** *or* **take umbrage**). [2] the foliage of trees, considered as providing shade. [3] *Rare* shadow or shade. [4] *Archaic* a shadow or semblance.
▷HISTORY C15: from Old French *umbrage*, from Latin *umbrāticus* relating to shade, from *umbra* shade, shadow

umbrageous (ʌmˈbreɪdʒəs) ADJECTIVE shady or shading.
▸**umˈbrageously** ADVERB ▸**umˈbrageousness** NOUN

umbrella (ʌmˈbrɛlə) NOUN [1] a portable device used for protection against rain, snow, etc., and consisting of a light canopy supported on a collapsible metal frame mounted on a central rod. [2] the flattened cone-shaped contractile body of a jellyfish or other medusa. [3] a protective shield or screen, esp of aircraft or gunfire. [4] anything that has the effect of a protective screen or cover. [5] **a** any system or agency that provides centralized organization or general cover for a group of related companies, organizations, etc.: *dance umbrella*. **b** (*as modifier*): *an umbrella fund; umbrella group*.
▷HISTORY C17: from Italian *ombrella*, diminutive of *ombra* shade; see UMBRA
▸**umˈbrella-ˌlike** ADJECTIVE

umbrella bird NOUN a black tropical American passerine bird, *Cephalopterus ornatus*, having a large overhanging crest and a long feathered wattle: family *Cotingidae* (cotingas).

umbrella pine NOUN another name for **stone pine**.

umbrella plant NOUN an African sedge, *Cyperus alternifolius*, having large umbrella-like whorls of slender leaves: widely grown as an ornamental water plant.

umbrella stand NOUN an upright rack or stand for umbrellas.

umbrella tree NOUN [1] a North American magnolia, *Magnolia tripetala*, having long leaves clustered into an umbrella formation at the ends of the branches and unpleasant-smelling white flowers. [2] Also called: **umbrella bush**. any of various other trees or shrubs having leaves shaped like an umbrella or growing in an umbrella-like cluster.

Umbria (ˈʌmbrɪə; *Italian* ˈumbrja) NOUN a mountainous region of central Italy, in the valley of the Tiber. Pop.: 835 488 (2001 est.). Area: 8456 sq. km (3265 sq. miles).

Umbrian (ˈʌmbrɪən) ADJECTIVE [1] of or relating to Umbria, its inhabitants, their dialect of Italian, or the ancient language once spoken there. [2] of or relating to a Renaissance school of painting that included Raphael. ◆ NOUN [3] a native or inhabitant of Umbria. [4] an extinct language of ancient S Italy, belonging to the Italic branch of the Indo-European family. See also **Osco-Umbrian**.

Umbriel (ˈʌmbrɪəl) NOUN one of the main satellites of Uranus.

umfazi (ʊmˈfɑːzɪ) NOUN *South African* an African married woman.
▷HISTORY Nguni

umiak *or* **oomiak** (ˈuːmɪˌæk) NOUN a large open boat made of stretched skins, used by Eskimos. Compare **kayak**.
▷HISTORY C18: from Greenland Eskimo: boat for the use of women

UMIST (ˈjuːˌmɪst) NOUN ACRONYM FOR University of Manchester Institute of Science and Technology.

umlaut (ˈʊmlaʊt) NOUN [1] the mark (¨) placed over a vowel in some languages, such as German, indicating modification in the quality of the vowel. Compare **diaeresis**. [2] (esp in Germanic languages) the change of a vowel within a word brought about by the assimilating influence of a vowel or semivowel in a preceding or following syllable.
▷HISTORY C19: German, from *um* around (in the sense of changing places) + *Laut* sound

umlungu (ʊmˈlʊŋgʊ) NOUN *South African* a white man.
▷HISTORY Nguni: a white man

Ummah (ˈʊmə) NOUN the Muslim community throughout the world.
▷HISTORY from Arabic: community

umpie *or* **umpy** (ˈʌmpɪ) NOUN, *plural* **umpies**. *Austral* an informal word for **umpire**.

umpire (ˈʌmpaɪə) NOUN [1] an official who rules on the playing of a game, as in cricket or baseball. [2] a person who rules on or judges disputes between contesting parties. ◆ VERB [3] to act as umpire in (a game, dispute, or controversy).
▷HISTORY C15: by mistaken division from *a noumpere*, from Old French *nomper* not one of a pair, from *nom-*, *non-* not + *per* equal, PEER[1]
▸ˈ**umpireship** *or* ˈ**umpirage** NOUN

umpteen (ˌʌmpˈtiːn) DETERMINER *Informal* **a** very many: *umpteen things to do*. **b** (*as pronoun*): *umpteen of them came*.
▷HISTORY C20: from *umpty* a great deal (perhaps from *-enty* as in *twenty*) + *-teen* ten
▸ˌ**umpˈteenth** NOUN, ADJECTIVE

Umtali (ʊmˈtɑːlɪ) NOUN the former name (until 1982) of **Mutare**.

Umtata (ʌmˈtɑːtə) NOUN a city in South Africa, in Eastern Cape province; the capital of the former Transkei Bantu homeland. Pop.: 80 000 (latest est.).

umwelt (ˈʊmvɛlt) NOUN *Biology, psychol* the environmental factors, collectively, that are capable of affecting the behaviour of an animal or individual.
▷HISTORY C20: from German *Umwelt* environment

UN ABBREVIATION FOR United Nations.

un-[1] PREFIX (*freely used with adjectives, participles, and their derivative adverbs and nouns: less frequently used with certain other nouns*) not; contrary to; opposite of: *uncertain; uncomplaining; unemotionally; untidiness; unbelief; unrest; untruth*.
▷HISTORY from Old English *on-*, *un-*; related to Gothic *on-*, German *un-*, Latin *in-*

un-[2] PREFIX FORMING VERBS [1] denoting reversal of an action or state: *uncover; untangle*. [2] denoting removal from, release, or deprivation: *unharness; unman; unthrone*. [3] (intensifier): *unloose*.
▷HISTORY from Old English *un-*, *on-*; related to Gothic *and-*, German *ent-*, Latin *ante*

ʼun *or* **un** (ən) PRONOUN a spelling of **one** intended to reflect a dialectal or informal pronunciation: *that's a big ʼun*.

UNA (in Britain) ABBREVIATION FOR United Nations Association.

unabashed (ˌʌnəˈbæʃt) ADJECTIVE not ashamed, embarrassed, or ill at ease.

unabated (ˌʌnəˈbeɪtɪd) ADJECTIVE without losing any original force or violence; undiminished.
▸ˌ**unaˈbatedly** ADVERB

unable (ʌnˈeɪbᵊl) ADJECTIVE [1] (*postpositive*; foll by *to*) lacking the necessary power, ability, or authority (to do something); not able. [2] *Archaic* incompetent.

unabridged (ˌʌnəˈbrɪdʒd) ADJECTIVE (of a book, speech, etc.) not reduced in length by condensing.

unacceptable (ˌʌnəkˈsɛptəbᵊl) ADJECTIVE [1] not satisfactory; inadequate: *the standard was wholly unacceptable*. [2] intolerable: *hitting children is unacceptable*.

unaccommodated (ˌʌnəˈkɒməˌdeɪtɪd) ADJECTIVE [1] not suitable or apt; not adapted. [2] unprovided for.

unaccompanied (ˌʌnəˈkʌmpənɪd) ADJECTIVE [1] not accompanied. [2] *Music* **a** (of an instrument) playing alone. **b** (of music for a group of singers) without instrumental accompaniment.

unaccomplished (ˌʌnəˈkɒmplɪʃt) ADJECTIVE [1] not accomplished or finished. [2] lacking accomplishments.

unaccountable (ˌʌnəˈkaʊntəbᵊl) ADJECTIVE [1] allowing of no explanation; inexplicable. [2] puzzling; extraordinary: *an unaccountable fear of hamburgers*. [3] not accountable or answerable to.
▸ˌ**unacˈcountableness** *or* ˌ**unacˌcountaˈbility** NOUN
▸ˌ**unacˈcountably** ADVERB

unaccounted (ˌʌnəˈkaʊntɪd) ADJECTIVE (usually followed by *for*) [1] missing: *as many as 100 people are unaccounted for*. [2] not included in an account: *70 million dollars of unaccounted money*. [3] not explained adequately: *unaccounted friendliness*.

unaccustomed (ˌʌnəˈkʌstəmd) ADJECTIVE [1] (foll by *to*) not used (to): *unaccustomed to pain*. [2] not familiar; strange or unusual.
▸ˌ**unacˈcustomedness** NOUN

unacknowledged (ˌʌnəkˈnɒlɪdʒd) ADJECTIVE not having been acknowledged or recognized: *unacknowledged legislators of the world*.

una corda (ˈuːnə ˈkɔːdə) ADJECTIVE, ADVERB *Music* (of the piano) to be played with the soft pedal depressed.
▷HISTORY Italian, literally: one string; the pedal moves the mechanism so that only one string of the three tuned to each note is struck by the hammer

unacquainted (ˌʌnəˈkweɪntɪd) ADJECTIVE [1] not familiar or conversant with (someone or something). [2] (of people) not having met or been introduced.

unaddressed (ˌʌnəˈdrɛst) ADJECTIVE (of a letter, package, etc.) not having an address.

unadopted (ˌʌnəˈdɒptɪd) ADJECTIVE [1] (of a child) not adopted. [2] *Brit* (of a road, etc.) not maintained by a local authority.

unadorned (ˌʌnəˈdɔːnd) ADJECTIVE not decorated; plain: *a bare unadorned style*.

unadulterated (ˌʌnəˈdʌltəreɪtɪd) ADJECTIVE not debased or made impure.

unadventurous (ˌʌnədˈvɛntʃərəs) ADJECTIVE not daring or enterprising.

unadvised (ˌʌnədˈvaɪzd) ADJECTIVE [1] rash or unwise. [2] not having received advice.
▸**unadvisedly** (ˌʌnədˈvaɪzɪdlɪ) ADVERB ▸ˌ**unadˈvisedness** NOUN

unaffected[1] (ˌʌnəˈfɛktɪd) ADJECTIVE unpretentious, natural, or sincere.
▸ˌ**unafˈfectedly** ADVERB ▸ˌ**unafˈfectedness** NOUN

unaffected[2] (ˌʌnəˈfɛktɪd) ADJECTIVE not affected.

unaffiliated (ˌʌnəˈfɪlɪˌeɪtɪd) ADJECTIVE not officially connected or associated with an organization.

unafraid (ˌʌnəˈfreɪd) ADJECTIVE (*postpositive*; often followed by *of*) not frightened: *unafraid to break new ground*.

unaided (ʌnˈeɪdɪd) ADJECTIVE without having received any help.

Unalaska Island (ˌuːnəˈlæskə) NOUN a large volcanic island in SW Alaska, in the Aleutian Islands. Length: 120 km (75 miles). Greatest width: about 40 km (25 miles).

unalienable (ʌnˈeɪljənəbᵊl) ADJECTIVE *Law* a variant of **inalienable**.

unalloyed (ˌʌnəˈlɔɪd) ADJECTIVE not mixed or intermingled with any other thing; pure: *unalloyed metal; unalloyed pleasure*.

unalterable (ʌnˈɔːltərəbᵊl, -ˈɔːltrəbᵊl) ADJECTIVE (of a condition, truth, etc.) unable to be changed or altered.

unaltered (ʌnˈɔːltəd) ADJECTIVE not altered; unchanged.

unambiguous (ˌʌnæmˈbɪgjʊəs) ADJECTIVE not ambiguous; clear: *an unambiguous message*.

unambitious (ˌʌnæmˈbɪʃəs) ADJECTIVE lacking in ambition: *they were unambitious for their daughters*.

un-American ADJECTIVE [1] not in accordance

with the aims, ideals, customs, etc., of the US. [2] against the interests of the US.
▸ **ˌun-Aˈmericanˌism** NOUN

unamused (ˌʌnəˈmjuːzd) ADJECTIVE not entertained, diverted, or laughing: *they looked on, unamused.*

unaneled (ˌʌnəˈniːld) ADJECTIVE *Archaic* not having received extreme unction.
▷HISTORY C17: from UN-[1] + ANELE

unanimous (juːˈnænɪməs) ADJECTIVE [1] in complete or absolute agreement. [2] characterized by complete agreement: *a unanimous decision.*
▷HISTORY C17: from Latin *ūnanimus* from *ūnus* one + *animus* mind
▸**uˈnanimously** ADVERB ▸**unanimity** (ˌjuːnəˈnɪmɪtɪ) *or* **uˈnanimousness** NOUN

unannounced (ˌʌnəˈnaʊnst) ADJECTIVE not made known publicly or declared in advance: *an unannounced visit.*

unanswerable (ʌnˈɑːnsərəbᵊl) ADJECTIVE [1] incapable of being refuted. [2] (of a question) not admitting of any answer.
▸**unˈanswerableness** NOUN ▸**unˈanswerably** ADVERB

unanswered (ʌnˈɑːnsəd) ADJECTIVE not answered or replied to: *many unanswered questions.*

unanticipated (ˌʌnænˈtɪsɪˌpeɪtəd) ADJECTIVE not anticipated; unforeseen.

unappealable (ˌʌnəˈpiːləbᵊl) ADJECTIVE *Law* (of a judgment, etc.) not capable of being appealed against.
▸**ˌunapˈpealableness** NOUN ▸**ˌunapˈpealably** ADVERB

unappealing (ˌʌnəˈpiːlɪŋ) ADJECTIVE not attractive or pleasing.

unappetizing *or* **unappetising** (ʌnˈæpɪˌtaɪzɪŋ) ADJECTIVE [1] (of food) not pleasing or stimulating to the appetite. [2] (of a prospect, person, etc.) not appealing or attractive: *unappetizing to investors.*

unappreciated (ˌʌnəˈpriːʃɪˌeɪtɪd, -sɪ-) ADJECTIVE not given or shown thanks or gratitude.
▸**ˌunapˈpreciative** ADJECTIVE

unapproachable (ˌʌnəˈprəʊtʃəbᵊl) ADJECTIVE [1] discouraging intimacy, friendliness, etc.; aloof. [2] inaccessible. [3] not to be rivalled.
▸**ˌunapˈproachableness** NOUN ▸**ˌunapˈproachably** ADVERB

unappropriated (ˌʌnəˈprəʊprɪˌeɪtɪd) ADJECTIVE [1] not set aside for specific use. [2] *Accounting* designating that portion of the profits of a business enterprise that is retained in the business and not withdrawn by the proprietor. [3] (of property) not having been taken into any person's possession or control.

unapproved (ˌʌnəˈpruːvd) ADJECTIVE not having been given approval or sanction.

unapt (ʌnˈæpt) ADJECTIVE [1] (*usually postpositive; often foll by for*) not suitable or qualified; unfitted. [2] mentally slow. [3] (*postpositive; may take an infinitive*) not disposed or likely (to).
▸**unˈaptly** ADVERB ▸**unˈaptness** NOUN

unarguable (ʌnˈɑːgjʊəbᵊl) ADJECTIVE [1] incapable of being argued. [2] incontestable; indisputable.
▸**unˈarguably** ADVERB

unarm (ʌnˈɑːm) VERB a less common word for **disarm.**

unarmed (ʌnˈɑːmd) ADJECTIVE [1] without weapons. [2] (of animals and plants) having no claws, prickles, spines, thorns, or similar structures. [3] of or relating to a projectile that does not use a detonator to initiate explosive action.

unary (ˈjuːnərɪ) ADJECTIVE consisting of, or affecting, a single element or component; monadic.
▷HISTORY C16 (in the obsolete sense: a unit): from Latin *unus* one + -ARY

unashamed (ˌʌnəˈʃeɪmd) ADJECTIVE [1] lacking moral restraints. [2] not embarrassed, contrite, or apologetic.
▸**unashamedly** (ˌʌnəˈʃeɪmɪdlɪ) ADVERB ▸**ˌunaˈshamedness** NOUN

unasked (ʌnˈɑːskt) ADJECTIVE [1] not requested or demanded. [2] not invited.

unassailable (ˌʌnəˈseɪləbᵊl) ADJECTIVE [1] not able to be attacked. [2] undeniable or irrefutable.
▸**ˌunasˈsailableness** NOUN ▸**ˌunasˈsailably** ADVERB

unassisted (ˌʌnəˈsɪstɪd) ADJECTIVE without aid or help; alone.

unassuming (ˌʌnəˈsjuːmɪŋ) ADJECTIVE modest or unpretentious.
▸**ˌunasˈsumingly** ADVERB ▸**ˌunasˈsumingness** NOUN

unattached (ˌʌnəˈtætʃt) ADJECTIVE [1] not connected with any specific thing, body, group, etc.; independent. [2] not engaged or married. [3] (of property) not seized or held as security or in satisfaction of a judgment.

unattainable (ˌʌnəˈteɪnəbᵊl) ADJECTIVE not achievable or accomplishable: *an unattainable goal.*

unattended (ˌʌnəˈtendɪd) ADJECTIVE [1] not looked after or cared for. [2] unaccompanied or alone. [3] not listened to.

unattractive (ˌʌnəˈtræktɪv) ADJECTIVE [1] not appealing to the senses or mind through beauty, form, character, etc. [2] not arousing interest: *an unattractive proposition.*

unattributed (ˌʌnəˈtrɪbjuːtɪd) ADJECTIVE not having been ascribed or attributed (to someone).
▸**ˌunatˈtributable** ADJECTIVE

unau (ˈjuːnaʊ) NOUN another name for the **two-toed sloth** (see **sloth** (sense 1)).
▷HISTORY C18: via French from Tupi

unauthorized *or* **unauthorised** (ʌnˈɔːθəˌraɪzd) ADJECTIVE not having official permission.

unavailable (ˌʌnəˈveɪləbᵊl) ADJECTIVE not obtainable or accessible: *unavailable for comment.*

unavailing (ˌʌnəˈveɪlɪŋ) ADJECTIVE useless or futile.
▸**ˌunaˈvailingly** ADVERB

unavoidable (ˌʌnəˈvɔɪdəbᵊl) ADJECTIVE [1] unable to be avoided; inevitable. [2] *Law* not capable of being declared null and void.
▸**ˌunaˌvoidaˈbility** *or* **ˌunaˈvoidableness** NOUN
▸**ˌunaˈvoidably** ADVERB

unaware (ˌʌnəˈwɛə) ADJECTIVE [1] (*postpositive*) not aware or conscious (of): *unaware of the danger he ran across the road.* [2] not fully cognizant of what is going on in the world: *he's the most unaware person I've ever met.* ◆ ADVERB [3] a variant of **unawares.**
▸**ˌunaˈwarely** ADVERB ▸**ˌunaˈwareness** NOUN

unawares (ˌʌnəˈwɛəz) ADVERB [1] without prior warning or plan; unexpectedly: *she caught him unawares.* [2] without being aware of or knowing: *he lost it unawares.*

unbacked (ʌnˈbækt) ADJECTIVE [1] (of a book, chair, etc.) not having a back. [2] bereft of support, esp on a financial basis. [3] (of a horse) **a** not supported by bets. **b** never having been ridden.

unbalance (ʌnˈbæləns) VERB (*tr*) [1] to upset the equilibrium or balance of. [2] to disturb the mental stability of (a person or his mind). ◆ NOUN [3] imbalance or instability.

unbalanced (ʌnˈbælənst) ADJECTIVE [1] lacking balance. [2] irrational or unsound; erratic. [3] mentally disordered or deranged. [4] biased; one-sided: *unbalanced reporting.* [5] (in double-entry book-keeping) not having total debit balances equal to total credit balances. [6] *Electronics* (of signals or circuitry) not symmetrically disposed about earth or zero reference potential.

unbar (ʌnˈbɑː) VERB **-bars, -barring, -barred.** (*tr*) [1] to take away a bar or bars from. [2] to unfasten bars, locks, etc., from (a door); open.

unbated (ʌnˈbeɪtɪd) ADJECTIVE [1] a less common spelling of **unabated.** [2] *Archaic* (of a sword, lance, etc.) not covered with a protective button.

unbearable (ʌnˈbɛərəbᵊl) ADJECTIVE not able to be borne or endured.
▸**unˈbearableness** NOUN ▸**unˈbearably** ADVERB

unbeatable (ʌnˈbiːtəbᵊl) ADJECTIVE unable to be defeated or outclassed; surpassingly excellent.

unbeaten (ʌnˈbiːtᵊn) ADJECTIVE [1] having suffered no defeat. [2] not worn down; untrodden. [3] not mixed or stirred by beating: *unbeaten eggs.* [4] not beaten or struck.

unbecoming (ˌʌnbɪˈkʌmɪŋ) ADJECTIVE [1] unsuitable or inappropriate, esp through being unattractive: *an unbecoming hat.* [2] (when *postpositive,* usually foll by *of* or an object) not proper or seemly (for): *manners unbecoming a lady.*
▸**ˌunbeˈcomingly** ADVERB ▸**ˌunbeˈcomingness** NOUN

unbeknown (ˌʌnbɪˈnəʊn) ADVERB [1] (*sentence modifier;* foll by *to*) Also (esp Brit): **unbeknownst.** without the knowledge (of a person): *unbeknown to him she had left the country.* ◆ ADJECTIVE [2] (*postpositive;* usually foll by *to*) *Rare* not known (to).
▷HISTORY C17: from the archaic *beknown* known; see BE-, KNOW

unbelief (ˌʌnbɪˈliːf) NOUN disbelief or rejection of belief.

unbelievable (ˌʌnbɪˈliːvəbᵊl) ADJECTIVE unable to be believed; incredible or astonishing.
▸**ˌunbeˌlievaˈbility** *or* **ˌunbeˈlievableness** NOUN

unbelievably (ˌʌnbɪˈliːvəblɪ) ADVERB [1] in a manner that is hard to believe; astonishingly: *it gets unbelievably hot.* [2] (*sentence modifier*) it is hard to believe that; incredibly: *unbelievably he remained utterly cheerful.*

unbeliever (ˌʌnbɪˈliːvə) NOUN a person who does not believe or withholds belief, esp in religious matters.

unbelieving (ˌʌnbɪˈliːvɪŋ) ADJECTIVE [1] not believing; sceptical. [2] proceeding from or characterized by scepticism.
▸**ˌunbeˈlievingly** ADVERB ▸**ˌunbeˈlievingness** NOUN

unbelt (ʌnˈbɛlt) VERB (*tr*) [1] to unbuckle the belt of (a garment). [2] to remove (something) from a belt.

unbend (ʌnˈbɛnd) VERB **-bends, -bending, -bent.** [1] to release or be released from the restraints of formality and ceremony. [2] *Informal* to relax (the mind) or (of the mind) to become relaxed. [3] to become or be made straightened out from an originally bent shape or position. [4] (*tr*) *Nautical* **a** to remove (a sail) from a stay, mast, yard, etc. **b** to untie (a rope, etc.) or cast (a cable) loose.
▸**unˈbendable** ADJECTIVE

unbending (ʌnˈbɛndɪŋ) ADJECTIVE [1] rigid or inflexible. [2] characterized by sternness or severity: *an unbending rule.*
▸**unˈbendingly** ADVERB ▸**unˈbendingness** NOUN

unbent (ʌnˈbɛnt) VERB [1] the past tense and past participle of **unbend.** ◆ ADJECTIVE [2] not bent or bowed. [3] not compelled to yield or give way by force.

unbiased *or* **unbiassed** (ʌnˈbaɪəst) ADJECTIVE [1] having no bias or prejudice; fair or impartial. [2] *Statistics* **a** (of a sample) not affected by any extraneous factors, conflated variables, or selectivity which influence its distribution; random. **b** (of an estimator) having an expected value equal to the parameter being estimated; having zero bias. **c** Also called: **discriminatory.** (of a significance test). having a power greater than the predetermined significance level.
▸**unˈbiasedly** *or* **unˈbiassedly** ADVERB ▸**unˈbiasedness** *or* **unˈbiassedness** NOUN

unbidden (ʌnˈbɪdᵊn) ADJECTIVE [1] not ordered or commanded; voluntary or spontaneous. [2] not invited or asked.

unbind (ʌnˈbaɪnd) VERB **-binds, -binding, -bound.** (*tr*) [1] to set free from restraining bonds or chains; release. [2] to unfasten or make loose (a bond, tie, etc.).

unbirthday (ˌʌnˈbɜːθdeɪ) NOUN *Brit jocular* **a** any day other than one's birthday. **b** (*as modifier*): *an unbirthday present.*
▷HISTORY C19: coined by Lewis Carroll in *Through the Looking-Glass*

unbleached (ʌnˈbliːtʃt) ADJECTIVE not having been made or become white or lighter through exposure to sunlight or by the action of chemical agents, etc.

unblemished (ʌnˈblɛmɪʃt) ADJECTIVE not blemished or tarnished in any way.

unblenched (ʌnˈblɛntʃt) ADJECTIVE *Obsolete* undismayed.
▷HISTORY C17: from UN-[1] + BLENCH[1]

unblessed (ʌnˈblɛst) ADJECTIVE [1] deprived of blessing. [2] unhallowed, cursed, or evil. [3] unhappy or wretched.
▸**unblessedness** (ʌnˈblɛsɪdnɪs) NOUN

unblinking (ʌnˈblɪŋkɪŋ) ADJECTIVE [1] without blinking. [2] showing no visible response or emotion. [3] not wavering through trepidation or fear.
▸**unˈblinkingly** ADVERB

unblock (ʌnˈblɒk) VERB (*tr*) to remove a blockage from (a pipe, etc.).

unblown (ʌnˈbləʊn) ADJECTIVE [1] *Archaic* (of a flower) still in the bud. [2] not blown.

unblushing (ʌnˈblʌʃɪŋ) ADJECTIVE immodest or shameless.
▸**unˈblushingly** ADVERB ▸**unˈblushingness** NOUN

unbolt (ʌnˈbəʊlt) VERB (*tr*) [1] to unfasten a bolt of (a door). [2] to undo (the nut) on a bolt.

unbolted (ʌnˈbəʊltɪd) ADJECTIVE (of grain, meal, or flour) not sifted.

unboned (ʌnˈbəʊnd) ADJECTIVE 1 (of meat, fish, etc.) not having had the bones removed. 2 (of animals) having no bones.

unborn (ʌnˈbɔːn) ADJECTIVE 1 not yet born or brought to birth. 2 still to come in the future: *the unborn world.*

unbosom (ʌnˈbʊzəm) VERB (*tr*) to relieve (oneself) of (secrets, etc.) by telling someone.
▷HISTORY C16: from UN-² + BOSOM (in the sense: seat of the emotions); compare Dutch *ontboezemen*
▸**unˈbosomer** NOUN

unbound (ʌnˈbaʊnd) VERB 1 the past tense and past participle of **unbind.** ◆ ADJECTIVE 2 (of a book) not bound within a cover. 3 not restrained or tied down by bonds. 4 (of a morpheme) able to form a word by itself; free.

unbounded (ʌnˈbaʊndɪd) ADJECTIVE having no boundaries or limits.
▸**unˈboundedly** ADVERB ▸**unˈboundedness** NOUN

unbowed (ʌnˈbaʊd) ADJECTIVE 1 not bowed or bent. 2 free or unconquered.

unbrace (ʌnˈbreɪs) VERB (*tr*) 1 to remove tension or strain from; relax. 2 to remove a brace or braces from.

unbreakable (ʌnˈbreɪkəbᵊl) ADJECTIVE not able to be broken.

unbred (ʌnˈbrɛd) ADJECTIVE 1 a less common word for **ill-bred.** 2 not taught or instructed. 3 *Obsolete* not born.

unbridle (ʌnˈbraɪdᵊl) VERB (*tr*) 1 to remove the bridle from (a horse). 2 to remove all controls or restraints from.

unbridled (ʌnˈbraɪdᵊld) ADJECTIVE 1 with all restraints removed. 2 (of a horse, etc.) wearing no bridle.
▸**unˈbridledly** ADVERB ▸**unˈbridledness** NOUN

unbroken (ʌnˈbrəʊkən) ADJECTIVE 1 complete or whole. 2 continuous or incessant. 3 undaunted in spirit. 4 (of animals, esp horses) not tamed; wild. 5 not disturbed or upset: *the unbroken silence of the afternoon.* 6 (of a record, esp at sport) not improved upon. 7 (of a contract, law, etc.) not broken or infringed.
▸**unˈbrokenly** ADVERB ▸**unˈbrokenness** NOUN

unbundle (ʌnˈbʌndᵊl) VERB (*tr*) *Computing* to separate (hardware from software) for sales purposes.

unbundling (ʌnˈbʌndlɪŋ) NOUN *Commerce* the takeover of a large conglomerate with a view to retaining the core business and selling off some of the subsidiaries to help finance the takeover.

unburden (ʌnˈbɜːdᵊn) VERB (*tr*) 1 to remove a load or burden from. 2 to relieve or make free (one's mind, oneself, etc.) of a worry, trouble, etc., by revelation or confession. ◆ Archaic spelling: **unburthen** (ʌnˈbɜːðən).

unbutton (ʌnˈbʌtᵊn) VERB 1 to undo by unfastening (the buttons) of (a garment). 2 *Informal* to release or relax (oneself, tension, etc.).

unbuttoned (ʌnˈbʌtᵊnd) ADJECTIVE 1 with buttons not fastened. 2 *Informal* uninhibited; unrestrained: *hours of unbuttoned self-revelation.*

uncaged (ʌnˈkeɪdʒd) ADJECTIVE at liberty.

uncalled-for (ˌʌnˈkɔːldfɔː) ADJECTIVE unnecessary or unwarranted.

uncanny (ʌnˈkænɪ) ADJECTIVE 1 characterized by apparently supernatural wonder, horror, etc. 2 beyond what is normal or expected: *an uncanny accuracy.*
▸**unˈcannily** ADVERB ▸**unˈcanniness** NOUN

uncap (ʌnˈkæp) VERB **-caps, -capping, -capped.** 1 (*tr*) to remove a cap or top from (a container): *to uncap a bottle.* 2 to remove a cap from (the head).

uncared-for (ˌʌnˈkɛədfɔː) ADJECTIVE not cared for; neglected.

uncaused (ʌnˈkɔːzd) ADJECTIVE *Now rare* not brought into existence by any cause; spontaneous or natural.

unceasing (ʌnˈsiːsɪŋ) ADJECTIVE not ceasing or ending.
▸**unˈceasingly** ADVERB ▸**unˈceasingness** NOUN

uncensored (ʌnˈsɛnsəd) ADJECTIVE (of a publication, film, letter, etc.) not having been banned or edited.

unceremonious (ˌʌnsɛrɪˈməʊnɪəs) ADJECTIVE without ceremony; informal, abrupt, rude, or undignified.
▸**ˌunceremoniously** ADVERB ▸**ˌunceremoniousness** NOUN

uncertain (ʌnˈsɜːtᵊn) ADJECTIVE 1 not able to be accurately known or predicted: *the issue is uncertain.* 2 (when *postpositive,* often foll by *of*) not sure or confident (about): *a man of uncertain opinion.* 3 not precisely determined, established, or decided: *uncertain plans.* 4 not to be depended upon; unreliable: *an uncertain vote.* 5 liable to variation; changeable: *the weather is uncertain.* 6 **in no uncertain terms. a** unambiguously. **b** forcefully.
▸**unˈcertainly** ADVERB ▸**unˈcertainness** NOUN

uncertainty (ʌnˈsɜːtᵊntɪ) NOUN, *plural* **-ties.** 1 Also called: **uncertainness.** the state or condition of being uncertain. 2 an uncertain matter, contingency, etc.

uncertainty principle NOUN **the.** the principle that energy and time or position and momentum of a quantum mechanical system, cannot both be accurately measured simultaneously. The product of their uncertainties is always greater than or of the order of *h*, where *h* is the Planck constant. Also called: **Heisenberg uncertainty principle, indeterminacy principle.**

unchain (ʌnˈtʃeɪn) VERB (*tr*) 1 to remove a chain or chains from. 2 to set at liberty; make free.

unchallenged (ʌnˈtʃælɪndʒd) ADJECTIVE not having been challenged or questioned: *thirty years of unchallenged power.*
▸**unˈchallengeable** ADJECTIVE

unchancy (ʌnˈtʃɑːnsɪ) ADJECTIVE *Scot* unlucky, ill-omened, or dangerous. Compare **wanchancy.**

unchangeable (ʌnˈtʃeɪndʒəbᵊl) ADJECTIVE not capable of being changed or altered.

unchanged (ʌnˈtʃeɪndʒd) ADJECTIVE not altered or different in any way.

unchanging (ʌnˈtʃeɪndʒɪŋ) ADJECTIVE remaining the same; constant: *an unchanging nature.*

uncharacteristic (ˌʌnkærɪktəˈrɪstɪk) ADJECTIVE not typical or usual.

uncharged (ʌnˈtʃɑːdʒd) ADJECTIVE 1 (of land or other property) not subject to a charge. 2 having no electric charge; neutral. 3 *Archaic* (of a firearm) not loaded.

uncharitable (ʌnˈtʃærɪtəbᵊl) ADJECTIVE (of a person, remark, etc.) unkind or lacking in generosity: *an uncharitable criticism.*

uncharted (ʌnˈtʃɑːtɪd) ADJECTIVE (of a physical or nonphysical region or area) not yet mapped, surveyed, or investigated: *uncharted waters; the uncharted depths of the mind.*

unchartered (ʌnˈtʃɑːtəd) ADJECTIVE 1 not authorized by charter; unregulated. 2 unauthorized, lawless, or irregular.

> **Language note** Care should be taken not to use *unchartered* where *uncharted* is meant: *uncharted* (not *unchartered*) *territory.*

unchecked (ʌnˈtʃɛkt) ADJECTIVE 1 not prevented from continuing or growing: *unchecked population growth.* 2 not examined or inspected. ◆ ADVERB 3 without being stopped or hindered: *the virus could spread unchecked.* 4 without being examined or inspected: *our luggage passed unchecked through customs.*

unchristian (ʌnˈkrɪstʃən) ADJECTIVE 1 not in accordance with the principles or ethics of Christianity. 2 non-Christian or pagan.
▸**unˈchristianly** ADVERB

unchurch (ʌnˈtʃɜːtʃ) VERB (*tr*) 1 to excommunicate. 2 to remove church status from (a building).

uncial (ˈʌnsɪəl) ADJECTIVE 1 of, relating to, or written in majuscule letters, as used in Greek and Latin manuscripts of the third to ninth centuries, that resemble modern capitals, but are characterized by much greater curvature and inclination and general inequality of height. 2 pertaining to an inch or an ounce. 3 pertaining to the duodecimal system. ◆ NOUN 4 an uncial letter or manuscript.
▷HISTORY C17: from Late Latin *unciālēs litterae* letters an inch long, from Latin *unciālis,* from *uncia* one twelfth, inch, OUNCE¹
▸**ˈuncially** ADVERB

unciform (ˈʌnsɪˌfɔːm) ADJECTIVE 1 *Anatomy, zoology* having the shape of a hook. ◆ NOUN 2 Also called: **hamate bone.** *Anatomy* any hook-shaped structure or part, esp a small bone of the wrist (**unciform bone**).
▷HISTORY C18: from New Latin *unciformis,* from Latin *uncus* a hook

uncinariasis (ˌʌnsɪnəˈraɪəsɪs) NOUN the condition of being infested with hookworms; hookworm disease.
▷HISTORY C20: via New Latin *Uncināria,* from Late Latin *uncīnus* a hook, from Latin *uncus*

uncinate (ˈʌnsɪnɪt, -ˌneɪt) ADJECTIVE *Biology* 1 shaped like a hook: *the uncinate process of the ribs of certain vertebrates.* 2 of, relating to, or possessing uncini.
▷HISTORY C18: from Latin *uncīnātus,* from *uncīnus* a hook, from *uncus*

uncinus (ʌnˈsaɪnəs) NOUN, *plural* **-cini** (-ˈsaɪnaɪ). *Zoology* a small hooked structure, such as any of the hooked chaetae of certain polychaete worms.
▷HISTORY C19: from Late Latin: hook, from Latin *uncus*

uncircumcised (ʌnˈsɜːkəmˌsaɪzd) ADJECTIVE 1 not circumcised. 2 not Jewish; gentile. 3 *Theol* not purified.

uncircumcision (ˌʌnsɜːkəmˈsɪʒən) NOUN *Chiefly New Testament* the state of being uncircumcised.

uncivil (ʌnˈsɪvəl) ADJECTIVE 1 lacking civility or good manners. 2 an obsolete word for **uncivilized.**
▸**uncivility** (ˌʌnsɪˈvɪlɪtɪ) *or* **unˈcivilness** NOUN ▸**unˈcivilly** ADVERB

uncivilized *or* **uncivilised** (ʌnˈsɪvɪˌlaɪzd) ADJECTIVE 1 (of a tribe or people) not yet civilized, esp preliterate. 2 lacking culture or sophistication.
▸**uncivilizedly** *or* **uncivilisedly** (ʌnˈsɪvɪˌlaɪzɪdlɪ) ADVERB ▸**unˈciviˌlizedness** *or* **unˈciviˌlisedness** NOUN

unclad (ʌnˈklæd) ADJECTIVE having no clothes on; naked.

unclaimed (ʌnˈkleɪmd) ADJECTIVE not having been claimed: *£7 million in unclaimed prizes.*

unclasp (ʌnˈklɑːsp) VERB 1 (*tr*) to unfasten the clasp of (something). 2 to release one's grip (upon an object).

unclassified (ʌnˈklæsɪˌfaɪd) ADJECTIVE 1 not arranged in any specific order or grouping. 2 (of information) not possessing a security classification. 3 (of football results) not arranged in any special order or in divisions.

uncle (ˈʌŋkᵊl) NOUN 1 a brother of one's father or mother. 2 the husband of one's aunt. 3 a term of address sometimes used by children for a male friend of their parents. 4 *Slang* a pawnbroker. ◆ Related adjective: **avuncular.**
▷HISTORY C13: from Old French *oncle,* from Latin *avunculus;* related to Latin *avus* grandfather

unclean (ʌnˈkliːn) ADJECTIVE lacking moral, spiritual, ritual, or physical cleanliness.
▸**unˈcleanness** NOUN

uncleanly¹ (ʌnˈkliːnlɪ) ADVERB in an unclean manner.

uncleanly² (ʌnˈklɛnlɪ) ADJECTIVE characterized by an absence of cleanliness; unclean.
▸**unˈcleanliness** NOUN

unclear (ʌnˈklɪə) ADJECTIVE not clear or definite; ambiguous.
▸**unˈclearly** ADVERB ▸**unˈclearness** NOUN

Uncle Sam NOUN a personification of the government of the United States.
▷HISTORY C19: apparently a humorous interpretation of the letters stamped on army supply boxes during the War of 1812: *US*

Uncle Tom NOUN *Informal, derogatory* a Black whose behaviour towards Whites is regarded as obsequious and servile.
▷HISTORY C20: after the slave who is the main character of H. B. Stowe's novel *Uncle Tom's Cabin* (1852)
▸**Uncle Tomism** NOUN

unclog (ʌnˈklɒg) VERB **-clogs, -clogging, -clogged.** (*tr*) to remove an obstruction from (a drain, etc.).

unclose (ʌnˈkləʊz) VERB 1 to open or cause to

open. 2 to come or bring to light; reveal or be revealed.

unclothe (ʌn'kləʊð) VERB **-clothes, -clothing, -clothed** *or* **-clad.** (*tr*) 1 to take off garments from; strip. 2 to uncover or lay bare.

uncluttered (ʌn'klʌtəd) ADJECTIVE not having too many objects, details, etc.

unco[1] ('ʌŋkəʊ) *Scot* ◆ ADJECTIVE **uncoer, uncoest.** 1 unfamiliar, strange, or odd. 2 remarkable or striking. ◆ ADVERB 3 very; extremely. 4 narrow-minded, excessively religious, or self-righteous people. ◆ NOUN, *plural* **uncos** *or* **uncoes.** 5 a novel or remarkable person or thing. 6 *Obsolete* a stranger. 7 (*plural*) news.
▷HISTORY C15: variant of UNCOUTH

unco[2] ('ʌŋkəʊ) *Austral informal* ◆ ADJECTIVE 1 awkward; clumsy. ◆ NOUN, *plural* **uncos.** 2 an awkward or clumsy person.
▷HISTORY C20: shortened form of UNCOORDINATED

uncoil (ʌn'kɔɪl) VERB to unwind or become unwound; untwist.

uncoined (ʌn'kɔɪnd) ADJECTIVE (of a metal) not made into coin.

uncollected (ˌʌnkə'lɛktɪd) ADJECTIVE not having been called for, gathered, or collected.

uncomfortable (ʌn'kʌmftəb^{ə}l) ADJECTIVE 1 not comfortable. 2 feeling or causing discomfort or unease; disquieting.
▸**un'comfortableness** NOUN ▸**un'comfortably** ADVERB

uncommercial (ˌʌnkə'mɜːʃəl) ADJECTIVE 1 not concerned with commerce or trade. 2 not in accordance with the aims or principles of business or trade.

uncommitted (ˌʌnkə'mɪtɪd) ADJECTIVE not bound or pledged to a specific opinion, course of action, or cause.

uncommon (ʌn'kɒmən) ADJECTIVE 1 outside or beyond normal experience, conditions, etc.; unusual. 2 in excess of what is normal: *an uncommon liking for honey.* ◆ ADVERB 3 an archaic word for **uncommonly** (sense 2).
▸**un'commonness** NOUN

uncommonly (ʌn'kɒmənlɪ) ADVERB 1 in an uncommon or unusual manner or degree; rarely. 2 (intensifier): *you're uncommonly friendly.*

uncommunicative (ˌʌnkə'mjuːnɪkətɪv) ADJECTIVE disinclined to talk or give information or opinions.
▸**ˌuncom'municatively** ADVERB ▸**ˌuncom'municativeness** NOUN

uncompetitive (ˌʌnkəm'pɛtɪtɪv) ADJECTIVE not able or willing to compete.

uncomplaining (ˌʌnkəm'pleɪnɪŋ) ADJECTIVE not complaining or resentful; resigned.

uncomplicated (ʌn'kɒmplɪˌkeɪtɪd) ADJECTIVE not complicated; simple.

uncomplimentary (ˌʌnkɒmplɪ'mɛntərɪ, -trɪ) ADJECTIVE not conveying, containing, or resembling a compliment.

uncomprehending (ˌʌnkɒmprɪ'hɛndɪŋ) ADJECTIVE not able to understand; puzzled: *a long, uncomprehending look.*

uncompromising (ʌn'kɒmprəˌmaɪzɪŋ) ADJECTIVE not prepared to give ground or to compromise.
▸**un'comproˌmisingly** ADVERB ▸**un'comproˌmisingness** NOUN

unconcealed (ˌʌnkən'siːld) ADJECTIVE (of feelings, attitudes, etc.) not hidden or concealed; open.

unconcern (ˌʌnkən'sɜːn) NOUN apathy or indifference.

unconcerned (ˌʌnkən'sɜːnd) ADJECTIVE 1 lacking in concern or involvement. 2 not worried; untroubled.
▸**unconcernedly** (ˌʌnkən'sɜːnɪdlɪ) ADVERB
▸**ˌuncon'cernedness** NOUN

unconditional (ˌʌnkən'dɪʃən^{ə}l) ADJECTIVE 1 without conditions or limitations; total: *unconditional surrender.* 2 *Maths* (of an equality) true for all values of the variable: *(x+1)>x is an unconditional equality.*
▸**ˌuncon'ditionally** ADVERB ▸**ˌuncon'ditionalness** *or* **ˌunconˌdition'ality** NOUN

unconditioned (ˌʌnkən'dɪʃənd) ADJECTIVE 1 *Psychol* characterizing an innate reflex and the stimulus and response that form parts of it. Compare **conditioned** (sense 1). 2 *Metaphysics* unrestricted by conditions; infinite; absolute. 3 without limitations; unconditional.
▸**ˌuncon'ditionedness** NOUN

unconditioned response NOUN a reflex action innately elicited by a stimulus without the intervention of any learning process. Also called (esp formerly): **unconditioned reflex.** Compare **conditioned response.**

unconditioned stimulus NOUN *Psychol* any stimulus evoking an unlearnt response, esp in the context of classical conditioning, in which the conditioned stimulus is followed by the unconditioned one.

unconfined (ˌʌnkən'faɪnd) ADJECTIVE 1 not enclosed or restricted; free. 2 (of an emotion) not restricted or disguised: *unconfined joy.*

unconfirmed (ˌʌnkən'fɜːmd) ADJECTIVE not confirmed; uncorroborated: *unconfirmed reports.*

unconformable (ˌʌnkən'fɔːməb^{ə}l) ADJECTIVE 1 not conformable or conforming. 2 (of rock strata) consisting of a series of younger strata that do not succeed the underlying older rocks in age or in parallel position, as a result of a long period of erosion or nondeposition.
▸**ˌunconˌforma'bility** *or* **ˌuncon'formableness** NOUN
▸**ˌuncon'formably** ADVERB

unconformity (ˌʌnkən'fɔːmɪtɪ) NOUN, *plural* **-ties.** 1 lack of conformity. 2 the contact surface between younger and older rocks representing a discontinuity in the geological record. Most commonly it represents an erosional surface.

uncongenial (ˌʌnkən'dʒiːnjəl, -nɪəl) ADJECTIVE not friendly, pleasant, or agreeable.

unconnected (ˌʌnkə'nɛktɪd) ADJECTIVE 1 not linked; separate or independent. 2 disconnected or incoherent.
▸**ˌuncon'nectedly** ADVERB ▸**ˌuncon'nectedness** NOUN

unconscionable (ʌn'kɒnʃənəb^{ə}l) ADJECTIVE 1 unscrupulous or unprincipled: *an unconscionable liar.* 2 immoderate or excessive: *unconscionable demands.*
▸**un'conscionableness** NOUN ▸**un'conscionably** ADVERB

unconscious (ʌn'kɒnʃəs) ADJECTIVE 1 lacking normal sensory awareness of the environment; insensible. 2 not aware of one's actions, behaviour, etc.: *unconscious of his bad manners.* 3 characterized by lack of awareness or intention: *an unconscious blunder.* 4 coming from or produced by the unconscious: *unconscious resentment.* ◆ NOUN 5 *Psychoanal* the part of the mind containing instincts, impulses, images, and ideas that are not available for direct examination. See also **collective unconscious.** Compare **subconscious, preconscious.**
▸**un'consciously** ADVERB

unconsciousness (ʌn'kɒnʃəsnɪs) NOUN the state of being without normal sensory awareness; insensibility.

unconsecrated (ʌn'kɒnsɪˌkreɪtɪd) ADJECTIVE not having been made or declared sacred or holy.

unconsidered (ˌʌnkən'sɪdəd) ADJECTIVE 1 not considered; disregarded. 2 done without consideration.

unconstitutional (ˌʌnkɒnstɪ'tjuːʃən^{ə}l) ADJECTIVE at variance with or not permitted by a constitution.
▸**ˌunconstiˌtution'ality** NOUN

unconstitutional strike NOUN a stoppage of work which violates the dispute procedure agreed between the employer and the trade union or trade unions concerned.

unconstrained (ˌʌnkən'streɪnd) ADJECTIVE not having any constraints.

unconsummated (ʌn'kɒnsəˌmeɪtɪd) ADJECTIVE (of a marriage, relationship, etc.) not having been consummated.

uncontaminated (ˌʌnkən'tæmɪˌneɪtɪd) ADJECTIVE not having been polluted, infected, or made impure.

uncontested (ˌʌnkən'tɛstɪd) ADJECTIVE not having been challenged, called into question, or disputed.

uncontrollable (ˌʌnkən'trəʊləb^{ə}l) ADJECTIVE incapable of being controlled or managed.
▸**ˌunconˌtrolla'bility** *or* **ˌuncon'trollableness** NOUN
▸**ˌuncon'trollably** ADVERB

uncontrolled (ˌʌnkən'trəʊld) ADJECTIVE not controlled or regulated; uncurbed.

uncontroversial (ˌʌnkɒntrə'vɜːʃəl) ADJECTIVE not inspiring or causing controversy.

unconventional (ˌʌnkən'vɛnʃən^{ə}l) ADJECTIVE not conforming to accepted rules or standards.
▸**ˌunconˌvention'ality** NOUN ▸**ˌuncon'ventionally** ADVERB

unconverted (ˌʌnkən'vɜːtɪd) ADJECTIVE 1 not having been changed or adapted: *an unconverted barn.* 2 **a** not having changed one's beliefs, opinions, etc. **b** (*as collective noun;* preceded by *the*): *he'll be preaching to the unconverted.*

unconvinced (ˌʌnkən'vɪnst) ADJECTIVE not convinced or persuaded: *I remain unconvinced.*

unconvincing (ˌʌnkən'vɪnsɪŋ) ADJECTIVE not credible or plausible.

uncooked (ʌn'kʊkt) ADJECTIVE not cooked; raw: *uncooked meat or fish.*

uncool (ʌn'kuːl) ADJECTIVE *Slang* 1 unsophisticated; unfashionable. 2 excitable; tense; not cool.

uncoordinated (ˌʌnkəʊ'ɔːdɪˌneɪtɪd) ADJECTIVE 1 lacking order, system, or organization. 2 (of a person, action, etc.) lacking muscular or emotional coordination.

uncork (ʌn'kɔːk) VERB (*tr*) 1 to draw the cork from (a bottle, etc.). 2 to release or unleash (emotions, etc.).

uncorrected (ˌʌnkə'rɛktɪd) ADJECTIVE (of proofs, a transcript, etc.) not having been corrected or amended.

uncorroborated (ˌʌnkə'rɒbəˌreɪtɪd) ADJECTIVE (of evidence, a statement, etc.) lacking confirmation or evidence.

uncorrupted (ˌʌnkə'rʌptɪd) ADJECTIVE 1 not having been corrupted: *you're touchingly uncorrupted by power.* 2 not contaminated: *food that is uncorrupted by chemicals.*

uncountable (ʌn'kaʊntəb^{ə}l) ADJECTIVE 1 too many to be counted; innumerable. 2 *Linguistics* denoting a noun that does not refer to an isolable object. See **mass noun.**

uncounted (ʌn'kaʊntɪd) ADJECTIVE 1 unable to be counted; innumerable. 2 not counted.

uncouple (ʌn'kʌp^{ə}l) VERB 1 to disconnect or unfasten or become disconnected or unfastened. 2 (*tr*) to set loose; release.

uncouth (ʌn'kuːθ) ADJECTIVE lacking in good manners, refinement, or grace.
▷HISTORY Old English *uncūth,* from UN-[1] + *cūth* familiar; related to Old High German *kund* known, Old Norse *kunnr*
▸**un'couthly** ADVERB ▸**un'couthness** NOUN

uncovenanted (ʌn'kʌvənəntɪd) ADJECTIVE *Law* 1 not guaranteed or promised by a covenant. 2 not in accordance with or sanctioned by a covenant.

uncover (ʌn'kʌvə) VERB 1 (*tr*) to remove the cover, cap, top, etc., from. 2 (*tr*) to reveal or disclose: *to uncover a plot.* 3 to take off (one's head covering), esp as a mark of respect.

uncovered (ʌn'kʌvəd) ADJECTIVE 1 not covered; revealed or bare. 2 not protected by insurance, security, etc. 3 with hat removed as a mark of respect.

uncritical (ʌn'krɪtɪk^{ə}l) ADJECTIVE not containing or making severe or negative judgments.

uncrowded (ʌn'kraʊdɪd) ADJECTIVE (of a confined space, area, etc.) not containing too many people or things.

uncrowned (ʌn'kraʊnd) ADJECTIVE 1 having the power of royalty without the title. 2 not having yet assumed the crown. 3 **uncrowned king** *or* **queen.** a man or woman of high status among a certain group.

UNCTAD ABBREVIATION FOR United Nations Conference on Trade and Development.

unction ('ʌŋkʃən) NOUN 1 *Chiefly RC and Eastern Churches* the act of anointing with oil in sacramental ceremonies, in the conferring of holy orders. 2 excessive suavity or affected charm. 3 an ointment or unguent. 4 anything soothing or comforting.
▷HISTORY C14: from Latin *unctiō* an anointing, from *ungere* to anoint; see UNGUENT
▸**'unctionless** ADJECTIVE

unctuous ('ʌŋktjʊəs) ADJECTIVE 1 slippery or greasy. 2 affecting an oily charm.
▷HISTORY C14: from Medieval Latin *unctuōsus,* from Latin *unctum* ointment, from *ungere* to anoint

▸**unctuosity** (ˌʌŋktjʊˈɒsɪtɪ) *or* ˈ**unctuousness** NOUN ▸ˈ**unctuously** ADVERB

uncultivated (ʌnˈkʌltɪˌveɪtɪd) ADJECTIVE 1 (of a garden, fields, the earth, etc.) not having been tilled and prepared or planted. 2 (of a mind, person, etc) not improved by education.

uncultured (ʌnˈkʌltʃəd) ADJECTIVE lacking good taste, manners, upbringing, and education.

uncurl (ʌnˈkɜːl) VERB to move or cause to move out of a curled or rolled up position.

uncus (ˈʌŋkəs) NOUN, *plural* **unci** (ˈʌnsaɪ). *Zoology, anatomy* a hooked part or process, as in the human cerebrum.
▷HISTORY C19: from Latin: hook

uncustomary (ʌnˈkʌstəmərɪ, -təmrɪ) ADJECTIVE not in accordance with custom or habitual practice.

uncut (ʌnˈkʌt) ADJECTIVE 1 (of a book) not having the edges of its pages trimmed or slit. 2 (of a gemstone) not cut and faceted. 3 not abridged or shortened.

undamaged (ʌnˈdæmɪdʒd) ADJECTIVE not damaged: *the crops are undamaged.*

undamped (ʌnˈdæmpt) ADJECTIVE 1 (of an oscillating system) having unrestricted motion; not damped. 2 not repressed, discouraged, or subdued; undiminished.

undated (ʌnˈdeɪtɪd) ADJECTIVE (of a manuscript, letter, etc.) not having an identifying date.

undaunted (ʌnˈdɔːntɪd) ADJECTIVE not put off, discouraged, or beaten.
▸**unˈdauntedly** ADVERB ▸**unˈdauntedness** NOUN

undecagon (ʌnˈdɛkəˌgɒn) NOUN a polygon having eleven sides.
▷HISTORY C18: from Latin *undecim* eleven (from *unus* one + *decem* ten) + -GON

undeceive (ˌʌndɪˈsiːv) VERB (*tr*) to reveal the truth to (someone previously misled or deceived); enlighten.
▸ˌ**undeˈceivable** ADJECTIVE ▸ˌ**undeˈceiver** NOUN

undecided (ˌʌndɪˈsaɪdɪd) ADJECTIVE 1 not having made up one's mind. 2 (of an issue, problem, etc.) not agreed or decided upon.
▸ˌ**undeˈcidedly** ADVERB ▸ˌ**undeˈcidedness** NOUN

undeclared (ˌʌndɪˈklɛəd) ADJECTIVE not announced or acknowledged publicly.

undefeated (ˌʌndɪˈfiːtɪd) ADJECTIVE not having been defeated: *the undefeated champion.*

undefended (ˌʌndɪˈfɛndɪd) ADJECTIVE not having people to provide resistance against danger, attack, or harm.

undefined (ˌʌndɪˈfaɪnd) ADJECTIVE not defined or made clear: *the job has remained undefined.*
▸ˌ**undeˈfinable** ADJECTIVE

undemanding (ˌʌndɪˈmɑːndɪŋ) ADJECTIVE not requiring great patience, skill, attention, etc.: *an undemanding book.*

undemocratic (ˌʌndɛməˈkrætɪk) ADJECTIVE not characterized by, derived from, or relating to the principles of democracy.

undemonstrative (ˌʌndɪˈmɒnstrətɪv) ADJECTIVE tending not to show the feelings; of a reserved nature.
▸ˌ**undeˈmonstratively** ADVERB ▸ˌ**undeˈmonstrativeness** NOUN

undeniable (ˌʌndɪˈnaɪəbᵊl) ADJECTIVE 1 unquestionably or obviously true. 2 of unquestionable excellence: *a man of undeniable character.* 3 unable to be resisted or denied.
▸ˌ**undeˈniableness** NOUN

undeniably (ˌʌndɪˈnaɪəblɪ) ADVERB in an unquestionable or obvious manner; irrefutably.

under (ˈʌndə) PREPOSITION 1 directly below; on, to, or beneath the underside or base of: *under one's feet.* 2 less than: *under forty years.* 3 lower in rank than: *under a corporal.* 4 subject to the supervision, jurisdiction, control, or influence of. 5 subject to (conditions); in (certain circumstances). 6 within a classification of: *a book under theology.* 7 known by: *under an assumed name.* 8 planted with: *a field under corn.* 9 powered by: *under sail.* 10 *Astrology* during the period that the sun is in (a sign of the zodiac): *born under Aries.* ◆ ADVERB 11 below; to a position underneath something.
▷HISTORY Old English; related to Old Saxon, Gothic *undar,* Old High German *untar,* Old Norse *undir,* Latin *infra*

under- PREFIX 1 below or beneath: *underarm; underground.* 2 of lesser importance or lower rank: *undersecretary.* 3 to a lesser degree than is proper; insufficient or insufficiently: *undercharge; underemployed.* 4 indicating secrecy or deception: *underhand.*

underachieve (ˌundərəˈtʃiːv) VERB (*intr*) to fail to achieve a performance appropriate to one's age or talents.
▸ˌ**underaˈchiever** NOUN ▸ˌ**underaˈchievement** NOUN

underact (ˌʌndərˈækt) VERB *Theatre* to play (a role) without adequate emphasis. Compare **overact.**

underactive (ˌʌndərˈæktɪv) ADJECTIVE (of the thyroid or adrenal glands) not functioning at full capacity.

underage (ˌʌndərˈeɪdʒ) ADJECTIVE below the required or standard age, esp below the legal age for voting or drinking.

underarm (ˈʌndərˌɑːm) ADJECTIVE 1 (of a measurement) extending along the arm from wrist to armpit. 2 *Sport* of or denoting a style of throwing, bowling, or serving in which the hand is swung below shoulder level. 3 below the arm. ◆ ADVERB 4 in an underarm style.

underbelly (ˈʌndəˌbɛlɪ) NOUN, *plural* **-lies.** 1 the part of an animal's belly nearest to the ground. 2 a vulnerable or unprotected part, aspect, or region.

underbid (ˌʌndəˈbɪd) VERB **-bids, -bidding, -bid.** (*tr*) 1 to submit a bid lower than that of (others): *Irena underbid the other dealers.* 2 to submit an excessively low bid for. 3 *Bridge* to make a bid that will win fewer tricks than is justified by the strength of the hand: *he underbid his hand.*
▸ˈ**underˌbidder** NOUN

underbody (ˈʌndəˌbɒdɪ) NOUN, *plural* **-bodies.** the underpart of a body, as of an animal or motor vehicle.

underbred (ˌʌndəˈbrɛd) ADJECTIVE 1 of impure stock; not thoroughbred. 2 a less common word for **ill-bred.**
▸ˌ**underˈbreeding** NOUN

underbrush (ˈʌndəˌbrʌʃ) *or* **underbush** NOUN *Chiefly US and Canadian* undergrowth.

underbuy (ˌʌndəˈbaɪ) VERB **-buys, -buying, -bought.** 1 to buy (stock in trade) in amounts lower than required. 2 (*tr*) to buy at a price below that paid by (others). 3 (*tr*) to pay a price less than the true value for.

undercapitalize *or* **undercapitalise** (ˌʌndəˈkæpɪtəˌlaɪz) VERB to provide or issue capital for (a commercial enterprise) in an amount insufficient for efficient operation.

undercarriage (ˈʌndəˌkærɪdʒ) NOUN 1 Also called: **landing gear.** the assembly of wheels, shock absorbers, struts, etc., that supports an aircraft on the ground and enables it to take off and land. 2 the framework that supports the body of a vehicle, carriage, etc.

undercart (ˈʌndəˌkɑːt) NOUN *Brit informal* another name for **undercarriage** (sense 1).

undercharge (ˌʌndəˈtʃɑːdʒ) VERB 1 to charge too little (for). 2 (*tr*) to load (a gun, cannon, etc.) with an inadequate charge. ◆ NOUN 3 an insufficient charge.

underclass (ˈʌndəˌklɑːs) NOUN a class beneath the usual social scale consisting of the most disadvantaged people, such as the unemployed in inner cities.

underclay (ˈʌndəˌkleɪ) NOUN a grey or whitish clay rock containing fossilized plant roots and occurring beneath coal seams. When used as a refractory, it is known as fireclay.

underclothes (ˈʌndəˌkləʊðz) PLURAL NOUN a variant of **underwear.** Also called: **underclothing.**

undercoat (ˈʌndəˌkəʊt) NOUN 1 a coat of paint or other substance applied before the top coat. 2 a coat worn under an overcoat. 3 *Zoology* another name for **underfur.** 4 the US name for **underseal.** ◆ VERB 5 (*tr*) to apply an undercoat to (a surface).

undercool (ˌʌndəˈkuːl) VERB a less common word for **supercool.**

undercover (ˌʌndəˈkʌvə) ADJECTIVE done or acting in secret: *undercover operations.*

undercroft (ˈʌndəˌkrɒft) NOUN an underground chamber, such as a church crypt, often with a vaulted ceiling.
▷HISTORY C14: from *croft* a vault, cavern, from earlier *crofte,* ultimately from Latin *crypta* CRYPT

undercurrent (ˈʌndəˌkʌrənt) NOUN 1 a current that is not apparent at the surface or lies beneath another current. 2 an opinion, emotion, etc., lying beneath apparent feeling or meaning. ◆ Also called: **underflow.**

undercut VERB (ˌʌndəˈkʌt, ˈʌndəˌkʌt) **-cuts, -cutting, -cut.** 1 to charge less than (a competitor) in order to obtain trade. 2 to cut away the under part of (something). 3 *Sport* to hit (a ball) in such a way as to impart backspin. ◆ NOUN (ˈʌndəˌkʌt) 4 the act or an instance of cutting underneath. 5 a part that is cut away underneath. 6 a tenderloin of beef, including the fillet. 7 *Forestry, chiefly US and Canadian* a notch cut in a tree trunk, to ensure a clean break in felling. 8 *Sport* a stroke that imparts backspin to the ball.

underdaks (ˈʌndəˌdæks) PLURAL NOUN *Austral* an informal word for **underpants.**

underdevelop (ˌʌndədɪˈvɛləp) VERB (*tr*) *Photog* to process (a film, plate, or paper) in developer for less than the required time, or at too low a temperature, or in an exhausted solution.
▸ˌ**underdeˈvelopment** NOUN

underdeveloped (ˌʌndədɪˈvɛləpt) ADJECTIVE 1 immature or undersized. 2 relating to societies in which both the surplus capital and the social organization necessary to advance are lacking. 3 *Photog* (of a film, plate, or print) processed in developer for less than the required time, thus lacking in contrast.

underdog (ˈʌndəˌdɒg) NOUN 1 the competitor least likely to win a fight or contest. 2 a person in adversity or in a position of inferiority.

underdone (ˌʌndəˈdʌn) ADJECTIVE insufficiently or lightly cooked.

underdrain NOUN (ˈʌndəˌdreɪn) 1 a drain buried below agricultural land. ◆ VERB (ˌʌndəˈdreɪn) 2 to bury such drains below (agricultural land).
▸ˈ**underˌdrainage** NOUN

underdressed (ˌʌndəˈdrɛst) ADJECTIVE wearing clothes that are not elaborate or formal enough for a particular occasion.

underemployed (ˌʌndərɪmˈplɔɪd) ADJECTIVE not fully or adequately employed.
▸ˌ**underemˈployment** NOUN

underestimate VERB (ˌʌndərˈɛstɪˌmeɪt) (*tr*) 1 to make too low an estimate of: *he underestimated the cost.* 2 to think insufficiently highly of: *to underestimate a person.* ◆ NOUN (ˌʌndərˈɛstɪmɪt) 3 too low an estimate.
▸ˌ**underˌestiˈmation** NOUN

> **Language note** *Underestimate* is sometimes wrongly used where *overestimate* is meant: *the importance of his work cannot be overestimated* (not *cannot be underestimated*).

underexpose (ˌʌndərɪkˈspəʊz) VERB (*tr*) 1 *Photog* to expose (a film, plate, or paper) for too short a period or with insufficient light so as not to produce the required effect. 2 (*often passive*) to fail to subject to appropriate or expected publicity.

underexposure (ˌʌndərɪkˈspəʊʒə) NOUN 1 *Photog* **a** inadequate exposure to light. **b** an underexposed negative, print, or transparency. 2 insufficient attention or publicity.

underfeed VERB (ˌʌndəˈfiːd) **-feeds, -feeding, -fed.** (*tr*) 1 to give too little food to. 2 to supply (a furnace, engine, etc.) with fuel from beneath. ◆ NOUN (ˈʌndəˌfiːd) 3 an apparatus by which fuel, etc., is supplied from below.

underfelt (ˈʌndəˌfɛlt) NOUN thick felt laid between floorboards and carpet to increase insulation and resilience.

underfloor (ˈʌndəˌflɔː) ADJECTIVE situated beneath the floor: *underfloor heating.*

underflow (ˈʌndəˌfləʊ) NOUN 1 another word for **undercurrent.** 2 *Computing* a condition that occurs when arithmetic operations produce results too small to store in the available register.

underfoot (ˌʌndəˈfʊt) ADVERB 1 underneath the feet; on the ground. 2 in a position of subjugation or subservience. 3 in the way.

underfunded (ˌʌndəˈfʌndɪd) ADJECTIVE having or provided with insufficient funding.

underfur (ˈʌndəˌfɜː) NOUN the layer of dense soft fur occurring beneath the outer coarser fur in certain mammals, such as the otter and seal. Also called: **undercoat**.

undergarment (ˈʌndəˌgɑːmənt) NOUN any garment worn under the visible outer clothes, usually next to the skin.

undergird (ˌʌndəˈgɜːd) VERB **-girds, -girding, -girded** *or* **-girt**. *(tr)* to strengthen or reinforce by passing a rope, cable, or chain around the underside of (an object, load, etc.).
▷HISTORY C16: from UNDER- + GIRD[1]

underglaze (ˈʌndəˌgleɪz) ADJECTIVE 1 *Ceramics* applied to pottery or porcelain before the application of glaze. ◆ NOUN 2 a pigment, etc., applied in this way.

undergo (ˌʌndəˈgəʊ) VERB **-goes, -going, -went, -gone**. *(tr)* to experience, endure, or sustain: *to undergo a dramatic change of feelings*.
▷HISTORY Old English: earlier meanings were more closely linked with the senses of *under* and *go*
▸ **ˈunderˌgoer** NOUN

undergraduate (ˌʌndəˈgrædjʊɪt) NOUN a person studying in a university for a first degree. Sometimes shortened to: **undergrad**.
▸ **ˌunderˈgraduateship** NOUN

underground ADJECTIVE (ˈʌndəˌgraʊnd), ADVERB (ˌʌndəˈgraʊnd) 1 occurring, situated, used, or going below ground level: *an underground tunnel; an underground explosion*. 2 secret; hidden: *underground activities*. ◆ NOUN (ˈʌndəˌgraʊnd) 3 a space or region below ground level. 4 **a** a movement dedicated to overthrowing a government or occupation forces, as in the European countries occupied by the German army in World War II. **b** *(as modifier)*: *an underground group*. 5 (often preceded by *the*) an electric passenger railway operated in underground tunnels. US and Canadian equivalent: **subway**. 6 (usually preceded by *the*) **a** any avant-garde, experimental, or subversive movement in popular art, films, music, etc. **b** *(as modifier)*: *the underground press; underground music*.

underground railroad NOUN *(often capitals)* (in the pre-Civil War US) the system established by abolitionists to aid escaping slaves.

undergrown (ˈʌndəˌgrəʊn, ˌʌndəˈgrəʊn) ADJECTIVE 1 not having the expected height. 2 having undergrowth.

undergrowth (ˈʌndəˌgrəʊθ) NOUN 1 small trees, bushes, ferns, etc., growing beneath taller trees in a wood or forest. 2 the condition of being undergrown. 3 a growth of short fine hairs beneath longer ones; underfur.

underhand (ˈʌndəˌhænd) ADJECTIVE *also* **underhanded**. 1 clandestine, deceptive, or secretive. 2 *Sport* another word for **underarm**. ◆ ADVERB 3 in an underhand manner or style.

underhand chop NOUN *NZ* (in an axemen's competition) a chop where the axeman stands on the log, which is placed on the ground. Compare **standing chop**.

underhanded (ˌʌndəˈhændɪd) ADJECTIVE another word for **underhand** or **short-handed**.
▸ **ˌunderˈhandedly** ADVERB ▸ **ˌunderˈhandedness** NOUN

underhung (ˌʌndəˈhʌŋ) ADJECTIVE 1 (of the lower jaw) projecting beyond the upper jaw; undershot. 2 (of a sliding door, etc.) supported at its lower edge by a track or rail.

underinsured (ˌʌndərɪnˈʃʊəd) ADJECTIVE not having enough insurance to cover the cost of a loss.

underlaid (ˌʌndəˈleɪd) ADJECTIVE 1 laid underneath. 2 having an underlay or supporting layer underneath. ◆ VERB 3 the past tense and past participle of **underlay**.

underlay VERB (ˌʌndəˈleɪ) **-lays, -laying, -laid**. *(tr)* 1 to place (something) under or beneath. 2 to support by something laid beneath. 3 to achieve the correct printing pressure all over (a forme block) or to bring (a block) up to type height by adding material, such as paper, to the appropriate areas beneath it. ◆ NOUN (ˈʌndəˌleɪ) 4 a layer, lining, support, etc., laid underneath something else. 5 *Printing* material, such as paper, used to underlay a forme or block. 6 felt, rubber, etc., laid beneath a carpet to increase insulation and resilience.

underleaf (ˈʌndəˌliːf) NOUN (in liverworts) any of the leaves forming a row on the underside of the stem: usually smaller than the two rows of lateral leaves and sometimes absent.

underlet (ˌʌndəˈlɛt) VERB **-lets, -letting, -let**. *(tr)* 1 to let for a price lower than expected or justified. 2 a less common word for **sublet**.
▸ **ˈunderˌletter** NOUN

underlie (ˌʌndəˈlaɪ) VERB **-lies, -lying, -lay, -lain**. *(tr)* 1 to lie or be placed under or beneath. 2 to be the foundation, cause, or basis of: *careful planning underlies all our decisions*. 3 *Finance* to take priority over (another claim, liability, mortgage, etc.): *a first mortgage underlies a second*. 4 to be the root or stem from which (a word) is derived: *"happy" underlies "happiest"*.
▸ **ˈunderˌlier** NOUN

underline VERB (ˌʌndəˈlaɪn) *(tr)* 1 to put a line under. 2 to state forcibly; emphasize or reinforce. ◆ NOUN (ˈʌndəˌlaɪn) 3 a line underneath, esp under written matter.

underlinen (ˈʌndəˌlɪnən) NOUN underclothes, esp when made of linen.

underling (ˈʌndəlɪŋ) NOUN a subordinate or lackey.

underlying (ˌʌndəˈlaɪɪŋ) ADJECTIVE 1 concealed but detectable: *underlying guilt*. 2 fundamental; basic. 3 lying under. 4 *Finance* (of a claim, liability, etc.) taking precedence; prior.

undermentioned (ˈʌndəˌmɛnʃənd) ADJECTIVE mentioned below or subsequently.

undermine (ˌʌndəˈmaɪn) VERB *(tr)* 1 (of the sea, wind, etc.) to wear away the bottom or base of (land, cliffs, etc.). 2 to weaken gradually or insidiously: *their insults undermined her confidence*. 3 to tunnel or dig beneath.
▸ **ˌunderˈminer** NOUN

undermost (ˈʌndəˌməʊst) ADJECTIVE 1 being the furthest under; lowest. ◆ ADVERB 2 in the lowest place.

underneath (ˌʌndəˈniːθ) PREPOSITION, ADVERB 1 under; beneath. ◆ ADJECTIVE 2 lower. ◆ NOUN 3 a lower part, surface, etc.
▷HISTORY Old English *underneothan*, from UNDER + *neothan* below; related to Old Danish *underneden;* see BENEATH

undernourish (ˌʌndəˈnʌrɪʃ) VERB *(tr; usually passive)* to deprive of or fail to provide with nutrients essential for health and growth.
▸ **ˌunderˈnourishment** NOUN

underpaid (ˌʌndəˈpeɪd) ADJECTIVE not paid enough: *underpaid and overworked*.

underpainting (ˈʌndəˌpeɪntɪŋ) NOUN the first layer in a painting, indicating the design and main areas of light and shade.

underpants (ˈʌndəˌpænts) PLURAL NOUN a man's undergarment covering the body from the waist or hips to the top of the thighs or knees. Often shortened to: **pants**.

underpass (ˈʌndəˌpɑːs) NOUN 1 a section of a road that passes under another road, railway line, etc. 2 another word for **subway** (sense 1).

underpay (ˌʌndəˈpeɪ) VERB **-pays, -paying, -paid**. to pay (someone) insufficiently.
▸ **ˌunderˈpayment** NOUN

underpin (ˌʌndəˈpɪn) VERB **-pins, -pinning, -pinned**. *(tr)* 1 to support from beneath, esp by a prop, while avoiding damaging or weakening the superstructure: *to underpin a wall*. 2 to give corroboration, strength, or support to.

underpinning (ˈʌndəˌpɪnɪŋ) NOUN a structure of masonry, concrete, etc., placed beneath a wall to provide support.

underpinnings (ˈʌndəˌpɪnɪŋz) PLURAL NOUN any supporting structure or system.

underpitch vault (ˈʌndəˌpɪtʃ) NOUN *Architect* a vault that is intersected by one or more vaults of lower pitch.

underplay (ˌʌndəˈpleɪ) VERB 1 to play (a role) with restraint or subtlety. 2 to achieve (an effect) by deliberate lack of emphasis. 3 *(intr) Cards* to lead or follow suit with a lower card when holding a higher one.

underplot (ˈʌndəˌplɒt) NOUN 1 a subsidiary plot in a literary or dramatic work. 2 an undercover plot.

underpopulated (ˌʌndəˈpɒpjʊˌleɪtɪd) ADJECTIVE having a low population rate.

underpowered (ˌʌndəˈpaʊəd) ADJECTIVE lacking or low in power: *two-litre cars are underpowered*.

underprice (ˌʌndəˈpraɪs) VERB *(tr)* to price (an article for sale) at too low a level or amount.

underprivileged (ˌʌndəˈprɪvɪlɪdʒd) ADJECTIVE lacking the rights and advantages of other members of society; deprived.

underproduction (ˌʌndəprəˈdʌkʃən) NOUN *Commerce* production below full capacity or below demand.

underproof (ˌʌndəˈpruːf) ADJECTIVE (of a spirit) containing less than 57.1 per cent alcohol by volume.

underprop (ˌʌndəˈprɒp) VERB **-props, -propping, -propped**. *(tr)* to prop up from beneath.
▸ **ˈunderˌpropper** NOUN

underquote (ˌʌndəˈkwəʊt) VERB 1 to offer for sale (securities, goods, or services) at a price lower than the market price. 2 *(tr)* to quote a price lower than that quoted by (another).

underrate (ˌʌndəˈreɪt) VERB *(tr)* to underestimate.

undersaturated (ˌʌndəˈsætʃəˌreɪtɪd) ADJECTIVE (of an igneous rock) having a low silica content.

underscore VERB (ˌʌndəˈskɔː) *(tr)* 1 to draw or score a line or mark under. 2 to stress or reinforce. ◆ NOUN (ˈʌndəˌskɔː) 3 a line drawn under written matter.

undersea (ˈʌndəˌsiː) ADJECTIVE, ADVERB *also* **underseas** (ˌʌndəˈsiːz). below the surface of the sea.

underseal (ˈʌndəˌsiːl) *Brit* ◆ NOUN 1 a coating of a tar or rubber-based material applied to the underside of a motor vehicle to retard corrosion. US name: **undercoat**. ◆ VERB 2 *(tr)* to apply a coating of underseal to (a motor vehicle).

undersecretary (ˌʌndəˈsɛkrətrɪ) NOUN, *plural* **-taries**. 1 (in Britain) **a** any of various senior civil servants in certain government departments. **b** short for **undersecretary of state**: any of various high officials subordinate only to the minister in charge of a department. 2 (in the US) a high government official subordinate only to the secretary in charge of a department.
▸ **ˌunderˈsecretaryˌship** NOUN

undersell (ˌʌndəˈsɛl) VERB **-sells, -selling, -sold**. 1 to sell for less than the usual or expected price. 2 *(tr)* to sell at a price lower than that of (another seller). 3 *(tr)* to advertise (merchandise) with moderation or restraint.
▸ **ˌunderˈseller** NOUN

underset (ˈʌndəˌsɛt) NOUN 1 an ocean undercurrent. 2 an underlying vein of ore. ◆ VERB **-sets, -setting, -set**. 3 *(tr)* to support from underneath.

undersexed (ˌʌndəˈsɛkst) ADJECTIVE having weaker sex urges or responses than is considered normal.

undersheriff (ˈʌndəˌʃɛrɪf) NOUN a deputy sheriff.

undershirt (ˈʌndəˌʃɜːt) NOUN *Chiefly US and Canadian* an undergarment worn under a blouse or shirt. Brit name: **vest**.

undershoot (ˌʌndəˈʃuːt) VERB **-shoots, -shooting, -shot**. 1 (of a pilot) to cause (an aircraft) to land short of (a runway) or (of an aircraft) to land in this way. 2 to shoot a projectile so that it falls short of (a target).

undershorts (ˈʌndəˌʃɔːts) PLURAL NOUN another word for **shorts** (sense 2).

undershot (ˈʌndəˌʃɒt) ADJECTIVE 1 (of the lower jaw) projecting beyond the upper jaw; underhung. 2 (of a water wheel) driven by a flow of water that passes under the wheel rather than over it. ◆ Compare **overshot**.

undershrub (ˈʌndəˌʃrʌb) NOUN another name for **subshrub**.

underside (ˈʌndəˌsaɪd) NOUN the bottom or lower surface.

undersigned (ˈʌndəˌsaɪnd) NOUN 1 **the.** the person or persons who have signed at the foot of a document, statement, etc. ◆ ADJECTIVE 2 having signed one's name at the foot of a document, statement, etc. 3 (of a document) signed at the foot. 4 signed at the foot of a document.

undersized (ˌʌndəˈsaɪzd) ADJECTIVE of less than usual size.

underskirt (ˈʌndəˌskɜːt) NOUN any skirtlike garment worn under a skirt.

underslung (ˌʌndəˈslʌŋ) ADJECTIVE 1 suspended below a supporting member, esp (of a motor vehicle chassis) suspended below the axles. 2 having a low centre of gravity.

undersoil (ˈʌndəˌsɔɪl) NOUN another word for **subsoil** (sense 1a).

underspend VERB (ˌʌndəˈspɛnd) **-spends, -spending, -spent.** 1 to spend less than (one can afford or is allocated). ◆ NOUN (ˈʌndəˌspɛnd) 2 the amount by which someone or something is underspent.

understaffed (ˌʌndəˈstɑːft) ADJECTIVE not having enough staff: *her department is understaffed.*

understand (ˌʌndəˈstænd) VERB **-stands, -standing, -stood.** 1 (*may take a clause as object*) to know and comprehend the nature or meaning of: *I understand you; I understand what you mean.* 2 (*may take a clause as object*) to realize or grasp (something): *he understands your position.* 3 (*tr; may take a clause as object*) to assume, infer, or believe: *I understand you are thinking of marrying.* 4 (*tr*) to know how to translate or read: *can you understand Spanish?* 5 (*tr; may take a clause as object; often passive*) to accept as a condition or proviso: *it is understood that children must be kept quiet.* 6 (*tr*) to be sympathetic to or compatible with: *we understand each other.*
▷HISTORY Old English *understandan;* related to Old Frisian *understonda,* Middle High German *understān* step under; see UNDER, STAND
▸ˌ**under'standable** ADJECTIVE ▸ˌ**under'standably** ADVERB

understanding (ˌʌndəˈstændɪŋ) NOUN 1 the ability to learn, judge, make decisions, etc.; intelligence or sense. 2 personal opinion or interpretation of a subject: *my understanding of your predicament.* 3 a mutual agreement or compact, esp an informal or private one. 4 *Chiefly Brit* an unofficial engagement to be married. 5 *Philosophy, archaic* the mind, esp the faculty of reason. 6 **on the understanding that.** with the condition that; providing. ◆ ADJECTIVE 7 sympathetic, tolerant, or wise towards people. 8 possessing judgment and intelligence.
▸ˌ**under'standingly** ADVERB

understate (ˌʌndəˈsteɪt) VERB 1 to state (something) in restrained terms, often to obtain an ironic effect. 2 to state that (something, such as a number) is less than it is.

understatement (ˌʌndəˈsteɪtmənt) NOUN the act or an instance of stating something in restrained terms, or as less than it is.

understeer (ˈʌndəˌstɪə) VERB (*intr*) (of a vehicle) to turn less sharply, for a particular movement of the steering wheel, than anticipated.

understood (ˌʌndəˈstʊd) VERB 1 the past tense and past participle of **understand.** ◆ ADJECTIVE 2 implied or inferred. 3 taken for granted; assumed.

understorey (ˈʌndəˌstɔːrɪ) NOUN a lower tier of shrubs and small trees under the main canopy of forest trees.

understrapper (ˈʌndəˌstræpə) NOUN a less common word for **underling.**
▷HISTORY C18: from STRAP (in the archaic sense: to work hard)

understudy (ˈʌndəˌstʌdɪ) VERB **-studies, -studying, -studied.** 1 (*tr*) to study (a role or part) so as to be able to replace the usual actor or actress if necessary. 2 to act as understudy to (an actor or actress). ◆ NOUN, *plural* **-studies.** 3 an actor or actress who studies a part so as to be able to replace the usual actor or actress if necessary. 4 anyone who is trained to take the place of another in case of need.

undertake (ˌʌndəˈteɪk) VERB **-takes, -taking, -took, -taken.** 1 (*tr*) to contract to or commit oneself to (something) or (to do something): *to undertake a job; to undertake to deliver the goods.* 2 (*tr*) to attempt to; agree to start. 3 (*tr*) to take (someone) in charge. 4 (*intr; foll by for*) *Archaic* to make oneself responsible (for). 5 (*tr*) to promise.

undertaker (ˈʌndəˌteɪkə) NOUN a person whose profession is the preparation of the dead for burial or cremation and the management of funerals; funeral director.

undertaking (ˈʌndəˌteɪkɪŋ) NOUN 1 something undertaken; task, venture, or enterprise. 2 an agreement to do something. 3 the business of an undertaker. 4 *Informal* the practice of overtaking on an inner lane a vehicle which is travelling in an outer lane.

under the table ADJECTIVE 1 (**under-the-table** *when prenominal*) done illicitly and secretly. 2 *Slang* drunk.

underthings (ˈʌndəˌθɪŋz) PLURAL NOUN girls' or women's underwear.

underthrust (ˈʌndəˌθrʌst) NOUN *Geology* a reverse fault in which the rocks on the lower surface of a fault plane have moved under the relatively static rocks on the upper surface. Compare **overthrust.**

undertime (ˈʌndəˌtaɪm) NOUN *Informal* the time spent by an employee at work in non-work-related activities like socializing, surfing the Internet, making personal telephone calls, etc.

undertint (ˈʌndəˌtɪnt) NOUN a slight, subdued, or delicate tint.

undertone (ˈʌndəˌtəʊn) NOUN 1 a quiet or hushed tone of voice. 2 an underlying tone or suggestion in words or actions: *his offer has undertones of dishonesty.* 3 a pale or subdued colour.

undertook (ˌʌndəˈtʊk) VERB the past tense of **undertake.**

undertow (ˈʌndəˌtəʊ) NOUN 1 the seaward undercurrent following the breaking of a wave on the beach. 2 any strong undercurrent flowing in a different direction from the surface current.

undertrick (ˈʌndəˌtrɪk) NOUN *Bridge* a trick by which a declarer falls short of making his contract.

undertrump (ˌʌndəˈtrʌmp) VERB (*intr*) *Cards* to play a lower trump on a trick to which a higher trump has already been played.

undervalue (ˌʌndəˈvæljuː) VERB **-values, -valuing, -valued.** (*tr*) to value at too low a level or price.
▸ˌ**underˌvalu'ation** NOUN ▸ˌ**under'valuer** NOUN

undervest (ˈʌndəˌvɛst) NOUN *Brit* another name for **vest** (sense 1).

underwater (ˈʌndəˈwɔːtə) ADJECTIVE 1 being, occurring, or going under the surface of the water, esp the sea: *underwater exploration.* 2 *Nautical* below the water line of a vessel. 3 (of a stock option or other asset) having a market value below its purchase value. ◆ ADVERB 4 beneath the surface of the water.

under way ADJECTIVE (*postpositive*) 1 in progress; in operation: *the show was under way.* 2 *Nautical* in motion.

underwear (ˈʌndəˌwɛə) NOUN clothing worn under the outer garments, usually next to the skin. Also called: **underclothes.**

underweight (ˌʌndəˈweɪt) ADJECTIVE 1 weighing less than is average, expected, or healthy. 2 *Finance* **a** having a lower proportion of one's investments in a particular sector of the market than the size of that sector relative to the total market would suggest. **b** (of a fund etc.) disproportionately invested in this way: *pension funds have become underweight of equities.*

underwent (ˌʌndəˈwɛnt) VERB the past tense of **undergo.**

underwhelm (ˌʌndəˈwɛlm) VERB (*tr*) to make no positive impact or impression on; disappoint.
▷HISTORY C20: originally a humorous coinage based on *overwhelm*

underwhelming (ˌʌndəˈwɛlmɪŋ) ADJECTIVE failing to make a positive impact or impression; disappointing.

underwing (ˈʌndəˌwɪŋ) NOUN 1 the hind wing of an insect, esp when covered by the forewing. 2 See **red underwing, yellow underwing.**

underwood (ˈʌndəˌwʊd) NOUN a less common word for **undergrowth.**

underworld (ˈʌndəˌwɜːld) NOUN 1 **a** criminals and their associates considered collectively. **b** (*as modifier*): *underworld connections.* 2 *Greek and Roman myth* the regions below the earth's surface regarded as the abode of the dead; Hades. Related adjectives: **chtonian, chthonic.**

underwrite (ˈʌndəˌraɪt, ˌʌndəˈraɪt) VERB **-writes, -writing, -wrote, -written.** (*tr*) 1 *Finance* to undertake to purchase at an agreed price any unsold portion of (a public issue of shares, etc.). 2 to accept financial responsibility for (a commercial project or enterprise). 3 *Insurance* **a** to sign and issue (an insurance policy) thus accepting liability if specified losses occur. **b** to insure (a property or risk). **c** to accept liability up to (a specified amount) in an insurance policy. 4 to write (words, a signature, etc.) beneath (other written matter); subscribe. 5 to support or concur with (a decision, statement, etc.) by or as if by signature.

underwriter (ˈʌndəˌraɪtə) NOUN 1 a person or enterprise that underwrites public issues of shares, bonds, etc. 2 **a** a person or enterprise that underwrites insurance policies. **b** an employee or agent of an insurance company who assesses risks and determines the premiums payable.

undescended (ˌʌndɪˈsɛndɪd) ADJECTIVE (of the testes) remaining in the abdominal cavity rather than descending to lie in the scrotum.

undeserved (ˌʌndɪˈzɜːvd) ADJECTIVE not earned or merited; unwarranted: *an undeserved reputation.*

undesigned (ˌʌndɪˈzaɪnd) ADJECTIVE 1 (of an action) unintentional. 2 not yet designed.

undesigning (ˌʌndɪˈzaɪnɪŋ) ADJECTIVE (of a person) frank; straightforward.

undesirable (ˌʌndɪˈzaɪərəbᵊl) ADJECTIVE 1 not desirable or pleasant; objectionable. ◆ NOUN 2 a person or thing that is considered undesirable.
▸ˌ**undeˌsira'bility** *or* ˌ**unde'sirableness** NOUN
▸ˌ**unde'sirably** ADVERB

undetected (ˌʌndɪˈtɛktɪd) ADJECTIVE not perceived, noticed, or discovered: *the fake bomb passed undetected.*

undetermined (ˌʌndɪˈtɜːmɪnd) ADJECTIVE 1 not yet resolved; undecided. 2 not known or discovered.

undeterred (ˌʌndɪˈtɜːd) ADJECTIVE not discouraged or dissuaded.

undeveloped (ˌʌndɪˈvɛləpt) ADJECTIVE not having developed or been developed.

undiagnosed (ˌʌndaɪəgˈnəʊzd) ADJECTIVE (of a medical condition, a problem, etc.) not having been identified.

undid (ʌnˈdɪd) VERB the past tense of **undo.**

undies (ˈʌndɪz) PLURAL NOUN *Informal* women's underwear.

undifferentiated (ˌʌndɪfəˈrɛnʃɪˌeɪtɪd) ADJECTIVE not having any distinguishing features: *an undifferentiated mass.*

undignified (ʌnˈdɪgnɪˌfaɪd) ADJECTIVE lacking in dignity.

undiluted (ˌʌndaɪˈluːtɪd) ADJECTIVE 1 not diluted with water or any other liquid: *undiluted fruit juice.* 2 not moderated or qualified in any way: *expressing undiluted pleasure.*

undiminished (ˌʌndɪˈmɪnɪʃt) ADJECTIVE not reduced or lessened.

undimmed (ʌnˈdɪmd) ADJECTIVE 1 (of eyes, light, etc.) still bright or shining. 2 (of enthusiasm, admiration, etc.) not diminished or lessened.

undine (ˈʌndiːn) NOUN any of various female water spirits.
▷HISTORY C17: from New Latin *undina,* from Latin *unda* a wave

undiplomatic (ˌʌndɪpləˈmætɪk) ADJECTIVE lacking in diplomacy.

undirected (ˌʌndɪˈrɛktɪd, -daɪ-) ADJECTIVE 1 lacking a clear purpose or objective. 2 (of a letter, parcel, etc.) having no address.

undisciplined (ʌnˈdɪsɪˌplɪnd) ADJECTIVE not exhibiting self-control or good behaviour.

undisclosed (ˌʌndɪsˈkləʊzd) ADJECTIVE not made known or revealed: *an undisclosed sum.*

undiscovered (ˌʌndɪˈskʌvəd) ADJECTIVE not discovered or encountered.

undisguised (ˌʌndɪsˈgaɪzd) ADJECTIVE not disguised or concealed: *with undisguised glee.*

undisputed (ˌʌndɪˈspjuːtɪd) ADJECTIVE not challenged or questioned; accepted: *of undisputed importance.*

undisputed world champion NOUN *Boxing* a boxer who holds the World Boxing Association, the World Boxing Council, the World Boxing Organization, and the International Boxing Federation world championship titles simultaneously.

undistinguished (ˌʌndɪˈstɪŋgwɪʃt) ADJECTIVE 1 not particularly good or bad: *an undistinguished* *career.* [2] without distinction: *undistinguished features.*

undistributed (ˌʌndɪsˈtrɪbjʊtɪd) ADJECTIVE [1] *Logic* (of a term) referring only to some members of the class designated by the term, as *doctors* in *some doctors are overworked.* [2] *Business* (of a profit) not paid in dividends to the shareholders of a company but retained to help finance its trading.

undisturbed (ˌʌndɪˈstɜːbd) ADJECTIVE not disturbed; uninterrupted: *lots of undisturbed sleep.*

undivided (ˌʌndɪˈvaɪdɪd) ADJECTIVE [1] not divided into parts or groups. [2] concentrated on one object, idea, etc.: *undivided attention.*

undo (ʌnˈduː) VERB **-does, -doing, -did, -done.** (*mainly tr*) [1] (*also intr*) to untie, unwrap, or open or become untied, unwrapped, etc. [2] to reverse the effects of. [3] to cause the downfall of. [4] *Obsolete* to explain or solve.
▸**unˈdoer** NOUN

undoing (ʌnˈduːɪŋ) NOUN [1] ruin; downfall. [2] the cause of downfall: *drink was his undoing.*

undone[1] (ʌnˈdʌn) ADJECTIVE not done or completed; unfinished.

undone[2] (ʌnˈdʌn) ADJECTIVE [1] ruined; destroyed. [2] unfastened; untied.

undoubted (ʌnˈdaʊtɪd) ADJECTIVE beyond doubt; certain or indisputable.

undoubtedly (ʌnˈdaʊtɪdlɪ) ADVERB [1] certainly or definitely; unquestionably: *he is undoubtedly talented.* [2] (*sentence modifier*) without doubt; certainly or indisputably: *undoubtedly there will be changes.*

undreamed (ʌnˈdriːmd) *or* **undreamt** (ʌnˈdrɛmt) ADJECTIVE (often foll by *of*) not thought of, conceived, or imagined.

undress VERB (ʌnˈdrɛs) [1] to take off clothes from (oneself or another). [2] (*tr*) to strip of ornamentation. [3] (*tr*) to remove the dressing from (a wound). ◆ NOUN (ʌnˈdrɛs) [4] partial or complete nakedness. [5] informal or normal working clothes or uniform. ◆ ADJECTIVE (ˈʌndrɛs) [6] characterized by or requiring informal or normal working dress or uniform.

undressed (ʌnˈdrɛst) ADJECTIVE [1] partially or completely naked. [2] (of an animal hide) not fully processed. [3] (of food, esp salad) not prepared with sauce or dressing.

undrinkable (ʌnˈdrɪŋkəb(ə)l) ADJECTIVE not pleasant or safe enough to be drunk.

UNDRO (ˈʌnˌdrəʊ) NOUN ACRONYM FOR United Nations Disaster Relief Organization.

undue (ʌnˈdjuː) ADJECTIVE [1] excessive or unwarranted. [2] unjust, improper, or illegal. [3] (of a debt, bond, etc.) not yet payable.

> **Language note** The use of *undue* in sentences such as *there is no cause for undue alarm* is redundant and should be avoided.

undulant (ˈʌndjʊlənt) ADJECTIVE *Rare* resembling waves; undulating.
▸**ˈundulance** NOUN

undulant fever NOUN another name for **brucellosis.**
▷**HISTORY** C19: so called because the fever symptoms are intermittent

undulate VERB (ˈʌndjʊˌleɪt) [1] to move or cause to move in waves or as if in waves. [2] to have or provide with a wavy form or appearance. ◆ ADJECTIVE (ˈʌndjʊlɪt, -ˌleɪt) *also* **undulated.** [3] having a wavy or rippled appearance, margin, or form: *an undulate leaf.*
▷**HISTORY** C17: from Latin *undulātus,* from *unda* a wave
▸**ˈunduˌlator** NOUN

undulation (ˌʌndjʊˈleɪʃən) NOUN [1] the act or an instance of undulating. [2] any wave or wavelike form, line, etc.

undulatory (ˈʌndjʊlətərɪ, -trɪ) ADJECTIVE [1] caused by or characterized by waves or undulations. [2] having a wavelike motion or form.

unduly (ʌnˈdjuːlɪ) ADVERB [1] immoderately; excessively. [2] in contradiction of moral or legal standards.

undying (ʌnˈdaɪɪŋ) ADJECTIVE unending; eternal.
▸**unˈdyingly** ADVERB

unearned (ʌnˈɜːnd) ADJECTIVE [1] not deserved. [2] not yet earned.

unearned income NOUN income from property, investment, etc., comprising rent, interest, and dividends.

unearned increment NOUN a rise in the market value of landed property resulting from general economic factors.

unearth (ʌnˈɜːθ) VERB (*tr*) [1] to dig up out of the earth. [2] to reveal or discover, esp by exhaustive searching.

unearthly (ʌnˈɜːθlɪ) ADJECTIVE [1] ghostly; eerie; weird: *unearthly screams.* [2] heavenly; sublime: *unearthly music.* [3] ridiculous or unreasonable (esp in the phrase **unearthly hour**).
▸**unˈearthliness** NOUN

uneasy (ʌnˈiːzɪ) ADJECTIVE [1] (of a person) anxious; apprehensive. [2] (of a condition) precarious; uncomfortable: *an uneasy truce.* [3] (of a thought, etc.) disturbing; disquieting.
▸**unˈease** NOUN ▸**unˈeasily** ADVERB ▸**unˈeasiness** NOUN

uneatable (ʌnˈiːtəb(ə)l) ADJECTIVE not pleasant or safe enough to be eaten.

uneaten (ʌnˈiːt(ə)n) ADJECTIVE (of food) not having been consumed; leftover.

uneconomic (ˌʌniːkəˈnɒmɪk, ˌʌnɛkə-) ADJECTIVE not economic; not profitable.

uneconomical (ˌʌniːkəˈnɒmɪk(ə)l, ˌʌnɛkə-) ADJECTIVE not economical; wasteful.

unedifying (ʌnˈɛdɪˌfaɪɪŋ) ADJECTIVE not having the result of improving morality, intellect, etc.

uneducated (ʌnˈɛdjʊˌkeɪtɪd) ADJECTIVE not having been educated to a good standard: *poor uneducated people.*

UNEF (ˈjuːˌnɛf) NOUN ACRONYM FOR United Nations Emergency Force.

unelectable (ˌʌnɪˈlɛktəb(ə)l) ADJECTIVE (of a political party, candidate, etc.) not likely to be elected.

unembarrassed (ʌnɪmˈbærəst) ADJECTIVE not embarrassed, disconcerted, or flustered.

unemotional (ˌʌnɪˈməʊʃən(ə)l) ADJECTIVE lacking in strong feeling.

unemployable (ˌʌnɪmˈplɔɪəb(ə)l) ADJECTIVE unable or unfit to keep a job.
▸ˌ**unemˌployaˈbility** NOUN

unemployed (ˌʌnɪmˈplɔɪd) ADJECTIVE [1] **a** without remunerative employment; out of work. **b** (*as collective noun; preceded by the*): *the unemployed.* [2] not being used; idle.

unemployment (ˌʌnɪmˈplɔɪmənt) NOUN [1] the condition of being unemployed. [2] the number of unemployed workers, often as a percentage of the total labour force.

unemployment benefit NOUN [1] (in Britain, formerly) a regular payment to a person who is out of work: replaced by jobseeker's allowance in 1996. Informal term: **dole.** [2] (in New Zealand) a means-tested monetary benefit paid weekly by the Social Security Department to the unemployed.

unemployment compensation NOUN (in the US) payment by a governmental agency to unemployed people.

unencumbered (ˌʌnɪnˈkʌmbəd) ADJECTIVE not burdened, impeded, or hampered.

unending (ʌnˈɛndɪŋ) ADJECTIVE having or seeming to have no end; interminable.

unendurable (ˌʌnɪnˈdjʊrəb(ə)l) ADJECTIVE not able to be undergone or tolerated; insufferable.

unenforced (ˌʌnɪnˈfɔːst) ADJECTIVE (of a law, decision, etc.) not having been imposed or enforced.

unenlightened (ˌʌnɪnˈlaɪt(ə)nd) ADJECTIVE not well-informed, tolerant, or rational: *a most backward, unenlightened nation.*

unentered (ʌnˈɛntəd) ADJECTIVE [1] not having been entered previously. [2] (of hounds) not having been put into a pack yet.

unenthusiastic (ˌʌnɪnθjuːzɪˈæstɪk) ADJECTIVE lacking in enthusiasm.

unenviable (ʌnˈɛnvɪəb(ə)l) ADJECTIVE not to be envied: *the unenviable task.*

unequal (ʌnˈiːkwəl) ADJECTIVE [1] not equal in quantity, size, rank, value, etc. [2] (foll by *to*) inadequate; insufficient. [3] not evenly balanced. [4] (of character, quality, etc.) irregular; varying; inconsistent. [5] (of a contest, etc.) having competitors of different ability. [6] *Obsolete* unjust.
▸**unˈequally** ADVERB

unequalled *or US* **unequaled** (ʌnˈiːkwəld) ADJECTIVE not equalled; unparalleled or unrivalled; supreme.

unequipped (ˌʌnɪˈkwɪpt) ADJECTIVE not furnished with the necessary supplies, abilities, etc.

unequivocal (ˌʌnɪˈkwɪvək(ə)l) ADJECTIVE not ambiguous; plain.
▸ˌ**uneˈquivocally** ADVERB ▸ˌ**uneˈquivocalness** NOUN

unerring (ʌnˈɜːrɪŋ) ADJECTIVE [1] not missing the mark or target. [2] consistently accurate; certain.
▸**unˈerringly** ADVERB ▸**unˈerringness** NOUN

UNESCO (juːˈnɛskəʊ) NOUN ACRONYM FOR United Nations Educational, Scientific, and Cultural Organization: an agency of the United Nations that sponsors programmes to promote education, communication, the arts, etc.

unescorted (ˌʌnɪsˈkɔːtɪd) ADJECTIVE not accompanied by an escort.

unessential (ˌʌnɪˈsɛnʃəl) ADJECTIVE [1] a less common word for **inessential.** ◆ NOUN [2] something that is not essential.
▸ˌ**unesˈsentially** ADVERB

unethical (ʌnˈɛθɪk(ə)l) ADJECTIVE not ethical; improper: *companies involved in unethical practices.*

uneven (ʌnˈiːvən) ADJECTIVE [1] (of a surface, etc.) not level or flat. [2] spasmodic or variable. [3] not parallel, straight, or horizontal. [4] not fairly matched: *an uneven race.* [5] *Archaic* not equal. [6] *Obsolete* unjust.
▸**unˈevenly** ADVERB ▸**unˈevenness** NOUN

uneventful (ˌʌnɪˈvɛntfʊl) ADJECTIVE ordinary, routine, or quiet.
▸ˌ**uneˈventfully** ADVERB ▸ˌ**uneˈventfulness** NOUN

unexampled (ˌʌnɪgˈzɑːmp(ə)ld) ADJECTIVE without precedent or parallel.

unexceptionable (ˌʌnɪkˈsɛpʃənəb(ə)l) ADJECTIVE beyond criticism or objection.
▸ˌ**unexˈceptionableness** *or* ˌ**unexˌceptionaˈbility** NOUN
▸ˌ**unexˈceptionably** ADVERB

unexceptional (ˌʌnɪkˈsɛpʃən(ə)l) ADJECTIVE [1] usual, ordinary, or normal. [2] subject to or allowing no exceptions. [3] *Not standard* another word for **unexceptionable.**
▸ˌ**unexˈceptionally** ADVERB

unexcited (ˌʌnɪkˈsaɪtɪd) ADJECTIVE [1] not aroused to pleasure, interest, agitation, etc. [2] (of an atom, molecule, etc.) remaining in its ground state.

unexciting (ˌʌnɪkˈsaɪtɪŋ) ADJECTIVE not interesting, stirring, or stimulating: *unexciting but likable.*

unexpected (ˌʌnɪkˈspɛktɪd) ADJECTIVE surprising or unforeseen.
▸ˌ**unexˈpectedly** ADVERB ▸ˌ**unexˈpectedness** NOUN

unexperienced (ˌʌnɪkˈspɪərɪənst) ADJECTIVE [1] (of a situation, sensation, fact, etc.) not having been undergone or known by experience. [2] inexperienced.

unexplained (ˌʌnɪkˈspleɪnd) ADJECTIVE not explained or understood: *unexplained phenomena.*
▸ˌ**unexˈplainable** ADJECTIVE

unexploited (ˌʌnɪksˈplɔɪtɪd) ADJECTIVE (of resources) not being used effectively: *rich with unexploited minerals.*

unexplored (ˌʌnɪkˈsplɔːd) ADJECTIVE not having been explored.

unexposed (ˌʌnɪkˈspəʊzd) ADJECTIVE [1] not having been exhibited or brought to public notice. [2] (of a slide, photograph, etc.) not having been subjected to the exposure process.

unexpressed (ˌʌnɪkˈsprɛst) ADJECTIVE [1] not expressed or said. [2] understood without being expressed.

unexpurgated (ʌnˈɛkspəˌgeɪtɪd) ADJECTIVE (of a book, text, etc.) not amended or censored by removing potentially offensive material.

unfailing (ʌnˈfeɪlɪŋ) ADJECTIVE [1] not failing; unflagging. [2] continuous or unceasing. [3] sure; certain.
▸**unˈfailingly** ADVERB ▸**unˈfailingness** NOUN

unfair (ʌnˈfɛə) ADJECTIVE [1] characterized by inequality or injustice. [2] dishonest or unethical.
▸**unˈfairly** ADVERB ▸**unˈfairness** NOUN

unfaithful (ʌnˈfeɪθfʊl) ADJECTIVE [1] not true to a

promise, vow, etc. 2 not true to a wife, husband, lover, etc., esp in having sexual intercourse with someone else. 3 inaccurate; inexact; unreliable; untrustworthy: *unfaithful copy.* 4 *Obsolete* not having religious faith; infidel. 5 *Obsolete* not upright; dishonest.
▸**un'faithfully** ADVERB ▸**un'faithfulness** NOUN

unfamiliar (ˌʌnfəˈmɪljə) ADJECTIVE 1 not known or experienced; strange. 2 (*postpositive; foll by* with) not familiar.
▸**unfamiliarity** (ˌʌnfəˌmɪlɪˈærɪtɪ) NOUN ▸**ˌunfa'miliarly** ADVERB

unfashionable (ʌnˈfæʃənəbᵊl) ADJECTIVE not fashionable: *dull unfashionable clothes; an unfashionable view.*

unfasten (ʌnˈfɑːsᵊn) VERB to undo, untie, or open or become undone, untied, or opened.

unfathered (ʌnˈfɑːðəd) ADJECTIVE 1 having no known father. 2 of unknown or uncertain origin. 3 *Archaic* fatherless.

unfathomable (ʌnˈfæðəməbᵊl) ADJECTIVE 1 incapable of being fathomed; immeasurable. 2 incomprehensible.
▸**un'fathomableness** NOUN ▸**un'fathomably** ADVERB

unfavourable *or US* **unfavorable** (ʌnˈfeɪvərəbᵊl, -ˈfeɪvrə-) ADJECTIVE not favourable; adverse or inauspicious.
▸**un'favourableness** *or (US)* **un'favorableness** NOUN ▸**un'favourably** *or (US)* **un'favorably** ADVERB

unfavoured *or US* **unfavored** (ʌnˈfeɪvəd) ADJECTIVE 1 not regarded with especial kindness or approval: *unvalued and unfavoured daughter.* 2 not regarded with partiality or favouritism: *the unfavoured far side of the course.*

unfazed (ʌnˈfeɪzd) ADJECTIVE *Informal* not disconcerted; unperturbed.

unfeasible (ʌnˈfiːzəbᵊl) ADJECTIVE not able to be done or put into effect; impossible.

Unfederated Malay States (ʌnˈfɛdəˌreɪtɪd) PLURAL NOUN a former group of native states in the Malay Peninsula that became British protectorates between 1885 and 1909. All except Brunei joined the Malayan Union (later Federation of Malaya) in 1946. Brunei joined the Federation of Malaysia in 1963.

unfeeling (ʌnˈfiːlɪŋ) ADJECTIVE 1 without sympathy; callous. 2 without physical feeling or sensation.
▸**un'feelingly** ADVERB ▸**un'feelingness** NOUN

unfertilized *or* **unfertilised** (ʌnˈfɜːtɪˌlaɪzd) ADJECTIVE (of an animal, plant, or egg cell) not fertilized: *an unfertilized ovum.*

unfetter (ʌnˈfɛtə) VERB (*tr*) 1 to release from fetters, bonds, etc. 2 to release from restraint or inhibition.

unfettered (ʌnˈfɛtəd) ADJECTIVE released from physical or mental bonds; unrestrained.

unfilled (ʌnˈfɪld) ADJECTIVE 1 (of a container, receptacle, etc.) not having become or been made full: *unfilled stomachs.* 2 (of a job, role, etc.) not occupied. 3 (of a cake, doughnut, etc) with no filling: *unfilled choux pastry will freeze.*

unfiltered (ʌnˈfɪltəd) ADJECTIVE 1 (of oil, coffee, smoke, etc.) not having been passed through a filter. 2 not having been toned down, censored, or edited: *unfiltered news sources.* 3 (of a cigarette) not having a filter tip.

unfinished (ʌnˈfɪnɪʃt) ADJECTIVE 1 incomplete or imperfect. 2 (of paint, polish, varnish, etc.) without an applied finish; rough. 3 (of fabric) unbleached or not processed. 4 (of fabric) with a short nap.

unfit (ʌnˈfɪt) ADJECTIVE 1 (*postpositive; often foll by* for) unqualified, incapable, or incompetent: *unfit for military service.* 2 (*postpositive; often foll by* for) unsuitable or inappropriate: *the ground was unfit for football.* 3 in poor physical condition.
▸**un'fitness** NOUN

unfitted (ʌnˈfɪtɪd) ADJECTIVE unsuitable: *unused to and unfitted for any form of manual labour.*

unfix (ʌnˈfɪks) VERB (*tr*) 1 to unfasten, detach, or loosen. 2 to unsettle or disturb.

unflagging (ʌnˈflægɪŋ) ADJECTIVE not declining in strength or vigour; tireless.

unflappable (ʌnˈflæpəbᵊl) ADJECTIVE *Informal* hard to upset; imperturbable; calm; composed.
▸**unˌflappa'bility** *or* **un'flappableness** NOUN ▸**un'flappably** ADVERB

unflattering (ʌnˈflætərɪŋ) ADJECTIVE not flattering: *in an unflattering light.*

unfledged (ʌnˈflɛdʒd) ADJECTIVE 1 (of a young bird) not having developed adult feathers. 2 immature and undeveloped.

unflinching (ʌnˈflɪntʃɪŋ) ADJECTIVE not shrinking from danger, difficulty, etc.
▸**un'flinchingly** ADVERB

unfold (ʌnˈfəʊld) VERB 1 to open or spread out or be opened or spread out from a folded state. 2 to reveal or be revealed: *the truth unfolds.* 3 to develop or expand or be developed or expanded.
▸**un'folder** NOUN

unforced (ʌnˈfɔːst) ADJECTIVE not forced or having been forced: *unforced errors.*

unforeseeable (ˌʌnfɔːˈsiːəbᵊl) ADJECTIVE not able to be foreseen or known beforehand.

unforeseen (ˌʌnfɔːˈsiːn) ADJECTIVE not seen or known beforehand; unanticipated.

unforgettable (ˌʌnfəˈgɛtəbᵊl) ADJECTIVE impossible to forget; highly memorable.
▸**ˌunfor'gettably** ADVERB

unforgivable (ˌʌnfəˈgɪvəbᵊl) ADJECTIVE so bad as to be unable to be excused or pardoned.

unforgiving (ˌʌnfəˈgɪvɪŋ) ADJECTIVE 1 not willing to forgive; unmerciful. 2 (of a machine, system, etc.) allowing little or no opportunity for mistakes to be corrected. 3 harsh and unremitting: *an unforgiving and desolate landscape.*

unformed (ʌnˈfɔːmd) ADJECTIVE 1 shapeless. 2 immature.

unforthcoming (ˌʌnfɔːθˈkʌmɪŋ) ADJECTIVE not inclined to talk about something: *she was unforthcoming about her past.*

unfortunate (ʌnˈfɔːtʃənɪt) ADJECTIVE 1 causing or attended by misfortune. 2 unlucky, unsuccessful, or unhappy: *an unfortunate character.* 3 regrettable or unsuitable: *an unfortunate speech.* ◆ NOUN 4 an unlucky person.
▸**un'fortunately** ADVERB ▸**un'fortunateness** NOUN

unfortunately (ʌnˈfɔːtʃənɪtlɪ) ADVERB (*sentence modifier*) it is regrettable that; unluckily.

unfounded (ʌnˈfaʊndɪd) ADJECTIVE 1 (of ideas, allegations, etc.) baseless; groundless. 2 not yet founded or established.
▸**un'foundedly** ADVERB ▸**un'foundedness** NOUN

unfranked income (ʌnˈfræŋkt) NOUN any income from an investment that does not qualify as franked investment income.

unfreeze (ʌnˈfriːz) VERB **-freezes, -freezing, -froze, -frozen.** 1 to thaw or cause to thaw. 2 (*tr*) to relax governmental restrictions on (wages, prices, credit, etc.) or on the manufacture or sale of (goods, etc.).

unfriended (ʌnˈfrɛndɪd) ADJECTIVE *Now rare* without a friend or friends; friendless.

unfriendly (ʌnˈfrɛndlɪ) ADJECTIVE **-lier, -liest.** 1 not friendly; hostile. 2 unfavourable or disagreeable. ◆ ADVERB 3 *Rare* in an unfriendly manner.
▸**un'friendliness** NOUN

unfrock (ʌnˈfrɒk) VERB (*tr*) to deprive (a person in holy orders) of ecclesiastical status.

unfruitful (ʌnˈfruːtfʊl) ADJECTIVE 1 barren, unproductive, or unprofitable. 2 failing to produce or develop into fruit.
▸**un'fruitfully** ADVERB ▸**un'fruitfulness** NOUN

unfulfilled (ˌʌnfʊlˈfɪld) ADJECTIVE 1 not completed or achieved: *unfulfilled ambitions.* 2 not having achieved one's potential or desires.

unfunded debt (ʌnˈfʌndɪd) NOUN a short-term floating debt not represented by bonds.

unfunny (ʌnˈfʌnɪ) ADJECTIVE **-nier, -niest.** not funny: *obscene and unfunny jokes.*

unfurl (ʌnˈfɜːl) VERB to unroll, unfold, or spread out or be unrolled, unfolded, or spread out from a furled state.

unfurnished (ʌnˈfɜːnɪʃt) ADJECTIVE (of a room, property, etc.) not having any furniture.

unfussy (ʌnˈfʌsɪ) ADJECTIVE **unfussier, unfussiest.** 1 not characterized by overelaborate detail. 2 not particular: *he's unfussy about which grievances he exploits.*

ungainly (ʌnˈgeɪnlɪ) ADJECTIVE **-lier, -liest.** 1 lacking grace when moving. 2 difficult to move or use; unwieldy. 3 *Rare* crude or coarse. ◆ ADVERB 4 *Rare* clumsily.
▷**HISTORY** C17: from UN-[1] + obsolete or dialect GAINLY graceful
▸**un'gainliness** NOUN

Ungava (ʊŋˈgeɪvə, -ˈgɑː-) NOUN a sparsely inhabited region of NE Canada, in N Quebec east of Hudson Bay: part of the Labrador peninsula: rich mineral resources. Area: 911 110 sq. km (351 780 sq. miles).

ungenerous (ʌnˈdʒɛnərəs, -ˈdʒɛnrəs) ADJECTIVE not willing and liberal in giving away one's money, time, etc.

unglamorous (ʌnˈglæmərəs) ADJECTIVE lacking in glamour, allure, or fascination: *the unglamorous side of the music business.*

ungodly (ʌnˈgɒdlɪ) ADJECTIVE **-lier, -liest.** 1 **a** wicked; sinful. **b** (*as collective noun; preceded by* the): *the ungodly.* 2 *Informal* unseemly; outrageous (esp in the phrase **an ungodly hour**).
▸**un'godliness** NOUN

ungotten (ʌnˈgɒtᵊn) ADJECTIVE *Archaic* not obtained or won.

ungovernable (ʌnˈgʌvənəbᵊl) ADJECTIVE not able to be disciplined, restrained, etc.: *an ungovernable temper.*
▸**un'governableness** NOUN ▸**un'governably** ADVERB

ungracious (ʌnˈgreɪʃəs) ADJECTIVE not characterized by or showing kindness and courtesy.

ungrammatical (ˌʌngrəˈmætɪkᵊl) ADJECTIVE (of a sentence) not regarded as correct by native speakers of the language.

ungrateful (ʌnˈgreɪtfʊl) ADJECTIVE 1 not grateful or thankful. 2 unrewarding or unpleasant; thankless. 3 (of land) failing to increase fertility in response to cultivation.
▸**un'gratefully** ADVERB ▸**un'gratefulness** NOUN

ungrudging (ʌnˈgrʌdʒɪŋ) ADJECTIVE liberal; unstinted; willing: *ungrudging support.*
▸**un'grudgingly** ADVERB

ungual (ˈʌŋgwəl) *or* **ungular** (ˈʌŋgjʊlə) ADJECTIVE 1 of, relating to, or affecting the fingernails or toenails. 2 of or relating to an unguis.
▷**HISTORY** C19: from Latin *unguis* nail, claw

unguarded (ʌnˈgɑːdɪd) ADJECTIVE 1 unprotected; vulnerable. 2 guileless; open; frank. 3 incautious or careless.
▸**un'guardedly** ADVERB ▸**un'guardedness** NOUN

unguent (ˈʌŋgwənt) NOUN a less common name for an **ointment**.
▷**HISTORY** C15: from Latin *unguentum,* from *unguere* to anoint
▸**'unguentary** ADJECTIVE

unguiculate (ʌŋˈgwɪkjʊlɪt, -ˌleɪt) ADJECTIVE 1 (of mammals) having claws or nails. 2 (of petals) having a clawlike base. ◆ NOUN 3 an unguiculate mammal.
▷**HISTORY** C19: from New Latin *unguiculātus,* from Latin *unguiculus,* diminutive of *unguis* nail, claw

unguided (ʌnˈgaɪdɪd) ADJECTIVE 1 (of a missile, bomb, etc.) not having a flight path controlled either by radio signals or internal preset or self-actuating homing devices. 2 without a guide: *guided and unguided hikes.*

unguinous (ˈʌŋgwɪnəs) ADJECTIVE *Obsolete* fatty; greasy; oily.
▷**HISTORY** C17: from Latin *unguinōsus* oily, from *unguin-, unguen* a fatty substance, from *unguere* to anoint, besmear

unguis (ˈʌŋgwɪs) NOUN, *plural* **-gues** (-gwiːz). 1 a nail, claw, or hoof, or the part of the digit giving rise to it. 2 the clawlike base of certain petals.
▷**HISTORY** C18: from Latin

ungula (ˈʌŋgjʊlə) NOUN, *plural* **-lae** (-ˌliː). 1 *Maths* a truncated cone, cylinder, etc. 2 a rare word for **hoof**.
▷**HISTORY** C18: from Latin: hoof, from *unguis* nail
▸**'ungular** ADJECTIVE

ungulate (ˈʌŋgjʊlɪt, -ˌleɪt) NOUN any of a large group of mammals all of which have hooves: divided into odd-toed ungulates (see **perissodactyl**) and even-toed ungulates (see **artiodactyl**).
▷**HISTORY** C19: from Late Latin *ungulātus* having hooves, from UNGULA

unguligrade (ˈʌŋgjʊlɪˌgreɪd) ADJECTIVE (of horses, etc.) walking on hooves.
▷**HISTORY** C19: from Latin *ungula* hoof + -GRADE

unhair (ʌnˈhɛə) VERB to remove the hair from (a hide).

unhallow (ʌnˈhæləʊ) VERB (*tr*) *Archaic* to desecrate.

unhallowed (ʌnˈhæləʊd) ADJECTIVE 1 not consecrated or holy: *unhallowed ground.* 2 sinful or profane.

unhampered (ʌnˈhæmpəd) ADJECTIVE allowed to move or progress freely.

unhand (ʌnˈhænd) VERB (*tr*) *Archaic or literary* to release from the grasp.

unhandy (ʌnˈhændɪ) ADJECTIVE 1 not skilful with one's hands; clumsy; awkward. 2 inconvenient.

unhappy (ʌnˈhæpɪ) ADJECTIVE **-pier, -piest.** 1 not joyful; sad or depressed. 2 unfortunate or wretched: *an unhappy fellow.* 3 tactless or inappropriate: *an unhappy remark.* 4 *Archaic* unfavourable.
▸**unˈhappily** ADVERB ▸**unˈhappiness** NOUN

unharmed (ʌnˈhɑːmd) ADJECTIVE not having sustained physical, moral, or mental injury.

unharness (ʌnˈhɑːnɪs) VERB (*tr*) 1 to remove the harness from (a horse, etc.). 2 *Archaic* to remove the armour from.

unhatched (ʌnˈhætʃt) ADJECTIVE 1 (of an egg) not having broken to release the fully developed young. 2 (of a bird, snake, etc.) not having emerged from the egg. 3 (of a plan, mission, etc.) not having been fully developed or carried out.

UNHCR ABBREVIATION FOR United Nations High Commissioner for Refugees.

unhealed (ʌnˈhiːld) ADJECTIVE not having healed physically, mentally, or emotionally.

unhealthy (ʌnˈhɛlθɪ) ADJECTIVE **-healthier, -healthiest.** 1 characterized by ill-health; sick; unwell. 2 characteristic of, conducive to, or resulting from ill-health: *an unhealthy complexion; an unhealthy atmosphere.* 3 morbid or unwholesome. 4 *Informal* dangerous; risky.
▸**unˈhealthily** ADVERB ▸**unˈhealthiness** NOUN

unheard (ʌnˈhɜːd) ADJECTIVE 1 not heard; not perceived by the ear. 2 not listened to or granted a hearing: *his warning went unheard.* 3 *Archaic* unheard-of.

unheard-of ADJECTIVE 1 previously unknown: *an unheard-of actress.* 2 without precedent: *an unheard-of treatment.* 3 highly offensive: *unheard-of behaviour.*

unheated (ʌnˈhiːtɪd) ADJECTIVE not having been warmed up.

unheeded (ʌnˈhiːdɪd) ADJECTIVE noticed or heard but disregarded.

unhelm (ʌnˈhɛlm) VERB to remove the helmet of (oneself or another).
▷**HISTORY** C15: from UN-[2] + HELM[2]

unhelpful (ʌnˈhɛlpfʊl) ADJECTIVE not serving a useful function.

unheralded (ʌnˈhɛrəldɪd) ADJECTIVE not previously announced, notified, or expected.

unhesitating (ʌnˈhɛzɪˌteɪtɪŋ) ADJECTIVE 1 steadfast; unwavering: *unhesitating loyalty.* 2 without hesitation; prompt.
▸**unˈhesiˌtatingly** ADVERB

unhindered (ʌnˈhɪndəd) ADJECTIVE without hindrance: *he could proceed unhindered.*

unhinge (ʌnˈhɪndʒ) VERB (*tr*) 1 to remove (a door, gate, etc.) from its hinges. 2 to derange or unbalance (a person, his mind, etc.). 3 to disrupt or unsettle (a process or state of affairs). 4 (usually foll by *from*) to detach or dislodge.

unhip (ʌnˈhɪp) ADJECTIVE **unhipper, unhippest.** *Slang* not at all fashionable or up to date: *my terminally unhip parents.*

unholy (ʌnˈhəʊlɪ) ADJECTIVE **-lier, -liest.** 1 not holy or sacred. 2 immoral or depraved. 3 *Informal* outrageous or unnatural: *an unholy alliance.*
▸**unˈholiness** NOUN

unhook (ʌnˈhʊk) VERB 1 (*tr*) to remove (something) from a hook. 2 (*tr*) to unfasten the hook of (a dress, etc.). 3 (*intr*) to become unfastened or be capable of unfastening: *the dress wouldn't unhook.*

unhoped-for (ˌʌnˈhəʊptfɔː) ADJECTIVE (esp of something pleasant) not anticipated; unexpected.

unhorse (ʌnˈhɔːs) VERB (*tr*) 1 (*usually passive*) to knock or throw from a horse. 2 to overthrow or dislodge, as from a powerful position. 3 *Now rare* to unharness horses from (a carriage, etc.).

unhouseled (ʌnˈhaʊzəld) ADJECTIVE *Archaic* not having received the Eucharist.
▷**HISTORY** C16: from *un-* + obsolete *housel* to administer the sacrament, from Old English *hūsl* (n), *hūslian* (vb), of unknown origin

unhurried (ʌnˈhʌrɪd) ADJECTIVE leisurely or deliberate: *an unhurried walk.*
▸**unˈhurriedly** ADVERB

unhurt (ʌnˈhɜːt) ADJECTIVE not having sustained any injury.

unhygienic (ˌʌnhaɪˈdʒiːnɪk) ADJECTIVE not promoting health or cleanliness; unsanitary.

uni (ˈjuːnɪ) NOUN *Informal* short for **university.**

uni- COMBINING FORM consisting of, relating to, or having only one: *unilateral; unisexual.*
▷**HISTORY** from Latin *ūnus* one

Uniat (ˈjuːnɪˌæt) *or* **Uniate** (ˈjuːnɪɪt, -ˌeɪt) ADJECTIVE 1 designating any of the Eastern Churches that retain their own liturgy but submit to papal authority. ◆ NOUN 2 a member of one of these Churches.
▷**HISTORY** C19: from Russian *uniyat,* from Polish *unja* union, from Late Latin *ūniō;* see UNION
▸**ˈUniˌatism** NOUN

uniaxial (ˌjuːnɪˈæksɪəl) ADJECTIVE 1 (esp of plants) having an unbranched main axis. 2 (of a crystal) having only one direction along which double refraction of light does not occur.
▸**ˌuniˈaxially** ADVERB

unicameral (ˌjuːnɪˈkæmərəl) ADJECTIVE of or characterized by a single legislative chamber.
▸**ˌuniˈcameralism** NOUN ▸**ˌuniˈcameralist** NOUN
▸**ˌuniˈcamerally** ADVERB

UNICEF (ˈjuːnɪˌsɛf) NOUN ACRONYM FOR United Nations Children's Fund (formerly, United Nations International Children's Emergency Fund): an agency of the United Nations that administers programmes to aid education and child and maternal health in developing countries.

unicellular (ˌjuːnɪˈsɛljʊlə) ADJECTIVE (of organisms, such as protozoans and certain algae) consisting of a single cell.
▸**ˌuniˌcelluˈlarity** NOUN

unicolour *or US* **unicolor** (ˈjuːnɪˌkʌlə) ADJECTIVE of one colour; monochromatic.

unicorn (ˈjuːnɪˌkɔːn) NOUN 1 an imaginary creature usually depicted as a white horse with one long spiralled horn growing from its forehead. 2 *Old Testament* a two-horned animal, thought to be either the rhinoceros or the aurochs: (Deuteronomy 33:17): mistranslation in the Authorized Version of the original Hebrew.
▷**HISTORY** C13: from Old French *unicorne,* from Latin *ūnicornis* one-horned, from *ūnus* one + *cornu* a horn

unicostate (ˌjuːnɪˈkɒsteɪt) ADJECTIVE *Biology* having only one rib or riblike part: *unicostate leaves.*

unicycle (ˈjuːnɪˌsaɪkəl) NOUN a one-wheeled vehicle driven by pedals, esp one used in a circus, etc. Also called: **monocycle.**
▷**HISTORY** from UNI- + CYCLE, on the model of TRICYCLE
▸**ˈuniˌcyclist** NOUN

unidentified (ˌʌnaɪˈdɛntɪˌfaɪd) ADJECTIVE not identified or recognized: *an unidentified man.*
▸**ˌuniˈdentiˌfiable** ADJECTIVE

unidirectional (ˌjuːnɪdɪˈrɛkʃənəl, -daɪ-) ADJECTIVE having, moving in, or operating in only one direction.

UNIDO (juːˈniːdəʊ) NOUN ACRONYM FOR United Nations Industrial Development Organization.

UniFi *or* **UNiFI** (ˈjuːnɪˌfaɪ) NOUN ACRONYM FOR Union Finance, a finance sector union.
▷**HISTORY** C20: from UNI(ON) + FI(NANCE)

unific (juːˈnɪfɪk) ADJECTIVE *Rare* unifying; uniting.

unification (ˌjuːnɪfɪˈkeɪʃən) NOUN 1 an act, instance, or process of uniting. 2 the state of being united.

Unification Church NOUN a religious sect founded in 1954 by Sun Myung Moon (born 1920), S Korean industrialist and religious leader. See also **Moonie.**

unified atomic mass unit NOUN another name for **atomic mass unit.**

unified field theory NOUN any theory capable of describing in one set of equations the properties of gravitational fields, electromagnetic fields, and strong and weak nuclear interactions. No satisfactory theory has yet been found.

unified screw thread NOUN a screw thread system introduced for defence equipment (1939–44), in which the thread form and pitch were a compromise between British Standard Whitworth and American Standard Sellers: adopted by the International Standards Organization.

unifilar (ˌjuːnɪˈfaɪlə) ADJECTIVE *Rare* composed of, having, or using only one wire, thread, filament, etc.
▷**HISTORY** from UNI- + Latin *fīlum* thread; see FILAMENT, FILAR

unifoliate (ˌjuːnɪˈfəʊlɪɪt, -ˌeɪt) ADJECTIVE having a single leaf or leaflike part.

unifoliolate (ˌjuːnɪˈfəʊlɪəˌleɪt) ADJECTIVE (of a compound leaf) having only one leaflet.

uniform (ˈjuːnɪˌfɔːm) NOUN 1 a prescribed identifying set of clothes for the members of an organization, such as soldiers or schoolchildren. 2 a single set of such clothes. 3 a characteristic feature or fashion of some class or group. 4 *Informal* a police officer who wears a uniform. ◆ ADJECTIVE 5 unchanging in form, quality, quantity, etc.; regular: *a uniform surface.* 6 identical; alike or like: *a line of uniform toys.* ◆ VERB (*tr*) 7 to fit out (a body of soldiers, etc.) with uniforms. 8 to make uniform.
▷**HISTORY** C16: from Latin *ūniformis,* from *ūnus* one + *forma* shape
▸**ˈuniˌformly** ADVERB ▸**ˈuniˌformness** NOUN

Uniform (ˈjuːnɪˌfɔːm) NOUN *Communications* a code word for the letter *u.*

Uniform Business Rate NOUN a local tax in the UK paid by businesses, based on a local valuation of their premises and a rate fixed by central government that applies throughout the country. Abbreviation: **UBR.**

uniformitarian (ˌjuːnɪˌfɔːmɪˈtɛərɪən) ADJECTIVE 1 of or relating to uniformitarianism. 2 of, characterized by, or conforming to uniformity. ◆ NOUN 3 a supporter of a theory of uniformity or of uniformitarianism.

uniformitarianism (ˌjuːnɪˌfɔːmɪˈtɛərɪəˌnɪzəm) NOUN the concept that the earth's surface was shaped in the past by gradual processes, such as erosion, and by small sudden changes, such as earthquakes, of the type acting today rather than by the sudden divine acts, such as the flood survived by Noah (Genesis 6–8), demanded by the doctrine of catastrophism.

uniformity (ˌjuːnɪˈfɔːmɪtɪ) NOUN, *plural* **-ties.** 1 a state or condition in which everything is regular, homogeneous, or unvarying. 2 lack of diversity or variation, esp to the point of boredom or monotony; sameness.

unify (ˈjuːnɪˌfaɪ) VERB **-fies, -fying, -fied.** to make or become one; unite.
▷**HISTORY** C16: from Medieval Latin *ūnificāre,* from Latin *ūnus* one + *facere* to make
▸**ˈuniˌfiable** ADJECTIVE ▸**ˈuniˌfier** NOUN

unijugate (ˌjuːnɪˈdʒuːgɪt, -ˌgeɪt) ADJECTIVE (of a compound leaf) having only one pair of leaflets.

unilateral (ˌjuːnɪˈlætərəl) ADJECTIVE 1 of, having, affecting, or occurring on only one side. 2 involving or performed by only one party of several: *unilateral disarmament.* 3 *Law* (of contracts, obligations, etc.) made by, affecting, or binding one party only and not involving the other party in reciprocal obligations. 4 *Botany* having or designating parts situated or turned to one side of an axis. 5 *Sociol* relating to or tracing the line of descent through ancestors of one sex only. Compare **bilateral** (sense 5). 6 *Phonetics* denoting an (l) sound produced on one side of the tongue only.
▸**ˌuniˈlateralism** *or* **ˌuniˌlaterˈality** NOUN ▸**ˌuniˈlaterally** ADVERB

Unilateral Declaration of Independence NOUN a declaration of independence made by a dependent state without the assent of the protecting state. Abbreviation: **UDI.**

unilateral neglect NOUN a symptom of brain damage in which a person is unaware of one side of his body and of anything in the external world on the same side.

unilingual (ˌjuːnɪˈlɪŋgwəl) ADJECTIVE of or having only one language.
▸ **ˌuniˈlingualˌism** NOUN

uniliteral (ˌjuːnɪˈlɪtərəl) ADJECTIVE consisting of one letter.

unilocular (ˌjuːnɪˈlɒkjʊlə) ADJECTIVE (esp of a plant ovary or anther) having or consisting of a single chamber or cavity.

unimaginable (ˌʌnɪˈmædʒɪnəbᵊl) ADJECTIVE difficult or impossible to believe; inconceivable.
▸ **ˌunimˈaginably** ADVERB

unimaginative (ˌʌnɪˈmædʒɪnətɪv) ADJECTIVE lacking in imagination or imaginative thought; dull.
▸ **ˌunimˈaginatively** ADVERB

unimagined (ˌʌnɪˈmædʒɪnd) ADJECTIVE not having been conceived of: *a hitherto unimagined scale.*

Unimak Island (ˈjuːnɪˌmæk) NOUN an island in SW Alaska, in the Aleutian Islands. Length: 113 km (70 miles).

unimpaired (ˌʌnɪmˈpɛəd) ADJECTIVE not reduced or weakened in strength, quality, etc.

unimpeachable (ˌʌnɪmˈpiːtʃəbᵊl) ADJECTIVE unquestionable as to honesty, truth, etc.
▸ **ˌunimˌpeachaˈbility** *or* **ˌunimˈpeachableness** NOUN
▸ **ˌunimˈpeachably** ADVERB

unimpeded (ˌʌnɪmˈpiːdɪd) ADJECTIVE not impeded; unhindered.

unimportant (ˌʌnɪmˈpɔːtᵊnt) ADJECTIVE lacking in significance or value: *unimportant matters.*

unimpressed (ˌʌnɪmˈprɛst) ADJECTIVE not having a favourable opinion: *unimpressed by his arguments.*

unimpressive (ˌʌnɪmˈprɛsɪv) ADJECTIVE not capable of impressing, esp by size, magnificence, etc.: *an unimpressive performance.*

unimproved (ˌʌnɪmˈpruːvd) ADJECTIVE 1 not improved or made better. 2 (of land) not cleared, drained, cultivated, etc. 3 neglected; unused: *unimproved resources.*

unimproved value NOUN *NZ* the valuation of land for rating purposes, disregarding the value of buildings or other development.

unincorporated (ˌʌnɪnˈkɔːpəˌreɪtɪd) ADJECTIVE 1 *Law* lacking corporate status. 2 not unified or included.

unincorporated business NOUN a privately owned business, often owned by one person who has unlimited liability as the business is not legally registered as a company.

uninfected (ˌʌnɪnˈfɛktɪd) ADJECTIVE (of a person, wound, etc.) not having been contaminated with pathogenic microorganisms.

uninformed (ˌʌnɪnˈfɔːmd) ADJECTIVE not having knowledge or information about a situation, subject, etc.

uninhabitable (ˌʌnɪnˈhæbɪtəbᵊl) ADJECTIVE not capable of being lived in.

uninhabited (ˌʌnɪnˈhæbɪtɪd) ADJECTIVE (of a place) not having inhabitants: *an uninhabited island.*

uninhibited (ˌʌnɪnˈhɪbɪtɪd) ADJECTIVE lacking in inhibitions or restraint.

uninitiated (ˌʌnɪˈnɪʃɪeɪtɪd) ADJECTIVE **a** not having gained knowledge or experience of a particular subject or activity. **b** (*as collective noun*; preceded by *the*): *the uninitiated.*

uninjured (ʌnˈɪndʒəd) ADJECTIVE not having sustained any injury; unhurt.

uninspired (ˌʌnɪnˈspaɪəd) ADJECTIVE dull or ordinary; unimaginative: *an uninspired painting.*

uninspiring (ˌʌnɪnˈspaɪᵊrɪŋ) ADJECTIVE not stimulating or invigorating: *an uninspiring performance.*

uninsurable (ˌʌnɪnˈʃʊərəbᵊl, -ˈʃɔː) ADJECTIVE not eligible for insurance.

uninsured (ˌʌnɪnˈʃʊəd, -ˈʃɔːd) ADJECTIVE not covered by insurance: *uninsured motorists.*

unintellectual (ˌʌnɪntɪˈlɛktʃʊəl) ADJECTIVE 1 not expressing or enjoying mental activity. 2 not appealing to people with a developed intellect.

unintelligent (ˌʌnɪnˈtɛlɪdʒənt) ADJECTIVE 1 lacking intelligence; stupid; foolish. 2 not endowed with a mind or intelligence.
▸ **ˌuninˈtelligence** NOUN ▸ **ˌuninˈtelligently** ADVERB

unintelligible (ˌʌnɪnˈtɛlɪdʒɪbᵊl) ADJECTIVE not able to be understood; incomprehensible.

unintended (ˌʌnɪnˈtɛndɪd) ADJECTIVE not intended; unplanned.

unintentional (ˌʌnɪnˈtɛnʃənᵊl) ADJECTIVE not deliberate; accidental: *the killing had been unintentional.*
▸ **ˌuninˈtentionally** ADVERB

uninterested (ʌnˈɪntrɪstɪd, -tərɪs-) ADJECTIVE indifferent; unconcerned.
▸ **unˈinterestedly** ADVERB ▸ **unˈinterestedness** NOUN

> **Language note** See at **disinterested.**

uninteresting (ʌnˈɪntrɪstɪŋ, ʌnˈɪntərɪs-) ADJECTIVE not interesting; boring: *lifeless and uninteresting.*

uninterrupted (ˌʌnɪntəˈrʌptɪd) ADJECTIVE not broken, discontinued, or hindered: *an uninterrupted view.*

uninvited (ˌʌnɪnˈvaɪtɪd) ADJECTIVE not having been invited: *uninvited guests.*

uninviting (ˌʌnɪnˈvaɪtɪŋ) ADJECTIVE not tempting, alluring, or attractive.

uninvolved (ˌʌnɪnˈvɒlvd) ADJECTIVE not included or involved: *uninvolved bystanders.*

union (ˈjuːnjən) NOUN 1 the condition of being united, the act of uniting, or a conjunction formed by such an act. 2 an association, alliance, or confederation of individuals or groups for a common purpose, esp political. 3 agreement or harmony. 4 short for **trade union.** 5 the act or state of marriage or sexual intercourse. 6 a device on a flag representing union, such as another flag depicted in the top left corner. 7 a device for coupling or linking parts, such as pipes. 8 (*often capital*) **a** an association of students at a university or college formed to look after the students' interests, provide facilities for recreation, etc. **b** the building or buildings housing the facilities of such an organization. 9 Also called: **join.** *Maths* a set containing all members of two given sets. Symbol: ∪, as in A∪B. 10 (in 19th-century England) **a** a number of parishes united for the administration of poor relief. **b** a workhouse supported by such a combination. 11 *Textiles* a piece of cloth or fabric consisting of two different kinds of yarn. 12 (*modifier*) of or related to a union, esp a trade union.
▷HISTORY C15: from Church Latin *ūniō* oneness, from Latin *ūnus* one

Union (ˈjuːnjən) NOUN **the.** 1 *Brit* **a** the union of England and Wales from 1543. **b** the union of the English and Scottish crowns (1603–1707). **c** the union of England and Scotland from 1707. **d** the political union of Great Britain and Ireland (1801–1920). **e** the union of Great Britain and Northern Ireland from 1920. 2 *US* **a** the United States of America. **b** the northern states of the US during the Civil War. **c** (*as modifier*): *Union supporters.* 3 short for the **Union of South Africa.**

union card NOUN a membership card for a trade union.

union catalogue NOUN a catalogue listing every publication held at cooperating libraries.

Union flag NOUN the national flag of the United Kingdom, being a composite design composed of St George's Cross (England), Saint Andrew's Cross (Scotland), and Saint Patrick's Cross (Ireland). Often called: **Union Jack.**

unionism (ˈjuːnjəˌnɪzəm) NOUN 1 the principles of trade unions. 2 adherence to the principles of trade unions. 3 the principle or theory of any union.

Unionism (ˈjuːnjəˌnɪzəm) NOUN (*sometimes not capital*) the principles or adherence to the principles of Unionists.

unionist (ˈjuːnjənɪst) NOUN 1 a supporter or advocate of unionism or union. 2 a member of a trade union. ◆ ADJECTIVE 3 *Chiefly Brit* of or relating to union or unionism, esp trade unionism.
▸ **ˌunionˈistic** ADJECTIVE

Unionist (ˈjuːnjənɪst) NOUN 1 (*sometimes not capital*) **a** (before 1920) a supporter of the union of all Ireland and Great Britain. **b** (since 1920) a supporter of union between Britain and Northern Ireland. 2 a supporter of the US federal Union, esp during the Civil War. ◆ ADJECTIVE 3 of, resembling, or relating to Unionists.

Unionist Party NOUN (formerly, in Northern Ireland) the major Protestant political party, closely identified with union with Britain. It formed the Northern Ireland Government from 1920 to 1972. See also **Ulster Democratic Unionist Party, Ulster Unionist Council.**

unionize *or* **unionise** (ˈjuːnjəˌnaɪz) VERB 1 to organize (workers) into a trade union. 2 to join or cause to join a trade union. 3 (*tr*) to subject to the rules or codes of a trade union.
▸ **ˌunioniˈzation** *or* **ˌunioniˈsation** NOUN

Union Jack NOUN 1 a common name for **Union flag.** 2 (*often not capitals*) a national flag flown at the jackstaff of a vessel.

Union of South Africa NOUN the former name (1910–61) of the (Republic of) **South Africa.**

Union of Soviet Socialist Republics NOUN the official name of the former **Soviet Union.**

union pipes PLURAL NOUN another name for **uillean pipes.**

union shop NOUN (formerly) an establishment whose employment policy is governed by a contract between employer and a trade union permitting the employment of nonunion labour only on the condition that such labour joins the union within a specified time period. Compare **open shop, closed shop.**

union territory NOUN one of the 9 administrative territories that, with 21 states, make up the Indian Republic.

uniparous (juːˈnɪpərəs) ADJECTIVE 1 (of certain animals) producing a single offspring at each birth. 2 (of a woman) having borne only one child. 3 *Botany* (of a cyme) giving rise to only one branch from each flowering stem.

unipersonal (ˌjuːnɪˈpɜːsənᵊl) ADJECTIVE 1 existing in the form of only one person or being. Compare **tripersonal.** 2 (of a verb) existing or used in only one person; for example, *rain* is used only in the third person.
▸ **ˌuniˌpersonˈality** NOUN

uniplanar (ˌjuːnɪˈpleɪnə) ADJECTIVE situated in one plane.

unipod (ˈjuːnɪˌpɒd) NOUN a one-legged support, as for a camera.

unipolar (ˌjuːnɪˈpəʊlə) ADJECTIVE 1 of, concerned with, or having a single magnetic or electric pole. 2 (of a nerve cell) having a single process. 3 (of a transistor) utilizing charge carriers of one polarity only, as in a field-effect transistor. 4 (of nervous depression) occurring without accompanying bouts of mania. 5 dominated by one superpower, esp the United States. ◆ Compare **bipolar.**
▸ **unipolarity** (ˌjuːnɪpəʊˈlærɪtɪ) NOUN

unique (juːˈniːk) ADJECTIVE 1 being the only one of a particular type; single; sole. 2 without equal or like; unparalleled. 3 *Informal* very remarkable or unusual. 4 *Maths* **a** leading to only one result: *the sum of two integers is unique.* **b** having precisely one value: *the unique positive square root of 4 is 2.*
▷HISTORY C17: via French from Latin *ūnicus* unparalleled, from *ūnus* one
▸ **uˈniquely** ADVERB ▸ **uˈniqueness** NOUN

> **Language note** *Unique* is normally taken to describe an absolute state, i.e. one that cannot be qualified; thus something is either *unique* or *not unique;* it cannot be *rather unique* or *very unique.* However, *unique* is sometimes used informally to mean very remarkable or unusual and this makes it possible to use comparatives or intensifiers with it, although many people object to this use.

uniramous (ˌjuːnɪˈreɪməs) ADJECTIVE (esp of the appendages of crustaceans) consisting of a single branch; undivided. Also: **uniramose** (ˌjuːnɪˈreɪməʊs, -ræˈməʊs).

UNISA (juːˈniːsə) NOUN ACRONYM FOR University of South Africa.

uniseptate (ˌjuːnɪˈsɛpteɪt) ADJECTIVE *Biology* having only one partition or septum: *a uniseptate fruit.*

uniserial (ˌjuːnɪˈsɪərɪəl) ADJECTIVE in or relating to a single series.

uniseriate (ˌjuːnɪˈsɪərɪˌeɪt) ADJECTIVE *Botany* (of

parts, cells, etc.) arranged in a single row, layer, or series.

unisex ('ju:nɪˌsɛks) ADJECTIVE of or relating to clothing, a hairstyle, etc., that can be worn by either sex.
▷HISTORY C20: from UNI- + SEX

unisexual (ˌju:nɪ'sɛksjʊəl) ADJECTIVE 1 of or relating to one sex only. 2 (of some organisms) having either male or female reproductive organs but not both.
▸ˌuniˌsexu'ality NOUN ▸ˌuni'sexually ADVERB

unison ('ju:nɪsᵊn, -zᵊn) NOUN 1 *Music* **a** the interval between two sounds of identical pitch. **b** (*modifier*) played or sung at the same pitch: *unison singing*. 2 complete agreement; harmony (esp in the phrase **in unison**).
▷HISTORY C16: from Late Latin *ūnisonus*, from UNI- + *sonus* sound
▸u'nisonous *or* u'nisonal *or* u'nisonant ADJECTIVE

UNISON ('ju:nɪsᵊn) NOUN (in Britain) a trade union representing local government, health care, and other workers: formed in 1993 by the amalgamation of COHSE, NALGO, and NUPE.

unit ('ju:nɪt) NOUN 1 a single undivided entity or whole. 2 any group or individual, esp when regarded as a basic element of a larger whole. 3 a mechanical part or integrated assembly of parts that performs a subsidiary function: *a filter unit*. 4 a complete system, apparatus, or establishment that performs a specific function: *a production unit*. 5 a subdivision of a larger military formation. 6 Also called: **unit of measurement**. a standard amount of a physical quantity, such as length, mass, energy, etc., specified multiples of which are used to express magnitudes of that physical quantity: *the second is a unit of time*. 7 the amount of a drug, vaccine, etc., needed to produce a particular effect. 8 a standard measure used in calculating alcohol intake and its effect. 9 *Maths* **a** (*usually plural*) the first position in a place-value counting system, representing a single-digit number: *in the decimal system the number 27 has 7 units and 2 tens*. **b** (*modifier*) having a value defined as one for the system: *unit vector*. 10 Also called: **unit set**. *Maths, logic* a set having a single member. 11 short for **home unit**. 12 short for **stock unit**. 13 *NZ* a self-propelled railcar.
▷HISTORY C16: back formation from UNITY, perhaps on the model of *digit*

Unit. ABBREVIATION FOR Unitarian.

UNITA (ju:'ni:tə) NOUN ACRONYM FOR União Nacional para a Independencia Total de Angola.
▷HISTORY Portuguese: National Union for the Total Independence of Angola

unitarian (ˌju:nɪ'tɛərɪən) NOUN 1 a supporter of unity or centralization. ◆ ADJECTIVE 2 of or relating to unity or centralization. 3 another word for **unitary**.

Unitarian (ˌju:nɪ'tɛərɪən) NOUN 1 *Theol* a person who believes that God is one being and rejects the doctrine of the Trinity. 2 *Ecclesiast* an upholder of Unitarianism, esp a member of the Church (**Unitarian Church**) that embodies this system of belief. ◆ ADJECTIVE 3 of or relating to Unitarians or Unitarianism.

unitarianism (ˌju:nɪ'tɛərɪəˌnɪzəm) NOUN any unitary system, esp of government.

Unitarianism (ˌju:nɪ'tɛərɪəˌnɪzəm) NOUN a system of Christian belief that maintains the unipersonality of God, rejects the Trinity and the divinity of Christ, and takes reason, conscience, and character as the criteria of belief and practice.

unitary ('ju:nɪtərɪ, -trɪ) ADJECTIVE 1 of a unit or units. 2 based on or characterized by unity. 3 individual; whole. 4 of or relating to a system of government in which all governing authority is held by the central government. Compare **federal**.

unitary authority NOUN (in the United Kingdom) a district administered by a single tier of local government, esp those districts of England that became administratively independent of the county councils in 1996–98.

unitary matrix NOUN *Maths* a square matrix that is the inverse of its Hermitian conjugate.

unit cell NOUN *Crystallog* the smallest group of atoms, ions, or molecules that is characteristic of a particular crystal lattice.

unit character NOUN *Genetics* a character inherited as a single unit and dependent on a single gene.

unit cost NOUN the actual cost of producing one article.

unite¹ (ju:'naɪt) VERB 1 to make or become an integrated whole or a unity; combine. 2 to join, unify or be unified in purpose, action, beliefs, etc. 3 to enter or cause to enter into an association or alliance. 4 to adhere or cause to adhere; fuse. 5 (*tr*) to possess or display (qualities) in combination or at the same time: *he united charm with severity*. 6 *Archaic* to join or become joined in marriage.
▷HISTORY C15: from Late Latin *ūnīre*, from *ūnus* one
▸u'niter NOUN

unite² ('ju:naɪt, ju:'naɪt) NOUN an English gold coin minted in the Stuart period, originally worth 20 shillings.
▷HISTORY C17: from obsolete *unite* joined, alluding to the union of England and Scotland (1603)

united (ju:'naɪtɪd) ADJECTIVE 1 produced by two or more persons or things in combination or from their union or amalgamation: *a united effort*. 2 in agreement. 3 in association or alliance.
▸u'nitedly ADVERB ▸u'nitedness NOUN

United Arab Emirates PLURAL NOUN a group of seven emirates in SW Asia, on the Persian Gulf: consists of Abu Dhabi, Dubai, Sharjah, Ajman, Umm al Qaiwain, Ras el Khaimah, and Fujairah; a former British protectorate; became fully independent in 1971; consists mostly of flat desert, with mountains in the east; rich petroleum resources. Official language: Arabic. Official religion: Muslim. Currency: dirham. Capital: Abu Dhabi. Pop.: 3 108 000 (2001 est.). Area: 83 600 sq. km (32 300 sq. miles). Former name (until 1971): **Trucial States**. Abbreviation: **UAE**.

United Arab Republic NOUN the official name (1958–71) of **Egypt**.

United Arab States PLURAL NOUN a federation (1958–61) between the United Arab Republic and Yemen.

United Church of Canada NOUN the largest Protestant denomination in Canada, formed in the 1920s by incorporating some Presbyterians and most Methodists.

United Church of Christ NOUN a US Protestant denomination formed in 1957 from the Evangelical and Reformed Church and the Congregational Christian Church.

United Empire Loyalist NOUN *Canadian history* any of the American colonists who settled in Canada during or after the War of American Independence because of loyalty to the British Crown.

United Kingdom NOUN a kingdom of NW Europe, consisting chiefly of the island of Great Britain together with Northern Ireland: became the world's leading colonial power in the 18th century: the first country to undergo the Industrial Revolution. It became the **United Kingdom of Great Britain and Northern Ireland** in 1921, after the rest of Ireland became autonomous as the Irish Free State. Primarily it is a trading nation, the chief exports being manufactured goods; joined the Common Market (now the European Union) in January 1973. Official language: English; Gaelic, Welsh, and other minority languages. Religion: Christian majority. Currency: pound sterling. Capital: London. Pop.: 58 789 194 (2001). Area: 244 110 sq. km (94 251 sq. miles). Abbreviation: **UK**. See also **Great Britain**.

United Kingdom Overseas Territory NOUN See **UK Overseas Territory**.

United Kingdom Unionists NOUN (in Britain) a political party, based in Northern Ireland: non-sectarian but opposed to a united Ireland.

United Nations NOUN (*functioning as singular or plural*) 1 an international organization of independent states, with its headquarters in New York City, that was formed in 1945 to promote peace and international cooperation and security. Abbreviation: **UN**. 2 (in World War II) a coalition of 26 nations that signed a joint declaration in Jan. 1942, pledging their full resources to defeating the Axis powers.

United Party NOUN (formerly, in South Africa) the major opposition party, founded by General Smuts in 1934: the official Opposition in Parliament from 1948, the party was disbanded in 1977. See also **National Party, Progressive Federal Party**.

United Provinces PLURAL NOUN 1 a Dutch republic (1581–1795) formed by the union of the seven northern provinces of the Netherlands, which were in revolt against their suzerain, Philip II of Spain. 2 short for **United Provinces of Agra and Oudh**: the former name of **Uttar Pradesh**.

United Reformed Church NOUN (in England and Wales) a Protestant denomination formed from the union of the Presbyterian and Congregational churches in 1972.

United States of America NOUN (*functioning as singular or plural*) a federal republic mainly in North America consisting of 50 states and the District of Columbia: colonized principally by the English and French in the 17th century, the native Indians being gradually defeated and displaced; 13 colonies under British rule made the Declaration of Independence in 1776 and became the United States after the War of American Independence. The northern states defeated the South in the Civil War (1861–65). It is the world's most productive industrial nation and also exports agricultural products. It participated reluctantly in World Wars I and II but since the establishment of the United Nations in 1945 has played a major role in international affairs. It consists generally of the Rocky Mountains in the west, the Great Plains in the centre, the Appalachians in the east, deserts in the southwest, and coastal lowlands and swamps in the southeast. Language: predominantly English; Spanish is also widely spoken. Religion: Christian majority. Currency: dollar. Capital: Washington, D.C. Pop.: 286 067 000 (2001 est.). Area: 9 518 323 sq. km (3 675 031 sq. miles). Often shortened to: **United States**. Abbreviations: **U.S., U.S.A.**

unit factor NOUN *Genetics* the gene responsible for the inheritance of a unit character.

unitive ('ju:nɪtɪv) ADJECTIVE 1 tending to unite or capable of uniting. 2 characterized by unity.
▸'unitively ADVERB

unitize *or* **unitise** ('ju:nɪˌtaɪz) VERB (*tr*) *Finance* to convert (an investment trust) into a unit trust.
▸ˌuniti'zation *or* ˌuniti'sation NOUN

unit-linked policy NOUN a life-assurance policy the investment benefits of which are directly in proportion to the number of units in a unit trust purchased on the policyholder's behalf. Compare **traditional policy**.

unit magnetic pole NOUN the strength of a magnetic pole that will repel a similar pole 1 centimetre distant from it, in a vacuum, with a force of 1 dyne.

unit of account NOUN 1 *Economics* the function of money that enables the user to keep accounts, value transactions, etc. 2 a monetary denomination used for accounting purposes, etc., but not necessarily corresponding to any real currency: *the ECU is the unit of account of the European Monetary Fund*. Also called (esp US and Canadian): **money of account**. 3 the unit of currency of a country.

unit price NOUN a price for foodstuffs, etc., stated or shown as the cost per unit, as per pound, per kilogram, per dozen, etc.

unit pricing NOUN a system of pricing foodstuffs, etc., in which the cost of a single unit is shown to enable shoppers to see the advantage of buying multipacks.

unit process NOUN *Chemical engineering* any of a number of standard operations, such as filtration or distillation, that are widely used in various chemical and process industries.

unit trust NOUN *Brit* an investment trust that issues units for public sale, the holders of which are creditors and not shareholders with their interests represented by a trust company independent of the issuing agency.

unity ('ju:nɪtɪ) NOUN, *plural* **-ties**. 1 the state or quality of being one; oneness. 2 the act, state, or quality of forming a whole from separate parts. 3 something whole or complete that is composed of separate parts. 4 mutual agreement; harmony or concord: *the participants were no longer in unity*. 5 uniformity or constancy: *unity of purpose*. 6 *Maths* **a** the number or numeral one. **b** a quantity assuming the value of one: *the area of the triangle was regarded*

as unity. **c** the element of a set producing no change in a number following multiplication. [7] the arrangement of the elements in a work of art in accordance with a single overall design or purpose. [8] any one of the three principles of dramatic structure deriving from Aristotle's *Poetics* by which the action of a play should be limited to a single plot (unity of action), a single location (unity of place), and the events of a single day (unity of time).
▷HISTORY C13: from Old French *unité,* from Latin *ūnitās,* from *ūnus* one

unity of interest NOUN *Property law* the equal interest in property held by joint tenants.

unity ticket NOUN *Austral* a how-to-vote card in a union election associating Labor and Communist candidates.

Univ. University.

univalent (ˌjuːnɪˈveɪlənt, juːˈnɪvələnt) ADJECTIVE [1] (of a chromosome during meiosis) not paired with its homologue. [2] *Chem* another word for **monovalent.**
▸ˌuniˈvalency NOUN

univalve (ˈjuːnɪˌvælv) *Zoology* ◆ ADJECTIVE [1] relating to, designating, or possessing a mollusc shell that consists of a single piece (valve). ◆ NOUN [2] a gastropod mollusc or its shell.

universal (ˌjuːnɪˈvɜːsᵊl) ADJECTIVE [1] of, relating to, or typical of the whole of mankind or of nature. [2] common to, involving, or proceeding from all in a particular group. [3] applicable to or affecting many individuals, conditions, or cases; general. [4] existing or prevailing everywhere. [5] applicable or occurring throughout or relating to the universe; cosmic: *a universal constant.* [6] (esp of a language) capable of being used and understood by all. [7] embracing or versed in many fields of knowledge, activity, interest, etc. [8] *Machinery* designed or adapted for a range of sizes, fittings, or uses. [9] *Linguistics* (of a constraint in a formal grammar) common to the grammatical description of all human languages, actual or possible. [10] *Logic* (of a statement or proposition) affirming or denying something about every member of a class, as in *all men are wicked.* Compare **particular** (sense 6). ◆ NOUN [11] *Philosophy* **a** a general term or concept or the type such a term signifies. **b** a metaphysical entity taken to be the reference of a general term, as distinct from the class of individuals it describes. **c** a Platonic Idea or Aristotelian form. [12] *Logic* **a** a universal proposition, statement, or formula. **b** a universal quantifier. [13] a characteristic common to every member of a particular culture or to every human being. [14] short for **universal joint.**
▸ˌuniˈversalness NOUN

> **Language note** The use of *more universal* as in *his writings have long been admired by fellow scientists, but his latest book should have more universal appeal* is acceptable in modern English usage.

universal beam NOUN a broad-flanged rolled steel joist suitable for a stanchion (axial load) or beam (bending load).

universal class *or* **set** NOUN (in Boolean algebra) the class containing all points and including all other classes.

universal donor NOUN a person who has blood of group O and whose blood may be safely transfused to persons with most other blood types.

universal gas constant NOUN another name for **gas constant.**

universal grammar NOUN *Linguistics* (in Chomskyan transformation linguistics) the abstract limitations on the formal grammatical description of all human languages, actual or possible, that make them human languages.

universalism (ˌjuːnɪˈvɜːsəˌlɪzəm) NOUN [1] a universal feature or characteristic. [2] another word for **universality.** [3] *Social welfare* the principle that welfare services should be available to all by right, according to need, and not restricted by individual ability to pay, but funded by general contributions through taxes, rates, or national insurance payments.

Universalism (ˌjuːnɪˈvɜːsəˌlɪzəm) NOUN a system of religious beliefs maintaining that all men are predestined for salvation.
▸ˌUniˈversalist NOUN, ADJECTIVE

universalist (ˌjuːnɪˈvɜːsəlɪst) NOUN [1] a person who has a wide range of interests, knowledge, activities, etc. ◆ ADJECTIVE [2] characterized by universality.
▸ˌuniˌversalˈistic ADJECTIVE

universality (ˌjuːnɪvɜːˈsælɪtɪ) NOUN the state or quality of being universal.

universalizability *or* **universalisability** (ˌjuːnɪˌvɜːsəlaɪzəˈbɪlɪtɪ) NOUN *Ethics* [1] the thesis that any moral judgment must be equally applicable to every relevantly identical situation. [2] the Kantian principle that if a course of action cannot be universally adopted it must be morally impermissible.

universalize *or* **universalise** (ˌjuːnɪˈvɜːsəˌlaɪz) VERB *(tr)* to make universal.
▸ˌuniˌversaliˈzation *or* ˌuniˌversaliˈsation NOUN

universal joint *or* **coupling** NOUN a form of coupling between two rotating shafts allowing freedom of angular movement in all directions.

universally (ˌjuːnɪˈvɜːsəlɪ) ADVERB everywhere or in every case; without exception: *this principle applies universally.*

universal motor NOUN an electric motor capable of working on either direct current or single-phase alternating current at approximately the same speed and output.

universal quantifier NOUN *Logic* a formal device indicating that the open sentence that follows is true of every member of the relevant universe of interpretation, as $(\forall x)(Fx \rightarrow Gx)$ or $(x)(Fx \rightarrow Gx)$, literally, for everything, if it is an F it is a G, that is, all Fs are Gs. Usual symbol: ∀.

Universal Soul *or* **Spirit** NOUN *Hinduism* Brahman in its aspect as the sacred syllable Om, the eternal and spiritual principle that permeates the universe.

universal time NOUN [1] (from 1928) name adopted internationally for Greenwich Mean Time (measured from Greenwich midnight), now split into several slightly different scales, one of which (UT1) is used by astronomers. Abbreviation: **UT.** [2] Also called: **universal coordinated time.** an internationally agreed system for civil timekeeping introduced in 1960 and redefined in 1972 as an atomic timescale. Available from broadcast signals, it has a second equal to the International Atomic Time (TAI) second, the difference between UTC and TAI being an integral number of seconds with leap seconds inserted when necessary to keep it within 0.9 seconds of UT1. Abbreviation: **UTC.**

universe (ˈjuːnɪˌvɜːs) NOUN [1] *Astronomy* the aggregate of all existing matter, energy, and space. [2] human beings collectively. [3] a province or sphere of thought or activity. [4] *Statistics* another word for **population** (sense 7).
▷HISTORY C16: from French *univers,* from Latin *ūniversum* the whole world, from *ūniversus* all together, from UNI- + *vertere* to turn

universe of discourse NOUN *Logic* the complete range of objects, events, attributes, relations, ideas, etc., that are expressed, assumed, or implied in a discussion.

university (ˌjuːnɪˈvɜːsɪtɪ) NOUN, *plural* **-ties.** [1] an institution of higher education having authority to award bachelors' and higher degrees, usually having research facilities. [2] the buildings, members, staff, or campus of a university.
▷HISTORY C14: from Old French *universite,* from Medieval Latin *universitās* group of scholars, from Late Latin: guild, society, body of men, from Latin: whole, totality, universe

university entrance NOUN (in New Zealand) **a** an examination taken by pupils of postprimary schools. **b** the certificate issued to a successful candidate. ◆ Abbreviation: **UE.**

univocal (ˌjuːnɪˈvəʊkᵊl) ADJECTIVE [1] unambiguous or unmistakable. ◆ NOUN [2] a word or term that has only one meaning.
▸ˌuniˈvocally ADVERB

UNIX (ˈjuːnɪks) NOUN *Trademark* a multi-user multitasking operating system found on many types of computer.

unjust (ʌnˈdʒʌst) ADJECTIVE not in accordance with accepted standards of fairness or justice; unfair.
▸unˈjustly ADVERB ▸unˈjustness NOUN

unjustifiable (ʌnˈdʒʌstɪˌfaɪəbᵊl) ADJECTIVE not capable of being justified.
▸unˈjustiˌfiably ADVERB

unjustified (ʌnˈdʒʌstɪˌfaɪd) ADJECTIVE not justified or vindicated: *an entirely unjustified attack.*

unkempt (ʌnˈkɛmpt) ADJECTIVE [1] (of the hair) uncombed; dishevelled. [2] ungroomed; slovenly: *unkempt appearance.* [3] *Archaic* crude or coarse.
▷HISTORY Old English *uncembed;* from UN-[1] + *cembed,* past participle of *cemban* to COMB; related to Old Saxon *kembian,* Old High German *kemben* to comb
▸unˈkemptly ADVERB ▸unˈkemptness NOUN

unkenned (ʌnˈkɛnd) *or* **unkent** (ʌnˈkɛnt) ADJECTIVE *Scot and N English dialect* unknown.
▷HISTORY C14: from UN-[1] + KEN

unkennel (ʌnˈkɛnᵊl) VERB **-nels, -nelling, -nelled** *or US* **-nels, -neling, -neled.** *(tr)* [1] to release from a kennel. [2] to drive from a hole or lair. [3] *Rare* to bring to light.

unkind (ʌnˈkaɪnd) ADJECTIVE [1] lacking kindness; unsympathetic or cruel. [2] *Archaic or dialect* **a** (of weather) unpleasant. **b** (of soil) hard to cultivate.
▸unˈkindly ADVERB ▸unˈkindness NOUN

unknit (ʌnˈnɪt) VERB **-knits, -knitting, -knitted** *or* **-knit.** [1] to make or become undone, untied, or unravelled. [2] *(tr)* to loosen, weaken, or destroy: *to unknit an alliance.* [3] *(tr) Rare* to smooth out (a wrinkled brow).

unknowable (ʌnˈnəʊəbᵊl) ADJECTIVE [1] incapable of being known or understood. [2] **a** beyond human understanding. **b** *(as noun): the unknowable.*
▸unˈknowableness *or* unˌknowaˈbility NOUN
▸unˈknowably ADVERB

Unknowable (ʌnˈnəʊəbᵊl) NOUN **the.** *Philosophy* the ultimate reality that underlies all phenomena but cannot be known.

unknowing (ʌnˈnəʊɪŋ) ADJECTIVE [1] not knowing; ignorant. [2] *(postpositive;* often foll by *of)* without knowledge or unaware (of).
▸unˈknowingly ADVERB

unknown (ʌnˈnəʊn) ADJECTIVE [1] not known, understood, or recognized. [2] not established, identified, or discovered: *an unknown island.* [3] not famous; undistinguished: *some unknown artist.* [4] **unknown quantity.** a person or thing whose action, effect, etc., is unknown or unpredictable. ◆ NOUN [5] an unknown person, quantity, or thing. [6] *Maths* a variable, or the quantity it represents, the value of which is to be discovered by solving an equation; a variable in a conditional equation: $3y = 4x + 5$ *is an equation in two unknowns.*
▸unˈknownness NOUN

Unknown Soldier *or* **Warrior** NOUN (in various countries) an unidentified soldier who has died in battle and for whom a tomb is established as a memorial to other unidentified dead of the nation's armed forces.

unlace (ʌnˈleɪs) VERB *(tr)* [1] to loosen or undo the lacing of (shoes, garments, etc.). [2] to unfasten or remove garments of (oneself or another) by or as if by undoing lacing.

unlade (ʌnˈleɪd) VERB a less common word for **unload.**

unlamented (ˌʌnləˈmɛntɪd) ADJECTIVE not missed, regretted, or grieved over: *his late unlamented father.*

unlash (ʌnˈlæʃ) VERB *(tr)* to untie or unfasten.

unlatch (ʌnˈlætʃ) VERB to open or unfasten or come open or unfastened by the lifting or release of a latch.

unlawful (ʌnˈlɔːfʊl) ADJECTIVE [1] illegal. [2] illicit; immoral: *unlawful love.* [3] an archaic word for **illegitimate.**
▸unˈlawfully ADVERB ▸unˈlawfulness NOUN

unlawful assembly NOUN *Law* a meeting of three or more people with the intent of carrying out any unlawful purpose.

unlay (ʌnˈleɪ) VERB **-lays, -laying, -laid.** *(tr)* to untwist (a rope or cable) to separate its strands.

unlead (ʌnˈlɛd) VERB *(tr)* [1] to strip off lead. [2] *Printing* to remove the leads or spaces from between (lines of type).

unleaded (ʌnˈlɛdɪd) ADJECTIVE [1] (of petrol) containing a reduced amount of tetraethyl lead, in order to reduce environmental pollution. [2] not covered or weighted with lead. [3] *Printing* (of lines of type, etc.) not spaced or separated with leads; solid. ◆ NOUN [4] petrol containing a reduced amount of tetraethyl lead.

unlearn (ʌn'lɜːn) VERB **-learns, -learning, -learned** (-'lɜːnd) *or* **-learnt.** to try to forget (something learnt) or to discard (accumulated knowledge).

unlearned (ʌn'lɜːnɪd) ADJECTIVE ignorant or untaught.
▸**un'learnedly** ADVERB

unlearnt (ʌn'lɜːnt) *or* **unlearned** (ʌn'lɜːnd) ADJECTIVE [1] denoting knowledge or skills innately present and therefore not learnt. [2] not learnt or taken notice of: *unlearnt lessons.*

unleash (ʌn'liːʃ) VERB *(tr)* [1] to release from or as if from a leash. [2] to free from restraint or control.

unleavened (ʌn'lɛvənd) ADJECTIVE (of bread, biscuits, etc.) made from a dough containing no yeast or leavening.

unless (ʌn'lɛs) CONJUNCTION [1] *(subordinating)* except under the circumstances that; except on the condition that: *they'll sell it unless he hears otherwise.* ◆ PREPOSITION [2] *Rare* except.
▷**HISTORY** C14: *onlesse,* from *on* ON + *lesse* LESS; compare French *à moins que,* literally: at less than

unlettered (ʌn'lɛtəd) ADJECTIVE [1] uneducated; illiterate. [2] not marked with letters: *an unlettered tombstone.*

unlevel (ʌn'lɛvᵊl) ADJECTIVE [1] not level. [2] unfair or inequitable; giving one person or group an unfair advantage: *an unlevel playing field.*

unlicensed (ʌn'laɪsənst) ADJECTIVE [1] having no licence: *an unlicensed restaurant.* [2] without permission; unauthorized. [3] unrestrained or lawless.

unlike (ʌn'laɪk) ADJECTIVE [1] not alike; dissimilar or unequal; different. [2] *Archaic* unlikely. ◆ PREPOSITION [3] not like; not typical of: *unlike his father he lacks intelligence.*
▸**un'likeness** NOUN

unlikely (ʌn'laɪklɪ) ADJECTIVE not likely; improbable.
▸**un'likeliness** *or* **un'likelihood** NOUN

unlimber (ʌn'lɪmbə) VERB [1] *(tr)* to disengage (a gun) from its limber. [2] to prepare (something) for use.

unlimited (ʌn'lɪmɪtɪd) ADJECTIVE [1] without limits or bounds: *unlimited knowledge.* [2] not restricted, limited, or qualified: *unlimited power.* [3] *Finance Brit* **a** (of liability) not restricted to any unpaid portion of nominal capital invested in a business. **b** (of a business enterprise) having owners with such unlimited liability.
▸**un'limitedly** ADVERB ▸**un'limitedness** NOUN

unlined (ʌn'laɪnd) ADJECTIVE [1] not having any lining. [2] (of paper) not marked with lines.

unlisted (ʌn'lɪstɪd) ADJECTIVE [1] not entered on a list. [2] *US and Canadian* (of a telephone number or telephone subscriber) not listed in a telephone directory. Brit term: **ex-directory.**

unlisted securities market NOUN a market on the London Stock Exchange, established in 1981, for trading in shares of smaller companies, who do not wish to comply with the requirements for a full listing. Abbreviation: **USM.**

unlistenable (ʌn'lɪsᵊnəbᵊl) ADJECTIVE impossible or unpleasant to listen to.

unlit (ʌn'lɪt) ADJECTIVE [1] not having lighting; unilluminated: *avoid unlit streets after dark.* [2] not having been ignited: *tapping his unlit cigarette.*

unlive (ʌn'lɪv) VERB *(tr)* to live so as to nullify, undo, or live down (past events or times).

unload (ʌn'ləʊd) VERB [1] to remove a load or cargo from (a ship, lorry, etc.). [2] to discharge (cargo, freight, etc.). [3] *(tr)* to relieve of a burden or troubles. [4] *(tr)* to give vent to (anxiety, troubles, etc.). [5] *(tr)* to get rid of or dispose of (esp surplus goods). [6] *(tr)* to remove the charge of ammunition from (a firearm).
▸**un'loader** NOUN

unlock (ʌn'lɒk) VERB [1] *(tr)* to unfasten (a lock, door, etc.). [2] *(tr)* to open, release, or let loose. [3] *(tr)* to disclose or provide the key to: *unlock a puzzle.* [4] *(intr)* to become unlocked.
▸**un'lockable** ADJECTIVE

unlocked (ʌn'lɒkt) ADJECTIVE not locked: *all those unlocked cars.*

unlooked-for (ˌʌn'lʊktfɔː) ADJECTIVE unexpected; unforeseen.

unloose (ʌn'luːs) *or* **unloosen** VERB *(tr)* [1] to set free; release. [2] to loosen or relax (a hold, grip, etc.). [3] to unfasten or untie.

unlovable *or* **unloveable** (ʌn'lʌvəbᵊl) ADJECTIVE not attracting or deserving love.

unloved (ʌn'lʌvd) ADJECTIVE not loved or cared for: *feeling neglected and unloved.*

unlovely (ʌn'lʌvlɪ) ADJECTIVE [1] unpleasant in appearance. [2] unpleasant in character.
▸**un'loveliness** NOUN

unloving (ʌn'lʌvɪŋ) ADJECTIVE not feeling or showing love and affection.

unlucky (ʌn'lʌkɪ) ADJECTIVE [1] characterized by misfortune or failure: *an unlucky person; an unlucky chance.* [2] ill-omened; inauspicious: *an unlucky date.* [3] regrettable; disappointing. [4] *Brit dialect* causing trouble; mischievous.
▸**un'luckily** ADVERB ▸**un'luckiness** NOUN

unmade (ʌn'meɪd) VERB [1] the past tense and past participle of **unmake.** ◆ ADJECTIVE [2] not yet made. [3] existing without having been made or created. [4] *Falconry* another word for **unmanned** (sense 4).

unmake (ʌn'meɪk) VERB **-makes, -making, -made.** *(tr)* [1] to undo or destroy. [2] to depose from office, rank, or authority. [3] to alter the nature of.
▸**un'maker** NOUN

unman (ʌn'mæn) VERB **-mans, -manning, -manned.** *(tr)* [1] to cause to lose courage or nerve. [2] to make effeminate. [3] to remove the men from. [4] *Archaic* to deprive of human qualities.

unmanageable (ʌn'mænɪdʒəbᵊl) ADJECTIVE difficult or impossible to control, use, or manipulate.

unmanly (ʌn'mænlɪ) ADJECTIVE [1] not masculine or virile. [2] ignoble, cowardly, or dishonourable.
▸**un'manliness** NOUN

unmanned (ʌn'mænd) ADJECTIVE [1] lacking personnel or crew: *an unmanned ship.* [2] (of aircraft, spacecraft, etc.) operated by automatic or remote control. [3] uninhabited. [4] *Falconry* (of a hawk or falcon) not yet trained to accept humans.

unmannered (ʌn'mænəd) ADJECTIVE [1] without good manners; coarse; rude. [2] not affected; without mannerisms.

unmannerly (ʌn'mænəlɪ) ADJECTIVE [1] lacking manners; discourteous. ◆ ADVERB [2] *Archaic* rudely; discourteously.
▸**un'mannerliness** NOUN

unmarked (ʌn'mɑːkt) ADJECTIVE [1] not carrying a mark or marks: *an unmarked police car.* [2] not noticed or observed.

unmarried (ʌn'mærɪd) ADJECTIVE [1] not married: *an unmarried mother.* [2] *Films* denoting a print of a cinematograph film in which the picture and sound recordings are on separate reels.

unmask (ʌn'mɑːsk) VERB [1] to remove (the mask or disguise) from (someone or oneself). [2] to appear or cause to appear in true character. [3] *(tr) Military* to make evident the presence of (weapons), either by firing or by the removal of camouflage, etc.
▸**un'masker** NOUN

unmatched (ʌn'mætʃt) ADJECTIVE [1] not equalled: *a landscape of unmatched beauty.* [2] (of socks, clothes, etc.) not matching: *unmatched dresses and stockings.*

unmeaning (ʌn'miːnɪŋ) ADJECTIVE [1] having no meaning. [2] showing no intelligence; vacant: *an unmeaning face.*
▸**un'meaningly** ADVERB ▸**un'meaningness** NOUN

unmeant (ʌn'mɛnt) ADJECTIVE unintentional; accidental.

unmeasured (ʌn'mɛʒəd) ADJECTIVE [1] measureless; limitless. [2] unrestrained; unlimited or lavish. [3] *Music* without bar lines and hence without a fixed pulse.
▸**un'measurable** ADJECTIVE ▸**un'measurableness** NOUN
▸**un'measurably** ADVERB ▸**un'measuredly** ADVERB

unmeet (ʌn'miːt) ADJECTIVE *Literary or archaic* not meet; unsuitable.
▸**un'meetly** ADVERB ▸**un'meetness** NOUN

unmemorable (ʌn'mɛmərəbᵊl, ʌn'mɛmrə-) ADJECTIVE not worth remembering or easily remembered.

unmentionable (ʌn'mɛnʃənəbᵊl) ADJECTIVE **a** unsuitable or forbidden as a topic of conversation. **b** *(as noun): the unmentionable.*
▸**un'mentionableness** NOUN ▸**un'mentionably** ADVERB

unmentionables (ʌn'mɛnʃənəbᵊlz) PLURAL NOUN *Chiefly humorous* underwear.

unmentioned (ʌn'mɛnʃənd) ADJECTIVE not referred to or spoken about.

unmerciful (ʌn'mɜːsɪfʊl) ADJECTIVE [1] showing no mercy; relentless. [2] extreme or excessive.
▸**un'mercifully** ADVERB ▸**un'mercifulness** NOUN

unmerited (ʌn'mɛrɪtɪd) ADJECTIVE not merited or deserved.

unmindful (ʌn'maɪndfʊl) ADJECTIVE *(usually postpositive* and foll by *of)* careless, heedless, or forgetful.
▸**un'mindfully** ADVERB ▸**un'mindfulness** NOUN

unmissable (ʌn'mɪsəbᵊl) ADJECTIVE (of a film, television programme, etc.) so good that it should not be missed.

unmistakable *or* **unmistakeable** (ˌʌnmɪs'teɪkəbᵊl) ADJECTIVE not mistakable; clear, obvious, or unambiguous.
▸**ˌunmis'takableness** *or* **ˌunmis'takeableness** NOUN
▸**ˌunmis'takably** *or* **ˌunmis'takeably** ADVERB

unmitigated (ʌn'mɪtɪˌgeɪtɪd) ADJECTIVE [1] not diminished in intensity, severity, etc. [2] *(prenominal)* (intensifier): *an unmitigated disaster.*
▸**un'mitiˌgatedly** ADVERB

unmolested (ˌʌnmə'lɛstɪd) ADJECTIVE not having been disturbed, accosted, or attacked.

unmoor (ʌn'mʊə, -'mɔː) VERB *Nautical* [1] to weigh the anchor or drop the mooring of (a vessel). [2] *(tr)* to reduce the mooring of (a vessel) to one anchor.

unmoral (ʌn'mɒrəl) ADJECTIVE outside morality; amoral.
▸**unmorality** (ˌʌnmɒ'rælɪtɪ) NOUN ▸**un'morally** ADVERB

unmoved (ʌn'muːvd) ADJECTIVE [1] not affected emotionally. [2] unchanged: *share price remained unmoved.*

unmoving (ʌn'muːvɪŋ) ADJECTIVE [1] not in motion: *the unmoving sea.* [2] still or constant: *an invisible but unmoving point.*

unmurmuring (ʌn'mɜːmərɪŋ) ADJECTIVE not complaining.

unmusical (ʌn'mjuːzɪkᵊl) ADJECTIVE [1] not musical or harmonious. [2] not talented in or appreciative of music.
▸**un'musically** ADVERB ▸**un'musicalness** NOUN

unmuzzle (ʌn'mʌzᵊl) VERB *(tr)* [1] to take the muzzle off (a dog, etc.). [2] to free from control or censorship.

unnamed (ʌn'neɪmd) ADJECTIVE [1] having no name. [2] not mentioned by name: *the culprit shall remain unnamed.*

unnatural (ʌn'nætʃərəl, -'nætʃrəl) ADJECTIVE [1] contrary to nature; abnormal. [2] not in accordance with accepted standards of behaviour or right and wrong: *unnatural love.* [3] uncanny; supernatural: *unnatural phenomena.* [4] affected or forced: *an unnatural manner.* [5] inhuman or monstrous; wicked: *an unnatural crime.* [6] *Obsolete* illegitimate.
▸**un'naturally** ADVERB ▸**un'naturalness** NOUN

unnecessary (ʌn'nɛsɪsərɪ, -ɪsrɪ) ADJECTIVE not necessary.
▸**un'necessarily** ADVERB ▸**un'necessariness** NOUN

unnerve (ʌn'nɜːv) VERB *(tr)* to cause to lose courage, strength, confidence, self-control, etc.

unnoticeable (ʌn'nəʊtɪsəbᵊl) ADJECTIVE not easily seen or detected; imperceptible.
▸**un'noticeably** ADVERB

unnoticed (ʌn'nəʊtɪst) ADJECTIVE not perceived or observed.

unnumbered (ʌn'nʌmbəd) ADJECTIVE [1] countless; innumerable. [2] not counted or assigned a number.

UNO ABBREVIATION FOR United Nations Organization.

unobserved (ˌʌnəb'zɜːvd) ADJECTIVE not seen or perceived.

unobstructed (ˌʌnəb'strʌktɪd) ADJECTIVE (of a passageway, view, etc.) not blocked by any object.

unobtainable (ˌʌnəb'teɪnəbᵊl) ADJECTIVE not able to be obtained.

unobtrusive (ˌʌnəbˈtruːsɪv) ADJECTIVE not noticeable or conspicuous.
▸ **ˌunobˈtrusively** ADVERB

unoccupied (ʌnˈɒkjʊˌpaɪd) ADJECTIVE [1] (of a building) without occupants. [2] unemployed or idle. [3] (of an area or country) not overrun by foreign troops.

unofficial (ˌʌnəˈfɪʃəl) ADJECTIVE [1] not official or formal: *an unofficial engagement.* [2] not confirmed officially: *an unofficial report.* [3] (of a strike) not approved by the strikers' trade union. [4] (of a medicinal drug) not listed in a pharmacopoeia.
▸ **ˌunofˈficially** ADVERB

unopened (ʌnˈəʊpənd) ADJECTIVE closed, barred, or sealed: *an unopened bottle of whisky.*

unopposed (ˌʌnəˈpəʊzd) ADJECTIVE not opposed: *elected unopposed as party president.*

unorganized *or* **unorganised** (ʌnˈɔːgəˌnaɪzd) ADJECTIVE [1] not arranged into an organized system, structure, or unity. [2] (of workers) not unionized. [3] nonliving; inorganic.

unoriginal (ˌʌnəˈrɪdʒɪnᵊl) ADJECTIVE not fresh and unusual.

unorthodox (ʌnˈɔːθəˌdɒks) ADJECTIVE not conventional in belief, behaviour, custom, etc.
▸ **unˈorthoˌdoxly** ADVERB

unpack (ʌnˈpæk) VERB [1] to remove the packed contents of (a case, trunk, etc.). [2] (*tr*) to take (something) out of a packed container. [3] (*tr*) to remove a pack from; unload: *to unpack a mule.*
▸ **unˈpacker** NOUN

unpaged (ʌnˈpeɪdʒd) ADJECTIVE (of a book) having no page numbers.

unpaid (ʌnˈpeɪd) ADJECTIVE [1] (of a bill, debt, etc.) not yet paid. [2] working without pay. [3] having wages outstanding.

unpalatable (ʌnˈpælətəbᵊl) ADJECTIVE [1] unpleasant to taste. [2] difficult to accept: *the unpalatable truth.*

unparalleled (ʌnˈpærəˌlɛld) ADJECTIVE unmatched; unequalled.

unpardonable (ʌnˈpɑːdᵊnəbᵊl) ADJECTIVE not excusable; disgraceful.

unparliamentary (ˌʌnpɑːləˈmɛntərɪ, -trɪ) ADJECTIVE not consistent with parliamentary procedure or practice.
▸ **ˌunparliaˈmentarily** ADVERB ▸ **ˌunparliaˈmentariness** NOUN

unpasteurized *or* **unpasteurised** (ʌnˈpæstəˌraɪzd, -stjə-, ʌnˈpɑː-) ADJECTIVE (of milk, beer, etc.) not subjected to pasteurization.

unpatriotic (ˌʌnpeɪtrɪˈɒtɪk, ˌʌnpæ-) ADJECTIVE not enthusiastically supporting one's country and its ways of life.

unpaved (ʌnˈpeɪvd) ADJECTIVE not covered in paving.

unpeg (ʌnˈpɛg) VERB **-pegs, -pegging, -pegged.** (*tr*) [1] to remove the peg or pegs from, esp to unfasten. [2] to allow (prices, wages, etc.) to rise and fall freely.

unpeople (ʌnˈpiːpᵊl) VERB (*tr*) to empty of people.

unperforated (ʌnˈpɜːfəˌreɪtɪd) ADJECTIVE (of a stamp) not provided with perforations.

unperson (ˈʌnpɜːsᵊn) NOUN a person whose existence is officially denied or ignored.

unpersuaded (ˌʌnpəˈsweɪdɪd) ADJECTIVE not having been induced, urged, or prevailed upon successfully.

unperturbed (ˌʌnpəˈtɜːbd) ADJECTIVE not disturbed or troubled: *unperturbed by the prospect of a fight.*

unpick (ʌnˈpɪk) VERB (*tr*) [1] to undo (the stitches) of (a piece of sewing). [2] to unravel or undo (a garment, etc.). [3] *Obsolete* to open (a door, lock, etc.) by picking.

unpicked (ʌnˈpɪkt) ADJECTIVE (of knitting, sewing, etc.) having been unravelled or picked out.

unpin (ʌnˈpɪn) VERB **-pins, -pinning, -pinned.** (*tr*) [1] to remove a pin or pins from. [2] to unfasten by removing pins.

unplaced (ʌnˈpleɪst) ADJECTIVE [1] not given or put in a particular place. [2] *Horse racing* not in the first three (sometimes four) runners in a race.

unplanned (ʌnˈplænd) ADJECTIVE not planned: *an unplanned baby.*

unplayable (ʌnˈpleɪəbᵊl) ADJECTIVE [1] not able to be played: *an almost unplayable ball.* [2] not able to be played on: *unplayable pitches.*

unpleasant (ʌnˈplɛzᵊnt) ADJECTIVE not pleasant or agreeable.
▸ **unˈpleasantly** ADVERB

unpleasantness (ʌnˈplɛzᵊntnɪs) NOUN [1] the state or quality of being unpleasant. [2] an unpleasant event, situation, etc. [3] a disagreement or quarrel.

unplug (ʌnˈplʌg) VERB **-plugs, -plugging, -plugged.** (*tr*) [1] to disconnect (an electrical appliance) by taking the plug out of the socket. [2] to remove a plug or obstruction from.

unplugged (ʌnˈplʌgd) ADJECTIVE (of a performer or performance of popular music) using acoustic rather than electric instruments: *Eric Clapton unplugged; an unplugged version of the song.*

unplumbed (ʌnˈplʌmd) ADJECTIVE [1] unfathomed; unsounded. [2] not understood in depth. [3] (of a building) having no plumbing.

unpolitic (ʌnˈpɒlɪtɪk) ADJECTIVE another word for **impolitic.**

unpolled (ʌnˈpəʊld) ADJECTIVE [1] not included in an opinion poll. [2] not having voted. [3] *US* not registered for an election: *unpolled votes.*

unpolluted (ˌʌnpəˈluːtɪd) ADJECTIVE [1] not affected or contaminated by pollution. [2] untainted; pure: *unpolluted by the corruption of Europe.*

unpopular (ʌnˈpɒpjʊlə) ADJECTIVE not popular with an individual or group of people.
▸ **unpopularity** (ˌʌnpɒpjʊˈlærɪtɪ) NOUN ▸ **unˈpopularly** ADVERB

unpractical (ʌnˈpræktɪkᵊl) ADJECTIVE another word for **impractical.**
▸ **ˌunpractiˈcality** *or* **unˈpracticalness** NOUN
▸ **unˈpractically** ADVERB

unpractised *or US* **unpracticed** (ʌnˈpræktɪst) ADJECTIVE [1] without skill, training, or experience. [2] not used or done often or repeatedly. [3] not yet tested.

unprecedented (ʌnˈprɛsɪˌdɛntɪd) ADJECTIVE having no precedent; unparalleled.
▸ **unˈpreceˌdentedly** ADVERB

unpredictable (ˌʌnprɪˈdɪktəbᵊl) ADJECTIVE not capable of being predicted; changeable.
▸ **ˌunpreˌdictaˈbility** *or* **ˌunpreˈdictableness** NOUN
▸ **ˌunpreˈdictably** ADVERB

unprejudiced (ʌnˈprɛdʒʊdɪst) ADJECTIVE not prejudiced or biased; impartial.
▸ **unˈprejudicedly** ADVERB

unpremeditated (ˌʌnprɪˈmɛdɪˌteɪtɪd) ADJECTIVE not planned beforehand; spontaneous.
▸ **ˌunpreˈmediˌtatedly** ADVERB ▸ **ˌunpreˌmediˈtation** NOUN

unprepared (ˌʌnprɪˈpɛəd) ADJECTIVE [1] having made inadequate preparations. [2] not made ready or prepared. [3] done without preparation; extemporaneous.
▸ **ˌunpreˈparedly** ADVERB ▸ **ˌunpreˈparedness** NOUN

unprepossessing (ˌʌnpriːpəˈzɛsɪŋ) ADJECTIVE not creating a favourable impression; unattractive.

unpretentious (ˌʌnprɪˈtɛnʃəs) ADJECTIVE not making claim to distinction or importance undeservedly.

unpriced (ʌnˈpraɪst) ADJECTIVE [1] having no fixed or marked price. [2] *Poetic* beyond price; priceless.

unprincipled (ʌnˈprɪnsɪpᵊld) ADJECTIVE [1] lacking moral principles; unscrupulous. [2] (foll by *in*) *Archaic* not versed in the principles of (a subject).
▸ **unˈprincipledness** NOUN

unprintable (ʌnˈprɪntəbᵊl) ADJECTIVE unsuitable for printing for reasons of obscenity, libel, bad taste, etc.
▸ **unˈprintableness** NOUN ▸ **unˈprintably** ADVERB

unprocessed (ʌnˈprəʊsest) ADJECTIVE (of food, oil, etc.) not having undergone a process to preserve or purify.

unproductive (ˌʌnprəˈdʌktɪv) ADJECTIVE [1] (often foll by *of*) not productive of (anything). [2] not producing goods and services with exchange value.
▸ **ˌunproˈductively** ADVERB ▸ **ˌunproˈductiveness** NOUN

unprofessional (ˌʌnprəˈfɛʃənᵊl) ADJECTIVE [1] contrary to the accepted code of conduct of a profession. [2] amateur. [3] not belonging to or having the required qualifications for a profession.
▸ **ˌunproˈfessionally** ADVERB

unprofitable (ʌnˈprɒfɪtəbᵊl) ADJECTIVE [1] not making a profit. [2] not fruitful or beneficial.
▸ **unˌprofitaˈbility** *or* **unˈprofitableness** NOUN
▸ **unˈprofitably** ADVERB

unpromising (ʌnˈprɒmɪsɪŋ) ADJECTIVE not showing any promise of favourable development or future success.

unprompted (ʌnˈprɒmptɪd) ADJECTIVE without prompting; spontaneous.

unpronounceable (ˌʌnprəˈnaʊnsəbᵊl) ADJECTIVE not able to be uttered or articulated.

unprotected (ˌʌnprəˈtɛktɪd) ADJECTIVE not protected or safe from trouble, harm, etc.: *an unprotected position.*

unprotected sex NOUN an act of sexual intercourse or sodomy performed without the use of a condom thus involving the risk of sexually transmitted diseases.

unprotesting (ˌʌnprəˈtɛstɪŋ) ADJECTIVE without complaint or disagreement.

unproved (ʌnˈpruːvd) ADJECTIVE not having been established as true, valid, or possible.

unproven (ʌnˈpruːvᵊn) ADJECTIVE [1] not established as true by evidence or demonstration: *unproven allegations.* [2] (of a new product, system, treatment, etc.) not tried or tested.

unprovided (ˌʌnprəˈvaɪdɪd) ADJECTIVE (*postpositive*) [1] (foll by *with*) not provided or supplied. [2] (often foll by *for*) not prepared or ready. [3] **unprovided for.** without income or means.
▸ **ˌunproˈvidedly** ADVERB

unprovoked (ʌnprəˈvəʊkt) ADJECTIVE not provoked by anything done or said.

unpublished (ˌʌnˈpʌblɪʃt) ADJECTIVE [1] not available in print for distribution and sale. [2] having no written work issued for publication: *an unpublished undergraduate.*

unpunished (ʌnˈpʌnɪʃt) ADJECTIVE not receiving or having received a penalty or sanction as punishment for any crime or offence.

unputdownable (ˌʌnpʊtˈdaʊnəbᵊl) ADJECTIVE (of a book, esp a novel) so gripping as to be read right through at one sitting.

unqualified (ʌnˈkwɒlɪˌfaɪd) ADJECTIVE [1] lacking the necessary qualifications. [2] not restricted or modified: *an unqualified criticism.* [3] (*usually prenominal*) (intensifier): *an unqualified success.*
▸ **unˈqualiˌfiable** ADJECTIVE ▸ **unˈqualiˌfiedly** ADVERB
▸ **unˈqualiˌfiedness** NOUN

unquantifiable (ʌnˈkwɒntɪˌfaɪəbᵊl) ADJECTIVE not capable of being quantified.

unquestionable (ʌnˈkwɛstʃənəbᵊl) ADJECTIVE [1] indubitable or indisputable. [2] not admitting of exception or qualification: *an unquestionable decision.*
▸ **unˌquestionaˈbility** *or* **unˈquestionableness** NOUN

unquestionably (ʌnˈkwɛstʃənəblɪ) ADVERB [1] indisputably; definitely: *an unquestionably great club.* [2] (*sentence modifier*) without a doubt; certainly: *unquestionably there were costs incurred.*

unquestioned (ʌnˈkwɛstʃənd) ADJECTIVE [1] accepted without question. [2] not admitting of doubt or question: *unquestioned power.* [3] not questioned or interrogated. [4] *Rare* not examined or investigated.

unquestioning (ʌnˈkwɛstʃənɪŋ) ADJECTIVE accepting something without expressing doubt or uncertainty.

unquiet (ʌnˈkwaɪət) *Chiefly literary* ◆ ADJECTIVE [1] characterized by disorder, unrest, or tumult: *unquiet times.* [2] anxious; uneasy. ◆ NOUN [3] a state of unrest.
▸ **unˈquietly** ADVERB ▸ **unˈquietness** NOUN

unquote (ʌnˈkwəʊt) INTERJECTION [1] an expression used parenthetically to indicate that the preceding quotation is finished. ◆ VERB [2] to close (a quotation), esp in printing.

unravel (ʌnˈrævᵊl) VERB **-els, -elling, -elled** *or US* **-els, -eling, -eled.** [1] (*tr*) to reduce (something knitted or woven) to separate strands. [2] (*tr*) to undo or untangle (something tangled or knotted). [3] (*tr*) to explain or solve: *the mystery was unravelled.* [4] (*intr*) to become unravelled.
▸ **unˈraveller** NOUN ▸ **unˈravelment** NOUN

unreactive (ˌʌnrɪˈæktɪv) ADJECTIVE (of a substance) not readily partaking in chemical reactions.

unread (ʌnˈrɛd) ADJECTIVE [1] (of a book, newspaper, etc.) not yet read. [2] (of a person) having read little. [3] (*postpositive;* foll by *in*) not versed (in a specified field).

unreadable (ʌnˈriːdəb^{ə}l) ADJECTIVE [1] illegible; undecipherable. [2] difficult or tedious to read.
▸**unˌreadaˈbility** *or* **unˈreadableness** NOUN ▸**unˈreadably** ADVERB

unready (ʌnˈrɛdɪ) ADJECTIVE [1] not ready or prepared. [2] slow or hesitant to see or act. [3] *Archaic* not dressed.
▸**unˈreadily** ADVERB ▸**unˈreadiness** NOUN

unreal (ʌnˈrɪəl) ADJECTIVE [1] imaginary or fanciful or seemingly so: *an unreal situation.* [2] having no actual existence or substance. [3] insincere or artificial.
▸**unˈreally** ADVERB

unrealistic (ˌʌnrɪəˈlɪstɪk) ADJECTIVE not realistic: *unrealistic expectations.*

unreality (ˌʌnrɪˈælɪtɪ) NOUN [1] the quality or state of being unreal, fanciful, or impractical. [2] something that is unreal.

unrealized *or* **unrealised** (ʌnˈrɪəˌlaɪzd) ADJECTIVE (of an amibition, hope, goal, etc.) not attained or brought to fruition.

unreason (ʌnˈriːz^{ə}n) NOUN [1] irrationality or madness. [2] something that lacks or is contrary to reason. [3] lack of order; chaos. ◆ VERB [4] (*tr*) to deprive of reason.

unreasonable (ʌnˈriːznəb^{ə}l) ADJECTIVE [1] immoderate; excessive: *unreasonable demands.* [2] refusing to listen to reason. [3] lacking reason or judgment.
▸**unˈreasonableness** NOUN ▸**unˈreasonably** ADVERB

unreasonable behaviour NOUN *Law* conduct by a spouse sufficient to cause the irretrievable breakdown of a marriage.

unreasoning (ʌnˈriːzənɪŋ) ADJECTIVE not controlled by reason; irrational.
▸**unˈreasoningly** ADVERB

unreckonable (ʌnˈrɛkənəb^{ə}l) ADJECTIVE incalculable; unlimited.

unrecognizable *or* **unrecognisable** (ʌnˈrɛkəgˌnaɪzəb^{ə}l) ADJECTIVE not able to be recognized or identified: *tiny unrecognizable fragments.*

unrecognized *or* **unrecognised** (ʌnˈrɛkəgˌnaɪzd) ADJECTIVE [1] not recognized or identified: *hitherto unrecognized planets.* [2] not given formal acknowledgment of legal status: *the unrecognized Communist Workers' Party.*

unreconstructed (ˌʌnriːkənsˈtrʌktɪd) ADJECTIVE *Chiefly US* unwilling to accept social and economic change, as exemplified by those White Southerners who refused to accept the Reconstruction after the Civil War.

unrecorded (ˌʌnrɪˈkɔːdɪd) ADJECTIVE not recorded on paper, tape, video tape, etc.

unreeve (ʌnˈriːv) VERB **-reeves, -reeving, -rove** *or* **-reeved.** *Nautical* to withdraw (a rope) from a block, thimble, etc.
▹HISTORY C17: from UN-^{2} + REEVE^2

unrefined (ˌʌnrɪˈfaɪnd) ADJECTIVE [1] (of substances such as petroleum, ores, and sugar) not processed into a pure or usable form. [2] coarse in manners or language.

unreflected (ˌʌnrɪˈflɛktɪd) ADJECTIVE [1] (foll by *on* or *upon*) not considered. [2] (of light, particles, etc., incident on a surface) not reflected; absorbed or transmitted.

unreflective (ˌʌnrɪˈflɛktɪv) ADJECTIVE not reflective or thoughtful; rash; unthinking.
▸**ˌunreˈflectively** ADVERB

unregenerate (ˌʌnrɪˈdʒɛnərɪt) ADJECTIVE *also* **unregenerated.** [1] unrepentant; unreformed. [2] obstinately adhering to one's own views. ◆ NOUN [3] an unregenerate person.
▸**ˌunreˈgeneracy** NOUN ▸**ˌunreˈgenerately** ADVERB

unregistered (ʌnˈrɛdʒɪstəd) ADJECTIVE not registered: *driving an unregistered vehicle.*

unregulated (ʌnˈrɛgjʊˌleɪtɪd) ADJECTIVE not regulated; uncontrolled.

unrehearsed (ˌʌnrɪˈhɜːst) ADJECTIVE (of a play, speech, etc.) not having been practised in advance.

unrelated (ˌʌnrɪˈleɪtɪd) ADJECTIVE [1] not connected or associated: *an unrelated incident.* [2] not connected by kinship or marriage.

unrelenting (ˌʌnrɪˈlɛntɪŋ) ADJECTIVE [1] refusing to relent or take pity; relentless; merciless. [2] not diminishing in determination, speed, effort, force, etc.
▸**ˌunreˈlentingly** ADVERB ▸**ˌunreˈlentingness** NOUN

unreliable (ˌʌnrɪˈlaɪəb^{ə}l) ADJECTIVE not reliable; untrustworthy: *an unreliable witness.*

unreligious (ˌʌnrɪˈlɪdʒəs) ADJECTIVE [1] another word for **irreligious.** [2] secular.
▸**ˌunreˈligiously** ADVERB

unremarkable (ˌʌnrɪˈmɑːkəb^{ə}l) ADJECTIVE not worthy of note or attention.

unremitting (ˌʌnrɪˈmɪtɪŋ) ADJECTIVE never slackening or stopping; unceasing; constant.
▸**ˌunreˈmittingly** ADVERB ▸**ˌunreˈmittingness** NOUN

unrepair (ˌʌnrɪˈpɛə) NOUN a less common word for **disrepair.**
▸**ˌunreˈpaired** ADJECTIVE

unrepeatable (ˌʌnrɪˈpiːtəb^{ə}l) ADJECTIVE [1] not capable of being repeated. [2] not fit to be repeated, esp due to swearing or lewdness: *his stories were unrepeatable.*

unrepentant (ˌʌnrɪˈpɛntənt) ADJECTIVE not repentant or contrite.

unreported (ˌʌnrɪˈpɔːtɪd) ADJECTIVE not reported or recorded: *unreported cases.*

unrepresentative (ˌʌnrɛprɪˈzɛntətɪv) ADJECTIVE not typical or representative.

unrepresented (ʌnrɛprɪˈzɛntɪd) ADJECTIVE **a** not having representation. **b** (*as collective noun;* preceded by *the*): *we intend to represent the unrepresented.*

unrequited (ˌʌnrɪˈkwaɪtɪd) ADJECTIVE (of love, affection, etc.) not reciprocated or returned.

unreserved (ˌʌnrɪˈzɜːvd) ADJECTIVE [1] without reserve; having an open manner. [2] without reservation. [3] not booked or bookable.
▸**unreservedly** (ˌʌnrɪˈzɜːvɪdlɪ) ADVERB ▸**ˌunreˈservedness** NOUN

unresisting (ˌʌnrɪˈzɪstɪŋ) ADJECTIVE not fighting against something or someone; yielding: *she lay unresisting beneath him.*

unresolved (ˌʌnrɪˈzɒlvd) ADJECTIVE (of a problem or dispute) not having been solved or concluded.

unresponsive (ˌʌnrɪˈspɒnsɪv) ADJECTIVE not reacting or responding to an action, question, suggestion, etc.

unrest (ʌnˈrɛst) NOUN [1] a troubled or rebellious state of discontent. [2] an uneasy or troubled state.

unrestrained (ˌʌnrɪˈstreɪnd) ADJECTIVE not restrained or checked; free or natural.
▸**unrestrainedly** (ˌʌnrɪˈstreɪnɪdlɪ) ADVERB

unrestricted (ˌʌnrɪˈstrɪktɪd) ADJECTIVE not restricted or limited in any way: *unrestricted access.*

unrevealed (ˌʌnrɪˈviːld) ADJECTIVE not having been disclosed, divulged, revealed, etc.
▸**ˌunreˈvealing** ADJECTIVE

unrewarded (ˌʌnrɪˈwɔːdɪd) ADJECTIVE not having received any reward or advantages.

unrewarding (ˌʌnrɪˈwɔːdɪŋ) ADJECTIVE not giving personal satisfaction.

unriddle (ʌnˈrɪd^{ə}l) VERB (*tr*) to solve or puzzle out.
▹HISTORY C16: from UN-^{2} + RIDDLE^1
▸**unˈriddler** NOUN

unrifled (ʌnˈraɪf^{ə}ld) ADJECTIVE (of a firearm or its bore) not rifled; smoothbore.

unrig (ʌnˈrɪg) VERB **-rigs, -rigging, -rigged.** [1] (*tr*) to strip (a vessel) of standing and running rigging. [2] *Archaic or dialect* to undress (someone or oneself).

unrighteous (ʌnˈraɪtʃəs) ADJECTIVE [1] **a** sinful; wicked. **b** (*as collective noun;* preceded by *the*): *the unrighteous.* [2] not fair or right; unjust.
▸**unˈrighteously** ADVERB ▸**unˈrighteousness** NOUN

unrip (ʌnˈrɪp) VERB **-rips, -ripping, -ripped.** (*tr*) [1] to rip open. [2] *Obsolete* to reveal; disclose.

unripe (ʌnˈraɪp) *or* **unripened** ADJECTIVE [1] not fully matured. [2] not fully prepared or developed; not ready. [3] *Obsolete* premature or untimely.
▸**unˈripeness** NOUN

unrivalled *or US* **unrivaled** (ʌnˈraɪv^{ə}ld) ADJECTIVE having no equal; matchless.

unroll (ʌnˈrəʊl) VERB [1] to open out or unwind (something rolled, folded, or coiled) or (of something rolled, etc.) to become opened out or unwound. [2] to make or become visible or apparent, esp gradually; unfold.

unromantic (ˌʌnrəʊˈmæntɪk) ADJECTIVE not of, related to, imbued with, or characterized by romance.

unroot (ʌnˈruːt) VERB (*tr*) *Chiefly US* a less common word for **uproot.**

unrounded (ʌnˈraʊndɪd) ADJECTIVE *Phonetics* articulated with the lips spread; not rounded.

unruffled (ʌnˈrʌf^{ə}ld) ADJECTIVE [1] unmoved; calm. [2] still: *the unruffled seas.*
▸**unˈruffledness** NOUN

unruly (ʌnˈruːlɪ) ADJECTIVE **-lier, -liest.** disposed to disobedience or indiscipline.
▸**unˈruliness** NOUN

unruly certificate NOUN an informal name for **certificate of unruliness.**

UNRWA (ˈʌnrə) NOUN ACRONYM FOR United Nations Relief and Works Agency.

unsaddle (ʌnˈsæd^{ə}l) VERB [1] to remove the saddle from (a horse, mule, etc.). [2] (*tr*) to unhorse.

unsaddling enclosure NOUN the area at a racecourse where horses are unsaddled after a race and often where awards are given to owners, trainers, and jockeys.

unsafe (ʌnˈseɪf) ADJECTIVE [1] not safe; perilous. [2] (of a criminal conviction) based on inadequate or false evidence.

unsaid (ʌnˈsɛd) ADJECTIVE not said or expressed; unspoken.

unsaleable *or US* **unsalable** (ʌnˈseɪləb^{ə}l) ADJECTIVE not capable of being sold.

unsalted (ʌnˈsɔːltɪd) ADJECTIVE not seasoned, preserved, or treated with salt: *unsalted peanuts.*

unsanctioned (ʌnˈsæŋkʃənd) ADJECTIVE not having been given permission or authorization.

unsanitary (ʌnˈsænɪtərɪ, -trɪ) ADJECTIVE not conducive to or promoting health; dirty or unhygienic.

unsatisfactory (ˌʌnsætɪsˈfæktərɪ, -trɪ) ADJECTIVE not adequate or suitable; unacceptable.

unsatisfied (ʌnˈsætɪsˌfaɪd) ADJECTIVE (of a person, demand, need, etc.) not satisfied or fulfilled: *an unsatisfied demand for fresh fruit.*

unsatisfying (ʌnˈsætɪsˌfaɪɪŋ) ADJECTIVE not fulfilling or satisfactory: *it was inherently unsatisfying work.*

unsaturated (ʌnˈsætʃəˌreɪtɪd) ADJECTIVE [1] not saturated. [2] (of a chemical compound, esp an organic compound) containing one or more double or triple bonds and thus capable of undergoing addition reactions. [3] (of a fat, esp a vegetable fat) containing a high proportion of fatty acids having double bonds. [4] (of a solution) containing less solute than a saturated solution.
▸**ˌunsatuˈration** NOUN

unsavoury *or US* **unsavory** (ʌnˈseɪvərɪ) ADJECTIVE [1] objectionable or distasteful: *an unsavoury character.* [2] disagreeable in odour or taste.
▸**unˈsavourily** *or* (*US*) **unˈsavorily** ADVERB ▸**unˈsavouriness** *or* (*US*) **unˈsavoriness** NOUN

unsay (ʌnˈseɪ) VERB **-says, -saying, -said.** (*tr*) to retract or withdraw (something said or written).

unscathed (ʌnˈskeɪðd) ADJECTIVE not harmed or injured.

unscented (ʌnˈsɛntɪd) ADJECTIVE not filled or impregnated with odour or fragrance.

unscheduled (ʌnˈʃɛdjuːld) ADJECTIVE not arranged or planned according to a programme, timetable, etc.

unschooled (ʌnˈskuːld) ADJECTIVE [1] having received no training or schooling. [2] spontaneous; natural: *unschooled talent.*

unscientific (ˌʌnsaɪənˈtɪfɪk) ADJECTIVE [1] not consistent with the methods or principles of science, esp lacking objectivity. [2] ignorant of science.
▸**ˌunscienˈtifically** ADVERB

unscramble (ʌnˈskræmb^{ə}l) VERB (*tr*) [1] to resolve from confusion or disorderliness. [2] to restore (a scrambled message) to an intelligible form.
▸**unˈscrambler** NOUN

unscratched (ʌnˈskrætʃt) ADJECTIVE quite unharmed.

unscreened (ʌnˈskriːnd) ADJECTIVE [1] not sheltered or concealed by a screen. [2] not passed through a screen; unsifted. [3] (of a film) not yet on show to the public. [4] not put through a security check.

unscrew (ʌnˈskruː) VERB [1] (*tr*) to draw or remove a screw from (an object). [2] (*tr*) to loosen (a screw, lid, etc.) by rotating continuously, usually in an anticlockwise direction. [3] (*intr*) (esp of an engaged threaded part) to become loosened or separated: *the lid wouldn't unscrew.*

unscripted (ʌnˈskrɪptɪd) ADJECTIVE (of a speech, play, etc.) not using or based on a script.

unscrupulous (ʌnˈskruːpjʊləs) ADJECTIVE without scruples; unprincipled.
▸**unˈscrupulously** ADVERB ▸**unˈscrupulousness** *or* **unscrupulosity** (ʌnˌskruːpjʊˈlɒsɪtɪ) NOUN

unseal (ʌnˈsiːl) VERB (*tr*) [1] to remove or break the seal of. [2] to reveal or free (something concealed or closed as if sealed): *to unseal one's lips.*
▸**unˈsealable** ADJECTIVE

unseam (ʌnˈsiːm) VERB (*tr*) to open or undo the seam of.

unseasonable (ʌnˈsiːzənəbᵊl) ADJECTIVE [1] (esp of the weather) inappropriate for the season. [2] untimely; inopportune.
▸**unˈseasonableness** NOUN ▸**unˈseasonably** ADVERB

unseasoned (ʌnˈsiːzənd) ADJECTIVE [1] (of persons) not sufficiently experienced: *unseasoned troops.* [2] not matured or seasoned: *unseasoned timber.* [3] (of food) not flavoured with seasoning.
▸**unˈseasonedness** NOUN

unseat (ʌnˈsiːt) VERB (*tr*) [1] to throw or displace from a seat, saddle, etc. [2] to depose from office or position.

unseaworthy (ʌnˈsiːwɜːðɪ) ADJECTIVE not in a fit condition or ready for a sea voyage.

unsecured (ˌʌnsɪˈkjʊəd) ADJECTIVE [1] *Finance* **a** (of a loan, etc.) secured only against general assets and not against a specific asset. **b** (of a creditor) having no security against a specific asset and with a claim inferior to those of secure creditors. [2] not made secure; loose.

unseeded (ʌnˈsiːdɪd) ADJECTIVE (of players in various sports) not assigned to a preferential position in the preliminary rounds of a tournament. See **seed** (sense 18).

unseeing (ʌnˈsiːɪŋ) ADJECTIVE with one's eyes open but not noticing or perceiving anything.

unseelie (ʌnˈsiːlɪ) PLURAL NOUN **the.** [1] evil malevolent fairies. ◆ ADJECTIVE [2] **a** of or belonging to the unseelie. **b** evil and malevolent like the unseelie: *unseelie wights.*
▷HISTORY Old English *unsǣlig*; compare SEELIE and SILLY

unseemly (ʌnˈsiːmlɪ) ADJECTIVE [1] not in good style or taste; unbecoming. [2] *Obsolete* unattractive. ◆ ADVERB [3] *Rare* in an unseemly manner.
▸**unˈseemliness** NOUN

unseen (ʌnˈsiːn) ADJECTIVE [1] not observed or perceived; invisible. [2] (of passages of writing) not previously seen or prepared. ◆ NOUN [3] *Chiefly Brit* a passage, not previously seen, that is presented to students for translation.

unselfconscious (ˌʌnselfˈkɒnʃəs) ADJECTIVE not unduly aware of oneself as the object of attention of others.

unselfish (ʌnˈselfɪʃ) ADJECTIVE not selfish or greedy; generous.
▸**unˈselfishly** ADVERB ▸**unˈselfishness** NOUN

unsentimental (ˌʌnsentɪˈmentᵊl) ADJECTIVE not tending to indulge the emotions excessively: *a frank and unsentimental account.*

unset (ʌnˈset) ADJECTIVE [1] not yet solidified or firm. [2] (of a gem) not yet in a setting. [3] (of textual matter) not yet composed.

unsettle (ʌnˈsetᵊl) VERB [1] (*usually tr*) to change or become changed from a fixed or settled condition. [2] (*tr*) to confuse or agitate (emotions, the mind, etc.).
▸**unˈsettlement** NOUN

unsettled (ʌnˈsetᵊld) ADJECTIVE [1] lacking order or stability: *an unsettled era.* [2] unpredictable; uncertain: *an unsettled climate.* [3] constantly changing or moving from place to place: *an unsettled life.* [4] (of controversy, etc.) not brought to an agreed conclusion. [5] (of debts, law cases, etc.) not disposed of. [6] (of regions, etc.) devoid of settlers.
▸**unˈsettledness** NOUN

unsex (ʌnˈseks) VERB (*tr*) *Chiefly literary* to deprive (a person) of the attributes of his or her sex, esp to make a woman more callous.

unshakable *or* **unshakeable** (ʌnˈʃeɪkəbᵊl) ADJECTIVE (of beliefs, convictions, etc.) utterly firm and unwavering.
▸**unˈshakableness** *or* **unˈshakeableness** NOUN
▸**unˈshakably** *or* **unˈshakeably** ADVERB

unshaken (ʌnˈʃeɪkᵊn) ADJECTIVE not disturbed or moved from a position or belief.

unshapen (ʌnˈʃeɪpᵊn) ADJECTIVE [1] having no definite shape; shapeless. [2] deformed; misshapen.

unshaven (ʌnˈʃeɪvᵊn) ADJECTIVE not having shaved or been shaven recently.

unsheathe (ʌnˈʃiːð) VERB (*tr*) to draw or pull out (something, esp a weapon) from a sheath or other covering.

unship (ʌnˈʃɪp) VERB **-ships, -shipping, -shipped.** [1] to be or cause to be unloaded, discharged, or disembarked from a ship. [2] (*tr*) *Nautical* to remove from a regular place: *to unship oars.*

unsighted (ʌnˈsaɪtɪd) ADJECTIVE [1] not sighted. [2] not having a clear view. [3] **a** (of a gun) not equipped with a sight. **b** (of a shot) not aimed by means of a sight.
▸**unˈsightedly** ADVERB

unsightly (ʌnˈsaɪtlɪ) ADJECTIVE unpleasant or unattractive to look at; ugly.
▸**unˈsightliness** NOUN

unsigned (ʌnˈsaɪnd) ADJECTIVE [1] not signed: *an unsigned typewritten note.* [2] not having a plus or minus sign. [3] *Computing* not having a bit representing a plus or minus sign.

unsinkable (ʌnˈsɪŋkəbᵊl) ADJECTIVE not capable of sinking or being sunk.

unsized[1] (ʌnˈsaɪzd) ADJECTIVE not made or sorted according to size.

unsized[2] (ʌnˈsaɪzd) ADJECTIVE (of a wall, etc.) not treated with size.

unskilful *or US* **unskillful** (ʌnˈskɪlfʊl) ADJECTIVE [1] lacking dexterity or proficiency. [2] (often foll by *in*) *Obsolete* ignorant (of).
▸**unˈskilfully** *or (US)* **unˈskillfully** ADVERB ▸**unˈskilfulness** *or (US)* **unˈskillfulness** NOUN

unskilled (ʌnˈskɪld) ADJECTIVE [1] not having or requiring any special skill or training: *unskilled workers; an unskilled job.* [2] having or displaying no skill; inexpert: *he is quite unskilled at dancing.*

unslaked lime (ʌnˈsleɪkt) NOUN another name for **calcium oxide.** Compare **slaked lime.**

unsling (ʌnˈslɪŋ) VERB **-slings, -slinging, -slung.** (*tr*) [1] to remove or release from a slung position. [2] to remove slings from.

unsmiling (ʌnˈsmaɪlɪŋ) ADJECTIVE not wearing or assuming a smile; serious.

unsnap (ʌnˈsnæp) VERB **-snaps, -snapping, -snapped.** (*tr*) to unfasten (the snap or catch) of (something).

unsnarl (ʌnˈsnɑːl) VERB (*tr*) to free from a snarl or tangle.

unsociable (ʌnˈsəʊʃəbᵊl) ADJECTIVE [1] (of a person) disinclined to associate or fraternize with others. [2] unconducive to social intercourse: *an unsociable neighbourhood.*
▸**unˌsociaˈbility** *or* **unˈsociableness** NOUN ▸**unˈsociably** ADVERB

unsocial (ʌnˈsəʊʃəl) ADJECTIVE [1] not social; antisocial. [2] (of the hours of work of certain jobs) falling outside the normal working day.

unsold (ʌnˈsəʊld) ADJECTIVE not sold: *quantities of unsold stock.*

unsolicited (ˌʌnsəˈlɪsɪtɪd) ADJECTIVE not requested or invited: *unsolicited advice.*

unsolved (ʌnˈsɒlvd) ADJECTIVE not having been solved or explained: *several unsolved murders.*
▸**unˈsolvable** ADJECTIVE

unsophisticated (ˌʌnsəˈfɪstɪˌkeɪtɪd) ADJECTIVE [1] lacking experience or worldly wisdom. [2] marked by a lack of refinement or complexity: *an unsophisticated machine.* [3] unadulterated or genuine.
▸**ˌunsoˈphistiˌcatedly** ADVERB ▸**ˌunsoˈphistiˌcatedness** *or* **ˌunsoˌphistiˈcation** NOUN

unsound (ʌnˈsaʊnd) ADJECTIVE [1] diseased, weak, or unstable: *of unsound mind.* [2] unreliable or fallacious: *unsound advice.* [3] lacking solidity, strength, or firmness: *unsound foundations.* [4] of doubtful financial or commercial viability: *an unsound enterprise.* [5] (of fruit, timber, etc.) not in an edible or usable condition.
▸**unˈsoundly** ADVERB ▸**unˈsoundness** NOUN

unsparing (ʌnˈspeərɪŋ) ADJECTIVE [1] not sparing or frugal; lavish; profuse. [2] showing harshness or severity; unmerciful.
▸**unˈsparingly** ADVERB ▸**unˈsparingness** NOUN

unspeak (ʌnˈspiːk) VERB **-speaks, -speaking, -spoke, -spoken.** an obsolete word for **unsay.**

unspeakable (ʌnˈspiːkəbᵊl) ADJECTIVE [1] incapable of expression in words: *unspeakable ecstasy.* [2] indescribably bad or evil. [3] not to be uttered: *unspeakable thoughts.*
▸**unˈspeakableness** NOUN ▸**unˈspeakably** ADVERB

unspecific (ˌʌnspɪˈsɪfɪk) ADJECTIVE not explicit, particular, or definite.

unspecified (ʌnˈspesɪˌfaɪd) ADJECTIVE not referred to or stated specifically.

unspectacular (ˌʌnspekˈtækjʊlə) ADJECTIVE not of or resembling a spectacle; unimpressive: *a steady if unspectacular performance.*

unsphere (ʌnˈsfɪə) VERB (*tr*) *Chiefly poetic* to remove from its, one's, etc., sphere or place.

unspoiled (ʌnˈspɔɪld) *or* **unspoilt** (ʌnˈspɔɪlt) ADJECTIVE (of a village, town, etc.) having an unaltered character.

unspoken (ʌnˈspəʊkən) ADJECTIVE [1] understood without needing to be spoken; tacit. [2] not uttered aloud.

unsporting (ʌnˈspɔːtɪŋ) ADJECTIVE not relating or conforming to sportsmanship; unfair.

unsportsmanlike (ʌnˈspɔːtsmənˌlaɪk) ADJECTIVE lacking in sportsmanship.

unspotted (ʌnˈspɒtɪd) ADJECTIVE [1] without spots or stains. [2] (esp of reputations) free from moral stigma or blemish.
▸**unˈspottedness** NOUN

unstable (ʌnˈsteɪbᵊl) ADJECTIVE [1] lacking stability, fixity, or firmness. [2] disposed to temperamental, emotional, or psychological variability. [3] (of a chemical compound) readily decomposing. [4] *Physics* **a** (of an elementary particle) having a very short lifetime. **b** spontaneously decomposing by nuclear decay; radioactive: *an unstable nuclide.* [5] *Electronics* (of an electrical circuit, mechanical body, etc.) having a tendency to self-oscillation.
▸**unˈstableness** NOUN ▸**unˈstably** ADVERB

unstarry (ʌnˈstɑːrɪ) ADJECTIVE not resembling or characteristic of a star from the entertainment world: *their simple unstarry ways.*

unstated (ʌnˈsteɪtɪd) ADJECTIVE not having been articulated or uttered.

unsteady (ʌnˈstedɪ) ADJECTIVE [1] not securely fixed: *an unsteady foothold.* [2] (of behaviour, etc.) lacking constancy; erratic. [3] without regularity: *an unsteady rhythm.* [4] (of a manner of walking, etc.) precarious or staggering, as from intoxication. ◆ VERB **-steadies, -steadying, -steadied.** [5] (*tr*) to make unsteady.
▸**unˈsteadily** ADVERB ▸**unˈsteadiness** NOUN

unsteel (ʌnˈstiːl) VERB (*tr*) to make (the heart, feelings, etc.) more gentle or compassionate.

unstep (ʌnˈstep) VERB **-steps, -stepping, -stepped.** (*tr*) *Nautical* to remove (a mast) from its step.

unsterile (ʌnˈsteraɪl) ADJECTIVE not free from living, esp pathogenic, microorganisms.

unstick (ʌnˈstɪk) VERB **-sticks, -sticking, -stuck.** (*tr*) to free or loosen (something stuck).

unstinting (ʌnˈstɪntɪŋ) ADJECTIVE not frugal or miserly; generous: *hard work and unstinting support.*

unstop (ʌnˈstɒp) VERB **-stops, -stopping, -stopped.** (*tr*) [1] to remove the stop or stopper from. [2] to free from any stoppage or obstruction; open. [3] to draw out the stops on (an organ).

unstoppable (ʌnˈstɒpəbᵊl) ADJECTIVE not capable of being stopped; extremely forceful.
▸**unˈstoppably** ADVERB

unstopped (ʌnˈstɒpt) ADJECTIVE [1] not obstructed or stopped up. [2] *Phonetics* denoting a speech sound for whose articulation the closure is not complete, as in the pronunciation of a vowel, fricative, or continuant. [3] *Prosody* (of verse) having the sense of the line carried over into the next. [4] (of an organ pipe or a string on a musical instrument) not stopped.

unstrained (ʌn'streɪnd) ADJECTIVE [1] not under strain; relaxed. [2] not cleared or separated by passing through a strainer.

unstratified (ʌn'strætɪˌfaɪd) ADJECTIVE (esp of igneous rocks and rock formations) not occurring in distinct layers or strata; not stratified.

unstreamed (ʌn'striːmd) ADJECTIVE *Brit education* (of children) not divided into groups or streams according to ability.

unstressed (ʌn'strɛst) ADJECTIVE [1] carrying relatively little stress; unemphasized. [2] *Phonetics* of, relating to, or denoting the weakest accent in a word or breath group, which in some languages, such as English or German, is also associated with a reduction in vowel quality to a centralized (i) or (a). [3] *Prosody* (of a syllable in verse) having no stress or accent.

unstriated (ʌn'straɪˌeɪtɪd) ADJECTIVE (of muscle) composed of elongated cells that do not have striations; smooth.

unstring (ʌn'strɪŋ) VERB **-strings, -stringing, -strung**. (*tr*) [1] to remove the strings of. [2] (of beads, pearls, etc.) to remove or take from a string. [3] to weaken or enfeeble emotionally (a person or his nerves).

unstriped (ʌn'straɪpt) ADJECTIVE (esp of smooth muscle) not having stripes; unstriated.

unstructured (ʌn'strʌktʃəd) ADJECTIVE [1] without formal structure or systematic organization. [2] without a preformed shape; (esp of clothes) loose; untailored.

unstrung (ʌn'strʌŋ) ADJECTIVE [1] emotionally distressed; unnerved. [2] (of a stringed instrument) with the strings detached.

unstuck (ʌn'stʌk) ADJECTIVE [1] freed from being stuck, glued, fastened, etc. [2] **come unstuck**. to suffer failure or disaster.

unstudied (ʌn'stʌdɪd) ADJECTIVE [1] natural; unaffected. [2] (foll by *in*) without knowledge or training.

unsubscribe (ˌʌnsəb'skraɪb) VERB (*intr*) to cancel a subscription, for example to an emailing service: *you can unsubscribe at the following URL*.

unsubstantial (ˌʌnsəb'stænʃəl) ADJECTIVE [1] lacking weight, strength, or firmness. [2] (esp of an argument) of doubtful validity. [3] of no material existence or substance; unreal.
▸ **ˌunsubˌstantiˈality** NOUN ▸ **ˌunsubˈstantially** ADVERB

unsubstantiated (ˌʌnsəb'stænʃɪˌeɪtɪd) ADJECTIVE not established as valid or genuine: *unsubstantiated allegations*.

unsubtle (ʌn'sʌtᵊl) ADJECTIVE not subtle; obvious or blatant.

unsuccessful (ˌʌnsək'sɛsfʊl) ADJECTIVE not having succeeded.
▸ **unsuccessfully** ADVERB

unsuitable (ʌn'suːtəbᵊl, ʌn'sjuːt-) ADJECTIVE not appropriate, suitable, or fit.

unsuited (ʌn'suːtɪd, ʌn'sjuː-) ADJECTIVE [1] not appropriate for a particular purpose: *temperamentally unsuited to his role*. [2] (of two people) not likely to have a successful relationship.

unsullied (ʌn'sʌlɪd) ADJECTIVE (of a reputation, etc.) not stained or tarnished.

unsung (ʌn'sʌŋ) ADJECTIVE [1] not acclaimed or honoured: *unsung deeds*. [2] not yet sung.

unsupervised (ʌn'suːpəˌvaɪzd, ʌn'sjuː-) ADJECTIVE without supervision: *playing unsupervised in the garden*.

unsupportable (ˌʌnsə'pɔːtəbᵊl) ADJECTIVE [1] not able to be supported. [2] not able to be defended: *unsupportable actions*.

unsupported (ˌʌnsə'pɔːtɪd) ADJECTIVE [1] not supported physically, financially, or emotionally: *unable to sit up unsupported*. [2] not upheld by evidence or facts; unsubstantiated.

unsure (ʌn'ʃʊə) ADJECTIVE [1] lacking assurance or self-confidence. [2] (*usually postpositive*) without sure knowledge; uncertain: *unsure of her agreement*. [3] precarious; insecure. [4] not certain or reliable.

unsurmountable (ˌʌnsɜː'maʊntəbᵊl) ADJECTIVE (of a problem, etc.) not capable of being solved or overcome.

unsurpassed (ˌʌnsɜː'pɑːst) ADJECTIVE superior in achievement or excellence to any other: *of an unsurpassed quality*.
▸ **ˌunsurˈpassable** ADJECTIVE

unsurprised (ˌʌnsə'praɪzd) ADJECTIVE not feeling amazement or wonder.

unsuspected (ˌʌnsə'spɛktɪd) ADJECTIVE [1] not under suspicion. [2] not known to exist.
▸ **ˌunsusˈpectedly** ADVERB ▸ **ˌunsusˈpectedness** NOUN

unsuspecting (ˌʌnsə'spɛktɪŋ) ADJECTIVE disposed to trust; not suspicious; trusting.
▸ **ˌunsusˈpectingly** ADVERB

unswear (ʌn'swɛə) VERB **-swears, -swearing, -swore, -sworn**. to retract or revoke (a sworn oath); abjure.

unsweetened (ʌn'swiːtᵊnd) ADJECTIVE not having any added sugar or other sweeteners.

unswerving (ʌn'swɜːvɪŋ) ADJECTIVE not turning aside; constant.

unsympathetic (ˌʌnsɪmpə'θɛtɪk) ADJECTIVE [1] not characterized by, feeling, or showing sympathy. [2] (when *postpositive*, often followed by *to* or *towards*) not showing agreement (with) or favour (towards).

untainted (ʌn'teɪntɪd) ADJECTIVE not tarnished, contaminated, or polluted: *he was untainted by the scandal*.

untalented (ʌn'tæləntɪd) ADJECTIVE lacking in talent: *an untalented but gorgeous actress*.

untamable *or* **untameable** (ʌn'teɪməbᵊl) ADJECTIVE (of an animal or person) not capable of being tamed, subdued, or made obedient.

untamed (ʌn'teɪmd) ADJECTIVE not cultivated, domesticated, or controlled: *beautiful untamed wilderness*.

untangle (ʌn'tæŋgᵊl) VERB (*tr*) [1] to free from a tangled condition. [2] to free from perplexity or confusion.

untapped (ʌn'tæpt) ADJECTIVE not yet used: *previously untapped resources*.

untarnished (ʌn'tɑːnɪʃt) ADJECTIVE [1] (of silver, etc.) not tarnished or discoloured. [2] not tainted or spoiled: *untarnished by graffiti*.

untaught (ʌn'tɔːt) ADJECTIVE [1] without training or education. [2] attained or achieved without instruction.

untaxed (ʌn'tækst) ADJECTIVE not subject to taxation.

unteach (ʌn'tiːtʃ) VERB **-teaches, -teaching, -taught**. (*tr*) *Rare* to cause to disbelieve (teaching).

untenable (ʌn'tɛnəbᵊl) ADJECTIVE [1] (of theories, propositions, etc.) incapable of being maintained, defended, or vindicated. [2] unable to be maintained against attack. [3] *Rare* (of a house, etc.) unfit for occupation.
▸ **unˌtenaˈbility** *or* **unˈtenableness** NOUN ▸ **unˈtenably** ADVERB

untended (ʌn'tɛndɪd) ADJECTIVE not cared for or attended to.

Unter den Linden (*German* 'ʊntər deːn 'lɪndən) NOUN the main street of Berlin, formerly in East Berlin, extending to the Brandenburg Gate.

Unterwalden (*German* 'ʊntərˌvaldən) NOUN a canton of central Switzerland, on Lake Lucerne: consists of the demicantons of **Nidwalden** (east) and **Obwalden** (west). Capitals: (Nidwalden) Stans; (Obwalden) Sarnen. Pop.: (Nidwalden) 37 700 (2000 est.); (Obwalden) 32 200 (2000 est.). Areas: (Nidwalden) 274 sq. km (107 sq. miles); (Obwalden) 492 sq. km (192 sq. miles).

untested (ʌn'tɛstɪd) ADJECTIVE not having been tested or examined.

untethered (ʌn'tɛðəd) ADJECTIVE not tied or limited with or as if with a tether.

unthink (ʌn'θɪŋk) VERB **-thinks, -thinking, -thought**. (*tr*) [1] to reverse one's opinion about. [2] to dispel from the mind.

unthinkable (ʌn'θɪŋkəbᵊl) ADJECTIVE [1] not to be contemplated; out of the question. [2] unimaginable; inconceivable. [3] unreasonable; improbable.
▸ **unˌthinkaˈbility** *or* **unˈthinkableness** NOUN ▸ **unˈthinkably** ADVERB

unthinking (ʌn'θɪŋkɪŋ) ADJECTIVE [1] lacking thoughtfulness; inconsiderate. [2] heedless; inadvertent: *it was done in an unthinking moment*. [3] not thinking or able to think.
▸ **unˈthinkingly** ADVERB ▸ **unˈthinkingness** NOUN

unthought-of (ʌn'θɔːtɒv) ADJECTIVE unimaginable; inconceivable.

unthread (ʌn'θrɛd) VERB (*tr*) [1] to draw out the thread or threads from (a needle, etc.). [2] to disentangle.

unthrone (ʌn'θrəʊn) VERB (*tr*) a less common word for **dethrone**.

untidy (ʌn'taɪdɪ) ADJECTIVE **-dier, -diest**. [1] not neat; slovenly. ◆ VERB **-dies, -dying, -died**. [2] (*tr*) to make untidy.
▸ **unˈtidily** ADVERB ▸ **unˈtidiness** NOUN

untie (ʌn'taɪ) VERB **-ties, -tying, -tied**. [1] to unfasten or free (a knot or something that is tied) or (of a knot or something that is tied) to become unfastened. [2] (*tr*) to free from constraint or restriction.

until (ʌn'tɪl) CONJUNCTION (*subordinating*) [1] up to (a time) that: *he laughed until he cried*. [2] (*used with a negative*) before (a time or event): *until you change, you can't go out*. ◆ PREPOSITION [3] (often preceded by *up*) in or throughout the period before: *he waited until six*. [4] (*used with a negative*) earlier than; before: *he won't come until tomorrow*.
▷ **HISTORY** C13 *untill*; related to Old High German *unt* unto, until, Old Norse *und*; see TILL[1]

> **Language note** The use of *until such time as* (as in *industrial action will continue until such time as our demands are met*) is unnecessary and should be avoided: *industrial action will continue until our demands are met*. See also at **till[1]**.

untimely (ʌn'taɪmlɪ) ADJECTIVE [1] occurring before the expected, normal, or proper time: *an untimely death*. [2] inappropriate to the occasion, time, or season: *his joking at the funeral was most untimely*. ◆ ADVERB [3] prematurely or inopportunely.
▸ **unˈtimeliness** NOUN

untiring (ʌn'taɪrɪŋ) ADJECTIVE (of a person or their actions) continuing or persisting without declining in strength or vigour.

untitled (ʌn'taɪtᵊld) ADJECTIVE [1] without a title: *an untitled manuscript*. [2] having no claim or title: *an untitled usurper*.

unto ('ʌntuː) PREPOSITION an archaic word for **to**.
▷ **HISTORY** C13: of Scandinavian origin; see UNTIL

untogether (ˌʌntə'gɛðə) ADJECTIVE *Slang* incompetent or badly organized; mentally or emotionally unstable.

untold (ʌn'təʊld) ADJECTIVE [1] incapable of description or expression: *untold suffering*. [2] incalculably great in number or quantity: *untold thousands*. [3] not told.

untouchable (ʌn'tʌtʃəbᵊl) ADJECTIVE [1] lying beyond reach. [2] above reproach, suspicion, or impeachment. [3] unable to be touched. ◆ NOUN [4] also called: **Dalit**. a member of the lowest class in India, whom those of the four main castes were formerly forbidden to touch.
▸ **unˌtouchaˈbility** NOUN

untouched (ʌn'tʌtʃt) ADJECTIVE [1] not used, handled, touched, etc. [2] not injured or harmed. [3] (*postpositive*) emotionally unmoved. [4] not changed, modified, or affected. [5] (of food or drink) left without being consumed. [6] not mentioned or referred to: *he left the subject untouched*.

untoward (ˌʌntə'wɔːd, ʌn'təʊəd) ADJECTIVE [1] characterized by misfortune, disaster, or annoyance. [2] not auspicious; adverse; unfavourable. [3] unseemly or improper. [4] out of the ordinary; out of the way. [5] *Archaic* refractory; perverse. [6] *Obsolete* awkward, ungainly, or uncouth.
▸ **ˌuntoˈwardly** ADVERB ▸ **ˌuntoˈwardness** NOUN

untrained (ʌn'treɪnd) ADJECTIVE not having been trained: *untrained volunteers*.

untrammelled *or US* **untrammeled** (ʌn'træmᵊld) ADJECTIVE not hindered or restricted in thought or action.

untranslated (ˌʌntræns'leɪtɪd, ˌʌntrænz-) ADJECTIVE not having been expressed or written down in another language or dialect.

untravelled *or US* **untraveled** (ʌnˈtrævᵊld) ADJECTIVE [1] (of persons) not having travelled widely; narrow or provincial. [2] (of a road) never travelled over.

untread (ʌnˈtrɛd) VERB **-treads, -treading, -trod, -trodden** *or* **-trod**. (*tr*) *Rare* to retrace (a course, path, etc.).

untreated (ʌnˈtriːtɪd) ADJECTIVE [1] (of an illness, etc.) not having been dealt with. [2] not having been processed in any way: *untreated sewage*.

untried (ʌnˈtraɪd) ADJECTIVE [1] not tried, attempted, or proved; untested. [2] not tried by a judge or court.

untroubled (ʌnˈtrʌblᵊd) ADJECTIVE not feeling, showing, or involving anxiety, worry, or discomfort.

untrue (ʌnˈtruː) ADJECTIVE [1] incorrect or false. [2] disloyal. [3] diverging from a rule, standard, or measure; inaccurate.
▸**unˈtrueness** NOUN ▸**unˈtruly** ADVERB

untruss (ʌnˈtrʌs) VERB [1] (*tr*) to release from or as if from a truss; unfasten. [2] *Obsolete* to undress.

untrustworthy (ʌnˈtrʌstˌwɜːðɪ) ADJECTIVE not worthy of being trusted: *untrustworthy witnesses*.

untruth (ʌnˈtruːθ) NOUN [1] the state or quality of being untrue. [2] a statement, fact, etc., that is not true.

untruthful (ʌnˈtruːθfʊl) ADJECTIVE [1] (of a person) given to lying. [2] diverging from the truth; untrue.
▸**unˈtruthfully** ADVERB ▸**unˈtruthfulness** NOUN

untuck (ʌnˈtʌk) VERB to become or cause to become loose or not tucked in: *to untuck the blankets*.

unturned (ʌnˈtɜːnd) ADJECTIVE not turned: *unturned pages*.

untutored (ʌnˈtjuːtəd) ADJECTIVE [1] without formal instruction or education. [2] lacking sophistication or refinement.

untypical (ʌnˈtɪpɪkᵊl) ADJECTIVE not representative or characteristic of a particular type, person, etc.

unusable (ʌnˈjuːzəbᵊl) ADJECTIVE not able or fit to be used.

unused ADJECTIVE [1] (ʌnˈjuːzd) not being or never having been made use of. [2] (ʌnˈjuːst) (*postpositive; foll by to*) not accustomed or used (to something).

unusual (ʌnˈjuːʒʊəl) ADJECTIVE out of the ordinary; uncommon; extraordinary: *an unusual design*.
▸**unˈusually** ADVERB ▸**unˈusualness** NOUN

unutterable (ʌnˈʌtərəbᵊl) ADJECTIVE incapable of being expressed in words.
▸**unˈutterableness** NOUN ▸**unˈutterably** ADVERB

unvaccinated (ʌnˈvæksɪˌneɪtɪd) ADJECTIVE (of a person or animal) not having been inoculated with a vaccine.

unvalued (ʌnˈvæljuːd) ADJECTIVE [1] not appreciated or valued. [2] not assessed or estimated as to price or valuation. [3] *Obsolete* of great value.

unvarnished (ʌnˈvɑːnɪʃt) ADJECTIVE not elaborated upon or glossed; plain and direct: *the unvarnished truth*.

unveil (ʌnˈveɪl) VERB [1] (*tr*) to remove the cover or shroud from, esp in the ceremonial unveiling of a monument, etc. [2] to remove the veil from (one's own or another person's face). [3] (*tr*) to make (something secret or concealed) known or public; divulge; reveal.

unveiling (ʌnˈveɪlɪŋ) NOUN [1] a ceremony involving the removal of a veil at the formal presentation of a statue, monument, etc., for the first time. [2] the presentation of something, esp for the first time.

unverified (ʌnˈvɛrɪˌfaɪd) ADJECTIVE not having been confirmed, substantiated, or proven to be true.
▸**unˈveriˌfiable** ADJECTIVE

unviable (ʌnˈvaɪəbᵊl) ADJECTIVE not capable of succeeding, esp financially: *the pit had proved economically unviable*.

unvoice (ʌnˈvɔɪs) VERB (*tr*) [1] to pronounce without vibration of the vocal cords. [2] another word for **devoice**.

unvoiced (ʌnˈvɔɪst) ADJECTIVE [1] not expressed or spoken. [2] articulated without vibration of the vocal cords; voiceless.

unwaged (ʌnˈweɪdʒd) ADJECTIVE of, relating to, or denoting a person who is not receiving pay because of either being unemployed or working in the home.

unwanted (ʌnˈwɒntɪd) ADJECTIVE not wanted or desired: *an unwanted pregnancy*.

unwarrantable (ʌnˈwɒrəntəbᵊl) ADJECTIVE incapable of vindication or justification.
▸**unˈwarrantableness** NOUN ▸**unˈwarrantably** ADVERB

unwarranted (ʌnˈwɒrəntɪd) ADJECTIVE [1] lacking justification or authorization. [2] another word for **unwarrantable.**

unwary (ʌnˈwɛərɪ) ADJECTIVE lacking caution or prudence; not vigilant or careful.
▸**unˈwarily** ADVERB ▸**unˈwariness** NOUN

unwashed (ʌnˈwɒʃt) ADJECTIVE [1] not washed. ◆ PLURAL NOUN [2] **the great unwashed.** *Informal and derogatory* the masses.

unwatched (ʌnˈwɒtʃt) ADJECTIVE (of an automatic device, such as a beacon) not manned.

unwavering (ʌnˈweɪvərɪŋ) ADJECTIVE not wavering or hesitant; resolute.

unwaxed (ʌnˈwækst) ADJECTIVE not treated with wax, esp of oranges or lemons, not sprayed with a protective coating of wax.

unwearied (ʌnˈwɪərɪd) ADJECTIVE [1] not abating or tiring. [2] not fatigued; fresh.
▸**unˈweariedly** ADVERB ▸**unˈweariedness** NOUN

unweighed (ʌnˈweɪd) ADJECTIVE [1] (of quantities purchased, etc.) not measured for weight. [2] (of statements, etc.) not carefully considered.

unwelcome (ʌnˈwɛlkəm) ADJECTIVE [1] (of persons) not welcome. [2] causing dissatisfaction or displeasure.
▸**unˈwelcomely** ADVERB ▸**unˈwelcomeness** NOUN

unwell (ʌnˈwɛl) ADJECTIVE (*postpositive*) not well; ill.

unwept (ʌnˈwɛpt) ADJECTIVE [1] not wept for or lamented. [2] *Rare* (of tears) not shed.

unwholesome (ʌnˈhəʊlsəm) ADJECTIVE [1] detrimental to physical or mental health: *an unwholesome climate*. [2] morally harmful or depraved: *unwholesome practices*. [3] indicative of illness, esp in appearance. [4] (esp of food) of inferior quality.
▸**unˈwholesomely** ADVERB ▸**unˈwholesomeness** NOUN

unwieldy (ʌnˈwiːldɪ) *or* **unwieldly** ADJECTIVE [1] too heavy, large, or awkwardly shaped to be easily handled. [2] ungainly; clumsy.
▸**unˈwieldily** *or* **unˈwieldlily** ADVERB ▸**unˈwieldiness** *or* **unˈwieldliness** NOUN

unwilled (ʌnˈwɪld) ADJECTIVE not intentional; involuntary.

unwilling (ʌnˈwɪlɪŋ) ADJECTIVE [1] unfavourably inclined; reluctant. [2] performed, given, or said with reluctance.
▸**unˈwillingly** ADVERB ▸**unˈwillingness** NOUN

unwind (ʌnˈwaɪnd) VERB **-winds, -winding, -wound.** [1] to slacken, undo, or unravel or cause to slacken, undo, or unravel. [2] (*tr*) to disentangle. [3] to make or become relaxed: *he finds it hard to unwind after a busy day at work*.
▸**unˈwindable** ADJECTIVE ▸**unˈwinder** NOUN

unwinking (ʌnˈwɪŋkɪŋ) ADJECTIVE vigilant; watchful.

unwinnable (ʌnˈwɪnəbᵊl) ADJECTIVE [1] not able to be won or achieved. [2] (of a seat in an election) not able to be taken from the incumbent or the incumbent's party.

unwise (ʌnˈwaɪz) ADJECTIVE lacking wisdom or prudence; foolish.
▸**unˈwisely** ADVERB ▸**unˈwiseness** NOUN

unwish (ʌnˈwɪʃ) VERB (*tr*) [1] to retract or revoke (a wish). [2] to desire (something) not to be or take place.

unwished (ʌnˈwɪʃt) ADJECTIVE not desired; unwelcome.

unwitnessed (ʌnˈwɪtnɪst) ADJECTIVE [1] without the signature or attestation of a witness. [2] not seen or observed.

unwitting (ʌnˈwɪtɪŋ) ADJECTIVE (*usually prenominal*) [1] not knowing or conscious. [2] not intentional; inadvertent.
▷**HISTORY** Old English *unwitende*, from UN-[1] + *witting*, present participle of *witan* to know; related to Old High German *wizzan* to know, Old Norse *vita*
▸**unˈwittingly** ADVERB ▸**unˈwittingness** NOUN

unwonted (ʌnˈwəʊntɪd) ADJECTIVE [1] out of the ordinary; unusual. [2] (usually foll by *to*) *Archaic* unaccustomed; unused.
▸**unˈwontedly** ADVERB ▸**unˈwontedness** NOUN

unworkable (ʌnˈwɜːkəbᵊl) ADJECTIVE not practicable or feasible.

unworldly (ʌnˈwɜːldlɪ) ADJECTIVE [1] not concerned with material values or pursuits. [2] lacking sophistication; naive. [3] not of this earth or world.
▸**unˈworldliness** NOUN

unworried (ʌnˈwʌrɪd) ADJECTIVE not anxious or uneasy.

unworthy (ʌnˈwɜːðɪ) ADJECTIVE [1] (often foll by *of*) not deserving or worthy. [2] (often foll by *of*) beneath the level considered befitting (to): *that remark is unworthy of you*. [3] lacking merit or value. [4] (of treatment) not warranted or deserved.
▸**unˈworthily** ADVERB ▸**unˈworthiness** NOUN

unwound (ʌnˈwaʊnd) VERB the past tense and past participle of **unwind.**

unwrap (ʌnˈræp) VERB **-wraps, -wrapping, -wrapped.** to remove the covering or wrapping from (something) or (of something wrapped) to have the covering come off.

unwritten (ʌnˈrɪtᵊn) ADJECTIVE [1] not printed or in writing. [2] effective only through custom; traditional. [3] without writing upon it.

unwritten law NOUN [1] the law based upon custom, usage, and judicial decisions, as distinguished from the enactments of a legislature, orders or decrees in writing, etc. [2] **the.** the tradition that a person may avenge any insult to family integrity, as used to justify criminal acts of vengeance.

unyielding (ʌnˈjiːldɪŋ) ADJECTIVE [1] not compliant, submissive, or flexible: *his unyielding attitude*. [2] not pliable or soft: *a firm and unyielding surface*.

unyoke (ʌnˈjəʊk) VERB [1] to release (an animal, etc.) from a yoke. [2] (*tr*) to set free; liberate. [3] (*tr*) to disconnect or separate. [4] (*intr*) *Archaic* to cease working.

unzip (ʌnˈzɪp) VERB **-zips, -zipping, -zipped.** to unfasten the zip of (a garment) or (of a zip or garment with a zip) to become unfastened: *her skirt unzipped as she sat down*.

up (ʌp) PREPOSITION [1] indicating movement from a lower to a higher position: *climbing up a mountain*. [2] at a higher or further level or position in or on: *soot up the chimney; a shop up the road*. ◆ ADVERB [3] (*often particle*) to an upward, higher, or erect position, esp indicating readiness for an activity: *looking up at the stars; up and doing something*. [4] (*particle*) indicating intensity or completion of an action: *he tore up the cheque; drink up now!* [5] to the place referred to or where the speaker is: *the man came up and asked the way*. [6] **a** to a more important place: *up to London*. **b** to a more northerly place: *up to Scotland*. **c** (of a member of some British universities) to or at university. **d** in a particular part of the country: *up north*. [7] appearing for trial: *up before the magistrate*. [8] having gained: *ten pounds up on the deal*. [9] higher in price: *coffee is up again*. [10] raised (for discussion, etc.): *the plan was up for consideration*. [11] taught: *well up in physics*. [12] (*functioning as imperative*) get, stand, etc., up: *up with you!* [13] **all up with.** *Informal* **a** over; finished. **b** doomed to die. [14] **up with.** (*functioning as imperative*) wanting the beginning or continuation of: *up with the monarchy!* [15] **something's up.** *Informal* something strange is happening. [16] **up against. a** touching. **b** having to cope with: *look what we're up against now*. [17] **up and running.** in operation; functioning properly. [18] **up for.** as a candidate or applicant for: *he's up for re-election again*. [19] **up for it.** *Informal* keen or willing to try something out or make a good effort: *it's a big challenge and I'm up for it*. [20] **up to. a** devising or scheming; occupied with: *she's up to no good*. **b** dependent or incumbent upon: *the decision is up to you*. **c** equal to (a challenge, etc.) or capable of (doing, etc.): *are you up to playing in the final?* **d** aware of: *up to a person's tricks*. **e** as far as: *up to his waist in mud*. **f** as many as: *up to two years waiting time*. **g** comparable with: *not up to your normal standard*. [21] **up top.** *Informal* in the head or mind. [22] **up yours.** *Slang* a vulgar expression of contempt or refusal. [23] **what's up?** *Informal* **a** what is the matter? **b** what is

happening? ◆ ADJECTIVE [24] (*predicative*) of a high or higher position. [25] (*predicative*) out of bed; awake: *the children aren't up yet.* [26] (*prenominal*) of or relating to a train or trains to a more important place or one regarded as higher: *the up platform.* [27] (*predicative*) over or completed: *the examiner announced that their time was up.* [28] (*predicative*) beating one's opponent by a specified amount: *three goals up by half-time.* ◆ VERB **ups, upping, upped.** [29] (*tr*) to increase or raise. [30] (*intr; foll by* and *with a verb*) *Informal* to do (something) suddenly, unexpectedly, etc.: *she upped and married someone else.* ◆ NOUN [31] high point; good or pleasant period (esp in the phrase **ups and downs**). [32] *Slang* another word (esp US) for **upper** (sense 9). [33] **on the up and up.** **a** trustworthy or honest. **b** *Brit* on the upward trend or movement: *our firm's on the up and up.*
▷**HISTORY** Old English *upp;* related to Old Saxon, Old Norse *up,* Old High German *ūf,* Gothic *iup*

> **Language note** The use of *up* before *until* is redundant and should be avoided: *the talks will continue until* (not *up until*) *23rd March.*

UP ABBREVIATION FOR: [1] United Press. [2] Uttar Pradesh.

up- PREFIX up, upper, or upwards: *uproot; upmost; upthrust; upgrade; uplift.*

up-anchor VERB (*intr*) *Nautical* to weigh anchor.

up-and-coming ADJECTIVE promising continued or future success; enterprising.

up-and-down ADJECTIVE [1] moving, executed, or formed alternately upwards and downwards. [2] *Chiefly US* very steep; vertical. ◆ ADVERB, PREPOSITION **up and down.** [3] backwards and forwards (along).

up-and-over ADJECTIVE (of a door, etc.) opened by being lifted and moved into a horizontal position.

up-and-under NOUN *Rugby League* a high kick forwards followed by a charge to the place where the ball lands.

Upanishad (uːˈpʌnɪʃəd, -ˌʃæd, juː-) NOUN *Hinduism* any of a class of the Sanskrit sacred books probably composed between 400 and 200 B.C. and embodying the mystical and esoteric doctrines of ancient Hindu philosophy.
▷**HISTORY** C19: from Sanskrit *upanisad* a sitting down near something, from *upa* near to + *ni* down + *sīdati* he sits
▸**Uˌpaniˈshadic** ADJECTIVE

upas (ˈjuːpəs) NOUN [1] a large moraceous tree of Java, *Antiaria toxicaria,* having whitish bark and poisonous milky sap. [2] the sap of this tree, used as an arrow poison. ◆ Also called: **antiar.**
▷**HISTORY** C19: from Malay: poison

upbeat (ˈʌpˌbiːt) NOUN [1] *Music* **a** a usually unaccented beat, esp the last in a bar. **b** the upward gesture of a conductor's baton indicating this. Compare **downbeat.** [2] an upward trend (in prosperity, etc.). ◆ ADJECTIVE [3] *Informal* marked by cheerfulness or optimism.

up-bow (ˈʌpˌbəʊ) NOUN a stroke of the bow from its tip to its nut on a stringed instrument. Compare **down-bow.**

upbraid (ʌpˈbreɪd) VERB (*tr*) [1] to reprove or reproach angrily. [2] to find fault with.
▷**HISTORY** Old English *upbregdan;* related to Danish *bebreide;* see UP, BRAID
▸**upˈbraider** NOUN ▸**upˈbraiding** NOUN ▸**upˈbraidingly** ADVERB

upbringing (ˈʌpˌbrɪŋɪŋ) NOUN the education of a person during his formative years. Also called: **bringing-up.**

upbuild (ʌpˈbɪld) VERB **-builds, -building, -built.** (*tr*) to build up; enlarge, increase, etc.
▸**upˈbuilder** NOUN

UPC ABBREVIATION FOR Universal Product Code: another name for **bar code.**

upcast (ˈʌpˌkɑːst) NOUN [1] material cast or thrown up. [2] a ventilation shaft through which air leaves a mine. Compare **downcast** (sense 3). [3] *Geology* (in a fault) the section of strata that has been displaced upwards. ◆ ADJECTIVE [4] directed or thrown upwards. ◆ VERB **-casts, -casting, -cast.** [5] (*tr*) to throw or cast up.

up close and personal ADVERB [1] intimately: *he got to know the prime minister up close and personal.* ◆ ADJECTIVE (**up-close-and-personal** *when prenominal*) [2] intimate: *up-close-and-personal interaction.*

upcoming (ˌʌpˈkʌmɪŋ) ADJECTIVE coming soon; forthcoming.

upcountry (ʌpˈkʌntrɪ) ADJECTIVE [1] of or coming from the interior of a country or region. [2] *Disparaging* lacking the sophistication associated with city-dwellers; countrified. ◆ NOUN [3] the interior part of a region or country. ◆ ADVERB [4] towards, in, or into the interior part of a country or region.

update VERB (ʌpˈdeɪt) (*tr*) [1] to bring up to date. ◆ NOUN (ˈʌpˌdeɪt) [2] the act of updating or something that is updated.
▸**upˈdateable** ADJECTIVE ▸**upˈdater** NOUN

updraught (ˈʌpˌdrɑːft) NOUN an upward movement of air or other gas.

upend (ʌpˈɛnd) VERB [1] to turn or set or become turned or set on end. [2] (*tr*) to affect or upset drastically.

upfront (ˈʌpˈfrʌnt) ADJECTIVE [1] *Informal* open, frank, honest. ◆ ADVERB, ADJECTIVE [2] (of money) paid out at the beginning of a business arrangement.

upgrade VERB (ʌpˈɡreɪd) (*tr*) [1] to assign or promote (a person or job) to a higher professional rank or position. [2] to raise in value, importance, esteem, etc. [3] to improve (a breed of livestock) by crossing with a better strain. ◆ NOUN (ˈʌpˌɡreɪd) [4] *US and Canadian* an upward slope. [5] **on the upgrade.** improving or progressing, as in importance, status, health, etc. ◆ ADJECTIVE [6] *US and Canadian* going or sloping upwards. ◆ ADVERB (ˈʌpˈɡreɪd) [7] *US and Canadian* up an incline, hill, or slope.
▸**upˈgrader** NOUN

upgrowth (ˈʌpˌɡrəʊθ) NOUN [1] the process of developing or growing upwards. [2] a result of evolution or growth.

upheaval (ʌpˈhiːvᵊl) NOUN [1] a strong, sudden, or violent disturbance, as in politics, social conditions, etc. [2] *Geology* another word for **uplift** (sense 7).

upheave (ʌpˈhiːv) VERB **-heaves, -heaving, -heaved** *or* **-hove.** [1] to heave or rise upwards. [2] *Geology* to thrust (land) upwards or (of land) to be thrust upwards. [3] (*tr*) to disturb violently; throw into disorder.

upheld (ʌpˈhɛld) VERB the past tense and past participle of **uphold.**

Up-Helly-Aa (ˌʌpˈhɛlɪɑː) NOUN a midwinter festival held in January in Shetland, originally a fire festival, but now a celebration of Shetland's Norse heritage, involving the ceremonial burning of a newly built Viking ship.
▷**HISTORY** from UP (in the sense: finished) + *haliday* a Scottish form of HOLIDAY

uphill (ˈʌpˈhɪl) ADJECTIVE [1] inclining, sloping, or leading upwards. [2] requiring arduous and protracted effort: *an uphill task.* ◆ ADVERB [3] up an incline or slope; upwards. [4] against difficulties. ◆ NOUN [5] a rising incline; ascent.

uphold (ʌpˈhəʊld) VERB **-holds, -holding, -held.** (*tr*) [1] to maintain, affirm, or defend against opposition or challenge. [2] to give moral support or inspiration to. [3] *Rare* to support physically. [4] to lift up.
▸**upˈholder** NOUN

upholster (ʌpˈhəʊlstə) VERB (*tr*) to fit (chairs, sofas, etc.) with padding, springs, webbing, and covering.

upholsterer (ʌpˈhəʊlstərə) NOUN a person who upholsters furniture as a profession.
▷**HISTORY** C17: from *upholster* small furniture dealer; see UPHOLD, -STER, -ER[1]

upholstery (ʌpˈhəʊlstərɪ) NOUN, *plural* **-steries.** [1] the padding, covering, etc., of a piece of furniture. [2] the business, work, or craft of upholstering.

uphroe (ˈjuːfrəʊ) NOUN *Nautical* a variant spelling of **euphroe.**

UPI ABBREVIATION FOR United Press International.

up-itself ADJECTIVE *Slang* pretentious or pompous.

upkeep (ˈʌpˌkiːp) NOUN [1] the act or process of keeping something in good repair, esp over a long period; maintenance. [2] the cost of maintenance.

upland (ˈʌplənd) NOUN [1] an area of high or relatively high ground. ◆ ADJECTIVE [2] relating to or situated in an upland.

upland cotton NOUN [1] a tropical American cotton plant, *Gossypium hirsutum,* widely cultivated for its fibre. [2] the fibre of this plant, or the fabric woven from it.

upland plover *or* **sandpiper** NOUN an American sandpiper, *Bartramia longicauda,* with a short slender bill and long tail.

uplift VERB (ʌpˈlɪft) (*tr*) [1] to raise; elevate; lift up. [2] to raise morally, spiritually, culturally, etc. [3] *Scot and NZ* to collect (a passenger, parcel, etc.); pick up. ◆ NOUN (ˈʌpˌlɪft) [4] the act, process, or result of lifting up. [5] the act or process of bettering moral, social or cultural conditions, etc. [6] **a** a brassiere for lifting and supporting the breasts. **b** (*as modifier*): *an uplift bra.* [7] the process or result of land being raised to a higher level, as during a period of mountain building.
▸**upˈlifter** NOUN

uplifting (ʌpˈlɪftɪŋ) ADJECTIVE acting to raise moral, spiritual, cultural, etc. levels.

uplighter (ˈʌpˌlaɪtə) NOUN a lamp or wall light designed or positioned to cast its light upwards.

uplink (ˈʌpˌlɪŋk) NOUN the transmitter on the ground that sends signals up to a communications satellite.

upload (ʌpˈləʊd) VERB (*tr*) to copy or transfer (data or a program) from one's own computer into the memory of another computer. Compare **download** (sense 1).

up-market ADJECTIVE relating to commercial products, services, etc., that are relatively expensive and of superior quality.

upmost (ˈʌpˌməʊst) ADJECTIVE another word for **uppermost.**

Upolu (uːˈpəʊluː) NOUN an island in the SW central Pacific, in Samoa. Chief town: Apia. Pop.: 116 248 (1991). Area: 1114 sq. km (430 sq. miles).

upon (əˈpɒn) PREPOSITION [1] another word for **on.** [2] indicating a position reached by going up: *climb upon my knee.* [3] imminent for: *the weekend was upon us again.*
▷**HISTORY** C13: from UP + ON

upper (ˈʌpə) ADJECTIVE [1] higher or highest in relation to physical position, wealth, rank, status, etc. [2] (*capital when part of a name*) lying farther upstream, inland, or farther north: *the upper valley of the Loire.* [3] (*capital when part of a name*) *Geology, archaeol* denoting the late part or division of a period, system, formation, etc.: *Upper Palaeolithic.* [4] *Maths* (of a limit or bound) greater than or equal to one or more numbers or variables. ◆ NOUN [5] the higher of two objects, people, etc. [6] the part of a shoe above the sole, covering the upper surface of the foot. [7] **on one's uppers.** extremely poor; destitute. [8] *Informal* any tooth of the upper jaw. [9] Also called (esp US): **up.** *Slang* any of various drugs having a stimulant or euphoric effect. Compare **downer.**

upper atmosphere NOUN *Meteorol* that part of the atmosphere above the troposphere.

Upper Austria NOUN a state of N Austria: first divided from Lower Austria in 1251. Capital: Linz. Pop.: 1 382 017 (2001). Area: 11 978 sq. km (4625 sq. miles). German name: **Oberösterreich.**

Upper Canada NOUN [1] *History* (from 1791–1841) the official name of the region of Canada lying southwest of the Ottawa River and north of the lower Great Lakes. Compare **Lower Canada.** [2] (esp in E Canada) another name for **Ontario.**

upper case *Printing* ◆ NOUN [1] the top half of a compositor's type case in which capital letters, reference marks, and accents are kept. ◆ ADJECTIVE (**upper-case** when prenominal) [2] of or relating to capital letters kept in this case and used in the setting or production of printed or typed matter. ◆ VERB **upper-case.** [3] (*tr*) to print with upper-case letters; capitalize.

upper chamber NOUN another name for an **upper house.**

upper class NOUN [1] the class occupying the highest position in the social hierarchy, esp the wealthy or the aristocracy. ◆ ADJECTIVE (**upper-class** when prenominal) [2] of or relating to the upper class. [3] *US education* of or relating to the junior or senior classes of a college or high school.

upper crust NOUN *Informal* the upper class.

uppercut (ˈʌpəˌkʌt) NOUN [1] a short swinging

upward blow with the fist delivered at an opponent's chin. ◆ VERB **-cuts, -cutting, -cut.** [2] to hit (an opponent) with an uppercut.

Upper Egypt NOUN one of the four main administrative districts of Egypt: extends south from Cairo to the Sudan.

upper hand NOUN **the.** the position of control; advantage (esp in the phrases **have** *or* **get the upper hand**).

upper house NOUN (*often capitals*) one of the two houses of a bicameral legislature. Also called: **upper chamber.** Compare **lower house.**

upper mordent NOUN another name for **inverted mordent.**

uppermost ('ʌpəˌməʊst) ADJECTIVE *also* **upmost.** [1] highest in position, power, importance, etc. ◆ ADVERB [2] in or into the highest position, etc.

Upper Palaeolithic NOUN [1] the latest of the three periods of the Palaeolithic, beginning about 40 000 B.C. and ending, in Europe, about 12 000 B.C.: characterized by the emergence of modern man, *Homo sapiens.* ◆ ADJECTIVE [2] of or relating to this period.

Upper Palatinate NOUN See **Palatinate.**

Upper Peninsula NOUN a peninsula in the northern US between Lakes Superior and Michigan, constituting the N part of the state of Michigan.

upper regions PLURAL NOUN **the.** *Chiefly literary* the sky; heavens.

upper school NOUN the senior pupils in a secondary school, usually those in the fourth and fifth years and above.

Upper Silesia NOUN a region of SW Poland, formerly ruled by Germany: coal mining and other heavy industry.

Upper Tunguska NOUN See **Tunguska.**

Upper Volta ('vɒltə) NOUN the former name (until 1984) of **Burkina-Faso.**

upper works PLURAL NOUN *Nautical* the parts of a vessel above the waterline when fully laden.

uppish ('ʌpɪʃ) ADJECTIVE *Brit informal* snobbish, arrogant, or presumptuous.
▷HISTORY C18: from UP + -ISH
▸**'uppishly** ADVERB ▸**'uppishness** NOUN

uppity ('ʌpɪtɪ) ADJECTIVE *Informal* [1] not yielding easily to persuasion or control. [2] another word for **uppish.**
▷HISTORY from UP + fanciful ending, perhaps influenced by -ITY

Uppsala *or* **Upsala** ('ʌpsɑːlə) NOUN a city in E central Sweden: the royal headquarters in the 13th century; Gothic cathedral (the largest in Sweden) and Sweden's oldest university (1477). Pop.: 188 478 (2000 est.).

upraise (ʌp'reɪz) VERB (*tr*) [1] *Chiefly literary* to lift up; elevate. [2] *Archaic* to praise; exalt.
▸**up'raiser** NOUN

uprate (ʌp'reɪt) VERB [1] raise the value, rate, or size of, upgrade. [2] *Photog* to increase the effective speed of (a film) by underexposing, usually up to two stops, and subsequently overdeveloping (pushing the processing).

uprear (ʌp'rɪə) VERB (*tr*) to lift up; raise.

upright ('ʌpˌraɪt) ADJECTIVE [1] vertical or erect. [2] honest, honourable, or just. ◆ ADVERB [3] vertically. ◆ NOUN [4] a vertical support, such as a stake or post. [5] short for **upright piano.** [6] the state of being vertical. ◆ VERB [7] (*tr*) to make upright.
▸**'upˌrightly** ADVERB ▸**'upˌrightness** NOUN

upright piano NOUN a piano which has a rectangular vertical case. Compare **grand piano.**

uprise VERB (ʌp'raɪz) **-rises, -rising, -rose, -risen.** [1] (*tr*) to rise up. ◆ NOUN ('ʌpˌraɪz) [2] another word for **rise** (senses 24, 25, 30).
▸**up'riser** NOUN

uprising ('ʌpˌraɪzɪŋ, ʌp'raɪzɪŋ) NOUN [1] a revolt or rebellion. [2] *Archaic* an ascent.

upriver ('ʌp'rɪvə) ADJECTIVE, ADVERB [1] towards or near the source of a river. ◆ NOUN [2] an area located upstream.

uproar ('ʌpˌrɔː) NOUN a commotion or disturbance characterized by loud noise and confusion; turmoil.

uproarious (ʌp'rɔːrɪəs) ADJECTIVE [1] causing or characterized by an uproar; tumultuous. [2] extremely funny; hilarious. [3] (of laughter) loud and boisterous.
▸**up'roariously** ADVERB ▸**up'roariousness** NOUN

uproot (ʌp'ruːt) VERB (*tr*) [1] to pull up by or as if by the roots. [2] to displace (a person or persons) from native or habitual surroundings. [3] to remove or destroy utterly.
▸**up'rootedness** NOUN ▸**up'rooter** NOUN

uprouse (ʌp'raʊz) VERB (*tr*) *Rare* to rouse or stir up; arouse.

uprush ('ʌpˌrʌʃ) NOUN an upward rush, as of consciousness.

upsadaisy ('ʌpsə'deɪzɪ) INTERJECTION a variant of **upsy-daisy.**

Upsala ('ʌpsɑːlə) NOUN a variant spelling of **Uppsala.**

ups and downs PLURAL NOUN alternating periods of good and bad fortune, high and low spirits, etc.

upscale ('ʌp'skeɪl) ADJECTIVE *Informal* of or for the upper end of an economic or social scale; up-market.

upset VERB (ʌp'sɛt) **-sets, -setting, -set.** (*mainly tr*) [1] (*also intr*) to tip or be tipped over; overturn, capsize, or spill. [2] to disturb the normal state, course, or stability of: *to upset the balance of nature.* [3] to disturb mentally or emotionally. [4] to defeat or overthrow, usually unexpectedly. [5] to make physically ill: *seafood always upsets my stomach.* [6] to thicken or spread (the end of a bar, rivet, etc.) by forging, hammering, or swagging. ◆ NOUN ('ʌpˌsɛt) [7] an unexpected defeat or reversal, as in a contest or plans. [8] a disturbance or disorder of the emotions, body, etc. [9] a tool used to upset a bar or rivet; swage. [10] a forging or bar that has been upset in preparation for further processing. ◆ ADJECTIVE (ʌp'sɛt) [11] overturned or capsized. [12] emotionally or physically disturbed or distressed. [13] disordered; confused. [14] defeated or overthrown.
▷HISTORY C14 (in the sense: to set up, erect; C19 in the sense: to overthrow); related to Middle High German *ūfsetzen* to put on, Middle Dutch *opzetten*
▸**up'settable** ADJECTIVE ▸**up'setter** NOUN ▸**up'setting** ADJECTIVE ▸**up'settingly** ADVERB

upset price ('ʌpˌsɛt) NOUN another name (esp Scot, US, and Canadian) for **reserve price.**

upsetting (ʌp'sɛtɪŋ) NOUN *Metallurgy* the process of hammering the end of a heated bar of metal so that its width is increased locally, as in the manufacture of bolts.

upshot ('ʌpˌʃɒt) NOUN [1] the final result; conclusion; outcome. [2] *Archery* the final shot in a match.
▷HISTORY C16: from UP + SHOT[1]

upside ('ʌpˌsaɪd) NOUN the upper surface or part.

upside down ADJECTIVE [1] (*usually postpositive;* **upside-down** when prenominal) turned over completely; inverted. [2] *Informal* confused; muddled; topsy-turvy: *an upside-down world.* ◆ ADVERB [3] in an inverted fashion. [4] in a chaotic or crazy manner.
▷HISTORY C16: variant, by folk etymology, of earlier *upsodown*
▸**ˌupside-'downness** NOUN

upside-down cake NOUN a sponge cake baked with sliced fruit at the bottom, then inverted before serving.

upsides ('ʌpˌsaɪdz) ADVERB *Informal, chiefly Brit* (foll by *with*) equal or level (with), as through revenge or retaliation.

upsilon ('ʌpsɪˌlɒn, juːp'saɪlən) NOUN the 20th letter in the Greek alphabet (Υ or υ) a vowel, transliterated as *y* or *u.*
▷HISTORY C17: from Medieval Greek *u psilon* simple *u,* name adopted for graphic *u* to avoid confusion with graphic *oi,* since pronunciation was the same for both in Late Greek

upskill ('ʌpˌskɪl) VERB (*tr*) *NZ* to improve the aptitude for work of (a person) by additional training.

upspring *Archaic or literary* ◆ VERB (ʌp'sprɪŋ) **-springs, -springing, -sprang** *or* **-sprung, -sprung.** [1] (*intr*) to spring up or come into existence. ◆ NOUN ('ʌpˌsprɪŋ) [2] a leap forwards or upwards. [3] the act of coming into existence.

upstage ('ʌp'steɪdʒ) ADVERB [1] on, at, or to the rear of the stage. ◆ ADJECTIVE [2] of or relating to the back half of the stage. [3] *Informal* haughty; supercilious; aloof. ◆ VERB (*tr*) [4] to move upstage of (another actor), thus forcing him to turn away from the audience. [5] *Informal* to draw attention to oneself from (someone else); steal the show from (someone). [6] *Informal* to treat haughtily. ◆ NOUN [7] the back half of the stage.

upstairs ('ʌp'stɛəz) ADVERB [1] up the stairs; to or on an upper floor or level. [2] *Informal* to or into a higher rank or office. [3] *Informal* in the mind: *a little weak upstairs.* [4] **kick upstairs.** *Informal* to promote to a higher rank or position, esp one that carries less power. ◆ NOUN (*functioning as singular or plural*) [5] **a** an upper floor or level. **b** (*as modifier*): *an upstairs room.* [6] *Brit informal, old-fashioned* the masters and mistresses of a household collectively, esp of a large house. Compare **downstairs** (sense 3).

upstanding (ʌp'stændɪŋ) ADJECTIVE [1] of good character. [2] upright and vigorous in build. [3] **be upstanding. a** (in a court of law) a direction to all persons present to rise to their feet before the judge enters or leaves the court. **b** (at a formal dinner) a direction to all persons present to rise to their feet for a toast.
▸**up'standingness** NOUN

upstart NOUN ('ʌpˌstɑːt) [1] **a** a person, group, etc., that has risen suddenly to a position of power or wealth. **b** (*as modifier*): *an upstart tyrant; an upstart family.* [2] **a** an arrogant or presumptuous person. **b** (*as modifier*): *his upstart ambition.* ◆ VERB (ʌp'stɑːt) [3] (*intr*) *Archaic* to start up, as in surprise, etc.

upstate ('ʌp'steɪt) *US* ◆ ADJECTIVE, ADVERB [1] towards, in, from, or relating to the outlying or northern sections of a state, esp of New York State. ◆ NOUN [2] the outlying, esp northern, sections of a state.
▸**'up'stater** NOUN

upstream ('ʌp'striːm) ADVERB, ADJECTIVE [1] in or towards the higher part of a stream; against the current. [2] (in the oil industry) of or for any of the stages prior to oil production, such as exploration or research. Compare **downstream** (sense 2).

upstretched (ʌp'strɛtʃt) ADJECTIVE (esp of the arms) stretched or raised up.

upstroke ('ʌpˌstrəʊk) NOUN [1] **a** an upward stroke or movement, as of a pen or brush. **b** the mark produced by such a stroke. [2] the upward movement of a piston in a reciprocating engine.

up-sum NOUN a summing-up.

upsurge VERB (ʌp'sɜːdʒ) [1] (*intr*) *Chiefly literary* to surge up. ◆ NOUN ('ʌpˌsɜːdʒ) [2] a rapid rise or swell.

upsweep NOUN ('ʌpˌswiːp) [1] a curve or sweep upwards. [2] *US and Canadian* an upswept hairstyle. ◆ VERB (ʌp'swiːp) **-sweeps, -sweeping, -swept.** [3] to sweep, curve, or brush or be swept, curved, or brushed upwards.

upswell (ʌp'swɛl) VERB **-swells, -swelling, -swelled, -swelled** *or* **-swollen.** *Rare* to swell up or cause to swell up.

upswing NOUN ('ʌpˌswɪŋ) [1] *Economics* a recovery period in the trade cycle. [2] an upward swing or movement or any increase or improvement. ◆ VERB (ʌp'swɪŋ) **-swings, -swinging, -swung.** [3] (*intr*) to swing or move up.

upsy-daisy ('ʌpsɪ'deɪzɪ) *or* **upsadaisy** INTERJECTION an expression, usually of reassurance, uttered as when someone, esp a child, stumbles or is being lifted up.
▷HISTORY C18 *up-a-daisy,* irregularly formed from UP (adv)

uptake ('ʌpˌteɪk) NOUN [1] a pipe, shaft, etc., that is used to convey smoke or gases, esp one that connects a furnace to a chimney. [2] *Mining* another term for **upcast** (sense 2). [3] taking up or lifting up. [4] the act of accepting or taking up something on offer or available. [5] **quick** (*or* **slow**) **on the uptake.** *Informal* quick (or slow) to understand or learn.

uptalk ('ʌpˌtɔːk) NOUN a style of speech in which every sentence ends with a rising tone, as if the speaker is always asking a question.

upter *or* **upta** ADJECTIVE *Austral slang* of poor quality; in disrepair.
▷HISTORY euphemistic: short for *up to shit*

upthrow ('ʌpˌθrəʊ) NOUN [1] *Geology* the upward movement of rocks on one side of a fault plane relative to rocks on the other side. [2] *Rare* an upward thrust or throw; upheaval.

upthrust ('ʌpˌθrʌst) NOUN 1 an upward push or thrust. 2 *Geology* a violent upheaval of the earth's surface.

uptick ('ʌptɪk) NOUN a rise or increase.

uptight (ʌp'taɪt) ADJECTIVE *Informal* 1 displaying tense repressed nervousness, irritability, or anger. 2 unable to give expression to one's feelings, personality, etc.

uptilt (ʌp'tɪlt) VERB (*tr*) to tilt up.

uptime ('ʌpˌtaɪm) NOUN *Commerce* time during which a machine, such as a computer, actually operates.

uptitling (ʌp'taɪtᵊlɪŋ) NOUN *Jocular* the practice of conferring grandiose job titles to employees performing relatively menial jobs.
▷HISTORY C20: from UP + TITLE (sense 4)

up-to-date ADJECTIVE **a** modern, current, or fashionable: *an up-to-date magazine.* **b** (*predicative*): *the magazine is up to date.*
▸**'up-to-'dately** ADVERB ▸**'up-to-'dateness** NOUN

uptown ('ʌp'taʊn) *US and Canadian* ◆ ADJECTIVE, ADVERB 1 towards, in, or relating to some part of a town that is away from the centre. ◆ NOUN 2 such a part of a town, esp a residential part.
▸**'up'towner** NOUN

upturn VERB (ʌp'tɜːn) 1 to turn or cause to turn up, over, or upside down. 2 (*tr*) to create disorder. 3 (*tr*) to direct upwards. ◆ NOUN ('ʌpˌtɜːn) 4 an upward turn, trend, or improvement. 5 an upheaval or commotion.

UPVC ABBREVIATION FOR unplasticized polyvinyl chloride. See also **PVC.**

upward ('ʌpwəd) ADJECTIVE 1 directed or moving towards a higher point or level. ◆ ADVERB 2 a variant of **upwards.**
▸**'upwardly** ADVERB ▸**'upwardness** NOUN

upwardly mobile ADJECTIVE (of a person or social group) moving or aspiring to move to a higher social class or to a position of increased status or power.

upward mobility NOUN *Sociol* the movement of an individual, social group, or class to a position of increased status or power. Compare **downward mobility.** See also **horizontal mobility, vertical mobility.**

upwards ('ʌpwədz) *or* **upward** ADVERB 1 from a lower to a higher place, level, condition, etc. 2 towards a higher level, standing, etc.

upwind ('ʌp'wɪnd) ADVERB 1 into or against the wind. 2 towards or on the side where the wind is blowing; windward. ◆ ADJECTIVE 3 going against the wind: *the upwind leg of the course.* 4 on the windward side: *the upwind side of the house has weathered.*

Ur (ɜː) NOUN an ancient city of Sumer located on a former channel of the Euphrates.

UR *Text messaging* ABBREVIATION FOR your.

ur- COMBINING FORM a variant of **uro-**[1] and **uro-**[2] before a vowel.

Ur- COMBINING FORM original, primitive: *Ursprache.*
▷HISTORY German

uracil ('jʊərəsɪl) NOUN *Biochem* a pyrimidine present in all living cells, usually in a combined form, as in RNA. Formula: $C_4H_4N_2O_2$.
▷HISTORY C20: from URO-[1] + ACETIC + -ILE

uraemia *or US* **uremia** (jʊ'riːmɪə) NOUN *Pathol* the accumulation of waste products, normally excreted in the urine, in the blood: causes severe headaches, vomiting, etc. Also called: **azotaemia.**
▷HISTORY C19: from New Latin, from Greek *ouron* urine + *haima* blood
▸**u'raemic** *or* (*US*) **u'remic** ADJECTIVE

uraeus (jʊ'riːəs) NOUN, *plural* **-uses.** the sacred serpent represented on the headdresses of ancient Egyptian kings and gods.
▷HISTORY C19: from New Latin, from Greek *ouraios,* from Egyptian *uro* asp

Ural ('jʊərəl; *Russian* u'ral) NOUN a river in central Russia, rising in the S Ural Mountains and flowing south to the Caspian Sea. Length: 2534 km (1575 miles).

Ural-Altaic NOUN 1 a postulated group of related languages consisting of the Uralic and Altaic families of languages. ◆ ADJECTIVE 2 of or relating to this group of languages, characterized by agglutination and vowel harmony.

Uralic (jʊ'rælɪk) *or* **Uralian** (jʊ'reɪlɪən) NOUN 1 a superfamily of languages consisting of the Finno-Ugric family together with Samoyed. See also **Ural-Altaic.** ◆ ADJECTIVE 2 of or relating to these languages.

uralite ('jʊərəˌlaɪt) NOUN an amphibole mineral, similar to hornblende, that replaces pyroxene in some igneous and metamorphic rocks.
▷HISTORY C19: from the URAL MOUNTAINS where it was first found + -ITE[1]
▸**uralitic** (ˌjʊərə'lɪtɪk) ADJECTIVE

Ural Mountains *or* **Urals** PLURAL NOUN a mountain system in W central Russia, extending over 2000 km (1250 miles) from the Arctic Ocean towards the Aral Sea: forms part of the geographical boundary between Europe and Asia; one of the richest mineral areas in the world, with many associated major industrial centres. Highest peak: Mount Narodnaya, 1894 m (6214 ft.).

uranalysis (ˌjʊərə'nælɪsɪs) NOUN, *plural* **-ses** (-ˌsiːz). *Med* a variant spelling of **urinalysis.**

Urania (jʊ'reɪnɪə) NOUN *Greek myth* 1 the Muse of astronomy. 2 another name of **Aphrodite.**
▷HISTORY C17: from Latin, from Greek *Ourania,* from *ouranios* heavenly, from *ouranos* heaven

Uranian (jʊ'reɪnɪən) NOUN 1 a hypothetical inhabitant of the planet Uranus. ◆ ADJECTIVE 2 of, occurring on, or relating to the planet Uranus. 3 of the heavens; celestial. 4 relating to astronomy; astronomical. 5 (as an epithet of Aphrodite) heavenly; spiritual. 6 of or relating to the Muse Urania.

uranic[1] (jʊ'rænɪk) ADJECTIVE of or containing uranium, esp in a high valence state.

uranic[2] (jʊ'rænɪk) ADJECTIVE *Obsolete* astronomical or celestial.
▷HISTORY C19: from Greek *ouranos* heaven

uranide ('jʊərəˌnaɪd) NOUN any element having an atomic number greater than that of protactinium.

uraninite (jʊ'rænɪˌnaɪt) NOUN a blackish heavy radioactive mineral consisting of uranium oxide in cubic crystalline form together with radium, lead, helium, etc.: occurs in coarse granite. Formula: UO_2.
▷HISTORY C19: see URANIUM, -IN, -ITE[1]

uranism ('jʊərænɪzəm) NOUN a rare word for **homosexuality** (esp male homosexuality).
▷HISTORY C20: from German *Uranismus,* from Greek *ouranios* heavenly, i.e. spiritual; compare URANIAN (sense 5)

uranite ('jʊərəˌnaɪt) NOUN any of various minerals containing uranium, esp torbernite or autunite.
▸**uranitic** (ˌjʊərə'nɪtɪk) ADJECTIVE

uranium (jʊ'reɪnɪəm) NOUN a radioactive silvery-white metallic element of the actinide series. It occurs in several minerals including pitchblende, carnotite, and autunite and is used chiefly as a source of nuclear energy by fission of the radioisotope **uranium-235.** Symbol: U; atomic no.: 92; atomic wt.: 238.0289; half-life of most stable isotope, ^{238}U:451 × 10^9 years; valency: 2-6; relative density: 18.95 (approx.); melting pt.: 1135°C; boiling pt.: 4134°C.
▷HISTORY C18: from New Latin, from URANUS[2]; from the fact that the element was discovered soon after the planet

uranium series NOUN *Physics* a radioactive series that starts with uranium-238 and proceeds by radioactive decay to lead-206.

urano- COMBINING FORM denoting the heavens: *uranography.*
▷HISTORY from Greek *ouranos*

uranography (ˌjʊərə'nɒgrəfɪ) NOUN *Obsolete* the branch of astronomy concerned with the description and mapping of the stars, galaxies, etc.
▸**ˌura'nographer** *or* **ˌura'nographist** NOUN ▸**uranographic** (ˌjʊərənə'græfɪk) *or* **ˌurano'graphical** ADJECTIVE

uranous ('jʊərənəs) ADJECTIVE of or containing uranium, esp in a low valence state.

Uranus[1] (jʊ'reɪnəs, 'jʊrənəs) NOUN *Greek myth* the personification of the sky, who, as a god, ruled the universe and fathered the Titans and Cyclopes on his wife and mother Gaea (earth). He was overthrown by his son Cronus.

Uranus[2] (jʊ'reɪnəs, 'jʊrənəs) NOUN one of the giant planets, the seventh planet from the sun, sometimes visible to the naked eye. It has about 15 satellites, a ring system, and an axis of rotation almost lying in the plane of the orbit. Mean distance from sun: 2870 million km; period of revolution around sun: 84 years; period of axial rotation: 17.23 hours; diameter and mass: 4 and 14.5 times that of earth respectively.
▷HISTORY C19: from Latin *Ūranus,* from Greek *Ouranos* heaven

uranyl ('jʊərənɪl) NOUN (*modifier*) of, consisting of, or containing the divalent ion UO_2^{2+} or the group $-UO_2$.
▷HISTORY C19: from URANIUM + -YL
▸**ˌura'nylic** ADJECTIVE

urate ('jʊəreɪt) NOUN any salt or ester of uric acid.
▸**uratic** (jʊ'rætɪk) ADJECTIVE

urban ('ɜːbᵊn) ADJECTIVE 1 of, relating to, or constituting a city or town. 2 living in a city or town. 3 (of music) emerging and developing in densely populated areas of large cities, esp those populated by people of African or Caribbean origin. ◆ Compare **rural.**
▷HISTORY C17: from Latin *urbānus,* from *urbs* city

urban area NOUN (in population censuses) a city area considered as the inner city plus built-up environs, irrespective of local body administrative boundaries.

urban blues NOUN (*sometimes functioning as singular*) an extrovert and rhythmic style of blues, usually accompanied by a band. Compare **country blues.**

urban district NOUN 1 (in England and Wales from 1888 to 1974 and Northern Ireland from 1898 to 1973) an urban division of an administrative county with an elected council in charge of housing and environmental services: usually made up of one or more thickly populated areas but lacking a borough charter. 2 (in the Republic of Ireland) any of 49 medium-sized towns with their own elected councils.

urbane (ɜː'beɪn) ADJECTIVE characterized by elegance or sophistication.
▷HISTORY C16: from Latin *urbānus* belonging to the town; see URBAN
▸**ur'banely** ADVERB ▸**ur'baneness** NOUN

urban guerrilla NOUN a guerrilla who operates in a town or city, engaging in terrorism, kidnapping, etc.

urbanism ('ɜːbəˌnɪzəm) NOUN *Chiefly US* 1 **a** the character of city life. **b** the study of this. 2 a less common term for **urbanization.**

urbanite ('ɜːbəˌnaɪt) NOUN a resident of an urban community; city dweller.

urbanity (ɜː'bænɪtɪ) NOUN, *plural* **-ties.** 1 the quality of being urbane. 2 (*usually plural*) civilities or courtesies.

urbanize *or* **urbanise** ('ɜːbəˌnaɪz) VERB (*tr*) (*usually passive*) **a** to make (esp a predominantly rural area or country) more industrialized and urban. **b** to cause the migration of an increasing proportion of (rural dwellers) into cities.
▸**ˌurbani'zation** *or* **ˌurbani'sation** NOUN

urban myth NOUN a story, esp one with a shocking or amusing ending, related as having actually happened, usu. to someone vaguely connected with the teller.

urban renewal NOUN the process of redeveloping dilapidated or no longer functional urban areas.

urbi et orbi *Latin* ('ɜːbɪ ɛt 'ɔːbɪ) ADVERB *RC Church* to the city and the world: a phrase qualifying the solemn papal blessing.

URC ABBREVIATION FOR United Reformed Church.

urceolate ('ɜːsɪəlɪt, -ˌleɪt) ADJECTIVE *Biology* shaped like an urn or pitcher: *an urceolate corolla.*
▷HISTORY C18: via New Latin *urceolātus,* from Latin *urceolus* diminutive of *urceus* a pitcher

urchin ('ɜːtʃɪn) NOUN 1 a mischievous roguish child, esp one who is young, small, or raggedly dressed. 2 See **sea urchin, heart urchin.** 3 an archaic or dialect name for a **hedgehog.** 4 either of the two cylinders in a carding machine that are covered with carding cloth. 5 *Obsolete* an elf or sprite.
▷HISTORY C13: *urchon,* from Old French *heriçon,* from Latin *ēricius* hedgehog, from *ēr,* related to Greek *khēr* hedgehog

urd (ɜːd) NOUN another name for **black gram** (see **gram**[2] (sense 1)).
▷HISTORY Hindi

urdé *or* **urdée** (ˈɜːdeɪ, -diː, -dɪ) ADJECTIVE *Heraldry* having points; pointed.
▷HISTORY C16 *urdee:* probably a misreading and misunderstanding of French *vidée* in the phrase *croix aiquissée et vidée* cross sharply pointed and reduced

Urdu (ˈʊəduː, ˈɜː-) NOUN an official language of Pakistan, also spoken in India. The script derives primarily from Persia. It belongs to the Indic branch of the Indo-European family of languages, being closely related to Hindi but containing many Arabic and Persian loan words.
▷HISTORY C18: from Hindustani (*zabāni*) *urdū* (language of the) camp, from Persian *urdū* camp, from Turkish *ordū*

-ure SUFFIX FORMING NOUNS [1] indicating act, process, or result: *seizure.* [2] indicating function or office: *legislature; prefecture.*
▷HISTORY from French, from Latin *-ūra*

urea (jʊˈrɪə) NOUN a white water-soluble crystalline compound with a saline taste and often an odour of ammonia, produced by protein metabolism and excreted in urine. A synthetic form is used as a fertilizer, animal feed, and in the manufacture of synthetic resins. Formula: $CO(NH_2)_2$. Also called: **carbamide.**
▷HISTORY C19: from New Latin, from French *urée,* from Greek *ouron* URINE
▸**uˈreal** *or* **uˈreic** ADJECTIVE

urea cycle NOUN the sequence of metabolic reactions leading in vertebrates to the synthesis of urea.

urea-formaldehyde resin NOUN any one of a class of rigid odourless synthetic materials that are made from urea and formaldehyde and are used in electrical fittings, adhesives, laminates, and finishes for textiles.

urease (ˈjʊərɪˌeɪs, -ˌeɪz) NOUN an enzyme occurring in many plants, esp fungi, that converts urea to ammonium carbonate.

uredium (jʊˈriːdɪəm) *or* **uredinium** (ˌjʊərɪˈdɪnɪəm) NOUN, *plural* **-dia** (-dɪə) *or* **-dinia** (-ˈdɪnɪə). a spore-producing body of some rust fungi in which uredospores are formed. Also called: **uredosorus.**
▷HISTORY C20: from New Latin, from UREDO
▸**uˈredial** ADJECTIVE

uredo (jʊˈriːdəʊ) NOUN, *plural* **uredines** (jʊˈriːdɪˌniːz). a less common name for **urticaria.**
▷HISTORY C18: from Latin: burning itch, from *ūrere* to burn

uredosorus (jʊˌriːdəʊˈsɔːrəs) NOUN, *plural* **-sori** (-ˈsɔːraɪ). another word for **uredium.**
▷HISTORY from UREDO + SORUS

uredospore (jʊˈriːdəʊˌspɔː) NOUN any of the brownish spores that are produced in each uredium of the rust fungi and spread the infection between hosts.

ureide (ˈjʊərɪˌaɪd) NOUN *Chem* [1] any of a class of organic compounds derived from urea by replacing one or more of its hydrogen atoms by organic groups. [2] any of a class of derivatives of urea and carboxylic acids, in which one or more of the hydrogen atoms have been replaced by acyl groups: includes the cyclic ureides, such as alloxan.

uremia (jʊˈriːmɪə) NOUN the usual US spelling of **uraemia.**
▸**uˈremic** ADJECTIVE

-uret SUFFIX formerly used to form the names of binary chemical compounds.
▷HISTORY from New Latin *-uretum*

ureter (jʊˈriːtə) NOUN the tube that conveys urine from the kidney to the urinary bladder or cloaca.
▷HISTORY C16: via New Latin from Greek *ourētēr,* from *ourein* to URINATE
▸**uˈreteral** *or* **ureteric** (ˌjʊərɪˈtɛrɪk) ADJECTIVE

urethane (ˈjʊərɪˌθeɪn) *or* **urethan** (ˈjʊərɪˌθæn) NOUN [1] short for **polyurethane.** [2] another name for **ethyl carbamate.**
▷HISTORY C19: from URO-[1] + ETHYL + -ANE

urethra (jʊˈriːθrə) NOUN, *plural* **-thrae** (-θriː) *or* **-thras.** the canal that in most mammals conveys urine from the bladder out of the body. In human males it also conveys semen.
▷HISTORY C17: via Late Latin from Greek *ourēthra,* from *ourein* to URINATE
▸**uˈrethral** ADJECTIVE

urethritis (ˌjʊərɪˈθraɪtɪs) NOUN inflammation of the urethra.
▷HISTORY C19: from New Latin, from Late Latin URETHRA
▸**urethritic** (ˌjʊərɪˈθrɪtɪk) ADJECTIVE

urethroscope (jʊˈriːθrəˌskəʊp) NOUN a medical instrument for examining the urethra.
▷HISTORY C20: see URETHRA, -SCOPE
▸**urethroscopic** (jʊˌriːθrəˈskɒpɪk) ADJECTIVE
▸**urethroscopy** (ˌjʊərɪˈθrɒskəpɪ) NOUN

uretic (jʊˈrɛtɪk) ADJECTIVE of or relating to the urine.
▷HISTORY C19: via Late Latin from Greek *ourētikos,* from *ouron* URINE

Urfa (ˈɜːfə) NOUN a city in SE Turkey: market centre. Pop.: 410 762 (1997). Ancient name: **Edessa.**

Urga (ˈɜːgə) NOUN the former name (until 1924) of **Ulan Bator.**

urge (ɜːdʒ) VERB [1] (*tr*) to plead, press, or move (someone to do something): *we urged him to surrender.* [2] (*tr; may take a clause as object*) to advocate or recommend earnestly and persistently; plead or insist on: *to urge the need for safety.* [3] (*tr*) to impel, drive, or hasten onwards: *he urged the horses on.* [4] (*tr*) *Archaic or literary* to stimulate, excite, or incite. ◆ NOUN [5] a strong impulse, inner drive, or yearning.
▷HISTORY C16: from Latin *urgēre*

urgent (ˈɜːdʒənt) ADJECTIVE [1] requiring or compelling speedy action or attention: *the matter is urgent; an urgent message.* [2] earnest and persistent.
▷HISTORY C15: via French from Latin *urgent-, urgens,* present participle of *urgēre* to URGE
▸**urgency** (ˈɜːdʒənsɪ) NOUN ▸**ˈurgently** ADVERB

-urgy NOUN COMBINING FORM indicating technology concerned with a specified material: *metallurgy.*
▷HISTORY from Greek *-urgia,* from *ergon* WORK

Uri (*German* ˈuːri) NOUN one of the original three cantons of Switzerland, in the centre of the country: mainly German-speaking and Roman Catholic. Capital: Altdorf. Pop.: 35 500 (2000 est.). Area: 1075 sq. km (415 sq. miles).

-uria NOUN COMBINING FORM indicating a diseased or abnormal condition of the urine: *dysuria; pyuria.*
▷HISTORY from Greek *-ouria,* from *ouron* urine
▸**-uric** ADJECTIVE COMBINING FORM

Uriah (jʊˈraɪə) NOUN *Old Testament* a Hittite officer, who was killed in battle on instructions from David so that he could marry Uriah's wife Bathsheba (II Samuel 11).

uric (ˈjʊərɪk) ADJECTIVE of, concerning, or derived from urine.
▷HISTORY C18: from URO-[1] + -IC

uric acid NOUN a white odourless tasteless crystalline product of protein metabolism, present in the blood and urine; 2,6,8-trihydroxypurine. Formula: $C_5H_4N_4O_3$.

uridine (ˈjʊərɪˌdiːn) NOUN *Biochem* a nucleoside present in all living cells in a combined form, esp in RNA.
▷HISTORY C20: from URO-[1] + -IDE + -INE[2]

uridylic acid (ˌjuːrɪˈdɪlɪk) NOUN a nucleotide consisting of uracil, ribose, and a phosphate group. It is a constituent of RNA. Also called: **uridine monophosphate.**

Uriel (ˈjʊərɪəl) NOUN one of the four chief angels in Jewish apocryphal writings.

Urim and Thummim (ˈjʊərɪm, ˈθʌmɪm) NOUN *Old Testament* two objects probably used as oracles and carried in the breastplate of the high priest (Exodus 28:30).
▷HISTORY C16: from Hebrew

urinal (jʊˈraɪnᵊl, ˈjʊərɪ-) NOUN [1] a sanitary fitting, esp one fixed to a wall, used by men for urination. [2] a room containing urinals. [3] any vessel for holding urine prior to its disposal.

urinalysis (ˌjʊərɪˈnælɪsɪs) *or* **uranalysis** NOUN, *plural* **-ses** (-ˌsiːz). *Med* analysis of the urine to test for the presence of disease by the presence of protein, glucose, ketones, cells, etc.

urinant (ˈjʊərɪnənt) ADJECTIVE *Heraldry* having the head downwards.
▷HISTORY C17: from Latin *ūrīnāri* to dive

urinary (ˈjʊərɪnərɪ) ADJECTIVE [1] *Anatomy* of or relating to urine or to the organs and structures that secrete and pass urine. ◆ NOUN, *plural* **-naries.** [2] a reservoir for urine. [3] another word for **urinal.**

urinary bladder NOUN a distensible membranous sac in which the urine excreted from the kidneys is stored.

urinate (ˈjʊərɪˌneɪt) VERB (*intr*) to excrete or void urine; micturate.
▸**ˌuriˈnation** NOUN ▸**ˈurinative** ADJECTIVE

urine (ˈjʊərɪn) NOUN the pale yellow slightly acid fluid excreted by the kidneys, containing waste products removed from the blood. It is stored in the urinary bladder and discharged through the urethra. Related adjective: **uretic.**
▷HISTORY C14: via Old French from Latin *ūrīna;* related to Greek *ouron,* Latin *ūrīnāre* to plunge under water

uriniferous (ˌjʊərɪˈnɪfərəs) ADJECTIVE conveying urine.

urinogenital (ˌjʊərɪnəʊˈdʒɛnɪtᵊl) ADJECTIVE another word for **urogenital** or **genitourinary.**

urinometer (ˌjʊərɪˈnɒmɪtə) NOUN *Med* an instrument for determining the specific gravity of urine.

urinous (ˈjʊərɪnəs) *or* **urinose** ADJECTIVE of, resembling, or containing urine.

URL ABBREVIATION FOR uniform resource locator; a standardized address of a location on the Internet, esp on the World Wide Web.

Urmia (ˈɜːmɪə) NOUN **Lake.** a shallow lake in NW Iran, at an altitude of 1300 m (4250 ft.): the largest lake in Iran, varying in area from 4000–6000 sq. km (1500–2300 sq. miles) between autumn and spring.

Urmston (ˈɜːmstən) NOUN a town in NW England, in Salford unitary authority, Greater Manchester. Pop.: 41 804 (1991).

urn (ɜːn) NOUN [1] a vaselike receptacle or vessel, esp a large bulbous one with a foot. [2] a vase used as a receptacle for the ashes of the dead. [3] a large vessel, usually of metal, with a tap, used for making and holding tea, coffee, etc. [4] *Botany* the spore-producing capsule of a moss.
▷HISTORY C14: from Latin *ūrna;* related to Latin *ūrere* to burn, *urceus* pitcher, Greek *hurkhē* jar
▸**ˈurnˌlike** ADJECTIVE

urnfield (ˈɜːnˌfiːld) NOUN [1] a cemetery full of individual cremation urns. ◆ ADJECTIVE [2] (of a number of Bronze Age cultures) characterized by cremation in urns, which began in E Europe about the second millennium B.C. and by the seventh century B.C. had covered almost all of mainland Europe.

urning (ˈɜːnɪŋ) NOUN a rare word for **homosexual** (esp a male homosexual).
▷HISTORY C20: from German, from URANIA (Aphrodite); compare URANISM

uro-[1] *or before a vowel* **ur-** COMBINING FORM indicating urine or the urinary tract: *urochrome; urogenital; urolith; urology.*
▷HISTORY from Greek *ouron* urine

uro-[2] *or before a vowel* **ur-** COMBINING FORM indicating a tail: *urochord; uropod; urostyle.*
▷HISTORY from Greek *oura*

urobilin (ˌjʊərəʊˈbaɪlɪn) NOUN a brownish pigment found in faeces and sometimes in urine. It is formed by oxidation of **urobilinogen,** a colourless substance produced by bacterial degradation of the bile pigment bilirubin in the intestine.

urochord (ˈjʊərəʊˌkɔːd) NOUN [1] the notochord of a larval tunicate, typically confined to the tail region. ◆ NOUN, ADJECTIVE [2] Also: **urochordate** (ˌjʊərəʊˈkɔːdeɪt). another word for **tunicate.**
▷HISTORY C19: from URO-[2] + *chord,* a variant of CORD
▸**ˌuroˈchordal** ADJECTIVE

urochrome (ˈjʊərəʊˌkrəʊm) NOUN the yellowish pigment that colours urine.
▷HISTORY C19: from URO-[1] + -CHROME

urodele (ˈjʊərəʊˌdiːl) NOUN [1] any amphibian of the order *Urodela,* having a long body and tail and four short limbs: includes the salamanders and newts. ◆ ADJECTIVE [2] of, relating to, or belonging to the *Urodela.*
▷HISTORY C19: from French *urodèle,* from URO-[2] + *-dèle,* from Greek *dēlos* evident

urodynamics (ˌjʊərəʊdaɪˈnæmɪks) NOUN (*functioning as singular*) the study and measurement of the flow of urine in the urinary tract.

urogenital (ˌjʊərəʊˈdʒɛnɪtᵊl) *or* **urinogenital** ADJECTIVE of or relating to the urinary and genital organs and their functions. Also: **genitourinary.**

urogenital system *or* **tract** NOUN *Anatomy* the urinary tract and reproductive organs.

urogenous (juˈrɒdʒɪnəs) ADJECTIVE [1] producing or derived from urine. [2] involved in the secretion and excretion of urine.

urography (juˈrɒgrəfɪ) NOUN another name for **pyelography.**

urolith (ˈjuərəulɪθ) NOUN *Pathol* a calculus in the urinary tract.
▷HISTORY from URO-¹ + Greek *lithos* stone
▸ ˌ**uroˈlithic** ADJECTIVE

urology (juˈrɒlədʒɪ) NOUN the branch of medicine concerned with the study and treatment of diseases of the urogenital tract.
▸**urologic** (ˌjuərəˈlɒdʒɪk) *or* ˌ**uroˈlogical** ADJECTIVE
▸**uˈrologist** NOUN

uropod (ˈjuərəuˌpɒd) NOUN the paired appendage that arises from the last segment of the body in lobsters and related crustaceans and forms part of the tail fan.
▷HISTORY C19: from URO-² + -POD
▸**uropodal** (juˈrɒpədᵊl) *or* **uˈropodous** ADJECTIVE

uropygial gland NOUN a gland, situated at the base of the tail in most birds, that secretes oil used in preening.

uropygium (ˌjuərəˈpɪdʒɪəm) NOUN the hindmost part of a bird's body, from which the tail feathers grow.
▷HISTORY C19: via New Latin from Greek *ouropugion,* from URO-² + *pugē* rump
▸ ˌ**uroˈpygial** ADJECTIVE

uroscopy (juˈrɒskəpɪ) NOUN *Med* examination of the urine. See also **urinalysis.**
▸**uroscopic** (ˌjuərəˈskɒpɪk) ADJECTIVE ▸**uˈroscopist** NOUN

urostyle (ˈjuərəuˌstaɪl) NOUN the bony rod forming the last segment of the vertebral column of frogs, toads, and related amphibians.
▷HISTORY C19: from URO-² + Greek *stulos* pillar

Urquhart Castle (ˈɜːkət) NOUN a castle near Drumnadrochit in Highland, Scotland: situated on Loch Ness.

Ursa Major (ˈɜːsə ˈmeɪdʒə) NOUN, *Latin genitive* **Ursae Majoris** (ˈɜːsiː məˈdʒɔːrɪs). an extensive conspicuous constellation in the N hemisphere, visible north of latitude 40°. The seven brightest stars form the **Plough**. A line through the two brightest stars points to the Pole Star lying in **Ursa Minor**. Also called: **the Great Bear, the Bear.**
▷HISTORY Latin: greater bear

Ursa Minor (ˈɜːsə ˈmaɪnə) NOUN, *Latin genitive* **Ursae Minoris** (ˈɜːsiː mɪˈnɔːrɪs). a small faint constellation, the brightest star of which is the Pole Star, lying 1° from the true celestial pole. Also called: **the Little Bear, the Bear,** (US and Canadian) **the Little Dipper.**
▷HISTORY Latin: lesser bear

ursine (ˈɜːsaɪn) ADJECTIVE of, relating to, or resembling a bear or bears.
▷HISTORY C16: from Latin *ursus* a bear

Ursprache *German* (ˈuːrʃpraːxə) NOUN any hypothetical extinct and unrecorded language reconstructed from groups of related recorded languages. For example, Germanic is an Ursprache reconstructed by comparison of English, Dutch, German, the Scandinavian languages, and Gothic; Indo-European is an Ursprache reconstructed by comparison of the Germanic group, Latin, Sanskrit, etc.
▷HISTORY from *ur-* primeval, original + *Sprache* language

Ursuline (ˈɜːsjuˌlaɪn) NOUN a member of an order of nuns devoted to teaching in the Roman Catholic Church: founded in 1537 at Brescia.
▷HISTORY C16: named after St Ursula, legendary British princess and martyr of the fourth or fifth century A.D., patron saint of St Angela Merici, who founded the order

Urtext *German* (ˈuːrtɛkst) NOUN [1] the earliest form of a text as established by linguistic scholars as a basis for variants in later texts still in existence. [2] an edition of a musical score showing the composer's intentions without later editorial interpolation.
▷HISTORY from *ur-* original + TEXT

urticaceous (ˌɜːtɪˈkeɪʃəs) ADJECTIVE of, relating to, or belonging to the *Urticaceae,* a family of plants, having small flowers and, in many species, stinging hairs: includes the nettles and pellitory.
▷HISTORY C18: via New Latin from Latin *urtīca* nettle, from *ūrere* to burn

urticaria (ˌɜːtɪˈkɛərɪə) NOUN a skin condition characterized by the formation of itchy red or whitish raised patches, usually caused by an allergy. Nontechnical names: **hives, nettle rash.**
▷HISTORY C18: from New Latin, from Latin *urtīca* nettle
▸ ˌ**urtiˈcarial** *or* ˌ**urtiˈcarious** ADJECTIVE

urticate (ˈɜːtɪˌkeɪt) ADJECTIVE [1] Also: **urticant** (ˈɜːtɪkənt). characterized by the presence of weals. ◆ VERB [2] to perform urtication.
▷HISTORY C19: from Medieval Latin *urtīcāre* to sting, from Latin *urtīca* a nettle

urtication (ˌɜːtɪˈkeɪʃən) NOUN [1] a burning or itching sensation. [2] another name for **urticaria.** [3] a former method of producing counterirritation of the skin by beating the area with nettles.

Uru. ABBREVIATION FOR Uruguay.

Uruapan (*Spanish* uˈrwapan) NOUN a city in SW Mexico, in Michoacán state: agricultural trading centre. Pop.: 227 000 (2000 est.).

Uruguay (ˈjuərəˌgwaɪ) NOUN a republic in South America, on the Atlantic: Spanish colonization began in 1624, followed by Portuguese settlement in 1680; revolted against Spanish rule in 1820 but was annexed by the Portuguese to Brazil; gained independence in 1825. It consists mainly of rolling grassy plains, low hills, and plateaus. Official language: Spanish. Religion: Roman Catholic majority. Currency: peso. Capital: Montevideo. Pop.: 3 303 000 (2001 est.). Area: 176 215 sq. km (68 037 sq. miles).

Uruguayan (ˌjuərəˈgwaɪən) ADJECTIVE [1] of or relating to Uruguay or its inhabitants. ◆ NOUN [2] a native or inhabitant of Uruguay.

Urumchi (uːˈruːmtʃɪ), **Urumqi,** *or* **Wu-lu-mu-ch'i** NOUN a city in NW China, capital of Xinjiang Uygur Autonomous Region: trading centre on a N route between China and central Asia. Pop.: 1 258 457 (1999 est.). Former name: **Tihwa.**

Urundi (uˈrundɪ) NOUN the former name (until 1962) of **Burundi.**

urus (ˈjuərəs) NOUN, *plural* **uruses.** another name for the **aurochs.**
▷HISTORY C17: from *ūrus,* of Germanic origin; compare Old High German *ūr,* Old Norse *urr,* Greek *ouros* aurochs

urushiol (ˈuːruʃɪˌɒl, uːˈruː-) NOUN a poisonous pale yellow liquid occurring in poison ivy and the lacquer tree.
▷HISTORY from Japanese *urushi* lacquer + -OL²

us¹ (ʌs) PRONOUN (*objective*) [1] refers to the speaker or writer and another person or other people: *don't hurt us; to decide among us.* [2] refers to all people or people in general: *this table shows us the tides.* [3] an informal word for **me¹**. *give us a kiss!* [4] a formal word for **me¹** used by editors, monarchs, etc. [5] *Chiefly US* a dialect word for **ourselves** when used as an indirect object: *we ought to get us a car.*
▷HISTORY Old English *ūs;* related to Old High German *uns,* Old Norse *oss,* Latin *nōs,* Sanskrit *nas* we

> **Language note** See at **me¹**.

us² THE INTERNET DOMAIN NAME FOR United States.

u.s. ABBREVIATION FOR: [1] ubi supra. [2] ut supra.

U.S. *or* **US** ABBREVIATION FOR United States.

U/S *Informal* ◆ ABBREVIATION FOR: [1] unserviceable. [2] useless.

USA [1] ABBREVIATION FOR United States Army. ◆ [2] INTERNATIONAL CAR REGISTRATION FOR United States of America.

U.S.A. *or* **USA** ABBREVIATION FOR United States of America.

usable *or* **useable** (ˈjuːzəbᵊl) ADJECTIVE able to be used.
▸ ˌ**usaˈbility** *or* ˌ**useaˈbility** *or* ˈ**usableness** *or* ˈ**useableness** NOUN ▸ˈ**usably** *or* ˈ**useably** ADVERB

USAF ABBREVIATION FOR United States Air Force.

usage (ˈjuːsɪdʒ, -zɪdʒ) NOUN [1] the act or a manner of using; use; employment. [2] constant use, custom, or habit. [3] something permitted or established by custom or practice. [4] what is actually said in a language, esp as contrasted with what is prescribed.
▷HISTORY C14: via Old French, from Latin *ūsus* USE (n)

usance (ˈjuːzəns) NOUN [1] *Commerce* the period of time permitted by commercial usage for the redemption of foreign bills of exchange. [2] *Rare* unearned income. [3] an obsolete word for **usage, usury** or **use.**
▷HISTORY C14: from Old French, from Medieval Latin *ūsantia,* from *ūsāre* to USE

USB ABBREVIATION FOR Universal Serial Bus: a standard for connection sockets on computers and other electronic equipment.

USDAW (ˈʌzˌdɔː) NOUN ACRONYM FOR Union of Shop, Distributive, and Allied Workers.

use VERB (juːz) (*tr*) [1] to put into service or action; employ for a given purpose: *to use a spoon to stir with.* [2] to make a practice or habit of employing; exercise: *he uses his brain.* [3] to behave towards: *to use a friend well.* [4] to behave towards in a particular way for one's own ends: *he uses people.* [5] to consume, expend, or exhaust: *the engine uses very little oil.* [6] *Chiefly US and Canadian* to partake of (alcoholic drink, drugs, etc.) or smoke (tobacco, marijuana, etc.). ◆ NOUN (juːs) [7] the act of using or the state of being used: *the carpet wore out through constant use.* [8] the ability, right, or permission to use. [9] the occasion to use; need: *I have no use for this paper.* [10] an instance or manner of using. [11] usefulness; advantage: *it is of no use to complain.* [12] custom; practice; habit: *long use has inured him to it.* [13] the purpose for which something is used; end. [14] *Christianity* a distinctive form of liturgical or ritual observance, esp one that is traditional in a Church or group of Churches. [15] the enjoyment of property, land, etc., by occupation or by deriving revenue or other benefit from it. [16] *Law* the beneficial enjoyment of property the legal title to which is held by another person as trustee. [17] *Law* an archaic word for **trust** (sense 7). [18] *Philosophy, logic, linguistics* the occurrence of an expression in such a context that it performs its own linguistic function rather than being itself referred to. In *"Fido" refers to Fido,* the name *Fido* is used only on the second occurrence, first being mentioned. Compare **mention** (sense 7). See also **material mode.** [19] **have no use for. a** to have no need of. **b** to have a contemptuous dislike for. [20] **make use of. a** to employ; use. **b** to exploit (a person). ◆ See also **used to, use up.**
▷HISTORY C13: from Old French *user* to use, from Latin *ūsus* having used, from *ūtī* to use

used (juːzd) ADJECTIVE bought or sold second-hand: *used cars.*

used to (juːst) ADJECTIVE [1] made familiar with; accustomed to: *I am used to hitchhiking.* ◆ VERB (*tr*) [2] (*takes an infinitive or implied infinitive*) used as an auxiliary to express habitual or accustomed actions, states, etc., taking place in the present but not continuing into the present: *I don't drink these days, but I used to; I used to fish here every day.*

> **Language note** The most common negative form of *used to* is *didn't used to* (or *didn't use to*), but in formal contexts *used not to* is preferred.

useful (ˈjuːsful) ADJECTIVE [1] able to be used advantageously, beneficially, or for several purposes; helpful or serviceable. [2] *Informal* commendable or capable: *a useful term's work.* ◆ NOUN [3] *Austral informal* an odd-jobman or general factotum.
▸ˈ**usefully** ADVERB ▸ˈ**usefulness** NOUN

useless (ˈjuːslɪs) ADJECTIVE [1] having no practical use or advantage. [2] *Informal* ineffectual, weak, or stupid: *he's useless at history.*
▸ˈ**uselessly** ADVERB ▸ˈ**uselessness** NOUN

user (ˈjuːzə) NOUN [1] *Law* **a** the continued exercise, use, or enjoyment of a right, esp in property. **b** a presumptive right based on long-continued use: *right of user.* [2] (*often in combination*) a person or thing that uses: *a road-user.* [3] *Informal* a drug addict.

user-defined key NOUN a key on the keyboard

of a computer that can be used to carry out any of a limited number of predefined actions as selected by the user.

user-friendly ADJECTIVE [1] easy to use or understand: *a user-friendly dictionary.* [2] (of a computer system) easily operated and understood by means of a straightforward guide in jargon-free language.
▸**user-friendliness** NOUN

use up VERB *(tr, adverb)* [1] to finish (a supply); consume completely. [2] to exhaust; wear out.

Ushant ('ʌʃənt) NOUN an island off the NW coast of France, at the tip of Brittany: scene of naval battles in 1778 and 1794 between France and Britain. Area: about 16 sq. km (6 sq. miles). French name: **Ouessant.**

U-shaped valley NOUN *Geology* a steep-sided valley caused by glacial erosion.

Ushas ('u:ʃəs) NOUN the Hindu goddess of the dawn.

usher ('ʌʃə) NOUN [1] an official who shows people to their seats, as in a church or theatre. [2] a person who acts as doorkeeper, esp in a court of law. [3] (in England) a minor official charged with maintaining order in a court of law. [4] an officer responsible for preceding persons of rank in a procession or introducing strangers at formal functions. [5] *Brit obsolete* a teacher. ◆ VERB *(tr)* [6] to conduct or escort, esp in a courteous or obsequious way. [7] (usually foll by *in*) to be a precursor or herald (of).
▹HISTORY C14: from Old French *huissier* doorkeeper, from Vulgar Latin *ustiārius* (unattested), from Latin *ostium* door

usherette (ˌʌʃə'rɛt) NOUN a woman assistant in a cinema, theatre, etc., who shows people to their seats.

Usk (ʌsk) NOUN a river in SE Wales, flowing southeast and south to the Bristol Channel. Length: 113 km (70 miles).

Üsküb ('ʊsku:b) NOUN the Turkish name (1392–1913) for **Skopje.**

Üsküdar (ˌu:sku:'dɑ:) NOUN a town in NW Turkey, across the Bosporus from Istanbul: formerly a terminus of caravan routes from Syria and Asia; base of the British army in the Crimean War. Pop.: 261 140 (latest est.). Former name: **Scutari.**

USM ABBREVIATION FOR: [1] *Stock Exchange* **unlisted securities market.** [2] underwater-to-surface missile.

USN ABBREVIATION FOR United States Navy.

Usnach *or* **Usnech** ('ʊʃnəx) NOUN (in Irish legend) the father of Naoise.

USO (in the US) ABBREVIATION FOR United Service Organization.

USP ABBREVIATION FOR unique selling proposition or unique selling point: a characteristic of a product that can be used in advertising to differentiate it from its competitors.

Uspallata Pass (ˌu:spə'lɑ:tə; *Spanish* uspa'ʎata) NOUN a pass over the Andes in S South America, between Mendoza (Argentina) and Santiago (Chile). Height: 3840 m (12 600 ft.). Also called: **La Cumbre.**

usquebaugh ('ʌskwɪˌbɔ:) NOUN [1] *Irish* the former name for **whiskey.** [2] *Scot* the former name for **whisky.** [3] an Irish liqueur flavoured with coriander.
▹HISTORY C16: from Irish Gaelic *uisce beathadh* or Scot Gaelic *uisge beatha* water of life

USS ABBREVIATION FOR: [1] United States Senate. [2] United States Ship.

USSR (formerly) ABBREVIATION FOR Union of Soviet Socialist Republics.

Ussuri (*Russian* ussu'ri) NOUN a river in E central Asia, flowing north, forming part of the Chinese border with Russia, to the Amur River. Length: about 800 km (500 miles).

Ustashi (u'stɑ:ʃɪ) NOUN (formerly) a terrorist organization of right-wing Yugoslav exiles dedicated to the overthrow of Communism in their homeland.
▹HISTORY from Serbo-Croat

Ústí nad Labem (*Czech* 'u:stji: nad 'labɛm) NOUN a port in the Czech Republic, on the Elbe River: textile and chemical industries. Pop.: 118 000 (1993).

Ust-Kamenogorsk (*Russian* ustjkəmɪna'gɔrsk) NOUN a city in E Kazakhstan: centre of a zinc-, lead-, and copper-mining area. Pop.: 311 000 (1999).

ustulation (ˌʌstjʊ'leɪʃən) NOUN the act or process of searing or burning.
▹HISTORY C17: from Late Latin *ustulāre,* from Latin *ūrere* to burn

Ustyurt *or* **Ust Urt** (*Russian* us'tjurt) NOUN an arid plateau in central Asia, between the Caspian and Aral seas in Kazakhstan and Uzbekistan. Area: about 238 000 sq. km (92 000 sq. miles).

usual ('ju:ʒʊəl) ADJECTIVE [1] of the most normal, frequent, or regular type; customary: *that's the usual sort of application to send.* ◆ NOUN [2] ordinary or commonplace events (esp in the phrase **out of the usual**). [3] **the usual.** *Informal* the habitual or usual drink, meal, etc.
▹HISTORY C14: from Late Latin *ūsuālis* ordinary, from Latin *ūsus* USE
▸'**usualness** NOUN

usually ('ju:ʒʊəlɪ) ADVERB *(sentence modifier)* customarily; at most times; in the ordinary course of events.

usufruct ('ju:sjʊˌfrʌkt) NOUN the right to use and derive profit from a piece of property belonging to another, provided the property itself remains undiminished and uninjured in any way.
▹HISTORY C17: from Late Latin *ūsūfrūctus,* from Latin *ūsus* use + *frūctus* enjoyment
▸ˌ**usu'fructuary** NOUN, ADJECTIVE

Usumbura (ˌu:zəm'bʊərə) NOUN the former name of **Bujumbura.**

usurer ('ju:ʒərə) NOUN [1] a person who lends funds at an exorbitant rate of interest. [2] *Obsolete* a moneylender.

usurp (ju:'zɜ:p) VERB to seize, take over, or appropriate (land, a throne, etc.) without authority.
▹HISTORY C14: from Old French *usurper,* from Latin *ūsūrpāre* to take into use, probably from *ūsus* use + *rapere* to seize
▸ˌ**usur'pation** NOUN ▸**u'surpative** *or* **u'surpatory** ADJECTIVE
▸**u'surper** NOUN

usury ('ju:ʒərɪ) NOUN, *plural* **-ries.** [1] the act or practice of loaning money at an exorbitant rate of interest. [2] an exorbitant or unlawfully high amount or rate of interest. [3] *Obsolete* moneylending.
▹HISTORY C14: from Medieval Latin *ūsūria,* from Latin *ūsūra* usage, from *ūsus* USE
▸**usurious** (ju:'ʒʊərɪəs) ADJECTIVE

USW *Radio* ABBREVIATION FOR ultrashort wave.

ut (ʌt, u:t) NOUN *Music* [1] the syllable used in the fixed system of solmization for the note C. [2] the first note of a hexachord in medieval music.
▹HISTORY C14: from Latin *ut;* see GAMUT

UT ABBREVIATION FOR: [1] universal time. [2] Utah.

Utah ('ju:tɔ:, 'ju:tɑ:) NOUN a state of the western US: settled by Mormons in 1847; situated in the Great Basin and the Rockies, with the Great Salt Lake in the northwest; mainly arid and mountainous. Capital: Salt Lake City. Pop.: 2 233 169 (2000). Area: 212 628 sq. km (82 096 sq. miles). Abbreviations: **Ut,** (with zip code) **UT.**

Utahan (ju:'tɔ:ən, -'tɑ:ən) ADJECTIVE [1] of or relating to Utah or its inhabitants. ◆ NOUN [2] a native or inhabitant of Utah.

UTC ABBREVIATION FOR universal time coordinated. See **universal time.**

ut dict. (in prescriptions) ABBREVIATION FOR as directed.
▹HISTORY from Latin *ut dictum*

ute (ju:t) NOUN *Austral and NZ informal* short for **utility** (sense 6).

Ute (ju:t, 'ju:tɪ) NOUN [1] *(plural* **Utes** *or* **Ute)** a member of a North American Indian people of Utah, Colorado, and New Mexico, related to the Aztecs. [2] the language of this people, belonging to the Shoshonean subfamily of the Uto-Aztecan family.

utensil (ju:'tɛnsəl) NOUN an implement, tool, or container for practical use: *writing utensils.*
▹HISTORY C14 *utensele,* via Old French from Latin *ūtēnsilia* necessaries, from *ūtēnsilis* available for use, from *ūtī* to use

uterine ('ju:təˌraɪn) ADJECTIVE [1] of, relating to, or affecting the uterus. [2] (of offspring) born of the same mother but not the same father: *uterine brothers.*

uterus ('ju:tərəs) NOUN, *plural* **uteri** ('ju:təˌraɪ). [1] *Anatomy* a hollow muscular organ lying within the pelvic cavity of female mammals. It houses the developing fetus and by contractions aids in its expulsion at parturition. Nontechnical name: **womb.** [2] the corresponding organ in other animals.
▹HISTORY C17: from Latin; compare Greek *hustera* womb, *hoderos* belly, Sanskrit *udara* belly

Utgard ('ʊtgɑ:d, 'u:t-) NOUN *Norse myth* one of the divisions of Jotunheim, land of the giants, ruled by Utgard-Loki.

Utgard-Loki NOUN *Norse myth* the giant king of Utgard.

Uther ('ju:θə) *or* **Uther Pendragon** NOUN (in Arthurian legend) a king of Britain and father of Arthur.

Utica ('ju:tɪkə) NOUN an ancient city on the N coast of Africa, northwest of Carthage.

utile ('ju:taɪl, -tɪl) ADJECTIVE an obsolete word for **useful.**
▹HISTORY C15: via Old French from Latin *ūtilis,* from *ūtī* to use

utilidor (ju:'tɪlɪˌdɔ:) NOUN *Canadian* an enclosed and insulated conduit for sewage and other utilities placed above the level of permafrost.

utilitarian (ju:ˌtɪlɪ'tɛərɪən) ADJECTIVE [1] of or relating to utilitarianism. [2] designed for use rather than beauty. ◆ NOUN [3] a person who believes in utilitarianism.

utilitarianism (ju:ˌtɪlɪ'tɛərɪəˌnɪzəm) NOUN *Ethics* [1] the doctrine that the morally correct course of action consists in the greatest good for the greatest number, that is, in maximizing the total benefit resulting, without regard to the distribution of benefits and burdens. [2] the theory that the criterion of virtue is utility.

utility (ju:'tɪlɪtɪ) NOUN, *plural* **-ties.** [1] **a** the quality of practical use; usefulness; serviceability. **b** *(as modifier): a utility fabric.* [2] something useful. [3] **a** a public service, such as the bus system; public utility. **b** *(as modifier): utility vehicle.* [4] *Economics* **a** the ability of a commodity to satisfy human wants. **b** the amount of such satisfaction. ◆ Compare **disutility.** [5] *Statistics* **a** a measure of the total benefit or disadvantage attaching to each of a set of alternative courses of action. **b** *(as modifier): utility function.* ◆ See also **expected utility, decision theory.** [6] Also called: **utility truck,** *informal* **ute.** *Austral and NZ* a small truck with an open body and low sides, often with a removable tarpaulin cover; pick-up. [7] a piece of computer software designed for a routine task, such as examining or copying files.
▹HISTORY C14: from Old French *utelite,* from Latin *ūtilitās* usefulness, from *ūtī* to use

utility function NOUN *Economics* a function relating specific goods and services in an economy to individual preferences.

utility man NOUN *Chiefly US* [1] a worker who is expected to serve in any of several capacities. [2] an actor who plays any of numerous small parts.

utility player NOUN *Sport* a player who is capable of playing competently in any of several positions.

utility room NOUN a room with equipment for domestic work like washing and ironing.

utility truck NOUN another name for **utility** (sense 6).

utility wear NOUN casual clothing that was originally intended for a particular activity, such as snowboarding or skiing.

utilize *or* **utilise** ('ju:tɪˌlaɪz) VERB *(tr)* to make practical or worthwhile use of.
▸'**utiˌlizable** *or* '**utiˌlisable** ADJECTIVE ▸ˌ**utili'zation** *or* ˌ**utili'sation** NOUN ▸'**utiˌlizer** *or* '**utiˌliser** NOUN

ut infra *Latin* (ʊt 'ɪnfrɑ:) as below.

uti possidetis ('ju:taɪ ˌpɒsɪ'di:tɪs) NOUN *International law* the rule that territory and other property remains in the hands of the belligerent state actually in possession at the end of a war unless otherwise provided for by treaty.
▹HISTORY from Latin, literally: as you possess

utmost ('ʌtˌməʊst) *or* **uttermost** ADJECTIVE *(prenominal)* [1] of the greatest possible degree or amount: *the utmost degree.* [2] at the furthest limit: *the utmost town on the peninsula.* ◆ NOUN [3] the greatest possible degree, extent, or amount: *he tried his utmost.*

▷HISTORY Old English *ūtemest,* from *ūte* out + *-mest* MOST

utmost good faith NOUN a principle used in insurance contracts, legally obliging all parties to reveal to the others any information that might influence the others' decision to enter into the contract. Also called: ***uberrima fides.***

Uto-Aztecan ('ju:təʊ'æztɛkən) NOUN [1] a family of North and Central American Indian languages including Nahuatl, Shoshone, Pima, and Ute. ◆ ADJECTIVE [2] of or relating to this family of languages or the peoples speaking them.

Utopia (ju:'təʊpɪə) NOUN *(sometimes not capital)* any real or imaginary society, place, state, etc., considered to be perfect or ideal.
▷HISTORY C16: from New Latin *Utopia* (coined by Sir Thomas More in 1516 as the title of his book that described an imaginary island representing the perfect society), literally: no place, from Greek *ou* not + *topos* a place

Utopian (ju:'təʊpɪən) *(sometimes not capital)* ADJECTIVE [1] of or relating to a perfect or ideal existence. ◆ NOUN [2] an idealistic social reformer.
▸**U'topianism** NOUN

utopian socialism NOUN *(sometimes capitals)* socialism established by the peaceful surrender of the means of production by capitalists moved by moral persuasion, example, etc.: the form of socialism advocated by Robert Owen, the Welsh industrialist and social reformer (1771–1858), Johann Gottlieb Fichte, the German philosopher (1762–1814), and others. Compare **scientific socialism.**

Utrecht (*Dutch* 'y:trɛxt; *English* 'ju:trɛkt) NOUN [1] a province of the W central Netherlands. Capital: Utrecht. Pop.: 1 107 800 (2000 est.). Area: 1362 sq. km (526 sq. miles). [2] a city in the central Netherlands, capital of Utrecht province: scene of the signing (1579) of the **Union of Utrecht** (the foundation of the later kingdom of the Netherlands) and of the **Treaty of Utrecht** (1713), ending the War of the Spanish Succession. Pop.: 232 718 (1999 est.).

utricle ('ju:trɪkᵊl) *or* **utriculus** (ju:'trɪkjʊləs) NOUN, *plural* **utricles** *or* **utriculi** (ju:'trɪkjʊˌlaɪ). [1] *Anatomy* the larger of the two parts of the membranous labyrinth of the internal ear. Compare **saccule.** [2] *Botany* the bladder-like one-seeded indehiscent fruit of certain plants, esp sedges.
▷HISTORY C18: from Latin *ūtriculus* diminutive of *ūter* bag
▸**u'tricular** *or* **u'triculate** ADJECTIVE

utriculitis (ju:ˌtrɪkjʊ'laɪtɪs) NOUN inflammation of the inner ear.

ut supra *Latin* (ʊt 'su:prɑ:) as above.

Uttaranchal ('ʊtə'ræntʃʌl) NOUN a state of N India, created in 2000 from the N part of Uttar Pradesh: in the Himalayas, rising to over 7500 m (25 000 ft); rice, tea, and timber. Capital: Dehra Dun. Pop.: 8 479 562 (2001). Area: 51 125 sq. km (19 739 sq. miles).

Uttar Pradesh ('ʊtə 'prɑ:dɛʃ) NOUN a state of N India: the most populous state; originated in 1877 with the merging of Agra and Oudh as the United Provinces; augmented by the states of Rampur, Benares, and Tehri-Garhwal in 1949; the N Himalayan region passed to the new state of Uttaranchal in 2000; now consists mostly of the Upper Ganges plain; agricultural. Capital: Lucknow. Pop.: 166 052 859 (2001). Area: 243 350 sq. km (93 933 sq. miles).

utter[1] ('ʌtə) VERB [1] to give audible expression to (something): *to utter a growl.* [2] *Criminal law* to put into circulation (counterfeit coin, forged banknotes, etc.). [3] *(tr)* to make publicly known; publish: *to utter slander.* [4] *Obsolete* to give forth, issue, or emit.
▷HISTORY C14: probably originally a commercial term, from Middle Dutch *ūteren* (modern Dutch *uiteren*) to make known; related to Middle Low German *ūtern* to sell, show
▸**'utterable** ADJECTIVE ▸**'utterableness** NOUN ▸**'utterer** NOUN ▸**'utterless** ADJECTIVE

utter[2] ('ʌtə) ADJECTIVE *(prenominal)* (intensifier): *an utter fool; utter bliss; the utter limit.*
▷HISTORY C15: from Old English *utera* outer, comparative of *ūte* OUT (adv); related to Old High German *ūzaro,* Old Norse *ūtri*

utterance[1] ('ʌtərəns) NOUN [1] something uttered, such as a statement. [2] the act or power of uttering or the ability to utter. [3] *Logic, philosophy* an element of spoken language, esp a sentence. Compare **inscription** (sense 4).

utterance[2] ('ʌtərəns) NOUN *Archaic or literary* the bitter end (esp in the phrase **to the utterance**).
▷HISTORY C13: from Old French *oultrance,* from *oultrer* to carry to excess, from Latin *ultrā* beyond

utter barrister NOUN *Law* the full title of a barrister who is not a Queen's Counsel. See also **junior** (sense 6).

utterly ('ʌtəlɪ) ADVERB (intensifier): *I'm utterly miserable.*

uttermost ('ʌtəˌməʊst) ADJECTIVE, NOUN a variant of **utmost.**

U-turn NOUN [1] a turn made by a vehicle in the shape of a U, resulting in a reversal of direction. [2] a complete change in direction of political or other policy.

UU ABBREVIATION FOR Ulster Unionist.

UV ABBREVIATION FOR ultraviolet.

UV-A *or* **UVA** ABBREVIATION FOR ultraviolet radiation with a range of 315–380 nanometres.

uvarovite (u:'vɑ:rəˌvaɪt) NOUN an emerald-green garnet found in chromium deposits: consists of calcium chromium silicate. Formula: $Ca_3Cr_2(SiO_4)_3$.
▷HISTORY C19: from German *Uvarovit;* named after Count Sergei S. *Uvarov* (1785–1855), Russian author and statesman

UV-B *or* **UVB** ABBREVIATION FOR ultraviolet radiation with a range of 280–315 nanometres.

uvea ('ju:vɪə) NOUN the part of the eyeball consisting of the iris, ciliary body, and choroid.
▷HISTORY C16: from Medieval Latin *ūvea,* from Latin *ūva* grape
▸**'uveal** *or* **'uveous** ADJECTIVE

uveitis (ˌju:vɪ'aɪtɪs) NOUN inflammation of the uvea.
▸**uveitic** (ˌju:vɪ'ɪtɪk) ADJECTIVE

UVF ABBREVIATION FOR Ulster Volunteer Force.

uvula ('ju:vjʊlə) NOUN, *plural* **-las** *or* **-lae** (-ˌli:). a small fleshy finger-like flap of tissue that hangs in the back of the throat and is an extension of the soft palate.
▷HISTORY C14: from Medieval Latin, literally: a little grape, from Latin *ūva* a grape

uvular ('ju:vjʊlə) ADJECTIVE [1] of or relating to the uvula. [2] *Phonetics* articulated with the uvula and the back of the tongue, such as the (r) sound of Parisian French. ◆ NOUN [3] a uvular consonant.
▸**'uvularly** ADVERB

uvulitis (ˌju:vjʊ'laɪtɪs) NOUN inflammation of the uvula.

UWIST ('ju:ˌwɪst) NOUN ACRONYM FOR University of Wales Institute of Science and Technology.

Uxbridge ('ʌksˌbrɪdʒ) NOUN a town in SE England, part of the Greater London borough of Hillingdon since 1965; chiefly residential; seat of Brunel University (1966).

Uxmal (*Spanish* uz'mal) NOUN an ancient ruined city in SE Mexico, in Yucatán: capital of the later Maya empire.

uxorial (ʌk'sɔ:rɪəl) ADJECTIVE of or relating to a wife: *uxorial influence.*
▷HISTORY C19: from Latin *uxor* wife
▸**ux'orially** ADVERB

uxoricide (ʌk'sɔ:rɪˌsaɪd) NOUN [1] the act of killing one's wife. [2] a man who kills his wife.
▷HISTORY C19: from Latin *uxor* wife + -CIDE
▸**uxˌori'cidal** ADJECTIVE

uxorious (ʌk'sɔ:rɪəs) ADJECTIVE excessively attached to or dependent on one's wife.
▷HISTORY C16: from Latin *uxōrius* concerning a wife, from *uxor* wife
▸**ux'oriously** ADVERB ▸**ux'oriousness** NOUN

uy THE INTERNET DOMAIN NAME FOR Uruguay.

uz THE INTERNET DOMAIN NAME FOR Uzbekistan.

UZ INTERNATIONAL CAR REGISTRATION FOR Uzbekistan.

Uzbek ('ʊzbɛk, 'ʌz-) NOUN [1] *(plural* **-beks** *or* **-bek**) a member of a Mongoloid people of Uzbekistan. [2] the language of this people, belonging to the Turkic branch of the Altaic family.

Uzbekistan (ˌʌzbɛkɪ'stɑ:n) NOUN a republic in central Asia: annexed by Russia in the 19th century, it became a separate Soviet Socialist republic in 1924 and gained independence in 1991; mining, textile, and chemical industries are important. Official language: Uzbek. Religion: believers are mainly Muslim. Currency: sum. Capital: Tashkent. Pop.: 25 155 000 (2001 est.). Area: 449 600 sq. km (173 546 sq. miles).

Uzi ('u:zɪ) NOUN a sub-machine gun of Israeli design.
▷HISTORY C20: after *Uziel Gal,* the Israeli army officer who designed it

Vv

v *or* **V** (viː) NOUN, *plural* **v's, V's** *or* **Vs.** 1 the 22nd letter and 17th consonant of the modern English alphabet. 2 a speech sound represented by this letter, in English usually a voiced labio-dental fricative, as in *vote.* 3 **a** something shaped like a V. **b** (*in combination*): *a V neck.* See also **V-sign.**

v SYMBOL FOR: 1 *Physics* velocity. 2 specific volume (of a gas).

V SYMBOL FOR: 1 (in transformational grammar) verb. 2 volume (capacity). 3 volt. 4 *Chem* vanadium. 5 luminous efficiency. 6 victory. ◆ 7 THE ROMAN NUMERAL FOR five. See **Roman numerals.** ◆ 8 INTERNATIONAL CAR REGISTRATION FOR Vatican City.

v. 1 verb. 2 verse. 3 version. 4 verso. 5 (*usually italic*) versus. 6 very. 7 vide. [Latin: see] 8 vocative. 9 volume. 10 von.

V. ABBREVIATION FOR: 1 Venerable. 2 (in titles) Very. 3 (in titles) Vice. 4 Viscount.

V-1 NOUN a robot bomb invented by the Germans in World War II: used esp to bombard London. It was propelled by a pulsejet. Also called: **doodlebug, buzz bomb, flying bomb.**
▷**HISTORY** from German *Vergeltungswaffe* revenge weapon

V-2 NOUN a rocket-powered ballistic missile invented by the Germans in World War II: used esp to bombard London. It used ethanol as fuel and liquid oxygen as the oxidizer.
▷**HISTORY** see V-1

V6 NOUN a car or internal-combustion engine having six cylinders arranged in the form of a V.

V8 NOUN a car or internal-combustion engine having eight cylinders arranged in the form of a V.

va THE INTERNET DOMAIN NAME FOR Holy See (Vatican State).

VA ABBREVIATION FOR: 1 (in the US) Veterans' Administration. 2 Vicar Apostolic. 3 Vice Admiral. 4 (Order of) Victoria and Albert. 5 Virginia. 6 **volt-ampere.**

Va. ABBREVIATION FOR Virginia.

v.a. ABBREVIATION FOR verb active.

Vaal (vɑːl) NOUN a river in South Africa, rising in the Drakensberg and flowing west to join the Orange River. Length: 1160 km (720 miles).

Vaasa (*Finnish* ˈvɑːsɑ) NOUN a port in W Finland, on the Gulf of Bothnia: the provisional capital of Finland (1918); textile industries. Pop.: 55 089 (1994). Former name: **Nikolainkaupunki.**

vac (væk) NOUN *Brit informal* short for **vacation.**

vacancy (ˈveɪkənsɪ) NOUN, *plural* **-cies.** 1 the state or condition of being vacant or unoccupied; emptiness. 2 an unoccupied post or office: *we have a vacancy in the accounts department.* 3 an unoccupied room in a boarding house, hotel, etc.: *put the "No Vacancies" sign in the window.* 4 lack of thought or intelligent awareness; inanity: *an expression of vacancy on one's face.* 5 *Physics* a defect in a crystalline solid caused by the absence of an atom, ion, or molecule from its position in the crystal lattice. 6 *Obsolete* idleness or a period spent in idleness.

vacant (ˈveɪkənt) ADJECTIVE 1 without any contents; empty. 2 (*postpositive; foll by of*) devoid (of something specified). 3 having no incumbent; unoccupied: *a vacant post.* 4 having no tenant or occupant: *a vacant house.* 5 characterized by or resulting from lack of thought or intelligent awareness: *a vacant stare.* 6 (of time, etc.) not allocated to any activity: *a vacant hour in one's day.* 7 spent in idleness or inactivity: *a vacant life.* 8 *Law* (of an estate, etc.) having no heir or claimant.
▷**HISTORY** C13: from Latin *vacāre* to be empty
▸ˈ**vacantly** ADVERB ▸ˈ**vacantness** NOUN

vacant possession NOUN ownership of an unoccupied house or property, any previous owner or tenant having departed.

vacate (vəˈkeɪt) VERB (*mainly tr*) 1 to cause (something) to be empty, esp by departing from or abandoning it: *to vacate a room.* 2 (*also intr*) to give up the tenure, possession, or occupancy of (a place, post, etc.); leave or quit. 3 *Law* **a** to cancel or rescind. **b** to make void or of no effect; annul.
▸**vaˈcatable** ADJECTIVE

vacation (vəˈkeɪʃən) NOUN 1 *Chiefly Brit* a period of the year when the law courts or universities are closed. 2 another word (esp US and Canadian) for **holiday.** 3 the act of departing from or abandoning property, etc. ◆ VERB 4 (*intr*) *US and Canadian* to take a vacation; holiday.
▷**HISTORY** C14: from Latin *vacātiō* freedom, from *vacāre* to be empty
▸**vaˈcationless** ADJECTIVE

vacationer (vəˈkeɪʃənə) *or* **vacationist** (vəˈkeɪʃənɪst) NOUN US and Canadian words for **holiday-maker.**

vaccinal (ˈvæksɪnəl) ADJECTIVE of or relating to vaccine or vaccination.

vaccinate (ˈvæksɪˌneɪt) VERB to inoculate (a person) with a vaccine so as to produce immunity against a specific disease.
▸ˈ**vacciˌnator** NOUN

vaccination (ˌvæksɪˈneɪʃən) NOUN 1 the act of vaccinating. 2 the scar left following inoculation with a vaccine.

vaccine (ˈvæksiːn) NOUN *Med* 1 a suspension of dead, attenuated, or otherwise modified microorganisms (viruses, bacteria, or rickettsiae) for inoculation to produce immunity to a disease by stimulating the production of antibodies. 2 (originally) a preparation of the virus of cowpox taken from infected cows and inoculated in humans to produce immunity to smallpox. 3 (*modifier*) of or relating to vaccination or vaccinia. 4 *Computing* a piece of software designed to detect and remove computer viruses from a system.
▷**HISTORY** C18: from New Latin *variolae vaccīnae* cowpox, title of medical treatise (1798) by Edward Jenner, from Latin *vacca* a cow

vaccinia (vækˈsɪnɪə) NOUN a technical name for **cowpox.**
▷**HISTORY** C19: New Latin, from Latin *vaccīnus* of cows
▸**vacˈcinial** ADJECTIVE

Vacherin (*French* vaʃrɛ̃) NOUN 1 a soft French or Swiss cheese made from cow's milk. 2 a dessert consisting of a meringue shell filled with whipped cream, ice cream, fruit, etc.
▷**HISTORY** from French *vache* cow, from Latin *vacca*

vacillate (ˈvæsɪˌleɪt) VERB (*intr*) 1 to fluctuate in one's opinions; be indecisive. 2 to sway from side to side physically; totter or waver.
▷**HISTORY** C16: from Latin *vacillāre* to sway, of obscure origin
▸ˌ**vacilˈlation** NOUN ▸ˈ**vacilˌlator** NOUN

vacillating (ˈvæsɪˌleɪtɪŋ) *or rarely* **vacillant** (ˈvæsɪlənt) ADJECTIVE inclined to waver; indecisive.
▸ˈ**vacilˌlatingly** ADVERB

vacua (ˈvækjʊə) NOUN a plural of **vacuum.**

vacuity (væˈkjuːɪtɪ) NOUN, *plural* **-ties.** 1 the state or quality of being vacuous; emptiness. 2 an empty space or void; vacuum. 3 a lack or absence of something specified: *a vacuity of wind.* 4 lack of normal intelligence or awareness; vacancy: *his stare gave an impression of complete vacuity.* 5 something, such as a statement, saying, etc., that is inane or pointless. 6 (in customs terminology) the difference in volume between the actual contents of a container and its full capacity.
▷**HISTORY** C16: from Latin *vacuitās* empty space, from *vacuus* empty

vacuole (ˈvækjʊˌəʊl) NOUN *Biology* a fluid-filled cavity in the cytoplasm of a cell.
▷**HISTORY** C19: from French, literally: little vacuum, from Latin VACUUM
▸**vacuolar** (ˌvækjʊˈəʊlə) ADJECTIVE ▸**vacuolate** (ˈvækjʊəlɪt, -ˌleɪt) ADJECTIVE ▸**vacuolation** (ˌvækjʊəˈleɪʃən) NOUN

vacuous (ˈvækjʊəs) ADJECTIVE 1 containing nothing; empty. 2 bereft of ideas or intelligence; mindless. 3 characterized by or resulting from vacancy of mind: *a vacuous gaze.* 4 indulging in no useful mental or physical activity; idle. 5 *Logic, maths* (of an operator or expression) having no import; idle: in (*x*) (*John is tall*) the quantifier (*x*) is vacuous.
▷**HISTORY** C17: from Latin *vacuus* empty, from *vacāre* to be empty
▸ˈ**vacuously** ADVERB ▸ˈ**vacuousness** NOUN

vacuum (ˈvækjʊəm) NOUN, *plural* **vacuums** *or* **vacua** (ˈvækjʊə). 1 a region containing no matter; free space. Compare **plenum** (sense 3). 2 a region in which gas is present at a low pressure. 3 the degree of exhaustion of gas within an enclosed space: *a high vacuum; a perfect vacuum.* 4 a sense or feeling of emptiness: *his death left a vacuum in her life.* 5 short for **vacuum cleaner.** 6 (*modifier*) of, containing, measuring, producing, or operated by a low gas pressure: *a vacuum tube; a vacuum brake.* ◆ VERB 7 to clean (something) with a vacuum cleaner: *to vacuum a carpet.*
▷**HISTORY** C16: from Latin: an empty space, from *vacuus* empty

vacuum activity NOUN *Ethology* instinctive behaviour occurring in the absence of the appropriate stimulus.

vacuum brake NOUN a brake system, used on British and many overseas railways, in which the brake is held off by a vacuum on one side of the brake-operating cylinder. If the vacuum is destroyed by controlled leakage of air or a disruptive emergency the brake is applied. It is now largely superseded by the Westinghouse brake system.

vacuum cleaner NOUN an electrical household appliance used for cleaning floors, carpets, furniture, etc., by suction.
▸**vacuum cleaning** NOUN

vacuum distillation NOUN distillation in which the liquid distilled is enclosed at a low pressure in order to reduce its boiling point.

vacuum flask NOUN an insulating flask that has double walls, usually of silvered glass, with an evacuated space between them. It is used for maintaining substances at high or low temperatures. Also called: **Thermos, Dewar flask.**

vacuum forming NOUN a process in which a sheet of warmed thermoplastic is shaped by placing it in a mould and applying suction.

vacuum frame NOUN *Printing* a machine from which the air is extracted in order to obtain close contact between the surfaces of two materials, e.g. the film and plate during platemaking.

vacuum gauge NOUN any of a number of instruments for measuring pressures below atmospheric pressure.

vacuum-packed ADJECTIVE packed in an airtight container or packet under low pressure in order to maintain freshness, prevent corrosion, etc.

vacuum pump NOUN a pump for producing a low gas pressure.

vacuum servo NOUN a servomechanism that is operated by the lowering of pressure in the intake duct of an internal-combustion engine.

vacuum tube *or* **valve** NOUN another name for **valve** (sense 3).

VAD 1 ABBREVIATION FOR **Voluntary Aid Detachment.** ◆ NOUN 2 a nurse serving in the Voluntary Aid Detachment.

vade mecum (ˈvɑːdɪ ˈmeɪkʊm) NOUN a handbook or other aid carried on the person for immediate use when needed.
▷**HISTORY** C17: from Latin, literally: go with me

Vadodara (wəˈdəʊdərə) NOUN a city in W India, in SE Gujurat: textile manufacturing. Pop.: 1 031 346 (1991). Former name (until 1976): **Baroda.**

vadose (ˈveɪdəʊs) ADJECTIVE of, relating to,

designating, or derived from water occurring above the water table: *vadose water; vadose deposits.*
▷HISTORY C19: from Latin *vadōsus* full of shallows, from *vadum* a ford

Vaduz (*German* fa'dʊts) NOUN the capital of Liechtenstein, in the Rhine valley: an old market town, dominated by a medieval castle, residence of the prince of Liechtenstein. Pop.: 5043 (2000 est.).

vag (væg) *Austral informal* ◆ NOUN [1] a vagrant. [2] **the vag.** the Vagrancy Act: *the police finally got him on the vag.* ◆ VERB **vags, vagging, vagged.** [3] (*tr*) to arrest (someone) for vagrancy.

vagabond ('vægəˌbɒnd) NOUN [1] a person with no fixed home. [2] an idle wandering beggar or thief. [3] (*modifier*) of or like a vagabond; shiftless or idle.
▷HISTORY C15: from Latin *vagābundus* wandering, from *vagārī* to roam, from *vagus* VAGUE
▸ **'vagaˌbondage** NOUN ▸ **'vagaˌbondish** ADJECTIVE
▸ **'vagaˌbondism** NOUN

vagal ('veɪgᵊl) ADJECTIVE *Anatomy* of, relating to, or affecting the vagus nerve: *vagal inhibition.*

vagarious (və'gɛərɪəs) ADJECTIVE *Rare* characterized or caused by vagaries; irregular or erratic.
▸ **va'gariously** ADVERB

vagary ('veɪgərɪ, və'gɛərɪ) NOUN, *plural* **-garies.** an erratic or outlandish notion or action; whim.
▷HISTORY C16: probably from Latin *vagārī* to roam; compare Latin *vagus* VAGUE

vagina (və'dʒaɪnə) NOUN, *plural* **-nas** *or* **-nae** (-niː). [1] the moist canal in most female mammals, including humans, that extends from the cervix of the uterus to an external opening between the labia minora. [2] *Anatomy, biology* any sheath or sheathlike structure, such as a leaf base that encloses a stem.
▷HISTORY C17: from Latin: sheath
▸ **vag'inal** ADJECTIVE

vaginate ('vædʒɪnɪt, -ˌneɪt) ADJECTIVE (esp of plant parts) having a sheath; sheathed: *a vaginate leaf.*

vaginectomy (ˌvædʒɪ'nɛktəmɪ) NOUN [1] surgical removal of all or part of the vagina. [2] surgical removal of part of the serous sheath surrounding the testis and epididymis.

vaginismus (ˌvædʒɪ'nɪzməs, -'nɪsməs) NOUN painful spasm of the vagina.
▷HISTORY C19: from New Latin, from VAGINA + *-ismus;* see -ISM

vaginitis (ˌvædʒɪ'naɪtɪs) NOUN inflammation of the vagina.

vagotomy (væ'gɒtəmɪ) NOUN, *plural* **-mies.** surgical division of the vagus nerve, performed to limit gastric secretion in patients with severe peptic ulcers.
▷HISTORY C19: from VAG(US) + -TOMY

vagotonia (ˌveɪgə'təʊnɪə) NOUN pathological overactivity of the vagus nerve, affecting various bodily functions controlled by this nerve.
▷HISTORY C19: from VAG(US) + *-tonia,* from Latin *tonus* tension, TONE

vagotropic (ˌveɪgə'trɒpɪk) ADJECTIVE *Physiol* (of a drug) affecting the activity of the vagus nerve.
▷HISTORY C20: from VAG(US) + -TROPIC

vagrancy ('veɪgrənsɪ) NOUN, *plural* **-cies.** [1] the state or condition of being a vagrant. [2] the conduct or mode of living of a vagrant.

vagrant ('veɪgrənt) NOUN [1] a person of no settled abode, income, or job; tramp. [2] a migratory animal that is off course. ◆ ADJECTIVE [3] wandering about; nomadic. [4] of, relating to, or characteristic of a vagrant or vagabond. [5] moving in an erratic fashion, without aim or purpose; wayward. [6] (of plants) showing uncontrolled or straggling growth. ◆ Archaic equivalent: **vagrom** ('veɪgrəm).
▷HISTORY C15: probably from Old French *waucrant* (from *wancrer* to roam, of Germanic origin), but also influenced by Old French *vagant* vagabond, from Latin *vagārī* to wander
▸ **'vagrantly** ADVERB ▸ **'vagrantness** NOUN

vague (veɪg) ADJECTIVE [1] (of statements, meaning, etc.) not explicit; imprecise: *vague promises.* [2] not clearly perceptible or discernible; indistinct: *a vague idea; a vague shape.* [3] not clearly or definitely established or known: *a vague rumour.* [4] (of a person or his expression) demonstrating lack of precision or clear thinking; absent-minded.
▷HISTORY C16: via French from Latin *vagus* wandering, of obscure origin
▸ **'vaguely** ADVERB ▸ **'vagueness** NOUN

vagus *or* **vagus nerve** ('veɪgəs) NOUN, *plural* **-gi** (-dʒaɪ). the tenth cranial nerve, which supplies the heart, lungs, and viscera.
▷HISTORY C19: from Latin *vagus* wandering

vahana ('vɑːhənə) NOUN *Indian myth* a vehicle.
▷HISTORY Hindi, from Sanskrit, from *vaha* to carry

vail¹ (veɪl) VERB (*tr*) *Obsolete* [1] to lower (something, such as a weapon), esp as a sign of deference or submission. [2] to remove (the hat, cap, etc.) as a mark of respect or meekness.
▷HISTORY C14 *valen,* from obsolete *avalen,* from Old French *avaler* to let fall, from Latin *ad vallem,* literally: to the valley, that is, down, from *ad* to + *vallis* VALLEY

vail² (veɪl) NOUN, VERB an archaic word for **avail.**

vail³ (veɪl) NOUN, VERB an archaic spelling of **veil.**

vain (veɪn) ADJECTIVE [1] inordinately proud of one's appearance, possessions, or achievements. [2] given to ostentatious display, esp of one's beauty. [3] worthless. [4] senseless or futile. ◆ NOUN [5] **in vain.** to no avail; fruitlessly. [6] **take someone's name in vain. a** to use the name of someone, esp God, without due respect or reverence. **b** *Jocular* to mention someone's name.
▷HISTORY C13: via Old French from Latin *vānus*
▸ **'vainly** ADVERB ▸ **'vainness** NOUN

vainglorious (ˌveɪn'glɔːrɪəs) ADJECTIVE boastful or vain; ostentatious.

vainglory (ˌveɪn'glɔːrɪ) NOUN [1] boastfulness or vanity. [2] ostentation.

vair (vɛə) NOUN [1] a fur, probably Russian squirrel, used to trim robes in the Middle Ages. [2] one of the two principal furs used on heraldic shields, conventionally represented by white and blue skins in alternate lines. Compare **ermine** (sense 3).
▷HISTORY C13: from Old French: of more than one colour, from Latin *varius* variegated, VARIOUS

Vaishnava ('vɪʃnəvə) NOUN *Hinduism* a member of a sect devoted to the cult of Vishnu, strongly anti-Brahminic and antipriestly in outlook and stressing devotion through image worship and simple ritual.
▷HISTORY from Sanskrit *vaisnava* of VISHNU
▸ **'Vaishnaˌvism** NOUN

Vaisya ('vaɪsjə, 'vaɪʃjə) NOUN the third of the four main Hindu castes, the traders.
▷HISTORY C18: from Sanskrit, literally: settler, from *viś* settlement

Vajrayana (ˌvʌdʒrʌ'jɑːnə) NOUN a school of Tantric Buddhism of India and Tibet.
▷HISTORY from Sanskrit: vehicle of the diamond or thunderbolt

Valais (*French* valɛ) NOUN a canton of S Switzerland: includes the entire valley of the upper Rhône and the highest peaks in Switzerland; produces a quarter of Switzerland's hydroelectricity. Capital: Sion. Pop.: 275 600 (2000 est.). Area: 5231 sq. km (2020 sq. miles). German name: **Wallis.**

valance ('væləns) NOUN a short piece of drapery hung along a shelf, canopy, or bed, or across a window, to hide structural detail.
▷HISTORY C15: perhaps named after VALENCE, France, town noted for its textiles
▸ **'valanced** ADJECTIVE

Valdai Hills (vɑːl'daɪ) PLURAL NOUN a region of hills and plateaus in NW Russia, between Moscow and St Petersburg. Greatest height: 346 m (1135 ft.).

Val-de-Marne (*French* valdəmarn) NOUN a department of N France, in Île-de-France region. Capital: Créteil. Pop.: 1 227 250 (1999). Area: 244 sq. km (95 sq. miles).

Valdivia (*Spanish* bal'diβja) NOUN a port in S Chile, on the **Valdivia River** about 19 km (12 miles) from the Pacific: developed chiefly by German settlers in the 1850s; university (1954). Pop.: 122 166 (1999 est.).

Val-d'Oise (*French* valdwaz) NOUN a department of N France, in Île-de-France region. Capital: Pontoise. Pop.: 1 105 464 (1999). Area: 1249 sq. km (487 sq. miles).

vale¹ (veɪl) NOUN a literary word for **valley.**
▷HISTORY C13: from Old French *val,* from Latin *vallis* valley

vale² *Latin* ('vɑːleɪ) SENTENCE SUBSTITUTE farewell; goodbye.

valediction (ˌvælɪ'dɪkʃən) NOUN [1] the act or an instance of saying goodbye. [2] any valedictory statement, speech, etc.
▷HISTORY C17: from Latin *valedīcere,* from *valē* farewell + *dīcere* to say

valedictorian (ˌvælɪdɪk'tɔːrɪən) ADJECTIVE *also* **valedictory.** [1] saying goodbye. [2] of or relating to a farewell or an occasion of farewell. ◆ NOUN [3] *US and Canadian* a person, usually the most outstanding graduate, who delivers a farewell speech at a graduation ceremony.

valedictory (ˌvælɪ'dɪktərɪ, -trɪ) NOUN, *plural* **-ries.** [1] a farewell address or speech. [2] *US and Canadian* a farewell speech delivered at a graduation ceremony, usually by the most outstanding graduate.

valence ('veɪləns) NOUN *Chem* [1] another name (esp US and Canadian) for **valency.** [2] the phenomenon of forming chemical bonds.

Valence (*French* valɑ̃s) NOUN a town in SE France, on the River Rhône. Pop.: 63 437 (1990).

valence band NOUN See **energy band.**

valence-conduction band NOUN See **energy band.**

Valencia (*Spanish* ba'lenθja) NOUN [1] a port in E Spain, capital of Valencia province, on the Mediterranean: the third largest city in Spain; capital of the Moorish kingdom of Valencia (1021–1238); university (1501). Pop.: 739 412 (1998 est.). Latin name: **Valentia** (və'lɛntɪə). [2] a region and former kingdom of E Spain, on the Mediterranean. [3] a city in N Venezuela: one of the two main industrial centres in Venezuela. Pop.: 1 338 833 (2000 est.).

Valenciennes¹ (ˌvælənsɪ'ɛn) NOUN a flat bobbin lace typically having scroll and floral designs and originally made of linen, now often cotton.
▷HISTORY named after VALENCIENNES², where it was originally made

Valenciennes² (*French* valɑ̃sjɛn) NOUN a town in N France, on the River Escaut: a coal-mining and heavy industrial centre. Pop.: 39 276 (1990).

valency ('veɪlənsɪ) *or esp US and Canadian* **valence** NOUN, *plural* **-cies** *or* **-ces.** [1] *Chem* a property of atoms or groups, equal to the number of atoms of hydrogen that the atom or group could combine with or displace in forming compounds. [2] *Linguistics* the number of satellite noun phrases with which a verb combines: *the English verb "give" takes a subject and two objects, so it has a valency of three.* [3] *Immunol* **a** the number of antigen-binding sites on an antibody molecule. **b** the number of antigen-binding sites with which an antigen can combine.
▷HISTORY C19: from Latin *valentia* strength, from *valēre* to be strong

valency electron NOUN *Chem* an electron in the outer shell of an atom, responsible for forming chemical bonds.

valency grammar NOUN a system of linguistic syntax, conceived by analogy with chemical valency, according to which verbs have valencies dependent on the number of noun phrases with which they combine. See **valency** (sense 2).

-valent ('veɪlənt) ADJECTIVE COMBINING FORM *Chem* having a specified valency: *bivalent; trivalent.*
▷HISTORY C19: from Latin *valentia;* see VALENCY

valentine ('vælənˌtaɪn) NOUN [1] a card or gift expressing love or affection, sent, often anonymously, to one's sweetheart or satirically to a friend, on Saint Valentine's Day. [2] a sweetheart selected for such a greeting.

Vale of Glamorgan (glə'mɔːgən) NOUN a county borough of S Wales, created in 1996 from parts of South Glamorgan and Mid Glamorgan. Administrative centre: Barry. Pop.: 119 293 (2001). Area: 295 sq. km (114 sq. miles).

valerian (və'lɪərɪən) NOUN [1] Also called: **allheal.** any of various Eurasian valerianaceous plants of the genus *Valeriana,* esp *V. officinalis,* having small white or pinkish flowers and a medicinal root. [2] a sedative drug made from the dried roots of *V. officinalis.*
▷HISTORY C14: via Old French from Medieval Latin

valeriana (*herba*) (herb) of *Valerius*, unexplained Latin personal name

valerianaceous (vəˌlɪərɪəˈneɪʃəs) ADJECTIVE of, relating to, or belonging to the *Valerianaceae*, a family of herbaceous plants having, in some genera, the calyx of the flower reduced to a ring of hairs: includes valerian, spikenard, and corn salad.
▷HISTORY C19: from New Latin; see VALERIAN

valeric (vəˈlɛrɪk, -ˈlɪərɪk) ADJECTIVE of, relating to, or derived from valerian.

valeric acid NOUN another name for **pentanoic acid.**

valet (ˈvælɪt, ˈvæleɪ) NOUN [1] a manservant who acts as personal attendant to his employer, looking after his clothing, serving his meals, etc. French name: **valet de chambre.** [2] a manservant who attends to the requirements of patrons in a hotel, passengers on board ship, etc.; steward. ◆ VERB **-ets, -eting, -eted.** [3] to act as a valet for (a person). [4] (*tr*) to clean the bodywork and interior of (a car) as a professional service.
▷HISTORY C16: from Old French *vaslet* page, from Medieval Latin *vassus* servant; see VASSAL

valeta *or* **veleta** (vəˈliːtə) NOUN a ballroom dance in triple time.
▷HISTORY from Spanish *veleta* weather vane

valet de chambre *French* (valɛ də ʃɑ̃brə) NOUN, *plural* ***valets de chambre*** (valɛ də ʃɑ̃brə). the full French term for **valet** (sense 1).

valet parking NOUN a system at hotels, airports, etc., in which patrons' cars are parked by a steward.

Valetta (vəˈlɛtə) NOUN a variant spelling of **Valletta.**

valetudinarian (ˌvælɪˌtjuːdɪˈnɛərɪən) *or* **valetudinary** (ˌvælɪˈtjuːdɪnərɪ) NOUN, *plural* **-narians** *or* **-naries.** [1] a person who is or believes himself to be chronically sick; invalid. [2] a person excessively worried about the state of his health; hypochondriac. ◆ ADJECTIVE [3] relating to, marked by, or resulting from poor health. [4] being a valetudinarian. [5] trying to return to a healthy state.
▷HISTORY C18: from Latin *valētūdō* state of health, from *valēre* to be well
▸ˌ**valeˌtudiˈnarianˌism** NOUN

valgus (ˈvælgəs) ADJECTIVE *Pathol* denoting a deformity in which the distal part of a limb is displaced or twisted away from the midline of the body. See **hallux valgus.**
▷HISTORY C19: from Latin: knock-kneed

Valhalla (vælˈhælə), **Walhalla, Valhall** (vælˈhæl, ˈvælhæl), *or* **Walhall** NOUN *Norse myth* the great hall of Odin where warriors who die as heroes in battle dwell eternally.
▷HISTORY C18: from Old Norse, from *valr* slain warriors + *höll* HALL

valiant (ˈvæljənt) ADJECTIVE [1] courageous, intrepid, or stout-hearted; brave. [2] marked by bravery or courage: *a valiant deed.*
▷HISTORY C14: from Old French *vaillant*, from *valoir* to be of value, from Latin *valēre* to be strong
▸ˈ**valiance** *or* ˈ**valiancy** NOUN ▸ˈ**valiantly** ADVERB

valid (ˈvælɪd) ADJECTIVE [1] having some foundation; based on truth. [2] legally acceptable: *a valid licence.* [3] **a** having legal force; effective. **b** having legal authority; binding. [4] having some force or cogency: *a valid point in a debate.* [5] *Logic* (of an inference or argument) having premises and conclusion so related that whenever the former are true the latter must also be true, esp (**formally valid**) when the inference is justified by the form of the premises and conclusion alone. Thus *Tom is a bachelor; therefore Tom is unmarried* is valid but not formally so, while *today is hot and dry; therefore today is hot* is formally valid. Compare **invalid**[2] (sense 2). [6] *Archaic* healthy or strong.
▷HISTORY C16: from Latin *validus* robust, from *valēre* to be strong
▸ˈ**validly** ADVERB ▸**validity** (vəˈlɪdɪtɪ) *or* ˈ**validness** NOUN

validate (ˈvælɪˌdeɪt) VERB (*tr*) [1] to confirm or corroborate. [2] to give legal force or official confirmation to; declare legally valid.
▸ˌ**valiˈdation** NOUN ▸ˈ**validatory** ADJECTIVE

valine (ˈveɪliːn, ˈvæl-) NOUN an essential amino acid; a component of proteins.
▷HISTORY C19: from VAL(ERIC ACID) + -INE[2]

valise (vəˈliːz) NOUN a small overnight travelling case.
▷HISTORY C17: via French from Italian *valigia*, of unknown origin

Valium (ˈvælɪəm) NOUN *Trademark* a brand of diazepam used as a tranquillizer. See also **benzodiazepine.**

Valkyrie, Walkyrie (vælˈkɪərɪ, ˈvælkɪərɪ), *or* **Valkyr** (ˈvælkɪə) NOUN *Norse myth* any of the beautiful maidens who serve Odin and ride over battlefields to claim the dead heroes and take them to Valhalla.
▷HISTORY C18: from Old Norse *Valkyrja*, from *valr* slain warriors + *köri* to CHOOSE
▸**Valˈkyrian** ADJECTIVE

Valladolid (*Spanish* baʎaðoˈlið) NOUN [1] a city in NW Spain: residence of the Spanish court in the 16th century; university (1346). Pop.: 319 946 (1998 est.). [2] the former name (until 1828) of **Morelia.**

vallation (vəˈleɪʃən) NOUN [1] the act or process of building fortifications. [2] a wall or rampart.
▷HISTORY C17: from Late Latin *vallātiō*, from *vallum* rampart

vallecula (vəˈlɛkjʊlə) NOUN, *plural* **-lae** (-ˌliː). [1] *Anatomy* any of various natural depressions or crevices, such as certain fissures of the brain. [2] *Botany* a small groove or furrow in a plant stem or fruit.
▷HISTORY C19: from Late Latin: little valley, from Latin *vallis* valley
▸**valˈlecular** *or* **valˈleculate** ADJECTIVE

Valle d'Aosta (*Italian* ˈvalle daˈɔsta) NOUN an autonomous region of NW Italy: under many different rulers until passing to the house of Savoy in the 11th century; established as an autonomous region in 1944. Capital: Aosta. Pop.: 120 343 (2000 est.). Area: 3263 sq. km (1260 sq. miles).

Valletta *or* **Valetta** (vəˈlɛtə) NOUN the capital of Malta, on the NE coast: founded by the Knights Hospitallers, after the victory over the Turks in 1565; became a major naval base after Malta's annexation by Britain (1814). Pop.: 7100 (1999 est.), with a conurbation of 102 000 (1999 est.).

valley (ˈvælɪ) NOUN [1] a long depression in the land surface, usually containing a river, formed by erosion or by movements in the earth's crust. [2] the broad area drained by a single river system: *the Thames valley.* [3] any elongated depression resembling a valley. [4] the junction of a roof slope with another or with a wall. [5] (*modifier*) relating to or proceeding by way of a valley: *a valley railway.*
▷HISTORY C13: from Old French *valee*, from Latin *vallis*

Valley Forge NOUN an area in SE Pennsylvania, northwest of Philadelphia: winter camp (1777–78) of Washington and the American Revolutionary Army.

Valley of Ten Thousand Smokes NOUN a volcanic region of SW Alaska, formed by the massive eruption of Mount Katmai in 1912; jets of steam issue from vents up to 45 m (150 ft.) across.

Vallombrosa (*Italian* vallomˈbroːsa) NOUN a village and resort in central Italy, in Tuscany region: 11th-century Benedictine monastery.

vallum (ˈvæləm) NOUN *Archaeol* a Roman rampart or earthwork.

Valois (*French* valwa) NOUN a historic region and former duchy of N France.

Valona (vəˈləʊnə) NOUN another name for **Vlorë.**

valonia (vəˈləʊnɪə) NOUN the acorn cups and unripe acorns of the Eurasian oak *Quercus aegilops*, used in tanning, dyeing, and making ink.
▷HISTORY C18: from Italian *vallonia*, ultimately from Greek *balanos* acorn

valorize *or* **valorise** (ˈvæləˌraɪz) VERB (*tr*) to fix and maintain an artificial price for (a commodity) by governmental action.
▷HISTORY C20: back formation from *valorization*; see VALOUR
▸ˌ**valoriˈzation** *or* ˌ**valoriˈsation** NOUN

valour *or US* **valor** (ˈvælə) NOUN courage or bravery, esp in battle.
▷HISTORY C15: from Late Latin *valor*, from *valēre* to be strong
▸ˈ**valorous** ADJECTIVE ▸ˈ**valorously** ADVERB

Valparaíso (*Spanish* balparaˈiso) NOUN a port in central Chile, on a wide bay of the Pacific: the third largest city and chief port of Chile; two universities. Pop.: 283 489 (1999 est.).

Valpolicella (ˌvælpɒlɪˈtʃɛlə; *Italian* valpoliˈtʃɛlla) NOUN a dry red table wine from the Veneto region of NE Italy.
▷HISTORY C20: named after a valley where it is produced

valse *French* (vals) NOUN another word, esp used in the titles of some pieces of music, for **waltz.**

valuable (ˈvæljʊəbᵊl) ADJECTIVE [1] having considerable monetary worth. [2] of considerable importance or quality: *a valuable friend; valuable information.* [3] able to be valued. ◆ NOUN [4] (*usually plural*) a valuable article of personal property, esp jewellery.
▸ˈ**valuableness** NOUN ▸ˈ**valuably** ADVERB

valuate (ˈvæljʊˌeɪt) VERB *US* another word for **value** (senses 10, 12) or **evaluate.**

valuation (ˌvæljʊˈeɪʃən) NOUN [1] the act of valuing, esp a formal assessment of the worth of property, jewellery, etc. [2] the price arrived at by the process of valuing: *the valuation of this property is considerable; I set a high valuation on technical ability.*
▸ˌ**valuˈational** ADJECTIVE ▸ˌ**valuˈationally** ADVERB

valuator (ˈvæljʊˌeɪtə) NOUN a person who estimates the value of objects, paintings, etc.; appraiser.

value (ˈvæljuː) NOUN [1] the desirability of a thing, often in respect of some property such as usefulness or exchangeability: worth, merit, or importance. [2] an amount, esp a material or monetary one, considered to be a fair exchange in return for a thing; assigned valuation: *the value of the picture is £10 000.* [3] reasonable or equivalent return; satisfaction: *value for money.* [4] precise meaning or significance. [5] (*plural*) the moral principles and beliefs or accepted standards of a person or social group: *a person with old-fashioned values.* [6] *Maths* **a** a particular magnitude, number, or amount: *the value of the variable was 7.* **b** the particular quantity that is the result of applying a function or operation for some given argument: *the value of the function for x=3 was 9.* [7] *Music* short for **time value.** [8] (in painting, drawing, etc.) **a** a gradation of tone from light to dark or of colour luminosity. **b** the relation of one of these elements to another or to the whole picture. [9] *Phonetics* the quality or tone of the speech sound associated with a written character representing it: *"g" has the value* (dʒ) *in English "gem.".* ◆ VERB **-ues, -uing, -ued.** (*tr*) [10] to assess or estimate the worth, merit, or desirability of; appraise. [11] to have a high regard for, esp in respect of worth, usefulness, merit, etc.; esteem or prize: *to value freedom.* [12] (foll by *at*) to fix the financial or material worth of (a unit of currency, work of art, etc.): *jewels valued at £40 000.*
▷HISTORY C14: from Old French, from *valoir*, from Latin *valēre* to be worth, be strong
▸ˈ**valuer** NOUN

value added NOUN the difference between the total revenues of a firm, industry, etc., and its total purchases from other firms, industries, etc. The aggregate of values added throughout an economy (**gross value added**) represents that economy's gross domestic product.

value-added tax NOUN (in Britain) the full name for **VAT.**

value date NOUN the exact date on which a financial transaction, esp in buying and selling foreign exchange, is deemed to take place: used for calculating exchange rates.

valued policy NOUN an insurance policy in which the amount payable in the event of a valid claim is agreed upon between the company and policyholder when the policy is issued and is not related to the actual value of a loss. Compare **open policy.**

value judgment NOUN a subjective assessment based on one's own code of values or that of one's class.

valueless (ˈvæljʊlɪs) ADJECTIVE having or possessing no value; worthless.
▸ˈ**valuelessness** NOUN

valuer (ˈvæljʊə) NOUN a person who assesses the monetary worth of a work of art, jewel, house, etc.; appraiser.

Valuer General NOUN *Austral* a state official who values properties for rating purposes.

valuta (vəˈluːtə) NOUN *Rare* the value of one currency in terms of its exchange rate with another.
▷HISTORY C20: from Italian, literally: VALUE

valvate (ˈvælveɪt) ADJECTIVE 1 furnished with a valve or valves. 2 functioning as or resembling a valve. 3 *Botany* **a** having or taking place by means of valves: *valvate dehiscence*. **b** (of petals or sepals in the bud) having the margins touching but not overlapping.

valve (vælv) NOUN 1 any device that shuts off, starts, regulates, or controls the flow of a fluid. 2 *Anatomy* a flaplike structure in a hollow organ, such as the heart, that controls the one-way passage of fluid through that organ. 3 Also called: **tube, vacuum tube.** an evacuated electron tube containing a cathode, anode, and, usually, one or more additional control electrodes. When a positive potential is applied to the anode, electrons emitted from the cathode are attracted to the anode, constituting a flow of current which can be controlled by a voltage applied to the grid to produce amplification, oscillation, etc. See also **diode** (sense 2), **triode** (sense 1), **tetrode, pentode.** 4 *Zoology* any of the separable pieces that make up the shell of a mollusc. 5 *Music* a device on some brass instruments by which the effective length of the tube may be varied to enable a chromatic scale to be produced. 6 *Botany* **a** any of the several parts that make up a dry dehiscent fruit, esp a capsule. **b** either of the two halves of a diatom cell wall. 7 *Archaic* a leaf of a double door or of a folding door.
▷HISTORY C14: from Latin *valva* a folding door
▸ˈ**valveless** ADJECTIVE ▸ˈ**valve,like** ADJECTIVE

valve gear NOUN a mechanism that operates the valves of a reciprocating engine, usually involving the use of cams, pushrods, rocker arms, etc.

valve-in-head engine NOUN the US name for **overhead-valve engine.**

valve spring NOUN 1 a helical spring used to hold closed a valve in the cylinder head of an internal-combustion engine. 2 any spring that closes a valve after it has been opened mechanically or by flow pressure.

valvular (ˈvælvjʊlə) ADJECTIVE 1 of, relating to, operated by, or having a valve or valves. 2 having the shape or function of a valve.

valvule (ˈvælvjuːl) *or* **valvelet** (ˈvælvlɪt) NOUN a small valve or a part resembling one.
▷HISTORY C18: from New Latin *valvula*, diminutive of VALVE

valvulitis (ˌvælvjʊˈlaɪtɪs) NOUN inflammation of a bodily valve, esp a heart valve.
▷HISTORY C19: from VALVULE + -ITIS

vambrace (ˈvæmbreɪs) NOUN a piece of armour used to protect the arm.
▷HISTORY C14: from Anglo-French *vauntbras*, from *vaunt-* (from Old French *avant-* fore-) + *bras* arm
▸ˈ**vambraced** ADJECTIVE

vamoose (vəˈmuːs) VERB (*intr*) *Slang, chiefly US* to leave a place hurriedly; decamp.
▷HISTORY C19: from Spanish *vamos* let us go, from Latin *vādere* to go, walk rapidly

vamp[1] (væmp) *Informal* ◆ NOUN 1 a seductive woman who exploits men by use of her sexual charms. ◆ VERB 2 to exploit (a man) in the fashion of a vamp.
▷HISTORY C20: short for VAMPIRE
▸ˈ**vamper** NOUN ▸ˈ**vampish** ADJECTIVE

vamp[2] (væmp) NOUN 1 something patched up to make it look new. 2 the reworking of a theme, story, etc. 3 an improvised accompaniment, consisting largely of chords. 4 the front part of the upper of a shoe. ◆ VERB 5 (*tr; often foll by up*) to give a vamp to; make a renovation of. 6 to improvise (an accompaniment) to (a tune).
▷HISTORY C13: from Old French *avantpié* the front part of a shoe (hence, something patched), from *avant-* fore- + *pié* foot, from Latin *pēs*
▸ˈ**vamper** NOUN

vampire (ˈvæmpaɪə) NOUN 1 (in European folklore) a corpse that rises nightly from its grave to drink the blood of the living. 2 See **vampire bat.** 3 a person who preys mercilessly upon others, such as a blackmailer. 4 See **vamp**[1] (sense 1). 5 *Theatre* a trapdoor on a stage.
▷HISTORY C18: from French, from German *Vampir*, from Magyar; perhaps related to Turkish *uber* witch, Russian *upyr* vampire
▸**vampiric** (væmˈpɪrɪk) *or* **vampirish** (ˈvæmpaɪərɪʃ) ADJECTIVE

vampire bat NOUN any bat, esp *Desmodus rotundus*, of the family *Desmodontidae* of tropical regions of Central and South America, having sharp incisor and canine teeth and feeding on the blood of birds and mammals. Compare **false vampire.**

vampirism (ˈvæmpaɪəˌrɪzəm) NOUN 1 belief in the existence of vampires. 2 the actions of vampires; bloodsucking. 3 the act of preying upon or exploiting others.

van[1] (væn) NOUN 1 short for **caravan** (sense 1). 2 a covered motor vehicle for transporting goods, etc., by road. 3 *Brit* a closed railway wagon in which the guard travels, for transporting goods, mail, etc. 4 *Brit* See **delivery van.**

van[2] (væn) NOUN short for **vanguard.**

van[3] (væn) NOUN *Tennis, chiefly Brit* short for **advantage** (sense 3). Usual US and Canadian word: **ad.**

van[4] (væn) NOUN 1 any device for winnowing corn. 2 an archaic or poetic word for **wing.**
▷HISTORY C17: variant of FAN[1]

Van (vɑːn) NOUN 1 a city in E Turkey, on Lake Van. Pop.: 226 965 (1997). 2 **Lake.** a salt lake in E Turkey, at an altitude of 1650 m (5400 ft.): fed by melting snow and glaciers. Area: 3737 sq. km (1433 sq. miles).

vanadate (ˈvænəˌdeɪt) NOUN any salt or ester of a vanadic acid.

vanadic (vəˈnædɪk, -ˈneɪdɪk) ADJECTIVE of or containing vanadium, esp in a trivalent or pentavalent state.

vanadic acid NOUN any one of various oxyacids of vanadium, such as H_3VO_4 (**orthovanadic acid**), HVO_4 (**metavanadic acid**), and $H_4V_2O_7$ (**pyrovanadic acid**), known chiefly in the form of their vanadate salts.

vanadinite (vəˈnædɪˌnaɪt) NOUN a red, yellow, or brownish mineral consisting of a chloride and vanadate of lead in hexagonal crystalline form. It results from weathering of lead ores in desert regions and is a source of vanadium. Formula: $Pb_5(VO_4)_3Cl$.

vanadium (vəˈneɪdɪəm) NOUN a toxic silvery-white metallic element occurring chiefly in carnotite and vanadinite and used in steel alloys, high-speed tools, and as a catalyst. Symbol: V; atomic no.: 23; atomic wt.: 50.9415; valency: 2–5; relative density: 6.11; melting pt.: 1910±10°C; boiling pt.: 3409°C.
▷HISTORY C19: New Latin, from Old Norse *Vanadis*, epithet of the goddess Freya + -IUM

vanadium steel NOUN *Engineering* steel containing up to 0.5 per cent vanadium, usually with 1.1–1.5 per cent chromium and 0.4–0.5 per cent carbon to increase its tensile strength and elasticity.

vanadous (ˈvænədəs) ADJECTIVE of or containing vanadium, esp in a divalent or trivalent state.

Van Allen belt (væn ˈælən) NOUN either of two regions of charged particles above the earth, the inner one extending from 2400 to 5600 kilometres above the earth and the outer one from 13 000 to 19 000 kilometres. The charged particles result from cosmic rays and are trapped by the earth's magnetic field.
▷HISTORY C20: named after its discoverer, James Alfred Van Allen (born 1914), US physicist

vanaspati (vəˈnæspətɪ) NOUN a hydrogenated vegetable fat commonly used in India as a substitute for butter.
▷HISTORY C20: the Sanskrit name of a forest plant, from *vana* forest + *pati* lord

vancomycin (ˌvænkəʊˈmaɪsɪn) NOUN an antibiotic effective against most Gram-positive organisms. It is given by intravenous infusions for serious infections that are resistant to other antibiotics.

Vancouver (vænˈkuːvə) NOUN 1 an island of SW Canada, off the SW coast of British Columbia: separated from the Canadian mainland by the Strait of Georgia and Queen Charlotte Sound, and from the US mainland by Juan de Fuca Strait; the largest island off the W coast of North America. Chief town: Victoria. Pop.: 461 575 (latest est.). Area: 32 137 sq. km (12 408 sq. miles). 2 a city in SW Canada, in SW British Columbia: Canada's chief Pacific port, named after Captain George Vancouver: university (1908). Pop.: 514 008 (1996), with a conurbation of 1 826 800 (1995). 3 **Mount.** a mountain on the border between Canada and Alaska, in the St Elias Mountains. Height: 4785 m (15 700 ft.).

vanda (ˈvændə) NOUN any epiphytic orchid of the E hemisphere genus *Vanda*, having white, mauve, blue, or greenish fragrant flowers.
▷HISTORY C19: New Latin, from Hindi *vandā* mistletoe, from Sanskrit

V and A (in Britain) ABBREVIATION FOR Victoria and Albert Museum.

vandal (ˈvændᵊl) NOUN **a** a person who deliberately causes damage or destruction to personal or public property. **b** (*as modifier*): *vandal instincts*.
▷HISTORY C17: from VANDAL, from Latin *Vandallus*, of Germanic origin

Vandal (ˈvændᵊl) NOUN a member of a Germanic people that raided Roman provinces in the 3rd and 4th centuries A.D. before devastating Gaul (406–409), conquering Spain and N Africa, and sacking Rome (455): crushed by Belisarius at Carthage (533).
▸**Vandalic** (vænˈdælɪk) ADJECTIVE ▸ˈ**Vandal,ism** NOUN

vandalism (ˈvændəˌlɪzəm) NOUN the wanton or deliberate destruction caused by a vandal or an instance of such destruction.
▸ˌ**vandalˈistic** *or* ˈ**vandalish** ADJECTIVE

vandalize *or* **vandalise** (ˈvændəˌlaɪz) VERB (*tr*) to destroy or damage (something) by an act of vandalism.

Van de Graaff generator (ˈvæn də ˌgrɑːf) NOUN a device for producing high electrostatic potentials (up to 15 million volts), consisting of a hollow metal sphere on which a charge is accumulated from a continuous moving belt of insulating material: used in particle accelerators.
▷HISTORY C20: named after R. J. *Van de Graaff* (1901–67), US physicist

Vandemonian (ˌvæn dəˈməʊnɪən) NOUN 1 a native or inhabitant of the former Van Diemen's Land (now Tasmania). ◆ ADJECTIVE 2 of or relating to Van Diemen's Land or its inhabitants.

Van der Hum (væn də hʌm) NOUN *South African* a liqueur with tangerine flavouring.
▷HISTORY of uncertain origin, but possibly derived from the humorous uncertainty of the name, equivalent of WHATSHISNAME

Van der Merwe (væn də ˈmɜːvə) NOUN *South African* a stereotypical figure humorously representating Boer stupidity and prejudice.
▷HISTORY C20: from a common Afrikaner surname

van der Waals equation (ˈvæn də ˌwɑːlz) NOUN an equation of state for a non-ideal gas that takes account of intermolecular forces and the volume occupied by the molecules of the gas.

van der Waals forces (ˈvæn də ˌwɑːlz) PLURAL NOUN weak electrostatic forces between atoms and molecules caused by transient distortions in the distribution of electrons in the interacting atoms or molecules.

Van Diemen Gulf (væn ˈdiːmən) NOUN an inlet of the Timor Sea in N Australia, in the Northern Territory.

Van Diemen's Land (væn ˈdiːmənz) NOUN the former name (1642–1855) of **Tasmania.**

Vandyke beard (ˈvændaɪk) NOUN a short pointed beard. Often shortened to: **Vandyke.**

Vandyke brown NOUN 1 **a** a moderate brown colour. **b** (*as adjective*): *a Vandyke-brown suit*. 2 any of various brown pigments, usually consisting of a mixture of ferric oxide and lampblack.

Vandyke collar *or* **cape** NOUN a large white collar with several very deep points. Often shortened to: **Vandyke.**

vane (veɪn) NOUN 1 Also called: **weather vane, wind vane.** a flat plate or blade of metal mounted on a vertical axis in an exposed position to indicate wind direction. 2 any one of the flat blades or sails forming part of the wheel of a windmill. 3 any flat or shaped plate used to direct fluid flow, esp a stator blade in a turbine, etc. 4 a fin or plate fitted to a projectile or missile to provide stabilization or guidance. 5 *Ornithol* the flat part of a feather, consisting of two rows of barbs on either side of the

shaft. [6] *Surveying* **a** a sight on a quadrant or compass. **b** the movable marker on a levelling staff.
▷**HISTORY** Old English *fana;* related to Old Saxon, Old High German *fano,* Old Norse *fani,* Latin *pannus* cloth
▸**vaned** ADJECTIVE ▸ˈ**vaneless** ADJECTIVE

Vänern (*Swedish* ˈvɛːnərn) NOUN **Lake.** a lake in SW Sweden: the largest lake in Sweden and W Europe; drains into the Kattegat. Area: 5585 sq. km (2156 sq. miles).

vanessid (vəˈnɛsɪd) NOUN [1] a butterfly belonging to any of several brightly coloured species, including admirals, tortoiseshells, and the Camberwell beauty, which with the fritillaries comprise the *Nymphalidae.* ◆ ADJECTIVE [2] of, relating to, or belonging to this group.
▷**HISTORY** C20: from New Latin *vanessa*

vang (væŋ) NOUN *Nautical* [1] a rope or tackle extended from the boom of a fore-and-aft mainsail to a deck fitting of a vessel when running, in order to keep the boom from riding up. [2] a guy extending from the end of a gaff to the vessel's rail on each side, used for steadying the gaff.
▷**HISTORY** C18: from Dutch, from *vangen* to catch

vanguard (ˈvænˌɡɑːd) NOUN [1] the leading division or units of a military force. [2] the leading position in any movement or field, or the people who occupy such a position: *the vanguard of modern literature.*
▷**HISTORY** C15: from Old French *avant-garde,* from *avant-* fore- + *garde* GUARD

vanilla (vəˈnɪlə) NOUN [1] any tropical climbing orchid of the genus *Vanilla,* esp *V. planifolia,* having spikes of large fragrant greenish-yellow flowers and long fleshy pods containing the seeds (beans). [2] the pod or bean of certain of these plants, used to flavour food, etc. [3] a flavouring extract prepared from vanilla beans and used in cooking. ◆ ADJECTIVE [4] flavoured with or as if with vanilla: *vanilla ice cream.* [5] *Slang* ordinary or conventional: *a vanilla kind of guy.*
▷**HISTORY** C17: from New Latin, from Spanish *vainilla* pod, from *vaina* a sheath, from Latin *vāgīna* sheath

vanillic (vəˈnɪlɪk) ADJECTIVE of, resembling, containing, or derived from vanilla or vanillin.

vanillin (ˈvænɪlɪn, vəˈnɪlɪn) NOUN a white crystalline aldehyde found in vanilla and many natural balsams and resins; 3-methoxy-4-hydroxybenzaldehyde. It is a by-product of paper manufacture and is used as a flavouring and in perfumes and pharmaceuticals. Formula: $(CH_3O)(OH)C_6H_3CHO$.

Vanir (ˈvɑːnɪə) NOUN *Norse myth* a race of ancient gods often locked in struggle with the Aesir. The most notable of them are Njord and his children Frey and Freya.
▷**HISTORY** from Old Norse *Vanr,* a fertility god

vanish (ˈvænɪʃ) VERB (*intr*) [1] to disappear, esp suddenly or mysteriously. [2] to cease to exist; fade away. [3] *Maths* to become zero. ◆ NOUN [4] *Phonetics, rare* the second and weaker of the two vowels in a falling diphthong.
▷**HISTORY** C14 *vanissen,* from Old French *esvanir,* from Latin *ēvānēscere* to evaporate, from *ē-* EX-[1] + *vānēscere* to pass away, from *vānus* empty
▸ˈ**vanisher** NOUN ▸ˈ**vanishingly** ADVERB

vanishing cream NOUN a cosmetic cream that is colourless once applied, used as a foundation for powder or as a cleansing or moisturizing cream.

vanishing point NOUN [1] the point to which parallel lines appear to converge in the rendering of perspective, usually on the horizon. [2] a point in space or time at or beyond which something disappears or ceases to exist.

vanity (ˈvænɪtɪ) NOUN, *plural* **-ties.** [1] the state or quality of being vain; excessive pride or conceit. [2] ostentation occasioned by ambition or pride. [3] an instance of being vain or something about which one is vain. [4] the state or quality of being valueless, futile, or unreal. [5] something that is worthless or useless. [6] *NZ* short for **vanity unit.**
▷**HISTORY** C13: from Old French *vanité,* from Latin *vānitās* emptiness, from *vānus* empty

vanity bag, case, *or* **box** NOUN a woman's small bag or hand case used to carry cosmetics, etc.

Vanity Fair NOUN (*often not capitals*) *Literary* the social life of a community, esp of a great city, or the world in general, considered as symbolizing worldly frivolity.
▷**HISTORY** from Bunyan's *The Pilgrim's Progress*

vanity plates PLURAL NOUN *Informal* personalized car numberplates.

vanity publishing NOUN the practice of the author of a book paying all or most of the costs of its publication.

vanity unit NOUN a hand basin built into a wooden Formica-covered or tiled top, usually with a built-in cupboard below it. Also called (trademark): **Vanitory unit** (ˈvænɪtərɪ).

vanquish (ˈvæŋkwɪʃ) VERB (*tr*) [1] to defeat or overcome in a battle, contest, etc.; conquer. [2] to defeat or overcome in argument or debate. [3] to conquer (an emotion).
▷**HISTORY** C14 *vanquisshen,* from Old French *venquis* vanquished, from *veintre* to overcome, from Latin *vincere*
▸ˈ**vanquishable** ADJECTIVE ▸ˈ**vanquisher** NOUN
▸ˈ**vanquishment** NOUN

vantage (ˈvɑːntɪdʒ) NOUN [1] a state, position, or opportunity affording superiority or advantage. [2] superiority or benefit accruing from such a position, state, etc. [3] *Tennis* short for **advantage.**
▷**HISTORY** C13: from Old French *avantage* ADVANTAGE
▸ˈ**vantageless** ADJECTIVE

vantage ground NOUN a position or condition affording superiority or advantage over or as if over an opponent.

vantage point NOUN a position or place that allows one a wide or favourable overall view of a scene or situation.

Vanua Levu (vɑːˈnuːə ˈlɛvuː) NOUN the second largest island of Fiji: mountainous. Area: 5535 sq. km (2137 sq. miles).

Vanuatu (ˈvænuːˌætuː) NOUN a republic comprising a group of islands in the W Pacific, W of Fiji: a condominium under Anglo-French joint rule from 1906; attained partial autonomy in 1978 and full independence in 1980 as a member of the Commonwealth. Its economy is based chiefly on copra. Official languages: Bislama; French; English. Religion: Christian majority. Currency: vatu. Capital: Vila (on Efate). Pop.: 195 000 (2001 est.). Area: about 14 760 sq. km (5700 sq. miles). Official name: **Republic of Vanuatu.** Former name (until 1980): **New Hebrides.**

vanward (ˈvænwəd) ADJECTIVE, ADVERB in or towards the front.

vapid (ˈvæpɪd) ADJECTIVE [1] bereft of strength, sharpness, flavour, etc.; flat. [2] boring or dull; lifeless: *vapid talk.*
▷**HISTORY** C17: from Latin *vapidus;* related to *vappa* tasteless or flat wine, and perhaps to *vapor* warmth
▸**vaˈpidity** NOUN ▸ˈ**vapidly** ADVERB ▸ˈ**vapidness** NOUN

vapor (ˈveɪpə) NOUN the US spelling of **vapour.**

vaporescence (ˌveɪpəˈrɛsəns) NOUN the production or formation of vapour.
▸ˌ**vaporˈescent** ADJECTIVE

vaporetto (ˌveɪpəˈrɛtəʊ; *Italian* vapoˈretto) NOUN, *plural* **-ti** (-tɪ; *Italian* -ti) *or* **-tos.** a steam-powered passenger boat, as used on the canals in Venice.
▷**HISTORY** Italian, from *vapore* a steamboat

vaporific (ˌveɪpəˈrɪfɪk) ADJECTIVE [1] producing, causing, or tending to produce vapour. [2] of, concerned with, or having the nature of vapour. [3] tending to become vapour; volatile. ◆ Also: **vaporous.**
▷**HISTORY** C18: from New Latin *vaporificus,* from Latin *vapor* steam + *facere* to make

vaporimeter (ˌveɪpəˈrɪmɪtə) NOUN an instrument for measuring vapour pressure, used to determine the volatility of oils or the amount of alcohol in alcoholic liquids.

vaporize *or* **vaporise** (ˈveɪpəˌraɪz) VERB [1] to change or cause to change into vapour or into the gaseous state. [2] to evaporate or disappear or cause to evaporate or disappear, esp suddenly. [3] to destroy or be destroyed by being turned into a gas as a result of extreme heat (for example, generated by a nuclear explosion).
▸ˈ**vaporˌizable** *or* ˈ**vaporˌisable** ADJECTIVE ▸ˌ**vaporiˈzation** *or* ˌ**vaporiˈsation** NOUN

vaporizer *or* **vaporiser** (ˈveɪpəˌraɪzə) NOUN [1] a substance that vaporizes or a device that causes vaporization. [2] *Med* a device that produces steam or atomizes medication for inhalation.

vaporous (ˈveɪpərəs) ADJECTIVE [1] resembling or full of vapour. [2] another word for **vaporific.** [3] lacking permanence or substance; ephemeral or fanciful. [4] given to foolish imaginings. [5] dulled or obscured by an atmosphere of vapour.
▸ˈ**vaporously** ADVERB ▸ˈ**vaporousness** *or* **vaporosity** (ˌveɪpəˈrɒsɪtɪ) NOUN

vapour *or US* **vapor** (ˈveɪpə) NOUN [1] particles of moisture or other substance suspended in air and visible as clouds, smoke, etc. [2] a gaseous substance at a temperature below its critical temperature. Compare **gas** (sense 3). [3] a substance that is in a gaseous state at a temperature below its boiling point. [4] *Rare* something fanciful that lacks substance or permanence. [5] **the vapours.** *Archaic* a depressed mental condition believed originally to be the result of vaporous exhalations from the stomach. ◆ VERB [6] to evaporate or cause to evaporate; vaporize. [7] (*intr*) to make vain empty boasts; brag.
▷**HISTORY** C14: from Latin *vapor*
▸ˈ**vapourable** *or* (*US*) ˈ**vaporable** ADJECTIVE
▸ˌ**vapouraˈbility** *or* (*US*) ˌ**vaporaˈbility** NOUN ▸ˈ**vapourer** *or* (*US*) ˈ**vaporer** NOUN ▸ˈ**vapourish** *or* (*US*) ˈ**vaporish** ADJECTIVE ▸ˈ**vapourless** *or* (*US*) ˈ**vaporless** ADJECTIVE
▸ˈ**vapour-ˌlike** *or* (*US*) ˈ**vapor-ˌlike** ADJECTIVE ▸ˈ**vapoury** *or* (*US*) ˈ**vapory** ADJECTIVE

vapour density NOUN the ratio of the density of a gas or vapour to that of hydrogen at the same temperature and pressure. See also **relative density.**

vapourer moth NOUN a tussock moth, *Orgyia antiqua,* of hedgerows and trees, the female of which is wingless and lays her eggs on her former cocoon.

vapour lock NOUN a stoppage in a pipe carrying a liquid caused by a bubble of gas, esp such a stoppage caused by vaporization of the petrol in the pipe feeding the carburettor of an internal-combustion engine.

vapour pressure NOUN *Physics* the pressure exerted by a vapour. The saturated vapour pressure is that exerted by a vapour in equilibrium with its solid or liquid phase at a particular temperature.

vapour trail NOUN a visible trail left by an aircraft flying at high altitude or through supercold air, caused by the deposition of water vapour in the engine exhaust as minute ice crystals. Also called: **condensation trail, contrail.**

var (vɑː) NOUN a unit of reactive power of an alternating current, equal to the product of the current measured in amperes and the voltage measured in volts.
▷**HISTORY** from *v(olt-)a(mperes) r(eactive)*

Var (*French* var) NOUN [1] a department of SE France, in Provence-Alpes-Côte-d'Azur region. Capital: Toulon. Pop.: 898 441 (1999). Area: 6023 sq. km (2349 sq. miles). [2] a river in SE France, flowing southeast and south to the Mediterranean near Nice. Length: about 130 km (80 miles).

VAR ABBREVIATION FOR visual aural range.

var. ABBREVIATION FOR: [1] variable. [2] variant. [3] variation. [4] variety. [5] various.

vara (ˈvɑːrə) NOUN a unit of length used in Spain, Portugal, and South America and having different values in different localities, usually between 32 and 43 inches (about 80 to 108 centimetres).
▷**HISTORY** C17: via Spanish from Latin: wooden trestle, from *vārus* crooked

varactor (ˈvɛəˌræktə) NOUN a semiconductor diode that acts as a voltage-dependent capacitor, being operated with a reverse bias. Compare **varistor.**
▷**HISTORY** C20: probably a blend of *variable reactor*

Varanasi (vəˈrɑːnəsɪ) NOUN a city in NE India, in SE Uttar Pradesh on the River Ganges: probably dates from the 13th century B.C.; an early centre of Aryan philosophy and religion; a major place of pilgrimage for Hindus, Jains, Sikhs, and Buddhists, with many ghats along the Ganges; seat of the Banaras Hindu University (1916), India's leading university, and the Sanskrit University (1957). Pop.: 929 270 (1991). Former names: **Benares, Banaras.**

Varangian (vəˈrændʒɪən) NOUN [1] one of the Scandinavians who invaded and settled parts of Russia and the Ukraine from the 8th to the 11th centuries, and who formed the bodyguard of the Byzantine emperor (**Varangian Guard**) in the late 10th

and 11th centuries. ◆ ADJECTIVE [2] of or relating to the Varangians.
▷HISTORY C18: from Medieval Latin *Varangus,* from Medieval Greek *Barangos,* from Old Norse *Væringi,* probably from *vār* pledge

Vardar (*Serbo-Croat* 'vardar) NOUN a river in S Europe, rising in W Macedonia and flowing northeast, then south past Skopje into Greece, where it is called the Axios and enters the Aegean at Thessaloníki. Length: about 320 km (200 miles).

varec ('værɛk) NOUN [1] another name for **kelp.** [2] the ash obtained from kelp.
▷HISTORY C17: from French, from Old Norse *wrek* (unattested); see WRECK

Varese (*Italian* va're:se) NOUN a historic city in N Italy, in Lombardy near Lake Varese: manufacturing centre, esp for leather goods. Pop.: 88 018 (1990).

varia ('vɛərɪə) PLURAL NOUN a collection or miscellany, esp of literary works.
▷HISTORY Latin, neuter plural of *varius* VARIOUS

variable ('vɛərɪəbᵊl) ADJECTIVE [1] liable to or capable of change: *variable weather.* [2] (of behaviour, opinions, emotions, etc.) lacking constancy; fickle. [3] *Maths* having a range of possible values. [4] (of a species, characteristic, etc.) liable to deviate from the established type. [5] (of a wind) varying its direction and intensity. [6] (of an electrical component or device) designed so that a characteristic property, such as resistance, can be varied: *variable capacitor.* ◆ NOUN [7] something that is subject to variation. [8] *Maths* **a** an expression that can be assigned any of a set of values. **b** a symbol, esp *x, y,* or *z,* representing an unspecified member of a class of objects, numbers, etc. See also **dependent variable, independent variable.** [9] *Logic* a symbol, esp *x, y, z,* representing any member of a class of entities. [10] *Computing* a named unit of storage that can be changed to any of a set of specified values during execution of a program. [11] *Astronomy* See **variable star.** [12] a variable wind. [13] (*plural*) a region where variable winds occur.
▷HISTORY C14: from Latin *variābilis* changeable, from *variāre* to diversify
▶ˌ**variaˈbility** *or* ˈ**variableness** NOUN ▶ˈ**variably** ADVERB

variable cost NOUN a cost that varies directly with output.

variable-density wind tunnel NOUN a closed-circuit wind tunnel entirely contained in a casing in which the pressure and therefore the density of the working fluid can be maintained at a preselected value.

variable-geometry *or* **variable-sweep** ADJECTIVE denoting an aircraft in which the wings are hinged to give the variable aspect ratio colloquially known as a **swing-wing.**

variable star NOUN any star that varies considerably in brightness, either irregularly or in regular periods. **Intrinsic variables,** in which the variation is a result of internal changes, include novae, supernovae, and pulsating stars. See also **eclipsing binary.**

variance ('vɛərɪəns) NOUN [1] the act of varying or the quality, state, or degree of being divergent; discrepancy. [2] an instance of diverging; dissension: *our variance on this matter should not affect our friendship.* [3] **at variance. a** (often foll by *with*) (of facts, etc.) not in accord; conflicting. **b** (of persons) in a state of dissension. [4] *Statistics* a measure of dispersion obtained by taking the mean of the squared deviations of the observed values from their mean in a frequency distribution. [5] a difference or discrepancy between two steps in a legal proceeding, esp between a statement in a pleading and the evidence given to support it. [6] (in the US and Canada) a licence or authority issued by the board of variance to contravene the usual rule, esp to build contrary to the provision of a zoning code. [7] *Chem* the number of degrees of freedom of a system, used in the phase rule. [8] *Accounting* the difference between actual and standard costs of production.

variant ('vɛərɪənt) ADJECTIVE [1] liable to or displaying variation. [2] differing from a standard or type: *a variant spelling.* [3] *Obsolete* not constant; fickle. ◆ NOUN [4] something that differs from a standard or type. [5] *Statistics* another word for **variate** (sense 1).

▷HISTORY C14: via Old French from Latin *variāns,* from *variāre* to diversify, from *varius* VARIOUS

variate ('vɛərɪɪt) NOUN [1] *Statistics* a random variable or a numerical value taken by it. [2] a less common word for **variant** (sense 4).
▷HISTORY C16: from Latin *variāre* to VARY

variation (ˌvɛərɪ'eɪʃən) NOUN [1] the act, process, condition, or result of changing or varying; diversity. [2] an instance of varying or the amount, rate, or degree of such change. [3] something that differs from a standard or convention. [4] *Music* **a** a repetition of a musical theme in which the rhythm, harmony, or melody is altered or embellished. **b** (*as modifier*): *variation form.* [5] *Biology* **a** a marked deviation from the typical form or function. **b** a characteristic or an organism showing this deviation. [6] *Astronomy* any change in or deviation from the mean motion or orbit of a planet, satellite, etc., esp a perturbation of the moon. [7] another word for **magnetic declination.** [8] *Ballet* a solo dance. [9] *Linguistics* any form of morphophonemic change, such as one involved in inflection, conjugation, or vowel mutation.
▶ˌ**variˈational** ADJECTIVE ▶ˌ**variˈationally** ADVERB

varicella (ˌværɪ'sɛlə) NOUN the technical name for **chickenpox.**
▷HISTORY C18: New Latin, irregular diminutive of VARIOLA
▶ˌ**variˈcellar** ADJECTIVE

varicellate (ˌværɪ'sɛlɪt, -eɪt) ADJECTIVE (of certain shells) marked on the surface with small ridges.
▷HISTORY C19: from New Latin *varicella,* diminutive of Latin *varix* dilated vein, VARIX

varicelloid (ˌværɪ'sɛlɔɪd) ADJECTIVE resembling chickenpox.

varices ('værɪˌsi:z) NOUN the plural of **varix.**

varico- *or before a vowel* **varic-** COMBINING FORM indicating a varix or varicose veins: *varicotomy.*
▷HISTORY from Latin *varix, varic-* distended vein

varicocele ('værɪkəʊˌsi:l) NOUN *Pathol* an abnormal distension of the veins of the spermatic cord in the scrotum.

varicoloured *or US* **varicolored** ('vɛərɪˌkʌləd) ADJECTIVE having many colours; variegated; motley.

varicose ('værɪˌkəʊs) ADJECTIVE of or resulting from varicose veins: *a varicose ulcer.*
▷HISTORY C18: from Latin *varicōsus,* from VARIX

varicose veins PLURAL NOUN a condition in which the superficial veins, esp of the legs, become tortuous, knotted, and swollen: caused by a defect in the venous valves or in the venous pump that normally moves the blood out of the legs when standing for long periods.

varicosis (ˌværɪ'kəʊsɪs) NOUN *Pathol* any condition characterized by distension of the veins.
▷HISTORY C18: from New Latin, from Latin: VARIX

varicosity (ˌværɪ'kɒsɪtɪ) NOUN, *plural* **-ties.** *Pathol* [1] the state, condition, or quality of being varicose. [2] an abnormally distended vein.

varicotomy (ˌværɪ'kɒtəmɪ) NOUN, *plural* **-mies.** surgical excision of a varicose vein.

varied ('vɛərɪd) ADJECTIVE [1] displaying or characterized by variety; diverse. [2] modified or altered: *the amount may be varied without notice.* [3] varicoloured; variegated.
▶ˈ**variedly** ADVERB ▶ˈ**variedness** NOUN

variegate ('vɛərɪˌgeɪt) VERB (*tr*) [1] to alter the appearance of, esp by adding different colours. [2] to impart variety to.
▷HISTORY C17: from Late Latin *variegāre,* from Latin *varius* diverse, VARIOUS + *agere* to make
▶ˌ**varieˈgation** NOUN

variegated ('vɛərɪˌgeɪtɪd) ADJECTIVE [1] displaying differently coloured spots, patches, streaks, etc. [2] (of foliage or flowers) having pale patches, usually as a result of mutation, infection, etc.

varietal (və'raɪɪtᵊl) ADJECTIVE [1] of, relating to, characteristic of, designating, or forming a variety, esp a biological variety. ◆ NOUN [2] a wine labelled with the name of the grape from which it is pressed.
▶**vaˈrietally** ADVERB

variety (və'raɪɪtɪ) NOUN, *plural* **-ties.** [1] the quality or condition of being diversified or various. [2] a collection of unlike things, esp of the same general group; assortment. [3] a different form or kind within a general category; sort: *varieties of behaviour.* [4] **a** *Taxonomy* a race whose distinct characters are insufficient to justify classification as a separate species; a subspecies. **b** *Horticulture, stockbreeding* a strain of animal or plant produced by artificial breeding. [5] **a** entertainment consisting of a series of short unrelated performances or acts, such as comedy turns, songs, dances, sketches, etc. **b** (*as modifier*): *a variety show.*
▷HISTORY C16: from Latin *varietās,* from VARIOUS

variety meat NOUN *Chiefly US* processed meat, such as sausage, or offal.

varifocal ('vɛərɪˌfəʊkᵊl) ADJECTIVE [1] *Optics* having a focus that can vary. [2] relating to a lens that is graduated to permit any length of vision between near and distant.

varifocals ('vɛərɪˌfəʊkᵊlz) PLURAL NOUN a pair of spectacles with varifocal lenses.

variform ('vɛərɪˌfɔ:m) ADJECTIVE varying in form or shape.
▶ˈ**variˌformly** ADVERB

vario- COMBINING FORM indicating variety or difference: *variometer.*
▷HISTORY from Latin *varius* VARIOUS

variola (və'raɪələ) NOUN the technical name for **smallpox.**
▷HISTORY C18: from Medieval Latin: disease marked by little spots, from Latin *varius* spotted
▶**vaˈriolar** ADJECTIVE

variolate ('vɛərɪəˌleɪt) VERB [1] (*tr*) to inoculate with the smallpox virus. ◆ ADJECTIVE [2] marked or pitted with or as if with the scars of smallpox.
▷HISTORY C18: from VARIOLA
▶ˌ**varioˈlation** *or* ˌ**varioliˈzation** *or* ˌ**varioliˈsation** NOUN

variole ('vɛərɪˌəʊl) NOUN any of the rounded masses that make up the rock variolite.
▷HISTORY C19: from French, from Medieval Latin; see VARIOLA

variolite ('vɛərɪəˌlaɪt) NOUN any basic igneous rock containing rounded bodies (varioles) consisting of radiating crystal fibres.
▷HISTORY C18: from VARIOLA, referring to the pockmarked appearance of the rock
▶**variolitic** (ˌvɛərɪə'lɪtɪk) ADJECTIVE

varioloid ('vɛərɪəˌlɔɪd) ADJECTIVE [1] resembling smallpox. ◆ NOUN [2] a mild form of smallpox occurring in persons with partial immunity.

variolous (və'raɪələs) ADJECTIVE relating to or resembling smallpox; variolar.

variometer (ˌvɛərɪ'ɒmɪtə) NOUN [1] an instrument for measuring variations in a magnetic field, used esp for studying the magnetic field of the earth. [2] *Electronics* a variable inductor consisting of a movable coil mounted inside and connected in series with a fixed coil. [3] a sensitive rate-of-climb indicator, used mainly in gliders.

variorum (ˌvɛərɪ'ɔ:rəm) ADJECTIVE [1] containing notes by various scholars or critics or various versions of the text: *a variorum edition.* ◆ NOUN [2] an edition or text of this kind.
▷HISTORY C18: from Latin phrase *ēditiō cum notīs variōrum* edition with the notes of various commentators

various ('vɛərɪəs) DETERMINER [1] **a** several different: *he is an authority on various subjects.* **b** *Not standard* (*as pronoun;* followed by *of*): *various of them came.* ◆ ADJECTIVE [2] of different kinds, though often within the same general category; diverse: *various occurrences; his disguises are many and various.* [3] (*prenominal*) relating to a collection of separate persons or things: *the various members of the club.* [4] displaying variety; many-sided: *his various achievements are most impressive.* [5] *Poetic* variegated. [6] *Obsolete* inconstant.
▷HISTORY C16: from Latin *varius* changing; perhaps related to Latin *vārus* crooked
▶ˈ**variously** ADVERB ▶ˈ**variousness** NOUN

Language note The use of *different* after *various* should be avoided: *the disease exists in various forms* (not *in various different forms*).

variscite ('værɪˌsaɪt) NOUN a green secondary mineral consisting of hydrated aluminium phosphate.
▷HISTORY from Medieval Latin *Variscia,* the district of Vogtland in Saxony

varistor (vəˈrɪstə) NOUN a two-electrode semiconductor device having a voltage-dependent nonlinear resistance. Compare **varactor.**
▷HISTORY C20: a blend of *variable resistor*

varitype (ˈvɛərɪˌtaɪp) VERB [1] to produce (copy) on a Varityper. ◆ NOUN [2] copy produced on a Varityper.
▸ **ˈvariˌtypist** NOUN

Varityper (ˈvɛərɪˌtaɪpə) NOUN *Trademark* a justifying typewriter used to produce copy in various type styles.

varix (ˈvɛərɪks) NOUN, *plural* **varices** (ˈværɪˌsi:z). *Pathol* **a** a tortuous dilated vein. See **varicose veins. b** Also called: **arterial varix, varix lymphaticus.** a similar condition affecting an artery or lymphatic vessel.
▷HISTORY C15: from Latin

varlet (ˈvɑ:lɪt) NOUN *Archaic* [1] a menial servant. [2] a knight's page. [3] a rascal.
▷HISTORY C15: from Old French, variant of *vallet* VALET

varletry (ˈvɑ:lɪtrɪ) NOUN *Archaic* [1] **the.** rabble; mob. [2] varlets collectively.

varmint (ˈvɑ:mɪnt) NOUN *Informal* an irritating or obnoxious person or animal.
▷HISTORY C16: dialect variant of *varmin* VERMIN

varna (ˈvɑ:nə) NOUN any of the four Hindu castes; Brahman, Kshatriya, Vaisya, or Sudra.
▷HISTORY from Sanskrit: class

Varna (*Bulgarian* ˈvarna) NOUN a port in NE Bulgaria, on the Black Sea: founded by Greeks in the 6th century B.C.; under the Ottoman Turks (1391–1878). Pop.: 299 801 (1999 est.). Former name (1949–56): **Stalin.**

varnish (ˈvɑ:nɪʃ) NOUN [1] Also called: **oil varnish.** a preparation consisting of a solvent, a drying oil, and usually resin, rubber, bitumen, etc., for application to a surface where it polymerizes to yield a hard glossy, usually transparent, coating. [2] a similar preparation consisting of a substance, such as shellac or cellulose ester, dissolved in a volatile solvent, such as alcohol. It hardens to a film on evaporation of the solvent. See also **spirit varnish.** [3] Also called: **natural varnish.** the sap of certain trees used to produce such a coating. [4] a smooth surface, coated with or as with varnish. [5] an artificial, superficial, or deceptively pleasing manner, covering, etc.; veneer. [6] *Chiefly Brit* another word for **nail polish.** ◆ VERB (*tr*) [7] to cover with varnish. [8] to give a smooth surface to, as if by painting with varnish. [9] to impart a more attractive appearance to. [10] to make superficially attractive.
▷HISTORY C14: from Old French *vernis,* from Medieval Latin *veronix* sandarac, resin, from Medieval Greek *berenikē,* perhaps from Greek *Berenikē,* city in Cyrenaica, Libya where varnishes were used
▸ **ˈvarnisher** NOUN

varnishing day NOUN (at an exhibition of paintings) the day before the opening when artists may varnish or retouch their pictures after they have been hung.

varnish tree NOUN any of various trees, such as the lacquer tree, yielding substances used to make varnish or lacquer.

varsity (ˈvɑ:sɪtɪ) NOUN, *plural* **-ties.** *Brit, NZ, and South African informal* short for **university**: formerly used esp at the universities of Oxford and Cambridge.

Varuna (ˈværʊnə, ˈvʌ-) NOUN *Hinduism* the ancient sky god, later the god of the waters and rain-giver. In earlier traditions he was also the all-seeing divine judge.

varus (ˈvɛərəs) ADJECTIVE *Pathol* denoting a deformity in which the distal part of a limb is turned inwards towards the midline of the body.
▷HISTORY C19: from Latin: bow-legged

varve (vɑ:v) NOUN *Geology* [1] a typically thin band of sediment deposited annually in glacial lakes, consisting of a light layer and a dark layer deposited at different seasons. [2] either of the layers of sediment making up this band.
▷HISTORY C20: from Swedish *varv* layer, from *varva,* from Old Norse *hverfa* to turn

vary (ˈvɛərɪ) VERB **varies, varying, varied.** [1] to undergo or cause to undergo change, alteration, or modification in appearance, character, form, attribute, etc. [2] to be different or cause to be different; be subject to change. [3] (*tr*) to give variety to. [4] (*intr;* foll by *from*) to differ, as from a convention, standard, etc. [5] (*intr*) to change in accordance with another variable: *her mood varies with the weather; pressure varies directly with temperature and inversely with volume.* [6] (*tr*) *Music* to modify (a theme) by the use of variation.
▷HISTORY C14: from Latin *variāre,* from *varius* VARIOUS
▸ **ˈvarying** ADJECTIVE ▸ **ˈvaryingly** ADVERB

vas (væs) NOUN, *plural* **vasa** (ˈveɪsə). *Anatomy, zoology* a vessel, duct, or tube that carries a fluid.
▷HISTORY C17: from Latin: vessel

vas- COMBINING FORM a variant of **vaso-** before a vowel.

vascular (ˈvæskjʊlə) ADJECTIVE *Biology, anatomy* of, relating to, or having vessels that conduct and circulate liquids: *a vascular bundle; the blood vascular system.*
▷HISTORY C17: from New Latin *vāsculāris,* from Latin: VASCULUM
▸ **vascularity** (ˌvæskjʊˈlærɪtɪ) NOUN ▸ **ˈvascularly** ADVERB

vascular bundle NOUN a longitudinal strand of vascular tissue in the stems and leaves of higher plants.

vascularization *or* **vascularisation** (ˌvæskjʊlәraɪˈzeɪʃən) NOUN the development of blood vessels in an organ or part.

vascular ray NOUN another name for **medullary ray.**

vascular tissue NOUN tissue of higher plants consisting mainly of xylem and phloem and occurring as a continuous system throughout the plant: it conducts water, mineral salts, and synthesized food substances and provides mechanical support. Also called: **conducting tissue.**

vasculitis (ˌvæskjʊˈlaɪtɪs) NOUN inflammation of the blood vessels.

vasculum (ˈvæskjʊləm) NOUN, *plural* **-la** (-lə) *or* **-lums.** a metal box used by botanists in the field for carrying botanical specimens.
▷HISTORY C19: from Latin: little vessel, from VAS

vas deferens (ˈvæs ˈdɛfəˌrɛnz) NOUN, *plural* **vasa deferentia** (ˈveɪsə ˌdɛfəˈrɛnʃɪə). *Anatomy* the duct that conveys spermatozoa from the epididymis to the urethra.
▷HISTORY C16: from New Latin, from Latin *vās* vessel + *dēferēns,* present participle of *dēferre* to bear away

vase (vɑ:z) NOUN a vessel used as an ornament or for holding cut flowers.
▷HISTORY C17: via French from Latin *vās* vessel

vasectomy (væˈsɛktəmɪ) NOUN, *plural* **-mies.** surgical removal of all or part of the vas deferens, esp as a method of contraception.

Vaseline (ˈvæsɪˌli:n) NOUN a trademark for **petrolatum.**

Vashti (ˈvæʃtaɪ) NOUN *Old Testament* the wife of the Persian king Ahasuerus: deposed for refusing to display her beauty before his guests (Esther 1–2). Douay spelling: **Vasthi.**

vaso- *or before a vowel* **vas-** COMBINING FORM [1] indicating a blood vessel: *vasodilator.* [2] indicating the vas deferens: *vasectomy.*
▷HISTORY from Latin *vās* vessel

vasoactive (ˌveɪzəʊˈæktɪv) ADJECTIVE affecting the diameter of blood vessels: *vasoactive peptides.*

vasoconstrictor (ˌveɪzəʊkənˈstrɪktə) NOUN [1] a drug, agent, or nerve that causes narrowing (**vasoconstriction**) of the walls of blood vessels. ◆ ADJECTIVE [2] causing vasoconstriction.
▸ **ˌvasoconˈstrictive** ADJECTIVE

vasodilator (ˌveɪzəʊdaɪˈleɪtə) NOUN [1] a drug, agent, or nerve that can cause dilatation (**vasodilatation**) of the walls of blood vessels. ◆ ADJECTIVE [2] causing vasodilatation.

vasoinhibitor (ˌveɪzəʊɪnˈhɪbɪtə) NOUN any of a group of drugs that reduce or inhibit the action of the vasomotor nerves.
▸ **vasoinhibitory** (ˌveɪzəʊɪnˈhɪbɪtərɪ, -trɪ) ADJECTIVE

vasomotor (ˌveɪzəʊˈməʊtə) ADJECTIVE (of a drug, agent, nerve, etc.) relating to or affecting the diameter of blood vessels.

vasopressin (ˌveɪzəʊˈprɛsɪn) NOUN a polypeptide hormone secreted by the posterior lobe of the pituitary gland. It increases the reabsorption of water by the kidney tubules and increases blood pressure by constricting the arteries. Also called: **antidiuretic hormone.** Chemical name: **beta-hypophamine.** Compare **oxytocin.**
▷HISTORY from *Vasopressin,* a trademark

vasopressor (ˌveɪzəʊˈprɛsə) *Med* ◆ ADJECTIVE [1] causing an increase in blood pressure by constricting the arteries. ◆ NOUN [2] a substance that has such an effect.

vasovagal syncope (ˌveɪzəʊˈveɪgəl) NOUN a faint brought on by excessive activity of the vagus nerve, causing the heart to slow and the blood pressure to fall. It can be caused by fear, choking, or stomach cramps and has no lasting effects.

vassal (ˈvæsᵊl) NOUN [1] (in feudal society) a man who entered into a personal relationship with a lord to whom he paid homage and fealty in return for protection and often a fief. A **great vassal** was in vassalage to a king and a **rear vassal** to a great vassal. [2] **a** a person, nation, etc., in a subordinate, suppliant, or dependent position relative to another. **b** (*as modifier*): *vassal status.* ◆ ADJECTIVE [3] of or relating to a vassal.
▷HISTORY C14: via Old French from Medieval Latin *vassallus,* from *vassus* servant, of Celtic origin; compare Welsh *gwas* boy, Old Irish *foss* servant
▸ **ˈvassal-less** ADJECTIVE

vassalage (ˈvæsəlɪdʒ) NOUN [1] (esp in feudal society) **a** the condition of being a vassal or the obligations to which a vassal was liable. **b** the relationship between a vassal and his lord. [2] subjection, servitude, or dependence in general. [3] *Rare* vassals collectively.

vassalize *or* **vassalise** (ˈvæsəˌlaɪz) VERB (*tr*) to make a vassal of.

vast (vɑ:st) ADJECTIVE [1] unusually large in size, extent, degree, or number; immense. [2] (*prenominal*) (intensifier): *in vast haste.* ◆ NOUN [3] **the vast.** *Chiefly poetic* immense or boundless space. [4] *Brit dialect* a very great amount or number.
▷HISTORY C16: from Latin *vastus* deserted
▸ **ˈvastity** NOUN ▸ **ˈvastly** ADVERB ▸ **ˈvastness** NOUN

Västerås (*Swedish* vestərˈo:s) NOUN a city in central Sweden, on Lake Mälar: Sweden's largest inland port; site of several national parliaments in the 16th century. Pop.: 125 433 (2000 est.).

vastitude (ˈvɑ:stɪˌtju:d) NOUN *Rare* [1] the condition or quality of being vast. [2] a vast space, expanse, extent, etc.

vasty (ˈvɑ:stɪ) ADJECTIVE **vastier, vastiest.** an archaic or poetic word for **vast.**

vat (væt) NOUN [1] a large container for holding or storing liquids. [2] *Chem* a preparation of reduced vat dye. ◆ VERB **vats, vatting, vatted.** [3] (*tr*) to place, store, or treat in a vat.
▷HISTORY Old English *fæt;* related to Old Frisian *fet,* Old Saxon, Old Norse *fat,* Old High German *faz*

VAT (*sometimes* væt) (in Britain) ABBREVIATION FOR value-added tax: a tax levied on the difference between the cost of materials and the selling price of a commodity or service.

Vat. ABBREVIATION FOR Vatican.

vat dye NOUN a dye, such as indigo, that is applied by first reducing it to its leuco base, which is soluble in alkali, and then regenerating the insoluble dye by oxidation in the fibres of the material.
▸ **ˈvat-ˌdyed** ADJECTIVE

vatic (ˈvætɪk) ADJECTIVE *Rare* of, relating to, or characteristic of a prophet; oracular.
▷HISTORY C16: from Latin *vātēs* prophet

Vatican (ˈvætɪkən) NOUN [1] **a** the palace of the popes in Rome and their principal residence there since 1377, which includes administrative offices, a library, museum, etc., and is attached to the basilica of St Peter's. **b** (*as modifier*): *the Vatican Council.* [2] **a** the authority of the Pope and the papal curia. **b** (*as modifier*): *a Vatican edict.*
▷HISTORY C16: from Latin *Vāticānus mons* Vatican hill, on the western bank of the Tiber, of Etruscan origin

Vatican City NOUN an independent state forming an enclave in Rome, with extraterritoriality over 12 churches and palaces in Rome: the only remaining Papal State; independence recognized by the Italian government in 1929; contains St Peter's Basilica and Square and the Vatican; the spiritual and administrative centre of the Roman Catholic Church. Languages: Italian and Latin. Currency: lira. Pop.: 1000 (1997 est.). Area: 44 hectares (109 acres). Italian name: **Città del Vaticano**. Also called: **the Holy See**.

Vaticanism ('vætɪkəˌnɪzəm) NOUN *Often derogatory* the authority and policies of the Pope and the papal curia, esp with regard to papal infallibility.

vaticide ('vætɪˌsaɪd) NOUN *Rare* **a** the murder of a prophet. **b** a person guilty of this.
▷HISTORY C18: from Latin *vātēs* prophet + -CIDE

vaticinate (vəˈtɪsɪˌneɪt) VERB *Rare* to foretell; prophesy.
▷HISTORY C17: from Latin *vāticinārī* from *vātēs* prophet + *canere* to foretell
▸**vaticination** (ˌvætɪsɪˈneɪʃən) NOUN ▸**va'tici,nator** NOUN ▸**vaticinal** (vəˈtɪsɪnᵊl) *or* **va'ticinatory** ADJECTIVE

Vättern (*Swedish* ˈvɛtərn) NOUN **Lake.** a lake in S central Sweden: the second largest lake in Sweden; linked to Lake Vänern by the Göta Canal; drains into the Baltic. Area: 1912 sq. km (738 sq. miles).

vatu ('vætuː) NOUN the standard monetary unit of Vanuatu.

vauch ('vɒtʃ) VERB (*intr*) *Southwest English dialect* to move fast.

Vaucluse (*French* voklyz) NOUN a department of SE France, in Provence-Alpes-Côte-d'Azur region. Capital: Avignon. Pop.: 499 685 (1999). Area: 3578 sq. km (1395 sq. miles).

Vaud (*French* vo) NOUN a canton of SW Switzerland: mountainous in the southeast; chief Swiss producer of wine. Capital: Lausanne. Pop.: 616 300 (2000 est.). Area: 3209 sq. km (1240 sq. miles). German name: **Waadt**.

vaudeville ('vəʊdəvɪl, 'vɔː-) NOUN [1] *Chiefly US and Canadian* variety entertainment consisting of short acts such as acrobatic turns, song-and-dance routines, animal acts, etc., popular esp in the early 20th century. Brit name: **music hall.** [2] a light or comic theatrical piece interspersed with songs and dances.
▷HISTORY C18: from French, from *vaudevire* satirical folk song, shortened from *chanson du vau de Vire* song of the valley of Vire, a district in Normandy where this type of song flourished

vaudevillian (ˌvəʊdəˈvɪlɪən, ˌvɔː-) NOUN *also* **vaudevillist.** [1] a person who writes for or performs in vaudeville. ◆ ADJECTIVE [2] of, characteristic of, or relating to vaudeville.

Vaudois ('vəʊdwɑː) PLURAL NOUN, *singular* **-dois.** [1] another name for the **Waldenses.** [2] the inhabitants of Vaud.

vault¹ (vɔːlt) NOUN [1] an arched structure that forms a roof or ceiling. [2] a room, esp a cellar, having an arched roof down to floor level. [3] a burial chamber, esp when underground. [4] a strongroom for the safe-deposit and storage of valuables. [5] an underground room or part of such a room, used for the storage of wine, food, etc. [6] *Anatomy* any arched or domed bodily cavity or space: *the cranial vault.* [7] something suggestive of an arched structure, as the sky. ◆ VERB [8] (*tr*) to furnish with or as if with an arched roof. [9] (*tr*) to construct in the shape of a vault. [10] (*intr*) to curve, arch, or bend in the shape of a vault.
▷HISTORY C14 *vaute,* from Old French, from Vulgar Latin *volvita* (unattested) a turn, probably from Latin *volvere* to roll
▸**'vault,like** ADJECTIVE

vault² (vɔːlt) VERB [1] to spring over (an object), esp with the aid of a long pole or with the hands resting on the object. [2] (*intr*) to do, achieve, or attain something as if by a leap: *he vaulted to fame on the strength of his discovery.* [3] *Dressage* to perform or cause to perform a curvet. ◆ NOUN [4] the act of vaulting. [5] *Dressage* a low leap; curvet.
▷HISTORY C16: from Old French *voulter* to turn, from Italian *voltare* to turn, from Vulgar Latin *volvitāre* (unattested) to turn, leap; see VAULT¹
▸**'vaulter** NOUN

vaulting¹ ('vɔːltɪŋ) NOUN one or more vaults in a building or such structures considered collectively.

vaulting² ('vɔːltɪŋ) ADJECTIVE (*prenominal*) [1] excessively confident; overreaching; exaggerated: *vaulting arrogance.* [2] used to vault: *a vaulting pole.*

vaunt (vɔːnt) VERB [1] (*tr*) to describe, praise, or display (one's success, possessions, etc.) boastfully. [2] (*intr*) *Rare or literary* to use boastful language; brag. ◆ NOUN [3] a boast. [4] *Archaic* ostentatious display.
▷HISTORY C14: from Old French *vanter,* from Late Latin *vānitāre* to brag, from Latin *vānus* VAIN
▸**'vaunter** NOUN

vaunt-courier NOUN *Archaic or poetic* a person or thing that goes in advance; forerunner; herald.
▷HISTORY C16: from French *avant-courrier;* see AVAUNT, COURIER

v. aux. ABBREVIATION FOR auxiliary verb.

Vauxhall ('vɒksˌhɔːl) NOUN [1] a district in London, on the south bank of the Thames. [2] Also called: **Vauxhall Gardens.** a public garden at Vauxhall, laid out in 1661; a fashionable meeting place and site of lavish entertainments. Closed in 1859.

vav (vɔːv) NOUN the sixth letter of the Hebrew alphabet (ו) transliterated as *v* or *w*. Also called: **waw.**
▷HISTORY from Hebrew *wāw* a hook

vavasor ('vævəˌsɔː) *or* **vavasour** ('vævəˌsʊə) NOUN (in feudal society) the noble or knightly vassal of a baron or great lord who also has vassals himself. Also: **vavassor.**
▷HISTORY C13: from Old French *vavasour,* perhaps contraction of Medieval Latin *vassus vassōrum* vassal of vassals; see VASSAL

va-va-voom (ˌvæˌvæˈvuːm) NOUN *Informal* the quality of being interesting, exciting, or sexually appealing.

vb ABBREVIATION FOR verb.

VB (in transformational grammar) ABBREVIATION FOR verbal constituent.

vc THE INTERNET DOMAIN NAME FOR Saint Vincent and the Grenadines.

VC ABBREVIATION FOR: [1] Vice-chairman. [2] Vice Chancellor. [3] Vice Consul. [4] Victoria Cross. [5] Vietcong.

V-chip NOUN a device within a television set that allows the set to be programmed not to receive transmissions that have been classified as containing sex, violence, or obscene language.

vCJD ABBREVIATION FOR **(new-)variant Creutzfeldt-Jakob disease.**

VCR ABBREVIATION FOR: [1] video cassette recorder. [2] visual control room (at an airfield).

vd ABBREVIATION FOR various dates.

VD ABBREVIATION FOR venereal disease.

V-Day NOUN a day nominated to celebrate victory, as in V-E Day or V-J Day in World War II.

VDC ABBREVIATION FOR Volunteer Defence Corps.

VDQS ABBREVIATION FOR vins délimités de qualité supérieure: on a bottle of French wine, indicates that it contains high-quality wine from an approved regional vineyard: the second highest French wine classification. Compare **AC,** ***vin de pays, vin de table.***

VDT *Computing* ABBREVIATION FOR visual display terminal.

VDU *Computing* ABBREVIATION FOR **visual display unit.**

ve THE INTERNET DOMAIN NAME FOR Venezuela.

've CONTRACTION OF have: *I've; you've.*

Veadar *Hebrew* ('viːəˌdɑː, 'veɪ-) NOUN *Judaism* another term for **Adar Sheni:** see **Adar.**
▷HISTORY from Hebrew *va'adhar,* literally: and Adar, that is, the extra Adar

veal (viːl) NOUN [1] the flesh of the calf used as food. [2] Also called: **veal calf.** a calf, esp one bred for eating. Related adjective: **vituline.**
▷HISTORY C14: from Old French *veel,* from Latin *vitellus* a little calf, from *vitulus* calf

vealer ('viːlə) NOUN [1] *US, Canadian, and Austral* another name for **veal** (sense 2). [2] *NZ* a young bovine animal of up to 14 months old grown for veal.

vector ('vɛktə) NOUN [1] Also called: **polar vector.** *Maths* a variable quantity, such as force, that has magnitude and direction and can be resolved into components that are odd functions of the coordinates. It is represented in print by a bold italic symbol: ***F*** or $\vec{F}$. Compare **pseudoscalar, pseudovector, scalar** (sense 1), **tensor** (sense 2). [2] *Maths* an element of a vector space. [3] Also called: **carrier.** *Pathol* an organism, esp an insect, that carries a disease-producing microorganism from one host to another, either within or on the surface of its body. [4] Also called: **cloning vector.** *Genetics* an agent, such as a bacteriophage or a plasmid, by means of which a fragment of foreign DNA is inserted into a host cell to produce a gene clone in genetic engineering. [5] the course or compass direction of an aircraft. [6] any behavioural influence, force, or drive. ◆ VERB (*tr*) [7] to direct or guide (a pilot, aircraft, etc.) by directions transmitted by radio. [8] to alter the direction of (the thrust of a jet engine) as a means of steering an aircraft.
▷HISTORY C18: from Latin: carrier, from *vehere* to convey
▸**vectorial** (vɛkˈtɔːrɪəl) ADJECTIVE ▸**vec'torially** ADVERB

vector field NOUN a region of space under the influence of some vector quantity, such as magnetic field strength, in which the quantity takes a unique vector value at every point of the region.

vector product NOUN the product of two vectors that is a pseudovector, whose magnitude is the product of the magnitudes of the given vectors and the sine of the angle between them. Its axis is perpendicular to the plane of the given vectors. Written: $\boldsymbol{A} \times \boldsymbol{B}$ or $\boldsymbol{A} \wedge \boldsymbol{B}$. Compare **scalar product.** Also called: **cross product.**

vector space NOUN *Maths* a mathematical structure consisting of a set of objects (**vectors**) associated with a field of objects (**scalars**), such that the set constitutes an Abelian group and a further operation, scalar multiplication, is defined in which the product of a scalar and a vector is a vector. See also **scalar multiplication.**

vector sum NOUN a vector whose length and direction are represented by the diagonal of a parallelogram whose sides represent the given vectors. See also **resultant.**

Veda ('veɪdə) NOUN any or all of the most ancient sacred writings of Hinduism, esp the Rig-Veda, Yajur-Veda, Sama-Veda, and Atharva-Veda.
▷HISTORY C18: from Sanskrit: knowledge; related to *veda* I know
▸**Vedaic** (vɪˈdeɪɪk) ADJECTIVE ▸**Vedaism** ('veɪdəˌɪzəm) NOUN

vedalia (vɪˈdeɪlɪə) NOUN an Australian ladybird, *Rodolia cardinalis,* introduced elsewhere to control the scale insect *Icerya purchasi,* which is a pest of citrus fruits.
▷HISTORY C20: from New Latin

Vedanta (vɪˈdɑːntə, -ˈdæn-) NOUN one of the six main philosophical schools of Hinduism, expounding the monism regarded as implicit in the Veda in accordance with the doctrines of the Upanishads. It teaches that only Brahman has reality, while the whole phenomenal world is the outcome of illusion (maya).
▷HISTORY C19: from Sanskrit, from VEDA + *ánta* end
▸**Ve'dantic** ADJECTIVE ▸**Ve'dantism** NOUN ▸**Ve'dantist** NOUN

V-E Day NOUN the day marking the Allied victory in Europe in World War II (May 8, 1945).

Vedda *or* **Veddah** ('vɛdə) NOUN, *plural* **-da, -das** *or* **-dah, -dahs.** a member of an aboriginal people of Sri Lanka, characterized by slender build, dark complexion, and wavy hair, noted for their Stone Age technology.
▷HISTORY C17: from Sinhalese: hunter, of Dravidian origin

Veddoid ('vɛdɔɪd) ADJECTIVE [1] of, relating to, or resembling the Vedda. ◆ NOUN [2] a Vedda. [3] a member of a postulated prehistoric race of S Asia, having slender build, dark complexion, and wavy hair: thought to be ancestors of the Vedda.

vedette (vɪˈdɛt) NOUN [1] Also called: **vedette boat.** *Naval* a small patrol vessel. [2] Also called: **vidette.** *Military* a mounted sentry posted forward of a formation's position.
▷HISTORY C17: from French, from Italian *vedetta* (influenced by *vedere* to see), from earlier *veletta,* perhaps from Spanish *vela* watch, from *velar* to keep vigil, from Latin *vigilāre*

Vedic ('veɪdɪk) ADJECTIVE [1] of or relating to the Vedas or the ancient form of Sanskrit in which they are written. [2] of or relating to the ancient Indo-European settlers in India, regarded as the originators of many of the traditions preserved in the Vedas. ◆ NOUN [3] the classical form of Sanskrit; the language of the Vedas.

veep (vi:p) NOUN *Informal* a vice president.
▷**HISTORY** C20: from the initials VP

veer[1] (vɪə) VERB [1] to alter direction (of); swing around. [2] (*intr*) to change from one position, opinion, etc., to another. [3] (*intr*) (of the wind) **a** to change direction clockwise in the northern hemisphere and anticlockwise in the southern. **b** *Nautical* to blow from a direction nearer the stern. Compare **haul** (sense 5). [4] *Nautical* to steer (a vessel) off the wind. ◆ NOUN [5] a change of course or direction.
▷**HISTORY** C16: from Old French *virer,* probably of Celtic origin; compare Welsh *gwyro* to diverge

veer[2] (vɪə) VERB (*tr;* often foll by *out* or *away*) *Nautical* to slacken or pay out (cable or chain).
▷**HISTORY** C16: from Dutch *vieren,* from Old High German *fieren* to give direction

veery ('vɪərɪ) NOUN, *plural* **veeries**. a tawny brown North American thrush, *Hylocichla fuscescens,* with a slightly spotted grey breast.
▷**HISTORY** C19: probably imitative of its note

veg (vɛdʒ) NOUN *Informal* a vegetable or vegetables.

Vega ('vi:gə) NOUN the brightest star in the constellation Lyra and one of the most conspicuous in the N hemisphere. It is part of an optical double star having a faint companion. Distance: 25.3 light years; spectral type: A0V.
▷**HISTORY** C17: from Medieval Latin, from Arabic (*al nasr*) *al wāqi,* literally: the falling (vulture), that is, the constellation Lyra

vegan ('vi:gən) NOUN a person who refrains from using any animal product whatever for food, clothing, or any other purpose.

vegeburger *or* **veggieburger** ('vɛdʒɪ,bɜ:gə) NOUN a flat cake of chopped seasoned vegetables and pulses that is grilled or fried and often served in a bread roll.

Vegemite ('vɛdʒɪ,maɪt) NOUN *Austral* [1] *Trademark* a vegetable extract used as a spread, flavouring, etc. [2] (*not capital*) *Informal* a child, esp one who is well-behaved. [3] **happy little vegemite.** *Informal* a person who is in good humour.

vegetable ('vɛdʒtəbəl) NOUN [1] any of various herbaceous plants having parts that are used as food, such as peas, beans, cabbage, potatoes, cauliflower, and onions. [2] *Informal* a person who has lost control of his mental faculties, limbs, etc., as from an injury, mental disease, etc. [3] **a** a dull inactive person. **b** (*as modifier*): *a vegetable life.* [4] (*modifier*) consisting of or made from edible vegetables: *a vegetable diet.* [5] (*modifier*) of, relating to, characteristic of, derived from, or consisting of plants or plant material: *vegetable oils; the vegetable kingdom.* [6] *Rare* any member of the plant kingdom.
▷**HISTORY** C14 (adj): from Late Latin *vegetābilis* animating, from *vegetāre* to enliven, from Latin *vegēre* to excite

vegetable butter NOUN any of a group of vegetable fats having the consistency of butter.

vegetable ivory NOUN [1] the hard whitish material obtained from the endosperm of the ivory nut: used to make buttons, ornaments, etc. [2] another name for the **ivory nut**.

vegetable kingdom NOUN another name for **plant kingdom**.

vegetable marrow NOUN [1] a cucurbitaceous plant, *Cucurbita pepo,* probably native to America but widely cultivated for its oblong green striped fruit, which is eaten as a vegetable. [2] Also called (in the US): **marrow squash.** the fruit of this plant. Often shortened to: **marrow.**

vegetable oil NOUN any of a group of oils that are esters of fatty acids and glycerol and are obtained from plants.

vegetable oyster NOUN another name for **salsify** (sense 1).

vegetable sheep NOUN *NZ* any of various species of the genus *Raoulia,* esp *R. mammillaris* or *R. eximia,* of New Zealand rocky mountains: a small low bush having white flowers and hairy leaves which, from a distance, make it look like a sheep.

vegetable silk NOUN any of various silky fibres obtained from the seed pods of certain plants. See also **kapok.**

vegetable sponge NOUN another name for **dishcloth gourd.**

vegetable tallow NOUN any of various types of tallow that are obtained from plants.

vegetable wax NOUN any of various waxes that occur on parts of certain plants, esp the trunks of certain palms, and prevent loss of water from the plant.

vegetal ('vɛdʒɪtəl) ADJECTIVE [1] of, relating to, or characteristic of vegetables or plant life. [2] of or relating to processes in plants and animals that do not involve sexual reproduction; vegetative.
▷**HISTORY** C15: from Late Latin *vegetāre* to quicken; see VEGETABLE

vegetarian (,vɛdʒɪ'tɛərɪən) NOUN [1] a person who advocates or practises vegetarianism. ◆ ADJECTIVE [2] relating to, advocating, or practising vegetarianism. [3] *Cookery* strictly, consisting of vegetables and fruit only, but usually including milk, cheese, eggs, etc.

vegetarianism (,vɛdʒɪ'tɛərɪə,nɪzəm) NOUN the principle or practice of excluding all meat and fish, and sometimes, in the case of vegans, all animal products (such as eggs, cheese, etc.) from one's diet.

vegetate ('vɛdʒɪ,teɪt) VERB (*intr*) [1] to grow like a plant; sprout. [2] to lead a life characterized by monotony, passivity, or mental inactivity. [3] *Pathol* (of a wart, polyp, etc.) to develop fleshy outgrowths.
▷**HISTORY** C17: from Late Latin *vegetāre* to invigorate

vegetation (,vɛdʒɪ'teɪʃən) NOUN [1] plant life as a whole, esp the plant life of a particular region. [2] the process of vegetating. [3] *Pathol* any abnormal growth, excrescence, etc. [4] a vegetative existence.
▸ **,vege'tational** ADJECTIVE ▸ **,vege'tatious** ADJECTIVE

vegetative ('vɛdʒɪtətɪv) ADJECTIVE [1] of, relating to, or denoting the nonreproductive parts of a plant, i.e. the stems, leaves, and roots, or growth that does not involve the reproductive parts. [2] (of reproduction) characterized by asexual processes. [3] of or relating to functions such as digestion, growth, and circulation rather than sexual reproduction. [4] (of a style of living) dull, stagnant, unthinking, or passive.
▸ **'vegetatively** ADVERB ▸ **'vegetativeness** NOUN

veggie ('vɛdʒɪ) NOUN, ADJECTIVE an informal word for **vegetarian.**

veggieburger ('vɛdʒɪ,bɜ:gə) NOUN a variant spelling of **vegeburger.**

vegie ('vɛdʒɪ) ADJECTIVE *Austral informal* (of school subjects) considered to be trivial; not academically taxing.

vego ('vɛdʒəʊ) *Austral informal* ◆ ADJECTIVE [1] vegetarian. ◆ NOUN, *plural* **vegos.** [2] a vegetarian.

veg out VERB **vegges, vegging, vegged.** (*intr, adverb*) *Slang* to relax in an inert passive way; vegetate: *vegging out in front of the television set.*

vehement ('vi:ɪmənt) ADJECTIVE [1] marked by intensity of feeling or conviction; emphatic. [2] (of actions, gestures, etc.) characterized by great energy, vigour, or force; furious.
▷**HISTORY** C15: from Latin *vehemēns* ardent; related to *vehere* to carry
▸ **'vehemence** NOUN ▸ **'vehemently** ADVERB

vehicle ('vi:ɪkəl) NOUN [1] any conveyance in or by which people or objects are transported, esp one fitted with wheels. [2] a medium for the expression, communication, or achievement of ideas, information, power, etc. [3] *Pharmacol* a therapeutically inactive substance mixed with the active ingredient to give bulk to a medicine. [4] Also called: **base.** a painting medium, such as oil, in which pigments are suspended. [5] (in the performing arts) a play, musical composition, etc., that enables a particular performer to display his talents. [6] a rocket excluding its payload.
▷**HISTORY** C17: from Latin *vehiculum,* from *vehere* to carry
▸**vehicular** (vɪ'hɪkjʊlə) ADJECTIVE

Veii ('vi:jaɪ) NOUN an ancient Etruscan city, northwest of Rome: destroyed by the Romans in 396 B.C.

veil (veɪl) NOUN [1] a piece of more or less transparent material, usually attached to a hat or headdress, used to conceal or protect a woman's face and head. [2] part of a nun's headdress falling round the face onto the shoulders. [3] something that covers, conceals, or separates; mask: *a veil of reticence.* [4] **the veil.** the life of a nun in a religious order and the obligations entailed by it. [5] **take the veil.** to become a nun. [6] Also called: **velum.** *Botany* a membranous structure, esp the thin layer of cells connecting the edge of a young mushroom cap with the stipe. [7] *Anatomy* another word for **caul.** [8] See **humeral veil.** ◆ VERB [9] (*tr*) to cover, conceal, or separate with or as if with a veil. [10] (*intr*) to wear or put on a veil.
▷**HISTORY** C13: from Norman French *veile,* from Latin *vēla* sails, pl of *vēlum* a covering
▸ **'veiler** NOUN ▸ **'veilless** ADJECTIVE ▸ **'veil-,like** ADJECTIVE

veiled (veɪld) ADJECTIVE [1] disguised: *a veiled insult.* [2] (of sound, tone, the voice, etc.) not distinct; muffled.
▸**veiledly** ('veɪlɪdlɪ) ADVERB

veiling ('veɪlɪŋ) NOUN a veil or the fabric used for veils.

vein (veɪn) NOUN [1] any of the tubular vessels that convey oxygen-depleted blood to the heart. Compare **pulmonary vein, artery.** Related adjective: **venous.** [2] any of the hollow branching tubes that form the supporting framework of an insect's wing. [3] any of the vascular strands of a leaf. [4] a clearly defined mass of ore, mineral, etc., filling a fault or fracture, often with a tabular or sheetlike shape. [5] an irregular streak of colour or alien substance in marble, wood, or other material. [6] a natural underground watercourse. [7] a crack or fissure. [8] a distinctive trait or quality in speech, writing, character, etc.; strain: *a vein of humour.* [9] a temporary disposition, attitude, or temper; mood: *the debate entered a frivolous vein.* [10] *Irish* a parting in hair. ◆ VERB (*tr*) [11] to diffuse over or cause to diffuse over in streaked patterns. [12] to fill, furnish, or mark with or as if with veins.
▷**HISTORY** C13: from Old French *veine,* from Latin *vēna*
▸ **'veinal** ADJECTIVE ▸ **'veinless** ADJECTIVE ▸ **'vein,like** ADJECTIVE ▸ **'veiny** ADJECTIVE

veining ('veɪnɪŋ) NOUN a pattern or network of veins or streaks.

veinlet ('veɪnlɪt) NOUN any small vein or venule.

veinstone ('veɪn,stəʊn) NOUN another word for **gangue.**

veinule ('veɪnju:l) NOUN a less common spelling of **venule.**

Vela ('vi:lə) NOUN, *Latin genitive* **Velorum** (vi:'lɔ:rəm). a constellation in the S hemisphere, close to Puppis and Carina and crossed by the Milky Way, that has four second-magnitude stars and a young bright pulsar.

velamen (və'leɪmen) NOUN, *plural* **-lamina** (-'læmɪnə). [1] the thick layer of dead cells that covers the aerial roots of certain orchids and aroids and absorbs moisture from the surroundings. [2] *Anatomy* another word for **velum.**
▷**HISTORY** C19: from Latin: a veil, from *vēlāre* to cover

velar ('vi:lə) ADJECTIVE [1] of, relating to, or attached to a velum: *velar tentacles.* [2] *Phonetics* articulated with the soft palate and the back of the tongue, as in the sounds (k), (g), or (ŋ).
▷**HISTORY** C18: from Latin *vēlāris,* from *vēlum* VEIL

velarium (vɪ'lɛərɪəm) NOUN, *plural* **-laria** (-'lɛərɪə). an awning used to protect the audience in ancient Roman theatres and amphitheatres.
▷**HISTORY** C19: from Latin, from *vēlāre* to cover

velarize *or* **velarise** ('vi:lə,raɪz) VERB (*tr*) *Phonetics* to pronounce or supplement the pronunciation of (a speech sound) with articulation at the soft palate, as in dark (l) in English *tall.*
▸ **,velari'zation** *or* **,velari'sation** NOUN

velate ('vi:lɪt, -leɪt) ADJECTIVE having or covered with velum.

Velcro ('vɛlkrəʊ) NOUN *Trademark* a fastening consisting of two strips of nylon fabric, one having tiny hooked threads and the other a coarse surface, that form a strong bond when pressed together.

veld *or* **veldt** (fɛlt, vɛlt) NOUN elevated open grassland in Southern Africa. See also **bushveld, highveld.** Compare **pampas, prairie, steppe.**
▷**HISTORY** C19: from Afrikaans, from earlier Dutch *veldt* FIELD

veldskoen ('fɛlt,skʊn, 'vɛlt-) NOUN an ankle-length boot of soft but strong rawhide.

▷HISTORY C19: from Afrikaans, from *vel* skin + *skoen* shoes

veleta (vəˈliːtə) NOUN a variant spelling of **valeta.**

veliger (ˈvɛlɪdʒə) NOUN the free-swimming larva of many molluscs, having a rudimentary shell and a ciliated velum used for feeding and locomotion.
▷HISTORY C19: from New Latin, from VELUM + -GER(OUS)

velites (ˈviːlɪˌtiːz) PLURAL NOUN light-armed troops in ancient Rome, drawn from the poorer classes.
▷HISTORY C17: from Latin, pl of *vēles* light-armed foot soldier; related to *volāre* to fly

velleity (vɛˈliːɪtɪ) NOUN, *plural* **-ties.** *Rare* 1 the weakest level of desire or volition. 2 a mere wish.
▷HISTORY C17: from New Latin *velleitās,* from Latin *velle* to wish

vellicate (ˈvɛlɪˌkeɪt) VERB *Rare* to twitch, pluck, or pinch.
▷HISTORY C17: from Latin *vellicāre,* from *vellere* to tear off
▸ˌ**velliˈcation** NOUN ▸ˈ**vellicative** ADJECTIVE

Vellore (vɛˈlɔː) NOUN a town in SE India, in NE Tamil Nadu: medical centre. Pop.: 175 061 (1991).

vellum (ˈvɛləm) NOUN 1 a fine parchment prepared from the skin of a calf, kid, or lamb. 2 a work printed or written on vellum. 3 a creamy coloured heavy paper resembling vellum. ◆ ADJECTIVE 4 made of or resembling vellum. 5 (of a book) bound in vellum.
▷HISTORY C15: from Old French *velin,* from *velin* of a calf, from *veel* VEAL

veloce (vɪˈləʊtʃɪ) ADJECTIVE, ADVERB *Music* to be played rapidly.
▷HISTORY from Italian, from Latin *vēlōx* quick

velocipede (vɪˈlɒsɪˌpiːd) NOUN 1 an early form of bicycle propelled by pushing along the ground with the feet. 2 any early form of bicycle or tricycle.
▷HISTORY C19: from French *vélocipède,* from Latin *vēlōx* swift + *pēs* foot
▸**veˈlociˌpedist** NOUN

velocity (vɪˈlɒsɪtɪ) NOUN, *plural* **-ties.** 1 speed of motion, action, or operation; rapidity; swiftness. 2 *Physics* a measure of the rate of motion of a body expressed as the rate of change of its position in a particular direction with time. It is measured in metres per second, miles per hour, etc. Symbol: *u, v, w.* 3 *Physics* (not in technical usage) another word for **speed** (sense 3).
▷HISTORY C16: from Latin *vēlōcitās,* from *vēlōx* swift; related to *volāre* to fly

velocity head NOUN the velocity of a fluid expressed in terms of the head or static pressure required to produce that velocity. It equals ρv/2 where ρ is the density of the fluid and v is the velocity. In hydrology the density of water can be written 1/G where G is the gravitational constant.

velocity modulation NOUN the modulation in velocity of a beam of electrons or ions caused by passing the beam through a high-frequency electric field, as in a cavity resonator.

velocity of circulation NOUN *Economics* the average number of times a unit of money is used in a given time, esp calculated as the ratio of the total money spent in that time to the total amount of money in circulation.

velodrome (ˈviːləˌdrəʊm, ˈvɛl-) NOUN an arena with a banked track for cycle racing.
▷HISTORY C20: from French *vélodrome,* from *vélo-* (from Latin *vēlōx* swift) + -DROME

velour *or* **velours** (vɛˈlʊə) NOUN any of various fabrics with a velvet-like finish, used for upholstery, coats, hats, etc.
▷HISTORY C18: from Old French *velous,* from Old Provençal *velos* velvet, from Latin *villosus* shaggy, from *villus* shaggy hair; compare Latin *vellus* a fleece

velouté (vəˈluːteɪ) NOUN a rich white sauce or soup made from stock, egg yolks, and cream.
▷HISTORY from French, literally: velvety, from Old French *velous;* see VELOUR

Velsen (*Dutch* ˈvɛlsə) NOUN a port in the W Netherlands, in North Holland at the mouth of the canal connecting Amsterdam with the North Sea: fishing and heavy industrial centre. Pop.: 63 617 (1994).

velum (ˈviːləm) NOUN, *plural* **-la** (-lə). 1 *Zoology* any of various membranous structures, such as the ciliated oral membrane of certain mollusc larvae or the veil-like membrane running around the rim of a jellyfish. 2 *Anatomy* any of various veil-like bodily structures, esp the soft palate. 3 *Botany* another word for **veil** (sense 6).
▷HISTORY C18: from Latin: veil

velure (vəˈlʊə) NOUN 1 velvet or a similar fabric. 2 a hatter's pad, used for smoothing silk hats.
▷HISTORY C16: from Old French *velour,* from Old French *velous;* see VELOUR

velutinous (vəˈluːtɪnəs) ADJECTIVE covered with short dense soft hairs: *velutinous leaves.*
▷HISTORY C19: from New Latin *velūtīnus* like velvet

velvet (ˈvɛlvɪt) NOUN 1 **a** a fabric of silk, cotton, nylon, etc., with a thick close soft usually lustrous pile. **b** (*as modifier*): *velvet curtains.* 2 anything with a smooth soft surface. 3 **a** smoothness; softness. **b** (*as modifier*): *velvet skin; a velvet night.* 4 the furry covering of the newly formed antlers of a deer. 5 *Slang, chiefly US* **a** gambling or speculative winnings. **b** a gain, esp when unexpectedly high. 6 **velvet glove.** gentleness or caution, often concealing strength or determination (esp in the phrase **an iron fist** *or* **hand in a velvet glove**).
▷HISTORY C14 *veluet,* from Old French *veluotte,* from *velu* hairy, from Vulgar Latin *villutus* (unattested), from Latin *villus* shaggy hair
▸ˈ**velvet-ˌlike** ADJECTIVE ▸ˈ**velvety** ADJECTIVE

velvet ant NOUN a solitary digger wasp of the family *Mutillidae.*
▷HISTORY C19: so named from the wingless female

velveteen (ˌvɛlvɪˈtiːn) NOUN 1 **a** a cotton fabric resembling velvet with a short thick pile, used for clothing, etc. **b** (*as modifier*): *velveteen trousers.* 2 (*plural*) trousers made of velveteen.
▸ˌ**velvetˈeened** ADJECTIVE

velvet revolution NOUN the peaceful overthrow of a government, esp a communist government, as occurred in Czechoslovakia in late 1989.

velvet scoter NOUN a European sea duck, *Melanitta fusca,* the male of which has a black plumage with white patches below the eyes and on the wings.

velvet shank NOUN a bright yellow edible basidiomycetous fungus, *Flammulina velutipes,* common on trunks, stumps, or branches of broad-leaved trees in winter.

velvet stout NOUN a less common name for **black velvet.**

Ven. ABBREVIATION FOR Venerable.

vena (ˈviːnə) NOUN, *plural* **-nae** (-niː). *Anatomy* a technical word for **vein.**
▷HISTORY C15: from Latin *vēna* VEIN

vena cava (ˈkeɪvə) NOUN, *plural* **venae cavae** (ˈkeɪviː). either one of the two large veins that convey oxygen-depleted blood to the heart.
▷HISTORY Latin: hollow vein

venal (ˈviːnᵊl) ADJECTIVE 1 easily bribed or corrupted; mercenary: *a venal magistrate.* 2 characterized by corruption: *a venal civilization.* 3 open to purchase, esp by bribery: *a venal contract.*
▷HISTORY C17: from Latin *vēnālis,* from *vēnum* sale
▸**veˈnality** NOUN ▸ˈ**venally** ADVERB

venatic (viːˈnætɪk) *or* **venatical** ADJECTIVE 1 of, relating to, or used in hunting. 2 (of people) engaged in or given to hunting.
▷HISTORY C17: from Latin *vēnāticus,* from *vēnārī* to hunt
▸**veˈnatically** ADVERB

venation (viːˈneɪʃən) NOUN 1 the arrangement of the veins in a leaf or in the wing of an insect. 2 such veins collectively.
▸**veˈnational** ADJECTIVE

vend (vɛnd) VERB 1 to sell or be sold. 2 to sell (goods) for a living. 3 (*tr*) *Rare* to utter or publish (an opinion, etc.).
▷HISTORY C17: from Latin *vendere,* contraction of *vēnum dare* to offer for sale
▸**vendition** (vɛnˈdɪʃən) NOUN

Venda[1] (ˈvɛndə) NOUN 1 (*plural* **-da** *or* **-das**) a member of a Negroid people of southern Africa, living chiefly in NE South Africa. 2 the language of this people, belonging to the Bantu group of the Niger-Congo family but not easily related to any other members of the group.

Venda[2] (ˈvɛndə) NOUN a former Bantu homeland in South Africa, near the Zimbabwe border; abolished in 1993. Capital: Thohoyandou.

vendace (ˈvɛndeɪs) NOUN, *plural* **-daces** *or* **-dace.** either of two small whitefish, *Coregonus vandesius* (**Lochmaben vendace**) or *C. gracilior* (**Cumberland vendace**), occurring in lakes in Scotland and NW England respectively. See also **powan.**
▷HISTORY C18: from New Latin *vandēsius,* from Old French *vandoise,* probably of Celtic origin

vendee (vɛnˈdiː) NOUN *Chiefly law* a person to whom something, esp real property, is sold; buyer.

Vendée (*French* vɑ̃de) NOUN a department of W France, in Pays-de-la-Loire region: scene of the **Wars of the Vendée,** a series of peasant-royalist insurrections (1793–95) against the Revolutionary government. Capital: La Roche-sur-Yon. Pop.: 539 664 (1999). Area: 7016 sq. km (2709 sq. miles).

Vendémiaire *French* (vɑ̃demjɛr) NOUN the month of the grape harvest: the first month of the French Revolutionary calendar, extending from Sept. 23 to Oct. 22.
▷HISTORY C18: from French, from Latin *vindēmia* vintage, from *vīnum* wine + *dēmere* to take away

vendetta (vɛnˈdɛtə) NOUN 1 a private feud, originally between Corsican or Sicilian families, in which the relatives of a murdered person seek vengeance by killing the murderer or some member of his family. 2 any prolonged feud, quarrel, etc.
▷HISTORY C19: from Italian, from Latin *vindicta,* from *vindicāre* to avenge; see VINDICATE
▸**venˈdettist** NOUN

vendible (ˈvɛndəbᵊl) ADJECTIVE 1 saleable or marketable. 2 *Obsolete* venal. ◆ NOUN 3 (*usually plural*) *Rare* a saleable object.
▸ˌ**vendiˈbility** *or* ˈ**vendibleness** NOUN

vending machine NOUN a machine that automatically dispenses consumer goods such as cigarettes, food, or petrol, when money is inserted. Also called: **automat.**

vendor (ˈvɛndɔː) *or* **vender** (ˈvɛndə) NOUN 1 *Chiefly law* a person who sells something, esp real property. 2 another name for **vending machine.**

vendor placing NOUN *Finance* a method of financing the purchase of one company by another in which the purchasing company pays for the target company in its own shares, on condition that the vendor places these shares with investors for cash payment.

vendue (ˈvɛndjuː) NOUN *US* a public sale; auction.
▷HISTORY C17: from Dutch *vendu,* from Old French *vendue* a sale, from *vendre* to sell, from Latin *vendere*

veneer (vɪˈnɪə) NOUN 1 a thin layer of wood, plastic, etc., with a decorative or fine finish that is bonded to the surface of a less expensive material, usually wood. 2 a superficial appearance, esp one that is pleasing: *a veneer of gentility.* 3 any facing material that is applied to a different backing material. 4 any one of the layers of wood that is used to form plywood. ◆ VERB (*tr*) 5 to cover (a surface) with a veneer. 6 to bond together (thin layers of wood) to make plywood. 7 to conceal (something) under a superficially pleasant surface.
▷HISTORY C17: from German *furnieren* to veneer, from Old French *fournir* to FURNISH
▸**veˈneerer** NOUN

veneering (vɪˈnɪərɪŋ) NOUN 1 material used as veneer or a veneered surface. 2 *Rare* a superficial show.

venepuncture (ˈvɛnɪˌpʌŋktʃə) NOUN a variant spelling of **venipuncture.**

venerable (ˈvɛnərəbᵊl) ADJECTIVE 1 (esp of a person) worthy of reverence on account of great age, religious associations, character, position, etc. 2 (of inanimate objects) hallowed or impressive on account of historical or religious association. 3 ancient: *venerable tomes.* 4 *RC Church* a title bestowed on a deceased person when the first stage of his canonization has been accomplished and his holiness has been recognized in a decree of the official Church. 5 *Church of England* a title given to an archdeacon.
▷HISTORY C15: from Latin *venerābilis,* from *venerārī* to venerate
▸ˌ**veneraˈbility** *or* ˈ**venerableness** NOUN ▸ˈ**venerably** ADVERB

venerate (ˈvɛnəˌreɪt) VERB (*tr*) 1 to hold in deep respect; revere. 2 to honour in recognition of qualities of holiness, excellence, wisdom, etc.
▷HISTORY C17: from Latin *venerārī,* from *venus* love
▸ˈ**venerˌator** NOUN

veneration (ˌvɛnəˈreɪʃən) NOUN [1] a feeling or expression of awe or reverence. [2] the act of venerating or the state of being venerated.
▸ˌ**venerˈational** ADJECTIVE ▸ˈ**venerativeness** NOUN

venereal (vɪˈnɪərɪəl) ADJECTIVE [1] of, relating to, or infected with venereal disease. [2] (of a disease) transmitted by sexual intercourse. [3] of, relating to, or involving the genitals. [4] of or relating to sexual intercourse or erotic desire; aphrodisiac.
▷HISTORY C15: from Latin *venereus* concerning sexual love, from *venus* sexual love, from VENUS[1]

venereal disease NOUN any of various diseases, such as syphilis or gonorrhoea, transmitted by sexual intercourse. Abbreviation: **VD.**

venereology (vɪˌnɪərɪˈɒlədʒɪ) NOUN the branch of medicine concerned with the study and treatment of venereal disease.
▸**veˌnereˈologist** NOUN

venery[1] (ˈvɛnərɪ, ˈviː-) NOUN *Archaic* the pursuit of sexual gratification.
▷HISTORY C15: from Medieval Latin *veneria,* from Latin *venus* love, VENUS[1]

venery[2] (ˈvɛnərɪ, ˈviː-) NOUN the art, sport, lore, or practice of hunting, esp with hounds; the chase.
▷HISTORY C14: from Old French *venerie,* from *vener* to hunt, from Latin *vēnārī*

venesection (ˈvɛnɪˌsɛkʃən) NOUN surgical incision into a vein.
▷HISTORY C17: from New Latin *vēnae sectiō;* see VEIN, SECTION

Veneti (vɛˈnɛtɪ, -taɪ) NOUN **the.** (*functioning as plural*) an ancient people who established themselves at the head of the Adriatic around 950 B.C., later becoming Roman subjects.

Venetia (vɪˈniːʃə) NOUN [1] the area of ancient Italy between the lower Po valley and the Alps: later a Roman province. [2] the territorial possessions of the medieval Venetian republic that were at the head of the Adriatic and correspond to the present-day region of Veneto and a large part of Friuli-Venezia Giulia.

Venetian (vɪˈniːʃən) ADJECTIVE [1] of, relating to, or characteristic of Venice or its inhabitants. ◆ NOUN [2] a native or inhabitant of Venice. [3] See **Venetian blind.** [4] (*sometimes not capital*) one of the tapes that join the slats of a Venetian blind. [5] a cotton or woollen cloth used for linings.

Venetian blind NOUN a window blind consisting of a number of horizontal slats whose angle may be altered to let in more or less light.

Venetian glass NOUN fine ornamental glassware made in or near Venice, esp at Murano.

Venetian red NOUN [1] natural or synthetic ferric oxide used as a red pigment. [2] **a** a moderate to strong reddish-brown colour. **b** (*as adjective*): *a Venetian-red coat.*

Venetic (vɪˈnɛtɪk) NOUN an ancient language of NE Italy, usually regarded as belonging to the Italic branch of the Indo-European family. It is recorded in about 200 inscriptions and was extinct by the 2nd century A.D.

Veneto (*Italian* ˈvɛːneto) NOUN a region of NE Italy, on the Adriatic: mountainous in the north with a fertile plain in the south, crossed by the Rivers Po, Adige, and Piave. Capital: Venice. Pop.: 4 511 714 (2000 est.). Area: 18 377 sq. km (7095 sq. miles). Also called: **Venezia-Euganea** (veˈnɛttsja euˈgaːnea).

Venez. ABBREVIATION FOR Venezuela.

Venezia (veˈnɛttsja) NOUN the Italian name for **Venice.**

Venezia Giulia (*Italian* ˈdʒuːlja) NOUN a former region of NE Italy at the N end of the Adriatic: divided between Yugoslavia and Italy after World War II; now divided between Italy and Slovenia.

Venezia Tridentina (*Italian* tridenˈtiːna) NOUN the former name (until 1947) of **Trentino-Alto Adige.**

Venezuela (ˌvɛnɪˈzweɪlə) NOUN [1] a republic in South America, on the Caribbean: colonized by the Spanish in the 16th century; independence from Spain declared in 1811 and won in 1819 after a war led by Simón Bolívar. It contains Lake Maracaibo and the northernmost chains of the Andes in the northwest, the Orinoco basin in the central part, and the Guiana Highlands in the south. Exports: petroleum, iron ore, and coffee. Official language: Spanish. Religion: Roman Catholic majority. Currency: bolívar. Capital: Caracas. Pop.: 24 632 000 (2001 est.). Area: 912 050 sq. km (352 142 sq. miles). Official name: **Bolivarian Republic of Venezuela.** [2] **Gulf of.** an inlet of the Caribbean in NW Venezuela: continues south as Lake Maracaibo.

Venezuelan (ˌvɛnɪˈzweɪlən) ADJECTIVE [1] of or relating to Venezuela or its inhabitants. ◆ NOUN [2] a native or inhabitant of Venezuela.

venge (vɛndʒ) VERB (*tr*) an archaic word for **avenge.**
▷HISTORY C13: from Old French *venger,* from Latin *vindicāre;* see VINDICATE

vengeance (ˈvɛndʒəns) NOUN [1] the act of or desire for taking revenge; retributive punishment. [2] **with a vengeance.** (intensifier): *the 70's have returned with a vengeance.*
▷HISTORY C13: from Old French, from *venger* to avenge, from Latin *vindicāre* to punish; see VINDICATE

vengeful (ˈvɛndʒfʊl) ADJECTIVE [1] desiring revenge; vindictive. [2] characterized by or indicating a desire for revenge: *a vengeful glance.* [3] inflicting or taking revenge: *with vengeful blows.*
▸ˈ**vengefully** ADVERB ▸ˈ**vengefulness** NOUN

venial (ˈviːnɪəl) ADJECTIVE easily excused or forgiven: *a venial error.*
▷HISTORY C13: via Old French from Late Latin *veniālis,* from Latin *venia* forgiveness; related to Latin *venus* love
▸ˌ**veniˈality** NOUN ▸ˈ**venially** ADVERB

venial sin NOUN *Christianity* a sin regarded as involving only a partial loss of grace. Compare **mortal sin.**

Venice (ˈvɛnɪs) NOUN a port in NE Italy, capital of Veneto region, built on over 100 islands and mud flats in the **Lagoon of Venice** (an inlet of the **Gulf of Venice** at the head of the Adriatic): united under the first doge in 697 A.D.; became an independent republic and a great commercial and maritime power, defeating Genoa, the greatest rival, in 1380; contains the Grand Canal and about 170 smaller canals, providing waterways for city transport. Pop.: 277 305 (2000 est.). Italian name: **Venezia.** Related adjective: **Venetian.**

venin (ˈvɛnɪn, ˈviː-) NOUN any of the poisonous constituents of animal venoms.
▷HISTORY C20: from French *ven(in)* poison + -IN

venipuncture *or* **venepuncture** (ˈvɛnɪˌpʌŋktʃə) NOUN *Med* the puncturing of a vein, esp to take a sample of venous blood or inject a drug.

venire facias (vɪˈnaɪrɪ ˈfeɪʃɪˌæs) NOUN *Law* (formerly) a writ directing a sheriff to summon suitable persons to form a jury.
▷HISTORY C15: Latin, literally: you must make come

venireman (vɪˈnaɪərɪmən) NOUN, *plural* **-men.** (in the US and formerly in England) a person summoned for jury service under a venire facias.

venison (ˈvɛnzən, ˈvɛnɪzᵊn, -sᵊn) NOUN [1] the flesh of a deer, used as food. [2] *Archaic* the flesh of any game animal used for food.
▷HISTORY C13: from Old French *venaison,* from Latin *vēnātiō* hunting, from *vēnārī* to hunt

Venite (vɪˈnaɪtɪ) NOUN [1] *Ecclesiast* the opening word of the 95th psalm, an invitatory prayer at matins. [2] a musical setting of this.
▷HISTORY Latin: come ye

Venlo *or* **Venloo** (*Dutch* ˈvɛnloː) NOUN a city in the SE Netherlands, in Limburg on the Maas River. Pop.: 63 820 (latest est.).

Venn diagram (vɛn) NOUN *Maths, logic* a diagram in which mathematical sets or terms of a categorial statement are represented by overlapping circles within a boundary representing the universal set, so that all possible combinations of the relevant properties are represented by the various distinct areas in the diagram.
▷HISTORY C19: named after John *Venn* (1834–1923), English logician

vennel (ˈvɛnᵊl) NOUN *Scot* a lane; alley.
▷HISTORY C15: from Old French *venelle,* from Latin *vēna* vein

venography (vɪˈnɒgrəfɪ) NOUN *Med* radiography of veins after injection of a contrast medium. Also called: **phlebography.**

venom (ˈvɛnəm) NOUN [1] a poisonous fluid secreted by such animals as certain snakes and scorpions and usually transmitted by a bite or sting. [2] malice; spite.
▷HISTORY C13: from Old French *venim,* from Latin *venēnum* poison, love potion; related to *venus* sexual love
▸ˈ**venomless** ADJECTIVE ▸ˈ**venomous** ADJECTIVE ▸ˈ**venomously** ADVERB ▸ˈ**venomousness** NOUN

venosclerosis (ˌviːnəʊsklɪˈrəʊsɪs) NOUN another name for **phlebosclerosis.**

venose (ˈviːnəʊs) ADJECTIVE [1] having veins; venous. [2] (of a plant) covered with veins or similar ridges.
▷HISTORY C17: via Latin *vēnōsus,* from *vēna* a VEIN

venosity (vɪˈnɒsɪtɪ) NOUN [1] an excessive quantity of blood in the venous system or in an organ or part. [2] an unusually large number of blood vessels in an organ or part.

venous (ˈviːnəs) ADJECTIVE [1] *Physiol* of or relating to the blood circulating in the veins. [2] of or relating to the veins.
▷HISTORY C17: see VENOSE
▸ˈ**venously** ADVERB ▸ˈ**venousness** NOUN

vent[1] (vɛnt) NOUN [1] a small opening for the passage or escape of fumes, liquids, etc. [2] the shaft of a volcano or an aperture in the earth's crust through which lava and gases erupt. [3] the external opening of the urinary or genital systems of lower vertebrates. [4] a small aperture at the breech of old guns through which the charge was ignited. [5] an exit, escape, or passage. [6] **give vent to.** to release (an emotion, passion, idea, etc.) in an utterance or outburst. ◆ VERB (*mainly tr*) [7] to release or give expression or utterance to (an emotion, idea, etc.): *he vents his anger on his wife.* [8] to provide a vent for or make vents in. [9] to let out (steam, liquid, etc.) through a vent.
▷HISTORY C14: from Old French *esventer* to blow out, from EX-[1] + *venter,* from Vulgar Latin *ventāre* (unattested) to be windy, from Latin *ventus* wind
▸ˈ**venter** NOUN ▸ˈ**ventless** ADJECTIVE

vent[2] (vɛnt) NOUN [1] a vertical slit at the back or both sides of a jacket. ◆ VERB [2] (*tr*) to make a vent or vents in (a jacket).
▷HISTORY C15: from Old French *fente* slit, from *fendre* to split, from Latin *findere* to cleave

ventage (ˈvɛntɪdʒ) NOUN [1] a small opening; vent. [2] a finger hole in a musical instrument such as a recorder.

ventail (ˈvɛnteɪl) NOUN (in medieval armour) a covering for the lower part of the face.
▷HISTORY C14: from Old French *ventaille* sluice, from *vent* wind, from Latin *ventus*

venter (ˈvɛntə) NOUN [1] *Anatomy, zoology* **a** the belly or abdomen of vertebrates. **b** a protuberant structure or part, such as the belly of a muscle. [2] *Botany* the swollen basal region of an archegonium, containing the developing ovum. [3] *Law* the womb. [4] **in venter.** *Law* conceived but not yet born.
▷HISTORY C16: from Latin

vent gleet NOUN *Vet science* inflammation of the cloaca in poultry, characterized by a yellowish discharge accompanied by local swelling and congestion.

ventifact (ˈvɛntɪˌfækt) NOUN *Geology* a pebble that has been shaped by wind-blown sand.

ventilate (ˈvɛntɪˌleɪt) VERB (*tr*) [1] to drive foul air out of (an enclosed area). [2] to provide with a means of airing. [3] to expose (a question, grievance, etc.) to public examination or discussion. [4] *Physiol* to oxygenate (the blood) in the capillaries of the lungs. [5] to winnow (grain).
▷HISTORY C15: from Latin *ventilāre* to fan, from *ventulus* diminutive of *ventus* wind
▸ˈ**ventilable** ADJECTIVE

ventilation (ˌvɛntɪˈleɪʃən) NOUN [1] the act or process of ventilating or the state of being ventilated. [2] an installation in a building that provides a supply of fresh air.
▸ˈ**ventiˌlative** ADJECTIVE ▸ˈ**ventiˌlatory** ADJECTIVE

ventilator (ˈvɛntɪˌleɪtə) NOUN [1] an opening or device, such as a fan, used to ventilate a room, building, etc. [2] *Med* a machine that maintains a flow of air into and out of the lungs of a patient who is unable to breathe normally.

Ventôse *French* (vɑ̃toz) NOUN the windy month: the sixth month of the French Revolutionary calendar, extending from Feb. 20 to March 21.

▷HISTORY C18: from Latin *ventōsus* full of wind, from *ventus* wind

ventouse (vɛnˈtuːs) NOUN an apparatus sometimes used to assist the delivery of a baby, consisting of a cup which is attached to the fetal head by suction, and a chain by which traction can be exerted in order to draw out the baby.
▷HISTORY C16: from Old French *ventose* a cupping glass

ventral (ˈvɛntrəl) ADJECTIVE 1 relating to the front part of the body; towards the belly. Compare **dorsal**. 2 of, relating to, or situated on the upper or inner side of a plant organ, esp a leaf, that is facing the axis.
▷HISTORY C18: from Latin *ventrālis,* from *venter* abdomen
▸ˈ**ventrally** ADVERB

ventral fin NOUN 1 another name for **pelvic fin.** 2 any unpaired median fin situated on the undersurface of fishes and some other aquatic vertebrates.

ventricle (ˈvɛntrɪkᵊl) NOUN *Anatomy* 1 a chamber of the heart, having thick muscular walls, that receives blood from the atrium and pumps it to the arteries. 2 any one of the four main cavities of the vertebrate brain, which contain cerebrospinal fluid. 3 any of various other small cavities in the body.
▷HISTORY C14: from Latin *ventriculus,* diminutive of *venter* belly

ventricose (ˈvɛntrɪˌkəʊs) ADJECTIVE 1 *Botany, zoology, anatomy* having a swelling on one side; unequally inflated: *the ventricose corolla of many labiate plants.* 2 another word for **corpulent.**
▷HISTORY C18: from New Latin *ventricōsus,* from Latin *venter* belly
▸**ventricosity** (ˌvɛntrɪˈkɒsɪtɪ) NOUN

ventricular (vɛnˈtrɪkjʊlə) ADJECTIVE 1 of, relating to, involving, or constituting a ventricle. 2 having a belly. 3 swollen or distended; ventricose.

ventriculography (vɛnˌtrɪkjʊˈlɒgrəfɪ) NOUN *Med* 1 radiography of the ventricles of the heart after injection of a contrast medium. 2 radiography of the ventricles of the brain after injection of air or a radiopaque material.

ventriculus (vɛnˈtrɪkjʊləs) NOUN, *plural* **-li** (-ˌlaɪ). 1 *Zoology* **a** the midgut of an insect, where digestion takes place. **b** the gizzard of a bird. 2 another word for **ventricle.**
▷HISTORY C18: from Latin, diminutive of *venter* belly

ventriloquism (vɛnˈtrɪləˌkwɪzəm) *or* **ventriloquy** NOUN the art of producing vocal sounds that appear to come from another source.
▷HISTORY C18: from Latin *venter* belly + *loquī* to speak
▸**ventriloquial** (ˌvɛntrɪˈləʊkwɪəl) *or* **ventriloqual** (vɛnˈtrɪləkwəl) ADJECTIVE ▸ˌ**ventriˈloquially** ADVERB
▸**venˈtriloquist** NOUN ▸**venˌtriloˈquistic** ADJECTIVE

ventriloquize *or* **ventriloquise** (vɛnˈtrɪləˌkwaɪz) VERB to produce (sounds) in the manner of a ventriloquist.

venture (ˈvɛntʃə) VERB 1 (*tr*) to expose to danger; hazard: *he ventured his life.* 2 (*tr*) to brave the dangers of (something): *I'll venture the seas.* 3 (*tr*) to dare (to do something): *does he venture to object?* 4 (*tr; may take a clause as object*) to express in spite of possible refutation or criticism: *I venture that he is not that honest.* 5 (*intr;* often foll by *out, forth,* etc.) to embark on a possibly hazardous journey, undertaking, etc.: *to venture forth upon the high seas.* ◆ NOUN 6 an undertaking that is risky or of uncertain outcome. 7 **a** a commercial undertaking characterized by risk of loss as well as opportunity for profit. **b** the merchandise, money, or other property placed at risk in such an undertaking. 8 something hazarded or risked in an adventure; stake. 9 *Archaic* chance or fortune. 10 **at a venture.** at random; by chance.
▷HISTORY C15: variant of *aventure* ADVENTURE
▸ˈ**venturer** NOUN

venture capital NOUN 1 capital that is provided for a new commercial enterprise by individuals or organizations other than those who own the new enterprise. 2 another name for **risk capital.**

Venture Scout *or* **Venturer** NOUN *Brit* a young man or woman, aged 16–20, who is a member of the senior branch of the Scouts. Former name: **Rover.** US equivalent: **Explorer.**

venturesome (ˈvɛntʃəsəm) *or* **venturous** (ˈvɛntʃərəs) ADJECTIVE 1 willing to take risks; daring. 2 hazardous.

Venturi tube NOUN 1 *Physics* a device for measuring fluid flow, consisting of a tube so constricted that the pressure differential produced by fluid flowing through the constriction gives a measure of the rate of flow. 2 Also called: **venturi.** a tube with a constriction used to reduce or control fluid flow, as one in the air inlet of a carburettor.
▷HISTORY C19: named after G. B. *Venturi* (1746–1822), Italian physicist

venue (ˈvɛnjuː) NOUN 1 *Law* **a** the place in which a cause of action arises. **b** the place fixed for the trial of a cause. **c** the locality from which the jurors must be summoned to try a particular cause. 2 a meeting place. 3 any place where an organized gathering, such as a rock concert or public meeting, is held. 4 *Chiefly US* a position in an argument.
▷HISTORY C14: from Old French, from *venir* to come, from Latin *venīre*

venule (ˈvɛnjuːl) NOUN 1 *Anatomy* any of the small branches of a vein that receives oxygen-depleted blood from the capillaries and returns it to the heart via the venous system. 2 any of the branches of a vein in an insect's wing.
▷HISTORY C19: from Latin *vēnula* diminutive of *vēna* VEIN
▸**venular** (ˈvɛnjʊlə) ADJECTIVE

Venus[1] (ˈviːnəs) NOUN 1 the Roman goddess of love. Greek counterpart: **Aphrodite.** 2 **mount of Venus.** See **mons veneris.**

Venus[2] (ˈviːnəs) NOUN 1 one of the inferior planets and the second nearest to the sun, visible as a bright morning or evening star. Its surface is extremely hot (over 400°C) and is completely shrouded by dense cloud. The atmosphere is principally carbon dioxide. Mean distance from sun: 108 million km; period of revolution around sun: 225 days; period of axial rotation: 244.3 days (retrograde motion); diameter and mass: 96.5 and 81.5 per cent that of earth respectively. 2 the alchemical name for **copper**[1].

Venusberg (ˈviːnəsˌbɜːg; *German* ˈveːnʊsbɛrk) NOUN a mountain in central Germany: contains caverns that, according to medieval legend, housed the palace of the goddess Venus.

Venusian (vɪˈnjuːzɪən) ADJECTIVE 1 of, occurring on, or relating to the planet Venus. ◆ NOUN 2 (in science fiction) an inhabitant of Venus.

Venus's flower basket NOUN any of several deep-sea sponges of the genus *Euplectella,* esp *E. aspergillum,* having a skeleton composed of interwoven glassy six-rayed spicules.

Venus's-flytrap *or* **Venus flytrap** NOUN an insectivorous plant, *Dionaea muscipula,* of Carolina, having hinged two-lobed leaves that snap closed when the sensitive hairs on the surface are touched: family *Droseraceae.* See also **sundew, pitcher plant, butterwort.**

Venus's-girdle NOUN a ctenophore, *Cestum veneris,* of warm seas, having an elongated ribbon-like body.

Venus's-hair NOUN a fragile maidenhair fern, *Adiantum capillus-veneris,* of tropical and subtropical America, having fan-shaped leaves and a black stem.

Venus shell NOUN a marine bivalve mollusc of the family Veneridae, typified by the intertidal *Venus gallina,* with somewhat rounded ribbed valves.

Venus's looking glass NOUN a purple-flowered campanulaceous plant, *Legousia hybrida,* of Europe, W Asia, and N Africa.

veracious (vɛˈreɪʃəs) ADJECTIVE 1 habitually truthful or honest. 2 accurate; precise.
▷HISTORY C17: from Latin *vērax,* from *vērus* true
▸**veˈraciously** ADVERB ▸**veˈraciousness** NOUN

veracity (vɛˈræsɪtɪ) NOUN, *plural* **-ties.** 1 truthfulness or honesty, esp when consistent or habitual. 2 precision; accuracy. 3 something true; a truth.
▷HISTORY C17: from Medieval Latin *vērācitās,* from Latin *vērax;* see VERACIOUS

Veracruz (ˌvɛrəˈkruːz; *Spanish* beraˈkruθ) NOUN 1 a state of E Mexico, on the Gulf of Mexico: consists of a hot humid coastal strip with lagoons, rising rapidly inland to the central plateau and Sierra Madre Oriental. Capital: Jalapa. Pop.: 6 901 111 (2000). Area: 72 815 sq. km (28 114 sq. miles). 2 the chief port of Mexico, in Veracruz state on the Gulf of Mexico. Pop.: 410 000 (2000 est.).

veranda *or* **verandah** (vəˈrændə) NOUN 1 a porch or portico, sometimes partly enclosed, along the outside of a building. 2 *NZ* a canopy sheltering pedestrians in a shopping street.
▷HISTORY C18: from Portuguese *varanda* railing; related to Hindi *varandā* railing
▸**veˈrandaed** *or* **veˈrandahed** ADJECTIVE

verapamil (vɪˈræpəˌmɪl) NOUN *Med* a calcium-channel blocker used in the treatment of angina pectoris, hypertension, and some types of irregular heart rhythm.

veratridine (vɪˈrætrɪˌdiːn) NOUN a yellowish-white amorphous alkaloid obtained from the seeds of sabadilla. Formula: $C_{36}H_{51}NO_{11}$.
▷HISTORY C20: from VERATR(INE) + -ID[3] + -INE[2]

veratrine (ˈvɛrəˌtriːn) *or* **veratrin** (ˈvɛrətrɪn) NOUN a white poisonous mixture obtained from the seeds of sabadilla, consisting of veratridine and several other alkaloids: formerly used in medicine as a counterirritant.
▷HISTORY C19: from Latin *vērātrum* hellebore + -INE[2]

verb (vɜːb) NOUN 1 (in traditional grammar) any of a large class of words in a language that serve to indicate the occurrence or performance of an action, the existence of a state or condition, etc. In English, such words as *run, make, do,* and the like are verbs. 2 (in modern descriptive linguistic analysis) **a** a word or group of words that functions as the predicate of a sentence or introduces the predicate. **b** (*as modifier*): *a verb phrase.* ◆ Abbreviations: **vb, v.**
▷HISTORY C14: from Latin *verbum* a word
▸ˈ**verbless** ADJECTIVE

verbal (ˈvɜːbᵊl) ADJECTIVE 1 of, relating to, or using words, esp as opposed to ideas, etc.: *merely verbal concessions.* 2 oral rather than written: *a verbal agreement.* 3 verbatim; literal: *an almost verbal copy.* 4 *Grammar* of or relating to verbs or a verb. ◆ NOUN 5 *Grammar* another word for **verbid.** 6 (*plural*) *Slang* abuse or invective: *new forms of on-field verbals.* 7 (*plural*) *Slang* a criminal's admission of guilt on arrest. ◆ VERB **-bals, -balling, -balled.** (*tr*) 8 *Slang* (of the police) to implicate (someone) in a crime by quoting alleged admission of guilt in court.
▸ˈ**verbally** ADVERB

verbalism (ˈvɜːbəˌlɪzəm) NOUN 1 a verbal expression; phrase or word. 2 an exaggerated emphasis on the importance of words by the uncritical acceptance of assertions in place of explanations, the use of rhetorical style, etc. 3 a statement lacking real content, esp a cliché.

verbalist (ˈvɜːbəlɪst) NOUN 1 a person who deals with words alone, rather than facts, ideas, feeling, etc. 2 a person skilled in the use of words.

verbalize *or* **verbalise** (ˈvɜːbəˌlaɪz) VERB 1 to express (an idea, feeling, etc.) in words. 2 to change (any word that is not a verb) into a verb or derive a verb from (any word that is not a verb). 3 (*intr*) to be verbose.
▸ˌ**verbaliˈzation** *or* ˌ**verbaliˈsation** NOUN ▸ˈ**verbalˌizer** *or* ˈ**verbalˌiser** NOUN

verbal noun NOUN a noun derived from a verb, such as *smoking* in the sentence *smoking is bad for you.* See also **gerund.**

verbascum (vɜːˈbæskəm) NOUN See **mullein.**
▷HISTORY Latin: mullein

verbatim (vɜːˈbeɪtɪm) ADVERB, ADJECTIVE using exactly the same words; word for word.
▷HISTORY C15: from Medieval Latin: word by word, from Latin *verbum* word

verbena (vɜːˈbiːnə) NOUN 1 any plant of the verbenaceous genus *Verbena,* chiefly of tropical and temperate America, having red, white, or purple fragrant flowers: much cultivated as garden plants. See also **vervain.** 2 any of various similar or related plants, esp the lemon verbena.
▷HISTORY C16: via Medieval Latin, from Latin: sacred bough used by the priest in religious acts, VERVAIN

verbenaceous (ˌvɜːbɪˈneɪʃəs) ADJECTIVE of, relating to, or belonging to the *Verbenaceae,* a family of herbaceous and climbing plants, shrubs, and trees, mostly of warm and tropical regions, having

tubular typically two-lipped flowers: includes teak, lantana, vervain, and verbena.
▷**HISTORY** C19: from New Latin *Verbēnāceae,* from Medieval Latin: VERBENA

verbiage ('vɜːbɪɪdʒ) NOUN [1] the excessive and often meaningless use of words; verbosity. [2] *Rare* diction; wording.
▷**HISTORY** C18: from French, from Old French *verbier* to chatter, from *verbe* word, from Latin *verbum*

verbid ('vɜːbɪd) NOUN *Grammar* any nonfinite form of a verb or any nonverbal word derived from a verb: *participles, infinitives, and gerunds are all verbids.*

verbify ('vɜːbɪˌfaɪ) VERB **-fies, -fying, -fied**. another word for **verbalize** (senses 2, 3).
▸ **ˌverbifiˈcation** NOUN

verbose (vɜːˈbəʊs) ADJECTIVE using or containing an excess of words, so as to be pedantic or boring; prolix.
▷**HISTORY** C17: from Latin *verbōsus* from *verbum* word
▸**verˈbosely** ADVERB ▸**verbosity** (vɜːˈbɒsɪtɪ) *or* **verˈboseness** NOUN

verboten *German* (fɛrˈboːtən) ADJECTIVE forbidden; prohibited.

verb phrase NOUN *Grammar* a constituent of a sentence that contains the verb and any direct and indirect objects but not the subject. It is a controversial question in grammatical theory whether or not this constituent is to be identified with the predicate of the sentence. Abbreviation: **VP.**

verb. sap. *or* **sat.** ABBREVIATION FOR verbum sapienti sat est.
▷**HISTORY** Latin: a word is enough to the wise

Vercelli (*Italian* verˈtʃɛlli) NOUN a city in NW Italy, in Piedmont: an ancient Ligurian and later Roman city; has an outstanding library of manuscripts (notably the *Codex Vercellensis,* dating from the 10th century). Pop.: 50 313 (1990).

verdant ('vɜːdᵊnt) ADJECTIVE [1] covered with green vegetation. [2] (of plants, etc.) green in colour. [3] immature or unsophisticated; green.
▷**HISTORY** C16: from Old French *verdoyant,* from *verdoyer* to become green, from Old French *verd* green, from Latin *viridis,* from *virēre* to be green
▸ **ˈverdancy** NOUN ▸ **ˈverdantly** ADVERB

verd antique (vɜːd) NOUN [1] a dark green mottled impure variety of serpentine marble. [2] any of various similar marbles or stones. [3] another name for **verdigris.**
▷**HISTORY** C18: from French, from Italian *verde antico* ancient green

Verde (vɜːd) NOUN **Cape.** a cape in Senegal, near Dakar: the westernmost point of Africa. See also **Cape Verde.**

verderer ('vɜːdərə) NOUN *English legal history* a judicial officer responsible for the maintenance of law and order in the royal forests.
▷**HISTORY** C16: from Anglo-French, from Old French *verdier,* from *verd* green, from Latin *viridis;* compare Latin *viridārium* plantation of trees

verdict ('vɜːdɪkt) NOUN [1] the findings of a jury on the issues of fact submitted to it for examination and trial; judgment. [2] any decision, judgment, or conclusion.
▷**HISTORY** C13: from Medieval Latin *vērdictum,* from Latin *vērē dictum* truly spoken, from *vērus* true + *dīcere* to say

verdigris ('vɜːdɪgrɪs) NOUN [1] a green or bluish patina formed on copper, brass, or bronze and consisting of a basic salt of copper containing both copper oxide and a copper salt. [2] a green or blue crystalline substance obtained by the action of acetic acid on copper and used as a fungicide and pigment; basic copper acetate.
▷**HISTORY** C14: from Old French *vert de Grice* green of Greece

verdigris toadstool NOUN a basidiomycetous fungus, *Stropharia aeruginosa,* having a distinctive and unusual blue-green cap and paler shaggy stem.

verdin ('vɜːdɪn) NOUN a small W North American tit, *Auriparus flaviceps,* having a grey plumage with a yellow head.
▷**HISTORY** French: yellowhammer

Verdun (*French* vɛrdœ̃; *English* 'vɛədʌn) NOUN [1] a fortified town in NE France, on the Meuse: scene of the longest and most severe battle (1916) of World War I, in which the French repelled a powerful German offensive. Pop.: 23 430 (1990). Ancient name: **Verodunum** (ˌverəˈdjuːnəm). [2] **Treaty of.** an agreement reached in 843 A.D. by three grandsons of Charlemagne, dividing his empire into an E kingdom (later Germany), a W kingdom (later France), and a middle kingdom (containing what became the Low Countries, Lorraine, Burgundy, and N Italy).

verdure ('vɜːdʒə) NOUN [1] flourishing green vegetation or its colour. [2] a condition of freshness or healthy growth.
▷**HISTORY** C14: from Old French *verd* green, from Latin *viridis*
▸ **ˈverdured** ADJECTIVE ▸ **ˈverdurous** ADJECTIVE

verecund ('vɛrɪˌkʌnd) ADJECTIVE *Rare* shy or modest.
▷**HISTORY** C16: from Latin *verēcundus* diffident, from *verērī* to fear

Vereeniging (fəˈriːnɪkɪŋ, və-) NOUN a city in E South Africa: scene of the signing (1902) of the treaty ending the Boer War. Pop. (urban area): 346 780 (1996).

verge¹ (vɜːdʒ) NOUN [1] an edge or rim; margin. [2] a limit beyond which something occurs; brink: *on the verge of ecstasy.* [3] *Brit* a grass border along a road. [4] an enclosing line, belt, or strip. [5] *Architect* the edge of the roof tiles projecting over a gable. [6] *Architect* the shaft of a classical column. [7] an enclosed space. [8] *Horology* the spindle of a balance wheel in a vertical escapement, found only in very early clocks. [9] *English legal history* **a** the area encompassing the royal court that is subject to the jurisdiction of the Lord High Steward. **b** a rod or wand carried as a symbol of office or emblem of authority, as in the Church. **c** a rod held by a person swearing fealty to his lord on becoming a tenant, esp of copyhold land. ◆ VERB [10] (*intr;* foll by *on*) to be near (to): *to verge on chaos.* [11] (when *intr,* sometimes foll by *on*) to serve as the edge of (something): *this narrow strip verges the road.*
▷**HISTORY** C15: from Old French, from Latin *virga* rod

verge² (vɜːdʒ) VERB (*intr;* foll by *to* or *towards*) to move or incline in a certain direction.
▷**HISTORY** C17: from Latin *vergere*

vergeboard ('vɜːdʒˌbɔːd) NOUN another name for **bargeboard.**

vergence ('vɜːdʒəns) NOUN the inward or outward turning movement of the eyes in convergence or divergence.
▷**HISTORY** C19: from VERGE² + -ENCE

verger ('vɜːdʒə) NOUN *Chiefly Church of England* [1] a church official who acts as caretaker and attendant, looking after the interior of a church and often the vestments and church furnishings. [2] an official who carries the verge or rod of office before a bishop, dean, or other dignitary in ceremonies and processions.
▷**HISTORY** C15: from Old French, from *verge,* from Latin *virga* rod, twig

Vergilian (vəˈdʒɪlɪən) ADJECTIVE a variant spelling of **Virgilian.**

verglas ('vɛəglɑː) NOUN, *plural* **-glases** (-glɑː, -glɑːz). a thin film of ice on rock.
▷**HISTORY** from Old French *verre-glaz* glass-ice, from *verre* glass (from Latin *vitrum*) + *glaz* ice (from Late Latin *glacia,* from Latin *glaciēs*)

veridical (vɪˈrɪdɪkᵊl) ADJECTIVE [1] truthful. [2] *Psychol* of or relating to revelations in dreams, hallucinations, etc., that appear to be confirmed by subsequent events.
▷**HISTORY** C17: from Latin *vēridicus,* from *vērus* true + *dīcere* to say
▸**veˌridiˈcality** NOUN ▸**veˈridically** ADVERB

veriest ('vɛrɪɪst) ADJECTIVE *Archaic* (intensifier): *the veriest coward.*

verification (ˌvɛrɪfɪˈkeɪʃən) NOUN [1] establishment of the correctness of a theory, fact, etc. [2] evidence that provides proof of an assertion, theory, etc. [3] *Law* **a** (formerly) a short affidavit at the end of a pleading stating the pleader's readiness to prove his assertions. **b** confirmatory evidence.
▸ **ˈverifiˌcative** *or* **ˈverifiˌcatory** ADJECTIVE

verification principle NOUN (in the philosophy of the logical positivists) the doctrine that nontautologous statements are meaningful only if it is in principle possible to establish empirically whether they are true or false.

verify ('vɛrɪˌfaɪ) VERB **-fies, -fying, -fied.** (*tr*) [1] to prove to be true; confirm; substantiate. [2] to check or determine the correctness or truth of by investigation, reference, etc. [3] *Law* to add a verification to (a pleading); substantiate or confirm (an oath).
▷**HISTORY** C14: from Old French *verifier,* from Medieval Latin *vērificāre,* from Latin *vērus* true + *facere* to make
▸ **ˈveriˌfiable** ADJECTIVE ▸ **ˈveriˌfiableness** NOUN
▸ **ˈveriˌfiably** ADVERB ▸ **ˈveriˌfier** NOUN

verily ('vɛrɪlɪ) ADVERB (*sentence modifier*) *Archaic* in truth; truly: *verily, thou art a man of God.*
▷**HISTORY** C13: from VERY + -LY²

verisimilar (ˌvɛrɪˈsɪmɪlə) ADJECTIVE appearing to be true; probable; likely.
▷**HISTORY** C17: from Latin *vērīsimilis,* from *vērus* true + *similis* like
▸ **ˌveriˈsimilarly** ADVERB

verisimilitude (ˌvɛrɪsɪˈmɪlɪˌtjuːd) NOUN [1] the appearance or semblance of truth or reality; quality of seeming true. [2] something that merely seems to be true or real, such as a doubtful statement.
▷**HISTORY** C17: from Latin *vērisimilitūdō,* from *vērus* true + *similitūdō* SIMILITUDE

verism ('vɪərɪzəm) NOUN extreme naturalism in art or literature.
▷**HISTORY** C19: from Italian *verismo,* from *vero* true, from Latin *vērus*
▸ **ˈverist** NOUN, ADJECTIVE ▸**veˈristic** ADJECTIVE

verismo (vɛˈrɪzməʊ; *Italian* veˈrismo) NOUN *Music* a school of composition that originated in Italian opera towards the end of the 19th century, drawing its themes from real life and emphasizing naturalistic elements. Its chief exponent was Giacomo Puccini (1858–1924).
▷**HISTORY** C19: from Italian; see VERISM

veritable ('vɛrɪtəbᵊl) ADJECTIVE (*prenominal*) [1] (intensifier; usually qualifying a word used metaphorically): *he's a veritable swine!* [2] *Rare* genuine or true; proper: *I require veritable proof.*
▷**HISTORY** C15: from Old French, from *vérité* truth; see VERITY
▸ **ˈveritableness** NOUN ▸ **ˈveritably** ADVERB

vérité ('vɛriːˌteɪ; *French* verite) ADJECTIVE involving a high degree of realism or naturalism: *a vérité look at David Bowie.* See also **cinéma vérité.**
▷**HISTORY** French, literally: truth

verity ('vɛrɪtɪ) NOUN, *plural* **-ties.** [1] the quality or state of being true, real, or correct. [2] a true principle, statement, idea, etc.; a truth or fact.
▷**HISTORY** C14: from Old French *vérité,* from Latin *vēritās,* from *vērus* true

verjuice ('vɜːˌdʒuːs) NOUN [1] **a** the acid juice of unripe grapes, apples, or crab apples, formerly much used in making sauces, etc. **b** (*as modifier*): *verjuice sauce.* [2] *Rare* **a** sourness or sharpness of temper, looks, etc. **b** (*as modifier*): *a verjuice old wife.* ◆ VERB [3] (*tr*) *Rare* to make sour; embitter.
▷**HISTORY** C14: from Old French *vert jus* green (unripe) juice, from Old French *vert* green (from Latin *viridis*) + *jus* juice (from Latin *jūs*)

Verkhne-Udinsk (*Russian* ˈvjerxnɪuˈdjinsk) NOUN the former name (until 1934) of **Ulan-Ude.**

verkrampte (fəˈkrɑmtə) NOUN (in South Africa) **a** (during apartheid) an Afrikaner Nationalist who opposed any changes toward liberal trends in government policy, esp relating to racial questions. **b** (*as modifier*): *verkrampte politics.* ◆ Compare **verligte.**
▷**HISTORY** C20: from Afrikaans (adj), literally: restricted

verlan (*French* vɛrlɑ̃) NOUN a variety of French slang in which the syllables are inverted, such as *meuf* for *femme,* and also incorporating Arabic words and phrases.
▷**HISTORY** C20: from inverting the syllables of the French word *l'envers* meaning the other way round

verligte (fəˈləxtə) NOUN (in South Africa) **a** (during apartheid) a person of any of the White political parties who supported liberal trends in government policy. **b** (*as modifier*): *verligte politics.* ◆ Compare **verkrampte.**
▷**HISTORY** C20: from Afrikaans (adj), literally: enlightened

vermeil ('vɜːmeɪl) NOUN [1] gilded silver, bronze,

or other metal, used esp in the 19th century. [2] **a** vermilion. **b** (*as adjective*): *vermeil shoes.*
▷HISTORY C15: from Old French, from Late Latin *vermiculus* insect (of the genus *Kermes*) or the red dye prepared from it, from Latin: little worm

vermi- COMBINING FORM worm: *vermicide; vermiform; vermifuge.*
▷HISTORY from Latin *vermis* worm

vermicelli (ˌvɜːmɪˈsɛlɪ; *Italian* vermiˈtʃɛlli) NOUN [1] very fine strands of pasta, used in soups. [2] tiny chocolate strands used to coat cakes, etc.
▷HISTORY C17: from Italian: little worms, from *verme* a worm, from Latin *vermis*

vermicide (ˈvɜːmɪˌsaɪd) NOUN any substance used to kill worms.
▸**ˌvermiˈcidal** ADJECTIVE

vermicular (vɜːˈmɪkjʊlə) ADJECTIVE [1] resembling the form, markings, motion, or tracks of worms. [2] of or relating to worms or wormlike animals.
▷HISTORY C17: from Medieval Latin *vermiculāris*, from Latin *vermiculus*, diminutive of *vermis* worm
▸**verˈmicularly** ADVERB

vermiculate VERB (vɜːˈmɪkjʊˌleɪt) [1] (*tr*) to decorate with wavy or wormlike tracery or markings. ◆ ADJECTIVE (vɜːˈmɪkjʊlɪt, -ˌleɪt) [2] vermicular; sinuous. [3] worm-eaten or appearing as if worm-eaten. [4] (of thoughts, etc.) insinuating; subtly tortuous.
▷HISTORY C17: from Latin *vermiculātus* in the form of worms, from *vermis* worm

vermiculation (vɜːˌmɪkjʊˈleɪʃən) NOUN [1] *Physiol* any wormlike movement, esp of the intestines; peristalsis. [2] decoration consisting of wormlike carving or marks. [3] the state of being worm-eaten.

vermiculite (vɜːˈmɪkjʊˌlaɪt) NOUN any of a group of micaceous minerals consisting mainly of hydrated silicate of magnesium, aluminium, and iron: on heating they expand and exfoliate and in this form are used in heat and sound insulation, fireproofing, and as a bedding medium for young plants.
▷HISTORY C19: from VERMICUL(AR) + -ITE[1]

vermiform (ˈvɜːmɪˌfɔːm) ADJECTIVE resembling a worm.

vermiform appendix *or* **process** NOUN a wormlike pouch extending from the lower end of the caecum in some mammals. In man it is vestigial. Also called: **appendix.**

vermifuge (ˈvɜːmɪˌfjuːdʒ) NOUN any drug or agent able to destroy or expel intestinal worms; an anthelmintic.
▸**vermifugal** (ˌvɜːmɪˈfjuːgəl) ADJECTIVE

vermilion *or* **vermillion** (vəˈmɪljən) NOUN [1] **a** a bright red to reddish-orange colour. **b** (*as adjective*): *a vermilion car.* [2] mercuric sulphide, esp when used as a bright red pigment; cinnabar.
▷HISTORY C13: from Old French *vermeillon*, from VERMEIL

vermin (ˈvɜːmɪn) NOUN [1] (*functioning as plural*) small animals collectively, esp insects and rodents, that are troublesome to man, domestic animals, etc. [2] (*plural* **-min**) an unpleasant, obnoxious, or dangerous person.
▷HISTORY C13: from Old French *vermine*, from Latin *vermis* a worm

vermination (ˌvɜːmɪˈneɪʃən) NOUN the spreading of or infestation with vermin.

verminous (ˈvɜːmɪnəs) ADJECTIVE relating to, infested with, or suggestive of vermin.
▸**ˈverminously** ADVERB ▸**ˈverminousness** NOUN

vermis (ˈvɜːmɪs) NOUN, *plural* **-mes** (-miːz). *Anatomy* the middle lobe connecting the two halves of the cerebellum.
▷HISTORY C19: via New Latin from Latin: worm

vermivorous (vɜːˈmɪvərəs) ADJECTIVE (of certain animals) feeding on worms.

Vermont (vɜːˈmɒnt) NOUN a state in the northeastern US: crossed from north to south by the Green Mountains; bounded on the east by the Connecticut River and by Lake Champlain in the northwest. Capital: Montpelier. Pop.: 608 827 (2000). Area: 24 887 sq. km (9609 sq. miles). Abbreviations: **Vt**, (with zip code) **VT.**

Vermonter (vɜːˈmɒntə) NOUN a native or inhabitant of Vermont.

vermouth (ˈvɜːməθ, vəˈmuːθ) NOUN any of several wines containing aromatic herbs and some other flavourings.
▷HISTORY C19: from French, from German *Wermut* WORMWOOD (absinthe)

vernacular (vəˈnækjʊlə) NOUN [1] **the.** the commonly spoken language or dialect of a particular people or place. [2] a local style of architecture, in which ordinary houses are built: *this architect has re-created a true English vernacular.* ◆ ADJECTIVE [3] relating to, using, or in the vernacular. [4] designating or relating to the common name of an animal or plant. [5] built in the local style of ordinary houses, rather than a grand architectural style.
▷HISTORY C17: from Latin *vernāculus* belonging to a household slave, from *verna* household slave
▸**verˈnacularly** ADVERB

vernacularism (vəˈnækjʊləˌrɪzəm) NOUN the use of the vernacular or a term in the vernacular.

vernal (ˈvɜːnəl) ADJECTIVE [1] of or occurring in spring. [2] *Poetic* of or characteristic of youth; fresh.
▷HISTORY C16: from Latin *vernālis*, from *vēr* spring
▸**ˈvernally** ADVERB

vernal equinox NOUN [1] the time at which the sun crosses the plane of the equator towards the relevant hemisphere, making day and night of equal length. It occurs about March 21 in the N hemisphere (Sept. 23 in the S hemisphere). [2] **a** *Astronomy* the point, lying in the constellation Pisces, at which the sun's ecliptic intersects the celestial equator. **b** the time at which this occurs as the sun travels south to north (March 21).

vernal grass NOUN any of various Eurasian grasses of the genus *Anthoxanthum*, such as *A. odoratum* (**sweet vernal grass**), having the fragrant scent of coumarin.

vernalize *or* **vernalise** (ˈvɜːnəˌlaɪz) VERB to subject ungerminated or germinating seeds to low temperatures, which is essential for many (plants) of temperate environments to ensure germination in some species and flowering in others.
▸**ˌvernaliˈzation** *or* **ˌvernaliˈsation** NOUN

vernation (vɜːˈneɪʃən) NOUN the way in which leaves are arranged in the bud.
▷HISTORY C18: from New Latin *vernātiō*, from Latin *vernāre* to be springlike, from *vēr* spring

Verner's law (ˈvɜːnəz) NOUN *Linguistics* a modification of Grimm's Law accommodating some of its exceptions. It states that noninitial voiceless fricatives in Proto-Germanic occurring as a result of Grimm's law became voiced fricatives if the previous syllable had been unstressed in Proto-Indo-European.
▷HISTORY C19: named after Karl Adolph *Verner* (1846–96), Danish philologist, who formulated it
▸**Vernerian** (vɜːˈnɛərɪən) ADJECTIVE

vernier (ˈvɜːnɪə) NOUN [1] a small movable scale running parallel to the main graduated scale in certain measuring instruments, such as theodolites, used to obtain a fractional reading of one of the divisions on the main scale. [2] an auxiliary device for making a fine adjustment to an instrument, usually by means of a fine screw thread. [3] (*modifier*) relating to or fitted with a vernier: *a vernier scale; a vernier barometer.*
▷HISTORY C18: named after Paul *Vernier* (1580–1637), French mathematician, who described the scale

vernier rocket NOUN another name for **thruster** (sense 2).

vernissage (ˌvɜːnɪˈsɑːʒ) NOUN [1] a preview or the opening or first day of an exhibition of paintings. [2] another term for **varnishing day.**
▷HISTORY French, from *vernis* VARNISH

Vernoleninsk (*Russian* virnalɪˈnjiːnsk) NOUN the former name of **Nikolayev.**

Verny (*Russian* ˈvjɛrnɪj) NOUN a former name (until 1927) of **Alma-Ata.**

Verona (vəˈrəʊnə; *Italian* veˈroːna) NOUN a city in N Italy, in Veneto on the Adige River: strategically situated at the junction of major routes between Italy and N Europe; became a Roman colony (89 B.C.); under Austrian rule (1797–1866); many Roman remains. Pop.: 255 268 (2000 est.).
▸**Veronese** (ˌvɛrəˈniːz) ADJECTIVE, NOUN

Veronal (ˈvɛrənəl) NOUN a trademark for **barbital.**

veronica[1] (vəˈrɒnɪkə) NOUN any scrophulariaceous plant of the genus *Veronica*, esp the speedwells, of temperate and cold regions, having small blue, pink, or white flowers and flattened notched fruits.
▷HISTORY C16: from Medieval Latin, perhaps from the name *Veronica*

veronica[2] (vəˈrɒnɪkə) NOUN *RC Church* [1] the representation of the face of Christ that, according to legend, was miraculously imprinted upon the headcloth that Saint Veronica offered him on his way to his crucifixion. [2] the cloth itself. [3] any similar representation of Christ's face.

veronica[3] (vəˈrɒnɪkə) NOUN *Bullfighting* a pass in which the matador slowly swings the cape away from the charging bull.
▷HISTORY from Spanish, from the name *Veronica*

verra (ˈvɛrə) ADJECTIVE, ADVERB a Scot word for **very.**

verruca (vɛˈruːkə) NOUN, *plural* **-cae** (-siː) *or* **-cas.** [1] *Pathol* a wart, esp one growing on the hand or foot. [2] *Biology* a wartlike outgrowth, as in certain plants or on the skin of some animals.
▷HISTORY C16: from Latin: wart

verrucose (ˈvɛrʊˌkəʊs) *or* **verrucous** (ˈvɛrʊkəs, vɛˈruːkəs) ADJECTIVE *Botany* covered with warty processes.
▷HISTORY C17: from Latin *verrūcōsus* full of warts, from *verrūca* a wart
▸**verrucosity** (ˌvɛrʊˈkɒsɪtɪ) NOUN

vers ABBREVIATION FOR versed sine.

Versailles (vɛəˈsaɪ, -ˈseɪlz; *French* vɛrsaj) NOUN [1] a city in N central France, near Paris: site of an elaborate royal residence built for Louis XIV; seat of the French kings (1682–1789). Pop.: 87 789 (1990). [2] **Treaty of Versailles. a** the treaty of 1919 imposed upon Germany by the Allies (except for the US and the Soviet Union): the most important of the five peace treaties that concluded World War I. **b** another name for the (Treaty of) **Paris** of 1783.

versant (ˈvɜːsənt) NOUN [1] *Rare* the side or slope of a mountain or mountain range. [2] the slope of a region.
▷HISTORY C19: from French, from *verser* to turn, from Latin *versāre*

versatile (ˈvɜːsəˌtaɪl) ADJECTIVE [1] capable of or adapted for many different uses, skills, etc. [2] variable or changeable. [3] *Botany* (of an anther) attached to the filament by a small area so that it moves freely in the wind. [4] *Zoology* able to turn forwards and backwards: *versatile antennae.*
▷HISTORY C17: from Latin *versātilis* moving around, from *versāre* to turn
▸**ˈversaˌtilely** ADVERB ▸**versatility** (ˌvɜːsəˈtɪlɪtɪ) NOUN

vers de société *French* (vɛr də sɔsjete) NOUN light, witty, and polished verse.
▷HISTORY literally: society verse

verse (vɜːs) NOUN [1] (not in technical usage) a stanza or other short subdivision of a poem. [2] poetry as distinct from prose. [3] **a** a series of metrical feet forming a rhythmic unit of one line. **b** (*as modifier*): *verse line.* [4] a specified type of metre or metrical structure: *iambic verse.* [5] one of the series of short subsections into which most of the writings in the Bible are divided. [6] a metrical composition; poem. ◆ VERB [7] a rare word for **versify.**
▷HISTORY Old English *vers*, from Latin *versus* a furrow, literally: a turning (of the plough), from *vertere* to turn

versed (vɜːst) ADJECTIVE (*postpositive; foll by in*) thoroughly knowledgeable (about), acquainted (with), or skilled (in).

versed sine NOUN a trigonometric function equal to one minus the cosine of the specified angle. Abbreviation: **vers.**
▷HISTORY C16: from New Latin *sinus versus*, from SINE[1] + *versus* turned, from *vertere* to turn

versicle (ˈvɜːsɪkəl) NOUN [1] a short verse. [2] a short sentence recited or sung by the minister at a liturgical ceremony and responded to by the choir or congregation.
▷HISTORY C14: from Latin *versiculus* a little line, from *versus* VERSE

versicolour *or US* **versicolor** (ˈvɜːsɪˌkʌlə) ADJECTIVE of variable or various colours.
▷HISTORY C18: from Latin *versicolor*, from *versāre* to turn + *color* COLOUR

versicular (vɜːˈsɪkjʊlə) ADJECTIVE *Rare* of, relating to, or consisting of verses or versicles.

versification (ˌvɜːsɪfɪˈkeɪʃən) NOUN [1] the

technique or art of versifying. 2 the form or metrical composition of a poem. 3 a metrical version of a prose text.

versify (ˈvɜːsɪˌfaɪ) VERB **-fies, -fying, -fied.** 1 (*tr*) to render (something) into metrical form or verse. 2 (*intr*) to write in verse.
▷**HISTORY** C14: from Old French *versifier,* from Latin *versificāre,* from *versus* VERSE + *facere* to make
▸ **ˈversiˌfier** NOUN

version (ˈvɜːʃən, -ʒən) NOUN 1 an account of a matter from a certain point of view, as contrasted with others: *his version of the accident is different from the policeman's.* 2 a translation, esp of the Bible, from one language into another. 3 a variant form of something; type. 4 an adaptation, as of a book or play into a film. 5 *Med* manual turning of a fetus to correct an irregular position within the uterus. 6 *Pathol* an abnormal displacement of the uterus characterized by a tilting forwards (**anteversion**), backwards (**retroversion**), or to either side (**lateroversion**).
▷**HISTORY** C16: from Medieval Latin *versiō* a turning, from Latin *vertere* to turn
▸ **ˈversional** ADJECTIVE

versioning (ˈvɜːʃənɪŋ) NOUN the adaptation of classic literary texts for film, which often involves updating or changing the setting.

vers libre *French* (vɛr librə) NOUN (in French poetry) another term for **free verse.**

verso (ˈvɜːsəʊ) NOUN, *plural* **-sos.** 1 **a** the back of a sheet of printed paper. **b** Also called: **reverso.** the left-hand pages of a book, bearing the even numbers. Compare **recto.** 2 the side of a coin opposite to the obverse; reverse.
▷**HISTORY** C19: from the New Latin phrase *versō foliō* the leaf having been turned, from Latin *vertere* to turn + *folium* a leaf

verst (vɛəst, vɜːst) NOUN a unit of length, used in Russia, equal to 1.067 kilometres (0.6629 miles).
▷**HISTORY** C16: from French *verste* or German *Werst,* from Russian *versta* line

versus (ˈvɜːsəs) PREPOSITION 1 (esp in a competition or lawsuit) against; in opposition to. Abbreviation: **v,** (esp US) **vs.** 2 as opposed to; in contrast with.
▷**HISTORY** C15: from Latin: turned (in the direction of), opposite, from *vertere* to turn

vert (vɜːt) NOUN 1 *English legal history* **a** the right to cut green wood in a forest. **b** the wood itself. 2 *Heraldry* **a** the colour green. **b** (*as adjective, usually postpositive*): *a table vert.*
▷**HISTORY** C15: from Old French *verd,* from Latin *viridis* green, from *virēre* to grow green

vert. ABBREVIATION FOR vertical.

vertebra (ˈvɜːtɪbrə) NOUN, *plural* **-brae** (-briː) *or* **-bras.** one of the bony segments of the spinal column.
▷**HISTORY** C17: from Latin: joint of the spine, from *vertere* to turn
▸ **ˈvertebral** ADJECTIVE ▸ **ˈvertebrally** ADVERB

vertebral column NOUN another name for **spinal column.**

vertebrate (ˈvɜːtɪˌbreɪt, -brɪt) NOUN 1 any chordate animal of the subphylum *Vertebrata,* characterized by a bony or cartilaginous skeleton and a well-developed brain: the group contains fishes, amphibians, reptiles, birds, and mammals. ◆ ADJECTIVE 2 of, relating to, or belonging to the subphylum *Vertebrata.*

vertebration (ˌvɜːtɪˈbreɪʃən) NOUN the formation of vertebrae or segmentation resembling vertebrae.

vertex (ˈvɜːtɛks) NOUN, *plural* **-texes** *or* **-tices** (-tɪˌsiːz). 1 the highest point. 2 *Maths* **a** the point opposite the base of a figure. **b** the point of intersection of two sides of a plane figure or angle. **c** the point of intersection of a pencil of lines or three or more planes of a solid figure. 3 *Astronomy* a point in the sky towards which a star stream appears to move. 4 *Anatomy* the crown of the head.
▷**HISTORY** C16: from Latin: highest point, from *vertere* to turn

vertical (ˈvɜːtɪkᵊl) ADJECTIVE 1 at right angles to the horizon; perpendicular; upright: *a vertical wall.* Compare **horizontal** (sense 1). 2 extending in a perpendicular direction. 3 at or in the vertex or zenith; directly overhead. 4 *Economics* of or relating to associated or consecutive, though not identical, stages of industrial activity: *vertical integration; vertical amalgamation.* 5 of or relating to the vertex. 6 *Anatomy* of, relating to, or situated at the top of the head (vertex). ◆ NOUN 7 a vertical plane, position, or line. 8 a vertical post, pillar, or other structural member.
▷**HISTORY** C16: from Late Latin *verticālis,* from Latin VERTEX
▸ **ˌvertiˈcality** NOUN ▸ **ˈvertically** ADVERB

vertical angles PLURAL NOUN *Geometry* the pair of equal angles between a pair of intersecting lines; opposite angles. Also called: **vertically opposite angles.**

vertical circle NOUN *Astronomy* a great circle on the celestial sphere passing through the zenith and perpendicular to the horizon.

vertical grouping NOUN another term for **family grouping.**

vertical mobility NOUN *Sociol* the movement of individuals or groups to positions in society that involve a change in class, status, and power. Compare **horizontal mobility.** See also **upward mobility, downward mobility.**

vertical stabilizer NOUN the US name for **fin¹** (sense 3a).

vertical union NOUN another name (esp US) for **industrial union.**

vertices (ˈvɜːtɪˌsiːz) NOUN a plural of **vertex** (in technical and scientific senses only).

verticil (ˈvɜːtɪsɪl) NOUN *Biology* a circular arrangement of parts about an axis, esp leaves around a stem.
▷**HISTORY** C18: from Latin *verticillus* whorl (of a spindle), from VERTEX

verticillaster (ˌvɜːtɪsɪˈlæstə) NOUN *Botany* an inflorescence, such as that of the dead-nettle, that resembles a whorl but consists of two crowded cymes on either side of the stem.
▷**HISTORY** C19: from New Latin; see VERTICIL, -ASTER
▸ **verticillastrate** (ˌvɜːtɪsɪˈlæsˌtreɪt, -trɪt) ADJECTIVE

verticillate (vɜːˈtɪsɪlɪt, -ˌleɪt, ˌvɜːtɪˈsɪleɪt) ADJECTIVE *Biology* having or arranged in whorls or verticils.
▸ **verˈticillately** ADVERB ▸ **verˌticilˈlation** NOUN

vertiginous (vɜːˈtɪdʒɪnəs) ADJECTIVE 1 of, relating to, or having vertigo. 2 producing dizziness. 3 whirling. 4 changeable; unstable.
▷**HISTORY** C17: from Latin *vertīginōsus,* from VERTIGO
▸ **verˈtiginously** ADVERB ▸ **verˈtiginousness** NOUN

vertigo (ˈvɜːtɪˌgəʊ) NOUN, *plural* **vertigoes** *or* **vertigines** (vɜːˈtɪdʒɪˌniːz). *Pathol* a sensation of dizziness or abnormal motion resulting from a disorder of the sense of balance.
▷**HISTORY** C16: from Latin: a whirling round, from *vertere* to turn

vertu (vɜːˈtuː) NOUN a variant spelling of **virtu.**

Vertumnus (vɜːˈtʌmnəs) *or* **Vortumnus** NOUN a Roman god of gardens, orchards, and seasonal change.
▷**HISTORY** from Latin, from *vertere* to turn, change

Verulamium (ˌvɛruˈleɪmɪəm) NOUN the Latin name of **Saint Albans.**

vervain (ˈvɜːveɪn) NOUN any of several verbenaceous plants of the genus *Verbena,* having square stems and long slender spikes of purple, blue, or white flowers.
▷**HISTORY** C14: from Old French *verveine,* from Latin *verbēna* sacred bough; see VERBENA

verve (vɜːv) NOUN 1 great vitality, enthusiasm, and liveliness; sparkle. 2 a rare word for **talent.**
▷**HISTORY** C17: from Old French: garrulity, from Latin *verba* words, chatter

vervet (ˈvɜːvɪt) NOUN a variety of a South African guenon monkey, *Cercopithecus aethiops,* having dark hair on the hands and feet and a reddish patch beneath the tail. Compare **green monkey, grivet.**
▷**HISTORY** C19: from French, from *vert* green, but influenced by GRIVET

very (ˈvɛrɪ) ADVERB 1 (intensifier) used to add emphasis to adjectives that are able to be graded: *very good; very tall.* ◆ ADJECTIVE (*prenominal*) 2 (intensifier) used with nouns preceded by a definite article or possessive determiner, in order to give emphasis to the significance, appropriateness or relevance of a noun in a particular context, or to give exaggerated intensity to certain nouns: *the very man I want to see; his very name struck terror; the very back of the room.* 3 (intensifier) used in metaphors to emphasize the applicability of the image to the situation described: *he was a very lion in the fight.* 4 *Archaic* **a** real or true; genuine: *the very living God.* **b** lawful: *the very vengeance of the gods.*
▷**HISTORY** C13: from Old French *verai* true, from Latin *vērax* true, from *vērus* true

Language note In strict usage adverbs of degree such as *very, too, quite, really,* and *extremely* are used only to qualify adjectives: *he is very happy; she is too sad.* By this rule, these words should not be used to qualify past participles that follow the verb *to be,* since they would then be technically qualifying verbs. With the exception of certain participles, such as *tired* or *disappointed,* that have come to be regarded as adjectives, all other past participles are qualified by adverbs such as *much, greatly, seriously,* or *excessively: he has been much* (not *very*) *inconvenienced; she has been excessively* (not *too*) *criticized.*

very high frequency NOUN a radio-frequency band or radio frequency lying between 30 and 300 megahertz. Abbreviation: **VHF.**

very large-scale integration NOUN *Computing* the process of fabricating a few thousand logic gates or more in a single integrated circuit. Abbreviation: **VLSI.**

Very light (ˈvɛrɪ) NOUN a coloured flare fired from a special pistol (**Very pistol**) for signalling at night, esp at sea.
▷**HISTORY** C19: named after Edward W. *Very* (1852–1910), US naval ordnance officer

very low frequency NOUN a radio-frequency band or radio frequency lying between 3 and 30 kilohertz. Abbreviation: **VLF.**

Very Reverend NOUN a title of respect for a variety of ecclesiastical officials, such as deans and the superiors of some religious houses.

vesica (ˈvɛsɪkə) NOUN, *plural* **-cae** (-ˌsiː). 1 *Anatomy* a technical name for **bladder** (sense 1). 2 (in medieval sculpture and painting) an aureole in the shape of a pointed oval.
▷**HISTORY** C17: from Latin: bladder, sac, blister

vesical (ˈvɛsɪkᵊl) ADJECTIVE of or relating to a vesica, esp the urinary bladder.

vesicant (ˈvɛsɪkənt) *or* **vesicatory** (ˈvɛsɪˌkeɪtərɪ) NOUN, *plural* **-cants** *or* **-catories.** 1 any substance that causes blisters, used in medicine and in chemical warfare. ◆ ADJECTIVE 2 acting as a vesicant.
▷**HISTORY** C19: see VESICA

vesicate (ˈvɛsɪˌkeɪt) VERB to blister.
▷**HISTORY** C17: from New Latin *vēsīcāre* to blister; see VESICA
▸ **ˌvesiˈcation** NOUN

vesicle (ˈvɛsɪkᵊl) NOUN 1 *Pathol* **a** any small sac or cavity, esp one containing serous fluid. **b** a blister. 2 *Geology* a rounded cavity within a rock formed during solidification by expansion of the gases present in the magma. 3 *Botany* a small bladder-like cavity occurring in certain seaweeds and aquatic plants. 4 any small cavity or cell.
▷**HISTORY** C16: from Latin *vēsīcula,* diminutive of VESICA
▸ **vesicular** (vɛˈsɪkjʊlə) ADJECTIVE ▸ **veˈsicularly** ADVERB

vesiculate VERB (vɛˈsɪkjʊˌleɪt) 1 to make (an organ or part) vesicular or (of an organ or part) to become vesicular. ◆ ADJECTIVE (vɛˈsɪkjʊlɪt, -ˌleɪt) 2 containing, resembling, or characterized by a vesicle or vesicles.
▸ **veˌsicuˈlation** NOUN

vesper (ˈvɛspə) NOUN 1 an evening prayer, service, or hymn. 2 an archaic word for **evening.** 3 (*modifier*) of or relating to vespers. ◆ See also **vespers.**
▷**HISTORY** C14: from Latin: evening, the evening star; compare Greek *hesperos* evening; see WEST

Vesper (ˈvɛspə) NOUN the planet Venus, when appearing as the evening star.

vesperal (ˈvɛspərəl) NOUN *Christianity* 1 a liturgical book containing the prayers, psalms, and hymns used at vespers. 2 the part of the antiphonary containing these. 3 a cloth laid over the altar cloth between offices or services.

vespers (ˈvɛspəz) NOUN (*functioning as singular or plural*) 1 *Chiefly RC Church* the sixth of the seven canonical hours of the divine office, originally fixed for the early evening and now often made a public service on Sundays and major feast days. 2 another word for **evensong** (sense 1).

vespertilionine (ˌvɛspəˈtɪlɪəˌnaɪn, -nɪn) ADJECTIVE of, relating to, or belonging to the *Vespertilionidae,* a family of common and widespread bats.
▷HISTORY C17: from Latin *vespertīliō* a bat, from *vesper* evening
▸**vespertilionid** (ˌvɛspəˈtɪlɪənɪd) ADJECTIVE, NOUN

vespertine (ˈvɛspəˌtaɪn) ADJECTIVE 1 *Botany, zoology* appearing, opening, or active in the evening: *vespertine flowers.* 2 occurring in the evening or (esp of stars) appearing or setting in the evening.

vespiary (ˈvɛspɪərɪ) NOUN, *plural* **-aries.** a nest or colony of social wasps or hornets.
▷HISTORY C19: from Latin *vespa* a wasp, on the model of *apiary*

vespid (ˈvɛspɪd) NOUN 1 any hymenopterous insect of the family *Vespidae,* including the common wasps and hornets. ◆ ADJECTIVE 2 of, relating to, or belonging to the family *Vespidae.*
▷HISTORY C19: from New Latin *Vespidae,* from Latin *vespa* a wasp

vespine (ˈvɛspaɪn) ADJECTIVE of, relating to, or resembling a wasp or wasps.
▷HISTORY C19: from Latin *vespa* a wasp

vessel (ˈvɛsᵊl) NOUN 1 any object used as a container, esp for a liquid. 2 a passenger or freight-carrying ship, boat, etc. 3 an aircraft, esp an airship. 4 *Anatomy* a tubular structure that transports such body fluids as blood and lymph. 5 *Botany* a tubular element of xylem tissue consisting of a row of cells in which the connecting cell walls have broken down. 6 *Rare* a person regarded as an agent or vehicle for some purpose or quality: *she was the vessel of the Lord.*
▷HISTORY C13: from Old French *vaissel,* from Late Latin *vascellum* urn, from Latin *vās* vessel

vest (vɛst) NOUN 1 an undergarment covering the body from the shoulders to the hips, made of cotton, nylon, etc. US and Canadian equivalent: **T-shirt, undershirt.** Austral equivalent: **singlet.** 2 a similar sleeveless garment worn as outerwear. Austral equivalent: **singlet.** 3 the usual US, Canadian, and Austral word for **waistcoat.** 4 *Obsolete* any form of dress, esp a long robe. ◆ VERB 5 (*tr;* foll by *in*) to place or settle (power, rights, etc., in): *power was vested in the committee.* 6 (*tr;* foll by *with*) to bestow or confer (on): *the company was vested with authority.* 7 (usually foll by *in*) to confer (a right, title, property, etc., upon) or (of a right, title, etc.) to pass (to) or devolve (upon). 8 (*tr*) to clothe or array. 9 (*intr*) to put on clothes, ecclesiastical vestments, etc.
▷HISTORY C15: from Old French *vestir* to clothe, from Latin *vestīre,* from *vestis* clothing
▸ˈ**vestless** ADJECTIVE ▸ˈ**vestˌlike** ADJECTIVE

vesta (ˈvɛstə) NOUN a short friction match, usually of wood.
▷HISTORY C19: named after the goddess; see VESTA¹

Vesta¹ (ˈvɛstə) NOUN the Roman goddess of the hearth and its fire. In her temple a perpetual flame was tended by the vestal virgins. Greek counterpart: **Hestia.**

Vesta² (ˈvɛstə) NOUN the brightest of the four largest asteroids. Diameter: about 530 km (240 miles).
▷HISTORY C19: named after the goddess; see VESTA¹

vestal (ˈvɛstᵊl) ADJECTIVE 1 chaste or pure; virginal. 2 of or relating to the Roman goddess Vesta. ◆ NOUN 3 a chaste woman; virgin. 4 a rare word for **nun¹** (sense 1).

vestal virgin NOUN (in ancient Rome) one of the four, later six, virgin priestesses whose lives were dedicated to Vesta and to maintaining the sacred fire in her temple.

vested (ˈvɛstɪd) ADJECTIVE *Property law* having a present right to the immediate or future possession and enjoyment of property. Compare **contingent.**

vested interest NOUN 1 *Property law* an existing and disposable right to the immediate or future possession and enjoyment of property. 2 a strong personal concern in a state of affairs, system, etc., usually resulting in private gain. 3 a person or group that has such an interest.

vestiary (ˈvɛstɪərɪ) NOUN, *plural* **-aries.** 1 *Obsolete* a room for storing clothes or dressing in, such as a vestry. ◆ ADJECTIVE 2 *Rare* of or relating to clothes.
▷HISTORY C17: from Late Latin *vestiārius,* from *vestis* clothing

vestibular system NOUN the sensory mechanism in the inner ear that detects movement of the head and helps to control balance.

vestibule (ˈvɛstɪˌbjuːl) NOUN 1 a small entrance hall or anteroom; lobby. 2 any small bodily cavity or space at the entrance to a passage or canal.
▷HISTORY C17: from Latin *vestibulum*
▸**vestibular** (vɛˈstɪbjʊlə) ADJECTIVE

vestibulocochlear nerve (vɛˌstɪbjʊlə ˈkɒklɪə) NOUN either one of the eight pairs of cranial nerves that supply the cochlea and semicircular canals of the internal ear and contribute to the sense of hearing. Formerly called: **acoustic nerve.**

vestige (ˈvɛstɪdʒ) NOUN 1 a small trace, mark, or amount; hint: *a vestige of truth; no vestige of the meal.* 2 *Biology* an organ or part of an organism that is a small nonfunctioning remnant of a functional organ in an ancestor.
▷HISTORY C17: via French from Latin *vestīgium* track

vestigial (vɛˈstɪdʒɪəl) ADJECTIVE 1 of, relating to, or being a vestige. 2 (of certain organs or parts of organisms) having attained a simple structure and reduced size and function during the evolution of the species: *the vestigial pelvic girdle of a snake.*
▸**vesˈtigially** ADVERB

Vestmannaeyjar (ˌvestmænˈeɪjɑː) NOUN a group of islands off the S coast of Iceland: they include the island of Surtsey (emerged 1963) and the volcano Helgafell (erupted 1974). Pop.: 4888 (1994). English name: **Vestmann Islands.**

vestment (ˈvɛstmənt) NOUN 1 a garment or robe, esp one denoting office, authority, or rank. 2 any of various ceremonial garments worn by the clergy at religious services.
▷HISTORY C13: from Old French *vestiment,* from Latin *vestīmentum* clothing, from *vestīre* to clothe
▸**vestmental** (vɛstˈmɛntᵊl) ADJECTIVE

vest-pocket NOUN (*modifier*) *Chiefly US* small enough to fit into a waistcoat pocket.

vestry (ˈvɛstrɪ) NOUN, *plural* **-tries.** 1 a room in or attached to a church in which vestments, sacred vessels, etc., are kept. 2 a room in or attached to some churches, used for Sunday school, meetings, etc. 3 *Church of England* **a** a meeting of all the members of a parish or their representatives, to transact the official business of the parish. **b** the body of members meeting for this; the parish council. 4 *Episcopalian* (*US*) *and Anglican* (*Canadian*) *Churches* a committee of vestrymen chosen by the congregation to manage the temporal affairs of their church.
▷HISTORY C14: probably from Old French *vestiarie;* see VEST
▸ˈ**vestral** ADJECTIVE

vestryman (ˈvɛstrɪmən) NOUN, *plural* **-men.** a member of a church vestry.

vesture (ˈvɛstʃə) NOUN 1 *Archaic* a garment or something that seems like a garment: *a vesture of cloud.* 2 *Law* **a** everything except trees that grows on the land. **b** a product of the land, such as grass, wheat, etc. ◆ VERB 3 (*tr*) *Archaic* to clothe.
▷HISTORY C14: from Old French, from *vestir,* from Latin *vestīre,* from *vestis* clothing
▸ˈ**vestural** ADJECTIVE

vesuvian (vɪˈsuːvɪən) NOUN 1 (esp formerly) a match for lighting cigars; fusee. 2 another name for **vesuvianite.**
▷HISTORY C18 (the mineral), C19 (the match): both named after VESUVIUS

vesuvianite (vɪˈsuːvɪəˌnaɪt) NOUN a green, brown, or yellow mineral consisting of a hydrated silicate of calcium, magnesium, iron, and aluminium: it occurs as tetragonal crystals in limestones and is used as a gemstone. Formula: $Ca_{10}(Mg,Fe)_2Al_4Si_9O_{34}(OH)_4$. Also called: **idocrase, vesuvian.**
▷HISTORY C19: first found in the lava of VESUVIUS

Vesuvius (vɪˈsuːvɪəs) NOUN a volcano in SW Italy, on the Bay of Naples: first recorded eruption in 79 A.D., which destroyed Pompeii, Herculaneum, and Stabiae; numerous eruptions since then. Average height: 1220 m (4003 ft.). Italian name: **Vesuvio** (veˈzuːvjo).

vet¹ (vɛt) NOUN 1 short for **veterinary surgeon.** ◆ VERB **vets, vetting, vetted.** 2 (*tr*) *Chiefly Brit* to make a prior examination and critical appraisal of (a person, document, scheme, etc.): *the candidates were well vetted.* See also **positive vetting.** 3 to examine, treat, or cure (an animal).

vet² (vɛt) NOUN *US and Canadian* short for **veteran** (senses 2, 3).

vet. ABBREVIATION FOR: 1 veteran. 2 veterinarian. 3 veterinary. ◆ Also (for senses 2, 3): **veter.**

vetch (vɛtʃ) NOUN 1 any of various climbing leguminous plants of the temperate genus *Vicia,* esp *V. sativa,* having pinnate leaves, typically blue or purple flowers, and tendrils on the stems. 2 any of various similar and related plants, such as *Lathyrus sativus,* cultivated in parts of Europe, and the kidney vetch. 3 the beanlike fruit of any of these plants.
▷HISTORY C14 *fecche,* from Old French *veche,* from Latin *vicia*

vetchling (ˈvɛtʃlɪŋ) NOUN any of various leguminous tendril-climbing plants of the genus *Lathyrus,* esp *L. pratensis* (**meadow vetchling**), mainly of N temperate regions, having winged or angled stems and showy flowers. See also **sweet pea.**

veteran (ˈvɛtərən, ˈvɛtrən) NOUN 1 **a** a person or thing that has given long service in some capacity. **b** (*as modifier*): *veteran firemen.* 2 **a** a soldier who has seen considerable active service. **b** (*as modifier*): *veteran soldier.* 3 *US and Canadian* a person who has served in the military forces. 4 See **veteran car.**
▷HISTORY C16: from Latin *veterānus,* from *vetus* old

veteran car NOUN *Brit* a car constructed before 1919, esp one constructed before 1905. Compare **classic car, vintage car.**

Veterans Day NOUN the US equivalent of **Armistice Day.**

veterinarian (ˌvɛtərɪˈnɛərɪən, ˌvɛtrɪ-) NOUN the US and Canadian term for **veterinary surgeon.**

veterinary (ˈvɛtərɪnərɪ, ˈvɛtrɪnrɪ) ADJECTIVE of or relating to veterinary medicine.
▷HISTORY C18: from Latin *veterīnārius* concerning draught animals, from *veterīnae* draught animals; related to *vetus* mature (hence able to bear a burden)

veterinary medicine *or* **science** NOUN the branch of medicine concerned with the health of animals and the treatment of injuries or diseases that affect them.

veterinary surgeon NOUN *Brit* a person suitably qualified and registered to practise veterinary medicine. US and Canadian term: **veterinarian.**

vetiver (ˈvɛtɪvə) NOUN 1 a tall hairless grass, *Vetiveria zizanioides,* of tropical and subtropical Asia, having aromatic roots and stiff long narrow ornamental leaves. 2 the root of this plant used for making screens, mats, etc., and yielding a fragrant oil used in perfumery, medicine, etc.
▷HISTORY C19: from French *vétiver,* from Tamil *vettivēru*

veto (ˈviːtəʊ) NOUN, *plural* **-toes.** 1 the power to prevent legislation or action proposed by others; prohibition: *the presidential veto.* 2 the exercise of this power. 3 Also called: **veto message.** *US government* a document containing the reasons why a chief executive has vetoed a measure. ◆ VERB **-toes, -toing, -toed.** (*tr*) 4 to refuse consent to (a proposal, esp a government bill). 5 to prohibit, ban, or forbid: *her parents vetoed her trip.*
▷HISTORY C17: from Latin: I forbid, from *vetāre* to forbid
▸ˈ**vetoer** NOUN ▸ˈ**vetoless** ADJECTIVE

vex (vɛks) VERB (*tr*) 1 to anger or annoy. 2 to confuse; worry. 3 *Archaic* to agitate.
▷HISTORY C15: from Old French *vexer,* from Latin *vexāre* to jolt (in carrying), from *vehere* to convey
▸ˈ**vexer** NOUN ▸ˈ**vexing** ADJECTIVE ▸ˈ**vexingly** ADVERB

vexation (vɛkˈseɪʃən) NOUN 1 the act of vexing or the state of being vexed. 2 something that vexes.

vexatious (vɛkˈseɪʃəs) ADJECTIVE 1 vexing or tending to vex. 2 vexed. 3 *Law* (of a legal action or proceeding) instituted without sufficient grounds, esp so as to cause annoyance or embarrassment to the defendant: *vexatious litigation.*
▸**vexˈatiously** ADVERB ▸**vexˈatiousness** NOUN

vexed (vɛkst) ADJECTIVE 1 annoyed, confused, or agitated. 2 much debated and discussed (esp in the phrase **a vexed question**).
▸**vexedly** (ˈvɛksɪdlɪ) ADVERB ▸ˈ**vexedness** NOUN

vexillology (ˌvɛksɪˈlɒlədʒɪ) NOUN the study and collection of information about flags.
▷HISTORY C20: from Latin *vexillum* flag + -LOGY
▸ˌvexilˈlologist NOUN

vexillum (vɛkˈsɪləm) NOUN, *plural* **-la** (-lə). [1] *Ornithol* the vane of a feather. [2] *Botany* another name for **standard** (sense 16).
▷HISTORY C18: from Latin: banner, perhaps from *vēlum* sail
▸ˈ**vexillary** *or* **vexˈillar** ADJECTIVE ▸ˈ**vexillate** ADJECTIVE

VF ABBREVIATION FOR **video frequency**.

vg[1] ABBREVIATION FOR very good.

vg[2] THE INTERNET DOMAIN NAME FOR British Virgin Islands.

VG ABBREVIATION FOR Vicar General.

VGA ABBREVIATION FOR video graphics display; a computing standard that has a resolution of 640 × 480 pixels with 16 colours or of 320 × 200 pixels with 256 colours. **SVGA** (**super VGA**) is a later version with higher spatial and colour resolution, esp 800 × 600 pixels with 256 colours.

VHF *or* **vhf** *Radio* ABBREVIATION FOR **very high frequency**.

VHS *Trademark* ABBREVIATION FOR video home system: a video cassette recording system using ½″ magnetic tape.

vi[1] ABBREVIATION FOR vide infra.

vi[2] THE INTERNET DOMAIN NAME FOR US Virgin Islands.

VI ABBREVIATION FOR Virgin Islands.

via (ˈvaɪə) PREPOSITION by way of; by means of; through: *to London via Paris*.
▷HISTORY C18: from Latin *viā*, from *via* way

viable (ˈvaɪəbᵊl) ADJECTIVE [1] capable of becoming actual, useful, etc.; practicable: *a viable proposition*. [2] (of seeds, eggs, etc.) capable of normal growth and development. [3] (of a fetus) having reached a stage of development at which further development can occur independently of the mother.
▷HISTORY C19: from French, from *vie* life, from Latin *vīta*
▸ˌ**viaˈbility** NOUN

Via Dolorosa (ˈviːə ˌdɒləˈrəʊsə) NOUN [1] the route followed by Christ from the place of his condemnation to Calvary for his crucifixion. [2] an arduous or distressing course or experience.
▷HISTORY Latin, literally: sorrowful road

viaduct (ˈvaɪəˌdʌkt) NOUN a bridge, esp for carrying a road or railway across a valley, etc., consisting of a set of arches supported by a row of piers or towers.
▷HISTORY C19: from Latin *via* way + *dūcere* to bring, on the model of *aqueduct*

Viagra (vaɪˈægrə, viː-) NOUN *Trademark* a drug, sildenafil, that allows increased blood flow into the penis; used to treat erectile impotence in men.

vial (ˈvaɪəl, vaɪl) NOUN a less common variant of **phial**.
▷HISTORY C14 *fiole*, from Old French, from Old Provençal *fiola*, from Latin *phiala*, from Greek *phialē*; see PHIAL

via media *Latin* (ˈvaɪə ˈmiːdɪə) NOUN a compromise between two extremes; middle course.

viand (ˈviːənd, ˈvaɪ-) NOUN [1] a type of food, esp a delicacy. [2] (*plural*) provisions.
▷HISTORY C14: from Old French *viande*, ultimately from Latin *vīvenda* things to be lived on, from *vīvere* to live

Viareggio (*Italian* viaˈreddʒo) NOUN a town and resort in W Italy, in Tuscany on the Ligurian Sea. Pop.: 50 310 (latest est.).

viatical (vaɪˈætɪkᵊl) ADJECTIVE [1] of or denoting a road or a journey. [2] *Botany* (of a plant) growing by the side of a road.
▷HISTORY C19: from Latin *viāticus* belonging to a journey + -AL[1]

viatical settlement NOUN the purchase by a charity of a life assurance policy owned by a person with only a short time to live, to enable that person to use the proceeds during his or her lifetime. See also **death futures**.

viaticum (vaɪˈætɪkəm) NOUN, *plural* **-ca** (-kə) *or* **-cums**. [1] *Christianity* Holy Communion as administered to a person dying or in danger of death. [2] *Rare* provisions or a travel allowance for a journey.
▷HISTORY C16: from Latin, from *viāticus* belonging to a journey, from *viāre* to travel, from *via* way

viator (vaɪˈeɪtɔː) NOUN, *plural* **viatores** (ˌvaɪəˈtɔːriːz). *Rare* a traveller.
▷HISTORY C16: from Latin, from *viāre* to travel

vibe (vaɪb) NOUN *Slang* a feeling or flavour of the kind specified: *a 1970s vibe*.
▷HISTORY from VIBRATION

vibes (vaɪbz) PLURAL NOUN [1] *Informal* (esp in jazz) short for **vibraphone.** [2] *Slang* short for **vibrations.**

vibey (ˈvaɪbɪ) ADJECTIVE **vibier, vibiest**. *Slang* lively and vibrant.

vibist (ˈvaɪbɪst) NOUN *Informal* a person who plays a vibraphone in a jazz band or group.

Viborg NOUN [1] (ˈviːbɔrj) the Swedish name for **Vyborg.** [2] (*Danish* ˈvibɔr) a town in N central Denmark, in Jutland: formerly a royal town and capital of Jutland. Pop.: 29 455 (1990).

vibraculum (vaɪˈbrækjʊləm) NOUN, *plural* **-la** (-lə). *Zoology* any of the specialized bristle-like polyps in certain bryozoans, the actions of which prevent parasites from settling on the colony.
▷HISTORY C19: from New Latin, from Latin *vibrāre* to brandish
▸**viˈbracular** ADJECTIVE ▸**viˈbracuˌloid** ADJECTIVE

Vibram (ˈvaɪbrəm) NOUN *Trademark* a special type of moulded rubber sole, widely used for climbing and walking boots.
▷HISTORY C20: from *Vi(tale) Bram(ini)*, Italian climber who devised the product

vibrant (ˈvaɪbrənt) ADJECTIVE [1] characterized by or exhibiting vibration; pulsating or trembling. [2] giving an impression of vigour and activity. [3] caused by vibration; resonant. [4] *Phonetics* trilled or rolled. ◆ NOUN [5] a vibrant speech sound, such as a trilled (r).
▷HISTORY C16: from Latin *vibrāre* to agitate
▸ˈ**vibrancy** NOUN ▸ˈ**vibrantly** ADVERB

vibraphone (ˈvaɪbrəˌfəʊn) *or esp US* **vibraharp** (ˈvaɪbrəˌhɑːp) NOUN a percussion instrument, used esp in jazz, consisting of a set of metal bars placed over tubular metal resonators, which are made to vibrate electronically.
▸ˈ**vibraˌphonist** NOUN

vibrate (vaɪˈbreɪt) VERB [1] to move or cause to move back and forth rapidly; shake, quiver, or throb. [2] (*intr*) to oscillate. [3] to send out (a sound) by vibration; resonate or cause to resonate. [4] (*intr*) to waver. [5] *Physics* to undergo or cause to undergo an oscillatory or periodic process, as of an alternating current; oscillate. [6] (*intr*) *Rare* to respond emotionally; thrill.
▷HISTORY C17: from Latin *vibrāre*
▸**vibratile** (ˈvaɪbrəˌtaɪl) ADJECTIVE ▸**viˈbrating** ADJECTIVE ▸**viˈbratingly** ADVERB ▸ˈ**vibratory** ADJECTIVE

vibration (vaɪˈbreɪʃən) NOUN [1] the act or an instance of vibrating. [2] *Physics* **a** a periodic motion about an equilibrium position, such as the regular displacement of air in the propagation of sound. **b** a single cycle of such a motion. [3] the process or state of vibrating or being vibrated.
▸**viˈbrational** ADJECTIVE ▸**viˈbrationless** ADJECTIVE

vibrations (vaɪˈbreɪʃənz) PLURAL NOUN *Slang* [1] instinctive feelings supposedly influencing human communication. [2] a characteristic atmosphere felt to be emanating from places or objects. ◆ Often shortened to: **vibes.**

vibration white finger NOUN a condition affecting workers using vibrating machinery, which causes damage to the blood vessels and nerves of the fingers and leads to a permanent loss of feeling.

vibrato (vɪˈbrɑːtəʊ) NOUN, *plural* **-tos.** *Music* [1] a slight, rapid, and regular fluctuation in the pitch of a note produced on a stringed instrument by a shaking movement of the hand stopping the strings. [2] an oscillatory effect produced in singing by fluctuation in breath pressure or pitch. ◆ Compare **tremolo.**
▷HISTORY C19: from Italian, from Latin *vibrāre* to VIBRATE

vibrator (vaɪˈbreɪtə) NOUN [1] **a** a device for producing a vibratory motion, such as one used in massage or in the distribution of wet concrete in moulds. **b** such a device with a vibrating part or tip, used as a dildo. [2] a device in which a vibrating conductor interrupts a circuit to produce a pulsating current from a steady current, usually so that the current can then be amplified or the voltage transformed. See also **chopper** (sense 6).

vibrio (ˈvɪbrɪˌəʊ) NOUN, *plural* **-os.** any curved or spiral rodlike Gram-negative bacterium of the genus *Vibrio*, including *V. cholerae*, which causes cholera: family *Spirillaceae*.
▷HISTORY C19: from New Latin, from Latin *vibrāre* to VIBRATE
▸ˈ**vibriˌoid** ADJECTIVE

vibrissa (vaɪˈbrɪsə) NOUN, *plural* **-sae** (-siː). (*usually plural*) [1] any of the bristle-like sensitive hairs on the face of many mammals; a whisker. [2] any of the specialized bristle-like feathers around the beak in certain insectivorous birds.
▷HISTORY C17: from Latin, probably from *vibrāre* to shake
▸**viˈbrissal** ADJECTIVE

vibronic (vaɪˈbrɒnɪk) ADJECTIVE *Physics* of, concerned with, or involving both electronic and vibrational energy levels of a molecule: *a vibronic spectrum; a vibronic transition*.
▷HISTORY C20: from *vibr(atory + electr)onic*

Vibropac block (ˈvaɪbrəʊˌpæk) NOUN *Trademark, NZ* a precast concrete building block.

viburnum (vaɪˈbɜːnəm) NOUN [1] any of various temperate and subtropical caprifoliaceous shrubs or trees of the genus *Viburnum*, such as the wayfaring tree, having small white flowers and berry-like red or black fruits. [2] the dried bark of several species of this tree, sometimes used in medicine.
▷HISTORY C18: from Latin: wayfaring tree

vicar (ˈvɪkə) NOUN [1] *Church of England* **a** (in Britain) a clergyman appointed to act as priest of a parish from which, formerly, he did not receive tithes but a stipend. **b** a clergyman who acts as assistant to or substitute for the rector of a parish at Communion. **c** (in the US) a clergyman in charge of a chapel. [2] *RC Church* a bishop or priest representing the pope or the ordinary of a diocese and exercising a limited jurisdiction. [3] Also called: **lay vicar, vicar choral.** *Church of England* a member of a cathedral choir appointed to sing certain parts of the services. [4] a person appointed to do the work of another.
▷HISTORY C13: from Old French *vicaire*, from Latin *vicārius* (n) a deputy, from *vicārius* (adj) VICARIOUS
▸ˈ**vicarly** ADJECTIVE

vicarage (ˈvɪkərɪdʒ) NOUN [1] the residence or benefice of a vicar. [2] a rare word for **vicariate** (sense 1).

vicar apostolic NOUN *RC Church* a titular bishop having jurisdiction in non-Catholic or missionary countries where the normal hierarchy has not yet been established.

vicar forane (fɒˈreɪn) NOUN, *plural* **vicars forane.** *RC Church* a priest or bishop appointed by the ordinary of the diocese to exercise a limited jurisdiction in a locality at some distance from the ordinary's official see.
▷HISTORY *forane*, from Late Latin *forāneus* in a foreign land, from Latin *forās* outside

vicar general NOUN, *plural* **vicars general**. an official, usually a layman, appointed to assist the bishop of a diocese in discharging his administrative or judicial duties.

vicarial (vɪˈkɛərɪəl, vaɪ-) ADJECTIVE [1] of or relating to a vicar, vicars, or a vicariate. [2] holding the office of a vicar. [3] vicarious: used esp of certain ecclesiastical powers.

vicariant (vɪˈkɛərɪənt, vaɪ-) NOUN any of several closely related species, races, etc., each of which exists in a separate geographical area: assumed to have originated from a single population that became dispersed by geological events.
▷HISTORY C20: from Latin *vicārius* (see VICAR) + -ANT
▸**viˈcariance** NOUN

vicariate (vɪˈkɛərɪɪt, vaɪ-) NOUN [1] Also called: **vicarship** (ˈvɪkəʃɪp). the office, rank, or authority of a vicar. [2] the district that a vicar holds as his pastoral charge.

vicarious (vɪˈkɛərɪəs, vaɪ-) ADJECTIVE [1] obtained or undergone at second hand through sympathetic participation in another's experiences. [2] suffered, undergone, or done as the substitute for another: *vicarious punishment*. [3] delegated: *vicarious authority*. [4] taking the place of another. [5] *Pathol* (of menstrual bleeding) occurring at an abnormal site. See **endometriosis.**

▷HISTORY C17: from Latin *vicārius* substituted, from *vicis* interchange; see VICE[3], VICISSITUDE
▸viˈcariously ADVERB ▸viˈcariousness NOUN

Vicar of Bray (breɪ) NOUN [1] a person who changes his or her views or allegiances in accordance with what is suitable at the time. [2] Also called: **In Good King Charles's Golden Days.** a ballad in which a vicar of the Stuart period changes faith to keep his living.
▷HISTORY from a vicar (Simon Aleyn) of the parish of Bray in Berkshire during Henry VIII's reign who changed his faith to Catholic when Mary I was on the throne and back to Protestant when Elizabeth I succeeded and so retained his living

Vicar of Christ NOUN *RC Church* the pope when regarded as Christ's earthly representative.

vice[1] (vaɪs) NOUN [1] an immoral, wicked, or evil habit, action, or trait. [2] habitual or frequent indulgence in pernicious, immoral, or degrading practices. [3] a specific form of pernicious conduct, esp prostitution or sexual perversion. [4] a failing or imperfection in character, conduct, etc.: *smoking is his only vice.* [5] *Pathol, obsolete* any physical defect or imperfection. [6] a bad trick or disposition, as of horses, dogs, etc.
▷HISTORY C13: via Old French from Latin *vitium* a defect
▸ˈviceless ADJECTIVE

vice[2] *or US (often)* **vise** (vaɪs) NOUN [1] an appliance for holding an object while work is done upon it, usually having a pair of jaws. ◆ VERB [2] *(tr)* to grip (something) with or as if with a vice.
▷HISTORY C15: from Old French *vis* a screw, from Latin *vītis* vine, plant with spiralling tendrils (hence the later meaning)
▸ˈviceˌlike *or (US (often))* ˈviseˌlike ADJECTIVE

vice[3] (vaɪs) ADJECTIVE [1] **a** *(prenominal)* serving in the place of or as a deputy for. **b** *(in combination)*: *viceroy.* ◆ NOUN [2] *Informal* a person who serves as a deputy to another.
▷HISTORY C18: from Latin *vice,* from *vicis* interchange

vice[4] (ˈvaɪsɪ) PREPOSITION instead of; as a substitute for.
▷HISTORY C16: from Latin, ablative of *vicis* change

Vice (vaɪs) NOUN (in English morality plays) a character personifying a particular vice or vice in general.

vice admiral NOUN a commissioned officer of flag rank in certain navies, junior to an admiral and senior to a rear admiral.
▸ˌvice-ˈadmiralty NOUN

vice-chairman NOUN, *plural* **-men.** a person who deputizes for a chairman and serves in his place during his absence or indisposition.
▸ˌvice-ˈchairmanship NOUN

vice chancellor NOUN [1] the chief executive or administrator at some British universities. Compare **chancellor** (sense 3). [2] (in the US) a judge in courts of equity subordinate to the chancellor. [3] (formerly in England) a senior judge of the court of chancery who acted as assistant to the Lord Chancellor. [4] a person serving as the deputy of a chancellor.
▸ˌvice-ˈchancellorship NOUN

vice-county NOUN, *plural* **-counties.** any of the geographical units into which the British Isles are divided for purposes of botanical and zoological recording, corresponding wherever possible to county boundaries.

vicegerent (ˌvaɪsˈdʒɛrənt) NOUN [1] a person appointed to exercise all or some of the authority of another, esp the administrative powers of a ruler; deputy. [2] *RC Church* the pope or any other representative of God or Christ on earth, such as a bishop. ◆ ADJECTIVE [3] invested with or characterized by delegated authority.
▷HISTORY C16: from New Latin *vicegerēns,* from VICE[3] + Latin *gerere* to manage
▸ˌviceˈgeral ADJECTIVE ▸ˌviceˈgerency NOUN

vicenary (ˈvɪsɪnərɪ) ADJECTIVE [1] relating to or consisting of 20. [2] *Maths* having or using a base 20.
▷HISTORY C17 (in the sense: one who has charge over twenty persons): from Latin *vīcēnārius,* from *vīcēnī* twenty each, from *vīgintī* twenty

vicennial (vɪˈsɛnɪəl) ADJECTIVE [1] occurring every 20 years. [2] relating to or lasting for a period of 20 years.
▷HISTORY C18: from Late Latin *vīcennium* period of twenty years, from Latin *vīciēs* twenty times + *-ennium,* from *annus* year

Vicenza (*Italian* viˈtʃɛntsa) NOUN a city in NE Italy, in Veneto: home of the 16th-century architect Andrea Palladio and site of some of his finest works. Pop.: 109 738 (2000 est.).

vice president NOUN an officer ranking immediately below a president and serving as his deputy. A vice president takes the president's place during his absence or incapacity, after his death, and in certain other circumstances. Abbreviations: **VP, V. Pres.**
▸ˌvice-ˈpresidency NOUN ▸ˌvice-ˌpresiˈdential ADJECTIVE

viceregal (ˌvaɪsˈriːgᵊl) ADJECTIVE [1] of or relating to a viceroy or his viceroyalty. [2] *Chiefly Austral and NZ* of or relating to a governor or governor general.
▸ˌviceˈregally ADVERB

viceregal assent NOUN *Austral* the formal signing of an act of parliament by a governor general, by which it becomes law.

vicereine (ˌvaɪsˈreɪn) NOUN [1] the wife of a viceroy. [2] a female viceroy.
▷HISTORY C19: from French, from VICE[3] + *reine* queen, from Latin *rēgīna*

viceroy (ˈvaɪsrɔɪ) NOUN a governor of a colony, country, or province who acts for and rules in the name of his sovereign or government. Related adjective: **viceregal.**
▷HISTORY C16: from French, from VICE[3] + *roy* king, from Latin *rex*
▸ˈviceroyˌship NOUN

viceroyalty (ˌvaɪsˈrɔɪəltɪ) NOUN, *plural* **-ties.** [1] the office, authority, or dignity of a viceroy. [2] the domain governed by a viceroy. [3] the term of office of a viceroy.

vice squad NOUN a police division to which is assigned the enforcement of gaming and prostitution laws.

vice versa (ˈvaɪsɪ ˈvɜːsə) ADVERB with the order reversed; the other way around.
▷HISTORY C17: from Latin: relations being reversed, from *vicis* change + *vertere* to turn

Vichy (*French* viʃi; *English* ˈviːʃiː) NOUN a town and spa in central France, on the River Allier: seat of the collaborationist government under Marshal Pétain (1940–44); mineral waters bottled for export. Pop.: 28 048 (1990). Latin name: **Vicus Calidus** (ˈviːkəs ˈkælɪdəs).

vichyssoise (*French* viʃiswaz) NOUN a thick soup made from leeks, potatoes, chicken stock, and cream, usually served chilled.
▷HISTORY French, from *(crème) Vichyssoise (glacée)* (ice-cold cream) from Vichy

vichy water NOUN [1] *(sometimes capital)* a natural mineral water from springs at Vichy in France, reputed to be beneficial to the health. [2] any sparkling mineral water resembling this. ◆ Often shortened to: **vichy.**

vicinage (ˈvɪsənɪdʒ) NOUN *Now rare* [1] the residents of a particular neighbourhood. [2] a less common word for **vicinity.**
▷HISTORY C14: from Old French *vicenage,* from *vicin* neighbouring, from Latin *vīcīnus;* see VICINITY

vicinal (ˈvɪsɪnᵊl) ADJECTIVE [1] neighbouring. [2] (esp of roads) of or relating to a locality or neighbourhood. [3] *Chem* relating to or designating two adjacent atoms to which groups are attached in a chain.
▷HISTORY C17: from Latin *vīcīnālis* nearby, from *vīcīnus,* from *vīcus* a neighbourhood

vicinity (vɪˈsɪnɪtɪ) NOUN, *plural* **-ties.** [1] a surrounding, adjacent, or nearby area; neighbourhood. [2] the fact or condition of being close in space or relationship.
▷HISTORY C16: from Latin *vīcīnitās,* from *vīcīnus* neighbouring, from *vīcus* village

vicious (ˈvɪʃəs) ADJECTIVE [1] wicked or cruel; villainous: *a vicious thug.* [2] characterized by violence or ferocity: *a vicious blow.* [3] *Informal* unpleasantly severe; harsh: *a vicious wind.* [4] characterized by malice: *vicious lies.* [5] (esp of dogs, horses, etc.) ferocious or hostile; dangerous. [6] characterized by or leading to vice. [7] invalidated by defects; unsound: *a vicious inference.* [8] *Obsolete* noxious or morbid: *a vicious exhalation.*
▷HISTORY C14: from Old French *vicieus,* from Latin *vitiōsus* full of faults, from *vitium* a defect
▸ˈviciously ADVERB ▸ˈviciousness NOUN

vicious circle NOUN [1] Also: **vicious cycle.** a situation in which an attempt to resolve one problem creates new problems that lead back to the original situation. [2] *Logic* **a** a form of reasoning in which a conclusion is inferred from premises the truth of which cannot be established independently of that conclusion. **b** an explanation given in terms that cannot be understood independently of that which was to be explained. **c** a situation in which some statement is shown to entail its negation and vice versa, as *this statement is false* is true only if false and false only if true. [3] *Med* a condition in which one disease or disorder causes another, which in turn aggravates the first condition.

vicissitude (vɪˈsɪsɪˌtjuːd) NOUN [1] variation or mutability in nature or life, esp successive alternation from one condition or thing to another. [2] a variation in circumstance, fortune, character, etc.
▷HISTORY C16: from Latin *vicissitūdō,* from *vicis* change, alternation
▸viˌcissiˈtudinary *or* viˌcissiˈtudinous ADJECTIVE

Vicksburg (ˈvɪksˌbɜːg) NOUN a city in W Mississippi, on the Mississippi River: site of one of the most decisive campaigns (1863) of the American Civil War, in which the Confederates were besieged for nearly seven weeks before capitulating. Pop.: 20 908 (1990).

vicomte (*French* vikɔ̃t) *or feminine* **vicomtesse** (*French* vikɔ̃tɛs) NOUN a French noble holding a rank corresponding to that of a British viscount or viscountess.

Victa (ˈvɪktə) NOUN *Trademark, Austral* a type of rotary lawnmower first manufactured in 1952.
▷HISTORY C20: named after Mervyn Victor Richardson, who invented it

victim (ˈvɪktɪm) NOUN [1] a person or thing that suffers harm, death, etc., from another or from some adverse act, circumstance, etc.: *victims of tyranny.* [2] a person who is tricked or swindled; dupe. [3] a living person or animal sacrificed in a religious rite.
▷HISTORY C15: from Latin *victima*

victimize *or* **victimise** (ˈvɪktɪˌmaɪz) VERB *(tr)* [1] to punish or discriminate against selectively or unfairly. [2] to make a victim of. [3] to kill as or in a manner resembling a sacrificial victim.
▸ˌvictimiˈzation *or* ˌvictimiˈsation NOUN ▸ˈvictimˌizer *or* ˈvictimˌiser NOUN

victimless crime (ˈvɪktɪmləs) NOUN a type of crime, such as insurance fraud, regarded by some people as being excusable because the victim is the state or an organization, rather than an individual.

victimology (ˌvɪktɪˈmɒlədʒɪ) NOUN the study of the psychological effects experienced by the victims of crime.
▸ˌvictiˈmologist NOUN

victor (ˈvɪktə) NOUN [1] **a** a person, nation, etc., that has defeated an adversary in war, etc. **b** *(as modifier)*: *the victor army.* [2] the winner of any contest, conflict, or struggle.
▷HISTORY C14: from Latin, from *vincere* to conquer

Victor (ˈvɪktə) NOUN *Communications* a code word for the letter *v.*

victoria (vɪkˈtɔːrɪə) NOUN [1] a light four-wheeled horse-drawn carriage with a folding hood, two passenger seats, and a seat in front for the driver. [2] Also called: **victoria plum.** *Brit* a large sweet variety of plum, red and yellow in colour. [3] any South American giant water lily of the genus *Victoria,* having very large floating leaves and large white, red, or pink fragrant flowers: family *Nymphaeaceae.*
▷HISTORY C19: all named after Victoria (1819–1901), queen of the United Kingdom (1837–1901) and empress of India (1876–1901)

Victoria[1] (vɪkˈtɔːrɪə) NOUN [1] a state of SE Australia: part of New South Wales colony until 1851; semiarid in the northwest, with the Great Dividing Range in the centre and east and the Murray River along the N border. Capital: Melbourne. Pop.: 4 712 170 (1999 est.). Area: 227 620 sq. km (87 884 sq. miles). [2] **Lake.** Also called: **Victoria Nyanza.** a lake in East Africa, in Tanzania, Uganda, and Kenya, at an altitude of 1134 m (3720 ft.): the largest lake in Africa and second largest in the world; drained by the Victoria Nile. Area: 69 485 sq. km (26 828 sq. miles). 3 a port in SW Canada, capital of British Columbia, on Vancouver Island: founded in 1843 by the Hudson's Bay Company; made capital of British Columbia in 1868; university (1963). Pop.: 287 897 (1991). 4 the capital of the Seychelles, a port on NE Mahé. Pop.: 24 701 (1997). 5 an urban area in S China, part of Hong Kong, on N Hong Kong Island: financial and administrative district; university (1911). Pop.: 595 000 (latest est.). 6 **Mount.** a mountain in SE Papua New Guinea: the highest peak of the Owen Stanley Range. Height: 4073 m (13 363 ft.).

Victoria² (vɪkˈtɔːrɪə) NOUN the Roman goddess of victory. Greek counterpart: **Nike.**

Victoria and Albert Museum NOUN a museum of the fine and applied arts in London, originating from 1856 and given its present name and site in 1899. Abbreviation: **V and A.**

Victoria Cross NOUN the highest decoration for gallantry in the face of the enemy awarded to the British and Commonwealth armed forces: instituted in 1856 by Queen Victoria.

Victoria Day NOUN the Monday preceding May 24: observed in Canada as a national holiday in commemoration of the birthday of Queen Victoria.

Victoria Desert NOUN See **Great Victoria Desert.**

Victoria Falls PLURAL NOUN a waterfall on the border between Zimbabwe and Zambia, on the Zambezi River. Height: about 108 m (355 ft.). Width: about 1400 m (4500 ft.).

Victoria Island NOUN a large island in the Canadian Arctic, in Nunavut and the Northwest Territories. Area: about 212 000 sq. km (82 000 sq. miles).

Victoria Land NOUN a section of Antarctica, largely in the Ross Dependency on the Ross Sea.

Victorian (vɪkˈtɔːrɪən) ADJECTIVE 1 of, relating to, or characteristic of Victoria (1819–1901), queen of the United Kingdom (1837–1901) and empress of India (1876–1901), or the period of her reign. 2 exhibiting the characteristics popularly attributed to the Victorians, esp prudery, bigotry, or hypocrisy. Compare **Victorian values.** 3 denoting, relating to, or having the style of architecture used in England during the reign of Queen Victoria, characterized by massive construction and elaborate ornamentation. 4 of or relating to Victoria (the state or any of the cities). ◆ NOUN 5 a person who lived during the reign of Queen Victoria. 6 an inhabitant of Victoria (the state or any of the cities).
▸**Vicˈtorian,ism** NOUN

Victoriana (vɪk,tɔːrɪˈɑːnə) PLURAL NOUN objects, ornaments, etc., of the Victorian period.

Victoria Nile NOUN See **Nile.**

Victorian values PLURAL NOUN qualities considered to characterize the Victorian period, including enterprise and initiative and the importance of the family. Compare **Victorian** (sense 2).

victorious (vɪkˈtɔːrɪəs) ADJECTIVE 1 having defeated an adversary: *the victorious nations.* 2 of, relating to, indicative of, or characterized by victory: *a victorious conclusion.*
▸**vicˈtoriously** ADVERB ▸**vicˈtoriousness** NOUN

victory (ˈvɪktərɪ) NOUN, *plural* **-ries.** 1 final and complete superiority in a war. 2 a successful military engagement. 3 a success attained in a contest or struggle or over an opponent, obstacle, or problem. 4 the act of triumphing or state of having triumphed.
▷HISTORY C14: from Old French *victorie,* from Latin *victōria,* from *vincere* to subdue

Victory (ˈvɪktərɪ) NOUN another name (in English) for the Roman goddess **Victoria** or the Greek **Nike.**

victory roll NOUN a roll of an aircraft made by a pilot to announce or celebrate the shooting down of an enemy plane or other cause for celebration.

victual (ˈvɪtᵊl) VERB **-uals, -ualling, -ualled** *or US* **-uals, -ualing, -ualed.** 1 to supply with or obtain victuals. 2 (*intr*) *Rare* (esp of animals) to partake of victuals. ◆ See also **victuals.**
▷HISTORY C14: from Old French *vitaille,* from Late Latin *victūalia* provisions, from Latin *victūālis* concerning food, from *victus* sustenance, from *vīvere* to live
▸**ˈvictual-less** ADJECTIVE

victualage (ˈvɪtəlɪdʒ) NOUN a rare word for **victuals.**

victualler (ˈvɪtələ, ˈvɪtlə) NOUN 1 a supplier of victuals, as to an army; sutler. 2 *Brit* a licensed purveyor of spirits; innkeeper. 3 a supply ship, esp one carrying foodstuffs.

victuals (ˈvɪtᵊlz) PLURAL NOUN (*sometimes singular*) food or provisions.

vicuña (vɪˈkuːnjə) *or* **vicuna** (vɪˈkjuːnə) NOUN 1 a tawny-coloured cud-chewing Andean artiodactyl mammal, *Vicugna vicugna,* similar to the llama: family *Camelidae.* 2 the fine light cloth made from the wool obtained from this animal.
▷HISTORY C17: from Spanish *vicuña,* from Quechuan *wikúña*

vid (vɪd) NOUN *Informal* short for **video** (sense 4).

vide (ˈvaɪdɪ) (used to direct a reader to a specified place in a text, another book, etc.) refer to, see (often in the phrases **vide ante** (see before), **vide infra** (see below), **vide post** (see after), **vide supra** (see above), **vide ut supra** (see as above), etc.). Abbreviation: **v, vid.**
▷HISTORY C16: from Latin

videlicet (vɪˈdiːlɪ,sɛt) ADVERB namely: used to specify items, examples, etc. Abbreviation: **viz.**
▷HISTORY C15: from Latin

video (ˈvɪdɪ,əʊ) ADJECTIVE 1 relating to or employed in the transmission or reception of a televised image. 2 of, concerned with, or operating at video frequencies. ◆ NOUN, *plural* **-os.** 3 the visual elements of a television broadcast. 4 a film recorded on a video cassette. 5 short for **video cassette, video cassette recorder.** 6 *US* an informal name for **television.** ◆ VERB **videos, videoing, videoed.** 7 to record (a television programme, etc.) on a video cassette recorder. ◆ Compare **audio.**
▷HISTORY C20: from Latin *vidēre* to see, on the model of AUDIO

video cassette NOUN a cassette containing video tape.

video cassette recorder NOUN a tape recorder for vision and sound signals using magnetic tape in closed plastic cassettes: used for recording and playing back television programmes and films. Often shortened to: **video.** Abbreviation: **VCR.**

video conferencing NOUN a facility enabling participants in distant locations to take part in a conference by means of electronic sound and video communication.

videodisk (ˈvɪdɪəʊ,dɪsk) NOUN another name for **optical disc.**

videofit (ˈvɪdɪəʊ,fɪt) NOUN a computer-generated picture of a person sought by the police, created by combining facial characteristics on the basis of witnesses' descriptions.
▷HISTORY C20: from VIDEO + (PHOTO)FIT

video frequency NOUN the frequency of a signal conveying the image and synchronizing pulses in a television broadcasting system. It lies in the range from about 50 hertz to 8 megahertz.

video game NOUN any of various games that can be played by using an electronic control to move points of light or graphical symbols on the screen of a visual display unit.

videography (,vɪdɪˈɒgrəfɪ) NOUN the art, practice, or occupation of making videos.
▸**,videˈographer** NOUN

video jockey NOUN a person who introduces and plays videos, esp of pop songs, on a television programme.

video nasty NOUN a film, usually specially made for video, that is explicitly horrific, brutal, and pornographic.

videophone (ˈvɪdɪə,fəʊn) NOUN a telephonic device in which there is both verbal and visual communication between parties.
▸**videophonic** (,vɪdɪəˈfɒnɪk) ADJECTIVE

video referee NOUN *Rugby* an additional referee during a televised game who is able to examine video playback to determine whether or not a try has been legitimately scored.

video tape NOUN 1 magnetic tape used mainly for recording the vision and sound signals of a television programme or film for subsequent transmission. ◆ VERB **video-tape.** 2 to record (a programme, film, etc.) on video tape.

video tape recorder NOUN a tape recorder for vision signals and sometimes accompanying sound, using magnetic tape on open spools: used in television broadcasting. Abbreviation: **VTR.**

Videotex (ˈvɪdɪəʊ,tɛks) NOUN *Trademark* an information system that displays information from a distant computer on a television screen. See also **Teletext, Viewdata.**

videotext (ˈvɪdɪəʊ,tɛkst) NOUN a means of providing a written or graphical representation of computerized information on a television screen.

vidette (vɪˈdɛt) NOUN a variant spelling of **vedette.**

Vidhan Sabha (vɪˈdɑːn ˈsʌbə) NOUN the legislative assembly of any of the states of India.
▷HISTORY Hindi, from *vidhan* law + *sabha* assembly

vidicon (ˈvɪdɪ,kɒn) NOUN a small television camera tube, used in closed-circuit television and outside broadcasts, in which incident light forms an electric charge pattern on a photoconductive surface. Scanning by a low-velocity electron beam discharges the surface, producing a current in an adjacent conducting layer. See also **Plumbicon.**
▷HISTORY C20: from VID(EO) + ICON(OSCOPE)

vie (vaɪ) VERB **vies, vying, vied.** 1 (*intr;* foll by *with* or *for*) to contend for superiority or victory (with) or strive in competition (for). 2 (*tr*) *Archaic* to offer, exchange, or display in rivalry.
▷HISTORY C15: probably from Old French *envier* to challenge, from Latin *invītāre* to INVITE
▸**ˈvier** NOUN ▸**ˈvying** ADJECTIVE, NOUN

Vienna (vɪˈɛnə) NOUN the capital and the smallest state of Austria, in the northeast on the River Danube: seat of the Hapsburgs (1278-1918); residence of the Holy Roman Emperor (1558–1806); withstood sieges by Turks in 1529 and 1683; political and cultural centre in the 18th and 19th centuries, having associations with many composers; university (1365). Pop.: 1 562 676 (2001). Area: 1075 sq. km (415 sq. miles). German name: **Wien.**

Vienna Union *or* **International** NOUN **the.** an international conference of socialists who came together in Vienna in 1921 in an attempt to reconstruct a united International by offering an alternative to the right-wing remnant of the Second International and to the Comintern: merged into the Labour and Socialist International in 1923. Also called: **Two-and-a-half International.**

Vienne (*French* vjɛn) NOUN 1 a department of W central France, in Poitou-Charentes region. Capital: Poitiers. Pop.: 399 024 (1999). Area: 7044 sq. km (2747 sq. miles). 2 a town in SE France, on the River Rhône: extensive Roman remains. Ancient name: **Vienna.** 3 a river in SW central France, flowing west and north to the Loire below Chinon. Length: over 350 km (200 miles).

Viennese (,vɪəˈniːz) ADJECTIVE 1 of, relating to, or characteristic of Vienna. ◆ NOUN, *plural* **-nese.** 2 a native or inhabitant of Vienna.

Vientiane (,vjɛntɪˈɑːn) NOUN the administrative capital of Laos, in the south near the border with Thailand: capital of the kingdom of Vientiane from 1707 until taken by the Thais in 1827. Pop.: 534 000 (1999 est.).

Vierwaldstättersee (fiːrˈvaltʃtɛtər,zeː) NOUN the German name for (Lake) **Lucerne.**

vies (fiːs) ADJECTIVE *South African slang* angry, furious, or disgusted.
▷HISTORY Afrikaans

vi et armis *Latin* (ˈvaɪ ɛt ˈɑːmɪs) NOUN *Legal history* a kind of trespass accompanied by force and violence.
▷HISTORY literally: by force and arms

Vietcong (,vjɛtˈkɒŋ) *or* **Viet Cong** NOUN (in the Vietnam War) 1 the Communist-led guerrilla force and revolutionary army of South Vietnam; the armed forces of the National Liberation Front of South Vietnam. 2 a member of these armed forces. 3 (*modifier*) of or relating to the Vietcong or a Vietcong.
▷HISTORY from Vietnamese *Viet Nam Cong San* Vietnamese Communist

Vietminh (ˌvjɛtˈmɪn) *or* **Viet Minh** NOUN [1] a Vietnamese organization led by Ho Chi Minh that first fought the Japanese and then the French (1941–54) in their attempt to achieve national independence. [2] a member or group of members of this organization, esp in the armed forces. [3] (*modifier*) of or relating to this organization or to its members.
▷HISTORY from Vietnamese *Viet Nam Doc Lap Dong Minh Hoi* Vietnam League of Independence

Vietnam (ˌvjɛtˈnæm) *or* **Viet Nam** NOUN a republic in SE Asia: an ancient empire, conquered by France in the 19th century; occupied by Japan (1940–45) when the Communist-led Vietminh began resistance operations that were continued against restored French rule after 1945. In 1954 the country was divided along the 17th parallel, establishing North Vietnam (under the Vietminh) and South Vietnam (under French control), the latter becoming the independent **Republic of Vietnam** in 1955. From 1959 the country was dominated by war between the Communist Vietcong, supported by North Vietnam, and the South Vietnamese government; increasing numbers of US forces were brought to the aid of the South Vietnamese army until a peace agreement (1973) led to the withdrawal of US troops; further fighting led to the eventual defeat of the South Vietnamese government in March 1975 and in 1976 an elected National Assembly proclaimed the reunification of the country. Official language: Vietnamese. Religion: Buddhist majority. Currency: dong. Capital: Hanoi. Pop.: 79 939 000 (2001 est.). Area: 331 041 sq. km (127 816 sq. miles). Official name: **Socialist Republic of Vietnam.**

Vietnamese (ˌvjɛtnəˈmiːz) ADJECTIVE [1] of, relating to, or characteristic of Vietnam, its people, or their language. ◆ NOUN [2] (*plural* **-ese**) a native or inhabitant of Vietnam. [3] the language of Vietnam, probably related to the Mon-Khmer languages.

Vietnamization *or* **Vietnamisation** (ˌvjɛtnəmaɪˈzeɪʃən) NOUN (in the Vietnam War) a US government policy of transferring the tasks of fighting and directing the war to the government and forces of South Vietnam.

vieux jeu *French* (vjø ʒø) ADJECTIVE old-fashioned.
▷HISTORY literally: old game

view (vjuː) NOUN [1] the act of seeing or observing; an inspection. [2] vision or sight, esp range of vision: *the church is out of view.* [3] a scene, esp of a fine tract of countryside: *the view from the top was superb.* [4] a pictorial representation of a scene, such as a photograph. [5] (*sometimes plural*) opinion; thought: *my own view on the matter differs from yours.* [6] chance or expectation: *the policy has little view of success.* [7] (foll by *to*) a desired end or intention: *he has a view to securing further qualifications.* [8] a general survey of a topic, subject, etc.: *a comprehensive view of Shakespearean literature.* [9] visual aspect or appearance: *they look the same in outward view.* [10] *Law* **a** a formal inspection by a jury of the place where an alleged crime was committed. **b** a formal inspection of property in dispute. [11] a sight of a hunted animal before or during the chase. [12] **in view of.** taking into consideration. [13] **on view.** exhibited to the public gaze. [14] **take a dim** *or* **poor view of.** to regard (something) with disfavour or disapproval. [15] **with a view to. a** with the intention of. **b** in anticipation or hope of. ◆ VERB [16] (*tr*) to look at. [17] (*tr*) to consider in a specified manner: *they view the growth of Communism with horror.* [18] (*tr*) to examine or inspect carefully: *to view the accounts.* [19] (*tr*) to survey mentally; contemplate: *to view the difficulties.* [20] to watch (television). [21] (*tr*) to sight (a hunted animal) before or during the chase.
▷HISTORY C15: from Old French *veue,* from *veoir* to see, from Latin *vidēre*
▸ˈ**viewable** ADJECTIVE

Viewdata (ˈvjuːˌdeɪtə) NOUN *Trademark* an interactive form of Videotext that sends information from a distant computer along telephone lines, enabling shopping, booking theatre and airline tickets, and banking transactions to be conducted from the home.

viewer (ˈvjuːə) NOUN [1] a person who views something, esp television. [2] any optical device by means of which something is viewed, esp one used for viewing photographic transparencies. [3] *Law* a person appointed by a court to inspect and report upon property, etc.
▸ˈ**viewership** NOUN

viewfinder (ˈvjuːˌfaɪndə) NOUN a device on a camera, consisting of a lens system and sometimes a ground-glass screen, enabling the user to see what will be included in his photograph. Sometimes shortened to: **finder.**

view halloo INTERJECTION [1] a huntsman's cry uttered when the quarry is seen breaking cover or shortly afterwards. ◆ NOUN [2] a shout indicating an abrupt appearance.

viewing (ˈvjuːɪŋ) NOUN [1] the act of watching television. [2] television programmes collectively: *late-night viewing.*

viewless (ˈvjuːlɪs) ADJECTIVE [1] (of windows, etc.) not affording a view. [2] having no opinions. [3] *Poetic* invisible.

viewpoint (ˈvjuːˌpɔɪnt) NOUN [1] the mental attitude that determines a person's opinions or judgments; point of view. [2] a place from which something can be viewed.

viewy (ˈvjuːɪ) ADJECTIVE **viewier, viewiest.** *Informal, rare* [1] having fanciful opinions or ideas; visionary. [2] characterized by ostentation; showy.
▸ˈ**viewiness** NOUN

VIFF (vɪf) NOUN a technique used in flying VTOL aircraft to change direction suddenly by swivelling the jet engine nozzles.
▷HISTORY C20: *v(ectoring) i(n) f(orward) f(light)*

vig (vɪg) NOUN *US slang* the interest on a loan that is paid to a moneylender.
▷HISTORY C20: short for *vigorish,* prob. via Yiddish from Russian *vyigrysh* profit, winnings

vigesimal (vaɪˈdʒɛsɪməl) ADJECTIVE [1] relating to or based on the number 20. [2] taking place or proceeding in intervals of 20. [3] twentieth.
▷HISTORY C17: from Latin *vīgēsimus,* variant (influenced by *vīgintī* twenty) of *vīcēsimus* twentieth

vigia (ˈvɪdʒɪə) NOUN *Nautical* a navigational hazard marked on a chart although its existence and nature has not been confirmed.
▷HISTORY C19: from Spanish *vigía* reef, from Latin *vigilāre* to keep watch

vigil (ˈvɪdʒɪl) NOUN [1] a purposeful watch maintained, esp at night, to guard, observe, pray, etc. [2] the period of such a watch. [3] *RC Church, Church of England* the eve of certain major festivals, formerly observed as a night spent in prayer: often marked by fasting and abstinence and a special Mass and divine office. [4] a period of sleeplessness; insomnia.
▷HISTORY C13: from Old French *vigile,* from Medieval Latin *vigilia* watch preceding a religious festival, from Latin: vigilance, from *vigil* alert, from *vigēre* to be lively

vigilance (ˈvɪdʒɪləns) NOUN [1] the fact, quality, or condition of being vigilant. [2] the abnormal state or condition of being unable to sleep.

vigilance committee NOUN (in the US) a self-appointed body of citizens organized to maintain order, punish crime, etc., where an efficient system of courts does not exist.

vigilant (ˈvɪdʒɪlənt) ADJECTIVE keenly alert to or heedful of trouble or danger, as while others are sleeping or unsuspicious.
▷HISTORY C15: from Latin *vigilāns* keeping awake, from *vigilāre* to be watchful; see VIGIL
▸ˈ**vigilantly** ADVERB ▸ˈ**vigilantness** NOUN

vigilante (ˌvɪdʒɪˈlæntɪ) NOUN [1] one of an organized group of citizens who take upon themselves the protection of their district, properties, etc. [2] Also called: **vigilance man.** *US* a member of a vigilance committee.
▷HISTORY C19: from Spanish, from Latin *vigilāre* to keep watch

vigilantism (ˌvɪdʒɪˈlæntɪzəm) NOUN *US* the methods, conduct, attitudes, etc., associated with vigilantes, esp militancy, bigotry, or suspiciousness.

vigil light NOUN *Chiefly RC Church* [1] a small candle lit as an act of personal devotion before a shrine or statue, usually in a church. [2] a small lamp kept permanently burning before such a shrine or statue.

Vigil Mass NOUN *RC Church* a Mass held on Saturday evening, attendance at which fulfils one's obligation to attend Mass on Sunday.

vigneron (ˈviːnjərɒn; *French* viɲrɔ̃) NOUN a person who grows grapes for winemaking.
▷HISTORY French, from *vigne* vine

vignette (vɪˈnjɛt) NOUN [1] a small illustration placed at the beginning or end of a book or chapter. [2] a short graceful literary essay or sketch. [3] a photograph, drawing, etc., with edges that are shaded off. [4] *Architect* a carved ornamentation that has a design based upon tendrils, leaves, etc. [5] any small endearing scene, view, picture, etc. ◆ VERB (*tr*) [6] to finish (a photograph, picture, etc.) with a fading border in the form of a vignette. [7] **a** to decorate with vignettes. **b** to portray in or as in a vignette.
▷HISTORY C18: from French, literally: little vine, from *vigne* VINE; with reference to the vine motif frequently used in embellishments to a text
▸viˈ**gnettist** NOUN

vignetting (vɪˈnjɛtɪŋ) NOUN [1] the technique of producing a photographic vignette, esp a portrait, by progressively reducing the amount of light falling on the photographic surface towards the edges. [2] the reduction in area of a light beam passing through a camera lens as the obliquity of the beam is increased.

Vigo (ˈviːgəʊ; *Spanish* ˈbigo) NOUN a port in NW Spain, in Galicia on **Vigo Bay** (an inlet of the Atlantic): site of a British and Dutch naval victory (1702) over the French and Spanish. Pop.: 283 110 (1998 est.).

vigoro (ˈvɪgəˌrəʊ) NOUN *Austral sport* a women's game similar to cricket with paddle-shaped bats, introduced into Australia in 1919 by its British inventor J. J. Grant.
▷HISTORY C20: from VIGOUR

vigorous (ˈvɪgərəs) ADJECTIVE [1] endowed with bodily or mental strength or vitality; robust. [2] displaying, involving, characterized by, or performed with vigour: *vigorous growth.*
▸ˈ**vigorously** ADVERB ▸ˈ**vigorousness** NOUN

vigour *or US* **vigor** (ˈvɪgə) NOUN [1] exuberant and resilient strength of body or mind; vitality. [2] substantial effective energy or force: *the vigour of the tempest.* [3] forcefulness; intensity: *the vigour of her complaints.* [4] the capacity for survival or strong healthy growth in a plant or animal: *hybrid vigour.* [5] the most active period or stage of life, manhood, etc.; prime. [6] *Chiefly US* legal force or effectiveness; validity (esp in the phrase **in vigour**).
▷HISTORY C14: from Old French *vigeur,* from Latin *vigor* activity, from *vigēre* to be lively

vihuela (*Spanish* biˈwela) NOUN an obsolete plucked stringed instrument of Spain, related to the guitar.
▷HISTORY from Spanish

Viipuri (ˈviːpuri) NOUN the Finnish name for **Vyborg.**

Vijayawada (ˌviːdʒaɪəˈwɑːdə) NOUN a town in SE India, in E central Andra Pradesh on the Krishna River: Hindu pilgrimage centre. Pop.: 701 827 (1991). Former name: **Bezwada.**

Viking (ˈvaɪkɪŋ) NOUN (*sometimes not capital*) [1] Also called: **Norseman, Northman.** any of the Danes, Norwegians, and Swedes who raided by sea most of N and W Europe from the 8th to the 11th centuries, later often settling, as in parts of Britain. [2] any sea rover, plunderer, or pirate. [3] either of two unmanned American spacecraft that reached Mars in 1976. [4] (*modifier*) of, relating to, or characteristic of a Viking or Vikings: *a Viking ship.*
▷HISTORY C19: from Old Norse *víkingr,* probably from *vík* creek, sea inlet + *-ingr* (see -ING[3]); perhaps related to Old English *wīc* camp

vilayet (vɪˈlɑːjɛt) NOUN a major administrative division of Turkey.
▷HISTORY C19: from Turkish, from Arabic *wilāyat,* from *walīy* governor

vile (vaɪl) ADJECTIVE [1] abominably wicked; shameful or evil: *the vile development of slavery appalled them.* [2] morally despicable; ignoble: *vile accusations.* [3] disgusting to the senses or emotions; foul: *a vile smell; vile epithets.* [4] tending to humiliate or degrade: *only slaves would perform such vile tasks.* [5] unpleasant or bad: *vile weather.* [6] paltry: *a vile reward.*
▷HISTORY C13: from Old French *vil,* from Latin *vīlis* cheap
▸ˈ**vilely** ADVERB ▸ˈ**vileness** NOUN

vilify ('vɪlɪˌfaɪ) VERB **-fies, -fying, -fied.** (*tr*) 1 to revile with abusive or defamatory language; malign: *he was vilified in the tabloid press.* 2 *Rare* to make vile; debase; degrade.
▷**HISTORY** C15: from Late Latin *vīlificāre,* from Latin *vīlis* worthless + *facere* to make
▸**vilification** (ˌvɪlɪfɪ'keɪʃən) NOUN ▸**'viliˌfier** NOUN

vilipend ('vɪlɪˌpɛnd) VERB (*tr*) *Rare* 1 to treat or regard with contempt. 2 to speak slanderously or slightingly of.
▷**HISTORY** C15: from Late Latin *vīlipendere,* from Latin *vīlis* worthless + *pendere* to esteem
▸**'viliˌpender** NOUN

villa ('vɪlə) NOUN 1 (in ancient Rome) a country house, usually consisting of farm buildings and residential quarters around a courtyard. 2 a large and usually luxurious country residence. 3 *Brit* a detached or semidetached suburban house. 4 *NZ* a medium-sized suburban house standing in its own grounds.
▷**HISTORY** C17: via Italian from Latin; related to Latin *vīcus* a village
▸**'villa-ˌlike** ADJECTIVE

Villach (*German* 'fɪlax) NOUN a city in S central Austria, on the Drava River: nearby hot mineral springs. Pop.: 54 640 (1991).

village ('vɪlɪdʒ) NOUN 1 a small group of houses in a country area, larger than a hamlet. 2 the inhabitants of such a community collectively. 3 an incorporated municipality smaller than a town in various parts of the US and Canada. 4 a group of habitats of certain animals. 5 *NZ* a self-contained city area having its own shops, etc. 6 (*modifier*) of, relating to, or characteristic of a village: *a village green.*
▷**HISTORY** C15: from Old French, from *ville* farm, from Latin: VILLA
▸**'village-ˌlike** ADJECTIVE

village college NOUN *Brit* a centre, often for a group of villages, with educational and recreational facilities for the whole neighbourhood. Also called: **community college.**

villager ('vɪlɪdʒə) NOUN 1 an inhabitant of a village. ◆ ADJECTIVE 2 *E African* backward, unsophisticated, or illiterate.

Villahermosa (*Spanish* biʎaer'mosa) NOUN a town in E Mexico, capital of Tabasco state: university (1959). Pop.: 330 605 (2000 est.). Former name: **San Juan Bautista.**

villa home NOUN *Austral* one of a set of suburban bungalows built compactly on the one allotment, esp on the former site of a single bungalow.

villain ('vɪlən) NOUN 1 a wicked or malevolent person. 2 (in a novel, play, film, etc.) the main evil character and antagonist to the hero. 3 *Often jocular* a mischievous person; rogue. 4 *Brit police slang* a criminal. 5 *History* a variant spelling of **villein.** 6 *Obsolete* an uncouth person; boor.
▷**HISTORY** C14: from Old French *vilein* serf, from Late Latin *vīllānus* worker on a country estate, from Latin: VILLA
▸**'villainess** FEMININE NOUN

villainage ('vɪlənɪdʒ) NOUN a variant spelling of **villeinage.**

villainous ('vɪlənəs) ADJECTIVE 1 of, like, or appropriate to a villain. 2 very bad or disagreeable: *a villainous climate.*
▸**'villainously** ADVERB ▸**'villainousness** NOUN

villainy ('vɪlənɪ) NOUN, *plural* **-lainies.** 1 conduct befitting a villain; vicious behaviour or action. 2 an evil, abhorrent, or criminal act or deed. 3 the fact or condition of being villainous. 4 *English history* a rare word for **villeinage.**

villanella (ˌvɪlə'nɛlə) NOUN, *plural* **-las.** a type of part song originating in Naples during the 16th century.
▷**HISTORY** C16: from Italian, from *villano* rustic, from Late Latin *vīllānus;* see VILLAIN

villanelle (ˌvɪlə'nɛl) NOUN a verse form of French origin consisting of 19 lines arranged in five tercets and a quatrain. The first and third lines of the first tercet recur alternately at the end of each subsequent tercet and both together at the end of the quatrain.
▷**HISTORY** C16: from French, from Italian VILLANELLA

Villanovan (ˌvɪlə'nəʊvᵊn) ADJECTIVE 1 of or relating to an early Iron Age culture near Bologna, Italy, characterized by the use of bronze and the primitive use of iron. ◆ NOUN 2 a member of this culture.
▷**HISTORY** C19: named after the NE Italian town of *Villanova,* where the first remains of the culture were excavated in 1853

villatic (vɪ'lætɪk) ADJECTIVE *Literary* of or relating to a villa, village, or farm; rustic; rural.
▷**HISTORY** C17: from Latin *vīllatīcus,* from *villa* a farm

-ville NOUN AND ADJECTIVE COMBINING FORM *Slang, chiefly US* (denoting) a place, condition, or quality with a character as specified: *dragsville; squaresville.*

villein *or* **villain** ('vɪlən) NOUN (in medieval Europe) a peasant personally bound to his lord, to whom he paid dues and services, sometimes commuted to rents, in return for his land.
▷**HISTORY** C14: from Old French *vilein* serf; see VILLAIN

villeinage *or* **villainage** ('vɪlənɪdʒ) NOUN (in medieval Europe) 1 the status and condition of a villein. 2 the tenure by which a villein held his land.

Villeurbanne (*French* vijœrban) NOUN a town in E France: an industrial suburb of E Lyons. Pop.: 119 848 (1990).

villi ('vɪlaɪ) NOUN the plural of **villus.**

villiform ('vɪlɪˌfɔːm) ADJECTIVE having the form of a villus or a series of villi.
▷**HISTORY** C19: from New Latin *villiformis,* from Latin *villus* shaggy hair + -FORM

villosity (vɪ'lɒsɪtɪ) NOUN, *plural* **-ties.** 1 the state of being villous. 2 a villous coating or surface. 3 a villus or a collection of villi.

villous ('vɪləs) ADJECTIVE 1 (of plant parts) covered with long hairs. 2 of, relating to, or having villi.
▷**HISTORY** C14: from Latin *villōsus,* from *villus* tuft of hair
▸**'villously** ADVERB

villus ('vɪləs) NOUN, *plural* **villi** ('vɪlaɪ). (*usually plural*) 1 *Zoology, anatomy* any of the numerous finger-like projections of the mucous membrane lining the small intestine of many vertebrates. 2 any similar membranous process, such as any of those in the mammalian placenta. 3 *Botany* any of various hairlike outgrowths, as from the stem of a moss.
▷**HISTORY** C18: from Latin: shaggy hair

Vilnius *or* **Vilnyus** ('vɪlnɪʊs) NOUN the capital of Lithuania: passed to Russia in 1795; under Polish rule (1920–39); university (1578); an industrial and commercial centre. Pop.: 577 969 (2000 est.). Russian name: **Vilna** ('vilna). Polish name: **Wilno.**

vim (vɪm) NOUN *Slang* exuberant vigour and energy.
▷**HISTORY** C19: from Latin, from *vīs;* related to Greek *is* strength

vimen ('vaɪmɛn) NOUN, *plural* **vimina** ('vɪmɪnə). *Botany, now rare* a long flexible shoot that occurs in certain plants.
▷**HISTORY** C19: from Latin: a pliant twig, osier

Viminal ('vɪmɪnᵊl) NOUN one of the seven hills on which ancient Rome was built.
▷**HISTORY** from Latin *Vīminālis Collis* the Viminal Hill, from *vīminālis* of osiers, from *vīmen* an osier, referring to the willow grove on the hill

vimineous (vɪ'mɪnɪəs) ADJECTIVE *Botany, now rare* having, producing, or resembling long flexible shoots.
▷**HISTORY** C17: from Latin *vīmineus* made of osiers, from *vīmen* flexible shoot

vin- COMBINING FORM a variant of **vini-** before a vowel.

vina ('viːnə) NOUN a stringed musical instrument, esp of India, related to the sitar.
▷**HISTORY** C18: from Hindi *bīnā,* from Sanskrit *vīṇā*

vinaceous (vaɪ'neɪʃəs) ADJECTIVE 1 of, relating to, or containing wine. 2 having a colour suggestive of red wine.
▷**HISTORY** C17: from Late Latin *vīnāceus,* from Latin *vīnum* wine

Viña del Mar (*Spanish* 'biɲa ðɛl 'mar) NOUN a city and resort in central Chile, just north of Valparaíso on the Pacific: the second largest city of Chile. Pop.: 330 736 (1999 est.).

vinaigrette (ˌvɪneɪ'grɛt) NOUN 1 Also called: **vinegarette.** a small decorative bottle or box with a perforated top, used for holding smelling salts, etc. 2 Also called: **vinaigrette sauce.** a salad dressing made from oil and vinegar with seasonings; French dressing. ◆ ADJECTIVE 3 served with vinaigrette.
▷**HISTORY** C17: from French, from *vinaigre* VINEGAR

vinasse (vɪ'næs) NOUN the residue left in a still after distilling spirits, esp brandy.
▷**HISTORY** C20: from French

vinblastine (vɪn'blæstiːn) NOUN a cytotoxic drug used in the treatment of lymphomas, derived as an alkaloid from the tropical shrub Madagascar periwinkle (*Vinca rosea*).
▷**HISTORY** C20: shortened from *vincaleukoblastine,* from VINCA + *leukoblast,* from *leukocyte* + -BLAST + -INE[2]

vinca ('vɪŋkə) NOUN See **periwinkle[2].**
▷**HISTORY** New Latin, from Latin *pervinca* periwinkle

vinca alkaloid NOUN *Med* any of a group of alkaloids obtained from the periwinkle *Vinca rosea,* such as vinblastine and vincristine, that interfere with cell division and are used in the treatment of cancer.

Vincennes (*French* vɛ̃sɛn; *English* vɪn'sɛnz) NOUN a suburb of E Paris: 14th-century castle. Pop.: 45 000 (latest est.).

Vincent's angina *or* **disease** ('vɪnsənts) NOUN an ulcerative bacterial infection of the mouth, esp involving the throat and tonsils.
▷**HISTORY** C20: named after J. H. *Vincent* (died 1950), French bacteriologist

vincible ('vɪnsɪbᵊl) ADJECTIVE *Rare* capable of being defeated or overcome.
▷**HISTORY** C16: from Latin *vincibilis,* from *vincere* to conquer
▸**ˌvinci'bility** *or* **'vincibleness** NOUN

vincristine (vɪn'krɪstiːn) NOUN a cytotoxic drug used in the treatment of leukaemia, derived as an alkaloid from the tropical shrub Madagascar periwinkle (*Vinca rosea*).
▷**HISTORY** C20: from New Latin VINCA + Latin *crista* crest + -INE[2]

vinculum ('vɪŋkjʊləm) NOUN, *plural* **-la** (-lə). 1 a horizontal line drawn above a group of mathematical terms, used as an alternative to parentheses in mathematical expressions, as in $x + \overline{y - z}$ *which is equivalent to* $x + (y - z)$. 2 *Anatomy* **a** any bandlike structure, esp one uniting two or more parts. **b** another name for **ligament.** 3 *Rare* a unifying bond; tie.
▷**HISTORY** C17: from Latin: bond, from *vincīre* to bind

vindaloo (ˌvɪndə'luː) NOUN, *plural* **-loos.** a type of very hot Indian curry.
▷**HISTORY** C20: perhaps from Portuguese *vin d'alho* wine and garlic sauce

vin de pays *French* (vɛ̃ də pei) NOUN, *plural* ***vins de pays*** (vɛ̃ də pei). the third highest French wine classification: indicates that the wine meets certain requirements concerning area of production, strength, etc. Also called: **vin du pays.** Abbreviation: **VDP.** Compare **AC, VDQS, *vin de table.***
▷**HISTORY** literally: local wine

vin de table *French* (vɛ̃ də tablə) NOUN, *plural* ***vins de table*** (vɛ̃ də tablə). the classification given to a French wine that does not meet the requirements of any of the three higher classifications. Compare **AC, VDQS, *vin de pays.***
▷**HISTORY** literally: table wine

Vindhya Pradesh ('vɪndjə) NOUN a former state of central India: merged with the reorganized Madhya Pradesh in 1956.

Vindhya Range *or* **Mountains** NOUN a mountain range in central India: separates the Ganges basin from the Deccan, marking the limits of northern and peninsular India. Greatest height: 1113 m (3651 ft.).

vindicable ('vɪndɪkəbᵊl) ADJECTIVE capable of being vindicated; justifiable.
▸**ˌvindica'bility** NOUN

vindicate ('vɪndɪˌkeɪt) VERB (*tr*) 1 to clear from guilt, accusation, blame, etc., as by evidence or argument. 2 to provide justification for: *his promotion vindicated his unconventional attitude.* 3 to uphold, maintain, or defend (a cause, etc.): *to vindicate a claim.* 4 *Roman law* to bring an action to regain possession of (property) under claim of legal title. 5 *Rare* to claim, as for oneself or another. 6 *Obsolete* to take revenge on or for; punish. 7 *Obsolete* to set free.

▷HISTORY C17: from Latin *vindicāre,* from *vindex* claimant
▸ **'vindi,cator** NOUN ▸ **'vindi,catory** ADJECTIVE

vindication (,vɪndɪ'keɪʃən) NOUN [1] the act of vindicating or the condition of being vindicated. [2] a means of exoneration from an accusation. [3] a fact, evidence, circumstance, etc., that serves to vindicate a theory or claim.

vindictive (vɪn'dɪktɪv) ADJECTIVE [1] disposed to seek vengeance. [2] characterized by spite or rancour. [3] *English law* (of damages) in excess of the compensation due to the plaintiff and imposed in punishment of the defendant.
▷HISTORY C17: from Latin *vindicta* revenge, from *vindicāre* to VINDICATE
▸ **vin'dictively** ADVERB ▸ **vin'dictiveness** NOUN

vin du pays *French* (vɛ̃ du pei) NOUN, *plural* ***vins du pays***. a variant spelling of ***vin de pays***

vine (vaɪn) NOUN [1] any of various plants, esp the grapevine, having long flexible stems that creep along the ground or climb by clinging to a support by means of tendrils, leafstalks, etc. [2] the stem of such a plant.
▷HISTORY C13: from Old French *vine,* from Latin *vīnea* vineyard, from *vīneus* belonging to wine, from *vīnum* wine
▸ **vined** ADJECTIVE ▸ **'vineless** ADJECTIVE ▸ **'vine,like** ADJECTIVE ▸ **'viny** ADJECTIVE

vinedresser ('vaɪn,drɛsə) NOUN a person who prunes, tends, or cultivates grapevines.

vinegar ('vɪnɪgə) NOUN [1] a sour-tasting liquid consisting of impure dilute acetic acid, made by oxidation of the ethyl alcohol in beer, wine, or cider. It is used as a condiment or preservative. [2] sourness or peevishness of temper, countenance, speech, etc. [3] *Pharmacol* a medicinal solution in dilute acetic acid. [4] *US and Canadian informal* vitality. ◆ VERB [5] *(tr)* to apply vinegar to.
▷HISTORY C13: from Old French *vinaigre,* from *vin* WINE + *aigre* sour, from Latin *acer* sharp
▸ **'vinegarish** ADJECTIVE ▸ **'vinegar-,like** ADJECTIVE

vinegar eel NOUN a nematode worm, *Anguillula aceti,* that feeds on the organisms that cause fermentation in vinegar and other liquids. Also called: **vinegar worm, eelworm.**

vinegarette (,vɪnɪgə'rɛt) NOUN a variant spelling of **vinaigrette** (sense 1).

vinegar fly NOUN any of various dipterous flies of the genus *Drosophila*. See **drosophila.**

vinegarroon (,vɪnɪgə'ru:n) NOUN a large whip scorpion, *Mastigoproctus giganteus,* of the southwestern US and Mexico that emits a vinegary odour when alarmed.
▷HISTORY from Mexican Spanish *vinagrón,* from Spanish *vinagre* VINEGAR

vinegary ('vɪnɪgərɪ) ADJECTIVE [1] containing vinegar; tasting of or like vinegar. [2] bad-tempered, sour, or peevish.

vinery ('vaɪnərɪ) NOUN, *plural* **-eries.** [1] a hothouse for growing grapes. [2] another name for a **vineyard.** [3] vines collectively.

vineyard ('vɪnjəd) NOUN a plantation of grapevines, esp where wine grapes are produced.
▷HISTORY Old English *wīngeard;* see VINE, YARD[2]; related to Old High German *wīngart,* Old Norse *vingarthr*
▸ **'vineyardist** NOUN

vingt-et-un *French* (vɛ̃teœ̃) NOUN another name for **pontoon**[2].
▷HISTORY literally: twenty-one

vinho verde (,vi:njəʊ 'vɜ:dɪ) NOUN any of a variety of light, slightly sharp-tasting wines made from early-picked grapes in the Minho region of NW Portugal.
▷HISTORY Portuguese, literally: green (or young) wine

vini- *or before a vowel* **vin-** COMBINING FORM indicating wine: *viniculture.*
▷HISTORY from Latin *vīnum*

vinic ('vaɪnɪk, 'vɪnɪk) ADJECTIVE of, relating to, or contained in wine.
▷HISTORY C19: from Latin *vīnum* wine

viniculture ('vɪnɪ,kʌltʃə) NOUN the process or business of growing grapes and making wine.
▸ **,vini'cultural** ADJECTIVE ▸ **,vini'culturist** NOUN

viniferous (vɪ'nɪfərəs) ADJECTIVE wine-producing.

vinificator ('vɪnɪfɪ,keɪtə) NOUN a condenser that collects the alcohol vapour escaping from fermenting wine.
▷HISTORY C19: from Latin *vīnum* wine + *facere* to make

vino ('vi:nəʊ) NOUN, *plural* **-nos.** an informal word for **wine.**
▷HISTORY jocular use of Italian or Spanish *vino*

vin ordinaire *French* (vɛ̃n ɔrdinɛr) NOUN, *plural* ***vins ordinaires*** (vɛ̃z ɔrdinɛr). cheap table wine, esp French.

vinosity (vɪ'nɒsɪtɪ) NOUN the distinctive and essential quality and flavour of wine.
▷HISTORY C17: from Late Latin *vīnōsitas,* from Latin *vīnōsus* VINOUS

vinous ('vaɪnəs) ADJECTIVE [1] of, relating to, or characteristic of wine. [2] indulging in or indicative of indulgence in wine: *a vinous complexion.*
▷HISTORY C17: from Latin *vīnōsus,* from *vīnum* WINE

vintage ('vɪntɪdʒ) NOUN [1] the wine obtained from a harvest of grapes, esp in an outstandingly good year, referred to by the year involved, the district, or the vineyard. [2] the harvest from which such a wine is obtained. [3] **a** the harvesting of wine grapes. **b** the season of harvesting these grapes or for making wine. [4] a time of origin: *a car of Edwardian vintage.* [5] *Informal* a group of people or objects of the same period: *a fashion of last season's vintage.* ◆ ADJECTIVE [6] (of wine) of an outstandingly good year. [7] representative of the best and most typical: *vintage Shakespeare.* [8] of lasting interest and importance; venerable; classic: *vintage films.* [9] old-fashioned; dated. ◆ VERB [10] *(tr)* to gather (grapes) or make (wine).
▷HISTORY C15: from Old French *vendage* (influenced by *vintener* VINTNER), from Latin *vindēmia,* from *vīnum* WINE, grape + *dēmere* to take away (from *dē-* away + *emere* to take)

vintage car NOUN *Chiefly Brit* an old car, esp one constructed between 1919 and 1930. Compare **classic car, veteran car.**

vintager ('vɪntɪdʒə) NOUN a grape harvester.

vintner ('vɪntnə) NOUN a wine merchant.
▷HISTORY C15: from Old French *vinetier,* from Medieval Latin *vīnētārius,* from Latin *vīnētum* vineyard, from *vīnum* WINE

vinyl ('vaɪnɪl) NOUN [1] *(modifier)* of, consisting of, or containing the monovalent group of atoms CH_2CH-: *a vinyl polymer; vinyl chloride.* [2] *(modifier)* of, consisting of, or made of a vinyl resin: *a vinyl raincoat.* [3] any vinyl polymer, resin, or plastic, esp PVC. [4] (collectively) conventional records made of vinyl as opposed to compact discs.
▷HISTORY C19: from VINI- + -YL

vinyl acetate NOUN a colourless volatile liquid unsaturated ester that polymerizes readily in light and is used for making polyvinyl acetate. Formula: CH_2:$CHOOCCH_3$.

vinyl chloride NOUN a colourless flammable gaseous unsaturated compound made by the chlorination of ethylene and used as a refrigerant and in the manufacture of PVC; chloroethylene; chloroethene. Formula: CH_2:CHCl.

vinylidene (vaɪ'nɪlɪ,di:n) NOUN *(modifier)* of, consisting of, or containing the group CH_2:C: *a vinylidene group or radical; vinylidene chloride; a vinylidene resin.*
▷HISTORY C20: from VINYL + -IDE + -ENE

vinyl resin *or* **polymer** NOUN any one of a class of thermoplastic materials, esp PVC and polyvinyl acetate, made by polymerizing vinyl compounds.

viol ('vaɪəl) NOUN any of a family of stringed musical instruments that preceded the violin family, consisting of a fretted fingerboard, a body rather like that of a violin but having a flat back and six strings, played with a curved bow. They are held between the knees when played and have a quiet yet penetrating tone; they were much played, esp in consorts, in the 16th and 17th centuries.
▷HISTORY C15: from Old French *viole,* from Old Provençal *viola;* see VIOLA[1]

viola[1] (vɪ'əʊlə) NOUN [1] a bowed stringed instrument, the alto of the violin family; held beneath the chin when played. It is pitched and tuned an octave above the cello. [2] any of various instruments of the viol family, such as the viola da gamba.
▷HISTORY C18: from Italian *viola,* probably from Old Provençal *viola,* of uncertain origin; perhaps related to Latin *vītulārī* to rejoice

viola[2] ('vaɪələ, vaɪ'əʊ-) NOUN any temperate perennial herbaceous plant of the violaceous genus *Viola,* the flowers of which have showy irregular petals, white, yellow, blue, or mauve in colour. See also **violet** (sense 1), **pansy** (sense 1).
▷HISTORY C15: from Latin: violet

violaceous (,vaɪə'leɪʃəs) ADJECTIVE [1] of, relating to, or belonging to the *Violaceae,* a family of herbaceous plants and shrubs including the violets and pansies. [2] of the colour violet.
▷HISTORY C17: from Latin *violāceus,* from *viola* VIOLET

viola clef NOUN another term for **alto clef.**

viola da braccio (vɪ'əʊlə də 'brætʃɪ,əʊ) NOUN [1] an old name for **viola**[1] (sense 1). [2] a type of viol held on the shoulder, from which the modern viola was developed.
▷HISTORY from Italian, literally: viol for the arm

viola da gamba (vɪ'əʊlə də 'gæmbə) NOUN the second largest and lowest member of the viol family. See **viol.**
▷HISTORY C18: from Italian, literally: viol for the leg

viola d'amore (vɪ'əʊlə dæ'mɔ:rɪ) NOUN an instrument of the viol family having no frets, seven strings, and a set of sympathetic strings. It was held under the chin when played.
▷HISTORY C18: from Italian, literally: viol of love

violate ('vaɪə,leɪt) VERB *(tr)* [1] to break, disregard, or infringe (a law, agreement, etc.). [2] to rape or otherwise sexually assault. [3] to disturb rudely or improperly; break in upon. [4] to treat irreverently or disrespectfully; outrage: *he violated a sanctuary.* [5] *Obsolete* to mistreat physically. ◆ ADJECTIVE [6] *Archaic* violated or dishonoured.
▷HISTORY C15: from Latin *violāre* to do violence to, from *vīs* strength
▸ **'violable** ADJECTIVE ▸ **,viola'bility** *or* **'violableness** NOUN ▸ **'violably** ADVERB ▸ **,vio'lation** NOUN ▸ **'violative** ADJECTIVE ▸ **'vio,lator** *or* **'vio'later** NOUN

violence ('vaɪələns) NOUN [1] the exercise or an instance of physical force, usually effecting or intended to effect injuries, destruction, etc. [2] powerful, untamed, or devastating force: *the violence of the sea.* [3] great strength of feeling, as in language, etc.; fervour. [4] an unjust, unwarranted, or unlawful display of force, esp such as tends to overawe or intimidate. [5] **do violence to. a** to inflict harm upon; damage or violate: *they did violence to the prisoners.* **b** to distort or twist the sense or intention of: *the reporters did violence to my speech.*
▷HISTORY C13: via Old French from Latin *violentia* impetuosity, from *violentus* VIOLENT

violent ('vaɪələnt) ADJECTIVE [1] marked or caused by great physical force or violence: *a violent stab.* [2] (of a person) tending to the use of violence, esp in order to injure or intimidate others. [3] marked by intensity of any kind: *a violent clash of colours.* [4] characterized by an undue use of force; severe; harsh. [5] caused by or displaying strong or undue mental or emotional force: *a violent tongue.* [6] tending to distort the meaning or intent: *a violent interpretation of the text.*
▷HISTORY C14: from Latin *violentus,* probably from *vīs* strength
▸ **'violently** ADVERB

violent storm NOUN a wind of force 11 on the Beaufort scale, reaching speeds of 64–72 mph.

violet ('vaɪəlɪt) NOUN [1] any of various temperate perennial herbaceous plants of the violaceous genus *Viola,* such as *V. odorata* (**sweet** (or **garden**) **violet**), typically having mauve or bluish flowers with irregular showy petals. [2] any other plant of the genus *Viola,* such as the wild pansy. [3] any of various similar but unrelated plants, such as the African violet. [4] **a** any of a group of colours that vary in saturation but have the same purplish-blue hue. They lie at one end of the visible spectrum, next to blue; approximate wavelength range 445–390 nanometres. **b** *(as adjective)*: *a violet dress.* [5] a dye or pigment of or producing these colours. [6] violet clothing: *dressed in violet.* [7] **shrinking violet.** *Informal* a shy person.
▷HISTORY C14: from Old French *violete* a little violet, from *viole,* from Latin *viola* violet
▸ **'violet-,like** ADJECTIVE

violin (ˌvaɪəˈlɪn) NOUN a bowed stringed instrument, the highest member of the violin family, consisting of a fingerboard, a hollow wooden body with waisted sides, and a sounding board connected to the back by means of a soundpost that also supports the bridge. It has two f-shaped sound holes cut in the belly. The instrument, noted for its fine and flexible tone, is the most important of the stringed instruments. It is held under the chin when played. Range: roughly three and a half octaves upwards from G below middle C.
▷HISTORY C16: from Italian *violino* a little viola, from VIOLA[1]

violinist (ˌvaɪəˈlɪnɪst) NOUN a person who plays the violin.

violist[1] (vɪˈəʊlɪst) NOUN *US* a person who plays the viola.

violist[2] (ˈvaɪəlɪst) NOUN a person who plays the viol.

violoncello (ˌvaɪələnˈtʃɛləʊ) NOUN, *plural* **-los**. the full name for **cello**.
▷HISTORY C18: from Italian, from VIOLONE + *-cello*, diminutive suffix
▸ ˌ**violonˈcellist** NOUN

violone (ˈvaɪəˌləʊn) NOUN the double-bass member of the viol family lying an octave below the viola da gamba. It corresponds to the double bass in the violin family.
▷HISTORY C18: from Italian, from VIOLA[1] + *-one*, augmentative suffix

VIP ABBREVIATION FOR: 1 very important person. 2 visually impaired person. 3 vasoactive intestinal peptide: a polypeptide secreted by the small intestine during digestion and also found in the brain as a neurotransmitter: large amounts in the blood cause diarrhoea.

viper (ˈvaɪpə) NOUN 1 any venomous Old World snake of the family *Viperidae*, esp any of the genus *Vipera* (the adder and related forms), having hollow fangs in the upper jaw that are used to inject venom. 2 any of various other snakes, such as the horned viper. 3 See **pit viper.** 4 a malicious or treacherous person.
▷HISTORY C16: from Latin *vīpera*, perhaps from *vīvus* living + *parere* to bear, referring to a tradition that the viper was viviparous
▸ ˈ**viper-ˌlike** ADJECTIVE

viperous (ˈvaɪpərəs) *or* **viperish** ADJECTIVE 1 Also: **viperine** (ˈvaɪpəˌraɪn). of, relating to, or resembling a viper. 2 malicious.
▸ ˈ**viperously** *or* ˈ**viperishly** ADVERB

viper's bugloss NOUN 1 Also called (US): **blueweed.** a Eurasian boraginaceous weed, *Echium vulgare*, having blue flowers and pink buds. 2 Also called: (Austral) **Paterson's curse,** (South Australia) **Salvation Jane.** a related plant, *E. plantagineum*, that has purple flowers and is naturalized in Australia and New Zealand. See also **echium.**

VIR ABBREVIATION FOR Victoria Imperatrix Regina.
▷HISTORY Latin: Victoria, Empress and Queen

viraemia *or US* **viremia** (vaɪˈriːmɪə) NOUN a condition in which virus particles circulate and reproduce in the bloodstream.

virago (vɪˈrɑːgəʊ) NOUN, *plural* **-goes** *or* **-gos.** 1 a loud, violent, and ill-tempered woman; scold; shrew. 2 *Archaic* a strong, brave, or warlike woman; amazon.
▷HISTORY Old English, from Latin: a manlike maiden, from *vir* a man
▸ **viraginous** (vɪˈrædʒɪnəs) ADJECTIVE ▸ **viˈrago-ˌlike** ADJECTIVE

viral (ˈvaɪrəl) ADJECTIVE of, relating to, or caused by a virus.

viral marketing NOUN 1 a direct marketing technique in which a company persuades Internet users to forward its publicity material in E-mails (usually by including jokes, games, video clips, etc.). 2 a marketing strategy in which conventional media are eschewed in favour of various techniques designed to generate word-of-mouth publicity, in the hope of creating a fad or craze.

Vir Chakra (ˈviːr ˈtʃʌkrə) NOUN an award made to distinguished soldiers by the Government of India.
▷HISTORY Hindi: *vir* brave man + *chakra* wheel

virelay (ˈvɪrɪˌleɪ) NOUN 1 an old French verse form, rarely used in English, consisting of short lines arranged in stanzas having only two rhymes, and two opening lines recurring at intervals. 2 any of various similar forms.
▷HISTORY C14: from Old French *virelai*, probably from *vireli* (associated with *lai* LAY[4]), meaningless word used as a refrain

virement (ˈvaɪəmənt, ˈvɪəmɑ̃) NOUN an administrative transfer of funds from one part of a budget to another.
▷HISTORY from French, from Middle French: act of turning, from *virer* to turn

viremia (vaɪˈriːmɪə) NOUN the usual US spelling of **viraemia.**

vireo (ˈvɪrɪəʊ) NOUN, *plural* **vireos.** any insectivorous American songbird of the family *Vireonidae*, esp those of the genus *Vireo*, having an olive-grey back with pale underparts.
▷HISTORY C19: from Latin: a bird, probably a greenfinch; compare *virēre* to be green

virescence (vɪˈrɛsəns) NOUN 1 (in plants) the process of becoming green, esp by the action of disease, etc., in parts not normally green. 2 the condition of being or the process of becoming green.
▷HISTORY C19: see VIRESCENT

virescent (vɪˈrɛsᵊnt) ADJECTIVE greenish or becoming green.
▷HISTORY C19: from Latin *virescere* to grow green, from *virēre* to be green

virga (ˈvɜːgə) NOUN (*sometimes functioning as plural*) *Meteorol* wisps of rain or snow, seen trailing from clouds, that evaporate before reaching the earth.
▷HISTORY C20: from Latin: streak

virgate[1] (ˈvɜːgɪt, -geɪt) ADJECTIVE long, straight, and thin; rod-shaped: *virgate stems.*
▷HISTORY C19: from Latin *virgātus* made of twigs, from *virga* a rod

virgate[2] (ˈvɜːgɪt, -geɪt) NOUN *Brit* an obsolete measure of land area, usually taken as equivalent to 30 acres.
▷HISTORY C17: from Medieval Latin *virgāta* (*terrae*) a rod's measurement (of land), from Latin *virga* rod; the phrase is a translation of Old English *gierd landes* a yard of land

Virgilian *or* **Vergilian** (vəˈdʒɪlɪən) ADJECTIVE of or relating to Virgil (Latin name *Publius Vergilius Maro.*), the Roman poet (70–19 B.C.).

virgin (ˈvɜːdʒɪn) NOUN 1 a person, esp a woman, who has never had sexual intercourse. 2 an unmarried woman who has taken a religious vow of chastity in order to dedicate herself totally to God. 3 any female animal that has never mated. 4 a female insect that produces offspring by parthenogenesis. 5 a person who is new to or inexperienced in a specified field: *a political virgin.* ◆ ADJECTIVE (*usually prenominal*) 6 of, relating to, resembling, suitable for, or characteristic of a virgin or virgins; chaste. 7 pure and natural, uncorrupted, unsullied, or untouched: *virgin purity.* 8 not yet cultivated, explored, exploited, etc., by man: *virgin territories.* 9 being the first or happening for the first time. 10 (of vegetable oils) obtained directly by the first pressing of fruits, leaves, or seeds of plants without applying heat. 11 (of a metal) made from an ore rather than from scrap. 12 occurring naturally in a pure and uncombined form: *virgin silver.* 13 *Physics* (of a neutron) not having experienced a collision.
▷HISTORY C13: from Old French *virgine*, from Latin *virgō* virgin

Virgin[1] (ˈvɜːdʒɪn) NOUN 1 **the.** See **Virgin Mary.** 2 a statue or other artistic representation of the Virgin Mary.

Virgin[2] (ˈvɜːdʒɪn) NOUN **the.** the constellation Virgo, the sixth sign of the zodiac.

virginal[1] (ˈvɜːdʒɪnᵊl) ADJECTIVE 1 of, relating to, characterized by, proper to, or maintaining a state of virginity; chaste. 2 extremely pure or fresh; untouched; undefiled.
▷HISTORY C15: from Latin *virginālis* maidenly, from *virgō* virgin
▸ ˈ**virginally** ADVERB

virginal[2] (ˈvɜːdʒɪnᵊl) NOUN (*often plural*) a smaller version of the harpsichord, but oblong in shape, having one manual and no pedals.
▷HISTORY C16: probably from Latin *virginālis* VIRGINAL[1], perhaps because it was played largely by young ladies
▸ ˈ**virginalist** NOUN

virgin birth NOUN another name for **parthenogenesis** (sense 2).

Virgin Birth NOUN the doctrine that Jesus Christ had no human father but was conceived solely by the direct intervention of the Holy Spirit so that Mary remained miraculously a virgin during and after his birth.

virgin forest NOUN a forest in its natural state, before it has been explored or exploited by man.

Virginia[1] (vəˈdʒɪnɪə) NOUN (*sometimes not capital*) a type of flue-cured tobacco grown originally in Virginia.

Virginia[2] (vəˈdʒɪnɪə) NOUN a state of the eastern US, on the Atlantic: site of the first permanent English settlement in North America; consists of a low-lying deeply indented coast rising inland to the Piedmont plateau and the Blue Ridge Mountains. Capital: Richmond. Pop.: 7 078 515 (1997 est.). Area: 103 030 sq. km (39 780 sq. miles). Abbreviations: **Va,** (with zip code) **VA.**

Virginia creeper NOUN 1 Also called (US): **American ivy, woodbine.** a vitaceous woody vine, *Parthenocissus quinquefolia*, of North America, having tendrils with adhesive tips, bluish-black berry-like fruits, and compound leaves that turn red in autumn: widely planted for ornament. 2 Also called: **Japanese ivy.** a similar related plant, *Parthenocissus tricuspidata*, of SE Asia, having trilobed leaves and purple berries. US name: **Boston ivy.**

Virginia deer NOUN another name for **white-tailed deer.**

Virginian (vəˈdʒɪnɪən) ADJECTIVE 1 of or relating to Virginia or its inhabitants. ◆ NOUN 2 a native or inhabitant of Virginia.

Virginia reel NOUN 1 an American country dance. 2 music written for or in the manner of this dance.

Virginia stock NOUN a Mediterranean plant, *Malcolmia maritima*, cultivated for its white and pink flowers: family *Brassicaceae* (crucifers).

Virgin Islands PLURAL NOUN a group of about 100 small islands (14 inhabited) in the Caribbean, east of Puerto Rico: discovered by Columbus (1493); consists of the British Virgin Islands in the east and the Virgin Islands of the United States in the west and south. Pop.: 141 000 (1999 est.). Area: 497 sq. km (192 sq. miles).

Virgin Islands of the United States PLURAL NOUN a territory of the US in the Caribbean, consisting of islands west and south of the British Virgin Islands: purchased from Denmark in 1917 for their strategic importance. Capital: Charlotte Amalie. Pop.: 122 000 (2001 est.). Area: 344 sq. km (133 sq. miles). Former name: **Danish West Indies.**

virginity (vəˈdʒɪnɪtɪ) NOUN 1 the condition or fact of being a virgin; maidenhood; chastity. 2 the condition of being untouched, unsullied, etc.

virginium (vəˈdʒɪnɪəm) NOUN *Chem* a former name for **francium.**

Virgin Mary NOUN Mary, the mother of Christ. Also called: **the Virgin.**

virgin's-bower NOUN any of several American clematis plants, esp *Clematis virginiana*, of E North America, which has clusters of small white flowers.

virgin soil NOUN 1 soil that has not been cultivated before. 2 a person or thing that is as yet undeveloped.

virgin wool NOUN wool that is being processed or woven for the first time.

Virgo (ˈvɜːgəʊ) NOUN, *Latin genitive* **Virginis** (ˈvɜːdʒɪnɪs). 1 *Astronomy* a large zodiacal constellation on the celestial equator, lying between Leo and Libra. It contains the star Spica and a cluster of several thousand galaxies, the **Virgo cluster,** lying 50 million light years away and itself containing the intense radio source Virgo A, which is the closest active galaxy. 2 *Astrology* **a** Also called: **the Virgin.** the sixth sign of the zodiac, symbol ♍, having a mutable earth classification and ruled by the planet Mercury. The sun is in this sign between about Aug. 23 and Sept. 22. **b** Also called: **Virgoan** (vɜːˈgəʊən). a person born when the sun is in this sign. ◆ ADJECTIVE 3 Also: **Virgoan.** *Astrology* born under or characteristic of Virgo.

▷HISTORY C14: from Latin

virgo intacta ('vɜːɡəʊ ɪn'tæktə) NOUN a girl or woman whose hymen has not been broken.
▷HISTORY Latin, literally: untouched virgin

virgulate ('vɜːɡjʊlɪt, -ˌleɪt) ADJECTIVE rod-shaped or rodlike.
▷HISTORY C19: from Latin *virgula* a little rod, from *virga* rod

virgule ('vɜːɡjuːl) NOUN *Printing* another name for **solidus.**
▷HISTORY C19: from French: comma, from Latin *virgula* a little rod, from *virga* rod

viridescent (ˌvɪrɪ'dɛsᵊnt) ADJECTIVE greenish or tending to become green.
▷HISTORY C19: from Late Latin *viridescere* to grow green, from Latin *viridis* green
▸ˌ**viri'descence** NOUN

viridian (vɪ'rɪdɪən) NOUN a green pigment consisting of a hydrated form of chromic oxide.
▷HISTORY C19: from Latin *viridis* green

viridity (vɪ'rɪdɪtɪ) NOUN 1 the quality or state of being green; greenness; verdancy. 2 innocence, youth, or freshness.
▷HISTORY C15: from Latin *viriditās,* from *viridis* green

virile ('vɪraɪl) ADJECTIVE 1 of, relating to, or having the characteristics of an adult male. 2 (of a male) possessing high sexual drive and capacity for sexual intercourse. 3 of or capable of copulation or procreation. 4 strong, forceful, or vigorous.
▷HISTORY C15: from Latin *virīlis* manly, from *vir* a man; related to Old English *wer* man and probably to Latin *vis* strength
▸**virility** (vɪ'rɪlɪtɪ) NOUN

virilism ('vɪrɪˌlɪzəm) NOUN *Med* the abnormal development in a woman of male secondary sex characteristics.

virilization *or* **virilisation** (ˌvɪrɪlaɪ'zeɪʃən) NOUN the development of adult male physical characteristics in a female or a young boy.

virino (vɪ'riːnəʊ) NOUN an entity postulated to be the causative agent of BSE and related diseases, said to consist of a fragment of nucleic acid surrounded by a protein coat derived from the host cell.
▷HISTORY C20: from VIRUS + *-ino* diminutive form

virion ('vaɪrɪən) NOUN a virus in infective form, consisting of an RNA particle within a protein covering.
▷HISTORY C20: from VIR(US) + ION

viroid ('vaɪrɔɪd) NOUN any of various infective RNA particles, smaller than a virus and known to cause some plant diseases.
▷HISTORY C20: from VIR(US) + -OID

virology (vaɪ'rɒlədʒɪ) NOUN the branch of medicine concerned with the study of viruses and the diseases they cause.
▸**virological** (ˌvaɪrə'lɒdʒɪkᵊl) ADJECTIVE ▸**vi'rologist** NOUN

virtu *or* **vertu** (vɜː'tuː) NOUN 1 a taste or love for curios or works of fine art; connoisseurship. 2 such objects collectively. 3 the quality of being rare, beautiful, or otherwise appealing to a connoisseur (esp in the phrases **articles of virtu; objects of virtu**).
▷HISTORY C18: from Italian *virtù;* see VIRTUE

virtual ('vɜːtʃʊəl) ADJECTIVE 1 having the essence or effect but not the appearance or form of: *a virtual revolution.* 2 *Physics* being, relating to, or involving a virtual image: *a virtual focus.* 3 *Computing* of or relating to virtual storage: *virtual memory.* 4 of or relating to a computer technique by which a person, wearing a headset or mask, has the experience of being in an environment created by the computer, and of interacting with and causing changes in it. 5 *Rare* capable of producing an effect through inherent power or virtue. 6 *Physics* designating or relating to a particle exchanged between other particles that are interacting by a field of force: *a virtual photon.* See also **exchange force.**
▷HISTORY C14: from Medieval Latin *virtuālis* effective, from Latin *virtūs* VIRTUE

virtual human NOUN a computer-generated moving image of a human being, used esp in films as an extra in large crowd scenes.

virtual image NOUN an optical image formed by the apparent divergence of rays from a point, rather than their actual divergence from a point.

virtuality (ˌvɜːtjʊ'ælɪtɪ) NOUN virtual reality.

virtually ('vɜːtʃʊəlɪ) ADVERB in effect though not in fact; practically; nearly.

virtual reality NOUN a computer-generated environment that, to the person experiencing it, closely resembles reality. Abbreviation: **VR.** See also **virtual** (sense 4).

virtual storage *or* **memory** NOUN a computer system in which the size of the memory is effectively increased by automatically transferring sections of a program from a large capacity backing store, such as a disk, into the smaller core memory as they are required.

virtue ('vɜːtjuː, -tʃuː) NOUN 1 the quality or practice of moral excellence or righteousness. 2 a particular moral excellence: *the virtue of tolerance.* 3 any of the cardinal virtues (prudence, justice, fortitude, and temperance) or theological virtues (faith, hope, and charity). 4 any admirable quality, feature, or trait. 5 chastity, esp in women. 6 *Archaic* an effective, active, or inherent power or force. 7 **by** *or* **in virtue of.** on account of or by reason of. 8 **make a virtue of necessity.** to acquiesce in doing something unpleasant with a show of grace because one must do it in any case.
▷HISTORY C13 *vertu,* from Old French, from Latin *virtūs* manliness, courage, from *vir* man
▸'**virtueless** ADJECTIVE

virtues ('vɜːtjuːz, -tʃuːz) PLURAL NOUN *(often capital)* the fifth of the nine orders into which the angels are traditionally divided in medieval angelology.

virtuoso (ˌvɜːtjʊ'əʊzəʊ, -səʊ) NOUN, *plural* **-sos** *or* **-si** (-siː). 1 a consummate master of musical technique and artistry. 2 a person who has a masterly or dazzling skill or technique in any field of activity. 3 a connoisseur, dilettante, or collector of art objects. 4 *Obsolete* a scholar or savant. 5 *(modifier)* showing masterly skill or brilliance: *a virtuoso performance.*
▷HISTORY C17: from Italian: skilled, from Late Latin *virtuōsus* good, virtuous; see VIRTUE
▸**virtuosic** (ˌvɜːtjʊ'ɒsɪk) ADJECTIVE ▸ˌ**virtu'osity** NOUN

virtuous ('vɜːtʃʊəs) ADJECTIVE 1 characterized by or possessing virtue or moral excellence; righteous; upright. 2 (of women) chaste or virginal.
▸'**virtuously** ADVERB ▸'**virtuousness** NOUN

virulence ('vɪrʊləns) *or* **virulency** NOUN 1 the quality of being virulent. 2 the capacity of a microorganism for causing disease.

virulent ('vɪrʊlənt) ADJECTIVE 1 **a** (of a microorganism) extremely infective. **b** (of a disease) having a rapid course and violent effect. 2 extremely poisonous, injurious, etc. 3 extremely bitter, hostile, etc.
▷HISTORY C14: from Latin *vīrulentus* full of poison, from *vīrus* poison; see VIRUS
▸'**virulently** ADVERB

virus ('vaɪrəs) NOUN, *plural* **-ruses.** 1 any of a group of submicroscopic entities consisting of a single nucleic acid chain surrounded by a protein coat and capable of replication only within the cells of living organisms: many are pathogenic. 2 *Informal* a disease caused by a virus. 3 any corrupting or infecting influence. 4 *Computing* an unauthorized program that inserts itself into a computer system and then propagates itself to other computers via networks or disks; when activated it interferes with the operation of the computer.
▷HISTORY C16: from Latin: slime, poisonous liquid; related to Old English *wāse* marsh, Greek *ios* poison
▸'**virus-ˌlike** ADJECTIVE

vis *Latin* (vɪs) NOUN, *plural* ***vires*** ('vaɪriːz). power, force, or strength.

Vis. ABBREVIATION FOR Viscount *or* Viscountess.

visa ('viːzə) NOUN, *plural* **-sas.** 1 an endorsement in a passport or similar document, signifying that the document is in order and permitting its bearer to travel into or through the country of the government issuing it. 2 any sign or signature of approval. ◆ VERB **-sas, -saing, -saed.** *(tr)* 3 to enter a visa into (a passport). 4 to endorse or ratify.
▷HISTORY C19: via French from Latin *vīsa* things seen, from *vīsus,* past participle of *vidēre* to see

visage ('vɪzɪdʒ) NOUN *Chiefly literary* 1 face or countenance. 2 appearance; aspect.
▷HISTORY C13: from Old French: aspect, from *vis* face, from Latin *vīsus* appearance, from *vidēre* to see

-visaged ADJECTIVE *(in combination)* having a visage as specified: *flat-visaged.*

visagiste (ˌviːzɑː'ʒiːst) NOUN a person who designs and applies face make-up; make-up artist.
▷HISTORY C20: from French, from *visage* face + *-iste* -ist

vis-à-vis (ˌviːzɑː'viː) PREPOSITION 1 in relation to; regarding. 2 face to face with; opposite. ◆ ADVERB, ADJECTIVE 3 face to face; opposite. ◆ NOUN, *plural* **vis-à-vis.** 4 a person or thing that is situated opposite to another. 5 a person who corresponds to another in office, capacity, etc.; counterpart. 6 an upholstered sofa; tête-à-tête. 7 a type of horse-drawn carriage in which the passengers sit opposite one another. 8 a coin having an obverse upon which two portraits appear facing each other.
▷HISTORY C18: French, from *vis* face

Visayan (vɪ'sɑːjən) *or* **Bisayan** NOUN, *plural* **-yans** *or* **-yan.** 1 a member of the most numerous indigenous people of the Philippines. ◆ ADJECTIVE 2 of or relating to this people.

Visayan Islands PLURAL NOUN a group of seven large and several hundred small islands in the central Philippines. Chief islands: Negros and Panay. Pop.: 13 041 000 (1990). Area: about 61 000 sq. km (23 535 sq. miles). Spanish name: **Bisayas.**

Visc. ABBREVIATION FOR Viscount *or* Viscountess.

viscacha *or* **vizcacha** (vɪs'kætʃə) NOUN 1 a gregarious burrowing hystricomorph rodent, *Lagostomus maximus,* of southern South America, similar to but larger than the chinchillas: family *Chinchillidae.* 2 **mountain viscacha.** another name for **mountain chinchilla** (see **chinchilla** (sense 3)).
▷HISTORY C17: from Spanish, from Quechuan *wiskácha*

viscaria (vɪs'kɛərɪə) NOUN any plant of the Eurasian perennial genus *Viscaria,* closely related to genus *Lychnis,* in which it is sometimes included: low-growing, with pink, white, or purple flowers: family *Carophyllaceae.*
▷HISTORY New Latin, from *viscum* birdlime (from the viscid stems)

viscera ('vɪsərə) PLURAL NOUN, *singular* **viscus** ('vɪskəs). 1 *Anatomy* the large internal organs of the body collectively, esp those in the abdominal cavity. Related adjective: **splanchnic.** 2 (less formally) the intestines; guts.
▷HISTORY C17: from Latin: entrails, pl of *viscus* internal organ

visceral ('vɪsərəl) ADJECTIVE 1 of, relating to, or affecting the viscera. 2 characterized by intuition or instinct rather than intellect.
▸'**viscerally** ADVERB

visceromotor ('vɪsərəʊˌməʊtə) ADJECTIVE *Physiol* relating to or controlling movements of the viscera.

viscerotonia (ˌvɪsərəʊ'təʊnɪə) NOUN a personality type characterized by hedonism and conviviality: said to be correlated with an endomorph body type. Compare **cerebrotonia, somatotonia.**

viscid ('vɪsɪd) ADJECTIVE 1 cohesive and sticky; glutinous; viscous. 2 (esp of a leaf) covered with a sticky substance.
▷HISTORY C17: from Late Latin *viscidus* sticky, from Latin *viscum* mistletoe or birdlime
▸**vis'cidity** *or* '**viscidness** NOUN ▸'**viscidly** ADVERB

viscoelastic (ˌvɪskəʊɪ'læstɪk) ADJECTIVE *Physics* (of a solid or liquid) exhibiting both viscous and elastic behaviour when deformed.
▸ˌ**viscoelas'ticity** NOUN

viscoid ('vɪskɔɪd) *or* **viscoidal** (vɪs'kɔɪdᵊl) ADJECTIVE (of a fluid) somewhat viscous.

viscometer (vɪs'kɒmɪtə) *or* **viscosimeter** (ˌvɪskəʊ'sɪmɪtə) NOUN any device for measuring viscosity.
▸**viscometric** (ˌvɪskə'mɛtrɪk) *or* ˌ**visco'metrical** ADJECTIVE
▸**vis'cometry** NOUN

viscose ('vɪskəʊs) NOUN 1 **a** a viscous orange-brown solution obtained by dissolving cellulose in sodium hydroxide and carbon disulphide. It can be converted back to cellulose by an acid, as in the manufacture of rayon and cellophane. **b** *(as modifier)*: *viscose rayon.* 2 rayon made from this material. ◆ ADJECTIVE 3 another word for **viscous.**

▹HISTORY C19: from Late Latin *viscōsus* full of birdlime, sticky, from *viscum* birdlime; see VISCID

viscosity (vɪs'kɒsɪtɪ) NOUN, *plural* **-ties.** [1] the state or property of being viscous. [2] *Physics* **a** the extent to which a fluid resists a tendency to flow. **b** Also called: **absolute viscosity.** a measure of this resistance, equal to the tangential stress on a liquid undergoing streamline flow divided by its velocity gradient. It is measured in newton seconds per metre squared. Symbol: η. See also **kinematic viscosity, specific viscosity.**

viscount ('vaɪkaʊnt) NOUN [1] (in the British Isles) a nobleman ranking below an earl and above a baron. [2] (in various countries) a son or younger brother of a count. See also **vicomte.** [3] (in medieval Europe) the deputy of a count.
▹HISTORY C14: from Old French *visconte,* from Medieval Latin *vicecomes,* from Late Latin *vice-* VICE[3] + *comes* COUNT[2]

viscountcy ('vaɪkaʊntsɪ) *or* **viscounty** NOUN the rank or position of a viscount.

viscountess ('vaɪkaʊntɪs) NOUN [1] the wife or widow of a viscount. [2] a woman who holds the rank of viscount in her own right.

viscous ('vɪskəs) *or* **viscose** ADJECTIVE [1] (of liquids) thick and sticky; viscid. [2] having or involving viscosity.
▹HISTORY C14: from Late Latin *viscōsus;* see VISCOSE
▸**'viscously** ADVERB ▸**'viscousness** NOUN

viscous flow NOUN another name for **streamline flow.**

viscus ('vɪskəs) NOUN the singular of **viscera.**

vise (vaɪs) NOUN, VERB *US* a variant spelling of **vice[2]**.

Vishnu ('vɪʃnuː) NOUN *Hinduism* the Pervader or Sustainer, originally a solar deity occupying a secondary place in the Hindu pantheon, later one of the three chief gods, the second member of the Trimurti, and, later still, the saviour appearing in many incarnations.
▹HISTORY C17: from Sanskrit *Viṣṇu,* literally: the one who works everywhere
▸**'Vishnuism** NOUN

visibility (ˌvɪzɪ'bɪlɪtɪ) NOUN [1] the condition or fact of being visible. [2] clarity of vision or relative possibility of seeing. [3] the range of vision: *visibility is 500 yards.*

visible ('vɪzɪb^{ə}l) ADJECTIVE [1] capable of being perceived by the eye. [2] capable of being perceived by the mind; evident: *no visible dangers.* [3] available: *the visible resources.* [4] (of an index or file) using a flexible display system for the contents. [5] of or relating to the balance of trade: *visible transactions.* [6] represented by visible symbols. ◆ NOUN [7] a visible item of trade; product.
▹HISTORY C14: from Latin *vīsibilis,* from *vidēre* to see
▸**'visibleness** NOUN ▸**'visibly** ADVERB

visible balance NOUN another name for **balance of trade.**

visible radiation NOUN electromagnetic radiation that causes the sensation of sight; light. It has wavelengths between about 380 and 780 nanometres.

visible speech NOUN a system of phonetic notation invented by Alexander Melville Bell (1819–1905) that utilized symbols based on the schematic representation of the articulations used for each speech sound.

Visigoth ('vɪzɪˌgɒθ) NOUN a member of the western group of the Goths, who were driven into the Balkans in the late 4th century A.D. Moving on, they sacked Rome (410) and established a kingdom in present-day Spain and S France that lasted until 711.
▹HISTORY C17: from Late Latin *Visigothī* (pl), of Germanic origin, *visi-* perhaps meaning: west
▸ˌ**Visi'gothic** ADJECTIVE

vision ('vɪʒən) NOUN [1] the act, faculty, or manner of perceiving with the eye; sight. [2] **a** the image on a television screen. **b** (*as modifier*): *vision control.* [3] the ability or an instance of great perception, esp of future developments: *a man of vision.* [4] a mystical or religious experience of seeing some supernatural event, person, etc.: *the vision of St John of the Cross.* [5] that which is seen, esp in such a mystical experience. [6] (*sometimes plural*) a vivid mental image produced by the imagination: *he had visions of becoming famous.* [7] a person or thing of extraordinary beauty. [8] the stated aims and objectives of a business or other organization. ◆ VERB [9] (*tr*) to see or show in or as if in a vision.
▹HISTORY C13: from Latin *vīsiō* sight, from *vidēre* to see
▸**'visionless** ADJECTIVE

visional ('vɪʒən^{ə}l) ADJECTIVE of, relating to, or seen in a vision, apparition, etc.
▸**'visionally** ADVERB

visionary ('vɪʒənərɪ) ADJECTIVE [1] marked by vision or foresight: *a visionary leader.* [2] incapable of being realized or effected; unrealistic. [3] (of people) characterized by idealistic or radical ideas, esp impractical ones. [4] given to having visions. [5] of, of the nature of, or seen in visions. ◆ NOUN, *plural* **-aries.** [6] a visionary person.
▸**'visionariness** NOUN

vision mixer NOUN *Television* [1] the person who selects and manipulates the television signals from cameras, film, and other sources, to make the composite programme. [2] the equipment used for vision mixing.

visit ('vɪzɪt) VERB **-its, -iting, -ited.** [1] to go or come to see (a person, place, etc.). [2] to stay with (someone) as a guest. [3] to go or come to (an institution, place, etc.) for the purpose of inspecting or examining. [4] (*tr*) (of a disease, disaster, etc.) to assail; afflict. [5] (*tr;* foll by *upon* or *on*) to inflict (punishment, etc.): *the judge visited his full anger upon the defendant.* [6] (*tr;* usually foll by *with*) *Archaic* to afflict or plague (with punishment, etc.). [7] (often foll by *with*) *US and Canadian informal* to chat or converse (with someone). ◆ NOUN [8] the act or an instance of visiting. [9] a stay as a guest. [10] a professional or official call. [11] a formal call for the purpose of inspection or examination. [12] *International law* the right of an officer of a belligerent state to stop and search neutral ships in war to verify their nationality and ascertain whether they carry contraband: *the right of visit and search.* [13] *US and Canadian informal* a friendly talk or chat.
▹HISTORY C13: from Latin *vīsitāre* to go to see, from *vīsere* to examine, from *vidēre* to see
▸**'visitable** ADJECTIVE

visitant ('vɪzɪtənt) NOUN [1] a supernatural being; ghost; apparition. [2] a visitor or guest, usually from far away. [3] a pilgrim or tourist. [4] Also called: **visitor.** a migratory bird that is present in a particular region only at certain times: *a summer visitant.* ◆ ADJECTIVE [5] *Archaic* paying a visit; visiting.
▹HISTORY C16: from Latin *vīsitāns* going to see, from *vīsitāre;* see VISIT

visitation (ˌvɪzɪ'teɪʃən) NOUN [1] an official call or visit for the purpose of inspecting or examining an institution, esp such a visit made by a bishop to his diocese. [2] a visiting of punishment or reward from heaven. [3] any disaster or catastrophe: *a visitation of the plague.* [4] an appearance or arrival of a supernatural being. [5] any call or visit. [6] *Informal* an unduly prolonged social call.
▸ˌ**visit'ational** ADJECTIVE

Visitation (ˌvɪzɪ'teɪʃən) NOUN [1] **a** the visit made by the Virgin Mary to her cousin Elizabeth (Luke 1:39–56). **b** the Church festival commemorating this, held on July 2. [2] a religious order of nuns, the **Order of the Visitation,** founded in 1610 by St Francis of Sales and dedicated to contemplation and the cultivation of humility, gentleness, and sisterly love.

visitatorial (ˌvɪzɪtə'tɔːrɪəl) *or* **visitorial** ADJECTIVE [1] of, relating to, or for an official visitation or visitor. [2] empowered to make official visitations.

visiting card NOUN another term for **calling card.**

visiting fireman NOUN *US informal* a visitor whose presence is noticed because he is an important figure, a lavish spender, etc.

visiting nurse NOUN (in the US) a registered nurse employed by a community, hospital, etc., to visit and nurse the sick in their homes or to promote public health.

visiting professor NOUN a professor invited to teach in a college or university other than his own, often in another country, for a certain period, such as a term or year.

visitor ('vɪzɪtə) NOUN [1] a person who pays a visit; caller, guest, tourist, etc. [2] another name for **visitant** (sense 4).
▸ˌ**visi'torial** ADJECTIVE

visitor centre NOUN another term for **interpretive centre.**

visitor's passport NOUN (formerly, in Britain) a passport, valid for one year and for certain countries only, that could be purchased from post offices. Also called: **British Visitor's Passport.**

vis major ('vɪs 'meɪdʒə) NOUN See **force majeure.**
▹HISTORY from Latin, literally: greater force

visor *or* **vizor** ('vaɪzə) NOUN [1] a transparent flap on a helmet that can be pulled down to protect the face. [2] a piece of armour fixed or hinged to the helmet to protect the face and with slits for the eyes. [3] another name for **peak** (on a cap). [4] a small movable screen used as protection against glare from the sun, esp one attached above the windscreen of a motor vehicle. [5] *Archaic or literary* a mask or any other means of disguise or concealment. ◆ VERB [6] (*tr*) to cover, provide, or protect with a visor; shield.
▹HISTORY C14: from Anglo-French *viser,* from Old French *visiere,* from *vis* face; see VISAGE
▸**'visored** *or* **'vizored** ADJECTIVE ▸**'visorless** *or* **'vizorless** ADJECTIVE

vista ('vɪstə) NOUN [1] a view, esp through a long narrow avenue of trees, buildings, etc., or such a passage or avenue itself; prospect: *a vista of arches.* [2] a comprehensive mental view of a distant time or a lengthy series of events: *the vista of the future.*
▹HISTORY C17: from Italian: a view, from *vedere* to see, from Latin *vidēre*
▸**'vistaed** ADJECTIVE ▸**'vistaless** ADJECTIVE

VISTA ('vɪstə) NOUN (in the US) ◆ ACRONYM FOR Volunteers in Service to America; an organization of volunteers established by the Federal government to assist the poor.

Vistula ('vɪstjʊlə) NOUN [1] a river in central and N Poland, rising in the Carpathian Mountains and flowing generally north and northwest past Warsaw and Torun, then northeast to enter the Baltic via an extensive delta region. Length: 1090 km (677 miles). Polish name: **Wisla.** German name: **Weichsel.** [2] **Lagoon.** a shallow lagoon on the SW coast of the Baltic Sea, between Danzig and Kaliningrad, crossed by the border between Poland and Russia. German name: **Frisches Haff.** Polish name: **Wislany Zalew.** Russian name: **Vislinsky Zaliv.**

visual ('vɪʒʊəl, -zjʊ-) ADJECTIVE [1] of, relating to, done by, or used in seeing: *visual powers; visual steering.* [2] another word for **optical.** [3] capable of being seen; visible. [4] of, occurring as, or induced by a mental image. ◆ NOUN [5] a sketch to show the proposed layout of an advertisement, as in a newspaper. [6] (*often plural*) a photograph, film, or other display material.
▹HISTORY C15: from Late Latin *vīsuālis,* from Latin *vīsus* sight, from *vidēre* to see
▸**'visually** ADVERB

visual aids PLURAL NOUN devices, such as films, slides, models, and blackboards, that display in visual form material to be understood or remembered.

visual angle NOUN the angle subtended by an object at the lens of the eye.

visual arts PLURAL NOUN the arts of painting, sculpting, photography, etc., as opposed to music, drama, and literature.

visual display unit NOUN *Computing* a device with a screen that displays characters or graphics representing data in a computer memory. It usually has a keyboard or light pen for the input of information or inquiries. Abbreviation: **VDU.**

visual field NOUN the whole extent of the image falling on the retina when the eye is fixating a given point in space.

visualization *or* **visualisation** (ˌvɪʒʊəlaɪ'zeɪʃən, -zjʊ-) NOUN [1] the act or an instance of visualizing. [2] a technique involving focusing on positive mental images in order to achieve a particular goal.

visualize *or* **visualise** ('vɪʒʊəˌlaɪz, -zjʊ-) VERB [1] to form a mental image of (something incapable of being viewed or not at that moment visible). [2] *Med* to view by means of an X-ray the outline of (a bodily organ, structure, or part).
▸**'visualˌizer** *or* **'visualˌiser** NOUN

visually handicapped ADJECTIVE **a** unable to carry out normal activities because of defects of vision, including blindness. **b** (*as collective noun; preceded by the*): *the visually handicapped.*
▸**visual handicap** NOUN

visually impaired ADJECTIVE **a** having any defect of vision, whether disabling or not. **b** (*as collective noun; preceded by the*): *the visually impaired.* ◆ Compare **partially sighted.**
▸**visual impairment** NOUN

visual magnitude NOUN *Astronomy* the magnitude of a star as determined by visual observation. Compare **photoelectric magnitude.**

visual purple NOUN another name for **rhodopsin.**

visual violet NOUN another name for **iodopsin.**

vita ('viːtə, 'vaɪ-) NOUN, *plural* **vitae** ('viːtaɪ, 'vaɪtiː). *US and Canadian* a less common term for **curriculum vitae.**
▷HISTORY from Latin: life

vitaceous (vaɪ'teɪʃəs) ADJECTIVE of, relating to, or belonging to the *Vitaceae,* a family of tropical and subtropical flowering plants having a climbing habit and berry-like fruits: includes the grapevine and Virginia creeper.
▷HISTORY C19: via New Latin *Vītāceae,* from Latin: vine

vital ('vaɪtᵊl) ADJECTIVE 1 essential to maintain life: *the lungs perform a vital function.* 2 forceful, energetic, or lively: *a vital person.* 3 of, relating to, having, or displaying life: *a vital organism.* 4 indispensable or essential: *books vital to this study.* 5 of great importance; decisive: *a vital game.* 6 *Archaic* influencing the course of life, esp negatively: *a vital treachery.* ◆ NOUN 7 (*plural*) **a** the bodily organs, such as the brain, liver, heart, lungs, etc., that are necessary to maintain life. **b** the organs of reproduction, esp the male genitals. 8 (*plural*) the essential elements of anything.
▷HISTORY C14: via Old French from Latin *vītālis* belonging to life, from *vīta* life
▸**'vitally** ADVERB

vital capacity NOUN *Physiol* the volume of air that can be exhaled from the lungs after the deepest possible breath has been taken: a measure of lung function.

vital force NOUN (esp in early biological theory) a hypothetical force, independent of physical and chemical forces, regarded as being the causative factor of the evolution and development of living organisms.

vitalism ('vaɪtəˌlɪzəm) NOUN the philosophical doctrine that the phenomena of life cannot be explained in purely mechanical terms because there is something immaterial which distinguishes living from inanimate matter. Compare **dynamism, mechanism.**
▸**'vitalist** NOUN, ADJECTIVE ▸**ˌvital'istic** ADJECTIVE

vitality (vaɪ'tælɪtɪ) NOUN, *plural* **-ties.** 1 physical or mental vigour, energy, etc. 2 the power or ability to continue in existence, live, or grow: *the vitality of a movement.* 3 a less common name for **vital force.**

vitalize *or* **vitalise** ('vaɪtəˌlaɪz) VERB (*tr*) to make vital, living, or alive; endow with life or vigour.
▸**ˌvitali'zation** *or* **ˌvitali'sation** NOUN ▸**'vitalˌizer** *or* **'vitalˌiser** NOUN

vital signs PLURAL NOUN *Med* indications that a person is still alive. Vital signs include a heartbeat, a pulse that can be felt, breathing, and body temperature.

vital staining NOUN the technique of treating living cells and tissues with dyes that do not immediately kill them, facilitating observation with a microscope.

vital statistics PLURAL NOUN 1 quantitative data concerning human life or the conditions and aspects affecting it, such as the death rate. 2 *Informal* the measurements of a woman's bust, waist, and hips.

vitamin ('vɪtəmɪn, 'vaɪ-) NOUN any of a group of substances that are essential, in small quantities, for the normal functioning of metabolism in the body. They cannot usually be synthesized in the body but they occur naturally in certain foods: insufficient supply of any particular vitamin results in a deficiency disease.
▷HISTORY C20 *vit-* from Latin *vīta* life + *-amin* from AMINE; so named by Casimir *Funk* (1884–1967), US biochemist who believed the substances to be amines
▸**ˌvita'minic** ADJECTIVE

vitamin A NOUN a fat-soluble yellow unsaturated alcohol occurring in green and yellow vegetables (esp carrots), butter, egg yolk, and fish-liver oil (esp halibut oil). It is essential for the prevention of night blindness and the protection of epithelial tissue. Formula: $C_{20}H_{30}O$. Also called: **vitamin A_1, retinol.**

vitamin A_2 NOUN a vitamin that occurs in the tissues of freshwater fish and has a function similar to that of vitamin A. Formula: $C_{20}H_{28}O$. Also called: **dehydroretinol.**

vitamin B NOUN, *plural* **B vitamins.** any of the vitamins in the vitamin B complex.

vitamin B_1 NOUN another name for **thiamine.**

vitamin B_2 NOUN another name for **riboflavin.**

vitamin B_6 NOUN another name for **pyridoxine.**

vitamin B_{12} NOUN another name for **cyanocobalamin.**

vitamin B complex NOUN a large group of water-soluble vitamins occurring esp in liver and yeast: includes thiamine, riboflavin, nicotinic acid, pyridoxine, pantothenic acid, biotin, choline, folic acid, and cyanocobalamin. Sometimes shortened to: **B complex.**

vitamin C NOUN another name for **ascorbic acid.**

vitamin D NOUN, *plural* **D vitamins.** any of the fat-soluble vitamins, including calciferol and cholecalciferol, occurring in fish-liver oils (esp cod-liver oil), milk, butter, and eggs: used in the treatment of rickets and osteomalacia.

vitamin D_1 NOUN the first isolated form of vitamin D, consisting of calciferol and its precursor, lumisterol.

vitamin D_2 NOUN another name for **calciferol.**

vitamin D_3 NOUN another name for **cholecalciferol.**

vitamin E NOUN another name for **tocopherol.**

vitamin G NOUN another name (esp US and Canadian) for **riboflavin.**

vitamin H NOUN another name (esp US and Canadian) for **biotin.**

vitamin K NOUN, *plural* **K vitamins.** any of the fat-soluble vitamins, including phylloquinone and the menaquinones, which are essential for the normal clotting of blood.

vitamin K_1 NOUN another name for **phylloquinone.**

vitamin K_2 NOUN another name for **menaquinone.**

vitamin K_3 NOUN a former name for **menadione.**

vitamin P NOUN, *plural* **P vitamins.** any of a group of water-soluble crystalline substances occurring mainly in citrus fruits, blackcurrants, and rosehips: they regulate the permeability of the blood capillaries. Also called: **citrin, bioflavonoid.**

Vitaphone ('vaɪtəˌfəʊn) NOUN *Trademark* an early technique in commercial film-making in which the accompanying sound was produced by discs.

vitascope ('vaɪtəˌskəʊp) NOUN an early type of film projector.
▷HISTORY C19: from Latin *vīta* life + -SCOPE

vitellin (vɪ'tɛlɪn) NOUN *Biochem* a phosphoprotein that is the major protein in egg yolk.
▷HISTORY C19: from VITELLUS + -IN

vitelline (vɪ'tɛlɪn, -aɪn) ADJECTIVE *Zoology* 1 of or relating to the yolk of an egg: *the vitelline gland.* 2 having the yellow colour of an egg yolk.
▷HISTORY C15: from Medieval Latin *vitellīnus,* from Latin *vitellus* the yolk of an egg; see VITELLUS

vitelline membrane NOUN *Zoology* a membrane that surrounds a fertilized ovum and prevents the entry of other spermatozoa.

vitellogenic (ˌvɪtələʊ'dʒɛnɪk) *or* **vitelligenous** (ˌvɪtə'lɪdʒɪnəs) ADJECTIVE *Zoology* producing or stimulating the formation of yolk.
▷HISTORY C20: from VITELLUS + -GENIC
▸**ˌvitello'genesis** NOUN

vitellus (vɪ'tɛləs) NOUN, *plural* **-luses** *or* **-li** (-laɪ). *Zoology, rare* the yolk of an egg.
▷HISTORY C18: from Latin, literally: little calf, later: yolk of an egg, from *vitulus* calf

vitiate ('vɪʃɪˌeɪt) VERB (*tr*) 1 to make faulty or imperfect. 2 to debase, pervert, or corrupt. 3 to destroy the force or legal effect of (a deed, etc.): *to vitiate a contract.*
▷HISTORY C16: from Latin *vitiāre* to injure, from *vitium* a fault
▸**'vitiable** ADJECTIVE ▸**ˌviti'ation** NOUN ▸**'vitiˌator** NOUN

viticulture ('vɪtɪˌkʌltʃə) NOUN 1 the science, art, or process of cultivating grapevines. 2 the study of grapes and the growing of grapes.
▷HISTORY C19: *viti-,* from Latin *vītis* vine
▸**ˌviti'cultural** ADJECTIVE ▸**ˌviti'culturer** *or* **ˌviti'culturist** NOUN

Viti Levu ('viːtɪ 'lɛvuː) NOUN the largest island of Fiji: mountainous. Chief town (and capital of the state): Suva. Pop.: 340 560 (latest est.) Area: 10 386 sq. km (4010 sq. miles).

vitiligo (ˌvɪtɪ'laɪgəʊ) NOUN another name for **leucoderma.**
▷HISTORY C17: from Latin: a skin disease, probably from *vitium* a blemish

vitrain ('vɪtreɪn) NOUN a type of coal occurring as horizontal glassy bands of a nonsoiling friable material.
▷HISTORY C20: from Latin *vitrum* glass + *-ain,* as in FUSAIN

vitreous ('vɪtrɪəs) ADJECTIVE 1 of, relating to, or resembling glass. 2 made of, derived from, or containing glass. 3 of or relating to the vitreous humour or vitreous body.
▷HISTORY C17: from Latin *vitreus* made of glass, from *vitrum* glass; probably related to *vidēre* to see
▸**'vitreously** ADVERB

vitreous body NOUN a transparent gelatinous substance, permeated by fine fibrils, that fills the interior of the eyeball between the lens and the retina.

vitreous humour NOUN the aqueous fluid contained within the interstices of the vitreous body.

vitreous silica NOUN another name for **silica glass.**

vitrescence (vɪ'trɛsəns) NOUN 1 the quality or condition of being or becoming vitreous. 2 the process of producing a glass or turning a crystalline material into glass.

vitrescent (vɪ'trɛsᵊnt) ADJECTIVE 1 tending to turn into glass. 2 capable of being transformed into glass.

vitric ('vɪtrɪk) ADJECTIVE of, relating to, resembling, or having the nature of glass; vitreous.

vitrification (ˌvɪtrɪfɪ'keɪʃən) NOUN 1 the process or act of vitrifying or the state of being vitrified. 2 something that is or has been vitrified.

vitriform ('vɪtrɪˌfɔːm) ADJECTIVE having the form or appearance of glass.

vitrify ('vɪtrɪˌfaɪ) VERB **-fies, -fying, -fied.** to convert or be converted into glass or a glassy substance.
▷HISTORY C16: from French *vitrifier,* from Latin *vitrum* glass
▸**'vitriˌfiable** ADJECTIVE ▸**ˌvitriˌfia'bility** NOUN

vitrine ('vɪtriːn) NOUN a glass display case or cabinet for works of art, curios, etc.
▷HISTORY C19: from French, from *vitre* pane of glass, from Latin *vitrum* glass

vitriol ('vɪtrɪˌɒl) NOUN 1 another name for **sulphuric acid.** 2 any one of a number of sulphate salts, such as ferrous sulphate (**green vitriol**), copper sulphate (**blue vitriol**), or zinc sulphate (**white vitriol**). 3 speech, writing, etc., displaying rancour, vituperation, or bitterness. ◆ VERB **-ols, -oling, -oled** *or* **-olling, -olled.** (*tr*) 4 to attack or injure with or as if with vitriol. 5 to treat with vitriol.
▷HISTORY C14: from Medieval Latin *vitriolum,* from Late Latin *vitriolus* glassy, from Latin *vitrum* glass, referring to the glossy appearance of the sulphates

vitriolic (ˌvɪtrɪ'ɒlɪk) ADJECTIVE 1 (of a substance, esp a strong acid) highly corrosive. 2 severely bitter or caustic; virulent: *vitriolic criticism.*

vitriolize *or* **vitriolise** ('vɪtrɪəˌlaɪz) VERB (*tr*) 1 to convert into or treat with vitriol. 2 to burn or injure with vitriol.
▸**ˌvitrioli'zation** *or* **ˌvitrioli'sation** NOUN

vitta ('vɪtə) NOUN, *plural* **-tae** (-tiː). 1 any of numerous tubelike cavities containing oil or resin that occur in the fruits of certain plants, esp of parsley and other umbellifers. 2 *Biology* a band or stripe of colour.
▷HISTORY C17: from Latin: headband; related to *viēre* to plait
▸**'vittate** ADJECTIVE

vittle ('vɪtᵊl) NOUN, VERB an obsolete or dialect spelling of **victual.**

vituline ('vɪtjʊˌlaɪn, -lɪn) ADJECTIVE of or resembling a calf or veal.
▷HISTORY C17: from Latin *vitulīnus,* from *vitulus* a calf

vituperate (vɪ'tju:pəˌreɪt) VERB to berate or rail (against) abusively; revile.
▷HISTORY C16: from Latin *vituperāre* to blame, from *vitium* a defect + *parāre* to make
▸**vi'tuperˌator** NOUN

vituperation (vɪˌtju:pə'reɪʃən) NOUN 1 abusive language or venomous censure. 2 the act of vituperating.
▸**vituperative** (vɪ'tju:pərətɪv, -prətɪv) ADJECTIVE
▸**vi'tuperatively** ADVERB

viva¹ ('vi:və) INTERJECTION long live; up with (a specified person or thing).
▷HISTORY C17: from Italian, literally: may (he) live! from *vivere* to live, from Latin *vīvere*

viva² ('vaɪvə) *Brit* ◆ NOUN 1 an oral examination. ◆ VERB **-vas, -vaing, -vaed.** (*tr*) 2 to examine orally.
▷HISTORY shortened from VIVA VOCE

vivace (vɪ'vɑ:tʃɪ) ADJECTIVE, ADVERB *Music* to be performed in a brisk lively manner.
▷HISTORY C17: from Italian, from Latin *vīvax* long-lived, vigorous, from *vīvere* to live

vivacious (vɪ'veɪʃəs) ADJECTIVE 1 full of high spirits and animation; lively or vital. 2 *Obsolete* having or displaying tenacity of life.
▷HISTORY C17: from Latin *vīvax* lively; see VIVACE
▸**vi'vaciously** ADVERB ▸**vi'vaciousness** NOUN

vivacity (vɪ'væsɪtɪ) NOUN, *plural* **-ties.** 1 the quality or condition of being vivacious. 2 (*often plural*) *Rare* a vivacious act or expression.

vivandière *French* (vivɑ̃djɛr) NOUN (formerly) a female sutler or victualler offering extra provisions and spirits to soldiers, esp those of the French and British armies.
▷HISTORY C16: see VIAND

vivarium (vaɪ'vɛərɪəm) NOUN, *plural* **-iums** *or* **-ia** (-ɪə). a place where live animals are kept under natural conditions for study, research, etc.
▷HISTORY C16: from Latin: enclosure where live fish or game are kept, from *vīvus* alive

viva voce ('vaɪvə 'vəʊtʃɪ) ADVERB, ADJECTIVE 1 by word of mouth. ◆ NOUN, VERB 2 the full form of **viva².**
▷HISTORY C16: from Medieval Latin, literally: with living voice

vive (vi:v) INTERJECTION long live; up with (a specified person or thing).
▷HISTORY from French

viverrine (vaɪ'verəɪn) ADJECTIVE 1 of, relating to, or belonging to the *Viverridae,* a family of small to medium-sized predatory mammals of Eurasia and Africa, including genets, civets and mongooses: order *Carnivora* (carnivores). ◆ NOUN 2 any animal belonging to the family *Viverridae.*
▷HISTORY C19: from New Latin *viverrīnus,* from Latin *viverra* a ferret

Vivian ('vɪvɪən) NOUN (in Arthurian legend) the mistress of Merlin, sometimes identified with the **Lady of the Lake.**

vivid ('vɪvɪd) ADJECTIVE 1 (of a colour) very bright; having a very high saturation or purity; produced by a pure or almost pure colouring agent. 2 brilliantly coloured: *vivid plumage.* 3 conveying to the mind striking realism, freshness, or trueness to life; graphic: *a vivid account.* 4 (of a recollection, memory, etc.) remaining distinct in the mind. 5 (of the imagination, etc.) prolific in the formation of lifelike images. 6 making a powerful impact on the emotions or senses: *a vivid feeling of shame.* 7 uttered, operating, or acting with vigour: *vivid expostulations.* 8 full of life or vitality: *a vivid personality.*
▷HISTORY C17: from Latin *vīvidus* animated, from *vīvere* to live
▸**'vividly** ADVERB ▸**'vividness** NOUN

vivify ('vɪvɪˌfaɪ) VERB **-fies, -fying, -fied.** (*tr*) 1 to bring to life; animate. 2 to make more vivid or striking.
▷HISTORY C16: from Late Latin *vīvificāre,* from Latin *vīvus* alive + *facere* to make
▸**ˌvivifi'cation** NOUN ▸**'viviˌfier** NOUN

viviparous (vɪ'vɪpərəs) ADJECTIVE 1 (of animals) producing offspring that as embryos develop within and derive nourishment from the body of the female parent. Compare **oviparous, ovoviviparous.** 2 (of plants) producing bulbils or young plants instead of flowers. 3 (of seeds) germinating before separating from the parent plant.
▷HISTORY C17: from Latin *vīviparus,* from *vīvus* alive + *parere* to bring forth
▸**viviparity** (ˌvɪvɪ'pærɪtɪ) *or* **vi'vipary** *or* **vi'viparism** *or* **vi'viparousness** NOUN ▸**vi'viparously** ADVERB

vivisect ('vɪvɪˌsɛkt, ˌvɪvɪ'sɛkt) VERB to subject (an animal) to vivisection.
▷HISTORY C19: back formation from VIVISECTION
▸**'viviˌsector** NOUN

vivisection (ˌvɪvɪ'sɛkʃən) NOUN the act or practice of performing experiments on living animals, involving cutting into or dissecting the body.
▷HISTORY C18: from *vivi-,* from Latin *vīvus* living + SECTION, as in DISSECTION
▸**ˌvivi'sectional** ADJECTIVE ▸**ˌvivi'sectionally** ADVERB

vivisectionist (ˌvɪvɪ'sɛkʃənɪst) NOUN 1 a person who practises vivisection. 2 a person who advocates the practice of vivisection as being useful or necessary to science.

vivo ('vi:vəʊ) ADJECTIVE, ADVERB *Music* (*in combination*) with life and vigour: *allegro vivo.*
▷HISTORY Italian: lively

vixen ('vɪksən) NOUN 1 a female fox. 2 a quarrelsome or spiteful woman.
▷HISTORY C15 *fixen;* related to Old English *fyxe,* feminine of FOX; compare Old High German *fuhsīn*
▸**'vixenish** ADJECTIVE ▸**'vixenishly** ADVERB ▸**'vixenishness** NOUN ▸**'vixenly** ADVERB, ADJECTIVE

Viyella (vaɪ'ɛlə) NOUN *Trademark* a soft fabric made of wool and cotton, used esp for blouses and shirts.

viz ABBREVIATION FOR videlicet.

vizard ('vɪzəd) NOUN *Archaic or literary* a means of disguise; mask; visor.
▷HISTORY C16: variant of VISOR
▸**'vizarded** ADJECTIVE

vizcacha (vɪs'kætʃə) NOUN a variant spelling of **viscacha.**

vizier (vɪ'zɪə) NOUN a high official in certain Muslim countries, esp in the former Ottoman Empire. Viziers served in various capacities, such as that of provincial governor or chief minister to the sultan.
▷HISTORY C16: from Turkish *vezīr,* from Arabic *wazīr* porter, from *wazara* to bear a burden
▸**vi'zierial** *or* **vi'zirial** ADJECTIVE ▸**vi'ziership** NOUN

vizierate (vɪ'zɪərɪt, -eɪt) NOUN 1 the position, rank, or authority of a vizier. 2 the term of office of a vizier.

vizor ('vaɪzə) NOUN, VERB a variant spelling of **visor.**

vizsla ('vɪʒlə) NOUN a breed of Hungarian hunting dog with a smooth rusty-gold coat.
▷HISTORY C20: named after *Vizsla,* Hungary

VJ ABBREVIATION FOR: 1 video jockey. 2 *Austral* Vaucluse Junior: a type of small yacht.

V-J Day NOUN the day marking the Allied victory over Japan in World War II (Aug. 15, 1945).

vl ABBREVIATION FOR variant reading.
▷HISTORY from Latin *varia lectio*

VL ABBREVIATION FOR Vulgar Latin.

VLA *Astronomy* ABBREVIATION FOR very large array.

Vlach (vlɑ:k) *or* **Walach** ('wɑ:lɒk) NOUN 1 a member of a people scattered throughout SE Europe in the early Middle Ages, speaking a Romanic dialect. ◆ ADJECTIVE 2 of or relating to Vlachs or their dialect.

Vladikavkaz (*Russian* vlədikaf'kas) NOUN a city in S Russia, capital of the North Ossetian Republic on the N slopes of the Caucasus. Pop.: 310 600 (1999 est.). Former names: **Dzaudzhikau** (1944–54), **Ordzhonikidze** (1954–91).

Vladivostok (ˌvlædɪ'vɒstɒk; *Russian* vlədivas'tɔk) NOUN a port in SE Russia, on the Sea of Japan: terminus of the Trans-Siberian Railway; the main Russian Pacific naval base since 1872 and chief commercial and civilian Russian port in the Far East; university (1956). Pop.: 613 100 (1999 est.).

VLBI *Astronomy* ABBREVIATION FOR very long baseline interferometry.

VLCC ABBREVIATION FOR very large crude carrier: an oil tanker with a capacity between 200 000 and 400 000 tons.

vlei (fleɪ, vleɪ) NOUN 1 *South African* an area of low marshy ground, esp one that feeds a stream. 2 *Northern US dialect* a marsh.
▷HISTORY C19: from Afrikaans (for sense 1); from obsolete N American Dutch dialect (for sense 2): VALLEY

VLF *or* **vlf** *Radio* ABBREVIATION FOR **very low frequency.**

Vlissingen ('vlɪsɪŋə) NOUN the Dutch name for **Flushing.**

Vlorë (*Albanian* 'vlorə) *or* **Vlonë** (*Albanian* 'vlonə) NOUN a port in SW Albania, on the **Bay of Vlorë:** under Turkish rule from 1462 until Albanian independence was declared here in 1912. Pop.: 76 000 (1991 est.). Ancient name: **Avlona.** Also called: **Valona.**

VLSI *Computing* ABBREVIATION FOR **very large-scale integration.**

Vltava (*Czech* 'vltava) NOUN a river in the Czech Republic, rising in the Bohemian Forest and flowing generally southeast and then north to the River Elbe near Melnik. Length: 434 km (270 miles). German name: **Moldau.**

VMD ABBREVIATION FOR Doctor of Veterinary Medicine.
▷HISTORY Latin *veterinariae medicinae doctor*

VMI ABBREVIATION FOR vendor managed inventory: an inventory management system in which a supplier assumes responsibility for the timely replenishment of a customer's stock.

vn THE INTERNET DOMAIN NAME FOR Vietnam.

VN INTERNATIONAL CAR REGISTRATION FOR Vietnam.

V neck NOUN a neck on a garment that comes down to a point on the throat or chest, resembling the shape of the letter "V".
▸**'V-ˌneck** *or* **'V-ˌnecked** ADJECTIVE

VO ABBREVIATION FOR: 1 very old: used to imply that a brandy or whisky is old, now often extended to port and other dessert wines. 2 **Royal Victorian Order.**

vo. ABBREVIATION FOR verso.

voc. *or* **vocat.** ABBREVIATION FOR vocative.

vocab ('vəʊkæb) NOUN short for **vocabulary.**

vocable ('vəʊkəbᵊl) NOUN 1 any word, either written or spoken, regarded simply as a sequence of letters or spoken sounds, irrespective of its meaning. 2 a vocal sound; vowel. ◆ ADJECTIVE 3 capable of being uttered.
▷HISTORY C16: from Latin *vocābulum* a designation, from *vocāre* to call
▸**'vocably** ADVERB

vocabulary (və'kæbjʊlərɪ) NOUN, *plural* **-laries.** 1 a listing, either selective or exhaustive, containing the words and phrases of a language, with meanings or translations into another language; glossary. 2 the aggregate of words in the use or comprehension of a specified person, class, profession, etc. 3 all the words contained in a language. 4 a range or system of symbols, qualities, or techniques constituting a means of communication or expression, as any of the arts or crafts: *a wide vocabulary of textures and colours.*
▷HISTORY C16: from Medieval Latin *vocābulārium,* from *vocābulārius* concerning words, from Latin *vocābulum* VOCABLE

vocal ('vəʊkᵊl) ADJECTIVE 1 of, relating to, or designed for the voice: *vocal music.* 2 produced or delivered by the voice: *vocal noises.* 3 connected with an attribute or the production of the voice: *vocal organs.* 4 frequently disposed to outspoken speech, criticism, etc.: *a vocal minority.* 5 full of sound or voices: *a vocal assembly.* 6 endowed with a voice. 7 eloquent or meaningful. 8 *Phonetics* **a** of or relating to a speech sound. **b** of or relating to a voiced speech sound, esp a vowel. ◆ NOUN 9 a piece of jazz or pop music that is sung. 10 a performance of such a piece of music.
▷HISTORY C14: from Latin *vōcālis* possessed of a voice, from *vōx* voice
▸**vocality** (vəʊ'kælɪtɪ) NOUN ▸**'vocally** ADVERB

vocal cords PLURAL NOUN either of two pairs of mucomembranous folds in the larynx. The upper pair (**false vocal cords**) are not concerned with vocal production; the lower pair (**true vocal cords** or **vocal folds**) can be made to vibrate and produce sound when air from the lungs is forced over them. See also **glottis.** Related adjective: **glottal.**

vocal folds PLURAL NOUN See **vocal cords.**

vocalic (vəʊˈkælɪk) ADJECTIVE *Phonetics* of, relating to, or containing a vowel or vowels.

vocalise (ˌvəʊkəˈliːz) NOUN a musical passage sung upon one vowel as an exercise to develop flexibility and control of pitch and tone; solfeggio.

vocalism (ˈvəʊkəˌlɪzəm) NOUN [1] the exercise of the voice, as in singing or speaking. [2] singing, esp in respect to technique or skill. [3] *Phonetics* **a** a voiced speech sound, esp a vowel. **b** a system of vowels as used in a language.

vocalist (ˈvəʊkəlɪst) NOUN a singer, esp one who regularly appears with a jazz band or pop group.

vocalize *or* **vocalise** (ˈvəʊkəˌlaɪz) VERB [1] to express with or use the voice; articulate (a speech, song, etc.). [2] (*tr*) to make vocal or articulate. [3] (*tr*) *Phonetics* **a** to articulate (a speech sound) with voice. **b** to change (a consonant) into a vowel. [4] another word for **vowelize.** [5] (*intr*) to sing a melody on a vowel, etc.
▸ ˌ**vocaliˈzation** *or* ˌ**vocaliˈsation** NOUN ▸ ˈ**vocalˌizer** *or* ˈ**vocalˌiser** NOUN

vocal sac NOUN *Zoology* either of the loose folds of skin on each side of the mouth in many male frogs that can be inflated and act as resonators.

vocal score NOUN a musical score that shows voice parts in full and orchestral parts in the form of a piano transcription.

vocation (vəʊˈkeɪʃən) NOUN [1] a specified occupation, profession, or trade. [2] **a** a special urge, inclination, or predisposition to a particular calling or career, esp a religious one. **b** such a calling or career.
▷HISTORY C15: from Latin *vocātiō* a calling, from *vocāre* to call

vocational (vəʊˈkeɪʃənᵊl) ADJECTIVE [1] of or relating to a vocation or vocations. [2] of or relating to applied educational courses concerned with skills needed for an occupation, trade, or profession: *vocational training.*
▸ **voˈcationally** ADVERB

vocational guidance NOUN a guidance service based on psychological tests and interviews to find out what career or occupation may best suit a person.

vocative (ˈvɒkətɪv) ADJECTIVE [1] relating to, used in, or characterized by calling. [2] *Grammar* denoting a case of nouns, in some inflected languages, used when the referent of the noun is being addressed. ◆ NOUN [3] *Grammar* **a** the vocative case. **b** a vocative noun or speech element.
▷HISTORY C15: from Latin phrase *vocātīvus cāsus* the calling case, from *vocāre* to call
▸ ˈ**vocatively** ADVERB

voces (ˈvəʊsiːz) NOUN the plural of **vox.**

vociferant (vəʊˈsɪfərənt) ADJECTIVE [1] a less common word for **vociferous.** ◆ NOUN [2] *Rare* a vociferous person.
▷HISTORY C17: from Latin *vōciferārī* to bawl; see VOCIFERATE
▸ **voˈciferance** NOUN

vociferate (vəʊˈsɪfəˌreɪt) VERB to exclaim or cry out about (something) clamorously, vehemently, or insistently.
▷HISTORY C17: from Latin *vōciferārī* to clamour, from *vōx* voice + *ferre* to bear
▸ **voˌciferˈation** NOUN ▸ **voˈciferˌator** NOUN

vociferous (vəʊˈsɪfərəs) ADJECTIVE [1] characterized by vehemence, clamour, or noisiness: *vociferous protests.* [2] making an outcry or loud noises; clamorous: *a vociferous mob.*
▸ **voˈciferously** ADVERB ▸ **voˈciferousness** NOUN

vocoder (ˈvəʊˌkəʊdə) NOUN *Music* a type of synthesizer that uses the human voice as an oscillator.

vodka (ˈvɒdkə) NOUN an alcoholic drink originating in Russia, made from grain, potatoes, etc., usually consisting only of rectified spirit and water.
▷HISTORY C19: from Russian, diminutive of *voda* water; related to Sanskrit *udan* water, Greek *hudōr*

voe (vəʊ; *Scot* vo) NOUN (in Orkney and Shetland) a small bay or narrow creek.
▷HISTORY C17: from Old Norse *vagr*

voema (ˈvʊmə) NOUN *South African informal* vigour or energy.
▷HISTORY C20: Afrikaans

voetsek *or* **voetsak** (ˈfʊtsɑk, ˈvʊt-) INTERJECTION *South African offensive, informal* an expression of dismissal or rejection.
▷HISTORY C19: Afrikaans, from Dutch *voort se ek* forward, I say, commonly applied to animals

voetstoots *or* **voetstoets** (ˈfʊtstʊts, ˈvʊt-) *South African* ◆ ADJECTIVE [1] denoting a sale in which the vendor is freed from all responsibility for the condition of the goods being sold. ◆ ADVERB [2] without responsibility for the condition of the goods sold.
▷HISTORY from Afrikaans *voetstoots* as it is

vogue (vəʊg) NOUN [1] the popular style at a specified time (esp in the phrase **in vogue**). [2] a period of general or popular usage or favour: *the vogue for such dances is now over.* ◆ ADJECTIVE [3] (*usually prenominal*) popular or fashionable: *a vogue word.*
▷HISTORY C16: from French: a rowing, fashion, from Old Italian *voga,* from *vogare* to row, of unknown origin
▸ ˈ**voguish** ADJECTIVE

vogueing (ˈvəʊgɪŋ) NOUN a dance style of the late 1980s, in which a fashion model's movements and postures are imitated in a highly stylized manner.
▷HISTORY C20: from *Vogue* magazine

Vogul (ˈvəʊgᵊl) NOUN [1] (*plural* **-gul** *or* **-guls**) a member of a people living in W Siberia and NE Europe. [2] the language of this people, belonging to the Finno-Ugric family: related to Hungarian.

voice (vɔɪs) NOUN [1] the sound made by the vibration of the vocal cords, esp when modified by the resonant effect of the tongue and mouth. See also **speech.** Related adjective: **vocal.** [2] the natural and distinctive tone of the speech sounds characteristic of a particular person: *nobody could mistake his voice.* [3] the condition, quality, effectiveness, or tone of such sounds: *a hysterical voice.* [4] the musical sound of a singing voice, with respect to its quality or tone: *she has a lovely voice.* [5] the ability to speak, sing, etc.: *he has lost his voice.* [6] a sound resembling or suggestive of vocal utterance: *the voice of the sea; the voice of hard experience.* [7] written or spoken expression, as of feeling, opinion, etc. (esp in the phrase **give voice to**). [8] a stated choice, wish, or opinion or the power or right to have an opinion heard and considered: *to give someone a voice in a decision.* [9] an agency through which is communicated another's purpose, policy, etc.: *such groups are the voice of our enemies.* [10] *Music* **a** musical notes produced by vibrations of the vocal cords at various frequencies and in certain registers: *a tenor voice.* **b** (in harmony) an independent melodic line or part: *a fugue in five voices.* [11] *Phonetics* the sound characterizing the articulation of several speech sounds, including all vowels or sonants, that is produced when the vocal cords make loose contact with each other and are set in vibration by the breath as it forces its way through the glottis. [12] *Grammar* a category of the verb or verbal inflections that expresses whether the relation between the subject and the verb is that of agent and action, action and recipient, or some other relation. See **active** (sense 5), **passive** (sense 5), **middle** (sense 5). [13] *Obsolete* rumour. [14] (foll by *of*) *Obsolete* fame; renown. [15] **in voice.** in a condition to sing or speak well. [16] **out of voice.** with the voice temporarily in a poor condition, esp for singing. [17] **with one voice.** unanimously. ◆ VERB (*tr*) [18] to utter in words; give expression to: *to voice a complaint.* [19] to articulate (a speech sound) with voice. [20] *Music* to adjust (a wind instrument or organ pipe) so that it conforms to the correct standards of tone colour, pitch, etc. [21] to provide the voice for (a puppet or cartoon character) in an animated film.
▷HISTORY C13: from Old French *voiz,* from Latin *vōx*
▸ ˈ**voicer** NOUN

voice box NOUN [1] another word for the **larynx.** Related adjective: **laryngeal.** [2] Also called: **talkbox.** an electronic guitar attachment with a tube into the player's mouth to modulate the sound vocally.

voiced (vɔɪst) ADJECTIVE [1] declared or expressed by the voice. [2] (*in combination*) having a voice as specified: *loud-voiced.* [3] *Phonetics* articulated with accompanying vibration of the vocal cords: *in English* (b) *is a voiced consonant.* Compare **voiceless.**

voiceful (ˈvɔɪsful) ADJECTIVE *Poetic* [1] endowed with a voice, esp of loud quality. [2] full of voices.
▸ ˈ**voicefulness** NOUN

voice input NOUN the control and operation of computer systems by spoken commands.

voice-leading (ˈvɔɪsˌliːdɪŋ) NOUN *US* another term for **part-writing.**

voiceless (ˈvɔɪslɪs) ADJECTIVE [1] without a voice; mute. [2] not articulated: *voiceless misery.* [3] lacking a musical voice. [4] silent. [5] without the power or right to express an opinion. [6] *Phonetics* articulated without accompanying vibration of the vocal cords: *in English* (p) *is a voiceless consonant.*
▸ ˈ**voicelessly** ADVERB ▸ ˈ**voicelessness** NOUN

voice mail NOUN an electronic system for the transfer and storage of telephone messages, which can then be dealt with by the user at his or her convenience.

voice-over NOUN the voice of an unseen commentator heard during a film, television programme, etc.

voice part NOUN a melodic line written for the voice.

voiceprint (ˈvɔɪsˌprɪnt) NOUN a graphic representation of a person's voice recorded electronically, usually having time plotted along the horizontal axis and the frequency of the speech on the vertical axis.

voice recognition NOUN the control of a computer system by a voice or voices that the computer has been instructed to accept.

voice response NOUN output of information from a computer system in the form of speech rather than displayed text.

voice vote NOUN a vote taken in a legislative body by calling for the ayes and the noes and estimating which faction is more numerous from the volume of the noise.

void (vɔɪd) ADJECTIVE [1] without contents; empty. [2] not legally binding: *null and void.* [3] (of an office, house, position, etc.) without an incumbent; unoccupied. [4] (*postpositive;* foll by *of*) destitute or devoid: *void of resources.* [5] having no effect; useless: *all his efforts were rendered void.* [6] (of a card suit or player) having no cards in a particular suit: *his spades were void.* ◆ NOUN [7] an empty space or area: *the huge desert voids of Asia.* [8] a feeling or condition of loneliness or deprivation: *his divorce left him in a void.* [9] a lack of any cards in one suit: *to have a void in spades.* [10] Also called: **counter.** the inside area of a character of type, such as the inside of an *o.* ◆ VERB (*mainly tr*) [11] to make ineffective or invalid. [12] to empty (contents, etc.) or make empty of contents. [13] (*also intr*) to discharge the contents of (the bowels or urinary bladder). [14] *Archaic* to vacate (a place, room, etc.). [15] *Obsolete* to expel.
▷HISTORY C13: from Old French *vuide,* from Vulgar Latin *vocītus* (unattested), from Latin *vacuus* empty, from *vacāre* to be empty
▸ ˈ**voider** NOUN ▸ ˈ**voidness** NOUN

voidable (ˈvɔɪdəbᵊl) ADJECTIVE [1] capable of being voided. [2] capable of being made of no legal effect or made void.
▸ ˈ**voidableness** NOUN

voidance (ˈvɔɪdᵊns) NOUN [1] an annulment, as of a contract. [2] the condition of being vacant, as an office, benefice, etc. [3] the act of voiding, ejecting, or evacuating.
▷HISTORY C14: variant of AVOIDANCE

voided (ˈvɔɪdɪd) ADJECTIVE [1] *Heraldry* (of a design) with a hole in the centre of the same shape as the design: *a voided lozenge.* [2] *Rare* having a void or made void.

voile (vɔɪl; *French* vwal) NOUN a light semitransparent fabric of silk, rayon, cotton, etc., used for dresses, scarves, shirts, etc.
▷HISTORY C19: from French: VEIL

Voiotia (*Greek* vjɔˈtiːa) NOUN a department of E central Greece: corresponds to ancient Boeotia and part of ancient Phocis. Pop.: 134 108 (1991). Area: 3173 sq. km (1225 sq. miles). Modern Greek name: **Boeotia.**

voir dire (vwɑː ˈdɪə) NOUN *Law* [1] the preliminary examination on oath of a proposed witness by the judge. [2] the oath administered to such a witness.
▷HISTORY C17: from Old French: to speak the truth

voix céleste (vwɑː seˈlɛst) NOUN an organ stop which produces a tremolo effect through the acoustic phenomenon of beats.

▷HISTORY from French: heavenly voice

vol. ABBREVIATION FOR: [1] volcano. [2] volume. [3] volunteer.

Volans ('vəʊlænz) NOUN, *Latin genitive* **Volantis** (vəʊ'læntɪs). a small constellation in the S hemisphere lying between Carina and Hydrus.
▷HISTORY C19: from Latin, literally: flying, from *volāre* to fly

volant ('vəʊlənt) ADJECTIVE [1] (*usually postpositive*) *Heraldry* in a flying position. [2] *Rare* flying or capable of flight. [3] *Poetic* moving lightly or agilely; nimble.
▷HISTORY C16: from French: flying, from *voler* to fly, from Latin *volāre*

Volapuk *or* **Volapük** ('vɒlə,pʊk) NOUN an artificial language based on English, French, German, Latin, etc., invented by Johann Schleyer (1831–1912) in 1880.
▷HISTORY C19: from *vol,* based on WORLD + euphonic *-a-* + *pük* speech, based on SPEAK

volar ('vəʊlə) ADJECTIVE *Anatomy* of or relating to the palm of the hand or the sole of the foot.
▷HISTORY C19: from Latin *vola* hollow of the hand, palm, sole of the foot

volatile ('vɒlə,taɪl) ADJECTIVE [1] (of a substance) capable of readily changing from a solid or liquid form to a vapour; having a high vapour pressure and a low boiling point. [2] (of persons) disposed to caprice or inconstancy; fickle; mercurial. [3] (of circumstances) liable to sudden, unpredictable, or explosive change. [4] lasting only a short time: *volatile business interests.* [5] *Computing* (of a memory) not retaining stored information when the power supply is cut off. [6] *Obsolete* flying or capable of flight; volant. ◆ NOUN [7] a volatile substance. [8] *Rare* a winged creature.
▷HISTORY C17: from Latin *volātilis* flying, from *volāre* to fly
▸**'volatileness** *or* **volatility** (,vɒlə'tɪlɪtɪ) NOUN

volatile oil NOUN another name for **essential oil.**

volatile salt NOUN another name for **sal volatile.**

volatilize *or* **volatilise** (vɒ'lætɪ,laɪz) VERB to change or cause to change from a solid or liquid to a vapour.
▸**vo'lati,lizable** *or* **vo'lati,lisable** ADJECTIVE ▸**vo,latiliz'ation** *or* **vo,latilis'ation** NOUN

vol-au-vent (*French* vɔlovɑ̃) NOUN a very light puff pastry case filled either with a savoury mixture in a richly flavoured sauce or sometimes with fruit.
▷HISTORY C19: from French, literally: flight in the wind

volcanic (vɒl'kænɪk) ADJECTIVE [1] of, relating to, produced by, or characterized by the presence of volcanoes: *a volcanic region.* [2] suggestive of or resembling an erupting volcano: *a volcanic era.* [3] another word for **extrusive** (sense 2).
▸**vol'canically** ADVERB ▸**volcanicity** (,vɒlkə'nɪsɪtɪ) NOUN

volcanic bomb NOUN See **bomb** (sense 4).

volcanic glass NOUN any of several glassy volcanic igneous rocks, such as obsidian and pitchstone.

volcanism ('vɒlkə,nɪzəm) *or* **vulcanism** NOUN those processes collectively that result in the formation of volcanoes and their products.

volcanize *or* **volcanise** ('vɒlkə,naɪz) VERB (*tr*) to subject to the effects of or change by volcanic heat.
▸**,volcani'zation** *or* **,volcani'sation** NOUN

volcano (vɒl'keɪnəʊ) NOUN, *plural* **-noes** *or* **-nos.** [1] an opening in the earth's crust from which molten lava, rock fragments, ashes, dust, and gases are ejected from below the earth's surface. [2] a mountain formed from volcanic material ejected from a vent in a central crater.
▷HISTORY C17: from Italian, from Latin *Volcānus* VULCAN[1], whose forges were believed to be responsible for volcanic rumblings

Volcano Islands PLURAL NOUN a group of three volcanic islands in the W Pacific, about 1100 km (700 miles) south of Japan: the largest is Iwo Jima, taken by US forces in 1945 and returned to Japan in 1968. Area: about 28 sq. km (11 sq. miles). Japanese name: **Kazan Retto.**

volcanology (,vɒlkə'nɒlədʒɪ) *or* **vulcanology** NOUN the study of volcanoes and volcanic phenomena.
▸**volcanological** (,vɒlkənə'lɒdʒɪkəl) *or* **,vulcano'logical** ADJECTIVE ▸**,volcan'ologist** *or* **,vulcan'ologist** NOUN

vole[1] (vəʊl) NOUN any of numerous small rodents of the genus *Microtus* and related genera, mostly of Eurasia and North America and having a stocky body, short tail, and inconspicuous ears: family *Cricetidae*. See also **water vole.**
▷HISTORY C19: short for *volemouse,* from Old Norse *vollr* field + *mus* MOUSE; related to Icelandic *vollarmus*

vole[2] (vəʊl) NOUN (in some card games, such as écarté) the taking of all the tricks in a deal, thus scoring extra points.
▷HISTORY C17: from French, from *voler* to fly, from Latin *volāre*

Volga ('vɒlgə) NOUN a river in W Russia, rising in the Valdai Range and flowing through a chain of small lakes to the Rybinsk Reservoir and south to the Caspian Sea through Volgograd: the longest river in Europe. Length: 3690 km (2293 miles).

Volgograd (*Russian* vəlga'grat; *English* 'vɒlgə,græd) NOUN a port in SW Russia, on the River Volga: scene of a major engagement (1918) during the civil war and again in World War II (1942–43), in which the German forces were defeated; major industrial centre. Pop.: 1 000 000 (1999 est.). Former names: **Tsaritsyn** (until 1925), **Stalingrad** (1925–61).

volitant ('vɒlɪtənt) ADJECTIVE [1] flying or moving about rapidly. [2] capable of flying.
▷HISTORY C19: from Latin *volitāre* to flit, from *volāre* to fly

volition (və'lɪʃən) NOUN [1] the act of exercising the will: *of one's own volition.* [2] the faculty or capability of conscious choice, decision, and intention; the will. [3] the resulting choice or resolution. [4] *Philosophy* an act of will as distinguished from the physical movement it intends to bring about.
▷HISTORY C17: from Medieval Latin *volitiō,* from Latin *vol-* as in *volō* I will, present stem of *velle* to wish
▸**vo'litional** *or* **vo'litionary** ADJECTIVE ▸**vo'litionally** ADVERB

volitive ('vɒlɪtɪv) ADJECTIVE [1] of, relating to, or emanating from the will. [2] *Grammar* another word for **desiderative.**

volk (fɒlk) NOUN *South African* the people or nation, esp the nation of Afrikaners.
▷HISTORY Afrikaans

Völkerwanderung *German* ('fœlkərvandərʊŋ) NOUN the migration of peoples, esp of Germanic and Slavic peoples into S and W Europe from 2nd to 11th centuries.
▷HISTORY literally: nations wandering, German translation of Latin *migrātiō gentium*

Volkslied *German* ('fɔlksli:t) NOUN, *plural* **-lieder** (-li:dər). a type of popular German folk song.
▷HISTORY literally: folk song

Volksraad ('fɒlks,rɑ:t) NOUN *South African* the legislative assembly of the Boer republics in South Africa during the latter half of the 19th century.
▷HISTORY Afrikaans *volk* people + *raad* council

volley ('vɒlɪ) NOUN [1] the simultaneous discharge of several weapons, esp firearms. [2] the projectiles or missiles so discharged. [3] a burst of oaths, protests, etc., occurring simultaneously or in rapid succession. [4] *Sport* a stroke, shot, or kick at a moving ball before it hits the ground. Compare **half volley.** [5] *Cricket* the flight of such a ball or the ball itself. [6] the simultaneous explosion of several blastings of rock. ◆ VERB [7] to discharge (weapons, etc.) in or as if in a volley or (of weapons, etc.) to be discharged. [8] (*tr*) to utter vehemently or sound loudly and continuously. [9] (*tr*) *Sport* to strike or kick (a moving ball) before it hits the ground. [10] (*intr*) to issue or move rapidly or indiscriminately.
▷HISTORY C16: from French *volée* a flight, from *voler* to fly, from Latin *volāre*
▸**'volleyer** NOUN

volleyball ('vɒlɪ,bɔ:l) NOUN [1] a game in which two teams hit a large ball back and forth over a high net with their hands. [2] the ball used in this game.

Vologda (*Russian* 'vɔləgdə) NOUN an industrial city in W central Russia. Pop.: 304 300 (1999 est.).

Vólos (*Greek* 'vɔlɔs) NOUN a port in E Greece, in Thessaly on the **Gulf of Volos** (an inlet of the Aegean): the third largest port in Greece. Pop.: 70 000 (latest est.).

volost ('vəʊlɒst) NOUN [1] (in the former Soviet Union) a rural soviet. [2] (in tsarist Russia) a peasant community consisting of several villages or hamlets.
▷HISTORY from Russian

vols. ABBREVIATION FOR volumes.

Volsci ('vɒlski:) PLURAL NOUN a warlike people of ancient Latium, subdued by Rome in the fifth and fourth centuries B.C.

Volscian ('vɒlskɪən) NOUN [1] a member of the Volsci. [2] the extinct language of the Volsci, closely related to Umbrian. ◆ ADJECTIVE [3] of or relating to the Volsci or their language.

Volsung ('vɒlsʊŋ) NOUN [1] a great hero of Norse and Germanic legend and poetry who gave his name to a race of warriors; father of Sigmund and Signy. [2] any member of his family.

Volsunga Saga ('vɒlsʊŋgə) NOUN a 13th-century Icelandic saga about the family of the Volsungs and the deeds of Sigurd, related in theme and story to the Nibelungenlied.

volt[1] (vəʊlt) NOUN the derived SI unit of electric potential; the potential difference between two points on a conductor carrying a current of 1 ampere, when the power dissipated between these points is 1 watt. Symbol: V.
▷HISTORY C19: named after Count Alessandro *Volta* (1745–1827), Italian physicist

volt[2] *or* **volte** (vɒlt) NOUN [1] a small circle of determined size executed in dressage. [2] a leap made in fencing to avoid an opponent's thrust.
▷HISTORY C17: from French *volte,* from Italian *volta* a turn, ultimately from Latin *volvere* to turn

volta ('vɒltə; *Italian* 'vɔlta) NOUN, *plural* **-te** (*Italian* -te). [1] a quick-moving Italian dance popular during the 16th and 17th centuries. [2] a piece of music written for or in the rhythm of this dance, in triple time.
▷HISTORY C17: from Italian: turn; see VOLT[2]

Volta ('vɒltə) NOUN [1] a river in W Africa, formed by the confluence of the **Black Volta** and the **White Volta** in N central Ghana: flows south to the Bight of Benin: the chief river of Ghana. Length: 480 km (300 miles); (including the Black Volta) 1600 km (1000 miles). [2] **Lake.** an artificial lake in Ghana, extending 408 km (250 miles) upstream from the **Volta River Dam** on the Volta River: completed in 1966. Area: 8482 sq. km (3275 sq. miles).

voltage ('vəʊltɪdʒ) NOUN an electromotive force or potential difference expressed in volts.

voltage divider NOUN another name for a **potential divider.**

voltaic (vɒl'teɪɪk) ADJECTIVE another word for **galvanic** (sense 1).

Voltaic (vɒl'teɪɪk) ADJECTIVE [1] of or relating to Burkina-Faso, formerly known as Upper Volta. [2] denoting, belonging to, or relating to the Gur group of African languages. ◆ NOUN [3] this group of languages. See also **Gur.**

voltaic cell NOUN another name for **primary cell.**

voltaic couple NOUN *Physics* a pair of dissimilar metals in an electrolyte with a potential difference between the metals resulting from chemical action.

voltaic pile NOUN an early form of battery consisting of a pile of paired plates of dissimilar metals, such as zinc and copper, each pair being separated from the next by a pad moistened with an electrolyte. Also called: **pile, galvanic pile, Volta's pile.**

Voltairean *or* **Voltairian** (vɒl'tɛərɪən, vəʊl-) ADJECTIVE of or relating to Voltaire (pseudonym of *François Marie Arouet*), the French writer (1694–1778).

voltaism ('vɒltə,ɪzəm) NOUN another name for **galvanism.**

voltameter (vɒl'tæmɪtə) NOUN another name for **coulometer.**
▸**voltametric** (,vɒltə'mɛtrɪk) ADJECTIVE

voltammeter (,vəʊlt'æm,mi:tə) NOUN a dual-purpose instrument that can measure both potential difference and electric current, usually in volts and amperes respectively.

volt-ampere ('vəʊlt'æmpɛə) NOUN the product of the potential in volts across an electrical circuit and the resultant current in amperes. Abbreviation: **VA.**

volte (vɒlt) NOUN a variant spelling of **volt**[2].

volte-face ('vɒlt'fɑ:s) NOUN, *plural* **volte-face.** [1] a reversal, as in opinion or policy. [2] a change of

position so as to look, lie, etc., in the opposite direction.
▷**HISTORY** C19: from French, from Italian *volta-faccia*, from *volta* a turn + *faccia* face

voltmeter ('vəʊlt,miːtə) NOUN an instrument for measuring potential difference or electromotive force.

Volturno (*Italian* vol'turno) NOUN a river in S central Italy, flowing southeast and southwest to the Tyrrhenian Sea: scene of a battle (1860) during the wars for Italian unity, in which Garibaldi defeated the Neapolitans; German line of defence during World War II. Length: 175 km (109 miles).

voluble ('vɒljʊbᵊl) ADJECTIVE [1] talking easily, readily, and at length; fluent. [2] *Archaic* easily turning or rotating, as on an axis. [3] *Rare* (of a plant) twining or twisting.
▷**HISTORY** C16: from Latin *volūbilis* turning readily, fluent, from *volvere* to turn
▸**,volu'bility** *or* **'volubleness** NOUN ▸**'volubly** ADVERB

volume ('vɒljuːm) NOUN [1] the magnitude of the three-dimensional space enclosed within or occupied by an object, geometric solid, etc. Symbol: *V*. [2] a large mass or quantity: *the volume of protest*. [3] an amount or total: *the volume of exports*. [4] fullness or intensity of tone or sound. [5] the control on a radio, etc., for adjusting the intensity of sound. [6] a bound collection of printed or written pages; book. [7] any of several books either bound in an identical format or part of a series. [8] the complete set of issues of a periodical over a specified period, esp one year. [9] *History* a roll or scroll of parchment, papyrus, etc. [10] **speak volumes.** to convey much significant information. ◆ Abbreviations (for senses 6–8): **v, vol.**
▷**HISTORY** C14: from Old French *volum*, from Latin *volūmen* a roll, book, from *volvere* to roll up

volumed ('vɒljuːmd) ADJECTIVE [1] (of literary works) **a** consisting of or being in volumes. **b** (*in combination*): *a three-volumed history*. [2] *Rare* having bulk or volume. [3] *Poetic* forming a rounded mass.

volumeter (vɒ'ljuːmɪtə) NOUN any instrument for measuring the volume of a solid, liquid, or gas.

volumetric (,vɒljʊ'mɛtrɪk) ADJECTIVE of, concerning, or using measurement by volume: *volumetric analysis*. Compare **gravimetric.**
▸**,volu'metrically** ADVERB ▸**volumetry** (vɒ'ljuːmɪtrɪ) NOUN

volumetric analysis NOUN *Chem* [1] quantitative analysis of liquids or solutions by comparing the volumes that react with known volumes of standard reagents, usually by titration. Compare **gravimetric analysis.** [2] quantitative analysis of gases by volume.

volumetric displacement NOUN the volume of air per revolution that passes through a mechanical pump when the pressure at the intake and the exhaust is the same as that of the atmosphere. Also called: **swept volume.**

volumetric efficiency NOUN [1] the ratio of fluid delivered by a piston or ram pump per stroke to the displacement volume of the piston or ram. [2] the ratio of air or gas-air mixture drawn into the cylinder of an internal-combustion engine to the volumetric displacement of the piston.

voluminous (və'luːmɪnəs) ADJECTIVE [1] of great size, quantity, volume, or extent. [2] (of writing) consisting of or sufficient to fill volumes. [3] prolific in writing or speech. [4] *Obsolete* winding.
▷**HISTORY** C17: from Late Latin *volūminōsus* full of windings, from *volūmen* VOLUME
▸**voluminosity** (və,luːmɪ'nɒsɪtɪ) *or* **vo'luminousness** NOUN ▸**vo'luminously** ADVERB

voluntarism ('vɒləntə,rɪzəm) NOUN [1] *Philosophy* the theory that the will rather than the intellect is the ultimate principle of reality. [2] a doctrine or system based on voluntary participation in a course of action. [3] the belief that the state, government, and the law should not interfere with the procedures of collective bargaining and of trade union organization. [4] another name for **voluntaryism.**
▸**'voluntarist** NOUN, ADJECTIVE ▸**,volunta'ristic** ADJECTIVE

voluntary ('vɒləntərɪ, -trɪ) ADJECTIVE [1] performed, undertaken, or brought about by free choice, willingly, or without being asked: *a voluntary donation*. [2] (of persons) serving or acting in a specified function of one's own accord and without compulsion or promise of remuneration: *a voluntary social worker*. [3] done by, composed of, or functioning with the aid of volunteers: *a voluntary association*. [4] endowed with, exercising, or having the faculty of willing: *a voluntary agent*. [5] arising from natural impulse; spontaneous: *voluntary laughter*. [6] *Law* **a** acting or done without legal obligation, compulsion, or persuasion. **b** made without payment or recompense in any form: *a voluntary conveyance*. [7] (of the muscles of the limbs, neck, etc.) having their action controlled by the will. [8] maintained or provided by the voluntary actions or contributions of individuals and not by the state: *voluntary schools; the voluntary system*. ◆ NOUN, *plural* **-taries.** [9] *Music* a composition or improvisation, usually for organ, played at the beginning or end of a church service. [10] work done without compulsion. [11] *Obsolete* a volunteer, esp in an army.
▷**HISTORY** C14: from Latin *voluntārius*, from *voluntās* will, from *velle* to wish
▸**volun'tarily** ADVERB ▸**'voluntariness** NOUN

Voluntary Aid Detachment NOUN (in World War I) an organization of British women volunteers who assisted in military hospitals and ambulance duties. Abbreviation: **VAD.**

voluntary arrangement NOUN *Law* a procedure enabling an insolvent company to come to an arrangement with its creditors and resolve its financial problems, often in compliance with a court order.

voluntaryism ('vɒləntərɪ,ɪzəm, -trɪ-) *or* **voluntarism** NOUN [1] the principle of supporting churches, schools, and various other institutions by voluntary contributions rather than with state funds. [2] any system based on this principle.
▸**'voluntaryist** *or* **'voluntarist** NOUN

voluntary retailer NOUN another name for **symbol retailer.**

volunteer (,vɒlən'tɪə) NOUN [1] **a** a person who performs or offers to perform voluntary service. **b** (*as modifier*): *a volunteer system; volunteer advice*. [2] a person who freely undertakes military service, esp temporary or special service. [3] *Law* **a** a person who does some act or enters into a transaction without being under any legal obligation to do so and without being promised any remuneration for his services. **b** *Property law* a person to whom property is transferred without his giving any valuable consideration in return, as a legatee under a will. [4] **a** a plant that grows from seed that has not been deliberately sown. **b** (*as modifier*): *a volunteer plant*. ◆ VERB [5] to offer (oneself or one's services) for an undertaking by choice and without request or obligation. [6] (*tr*) to perform, give, or communicate voluntarily: *to volunteer help; to volunteer a speech*. [7] (*intr*) to enlist voluntarily for military service.
▷**HISTORY** C17: from French *volontaire*, from Latin *voluntārius* willing; see VOLUNTARY

volunteer bureau NOUN (*often capitals*) (in Britain) *Social welfare* an agency that matches up people wishing to do voluntary work with appropriate voluntary organizations.

volunteerism (,vɒlən'tɪərɪzəm) NOUN the principle of donating time and energy for the benefit of other people in the community as a social responsibility rather than for any financial reward.

Volunteers of America PLURAL NOUN a religious body aimed at reform and relief of human need and resembling the Salvation Army in organization and tenets, founded in New York City in 1896 by Ballington Booth.

voluptuary (və'lʌptjʊərɪ) NOUN, *plural* **-aries.** [1] a person devoted or addicted to luxury and sensual pleasures. ◆ ADJECTIVE [2] of, relating to, characterized by, or furthering sensual gratification or luxury.
▷**HISTORY** C17: from Late Latin *voluptuārius* delightful, from Latin *voluptās* pleasure

voluptuous (və'lʌptjʊəs) ADJECTIVE [1] relating to, characterized by, or consisting of pleasures of the body or senses; sensual. [2] disposed, devoted, or addicted to sensual indulgence or luxurious pleasures. [3] provocative and sexually alluring, esp through shapeliness or fullness: *a voluptuous woman*.
▷**HISTORY** C14: from Latin *voluptuōsus* full of gratification, from *voluptās* pleasure
▸**vo'luptuously** ADVERB ▸**vo'luptuousness** NOUN

volute ('vɒljuːt, və'luːt) NOUN [1] a spiral or twisting turn, form, or object; spiral; whorl. [2] Also called: **helix.** a carved ornament, esp as used on an Ionic capital, that has the form of a spiral scroll. [3] any of the whorls of the spirally coiled shell of a snail or similar gastropod mollusc. [4] any tropical marine gastropod mollusc of the family *Volutidae*, typically having a spiral shell with beautiful markings. [5] a tangential part, resembling the volute of a snail's shell, that collects the fluids emerging from the periphery of a turbine, impeller pump, etc. ◆ ADJECTIVE *also* **voluted** (və'luːtɪd). [6] having the form of a volute; spiral. [7] *Machinery* moving in a spiral path.
▷**HISTORY** C17: from Latin *volūta* a spiral decoration, from *volūtus* rolled, from *volvere* to roll up

volution (və'luːʃən) NOUN [1] a rolling, revolving, or spiral form or motion. [2] a whorl of a spiral gastropod shell.

volva ('vɒlvə) NOUN, *plural* **-vae** (-viː) *or* **-vas.** *Botany* a cup-shaped structure that sheathes the base of the stalk of certain mushrooms.
▷**HISTORY** C18: from Latin: a covering, from *volvere* to wrap
▸**volvate** ('vɒlvɪt, -veɪt) ADJECTIVE

volvox ('vɒlvɒks) NOUN any freshwater flagellate protozoan of the genus *Volvox*, occurring in colonies in the form of hollow multicellular spheres.
▷**HISTORY** C18: from New Latin, from Latin *volvere* to roll

volvulus ('vɒlvjʊləs) NOUN, *plural* **-luses.** *Pathol* an abnormal twisting of the intestines causing obstruction.
▷**HISTORY** C17: from New Latin, from Latin *volvere* to twist

vomer ('vəʊmə) NOUN the thin flat bone forming part of the separation between the nasal passages in mammals.
▷**HISTORY** C18: from Latin: ploughshare
▸**vomerine** ('vəʊmə,raɪn, -rɪn, 'vɒm-) ADJECTIVE

vomit ('vɒmɪt) VERB **-its, -iting, -ited.** [1] to eject (the contents of the stomach) through the mouth as the result of involuntary muscular spasms of the stomach and oesophagus. [2] to eject or be ejected forcefully; spew forth. ◆ NOUN [3] the matter ejected in vomiting. [4] the act of vomiting. [5] a drug or agent that induces vomiting; emetic.
▷**HISTORY** C14: from Latin *vomitāre* to vomit repeatedly, from *vomere* to vomit
▸**'vomiter** NOUN

vomit comet NOUN *Informal* an aircraft that dives suddenly in altitude, simulating freefall, in order to allow astronauts to experience the nausea that can affect people in a gravity-free environment.

vomitory ('vɒmɪtərɪ, -trɪ) ADJECTIVE [1] Also: **vomitive** ('vɒmɪtɪv). causing vomiting; emetic. ◆ NOUN, *plural* **-ries.** [2] Also called: **vomitive.** a vomitory agent. [3] *Rare* a container for receiving vomitus. [4] Also called: **vomitorium** (,vɒmɪ'tɔːrɪəm). a passageway in an ancient Roman amphitheatre that connects an outside entrance to a tier of seats. [5] an opening through which matter is ejected.

vomitous ('vɒmɪtəs) ADJECTIVE [1] arousing feelings of disgust: *a vomitous ending*. [2] relating or connected to feeling or being sick: *a vomitous night on the town*.

vomiturition (,vɒmɪtjʊ'rɪʃən) NOUN the act of retching.

vomitus ('vɒmɪtəs) NOUN, *plural* **-tuses.** [1] matter that has been vomited. [2] the act of vomiting.
▷**HISTORY** Latin: a vomiting

voodoo ('vuːduː) NOUN, *plural* **-doos.** [1] Also called: **voodooism.** a religious cult involving witchcraft and communication by trance with ancestors and animistic deities, common in Haiti and other Caribbean islands. [2] a person who practises voodoo. [3] a charm, spell, or fetish involved in voodoo worship and ritual. ◆ ADJECTIVE [4] relating to or associated with voodoo. ◆ VERB **-doos, -dooing, -dooed.** [5] (*tr*) to affect by or as if by the power of voodoo.
▷**HISTORY** C19: from Louisiana French *voudou*, ultimately of West African origin; compare Ewe *vodu* guardian spirit
▸**'voodooist** NOUN ▸**,voodoo'istic** ADJECTIVE

voorkamer ('fʊə,kɑːmə) NOUN *South African* the

front room, esp of a Cape Dutch house or farmhouse.
▷HISTORY from Afrikaans *voor* front + *kamer* room

voorskot ('fʊəˌskɒt) NOUN *South African* advance payment made to a farmer for crops. Compare **agterskot.**
▷HISTORY C20: Afrikaans, from *voor* before + *skot* shot, payment

Voortrekker ('fʊəˌtrɛkə, 'vʊə-) NOUN (in South Africa) 1 one of the original Afrikaner settlers of the Transvaal and the Orange Free State who migrated from the Cape Colony in the 1830s. 2 a member of the Afrikaner youth movement founded in 1931.
▷HISTORY C19: from Dutch, from *voor-* FORE- + *trekken* to TREK

voracious (vɒ'reɪʃəs) ADJECTIVE 1 devouring or craving food in great quantities. 2 very eager or unremitting in some activity: *voracious reading.*
▷HISTORY C17: from Latin *vorāx* swallowing greedily, from *vorāre* to devour
▸**vo'raciously** ADVERB ▸**voracity** (vɒ'ræsɪtɪ) *or* **vo'raciousness** NOUN

Vorarlberg (*German* 'fo:rarlbɛrk) NOUN a mountainous state of W Austria. Capital: Bregenz. Pop.: 351 565 (2001). Area: 2601 sq. km (1004 sq. miles).

Vorlage *German* ('fo:rla:gə) NOUN *Skiing* a position in which a skier leans forward but keeps his heels on the skis.
▷HISTORY from *vor* before, in front of + *Lage* position, stance

-vorous ADJECTIVE COMBINING FORM feeding on or devouring: *carnivorous.*
▷HISTORY from Latin *-vorus;* related to *vorāre* to swallow up, DEVOUR
▸**-vore** NOUN COMBINING FORM

vortex ('vɔ:tɛks) NOUN, *plural* **-texes** *or* **-tices** (-tɪˌsi:z). 1 a whirling mass or rotary motion in a liquid, gas, flame, etc., such as the spiralling movement of water around a whirlpool. 2 any activity, situation, or way of life regarded as irresistibly engulfing.
▷HISTORY C17: from Latin: a whirlpool; variant of VERTEX
▸**vortical** ('vɔ:tɪkᵊl) ADJECTIVE ▸**'vortically** ADVERB

vortex drag NOUN See **trailing vortex drag.**

vortex ring NOUN a stable perturbation in a fluid that takes the form of a torus in which the flow rotates in the section of the torus so that the pressure difference between the inside and outside of the torus balances body forces. The best-known vortex ring is a smoke ring.

vortex shedding NOUN the process by which vortices formed continuously by the aerodynamic conditions associated with a solid body in a gas or air stream are carried downstream by the flow in the form of a vortex street. See also **vortex street.**

vortex street NOUN a regular stream of vortices or parallel streams of vortices carried downstream by the flow of a fluid over a body. These are sometimes made visible by vapour condensation as in the vortex trails from the wing tips of an aeroplane. See also **Kármán vortex street, vortex shedding.**

vorticella (ˌvɔ:tɪ'sɛlə) NOUN, *plural* **-lae** (-li:). any protozoan of the genus *Vorticella,* consisting of a goblet-shaped ciliated cell attached to the substratum by a long contractile stalk.
▷HISTORY C18: from New Latin, literally: a little eddy, from VORTEX

vorticism ('vɔ:tɪˌsɪzəm) NOUN an art movement in England initiated in 1913 by Wyndham Lewis, the British painter, novelist, and critic (1884–1957), combining the techniques of cubism with the concern for the problems of the machine age evinced in futurism.
▷HISTORY C20: referring to the "vortices" of modern life on which the movement was based
▸**'vorticist** NOUN

vorticose ('vɔ:tɪˌkəʊs) ADJECTIVE *Rare* rotating quickly; whirling.
▷HISTORY C18: from Latin *vorticōsus,* variant of *verticōsus* full of whirlpools; see VERTEX

vortiginous (vɔ:'tɪdʒɪnəs) ADJECTIVE like a vortex; vortical; whirling.
▷HISTORY C17: variant of VERTIGINOUS

Vortumnus (vɔ:'tʌmnəs) NOUN a variant spelling of **Vertumnus.**

Vosges (*French* voʒ) NOUN 1 a mountain range in E France, west of the Rhine valley. Highest peak: 1423 m (4672 ft.). 2 a department of NE France, in Lorraine region. Capital: Épinal. Pop.: 380 952 (1999). Area: 5903 sq. km (2302 sq. miles).

Vostok ('vɒstɒk) NOUN any of six manned Soviet spacecraft made to orbit the earth. **Vostok 1,** launched in April 1961, carried Yuri Gagarin, the first man in space; **Vostok 6** carried Valentina Tereshkova, the first woman in space.

vostro account ('vɒstrəʊ) NOUN a bank account held by a foreign bank with a British bank, usually in sterling. Compare **nostro account.**

votary ('vəʊtərɪ) NOUN, *plural* **-ries.** *also* **votarist.** 1 *RC Church, Eastern Churches* a person, such as a monk or nun, who has dedicated himself or herself to religion by taking vows. 2 a devoted adherent of a religion, cause, leader, pursuit, etc. ◆ ADJECTIVE 3 ardently devoted to the services or worship of God, a deity, or a saint.
▷HISTORY C16: from Latin *vōtum* a vow, from *vovēre* to vow
▸**'votaress** *or* **'votress** FEMININE NOUN

vote (vəʊt) NOUN 1 an indication of choice, opinion, or will on a question, such as the choosing of a candidate, by or as if by some recognized means, such as a ballot: *10 votes for Jones.* 2 the opinion of a group of persons as determined by voting: *it was put to the vote; do not take a vote; it came to a vote.* 3 a body of votes or voters collectively: *the Jewish vote.* 4 the total number of votes cast: *the vote decreased at the last election.* 5 the ticket, ballot, etc., by which a vote is expressed. 6 **a** the right to vote; franchise; suffrage. **b** a person regarded as the embodiment of this right. 7 a means of voting, such as a ballot. 8 *Chiefly Brit* a grant or other proposition to be voted upon. ◆ VERB 9 (when *tr, takes a clause as object or an infinitive*) to express or signify (one's preference, opinion, or will) (for or against some question, etc.): *to vote by ballot; we voted that it was time to adjourn; vote for me!* 10 (*intr*) to declare oneself as being (something or in favour of something) by exercising one's vote: *to vote socialist.* 11 (*tr;* foll by *into* or *out of,* etc.) to appoint or elect (a person to or from a particular post): *they voted him into the presidency; he was voted out of office.* 12 (*tr*) to determine the condition of in a specified way by voting: *the court voted itself out of existence.* 13 (*tr*) to authorize, confer, or allow by voting: *vote us a rise.* 14 (*tr*) *Informal* to declare by common opinion: *the party was voted a failure.* 15 (*tr*) to influence or control the voting of: *do not try to vote us!*
▷HISTORY C15: from Latin *vōtum* a solemn promise, from *vovēre* to vow
▸**'votable** *or* **'voteable** ADJECTIVE ▸**'voteless** ADJECTIVE

vote down VERB (*tr, adverb*) to decide against or defeat in a vote: *the bill was voted down.*

vote of no confidence NOUN *Parliament* a vote on a motion put by the Opposition censuring an aspect of the Government's policy; if the motion is carried the Government is obliged to resign. Also called: **vote of censure.**

voter ('vəʊtə) NOUN a person who can or does vote.

voting machine NOUN (esp in the US) a machine at a polling station that voters operate to register their votes and that mechanically or electronically counts all votes cast.

votive ('vəʊtɪv) ADJECTIVE 1 offered, given, undertaken, performed or dedicated in fulfilment of or in accordance with a vow. 2 *RC Church* optional; not prescribed; having the nature of a voluntary offering: *a votive Mass; a votive candle.*
▷HISTORY C16: from Latin *vōtīvus* promised by a vow, from *vōtum* a vow
▸**'votively** ADVERB ▸**'votiveness** NOUN

Votyak ('vəʊtɪˌæk) NOUN 1 (*plural* **-aks** *or* **-ak**) a member of a Finnish people living chiefly in the Udmurt Autonomous Republic, between the Volga and the Urals. 2 Also called: **Udmurt.** the language of this people, belonging to the Finno-Ugric family.

vouch (vaʊtʃ) VERB 1 (*intr;* usually foll by *for*) to give personal assurance; guarantee: *I'll vouch for his safety.* 2 (when *tr, usually takes a clause as object;* when *intr,* usually foll by *for*) to furnish supporting evidence (for) or function as proof (of). 3 (*tr*) *English legal history* to summon (a person who had warranted title to land) to defend that title or give up land of equal value. 4 (*tr*) *Archaic* to cite (authors, principles, etc.) in support of something. 5 (*tr*) *Obsolete* to assert. ◆ NOUN 6 *Obsolete* the act of vouching; assertion or allegation.
▷HISTORY C14: from Old French *vocher* to summon, ultimately from Latin *vocāre* to call

voucher ('vaʊtʃə) NOUN 1 a document serving as evidence for some claimed transaction, as the receipt or expenditure of money. 2 *Brit* a ticket or card serving as a substitute for cash: *a gift voucher.* 3 a person or thing that vouches for the truth of some statement, etc. 4 any of certain documents that various groups of British nationals born outside Britain must obtain in order to settle in Britain. 5 *English law, obsolete* **a** the summoning into court of a person to warrant a title to property. **b** the person so summoned.
▷HISTORY C16: from Anglo-French, noun use of Old French *voucher* to summon; see VOUCH

vouchsafe (ˌvaʊtʃ'seɪf) VERB (*tr*) 1 to give or grant or condescend to give or grant: *she vouchsafed no reply; he vouchsafed me no encouragement.* 2 (*may take a clause as object or an infinitive*) to agree, promise, or permit, often graciously or condescendingly: *he vouchsafed to come yesterday.* 3 *Obsolete* **a** to warrant as being safe. **b** to bestow as a favour (upon).
▷HISTORY C14 *vouchen sauf;* see VOUCH, SAFE
▸**ˌvouch'safement** NOUN

vouge (vu:ʒ) NOUN a form of pike or halberd used by foot soldiers in the 14th century and later.
▷HISTORY from Old French *voulge, vouge* (Medieval Latin *vanga*), of obscure origin

voussoir (vu:'swɑ:) NOUN a wedge-shaped stone or brick that is used with others to construct an arch or vault.
▷HISTORY C18: from French, from Vulgar Latin *volsōrium* (unattested), ultimately from Latin *volvere* to turn, roll

Vouvray ('vu:vreɪ; *French* vuvrɛ) NOUN a dry white wine, which can be still, sparkling, or semisparkling, produced around Touraine in the Loire Valley.

vow (vaʊ) NOUN 1 a solemn or earnest pledge or promise binding the person making it to perform a specified act or behave in a certain way. 2 a solemn promise made to a deity or saint, by which the promiser pledges himself to some future act, course of action, or way of life. 3 **take vows.** to enter a religious order and commit oneself to its rule of life by the vows of poverty, chastity, and obedience, which may be taken for a limited period as **simple vows** or as a perpetual and still more solemn commitment as **solemn vows.** ◆ VERB 4 (*tr; may take a clause as object or an infinitive*) to pledge, promise, or undertake solemnly: *he vowed that he would continue; he vowed to return.* 5 (*tr*) to dedicate or consecrate to God, a deity, or a saint. 6 (*tr; usually takes a clause as object*) to assert or swear emphatically. 7 (*intr*) *Archaic* to declare solemnly.
▷HISTORY C13: from Old French *vou,* from Latin *vōtum* a solemn promise, from *vovēre* to vow
▸**'vower** NOUN ▸**'vowless** ADJECTIVE

vowel ('vaʊəl) NOUN 1 *Phonetics* a voiced speech sound whose articulation is characterized by the absence of friction-causing obstruction in the vocal tract, allowing the breath stream free passage. The timbre of a vowel is chiefly determined by the position of the tongue and the lips. 2 a letter or character representing a vowel.
▷HISTORY C14: from Old French *vouel,* from Latin *vocālis littera* a vowel, from *vocālis* sonorous, from *vox* a voice
▸**'vowel-less** ADJECTIVE ▸**'vowel-ˌlike** ADJECTIVE

vowel gradation NOUN another name for **ablaut.** See **gradation** (sense 5).

vowelize *or* **vowelise** ('vaʊəˌlaɪz) VERB (*tr*) to mark the vowel points in (a Hebrew word or text). Also: **vocalize.**
▸**ˌvoweli'zation** *or* **ˌvoweli'sation** NOUN

vowel mutation NOUN another name for **umlaut.**

vowel point NOUN any of several marks or points placed above or below consonants, esp those evolved for Hebrew or Arabic, in order to indicate vowel sounds.

vox (vɒks) NOUN, *plural* **voces** ('vəʊsi:z). a voice or sound.
▷HISTORY Latin: voice

vox angelica (æn'dʒɛlɪkə) NOUN an organ stop with a soft tone, often similar to the voix céleste.
▷**HISTORY** C18: from Latin: angelic voice

vox humana (hjuː'mɑːnə) NOUN a reed stop on an organ supposedly imitative of the human voice.
▷**HISTORY** C18: from Latin: human voice

vox pop NOUN interviews with members of the public on a radio or television programme.
▷**HISTORY** C20: shortened from VOX POPULI

vox populi ('pɒpjʊˌlaɪ) NOUN the voice of the people; popular or public opinion.
▷**HISTORY** Latin

voyage ('vɔɪɪdʒ) NOUN [1] a journey, travel, or passage, esp one to a distant land or by sea or air. [2] *Obsolete* an ambitious project. ◆ VERB [3] to travel over or traverse (something): *we will voyage to Africa.*
▷**HISTORY** C13: from Old French *veiage,* from Latin *viāticum* provision for travelling, from *viāticus* concerning a journey, from *via* a way
▸ **'voyager** NOUN

voyage charter NOUN the hire of a ship or aircraft for a specified number of voyages. Compare **time charter.**

Voyager ('vɔɪədʒə) NOUN either of two US spacecraft that studied the outer solar system; **Voyager 1** visited Jupiter (1979) and Saturn (1980), **Voyager 2** visited Jupiter (1979) and Saturn (1981) and made the first flyby of Uranus (1986) and Neptune (1989).

voyageur (ˌvɔɪə'dʒɜː) NOUN *Canadian* [1] *History* a boatman employed by one of the early fur-trading companies, esp in the interior. [2] a woodsman, guide, trapper, boatman, or explorer, esp in the North.
▷**HISTORY** C19: from French: traveller, from *voyager* to VOYAGE

voyeur (vwaɪ'ɜː; *French* vwajœr) NOUN a person who obtains sexual pleasure or excitement from the observation of someone undressing, having intercourse, etc.
▷**HISTORY** C20: French, literally: one who sees, from *voir* to see, from Latin *vidēre*
▸ **vo'yeurism** NOUN ▸ **ˌvoyeur'istic** ADJECTIVE
▸ **ˌvoyeur'istically** ADVERB

VP ABBREVIATION FOR: [1] Vice President. [2] **verb phrase.**

VPL *Jocular* ABBREVIATION FOR visible panty line.

VR ABBREVIATION FOR: [1] variant reading. [2] Victoria Regina. [Latin: Queen Victoria] [3] virtual reality. [4] Volunteer Reserve.

vraisemblance (ˌvreɪsɒm'blɒns; *French* vrɛsɑ̃blɑ̃s) NOUN verisimilitude; appearance of truth.
▷**HISTORY** French, from *vrai* true + SEMBLANCE

V. Rev. ABBREVIATION FOR Very Reverend.

VRI ABBREVIATION FOR Victoria Regina et Imperatrix.
▷**HISTORY** Latin: Victoria, Queen and Empress

vroom (vruːm, vrʊm) INTERJECTION an exclamation imitative of a car engine revving up, as for high-speed motor racing.

vrou (fraʊ) NOUN *South African* a woman or wife.
▷**HISTORY** Afrikaans

vs ABBREVIATION FOR versus.

VS ABBREVIATION FOR Veterinary Surgeon.

v.s. ABBREVIATION FOR vide supra. See **vide.**

vsb ABBREVIATION FOR vestigial sideband: a transmission in an amplitude-modulated signal in which one complete sideband is transmitted, but only part of the other.

V-sign NOUN [1] (in Britain) an offensive gesture made by sticking up the index and middle fingers with the palm of the hand inwards as an indication of contempt, defiance, etc. [2] a similar gesture with the palm outwards meaning victory or peace.

VSO ABBREVIATION FOR: [1] very superior old: used to indicate that a brandy, port, etc., is between 12 and 17 years old. [2] (in Britain) Voluntary Service Overseas: an organization that sends young volunteers to use and teach their skills in developing countries.

VSOP ABBREVIATION FOR very special (or superior) old pale: used to indicate that a brandy, port, etc., is between 20 and 25 years old.

Vt. *or* **VT** ABBREVIATION FOR Vermont.

VTOL ('viːtɒl) NOUN [1] vertical takeoff and landing; a system in which an aircraft can take off and land vertically. [2] an aircraft that uses this system. Compare **STOL.**

VTR ABBREVIATION FOR video tape recorder.

V-type engine NOUN a type of internal-combustion engine having two cylinder blocks attached to a single crankcase, the angle between the two blocks forming a V.

vu THE INTERNET DOMAIN NAME FOR Vanuatu.

vug, vugg, *or* **vugh** (vʌg) NOUN *Mining* a small cavity in a rock or vein, usually lined with crystals.
▷**HISTORY** C19: from Cornish *vooga* cave
▸ **'vuggy** *or* **'vughy** ADJECTIVE

Vulcan[1] ('vʌlkən) NOUN the Roman god of fire and metalworking. Greek counterpart: **Hephaestus.**
▸ **Vulcanian** (vʌl'keɪnɪən) ADJECTIVE

Vulcan[2] ('vʌlkən) NOUN a hypothetical planet once thought to lie within the orbit of Mercury.
▸ **Vulcanian** (vʌl'keɪnɪən) ADJECTIVE

vulcanian (vʌl'keɪnɪən) ADJECTIVE *Geology* **a** of or relating to a volcanic eruption characterized by the explosive discharge of fine ash and large irregular fragments of solidified or viscous lava. **b** a less common word for **volcanic.**

vulcanism ('vʌlkəˌnɪzəm) NOUN a variant spelling of **volcanism.**

vulcanite ('vʌlkəˌnaɪt) NOUN a hard usually black rubber produced by vulcanizing natural rubber with large amounts of sulphur. It is resistant to chemical attack: used for chemical containers, electrical insulators, etc. Also called: **ebonite.**

vulcanize *or* **vulcanise** ('vʌlkəˌnaɪz) VERB *(tr)* [1] to treat (rubber) with sulphur or sulphur compounds under heat and pressure to improve elasticity and strength or to produce a hard substance such as vulcanite. [2] to treat (substances other than rubber) by a similar process in order to improve their properties.
▸ **'vulcanˌizable** *or* **'vulcanˌisable** ADJECTIVE
▸ **ˌvulcani'zation** *or* **ˌvulcani'sation** NOUN ▸ **'vulcanˌizer** *or* **'vulcanˌiser** NOUN

vulcanology (ˌvʌlkə'nɒlədʒɪ) NOUN a variant spelling of **volcanology.**
▸ **vulcanological** (ˌvʌlkənə'lɒdʒɪkᵊl) ADJECTIVE
▸ **ˌvulcan'ologist** NOUN

Vulg. ABBREVIATION FOR Vulgate.

vulgar ('vʌlgə) ADJECTIVE [1] marked by lack of taste, culture, delicacy, manners, etc.: *vulgar behaviour; vulgar language.* [2] *(often capital; usually prenominal)* denoting a form of a language, esp of Latin, current among common people, esp at a period when the formal language is archaic and not in general spoken use. [3] *Archaic* **a** of, relating to, or current among the great mass of common people, in contrast to the educated, cultured, or privileged; ordinary. **b** *(as collective noun;* preceded by *the): the vulgar.*
▷**HISTORY** C14: from Latin *vulgāris* belonging to the multitude, from *vulgus* the common people
▸ **'vulgarly** ADVERB

vulgar fraction NOUN another name for **simple fraction.**

vulgarian (vʌl'gɛərɪən) NOUN a vulgar person, esp one who is rich or has pretensions to good taste.

vulgarism ('vʌlgəˌrɪzəm) NOUN [1] a coarse, crude, or obscene expression. [2] a word or phrase found only in the vulgar form of a language. [3] another word for **vulgarity.**

vulgarity (vʌl'gærɪtɪ) NOUN, *plural* **-ties.** [1] the condition of being vulgar; lack of good manners. [2] a vulgar action, phrase, etc.

vulgarize *or* **vulgarise** ('vʌlgəˌraɪz) VERB *(tr)* [1] to make commonplace or vulgar; debase. [2] to make (something little known or difficult to understand) widely known or popular among the public; popularize.
▸ **ˌvulgari'zation** *or* **ˌvulgari'sation** NOUN ▸ **'vulgarˌizer** *or* **'vulgarˌiser** NOUN

Vulgar Latin NOUN any of the dialects of Latin spoken in the Roman Empire other than classical Latin. The Romance languages developed from them.

vulgate ('vʌlgeɪt, -gɪt) *Rare* ◆ NOUN [1] a commonly recognized text or version. [2] everyday or informal speech; the vernacular. ◆ ADJECTIVE [3] generally accepted; common.

Vulgate ('vʌlgeɪt, -gɪt) NOUN **a** (from the 13th century onwards) the fourth-century version of the Bible produced by Jerome, partly by translating the original languages, and partly by revising the earlier Latin text based on the Greek versions. **b** *(as modifier): the Vulgate version.*
▷**HISTORY** C17: from Medieval Latin *Vulgāta,* from Late Latin *vulgāta editiō* popular version (of the Bible), from Latin *vulgāre* to make common, from *vulgus* the common people

vulnerable ('vʌlnərəbᵊl) ADJECTIVE [1] capable of being physically or emotionally wounded or hurt. [2] open to temptation, persuasion, censure, etc. [3] liable or exposed to disease, disaster, etc. [4] *Military* liable or exposed to attack. [5] *Bridge* (of a side who have won one game towards rubber) subject to increased bonuses or penalties.
▷**HISTORY** C17: from Late Latin *vulnerābilis,* from Latin *vulnerāre* to wound, from *vulnus* a wound
▸ **ˌvulnera'bility** *or* **'vulnerableness** NOUN ▸ **'vulnerably** ADVERB

vulnerary ('vʌlnərərɪ) *Med* ◆ ADJECTIVE [1] of, relating to, or used to heal a wound. ◆ NOUN, *plural* **-aries.** [2] a vulnerary drug or agent.
▷**HISTORY** C16: from Latin *vulnerārius* belonging to wounds, from *vulnus* a wound

Vulpecula (vʌl'pɛkjʊlə) NOUN, *Latin genitive* **Vulpeculae** (vʌl'pɛkjʊˌliː). a faint constellation in the N hemisphere lying between Cygnus and Aquila.
▷**HISTORY** C19: from Latin: a little fox, from *vulpēs* a fox

vulpine ('vʌlpaɪn) ADJECTIVE [1] Also: **vulpecular** (vʌl'pɛkjʊlə). of, relating to, or resembling a fox. [2] possessing the characteristics often attributed to foxes; crafty, clever, etc.
▷**HISTORY** C17: from Latin *vulpīnus* foxlike, from *vulpēs* a fox

vulture ('vʌltʃə) NOUN [1] any of various very large diurnal birds of prey of the genera *Neophron, Gyps, Gypaetus,* etc., of Africa, Asia, and warm parts of Europe, typically having broad wings and soaring flight and feeding on carrion: family *Accipitridae* (hawks). See also **griffon**[1] (sense 2), **lammergeier.** [2] any similar bird of the family *Cathartidae* of North, Central, and South America. See also **condor, turkey buzzard.** [3] a person or thing that preys greedily and ruthlessly on others, esp the helpless.
▷**HISTORY** C14: from Old French *voltour,* from Latin *vultur;* perhaps related to Latin *vellere* to pluck, tear
▸ **'vulture-ˌlike** ADJECTIVE

vulturine ('vʌltʃəˌraɪn) ADJECTIVE [1] of, relating to, or resembling a vulture. [2] Also: **vulturous.** rapacious, predatory, or greedy.

vulva ('vʌlvə) NOUN, *plural* **-vae** (-viː) *or* **-vas.** the external genitals of human females, including the labia, mons veneris, clitoris, and the vaginal orifice.
▷**HISTORY** C16: from Latin: covering, womb, matrix
▸ **'vulval** *or* **'vulvar** *or* **vulvate** ('vʌlveɪt) ADJECTIVE
▸ **vulviform** ('vʌlvɪˌfɔːm) ADJECTIVE

vulvitis (vʌl'vaɪtɪs) NOUN inflammation of the vulva.

vulvovaginitis (ˌvʌlvəʊˌvædʒɪ'naɪtɪs) NOUN inflammation of the vulva and vagina or of the small glands **(vulvovaginal glands)** on either side of the lower part of the vagina.

vutty ('vʌtɪ) ADJECTIVE **vuttier, vuttiest.** *Southwest English dialect* dirty.

vv ABBREVIATION FOR vice versa.

VW ABBREVIATION FOR: [1] Very Worshipful. [2] Volkswagen.

VX NOUN a US lethal nerve gas.

Vyborg (*Russian* 'vibərk) NOUN a port in NW Russia, at the head of **Vyborg Bay** (an inlet of the Gulf of Finland): belonged to Finland (1918–40). Pop.: 80 000 (latest est.). Finnish name: **Viipuri.** Swedish name: **Viborg.**

vying ('vaɪɪŋ) VERB [1] the present participle of **vie.** ◆ ADJECTIVE [2] competing: *two vying patriarchs.*

Ww

w *or* **W** ('dʌbᵊl,juː) NOUN, *plural* **w's, W's** *or* **Ws**. 1 the 23rd letter and 18th consonant of the modern English alphabet. 2 a speech sound represented by this letter, in English usually a bilabial semivowel, as in *web*.

W SYMBOL FOR: 1 watt. 2 West. 3 *Physics* work. 4 *Chem* tungsten. [from New Latin *wolframium,* from German *Wolfram*] 5 women's (size).

W8 *Text messaging* ABBREVIATION FOR wait.

w. ABBREVIATION FOR: 1 week. 2 weight. 3 width. 4 wife. 5 with. 6 *Cricket* **a** wide. **b** wicket.

W. ABBREVIATION FOR: 1 Wales. 2 Welsh.

WA ABBREVIATION FOR: 1 Washington (state). 2 Western Australia.

WAAAF (formerly) ABBREVIATION FOR Women's Auxiliary Australian Air Force.

WAAC (wæk) NOUN (formerly) 1 ACRONYM FOR Women's Army Auxiliary Corps. 2 Also called: **waac.** a member of this corps.

Waadt (vat) NOUN the German name for **Vaud.**

WAAF (wæf) NOUN (formerly) 1 ACRONYM FOR **a** Women's Auxiliary Air Force. **b** Women's Auxiliary Australian Air Force. 2 Also called: **Waaf.** a member of either of these forces.

Waal (*Dutch* waːl) NOUN a river in the central Netherlands: the S branch of the Lower Rhine. Length: 84 km (52 miles).

Wabash ('wɔːbæʃ) NOUN a river in the E central US, rising in W Ohio and flowing west and southwest to join the Ohio River in Indiana. Length: 764 km (475 miles).

wabbit ('wæbɪt) ADJECTIVE *Scot* weary; exhausted.
▷**HISTORY** C19: from earlier *wobart* withered, feeble

wabble ('wɒbᵊl) VERB, NOUN a variant spelling of **wobble.**
▸ '**wabbler** NOUN ▸ '**wabbly** ADJECTIVE

wack (wæk) *or* **wacker** ('wækə) NOUN *Liverpool and Midlands dialect* friend; pal: used chiefly as a term of address.
▷**HISTORY** perhaps from dialect *wack* or *whack* to share out, hence one who shares, a friend

wacke ('wækə) NOUN *Obsolete* any of various soft earthy rocks that resemble or are derived from basaltic rocks.
▷**HISTORY** C18: from German: rock, gravel, basalt

wacko ('wækəʊ) *Informal* ◆ ADJECTIVE 1 mad or eccentric. ◆ NOUN, *plural* **wackos.** 2 a mad or eccentric person.
▷**HISTORY** C20: back formation from WACKY

wacky ('wækɪ) ADJECTIVE **wackier, wackiest.** *Slang* eccentric, erratic, or unpredictable.
▷**HISTORY** C19 (in dialect sense: a fool, an eccentric): from WHACK (hence, a *whacky,* a person who behaves as if he had been whacked on the head)
▸ '**wackily** ADVERB ▸ '**wackiness** NOUN

wad¹ (wɒd) NOUN 1 a small mass or ball of fibrous or soft material, such as cotton wool, used esp for packing or stuffing. 2 **a** a plug of paper, cloth, leather, etc., pressed against a charge to hold it in place in a muzzle-loading cannon. **b** a disc of paper, felt, pasteboard, etc., used to hold in place the powder and shot in a shotgun cartridge. 3 a roll or bundle of something, esp of banknotes. 4 *US and Canadian slang* a large quantity, esp of money. 5 *Brit dialect* a bundle of hay or straw. 6 *Brit military slang* a bun: *char and a wad.* ◆ VERB **wads, wadding, wadded.** 7 to form (something) into a wad. 8 (*tr*) to roll into a wad or bundle. 9 (*tr*) **a** to hold (a charge) in place with a wad. **b** to insert a wad into (a gun). 10 (*tr*) to pack or stuff with wadding; pad.
▷**HISTORY** C14: from Late Latin *wadda;* related to German *Watte* cotton wool
▸ '**wadder** NOUN

wad² (wɒd) NOUN a soft dark earthy amorphous material consisting of decomposed manganese minerals: occurs in damp marshy areas.
▷**HISTORY** C17: of unknown origin

Wadai (wɑː'daɪ) NOUN a former independent sultanate of NE central Africa: now the E part of Chad.

Waddenzee (*Dutch* 'wɑdənzeː) NOUN the part of the North Sea between the Dutch mainland and the West Frisian Islands.

Waddesdon Manor ('wɒdzdən) NOUN a mansion near Aylesbury in Buckinghamshire: built (1880–89) in the French style for the Rothschild family: noted for its furnishings and collections of porcelain and paintings.

wadding ('wɒdɪŋ) NOUN 1 **a** any fibrous or soft substance used as padding, stuffing, etc., esp sheets of carded cotton prepared for the purpose. **b** a piece of this. 2 material for wads used in cartridges or guns.

waddle ('wɒdᵊl) VERB (*intr*) 1 to walk with short steps, rocking slightly from side to side. ◆ NOUN 2 a swaying gait or motion.
▷**HISTORY** C16: probably frequentative of WADE
▸ '**waddler** NOUN ▸ '**waddling** ADJECTIVE ▸ '**waddly** ADJECTIVE

waddy ('wɒdɪ) NOUN, *plural* **-dies.** 1 a heavy wooden club used as a weapon by native Australians. ◆ VERB **-dies, -dying, -died.** 2 (*tr*) to hit with a waddy.
▷**HISTORY** C19: from a native Australian language, perhaps based on English WOOD¹

wade (weɪd) VERB 1 to walk with the feet immersed in (water, a stream, etc.): *the girls waded the river at the ford.* 2 (*intr;* often foll by *through*) to proceed with difficulty: *to wade through a book.* 3 (*intr;* foll by *in* or *into*) to attack energetically. ◆ NOUN 4 the act or an instance of wading.
▷**HISTORY** Old English *wadan;* related to Old Frisian *wada,* Old High German *watan,* Old Norse *vatha,* Latin *vadum* FORD
▸ '**wadable** *or* '**wadeable** ADJECTIVE

wader ('weɪdə) NOUN 1 a person or thing that wades. 2 Also called: **wading bird.** any of various long-legged birds, esp those of the order *Ciconiiformes* (herons, storks, etc.), that live near water and feed on fish, etc. 3 a Brit name for **shore bird.**

waders ('weɪdəz) PLURAL NOUN long waterproof boots, sometimes extending to the chest like trousers, worn by anglers.

wadi *or* **wady** ('wɒdɪ) NOUN, *plural* **-dies.** a watercourse in N Africa and Arabia, dry except in the rainy season.
▷**HISTORY** C19: from Arabic

Wadi Halfa ('wɒdɪ 'hælfə) NOUN a town in the N Sudan that was partly submerged by Lake Nasser: an important archaeological site.

wadmal ('wɒdməl) NOUN a coarse thick woollen fabric, formerly woven esp in Orkney and Shetland, for outer garments.
▷**HISTORY** C14: from Old Norse *vathmal,* from *vath* cloth + *mal* measure

Wad Medani (wɑːd mɪ'dɑːniː) NOUN a town in the E Sudan, on the Blue Nile: headquarters of the Gezira irrigation scheme; agricultural research centre. Pop.: 218 714 (1993).

wadset ('wɒd,sɛt) *Scots law* ◆ NOUN 1 another name for **mortgage.** ◆ VERB **-sets, -setting, -setted.** 2 (*tr*) to pledge or mortgage.
▷**HISTORY** C14: *wad,* a Scottish variant of WED + SET¹; compare Old English *wedd settan* to deposit a pledge

Wafd (wɒft) NOUN a nationalist Egyptian political party: founded in 1924 and dissolved in 1952.
▷**HISTORY** Arabic: deputation
▸ '**Wafdist** NOUN, ADJECTIVE

wafer ('weɪfə) NOUN 1 a thin crisp sweetened biscuit with different flavourings, served with ice cream, etc. 2 *Christianity* a thin disc of unleavened bread used in the Eucharist as celebrated by the Western Church. 3 *Pharmacol* an envelope of rice paper enclosing a medicament. 4 *Electronics* a large single crystal of semiconductor material, such as silicon, on which numerous integrated circuits are manufactured and then separated. 5 a small thin disc of adhesive material used to seal letters, documents, etc. ◆ VERB 6 (*tr*) to seal, fasten, or attach with a wafer.
▷**HISTORY** C14: from Old Northern French *waufre,* from Middle Low German *wāfel;* related to WAFFLE¹
▸ '**wafer-,like** *or* '**wafery** ADJECTIVE

waff (wæf, wɑːf) NOUN *Scot and northern English dialect* 1 a gust or puff of air. 2 a glance; glimpse. ◆ VERB 3 to flutter or cause to flutter.
▷**HISTORY** C16: Scottish and northern English variant of WAVE

waffle¹ ('wɒfᵊl) NOUN **a** a crisp golden-brown pancake with deep indentations on both sides. **b** (*as modifier*): *waffle iron.*
▷**HISTORY** C19: from Dutch *wafel* (earlier *wæfel*), of Germanic origin; related to Old High German *wabo* honeycomb

waffle² ('wɒfᵊl) *Informal, chiefly Brit* ◆ VERB 1 (*intr;* often foll by *on*) to speak or write in a vague and wordy manner: *he waffled on for hours.* ◆ NOUN 2 vague and wordy speech or writing.
▷**HISTORY** C19: of unknown origin
▸ '**waffler** NOUN ▸ '**waffling** ADJECTIVE, NOUN ▸ '**waffly** ADJECTIVE

waft (wɑːft, wɒft) VERB 1 to carry or be carried gently on or as if on the air or water. ◆ NOUN 2 the act or an instance of wafting. 3 something, such as a scent, carried on the air. 4 a wafting motion. 5 Also called: **waif.** *Nautical* (formerly) a signal flag hoisted furled to signify various messages depending on where it was flown.
▷**HISTORY** C16 (in obsolete sense: to convey by ship): back formation from C15 *wafter* a convoy vessel, from Middle Dutch *wachter* guard, from *wachten* to guard; influenced by WAFF
▸ '**waftage** NOUN

wafter ('wɑːftə, 'wɒf-) NOUN a device that causes a draught.

wafture ('wɑːftʃə, 'wɒf-) NOUN *Archaic* 1 the act of wafting or waving. 2 anything that is wafted.

wag¹ (wæg) VERB **wags, wagging, wagged.** 1 to move or cause to move rapidly and repeatedly from side to side or up and down. 2 to move (the tongue) or (of the tongue) to be moved rapidly in talking, esp in idle gossip. 3 to move (the finger) or (of the finger) to be moved from side to side, in or as in admonition. 4 *Slang* to play truant (esp in the phrase **wag it**). ◆ NOUN 5 the act or an instance of wagging.
▷**HISTORY** C13: from Old English *wagian* to shake; compare Old Norse *vagga* cradle

wag² (wæg) NOUN a humorous or jocular person; wit.
▷**HISTORY** C16: of uncertain origin
▸ '**waggery** NOUN ▸ '**waggish** ADJECTIVE ▸ '**waggishly** ADVERB ▸ '**waggishness** NOUN

WAG INTERNATIONAL CAR REGISTRATION FOR (West Africa) Gambia.

wage (weɪdʒ) NOUN 1 **a** (*often plural*) payment in return for work or services, esp that made to workmen on a daily, hourly, weekly, or piece-work basis. Compare **salary. b** (*as modifier*): *wage freeze.* 2 (*plural*) *Economics* the portion of the national income accruing to labour as earned income, as contrasted with the unearned income accruing to capital in the form of rent, interest, and dividends. 3 (*often plural*) recompense, return, or yield. 4 an obsolete word for **pledge.** ◆ VERB (*tr*) 5 to engage in. 6 *Obsolete* to pledge or wager. 7 *Archaic* another word for **hire** (senses 1, 2).
▷**HISTORY** C14: from Old Northern French *wagier* to pledge, from *wage,* of Germanic origin; compare Old English *weddian* to pledge, WED
▸ '**wageless** ADJECTIVE ▸ '**wagelessness** NOUN

wage determination NOUN the process of

setting wage rates or establishing wage structures in particular situations.

wage differential NOUN the difference in wages between workers with different skills in the same industry or between those with comparable skills in different industries or localities.

wage earner *or US* **wage worker** NOUN 1 a person who works for wages, esp as distinguished from one paid a salary. 2 the person who earns money to support a household by working.

wage incentive NOUN additional wage payments intended to stimulate improved work performance.

wager ('weɪdʒə) NOUN 1 an agreement or pledge to pay an amount of money as a result of the outcome of an unsettled matter. 2 an amount staked on the outcome of such a matter or event. 3 **wager of battle.** (in medieval Britain) a pledge to do battle for a cause, esp to decide guilt or innocence by single combat. 4 **wager of law.** *English legal history* a form of trial in which the accused offered to make oath of his innocence, supported by the oaths of 11 of his neighbours declaring their belief in his statements. ◆ VERB 5 (when *tr, may take a clause as object*) to risk or bet (something) on the outcome of an unsettled matter. 6 (*tr*) *History* to pledge oneself to (battle).
▷HISTORY C14: from Anglo-French *wageure* a pledge, from Old Northern French *wagier* to pledge; see WAGE
▸ **'wagerer** NOUN

wage scale NOUN 1 a schedule of wages paid to workers for various jobs in an industry, company, etc. 2 an employer's schedule of wages.

wages council NOUN (formerly, in Britain) a statutory body empowered to fix minimum wages in an industry; abolished in 1994.

wage slave NOUN *Ironic* a person dependent on a wage or salary.

wagga ('wɒgə) NOUN *Austral* a blanket or bed covering made out of sacks stitched together.
▷HISTORY C19: named after WAGGA WAGGA

Wagga Wagga ('wɒgə 'wɒgə) NOUN a city in SE Australia, in New South Wales on the Murrumbidgee River: agricultural trading centre. Pop.: 50 380 (latest est.).

waggle ('wægᵊl) VERB 1 to move or cause to move with a rapid shaking or wobbling motion. ◆ NOUN 2 a rapid shaking or wobbling motion.
▷HISTORY C16: frequentative of WAG[1]
▸ **'wagglingly** ADVERB ▸ **'waggly** ADJECTIVE

waggler ('wæglə) NOUN *Angling* a float only the bottom of which is attached to the line.

waggon ('wægən) NOUN, VERB a variant spelling (esp Brit) of **wagon.**

Wagnerian (vɑːg'nɪərɪən) ADJECTIVE 1 of or suggestive of the dramatic musical compositions of Richard Wagner, the German romantic composer (1813–83), their massive scale, dramatic and emotional intensity, etc. 2 denoting or relating to a singer who has a voice suitable for singing Wagner. 3 of or relating to a big, powerful, or domineering woman: *a Wagnerian maiden.* ◆ NOUN *also* **Wagnerite.** 4 a follower or disciple of the music or theories of Richard Wagner.

wagon *or* **waggon** ('wægən) NOUN 1 any of various types of wheeled vehicles, ranging from carts to lorries, esp a vehicle with four wheels drawn by a horse, tractor, etc., and used for carrying crops, heavy loads, etc. 2 *Brit* a railway freight truck, esp an open one. 3 *US and Canadian* a child's four-wheeled cart. 4 *US and Canadian* a police van for transporting prisoners and those arrested. 5 *Chiefly US and Canadian* See **station wagon.** 6 an obsolete word for **chariot.** 7 **on** (*or* **off**) **the wagon.** *Informal* abstaining (or no longer abstaining) from alcoholic drinks. ◆ VERB 8 (*tr*) to transport by wagon.
▷HISTORY C16: from Dutch *wagen* WAIN
▸ **'wagonless** *or* **'waggonless** ADJECTIVE

Wagon *or* **Waggon** ('wægən) NOUN **the.** another name for the **Plough.**

wagoner *or* **waggoner** ('wægənə) NOUN a person who drives a wagon.

wagonette *or* **waggonette** (ˌwægə'nɛt) NOUN a light four-wheeled horse-drawn vehicle with two lengthwise seats facing each other behind a crosswise driver's seat.

wagon-lit (*French* vagɔ̃li) NOUN, *plural* **wagons-lits** (vagɔ̃li). 1 a sleeping car on a European railway. 2 a compartment on such a car.
▷HISTORY C19: from French, from *wagon* railway coach + *lit* bed

wagonload *or* **waggonload** ('wægənˌləʊd) NOUN the load that is or can be carried by a wagon.

wagon soldier NOUN *US slang* a soldier belonging to the field artillery.

wagon train NOUN a supply train of horses and wagons, esp one going over rough terrain.

wagon vault NOUN another name for **barrel vault.**

Wagram (*German* 'vaːgram) NOUN a village in NE Austria: scene of the defeat of the Austrians by Napoleon in 1809.

wagtail ('wægˌteɪl) NOUN any of various passerine songbirds of the genera *Motacilla* and *Dendronanthus,* of Eurasia and Africa, having a very long tail that wags when the bird walks: family *Motacillidae.*

Wahhabi *or* **Wahabi** (wə'hɑːbɪ) NOUN, *plural* **-bis.** a member of a strictly conservative Muslim sect founded in the 18th century with the aim of eliminating all innovations later than the 3rd century of Islam.
▸ **Wah'habism** *or* **Wa'habism** NOUN

wahine (wɑː'hiːnɪ) NOUN (esp in the Pacific islands) a Polynesian or Maori woman, esp a girlfriend or wife.
▷HISTORY C19: from Maori and Hawaiian

wahoo[1] (wɑː'huː, 'wɑːhuː) NOUN, *plural* **-hoos.** an elm, *Ulmus alata,* of SE North America having twigs with winged corky edges. Also called: **winged elm.**
▷HISTORY from Creek *ŭhawhu* cork elm

wahoo[2] (wɑː'huː, 'wɑːhuː) NOUN, *plural* **-hoos.** an E North American shrub or small tree, *Euonymus atropurpureus,* with scarlet capsules and seeds. Also called: **burning bush.**
▷HISTORY C19: from Dakota *wāhu* arrowwood

wahoo[3] (wɑː'huː, 'wɑːhuː) NOUN, *plural* **-hoos.** a large fast-moving food and game fish, *Acanthocybium solandri,* of tropical seas: family *Scombridae* (mackerels and tunnies).
▷HISTORY of unknown origin

wah-wah ('wɑːˌwɑː) NOUN 1 the sound made by a trumpet, cornet, etc., when the bell is alternately covered and uncovered: much used in jazz. 2 an electronic attachment for an electric guitar, etc., that simulates this effect.
▷HISTORY C20: of imitative origin

waif (weɪf) NOUN 1 a person, esp a child, who is homeless, friendless, or neglected. 2 anything found and not claimed, the owner being unknown. 3 *Nautical* another name for **waft** (sense 5). 4 *Law, obsolete* a stolen article thrown away by a thief in his flight and forfeited to the Crown or to the lord of the manor.
▷HISTORY C14: from Anglo-Norman, variant of Old Northern French *gaif,* of Scandinavian origin; related to Old Norse *veif* a flapping thing
▸ **'waifˌlike** ADJECTIVE

Waikaremoana (waɪˈkɒrəməʊˌɑːnə) NOUN **Lake.** a lake in the North Island of New Zealand in a dense bush setting. Area: about 55 sq. km (21 sq. miles).

Waikato ('waɪˌkɑːtəʊ) NOUN the longest river in New Zealand, flowing northwest across North Island to the Tasman Sea. Length: 350 km (220 miles).

Waikiki ('waɪkɪˌkiː, ˌwaɪkɪ'kiː) NOUN a resort area in Hawaii, on SE Oahu: a suburb of Honolulu.

wail (weɪl) VERB 1 (*intr*) to utter a prolonged high-pitched cry, as of grief or misery. 2 (*intr*) to make a sound resembling such a cry: *the wind wailed in the trees.* 3 (*tr*) to lament, esp with mournful sounds. ◆ NOUN 4 a prolonged high-pitched mournful cry or sound.
▷HISTORY C14: of Scandinavian origin; related to Old Norse *væla* to wail, Old English *wā* WOE
▸ **'wailer** NOUN ▸ **'wailful** ADJECTIVE ▸ **'wailfully** ADVERB

Wailing Wall NOUN another name for **Western Wall.**

wain (weɪn) NOUN *Chiefly poetic* a farm wagon or cart.
▷HISTORY Old English *wægn;* related to Old Frisian *wein,* Old Norse *vagn*

wainscot ('weɪnskət) NOUN 1 Also called: **wainscoting** *or* **wainscotting.** a lining applied to the walls of a room, esp one of wood panelling. 2 the lower part of the walls of a room, esp when finished in a material different from the upper part. 3 fine quality oak used as wainscot. ◆ VERB 4 (*tr*) to line (a wall of a room) with a wainscot.
▷HISTORY C14: from Middle Low German *wagenschot,* perhaps from *wagen* WAGON + *schot* planking, related to German *Scheit* piece of wood

wainwright ('weɪnˌraɪt) NOUN a person who makes wagons.

wairsh (werʃ) ADJECTIVE *Scot* a variant spelling of **wersh.**

waist (weɪst) NOUN 1 *Anatomy* the constricted part of the trunk between the ribs and hips. 2 the part of a garment covering the waist. 3 the middle part of an object that resembles the waist in narrowness or position. 4 the middle part of a ship. 5 Also called: **centre section.** the middle section of an aircraft fuselage. 6 the constriction between the thorax and abdomen in wasps and similar insects.
▷HISTORY C14: origin uncertain; related to Old English *wæstm* WAX[2]
▸ **'waistless** ADJECTIVE

waistband ('weɪstˌbænd) NOUN an encircling band of material to finish and strengthen a skirt or trousers at the waist.

waistcloth ('weɪstˌklɒθ) NOUN *Obsolete* another word for **loincloth.**

waistcoat ('weɪsˌkəʊt) NOUN 1 a man's sleeveless waistlength garment worn under a suit jacket, usually buttoning up the front. US and Canadian name: **vest.** 2 a man's garment worn under a doublet in the 16th century.
▸ **'waistˌcoated** ADJECTIVE

waisted ('weɪstɪd) ADJECTIVE **a** having a waist or waistlike part: *a waisted air-gun pellet.* **b** (*in combination*): *high-waisted.*

waistline ('weɪstˌlaɪn) NOUN 1 a line or indentation around the body at the narrowest part of the waist. 2 the intersection of the bodice and the skirt of a dress, etc., or the level of this: *a low waistline.*

wait (weɪt) VERB 1 (when *intr,* often foll by *for, until,* or *to*) to stay in one place or remain inactive in expectation (of something); hold oneself in readiness (for something). 2 to delay temporarily or be temporarily delayed: *that work can wait.* 3 (when *intr,* usually foll by *for*) (of things) to be in store (for a person): *success waits for you in your new job.* 4 (*intr*) to act as a waiter or waitress. ◆ NOUN 5 the act or an instance of waiting. 6 a period of waiting. 7 (*plural*) *Rare* a band of musicians who go around the streets, esp at Christmas, singing and playing carols. 8 an interlude or interval between two acts or scenes in a play, etc. 9 **lie in wait.** to prepare an ambush (for someone). ◆ See also **wait on, wait up.**
▷HISTORY C12: from Old French *waitier;* related to Old High German *wahtēn* to WAKE[1]

wait-a-bit NOUN any of various plants having sharp hooked thorns or similar appendages, esp the greenbrier and the grapple plant.

Waitangi Day (waɪ'tʌŋiː) NOUN the national day of New Zealand (Feb. 6), commemorating the signing of the **Treaty of Waitangi** (1840) by Maori chiefs and a representative of the British Government. The treaty provided the basis for the British annexation of New Zealand.

Waitangi Tribunal NOUN (in New Zealand) a government tribunal empowered to examine and make recommendations on Maori claims under the Treaty of Waitangi.

wait-a-while NOUN (in Australia) another name for **rattan** (sense 1).

waiter ('weɪtə) NOUN 1 a man whose occupation is to serve at table, as in a restaurant. 2 an attendant at the London Stock Exchange or Lloyd's who carries messages: the modern equivalent of waiters who performed these duties in the 17th-century London coffee houses in which these institutions originated. 3 a person who waits. 4 a tray or salver on which dishes, etc., are carried.

waiting game NOUN the postponement of action or decision in order to gain the advantage.

waiting list NOUN a list of people waiting to obtain some object, treatment, status, etc.

waiting room NOUN a room in which people may wait, as at a railway station, doctor's or dentist's office, etc.

wait on VERB (*intr, preposition*) [1] to serve at the table of. [2] to act as an attendant or servant to. [3] *Archaic* to visit. ◆ INTERJECTION [4] *Austral and NZ* stop! hold on! ◆ Also (for senses 1, 2, 3): **wait upon.**

waitress ('weɪtrɪs) NOUN [1] a woman who serves at table, as in a restaurant. ◆ VERB [2] (*intr*) to act as a waitress.

wait up VERB (*intr, adverb*) [1] to delay going to bed in order to await some event. [2] *Informal, chiefly US and Canadian* to halt and pause in order that another person may catch up.

waive (weɪv) VERB (*tr*) [1] to set aside or relinquish: *to waive one's right to something.* [2] to refrain from enforcing (a claim) or applying (a law, penalty, etc.). [3] to defer.
▷HISTORY C13: from Old Northern French *weyver,* from *waif* abandoned; see WAIF

waiver ('weɪvə) NOUN [1] the voluntary relinquishment, expressly or by implication, of some claim or right. [2] the act or an instance of relinquishing a claim or right. [3] a formal statement in writing of such relinquishment.
▷HISTORY C17: from Old Northern French *weyver* to relinquish, WAIVE

waka ('wɔːkə) NOUN *NZ* [1] a Maori canoe, usually made from a tree trunk. [2] a tribal group claiming descent from the first Maori settlers in New Zealand.
▷HISTORY Maori

Wakashan (wɑː'kæʃən, 'wɔːkə,ʃɑːn) NOUN [1] a family of North American Indian languages of British Columbia and Washington, including Kwakiutl and Nootka. [2] a speaker of any of these languages.

Wakayama (,wækə'jɑːmə) NOUN an industrial city in S Japan, on S Honshu. Pop.: 393 951 (1995).

wake[1] (weɪk) VERB **wakes, waking, woke, woken.** [1] (often foll by *up*) to rouse or become roused from sleep. [2] (often foll by *up*) to rouse or become roused from inactivity. [3] (*intr; often foll by to* or *up to*) to become conscious or aware: *at last he woke to the situation.* [4] (*intr*) to be or remain awake. [5] *Dialect* to hold a wake over (a corpse). [6] *Archaic or dialect* to keep watch over. [7] **wake up and smell the coffee.** *Informal* to face up to reality, especially in an unpleasant situation. ◆ NOUN [8] a watch or vigil held over the body of a dead person during the night before burial. [9] (in Ireland) festivities held after a funeral. [10] the patronal or dedication festival of English parish churches. [11] a solemn or ceremonial vigil. [12] (*usually plural*) an annual holiday in any of various towns in northern England, when the local factory or factories close, usually for a week or two weeks. [13] *Rare* the state of being awake.
▷HISTORY Old English *wacian;* related to Old Frisian *wakia,* Old High German *wahtēn*
▸'**waker** NOUN

> **Language note** Where there is an object and the sense is the literal one *wake (up)* and *waken* are the commonest forms: *I wakened him; I woke him (up).* Both verbs are also commonly used without an object: *I woke up. Awake* and *awaken* are preferred to other forms of *wake* where the sense is a figurative one: *he awoke to the danger.*

wake[2] (weɪk) NOUN [1] the waves or track left by a vessel or other object moving through water. [2] the track or path left by anything that has passed: *wrecked houses in the wake of the hurricane.*
▷HISTORY C16: of Scandinavian origin; compare Old Norse *vaka, vök* hole cut in ice, Swedish *vak,* Danish *vaage;* perhaps related to Old Norse *vökr,* Middle Dutch *wak* wet

wakeboarding ('weɪk,bɔːdɪŋ) NOUN the sport of riding over water on a short surfboard and performing stunts while holding a rope towed by a speedboat.

Wakefield ('weɪk,fiːld) NOUN [1] a city in N England, in Wakefield unitary authority, West Yorkshire: important since medieval times as an agricultural and textile centre. Pop.: 73 955 (1991). [2] a unitary authority in N England, in West Yorkshire. Pop.: 315 173 (2001). Area: 333 sq. km (129 sq. miles).

wakeful ('weɪkfʊl) ADJECTIVE [1] unable or unwilling to sleep. [2] sleepless. [3] alert.
▸'**wakefully** ADVERB ▸'**wakefulness** NOUN

Wake Island NOUN an atoll in the N central Pacific: claimed by the US in 1899; developed as a civil and naval air station in the late 1930s. Area: 8 sq. km (3 sq. miles).

wakeless ('weɪklɪs) ADJECTIVE (of sleep) deep or unbroken.

waken ('weɪkən) VERB to rouse or be roused from sleep or some other inactive state.
▸'**wakener** NOUN

> **Language note** See at **wake**[1].

wake-robin NOUN [1] any of various North American herbaceous plants of the genus *Trillium,* such as *T. grandiflorum,* having a whorl of three leaves and three-petalled solitary flowers: family *Trilliaceae.* [2] *US* any of various aroid plants, esp the cuckoopint.

wake-up NOUN [1] *Austral informal* an alert or intelligent person. [2] **be a wake-up to.** *Austral informal* to be fully alert to (a person, thing, action, etc.).

wake-up call NOUN [1] a telephone call that wakes a person from sleep. [2] an event that alerts people to a danger or difficulty.

WAL INTERNATIONAL CAR REGISTRATION FOR Sierra Leone.
▷HISTORY from *W(est) A(frica) L(eone)*

Walach ('wɑːlɒk) NOUN, ADJECTIVE a variant spelling of **Vlach.**

Walachia *or* **Wallachia** (wɒ'leɪkɪə) NOUN a former principality of SE Europe: a vassal state of the Ottoman Empire from the 15th century until its union with Moldavia in 1859, subsequently forming present-day Romania.

Walachian *or* **Wallachian** (wɒ'leɪkɪən) ADJECTIVE [1] of or relating to the former SE European principality of Walachia (now part of Romania) or its inhabitants. ◆ NOUN [2] a native or inhabitant of Walachia.

Wałbrzych (*Polish* 'vaubʒix) NOUN an industrial city in SW Poland. Pop.: 136 923 (1999 est.). German name: **Waldenburg.**

Walcheren (*Dutch* 'wɑlxərə) NOUN an island in the SW Netherlands, in the Scheldt estuary: administratively part of Zeeland province; suffered severely in World War II, when the dykes were breached, and again in the floods of 1953. Area: 212 sq. km (82 sq. miles).

Waldenburg ('valdənbʊrk) NOUN the German name for **Wałbrzych.**

Waldenses (wɒl'dɛnsiːz) PLURAL NOUN the members of a small sect founded as a reform movement within the Roman Catholic Church by Peter Waldo, a merchant of Lyons in the late 12th century, which in the 16th century joined the Reformation movement. Also called: **Vaudois.**
▸**Waldensian** (wɒl'dɛnsɪən) NOUN, ADJECTIVE

waldgrave ('wɔːld,greɪv) NOUN (in medieval Germany) an officer with jurisdiction over a royal forest.
▷HISTORY from German *Waldgraf,* from *Wald* forest + *Graf* count

waldo ('wɔːldəʊ) NOUN, *plural* **-dos** *or* **-does.** a gadget for manipulating objects by remote control.
▷HISTORY C20: named after *Waldo* F. Jones, inventor in a science-fiction story by Robert Heinlein

Waldorf salad ('wɔːldɔːf) NOUN a salad of diced apples, celery, and walnuts mixed with mayonnaise.
▷HISTORY C20: named after the *Waldorf-Astoria Hotel* in New York City

waldsterben ('wɔːld,stɜːbən) NOUN *Ecology* the symptoms of tree decline in central Europe from the 1970s, considered to be caused by atmospheric pollution.
▷HISTORY C20: from German *Wald* forest + *sterben* to die

wale[1] (weɪl) NOUN [1] the raised mark left on the skin after the stroke of a rod or whip. [2] **a** the weave or texture of a fabric, such as the ribs in corduroy. **b** a vertical row of stitches in knitting. Compare **course** (sense 14). [3] *Nautical* **a** a ridge of planking along the rail of a ship. **b** See **gunwale.** ◆ VERB (*tr*) [4] to raise a wale or wales on by striking. [5] to weave with a wale.
▷HISTORY Old English *walu* WEAL[1]; related to Old Norse *vala* knuckle, Dutch *wäle*

wale[2] (weɪl) *Scot and northern English dialect* ◆ NOUN [1] a choice. [2] anything chosen as the best. ◆ ADJECTIVE [3] choice. ◆ VERB [4] (*tr*) to choose.
▷HISTORY C14: from Old Norse *val* choice, related to German *Wahl*

Waler ('weɪlə) NOUN *Chiefly Austral* a saddle horse originating in New South Wales.
▷HISTORY C19: from *Wales,* in *New South Wales*

Wales (weɪlz) NOUN a principality that is part of the United Kingdom, in the west of Great Britain; conquered by the English in 1282; parliamentary union with England took place in 1536: a separate Welsh Assembly with limited powers was established in 1999. Wales consists mainly of moorlands and mountains and has an economy that is chiefly agricultural, with an industrial and former coal-mining area in the south. Capital: Cardiff. Pop.: 2 903 085 (2001). Area: 20 768 sq. km (8017 sq. miles). Welsh name: **Cymru.** Medieval Latin name: **Cambria.**

Walfish Bay ('wɔːlfɪʃ) NOUN a variant spelling of **Walvis Bay.**

Walhalla (wæl'hælə, væl-) *or* **Walhall** (wæl'hæl, væl-) NOUN variants of **Valhalla.**

walk (wɔːk) VERB [1] (*intr*) to move along or travel on foot at a moderate rate; advance in such a manner that at least one foot is always on the ground. [2] (*tr*) to pass through, on, or over on foot, esp habitually. [3] (*tr*) to cause, assist, or force to move along at a moderate rate: *to walk a dog.* [4] (*tr*) to escort or conduct by walking: *to walk someone home.* [5] (*intr*) (of ghosts, spirits, etc.) to appear or move about in visible form. [6] (of inanimate objects) to move or cause to move in a manner that resembles walking. [7] (*intr*) to follow a certain course or way of life: *to walk in misery.* [8] (*tr*) to bring into a certain condition by walking: *I walked my shoes to shreds.* [9] (*tr*) to measure, survey, or examine by walking. [10] (*intr*) *Basketball* to take more than two steps without passing or dribbling the ball. [11] to disappear or be stolen: *where's my pencil? It seems to have walked.* [12] (*intr*) *Slang, chiefly US* (in a court of law) to be acquitted or given a noncustodial sentence. [13] **walk it.** to win easily. [14] **walk the plank.** See **plank** (sense 4). [15] **walk on air.** to be delighted or exhilarated. [16] **walk tall.** *Informal* to have self-respect or pride. [17] **walk the streets. a** to be a prostitute. **b** to wander round a town or city, esp when looking for work or having nowhere to stay. [18] **walk the talk.** *Informal* to put theory into practice. ◆ NOUN [19] the act or an instance of walking. [20] the distance or extent walked. [21] a manner of walking; gait. [22] a place set aside for walking; promenade. [23] a chosen profession or sphere of activity (esp in the phrase **walk of life**). [24] a foot race in which competitors walk. [25] **a** an arrangement of trees or shrubs in widely separated rows. **b** the space between such rows. [26] an enclosed ground for the exercise or feeding of domestic animals, esp horses. [27] *Chiefly Brit* the route covered in the course of work, as by a tradesman or postman. [28] a procession; march: *Orange walk.* [29] *Obsolete* the section of a forest controlled by a keeper. ◆ See also **walk away, walk into, walk off, walk out, walkover, walk through.**
▷HISTORY Old English *wealcan;* related to Old High German *walchan,* Sanskrit *valgati* he moves
▸'**walkable** ADJECTIVE

walkabout ('wɔːkə,baʊt) NOUN [1] a periodic nomadic excursion into the Australian bush made by a native Australian. [2] a walking tour. [3] *Chiefly journalistic* an occasion when celebrities, royalty, etc., walk among and meet the public. [4] **go walkabout.** *Austral* **a** to wander through the bush. **b** *Informal* to be lost or misplaced. **c** *Informal* to lose one's concentration.

walk away VERB (*intr, adverb*) [1] to leave, esp callously and disregarding someone else's distress. [2] **walk away with.** to achieve or win easily.

walker ('wɔːkə) NOUN [1] a person who walks. [2] Also called: **baby walker.** a tubular frame on wheels or castors to support a baby learning to walk. [3] a similar support for walking, often with rubber feet, for use by disabled or infirm people. [4] a woman's escort at a social event: *let me introduce my walker for tonight.*

walkie-talkie *or* **walky-talky** (ˌwɔːkɪˈtɔːkɪ) NOUN, *plural* **-talkies.** a small combined radio transmitter and receiver, usually operating on shortwave, that can be carried around by one person: widely used by the police, medical services, etc.

walk-in ADJECTIVE [1] (of a cupboard) large enough to allow a person to enter and move about in. [2] *US* (of a building or apartment) located so as to admit of direct access from the street. [3] (of a flat or house) in a suitable condition for immediate occupation.

walking (ˈwɔːkɪŋ) ADJECTIVE (of a person) considered to possess the qualities of something inanimate as specified: *he is a walking encyclopedia.*

walking bass (beɪs) NOUN *Jazz* a simple accompaniment played by the double bass at medium tempo, usually consisting of ascending and descending tones or semitones, one to each beat.

walking bus NOUN a group of school children walking together along an agreed route to and from school, accompanied by adults, with children joining and leaving the group at pre-arranged points.

walking delegate NOUN [1] (in the US) an agent appointed by a trade union to visit branches, check whether agreements are observed, and negotiate with employers. [2] (in New Zealand) a trade union official who visits dispersed working areas on a wharf.

walking dragline NOUN a very large-capacity dragline mounted on feet or pads instead of tracks. See **dragline** (sense 2).

walking fern *or* **leaf** NOUN a North American fern, *Camptosorus rhizophyllus,* having sword-shaped fronds, the tips of which take root when in contact with the ground: family *Aspleniaceae.*

walking papers PLURAL NOUN *Slang, chiefly US and Canadian* notice of dismissal.

walking stick NOUN [1] a stick or cane carried in the hand to assist walking. [2] the usual US name for **stick insect.**

walk into VERB *(intr, preposition)* to meet with unwittingly: *to walk into a trap.*

Walkman (ˈwɔːkmən) NOUN *Trademark* a small portable cassette player with light headphones.

walk off VERB [1] *(intr)* to depart suddenly. [2] *(tr, adverb)* to get rid of by walking: *to walk off an attack of depression.* [3] **walk (a person) off his feet.** to make (someone) walk so fast or far that he or she is exhausted. [4] **walk off with. a** to steal. **b** to win, esp easily.

walk-on NOUN [1] **a** a small part in a play or theatrical entertainment, esp one without any lines. **b** *(as modifier): a walk-on part.* ◆ ADJECTIVE [2] (of an aircraft or air service) having seats to be booked immediately before departure rather than in advance.

walk out VERB *(intr, adverb)* [1] to leave without explanation, esp in anger. [2] to go on strike. [3] **walk out on.** *Informal* to abandon or desert. [4] **walk out with.** *Brit obsolete or dialect* to court or be courted by. ◆ NOUN **walkout.** [5] a strike by workers. [6] the act of leaving a meeting, conference, etc., as a protest.

walkover (ˈwɔːkˌəʊvə) NOUN [1] *Informal* an easy or unopposed victory. [2] *Horse racing* **a** the running or walking over the course by the only contestant entered in a race at the time of starting. **b** a race won in this way. ◆ VERB **walk over.** *(intr, mainly preposition)* [3] *(also adverb)* to win a race by a walkover. [4] *Informal* to beat (an opponent) conclusively or easily. [5] *Informal* to take advantage of (someone).

walkshorts (ˈwɔːkˌʃɔːts) PLURAL NOUN *NZ* smart shorts for men.

walk socks PLURAL NOUN *NZ* men's knee-length stockings.

walk through *Theatre* ◆ VERB [1] *(tr)* to act or recite (a part) in a perfunctory manner, as at a first rehearsal. ◆ NOUN **walk-through.** [2] a rehearsal of a part.

walk-up NOUN *US and Canadian informal* **a** a block of flats having no lift. **b** *(as modifier): a walk-up block.*

walkway (ˈwɔːkˌweɪ) NOUN [1] a path designed, and sometimes landscaped, for pedestrian use. [2] a passage or path connecting buildings. [3] a passage or path, esp one for walking over machinery, etc.

Walkyrie (vælˈkɪərɪ, ˈvælkɪərɪ) NOUN a variant spelling of **Valkyrie.**

wall (wɔːl) NOUN [1] **a** a vertical construction made of stone, brick, wood, etc., with a length and height much greater than its thickness, used to enclose, divide, or support. **b** *(as modifier): wall hangings.* Related adjective: **mural.** [2] *(often plural)* a structure or rampart built to protect and surround a position or place for defensive purposes. [3] *Anatomy* any lining, membrane, or investing part that encloses or bounds a bodily cavity or structure: *abdominal wall.* Technical name: **paries.** Related adjective: **parietal.** [4] *Mountaineering* a vertical or almost vertical smooth rock face. [5] anything that suggests a wall in function or effect: *a wall of fire; a wall of prejudice.* [6] **bang one's head against a brick wall.** to try to achieve something impossible. [7] **drive** (*or* **push**) **to the wall.** to force into an awkward situation. [8] **go to the wall.** to be ruined; collapse financially. [9] **go** (*or* **drive**) **up the wall.** *Slang* to become (or cause to become) crazy or furious. [10] **have one's back to the wall.** to be in a very difficult situation. [11] See **off-the-wall.** [12] See **wall-to-wall.** ◆ VERB *(tr)* [13] to protect, provide, or confine with or as if with a wall. [14] (often foll by *up*) to block (an opening) with a wall. [15] (often foll by *in* or *up*) to seal by or within a wall or walls.
▷**HISTORY** Old English *weall,* from Latin *vallum* palisade, from *vallus* stake
▸**walled** ADJECTIVE ▸**ˈwall-less** ADJECTIVE ▸**ˈwall-ˌlike** ADJECTIVE

wallaby (ˈwɒləbɪ) NOUN, *plural* **-bies** *or* **-by.** [1] any of various herbivorous marsupials of the genera *Lagorchestes* (**hare wallabies**), *Petrogale* (**rock wallabies**), *Protemnodon,* etc., of Australia and New Guinea, similar to but smaller than kangaroos: family *Macropodidae.* [2] **on the wallaby (track).** *Austral slang* (of a person) wandering about looking for work.
▷**HISTORY** C19: from native Australian *wolabā*

Wallaby (ˈwɒləbɪ) NOUN, *plural* **-bies.** a member of the international Rugby Union football team of Australia.

Wallace's line NOUN the hypothetical boundary between the Oriental and Australasian zoogeographical regions, which runs between the Indonesian islands of Bali and Lombok, through the Macassar Strait, and SE of the Philippines.
▷**HISTORY** C20: named after Alfred Russel *Wallace* (1823–1913), British naturalist

Wallachia (wɒˈleɪkɪə) NOUN a variant spelling of **Walachia.**

Wallachian (wɒˈleɪkɪən) ADJECTIVE, NOUN a variant spelling of **Walachian.**

wallah *or* **walla** (ˈwɒlə) NOUN *(usually in combination) Informal* a person involved with or in charge of (a specified thing): *the book wallah.*
▷**HISTORY** C18: from Hindi *-wālā* from Sanskrit *pāla* protector

wallaroo (ˌwɒləˈruː) NOUN, *plural* **-roos** *or* **-roo.** a large stocky Australian kangaroo, *Macropus* (or *Osphranter*) *robustus,* of rocky regions.
▷**HISTORY** C19: from native Australian *wolarū*

Wallasey (ˈwɒləsɪ) NOUN a town in NW England, in Wirral unitary authority, Merseyside; near the mouth of the River Mersey, opposite Liverpool. Pop.: 60 895 (1991).

wall bars PLURAL NOUN a series of horizontal bars attached to a wall and used in gymnastics.

wallboard (ˈwɔːlˌbɔːd) NOUN a thin board made of materials, such as compressed wood fibres or gypsum plaster, between stiff paper, and used to cover walls, partitions, etc.

wall brown NOUN any of three species of brown butterfly, esp the common *Lasiommata megera,* that habitually sun themselves on rocks and walls.

wall creeper NOUN a pink-and-grey woodpecker-like songbird, *Tichodroma muraria,* of Eurasian mountain regions: family *Sittidae* (nuthatches).

walled plain NOUN any of the largest of the lunar craters, having diameters between 50 and 300 kilometres.

wallet (ˈwɒlɪt) NOUN [1] a small folding case, usually of leather, for holding paper money, documents, etc. [2] a bag used to carry tools. [3] *Archaic, chiefly Brit* a rucksack or knapsack.
▷**HISTORY** C14: of Germanic origin; compare Old English *weallian,* Old High German *wallōn* to roam, German *wallen* to go on a pilgrimage

walleye (ˈwɔːlˌaɪ) NOUN, *plural* **-eyes** *or* **-eye.** [1] a divergent squint. [2] opacity of the cornea. [3] an eye having a white or light-coloured iris. [4] (in some collies) an eye that is particoloured white and blue. [5] Also called: **walleyed pike.** a North American pikeperch, *Stizostedion vitreum,* valued as a food and game fish. [6] any of various other fishes having large staring eyes.
▷**HISTORY** back formation from earlier *walleyed,* from Old Norse *vagleygr,* from *vage,* perhaps: a film over the eye (compare Swedish *vagel* sty in the eye) + *-eygr* -eyed, from *auga* eye; modern form influenced by WALL
▸**ˈwallˌeyed** ADJECTIVE

wallflower (ˈwɔːlˌflaʊə) NOUN [1] Also called: **gillyflower.** a plant, *Cheiranthus cheiri,* of S Europe, grown for its clusters of yellow, orange, brown, red, or purple fragrant flowers and naturalized on old walls, cliffs, etc.: family *Brassicaceae* (crucifers). [2] any of numerous other crucifers of the genera *Cheiranthus* and *Erysimum,* having orange or yellow flowers. [3] *Informal* a person who stays on the fringes of a dance or party on account of lacking a partner or being shy.

wall fruit NOUN fruit grown on trees trained against a wall for the shelter and warmth it provides.

wall game NOUN a type of football played at Eton against a wall.

wallies (ˈwælɪz) PLURAL NOUN *Central Scot dialect* false teeth; dentures.
▷**HISTORY** see WALLY[2]

Wallis (ˈvalɪs) NOUN the German name for **Valais.**

Wallis and Futuna Islands (ˈwɒlɪs, fuːˈtjuːnə) PLURAL NOUN a French overseas territory in the SW Pacific, west of Samoa. Capital: Mata-Utu. Pop.: 14 400 (1993 est.). Area: 367 sq. km (143 sq. miles).

wall knot NOUN a knot forming a knob at the end of a rope, made by unwinding the strands and weaving them together.

wall lizard NOUN a small mottled grey lizard, *Lacerta muralis,* of Europe, N Africa, and SW Asia: family *Lacertidae.*

wall mustard NOUN another name for **stinkweed** (sense 1).

wall of death NOUN (at a fairground) a giant cylinder round the inside walls of which a motorcyclist rides.

Walloon (wɒˈluːn) NOUN [1] a member of a French-speaking people living chiefly in S Belgium and adjacent parts of France. Compare **Fleming**[1]. [2] the French dialect of Belgium. ◆ ADJECTIVE [3] of, relating to, or characteristic of the Walloons or their dialect.
▷**HISTORY** C16: from Old French *Wallon,* from Medieval Latin: foreigner, of Germanic origin; compare Old English *wealh* foreign, WELSH[1]

Walloon Brabant NOUN a province of central Belgium, formed in 1995 from the S part of Brabant province: densely populated and intensively farmed, with large industrial centres. Pop.: 349 884 (2000 est.). Area: 1091 sq. km (421 sq. miles).

wallop (ˈwɒləp) VERB **-lops, -loping, -loped.** [1] *(tr) Informal* to beat soundly; strike hard. [2] *(tr) Informal* to defeat utterly. [3] *(intr) Dialect* to move in a clumsy manner. [4] *(intr)* (of liquids) to boil violently. ◆ NOUN [5] *Informal* a hard blow. [6] *Informal* the ability to hit powerfully, as of a boxer. [7] *Informal* a forceful impression. [8] *Brit* a slang word for **beer.** ◆ VERB, NOUN [9] an obsolete word for **gallop.**
▷**HISTORY** C14: from Old Northern French *waloper* to gallop, from Old French *galoper,* of unknown origin

walloper (ˈwɒləpə) NOUN [1] a person or thing that wallops. [2] *Austral slang* a policeman.

walloping (ˈwɒləpɪŋ) *Informal* ◆ NOUN [1] a

thrashing. ◆ ADJECTIVE [2] (intensifier): *a walloping drop in sales.*

wallow ('wɒləʊ) VERB *(intr)* [1] (esp of certain animals) to roll about in mud, water, etc., for pleasure. [2] to move about with difficulty. [3] to indulge oneself in possessions, emotion, etc.: *to wallow in self-pity.* [4] (of smoke, waves, etc.) to billow. ◆ NOUN [5] the act or an instance of wallowing. [6] a muddy place or depression where animals wallow.
▷HISTORY Old English *wealwian* to roll (in mud); related to Latin *volvere* to turn, Greek *oulos* curly, Russian *valun* round pebble
▸'**wallower** NOUN

wallpaper ('wɔːlˌpeɪpə) NOUN [1] paper usually printed or embossed with designs for pasting onto walls and ceilings. [2] **a** something pleasant but bland which serves as an unobtrusive background. **b** *(as modifier)*: *wallpaper music.* ◆ VERB [3] *Computing* a graphics file that can be displayed in certain applications behind or around the main dialogue boxes, working display areas, etc., for decoration. [4] to cover (a surface) with wallpaper.

wall pass NOUN *Soccer* a movement in which one player passes the ball to another and sprints forward to receive the quickly played return. Also called: **one-two.**

wall pellitory NOUN See **pellitory** (sense 1).

wall pepper NOUN a small Eurasian crassulaceous plant, *Sedum acre,* having creeping stems, yellow flowers, and acrid-tasting leaves.

wall plate NOUN a horizontal timber member placed along the top of a wall to support the ends of joists, rafters, etc., and distribute the load.

wallposter ('wɔːlˌpəʊstə) NOUN (in China) a bulletin or political message painted in large characters on walls.

wall rock NOUN rock that is immediately adjacent to a mineral vein, fault, or igneous intrusion.

wall rocket NOUN any of several yellow-flowered European plants of the genus *Diplotaxis,* such as *D. muralis,* that grow on old walls and in waste places: family *Brassicaceae* (crucifers).

wall rue NOUN a delicate fern, *Asplenium ruta-muraria,* that grows in rocky crevices and walls in North America and Eurasia.

Wallsend ('wɔːlzˌɛnd) NOUN a town in NE England, in North Tyneside unitary authority, Tyne and Wear: situated on the River Tyne at the E end of Hadrian's Wall. Pop.: 45 280 (1991).

Wall Street NOUN a street in lower Manhattan, New York, where the Stock Exchange and major banks are situated, regarded as the embodiment of American finance.

wall-to-wall ADJECTIVE [1] (of carpeting) completely covering a floor. [2] *Informal* as far as the eye can see; widespread: *wall-to-wall sales in the high street shops.*

wally¹ ('weɪlɪ) ADJECTIVE *Scot archaic* [1] fine, pleasing, or splendid. [2] robust or strong.
▷HISTORY C16: of obscure origin

wally² ('wælɪ) ADJECTIVE *Central Scot dialect* [1] made of china: *a wally dug; a wally vase.* [2] lined with ceramic tiles: *a wally close.* ◆ See also **wallies.**
▷HISTORY from obsolete dialect *wallow* faded, adjectival use of *wallow* to fade, from Old English *wealwian*

wally³ ('wɒlɪ) NOUN, *plural* **-lies.** *Slang* a stupid person.
▷HISTORY C20: shortened form of the given name *Walter*

walnut ('wɔːlˌnʌt) NOUN [1] any juglandaceous deciduous tree of the genus *Juglans,* of America, SE Europe, and Asia, esp *J. regia,* which is native to W Asia but introduced elsewhere. They have aromatic leaves and flowers in catkins and are grown for their edible nuts and for their wood. [2] the nut of any of these trees, having a wrinkled two-lobed seed and a hard wrinkled shell. [3] the wood of any of these trees, used in making furniture, panelling, etc. [4] a light yellowish-brown colour. ◆ ADJECTIVE [5] made from the wood of a walnut tree: *a walnut table.* [6] of the colour walnut.
▷HISTORY Old English *walh-hnutu,* literally: foreign nut; compare Old French *noux gauge* walnut, probably translation of Vulgar Latin phrase *nux gallica* (unattested) Gaulish (hence, foreign) nut

walnut oil NOUN an oil pressed from walnuts and used in cooking, esp in salad dressings.

Walpurgis Night (væl'pʊəgɪs) NOUN the eve of May 1, believed in German folklore to be the night of a witches' sabbath on the Brocken, in the Harz Mountains.
▷HISTORY C19: translation of German *Walpurgisnacht,* the eve of the feast day of St Walpurga, 8th-century abbess in Germany

walrus ('wɔːlrəs, 'wɒl-) NOUN, *plural* **-ruses** *or* **-rus.** a pinniped mammal, *Odobenus rosmarus,* of northern seas, having a tough thick skin, upper canine teeth enlarged as tusks, and coarse whiskers and feeding mainly on shellfish: family *Odobenidae.*
▷HISTORY C17: probably from Dutch, from Scandinavian; compare Old Norse *hrosshvalr* (literally: horse whale) and Old English *horschwæl;* see HORSE, WHALE

walrus moustache NOUN a long thick moustache drooping at the ends.

Walsall ('wɔːlsɔːl) NOUN [1] an industrial town in central England, in Walsall unitary authority, West Midlands: engineering, electronics. Pop.: 174 739 (1991). [2] a unitary authority in central England, in the West Midlands. Pop.: 253 502 (2001). Area: 106 sq. km (41 sq. miles).

Walsingham ('wɔːlsɪŋəm) NOUN a village in E England, in Norfolk: remains of a medieval priory; site of the shrine of Our Lady of Walsingham.

Waltham Forest ('wɔːlθəm) NOUN a borough of NE Greater London. Pop.: 218 277 (2001). Area: 40 sq. km (15 sq. miles).

waltz (wɔːls) NOUN [1] a ballroom dance in triple time in which couples spin around as they progress round the room. [2] a piece of music composed for or in the rhythm of this dance. ◆ VERB [3] to dance or lead (someone) in or as in a waltz: *he waltzed her off her feet.* [4] *(intr)* to move in a sprightly and self-assured manner. [5] *(intr) Informal* to succeed easily.
▷HISTORY C18: from German *Walzer,* from Middle High German *walzen* to roll; compare WELTER
▸'**waltz,like** ADJECTIVE

waltzer ('wɔːlsə) NOUN [1] a person who waltzes. [2] a fairground roundabout on which people are spun round and moved up and down as it revolves about a central axis.

waltz Matilda VERB *Austral* See **Matilda.**

Walvis Bay ('wɔːlvɪs) *or* **Walfish Bay** NOUN a port in Namibia, on the Atlantic: formed an exclave of South Africa, covering an area of 1124 sq. km (434 sq. miles) with its hinterland, but has been administered by Namibia since 1992; formally returned to Namibia in 1994; chief port of Namibia and rich fishing centre. Pop. (urban area): 23 000 (1992 est.).

wambenger (wɒm'bɛŋə) NOUN *Austral* another name for **tuan²**.
▷HISTORY from a native Australian language

wamble ('wɒmbəl) *Dialect, chiefly Brit* ◆ VERB *(intr)* [1] to move unsteadily. [2] to twist the body. [3] to feel nausea. ◆ NOUN [4] an unsteady movement. [5] a sensation of nausea.
▷HISTORY C14 *wamelen* to feel ill, perhaps of Scandinavian origin; compare Norwegian *vamla* to stagger
▸'**wambliness** NOUN ▸'**wambly** ADJECTIVE

wame (weɪm) NOUN *Scot and northern English dialect* the belly, abdomen, or womb.
▷HISTORY C14: northern variant of WOMB

wammul ('wæməl) NOUN *Midland English dialect* a dog.

wampum ('wɒmpəm) NOUN [1] (formerly) money used by North American Indians, made of cylindrical shells strung or woven together, esp white shells rather than the more valuable black or purple ones. [2] *US and Canadian informal* money or wealth. ◆ Also called: **peag, peage.**
▷HISTORY C17: short for *wampumpeag,* from Narraganset *wampompeag,* from *wampan* light + *api* string + *-ag* plural suffix

wan (wɒn) ADJECTIVE **wanner, wannest.** [1] unnaturally pale esp from sickness, grief, etc. [2] characteristic or suggestive of ill health, unhappiness, etc. [3] (of light, stars, etc.) faint or dim. ◆ VERB **wans, wanning, wanned.** [4] to make or become wan.
▷HISTORY Old English *wann* dark; related to *wanian* to WANE
▸'**wanly** ADVERB ▸'**wanness** NOUN

WAN ABBREVIATION FOR: [1] **wide area network.** ◆ [2] INTERNATIONAL CAR REGISTRATION FOR (West Africa) Nigeria.

wanchancy (wɒn'tʃænsɪ) ADJECTIVE *Scot* [1] unlucky. [2] dangerous; risky. [3] uncanny; eerie. ◆ Compare **unchancy.**
▷HISTORY C18: from *wanchance* ill luck, from *wan-* prefix expressing negation or privation + CHANCE

Wanchüan *or* **Wan-ch'uan** (ˌwæntʃʊ'ɑːn) NOUN a former name of **Zhangjiakou.**

wand (wɒnd) NOUN [1] a slender supple stick or twig. [2] a thin rod carried as a symbol of authority. [3] a rod used by a magician, water diviner, etc. [4] *Informal* a conductor's baton. [5] *Archery* a marker used to show the distance at which the archer stands from the target. [6] a hand-held electronic device, such as a light pen or bar-code reader, which is pointed at or passed over an item to read the data stored there.
▷HISTORY C12: from Old Norse *vǫndr;* related to Gothic *wandus* and English WEND
▸'**wand,like** ADJECTIVE

wander ('wɒndə) VERB *(mainly intr)* [1] *(also tr)* to move or travel about, in, or through (a place) without any definite purpose or destination. [2] to proceed in an irregular course; meander. [3] to go astray, as from a path or course. [4] (of the mind, thoughts, etc.) to lose concentration or direction. [5] to think or speak incoherently or illogically. ◆ NOUN [6] the act or an instance of wandering.
▷HISTORY Old English *wandrian;* related to Old Frisian *wandria,* Middle Dutch, Middle High German *wanderen*
▸'**wanderer** NOUN ▸'**wandering** ADJECTIVE, NOUN
▸'**wanderingly** ADVERB

wandering albatross NOUN a large albatross, *Diomedea exulans,* having a very wide wingspan and a white plumage with black wings.

wandering Jew NOUN [1] any of several related creeping or trailing plants of tropical America, esp *Tradescantia fluminensis* and *Zebrina pendula:* family *Commelinaceae.* [2] *Austral* a similar creeping plant of the genus *Commelina.*

Wandering Jew NOUN (in medieval legend) a character condemned to roam the world eternally because he mocked Christ on the day of the Crucifixion.

Wanderjahr *German* ('vandərjaːr) NOUN, *plural* ***-jahre*** (-jaːrə). (formerly) a year in which an apprentice travelled to improve his skills.
▷HISTORY German, literally: wander year

wanderlust ('wɒndəˌlʌst) NOUN a great desire to travel and rove about.
▷HISTORY German, literally: wander desire

wanderoo (ˌwɒndə'ruː) NOUN, *plural* **-deroos.** a macaque monkey, *Macaca silenus,* of India and Sri Lanka, having black fur with a ruff of long greyish fur on each side of the face.
▷HISTORY C17: from Sinhalese *vanduru* monkeys, literally: forest-dwellers, from Sanskrit *vānara* monkey, from *vana* forest

wander plug NOUN an electrical plug on the end of a flexible wire, for insertion into any of a number of sockets.

wandoo ('wɒnduː) NOUN a eucalyptus tree, *Eucalyptus wandoo,* of W Australia, having white bark and durable wood.
▷HISTORY from a native Australian language

Wandsworth ('wɒnzwəθ) NOUN a borough of S Greater London, on the River Thames. Pop.: 260 383 (2001). Area: 35 sq. km (13 sq. miles).

wane (weɪn) VERB *(intr)* [1] (of the moon) to show a gradually decreasing portion of illuminated surface, between full moon and new moon. Compare **wax²** (sense 2). [2] to decrease gradually in size, strength, power, etc. [3] to draw to a close. ◆ NOUN [4] a decrease, as in size, strength, power, etc. [5] the period during which the moon wanes. [6] the act or an instance of drawing to a close. [7] a rounded surface or defective edge of a plank, where the bark was. [8] **on the wane.** in a state of decline.
▷HISTORY Old English *wanian* (vb); related to *wan-,* prefix indicating privation, *wana* defect, Old Norse *vana*
▸'**waney** *or* '**wany** ADJECTIVE

Wanganui (ˌwɒŋəˈnuːɪ) NOUN a port in New Zealand, on SW North Island: centre for a dairy-farming and sheep-rearing district. Pop.: 42 200 (1995 est.).

wangle (ˈwæŋgᵊl) *Informal* ◆ VERB [1] (*tr*) to use devious or illicit methods to get or achieve (something) for (oneself or another): *he wangled himself a salary increase.* [2] to manipulate or falsify (a situation, action, etc.). ◆ NOUN [3] the act or an instance of wangling.
▷**HISTORY** C19: originally printers' slang, perhaps a blend of WAGGLE and dialect *wankle* wavering, from Old English *wancol;* compare Old High German *wankōn* to waver
▸ˈ**wangler** NOUN

Wanhsien *or* **Wan-Hsien** (ˈwænˈʃjɛn) NOUN a variant transliteration of the Chinese name for **Wanxian.**

wank (wæŋk) *Slang* ◆ VERB [1] (*intr*) to masturbate. ◆ NOUN [2] an instance of wanking. ◆ ADJECTIVE [3] bad, useless, or worthless.
▷**HISTORY** of uncertain origin

Wankel engine (ˈwæŋkᵊl) NOUN a type of four-stroke internal-combustion engine without reciprocating parts. It consists of one or more approximately elliptical combustion chambers within which a curved triangular-shaped piston rotates, by the explosion of compressed gas, dividing the combustion chamber into three gastight sections.
▷**HISTORY** C20: named after Felix *Wankel* (1902–88), German engineer who invented it

wanker (ˈwæŋkə) NOUN *Slang* [1] a person who wanks; masturbator. [2] a worthless fellow.

Wankie (ˈwɑːŋkɪ) NOUN the former name (until 1982) of **Hwange.**

wanky (ˈwæŋkɪ) ADJECTIVE *Slang* pretentious.

wanna (ˈwɒnə) VERB a spelling of **want to** intended to reflect a dialectal or informal pronunciation: *I wanna go home.*

wannabe *or* **wannabee** (ˈwɒnəˌbiː) NOUN *Informal* **a** a person who desires to be, or be like, someone or something else. **b** (*as modifier*): *a wannabe film star.*
▷**HISTORY** C20: phonetic shortening of *want to be*

Wanne-Eickel (*German* ˈvanəˈaikəl) NOUN an industrial town in W Germany, in North Rhine-Westphalia on the Rhine-Herne Canal: formed in 1926 by the merging of two townships. Pop.: 98 800 (latest est.).

want¹ (wɒnt) VERB [1] (*tr*) to feel a need or longing for: *I want a new hat.* [2] (*when tr, may take a clause as object or an infinitive*) to wish, need, or desire (something or to do something): *he wants to go home.* [3] (*intr;* usually used with a negative and often foll by *for*) to be lacking or deficient (in something necessary or desirable): *the child wants for nothing.* [4] (*tr*) to feel the absence of: *lying on the ground makes me want my bed.* [5] (*tr*) to fall short by (a specified amount). [6] (*tr*) *Chiefly Brit* to have need of or require (doing or being something): *your shoes want cleaning.* [7] (*intr*) to be destitute. [8] (*tr; often passive*) to seek or request the presence of: *you're wanted upstairs.* [9] (*intr*) to be absent. [10] (*tr; takes an infinitive*) *Informal* should or ought (to do something): *you don't want to go out so late.* [11] **want in** (*or* **out**). *Informal* to wish to be included in (or excluded from) a venture. ◆ NOUN [12] the act or an instance of wanting. [13] anything that is needed, desired, or lacked: *to supply someone's wants.* [14] a lack, shortage, or absence: *for want of common sense.* [15] the state of being in need; destitution: *the state should help those in want.* [16] a sense of lack; craving.
▷**HISTORY** C12 (vb, in the sense: it is lacking), C13 (n): from Old Norse *vanta* to be deficient; related to Old English *wanian* to WANE
▸ˈ**wanter** NOUN

want² (wɒnt) NOUN *English dialect* a mole.
▷**HISTORY** Old English *wand*

want ad NOUN *Informal* a classified advertisement in a newspaper, magazine, etc., for something wanted, such as property or employment.

wanted (ˈwɒntɪd) ADJECTIVE being searched for by the police in connection with a crime that has been committed.

wanting (ˈwɒntɪŋ) ADJECTIVE (*postpositive*) [1] lacking or absent; missing. [2] not meeting requirements or expectations: *you have been found wanting.* ◆ PREPOSITION [3] without. [4] *Archaic* minus.

want knap NOUN *Southwest English dialect* a mole hill.

WAN2TLK *Text messaging* ABBREVIATION FOR want to talk?

wanton (ˈwɒntən) ADJECTIVE [1] dissolute, licentious, or immoral. [2] without motive, provocation, or justification: *wanton destruction.* [3] maliciously and unnecessarily cruel or destructive. [4] unrestrained: *wanton spending.* [5] *Archaic or poetic* playful or capricious. [6] *Archaic* (of vegetation, etc.) luxuriant or superabundant. ◆ NOUN [7] a licentious person, esp a woman. [8] a playful or capricious person. ◆ VERB [9] (*intr*) to behave in a wanton manner. [10] (*tr*) to squander or waste.
▷**HISTORY** C13 *wantowen* (in the obsolete sense: unmanageable, unruly): from *wan-* (prefix equivalent to UN-¹; related to Old English *wanian* to WANE) + *-towen,* from Old English *togen* brought up, from *tēon* to bring up
▸ˈ**wantonly** ADVERB ▸ˈ**wantonness** NOUN

Wanxian, Wanhsien, *or* **Wan-Hsien** (ˈwænˈʃjɛn) NOUN an inland port in central China, in E Sichuan province, on the Yangtze River. Pop.: 156 823 (1990 est.).

WAP (wæp) NOUN ACRONYM FOR Wireless Application Protocol: a global application that enables mobile phone users to access the Internet and other information services.

wapentake (ˈwɒpənˌteɪk, ˈwæp-) NOUN *English legal history* a subdivision of certain shires or counties, esp in the Midlands and North of England, corresponding to the hundred in other shires.
▷**HISTORY** Old English *wǣpen(ge)tæc,* from Old Norse *vápnatak,* from *vápn* WEAPON + *tak* TAKE

wapiti (ˈwɒpɪtɪ) NOUN, *plural* **-tis.** a large deer, *Cervus canadensis,* with large much-branched antlers, native to North America and now also common in the South Island of New Zealand. Also called: **American elk.**
▷**HISTORY** C19: from Shawnee, literally: white deer, from *wap* (unattested) white; from the animal's white tail and rump

wappenshaw (ˈwæpənʃɔː, ˈwɒp-) NOUN (formerly) a muster of men in a particular area in Scotland to show that they were properly armed.
▷**HISTORY** C16: from Northern English *wapen,* from Old Norse *vápn* WEAPON + *schaw* SHOW

war (wɔː) NOUN [1] open armed conflict between two or more parties, nations, or states. Related adjectives: **belligerent, martial.** [2] a particular armed conflict: *the 1973 war in the Middle East.* [3] the techniques of armed conflict as a study, science, or profession. [4] any conflict or contest: *a war of wits; the war against crime.* [5] (*modifier*) of, relating to, resulting from, or characteristic of war: *a war hero; war damage; a war story.* [6] **to have had a good war.** to have made the most of the opportunities presented to one during wartime. [7] **in the wars.** *Informal* (esp of a child) hurt or knocked about, esp as a result of quarrelling and fighting. ◆ VERB **wars, warring, warred.** [8] (*intr*) to conduct a war.
▷**HISTORY** C12: from Old Northern French *werre* (variant of Old French *guerre*), of Germanic origin; related to Old High German *werra*

War. ABBREVIATION FOR Warwickshire.

waragi (ˈwaragɪ, -dʒɪ) NOUN a Ugandan alcoholic drink made from bananas.
▷**HISTORY** from Luganda

Warangal (ˈwʌrəngəl) NOUN a city in S central India, in N Andhra Pradesh: capital of a 12th-century Hindu kingdom. Pop.: 447 657 (1991).

waratah (ˌwɒrəˈtɑː, ˈwɒrətɑː) NOUN *Austral* a proteaceous shrub, *Telopea speciosissima,* the floral emblem of New South Wales, having dark green leaves and large clusters of crimson flowers.
▷**HISTORY** from a native Australian language

warb (wɔːb) NOUN *Austral slang* a dirty or insignificant person.
▷**HISTORY** C20: of unknown origin
▸ˈ**warby** ADJECTIVE

war baby NOUN a child born in wartime, esp the illegitimate child of a soldier.

War Between the States NOUN the American Civil War.

warble¹ (ˈwɔːbᵊl) VERB [1] to sing (words, songs, etc.) with trills, runs, and other embellishments. [2] (*tr*) to utter in a song. [3] *US* another word for **yodel.** ◆ NOUN [4] the act or an instance of warbling.
▷**HISTORY** C14: via Old French *werbler* from Germanic; compare Frankish *hwirbilōn* (unattested), Old High German *wirbil* whirlwind; see WHIRL

warble² (ˈwɔːbᵊl) NOUN *Vet science* [1] a small lumpy abscess under the skin of cattle caused by infestation with larvae of the warble fly. [2] a hard tumorous lump of tissue on a horse's back, caused by prolonged friction of a saddle.
▷**HISTORY** C16: of uncertain origin
▸ˈ**warbled** ADJECTIVE

warble fly NOUN any of various hairy beelike dipterous flies of the genus *Hypoderma* and related genera, the larvae of which produce warbles in cattle: family *Oestridae.*

warbler (ˈwɔːblə) NOUN [1] a person or thing that warbles. [2] any small active passerine songbird of the Old World subfamily *Sylviinae:* family *Muscicapidae.* They have a cryptic plumage and slender bill and are arboreal insectivores. [3] Also called: **wood warbler.** any small bird of the American family *Parulidae,* similar to the Old World forms but often brightly coloured.

war bonnet NOUN a headband with trailing feathers, worn by certain North American Indian warriors as a headdress.

war bride NOUN a soldier's bride met as a result of troop movements in wartime, esp a foreign national.

warchalking (ˈwɔːtʃɔːkɪŋ) NOUN the practice of marking chalk symbols on walls and pavements at places where local wireless Internet connections may be obtained for free via a computer, usually without permission.
▸ˈ**warchalker** NOUN
▷**HISTORY** C21: from w(ireless) a(cess) r(evolution) + gerund of of CHALK

war chest NOUN a fund collected for a specific purpose, such as an election campaign.

war correspondent NOUN a journalist who reports on a war from the scene of action.

war crime NOUN a crime committed in wartime in violation of the accepted rules and customs of war, such as genocide, ill-treatment of prisoners of war, etc.
▸**war criminal** NOUN

war cry NOUN [1] a rallying cry used by combatants in battle. [2] a cry, slogan, etc., used to rally support for a cause.

ward (wɔːd) NOUN [1] (in many countries) a district into which a city, town, parish, or other area is divided for administration, election of representatives, etc. [2] a room in a hospital, esp one for patients requiring similar kinds of care: *a maternity ward.* [3] one of the divisions of a prison. [4] an open space enclosed within the walls of a castle. [5] *Law* **a** Also called: **ward of court.** a person, esp a minor or one legally incapable of managing his own affairs, placed under the control or protection of a guardian or of a court. **b** guardianship, as of a minor or legally incompetent person. [6] the state of being under guard or in custody. [7] a person who is under the protection or in the custody of another. [8] a means of protection. [9] **a** an internal ridge or bar in a lock that prevents an incorrectly cut key from turning. **b** a corresponding groove cut in a key. [10] a less common word for **warden¹.** ◆ VERB [11] (*tr*) *Archaic* to guard or protect. ◆ See also **ward off.**
▷**HISTORY** Old English *weard* protector; related to Old High German *wart,* Old Saxon *ward,* Old Norse *vorthr.* See GUARD
▸ˈ**wardless** ADJECTIVE

-ward SUFFIX [1] (*forming adjectives*) indicating direction towards: *a backward step; heavenward progress.* [2] (*forming adverbs*) a variant and the usual US and Canadian form of **-wards.**
▷**HISTORY** Old English *-weard* towards

war dance NOUN [1] a ceremonial dance performed before going to battle or after victory, esp by certain North American Indian peoples. [2] a dance representing warlike action.

warded ('wɔːdɪd) ADJECTIVE (of locks, keys, etc.) having wards.

warden[1] ('wɔːdᵊn) NOUN [1] a person who has the charge or care of something, esp. a building, or someone. [2] *Archaic* any of various public officials, esp. one responsible for the enforcement of certain regulations. [3] *Chiefly US and Canadian* the chief officer in charge of a prison. [4] *Brit* the principal or president of any of various universities or colleges. [5] See **churchwarden** (sense 1).
▷HISTORY C13: from Old Northern French *wardein,* from *warder* to guard, of Germanic origin; see GUARD
▸ **'wardenry** NOUN

warden[2] ('wɔːdᵊn) NOUN a variety of pear that has crisp firm flesh and is used for cooking.
▷HISTORY C15: of obscure origin

warder[1] ('wɔːdə) *or feminine* **wardress** NOUN [1] *Chiefly Brit* an officer in charge of prisoners in a jail. [2] a person who guards or has charge of something.
▷HISTORY C14: from Anglo-French *wardere,* from Old French *warder* to GUARD, of Germanic origin
▸ **'wardership** NOUN

warder[2] ('wɔːdə) NOUN (formerly) a staff or truncheon carried by a ruler as an emblem of authority and used to signal his wishes or intentions.
▷HISTORY C15: perhaps from Middle English *warden* to WARD

ward heeler NOUN *US politics, disparaging* a party worker who canvasses votes and performs chores for a political boss. Also called: **heeler.**

wardian case ('wɔːdɪən) NOUN a type of glass container used for housing delicate ferns and similar plants.
▷HISTORY C19: named after N. B. *Ward* (died 1868), English botanist

wardmote ('wɔːdməʊt) NOUN *Brit* an assembly of the citizens or liverymen of a ward.
▷HISTORY C14: see WARD, MOOT

ward off VERB (*tr, adverb*) to turn aside or repel; avert.

Wardour Street ('wɔːdə) NOUN [1] a street in Soho where many film companies have their London offices: formerly noted for shops selling antiques and mock antiques. [2] **Wardour Street English.** affectedly archaic speech or writing.

wardrobe ('wɔːdrəʊb) NOUN [1] a tall closet or cupboard, with a rail or hooks on which to hang clothes. [2] the total collection of articles of clothing belonging to one person. [3] the collection of costumes belonging to a theatre or theatrical company.
▷HISTORY C14: from Old Northern French *warderobe,* from *warder* to GUARD + *robe* ROBE

wardrobe mistress NOUN a person responsible for maintaining and sometimes making the costumes in a theatre.

wardrobe trunk NOUN a large upright rectangular travelling case, usually opening longitudinally, with one side having a hanging rail, the other having drawers or compartments.

wardroom ('wɔːdˌruːm, -ˌrʊm) NOUN [1] the quarters assigned to the officers (except the captain) of a warship. [2] the officers of a warship collectively, excepting the captain.

-wards *or* **-ward** SUFFIX FORMING ADVERBS indicating direction towards: *a step backwards; to sail shorewards.* Compare **-ward.**
▷HISTORY Old English *-weardes* towards

wardship ('wɔːdʃɪp) NOUN the state of being a ward.

ware[1] (wɛə) NOUN (*often in combination*) [1] (*functioning as singular*) articles of the same kind or material: *glassware; silverware.* [2] porcelain or pottery of a specified type: *agateware; jasper ware.* ◆ See also **wares.**
▷HISTORY Old English *waru;* related to Old Frisian *were,* Old Norse *vara,* Middle Dutch *Ware*

ware[2] (wɛə) *Archaic* ◆ VERB [1] another word for **beware.** ◆ ADJECTIVE [2] another word for **wary** or **wise**[1].
▷HISTORY Old English *wær;* related to Old Saxon, Old High German *giwar,* Old Norse *varr,* Gothic *war,* Latin *vereor.* See AWARE, BEWARE

ware[3] (wɛə) VERB (*tr*) *Northern Brit dialect* to spend or squander.
▷HISTORY C15: of Scandinavian origin; related to Icelandic *verja*

warehouse NOUN ('wɛəˌhaʊs) [1] a place where goods are stored prior to their use, distribution, or sale. [2] See **bonded warehouse.** [3] *Chiefly Brit* a large commercial, esp wholesale, establishment. ◆ VERB ('wɛəˌhaʊz, -ˌhaʊs) [4] (*tr*) to store or place in a warehouse, esp a bonded warehouse.

warehouseman ('wɛəˌhaʊsmən) NOUN, *plural* **-men.** a person who manages, is employed in, or owns a warehouse.

warehousing ('wɛəˌhaʊzɪŋ) NOUN *Stock Exchange* an attempt to maintain the price of a company's shares or to gain a significant stake in a company without revealing the true identity of the purchaser. Shares are purchased through an insurance company, a unit trust, or nominees.

wares (wɛəz) PLURAL NOUN [1] articles of manufacture considered as being for sale. [2] any talent or asset regarded as a commercial or saleable commodity. [3] (*Caribbean*) earthenware.

war establishment NOUN the full wartime complement of men, equipment, and vehicles of a military unit.

warfare ('wɔːˌfɛə) NOUN [1] the act, process, or an instance of waging war. [2] conflict, struggle, or strife.

warfarin ('wɔːfərɪn) NOUN a crystalline insoluble optically active compound, used as a rodenticide and, in the form of its sodium salt, as a medical anticoagulant. Formula: $C_{19}H_{16}O_4$.
▷HISTORY C20: from the patent owners *W(isconsin) A(lumni) R(esearch) F(oundation)* + (COUM)ARIN

war game NOUN [1] a notional tactical exercise for training military commanders, in which no military units are actually deployed. [2] a game in which model soldiers are used to create battles, esp past battles, in order to study tactics.

warhead ('wɔːˌhɛd) NOUN the part of the fore end of a missile or projectile that contains explosives.

warhorse ('wɔːˌhɔːs) NOUN [1] a horse used in battle. [2] *Informal* a veteran soldier, politician, or elderly person, esp one who is aggressive.

warison ('wærɪsən) NOUN (esp formerly) a bugle note used as an order to a military force to attack.
▷HISTORY C13: from Old Northern French, from *warir* to protect, of Germanic origin; compare Old English *warian* to defend

wark (wɑːrk, wɔːrk) NOUN a Scot word for **work.**

Warks ABBREVIATION FOR Warwickshire.

Warley ('wɔːlɪ) NOUN an industrial town in W central England, in Sandwell unitary authority, West Midlands: formed in 1966 by the amalgamation of Smethwick, Oldbury, and Rowley Regis. Pop.: 145 542 (1991).

warlike ('wɔːˌlaɪk) ADJECTIVE [1] of, relating to, or used in war. [2] hostile or belligerent. [3] fit or ready for war.

warlock ('wɔːˌlɒk) NOUN [1] a man who practises black magic; sorcerer. [2] a fortune-teller, conjuror, or magician.
▷HISTORY Old English *wǣrloga* oath breaker, from *wǣr* oath + *-loga* liar, from *lēogan* to LIE[1]

warlord ('wɔːˌlɔːd) NOUN a military leader of a nation or part of a nation, esp one who is accountable to nobody when the central government is weak: *the Chinese warlords.*

Warlpiri ('walpri) NOUN an Aboriginal language of central Australia.

warm (wɔːm) ADJECTIVE [1] characterized by or having a moderate degree of heat; moderately hot. [2] maintaining or imparting heat: *a warm coat.* [3] having or showing ready affection, kindliness, etc.: *a warm personality.* [4] lively, vigorous, or passionate: *a warm debate.* [5] cordial or enthusiastic; ardent: *warm support.* [6] quickly or easily aroused: *a warm temper.* [7] (of colours) predominantly red or yellow in tone. [8] (of a scent, trail, etc.) recently made; strong. [9] near to finding a hidden object or discovering or guessing facts, as in children's games. [10] *Informal* uncomfortable or disagreeable, esp because of the proximity of danger. ◆ VERB [11] (sometimes foll by *up*) to raise or be raised in temperature; make or become warm or warmer. [12] (when *intr,* often foll by *to*) to make or become excited, enthusiastic, etc. (about): *he warmed to the idea of buying a new car.* [13] (*intr;* often foll by *to*) to feel affection, kindness, etc. (for someone): *I warmed to her mother from the start.* [14] (*tr*) *Brit* to give a caning to: *I'll warm you in a minute.* ◆ NOUN [15] *Informal* a warm place or area: *come into the warm.* [16] *Informal* the act or an instance of warming or being warmed. ◆ See also **warm over, warm up.**
▷HISTORY Old English *wearm;* related to Old Frisian, Old Saxon *warm,* Old Norse *varmr*
▸ **'warmer** NOUN ▸ **'warmish** ADJECTIVE ▸ **'warmly** ADVERB
▸ **'warmness** NOUN

warm-blooded ADJECTIVE [1] ardent, impetuous, or passionate. [2] (of birds and mammals) having a constant body temperature, usually higher than the temperature of the surroundings. Technical name: **homoiothermic.**
▸ **ˌwarm-'bloodedness** NOUN

warm-down NOUN light exercises performed to aid recovery from strenuous physical activity.

war memorial NOUN a monument, usually an obelisk or cross, to those who die in a war, esp those from a particular locality.

warm front NOUN *Meteorol* the boundary between a warm air mass and the cold air above which it is rising, at a less steep angle than at the cold front. Compare **cold front, occluded front.**

warm-hearted ADJECTIVE kindly, generous, forgiving, or readily sympathetic.
▸ **ˌwarm-'heartedly** ADVERB ▸ **ˌwarm-'heartedness** NOUN

warming pan NOUN a pan, often of copper and having a long handle, filled with hot coals or hot water and formerly drawn over the sheets to warm a bed.

warmonger ('wɔːˌmʌŋgə) NOUN a person who fosters warlike ideas or advocates war.
▸ **'warˌmongering** NOUN

warm over VERB (*tr, adverb*) [1] *US and Canadian* to reheat (food). [2] *Informal* to present (an idea, etc.) again, esp without freshness or originality.

warm sector NOUN *Meteorol* a wedge of warm air between the warm and cold fronts of a depression, which is eventually occluded. See also **cold front, warm front.**

warmth (wɔːmθ) NOUN [1] the state, quality, or sensation of being warm. [2] intensity of emotion: *he denied the accusation with some warmth.* [3] affection or cordiality.

warm up VERB (*adverb*) [1] to make or become warm or warmer. [2] (*intr*) to exercise in preparation for and immediately before a game, contest, or more vigorous exercise. [3] to get ready for something important; prepare. [4] to run or operate (an engine, etc.) until the normal working temperature or condition is attained, or (of an engine, etc.) to undergo this process. [5] to make or become more animated or enthusiastic: *the party warmed up when Tom came.* [6] to reheat (already cooked food) or (of such food) to be reheated. [7] (*tr*) to make (an audience) relaxed and receptive before a show, esp a television comedy show. ◆ NOUN **warm-up.** [8] the act or an instance of warming up. [9] a preparatory exercise routine.

warn (wɔːn) VERB [1] to notify or make (someone) aware of danger, harm, etc. [2] (*tr; often takes a negative and an infinitive*) to advise or admonish (someone) as to action, conduct, etc.: *I warn you not to do that again.* [3] (*takes a clause as object or an infinitive*) to inform (someone) in advance: *he warned them that he would arrive late.* [4] (*tr;* usually foll by *away, off,* etc.) to give notice to go away, be off, etc.: *he warned the trespassers off his ground.*
▷HISTORY Old English *wearnian;* related to Old High German *warnēn,* Old Norse *varna* to refuse
▸ **'warner** NOUN

warning ('wɔːnɪŋ) NOUN [1] a hint, intimation, threat, etc., of harm or danger. [2] advice to beware or desist. [3] an archaic word for **notice** (sense 6). ◆ ADJECTIVE [4] (*prenominal*) intended or serving to warn: *a warning look.* [5] (of the coloration of certain distasteful or poisonous animals) having conspicuous markings, which predators recognize and learn to avoid; aposematic.
▸ **'warningly** ADVERB

War of American Independence NOUN the conflict following the revolt of the North American colonies against British rule, particularly on the issue of taxation. Hostilities began in 1775 when British and American forces clashed at Lexington and Concord. Articles of Confederation agreed in the Continental Congress in 1777 provided for a confederacy to be known as the United States of America. The war was effectively ended with the surrender of the British at Yorktown in 1781 and peace was signed at Paris in Sept. 1783. Also called: **American Revolution** *or* **Revolutionary War.**

War of 1812 NOUN a war between Great Britain and the US, fought chiefly along the Canadian border (1812–14).

War Office NOUN *Brit* (formerly) **a** the department of state responsible for the British Army, now part of the Ministry of Defence. **b** the premises of this department in Whitehall, London.

war of nerves NOUN the use of psychological tactics against an opponent, such as shattering his morale by the use of propaganda.

War of Secession NOUN another name for the (American) **Civil War.**

War of the Austrian Succession NOUN the war (1740–48) fought by Austria, Britain, and the Netherlands against Prussia, France, and Spain in support of the right of succession of Maria Theresa to the Austrian throne and against the territorial aims of Prussia.

War of the Grand Alliance NOUN the war (1689–97) waged by the Grand Alliance, led by Britain, the Netherlands, and Austria, against Louis XIV of France, following his invasion (1688) of the Palatinate.

War of the Spanish Succession NOUN the war (1701–14) between Austria, Britain, Prussia, and the Netherlands on the one side and France, Spain, and Bavaria on the other over the disputed succession to the Spanish throne.

warp (wɔːp) VERB [1] to twist or cause to twist out of shape, as from heat, damp, etc. [2] to turn or cause to turn from a true, correct, or proper course. [3] to pervert or be perverted. [4] (*tr*) to prepare (yarn) as a warp. [5] *Nautical* to move (a vessel) by hauling on a rope fixed to a stationary object ashore or (of a vessel) to be moved thus. [6] (*tr*) (formerly) to curve or twist (an aircraft wing) in order to assist control in flight. [7] (*tr*) to flood (land) with water from which alluvial matter is deposited. ◆ NOUN [8] the state or condition of being twisted out of shape. [9] a twist, distortion, or bias. [10] a mental or moral deviation. [11] the yarns arranged lengthways on a loom, forming the threads through which the weft yarns are woven. [12] the heavy threads used to reinforce the rubber in the casing of a pneumatic tyre. [13] *Nautical* a rope used for warping a vessel. [14] alluvial sediment deposited by water.
▷**HISTORY** Old English *wearp* a throw; related to Old High German *warf,* Old Norse *varp* throw of a dragging net, Old English *weorpan* to throw
▸ **ˈwarpage** NOUN ▸ **warped** ADJECTIVE ▸ **ˈwarper** NOUN

war paint NOUN [1] painted decoration of the face and body applied by certain North American Indians before battle. [2] *Informal* finery or regalia. [3] *Informal* cosmetics.

warpath (ˈwɔːˌpɑːθ) NOUN [1] the route taken by North American Indians on a warlike expedition. [2] **on the warpath. a** preparing to engage in battle. **b** *Informal* in a state of anger.

warplane (ˈwɔːˌpleɪn) NOUN any aircraft designed for and used in warfare. Also called (US): **battle plane.**

warrant (ˈwɒrənt) NOUN [1] anything that gives authority for an action or decision; authorization; sanction. [2] a document that certifies or guarantees, such as a receipt for goods stored in a warehouse, a licence, or a commission. [3] *Law* an authorization issued by a magistrate or other official allowing a constable or other officer to search or seize property, arrest a person, or perform some other specified act. [4] (in certain armed services) the official authority for the appointment of warrant officers. [5] a security that functions as a stock option by giving the owner the right to buy ordinary shares in a company at a specified date, often at a specified price. ◆ VERB (*tr*) [6] to guarantee the quality, condition, etc., of (something). [7] to give authority or power to. [8] to attest to or assure the character, worthiness, etc., of. [9] to guarantee (a purchaser of merchandise) against loss of, damage to, or misrepresentation concerning the merchandise. [10] *Law* to guarantee (the title to an estate or other property). [11] to declare boldly and confidently.
▷**HISTORY** C13: from Anglo-French *warrant,* variant of Old French *guarant,* from *guarantir* to guarantee, of Germanic origin; compare GUARANTY
▸ **ˈwarrantable** ADJECTIVE ▸ **ˌwarrantaˈbility** NOUN ▸ **ˈwarrantably** ADVERB ▸ **ˈwarranter** NOUN ▸ **ˈwarrantless** ADJECTIVE

warrantee (ˌwɒrənˈtiː) NOUN a person to whom a warranty is given.

warrant officer NOUN an officer in certain armed services who holds a rank between those of commissioned and noncommissioned officers. In the British army, the rank has two classes: see **regimental sergeant major, company sergeant major.**

Warrant of Fitness NOUN *NZ* a six-monthly certificate required for motor vehicles certifying mechanical soundness.

warrantor (ˈwɒrənˌtɔː) NOUN an individual or company that provides a warranty.

warrant sale NOUN *Scots law* a sale of someone's personal belongings or household effects that have been seized to meet unpaid debts.

warranty (ˈwɒrəntɪ) NOUN, *plural* **-ties.** [1] *Property law* a covenant, express or implied, by which the vendor of real property vouches for the security of the title conveyed. [2] *Contract law* an express or implied term in a contract, such as an undertaking that goods contracted to be sold shall meet specified requirements as to quality, etc. [3] *Insurance law* an undertaking by the party insured that the facts given regarding the risk are as stated. [4] the act of warranting.
▷**HISTORY** C14: from Anglo-French *warantie,* from *warantir* to warrant, variant of Old French *guarantir;* see WARRANT

warren (ˈwɒrən) NOUN [1] a series of interconnected underground tunnels in which rabbits live. [2] a colony of rabbits. [3] an overcrowded area or dwelling. [4] **a** *Chiefly Brit* an enclosed place where small game animals or birds are kept, esp for breeding, or a part of a river or lake enclosed by nets in which fish are kept (esp in the phrase **beasts** or **fowls of warren**). **b** *English legal history* a franchise permitting one to keep animals, birds, or fish in this way.
▷**HISTORY** C14: from Anglo-French *warenne,* of Germanic origin; compare Old High German *werien* to preserve

Warren (ˈwɒrən) NOUN a city in the US, in SE Michigan, northeast of Detroit. Pop.: 138 078 (1996 est.).

warrener (ˈwɒrənə) NOUN *Obsolete* a gamekeeper or keeper of a warren (sense 4).

warrigal (ˈwɒrɪgæl) *Austral* ◆ NOUN [1] a dingo. [2] another word for **brumby.** ◆ ADJECTIVE [3] untamed or wild.
▷**HISTORY** C19: from a native Australian language

Warrington (ˈwɒrɪŋtən) NOUN [1] an industrial town in NW England, in Warrington unitary authority, Cheshire on the River Mersey: dates from Roman times. Pop.: 81 812 (1991 est.). [2] a unitary authority in NW England, in N Cheshire. Pop.: 191 084 (2001). Area: 176 sq. km (68 sq. miles).

warrior (ˈwɒrɪə) NOUN **a** a person engaged in, experienced in, or devoted to war. **b** (*as modifier*): *a warrior nation.*
▷**HISTORY** C13: from Old Northern French *werreieor,* from *werre* WAR

Warsaw (ˈwɔːsɔː) NOUN the capital of Poland, in the E central part on the River Vistula: became capital at the end of the 16th century; almost completely destroyed in World War II as the main centre of the Polish resistance movement; rebuilt within about six years; university (1818); situated at the junction of important trans-European routes. Pop.: 1 618 468 (1999 est.). Polish name: **Warszawa** (varˈʃava).

Warsaw Pact NOUN a military treaty and association of E European countries, formed in 1955 by the Soviet Union, Bulgaria, Czechoslovakia, East Germany, Hungary, Poland, and Romania: East Germany left in 1990; the remaining members dissolved the Pact in 1991.

warship (ˈwɔːˌʃɪp) NOUN a vessel armed, armoured, and otherwise equipped for naval warfare.

Wars of the Roses PLURAL NOUN the conflicts in England (1455–85) centred on the struggle for the throne between the house of York (symbolized by the white rose) and the house of Lancaster (of which one badge was the red rose).

wart (wɔːt) NOUN [1] Also called: **verruca.** *Pathol* any firm abnormal elevation of the skin caused by a virus. [2] *Botany* a small rounded outgrowth. [3] **warts and all.** with all blemishes evident.
▷**HISTORY** Old English *weart(e)*; related to Old High German *warza,* Old Norse *varta*
▸ **ˈwarted** ADJECTIVE ▸ **ˈwartˌlike** ADJECTIVE ▸ **ˈwarty** ADJECTIVE

Warta (*Polish* ˈvarta) NOUN a river in Poland, flowing generally north and west across the whole W Polish Plain to the River Oder. Length: 808 km (502 miles).

Wartburg (*German* ˈvartbʊrk) NOUN a medieval castle in central Germany, in Thuringia southwest of Eisenach: residence of Luther (1521–22) when he began his German translation of the New Testament.

wart cress NOUN either of two prostrate annuals, *Coronopus squamatus* and *C. didymus,* having small white flowers: family *Brassicaceae* (crucifers). Also called: **swine's cress.**

warthog (ˈwɔːthɒg) NOUN a wild pig, *Phacochoerus aethiopicus,* of southern and E Africa, having heavy tusks, wartlike protuberances on the face, and a mane of coarse hair.

wartime (ˈwɔːˌtaɪm) NOUN **a** a period or time of war. **b** (*as modifier*): *wartime conditions.*

war whoop NOUN the yell or howl uttered, esp by North American Indians, while making an attack.

Warwick (ˈwɒrɪk) NOUN a town in central England, administrative centre of Warwickshire, on the River Avon: 14th-century castle, with collections of armour and waxworks: the university of Warwick (1965) is in Coventry. Pop.: 22 476 (1991).

Warwickshire (ˈwɒrɪkˌʃɪə, -ʃə) NOUN a county of central England: until 1974, when the West Midlands metropolitan county was created, it contained one of the most highly industrialized regions in the world, centred on Birmingham. Administrative centre: Warwick. Pop.: 505 885 (2001). Area: 1981 sq. km (765 sq. miles).

wary (ˈwɛərɪ) ADJECTIVE **warier, wariest.** [1] watchful, cautious, or alert. [2] characterized by caution or watchfulness.
▷**HISTORY** C16: from WARE[2] + -Y[1]
▸ **ˈwarily** ADVERB ▸ **ˈwariness** NOUN

warzone (ˈwɔːˌzəʊn) NOUN an area where a war is taking place or there is some other violent conflict.

was (wɒz; *unstressed* wəz) VERB (used with *I, he, she, it,* and with singular nouns) [1] the past tense (indicative mood) of **be.** [2] *Not standard* a form of the subjunctive mood used in place of *were,* esp in conditional sentences: *if the film was to be with you, would you be able to process it?*
▷**HISTORY** Old English *wæs,* from *wesan* to be; related to Old Frisian, Old High German *was,* Old Norse *var*

wasabi (wəˈsɑːbɪ) NOUN [1] a Japanese cruciferous plant, *Eutrema Wasabi,* cultivated for its thick green pungent root. [2] the root of this plant, esp in paste or powder form, used as a condiment in Japanese cookery.
▷**HISTORY** Japanese

Wasatch Range (ˈwɔːsætʃ) NOUN a mountain range in the W central US, in N Utah and SE Idaho. Highest peak: Mount Timpanogos, 3581 m (11 750 ft.).

wash (wɒʃ) VERB [1] to apply water or other liquid, usually with soap, to (oneself, clothes, etc.) in order to cleanse. [2] (*tr;* often foll by *away, from, off,* etc.) to remove by the application of water or other liquid and usually soap: *she washed the dirt from her clothes.* [3] (*intr*) to be capable of being washed without damage or loss of colour. [4] (of an animal such as a cat) to cleanse (itself or another animal) by licking. [5] (*tr*) to cleanse from pollution or defilement. [6] (*tr*) to make wet or moist. [7] (often foll by *away,* etc.) to move or be moved by water: *the flood washed away the bridge.* [8] (esp of waves) to flow or sweep against or over (a surface or object), often with a lapping sound. [9] to form by erosion or be eroded: *the stream washed a ravine in the hill.* [10] (*tr*) to apply a thin coating of paint, metal, etc., to.

[11] (*tr*) to separate (ore, precious stones, etc.) from (gravel, earth, or sand) by immersion in water. [12] (*intr; usually used with a negative*) *Informal, chiefly Brit* to admit of testing or proof: *your excuses won't wash.* [13] **wash one's hands. a** *Euphemistic* to go to the lavatory. **b** (usually foll by *of*) to refuse to have anything more to do (with). ◆ NOUN [14] the act or process of washing; ablution. [15] a quantity of articles washed together. [16] a preparation or thin liquid used as a coating or in washing: *a thin wash of paint; a hair wash.* [17] *Med* **a** any medicinal or soothing lotion for application to a part of the body. **b** (*in combination*): *an eyewash.* [18] the flow of water, esp waves, against a surface, or the sound made by such a flow. [19] **a** the technique of making wash drawings. **b** See **wash drawing.** [20] the erosion of soil by the action of flowing water. [21] a mass of alluvial material transported and deposited by flowing water. [22] land that is habitually washed by tidal or river waters. [23] the disturbance in the air or water produced at the rear of an aircraft, boat, or other moving object. [24] gravel, earth, etc., from which valuable minerals may be washed. [25] waste liquid matter or liquid refuse, esp as fed to pigs; swill. [26] an alcoholic liquid resembling strong beer, resulting from the fermentation of wort in the production of whisky. [27] **come out in the wash.** *Informal* to become known or apparent in the course of time. ◆ See also **wash down, wash out, wash up.**

▷HISTORY Old English *wæscan, waxan;* related to Old High German *wascan;* see WATER

Wash (wɒʃ) NOUN **the.** a shallow inlet of the North Sea on the E coast of England, between Lincolnshire and Norfolk.

Wash. ABBREVIATION FOR Washington.

washable (ˈwɒʃəbᵊl) ADJECTIVE (esp of fabrics or clothes) capable of being washed without deteriorating.
▸ ˌ**washaˈbility** NOUN

wash-and-wear ADJECTIVE (of fabrics, garments, etc.) requiring only light washing, short drying time, and little or no ironing.

washaway (ˈwɒʃəˌweɪ) NOUN *Austral* another word for **washout** (sense 4).

washbasin (ˈwɒʃˌbeɪsᵊn) NOUN a basin or bowl for washing the face and hands. Also called: **washbowl.**

washboard (ˈwɒʃˌbɔːd) NOUN [1] a board having a surface, usually of corrugated metal, on which esp formerly, clothes were scrubbed. [2] such a board used as a rhythm instrument played with the fingers in skiffle, Country and Western music, etc. [3] a less common US word for **skirting board.** [4] *Nautical* **a** a vertical planklike shield fastened to the gunwales of a boat to prevent water from splashing over the side. **b** Also called: **splashboard.** a shield under a port for the same purpose.

washcloth (ˈwɒʃˌklɒθ) NOUN [1] another name for **dishcloth.** [2] the US and Canadian word for **face cloth.**

washday (ˈwɒʃˌdeɪ) NOUN a day on which clothes and linen are washed, often the same day each week.

wash down VERB (*tr, adverb*) [1] to wash completely, esp from top to bottom. [2] to take drink with or after (food or another drink).

wash drawing NOUN a pen-and-ink drawing that has been lightly brushed over with water to soften the lines.

washed out ADJECTIVE (**washed-out** when prenominal) [1] faded or colourless. [2] exhausted, esp when being pale in appearance.

washed up ADJECTIVE (**washed-up** when prenominal) *Informal, chiefly US, Canadian, and NZ* [1] no longer useful, successful, hopeful, etc.: *our hopes for the new deal are all washed up.* [2] exhausted.

washer (ˈwɒʃə) NOUN [1] a person or thing that washes. [2] a flat ring or drilled disc of metal used under the head of a bolt or nut to spread the load when tightened. [3] any flat ring of rubber, felt, metal, etc., used to provide a seal under a nut or in a tap or valve seat. [4] See **washing machine.** [5] *Chemical engineering* a device for cleaning or washing gases or vapours; scrubber. [6] *Austral* a face cloth; flannel.

washerwoman (ˈwɒʃəˌwʊmən), **washwoman,** *or masculine* **washerman** NOUN, *plural* **-women** *or* **-men.** a person who washes clothes for a living.

washery (ˈwɒʃərɪ) NOUN a plant at a mine where water or other liquid is used to remove dirt from a mineral, esp coal.

wash house NOUN (formerly) a building or outbuilding in which laundry was done.

washin (ˈwɒʃɪn) NOUN *Aeronautics* an increase in the angle of attack of an aircraft wing towards the wing tip.
▷HISTORY C20: from WASH (flow) + IN

washing (ˈwɒʃɪŋ) NOUN [1] articles that have been or are to be washed together on a single occasion. [2] liquid in which an article has been washed. [3] something, such as gold dust or metal ore, that has been obtained by washing. [4] a thin coat of something applied in liquid form.

washing machine NOUN a mechanical apparatus, usually powered by electricity, for washing clothing, linens, etc.

washing powder NOUN powdered detergent for washing fabrics.

washing soda NOUN the crystalline decahydrate of sodium carbonate, esp when used as a cleansing agent.

Washington (ˈwɒʃɪŋtən) NOUN [1] a state of the northwestern US, on the Pacific: consists of the Coast Range and the Olympic Mountains in the west and the Columbia Plateau in the east. Capital: Olympia. Pop.: 5 894 121 (2000). Area: 172 416 sq. km (66 570 sq. miles). Abbreviations: **Wash,** (with zip code) **WA.** [2] the capital of the US, coextensive with the District of Columbia and situated near the E coast on the Potomac River: site chosen by President Washington in 1790; contains the White House and the Capitol; a major educational and administrative centre. Pop.: 572 059 (2000). Also called: **Washington, DC.** [3] a town in Tyne and Wear: designated a new town in 1964. Pop.: 56 848 (1991). [4] **Mount.** a mountain in N New Hampshire, in the White Mountains: the highest peak in the northeast US; noted for extreme weather conditions. Height: 1917 m (6288 ft.). [5] **Lake.** a lake in W Washington, forming the E boundary of the city of Seattle: linked by canal with Puget Sound. Length: about 32 km (20 miles). Width: 6 km (4 miles).

Washingtonian (ˌwɒʃɪŋˈtəʊnɪən) ADJECTIVE [1] of or relating to the city or state of Washington or their inhabitants. ◆ NOUN [2] a native or inhabitant of the city or state of Washington.

Washington palm NOUN a palm tree, *Washingtonia filifera,* of California and Florida, having large fan-shaped leaves and small black fruits. Also called: **desert palm.**

washing-up NOUN *Brit* [1] the washing of dishes, cutlery, etc., after a meal. [2] dishes and cutlery waiting to be washed up. [3] (*as modifier*): *a washing-up machine.*

wash out VERB (*adverb*) [1] (*tr*) to wash (the inside of something) so as to remove (dirt). [2] Also: **wash off.** to remove or be removed by washing: *grass stains don't wash out easily.* [3] (*tr*) to cancel or abandon (a sporting event). ◆ NOUN **washout.** [4] *Geology* **a** erosion of the earth's surface by the action of running water. **b** a narrow channel produced by this erosion. [5] *Informal* **a** a total failure or disaster. **b** an incompetent person. [6] a sporting or social event that is cancelled due to rain. [7] *Aeronautics* a decrease in the angle of attack of an aircraft wing towards the wing tip.

washrag (ˈwɒʃˌræg) NOUN *US* another word for **flannel** (sense 4).

washroom (ˈwɒʃˌruːm, -ˌrʊm) NOUN [1] a room, esp in a factory or office block, in which lavatories, washbasins, etc., are situated. [2] *US and Canadian* a euphemism for **lavatory.**

wash sale NOUN *US* the illegal stock-exchange practice of buying and selling the same securities at an inflated price through a colluding broker to give the impression that the security has a strong market.

washstand (ˈwɒʃˌstænd) NOUN a piece of furniture designed to hold a basin, etc., for washing the face and hands.

washtub (ˈwɒʃˌtʌb) NOUN a tub or large container used for washing anything, esp clothes.

wash up VERB (*adverb*) [1] *Chiefly Brit* to wash (dishes, cutlery, etc.) after a meal. [2] (*intr*) *US* to wash one's face and hands. ◆ NOUN **washup.** [3] *Austral* the end, outcome of a process: *in the washup, three candidates were elected.*

washwoman (ˈwɒʃˌwʊmən) NOUN, *plural* **-women.** a less common word for **washerwoman.**

washy (ˈwɒʃɪ) ADJECTIVE **washier, washiest.** [1] overdiluted, watery, or weak. [2] lacking intensity or strength.
▸ ˈ**washily** ADVERB ▸ ˈ**washiness** NOUN

wasn't (ˈwɒzᵊnt) VERB CONTRACTION OF was not.

wasp (wɒsp) NOUN [1] any social hymenopterous insect of the family *Vespidae,* esp *Vespula vulgaris* (**common wasp**), typically having a black-and-yellow body and an ovipositor specialized for stinging. See also **potter wasp, hornet.** Related adjective: **vespine.** [2] any of various solitary hymenopterans, such as the digger wasp and gall wasp.
▷HISTORY Old English *wæsp;* related to Old Saxon *waspa,* Old High German *wefsa,* Latin *vespa*
▸ ˈ**waspˌlike** ADJECTIVE ▸ ˈ**waspy** ADJECTIVE ▸ ˈ**waspily** ADVERB ▸ ˈ**waspiness** NOUN

Wasp *or* **WASP** (wɒsp) NOUN (in the US) ACRONYM FOR White Anglo-Saxon Protestant: a person descended from N European, usually Protestant stock, forming a group often considered the most dominant, privileged, and influential in American society.
▸ ˈ**Waspy** ADJECTIVE

waspish (ˈwɒspɪʃ) ADJECTIVE [1] relating to or suggestive of a wasp. [2] easily annoyed or angered.
▸ ˈ**waspishly** ADVERB ▸ ˈ**waspishness** NOUN

wasp waist NOUN a very slender waist, esp one that is tightly corseted.
▸ ˈ**wasp-ˌwaisted** ADJECTIVE

wassail (ˈwɒseɪl) NOUN [1] (formerly) a toast or salutation made to a person at festivities. [2] a festivity when much drinking takes place. [3] alcoholic drink drunk at such a festivity, esp spiced beer or mulled wine. [4] the singing of Christmas carols, going from house to house. [5] *Archaic* a drinking song. ◆ VERB [6] to drink the health of (a person) at a wassail. [7] (*intr*) to go from house to house singing carols at Christmas.
▷HISTORY C13: from Old Norse *ves heill* be in good health; related to Old English *wes hāl;* see HALE[1]
▸ ˈ**wassailer** NOUN

Wassermann test *or* **reaction** (ˈwæsəmən; *German* ˈvasərman) NOUN *Med* a diagnostic test for syphilis. See **complement fixation test.**
▷HISTORY C20: named after August von *Wassermann* (1866–1925), German bacteriologist

wassup (wɒˈsʌp) SENTENCE SUBSTITUTE *Slang* what is happening?
▷HISTORY C20: from *what's up?*

wast (wɒst; *unstressed* wəst) VERB *Archaic or dialect* (used with the pronoun *thou* or its relative equivalent) a singular form of the past tense (indicative mood) of **be.**

wastage (ˈweɪstɪdʒ) NOUN [1] anything lost by wear or waste. [2] the process of wasting. [3] reduction in size of a workforce by retirement, voluntary resignation, etc. (esp in the phrase **natural wastage**).

> **Language note** *Waste* and *wastage* are to some extent interchangeable, but many people think that *wastage* should not be used to refer to loss resulting from human carelessness, inefficiency, etc.: *a waste* (not *a wastage*) *of time/money/effort* etc.

waste (weɪst) VERB [1] (*tr*) to use, consume, or expend thoughtlessly, carelessly, or to no avail. [2] (*tr*) to fail to take advantage of: *to waste an opportunity.* [3] (when *intr,* often foll by *away*) to lose or cause to lose bodily strength, health, etc. [4] to exhaust or become exhausted. [5] (*tr*) to ravage. [6] (*tr*) *Informal* to murder or kill: *I want that guy wasted by tomorrow.* ◆ NOUN [7] the act of wasting or state of being wasted. [8] a failure to take advantage of something. [9] anything unused or not used to full advantage. [10] anything or anyone rejected as useless, worthless, or in excess of what is required. [11] garbage, rubbish, or trash. [12] a land or region that is devastated or ruined. [13] a land or region that is wild or uncultivated. [14] *Physiol* **a** the useless

products of metabolism. **b** indigestible food residue. [15] disintegrated rock material resulting from erosion. [16] *Law* reduction in the value of an estate caused by act or neglect, esp by a life-tenant. ◆ ADJECTIVE [17] rejected as useless, unwanted, or worthless. [18] produced in excess of what is required. [19] not cultivated, inhabited, or productive: *waste land*. [20] **a** of or denoting the useless products of metabolism. **b** of or denoting indigestible food residue. [21] destroyed, devastated, or ruined. [22] designed to contain or convey waste products. [23] **lay waste.** to devastate or destroy.
▷HISTORY C13: from Anglo-French *waster,* from Latin *vastāre* to lay waste, from *vastus* empty
▸ˈ**wastable** ADJECTIVE

wastebasket (ˈweɪstˌbɑːskɪt) NOUN another term (esp US and Canadian) for **wastepaper basket.**

wasted (ˈweɪstɪd) ADJECTIVE [1] not exploited or taken advantage of: *a wasted opportunity*. [2] useless or unprofitable: *wasted effort*. [3] physically enfeebled and emaciated: *a thin wasted figure*. [4] *Slang* showing signs of habitual drug abuse.

waste disposal unit NOUN an electrically operated fitment in the plughole of a kitchen sink that breaks up food refuse so that it goes down the waste pipe.

wasteful (ˈweɪstfʊl) ADJECTIVE [1] tending to waste or squander; extravagant. [2] causing waste, destruction, or devastation.
▸ˈ**wastefully** ADVERB ▸ˈ**wastefulness** NOUN

waste heat recovery NOUN the use of heat that is produced in a thermodynamic cycle, as in a furnace, combustion engine, etc., in another process, such as heating feedwater or air.

wasteland (ˈweɪstˌlænd) NOUN [1] a barren or desolate area of land, not or no longer used for cultivation or building. [2] a region, period in history, etc., that is considered spiritually, intellectually, or aesthetically barren or desolate: *American television is a cultural wasteland*.

wastelot (ˈweɪstˌlɒt) NOUN *Chiefly Canadian* a piece of waste ground in a city.

wastepaper (ˈweɪstˌpeɪpə) NOUN paper discarded after use.

wastepaper basket *or* **bin** NOUN an open receptacle for paper and other dry litter. Usual US and Canadian word: **wastebasket.**

waste pipe NOUN a pipe to take excess or used water away, as from a sink to a drain.

waster (ˈweɪstə) NOUN [1] a person or thing that wastes. [2] a ne'er-do-well; wastrel. [3] an article spoiled in manufacture.

wasteweir (ˈweɪstˌwɪə) NOUN another name for **spillway.**

wasting (ˈweɪstɪŋ) ADJECTIVE (*prenominal*) reducing the vitality, strength, or robustness of the body: *a wasting disease*.
▸ˈ**wastingly** ADVERB

wasting asset NOUN an unreplaceable business asset of limited life, such as a coal mine or an oil well.

wastrel (ˈweɪstrəl) NOUN [1] a wasteful person; spendthrift; prodigal. [2] an idler or vagabond.

Wast Water (wɒst) NOUN a lake in NW England, in Cumbria in the Lake District. Length: 5 km (3 miles).

wat (wɑːt) NOUN a Thai Buddhist monastery or temple.
▷HISTORY Thai, from Sanskrit *vāta* enclosure

watap (wæˈtɑːp, wɑː-) NOUN a stringy thread made by North American Indians from the roots of various conifers and used for weaving and sewing.
▷HISTORY C18: from Canadian French, from Cree *watapiy*

watch (wɒtʃ) VERB [1] to look at or observe closely or attentively. [2] (*intr;* foll by *for*) to wait attentively or expectantly. [3] to guard or tend (something) closely or carefully. [4] (*intr*) to keep vigil. [5] (*tr*) to maintain an interest in: *to watch the progress of a child at school*. [6] **watch it!** be careful! look out! ◆ NOUN [7] **a** a small portable timepiece, usually worn strapped to the wrist (a **wristwatch**) or in a waistcoat pocket. **b** (*as modifier*): *a watch spring*. [8] the act or an instance of watching. [9] a period of vigil, esp during the night. [10] (formerly) one of a set of periods of any of various lengths into which the night was divided. [11] *Nautical* **a** any of the usually four-hour periods beginning at midnight and again at noon during which part of a ship's crew are on duty. **b** those officers and crew on duty during a specified watch. [12] the period during which a guard is on duty. [13] (formerly) a watchman or band of watchmen. [14] **on the watch.** on the lookout; alert. ◆ See also **watch out.**
▷HISTORY Old English *wæccan* (vb), *wæcce* (n); related to WAKE[1]

-watch SUFFIX OF NOUNS indicating a regular television programme or newspaper feature on the topic specified: *Crimewatch*.

watchable (ˈwɒtʃəbᵊl) ADJECTIVE [1] capable of being watched. [2] interesting, enjoyable, or entertaining: *a watchable television documentary*.

watchband (ˈwɒtʃˌbænd) NOUN a US, Canadian, and Austral word for **watchstrap.**

watch cap NOUN a knitted navy-blue woollen cap worn by seamen in cold weather.

watchcase (ˈwɒtʃˌkeɪs) NOUN a protective case for a watch, generally of metal such as gold, silver, brass, or gunmetal.

watch chain NOUN a chain used for fastening a pocket watch to the clothing. See also **fob**[1].

Watch Committee NOUN *Brit history* a local government committee composed of magistrates and representatives of the county borough council responsible for the efficiency of the local police force.

watchdog (ˈwɒtʃˌdɒɡ) NOUN [1] a dog kept to guard property. [2] **a** a person or group of persons that acts as a protector or guardian against inefficiency, illegal practices, etc. **b** (*as modifier*): *a watchdog committee*.

watcher (ˈwɒtʃə) NOUN [1] a person who watches. [2] a person who maintains a vigil at the bedside of an invalid. [3] *US* a representative of a candidate or party stationed at a poll on election day to watch out for fraud.

watch fire NOUN a fire kept burning at night as a signal or for warmth and light by a person keeping watch.

watchful (ˈwɒtʃfʊl) ADJECTIVE [1] vigilant or alert. [2] *Archaic* not sleeping.
▸ˈ**watchfully** ADVERB ▸ˈ**watchfulness** NOUN

watch-glass NOUN [1] a curved glass disc that covers the dial of a watch. [2] a similarly shaped piece of glass used in laboratories for evaporating small samples of a solution, etc.

watchmaker (ˈwɒtʃˌmeɪkə) NOUN a person who makes or mends watches.
▸ˈ**watchˌmaking** NOUN

watchman (ˈwɒtʃmən) NOUN, *plural* **-men.** [1] a person employed to guard buildings or property. [2] (formerly) a man employed to patrol or guard the streets at night.

watch night NOUN (in Protestant churches) [1] **a** the night of December 24, during which a service is held to mark the arrival of Christmas Day. **b** the night of December 31, during which a service is held to mark the passing of the old year and the beginning of the new. [2] the service held on either of these nights.

watch out VERB [1] (*intr, adverb*) to be careful or on one's guard. ◆ NOUN **watchout.** [2] a less common word for **lookout** (sense 1).

watchstrap (ˈwɒtʃˌstræp) NOUN a strap of leather, cloth, etc., attached to a watch for fastening it around the wrist. Also called (US and Canadian): **watchband.**

watchtower (ˈwɒtʃˌtaʊə) NOUN a tower on which a sentry keeps watch.

watchword (ˈwɒtʃˌwɜːd) NOUN [1] another word for **password.** [2] a rallying cry or slogan.

water (ˈwɔːtə) NOUN [1] a clear colourless tasteless odourless liquid that is essential for plant and animal life and constitutes, in impure form, rain, oceans, rivers, lakes, etc. It is a neutral substance, an effective solvent for many compounds, and is used as a standard for many physical properties. Formula: H_2O. Related adjective: **aqueous.** Related combining forms: **hydro-, aqua-.** [2] **a** any body or area of this liquid, such as a sea, lake, river, etc. **b** (*as modifier*): *water sports; water transport; a water plant*. Related adjective: **aquatic.** [3] the surface of such a body or area: *fish swam below the water*. [4] any form or variety of this liquid, such as rain. [5] See **high water, low water.** [6] any of various solutions of chemical substances in water: *lithia water; ammonia water*. [7] *Physiol* **a** any fluid secreted from the body, such as sweat, urine, or tears. **b** (*usually plural*) the amniotic fluid surrounding a fetus in the womb. [8] a wavy lustrous finish on some fabrics, esp silk. [9] *Archaic* the degree of brilliance in a diamond. See also **first water.** [10] excellence, quality, or degree (in the phrase **of the first water**). [11] *Finance* **a** capital stock issued without a corresponding increase in paid-up capital, so that the book value of the company's capital is not fully represented by assets or earning power. **b** the fictitious or unrealistic asset entries that reflect such inflated book value of capital. [12] (*modifier*) *Astrology* of or relating to the three signs of the zodiac Cancer, Scorpio, and Pisces. Compare **air** (sense 20), **earth** (sense 10), **fire** (sense 24). [13] **above the water.** *Informal* out of trouble or difficulty, esp financial trouble. [14] **hold water.** to prove credible, logical, or consistent: *the alibi did not hold water*. [15] **in deep water.** in trouble or difficulty. [16] **make water. a** to urinate. **b** (of a boat, hull, etc.) to let in water. [17] **pass water.** to urinate. [18] **test the water.** See **test**[1] (sense 5). [19] **throw** (*or* **pour**) **cold water on.** *Informal* to be unenthusiastic about or discourage. [20] **water under the bridge.** events that are past and done with. ◆ VERB [21] (*tr*) to sprinkle, moisten, or soak with water. [22] (*tr;* often foll by *down*) to weaken by the addition of water. [23] (*intr*) (of the eyes) to fill with tears. [24] (*intr*) (of the mouth) to salivate, esp in anticipation of food (esp in the phrase **make one's mouth water**). [25] (*tr*) to irrigate or provide with water: *to water the land; he watered the cattle*. [26] (*intr*) to drink water. [27] (*intr*) (of a ship, etc.) to take in a supply of water. [28] (*tr*) *Finance* to raise the par value of (issued capital stock) without a corresponding increase in the real value of assets. [29] (*tr*) to produce a wavy lustrous finish on (fabrics, esp silk). ◆ See also **water down.**
▷HISTORY Old English *wæter,* of Germanic origin; compare Old Saxon *watar,* Old High German *wazzar,* Gothic *watō,* Old Slavonic *voda;* related to Greek *hudor*
▸ˈ**waterer** NOUN ▸ˈ**waterish** ADJECTIVE ▸ˈ**waterless** ADJECTIVE ▸ˈ**water-ˌlike** ADJECTIVE

waterage (ˈwɔːtərɪdʒ) NOUN *Brit* the transportation of cargo by means of ships, or the charges for such transportation.

water back NOUN the US name for **back boiler.**

water bag NOUN a bag, sometimes made of skin, leather, etc., but in Australia usually canvas, for holding, carrying, and keeping water cool.

water bailiff NOUN an official responsible for enforcing laws on river management and fishing.

water-bath NOUN *Chem* a vessel containing heated water, used for heating substances.

water bear NOUN another name for a **tardigrade.**

water bed NOUN a waterproof mattress filled with water.

water beetle NOUN any of various beetles of the families *Dysticidae, Hydrophilidae,* etc., that live most of the time in freshwater ponds, rivers, etc. See **whirligig beetle.**

water bird NOUN any aquatic bird, including the wading and swimming birds.

water biscuit NOUN a thin crisp plain biscuit, usually served with butter or cheese.

water blister NOUN a blister containing watery or serous fluid, without any blood or pus.

water boatman NOUN any of various aquatic bugs of the families *Notonectidae* and *Corixidae,* having a flattened body and oarlike hind legs, adapted for swimming.

waterborne (ˈwɔːtəˌbɔːn) ADJECTIVE [1] floating or travelling on water. [2] (of a disease, etc.) transported or transmitted by water.

water bottle NOUN any of various types of container for drinking water, such as a skin or leather bag used in some countries, a glass bottle for table use, or a flask used by soldiers or travellers.

waterbrain (ˈwɔːtəˌbreɪn) NOUN *Vet science* an archaic name for **gid.**

water brash NOUN *Pathol* another term for **heartburn.**

waterbuck (ˈwɔːtəˌbʌk) NOUN any of various antelopes of the genus *Kobus,* esp *K. ellipsiprymnus,* of swampy areas of Africa, having long curved ridged horns.

water buffalo *or* **ox** NOUN a member of the cattle tribe, *Bubalus bubalis,* of swampy regions of S Asia, having widely spreading back-curving horns. Domesticated forms are used as draught animals. Also called: **Asiatic buffalo, Indian buffalo, carabao.**

water bug NOUN any of various heteropterous insects adapted to living in the water or on its surface, esp any of the family *Belostomatidae* (**giant water bugs**), of North America, India, and southern Africa, which have flattened hairy legs.

water butt NOUN a barrel for collecting rainwater, esp from a drainpipe.

water cannon NOUN an apparatus for pumping water through a nozzle at high pressure, used in quelling riots.

Water Carrier *or* **Bearer** NOUN **the.** the constellation Aquarius, the 11th sign of the zodiac.

water chestnut NOUN [1] Also called: **water caltrop.** a floating aquatic onagraceous plant, *Trapa natans,* of Asia, having four-pronged edible nutlike fruits. [2] **Chinese water chestnut.** a Chinese cyperaceous plant, *Eleocharis tuberosa,* with an edible succulent corm. [3] the corm of the Chinese water chestnut, used in Oriental cookery.

water chinquapin NOUN a North American aquatic plant, *Nelumbo lutea,* having large umbrella-shaped leaves, pale yellow flowers, and edible nutlike seeds: family *Nelumbonaceae.* Compare **chinquapin.**

water clock *or* **glass** NOUN any of various devices for measuring time that use the escape of water as the motive force.

water closet NOUN [1] a lavatory flushed by water. [2] a small room that has a lavatory. ◆ Usually abbreviated to: **WC.**

watercolour *or US* **watercolor** (ˈwɔːtəˌkʌlə) NOUN [1] **a** Also called: **pure watercolour.** water-soluble pigment, applied in transparent washes and without the admixture of white pigment in the lighter tones. **b** any water-soluble pigment, including opaque kinds such as gouache and tempera. [2] **a** a painting done in watercolours. **b** (*as modifier*): *a watercolour masterpiece.* [3] the art or technique of painting with such pigments.
▸ **ˈwaterˌcolourist** *or (US)* **ˈwaterˌcolorist** NOUN

water-cool VERB (*tr*) to cool (an engine, etc.) by a flow of water circulating in an enclosed jacket. Compare **air-cool.**
▸ **ˈwater-ˌcooled** ADJECTIVE ▸ **ˈwater-ˌcooling** ADJECTIVE

water cooler NOUN [1] a device for cooling and dispensing drinking water. ◆ MODIFIER **water-cooler.** [2] *US informal* indicating the kind of informal conversation among office staff that takes place at such a dispenser: *water-cooler conversations.*

watercourse (ˈwɔːtəˌkɔːs) NOUN [1] a stream, river, or canal. [2] the channel, bed, or route along which this flows.

watercraft (ˈwɔːtəˌkrɑːft) NOUN [1] a boat or ship or such vessels collectively. [2] skill in handling boats or in water sports.

water crake NOUN another name for **spotted crake** and **dipper** (the bird).

watercress (ˈwɔːtəˌkrɛs) NOUN [1] an Old World plant, *Nasturtium officinale,* of clear ponds and streams, having pungent leaves that are used in salads and as a garnish: family *Brassicaceae* (crucifers). [2] any of several similar or related plants.

water cure NOUN [1] *Med* a nontechnical name for **hydropathy** or **hydrotherapy.** [2] *Informal* a form of torture in which the victim is forced to drink very large amounts of water.

water cycle NOUN the circulation of the earth's water, in which water evaporates from the sea into the atmosphere, where it condenses and falls as rain or snow, returning to the sea by rivers or returning to the atmosphere by evapotranspiration. Also called: **hydrologic cycle.**

water diviner NOUN *Brit* a person able to locate the presence of water, esp underground, with a divining rod. US name: **waterfinder.**

water dog NOUN [1] a dog trained to hunt in water. [2] *Informal* a dog or person who enjoys going in or on the water.

water down VERB (*tr, adverb*) [1] to dilute or weaken with water. [2] to modify or adulterate, esp so as to omit anything harsh, unpleasant, or offensive: *to water down the truth.*
▸ **ˌwatered-ˈdown** ADJECTIVE

water dropwort NOUN See **dropwort** (sense 2).

waterfall (ˈwɔːtəˌfɔːl) NOUN a cascade of falling water where there is a vertical or almost vertical step in a river.

water flea NOUN any of numerous minute freshwater branchiopod crustaceans of the order *Cladocera,* which swim by means of hairy branched antennae. See also **daphnia.**

Waterford (ˈwɔːtəfəd) NOUN [1] a county of S Republic of Ireland, in Munster province on the Atlantic: mountainous in the centre and in the northwest. County town: Waterford. Pop.: 94 680 (1996). Area: 1838 sq. km (710 sq. miles). [2] a port in S Republic of Ireland, county town of Co. Waterford: famous glass industry; fishing. Pop.: 42 540 (1996).

waterfowl (ˈwɔːtəˌfaʊl) NOUN [1] any aquatic freshwater bird, esp any species of the family *Anatidae* (ducks, geese, and swans). [2] such birds collectively.

waterfront (ˈwɔːtəˌfrʌnt) NOUN the area of a town or city alongside a body of water, such as a harbour or dockyard.

water gap NOUN a deep valley in a ridge, containing a stream.

water gas NOUN a mixture of hydrogen and carbon monoxide produced by passing steam over hot carbon, used as a fuel and raw material. See also **producer gas.**

water gate NOUN [1] a gate in a canal, leat, etc. that can be opened or closed to control the flow of water. [2] a gate through which access may be gained to a body of water.

Watergate (ˈwɔːtəˌgeɪt) NOUN [1] an incident during the 1972 US presidential campaign, when a group of agents employed by the re-election organization of President Richard Nixon were caught breaking into the Democratic Party headquarters in the Watergate building, Washington, DC. The consequent political scandal was exacerbated by attempts to conceal the fact that senior White House officials had approved the burglary, and eventually forced the resignation of President Nixon. [2] any similar public scandal, esp involving politicians or a possible cover-up. See also **-gate.**

water gauge NOUN an instrument that indicates the presence or the quantity of water in a tank, reservoir, or boiler feed. Also called: **water glass.**

water glass NOUN [1] a viscous syrupy solution of sodium silicate in water: used as a protective coating for cement and a preservative, esp for eggs. [2] another name for **water clock** or **water gauge.**

water gum NOUN [1] any of several gum trees, esp *Nyssa biflora* (or *tupelo*), of swampy areas of North America: family *Nyssaceae.* [2] any of several Australian myrtaceous trees, esp *Tristania laurina,* of swampy ground.

water gun NOUN another term (esp US) for **water pistol.**

water hammer NOUN a sharp concussion produced when the flow of water in a pipe is suddenly blocked.

water hemlock NOUN another name for **cowbane** (sense 1).

water hen NOUN another name for **gallinule.**

water hole NOUN [1] a depression, such as a pond or pool, containing water, esp one used by animals as a drinking place. [2] a source of drinking water in a desert.

water hyacinth NOUN a floating aquatic plant, *Eichhornia crassipes,* of tropical America, having showy bluish-purple flowers and swollen leafstalks: family *Pontederiaceae.* It forms dense masses in rivers, ponds, etc., and is a serious problem in the southern US, Australia, and parts of Africa.

water ice NOUN an ice cream made from a frozen sugar syrup flavoured with fruit juice or purée; sorbet.

watering can NOUN a container with a handle and a spout with a perforated nozzle used to sprinkle water over plants.

watering hole NOUN [1] a pool where animals drink; water hole. [2] *Facetious slang* a pub.

watering place NOUN [1] a place where drinking water for men or animals may be obtained. [2] *Brit* a spa. [3] *Brit* a seaside resort.

watering pot NOUN another name (US) for **watering can.**

water intoxication NOUN a nontechnical name for **hyponatraemia.**

water jacket NOUN a water-filled envelope or container surrounding a machine, engine, or part for cooling purposes, esp the casing around the cylinder block of a pump or internal-combustion engine. Compare **air jacket.**

water jump NOUN a ditch, brook, or pond over which athletes or horses must jump in a steeplechase or similar contest.

water level NOUN [1] the level reached by the surface of a body of water. [2] the water line of a boat or ship.

water lily NOUN [1] any of various aquatic plants of the genus *Nymphaea* and related genera, of temperate and tropical regions, having large leaves and showy flowers that float on the surface of the water: family *Nymphaeaceae.* [2] any of various similar and related plants, such as the yellow water lily.

water line NOUN [1] a line marked at the level around a vessel's hull to which the vessel will be immersed when afloat. [2] a line marking the level reached by a body of water.

waterlogged (ˈwɔːtəˌlɒgd) ADJECTIVE [1] saturated with water. [2] (of a vessel still afloat) having taken in so much water as to be unmanageable.

Waterloo (ˌwɔːtəˈluː) NOUN [1] a small town in central Belgium, in Walloon Brabant province south of Brussels: battle (1815) fought nearby in which British and Prussian forces under the Duke of Wellington and Blücher routed the French under Napoleon. Pop.: 17 800 (latest est.). [2] a total or crushing defeat (esp in **meet one's Waterloo**).

water louse NOUN an aquatic isopod of the genus *Asellus,* common in weedy water. Also called: **water slater.**

water main NOUN a principal supply pipe in an arrangement of pipes for distributing water.

waterman (ˈwɔːtəmən) NOUN, *plural* **-men.** a skilled boatman.
▸ **ˈwatermanˌship** NOUN

watermark (ˈwɔːtəˌmɑːk) NOUN [1] a distinguishing mark impressed on paper during manufacture, visible when the paper is held up to the light. [2] another word for **water line** (senses 1, 2). ◆ VERB (*tr*) [3] to mark (paper) with a watermark.

water meadow NOUN a meadow that remains fertile by being periodically flooded by a stream.

water measurer NOUN a slender heteropterous bug, *Hydrometra stagnorum,* that has a greatly elongated head and is found on still or sluggish water where it preys on water fleas, mosquito larvae, etc.

watermelon (ˈwɔːtəˌmɛlən) NOUN [1] an African melon, *Citrullus vulgaris,* widely cultivated for its large edible fruit. [2] the fruit of this plant, which has a hard green rind and sweet watery reddish flesh.

water meter NOUN a device for measuring the quantity or rate of water flowing through a pipe.

water milfoil NOUN any of various pond plants of the genus *Myriophyllum,* having feathery underwater leaves and small inconspicuous flowers: family *Haloragidaceae.*

water mill NOUN a mill operated by a water wheel.

water mint NOUN a Eurasian mint plant, *Mentha aquatica,* of marshy places, having scented leaves and whorls of small flowers.

water moccasin NOUN a large dark grey venomous snake, *Agkistrodon piscivorus,* of swamps in the southern US: family *Crotalidae* (pit vipers). Also called: **cottonmouth.**

water nymph NOUN [1] any fabled nymph of the water, such as the Naiad, Nereid, or Oceanid of

Greek mythology. [2] any of various aquatic plants, esp a water lily or a naiad.

water of crystallization NOUN water present in the crystals of certain compounds. It is chemically combined in stoichiometric amounts, usually by coordinate or hydrogen bonds, but can often be easily expelled.

water ouzel NOUN another name for **dipper** (the bird).

water ox NOUN another term for **water buffalo.**

water paint NOUN any water-based paint, such as an emulsion or an acrylic paint.

water parting NOUN another term (esp US) for **watershed** (sense 1).

water pepper NOUN any of several polygonaceous plants of the genus *Polygonum,* esp *P. hydropiper,* of marshy regions, having reddish stems, clusters of small greenish flowers, and acrid-tasting leaves.

water pimpernel NOUN another name for **brookweed.**

water pipe NOUN [1] a pipe for water. [2] another name for **hookah.**

water pistol NOUN a toy pistol that squirts a stream of water or other liquid. Also called (US): **water gun.**

water plantain NOUN any of several marsh plants of the genus *Alisma,* esp *A. plantago-aquatica,* of N temperate regions and Australia, having clusters of small white or pinkish flowers and broad pointed leaves: family *Alismataceae.*

water polo NOUN a game played in water by two teams of seven swimmers in which each side tries to throw or propel an inflated ball into the opponents' goal.

water power NOUN [1] the power latent in a dynamic or static head of water as used to drive machinery, esp for generating electricity. [2] a source of such power, such as a drop in the level of a river, etc. [3] the right to the use of water for such a purpose, as possessed by a water mill.

waterproof ('wɔːtəˌpruːf) ADJECTIVE [1] not penetrable by water. Compare **water-repellent, water-resistant.** ◆ NOUN [2] *Chiefly Brit* a waterproof garment, esp a raincoat. ◆ VERB *(tr)* [3] to make (a fabric, item of clothing, etc.) waterproof.

water purslane NOUN [1] an onagraceous marsh plant, *Ludwigia palustris,* of temperate and warm regions, having reddish stems and small greenish flowers. [2] any of several lythraceous plants of wet places that resemble purslane, such as *Peplis portula* of Europe, which has small pinkish flowers, and *Didiplis diandris* of North America, which has small greenish flowers.

water rail NOUN a large Eurasian rail, *Rallus aquaticus,* of swamps, ponds, etc., having a long red bill.

water rat NOUN [1] any of several small amphibious rodents, esp the water vole or the muskrat. [2] any of various amphibious rats of the subfamily *Hydromyinae,* of New Guinea, the Philippines, and Australia. [3] *Informal* a person who is very fond of water sports.

water-repellent ADJECTIVE (of fabrics, garments, etc.) having a finish that resists the absorption of water.

water-resistant ADJECTIVE (esp of fabrics) designed to resist but not entirely prevent the penetration of water.

water right NOUN the right to make use of a water supply, as for irrigation.

water sapphire NOUN a deep blue variety of the mineral cordierite that occurs in Sri Lanka: used as a gemstone.

waterscape ('wɔːtəˌskeɪp) NOUN a picture, view, or representation of a body of water.

water scorpion NOUN any of various long-legged aquatic insects of the heteropterous family *Nepidae,* which breathe by means of a long spinelike tube that projects from the rear of the body and penetrates the surface of the water.

water seal NOUN a small amount of water contained in the trap of a drain to prevent the passage of foul smells.

watershed ('wɔːtəˌʃɛd) NOUN [1] the dividing line between two adjacent river systems, such as a ridge. [2] an important period or factor that serves as a dividing line.

water shield NOUN [1] a North American nymphaeaceous plant, *Brasenia schreberi,* with floating oval leaves and purple flowers. [2] any of several similar and related plants of the genus *Cabomba.*

water shrew NOUN either of two small amphibious shrews, *Neomys fodiens* (**European water shrew**) or *N. anomalus* (**Mediterranean water shrew**), having a dark pelage with paler underparts.

water-sick ADJECTIVE (of land) made infertile or uncultivable by excessive irrigation.

waterside ('wɔːtəˌsaɪd) NOUN **a** the area of land beside a body of water. **b** (*as modifier*): *waterside houses.*

watersider ('wɔːtəˌsaɪdə) NOUN *Austral and NZ* a wharf labourer.

water-ski NOUN *also* **water ski.** [1] a type of ski used for planing or gliding over water. ◆ VERB **-skis, -skiing, -skied** *or* **-ski'd.** [2] *(intr)* to ride over water on a water-ski or water-skis while holding a rope towed by a speedboat.
▸ **'water-ˌskier** NOUN ▸ **'water-ˌskiing** NOUN

water snake NOUN any of various colubrid snakes that live in or near water, esp any of numerous harmless North American snakes of the genus *Natrix,* such as *N. sipedon.*

water-soak VERB *(tr)* to soak or drench with or in water.

water softener NOUN [1] any substance that lessens the hardness of water, usually by precipitating or absorbing calcium and magnesium ions. [2] a tank, apparatus, or chemical plant that is used to filter or treat water to remove chemicals that cause hardness.

water soldier NOUN an aquatic plant, *Stratiotes aloides,* of Europe and NW Asia, having rosettes of large leaves and large three-petalled white flowers: family *Hydrocharitaceae.*

water spaniel NOUN either of two large curly-coated breeds of spaniel (the Irish and the American), which are used for hunting waterfowl. See also **Irish water spaniel.**

water spider NOUN a Eurasian spider, *Argyroneta aquatica,* that spins a web in the form of an air-filled chamber in which it lives submerged in streams and ponds.

water splash NOUN a place where a stream runs over a road.

water sports PLURAL NOUN [1] various sports, such as swimming, water-skiing, or windsurfing, that take place in or on water. [2] *Slang* sexual practices that involve urination.

waterspout ('wɔːtəˌspaʊt) NOUN [1] *Meteorol* **a** a tornado occurring over water that forms a column of water and mist extending between the surface and the clouds above. **b** a sudden downpour of heavy rain. [2] a pipe or channel through which water is discharged, esp one used for drainage from the gutters of a roof.

water starwort NOUN See **starwort** (sense 2).

water stick insect NOUN a slender sticklike flightless water bug, *Ranatra linearis,* that is predatory on small creatures such as water fleas.

water strider *or* **skater** NOUN another name for a **pond-skater.**

water supply NOUN [1] an arrangement of reservoirs, purification plant, distribution pipes, etc., for providing water to a community. [2] the supply of treated and purified water for a community.

water system NOUN [1] a river and all its tributaries. [2] a system for supplying water to a community.

water table NOUN [1] the surface of the water-saturated part of the ground, usually following approximately the contours of the overlying land surface. [2] an offset or string course that has a moulding designed to throw rainwater clear of the wall below.

water thrush NOUN either of two North American warblers, *Seiurus motacilla* or *S. noveboracensis,* having a brownish back and striped underparts and occurring near water.

watertight ('wɔːtəˌtaɪt) ADJECTIVE [1] not permitting the passage of water either in or out: *a watertight boat.* [2] without loopholes: *a watertight argument.* [3] kept separate from other subjects or influences: *different disciplines are often thought of in watertight compartments.*
▸ **'waterˌtightness** NOUN

water torture NOUN any of various forms of torture using water, esp one in which water drips or is slowly poured onto the victim's forehead.

water tower NOUN a reservoir or storage tank mounted on a tower-like structure at the summit of an area of high ground in a place where the water pressure would otherwise be inadequate for distribution at a uniform pressure.

water tube boiler NOUN a steam generator consisting of water drums and steam drums connected by banks of tubes through which the water is circulated. The tubes are exposed to the hot gases of the furnace and the heat transfer rate is high.

water vapour NOUN water in the gaseous state, esp when due to evaporation at a temperature below the boiling point. Compare **steam.**

water vole NOUN a large amphibious vole, *Arvicola terrestris,* of Eurasian river banks: family *Cricetidae.* Also called: **water rat.**

water wagtail NOUN another name for **pied wagtail.**

waterway ('wɔːtəˌweɪ) NOUN a river, canal, or other navigable channel used as a means of travel or transport.

waterweed ('wɔːtəˌwiːd) NOUN [1] any of various weedy aquatic plants. [2] another name for **pondweed** (sense 2).

water wheel NOUN [1] a simple water-driven turbine consisting of a wheel having vanes set axially across its rim, used to drive machinery. [2] a wheel with buckets attached to its rim for raising water from a stream, pond, etc.

water wings PLURAL NOUN an inflatable rubber device shaped like a pair of wings, which is placed round the front of the body and under the arms of a person learning to swim.

water witch NOUN a person who claims the ability to detect water underground by means of a divining rod.

waterworks ('wɔːtəˌwɜːks) NOUN [1] (*functioning as singular*) an establishment for storing, purifying, and distributing water for community supply. [2] (*functioning as plural*) a display of water in movement, as in fountains. [3] (*functioning as plural*) *Brit informal euphemism* the urinary system, esp with reference to its normal functioning: *he has trouble with his waterworks.* [4] (*functioning as plural*) *Informal* crying; tears.

waterworn ('wɔːtəˌwɔːn) ADJECTIVE worn smooth by the action or passage of water.

watery ('wɔːtərɪ) ADJECTIVE [1] relating to, consisting of, containing, or resembling water. [2] discharging or secreting water or a water-like fluid: *a watery wound.* [3] tearful; weepy. [4] insipid, thin, or weak.
▸ **'wateriness** NOUN

Watford ('wɒtfəd) NOUN a town in SE England, in SW Hertfordshire: light industries, services. Pop.: 113 080 (1991).

Watling Island ('wɒtlɪŋ) NOUN another name for **San Salvador Island.**

watt (wɒt) NOUN the derived SI unit of power, equal to 1 joule per second; the power dissipated by a current of 1 ampere flowing across a potential difference of 1 volt. 1 watt is equivalent to 1.341×10^{-3} horsepower. Symbol: W.
▷ **HISTORY** C19: named after James Watt (1736–1819), Scottish engineer and inventor

wattage ('wɒtɪdʒ) NOUN [1] power, esp electric power, measured in watts. [2] the power rating, measured in watts, of an electrical appliance.

Watteau back NOUN a section at the back of a woman's dress that is caught in pleats or gathers at the neck and falls unbelted to the floor.

Wattenscheid (*German* 'vatənʃait) NOUN an industrial town in NW Germany, in North Rhine-Westphalia east of Essen. Pop.: 81 200 (latest est.).

watt-hour NOUN a unit of energy equal to a power

of one watt operating for one hour. 1 watt-hour equals 3600 joules.

wattle[1] ('wɒtᵊl) NOUN [1] a frame of rods or stakes interwoven with twigs, branches, etc., esp when used to make fences. [2] the material used in such a construction. [3] a loose fold of skin, often brightly coloured, hanging from the neck or throat of certain birds, lizards, etc. [4] any of various chiefly Australian acacia trees having spikes of small brightly coloured flowers and flexible branches, which were used by early settlers for making fences. See also **golden wattle.** [5] a southern African caesalpinaceous tree, *Peltophorum africanum,* with yellow flowers. ◆ VERB *(tr)* [6] to construct from wattle. [7] to bind or frame with wattle. [8] to weave or twist (branches, twigs, etc.) into a frame. ◆ ADJECTIVE [9] made of, formed by, or covered with wattle.
▷**HISTORY** Old English *watol;* related to *wethel* wrap, Old High German *wadal,* German *Wedel*
▸'**wattled** ADJECTIVE

wattle[2] ('wɒtᵊl) ADJECTIVE *Midland English dialect* of poor quality.

wattle and daub NOUN **a** a form of wall construction consisting of interwoven twigs plastered with a mixture of clay, lime, water, and sometimes dung and chopped straw. **b** *(as modifier): a wattle-and-daub hut.*

wattlebird ('wɒtᵊl,bɜːd) NOUN [1] any of various Australian honeyeaters of the genus *Anthochaera,* such as *A. paradoxa* (**yellow wattlebird**), that have red or yellow wattles on both sides of the head. [2] any arboreal New Zealand songbird of the family *Callaeidae,* having wattles on both sides of the bill.

wattmeter ('wɒt,miːtə) NOUN a meter for measuring electric power in watts.

Watusi (wə'tuːzɪ) *or* **Watutsi** (wə'tʊtsɪ) NOUN, *plural* **-sis** *or* **-si.** a member of a cattle-owning Negroid people of Rwanda and Burundi in Africa.

wauk[1] (wɔːk) VERB a Scot word for **wake[1]**.

wauk[2] *or* **waulk** (wɔːk) VERB *(tr) Scot* to full (cloth).
▷**HISTORY** C15: variant of WALK

waul *or* **wawl** (wɔːl) VERB *(intr)* to cry or wail plaintively like a cat.
▷**HISTORY** C16: of imitative origin

waur[1] (wɔːr) ADJECTIVE, NOUN, ADVERB a Scot word for **worse.**

waur[2] (wɔːr) ADJECTIVE a Scot word for **wary.**

wave (weɪv) VERB [1] to move or cause to move freely to and fro: *the banner waved in the wind.* [2] *(intr)* to move the hand to and fro as a greeting. [3] to signal or signify by or as if by waving something. [4] *(tr)* to direct to move by or as if by waving something: *he waved me on.* [5] to form or be formed into curves, undulations, etc. [6] *(tr)* to give a wavy or watered appearance to (silk, etc.). [7] *(tr)* to set waves in (the hair). ◆ NOUN [8] one of a sequence of ridges or undulations that moves across the surface of a body of a liquid, esp the sea: created by the wind or a moving object and gravity. [9] any undulation on or at the edge of a surface reminiscent of such a wave: *a wave across the field of corn.* [10] **the waves.** the sea. [11] anything that suggests the movement of a wave, as by a sudden rise: *a crime wave.* [12] a widespread movement that advances in a body: *a wave of settlers swept into the country.* [13] the act or an instance of waving. [14] *Physics* an oscillation propagated through a medium or space such that energy is periodically interchanged between two kinds of disturbance. For example, an oscillating electric field generates a magnetic oscillation and vice versa, hence an electromagnetic wave is produced. Similarly a wave on a liquid comprises vertical and horizontal displacements. See also **antinode, longitudinal wave, node, standing wave, transverse wave.** [15] *Physics* a graphical representation of a wave obtained by plotting the magnitude of the disturbance against time at a particular point in the medium or space; waveform. [16] a prolonged spell of some weather condition: *a heat wave.* [17] an undulating curve or series of curves or loose curls in the hair. [18] an undulating pattern or finish on a fabric. [19] short for **wave moth.** [20] **make waves.** to cause trouble; disturb the status quo. [21] **ride the wave.** *US slang* to enjoy a period of success and good fortune.
▷**HISTORY** Old English *wafian* (vb); related to Old High German *weban* to WEAVE, Old Norse *vafra;* see WAVER; C16 (n) changed from earlier *wāwe,* probably from Old English *wǣg* motion; compare WAG[1]
▸'**waveless** ADJECTIVE ▸'**wave,like** ADJECTIVE

waveband ('weɪv,bænd) NOUN a range of wavelengths or frequencies used for a particular type of radio transmission.

wave-cut platform NOUN a flat surface at the base of a cliff formed by erosion by waves.

wave down VERB *(tr, adverb)* to signal with a wave to (a driver or vehicle) to stop.

wave energy NOUN energy obtained by harnessing wave power.

wave equation NOUN *Physics* a partial differential equation describing wave motion. It has the form $\nabla^2\phi = (1/c^2) \times (\partial^2\phi/\partial t^2)$, where ∇^2 is the Laplace operator, *t* the time, *c* the speed of propagation, and ϕ is a function characterizing the displacement of the wave.

waveform ('weɪv,fɔːm) NOUN *Physics* the shape of the graph of a wave or oscillation obtained by plotting the value of some changing quantity against time.

wavefront ('weɪv,frʌnt) NOUN *Physics* a surface associated with a propagating wave and passing through all points in the wave that have the same phase. It is usually perpendicular to the direction of propagation.

wave function NOUN *Physics* a mathematical function of position and generally time, used in wave mechanics to describe the state of a physical system. Symbol: ψ.

waveguide ('weɪv,gaɪd) NOUN *Electronics* a solid rod of dielectric or a hollow metal tube, usually of rectangular cross section, used as a path to guide microwaves.

wavelength ('weɪv,lɛŋθ) NOUN [1] the distance, measured in the direction of propagation, between two points of the same phase in consecutive cycles of a wave. Symbol: λ. [2] the wavelength of the carrier wave used by a particular broadcasting station. [3] **on someone's** (*or* **the same**) **wavelength.** *Informal* having similar views, feelings, or thoughts (as someone else).

wavelet ('weɪvlɪt) NOUN a small wave.

wavellite ('weɪvə,laɪt) NOUN a greyish-white, yellow, or brown mineral consisting of hydrated basic aluminium phosphate in radiating clusters of small orthorhombic crystals. Formula: $Al_3(PO_4)_2(OH)_3.5H_2O$.
▷**HISTORY** C19: named after William *Wavell* (died 1829), English physician

wave mechanics NOUN *(functioning as singular) Physics* the formulation of quantum mechanics in which the behaviour of systems, such as atoms, is described in terms of their wave functions.

wavemeter ('weɪv,miːtə) NOUN an instrument for measuring the frequency or wavelength of radio waves.

wave moth NOUN any of several small geometrid moths with wavy markings, such as the **common wave** (*Deilinia exanthemata*), with grey-marked wings, and the lighter **common white wave** (*D. pusaria*). Often shortened to: **wave.**

wave number NOUN *Physics* the reciprocal of the wavelength of a wave. Symbol: ν, σ.

waveoff ('weɪv,ɒf) NOUN a signal or instruction to an aircraft not to land.

wave power NOUN power extracted from the motion of sea waves at the coast.

waver ('weɪvə) VERB *(intr)* [1] to be irresolute; hesitate between two possibilities. [2] to become unsteady. [3] to fluctuate or vary. [4] to move back and forth or one way and another. [5] (of light) to flicker or flash. ◆ NOUN [6] the act or an instance of wavering.
▷**HISTORY** C14: from Old Norse *vafra* to flicker; related to German *wabern* to move about
▸'**waverer** NOUN ▸'**wavering** ADJECTIVE ▸'**waveringly** ADVERB

WAVES *or* **Waves** (weɪvz) NOUN (in the US) ACRONYM FOR Women Accepted for Volunteer Emergency Service; the women's reserve of the US navy.

wave speed *or* **velocity** NOUN other names for **phase speed.**

wave theory NOUN [1] the theory proposed by Huygens that light is transmitted by waves. [2] any theory that light or other radiation is transmitted as waves. See **electromagnetic wave.** ◆ Compare **corpuscular theory.**

wave train NOUN *Physics* a series of waves travelling in the same direction and spaced at regular intervals.

wavey ('weɪvɪ) NOUN *Canadian* a snow goose or other wild goose. Also called: **wawa.**
▷**HISTORY** via Canadian French from Algonquian (Cree *wehwew*)

wavy ('weɪvɪ) ADJECTIVE **wavier, waviest.** [1] abounding in or full of waves. [2] moving or proceeding in waves or undulations. [3] (of hair) set in or having waves and curls. [4] unstable or wavering.
▸'**wavily** ADVERB ▸'**waviness** NOUN

waw (wɔː) NOUN another name for **vav.**

wawa[1] ('wɑː,wɑː) *Canadian W coast slang* ◆ NOUN [1] speech; language. ◆ VERB [2] *(intr)* to speak.
▷**HISTORY** C19: from Chinook Jargon; probably of imitative origin

wawa[2] ('wɑː,wɑː, 'wɑːwə) NOUN *Canadian* a variant of **wavey.**

wawl (wɔːl) VERB a variant spelling of **waul.**

wax[1] (wæks) NOUN [1] any of various viscous or solid materials of natural origin: characteristically lustrous, insoluble in water, and having a low softening temperature, they consist largely of esters of fatty acids. [2] any of various similar substances, such as paraffin wax or ozocerite, that have a mineral origin and consist largely of hydrocarbons. [3] short for **beeswax** or **sealing wax.** [4] *Physiol* another name for **cerumen.** [5] a resinous preparation used by shoemakers to rub on thread. [6] **bone wax.** a mixture of wax, oil, and carbolic acid applied to the cut surface of a bone to prevent bleeding. [7] any substance or object that is pliable or easily moulded: *he was wax in the hands of the political bosses.* [8] *(modifier)* made of or resembling wax: *a wax figure.* [9] the act or an instance of removing body hair by coating it with warm wax, applying a strip or fabric, and then remvoing the fabric sharply, thereby plucking the hairs out by their roots. ◆ VERB [10] to remove (body hair) by means of a wax treatment. [11] *(tr)* to coat, polish, etc., with wax.
▷**HISTORY** Old English *weax,* related to Old Saxon, Old High German *wahs,* Old Norse *vax*
▸'**waxer** NOUN ▸'**wax,like** ADJECTIVE

wax[2] (wæks) VERB *(intr)* [1] to become larger, more powerful, etc. [2] (of the moon) to show a gradually increasing portion of illuminated surface, between new moon and full moon. Compare **wane** (sense 1). [3] *Archaic* to become as specified: *the time waxed late.*
▷**HISTORY** Old English *weaxan;* related to Old Frisian *waxa,* Old Saxon, Old High German *wahsan,* Gothic *wahsjan*

wax[3] (wæks) NOUN *Brit informal old-fashioned* a fit of rage or temper: *he's in a wax today.*
▷**HISTORY** of obscure origin; perhaps from the phrase *to wax angry*

wax bean NOUN *US* any of certain string beans that have yellow waxy pods and are grown in the US.

waxberry ('wæksbərɪ, -brɪ) NOUN, *plural* **-ries.** the waxy fruit of the wax myrtle or the snowberry.

waxbill ('wæks,bɪl) NOUN any of various chiefly African finchlike weaverbirds of the genus *Estrilda* and related genera, having a brightly coloured bill and plumage.

wax cap NOUN any fungus of the basidiomycetous family Hygrophoraceae, having thick waxy gills. Many are brightly coloured, like the **parrot toadstool** (*Hygrophorus psittacinus*), which is yellow with a covering of green slime, and the orange-red *H. conicus.*

waxcloth ('wæks,klɒθ) NOUN [1] another name for **oilcloth.** [2] another name for **linoleum.**

waxen[1] ('wæksən) ADJECTIVE [1] made of, treated with, or covered with wax. [2] resembling wax in colour or texture.

waxen[2] ('wæksən) VERB *Archaic* a past participle of **wax[2].**

waxeye ('wæks,aɪ) NOUN *Austral and NZ* another name for **white-eye.**

wax flower NOUN *Austral* any of several rutaceous shrubs of the genus *Eriostemon,* having waxy pink-white five-petalled flowers.

wax insect NOUN any of various scale insects that secrete wax or a waxy substance, esp the oriental species *Ceroplastes ceriferus,* which produces Chinese wax.

wax light NOUN a candle or taper of wax.

wax moth NOUN a brown pyralid moth, *Galleria mellonella,* the larvae of which feed on the combs of beehives. Also called: **honeycomb moth, bee moth.**

wax myrtle NOUN a shrub, *Myrica cerifera,* of SE North America, having evergreen leaves and a small berry-like fruit with a waxy coating: family *Myricaceae*. Also called: **bayberry, candleberry, waxberry.**

wax palm NOUN 1 a tall Andean palm tree, *Ceroxylon andicola,* having pinnate leaves that yield a resinous wax used in making candles. 2 another name for **carnauba** (sense 1).

wax paper NOUN paper treated or coated with wax or paraffin to make it waterproof.

waxplant ('wæks,plɑ:nt) NOUN 1 a climbing asclepiadaceous shrub, *Hoya carnosa,* of E Asia and Australia, having fleshy leaves and clusters of small waxy white pink-centred flowers. 2 any of various similar plants of the genus *Hoya.*

wax tree NOUN a Japanese anacardiaceous tree, *Rhus succedanea,* having white berries that yield wax.

waxwing ('wæks,wɪŋ) NOUN any of several gregarious passerine songbirds of the genus *Bombycilla,* esp *B. garrulus,* having red waxy wing tips and crested heads: family *Bombycillidae.*

waxwork ('wæks,wɜ:k) NOUN 1 an object reproduced in wax, esp as an ornament. 2 a life-size lifelike figure, esp of a famous person, reproduced in wax. 3 *(plural; functioning as singular or plural)* a museum or exhibition of wax figures or objects.
▸ **'wax,worker** NOUN

waxy[1] ('wæksɪ) ADJECTIVE **waxier, waxiest.** 1 resembling wax in colour, appearance, or texture. 2 made of, covered with, or abounding in wax.
▸ **'waxily** ADVERB ▸ **'waxiness** NOUN

waxy[2] ('wæksɪ) ADJECTIVE **waxier, waxiest.** *Brit informal old-fashioned* bad-tempered or irritable; angry.

way (weɪ) NOUN 1 a manner, method, or means: *a way of life; a way of knowing.* 2 a route or direction: *the way home.* 3 **a** a means or line of passage, such as a path or track. **b** *(in combination)*: *waterway.* 4 space or room for movement or activity (esp in the phrases **make way, in the way, out of the way**). 5 distance, usually distance in general: *you've come a long way.* 6 a passage or journey: *on the way.* 7 characteristic style or manner: *I did it in my own way.* 8 *(often plural)* habits; idiosyncrasies: *he has some offensive ways.* 9 an aspect of something; particular: *in many ways he was right.* 10 **a** a street in or leading out of a town. **b** *(capital when part of a street name)*: *Icknield Way.* 11 something that one wants in a determined manner (esp in the phrases **get** *or* **have one's** (**own**) **way**). 12 the experience or sphere in which one comes into contact with things (esp in the phrase **come one's way**). 13 *Informal* a state or condition, usually financial or concerning health (esp in the phrases **in a good** (*or* **bad**) **way**). 14 *Informal* the area or direction of one's home: *drop in if you're ever over my way.* 15 movement of a ship or other vessel. 16 a right of way in law. 17 a guide along which something can be moved, such as the surface of a lathe along which the tailstock slides. 18 *(plural)* the wooden or metal tracks down which a ship slides to be launched. 19 a course of life including experiences, conduct, etc.: *the way of sin.* 20 *Archaic* calling or trade. 21 **by the way.** *(sentence modifier)* in passing or incidentally. 22 **by way of. a** via. **b** serving as: *by way of introduction.* **c** in the state or condition of: *by way of being an artist.* 23 **each way.** (of a bet) laid on a horse, dog, etc., to win or gain a place. 24 **give way. a** to collapse or break down. **b** to withdraw or yield. 25 **give way to. a** to step aside for or stop for. **b** to give full rein to (emotions, etc.). 26 **go out of one's way.** to take considerable trouble or inconvenience oneself. 27 **have a way with.** to have such a manner or skill as to handle successfully. 28 **have it both ways.** to enjoy two things that would normally contradict each other or be mutually exclusive. 29 **in a way.** in some respects. 30 **in no way.** not at all. 31 **lead the way. a** to go first. **b** to set an example or precedent. 32 **make one's way. a** to proceed or advance. **b** to achieve success in life. 33 **no way.** *Informal* that is impossible. 34 **on the way out.** *Informal* **a** becoming unfashionable, obsolete, etc. **b** dying. 35 **out of the way. a** removed or dealt with so as to be no longer a hindrance. **b** remote. **c** unusual and sometimes improper. 36 **pay one's way.** See **pay** (sense 11). 37 **see one's way** (**clear**). to find it possible and be willing (to do something). 38 **the way.** *Irish* so that: *I left early the way I would avoid the traffic.* 39 **under way.** having started moving or making progress. ◆ ADVERB 40 *Informal* **a** at a considerable distance or extent: *way over yonder.* **b** very far: *they're way up the mountain.* 41 *Informal* by far; considerably: *way better.* 42 *Slang* truly; genuinely: *they have a way cool site.*
▹ HISTORY Old English *weg;* related to Old Frisian *wei,* Old Norse *vegr,* Gothic *wigs*

waybill ('weɪ,bɪl) NOUN a document attached to goods in transit specifying their nature, point of origin, and destination as well as the route to be taken and the rate to be charged.

way-cool ADJECTIVE *Informal* outstanding; excellent; marvellous.

wayfarer ('weɪ,fɛərə) NOUN a person who goes on a journey.
▸ **'way,faring** NOUN, ADJECTIVE

wayfaring tree NOUN a caprifoliaceous shrub, *Viburnum lantana,* of Europe and W Asia, having white flowers and berries that turn from red to black.

Wayland *or* **Wayland Smith** ('weɪlənd) NOUN a smith, artificer, and king of the elves in European folklore. Scandinavian name: **Völund.** German name: **Wieland.**

waylay (weɪ'leɪ) VERB **-lays, -laying, -laid.** *(tr)* 1 to lie in wait for and attack. 2 to await and intercept unexpectedly.
▹ HISTORY C16: from WAY + LAY[1]
▸ **way'layer** NOUN

wayleave ('weɪ,li:v) NOUN access to property granted by a landowner for payment, for example to allow a contractor access to a building site.

wayleggo (,weɪlɛ'gəʊ) INTERJECTION *NZ* away here! let go!; a shepherd's call to a dog on completion of a task.

waymark ('weɪ,mɑ:k) NOUN a symbol or signpost marking the route of a footpath.

waymarked ('weɪ,mɑ:kt) ADJECTIVE marked or identified with waymarks.

way-out ADJECTIVE *Informal* 1 extremely unconventional or experimental; avant-garde. 2 excellent or amazing.

-ways SUFFIX FORMING ADVERBS indicating direction or manner: *sideways.*
▹ HISTORY Old English *weges,* literally: of the way, from *weg* WAY

ways and means PLURAL NOUN 1 the revenues and methods of raising the revenues needed for the functioning of a state or other political unit. 2 *(usually capital)* a standing committee of the US House of Representatives that supervises all financial legislation. 3 the methods and resources for accomplishing some purpose.

wayside ('weɪ,saɪd) NOUN 1 **a** the side or edge of a road. **b** *(modifier)* situated by the wayside: *a wayside inn.* 2 **fall by the wayside.** to cease or fail to continue doing something: *of the nine starters, three fell by the wayside.* 3 **go by the wayside.** to be put aside on account of something more urgent.

wayward ('weɪwəd) ADJECTIVE 1 wanting to have one's own way regardless of the wishes or good of others. 2 capricious, erratic, or unpredictable.
▹ HISTORY C14: changed from *awayward* turned or turning away
▸ **'waywardly** ADVERB ▸ **'waywardness** NOUN

wayworn ('weɪ,wɔ:n) ADJECTIVE *Rare* worn or tired by travel.

wayzgoose ('weɪz,gu:s) NOUN a works outing made annually by a printing house.
▹ HISTORY C18: from earlier *waygoose,* of unknown origin

Waziristan (wə,zɪərɪ'stɑ:n) NOUN a mountainous region of N Pakistan, on the border with Afghanistan.

wazzock ('wæzək) NOUN *Brit informal* a foolish or annoying person.
▹ HISTORY C20: of unknown origin

wb ABBREVIATION FOR: 1 water ballast. 2 Also: **W/B, WB.** waybill. 3 westbound.

Wb *Physics* SYMBOL FOR weber.

WB *Text messaging* ABBREVIATION FOR welcome back.

WBA ABBREVIATION FOR World Boxing Association.

WBC ABBREVIATION FOR World Boxing Council.

WBO ABBREVIATION FOR World Boxing Organization.

W boson NOUN *Physics* another name for **W particle.**

WBU ABBREVIATION FOR World Boxing Union.

wc ABBREVIATION FOR: 1 water closet. 2 without charge.

WC ABBREVIATION FOR: 1 water closet. 2 (in London postal code) West Central.

WCC ABBREVIATION FOR **World Council of Churches.**

wd ABBREVIATION FOR: 1 ward. 2 wood. 3 word.

WD ABBREVIATION FOR: 1 War Department. 2 Works Department. ◆ 3 INTERNATIONAL CAR REGISTRATION FOR (Windward Islands) Dominica.

WDA ABBREVIATION FOR Welsh Development Agency.

WDM *or* **wdm** ABBREVIATION FOR wavelength division multiplex: a system in which several independent signals may be sent down an optical fibre link by monitoring them on light-carriers of different wavelengths.

we (wi:) PRONOUN *(subjective)* 1 refers to the speaker or writer and another person or other people: *we should go now.* 2 refers to all people or people in general: *the planet on which we live.* 3 **a** a formal word for **I**[1] used by editors or other writers, and formerly by monarchs. **b** *(as noun)*: *he uses the royal we in his pompous moods.* 4 *Informal* used instead of *you* with a tone of persuasiveness, condescension, or sarcasm: *how are we today?*
▹ HISTORY Old English *wē,* related to Old Saxon *wī,* Old High German *wir,* Old Norse *vēr,* Danish, Swedish *vi,* Sanskrit *vayam*

WEA (in Britain) ABBREVIATION FOR Workers' Educational Association.

weak (wi:k) ADJECTIVE 1 lacking in physical or mental strength or force; frail or feeble. 2 liable to yield, break, or give way: *a weak link in a chain.* 3 lacking in resolution or firmness of character. 4 lacking strength, power, or intensity: *a weak voice.* 5 lacking strength in a particular part: *a team weak in defence.* 6 **a** not functioning as well as normal: *weak eyes.* **b** easily upset: *a weak stomach.* 7 lacking in conviction, persuasiveness, etc.: *a weak argument.* 8 lacking in political or strategic strength: *a weak state.* 9 lacking the usual, full, or desirable strength of flavour: *weak tea.* 10 *Grammar* **a** denoting or belonging to a class of verbs, in certain languages including the Germanic languages, whose conjugation relies on inflectional endings rather than internal vowel gradation, as *look, looks, looking, looked.* **b** belonging to any part-of-speech class, in any of various languages, whose inflections follow the more regular of two possible patterns. Compare **strong** (sense 13). 11 (of a syllable) not accented or stressed. 12 (of a fuel-air mixture) containing a relatively low proportion of fuel. Compare **rich** (sense 13). 13 *Photog* having low density or contrast; thin. 14 (of an industry, market, currency, securities, etc.) falling in price or characterized by falling prices.
▹ HISTORY Old English *wāc* soft, miserable; related to Old Saxon *wēk,* Old High German *weih,* Old Norse *veikr*
▸ **'weakish** ADJECTIVE ▸ **'weakishly** ADVERB ▸ **'weakishness** NOUN

weaken ('wi:kən) VERB to become or cause to become weak or weaker.
▸ **'weakener** NOUN

weaker sex ('wi:kə) NOUN the female sex.

weakest link NOUN **the.** *Brit* the person who is making the least contribution to the collective achievement of the group.
▹ HISTORY C20: from the British television quiz of the same name

weakfish ('wiːkˌfɪʃ) NOUN, *plural* **-fish** *or* **-fishes**. any of several sciaenid sea trouts, esp *Cynoscion regalis*, a food and game fish of American Atlantic coastal waters.

weak interaction *or* **force** NOUN *Physics* an interaction between elementary particles that is responsible for certain decay processes, operates at distances less than about 10^{-15} metres, and is 10^{12} times weaker than the strong interaction. The weak interaction and electromagnetic interactions are now described by the unifying electroweak theory. Also called: **weak nuclear interaction** *or* **force.** See **interaction** (sense 2), **electroweak interaction.**

weak-kneed ADJECTIVE *Informal* yielding readily to force, persuasion, intimidation, etc.
▸ **ˌweak-ˈkneedly** ADVERB ▸ **ˌweak-ˈkneedness** NOUN

weakling ('wiːklɪŋ) NOUN a person or animal that is lacking in strength or weak in constitution or character.

weakly ('wiːklɪ) ADJECTIVE **-lier, -liest.** 1 sickly; feeble. ◆ ADVERB 2 in a weak or feeble manner.
▸ **ˈweakliness** NOUN

weak-minded ADJECTIVE 1 lacking in stability of mind or character. 2 another word for **feeble-minded.**
▸ **ˌweak-ˈmindedly** ADVERB ▸ **ˌweak-ˈmindedness** NOUN

weakness ('wiːknɪs) NOUN 1 the state or quality of being weak. 2 a deficiency or failing, as in a person's character. 3 a self-indulgent fondness or liking: *a weakness for chocolates.*

weak sister NOUN *US informal* a person in a group who is regarded as weak or unreliable.

weak-willed ADJECTIVE lacking strength of will.

weal¹ (wiːl) NOUN a raised mark on the surface of the body produced by a blow. Also called: **wale, welt, wheal.**
▷HISTORY C19: variant of WALE¹, influenced in form by WHEAL

weal² (wiːl) NOUN 1 *Archaic* prosperity or wellbeing (now esp in the phrases **the public weal, the common weal**). 2 *Obsolete* the state. 3 *Obsolete* wealth.
▷HISTORY Old English *wela;* related to Old Saxon *welo,* Old High German *wolo*

weald (wiːld) NOUN *Brit archaic* open or forested country.
▷HISTORY Old English; related to Old Saxon, Old High German *wald,* Old Norse *vollr,* probably related to WILD

Weald (wiːld) NOUN **the.** a region of SE England, in Kent, Surrey, and East and West Sussex between the North Downs and the South Downs: formerly forested.

wealth (wɛlθ) NOUN 1 a large amount of money and valuable material possessions. 2 the state of being rich. 3 a great profusion: *a wealth of gifts.* 4 *Economics* all goods and services with monetary, exchangeable, or productive value.
▷HISTORY C13 *welthe,* from WEAL²; related to WELL¹
▸ **ˈwealthless** ADJECTIVE

wealth tax NOUN a tax on personal property; capital levy.

wealthy ('wɛlθɪ) ADJECTIVE **wealthier, wealthiest.** 1 possessing wealth; affluent; rich. 2 of, characterized by, or relating to wealth. 3 abounding: *wealthy in friends.*
▸ **ˈwealthily** ADVERB ▸ **ˈwealthiness** NOUN

wean¹ (wiːn) VERB (*tr*) 1 to cause (a child or young mammal) to replace mother's milk by other nourishment. 2 (usually foll by *from*) to cause to desert former habits, pursuits, etc.
▷HISTORY Old English *wenian* to accustom; related to German *gewöhnen* to get used to
▸ **ˈweaning** NOUN

wean² (weɪn, wiːn) NOUN *Scot and northern English dialect* a child; infant.
▷HISTORY a contraction of *wee ane* or perhaps a shortened form of WEANLING

weaner ('wiːnə) NOUN 1 a person or thing that weans. 2 a pig that has just been weaned and weighs less than 40 kg. 3 *Austral and NZ* a lamb, pig, or calf in the year in which it is weaned.

weanling ('wiːnlɪŋ) NOUN **a** a child or young animal recently weaned. **b** (*as modifier*): *a weanling calf.*
▷HISTORY C16: from WEAN¹ + -LING¹

weapon ('wɛpən) NOUN 1 an object or instrument used in fighting. 2 anything that serves to outwit or get the better of an opponent: *his power of speech was his best weapon.* 3 any part of an animal that is used to defend itself, to attack prey, etc., such as claws, teeth, horns, or a sting. 4 a slang word for **penis.**
▷HISTORY Old English *wǣpen;* related to Old Norse *vápn,* Old Frisian *wēpen,* Old High German *wāffan*
▸ **ˈweaponed** ADJECTIVE ▸ **ˈweaponless** ADJECTIVE

weaponeer (ˌwɛpəˈnɪə) NOUN a person associated with the use or maintenance of weapons, esp nuclear weapons.

weaponize *or* **weaponise** ('wɛpəˌnaɪz) VERB (*tr*) to adapt (a chemical, bacillus, etc.) in such a way that it can be used as a weapon.

weaponry ('wɛpənrɪ) NOUN weapons regarded collectively.

weapon system NOUN *Military* a weapon and the components necessary to its proper function, such as targeting and guidance devices.

wear¹ (wɛə) VERB **wears, wearing, wore, worn.** 1 (*tr*) to carry or have (a garment, etc.) on one's person as clothing, ornament, etc. 2 (*tr*) to carry or have on one's person habitually: *she wears a lot of red.* 3 (*tr*) to have in one's aspect: *to wear a smile.* 4 (*tr*) to display, show, or fly: *a ship wears its colours.* 5 to deteriorate or cause to deteriorate by constant use or action. 6 to produce or be produced by constant rubbing, scraping, etc.: *to wear a hole in one's trousers.* 7 to bring or be brought to a specified condition by constant use or action: *to wear a tyre to shreds.* 8 (*intr*) to submit to constant use or action in a specified way: *his suit wears well.* 9 (*tr*) to harass or weaken. 10 (when *intr,* often foll by *on*) (of time) to pass or be passed slowly. 11 (*tr*) *Brit slang* to accept: *Larry won't wear that argument.* 12 **wear ship.** to change the tack of a sailing vessel, esp a square-rigger, by coming about so that the wind passes astern. ◆ NOUN 13 the act of wearing or state of being worn. 14 **a** anything designed to be worn: *leisure wear.* **b** (*in combination*): *nightwear.* 15 deterioration from constant or normal use or action. 16 the quality of resisting the effects of constant use. ◆ See also **wear down, wear off, wear out.**
▷HISTORY Old English *werian;* related to Old High German *werien,* Old Norse *verja,* Gothic *vasjan*
▸ **ˈwearer** NOUN

wear² (wɛə) VERB **wears, wearing, wore, worn.** *Nautical* to tack by gybing instead of by going through stays.
▷HISTORY C17: from earlier *weare,* of unknown origin

Wear (wɪə) NOUN a river in NE England, rising in NW Durham and flowing southeast then northeast to the North Sea at Sunderland. Length: 105 km (65 miles).

wearable ('wɛərəbᵊl) ADJECTIVE 1 suitable for wear or able to be worn. ◆ NOUN 2 (*often plural*) any garment that can be worn.
▸ **ˌwearaˈbility** NOUN

wear and tear NOUN damage, depreciation, or loss resulting from ordinary use.

wear down VERB (*adverb*) 1 to consume or be consumed by long or constant wearing, rubbing, etc. 2 to overcome or be overcome gradually by persistent effort.

weariless ('wɪərɪlɪs) ADJECTIVE not wearied or able to be wearied.
▸ **ˈwearilessly** ADVERB

wearing ('wɛərɪŋ) ADJECTIVE causing fatigue or exhaustion; tiring.
▸ **ˈwearingly** ADVERB

wearing course NOUN the top layer of a road that carries the traffic; road surface. Also called: **carpet, topping.**

wearisome ('wɪərɪsəm) *or* **weariful** ADJECTIVE causing fatigue or annoyance; tedious.
▸ **ˈwearisomely** *or* **ˈwearifully** ADVERB ▸ **ˈwearisomeness** *or* **ˈwearifulness** NOUN

wear off VERB (*adverb*) 1 (*intr*) to decrease in intensity gradually: *the pain will wear off in an hour.* 2 to disappear or cause to disappear gradually through exposure, use, etc.: *the pattern on the ring had been worn off.*

wear out VERB (*adverb*) 1 to make or become unfit or useless through wear. 2 (*tr*) to exhaust or tire.

wearproof ('wɛəˌpruːf) ADJECTIVE resistant to damage from normal wear or usage.

weary ('wɪərɪ) ADJECTIVE **-rier, -riest.** 1 tired or exhausted. 2 causing fatigue or exhaustion. 3 caused by or suggestive of weariness: *a weary laugh.* 4 (*postpositive;* often foll by *of* or *with*) discontented or bored, esp by the long continuance of something. ◆ VERB **-ries, -rying, -ried.** 5 to make or become weary. 6 to make or become discontented or impatient, esp by the long continuance of something.
▷HISTORY Old English *wērig;* related to Old Saxon *wōrig,* Old High German *wuorag* drunk, Greek *hōrakian* to faint
▸ **ˈwearily** ADVERB ▸ **ˈweariness** NOUN ▸ **ˈwearying** ADJECTIVE ▸ **ˈwearyingly** ADVERB

weasand ('wiːzənd) NOUN a former name for the **trachea.**
▷HISTORY Old English *wǣsend, wāsend;* related to Old Frisian *wāsenda,* Old High German *weisont* vein, Danish *vissen*

weasel ('wiːzᵊl) NOUN, *plural* **-sels** *or* **-sel.** 1 any of various small predatory musteline mammals of the genus *Mustela* and related genera, esp *M. nivalis* (**European weasel**), having reddish-brown fur, an elongated body and neck, and short legs. 2 *Informal* a sly or treacherous person. 3 *Chiefly US* a motor vehicle for use in snow, esp one with caterpillar tracks.
▷HISTORY Old English *weosule, wesle;* related to Old Norse *visla,* Old High German *wisula,* Middle Dutch *wesel*
▸ **ˈweaselly** ADJECTIVE

weasel out VERB (*intr, adverb*) *Informal* 1 to go back on a commitment. 2 to evade a responsibility, esp in a despicable manner.

weasel words PLURAL NOUN *Informal* intentionally evasive or misleading speech; equivocation.
▷HISTORY C20: alluding to the weasel's supposed ability to suck an egg out of its shell without seeming to break the shell
▸ **ˈweasel-ˌworded** ADJECTIVE

weather ('wɛðə) NOUN 1 **a** the day-to-day meteorological conditions, esp temperature, cloudiness, and rainfall, affecting a specific place. Compare **climate** (sense 1). **b** (*modifier*) relating to the forecasting of weather: *a weather ship.* 2 a prevailing state or condition. 3 **make heavy weather. a** (of a vessel) to roll and pitch in heavy seas. **b** (foll by *of*) to carry out with great difficulty or unnecessarily great effort. 4 **under the weather.** *Informal* **a** not in good health. **b** intoxicated. ◆ ADJECTIVE 5 (*prenominal*) on or at the side or part towards the wind; windward: *the weather anchor.* Compare **lee** (sense 4). ◆ VERB 6 to expose or be exposed to the action of the weather. 7 to undergo or cause to undergo changes, such as discoloration, due to the action of the weather. 8 (*intr*) to withstand the action of the weather. 9 (when *intr,* foll by *through*) to endure (a crisis, danger, etc.). 10 (*tr*) to slope (a surface, such as a roof, sill, etc.) so as to throw rainwater clear. 11 (*tr*) to sail to the windward of: *to weather a point.*
▷HISTORY Old English *weder;* related to Old Saxon *wedar,* Old High German *wetar,* Old Norse *vethr*
▸ **ˌweatheraˈbility** NOUN ▸ **ˈweatherer** NOUN

weather-beaten ADJECTIVE 1 showing signs of exposure to the weather. 2 tanned or hardened by exposure to the weather.

weatherboard ('wɛðəˌbɔːd) NOUN 1 a timber board, with a groove (rabbet) along the front of its top edge and along the back of its lower edge, that is fixed horizontally with others to form an exterior cladding on a wall or roof. Compare **clapboard.** 2 a sloping timber board fixed at the bottom of a door to deflect rain. 3 the windward side of a vessel. 4 Also called: **weatherboard house.** *Chiefly Austral and NZ* a house having walls made entirely of weatherboarding.

weatherboarding ('wɛðəˌbɔːdɪŋ) NOUN 1 an area or covering of weatherboards. 2 weatherboards collectively.

weather-bound ADJECTIVE (of a vessel, aircraft, etc.) delayed by bad weather.

weathercock ('wɛðəˌkɒk) NOUN 1 a weather vane in the form of a cock. 2 a person who is fickle or changeable. ◆ VERB 3 (*intr*) (of an aircraft) to turn or tend to turn into the wind.

weathered ('wɛðəd) ADJECTIVE 1 affected by exposure to the action of the weather. 2 (of rocks and rock formations) eroded, decomposed, or otherwise altered by the action of water, wind, frost, heat, etc. 3 (of a sill, roof, etc.) having a sloped surface so as to allow rainwater to run off. 4 (of wood) artificially stained so as to appear weather-beaten.

weather eye NOUN 1 the vision of a person trained to observe changes in the weather. 2 *Informal* an alert or observant gaze. 3 **keep one's weather eye open.** to stay on the alert.

weatherglass ('wɛðə,glɑːs) NOUN (*not in technical use*) any of various instruments, esp a barometer, that measure atmospheric conditions.

weather house NOUN a model house with two human figures, one that comes out to foretell bad weather and the other to foretell good weather.

weathering ('wɛðərɪŋ) NOUN the mechanical and chemical breakdown of rocks by the action of rain, snow, cold, etc.

weatherly ('wɛðəlɪ) ADJECTIVE (of a sailing vessel) making very little leeway when close-hauled, even in a stiff breeze.
▸ **'weatherliness** NOUN

weatherman ('wɛðə,mæn) NOUN, *plural* **-men.** a person who forecasts the weather, esp one who works in a meteorological office.

Weatherman ('wɛðə,mæn) NOUN, *plural* **-men.** *US* a member of a militant revolutionary group active in the US during the 1970s.
▷HISTORY C20: name adopted from a line in Bob Dylan's song "Subterranean Homesick Blues": "You don't need a weatherman To know which way the wind blows."

weather map *or* **chart** NOUN a synoptic chart showing weather conditions, compiled from simultaneous observations taken at various weather stations.

weatherproof ('wɛðə,pruːf) ADJECTIVE 1 designed or able to withstand exposure to weather without deterioration. ◆ VERB 2 (*tr*) to render (something) weatherproof.
▸ **'weather,proofness** NOUN

weather station NOUN one of a network of meteorological observation posts where weather data is recorded.

weather strip NOUN a thin strip of compressible material, such as spring metal, felt, etc., that is fitted between the frame of a door or window and the opening part to exclude wind and rain. Also called: **weatherstripping.**

weather vane NOUN a vane designed to indicate the direction in which the wind is blowing.

weather window NOUN a limited interval when weather conditions can be expected to be suitable for a particular project, such as laying offshore pipelines, reaching a high mountain summit, launching a satellite, etc.

weather-wise ADJECTIVE 1 skilful or experienced in predicting weather conditions. 2 skilful or experienced in predicting trends in public opinion, reactions, etc.

weatherworn ('wɛðə,wɔːn) ADJECTIVE another word for **weather-beaten.**

weave (wiːv) VERB **weaves, weaving, wove** *or* **weaved; woven** *or* **weaved.** 1 to form (a fabric) by interlacing (yarn, etc.), esp on a loom. 2 (*tr*) to make or construct by such a process: *to weave a shawl.* 3 (*tr*) to make or construct (an artefact, such as a basket) by interlacing (a pliable material, such as cane). 4 (of a spider) to make (a web). 5 (*tr*) to construct by combining separate elements into a whole. 6 (*tr*; often foll by *in, into, through,* etc.) to introduce: *to weave factual details into a fiction.* 7 to create (a way, etc.) by moving from side to side: *to weave through a crowd.* 8 (*intr*) *Vet science* (of a stabled horse) to swing the head, neck, and body backwards and forwards. 9 **get weaving.** *Informal* to hurry; start to do something. ◆ NOUN 10 the method or pattern of weaving or the structure of a woven fabric.
▷HISTORY Old English *wefan;* related to Old High German *weban,* Old Norse *vefa,* Greek *hyphos,* Sanskrit *vābhis;* compare WEB, WEEVIL, WASP
▸ **'weaving** NOUN

weaver ('wiːvə) NOUN 1 a person who weaves, esp as a means of livelihood. 2 short for **weaverbird.**

weaverbird ('wiːvə,bɜːd) *or* **weaver** NOUN 1 any small Old World passerine songbird of the chiefly African family *Ploceidae,* having a short thick bill and a dull plumage and building covered nests: includes the house sparrow and whydahs. 2 any similar bird of the family *Estrildidae,* of warm regions of the Old World: includes the waxbills, grassfinches, and Java sparrow. Also called: **weaver finch.**

weaver's hitch *or* **knot** NOUN another name for **sheet bend.**

web (wɛb) NOUN 1 any structure, construction, fabric, etc., formed by or as if by weaving or interweaving. Related adjective: **retiary.** 2 a mesh of fine tough scleroprotein threads built by a spider from a liquid secreted from its spinnerets and used to trap insects. See also **cobweb** (sense 1). 3 a similar network of threads spun by certain insect larvae, such as the silkworm. 4 a fabric, esp one in the process of being woven. 5 a membrane connecting the toes of some aquatic birds or the digits of such aquatic mammals as the otter. 6 the vane of a bird's feather. 7 *Architect* the surface of a ribbed vault that lies between the ribs. 8 the central section of an I-beam or H-beam that joins the two flanges of the beam. 9 any web-shaped part of a casting used for reinforcement. 10 the radial portion of a crank that connects the crankpin to the crankshaft. 11 a thin piece of superfluous material left attached to a forging; fin. 12 **a** a continuous strip of paper as formed on a paper machine or fed from a reel into some printing presses. **b** (*as modifier*): *web offset; a web press.* 13 the woven edge, without pile, of some carpets. 14 **a** (*often capital;* preceded by *the*) short for **World Wide Web. b** (*as modifier*): *a web site; web pages.* 15 any structure, construction, etc., that is intricately formed or complex: *a web of intrigue.* ◆ VERB **webs, webbing, webbed.** 16 (*tr*) to cover with or as if with a web. 17 (*tr*) to entangle or ensnare. 18 (*intr*) to construct a web.
▷HISTORY Old English *webb;* related to Old Saxon, Old High German *webbi,* Old Norse *vefr*
▸ **'webless** ADJECTIVE ▸ **'web,like** ADJECTIVE

web-based ADJECTIVE of, relating to, or using the World Wide Web: *web-based applications.*

webbed (wɛbd) ADJECTIVE 1 (of the feet of certain animals) having the digits connected by a thin fold of skin; palmate. 2 having, consisting of, or resembling a web.

webbie ('wɛbɪ) NOUN *Informal* a person who is well versed in the use the World Wide Web.

webbing ('wɛbɪŋ) NOUN 1 a strong fabric of hemp, cotton, jute, etc., woven in strips and used under springs in upholstery or for straps, etc. 2 the skin that unites the digits of a webbed foot. 3 anything that forms a web.

webby ('wɛbɪ) ADJECTIVE **-bier, -biest.** of, relating to, resembling, or consisting of a web.

webcam ('wɛb,kæm) NOUN a camera that transmits still or moving images over the Internet.

webcast ('wɛb,kɑːst) NOUN a broadcast of an event over the World Wide Web: *a live webcast of the game.*

weber ('veɪbə) NOUN the derived SI unit of magnetic flux; the flux that, when linking a circuit of one turn, produces in it an emf of 1 volt as it is reduced to zero at a uniform rate in one second. 1 weber is equivalent to 10^8 maxwells. Symbol: Wb.
▷HISTORY C20: named after Wilhelm Eduard *Weber* (1804–91), German physicist

webfoot ('wɛb,fʊt) NOUN 1 *Zoology* a foot having the toes connected by folds of skin. 2 *Anatomy* a foot having an abnormal membrane connecting adjacent toes.

web-footed *or* **web-toed** ADJECTIVE (of certain animals) having webbed feet that facilitate swimming.

weblish ('wɛblɪʃ) NOUN *Informal* the shorthand form of English that is used in text messaging, chat rooms, etc.
▷HISTORY C20: WEB (sense 14) + (ENG)LISH

weblog ('wɛb,lɒg) NOUN a journal written on-line and accessible to users of the Internet. Also: **blog.**

webmaster ('wɛb,mɑːstə) NOUN a person responsible for the administration of a website on the World Wide Web.

website ('wɛb,saɪt) NOUN a group of connected pages on the World Wide Web containing information on a particular subject.

web spinner NOUN any small fragile dull-coloured typically tropical insect of the order *Embioptera,* which has biting mouthparts and constructs silken tunnels in which to live.

webster ('wɛbstə) NOUN an archaic word for **weaver** (sense 1).
▷HISTORY Old English *webbestre,* from *webba* a weaver, from *webb* WEB

webwheel ('wɛb,wiːl) NOUN 1 a wheel containing a plate or web instead of spokes. 2 a wheel of which the rim, spokes, and centre are in one piece.

wed (wɛd) VERB **weds, wedding, wedded** *or* **wed.** 1 to take (a person of the opposite sex) as a husband or wife; marry. 2 (*tr*) to join (two people) in matrimony. 3 (*tr*) to unite closely.
▷HISTORY Old English *weddian;* related to Old Frisian *weddia,* Old Norse *vethja,* Gothic *wadi* pledge

we'd (wiːd; *unstressed* wɪd) CONTRACTION OF we had *or* we would.

Wed. ABBREVIATION FOR Wednesday.

wedded ('wɛdɪd) ADJECTIVE 1 of marriage: *wedded bliss.* 2 firmly in support of an idea or institution: *wedded to the virtues of capitalism.*

Weddell Sea ('wɛdᵊl) NOUN an arm of the S Atlantic in Antarctica.

wedding ('wɛdɪŋ) NOUN 1 **a** the act of marrying or the celebration of a marriage. **b** (*as modifier*): *wedding day.* 2 the anniversary of a marriage (in such combinations as **silver wedding** or **diamond wedding**). 3 the combination or blending of two separate elements.

wedding breakfast NOUN the meal usually served after a wedding ceremony or just before the bride and bridegroom leave for their honeymoon.

wedding cake NOUN a rich fruit cake, with one, two, or more tiers, covered with almond paste and decorated with royal icing, which is served at a wedding reception.

wedding ring NOUN a band ring with parallel sides, typically of precious metal, worn to indicate married status.

wedeln ('veɪdəln) NOUN a succession of high-speed turns performed in skiing.
▷HISTORY from German, literally: to wag

wedge (wɛdʒ) NOUN 1 a block of solid material, esp wood or metal, that is shaped like a narrow V in cross section and can be pushed or driven between two objects or parts of an object in order to split or secure them. 2 any formation, structure, or substance in the shape of a wedge: *a wedge of cheese.* 3 something such as an idea, action, etc., that tends to cause division. 4 a shoe with a wedge heel. 5 *Golf* a club with a face angle of more than 50°, used for bunker shots (**sand wedge**) or pitch shots (**pitching wedge**). 6 a wedge-shaped extension of the high pressure area of an anticyclone, narrower than a ridge. 7 *Mountaineering* a wedge-shaped device, formerly of wood, now usually of hollow steel, for hammering into a crack to provide an anchor point. 8 any of the triangular characters used in cuneiform writing. 9 (formerly) a body of troops formed in a V-shape. 10 *Photog* a strip of glass coated in such a way that it is clear at one end but becomes progressively more opaque towards the other end: used in making measurements of transmission density. 11 *Brit slang* a bribe. 12 **thin end of the wedge.** anything unimportant in itself that implies the start of something much larger. ◆ VERB 13 (*tr*) to secure with or as if with a wedge. 14 to squeeze or be squeezed like a wedge into a narrow space. 15 (*tr*) to force apart or divide with or as if with a wedge.
▷HISTORY Old English *wecg;* related to Old Saxon *weggi,* Old High German *wecki,* Old Norse *veggr* wall
▸ **'wedge,like** ADJECTIVE ▸ **'wedgy** ADJECTIVE

wedge heel NOUN 1 a raised shoe heel with the heel and sole forming a solid block. 2 a shoe with such a heel.

wedge-tailed eagle NOUN a large brown Australian eagle, *Aquila audax,* having a wedge-shaped tail and a wingspan of 3 m. Also called: **eaglehawk.**

Wedgwood ('wɛdʒwʊd) [1] *Trademark* **a** pottery produced, esp during the late 18th and early 19th centuries, at the Wedgwood factories. **b** such pottery having applied classical decoration in white on a blue or other coloured ground. ADJECTIVE [2] relating to or characteristic of such pottery: *Wedgwood blue.*

Wedgwood blue NOUN **a** a pale blue or greyish-blue colour. **b** (*as adjective*): *a Wedgwood-blue door.*

wedlock ('wɛdlɒk) NOUN [1] the state of being married. [2] **born out of wedlock.** born when one's parents are not legally married.
▷**HISTORY** Old English *wedlāc,* from *wedd* pledge + *-lāc,* suffix denoting activity, perhaps from *lāc* game, battle (related to Gothic *laiks* dance, Old Norse *leikr*)

Wednesday ('wɛnzdɪ) NOUN the fourth day of the week; third day of the working week.
▷**HISTORY** Old English *Wōdnes dæg* Woden's day, translation of Latin *mercurii dies* Mercury's day; related to Old Frisian *wōnsdei,* Middle Dutch *wōdensdach* (Dutch *woensdag*)

wee[1] (wi:) ADJECTIVE [1] very small; tiny; minute. ◆ NOUN [2] *Chiefly Scot* a short time (esp in the phrase **bide a wee.**).
▷**HISTORY** C13: from Old English *wǣg* WEIGHT

wee[2] (wi:) *Brit, Austral, and NZ informal* ◆ NOUN [1] **a** the act or an instance of urinating. **b** urine. ◆ VERB [2] (*intr*) to urinate. ◆ Also: **wee-wee.**
▷**HISTORY** of unknown origin

weed[1] (wi:d) NOUN [1] any plant that grows wild and profusely, esp one that grows among cultivated plants, depriving them of space, food, etc. [2] *Slang* **a the weed.** tobacco. **b** marijuana. [3] *Informal* a thin or unprepossessing person. [4] an inferior horse, esp one showing signs of weakness of constitution. ◆ VERB [5] to remove (useless or troublesome plants) from (a garden, etc.).
▷**HISTORY** Old English *weod;* related to Old Saxon *wiod,* Old High German *wiota* fern
▸'**weeder** NOUN ▸'**weedless** ADJECTIVE ▸'**weed,like** ADJECTIVE

weed[2] (wi:d) NOUN *Rare* a black crepe band worn to indicate mourning. See also **weeds.**
▷**HISTORY** Old English *wǣd, wēd;* related to Old Saxon *wād,* Old High German *wāt,* Old Norse *vāth*

weedkiller ('wi:d,kɪlə) NOUN a substance, usually a chemical or hormone, used for killing weeds.

weed out VERB (*tr, adverb*) to separate out, remove, or eliminate (anything unwanted): *to weed out troublesome students.*

weeds (wi:dz) PLURAL NOUN [1] Also called: **widow's weeds.** a widow's black mourning clothes. [2] *Obsolete* any clothing.
▷**HISTORY** pl of WEED[2]

weedy ('wi:dɪ) ADJECTIVE **weedier, weediest.** [1] full of or containing weeds: *weedy land.* [2] (of a plant) resembling a weed in rapid or straggling growth. [3] *Informal* thin or weakly in appearance.
▸'**weedily** ADVERB ▸'**weediness** NOUN

Wee Free NOUN *Informal often derogatory* a member of the minority of the Free Church of Scotland that refused to be joined with the United Free Church in 1900.

week (wi:k) NOUN [1] a period of seven consecutive days, esp, one beginning with Sunday. Related adjective: **hebdomadal.** [2] a period of seven consecutive days beginning from or including a specified day: *Easter week; a week from Wednesday.* [3] the period of time within a week devoted to work. [4] a week devoted to the celebration of a cause. ◆ ADVERB [5] *Chiefly Brit* seven days before or after a specified day: *I'll visit you Wednesday week.*
▷**HISTORY** Old English *wice, wicu, wucu;* related to Old Norse *vika,* Gothic *wikō* order

weekday ('wi:k,deɪ) NOUN any day of the week other than Sunday and, often, Saturday.

weekend NOUN (,wi:k'ɛnd) [1] **a** the end of the week, esp the period from Friday night until the end of Sunday. **b** (*as modifier*): *a weekend party.* ◆ VERB ('wi:k,ɛnd) [2] (*intr*) *Informal* to spend or pass a weekend. ◆ See also **weekends.**

weekender (,wi:k'ɛndə) NOUN [1] a person spending a weekend holiday in a place, esp habitually. [2] *Austral* a house, shack, etc., occupied only at weekends, for holidays, etc.

weekends (,wi:k'ɛndz) ADVERB *Informal* at the weekend, esp regularly or during every weekend.

weekly ('wi:klɪ) ADJECTIVE [1] happening or taking place once a week or every week. [2] determined or calculated by the week. ◆ ADVERB [3] once a week or every week. ◆ NOUN, *plural* **-lies.** [4] a newspaper or magazine issued every week.

weeknight ('wi:k,naɪt) NOUN the evening or night of a weekday.

weel (wi:l) ADVERB, ADJECTIVE, INTERJECTION, SENTENCE CONNECTOR a Scot word for **well**[1].

ween (wi:n) VERB *Archaic* to think or imagine (something).
▷**HISTORY** Old English *wēnan;* related to Old Saxon *wānian,* Gothic *wēnjan,* German *wähnen* to assume wrongly

weeny ('wi:nɪ) *or* **weensy** ('wi:nzɪ) ADJECTIVE **-nier, -niest** *or* **-sier, -siest.** *Informal* very small; tiny.
▷**HISTORY** C18: from WEE[1] with the ending *-ny* as in TINY

weeny-bopper NOUN *Informal* a child of 8 to 12 years, esp a girl, who is a keen follower of pop music.
▷**HISTORY** C20: formed on the model of TEENYBOPPER, from *weeny,* as in *teeny-weeny* very small

weep (wi:p) VERB **weeps, weeping, wept.** [1] to shed (tears) as an expression of grief or unhappiness. [2] (*tr;* foll by *out*) to utter, shedding tears. [3] (when *intr,* foll by *for*) to mourn or lament (for something). [4] to exude (drops of liquid). [5] (*intr*) (of a wound, etc.) to exude a watery or serous fluid. ◆ NOUN [6] a spell of weeping.
▷**HISTORY** Old English *wēpan;* related to Gothic *wōpjan,* Old High German *wuofan,* Old Slavonic *vabiti* to call

weeper ('wi:pə) NOUN [1] a person who weeps, esp a hired mourner. [2] something worn as a sign of mourning. [3] a hole through a wall, to allow water to drain away.

weeping ('wi:pɪŋ) ADJECTIVE (of plants) having slender hanging branches.
▸'**weepingly** ADVERB

weeping ivy NOUN a climbing plant, *Ficus benjamina,* of the fig family, grown as a greenhouse or house plant for its graceful glossy leaves on slender drooping branches.

weeping willow NOUN a hybrid willow tree, *Salix alba* × *S. babylonica,* known as *S. alba* var. *tristis,* having long hanging branches: widely planted for ornament.

weepy ('wi:pɪ) *Informal* ◆ ADJECTIVE **weepier, weepiest.** [1] liable or tending to weep. ◆ NOUN, *plural* **weepies.** [2] a romantic and sentimental film or book.
▸'**weepily** ADVERB ▸'**weepiness** NOUN

weever ('wi:və) NOUN any small marine percoid fish of the family *Trachinidae,* such as *Trachinus vipera* of European waters, having venomous spines around the gills and the dorsal fin.
▷**HISTORY** C17: from Old Northern French *wivre* viper, ultimately from Latin *vīpera* VIPER

weevil ('wi:vɪl) NOUN [1] Also called: **snout beetle.** any beetle of the family *Curculionidae,* having an elongated snout (rostrum): they are pests, feeding on plants and plant products. See also **boll weevil.** [2] Also called: **pea** *or* **bean weevil.** any of various beetles of the family *Bruchidae* (or *Lariidae*), the larvae of which live in the seeds of leguminous plants. [3] any of various similar or related beetles.
▷**HISTORY** Old English *wifel;* related to Old High German *wibil;* compare Old Norse *tordȳfill* dungbeetle
▸'**weevily** ADJECTIVE

wee-wee NOUN, VERB a variant of **wee**[2].

w.e.f. ABBREVIATION FOR with effect from.

weft (wɛft) NOUN the yarn woven across the width of the fabric through the lengthwise warp yarn. Also called: **filling, woof.**
▷**HISTORY** Old English, related to Old Norse *veptr;* see WEAVE

Wehrmacht *German* ('ve:r,maxt) NOUN the armed services of the German Third Reich from 1935 to 1945.
▷**HISTORY** from *Wehr* defence + *Macht* force

Weichsel ('vaiksəl) NOUN the German name for the **Vistula** (sense 1).

weigela (waɪ'gi:lə, -'dʒi:-, 'waɪgɪlə) NOUN any caprifoliaceous shrub of the Asian genus *Weigela,* having clusters of pink, purple, red, or white showy bell-shaped flowers.
▷**HISTORY** C19: from New Latin, named after C. E. *Weigel* (1748–1831), German physician

weigh[1] (weɪ) VERB [1] (*tr*) to measure the weight of. [2] (*intr*) to have weight or be heavy: *she weighs more than her sister.* [3] (*tr;* often foll by *out*) to apportion according to weight. [4] (*tr*) to consider carefully: *to weigh the facts of a case.* [5] (*intr*) to be influential: *his words weighed little with the jury.* [6] (*intr;* often foll by *on*) to be oppressive or burdensome (to). [7] *Obsolete* to regard or esteem. [8] **weigh anchor.** to raise a vessel's anchor or (of a vessel) to have its anchor raised preparatory to departure. ◆ See also **weigh down, weigh in, weigh up.**
▷**HISTORY** Old English *wegan;* related to Old Frisian *wega,* Old Norse *vega,* Gothic *gawigan,* German *wiegen*
▸'**weighable** ADJECTIVE ▸'**weigher** NOUN

weigh[2] (weɪ) NOUN **under weigh.** a variant spelling of **under way.**
▷**HISTORY** C18: variation due to the influence of phrases such as *to weigh anchor*

weighbridge ('weɪ,brɪdʒ) NOUN a machine for weighing vehicles, etc., by means of a metal plate set into a road.

weigh down VERB (*adverb*) to press (a person) down by or as if by weight: *his troubles weighed him down.*

weigh in VERB (*intr, adverb*) [1] **a** (of a boxer or wrestler) to be weighed before a bout. **b** (of a jockey) to be weighed after, or sometimes before, a race. [2] *Informal* to contribute, as in a discussion, etc.: *he weighed in with a few sharp comments.* ◆ NOUN **weigh-in.** [3] the act of checking a competitor's weight, as in boxing, horse racing, etc.

weight (weɪt) NOUN [1] a measure of the heaviness of an object; the amount anything weighs. [2] *Physics* the vertical force experienced by a mass as a result of gravitation. It equals the mass of the body multiplied by the acceleration of free fall. Its units are units of force (such as newtons or poundals) but is often given as a mass unit (kilogram or pound). Symbol: *W.* [3] a system of units used to express the weight of a substance: *troy weight.* [4] a unit used to measure weight: *the kilogram is the weight used in the metric system.* [5] any mass or heavy object used to exert pressure or weigh down. [6] an oppressive force: *the weight of cares.* [7] any heavy load: *the bag was such a weight.* [8] the main or greatest force: preponderance: *the weight of evidence.* [9] importance, influence, or consequence: *his opinion carries weight.* [10] *Statistics* one of a set of coefficients assigned to items of a frequency distribution that are analysed in order to represent the relative importance of the different items. [11] *Printing* the apparent blackness of a printed typeface. [12] *Slang* a pound of a drug, esp cannabis. [13] **pull one's weight.** *Informal* to do one's full or proper share of a task. [14] **throw one's weight around.** *Informal* to act in an overauthoritarian or aggressive manner. ◆ VERB (*tr*) [15] to add weight to. [16] to burden or oppress. [17] to add importance, value, etc., to one side rather than another; bias; favour: *a law weighted towards landlords.* [18] *Statistics* to attach a weight or weights to. [19] to make (fabric, threads, etc.) heavier by treating with mineral substances, etc.
▷**HISTORY** Old English *wiht;* related to Old Frisian, Middle Dutch *wicht,* Old Norse *vētt,* German *Gewicht*
▸'**weighter** NOUN

weighted average NOUN an average calculated by taking into account not only the frequencies of the values of a variable but also some other factor such as their variance. The weighted average of observed data is the result of dividing the sum of the products of each observed value, the number of times it occurs, and this other factor by the total number of observations.

weighting ('weɪtɪŋ) NOUN [1] a factor by which some quantity is multiplied in order to make it comparable with others. See also **weighted average.** [2] an increase in some quantity, esp an additional allowance paid to compensate for higher living costs: *a London weighting.*

weightless ('weɪtləs) ADJECTIVE 1 (of a body) having no actual weight; a state in which an object has no actual weight (because it is in space and unaffected by gravitational attraction) or no apparent weight (because the gravitational attraction equals the centripetal force and the object is in free fall). 2 *Business* **a** (of economic activity) based on the supply of information and ideas rather than trade in physical goods: *the weightless economy*. **b** (of a company) having very few physical assets: *weightless dot.coms*.
▸ **'weightlessness** NOUN

weightlessness ('weɪtlɪsnɪs) NOUN a state in which an object has no actual weight (because it is in space and unaffected by gravitational attraction) or no apparent weight (because the gravitational attraction equals the centripetal force and the object is in free fall).
▸ **'weightless** ADJECTIVE

weightlifting ('weɪtˌlɪftɪŋ) NOUN the sport of lifting barbells of specified weights in a prescribed manner for competition or exercise.
▸ **'weightˌlifter** NOUN

weight training NOUN physical exercise involving lifting weights to improve muscle performance.

weight watcher NOUN a person who tries to lose weight, esp by dieting.

Weightwatchers ('weɪtˌwɒtʃəz) NOUN (*functioning as singular*) *Trademark* an organization that assists people who want to lose weight.

weighty ('weɪtɪ) ADJECTIVE **weightier, weightiest.** 1 having great weight. 2 important or momentous. 3 causing anxiety or worry.
▸ **'weightily** ADVERB ▸ **'weightiness** NOUN

weigh up VERB (*tr, adverb*) to make an assessment of (a person, situation, etc.); judge.

Weihai *or* **Wei-hai** ('weɪ'haɪ) NOUN a port in NE China, in NE Shandong on the Yellow Sea: leased to Britain as a naval base (1898–1930). Pop.: 287 872 (1999 est.). Also called: **Weihaiwei** (ˌweɪ'haɪˌweɪ).

Weil's disease (vaɪlz) NOUN another name for **leptospirosis.**
▷**HISTORY** named after Adolf *Weil* (1848–1916), German physician

Weimar (*German* 'vaimar) NOUN a city in E central Germany, in Thuringia: a cultural centre in the 18th and early 19th century; scene of the adoption (1919) of the constitution of the Weimar Republic. Pop.: 59 100 (1991).

Weimaraner ('vaɪməˌrɑːnə, 'waɪməˌrɑː-) NOUN a breed of hunting dog, having a very short sleek grey coat and short tail.
▷**HISTORY** C20: named after WEIMAR, where the breed was developed

Weimar Republic NOUN the German republic that existed from 1919 to Hitler's accession to power in 1933.

weir (wɪə) NOUN 1 a low dam that is built across a river to raise the water level, divert the water, or control its flow. 2 a series of traps or enclosures placed in a stream to catch fish.
▷**HISTORY** Old English *wer;* related to Old Norse *ver,* Old Frisian *were,* German *Wehr*

weird (wɪəd) ADJECTIVE 1 suggestive of or relating to the supernatural; eerie. 2 strange or bizarre. 3 *Archaic* of or relating to fate or the Fates. ◆ NOUN 4 *Archaic, chiefly Scot* **a** fate or destiny. **b** one of the Fates. 5 **dree one's weird.** *Scot* See **dree.** ◆ VERB 6 (*tr*) *Scot* to destine or ordain by fate; predict. ◆ See also **weird out.**
▷**HISTORY** Old English (*ge*)*wyrd* destiny; related to *weorthan* to become, Old Norse *urthr* bane, Old Saxon *wurd;* see WORTH[2]
▸ **'weirdly** ADVERB ▸ **'weirdness** NOUN

weirdo ('wɪədəʊ) *or* **weirdie** ('wɪədɪ) NOUN, *plural* **-dos** *or* **-dies.** *Informal* a person who behaves in a bizarre or eccentric manner.

weird out VERB (*tr, adverb*) *Informal* to cause (someone) to feel afraid or uncomfortable: *his unstable behaviour was weirding me out.*

weird sisters PLURAL NOUN 1 another name for the **Fates.** 2 *Norse myth* another name for the **Norns** (see **Norn**[1]).

Weismannism ('vaɪsmənˌɪzəm) NOUN the doctrine of the continuity of the germ plasm. This theory of heredity states that all inheritable characteristics are transmitted by the reproductive cells and that characteristics acquired during the lifetime of the organism are not inherited.
▷**HISTORY** C19: named after August *Weismann* (1834–1914), German biologist

Weisshorn ('vaɪsˌhɔːn) NOUN a mountain in S Switzerland, in the Pennine Alps. Height: 4505 m (14 781 ft.).

weka ('weɪkə, 'wiːkə) NOUN any flightless New Zealand rail of the genus *Gallirallus,* having a mottled brown plumage and rudimentary wings. Also called: **Maori hen, wood hen.**
▷**HISTORY** C19: from Maori, of imitative origin

welch (welʃ) VERB a variant spelling of **welsh.**
▸ **'welcher** NOUN

Welch (welʃ) ADJECTIVE an archaic spelling of **Welsh**[1].

welcome ('welkəm) ADJECTIVE 1 gladly and cordially received or admitted: *a welcome guest.* 2 bringing pleasure or gratitude: *a welcome gift.* 3 freely permitted or invited: *you are welcome to call.* 4 under no obligation (only in such phrases as **you're welcome** or **he's welcome**, as conventional responses to thanks). ◆ SENTENCE SUBSTITUTE 5 an expression of cordial greeting, esp to a person whose arrival is desired or pleasing. ◆ NOUN 6 the act of greeting or receiving a person or thing; reception: *the new theory had a cool welcome.* 7 **wear out one's welcome.** to come more often or stay longer than is acceptable or pleasing. ◆ VERB (*tr*) 8 to greet the arrival of (visitors, guests, etc.) cordially or gladly. 9 to receive or accept, esp gladly.
▷**HISTORY** C12: changed (through influence of WELL[1]) from Old English *wilcuma* (agent noun referring to a welcome guest), *wilcume* (a greeting of welcome), from *wil* WILL[2] + *cuman* to COME
▸ **'welcomely** ADVERB ▸ **'welcomeness** NOUN ▸ **'welcomer** NOUN

weld[1] (weld) VERB 1 (*tr*) to unite (pieces of metal or plastic) together, as by softening with heat and hammering or by fusion. 2 to bring or admit of being brought into close association or union. ◆ NOUN 3 a joint formed by welding.
▷**HISTORY** C16: variant probably based on past participle of WELL[2] in obsolete sense to boil, heat
▸ **'weldable** ADJECTIVE ▸ **ˌwelda'bility** NOUN ▸ **'welder** *or* **'weldor** NOUN ▸ **'weldless** ADJECTIVE

weld[2] (weld), **wold,** *or* **woald** (wəʊld) NOUN 1 a yellow dye obtained from the plant dyer's rocket. 2 another name for **dyer's rocket.**
▷**HISTORY** C14: from Low German; compare Middle Low German *walde, waude,* Dutch *wouw*

welding rod NOUN *Electrical engineering* filler metal supplied in the form of a rod, usually coated with flux.

welfare ('welˌfɛə) NOUN 1 health, happiness, prosperity, and well-being in general. 2 **a** financial and other assistance given to people in need. **b** (*as modifier*): *welfare services.* 3 Also called: **welfare work.** plans or work to better the social or economic conditions of various underprivileged groups. 4 **the welfare.** *Informal, chiefly Brit* the public agencies involved with giving such assistance. 5 **on welfare.** *Chiefly US and Canadian* in receipt of financial aid from a government agency or other source.
▷**HISTORY** C14: from the phrase *wel fare;* related to Old Norse *velferth,* German *Wohlfahrt;* see WELL[1], FARE

welfare economics NOUN (*functioning as singular*) the aspects of economic theory concerned with the welfare of society and priorities to be observed in the allocation of resources.

welfare state NOUN 1 a system in which the government undertakes the chief responsibility for providing for the social and economic security of its population, usually through unemployment insurance, old-age pensions, and other social-security measures. 2 a social system characterized by such policies.

welfarism ('welˌfɛərɪzəm) NOUN policies or attitudes associated with a welfare state.
▸ **'welˌfarist** NOUN

welkin ('welkɪn) NOUN *Archaic* the sky, heavens, or upper air.
▷**HISTORY** Old English *wolcen, welcen;* related to Old Frisian *wolken,* Old Saxon, Old High German *wolcan*

Welkom ('welkəm, 'vel-) NOUN a town in central South Africa; developed rapidly following the discovery of gold. Pop.: 203 296 (1996).

well[1] (wel) ADVERB **better, best.** 1 (*often used in combination*) in a satisfactory manner: *the party went very well.* 2 (*often used in combination*) in a good, skilful, or pleasing manner: *she plays the violin well.* 3 in a correct or careful manner: *listen well to my words.* 4 in a comfortable or prosperous manner: *to live well.* 5 (*usually used with auxiliaries*) suitably; fittingly: *you can't very well say that.* 6 intimately: *I knew him well.* 7 in a kind or favourable manner: *she speaks well of you.* 8 to a great or considerable extent; fully: *to be well informed.* 9 by a considerable margin: *let me know well in advance.* 10 (preceded by *could, might,* or *may*) indeed: *you may well have to do it yourself.* 11 *Informal* (intensifier): *well safe.* 12 **all very well.** used ironically to express discontent, dissent, etc. 13 **as well. a** in addition; too. **b** (preceded by *may* or *might*) with equal effect: *you might as well come.* 14 **as well as.** in addition to. 15 (**just**) **as well.** preferable or advisable: *it would be just as well if you paid me now.* 16 **just leave well** (**enough**) **alone.** to refrain from interfering with something that is satisfactory. 17 **well and good.** used to indicate calm acceptance, as of a decision: *if you accept my offer, well and good.* 18 **well up in.** well acquainted with (a particular subject); knowledgeable about. ◆ ADJECTIVE (*usually postpositive*) 19 (when *prenominal, usually used with a negative*) in good health: *I'm very well, thank you; he's not a well man.* 20 satisfactory, agreeable, or pleasing. 21 prudent; advisable: *it would be well to make no comment.* 22 prosperous or comfortable. 23 fortunate or happy: *it is well that you agreed to go.* ◆ INTERJECTION 24 **a** an expression of surprise, indignation, or reproof. **b** an expression of anticipation in waiting for an answer or remark. ◆ SENTENCE CONNECTOR 25 an expression used to preface a remark, gain time, etc.: *well, I don't think I will come.*
▷**HISTORY** Old English *wel;* related to Old High German *wala, wola* (German *wohl*), Old Norse *val,* Gothic *waila*

well[2] (wel) NOUN 1 a hole or shaft that is excavated, drilled, bored, or cut into the earth so as to tap a supply of water, oil, gas, etc. 2 a natural pool where ground water comes to the surface. 3 **a** a cavity, space, or vessel used to contain a liquid. **b** (*in combination*): *an inkwell.* 4 an open shaft through the floors of a building, such as one used for a staircase. 5 a deep enclosed space in a building or between buildings that is open to the sky to permit light and air to enter. 6 **a** a bulkheaded compartment built around a ship's pumps for protection and ease of access. **b** another word for **cockpit.** 7 a perforated tank in the hold of a fishing boat for keeping caught fish alive. 8 (in England) the open space in the centre of a law court. 9 a source, esp one that provides a continuous supply: *he is a well of knowledge.* ◆ VERB 10 to flow or cause to flow upwards or outwards: *tears welled from her eyes.*
▷**HISTORY** Old English *wella;* related to Old High German *wella* (German *Welle* wave), Old Norse *vella* boiling heat

we'll (wiːl) CONTRACTION OF we will *or* we shall.

well-accepted ADJECTIVE (**well accepted** when postpositive) generally considered as true or correct.

well-accustomed ADJECTIVE (**well accustomed** when postpositive) sufficiently used to: *well-accustomed to desert conditions.*

well-acquainted ADJECTIVE (**well acquainted** when postpositive) having a good knowledge or understanding of someone or something: *well acquainted with Milton.*

well-acted ADJECTIVE (**well acted** when postpositive) (of a play, film, dramatic part, etc.) performed in a skilful manner.

well-adapted ADJECTIVE (**well adapted** when postpositive) having been made or adjusted to fit suitably into an environment, situation, etc.

well-adjusted ADJECTIVE (**well adjusted** when postpositive) mentally and emotionally stable.

well-advertised ADJECTIVE (**well advertised** when postpositive) advertised widely or interestingly in order to elicit interest.

well-advised ADJECTIVE (**well advised** when

postpositive) 1 acting with deliberation or reason. 2 well thought out; considered: *a well-advised plan.*

well-affected ADJECTIVE (**well affected** when postpositive) favourably disposed (towards); steadfast or loyal.

well-aimed ADJECTIVE (**well aimed** when postpositive) 1 (of a missile, punch, etc.) having been pointed or directed accurately at a person or object: *a well-aimed, precise blow.* 2 (of a comment, criticism, etc.) obviously and accurately directed at a person, object, etc.: *a well-aimed expression of contempt.*

well-aired ADJECTIVE (**well aired** when postpositive) (of bedding, clothes, a room, etc.) having been hung up or ventilated to allow air to circulate.

Welland Canal ('wɛlənd) NOUN a canal in S Canada, in Ontario, linking Lake Erie to Lake Ontario: part of the St Lawrence Seaway, with eight locks. Length: 44 km (28 miles). Also called: **Welland Ship Canal.**

well-appointed ADJECTIVE (**well appointed** when postpositive) well equipped or furnished; properly supplied.

well-argued ADJECTIVE (**well argued** when postpositive) having been reasoned, proposed, or debated convincingly.

well-armed ADJECTIVE (**well armed** when postpositive) 1 having many or good weapons: *well-armed forces.* 2 suitably prepared in advance: *well-armed for an argument.*

well-arranged ADJECTIVE (**well arranged** when postpositive) having been put into a good systematic or decorative order.

well-attended ADJECTIVE (**well attended** when postpositive) (of an event, meeting, etc.) attended by a large or regular audience or group of participants: *evening mass is well attended.*

well-attested ADJECTIVE (**well attested** when postpositive) widely affirmed as correct or true.

well-aware ADJECTIVE (**well aware** when postpositive) having knowledge or awareness: *well-aware of the problems.*

wellaway ('wɛlə'weɪ) INTERJECTION *Archaic* woe! alas!

▷**HISTORY** Old English, from *wei lā wei,* variant of *wā lā wā,* literally: woe! lo woe

well-balanced ADJECTIVE (**well balanced** when postpositive) 1 having good balance or proportions. 2 of balanced mind; sane or sensible.

well-behaved ADJECTIVE (**well behaved** when postpositive) conducting onself in a satisfactory manner.

wellbeing ('wɛl'biːɪŋ) NOUN the condition of being contented, healthy, or successful; welfare.

well-blessed ADJECTIVE (**well blessed** when postpositive) having been generously endowed with a talent, beauty, etc.

well-born ADJECTIVE (**well born** when postpositive) having been born into a wealthy or upper-class family.

well-bred ADJECTIVE (**well bred** when postpositive) 1 Also: **well-born.** of respected or noble lineage. 2 indicating good breeding: *well-bred manners.* 3 of good thoroughbred stock: *a well-bred spaniel.*

well-built ADJECTIVE (**well built** when postpositive) 1 large or ample: *a well-built lady.* 2 having a good, strong construction: *well-built houses.*

well-chosen ADJECTIVE (**well chosen** when postpositive) carefully selected to produce a desired effect; apt: *a few well-chosen words may be more effective than a long speech.*

well-clothed ADJECTIVE (**well clothed** when postpositive) dressed in good quality clothes.

well-concealed ADJECTIVE (**well concealed** when postpositive) hidden or concealed in a skilful, satisfactory, or careful manner.

well-conditioned ADJECTIVE (**well conditioned** when postpositive) (of a person or animal's body, hair, etc.) in a good or healthy condition.

well-conducted ADJECTIVE (**well conducted** when postpositive) 1 (of research, business, an operation, etc.) led, conducted, or carried out in a satisfactory manner. 2 (of a person or animal) behaving in a satisfactory manner: *well-conducted, tidy creatures.*

well-connected ADJECTIVE (**well connected** when postpositive) having influential or important relatives or friends.

well-considered ADJECTIVE (**well considered** when postpositive) having been thought about carefully.

well-constructed ADJECTIVE (**well constructed** when postpositive) made or having been made to a high standard of workmanship and safety.

well-controlled ADJECTIVE (**well controlled** when postpositive) regulated, operated, or restrained successfully or strictly: *well-controlled research work.*

well-cooked ADJECTIVE (**well cooked** when postpositive) 1 having been cooked with skill so as to be pleasant to eat. 2 (of meat) having been cooked thoroughly.

well-covered ADJECTIVE (**well covered** when postpositive) 1 satisfactorily or pleasantly provided with a covering. 2 (of news, etc.) having been given sufficient coverage: *child abuse is well covered.*

well-cultivated ADJECTIVE (**well cultivated** when postpositive) 1 (of land, plants, etc.) tilled, planted, or maintained in a satisfactory manner. 2 (of a trait, talent, etc.) fostered or improved by study or practice: *his well-cultivated sarcasm.*

well-defended ADJECTIVE (**well defended** when postpositive) having sufficient defences against attack.

well-defined ADJECTIVE (**well defined** when postpositive) clearly delineated, described, or determined.

well-demonstrated ADJECTIVE (**well demonstrated** when postpositive) (of an ability, fact, idea, etc.) shown, manifested, or proved convincingly or thoroughly.

well-described ADJECTIVE (**well described** when postpositive) (of a scene, picture, incident, etc.) having been skillfully represented or expressed in words.

well-deserved ADJECTIVE (**well deserved** when postpositive) fully merited: *a well-deserved reputation.*

well-developed ADJECTIVE (**well developed** when postpositive) carefully or extensively elaborated or evolved.

well-disciplined ADJECTIVE (**well disciplined** when postpositive) having been strictly trained or conditioned to ensure good behaviour, orderliness, etc.

well-disposed ADJECTIVE (**well disposed** when postpositive) inclined to be sympathetic, kindly, or friendly: *he was never well disposed towards her relatives.*

well-documented ADJECTIVE (**well documented** when postpositive) widely recorded or recounted: *a well-documented fact.*

well-done ADJECTIVE (**well done** when postpositive) 1 (of food, esp meat) cooked thoroughly. 2 made or accomplished satisfactorily.

well-dressed ADJECTIVE (**well dressed** when postpositive) neatly, expensively, or fashionably attired.

well dressing NOUN the decoration of wells with flowers, etc.: a traditional annual ceremony of great antiquity in some parts of Britain, originally associated with the cult of water deities.

well-earned ADJECTIVE (**well earned** when postpositive) fully deserved: *a well-earned rest.*

well-endowed ADJECTIVE (**well endowed** when postpositive) 1 having a large supply of money, resources, etc. 2 *Informal* having a large penis. 2 *Informal* having large breasts.

well-equipped ADJECTIVE (**well equipped** when postpositive) having sufficient equipment, supplies, or abilities.

well-established ADJECTIVE (**well established** when postpositive) 1 having permanence or security in a certain place, condition, job, etc: *a well-established brand.* 2 well-known or validated: *a well-established fact.*

well-favoured ADJECTIVE (**well favoured** when postpositive) having good features; good-looking.

well-fed ADJECTIVE (**well fed** when postpositive) 1 having a nutritious diet; well nourished. 2 plump; fat.

well-financed ADJECTIVE (**well financed** when postpositive) having received or receiving a sufficient amount of funds.

well-finished ADJECTIVE (**well finished** when postpositive) (of a garment, piece of furniture, interior decoration, etc.) completed with a high degree of attention to detail and surface appearance: *the woodwork is well finished.*

well-fitted ADJECTIVE (**well fitted** when postpositive) 1 (of clothes, a lid, etc.) fitting closely or comfortably. 2 (of a room, boat, etc.) having been installed with good quality storage, appliances, etc.

well-formed ADJECTIVE (**well formed** when postpositive) *Logic, linguistics* (of a formula, expression, etc.) constructed in accordance with the syntactic rules of a particular system; grammatically correct.

▸**well-formedness** NOUN

well-fortified ADJECTIVE (**well fortified** when postpositive) 1 (of a position, garrison, city, etc.) having been made defensible. 2 (of a person) having strengthened oneself or been strengthened physically, mentally, or morally: *the police were well fortified with steaming mugs of tea.*

well-found ADJECTIVE (**well found** when postpositive) furnished or supplied with all or most necessary things.

well-founded ADJECTIVE (**well founded** when postpositive) having good grounds: *well-founded rumours.*

well-furnished ADJECTIVE (**well furnished** when postpositive) 1 (of a room, house, etc.) fitted out or decorated with attractive or good quality furniture, carpets, etc.: *well furnished with tapestries and porcelain.* 2 amply stocked, equipped, or supplied: *he was well furnished with notebooks.*

well-governed ADJECTIVE (**well governed** when postpositive) (of a political unit, organization, nation, etc.) directed and controlled efficiently or satisfactorily.

well-groomed ADJECTIVE (**well groomed** when postpositive) 1 (of a person) having a tidy pleasing appearance. 2 kept tidy and neat: *a well-groomed garden.* 3 (of an animal) well turned out and tended: *a well-groomed horse.*

well-grounded ADJECTIVE (**well grounded** when postpositive) 1 well instructed in the basic elements of a subject. 2 another term for **well-founded.**

well-guarded ADJECTIVE (**well guarded** when postpositive) 1 having sufficient protection from danger or harm. 2 kept private or out of the public eye: *well-guarded secrets.*

well-handled ADJECTIVE (**well handled** when postpositive) 1 having been managed successfully: *a well-handled merger.* 2 operated or employed skillfully: *a well-handled vehicle.*

wellhead ('wɛl,hɛd) NOUN 1 the source of a well or stream. 2 a source, fountainhead, or origin.

well-heeled ADJECTIVE (**well heeled** when postpositive) *Informal* rich; prosperous; wealthy.

well-hidden ADJECTIVE (**well hidden** when postpositive) having been concealed to make discovery difficult or impossible.

well-hung ADJECTIVE (**well hung** when postpositive) 1 (of game) hung for a sufficient length of time. 2 *Slang* (of a man) having large genitals.

wellies ('wɛlɪz) PLURAL NOUN *Brit informal* Wellington boots.

well-illustrated ADJECTIVE (**well illustrated** when postpositive) 1 having good illustrations: *a well-illustrated book.* 2 clarified or explained with good examples: *a well-illustrated review of current literature.*

well in ADJECTIVE (*postpositive;* often foll by *with*) *Informal* on good terms or favourably placed (with): *the foreman was well in with the management.*

well-informed ADJECTIVE (**well informed** when postpositive) 1 having knowledge about a great variety of subjects: *he seems to be a well-informed person.* 2 possessing reliable information on a particular subject.

Wellingborough ('wɛlɪŋbərə, -brə) NOUN a town in central England, in Northamptonshire. Pop.: 41 602 (1991).

Wellington ('wɛlɪŋtən) NOUN 1 an administrative district, formerly a province, of New Zealand, on SW North Island: major livestock producer in New

Zealand. Capital: Wellington. Pop.: 424 461 (2001). Area: 28 153 sq. km (10 870 sq. miles). [2] the capital city of New Zealand. Its port, historically Port Nicholson, on **Wellington Harbour** has a car and rail ferry link between the North and South Islands; university (1899). Pop.: 166 700 (1999 est.).

Wellington boots PLURAL NOUN [1] Also called: **gumboots, wellingtons.** *Brit* knee-length or calf-length rubber or rubberized boots, worn esp in wet conditions. Often shortened to: **wellies.** [2] military leather boots covering the front of the knee but cut away at the back to allow easier bending of the knee.
▷HISTORY C19: named after the 1st Duke of *Wellington*

wellingtonia (ˌwɛlɪŋˈtəʊnɪə) NOUN another name for **big tree.**
▷HISTORY C19: named after the 1st Duke of *Wellington*

well-intentioned ADJECTIVE (**well intentioned** when postpositive) having or indicating benevolent intentions, usually with unfortunate results.

well-judged ADJECTIVE (**well judged** when postpositive) showing careful consideration or skill.

well-justified ADJECTIVE (**well justified** when postpositive) having been shown, proved, or validated satisfactorily.

well-kept ADJECTIVE (**well kept** when postpositive) maintained in good condition: *the front lawns are well kept.*

well-knit ADJECTIVE (**well knit** when postpositive) strong, firm, or sturdy.

well-known ADJECTIVE (**well known** when postpositive) [1] widely known; famous; celebrated. [2] known fully or clearly.

well-liked ADJECTIVE (**well liked** when postpositive) liked by many people; popular.

well-loved ADJECTIVE (**well loved** when postpositive) loved by many people; very popular.

well-made ADJECTIVE (**well made** when postpositive) made to a good or high standard.

well-man NOUN, *plural* **-men. a** a healthy man who attends a clinic or surgery to ensure that his general health, lifestyle, and sexual performance are satisfactory. **b** (*as modifier*): *a well-man clinic.*

well-managed ADJECTIVE (**well managed** when postpositive) administered or controlled in a competent or successful manner.

well-mannered ADJECTIVE (**well mannered** when postpositive) having good manners; courteous; polite.

well-marked ADJECTIVE (**well marked** when postpositive) (of a path, trail, landmark, etc.) clearly indicated or signposted.

well-matched ADJECTIVE (**well matched** when postpositive) [1] (of two people) likely to have a successful relationship. [2] (of two teams or competitors) likely to compete on an even level. [3] (of two or a pair) looking or functioning well together: *well-matched roan ponies.*

well-meaning ADJECTIVE (**well meaning** when postpositive) having or indicating good or benevolent intentions, usually with unfortunate results.

well-merited ADJECTIVE (**well merited** when postpositive) fully deserved or merited.

well-mixed ADJECTIVE (**well mixed** when postpositive) (of ingredients, constituents, etc.) formed or blended together thoroughly.

well-motivated ADJECTIVE (**well motivated** when postpositive) (of a person, intention, etc.) have sufficient incentive, desire, or drive.

wellness (ˈwɛlnəs) NOUN the state of being in good physical and mental health.

well-nigh ADVERB nearly; almost: *it's well-nigh three o'clock.*

well-off ADJECTIVE (**well off** when postpositive) [1] in a comfortable or favourable position or state. [2] financially well provided for; moderately rich.

well-oiled ADJECTIVE (**well oiled** when postpositive) *Informal* drunk.

well-ordered ADJECTIVE *Logic, maths* (of a relation) having the property that every nonempty subset of its field has a least member under the relation: *less than* is well-ordered on the natural numbers but not on the reals, since an open set has no least member.

well-organized *or* **well-organised** ADJECTIVE (**well organized** *or* **well organised** when postpositive) having good organization; orderly and efficient: *a well-organized individual.*

well-padded ADJECTIVE (**well padded** when postpositive) (of a person) corpulent; portly; fat.

well-paid ADJECTIVE (**well paid** when postpositive) receiving or involving good remuneration.

well-placed ADJECTIVE (**well placed** when postpositive) having an advantageous position.

well-planned ADJECTIVE (**well planned** when postpositive) (of an event, project, etc.) suitably devised or drafted in advance to ensure success.

well-played ADJECTIVE (**well played** when postpositive) (of a piece of music, game, etc.) skilfully or pleasingly executed.

well-pleased ADJECTIVE (**well pleased** when postpositive) very happy or satisfied: *well pleased with the outcome of the meeting.*

well-practised ADJECTIVE (**well practised** when postpositive) having or having been habitually or frequently practised in order to improve skill or quality.

well-prepared ADJECTIVE (**well prepared** when postpositive) suitably prepared in advance.

well-preserved ADJECTIVE (**well preserved** when postpositive) [1] kept in a good condition. [2] continuing to appear youthful: *she was a well-preserved old lady.*

well-proportioned ADJECTIVE (**well proportioned** when postpositive) having the correct or desirable relationship between constituent parts with respect to size, number, or degree.

well-protected ADJECTIVE (**well protected** when postpositive) having suitable defence against attack, harm, etc.

well-provided ADJECTIVE (**well provided** when postpositive) [1] having been furnished or supplied with a sufficient amount. [2] (followed by *for*) having been supplied with sufficient means of support, esp financially.

well-qualified ADJECTIVE (**well qualified** when postpositive) having good or excellent qualifications.

well-read (ˈwɛlˈrɛd) ADJECTIVE (**well read** when postpositive) having read widely and intelligently; erudite.

well-reasoned ADJECTIVE (**well reasoned** when postpositive) logically argued with skill or care.

well-received ADJECTIVE (**well received** when postpositive) having been greeted or reviewed with approval: *his well-received books.*

well-recommended ADJECTIVE (**well recommended** when postpositive) highly praised or commended: *a popular and well-recommended book.*

well-regarded ADJECTIVE (**well regarded** when postpositive) considered to be good morally, professionally, etc.; esteemed: *a well-regarded local MP.*

well-regulated ADJECTIVE (**well regulated** when postpositive) (of a business, military outfit, routine, etc.) controlled or supervised to conform to rules, regulations, tradition, etc.: *a well-regulated militia.*

well-rehearsed ADJECTIVE (**well rehearsed** when postpositive) (of a play, speech, excuse, etc.) sufficiently practised or prepared in advance to ensure a good performance.

well-remembered ADJECTIVE (**well remembered** when postpositive) recalled or having been recalled with affection, nostalgia, or vividness.

well-represented ADJECTIVE (**well represented** when postpositive) having good or sufficient representation.

well-respected ADJECTIVE (**well respected** when postpositive) held in high respect; esteemed.

well-rounded ADJECTIVE (**well rounded** when postpositive) [1] rounded in shape or well developed: *a well-rounded figure.* [2] full, varied, and satisfying: *a well-rounded life.* [3] well planned and balanced: *a well-rounded programme.*

Wells (wɛlz) NOUN a city in SW England, in Somerset: 12th-century cathedral. Pop.: 9763 (1991).

well-satisfied ADJECTIVE (**well satisfied** when postpositive) fully convinced of or happy.

well-schooled ADJECTIVE (**well schooled** when postpositive) having been trained or educated sufficiently, as in a school: *well-schooled ponies.*

well-seasoned ADJECTIVE (**well seasoned** when postpositive) [1] (of food) flavoured pleasantly or generously with herbs, salt, pepper, or spices. [2] (of timber) prepared and dried skilfully or thoroughly. [3] (of a person) matured or experienced.

well-secured ADJECTIVE (**well secured** when postpositive) having been made fast or firm: *well secured with steel brackets.*

well-set ADJECTIVE (**well set** when postpositive) [1] firmly established. [2] (of a person) strongly built.

well-shaped ADJECTIVE (**well shaped** when postpositive) (of physical attributes) having a good shape aesthetically or for a certain function: *her well-shaped teeth.*

well-situated ADJECTIVE (**well situated** when postpositive) [1] having a good position or site: *a well-situated airport.* [2] in a good position or situation to carry something out: *he was well situated as president.* [3] having sufficient funds; well-off.

well-spent ADJECTIVE (**well spent** when postpositive) (of time or money) usefully or profitably spent or expended.

well-spoken ADJECTIVE (**well spoken** when postpositive) [1] having a clear, articulate, and socially acceptable accent and way of speaking. [2] spoken satisfactorily or pleasingly.

wellspring (ˈwɛlˌsprɪŋ) NOUN [1] the source of a spring or stream; fountainhead. [2] a source of continual or abundant supply.
▷HISTORY Old English *welspryng, wylspring;* see WELL[2], SPRING

well-stacked ADJECTIVE (**well stacked** when postpositive) *Brit slang* (of a woman) of voluptuous proportions.

well-stocked ADJECTIVE (**well stocked** when postpositive) having or containing sufficient goods, wares, food, etc.

well-suited ADJECTIVE (**well suited** when postpositive) [1] appropriate for a particular purpose. [2] (of two people) likely to have a successful relationship.

well-supplied ADJECTIVE (**well supplied** when postpositive) provided or furnished with a sufficient amount.

well-supported ADJECTIVE (**well supported** when postpositive) [1] having good physical support: *a sofa in which your back is well supported.* [2] having a lot of support or encouragement: *friendly matches were less well supported.* [3] substantially upheld by evidence or facts: *many well-supported theories.*

well sweep NOUN a device for raising buckets from and lowering them into a well, consisting of a long pivoted pole, the bucket being attached to one end by a long rope.

well-taught ADJECTIVE (**well taught** when postpositive) having been shown, tutored, or instructed in a successful manner.

well-tempered ADJECTIVE (**well tempered** when postpositive) (of a musical scale or instrument) conforming to the system of equal temperament. See **temperament** (sense 4).

well-thought-of ADJECTIVE (**well thought of** when postpositive) having a good reputation; respected.

well-thought-out ADJECTIVE (**well thought out** when postpositive) carefully planned.

well-thumbed ADJECTIVE (**well thumbed** when postpositive) (of a copy of a book) having the pages marked from frequent turning.

well-timed ADJECTIVE (**well timed** when postpositive) happening or scheduled to happen at an appropriate or suitable time.

well-to-do ADJECTIVE moderately wealthy.

well-trained ADJECTIVE (**well trained** when postpositive) having gained satisfactory training.

well-travelled ADJECTIVE (**well travelled** when postpositive) having travelled far and wide.

well-treated ADJECTIVE (**well treated** when postpositive) not subjected to threats, harm, or other bad treatment: *hostages were well treated.*

well-tried ADJECTIVE (**well tried** when postpositive) repeatedly and exhaustively attempted or tried.

well-trodden ADJECTIVE (**well trodden** when

postpositive) (of a path, route, etc.) much frequented or used by walkers, travellers, etc.

well-turned ADJECTIVE (**well turned** when postpositive) 1 (of a phrase, speech, etc.) apt and pleasingly sonorous. 2 having a pleasing shape: *a well-turned leg.*

well-understood ADJECTIVE (**well understood** when postpositive) widely or sufficiently understood or comprehended.

well-upholstered ADJECTIVE (**well upholstered** when postpositive) *Informal* (of a person) fat.

well-used ADJECTIVE (**well used** when postpositive) used or employed often or for a long time; well-worn.

well-versed ADJECTIVE (**well versed** when postpositive) comprehensively knowledgeable (about), acquainted (with), or skilled (in).

well-wisher NOUN a person who shows benevolence or sympathy towards a person, cause, etc.
▸ **'well-,wishing** ADJECTIVE, NOUN

well-woman NOUN, *plural* **-women.** *Social welfare* **a** a woman who, although not ill, attends a health-service clinic for preventive monitoring, health education, and advice. **b** (*as modifier*): *well-woman clinic.*

well-wooded ADJECTIVE (**well wooded** when postpositive) having abundant trees, shrubs, grasses, etc: *a well-wooded escarpment.*

well-worn ADJECTIVE (**well worn** when postpositive) 1 so much used as to be affected by wear: *a well-worn coat.* 2 used too often; hackneyed: *a well-worn phrase.*

well-written ADJECTIVE (**well written** when postpositive) composed in a competent, and often entertaining, style.

well-wrought ADJECTIVE (**well wrought** when postpositive) shaped, formed, or decorated with skill.

welly ('wɛlɪ) NOUN 1 (*plural* **-lies**) *Informal* Also called: **welly boot.** a Wellington boot. 2 *Slang* energy, concentration, or commitment (esp in the phrase **give it some welly**).

Wels (*German* vɛls) NOUN an industrial city in N central Austria, in Upper Austria. Pop.: 52 594 (1991).

Welsbach burner ('wɛlzbæk; *German* 'vɛlsbax) NOUN *Trademark* a type of gaslight in which a mantle containing thorium and cerium compounds becomes incandescent when heated by a gas flame.
▹**HISTORY** C19: named after Carl Auer, Baron von *Welsbach* (1858–1929), Austrian chemist, who invented it

welsh *or* **welch** (wɛlʃ) VERB (*intr;* often foll by *on*) *Slang* 1 to fail to pay a gambling debt. 2 to fail to fulfil an obligation.
▹**HISTORY** C19: of unknown origin
▸ **'welsher** *or* **'welcher** NOUN

Welsh[1] (wɛlʃ) ADJECTIVE 1 of, relating to, or characteristic of Wales, its people, their Celtic language, or their dialect of English. ◆ NOUN 2 a language of Wales, belonging to the S Celtic branch of the Indo-European family. Welsh shows considerable diversity between dialects. 3 **the Welsh.** (*functioning as plural*) the natives or inhabitants of Wales collectively. ◆ Also (rare): **Welch.**
▹**HISTORY** Old English *Wēlisc, Wǣlisc;* related to *wealh* foreigner, Old High German *walahisc* (German *welsch*), Old Norse *valskr,* Latin *Volcae*

Welsh[2] (wɛlʃ) NOUN a white long-bodied lop-eared breed of pig, kept chiefly for bacon.

Welsh Black NOUN a breed of black cattle originally from N Wales that are bred for both meat and milk.

Welsh corgi NOUN another name for **corgi.**

Welsh dresser NOUN a sideboard with drawers and cupboards below and open shelves above.

Welsh harp NOUN a type of harp in which the strings are arranged in three rows, used esp for the accompaniment of singing, improvisation on folk tunes, etc.

Welshman ('wɛlʃmən) *or feminine* **Welshwoman** NOUN, *plural* **-men** *or* **-women.** a native or inhabitant of Wales.

Welshman's button NOUN an angler's name for a species of caddis fly, *Sericostoma personatum.*

Welsh Mountain NOUN a common breed of small hardy sheep kept mainly in the mountains of Wales.

Welsh mountain pony NOUN a small sturdy but graceful breed of pony used mostly for riding, originally from Wales.

Welsh poppy NOUN a perennial W European papaveraceous plant, *Meconopsis cambrica,* with large yellow flowers.

Welsh rabbit NOUN a savoury dish consisting of melted cheese sometimes mixed with milk, seasonings, etc., on hot buttered toast. Also called: **Welsh rarebit, rarebit.**
▹**HISTORY** C18: a fanciful coinage; *rarebit* is a later folk-etymological variant

Welsh springer spaniel NOUN See **springer spaniel.**

Welsh terrier NOUN a wire-haired breed of terrier with a black-and-tan coat.

welt (wɛlt) NOUN 1 a raised or strengthened seam or edge, sewn in or on a knitted garment. 2 another word for **weal**[1]. 3 (in shoemaking) a strip of leather, etc., put in between the outer sole and the inner sole and upper. ◆ VERB (*tr*) 4 to put a welt in (a garment, etc.). 5 to beat or flog soundly.
▹**HISTORY** C15: origin unknown

Weltanschauung *German* ('vɛltanʃauuŋ) NOUN a comprehensive view or personal philosophy of human life and the universe.
▹**HISTORY** from *Welt* world + *Anschauung* view

welter ('wɛltə) VERB (*intr*) 1 to roll about, writhe, or wallow. 2 (esp of the sea) to surge, heave, or toss. 3 to lie drenched in a liquid, esp blood. ◆ NOUN 4 a rolling motion, as of the sea. 5 a confused mass; jumble.
▹**HISTORY** C13: from Middle Low German, Middle Dutch *weltern;* related to Old High German *walzan, welzen* to roll

welterweight ('wɛltə,weɪt) NOUN 1 **a** a professional boxer weighing 140–147 pounds (63.5–66.5 kg). **b** an amateur boxer weighing 63.5–67 kg (140–148 pounds). **c** (*as modifier*): *a great welterweight era.* 2 a wrestler in a similar weight category (usually 154–172 pounds (70–78 kg)).

Weltpolitik *German* ('vɛltpoliti:k) NOUN the policy of participation in world affairs.
▹**HISTORY** literally: world politics

Weltschmerz *German* ('vɛltʃmɛrts) NOUN sadness or melancholy at the evils of the world; world-weariness.
▹**HISTORY** literally: world pain

welwitschia (wɛl'wɪtʃɪə) NOUN a gymnosperm plant, *Welwitschia mirabilis,* of the Namib Desert in SW Africa, consisting of two large woody leaves lying on the ground with a conelike structure arising between them: phylum *Gnetophyta.*
▹**HISTORY** C19: named after F. M. J. *Welwitsch* (1807–72), Portuguese botanist, born in Austria

Welwyn Garden City ('wɛlɪn) NOUN a town in SE England, in Hertfordshire: established (1920) as a planned industrial and residential community. Pop.: 42 087 (1991).

Wembley ('wɛmblɪ) NOUN part of the Greater London borough of Brent: site of the English national soccer stadium.

wen[1] (wɛn) NOUN 1 *Pathol* a sebaceous cyst, esp one occurring on the scalp. 2 a large overcrowded city (esp London in the phrase **the great wen**).
▹**HISTORY** Old English *wenn;* related to Danish dialect *van, væne,* Dutch *wenn*

wen[2] (wɛn) NOUN a rune having the sound of Modern English *w.*
▹**HISTORY** Old English *wen, wyn*

wench (wɛntʃ) NOUN 1 a girl or young woman, esp a buxom or lively one: now used facetiously. 2 *Archaic* a female servant. 3 *Archaic* a prostitute. ◆ VERB (*intr*) 4 *Archaic* to frequent the company of prostitutes.
▹**HISTORY** Old English *wencel* child, from *wancol* weak; related to Old High German *wanchal, wankōn*
▸ **'wencher** NOUN

wend (wɛnd) VERB to direct (one's course or way); travel.
▹**HISTORY** Old English *wendan;* related to Old High German *wenten,* Gothic *wandjan;* see WIND[2]

Wend (wɛnd) NOUN (esp in medieval European history) a Sorb; a member of the Slavonic people who inhabited the area between the Rivers Saale and Oder in the early Middle Ages and were conquered by Germanic invaders by the 12th century. See also **Lusatia.**

wendigo ('wɛndɪ,gəʊ) *or* **windigo** ('wɪndɪ,gəʊ) NOUN *Canadian* 1 (*plural* **-gos**) (among Algonquian Indians) an evil spirit or cannibal. 2 (*plural* **-go** *or* **-gos**) another name for **splake.**
▹**HISTORY** from Algonquian: evil spirit or cannibal

Wendish ('wɛndɪʃ) ADJECTIVE 1 of or relating to the Wends. ◆ NOUN 2 the West Slavonic language of the Wends. See also **Sorbian.**

Wendy house ('wɛndɪ) NOUN a small model house that children can enter and play in.
▹**HISTORY** C20: named after the house built for *Wendy,* the girl in J. M. Barrie's play *Peter Pan* (1904)

wensleydale ('wɛnzlɪ,deɪl) NOUN 1 a type of white cheese with a flaky texture. 2 a breed of sheep with long woolly fleece.
▹**HISTORY** named after *Wensleydale,* North Yorkshire

went (wɛnt) VERB the past tense of **go.**

wentletrap ('wɛntᵊl,træp) NOUN any marine gastropod mollusc of the family *Epitoniidae,* having a long pointed pale-coloured longitudinally ridged shell.
▹**HISTORY** C18: from Dutch *winteltrap* spiral shell, from *wintel,* earlier *windel,* from *wenden* to wind + *trap* a step, stairs

Wentworth scale NOUN *Geology* a scale for specifying the sizes (diameters) of sedimentary particles, ranging from clay particles (less than 1/256 mm) to boulders (over 256 mm).
▹**HISTORY** after C. K. *Wentworth* (1891–1969), US geologist

Wenzhou, Wen-chou, *or* **Wenchow** ('wɛn'tʃu:) NOUN a port in SE China, in Zhejiang province: noted for its historic buildings. Pop.: 512 523 (1999 est.).

wept (wɛpt) VERB the past tense and past participle of **weep.**

were (wɜ:; *unstressed* wə) VERB the plural form of the past tense (indicative mood) of **be** and the singular form used with *you.* It is also used as a subjunctive, esp in conditional sentences.
▹**HISTORY** Old English *wērun, wǣron* past tense plural of *wesan* to be; related to Old Norse *vera,* Old Frisian *weria,* Old High German *werōn* to last

> **Language note** *Were,* as a remnant of the past subjunctive in English, is used in formal contexts in clauses expressing hypotheses (*if he were to die, she would inherit everything*), suppositions contrary to fact (*if I were you, I would be careful*), and desire (*I wish he were there now*). In informal speech, however, *was* is often used instead.

we're (wɪə) CONTRACTION OF we are.

weren't (wɜ:nt) VERB CONTRACTION OF were not.

werewolf ('wɪə,wʊlf, 'wɛə-) NOUN, *plural* **-wolves.** a person fabled in folklore and superstition to have been changed into a wolf by being bewitched or said to be able to assume wolf form at will.
▹**HISTORY** Old English *werewulf,* from *wer* man + *wulf* WOLF; related to Old High German *werwolf,* Middle Dutch *weerwolf*

wergild, weregild ('wɜ:,gɪld, 'wɛə-), *or* **wergeld** ('wɜ:,gɛld, 'wɛə-) NOUN the price set on a man's life in successive Anglo-Saxon and Germanic law codes, to be paid as compensation by his slayer.
▹**HISTORY** Old English *wergeld,* from *wer* man (related to Old Norse *ver,* Latin *vir*) + *gield* tribute (related to Gothic *gild,* Old High German *gelt* payment); see YIELD

wernerite ('wɜ:nə,raɪt) NOUN another name for **scapolite.**
▹**HISTORY** C19: named after Abraham Gottlieb *Werner* (1749–1817), German geologist

wero ('wɜ:rəʊ) NOUN *NZ* the challenge made by an armed Maori warrior to a visitor to a marae.
▹**HISTORY** Maori

werris ('wɛrɪs) NOUN *Austral* a slang word for **urination.**
▹**HISTORY** shortened from *Werris Creek,* rhyming slang for LEAK meaning urination

wersh (wɜːʃ; *Scot* wɛrʃ) ADJECTIVE *Scot* [1] tasteless; insipid. [2] sour; bitter.
▷HISTORY C16: perhaps alteration of dialect *wearish,* probably of Germanic origin

wert (wɜːt; *unstressed* wət) VERB *Archaic or dialect* (used with the pronoun *thou* or its relative equivalent) a singular form of the past tense (indicative mood) of **be.**

Wesak (wɛsʌk) NOUN *Buddhism* a festival in May celebrating the birth, enlightenment, and death of the Buddha.
▷HISTORY Sinhalese

Weser (*German* 'veːzər) NOUN a river in NW Germany: flows northwest to the North Sea at Bremerhaven and is linked by the Mittelland Canal to the Ems, Rhine, and Elbe waterways. Length: 477 km (196 miles).

Wesermünde (*German* veːzər'myndə) NOUN the former name (until 1947) of **Bremerhaven.**

weskit ('wɛskɪt) NOUN an informal word for **waistcoat.**

Wesleyan ('wɛzlɪən) ADJECTIVE [1] of, relating to, or deriving from John Wesley, the English preacher and founder of Methodism (1703–91). [2] of, relating to, or characterizing Methodism, esp in its original form or as upheld by the branch of the Methodist Church known as the **Wesleyan Methodists.** ◆ NOUN [3] a follower of John Wesley. [4] a member of the Methodist Church or (formerly) of the Wesleyan Methodists.
▸**'Wesleyanism** NOUN

Wessex ('wɛsɪks) NOUN [1] an Anglo-Saxon kingdom in S and SW England that became the most powerful English kingdom by the 10th century A.D. [2] **a** (in Thomas Hardy's works) the southwestern counties of England, esp Dorset. **b** (*as modifier*): *Wessex Poems.*

Wessi ('vɛsɪ; *German* 'vɛsi) NOUN *Informal* a native, inhabitant, or citizen of that part of Germany that was formerly West Germany.
▷HISTORY C20: from German *westdeutsch* West German

west (wɛst) NOUN [1] one of the four cardinal points of the compass, 270° clockwise from north and 180° from east. [2] the direction along a parallel towards the sunset, at 270° clockwise from north. [3] **the west.** (*often capital*) any area lying in or towards the west. Related adjectives: **Hesperian, Occidental.** [4] *Cards* (*usually capital*) the player or position at the table corresponding to west on the compass. ◆ ADJECTIVE [5] situated in, moving towards, or facing the west. [6] (esp of the wind) from the west. ◆ ADVERB [7] in, to, or towards the west. [8] *Archaic* (of the wind) from the west. [9] **go west.** *Informal* **a** to be lost or destroyed irrevocably. **b** to die. ◆ Symbol: W.
▷HISTORY Old English; related to Old Norse *vestr,* Sanskrit *avástāt,* Latin *vesper* evening, Greek *hésperos*

West (wɛst) NOUN **the.** [1] the western part of the world contrasted historically and culturally with the East or Orient; the Occident. [2] (formerly) the non-Communist countries of Europe and America contrasted with the Communist states of the East. Compare **East** (sense 2). [3] (in the US) **a** that part of the US lying approximately to the west of the Mississippi. **b** (during the Colonial period) the region outside the 13 colonies, lying mainly to the west of the Alleghenies. [4] (in the ancient and medieval world) the Western Roman Empire and, later, the Holy Roman Empire. ◆ ADJECTIVE [5] **a** of or denoting the western part of a specified country, area, etc. **b** (*as part of a name*): *the West Coast.*

West Atlantic NOUN [1] the W part of the Atlantic Ocean, esp the N Atlantic around North America. [2] a branch of the Niger-Congo family of African languages, spoken in Senegal and in scattered areas eastwards, including Fulani and Wolof. ◆ ADJECTIVE [3] relating to or belonging to this group of languages.

West Bank NOUN **the.** an autonomous Palestinian region in the Middle East on the W bank of the River Jordan, comprising the hills of Judaea and Samaria and part of Jerusalem: formerly part of Palestine: became part of Jordan after the ceasefire of 1949: occupied by Israel since the 1967 Arab-Israeli War. In 1993 a peace treaty between Israel and the Palestinian Liberation Organization provided for the West Bank to become a self-governing Palestinian area; a new Palestinian National Authority assumed control of parts of the territory in 1994–95, but subsequent talks broke down and Israel reoccupied much of this in 2001–02. Pop.: 1 949 000 (2000 est.). Area: 5879 sq. km (2270 sq. miles).

West Bengal NOUN a state of E India, on the Bay of Bengal: formed in 1947 from the Hindu area of Bengal; additional territories added in 1950 (Cooch Behar), 1954 (Chandernagor), and 1956 (part of Bihar); mostly low-lying and crossed by the Hooghly River. Capital: Calcutta. Pop.: 80 221 171 (2001). Area: 88 752 sq. km (34 260 sq. miles).

West Berkshire NOUN a unitary authority in S England, in Berkshire. Pop.: 144 445 (2001). Area: 705 sq. km (272 sq. miles).

West Berlin NOUN (formerly) the part of Berlin under US, British, and French control.
▸**West Berliner** NOUN

West Berliner NOUN a native or inhabitant of the part of Berlin formerly under US, British, and French control.

westbound ('wɛst,baʊnd) ADJECTIVE going or leading towards the west.

West Bromwich ('brɒmɪdʒ, -ɪtʃ) NOUN a town in central England, in Sandwell unitary authority, West Midlands: industrial centre. Pop.: 146 386 (1991).

west by north NOUN [1] one point on the compass north of west, 281° 15′ clockwise from north. ◆ ADJECTIVE, ADVERB [2] in, from, or towards this direction.

west by south NOUN [1] one point on the compass south of west, 258° 45′ clockwise from north. ◆ ADJECTIVE, ADVERB [2] in, from, or towards this direction.

West Coast jazz NOUN a type of cool jazz displaying a soft intimate sound, regular rhythms, and a tendency to incorporate academic classical devices into jazz, such as fugue.

West Country NOUN **the.** the southwest of England, esp Cornwall, Devon, and Somerset.

West Dunbartonshire NOUN a council area of W central Scotland, on Loch Lomond and the Clyde estuary: corresponds to part of the historical county of Dunbartonshire; part of Strathclyde Region from 1975 to 1996: engineering industries. Administrative centre: Dumbarton. Pop.: 93 378 (2001). Area: 162 sq. km (63 sq. miles).

West End NOUN **the.** a part of W central London containing the main shopping and entertainment areas.

wester ('wɛstə) VERB [1] (*intr*) (of the sun, moon, or a star) to move or appear to move towards the west. ◆ NOUN [2] a strong wind or storm from the west.

westering ('wɛstərɪŋ) ADJECTIVE *Poetic* moving towards the west: *the westering star.*

Westerlies ('wɛstəlɪz) PLURAL NOUN *Meteorol* the prevailing winds blowing from the west on the poleward sides of the horse latitudes, often bringing depressions and anticyclones.

westerly ('wɛstəlɪ) ADJECTIVE [1] of, relating to, or situated in the west. ◆ ADVERB, ADJECTIVE [2] towards or in the direction of the west. [3] (esp of the wind) from the west. ◆ NOUN, *plural* **-lies.** [4] a wind blowing from the west.
▸**'westerliness** NOUN

western ('wɛstən) ADJECTIVE [1] situated in or towards or facing the west. [2] going or directed to or towards the west. [3] (of a wind, etc.) coming or originating from the west. [4] native to, inhabiting, or growing in the west. [5] *Music* See **country and western.**

Western ('wɛstən) ADJECTIVE [1] of, relating to, or characteristic of the West as opposed to the Orient. [2] (formerly) of, relating to, or characteristic of the Americas and the parts of Europe not under Communist rule. [3] of, relating to, or characteristic of the western states of the US. ◆ NOUN [4] a film, book, etc., concerned with life in the western states of the US, esp during the era of exploration and early development.

Western Australia NOUN a state of W Australia: mostly an arid undulating plateau, with the Great Sandy Desert, Gibson Desert, and Great Victoria Desert in the interior; settlement concentrated in the southwest; rich mineral resources. Capital: Perth. Pop.: 1 861 020 (1999 est.). Area: 2 527 636 sq. km (975 920 sq. miles).

Western Cape NOUN a province of W South Africa, created in 1994 from the SW part of Cape Province: agriculture (esp fruit), wine making, fishing, various industries in Cape Town. Capital: Cape Town. Pop.: 4 170 970 (1999 est.). Area: 129 370 sq. km (49 950 sq. miles). Also called: **Western Province.**

Western Church NOUN [1] the part of Christendom that derives its liturgy, discipline, and traditions principally from the patriarchate of Rome, as contrasted with the part that derives these from the other ancient patriarchates, esp that of Constantinople. [2] the Roman Catholic Church, sometimes together with the Anglican Communion of Churches.

westerner ('wɛstənə) NOUN (*sometimes capital*) a native or inhabitant of the west of any specific region, esp of the western states of the US or of the western hemisphere.

Western Ghats PLURAL NOUN a mountain range in W peninsular India, parallel to the Malabar coast of the Arabian Sea. Highest peak: Anai Mudi, 2695 m (8841 ft.).

western hemisphere NOUN (*often capitals*) [1] that half of the globe containing the Americas, lying to the west of the Greenwich or another meridian. [2] the lands contained in this, esp the Americas.

western hemlock NOUN a North American coniferous evergreen tree, *Tsuga heterophylla,* having hanging branches and oblong cones: family *Pinaceae.*

Western Isles NOUN (*functioning as singular or plural*) [1] an island authority in W Scotland, consisting of the Outer Hebrides; created in 1975. Administrative centre: Stornoway. Pop.: 26 502 (2001). Area: 2900 sq. km (1120 sq. miles). Gaelic name: **Eileen Siar.** [2] Also called: **Western Islands.** another name for the **Hebrides.**

Western Isles pony NOUN a breed of large pony, typically grey, with a dense waterproof coat. The only surviving variety is the Eriskay pony.

westernism ('wɛstə,nɪzəm) NOUN a word, habit, practice, etc., characteristic of western people or of the American West.

westernize *or* **westernise** ('wɛstə,naɪz) VERB (*tr*) to influence or make familiar with the customs, practices, etc., of the West.
▸**,westerni'zation** *or* **,westerni'sation** NOUN

western larch NOUN a North American larch, *Larix occidentalis,* having oval cones and found mainly in S British Columbia.

westernmost ('wɛstən,məʊst) ADJECTIVE situated or occurring farthest west.

Western Ocean NOUN (formerly) another name for the **Atlantic Ocean.**

Western Province NOUN another name for **Western Cape.**

western red cedar NOUN [1] a large North American arbor vitae, *Thuja plicata,* found along and near the Pacific coast. [2] the wood of this tree, used by North American Indians for building and for carving totem poles.

western roll NOUN a technique in high-jumping in which the jumper executes a half-turn of the body to clear the bar.

Western Roman Empire NOUN the westernmost of the two empires created by the division of the later Roman Empire, esp after its final severance from the Eastern Roman Empire (395 A.D.). Also called: **Western Empire.**

Western Sahara NOUN a disputed region of NW Africa, on the Atlantic: mainly desert; rich phosphate deposits; a Spanish overseas province from 1958 to 1975; partitioned in 1976 between Morocco and Mauritania who faced growing resistance from the Polisario Front, an organization aiming for the independence of the region as the Democratic Saharan Arab Republic. Mauritania renounced its claim in 1979 and it was taken over by Morocco. Polisario agreed to a UN-brokered cease-fire in 1991 but attempts to settle the status of the region have failed. Pop.: 288 000 (1998 est.). Area: 266 000 sq. km (102 680 sq. miles). Former name (until 1975): **Spanish Sahara.**

Western Samoa NOUN See **Samoa** (sense 1).

western swing NOUN a 1930s jazz-influenced style of country music.

Western Wall NOUN *Judaism* a wall in Jerusalem, the last extant part of the Temple of Herod, held sacred by Jews as a place of prayer and pilgrimage. Also called: **Wailing Wall.**

Westfalen (vɛst'fa:lən) NOUN the German name for **Westphalia.**

West Flanders NOUN a province of W Belgium: the country's chief agricultural province. Capital: Bruges. Pop.: 1 128 774 (2000 est.). Area: 3132 sq. km (1209 sq. miles).

West German ADJECTIVE 1 of or relating to the former republic of West Germany (now part of Germany) or its inhabitants. ◆ NOUN 2 a native or inhabitant of the former West Germany.

West Germanic NOUN a subbranch of the Germanic languages that consists of English, Frisian, Dutch, Flemish, Afrikaans, Low German, German, Yiddish, and their associated dialects.

West Germany NOUN a former republic in N central Europe, on the North Sea: established in 1949 from the zones of Germany occupied by the British, Americans, and French after the defeat of Nazi Germany; a member of the European Community; reunited with East Germany in 1990. Official name: **Federal Republic of Germany.** See also **Germany.**

West Glamorgan NOUN a former county in S Wales, formed in 1974 from part of Glamorgan and the county borough of Swansea: replaced in 1996 by the county of Swansea and the county borough of Neath Port Talbot.

West Highland white terrier NOUN a small pure white terrier having a hard straight coat and erect ears and tail.

West Indian ADJECTIVE 1 of or relating to the West Indies, its inhabitants, or their language or culture. 2 native to or derived from the West Indies. ◆ NOUN 3 a native or inhabitant of the West Indies. 4 a person of West Indian descent.

West Indies ('ɪndɪz) PLURAL NOUN an archipelago off Central America, extending over 2400 km (1500 miles) in an arc from the peninsula of Florida to Venezuela, separating the Caribbean Sea from the Atlantic Ocean: consists of the Greater Antilles, the Lesser Antilles, and the Bahamas; largest island is Cuba. Area: over 235 000 sq. km (91 000 sq. miles). Also called: **the Caribbean.**

westing ('wɛstɪŋ) NOUN *Navigation* movement, deviation, or distance covered in a westerly direction, esp as expressed in the resulting difference in longitude.

Westinghouse brake ('wɛstɪŋˌhaʊs) NOUN a braking system, invented by Westinghouse in 1872 and adopted by US railways, in which the brakes are held off by compressed air in the operating cylinder: controlled leakage of the air or a disruptive emergency causes the brakes to be applied. The system is used on most heavy vehicles and is replacing the vacuum system on many railways.
▷HISTORY named after George *Westinghouse* (1846–1914), US inventor and manufacturer

West Irian NOUN the English name for **Irian Jaya.**

West Lothian NOUN a council area and historical county of central Scotland, on the Firth of Forth: became part of Lothian region in 1975: reinstated as an independent authority (with revised boundaries) in 1996: agriculture, oil-refining. Administrative centre: Livingston. Pop.: 158 714 (1996 est.). Area: 425 sq. km (164 sq. miles).

Westm. ABBREVIATION FOR Westminster.

Westmeath (ˌwest'mi:ð) NOUN a county of N central Republic of Ireland, in Leinster province: mostly low-lying, with many lakes and bogs. County town: Mullingar. Pop.: 63 314 (1996). Area: 1764 sq. km (681 sq. miles).

West Midlands NOUN (*functioning as singular or plural*) a metropolitan county of central England, administered since 1986 by the unitary authorities of Wolverhampton, Walsall, Dudley, Sandwell, Birmingham, Solihull, and Coventry. Area: 899 sq. km (347 sq. miles).

Westminster ('wɛstˌmɪnstə) NOUN 1 Also called: **City of Westminster.** a borough of Greater London, on the River Thames: contains the Houses of Parliament, Westminster Abbey, and Buckingham Palace. Pop.: 181 279 (2001). Area: 22 sq. km (8 sq. miles). 2 the Houses of Parliament at Westminster.

Westminster Abbey NOUN a Gothic church in London: site of a Benedictine monastery (1050–65); scene of the coronations of almost all English monarchs since William I.

Westmorland ('wɛstmələnd, 'wɛsmə-) NOUN (until 1974) a county of NW England, now part of Cumbria.

West Nile fever NOUN a viral disease, caused by a flavivirus and spread by a mosquito (*Culex pipiens*), that results in encephalitis.

west-northwest NOUN 1 the point on the compass or the direction midway between west and northwest, 292° 30′ clockwise from north. ◆ ADJECTIVE, ADVERB 2 in, from, or towards this direction. ◆ Symbol: WNW.

Weston standard cell ('wɛstən) NOUN a primary cell used as a standard of emf, producing 1.018636 volts: consists of a mercury anode and a cadmium amalgam cathode in an electrolyte of saturated cadmium sulphate. Former name: **cadmium cell.**
▷HISTORY C20: from a trademark

Weston-super-Mare ('wɛstənˌsu:pə'mɛə, -ˌsju:-) NOUN a town and resort in SW England, in North Somerset unitary authority, Somerset, on the Bristol Channel. Pop.: 69 372 (1991).

West Pakistan NOUN the former name (until the end of 1971) of **Pakistan.**

Westphalia (wɛst'feɪlɪə) NOUN a historic region of NW Germany, now mostly in the state of North Rhine-Westphalia. German name: **Westfalen.**

Westphalian (wɛst'feɪlɪən) ADJECTIVE 1 of or relating to the historic German region of Westphalia or its inhabitants. ◆ NOUN 2 a native or inhabitant of Westphalia.

West Point NOUN the US Army installation in New York State that houses the US Military Academy.

West Prussia NOUN a former province of NE Prussia, on the Baltic: assigned to Poland in 1945. German name: **Westpreussen** ('vɛstprɔysən).

West Riding NOUN (until 1974) an administrative division of Yorkshire, now part of West Yorkshire, North Yorkshire, Cumbria, and Lancashire.

West Saxon (in Anglo-Saxon England) ADJECTIVE 1 of or relating to Wessex, its inhabitants, or their dialect. ◆ NOUN 2 the dialect of Old English spoken in Wessex: the chief literary dialect of Old English. See also **Anglian, Kentish.** 3 an inhabitant of Wessex.

west-southwest NOUN 1 the point on the compass or the direction midway between southwest and west, 247° 30′ clockwise from north. ◆ ADJECTIVE, ADVERB 2 in, from, or towards this direction. ◆ Symbol: WSW.

West Sussex NOUN a county of SE England, comprising part of the former county of Sussex: mainly low-lying, with the South Downs in the S. Administrative centre: Chichester. Pop.: 753 612 (2001). Area: 1989 sq. km (768 sq. miles).

West Virginia NOUN a state of the eastern US: part of Virginia until the outbreak of the American Civil War (1861); consists chiefly of the Allegheny Plateau; bounded on the west by the Ohio River; coal-mining. Capital: Charleston. Pop.: 1 808 344 (1997 est.). Area: 62 341 sq. km (24 070 sq. miles). Abbreviations: **W. Va,** (with zip code) **WV.**

West Virginian ADJECTIVE 1 of or relating to the state of West Virginia or its inhabitants. ◆ NOUN 2 a native or inhabitant of West Virginia.

westward ('wɛstwəd) ADJECTIVE 1 moving, facing, or situated in the west. ◆ ADVERB 2 Also: **westwards.** towards the west. ◆ NOUN 3 the westward part, direction, etc.; the west.
▸ **'westwardly** ADJECTIVE, ADVERB

West Yorkshire NOUN a metropolitan county of N England, administered since 1986 by the unitary authorities of Bradford, Leeds, Calderdale, Kirklees, and Wakefield. Area: 2039 sq. km (787 sq. miles).

wet (wet) ADJECTIVE **wetter, wettest.** 1 moistened, covered, saturated, etc., with water or some other liquid. 2 not yet dry or solid: *wet varnish.* 3 rainy, foggy, misty, or humid: *wet weather.* 4 employing a liquid, usually water: *a wet method of chemical analysis.* 5 *Chiefly US and Canadian* characterized by or permitting the free sale of alcoholic beverages: *a wet state.* 6 *Brit informal* feeble or foolish. 7 **wet behind the ears.** *Informal* immature or inexperienced; naive. ◆ NOUN 8 wetness or moisture. 9 damp or rainy weather. 10 *Brit informal* a Conservative politician who is considered not to be a hard-liner. Compare **dry** (sense 21). 11 *Brit informal* a feeble or foolish person. 12 *Chiefly US and Canadian* a person who advocates free sale of alcoholic beverages. 13 **the wet.** *Austral* (in northern and central Australia) the rainy season. ◆ VERB **wets, wetting, wet** *or* **wetted.** 14 to make or become wet. 15 to urinate on (something). 16 (*tr*) *Dialect* to prepare (tea) by boiling or infusing. 17 **wet one's whistle.** *Informal* to take an alcoholic drink.
▷HISTORY Old English *wǣt;* related to Old Frisian *wēt,* Old Norse *vātr,* Old Slavonic *vedro* bucket
▸ **'wetly** ADVERB ▸ **'wetness** NOUN ▸ **ˌwetta'bility** NOUN ▸ **'wettable** ADJECTIVE ▸ **'wetter** NOUN ▸ **'wettish** ADJECTIVE

weta ('wɛtə) NOUN any of various wingless insects of the family *Stenopelmatidae* of New Zealand, with long spiny legs.
▷HISTORY Maori

wet-and-dry-bulb thermometer NOUN another name for **psychrometer.**

wetback ('wetˌbæk) NOUN *US informal* a Mexican labourer who enters the US illegally.

wet blanket NOUN *Informal* a person whose low spirits or lack of enthusiasm have a depressing effect on others.

wet-bulb thermometer NOUN a thermometer the bulb of which is covered by a moist muslin bag, used together with a dry-bulb thermometer to measure humidity.

wet cell NOUN a primary cell in which the electrolyte is a liquid. Compare **dry cell.**

wet dream NOUN an erotic dream accompanied by an emission of semen during or just after sleep.

wet fish NOUN **a** fresh fish as opposed to frozen or cooked fish. **b** (*as modifier*): *a wet-fish shop.*

wet fly NOUN *Angling* **a** an artificial fly designed to float or ride below the water surface. **b** (*as modifier*): *wet-fly fishing.* ◆ Compare **dry fly.**

wether ('wɛðə) NOUN a male sheep, esp a castrated one.
▷HISTORY Old English *hwæther;* related to Old Frisian *hweder,* Old High German *hwedar,* Old Norse *hvatharr*

wetland ('wɛtlənd) NOUN (*sometimes plural*) **a** an area of swampy or marshy land, esp considered as part of an ecological system. **b** (*as modifier*): *wetland species.*

wet look NOUN a shiny finish given to certain clothing and footwear materials, esp plastic and leather.

wet nurse NOUN 1 a woman hired to suckle the child of another. ◆ VERB **wet-nurse.** (*tr*) 2 to act as a wet nurse to (a child). 3 *Informal* to attend with great devotion.

wet pack NOUN *Med* a hot or cold damp sheet or blanket for wrapping around a patient.

wet rot NOUN 1 a state of decay in timber caused by various fungi, esp *Coniophora puteana.* The hyphal strands of the fungus are seldom visible and affected timber turns dark brown. 2 any of the fungi causing this decay.

wet steam NOUN steam, usually low-pressure, that contains water droplets in suspension.

wet suit NOUN a close-fitting rubber suit used by skin divers, yachtsmen, etc., to retain body heat when they are immersed in water or sailing in cold weather.

Wetterhorn (*German* 'vɛtərˌhɔrn) NOUN a mountain in S Switzerland, in the Bernese Alps. Height: 3701 m (12 143 ft.).

wettie ('wɛtɪ) NOUN *NZ informal* a wetsuit.

wetting agent NOUN *Chem* any substance added to a liquid to lower its surface tension and thus increase its ability to spread across or penetrate into a solid.

WEU ABBREVIATION FOR Western European Union.

we've (wi:v) CONTRACTION OF we have.

Wexford ('wɛksfəd) NOUN 1 a county of SE Republic of Ireland, in Leinster province on the Irish Sea: the first Irish county to be colonized from

England; mostly low-lying and fertile. County town: Wexford. Pop.: 104 371 (1996). Area: 2352 sq. km (908 sq. miles). 2 a port in SE Republic of Ireland, county town of Co. Wexford: sacked by Oliver Cromwell in 1649. Pop.: 9540 (1991).

Weymouth (ˈweɪməθ) NOUN a port and resort in S England, in Dorset on the English Channel: administratively part of the borough of **Weymouth and Melcombe** Regis. Pop. (with Melcombe Regis): 53 235 (1991).

wf ABBREVIATION FOR: 1 **wrong fount.** ◆ 2 THE INTERNET DOMAIN NAME FOR Wallis and Futuna Islands.

WFF *Logic* ABBREVIATION FOR well-formed formula.

WFTU ABBREVIATION FOR World Federation of Trade Unions.

wg *or* **WG** ABBREVIATION FOR: 1 water gauge. 2 wire gauge.

WG INTERNATIONAL CAR REGISTRATION FOR (Windward Islands) Grenada.

wha (hwɔː) *or* **whae** (hwe) PRONOUN a Scot word for **who.**

whack (wæk) VERB *(tr)* 1 to strike with a sharp resounding blow. 2 *(usually passive) Brit informal* to exhaust completely. ◆ NOUN 3 *(tr) US slang* to murder: *if you were out of line you got whacked.* 4 a sharp resounding blow or the noise made by such a blow. 5 *Informal* a share or portion. 6 *Informal* a try or attempt (esp in the phrase **have a whack at**). 7 **out of whack.** *Informal* out of order; unbalanced: *the whole system is out of whack.* ◆ INTERJECTION 8 an exclamation imitating the noise of a sharp resounding blow.
▷HISTORY C18: perhaps a variant of THWACK, ultimately of imitative origin
▸ˈ**whacker** NOUN

whacking (ˈwækɪŋ) *Informal, chiefly Brit* ◆ ADJECTIVE 1 enormous. ◆ ADVERB 2 (intensifier): *a whacking big lie.*

whack off VERB *(intr, adverb) Slang* to masturbate.

whacky (ˈwækɪ) ADJECTIVE **whackier, whackiest.** *US slang* a variant spelling of **wacky.**

whakapapa (ˈhwækəpæpə, ˈfæk-) NOUN *NZ* genealogy; family tree.
▷HISTORY Maori

whale[1] (weɪl) NOUN, *plural* **whales** *or* **whale.** 1 any of the larger cetacean mammals, excluding dolphins, porpoises, and narwhals. They have flippers, a streamlined body, and a horizontally flattened tail and breathe through a blowhole on the top of the head. Related adjective: **cetacean.** 2 any cetacean mammal. See also **toothed whale, whalebone whale.** 3 *Slang* a gambler who has the capacity to win and lose large sums of money in a casino. 4 **a whale of a.** *Informal* an exceptionally large, fine, etc., example of a (person or thing): *we had a whale of a time on holiday.*
▷HISTORY Old English *hwæl;* related to Old Saxon, Old High German *hwal,* Old Norse *hvalr,* Latin *squalus* seapig

whale[2] (weɪl) VERB *(tr)* to beat or thrash soundly.
▷HISTORY C18: variant of WALE[1]

whaleback (ˈweɪlˌbæk) NOUN 1 something shaped like the back of a whale. 2 a steamboat having a curved upper deck.

whaleboat (ˈweɪlˌbəʊt) NOUN a narrow boat from 20 to 30 feet long having a sharp prow and stern, formerly used in whaling. Also called: **whaler.**

whalebone (ˈweɪlˌbəʊn) NOUN 1 Also called: **baleen.** a horny elastic material forming a series of numerous thin plates that hang from the upper jaw on either side of the palate in the toothless (whalebone) whales and strain plankton from water entering the mouth. 2 a thin strip of this substance, used in stiffening corsets, bodices, etc.

whalebone whale NOUN any whale belonging to the cetacean suborder *Mysticeti,* having a double blowhole and strips of whalebone between the jaws instead of teeth: includes the rorquals, right whales, and the blue whale. Compare **toothed whale.**

whale catcher NOUN a vessel engaged in the actual harpooning of whales.

whale oil NOUN oil obtained either from the blubber of whales (train oil) or the head of the sperm whale (sperm oil).

whaler (ˈweɪlə) NOUN 1 Also called (US): **whaleman.** a person employed in whaling. 2 a vessel engaged in whaling. See **factory ship, whale catcher.** 3 another word for **whaleboat.** 4 *Austral* a nomad surviving in the bush without working.

whaler shark NOUN *Austral* a large voracious shark, *Galeolamna macrurus,* of E. Australian waters.

whale shark NOUN a large spotted whalelike shark, *Rhincodon typus,* of warm seas, that feeds on plankton and small animals: family *Rhincodontidae.*

whaling (ˈweɪlɪŋ) NOUN 1 the work or industry of hunting and processing whales for food, oil, etc. ◆ ADVERB 2 *Informal* (intensifier): *a whaling good time.*

wham (wæm) NOUN 1 a forceful blow or impact or the sound produced by such a blow or impact. ◆ INTERJECTION 2 an exclamation imitative of this sound. ◆ VERB **whams, whamming, whammed.** 3 to strike or cause to strike with great force.
▷HISTORY C20: of imitative origin

whammy (ˈwæmɪ) NOUN, *plural* **-mies.** 1 something which has great, often negative, impact: *the double whammy of high interest rates and low wage increases.* 2 an evil spell or curse: *she was convinced he had put the whammy on her.*
▷HISTORY C20: WHAM + -Y[2]

whanau (ˈfɑːnaʊ) NOUN *NZ* (in Maori societies) a family, esp an extended family.
▷HISTORY Maori

whang[1] (wæŋ) VERB 1 to strike or be struck so as to cause a resounding noise. ◆ NOUN 2 the resounding noise produced by a heavy blow. 3 a heavy blow.
▷HISTORY C19: of imitative origin

whang[2] (wæŋ) NOUN *Scot* 1 a leather thong. ◆ VERB 2 *(tr)* to strike with or as if with a thong.
▷HISTORY C17: variant of THONG

Whangarei (ˌwɑːŋɑːˈreɪ) NOUN a port in New Zealand, the northernmost city of North Island: oil refinery. Pop.: 44 800 (1994).

whangee (wæŋˈiː) NOUN 1 any tall woody grass of the S and SE Asian genus *Phyllostachys,* grown for its stems, which are used for bamboo canes and as a source of paper pulp. 2 a cane or walking stick made from the stem of any of these plants.
▷HISTORY C19: probably from Chinese (Mandarin) *huangli,* from *huang* yellow + *li* bamboo cane

whap (wɒp) VERB **whaps, whapping, whapped,** NOUN a less common spelling of **whop.**

whare (ˈwɔːrɪ; *Maori* ˈfɒrɛ) NOUN *NZ* 1 a Maori hut or dwelling place. 2 any simple dwelling place, esp at a beach or in the bush.
▷HISTORY from Maori

wharepuni (ˈfɒrɛˌpʊnɪ) NOUN *NZ* another name for **meeting house** (sense 2).

whare wanaga (ˈfɒrɛ wəˈnɑːgə) NOUN *NZ* a university.
▷HISTORY Maori

wharf (wɔːf) NOUN, *plural* **wharves** (wɔːvz) *or* **wharfs.** 1 a platform of timber, stone, concrete, etc., built parallel to the waterfront at a harbour or navigable river for the docking, loading, and unloading of ships. 2 **the wharves.** *NZ* the working area of a dock. 3 an obsolete word for **shore**[1]. ◆ VERB *(tr)* 4 to moor or dock at a wharf. 5 to provide or equip with a wharf or wharves. 6 to store or unload on a wharf.
▷HISTORY Old English *hwearf* heap; related to Old Saxon *hwarf,* Old High German *hwarb* a turn, Old Norse *hvarf* circle

wharfage (ˈwɔːfɪdʒ) NOUN 1 accommodation for ships at wharves. 2 a charge for use of a wharf. 3 wharves collectively.

wharfie (ˈwɔːfɪ) NOUN *Austral and NZ* a wharf labourer; docker.

wharfinger (ˈwɔːfɪndʒə) NOUN an owner or manager of a wharf.
▷HISTORY C16: probably alteration of *wharfager* (see WHARFAGE, -ER[1]); compare HARBINGER

wharf rat NOUN 1 any rat, usually a brown rat, that infests wharves. 2 *Informal* a person who haunts wharves, usually for dishonest purposes.

wharve (wɔːv) NOUN a wooden disc or wheel on a shaft serving as a flywheel or pulley.
▷HISTORY Old English *hweorfa,* from *hweorfan* to revolve; related to Old Saxon *hwervo* axis, Old High German *hwerbo* a turn

what (wɒt; *unstressed* wət) DETERMINER 1 **a** used with a noun in requesting further information about the identity or categorization of something: *what job does he do?* **b** *(as pronoun): what is her address?* **c** *(used in indirect questions): does he know what man did this?; tell me what he said.* 2 **a** the (person, thing, persons, or things) that: *we photographed what animals we could see.* **b** *(as pronoun): bring me what you've written; come what may.* 3 (intensifier; used in exclamations): *what a good book!* ◆ ADVERB 4 in what respect? to what degree?: *what do you care?* ◆ PRONOUN 5 *Not standard* which, who, or that, when used as relative pronouns: *this is the man what I saw in the park yesterday.* 6 **what about.** what do you think, know, feel, etc., concerning? 7 **what for. a** for what purpose? why? **b** *Informal* a punishment or reprimand (esp in the phrase **give (a person) what for**). 8 **what have you.** someone, something, or somewhere unknown or unspecified: *cars, motorcycles, or what have you.* 9 **what if. a** what would happen if? **b** what difference would it make if? 10 **what matter.** what does it matter? 11 **what's what.** *Informal* the true or real state of affairs. ◆ INTERJECTION 12 *Informal* don't you think? don't you agree?: *splendid party, what?*
▷HISTORY Old English *hwæt;* related to Old Frisian *whet,* Old High German *hwaz* (German *was*), Old Norse *hvatr*

> **Language note** The use of *are* in sentences such as *what we need are more doctors* is common, although many people think *is* should be used: *what we need is more doctors.*

whatever (wɒtˈɛvə, wət-) PRONOUN 1 everything or anything that: *do whatever he asks you to.* 2 no matter what: *whatever he does, he is forgiven.* 3 *Informal* an unknown or unspecified thing or things: *take a hammer, chisel, or whatever.* 4 an intensive form of *what,* used in questions: *whatever can he have said to upset her so much?* ◆ DETERMINER 5 an intensive form of *what: use whatever tools you can get hold of.* ◆ ADJECTIVE 6 *(postpositive)* absolutely; whatsoever: *I saw no point whatever in continuing.* ◆ INTERJECTION 7 *Informal* an expression used to show indifference or dismissal.

what-if NOUN *Informal* a hypothetical question; speculation: *one of the great what-ifs of modern history.*

whatnot (ˈwɒtˌnɒt) NOUN 1 Also called: **what-d'you-call-it.** *Informal* a person or thing the name of which is unknown, temporarily forgotten, or deliberately overlooked. 2 *Informal* unspecified assorted material. 3 a portable stand with shelves, used for displaying ornaments, etc.

whatsit (ˈwɒtsɪt), **whatsitsname,** *or masculine* **whatshisname,** *feminine* **whatshername** NOUN *Informal* a person or thing the name of which is unknown, temporarily forgotten, or deliberately overlooked.

whatsoever (ˌwɒtsəʊˈɛvə) ADJECTIVE 1 *(postpositive)* at all: used as an intensifier with indefinite pronouns and determiners such as *none, any, no one, anybody,* etc. 2 an archaic word for **whatever.**

whaup (wɔːp; *Scot* hwɔːp) NOUN *Chiefly Scot* a popular name for the **curlew.**
▷HISTORY C16: related to Old English *huilpe,* ultimately imitative of the bird's cry; compare Low German *regenwilp* sandpiper

whaur (hwɔːr) ADVERB, PRONOUN, CONJUNCTION, NOUN a Scot word for **where.**

wheal (wiːl) NOUN a variant spelling of **weal**[1].

wheat (wiːt) NOUN 1 any annual or biennial grass of the genus *Triticum,* native to the Mediterranean region and W Asia but widely cultivated, having erect flower spikes and light brown grains. 2 the grain of any of these grasses, used in making flour, pasta, etc. ◆ See also **emmer, durum.**
▷HISTORY Old English *hwǣte,* related to Old Frisian, Old Saxon *hwēti,* Old High German *hweizi,* Old Norse *hveiti;* see WHITE

wheat beer NOUN any of various beers brewed using a mixture of wheat malt and barley malt.

wheatear (ˈwiːtˌɪə) NOUN any small northern songbird of the genus *Oenanthe,* esp *O. oenanthe,* a species having a pale grey back, black wings and tail, white rump, and pale brown underparts: subfamily *Turdinae* (thrushes).
▷HISTORY C16: back formation from *wheatears* (wrongly taken as plural), probably from WHITE +

ARSE; compare Dutch *witstaart,* French *culblanc* white tail

wheaten ('wiːt^{ə}n) ADJECTIVE 1 made of the grain or flour of wheat: *wheaten bread.* 2 of a pale yellow colour.

wheat germ NOUN the vitamin-rich embryo of the wheat kernel, which is largely removed before milling and is used in cereals, as a food supplement, etc.

wheatgrass ('wiːtgrɑːs) NOUN another name for **couch grass.**

wheatmeal ('wiːt,miːl) NOUN **a** a brown flour intermediate between white flour and wholemeal flour. **b** (*as modifier*): *a wheatmeal loaf.*

wheat rust NOUN 1 a rust fungus, *Puccinia graminis,* that attacks cereals, esp wheat, and the barberry. 2 the disease caused by this fungus.

Wheatstone bridge ('wiːtstən) NOUN a device for determining the value of an unknown resistance by comparison with a known standard resistance.
▷HISTORY C19: named after Sir Charles *Wheatstone* (1802–75), British physicist and inventor

wheatworm ('wiːt,wɜːm) NOUN a parasitic nematode worm, *Anguina tritici,* that forms galls in the seeds of wheat.

whee (wiː) INTERJECTION an exclamation of joy, thrill, etc.

wheedle ('wiːd^{ə}l) VERB 1 to persuade or try to persuade (someone) by coaxing words, flattery, etc. 2 (*tr*) to obtain by coaxing and flattery: *she wheedled some money out of her father.*
▷HISTORY C17: perhaps from German *wedeln* to wag one's tail, from Old High German *wedil, wadil* tail
▸'**wheedler** NOUN ▸'**wheedling** ADJECTIVE ▸'**wheedlingly** ADVERB

wheel (wiːl) NOUN 1 a solid disc, or a circular rim joined to a hub by radial or tangential spokes, that is mounted on a shaft about which it can turn, as in vehicles and machines. 2 anything like a wheel in shape or function. 3 a device consisting of or resembling a wheel or having a wheel as its principal component: *a steering wheel; a water wheel.* 4 (usually preceded by *the*) a medieval torture consisting of a wheel to which the victim was tied and then had his limbs struck and broken by an iron bar. 5 short for **wheel of fortune** or **potter's wheel.** 6 the act of turning. 7 a pivoting movement of troops, ships, etc. 8 a type of firework coiled to make it rotate when let off. 9 a set of short rhyming lines, usually four or five in number, forming the concluding part of a stanza. Compare **bob**^{2} (sense 7). 10 the disc in which the ball is spun in roulette. 11 *US and Canadian* an informal word for **bicycle.** 12 *Archaic* a refrain. 13 *Informal, chiefly US and Canadian* a person of great influence (esp in the phrase **big wheel**). 14 **at the wheel. a** driving or steering a vehicle or vessel. **b** in charge. ◆ VERB 15 (when *intr* sometimes foll by *about* or *round*) to turn or cause to turn on or as if on an axis. 16 to move or cause to move on or as if on wheels; roll. 17 (*tr*) to perform with or in a circular movement. 18 (*tr*) to provide with a wheel or wheels. 19 (*intr;* often foll by *about*) to change one's mind or opinion. 20 **wheel and deal.** *Informal* to be a free agent, esp to advance one's own interests. ◆ See also **wheels.**
▷HISTORY Old English *hweol, hweowol;* related to Old Norse *hvēl,* Greek *kuklos,* Middle Low German *wēl,* Dutch *wiel*
▸'**wheel-less** ADJECTIVE

wheel and axle NOUN a simple machine for raising weights in which a rope unwinding from a wheel is wound onto a cylindrical drum or shaft coaxial with or joined to the wheel to provide mechanical advantage.

wheel animalcule NOUN another name for **rotifer.**

wheelbarrow ('wiːl,bærəʊ) NOUN 1 a simple vehicle for carrying small loads, typically being an open container supported by a wheel at the front and two legs and two handles behind. ◆ VERB 2 (*tr*) to convey in a wheelbarrow.

wheelbase ('wiːl,beɪs) NOUN the distance between the front and back axles of a motor vehicle.

Wheel Blacks PLURAL NOUN **the.** the international wheelchair rugby football team of New Zealand.
▷HISTORY C20: allusion to ALL BLACKS

wheel bug NOUN a large predatory North American heteropterous insect, *Arilus cristatus,* having a semicircular thoracic projection: family *Reduviidae* (assassin bugs).

wheelchair ('wiːl,tʃɛə) NOUN *Med* a special chair mounted on large wheels, for use by invalids or others for whom walking is impossible or temporarily inadvisable.

wheelchair housing NOUN *Social welfare* housing designed or adapted for a chairbound person. See also **mobility housing.**

wheel clamp NOUN a device fixed onto one wheel of an illegally parked car in order to immobilize it. The driver has to pay to have it removed.

wheeled (wiːld) ADJECTIVE **a** having or equipped with a wheel or wheels. **b** (*in combination*): *four-wheeled.*

wheeler ('wiːlə) NOUN 1 Also called: **wheel horse.** a horse or other draught animal nearest the wheel. 2 (*in combination*) something equipped with a specified sort or number of wheels: *a three-wheeler.* 3 a person or thing that wheels.

wheeler-dealer NOUN *Informal* a person who wheels and deals.

wheel horse NOUN 1 another word for **wheeler** (sense 1). 2 *US and Canadian* a person who works steadily or hard.

wheelhouse ('wiːl,haʊs) NOUN another term for **pilot house.**

wheelie ('wiːlɪ) NOUN, *plural* **-ies.** a manoeuvre on a bicycle or motorbike in which the front wheel is raised off the ground.

wheelie bin *or* **wheely bin** NOUN a large container for rubbish, esp one used by a household, mounted on wheels so that it can be moved more easily.

wheel lock NOUN 1 a gunlock formerly in use in which the firing mechanism was activated by sparks produced by friction between a small steel wheel and a flint. 2 a gun having such a lock.

wheel man NOUN 1 a cyclist. 2 Also called: **wheelsman.** *US* a helmsman.

wheel of fortune NOUN (in mythology and literature) a revolving device spun by a deity of fate selecting random changes in the affairs of man. Often shortened to: **wheel.**

wheels (wiːlz) PLURAL NOUN 1 the main directing force behind an organization, movement, etc.: *the wheels of government.* 2 an informal word for **car.** 3 **wheels within wheels.** a series of intricately connected events, plots, etc.

wheel window NOUN another name for **rose window.**

wheel wobble NOUN an oscillation of the front wheels of a vehicle caused by a defect in the steering gear, unbalanced wheels, etc.

wheelwork ('wiːl,wɜːk) NOUN an arrangement of wheels in a machine, esp a train of gears.

wheelwright ('wiːl,raɪt) NOUN a person who makes or mends wheels as a trade.

wheen (wiːn; *Scot* hwiːn) DETERMINER *Scot and northern English dialect* 1 few; some. 2 (preceded by *a*) **a** a small number of. **b** a good number of. **c** (*as pronoun; functioning as plural*): *a wheen of years.*
▷HISTORY Old English *hwēne,* instrumental of *hwōn* few, a few

wheesh (hwiːʃ) *or* **wheesht** (hwiːʃt) *Scot* ◆ INTERJECTION 1 a plea or demand for silence; hush. ◆ VERB 2 to silence (a person, noise, etc.) or to be silent. ◆ NOUN 3 silence; hush. 4 **haud your wheesht!** be silent! hush!
▷HISTORY of imitative origin; compare HUSH^{1}

wheeze (wiːz) VERB 1 to breathe or utter (something) with a rasping or whistling sound. 2 (*intr*) to make or move with a noise suggestive of wheezy breathing. ◆ NOUN 3 a husky, rasping, or whistling sound or breathing. 4 *Brit slang* a trick, idea, or plan (esp in the phrase **good wheeze**). 5 *Informal* a hackneyed joke or anecdote.
▷HISTORY C15: probably from Old Norse *hvæsa* to hiss
▸'**wheezer** NOUN ▸'**wheezy** ADJECTIVE ▸'**wheezily** ADVERB ▸'**wheeziness** NOUN

whelk^{1} (wɛlk) NOUN any carnivorous marine gastropod mollusc of the family *Buccinidae,* of coastal waters and intertidal regions, having a strong snail-like shell.
▷HISTORY Old English *weoloc;* related to Middle Dutch *willok,* Old Norse *vil* entrails

whelk^{2} (wɛlk) NOUN a raised lesion on the skin; wheal.
▷HISTORY Old English *hwylca,* of obscure origin
▸'**whelky** ADJECTIVE

whelm (wɛlm) VERB (*tr*) *Archaic* 1 to engulf entirely with or as if with water. 2 another word for **overwhelm.**
▷HISTORY C13: *whelmen* to turn over, of uncertain origin

whelp (wɛlp) NOUN 1 a young offspring of certain animals, esp of a wolf or dog. 2 *Disparaging* a young man or youth. 3 *Jocular* a young child. 4 *Nautical* any of the ridges, parallel to the axis, on the drum of a capstan to keep a rope, cable, or chain from slipping. ◆ VERB 5 (of an animal or, disparagingly, a woman) to give birth to (young).
▷HISTORY Old English *hwelp(a);* related to Old High German *hwelf,* Old Norse *hvelpr,* Danish *hvalp*

when (wɛn) ADVERB 1 **a** at what time? over what period?: *when is he due?* **b** (*used in indirect questions*): *ask him when he's due.* 2 **say when.** to state when an action is to be stopped or begun, as when someone is pouring a drink. 3 (*subordinating*) at a time at which; at the time at which; just as; after: *I found it easily when I started to look seriously.* 4 although: *he drives when he might walk.* 5 considereing the fact that: *how did you pass the exam when you'd not worked for it?* 6 at which (time); over which (period): *an age when men were men.* ◆ NOUN 7 (*usually plural*) a question as to the time of some occurrence.
▷HISTORY Old English *hwanne, hwænne;* related to Old High German *hwanne, hwenne,* Latin *cum*

> **Language note** *When* should not be used loosely as a substitute for *in which* after a noun which does not refer to a period of time: *paralysis is a condition in which* (not *when*) *parts of the body cannot be moved.*

whenas (wɛn'æz) CONJUNCTION 1 *Archaic* **a** when; whenever. **b** inasmuch as; while. 2 *Obsolete* whereas; although.

whence (wɛns) *Archaic or formal* ◆ ADVERB 1 from what place, cause, or origin? ◆ PRONOUN 2 (*subordinating*) from what place, cause, or origin.
▷HISTORY C13 *whannes,* adverbial genitive of Old English *hwanon;* related to Old Frisian *hwana,* Old High German *hwanan*

> **Language note** The expression *from whence* should be avoided, since *whence* already means from which place: *the tradition whence* (not *from whence*) *such ideas flowed.*

whencesoever (,wɛnssəʊ'ɛvə) CONJUNCTION (*subordinating*), ADVERB *Archaic* out of whatsoever place, cause, or origin.

whene'er (wɛn'ɛə) ADVERB, CONJUNCTION a poetic contraction of **whenever.**

whenever (wɛn'ɛvə) CONJUNCTION 1 (*subordinating*) at every or any time that; when: *I laugh whenever I see that.* ◆ ADVERB *also* **when ever.** 2 no matter when: *it'll be here, whenever you decide to come for it.* 3 *Informal* at an unknown or unspecified time: *I'll take it if it comes today, tomorrow, or whenever.* 4 an intensive form of *when,* used in questions: *whenever did he escape?*

whensoever (,wɛnsəʊ'ɛvə) CONJUNCTION, ADVERB *Rare* an intensive form of **whenever.**

whenua (fɛn'uə) NOUN *NZ* land.
▷HISTORY Maori

whenwe ('wɛnwiː) NOUN *South African informal* a White immigrant from Zimbabwe, caricatured as being tiresomely over-reminiscent of happier times.
▷HISTORY C20: from WHEN + WE

where (wɛə) ADVERB 1 **a** in, at, or to what place, point, or position?: *where are you going?* **b** (*used in indirect questions*): *I don't know where they are.* 2 in, at, or to which (place): *the hotel where we spent our honeymoon.* 3 (*subordinating*) in the place at which: *where we live it's always raining.* ◆ NOUN 4 (*usually*

plural) a question as to the position, direction, or destination of something.
▷**HISTORY** Old English *hwǣr, hwār(a)*; related to Old Frisian *hwēr*, Old Saxon, Old High German *hwār*, Old Norse, Gothic *hvar*

> **Language note** It was formerly considered incorrect to use *where* as a substitute for *in which* after a noun which did not refer to a place or position, but this use has now become acceptable: *we now have a situation where/in which no further action is needed.*

whereabouts (ˈwɛərəˌbaʊts) ADVERB [1] Also: **whereabout.** at what approximate location or place; where: *whereabouts are you?* [2] *Obsolete* about or concerning which. ◆ NOUN [3] *(functioning as singular or plural)* the place, esp the approximate place, where a person or thing is.

whereafter (ˌwɛərˈɑːftə) SENTENCE CONNECTOR *Archaic or formal* after which.

whereas (wɛərˈæz) CONJUNCTION [1] *(coordinating)* but on the other hand: *I like to go swimming whereas Sheila likes to sail.* ◆ SENTENCE CONNECTOR [2] (in formal documents to begin sentences) it being the case that; since.

whereat (wɛərˈæt) *Archaic* ◆ ADVERB [1] at or to which place. ◆ SENTENCE CONNECTOR [2] upon which occasion.

whereby (wɛəˈbaɪ) PRONOUN [1] by or because of which: *the means whereby he took his life.* ◆ ADVERB [2] *Archaic* how? by what means?: *whereby does he recognize me?*

where'er (wɛərˈɛə) ADVERB, CONJUNCTION a poetic contraction of **wherever.**

wherefore (ˈwɛəˌfɔː) NOUN [1] *(usually plural)* an explanation or reason (esp in the phrase **the whys and wherefores**). ◆ ADVERB [2] *Archaic* for what reason? why? ◆ SENTENCE CONNECTOR [3] *Archaic or formal* for which reason: used as an introductory word in legal preambles.

wherefrom (wɛəˈfrɒm) *Archaic* ◆ ADVERB [1] from what or where? whence? ◆ PRONOUN [2] from which place; whence.

wherein (wɛərˈɪn) *Archaic or formal* ◆ ADVERB [1] in what place or respect? ◆ PRONOUN [2] in which place, thing, etc.

whereinto (wɛərˈɪntuː) *Archaic* ◆ ADVERB [1] into what place? ◆ PRONOUN [2] into which place.

whereof (wɛərˈɒv) *Archaic or formal* ◆ ADVERB [1] of what or which person or thing? ◆ PRONOUN [2] of which (person or thing): *the man whereof I speak is no longer alive.*

whereon (wɛərˈɒn) *Archaic* ◆ ADVERB [1] on what thing or place? ◆ PRONOUN [2] on which thing, place, etc.

wheresoever (ˌwɛəsəʊˈɛvə) CONJUNCTION *(subordinating)*, ADVERB, PRONOUN *Rare* an intensive form of **wherever.**

whereto (wɛəˈtuː) *Archaic or formal* ◆ ADVERB [1] towards what (place, end, etc.)? ◆ PRONOUN [2] to which. ◆ Also (archaic): **whereunto.**

whereupon (ˌwɛərəˈpɒn) SENTENCE CONNECTOR [1] at which; at which point; upon which. ◆ ADVERB [2] *Archaic* upon what?

wherever (wɛərˈɛvə) PRONOUN [1] at, in, or to every place or point which; where: *wherever she went, he would be there.* [2] *(subordinating)* in, to, or at whatever place: *wherever we go the weather is always bad.* ◆ ADVERB *also* **where ever.** [3] no matter where: *I'll find you, wherever you are.* [4] *Informal* at, in, or to an unknown or unspecified place: *I'll go anywhere to escape: London, Paris, or wherever.* [5] an intensive form of *where*, used in questions: *wherever can they be?*

wherewith (wɛəˈwɪθ, -ˈwɪð) *Archaic or formal* ◆ PRONOUN [1] *(often foll by an infinitive)* with or by which: *the pen wherewith I am wont to write.* [2] something with which: *I have not wherewith to buy my bread.* ◆ ADVERB [3] with what? ◆ SENTENCE CONNECTOR [4] with or after that; whereupon.

wherewithal NOUN (ˈwɛəwɪðˌɔːl) [1] **the wherewithal.** necessary funds, resources, or equipment (for something or to do something): *these people lack the wherewithal for a decent existence.* ◆ PRONOUN (ˌwɛəwɪðˈɔːl) [2] a less common word for **wherewith** (senses 1, 2).

wherret (ˈwɛrət) *Dialect* ◆ VERB [1] *(tr)* to strike (someone) a blow. ◆ NOUN [2] a blow, esp a slap on the face; stroke.
▷**HISTORY** probably of imitative origin

wherrit (ˈwɛrɪt) VERB [1] to worry or cause to worry. [2] *(intr)* to complain or moan.
▷**HISTORY** perhaps from *thwert*, obsolete variant of THWART; compare WORRIT

wherry (ˈwɛrɪ) NOUN, *plural* **-ries.** [1] any of certain kinds of half-decked commercial boats, such as barges, used in Britain. [2] a light rowing boat used in inland waters and harbours.
▷**HISTORY** C15: origin unknown
▸ˈ**wherryman** NOUN

whet (wɛt) VERB **whets, whetting, whetted.** *(tr)* [1] to sharpen, as by grinding or friction. [2] to increase or enhance (the appetite, desire, etc.); stimulate. ◆ NOUN [3] the act of whetting. [4] a person or thing that whets.
▷**HISTORY** Old English *hwettan;* related to *hvæt* sharp, Old High German *hwezzen*, Old Norse *hvetja*, Gothic *hvatjan*
▸ˈ**whetter** NOUN

whether (ˈwɛðə) CONJUNCTION [1] *(subordinating)* used to introduce an indirect question or a clause after a verb expressing or implying doubt or choice in order to indicate two or more alternatives, the second or last of which is introduced by *or* or *or whether*: *he doesn't know whether she's in Britain or whether she's gone to France.* [2] *(subordinating; often foll by or not)* used to introduce any indirect question: *he was not certain whether his friend was there or not.* [3] *(coordinating)* another word for **either** (sense 3). *any man, whether liberal or conservative, would agree with me.* [4] *(coordinating) Archaic* used to introduce a direct question consisting of two alternatives, the second of which is introduced by *or* or *or whether*: *whether does he live at home or abroad.* [5] **whether or no. a** used as a conjunction as a variant of **whether** (sense 1). **b** under any circumstances: *he will be here tomorrow, whether or no.* [6] **whether…or** (**whether**). if on the one hand…or even if on the other hand: *you'll eat that, whether you like it or not.* ◆ DETERMINER, PRONOUN [7] *Obsolete* which (of two): used in direct or indirect questions.
▷**HISTORY** Old English *hwæther, hwether;* related to Old Frisian *hweder, hoder*, Old High German *hwedar*, Old Norse *hvatharr, hvarr*, Gothic *hwathar*

whetstone (ˈwɛtˌstəʊn) NOUN [1] a stone used for sharpening edged tools, knives, etc. [2] something that sharpens.

whew (hwjuː) INTERJECTION an exclamation or sharply exhaled breath expressing relief, surprise, delight, etc.

whey (weɪ) NOUN the watery liquid that separates from the curd when the milk is clotted, as in making cheese.
▷**HISTORY** Old English *hwæg;* related to Middle Low German *wei, heie*, Dutch *hui*
▸ˈ**wheyey** *or* ˈ**wheyish** *or* ˈ**whey,like** ADJECTIVE

wheyface (ˈweɪˌfeɪs) NOUN [1] a pale bloodless face. [2] a person with such a face.
▸ˈ**whey,faced** ADJECTIVE

whf ABBREVIATION FOR wharf.

which (wɪtʃ) DETERMINER [1] **a** used with a noun in requesting that its referent be further specified, identified, or distinguished from the other members of a class: *which house did you want to buy?* **b** *(as pronoun)*: *which did you find?* **c** *(used in indirect questions)*: *I wondered which apples were cheaper.* [2] **a** whatever of a class; whichever: *bring which car you want.* **b** *(as pronoun)*: *choose which of the cars suit you.* [3] used in relative clauses with inanimate antecedents: *the house, which is old, is in poor repair.* [4] as; and that: used in relative clauses with verb phrases or sentences as their antecedents: *he died of cancer, which is what I predicted.* [5] **the which.** *Archaic* a longer form of **which**, often used as a sentence connector
▷**HISTORY** Old English *hwelc, hwilc;* related to Old High German *hwelīh* (German *welch*), Old Norse *hvelīkr*, Gothic *hvileiks*, Latin *quis, quid*

> **Language note** See at **that.**

whichever (wɪtʃˈɛvə) DETERMINER [1] **a** any (one, two, etc., out of several): *take whichever car you like.* **b** *(as pronoun)*: *choose whichever appeals to you.* [2] **a** no matter which (one or ones): *whichever card you pick you'll still be making a mistake.* **b** *(as pronoun)*: *it won't make any difference, whichever comes first.*

whichsoever (ˌwɪtʃsəʊˈɛvə) PRONOUN an archaic or formal word for **whichever.**

whicker (ˈwɪkə) VERB *(intr)* (of a horse) to whinny or neigh; nicker.
▷**HISTORY** C17: of imitative origin

whidah (ˈwɪdə) NOUN a variant spelling of **whydah.**

whiff[1] (wɪf) NOUN [1] a passing odour. [2] a brief gentle gust of air. [3] a single inhalation or exhalation from the mouth or nose. ◆ VERB [4] to come, convey, or go in whiffs; puff or waft. [5] to take in or breathe out (tobacco smoke, air, etc.). [6] *(tr)* to sniff or smell. [7] *(intr) Brit slang* to have an unpleasant smell; stink.
▷**HISTORY** C16: of imitative origin
▸ˈ**whiffer** NOUN

whiff[2] (wɪf) NOUN *Chiefly Brit* a narrow clinker-built skiff having outriggers, for one oarsman.
▷**HISTORY** C19: special use of WHIFF[1]

whiffle (ˈwɪfᵊl) VERB [1] *(intr)* to think or behave in an erratic or unpredictable way. [2] to blow or be blown fitfully or in gusts. [3] *(intr)* to whistle softly.
▷**HISTORY** C16: frequentative of WHIFF[1]

whiffler[1] (ˈwɪflə) NOUN a person who whiffles.

whiffler[2] (ˈwɪflə) NOUN *Archaic* an attendant who cleared the way for a procession.
▷**HISTORY** C16: from *wifle* battle-axe, from Old English *wifel*, of Germanic origin; the attendants originally carried weapons to clear the way

whiffletree (ˈwɪfᵊlˌtriː) NOUN another name (esp US) for **swingletree.**
▷**HISTORY** C19: variant of WHIPPLETREE

whiffy (ˈwɪfɪ) ADJECTIVE **-fier, -fiest.** *Slang* smelly.

Whig (wɪg) NOUN [1] a member of the English political party or grouping that in 1679–80 opposed the succession to the throne of James, Duke of York (1633–1701; king of England and Ireland as James II, and of Scotland as James VII, 1685–88), on the grounds that he was a Catholic. Standing for a limited monarchy, the Whigs represented the great aristocracy and the moneyed middle class for the next 80 years. In the late 18th and early 19th centuries the Whigs represented the desires of industrialists and Dissenters for political and social reform. The Whigs provided the core of the Liberal Party. [2] (in the US) a supporter of the War of American Independence. Compare **Tory.** [3] a member of the American political party that opposed the Democrats from about 1834 to 1855 and represented propertied and professional interests. [4] a conservative member of the Liberal Party in Great Britain. [5] a person who advocates and believes in an unrestricted laissez-faire economy. [6] *History* a 17th-century Scottish Presbyterian, esp one in rebellion against the Crown. ◆ ADJECTIVE [7] of, characteristic of, or relating to Whigs.
▷**HISTORY** C17: probably shortened from *whiggamore*, one of a group of 17th-century Scottish rebels who joined in an attack on Edinburgh known as *the whiggamore raid;* probably from Scottish *whig* to drive (of obscure origin) + *more, mer, maire* horse, MARE[1]
▸ˈ**Whiggery** *or* ˈ**Whiggism** NOUN ▸ˈ**Whiggish** ADJECTIVE
▸ˈ**Whiggishly** ADVERB ▸ˈ**Whiggishness** NOUN

whigmaleerie (ˌhwɪgməˈliːrɪ) NOUN *Scot* [1] a trinket, whimsical ornament, or trifle. [2] a whim or caprice.
▷**HISTORY** C18: of unknown origin

while (waɪl) CONJUNCTION *also* **whilst** (waɪlst). [1] *(subordinating)* at the same time that: *please light the fire while I'm cooking.* [2] *(subordinating)* all the time that: *I stay inside while it's raining.* [3] *(subordinating)* in spite of the fact that: *while I agree about his brilliance I still think he's rude.* [4] *(coordinating)* whereas; and in contrast: *flats are expensive, while houses are cheap.* [5] *(subordinating; used with a gerund)* during the activity of: *while walking I often whistle.* ◆ PREPOSITION, CONJUNCTION [6] *Scot and northern English dialect* another word for **until**: *you'll have to wait while Monday for these sheets; you'll never make any progress while you listen to me.* ◆ NOUN [7] *(usually used in adverbial phrases)* a period or interval of time: *once in a long while.* [8] trouble or time (esp in the phrase **worth one's while**): *it's hardly worth your while to begin*

work today. 9 **the while.** at that time: *he was working the while.* ◆ See also **whiles.**
▷HISTORY Old English *hwīl;* related to Old High German *hwīla* (German *Weile*), Gothic *hveila,* Latin *quiēs* peace, *tranquīlus* TRANQUIL

Language note It was formerly considered incorrect to use *while* to mean *in spite of the fact that* or *whereas*, but these uses have now become acceptable.

while away VERB *(tr, adverb)* to pass (time) idly and usually pleasantly.

whiles (waɪlz; *Scot* hwəɪlz) *Archaic or dialect* ◆ ADVERB 1 at times; occasionally. ◆ CONJUNCTION 2 while; whilst.

whilk (hwɪlk) PRONOUN an archaic and dialect word for **which.**

whilom ('waɪləm) *Archaic* ◆ ADVERB 1 formerly; once. ◆ ADJECTIVE 2 *(prenominal)* one-time; former.
▷HISTORY Old English *hwīlum,* dative plural of *hwīl* WHILE; related to Old High German *hwīlōm,* German *weiland* of old

whilst (waɪlst) CONJUNCTION *Chiefly Brit* another word for **while** (senses 1–5).
▷HISTORY C13: from WHILES + *-t* as in *amidst*

whim (wɪm) NOUN 1 a sudden, passing, and often fanciful idea; impulsive or irrational thought. 2 a horse-drawn winch formerly used in mining to lift ore or water.
▷HISTORY C17: from WHIM-WHAM

whimbrel ('wɪmbrəl) NOUN a small European curlew, *Numenius phaeopus,* with a striped head.
▷HISTORY C16: from dialect *whimp* or from WHIMPER, alluding to its cry

whimper ('wɪmpə) VERB 1 *(intr)* to cry, sob, or whine softly or intermittently. 2 to complain or say (something) in a whining plaintive way. ◆ NOUN 3 a soft plaintive whine.
▷HISTORY C16: from dialect *whimp,* of imitative origin
▸'**whimperer** NOUN ▸'**whimpering** NOUN ▸'**whimperingly** ADVERB

whimsical ('wɪmzɪkəl) ADJECTIVE 1 spontaneously fanciful or playful. 2 given to whims; capricious. 3 quaint, unusual, or fantastic.
▸**whimsicality** (ˌwɪmzɪ'kælɪtɪ) NOUN ▸'**whimsically** ADVERB ▸'**whimsicalness** NOUN

whimsy *or* **whimsey** ('wɪmzɪ) NOUN, *plural* **-sies** *or* **-seys.** 1 a capricious idea or notion. 2 light or fanciful humour. 3 something quaint or unusual. ◆ ADJECTIVE **-sier, -siest.** 4 quaint, comical, or unusual, often in a tasteless way.
▷HISTORY C17: from WHIM; compare FLIMSY

whim-wham NOUN *Archaic* something fanciful; a trifle.
▷HISTORY C16: of unknown origin; compare FLIMFLAM

whin[1] (wɪn) NOUN another name for **gorse.**
▷HISTORY C11: from Scandinavian; compare Old Danish *hvine* (*græs*), Norwegian *hvine,* Swedish *hven*

whin[2] (wɪn) NOUN short for **whinstone.**
▷HISTORY C14: *quin,* of obscure origin

whinchat ('wɪnˌtʃæt) NOUN an Old World songbird, *Saxicola rubetra,* having a mottled brown-and-white plumage with pale cream underparts: subfamily *Turdinae* (thrushes).
▷HISTORY C17: from WHIN[1] + CHAT[1]

whine (waɪn) NOUN 1 a long high-pitched plaintive cry or moan. 2 a continuous high-pitched sound. 3 a peevish complaint, esp one repeated. ◆ VERB 4 to make a whine or utter in a whine.
▷HISTORY Old English *hwīnan;* related to Old Norse *hvīna,* Swedish *hvija* to scream
▸'**whiner** NOUN ▸'**whining** ADJECTIVE ▸'**whiningly** ADVERB

whinge (wɪndʒ) *Informal* ◆ VERB **whinges, whingeing, whinged.** *(intr)* 1 to cry in a fretful way. 2 to complain. ◆ NOUN 3 a complaint.
▷HISTORY from a Northern variant of Old English *hwinsian* to whine; related to Old High German *winsan, winisan,* whence Middle High German *winsen*
▸'**whingeing** NOUN, ADJECTIVE ▸'**whinger** NOUN

whinny ('wɪnɪ) VERB **-nies, -nying, -nied.** *(intr)* 1 (of a horse) to neigh softly or gently. 2 to make a sound resembling a neigh, such as a laugh. ◆ NOUN, *plural* **-nies.** 3 a gentle or low-pitched neigh.
▷HISTORY C16: of imitative origin

whinstone ('wɪnˌstəʊn) NOUN any dark hard fine-grained rock, such as basalt.
▷HISTORY C16: from WHIN[2] + STONE

whiny ('waɪnɪ) ADJECTIVE **whinier, whiniest.** 1 high-pitched and plaintive. 2 peevish; complaining.

whip (wɪp) VERB **whips, whipping, whipped.** 1 to strike (a person or thing) with several strokes of a strap, rod, etc. 2 *(tr)* to punish by striking in this manner. 3 *(tr; foll by out, away,* etc.) to pull, remove, etc., with sudden rapid motion: *to whip out a gun.* 4 *(intr; foll by down, into, out of,* etc.) *Informal* to come, go, etc., in a rapid sudden manner: *they whipped into the bar for a drink.* 5 to strike or be struck as if by whipping: *the tempest whipped the surface of the sea.* 6 *(tr)* to criticize virulently. 7 *(tr)* to bring, train, etc., forcefully into a desired condition (esp in the phrases **whip into line** and **whip into shape**). 8 *(tr) Informal* to overcome or outdo: *I know when I've been whipped.* 9 *(tr; often foll by on, out,* or *off)* to drive, urge, compel, etc., by or as if by whipping. 10 *(tr)* to wrap or wind (a cord, thread, etc.) around (a rope, cable, etc.) to prevent chafing or fraying. 11 *(tr) Nautical* to hoist by means of a rope through a single pulley. 12 *(tr)* (in fly-fishing) to cast the fly repeatedly onto (the water) in a whipping motion. 13 *(tr)* (in sewing) to join, finish, or gather with whipstitch. 14 to beat (eggs, cream, etc.) with a whisk or similar utensil to incorporate air and produce expansion. 15 *(tr)* to spin (a top). 16 *(tr) Informal* to steal: *he whipped her purse.* ◆ NOUN 17 a device consisting of a lash or flexible rod attached at one end to a stiff handle and used for driving animals, inflicting corporal punishment, etc. 18 a whipping stroke or motion. 19 a person adept at handling a whip, as a coachman, etc. 20 (in a legislative body) **a** a member of a party chosen to organize and discipline the members of his faction, esp in voting and to assist in the arrangement of the business. **b** a call issued to members of a party, insisting with varying degrees of urgency upon their presence or loyal voting behaviour. **c** (in the British Parliament) a schedule of business sent to members of a party each week. Each item on it is underlined to indicate its importance: one line means that no division is expected, two lines means that the item is fairly important, and three lines means that the item is very important and every member must attend and vote according to the party line. 21 an apparatus for hoisting, consisting of a rope, pulley, and snatch block. 22 any of a variety of desserts made from egg whites or cream beaten stiff, sweetened, and flavoured with fruit, fruit juice, etc. 23 See **whipper-in.** 24 a windmill vane. 25 transient elastic movement of a structure or part when subjected to sudden release of load or dynamic excitation. 26 a percussion instrument consisting of two strips of wood, joined forming the shape of a V, and clapped loudly together. 27 flexibility, as in the shaft of a golf club, etc. 28 a ride in a funfair involving bumper cars that move with sudden jerks. 29 a wrestling throw in which a wrestler seizes his opponent's arm and spins him to the floor. 30 **a fair crack of the whip.** *Informal* a fair chance or opportunity. ◆ See also **whip in, whip-round, whips, whip up.**
▷HISTORY C13: perhaps from Middle Dutch *wippen* to swing; related to Middle Dutch *wipfen* to dance, German *Wipfel* tree top
▸'**whipˌlike** ADJECTIVE ▸'**whipper** NOUN

whipbird ('wɪpˌbɜːd) NOUN *Austral* 1 any of several birds of the genus *Psophodes,* esp *P. olivaceus* (**eastern whipbird**) and *P. nigrogularis* (**black-throated whipbird**), having a whistle ending in a whipcrack note. 2 any of various other birds, such as *Pachycephala pectoralis* and *P. rufiventris* (**mock whipbird**).

whipcord ('wɪpˌkɔːd) NOUN 1 a strong worsted or cotton fabric with a diagonally ribbed surface. 2 a closely twisted hard cord used for the lashes of whips, etc.

whip graft NOUN *Horticulture* a graft made by inserting a tongue cut on the sloping base of the scion into a slit on the sloping top of the stock.

whip hand NOUN (usually preceded by *the*) 1 (in driving horses) the hand holding the whip. 2 advantage or dominating position.

whip in VERB *(adverb)* 1 *(intr)* to perform the duties of a whipper-in to a pack of hounds. 2 *(tr) Chiefly US* to keep (members of a political party, etc.) together.

whiplash ('wɪpˌlæʃ) NOUN 1 a quick lash or stroke of a whip or like that of a whip. 2 *Med* See **whiplash injury.**

whiplash injury NOUN *Med, informal* any injury to the neck resulting from a sudden thrusting forwards and snapping back of the unsupported head. Technical name: **hyperextension-hyperflexion injury.**

whipper-in NOUN, *plural* **whippers-in.** a person employed to assist the huntsman managing the hounds.

whippersnapper ('wɪpəˌsnæpə) NOUN an insignificant but pretentious or cheeky person, often a young one. Also called: **whipster.**
▷HISTORY C17: probably from *whipsnapper* a person who snaps whips, influenced by earlier *snippersnapper,* of obscure origin

whippet ('wɪpɪt) NOUN a small slender breed of dog similar to a greyhound in appearance.
▷HISTORY C16: of uncertain origin; perhaps based on the phrase *whip it!* move quickly!

whipping ('wɪpɪŋ) NOUN 1 a thrashing or beating with a whip or similar implement. 2 cord or twine used for binding or lashing.

whipping boy NOUN a person of little importance who is blamed for the errors, incompetence, etc., of others, esp his superiors; scapegoat.
▷HISTORY C17: originally referring to a boy who was educated with a prince and who received punishment for any faults committed by the prince

whipping cream NOUN cream that contains just enough butterfat to allow it to be whipped until stiff.

whippletree ('wɪpəlˌtriː) NOUN another name for **swingletree.**
▷HISTORY C18: apparently from WHIP

whippoorwill ('wɪpʊˌwɪl) NOUN a nightjar, *Caprimulgus vociferus,* of North and Central America, having a dark plumage with white patches on the tail.
▷HISTORY C18: imitative of its cry

whip-round *Informal, chiefly Brit* ◆ NOUN 1 an impromptu collection of money. ◆ VERB **whip round.** 2 *(intr, adverb)* to make such a collection of money.

whips (wɪps) PLURAL NOUN (often foll by *of*) *Austral informal* a large quantity: *I've got whips of cash at the moment.*

whipsaw ('wɪpˌsɔː) NOUN 1 any saw with a flexible blade, such as a bandsaw. ◆ VERB **-saws, -sawing, -sawed, -sawed** *or* **-sawn.** *(tr)* 2 to saw with a whipsaw. 3 *US* to defeat in two ways at once.

whip scorpion NOUN any nonvenomous arachnid of the order *Uropygi* (or *Pedipalpi*), typically resembling a scorpion but lacking a sting. See also **vinegarroon.**

whip snake NOUN 1 any of several long slender fast-moving nonvenomous snakes of the colubrid genus *Coluber,* such as *C. hippocrepis* (**horseshoe whipsnake**) of Eurasia. 2 any of various other slender nonvenomous snakes, such as *Masticophis flagellum* (**coachwhip snake**) of the US.

whipstall ('wɪpˌstɔːl) NOUN a stall in which an aircraft goes into a nearly vertical climb, pauses, slips backwards momentarily, and drops suddenly with its nose down.

whipstitch ('wɪpˌstɪtʃ) NOUN 1 a sewing stitch passing over an edge. 2 *US slang* an instant; moment. ◆ VERB 3 *(tr)* to sew (an edge) using whipstitch; overcast.

whipstock ('wɪpˌstɒk) NOUN a whip handle.

whiptail wallaby ('wɪpˌteɪl) NOUN a wallaby of NE Australia, *Macropus parryi,* with a long slender tail.

whip up VERB *(tr, adverb)* 1 to excite; arouse: *to whip up a mob; to whip up discontent.* 2 *Informal* to prepare quickly: *to whip up a meal.*

whipworm ('wɪpˌwɜːm) NOUN any of several parasitic nematode worms of the genus *Trichuris,* esp *T. trichiura,* having a whiplike body and living in the intestines of mammals.

whir *or* **whirr** (wɜː) NOUN 1 a prolonged soft swish or buzz, as of a motor working or wings flapping. 2 a bustle or rush. ♦ VERB **whirs** *or* **whirrs, whirring, whirred.** 3 to make or cause to make a whir.
▷HISTORY C14: probably from Scandinavian; compare Norwegian *kvirra,* Danish *hvirre;* see WHIRL

whirl (wɜːl) VERB 1 to spin, turn, or revolve or cause to spin, turn, or revolve. 2 (*intr*) to turn around or away rapidly. 3 (*intr*) to have a spinning sensation, as from dizziness, etc. 4 to move or drive or be moved or driven at high speed. ♦ NOUN 5 the act or an instance of whirling; swift rotation or a rapid whirling movement. 6 a condition of confusion or giddiness: *her accident left me in a whirl.* 7 a swift round, as of events, meetings, etc. 8 a tumult; stir. 9 *Informal* a brief trip, dance, etc. 10 **give (something) a whirl.** *Informal* to attempt or give a trial to (something).
▷HISTORY C13: from Old Norse *hvirfla* to turn about; related to Old High German *wirbil* whirlwind
▶ **'whirler** NOUN ▶ **'whirling** ADJECTIVE ▶ **'whirlingly** ADVERB

whirlabout ('wɜːlə,baʊt) NOUN 1 anything that whirls around; whirligig. 2 the act or an instance of whirling around.

whirligig ('wɜːlɪ,gɪg) NOUN 1 any spinning toy, such as a top. 2 another name for **merry-go-round.** 3 anything that whirls about, spins, or moves in a circular or giddy way: *the whirligig of social life.* 4 another name for **windmill** (the toy).
▷HISTORY C15: *whirlegigge,* from WHIRL + GIG[1]

whirligig beetle NOUN any flat-bodied water beetle of the family *Gyrinidae,* which circles rapidly on the surface of the water.

whirlpool ('wɜːl,puːl) NOUN 1 a powerful circular current or vortex of water, usually produced by conflicting tidal currents or by eddying at the foot of a waterfall. 2 something resembling a whirlpool in motion or the power to attract into its vortex. 3 short for **whirlpool bath.**

whirlpool bath NOUN a bath having a device for maintaining the water in a swirling motion.

whirlwind ('wɜːl,wɪnd) NOUN 1 a column of air whirling around and towards a more or less vertical axis of low pressure, which moves along the land or ocean surface. 2 **a** a motion or course resembling this, esp in rapidity. **b** (*as modifier*): *a whirlwind romance.* 3 an impetuously active person.

whirlybird ('wɜːlɪ,bɜːd) NOUN an informal word for **helicopter.**

whish (wɪʃ) NOUN, VERB a less common word for **swish.**

whisht (hwɪʃt) *or* **whist** (hwɪst) *Scot* ♦ INTERJECTION 1 hush! be quiet! ♦ ADJECTIVE 2 silent or still. ♦ VERB 3 to make or become silent. ♦ See also **wheesh.**
▷HISTORY C14: compare HIST; also obsolete v. *whist* to become silent

whisk (wɪsk) VERB 1 (*tr;* often foll by *away* or *off*) to brush, sweep, or wipe off lightly. 2 (*tr*) to move, carry, etc., with a light or rapid sweeping motion: *the taxi whisked us to the airport.* 3 (*intr*) to move, go, etc., quickly and nimbly: *to whisk downstairs for a drink.* 4 (*tr*) to whip (eggs, cream, etc.) to a froth. ♦ NOUN 5 the act of whisking. 6 a light rapid sweeping movement or stroke. 7 a utensil, often incorporating a coil of wires, for whipping eggs, etc. 8 a small brush or broom. 9 a small bunch or bundle, as of grass, straw, etc.
▷HISTORY C14: from Old Norse *visk* wisp; related to Middle Dutch *wisch,* Old High German *wisc*

whisker ('wɪskə) NOUN 1 any of the stiff sensory hairs growing on the face of a cat, rat, or other mammal. Technical name: **vibrissa.** 2 any of the hairs growing on a person's face, esp on the cheeks or chin. 3 (*plural*) a beard or that part of it growing on the sides of the face. 4 (*plural*) *Informal* a moustache. 5 Also called: **whisker boom, whisker pole.** any light spar used for extending the clews of a sail, esp in light airs. 6 *Chem* a very fine filamentary crystal having greater strength than the bulk material since it is a single crystal. Such crystals often show unusual electrical properties. 7 a person or thing that whisks. 8 a narrow margin; a small distance: *he escaped death by a whisker.*

whiskered ('wɪskəd) ADJECTIVE having whiskers.

whiskery ('wɪskərɪ) ADJECTIVE **-skerier, -skeriest.** 1 having whiskers. 2 old; unkempt.

whiskey ('wɪskɪ) NOUN the usual Irish and US spelling of **whisky.**

Whiskey ('wɪskɪ) NOUN *Communications* a code word for the letter *w.*

whiskey sour NOUN *US* a mixed drink of whisky and lime or lemon juice, sometimes sweetened.

whisky ('wɪskɪ) NOUN, *plural* **-kies.** a spirit made by distilling fermented cereals, which is matured and often blended.
▷HISTORY C18: shortened from *whiskybae,* from Scottish Gaelic *uisge beatha,* literally: water of life; see USQUEBAUGH

whisky mac NOUN *Brit* a drink consisting of whisky and ginger wine.

whisper ('wɪspə) VERB 1 to speak or utter (something) in a soft hushed tone, esp without vibration of the vocal cords. 2 (*intr*) to speak secretly or furtively, as in promoting intrigue, gossip, etc. 3 (*intr*) (of leaves, trees, etc.) to make a low soft rustling sound. 4 (*tr*) to utter or suggest secretly or privately: *to whisper treason.* ♦ NOUN 5 a low soft voice: *to speak in a whisper.* 6 something uttered in such a voice. 7 a low soft rustling sound. 8 a trace or suspicion. 9 *Informal* a rumour or secret.
▷HISTORY Old English *hwisprian;* related to Old Norse *hvīskra,* Old High German *hwispalōn,* Dutch *wispern*

whisperer ('wɪspərə) NOUN 1 a person or thing that whispers. 2 a person who is able to tame or control animals, esp by talking to them in gentle tones: *a horse whisperer.*

whispering campaign NOUN the organized diffusion by word of mouth of defamatory rumours designed to discredit a person, group, etc.

whispering gallery NOUN a gallery or dome with acoustic characteristics such that a sound made at one point is audible at distant points.

whist[1] (wɪst) NOUN a card game for four in which the two sides try to win the balance of the 13 tricks: forerunner of bridge.
▷HISTORY C17: perhaps changed from WHISK, referring to the sweeping up or whisking up of the tricks

whist[2] (hwɪst) INTERJECTION, ADJECTIVE, VERB a variant of **whisht.**

whist drive NOUN a social gathering where whist is played; the winners of each hand move to different tables to play the losers of the previous hand.

whistle ('wɪsᵊl) VERB 1 to produce (shrill or flutelike musical sounds), as by passing breath through a narrow constriction most easily formed by the pursed lips: *he whistled a melody.* 2 (*tr*) to signal, summon, or command by whistling or blowing a whistle: *the referee whistled the end of the game.* 3 (of a kettle, train, etc.) to produce (a shrill sound) caused by the emission of steam through a small aperture. 4 (*intr*) to move with a whistling sound caused by rapid passage through the air. 5 (of animals, esp birds) to emit (a shrill sound) resembling human whistling. 6 **whistle in the dark.** to try to keep up one's confidence in spite of fear. ♦ See also **whistle for, whistle up.** ♦ NOUN 7 a device for making a shrill high-pitched sound by means of air or steam under pressure. 8 a shrill sound effected by whistling. 9 a whistling sound, as of a bird, bullet, the wind, etc. 10 a signal, warning, command, etc., transmitted by or as if by a whistle. 11 the act of whistling. 12 *Music* any pipe that is blown down its end and produces sounds on the principle of a flue pipe, usually having as a mouthpiece a fipple cut in the side. 13 **wet one's whistle.** *Informal* to take an alcoholic drink. 14 **blow the whistle.** (usually foll by *on*) *Informal* **a** to inform (on). **b** to bring a stop (to).
▷HISTORY Old English *hwistlian;* related to Old Norse *hvīsla*

whistle-blower NOUN *Informal* a person who informs on someone or puts a stop to something.

whistle for VERB (*intr, preposition*) *Informal* to seek or expect in vain.

whistler ('wɪslə) NOUN 1 a person or thing that whistles. 2 *Radio* an atmospheric disturbance picked up by radio receivers, characterized by a whistling sound of decreasing pitch. It is caused by the electromagnetic radiation produced by lightning. 3 any of various birds having a whistling call, such as certain Australian flycatchers (see **thickhead** (sense 2)) and the goldeneye. 4 any of various North American marmots of the genus *Marmota,* esp *M. caligata* (**hoary marmot**). 5 *Vet science* a horse affected with an abnormal respiratory noise, resembling whistling. 6 *Informal* a referee.

whistle stop NOUN 1 *US and Canadian* **a** a minor railway station where trains stop only on signal. **b** a small town having such a station. 2 **a** a brief appearance in a town, esp by a political candidate to make a speech, shake hands, etc. **b** (*as modifier*): *a whistle-stop tour.* ♦ VERB **whistle-stop, -stops, -stopping, -stopped.** 3 (*intr*) to campaign for office by visiting many small towns to give short speeches.

whistle up VERB (*tr, adverb*) to call or summon (a person or animal) by whistling.

whistling ('wɪslɪŋ) NOUN *Vet science* a breathing defect of horses characterized by a high-pitched sound with each intake of air. Compare **roaring** (sense 6).

whistling swan NOUN a white North American swan, *Cygnus columbianus,* with a black bill and straight neck. Compare **mute swan.**

whit (wɪt) NOUN (*usually used with a negative*) the smallest particle; iota; jot: *he has changed not a whit.*
▷HISTORY C15: probably variant of WIGHT[1]

Whit (wɪt) NOUN 1 See **Whitsuntide.** ♦ ADJECTIVE 2 of or relating to Whitsuntide.

Whitby ('wɪtbɪ) NOUN a fishing port and resort in NE England, in E North Yorkshire at the mouth of the River Esk: an important ecclesiastical centre in Anglo-Saxon times; site of an abbey founded in 656. See also **Synod of Whitby.** Pop.: 13 640 (1991).

white (waɪt) ADJECTIVE 1 having no hue due to the reflection of all or almost all incident light. Compare **black** (sense 1). 2 (of light, such as sunlight) consisting of all the colours of the spectrum or produced by certain mixtures of three additive primary colours, such as red, green, and blue. 3 comparatively white or whitish-grey in colour or having parts of this colour: *white clover.* 4 (of an animal) having pale-coloured or white skin, fur, or feathers. 5 bloodless or pale, as from pain, emotion, etc. 6 (of hair, a beard, etc.) silvery or grey, usually from age. 7 benevolent or without malicious intent: *white magic.* 8 colourless or transparent: *white glass.* 9 capped with or accompanied by snow: *a white Christmas.* 10 (*sometimes capital*) counterrevolutionary, very conservative, or royalist. Compare **Red** (sense 2). 11 blank, as an unprinted area of a page. 12 (of wine) made from pale grapes or from black grapes separated from their skins. 13 **a** (of coffee or tea) with milk or cream. **b** (of bread) made with white flour. 14 *Physics* having or characterized by a continuous distribution of energy, wavelength, or frequency: *white noise.* 15 *Informal* honourable or generous. 16 (of armour) made completely of iron or steel (esp in the phrase **white harness**). 17 *Rare* morally unblemished. 18 *Rare* (of times, seasons, etc.) auspicious; favourable. 19 *Poetic or archaic* having a fair complexion; blond. 20 **bleed white.** to deprive slowly of resources. 21 **whiter than white. a** extremely clean and white. **b** *Informal* very pure, honest, and moral. ♦ NOUN 22 a white colour. 23 the condition or quality of being white; whiteness. 24 the white or lightly coloured part or area of something. 25 (usually preceded by *the*) the viscous fluid that surrounds the yolk of a bird's egg, esp a hen's egg; albumen. 26 *Anatomy* the white part (sclera) of the eyeball. 27 any of various butterflies of the family *Pieridae.* See **large white, small white, cabbage white.** 28 *Chess, draughts* **a** a white or light-coloured piece or square. **b** (*usually capital*) the player playing with such pieces. 29 anything that has or is characterized by a white colour, such as a white paint or pigment, a white cloth, a white ball in billiards. 30 an unprinted area of a page. 31 *Archery* **a** the outer ring of the target, having the lowest score. **b** a shot or arrow hitting this ring. 32 *Poetic* fairness of complexion. 33 **in the white.** (of wood or furniture) left unpainted or unvarnished. ♦ VERB 34 (usually foll by *out*) to create or leave white spaces in (printed or other matter). 35 *Obsolete* to make or become white. ♦ See also **white out, whites.**

▷**HISTORY** Old English *hwīt;* related to Old Frisian *hwīt,* Old Saxon *hwīt,* Old Norse *hvītr,* Gothic *hveits,* Old High German *hwīz* (German *weiss*)
▸ **'whitely** ADVERB ▸ **'whiteness** NOUN ▸ **'whitish** ADJECTIVE

White (waɪt) NOUN 1 a member of the Caucasoid race. 2 a person of European ancestry. ◆ ADJECTIVE 3 denoting or relating to a White or Whites.

white admiral NOUN a nymphalid butterfly, *Limenitis camilla,* of Eurasia, having brown wings with white markings. See also **red admiral.**

white alkali NOUN 1 refined sodium carbonate. 2 any of several mineral salts, esp sodium sulphate, sodium chloride, and magnesium sulphate, that often appear on the surface of soils as a whitish layer in dry conditions.

white ant NOUN another name for **termite.**

white area NOUN an area of land for which no specific planning proposal has been adopted.

White Australia policy NOUN *History* an unofficial term for an immigration policy designed to restrict the entry of coloured people into Australia.

whitebait ('waɪtˌbeɪt) NOUN 1 the young of herrings, sprats, etc., cooked and eaten whole as a delicacy. 2 any of various small silvery fishes, such as *Galaxias attenuatus* of Australia and New Zealand and *Allosmerus elongatus* of North American coastal regions of the Pacific.
▷**HISTORY** C18: from its formerly having been used as bait

whitebeam ('waɪtˌbiːm) NOUN 1 a N temperate rosaceous tree, *Sorbus aria,* having leaves with dense white hairs on the undersurface and hard timber. 2 any of several similar and closely related trees.

white bear NOUN another name for **polar bear.**

white birch NOUN any of several birch trees with white bark, such as the silver birch of Europe and the paper birch of North America. See also **birch** (sense 1).

white blood cell NOUN a nontechnical name for **leucocyte.**

whiteboard ('waɪtˌbɔːd) NOUN 1 a shiny white surface that can be wiped clean after being used for writing or drawing on, used esp in teaching. 2 a large screen used to project computer images to a group of people.

white book NOUN an official government publication in some countries.

Whiteboy ('waɪtbɔɪ) NOUN *Irish history* a member of a secret society of violent agrarian protest, formed around 1760.
▷**HISTORY** C18: adopted from the earlier use of the phrase as a term of endearment for a boy or man

white bryony NOUN a climbing herbaceous cucurbitaceous plant, *Bryonia dioica,* of Europe and North Africa, having greenish flowers and red berries. Also called: **red bryony.** See also **black bryony, bryony.**

whitecap ('waɪtˌkæp) NOUN 1 a wave with a white broken crest. 2 *US* a member of a vigilante organization that attempts to control a community.

white cedar NOUN 1 a coniferous tree, *Chamaecyparis thyoides,* of swampy regions in North America, having scalelike leaves and boxlike cones: family *Cupressaceae.* See also **cypress**[1] (sense 2). 2 the wood of this tree, which is used for building boats, etc. 3 a coniferous tree, *Thuja occidentalis,* of NE North America, having scalelike leaves: family *Cupressaceae.* See also **arbor vitae.** 4 the wood of this tree, much used for telegraph poles.

Whitechapel ('waɪtˌtʃæpᵊl) NOUN *Billiards* the act of potting one's opponent's white ball.
▷**HISTORY** C19: slang use of *Whitechapel,* a district of London

white clover NOUN a Eurasian clover plant, *Trifolium repens,* with rounded white flower heads: cultivated as a forage plant.

white coal NOUN water, esp when flowing and providing a potential source of usable power.

white cockatoo NOUN another name for **sulphur-crested cockatoo.**

white-collar ADJECTIVE of, relating to, or designating nonmanual and usually salaried workers employed in professional and clerical occupations: *white-collar union.* Compare **blue-collar, pink-collar.**

white currant NOUN a cultivated N temperate shrub, *Ribes sativum,* having small rounded white edible berries: family *Grossulariaceae.*

whitedamp ('waɪtˌdæmp) NOUN a mixture of poisonous gases, mainly carbon monoxide, occurring in coal mines. See also **afterdamp.**

whited sepulchre ('waɪtɪd) NOUN a hypocrite.
▷**HISTORY** from Matthew 23:27

white dwarf NOUN one of a large class of small faint stars of enormous density (on average 10^8 kg/m^3) with diameters only about 1 per cent that of the sun, and masses less than the Chandrasekhar limit (about 1.4 solar masses). It is thought to mark the final stage in the evolution of a sun-like star.

white elephant NOUN 1 a rare albino or pale grey variety of the Indian elephant, regarded as sacred in parts of S Asia. 2 a possession that is unwanted by its owner. 3 an elaborate venture, construction, etc., that proves useless. 4 a rare or valuable possession the upkeep of which is very expensive.

White Ensign NOUN the ensign of the Royal Navy and the Royal Yacht Squadron, having a red cross on a white background with the Union Jack at the upper corner of the vertical edge alongside the hoist. Compare **Red Ensign, Blue Ensign.**

white-eye NOUN 1 Also called (NZ): **blighty, silvereye, waxeye.** any songbird of the family *Zosteropidae* of Africa, Australia, New Zealand, and Asia, having a greenish plumage with a white ring around each eye. 2 any of certain other birds having a white ring or patch around the eye.

white feather NOUN 1 a symbol or mark of cowardice. 2 **show the white feather.** to act in a cowardly manner.
▷**HISTORY** from the belief that a white feather in a gamecock's tail was a sign of a poor fighter

white finger NOUN a condition of a finger that results in a white appearance caused by a spasm of the blood vessels. It occurs with Raynaud's disease and with the long-term use of percussion tools.

whitefish ('waɪtˌfɪʃ) NOUN, *plural* **-fish** *or* **-fishes.** any herring-like salmonoid food fish of the genus *Coregonus* and family *Coregonidae,* typically of deep cold lakes of the N hemisphere, having large silvery scales and a small head.

white fish NOUN (in the British fishing industry) any edible marine fish or invertebrate in which the main reserves of fat are in the liver, excluding herring, trout, sprat, mackerel, salmon, and shellfish.

white flag NOUN a white flag or a piece of white cloth hoisted to signify surrender or request a truce.

white flight NOUN the departure of white residents from areas where non-Whites are settling.

white flint NOUN another name for **flint** (sense 4).

white flour NOUN flour that consists substantially of the starchy endosperm of wheat, most of the bran and the germ having been removed by the milling process.

whitefly ('waɪtˌflaɪ) NOUN, *plural* **-flies.** any hemipterous insect of the family *Aleyrodidae,* typically having a body covered with powdery wax. Many are pests of greenhouse crops.

white-footed mouse NOUN any of various mice of the genus *Peromyscus,* esp *P. leucopus,* of North and Central America, having brownish fur with white underparts: family *Cricetidae.* See also **deer mouse.**

white fox NOUN another name for **arctic fox.**

white friar NOUN a Carmelite friar, so called because of the white cloak that forms part of the habit of this order.

white frost NOUN another term for **hoarfrost.**

white gold NOUN any of various white lustrous hard-wearing alloys containing gold together with platinum and palladium and sometimes smaller amounts of silver, nickel, or copper: used in jewellery.

white goods PLURAL NOUN 1 *Marketing* large household appliances, such as refrigerators, cookers. Compare **brown goods.** 2 household linen such as sheets, towels, tablecloths, etc.

white gum NOUN any of various Australian eucalyptus trees with whitish bark.

white-haired boy *or* **white-headed boy** NOUN a favourite; darling.

Whitehall (ˌwaɪt'hɔːl) NOUN 1 a street in London stretching from Trafalgar Square to the Houses of Parliament: site of the main government offices. 2 the British Government or its central administration.

white hat NOUN *Informal* **a** a computer hacker who is hired by an organization to undertake nonmalicious hacking work in order to discover computer-security flaws. **b** (*as modifier*): *a white-hat hacker.* Compare **black hat.**

white heat NOUN 1 intense heat or a very high temperature, characterized by emission of white light. 2 *Informal* a state of intense excitement or activity.

white hope NOUN *Informal* a person who is expected to bring honour or glory to his group, team, etc.

white horse NOUN 1 the outline of a horse carved into the side of a chalk hill, usually dating to the Neolithic, Bronze, or Iron Ages, such as that at Uffington, Berkshire. 2 (*usually plural*) a wave with a white broken crest.

Whitehorse ('waɪtˌhɔːs) NOUN a town in NW Canada: capital of the Yukon Territory. Pop.: 22 884 (1995 est.).

white-hot ADJECTIVE 1 at such a high temperature that white light is emitted. 2 *Informal* in a state of intense emotion.

White House NOUN **the.** 1 the official Washington residence of the president of the US. 2 the US presidency.

white knight NOUN a champion or rescuer, esp a person or organization that rescues a company from financial difficulties, an unwelcome takeover bid, etc.

white-knuckle ADJECTIVE causing or experiencing fear or anxiety: *a white-knuckle ride.*

white lady NOUN 1 a cocktail consisting of gin, Cointreau, and lemon juice. 2 *Austral informal* methylated spirits as a drink, sometimes mixed with shoe polish or other additives.

white lead (lɛd) NOUN 1 Also called: **ceruse.** a white solid usually regarded as a mixture of lead carbonate and lead hydroxide; basic lead carbonate: used in paint and in making putty and ointments for the treatment of burns. Formula: $2PbCO_3.Pb(OH)_2$. 2 either of two similar white pigments based on lead sulphate or lead silicate. 3 a type of putty made by mixing white lead with boiled linseed oil.

white lead ore (lɛd) NOUN another name for **cerussite.**

white leather NOUN leather that has been treated with a chemical, such as alum or salt, to make it white. Also called: **whitleather** ('wɪtlɛðə).

white leg NOUN another name for **milk leg.**

white lias NOUN a type of rock composed of pale-coloured limestones and marls. See also **Lias.**

white lie NOUN a minor or unimportant lie, esp one uttered in the interests of tact or politeness.

white light NOUN light that contains all the wavelengths of visible light at approximately equal intensities, as in sunlight or the light from white-hot solids.

white line NOUN 1 a line or strip of white in the centre of a road to separate traffic going in different directions. 2 a white lamination in the hoof of a horse.

white list NOUN a list of countries considered to pose an insignificant threat to human rights, from which applications for political asylum are presumed to be unfounded.

white-livered ADJECTIVE 1 lacking in spirit or courage. 2 pallid and unhealthy in appearance.

White man's burden NOUN the supposed duty of the White race to bring education and Western culture to the non-White inhabitants of their colonies.

white matter NOUN the whitish tissue of the brain and spinal cord, consisting mainly of myelinated nerve fibres. Technical name: **substantia alba.** Compare **grey matter.**

white meat NOUN any meat that is light in

colour, such as veal or the breast of turkey. Compare **red meat.**

white metal NOUN any of various alloys, such as Babbitt metal, used for bearings. Also called: **antifriction metal.**

white meter NOUN *Brit obsolete* an electricity meter used to record the consumption of off-peak electricity.

White Mountains PLURAL NOUN [1] a mountain range in the US, chiefly in N New Hampshire: part of the Appalachians. Highest peak: Mount Washington, 1917 m (6288 ft.). [2] a mountain range in the US, in E California and SW Nevada. Highest peak: White Mountain, 4342 m (14 246 ft.).

white mustard NOUN a Eurasian plant, *Brassica hirta* (or *Sinapis alba*), having clusters of yellow flowers and pungent seeds from which the condiment mustard is made: family *Brassicaceae* (crucifers).

whiten ('waɪt^{ə}n) VERB to make or become white or whiter; bleach.
▸ **'whitening** NOUN

whitener ('waɪt^{ə}nə) NOUN [1] a substance that makes something white or whiter. [2] a powdered substitute for milk or cream, used in coffee or tea.

White Nile NOUN See **Nile.**

white noise NOUN **a** sound or electrical noise that has a relatively wide continuous range of frequencies of uniform intensity. **b** noise containing all frequencies rising in level by six decibels every octave.

white oak NOUN [1] a large oak tree, *Quercus alba,* of E North America, having pale bark, leaves with rounded lobes, and heavy light-coloured wood. [2] any of several other oaks, such as the roble.

white out VERB *(adverb)* [1] *(intr)* to lose or lack daylight visibility owing to snow or fog. [2] *(tr)* to create or leave white spaces in (printed or other matter). [3] *(tr)* to delete (typewritten words or characters) with a white correcting fluid. ◆ NOUN **whiteout.** [4] an atmospheric condition consisting of loss of visibility and sense of distance and direction due to a uniform whiteness of a heavy cloud cover and snow-covered ground, which reflects almost all the light it receives.

white paper NOUN *(often capitals)* an official government report in any of a number of countries, including Britain, Australia, New Zealand, and Canada, which sets out the government's policy on a matter that is or will come before Parliament.

white pepper NOUN a condiment, less pungent than black pepper, made from the husked dried beans of the pepper plant *Piper nigrum,* used either whole or ground.

white pine NOUN [1] a North American coniferous tree, *Pinus strobus,* having blue-green needle-like leaves, hanging brown cones, and rough bark: family *Pinaceae.* [2] the light-coloured wood of this tree, much used commercially. [3] another name for **kahikatea.**

white plague NOUN *Informal* tuberculosis of the lungs.

white poplar NOUN [1] Also called: **abele.** a Eurasian salicaceous tree, *Populus alba,* having leaves covered with dense silvery-white hairs. [2] another name for **tulipwood** (sense 1).

white potato NOUN another name for **potato** (sense 1).

white propaganda NOUN propaganda that comes from the source it claims to come from. Compare **black propaganda, grey propaganda.**

white pudding NOUN (in Britain) a kind of sausage made like black pudding but without pigs' blood.

white rainbow NOUN another name for **fogbow.**

white rat NOUN a white variety of the brown rat (*Rattus norvegicus*), used extensively in scientific research.

white rose NOUN *English history* a widely used emblem or badge of the House of York. See also **Wars of the Roses, red rose.**

White Russia NOUN another name for **Belarus.**

White Russian ADJECTIVE, NOUN another term for **Belarussian.**

whites (waɪts) PLURAL NOUN [1] household linen or cotton goods, such as sheets. [2] white or off-white clothing, such as that worn for playing cricket. [3] an informal name for **leucorrhoea.**

white sale NOUN a sale of household linens at reduced prices.

white sapphire NOUN a white pure variety of corundum, used as a gemstone.

white sauce NOUN a thick sauce made from flour, butter, seasonings, and milk or stock.

White Sea NOUN an almost landlocked inlet of the Barents Sea on the coast of NW Russia. Area: 90 000 sq. km (34 700 sq. miles).

white settler NOUN a well-off incomer to a district who takes advantage of what it has to offer without regard to the local inhabitants.
▹ **HISTORY** C20: from earlier colonial sense

white slave NOUN a girl or woman forced or sold into prostitution.
▸ **white slavery** NOUN

white-slaver NOUN a person who procures or forces women to become prostitutes.

whitesmith ('waɪtˌsmɪθ) NOUN a person who finishes and polishes metals, particularly tin plate and galvanized iron.

white spirit NOUN a colourless liquid obtained from petroleum and used as a substitute for turpentine.

white spruce NOUN a N North American spruce tree, *Picea glauca,* having grey bark, pale brown oblong cones, and bluish-green needle-like leaves.

white squall NOUN a violent highly localized weather disturbance at sea, in which the surface of the water is whipped to a white spray by the winds.

white stick NOUN a walking stick used by a blind person for feeling the way: painted white as a sign to others that the person is blind.

White supremacy NOUN the theory or belief that White people are innately superior to people of other races.
▸ **White supremacist** NOUN, ADJECTIVE

white-tailed deer NOUN a deer, *Odocoileus virginianus,* of North America and N South America: the coat varies in colour, being typically reddish-brown in the summer, and the tail is white. Also called: **Virginia deer.**

whitethorn ('waɪtˌθɔːn) NOUN another name for **hawthorn.**

whitethroat ('waɪtˌθrəʊt) NOUN either of two Old World warblers, *Sylvia communis* or *S. curruca* (**lesser whitethroat**), having a greyish-brown plumage with a white throat and underparts.

white tie NOUN [1] a white bow tie worn as part of a man's formal evening dress. [2] **a** formal evening dress for men. **b** *(as modifier): a white-tie occasion.*

white toast NOUN *Canadian* toasted white bread.

white trash NOUN *Disparaging* **a** poor White people living in the US, esp the South. **b** *(as modifier): white-trash culture.*

White Van Man NOUN *Informal, derogatory* a male van driver, often of a white van, whose driving is selfish and aggressive.

white vitriol NOUN another name for **zinc sulphate.**

White Volta NOUN a river in W Africa, rising in N Burkina-Faso flowing southwest and south to join the Black Volta in central Ghana and form the Volta River. Length: about 885 km (550 miles).

whitewall ('waɪtˌwɔːl) NOUN a pneumatic tyre having white sidewalls.

white walnut NOUN another name for **butternut** (senses 1–4).

whitewash ('waɪtˌwɒʃ) NOUN [1] a substance used for whitening walls and other surfaces, consisting of a suspension of lime or whiting in water, often with other substances, such as size, added. [2] *Informal* deceptive or specious words or actions intended to conceal defects, gloss over failings, etc. [3] *Informal* a defeat in a sporting contest in which the loser is beaten in every match, game, etc. in a series: *they face the prospect of a whitewash in the five-test series.* ◆ VERB *(tr)* [4] to cover or whiten with whitewash. [5] *Informal* to conceal, gloss over, or suppress. [6] *Informal* to defeat (an opponent or opposing team) by winning every match in a series.
▸ **'whiteˌwasher** NOUN

white water NOUN [1] a stretch of water with a broken foamy surface, as in rapids. [2] light-coloured sea water, esp over shoals or shallows.

whitewater rafting NOUN the sport of rafting down fast-flowing rivers, esp over rapids.

white whale NOUN a small white toothed whale, *Delphinapterus leucas,* of northern waters: family *Monodontidae.* Also called: **beluga.**

whitewood ('waɪtˌwʊd) NOUN [1] any of various trees with light-coloured wood, such as the tulip tree, basswood, and cottonwood. [2] the wood of any of these trees.

whitey *or* **whity** ('waɪtɪ) NOUN *Chiefly US* (used contemptuously by Black people) a White man.

whither ('wɪðə) *Archaic or poetic* ◆ ADVERB [1] to what place? [2] to what end or purpose? ◆ CONJUNCTION [3] to whatever place, purpose, etc.
▹ **HISTORY** Old English *hwider, hwæder;* related to Gothic *hvadrē;* modern English form influenced by HITHER

whithersoever (ˌwɪðəsəʊˈɛvə) ADVERB, CONJUNCTION *Archaic or poetic* to whichever place.

whitherward ('wɪðəwəd) ADVERB *Archaic or poetic* in which direction.

whiting^{1} ('waɪtɪŋ) NOUN [1] an important gadoid food fish, *Merlangius* (or *Gadus*) *merlangus,* of European seas, having a dark back with silvery sides and underparts. [2] any of various similar fishes, such as *Merluccius bilinearis,* a hake of American Atlantic waters, and any of several Atlantic sciaenid fishes of the genus *Menticirrhus.* [3] *Austral* any of several marine food fishes of the genus *Sillago.* [4] **whiting pout.** another name for **bib** (the fish).
▹ **HISTORY** C15: perhaps from Old English *hwītling;* related to Middle Dutch *wijting.* See WHITE, -ING^{3}

whiting^{2} ('waɪtɪŋ) NOUN white chalk that has been ground and washed, used in making whitewash, metal polish, etc. Also called: **whitening.**

Whitley Bay ('wɪtlɪ) NOUN a resort in NE England, in North Tyneside unitary authority, Tyne and Wear, on the North Sea. Pop.: 33 335 (1991).

Whitley Council NOUN any of a number of organizations made up of representatives of employees and employers for joint consultation on and settlement of industrial relations and conditions for a particular industry or service.
▹ **HISTORY** C20: named after J. H. *Whitley* (1866–1935), chairman of the committee that recommended setting up such councils (1917)

whitlow ('wɪtləʊ) NOUN any pussy inflammation of the end of a finger or toe.
▹ **HISTORY** C14: changed from *whitflaw,* from WHITE + FLAW^{1}

whitlow grass NOUN any of various plants of the genera *Draba* and *Erophila,* once thought to cure whitlows: family *Brassicaceae* (crucifers).

Whit Monday NOUN the Monday following Whit Sunday.

Whitney ('wɪtnɪ) NOUN **Mount.** a mountain in E California: the highest peak in the Sierra Nevada Mountains and in continental US (excluding Alaska). Height: 4418 m (14 495 ft.).

Whitsun ('wɪts^{ə}n) NOUN [1] short for **Whitsuntide.** ◆ ADJECTIVE [2] of or relating to Whit Sunday or Whitsuntide.

Whitsunday (ˌhwɪtˈsʌndɪ, ˌwɪt-) NOUN (in Scotland) May 15, one of the four quarter days.

Whit Sunday NOUN the seventh Sunday after Easter, observed as a feast in commemoration of the descent of the Holy Spirit on the apostles 50 days after Easter. Also called: **Pentecost.**
▹ **HISTORY** Old English *hwīta sunnandæg* white Sunday, probably named after the ancient custom of wearing white robes at or after baptism

Whitsuntide ('wɪts^{ə}nˌtaɪd) NOUN the week that begins with Whit Sunday, esp the first three days.

whitter ('wɪtə) VERB, NOUN a variant spelling of **witter.**

whittle ('wɪt^{ə}l) VERB [1] to cut or shave strips or pieces from (wood, a stick, etc.), esp with a knife. [2] *(tr)* to make or shape by paring or shaving. [3] *(tr;* often foll by *away, down, off,* etc.) to reduce, destroy, or wear away gradually. [4] *Northern English dialect (intr)* to complain or worry about something

continually. ◆ NOUN 5 *Brit dialect* a knife, esp a large one.
▷HISTORY C16: variant of C15 *thwittle* large knife, from Old English *thwitel*, from *thwītan* to cut; related to Old Norse *thveitr* cut, *thveita* to beat
▸ **'whittler** NOUN

whittlings ('wɪtlɪŋz) PLURAL NOUN chips or shavings whittled off from an object.

whittret ('wɪtrət) *or* **whitrick** ('wɪtrɪk) NOUN *Dialect* a male weasel.
▷HISTORY Old English *whytrate, whittratt;* perhaps from *hwīt* WHITE + *rætt* RAT

Whitworth screw thread ('wɪtwəθ) NOUN a thread form and system of standard sizes, proposed by Whitworth in 1841 and adopted as standard in the UK, having a flank angle of 55° and a rounded top and foot.
▷HISTORY named after Sir Joseph *Whitworth* (1803–87), English engineer

whity ('waɪtɪ) NOUN, *plural* **whities.** 1 *Informal* a variant spelling of **whitey.** ◆ ADJECTIVE 2 **a** whitish in colour. **b** (*in combination*): *whity-brown.*

whizz *or* **whiz** (wɪz) VERB **whizzes, whizzing, whizzed.** 1 to make or cause to make a loud humming or buzzing sound. 2 to move or cause to move with such a sound. 3 (*intr*) *Informal* to move or go rapidly. ◆ NOUN 4 a loud humming or buzzing sound. 5 *Informal* a person who is extremely skilful at some activity. 6 a slang word for **amphetamine.** 7 **take a whizz.** *US informal* to urinate.
▷HISTORY C16: of imitative origin

whizz-bang *or* **whiz-bang** NOUN 1 a small-calibre World War I shell that, when discharged, travelled at such a high velocity that the sound of its flight was heard only an instant, if at all, before the sound of its explosion. ◆ ADJECTIVE 2 *Informal* excellent or first-rate.

whizz kid, whiz kid, *or* **wiz kid** NOUN *Informal* a person who is outstandingly successful for his or her age.
▷HISTORY C20: from WHIZZ, perhaps influenced by WIZARD

whizzy ('wɪzɪ) ADJECTIVE *Informal* using sophisticated technology to produce vivid effects: *a whizzy new computer game.*

who (hu:) PRONOUN 1 which person? what person? used in direct and indirect questions: *he can't remember who did it; who met you?* 2 used to introduce relative clauses with antecedents referring to human beings: *the people who lived here have left.* 3 the one or ones who; whoever: *bring who you want.*
▷HISTORY Old English *hwā;* related to Old Saxon *hwē*, Old High German *hwer,* Gothic *hvas,* Lithuanian *kàs,* Danish *hvo*

> **Language note** See at **whom.**

WHO ABBREVIATION FOR **World Health Organization.**

whoa (wəʊ) INTERJECTION a command used esp to horses to stop or slow down.
▷HISTORY C19: variant of HO[1]

who'd (hu:d) CONTRACTION OF who had *or* who would.

who-does-what ADJECTIVE (of a dispute, strike, etc.) relating to the separation of kinds of work performed by different trade unions.

whodunnit *or* **whodunit** (hu:'dʌnɪt) NOUN *Informal* a novel, play, etc., concerned with a crime, usually murder.

whoever (hu:'ɛvə) PRONOUN 1 any person who; anyone that: *whoever wants it can have it.* 2 no matter who: *I'll come round tomorrow, whoever may be here.* 3 an intensive form of *who,* used in questions: *whoever could have thought that?* 4 *Informal* an unknown or unspecified person: *give those to John, or Cathy, or whoever.*

whole (həʊl) ADJECTIVE 1 containing all the component parts necessary to form a total; complete: *a whole apple.* 2 constituting the full quantity, extent, etc. 3 uninjured or undamaged. 4 healthy. 5 having no fractional or decimal part; integral: *a whole number.* 6 of, relating to, or designating a relationship established by descent from the same parents; full: *whole brothers.* 7 **out of whole cloth.** *US and Canadian informal* entirely without a factual basis. ◆ ADVERB 8 in an undivided or unbroken piece: *to swallow a plum whole.* ◆ NOUN 9 all the parts, elements, etc., of a thing. 10 an assemblage of parts viewed together as a unit. 11 a thing complete in itself. 12 **as a whole.** considered altogether; completely. 13 **on the whole. a** taking all things into consideration. **b** in general.
▷HISTORY Old English *hāl, hǣl;* related to Old Frisian *hāl, hēl,* Old High German *heil,* Gothic *hails;* compare HALE[1]
▸ **'wholeness** NOUN

whole blood NOUN blood obtained from a donor for transfusion from which none of the elements has been removed.

wholefood ('həʊl,fu:d) NOUN (*sometimes plural*) **a** food that has been refined or processed as little as possible and is eaten in its natural state, such as brown rice, wholemeal flour, etc. **b** (*as modifier*): *a wholefood restaurant.*

whole gale NOUN a wind of force ten on the Beaufort scale.

wholehearted (,həʊl'hɑ:tɪd) ADJECTIVE done, acted, given, etc., with total sincerity, enthusiasm, or commitment.
▸ **,whole'heartedly** ADVERB ▸ **,whole'heartedness** NOUN

whole hog NOUN *Slang* the whole or total extent (esp in the phrase **go the whole hog**).

wholemeal ('həʊl,mi:l) ADJECTIVE *Brit* (of flour, bread, etc.) made from the entire wheat kernel. US and Canadian term: **whole-wheat.**

whole milk NOUN milk from which no constituent has been removed. Compare **skimmed milk.**

whole note NOUN the usual US and Canadian name for **semibreve.**

whole number NOUN 1 an integer. 2 a natural number.

wholesale ('həʊl,seɪl) NOUN 1 the business of selling goods to retailers in larger quantities than they are sold to final consumers but in smaller quantities than they are purchased from manufacturers. Compare **retail** (sense 1). 2 **at wholesale. a** in large quantities. **b** at wholesale prices. ◆ ADJECTIVE 3 of, relating to, or engaged in such business. 4 made, done, etc., on a large scale or without discrimination. ◆ ADVERB 5 on a large scale or without discrimination. ◆ VERB 6 to sell (goods) at wholesale.
▸ **'whole,saler** NOUN

wholesale price index NOUN an indicator of price changes in the wholesale market.

wholesome ('həʊlsəm) ADJECTIVE 1 conducive to health or physical wellbeing. 2 conducive to moral wellbeing. 3 characteristic or suggestive of health or wellbeing, esp in appearance.
▷HISTORY C12: from WHOLE (healthy) + -SOME[1]; related to German *heilsam* healing
▸ **'wholesomely** ADVERB ▸ **'wholesomeness** NOUN

whole tone *or US and Canadian* **whole step** NOUN an interval of two semitones; a frequency difference of 200 cents in the system of equal temperament. Often shortened to: **tone.**

whole-tone scale NOUN either of two scales produced by commencing on one of any two notes a chromatic semitone apart and proceeding upwards or downwards in whole tones for an octave. Such a scale, consisting of six degrees to the octave, is used by Debussy and subsequent composers.

whole-wheat ADJECTIVE another term (esp US and Canadian) for **wholemeal.**

who'll (hu:l) CONTRACTION OF who will *or* who shall.

wholly ('həʊllɪ) ADVERB 1 completely, totally, or entirely. 2 without exception; exclusively.

whom (hu:m) PRONOUN the objective form of *who,* used when *who* is not the subject of its own clause: *whom did you say you had seen?; he can't remember whom he saw.*
▷HISTORY Old English *hwām,* dative of *hwā* WHO

> **Language note** It was formerly considered correct to use *whom* whenever the objective form of *who* was required. This is no longer thought to be necessary and the objective form *who* is now commonly used, even in formal writing: *there were several people there who he had met before.* *Who* cannot be used directly after a preposition – the preposition is usually displaced, as in *the man (who) he sold his car to.* In formal writing *whom* is preferred in sentences like these: *the man to whom he sold his car.* There are some types of sentence in which *who* cannot be used: *the refugees, many of whom were old and ill, were allowed across the border.*

whomever (hu:m'ɛvə) PRONOUN the objective form of *whoever*: *I'll hire whomever I can find.*

whomsoever (,hu:msəʊ'ɛvə) PRONOUN *Archaic or formal* the objective form of *whosoever*: *to whomsoever it may concern.*

whoop (wu:p) VERB 1 to utter (speech) with loud cries, as of enthusiasm or excitement. 2 *Med* to cough convulsively with a crowing sound made at each inspiration. 3 (of certain birds) to utter (a hooting cry). 4 (*tr*) to urge on or call with or as if with whoops. 5 (wʊp, wu:p) **whoop it up.** *Informal* **a** to indulge in a noisy celebration. **b** *US* to arouse enthusiasm. ◆ NOUN 6 a loud cry, esp one expressing enthusiasm or excitement. 7 *Med* the convulsive crowing sound made during a paroxysm of whooping cough. 8 **not worth a whoop.** *Informal* worthless. ◆ See also **whoops.**
▷HISTORY C14: of imitative origin

whoopee *Informal* ◆ INTERJECTION (wʊ'pi:) 1 an exclamation of joy, excitement, etc. ◆ NOUN ('wʊpi:) 2 **make whoopee. a** to engage in noisy merrymaking. **b** to make love.

whoopee cushion NOUN a joke cushion that emits a sound like the breaking of wind when someone sits on it.

whooper *or* **whooper swan** ('wu:pə) NOUN a large white Old World swan, *Cygnus cygnus,* having a black bill with a yellow base and a noisy whooping cry.

whooping cough ('hu:pɪŋ) NOUN an acute infectious disease characterized by coughing spasms that end with a shrill crowing sound on inspiration: caused by infection with the bacillus *Bordetella pertussis.* Technical name: **pertussis.**

whooping crane NOUN a rare North American crane, *Grus americana,* having a white plumage with black wings and a red naked face.

whoops (wʊps) INTERJECTION an exclamation of surprise, as when a person falls over, or of apology.

whoosh *or* **woosh** (wʊʃ) NOUN 1 a hissing or rushing sound. 2 a rush of emotion: *a whoosh of happiness.* ◆ VERB 3 (*intr*) to make or move with a hissing or rushing sound.

whop, wop, *or less commonly* **whap** (wɒp) *Informal* ◆ VERB **whops, whopping, whopped.** 1 (*tr*) to strike, beat, or thrash. 2 (*tr*) to defeat utterly. 3 (*intr*) to drop or fall. ◆ NOUN 4 a heavy blow or the sound made by such a blow.
▷HISTORY C14: variant of *wap,* perhaps of imitative origin

whopper ('wɒpə) NOUN *Informal* 1 anything uncommonly large of its kind. 2 a big lie.
▷HISTORY C18: from WHOP

whopping ('wɒpɪŋ) ADJECTIVE *Informal* uncommonly large.

whore (hɔ:) NOUN 1 a prostitute or promiscuous woman: often a term of abuse. ◆ VERB (*intr*) 2 to be or act as a prostitute. 3 (of a man) to have promiscuous sexual relations, esp with prostitutes. 4 (often foll by *after*) to seek that which is immoral, idolatrous, etc.
▷HISTORY Old English *hōre;* related to Old Norse *hōra,* Old High German *hvora,* Latin *carus* dear
▸ **'whorish** ADJECTIVE ▸ **'whorishly** ADVERB ▸ **'whorishness** NOUN

whoredom ('hɔ:dəm) NOUN 1 the activity of whoring or state of being a whore. 2 a biblical word for **idolatry.**

whorehouse ('hɔ:,haʊs) NOUN another word for **brothel.**

whoremaster ('hɔ:,mɑ:stə) NOUN *Archaic* a person who consorts with or procures whores.
▸ **'whore,mastery** NOUN

whoremonger ('hɔ:,mʌŋgə) NOUN a person who consorts with whores; lecher.
▸ **'whore,mongery** NOUN

whoreson ('hɔːsən) *Archaic* ◆ NOUN [1] a bastard. [2] a scoundrel; wretch. ◆ ADJECTIVE [3] vile or hateful.

whorl (wɜːl) NOUN [1] *Botany* a radial arrangement of three or more petals, stamens, leaves, etc., around a stem. [2] *Zoology* a single turn in a spiral shell. [3] one of the basic patterns of the human fingerprint, formed by several complete circular ridges one inside another. Compare **arch**[1] (sense 4b), **loop**[1] (sense 10a). [4] anything shaped like a coil.
▷HISTORY C15: probably variant of *wherville* WHIRL, influenced by Dutch *worvel*
▸**whorled** ADJECTIVE

whortleberry ('wɜːtᵊlˌbɛrɪ) NOUN, *plural* **-ries**. [1] Also called **huckleberry** and (dialect) **hurt, whort.** A small Eurasian ericaceous shrub, *Vaccinium myrtillus*, greenish-pink flowers and edible sweet blackish berries. [2] the fruit of this shrub. [3] **bog whortleberry.** a related plant, *V. uliginosum*, of mountain regions, having pink flowers and black fruits.
▷HISTORY C16: southwestern English dialect form of *hurtleberry;* of unknown origin

who's (huːz) CONTRACTION OF who is.

whose (huːz) DETERMINER [1] **a** of whom? belonging to whom? used in direct and indirect questions: *I told him whose fault it was; whose car is this?* **b** (*as pronoun*): *whose is that?* [2] of whom; belonging to whom; of which; belonging to which: used as a relative pronoun: *a house whose windows are broken.*
▷HISTORY Old English *hwæs,* genitive of *hwā* WHO and *hwæt* WHAT

whoso ('huːsəʊ) PRONOUN an archaic word for **whoever.**

whosoever (ˌhuːsəʊ'ɛvə) PRONOUN an archaic or formal word for **whoever.**

who's who NOUN a book or list containing the names and short biographies of famous people.

WH question NOUN a question in English to which an appropriate answer is to give information rather than to answer "yes" or "no": typically introduced by the word *who, which, what, where, when,* or *how.* Also called: **information question.**

Whr ABBREVIATION FOR watt-hour.

whsle ABBREVIATION FOR wholesale.

whump (wʌmp) NOUN *Informal* a dull thud.
▷HISTORY C19: of imitative origin

whup (wʌp, wʊp) VERB **whups, whupping, whupped.** (*tr*) *Chiefly US informal* to defeat totally; overwhelm.
▷HISTORY C19: variant of WHIP

why (waɪ) ADVERB [1] **a** for what reason, purpose, or cause?: *why are you here?* **b** (*used in indirect questions*): *tell me why you're here.* ◆ PRONOUN [2] for or because of which: *there is no reason why he shouldn't come.* ◆ NOUN, *plural* **whys.** [3] (*usually plural*) the reason, purpose, or cause of something (esp in the phrase **the whys and wherefores**). ◆ INTERJECTION [4] an introductory expression of surprise, disagreement, indignation, etc.: *why, don't be silly!*
▷HISTORY Old English *hwī;* related to Old Norse *hvī,* Gothic *hveileiks* what kind of, Latin *quī*

Whyalla (waɪ'ælə) NOUN a port in S South Australia, on Spencer Gulf: iron and steel and shipbuilding industries. Pop.: 25 526 (1991).

whydah *or* **whidah** ('wɪdə) NOUN any of various predominantly black African weaverbirds of the genus *Vidua* and related genera, the males of which grow very long tail feathers in the breeding season. Also called: **whydah bird, whidah bird, widow bird.**
▷HISTORY C18: after the name of a town in Benin

whydunnit *or* **whydunit** (ˌwaɪˈdʌnɪt) NOUN *Informal* a novel, film, etc., concerned with the motives of the criminal rather than his or her identity.

WI ABBREVIATION FOR: [1] West Indian. [2] West Indies. [3] Wisconsin. [4] (in Britain) **Women's Institute.**

wibble ('wɪbᵊl) VERB (*intr*) *Informal* [1] to wobble. [2] (often followed by *on*) to speak or write in a vague or wordy manner.
▷HISTORY C19: from *wibble-wobble,* reduplication of WOBBLE

Wicca ('wɪkə) NOUN (*sometimes not capital*) the cult or practice of witchcraft.
▷HISTORY C20: revival of Old English *wicca* witch
▸'**Wiccan** NOUN, ADJECTIVE

Wichita ('wɪtʃɪˌtɔː) NOUN a city in S Kansas, on the Arkansas River: the largest city in the state; two universities. Pop.: 344 284 (2000).

wick[1] (wɪk) NOUN [1] a cord or band of loosely twisted or woven fibres, as in a candle, cigarette lighter, etc., that supplies fuel to a flame by capillary action. [2] **get on (someone's) wick.** *Brit slang* to cause irritation to (a person).
▷HISTORY Old English *weoce;* related to Old High German *wioh,* Middle Dutch *wēke* (Dutch *wiek*)
▸'**wicking** NOUN

wick[2] (wɪk) NOUN *Archaic* a village or hamlet.
▷HISTORY Old English *wīc;* related to *-wich* in place names, Latin *vīcus,* Greek *oîkos*

wick[3] (wɪk) ADJECTIVE *Northern English dialect* [1] lively or active. [2] alive or crawling: *a dog wick with fleas.*
▷HISTORY dialect variant of QUICK alive

Wick (wɪk) NOUN a town in N Scotland, in Highland, at the head of **Wick Bay** (an inlet of the North Sea). Pop.: 7681 (1991).

wicked ('wɪkɪd) ADJECTIVE [1] **a** morally bad in principle or practice. **b** (*as collective noun;* preceded by *the*): *the wicked.* [2] mischievous or roguish, esp in a playful way: *a wicked grin.* [3] causing injury or harm. [4] troublesome, unpleasant, or offensive. [5] *Slang* very good.
▷HISTORY C13: from dialect *wick,* from Old English *wicca* sorcerer, *wicce* WITCH[1]
▸'**wickedly** ADVERB ▸'**wickedness** NOUN

wicker ('wɪkə) NOUN [1] a slender flexible twig or shoot, esp of willow. [2] short for **wickerwork.** ◆ ADJECTIVE [3] made, consisting of, or constructed from wicker.
▷HISTORY C14: from Scandinavian; compare Swedish *viker,* Danish *viger* willow, Swedish *vika* to bend

wickerwork ('wɪkəˌwɜːk) NOUN **a** a material consisting of wicker. **b** (*as modifier*): *a wickerwork chair.*

wicket ('wɪkɪt) NOUN [1] a small door or gate, esp one that is near to or part of a larger one. [2] *US* a small window or opening in a door, esp one fitted with a grating or glass pane, used as a means of communication in a ticket office, bank, etc. [3] a small sluicegate, esp one in a canal lock gate or by a water wheel. [4] *US* a croquet hoop. [5] **a** *Cricket* either of two constructions, placed 22 yards apart, consisting of three pointed stumps stuck parallel in the ground with two wooden bails resting on top, at which the batsman stands. **b** the strip of ground between these. **c** a batsman's turn at batting or the period during which two batsmen bat: *a third-wicket partnership.* **d** the act or instance of a batsman being got out: *the bowler took six wickets.* [6] **keep wicket.** to act as a wicketkeeper. [7] **on a good, sticky,** etc., **wicket.** *Informal* in an advantageous, awkward, etc., situation.
▷HISTORY C18: from Old Northern French *wiket;* related to Old Norse *vikja* to move

wicketkeeper ('wɪkɪtˌkiːpə) NOUN *Cricket* the player on the fielding side positioned directly behind the wicket.

wicket maiden NOUN *Cricket* an over in which no runs are scored with the bat and at least one wicket is taken by the bowler. See also **maiden over.**

wickiup, wikiup, *or* **wickyup** ('wɪkɪˌʌp) NOUN *US and Canadian* a crude shelter made of brushwood, mats, or grass and having an oval frame, esp of a kind used by nomadic Indians now in Oklahoma and neighbouring states of the US.
▷HISTORY C19: from Sac, Fox, and Kickapoo *wikiyap;* compare WIGWAM

Wicklow ('wɪkləʊ) NOUN [1] a county of E Republic of Ireland, in Leinster province on the Irish Sea: consists of a coastal strip rising inland to the **Wicklow Mountains;** mainly agricultural, with several resorts. County town: Wicklow. Pop.: 102 683 (1996). Area: 2025 sq. km (782 sq. miles). [2] a port in E Republic of Ireland, county town of Co. Wicklow. Pop.: 5850 (1991).

wickthing ('wɪkˌθɪŋ) NOUN *Lancashire dialect* a creeping animal, such as a woodlouse.
▷HISTORY from WICK[3] + THING[1]

wicopy ('wɪkəpɪ) NOUN, *plural* **-pies.** *US* any of various North American trees, shrubs, or herbaceous plants, esp the leatherwood, various willowherbs, and the basswood.
▷HISTORY C18: from Cree *wikupiy* inner bark, willow bark

widdershins ('wɪdəˌʃɪnz; *Scot* 'wɪdər-) ADVERB *Chiefly Scot* a variant spelling of **withershins.**

widdle ('wɪdᵊl) *Brit informal* ◆ VERB [1] (*intr*) to urinate. ◆ NOUN [2] urine. [3] an act or instance of urinating.
▷HISTORY C20: from PIDDLE

wide (waɪd) ADJECTIVE [1] having a great extent from side to side. [2] of vast size or scope; spacious or extensive. [3] **a** (*postpositive*) having a specified extent, esp from side to side: *two yards wide.* **b** (*in combination*) covering or extending throughout: *nationwide.* [4] distant or remote from the desired point, mark, etc.: *your guess is wide of the mark.* [5] (of eyes) opened fully. [6] loose, full, or roomy: *wide trousers.* [7] exhibiting a considerable spread, as between certain limits: *a wide variation.* [8] *Phonetics* another word for **lax** (sense 4) or **open** (sense 34). ◆ ADVERB [9] over an extensive area: *to travel far and wide.* [10] to the full extent: *he opened the door wide.* [11] far from the desired point, mark, etc. ◆ NOUN [12] (in cricket) a bowled ball that is outside the batsman's reach and scores a run for the batting side. [13] *Archaic or poetic* a wide space or extent. [14] **to the wide.** completely.
▷HISTORY Old English *wīd;* related to Old Norse *vīthr,* Old High German *wīt*
▸'**widely** ADVERB ▸'**wideness** NOUN ▸'**widish** ADJECTIVE

wide-angle lens NOUN a lens system on a camera that can cover an angle of view of 60° or more and therefore has a fairly small focal length. See also **fisheye lens.**

wide area network NOUN *Computing* a network of computers interconnected over large distances, often by optical fibres or microwave communications. Abbreviation: **WAN.**

wide-awake ADJECTIVE (**wide awake** when postpositive) [1] fully awake. [2] keen, alert, or observant. ◆ NOUN [3] Also called: **wide-awake hat.** a hat with a low crown and very wide brim.
▸'**wide-a'wakeness** NOUN

wide-body ADJECTIVE (of an aircraft) having a wide fuselage, esp wide enough to contain three rows of seats abreast.

wide boy NOUN *Brit slang* a man who is prepared to use unscrupulous methods to progress or make money.

wide-eyed ADJECTIVE innocent or credulous.

widen ('waɪdᵊn) VERB to make or become wide or wider.
▸'**widener** NOUN

wide-open ADJECTIVE (**wide open** when postpositive) [1] open to the full extent. [2] (*postpositive*) exposed to attack; vulnerable. [3] uncertain as to outcome. [4] *US informal* (of a town or city) lax in the enforcement of certain laws, esp those relating to the sale and consumption of alcohol, gambling, the control of vice, etc.

wide receiver NOUN *American football* a player whose function is to catch long passes from the quarterback.

widescreen ('waɪdˌskriːn) ADJECTIVE of or relating to a form of film projection or television broadcasting in which the screen has much greater width than height.

widespread ('waɪdˌsprɛd) ADJECTIVE [1] extending over a wide area. [2] accepted by or occurring among many people.

widgeon ('wɪdʒən) NOUN a variant spelling of **wigeon.**

widget ('wɪdʒɪt) NOUN [1] *Informal* any small mechanism or device, the name of which is unknown or temporarily forgotten. [2] a small device in a beer can which, when the can is opened, releases nitrogen gas into the beer, giving it a head.
▷HISTORY C20: changed from GADGET

widgie ('wɪdʒɪ) NOUN *Austral slang* a female larrikin or bodgie.
▷HISTORY C20: alteration of BODGIE

Widnes ('wɪdnɪs) NOUN a town in NW England, in Halton unitary authority, N Cheshire, on the River Mersey: chemical industry. Pop.: 57 162 (1991).

widow ('wɪdəʊ) NOUN [1] a woman who has survived her husband, esp one who has not remarried. [2] (*usually with a modifier*) *Informal* a

woman whose husband frequently leaves her alone while he indulges in a sport, etc.: *a golf widow.* 3 *Printing* a short line at the end of a paragraph, esp one that occurs as the top line of a page or column. Compare **orphan** (sense 3). 4 (in some card games) an additional hand or set of cards exposed on the table. ◆ VERB (*tr; usually passive*) 5 to cause to become a widow. 6 to deprive of something valued or desirable.
▷HISTORY Old English *widuwe;* related to German *Witwe,* Latin *vidua* (feminine of *viduus* deprived), Sanskrit *vidhavā*
▸ **ˈwidowhood** NOUN

widow bird NOUN another name for **whydah.**

widower (ˈwɪdəʊə) NOUN a man whose wife has died and who has not remarried.

widow's benefit NOUN (in the British National Insurance scheme) a former weekly payment made to a widow.

widow's cruse NOUN an endless or unfailing source of supply.
▷HISTORY allusion to I Kings 17:16

widow's mite NOUN a small contribution given by a person who has very little.
▷HISTORY allusion to Mark 12:43

widow's peak NOUN a V-shaped point in the hairline in the middle of the forehead.
▷HISTORY from the belief that it presaged early widowhood

widow woman NOUN *Archaic or dialect* another term for **widow** (sense 1).

width (wɪdθ) NOUN 1 the linear extent or measurement of something from side to side, usually being the shortest dimension or (for something fixed) the shortest horizontal dimension. 2 the state or fact of being wide. 3 a piece or section of something at its full extent from side to side: *a width of cloth.* 4 the distance across a rectangular swimming bath, as opposed to its length.
▷HISTORY C17: from WIDE + -TH[1], analogous to BREADTH

widthwise (ˈwɪdθˌwaɪz) *or* **widthways** (ˈwɪdθˌweɪz) ADVERB in the direction of the width; from side to side.

Wieland (ˈviːlant) NOUN the German name for **Wayland.**

wield (wiːld) VERB (*tr*) 1 to handle or use (a weapon, tool, etc.). 2 to exert or maintain (power or authority). 3 *Obsolete* to rule.
▷HISTORY Old English *wieldan, wealdan;* related to Old Norse *valda,* Old Saxon *waldan,* German *walten,* Latin *valēre* to be strong
▸ **ˈwieldable** ADJECTIVE ▸ **ˈwielder** NOUN

wieldy (ˈwiːldɪ) ADJECTIVE **wieldier, wieldiest.** easily handled, used, or managed.

Wien (viːn) NOUN the German name for **Vienna.**

wiener (ˈwiːnə) *or* **wienerwurst** (ˈwiːnəˌwɜːst) NOUN *US and Canadian* a kind of smoked beef or pork sausage, similar to a frankfurter. Also called: **wienie, weenie** (ˈwiːnɪ).
▷HISTORY C20: shortened from German *Wiener Wurst* Viennese sausage

Wiener Neustadt (*German* ˈviːnər ˈnɔyʃtat) NOUN a city in E Austria, in Lower Austria. Pop.: 35 268 (1991).

Wiener schnitzel (ˈviːnə ˈʃnɪtsəl) NOUN a large thin escalope of veal, coated in egg and crumbs, fried, and traditionally served with a garnish.
▷HISTORY German: Viennese cutlet

Wiesbaden (*German* ˈviːsbaːdən) NOUN a city in W Germany, capital of Hesse state: a spa resort since Roman times. Pop.: 268 200 (1999 est.). Latin name: **Aquae Mattiacorum** (ˈækwiː ˌmætjəˈkaʊrəm).

wife (waɪf) NOUN, *plural* **wives** (waɪvz). 1 a man's partner in marriage; a married woman. Related adjective: **uxorial.** 2 an archaic or dialect word for **woman.** 3 **take to wife.** to marry (a woman).
▷HISTORY Old English *wīf;* related to Old Norse *vīf* (perhaps from *vīfathr* veiled), Old High German *wīb* (German *Weib*)
▸ **ˈwifehood** NOUN ▸ **ˈwifeless** ADJECTIVE ▸ **ˈwifeˌlike** ADJECTIVE ▸ **ˈwifeliness** NOUN ▸ **ˈwifely** ADJECTIVE

wife-beater NOUN a man who hits his wife.
▸ **ˈwife-ˌbeating** NOUN

wife swapping NOUN **a** the temporary exchange of wives between married couples for sexual relations. **b** (*as modifier*): *a wife-swapping party.*

wig (wɪg) NOUN 1 an artificial head of hair, either human or synthetic, worn to disguise baldness, as part of a theatrical or ceremonial dress, as a disguise, or for adornment. ◆ VERB **wigs, wigging, wigged.** (*tr*) 2 *Obsolete* to furnish with a wig. 3 *Brit slang* to berate severely. ◆ See also **wig out.**
▷HISTORY C17: shortened from PERIWIG
▸ **wigged** ADJECTIVE ▸ **ˈwigless** ADJECTIVE ▸ **ˈwigˌlike** ADJECTIVE

Wig. ABBREVIATION FOR Wigtownshire.

Wigan (ˈwɪgən) NOUN 1 an industrial town in NW England, in Wigan unitary authority, Greater Manchester: former coal-mining centre. Pop.: 85 819 (1991). 2 a unitary authority in NW England, in Greater Manchester. Pop.: 301 417 (2001). Area: 199 sq. km (77 sq. miles).

wigeon *or* **widgeon** (ˈwɪdʒən) NOUN 1 a Eurasian duck, *Anas penelope,* of marshes, swamps, etc., the male of which has a reddish-brown head and chest and grey and white back and wings. 2 **American wigeon.** Also called: **baldpate.** a similar bird, *Anas americana,* of North America, the male of which has a white crown.
▷HISTORY C16: of uncertain origin

wigger *or* **wigga** (ˈwɪgə) NOUN *Slang* a white youth who adopts black youth culture by adopting its speech, wearing its clothes, and listening to its music.
▷HISTORY C20: from a blend of WHITE + NIGGER

wigging (ˈwɪgɪŋ) NOUN 1 *Brit slang* a rebuke or reprimand. 2 *NZ* the shearing of wool from the head of a sheep.

wiggle (ˈwɪgᵊl) VERB 1 to move or cause to move with jerky movements, esp from side to side. ◆ NOUN 2 the act or an instance of wiggling. 3 **get a wiggle on.** *Slang, chiefly US* to hurry up.
▷HISTORY C13: from Middle Low German, Middle Dutch *wiggelen*
▸ **ˈwiggler** NOUN ▸ **ˈwiggly** ADJECTIVE

wiggle room NOUN *Informal* scope for freedom of action or thought.

wight[1] (waɪt) NOUN *Archaic* a human being.
▷HISTORY Old English *wiht;* related to Old Frisian *āwet* something, Old Norse *vættr* being, Gothic *waihts* thing, German *Wicht* small person

wight[2] (waɪt) ADJECTIVE *Archaic* strong and brave; valiant.
▷HISTORY C13: from Old Norse *vigt;* related to Old English *wīg* battle, Latin *vincere* to conquer

Wight (waɪt) NOUN **Isle of.** an island and county of S England in the English Channel. Administrative centre: Newport. Pop.: 132 719 (2001). Area: 380 sq. km (147 sq. miles).

wig out VERB (*intr, adverb*) *Informal* to become extremely excited.
▷HISTORY C20: from BIGWIG

Wigtownshire (ˈwɪgtənˌʃɪə, -ʃə) NOUN (until 1975) a county of SW Scotland, now part of Dumfries and Galloway.

wigwag (ˈwɪgˌwæg) VERB **-wags, -wagging, -wagged.** 1 to move (something) back and forth. 2 to communicate with (someone) by means of a flag semaphore. ◆ NOUN 3 **a** a system of communication by flag semaphore. **b** the message signalled.
▷HISTORY C16: from obsolete *wig,* probably short for WIGGLE + WAG[1]
▸ **ˈwigˌwagger** NOUN

wigwam (ˈwɪgˌwæm) NOUN 1 any dwelling of the North American Indians, esp one made of bark, rushes, or skins spread over or enclosed by a set of arched poles lashed together. Compare **tepee.** 2 a similar structure for children.
▷HISTORY from Abnaki and Massachuset *wīkwām,* literally: their abode

wikiup (ˈwɪkɪˌʌp) NOUN a variant spelling of **wickiup.**

wilco (ˈwɪlˌkəʊ) INTERJECTION an expression in signalling, telecommunications, etc., indicating that a message just received will be complied with. Compare **roger.**
▷HISTORY C20: abbreviation for *I will comply*

Wilcoxon test (wɪlˈkɒksᵊn) NOUN **a** Also called: **Wilcoxon matched-pairs signed-ranks test.** a statistical test for the relative size of the scores of the same or matched subjects under two experimental conditions by comparing the distributions for positive and negative differences of the ranks of their absolute values. **b Wilcoxon Mann-Whitney test.** See **Mann-Whitney test.**
▷HISTORY named after Frank *Wilcoxon* (1892–1965), Irish mathematician and statistician

wild (waɪld) ADJECTIVE 1 (of animals) living independently of man; not domesticated or tame. 2 (of plants) growing in a natural state; not cultivated. 3 uninhabited or uncultivated; desolate: *a wild stretch of land.* 4 living in a savage or uncivilized way: *wild tribes.* 5 lacking restraint: *wild merriment.* 6 of great violence or intensity: *a wild storm.* 7 disorderly or chaotic: *wild thoughts; wild talk.* 8 dishevelled; untidy: *wild hair.* 9 in a state of extreme emotional intensity: *wild with anger.* 10 reckless: *wild speculations.* 11 not calculated; random: *a wild guess.* 12 unconventional; fantastic; crazy: *wild friends.* 13 (*postpositive;* foll by *about*) *Informal* intensely enthusiastic or excited. 14 (of a card, such as a joker or deuce in some games) able to be given any value the holder pleases: *jacks are wild.* 15 **wild and woolly. a** a rough; untamed; barbarous. **b** (of theories, plans, etc.) not fully thought out. ◆ ADVERB 16 in a wild manner. 17 **run wild. a** to grow without cultivation or care. **b** to behave without restraint. ◆ NOUN 18 (*often plural*) a desolate, uncultivated, or uninhabited region. 19 **the wild. a** a free natural state of living. **b** the wilderness.
▷HISTORY Old English *wilde;* related to Old Saxon, Old High German *wildi,* Old Norse *villr,* Gothic *wiltheis*
▸ **ˈwildish** ADJECTIVE ▸ **ˈwildly** ADVERB ▸ **ˈwildness** NOUN

wild boar NOUN a wild pig, *Sus scrofa,* of parts of Europe and central Asia, having a pale grey to black coat, thin legs, a narrow body, and prominent tusks.

wild brier NOUN another name for **wild rose.**

wild card NOUN 1 See **wild** (sense 14). 2 *Sport* a player or team that has not qualified for a competition but is allowed to take part, at the organizers' discretion, after all the regular places have been taken. 3 an unpredictable element in a situation. 4 *Computing* a symbol that can represent any character or group of characters, as in a filename.

wild carrot NOUN an umbelliferous plant, *Daucus carota,* of temperate regions, having clusters of white flowers and hooked fruits.

wildcat (ˈwaɪldˌkæt) NOUN, *plural* **-cats** *or* **-cat.** 1 a wild European cat, *Felis silvestris,* that resembles the domestic tabby but is larger and has a bushy tail. 2 any of various other felines, esp of the genus *Lynx,* such as the lynx and the caracal. 3 *US and Canadian* another name for **bobcat.** 4 *Informal* a savage or aggressive person. 5 an exploratory drilling for petroleum or natural gas. 6 *US and Canadian* an unsound commercial enterprise. 7 the US and Canadian name for **light engine.** 8 (*modifier*) *US and Canadian* **a** of or relating to an unsound business enterprise: *wildcat stock.* **b** financially or commercially unsound: *a wildcat project.* 9 (*modifier*) *US and Canadian* (of a train) running without permission or outside the timetable. ◆ VERB **-cats, -catting, -catted.** 10 (*intr*) to drill for petroleum or natural gas in an area having no known reserves.
▸ **ˈwildˌcatting** NOUN, ADJECTIVE

wildcat strike NOUN a strike begun by workers spontaneously or without union approval.

wildcatter (ˈwaɪldˌkætə) NOUN *US and Canadian informal* a prospector for oil or ores in areas having no proved resources.

wild celery NOUN a strongly scented umbelliferous plant, *Apium graveolens,* of temperate regions: the ancestor of cultivated celery. Archaic name: **smallage.**

wild cherry NOUN another name for **gean** (sense 1).

wild dog NOUN another name for **dingo.**

wildebeest (ˈwɪldɪˌbiːst, ˈvɪl-) NOUN, *plural* **-beests** *or* **-beest.** another name for **gnu.**
▷HISTORY C19: from Afrikaans, literally: wild beast

wilder (ˈwɪldə) VERB *Archaic* 1 to lead or be led astray. 2 to bewilder or become bewildered.
▷HISTORY C17: of uncertain origin
▸ **ˈwilderment** NOUN

wilderness ('wɪldənɪs) NOUN [1] a wild, uninhabited, and uncultivated region. [2] any desolate tract or area. [3] a confused mass or collection. [4] **a voice (crying) in the wilderness.** a person, group, etc., making a suggestion or plea that is ignored. [5] **in the wilderness.** no longer having influence, recognition, or publicity.
▷HISTORY Old English *wildēornes,* from *wildēor* wild beast (from WILD + *dēor* beast, DEER) + -NESS; related to Middle Dutch *wildernisse,* German *Wildernis*

Wilderness ('wɪldənɪs) NOUN **the.** the barren regions to the south and east of Palestine, esp those in which the Israelites wandered before entering the Promised Land and in which Christ fasted for 40 days and nights.

wild-eyed ADJECTIVE [1] glaring in an angry, distracted, or wild manner. [2] ill-conceived or totally impracticable.

wildfire ('waɪld,faɪə) NOUN [1] a highly flammable material, such as Greek fire, formerly used in warfare. [2] **a** a raging and uncontrollable fire. **b** anything that is disseminated quickly (esp in the phrase **spread like wildfire**). [3] lightning without audible thunder. [4] another name for **will-o'-the-wisp.**

wild flower NOUN [1] Also: **wildflower.** any flowering plant that grows in an uncultivated state. [2] the flower of such a plant.

wildfowl ('waɪld,faʊl) NOUN [1] any bird that is hunted by man, esp any duck or similar aquatic bird. [2] such birds collectively.
▸**'wild,fowler** NOUN ▸**'wild,fowling** ADJECTIVE, NOUN

Wild Geese NOUN **the.** the Irish expatriates who served as professional soldiers with the Catholic powers of Europe, esp France, from the late 17th to the early 20th centuries.

wild ginger NOUN a North American plant, *Asarum canadense,* having a solitary brownish flower and an aromatic root: family *Aristolochiaceae*. See also **asarabacca, asarum.**

wild-goose chase NOUN an absurd or hopeless pursuit, as of something unattainable.

wild hyacinth NOUN another name for **bluebell** (sense 1).

wild indigo NOUN any of several North American leguminous plants of the genus *Baptisia,* esp *B. tinctoria,* which has yellow flowers and three-lobed leaves.

wilding ('waɪldɪŋ) NOUN [1] an uncultivated plant, esp the crab apple, or a cultivated plant that has become wild. [2] a wild animal. ◆ Also called: **wildling.**

wild Irishman NOUN *NZ* another name for **matagouri.**

wild lettuce NOUN any of several uncultivated lettuce plants, such as *Lactuca serriola* (or *L. scariola*) of Eurasia and *L. canadensis* (**horseweed**) of North America, which grow as weeds and have yellow or blue flowers, milky juice in the stem, and prickly leaves: family *Asteraceae* (composites).

wildlife ('waɪld,laɪf) NOUN wild animals and plants collectively.

wild liquorice NOUN [1] another name for *Astragalus glycyphyllos:* see **milk vetch.** [2] another name for **liquorice** (sense 1). [3] a North American plant, *Glycyrrhiza lepidota,* that is related to true liquorice and has similar properties.

wild man NOUN [1] a savage. [2] an extremist in politics.

wild mustard NOUN another name for **charlock** (sense 1).

wild oat NOUN any of several temperate annual grasses of the genus *Avena,* esp *A. fatua,* that grow as weeds and have long bristles on their flower spikes.

wild oats PLURAL NOUN *Slang* the indiscretions of youth, esp dissoluteness before settling down (esp in the phrase **sow one's wild oats**).

wild olive NOUN any of various trees or shrubs that resemble the olive tree or bear olive-like fruits, esp the oleaster.

wild pansy NOUN [1] Also called: **heartsease, love-in-idleness,** and (in the US) **Johnny-jump-up.** a Eurasian violaceous plant, *Viola tricolor,* having purple, yellow, and pale mauve spurred flowers. [2] any of various similar plants of the genus *Viola.*

wild parsley NOUN any of various uncultivated umbelliferous plants that resemble parsley.

wild parsnip NOUN a strong-smelling umbelliferous plant, *Pastinaca sativa,* that has an inedible root: the ancestor of the cultivated parsnip.

wild rice NOUN another name for **Indian rice.**

wild rose NOUN any of numerous roses, such as the dogrose and sweetbrier, that grow wild and have flowers with only one whorl of petals.

wild rubber NOUN rubber obtained from uncultivated rubber trees.

wild rye NOUN any of various perennial grasses of the N temperate genus *Elymus,* resembling cultivated rye in having paired bristly ears or spikes and flat leaves.

wild silk NOUN [1] silk produced by wild silkworms. [2] a fabric made from this, or from short fibres of silk designed to imitate it.

wild Spaniard NOUN any of various subalpine perennials of the genus *Aciphylla* of New Zealand, with sharp leaves. Often shortened to: **Spaniard.**

wild track NOUN a soundtrack recorded other than with a synchronized picture, usually carrying sound effects, random dialogue, etc.

wild type NOUN *Biology* the typical form of a species of organism resulting from breeding under natural conditions.

wild water NOUN **a** turbulent water in a river, esp as an area for navigating in a canoe as a sport. **b** (*as modifier*): *wild-water racing.*

Wild West NOUN the western US during its settlement, esp with reference to its frontier lawlessness.

Wild West show NOUN *US* a show or circus act presenting feats of horsemanship, shooting, etc.

wildwood ('waɪld,wʊd) NOUN *Archaic* a wood or forest growing in a natural uncultivated state.

wile (waɪl) NOUN [1] trickery, cunning, or craftiness. [2] (*usually plural*) an artful or seductive trick or ploy. ◆ VERB [3] (*tr*) to lure, beguile, or entice.
▷HISTORY C12: from Old Norse *vel* craft; probably related to Old French *wīle,* Old English *wīgle* magic. See GUILE

wilful *or US* **willful** ('wɪlfʊl) ADJECTIVE [1] intent on having one's own way; headstrong or obstinate. [2] intentional: *wilful murder.*
▸**'wilfully** *or* (*US*) **'willfully** ADVERB ▸**'wilfulness** *or* (*US*) **'willfulness** NOUN

wilga ('wɪlgə) NOUN a small drought-resistant tree, *Geijera parviflora,* of Australia, having hard aromatic wood, white flowers, and foliage that resembles that of the willow.
▷HISTORY C19: from a native Australian language

Wilhelmshaven (*German* vɪlhelms'ha:fən) NOUN a port and resort in NW Germany, in Lower Saxony: founded in 1853; was the chief German North Sea naval base until 1945; a major oil port. Pop.: 91 150 (1991).

Wilhelmstrasse (*German* 'vɪlhɛlmʃtra:sə) NOUN [1] a street in the centre of Berlin, where the German foreign office and other government buildings were situated until 1945. [2] Germany's ministry of foreign affairs until 1945.

Wilkes Land NOUN a region in Antarctica south of Australia, on the Indian Ocean.

will[1] (wɪl) VERB, *past* **would.** (takes an infinitive without *to* or an implied infinitive) used as an auxiliary. [1] (esp with *you, he, she, it, they,* or a noun as subject) to make the future tense. Compare **shall** (sense 1). [2] to express resolution on the part of the speaker: *I will buy that radio if it's the last thing I do.* [3] to indicate willingness or desire: *will you help me with this problem?* [4] to express compulsion, as in commands: *you will report your findings to me tomorrow.* [5] to express capacity or ability: *this rope will support a load.* [6] to express probability or expectation on the part of the speaker: *that will be Jim telephoning.* [7] to express customary practice or inevitability: *boys will be boys.* [8] (*with the infinitive always implied*) to express desire: usually in polite requests: *stay if you will.* [9] **what you will.** whatever you like. [10] **will do.** *Informal* a declaration of willingness to do what is requested.
▷HISTORY Old English *willan;* related to Old Saxon *willian,* Old Norse *vilja,* Old High German *wollen,* Latin *velle* to wish, will

Language note See at **shall.**

will[2] (wɪl) NOUN [1] the faculty of conscious and deliberate choice of action; volition. Related adjectives: **voluntary, volitive.** [2] the act or an instance of asserting a choice. [3] **a** the declaration of a person's wishes regarding the disposal of his or her property after death. Related adjective: **testamentary. b** a revocable instrument by which such wishes are expressed. [4] anything decided upon or chosen, esp by a person in authority; desire; wish. [5] determined intention: *where there's a will there's a way.* [6] disposition or attitude towards others: *he bears you no ill will.* [7] **at will.** at one's own desire, inclination, or choice. [8] **with a will.** heartily; energetically. [9] **with the best will in the world.** even with the best of intentions. ◆ VERB (*mainly tr; often takes a clause as object or an infinitive*) [10] (*also intr*) to exercise the faculty of volition in an attempt to accomplish (something): *he willed his wife's recovery from her illness.* [11] to give (property) by will to a person, society, etc.: *he willed his art collection to the nation.* [12] (*also intr*) to order or decree: *the king wills that you shall die.* [13] to choose or prefer: *wander where you will.* [14] to yearn for or desire: *to will that one's friends be happy.*
▷HISTORY Old English *willa;* related to Old Norse *vili,* Old High German *willeo* (German *Wille*), Gothic *wilja,* Old Slavonic *volja*
▸**'willer** NOUN

willable ('wɪləbᵊl) ADJECTIVE able to be wished or determined by the will.

willed (wɪld) ADJECTIVE (*in combination*) having a will as specified: *weak-willed.*

willemite ('wɪlə,maɪt) NOUN a secondary mineral consisting of zinc silicate in hexagonal crystalline form. It is white, colourless, or coloured by impurities and is found in veins of zinc ore. Formula: Zn_2SiO_4.
▷HISTORY C19: from Dutch *willemit,* named after *Willem* I of the Netherlands (1772–1834)

Willemstad (*Dutch* 'wɪləmstɑt) NOUN the capital of the Netherlands Antilles, a port on the SW coast of Curaçao: important for refining Venezuelan oil. Pop.: 123 000 (1999 est.).

willet ('wɪlɪt) NOUN a large American shore bird, *Catoptrophorus semipalmatus,* having a long stout bill, long legs, and a grey plumage with black-and-white wings: family *Scolopacidae* (sandpipers, etc.), order *Charadriiformes.*
▷HISTORY short for *pill-will-willet* imitation of its cry

willful ('wɪlfʊl) ADJECTIVE the US spelling of **wilful.**

Williamsburg ('wɪljəmz,bɜ:g) NOUN a city in SE Virginia: the capital of Virginia (1693–1779); the restoration of large sections of the colonial city was begun in 1926. Pop.: 11 530 (1990).

Williams pear NOUN a variety of pear that has large yellow juicy sweet fruit. Also called: **William's Bon Chrétien.**

willies ('wɪlɪz) PLURAL NOUN **the.** *Slang* nervousness, jitters, or fright (esp in the phrase **give** (*or* **get**) **the willies**).
▷HISTORY C20: of unknown origin

willing ('wɪlɪŋ) ADJECTIVE [1] favourably disposed or inclined; ready. [2] cheerfully or eagerly compliant. [3] done, given, accepted, etc., freely or voluntarily.
▸**'willingly** ADVERB ▸**'willingness** NOUN

willing horse NOUN a person prepared to work hard.

williwaw ('wɪlɪ,wɔ:) NOUN *US and Canadian* [1] a sudden strong gust of cold wind blowing offshore from a mountainous coast, as in the Strait of Magellan. [2] a state of great turmoil.
▷HISTORY C19: of unknown origin

will-o'-the-wisp (,wɪləðə'wɪsp) NOUN [1] Also called: **friar's lantern, ignis fatuus, jack-o'-lantern.** a pale flame or phosphorescence sometimes seen over marshy ground at night. It is believed to be due to the spontaneous combustion of methane or other hydrocarbons originating from decomposing organic matter. [2] a person or thing that is elusive or allures and misleads.
▷HISTORY C17: originally *Will with the wisp,* from

Will short for *William* and *wisp* in former sense of a twist of hay or straw burning as a torch
▸ **ˌwill-o'-the-ˈwispish** *or* **ˌwill-o'-the-ˈwispy** ADJECTIVE

willow (ˈwɪləʊ) NOUN 1 any of numerous salicaceous trees and shrubs of the genus *Salix,* such as the weeping willow and osiers of N temperate regions, which have graceful flexible branches, flowers in catkins, and feathery seeds. 2 the whitish wood of certain of these trees. 3 something made of willow wood, such as a cricket or baseball bat. 4 a machine having a system of revolving spikes for opening and cleaning raw textile fibres.
▷HISTORY Old English *welig;* related to *wilige* wicker basket, Old Saxon *wilgia,* Middle High German *wilge,* Greek *helikē* willow, *helix* twisted
▸ **ˈwillowish** *or* **ˈwillow-ˌlike** ADJECTIVE

willow fly NOUN a stonefly, *Leuctra geniculata,* of the English chalk streams, esteemed by trout and therefore by anglers.

willow grouse NOUN a N European grouse, *Lagopus lagopus,* with a reddish-brown plumage and white wings: now regarded as the same species as the red grouse (*L. lagopus scoticus*) of Britain.

willowherb (ˈwɪləʊˌhɜːb) NOUN 1 any of various temperate and arctic onagraceous plants of the genus *Epilobium,* having narrow leaves, terminal clusters of pink, purplish, or white flowers, and willow-like feathery seeds. 2 short for **rosebay willowherb** (see **rosebay**). 3 (not in botanical usage) another name for **purple loosestrife** (see **loosestrife**). 4 **hairy willowherb.** See **codlins-and-cream.**

willow pattern NOUN **a** a pattern incorporating a willow tree, river, bridge, and figures, typically in blue on a white ground, used on pottery and porcelain. **b** (*as modifier*): *a willow-pattern plate.*

Willow South NOUN a city in S Alaska, about 113 km (70 miles) northwest of Anchorage: chosen as the site of the projected new state capital in 1976.

willow tit NOUN a small tit, *Parus montanus,* of marshy woods in Europe, having a greyish-brown body and dull black crown.

willow warbler NOUN an Old World warbler, *Phylloscopus trochilis,* of Eurasian woodlands.

willowy (ˈwɪləʊɪ) ADJECTIVE 1 slender and graceful. 2 flexible or pliant. 3 covered or shaded with willows.

willpower (ˈwɪlˌpaʊə) NOUN 1 the ability to control oneself and determine one's actions. 2 firmness of will.

willy (ˈwɪlɪ) NOUN *Brit informal* a childish or jocular term for **penis.**

willy-nilly (ˈwɪlɪˈnɪlɪ) ADVERB 1 whether desired or not. ◆ ADJECTIVE 2 occurring or taking place whether desired or not.
▷HISTORY Old English *wile hē, nyle hē,* literally: will he or will he not; *nyle,* from *ne* not + *willan* to WILL[1]

willy wagtail NOUN *Austral* a black-and-white flycatcher, *Rhipidura leucophrys,* having white feathers over the brows.

willy-willy (ˈwɪlɪˈwɪlɪ) NOUN *Austral* a tropical cyclone or duststorm.
▷HISTORY from a native Australian language

Wilmington (ˈwɪlmɪŋtən) NOUN a port in N Delaware, on the Delaware River: industrial centre. Pop.: 75 838 (2000).

Wilno (ˈviːlnɔ) NOUN the Polish name for **Vilnius.**

Wilson cloud chamber NOUN the full name for **cloud chamber.**

Wilson's petrel NOUN a common storm petrel, *Oceanites oceanicus,* that breeds around Antarctica but is often seen in the Atlantic. See **storm petrel.**

Wilson's snipe NOUN another name for the **common snipe.** See **snipe** (sense 1).

wilt[1] (wɪlt) VERB 1 to become or cause to become limp, flaccid, or drooping: *insufficient water makes plants wilt.* 2 to lose or cause to lose courage, strength, etc. ◆ NOUN 3 the act of wilting or state of becoming wilted. 4 any of various plant diseases characterized by permanent wilting, usually caused by fungal parasites attacking the roots.
▷HISTORY C17: perhaps variant of *wilk* to wither, from Middle Dutch *welken*

wilt[2] (wɪlt) VERB *Archaic or dialect* (used with the pronoun *thou* or its relative equivalent) a singular form of the present tense (indicative mood) of **will**[1].

Wilton (ˈwɪltən) NOUN a kind of carpet with a close velvet pile of cut loops.
▷HISTORY C18: named after *Wilton,* Wiltshire, noted for carpet manufacture

Wilton House NOUN a mansion in Wilton in Wiltshire: built for the 1st Earl of Pembroke in the 16th century; rebuilt after a fire in 1647 by Inigo Jones and John Webb; altered in the 19th century by James Wyatt; landscaped grounds include a famous Palladian bridge.

Wilts (wɪlts) ABBREVIATION FOR Wiltshire.

Wiltshire (ˈwɪltʃə, -ˌʃɪə) NOUN a county of S England, consisting mainly of chalk uplands, with Salisbury Plain in the south and the Marlborough Downs in the north; prehistoric remains (at Stonehenge and Avebury): the geographical and ceremonial county includes Swindon unitary authority (established in 1997). Administrative centre: Trowbridge. Pop. (excluding Swindon): 432 973 (2001). Area (excluding Swindon): 3481 sq. km (1344 sq. miles).

Wiltshire Horn NOUN a breed of medium-sized sheep having horns in both male and female, originating from the Chalk Downs, England.

wily (ˈwaɪlɪ) ADJECTIVE **wilier, wiliest.** characterized by or proceeding from wiles; sly or crafty.
▸ **ˈwiliness** NOUN

wimble (ˈwɪmbᵊl) NOUN 1 any of a number of hand tools, such as a brace and bit or a gimlet, used for boring holes. ◆ VERB 2 to bore (a hole) with or as if with a wimble.
▷HISTORY C13: from Middle Dutch *wimmel* auger

Wimbledon (ˈwɪmbᵊldən) NOUN part of the Greater London borough of Merton: headquarters of the All England Lawn Tennis Club since 1877 and the site of the annual international tennis championships.

wimp (wɪmp) NOUN *Informal* a feeble ineffective person. ◆ See also **wimp out.**
▷HISTORY C20: of unknown origin
▸ **ˈwimpish** *or* **ˈwimpy** ADJECTIVE

WIMP (wɪmp) ACRONYM FOR: 1 windows, icons, menus (*or* mice), pointers: denoting a type of user-friendly screen display used on small computers: *a WIMP system.* 2 *Physics* weakly interacting massive particle.

wimple (ˈwɪmpᵊl) NOUN 1 a piece of cloth draped around the head to frame the face, worn by women in the Middle Ages and still a part of the habit of some nuns. 2 *Scot* a curve or bend, as in a river. ◆ VERB 3 *Rare* to ripple or cause to ripple or undulate. 4 (*tr*) *Archaic* to cover with or put a wimple on. 5 *Archaic* (esp of a veil) to lie or cause to lie in folds or pleats.
▷HISTORY Old English *wimpel;* related to Old Saxon *wimpal,* Middle Dutch *wumpel,* Middle High German *bewimpfen* to veil

wimp out VERB (*intr, adverb*) *Informal* to fail to do or complete something through fear or lack of conviction.

Wimshurst machine (ˈwɪmzhɜːst) NOUN a type of electrostatic generator with two parallel insulating discs revolving in different directions, each being in contact with a thin metal wiper that produces a charge on the disc: usually used for demonstration purposes.
▷HISTORY C19: named after J. *Wimshurst* (1832–1903), English engineer

win[1] (wɪn) VERB **wins, winning, won.** 1 (*intr*) to achieve first place in a competition. 2 (*tr*) to gain or receive (a prize, first place, etc.) in a competition. 3 (*tr*) to succeed in or gain (something) with an effort: *we won recognition.* 4 **win one's spurs. a** to achieve recognition in some field of endeavour. **b** *History* to be knighted. 5 to gain victory or triumph in (a battle, argument, etc.). 6 (*tr*) to earn or procure (a living, etc.) by work. 7 (*tr*) to take possession of, esp violently; capture: *the Germans never won Leningrad.* 8 (when *intr,* foll by *out, through,* etc.) to reach with difficulty (a desired condition or position) or become free, loose, etc., with effort: *the boat won the shore; the boat won through to the shore.* 9 (*tr*) to turn someone into (a supporter, enemy, etc.): *you have just won an ally.* 10 (*tr*) to gain (the sympathy, loyalty, etc.) of someone. 11 (*tr*) to obtain (a woman, etc.) in marriage. 12 (*tr*) **a** to extract (ore, coal, etc.) from a mine. **b** to extract (metal or other minerals) from ore. **c** to discover and make (a mineral deposit) accessible for mining. 13 **you can't win.** *Informal* an expression of resignation after an unsuccessful attempt to overcome difficulties. ◆ NOUN 14 *Informal* a success, victory, or triumph. 15 profit; winnings. 16 the act or fact of reaching the finishing line or post first. ◆ See also **win out.**
▷HISTORY Old English *winnan;* related to Old Norse *vinna,* German *gewinnen*
▸ **ˈwinnable** ADJECTIVE

win[2] (wɪn) VERB **wins, winning, won** *or* **winned.** (*tr*) *Irish, Scot, and northern English dialect* 1 to dry (grain, hay, peat, etc.) by exposure to sun and air. 2 a less common word for **winnow.**
▷HISTORY Old English, perhaps a variant of WINNOW

wince[1] (wɪns) VERB 1 (*intr*) to start slightly, as with sudden pain; flinch. ◆ NOUN 2 the act of wincing.
▷HISTORY C18 (earlier (C13) meaning: to kick): via Old French *wencier, guenchir* to avoid, from Germanic; compare Old Saxon *wenkian,* Old High German *wenken*
▸ **ˈwincer** NOUN

wince[2] (wɪns) NOUN a roller for transferring pieces of cloth between dyeing vats.
▷HISTORY C17: variant of WINCH

wincey (ˈwɪnsɪ) NOUN *Brit* a plain- or twill-weave cloth, usually having a cotton or linen warp and a wool filling.
▷HISTORY C19: of Scottish origin, probably an alteration of *woolsey* as in LINSEY-WOOLSEY

winceyette (ˌwɪnsɪˈɛt) NOUN *Brit* a plain-weave cotton fabric with slightly raised two-sided nap.

winch[1] (wɪntʃ) NOUN 1 a windlass driven by a hand- or power-operated crank. 2 a hand- or power-operated crank by which a machine is driven. ◆ VERB 3 (*tr; often foll by up or in*) to pull (in a rope) or lift (a weight) using a winch.
▷HISTORY Old English *wince* pulley; related to WINK[1]
▸ **ˈwincher** NOUN

winch[2] (wɪntʃ) VERB (*intr*) an obsolete word for **wince**[1].

winchester (ˈwɪntʃɪstə) NOUN (*sometimes capital*) a large cylindrical bottle with a narrow neck used for transporting chemicals. It contains about 2.5 litres.
▷HISTORY after *Winchester,* Hampshire

Winchester (ˈwɪntʃɪstə) NOUN a city in S England, administrative centre of Hampshire: a Romano-British town; Saxon capital of Wessex; 11th-century cathedral; site of **Winchester College** (1382), English public school. Pop.: 36 121 (1991).

Winchester disk NOUN a type of hard disk in which disks are permanently sealed, together with read-write heads, in an airtight container to keep dust out.
▷HISTORY C20: named after the 3030 WINCHESTER RIFLE, as the original device would have had 3030 as its IBM number

Winchester rifle NOUN *Trademark* a breech-loading lever-action repeating rifle with a tubular magazine under the barrel. Often shortened to: **Winchester.**
▷HISTORY C19: named after O. F. *Winchester* (1810–80), US manufacturer

wind[1] (wɪnd) NOUN 1 a current of air, sometimes of considerable force, moving generally horizontally from areas of high pressure to areas of low pressure. See also **Beaufort scale.** Related adjective: **aeolian.** 2 *Chiefly poetic* the direction from which a wind blows, usually a cardinal point of the compass. 3 air artificially moved, as by a fan, pump, etc. 4 any sweeping and destructive force. 5 a trend, tendency, or force: *the winds of revolution.* 6 *Informal* a hint; suggestion: *we got wind that you were coming.* 7 something deemed insubstantial: *his talk was all wind.* 8 breath, as used in respiration or talk: *you're just wasting wind.* 9 (often used in sports) the power to breathe normally: *his wind is weak.* See also **second wind.** 10 *Music* **a** a wind instrument or wind instruments considered collectively. **b** (*often plural*) the musicians who play wind instruments in an orchestra. **c** (*modifier*) of, relating to, or composed of wind instruments: *a wind ensemble.* 11 an informal name for **flatus.** 12 the air on which the scent of an animal is carried to hounds or on which the scent of a hunter is carried to his quarry. 13 **between wind and water. a** the part of a vessel's hull below the

water line that is exposed by rolling or by wave action. **b** any point particularly susceptible to attack or injury. 14 **break wind.** to release intestinal gas through the anus. 15 **get** *or* **have the wind up.** *Informal* to become frightened. 16 **have in the wind.** to be in the act of following (quarry) by scent. 17 **how** *or* **which way the wind blows** *or* **lies.** what appears probable. 18 **in the wind.** about to happen. 19 **in the wind** *or* **three sheets in the wind.** *Informal* intoxicated; drunk. 20 **in the teeth** (*or* **eye**) **of the wind.** directly into the wind. 21 **into the wind.** against the wind or upwind. 22 **off the wind.** *Nautical* away from the direction from which the wind is blowing. 23 **on the wind.** *Nautical* as near as possible to the direction from which the wind is blowing. 24 **put the wind up.** *Informal* to frighten or alarm. 25 **raise the wind.** *Brit informal* to obtain the necessary funds. 26 **sail close** *or* **near to the wind. a** to come near the limits of danger or indecency. **b** to live frugally or manage one's affairs economically. 27 **take the wind out of someone's sails.** to destroy someone's advantage; disconcert or deflate. ◆ VERB (*tr*) 28 to cause (someone) to be short of breath: *the blow winded him.* 29 **a** to detect the scent of. **b** to pursue (quarry) by following its scent. 30 to cause (a baby) to bring up wind after feeding by patting or rubbing on the back. 31 to expose to air, as in drying, ventilating, etc.
▷HISTORY Old English *wind;* related to Old High German *wint,* Old Norse *vindr,* Gothic *winds,* Latin *ventus*
▸ **'windless** ADJECTIVE ▸ **'windlessly** ADVERB
▸ **'windlessness** NOUN

wind[2] (waɪnd) VERB **winds, winding, wound.** 1 (often foll by *around, about,* or *upon*) to turn or coil (string, cotton, etc.) around some object or point or (of string, etc.) to be turned etc., around some object or point: *he wound a scarf around his head.* 2 (*tr*) to twine, cover, or wreathe by or as if by coiling, wrapping, etc.; encircle: *we wound the body in a shroud.* 3 (*tr;* often foll by *up*) to tighten the spring of (a clockwork mechanism). 4 (*tr;* foll by *off*) to remove by uncoiling or unwinding. 5 (*usually intr*) to move or cause to move in a sinuous, spiral, or circular course: *the river winds through the hills.* 6 (*tr*) to introduce indirectly or deviously: *he is winding his own opinions into the report.* 7 (*tr*) to cause to twist or revolve: *he wound the handle.* 8 (*tr;* usually foll by *up* or *down*) to move by cranking: *please wind up the window.* 9 (*tr*) to haul, lift, or hoist (a weight, etc.) by means of a wind or windlass. 10 (*intr*) (of a board, etc.) to be warped or twisted. 11 (*intr*) *Archaic* to proceed deviously or indirectly. ◆ NOUN 12 the act of winding or state of being wound. 13 a single turn, bend, etc.: *a wind in the river.* 14 Also called: **winding.** a twist in a board or plank. ◆ See also **wind down, wind up.**
▷HISTORY Old English *windan;* related to Old Norse *vinda,* Old High German *wintan* (German *winden*)
▸ **'windable** ADJECTIVE

wind[3] (waɪnd) VERB **winds, winding, winded** *or* **wound.** (*tr*) *Poetic* to blow (a note or signal) on (a horn, bugle, etc.).
▷HISTORY C16: special use of WIND[1]

windage ('wɪndɪdʒ) NOUN 1 **a** a deflection of a projectile as a result of the effect of the wind. **b** the degree of such deflection. **c** the extent to which it is necessary to adjust the wind gauge of a gun sight in order to compensate for such deflection. 2 the difference between a firearm's bore and the diameter of its projectile. 3 *Nautical* the exposed part of the hull of a vessel responsible for wind resistance. 4 the retarding force upon a rotating machine resulting from the drag of the air.

windbag ('wɪnd,bæg) NOUN 1 *Slang* a voluble person who has little of interest to communicate. 2 the bag in a set of bagpipes, which provides a continuous flow of air to the pipes.

windbaggery ('wɪnd,bægərɪ) NOUN *Informal* lengthy talk or discussion with little or no interesting content.

windbill ('wɪnd,bɪl) NOUN an informal name for **accommodation bill.**

windblown ('wɪnd,bləʊn) ADJECTIVE 1 blown by the wind. 2 (of a woman's hair style) cut short and combed to look as though it has been dishevelled by the wind. 3 (of trees, shrubs, etc.) growing in a shape determined by the prevailing winds. 4 *NZ* (of trees) felled by the wind.

wind-borne ADJECTIVE (esp of plant seeds or pollen) transported by wind.

windbound ('wɪnd,baʊnd) ADJECTIVE (of a sailing vessel) prevented from sailing by an unfavourable wind.

windbreak ('wɪnd,breɪk) NOUN a fence, line of trees, etc., serving as a protection from the wind by breaking its force.

wind-broken ADJECTIVE (of a horse) asthmatic or heaving.

windburn ('wɪnd,bɜːn) NOUN irritation and redness of the skin caused by prolonged exposure to winds of high velocity.
▸ **'wind,burnt** *or* **'wind,burned** ADJECTIVE

windcheater ('wɪnd,tʃiːtə) NOUN a warm jacket, usually with a close-fitting knitted neck, cuffs, and waistband. Also called: **windjammer.** US name (trademark): **Windbreaker** ('wɪnd,breɪkə). Austral name (trademark): **Windcheater.**

wind chest (wɪnd) NOUN a box in an organ in which air from the bellows is stored under pressure before being supplied to the pipes or reeds.

wind-chill (wɪnd-) NOUN **a** the serious chilling effect of wind and low temperature: it is measured on a scale that runs from hot to fatal to life and allows for varying combinations of air temperature and wind speed. **b** (*as modifier*): *wind-chill factor.*

wind chimes (wɪnd) PLURAL NOUN a decorative arrangement of small discs of metal, shell, etc., hung near a window or door, that shake together with a tinkling sound in a draught.

wind cone (wɪnd) NOUN another name for **windsock.**

wind down (waɪnd) VERB (*adverb*) 1 (*tr*) to lower or move down by cranking. 2 (*intr*) (of a clock spring) to become slack. 3 (*intr*) to diminish gradually in force or power; relax.

winded ('wɪndɪd) ADJECTIVE 1 out of breath, as from strenuous exercise. 2 (*in combination*) having breath or wind as specified: *broken-winded; short-winded.*

winder ('waɪndə) NOUN 1 a person or device that winds, as an engine for hoisting the cages in a mine shaft or a device for winding the yarn in textile manufacture. 2 an object, such as a bobbin, around which something is wound. 3 a knob or key used to wind up a clock, watch, or similar mechanism. 4 any plant that twists itself around a support. 5 a step of a spiral staircase.

Windermere ('wɪndə,mɪə) NOUN **Lake.** a lake in NW England, in Cumbria in the SE part of the Lake District: the largest lake in England. Length: 17 km (10.5 miles).

windfall ('wɪnd,fɔːl) NOUN 1 a piece of unexpected good fortune, esp financial gain. 2 something blown down by the wind, esp a piece of fruit. 3 *Chiefly US and Canadian* a plot of land covered with trees blown down by the wind.

windfall tax NOUN a tax levied on an organization considered to have made excessive profits, esp a privatized utility company that has exploited a monopoly.

wind farm NOUN a large group of wind-driven generators for electricity supply.

windflower ('wɪnd,flaʊə) NOUN any of various anemone plants, such as the wood anemone.

windgall ('wɪnd,gɔːl) NOUN *Vet science* a soft swelling in the area of the fetlock joint of a horse.
▷HISTORY C16: from WIND[1] + GALL[2]
▸ **'wind,galled** ADJECTIVE

wind gap (wɪnd) NOUN a narrow dry valley on a mountain or ridge.

wind gauge (wɪnd) NOUN 1 another name for **anemometer** (sense 1). 2 a scale on a gun sight indicating the amount of deflection necessary to allow for windage. 3 *Music* a device for measuring the wind pressure in the bellows of an organ.

wind harp (wɪnd) NOUN a less common name for **aeolian harp.**

Windhoek ('wɪnt,hʊk, 'vɪnt-) NOUN the capital of Namibia, in the centre, at an altitude of 1654 m (5428 ft.): formerly the capital of German South West Africa. Pop.: 169 000 (1997 est.).

windhover ('wɪnd,hɒvə) NOUN *Brit* a dialect name for a **kestrel.**

Windies ('wɪndɪz) PLURAL NOUN *Informal* **the.** the international cricket team of the West Indies.
▷HISTORY from the abbreviation *W. Indies*

windigo ('wɪndɪ,gəʊ) NOUN a variant of **wendigo.**

winding ('waɪndɪŋ) NOUN 1 a curving or sinuous course or movement. 2 anything that has been wound or wrapped around something. 3 a particular manner or style in which something has been wound. 4 a curve, bend, or complete turn in wound material, a road, etc. 5 (*often plural*) devious thoughts or behaviour: *the tortuous windings of political argumentation.* 6 one or more turns of wire forming a continuous coil through which an electric current can pass, as used in transformers, generators, etc. 7 another name for **wind[2]** (sense 14). 8 a coil of tubing in certain brass instruments, esp the French horn. ◆ ADJECTIVE 9 curving; sinuous: *a winding road.*
▸ **'windingly** ADVERB

winding drum ('waɪndɪŋ) NOUN a rotating drum usually grooved to nest a wire rope which is wound onto it as part of the mechanism of a hoist.

winding sheet NOUN a sheet in which a corpse is wrapped for burial; shroud.

winding staircase NOUN another word for **spiral staircase.**

winding-up NOUN the process of finishing or closing something, esp the process of closing down a business.

wind instrument (wɪnd) NOUN any musical instrument sounded by the breath, such as the woodwinds and brass instruments of an orchestra.

windjammer ('wɪnd,dʒæmə) NOUN 1 a large merchant sailing ship. 2 another name for **windcheater.**

windlass ('wɪndləs) NOUN 1 a machine for raising weights by winding a rope or chain upon a barrel or drum driven by a crank, motor, etc. ◆ VERB 2 (*tr*) to raise or haul (a weight, etc.) by means of a windlass.
▷HISTORY C14: from Old Norse *vindáss,* from *vinda* to WIND[2] + *ass* pole; related to Old French *guindas,* Middle Low German, Dutch *windas*

windlestraw ('wɪndᵊl,strɔː) NOUN *Irish, Scot, and English dialect* 1 the dried stalk of any of various grasses. 2 anything weak or feeble, esp a thin unhealthy person.
▷HISTORY Old English *windelstrēaw,* from *windel* basket, from *windan* to WIND[2] + *strēaw* STRAW[1]

wind machine (wɪnd) NOUN a machine used, esp in the theatre, to produce wind or the sound of wind.

windmill ('wɪnd,mɪl, 'wɪn,mɪl) NOUN 1 a machine for grinding or pumping driven by a set of adjustable vanes or sails that are caused to turn by the force of the wind. 2 the set of vanes or sails that drives such a mill. 3 Also called: **whirligig.** *Brit* a toy consisting of plastic or paper vanes attached to a stick in such a manner that they revolve like the sails of a windmill. US and Canadian name: **pinwheel.** 4 an imaginary opponent or evil (esp in the phrase **tilt at** *or* **fight windmills**). 5 a small air-driven propeller fitted to a light aircraft to drive auxiliary equipment. Compare **ram-air turbine.** 6 an informal name for **helicopter.** 7 an informal name for **propeller** (sense 1). ◆ VERB 8 to move or cause to move like the arms of a windmill. 9 an informal name for **accommodation bill.** 10 (*intr*) (of an aircraft propeller, rotor of a turbine, etc.) to rotate as a result of the force of a current of air rather than under power.

window ('wɪndəʊ) NOUN 1 a light framework, made of timber, metal, or plastic, that contains glass or glazed opening frames and is placed in a wall or roof to let in light or air or to see through. Related adjective: **fenestral.** 2 an opening in the wall or roof of a building that is provided to let in light or air or to see through. 3 See **windowpane.** 4 the display space in and directly behind a shop window: *the dress in the window.* 5 any opening or structure resembling a window in function or appearance, such as the transparent area of an envelope revealing an address within. 6 an opportunity to see or understand something usually unseen: *a window on the workings of Parliament.* 7 a period of unbooked time in a diary, schedule, etc. 8 short for **launch window** or **weather window.** 9 *Physics* a region of the spectrum in

which a medium transmits electromagnetic radiation. See also **radio window.** [10] *Computing* an area of a VDU display that may be manipulated separately from the rest of the display area; typically different files can be displayed simultaneously in different overlapping windows. [11] (*modifier*) of or relating to a window or windows: *a window ledge.* [12] **out of the window.** *Informal* dispensed with; disregarded. ◆ VERB [13] (*tr*) to furnish with or as if with windows.
▷HISTORY C13: from Old Norse *vindauga,* from *vindr* WIND[1] + *auga* EYE[1]

window box NOUN [1] a long narrow box, placed on or outside a windowsill, in which plants are grown. [2] either of a pair of vertical boxes, attached to the sides of a sash window frame, that enclose a sash cord and counterbalancing weight.

window-dresser NOUN a person employed to design and build up a display in a shop window.

window-dressing NOUN [1] the ornamentation of shop windows, designed to attract customers. [2] the pleasant, showy, or false aspect of an idea, policy, etc., which is stressed to conceal the real or unpleasant nature; façade.

window envelope NOUN a type of envelope, esp for business use, having a transparent area that reveals the address within.

windowpane (ˈwɪndəʊˌpeɪn) NOUN a sheet of glass in a window.

window sash NOUN a glazed window frame, esp one that opens.

window seat NOUN [1] a seat below a window, esp in a bay window. [2] a seat beside a window in a bus, train, etc.

window-shop VERB **-shops, -shopping, -shopped.** (*intr*) to look at goods in shop windows without buying them.
▸ **ˈwindow-ˌshopper** NOUN ▸ **ˈwindow-ˌshopping** NOUN

windowsill (ˈwɪndəʊˌsɪl) NOUN a sill below a window.

window tax NOUN *History* a tax on windows in houses levied between 1696 and 1851.

windpipe (ˈwɪndˌpaɪp) NOUN a nontechnical name for **trachea** (sense 1). Related adjective: **tracheal.**

wind-pollinated ADJECTIVE (of certain plants) pollinated by wind-borne pollen.
▸ **ˈwind-ˌpolliˈnation** NOUN

wind power (wɪnd) NOUN power produced from windmills and wind turbines.

Wind River Range (wɪnd) NOUN a mountain range in W Wyoming: one of the highest ranges of the central Rockies. Highest peak: Gannet Peak, 4202 m (13 785 ft.).

wind rose (wɪnd) NOUN a diagram with radiating lines showing the frequency and strength of winds from each direction affecting a specific place.

windrow (ˈwɪndˌrəʊ, ˈwɪnˌrəʊ) NOUN [1] a long low ridge or line of hay or a similar crop, designed to achieve the best conditions for drying or curing. [2] a line of leaves, snow, dust, etc., swept together by the wind. ◆ VERB [3] (*tr*) to put (hay or a similar crop) into windrows.
▸ **ˈwindˌrower** NOUN

windsail (ˈwɪndˌseɪl) NOUN [1] a sail rigged as an air scoop over a hatch or companionway to catch breezes and divert them below. [2] any of the vanes or sails of a windmill.

wind scale (wɪnd) NOUN a numerical scale of wind force, such as the Beaufort scale.

Windscale (ˈwɪndˌskeɪl) NOUN the former name of **Sellafield.**

windscreen (ˈwɪndˌskriːn) NOUN *Brit* the sheet of flat or curved glass that forms a window of a motor vehicle, esp the front window. US and Canadian name: **windshield.**

windscreen wiper NOUN *Brit* an electrically operated blade with a rubber edge that wipes a windscreen clear of rain, snow, etc. US and Canadian name: **windshield wiper.**

wind shake (wɪnd) NOUN a crack between the annual rings in wood: caused by strong winds bending the tree trunk.

wind shear (wɪnd) NOUN stress on an aircraft in an area in which winds of different speeds and directions are close together.

windshield (ˈwɪndˌʃiːld) NOUN [1] the US and Canadian name for **windscreen.** [2] an object designed to shield something from the wind.

windsock (ˈwɪndˌsɒk) NOUN a truncated cone of textile mounted on a mast so that it is free to rotate about a vertical axis: used, esp at airports, to indicate the local wind direction. Also called: **air sock, drogue, wind sleeve, wind cone.**

Windsor (ˈwɪnzə) NOUN [1] a town in S England, in Windsor and Maidenhead unitary authority, Berkshire, on the River Thames, linked by bridge with Eton: site of **Windsor Castle**, residence of English monarchs since its founding by William the Conqueror; **Old Windsor**, royal residence in the time of Edward the Confessor, is 3 km (2 miles) southeast. Pop.: 30 136 (1991). Official name: **New Windsor.** [2] a city in SE Canada, in S Ontario on the Detroit River opposite Detroit: motor-vehicle manufacturing; university (1963). Pop.: 197 694 (1996).

Windsor and Maidenhead NOUN a unitary authority in S England, in Berkshire. Pop.: 133 606 (2001). Area: 197 sq. km (76 sq. miles).

Windsor chair NOUN a simple wooden chair, popular in England and America from the 18th century, usually having a shaped seat, splayed legs, and a back of many spindles.

Windsor knot NOUN a wide triangular knot, produced by making extra turns in tying a tie.

Windsor rocker NOUN *US and Canadian* a Windsor chair on rockers.

Windsor tie NOUN a wide silk tie worn in a floppy bow.

windstorm (ˈwɪndˌstɔːm) NOUN a storm consisting of violent winds.

wind-sucking NOUN a harmful habit of horses in which the animal arches its neck and swallows a gulp of air.
▸ **ˈwindˌsucker** NOUN

windsurf (ˈwɪndˌsɜːf) VERB (*intr*) to take part in the sport of windsurfing.
▸ **ˈwindˌsurfer** NOUN

windsurfing (ˈwɪndˌsɜːfɪŋ) NOUN the sport of sailing standing up on a sailboard that is equipped with a mast, sail, and wishbone boom. Also called: **boardsailing, sailboarding.**

wind surge (wɪnd) NOUN a wind-induced rise in the water level at the coast or the shore of an inland expanse of water. It has a definite frequency and if this is close to the tidal frequency serious flooding can result.

windswept (ˈwɪndˌswɛpt) ADJECTIVE [1] open to or swept by the wind. [2] another word for **windblown** (sense 2).

wind tee (wɪnd) NOUN a large weather vane shaped like a *T,* located at an airfield to indicate the wind direction.

wind tunnel (wɪnd) NOUN a chamber for testing the aerodynamic properties of aircraft, aerofoils, etc., in which a current of air can be maintained at a constant velocity.

wind up (waɪnd) VERB (*adverb*) [1] to bring to or reach a conclusion: *he wound up the proceedings.* [2] (*tr*) to tighten the spring of (a clockwork mechanism). [3] (*tr; usually passive*) *Informal* to make nervous, tense, etc.; excite: *he was all wound up before the big fight.* [4] (*tr*) to roll (thread, etc.) into a ball. [5] an informal word for **liquidate** (sense 2). [6] (*intr*) *Informal* to end up (in a specified state): *you'll wind up without any teeth.* [7] (*tr; usually passive*) to involve; entangle: *they were wound up in three different scandals.* [8] (*tr*) to hoist or haul up. [9] (*tr*) *Brit slang* to tease (someone). ◆ NOUN **wind-up.** [10] the act of concluding. [11] the finish; end. [12] *Brit slang* an act or instance of teasing: *she just thinks it's a big wind-up.*

windward (ˈwɪndwəd) *Chiefly nautical* ◆ ADJECTIVE [1] of, in, or moving to the quarter from which the wind blows. [2] **to windward of.** advantageously situated with respect to. ◆ NOUN [3] the windward point. [4] the side towards the wind. ◆ ADVERB [5] towards the wind. ◆ Compare **leeward.**

Windward Islands PLURAL NOUN [1] a group of islands in the SE Caribbean, in the Lesser Antilles: consists of the French Overseas Department of Martinique and the independent states of Grenada, St Lucia, and St Vincent and the Grenadines. [2] a group of islands in the S Pacific, in French Polynesia in the W Society Archipelago: Moorea, Maio (Tubuai Manu), and Mehetia and Tetiaoro. Pop.: 162 686 (1996). French name: **Îles du Vent.**

Windward Passage NOUN a strait in the Caribbean, between E Cuba and NW Haiti. Width: 80 km (50 miles).

windy (ˈwɪndɪ) ADJECTIVE **windier, windiest.** [1] of, characterized by, resembling, or relating to wind; stormy. [2] swept by or open to powerful winds. [3] marked by or given to empty, prolonged, and often boastful speech; bombastic: *windy orations.* [4] void of substance. [5] an informal word for **flatulent.** [6] *Slang* afraid; frightened; nervous.
▸ **ˈwindily** ADVERB ▸ **ˈwindiness** NOUN

Windy City NOUN, NOUN **the.** *Informal* Chicago, Illinois.

wine (waɪn) NOUN [1] **a** an alcoholic drink produced by the fermenting of grapes with water and sugar. Related adjectives: **vinaceous, vinous. b** an alcoholic drink produced in this way from other fruits, flowers, etc.: *elderberry wine.* [2] **a** a dark red colour, sometimes with a purplish tinge. **b** (*as adjective*): *wine-coloured.* [3] anything resembling wine in its intoxicating or invigorating effect. [4] *Pharmacol, obsolete* fermented grape juice containing medicaments. [5] **Adam's wine.** *Brit* a dialect word for **water.** [6] **new wine in old bottles.** something new added to or imposed upon an old or established order. ◆ VERB [7] (*intr*) to drink wine. [8] **wine and dine.** to entertain or be entertained with wine and fine food.
▷HISTORY Old English *wīn,* from Latin *vīnum;* related to Greek *oinos,* of obscure origin
▸ **ˈwineless** ADJECTIVE

wine bar NOUN a bar in a restaurant, etc., or an establishment that specializes in serving wine and usually food.

wineberry (ˈwaɪnˌbɛrɪ) NOUN, *plural* **-ries.** another name for **mako**[2] (sense 1).

winebibber (ˈwaɪnˌbɪbə) NOUN a person who drinks a great deal of wine.
▸ **ˈwineˌbibbing** NOUN

wine box NOUN wine sold in a cubic carton, usually of three-litre capacity, having a plastic lining and a tap for dispensing.

wine cellar NOUN [1] a place, such as a dark cool cellar, where wine is stored. [2] the stock of wines stored there.

wine cooler NOUN [1] a bucket-like vessel containing ice in which a bottle of wine is placed to be cooled. [2] the full name for **cooler** (sense 3).

wine gallon NOUN *Brit* a former unit of capacity equal to 231 cubic inches.

wineglass (ˈwaɪnˌglɑːs) NOUN [1] a glass drinking vessel, typically having a small bowl on a stem, with a flared foot. [2] Also called: **wineglassful.** the amount that such a glass will hold.

wine grower NOUN a person engaged in cultivating vines in order to make wine.
▸ **wine growing** NOUN

wine palm NOUN any of various palm trees, the sap of which is used, esp when fermented, as a drink. See **toddy** (sense 2). Also called: **toddy palm.**

winepress (ˈwaɪnˌprɛs) NOUN any equipment used for squeezing the juice from grapes in order to make wine.

winery (ˈwaɪnərɪ) NOUN, *plural* **-eries.** *Chiefly US and Canadian* a place where wine is made.

wineskin (ˈwaɪnˌskɪn) NOUN the skin of a sheep or goat sewn up and used as a holder for wine.

wine tasting NOUN an occasion for sampling a number of wines.
▸ **wine taster** NOUN

winey *or* **winy** (ˈwaɪnɪ) ADJECTIVE having the taste or qualities of wine.

wing (wɪŋ) NOUN [1] either of the modified forelimbs of a bird that are covered with large feathers and specialized for flight in most species. [2] one of the organs of flight of an insect, consisting of a membranous outgrowth from the thorax containing a network of veins. [3] either of the organs of flight in certain other animals, esp the forelimb of a bat. [4] **a** a half of the main supporting surface on an aircraft, confined to one side of it. **b** the full span of the main supporting surface on both sides of an aircraft. **c** an aircraft

designed as one complete wing. **d** a position in flight formation, just to the rear and to one side of an aircraft. 5 **a** an organ or apparatus resembling a wing. **b** *Anatomy* any bodily structure resembling a wing: *the wings of a sphenoid bone*. Technical name: **ala.** 6 anything suggesting a wing in form, function, or position, such as a sail of a windmill or a ship. 7 *Botany* **a** either of the lateral petals of a sweetpea or related flower. **b** any of various outgrowths of a plant part, esp the process on a wind-dispersed fruit or seed. 8 a means or cause of flight or rapid motion; flight: *fear gave wings to his feet*. 9 the act or manner of flying: *a bird of strong wing*. 10 *Brit* the part of a car body that surrounds the wheels. US and Canadian name: **fender.** 11 any affiliate of or subsidiary to a parent organization. 12 *Sport* **a** either of the two sides of the pitch near the touchline. **b** a player stationed in such a position; winger. 13 a faction or group within a political party or other organization. See also **left wing, right wing.** 14 a part of a building that is subordinate to the main part. 15 (*plural*) the space offstage to the right or left of the acting area in a theatre. 16 **in the wings.** ready to step in when needed. 17 *Fortifications* a side connecting the main fort and an outwork. 18 a folding panel, as of a double door or a movable partition. 19 either of the two pieces that project forwards from the sides of some chairbacks. 20 the US name for **quarterlight.** 21 a surface fitted to a racing car to produce aerodynamic download to hold it on the road at high speed. 22 (*plural*) an insignia in the form of stylized wings worn by a qualified aircraft pilot. 23 a tactical formation in some air forces, consisting of two or more squadrons. 24 any of various flattened organs or extensions in lower animals, esp when used in locomotion. 25 the side of a hold alongside a ship's hull. 26 the outside angle of the cutting edge on the share and mouldboard of a plough. 27 a jetty or dam for narrowing a channel of water. 28 **on a wing and a prayer.** with only the slightest hope of succeeding. 29 **on the wing. a** flying. **b** travelling. **c** about to leave. 30 **take wing. a** to lift off or fly away. **b** to depart in haste. **c** to become joyful. 31 **under one's wing.** in one's care or tutelage. 32 **clip (someone's) wings. a** to restrict (someone's) freedom. **b** to thwart (someone's) ambition. 33 **on wings.** flying or as if flying. 34 **spread** *or* **stretch one's wings.** to make full use of one's abilities. ◆ VERB (*mainly tr*) 35 (*also intr*) to make (one's way) swiftly on or as if on wings. 36 to shoot or wound (a bird, person, etc.) superficially, in the wing or arm, etc. 37 to cause to fly or move swiftly: *to wing an arrow*. 38 to fit (an arrow) with a feather. 39 to provide with wings. 40 (of buildings, altars, etc.) to provide with lateral extensions. 41 **wing it.** *Informal* to accomplish or perform something without full preparation or knowledge; improvise.
▷HISTORY C12: from Scandinavian; compare Old Norse *vængir* (plural), Norwegian *veng*
▸ **'wing,like** ADJECTIVE

wing and wing ADVERB with sails extended on both sides by booms.

wing beat NOUN a complete cycle of moving the wing by a bird when flying.

wing bow (bəʊ) NOUN a distinctive band of colour marking the wing of a bird.

wing-case NOUN the nontechnical name for **elytron.**

wing chair NOUN an easy chair having wings on each side of the back.

wing collar NOUN a stiff turned-up shirt collar worn with the points turned down over the tie.

wing commander NOUN an officer holding commissioned rank in certain air forces, such as the Royal Air Force: junior to a group captain and senior to a squadron leader.

wing covert NOUN any of the covert feathers of the wing of a bird, occurring in distinct rows.

wingding ('wɪŋ,dɪŋ) NOUN *Slang, chiefly US and Canadian* 1 **a** a noisy lively party or festivity. **b** (*as modifier*): *a real wingding party*. 2 a real or pretended fit or seizure.
▷HISTORY C20: of unknown origin

winged (wɪŋd) ADJECTIVE 1 furnished with wings: *winged god; winged horse*. 2 flying straight and true as if by wing: *winged words*.

winger ('wɪŋə) NOUN *Sport* a player stationed on the wing.

wing-footed ADJECTIVE *Archaic* fleet; swift.

wingless ('wɪŋlɪs) ADJECTIVE 1 having no wings or vestigial wings. 2 designating primitive insects of the subclass *Apterygota*, characterized by small size, lack of wings, and larvae resembling the adults: includes the springtails and bristletails.
▸ **'winglessness** NOUN

winglet ('wɪŋlɪt) NOUN 1 a small wing, esp the bastard wing of a bird. 2 a small wing placed at the tip of the main wing of an aircraft and perpendicular to it designed to reduce the aircraft's vortex drag.

wing loading NOUN the total weight of an aircraft divided by its wing area.

wingman ('wɪŋmæn) NOUN, *plural* **-men.** a player in the wing position in Australian Rules.

wing nut NOUN a threaded nut tightened by hand by means of two flat lugs or wings projecting from the central body. Also called: **butterfly nut.**

wingover ('wɪŋ,əʊvə) NOUN a manoeuvre in which the direction of flight of an aircraft is reversed by putting it into a climbing turn until nearly stalled, the nose then being allowed to fall while continuing the turn.

wing shot NOUN 1 a shot taken at a bird in flight. 2 an expert at shooting birds in flight.

wingspan ('wɪŋ,spæn) *or* **wingspread** ('wɪŋ,sprɛd) NOUN the distance between the wing tips of an aircraft, bird, etc.

wing tip NOUN the outermost edge of a wing.

wink[1] (wɪŋk) VERB 1 (*intr*) to close and open one eye quickly, deliberately, or in an exaggerated fashion to convey friendliness, etc. 2 to close and open (an eye or the eyes) momentarily. 3 (*tr; foll by away, back*, etc.) to force away (tears, etc.) by winking. 4 (*tr*) to signal with a wink. 5 (*intr*) (of a light) to gleam or flash intermittently. ◆ NOUN 6 a winking movement, esp one conveying a signal, etc., or such a signal. 7 an interrupted flashing of light. 8 a brief moment of time; instant. 9 *Informal* the smallest amount, esp of sleep. See also **forty winks.** 10 **tip the wink.** *Brit informal* to give a hint.
▷HISTORY Old English *wincian;* related to Old Saxon *wincon,* Old High German *winchan,* German *winken* to wave. See WENCH, WINCH

wink[2] (wɪŋk) NOUN a disc used in the game of tiddlywinks.
▷HISTORY C20: shortened from TIDDLYWINKS

wink at VERB (*intr, preposition*) to connive at; disregard: *the authorities winked at corruption*.

winker ('wɪŋkə) NOUN 1 a person or thing that winks. 2 *US and Canadian slang English dialect* an eye, eyelash, or eyelid. 3 another name for **blinker** (sense 1).

winkle ('wɪŋkᵊl) NOUN 1 See **periwinkle**[1]. ◆ VERB 2 (*tr; usually foll by out, out of*, etc.) *Informal, chiefly Brit* to extract or prise out.
▷HISTORY C16: shortened from PERIWINKLE[1]

winkle-pickers PLURAL NOUN shoes or boots with very pointed narrow toes, popular in the mid-20th century.

winnard ('wɪnəd) NOUN *Southwest English dialect* a heron.

Winnebago (,wɪnɪ'beɪgəʊ) NOUN 1 **Lake.** a lake in E Wisconsin, fed and drained by the Fox river: the largest lake in the state. Area: 557 sq. km (215 sq. miles). 2 (*plural* **-gos** *or* **-go**) a member of a North American Indian people living in Wisconsin and Nebraska. 3 the language of this people, belonging to the Siouan family.

winner ('wɪnə) NOUN 1 a person or thing that wins. 2 *Informal* a person or thing that seems sure to win or succeed.

winner's enclosure *or* **circle** NOUN See **unsaddling enclosure.**

winning ('wɪnɪŋ) ADJECTIVE 1 (of a person, character, etc.) charming, engaging, or attractive: *winning ways; a winning smile*. 2 gaining victory: *the winning stroke*. ◆ NOUN 3 **a** a shaft or seam of coal. **b** the extraction of coal or ore from the ground. 4 (*plural*) money, prizes, or valuables won, esp in gambling.
▸ **'winningly** ADVERB ▸ **'winningness** NOUN

winning gallery NOUN *Real Tennis* the gallery farthest from the net on either side of the court, into which any shot played wins a point.

winning opening NOUN *Real Tennis* the grille, dedans, or winning gallery, into which any shot played wins a point.

winning post NOUN the post marking the finishing line on a racecourse.

Winnipeg ('wɪnɪ,pɛg) NOUN 1 a city in S Canada, capital of Manitoba at the confluence of the Assiniboine and Red Rivers: University of Manitoba (1877) and University of Winnipeg (1871). Pop.: 618 477 (1996). 2 **Lake.** a lake in S Canada, in Manitoba: drains through the Nelson River into Hudson Bay. Area: 23 553 sq. km (9094 sq. miles).

Winnipeg couch NOUN *Canadian* a couch with no arms or back, opening out into a double bed.

Winnipegger ('wɪnɪ,pɛgə) NOUN a native or inhabitant of Winnipeg.

Winnipegosis (,wɪnɪpə'gəʊsɪs) NOUN **Lake.** a lake in S Canada, in W Manitoba. Area: 5400 sq. km (2086 sq. miles).

winnow ('wɪnəʊ) VERB 1 to separate (grain) from (chaff) by means of a wind or current of air. 2 (*tr*) to examine in order to select the desirable elements. 3 (*tr*) *Archaic* to beat (the air) with wings. 4 (*tr*) *Rare* to blow upon; fan. ◆ NOUN 5 **a** a device for winnowing. **b** the act or process of winnowing.
▷HISTORY Old English *windwian;* related to Old High German *wintōn,* Gothic *diswinthjan,* Latin *ventilāre.* See WIND[1]
▸ **'winnower** NOUN

wino ('waɪnəʊ) NOUN, *plural* **-os.** *Informal* a person who habitually drinks wine as a means of getting drunk.

win out VERB (*intr, adverb*) *Informal* to succeed or prevail as if in a contest: *sanity rarely wins out over prejudice*.

win over VERB (*tr, adverb*) to gain the support or consent of (someone). Also: **win round.**

winsome ('wɪnsəm) ADJECTIVE charming; winning; engaging: *a winsome smile*.
▷HISTORY Old English *wynsum,* from *wynn* joy (related to Old High German *wunnia,* German *Wonne*) + *-sum* -SOME[1]
▸ **'winsomely** ADVERB ▸ **'winsomeness** NOUN

Winston-Salem ('wɪnstən'seɪləm) NOUN a city in N central North Carolina: formed in 1913 by the uniting of Salem and Winston; a major tobacco manufacturing centre. Pop.: 185 776 (2000).

winter ('wɪntə) NOUN 1 **a** (*sometimes capital*) the coldest season of the year, between autumn and spring, astronomically from the December solstice to the March equinox in the N hemisphere and at the opposite time of year in the S hemisphere. **b** (*as modifier*): *winter pasture*. 2 the period of cold weather associated with the winter. 3 a time of decline, decay, etc. 4 *Chiefly poetic* a year represented by this season: *a man of 72 winters*. Related adjectives: **brumal, hibernal, hiemal.** ◆ VERB 5 (*intr*) to spend the winter in a specified place. 6 to keep or feed (farm animals, etc.) during the winter or (of farm animals) to be kept or fed during the winter.
▷HISTORY Old English; related to Old Saxon, Old High German *wintar,* Old Norse *vetr,* Gothic *wintrus*
▸ **'winterer** NOUN ▸ **'winterish** *or* **'winter-,like** ADJECTIVE
▸ **'winterless** ADJECTIVE

winter aconite NOUN a small Old World ranunculaceous herbaceous plant, *Eranthis hyemalis,* cultivated for its yellow flowers, which appear early in spring.

winterbourne ('wɪntə,bɔːn) NOUN a stream flowing only after heavy rainfall, esp in winter.
▷HISTORY Old English *winterburna;* see WINTER, BURN[2]

winter cherry NOUN 1 a Eurasian solanaceous plant, *Physalis alkekengi,* cultivated for its ornamental inflated papery orange-red calyx. 2 the calyx of this plant. ◆ See also **Chinese lantern, ground cherry.**

wintercress ('wɪntə,krɛs) NOUN 1 a bitter-tasting yellow-flowered perennial, *Barbarea vulgaris,* somewhat resembling mustard. 2 a commercial hybrid, *Rorippa × sterilis,* between watercress and *R. microphylla*.

winterfeed ('wɪntə,fiːd) VERB **-feeds, -feeding, -fed.**

to feed (livestock) in winter when the grazing is not rich enough.

winter garden NOUN [1] a garden of evergreen plants and plants that flower in winter. [2] a conservatory in which flowers are grown in winter.

wintergreen (ˈwɪntəˌgriːn) NOUN [1] Also called: **boxberry, checkerberry, teaberry, spiceberry, partridgeberry.** any of several evergreen ericaceous shrubs of the genus *Gaultheria,* esp *G. procumbens,* of E North America, which has white bell-shaped flowers and edible red berries. [2] **oil of wintergreen.** an aromatic compound, formerly made from this and various other plants but now synthesized: used medicinally and for flavouring. [3] any of various plants of the genus *Pyrola,* such as *P. minor* (**common wintergreen**), of temperate and arctic regions, having rounded leaves and small pink globose flowers: family *Pyrolaceae.* Usual US name: **shinleaf.** [4] any of several plants of the genera *Orthilia* and *Moneses:* family *Pyrolaceae.* [5] **chickweed wintergreen.** a primulaceous plant, *Trientalis europaea,* of N Europe and N Asia, having white flowers and leaves arranged in a whorl.
▷HISTORY C16: from Dutch *wintergroen* or German *Wintergrün;* see WINTER, GREEN

winter hedge NOUN *West Yorkshire, south Lancashire, and Derbyshire dialect* a clothes horse.
▷HISTORY so called in contrast to a hedge on which clothes are dried in summer

winter heliotrope NOUN a creeping perennial, *Petasites fragrans,* related to the butterbur, having lilac to heliotrope coloured flowers smelling of vanilla: found chiefly on road verges.

winterize *or* **winterise** (ˈwɪntəˌraɪz) VERB (*tr*) *US and Canadian* to prepare (a house, car, etc.) to withstand winter conditions.
▸ˌ**winteriˈzation** *or* ˌ**winteriˈsation** NOUN

winter jasmine NOUN a jasmine shrub, *Jasminum nudiflorum,* widely cultivated for its winter-blooming yellow flowers.

winterkill (ˈwɪntəˌkɪl) VERB *Chiefly US and Canadian* to kill (crops or other plants) by exposure to frost, cold, etc., or (of plants) to die by this means.
▸ˈ**winterˌkilling** ADJECTIVE, NOUN

winter melon NOUN a variety of muskmelon, *Cucumis melo inodorus,* that has sweet fruit with pale orange flesh and an unridged rind. Also called: **Persian melon.**

winter moth NOUN a brown geometrid moth, *Operophtera brumata,* of which the male is often seen against lighted windows in winter, the female being wingless.

Winter Olympic Games NOUN (*functioning as singular or plural*) an international contest of winter sports, esp skiing, held every four years. Also called: **Winter Olympics.**

winter quarters PLURAL NOUN housing or accommodation for the winter, esp for military personnel.

winter rose NOUN another name for **Christmas rose.**

winter solstice NOUN [1] the time at which the sun is at its southernmost point in the sky (northernmost point in the S hemisphere) appearing at noon at its lowest altitude above the horizon. It occurs about December 22 (June 21 in the S hemisphere). [2] *Astronomy* the point on the celestial sphere, opposite the **summer solstice,** at which the ecliptic is furthest south from the celestial equator. Right ascension: 18 hours; declination: –23.5°.

winter sports PLURAL NOUN sports held in the open air on snow or ice, esp skiing.

Winterthur (*German* ˈvɪntərtuːr) NOUN an industrial town in NE central Switzerland, in Zürich canton: has the largest technical college in the country. Pop.: 88 168 (1994).

wintertime (ˈwɪntəˌtaɪm) NOUN the winter season. Also (archaic): ˌ**winterˌtide.**

Winter War NOUN the war of the winter of 1939–40 between Finland and the USSR after which the Finns surrendered the Karelian Isthmus to the USSR.

winterweight (ˈwɪntəˌweɪt) ADJECTIVE (of clothes) suitable in weight for wear in the winter; relatively heavy.

winter wheat NOUN a type of wheat that is planted in the autumn and is harvested the following summer.

wintry (ˈwɪntrɪ), **wintery** (ˈwɪntərɪ, -trɪ), *or less commonly* **winterly** ADJECTIVE **-trier, -triest.** [1] (esp of weather) of or characteristic of winter. [2] lacking cheer or warmth; bleak.
▸ˈ**wintrily** ADVERB ▸ˈ**wintriness** *or* ˈ**winteriness** *or* (*less commonly*) ˈ**winterliness** NOUN

win-win ADJECTIVE guaranteeing a favourable outcome for everyone involved: *a win-win situation for NATO.*
▷HISTORY C20: modelled on NO-WIN

winy (ˈwaɪnɪ) ADJECTIVE **winier, winiest.** a variant spelling of **winey.**

winze (wɪnz) NOUN *Mining* a steeply inclined shaft, as for ventilation between levels.
▷HISTORY C18: from earlier *winds,* probably from C14 *wynde* windlass, from Middle Dutch or Middle Low German *winde;* related to Danish *vinde* pulley

wipe (waɪp) VERB (*tr*) [1] to rub (a surface or object) lightly, esp with (a cloth, hand, etc.), as in removing dust, water, grime, etc. [2] (usually foll by *off, away, from, up,* etc.) to remove by or as if by rubbing lightly: *he wiped the dirt from his hands.* [3] to eradicate or cancel (a thought, memory, etc.). [4] to erase a recording from (an audio or video tape). [5] *Austral informal* to abandon or reject (a person). [6] to apply (oil, grease, etc.) by wiping. [7] to form (a joint between two lead pipes) with solder or soft lead. [8] **wipe the floor with (someone).** *Informal* to defeat decisively. ◆ NOUN [9] the act or an instance of wiping. [10] (in film editing) an effect causing the transition from one scene to the next in which the image of the first scene appears to be wiped off the screen by that of the second. [11] *Dialect* a sweeping blow or stroke. [12] *Brit dialect* a gibe or jeer. [13] *Obsolete* a slang name for **handkerchief.**
▷HISTORY Old English *wīpian,* related to Middle Low German *wīpen, wīp* bundle (of cloth), Old High German *wīffa, wīfan* to wind, Gothic *weipan* to wreathe

wipe out VERB (*adverb*) [1] (*tr*) to destroy completely; eradicate. [2] (*tr*) *Informal* to murder or kill. [3] (*intr*) to fall or jump off a surfboard or skateboard. ◆ NOUN **wipeout.** [4] an act or instance of wiping out. [5] the interference of one radio signal by another so that reception is impossible.

wiper (ˈwaɪpə) NOUN [1] any piece of cloth, such as a handkerchief, towel, etc., used for wiping. [2] a cam rotated to ease a part and allow it to fall under its own weight, as used in stamping machines, etc. [3] See **windscreen wiper.** [4] *Electrical engineering* a movable conducting arm, esp one in a switching or selecting device, that makes contact with a row or ring of contacts.

WIPO *or* **Wipo** (ˈwaɪpəʊ) NOUN ACRONYM FOR World Intellectual Property Organization.

wire (waɪə) NOUN [1] a slender flexible strand or rod of metal. [2] a cable consisting of several metal strands twisted together. [3] a flexible metallic conductor, esp one made of copper, usually insulated, and used to carry electric current in a circuit. [4] (*modifier*) of, relating to, or made of wire: *a wire fence; a wire stripper.* [5] anything made of wire, such as wire netting, a barbed wire fence, etc. [6] a long continuous wire or cable connecting points in a telephone or telegraph system. [7] *Old-fashioned* **a** an informal name for **telegram** or **telegraph. b the wire.** an informal name for **telephone.** [8] a metallic string on a guitar, piano, etc. [9] *Horse racing, chiefly US and Canadian* the finishing line on a racecourse. [10] a wire-gauze screen upon which pulp is spread to form paper during the manufacturing process. [11] anything resembling a wire, such as a hair. [12] a snare made of wire for rabbits and similar animals. [13] **(down) to the wire.** *Informal* right up to the last moment. [14] **get in under the wire.** *Informal, chiefly US and Canadian* to accomplish something with little time to spare. [15] **get one's wires crossed.** *Informal* to misunderstand. [16] **pull wires.** *Chiefly US and Canadian* to exert influence behind the scenes, esp through personal connections; pull strings. [17] **take (it) to the wire.** to compete to the bitter end to win a competition or title. ◆ VERB (*mainly tr*) [18] (*also intr*) to send a telegram to (a person or place). [19] to send (news, a message, etc.) by telegraph. [20] to equip (an electrical system, circuit, or component) with wires. [21] to fasten or furnish with wire. [22] (often foll by *up*) to provide (an area) with fibre optic cabling to receive cable television. [23] to string (beads, etc.) on wire. [24] *Croquet* to leave (a player's ball) so that a hoop or peg lies between it and the other balls. [25] to snare with wire. [26] **wire in.** *Informal* to set about (something, esp food) with enthusiasm.
▷HISTORY Old English *wīr;* related to Old High German *wiara,* Old Norse *vīra,* Latin *viriae* bracelet
▸ˈ**wireˌlike** ADJECTIVE

wire brush NOUN a brush having wire bristles, used for cleaning metal, esp for removing rust, or for brushing against a cymbal.

wire cloth NOUN a mesh or netting woven from fine wire, used in window screens, strainers, etc.

wired (waɪəd) ADJECTIVE *Informal* [1] edgy from stimulant intake. [2] excited, nervous, or tense. [3] using computers to send and receive information, esp via the Internet.

wiredraw (ˈwaɪəˌdrɔː) VERB **-draws, -drawing, -drew, -drawn.** to convert (metal) into wire by drawing through successively smaller dies.

wire entanglement NOUN a barrier or obstruction of barbed wire used in warfare.

wire-gauge NOUN [1] a flat plate with slots in which standard wire sizes can be measured. [2] a standard system of sizes for measuring the diameters of wires.

wire gauze NOUN a stiff meshed fabric woven of fine wires.

wire glass NOUN a sheet glass that contains a layer of reinforcing wire netting within it.

wire grass NOUN any of various grasses, such as Bermuda grass, that have tough wiry roots or rhizomes.

wire-guided ADJECTIVE (of a missile) controlled by signals transmitted through fine wires uncoiled during the missile's flight.

wire-haired ADJECTIVE (of an animal) having a rough wiry coat.

wireless (ˈwaɪəlɪs) NOUN, VERB *Chiefly Brit old-fashioned* another word for **radio.**

wireless telegraphy NOUN another name for **radiotelegraphy.**

wireless telephone NOUN another name for **radiotelephone.**
▸**wireless telephony** NOUN

wireman (ˈwaɪəmən) NOUN, *plural* **-men.** *Chiefly US* a person who installs and maintains electric wiring, cables, etc.

wire netting NOUN a net made of wire, often galvanized, that is used for fencing, as a light reinforcement, etc.

wirephoto (ˈwaɪəˌfəʊtəʊ) NOUN, *plural* **-tos.** a facsimile of a photograph transmitted electronically via a telephone system.

wirepuller (ˈwaɪəˌpʊlə) NOUN *Chiefly US and Canadian* a person who uses private or secret influence for his own ends.
▸ˈ**wireˌpulling** NOUN

wirer (ˈwaɪərə) NOUN a person who sets or uses wires to snare rabbits and similar animals.

wire recorder NOUN an early type of magnetic recorder in which sounds were recorded on a thin steel wire magnetized by an electromagnet. Compare **tape recorder.**
▸**wire recording** NOUN

wire rope NOUN rope made of strands of wire twisted together.

wire service NOUN *Chiefly US and Canadian* an agency supplying news, etc., to newspapers, radio and television stations, etc.

wiretap (ˈwaɪəˌtæp) VERB **-taps, -tapping, -tapped.** to make a connection to a telegraph or telephone wire in order to obtain information secretly.
▸ˈ**wireˌtapper** NOUN ▸ˈ**wireˌtapping** NOUN

wirewalker (ˈwaɪəˌwɔːkə) NOUN *Chiefly US* another name for **tightrope walker.**

wire wheel NOUN [1] a wheel in which the rim is held to the hub by wire spokes, esp one used on a sports car. Compare **disc wheel.** [2] a power-driven rotary wire brush for scaling or burnishing.

wire wool NOUN a mass of fine wire used for cleaning and scouring.

wirework (ˈwaɪəˌwɜːk) NOUN [1] functional or

decorative work made of wire. 2 objects made of wire, esp netting. 3 the work performed by acrobats on a tightrope.

wireworks ('waɪə,wɜːks) NOUN *(functioning as singular or plural)* a factory where wire or articles of wire are made.

wireworm ('waɪə,wɜːm) NOUN the wormlike larva of various elaterid beetles, which feeds on the roots of many crop plants and is a serious agricultural pest.

wire-wove ADJECTIVE 1 of, relating to, or comprising a high-grade glazed paper, usually for writing. 2 woven of wire.

wirilda (wə'rɪldə) NOUN an acacia tree, *Acacia retinoides,* of SE Australia with edible seeds.
▷HISTORY from a native Australian language

wiring ('waɪərɪŋ) NOUN 1 the network of wires used in an electrical system, device, or circuit. 2 the quality or condition of such a network. ◆ ADJECTIVE 3 used in wiring.

wirra ('wɪrə) INTERJECTION *Irish* an exclamation of sorrow or deep concern.
▷HISTORY C19: shortened from Irish Gaelic *a Muire!* O Mary! as invocation to the Virgin Mary

wirrah ('wɪrə) NOUN a saltwater fish, *Acanthistius serratus,* of Australia, with bright blue spots.
▷HISTORY from a native Australian language

Wirral ('wɪrəl) NOUN 1 **the.** a peninsula in NW England between the estuaries of the Rivers Mersey and Dee. 2 a unitary authority in NW England, in Merseyside. Pop.: 312 289 (2001). Area: 158 sq. km (61 sq. miles).

wiry ('waɪərɪ) ADJECTIVE **wirier, wiriest.** 1 (of people or animals) slender but strong in constitution. 2 made of or resembling wire, esp in stiffness: *wiry hair.* 3 (of a sound) produced by or as if by a vibrating wire.
▸**'wirily** ADVERB ▸**'wiriness** NOUN

wis (wɪs) VERB *Archaic* to know or suppose (something).
▷HISTORY C17: a form derived from IWIS, mistakenly interpreted as *I wis* I know, as if from Old English *witan* to know

Wis. ABBREVIATION FOR Wisconsin.

Wisbech ('wɪzbiːtʃ) NOUN a town in E England, in N Cambridgeshire: market-gardening. Pop.: 24 981 (1991).

Wisconsin (wɪs'kɒnsɪn) NOUN 1 a state of the N central US, on Lake Superior and Lake Michigan: consists of an undulating plain, with uplands in the north and west; over 168 m (550 ft.) above sea level along the shore of Lake Michigan. Capital: Madison. Pop.: 5 363 675 (2000). Area: 141 061 sq. km (54 464 sq. miles). Abbreviations: **Wis,** (with zip code) **WI.** 2 a river in central and SW Wisconsin, flowing south and west to the Mississippi. Length: 692 km (430 miles).

Wisconsinite (wɪs'kɒnsɪ,naɪt) NOUN a native or inhabitant of Wisconsin.

Wisd. ABBREVIATION FOR Wisdom of Solomon.

wisdom ('wɪzdəm) NOUN 1 the ability or result of an ability to think and act utilizing knowledge, experience, understanding, common sense, and insight. 2 accumulated knowledge, erudition, or enlightenment. 3 *Archaic* a wise saying or wise sayings or teachings. 4 *Obsolete* soundness of mind. ◆ Related adjective: **sagacious.**
▷HISTORY Old English *wīsdōm;* see WISE[1], -DOM

Wisdom of Jesus, the Son of Sirach ('saɪræk) NOUN **the.** another name for **Ecclesiasticus.**

Wisdom of Solomon NOUN a book of the Apocrypha, probably written about 50 B.C., addressed primarily to Jews who were under the influence of Hellenistic learning.

wisdom tooth NOUN 1 any of the four molar teeth, one at the back of each side of the jaw, that are the last of the permanent teeth to erupt. Technical name: **third molar.** 2 **cut one's wisdom teeth.** to arrive at the age of discretion.

wise[1] (waɪz) ADJECTIVE 1 possessing, showing, or prompted by wisdom or discernment. 2 prudent; sensible. 3 shrewd; crafty: *a wise plan.* 4 well-informed; erudite. 5 aware, informed, or knowing (esp in the phrase **none the wiser**). 6 *Slang (postpositive;* often foll by *to)* in the know, esp possessing inside information (about). 7 *Archaic* possessing powers of magic. 8 *Slang, chiefly US and Canadian* cocksure or insolent. 9 **be** *or* **get wise.** (often foll by *to) Informal* to be or become aware or informed (of something) or to face up (to facts). 10 **put wise.** (often foll by *to) Slang* to inform or warn (of). ◆ VERB 11 See **wise up.**
▷HISTORY Old English *wīs;* related to Old Norse *vīss,* Gothic *weis,* German *weise*
▸**'wisely** ADVERB ▸**'wiseness** NOUN

wise[2] (waɪz) NOUN *Archaic* way, manner, fashion, or respect (esp in the phrases **any wise, in no wise**).
▷HISTORY Old English *wīse* manner; related to Old Saxon *wīsa,* German *Weise,* Old Norse *vīsa* verse, Latin *vīsus* face

-wise ADVERB COMBINING FORM 1 Also: **-ways.** indicating direction or manner: *clockwise; likewise.* 2 with reference to: *profitwise; businesswise.*
▷HISTORY Old English *-wisan;* see WISE[2]

wiseacre ('waɪz,eɪkə) NOUN 1 a person who wishes to seem wise. 2 a wise person: often used facetiously or contemptuously.
▷HISTORY C16: from Middle Dutch *wijsseggher* soothsayer; related to Old High German *wīssaga,* German *Weissager.* See WISE[1], SAY

wiseass ('waɪzæs) NOUN *Informal* **a** a person who thinks he or she is being witty or clever. **b** *(as modifier): some wiseass kid at the back of the class.*

wisecrack ('waɪz,kræk) *Informal* ◆ NOUN 1 a flippant gibe or sardonic remark. ◆ VERB 2 to make a wisecrack.
▸**'wise,cracker** NOUN

wise guy NOUN 1 *Informal* a person who is given to making conceited, sardonic, or insolent comments. *Informal* 2 *US* a member of the Mafia.

wisent ('wiːzᵊnt) NOUN another name for **European bison.** See **bison** (sense 2).
▷HISTORY German, from Old High German *wisunt* BISON

wise up VERB *(adverb)* 1 *Slang* (often foll by *to)* to become or cause to become aware or informed (of). 2 *(tr)* to make more intellectually demanding or sophisticated.

wish (wɪʃ) VERB 1 (when *tr, takes a clause as object or an infinitive;* when *intr,* often foll by *for)* to want or desire (something, often that which cannot be or is not the case): *I wish I lived in Italy; to wish for peace.* 2 *(tr)* to feel or express a desire or hope concerning the future or fortune of: *I wish you well.* 3 *(tr)* to desire or prefer to be as specified. 4 *(tr)* to greet as specified; bid: *he wished us good afternoon.* 5 *(tr) Formal* to order politely: *I wish you to come at three o'clock.* ◆ NOUN 6 the act of wishing; the expression of some desire or mental inclination: *to make a wish.* 7 something desired or wished for: *he got his wish.* 8 *(usually plural)* expressed hopes or desire, esp for someone's welfare, health, etc. 9 *(often plural) Formal* a polite order or request. ◆ See also **wish on.**
▷HISTORY Old English *wӯscan;* related to Old Norse *öskja,* German *wünschen,* Dutch *wenschen*
▸**'wisher** NOUN ▸**'wishless** ADJECTIVE

wishbone ('wɪʃ,bəʊn) NOUN the V-shaped bone above the breastbone in most birds consisting of the fused clavicles; furcula.
▷HISTORY C17: from the custom of two people breaking apart the bone after eating: the person with the longer part makes a wish

wishbone boom NOUN a boom on a sailboard having two arms that are joined at the mast and at the foot of the sail. The windsurfer holds onto it for support and to steer the sailboard.

wishful ('wɪʃfʊl) ADJECTIVE having wishes or characterized by wishing.
▸**'wishfully** ADVERB ▸**'wishfulness** NOUN

wish fulfilment NOUN (in Freudian psychology) any successful attempt to fulfil a wish stemming from the unconscious mind, whether in fact, in fantasy, or by such disguised means as sublimation. See also **pleasure principle.**

wishful thinking NOUN the erroneous belief that one's wishes are in accordance with reality.
▸**wishful thinker** NOUN

wish list NOUN a list of things desired by a person or organization: *the Polish government's wish list.*

wish on VERB *(tr, preposition)* to hope that (someone or something) should be imposed (on someone); foist: *I wouldn't wish my cold on anyone.*

wisht (wɪʃt) INTERJECTION a variant of **whisht.**

wish-wash NOUN *Informal* 1 any thin weak drink. 2 rubbishy talk or writing.

wishy-washy ('wɪʃɪ,wɒʃɪ) ADJECTIVE *Informal* 1 lacking in substance, force, colour, etc. 2 watery; thin.
▸**'wishy-,washily** ADVERB ▸**'wishy-,washiness** NOUN

Wisła ('viswa) NOUN the Polish name for **Vistula** (sense 1).

Wislany Zalew *(Polish* viʃ'laːni 'zaːlɛf) NOUN the Polish name for the **Vistula** (sense 2).

Wismar *(German* 'vɪsmar) NOUN a port in NE Germany, on an inlet of the Baltic, in Mecklenburg-West Pomerania: shipbuilding industries. Pop.: 54 470 (1991).

wisp (wɪsp) NOUN 1 a thin, light, delicate, or fibrous piece or strand, such as a streak of smoke or a lock of hair. 2 a small bundle, as of hay or straw. 3 anything slender and delicate: *a wisp of a girl.* 4 a mere suggestion or hint. 5 a flock of birds, esp snipe. ◆ VERB 6 *(intr;* often foll by *away)* to move or act like a wisp. 7 *(tr) Chiefly Brit dialect* to twist into a wisp. 8 *(tr) Chiefly Brit* to groom (a horse) with a wisp of straw, etc.
▷HISTORY C14: variant of *wips,* of obscure origin; compare WIPE
▸**'wisp,like** ADJECTIVE

wispy ('wɪspɪ) ADJECTIVE **wispier, wispiest.** wisplike; delicate, faint, light, etc.
▸**'wispily** ADVERB ▸**'wispiness** NOUN

wist (wɪst) VERB *Archaic* the past tense and past participle of **wit**[2].

wisteria (wɪ'stɪərɪə) NOUN any twining leguminous woody climbing plant of the genus *Wisteria,* of E Asia and North America, having blue, purple, or white flowers in large drooping clusters.
▷HISTORY C19: from New Latin, named after Caspar Wistar (1761–1818), American anatomist

wistful ('wɪstfʊl) ADJECTIVE sadly pensive, esp about something yearned for.
▸**'wistfully** ADVERB ▸**'wistfulness** NOUN

wit[1] (wɪt) NOUN 1 the talent or quality of using unexpected associations between contrasting or disparate words or ideas to make a clever humorous effect. 2 speech or writing showing this quality. 3 a person possessing, showing, or noted for such an ability, esp in repartee. 4 practical intelligence (esp in the phrase **have the wit to**). 5 *Scot and northern English dialect* information or knowledge (esp in the phrase **get wit of**). 6 *Archaic* mental capacity or a person possessing it. 7 *Obsolete* the mind or memory. ◆ See also **wits.**
▷HISTORY Old English *witt;* related to Old Saxon *giwitt,* Old High German *wizzi* (German *Witz*), Old Norse *vit,* Gothic *witi.* See WIT[2]

wit[2] (wɪt) VERB 1 *Archaic* to be or become aware of (something). ◆ ADVERB 2 **to wit.** that is to say; namely (used to introduce statements, as in legal documents).
▷HISTORY Old English *witan;* related to Old High German *wizzan* (German *wissen*), Old Norse *vita,* Latin *vidēre* to see

witan ('wɪtᵊn) NOUN (in Anglo-Saxon England) 1 an assembly of higher ecclesiastics and important laymen, including king's thegns, that met to counsel the king on matters such as judicial problems. 2 the members of this assembly. ◆ Also called: **witenagemot.**
▷HISTORY Old English *witan,* plural of *wita* wise man; see WIT[2], WITNESS

witblits ('vɪt,blɪts) NOUN *South African* an extremely potent illegally distilled spirit.
▷HISTORY from Afrikaans *wit* white + *blits* lightning

witch[1] (wɪtʃ) NOUN 1 a person, usually female, who practises or professes to practise magic or sorcery, esp black magic, or is believed to have dealings with the devil. 2 an ugly or wicked old woman. 3 a fascinating or enchanting woman. 4 short for **water witch.** ◆ VERB 5 *(tr)* to cause or change by or as if by witchcraft. 6 a less common word for **bewitch.**
▷HISTORY Old English *wicca;* related to Middle Low German *wicken* to conjure, Swedish *vicka* to move to and fro
▸**'witch,like** ADJECTIVE

witch[2] (wɪtʃ) NOUN a flatfish, *Pleuronectes* (or *Glyptocephalus) cynoglossus,* of N Atlantic coastal waters, having a narrow greyish-brown body

marked with tiny black spots: family *Pleuronectidae* (plaice, flounders, etc.).
▷**HISTORY** C19: perhaps from WITCH[1], alluding to the appearance of the fish

witch- *or* **wych-** PREFIX having pliant branches: *witchweed.*
▷**HISTORY** Old English *wice* and *wic;* probably from Germanic *wik-* bend

witchcraft ('wɪtʃˌkrɑːft) NOUN 1 the art or power of bringing magical or preternatural power to bear or the act or practice of attempting to do so. 2 the influence of magic or sorcery. 3 fascinating or bewitching influence or charm.

witch doctor NOUN 1 Also called: **shaman, medicine man.** a man in certain societies, esp preliterate ones, who appears to possess magical powers, used esp to cure sickness but also to harm people. 2 a person who seeks out or hunts witches in some African tribal cultures.

witch-elm NOUN a variant spelling of **wych-elm.**

witchery ('wɪtʃərɪ) NOUN, *plural* **-eries.** 1 the practice of witchcraft. 2 magical or bewitching influence or charm.

witches'-broom, witchbroom ('wɪtʃˌbruːm), *or* **witches'-besom** NOUN a dense abnormal growth of shoots on a tree or other woody plant, usually caused by parasitic fungi of the genus *Taphrina.*

witches' butter NOUN See **jelly fungus.**

witches' Sabbath NOUN See **Sabbath** (sense 4).

witchetty grub ('wɪtʃɪtɪ) NOUN the wood-boring edible larva of certain Australian moths and beetles.
▷**HISTORY** C19: *witchetty,* from a native Australian language

witch hazel *or* **wych-hazel** NOUN 1 any of several trees and shrubs of the genus *Hamamelis,* esp *H. virginiana,* of North America, having ornamental yellow flowers and medicinal properties: family *Hamamelidaceae.* 2 an astringent medicinal solution containing an extract of the bark and leaves of *H. virginiana,* applied to treat bruises, inflammation, etc.

witch-hunt NOUN a rigorous campaign to round up or expose dissenters on the pretext of safeguarding the welfare of the public.
▸'**witch-ˌhunter** NOUN ▸'**witch-ˌhunting** NOUN, ADJECTIVE

witching ('wɪtʃɪŋ) ADJECTIVE 1 relating to or appropriate for witchcraft. 2 *Now rare* bewitching. ◆ NOUN 3 witchcraft; magic.
▸'**witchingly** ADVERB

witching hour NOUN **the.** the hour at which witches are supposed to appear, usually midnight.

witch of Agnesi (ɑːn'jeɪzɪ) NOUN *Maths* a plane curve, symmetrical about the *y*-axis, having the equation $x^2y = 4a^2(2a-y)$. Sometimes shortened to: **witch.**
▷**HISTORY** C19: named after Maria Gaetana *Agnesi* (1718–99), Italian mathematician and philosopher; probably so called from the resemblance of the curve to the outline of a witch's hat

witchweed ('wɪtʃˌwiːd) NOUN any of several scrophulariaceous plants of the genus *Striga,* esp *S. hermonthica,* that are serious pests of grain crops in parts of Africa and Asia.

witenagemot (ˌwɪtɪnəgɪ'məʊt) NOUN another word for **witan.**
▷**HISTORY** Old English *witena,* genitive plural of *wita* councillor + *gemōt* meeting, MOOT

with (wɪð, wɪθ) PREPOSITION 1 using; by means of: *he killed her with an axe.* 2 accompanying; in the company of: *the lady you were with.* 3 possessing; having: *a man with a red moustache.* 4 concerning or regarding: *be patient with her.* 5 in spite of: *with all his talents, he was still humble.* 6 used to indicate a time or distance by which something is away from something else: *with three miles to go, he collapsed.* 7 in a manner characterized by: *writing with abandon.* 8 caused or prompted by: *shaking with rage.* 9 often used with a verb indicating a reciprocal action or relation between the subject and the preposition's object: *agreeing with me; chatting with the troops.* 10 **not with you.** *Informal* not able to grasp or follow what you are saying. 11 **with it.** *Informal* **a** fashionable; in style. **b** comprehending what is happening or being said. 12 **with that.** after that; having said or done that.
▷**HISTORY** Old English; related to Old Norse *vith,* Gothic *withra,* Latin *vitricus* stepfather, Sanskrit *vitarám* wider

withal (wɪ'ðɔːl) ADVERB 1 *Literary* as well; likewise. 2 *Literary* nevertheless. 3 *Archaic* therewith. ◆ PREPOSITION 4 (*postpositive*) an archaic word for **with.**
▷**HISTORY** C12: from WITH + ALL

withdraw (wɪð'drɔː) VERB **-draws, -drawing, -drew, -drawn.** 1 (*tr*) to take or draw back or away; remove. 2 (*tr*) to remove from deposit or investment in a bank, building society, etc. 3 (*tr*) to retract or recall (a statement, promise, etc.). 4 (*intr*) to retire or retreat: *the troops withdrew.* 5 (*intr;* often foll by *from*) to back out (of) or depart (from): *he withdrew from public life.* 6 (*intr*) to detach oneself socially, emotionally, or mentally.
▷**HISTORY** C13: from WITH (in the sense: away from) + DRAW
▸**with'drawable** ADJECTIVE ▸**with'drawer** NOUN

withdrawal (wɪð'drɔːəl) NOUN 1 an act or process of withdrawing; retreat, removal, or detachment. 2 the period a drug addict goes through following abrupt termination in the use of narcotics, usually characterized by physical and mental symptoms (**withdrawal symptoms**).

withdrawing room NOUN an archaic term for **drawing room.**

withdrawn (wɪð'drɔːn) VERB 1 the past participle of **withdraw.** ◆ ADJECTIVE 2 unusually reserved, introverted, or shy. 3 secluded or remote.
▸**with'drawnness** NOUN

withdrew (wɪð'druː) VERB the past tense of **withdraw.**

withe (wɪθ, wɪð, waɪð) NOUN 1 a strong flexible twig, esp of willow, suitable for binding things together; withy. 2 a band or rope of twisted twigs or stems. 3 a handle made of elastic material, fitted on some tools to reduce the shock during use. 4 a wall with a thickness of half a brick, such as a leaf of a cavity wall, or a division between two chimney flues. ◆ VERB 5 (*tr*) to bind with withes.
▷**HISTORY** Old English *withthe;* related to Old Norse *vithja,* Old High German *witta, widi,* Gothic *wida*

wither ('wɪðə) VERB 1 (*intr*) (esp of a plant) to droop, wilt, or shrivel up. 2 (*intr;* often foll by *away*) to fade or waste: *all hope withered away.* 3 (*intr*) to decay, decline, or disintegrate. 4 (*tr*) to cause to wilt, fade, or lose vitality. 5 (*tr*) to abash, esp with a scornful look. 6 (*tr*) to harm or damage.
▷**HISTORY** C14: perhaps variant of WEATHER (vb); related to German *verwittern* to decay
▸'**withered** ADJECTIVE ▸'**witherer** NOUN ▸'**withering** ADJECTIVE ▸'**witheringly** ADVERB

witherite ('wɪðəˌraɪt) NOUN a white, grey, or yellowish mineral consisting of barium carbonate in orthorhombic crystalline form: occurs in veins of lead ore. Formula: $BaCO_3$.
▷**HISTORY** C18: named after W. *Withering* (1741–99), English scientist, who first described it

withers ('wɪðəz) PLURAL NOUN the highest part of the back of a horse, behind the neck between the shoulders.
▷**HISTORY** C16: short for *widersones,* from *wider* WITH + *-sones,* perhaps variant of SINEW; related to German *Widerrist,* Old English *withre* resistance

withershins ('wɪðəˌʃɪnz; *Scot* 'wɪðər-) *or* **widdershins** ADVERB *Chiefly Scot* 1 in the direction contrary to the apparent course of the sun; anticlockwise. 2 in a direction contrary to the usual; in the wrong direction. Compare **deasil.**
▷**HISTORY** C16: from Middle Low German *weddersinnes,* from Middle High German, literally: opposite course, from *wider* against + *sinnes,* genitive of *sin* course

withhold (wɪð'həʊld) VERB **-holds, -holding, -held.** 1 (*tr*) to keep back; refrain from giving: *he withheld his permission.* 2 (*tr*) to hold back; restrain. 3 (*tr*) to deduct (taxes, etc.) from a salary or wages. 4 (*intr;* usually foll by *from*) to refrain or forbear.
▸**with'holder** NOUN

withholding tax NOUN 1 tax deducted at source from income, esp from dividends, paid to nonresidents of a country, which may be reclaimed if a double-taxation agreement exists between the country in which the income is paid and the country of residence of the recipient. 2 *US* a portion of an employee's tax liability paid directly to the government by the employer.

within (wɪ'ðɪn) PREPOSITION 1 in; inside; enclosed or encased by. 2 before (a period of time) has elapsed: *within a week.* 3 not beyond the limits of; not differing by more than (a specified amount) from: *live within your means; within seconds of the world record.* ◆ ADVERB 4 *Formal* inside; internally.

withindoors ('wɪðɪn'dɔːz) ADVERB an obsolete word for **indoors.**

within-subjects design NOUN (*modifier*) *Statistics* (of an experiment) concerned with measuring the value of the dependent variable for the same subjects under the various experimental conditions. Compare **between-subjects design, matched-pairs design.**

without (wɪ'ðaʊt) PREPOSITION 1 not having: *a traveller without much money.* 2 not accompanied by: *he came without his wife.* 3 not making use of: *it is not easy to undo screws without a screwdriver.* 4 (*foll by a verbal noun or noun phrase*) not, while not, or after not: *she can sing for two minutes without drawing breath.* 5 *Archaic* on the outside of. ◆ ADVERB 6 *Formal* outside; outwardly. ◆ CONJUNCTION 7 *Not standard* unless: *don't come without you have some money.*

withoutdoors ('wɪðaʊt'dɔːz) ADVERB an obsolete word for **outdoors.**

withstand (wɪð'stænd) VERB **-stands, -standing, -stood.** 1 (*tr*) to stand up to forcefully; resist. 2 (*intr*) to remain firm in endurance or opposition.
▸**with'stander** NOUN

withy ('wɪðɪ) NOUN, *plural* **withies.** 1 a variant spelling of **withe** (senses 1, 2). 2 a willow tree, esp an osier. ◆ ADJECTIVE 3 (of people) tough and agile. 4 *Rare* resembling a withe in strength or flexibility.
▷**HISTORY** Old English *wīdig(e);* related to Old Norse *vīthir,* Old High German *wīda,* Latin *vītis* vine, Sanskrit *vītika* fetter. See WITHE, WIRE

witless ('wɪtlɪs) ADJECTIVE lacking wit, intelligence, or sense; stupid.
▸'**witlessly** ADVERB ▸'**witlessness** NOUN

witling ('wɪtlɪŋ) NOUN *Archaic* a person who thinks himself witty.

witness ('wɪtnɪs) NOUN 1 a person who has seen or can give first-hand evidence of some event. 2 a person or thing giving or serving as evidence. 3 a person who testifies, esp in a court of law, to events or facts within his own knowledge. 4 a person who attests to the genuineness of a document, signature, etc., by adding his own signature. 5 **bear witness. a** to give written or oral testimony. **b** to be evidence or proof of. ◆ Related adjective: **testimonial.** ◆ VERB 6 (*tr*) to see, be present at, or know at first hand. 7 to give or serve as evidence (of). 8 (*tr*) to be the scene or setting of: *this field has witnessed a battle.* 9 (*intr*) to testify, esp in a court of law, to events within a person's own knowledge. 10 (*tr*) to attest to the genuineness of (a document, signature, etc.) by adding one's own signature.
▷**HISTORY** Old English *witnes* (meaning both *testimony* and *witness*), from *witan* to know, WIT[2] + -NESS; related to Old Norse *vitni*
▸'**witnessable** ADJECTIVE ▸'**witnesser** NOUN

witness box *or esp US* **witness stand** NOUN the place in a court of law in which witnesses stand to give evidence.

wits (wɪts) PLURAL NOUN 1 (*sometimes singular*) the ability to reason and act, esp quickly (esp in the phrase **have one's wits about one**). 2 (*sometimes singular*) right mind, sanity (esp in the phrase **out of one's wits**). 3 **at one's wits' end.** at a loss to know how to proceed. 4 **five wits.** *Obsolete* the five senses or mental faculties. 5 **live by one's wits.** to gain a livelihood by craftiness rather than by hard work.

Wits (wɪts) (South African, informal) NOUN SHORT FOR University of the Witwatersrand.

Witsie ('wɪtsɪ; *Afrikaans* 'vətsɪ) NOUN *South African informal* a student at the University of Witwatersrand, Johannesburg, esp one representing the University in a sport.

-witted ADJECTIVE (*in combination*) having wits or intelligence as specified: *slow-witted; dim-witted.*

Wittenberg (*German* 'vɪtənbɛrk; *English* 'wɪtənˌbɜːg) NOUN a city in E Germany, on the River Elbe, in Brandenburg: Martin Luther, as a philosophy teacher at Wittenberg university, began the Reformation here in 1517 by nailing his 95 theses to the doors of a church. Pop.: 87 000 (1991).

witter ('wɪtə) *Informal* ♦ VERB [1] (*intr*, often foll by *on*) to chatter or babble pointlessly or at unnecessary length. ♦ NOUN [2] pointless chat; chatter.
▷HISTORY C20: from dialect; compare TWITTER

Wittgensteinian ('vɪtgənˌʃtaɪnɪən, -ˌstaɪnɪən) ADJECTIVE (of a philosophical position or argument) derived from or related to the work of Ludwig Wittgenstein, the Austrian-born British philosopher (1889–1951), and esp the later work in which he attacks essentialism and stresses the open texture and variety of use of ordinary language.

witticism ('wɪtɪˌsɪzəm) NOUN a clever or witty remark.
▷HISTORY C17: from WITTY; coined by Dryden (1677) by analogy with *criticism*

witting ('wɪtɪŋ) ADJECTIVE *Rare* [1] deliberate; intentional: *a witting insult.* [2] aware; knowing.
▸ **'wittingly** ADVERB

wittol ('wɪtᵊl) NOUN *Obsolete* a man who tolerates his wife's unfaithfulness.
▷HISTORY C15 *wetewold*, from *witen* to know (see WIT[2]) + *-wold*, perhaps from *cokewold* CUCKOLD

witty ('wɪtɪ) ADJECTIVE **-tier, -tiest.** [1] characterized by clever humour or wit. [2] *Archaic or dialect* intelligent or sensible.
▸ **'wittily** ADVERB ▸ **'wittiness** NOUN

Witwatersrand (wɪt'wɔːtəzˌrænd; *Afrikaans* vət'vɑːtərs'rant) NOUN a rocky ridge in NE South Africa: contains the richest gold deposits in the world, also coal and manganese; chief industrial centre is Johannesburg. Height: 1500–1800 m (5000–6000 ft.). Also called: **the Rand, the Reef.**

wive (waɪv) VERB *Archaic* [1] to marry (a woman). [2] (*tr*) to supply with a wife.
▷HISTORY Old English *gewīfian*, from *wīf* WIFE

wivern ('waɪvən) NOUN a less common spelling of **wyvern.**

wives (waɪvz) NOUN the plural of **wife.**

wiz (wɪz) NOUN *Informal* a variant spelling of **whizz** (sense 6).

wizard ('wɪzəd) NOUN [1] a male witch or a man who practises or professes to practise magic or sorcery. [2] a person who is outstandingly clever in some specified field; expert. [3] *Obsolete* a wise man. [4] *Computing* a computer program that guides a user through a complex task. ♦ ADJECTIVE [5] *Informal, chiefly Brit* superb; outstanding. [6] of or relating to a wizard or wizardry.
▷HISTORY C15: variant of *wissard*, from WISE[1] + -ARD
▸ **'wizardly** ADJECTIVE

wizardry ('wɪzədrɪ) NOUN the art, skills, and practices of a wizard, sorcerer, or magician.

wizen[1] ('wɪzᵊn) VERB [1] to make or become shrivelled. ♦ ADJECTIVE [2] a variant of **wizened.**
▷HISTORY Old English *wisnian*; related to Old Norse *visna*, Old High German *wesanēn*

wizen[2] ('wiːzᵊn) NOUN an archaic word for **weasand** (the gullet).

wizened ('wɪzᵊnd) *or* **wizen** ADJECTIVE shrivelled, wrinkled, or dried up, esp with age.

wk ABBREVIATION FOR: [1] (*plural* **wks**) week. [2] work. [3] weak.

WK *Text messaging* ABBREVIATION FOR week.

wkly ABBREVIATION FOR weekly.

WKND *Text messaging* ABBREVIATION FOR weekend.

WL INTERNATIONAL CAR REGISTRATION FOR (Windward Islands) St Lucia.

WLM ABBREVIATION FOR women's liberation movement.

WLTM ABBREVIATION FOR would like to meet: used in lonely hearts columns and personal advertisements.

WMD ABBREVIATION FOR weapon(s) of mass destruction.

wmk ABBREVIATION FOR watermark.

WMO ABBREVIATION FOR World Meteorological Organization.

WNW SYMBOL FOR west-northwest.

wo (wəʊ) NOUN, *plural* **wos.** an archaic spelling of **woe.**

WO ABBREVIATION FOR: [1] War Office. [2] Warrant Officer. [3] wireless operator.

w/o ABBREVIATION FOR: [1] without. [2] written off.

woad (wəʊd) NOUN [1] a European plant, *Isatis tinctoria*, formerly cultivated for its leaves, which yield a blue dye: family *Brassicaceae* (crucifers). See also **dyer's-weed, dyer's rocket.** [2] the dye obtained from this plant, used esp by the ancient Britons, as a body dye.
▷HISTORY Old English *wād*; related to Old High German *weit*; Middle Dutch *wēd*, Latin *vitrum*

woaded ('wəʊdɪd) ADJECTIVE coloured blue with woad.

woadwaxen ('wəʊdˌwæksən) NOUN another name for **dyer's-greenweed.**

woald (wəʊld) NOUN another name for **weld**[2].

wobbegong ('wɒbɪˌgɒŋ) NOUN an Australian carpet shark, *Orectolobus maculatus*, with brown-and-white skin.
▷HISTORY from a native Australian language

wobble ('wɒbᵊl) VERB [1] (*intr*) to move, rock, or sway unsteadily. [2] (*intr*) to tremble or shake: *her voice wobbled with emotion.* [3] (*intr*) to vacillate with indecision. [4] (*tr*) to cause to wobble. ♦ NOUN [5] a wobbling movement, motion, or sound. ♦ Also: **wabble.**
▷HISTORY C17: variant of *wabble*, from Low German *wabbeln*; related to Middle High German *wabelen* to WAVER
▸ **'wobbler** NOUN

wobble board NOUN *Austral* a piece of fibreboard used as a musical instrument, producing a characteristic sound when flexed.

wobble plate NOUN another name for **swash plate.**

wobbly ('wɒblɪ) ADJECTIVE **-blier, -bliest.** [1] unsteady. [2] trembling, shaking. ♦ NOUN [3] **throw a wobbly.** *Slang* to become suddenly very agitated or angry.
▸ **'wobbliness** NOUN

Wobbly ('wɒblɪ) NOUN, *plural* **-blies.** a member of the Industrial Workers of the World.

Woburn Abbey ('wəʊbən) NOUN a mansion in Woburn in Bedfordshire: originally an abbey; rebuilt in the 17th century for the Dukes of Bedford, altered by Henry Holland in the 18th century; deer park landscaped by Humphrey Repton.

Woden *or* **Wodan** ('wəʊdᵊn) NOUN the foremost Anglo-Saxon god. Norse counterpart: **Odin.**
▷HISTORY Old English *Wōden*; related to Old Norse *thinn*, Old High German *Wuotan*, German *Wotan*; see WEDNESDAY

wodge (wɒdʒ) NOUN *Brit informal* a thick lump or chunk cut or broken off something.
▷HISTORY C20: alteration of WEDGE

woe (wəʊ) NOUN [1] *Literary* intense grief or misery. [2] (*often plural*) affliction or misfortune. [3] **woe betide (someone).** misfortune will befall (someone): *woe betide you if you arrive late.* ♦ INTERJECTION [4] Also: **woe is me.** *Archaic* an exclamation of sorrow or distress.
▷HISTORY Old English *wā, wǣ*; related to Old Saxon, Old High German *wē*, Old Norse *vei*, Gothic *wai*, Latin *vae*, Sanskrit *uvē*; see WAIL

woebegone ('wəʊbɪˌgɒn) ADJECTIVE [1] sorrowful or sad in appearance. [2] *Archaic* afflicted with woe.
▷HISTORY C14: from a phrase such as *me is wo begon* woe has beset me

woeful ('wəʊfᵊl) ADJECTIVE [1] expressing or characterized by sorrow. [2] bringing or causing woe. [3] pitiful; miserable: *a woeful standard of work.*
▸ **'woefully** ADVERB ▸ **'woefulness** NOUN

wof (wɒf) NOUN *Austral slang* a fool; idiot.
▷HISTORY from *w(aste) o(f) f(lesh)*

WOF (in New Zealand) ABBREVIATION FOR **Warrant of Fitness.**

wog[1] (wɒg) NOUN *Brit slang derogatory* a foreigner, esp one who is not White.
▷HISTORY probably from GOLLIWOG

wog[2] (wɒg) NOUN *Slang, chiefly Austral* influenza or any similar illness.
▷HISTORY C20: of unknown origin

woggle ('wɒgᵊl) NOUN the ring of leather through which a Scout neckerchief is threaded.
▷HISTORY C20: of unknown origin

wok (wɒk) NOUN a large metal Chinese cooking pot having a curved base like a bowl and traditionally with a wooden handle.
▷HISTORY from Chinese (Cantonese)

woke (wəʊk) VERB a past tense of **wake.**

woken ('wəʊkən) VERB a past participle of **wake.**

Woking ('wəʊkɪŋ) NOUN a town in SE England, in central Surrey: mainly residential. Pop.: 98 138 (1991).

Wokingham NOUN a unitary authority in SE England, in Berkshire. Pop.: 150 257 (2001). Area: 179 sq. km (69 sq. miles).

wokka board ('wɒkə) NOUN *Austral* another name for **wobble board.**

wold[1] (wəʊld) NOUN *Chiefly literary* a tract of open rolling country, esp upland.
▷HISTORY Old English *weald* bush; related to Old Saxon *wald*, German *Wald* forest, Old Norse *vollr* ground; see WILD

wold[2] (wəʊld) NOUN another name for **weld**[2].

Wolds (wəʊldz) PLURAL NOUN **the.** a range of chalk hills in NE England: consists of the **Yorkshire Wolds** to the north, separated from the **Lincolnshire Wolds** by the Humber estuary.

wolf (wʊlf) NOUN, *plural* **wolves** (wʊlvz). [1] a predatory canine mammal, *Canis lupus*, which hunts in packs and was formerly widespread in North America and Eurasia but is now less common. See also **timber wolf.** Related adjective: **lupine.** [2] any of several similar and related canines, such as the red wolf and the coyote (**prairie wolf**). [3] the fur of any such animal. [4] **Tasmanian wolf.** another name for the **thylacine.** [5] a voracious, grabbing, or fiercely cruel person or thing. [6] *Informal* a man who habitually tries to seduce women. [7] *Informal* the destructive larva of any of various moths and beetles. [8] Also called: **wolf note.** *Music* **a** an unpleasant sound produced in some notes played on the violin, cello, etc., owing to resonant vibrations of the belly. **b** an out-of-tune effect produced on keyboard instruments accommodated esp to the system of mean-tone temperament. See **temperament** (sense 4). [9] **cry wolf.** to give a false alarm. [10] **keep the wolf from the door.** to ward off starvation or privation. [11] **lone wolf.** a person or animal who prefers to be alone. [12] **throw to the wolves.** to abandon or deliver to destruction. [13] **wolf in sheep's clothing.** a malicious person in a harmless or benevolent disguise. ♦ VERB [14] (*tr*; often foll by *down*) to gulp (down). [15] (*intr*) to hunt wolves.
▷HISTORY Old English *wulf*; related to Old High German *wolf*, Old Norse *ulfr*, Gothic *wulfs*, Latin *lupus* and *vulpēs* fox
▸ **'wolfish** ADJECTIVE ▸ **'wolfˌlike** ADJECTIVE

Wolf Cub NOUN *Brit* the former name for **Cub Scout.**

Wolfenden Report ('wʊlfəndən) NOUN a study produced in 1957 by the Committee on Homosexual Offences and Prostitution in Britain, which recommended that homosexual relations between consenting adults be legalized.
▷HISTORY C20: named after Baron John Frederick *Wolfenden* (1906–85), who chaired the Committee

wolfer ('wʊlfə) NOUN a less common spelling of **wolver.**

Wolffian body ('vɒlfɪən) NOUN *Embryol* another name for **mesonephros.**
▷HISTORY C19: named after K. F. *Wolff* (1733–94), German embryologist

wolffish ('wʊlfˌfɪʃ) NOUN, *plural* **-fish** *or* **-fishes.** any large northern deep-sea blennioid fish of the family *Anarhichadidae*, such as *Anarhichas lupus*. They have large sharp teeth and no pelvic fins and are used as food fishes. Also called: **catfish.**

wolfhound ('wʊlfˌhaʊnd) NOUN the largest breed of dog, used formerly to hunt wolves.

wolfram ('wʊlfrəm) NOUN another name for **tungsten.**
▷HISTORY C18: from German, originally perhaps from the proper name, *Wolfram*, used pejoratively of tungsten because it was thought inferior to tin

wolframite ('wʊlfrəˌmaɪt) NOUN a black to reddish-brown mineral consisting of tungstates of iron and manganese in monoclinic crystalline form: it occurs mainly in quartz veins and is the chief ore of tungsten. Formula: $(Fe,Mn)WO_4$.

Wolf-Rayet star ('wʊlf'reɪət) NOUN any of a small class of very hot intensely luminous stars surrounded by a rapidly expanding envelope of gas.
▷HISTORY C19: named after Charles *Wolf* (1827–

1918) and Georges *Rayet* (1839–1906), French astronomers

wolfsbane *or* **wolf's-bane** ('wʊlfsˌbeɪn) NOUN any of several poisonous N temperate plants of the ranunculaceous genus *Aconitum,* esp *A. lycoctonum,* which has yellow hoodlike flowers.

Wolfsburg (*German* 'vɔlfsbʊrk) NOUN a city in N central Germany, in Lower Saxony: founded in 1938; motor-vehicle industry. Pop.: 122 200 (1999 est.).

wolf spider NOUN any spider of the family *Lycosidae,* which chase their prey to catch it. Also called: **hunting spider.**

wolf whistle NOUN 1 a whistle made by a man to express admiration of a woman's appearance. ◆ VERB **wolf-whistle.** 2 (when *intr,* sometimes foll by *at*) to make such a whistle (at someone).

wollastonite ('wʊləstəˌnaɪt) NOUN a white or grey mineral consisting of calcium silicate in triclinic crystalline form: occurs in metamorphosed limestones. Formula: $CaSiO_3$.
▷HISTORY C19: named after W. H. *Wollaston* (1766–1828), English physicist

Wollongong ('wʊlənˌgɒŋ) NOUN a city in E Australia, in E New South Wales on the Pacific: an early centre of dairy farming; now a coal-mining and heavy industrial centre. Pop.: 185 397 (1998 est.).

wolly ('wɒlɪ) NOUN, *plural* **-lies.** *East London dialect* a pickled cucumber or olive.
▷HISTORY perhaps from OLIVE

Wolof ('wɒlɒf) NOUN 1 (*plural* **-of** *or* **-ofs**) a member of a Negroid people of W Africa living chiefly in Senegal. 2 the language of this people, belonging to the West Atlantic branch of the Niger-Congo family.

wolver ('wʊlvə) *or* **wolfer** NOUN a person who hunts wolves.

Wolverhampton (ˌwʊlvə'hæmptən) NOUN 1 a city in W central England, in Wolverhampton unitary authority, West Midlands: iron and steel foundries; university (1992). Pop.: 257 943 (1991). 2 a unitary authority in W central England, in the West Midlands. Pop.: 236 573 (2001). Area: 69 sq. km (27 sq. miles).

wolverine ('wʊlvəˌriːn) NOUN a large musteline mammal, *Gulo gulo,* of northern forests of Eurasia and North America having dark very thick water-resistant fur. Also called: **glutton.**
▷HISTORY C16 *wolvering,* from WOLF + -ING[3] (later altered to *-ine*)

wolves (wʊlvz) NOUN the plural of **wolf.**

woman ('wʊmən) NOUN, *plural* **women** ('wɪmɪn). 1 an adult female human being. 2 (*modifier*) female or feminine: *a woman politician; woman talk.* 3 women collectively; womankind. 4 (usually preceded by *the*) feminine nature or feelings: *babies bring out the woman in her.* 5 a female servant or domestic help. 6 a man considered as having supposed female characteristics, such as meekness or timidity. 7 *Informal* a wife, mistress, or girlfriend. 8 **the little woman.** *Informal* one's wife. 9 **woman of the streets.** a prostitute. ◆ VERB (*tr*) 10 *Rare* to provide with women. 11 *Obsolete* to make effeminate. ◆ Related prefixes **gyno-, gynaeco-.**
▷HISTORY Old English *wīfmann, wimman;* from WIFE + MAN (human being)
▸'**womanless** ADJECTIVE ▸'**woman-**ˌ**like** ADJECTIVE

womanhood ('wʊmənˌhʊd) NOUN 1 the state or quality of being a woman or being womanly. 2 women collectively.

womanish ('wʊmənɪʃ) ADJECTIVE 1 having qualities or characteristics regarded as unsuitable to a strong character of either sex, esp a man. 2 characteristic of or suitable for a woman.
▸'**womanishly** ADVERB ▸'**womanishness** NOUN

womanize *or* **womanise** ('wʊməˌnaɪz) VERB 1 (*intr*) (of a man) to indulge in many casual affairs with women; philander. 2 (*tr*) to make effeminate.
▸'**woman**ˌ**izer** *or* '**woman**ˌ**iser** NOUN ▸'**woman**ˌ**izing** *or* '**woman**ˌ**ising** NOUN, ADJECTIVE

womankind ('wʊmənˌkaɪnd) NOUN the female members of the human race; women collectively.

womanly ('wʊmənlɪ) ADJECTIVE 1 possessing qualities, such as warmth, attractiveness, etc., generally regarded as typical of a woman, esp a mature woman. 2 characteristic of or belonging to a woman.
▸'**womanliness** NOUN

womb (wuːm) NOUN 1 the nontechnical name for **uterus.** Related adjective: **uterine.** 2 a hollow space enclosing something, esp when dark, warm, or sheltering. 3 a place where something is conceived: *the Near East is the womb of western civilization.* 4 *Obsolete* the belly.
▷HISTORY Old English *wamb;* related to Old Norse *vomb,* Gothic *wamba,* Middle Low German *wamme,* Swedish *våmm*
▸**wombed** ADJECTIVE ▸'**womblike** ADJECTIVE

wombat ('wɒmbæt) NOUN any of various burrowing herbivorous Australian marsupials, esp *Vombatus ursinus,* constituting the family *Vombatidae* and having short limbs, a heavy body, and coarse dense fur.
▷HISTORY C18: from a native Australian language

women ('wɪmɪn) NOUN the plural of **woman.**

womenfolk ('wɪmɪnˌfəʊk) *or sometimes US* **womenfolks** PLURAL NOUN 1 women collectively. 2 a group of women, esp the female members of one's family.

Women's Institute NOUN (in Britain and Commonwealth countries) a society for women interested in the problems of the home and in engaging in social activities.

Women's Liberation NOUN a movement directed towards the removal of attitudes and practices that preserve inequalities based upon the assumption that men are superior to women. Also called: **women's lib.**

Women's Movement NOUN a grass-roots movement of women concerned with women's liberation. See **Women's Liberation.**

women's refuge NOUN *Social welfare* a house where battered women and their children can go for protection from their oppressors.

Women's Royal Voluntary Service NOUN a British auxiliary service organized in 1938 as the Women's Voluntary Service for work in air raids and civil defence: active throughout World War II and since 1945 in providing support services for those in need: became the Women's Royal Voluntary Service in 1966. Abbreviation: **WRVS.**

women's studies PLURAL NOUN courses in history, literature, psychology, etc., that are particularly concerned with women's roles, experiences, and achievements.

women's suffrage NOUN the right of women to vote. See also **suffragette.**

womera ('wʊmərə) NOUN a variant spelling of **woomera.**

wommit ('wɒmɪt) NOUN *Southern English dialect* a foolish person.

won[1] (wʌn) VERB the past tense of **win**[1].

won[2] (wɒn) NOUN, *plural* **won.** 1 the standard monetary unit of North Korea, divided into 100 chon. 2 the standard monetary unit of South Korea, divided into 100 chon. ◆ Also called: **hwan.**
▷HISTORY Korean *wŏn*

won[3] (wʌn, wʊn, wəʊn) VERB **wons, wonning, wonned.** (*intr*) *Archaic* to live or dwell.
▷HISTORY Old English *wunian* to become accustomed to; related to WIN[1]

wonder ('wʌndə) NOUN 1 the feeling excited by something strange; a mixture of surprise, curiosity, and sometimes awe. 2 something that causes such a feeling, such as a miracle. 3 See **Seven Wonders of the World.** 4 (*modifier*) exciting wonder by virtue of spectacular results achieved, feats performed, etc.: *a wonder drug; a wonder horse.* 5 **do** *or* **work wonders.** to achieve spectacularly fine results. 6 **for a wonder.** surprisingly or amazingly. 7 **nine days' wonder.** a subject that arouses general surprise or public interest for a short time. 8 **no wonder.** (*sentence connector*) (I am) not surprised at all (that): *no wonder he couldn't come.* 9 **small wonder.** (*sentence connector*) (I am) hardly surprised (that): *small wonder he couldn't make it tonight.* ◆ VERB (when *tr, may take a clause as object*) 10 (when *intr,* often foll by *about*) to indulge in speculative inquiry, often accompanied by an element of doubt (concerning something): *I wondered about what she said; I wonder what happened.* 11 (when *intr,* often foll by *at*) to be amazed (at something): *I wonder at your impudence.*
▷HISTORY Old English *wundor;* related to Old Saxon *wundar,* Old Norse *undr,* German *Wunder*
▸'**wonderer** NOUN ▸'**wonderless** ADJECTIVE

wonderful ('wʌndəfʊl) ADJECTIVE 1 exciting a feeling of wonder; marvellous or strange. 2 extremely fine; excellent.
▸'**wonderfully** ADVERB ▸'**wonderfulness** NOUN

wonderland ('wʌndəˌlænd) NOUN 1 an imaginary land of marvels or wonders. 2 an actual place or scene of great or strange beauty or wonder.

wonderment ('wʌndəmənt) NOUN 1 rapt surprise; awe. 2 puzzled interest. 3 something that excites wonder.

wonderwork ('wʌndəˌwɜːk) NOUN something done or made that excites wonder; miracle or wonder.
▸'**wonder-**ˌ**worker** NOUN ▸'**wonder-**ˌ**working** NOUN, ADJECTIVE

wondrous ('wʌndrəs) *Archaic or literary* ◆ ADJECTIVE 1 exciting wonder; marvellous. ◆ ADVERB 2 (intensifier): *it is wondrous cold.*
▸'**wondrously** ADVERB ▸'**wondrousness** NOUN

wonga ('wɒŋgə) NOUN *Brit informal* money.
▷HISTORY C20: possibly from Romany *wongar* coal

wonga-wonga ('wɒŋə'wɒŋə) NOUN 1 Also called: **wonga pigeon.** a large Australian pigeon, *Leucosarcia melanoleuca.* 2 an Australian evergreen vine of the genus *Pandorea* or *Tecoma,* esp *T. australis.*
▷HISTORY from a native Australian language

wonk (wɒŋk) NOUN *Informal* a person who is obsessively interested in a specified subject: *a foreign policy wonk.*
▷HISTORY C20: of uncertain origin

wonky ('wɒŋkɪ) ADJECTIVE **-kier, -kiest.** *Brit informal* 1 shaky or unsteady. 2 not in correct alignment; askew. 3 liable to break down or develop a fault.
▷HISTORY C20: variant of dialect *wanky,* from Old English *wancol*

Wŏnsan ('wɒn'sæn) NOUN a port in SE North Korea, on the Sea of Japan: oil refineries. Pop.: 274 000 (latest est.).

wont (wəʊnt) ADJECTIVE 1 (*postpositive*) accustomed (to doing something): *he was wont to come early.* ◆ NOUN 2 a manner or action habitually employed by or associated with someone (often in the phrases **as is my wont, as is his wont,** etc.). ◆ VERB 3 (when *tr, usually passive*) to become or cause to become accustomed.
▷HISTORY Old English *gewunod,* past participle of *wunian* to be accustomed to; related to Old High German *wunēn* (German *wohnen*), Old Norse *una* to be satisfied; see WEAN[1], WISH, WINSOME

won't (wəʊnt) VERB CONTRACTION OF will not.

wonted ('wəʊntɪd) ADJECTIVE 1 (*postpositive*) accustomed or habituated (to doing something). 2 (*prenominal*) customary; usual: *she is in her wonted place.*

won ton ('wɒn 'tɒn) NOUN *Chinese cookery* 1 a dumpling filled with spiced minced pork, usually served in soup. 2 soup containing such dumplings.
▷HISTORY from Chinese (Cantonese) *wan t'an* pastry

woo (wuː) VERB **woos, wooing, wooed.** 1 to seek the affection, favour, or love of (a woman) with a view to marriage. 2 (*tr*) to seek after zealously or hopefully: *to woo fame.* 3 (*tr*) to bring upon oneself (good or evil results) by one's own action. 4 (*tr*) to beg or importune (someone).
▷HISTORY Old English *wōgian,* of obscure origin
▸'**wooer** NOUN ▸'**wooing** NOUN

wood[1] (wʊd) NOUN 1 the hard fibrous substance consisting of xylem tissue that occurs beneath the bark in trees, shrubs, and similar plants. Related adjectives: **ligneous, xyloid.** 2 the trunks of trees that have been cut and prepared for use as a building material. 3 a collection of trees, shrubs, herbs, grasses, etc., usually dominated by one or a few species of tree: usually smaller than a forest: *an oak wood.* Related adjective: **sylvan.** 4 fuel; firewood. 5 *Golf* **a** a long-shafted club with a broad wooden or metal head, used for driving: numbered from 1 to 7 according to size, angle of face, etc. **b** (*as modifier*): *a wood shot.* 6 *Tennis, squash, badminton* the frame of a racket: *he hit a winning shot off the wood.* 7 one of the biased wooden bowls used in the game of bowls. 8 *Music* short for **woodwind.** See also **woods** (sense 3). 9 **a** casks, barrels, etc., made of wood. **b**

from the wood. (of a beverage) from a wooden container rather than a metal or glass one. 10 **have (got) the wood on.** *Austral and NZ informal* to have an advantage over. 11 **out of the wood** *or* **woods.** clear of or safe from dangers or doubts: *we're not out of the wood yet.* 12 **see the wood for the trees.** (*used with a negative*) to obtain a general view of a situation, problem, etc., without allowing details to cloud one's analysis: *he can't see the wood for the trees.* 13 (*modifier*) made of, used for, employing, or handling wood: *a wood fire.* 14 (*modifier*) dwelling in, concerning, or situated in a wood: *a wood nymph.* ◆ VERB 15 (*tr*) to plant a wood upon. 16 to supply or be supplied with fuel or firewood. ◆ See also **woods.**
▷HISTORY Old English *widu, wudu;* related to Old High German *witu,* Old Norse *vithr*
▸ˈ**woodless** ADJECTIVE

wood[2] (wʊd) ADJECTIVE *Obsolete* raging or raving like a maniac.
▷HISTORY Old English *wōd;* related to Old High German *wuot* (German *Wut*), Old Norse *ōthr,* Gothic *wōths,* Latin *vātēs* seer

wood alcohol NOUN another name for **methanol.**

wood-and-water joey NOUN *Austral informal* a person employed to carry out menial tasks.
▷HISTORY from the biblical phrase "hewers of wood and drawers of water" (Joshua 9:21) and JOEY

wood anemone NOUN any of several woodland anemone plants, esp *Anemone quinquefolia* of E North America and *A. nemorosa* of Europe, having finely divided leaves and solitary white flowers. Also called: **windflower.**

wood ant NOUN a reddish-brown European ant, *Formica rufa,* typically living in anthills in woodlands.

wood avens NOUN another name for **herb bennet.**

woodbine (ˈwuːdˌbaɪn) NOUN 1 a honeysuckle, *Lonicera periclymenum,* of Europe, SW Asia, and N Africa, having fragrant creamy flowers. 2 **American woodbine.** a related North American plant, *L. caprifolium.* 3 *US* another name for **Virginia creeper** (sense 1). 4 *Austral obsolete slang* an Englishman.
▷HISTORY sense 4 from the English brand of cigarettes so named

wood block NOUN 1 a small rectangular flat block of wood that is laid with others as a floor surface. 2 *Music* another word for **Chinese block.**

woodborer (ˈwʊdˌbɔːrə) NOUN 1 any of various beetles of the families *Anobiidae, Buprestidae,* etc., the larvae of which bore into and damage wood. 2 any of various other unrelated invertebrates that bore into wood.

woodcarving (ˈwʊdˌkɑːvɪŋ) NOUN 1 the act of carving wood, esp as an art form. 2 a work of art produced by carving wood.
▸ˈ**woodˌcarver** NOUN

woodchat *or* **woodchat shrike** (ˈwʊdˌtʃæt) NOUN a songbird, *Lanius senator,* of Europe and N Africa, having a black-and-white plumage with a reddish-brown crown and a hooked bill: family *Laniidae* (shrikes).

woodchop (ˈwʊdˌtʃɒp) NOUN *Austral* a wood-chopping competition, esp at a show.

woodchuck (ˈwʊdˌtʃʌk) NOUN a North American marmot, *Marmota monax,* having coarse reddish-brown fur. Also called: **groundhog.**
▷HISTORY C17: by folk etymology from Cree *otcheck* fisher, marten

wood coal NOUN another name for **lignite** or **charcoal.**

woodcock (ˈwʊdˌkɒk) NOUN 1 an Old World game bird, *Scolopax rusticola,* resembling the snipe but larger and having shorter legs and neck: family *Scolopacidae* (sandpipers, etc.), order *Charadriiformes.* 2 a related North American bird, *Philohela minor.* 3 *Obsolete* a simpleton.

woodcraft (ˈwʊdˌkrɑːft) NOUN *Chiefly US and Canadian* 1 ability and experience in matters concerned with living in a wood or forest. 2 ability or skill at woodwork, carving, etc. 3 skill in caring for trees.
▸ˈ**woodˌcraftsman** NOUN

woodcut (ˈwʊdˌkʌt) NOUN 1 a block of wood cut along the grain and with a design, illustration, etc., incised with a knife, from which prints are made. 2 a print from a woodcut.

woodcutter (ˈwʊdˌkʌtə) NOUN 1 a person who fells trees or chops wood. 2 a person who makes woodcuts.
▸ˈ**woodˌcutting** NOUN

wood duck NOUN a duck, *Aix sponsa,* of wooded swamps, lakes, etc., in North America, having a very brightly coloured plumage in the male.

wooded (ˈwʊdɪd) ADJECTIVE 1 covered with or abounding in woods or trees. 2 (*in combination*) having wood of a specified character: *a soft-wooded tree.*

wooden (ˈwʊdᵊn) ADJECTIVE 1 made from or consisting of wood. 2 awkward or clumsy. 3 bereft of spirit or animation: *a wooden expression.* 4 obstinately unyielding: *a wooden attitude.* 5 mentally slow or dull. 6 not highly resonant: *a wooden thud.* ◆ VERB 7 (*tr*) *Austral slang* to fell or kill (a person or animal).
▸ˈ**woodenly** ADVERB ▸ˈ**woodenness** NOUN

wood engraving NOUN 1 the art of engraving pictures or designs on wood for printing by incising them with a burin on a block of wood cut across the grain. 2 a block of wood so engraved or a print taken from it.
▸**wood engraver** NOUN

woodenhead (ˈwʊdᵊnˌhɛd) NOUN *Informal* a dull, foolish, or unintelligent person.
▸ˌ**woodenˈheaded** ADJECTIVE ▸ˌ**woodenˈheadedness** NOUN

Wooden Horse NOUN another name for the **Trojan Horse** (sense 1).

wooden spoon NOUN a booby prize, esp in sporting contests.

wooden tongue *or* **woody tongue** NOUN *Vet science* the nontechnical name for **actino bacillosis.**

woodentop (ˈwʊdᵊnˌtɒp) NOUN *Brit informal* a dull, foolish, or unintelligent person.

woodfree (ˈwʊdˌfriː) ADJECTIVE (of high-quality paper) made from pulp that has been treated chemically, removing impurities.

woodgrouse (ˈwʊdˌgraʊs) NOUN another name for **capercaillie.**

wood hedgehog NOUN a pale buff basidiomycetous fungus, *Hydnum repandum,* found in broad-leaved woodlands having a spiny underside to the cap.

woodhen (ˈwʊdˌhɛn) NOUN *NZ* another name for **weka.**

wood hyacinth NOUN another name for **bluebell** (sense 1).

wood ibis NOUN any of several storks having a downward-curved bill, esp *Mycteria americana* of America and *Ibis ibis* of Africa.

woodland (ˈwʊdlənd) NOUN **a** land that is mostly covered with woods or dense growths of trees and shrubs. **b** (*as modifier*): *woodland fauna.*
▸ˈ**woodlander** NOUN

woodlark (ˈwʊdˌlɑːk) NOUN an Old World lark, *Lullula arborea,* similar to but slightly smaller than the skylark.

woodlot (ˈwʊdˌlɒt) NOUN an area restricted to the growing of trees. Also called (esp Canadian): **bush lot.**

woodlouse (ˈwʊdˌlaʊs) NOUN, *plural* **-lice** (-ˌlaɪs). any of various small terrestrial isopod crustaceans of the genera *Oniscus, Porcellio,* etc., which have a flattened segmented body and occur in damp habitats. See also **pill bug.**

woodman (ˈwʊdmən) NOUN, *plural* **-men.** 1 a person who looks after and fells trees used for timber. 2 another word for **woodsman.** 3 *Obsolete* a hunter who is knowledgeable about woods and the animals living in them.

woodnote (ˈwʊdˌnəʊt) NOUN a natural musical note or song, like that of a wild bird.

wood nymph NOUN one of a class of nymphs fabled to inhabit the woods, such as a dryad.

wood opal NOUN a form of petrified wood impregnated by common opal.

wood owl NOUN another name for **tawny owl.**

woodpecker (ˈwʊdˌpɛkə) NOUN any climbing bird of the family *Picidae,* typically having a brightly coloured plumage and strong chisel-like bill with which they bore into trees for insects: order *Piciformes.*

wood pigeon NOUN a large Eurasian pigeon, *Columba palumbus,* having white patches on the wings and neck. Also called: **ringdove, cushat.**

woodpile (ˈwʊdˌpaɪl) NOUN 1 a pile or heap of firewood. 2 **nigger in the woodpile.** See **nigger** (sense 3).

wood pitch NOUN the dark viscid residue left after the distillation of wood tar: used as a binder in briquettes.

wood preservative NOUN a coating applied to timber as a protection against decay, insects, weather, etc.

woodprint (ˈwʊdˌprɪnt) NOUN another name for **woodcut** (sense 2).

wood pulp NOUN 1 wood that has been ground to a fine pulp for use in making newsprint and other cheap forms of paper, and in the production of hardboard. 2 finely pulped wood that has been digested by a chemical, such as caustic soda, and sometimes bleached: used in making paper.

wood rat NOUN another name for **pack rat.**

woodruff (ˈwʊdrʌf) NOUN any of several rubiaceous plants of the genus *Galium,* esp *G. odoratum* (**sweet woodruff**), of Eurasia, which has small sweet-scented white flowers and whorls of narrow fragrant leaves used to flavour wine and liqueurs and in perfumery.
▷HISTORY Old English *wudurofe,* from WOOD[1] + *rōfe,* related to Old High German *ruoba,* Middle Low German *rōve* (beet)root, Latin *rāpere* to creep

Woodruff key (ˈwʊdrʌf) NOUN *Engineering* a semicircular key restrained in a curved keyway in a shaft.
▷HISTORY C19: named after the *Woodruff Manufacturing Co,* in Hartford, Connecticut, who first manufactured it in 1892

woodrush (ˈwʊdˌrʌʃ) NOUN any of various juncaceous plants of the genus *Luzula,* chiefly of cold and temperate regions of the N hemisphere, having grasslike leaves and small brown flowers.

woods (wʊdz) PLURAL NOUN 1 closely packed trees forming a forest or wood, esp a specific one. 2 another word for **backwoods** (sense 2). 3 the woodwind instruments in an orchestra. See also **wood[1]** (sense 8). 4 **neck of the woods.** *Informal* an area or locality: *a quiet neck of the woods.*

Woods NOUN **Lake of the.** See **Lake of the Woods.**

wood sage NOUN a downy labiate perennial, *Teucrium scorodonia,* having spikes of green-yellow flowers: common on acid heath and scree in Europe and naturalized in North America.

woodscrew (ˈwʊdˌskruː) NOUN a metal screw that tapers to a point so that it can be driven into wood by a screwdriver.

Woodser (ˈwʊdzə) NOUN See **Jimmy Woodser.**

woodshed (ˈwʊdˌʃɛd) NOUN a small outbuilding where firewood, garden tools, etc., are stored.

woodsia (ˈwʊdzɪə) NOUN any small fern of the genus *Woodsia,* of temperate and cold regions, having tufted rhizomes and numerous wiry fronds: family *Polypodiaceae.*

woodsman (ˈwʊdzmən) NOUN, *plural* **-men.** a person who lives in a wood or who is skilled in woodcraft. Also called: **woodman.**

wood sorrel NOUN a Eurasian plant, *Oxalis acetosella,* having trifoliate leaves, an underground creeping stem, and white purple-veined flowers: family *Oxalidaceae.*

wood spirit NOUN *Chem* another name for **methanol.**

Woodstock (ˈwʊdstɒk) NOUN a town in New York State, the site of a large rock festival in August 1969. Pop.: 1870 (1990).

wood sugar NOUN *Chem* another name for **xylose.**

woodswallow (ˈwʊdˌswɒləʊ) NOUN any of several insectivorous birds of the genus *Artamus* of Australia.

woodsy (ˈwʊdzɪ) ADJECTIVE **woodsier, woodsiest.** *US and Canadian informal* of, reminiscent of, or connected with woods.

wood tar NOUN any tar produced by the destructive distillation of wood: used in producing tarred cord and rope and formerly in medicine as disinfectants and antiseptics.

wood vinegar NOUN another name for **pyroligneous acid.**

wood warbler NOUN 1 a European woodland warbler, *Phylloscopus sibilatrix,* with a dull yellow plumage. 2 another name for the **American warbler.** See **warbler** (sense 3).

wood wasp NOUN another name for the **horntail.**

woodwaxen ('wʊd,wæksᵊn) NOUN another name for **dyer's-greenweed.**

woodwind ('wʊd,wɪnd) *Music* ◆ ADJECTIVE 1 of, relating to, or denoting a type of wind instrument, excluding the brass instruments, formerly made of wood but now often made of metal, such as the flute or clarinet. ◆ NOUN 2 *(functioning as plural)* woodwind instruments collectively.

wood woollyfoot ('wʊlɪ,fʊt) NOUN a common yellowish basidiomycetous fungus, *Collybia peronata,* of broad-leaved woodland, having a hairy tuft at the foot of the stem.

woodwork ('wʊd,wɜ:k) NOUN 1 the art, craft, or skill of making things in wood; carpentry. 2 components made of wood, such as doors, staircases, etc.

woodworker ('wʊd,wɜ:kə) NOUN a person who works in wood, such as a carpenter, joiner, or cabinet-maker.

woodworking ('wʊd,wɜ:kɪŋ) NOUN 1 the process of working wood. ◆ ADJECTIVE 2 of, relating to, or used in woodworking.

woodworm ('wʊd,wɜ:m) NOUN 1 any of various insect larvae that bore into wooden furniture, beams, etc., esp the larvae of the furniture beetle, *Anobium punctatum,* and the deathwatch beetle. 2 the condition caused in wood by any of these larvae.

woody ('wʊdɪ) ADJECTIVE **woodier, woodiest.** 1 abounding in or covered with forest or woods. 2 connected with, belonging to, or situated in a wood. 3 consisting of or containing wood or lignin: *woody tissue; woody stems.* 4 resembling wood in hardness or texture.
▸ **'woodiness** NOUN

woodyard ('wʊd,jɑ:d) NOUN a place where timber is cut and stored.

woody nightshade NOUN a scrambling woody Eurasian solanaceous plant, *Solanum dulcamara,* having purple flowers with recurved petals and a protruding cone of yellow anthers and producing poisonous red berry-like fruits. Also called: **bittersweet.**

woof¹ (wu:f) NOUN 1 the crosswise yarns that fill the warp yarns in weaving; weft. 2 a woven fabric or its texture.
▹HISTORY Old English *ōwef,* from *ō-,* perhaps from ON, + *wef* WEB (see WEAVE); modern form influenced by WARP

woof² (wʊf) INTERJECTION 1 an imitation of the bark or growl of a dog. ◆ VERB 2 *(intr)* (of dogs) to bark or growl.

woofer ('wu:fə) NOUN a loudspeaker used in high-fidelity systems for the reproduction of low audio frequencies.

woofter ('wʊftə, 'wu:ftə) NOUN *Derogatory slang* a male homosexual.

Wookey Hole ('wʊkɪ həʊl) NOUN a village in SW England, in Somerset, near Wells: noted for the nearby limestone cave in which prehistoric remains have been found. Pop.: 1000 (latest est.).

wool (wʊl) NOUN 1 the outer coat of sheep, yaks, etc., which consists of short curly hairs. 2 yarn spun from the coat of sheep, etc., used in weaving, knitting, etc. 3 **a** cloth or a garment made from this yarn. **b** *(as modifier)*: *a wool dress.* 4 any of certain fibrous materials: *glass wool; steel wool.* 5 *Informal* short thick curly hair. 6 a tangled mass of soft fine hairs that occurs in certain plants. 7 **dyed in the wool.** confirmed in one's beliefs or opinions. 8 **pull the wool over someone's eyes.** to deceive or delude someone.
▹HISTORY Old English *wull;* related to Old Frisian, Middle Dutch *wulle,* Old High German *wolla* (German *Wolle*), Old Norse *ull,* Latin *lāna* and *vellus* fleece
▸ **'wool-,like** ADJECTIVE

wool bale NOUN *Austral and NZ* a standard-sized jute, flax, etc., cubical container of compressed wool weighing over 100 kg when containing fleece or lamb's wool and weighing 204 kg when containing oddments.

wool cheque NOUN *NZ* the annual return for a sheep farmer.

wool classing NOUN *Austral and NZ* the grading and grouping together of similar types of wool.

wool clip NOUN the total amount of wool shorn from a particular flock, or from flocks in a particular region or country, in one year.

wool fat *or* **grease** NOUN another name for **lanolin.**

woolfell ('wʊl,fɛl) NOUN *Obsolete* the skin of a sheep or similar animal with the fleece still attached.

woolgathering ('wʊl,gæðərɪŋ) NOUN idle or absent-minded indulgence in fantasy; daydreaming.
▸ **'wool,gatherer** NOUN

woolgrower ('wʊl,grəʊə) NOUN a person who keeps sheep for their wool.
▸ **'wool,growing** NOUN, ADJECTIVE

woolled (wʊld) ADJECTIVE 1 (of animals) having wool. 2 having wool as specified: *coarse-woolled.*

woollen *or US* **woolen** ('wʊlən) ADJECTIVE 1 relating to or consisting partly or wholly of wool. ◆ NOUN 2 *(often plural)* a garment or piece of cloth made wholly or partly of wool, esp a knitted one.

woolly *or sometimes US* **wooly** ('wʊlɪ) ADJECTIVE **woollier, woolliest** *or sometimes US* **woolier, wooliest.** 1 consisting of, resembling, or having the nature of wool. 2 covered or clothed in wool or something resembling it. 3 lacking clarity or substance: *woolly thinking.* 4 *Botany* covered with long soft whitish hairs: *woolly stems.* 5 *US* recalling the rough and lawless period of the early West of America (esp in the phrase **wild and woolly**). ◆ NOUN, *plural* **woollies** *or sometimes US* **woolies.** 6 *(often plural)* a garment, such as a sweater, made of wool or something similar. 7 *Western US and Austral (usually plural)* an informal word for **sheep.**
▸ **'woollily** ADVERB ▸ **'woolliness** NOUN

woolly bear NOUN the caterpillar of any of various tiger moths, esp *Arctia caja* of Europe and *Isia isabella* of North America, having a dense covering of soft hairs.

woollybutt ('wʊlɪ,bʌt) NOUN *Austral* any of several eucalyptus trees, esp *Eucalyptus longifolia,* having loose fibrous bark around the base of the trunk.

woolly-minded ADJECTIVE showing a vague or muddled way of thinking.

woolpack ('wʊl,pæk) NOUN 1 the cloth or canvas wrapping used to pack a bale of wool. 2 a bale of wool.

woolsack ('wʊl,sæk) NOUN 1 a sack containing or intended to contain wool. 2 (in Britain) the seat of the Lord Chancellor in the House of Lords, formerly made of a large square sack of wool.

woolshed ('wʊl,ʃɛd) NOUN *Austral and NZ* a shearing shed.

wool-sorter's disease NOUN another name for **anthrax.**

wool stapler NOUN a person who sorts wool into different grades or classifications.
▸ **'wool-,stapling** NOUN, ADJECTIVE

wool store NOUN *Austral and NZ* a building where bales of wool are stored and made available to prospective buyers for inspection.

wool table NOUN *NZ* a slatted wooden table in a shearing shed where fleeces are skirted and classed.

woomera *or* **womera** ('wʊmərə) NOUN *Austral* a type of notched stick used by native Australians to increase leverage and propulsion in the throwing of a spear.
▹HISTORY from a native Australian language

Woomera ('wʊmərə) NOUN a town in South Australia: site of the Long Range Weapons Establishment. Pop.: 1660 (latest est.).

Woop Woop ('wu:p ,wu:p) NOUN *Austral slang* a jocular name for any backward or remote town or district.

woorali (wʊ'rɑ:lɪ) NOUN a less common name for **curare.**
▹HISTORY C18: from the native S American name

woosh (wʊʃ) NOUN, VERB a variant spelling of **whoosh.**

woozy ('wu:zɪ) ADJECTIVE **woozier, wooziest.** *Informal* 1 dazed or confused. 2 experiencing dizziness, nausea, etc.
▹HISTORY C19: perhaps from a blend of *woolly* + *muzzy* or *dizzy*
▸ **'woozily** ADVERB ▸ **'wooziness** NOUN

wop¹ (wɒp) NOUN *Slang derogatory* a member of a Latin people, esp an Italian.
▹HISTORY C20: probably from southern Italian dialect *guappo* dandy, braggart, from Spanish *guapo*

wop² (wɒp) VERB **wops, wopping, wopped.** NOUN a variant spelling of **whop.**

wop-wops ('wɒp,wɒps) NOUN *(functioning as plural or singular)* **the.** *NZ informal* the backblocks; the back of beyond.

Worcester ('wʊstə) NOUN 1 a cathedral city in W central England, the administrative centre of Worcestershire on the River Severn: scene of the battle (1651) in which Charles II was defeated by Cromwell. Pop.: 82 661 (1991). 2 an industrial city in the US, in central Massachusetts: Clark University (1887). Pop.: 172 648 (2000). 3 a town in S South Africa; centre of a fruit-growing region. Pop.: 60 324 (1990).

Worcester china *or* **porcelain** NOUN porcelain articles made in Worcester (England) from 1751 in a factory that became, in 1862, the Royal Worcester Porcelain Company. Sometimes shortened to: **Worcester.**

Worcester sauce *or* **Worcestershire sauce** NOUN a commercially prepared piquant sauce, made from a basis of soy sauce, with vinegar, spices, etc.

Worcestershire ('wʊstə,ʃɪə, -ʃə) NOUN a county of W central England, formerly (1974–98) part of Hereford and Worcester. Administrative centre: Worcester. Pop.: 542 107 (2001). Area: 1742 sq. km (674 sq. miles).

Worcs ABBREVIATION FOR Worcestershire.

word (wɜ:d) NOUN 1 one of the units of speech or writing that native speakers of a language usually regard as the smallest isolable meaningful element of the language, although linguists would analyse these further into morphemes. Related adjective: **lexical, verbal.** 2 an instance of vocal intercourse; chat, talk, or discussion: *to have a word with someone.* 3 an utterance or expression, esp a brief one: *a word of greeting.* 4 news or information: *he sent word that he would be late.* 5 a verbal signal for action; command: *when I give the word, fire!* 6 an undertaking or promise: *I give you my word; he kept his word.* 7 an autocratic decree or utterance; order: *his word must be obeyed.* 8 a watchword or slogan, as of a political party: *the word now is "freedom".* 9 *Computing* a set of bits used to store, transmit, or operate upon an item of information in a computer, such as a program instruction. 10 **as good as one's word.** doing what one has undertaken or promised to do. 11 **at a word.** at once. 12 **by word of mouth.** orally rather than by written means. 13 **in a word.** briefly or in short. 14 **my word! a** an exclamation of surprise, annoyance, etc. **b** *Austral* an exclamation of agreement. 15 **of one's word.** given to or noted for keeping one's promises: *I am a man of my word.* 16 **put in a word** *or* **good word for.** to make favourable mention of (someone); recommend. 17 **take someone at his** *or* **her word.** to assume that someone means, or will do, what he or she says: *when he told her to go, she took him at his word and left.* 18 **take someone's word for it.** to accept or believe what someone says. 19 **the last word. a** the closing remark of a conversation or argument, esp a remark that supposedly settles an issue. **b** the latest or most fashionable design, make, or model: *the last word in bikinis.* **c** the finest example (of some quality, condition, etc.): *the last word in luxury.* 20 **the word.** the proper or most fitting expression: *cold is not the word for it, it's freezing!* 21 **upon my word! a** *Archaic* on my honour. **b** an exclamation of surprise, annoyance, etc. 22 **word for word. a** (of a report, transcription, etc.) using exactly the same words as those employed in the situation being reported; verbatim. **b** translated by substituting each word in the new text for each corresponding word in the original rather than by general sense. 23 **word of honour.** a promise; oath. 24 *(modifier)* of, relating to, or consisting of words: *a word list.* ◆ VERB 25 *(tr)* to state in words, usually specially selected ones; phrase. 26 *(tr; often foll by up) Austral informal* to inform or advise (a person). ◆ See also **words.**
▹HISTORY Old English *word;* related to Old High German *wort,* Old Norse *orth,* Gothic *waurd,* Latin *verbum,* Sanskrit *vratá* command

Word (wɜːd) NOUN **the.** [1] *Christianity* the 2nd person of the Trinity. [2] Scripture, the Bible, or the Gospels as embodying or representing divine revelation. Often called: **the Word of God.**
▷HISTORY translation of Greek *logos,* as in John 1:1

-word NOUN COMBINING FORM (*preceded by* **the** and an initial letter) a euphemistic way of referring to a word by its first letter because it is considered to be in some way unmentionable by the user: *the C-word, meaning cancer.*

wordage (ˈwɜːdɪdʒ) NOUN words considered collectively, esp a quantity of words.

word association NOUN an early method of psychoanalysis in which the patient thinks of the first word that comes into consciousness on hearing a given word. In this way it was claimed that aspects of the unconscious could be revealed before defence mechanisms intervene.

word blindness NOUN the nontechnical name for **alexia** and **dyslexia.**
▸ **ˈword-ˌblind** ADJECTIVE

wordbook (ˈwɜːdˌbʊk) NOUN [1] a book containing words, usually with their meanings. [2] a libretto for an opera.

wordbreak (ˈwɜːdˌbreɪk) NOUN *Printing* the point at which a word is divided when it runs over from one line of print to the next.

word class NOUN *Linguistics* a form class in which the members are words. See **part of speech.**

word deafness NOUN loss of ability to understand spoken words, esp as the result of a cerebral lesion. Also called: **auditory aphasia.**
▸ **ˈword-ˌdeaf** ADJECTIVE

word game NOUN any game involving the formation, discovery, or alteration of a word or words.

wording (ˈwɜːdɪŋ) NOUN [1] the way in which words are used to express a statement, report, etc., esp a written one. [2] the words themselves, as used in a written statement or a sign.

wordless (ˈwɜːdlɪs) ADJECTIVE [1] inarticulate or silent. [2] *Music* of or relating to vocal music that is not provided with an articulated text: *a wordless chorus.*
▸ **ˈwordlessly** ADVERB ▸ **ˈwordlessness** NOUN

word order NOUN the arrangement of words in a phrase, clause, or sentence. In many languages, including English, word order plays an important part in determining meanings expressed in other languages by inflections.

word-perfect *or US* **letter-perfect** ADJECTIVE [1] correct in every detail. [2] (of a speech, part in a play, etc.) memorized perfectly. [3] (of a speaker, actor, etc.) knowing one's speech, role, etc., perfectly.

word picture NOUN a verbal description, esp a vivid one.

wordplay (ˈwɜːdˌpleɪ) NOUN verbal wit based on the meanings and ambiguities of words; puns, clever repartee, etc.

word processing NOUN the composition of documents using a computer system to input, edit, store, and print them.

word processor NOUN **a** a computer program that performs word processing. **b** a computer system designed for word processing.

words (wɜːdz) PLURAL NOUN [1] the text of a part of an actor, etc. [2] the text or lyrics of a song, as opposed to the music. [3] angry speech (esp in the phrase **have words with someone**). [4] **eat one's words.** to retract a statement. [5] **for words.** (preceded by *too* and an adjective or adverb) indescribably; extremely: *the play was too funny for words.* [6] **have no words for.** to be incapable of describing. [7] **in other words.** expressing the same idea but differently. [8] **in so many words.** explicitly or precisely. [9] **of many** (*or* **few**) **words.** (not) talkative. [10] **put into words.** to express in speech or writing as well as thought. [11] **say a few words.** to give a brief speech. [12] **take the words out of one's** (*or* **someone's**) **mouth.** to say exactly what someone else was about to say. [13] **words fail me.** I am too happy, sad, amazed, etc., to express my thoughts.

wordsearch (ˈwɜːdˌsɜːtʃ) NOUN a puzzle made up of letters arranged in a grid which contains a number of hidden words running in various directions.

wordsmith (ˈwɜːdˌsmɪθ) NOUN a person skilled in using words.

word square NOUN a puzzle in which the player must fill a square grid with words that read the same across as down.

word stress NOUN the stress accent on the syllables of individual words either in a sentence or in isolation.

word wrapping NOUN *Computing* the automatic shifting of a word at the end of a line to a new line in order to keep within preset margins.

wordy (ˈwɜːdɪ) ADJECTIVE **wordier, wordiest.** [1] using, inclined to use, or containing an excess of words: *a wordy writer; a wordy document.* [2] of the nature of or relating to words; verbal.
▸ **ˈwordily** ADVERB ▸ **ˈwordiness** NOUN

wore (wɔː) VERB the past tense of **wear.**

work (wɜːk) NOUN [1] physical or mental effort directed towards doing or making something. [2] paid employment at a job or a trade, occupation, or profession. [3] a duty, task, or undertaking. [4] something done, made, etc., as a result of effort or exertion: *a work of art.* [5] materials or tasks on which to expend effort or exertion. [6] another word for **workmanship** (sense 3). [7] the place, office, etc., where a person is employed. [8] any piece of material that is undergoing a manufacturing operation or process; workpiece. [9] **a** decoration or ornamentation, esp of a specified kind. **b** (*in combination*): *wirework; woolwork.* [10] an engineering structure such as a bridge, building, etc. [11] *Physics* the transfer of energy expressed as the product of a force and the distance through which its point of application moves in the direction of the force. Abbreviations: ***W, w.*** [12] a structure, wall, etc., built or used as part of a fortification system. [13] **at work. a** at one's job or place of employment. **b** in action; operating. [14] **make short work of.** *Informal* to handle or dispose of very quickly. [15] (*modifier*) of, relating to, or used for work: *work clothes; a work permit.* ◆ VERB [16] (*intr*) to exert effort in order to do, make, or perform something. [17] (*intr*) to be employed. [18] (*tr*) to carry on operations, activity, etc., in (a place or area): *that salesman works the southern region.* [19] (*tr*) to cause to labour or toil: *he works his men hard.* [20] to operate or cause to operate, esp properly or effectively: *to work a lathe; that clock doesn't work.* [21] (*tr*) to till or cultivate (land). [22] to handle or manipulate or be handled or manipulated: *to work dough.* [23] to shape, form, or process or be shaped, formed, or processed: *to work copper.* [24] to reach or cause to reach a specific condition, esp gradually: *the rope worked loose.* [25] (*tr*) *Chiefly US and Canadian* to solve (a mathematical problem). [26] (*intr*) to move in agitation: *his face worked with anger.* [27] (*tr; often foll by up*) to provoke or arouse: *to work someone into a frenzy.* [28] (*tr*) to effect or accomplish: *to work one's revenge.* [29] to make (one's way) with effort: *he worked his way through the crowd.* [30] (*tr*) to make or decorate by hand in embroidery, tapestry, etc.: *she was working a sampler.* [31] (*intr*) (of a mechanism) to move in a loose or otherwise imperfect fashion. [32] (*intr*) (of liquids) to ferment, as in brewing. [33] (*tr*) *Informal* to manipulate or exploit to one's own advantage. [34] (*tr*) *Slang* to cheat or swindle. ◆ See also **work back, work in, work off, work on, work out, work over, works, work up.**
▷HISTORY Old English *weorc* (n), *wircan, wyrcan* (vb); related to Old High German *wurchen,* German *wirken,* Old Norse *yrkja,* Gothic *waurkjan*
▸ **ˈworkless** ADJECTIVE ▸ **ˈworklessness** NOUN

workable (ˈwɜːkəbᵊl) ADJECTIVE [1] practicable or feasible. [2] able to be worked.
▸ **ˌworkaˈbility** *or* **ˈworkableness** NOUN

workaday (ˈwɜːkəˌdeɪ) ADJECTIVE (*usually prenominal*) [1] being a part of general human experience; ordinary. [2] suitable for working days; everyday or practical.

workaholic (ˌwɜːkəˈhɒlɪk) NOUN **a** a person obsessively addicted to work. **b** (*as modifier*): *workaholic behaviour.*
▷HISTORY C20: from WORK + -HOLIC, coined in 1971 by Wayne Oates, US author

workaround (ˈwɜːkəˌraʊnd) NOUN a method of circumventing or overcoming a problem in a computer program or system.

work back VERB (*intr, adverb*) *Austral informal* to work overtime.

workbag (ˈwɜːkˌbæg) NOUN a container for implements, tools, or materials, esp sewing equipment. Also called: **work basket, workbox.**

workbench (ˈwɜːkˌbentʃ) NOUN a heavy table at which work is done by a carpenter, mechanic, toolmaker, etc.

workbook (ˈwɜːkˌbʊk) NOUN [1] an exercise book or textbook used for study, esp a textbook with spaces for answers. [2] a book of instructions for some process. [3] a book in which is recorded all work done or planned.

work camp NOUN a camp set up for young people who voluntarily do manual work on a worthwhile project.

workday (ˈwɜːkˌdeɪ) NOUN [1] the usual US term for **working day.** ◆ ADJECTIVE [2] another word for **workaday.**

worked (wɜːkt) ADJECTIVE made or decorated with evidence of workmanship; wrought, as with embroidery or tracery.

worked up ADJECTIVE agitated or excited.

worker (ˈwɜːkə) NOUN [1] a person or thing that works, usually at a specific job: *a good worker; a research worker.* [2] an employee in an organization, as opposed to an employer or manager. [3] a manual labourer or other employee working in a manufacturing or other industry. [4] any other member of the working class. [5] a sterile female member of a colony of bees, ants, or wasps that forages for food, cares for the larvae, etc.
▸ **ˈworkerless** ADJECTIVE

worker director NOUN a worker elected to the governing board of a business concern to represent the interests of the employees in decision making.

worker participation NOUN a process by which subordinate employees, either individually or collectively, become involved in one or more aspects of organizational decision making within the enterprises in which they work.

worker-priest NOUN a Roman Catholic priest who has full-time or part-time employment in a secular job to be more closely in touch with the problems of the laity.

workers' cooperative NOUN See **cooperative** (sense 4).

work ethic NOUN a belief in the moral value of work (often in the phrase **Protestant work ethic**).

workfare (ˈwɜːkˌfɛə) NOUN a scheme under which the government of a country requires unemployed people to do community work or undergo job training in return for social-security payments.
▷HISTORY C20: from WORK + (WEL)FARE

workfolk (ˈwɜːkˌfəʊk) *or informal US* **workfolks** PLURAL NOUN working people, esp labourers on a farm.

workforce (ˈwɜːkˌfɔːs) NOUN [1] the total number of workers employed by a company on a specific job, project, etc. [2] the total number of people who could be employed: *the country's workforce is growing rapidly.*

work function NOUN [1] *Physics* the minimum energy required to transfer an electron from a point within a solid to a point just outside its surface. Symbol: ϕ *or* Φ. [2] *Thermodynamics* another name (not now used because of confusion with sense 1) for **Helmholtz function.**

work-harden VERB (*tr*) to increase the strength or hardness of (a metal) by a mechanical process, such as tension, compression, or torsion.
▸ **ˈwork-ˌhardening** NOUN

workhorse (ˈwɜːkˌhɔːs) NOUN [1] a horse used for nonrecreational activities. [2] *Informal* a person who takes on the greatest amount of work in a project or job.

workhouse (ˈwɜːkˌhaʊs) NOUN [1] (formerly in England) an institution maintained at public expense where able-bodied paupers did unpaid work in return for food and accommodation. [2] (in the US) a prison for petty offenders serving short sentences at manual labour.

work in VERB (*adverb*) [1] to insert or become inserted: *she worked the patch in carefully.* [2] (*tr*) to find space for: *I'll work this job in during the day.* ◆ NOUN **work-in.** [3] a form of industrial action in which a factory that is to be closed down is occupied and run by its workers.

working ('wɜːkɪŋ) NOUN 1 the operation or mode of operation of something. 2 the act or process of moulding something pliable. 3 a convulsive or jerking motion, as from excitement. 4 (*often plural*) a part of a mine or quarry that is being or has been worked. 5 (*plural*) the whole system of excavations in a mine. 6 a record of the steps by which the result of a calculation or the solution of a problem is obtained: *all working is to be submitted to the examiners.* 7 *Rare* slow advance against or as if against resistance. ♦ ADJECTIVE (*prenominal*) 8 relating to or concerned with a person or thing that works: *a working man.* 9 concerned with, used in, or suitable for work: *working clothes.* 10 (of a meal or occasion) during which business discussions are carried on: *working lunch; working breakfast.* 11 capable of being operated or used: *a working model.* 12 sufficiently large or accurate to be useful or to accomplish a desired end: *a working majority; a working knowledge of German.* 13 (of a theory, etc.) providing a basis, usually a temporary one, on which operations or procedures may be carried out.

working bee NOUN *NZ* a voluntary group doing a job for charity.

working capital NOUN 1 *Accounting* current assets minus current liabilities. 2 current or liquid assets. 3 that part of the capital of a business enterprise available for operations.

working class NOUN 1 Also called: **proletariat.** the social stratum, usually of low status, that consists of those who earn wages, esp as manual workers. Compare **lower class, middle class, upper class.** ♦ ADJECTIVE **working-class.** 2 of, relating to, or characteristic of the working class.

working day *or esp US* **workday** NOUN 1 a day on which work is done, esp for an agreed or stipulated number of hours in return for a salary or wage. 2 the part of the day allocated to work: *a seven-hour working day.* 3 (*often plural*) *Commerce* any day of the week except Sunday, public holidays, and, in some cases, Saturday.

working dog NOUN a dog of suitable breed or training kept for its practical use, such as herding sheep, rather than as a pet or for showing.

working drawing NOUN a scale drawing of a part or assembly that provides a guide for manufacture.

Working Families Tax Credit NOUN (in Britain) a means-tested allowance paid to single parents or families who have at least one dependent child, who work at least 16 hours per week, and whose earnings are low. It replaced family credit.

working girl NOUN 1 a girl or woman who works, esp one who supports herself. 2 *Informal* a prostitute.

working memory NOUN *Psychol* the current contents of consciousness.

working papers PLURAL NOUN 1 papers or notes showing the intermediate stages of a proposal, solution, etc., arrived at or being worked on. 2 legal documents that certain people in some countries must possess to be allowed to work.

working party NOUN 1 a committee established to investigate a problem, question, etc. 2 a group of soldiers or prisoners assigned to perform some manual task or duty.

working substance *or* **fluid** NOUN the fluid, esp water, steam, or compressed air, that operates an engine, refrigerator, etc.

working week *or esp US and Canadian* **workweek** ('wɜːkˌwiːk) NOUN the number of hours or days in a week actually or officially allocated to work: *a four-day working week.*

work-in-progress NOUN *Book-keeping* the value of work begun but not completed, as shown in a profit-and-loss account.

workload ('wɜːkˌləʊd) NOUN the amount of work to be done, esp in a specified period by a person, machine, etc.

workman ('wɜːkmən) NOUN, *plural* **-men.** 1 a man who is employed in manual labour or who works an industrial machine. 2 a craftsman of skill as specified: *a bad workman.*

workmanlike ('wɜːkmənˌlaɪk) *or less commonly* **workmanly** ('wɜːkmənlɪ) ADJECTIVE appropriate to or befitting a good workman.

workmanship ('wɜːkmənʃɪp) NOUN 1 the art or skill of a workman. 2 the art or skill with which something is made or executed. 3 the degree of art or skill exhibited in the finished product. 4 the piece of work so produced.

workmate ('wɜːkˌmeɪt) NOUN a person who works with another; fellow worker.

workmen's compensation *or* **worker's compensation** NOUN compensation for death, injury, or accident suffered by a workman in the course of his employment and paid to him or his dependents.

work of art NOUN 1 a piece of fine art, such as a painting or sculpture. 2 something that may be likened to a piece of fine art, esp in beauty, intricacy, etc.

work off VERB (*tr, adverb*) 1 to get rid of or dissipate, as by effort: *he worked off some of his energy by digging the garden.* 2 to discharge (a debt) by labour rather than payment.

work on VERB (*intr, preposition*) to persuade or influence or attempt to persuade or influence.

work out VERB (*adverb*) 1 (*tr*) to achieve or accomplish by effort. 2 (*tr*) to solve or find out by reasoning or calculation: *to work out an answer; to work out a sum.* 3 (*tr*) to devise or formulate: *to work out a plan.* 4 (*intr*) to prove satisfactory or effective: *did your plan work out?* 5 (*intr*) to happen as specified: *it all worked out well.* 6 (*intr*) to take part in physical exercise, as in training. 7 (*tr*) to remove all the mineral in (a mine, body of ore, etc.) that can be profitably exploited. 8 (*intr; often foll by to or at*) to reach a total: *your bill works out at a pound.* 9 (*tr*) *Informal* to understand the real nature of: *I shall never work you out.* ♦ NOUN **work-out.** 10 a session of physical exercise, esp for training or practice.

work over VERB 1 (*tr, adverb*) to do again; repeat. 2 (*intr, preposition*) to examine closely and thoroughly. 3 (*tr, adverb*) *Slang* to assault or thrash.

workpeople ('wɜːkˌpiːpᵊl) PLURAL NOUN the working members of a population, esp those employed in manual tasks.

workpiece ('wɜːkˌpiːs) NOUN a piece of metal or other material that is in the process of being worked on or made or has actually been cut or shaped by a hand tool or machine.

workplace ('wɜːkˌpleɪs) NOUN a place, such as a factory or office, where people work.

workroom ('wɜːkˌruːm, -ˌrʊm) NOUN 1 a room in which work, usually manual labour, is done. 2 a room in a house set aside for a hobby, such as sewing.

works (wɜːks) PLURAL NOUN 1 (*often functioning as singular*) a place where a number of people are employed, such as a factory. 2 the sum total of a writer's or artist's achievements, esp when considered together: *the works of Shakespeare.* 3 the deeds of a person, esp virtuous or moral deeds performed as religious acts: *works of charity.* 4 the interior parts of the mechanism of a machine, etc.: *the works of a clock.* 5 **in the works.** *Informal* in preparation. 6 **spanner in the works.** See **spanner** (sense 2). 7 **the works.** *Slang* **a** full or extreme treatment. **b** a very violent physical beating: *to give someone the works.* 8 *Slang* a syringe. 9 (*modifier*) of or denoting a racing car, etc., that is officially entered by a manufacturer in an event: *a works entry.*

works council NOUN *Chiefly Brit* 1 a council composed of both employer and employees convened to discuss matters of common interest concerning a factory, plant, business policy, etc., not covered by regular trade union agreements. 2 a body representing the workers of a plant, factory, etc., elected to negotiate with the management about working conditions, wages, etc. ♦ Also called: **works committee.**

work-sharing NOUN an arrangement whereby one full-time job may be carried out by two people working part time.
▸ **'work-ˌsharer** NOUN

worksheet ('wɜːkˌʃiːt) NOUN 1 a sheet of paper used for the preliminary or rough draft of a problem, design, etc. 2 a piece of paper recording work being planned or already in progress. 3 a sheet of paper containing exercises to be completed by a pupil or student.

workshop ('wɜːkˌʃɒp) NOUN 1 a room or building in which manufacturing or other forms of manual work are carried on. 2 a room in a private dwelling, school, etc., set aside for crafts. 3 a group of people engaged in study or work on a creative project or subject: *a music workshop.* ♦ VERB 4 (*tr*) to perform (a play) with no costumes, set, or musical accompaniment.

workshy ('wɜːkˌʃaɪ) ADJECTIVE not inclined to work.

Worksop ('wɜːksɒp) NOUN a town in N central England, in N Nottinghamshire. Pop.: 37 247 (1991).

work station NOUN 1 an area in an office where one person works. 2 *Computing* a device or component of an electronic office system consisting of a display screen and keyboard used to handle electronic office work.

work-study NOUN an examination of ways of finding the most efficient method of doing a job, esp in terms of time and effort.

worktable ('wɜːkˌteɪbᵊl) NOUN **a** any table at which writing, sewing, or other work may be done. **b** (in English cabinetwork) a small elegant table fitted with sewing accessories.

work through VERB (*tr, adverb*) *Psychol* to resolve (a problem, esp an emotional one), by thinking about it repeatedly and hence lessening its intensity either by gaining insight or by becoming bored by it.

worktop ('wɜːkˌtɒp) NOUN a surface in a kitchen, often of heat-resistant laminated plastic, that is used for food preparation.

work-to-rule NOUN 1 a form of industrial action in which employees adhere strictly to all the working rules laid down by their employers, with the deliberate intention of reducing the rate of working. ♦ VERB **work to rule.** 2 (*intr*) to decrease the rate of working by this means.

work up VERB (*tr, mainly adverb*) 1 to arouse the feelings of; excite. 2 to cause to grow or develop: *to work up a hunger.* 3 (*also preposition*) to move or cause to move gradually upwards. 4 to manipulate or mix into a specified object or shape. 5 to gain knowledge of or skill at (a subject).

workwear ('wɜːkˌwɛə) NOUN clothes, such as overalls, as worn for work in a factory, shop, etc.; working clothes.

workweek ('wɜːkˌwiːk) NOUN the usual US and Canadian term for **working week.**

world (wɜːld) NOUN 1 the earth as a planet, esp including its inhabitants. 2 mankind; the human race. 3 people generally; the public: *in the eyes of the world.* 4 social or public life: *to go out into the world.* 5 the universe or cosmos; everything in existence. 6 a complex united whole regarded as resembling the universe. 7 any star or planet, esp one that might be inhabited. 8 (*often capital*) a division or section of the earth, its history, or its inhabitants: *the Western World; the Ancient World; the Third World.* 9 an area, sphere, or realm considered as a complete environment: *the animal world.* 10 any field of human activity or way of life or those involved in it: *the world of television.* 11 a period or state of existence: *the next world.* 12 the total circumstances and experience of an individual that make up his life, esp that part of it relating to happiness: *you have shattered my world.* 13 a large amount, number, or distance: *worlds apart.* 14 worldly or secular life, ways, or people. 15 *Logic* See **possible world.** 16 **all the world and his wife.** a large group of people of various kinds. 17 **bring into the world. a** (of a midwife, doctor, etc.) to deliver (a baby). **b** to give birth to. 18 **come into the world.** to be born. 19 **dead to the world.** *Informal* unaware of one's surroundings, esp fast asleep or very drunk. 20 **for the world.** (*used with a negative*) for any inducement, however great. 21 **for all the world.** in every way; exactly. 22 **give to the world.** to publish. 23 **in the world.** (*usually used with a negative*) (intensifier): *no-one in the world can change things.* 24 **man** (*or* **woman**) **of the world.** a man (or woman) experienced in social or public life. 25 **not long for this world.** nearing death. 26 **on top of the world.** *Informal* exultant, elated, or very happy. 27 *Informal* wonderful; excellent. 28 **set the world on fire.** to be exceptionally or sensationally successful. 29 **the best of both worlds.** the benefits from two different or

opposed ways of life, philosophies, etc. 30 **think the world of.** to be extremely fond of or hold in very high esteem. 31 **world of one's own.** a state of mental detachment from other people. 32 **world without end.** for ever. 33 (*modifier*) of or concerning most or all countries; worldwide: *world politics; a world record.* 34 (*in combination*) throughout the world: *world-famous.*
▷HISTORY Old English *w(e)orold,* from *wer* man + *ald* age, life; related to Old Frisian *warld, wrald,* Old Norse *verold,* Old High German *wealt* (German *Welt*)

World Bank NOUN an international cooperative organization established in 1945 under the Bretton Woods Agreement to assist economic development, esp of backward nations, by the advance of loans guaranteed by member governments. Officially called: **International Bank for Reconstruction and Development.**

World Bank Group NOUN the collective name for the International Bank for Reconstruction and Development, the International Finance Corporation, and the International Development Association, whose headquarters are all in Washington.

world-beater NOUN a person or thing that surpasses all others in its category; champion.
▸ **'world-,beating** NOUN, ADJECTIVE

world-class ADJECTIVE of or denoting someone with a skill or attribute that puts him or her in the highest class in the world: *a world-class swimmer.*

World Council of Churches NOUN the ecumenical fellowship of Churches other than the Roman Catholic Church, formally constituted at Amsterdam in 1948 for coordinated action in theological, ecclesiastical, and secular matters.

World Court NOUN another name for **International Court of Justice.**

World Cup NOUN an international competition held between national teams in various sports, most notably association football.

World Health Organization NOUN an agency of the United Nations, established in 1948 with headquarters in Geneva, responsible for coordinating international health activities, aiding governments in improving health services, etc. Abbreviation: **WHO.**

world language NOUN 1 a language spoken and known in many countries, such as English. 2 an artificial language for international use, such as Esperanto.

world-line NOUN *Physics* a line on a space–time path that shows the path of a body.

worldling ('wɜːldlɪŋ) NOUN a person who is primarily concerned with worldly matters or material things.

worldly ('wɜːldlɪ) ADJECTIVE **-lier, -liest.** 1 not spiritual; mundane or temporal. 2 Also: **worldly-minded.** absorbed in or concerned with material things or matters that are immediately relevant. 3 Also: **worldly-wise.** versed in the ways of the world; sophisticated. 4 *Archaic* existing on or relating to the earth. 5 *Obsolete* secular; lay. ◆ ADVERB 6 *Archaic* in a worldly manner.
▸ **'worldliness** NOUN

world music NOUN popular music of various ethnic origins and styles outside the tradition of Western pop and rock music.

world power NOUN a state that possesses sufficient power to influence events throughout the world.

World Series *or* **World's Series** NOUN *Baseball* (in the US and Canada) a best-of-seven playoff for the world championship between the two winning teams in the major leagues at the end of the season.

world-shaking ADJECTIVE of enormous significance; momentous.

World Trade Center NOUN a former building complex, at 417 m (1368 ft) the tallest in the US, that stood in Manhattan, New York, from 1974 until its destruction in the terrorist attack of September 11 2001, in which some 2800 people were killed. Abbreviation: **WTC.**

World Trade Organization NOUN an international body concerned with promoting and regulating trade between its member states; established in 1995 as a successor to GATT.

world-view NOUN another word for **Weltanschauung.**

World War I NOUN the war (1914–18), fought mainly in Europe and the Middle East, in which the Allies (principally France, Russia, Britain, Italy after 1915, and the US after 1917) defeated the Central Powers (principally Germany, Austria-Hungary, and Turkey). The war was precipitated by the assassination of Austria's crown prince (Archduke Franz Ferdinand) at Sarajevo on June 28, 1914 and swiftly developed its major front in E France, where millions died in static trench warfare. After the October Revolution (1917) the Bolsheviks ended Russian participation in the war (Dec. 15, 1917). The exhausted Central Powers agreed to an armistice on Nov. 11, 1918 and quickly succumbed to internal revolution, before being forced to sign the Treaty of Versailles (June 28, 1919) and other treaties. Also called: **First World War, Great War.**

World War II NOUN the war (1939–45) in which the Allies (principally Britain, the Soviet Union, and the US) defeated the Axis powers (principally Germany, Italy, and Japan). Britain and France declared war on Germany (Sept. 3, 1939) as a result of the German invasion of Poland (Sept. 1, 1939). Italy entered the war on June 10, 1940 shortly before the collapse of France (armistice signed June 22, 1940). On June 22, 1941 Germany attacked the Soviet Union and on Dec. 7, 1941 the Japanese attacked the US at Pearl Harbor. On Sept. 8, 1943 Italy surrendered, the war in Europe ending on May 7, 1945 with the unconditional surrender of the Germans. The Japanese capitulated on Aug. 14, 1945 as a direct result of the atomic bombs dropped by the Americans on Hiroshima and Nagasaki. Also called: **Second World War.**

world-weary ADJECTIVE no longer finding pleasure in living; tired of the world.
▸ **'world-,weariness** NOUN

worldwide ('wɜːld'waɪd) ADJECTIVE applying or extending throughout the world; universal.

World Wide Web NOUN *Computing* a vast network of linked hypertext files, stored on computers throughout the world, that can provide a computer user with information on a huge variety of subjects. Abbreviation: **WWW.**

worm (wɜːm) NOUN 1 any of various invertebrates, esp the annelids (earthworms, etc.), nematodes (roundworms), and flatworms, having a slender elongated body. Related adjective: **vermicular.** 2 any of various insect larvae having an elongated body, such as the silkworm and wireworm. 3 any of various unrelated animals that resemble annelids, nematodes, etc., such as the glow-worm and shipworm. 4 a gnawing or insinuating force or agent that torments or slowly eats away. 5 a wretched or spineless person. 6 anything that resembles a worm in appearance or movement. 7 a shaft on which a helical groove has been cut, as in a gear arrangement in which such a shaft meshes with a toothed wheel. 8 a spiral pipe cooled by air or flowing water, used as a condenser in a still. 9 a nontechnical name for **lytta.** 10 *Anatomy* any wormlike organ, structure, or part, such as the middle lobe of the cerebellum (*vermis cerebelli*). Technical name: **vermis.** 11 *Computing* a program that duplicates itself many times in a network and prevents its destruction. It often carries a logic bomb or virus. ◆ VERB 12 to move, act, or cause to move or act with the slow sinuous movement of a worm. 13 (foll by *in, into, out of,* etc.) to make (one's way) slowly and stealthily; insinuate (oneself). 14 (*tr;* often foll by *out of* or *from*) to extract (information, a secret, etc.) from by persistent questioning. 15 (*tr*) to free from or purge of worms. 16 (*tr*) *Nautical* to wind yarn around (a rope) so as to fill the spaces between the strands and render the surface smooth for parcelling and serving. ◆ See also **worms.**
▷HISTORY Old English *wyrm;* related to Old Frisian *wirm,* Old High German *wurm,* Old Norse *ormr,* Gothic *waurms,* Latin *vermis,* Greek *romos* woodworm
▸ **'wormer** NOUN ▸ **'worm,like** *or* **'wormish** ADJECTIVE

WORM (wɜːm) NOUN *Computing* ACRONYM FOR write once read many times: an optical disk that enables users to store data but not change it.

wormcast ('wɜːm,kɑːst) NOUN a coil of earth or sand that has been egested by a burrowing earthworm or lugworm.

worm conveyor NOUN another name for **screw conveyor.**

worm-eaten ADJECTIVE 1 eaten into by worms: *a worm-eaten table.* 2 decayed; rotten. 3 old-fashioned; antiquated.

wormery ('wɜːmərɪ) NOUN, *plural* **-eries.** 1 a piece of apparatus, having a glass side or sides, in which worms are kept for study. 2 a container in which worms are kept, esp one in which they consume household waste and convert it into compost.

wormfly ('wɜːm,flaɪ) NOUN *Angling* a type of lure dressed on a double hook, the barbs of which sit one above the other and back-to-back.

worm gear NOUN 1 a device consisting of a threaded shaft (**worm**) that mates with a gearwheel (**worm wheel**) so that rotary motion can be transferred between two shafts at right angles to each other. 2 Also called: **worm wheel.** a gearwheel driven by a threaded shaft or worm.

wormhole ('wɜːm,həʊl) NOUN 1 a hole made by a worm in timber, plants, etc. 2 *Physics* a tunnel in the geometry of space–time postulated to connect different parts of the universe.
▸ **'worm,holed** ADJECTIVE

worm lizard NOUN any wormlike burrowing legless lizard of the family *Amphisbaenidae,* of Africa, South and Central America, and S Europe.

worms (wɜːmz) NOUN (*functioning as singular*) any disease or disorder, usually of the intestine, characterized by infestation with parasitic worms.

Worms (wɜːmz; *German* vɔrms) NOUN a city in SW Germany, in Rhineland-Palatinate on the Rhine: famous as the seat of imperial diets, notably that of 1521, before which Luther defended his doctrines in the presence of Charles V; river port and manufacturing centre with a large wine trade. Pop.: 77 430 (1991).

wormseed ('wɜːm,siːd) NOUN 1 any of various plants having seeds or other parts used in medicine to treat worm infestation, esp an American chenopodiaceous plant, *Chenopodium anthelminticum* (or *C. ambrosioides*) (**American wormseed**), and the santonica plant. 2 the part of any of these plants that is used as an anthelmintic.

worm's eye view NOUN a view seen from below or from a more lowly or humble point.

wormwood ('wɜːm,wʊd) NOUN 1 Also called: **absinthe.** any of various plants of the chiefly N temperate genus *Artemisia,* esp *A. absinthium,* a European plant yielding a bitter extract used in making absinthe: family *Asteraceae* (composites). 2 something that embitters, such as a painful experience.
▷HISTORY C15: changed (through influence of WORM and WOOD[1]) from Old English *wormōd, wermōd;* related to Old High German *wermuata,* German *Wermut;* see VERMOUTH

wormy ('wɜːmɪ) ADJECTIVE **wormier, wormiest.** 1 worm-infested or worm-eaten. 2 resembling a worm in appearance, ways, or condition. 3 (of wood) having irregular small tunnels bored into it and tracked over its surface, made either by worms or artificially. 4 low or grovelling.
▸ **'worminess** NOUN

worn (wɔːn) VERB 1 the past participle of **wear.** ◆ ADJECTIVE 2 affected, esp adversely, by long use or action: *a worn suit.* 3 haggard; drawn. 4 exhausted; spent.
▸ **'wornness** NOUN

worn-out ADJECTIVE (**worn out** when postpositive) 1 worn or used until threadbare, valueless, or useless. 2 exhausted; very weary.

worried well NOUN **the.** *Informal* the people who do not need medical treatment, but who visit the doctor to be reassured, or with emotional problems.

worriment ('wʌrɪmənt) NOUN *Informal, chiefly US and Canadian* anxiety or the trouble that causes it; worry.

worrisome ('wʌrɪsəm) ADJECTIVE 1 causing worry; vexing. 2 tending to worry.
▸ **'worrisomely** ADVERB

worrit ('wʌrɪt) VERB (*tr*) *Dialect* to tease or worry.
▷HISTORY probably variant of WORRY, but compare WHERRIT

worry ('wʌrɪ) VERB **-ries, -rying, -ried.** 1 to be or

cause to be anxious or uneasy, esp about something uncertain or potentially dangerous. 2 (*tr*) to disturb the peace of mind of; bother: *don't worry me with trivialities*. 3 (*intr*; often foll by *along* or *through*) to proceed despite difficulties. 4 (*intr*; often foll by *away*) to struggle or work: *to worry away at a problem*. 5 (*tr*) (of a dog, wolf, etc.) to lacerate or kill by biting, shaking, etc. 6 (when *intr*, foll by *at*) to bite, tear, or gnaw (at) with the teeth: *a dog worrying a bone*. 7 (*tr*) to move as specified, esp by repeated pushes: *they worried the log into the river*. 8 (*tr*) to touch or poke repeatedly and idly. 9 *Obsolete* to choke or cause to choke. 10 **not to worry.** *Informal* you need not worry. ◆ NOUN, *plural* **-ries.** 11 a state or feeling of anxiety. 12 a person or thing that causes anxiety. 13 an act of worrying.
▷HISTORY Old English *wyrgan*; related to Old Frisian *wergia* to kill, Old High German *wurgen* (German *(er)würgen* to strangle), Old Norse *virgill*, *urga* rope
▸ˈ**worried** ADJECTIVE ▸ˈ**worriedly** ADVERB ▸ˈ**worrying** ADJECTIVE ▸ˈ**worryingly** ADVERB

worry beads PLURAL NOUN a string of beads that when fingered or played with supposedly relieves nervous tension.

worryguts (ˈwʌrɪˌgʌts) *or* **worrywart** (ˈwʌrɪˌwɔːt) NOUN *Informal* a person who tends to worry, esp about insignificant matters.

worse (wɜːs) ADJECTIVE 1 the comparative of **bad.** 2 **none the worse for.** not harmed by (adverse events or circumstances). 3 **the worse for wear. a** shabby or worn. **b** a slang term for **drunk.** 4 **worse luck!** *Informal* unhappily; unfortunately. 5 (*postpositive*) **worse off.** in a worse, esp a worse financial, condition. ◆ NOUN 6 something that is worse. 7 **for the worse.** into a less desirable or inferior state or condition: *a change for the worse*. 8 **go from bad to worse.** to deteriorate even more. ◆ ADVERB 9 in a more severe or unpleasant manner. 10 in a less effective or successful manner.
▷HISTORY Old English *wiersa*; related to Old Frisian *werra*, Old High German *wirsiro*, Old Norse *verri*, Gothic *wairsiza*

worsen (ˈwɜːsᵊn) VERB to grow or cause to grow worse.

worser (ˈwɜːsə) ADJECTIVE an archaic or nonstandard word for **worse.**

worship (ˈwɜːʃɪp) VERB **-ships, -shipping, -shipped** *or US* **-ships, -shiping, -shiped.** 1 (*tr*) to show profound religious devotion and respect to; adore or venerate (God or any person or thing considered divine). 2 (*tr*) to be devoted to and full of admiration for. 3 (*intr*) to have or express feelings of profound adoration. 4 (*intr*) to attend services for worship. 5 (*tr*) *Obsolete* to honour. ◆ NOUN 6 religious adoration or devotion. 7 the formal expression of religious adoration; rites, prayers, etc. 8 admiring love or devotion. 9 *Archaic* dignity or standing.
▷HISTORY Old English *weorthscipe*, from WORTH¹ + -SHIP
▸ˈ**worshipable** ADJECTIVE ▸ˈ**worshipper** NOUN

Worship (ˈwɜːʃɪp) NOUN *Chiefly Brit* (preceded by *Your*, *His*, or *Her*) a title used to address or refer to a mayor, magistrate, or a person of similar high rank.

worshipful (ˈwɜːʃɪpfʊl) ADJECTIVE 1 feeling or showing reverence or adoration. 2 (*often capital*) *Chiefly Brit* a title used to address or refer to various people or bodies of distinguished rank, such as mayors and certain ancient companies of the City of London.
▸ˈ**worshipfully** ADVERB ▸ˈ**worshipfulness** NOUN

worst (wɜːst) ADJECTIVE 1 the superlative of **bad.** ◆ ADVERB 2 in the most extreme or bad manner or degree. 3 least well, suitably, or acceptably. 4 (*in combination*) in or to the smallest degree or extent; least: *worst-loved*. ◆ NOUN 5 **the worst.** the least good or most inferior person, thing, or part in a group, narrative, etc. 6 (often preceded by *at*) the most poor, unpleasant, or unskilled quality or condition: *television is at its worst these days*. 7 the greatest amount of damage or wickedness of which a person or group is capable: *the invaders came and did their worst*. 8 the weakest effort or poorest achievement that a person or group is capable of making: *the applicant did his worst at the test because he did not want the job*. 9 **the worst. a** in the least favourable interpretation or view. **b** under the least favourable conditions. 10 **if the worst comes to the worst.** if all the more desirable alternatives become impossible or if the worst possible thing happens. 11 **come off worst** *or* **get the worst of it.** to enjoy the least benefit from an issue or be defeated in it. ◆ VERB 12 (*tr*) to get the advantage over; defeat or beat.
▷HISTORY Old English *wierrest*; related to Old Frisian *wersta*, Old Saxon, Old High German *wirsisto*, Old Norse *verstr*

worst case NOUN **a** a situation in which the most unfavourable conditions prevail. **b** (*as modifier*): *a worst-case projection of a massive accident*.

worsted (ˈwʊstɪd) NOUN 1 a closely twisted yarn or thread made from combed long-staple wool. 2 a fabric made from this, with a hard smooth close-textured surface and no nap. 3 (*modifier*) made of this yarn or fabric: *a worsted suit*.
▷HISTORY C13: named after *Worstead*, a district in Norfolk

wort (wɜːt) NOUN 1 (*in combination*) any of various unrelated plants, esp ones formerly used to cure diseases: *liverwort*; *spleenwort*. 2 the sweet liquid obtained from the soaked mixture of warm water and ground malt, used to make a malt liquor.
▷HISTORY Old English *wyrt* root, related to Old High German *warz*, Gothic *waurts* root

worth¹ (wɜːθ) ADJECTIVE (governing a noun with prepositional force) 1 worthy of; meriting or justifying: *it's not worth discussing*; *an idea worth some thought*. 2 having a value of: *the book is worth 30 pounds*. 3 **for all one is worth.** to the utmost; to the full extent of one's powers or ability. 4 **worth one's weight in gold.** extremely helpful, kind, etc. ◆ NOUN 5 high quality; excellence. 6 value, price. 7 the amount or quantity of something of a specified value: *five pounds worth of petrol*.
▷HISTORY Old English *weorth*; related to Old Saxon, Old High German *werth* (German *Wert*), Old Norse *verthr*, Gothic *wairths*

worth² (wɜːθ) VERB (*intr*) *Archaic* to happen or betide (esp in the phrase **woe worth the day**).
▷HISTORY Old English *weorthan*; related to Old Frisian *wertha*, Old Saxon, Old High German *werthan* (German *werden*), Old Norse *vertha*, Gothic *wairthan*, Latin *vertere* to turn

Worthing (ˈwɜːðɪŋ) NOUN a resort in S England, in West Sussex on the English Channel. Pop.: 95 732 (1991).

worthless (ˈwɜːθlɪs) ADJECTIVE 1 without practical value or usefulness. 2 without merit; good-for-nothing.
▸ˈ**worthlessly** ADVERB ▸ˈ**worthlessness** NOUN

worthwhile (ˌwɜːθˈwaɪl) ADJECTIVE sufficiently important, rewarding, or valuable to justify time or effort spent.

worthy (ˈwɜːðɪ) ADJECTIVE **-thier, -thiest.** 1 (*postpositive*; often foll by *of* or an infinitive) having sufficient merit or value (for something or someone specified); deserving. 2 having worth, value, or merit. ◆ NOUN, *plural* **-thies.** 3 *Often facetious* a person of distinguished character, merit, or importance.
▸ˈ**worthily** ADVERB ▸ˈ**worthiness** NOUN

wot (wɒt) VERB *Archaic or dialect* (used with *I*, *she*, *he*, *it*, or a singular noun) a form of the present tense (indicative mood) of **wit²**.

Wotan (ˈvəʊtɑːn, ˈvɔː-) NOUN the supreme god in Germanic mythology. Norse counterpart: **Odin.**

wotcher (ˈwɒtʃə) SENTENCE SUBSTITUTE a slang term of greeting (esp in the phrase **wotcher cock!**).
▷HISTORY C19: Cockney for *what cheer?*

would (wʊd; *unstressed* wəd) VERB (takes an infinitive without *to* or an implied infinitive) used as an auxiliary. 1 to form the past tense or subjunctive mood of **will¹**. 2 (with *you*, *he*, *she*, *it*, *they*, or a noun as subject) to indicate willingness or desire in a polite manner: *would you help me, please?* 3 to describe a past action as being accustomed or habitual: *every day we would go for walks*. 4 I wish: *would that he were here*.

Language note See at **should.**

would-be ADJECTIVE (*prenominal*) 1 *Usually derogatory* wanting or professing to be: *a would-be politician*. 2 intended to be: *would-be generosity*. ◆ NOUN 3 *Derogatory* a person who wants or professes to be something that he is not.

wouldn't (ˈwʊdᵊnt) VERB CONTRACTION OF would not.

wouldst (wʊdst) VERB *Archaic or dialect* (used with the pronoun *thou* or its relative equivalent) a singular form of the past tense of **will¹**.

Woulfe bottle (wʊlf) NOUN *Chem* a bottle with more than one neck, used for passing gases through liquids.
▷HISTORY C18: named after Peter *Woulfe* (?1727–1803), English chemist

wound¹ (wuːnd) NOUN 1 any break in the skin or an organ or part as the result of violence or a surgical incision. 2 an injury to plant tissue. 3 any injury or slight to the feelings or reputation. ◆ VERB 4 to inflict a wound or wounds upon (someone or something).
▷HISTORY Old English *wund*; related to Old Frisian *wunde*, Old High German *wunta* (German *Wunde*), Old Norse *und*, Gothic *wunds*
▸ˈ**woundable** ADJECTIVE ▸ˈ**wounder** NOUN ▸ˈ**wounding** ADJECTIVE ▸ˈ**woundingly** ADVERB ▸ˈ**woundless** ADJECTIVE

wound² (waʊnd) VERB the past tense and past participle of **wind²**.

wounded (ˈwuːndɪd) ADJECTIVE 1 **a** suffering from wounds; injured, esp in a battle or fight. **b** (*as collective noun*; preceded by *the*): *the wounded*. 2 (of feelings) damaged or hurt.

woundwort (ˈwuːndˌwɜːt) NOUN 1 any of various plants of the genus *Stachys*, such as *S. arvensis* (**field woundwort**), having purple, scarlet, yellow, or white flowers and formerly used for dressing wounds: family *Lamiaceae* (labiates). 2 any of various other plants used in this way.

wove (wəʊv) VERB a past tense of **weave.**

woven (ˈwəʊvᵊn) VERB a past participle of **weave.**

wove paper NOUN paper with a very faint mesh impressed on it by the dandy roller on the paper-making machine. Compare **laid paper.**

wow¹ (waʊ) INTERJECTION 1 an exclamation of admiration, amazement, etc. ◆ NOUN 2 *Slang* a person or thing that is amazingly successful, attractive, etc. ◆ VERB 3 (*tr*) *Slang* to arouse great enthusiasm in.
▷HISTORY C16: originally Scottish, expressive of surprise, amazement, etc.

wow² (waʊ, wəʊ) NOUN a slow variation or distortion in pitch that occurs at very low audio frequencies in sound-reproducing systems, such as a record player, usually due to variation in speed of the turntable, etc. See also **flutter** (sense 14).
▷HISTORY C20: of imitative origin

WOW ABBREVIATION FOR waiting on weather: used esp in the oil industry.

wowser (ˈwaʊzə) NOUN *Austral and NZ slang* 1 a fanatically puritanical person. 2 a teetotaller.
▷HISTORY C20: from English dialect *wow* to whine, complain

WP ABBREVIATION FOR: 1 weather permitting. 2 word processing. 3 word processor. 4 (in South Africa) Western (Cape) Province.

WPA (in the US) ABBREVIATION FOR Work Projects Administration or Works Progress Administration.

W particle NOUN *Physics* a type of elementary particle with either a positive or negative charge considered to transmit the weak interaction between other elementary particles. W particles have a rest mass of 1.435×10^{-25} kg. Also called: **W boson.** See also **Z particle.**

WPB *or* **wpb** ABBREVIATION FOR waste paper basket.

WPC (in Britain) ABBREVIATION FOR woman police constable.

wpm ABBREVIATION FOR words per minute.

WR ABBREVIATION FOR Western Region.

Wraac (ræk) NOUN a member of the Women's Royal Australian Army Corps.

WRAAC ABBREVIATION FOR Women's Royal Australian Army Corps.

WRAAF ABBREVIATION FOR Women's Royal Australian Air Force.

WRAC (in Britain) ABBREVIATION FOR Women's Royal Army Corps.

wrack¹ *or* **rack** (ræk) NOUN 1 collapse or destruction (esp in the phrase **wrack and ruin**). 2 something destroyed or a remnant of such. ◆ VERB 3 a variant spelling of **rack¹**.
▷HISTORY Old English *wræc* persecution, misery;

related to Gothic *wraka,* Old Norse *rāk*. Compare WRECK, WRETCH

> **Language note** The use of the spelling *wrack* rather than *rack* in sentences such as *she was wracked by grief* or *the country was wracked by civil war* is very common but is thought by many people to be incorrect.

wrack[2] (ræk) NOUN [1] seaweed or other marine vegetation that is floating in the sea or has been cast ashore. [2] any of various seaweeds of the genus *Fucus,* such as *F. serratus* (**serrated wrack**). [3] *Literary or dialect* **a** a wreck or piece of wreckage. **b** a remnant or fragment of something destroyed.
▷HISTORY C14 (in the sense: a wrecked ship, wreckage, hence later applied to marine vegetation washed ashore): perhaps from Middle Dutch *wrak* wreckage; the term corresponds to Old English *wræc* WRACK[1]

WRAF (in Britain) ABBREVIATION FOR Women's Royal Air Force.

wraith (reɪθ) NOUN [1] the apparition of a person living or thought to be alive, supposed to appear around the time of his death. [2] a ghost or any apparition. [3] an insubstantial copy of something. [4] something pale, thin, and lacking in substance, such as a column of smoke.
▷HISTORY C16: Scottish, of unknown origin
▸ **'wraith,like** ADJECTIVE

Wran (ræn) NOUN a member of the Women's Royal Australian Naval Service.

wrang (ræŋ) ADJECTIVE, ADVERB, NOUN, VERB a Scot word for **wrong**.

Wrangel Island ('ræŋgəl) NOUN an island in the Arctic Ocean, off the coast of the extreme NE of Russia: administratively part of Russia; mountainous and mostly tundra. Area: about 7300 sq. km (2800 sq. miles).

Wrangell ('ræŋgəl) NOUN **Mount.** a mountain in S Alaska, in the W Wrangell Mountains. Height: 4269 m (14 005 ft.).

Wrangell Mountains PLURAL NOUN a mountain range in SE Alaska, extending into the Yukon, Canada. Highest peak: Mount Blackburn, 5037 m (16 523 ft.).

wrangle ('ræŋgəl) VERB [1] (*intr*) to argue, esp noisily or angrily. [2] (*tr*) to encourage, persuade, or obtain by argument. [3] (*tr*) *Western US and Canadian* to herd (cattle or horses). ◆ NOUN [4] a noisy or angry argument.
▷HISTORY C14: from Low German *wrangeln;* related to Norwegian *vrangla*

wrangler ('ræŋglə) NOUN [1] one who wrangles. [2] *Western US and Canadian* a herder; cowboy. [3] a person who handles or controls animals involved in the making of a film or television programme: *a snake wrangler.* [4] *Brit* (at Cambridge University) a candidate who has obtained first-class honours in Part II of the mathematics tripos. The wrangler with the highest marks is called the **senior wrangler**.

WRANS ABBREVIATION FOR Women's Royal Australian Naval Service.

wrap (ræp) VERB **wraps, wrapping, wrapped.** (*mainly tr*) [1] to fold or wind (paper, cloth, etc.) around (a person or thing) so as to cover. [2] (often foll by *up*) to fold paper, etc., around to fasten securely. [3] to surround or conceal by surrounding. [4] to enclose, immerse, or absorb: *wrapped in sorrow.* [5] to fold, wind, or roll up. [6] (*intr;* often foll by *about, around,* etc.) to be or become wound or extended. [7] to complete the filming of (a motion picture or television programme). [8] (often foll by *up*) Also: **rap.** *Austral informal* to praise (someone). ◆ NOUN [9] a garment worn wrapped around the body, esp the shoulders, such as a shawl or cloak. [10] short for **wrapround** (sense 5). [11] a type of sandwich consisting of a tortilla wrapped round a filling. [12] *Chiefly US* wrapping or a wrapper. [13] *Brit slang* a small package of an illegal drug in powder form: *a wrap of heroin.* [14] Also called: **rap.** *Austral informal* a commendation. [15] **a** the end of a working day during the filming of a motion picture or television programme. **b** the completion of filming of a motion picture or television programme. [16] **keep under wraps.** to keep secret. [17] **take the wraps off.** to reveal.
▷HISTORY C14: origin unknown

wraparound ('ræpə,raʊnd) NOUN *Computing* another name for **word wrapping.**

wrapover ('ræp,əʊvə) *or* **wrapround** ADJECTIVE [1] (of a garment, esp a skirt) not sewn up at one side, but worn wrapped round the body and fastened so that the open edges overlap. ◆ NOUN [2] such a garment.

wrapped (ræpt) VERB [1] the past tense and past participle of **wrap.** ◆ ADJECTIVE [2] *Austral and NZ informal* a variant spelling of **rapt**[2]. [3] **wrapped up.** *Informal* **a** completely absorbed or engrossed in. **b** implicated or involved in.

wrapper ('ræpə) NOUN [1] the cover, usually of paper or cellophane, in which something is wrapped. [2] a dust jacket of a book. [3] the ripe firm tobacco leaf forming the outermost portion of a cigar and wound around its body. [4] a loose negligee or dressing gown, esp in the 19th century.

wrapping ('ræpɪŋ) NOUN the material used to wrap something.

wrapround ('ræp,raʊnd) *or* **wraparound** ('ræpə,raʊnd) ADJECTIVE [1] made so as to be wrapped round something: *a wrapround skirt.* [2] surrounding, curving round, or overlapping. [3] curving round in one continuous piece: *a wrapround windscreen.* ◆ NOUN [4] *Printing* a flexible plate of plastic, metal, or rubber that is made flat but used wrapped round the plate cylinder of a rotary press. [5] Also called: **outsert.** *Printing* a separately printed sheet folded around a section for binding. Sometimes shortened to: **wrap.** [6] a slip of paper folded round the dust jacket of a book to announce a price reduction, special offer, etc. [7] another name for **wrapover.**

wrap up VERB (*adverb*) [1] (*tr*) to fold paper around. [2] to put warm clothes on. [3] (*usually imperative*) *Slang* to be silent. [4] (*tr*) *Informal* **a** to settle the final details of. **b** to make a summary of.

wrasse (ræs) NOUN any marine percoid fish of the family *Labridae,* of tropical and temperate seas, having thick lips, strong teeth, and usually a bright coloration: many are used as food fishes.
▷HISTORY C17: from Cornish *wrach;* related to Welsh *gwrach* old woman

wrath (rɒθ) NOUN [1] angry, violent, or stern indignation. [2] divine vengeance or retribution. [3] *Archaic* a fit of anger or an act resulting from anger. ◆ ADJECTIVE [4] *Obsolete* incensed; angry.
▷HISTORY Old English *wrǣththu;* see WROTH
▸ **'wrathless** ADJECTIVE

Wrath (rɒθ, rɔːθ) NOUN **Cape.** a promontory at the NW extremity of the Scottish mainland.

wrathful ('rɒθfʊl) ADJECTIVE [1] full of wrath; raging or furious. [2] resulting from or expressing wrath. ◆ Also (informal): **wrathy.**
▸ **'wrathfully** ADVERB ▸ **'wrathfulness** NOUN

wreak (riːk) VERB (*tr*) [1] to inflict (vengeance, etc.) or to cause (chaos, etc.): *to wreak havoc on the enemy.* [2] to express, or gratify (anger, hatred, etc.). [3] *Archaic* to take vengeance for.
▷HISTORY Old English *wrecan;* related to Old Frisian *wreka,* Old High German *rehhan* (German *rächen*), Old Norse *reka,* Latin *urgēre* to push
▸ **'wreaker** NOUN

> **Language note** See at **wrought.**

wreath (riːθ) NOUN, *plural* **wreaths** (riːðz, riːθs). [1] a band of flowers or foliage intertwined into a ring, usually placed on a grave as a memorial or worn on the head as a garland or a mark of honour. [2] any circular or spiral band or formation. [3] a spiral or circular defect appearing in porcelain and glassware.
▷HISTORY Old English *wrǣth, wrǣd;* related to Middle Low German *wrēden* to twist. See WRITHE
▸ **'wreathless** ADJECTIVE ▸ **'wreath,like** ADJECTIVE

wreathe (riːð) VERB [1] to form into or take the form of a wreath by intertwining or twisting together. [2] (*tr*) to decorate, crown, or encircle with wreaths. [3] to move or cause to move in a twisting way: *smoke wreathed up to the ceiling.*
▷HISTORY C16: perhaps back formation from *wrēthen,* from Old English *writhen,* past participle of *wrīthan* to WRITHE; see WREATH

wreck (rɛk) VERB [1] to involve in or suffer disaster or destruction. [2] (*tr*) to cause the wreck of (a ship). ◆ NOUN [3] **a** the accidental destruction of a ship at sea. **b** the ship so destroyed. [4] *Maritime law* goods cast ashore from a wrecked vessel. [5] a person or thing that has suffered ruin or dilapidation. [6] Also called: **wreckage.** the remains of something that has been destroyed. [7] Also called: **wreckage.** the act of wrecking or the state of being wrecked; ruin or destruction.
▷HISTORY C13: from Scandinavian; compare Icelandic *rek.* See WRACK[2], WREAK

wrecked (rɛkt) ADJECTIVE *Slang* in a state of intoxication, stupor, or euphoria, induced by drugs or alcohol.

wrecker ('rɛkə) NOUN [1] a person or thing that ruins or destroys. [2] *Chiefly US and Canadian* a person whose job is to demolish buildings or dismantle cars. [3] (formerly) a person who lures ships to destruction to plunder the wreckage. [4] a US and Canadian name for **breakdown van.**

wreckfish ('rɛk,fɪʃ) NOUN, *plural* **-fish** *or* **-fishes.** another name for **stone bass.**
▷HISTORY so called because it is often found near wrecked ships

wreckful ('rɛkfʊl) ADJECTIVE *Poetic* causing wreckage.

wrecking bar NOUN a short crowbar, forked at one end and slightly angled at the other to make a fulcrum.

Wrekin ('riːkɪn) NOUN [1] **the.** an isolated hill in the English Midlands in Telford and Wrekin unitary authority, Shropshire. Height: 400 m (1335 ft.). [2] (**all**) **round the Wrekin.** *Midland English dialect* the long way round: *he went all round the Wrekin instead of explaining clearly.*

wren (rɛn) NOUN [1] any small brown passerine songbird of the chiefly American family *Troglodytidae,* esp *Troglodytes troglodytes* (**wren** in Britain, **winter wren** in the US and Canada). They have a slender bill and feed on insects. [2] any of various similar birds of the families *Muscicapidae* (Australian warblers), *Xenicidae* (New Zealand wrens), etc.
▷HISTORY Old English *wrenna, werna;* related to Old High German *wrendo, rentilo,* Old Norse *rindill*

Wren (rɛn) NOUN *Informal* (in Britain and certain other nations) a member of the Women's Royal Naval Service.
▷HISTORY C20: from the abbreviation *WRNS*

wrench (rɛntʃ) VERB [1] to give (something) a sudden or violent twist or pull esp so as to remove (something) from that to which it is attached: *to wrench a door off its hinges.* [2] (*tr*) to twist suddenly so as to sprain (a limb): *to wrench one's ankle.* [3] (*tr*) to give pain to. [4] (*tr*) to twist from the original meaning or purpose. [5] (*intr*) to make a sudden twisting motion. ◆ NOUN [6] a forceful twist or pull. [7] an injury to a limb, caused by twisting. [8] sudden pain caused esp by parting. [9] a parting that is difficult or painful to make. [10] a distorting of the original meaning or purpose. [11] a spanner, esp one with adjustable jaws. See also **torque wrench.**
▷HISTORY Old English *wrencan;* related to Old High German *renken,* Lithuanian *rangyti* to twist. See WRINKLE[1]

wrest (rɛst) VERB (*tr*) [1] to take or force away by violent pulling or twisting. [2] to seize forcibly by violent or unlawful means. [3] to obtain by laborious effort. [4] to distort in meaning, purpose, etc. ◆ NOUN [5] the act or an instance of wresting. [6] *Archaic* a small key used to tune a piano or harp.
▷HISTORY Old English *wrǣstan;* related to Old Norse *reista.* See WRITHE
▸ **'wrester** NOUN

wrestle ('rɛsəl) VERB [1] to fight (another person) by holding, throwing, etc., without punching with the closed fist. [2] (*intr*) to participate in wrestling. [3] (when *intr,* foll by *with* or *against*) to fight with (a person, problem, or thing): *wrestle with one's conscience.* [4] (*tr*) to move laboriously, as with wrestling movements. [5] (*tr*) *US and Canadian* to throw (an animal) for branding. ◆ NOUN [6] the act of wrestling. [7] a struggle or tussle.
▷HISTORY Old English *wrǣstlian;* related to Middle Dutch *wrastelen* (Dutch *worstelen*), Old Norse *rost* current, race
▸ **'wrestler** NOUN

wrestling ('rɛslɪŋ) NOUN any of certain sports in which the contestants fight each other according to various rules governing holds and usually forbidding blows with the closed fist. The principal object is to overcome the opponent either by throwing or pinning him to the ground or by causing him to submit. See **freestyle, Graeco-Roman, sumo.**

wrest pin NOUN (on a piano, harp, etc.) a pin around which one end of a string is wound: it may be turned by means of a tuning key to alter the tension of the string. In a piano the wrest pin is embedded in the **wrest plank.**

wretch (rɛtʃ) NOUN 1 a despicable person. 2 a person pitied for his misfortune.
▷HISTORY Old English *wrecca;* related to Old Saxon *wrekkeo,* Old High German *reccheo* (German *Recke* warrior), Old Norse *rek(n)ingr*

wretched (ˈrɛtʃɪd) ADJECTIVE 1 in poor or pitiful circumstances. 2 characterized by or causing misery. 3 despicable; base. 4 poor, inferior, or paltry. 5 (*prenominal*) (intensifier qualifying something undesirable): *a wretched nuisance.*
▸ **ˈwretchedly** ADVERB ▸ **ˈwretchedness** NOUN

Wrexham (ˈrɛksəm) NOUN 1 a town in N Wales, in Wrexham county borough: seat of the Roman Catholic bishopric of Wales (except the former Glamorganshire); formerly noted for coal-mining. Pop.: 40 614 (1991). 2 a county borough in NE Wales, created in 1996 from part of Clwyd. Pop.: 128 477 (2001). Area: 500 sq. km (193 sq. miles).

wrick (rɪk) VERB a variant spelling (chiefly Brit) of **rick**[2].
▷HISTORY C19: earlier *rick;* perhaps from Middle Low German *wricken* to move jerkily, sprain

wrier *or* **wryer** (ˈraɪə) ADJECTIVE the comparative of **wry.**

wriest *or* **wryest** (ˈraɪɪst) ADJECTIVE the superlative of **wry.**

wriggle (ˈrɪgᵊl) VERB 1 to make or cause to make twisting movements. 2 (*intr*) to progress by twisting and turning. 3 (*intr; foll by into or out of*) to manoeuvre oneself by clever or devious means: *wriggle out of an embarrassing situation.* ◆ NOUN 4 a wriggling movement or action. 5 a sinuous marking or course.
▷HISTORY C15: from Middle Low German; compare Dutch *wriggelen*
▸ **ˈwriggler** NOUN ▸ **ˈwriggly** ADJECTIVE

wright (raɪt) NOUN (*now chiefly in combination*) a person who creates, builds, or repairs something specified: *a playwright; a shipwright.*
▷HISTORY Old English *wryhta, wyrhta;* related to Old Frisian *wrichta,* Old Saxon, Old High German *wurhtio.* See WORK

wring (rɪŋ) VERB **wrings, wringing, wrung.** 1 (often foll by *out*) to twist and compress to squeeze (a liquid) from (cloth, etc.). 2 (*tr*) to twist forcibly: *wring its neck.* 3 (*tr*) to clasp and twist (one's hands), esp in anguish. 4 (*tr*) to distress: *wring one's heart.* 5 (*tr*) to grip (someone's hand) vigorously in greeting. 6 (*tr*) to obtain by or as if by forceful means: *wring information out of.* 7 (*intr*) to writhe with or as if with pain. 8 **wringing wet.** soaking; drenched. ◆ NOUN 9 an act or the process of wringing.
▷HISTORY Old English *wringan;* related to Old High German *ringan* (German *wringen*), Gothic *wrungō* snare. See WRANGLE, WRONG

wringer (ˈrɪŋə) NOUN another name for **mangle**[2] (sense 1).

wring together VERB (*tr, adverb*) *Engineering* to join (two smooth flat surfaces, esp slip gauges) by hand pressure and a slight twisting movement.

wrinkle[1] (ˈrɪŋkᵊl) NOUN 1 a slight ridge in the smoothness of a surface, such as a crease in the skin as a result of age. ◆ VERB 2 to make or become wrinkled, as by crumpling, creasing, or puckering.
▷HISTORY C15: back formation from *wrinkled,* from Old English *gewrinclod,* past participle of *wrinclian* to wind around; related to Swedish *vrinka* to sprain, Lithuanian *reñgti* to twist. See WRENCH
▸ **ˈwrinkleless** ADJECTIVE ▸ **ˈwrinkly** ADJECTIVE

wrinkle[2] (ˈrɪŋkᵊl) NOUN *Informal* a clever or useful trick, hint, or dodge.
▷HISTORY Old English *wrenc* trick; related to Middle Low German *wrank* struggle, Middle High German *ranc* sudden turn. See WRENCH

wrinklies (ˈrɪŋklɪz) PLURAL NOUN *Informal derogatory* old people.

wrist (rɪst) NOUN 1 *Anatomy* the joint between the forearm and the hand. Technical name: **carpus.** 2 the part of a sleeve or glove that covers the wrist. 3 *Machinery* **a** See **wrist pin. b** a joint in which a wrist pin forms the pivot.
▷HISTORY Old English; related to Old High German, Old Norse *rist.* See WRIGGLE, WRY

wristband (ˈrɪst,bænd) NOUN 1 a band around the wrist, esp one attached to a watch or forming part of a long sleeve. 2 a sweatband around the wrist.

wrist-drop NOUN paralysis of the extensor muscles of the wrist and fingers.

wristlet (ˈrɪstlɪt) NOUN a band or bracelet worn around the wrist.

wristlock (ˈrɪst,lɒk) NOUN a wrestling hold in which a wrestler seizes his opponent's wrist and exerts pressure against the joints of his hand, arm, or shoulder.

wrist pin NOUN 1 a cylindrical boss or pin attached to the side of a wheel parallel with the axis, esp one forming a bearing for a crank. 2 the US and Canadian name for **gudgeon pin.**

wristwatch (ˈrɪst,wɒtʃ) NOUN a watch worn strapped around the wrist.

wristy (ˈrɪstɪ) ADJECTIVE (of a player's style of hitting the ball in cricket, tennis, etc.) characterized by considerable movement of the wrist.

writ[1] (rɪt) NOUN 1 *Law* (formerly) a document under seal, issued in the name of the Crown or a court, commanding the person to whom it is addressed to do or refrain from doing some specified act. Official name: **claim.** 2 *Archaic* a piece or body of writing: *Holy Writ.*
▷HISTORY Old English; related to Old Norse *rit,* Gothic *writs* stroke, Old High German *riz* (German *Riss* a tear). See WRITE

writ[2] (rɪt) VERB 1 *Archaic or dialect* a past tense and past participle of **write.** 2 **writ large.** plain to see; very obvious.

write (raɪt) VERB **writes, writing, wrote, written.** 1 to draw or mark (symbols, words, etc.) on a surface, usually paper, with a pen, pencil, or other instrument. 2 to describe or record (ideas, experiences, etc.) in writing. 3 to compose (a letter) to or correspond regularly with (a person, organization, etc.). 4 (*tr; may take a clause as object*) to say or communicate by letter: *he wrote that he was on his way.* 5 (*tr*) *Informal, chiefly US and Canadian* to send a letter to (a person, etc.). 6 to write (words) in cursive as opposed to printed style. 7 (*tr*) to be sufficiently familiar with (a specified style, language, etc.) to use it in writing. 8 to be the author or composer of (books, music, etc.). 9 (*tr*) to fill in the details for (a document, form, etc.). 10 (*tr*) to draw up or draft. 11 (*tr*) to produce by writing: *he wrote ten pages.* 12 (*tr*) to show clearly: *envy was written all over his face.* 13 (*tr*) to spell, inscribe, or entitle. 14 (*tr*) to ordain or prophesy: *it is written.* 15 (*tr*) to sit (an examination). 16 (*intr*) to produce writing as specified. 17 *Computing* to record (data) in a location in a storage device. Compare **read**[1] (sense 16). 18 (*tr*) See **underwrite** (sense 3a). ◆ See also **write down, write in, write off, write out, write up.**
▷HISTORY Old English *wrītan* (originally: to scratch runes into bark); related to Old Frisian *wrīta,* Old Norse *rīta,* Old High German *rīzan* (German *reissen* to tear)
▸ **ˈwritable** ADJECTIVE

write down VERB (*adverb*) 1 (*tr*) to set down in writing. 2 (*tr*) to harm or belittle by writing about (a person) in derogatory terms. 3 (*intr; foll by to or for*) to write in a simplified way (to a supposedly less cultured readership). 4 (*tr*) *Accounting* to decrease the book value of (an asset). ◆ NOUN **write-down.** 5 *Accounting* a reduction made in the book value of an asset.

write in VERB (*tr*) 1 to insert in (a document, form, etc.) in writing. 2 (*adverb*) *US* **a** to vote for (a person not on a ballot) by writing in his name. **b** to cast (a vote) for such a person by writing in his name. ◆ NOUN **write-in** *US.* 3 the act of voting for a person by writing his name on a ballot. 4 a candidate or vote that has been written in. 5 (*as modifier*): *a write-in campaign.*

write off VERB (*tr, adverb*) 1 *Accounting* **a** to cancel (a bad debt or obsolete asset) from the accounts. **b** to consider (a transaction, etc.) as a loss or set off (a loss) against revenues. **c** to depreciate (an asset) by periodic charges. **d** to charge (a specified amount) against gross profits as depreciation of an asset. 2 to cause or acknowledge the complete loss of. 3 to send a written order for (something): *she wrote off for a brochure.* 4 *Informal* to damage (something, esp a car) beyond repair. ◆ NOUN **write-off.** 5 *Accounting* **a** the act of cancelling a bad debt or obsolete asset from the accounts. **b** the bad debt or obsolete asset cancelled. **c** the amount cancelled against gross profits, corresponding to the book value of the bad debt or obsolete asset. 6 *Informal* something damaged beyond repair, esp a car.

write out VERB (*tr, adverb*) 1 to put into writing or reproduce in full form in writing. 2 to exhaust (oneself or one's creativity) by excessive writing. 3 to remove (a character) from a television or radio series.

writer (ˈraɪtə) NOUN 1 a person who writes books, articles, etc., esp as an occupation. 2 the person who has written something specified. 3 a person who is able to write or write well. 4 a scribe or clerk. 5 a composer of music. 6 *Scot* a legal practitioner, such as a notary or solicitor. 7 **Writer to the Signet.** (in Scotland) a member of an ancient society of solicitors, now having the exclusive privilege of preparing crown writs.

writerly (ˈraɪtəlɪ) ADJECTIVE of or characteristic of a writer; literary.

writer's cramp NOUN a muscular spasm or temporary paralysis of the muscles of the thumb and first two fingers caused by prolonged writing.

write up VERB (*tr, adverb*) 1 to describe fully, complete, or bring up to date in writing: *write up a diary.* 2 to praise or bring to public notice in writing. 3 *Accounting, US* **a** to place an excessively high value on (an asset). **b** to increase the book value of (an asset) in order to reflect more accurately its current worth in the market. ◆ NOUN **write-up.** 4 a published account of something, such as a review in a newspaper or magazine. 5 *Accounting US* **a** an excessive or illegally high valuation of corporate assets. **b** a raising of the book value of an asset.

writhe (raɪð) VERB 1 to twist or squirm in or as if in pain. 2 (*intr*) to move with such motions. 3 (*intr*) to suffer acutely from embarrassment, revulsion, etc. ◆ NOUN 4 the act or an instance of writhing.
▷HISTORY Old English *wrīthan;* related to Old High German *rīdan,* Old Norse *rītha.* See WRATH, WREATH, WRIST, WROTH
▸ **ˈwrither** NOUN

writhen (ˈrɪðən) *Archaic or poetic* ◆ VERB 1 a past participle of **writhe.** ◆ ADJECTIVE 2 twisted; distorted.

writing (ˈraɪtɪŋ) NOUN 1 a group of letters or symbols written or marked on a surface as a means of communicating ideas by making each symbol stand for an idea, concept, or thing (see **ideogram**), by using each symbol to represent a set of sounds grouped into syllables (**syllabic writing**), or by regarding each symbol as corresponding roughly or exactly to each of the sounds in the language (**alphabetic writing**). 2 short for **handwriting.** 3 anything expressed in letters, esp a literary composition. 4 the work of a writer. 5 literary style, art, or practice. 6 written form: *give it to me in writing.* 7 (*modifier*) related to or used in writing: *writing ink.* 8 **writing on the wall.** a sign or signs of approaching disaster.
▷HISTORY sense 8: allusion to Daniel 5:5

writing case NOUN a portable folder with compartments for holding writing materials.

writing desk NOUN a piece of furniture with a writing surface and drawers and compartments for papers, writing materials, etc.

writing paper NOUN paper sized to take writing ink and used for letters and other manuscripts.

Writings (ˈraɪtɪŋz) PLURAL NOUN **the.** another term for the **Hagiographa.**

writing table NOUN a table designed or used for writing at.

writ of execution NOUN *Law* a writ ordering that a judgment be enforced.

written (ˈrɪtᵊn) VERB 1 the past participle of **write.** ◆ ADJECTIVE 2 taken down in writing; transcribed: *written evidence; the written word.* Compare **spoken** (sense 2).

Written Law NOUN *Judaism* another name for the **Torah**.

WRNS ABBREVIATION FOR Women's Royal Naval Service. See also **Wren**[1].

wrnt ABBREVIATION FOR warrant.

Wrocław (*Polish* 'vrɔtswaf) NOUN an industrial city in SW Poland, on the River Oder: passed to Austria (1527) and to Prussia (1741); returned to Poland in 1945. Pop.: 637 877 (1999 est.). German name: **Breslau**.

wrong (rɒŋ) ADJECTIVE 1 not correct or truthful: *the wrong answer.* 2 acting or judging in error: *you are wrong to think that.* 3 (*postpositive*) immoral; bad: *it is wrong to cheat.* 4 deviating from or unacceptable to correct or conventional laws, usage, etc. 5 not intended or wanted: *the wrong road.* 6 (*postpositive*) not working properly; amiss: *something is wrong with the engine.* 7 (of a side, esp of a fabric) intended to face the inside so as not to be seen. 8 **get on the wrong side of** *or* (*US*) **get in wrong with**. *Informal* to come into disfavour with. 9 **go down the wrong way**. (of food) to pass into the windpipe instead of the gullet. ◆ ADVERB 10 in the wrong direction or manner. 11 **go wrong**. **a** to turn out other than intended. **b** to make a mistake. **c** (of a machine, etc.) to cease to function properly. **d** to go astray morally. 12 **get wrong**. **a** to fail to understand properly. **b** to fail to provide the correct answer to. ◆ NOUN 13 a bad, immoral, or unjust thing or action. 14 *Law* **a** an infringement of another person's rights, rendering the offender liable to a civil action, as for breach of contract or tort: *a private wrong.* **b** a violation of public rights and duties, affecting the community as a whole and actionable at the instance of the Crown: *a public wrong.* 15 **in the wrong**. mistaken or guilty. ◆ VERB (*tr*) 16 to treat unjustly. 17 to discredit, malign, or misrepresent. 18 to seduce or violate.
▷HISTORY Old English *wrang* injustice, from Old Norse *vrang;* see WRING
▸'**wronger** NOUN ▸'**wrongly** ADVERB ▸'**wrongness** NOUN

wrongdoer ('rɒŋˌduːə) NOUN a person who acts immorally or illegally.

wrongdoing ('rɒŋˌduːɪŋ) NOUN the act or an instance of doing something immoral or illegal.

wrong-foot VERB (*tr*) 1 *Sport* to play a shot in such a way as to cause (one's opponent) to be off balance. 2 to take by surprise so as to place in an embarrassing or disadvantageous situation.

wrong fount NOUN *Printing* an error in which a type of the wrong face or size is used. Abbreviation: **wf**.

wrongful ('rɒŋfʊl) ADJECTIVE immoral, unjust, or illegal.
▸'**wrongfully** ADVERB ▸'**wrongfulness** NOUN

wrong-headed ADJECTIVE 1 constantly wrong in judgment. 2 foolishly stubborn; obstinate.
▸ˌ**wrong-'headedly** ADVERB ▸ˌ**wrong-'headedness** NOUN

wrong number NOUN a telephone number wrongly connected or dialled in error or the person so contacted.

wrong 'un NOUN *Informal* 1 a dishonest or unscrupulous person. 2 *Cricket, chiefly Austral* another term for **googly**.

wrote (rəʊt) VERB the past tense of **write**.

wroth (rəʊθ, rɒθ) ADJECTIVE *Archaic or literary* angry; irate.
▷HISTORY Old English *wrāth;* related to Old Saxon *wrēth,* Old Norse *reithr,* Old High German *reid* curly haired

wrought (rɔːt) VERB 1 *Archaic* a past tense and past participle of **work**. ◆ ADJECTIVE 2 *Metallurgy* shaped by hammering or beating. 3 (*often in combination*) formed, fashioned, or worked as specified: *well-wrought.* 4 decorated or made with delicate care.
▷HISTORY C16: variant of *worht,* from Old English *geworht,* past participle of (*ge*)*wyrcan* to WORK

> **Language note** *Wrought* is sometimes used as if it were the past tense and past participle of *wreak* as in *the hurricane wrought havoc in coastal areas.* Many people think this use is incorrect.

wrought iron NOUN **a** a pure form of iron having a low carbon content and a fibrous microstructure. It is made by various processes and is often used for decorative work. **b** (*as modifier*): *wrought-iron gates.*

wrought-up ADJECTIVE agitated or excited.

wrung (rʌŋ) VERB the past tense and past participle of **wring**.

WRVS ABBREVIATION FOR **Women's Royal Voluntary Service**.

wry (raɪ) ADJECTIVE **wrier, wriest** *or* **wryer, wryest**. 1 twisted, contorted, or askew. 2 (of a facial expression) produced or characterized by contorting of the features, usually indicating dislike. 3 drily humorous; sardonic. 4 warped, misdirected, or perverse. 5 (of words, thoughts, etc.) unsuitable or wrong. ◆ VERB **wries, wrying, wried**. 6 (*tr*) to twist or contort.
▷HISTORY C16: from dialect *wry* to twist, from Old English *wrīgian* to turn; related to Old Frisian *wrīgia* to bend, Old Norse *riga* to move, Middle Low German *wrīch* bent, stubborn
▸'**wryly** ADVERB ▸'**wryness** NOUN

wrybill ('raɪˌbɪl) NOUN a New Zealand plover, *Anarhynchus frontalis,* having its bill deflected to one side enabling it to search for food beneath stones.

wryneck ('raɪˌnɛk) NOUN 1 either of two cryptically coloured Old World woodpeckers, *Jynx torquilla* or *J. ruficollis,* which do not drum on trees. 2 another name for **torticollis**. 3 *Informal* a person who has a twisted neck.

ws THE INTERNET DOMAIN NAME FOR Western Samoa.

WSSD ABBREVIATION FOR World Summit on Sustainable Development, an intergovernmental conference held in Johannesburg in 2002.

WST (in Australia) ABBREVIATION FOR Western Standard Time.

WSW SYMBOL FOR west-southwest.

wt. ABBREVIATION FOR weight.

WTC ABBREVIATION FOR **World Trade Center**.

WTG *Text messaging* ABBREVIATION FOR way to go!

WTO ABBREVIATION FOR **World Trade Organization**.

Wu (wuː) NOUN a group of dialects of Chinese spoken around the Yangtze delta.

Wuchang *or* **Wu-ch'ang** ('wuː'tʃæŋ) NOUN a former city of E central China: now a part of Wuhan.

wudu (wudu) NOUN *Islam* the practice of ritual washing before daily prayer.
▷HISTORY from Arabic

Wuhan ('wuː'hæn) NOUN a city in SE China, in Hubei province, at the confluence of the Han and Yangtze Rivers: formed in 1950 by the union of the cities of Hanyang, Hankou, and Wuchang (the Han Cities); river port and industrial centre; university (1913). Pop.: 3 911 824 (2000).

Wuhsien ('wuː'ʃjɛn) NOUN another name for **Suzhou**.

Wuhu ('wuː'huː) NOUN a port in E China, in E Anhui province on the Yangtze River. Pop.: 495 765 (1999 est.).

wulfenite ('wʊlfəˌnaɪt) NOUN a yellow, orange, red, or grey lustrous secondary mineral consisting of lead molybdate in the form of platelike tetragonal crystals. It occurs with lead ores and is a source of molybdenum. Formula: $PbMoO_4$.
▷HISTORY C19: from German *Wulfenit,* named after F. X. von *Wulfen* (1728–1805), Austrian mineralogist

Wu-lu-mu-ch'i ('wuː'luː'muː'tʃiː) NOUN a variant of **Urumchi**.

wunderkind ('wʌndəˌkɪnd; *German* 'vʊndərˌkɪnt) NOUN, *plural* **-kinds** *or* **-kinder** (*German* -kɪndər). 1 a child prodigy. 2 a person who is exceptionally successful in his field while still young.
▷HISTORY C20: German, literally: wonder child

Wuppertal (*German* 'vʊpərtaːl) NOUN a city in W Germany, in North Rhine-Westphalia state on the **Wupper River** (a Rhine tributary): formed in 1929 from the amalgamation of the towns of Barmen and Elberfeld and other smaller towns; textile centre. Pop.: 370 700 (1999 est.).

wurley *or* **wurlie** ('wɜːlɪ) NOUN *Austral* an Aboriginal hut.
▷HISTORY from a native Australian language

Würm (vʊəm, wɜːm) NOUN the fourth and final Pleistocene glaciation in Alpine Europe. See also **Günz, Riss, Mindel**.
▷HISTORY C20: named after the river *Würm* in Bavaria, Germany

wurst (wɜːst, wʊəst, vʊəst) NOUN a large sausage, esp of a type made in Germany, Austria, etc.
▷HISTORY from German, literally: something rolled; related to Latin *vertere* to turn

Württemberg ('vɜːtəmˌbɜːg; *German* 'vyrtəmbɛrk) NOUN a historic region and former state of S Germany; since 1952 part of the state of Baden-Württemberg.

Würzburg ('vɜːtsˌbɜːg; *German* 'vyrtsbʊrk) NOUN a city in S central Germany, in NW Bavaria on the River Main: university (1582). Pop.: 126 000 (1999 est.).

wus (wʌs) NOUN *South Wales dialect* a casual term of address: *fancy a drink, wus?*
▷HISTORY from Welsh *was,* variant of *gwas* servant

wuss (wʊs) *or* **wussy** ('wʊsɪ) NOUN, *plural* **wusses** *or* **wussies**. *Slang, chiefly US* a feeble or effeminate person.
▷HISTORY C20: perhaps from PUSSY[1] (cat)

wuthering ('wʌðərɪŋ) ADJECTIVE *Northern English dialect* 1 (of a wind) blowing strongly with a roaring sound. 2 (of a place) characterized by such a sound.
▷HISTORY variant of *whitherin,* from *whither* blow, from Old Norse *hvithra;* related to *hvitha* squall of wind, Old English *hweothu* wind

Wutsin ('wuː'tsɪn) NOUN the former name (until 1949) of **Zangzhou** (sense 1).

Wuxi, Wusih, *or* **Wu-hsi** ('wuː'ʃiː, -'siː) NOUN a city in E China, in S Jiangsu province on the Grand Canal: textile industry. Pop.: 940 858 (1999 est.).

WV 1 ABBREVIATION FOR West Virginia. ◆ 2 INTERNATIONAL CAR REGISTRATION FOR (Windward Islands) St Vincent.

W. Va. ABBREVIATION FOR West Virginia.

WVS (formerly, in Britain) ABBREVIATION FOR Women's Voluntary Service, since 1966 **WRVS**.

WWI ABBREVIATION FOR World War One.

WWII ABBREVIATION FOR World War Two.

WWF ABBREVIATION FOR Worldwide Fund for Nature.

WWW ABBREVIATION FOR **World Wide Web**.

WY *or* **Wy.** ABBREVIATION FOR Wyoming.

Wyandotte ('waɪənˌdɒt) NOUN a heavy American breed of domestic fowl with many different varieties.
▷HISTORY C19: from *Wyandot,* a N American Indian people

wych- PREFIX a variant of **witch-**.

wych-elm *or* **witch-elm** ('wɪtʃˌɛlm) NOUN 1 Eurasian elm tree, *Ulmus glabra,* having a rounded shape, longish pointed leaves, clusters of small flowers, and winged fruits. 2 the wood of this tree.
▷HISTORY C17: from Old English *wice* wych-elm

wych-hazel NOUN a variant spelling of **witch hazel**.

Wycliffite *or* **Wyclifite** ('wɪklɪˌfaɪt) *English history* ◆ NOUN 1 a follower of John Wycliffe, the English religious reformer (?1330–84), or an adherent of his religious ideas; a Lollard. ◆ ADJECTIVE 2 of or relating to Wycliffe, his followers, or his religious ideas.

Wye (waɪ) NOUN a river in E Wales and W England, rising in Powys and flowing southeast into Herefordshire, then south to the Severn estuary. Length: 210 km (130 miles).

Wykehamist ('wɪkəmɪst) NOUN a pupil or former pupil of Winchester College.

wynd (waɪnd) NOUN *Scot* a narrow lane or alley.
▷HISTORY C15: from the stem of WIND[2]

Wyo. ABBREVIATION FOR Wyoming.

Wyoming (waɪ'əʊmɪŋ) NOUN a state of the western US: consists largely of ranges of the Rockies in the west and north, with part of the Great Plains in the east and several regions of hot springs. Capital: Cheyenne. Pop.: 493 782 (2000). Area: 253 597 sq. km (97 914 sq. miles). Abbreviations: **Wyo, Wy,** (with zip code) **WY**.

Wyomingite (waɪ'əʊmɪŋˌaɪt) NOUN a native or inhabitant of Wyoming.

WYSIWYG ('wɪzɪˌwɪg) NOUN, ADJECTIVE *Computing* ACRONYM FOR what you see is what you get: referring to what is displayed on the screen being the same as what will be printed out.

wyvern *or less commonly* **wivern** ('waɪvən) NOUN a heraldic beast having a serpent's tail and a dragon's head and a body with wings and two legs.
▷HISTORY C17: variant of earlier *wyver,* from Old French, from Latin *vīpera* VIPER

Xx

x *or* **X** (ɛks) NOUN, *plural* **x's, X's** *or* **Xs.** [1] the 24th letter and 19th consonant of the modern English alphabet. [2] a speech sound sequence represented by this letter, in English pronounced as *ks* or *gz* or, in initial position, *z,* as in *xylophone.*

x SYMBOL FOR: [1] *Commerce, banking, finance* ex. [2] *Maths* the *x*-axis or a coordinate measured along the *x*-axis in a Cartesian coordinate system. [3] an algebraic variable.

X SYMBOL FOR: [1] (formerly, in Britain) **a** indicating a film that may not be publicly shown to anyone under 18. Since 1982 replaced by symbol 18. **b** (*as modifier*): *an X film.* [2] denoting any unknown, unspecified, or variable factor, number, person, or thing. [3] (on letters, cards, etc.) denoting a kiss. [4] (on ballot papers, etc.) indicating choice. [5] (on examination papers, etc.) indicating error. [6] for Christ; Christian. [from the form of the Greek letter khi (X), first letter of *Khristos* Christ] ◆ [7] THE ROMAN NUMERAL FOR ten. See **Roman numerals.**

xanthan gum ('zæn,θæn) NOUN a complex polysaccharide exuded by colonies of the bacterium *Xanthomonas campestris:* used as a food additive in salad dressings, dairy products, etc.

xanthate ('zænθeɪt) NOUN any salt or ester of xanthic acid.
▸**xan'thation** NOUN

xanthein ('zænθiɪn) NOUN the soluble part of the yellow pigment that is found in the cell sap of some flowers.

xanthene ('zænθi:n) NOUN a yellowish crystalline heterocyclic compound used as a fungicide; benzo-1,4-pyran. Its molecular structural unit is found in many dyes, such as rhodamine and fluorescein. Formula: $CH_2(C_6H_4)_2O$.

Xanthian ('zænθɪən) ADJECTIVE of or relating to the ancient Lycian city of Xanthus or its inhabitants.

xanthic ('zænθɪk) ADJECTIVE [1] of, containing, or derived from xanthic acid. [2] *Botany, rare* having a yellow colour.

xanthic acid NOUN any of a class of organic sulphur-containing acids with the general formula ROC(S)SH, where R is an organic group. Their salts are the xanthates.

xanthin ('zænθɪn) NOUN any of a group of yellow or orange carotene derivatives that occur in the fruit and flowers of certain plants.

xanthine ('zænθi:n, -θaɪn) NOUN [1] a crystalline compound related in structure to uric acid and found in urine, blood, certain plants, and certain animal tissues. Formula: $C_5H_4N_4O_2$. [2] any substituted derivative of xanthine, esp one of the three pharmacologically active methylated xanthines, caffeine, theophylline, or theobromine, which act as stimulants and diuretics.

Xanthippe (zæn'θɪpɪ) *or* **Xantippe** (zæn'tɪpɪ) NOUN any nagging, peevish, or irritable woman.
▷**HISTORY** from Xanthippe, the proverbially scolding and quarrelsome wife of Socrates

xanthism ('zæn,θɪzəm) NOUN a condition of skin, fur, or feathers in which yellow coloration predominates.

xantho- *or before a vowel* **xanth-** COMBINING FORM indicating yellow: *xanthophyll.*
▷**HISTORY** from Greek *xanthos*

xanthochroid ('zænθəʊ,krɔɪd) ADJECTIVE *Rare* of, relating to, or designating races having light-coloured hair and a pale complexion.
▷**HISTORY** C19: New Latin *xanthochroi,* from XANTHO- + Greek *ōkhros* pale

xanthochroism (zæn'θɒkrəʊ,ɪzəm) NOUN a condition in certain animals, esp aquarium goldfish, in which all skin pigments other than yellow and orange disappear.
▷**HISTORY** C19: from Greek *xanthokhro(os)* yellow-skinned (from *xanthos* yellow + *khroia* skin) + -ISM

xanthoma (zæn'θəʊmə) NOUN *Pathol* the presence in the skin of fatty yellow or brownish plaques or nodules, esp on the eyelids, caused by a disorder of lipid metabolism.

xanthophyll *or esp US* **xanthophyl** ('zænθəʊfɪl) NOUN any of a group of yellow carotenoid pigments occurring in plant and animal tissue.
▸**,xantho'phyllous** ADJECTIVE

xanthous ('zænθəs) ADJECTIVE of, relating to, or designating races with yellowish hair and a light complexion.

Xanthus ('zænθəs) NOUN the chief city of ancient Lycia in SW Asia Minor: source of some important antiquities.

***x*-axis** NOUN a reference axis, usually horizontal, of a graph or two- or three-dimensional Cartesian coordinate system along which the *x*-coordinate is measured.

X-chromosome NOUN the sex chromosome that occurs in pairs in the diploid cells of the females of many animals, including humans, and as one of a pair with the Y-chromosome in those of males. Compare **Y-chromosome.**

Xe THE CHEMICAL SYMBOL FOR xenon.

xebec, zebec, *or* **zebeck** ('zi:bɛk) NOUN a small three-masted Mediterranean vessel with both square and lateen sails, formerly used by Algerian pirates and later used for commerce.
▷**HISTORY** C18: earlier *chebec* from French, ultimately from Arabic *shabbāk;* present spelling influenced by Catalan *xabec,* Spanish *xabeque* (now *jabeque*)

xenia ('zi:nɪə) NOUN *Botany* the influence of pollen upon the form of the fruit developing after pollination.
▷**HISTORY** C19: from New Latin, from Greek: hospitality, from *xenos* guest
▸**'xenial** ADJECTIVE

Xenical ('zɛnɪkəl) NOUN *Trademark* a drug that reduces the ability to absorb fats; used in the medical treatment of obesity.

xeno- *or before a vowel* **xen-** COMBINING FORM indicating something strange, different, or foreign: *xenogamy.*
▷**HISTORY** from Greek *xenos* strange

xenocryst ('zɛnə,krɪst) NOUN a crystal included within an igneous rock as the magma cooled but not formed from it.
▷**HISTORY** C20: from XENO- + CRYST(AL)

xenogamy (zɛ'nɒgəmɪ) NOUN *Botany* another name for **cross-fertilization.**
▸**xe'nogamous** ADJECTIVE

xenogeneic (,zɛnəʊdʒɪ'neɪɪk) ADJECTIVE *Med* derived from an individual of a different species: *a xenogeneic tissue graft.*

xenogenesis (,zɛnə'dʒɛnɪsɪs) NOUN [1] the supposed production of offspring completely unlike either parent. [2] another name for **abiogenesis** or **alternation of generations.**
▸**xenogenetic** (,zɛnəʊdʒɪ'nɛtɪk) *or* **,xeno'genic** ADJECTIVE

xenoglossia (,zɛnə'glɒsɪə) *or* **xenoglossy** ('zɛnə,glɒsɪ) NOUN an ability claimed by some mediums, clairvoyants, etc., to speak a language with which they are unfamiliar.
▷**HISTORY** C20: from Greek, from XENO- + Attic Greek *glossa* tongue, language

xenograft ('zɛnəʊ,grɑ:ft) NOUN another word for **heterograft.**

xenolith ('zɛnəlɪθ) NOUN a fragment of rock differing in origin, composition, structure, etc., from the igneous rock enclosing it.
▸**,xeno'lithic** ADJECTIVE

xenomorphic (,zɛnə'mɔ:fɪk) ADJECTIVE (of a mineral constituent of an igneous rock) not having its characteristic crystal shape because of deforming pressure from adjacent minerals.
▸**,xeno'morphically** ADVERB

xenon ('zɛnɒn) NOUN a colourless odourless gaseous element occurring in trace amounts in air; formerly considered inert it is now known to form compounds and is used in radio valves, stroboscopic and bactericidal lamps, and bubble chambers. Symbol: Xe; atomic no.: 54; atomic wt.: 131.29; valency: 0; density: 5.887 kg/m^3; melting pt.: –111.76°C; boiling pt.: –108.0°C.
▷**HISTORY** C19: from Greek: something strange

xenophile ('zɛnə,faɪl) NOUN a person who likes foreigners or things foreign.
▷**HISTORY** C19: from Greek, from XENO- + -PHILE

xenophobe ('zɛnə,fəʊb) NOUN a person who hates or fears foreigners or strangers.
▷**HISTORY** C20: from Greek, from XENO- + -PHOBE

xenophobia (,zɛnə'fəʊbɪə) NOUN hatred or fear of foreigners or strangers or of their politics or culture.
▸**,xeno'phobic** ADJECTIVE

xenotransplant ('zɛnəʊ,træns,plɑ:nt) NOUN *Surgery* an operation in which an organ or tissue is transferred from one animal to another of a different species.
▸**'xeno,transplan,tation** NOUN

xeranthemum (zɪə'rænθəməm) NOUN any of a Mediterranean genus of plants having flower heads that are dry and retain their colour and shape for years: family *Asteraceae* (composites). See also **immortelle.**
▷**HISTORY** C18: New Latin, from Greek XERO- + *anthemon* flower

xerarch ('zɪərɑ:k) ADJECTIVE *Ecology* (of a sere) having its origin in a dry habitat.
▷**HISTORY** from XER(O)- + Greek *arkhē* a beginning, from *arkhein* to begin

Xeres (*Spanish* 'xerɛθ) NOUN the former name of **Jerez.**

xeric ('zɪərɪk) ADJECTIVE *Ecology* of, relating to, or growing in dry conditions.
▸**'xerically** ADVERB

xero- *or before a vowel* **xer-** COMBINING FORM indicating dryness: *xeroderma.*
▷**HISTORY** from Greek *xēros* dry

xeroderma (,zɪərəʊ'dɜ:mə) *or* **xerodermia** (,zɪərəʊ'dɜ:mɪə) NOUN *Pathol* [1] any abnormal dryness of the skin as the result of diminished secretions from the sweat or sebaceous glands. [2] another name for **ichthyosis.**
▸**xerodermatic** (,zɪərəʊdə'mætɪk) *or* **,xero'dermatous** ADJECTIVE

xerography (zɪ'rɒgrəfɪ) NOUN a photocopying process in which an electrostatic image is formed on a selenium plate or cylinder. The plate or cylinder is dusted with a resinous powder, which adheres to the charged regions, and the image is then transferred to a sheet of paper on which it is fixed by heating.
▸**xe'rographer** NOUN ▸**xerographic** (,zɪərə'græfɪk) ADJECTIVE ▸**,xero'graphically** ADVERB

xeromorphic (,zɪərə'mɔ:fɪk) ADJECTIVE (of plants or plant parts) having characteristics that serve as protection against excessive loss of water.

xerophilous (zɪ'rɒfɪləs) ADJECTIVE (of plants or animals) adapted for growing or living in dry surroundings.
▸**xerophile** ('zɪərəʊ,faɪl) NOUN ▸**xe'rophily** NOUN

xerophthalmia (,zɪərɒf'θælmɪə) NOUN *Pathol* excessive dryness of the cornea and conjunctiva, caused by a deficiency of vitamin A. Also called: **xeroma** (zɪ'rəʊmə).
▸**,xeroph'thalmic** ADJECTIVE

xerophyte ('zɪərə,faɪt) NOUN a xerophilous plant, such as a cactus.
▸**xerophytic** (,zɪərə'fɪtɪk) ADJECTIVE ▸**,xero'phytically** ADVERB ▸**'xero,phytism** NOUN

xerosere ('zɪərə,sɪə) NOUN *Ecology* a sere that originates in dry surroundings.

xerosis (zɪ'rəʊsɪs) NOUN *Pathol* abnormal dryness of bodily tissues, esp the skin, eyes, or mucous membranes.
▸**xerotic** (zɪ'rɒtɪk) ADJECTIVE

xerostomia (ˌzi:rəˈstəʊmɪə) NOUN abnormal lack of saliva; dryness of the mouth.
▷HISTORY C19: from XERO- + -STOM(E) + -IA

Xerox (ˈzɪərɒks) NOUN 1 *Trademark* **a** a xerographic copying process. **b** a machine employing this process. **c** a copy produced by this process. ◆ VERB 2 to produce a copy of (a document, illustration, etc.) by this process.

x-height NOUN *Printing* the height of lower case letters of a typeface, without ascenders or descenders.

Xhosa (ˈkɔ:sə) NOUN 1 (*plural* **-sa** *or* **-sas**) a member of a cattle-rearing Negroid people of southern Africa, living chiefly in South Africa. 2 the language of this people, belonging to the Bantu group of the Niger-Congo family: closely related to Swazi and Zulu and characterized by several clicks in its sound system.
▸**ˈXhosan** ADJECTIVE

xi (zaɪ, saɪ, ksaɪ, ksi:) NOUN, *plural* **xis**. the 14th letter in the Greek alphabet (Ξ, ξ), a composite consonant, transliterated as *x*.

Xi, Hsi, *or* **Si** (ʃi:) NOUN a river in S China, rising in Yünnan province and flowing east to the Canton delta on the South China Sea: the main river system of S China. Length: about 1900 km (1200 miles).

Xiamen (ˈʃjɑ:ˈmɛn) NOUN a variant transliteration of the Chinese name for **Amoy**.

Xi An, Hsian, *or* **Sian** (ʃjɑ:n) NOUN an industrial city in central China, capital of Shaanxi province: capital of China for 970 years at various times between the 3rd century B.C. and the 10th century A.D.; seat of the Northwestern University (1937). Pop.: 2 294 790 (1999 est.). Former name: **Siking**.

Xiang, Hsiang, *or* **Siang** (ʃjɑ:ŋ) NOUN 1 a river in SE central China, rising in NE Guangxi Zhuang and flowing northeast and north to Dongting Lake. Length: about 1150 km (715 miles). 2 a river in S China, rising in SE Yünnan and flowing generally east to the Hongxiu (the upper course of the Xi River). Length: about 800 km (500 miles).

Xiangtan *or* **Siangtan** (ˈʃjɑ:ŋˈtɑ:n) NOUN a city in S central China, in NE Hunan on the Xiang River: centre of a region noted for tea production. Pop.: 518 783 (1999 est.).

Xingú (*Portuguese* ʃiŋˈgu) NOUN a river in central Brazil, rising on the Mato Grosso plateau and flowing north to the Amazon delta, with over 650 km (400 miles) of rapids in its middle course. Length: 1932 km (1200 miles).

Xining, Hsining, *or* **Sining** (ˈʃi:ˈnɪŋ) NOUN a city in W China, capital of Qinghai province, at an altitude of 2300 m (7500 ft.). Pop.: 604 812 (1999 est.).

Xinjiang Uygur (ˈʃɪnˈdʒjæŋ ˈwi:gʊə) *or* **Sinkiang-Uighur Autonomous Region** NOUN an administrative division of NW China: established in 1955 for the Uygur ethnic minority, with autonomous subdivisions for other small minorities; produces over half China's wool and contains valuable mineral resources. Capital: Urumqi. Pop.: 19 250 000 (2000 est.). Area: 1 646 799 sq. km (635 829 sq. miles).

xiphi- *or before a vowel* **xiph-** COMBINING FORM indicating a sword, esp something shaped like or resembling a sword: *xiphisternum; xiphoid*.
▷HISTORY from Greek *xiphos* sword

xiphisternum (ˌzɪfɪˈstɜ:nəm) NOUN, *plural* **-na** (-nə). *Anatomy, zoology* the cartilaginous process forming the lowermost part of the breastbone (sternum). Also called: **xiphoid, xiphoid process**.

xiphoid (ˈzɪfɔɪd) ADJECTIVE 1 *Biology* shaped like a sword. 2 of or relating to the xiphisternum. ◆ NOUN 3 Also called: **xiphoid process**. another name for **xiphisternum**.

xiphosuran (ˌzɪfəˈsjʊərən) NOUN 1 any chelicerate arthropod of the subclass *Xiphosura*, including the horseshoe crabs and many extinct forms. ◆ ADJECTIVE 2 of, relating to, or belonging to the subclass *Xiphosura*.
▷HISTORY C19: from New Latin *Xiphosura*, irregularly from Greek *xiphos* sword + *oura* tail

Xizang Autonomous Region (ˈʃi:ˈzæŋ) NOUN the Pinyin transliteration of the Chinese name for **Tibet**.

XL SYMBOL FOR extra large.

XLNT *Text messaging* ABBREVIATION FOR excellent.

Xmas (ˈɛksməs, ˈkrɪsməs) NOUN *Informal* short for **Christmas**.
▷HISTORY C16: from symbol X for Christ + -MAS

Xn *or* **Xtian** ABBREVIATION FOR Christian.

Xnty *or* **Xty** ABBREVIATION FOR Christianity.

XO *US* ABBREVIATION FOR executive officer.

xoanon (ˈzəʊəˌnɒn) NOUN, *plural* **-na** (-nə). a primitive image of a god, carved, esp originally, in wood, and supposed to have fallen from heaven.
▷HISTORY C18: from Greek, from *xuō* to scrape, smooth

Xochimilco (ˌkɒtʃɪˈmɪlkəʊ) NOUN a town in central Mexico, on Lake Xochimilco: noted for its floating gardens. Pop.: 271 020 (1990).

XP NOUN the Christian monogram made up of the Greek letters *khi* and *rho*, the first two letters of *Khristos*, the Greek form of Christ's name.

x-radiation NOUN another term for **X-ray**.

X-rated ADJECTIVE 1 (formerly, in Britain) (of a film) considered suitable for viewing by adults only. 2 *Informal* involving bad language, violence, or sex: *an X-rated conversation*.

X-ray *or* **x-ray** NOUN 1 **a** electromagnetic radiation emitted when matter is bombarded with fast electrons. X-rays have wavelengths shorter than that of ultraviolet radiation, that is less than about 1×10^{-8} metres. They extend to indefinitely short wavelengths, but below about 1×10^{-11} metres they are often called gamma radiation. **b** (*as modifier*): *X-ray astronomy*. 2 a picture produced by exposing photographic film to X-rays: used in medicine as a diagnostic aid as parts of the body, such as bones, absorb X-rays and so appear as opaque areas on the picture. 3 (*usually capital*) *Communications* a code word for the letter *x*. ◆ VERB (*tr*) 4 to photograph (part of the body, etc.) using X-rays. 5 to treat or examine by means of X-rays.
▷HISTORY C19: partial translation of German *X-Strahlen* (from *Strahl* ray), coined in 1895 by W. K. *Röntgen* (1845–1923), German physicist

X-ray astronomy NOUN the branch of astronomy concerned with the detection and measurement of X-rays emitted by certain celestial bodies. As X-rays are absorbed by the atmosphere, satellites and rockets are used.

X-ray binary NOUN a binary star that is an intense source of X-rays and is composed of a normal star in close orbit with a white dwarf, neutron star, or black hole.

X-ray crystallography NOUN the study and practice of determining the structure of a crystal by passing a beam of X-rays through it and observing and analysing the diffraction pattern produced.

X-ray diffraction NOUN the scattering of X-rays on contact with matter, resulting in changes in radiation intensity, which is used for studying atomic structure.

X-ray therapy NOUN *Med* the therapeutic use of X-rays.

X-ray tube NOUN an evacuated tube containing a metal target onto which is directed a beam of electrons at high energy for the generation of X-rays.

Xt ABBREVIATION FOR Christ.
▷HISTORY representing the initial letter (chi) and the t (tau) of Greek *Khristos*

xu (tʃʊ) NOUN a monetary unit of Vietnam worth one hundredth of a dông.

x-unit NOUN a unit of length equal to $0.100\,202 \times 10^{-12}$ metre, for expressing the wavelengths of X-rays and gamma rays.

Xuthus (ˈzu:θəs) NOUN *Greek myth* a son of Hellen, regarded as an ancestor of the Ionian Greeks through his son Ion.

XUV ABBREVIATION FOR extreme ultraviolet: involving radiation bridging the gap between X-rays and ultraviolet radiation: *XUV astronomy; XUV waveband*. Also: **EUV**.

Xuzhou (ˈʃu:ˈdʒəʊ), **Hsü-chou,** *or* **Süchow** NOUN a city in N central China, in NW Jiangsu province: scene of a decisive battle (1949) in which the Communists defeated the Nationalists. Pop.: 1 044 729 (1999 est.).

xylan (ˈzaɪlæn) NOUN *Biochem* a yellow polysaccharide consisting of xylose units: occurs in straw husks and other woody tissue.

xylem (ˈzaɪləm, -lɛm) NOUN a plant tissue that conducts water and mineral salts from the roots to all other parts, provides mechanical support, and forms the wood of trees and shrubs. It is of two types (see **protoxylem, metaxylem**), both of which are made up mainly of vessels and tracheids.
▷HISTORY C19: from Greek *xulon* wood

xylene (ˈzaɪli:n) NOUN an aromatic hydrocarbon existing in three isomeric forms, all three being colourless flammable volatile liquids used as solvents and in the manufacture of synthetic resins, dyes, and insecticides; dimethylbenzene. Formula: $C_6H_4(CH_3)_2$. Also called: **xylol**.

xylidine (ˈzaɪlɪˌdi:n, -ˌdaɪn, ˈzɪlɪ-) NOUN 1 a mixture of six isomeric amines derived from xylene and used in dyes. Formula: $(CH_3)_2C_6H_3NH_2$. 2 any one of these isomers.

xylo- *or before a vowel* **xyl-** COMBINING FORM 1 indicating wood: *xylophone*. 2 indicating xylene: *xylidine*.
▷HISTORY from Greek *xulon* wood

xylocarp (ˈzaɪləˌkɑ:p) NOUN *Botany* a fruit, such as a coconut, having a hard woody pericarp.
▸**ˌxyloˈcarpous** ADJECTIVE

xylogenous (zaɪˈlɒdʒɪnəs) ADJECTIVE *Biology* living in or on wood. Also: **xylophilous** (zaɪˈlɒfɪləs).

xylograph (ˈzaɪləˌgrɑ:f, -ˌgræf) NOUN 1 an engraving in wood. 2 a print taken from a wood block. ◆ VERB 3 (*tr*) to print (a design, illustration, etc.) from a wood engraving.

xylography (zaɪˈlɒgrəfɪ) NOUN the art, craft, or process of printing from wooden blocks.
▸**xyˈlographer** NOUN ▸**xylographic** (ˌzaɪləˈgræfɪk) *or* **ˌxyloˈgraphical** ADJECTIVE

xyloid (ˈzaɪlɔɪd) ADJECTIVE *Botany* of, relating to, or resembling wood; woody.

xylol (ˈzaɪlɒl) NOUN another name (not in technical usage) for **xylene**.

xylophagous (zaɪˈlɒfəgəs) ADJECTIVE (of certain insects, crustaceans, etc.) feeding on or living within wood.

xylophone (ˈzaɪləˌfəʊn) NOUN *Music* a percussion instrument consisting of a set of wooden bars of graduated length. It is played with hard-headed hammers.
▷HISTORY C19: from XYLO- + -PHONE
▸**xylophonic** (ˌzaɪləˈfɒnɪk) ADJECTIVE ▸**xylophonist** (zaɪˈlɒfənɪst) NOUN

xylorimba (ˌzaɪləˈrɪmbə) NOUN a large xylophone with an extended range of five octaves.
▷HISTORY C20: XYLO(PHONE) + (MA)RIMBA

xylose (ˈzaɪləʊz, -ləʊs) NOUN a white crystalline dextrorotatory sugar found in the form of xylan in wood and straw. It is extracted by hydrolysis with acids and used in dyeing, tanning, and in foods for diabetics. Formula: $C_5H_{10}O_5$.

xylotomous (zaɪˈlɒtəməs) ADJECTIVE (of certain insects, insect larvae, etc.) cutting or boring into wood.

xylotomy (zaɪˈlɒtəmɪ) NOUN the preparation of sections of wood for examination by microscope.
▸**xyˈlotomist** NOUN

xylyl (ˈzaɪlɪl) NOUN (*modifier*) of, containing, or denoting the group of atoms $(CH_3)_2C_6H_3$-, derived from xylene.

xyst (zɪst), **xystus,** *or* **xystos** (ˈzɪstəs) NOUN 1 a long portico, esp one used in ancient Greece for athletics. 2 (in ancient Rome) a covered garden walk or one lined with trees.
▷HISTORY C17: from Latin *xystus*, from Greek *xustos*, literally: smoothed, polished (area), from *xuein* to scrape, make smooth

xyster (ˈzɪstə) NOUN a surgical instrument for scraping bone; surgical rasp or file.
▷HISTORY C17: via New Latin from Greek: tool for scraping, from *xuein* to scrape, make smooth

Yy

y *or* **Y** (waɪ) NOUN, *plural* **y's, Y's** *or* **Ys.** [1] the 25th letter of the modern English alphabet. [2] a speech sound represented by this letter, in English usually a semivowel, as in *yawn,* or a vowel, as in *symbol* or *shy.* [3] **a** something shaped like a Y. **b** (*in combination*): *a Y-cross.*

y *Maths* SYMBOL FOR: [1] the *y*-axis or a coordinate measured along the *y*-axis in a Cartesian coordinate system. [2] an algebraic variable.

Y SYMBOL FOR: [1] any unknown, unspecified, or variable factor, number, person, or thing. [2] *Chem* yttrium. [3] *Currency* **a** yen. **b** yuan.

y. ABBREVIATION FOR year.

Y. ABBREVIATION FOR YMCA or YWCA.

-y[1] *or* **-ey** SUFFIX FORMING ADJECTIVES [1] (*from nouns*) characterized by; consisting of; filled with; relating to; resembling: *sunny; sandy; smoky; classy.* [2] (*from verbs*) tending to; acting or existing as specified: *leaky; shiny.*
▷**HISTORY** from Old English *-ig, -ǣg*

-y[2]**, -ie,** *or* **-ey** SUFFIX OF NOUNS *Informal* [1] denoting smallness and expressing affection and familiarity: *a doggy; a granny; Jamie.* [2] a person or thing concerned with or characterized by being: *a groupie; a fatty.*
▷**HISTORY** C14: from Scottish *-ie, -y,* familiar suffix occurring originally in names, as in *Jamie* (*James*)

-y[3] SUFFIX FORMING NOUNS [1] (*from verbs*) indicating the act of doing what is indicated by the verbal element: *inquiry.* [2] (*esp with combining forms of Greek, Latin, or French origin*) indicating state, condition, or quality: *geography; jealousy.*
▷**HISTORY** from Old French *-ie,* from Latin *-ia*

yabba (ˈjæbə) NOUN *Slang* a form of methamphetamine.
▷**HISTORY** C20: of unknown origin

yabber (ˈjæbə) *Informal, chiefly Austral* ◆ VERB [1] (*intr*) to talk or jabber. ◆ NOUN [2] talk or jabber.
▷**HISTORY** C19: from a native Australian language *yabba* talk, probably influenced by JABBER

yabby *or* **yabbie** (ˈjæbɪ) *Austral* ◆ NOUN, *plural* **-bies.** [1] a small freshwater crayfish of the genus *Cherax,* esp *C. destructor.* [2] Also called: **nipper.** a marine prawn used as bait. ◆ VERB **-bies, -bying, -bied.** [3] (*intr*) to go out to catch yabbies.
▷**HISTORY** from a native Australian language

Yablonovy Mountains (*Russian* ˈjabləṇəvij) PLURAL NOUN a mountain range in Siberia. Highest peak: 1680 m (5512 ft.). Also called: **Yablonoi Mountains** (ˈjɑːbləˌnɔɪ).

yacca *or* **yacka** (ˈjækə) NOUN *Austral* another word for **black boy.**
▷**HISTORY** from a native Australian language

yacht (jɒt) NOUN [1] a vessel propelled by sail or power, used esp for pleasure cruising, racing, etc. [2] short for **sand yacht** or **ice yacht.** ◆ VERB [3] (*intr*) to sail or cruise in a yacht.
▷**HISTORY** C16: from obsolete Dutch *jaghte,* short for *jahtschip,* from *jagen* to chase + *schip* SHIP

yachtie (ˈjɒtɪ) NOUN *Austral and NZ informal* a yachtsman; sailing enthusiast.

yachting (ˈjɒtɪŋ) NOUN **a** the sport or practice of navigating a yacht. **b** (*as modifier*): *yachting clothes.*

yachtsman (ˈjɒtsmən) *or feminine* **yachtswoman** NOUN, *plural* **-men** *or* **-women.** a person who sails a yacht or yachts.
▸**ˈyachtsmanˌship** NOUN

yack (jæk) NOUN, VERB a variant spelling of **yak**[2].

yackety-yak (ˌjækɪtɪˈjæk) NOUN *Slang* noisy, continuous, and trivial talk or conversation. Sometimes shortened to: **yak.**
▷**HISTORY** of imitative origin

yad (jɑd) NOUN *Judaism* a hand-held pointer used for reading the sefer torah.
▷**HISTORY** Hebrew

yadda yadda yadda *or* **yada yada yada** (ˌjædəjædəˈjædə) NOUN *US slang* tedious or long-winded talk.
▷**HISTORY** C20: of uncertain origin; possibly imitative of the sound of someone talking at length in a dull manner

yae (je) ADJECTIVE *Scot* a variant of **ae.**

yaffle (ˈjæfᵊl) NOUN another name for **green woodpecker.**
▷**HISTORY** C18: imitative of its cry

Yafo (ˈjɑːfɔː) NOUN transliteration of the Hebrew name for **Jaffa** (sense 1).

Yagi aerial (ˈjɑːgɪ, ˈjægɪ) NOUN a highly directional aerial, used esp in television and radio astronomy, consisting of three or more elements lying parallel to each other, the principal direction of radiation being along the line of the centres.
▷**HISTORY** C20: named after Hidetsugu *Yagi* (1886–1976), Japanese engineer

yah (jɑː, jeə) SENTENCE SUBSTITUTE [1] an informal word for **yes,** often used to indicate derision or contempt ◆ INTERJECTION [2] an exclamation of derision or disgust.

Yah (jɑː) NOUN *Brit informal* an affected upper-class person.
▷**HISTORY** C20: from *yah,* the spoken form of YES supposedly used by upper-class British people

Yahata (ˈjɑːhɑːˌtɑː) NOUN a variant of **Yawata.**

yahoo (jəˈhuː) NOUN, *plural* **-hoos.** a crude, brutish, or obscenely coarse person.
▷**HISTORY** C18: from the name of a race of brutish creatures resembling men in Jonathan Swift's *Gulliver's Travels* (1726)
▸**yaˈhooism** NOUN

Yahrzeit (ˈjɔːtsaɪt) NOUN *Judaism* the anniversary of the death of a close relative, on which it is customary to kindle a light and recite the Kaddish and also, in some communities, to observe a fast.
▷**HISTORY** Yiddish, from Middle High German *järzīt* anniversary; see YEAR, TIDE[1]

Yahweh, Jahweh (ˈjɑːweɪ), **Yahveh,** *or* **Jahveh** (ˈjɑːveɪ) NOUN *Old Testament* a vocalization of the Tetragrammaton, used esp by Christian theologians.
▷**HISTORY** from Hebrew, from YHVH, with conjectural vowels; perhaps related to *hāwāh* to be; see also JEHOVAH

Yahwism, Jahwism (ˈjɑːwɪzəm), **Yahvism,** *or* **Jahvism** (ˈjɑːvɪzəm) NOUN the use of the name Yahweh, esp in parts of the Old Testament, as the personal name of God.

Yahwist, Jahwist (ˈjɑːwɪst), **Yahvist,** *or* **Jahvist** (ˈjɑːvɪst) NOUN *Bible* **the. a** the conjectured author or authors of the earliest of four main sources or strands of tradition of which the Pentateuch is composed and in which God is called *Yahweh* throughout. **b** (*as modifier*): *the Yahwist source.*

Yahwistic, Jahwistic (jɑːˈwɪstɪk), **Yahvistic,** *or* **Jahvistic** (jɑːˈvɪstɪk) ADJECTIVE *Bible* of or relating to Yahwism, the Yahwist, or Yahweh.

Yajur-Veda (ˈjʌdʒʊəˈveɪdə) NOUN *Hinduism* the second Veda, consisting of prayers and sacrificial formulas primarily for use by the priests.
▷**HISTORY** from Sanskrit, from *yajur* sacred, holy (compare Greek *hagios* holy) + VEDA

yak[1] (jæk) NOUN a wild and domesticated type of cattle, *Bos grunniens,* of Tibet, having long horns and long shaggy hair.
▷**HISTORY** C19: from Tibetan *gyag*

yak[2] (jæk) *Slang* ◆ NOUN [1] noisy, continuous, and trivial talk or conversation. ◆ VERB **yaks, yakking, yakked.** [2] (*intr*) to chatter or talk in this way; jabber. Also: **yakety-yak** (ˌjækɪtɪˈjæk).
▷**HISTORY** C20: of imitative origin

yakitori (ˌjækɪˈtɔːrɪ) NOUN a Japanese dish consisting of small pieces of chicken skewered and grilled.
▷**HISTORY** Japanese, from *yaki* grilled + *tori* bird

yakka, yakker, *or* **yacker** (ˈjækə) NOUN *Austral and NZ informal* work.
▷**HISTORY** C19: from a native Australian language

Yakut (jæˈkut) NOUN [1] (*plural* **-kuts** *or* **-kut**) a native or inhabitant of the Sakha Republic, in Russia. [2] the language of this people, belonging to the Turkic branch of the Altaic family.

Yakut Republic NOUN the former name of the **Sakha Republic.**

Yakutsk (*Russian* jɪˈkutsk) NOUN a port in E Russia, capital of the Sakha Republic, on the Lena River. Pop.: 195 500 (1999 est.).

yakuza (jəˈkuːzə) NOUN, *plural* **-kuza.** [1] **the.** a Japanese criminal organization involved in illegal gambling, extortion, gun-running, etc. [2] a member of this organization.
▷**HISTORY** C20: from Japanese *ya* eight + *ku* nine + *za* three, the worst hand in a game of cards

Yale lock (jeɪl) NOUN *Trademark* a type of cylinder lock using a flat serrated key.

Yalta (*Russian* ˈjaltə) NOUN a port and resort in the S Ukraine, in the Crimea on the Black Sea: scene of a conference (1945) between Churchill, Roosevelt, and Stalin, who met to plan the final defeat and occupation of Nazi Germany. Pop.: 89 000 (latest est.).

Yalu (ˈjɑːˌluː) NOUN a river in E Asia, rising in N North Korea and flowing southwest to Korea Bay, forming a large part of the border between North Korea and NE China. Length: 806 km (501 miles).

yam (jæm) NOUN [1] any of various twining plants of the genus *Dioscorea,* of tropical and subtropical regions, cultivated for their edible tubers: family *Dioscoreaceae.* [2] the starchy tuber of any of these plants, which is eaten as a vegetable. [3] *Southern US* any of certain large varieties of sweet potato. [4] a former Scot name for the (common) **potato.**
▷**HISTORY** C17: from Portuguese *inhame,* ultimately of West African origin; compare Senegal *nyami* to eat

yamen (ˈjɑːmɛn) NOUN (in imperial China) the office or residence of a public official.
▷**HISTORY** C19: from Chinese, from *ya* general's office + *měn* gate

Yamim Nora'im (jɑˈmim nɔrɑˈim) *or* **Yomim Noro'im** (ˈjɔmim nəʊˈroim) PLURAL NOUN another name for **High Holidays.**
▷**HISTORY** Hebrew, literally: Days of Awe

yammer (ˈjæmə) *Informal* ◆ VERB [1] to utter or whine in a complaining or peevish manner. [2] to make (a complaint) loudly or persistently. [3] (*intr*) (esp of an animal) to howl or wail plaintively or distressingly; yelp or yowl. ◆ NOUN [4] a yammering sound, wail, or utterance. [5] nonsense; jabber.
▷**HISTORY** Old English *geōmrian* to grumble, complain; related to Old High German *iāmar* misery, lamentation, Old Norse *amra* to howl
▸**ˈyammerer** NOUN

Yamoussoukro (ˌjæmuˈsuːkrəʊ) NOUN the capital of the Côte d'Ivoire, situated in the S centre of the country. It replaced Abidjan as capital in 1983. Pop.: 110 000 (1995 est.).

yampy (ˈjæmpɪ) NOUN *Midland English dialect* a foolish person.

Yanan (ˈjænˈæn) *or* **Yenan** NOUN a city in NE China, in N Shaanxi province: political and military capital of the Chinese Communists (1935–49). Pop.: 133 226 (1999 est.). Also called: **Fushih.**

Yang (jæŋ) NOUN See **Yin and Yang.**

Yangon (jæŋˈgɒn) NOUN the capital and chief port of Myanmar (formerly Burma): an industrial city and transport centre; dominated by the gold-covered Shwe Dagon pagoda, 112 m (368 ft.) high. Pop. (urban area): 3 361 700 (1993 est.). Former name (until 1989): **Rangoon.**

Yangtze (ˈjæŋtsɪ, ˈjæŋktsɪ) NOUN the longest river in China, rising in SE Qinghai province and flowing east to the East China Sea near Shanghai: a major commercial waterway in one of the most densely populated areas of the world. Work on the **Yangtze dam** near Yichang, the world's biggest hydroelectric and flood-control project, began in 1994. Length: 5528 km (3434 miles). Also called: **Yangtze Jiang, Chang Jiang, Chang.**

Yanina (ˈjɑːnɪnə) NOUN a variant spelling of **Ioánnina.**

yank (jæŋk) VERB [1] to pull, jerk, or move with a sharp movement; tug. ◆ NOUN [2] a sharp jerking movement; tug.
▷HISTORY C19: of unknown origin

Yank (jæŋk) NOUN [1] a slang word for an American. [2] *US informal* short for **Yankee.**

Yankee (ˈjæŋkɪ) *or informal* **Yank** NOUN [1] *Often disparaging* a native or inhabitant of the US; American. [2] a native or inhabitant of New England. [3] a native or inhabitant of the Northern US, esp a Northern soldier in the Civil War. [4] *Communications* a code word for the letter *y*. [5] *Finance* a bond issued in the US by a foreign borrower. ◆ ADJECTIVE [6] of, relating to, or characteristic of Yankees.
▷HISTORY C18: perhaps from Dutch *Jan Kees* John Cheese, nickname used derisively by Dutch settlers in New York to designate English colonists in Connecticut

Yankee Doodle NOUN [1] an American song, popularly regarded as a characteristically national melody. [2] another name for **Yankee.**

Yankeeism (ˈjæŋkɪɪzəm) NOUN [1] Yankee character, behaviour, or attitudes. [2] a typical Yankee word, expression, or trait.

Yantai (ˈjænˈtaɪ), **Yentai,** *or* **Yen-t'ai** NOUN a port in E China, in NE Shandong. Pop.: 452 127 (1990 est.). Also called: **Chefoo.**

Yaoundé *or* **Yaunde** (*French* jaunde) NOUN the capital of Cameroon, in the southwest: University of Cameroon (1962). Pop.: 800 000 (1992 est.).

yap (jæp) VERB **yaps, yapping, yapped.** (*intr*) [1] (of a dog) to bark in quick sharp bursts; yelp. [2] *Informal* to talk at length in an annoying or stupid way; jabber. ◆ NOUN [3] a high-pitched or sharp bark; yelp. [4] *Slang* annoying or stupid speech; jabber. [5] *Slang* a derogatory word for **mouth.** ◆ INTERJECTION [6] (*usually reiterated*) an imitation or representation of the sound of a dog yapping or people jabbering.
▷HISTORY C17: of imitative origin
▸ˈ**yapper** NOUN ▸ˈ**yappy** ADJECTIVE

Yap (jɑːp, jæp) NOUN a group of four main islands in the W Pacific, in the W Caroline Islands: administratively a district of the US Trust Territory of the Pacific Islands from 1947; became self-governing in 1979 as part of the Federated States of Micronesia; important Japanese naval base in World War II. Pop.: 12 055 (1999 est.). Area: 101 sq. km (39 sq. miles).

yapon (ˈjɔːpᵊn) NOUN a variant spelling of **yaupon.**

Yapurá (japuˈra) NOUN the Spanish name for **Japurá.**

Yaqui (*Spanish* ˈjaki) NOUN a river in NW Mexico, rising near the border with the US and flowing south to the Gulf of California. Length: about 676 km (420 miles).

yarborough (ˈjɑːbərə, -brə) NOUN *Bridge, whist* a hand of 13 cards in which no card is higher than nine.
▷HISTORY C19: supposed to be named after the second Earl of *Yarborough* (1809–62), who is said to have bet a thousand to one against the occurrence of such a hand

yard¹ (jɑːd) NOUN [1] a unit of length equal to 3 feet and defined in 1963 as exactly 0.9144 metre. Abbreviation: **yd.** [2] a cylindrical wooden or hollow metal spar, tapered at the ends, slung from a mast of a square-rigged or lateen-rigged vessel and used for suspending a sail. [3] short for **yardstick** (sense 2). [4] **put in the hard yards.** *Austral informal* to make a great effort to achieve an end.
▷HISTORY Old English *gierd* rod, twig; related to Old Frisian *jerde,* Old Saxon *gerdia,* Old High German *gertia,* Old Norse *gaddr*

yard² (jɑːd) NOUN [1] a piece of enclosed ground, usually either paved or laid with concrete and often adjoining or surrounded by a building or buildings. [2] **a** an enclosed or open area used for some commercial activity, for storage, etc.: *a railway yard.* **b** (*in combination*): *a brickyard; a shipyard.* [3] a US and Canadian word for **garden** (sense 1). [4] an area having a network of railway tracks and sidings, used for storing rolling stock, making up trains, etc. [5] *US and Canadian* the winter pasture of deer, moose, and similar animals. [6] *Austral and NZ* an enclosed area used to draw off part of a herd, etc. [7] *NZ* short for **saleyard** or **stockyard.** ◆ VERB (*tr*) [8] to draft (animals), esp to a saleyard.
▷HISTORY Old English *geard;* related to Old Saxon *gard,* Old High German *gart,* Old Norse *garthr* yard, Gothic *gards* house, Old Slavonic *gradu* town, castle, Albanian *garth* hedge

Yard (jɑːd) NOUN **the.** *Brit informal* short for **Scotland Yard.**

yardage¹ (ˈjɑːdɪdʒ) NOUN a length measured in yards.

yardage² (ˈjɑːdɪdʒ) NOUN [1] the use of a railway yard in the transportation of cattle. [2] the charge for this.

yardarm (ˈjɑːdˌɑːm) NOUN *Nautical* the two tapering outer ends of a ship's yard.

yardbird (ˈjɑːdˌbɜːd) NOUN *US military* an inexperienced, untrained, or clumsy soldier, esp one employed on menial duties.

yard grass NOUN an Old World perennial grass, *Eleusine indica,* with prostrate leaves, growing as a troublesome weed on open ground, yards, etc. Also called: **wire grass.**

Yardie (ˈjɑːdɪ) NOUN a member of a Black criminal syndicate originally based in Jamaica.
▷HISTORY C20: from Jamaican dialect *yard* home or (by expatriate Jamaicans) Jamaica

yarding (ˈjɑːdɪŋ) NOUN a group of animals displayed for sale: *a good yarding.*

yard of ale NOUN [1] the beer or ale contained in a narrow horn-shaped drinking glass, usually about one yard long and holding between two and three pints. [2] such a drinking glass itself.

yardstick (ˈjɑːdˌstɪk) NOUN [1] a measure or standard used for comparison: *on what kind of yardstick is he basing his criticism?* [2] a graduated stick, one yard long, used for measurement.

yare (jɛə) ADJECTIVE **yarer, yarest.** [1] *Archaic or dialect* ready, brisk, or eager. [2] (of a vessel) answering swiftly to the helm; easily handled. ◆ ADVERB [3] *Obsolete* readily or eagerly.
▷HISTORY Old English *gearu* ready; related to Old Saxon, Old High German *garo* ready, prepared, Old Norse *gorr*
▸ˈ**yarely** ADVERB

yark (jɑːk) VERB (*tr*) *Archaic or dialect* to make ready.
▷HISTORY Old English

Yarkand (ˌjɑːˈkænd) NOUN another name for **Shache.**

Yarmouth (ˈjɑːməθ) NOUN short for **Great Yarmouth.**

yarmulke (ˈjɑːməlkə) NOUN *Judaism* a skullcap worn by orthodox male Jews at all times, and by others during prayer.
▷HISTORY from Yiddish, from Ukrainian and Polish *yarmulka* cap, probably from Turkish *yağmurluk* raincoat, from *yağmur* rain

yarn (jɑːn) NOUN [1] a continuous twisted strand of natural or synthetic fibres, used in weaving, knitting, etc. [2] *Informal* a long and often involved story or account, usually telling of incredible or fantastic events. [3] **spin a yarn.** *Informal* **a** to tell such a story. **b** to make up or relate a series of excuses. ◆ VERB [4] (*intr*) to tell such a story or stories.
▷HISTORY Old English *gearn;* related to Old High German *garn* yarn, Old Norse *görn* gut, Greek *khordē* string, gut

yarn-dyed ADJECTIVE (of fabric) dyed while still in yarn form, before being woven. Compare **piece-dyed.**

Yaroslavl (*Russian* jɪraˈslavlj) NOUN a city in W Russia, on the River Volga: a major trading centre since early times and one of the first industrial centres in Russia; textile industries were established in the 18th century. Pop.: 620 600 (1995 est.).

yarraman (ˈjærəmən) NOUN, *plural* **-mans** *or* **-men.** *Austral* a horse.
▷HISTORY C19: from a native Australian language

yarran (ˈjærən) NOUN a small hardy tree, *Acacia homalophylla,* of inland Australia: useful as fodder and for firewood.
▷HISTORY from a native Australian language

Yarra River (ˈjærə) NOUN a river in SE Australia, rising in the Great Dividing Range and flowing west and southwest through Melbourne to Port Phillip Bay. Length: 250 km (155 miles).

yarrow (ˈjærəʊ) NOUN any of several plants of the genus *Achillea,* esp *A. millefolium,* of Eurasia, having finely dissected leaves and flat clusters of white flower heads: family *Asteraceae* (composites). Also called: **milfoil.** See also **sneezewort.**
▷HISTORY Old English *gearwe;* related to Old High German *garwa,* Dutch *gerwe*

yashmak *or* **yashmac** (ˈjæʃmæk) NOUN the face veil worn by Muslim women when in public.
▷HISTORY C19: from Arabic

yataghan (ˈjætəgən) *or* **ataghan** NOUN a Turkish sword with a curved single-edged blade.
▷HISTORY C19: from Turkish *yatağan*

yate (jeɪt) NOUN *Austral* any of several small eucalyptus trees, esp *Eucalyptus cornuta,* yielding a very hard timber.
▷HISTORY from a native Australian language

Yathrib (ˈjæθrɪb) NOUN the ancient Arabic name for **Medina.**

yatter (ˈjætə; *Scot* ˈjɑtər) *Scot* ◆ VERB (*intr*) [1] to talk at length; chatter. ◆ NOUN [2] continuous chatter.
▷HISTORY of imitative origin

Yaunde (*French* jaunde) NOUN a variant spelling of **Yaoundé.**

yaup (jɔːp) VERB, NOUN a variant spelling of **yawp.**
▸ˈ**yauper** NOUN

yaupon *or* **yapon** (ˈjɔːpᵊn) NOUN a southern US evergreen holly shrub, *Ilex vomitoria,* with spreading branches, scarlet fruits, and oval leaves: used as a substitute for tea.
▷HISTORY from Catawba *yopun* shrub, diminutive of *yop* tree

yautia (ˈjɔːtɪə) NOUN [1] any of several Caribbean aroid plants of the genus *Xanthosoma,* such as *X. sagittifolium,* cultivated for their edible leaves and underground stems. [2] the leaves or underground stems of these plants, which can be eaten as vegetables.
▷HISTORY C19: American Spanish, from Taino

Yavarí (jaβaˈri) NOUN the Spanish name for **Javari.**

yaw (jɔː) VERB [1] (*intr*) (of an aircraft, missile, etc.) to turn about its vertical axis. Compare **pitch¹** (sense 11), **roll** (sense 14). [2] (*intr*) (of a ship, etc.) to deviate temporarily from a straight course. [3] (*tr*) to cause (an aircraft, ship, etc.) to yaw. ◆ NOUN [4] the angular movement of an aircraft, missile, etc., about its vertical axis. [5] the deviation of a vessel from a straight course.
▷HISTORY C16: of unknown origin

Yawata (ˈjɑːwɑːˌtɑː) *or* **Yahata** NOUN a former city in Japan, on N Kyushu: merged with Moji, Kokura, Tobata, and Wakamatsu in 1963 to form **Kitakyushu.**

yawl¹ (jɔːl) NOUN [1] a two-masted sailing vessel, rigged fore-and-aft, with a large mainmast and a small mizzenmast stepped aft of the rudderpost. Compare **ketch, sloop.** [2] a ship's small boat, usually rowed by four or six oars.
▷HISTORY C17: from Dutch *jol* or Middle Low German *jolle,* of unknown origin

yawl² (jɔːl) VERB (*intr*) *Brit dialect* to howl, weep, or scream harshly; yowl.
▷HISTORY C14: from Low German *jaulen;* see YOWL

yawn (jɔːn) VERB [1] (*intr*) to open the mouth wide and take in air deeply, often as in involuntary reaction to tiredness, sleepiness, or boredom. [2] (*tr*) to express or utter while yawning. [3] (*intr*) to be open wide as if threatening to engulf (someone or something): *the mine shaft yawned below.* ◆ NOUN [4] the act or an instance of yawning.
▷HISTORY Old English *gionian;* related to Old Saxon *ginōn,* Old High German *ginēn* to yawn, Old Norse *gjā* gap
▸ˈ**yawner** NOUN ▸ˈ**yawning** ADJECTIVE ▸ˈ**yawningly** ADVERB

yawp (jɔːp) VERB (*intr*) [1] to gape or yawn, esp audibly. [2] to shout, cry, or talk noisily; bawl. [3] to bark, yelp, or yowl. ◆ NOUN [4] a shout, bark, yelp, or cry. [5] *US and Canadian* a noisy, foolish, or raucous utterance.
▷HISTORY C15 *yolpen,* probably of imitative origin; see YAP, YELP

▸ˈ**yawper** NOUN

yaws (jɔːz) NOUN (*usually functioning as singular*) an infectious nonvenereal disease of tropical climates with early symptoms resembling syphilis, characterized by red skin eruptions and, later, pain in the joints: it is caused by the spiral bacterium *Treponema pertenue*. Also called: **framboesia**.
▹HISTORY C17: of Carib origin

y-axis NOUN a reference axis, usually vertical, of a graph or two- or three-dimensional Cartesian coordinate system along which the *y*-coordinate is measured.

yay (jeɪ) INTERJECTION *Informal* an exclamation indicating approval, congratulation, or triumph.
▹HISTORY C20: perhaps from YEAH

Yazd (jɑːzd) *or* **Yezd** NOUN a city in central Iran: a major centre of silk weaving. Pop.: 326 776 (1996).

Yb THE CHEMICAL SYMBOL FOR ytterbium.

YBA ABBREVIATION FOR young British artist.

YC (in Britain) ABBREVIATION FOR Young Conservative.

Y-chromosome NOUN the sex chromosome that occurs as one of a pair with the X-chromosome in the diploid cells of the males of many animals, including humans. Compare **X-chromosome**.

yclept (ɪˈklɛpt) *Obsolete* ◆ VERB [1] a past participle of **clepe**. ◆ ADJECTIVE [2] having the name of; called.
▹HISTORY Old English *gecleopod*, past participle of *cleopian* to call

Y connection NOUN *Electrical engineering* a three-phase star connection.

yd *or* **yd.** ABBREVIATION FOR yard (measure).

ye[1] (jiː; *unstressed* jɪ) PRONOUN [1] *Archaic or dialect* refers to more than one person including the person addressed but not including the speaker. [2] Also: **ee** (iː). *Dialect* refers to one person addressed: *I tell ye*.
▹HISTORY Old English *gē*; related to Dutch *gij*, Old Norse *ēr*, Gothic *jus*

ye[2] (ðiː; *spelling pron* jiː) DETERMINER a form of **the**[1], in conjunction with other putative archaic spellings *ye olde oake*.
▹HISTORY from a misinterpretation of *the* as written in some Middle English texts. The runic letter thorn (Þ, representing *th*) was incorrectly transcribed as *y* because of a resemblance in their shapes

ye[3] THE INTERNET DOMAIN NAME FOR Yemen.

yea (jeɪ) SENTENCE SUBSTITUTE [1] a less common word for **aye** (yes). ◆ ADVERB [2] (*sentence modifier*) *Archaic or literary* indeed; truly: *yea, though my enemies spurn me, I shall prevail*.
▹HISTORY Old English *gēa*; related to Old Frisian *jē*, Old Saxon, Old Norse, Old High German *jā*, Gothic *jai*

yeah (jɛə) SENTENCE SUBSTITUTE an informal word for **yes**.

yean (jiːn) VERB (of a sheep or goat) to give birth to (offspring).
▹HISTORY Old English *geēanian*; related to Dutch *oonen* to bring forth young, Latin *agnus* lamb; see EWE

yeanling (ˈjiːnlɪŋ) NOUN the young of a goat or sheep.

year (jɪə) NOUN [1] Also called: **civil year**. the period of time, the **calendar year**, containing 365 days or in a **leap year** 366 days. It is based on the Gregorian calendar, being divided into 12 calendar months, and is reckoned from January 1 to December 31. [2] a period of twelve months from any specified date, such as one based on the four seasons. [3] a specific period of time, usually occupying a definite part or parts of a twelve-month period, used for some particular activity: *a school year*. [4] Also called: **astronomical year, tropical year**. the period of time, the **solar year**, during which the earth makes one revolution around the sun, measured between two successive vernal equinoxes: equal to 365.242 19 days. [5] the period of time, the **sidereal year**, during which the earth makes one revolution around the sun, measured between two successive conjunctions of a particular distant star: equal to 365.256 36 days. [6] the period of time, the **lunar year**, containing 12 lunar months and equal to 354.3671 days. [7] the period of time taken by a specified planet to complete one revolution around the sun: *the Martian year*. [8] (*plural*) age, esp old age: *a man of his years should be more careful*. [9] (*plural*) time: *in years to come*. [10] a group of pupils or students, who are taught or study together, divided into classes at school: *they are the best year we've ever had for history*. [11] **the year dot**. *Informal* as long ago as can be remembered. [12] **year and a day**. *English law* a period fixed by law to ensure the completion of a full year. It is applied for certain purposes, such as to determine the time within which wrecks must be claimed. [13] **year in, year out**. regularly or monotonously, over a long period. ◆ Related adjective: **annual**.
▹HISTORY Old English *gear*; related to Gothic *jēr*, Old Saxon, Old High German *jār*, Old Norse *ār* year, Polish *jar* springtime, Latin *hōrnus* of this year

> **Language note** In writing spans of years, it is important to choose a style that avoids ambiguity. The practice adopted in this dictionary is, in four-figure dates, to specify the last two digits of the second date if it falls within the same century as the first: *1801–08; 1850–51; 1899–1901*. In writing three-figure B.C. dates, it is advisable to give both dates in full: *159–156 B.C.*, not *159–56 B.C.* unless of course the span referred to consists of 103 years rather than three years. It is also advisable to specify B.C. or A.D. in years under 1000 unless the context makes this self-evident.

yearbook (ˈjɪəˌbʊk) NOUN an almanac or reference book published annually and containing details of events of the previous year.

yearling (ˈjɪəlɪŋ) NOUN [1] the young of any of various animals, including the antelope and buffalo, between one and two years of age. [2] a thoroughbred racehorse counted for racing purposes as being one year old until the second Jan. 1 following its birth. [3] **a** a bond that is intended to mature after one year. **b** (*as modifier*): *yearling bonds*. ◆ ADJECTIVE [4] being a year old.

yearlong (ˈjɪəˈlɒŋ) ADJECTIVE throughout a whole year.

yearly (ˈjɪəlɪ) ADJECTIVE [1] occurring, done, appearing, etc., once a year or every year; annual. [2] lasting or valid for a year; annual: *a yearly subscription*. ◆ ADVERB [3] once a year; annually. ◆ NOUN, *plural* **-lies**. [4] a publication, event, etc., that occurs once a year.

yearn (jɜːn) VERB (*intr*) [1] (usually foll by *for* or *after* or an infinitive) to have an intense desire or longing (for); pine (for). [2] to feel tenderness or affection.
▹HISTORY Old English *giernan*; related to Old Saxon *girnian*, Old Norse *girna*, Gothic *gairnjan*, Old High German *gerōn* to long for, Sanskrit *haryati* he likes
▸ˈ**yearner** NOUN

yearning (ˈjɜːnɪŋ) NOUN an intense or overpowering longing, desire, or need; craving.
▸ˈ**yearningly** ADVERB

year of grace NOUN any year of the Christian era, as dated from the presumed date of Christ's birth.

year-round ADJECTIVE open, in use, operating, etc., throughout the year.

yeast (jiːst) NOUN [1] any of various single-celled ascomycetous fungi of the genus *Saccharomyces* and related genera, which reproduce by budding and are able to ferment sugars: a rich source of vitamins of the B complex. [2] any yeastlike fungus, esp of the genus *Candida*, which can cause thrush in areas infected with it. [3] a commercial preparation containing yeast cells and inert material such as meal, used in raising dough for bread or for fermenting beer, whisky, etc. See also **brewer's yeast**. [4] a preparation containing yeast cells, used to treat diseases caused by vitamin B deficiency. [5] froth or foam, esp on beer. ◆ VERB [6] (*intr*) to froth or foam.
▹HISTORY Old English *giest*; related to Old Norse *jostr*, Old High German *jesan*, Swedish *esa*, Norwegian *asa*, Sanskrit *yasati*
▸ˈ**yeastless** ADJECTIVE ▸ˈ**yeast,like** ADJECTIVE

yeast cake NOUN *Chiefly US and Canadian* living yeast cells compressed with starch into a cake, for use in baking or brewing.

yeasty (ˈjiːstɪ) ADJECTIVE **yeastier, yeastiest**. [1] of, resembling, or containing yeast. [2] fermenting or causing fermentation. [3] tasting of or like yeast. [4] insubstantial or frivolous. [5] restless, agitated, or unsettled. [6] covered with or containing froth or foam.
▸ˈ**yeastily** ADVERB ▸ˈ**yeastiness** NOUN

yebo (ˈjebɑʊ) SENTENCE SUBSTITUTE *South African informal* an expression of affirmation.
▹HISTORY Zulu *yebo* yes, I agree

yegg (jɛg) NOUN *Slang, chiefly US* a burglar or safe-breaker.
▹HISTORY C20: perhaps from the surname of a burglar

Yeisk, Yeysk, *or* **Eisk** (*Russian* jejsk) NOUN a port and resort in SW Russia, on the Sea of Azov. Pop.: 86 300 (1991 est.).

Yekaterinburg *or* **Ekaterinburg** (*Russian* jɪkətɪrimˈburk) NOUN a city in NW Russia, in the Ural Mountains: scene of the execution (1918) of Nicholas II and his family; university (1920); one of the largest centres of heavy engineering in Russia. Pop.: 1 272 900 (1999 est.). Former name (1924–91): **Sverdlovsk**.

Yekaterinodar *or* **Ekaterinodar** (*Russian* jɪkətɪrinaˈdar) NOUN the former name (until 1920) of **Krasnodar**.

Yekaterinoslav *or* **Ekaterinoslav** (*Russian* jɪkətɪrinaˈslaf) NOUN the former name (1787–96, 1802–1926) of **Dnepropetrovsk**.

yeld (jɛld) ADJECTIVE *Scot and northern English dialect* [1] (of an animal) barren or too young to bear young. [2] (of a cow) not yielding milk.
▹HISTORY Old English *gelde* barren; related to GELD[1]

Yelisavetgrad *or* **Elisavetgrad** (*Russian* jɪlizaˈvjɛtgrət) NOUN the former name (until 1924) of **Kirovograd**.

Yelisavetpol *or* **Elisavetpol** (*Russian* jɪlizaˈvjɛtpəlj) NOUN the former name (until 1920) of **Kirovabad**.

yelk (jɛlk) NOUN a dialect word for **yolk** (of an egg).

yell (jɛl) VERB [1] to shout, scream, cheer, or utter in a loud or piercing way. ◆ NOUN [2] a loud piercing inarticulate cry, as of pain, anger, or fear. [3] *US and Canadian* a rhythmic cry of words or syllables, used in cheering in unison.
▹HISTORY Old English *giellan*; related to Old Saxon *gellon*, Old High German *gellan*, Old Norse *gjalla*; see NIGHTINGALE
▸ˈ**yeller** NOUN

yellow (ˈjɛləʊ) NOUN [1] any of a group of colours that vary in saturation but have the same hue. They lie in the approximate wavelength range 585–575 nanometres. Yellow is the complementary colour of blue and with cyan and magenta forms a set of primary colours. Related adjective: **xanthous**. [2] a pigment or dye of or producing these colours. [3] yellow cloth or clothing: *dressed in yellow*. [4] the yolk of an egg. [5] a yellow ball in snooker, etc. [6] any of a group of pieridine butterflies the males of which have yellow or yellowish wings, esp the clouded yellows (*Colias* spp.) and the brimstone. ◆ ADJECTIVE [7] of the colour yellow. [8] yellowish in colour or having parts or marks that are yellowish: *yellow jasmine*. [9] having a yellowish skin; Mongoloid. [10] *Informal* cowardly or afraid. [11] offensively sensational, as a cheap newspaper (esp in the phrase **yellow press**). ◆ VERB [12] to make or become yellow. ◆ See also **yellows**.
▹HISTORY Old English *geolu*; related to Old Saxon, Old High German *gelo*, Old Norse *gulr*, Latin *helvus*
▸ˈ**yellowish** ADJECTIVE ▸ˈ**yellowly** ADVERB ▸ˈ**yellowness** NOUN ▸ˈ**yellowy** ADJECTIVE

yellow archangel NOUN See **archangel** (sense 3).

yellowbark (ˈjɛləʊˌbɑːk) NOUN another name for **calisaya**.

yellow belly NOUN *Dialect* a native of Lincolnshire, esp of the fens.

yellow-belly NOUN, *plural* **-lies**. [1] a slang word for **coward**. [2] *Austral* another name for **callop**.

yellow bile NOUN *Archaic* one of the four bodily humours, choler.

yellowbird (ˈjɛləʊˌbɜːd) NOUN any of various birds having a yellow plumage, such as the American goldfinch.

yellow box NOUN *Austral* a large Australian eucalyptus tree, *Eucalyptus melliodora*.

yellow brain fungus NOUN See **jelly fungus**.

yellow cake NOUN *Informal* semirefined uranium ore.

yellow card *Sport* ◆ NOUN 1 a card of a yellow colour displayed by a referee to indicate that a player has been officially cautioned for some offence. ◆ VERB **yellow-card.** 2 *(tr)* to caution (a player) officially for some offence. ◆ ADJECTIVE 3 serving as a warning; intended to warn: *a yellow card system is in place.*

yellow cress NOUN any of various species of cress *(Rorippa)* that are related to watercress and have yellow flowers. They are not confined to water margins and some are garden weeds.

yellow-dog contract NOUN *US* a contract with an employer, now illegal, in which an employee agreed not to join a trade union during his employment.
▷**HISTORY** C20: from US *yellow-dog* anti-trade union, from *yellow dog* mongrel, contemptible person

yellow fever NOUN an acute infectious disease of tropical and subtropical climates, characterized by fever, haemorrhages, vomiting of blood, and jaundice: caused by a virus transmitted by the bite of a female mosquito of the species *Aedes aegypti.* Also called: **yellow jack, black vomit.**

yellow flag NOUN 1 another name for **quarantine flag.** 2 See **flag**[2] (sense 1).

yellowhammer ('jɛləʊˌhæmə) NOUN 1 a European bunting, *Emberiza citrinella,* having a yellowish head and body and brown streaked wings and tail. 2 *US and Canadian* an informal name for the **yellow-shafted flicker**, an American woodpecker (see **flicker**[2]).
▷**HISTORY** C16: of uncertain origin

yellowhead ('jɛləʊˌhed) NOUN a small bush bird, *Mohoua ochrocephala,* of South Island, New Zealand, having a yellow head and breast.

yellow jack NOUN 1 *Pathol* another name for **yellow fever.** 2 another name for **quarantine flag.** 3 any of certain large yellowish carangid food fishes, esp *Caranx bartholomaei,* of warm and tropical Atlantic waters.

yellow jacket NOUN *US and Canadian* any of several social wasps of the genus *Vespa,* having yellow markings on the body.

yellow jasmine NOUN a climbing shrub, *Gelsemium sempervirens,* of the southeastern US, having fragrant funnel-shaped yellow flowers: family *Loganiaceae.* See also **gelsemium.**

yellow jersey NOUN (in the Tour de France) a yellow jersey awarded as a trophy to the cyclist with the fastest time in each stage of the race.

yellow journalism NOUN the type of journalism that relies on sensationalism and lurid exaggeration to attract readers.
▷**HISTORY** C19: perhaps shortened from the phrase *Yellow Kid journalism,* referring to the *Yellow Kid,* a cartoon (1895) in the *New York World,* a newspaper having a reputation for sensationalism

Yellowknife ('jɛləʊˌnaɪf) NOUN a city in N Canada, capital of the Northwest Territories on Great Slave Lake. Pop.: 15 179 (1991).

yellowlegs ('jɛləʊˌlegz) NOUN *(functioning as singular)* either of two North American sandpipers, *Tringa melanoleuca* (or *Totanus melanoleucus*) (**greater yellowlegs**) or *T. flavipes* (**lesser yellowlegs**), having bright yellow legs.

yellow line NOUN *Brit* a yellow line painted along the edge of a road indicating waiting restrictions.

yellow metal NOUN 1 a type of brass having about 60 per cent copper and 40 per cent zinc. 2 another name for **gold.**

Yellow Pages PLURAL NOUN *Trademark* a classified telephone directory, often printed on yellow paper, that lists subscribers by the business or service provided.

yellow peril NOUN the power or alleged power of Asiatic peoples, esp the Chinese, to threaten or destroy the supremacy of White or Western civilization.

yellow poplar NOUN another name for **tulip tree** (sense 1) or **tulipwood** (sense 1).

yellow rain NOUN a type of yellow precipitation described in parts of SE Asia and alleged by some to be evidence of chemical warfare using mycotoxins.

yellow rattle NOUN See **rattle**[1] (sense 10).

Yellow River NOUN the second longest river in China, rising in SE Qinghai and flowing east, south, and east again to the Gulf of Bohai south of Tianjin; it has changed its course several times in recorded history. Length: about 4350 km (2700 miles). Chinese name: **Hwang Ho.**

yellows ('jɛləʊz) NOUN *(functioning as singular)* 1 any of various fungal or viral diseases of plants, characterized by yellowish discoloration and stunting. 2 *Vet science* another name for **jaundice.**

yellow sally NOUN an angler's name for either of two small yellow stoneflies: *Isoperla grammatica* of chalk streams and *Chloroperla torrentium* of upland streams.

Yellow Sea NOUN a shallow arm of the Pacific between Korea and NE China. Area: about 466 200 sq. km (180 000 sq. miles). Chinese name: **Hwang Hai.**

yellow spot NOUN *Anatomy* another name for **macula lutea.**

Yellowstone ('jɛləʊˌstəʊn) NOUN a river rising in N Wyoming and flowing north through Yellowstone National Park, then east to the Missouri. Length: 1080 km (671 miles).

Yellowstone Falls PLURAL NOUN a waterfall in NW Wyoming, in Yellowstone National Park on the Yellowstone River.

Yellowstone National Park NOUN a national park in the NW central US, mostly in NW Wyoming: the oldest and largest national park in the US, containing unusual geological formations and geysers. Area: 8956 sq. km (3458 sq. miles).

yellow streak NOUN *Informal* a cowardly or weak trait, characteristic, or flaw in a person's nature.

yellowtail ('jɛləʊˌteɪl) NOUN, *plural* **-tails** *or* **-tail.** 1 a carangid game fish, *Seriola dorsalis,* of coastal waters of S California and Mexico, having a yellow tail fin. 2 any of various similar fishes. 3 Also called: **yellowtail moth.** another name for **goldtail moth.** 4 *Austral* another word for **yellowtail kingfish.**

yellowtail kingfish NOUN a large carangid game fish, *Seriola grandis,* of S Australian waters. Also called: **yellowtail.**

yellow underwing NOUN any of several species of noctuid moths (*Noctua* and *Anarta* species), the hind wings of which are yellow with a black bar.

yellow water lily NOUN an aquatic nymphaeaceous plant, *Nuphar lutea,* of Europe and N Asia, having floating heart-shaped leaves and yellow flowers. Also called: **brandy bottle.**

yellowweed ('jɛləʊˌwiːd) NOUN any of various yellow-flowered plants, such as the ragwort in Europe and some species of goldenrod in the US.

yellowwood ('jɛləʊˌwʊd) NOUN 1 Also called (US): **gopherwood.** any of several leguminous trees of the genus *Cladrastis,* esp *C. lutea,* of the southeastern US, having clusters of white flowers and yellow wood yielding a yellow dye. 2 Also called: **West Indian satinwood.** a rutaceous tree, *Zanthoxylum flavum,* of the Caribbean, with smooth hard wood. 3 any of several other trees with yellow wood, esp *Podocarpus falcatus,* a conifer of southern Africa: family *Podocarpaceae.* 4 the wood of any of these trees.

yellowwort ('jɛləʊˌwɜːt) NOUN a gentianaceous perennial, *Blackstonia perfoliata,* that is related to centaury and has waxy grey foliage and yellow flowers: characteristically found on chalk turf.

yellow-yite NOUN a Scot word for **yellowhammer** (sense 1). Also called: **yite, yitie.**

yelp (jɛlp) VERB *(intr)* 1 (esp of a dog) to utter a sharp or high-pitched cry or bark, often indicating pain. ◆ NOUN 2 a sharp or high-pitched cry or bark.
▷**HISTORY** Old English *gielpan* to boast; related to Low German *galpen* to croak, Danish *gylpe* to croak
▸ **'yelper** NOUN

Yemen ('jɛmən) NOUN a republic in SW Arabia, on the Red Sea and the Gulf of Aden: formed in 1990 from the union of North Yemen and South Yemen: consists of arid coastal lowlands, rising to fertile upland valleys and mountains in the west and to the Hadhramaut plateau in the SE: the north and east contains part of the Great Sandy Desert. Official language: Arabic. Official religion: Muslim. Currency: riyal. Capital: San'a. Pop.: 18 078 000 (2001 est.). Area (including territory claimed by Yemen along the undemarcated eastern border with Saudi Arabia): 472 099 sq. km (182 278 sq. miles). Official name: **Yemen Republic.** See also **North Yemen, South Yemen.**

Yemeni ('jɛmənɪ) ADJECTIVE 1 of or relating to Yemen or its inhabitants. ◆ NOUN 2 a native or inhabitant of Yemen.

yemmer ('jɛmə) NOUN a southwest English form of **ember.**

yen[1] (jɛn) NOUN, *plural* **yen.** the standard monetary unit of Japan, (notionally) divided into 100 sen.
▷**HISTORY** C19: from Japanese *en,* from Chinese *yüan* circular object, dollar

yen[2] (jɛn) *Informal* ◆ NOUN 1 a passionate, ardent, or intense longing or desire. ◆ VERB **yens, yenning, yenned.** 2 *(intr)* to yearn.
▷**HISTORY** perhaps from Chinese (Cantonese) *yăn* a craving, addiction

Yenan ('jɛn'æn) NOUN a variant transliteration of the Chinese name for **Yanan.**

Yenisei *or* **Yenisey** (ˌjɛnɪ'seɪ; *Russian* jɪni'sjej) NOUN a river in central Russia, in central Siberia, formed by the confluence of two headstreams in the Tuva Republic: flows west and north to the Arctic Ocean; the largest river in volume in Russia. Length: 4129 km (2566 miles).

Yentai *or* **Yen-t'ai** ('jɛn'taɪ) NOUN a variant transliteration of the Chinese name for **Yantai.**

yeoman ('jəʊmən) NOUN, *plural* **-men.** 1 *History* **a** a member of a class of small freeholders of common birth who cultivated their own land. **b** an assistant or other subordinate to an official, such as a sheriff, or to a craftsman or trader. **c** an attendant or lesser official in a royal or noble household. 2 (in Britain) another name for **yeoman of the guard.** 3 *(modifier)* characteristic of or relating to a yeoman. 4 a petty officer or noncommissioned officer in the Royal Navy or Marines in charge of signals.
▷**HISTORY** C15: perhaps from *yongman* young man

yeomanly ('jəʊmənlɪ) ADJECTIVE 1 of, relating to, or like a yeoman. 2 having the virtues attributed to yeomen, such as staunchness, loyalty, and courage. ◆ ADVERB 3 in a yeomanly manner, as in being brave, staunch, or loyal.

yeoman of the guard NOUN a member of the bodyguard (**Yeomen of the Guard**) of the English monarch. This unit was founded in 1485 and now retains ceremonial functions only.

yeomanry ('jəʊmənrɪ) NOUN 1 yeomen collectively. 2 (in Britain) a volunteer cavalry force, organized in 1761 for home defence: merged into the Territorial Army in 1907.

yep (jɛp) SENTENCE SUBSTITUTE an informal word for **yes.**

yerba *or* **yerba maté** ('jɜːbə, 'jɜːbə) NOUN another name for **maté.**
▷**HISTORY** from Spanish *yerba maté* herb maté

Yerevan (*Russian* jɪrɪ'van) NOUN the capital of Armenia: founded in the 8th century B.C.; an industrial city and a main focus of trade routes since ancient times; university. Pop.: 1 248 700 (1995 est.). Also called: **Erevan** *or* **Erivan.**

Yerwa-Maiduguri ('jɜːwəˌmaɪdʊ'guːrɪ) NOUN another name for **Maiduguri.**

yes (jɛs) SENTENCE SUBSTITUTE 1 used to express acknowledgment, affirmation, consent, agreement, or approval or to answer when one is addressed. 2 used, often with interrogative intonation, to signal someone to speak or keep speaking, enter a room, or do something. ◆ NOUN 3 an answer or vote of *yes.* 4 *(often plural)* a person who votes in the affirmative. ◆ Compare **no**[1].
▷**HISTORY** Old English *gēse,* from *iā sīe* may it be; see YEA

yeshiva (jə'ʃiːvə; *Hebrew* jə'ʃiːva) NOUN **pl, -vahs** *or* **-voth** (*Hebrew* -vɔt). 1 a traditional Jewish school devoted chiefly to the study of rabbinic literature and the Talmud. 2 a school run by Orthodox Jews for children of primary school age, providing both religious and secular instruction.
▷**HISTORY** from Hebrew *yĕshībhāh* a sitting, seat, hence, an academy

Yeşil Irmak (jɛ'ʃiːl ɪə'mɑːk) NOUN a river in N Turkey, flowing northwest to the Black Sea. Length: 418 km (260 miles). Ancient name: **Iris.**

Yeşilköy (jɛ'ʃilˌkœɪ) NOUN the Turkish name for **San Stefano.**

yes man NOUN a servile, submissive, or

acquiescent subordinate, assistant, or associate; sycophant.

yes/no question NOUN *Grammar* a question inviting the answer "yes" or "no". Compare **WH question.**

yester ('jɛstə) ADJECTIVE *Archaic* of or relating to yesterday: *yester sun.* Also: **yestern** ('jɛstən).
▷HISTORY Old English *geostror;* related to Old High German *gestaron,* Gothic *gistra,* Old Norse *ī gær*

yester- PREFIX [1] indicating the day before today: *yesterday.* [2] indicating a period of time before the present one: *yesteryear.*
▷HISTORY Old English *geostran;* compare German *gestern,* Latin *hesternus* of yesterday

yesterday ('jɛstədɪ, -ˌdeɪ) NOUN [1] the day immediately preceding today. [2] (*often plural*) the recent past. ◆ ADVERB [3] on or during the day before today. [4] in the recent past.

yesteryear ('jɛstəˌjɪə) *Formal or literary* ◆ NOUN [1] last year or the past in general. ◆ ADVERB [2] during last year or the past in general.

yestreen (jɛ'stri:n) ADVERB *Scot* yesterday evening.
▷HISTORY C14: from YEST(E)R- + E(V)EN[2]

yet (jɛt) SENTENCE CONNECTOR [1] nevertheless; still; in spite of that: *I want to and yet I haven't the courage; she is strange yet kind.* ◆ ADVERB [2] (*usually used with a negative or interrogative*) so far; up until then or now: *they're not home yet; is it teatime yet?* [3] (often preceded by *just; usually used with a negative*) now (as contrasted with later): *we can't stop yet.* [4] (*often used with a comparative*) even; still: *yet more potatoes for sale; yet another problem family.* [5] eventually, in spite of everything: *we'll convince him yet.* [6] **as yet.** so far; up until then or now.
▷HISTORY Old English *gēta;* related to Old Frisian *jēta*

yeti ('jɛtɪ) NOUN another term for **abominable snowman.**
▷HISTORY C20: from Tibetan

yett (jɛt) NOUN *Scot* a gate or door.
▷HISTORY Old English variant of GATE[1]

yettie ('jɛtɪ) NOUN ACRONYM FOR young, entrepreneurial, and technology-based (person).

yew (ju:) NOUN [1] any coniferous tree of the genus *Taxus,* of the Old World and North America, esp *T. baccata,* having flattened needle-like leaves, fine-grained elastic wood, and solitary seeds with a red waxy aril resembling berries: family *Taxaceae.* [2] the wood of any of these trees, used to make bows for archery. [3] *Archery* a bow made of yew.
▷HISTORY Old English *īw;* related to Old High German *īwa,* Old Norse *ȳr* yew, Latin *ūva* grape, Russian *iva* willow

Yeysk (*Russian* jejsk) NOUN a variant spelling of **Yeisk.**

Yezd (jezd) NOUN a variant of **Yazd.**

Yezidis ('jɛzɪdɪz) PLURAL NOUN a religious sect found in the Kurdish areas of Iraq, Turkey, and Syria, whose beliefs combine elements of Zoroastrianism, Islam, Christianity, and other religions; in addition to believing in a Supreme God, the Yezidi worship seven angels, among whom is the devil, who is believed to have repented and been pardoned and reinstated as chief angel.
▷HISTORY C19: perhaps from *Yazid* or *Ezid* a name for God

Y-fronts PLURAL NOUN *Trademark* boys' or men's underpants having a front opening within an inverted Y shape.

Ygerne (i:'gɛən) NOUN a variant of **Igraine.**

Yggdrasil, Ygdrasil, *or* **Igdrasil** ('ɪgdrəsɪl) NOUN *Norse myth* the ash tree that was thought to overshadow the whole world, binding together earth, heaven, and hell with its roots and branches.
▷HISTORY Old Norse (probably meaning: Uggr's horse), from *Uggr* a name of Odin, from *yggr, uggr* frightful + *drasill* horse, of obscure origin

YHA ABBREVIATION FOR Youth Hostels Association.

YHVH, YHWH, JHVH, *or* **JHWH** *Old Testament* the letters of the **Tetragrammaton.** See also **Yahweh, Jehovah.**

Yibin ('ji:'bɪn) *or* **I-pin** NOUN a port in S central China, in Sichuan province: a commercial centre. Pop.: 288 039 (1999 est.).

Yichang ('ji:'tʃæŋ), **Ichang,** *or* **I-ch'ang** NOUN a port in S central China, in Hubei province on the Yangtze River 1600 km (1000 miles) from the East China Sea: the Yangtze dam, the world's biggest hydroelectric and flood-control project, is being constructed nearby. Pop.: 481 277 (1999 est.).

yid (jɪd) NOUN *Slang* a derogatory word for a Jew.
▷HISTORY C20: probably from *Yiddish,* from Middle High German *Jude* JEW

Yiddish ('jɪdɪʃ) NOUN [1] a language spoken as a vernacular by Jews in Europe and elsewhere by Jewish emigrants, usually written in the Hebrew alphabet. Historically, it is a dialect of High German with an admixture of words of Hebrew, Romance, and Slavonic origin, developed in central and E Europe during the Middle Ages. ◆ ADJECTIVE [2] in or relating to this language.
▷HISTORY C19: from German *jüdisch,* from *Jude* JEW

Yiddisher ('jɪdɪʃə) ADJECTIVE [1] in or relating to Yiddish. [2] Jewish. ◆ NOUN [3] a speaker of Yiddish; Jew.

yield (ji:ld) VERB [1] to give forth or supply (a product, result, etc.), esp by cultivation, labour, etc.; produce or bear. [2] (*tr*) to furnish as a return: *the shares yielded three per cent.* [3] (*tr;* often foll by *up*) to surrender or relinquish, esp as a result of force, persuasion, etc. [4] (*intr;* sometimes foll by *to*) to give way, submit, or surrender, as through force or persuasion: *she yielded to his superior knowledge.* [5] (*intr;* often foll by *to*) to agree; comply; assent: *he eventually yielded to their request for money.* [6] (*tr*) to grant or allow; concede: *to yield right of way.* [7] (*tr*) *Obsolete* to pay or repay: *God yield thee!* ◆ NOUN [8] the result, product, or amount yielded. [9] the profit or return, as from an investment or tax. [10] the annual income provided by an investment, usually expressed as a percentage of its cost or of its current value: *the yield on these shares is 15 per cent at today's market value.* [11] the energy released by the explosion of a nuclear weapon expressed in terms of the amount of TNT necessary to produce the same energy. [12] *Chem* the quantity of a specified product obtained in a reaction or series of reactions, usually expressed as a percentage of the quantity that is theoretically obtainable.
▷HISTORY Old English *gieldan;* related to Old Frisian *jelda,* Old High German *geltan,* Old Norse *gjalda,* Gothic *gildan*
▸ **'yieldable** ADJECTIVE ▸ **'yielder** NOUN

yielding ('ji:ldɪŋ) ADJECTIVE [1] compliant, submissive, or flexible. [2] pliable or soft: *a yielding material.*
▸ **'yieldingly** ADVERB ▸ **'yieldingness** NOUN

yield point NOUN the stress at which an elastic material under increasing stress ceases to behave elastically; under conditions of tensile strength the elongation is no longer proportional to the increase in stress. Also called: **yield stress, yield strength.**

yield stress NOUN the stress level at which a metal or other material ceases to behave elastically. The stress divided by the strain is no longer constant. The point at which this occurs is known as the yield point. Compare **proof stress.**

yike (jaɪk) *Austral informal, archaic* ◆ NOUN [1] an argument, squabble, or fight. ◆ VERB (*intr*) [2] to argue, squabble, or fight.
▷HISTORY origin unknown

yikes ('jaiks) INTERJECTION *Informal* an expression of surprise, fear, or alarm.

yin (jɪn) DETERMINER, PRONOUN, NOUN a Scot word for **one.**

Yin and Yang (jɪn) NOUN two complementary principles of Chinese philosophy: Yin is negative, dark, and feminine, Yang positive, bright, and masculine. Their interaction is thought to maintain the harmony of the universe and to influence everything within it.
▷HISTORY from Chinese (Peking) *yin* dark + *yang* bright

Yinchuan, Yin-ch'uan, *or* **Yinchwan** ('jɪn'tʃwa:n) NOUN a city in N central China, capital of the Ningxia Hui AR, on the Yellow River. Pop.: 469 180 (1999 est.).

Yingkou *or* **Yingkow** ('jɪŋ'kau) NOUN a port in NE China, in SW Liaoning province: a major shipping centre for Manchuria. Pop.: 498 300 (1999 est.).

Yinglish ('jɪŋglɪʃ) NOUN a dialect of English spoken esp by Jewish immigrants to New York, and heavily influenced by Yiddish constructions and loan words. Also: **Yenglish.**
▷HISTORY from YI(DDISH) + (E)NGLISH

yipes ('jaips) INTERJECTION *Informal* an expression of surprise, fear, or alarm.

yippee (jɪ'pi:) INTERJECTION an exclamation of joy, pleasure, anticipation, etc.

yips (jɪps) PLURAL NOUN **the.** *Informal* (in sport, originally esp golf) nervous twitching or tension that destroys concentration and spoils performance.
▷HISTORY C20: of unknown origin

yite (jəɪt) *or* **yitie** ('jəɪtɪ) NOUN Scot words for **yellowhammer** (sense 1). Also called: **yellow-yite.**
▷HISTORY C19: of unknown origin

yitten ('jɪtᵊn) ADJECTIVE *Northern English dialect* frightened.

Yizkor ('jizkor) NOUN *Judaism* a memorial prayer included in the liturgy for certain festivals.
▷HISTORY from Hebrew, literally: let him remember

Y2K NOUN *Informal* another name for the year 2000 A.D. (esp referring to the millennium bug).
▷HISTORY C20: Y(EAR) + 2 + K (in the sense: thousand)

-yl SUFFIX OF NOUNS (in chemistry) indicating a group or radical: *methyl; carbonyl.*
▷HISTORY from Greek *hulē* wood, matter

ylang-ylang *or* **ilang-ilang** (ˌi:læŋ'i:læŋ) NOUN [1] an aromatic Asian tree, *Cananga odorata* (or *Canangium odoratum*), with fragrant greenish-yellow flowers yielding a volatile oil: family *Annonaceae.* [2] the oil obtained from this tree, used in perfumery.
▷HISTORY C19: from Tagalog *ilang-ilang*

ylem ('aɪləm) NOUN the original matter from which the basic elements are said to have been formed following the explosion postulated in the big bang theory of cosmology.
▷HISTORY Middle English, from Old French *ilem,* from Latin *hȳlē* stuff, matter, from Greek *hulē* wood, matter

Y-level NOUN *Surveying* a level mounted on a Y-shaped support that can be rotated.

YMCA ABBREVIATION FOR Young Men's Christian Association.

YMHA ABBREVIATION FOR Young Men's Hebrew Association.

Ymir ('i:mɪə) *or* **Ymer** ('i:mə) NOUN *Norse myth* the first being and forefather of the giants. He was slain by Odin and his brothers, who made the earth from his flesh, the water from his blood, and the sky from his skull.

-yne SUFFIX FORMING NOUNS denoting an organic chemical containing a triple bond: *alkyne.*
▷HISTORY alteration of -INE[2]

yo (jəʊ) SENTENCE SUBSTITUTE an expression used as a greeting, to attract someone's attention, etc.
▷HISTORY C20: of unknown origin

yob (jɒb) *or* **yobbo** ('jɒbəʊ) NOUN, *plural* **yobs** *or* **yobbos.** *Brit slang* an aggressive and surly youth, esp a teenager.
▷HISTORY C19: perhaps back slang for BOY

yobbery ('jɒbərɪ) NOUN *Brit slang* behaviour typical of aggressive surly youths.

yobbish ('jɒbɪʃ) ADJECTIVE *Brit slang* typical of aggressive surly youths; vulgar or unrefined.

yod *or* **yodh** (jud) NOUN the tenth letter in the Hebrew alphabet (י), transliterated as *y.*
▷HISTORY C18: from Hebrew, literally: hand

yodel ('jəʊdᵊl) NOUN [1] an effect produced in singing by an abrupt change of register from the chest voice to falsetto, esp in popular folk songs of the Swiss Alps. ◆ VERB **-dels, -delling, -delled** *or US* **-dels, -deling, -deled.** [2] to sing (a song) in which a yodel is used.
▷HISTORY C19: from German *jodeln,* of imitative origin
▸ **'yodeller** NOUN

yodle ('jəʊdᵊl) NOUN a variant spelling of **yodel.**
▸ **'yodler** NOUN

yoga ('jəʊgə) NOUN (*often capital*) [1] a Hindu system of philosophy aiming at the mystical union of the self with the Supreme Being in a state of complete awareness and tranquillity through certain physical and mental exercises. [2] any method by which such awareness and tranquillity are attained, esp a course of related exercises and postures designed to promote physical and spiritual

wellbeing. See **Astanga yoga, hatha yoga, power yoga, raja yoga, Sivananda yoga.**
▷HISTORY C19: from Sanskrit: a yoking, union, from *yunakti* he yokes
▸**yogic** ('jəʊgɪk) ADJECTIVE

yogh (jɒg) NOUN [1] a character (ȝ) used in Old and Middle English to represent a palatal fricative very close to the semivowel sound of Modern English *y*, as in Old English *ȝeong* (young). [2] this same character as used in Middle English for both the voiced and voiceless palatal fricatives; when final or in a closed syllable in medial position the sound approached that of German *ch* in *ich*, as in *knyȝt* (knight). After the 14th century this symbol became the modern consonantal (semivocalic) *y* when initial or commencing a syllable, and though no longer pronounced in medial position it is preserved in many words by a modern *gh*, as in *thought*.
▷HISTORY C14: perhaps from *yok* YOKE, referring to the letter's shape

yogi ('jəʊgɪ) NOUN, *plural* **-gis** *or* **-gin** (-gɪn). a person who is a master of yoga.
▸**yogini** (jəʊ'gi:ni:) FEMININE NOUN

yogurt *or* **yoghurt** ('jəʊgət, 'jɒg-) NOUN a thick custard-like food prepared from milk that has been curdled by bacteria, often sweetened and flavoured with fruit, chocolate, etc.
▷HISTORY C19: from Turkish *yoğurt*

Yogyakarta (ˌjəʊgjɑ:'kɑ:tɑ:, 'jɒg-), **Jogjakarta, Jokjakarta,** *or* **Djokjakarta** NOUN a city in S Indonesia, in central Java: seat of government of Indonesia (1946–49); university (1949). Pop.: 419 500 (1995 est.).

yo-heave-ho (ˌjəʊhi:v'həʊ) INTERJECTION a cry formerly used by sailors while pulling or lifting together in rhythm.

yohimbine (jəʊ'hɪmbi:n) NOUN an alkaloid found in the bark of the tree *Corynanthe yohimbe*. It is used in medicine as an adrenergic blocking agent. Formula: $C_{21}H_{26}N_2O_3$.
▷HISTORY C19: from Bantu *yohimbé* a tropical African tree + -INE[1]

yo-ho-ho INTERJECTION [1] an exclamation to call attention. [2] another word for **yo-heave-ho.**

yoicks (haɪk; *spelling pron* jɔɪks) INTERJECTION a cry used by huntsmen to urge on the hounds to the fox.

yoke (jəʊk) NOUN, *plural* **yokes** *or* **yoke.** [1] a wooden frame, usually consisting of a bar with an oxbow or similar collar-like piece at either end, for attaching to the necks of a pair of draught animals, esp oxen, so that they can be worked as a team. [2] something resembling a yoke in form or function, such as a frame fitting over a person's shoulders for carrying buckets suspended at either end. [3] a fitted part of a garment, esp around the neck, shoulders, and chest or around the hips, to which a gathered, pleated, flared, or unfitted part is attached. [4] an immense oppressive force or burden: *under the yoke of a tyrant*. [5] a pair of oxen or other draught animals joined together by a yoke. [6] a part, esp one of relatively thick cross section, that secures two or more components so that they move together. [7] a crosshead that transmits the drive of an opposed piston engine from the upper of a pair of linked pistons to the crankshaft through a connecting rod. [8] a steel framework around the formwork during the casting of concrete. [9] *Nautical* a crossbar fixed athwartships to the head of a rudderpost in a small boat, to which are attached ropes or cables for steering. [10] a Y-shaped cable, rope, or chain, used for holding, towing, etc. [11] (in the ancient world) a symbolic reconstruction of a yoke, consisting of two upright spears with a third lashed across them, under which conquered enemies were compelled to march, esp in Rome. [12] a mark, token, or symbol of slavery, subjection, or suffering. [13] *Now rare* a link, tie, or bond: *the yoke of love*. [14] *Brit dialect* a period of steady work, esp the time during which a ploughman and his team work at a stretch. [15] *Irish* any device, unusual object, or gadget: *where's the yoke for opening tins?* ◆ VERB [16] (*tr*) to secure or harness (a draught animal) to (a plough, vehicle, etc.) by means of a yoke. [17] to join or be joined by means of a yoke; couple, unite, or link. [18] (*tr*) *Obsolete* to oppress, burden, or enslave.
▷HISTORY Old English *geoc;* related to Old High German *ioh*, Old Norse *ok*, Gothic *juk*, Latin *iugum*, Sanskrit *yugam*
▸'**yokeless** ADJECTIVE

yokefellow ('jəʊkˌfeləʊ) NOUN *Archaic* a working companion.

yokel ('jəʊkᵊl) NOUN *Disparaging* (used chiefly by townspeople) a person who lives in the country, esp one who appears to be simple and old-fashioned.
▷HISTORY C19: perhaps from dialect *yokel* green woodpecker, yellowhammer
▸'**yokelish** ADJECTIVE

yoker ('jəʊkə) VERB (*intr*) *Northern English dialect* to spit.

Yokohama (ˌjəʊkəʊ'hɑ:mə) NOUN a port in central Japan, on SE Honshu on Tokyo Bay: a major port and the country's second largest city situated in the largest and most populous industrial region of Japan. Pop.: 3 307 408 (1995).

Yokosuka (ˌjəʊkəʊ'su:kə) NOUN a port in Japan, in SE Honshu: a major naval base with shipbuilding industries. Pop.: 432 202 (1995).

Yokozuna (ˌjəʊkəʊ'zu:nə) NOUN, *plural* **-na** *or* **-ni.** a grand champion sumo wrestler.
▷HISTORY from Japanese *yoko* across + *zuna* rope, from the sacred straw rope presented to the grand champion

yolk (jəʊk) NOUN [1] the substance in an animal ovum consisting of protein and fat that nourishes the developing embryo. Related adjective: **vitelline.** [2] a greasy substance secreted by the skin of a sheep and present in the fleece.
▷HISTORY Old English *geoloca*, from *geolu* YELLOW
▸'**yolkless** ADJECTIVE ▸'**yolky** ADJECTIVE

yolk sac NOUN *Zoology* [1] the membranous sac that is attached to the ventral surface of the embryos of birds, reptiles, and some fishes and contains yolk. [2] the corresponding part in the embryo of mammals, which contains no yolk.

Yom Kippur (jɒm 'kɪpə; *Hebrew* jɔm ki'pur) NOUN an annual Jewish holiday celebrated on Tishri 10 as a day of fasting, on which prayers of penitence are recited in the synagogue throughout the day. Also called: **Day of Atonement.**
▷HISTORY from Hebrew, from *yōm* day + *kippūr* atonement

Yom Kippur War NOUN a war in which Egypt and Syria launched a joint surprise attack on Israel on the Jewish festival of Yom Kippur (Oct. 6, 1973). It ended with a ceasefire (Oct. 25, 1973), Syrian forces having been repulsed, Egypt having reoccupied a belt of the Sinai desert on the E bank of the Suez Canal, and Israel having established a salient on the W bank of the Suez Canal.

yomp (jɒmp) VERB (*intr*) to walk or trek laboriously, esp heavily laden and over difficult terrain.
▷HISTORY C20: military slang, of uncertain origin

yom tov ('jɔm 'tɒv, 'jɒmtəv) NOUN, *plural* **yamin tovim** (jɑ'min tɔ'vim). *Judaism* a festival, esp that of Passover, Shabuoth, Sukkoth, or Rosh Hashana.

yon (jɒn) *or* **yond** (jɒnd) DETERMINER [1] *Chiefly Scot and northern English* **a** an archaic or dialect word for **that**: *yon man*. **b** (*as pronoun*): *yon's a fool*. [2] variants of **yonder.**
▷HISTORY Old English *geon;* related to Old Frisian *jen*, Old High German *jenēr*, Old Norse *enn*, Gothic *jains*

yonder ('jɒndə) ADVERB [1] at, in, or to that relatively distant place; over there. ◆ DETERMINER [2] being at a distance, either within view or as if within view: *yonder valleys*.
▷HISTORY C13: from Old English *geond* yond; related to Old Saxon *jendra*, Old High German *jenēr*, Gothic *jaind*

yoni ('jəʊnɪ) NOUN *Hinduism* [1] the female genitalia, regarded as a divine symbol of sexual pleasure and matrix of generation and the visible form of Sakti. [2] an image of these as an object of worship.
▷HISTORY C18: from Sanskrit, literally: vulva, womb

Yonkers ('jɒŋkəz) NOUN a city in SE New York State, near New York City on the Hudson River. Pop.: 196 308 (2000).

yonks (jɒŋks) PLURAL NOUN *Informal* a very long time; ages: *I haven't seen him for yonks*.
▷HISTORY C20: of unknown origin

Yonne (*French* jɔn) NOUN [1] a department of N central France, in Burgundy region. Capital: Auxerre. Pop.: 333 221 (1999). Area: 7461 sq. km (2910 sq. miles). [2] a river in N France, flowing generally northwest to the Seine at Montereau. Length: 290 km (180 miles).

yonnie ('jɒnɪ) NOUN *Austral children's slang* a stone.
▷HISTORY from a native Australian language

yoof (ju:f) NOUN *Informal* **a** a non-standard spelling of **youth**, used humorously or facetiously. **b** (*as modifier*): *yoof TV*.

yoo-hoo ('ju:ˌhu:) INTERJECTION a call to attract a person's attention.

YOP (jɒp) NOUN (formerly, in Britain) [1] **a** ACRONYM FOR Youth Opportunities Programme. **b** (*as modifier*): *a YOP scheme*. [2] Also called: **yopper.** *Informal* a young person employed through this government programme.

yore (jɔ:) NOUN [1] time long past (now only in the phrase **of yore**). ◆ ADVERB [2] *Obsolete* in the past; long ago.
▷HISTORY Old English *geāra*, genitive plural of *gēar* YEAR; see HOUR

york (jɔ:k) VERB (*tr*) *Cricket* to bowl or try to bowl (a batsman) by pitching the ball under or just beyond the bat.
▷HISTORY C19: back formation from YORKER

York (jɔ:k) NOUN [1] a walled city in NE England, in York unitary authority, North Yorkshire, on the River Ouse: the military capital of Roman Britain; capital of the N archiepiscopal province of Britain since 625, with a cathedral (the Minster) begun in 1154; noted for its cycle of medieval mystery plays; university (1963). Pop.: 104 100 (1994 est.). Latin name: **Eboracum.** [2] a unitary authority in NE England, in North Yorkshire. Pop.: 181 131 (1996 est.). Area: 272 sq. km (105 sq. miles). [3] **Cape.** a cape in NE Australia, in Queensland at the N tip of Cape York Peninsula, extending into Torres Strait: the northernmost point of Australia.

Yorke Peninsula (jɔ:k) NOUN a peninsula in South Australia, between Spencer Gulf and St Vincent Gulf: mainly agricultural with several coastal resorts.

yorker (jɔ:kə) NOUN *Cricket* a ball bowled so as to pitch just under or just beyond the bat.
▷HISTORY C19: probably named after the *Yorkshire* County Cricket Club

yorkie ('jɔ:kɪ) NOUN another name for **Yorkshire terrier.**

Yorkist ('jɔ:kɪst) *English history* ◆ NOUN [1] a member or adherent of the royal house of York, esp during the Wars of the Roses. ◆ ADJECTIVE [2] of, belonging to, or relating to the supporters or members of the house of York.

Yorks. (jɔ:ks) ABBREVIATION FOR Yorkshire.

Yorkshire ('jɔ:kˌʃɪə, -ʃə) NOUN a historic county of N England: the largest English county, formerly divided administratively into East, West, and North Ridings. In 1974 it was much reduced in size and divided into the new counties of North, West, and South Yorkshire: in 1996 the East Riding of Yorkshire was reinstated as a unitary authority and parts of the NE were returned to North Yorkshire for geographical and ceremonial purposes.

Yorkshire Dales PLURAL NOUN the valleys of the rivers flowing from the Pennines in W Yorkshire: chiefly Ribblesdale, Swaledale, Nidderdale, Wharfedale, and Wensleydale; tourist area. Also called: **the Dales.**

Yorkshire fog NOUN a common tufted grass, *Holcus lanatus,* having downy leaves and flower heads that are white or pink and branched, with spikelets carrying the flowers.

Yorkshire pudding NOUN *Chiefly Brit* a light puffy baked pudding made from a batter of flour, eggs, and milk, traditionally served with roast beef.

Yorkshire terrier NOUN a very small breed of terrier with a long straight glossy coat of steel-blue and tan. Also called: **yorkie.**

Yorktown ('jɔ:kˌtaʊn) NOUN a village in SE Virginia: scene of the surrender (1781) of the British under Cornwallis to the Americans under Washington at the end of the War of American Independence.

yorp (jɔ:p) VERB (*intr*) *Midland English dialect* to shout.

Yoruba ('jɒrubə) NOUN [1] (*plural* **-bas** *or* **-ba**) a member of a Negroid people of W Africa, living chiefly in the coastal regions of SW Nigeria: noted for their former city states and complex material culture, particularly as evidenced in their music, art, and sculpture. [2] the language of this people, belonging to the Kwa branch of the Niger-Congo family.
▸ **'Yoruban** ADJECTIVE

Yosemite Falls (jəʊ'sɛmɪtɪ) PLURAL NOUN a series of waterfalls in central California, in the Yosemite National Park, with a total drop of 770 m (2525 ft.): includes the **Upper Yosemite Falls,** 436 m (1430 ft.) high, and the **Lower Yosemite Falls,** 98 m (320 ft.) high.

Yosemite National Park NOUN a national park in central California, in the Sierra Nevada Mountains: contains the **Yosemite Valley,** at an altitude of about 1200 m (4000 ft.), with sheer walls rising about another 1200 m (4000 ft.). Area: 3061 sq. km (1182 sq. miles).

Yoshkar-Ola (*Russian* jaʃ'kara'la) NOUN a city in Russia, capital of the Mari El Republic. Pop.: 249 800 (1999 est.).

you (juː; *unstressed* jʊ) PRONOUN (*subjective or objective*) [1] refers to the person addressed or to more than one person including the person or persons addressed but not including the speaker: *you know better; the culprit is among you.* [2] Also: **one.** refers to an unspecified person or people in general: *you can't tell the boys from the girls.* [3] *Chiefly US* a dialect word for **yourself** or **yourselves** when used as an indirect object: *you should get you a wife now.* ◆ NOUN [4] *Informal* the personality of the person being addressed or something that expresses it: *that hat isn't really you.* [5] **you know what** *or* **who.** a thing or person that the speaker cannot or does not want to specify.
▷ **HISTORY** Old English *ēow,* dative and accusative of *gē* YE[1]; related to Old Saxon *eu,* Old High German *iu,* Gothic *izwis*

> **Language note** See at **me**[1].

you-all PRONOUN a US, esp Southern, word for **you**, esp when addressing more than one person

you'd (juːd; *unstressed* jʊd) CONTRACTION OF you had *or* you would.

you'll (juːl; *unstressed* jʊl) CONTRACTION OF you will *or* you shall.

young (jʌŋ) ADJECTIVE **younger** ('jʌŋgə), **youngest** ('jʌŋgɪst). [1] **a** having lived, existed, or been made or known for a relatively short time: *a young man; a young movement; a young country.* **b** (*as collective noun; preceded by the*): *the young.* [2] youthful or having qualities associated with youth; vigorous or lively: *she's very young for her age.* [3] of or relating to youth: *in my young days.* [4] having been established or introduced for a relatively short time: *a young member.* [5] in an early stage of progress or development; not far advanced: *the day was young.* [6] *Geography* **a** (of mountains) formed in the Alpine orogeny and still usually rugged in outline. **b** another term for **youthful** (sense 4). [7] (*often capital*) of or relating to a rejuvenated group or movement or one claiming to represent the younger members of the population, esp one adhering to a political ideology: *Young England; Young Socialists.* ◆ NOUN [8] (*functioning as plural*) offspring, esp young animals: *a rabbit with her young.* [9] **with young.** (of animals) pregnant.
▷ **HISTORY** Old English *geong;* related to Old Saxon, Old High German *iung,* Old Norse *ungr,* Latin *iuvenis,* Sanskrit *yuvan*
▸ **'youngish** ADJECTIVE

youngberry ('jʌŋbərɪ, -brɪ) NOUN, *plural* **-ries.** [1] a trailing bramble of the southwestern US that is a hybrid of a blackberry and dewberry with large sweet dark purple fruits. [2] the fruit of this plant.
▷ **HISTORY** C20: named after B. M. *Young,* US fruit-grower who was first to cultivate it (circa 1900)

young blood NOUN young, fresh, or vigorous new people, ideas, attitudes, etc.

Young Fogey NOUN a young or fairly young person who adopts the conservative values of an older generation.

young gun NOUN an up-and-coming young man, esp one considered as being assertive and confident.

Young Ireland NOUN a movement or party of Irish patriots in the 1840s who split with Daniel O'Connell because they favoured a more violent policy than that which he promoted.

young lady NOUN a girlfriend; sweetheart.

youngling ('jʌŋlɪŋ) NOUN *Literary* **a** a young person, animal, or plant. **b** (*as modifier*): *a youngling brood.*
▷ **HISTORY** Old English *geongling*

young man NOUN a boyfriend; sweetheart.

young offender institution NOUN (in Britain) a place where offenders aged 15 to 21 may be detained and given training, instruction, and work. Former names: **borstal, youth custody centre.**

Young's modulus NOUN a modulus of elasticity, applicable to the stretching of a wire etc., equal to the ratio of the applied load per unit area of cross section to the increase in length per unit length. Symbol: *E.*
▷ **HISTORY** C19: named after Thomas *Young* (1773–1829), English physicist, physician, and Egyptologist

youngster ('jʌŋstə) NOUN [1] a young person; child or youth. [2] a young animal, esp a horse.

Youngstown ('jʌŋz,taʊn) NOUN a city in NE Ohio: a major centre of steel production: university (1908). Pop.: 82 026 (2000).

Young Turk NOUN [1] a progressive, revolutionary, or rebellious member of an organization, political party, etc., esp one agitating for radical reform. [2] a member of an abortive reform movement in the Ottoman Empire, originally made up of exiles in W Europe who advocated liberal reforms. The movement fell under the domination of young Turkish army officers of a nationalist bent, who wielded great influence in the government between 1908 and 1918.

younker ('jʌŋkə) NOUN [1] *Archaic or literary* a young man; lad. [2] *Obsolete* a young gentleman or knight.
▷ **HISTORY** C16: from Dutch *jonker,* from Middle Dutch *jonc* YOUNG

your (jɔː, jʊə; *unstressed* jə) DETERMINER [1] of, belonging to, or associated with you: *your nose; your house; your first taste of freedom.* [2] belonging to or associated with an unspecified person or people in general: *the path is on your left heading north; this lotion is for your head only.* [3] *Informal* used to indicate all things or people of a certain type: *your part-time worker is a problem.* [4] **your actual.** *Brit informal* (intensifier): *here is your actual automatic tin-opener.*
▷ **HISTORY** Old English *eower,* genitive of *gē* YE[1]; related to Old Frisian *jūwe,* Old Saxon *euwa,* Old High German *iuwēr*

you're (jʊə, jɔː; *unstressed* jə) CONTRACTION OF you are.

yours (jɔːz, jʊəz) PRONOUN [1] something or someone belonging to or associated in some way with you: *I've eaten yours.* [2] your family: *greetings to you and yours.* [3] used in conventional closing phrases at the end of a letter: *yours sincerely; yours faithfully.* [4] **of yours.** belonging to or associated with you. [5] **what's yours?** *Jocular* what would you like to drink?

yourself (jɔː'sɛlf, jʊə-) PRONOUN, *plural* **-selves.** [1] **a** the reflexive form of *you.* **b** (intensifier): *you yourself control your destiny.* [2] (*preceded by a copula*) your normal or usual self: *you're not yourself these days.*

yours truly PRONOUN an informal term for *I, myself,* or *me.*
▷ **HISTORY** from the conventional closing phrase used at the end of letters

yous *or* **youse** (juːz) PRONOUN *Dialect or not standard* refers to more than one person including the person or persons addressed but not including the speaker: *yous have all had it now; I'm fed up with yous.*

youth (juːθ) NOUN, *plural* **youths** (juːðz). [1] the quality or condition of being young, immature, or inexperienced: *his youth told against him in the contest.* [2] the period between childhood and maturity, esp adolescence and early adulthood. [3] the freshness, vigour, or vitality characteristic of young people: *youth shone out from her face.* [4] any period of early development: *the project was in its youth.* [5] a young person, esp a young man or boy. [6] young people collectively: *youth everywhere is rising in revolt.*
▷ **HISTORY** Old English *geogoth;* related to Old Frisian *jogethe,* Old High German *iugund,* Gothic *junda,* Latin *juventus*
▸ **'youthless** ADJECTIVE

Youth (juːθ) NOUN **Isle of.** an island in the NW Caribbean, south of Cuba: administratively part of Cuba from 1925. Chief town: Nueva Gerona. Pop.: 78 818 (1998 est.). Area: 3061 sq. km (1182 sq. miles). Former name: **Isle of Pines.** Spanish name: **Isla de la Juventud** ('izla ðe la xuβen'tuð).

youth club NOUN a centre providing leisure activities for young people, often associated with a church or community centre.

youth court NOUN a court that deals with juvenile offenders and children beyond parental control or in need of care. Former name: **juvenile court.**

youth custody NOUN (in Britain) a sentence of from four to eighteen months' detention passed on a person aged 15 to 21.

youth custody centre NOUN the former name for **young offender institution.**

youthful ('juːθfʊl) ADJECTIVE [1] of, relating to, possessing, or characteristic of youth. [2] fresh, vigorous, or active: *he's surprisingly youthful for his age.* [3] in an early stage of development: *a youthful culture.* [4] Also: **young.** (of a river, valley, or land surface) in the early stage of the cycle of erosion, characterized by steep slopes, lack of flood plains, and V-shaped valleys. Compare **mature** (sense 6), **old** (sense 18).
▸ **'youthfully** ADVERB ▸ **'youthfulness** NOUN

youth hostel NOUN one of a chain of inexpensive lodging places for young people travelling cheaply. Often shortened to: **hostel.**

Youth Training Scheme NOUN (formerly, in Britain) a scheme, run by the Training Agency, to provide vocational training for unemployed 16–17-year-olds. Abbreviation: **YTS.**

you've (juːv; *unstressed* jʊv) CONTRACTION OF you have.

yowe (jaʊ) NOUN a Scot word for **ewe.**

yowl (jaʊl) VERB [1] to express with or produce a loud mournful wail or cry; howl. ◆ NOUN [2] a loud mournful cry; wail or howl.
▷ **HISTORY** C13: from Old Norse *gaula;* related to German *jaulen;* see YAWL[2]
▸ **'yowler** NOUN

yo-yo ('jəʊjəʊ) NOUN, *plural* **-yos.** [1] a toy consisting of a spool attached to a string, the end of which is held while it is repeatedly spun out and reeled in. [2] *US and Canadian slang* a stupid person, esp one who is easily manipulated. ◆ VERB **yo-yos, yo-yoing, yo-yoed.** (*intr*) [3] *Informal* to change repeatedly from one position to another; fluctuate. ◆ ADJECTIVE [4] *Informal* changing repeatedly; fluctuating.
▷ **HISTORY** from Filipino *yo yo,* come come, a weapon consisting of a spindle attached to a thong

yo-yo dieting NOUN the practice of repeatedly going on slimming diets, and putting on weight in the interim.

Ypres (*French* iprə) NOUN a town in W Belgium, in W Flanders province near the border with France: scene of many sieges and battles, esp in World War I, when it was completely destroyed. Pop.: 21 400 (1991 est.). Flemish name: **Ieper.**

Yquem (iː'kɛm) NOUN a French vineyard of the Sauternes area of Bordeaux that produces a sweet white table wine. Also called: **Château d'Yquem.**

yr ABBREVIATION FOR: [1] (*plural* **yrs**) year. [2] younger. [3] your.

yrs ABBREVIATION FOR: [1] years. [2] yours.

Yser (*French* izɛr) NOUN a river in NW central Europe, rising in N France and flowing through SW Belgium to the North Sea: scene of battles in World War I. Length: 77 km (48 miles).

Yseult (ɪ'suːlt) NOUN a variant spelling of **Iseult.**

Yssel ('aɪsᵊl) NOUN a variant spelling of **IJssel.**

yt THE INTERNET DOMAIN NAME FOR Mayotte.

Yt THE FORMER CHEMICAL SYMBOL FOR yttrium (now **Y**).

YT *(esp in postal addresses)* ABBREVIATION FOR Yukon Territory.

YTS (in Britain) ABBREVIATION FOR (the former) **Youth Training Scheme.**

ytterbia (ɪ'tɜːbɪə) NOUN another name for **ytterbium oxide.**
▷HISTORY C19: New Latin, named after *Ytterby,* Swedish quarry where it was discovered

ytterbite (ɪ'tɜːbaɪt) NOUN another name for **gadolinite.**

ytterbium (ɪ'tɜːbɪəm) NOUN a soft malleable silvery element of the lanthanide series of metals that occurs in monazite and is used to improve the mechanical properties of steel. Symbol: Yb; atomic no.: 70; atomic wt.: 173.04; valency: 2 or 3; relative density: 6.903 (alpha), 6.966 (beta); melting pt.: 819°C; boiling pt.: 1196°C.
▷HISTORY C19: New Latin; see YTTERBIA

ytterbium oxide NOUN a colourless weakly basic hygroscopic substance used in certain alloys and ceramics. Formula: Yb_2O_3. Also called: **ytterbia.**

yttria ('ɪtrɪə) NOUN another name for **yttrium oxide.**
▷HISTORY C19: New Latin, named after *Ytterby;* see YTTERBIA

yttriferous (ɪ'trɪfərəs) ADJECTIVE containing or yielding yttrium.

yttrium ('ɪtrɪəm) NOUN a silvery metallic element occurring in monazite and gadolinite and used in various alloys, in lasers, and as a catalyst. Symbol: Y; atomic no.: 39; atomic wt.: 88.90585; valency: 3; relative density: 4.469; melting pt.: 1522°C; boiling pt.: 3338°C.
▷HISTORY C19: New Latin; see YTTERBIA
▸**'yttric** ADJECTIVE

yttrium metal NOUN *Chem* any one of a group of elements including yttrium and the related lanthanides, holmium, erbium, thulium, ytterbium, and lutecium.

yttrium oxide NOUN a colourless or white insoluble solid used mainly in incandescent mantles. Formula: Y_2O_3. Also called: **yttria.**

yu THE INTERNET DOMAIN NAME FOR Yugoslavia.

YU INTERNATIONAL CAR REGISTRATION FOR Serbia and Montenegro.
▷HISTORY from *Yugoslavia*

yuan ('juː'æn) NOUN, *plural* **-an.** the standard monetary unit of China, divided into 10 jiao and 100 fen. Also called: **renminbi, renminbi yuan.**
▷HISTORY from Chinese *yüan* round object; see YEN[1]

Yüan[1] ('juː'æn) ADJECTIVE of or relating to the Chinese porcelain produced during the Yüan imperial dynasty (1279–1368), characterized by the appearance of under-glaze blue-and-white ware.

Yüan[2] ('juː'æn) *or* **Yüen** ('juː'ɛn) NOUN a river in SE central China, rising in central Guizhou province and flowing northeast to Lake Tungting. Length: about 800 km (500 miles).

Yuan Tan ('juː'æn 'tæn) NOUN an annual Chinese festival marking the Chinese New Year. It can last over three days and includes the exchange of gifts, firework displays, and dancing.

Yucatán (ˌjuːkə'tɑːn; *Spanish* juka'tan) NOUN [1] a state of SE Mexico, occupying the N part of the Yucatán peninsula. Capital: Mérida. Pop.: 1 655 707 (2000). Area: 39 340 sq. km (15 186 sq. miles). [2] a peninsula of Central America between the Gulf of Mexico and the Caribbean, including the Mexican states of Campeche, Yucatán, and Quintana Roo, and part of Belize: a centre of Mayan civilization from about 100 B.C. to the 18th century. Area: about 181 300 sq. km (70 000 sq. miles).

Yucatán Channel NOUN a channel between W Cuba and the Yucatán peninsula.

yucca ('jʌkə) NOUN any of several plants of the genus *Yucca,* of tropical and subtropical America, having stiff lancelike leaves and spikes of white flowers: family *Agaraceae.* See also **Adam's-needle, Spanish bayonet.**
▷HISTORY C16: from American Spanish *yuca,* ultimately from an American Indian word

yuck *or* **yuk** (jʌk) INTERJECTION *Slang* an exclamation indicating contempt, dislike, or disgust.

yucko ('jʌkəʊ) *Austral slang* ◆ ADJECTIVE [1] disgusting; unpleasant. ◆ INTERJECTION [2] an exclamation of disgust.

yucky *or* **yukky** ('jʌkɪ) ADJECTIVE **yuckier, yuckiest** *or* **yukkier, yukkiest.** *Slang* disgusting; sickening; nasty.

Yuga ('jʊgə) NOUN (in Hindu cosmology) one of the four ages of mankind, together lasting over 4 million years and marked by a progressive decline in the vitality and morals of men.
▷HISTORY C18: from Sanskrit: yoke, race of men, era; see YOKE

yugarie ('juːgərɪ) NOUN a variant spelling of **eugarie.**

Yugo. ABBREVIATION FOR (the former) Yugoslavia.

Yugoslav *or* **Jugoslav** ('juːgəʊˌslɑːv) NOUN [1] (formerly) a native, inhabitant, or citizen of Yugoslavia (sense 1 or 2). [2] (not in technical use) another name for **Serbo-Croat** (the language). ◆ ADJECTIVE [3] (formerly) of, relating to, or characteristic of Yugoslavia (sense 1 or 2) or its people.

Yugoslavia *or* **Jugoslavia** (ˌjuːgəʊ'slɑːvɪə) NOUN [1] **Federal Republic of Yugoslavia.** a former country of SE Europe, comprising Serbia and Montenegro, that was formed in 1991 but not internationally recognized until 2000; it was replaced by the Union of Serbia and Montenegro in 2003. [2] a former country in SE Europe, on the Adriatic: established in 1918 from the independent states of Serbia and Montenegro, and regions that until World War I had belonged to Austria-Hungary (Croatia, Slovenia, and Bosnia-Herzegovina); the name was changed from Kingdom of Serbs, Croats, and Slovenes to Yugoslavia in 1929; German invasion of 1941–44 was resisted chiefly by a Communist group led by Tito, who declared a people's republic in 1945; it became the Socialist Federal Republic of Yugoslavia in 1963; in 1991 Slovenia, Croatia, and Bosnia-Herzegovina declared independence, followed by Macedonia in 1992; Serbia and Montenegro formed the Federal Republic of Yugoslavia, subsequently (2003) replaced by the Union of Serbia and Montenegro.

Yugoslavian *or* **Jugoslavian** (ˌjuːgəʊ'slɑːvɪən) ADJECTIVE [1] of or relating to Yugoslavia or its inhabitants. ◆ NOUN [2] a native or inhabitant of Yugoslavia.

Yukon ('juːkɒn) NOUN **the.** a territory of NW Canada, on the Beaufort Sea, between the Northwest Territories and Alaska: arctic and mountainous, reaching 6050 m (19 850 ft.) at Mount Logan, Canada's highest peak; mineral resources. Capital: Whitehorse. Pop.: 29 900 (2001 est.). Area: 536 327 sq. km (207 076 sq. miles). Abbreviation: **YT.**

Yukoner ('juːkɒnə) NOUN a native or inhabitant of the Yukon.

Yukon River NOUN a river in NW North America, rising in NW Canada on the border between the Yukon Territory and British Columbia: flows northwest into Alaska, US, and then southwest to the Bering Sea; navigable for about 2850 km (1775 miles) to Whitehorse. Length: 3185 km (1979 miles).

yulan ('juːlæn) NOUN a Chinese magnolia, *Magnolia denudata,* that is often cultivated for its showy white flowers.
▷HISTORY C19: from Chinese *yu* a gem + *lan* plant

yule (juːl) NOUN *(sometimes capital) Literary, archaic, or dialect* **a** Christmas, the Christmas season, or Christmas festivities. **b** *(in combination)*: *yuletide.*
▷HISTORY Old English *geōla,* originally a name of a pagan feast lasting 12 days; related to Old Norse *jōl,* Swedish *jul,* Gothic *jiuleis*

yule log NOUN a large log of wood traditionally used as the foundation of a fire in the hearth at Christmas.

Yuman ('juːmən) NOUN [1] a family of North American Indian languages spoken chiefly in Arizona, California, and Mexico. ◆ ADJECTIVE [2] relating to or belonging to this family of languages.

yummo ('jʌməʊ) *Austral slang* ◆ ADJECTIVE [1] tasty; delicious. ◆ INTERJECTION [2] an exclamation of delight or approval.

yummy ('jʌmɪ) *Slang* ◆ INTERJECTION [1] Also: **yum-yum.** an exclamation indicating pleasure or delight, as in anticipation of delicious food. ◆ ADJECTIVE **-mier, -miest.** [2] delicious, delightful, or attractive.
▷HISTORY C20: from *yum-yum,* of imitative origin

yummy mummy NOUN *Slang* an attractive woman who has had children.

Yünnan (juː'næn) NOUN a province of SW China: consists mainly of a plateau broken in the southeast by the Red and Black Rivers, with mountains in the west, rising over 5500 m (18 000 ft.); large deposits of tin, lead, zinc, and coal. Capital: Kunming. Pop.: 42 880 000 (2000 est.). Area: 436 200 sq. km (168 400 sq. miles).

yup (jʌp) SENTENCE SUBSTITUTE an informal word for **yes.**

Yupik ('juːpɪk) NOUN a western Eskimo, of Alaska or Asia. Compare **Inuit.**

yuppie *or* **yuppy** ('jʌpɪ) *(sometimes capital)* NOUN [1] an affluent young professional person. ◆ ADJECTIVE [2] typical of or reflecting the values characteristic of yuppies.
▷HISTORY C20: from *y(oung) u(rban)* or *up(wardly mobile) p(rofessional)* + -IE
▸**'yuppiedom** NOUN

yuppie disease *or* **flu** NOUN *Informal, sometimes considered offensive* any of a number of debilitating long-lasting viral disorders associated with stress, such as chronic fatigue syndrome, whose symptoms include muscle weakness, chronic tiredness, and depression.

yuppify ('jʌpɪˌfaɪ) VERB **-fies, -fying, -fied.** *(tr)* to make yuppie in nature.
▸**ˌyuppifi'cation** NOUN

Yurev *(Russian* 'jurjɪf) NOUN the former name (11th century until 1918) of **Tartu.**

yurt (jʊət) NOUN a circular tent consisting of a framework of poles covered with felt or skins, used by Mongolian and Turkic nomads of E and central Asia.
▷HISTORY from Russian *yurta,* of Turkic origin; compare Turkish *yurt* abode, home

Yuzovka *(Russian* 'juzəfkə) NOUN a former name (1872 until after the Revolution) of **Donetsk.**

YV INTERNATIONAL CAR REGISTRATION FOR Venezuela.

Yvelines *(French* ivlin) NOUN a department of N France, in Île de France region. Capital: Versailles. Pop.: 1 354 304 (1999). Area: 2271 sq. km (886 sq. miles).

YWCA ABBREVIATION FOR Young Women's Christian Association.

YWHA ABBREVIATION FOR Young Women's Hebrew Association.

ywis (ɪ'wɪs) ADVERB a variant spelling of **iwis.**

Zz

z *or* **Z** (zɛd; *US* zi:) NOUN, *plural* **z's, Z's** *or* **Zs.** [1] the 26th and last letter and the 20th consonant of the modern English alphabet. [2] a speech sound represented by this letter, in English usually a voiced alveolar fricative, as in *zip.* [3] **a** something shaped like a Z. **b** (*in combination*): *a Z-bend in a road.*

z *Maths* SYMBOL FOR: [1] the *z*-axis or a coordinate measured along the *z*-axis in a Cartesian or cylindrical coordinate system. [2] an algebraic variable.

Z SYMBOL FOR: [1] any unknown, variable, or unspecified factor, number, person, or thing. [2] *Chem* atomic number. [3] *Physics* impedance. [4] zone. [5] *Currency* zaïre. ◆ [6] INTERNATIONAL CAR REGISTRATION FOR Zambia.

za THE INTERNET DOMAIN NAME FOR South Africa.

ZA INTERNATIONAL CAR REGISTRATION FOR South Africa.
▷**HISTORY** from Afrikaans *Zuid Afrika*

Zaandam (*Dutch* za:n'dɑm) NOUN a former town in the W Netherlands, in North Holland: an important shipbuilding centre in the 17th century. It became part of Zaanstad in 1974.

Zaanstad (*Dutch* za:n'ʃtat) NOUN a port in the W Netherlands, in North Holland: formed (1974) from Zaandam, Koog a/d Zaan, Zaandijk, Wormerveer, Krommenie, Westzaan, and Assendelft; food and machinery industries. Pop.: 135 126 (1999 est.).

zabaglione (ˌzæbə'ljəʊnɪ) NOUN a light foamy dessert made of egg yolks, sugar, and marsala, whipped together and served warm in a glass.
▷**HISTORY** Italian; probably related to Late Latin *sabaia* Illyrian drink made from grain

Zabrze (*Polish* 'zabʒɛ) NOUN a city in SW Poland: a Prussian and German town from 1742 until 1945, when it passed to Poland; industrial centre in a coal-mining region. Pop.: 200 177 (1999 est.). German name: **Hindenburg.**

Zacatecas (*Spanish* θaka'tekas) NOUN [1] a state of N central Mexico, on the central plateau: rich mineral resources. Capital: Zacatecas. Pop.: 1 351 207 (2000). Area: 75 040 sq. km (28 973 sq. miles). [2] a city in N central Mexico, capital of Zacatecas state: silver mines Pop.: 113 780 (2000 est.).

Zacharias (ˌzækə'raɪəs), **Zachariah** (ˌzækə'raɪə), *or* **Zachary** ('zækərɪ) NOUN *New Testament* John the Baptist's father, who underwent a temporary period of dumbness for his lack of faith (Luke 1).

Zacynthus (zə'sɪnθəs, -'kɪn-) NOUN the Latin name for **Zante.**

zaffer *or* **zaffre** ('zæfə) NOUN impure cobalt oxide, used to impart a blue colour to enamels.
▷**HISTORY** C17: from Italian *zaffera;* perhaps related to Latin *sapphīrus* SAPPHIRE

Zagazig ('zægəˌzɪg) *or* **Zaqaziq** NOUN a city in NE Egypt, in the Nile Delta: major cotton market. Pop.: 267 351 (1996).

Zagreb ('zɑ:grɛb) NOUN the capital of Croatia, on the River Sava; gothic cathedral; university (1874); industrial centre. Pop.: 682 598 (2001). German name: **Agram.**

Zagreus ('zægrɪəs) NOUN *Greek myth* a young god whose cult came from Crete to Greece, where he was identified with Dionysus. The son of Zeus by either Demeter or Persephone, he was killed by the Titans at the behest of Hera.

Zagros Mountains ('zægrɒs) PLURAL NOUN a mountain range in S Iran: has Iran's main oilfields in its W central foothills. Highest peak: Zard Kuh, 4548 m (14 920 ft.).

zaibatsu ('zaɪbæt'su:) NOUN (*functioning as singular or plural*) the group or combine comprising a few wealthy families that controls industry, business, and finance in Japan.
▷**HISTORY** from Japanese, from *zai* wealth, from Chinese *ts'ai* + *batsu* family, person of influence, from Chinese *fa*

Zaïre (zɑ:'ɪə) NOUN [1] the former name (1971–97) of the (**Democratic Republic of**) **Congo** (sense 2). [2] (formerly) the Zaïrian name (1971–97) for the (River) **Congo.**

Zaïrian *or* **Zaïrean** (zɑ:'ɪərɪən) ADJECTIVE [1] of or relating to the former Zaïre (now the Democratic Republic of the Congo) or its inhabitants ◆ NOUN [2] a native or inhabitant of Zaïre

zakat ('zakat) NOUN *Islam* an annual tax on Muslims to aid the poor in the Muslim community.
▷**HISTORY** from Arabic *zakāt* alms

Zákinthos ('zakinˌθɔs) NOUN transliteration of the Modern Greek name for **Zante.**

zakuski *or* **zakouski** (zæ'kuskɪ) PLURAL NOUN, *singular* **-ka** (-kə). *Russian cookery* hors d'oeuvres, consisting of tiny open sandwiches spread with caviar, smoked sausage, etc., or a cold dish such as radishes in sour cream, all usually served with vodka.
▷**HISTORY** Russian, from *zakusit'* to have a snack

Zama ('zɑ:mə) NOUN the name of several ancient cities in N Africa, including the one near the site of Scipio's decisive defeat of Hannibal (202 B.C.).

Zambezi *or* **Zambese** (zæm'bi:zɪ) NOUN a river in S central and E Africa, rising in NW Zambia and flowing across E Angola back into Zambia, continuing south to the Caprivi Strip of Namibia, then east forming the Zambia–Zimbabwe border, and finally crossing Mozambique to the Indian Ocean: the fourth longest river in Africa. Length: 2740 km (1700 miles).

Zambezian (zæm'bi:zɪən) ADJECTIVE of or relating to the Zambezi River.

Zambia ('zæmbɪə) NOUN a republic in southern Africa: an early site of human settlement; controlled by the British South Africa Company by 1900 and unified as Northern Rhodesia in 1911; made a British protectorate in 1924; part of the Federation of Rhodesia and Nyasaland (1953–63), gaining independence as a member of the Commonwealth in 1964; important mineral exports, esp copper. Official language: English. Religion: Christian majority, animist minority. Currency: kwacha. Capital: Lusaka. Pop.: 9 770 000 (2001 est.). Area: 752 617 sq. km (290 587 sq. miles). Former name (until 1964): **Northern Rhodesia.**

Zambian ('zæmbɪən) ADJECTIVE [1] of or relating to Zambia or its inhabitants. ◆ NOUN [2] a native or inhabitant of Zambia.

Zamboanga (ˌzæmbəʊ'æŋgə) NOUN a port in the Philippines, on SW Mindanao on Basilan Strait: founded by the Spanish in 1635; tourist centre, with fisheries. Pop.: 135 000 (2000).

zambuck ('zæmbʌk) NOUN *Austral and NZ informal* a St John ambulance attendant, esp at a sports meeting.
▷**HISTORY** C20: from *Zam-Buck,* the trade name of an ointment which comes in a black-and-white container, black and white being the colours of the St John uniform

zamia ('zeɪmɪə) NOUN any cycadaceous plant of the genus *Zamia,* of tropical and subtropical America, having a short thick trunk, palmlike leaves, and short stout cones.
▷**HISTORY** C19: from New Latin, from Latin *zamiae,* erroneous reading of phrase *nucēs azāniae* pine cones, probably from Greek *azainein* to dry up

zamindar *or* **zemindar** (zəmi:n'dɑ:) NOUN (in India) the owner of an agricultural estate.
▷**HISTORY** via Hindi from Persian: landholder, from *zamīn* land + *-dār* holder

zamindari *or* **zemindari** (zəmi:n'dɑ:rɪ) NOUN, *plural* **-is.** (in India) a large agricultural estate.

Zamora (*Spanish* θa'mora) NOUN a city in NW central Spain, on the Douro River. Pop.: 58 560 (latest est.).

ZAMS ABBREVIATION FOR *Astronomy* zero age main sequence.

zamzawed ('zamˌzɒd) ADJECTIVE *Southwest English dialect* (of tea) having been left in the pot to stew.

zander ('zændə) NOUN, *plural* **zander** *or* **zanders.** a freshwater teleost pikeperch of Europe, *Stizostedion lucioperca,* valued as a food fish.

Zante ('zæntɪ) NOUN an island in the Ionian Sea, off the W coast of Greece: southernmost of the Ionian Islands; traditionally belonged to Ulysses, king of Ithaca. Pop.: 32 557 (1991). Area: 402 sq. km (155 sq. miles). Latin name: **Zacynthus.** Ancient Greek name: **Zakynthos** (zə'ku:nθɒs). Modern Greek name: **Zákinthos.**

zanthoxylum (zæn'θɒksɪləm) NOUN any rutaceous shrub or tree of the genus *Zanthoxylum,* of temperate and subtropical E Asia and North America: includes the prickly ash and the West Indian yellowwood (or satinwood).
▷**HISTORY** C19 *zantho-* variant of XANTHO- + Greek *xulon* wood

Zanu(PF) (ˌzænu: (ˌpi:'ɛf)) NOUN ACRONYM FOR Zimbabwe African National Union (Patriotic Front).

zany ('zeɪnɪ) ADJECTIVE **-nier, -niest.** [1] comical in an endearing way; imaginatively funny or comical, esp in behaviour. ◆ NOUN, *plural* **-nies.** [2] a clown or buffoon, esp one in old comedies who imitated other performers with ludicrous effect. [3] a ludicrous or foolish person.
▷**HISTORY** C16: from Italian *zanni,* from dialect (Venice and Lombardy) *Zanni,* nickname for *Giovanni* John; one of the traditional names for a clown
▶ **'zanily** ADVERB ▶ **'zaniness** NOUN ▶ **'zanyism** NOUN

Zanzibar (ˌzænzɪ'bɑ:) NOUN an island in the Indian Ocean, off the E coast of Africa: settled by Persians and Arabs from the 7th century onwards; became a flourishing trading centre for slaves, ivory, and cloves; made a British protectorate in 1890, becoming independent within the Commonwealth in 1963 and a republic in 1964; joined with Tanganyika in 1964 to form the United Republic of Tanzania. Pop.: 456 934 (1995 est.).

Zanzibari (ˌzænzɪ'bɑ:rɪ) ADJECTIVE [1] of or relating to Zanzibar or its inhabitants. ◆ NOUN [2] a native or inhabitant of Zanzibar.

zap (zæp) *Slang* ◆ VERB **zaps, zapping, zapped.** [1] (*tr*) to attack, kill, or destroy, as with a sudden bombardment. [2] (*intr*) to move quickly; rush. [3] (*tr*) *Computing* **a** to clear from the screen. **b** to erase. [4] (*intr*) *Television* to change channels rapidly by remote control. ◆ NOUN [5] energy, vigour, or pep. ◆ INTERJECTION [6] an exclamation used to express sudden or swift action.
▷**HISTORY** of imitative origin

zapateado *Spanish* (θapate'aðo) NOUN, *plural* **-dos** (-ðos). a Spanish dance with stamping and very fast footwork.
▷**HISTORY** from *zapatear* to tap with the shoe, from *zapato* shoe

Zaporozhye (*Russian* zəpa'rɔʒjɛ) NOUN a city in the E Ukraine on the Dnieper River: developed as a major industrial centre after the construction (1932) of the Dnieper hydroelectric station. Pop.: 863 100 (1998 est.). Former name (until 1921): **Aleksandrovsk.**

Zapotec ('zɑ:pəˌtɛk) NOUN [1] (*plural* **-tecs** *or* **-tec**) Also called: **Zapotecan** (ˌzæpəʊ'tɛkən, ˌzɑ:-). any member of a large tribe of central American Indians inhabiting S Mexico, esp the Mexican state of Oaxaca. [2] the group of languages spoken by this people. [3] Also: **Zapotecan.** of or relating to this people or their language.
▷**HISTORY** from Spanish *Zapoteca,* from Nahuatl *Tzapoteca,* literally: people of the land of the sapodillas, from *tzapotl* sapodilla

zappy ('zæpɪ) ADJECTIVE **zappier, zappiest.** *Slang* full of energy; snappy; zippy.

ZAPU ('zæpu:) NOUN ACRONYM FOR Zimbabwe African People's Union.

Zaqaziq ('zækəˌzɪk) NOUN a variant of **Zagazig.**

Zaragoza (*Spanish* θara'ɣoθa) NOUN a city in NE Spain, on the River Ebro: Roman colony established 25 B.C.; under Moorish rule (714–1118); capital of Aragon (12th–15th centuries); twice besieged by the French during the Peninsular War and captured (1809); university (1474). Pop.: 603 367 (1998 est.). Pre-Roman name: **Salduba.** Latin name: **Caesaraugusta.** English name: **Saragossa.**

zaratite ('zærəˌtaɪt) NOUN a green amorphous mineral consisting of hydrated nickel carbonate Formula: $Ni_3(CO_3)(OH)_4.4H_2O$.
▷HISTORY C19: from Spanish *zaratita,* named after G. *Zárate,* 19th-century Spaniard

zareba *or* **zareeba** (zə'ri:bə) NOUN (in northern E Africa, esp formerly) [1] a stockade or enclosure of thorn bushes around a village or campsite. [2] the area so protected or enclosed.
▷HISTORY C19: from Arabic *zarībah* cattlepen, from *zarb* sheepfold

zarf (zɑ:f) NOUN (esp in the Middle East) a holder, usually ornamental, for a hot coffee cup.
▷HISTORY from Arabic: container, sheath

Zaria ('zɑ:rɪə) NOUN a city in N central Nigeria: former capital of a Hausa state; agricultural trading centre; university (1962). Pop.: 379 200 (1997 est.).

Zarqa ('zɑ:kə) NOUN the second largest town in Jordan, northeast of Amman. Pop.: 344 524 (1994).

zarzuela (zɑ:'zweɪlə) NOUN [1] a type of Spanish vaudeville or operetta, usually satirical in nature. [2] a seafood stew.
▷HISTORY from Spanish, from *La Zarzuela,* name of the palace near Madrid where such vaudeville was first performed (1629)

zastruga (zə'stru:gə, zæ-) NOUN a variant spelling of **sastruga.**

zax (zæks) NOUN a variant of **sax**[1].

***z*-axis** NOUN a reference axis of a three-dimensional Cartesian coordinate system along which the *z*-coordinate is measured.

zayin ('zɑ:jɪn) NOUN the seventh letter of the Hebrew alphabet (ז), transliterated as *z.*
▷HISTORY from Hebrew, literally: weapon

zazen (zʌzɛn) NOUN (in Zen Buddhism) deep meditation undertaken whilst sitting upright with legs crossed.

ZB ABBREVIATION FOR zero balancing.

Z boson NOUN *Physics* another name for **Z particle.**

ZB station NOUN (in New Zealand) a radio station of a commercial network.

ZCC (in South Africa) ABBREVIATION FOR Zion Christian Church.

Z chart NOUN *Statistics* a chart often used in industry and constructed by plotting on it three series: monthly, weekly, or daily data, the moving annual total, and the cumulative total dating from the beginning of the current year.

Zea ('tsɛ:a) NOUN the Italian name for **Keos.**

zeal (zi:l) NOUN fervent or enthusiastic devotion, often extreme or fanatical in nature, as to a religious movement, political cause, ideal, or aspiration.
▷HISTORY C14: from Late Latin *zēlus,* from Greek *zēlos*

Zealand ('zi:lənd) NOUN the largest island of Denmark, separated from the island of Fyn by the Great Belt and from S Sweden by the Sound (both now spanned by road bridges). Chief town: Copenhagen. Pop.: 2 000 254 (1988 est.). Area: 7016 sq. km (2709 sq. miles). Danish name: **Sjælland.** German name: **Seeland.**

zealot ('zɛlət) NOUN an immoderate, fanatical, or extremely zealous adherent to a cause, esp a religious one.
▷HISTORY C16: from Late Latin *zēlōtēs,* from Greek, from *zēloun* to be zealous, from *zēlos* ZEAL

Zealot ('zɛlət) NOUN any of the members of an extreme Jewish sect or political party that resisted all aspects of Roman rule in Palestine in the 1st century A.D.

zealotry ('zɛlətrɪ) NOUN extreme or excessive zeal or devotion.

zealous ('zɛləs) ADJECTIVE filled with or inspired by intense enthusiasm or zeal; ardent; fervent.
▸**'zealously** ADVERB ▸**'zealousness** NOUN

zebec *or* **zebeck** ('zi:bɛk) NOUN variant spellings of **xebec.**

Zebedee ('zɛbɪˌdi:) NOUN *New Testament* the father of the apostles James and John (Matthew 4:21).

zebra ('zi:brə, 'zɛbrə) NOUN, *plural* **-ras** *or* **-ra.** any of several mammals of the horse family (*Equidae*), such as *Equus burchelli* (the **common zebra**), of southern and eastern Africa, having distinctive black-and-white striped hides.
▷HISTORY C16: via Italian from Old Spanish: wild ass, probably from Vulgar Latin *eciferus* (unattested) wild horse, from Latin *equiferus,* from *equus* horse + *ferus* wild
▸**'zebra-ˌlike** *or* **zebraic** (zɪ'breɪɪk) ADJECTIVE ▸**zebrine** ('zi:braɪn, 'zɛb-) *or* **'zebroid** ADJECTIVE

Zebra ('zi:brə, 'zɛbrə) NOUN *Finance* a noninterest-paying bond in which the accrued income is taxed annually rather than on redemption. Compare **zero** (sense 12).
▷HISTORY C20: from *zero-coupon bond*

zebra crossing NOUN *Brit* a pedestrian crossing marked on a road by broad alternate black and white stripes. Once on the crossing the pedestrian has right of way.

zebra finch NOUN any of various Australasian songbirds with zebra-like markings, such as the grassfinch *Poephila castanotis.*

zebra plant NOUN See **calathea.**

zebrawood ('zɛbrəˌwʊd, 'zi:-) NOUN [1] a tree, *Connarus guianensis,* of tropical America, Asia, and Africa, yielding striped hardwood used in cabinetwork: family *Connaraceae.* [2] any of various other trees or shrubs having striped wood. [3] the wood of any of these trees.

zebu ('zi:bu:) NOUN a domesticated ox, *Bos indicus,* having a humped back, long horns, and a large dewlap: used in India and E Asia as a draught animal.
▷HISTORY C18: from French *zébu,* perhaps of Tibetan origin

Zebulun ('zɛbjʊlən, zə'bju:-) NOUN *Old Testament* [1] the sixth son whom Leah bore to Jacob: one of the 12 patriarchs of Israel (Genesis 30:20). [2] the tribe descended from him. [3] the territory of this tribe, lying in lower Galilee to the north of Mount Carmel and to the east of the coastal plain. Douay spelling: **Zabulon** ('zæbjʊlən, zə'bju:-).

zecchino (zɛ'ki:nəʊ) NOUN, *plural* **-ni** (-nɪ). another word for **sequin** (the coin).
▷HISTORY C18: from Italian; see SEQUIN

Zech. *Bible* ABBREVIATION FOR Zechariah.

Zechariah (ˌzɛkə'raɪə) NOUN [1] *Old Testament* **a** a Hebrew prophet of the late 6th century B.C. **b** the book containing his oracles, which are chiefly concerned with the renewal of Israel after the exile as a national, religious, and messianic community with the restored Temple and rebuilt Jerusalem as its centre. Douay spelling: **Zacharias.** [2] a variant spelling of **Zachariah.** See **Zacharias.**

zed (zɛd) NOUN the Brit. spoken form of the letter *z.* US word: **zee.**
▷HISTORY C15: from Old French *zede,* via Late Latin from Greek *zēta*

Zedekiah (ˌzɛdə'kaɪə) NOUN *Old Testament* the last king of Judah, who died in captivity at Babylon. Douay spelling: **Sedecias** (ˌsɛdə'kaɪəs).

zedoary ('zɛdəʊərɪ) NOUN the dried rhizome of the tropical Asian plant *Curcuma zedoaria,* used as a stimulant and a condiment: family *Zingiberaceae.*
▷HISTORY C15: from Medieval Latin *zedoaria,* from Arabic *zadwār,* of Persian origin

zeds *or* **Zs** ('zɛdz) PLURAL NOUN *Informal* [1] sleep. [2] **catch a few zeds.** to have a nap.

zee (zi:) NOUN the US word for **zed** (letter *z*).

Zeebrugge (*Flemish* 'ze:bryxə; *English* 'zi:ˌbrʊgə) NOUN a port in NW Belgium, in W Flanders on the North Sea: linked by canal with Bruges; German submarine base in World War I.

Zeeland (*Dutch* 'ze:lɑnt; *English* 'zi:lənd) NOUN a province of the SW Netherlands: consists of a small area on the mainland together with a number of islands in the Scheldt estuary; mostly below sea level. Capital: Middelburg. Pop.: 371 900 (2000 est.). Area: 1787 sq. km (690 sq. miles).

Zeelander ('zi:ləndə) NOUN a native or inhabitant of the Dutch province of Zeeland.

Zeeman effect ('zi:mən) NOUN the splitting of a spectral line of a substance into several closely spaced lines when the substance is placed in a magnetic field.
▷HISTORY C20: named after Pieter *Zeeman* (1865–1943), Dutch physicist

zein ('zi:ɪn) NOUN a protein of the prolamine group occurring in maize and used in the manufacture of plastics, paper coatings, adhesives, etc.
▷HISTORY C19: from New Latin *zēa* maize, from Latin: a kind of grain, from Greek *zeia* barley

Zeist (zaɪst; *Dutch* zɛjst) NOUN a city in the central Netherlands, near Utrecht. Pop.: 59 258 (1994).

Zeitgeist *German* ('tsaitgaist) NOUN the spirit, attitude, or general outlook of a specific time or period, esp as it is reflected in literature, philosophy, etc.
▷HISTORY German, literally: time spirit; see TIDE[1], GHOST

zemindar (zəmi:n'dɑ:) NOUN a variant spelling of **zamindar.**
▸**zemin'dari** NOUN

zemstvo ('zɛmstvəʊ; *Russian* 'zjɛmstvə) NOUN, *plural* **-stvos.** (in tsarist Russia) an elective provincial or district council established in most provinces of Russia by Alexander II in 1864 as part of his reform policy.
▷HISTORY C19: from Russian, from *zemlya* land; related to Latin *humus* earth, Greek *khamai* on the ground

Zen (zɛn) *Buddhism* NOUN [1] a Japanese school, of 12th-century Chinese origin, teaching that contemplation of one's essential nature to the exclusion of all else is the only way of achieving pure enlightenment. [2] (*modifier*) of or relating to this school: *Zen Buddhism.*
▷HISTORY from Japanese, from Chinese *ch'an* religious meditation, from Pali *jhāna,* from Sanskrit *dhyāna*
▸**'Zenic** ADJECTIVE ▸**'Zenist** NOUN

zenana (zɛ'nɑ:nə) NOUN (in the East, esp in Muslim and Hindu homes) part of a house reserved for the women and girls of a household.
▷HISTORY C18: from Hindi *zanāna,* from Persian, from *zan* woman

Zend (zɛnd) NOUN [1] a former name for **Avestan.** [2] short for **Zend-Avesta.** [3] an exposition of the Avesta in the Middle Persian language (Pahlavi).
▷HISTORY C18: from Persian *zand* commentary, exposition; used specifically of the Middle Persian commentary on the Avesta, hence of the language of the Avesta itself
▸**'Zendic** ADJECTIVE

Zend-Avesta (ˌzɛndə'vɛstə) NOUN the Avesta together with the traditional interpretative commentary known as the Zend, esp as preserved in the Avestan language among the Parsees.
▷HISTORY from Avestan, representing *Avesta'-va-zend* Avesta with interpretation
▸**Zend-Avestaic** (ˌzɛndəvɛs'teɪɪk) ADJECTIVE

Zener diode ('zi:nə) NOUN a semiconductor diode that exhibits a sharp increase in reverse current at a well-defined reverse voltage: used as a voltage regulator.
▷HISTORY C20: named after C. M. *Zener* (1905–93), US physicist

zenith ('zɛnɪθ; *US* 'zi:nɪθ) NOUN [1] *Astronomy* the point on the celestial sphere vertically above an observer. [2] the highest point; peak; acme: *the zenith of someone's achievements.* ◆ Compare **nadir.**
▷HISTORY C17: from French *cenith,* from Medieval Latin, from Old Spanish *zenit,* based on Arabic *samt,* as in *samt arrās* path over one's head, from *samt* way, path + *al* the + *rās* head
▸**'zenithal** ADJECTIVE

zenithal projection NOUN a type of map projection in which part of the earth's surface is projected onto a plane tangential to it, either at one of the poles (**polar zenithal**), at the equator (**equatorial zenithal**), or between (**oblique zenithal**).

zenith telescope NOUN an instrument used to determine the latitude of stars, similar to the meridian circle but fitted with an extremely sensitive level and a declination micrometer.

zeolite ('zi:əˌlaɪt) NOUN [1] any of a large group of glassy secondary minerals consisting of hydrated aluminium silicates of calcium, sodium, or potassium: formed in cavities in lava flows and plutonic rocks. [2] any of a class of similar synthetic

materials used in ion exchange and as selective absorbents. See **molecular sieve**.
▷**HISTORY** C18 *zeo-*, from Greek *zein* to boil + -LITE; from the swelling up that occurs under the blowpipe
▸**zeolitic** (ˌziːəˈlɪtɪk) ADJECTIVE

Zeph. *Bible* ABBREVIATION FOR Zephaniah.

Zephaniah (ˌzɛfəˈnaɪə) NOUN *Old Testament* [1] a Hebrew prophet of the late 7th century B.C. [2] the book containing his oracles, which are chiefly concerned with the approaching judgment by God upon the sinners of Judah. Douay spelling: **Sophonias** (ˌsɒfəˈnaɪəs).

zephyr (ˈzɛfə) NOUN [1] a soft or gentle breeze. [2] any of several delicate soft yarns, fabrics, or garments, usually of wool.
▷**HISTORY** C16: from Latin *zephyrus*, from Greek *zephuros* the west wind; probably related to Greek *zophos* darkness, west

Zephyrus (ˈzɛfərəs) NOUN *Greek myth* the god of the west wind.

zeppelin (ˈzɛpəlɪn) NOUN (*sometimes capital*) a large cylindrical rigid airship built from 1900 to carry passengers, and used in World War I for bombing and reconnaissance.
▷**HISTORY** C20: named after Count Ferdinand von *Zeppelin* (1838–1917), German aeronautical pioneer, designer and manufacturer of airships

Zermatt (tserˈmat) NOUN a village and resort in S Switzerland, in Valais canton at the foot of the Matterhorn: cars are not allowed in the area. Pop.: 4200 (latest est.).

zero (ˈzɪərəʊ) NOUN, *plural* **-ros** *or* **-roes**. [1] the symbol 0, indicating an absence of quantity or magnitude; nought. Former name: **cipher**. [2] the integer denoted by the symbol 0; nought. [3] the cardinal number between +1 and –1. [4] nothing; nil. [5] a person or thing of no significance; nonentity. [6] the lowest point or degree: *his prospects were put at zero.* [7] the line or point on a scale of measurement from which the graduations commence. [8] **a** the temperature, pressure, etc., that registers a reading of zero on a scale. **b** the value of a variable, such as temperature, obtained under specified conditions. [9] a gunsight setting in which accurate allowance has been made for both windage and elevation for a specified range. [10] *Maths* **a** the cardinal number of a set with no members. **b** the identity element of addition. [11] *Linguistics* **a** an allomorph with no phonetic realization, as the plural marker of English *sheep*. **b** (*as modifier*): *a zero form.* [12] *Finance* Also called: **zero-coupon bond**. a bond that pays no interest, the equivalent being paid in its redemption value. Compare **Zebra**. ◆ ADJECTIVE [13] having no measurable quantity, magnitude, etc. [14] *Meteorol* **a** (of a cloud ceiling) limiting visibility to 15 metres (50 feet) or less. **b** (of horizontal visibility) limited to 50 metres (165 feet) or less. ◆ VERB **-roes, -roing, -roed**. [15] (*tr*) to adjust (an instrument, apparatus, etc.) so as to read zero or a position taken as zero. ◆ DETERMINER [16] *Informal, chiefly US* no (thing) at all: *this job has zero interest.*
▷**HISTORY** C17: from Italian, from Medieval Latin *zephirum*, from Arabic *sifr* empty, CIPHER

zero balancing NOUN a therapy involving the manipulation of the patient's skeletal structure in order to restore the balance of energy, relieve pain, and maintain well-being. Abbreviation: **ZB**.

zero defects PLURAL NOUN an aspect of total quality management that stresses the objective of error-free performance in providing goods or services.

zero-emission ADJECTIVE (of a motor vehicle) emitting no harmful pollutants.

zero gravity NOUN the state or condition of weightlessness.

zero grazing NOUN a type of dairy farming in which the cattle are fed with cut grass.

zero hour NOUN [1] *Military* the time set for the start of an attack or the initial stage of an operation. [2] *Informal* a critical time, esp at the commencement of an action.

zero in VERB (*adverb*) [1] (often foll by *on*) to bring (a weapon) to bear (on a target), as while firing repeatedly. [2] (*intr*; foll by *on*) *Informal* to bring one's attention to bear (on a problem, etc.). [3] (*intr*; foll by *on*) *Informal* to converge (upon): *the police zeroed in on the site of the crime.*

zero option NOUN (in international nuclear arms negotiations) an offer to remove all shorter-range nuclear missiles or, in the case of the **zero-zero option** all intermediate-range nuclear missiles, if the other side will do the same.

zero-rated ADJECTIVE (**zero rated** when postpositive) denoting goods on which the buyer pays no value-added tax although the seller can claim back any tax he has paid.

zero stage NOUN a solid-propellant rocket attached to a liquid-propellant rocket to provide greater thrust at liftoff.

zero-sum game NOUN (in game theory) a contest in which one person's loss is equal to the other person's gain.

zeroth (ˈzɪərəʊθ) ADJECTIVE denoting a term in a series that precedes the term otherwise regarded as the first term.
▷**HISTORY** C20: from ZERO + -TH[2]

zero tolerance NOUN **a** the policy of applying laws or penalties to even minor infringements of a code in order to reinforce its overall importance. **b** (*as modifier*): *a zero-tolerance policy on drugs.*

zest (zɛst) NOUN [1] invigorating or keen excitement or enjoyment: *a zest for living.* [2] added interest, flavour, or charm; piquancy: *her presence gave zest to the occasion.* [3] something added to give flavour or relish. [4] the peel or skin of an orange or lemon, used as flavouring in drinks, etc. ◆ VERB [5] (*tr*) to give flavour, interest, or piquancy to.
▷**HISTORY** C17: from French *zeste* peel of citrous fruits used as flavouring, of unknown origin
▸ˈ**zestful** ADJECTIVE ▸ˈ**zestfully** ADVERB ▸ˈ**zestfulness** NOUN ▸ˈ**zestless** ADJECTIVE ▸ˈ**zesty** ADJECTIVE

zester (ˈzɛstə) NOUN a kitchen utensil used to scrape fine shreds of peel from citrus fruits.

zeta (ˈziːtə) NOUN the sixth letter in the Greek alphabet (Z, ζ), a consonant, transliterated as *z*.
▷**HISTORY** from Greek, of Semitic origin; compare Hebrew *sādhē*

Zeta (ˈziːtə) NOUN (*foll by the genitive case of a specified constellation*) the sixth brightest star in a constellation: *Zeta Tauri.*

ZETA (ˈziːtə) NOUN a torus-shaped apparatus used for research in the 1950s and early 1960s on controlled thermonuclear reactions and plasma physics.
▷**HISTORY** C20: from *z*(*ero-*)*e*(*nergy*) *t*(*hermonuclear*) *a*(*pparatus*)

zetetic (zəˈtɛtɪk) ADJECTIVE proceeding by inquiry; investigating.
▷**HISTORY** C17: from New Latin, from Greek *zētētikos*, from *zēteō* to seek

Zetland (ˈzɛtlənd) NOUN the official name (until 1974) of **Shetland**.

zeugma (ˈzjuːgmə) NOUN a figure of speech in which a word is used to modify or govern two or more words although appropriate to only one of them or making a different sense with each, as in the sentence *Mr. Pickwick took his hat and his leave* (Charles Dickens).
▷**HISTORY** C16: via Latin from Greek: a yoking, from *zeugnunai* to yoke
▸**zeugmatic** (zjuːgˈmætɪk) ADJECTIVE ▸**zeugˈmatically** ADVERB

Zeus (zjuːs) NOUN the supreme god of the ancient Greeks, who became ruler of gods and men after he dethroned his father Cronus and defeated the Titans. He was the husband of his sister Hera and father by her and others of many gods, demigods, and mortals. He wielded thunderbolts and ruled the heavens, while his brothers Poseidon and Hades ruled the sea and underworld respectively. Roman counterpart: **Jupiter**.

Zhangjiakou (ˈdʒæŋˈdʒjækəʊ), **Changchiakow,** *or* **Changchiak'ou** NOUN a city in NE China, in NW Hebei province: a military centre, controlling the route to Mongolia, under the Ming and Manchu dynasties. Pop.: 660 504 (1999 est.). Former names: **Wanchüan, Kalgan**.

Zhangzhou (ˈdʒæŋˈdʒəʊ), **Changchow,** *or* **Ch'ang-chou** NOUN [1] a city in E China, in S Jiangsu province, on the Grand Canal: also known as **Wutsin** until 1949, when the 7th-century name was officially readopted. Pop.: 772 700 (1990 est.). [2] a city in SE China, in S Fujian province on the Saikoe River. Pop. 231 333 (1999 est.). Former name: **Lungki**.

Zhdanov (*Russian* ˈʒdanəf) NOUN the former name (1948–91) of **Mariupol**.

Zhejiang (ˈdʒɛˈdʒjæŋ) *or* **Chekiang** NOUN a province of E China: mountainous and densely populated; a cultural centre since the 12th century. Capital: Hangzhou. Pop.: 46 770 000 (2000 est.). Area: 102 000 sq. km (39 780 sq. miles).

Zhengzhou (ˈdʒʌŋˈdʒəʊ), **Chengchow,** *or* **Cheng-chou** NOUN a city in E central China, capital of Henan province; an administrative centre. Pop.: 1 465 069 (1999 est.).

Zhitomir (*Russian* ʒiˈtɔmir) NOUN a city in the central Ukraine; centre of an agricultural region. Pop. 297 700 (1998 est.).

zho (zəʊ) NOUN, *plural* **zhos** *or* **zho**. a variant spelling of **zo**.

Zhou (dʒəʊ) NOUN the Pinyin transliteration of the Chinese name for **Chou**.

Zhu Jiang (ˈdʒuː ˈdʒjæŋ), **Chu Chiang,** *or* **Chu Kiang** NOUN a river in SE China, in S Guangdong province, flowing southeast from Canton to the South China Sea. Length: about 177 km (110 miles). Also called: **Canton River, Pearl River**.

zibeline (ˈzɪbəˌlaɪn, -lɪn) NOUN [1] a sable or the fur of this animal. [2] a thick cloth made of wool or other animal hair, having a long nap and a dull sheen. ◆ ADJECTIVE [3] of, relating to, or resembling a sable.
▷**HISTORY** C16: from French, from Old Italian *zibellino*, ultimately of Slavonic origin; compare SABLE

zibet (ˈzɪbɪt) NOUN a large civet, *Viverra zibetha*, of S and SE Asia, having tawny fur marked with black spots and stripes.
▷**HISTORY** C16: from Medieval Latin *zibethum*, from Arabic *zabād* CIVET

Zibo (ˈziːˈbɔː), **Tzu-po,** *or* **Tzepo** NOUN a city in NE China, in Shandong province. Pop.: 1 458 000 (1999 est.).

zidovudine (zaɪˈdɒvjuˌdiːn) NOUN a drug that is used to treat AIDS. Also called: **AZT**.

Ziegler catalyst (ˈziːglə) NOUN any of a group of catalysts, such as titanium trichloride ($TiCl_3$) and aluminium alkyl ($Al(CH_3)_3$), that produce stereospecific polymers.
▷**HISTORY** C20: named after Carl *Ziegler* (1898–1973), German chemist

ziff (zɪf) NOUN *Austral informal* a beard.
▷**HISTORY** C20: of unknown origin

ziggurat (ˈzɪgʊˌræt), **zikkurat,** *or* **zikurat** (ˈzɪkʊˌræt) NOUN a type of rectangular temple tower or tiered mound erected by the Sumerians, Akkadians, and Babylonians in Mesopotamia. The tower of Babel is thought to be one of these.
▷**HISTORY** C19: from Assyrian *ziqqurati* summit, height

Zigong (ˈziːˈgʊŋ), **Tzekung,** *or* **Tzu-kung** NOUN an industrial city in W central China, in Sichuan. Pop.: 464 497 (1990 est.).

zigzag (ˈzɪgˌzæg) NOUN [1] a line or course characterized by sharp turns in alternating directions. [2] one of the series of such turns. [3] something having the form of a zigzag. ◆ ADJECTIVE [4] (*usually prenominal*) formed in or proceeding in a zigzag. [5] (of sewing machine stitches) produced in a zigzag by a swing needle used for joining stretch fabrics, neatening raw edges, etc. ◆ ADVERB [6] in a zigzag manner. ◆ VERB **-zags, -zagging, -zagged**. [7] to proceed or cause to proceed in a zigzag. [8] (*tr*) to form into a zigzag.
▷**HISTORY** C18: from French, from German *zickzack*, from *Zacke* point, jagged projection; see TACK[1]
▸ˈ**zigˌzaggedness** NOUN

zila, zilla, *or* **zillah** (ˈzɪlɑː) NOUN an administrative district in India.
▷**HISTORY** C19: from Hindi *dilah* division, from Arabic *dil'* part

zila parishad (ˈpʌrɪʃəd) NOUN a district council in India.
▷**HISTORY** Hindi, from *zila'* district (from Arabic *dil'* part) + *parishad* assembly, council

zilch (zɪltʃ) NOUN *Slang* [1] nothing. [2] *US and Canadian sport* nil.
▷**HISTORY** C20: of uncertain origin

zillion ('zɪljən) *Informal* ◆ NOUN, *plural* **-lions** *or* **-lion.** [1] (*often plural*) an extremely large but unspecified number, quantity, or amount: *zillions of flies in this camp.* ◆ DETERMINER [2] **a** amounting to a zillion: *a zillion different problems.* **b** (*as pronoun*): *I found a zillion under the sink.*
▷**HISTORY** on the model of *million*

Zilpah ('zɪlpə) NOUN *Old Testament* Leah's maidservant, who bore Gad and Asher to Jacob (Genesis 30:10–13).

Zimbabwe (zɪm'bɑ:bwɪ, -weɪ) NOUN [1] a country in SE Africa, formerly a self-governing British colony founded in 1890 by the British South Africa Company, which administered the country until a self-governing colony was established in 1923; joined with Northern Rhodesia (now Zambia) and Nyasaland (now Malawi) as the Federation of Rhodesia and Nyasaland from 1953 to 1963; made a unilateral declaration of independence under the leadership of Ian Smith in 1965 on the basis of White minority rule; proclaimed a republic in 1970; in 1976 the principle of Black majority rule was accepted and in 1978 a transitional government was set up; gained independence under Robert Mugabe in 1980; effectively a one-party state since 1987; a member of the Commonwealth. Official language: English. Religion: Christian majority. Currency: Zimbabwe dollar. Capital: Harare. Pop: 11 365 000 (2001 est.). Area: 390 624 sq. km (150 820 sq. miles). Former names: **Southern Rhodesia** (until 1964), **Rhodesia** (1964–79). [2] a ruined fortified settlement in Zimbabwe, which at its height, in the 15th century, was probably the capital of an empire covering SE Africa.

Zimbabwean (zɪm'bɑ:bwɪən, -weɪən) ADJECTIVE [1] of or relating to Zimbabwe or its inhabitants. ◆ NOUN [2] a native or inhabitant of Zimbabwe.

Zimmer ('zɪmə) NOUN *Trademark* another name for **walker** (sense 3). Also called: **Zimmer frame.**

zinc (zɪŋk) NOUN [1] a brittle bluish-white metallic element that becomes coated with a corrosion-resistant layer in moist air and occurs chiefly in sphalerite and smithsonite. It is a constituent of several alloys, esp brass and nickel-silver, and is used in die-casting, galvanizing metals, and in battery electrodes. Symbol: Zn; atomic no.: 30; atomic wt.: 65.39; valency: 2; relative density: 7.133; melting pt.: 419.58°C; boiling pt.: 907°C. [2] *Informal* corrugated galvanized iron.
▷**HISTORY** C17: from German *Zink*, perhaps from *Zinke* prong, from its jagged appearance in the furnace
▸**'zincic** *or* **'zincous** *or* **'zincoid** ADJECTIVE ▸**'zincky** *or* **'zincy** *or* **'zinky** ADJECTIVE

zincate ('zɪŋkeɪt) NOUN any of a class of salts derived from the amphoteric hydroxide of zinc, $Zn(OH)_2$, often thought of as the acid H_2ZnO_2.

zinc blende NOUN another name for **sphalerite.**

zinc chloride NOUN a white odourless soluble poisonous granular solid used in manufacturing parchment paper and vulcanized fibre and in preserving wood. It is also a soldering flux, embalming agent, and a medical astringent and antiseptic. Formula: $ZnCl_2$. Also called: **butter of zinc.**

zinciferous (zɪŋ'kɪfərəs) ADJECTIVE containing or yielding zinc.

zincite ('zɪŋkaɪt) NOUN a red or yellow mineral consisting of zinc oxide in hexagonal crystalline form. It occurs in metamorphosed limestone. Formula: ZnO.

zinckenite ('zɪŋkə,naɪt) NOUN a variant spelling of **zinkenite.**

zinco ('zɪŋkəʊ) NOUN, *plural* **-cos.** short for **zincograph** (sense 1).

zincograph ('zɪŋkə,grɑ:f, -,græf) NOUN [1] a printing plate made by zincography. [2] a print taken from such a plate.

zincography (zɪŋ'kɒgrəfɪ) NOUN the art or process of etching on zinc to form a printing plate.
▸**zin'cographer** NOUN ▸**zincographic** (,zɪŋkə'græfɪk) *or* **,zinco'graphical** ADJECTIVE

zinc ointment NOUN a medicinal ointment consisting of zinc oxide, petrolatum, and paraffin, used to treat certain skin diseases.

zinc oxide NOUN a white insoluble powder used as a pigment in paints (**zinc white** or **Chinese white**), cosmetics, glass, and printing inks. It is an antiseptic and astringent and is used in making zinc ointment. Formula: ZnO. Also called: **flowers of zinc, philosopher's wool.**

zinc sulphate NOUN a colourless soluble crystalline substance usually existing as the heptahydrate or monohydrate: used as a mordant, in preserving wood and skins, and in the electrodeposition of zinc. Formula: $ZnSO_4$. Also called: **white vitriol, zinc vitriol.**

zinc white NOUN another name for **Chinese white.**

zindabad ('zɪndɑ:,bɑ:d) VERB (*tr*) *Indian* long live: used as part of a slogan in India, Pakistan, etc. Compare **murdabad.**
▷**HISTORY** Hindi, from Persian

zine (zi:n) NOUN *Informal* a magazine or fanzine.

Zinfandel ('zɪnfən,dɛl) NOUN a Californian wine grape originally transplanted from Europe and producing a quick-maturing fruity red wine.
▷**HISTORY** C19: of unknown origin

zing (zɪŋ) NOUN *Informal* [1] a short high-pitched buzzing sound, as of a bullet or vibrating string. [2] vitality; zest. ◆ VERB [3] (*intr*) to make or move with or as if with a high-pitched buzzing sound.
▷**HISTORY** C20: of imitative origin

zingaro *Italian* ('dzingaro) *or feminine* ***zingara*** ('dzingara) NOUN, *plural* ***-ri*** (-ri) *or* ***-re*** (-re). an Italian Gypsy.
▷**HISTORY** C16: ultimately from Greek *Athinganoi*, name of an oriental people

zingiberaceous (,zɪndʒɪbə'reɪʃəs) ADJECTIVE of, relating to, or belonging to the *Zingiberaceae*, a family of tropical aromatic plants that typically have fleshy rhizomes and flowers in spikes or clusters: includes ginger and the plants yielding turmeric and cardamom.
▷**HISTORY** C19: via New Latin from *zingiber* GINGER

zingy (zɪŋɪ) ADJECTIVE **-gier, -giest.** *Informal* vibrant; energetic; lively.

zinjanthropus (zɪn'dʒænθrəpəs) NOUN a type of australopithecine, *Australopithecus boisei* (formerly *Zinjanthropus boisei*), remains of which were discovered in the Olduvai Gorge in Tanzania in 1959.
▷**HISTORY** C20: New Latin, from Arabic *Zinj* East Africa + Greek *anthrōpos* man

zinkenite *or* **zinckenite** ('zɪŋkə,naɪt) NOUN a steel-grey metallic mineral consisting of a sulphide of lead and antimony. Formula: $Pb_6Sb_{14}S_{27}$.
▷**HISTORY** C19: named after J. K. L. *Zincken* (1790–1862), German mineralogist

zinnia ('zɪnɪə) NOUN any annual or perennial plant of the genus *Zinnia*, of tropical and subtropical America, having solitary heads of brightly coloured flowers: family *Asteraceae* (composites).
▷**HISTORY** C18: named after J. G. *Zinn* (died 1759), German botanist

Zinovievsk (*Russian* zi'nɔvjɪfsk) NOUN a former name (1924–36) for **Kirovograd.**

Zion ('zaɪən) *or* **Sion** NOUN [1] the hill on which the city of Jerusalem stands. [2] *Judaism* **a** the ancient Israelites of the Bible. **b** the modern Jewish nation. **c** Israel as the national home of the Jewish people. [3] *Christianity* heaven regarded as the city of God and the final abode of his elect. [4] any form of social organization, way of life, or life after death regarded as an ultimate goal. [5] **a** a religious community or its site, regarded as chosen by God and under his special protection. **b** an ideal theocratic community, esp any of the Christian Churches regarded as such a community.

Zionism ('zaɪə,nɪzəm) NOUN [1] a political movement for the establishment and support of a national homeland for Jews in Palestine, now concerned chiefly with the development of the modern state of Israel. [2] a policy or movement for Jews to return to Palestine from the Diaspora.
▸**'Zionist** NOUN, ADJECTIVE ▸**,Zion'istic** ADJECTIVE

zip (zɪp) NOUN [1] **a** Also called: **zip fastener.** a fastening device operating by means of two parallel rows of metal or plastic teeth on either side of a closure that are interlocked by a sliding tab. US and Canadian term: **zipper. b** (*modifier*) having or equipped with such a device: *a zip bag.* [2] a short sharp whizzing sound, as of a passing bullet. [3] *Informal* energy; vigour; vitality. [4] *US slang* nothing. [5] *Sport, US and Canadian slang* nil. ◆ VERB **zips, zipping, zipped.** [6] (*tr;* often foll by *up*) to fasten (clothing, a bag, etc.) with a zip. [7] (*intr*) to move with a zip: *the bullet zipped past.* [8] (*intr;* often foll by *along, through,* etc.) to hurry; rush: *they zipped through town.*
▷**HISTORY** C19: of imitative origin

Zip (zɪp) NOUN *Trademark, NZ* an electric water heater.

Zipangu (zɪ'pæŋgu:) NOUN Marco Polo's name for **Cipango.**

zip code NOUN the US equivalent of **postcode.**
▷**HISTORY** C20: from *z(one) i(mprovement) p(lan)*

zip gun NOUN *US and Canadian slang* a crude homemade pistol, esp one powered by a spring or rubber band.

zip line NOUN a cable mechanism used for transportation across a river, gorge, etc.

zipper ('zɪpə) NOUN the US and Canadian word for **zip** (sense 1a).

zippered ('zɪpəd) ADJECTIVE provided or fastened with a zip.

zippy ('zɪpɪ) ADJECTIVE **-pier, -piest.** *Informal* full of energy; lively.

zircalloy (zɜ:k'ælɔɪ) NOUN an alloy of zirconium containing small amounts of tin, chromium, and nickel. It is used in pressurized-water reactors.

zircon ('zɜ:kɒn) NOUN a reddish-brown, grey, green, blue, or colourless hard mineral consisting of zirconium silicate in tetragonal crystalline form with hafnium and some rare earths as impurities. It occurs principally in igneous rocks and is an important source of zirconium, zirconia, and hafnia: it is used as a gemstone and a refractory. Formula: $ZrSiO_4$.
▷**HISTORY** C18: from German *Zirkon*, from French *jargon*, via Italian and Arabic, from Persian *zargūn* golden

zirconia (zɜ:'kəʊnɪə) NOUN another name (not in technical usage) for **zirconium oxide.**

zirconium (zɜ:'kəʊnɪəm) NOUN a greyish-white metallic element, occurring chiefly in zircon, that is exceptionally corrosion-resistant and has low neutron absorption. It is used as a coating in nuclear and chemical plants, as a deoxidizer in steel, and alloyed with niobium in superconductive magnets. Symbol: Zr; atomic no.: 40; atomic wt.: 91.224; valency: 2, 3, or 4; relative density: 6.506; melting pt.: 1855±2°C; boiling pt.: 4409°C.
▷**HISTORY** C19: from New Latin; see ZIRCON
▸**zirconic** (zɜ:'kɒnɪk) ADJECTIVE

zirconium oxide NOUN a white amorphous powder that is insoluble in water and highly refractory, used as a pigment for paints, a catalyst, and an abrasive. Formula: ZrO_2. Also called: **zirconia.**

zit (zɪt) NOUN *Slang* a pimple.
▷**HISTORY** of unknown origin

zither ('zɪðə) NOUN a plucked musical instrument consisting of numerous strings stretched over a resonating box, a few of which may be stopped on a fretted fingerboard.
▷**HISTORY** C19: from German, from Latin *cithara*, from Greek *kithara*
▸**'zitherist** NOUN

zizith ('tsɪtsɪs, tsi:'tsi:t) NOUN (*functioning as singular or plural*) *Judaism* a variant spelling of **tsitsith.**

zizz (zɪz) *Brit informal* ◆ NOUN [1] a short sleep; nap. ◆ VERB (*intr*) [2] to take a short sleep, snooze.
▷**HISTORY** C20: of imitative origin

Zl SYMBOL FOR zloty.

Zlatoust (*Russian* zləta'ust) NOUN a town in W Russia, on the Ay river: one of the chief metallurgical centres of the Urals since the 18th century. Pop.: 198 400 (1995 est.).

zloty ('zlɒtɪ) NOUN, *plural* **-tys** *or* **-ty.** the standard monetary unit of Poland, divided into 100 groszy.
▷**HISTORY** from Polish: golden, from *zlyoto* gold; related to Russian *zoloto* gold

zm THE INTERNET DOMAIN NAME FOR Zambia.

Zn THE CHEMICAL SYMBOL FOR zinc.

zo, zho, *or* **dzo** (zəʊ) NOUN, *plural* **zos, zhos, dzos** *or* **zo, zho, dzo.** a Tibetan breed of cattle, developed by crossing the yak with common cattle.
▷**HISTORY** C20: from Tibetan

zo- COMBINING FORM a variant of **zoo-** before a vowel.

zoa ('zəʊə) NOUN the plural of **zoon.**

-zoa SUFFIX FORMING PLURAL PROPER NOUNS indicating groups of animal organisms: *Metazoa.*
▷HISTORY from New Latin, from Greek *zōia,* plural of *zōion* animal, living being

zoaea (zəʊˈiːə) NOUN, *plural* **zoaeae** (zəʊˈiːiː) *or* **zoaeas.** a variant spelling of **zoea.**

Zoan (ˈzəʊæn) NOUN the Biblical name for **Tanis.**

zodiac (ˈzəʊdɪˌæk) NOUN 1 an imaginary belt extending 8° either side of the ecliptic, which contains the 12 **zodiacal constellations** and within which the moon and planets appear to move. It is divided into 12 equal areas, called **signs of the zodiac,** each named after the constellation which once lay in it. 2 *Astrology* a diagram, usually circular, representing this belt and showing the symbols, illustrations, etc., associated with each of the 12 signs of the zodiac, used to predict the future. 3 *Rare* a complete circuit; circle.
▷HISTORY C14: from Old French *zodiaque,* from Latin *zōdiacus,* from Greek *zōidiakos* (*kuklos*) (circle) of signs, from *zōidion* animal sign, carved figure, from *zōion* animal
▸**zodiacal** (zəʊˈdaɪəkəl) ADJECTIVE

zodiacal constellation NOUN any of the 12 constellations after which the signs of the zodiac are named: Aries, Taurus, Gemini, Cancer, Leo, Virgo, Libra, Scorpio, Sagittarius, Capricorn, Aquarius, or Pisces.

zodiacal light NOUN a very faint cone of light in the sky, visible in the east just before sunrise and in the west just after sunset. It is probably due to the reflection of sunlight from cosmic dust in the plane of the ecliptic.

zoea *or* **zoaea** (zəʊˈiːə) NOUN, *plural* **zoeae, zoaeae** (zəʊˈiːiː) *or* **zoeas, zoaeas.** the free-swimming larva of a crab or related crustacean, which has well-developed abdominal appendages and may bear one or more spines.
▷HISTORY C20: New Latin, from Greek *zōē* life

zoetrope (ˈzəʊɪˌtrəʊp) NOUN a cylinder-shaped toy with a sequence of pictures on its inner surface which, when viewed through the vertical slits spaced regularly around it while the toy is rotated, produce an illusion of animation.
▷HISTORY C19: Greek *zoe* life + *trope* turn

Zohar (ˈzəʊhɑː) NOUN *Judaism* a mystical work, consisting of a commentary on parts of the Pentateuch and the Hagiographa, probably composed in the 2nd century A.D.

zoic (ˈzəʊɪk) ADJECTIVE 1 relating to or having animal life. 2 *Geology* (of rocks, strata, etc.) containing fossilized animals.
▷HISTORY C19: from New Latin, from Greek *zōion* animal

-zoic ADJECTIVE AND NOUN COMBINING FORM indicating a geological era: *Palaeozoic.*
▷HISTORY from Greek *zōē* life + -IC

zoisite (ˈzɔɪˌsaɪt) NOUN a grey, brown, or pink mineral consisting of hydrated calcium aluminium silicate in orthorhombic crystalline form. Formula: $Ca_2Al_3(SiO_4)_3(OH)$.
▷HISTORY C19: from German *Zoisit;* named after Baron Sigismund *Zois* von Edelstein (1747–1819), Slovenian nobleman; see -ITE[1]

Zola Budd (bʌd) NOUN *South African informal* a black taxi or minibus.
▷HISTORY C20: after *Zola Budd* maiden name of Zola Pieterse (born 1966), South African athlete

Zollverein *German* (ˈtsɔlfɛrˌain) NOUN the customs union of German states organized in the early 1830s under Prussian auspices.
▷HISTORY C19: from *Zoll* tax, TOLL[2] + *Verein* union

Zomba (ˈzɒmbə) NOUN a city in S Malawi: the capital of Malawi until 1971. Pop.: 62 700 (1994 est.).

zombie *or* **zombi** (ˈzɒmbɪ) NOUN, *plural* **-bies** *or* **-bis.** 1 a person who is or appears to be lifeless, apathetic, or totally lacking in independent judgment; automaton. 2 a supernatural spirit that reanimates a dead body. 3 a corpse brought to life in this manner. 4 the snake god of voodoo cults in the West Indies, esp Haiti, and in scattered areas of the southern US. 5 the python god revered in parts of West Africa. 6 a piece of computer code which instructs an infected computer to send the virus on to other computer systems.
▷HISTORY from Kongo *zumbi* good-luck fetish
▸**ˈzombiism** NOUN

zonal (ˈzəʊnᵊl) *or less commonly* **zonary** (ˈzəʊnərɪ) ADJECTIVE of, relating to, or of the nature of a zone.
▸**ˈzonally** ADVERB

zonal soil NOUN soil having a profile determined mainly by the local climate and vegetation. Compare **azonal soil, intrazonal soil.**

zonate (ˈzəʊneɪt) *or* **zonated** ADJECTIVE marked with, divided into, or arranged in zones.

zonation (zəʊˈneɪʃən) NOUN arrangement in zones; zonate formation.

Zond (zɒnd) NOUN any of a series of unmanned Soviet spacecraft, first launched in 1964 as interplanetary space probes, the most successful of which, **Zond 3,** sent back photographs of the hidden side of the moon in 1965.

zone (zəʊn) NOUN 1 a region, area, or section characterized by some distinctive feature or quality. 2 a sphere of thought, disagreement, argument, etc. 3 an area subject to a particular political, military, or government function, use, or jurisdiction: *a demilitarized zone.* 4 (*often capital*) *Geography* one of the divisions of the earth's surface, esp divided into latitudinal belts according to temperature. See **Torrid Zone, Frigid Zone, Temperate Zone.** 5 *Geology* a distinctive layer or region of rock, characterized by particular fossils (**zone fossils**), metamorphism, structural deformity, etc. 6 *Ecology* an area, esp a belt of land, having a particular flora and fauna determined by the prevailing environmental conditions. 7 *Maths* a portion of a sphere between two parallel planes intersecting the sphere. 8 *Sport* **a** a period during which a competitor is performing particularly well: *Hingis is in the zone at the moment.* **b** (*modifier*) of or relating to competitive performance that depends on the mood or state of mind of the participant: *a zone player.* 9 *Archaic or literary* a girdle or belt. 10 *NZ* a section on a transport route; fare stage. 11 *NZ* a catchment area for pupils for a specific school. 12 **in the zone.** See: **zone** (sense 8). ◆ VERB (*tr*) 13 to divide into zones, as for different use, jurisdiction, activities, etc. 14 to designate as a zone. 15 to mark with or divide into zones. 16 *NZ* to establish (an area) as a zone for a specific school.
▷HISTORY C15: from Latin *zōna* girdle, climatic zone, from Greek *zōnē*
▸**ˈzoning** NOUN

zone of saturation NOUN the ground below the water table.

zone refining NOUN a technique for producing solids of extreme purity, esp for use in semiconductors. The material, in the form of a bar, is melted in one small region that is passed along the solid. Impurities concentrate in the melt and are moved to the end of the bar.

zonetime (ˈzəʊnˌtaɪm) NOUN the standard time of the time zone in which a ship is located at sea, each zone extending 7½° to each side of a meridian.

zonked (zɒŋkt) ADJECTIVE *Slang* 1 highly intoxicated from drugs or alcohol. 2 utterly exhausted.
▷HISTORY C20: of imitative origin

zonule (ˈzɒnjuːl) NOUN a small zone, band, or area.
▷HISTORY C19: from New Latin *zōnula* a little ZONE
▸**zonular** (ˈzɒnjʊlə) ADJECTIVE

zoo (zuː) NOUN, *plural* **zoos.** a place where live animals are kept, studied, bred, and exhibited to the public. Formal term: **zoological garden.**
▷HISTORY C19: shortened from *zoological gardens* (originally applied to those in London)

zoo- *or before a vowel* **zo-** COMBINING FORM indicating animals: *zooplankton.*
▷HISTORY from Greek *zōion* animal

zoobiotic (ˌzəʊəbaɪˈɒtɪk) ADJECTIVE *Biology* parasitic on or living in association with an animal.

zoochemistry (ˌzəʊəˈkɛmɪstrɪ) NOUN the branch of biochemistry that is concerned with the constituents of an animal's body.
▸**ˌzooˈchemical** ADJECTIVE

zoochorous (ˌzəʊəˈkɔːrəs) ADJECTIVE (of a plant) having the spores or seeds dispersed by animals.
▷HISTORY from ZOO- + -CHORE + -OUS
▸**ˈzooˌchore** NOUN

zoo doo NOUN compost made from the dung of zoo animals.

zoogeography (ˌzəʊədʒɪˈɒgrəfɪ) NOUN the branch of zoology concerned with the geographical distribution of animals.
▸**ˌzoogeˈographer** NOUN ▸**zoogeographic** (ˌzəʊəˌdʒɪəˈgræfɪk) *or* **ˌzooˌgeoˈgraphical** ADJECTIVE ▸**ˌzooˌgeoˈgraphically** ADVERB

zoogloea (ˌzəʊəˈgliːə) NOUN a mass of bacteria adhering together by a jelly-like substance derived from their cell walls.
▷HISTORY C19: ZOO- + New Latin *gloea* glue, from Greek *gloia*
▸**ˌzooˈgloeal** ADJECTIVE

zoography (zəʊˈɒgrəfɪ) NOUN the branch of zoology concerned with the description of animals.
▸**zoˈographer** NOUN ▸**zoographic** (ˌzəʊəˈgræfɪk) *or* **ˌzooˈgraphical** ADJECTIVE

zooid (ˈzəʊɔɪd) NOUN 1 any independent animal body, such as an individual of a coelenterate colony. 2 a motile cell or body, such as a gamete, produced by an organism.
▸**zoˈoidal** ADJECTIVE

zool. ABBREVIATION FOR: 1 zoological. 2 zoology.

zoolatry (zəʊˈɒlətrɪ) NOUN 1 (esp in ancient or primitive religions) the worship of animals as the incarnations of certain deities, symbols of particular qualities or natural forces, etc. 2 extreme or excessive devotion to animals, particularly domestic pets.
▸**zoˈolater** NOUN ▸**zoˈolatrous** ADJECTIVE

zoological garden NOUN the formal term for **zoo.**

zoology (zəʊˈɒlədʒɪ, zuː-) NOUN, *plural* **-gies.** 1 the study of animals, including their classification, structure, physiology, and history. 2 the biological characteristics of a particular animal or animal group. 3 the fauna characteristic of a particular region. 4 a book, treatise, etc., dealing with any aspect of the study of animals.
▸**zoological** (ˌzəʊəˈlɒdʒɪkᵊl, ˌzuːə-) ADJECTIVE ▸**zoˈologist** NOUN

zoom (zuːm) VERB 1 to make or cause to make a continuous buzzing or humming sound. 2 to move or cause to move with such a sound. 3 (*intr*) to move very rapidly; rush: *we zoomed through town.* 4 to cause (an aircraft) to climb briefly at an unusually steep angle, or (of an aircraft) to climb in this way. 5 (*intr*) (of prices) to rise rapidly. ◆ NOUN 6 the sound or act of zooming. 7 See **zoom lens.**
▷HISTORY C20: of imitative origin

zoometry (zəʊˈɒmɪtrɪ) NOUN the branch of zoology concerned with the relative length or size of the different parts of an animal or animals.
▸**zoometric** (ˌzəʊəˈmɛtrɪk) *or* **ˌzooˈmetrical** ADJECTIVE

zoom in VERB 1 (*intr, adverb*) *Photog, films, television* to increase rapidly the magnification of the image of a distant object by means of a zoom lens. 2 to examine the smallest details of a subject.

zoom lens NOUN a lens system that allows the focal length of a camera lens to be varied continuously without altering the sharpness of the image. See also **telephoto lens.**

zoomorphism (ˌzəʊəˈmɔːfɪzəm) NOUN 1 the conception or representation of deities in the form of animals. 2 the use of animal forms or symbols in art, literature, etc.
▸**ˌzooˈmorphic** ADJECTIVE

zoom out VERB (*intr, adverb*) 1 *Photog, films, television* to decrease rapidly the magnification of the image of a distant object by means of a zoom lens. 2 to consider the essential points, rather than the details of a subject.

zoon (ˈzəʊɒn) NOUN, *plural* **zoa** (ˈzəʊə) *or* **zoons.** a less common term for **zooid** (sense 1).
▷HISTORY C19: from New Latin, from Greek *zōion* animal; related to Greek *zōē* life
▸**zoˈonal** ADJECTIVE

-zoon NOUN COMBINING FORM indicating an individual animal or an independently moving entity derived from an animal: *spermatozoon.*
▷HISTORY from Greek *zōion* animal

zoonosis (zəʊˈɒnəsɪs, ˌzəʊəˈnəʊsɪs) NOUN, *plural* **-ses** (-siːz). *Pathol* any infection or disease that is transmitted to man from lower vertebrates.
▷HISTORY from ZOO- + Greek *nosos* disease

zoophagous (zəʊˈɒfəgəs) ADJECTIVE feeding on animals.

zoophile (ˈzəʊəˌfaɪl) NOUN a person who is devoted

to animals and their protection from practices such as vivisection.
▸**zoophilic** (ˌzəʊəˈfɪlɪk) ADJECTIVE

zoophilia (ˌzəʊəˈfɪlɪə) NOUN a morbid condition in which a person has a sexual attraction to animals; bestiality.

zoophilism (zəʊˈɒfɪˌlɪzəm) NOUN the tendency to be emotionally attached to animals.

zoophilous (zəʊˈɒfɪləs) ADJECTIVE 1 (of plants) pollinated by animals. 2 of, characterized by, or relating to zoophilism.

zoophobia (ˌzəʊəˈfəʊbɪə) NOUN an unusual or morbid dread of animals.
▸**zoophobous** (zəʊˈɒfəbəs) ADJECTIVE

zoophyte (ˈzəʊəˌfaɪt) NOUN any animal resembling a plant, such as a sea anemone.
▸**zoophytic** (ˌzəʊəˈfɪtɪk) *or* **ˌzooˈphytical** ADJECTIVE

zooplankton (ˌzəʊəˈplæŋktən) NOUN the animal constituent of plankton, which consists mainly of small crustaceans and fish larvae. Compare **phytoplankton.**

zooplasty (ˈzəʊəˌplæstɪ) NOUN the surgical transplantation to man of animal tissues.
▸**ˌzooˈplastic** ADJECTIVE

zoosperm (ˈzəʊəˌspɜːm) NOUN another word for **spermatozoon.**
▸**zoospermatic** (ˌzəʊəspɜːˈmætɪk) ADJECTIVE

zoosporangium (ˌzəʊəspɔːˈrændʒɪəm) NOUN, *plural* **-gia** (-dʒɪə). *Botany* a sporangium that produces zoospores.
▸**ˌzoospoˈrangial** ADJECTIVE

zoospore (ˈzəʊəˌspɔː) NOUN 1 an asexual spore of some algae and fungi that moves by means of flagella. 2 one of several spores produced in a saclike body (sporocyst) by some parasitic protozoans.
▸**ˌzooˈsporic** *or* **zoosporous** (zəʊˈɒspərəs, ˌzəʊəˈspɔːrəs) ADJECTIVE

zoosterol (zəʊˈɒstəˌrɒl) NOUN any of a group of animal sterols, such as cholesterol.

zootechnics (ˌzəʊəˈtɛknɪks) NOUN (*functioning as singular*) the science concerned with the domestication and breeding of animals.

zootomy (zəʊˈɒtəmɪ) NOUN the branch of zoology concerned with the dissection and anatomy of animals.
▸**zootomic** (ˌzəʊəˈtɒmɪk) *or* **ˌzooˈtomical** ADJECTIVE
▸**ˌzooˈtomically** ADVERB ▸**zoˈotomist** NOUN

zootoxin (ˌzəʊəˈtɒksɪn) NOUN a toxin, such as snake venom, that is produced by an animal. Compare **phytotoxin.**
▸**ˌzooˈtoxic** ADJECTIVE

zoot suit (zuːt) NOUN *Slang* a man's suit consisting of baggy trousers with very tapered bottoms and a long jacket with wide padded shoulders, popular esp in the US in the 1940s.
▷HISTORY C20: of uncertain origin; perhaps an arbitrary rhyme on *suit*
▸**ˈzoot-ˌsuiter** NOUN

zorbing (ˈzɔːbɪŋ) NOUN *Informal* the activity of travelling downhill inside a large air-cushioned hollow ball.
▷HISTORY C20 Z + ORB (sphere) + -ING[1]

zorbonaut (ˈzɔːbəˌnɔːt) NOUN *Jocular* a person who engages in the activity of zorbing.
▷HISTORY C20: from ZORB(ING) + -NAUT

zorilla (zəˈrɪlə) *or* **zorille** (zəˈrɪl) NOUN a skunk-like African musteline mammal, *Ictonyx striatus,* having a long black-and-white coat.
▷HISTORY C18: from French, from Spanish *zorrillo* a little fox, from *zorro* fox

Zoroastrian (ˌzɒrəʊˈæstrɪən) ADJECTIVE 1 of or relating to Zoroastrianism or Zoroaster. ◆ NOUN 2 a follower of Zoroaster or adherent of Zoroastrianism: in modern times a Gabar or a Parsee.

Zoroastrianism (ˌzɒrəʊˈæstrɪənˌɪzəm) *or* **Zoroastrism** NOUN the dualistic religion founded by the Persian prophet Zoroaster in the late 7th or early 6th centuries B.C. and set forth in the sacred writings of the Zend-Avesta. It is based on the concept of a continuous struggle between Ormazd (or Ahura Mazda), the god of creation, light, and goodness, and his arch enemy, Ahriman, the spirit of evil and darkness, and it includes a highly developed ethical code. Also called: **Mazdaism.**

zoster (ˈzɒstə) NOUN *Pathol* short for **herpes zoster.**
▷HISTORY C18: from Latin: shingles, from Greek *zōster* girdle

Zouave (zuːˈɑːv, zwɑːv) NOUN 1 (formerly) a member of a body of French infantry composed of Algerian recruits noted for their dash, hardiness, and colourful uniforms. 2 a member of any body of soldiers wearing a similar uniform or otherwise modelled on the French Zouaves, esp a volunteer in such a unit of the Union Army in the American Civil War.
▷HISTORY C19: from French, from *Zwāwa,* tribal name in Algeria

Zoug *or* **zug** NOUN the French name for **Zug.**

zouk (zuːk) NOUN a style of dance music that combines African and Latin American rhythms and uses electronic instruments and modern studio technology.
▷HISTORY C20: from West Indian Creole *zouk* to have a good time

zounds (zaʊndz) *or* **swounds** (zwaʊndz, zaʊndz) INTERJECTION *Archaic* a mild oath indicating surprise, indignation, etc.
▷HISTORY C16: euphemistic shortening of *God's wounds*

zoysia (ˈzɔɪzɪə) NOUN any creeping perennial grass of the genus *Zoysia,* of warm dry regions, having short stiffly pointed leaves: often used for lawns.
▷HISTORY C19: from New Latin, named after Karl von *Zois* (died 1800), German botanist

Z particle NOUN *Physics* a type of neutral elementary particle considered to transmit the weak interaction between other elementary particles. Z particles have a rest mass of 1.62557×10^{-25} kg. Also called: **Z boson.** See also **W particle.**

ZPG ABBREVIATION FOR zero population growth.

Zr THE CHEMICAL SYMBOL FOR zirconium.

ZRE INTERNATIONAL CAR REGISTRATION FOR Democratic Republic of Congo.
▷HISTORY from *Zaire*

zucchetto (tsuːˈkɛtəʊ, suː-, zuː-) NOUN, *plural* **-tos.** *RC Church* a small round skullcap worn by certain ecclesiastics and varying in colour according to the rank of the wearer, the Pope wearing white, cardinals red, bishops violet, and others black.
▷HISTORY C19: from Italian, from *zucca* a gourd, head, from Late Latin *cucutia* gourd, probably from Latin *cucurbita*

zucchini (tsuːˈkiːnɪ, zuː-) NOUN, *plural* **-ni** *or* **-nis.** the US and Canadian name for **courgette.**
▷HISTORY Italian, pl of *zucchino,* literally: a little gourd, from *zucca* gourd; see ZUCCHETTO

Zug (*German* tsuːk) NOUN 1 a canton of N central Switzerland: the smallest Swiss canton; mainly German-speaking and Roman Catholic; joined the Swiss Confederation in 1352. Capital: Zug. Pop.: 97 800 (2000 est.). Area: 239 sq. km (92 sq. miles). 2 a town in N central Switzerland, the capital of Zug canton, on Lake Zug. Pop.: 21 467 (1990). 3 **Lake.** a lake in N central Switzerland, in Zug and Schwyz cantons. Area: 39 sq. km (15 sq. miles). French name: **Zoug.**

Zugspitze (ˈtsuɡˌʃpɪtsə) NOUN a mountain peak in S Germany in the Bavarian Alps, on the Austrian border: the highest peak in Germany. Height: 2963 m (9721 ft.).

zugzwang (*German* ˈtsuːktsvaŋ) *Chess* ◆ NOUN 1 a position in which one player can move only with loss or severe disadvantage. ◆ VERB 2 (*tr*) to manoeuvre (one's opponent) into a zugzwang.
▷HISTORY from German, from *Zug* a pull, tug + *Zwang* force, compulsion

Zuider Zee *or* **Zuyder Zee** (ˈzaɪdə ˈziː; *Dutch* ˈzœidər ˈzeː) NOUN a former inlet of the North Sea in the N coast of the Netherlands sealed off from the sea by a dam in 1932, dividing it into the Waddenzee and the freshwater IJsselmeer, with several large areas under reclamation.

Zuidholland (zœitˈhɔlɑnt) NOUN the Dutch name for **South Holland.**

Zulu (ˈzuːluː) NOUN 1 (*plural* **-lus** *or* **-lu**) a member of a tall Negroid people of SE Africa, living chiefly in South Africa, who became dominant during the 19th century due to a warrior-clan system organized by the powerful leader, Shaka. 2 the language of this people, belonging to the Bantu group of the Niger-Congo family, closely related to Swazi and Xhosa. 3 *Communications* a code word for the letter *z.*
▷HISTORY from Zulu *amaZulu* people of the sky

Zululand (ˈzuːluˌlænd, ˈzuːluː-) NOUN a region of E South Africa, on the Indian Ocean; partly corresponds to KwaZulu/Natal. Chief town: Eshowe.

Zungaria (zʊŋˈɡɛərɪə) NOUN a variant transliteration of **Junggar Pendi.**

Zuñi (ˈzuːnjiː, ˈsuː-) NOUN 1 (*plural* **-ñis** *or* **-ñi**) a member of a North American Indian people of W New Mexico. 2 the language of this people, a member of the Penutian phylum of languages.
▸**ˈZuñian** ADJECTIVE, NOUN

Zürich (ˈzjʊərɪk; *German* ˈtsyːrɪç) NOUN 1 a canton of NE Switzerland: mainly Protestant and German-speaking Capital: Zürich. Pop.: 1 198 600 (2000 est.). Area: 1729 sq. km (668 sq. miles). 2 a city in NE Switzerland, the capital of Zürich canton, on Lake Zürich the largest city and industrial centre in Switzerland; centre of the Swiss Reformation; financial centre. Pop.: 336 821 (1999 est.). 3 **Lake.** a lake in N Switzerland, mostly in Zürich canton. Area: 89 sq. km (34 sq. miles).

Zuyder Zee (ˈzaɪdə ˈziː; *Dutch* ˈzœidər ˈzeː) NOUN a variant spelling of **Zuider Zee.**

zw THE INTERNET DOMAIN NAME FOR Zimbabwe.

ZW INTERNATIONAL CAR REGISTRATION FOR Zimbabwe.

Zwickau (*German* ˈtsvɪkau) NOUN a city in E Germany, in Saxony: Anabaptist movement founded here (1521); coal-mining and industrial centre. Pop.: 104 900 (1999 est.).

zwieback (ˈzwaɪˌbæk, ˈzwiː-; *German* ˈtsviːbak) NOUN a small type of rusk, which has been baked first as a loaf, then sliced and toasted, usually bought ready-made.
▷HISTORY German: twice-baked

Zwinglian (ˈzwɪŋɡlɪən, ˈswɪŋɡ-, ˈtsvɪŋ-) NOUN 1 an upholder of the religious doctrines or movement of the Swiss Reformation leader Ulrich Zwingli (1484–1531), who denied the Eucharistic presence, holding that the Communion was merely a commemoration of Christ's death. ◆ ADJECTIVE 2 of or relating to Zwingli, his religious movement, or his doctrines, esp his interpretation of the Eucharist.
▸**ˈZwinglianism** NOUN ▸**ˈZwinglianist** NOUN

zwischenzug (ˈzvɪʃənzuːɡ) NOUN *Chess* a tactical move interpolated into an exchange or series of exchanges to improve the outcome.
▷HISTORY C20: German: in-between move

zwitterion (ˈtsvɪtərˌaɪən) NOUN *Chem* an ion that carries both a positive and a negative charge.
▷HISTORY C20: from German *Zwitter* hermaphrodite + ION
▸**zwitterionic** (ˌtsvɪtəraɪˈɒnɪk) ADJECTIVE

Zwolle (*Dutch* ˈzwɔlə) NOUN a town in the central Netherlands, capital of Overijssel province. Pop.: 104 431 (1999 est.).

Zyban (ˈzaɪˌbæn) NOUN *Trademark* a drug that acts on the brain; used to help people give up smoking.

zydeco (ˈzaɪdəˌkəʊ) NOUN a type of Black Cajun music.

zygapophysis (ˌzɪɡəˈpɒfɪsɪs, ˌzaɪɡə-) NOUN, *plural* **-ses** (-ˌsiːz). *Anatomy, zoology* one of several processes on a vertebra that articulates with the corresponding process on an adjacent vertebra.
▷HISTORY C19: from ZYGO- + APOPHYSIS
▸**zygapophyseal** (ˌzɪɡæpəˈfɪzɪəl) ADJECTIVE

zygo- *or before a vowel* **zyg-** COMBINING FORM indicating a pair or a union: *zygodactyl; zygospore.*
▷HISTORY from Greek *zugon* yoke

zygodactyl (ˌzaɪɡəʊˈdæktɪl, ˌzɪɡə-) ADJECTIVE *also* **zygodactylous.** 1 (of the feet of certain birds) having the first and fourth toes directed backwards and the second and third forwards. ◆ NOUN 2 a zygodactyl bird. Compare **heterodactyl.**
▸**ˌzygoˈdactylism** NOUN

zygoma (zaɪˈɡəʊmə, zɪ-) NOUN, *plural* **-mata** (-mətə). another name for **zygomatic arch.**
▷HISTORY C17: via New Latin from Greek, from *zugon* yoke

zygomatic (ˌzaɪɡəʊˈmætɪk, ˌzɪɡ-) ADJECTIVE of or relating to the zygoma.

zygomatic arch NOUN the slender arch of bone that forms a bridge between the cheekbone and the temporal bone on each side of the skull of mammals. Also called: **zygoma.**

zygomatic bone NOUN either of two bones, one on each side of the skull, that form part of the side wall of the eye socket and part of the zygomatic arch; cheekbone. Also called: **malar, malar bone.**

zygomatic process NOUN a slender bony process of the temporal bone that forms part of the zygomatic arch.

zygomorphic (ˌzaɪgəʊˈmɔːfɪk, ˌzɪg-) *or* **zygomorphous** ADJECTIVE (of a flower) capable of being cut in only one plane so that the two halves are mirror images. See also **actinomorphic.**
▸**ˌzygoˈmorphism** *or* **ˈzygoˌmorphy** NOUN

zygomycete (ˌzaɪgəʊˈmaɪsiːt) NOUN any filamentous fungus of the phylum *Zygomycota* (or *Zygomycetes*), which reproduces sexually by means of zygospores includes the bread mould.
▸**ˌzygomyˈcetous** ADJECTIVE

zygophyllaceous (ˌzaɪgəʊfɪˈleɪʃəs, ˌzɪg-) ADJECTIVE of, relating to, or belonging to the *Zygophyllaceae*, an Old World family of flowering plants having pinnate leaves and capsules as fruits: includes the lignum vitae.

zygosis (zaɪˈgəʊsɪs, zɪ-) NOUN *Biology* another name for **conjugation.**
▸**zygose** (ˈzaɪgəʊs, ˈzɪg-) ADJECTIVE

zygospore (ˈzaɪgəʊˌspɔː, ˈzɪg-) NOUN a thick-walled sexual spore formed from the zygote of some fungi and algae.
▸**ˌzygoˈsporic** ADJECTIVE

zygote (ˈzaɪgəʊt, ˈzɪg-) NOUN [1] the cell resulting from the union of an ovum and a spermatozoon. [2] the organism that develops from such a cell.
▷**HISTORY** C19: from Greek *zugōtos* yoked, from *zugoun* to yoke
▸**zygotic** (zaɪˈgɒtɪk, zɪ-) ADJECTIVE ▸**zyˈgotically** ADVERB

zygotene (ˈzaɪgəˌtiːn, ˈzɪg-) NOUN the second stage of the prophase of meiosis, during which homologous chromosomes become associated in pairs (bivalents).

zymase (ˈzaɪmeɪs) NOUN a mixture of enzymes that is obtained as an extract from yeast and ferments sugars.

zymo- *or before a vowel* **zym-** COMBINING FORM indicating fermentation: *zymology.*
▷**HISTORY** from Greek *zumē* leaven

zymogen (ˈzaɪməʊˌdʒɛn) NOUN *Biochem* any of a group of compounds that are inactive precursors of enzymes and are activated by a kinase.

zymogenesis (ˌzaɪməʊˈdʒɛnɪsɪs) NOUN the conversion of a zymogen into an enzyme.

zymogenic (ˌzaɪməʊˈdʒɛnɪk) ADJECTIVE [1] of, or relating to a zymogen. [2] capable of causing zymogenesis.

zymology (zaɪˈmɒlədʒɪ) NOUN the chemistry of fermentation.
▸**zymologic** (ˌzaɪməʊˈlɒdʒɪk) *or* **ˌzymoˈlogical** ADJECTIVE
▸**zyˈmologist** NOUN

zymolysis (zaɪˈmɒlɪsɪs) NOUN the process of fermentation. Also called: **zymosis.**
▸**zymolytic** (ˌzaɪməʊˈlɪtɪk) ADJECTIVE

zymometer (zaɪˈmɒmɪtə) NOUN an instrument for estimating the degree of fermentation.

zymosis (zaɪˈməʊsɪs) NOUN, *plural* **-ses** (-siːz). [1] *Med* **a** any infectious disease. **b** the development process or spread of such a disease. [2] another name for **zymolysis.**

zymotic (zaɪˈmɒtɪk) ADJECTIVE [1] of, relating to, or causing fermentation. [2] relating to or caused by infection; denoting or relating to an infectious disease.
▸**zyˈmotically** ADVERB

zymurgy (ˈzaɪmɜːdʒɪ) NOUN the branch of chemistry concerned with fermentation processes in brewing, etc.

Zyrian (ˈzɪrɪən) NOUN [1] the language of the people of the Komi Autonomous Republic, belonging to the Finno-Ugric family; Komi. ◆ ADJECTIVE [2] of or relating to this language or its speakers.

Guide to the Text

Headword

champignon (tʃæmˈpɪnjən) NOUN any of various agaricaceous edible mushrooms, esp *Marasmius oreades* (**fairy ring champignon**) and the meadow mushroom.
▷**HISTORY** C16: from French, perhaps from Vulgar Latin *campīnus* (unattested) of the field, from Latin *campus* plain, field

Champigny-sur-Marne (*French* ʃɑ̃piɲisyrmarn) NOUN a suburb of Paris, on the River Marne. Pop.: 80 290 (latest est.).

Pronunciation — Sense number — Part of speech — Grammatical information

champion (ˈtʃæmpɪən) NOUN 1 **a** a person who has defeated all others in a competition: *a chess champion.* **b** (*as modifier*): *a champion team.* 2 **a** a plant or animal that wins first place in a show, etc. **b** (*as modifier*): *a champion marrow.* 3 a person who defends a person or cause: *champion of the underprivileged.* 4 (formerly) a warrior or knight who did battle for another, esp a king or queen, to defend their rights or honour. ◆ ADJECTIVE 5 *Northern English dialect* first rate; excellent. ◆ ADVERB 6 *Northern English dialect* very well; excellently. ◆ VERB (*tr*) 7 to support; defend: *we champion the cause of liberty.*
▷**HISTORY** C13: from Old French, from Late Latin *campiō*, from Latin *campus* field, battlefield

Definition

championship (ˈtʃæmpɪənˌʃɪp) NOUN 1 (*sometimes plural*) any of various contests held to determine a champion. 2 the title or status of being a champion. 3 support for or defence of a cause, person, etc.

Champlain (ʃæmˈpleɪn) NOUN **Lake.** a lake in the northeastern US, between the Green Mountains and the Adirondack Mountains: linked by the **Champlain Canal** to the Hudson River and by the Richelieu River to the St Lawrence; a major communications route in colonial times.

champlevé *French* (ʃɑ̃lve; *English* ˌʃæmpləˈveɪ) ADJECTIVE 1 of or relating to a process of enamelling by which grooves are cut into a metal base and filled with enamel colours. ◆ NOUN 2 an object enamelled by this process.
▷**HISTORY** C19: from *champ* field (level surface) + *levé* raised

Champs Elysées (ʃɒnz eɪˈliːzeɪ; *French* ʃɑ̃z elize) NOUN a major boulevard in Paris, leading from the Arc de Triomphe: site of the Elysées Palace and government offices.

Related word — Example — Idiom or phrase

chance (tʃɑːns) NOUN 1 **a** the unknown and unpredictable element that causes an event to result in a certain way rather than another, spoken of as a real force. **b** (*as modifier*): *a chance meeting.* Related adjective: **fortuitous.** 2 fortune; luck; fate. 3 an opportunity or occasion. 4 a risk; gamble: *you take a chance with his driving.* 5 the extent to which an event is likely to occur; probability. 6 an unpredicted event, esp a fortunate one: *that was quite a chance, finding him here.* 7 *Archaic* an unlucky event; mishap. 8 **by chance. a** accidentally: *he slipped by chance.* **b** perhaps: *do you by chance have a room?* 9 **(the) chances are....** it is likely (that) .... 10 **on the chance.** acting on the possibility; in case. 11 **the main chance.** the opportunity for personal gain (esp in the phrase **an eye to the main chance**). ◆ VERB 12 (*tr*) to risk; hazard: *I'll chance the worst happening.* 13 to happen by chance; be the case by chance: *I chanced to catch sight of her as she passed.* 14 **chance on** (*or* **upon**). to come upon by accident: *he chanced on the solution to his problem.* 15 **chance one's arm.** to attempt to do something although the chance of success may be slight.
▷**HISTORY** C13: from Old French *cheance*, from *cheoir* to fall, occur, from Latin *cadere*
▶ˈ**chanceful** ADJECTIVE ▶ˈ**chanceless** ADJECTIVE

chancel (ˈtʃɑːnsəl) NOUN the part of a church containing the altar, sanctuary, and choir, usually separated from the nave and transepts by a screen.
▷**HISTORY** C14: from Old French, from Latin *cancellī* (plural) lattice

Inflected forms

chancellery *or* **chancellory** (ˈtʃɑːnsələrɪ, -slərɪ) NOUN, *plural* **-leries** *or* **-lories.** 1 the building or room occupied by a chancellor's office. 2 the position, rank, or office of a chancellor. 3 *US* **a** the residence or office of an embassy or legation. **b** the office of a consulate. 4 *Brit* another name for a diplomatic **chancery.**

Pharmacy
Medicines information
December 2002.

HANDBOOK ON INJECTABLE DRUGS

12TH EDITION

LAWRENCE A. TRISSEL

25 YEARS IN PRINT

American Society of Health-System Pharmacists®

LAWRENCE A. TRISSEL, F.A.S.H.P., the author of the *Handbook on Injectable Drugs*, is Director, Clinical Pharmaceutics Research, Division of Pharmacy, The University of Texas, M. D. Anderson Cancer Center, Houston, Texas.

Any correspondence regarding this publication should be sent to the publisher, American Society of Health-System Pharmacists®, 7272 Wisconsin Avenue, Bethesda, MD 20814, attn: Special Publishing.

Produced by Special Publishing and the Publications Production Center of the American Society of Health-System Pharmacists
Managing Editor/Senior Project Editor: Bruce Hawkins
Development Editor: Mark Koenig
Project Assistant: Leah Carter

Cover Design: David A. Wade

ISBN: 1-58528-041-0

To the researchers who create the knowledge,
To the M&M's gang for 25 years of help,
and, as always,
To Pam for her continuing support

Now go, write it before them in a table,
and note it in a book, that it may be
for the time to come…
Isaiah 30:8

CONTENTS

ACKNOWLEDGMENTS

I would gratefully like to acknowledge the valuable contributions of the following individuals, who served as reviewers for the twelfth edition of the *Handbook on Injectable Drugs*:

TODD W. CANADA, Pharm.D., BCNSP, Clinical Specialist, Critical Care, Nutrition Support, Division of Pharmacy, The University of Texas, M. D. Anderson Cancer Center, Houston, Texas

N. PAULINE THOMAS PARKS, M.S., Consultant Pharmacist, Houston, Texas

---

In addition, I would like to acknowledge the contributions of the following individuals, who have served as reviewers for previous editions of the *Handbook* throughout its 25-year history:

MICHAEL A. ALLWOOD, Ph.D., F.R.Pharm.S.G.B.

DANIEL P. HAAS, M.S.

KAREN NAQUIN HALE, M.P.H.

JUDITH A. SMITH, Pharm.D.

PREFACE

The *Handbook on Injectable Drugs*, 12th edition, is the most recent contribution in this continuing series. With its publication, all previous editions are considered out of date.

For proper use of this reference work, the reader must review the *How to Use the Handbook* section that immediately follows this preface. This section will acquaint the user of the *Handbook* with its organization, content, structure, summarization strategy, interpretation of the information presented, and limitations of the published literature on which the *Handbook* is based. Without a good working knowledge of these points, the *Handbook* may not be used to its best advantage or even interpreted correctly.

The 12th edition of the *Handbook on Injectable Drugs* brings together a wealth of information on 301 parenteral drugs commercially available in the United States, plus 39 additional parenteral drugs available only in other countries. The information in the 12th edition is accumulated from 2350 references, including 151 new to this edition. As for each previous edition, the monographs have been completely updated. In addition to the updated monographs, 13 additional monographs on parenteral drugs available commercially in the United States that are new to this edition are presented. These include the following drugs:

- Alatrofloxacin mesylate
- Calcium acetate
- Dalteparin sodium
- Dolasetron mesylate
- Gatifloxacin
- Hetastarch 6% in lactated electrolyte injection
- Itraconazole
- Linezolid
- Rocuronium bromide
- Somatropin
- Sumatriptan succinate
- Tirofiban HCl
- Valproate sodium

In addition, the section on drugs available outside the United States has been completely updated and expanded. Nine new drug monographs are presented in this section, including:

- Alizapride HCl
- Flecainide acetate
- Fosfomycin disodium
- Fotemustine
- Hyoscine butylbromide
- Mexiletine HCl
- Nimodipine
- Papaveretum
- Pentoxifylline

In addition to the new and updated monographs in the 12th edition of the *Handbook*, the presentation style and format for the text portions of the monographs have been revised and standardized. The basic headings remain the same as in recent editions, but subheadings and text have been extensively reorganized for consistency throughout the book. The use of the reorganized and standardized subheadings is intended to aid the reader in locating information on specific topics more readily.

The tables of compatibility information, which are the most heavily used sections of the *Handbook*, have remained in the familiar easy-to-use format. The compatibility information for the subject drug in infusion solutions and with other drugs in admixtures, syringes, and during simultaneous administration through manifolds and Y-sites has been pre-sorted for the reader by category.

Heritage of the Handbook

With the 12th edition, the *Handbook on Injectable Drugs* marks its 25-year anniversary. But the involvement of the pharmacy profession with the issues surrounding parenteral drug compatibility is much older, extending back nearly 50 years. The first research paper published on this topic appeared in 1955 in the old *Bulletin of the American Society of Hospital Pharmacists*. Robert C. Bogash, then Director of the Pharmacy Department at Lenox Hill Hospital in New York City, wrote a paper entitled "Compatibilities and Incompatibilities of Some Parenteral Medications." In this groundbreaking paper, Mr. Bogash presented compatibility results on an array of parenteral drug combinations. This paper constitutes the earliest effort to compile such information for pharmacists to use. Mr. Bogash also noted the following obligation: "It is, therefore, the responsibility of the hospital pharmacist to be as fully aware of these [compatibility] phenomena as possible."

In subsequent years, a number of articles on drug compatibility and stability appeared, from both pharmacists and the pharmaceutical industry. In 1967, *Intravenous Therapy* by Jon T. Williams and Daniel F. Morovec was published. This book was the first compilation of parenteral drug compatibility in book form and the first to include tables of compatibility information along with text discussions.

Other early efforts at compiling parenteral drug stability and compatibility information included *Intravenous Additive Incompatibilities* in 1970 from the National Institutes of Health, Clinical Center, *Cutter* (now *King's*) *Guide to Parenteral Admixtures* in 1971, and the *Parenteral Drug Information Guide* in early 1974.

The experience of being the principal author on the *Parenteral Drug Information Guide* was valuable to me, although not for the excellence of the work. Indeed, reviews were mixed. Rather, the faults of this work served as a valuable learning experience, providing an understanding of problems and a focus on things to avoid.

In early 1975, I started over and began work on a new compilation that would become the *Handbook on Injectable Drugs*. The goal was to create the most comprehensive and complete compilation possible summarizing the original published research literature into a new concise, standardized format. The succeeding 20 months were spent compiling the text and tables for the first edition of the *Handbook*. I estimate that over 2400 hours of evenings, weekends, holidays, and vacation went into preparing the manuscript. In this pre-computer era, the manuscript had to be written in long hand (both text and tables) and then typed, corrected, and re-typed. My wife, Pam, had the unenviable job of typing all of those thousands of manuscript pages. The first four editions of the *Handbook* were prepared in this time-consuming and laborious manner—a process unimaginable in this computerized age. The first edition of the *Handbook* was prepared from the information in 297 references, was composed of 430 pages of material, and—at 6 inches by 9 inches— was truly handbook size. The first edition of the *Handbook on Injectable Drugs* appeared in January 1977. Thankfully, it received good reviews from journal editors and book reviewers, and, most importantly, approval by the pharmacists who were using it.

In my initial conceptualization of the project, I did not foresee in any way the vast growth of this work or its enduring nature. I could not have imagined that within a few years the *Handbook* would be found in most hospital and home care pharmacies in the United States and in much of the rest of the world as well. And I certainly did not think this project would become a life's work. But the *Handbook* has now been in continuous publication for 25 years—and counting. It has grown to incorporate the information from 2350 references based principally on laboratory research but also including observations from practice when the observations can be verified. Throughout the *Handbook's* 25-year publication history and twelve editions, the intent of this work has remained unchanged: to organize and summarize in a concise, standardized format the results of the primary research in parenteral drug stability and compatibility to facilitate its use in clinical practice settings for the benefit of our patients.

Envisioning the Next 25 Years

Recently, the safety of medications and medical care has been getting a lot of attention from both health care professionals and from the public, quite justifiably. While the profession of pharmacy has always been active in improving the medication use process and in improving pharmaceutical care, a more broadly based interest is certainly welcome and may be pivotal in creating effective improvements to the overall system.

One aspect of the safe use of parenteral drugs remains the assurance of the drug's pharmaceutical integrity, including stability and compatibility. Although few pharmacists would question this premise, the profession seems to be moving away from involvement with this issue, at least in the United States. De-emphasizing pharmaceutics, compounding, and other drug product related course work in schools of pharmacy, an apparent decrease in the publishing of parenteral drug stability and compatibility information in pharmacy journals, and the potential for a lack of new drug stability and compatibility researchers are a few examples that are emblematic of the changes.

Several decades ago, the profession of pharmacy, both practitioners and academicians, began actively conducting such research in response to the need for this information and the dearth of adequate information from drug manufacturers. Over the years, literally thousands of research projects have been conducted. Unfortunately, the ongoing decline of participation by the pharmacy profession in such research on drug stability and compatibility will result in an increasing number of drugs that have inadequate or no information beyond the official labeling. The pharmacy profession and pharmacy educators should consider the ramifications to patient care and a safe medication use process that this dwindling commitment represents. The assurance of pharmaceutical integrity in the clinical use environment, including drug stability and compatibility, is a responsibility that should not be ignored.

Note of Appreciation

I want to express my gratitude to the reviewers for the 12th edition of the *Handbook on Injectable Drugs*, Todd Canada and Pauline Thomas Parks. Working through a challenging review process in record time, they have made a great contribution toward making the *Handbook* a better reference. The commitment and effort that they had to put forth in performing the review is certainly appreciated. Thank you.

Thanks also go to Bruce Hawkins, Cynthia Reilly, and Mark Koenig of ASHP, as well as Luan Corrigan, who tackled the difficult editorial aspects of this 12th edition. I certainly recognize that this is a complicated manuscript and a difficult revision process at best. Your efforts and perseverance in bringing the 12th edition of the *Handbook on Injectable Drugs* into existence are greatly appreciated.

I also want to take the opportunity of this 25th-year edition to thank again Shelley Elliott, Johnna Hershey, Michael Soares, and James Caro, who helped so much with previous editions of the *Handbook*.

Special thanks go to those users of the *Handbook* who continue to make valuable suggestions for its improvement, call my attention to new articles and relevant information, and point out errors. I appreciate your interest and help. If any reader has input for improvement of the *Handbook*, please feel free to contact me through the publisher, the American Society of Health-System Pharmacists.

Finally, but most important, my deepest gratitude continues to go to my wife, Pam, whose forbearance in the face of this enormous time commitment is greatly appreciated. Her support makes it possible for me to undertake the demanding challenge the *Handbook* represents.

LAT
April 2002

HOW TO USE THE HANDBOOK

What Is the Handbook?

The *Handbook on Injectable Drugs* is a collection of summaries of information from the published literature on the pharmaceutics of parenteral medications as applied to the clinical setting. The *Handbook* is constructed from information derived from 2350 references with the information presented in the standardized structure described below. The purpose of the *Handbook* is to facilitate the use of this clinical pharmaceutics research by knowledgeable health care professionals for the benefit of patients. The summary information from published research is supplemented with information from the labeling of each product and from other references.

The information base summarized in the *Handbook on Injectable Drugs* is large and highly complex, requiring thoughtful consideration for proper use. The *Handbook* is not, nor should it be considered, elementary in nature or a primer. A single quick glance in a table is not adequate for proper interpretation of this highly complex information base. Proper interpretation includes the obvious need to consider and evaluate all relevant research information and results. Additionally, information on the formulation components, product attributes (especially pH), and the known stability behaviors of each parenteral drug, as well as the clinical situation of the patient, must be included in a thoughtful, reasoned evaluation of clinical pharmaceutics questions.

Who Should Use the Handbook?

The *Handbook on Injectable Drugs* is designed for use as a professional reference and guide to the literature on the clinical pharmaceutics of parenteral medications. The intended audience consists of knowledgeable health care professionals, particularly pharmacists, well versed in the formulation and clinical use of parenteral medications and who have the highly specialized knowledge base, training, and skills set necessary to interpret and apply the information. Practitioners who are not well versed in the formulation, essential properties, and clinical application of parenteral drugs should seek the assistance of more knowledgeable and experienced health care professionals to ensure patient safety.

Users of the *Handbook* must recognize that no reference work, including this one, can substitute for adequate decision-making by health care professionals. Proper clinical decisions must be made considering all aspects of the patient's condition and needs, with particular attention to the special demands imposed by parenteral medications. The *Handbook* cannot make decisions for its users. However, in knowledgeable hands, it is a valuable tool for the proper use of parenteral medications.

Organization of the Handbook

The *Handbook on Injectable Drugs* has been organized as a collection of monographs on each of 301 commercially available drugs. In addition, information on 39 drugs available outside the United States has been included. The monographs on the commercial drugs are arranged alphabetically by nonproprietary name. The names of the drugs follow the style of *USAN and the USP Dictionary of Drug Names*. Also included are some of the trade names and manufacturers of the drug products; this listing is not necessarily comprehensive and should not be considered an endorsement of any product or manufacturer.

All of the information included in the *Handbook* is referenced so that those who wish to study the original sources may find them. In addition, the *American Hospital Formulary Service* Classification System numbers have been included to facilitate the location of therapeutic information on the drugs.

The monographs have been divided into the subheadings described below:

Products—lists many of the sizes, strengths, volumes, and forms in which the drug is supplied, along with other components of the formulation. Instructions for reconstitution (when applicable) are included in this section.

The products cited do not necessarily constitute a comprehensive list of all available products. Rather, some common representative products are described. Furthermore, dosage forms, sizes, and container configurations of parenteral products may undergo significant changes during the lifespan of this edition of the *Handbook*.

Following the product descriptions, the pH of the drug products, the osmotic value(s) of the drug and/or dilutions (when available), and other product information such as the sodium content and definition of units are presented. In addition, the densities of solutions of various cytotoxic drugs have been added for use in quality assurance procedures that include a weight check in the preparation of these toxic products.

Practitioners have not always recognized the value and importance of incorporating product formulation information into the thought process that leads to their decision on handling drug compatibility and stability questions. However, consideration of the product information and formulation components as well as the properties and attributes of the products, especially pH, is essential to proper interpretation of the information presented in the *Handbook*.

Administration—includes route(s) by which the drug can be given, rates of administration (when applicable), and other related administration details.

The administration information is a condensation derived primarily from the product's official labeling and the *American Hospital Formulary Service*. For complete information, including dosage information sufficient for prescribing, the reader should refer to the official labeling and therapeutically comprehensive references such as the *American Hospital Formulary Service*.

Stability—describes the drug's stability and storage requirements. The storage condition terminology of *The United States Pharmacopeia*, 25th ed., is used in the *Handbook on Injectable Drugs*.

The United States Pharmacopeia defines controlled room temperature as "A temperature maintained thermostatically that encompasses the usual and customary working environment of 20 ° to 25 °; that results in a mean kinetic temperature calculated to be not more than 25 °; and that allows for excursions between 15 ° and 30 ° that are experienced in pharmacies, hospitals, and warehouses."[1] (All temperatures are Celsius.)

Protection from excessive heat is often required; excessive heat is defined as any temperature above 40 °C. Similarly, protection from freezing may be required for products that are subject to loss of strength or potency, or destructive alteration of their characteristics in addition to the risk of container breakage.[1]

Some products may require storage at a cool temperature, which is defined as any temperature between 8 and 15 °C, or a cold temperature, which is defined as any temperature not exceeding 8 °C. A refrigerator is defined as

Table 1.
Solution Compatibility

			Monograph drug name			
Solution	*Mfr*	*Mfr*	*Conc/L*	*Remarks*	*Ref*	*C/I*
(1)	(2)	(3)	(4)	(5)	(6)	(7)

1. Solution in which the test was conducted.
2. Manufacturer of the solution.
3. Manufacturer of the drug about which the monograph is written.
4. Concentration of the drug about which the monograph is written.
5. Description of the results of the test.
6. Reference to the original source of the information.
7. Designation of the compatibility (C) or incompatibility (I) of the test result according to conventional guidelines.

Table 2.
Additive Compatibility

			Monograph drug name					
Drug	*Mfr*	*Conc/L*	*Mfr*	*Conc/L*	*Test Soln*	*Remarks*	*Ref*	*C/I*
(1)	(2)	(3)	(4)	(5)	(6)	(7)	(8)	(9)

1. Test drug.
2. Manufacturer of the test drug.
3. Concentration of the test drug.
4. Manufacturer of the drug about which the monograph is written.
5. Concentration of the drug about which the monograph is written.
6. Infusion solution in which the test was conducted.
7. Description of the results of the test.
8. Reference to the original source of the information.
9. Designation of the compatibility (C) or incompatibility (I) of the test result according to conventional guidelines.

Table 3.
Drugs in Syringe Compatibility

			Monograph drug name				
Drug (in syringe)	*Mfr*	*Amt*	*Mfr*	*Amt*	*Remarks*	*Ref*	*C/I*
(1)	(2)	(3)	(4)	(5)	(6)	(7)	(8)

1. Test drug.
2. Manufacturer of the test drug.
3. Actual amount of the test drug.
4. Manufacturer of the drug about which the monograph is written.
5. Actual amount of the drug about which the monograph is written.
6. Description of the results of the test.
7. Reference to the original source of the information.
8. Designation of the compatibility (C) or incompatibility (I) of the test result according to conventional guidelines.

Table 4.
Y-Site Injection Compatibility (1:1 Mixture)

			Monograph drug name				
Drug	*Mfr*	*Conc*	*Mfr*	*Conc*	*Remarks*	*Ref*	*C/I*
(1)	(2)	(3)	(4)	(5)	(6)	(7)	(8)

1. Test drug.
2. Manufacturer of the test drug.
3. Concentration of the test drug prior to mixing at the Y-site.
4. Manufacturer of the drug about which the monograph is written.
5. Concentration of the drug about which the monograph is written prior to mixing at the Y-site.
6. Description of the results of the test.
7. Reference to the original source of the information.
8. Designation of the compatibility (C) or incompatibility (I) of the test result according to conventional guidelines.

a cold place in which the temperature is maintained thermostatically between 2 and 8 °C. Freezer storage refers to a place in which the temperature is maintained thermostatically between –25 and –10 °C.[1]

In addition to storage requirements, aspects of drug stability related to pH, freezing, and exposure to light are presented in this section. Also presented is information on repackaging of the drugs or their dilutions in container/closure systems other than the original package (e.g., prefilling into syringes or in ambulatory pumps). Sorption and filtration characteristics of the drugs are provided as well when this information is available. The information is derived principally from the primary published research literature and is supplemented by the product labeling and the *AHFS Drug Information*.

Compatibility Information—tabulates the results of published reports from primary research on the compatibility of the subject drug with infusion solutions and the other drugs. The various citations are listed alphabetically by solution or drug name; the information is completely cross-referenced among the monographs.

Four types of tables are utilized to present the available information, depending on the kind of test being reported. The first type is for information on the compatibility of a drug in various infusion solutions and is depicted in Table 1. The second type of table presents information on two or more drugs in intravenous solutions and is shown in Table 2. The third type of table is used for tests of two or more drugs in syringes and is shown in Table 3. The fourth table format is used for reports of simulated or actual injection into Y-sites and manifolds of administration sets and is shown in Table 4.

Many published articles, especially older ones, do not include all of the information necessary to complete the tables. However, the tables have been completed as fully as possible from the original articles.

Additional Compatibility Information—provides additional information and discussions of compatibility presented largely in narrative form. In addition to primary published research, the information in this section is derived from reliable secondary sources. Examples of such sources include the product labeling and the *AHFS Drug Information*. For information from secondary sources, the research on which the information is based is not available for review. However, the sources are sufficiently reliable that inclusion in the *Handbook* is warranted.

Other Information—contains any relevant auxiliary information concerning the drug which does not fall into the previous categories.

The Listing of Concentration

The concentrations of all admixtures in intravenous solutions in the tables have been indicated in terms of concentration per liter to facilitate comparison of the various studies. In some cases, this may result in amounts of the drug that are greater or lesser than those normally administered (as when the recommended dose is tested in 100 ml of vehicle), but the listings do accurately reflect the actual concentrations tested, expressed in standardized terms.

For studies involving syringes, the amounts actually used are indicated. The volumes are also listed if indicated in the original article.

For studies of actual or simulated Y-site injection of drugs, the concentrations are cited in terms of concentration per milliliter of each drug solution prior to mixing at the Y-site. Most published research reports have presented the drug concentrations in this manner, and the *Handbook* follows this convention. For those few published reports that presented the drug concentrations after mixing at the Y-site, the concentrations have been recalculated to be consistent with the more common presentation style to maintain the consistency of presentation in the *Handbook*. Note that the Y-Site Injection Compatibility table is designed with the assumption of a 1:1 mixture of the subject drug and infusion solution or admixture. For citations reporting other than a 1:1 mixture, the actual amounts tested are specifically noted.

Designating Compatibility or Incompatibility

Each summary of a published research report appearing in the Compatibility Information tables bears a compatibility indicator (***C***, ***I***, or ***?***). A report receives a designation of ***C*** when the study results indicate that compatibility of the test samples existed under the test conditions. If the study determined an incompatibility existed under the test conditions, then an ***I*** designation is assigned for the *Handbook* entry for that study result. Specific standardized guidelines are used to assign these compatibility designations. The citation is designated as a report of compatibility when results of the original article indicated one or more of the following criteria were met:

1. Physical or visual compatibility of the combination was reported (no visible or electronically detected indication of particulate formation, haze, precipitation, color change, or gas evolution).
2. Stability of the components for at least 24 hours in an admixture under the specified conditions was reported (decomposition of 10% or less).
3. Stability of the components for the entire test period, although in some cases it was less than 24 hours, was reported (time periods less than 24 hours have been noted).

The citation is designated as a report of incompatibility when the results of the original article indicated either or both of the following criteria were met:

1. A physical or visual incompatibility was reported (visible or electronically detected particulate formation, haze, precipitation, color change, or gas evolution).
2. Greater than 10% decomposition of one or more components in 24 hours or less under the specified conditions was reported (time periods of less than 24 hours have been noted in the table).

Reports of test results that do not clearly fit into the compatibility or incompatibility definitions cannot be designated as either. These are indicated with a question mark.

Although these criteria have become the conventional definitions of compatibility and incompatibility, the reader should recognize that the criteria may need to be tempered with professional judgment. Inflexible adherence to the compatibility designations should be avoided. Instead, they should be used as aids in the exercising of professional judgment.

Therapeutic incompatibilities or other drug interactions are not within the scope of the *Handbook* and have not been included.

Interpreting Compatibility Information in the Handbook

As mentioned above, the body of information summarized in the *Handbook* is large and complicated. With the possible exception of a report of immediate gross precipitation, it usually takes some degree of thoughtful consideration and judgment to properly evaluate and appropriately act on the research results that are summarized in this book.

Nowhere is the need for judgment more obvious than when apparently contradictory information appears in two or more published reports. The body of literature in drug–drug and drug–vehicle compatibility is replete with apparently contradictory results. Except for study results that have been documented later to be incorrect, the conflicting information has been included in the *Handbook* to provide practitioners with all of the information for their consideration. The conflicting information will be readily apparent to the reader because of the content of the Remarks section as well as the ***C***, ***I***, and ***?*** designations following each citation.

Many or most of the apparently conflicting citations may be the result of differing conditions or materials used in the studies. A variety of factors that can influence the compatibility and stability of drugs must be considered in evaluating such conflicting results, and absolute statements are often difficult or impossible to make. Differences in concentrations, buffering systems, preservatives, vehicles, temperatures, and order of mixing may all play a role. By reviewing a variety of reports, the user of the *Handbook* is better able to exercise professional judgment with regard to compatibility and stability.

The reader must guard against misinterpretation of research results, which may lead to extensions of compatibility and stability that are inappropriate. As an example, a finding of precipitate formation two hours after two drugs are mixed does not imply nor should it be interpreted to mean that the combination is compatible until that time point, when a sudden precipitation occurs. Rather, it should be interpreted to mean that precipitation occurred at some point between mixing and the first observation point at two hours. Such a result would lead to a designation of incompatibility in the *Handbook*.

Precipitation reports can be particularly troublesome for practitioners to deal with because of the variability of the time frames in which they may occur. Apart from combinations that repeatedly result in immediate precipitation, the formation of a precipitate can be unpredictable to some degree. Numerous examples of variable precipitation time frames can be found in the literature, including paclitaxel, etoposide, and sulfamethoxazole-trimethoprim in infusion solutions and calcium and phosphates precipitation in parenteral nutrition mixtures. Differing drug concentrations can also play a role in creating variability in results. A good example of this occurs with co-administered vancomycin HCl and beta-lactam antibiotics. Users of the information in the *Handbook* must always be aware that a marginally incompatible combination might exhibit precipitation earlier or later than that reported in the literature. It has been suggested that in many such cases, the precipitation is ultimately going to occur, it is just the timing that is in question. This is of particular importance for precipitate formation because of the potential for serious adverse clinical consequences, including death, which have occurred. Certainly, users of the *Handbook* information should always keep in mind and anticipate the possibility of precipitation and its clinical ramifications.

In addition, many research reports cite test solutions or concentrations that may not be appropriate for clinical use. An example would be a report of a drug's stability in unsterile water. Although the *Handbook* summary will accurately reflect the test solutions and conditions that existed in a study, it is certainly inappropriate to misinterpret a stability report like this as being an authorization to use the product clinically. In such cases, the researchers may have used the clinically inappropriate diluent to evaluate the drug's stability for extrapolation to a more suitable vehicle that is similar, or they may not have recognized that the diluent is clinically unsuitable. In either event, it is incumbent on the practitioner in the clinical setting to use professional judgment to apply the information in an appropriate manner and recognize what is not acceptable clinically.

Further, it should be noted that many of the citations designated incompatible are not absolute. While a particular admixture may incur more than 10% decomposition within 24 hours, the combination may be useful for a shorter time period. The concept of "utility time" or the time to 10% decomposition may be useful in these cases. Unfortunately, such information is often not available. Included in the Remarks columns of the tables are the amount of decomposition, the time period involved, and the temperature at which the study was conducted when this information is available.

Users of the *Handbook* information should always keep in mind that the information in the *Handbook* must be used as a tool and a guide to the research that has been conducted and published. It is not a replacement for thoughtfully considered professional judgment. It falls to the practitioner to interpret the information in light of the clinical situation, including the patient's needs and status. What is certain is that relying solely on the ***C*** or ***I*** designation without the application of professional judgment is inappropriate.

Limitations of the Literature

In addition to conflicting information, many of the published articles have provided only partial evaluations, not looking at all aspects of a drug's stability and compatibility. This is not surprising considering the complexity, difficulty, and costs of conducting such research. There are, in fact, some articles that do provide evaluations of both physical stability/compatibility and chemical stability. But others are devoted only to physical issues, while others examine only chemical stability. Although a finding of precipitation, haze, or other physical effect may constitute an incompatibility (unless transient), the lack of such changes does not rule out chemical deterioration. In some cases, drugs initially designated as compatible because of a lack of visual change were later shown to undergo chemical decomposition. Similarly, the determination of chemical stability does not rule out the presence of unacceptable levels of particulates and/or turbidity in the combination. In a classic case, the drugs leucovorin calcium and fluorouracil were determined to be chemically stable for extended periods by stability-indicating HPLC assays in several studies, but years later, repeated episodes of filter clogging led to the discovery of unacceptable quantities of particulates in combinations of these drugs. The reader must always bear in mind these possibilities when only partial information is available.

And, finally, contemporary practitioners have come to expect that the analytical methods used in reports on the chemical stability of drugs will be validated stability-indicating methods. However, many early studies used methods that were not demonstrated to be stability indicating.

Literature Search for Updating the Handbook

To gather the bulk of the published compatibility and stability information for updating the *Handbook*, a literature search is performed using the *International Pharmaceutical Abstracts* database. By using key terms (e.g., stability), a listing of candidate articles for inclusion in the *Handbook* is generated. From this list, truly relevant articles are selected. As a supplement to this automated literature searching, a manual search of the references of the articles is also conducted, and any articles not included previously are obtained. Although this labor-intensive approach yields a very high percentage of the relevant articles published in the world's literature, it is not 100% inclusive. Occasionally, users of the *Handbook* come across articles that were overlooked. The author encourages anyone who finds an article that has been missed to bring it to his attention.

Reference

1. *The United States Pharmacopeia*, 25th ed., United States Pharmacopeial Convention: Rockville, MD; 2002.

Solution Abbreviations

AA	Amino acids (percentage specified)
D	Dextrose solution (percentage unspecified)
D5LR	Dextrose 5% in Ringer's injection, lactated
D5R	Dextrose 5% in Ringer's injection
D–S	Dextrose–saline combinations
D2.5½S	Dextrose 2.5% in sodium chloride 0.45%
D2.5S	Dextrose 2.5% in sodium chloride 0.9%
D5¼S	Dextrose 5% in sodium chloride 0.225%
D5½S	Dextrose 5% in sodium chloride 0.45%
D5S	Dextrose 5% in sodium chloride 0.9%
D10S	Dextrose 10% in sodium chloride 0.9%
D5W	Dextrose 5% in water
D10W	Dextrose 10% in water

DXN–S	Dextran 6% in sodium chloride 0.9%
IDCM	Ionosol DCM
IG	Ionosol G
IM	Isolyte M
IP	Isolyte P
IS	Invert sugar
LR	Ringer's injection, lactated
NM	Normosol M
NR	Normosol R
NS	Sodium chloride 0.9%
PH	Protein hydrolysate
R	Ringer's injections
REF	Refrigeration
RT	Room temperature
S	Saline solution (percentage unspecified)
½S	Sodium chloride 0.45%
SL	Sodium lactate ⅙ M
TPN	Total parenteral nutrition solution
W	Sterile water for injection

Manufacturer and Compendium Abbreviations

AB	Abbott
ACC	American Critical Care
AD	Adria
AGT	Aguettant
AH	Allen & Hanburys
AHP	Ascot Hospital Pharmaceuticals
ALZ	Alza
AM	ASTA Medica
AMG	Amgen
AMR	American Regent
ANT	Antigen
AP	Asta-Pharma
APC	Apothecon
APP	American Pharmaceutical Partners
AQ	American Quinine
AR	Armour
ARC	American Red Cross
AS	Arnar-Stone
ASC	Ascot
AST	Astra
ASZ	AstraZeneca
AT	Alpha Therapeutic
AW	Asta Werke
AY	Ayerst
BA	Baxter
BAN	Banyu Pharmaceuticals
BAY	Bayer
BC	Bencard
BE	Beecham
BED	Bedford
BEL	R. Bellon
BFM	Bieffe Medital
BI	Boehringer Ingelheim
BK	Berk
BKN	Baker Norton
BM	Boehringer Mannheim
BMS	Bristol-Myers Squibb
BN	Breon
BP	British Pharmacopoeia[a]
BPC	British Pharmaceutical Codex[a]
BR	Bristol
BRN	B. Braun
BRT	Britianna
BT	Boots
BTK	Biotika
BV	Ben Venue
BW	Burroughs Wellcome
BX	Berlex
BY	Bayer
CA	Calmic
CE	Carlo Erba
CER	Cerenex
CET	Cetus
CH	Lab. Choay Societe Anonyme
CHI	Chiron
CL	Ciba
CL	Clintec
CN	Connaught
CNF	Centrafarm
CO	Cole
CP	Continental Pharma
CPP	CP Pharmaceuticals
CR	Critikon
CU	Cutter
CY	Cyanamid
DAK	Dakota
DB	David Bull Laboratories
DCC	Dupont Critical Care
DI	Dista
DIA	Diamant
DM	Dome
DME	Dupont Merck Pharma
DMX	Dumex
DRA	Dr. Rentschler Arzneimittel
DU	DuPont
DW	Delta West
EA	Eaton
EBE	Ebewe
EN	Endo
ES	Elkins-Sinn
EV	Evans
EX	Essex
FA	Farmitalia
FAU	Faulding
FC	Frosst & Cie
FED	Federa
FI	Fisons
FRE	Fresenius
FUJ	Fujisawa
GEI	Geistich Pharma
GEM	Geneva-Marsam
GEN	Genentech
GG	Geigy
GIL	Gilead
GIU	Giulini
GL	Glaxo
GNS	Gensia
GO	Goedecke
GRI	Grifols
GRP	Gruppo
GRU	Grunenthal
GW	Glaxo Wellcome
HC	Hillcross
HMR	Hoechst Marion Roussel
HO	Hoechst-Roussel
HR	Horner
HY	Hyland
ICI	ICI Pharmaceuticals
IMM	Immunex
IMS	IMS Ltd.
IN	Intra

IV	Ives
IVX	Ivex
IX	Invenex
JC	Janssen-Cilag
JN	Janssen
KA	Kabi
KN	Knoll
KP	Kabi Pharmacia
KV	Kabi-Vitrum
KY	Kyowa
LA	Lagap
LE	Lederle
LEM	Lemmon
LEO	Leo Laboratories
LI	Lilly
LY	Lyphomed
LZ	Labaz Laboratories
MA	Mallinckrodt
MAC	Maco Pharma
MAR	Marsam
MB	May & Baker
ME	Merck
MG	McGaw
MI	Miles
MJ	Mead Johnson
MN	McNeil
MMD	Marion Merrell Dow
MRD	Merrill-Dow
MRN	Merrill-National
MSD	Merck Sharp & Dohme
MUN	Mundi Pharma
MY	Maney
MYR	Mayrhofer Pharmazeutika
NA	National
NAP	NAPP Pharmaceuticals
NCI	National Cancer Institute
NE	Norwich-Eaton
NF	National Formulary[a]
NO	Nordic
NOV	Novo
OHM	Ohmeda
OM	Omega
OMJ	OMJ Pharmaceuticals
OMN	Ortho-McNeil
ON	Orion
OR	Organon
ORT	Ortho
PB	Pohl-Boskamp
PD	Parke-Davis
PE	Pentagone
PF	Pfizer
PFM	Pfrimmer
PH	Pharmacia
PHS	Pharmacience
PHT	Pharma-Tek
PHU	Pharmacia & Upjohn
PHX	Phoenix
PO	Poulenc
PR	Pasadena Research
PRK	Parkfields
PX	Pharmax
QLM	Qualimed Labs
QU	Quad
RB	Robins
RC	Roche
RI	Riker
RKC	Reckitt & Colman
ROR	Rorer
ROX	Roxane
RP	Rhone-Poulenc
RPR	Rhone-Poulenc Rorer
RR	Roerig
RS	Roussel
RU	Rugby
SA	Sankyo
SAN	Sanofi
SC	Schering
SCN	Schein
SCS	SCS Pharmaceuticals
SE	Searle
SEQ	Sequus
SER	Servier
SKB	SmithKline Beecham
SKF	Smith Kline & French
SM	Smith
SN	Smith + Nephew
SO	SoloPak
SQ	Squibb
SS	Sanofi-Synthelabo
ST	Sterilab
STP	Sterop
STR	Sterling
STS	Steris
STU	Stuart
SV	Savage
SW	Sanofi Winthrop
SX	Sabex
SY	Syntex
SYO	Synthelabo
SZ	Sandoz
TAK	Takeda
TAY	Taylor
TE	Teva
TL	Tillotts
TO	Torigian
TR	Travenol
UP	Upjohn
USB	US Bioscience
USP	United States Pharmacopeiea[a]
USV	USV Pharmaceuticals
VHA	VHA Plus
VI	Vitarine
VT	Vitrum
WAS	Wasserman
WAY	Wyeth-Ayerst
WB	Winthrop-Breon
WC	Warner-Chilcott
WED	Weddel
WEL	Wellcome
WI	Winthrop
WL	Warner Lambert
WY	Wyeth
YAM	Yamanouchi
ZEN	Zeneca

[a] *While reference to a compendium does not indicate the specific manufacturer of a product, it does help to indicate the formulation that was used in the test.*

Commercial Drug Monographs

ACETAZOLAMIDE SODIUM
AHFS 52:10

Products — Acetazolamide as the sodium salt is available in 500-mg vials with sodium hydroxide and, if necessary, hydrochloric acid to adjust the pH. Reconstitute the vial with at least 5 ml of sterile water for injection to yield a solution containing not more than 100 mg/ml. (4)

pH — Approximately 9.2 to 9.6. (1-11/00; 4)

Osmolality — The osmolality of acetazolamide sodium 500 mg was calculated for the following dilutions (1054):

	Osmolality (mOsm/kg)	
Diluent	50 ml	100 ml
Dextrose 5% in water	321	291
Sodium chloride	348	317

Sodium Content — 2.049 mEq/500 mg (calculated). (846)

Trade Name(s) — Diamox Sodium.

Administration — Administration by direct intravenous injection is preferred. Intramuscular injection is painful due to the alkaline pH and is not recommended. (1-11/00; 4)

Stability — Store intact vials at controlled room temperature. (4) The manufacturer states that the reconstituted solution is stable for three days if refrigerated or for 12 hours at room temperature. (1-11/00) Other information indicates that the reconstituted solution is stable for one week under refrigeration. However, because the product contains no preservatives, use of the solution within 24 hours after reconstitution is recommended. (4)

pH Effects — The stability of acetazolamide sodium in aqueous solution appears to decrease as the pH increases above 9. At pH 8.8, a 0.25-mg/ml solution retained 96% of the initial amount after three days at 25 °C; at pH 10.8 and 12.7, the remaining drug was 88 and 83%, respectively, after four days. (1230) Acetazolamide exhibits maximum stability at pH 4. (1424)

Freezing Solutions — Acetazolamide sodium (Lederle) 375 mg/L in dextrose 5% in water and sodium chloride 0.9% in PVC bags lost less than 3% after 44 days at −10 °C. (1085)

Sorption — Acetazolamide sodium (Lederle) 19 mg/L in sodium chloride 0.9% (Travenol) in PVC bags did not exhibit significant sorption to the plastic during one week of storage at room temperature (15 to 20 °C). (536)

Acetazolamide sodium (Lederle) 19 mg/L in sodium chloride 0.9% did not exhibit any loss due to sorption during a seven-hour simulated infusion through an infusion set (Travenol) consisting of a cellulose propionate burette chamber and 170 cm of PVC tubing. (606)

The drug was also tested as a simulated infusion over at least one hour by a syringe pump system. A glass syringe on a syringe pump was fitted with 20 cm of polyethylene tubing or 50 cm of Silastic tubing. No loss of drug due to sorption was observed with either tubing. (606)

A 25-ml aliquot of acetazolamide sodium (Lederle) 19 mg/L in sodium chloride 0.9% was stored in all-plastic syringes composed of polypropylene barrels and polyethylene plungers for 24 hours at room temperature in the dark. No loss due to sorption occurred. (606)

Compatibility Information

Solution Compatibility

Acetazolamide sodium

Solution	*Mfr*	*Mfr*	*Conc/L*	*Remarks*	*Ref*	*C/I*
Dextran 6% in dextrose 5%	AB	LE	375 mg	Physically compatible	3	C
Dextran 6% in sodium chloride 0.9%	AB	LE	375 mg	Physically compatible	3	C
Dextrose–Ringer's injection combinations	AB	LE	375 mg	Physically compatible	3	C
Dextrose–Ringer's injection, lactated, combinations	AB	LE	375 mg	Physically compatible	3	C
Dextrose–saline combinations	AB	LE	375 mg	Physically compatible	3	C
Dextrose 2½% in water	AB	LE	375 mg	Physically compatible	3	C
Dextrose 5% in water	AB	LE	375 mg	Physically compatible	3	C
	TR[a]	LE	375 mg	Physically compatible with 7% acetazolamide loss in 5 days at 25 °C and 5% loss in 44 days at 5 °C	1085	C
Dextrose 10% in water	AB	LE	375 mg	Physically compatible	3	C
Fructose 10% in sodium chloride 0.9%	AB	LE	375 mg	Physically compatible	3	C
Fructose 10% in water	AB	LE	375 mg	Physically compatible	3	C
Invert sugar 5 and 10% in sodium chloride 0.9%	AB	LE	375 mg	Physically compatible	3	C

Solution Compatibility (Cont.)

Acetazolamide sodium

Solution	*Mfr*	*Mfr*	*Conc/L*	*Remarks*	*Ref*	*C/I*
Invert sugar 5 and 10% in water	AB	LE	375 mg	Physically compatible	3	C
Ionosol products	AB	LE	375 mg	Physically compatible	3	C
Ringer's injection	AB	LE	375 mg	Physically compatible	3	C
Ringer's injection, lactated	AB	LE	375 mg	Physically compatible	3	C
Sodium chloride 0.45%	AB	LE	375 mg	Physically compatible	3	C
Sodium chloride 0.9%	AB	LE	375 mg	Physically compatible	3	C
	TR[a]	LE	375 mg	Physically compatible with 7% acetazolamide loss in 5 days at 25 °C and 5% loss in 44 days at 5 °C	1085	C
Sodium lactate ⅙ M	AB	LE	375 mg	Physically compatible	3	C

[a]*Tested in PVC containers.*

Additive Compatibility

Acetazolamide sodium

Drug	*Mfr*	*Conc/L*	*Mfr*	*Conc/L*	*Test Soln*	*Remarks*	*Ref*	*C/I*
Cimetidine HCl	SKF	3 g	LE	5 g	D5W	Physically compatible and cimetidine chemically stable for 24 hr at room temperature. Acetazolamide not tested	551	C
Ranitidine HCl	GL	50 mg and 2 g		5 g	D5W	Physically compatible and ranitidine chemically stable by HPLC for 24 hr at 25 °C. Acetazolamide not tested	1515	C

Y-Site Injection Compatibility (1:1 Mixture)

Acetazolamide sodium

Drug	*Mfr*	*Conc*	*Mfr*	*Conc*	*Remarks*	*Ref*	*C/I*
Diltiazem HCl	MMD	5 mg/ml	LE	100 mg/ml	Precipitate forms	1807	I
	MMD	1 mg/ml[b]	LE	100 mg/ml	Visually compatible	1807	C
TPN #203 and #204[a]			LE	100 mg/ml	White precipitate forms immediately	1974	I

[a]*Refer to Appendix I for the composition of parenteral nutrition solutions. TPN indicates a 2-in-1 admixture.*
[b]*Tested in sodium chloride 0.9%.*

Additional Compatibility Information

Acetazolamide sodium is stated to be physically incompatible with multivitamins (Astra). (1-11/00)

ACYCLOVIR SODIUM
AHFS 8:18

Products — Acyclovir sodium is available in vials containing 500 mg or 1 g of acyclovir as the sodium salt. Reconstitute the 500-mg vial with 10 ml and the 1-g vial with 20 ml of sterile water for injection; shake well to ensure complete dissolution. Do not use bacteriostatic water for injection containing parabens or benzyl alcohol for reconstitution. The acyclovir concentration in the reconstituted solution is 50 mg/ml; the reconstituted solution must be diluted to a concentration of 7 mg/ml or less for use. (2)

pH — The reconstituted solution has a pH of approximately 11 with a range of 10.5 to 11.6. (2; 4)

Osmolality — Acyclovir sodium (Glaxo Wellcome) 50 mg/ml in sterile water for injection has an osmolality of 348 mOsm/kg. (2043)

The osmolality of acyclovir sodium 500 mg was calculated for the following dilutions (1054):

	Osmolality (mOsm/kg)	
Diluent	50 ml	100 ml
Dextrose 5% in water	316	289
Sodium chloride 0.9%	342	316

The osmolality of acyclovir sodium 7 mg/ml was determined to be 278 mOsm/kg in dextrose 5% in water and 299 mOsm/kg in sodium chloride 0.9%. (1375)

Sodium Content — Acyclovir sodium (Glaxo Wellcome) contains 4.2 mEq of sodium per gram of drug. (4)

Trade Name(s) — Zovirax.

Administration — Acyclovir sodium is administered by slow intravenous infusion at concentrations of 7 mg/ml or less over a period of one hour. Rapid intravenous administration and administration by other routes must be avoided. (2; 4)

Stability — Intact vials of acyclovir sodium should be stored at controlled room temperature. The reconstituted solution should be used within 12 hours. Refrigeration of the reconstituted solution may cause a precipitate, but this precipitate will dissolve at room temperature, apparently without affecting potency. After dilution for administration, the dose may be stored at room temperature; it should be used within 24 hours. (2; 4) However, storage of acyclovir admixtures at room temperature does not guarantee that no precipitate will form. Precipitation has also been observed in acyclovir sodium infusions in PVC containers after a few days' storage at room temperature. (2190)

Acyclovir sodium reconstituted with bacteriostatic water for injection containing benzyl alcohol is as stable as when reconstituted with unpreserved sterile water for injection. However, the manufacturer recommends not using the benzyl alcohol-containing diluent because of concerns about the risks to neonates. The paraben-containing form of bacteriostatic water for injection must not be used for reconstitution because of the potential for precipitate formation. (4)

Precipitation — Short-term refrigerated storage of acyclovir sodium admixtures with concentrations exceeding 1 mg/ml may result in formation of a precipitate that redissolves upon warming to room temperature. However, such solutions should be used immediately after warming to room temperature because of the subsequent appearance of persistent microprecipitates. (2098)

Physical instability is the principal limitation to long-term storage of acyclovir sodium admixtures. Persistent subvisual microprecipitate formation as well as frank persistent precipitation may occur in variable time periods. Such precipitation has been reported to occur after as little as seven days and in varying time periods throughout a 35-day observation period; the appearance of a precipitate is not precisely predictable. (2098)

The formation of large amounts of subvisual particulates has been attributed to an interaction of the highly alkaline acyclovir sodium solution with PVC containers. Some increase in the number of particulates was observed in as little as one day, with substantial increases in seven days. When packaged in ethylene vinyl acetate (EVA) containers, no significant increase in subvisual particulates occurs, even after 28 days of storage. (2190)

Elastomeric Reservoir Pumps — Acyclovir sodium (Burroughs Wellcome) 5 mg/ml in both dextrose 5% in water and sodium chloride 0.9% was evaluated for binding potential to natural rubber elastomeric reservoirs (Baxter). No binding was found after storage for two weeks at 35 °C with gentle agitation. (2014)

Acyclovir sodium solutions in elastomeric reservoir pumps have been stated by the pump manufacturers to be stable for the following time periods refrigerated (REF) or at room temperature (RT) (31):

Pump Reservoir(s)	Conc.	REF	RT
Homepump; Homepump Eclipse	10 mg/ml[b]	30 days	10 days
Intermate HPC	1 to 10 mg/ml[a]		4 days
Intermate HPC	10 mg/ml[b]		29 days
Medflo	5 mg/ml[a,b]	37 days	37 days
ReadyMed	5 mg/ml[b]		7 days

[a] *In dextrose 5% in water.*
[b] *In sodium chloride 0.9%.*

Sorption — Acyclovir sodium (Glaxo Wellcome) 5 mg/ml in dextrose 5% in water and sodium chloride 0.9% packaged in PVC, polyethylene, and glass containers exhibited no loss due to sorption to any of the container types when stored at 4 and 22 °C for 24 hours protected from light. (2289) In another study, no binding to natural rubber elastomeric reservoirs was observed. (2014) See Elastomeric Reservoir Pumps above.

Central Venous Catheter — Acyclovir sodium (GlaxoWellcome) 1 mg/ml in dextrose 5% in water was found to be compatible with the ARROWg+ard Blue Plus (Arrow International) chlorhexidine-bearing triple-lumen central catheter. HPLC analysis was used to evaluate completeness of drug delivery through the catheter and the amount of chlorhexidine removed from the internal lumens. Essentially complete delivery of the drug was found with little or no drug loss occurring. Furthermore, chlorhexidine delivered from the catheter remained at trace amounts with no substantial increase due to the delivery of the drug through the catheter. (2335)

Compatibility Information

Solution Compatibility

Acyclovir sodium

Solution	Mfr	Mfr	Conc/L	Remarks	Ref	C/I
Dextrose 5% in water	TR[a]	BW	5 g	Visually compatible with no loss by HPLC in 37 days at 25 and 5 °C	1343	C
	BA[a]	BW	1 g	Physically compatible with no loss by HPLC after 35 days at 23 °C and after 35 days at 4 °C followed by 2 days at 23 °C protected from light	2098	C
	BA[a]	BW	7 g	Physically compatible with 3% or less loss by HPLC after 28 days at 23 °C protected from light. Subvisual microprecipitate forms by 35 days	2098	C
	BA[a]	BW	7 g	Precipitate forms on refrigeration that redissolves on warming. No loss by HPLC after 35 days at 4 °C protected from light, but subvisual precipitate forms after 2 more days at 23 °C	2098	C
	BA[a]	BW	10 g	Physically compatible with no loss by HPLC after 21 days at 23 °C protected from light. Subvisual microprecipitate forms in 28 days, and visible precipitate forms in 35 days	2098	C
	BA[a]	BW	10 g	Precipitate forms on refrigeration that redissolves on warming. No loss by HPLC after 35 days at 4 °C protected from light, but subvisual precipitate forms after 2 more days at 23 °C	2098	C
	BA[a], BRN[c]	GW	5 g	Visually compatible with little or no loss by HPLC in 24 hr at 4 and 22 °C	2289	C
Sodium chloride 0.9%	TR[a]	BW	5 g	No acyclovir loss by HPLC in 37 days at 25 and 5 °C. Storage at 5 °C resulted in white precipitate that dissolved on warming to 25 °C	1343	C
	BA[a]	BW	1, 7, 10 g	Physically compatible with no loss by HPLC after 7 days at 23 °C protected from light. Visible precipitate formed within 14 days	2098	C
	BA[a]	BW	1, 7, 10 g	Physically compatible with no loss by HPLC after 35 days at 4 °C followed by 2 days at 23 °C protected from light	2098	C
	BA[a]	WEL	2.5 and 5 g	No loss of acyclovir by HPLC in 28 days at 25 °C, but subvisual particulates increased significantly after 7 days due to interaction with PVC containers	2190	C
	BA[b]	WEL	2.5 and 5 g	No loss of acyclovir by HPLC and little or no change in subvisual particulates in 28 days at 25 °C in EVA containers	2190	C
	BA[a], BRN[c]	GW	5 g	Visually compatible with little or no loss by HPLC in 24 hr at 4 and 22 °C	2289	C

[a]Tested in PVC containers.
[b]Tested in ethylene vinyl acetate (EVA) containers.
[c]Tested in polyethylene and glass containers.

Additive Compatibility

Acyclovir sodium

Drug	Mfr	Conc/L	Mfr	Conc/L	Test Soln	Remarks	Ref	C/I
Dobutamine HCl	LI	1 g	BW	5 g	D5W	Discoloration developed in 25 min and cloudiness and brown color developed in 2 hr due to dobutamine oxidation. No acyclovir loss found	1343	I

Additive Compatibility (Cont.)

			Acyclovir sodium					
Drug	*Mfr*	*Conc/L*	*Mfr*	*Conc/L*	*Test Soln*	*Remarks*	*Ref*	*C/I*
Dopamine HCl	SO	1.6 g	BW	5 g	D5W	Yellow color developed in 1.5 hr due to dopamine oxidation. No acyclovir loss found	1343	I
Fluconazole	PF	1 g	BW	5 g	D5W	Visually compatible with no fluconazole loss by HPLC in 72 hr at 25 °C under fluorescent light. Acyclovir not tested	1677	C
Meropenem	ZEN	1 g	BW	5 g	NS	Visually compatible for 4 hr at room temperature	1994	C
	ZEN	20 g	BW	5 g	NS	Immediate precipitation	1994	I

Y-Site Injection Compatibility (1:1 Mixture)

			Acyclovir sodium				
Drug	*Mfr*	*Conc*	*Mfr*	*Conc*	*Remarks*	*Ref*	*C/I*
Allopurinol sodium	BW	3 mg/ml[b]	BW	7 mg/ml[b]	Physically compatible with no change in measured turbidity or increase in particle content in 4 hr at 22 °C	1686	C
Amifostine	USB	10 mg/ml[a]	BW	7 mg/ml[a]	Subvisual needles form in 1 hr. Visible particles form in 4 hr	1845	I
Amikacin sulfate	BR	5 mg/ml[a]	BW	5 mg/ml[a]	Physically compatible for 4 hr at 25 °C	1157	C
Amphotericin B cholesteryl sulfate complex	SEQ	0.83 mg/ml[a]	GW	7 mg/ml[a]	Physically compatible with little or no change in measured turbidity or increase in particle content in 4 hr at 23 °C under fluorescent light	2117	C
Ampicillin sodium	WY	20 mg/ml[b]	BW	5 mg/ml[a]	Physically compatible for 4 hr at 25 °C	1157	C
Amsacrine	NCI	1 mg/ml[a]	BW	7 mg/ml[a]	Immediate dark orange turbidity, becoming brownish orange in 1 hr	1381	I
Aztreonam	SQ	40 mg/ml[a]	BW	7 mg/ml[a]	White crystalline needles form immediately and become dense flocculent precipitate in 4 hr	1758	I
Cefamandole nafate	LI	20 mg/ml[a]	BW	5 mg/ml[a]	Physically compatible for 4 hr at 25 °C	1157	C
Cefazolin sodium	SKF	20 mg/ml[a]	BW	5 mg/ml[a]	Physically compatible for 4 hr at 25 °C	1157	C
Cefepime HCl	BMS	20 mg/ml[a]	BW	7 mg/ml[a]	Tiny crystals form in 4 hr	1689	I
Cefoperazone sodium	RR	20 mg/ml[a]	BW	5 mg/ml[a]	Physically compatible for 4 hr at 25 °C	1157	C
Cefotaxime sodium	HO	20 mg/ml[a]	BW	5 mg/ml[a]	Physically compatible for 4 hr at 25 °C	1157	C
Cefoxitin sodium	MSD	20 mg/ml[a]	BW	5 mg/ml[a]	Physically compatible for 4 hr at 25 °C	1157	C
Ceftazidime[g]	SKF	20 mg/ml[a]	BW	5 mg/ml[a]	Physically compatible for 4 hr at 25 °C	1157	C
Ceftizoxime sodium	SKF	20 mg/ml[a]	BW	5 mg/ml[a]	Physically compatible for 4 hr at 25 °C	1157	C
Ceftriaxone sodium	RC	20 mg/ml[a]	BW	5 mg/ml[a]	Physically compatible for 4 hr at 25 °C	1157	C
Cefuroxime sodium	GL	15 mg/ml[a]	BW	5 mg/ml[a]	Physically compatible for 4 hr at 25 °C	1157	C
Chloramphenicol sodium succinate	ES	20 mg/ml[a]	BW	5 mg/ml[a]	Physically compatible for 4 hr at 25 °C	1157	C
Cimetidine HCl	SKF	6 mg/ml[a]	BW	5 mg/ml[a]	Physically compatible for 4 hr at 25 °C	1157	C

Y-Site Injection Compatibility (1:1 Mixture) (Cont.)

Drug	Mfr	Conc	Acyclovir sodium Mfr	Acyclovir sodium Conc	Remarks	Ref	C/I
Cisatracurium besylate	GW	0.1 and 2 mg/ml[a]	BW	7 mg/ml[a]	Physically compatible with no change in measured turbidity or increase in particle content in 4 hr at 23 °C	2074	C
	GW	5 mg/ml[a]	BW	7 mg/ml[a]	White cloudiness forms immediately	2074	I
Clindamycin phosphate	UP	12 mg/ml[a]	BW	5 mg/ml[a]	Physically compatible for 4 hr at 25 °C	1157	C
Dexamethasone sodium phosphate	ES	0.2 mg/ml[a]	BW	5 mg/ml[a]	Physically compatible for 4 hr at 25 °C	1157	C
Diltiazem HCl	MMD	5 mg/ml	BW	5[a] and 7[b] mg/ml	Cloudiness and precipitate form	1807	I
	MMD	1 mg/ml[b]	BW	5[a] and 7[b] mg/ml	Visually compatible	1807	C
Dimenhydrinate	SE	1 mg/ml[a]	BW	5 mg/ml[a]	Physically compatible for 4 hr at 25 °C	1157	C
Diphenhydramine HCl	ES	1 mg/ml[a]	BW	5 mg/ml[a]	Physically compatible for 4 hr at 25 °C	1157	C
Dobutamine HCl	LI	1 mg/ml[a]	BW	5 mg/ml[a]	Solution turns cloudy and brown in 1 hr at 25 °C under fluorescent light	1157	I
Docetaxel	RPR	0.9 mg/ml[a]	GW	7 mg/ml[a]	Physically compatible with no change in measured turbidity or increase in particle content in 4 hr at 23 °C	2224	C
Dopamine HCl	AB	1.6 mg/ml[a]	BW	5 mg/ml[a]	Solution turns dark brown in 2 hr at 25 °C under fluorescent light	1157	I
Doxorubicin HCl liposome injection	SEQ	0.4 mg/ml[a]	GW	7 mg/ml[a]	Physically compatible with little or no change in measured turbidity and no increase in particle content in 4 hr at 23 °C	2087	C
Doxycycline hyclate	PF	1 mg/ml[a]	BW	5 mg/ml[a]	Physically compatible for 4 hr at 25 °C	1157	C
Erythromycin lactobionate	AB	4 mg/ml[a]	BW	5 mg/ml[a]	Physically compatible for 4 hr at 25 °C	1157	C
Etoposide phosphate	BR	5 mg/ml[a]	GW	7 mg/ml[a]	Physically compatible with no change in measured turbidity or increase in particle content in 4 hr at 23 °C	2218	C
Famotidine	ME	2 mg/ml[b]	BW	7 mg/ml[a]	Visually compatible for 4 hr at 22 °C	1936	C
Filgrastim	AMG	30 μg/ml[a]	BW	7 mg/ml[a]	Physically compatible with no change in measured turbidity or increase in particle content in 4 hr at 22 °C	1687	C
Fluconazole	RR	2 mg/ml	BW	10 mg/ml	Physically compatible for 24 hr at 25 °C	1407	C
Fludarabine phosphate	BX	1 mg/ml[a]	BW	7 mg/ml[a]	Darker color visible with high intensity light within 4 hr	1439	I
Foscarnet sodium	AST	24 mg/ml	BW	10 mg/ml	Immediate precipitation	1335	I
	AST	24 mg/ml	BW	7 mg/ml[c]	Acyclovir crystals form immediately	1393	I
Gatifloxacin	BMS	2 mg/ml[a]	APP	7 mg/ml[a]	Physically compatible with no change in measured haze or increase in particle content in 4 hr at 23 °C	2234	C
Gemcitabine HCl	LI	10 mg/ml[b]	GW	7 mg/ml[b]	Gross precipitation occurs immediately	2226	I
Gentamicin sulfate	TR	1.6 mg/ml[a]	BW	5 mg/ml[a]	Physically compatible for 4 hr at 25 °C	1157	C
Granisetron HCl	SKB	0.05 mg/ml[a]	BW	7 mg/ml[a]	Physically compatible with no change in measured turbidity or increase in particle content in 4 hr at 23 °C	2000	C

Y-Site Injection Compatibility (1:1 Mixture) (Cont.)

			Acyclovir sodium				
Drug	*Mfr*	*Conc*	*Mfr*	*Conc*	*Remarks*	*Ref*	*C/I*
Heparin sodium	ES	50 units/ml[a]	BW	5 mg/ml[a]	Physically compatible for 4 hr at 25 °C	1157	C
Hydrocortisone sodium succinate	LY	1 mg/ml[a]	BW	5 mg/ml[a]	Physically compatible for 4 hr at 25 °C	1157	C
Hydromorphone HCl	WB	0.04 mg/ml[a]	BW	5 mg/ml[a]	Physically compatible for 4 hr at 25 °C	1157	C
Idarubicin HCl	AD	1 mg/ml[b]	BW	5 mg/ml[b]	Haze forms and color changes immediately. Precipitate forms in 12 min	1525	I
Imipenem–cilastatin sodium	MSD	5 mg/ml[b]	BW	5 mg/ml[a]	Physically compatible for 4 hr at 25 °C	1157	C
Levofloxacin	OMN	5 mg/ml[a]	BW	50 mg/ml	Cloudy precipitate forms	2233	I
Linezolid	PHU	2 mg/ml[a]	APP	7 mg/ml[a]	Physically compatible with no change in measured turbidity or increase in particle content in 4 hr at 23 °C	2264	C
Lorazepam	WY	0.04 mg/ml[a]	BW	5 mg/ml[a]	Physically compatible for 4 hr at 25 °C	1157	C
Magnesium sulfate	LY	20 mg/ml[a]	BW	5 mg/ml[a]	Physically compatible for 4 hr at 25 °C	1157	C
Melphalan HCl	BW	0.1 mg/ml[b]	BW	7 mg/ml[b]	Physically compatible with no change in measured turbidity or increase in particle content in 3 hr at 22 °C	1557	C
Meperidine HCl	WB	1 mg/ml[a]	BW	5 mg/ml[a]	Physically compatible for 4 hr at 25 °C	1157	C
	AB	10 mg/ml	BW	5 mg/ml[a]	White crystalline precipitate forms within 1 hr at 25 °C under fluorescent light	1397	I
	WY	100 mg/ml	BW	5 mg/ml[c]	Visually compatible for 24 hr at room temperature in test tubes. No precipitate found on filter from Y-site delivery	2063	C
Meropenem	ZEN	1 mg/ml[b]	BW	5 mg/ml[d]	Visually compatible for 4 hr at room temperature	1994	C
	ZEN	50 mg/ml[b]	BW	5 mg/ml[d]	Precipitate forms	2068	I
Methylprednisolone sodium succinate	LY	0.8 mg/ml[a]	BW	5 mg/ml[a]	Physically compatible for 4 hr at 25 °C	1157	C
Metoclopramide HCl	ES	0.2 mg/ml[a]	BW	5 mg/ml[a]	Physically compatible for 4 hr at 25 °C	1157	C
Metronidazole	SE	5 mg/ml	BW	5 mg/ml[a]	Physically compatible for 4 hr at 25 °C	1157	C
Morphine sulfate	WB	0.08 mg/ml[a]	BW	5 mg/ml[a]	Physically compatible for 4 hr at 25 °C	1157	C
	AB	1 mg/ml	BW	5 mg/ml[a]	White crystalline precipitate forms within 2 hr at 25 °C under fluorescent light	1397	I
Multivitamins	LY	0.01 ml/ml[a]	BW	5 mg/ml[a]	Physically compatible for 4 hr at 25 °C	1157	C
Nafcillin sodium	WY	20 mg/ml[a]	BW	5 mg/ml[a]	Physically compatible for 4 hr at 25 °C	1157	C
Ondansetron HCl	GL	1 mg/ml[b]	BW	7 mg/ml[a]	Immediate precipitation	1365	I
Oxacillin sodium	BE	20 mg/ml[a]	BW	5 mg/ml[a]	Physically compatible for 4 hr at 25 °C	1157	C
Paclitaxel	NCI	1.2 mg/ml[a]	BW	7 mg/ml[a]	Physically compatible with no change in measured turbidity in 4 hr at 22 °C	1556	C
Penicillin G potassium	PF	40,000 units/ml[a]	BW	5 mg/ml[a]	Physically compatible for 4 hr at 25 °C	1157	C
Pentobarbital sodium	WY	2 mg/ml[a]	BW	5 mg/ml[a]	Physically compatible for 4 hr at 25 °C	1157	C
Perphenazine	SC	0.1 mg/ml[a]	BW	5 mg/ml[a]	Physically compatible for 4 hr at 25 °C	1157	C
Piperacillin sodium	LE	60 mg/ml[a]	BW	5 mg/ml[a]	Physically compatible for 4 hr at 25 °C	1157	C
Piperacillin sodium–tazobactam sodium	LE	40 + 5 mg/ml[a]	BW	7 mg/ml[a]	Particles form in 1 hr	1688	I

Y-Site Injection Compatibility (1:1 Mixture) (Cont.)

Drug	*Mfr*	*Conc*	Acyclovir sodium *Mfr*	*Conc*	*Remarks*	*Ref*	*C/I*
Potassium chloride	IX	0.04 mEq/ml[a]	BW	5 mg/ml[a]	Physically compatible for 4 hr at 25 °C	1157	C
Propofol	ZEN	10 mg/ml	BW	7 mg/ml[a]	Physically compatible for 1 hr at 23 °C with no increase in particle content	2066	C
Ranitidine HCl	GL	1 mg/ml[a]	BW	5 mg/ml[a]	Physically compatible for 4 hr at 25 °C	1157	C
Remifentanil HCl	GW	0.025 and 0.25 mg/ml[b]	BW	7 mg/ml[a]	Physically compatible with no change in measured turbidity or increase in particle content in 4 hr at 23 °C	2075	C
Sargramostim	IMM	10 µg/ml[b]	BW	7 mg/ml[b]	Few small white particles form in 4 hr	1436	I
Sodium bicarbonate	IX	0.5 mEq/ml[a]	BW	5 mg/ml[a]	Physically compatible for 4 hr at 25 °C	1157	C
Tacrolimus	FUJ	1 mg/ml[b]	BW	10 mg/ml[a]	Visually compatible for 24 hr at 25 °C	1630	C
Teniposide	BR	0.1 mg/ml[a]	BW	7 mg/ml[a]	Physically compatible with no subvisual haze or particle formation in 4 hr at 23 °C	1725	C
Theophylline	TR	1.6 mg/ml[a]	BW	5 mg/ml[a]	Physically compatible for 4 hr at 25 °C	1157	C
Thiotepa	IMM[e]	1 mg/ml[a]	BW	7 mg/ml[a]	Physically compatible with no change in measured turbidity or increase in particle content in 4 hr at 23 °C	1861	C
Ticarcillin disodium	TR	30 mg/ml[a]	BW	5 mg/ml[a]	Physically compatible for 4 hr at 25 °C	1157	C
TNA #218 to #226[f]			GW	7 mg/ml[a]	White precipitate forms immediately	2215	I
Tobramycin sulfate	DI	1.6 mg/ml[a]	BW	5 mg/ml[a]	Physically compatible for 4 hr at 25 °C	1157	C
TPN #203 and #204[f]			BW	7 mg/ml	White precipitate forms immediately	1974	I
TPN #212 to #215[f]			BW	7 mg/ml[a]	Crystalline needles form immediately, becoming a gross precipitate in 1 hr	2109	I
Trimethoprim–sulfamethoxazole	RC	0.8 + 4 mg/ml[a]	BW	5 mg/ml[a]	Physically compatible for 4 hr at 25 °C	1157	C
Vancomycin HCl	LI	5 mg/ml[a]	BW	5 mg/ml[a]	Physically compatible for 4 hr at 25 °C	1157	C
Vinorelbine tartrate	BW	1 mg/ml[b]	BW	7 mg/ml[b]	Heavy white precipitate forms immediately	1558	I
Zidovudine	BW	4 mg/ml[a]	BW	7 mg/ml[a]	Physically compatible for 4 hr at 25 °C under fluorescent light by visual and microscopic examination	1193	C

[a]*Tested in dextrose 5% in water.*
[b]*Tested in sodium chloride 0.9%.*
[c]*Tested in both dextrose 5% water and sodium chloride 0.9%.*
[d]*Tested in sterile water for injection.*
[e]*Lyophilized formulation tested.*
[f]*Refer to Appendix I for the composition of parenteral nutrition solutions. TNA indicates a 3-in-1 admixture, and TPN indicates a 2-in-1 admixture.*
[g]*Sodium carbonate–containing formulation tested.*

Additional Compatibility Information

Infusion Solutions — Recommended infusion solutions are dextrose 5% in water, sodium chloride 0.9%, dextrose 5%–sodium chloride combinations, and Ringer's injection, lactated. (857) Biologic or colloidal fluids are not recommended. (2)

If acyclovir sodium is diluted in solutions with dextrose concentrations greater than 10%, a yellow discoloration may appear. This discoloration does not affect the drug's potency. (4)

ADENOSINE
AHFS 24:04

Products — Adenosine is available under the name Adenocard IV as a 3-mg/ml solution in 2-ml vials and 2- and 4-ml disposable syringes for intravenous bolus injection. Adenosine is also available under the name Adenoscan as a 3-mg/ml solution in 20- and 30-ml vials for intravenous infusion only. Each of these products also contains sodium chloride 9 mg/ml. (2)

pH — Adenocard IV: from 4.5 to 7.5. Adenoscan: from 4.5 to 7.5. (2)

Trade Name(s) — Adenocard IV, Adenoscan.

Administration — Adenosine injections are administered intravenously. Adenocard IV is given as a rapid bolus injection by the peripheral intravenous route directly into a vein or into an intravenous line close to the patient and is followed by a sodium chloride 0.9% flush. Adenoscan is given by continuous peripheral intravenous infusion only. (2)

Stability — Intact containers of adenosine injections should be stored at controlled room temperatures of 15 to 30 °C. They should not be refrigerated, because of possible crystal formation. If crystallization occurs, let the solution warm to room temperature to dissolve the crystals. The solution must be clear prior to administration. (2)

Adenosine 6 μg/ml in sodium chloride 0.9% was packaged in 5-ml glass ampuls. Based on HPLC analysis of high-temperature-accelerated decomposition, it was projected that the drug solution would be stable for at least five years at 4 and 25 °C. (2115)

Adenosine 2 mg/ml in sodium chloride 0.9% was packaged in glass vials and stored for six months at temperatures ranging from 4 to 72 °C. HPLC analysis found no loss of adenosine in samples stored at 4, 22, and 37 °C. At the extreme temperatures of 60 and 72 °C, a 10% loss could be expected to occur in 250 and 91 days, respectively. (2277)

Syringes — Undiluted adenosine (Fujisawa) 3 mg/ml was packaged as 25 ml in 60-ml polypropylene syringes (Becton-Dickinson) and sealed with polyolefin tip caps (Sherwood Medical). The syringes were stored at 25, 5, and −15 °C. The solutions remained visually clear, and HPLC analysis showed no loss of adenosine in 7 days at 25 °C, 14 days at 5 °C, and 28 days at −15 °C. The drug's stability in glass vials was essentially identical under the same conditions. (2114)

Adenosine (Fujisawa) diluted to 0.75 mg/ml with several infusion solutions was packaged as 25 ml in 60-ml polypropylene syringes (Becton-Dickinson) and sealed with polyolefin tip caps (Sherwood Medical). The syringes were stored at 25, 5, and −15 °C. The solutions remained visually clear, and HPLC analysis showed no loss of adenosine in 14 days for dextrose 5% in lactated Ringer's and lactated Ringer's injection and 16 days for dextrose 5% in water and sodium chloride 0.9%. (2114)

Sorption — No loss due to sorption was found for adenosine (Fujisawa) undiluted at 3 mg/ml in polypropylene syringes and diluted to 0.75 mg/ml with infusion solutions in polypropylene syringes and PVC bags. (2114)

Compatibility Information

Solution Compatibility

Adenosine

Solution	*Mfr*	*Mfr*	*Conc/L*	*Remarks*	*Ref*	*C/I*
Dextrose 5% in Ringer's injection, lactated	BA[a]	FUJ	750 mg	Visually compatible with no loss by HPLC in 14 days at 25, 5, and −15 °C	2114	C
Dextrose 5% in water	BA[a]	FUJ	750 mg	Visually compatible with no loss by HPLC in 16 days at 25, 5, and −15 °C	2114	C
Ringer's injection, lactated	BA[a]	FUJ	750 mg	Visually compatible with no loss by HPLC in 14 days at 25, 5, and −15 °C	2114	C
Sodium chloride 0.9%	BA[a]	FUJ	750 mg	Visually compatible with no loss by HPLC in 16 days at 25, 5, and −15 °C	2114	C

[a] *Tested in PVC containers.*

ALATROFLOXACIN MESYLATE
AHFS 8:22

Products — Alatrofloxacin mesylate is available as a concentrated solution in 40- and 60-ml single-use vials. Each milliliter of the concentrated solution provides alatrofloxacin mesylate equivalent to trovafloxacin 5 mg and sodium hydroxide or hydrochloric acid to adjust pH in water for injection. The concentrated solution must be diluted prior to intravenous administration. (2)

pH — From 3.5 to 4.3. (2)

Trade Name(s) — Trovan I.V.

Administration — Alatrofloxacin mesylate is provided as a concentrated solution that must be diluted for administration by intravenous infusion. It should not be given by other routes of administration or by rapid or bolus intravenous administration. The drug should be diluted to a final concentration of 1 to 2 mg/ml using a compatible infusion solution. The diluted drug is infused over 60 minutes. (2)

Stability — Alatrofloxacin mesylate is a clear, colorless to slightly yellow solution. Intact vials should be stored at controlled room temperature between 15 and 30 °C and protected from light and freezing. (2)

Diluted to a concentration between 0.5 and 2 mg/ml, alatrofloxacin mesylate is physically and chemically stable in suitable infusion solutions for up to three days at room temperature and seven days under refrigeration. NOTE: Sodium chloride 0.9% and Ringer's injection, lactated are stated to be incompatible with alatrofloxacin mesylate and should not be used as diluents. See Additional Compatibility Information below.

Sorption—There is no difference in drug stability in glass and PVC intravenous infusion containers. (2)

Compatibility Information

Y-Site Injection Compatibility (1:1 Mixture)

			Alatrofloxacin mesylate				
Drug	*Mfr*	*Conc*	*Mfr*	*Conc*	*Remarks*	*Ref*	*C/I*
Amikacin sulfate	VHA	100 mg/ml[c]	PF	1.43 mg/ml[a]	Visually and microscopically compatible run through a Y-site over 25 min	2235	C
Aztreonam	SQ	40 mg/ml[b]	PF	1.43 mg/ml[a]	White precipitate forms	2235	I
Ceftazidime[d]	GW	40 mg/ml[b]	PF	1.43 mg/ml[a]	White precipitate forms	2235	I
Ceftriaxone sodium	RC	66.7 mg/ml[c]	PF	1.43 mg/ml[a]	White precipitate forms	2235	I
Cyclosporine	SZ	4.2 mg/ml[a]	PF	1.43 mg/ml[a]	Visually and microscopically compatible run through a Y-site over at least 60 min	2235	C
Dobutamine HCl	ES	4.2 mg/ml[a]	PF	1.43 mg/ml[a]	Microscopic particles form	2235	I
Dopamine HCl	AB	4.2 mg/ml[a]	PF	1.43 mg/ml[a]	Visually and microscopically compatible run through a Y-site over at least 60 min	2235	C
Droperidol	AMR	2.5 mg/ml	PF	1.43 mg/ml[a]	Visually and microscopically compatible when the droperidol is pushed through a Y-site over 2 min	2235	C
Famotidine	ME	2 mg/ml[e]	PF	1.43 mg/ml[a]	Microscopic particles form	2235	I
Fentanyl citrate	ES	0.05 mg/ml	PF	1.43 mg/ml[a]	Visually and microscopically compatible when the fentanyl citrate is pushed through a Y-site over 2 min	2235	C
Furosemide	AMR	10 mg/ml	PF	1.43 mg/ml[a]	White precipitate forms	2235	I
Gentamicin sulfate	FUJ	21 mg/ml[c]	PF	1.43 mg/ml[a]	Visually and microscopically compatible run through a Y-site over 25 min	2235	C
Heparin sodium	BA	100 units/ml[a]	PF	1.43 mg/ml[a]	Yellow precipitate forms	2235	I
Hetastarch in lactated electrolyte injection (Hextend)	AB	6%	PF	2 mg/ml[a]	Physically compatible with no change in measured turbidity or increase in particle content in 4 hr at 23 °C	2339	C
Insulin, regular	LI	1 unit/ml[b]	PF	1.43 mg/ml[a]	Microscopic particles form	2235	I
Ketorolac tromethamine	AB	15 mg/ml	PF	1.43 mg/ml[a]	Visually and microscopically compatible when the ketorolac is pushed through a Y-site over 20 sec	2235	C
Lorazepam	AB	0.1 mg/ml[a]	PF	1.43 mg/ml[a]	Visually and microscopically compatible run through a Y-site over at least 60 min	2235	C
Magnesium sulfate	AMR	20 mg/ml[b]	PF	1.43 mg/ml[a]	Microscopic particles form	2235	I

Y-Site Injection Compatibility (1:1 Mixture) (Cont.)

			Alatrofloxacin mesylate				
Drug	*Mfr*	*Conc*	*Mfr*	*Conc*	*Remarks*	*Ref*	*C/I*
Midazolam HCl	RC	0.5 mg/ml[b]	PF	1.43 mg/ml[a]	Visually and microscopically compatible run through a Y-site over at least 60 min	2235	I
Morphine sulfate	WY	1 mg/ml	PF	1.43 mg/ml[a]	Microscopic particles form	2235	I
Nitroglycerin	BA	0.2 mg/ml	PF	1.43 mg/ml[a]	Visually and microscopically compatible run through a Y-site over at least 60 min	2235	C
Ondansetron HCl	GL	2 mg/ml	PF	1.43 mg/ml[a]	Visually and microscopically compatible when the ondansetron HCl is pushed through a Y-site over 5 min	2235	C
Piperacillin sodium–tazobactam sodium	LE	40 + 5 mg/ml[c]	PF	1.43 mg/ml[a]	White precipitate forms	2235	I
Potassium chloride		0.02 mEq/ml[f]	PF	1.43 mg/ml[a]	Visually and microscopically compatible run through a Y-site over at least 60 min	2235	C
	BA	0.4 mEq/ml	PF	1.43 mg/ml[a]	Visually and microscopically compatible run through a Y-site over at least 60 min	2235	C
Propofol	ASZ	10 mg/ml	PF	2 mg/ml[a]	Physically compatible for 1 hr at 23 °C with no increase in particle content	1916	C
Ringer's injection, lactated	BA		PF	1.43 mg/ml[a]	Visually and microscopically compatible run through a Y-site over at least 60 min	2235	C
Sodium bicarbonate	AB	0.13 mEq/ml[a]	PF	1.43 mg/ml[a]	Visually and microscopically compatible run through a Y-site over at least 60 min	2235	C
Sodium chloride 0.45%	BA		PF	1.43 mg/ml[a]	Visually and microscopically compatible run through a Y-site over at least 60 min	2235	C
Ticarcillin disodium–clavulanate potassium	SKB	103.3 mg/ml[c]	PF	1.43 mg/ml[a]	Yellow precipitate forms	2235	I
Tobramycin sulfate	LI	21 mg/ml[c]	PF	1.43 mg/ml[a]	Visually and microscopically compatible run through a Y-site over at 33 min	2235	C
Vancomycin HCl	AB	4 mg/ml[b]	PF	1.43 mg/ml[a]	Visually and microscopically compatible run through a Y-site over at least 60 min	2235	C

[a] *Tested in dextrose 5% in water.*
[b] *Tested in sodium chloride 0.9%.*
[c] *Tested in sodium chloride 0.45%.*
[d] *Sodium carbonate—containing formulation tested.*
[e] *Diluent not specified.*
[f] *Tested in dextrose 5% in sodium chloride 0.45%.*

Additional Compatibility Information

Infusion Solutions — Alatrofloxacin mesylate in concentrations between 0.5 and 2 mg/ml is physically compatible and chemically stable for three days at room temperature and seven days under refrigeration in the following infusion solutions (2):

Dextrose 5% in Ringer's injection, lactated
Dextrose 5% in sodium chloride 0.2%
Dextrose 5% in sodium chloride 0.45%
Dextrose 5% in water
Sodium chloride 0.45%

Alatrofloxacin mesylate is physically incompatible with Ringer's injection, lactated and also sodium chloride 0.9% alone or in combination with other diluents. Precipitation may occur in these solutions. (2) The drug should not be mixed with or administered simultaneously with any solution containing magnesium, calcium, or other multivalent cations. (4)

Although longer-term exposure of alatrofloxacin mesylate to sodium chloride 0.9% and its combinations may result in precipitation, normal saline may be used as a flush before and after alatrofloxacin mesylate administration. (2)

Other Drugs — The manufacturer indicates that alatrofloxacin mesylate should not be mixed with or administered simultaneously through the same line with other drugs. If the drug is to be infused sequentially before or after other drugs through a common line, it is recommended that the line be flushed both before and after the alatrofloxacin mesylate is infused using a solution compatible with alatrofloxacin mesylate and the other drugs. (2)

ALBUMIN HUMAN
AHFS 16:00

Products — Albumin human is available in 20-, 50-, and 100-ml vials as a 25% aqueous solution. Each 100 ml of solution contains 25 g of serum albumin. Albumin human is also available as a 5% aqueous solution in 50-, 250-, 500-, and 1000-ml sizes. The products also contain sodium carbonate, sodium bicarbonate, sodium hydroxide, and/or acetic acid to adjust the pH. (1-8/00; 4) The products are heat-treated for inactivation of hepatitis viruses. Sodium caprylate and sodium *N*-acetyltryptophanate are added to the products as stabilizers to prevent denaturation during the heat treatment. (1-8/00; 2)

pH — From 6.4 to 7.4. (1-8/00; 4)

Sodium Content — From 130 to 160 mEq/L. (1-8/00; 4)

Trade Name(s) — Albuminar, Albutein, Albumarc, Buminate, Plasbumin.

Administration — Albumin human is administered intravenously either undiluted or diluted in an intravenous infusion solution. (1-8/00; 4)

Stability — Albumin human has been variously described as clear amber to deep orange-brown and as a transparent or slightly opalescent pale straw to dark brown solution. The solution should not be used if it is turbid or contains a deposit. Since it contains no preservative, the manufacturer recommends use within four hours after opening the vial. (1-8/00; 4) The expiration date is five years after issue from the manufacturer if the labeling recommends storage between 2 and 8 or 10 °C, or not more than three years after issue from the manufacturer if the labeling recommends storage at temperatures not greater than 30 or 37 °C. (4)

Freezing Solutions — Freezing the albumin human solutions may damage the container and result in contamination. (4) Exposure of albumin human to elevated temperatures of 55 and 70 °C results in increased degradation, including an increase in dimer formation and aggregation. (2295)

Compatibility Information

Solution Compatibility

Albumin human

Solution	*Mfr*	*Mfr*	*Conc/L*	*Remarks*	*Ref*	*C/I*
Dextran 6% in dextrose 5%	AB		5 g	Physically compatible	3	C
Dextran 6% in sodium chloride 0.9%	AB		5 g	Physically compatible	3	C
Dextrose–Ringer's injection combinations	AB		5 g	Physically compatible	3	C
Dextrose–Ringer's injection, lactated, combinations	AB		5 g	Physically compatible	3	C
Dextrose–saline combinations	AB		5 g	Physically compatible	3	C
Dextrose 2½% in water	AB		5 g	Physically compatible	3	C
Dextrose 5% in water	AB		5 g	Physically compatible	3	C
Dextrose 10% in water	AB		5 g	Physically compatible	3	C
Fructose 10% in sodium chloride 0.9%	AB		5 g	Physically compatible	3	C
Fructose 10% in water	AB		5 g	Physically compatible	3	C
Invert sugar 5 and 10% in sodium chloride 0.9%	AB		5 g	Physically compatible	3	C
Invert sugar 5 and 10% in water	AB		5 g	Physically compatible	3	C

Solution Compatibility (Cont.)

Albumin human

Solution	*Mfr*	*Mfr*	*Conc/L*	*Remarks*	*Ref*	*C/I*
Ionosol products (except as noted below)	AB		5 g	Physically compatible	3	C
Ionosol D-CM	AB		5 g	Haze or precipitate forms within 24 hr	3	I
Ringer's injection	AB		5 g	Physically compatible	3	C
Ringer's injection, lactated	AB		5 g	Physically compatible	3	C
Sodium chloride 0.45%	AB		5 g	Physically compatible	3	C
Sodium chloride 0.9%	AB		5 g	Physically compatible	3	C
Sodium lactate ⅙ M	AB		5 g	Physically compatible	3	C
TNA #232[a]			9.5 g	Microscopically observed emulsion disruption found with increased fat globule size in 48 hr at room temperature	2267	?
TNA #233[a]			9.5 g	Visually apparent emulsion disruption with creaming in as little as 4 hr at room temperature. Increased disruption attributed to the added effect of calcium and magnesium ions	2267	I
TNA #234[a]			18.2 g	Creaming and free oil formation visually observed in 24 hr at room temperature	2267	I
TNA #235[a]			18.2 g	Visually apparent emulsion disruption with creaming and free oil formation in as little as 4 hr at room temperature. Increased disruption attributed to the added effect of calcium and magnesium ions	2267	I

[a]*Refer to Appendix I for the composition of parenteral nutrition solutions. TNA indicates a 3-in-1 admixture.*

Additive Compatibility

Albumin human

Drug	*Mfr*	*Conc/L*	*Mfr*	*Conc/L*	*Test Soln*	*Remarks*	*Ref*	*C/I*
Verapamil HCl	KN	80 mg	ARC	25 g	D5W, NS	Cloudiness develops within 8 hr	764	I

Y-Site Injection Compatibility (1:1 Mixture)

Albumin human

Drug	*Mfr*	*Conc*	*Mfr*	*Conc*	*Remarks*	*Ref*	*C/I*
Diltiazem HCl	MMD	5 mg/ml	AR, AT	5 and 25%	Visually compatible	1807	C
Fat emulsion, intravenous (Intralipid)		20%		20%	Emulsion destabilization was evident immediately	2267	I
Lorazepam	WY	0.33 mg/ml[b]		200 mg/ml	Visually compatible for 24 hr at 22 °C	1855	C
Midazolam HCl	RC	5 mg/ml		200 mg/ml	White precipitate forms immediately	1855	I
Vancomycin HCl		20 mg/ml[a]		0.1 and 1%[b]	Heavy turbidity forms immediately and precipitate develops subsequently	1701	I
Verapamil HCl	LY	0.2 mg/ml[a]	HY	250 mg/ml[a]	Slight haze in 1 hr	1316	I
	LY	0.2 mg/ml[b]	HY	250 mg/ml[b]	Slight haze in 3 hr	1316	I

[a]*Tested in dextrose 5% in water.*
[b]*Tested in sodium chloride 0.9%.*

Additional Compatibility Information

Infusion Solutions — Dextrose 5% in water, dextrose 10% in water, and sodium chloride 0.9% have been recommended as infusion vehicles. Albumin human has been stated to be compatible with whole blood, plasma, and sodium lactate solutions as well as dextrose and sodium chloride injections. (4)

CAUTION—Substantial reduction in tonicity, creating the potential for fatal hemolysis and acute renal failure, may result from the use of sterile water as a diluent. The hemolysis and acute renal failure that result from the use of a sufficient volume of sterile water as a diluent may be life-threatening. (4; 1942; 2072; 2073)

Parenteral Nutrition Solutions — The addition of albumin human to parenteral nutrition solutions appears to result in visually compatible admixtures for 24 hours. However, occlusion of filters has occurred if the albumin human concentration exceeded 25 g/L (854) and, occasionally, even at concentrations of 19.4 and 10.8 g/L. (1634) Snyder studied the filtration of albumin human 25%, from several suppliers, through 0.22-μm filters using a syringe pump. Four products were filtered over 20 minutes, but the Armour product activated the occlusion alarm after only 3.2 minutes. Use of albumin human from suppliers other than Armour in parenteral nutrition solutions resulted in no additional occlusions or flow problems. (1634) However, Feldman and Bergman noted that although all U.S. manufacturers of albumin human and other plasma proteins use the same cold-alcohol fractionation process, batch-to-batch variations in polymer content occur within all manufacturers' products. Furthermore, parenteral nutrition solution composition, additives, filter composition, and kind of pump may affect flow rates as much as differences in batches or manufacturers. (1635)

Albumin human has also been found to increase the potential of parenteral nutrition solutions to support the growth of fungi and bacteria. Administration of albumin human separately was recommended. (573)

ALDESLEUKIN (INTERLEUKIN-2; IL-2) AHFS 10:00

Products — Aldesleukin is available in single-use vials containing 22 million I.U. (1.3 mg of protein). When reconstituted with 1.2 ml of sterile water for injection, each milliliter contains aldesleukin 18 million I.U. (1.1 mg) along with mannitol 50 mg, sodium dodecyl sulfate 0.18 mg, monobasic sodium phosphate 0.17 mg, and dibasic sodium phosphate 0.89 mg. During reconstitution, the sterile water for injection should be directed at the vial's sides. Swirl the contents gently to cause dissolution and avoid excess foaming. Do not shake the vial. (2)

Units — The biological potency of aldesleukin is determined by the lymphocyte proliferation bioassay and is expressed in International Units (I.U.). Aldesleukin 18 million I.U. equals 1.1 mg of protein. (2) During the development of aldesleukin, various unit systems were employed. However, the International Unit is now the standard measure of its activity.

pH — The reconstituted product has a pH of 7.2 to 7.8. (2)

Trade Name(s) — Proleukin.

Administration — Aldesleukin is administered intravenously; the reconstituted solution should be diluted in 50 ml of dextrose 5% in water and infused over 15 minutes. Inline filters should not be used. (2; 4) The drug should be diluted within the concentration range of 30 to 70 μg/ml for administration. Concentrations of aldesleukin below 30 μg/ml and above 70 μg/ml have shown increased variability in drug delivery. Dilution and drug delivery outside this concentration range should be avoided. (2)

Only dextrose 5% in water is recommended for intravenous infusion of aldesleukin. Reconstitution or dilution with sodium chloride 0.9% or bacteriostatic water for injection increases aggregation. (2; 4)

If aldesleukin concentrations less than 30 μg/ml are necessary for short-term intravenous infusion of 15 minutes, the manufacturer recommends diluting the dose in dextrose 5% in water that contains albumin human 0.1% to prevent variability in the stability and bioactivity of the drug. (4; 1890)

Stability — Aldesleukin is a white to off-white powder; it becomes a colorless to slightly yellow liquid when reconstituted. (2)

Intact vials should be stored under refrigeration and protected from light. (2) However, aldesleukin in intact vials is stable for at least two months at controlled room temperature. (1890) The reconstituted solution, as well as dilutions in infusion solutions for intravenous administration, should also be stored under refrigeration and protected from freezing. Intravenous infusions should be brought to room temperature before administration. (2)

The manufacturer indicates that reconstituted and diluted aldesleukin is stable for 48 hours when stored at room temperature or under refrigeration. Refrigeration is recommended because the product contains no antibacterial preservative. (2)

The manufacturer also states that reconstitution and dilution procedures other than those recommended may alter aldesleukin delivery and/or pharmacology and should not be used. (2)

Syringes — Aldesleukin (Cetus), reconstituted according to label directions, was evaluated for stability when stored in 1-ml plastic syringes (Becton-Dickinson). One- and 0.5-ml aliquots were drawn into these syringes and refrigerated for five days. The product was physically stable and retained activity by biological analysis (cell proliferation assay) throughout the study period. (1821)

Reconstituted aldesleukin diluted to a concentration of 220 μg/ml with dextrose 5% in water was repackaged aseptically as 1 ml drawn into tuberculin syringes and stored under refrigeration at 2 to 8 °C. The drug was found to be stable for the 14-day study period. (1890)

Ambulatory Pumps — For continuous intravenous infusion of aldesleukin in concentrations of 70 μg/ml or less via an ambulatory pump at the accompanying higher temperature of near 32 °C, the dose should be diluted in dextrose 5% in water to which albumin human at a concentration of 0.1% has been added to maintain aldesleukin stability. (1890) The albumin human helps keep aldesleukin in its microaggregate state and helps decrease sorption to surfaces, especially at concentrations below 10 μg/ml. (4) In the absence of albumin human, visually observed precipitation and loss of aldesleukin activity has been found. (1890) At concentrations greater than 70 and less than 100 μg/ml at 32 °C, aldesleukin is unstable whether albumin human is present or not. In an ambulatory pump at 32 °C at a concentration above 100 μg/ml, it is not necessary to add albumin human to maintain aldesleukin stability. (1890)

Aldesleukin (Cetus) 5 to 500 μg/ml in dextrose 5% in water was evaluated for stability in PVC containers during simulated administration from pumps (CADD-1, Pharmacia Deltec). At 100 to 500 μg/ml, aldesleukin was stable by biological analysis (cell proliferation assay) for six days at 32 °C and remained visually clear throughout the study period. At concentrations of 5 and 40 μg/ml, however, albumin human 0.1% was necessary to maintain physical stability. The aldesleukin solutions with albumin human remained clear and retained activity for six days at 32 °C. Without albumin human, precipitation occurred within a few hours. (1821)

Sorption — Aldesleukin in low concentrations, particularly less than 10 μg/ml, undergoes sorption to surfaces such as plastic bags, tubing, and administration devices. Addition of 0.1% albumin human to the solution decreases the extent of sorption. (4) Both glass and PVC containers have been used to infuse aldesleukin with comparable clinical results. However, drug delivery may be more consistent with PVC containers. (2; 4)

Filtration — Inline filters should not be used for aldesleukin. (2; 4)

Compatibility Information

Y-Site Injection Compatibility (1:1 Mixture)

IL-2

Drug	*Mfr*	*Conc*	*Mfr*	*Conc*	*Remarks*	*Ref*	*C/I*
Amikacin sulfate	BR	250 mg/ml	RC[c]	4800 I.U./ml[b]	Visually compatible and IL-2 activity by bioassay retained. Amikacin not tested	1552	C
Amphotericin B	SQ	1.6 mg/ml[a]	CHI	33,800 I.U./ml[a]	Visually compatible for 2 hr. Bioassay not possible	1857	C
Calcium gluconate	LY	100 mg/ml	CHI	33,800 I.U./ml[a]	Visually compatible with little or no loss of aldesleukin activity by bioassay	1857	C
Diphenhydramine HCl	SCN	50 mg/ml	CHI	33,800 I.U./ml[a]	Visually compatible for 2 hr. Bioassay not possible	1857	C
Dopamine HCl	ES	1.6 mg/ml[a]	CHI	33,800 I.U./ml[a]	Visually compatible with little or no loss of aldesleukin activity by bioassay	1857	C
Fat emulsion, intravenous	KA	20%	RC[c]	4800 I.U./ml[b]	Visually compatible and IL-2 activity by bioassay retained. Fat emulsion not tested	1552	C
Fluconazole	RR	2 mg/ml[a]	CHI	33,800 I.U./ml[a]	Visually compatible with little or no loss of aldesleukin activity by bioassay	1857	C
Foscarnet sodium	AST	24 mg/ml	CHI	33,800 I.U./ml[a]	Visually compatible with little or no loss of aldesleukin activity by bioassay	1857	C
Ganciclovir sodium	SY	10 mg/ml[a]	CHI	33,800 I.U./ml[a]	Aldesleukin bioactivity inhibited	1857	I
Gentamicin sulfate	ES	40 mg/ml	RC[c]	4800 I.U./ml[b]	Visually compatible and IL-2 activity by bioassay retained. Gentamicin not tested	1552	C
Heparin sodium	BA	100 units/ml	CHI	33,800 I.U./ml[a]	Visually compatible with little or no loss of aldesleukin activity by bioassay	1857	C
Lorazepam	WY	2 mg/ml	CHI	33,800 I.U./ml[a]	Globules form immediately	1857	I
Magnesium sulfate	LY	20 mg/ml[a]	CHI	33,800 I.U./ml[a]	Visually compatible with little or no loss of aldesleukin activity by bioassay	1857	C
Metoclopramide HCl	DU	5 mg/ml	CHI	33,800 I.U./ml[a]	Visually compatible with little or no loss of aldesleukin activity by bioassay	1857	C

Y-Site Injection Compatibility (1:1 Mixture) (Cont.)

			IL-2				
Drug	*Mfr*	*Conc*	*Mfr*	*Conc*	*Remarks*	*Ref*	*C/I*
Morphine sulfate	SCN	1 mg/ml	RC[c]	4800 I.U./ml[b]	Visually compatible and IL-2 activity by bioassay retained. Morphine not tested	1552	**C**
Ondansetron HCl	GL	0.7 mg/ml[a]	CHI	33,800 I.U./ml[a]	Visually compatible with little or no loss of aldesleukin activity by bioassay	1857	**C**
Pentamidine isethionate	FUJ	6 mg/ml[a]	CHI	33,800 I.U./ml[a]	Aldesleukin bioactivity inhibited	1857	**I**
Piperacillin sodium	LE	200 mg/ml	RC[c]	4800 I.U./ml[b]	Visually compatible and IL-2 activity by bioassay retained. Piperacillin not tested	1552	**C**
Potassium chloride	AB	0.2 mEq/ml	CHI	33,800 I.U./ml[a]	Visually compatible with little or no loss of aldesleukin activity by bioassay	1857	**C**
Prochlorperazine edisylate	SKB	5 mg/ml	CHI	33,800 I.U./ml[a]	Aldesleukin bioactivity inhibited	1857	**I**
Promethazine HCl	ES	25 mg/ml	CHI	33,800 I.U./ml[a]	Aldesleukin bioactivity inhibited	1857	**I**
Ranitidine HCl	AB	1 mg/ml[d]	CHI	33,800 I.U./ml[a]	Visually compatible with little or no loss of aldesleukin activity by bioassay	1857	**C**
Thiethylperazine malate	SZ	0.4 mg/ml[a]	CHI	33,800 I.U./ml[a]	Visually compatible with little or no loss of aldesleukin activity by bioassay	1857	**C**
Ticarcillin disodium	BE	200 mg/ml	RC[c]	4800 I.U./ml[b]	Visually compatible and IL-2 activity by bioassay retained. Ticarcillin not tested	1552	**C**
Tobramycin sulfate	LI	40 mg/ml	RC[c]	4800 I.U./ml[b]	Visually compatible and IL-2 activity by bioassay retained. Tobramycin not tested	1552	**C**
TPN #145[e]			RC[c]	4800 I.U./ml[b]	Visually compatible and IL-2 activity by bioassay retained	1552	**C**
Trimethoprim–sulfamethoxazole	BW	1.6 + 8 mg/ml[a]	CHI	33,800 I.U./ml[a]	Visually compatible with little or no loss of aldesleukin activity by bioassay	1857	**C**

[a] *Tested in dextrose 5% in water.*
[b] *Tested in sodium chloride 0.9%.*
[c] *The Roche product is a different form of IL-2 than the Chiron product.*
[d] *Tested in sodium chloride 0.45%.*
[e] *Refer to Appendix I for the composition of parenteral nutrition solutions. TPN indicates a 2-in-1 admixture.*

Additional Compatibility Information

Other Drugs — The manufacturer recommends that aldesleukin not be co-administered with other drugs in the same container. (2) Even so, the manufacturer also has stated that aldesleukin may be administered by simultaneous Y-site administration with vancomycin HCl. However, aldesleukin was stated to be incompatible with dopamine HCl, fluorouracil, potassium chloride, ondansetron HCl, and heparin sodium. (1890) This statement conflicts with other research cited above. (1857)

ALFENTANIL HCL
AHFS 28:08.08

Products — Alfentanil HCl is available at a concentration equivalent to alfentanil base 500 μg/ml with sodium chloride for isotonicity in 2-, 5-, 10-, and 20-ml ampuls. (1-7/98)

pH — From 4 to 6. (1-7/98)

Trade Name(s) — Alfenta.

Administration — Alfentanil HCl is administered by intravenous injection or infusion. For infusion, dilution to 25 to 80 μg/ml in a compatible solution has been utilized. (1-7/98)

Stability — Alfentanil HCl injection is stable at controlled room temperature when protected from light. (1-7/98)

Syringes — Alfentanil HCl (Janssen) 0.5 mg/ml in 5% dextrose injection was packaged in 20-ml polypropylene syringes (Becton-Dickinson) and stored at 20 °C exposed to light and at 8 °C for 16 weeks. The solutions were visually clear and colorless throughout the study. HPLC analysis found no loss of alfentanil HCl and no peaks for leached substances from the plastic syringes. (2191)

Alfentanil HCl (Janssen) 0.167 mg/ml in sodium chloride 0.9% packaged in polypropylene syringes (Sherwood) was physically stable and exhibited little or no loss by stability-indicating HPLC analysis in 24 hours stored at 4 and 23 °C. (2199)

Compatibility Information

Solution Compatibility

Alfentanil HCl

Solution	*Mfr*	*Mfr*	*Conc/L*	*Remarks*	*Ref*	*C/I*
Dextrose 5% in water	a	JN	500 mg	Visually compatible and no loss by HPLC in 16 weeks at 20 °C exposed to light and at 4 °C	2191	C

[a]*Packaged in 20-ml polypropylene syringes.*

Drugs in Syringe Compatibility

Alfentanil HCl

Drug (in syringe)	*Mfr*	*Amt*	*Mfr*	*Amt*	*Remarks*	*Ref*	*C/I*
Atracurium besylate	BW	10 mg/ml		0.5 mg/ml	Physically compatible and atracurium chemically stable for 24 hr at 5 and 30 °C	1694	C
Midazolam HCl	RC	0.2 mg/ml[a]	JN	0.5 mg/ml	Visually compatible with 8% midazolam and 2% alfentanil loss in 3 weeks at 20 °C exposed to light. No alfentanil loss and 7% midazolam loss in 4 weeks at 6 °C in the dark	2133	C
Ondansetron HCl	GW	1.33 mg/ml[a]	JN	0.167 mg/ml[a]	Physically compatible with no measured increase in particulates and little or no loss of either drug by HPLC in 24 hr at 4 or 23 °C	2199	C

[a]*Diluted with sodium chloride 0.9%.*

Y-Site Injection Compatibility (1:1 Mixture)

Alfentanil HCl

Drug	*Mfr*	*Conc*	*Mfr*	*Conc*	*Remarks*	*Ref*	*C/I*
Amphotericin B cholesteryl sulfate complex	SEQ	0.83 mg/ml[a]	JN	0.5 mg/ml	Gross precipitate forms	2117	I
Cisatracurium besylate	GW	0.1, 2, 5 mg/ml[a]	JN	0.125 mg/ml[a]	Physically compatible with no change in measured turbidity or increase in particle content in 4 hr at 23 °C	2074	C
Etomidate	AB	2 mg/ml	JN	0.5 mg/ml	Visually compatible for 7 days at 25 °C	1801	C
Gatifloxacin	BMS	2 mg/ml[a]	TAY	0.5 mg/ml	Physically compatible with no change in measured haze or increase in particle content in 4 hr at 23 °C	2234	C

Y-Site Injection Compatibility (1:1 Mixture) (Cont.)

Alfentanil HCl

Drug	*Mfr*	*Conc*	*Mfr*	*Conc*	*Remarks*	*Ref*	*C/I*
Hetastarch in lactated electrolyte injection (Hextend)	AB	6%	TAY	0.125 mg/ml[a]	Physically compatible with no change in measured turbidity or increase in particle content in 4 hr at 23 °C	2339	C
Linezolid	PHU	2 mg/ml	TAY	0.5 mg/ml	Physically compatible with no change in measured turbidity or increase in particle content in 4 hr at 23 °C	2264	C
Propofol	ZEN	10 mg/ml	JN	0.5 mg/ml	Physically compatible for 1 hr at 23 °C with no increase in particle content	2066	C
Remifentanil HCl	GW	0.025 and 0.25 mg/ml[b]	JN	0.125 mg/ml[a]	Physically compatible with no change in measured turbidity or increase in particle content in 4 hr at 23 °C	2075	C
Thiopental sodium	AB	25 mg/ml	JN	0.5 mg/ml	White pellets form within 24 hr at 25 °C	1801	I

[a]*Tested in dextrose 5% in water.*
[b]*Tested in sodium chloride 0.9%.*

Additional Compatibility Information

Infusion Solutions — The manufacturer states that alfentanil HCl is physically and chemically stable in dextrose 5% in sodium chloride 0.9%, Ringer's injection, lactated, dextrose 5% in water, and sodium chloride 0.9%. The recommended concentration range is 25 to 80 µg/ml. (1-7/98)

ALLOPURINOL SODIUM
AHFS 92:00

Products — Allopurinol sodium is available in single-use vials containing the equivalent of 500 mg of allopurinol in lyophilized form. Reconstitute with 25 ml of sterile water for injection to yield an almost colorless concentrated solution that is clear to slightly opalescent. (2)

pH — 11.1 to 11.8. (2)

Trade Name(s) — Aloprim.

Administration — The reconstituted solution must be diluted for use in sodium chloride 0.9% or dextrose 5% in water to a final concentration of no greater than 6 mg/ml. Sodium bicarbonate–containing solutions should not be used for this dilution. The diluted infusion is given as a single infusion daily or in equally divided infusions at 6-, 8-, or 12-hour intervals. The rate of infusion depends on the volume to be infused. (2)

Stability — Allopurinol sodium is supplied as a white lyophilized powder. The intact vials should be stored at controlled room temperature. Administration should begin within 10 hours of reconstitution. The reconstituted solution and diluted infusion solution should not be refrigerated. (2)

Compatibility Information

Y-Site Injection Compatibility (1:1 Mixture)

Allopurinol sodium

Drug	*Mfr*	*Conc*	*Mfr*	*Conc*	*Remarks*	*Ref*	*C/I*
Acyclovir sodium	BW	7 mg/ml[b]	BW	3 mg/ml[b]	Physically compatible with no change in measured turbidity or increase in particle content in 4 hr at 22 °C	1686	C

Y-Site Injection Compatibility (1:1 Mixture) (Cont.)

Drug	*Mfr*	*Conc*	Allopurinol sodium *Mfr*	*Conc*	*Remarks*	*Ref*	*C/I*
Amikacin sulfate	BR	5 mg/ml[b]	BW	3 mg/ml[b]	Crystals and flakes form within 1 hr	1686	**I**
Aminophylline	AB	2.5 mg/ml[b]	BW	3 mg/ml[b]	Physically compatible with no change in measured turbidity or increase in particle content in 4 hr at 22 °C	1686	C
Amphotericin B	SQ	0.6 mg/ml[a,b]	BW	3 mg/ml[b]	Natural haze of amphotericin B lost immediately	1686	**I**
Aztreonam	SQ	40 mg/ml[b]	BW	3 mg/ml[b]	Physically compatible with no change in measured turbidity or increase in particle content in 4 hr at 22 °C	1686	C
Bleomycin sulfate	BR	1 unit/ml[b]	BW	3 mg/ml[b]	Physically compatible with no change in measured turbidity or increase in particle content in 4 hr at 22 °C	1686	C
Bumetanide	RC	0.04 mg/ml[b]	BW	3 mg/ml[b]	Physically compatible with no change in measured turbidity or increase in particle content in 4 hr at 22 °C	1686	C
Buprenorphine HCl	RKC	0.04 mg/ml[b]	BW	3 mg/ml[b]	Physically compatible with no change in measured turbidity or increase in particle content in 4 hr at 22 °C	1686	C
Butorphanol tartrate	BR	0.04 mg/ml[b]	BW	3 mg/ml[b]	Physically compatible with no change in measured turbidity or increase in particle content in 4 hr at 22 °C	1686	C
Calcium gluconate	AMR	40 mg/ml[b]	BW	3 mg/ml[b]	Physically compatible with no change in measured turbidity or increase in particle content in 4 hr at 22 °C	1686	C
Carboplatin	BR	5 mg/ml[b]	BW	3 mg/ml[b]	Physically compatible with no change in measured turbidity or increase in particle content in 4 hr at 22 °C	1686	C
Carmustine	BR	1.5 mg/ml[b]	BW	3 mg/ml[b]	Gas evolves immediately	1686	**I**
Cefazolin sodium	GEM	20 mg/ml[b]	BW	3 mg/ml[b]	Physically compatible with no change in measured turbidity or increase in particle content in 4 hr at 22 °C	1686	C
Cefoperazone sodium	RR	40 mg/ml[b]	BW	3 mg/ml[b]	Physically compatible with no change in measured turbidity or increase in particle content in 4 hr at 22 °C	1686	C
Cefotaxime sodium	HO	20 mg/ml[b]	BW	3 mg/ml[b]	Tiny particles form immediately	1686	**I**
Cefotetan sodium	STU	20 mg/ml[b]	BW	3 mg/ml[b]	Physically compatible with no change in measured turbidity or increase in particle content in 4 hr at 22 °C	1686	C
Ceftazidime	LI[c]	40 mg/ml[b]	BW	3 mg/ml[b]	Physically compatible with no change in measured turbidity or increase in particle content in 4 hr at 22 °C	1686	C
Ceftizoxime sodium	FUJ	20 mg/ml[b]	BW	3 mg/ml[b]	Physically compatible with no change in measured turbidity or increase in particle content in 4 hr at 22 °C	1686	C
Ceftriaxone sodium	RC	20 mg/ml[b]	BW	3 mg/ml[b]	Physically compatible with no change in measured turbidity or increase in particle content in 4 hr at 22 °C	1686	C

Y-Site Injection Compatibility (1:1 Mixture) (Cont.)

Drug	*Mfr*	*Conc*	Allopurinol sodium *Mfr*	Allopurinol sodium *Conc*	*Remarks*	*Ref*	*C/I*
Cefuroxime sodium	GL	20 mg/ml[b]	BW	3 mg/ml[b]	Physically compatible with no change in measured turbidity or increase in particle content in 4 hr at 22 °C	1686	C
Chlorpromazine HCl	RU	2 mg/ml[b]	BW	3 mg/ml[b]	Heavy white turbidity and precipitate form immediately	1686	I
Cimetidine HCl	SKB	12 mg/ml[b]	BW	3 mg/ml[b]	Tiny crystals form in 1 hr and become large crystals in 4 hr	1686	I
Cisplatin	BR	1 mg/ml	BW	3 mg/ml[b]	Physically compatible with no change in measured turbidity or increase in particle content in 4 hr at 22 °C	1686	C
Clindamycin phosphate	AB	10 mg/ml[b]	BW	3 mg/ml[b]	Tiny particles form immediately and become more numerous over 4 hr	1686	I
Cyclophosphamide	MJ	10 mg/ml[b]	BW	3 mg/ml[b]	Physically compatible with no change in measured turbidity or increase in particle content in 4 hr at 22 °C	1686	C
Cytarabine	SCN	50 mg/ml	BW	3 mg/ml[b]	Tiny particles form within 4 hr	1686	I
Dacarbazine	MI	4 mg/ml[b]	BW	3 mg/ml[b]	Small particles form within 1 hr and become large pink pellets in 24 hr	1686	I
Dactinomycin	MSD	0.01 mg/ml[b]	BW	3 mg/ml[b]	Physically compatible with no change in measured turbidity or increase in particle content in 4 hr at 22 °C	1686	C
Daunorubicin HCl	WY	1 mg/ml[b]	BW	3 mg/ml[b]	Reddish-purple color and haze form immediately. Reddish-brown particles form within 1 hr	1686	I
Dexamethasone sodium phosphate	LY	1 mg/ml[b]	BW	3 mg/ml[b]	Physically compatible with no change in measured turbidity or increase in particle content in 4 hr at 22 °C	1686	C
Diphenhydramine HCl	PD	2 mg/ml[b]	BW	3 mg/ml[b]	Heavy white turbidity and precipitate form immediately	1686	I
Doxorubicin HCl	CET	2 mg/ml	BW	3 mg/ml[b]	Dark red color and haze form immediately. Reddish-brown particles form within 1 hr	1686	I
Doxorubicin HCl liposome injection	SEQ	0.4 mg/ml[a]	BW	3 mg/ml	Physically compatible with little or no change in measured turbidity and no increase in particle content in 4 hr at 23 °C	2087	C
Doxycycline hyclate	ES	1 mg/ml[b]	BW	3 mg/ml[b]	Small brown particles form immediately. Hazy brown solution with precipitate develops in 4 hr	1686	I
Droperidol	JN	0.4 mg/ml[b]	BW	3 mg/ml[b]	Heavy turbidity with particles forms immediately	1686	I
Enalaprilat	MSD	0.1 mg/ml[b]	BW	3 mg/ml[b]	Physically compatible with no change in measured turbidity or increase in particle content in 4 hr at 22 °C	1686	C
Etoposide	BR	0.4 mg/ml[b]	BW	3 mg/ml[b]	Physically compatible with no change in measured turbidity or increase in particle content in 4 hr at 22 °C	1686	C

Y-Site Injection Compatibility (1:1 Mixture) (Cont.)

Drug	Mfr	Conc	Allopurinol sodium Mfr	Allopurinol sodium Conc	Remarks	Ref	C/I
Famotidine	MSD	2 mg/ml[b]	BW	3 mg/ml[b]	Physically compatible with no change in measured turbidity or increase in particle content in 4 hr at 22 °C	1686	C
Floxuridine	RC	3 mg/ml[b]	BW	3 mg/ml[b]	Tiny particles form in 1 to 4 hr	1686	I
Fluconazole	RR	2 mg/ml	BW	3 mg/ml[b]	Physically compatible with no change in measured turbidity or increase in particle content in 4 hr at 22 °C	1686	C
Fludarabine phosphate	BX	1 mg/ml[b]	BW	3 mg/ml[b]	Physically compatible with no change in measured turbidity or increase in particle content in 4 hr at 22 °C	1686	C
Fluorouracil	RC	16 mg/ml[b]	BW	3 mg/ml[b]	Physically compatible with no change in measured turbidity or increase in particle content in 4 hr at 22 °C	1686	C
Furosemide	ES	3 mg/ml[b]	BW	3 mg/ml[b]	Physically compatible with no change in measured turbidity or increase in particle content in 4 hr at 22 °C	1686	C
Ganciclovir sodium	SY	20 mg/ml[b]	BW	3 mg/ml[b]	Physically compatible with no change in measured turbidity or increase in particle content in 4 hr at 22 °C	1686	C
Gentamicin sulfate	ES	5 mg/ml[b]	BW	3 mg/ml[b]	Hazy solution with crystals forms in 1 hr	1686	I
Granisetron HCl	SKB	0.05 mg/ml[a]	BW	3 mg/ml[a]	Physically compatible with no change in measured turbidity or increase in particle content in 4 hr at 23 °C	2000	C
Haloperidol lactate	MN	0.2 mg/ml[b]	BW	3 mg/ml[b]	Heavy turbidity forms immediately. Crystals form within 1 hr	1686	I
Heparin sodium	ES	100 units/ml[b]	BW	3 mg/ml[b]	Physically compatible with no change in measured turbidity or increase in particle content in 4 hr at 22 °C	1686	C
Hydrocortisone sodium phosphate	MSD	1 mg/ml[b]	BW	3 mg/ml[b]	Physically compatible with no change in measured turbidity or increase in particle content in 4 hr at 22 °C	1686	C
Hydrocortisone sodium succinate	UP	1 mg/ml[b]	BW	3 mg/ml[b]	Physically compatible with no change in measured turbidity or increase in particle content in 4 hr at 22 °C	1686	C
Hydromorphone HCl	KN	0.5 mg/ml[b]	BW	3 mg/ml[b]	Physically compatible with no change in measured turbidity or increase in particle content in 4 hr at 22 °C	1686	C
Hydroxyzine HCl	ES	4 mg/ml[b]	BW	3 mg/ml[b]	Heavy white turbidity and precipitate form immediately	1686	I
Idarubicin HCl	AD	0.5 mg/ml[b]	BW	3 mg/ml[b]	Reddish-purple color forms immediately. Particles form within 1 hr. Complete color loss in 24 hr	1686	I
Ifosfamide	MJ	25 mg/ml[b]	BW	3 mg/ml[b]	Physically compatible with no change in measured turbidity or increase in particle content in 4 hr at 22 °C	1686	C
Imipenem–cilastatin sodium	MSD	10 mg/ml[b]	BW	3 mg/ml[b]	Haze and particles form in 1 hr	1686	I

Y-Site Injection Compatibility (1:1 Mixture) (Cont.)

Drug	Mfr	Conc	Mfr	Conc	Remarks	Ref	C/I
			Allopurinol sodium				
Lorazepam	WY	0.1 mg/ml[b]	BW	3 mg/ml[b]	Physically compatible with no change in measured turbidity or increase in particle content in 4 hr at 22 °C	1686	C
Mannitol	BA	15%	BW	3 mg/ml[b]	Physically compatible with no change in measured turbidity or increase in particle content in 4 hr at 22 °C	1686	C
Mechlorethamine HCl	MSD	1 mg/ml	BW	3 mg/ml[b]	Haze and small particles form immediately and become numerous large particles in 4 hr	1686	I
Meperidine HCl	WY	4 mg/ml[b]	BW	3 mg/ml[b]	Tiny particles form immediately and increase in number over 4 hr	1686	I
Mesna	MJ	10 mg/ml[b]	BW	3 mg/ml[b]	Physically compatible with no change in measured turbidity or increase in particle content in 4 hr at 22 °C	1686	C
Methotrexate sodium	LE	15 mg/ml[b]	BW	3 mg/ml[b]	Physically compatible with no change in measured turbidity or increase in particle content in 4 hr at 22 °C	1686	C
Methylprednisolone sodium succinate	AB	5 mg/ml[b]	BW	3 mg/ml[b]	Haze forms in 1 hr with white precipitate in 24 hr	1686	I
Metoclopramide HCl	DU	5 mg/ml	BW	3 mg/ml[b]	Heavy white precipitate forms immediately	1686	I
Metronidazole	BA	5 mg/ml	BW	3 mg/ml[b]	Physically compatible with no change in measured turbidity or increase in particle content in 4 hr at 22 °C	1686	C
Minocycline HCl	LE	0.2 mg/ml[b]	BW	3 mg/ml[b]	Greenish-yellow color forms in 4 hr	1686	I
Mitoxantrone HCl	LE	0.5 mg/ml[b]	BW	3 mg/ml[b]	Physically compatible with no change in measured turbidity or increase in particle content in 4 hr at 22 °C	1686	C
Morphine sulfate	WI	1 mg/ml[b]	BW	3 mg/ml[b]	Physically compatible with no change in measured turbidity or increase in particle content in 4 hr at 22 °C	1686	C
Nalbuphine HCl	DU	10 mg/ml	BW	3 mg/ml[b]	Tiny particles form in 1 hr, becoming numerous crystals in 4 hr	1686	I
Netilmicin sulfate	SC	5 mg/ml[b]	BW	3 mg/ml[b]	Haze increases and flakes form in 1 hr	1686	I
Ondansetron HCl	GL	1 mg/ml[b]	BW	3 mg/ml[b]	Heavy turbidity forms immediately, becoming white flocculent precipitate	1686	I
Piperacillin sodium	LE	40 mg/ml[b]	BW	3 mg/ml[b]	Physically compatible with no change in measured turbidity or increase in particle content in 4 hr at 22 °C	1686	C
Plicamycin	MI	0.01 mg/ml[b]	BW	3 mg/ml[b]	Physically compatible with no change in measured turbidity or increase in particle content in 4 hr at 22 °C	1686	C
Potassium chloride	AB	0.1 mEq/ml[b]	BW	3 mg/ml[b]	Physically compatible with no change in measured turbidity or increase in particle content in 4 hr at 22 °C	1686	C
Prochlorperazine edisylate	SKB	0.5 mg/ml[b]	BW	3 mg/ml[b]	Heavy turbidity forms immediately	1686	I
Promethazine HCl	WY	2 mg/ml[b]	BW	3 mg/ml[b]	Heavy turbidity forms immediately, developing white particles in 4 hr	1686	I

Y-Site Injection Compatibility (1:1 Mixture) (Cont.)

Drug	Mfr	Conc	Mfr	Conc	Remarks	Ref	C/I
			Allopurinol sodium				
Ranitidine HCl	GL	2 mg/ml[b]	BW	3 mg/ml[b]	Physically compatible with no change in measured turbidity or increase in particle content in 4 hr at 22 °C	1686	C
Sodium bicarbonate	AB	1 mEq/ml	BW	3 mg/ml[b]	Small and large crystals form in 1 hr	1686	I
Streptozocin	UP	40 mg/ml[b]	BW	3 mg/ml[b]	Haze and small particles form in 1 hr and increase in 4 hr	1686	I
Teniposide	BR	0.1 mg/ml[a]	BW	3 mg/ml[a]	Physically compatible with no subvisual haze or particle formation in 4 hr at 23 °C	1725	C
Thiotepa	LE[d]	1 mg/ml[b]	BW	3 mg/ml[b]	Physically compatible with no change in measured turbidity or increase in particle content in 4 hr at 22 °C	1686	C
Ticarcillin disodium	BE	30 mg/ml[b]	BW	3 mg/ml[b]	Physically compatible with no change in measured turbidity or increase in particle content in 4 hr at 22 °C	1686	C
Ticarcillin disodium–clavulanate potassium	SKB	31 mg/ml[b]	BW	3 mg/ml[b]	Physically compatible with no change in measured turbidity or increase in particle content in 4 hr at 22 °C	1686	C
Tobramycin sulfate	LI	5 mg/ml[b]	BW	3 mg/ml[b]	Haze and crystals form in 1 hr	1686	I
Trimethoprim–sulfamethoxazole	ES	0.8 + 4 mg/ml[b]	BW	3 mg/ml[b]	Physically compatible with no change in measured turbidity or increase in particle content in 4 hr at 22 °C	1686	C
Vancomycin HCl	LY	10 mg/ml[b]	BW	3 mg/ml[b]	Physically compatible with no change in measured turbidity or increase in particle content in 4 hr at 22 °C	1686	C
Vinblastine sulfate	LI	0.12 mg/ml[b]	BW	3 mg/ml[b]	Physically compatible with no change in measured turbidity or increase in particle content in 4 hr at 22 °C	1686	C
Vincristine sulfate	LI	0.05 mg/ml[b]	BW	3 mg/ml[b]	Physically compatible with no change in measured turbidity or increase in particle content in 4 hr at 22 °C	1686	C
Vinorelbine tartrate	BW	1 mg/ml[b]	BW	3 mg/ml[b]	Heavy gelatinous white precipitate forms immediately	1686	I
Zidovudine	BW	4 mg/ml[b]	BW	3 mg/ml[b]	Physically compatible with no change in measured turbidity or increase in particle content in 4 hr at 22 °C	1686	C

[a] *Tested in dextrose 5% in water.*
[b] *Tested in sodium chloride 0.9%.*
[c] *Sodium carbonate–containing formulation tested.*
[d] *Powder fill formulation tested.*

ALTEPLASE
(t-PA)
AHFS 20:40

Products — Alteplase is available as a sterile lyophilized powder in 50- and 100-mg vials. The products contain (2):

Alteplase	50 mg	100 mg
L-Arginine	1.7 g	3.5 g
Phosphoric acid	0.5 g	1 g
Polysorbate 80	≤4 mg	≤11 mg

The pH may have been adjusted with phosphoric acid and/or sodium hydroxide. Intact 50-mg vials contain a vacuum, but the 100-mg vials do not. (2)

The alteplase vials are accompanied by 50- and 100-ml vials of sterile water for injection for the 50- and 100-mg sizes, respectively. Alteplase should be reconstituted with sterile water for injection only; do not use solutions containing preservatives. Use of the accompanying diluent results in a 1-mg/ml concentration. The manufacturer recommends use of a large bore needle to direct the stream into the lyophilized cake of the 50-mg vials. For the 100-mg vials, the special transfer device should be used. The vials should be swirled gently—not shaken—to dissolve the drug. Excessive agitation should be avoided. Although slight foaming may occur, the bubbles will dissipate after standing for several minutes. (2)

Specific Activity—Alteplase is a purified glycoprotein with a specific activity of 580,000 I.U./mg. The 50-mg vial contains 29 million I.U., and the 100-mg vial contains 58 million I.U. (2)

pH—Approximately 7.3. (2)

Osmolality—The product has an osmolality of 215 mOsm/kg. (2)

Trade Name(s)—Activase.

Administration — Alteplase is administered by intravenous infusion, directly after reconstitution to a 1-mg/ml concentration or diluted with an equal volume of sodium chloride 0.9% or dextrose 5% in water to a 0.5-mg/ml concentration. (2; 4) Dilution to a lower concentration may result in precipitation. (4; 1425)

Alteplase has been suggested as an effective and well-tolerated alternative to urokinase in catheter clearance (2328; 2329; 2330), although concerns about the stability of the solution have been raised. (2158)

Stability — Alteplase, an off-white lyophilized powder, becomes a colorless to pale yellow solution on reconstitution. Intact vials should be refrigerated or stored at room temperature with protection from extended exposure to light. The 50-mg vials should not be used unless a vacuum is present. (2)

Because alteplase has no bacteriostat, the manufacturer recommends reconstitution immediately before use. However, the solution may be administered within eight hours when stored at room temperature or under refrigeration. (2) Equal-volume dilutions (0.5 mg/ml) in dextrose 5% in water or sodium chloride 0.9% in either glass bottles or PVC containers are also stable for up to eight hours at room temperature. No other solutions should be used for dilution. (2) Exposure to light does not affect the potency of either reconstituted solutions of alteplase or dilutions in compatible infusion solutions. (2; 4)

Precipitation—Dilution of alteplase (Genentech) to 0.16 and 0.09 mg/ml in dextrose 5% in water (McGaw) resulted in precipitation immediately and in four hours, respectively, due to dilution of the arginine solubilizer. In sodium chloride 0.9%, dilution to 0.2 mg/ml did not result in precipitation. (1425)

pH Effects—Alteplase in solution is stable at pH 5 to 7.5. (4)

Freezing Solutions—A 50-mg vial of alteplase (Genentech), reconstituted with sterile water for injection to a concentration of 1 mg/ml, was diluted with balanced saline solution to a final concentration of 250 μg/ml. Then 0.3-ml (75 μg) portions of the diluted solution were drawn into 1-ml tuberculin syringes and frozen at −70 °C. Alteplase activity was retained for at least one year. (2157)

Sodium chloride 0.9% has also been suggested as a suitable diluent for alteplase solution for frozen storage. (1822)

However, others have objected to frozen storage of diluted alteplase solution. It was noted that the alteplase formulation has been designed for optimal stability, and dilution to a concentration lower than 500 μg/ml might adversely affect the drug's solubility by diluting the formulation's solubilizing components. Furthermore, it was noted that the calcium or magnesium salts contained in some diluents might interact with the phosphates present in the alteplase formulation to form a precipitate. Indeed, precipitated protein has been found in diluted alteplase after room temperature storage for 24 hours. Frozen storage at −20 °C with subsequent thawing has resulted in changed patterns of light scattering as well. It was recommended that dilution with balanced saline solution and storage of dilutions for any length of time at room temperature or frozen should be avoided. (2158)

Use of a diluent containing polysorbate 80, L-arginine, and phosphoric acid to reconstitute and dilute alteplase to 50 μg/ml is reported to permit frozen storage. Although the report did not specify the exact concentrations of the diluent components, it may have duplicated the alteplase vehicle after reconstitution. Use of this diluent for dilution prevented precipitation of the protein upon frozen storage at −20 °C. In addition, the activity in ophthalmic use was found to be unchanged after storage for six months in the frozen state. (2159)

Alteplase (Genentech) concentrations of 0.5, 1, and 2 mg/ml in sterile water for injection were packaged as 1 ml of solution in 5-ml polypropylene syringes and sealed with rubber tip caps. Sample syringes were stored frozen at −70 and −25 °C for up to 14 days as well as refrigerated at 2 °C. Frozen samples were thawed at room temperature and stored under refrigeration for determination of fibrinolytic activity. Fibrinolytic activity after frozen storage at both −70 and −25 °C remained near nominal initial concentrations for at least 14 days. Furthermore, the activity remained greater than 90% for up to 48 hours in all thawed samples subsequently stored at 2 °C and was comparable to the activity of refrigerated solutions that had never been frozen. However, substantial and unacceptable losses of activity occurred after 72 hours under refrigeration whether previously frozen or not. (2327)

Genentech evaluated the activity of alteplase 1 mg/ml when reconstituted with sterile water for injection, packaged in glass vials, and stored frozen at −20 °C for 32 days, followed by thawing at room temperature. The frozen alteplase solution remained physically and chemically comparable to newly reconstituted alteplase for at least eight hours at room temperature after thawing. (2328)

Compatibility Information

Solution Compatibility

Alteplase

Solution	Mfr	Mfr	Conc/L	Remarks	Ref	C/I
Dextrose 5% in water	MG	GEN	160 mg	Immediate precipitation	1425	I
	MG	GEN	90 mg	Precipitate forms in 4 hr	1425	I

Additive Compatibility

Alteplase

Drug	Mfr	Conc/L	Mfr	Conc/L	Test Soln	Remarks	Ref	C/I
Dobutamine HCl	LI	5 g	GEN	0.5 g	D5W, NS	Yellow discoloration and precipitate form	1856	I
Dopamine HCl	ACC	5 g	GEN	0.5 g	D5W, NS	About 30% alteplase clot-lysis activity loss in 24 hr at 25 °C	1856	I
Heparin sodium	ES	40,000 units	GEN	0.5 g	NS	Heparin interacts with alteplase. Opalescence forms within 5 min with peak intensity at 4 hr at 25 °C. Alteplase clot-lysis activity reduced slightly	1856	I
Lidocaine HCl	AST	4 g	GEN	0.5 g	D5W	Visually compatible with no alteplase clot-lysis activity loss in 24 hr at 25 °C	1856	C
	AST	4 g	GEN	0.5 g	NS	Visually compatible with 7% alteplase clot-lysis activity loss in 24 hr at 25 °C	1856	C
Morphine sulfate	WY	1 g	GEN	0.5 g	NS	Visually compatible with 5 to 8% alteplase clot-lysis activity loss in 24 hr at 25 °C	1856	C
Nitroglycerin	ACC	400 mg	GEN	0.5 g	D5W, NS	Visually compatible with 2% or less alteplase clot-lysis activity loss in 24 hr at 25 °C	1856	C

Y-Site Injection Compatibility (1:1 Mixture)

Alteplase

Drug	Mfr	Conc	Mfr	Conc	Remarks	Ref	C/I
Dobutamine HCl	LI	2 mg/ml[a]	GEN	1 mg/ml	Haze noted in 20 min by spectrophotometric examination and in 2 hr by visual examination	1340	I
Dopamine HCl	DU	8 mg/ml[a]	GEN	1 mg/ml	Haze noted in 4 hr by visual examination	1340	I
Heparin sodium	ES	100 units/ml[a]	GEN	1 mg/ml	Haze noted in 24 hr by visual examination. Erratic spectrophotometer readings	1340	I
Lidocaine HCl	AB	8 mg/ml[a]	GEN	1 mg/ml	Physically compatible for 6 days by spectrophotometric and visual examination	1340	C
Metoprolol tartrate	CI	1 mg/ml	GEN	1 mg/ml	Visually compatible with no alteplase clot-lysis activity loss in 24 hr at 25 °C	1856	C
Nitroglycerin	DU	0.2 mg/ml[a]	GEN	1 mg/ml	Haze noted in 24 hr by visual examination. Erratic spectrophotometer readings	1340	I
Propranolol HCl	AY	1 mg/ml	GEN	1 mg/ml	Visually compatible with 2% or less alteplase clot-lysis activity loss in 24 hr at 25 °C	1856	C

[a]*Tested in dextrose 5% in water.*

Additional Compatibility Information

Preservatives — Alteplase is stated to be incompatible with bacteriostatic water for injection because preservatives can interact with the alteplase molecule. (4)

AMIFOSTINE
AHFS 92:00

Products — Amifostine is available in vials containing, in lyophilized form, 500 mg of amifostine on the anhydrous basis. The vial contents are reconstituted with 9.7 ml of sodium chloride 0.9% to yield a solution containing amifostine 50 mg/ml. (2)

pH — Approximately 7. (234)

Trade Name(s) — Ethyol.

Administration — When used as a chemoprotectant in adults, amifostine is administered once daily as a 15-minute intravenous infusion. The infusion is started 30 minutes before chemotherapy. When used as a radioprotectant in adults, amifostine is administered once daily as a three-minute intravenous infusion started 15 to 30 minutes prior to radiation therapy. Patients should be well hydrated prior to intravenous infusion of amifostine and should maintain a supine position during the infusion. Only limited experience in administration to children or elderly patients is available. (2; 4)

Stability — The intact vials may be stored at controlled room temperatures of 20 to 25 °C. The manufacturer states that the reconstituted solution is chemically stable for 24 hours under refrigeration but only five hours at 25 °C. The product should not be used if cloudiness or a precipitate is observed. (2)

Admixed in PVC bags of sodium chloride 0.9%, amifostine concentrations between 5 and 40 mg/ml are also stable for 24 hours under refrigeration and five hours at 25 °C. The manufacturer does not recommend the use of infusion solutions other than sodium chloride 0.9%. (2; 4)

Compatibility Information

Y-Site Injection Compatibility (1:1 Mixture)

Drug	Mfr	Conc	Amifostine Mfr	Amifostine Conc	Remarks	Ref	C/I
Acyclovir sodium	BW	7 mg/ml[a]	USB	10 mg/ml[a]	Subvisual needles form in 1 hr. Visible particles form in 4 hr	1845	I
Amikacin sulfate	DU	5 mg/ml[a]	USB	10 mg/ml[a]	Physically compatible with no change in measured turbidity or increase in particle content in 4 hr at 23 °C	1845	C
Aminophylline	AMR	2.5 mg/ml[a]	USB	10 mg/ml[a]	Physically compatible with no change in measured turbidity or increase in particle content in 4 hr at 23 °C	1845	C
Amphotericin B	AD	0.6 mg/ml[a]	USB	10 mg/ml[a]	Turbidity forms immediately	1845	I
Ampicillin sodium	WY	20 mg/ml[b]	USB	10 mg/ml[a]	Physically compatible with no change in measured turbidity or increase in particle content in 4 hr at 23 °C	1845	C
Ampicillin sodium–sulbactam sodium	RR	20 + 10 mg/ml[b]	USB	10 mg/ml[a]	Physically compatible with no change in measured turbidity or increase in particle content in 4 hr at 23 °C	1845	C
Aztreonam	SQ	40 mg/ml[a]	USB	10 mg/ml[a]	Physically compatible with no change in measured turbidity or increase in particle content in 4 hr at 23 °C	1845	C
Bleomycin sulfate	MJ	1 unit/ml[b]	USB	10 mg/ml[a]	Physically compatible with no change in measured turbidity or increase in particle content in 4 hr at 23 °C	1845	C

Y-Site Injection Compatibility (1:1 Mixture) (Cont.)

Drug	Mfr	Conc	Amifostine Mfr	Amifostine Conc	Remarks	Ref	C/I
Bumetanide	RC	0.04 mg/ml[a]	USB	10 mg/ml[a]	Physically compatible with no change in measured turbidity or increase in particle content in 4 hr at 23 °C	1845	C
Buprenorphine HCl	RKC	0.04 mg/ml[a]	USB	10 mg/ml[a]	Physically compatible with no change in measured turbidity or increase in particle content in 4 hr at 23 °C	1845	C
Butorphanol tartrate	BR	0.04 mg/ml[a]	USB	10 mg/ml[a]	Physically compatible with no change in measured turbidity or increase in particle content in 4 hr at 23 °C	1845	C
Calcium gluconate	AMR	40 mg/ml[a]	USB	10 mg/ml[a]	Physically compatible with no change in measured turbidity or increase in particle content in 4 hr at 23 °C	1845	C
Carboplatin	BR	5 mg/ml[a]	USB	10 mg/ml[a]	Physically compatible with no change in measured turbidity or increase in particle content in 4 hr at 23 °C	1845	C
Carmustine	BR	1.5 mg/ml[a]	USB	10 mg/ml[a]	Physically compatible with no change in measured turbidity or increase in particle content in 4 hr at 23 °C	1845	C
Cefazolin sodium	MAR	20 mg/ml[a]	USB	10 mg/ml[a]	Physically compatible with no change in measured turbidity or increase in particle content in 4 hr at 23 °C	1845	C
Cefoperazone sodium	RR	40 mg/ml[a]	USB	10 mg/ml[a]	Haze forms immediately, becoming cloudy with microprecipitation in 4 hr	1845	I
Cefotaxime sodium	HO	20 mg/ml[a]	USB	10 mg/ml[a]	Physically compatible with no change in measured turbidity or increase in particle content in 4 hr at 23 °C	1845	C
Cefotetan disodium	STU	20 mg/ml[a]	USB	10 mg/ml[a]	Physically compatible with no change in measured turbidity or increase in particle content in 4 hr at 23 °C	1845	C
Cefoxitin sodium	MSD	20 mg/ml[a]	USB	10 mg/ml[a]	Physically compatible with no change in measured turbidity or increase in particle content in 4 hr at 23 °C	1845	C
Ceftazidime	LI[c]	40 mg/ml[a]	USB	10 mg/ml[a]	Physically compatible with no change in measured turbidity or increase in particle content in 4 hr at 23 °C	1845	C
Ceftizoxime sodium	FUJ	20 mg/ml[a]	USB	10 mg/ml[a]	Physically compatible with no change in measured turbidity or increase in particle content in 4 hr at 23 °C	1845	C
Ceftriaxone sodium	RC	20 mg/ml[a]	USB	10 mg/ml[a]	Physically compatible with no change in measured turbidity or increase in particle content in 4 hr at 23 °C	1845	C
Cefuroxime sodium	GL	30 mg/ml[a]	USB	10 mg/ml[a]	Physically compatible with no change in measured turbidity or increase in particle content in 4 hr at 23 °C	1845	C
Chlorpromazine HCl	SCN	2 mg/ml[a]	USB	10 mg/ml[a]	Subvisual haze forms immediately	1845	I
Cimetidine HCl	SKB	12 mg/ml[a]	USB	10 mg/ml[a]	Physically compatible with no change in measured turbidity or increase in particle content in 4 hr at 23 °C	1845	C

Y-Site Injection Compatibility (1:1 Mixture) (Cont.)

			Amifostine				
Drug	*Mfr*	*Conc*	*Mfr*	*Conc*	*Remarks*	*Ref*	*C/I*
Ciprofloxacin	MI	1 mg/ml[a]	USB	10 mg/ml[a]	Physically compatible with no change in measured turbidity or increase in particle content in 4 hr at 23 °C	1845	C
Cisplatin	BR	1 mg/ml	USB	10 mg/ml[a]	Subvisual haze forms in 4 hr	1845	I
Clindamycin phosphate	AST	10 mg/ml[a]	USB	10 mg/ml[a]	Physically compatible with no change in measured turbidity or increase in particle content in 4 hr at 23 °C	1845	C
Cyclophosphamide	MJ	10 mg/ml[a]	USB	10 mg/ml[a]	Physically compatible with no change in measured turbidity or increase in particle content in 4 hr at 23 °C	1845	C
Cytarabine	CET	50 mg/ml	USB	10 mg/ml[a]	Physically compatible with no change in measured turbidity or increase in particle content in 4 hr at 23 °C	1845	C
Dacarbazine	MI	4 mg/ml[a]	USB	10 mg/ml[a]	Physically compatible with no change in measured turbidity or increase in particle content in 4 hr at 23 °C	1845	C
Dactinomycin	ME	0.01 mg/ml[a]	USB	10 mg/ml[a]	Physically compatible with no change in measured turbidity or increase in particle content in 4 hr at 23 °C	1845	C
Daunorubicin HCl	WY	1 mg/ml[a]	USB	10 mg/ml[a]	Physically compatible with no change in measured turbidity or increase in particle content in 4 hr at 23 °C	1845	C
Dexamethasone sodium phosphate	AMR	1 mg/ml[a]	USB	10 mg/ml[a]	Physically compatible with no change in measured turbidity or increase in particle content in 4 hr at 23 °C	1845	C
Diphenhydramine HCl	PD	2 mg/ml[a]	USB	10 mg/ml[a]	Physically compatible with no change in measured turbidity or increase in particle content in 4 hr at 23 °C	1845	C
Dobutamine HCl	LI	4 mg/ml[a]	USB	10 mg/ml[a]	Physically compatible with no change in measured turbidity or increase in particle content in 4 hr at 23 °C	1845	C
Docetaxel	RPR	0.9 mg/ml[a]	ALZ	10 mg/ml[b]	Physically compatible with no change in measured turbidity or increase in particle content in 4 hr at 23 °C	2224	C
Dopamine HCl	AST	3.2 mg/ml[a]	USB	10 mg/ml[a]	Physically compatible with no change in measured turbidity or increase in particle content in 4 hr at 23 °C	1845	C
Doxorubicin HCl	CET	2 mg/ml	USB	10 mg/ml[a]	Physically compatible with no change in measured turbidity or increase in particle content in 4 hr at 23 °C	1845	C
Doxycycline hyclate	LY	1 mg/ml[a]	USB	10 mg/ml[a]	Physically compatible with no change in measured turbidity or increase in particle content in 4 hr at 23 °C	1845	C
Droperidol	JN	0.4 mg/ml[a]	USB	10 mg/ml[a]	Physically compatible with no change in measured turbidity or increase in particle content in 4 hr at 23 °C	1845	C
Enalaprilat	MSD	0.1 mg/ml[a]	USB	10 mg/ml[a]	Physically compatible with no change in measured turbidity or increase in particle content in 4 hr at 23 °C	1845	C

Y-Site Injection Compatibility (1:1 Mixture) (Cont.)

			Amifostine				
Drug	*Mfr*	*Conc*	*Mfr*	*Conc*	*Remarks*	*Ref*	*C/I*
Etoposide	BR	0.4 mg/ml[a]	USB	10 mg/ml[a]	Physically compatible with no change in measured turbidity or increase in particle content in 4 hr at 23 °C	1845	C
Famotidine	ME	2 mg/ml[a]	USB	10 mg/ml[a]	Physically compatible with no change in measured turbidity or increase in particle content in 4 hr at 23 °C	1845	C
Floxuridine	RC	3 mg/ml[a]	USB	10 mg/ml[a]	Physically compatible with no change in measured turbidity or increase in particle content in 4 hr at 23 °C	1845	C
Fluconazole	RR	2 mg/ml	USB	10 mg/ml[a]	Physically compatible with no change in measured turbidity or increase in particle content in 4 hr at 23 °C	1845	C
Fludarabine phosphate	BX	1 mg/ml[a]	USB	10 mg/ml[a]	Physically compatible with no change in measured turbidity or increase in particle content in 4 hr at 23 °C	1845	C
Fluorouracil	AD	16 mg/ml[a]	USB	10 mg/ml[a]	Physically compatible with no change in measured turbidity or increase in particle content in 4 hr at 23 °C	1845	C
Furosemide	AB	3 mg/ml[a]	USB	10 mg/ml[a]	Physically compatible with no change in measured turbidity or increase in particle content in 4 hr at 23 °C	1845	C
Ganciclovir sodium	SY	20 mg/ml[a]	USB	10 mg/ml[a]	Crystalline needles form immediately, becoming a dense flocculent precipitate in 1 hr	1845	I
Gemcitabine HCl	LI	10 mg/ml[b]	USB	10 mg/ml[b]	Physically compatible with no change in measured turbidity or increase in particle content in 4 hr at 23 °C	2226	C
Gentamicin sulfate	ES	5 mg/ml[a]	USB	10 mg/ml[a]	Physically compatible with no change in measured turbidity or increase in particle content in 4 hr at 23 °C	1845	C
Granisetron HCl	SKB	0.05 mg/ml[a]	USB	10 mg/ml[a]	Physically compatible with no change in measured turbidity or increase in particle content in 4 hr at 23 °C	2000	C
Haloperidol lactate	MN	0.2 mg/ml[a]	USB	10 mg/ml[a]	Physically compatible with no change in measured turbidity or increase in particle content in 4 hr at 23 °C	1845	C
Heparin sodium	ES	100 units/ml[a]	USB	10 mg/ml[a]	Physically compatible with no change in measured turbidity or increase in particle content in 4 hr at 23 °C	1845	C
Hydrocortisone sodium phosphate	MSD	1 mg/ml[a]	USB	10 mg/ml[a]	Physically compatible with no change in measured turbidity or increase in particle content in 4 hr at 23 °C	1845	C
Hydrocortisone sodium succinate	UP	1 mg/ml[a]	USB	10 mg/ml[a]	Physically compatible with no change in measured turbidity or increase in particle content in 4 hr at 23 °C	1845	C
Hydromorphone HCl	AST	0.5 mg/ml[a]	USB	10 mg/ml[a]	Physically compatible with no change in measured turbidity or increase in particle content in 4 hr at 23 °C	1845	C

Y-Site Injection Compatibility (1:1 Mixture) (Cont.)

			Amifostine				
Drug	*Mfr*	*Conc*	*Mfr*	*Conc*	*Remarks*	*Ref*	*C/I*
Hydroxyzine HCl	WI	4 mg/ml[a]	USB	10 mg/ml[a]	Subvisual haze forms immediately	1845	I
Idarubicin HCl	AD	0.5 mg/ml[a]	USB	10 mg/ml[a]	Increase in turbidity no greater than dilution with D5W alone. No change in particle content in 4 hr at 23 °C	1845	C
Ifosfamide	MJ	25 mg/ml[a]	USB	10 mg/ml[a]	Physically compatible with no change in measured turbidity or increase in particle content in 4 hr at 23 °C	1845	C
Imipenem–cilastatin sodium	MSD	10 mg/ml[a]	USB	10 mg/ml[a]	Physically compatible with no change in measured turbidity or increase in particle content in 4 hr at 23 °C	1845	C
Leucovorin calcium	LE	2 mg/ml[a]	USB	10 mg/ml[a]	Physically compatible with no change in measured turbidity or increase in particle content in 4 hr at 23 °C	1845	C
Lorazepam	WY	0.1 mg/ml[a]	USB	10 mg/ml[a]	Physically compatible with no change in measured turbidity or increase in particle content in 4 hr at 23 °C	1845	C
Magnesium sulfate	AST	100 mg/ml[a]	USB	10 mg/ml[a]	Physically compatible with no change in measured turbidity or increase in particle content in 4 hr at 23 °C	1845	C
Mannitol	BA	15%	USB	10 mg/ml[a]	Physically compatible with no change in measured turbidity or increase in particle content in 4 hr at 23 °C	1845	C
Mechlorethamine HCl	MSD	1 mg/ml	USB	10 mg/ml[a]	Physically compatible with no change in measured turbidity or increase in particle content in 4 hr at 23 °C	1845	C
Meperidine HCl	WY	4 mg/ml[a]	USB	10 mg/ml[a]	Physically compatible with no change in measured turbidity or increase in particle content in 4 hr at 23 °C	1845	C
Mesna	MJ	10 mg/ml[a]	USB	10 mg/ml[a]	Physically compatible with no change in measured turbidity or increase in particle content in 4 hr at 23 °C	1845	C
Methotrexate sodium	LE	15 mg/ml[a]	USB	10 mg/ml[a]	Physically compatible with no change in measured turbidity or increase in particle content in 4 hr at 23 °C	1845	C
Methylprednisolone sodium succinate	AB	5 mg/ml[a]	USB	10 mg/ml[a]	Physically compatible with no change in measured turbidity or increase in particle content in 4 hr at 23 °C	1845	C
Metoclopramide HCl	ES	5 mg/ml	USB	10 mg/ml[a]	Physically compatible with no change in measured turbidity or increase in particle content in 4 hr at 23 °C	1845	C
Metronidazole	BA	5 mg/ml	USB	10 mg/ml[a]	Physically compatible with no change in measured turbidity or increase in particle content in 4 hr at 23 °C	1845	C
Minocycline HCl	LE	0.2 mg/ml[a]	USB	10 mg/ml[a]	Bright yellow discoloration forms immediately	1845	I
Mitomycin	BR	0.5 mg/ml	USB	10 mg/ml[a]	Physically compatible with no change in measured turbidity or increase in particle content in 4 hr at 23 °C	1845	C

Y-Site Injection Compatibility (1:1 Mixture) (Cont.)

Drug	*Mfr*	*Conc*	Amifostine *Mfr*	Amifostine *Conc*	*Remarks*	*Ref*	*C/I*
Mitoxantrone HCl	LE	0.5 mg/ml[a]	USB	10 mg/ml[a]	Physically compatible with no change in measured turbidity or increase in particle content in 4 hr at 23 °C	1845	C
Morphine sulfate	AST	1 mg/ml[a]	USB	10 mg/ml[a]	Physically compatible with no change in measured turbidity or increase in particle content in 4 hr at 23 °C	1845	C
Nalbuphine HCl	AST	10 mg/ml	USB	10 mg/ml[a]	Physically compatible with no change in measured turbidity or increase in particle content in 4 hr at 23 °C	1845	C
Netilmicin sulfate	SC	5 mg/ml[a]	USB	10 mg/ml[a]	Physically compatible with no change in measured turbidity or increase in particle content in 4 hr at 23 °C	1845	C
Ondansetron HCl	GL	1 mg/ml[a]	USB	10 mg/ml[a]	Physically compatible with no change in measured turbidity or increase in particle content in 4 hr at 23 °C	1845	C
Piperacillin sodium	LE	40 mg/ml[a]	USB	10 mg/ml[a]	Physically compatible with no change in measured turbidity or increase in particle content in 4 hr at 23 °C	1845	C
Plicamycin	MI	0.01 mg/ml[a]	USB	10 mg/ml[a]	Physically compatible with no change in measured turbidity or increase in particle content in 4 hr at 23 °C	1845	C
Potassium chloride	AB	0.1 mEq/ml[a]	USB	10 mg/ml[a]	Physically compatible with no change in measured turbidity or increase in particle content in 4 hr at 23 °C	1845	C
Prochlorperazine edisylate	SN	0.5 mg/ml[a]	USB	10 mg/ml[a]	Immediate increase in subvisual haze	1845	I
Promethazine HCl	ES	2 mg/ml[a]	USB	10 mg/ml[a]	Physically compatible with no change in measured turbidity or increase in particle content in 4 hr at 23 °C	1845	C
Ranitidine HCl	GL	2 mg/ml[a]	USB	10 mg/ml[a]	Physically compatible with no change in measured turbidity or increase in particle content in 4 hr at 23 °C	1845	C
Sodium bicarbonate	AST	1 mEq/ml	USB	10 mg/ml[a]	Physically compatible with no change in measured turbidity or increase in particle content in 4 hr at 23 °C	1845	C
Streptozocin	UP	40 mg/ml[a]	USB	10 mg/ml[a]	Physically compatible with no change in measured turbidity or increase in particle content in 4 hr at 23 °C	1845	C
Teniposide	BR	0.1 mg/ml[a]	USB	10 mg/ml[a]	Physically compatible with no change in measured turbidity or increase in particle content in 4 hr at 23 °C	1845	C
Thiotepa	LE	1 mg/ml[a]	USB	10 mg/ml[a]	Physically compatible with no change in measured turbidity or increase in particle content in 4 hr at 23 °C	1845	C
Ticarcillin disodium	BE	30 mg/ml[a]	USB	10 mg/ml[a]	Physically compatible with no change in measured turbidity or increase in particle content in 4 hr at 23 °C	1845	C
Ticarcillin disodium–clavulanate potassium	SKB	31 mg/ml[a]	USB	10 mg/ml[a]	Physically compatible with no increase in measured turbidity or increase in particle content in 4 hr at 23 °C	1845	C

Y-Site Injection Compatibility (1:1 Mixture) (Cont.)

			Amifostine				
Drug	*Mfr*	*Conc*	*Mfr*	*Conc*	*Remarks*	*Ref*	*C/I*
Tobramycin sulfate	LI	5 mg/ml[a]	USB	10 mg/ml[a]	Physically compatible with no change in measured turbidity or increase in particle content in 4 hr at 23 °C	1845	C
Trimethoprim–sulfamethoxazole	ES	0.8 + 4 mg/ml[a]	USB	10 mg/ml[a]	Physically compatible with no change in measured turbidity or increase in particle content in 4 hr at 23 °C	1845	C
Trimetrexate glucuronate	USB	2 mg/ml[a]	USB	10 mg/ml[a]	Physically compatible with no change in measured turbidity or increase in particle content in 4 hr at 23 °C	1845	C
Vancomycin HCl	AB	10 mg/ml[a]	USB	10 mg/ml[a]	Physically compatible with no change in measured turbidity or increase in particle content in 4 hr at 23 °C	1845	C
Vinblastine sulfate	LI	0.12 mg/ml[a]	USB	10 mg/ml[a]	Physically compatible with no change in measured turbidity or increase in particle content in 4 hr at 23 °C	1845	C
Vincristine sulfate	LI	0.05 mg/ml[a]	USB	10 mg/ml[a]	Physically compatible with no change in measured turbidity or increase in particle content in 4 hr at 23 °C	1845	C
Zidovudine	BW	4 mg/ml[a]	USB	10 mg/ml[a]	Physically compatible with no change in measured turbidity or increase in particle content in 4 hr at 23 °C	1845	C

[a]*Tested in dextrose 5% in water.*
[b]*Tested in sodium chloride 0.9%.*
[c]*Sodium carbonate–containing formulation tested.*

AMIKACIN SULFATE
AHFS 8:12.02

Products — Amikacin sulfate is available in concentrations of 50, 62.5, and 250 mg/ml. These products also contain sodium metabisulfite, sodium citrate, and sodium hydroxide and/or sulfuric acid to adjust pH. (2; 29; 154)

pH — 4.5. (291) The range is 3.5 to 5.5. (4)

Osmolality — Amikacin sulfate (Apothecon) 250 mg/ml has an osmolality of 913 mOsm/kg; the 50-mg/ml concentration has an osmolality of 186 mOsm/kg. (2043)

The osmolality of amikacin sulfate 500 mg was calculated for the following dilutions (1054):

	Osmolality (mOsm/kg)	
Diluent	50 ml	100 ml
Dextrose 5% in water	353	319
Sodium chloride 0.9%	383	349

Sodium Content — The sodium content of amikacin sulfate 50 mg/ml is 0.064 mEq/ml; for the 250-mg/ml concentration, the sodium content is 0.319 mEq/ml. (291)

Trade Name(s) — Amikin.

Administration — Amikacin sulfate may be administered by intramuscular injection and intravenous infusion; for intravenous infusion 500 mg may be diluted in 100 to 200 ml of compatible infusion solution and administered to adults over 30 to 60 minutes. The diluent volume should be sufficient for drug infusion over one to two hours in infants and over 30 to 60 minutes in older children. (2; 4)

Stability — Amikacin sulfate is supplied as a colorless to pale yellow or light straw-colored solution which is stable for at least two years at controlled room temperature. (4) It was reported that aqueous solutions of amikacin sulfate in concentrations of 37.5 to 250 mg/ml retained greater than 90% potency for up to 36 months at 25 °C, 12 months at 37 °C, and three months at 56 °C. (291) Aqueous solutions of amikacin sulfate are subject to color darkening because of air oxidation. However, this change in color has no effect on potency. (291)

Amikacin sulfate (Bristol) in concentrations of 0.25 mg/ml and 5 mg/ml was found to be stable under the following conditions in almost all of the solutions listed under Compatibility Information (except as noted below) (292):

1. Stored for 60 days at 4 °C and then stored for 24 hours at 25 °C.
2. Frozen at −15 °C for 30 days, thawed, and then stored for 24 hours at 25 °C.
3. Frozen at −15 °C for 30 days, thawed, and then stored for 24 hours at 4 °C followed by 24 hours at 25 °C.

An exception to storage condition 1 was noted for amikacin sulfate 0.25 mg/ml in Normosol R in dextrose 5% in water. Greater than 10% potency loss of amikacin sulfate was noted within 24 hours of room temperature storage in this solution. The stability of the 5-mg/ml concentration was satisfactory under these conditions. If storage of the 0.25-mg/ml concentration at 4 °C was limited to 30 days, the amikacin sulfate potency was retained for 24 hours at 25 °C. (292)

Autoclaving—Autoclaving commercially available vials of amikacin sulfate of 50- and 250-mg/ml concentrations at 15 pounds pressure at 120 °C for 60 minutes resulted in no decrease in potency. (291)

Freezing Solutions—Amikacin sulfate (Bristol) 1 g/50 ml of dextrose 5% in water in PVC bags frozen at −20 °C for 30 days and then thawed by exposure to ambient temperature or microwave radiation had no evidence of precipitation or color change and showed 6% or less loss of potency as determined microbiologically. Subsequent storage of the admixture at room temperature for 24 hours also yielded a physically compatible solution which exhibited little or no additional loss of activity. (555)

Syringes—Amikacin sulfate (Bristol) 750 mg diluted with 1 ml of sodium chloride 0.9% to a final volume of 4 ml was stable, showing about a 2% loss when stored in polypropylene syringes (Becton-Dickinson) for 48 hours at 25 °C under fluorescent light. (1159)

Elastomeric Reservoir Pumps—Amikacin sulfate solutions in elastomeric reservoir pumps have been stated by the pump manufacturers to be stable for the following time periods frozen, refrigerated (REF), and at room temperature (RT) (31):

Pump Reservoir(s)	Conc.	Frozen	REF	RT
Homepump; Homepump Eclipse	10 mg/ml[b]	30 days	10 days	24 hr
Intermate	20 mg/ml[a]	30 days	10 days	24 hr
Medflo	5 mg/ml[a,b]	8 weeks	60 days	24 hr
ReadyMed	5 mg/ml[a,b]	30 days	60 days	24 hr

[a] *In dextrose 5% in water.*
[b] *In sodium chloride 0.9%.*

Sorption—Amikacin sulfate (Bristol-Myers Squibb) 10 mg/ml in dextrose 5% in water and in sodium chloride 0.9% was packaged in PVC bags (Macropharma) and in multilayer bags composed of polyethylene, polyamide, and polypropylene (Bieffe Medital). The solutions were delivered through PVC administration sets (Abbott) over one hour and evaluated for drug loss by HPLC analysis. No loss due to sorption to any of the plastic materials was found. (2269)

Central Venous Catheter—Amikacin sulfate (Apothecon) 1 mg/ml in dextrose 5% in water was found to be compatible with the ARROWg+ard Blue Plus (Arrow International) chlorhexidine-bearing triple-lumen central catheter. HPLC analysis was used to evaluate completeness of drug delivery through the catheter and the amount of chlorhexidine removed from the internal lumens. Delivery of the amikacin sulfate ranged from 92 to 98% of the initial concentration among the three lumens. Furthermore, chlorhexidine delivered from the catheter remained at trace amounts with no substantial increase due to the delivery of the drug through the catheter. (2335)

Compatibility Information

Solution Compatibility

Amikacin sulfate

Solution	*Mfr*	*Mfr*	*Conc/L*	*Remarks*	*Ref*	*C/I*
Dextran 75 6% in sodium chloride 0.9%	BA	BR	250 mg and 5 g	Physically compatible and potency retained for 24 hr at 25 °C	292	C
Dextrose 5% in Ringer's injection	BA	BR	250 mg and 5 g	Physically compatible and potency retained for 24 hr at 25 °C	292	C
Dextrose 5% in Ringer's injection, lactated	BA	BR	250 mg and 5 g	Physically compatible and potency retained for 24 hr at 25 °C	292	C
Dextrose 2½% in sodium chloride 0.45%	BA	BR	250 mg and 5 g	Physically compatible and potency retained for 24 hr at 25 °C	292	C
Dextrose 2½% in sodium chloride 0.9%	BA	BR	250 mg and 5 g	Physically compatible and potency retained for 24 hr at 25 °C	292	C
Dextrose 5% in sodium chloride 0.2%	BA	BR	250 mg and 5 g	Physically compatible and potency retained for 24 hr at 25 °C	292	C
Dextrose 5% in sodium chloride 0.33%	BA	BR	250 mg and 5 g	Physically compatible and potency retained for 24 hr at 25 °C	292	C

Solution Compatibility (Cont.)

Amikacin sulfate

Solution	*Mfr*	*Mfr*	*Conc/L*	*Remarks*	*Ref*	*C/I*
Dextrose 5% in sodium chloride 0.45%	BA	BR	250 mg and 5 g	Physically compatible and potency retained for 24 hr at 25 °C	292	C
Dextrose 5% in sodium chloride 0.9%	BA	BR	250 mg and 5 g	Physically compatible and potency retained for 24 hr at 25 °C	292	C
Dextrose 10% in sodium chloride 0.9%	BA	BR	250 mg and 5 g	Physically compatible and potency retained for 24 hr at 25 °C	292	C
Dextrose 5% in water	BA	BR	250 mg and 5 g	Physically compatible and potency retained for 24 hr at 25 °C	292	C
	TR[a]	BR	5 g	Physically compatible and potency retained for 24 hr at room temperature	518	C
	TR[a]	BR	20 g	Physically compatible and approximately 2 to 4% loss of potency in 24 hours at room temperature	555	C
	MG[b]	BR	4 g	Activity retained for 48 hr at 25 °C under fluorescent light	981	C
	AB[a]	BR	5 g	Visually compatible and potency by immunoassay retained for 48 hr at 25 °C under fluorescent light and 4 °C in the dark	1541	C
Dextrose 10% in water	BA	BR	250 mg and 5 g	Physically compatible and potency retained for 24 hr at 25 °C	292	C
	SO	BR	250 mg/ 21 ml[c]	Visually compatible with no amikacin loss by TDx in 30 days at 5 °C	1731	C
	SO	BR	500 mg/ 22 ml[c]	Visually compatible with no amikacin loss by TDx in 30 days at 5 °C	1731	C
Dextrose 20% in water	BA	BR	250 mg and 5 g	Physically compatible and potency retained for 24 hr at 25 °C	292	C
Invert sugar 10% in sodium chloride 0.9%	BA	BR	250 mg and 5 g	Physically compatible and potency retained for 24 hr at 25 °C	292	C
Invert sugar 10% in water	BA	BR	250 mg and 5 g	Physically compatible and potency retained for 24 hr at 25 °C	292	C
Mannitol 20% in water	BA	BR	250 mg and 5 g	Physically compatible and potency retained for 24 hr at 25 °C	292	C
Normosol M in dextrose 5% in water	AB	BR	250 mg and 5 g	Physically compatible and potency retained for 24 hr at 25 °C	292	C
Normosol R	AB	BR	250 mg and 5 g	Physically compatible and potency retained for 24 hr at 25 °C	292	C
Normosol R in dextrose 5% in water	AB	BR	250 mg and 5 g	Physically compatible and potency retained for 24 hr at 25 °C	292	C
Ringer's injection	BA	BR	250 mg and 5 g	Physically compatible and potency retained for 24 hr at 25 °C	292	C
Ringer's injection, lactated	BA	BR	250 mg and 5 g	Physically compatible and potency retained for 24 hr at 25 °C	292	C
Sodium chloride 0.25%	BA	BR	250 mg and 5 g	Physically compatible and potency retained for 24 hr at 25 °C	292	C
Sodium chloride 0.45%	BA	BR	250 mg and 5 g	Physically compatible and potency retained for 24 hr at 25 °C	292	C
Sodium chloride 0.9%	BA	BR	250 mg and 5 g	Physically compatible and potency retained for 24 hr at 25 °C	292	C
	TR[a]	BR	5 g	Physically compatible and potency retained for 24 hr at room temperature	518	C

Solution Compatibility (Cont.)

Amikacin sulfate

Solution	*Mfr*	*Mfr*	*Conc/L*	*Remarks*	*Ref*	*C/I*
	MG[b]	BR	4 g	Activity retained for 48 hr at 25 °C under fluorescent light	981	C
	AB[a]	BR	5 g	Visually compatible and potency by immunoassay retained for 48 hr at 25 °C under fluorescent light and 4 °C in the dark	1541	C
Sodium lactate ⅙ M	BA	BR	250 mg and 5 g	Physically compatible and potency retained for 24 hr at 25 °C	292	C
TPN #107[d]			150 mg	Physically compatible and amikacin activity retained for 24 hr at 21 °C by microbiological assay	1326	C

[a]Tested in PVC containers.
[b]Tested in glass containers.
[c]Tested as a concentrate in glass vials.
[d]Refer to Appendix I for the composition of parenteral nutrition solutions. TPN indicates a 2-in-1 admixture.

Additive Compatibility

Amikacin sulfate

Drug	*Mfr*	*Conc/L*	*Mfr*	*Conc/L*	*Test Soln*	*Remarks*	*Ref*	*C/I*
Aminophylline	SE	5 g	BR	5 g	LR, NS, R, SL	Physically compatible and amikacin potency retained for 24 hr at 25 °C. Aminophylline not analyzed	294	C
	SE	5 g	BR	5 g	D5LR, D5R, D5S, D5W, D10W, IS10	Greater than 10% amikacin decomposition after 8 hr but within 24 hr at 25 °C. Aminophylline not analyzed	294	I
Amobarbital sodium	LI	100 mg	BR	5 g	[a]	Physically compatible and potency of both retained for 24 hr at 25 °C	294	C
Amphotericin B	SQ	100 mg	BR	5 g	[a]	Immediate precipitate	293	I
Ampicillin sodium	BR	30 g	BR	5 g	[a]	Greater than 10% ampicillin decomposition in 4 hr at 25 °C	293	I
Ascorbic acid injection[b]	CO	5 g	BR	5 g	[a]	Physically compatible and potency of both retained for 24 hr at 25 °C	294	C
Bleomycin sulfate	BR	20 and 30 units	BR	1.25 g	NS	Physically compatible and bleomycin activity retained for 1 week at 4 °C. Amikacin not tested	763	C
Calcium chloride	UP	1 g	BR	5 g	[a]	Physically compatible and potency of both retained for 24 hr at 25 °C	294	C
Calcium gluconate	UP	500 mg	BR	5 g	[a]	Physically compatible and potency of both retained for 24 hr at 25 °C	294	C
Cefazolin sodium	LI	20 g	BR	5 g	[a]	Potency of both retained for at least 8 hr at 25 °C. Turbidity observed at 24 hr	293	I
Cefepime HCl	BR	40 g	BR	6 g	D5W, NS	Visually compatible with 6% cefepime loss by HPLC in 24 hr at room temperature and 4% loss in 7 days at 5 °C. No amikacin loss by bioassay	1681	C

Additive Compatibility (Cont.)

Amikacin sulfate

Drug	*Mfr*	*Conc/L*	*Mfr*	*Conc/L*	*Test Soln*	*Remarks*	*Ref*	*C/I*
Cefoxitin sodium	MSD	5 g	BR	5 g	D5S	9% cefoxitin decomposition at 25 °C and none at 5 °C over 48 hr. No amikacin decomposition at 25 °C and 1% at 5 °C over 48 hr	308	C
Chloramphenicol sodium succinate	PD	10 g	BR	5 g	[a]	Physically compatible and potency of both retained for 24 hr at 25 °C	293	C
Chlorothiazide sodium	MSD	10 mg	BR	5 g	[a]	Precipitate forms within 4 hr at 25 °C	294	I
Chlorpheniramine maleate	SC	40 mg	BR	5 g	[a]	Physically compatible and potency of both retained for 24 hr at 25 °C	294	C
Cimetidine HCl	SKF	1.5 g	BR	2.5 g	D5W	Physically compatible and cimetidine chemically stable for 24 hr at room temperature. Amikacin not tested	551	C
Ciprofloxacin	MI	1.6 g	BR	4.1 g	D5W, NS	Visually compatible and ciprofloxacin potency by HPLC and amikacin potency by immunoassay retained for 48 hr at 25 °C under fluorescent light	1541	C
Clindamycin phosphate	UP	6 g	BR	5 g	[a]	Physically compatible and amikacin potency retained for 24 hr at 25 °C. Clindamycin not analyzed	293	C
	UP	9 g	AB	4 g	D5W, NS[c]	Potency of both drugs retained for 48 hr at 25 °C under fluorescent light	981	C
Colistimethate sodium	WC	500 mg	BR	5 g	[a]	Physically compatible and amikacin potency retained for 24 hr at 25 °C. Colistimethate not analyzed	293	C
Dexamethasone sodium phosphate	MSD	40 mg	BR	5 g	[a]	Physically compatible and potency of both retained for 24 hr at 25 °C	294	C
	MSD	40 mg	BR	5 g	D2.5S	16% dexamethasone decomposition in 4 hr at 25 °C	294	I
Dimenhydrinate	SE	100 mg	BR	5 g	[a]	Physically compatible and potency of both retained for 24 hr at 25 °C	294	C
Diphenhydramine HCl	PD	100 mg	BR	5 g	[a]	Physically compatible and potency of both retained for 24 hr at 25 °C	294	C
Epinephrine HCl	PD	2.5 mg	BR	5 g	[a]	Physically compatible and potency of both retained for 24 hr at 25 °C	294	C
Ergonovine maleate	LI	0.2 mg	BR	5 g	[a]	Physically compatible and amikacin potency retained for 24 hr at 25 °C. Ergonovine not analyzed	294	C
Fluconazole	PF	1 g	BR	2.5 g	D5W	Visually compatible with no fluconazole loss by HPLC in 72 hr at 25 °C under fluorescent light. Amikacin not tested	1677	C
Furosemide	HO	160 mg	BR	2 g	D5W, NS	Transient cloudiness during admixture. Then physically compatible for 24 hr at 21 °C	876	C
Heparin sodium	AB	30,000 units	BR	5 g	[a]	Immediate precipitation	294	I
Hyaluronidase	SE	150 units	BR	5 g	[a]	Physically compatible and amikacin potency retained for 24 hr at 25 °C. Hyaluronidase not analyzed	294	C

Additive Compatibility (Cont.)

			Amikacin sulfate					
Drug	*Mfr*	*Conc/L*	*Mfr*	*Conc/L*	*Test Soln*	*Remarks*	*Ref*	*C/I*
Hydrocortisone sodium phosphate	MSD	250 mg	BR	5 g	[a]	Physically compatible and potency of both retained for 24 hr at 25 °C	294	C
Hydrocortisone sodium succinate	UP	200 mg	BR	5 g	[a]	Physically compatible and potency of both retained for 24 hr at 25 °C	294	C
Lincomycin HCl	UP	10 g	BR	5 g	[a]	Physically compatible and potency of both retained for 24 hr at 25 °C	293	C
Metaraminol bitartrate	BR	200 mg	BR	5 g	[a]	Physically compatible and potency of both retained for 24 hr at 25 °C	294	C
Metronidazole	RP	5 g[d]	BR	5 g		Physically compatible with little or no pH change for at least 12 hr at 23 °C	807	C
Metronidazole HCl with sodium bicarbonate	SE AB	5 g 50 mEq	BR	2.25 g	D5W, NS	Physically compatible for 48 hr	765	C
Norepinephrine bitartrate	WI	8 mg	BR	5 g	[a]	Physically compatible and potency of both retained for 24 hr at 25 °C	294	C
Oxacillin sodium	BR	2 g	BR	5 g	D5LR, D5R, D5S, D5W, D10W, IS10, LR, NS, R	Physically compatible and potency of both retained for 24 hr at 25 °C	293	C
	BR	2 g	BR	5 g	NR, SL	Oxacillin potency retained through 8 hr at 25 °C. Greater than 10% decomposition in 24 hr	293	I
Penicillin G potassium	LI	20 million units	BR	5 g	D5LR, D5R, D5S, D5W, D10W, LR, NS, R, SL	Physically compatible and potency of both retained for 24 hr at 25 °C	293	C
	LI	20 million units	BR	5 g	IG–D5W, IS10	Potency of penicillin retained through 8 hr at 25 °C. Greater than 10% decomposition in 24 hr	293	I
Pentobarbital sodium	AB	100 mg	BR	5 g	[a]	Physically compatible and potency of both retained for 24 hr at 25 °C	294	C
Phenobarbital sodium	LI	300 mg	BR	5 g	[a]	Physically compatible and potency of both retained for 24 hr at 25 °C	294	C
Phenytoin sodium	PD	250 mg	BR	5 g	[a]	Immediate precipitation	294	I
Phytonadione	MSD	200 mg	BR	5 g	[a]	Physically compatible and amikacin potency retained for 24 hr at 25 °C. Phytonadione not analyzed	294	C
Polymyxin B sulfate	BW	200 mg	BR	5 g	[a]	Physically compatible and amikacin potency retained for 24 hr at 25 °C. Polymyxin not analyzed	293	C
Potassium chloride	LI	3 g	BR	5 g	[a]	Physically compatible and potency of both retained for 24 hr at 25 °C	294	C
	LI	3 g	BR	5 g	DXN–S	14% amikacin decomposition in 4 hr at 25 °C	294	I

Additive Compatibility (Cont.)

			Amikacin sulfate					
Drug	*Mfr*	*Conc/L*	*Mfr*	*Conc/L*	*Test Soln*	*Remarks*	*Ref*	*C/I*
Prochlorperazine edisylate	SKF	20 mg	BR	5 g	[a]	Physically compatible and potency of both retained for 24 hr at 25 °C	294	C
Promethazine HCl	WY	100 mg	BR	5 g	[a]	Physically compatible and potency of both retained for 24 hr at 25 °C	294	C
Ranitidine HCl	GL	100 mg	BR	1 g	D5W	Physically compatible for 24 hr at ambient temperature under fluorescent light	1151	C
	GL	50 mg and 2 g		2.5 g	D5W	Physically compatible and ranitidine chemically stable by HPLC for 24 hr at 25 °C. Amikacin not tested	1515	C
Sodium bicarbonate	BR	15 g	BR	5 g	[a]	Physically compatible and potency of both retained for 24 hr at 25 °C	294	C
Succinylcholine chloride	SQ	2 g	BR	5 g	[a]	Physically compatible and potency of both retained for 24 hr at 25 °C	294	C
Thiopental sodium	AB	4 g	BR	5 g	[a]	Immediate precipitation	294	I
Vancomycin HCl	LI	2 g	BR	5 g	[a]	Physically compatible and amikacin potency retained for 24 hr at 25 °C. Vancomycin not analyzed	293	C
Verapamil HCl	KN	80 mg	BR	2 g	D5W, NS	Physically compatible for 24 hr	764	C
Vitamin B complex with C	AB	5 ml	BR	5 g	[a]	Red precipitate forms within 24 hr	294	I

[a]*Tested in the following solutions: D5R, D5LR, D5¼S, D5½S, D5S, D5W, D10W, IS10, NS, LR, R, and SL.*
[b]*Present as calcium ascorbate.*
[c]*Tested in glass containers.*
[d]*Minibags (100 ml) containing metronidazole 500 mg with disodium phosphate 150 mg, citric acid 44 mg, and sodium chloride 740 mg. This product differs from the Searle product.*

Drugs in Syringe Compatibility

			Amikacin sulfate				
Drug (in syringe)	*Mfr*	*Amt*	*Mfr*	*Amt*	*Remarks*	*Ref*	*C/I*
Clindamycin phosphate	UP	900 mg/ 6 ml	BR	750 mg/ 4 ml[a]	Physically compatible with little or no loss of either drug in 48 hr at 25 °C in polypropylene syringes	1159	C
Doxapram HCl	RB	400 mg/ 20 ml		100 mg/ 2 ml	Physically compatible with no doxapram loss in 24 hr	1177	C
Heparin sodium		2500 units/ 1 ml		100 mg	Turbidity or precipitate forms within 5 min	1053	I

[a]*Diluted to 4 ml with 1 ml of sodium chloride 0.9%.*

Y-Site Injection Compatibility (1:1 Mixture)

			Amikacin sulfate				
Drug	*Mfr*	*Conc*	*Mfr*	*Conc*	*Remarks*	*Ref*	*C/I*
Acyclovir sodium	BW	5 mg/ml[a]	BR	5 mg/ml[a]	Physically compatible for 4 hr at 25 °C	1157	C
Alatrofloxacin mesylate	PF	1.43 mg/ml[a]	VHA	100 mg/ml[e]	Visually and microscopically compatible run through a Y-site over 25 min	2235	C
Allopurinol sodium	BW	3 mg/ml[b]	BR	5 mg/ml[b]	Crystals and flakes form within 1 hr	1686	I

Y-Site Injection Compatibility (1:1 Mixture) (Cont.)

Drug	*Mfr*	*Conc*	*Mfr*	*Conc*	*Remarks*	*Ref*	*C/I*
			Amikacin sulfate				
Amifostine	USB	10 mg/ml[a]	DU	5 mg/ml[a]	Physically compatible with no change in measured turbidity or increase in particle content in 4 hr at 23 °C	1845	C
Amiodarone HCl	LZ	4 mg/ml[c]	BR	5 mg/ml[c]	Physically compatible for 4 hr at room temperature	1444	C
Amphotericin B cholesteryl sulfate complex	SEQ	0.83 mg/ml[a]	AB	5 mg/ml[a]	Gross precipitate forms	2117	I
Amsacrine	NCI	1 mg/ml[a]	BR	5 mg/ml[a]	Physically compatible for 4 hr at room temperature under fluorescent light	1381	C
Aztreonam	SQ	40 mg/ml[a]	BMS	5 mg/ml[a]	Physically compatible with no subvisual haze or particle formation in 4 hr at 23 °C	1758	C
Cefpirome sulfate	HO	50 mg/ml[d]	APC	0.5 mg/ml[d]	Visually and microscopically compatible with less than 6% cefpirome loss and less than 10% amikacin loss by HPLC in 8 hr at 23 °C	2044	C
Cisatracurium besylate	GW	0.1, 2, 5 mg/ml[a]	AB	5 mg/ml[a]	Physically compatible with no change in measured turbidity or increase in particle content in 4 hr at 23 °C	2074	C
Cyclophosphamide	MJ	20 mg/ml[a]	BR	5 mg/ml[a]	Physically compatible for 4 hr at 25 °C	1194	C
Dexamethasone sodium phosphate	AMR	4 mg/ml	SQ	50 mg/ml[e]	Visually compatible for 24 hr at room temperature in test tubes. No precipitate found on filter from Y-site delivery	2063	C
Diltiazem HCl	MMD	5 mg/ml	BR	5[b] and 250 mg/ml	Visually compatible	1807	C
Docetaxel	RPR	0.9 mg/ml[a]	AB	5 mg/ml[a]	Physically compatible with no change in measured turbidity or increase in particle content in 4 hr at 23 °C	2224	C
Enalaprilat	MSD	0.05 mg/ml[b]	BR	2 mg/ml[a]	Physically compatible for 24 hr at room temperature under fluorescent light	1355	C
Esmolol HCl	DCC	10 mg/ml[a]	BR	5 mg/ml[a]	Physically compatible for 24 hr at 22 °C	1169	C
Etoposide phosphate	BR	5 mg/ml[a]	APC	5 mg/ml[a]	Physically compatible with no change in measured turbidity or increase in particle content in 4 hr at 23 °C	2218	C
Filgrastim	AMG	30 μg/ml[a]	ES	5 mg/ml[a]	Physically compatible with no change in measured turbidity or increase in particle content in 4 hr at 22 °C	1687	C
	AMG	10[f] and 40[a] μg/ml	BMS	5 mg/ml[a]	Visually compatible with little or no loss of filgrastim activity by bioassay and amikacin by immunoassay in 4 hr at 25 °C	2060	C
Fluconazole	RR	2 mg/ml	BR	20 mg/ml	Physically compatible for 24 hr at 25 °C	1407	C
Fludarabine phosphate	BX	1 mg/ml[a]	BR	5 mg/ml[a]	Physically compatible for 4 hr at room temperature under fluorescent light	1439	C
Foscarnet sodium	AST	24 mg/ml	BR	20 mg/ml	Physically compatible for 24 hr at room temperature under fluorescent light	1335	C
Furosemide	HO	10 mg/ml	BR	2 mg/ml[c]	Physically compatible for 24 hr at 21 °C	876	C

Y-Site Injection Compatibility (1:1 Mixture) (Cont.)

Drug	*Mfr*	*Conc*	*Mfr*	*Conc*	*Remarks*	*Ref*	*C/I*
			Amikacin sulfate				
Gatifloxacin	BMS	2 mg/ml[a]	AB	5 mg/ml[a]	Physically compatible with no change in measured turbidity or increase in particle content in 4 hr at 23 °C	2234	**C**
Gemcitabine HCl	LI	10 mg/ml[b]	APC	5 mg/ml[b]	Physically compatible with no change in measured turbidity or increase in particle content in 4 hr at 23 °C	2226	**C**
Granisetron HCl	SKB	0.05 mg/ml[a]	AB	5 mg/ml[a]	Physically compatible with no change in measured turbidity or increase in particle content in 4 hr at 23 °C	2000	**C**
Hetastarch in lactated electrolyte injection (Hextend)	AB	6%	APC	5 mg/ml[a]	Physically compatible with no change in measured haze or increase in particle content in 4 hr at 23 °C	2339	**C**
Hetastarch in sodium chloride 0.9%	DCC	6%	BR	5 mg/ml[a]	Small crystals formed immediately after mixing and persisted for 4 hr	1313	**I**
Idarubicin HCl	AD	1 mg/ml[b]	BR	5 mg/ml[a]	Physically compatible for 24 hr at 25 °C	1525	**C**
IL-2	RC	4800 I.U./ml[b]	BR	250 mg/ml	Visually compatible and IL-2 activity by bioassay retained. Amikacin not tested	1552	**C**
Labetalol HCl	SC	1 mg/ml[a]	BR	5 mg/ml[a]	Physically compatible for 24 hr at 18 °C	1171	**C**
Levofloxacin	OMN	5 mg/ml	BED	50 mg/ml	Visually compatible for 4 hr at 24 °C under fluorescent light	2233	**C**
Linezolid	PHU	2 mg/ml	AB	5 mg/ml[a]	Physically compatible with no change in measured turbidity or increase in particle content in 4 hr at 23 °C	2264	**C**
Lorazepam	WY	0.33 mg/ml[b]	BMS	5 mg/ml	Visually compatible for 24 hr at 22 °C	1855	**C**
Magnesium sulfate	IX	16.7, 33.3, 66.7, 100 mg/ml[a]	BR	5 mg/ml[a]	Physically compatible for at least 4 hr at 32 °C	813	**C**
Melphalan HCl	BW	0.1 mg/ml[b]	BR	5 mg/ml[b]	Physically compatible with no change in measured turbidity or increase in particle content in 3 hr at 22 °C	1557	**C**
Midazolam HCl	RC	5 mg/ml	BMS	5 mg/ml	Visually compatible for 24 hr at 22 °C	1855	**C**
Morphine sulfate	WI	1 mg/ml[a]	BR	5 mg/ml[a]	Physically compatible for at least 4 hr at 25 °C under fluorescent light	987	**C**
Ondansetron HCl	GL	1 mg/ml[b]	BR	5 mg/ml[a]	Physically compatible for 4 hr at 22 °C	1365	**C**
Paclitaxel	NCI	1.2 mg/ml[a]	BR	5 mg/ml[a]	Physically compatible with no change in measured turbidity in 4 hr at 22 °C	1556	**C**
Perphenazine	SC	0.02 mg/ml[a]	BR	5 mg/ml[a]	Physically compatible for 4 hr at 25 °C	1155	**C**
Propofol	ZEN	10 mg/ml	DU	5 mg/ml[a]	White precipitate and yellow color form immediately	2066	**I**
Remifentanil HCl	GW	0.025 and 0.25 mg/ml[b]	AB	5 mg/ml[a]	Physically compatible with no change in measured turbidity or increase in particle content in 4 hr at 23 °C	2075	**C**
Sargramostim	IMM	10 μg/ml[b]	BR	5 mg/ml[b]	Physically compatible for 4 hr at 22 °C	1436	**C**
Teniposide	BR	0.1 mg/ml[a]	BR	5 mg/ml[a]	Physically compatible with no subvisual haze or particle formation in 4 hr at 23 °C	1725	**C**

Y-Site Injection Compatibility (1:1 Mixture) (Cont.)

Drug	Mfr	Conc	Amikacin sulfate Mfr	Amikacin sulfate Conc	Remarks	Ref	C/I
Thiotepa	IMM[g]	1 mg/ml[a]	DU	5 mg/ml[a]	Physically compatible with no change in measured turbidity or increase in particle content in 4 hr at 23 °C	1861	C
TNA #97 to #104[h]			BR	250 mg/ml	Broken fat emulsion with oil floating in admixtures	1324	I
TNA #218 to #226[h]			AB	5 mg/ml[a]	Visually compatible with no precipitate or emulsion damage apparent in 4 hr at 23 °C	2215	C
TPN #54[h]				250 mg/ml	Physically compatible and amikacin activity retained over 6 hr at 22 °C by microbiological assay	1045	C
TPN #61[h]		[i]	BR	37.5 mg/ 0.15 ml[j]	Physically compatible	1012	C
		[k]	BR	225 mg/0.9 ml[j]	Physically compatible	1012	C
TPN #91[h]		[l]		15 mg[m]	Physically compatible	1170	C
TPN #203 and #204[h]			APC	5 mg/ml	Visually compatible for 2 hr at 23 °C	1974	C
TPN #212 to #215[h]			AB	5 mg/ml[a]	Physically compatible with no change in measured turbidity or increase in particle content in 4 hr at 23 °C	2109	C
Vinorelbine tartrate	BW	1 mg/ml[b]	BR	5 mg/ml[b]	Physically compatible with no change in measured turbidity or increase in particle content in 4 hr at 22 °C	1558	C
Warfarin sodium	DU	0.1[c] and 2 mg/ml[n]	AB	5 mg/ml[c]	Physically compatible with no change in measured turbidity or increase in particle content in 24 hr at 23 °C	2011	C
Zidovudine	BW	4 mg/ml[a]	BR	4 mg/ml[a]	Physically compatible for 4 hr at 25 °C under fluorescent light by visual and microscopic examination	1193	C

[a] *Tested in dextrose 5% in water.*
[b] *Tested in sodium chloride 0.9%.*
[c] *Tested in both dextrose 5% in water and sodium chloride 0.9%.*
[d] *Tested in dextrose 5% in water, Ringer's injection, lactated, sodium chloride 0.45%, and sodium chloride 0.9%.*
[e] *Tested in sodium chloride 0.45%.*
[f] *Tested in dextrose 5% in water with albumin human 2 mg/ml.*
[g] *Lyophilized formulation tested.*
[h] *Refer to Appendix I for the composition of parenteral nutrition solutions. TNA indicates a 3-in-1 admixture, and TPN indicates a 2-in-1 admixture.*
[i] *Run at 21 ml/hr.*
[j] *Given over 30 minutes by syringe pump.*
[k] *Run at 94 ml/hr.*
[l] *Run at 10 ml/hr.*
[m] *Given over one hour by syringe pump.*
[n] *Tested in sterile water for injection.*

Additional Compatibility Information

Infusion Solutions — Amikacin sulfate 250 mg/L and 5 g/L is stable for 24 hours at room temperature in the following infusion solutions (2; 4):

Dextrose 5% in sodium chloride 0.2%
Dextrose 5% in sodium chloride 0.45%
Dextrose 5% in water
Normosol M in dextrose 5%
Normosol R in dextrose 5%
Plasma-Lyte 56 in dextrose 5%
Plasma-Lyte 148 in dextrose 5%
Ringer's injection, lactated
Sodium chloride 0.9%

Peritoneal Dialysis Solutions — Amikacin base (Bristol) 10 and 50 mg/L in peritoneal dialysis concentrate with 50% dextrose

(McGaw) retained about 70% of initial activity in seven hours and about 40 to 50% in 24 hours at room temperature as determined by microbiological assay. (1044)

Amikacin sulfate (Bristol) 25 µg/ml combined separately with the cephalosporins cefazolin sodium (Lilly), cefamandole nafate (Lilly), and cefoxitin sodium (MSD) at a concentration of 125 µg/ml in peritoneal dialysis solution (Dianeal 1.5%) exhibited enhanced rates of lethality to *Staphylococcus aureus, Escherichia coli,* and *Pseudomonas aeruginosa* compared to any of the drugs alone. (1623)

β-Lactam Antibiotics — In common with other aminoglycoside antibiotics, amikacin activity may be impaired by β-lactam antibiotics. This inactivation is dependent on concentration, temperature, and time of exposure. However, amikacin appears to be less affected by the β-lactam antibiotics than other aminoglycosides such as gentamicin and tobramycin.

Incubation of amikacin 10 mg/L in sodium chloride 0.9% with 500 mg/L of carbenicillin or ticarcillin at 37 °C for 24 hours resulted in about a 25% reduction in amikacin activity. When serum was substituted for the sodium chloride solution, only 10% or less reduction in activity was reported. However, when the drugs were buffered to pH 7.4 in aqueous solution, about a 30 to 40% loss of activity was noted. Ticarcillin appeared to affect the amikacin less than did carbenicillin. (574)

In another study, amikacin 10 and 20 µg/ml dissolved in human serum and incubated with carbenicillin and ticarcillin 100 to 600 µg/ml at 37 °C demonstrated greater rates of amikacin decomposition at the higher concentration of the penicillins. In 24 hours, little or no loss of amikacin activity occurred at 100 µg/ml, but about a 20% loss occurred at 600 µg/ml of carbenicillin. Approximately a 4% loss at 100 µg/ml to a 40% loss at 600 µg/ml occurred in 72 hours with carbenicillin. Ticarcillin affected amikacin less under these conditions. Little or no loss of amikacin activity occurred at the lower concentrations, but about a 10% loss occurred at 600 µg/ml in 72 hours. (575)

Both of these studies indicated that amikacin was more stable in the presence of carbenicillin and ticarcillin than other aminoglycosides. (574; 575) This relatively greater stability was also demonstrated in vivo in nephrectomized dogs. (576)

Flournoy noted the relative degree of inactivation of tobramycin, gentamicin, netilmicin, and amikacin 10 mg/L in serum when combined with carbenicillin 125 to 1000 mg/L over temperatures ranging from −20 to 42 °C. Tobramycin was more susceptible to inactivation than the others. Amikacin was the least susceptible, and gentamicin and netilmicin were similar in intermediate susceptibility to inactivation. (617)

Although piperacillin sodium and aminoglycosides act synergistically and have been used successfully clinically when recommended doses of each drug were administered, mixing piperacillin sodium directly in a syringe or infusion bottle with an aminoglycoside can result in substantial inactivation of the aminoglycoside. (740)

The inactivation of amikacin 10 µg/ml in sterile distilled water by several β-lactam antibiotics stored at 37 °C was reported by Jorgensen and Crawford. Ticarcillin 500 µg/ml caused a 16% amikacin loss in six hours, but no significant loss occurred at 100 µg/ml. Cephalothin and moxalactam 100 µg/ml caused a 16% amikacin loss, and a 500-µg/ml concentration of either drug caused a 30% loss. Amikacin was not inactivated by 500- or 100-µg/ml concentrations of penicillin G, carbenicillin, and cefotaxime. No loss of β-lactam antibiotic activity was detected in any combination. (973)

Cefotaxime sodium (Hoechst-Roussel) should not be mixed with aminoglycosides in the same solution, but they may be administered to the same patient separately. (2; 792) Cefotetan disodium is stated to be physically incompatible with aminoglycosides. (4)

Hale et al. evaluated piperacillin and carbenicillin, at concentrations of 62.5 to 1000 µg/ml in human serum in combination with amikacin, gentamicin, or tobramycin 10 µg/ml at 37 °C for up to 24 hours, by bioassay and radioimmunoassay. Penicillin concentrations of 62.5 and 125 µg/ml had relatively little effect on the aminoglycoside concentration, even after 24 hours. However, increasing the penicillin concentration to 250 or 500 µg/ml greatly increased decomposition. After 24 hours with carbenicillin 500 µg/ml, the amounts of aminoglycosides remaining were amikacin, 82%; gentamicin, 43%; and tobramycin, 27%. After 24 hours with piperacillin 500 µg/ml, the remaining concentrations were 95, 45, and 52%, respectively. Even greater inactivation occurred at 1000 µg/ml of the penicillins, including the essentially complete loss of tobramycin in 24 hours. The authors concluded that amikacin is much more resistant to inactivation than the other aminoglycosides tested and that carbenicillin appears to be somewhat more aggressive in its inactivation than piperacillin. (816)

Pickering and Rutherford evaluated several aminoglycosides combined with a number of penicillins. Gentamicin sulfate, netilmicin sulfate, and tobramycin sulfate 5 and 10 µg/ml and amikacin 10 and 20 µg/ml were combined in human serum with 125, 250, and 500 µg/ml of azlocillin, carbenicillin disodium, amdinocillin, mezlocillin, and piperacillin individually. Tobramycin and gentamicin sustained greater losses than netilmicin and amikacin at each of the penicillin concentrations. Significant decomposition of all aminoglycosides occurred in 24 hours at 37 °C at a penicillin concentration of 500 µg/ml. Tobramycin and gentamicin had losses of 40 to 60%, while 15 to 30% losses occurred for netilmicin. Amikacin sustained the least inactivation with losses of about 10 to 20%. At penicillin concentrations of 125 to 250 µg/ml, smaller losses of aminoglycosides were observed. (68)

To determine if spurious aminoglycoside levels could result from a delay in assaying blood samples, Tindula et al. evaluated the inactivation of amikacin 35 µg/ml and gentamicin and tobramycin 10 µg/ml in human serum by 400-µg/ml concentrations of several penicillins and cephalosporins. Samples were stored for 24 hours at room temperature and frozen at −20 °C. For the room temperature samples, cefazolin and cefamandole caused relatively little inactivation. Nafcillin, cephapirin, and cefoxitin caused moderate inactivation, 20% or less. Penicillin, ampicillin, carbenicillin, and ticarcillin generally caused 25% or more inactivation of gentamicin and tobramycin. Amikacin was somewhat less affected. Freezing samples at −20 °C retarded the reaction sufficiently to prevent significant inactivation of amikacin and gentamicin by any of the drugs. Freezing the tobramycin samples was satisfactory for most of the drugs except penicillin, ampicillin, and carbenicillin, which still exhibited a 15 to 20% loss in 24 hours. (824)

The inactivation of gentamicin, tobramycin, and amikacin, each 5 µg/ml, by seven β-lactam antibiotics, 250 and 500 µg/ml, in serum at 25 °C over 24 hours was studied using bioassay, enzyme-mediated immunoassay technique (EMIT), fluorescence polarization immunoassay (TDx), and radioimmunoassay. No inactivation of any aminoglycoside by the cephalosporins moxalactam, cefotaxime, and cefazolin occurred within the study period. Results with the penicillins varied, depending on the assay technique used. The bioassay was the most sensitive to loss, TDx and radioimmunoassay were intermediate, and EMIT was the least sensitive. Azlocillin, carbenicillin, mezlocillin, and piperacillin all caused variable but extensive inactivation (up to 70%) of gentamicin and tobramycin in 24 hours. Amikacin, however, had only minor losses compared to the other aminoglycosides. (654)

The comparative inactivation of five aminoglycosides by seven β-lactam antibiotics in human serum at 37 °C was reported by Riff and Thomason. Amikacin, followed by netilmicin, had the lowest degree of inactivation; tobramycin sustained the most pronounced losses. Gentamicin and kanamycin were intermediate in the extent of losses. The six penicillins that were tested all produced aminoglycoside inactivation; the greatest extent of inactivation was caused by carbenicillin followed by ticarcillin, penicillin G, oxacillin, methicillin, and ampicillin, in approximate descending order. Cephalothin produced minimal inactivation (5 to 10% in 24 hours). The rate of inactivation could be reduced by storage at 4 °C and further reduced by storage at −20 °C. The authors suggested processing blood samples rapidly to avoid inaccurate serum determinations. Storage of specimens at low temperature until analysis may be helpful. (1052)

Roberts et al. studied the stability of azlocillin sodium 500 mg/L combined with the aminoglycosides amikacin sulfate 20 mg/L, gentamicin sulfate 8 mg/L, and netilmicin sulfate 7.5 mg/L in peritoneal dialysis solution (Dianeal 1.36%) stored at 37 °C. No azlocillin sodium loss occurred by HPLC during the eight-hour study period. However, the aminoglycosides tested by EMIT showed 10% losses in about six hours for gentamicin sulfate and netilmicin sulfate and in about 30 minutes for amikacin sulfate. (1179)

The clinical significance of these interactions appears to be primarily confined to patients with renal failure. (218; 334; 361; 364; 616; 816; 847) Literature reports of greatly reduced aminoglycoside levels in such patients have appeared frequently. (363; 365–367; 614; 615; 962) In addition, the interaction may be clinically important if assays for aminoglycoside levels in serum are sufficiently delayed. (576; 618; 814; 824; 847; 1052)

Most authors believe that in vitro mixing of penicillins, such as ticarcillin disodium, with aminoglycoside antibiotics should be avoided but that clinical use of the drugs in combination can be of great value. It is generally recommended that the drugs be given separately in such combined therapy. (157; 218; 222; 224; 361; 364; 368–370)

Heparin — A white precipitate may result from the administration of amikacin sulfate through a heparinized intravenous cannula. (976) Flushing heparin locks with sterile water for injection or sodium chloride 0.9% before and after administering drugs incompatible with heparin has been recommended. (4)

Other Drugs — The manufacturer recommends that other drugs not be physically combined with amikacin sulfate but be administered separately. (2)

Other Information

Heating Plasma — Heating plasma samples to 56 °C for one hour to inactivate potential human immunodeficiency virus (HIV) content resulted in no amikacin loss as determined by TDx. (1615)

AMINO ACID INJECTION
AHFS 40:20

Products — Amino acid injections are supplied in a variety of concentrations and sizes, both alone and in kits with dextrose 50% injection. The approximate concentrations of amino acids and electrolytes in various representative solutions are listed in Table 1.

Administration — Parenteral nutrition solutions composed of amino acids and high-concentration dextrose, which are strongly hypertonic, may be safely administered only through an indwelling intravenous catheter with the tip in the superior vena cava; they are used for severely depleted patients or those requiring long-term therapy. For moderately depleted patients, parenteral nutrition solutions with dextrose concentrations of 5 to 10%, which are substantially less hypertonic, may be administered peripherally. (4; 154)

It has been recommended that administration sets used to administer lipid emulsions be changed within 24 hours of initiating infusion because of the potential for bacterial and fungal contamination. (2342)

The routine use of appropriate inline filters for the administration of parenteral nutrition has been recommended for patients requiring intensive or prolonged therapy, immunocompromised patients, neonates, children, and patients receiving home parenteral nutrition. Filtration is recommended to reduce intrinsic particulate burdens, protect patients from calcium phosphate or other precipitation, and reduce the risk from potential inadvertent microbial contamination. Inline filters should be positioned as close to the patient as possible. For non-lipid-containing (TPN, 2-in-1) parenteral nutrition, 0.2-μm filters, preferably endotoxin retaining, have been recommended. For lipid-containing (TNA, 3-in-1, AIO) parenteral nutrition, 1.2-μm filters have been recommended. (2346)

Stability — Solution containers should be visually inspected for cloudiness, haze, discoloration, precipitates, and bottle cracks and checked for the presence of vacuum before mixing and prior to administration. Only clear solutions should be administered. It is also recommended that the containers be protected from light until ready for use and from extremes of temperature such as freezing or over 40 °C. Because of the risk of microbiological contamination, manufacturers recommend storing mixed parenteral nutrition solutions for as little time as possible after preparation. Administration of a single bottle should not exceed 24 hours.

A study of the original FreAmine showed that the mixed solution was stable at 4 °C for 12 weeks. Increased temperature enhanced degradation. Decomposition due to the Maillard reaction is visible as a color change from the clear, light, pale yellow of the freshly prepared solution to yellow to red to dark brown. It was noted that the possibility of microbiological contamination limits the desirable storage time. It was recommended that solutions be stored under refrigeration and used as soon as possible after mixing. (186)

The previous study did not report on the stability of tryptophan because of variable and nonreproducible results. (186) In another study, it was shown that the tryptophan content of the original FreAmine was reduced approximately 20% by the presence of the sodium bisulfite 0.1% antioxidant. (187)

An evaluation of amino acid 4.25% injection with dextrose 25% (prepared from FreAmine II 8.5%), without additional additives, stored at 4 °C for two weeks showed little or no change in the con-

Table 1. Concentration of Amino Acids and Electrolytes in Selected Solutions

	Aminess 5.2%	Aminosyn 3.5%	Aminosyn 5%	Aminosyn 8.5%	Aminosyn II 7%	Aminosyn II 8.5%	Aminosyn II 10%	Aminosyn-HBC 7%	Aminosyn-PF 7%	Aminosyn-RF 5.2%	BranchAmin 4%
Protein equivalent (g/100 ml)	5.2	3.5	5	8.5	7	8.5	10	7	7	5.2	4
Total nitrogen (g/100 ml)	0.66	0.55	0.79	1.34	1.07	1.30	1.53	1.12	1.07	0.79	0.44
Osmolarity (mOsm/L)	416	357	500	850	612	742	873	665	586	475	316
pH	6.4	5.3	5.3	5.3	5–6.5	5–6.5	5–6.5	5.2	5.4	5.2	6.0
Essential Amino Acids (mg/100 ml)											
L-Histidine	412	105	150	260	210	255	300	154	220	429	
L-Isoleucine	525	252	360	620	462	561	660	789	534	462	1380
L-Leucine	825	329	470	810	700	850	1000	1576	831	726	1380
L-Lysine	600	252	360	624	735	893	1050	265	475	535	
L-Methionine	825	140	200	340	120	146	172	206	125	726	
L-Phenylalanine	825	154	220	380	209	253	298	228	300	726	
L-Threonine	375	182	260	460	280	340	400	272	360	330	
L-Tryptophan	188	56	80	150	140	170	200	88	125	165	
L-Valine	600	280	400	680	350	425	500	789	452	528	1240
Nonessential Amino Acids (mg/100 ml)											
L-Alanine		448	640	1100	695	844	993	660	490		
L-Arginine		343	490	850	713	865	1018	507	861	600	
L-Proline		300	430	750	505	614	722	448	570		
L-Serine		147	210	370	371	450	530	221	347		
L-Tyrosine		31	44	44				33	44		
N-Acetyl-L-tyrosine					189	230	270				
Glycine (aminoacetic acid)		448	640	1100	350	425	500	660	270		
L-Cysteine HCl • H2O											
Glutamic acid					517	627	738		576		
Aspartic acid					490	595	700		370		
Taurine									50		
Electrolytes (mEq/L)				[a]	[a]	[a]	[a]				
Sodium		7			31.3	33.3	45.3	7	3.4		
Potassium			5.4	5.4						5.4	
Magnesium											
Phosphorus											
Chloride				35							
Acetate	50	46	86	90	50.3	61.1	71.8	72	32.5	105	
Calcium											

[a]*Also available with added electrolytes.*

	FreAmine III 3% with electrolytes	FreAmine III 8.5%	FreAmine III 10%	FreAmine HBC 6.9%	HepatAmine 8%	NephrAmine 5.4%	Novamine 15%	ProcalAmine 3% with glycerin 3%	RenAmin 6.5%	Travasol 3.5% with electrolytes	Travasol 5.5%	Travasol 8.5%	Travasol 10%	TrophAmine 6%	TrophAmine 10%
	3	8.5	10	6.9	8	5.4	15	3	6.5	3.5	5.5	8.5	10	6	10
	0.46	1.3	1.53	0.97	1.2	0.64	2.37	0.46	1	0.59	0.93	1.43	1.65	0.93	1.55
	405	810	950	620	785	435	1388	735	600	450	569	880	998	525	875
	6.3–7	6–7	6–7	6–7	6–6.8	6–7	5.6	6.5–7	6.0	6.0	6.0	6.0	6.0	5–6	5–6
	85	240	280	160	240	250	894	85	420	154	241	372	480	290	480
	210	590	690	760	900	560	749	210	500	168	263	406	600	490	820
	270	770	910	1370	1100	880	1040	270	600	217	340	526	730	840	1400
	220	620	730	410	610	640	1180	220	450	203	318	492	580	490	820
	160	450	530	250	100	880	749	160	500	203	318	492	400	200	340
	170	480	560	320	100	880	1040	170	490	217	340	526	560	290	480
	120	340	400	200	450	400	749	120	380	147	230	356	420	250	420
	46	130	150	90	66	200	250	46	160	63	99	152	180	120	200
	200	560	660	880	840	640	960	200	820	161	252	390	580	470	780
	210	600	710	400	770		2170	210	560	728	1140	1760	2070	320	540
	290	810	950	580	600		1470	290	630	364	570	880	1150	730	1200
	340	950	1120	630	800		894	340	350	147	230	356	680	410	680
	180	500	590	330	500		592	180	300				500	230	380
							39		40	14	22	34	40	140	240
	420	1190	1400	330	900		1040	420	300	728	1140	1760	1030	220	360
	<20	<20	<20	<20	<20	<20		<20						<14	<16
							749							300	500
							434							190	320
														15	25
		[a]									[a]	[a]			
	35	10	10	10	10	5		35		25				5	5
	24.5							24		15					
	5							5		5					
	3.5	10	10		10			3.5		7.5					
	mmol	mmol	mmol		mmol			mmol		mmol					
	41	<3	<3	<3	<3	<3		41	31	25	22	34	40	<3	<3
	44	72	89	57	62	44	151	47	60	54	43	67	88	56	97
								3							

centrations of amino acids, including tryptophan, as well as pH. Particle counts were also normal over the period. When stored at 25 °C, approximately 6% tryptophan loss occurred, but no other changes were observed. (581)

In contrast, parenteral nutrition solutions composed of amino acids solution with ethanol and vitamins (Aminofusin, Pfrimmer) along with dextrose and a variety of electrolytes exhibited a darkening of color on storage at 37, 25, and 5 °C for 60 days. The rate of color change was less at the lowest temperature. A loss of ascorbic acid in the mixture was also demonstrated and was shown to be associated with the color changes. The rate of ascorbic acid decomposition was dependent on air space in the container and storage temperature. In addition, fine white crystals of calcium phosphate precipitated on day 12 at 25 and 37 °C and on day 25 at 5 °C. (580)

A photoreaction of the L-tryptophan in Nephramine essential amino acid injection was reported. The L-tryptophan in combination with bisulfite stabilizer, oxygen, and light yielded an indigo blue color. Although no toxicity was associated with the L-tryptophan degradation and blue color formation, it was recommended that Nephramine remain in its original carton until ready to be mixed with dextrose and that Nephramine mixtures be covered with amber, UV-light-resistant bags to retard the formation of the blue color. It was further noted that a slightly blue solution need not be changed for a colorless one, nor is it necessary to change a slightly blue filter for a white one. (579) However, it has been emphasized that the clinical importance of this reaction is largely undetermined and may not be entirely benign. (1055)

The effects of photoirradiation on a FreAmine II–dextrose 10% parenteral nutrition solution containing 1 ml/500 ml of multivitamins (USV) were evaluated. During simulated continuous administration to an infant at 0.156 ml/min, the amino acids did not change when the bottle, infusion tubing, and collection bottle were shielded with foil. Only 20 cm of tubing in the incubator was exposed to light. However, if the flow was stopped, a marked reduction in methionine (40%), tryptophan (44%), and histidine (22%) occurred in the solution exposed to light for 24 hours. In a similar solution without vitamins, only the tryptophan concentration decreased. The difference was attributed to the presence of riboflavin, a photosensitizer. The authors recommended administering the multivitamin separately and shielding from light. (833)

The stability of amino acids in a parenteral nutrition solution composed of amino acids 3.5%, dextrose 25%, and electrolytes in PVC bags was assessed at 4 and 25 °C over 30 days. No significant decreases of the amino acids occurred in the refrigerated samples. However, the sample stored at room temperature showed significant losses of methionine (10.2%) and arginine (8.2%) in 30 days. (1057)

The long-term stability of the components of a parenteral nutrition solution composed of amino acids, dextrose, electrolytes, and trace metals in PVC bags was determined over a six-month period of storage at 4 °C. None of the amino acids decomposed more than 10% during the first two months. However, at six months, all of the amino acids except tyrosine, lysine, and histidine had degraded by more than 10%; some losses exceeded 25%. The dextrose, electrolytes, and trace elements remained constant for the six-month period. Water loss through the PVC bag was only 0.2%. Visually the color remained unchanged. (1058)

The long-term stability of the components of six parenteral nutrition solutions containing variable amounts of amino acids, dextrose, electrolytes, trace elements, and vitamins, stored in PVC bags at 4 and 25 °C, was evaluated. No significant changes to the amino acids, dextrose, electrolytes, or trace elements were noted during 28 days. (1063)

Peroxide Formation— Potentially toxic peroxide is generated in parenteral nutrition admixtures as a reaction between oxygen and various components catalyzed by riboflavin in the presence of light. This is particularly true in neonatal formulations. (1650; 1653; 1947; 2306; 2309; 2316) Exposure of a neonatal parenteral nutrition admixture to ambient light resulted in the formation of peroxide concentrations up to 300 μM. Light protection from compounding through administration has been recommended as a more achievable approach to reduce the formation of peroxide than avoiding contact with oxygen. (2316)

Exposure of parenteral nutrition admixtures to light during phototherapy has been shown to generate substantially larger amounts of hydrogen peroxide. (2310) In a study of the rate of hydrogen peroxide formation in a TrophAmine 1%-based parenteral nutrition admixture exposed to light, levels of peroxide increased linearly for about eight hours and then reached a plateau at about 940 μM. A similar solution kept in the dark did not generate any detectable peroxide. A hydrogen peroxide concentration of as little as 25 μM has been shown to be lethal to 90% of human cells in culture. The authors speculated that additive hepatic oxidant injury over time might increase hepatic dysfunction as the duration of exposure to parenteral nutrition increases. The presence of sulfite antioxidants in the amino acids helps to reduce the formation of hydrogen peroxide, but the antioxidants are present in insufficient quantities to offer adequate protection. Shielding parenteral nutrition admixtures from light was recommended for neonatal administration. (2309)

The formation of toxic peroxides due to exposure of parenteral nutrition admixtures to light was reduced substantially by using colored administration sets. Both 2-in-1 and 3-in-1 parenteral nutrition admixtures exhibited little protection from peroxide formation when only the bag was shielded from light. Peroxide formation was two to three times higher using light-protected bags with clear tubing when compared to colored tubing. Shielding the parenteral nutrition bags from light and using black, yellow, or orange tubing would reduce peroxide loads down to about 100 μM. (2306)

Freezing Solutions— The acceptability of frozen storage of some parenteral nutrition solutions has been determined. Parenteral nutrition solutions composed of equal parts of Travasol 8.5% with electrolytes and dextrose 70% injection (final concentrations of amino acids and dextrose were 4.25 and 35%, respectively), in PVC containers were stored frozen at −20 °C for 60 days. Both overnight room temperature thawing and 30-minute microwave thawing were utilized. The results indicated that, with either thawing technique, the amino acids, electrolytes, and dextrose were unchanged after 60 days of frozen storage and subsequent thawing. (578)

Plasticizer Leaching— Mazur et al. reported that a parenteral nutrition solution containing an amino acid solution, dextrose, and electrolytes in a PVC bag did not leach measurable quantities of diethylhexyl phthalate (DEHP) plasticizer during 21 days of storage at 4 and 25 °C. However, addition of fat emulsion 10 or 20% to the formula caused detectable leaching of DEHP from the PVC containers stored for 48 hours. Higher DEHP levels were found in the 25 °C samples than in the 4 °C samples. The authors recommended limiting the use of lipid-containing parenteral nutrition admixtures to 24 to 36 hours. Use of non-PVC containers and tubing is another option to eliminate the problem of plasticizer leaching. (1430)

Compatibility Information

Solution Compatibility

Amino acid injection

Solution	*Mfr*	*Mfr*	*Conc/L*	*Remarks*	*Ref*	*C/I*
Fat emulsion 10%, intravenous	VT	MG	AA 8.5%	Mixed in equal parts. Physically compatible for 48 hr at 4 °C and room temperature	32	C
	CU	MG AB TR	8.5% 7% 8.5%	Mixed in equal parts. Physically compatible for 72 hr at room temperature	656	C
	VT		AA 10%	Mixed in equal parts. Changes observed in 20 min. Globule coalescence and creaming in 8 hr at 25 and 8 °C	825	I

Additive Compatibility

Amino acid injection

Drug	*Mfr*	*Conc/L*	*Mfr*	*Test Soln*	*Remarks*	*Ref*	*C/I*
Albumin human		9.5 g		TNA#232[a,i]	Microscopically observed emulsion disruption found with increased fat globule size in 48 hr at room temperature	2267	?
		9.5 g		TNA#233[a,i]	Visually apparent emulsion disruption with creaming in as little as 4 hr at room temperature. Increased disruption attributed to the added effect of calcium and magnesium ions	2267	I
		18.2 g		TNA#234[a,i]	Creaming and free oil formation visually observed in 24 hours at room temperature	2267	I
		18.2 g		TNA#235[a,i]	Visually apparent emulsion disruption with creaming and free oil formation in as little as 4 hr at room temperature. Increased disruption attributed to the added effect of calcium and magnesium ions	2267	I
Amikacin sulfate		150 mg		TPN #107[a]	Physically compatible and amikacin activity retained for 24 hr at 21 °C by microbiological assay	1326	C
Aminophylline	SE	500 mg	MG	AA 4.25%, D 25%	No increase in particulate matter in 24 hr at 4 °C	349	C
	SE	250 mg, 500 mg, 1 g, 1.5 g		TPN #25 to #27[a]	Physically compatible and aminophylline chemically stable for at least 24 hr at 25 °C	755	C
	SE	1 g		TPN #25 to #27[a]	Physically compatible and aminophylline chemically stable for at least 24 hr at 4 °C	755	C
	SE	1 g		TPN #28 to #30[a]	Physically compatible and aminophylline chemically stable for at least 24 hr at 25 °C	755	C
		29.3 mg		[b]	No significant change in aminophylline content over 24 hr at 24 to 26 °C	852	C
		284 and 638 mg		TNA #180[a]	Little or no theophylline loss by EMIT and no substantial increase in fat particle size in 24 hr at room temperature	1617	C
Amphotericin B	SQ	100 mg	MG	AA 4.25%, D 25%	Turbidity and fine yellow particles form	349	I

Additive Compatibility (Cont.)

Amino acid injection

Drug	*Mfr*	*Conc/L*	*Mfr*	*Test Soln*	*Remarks*	*Ref*	*C/I*
Ampicillin sodium	BR	1 g	MG	TPN #21[a]	Antibiotic potency retained for 24 hr at 4 °C	87	C
	BR	1 g	MG	TPN #21[a]	10% ampicillin decomposition in 6 hr and 25% decomposition in 24 hr at 25 °C	87	I
	BR	1 g	MG	AA 4.25%, D 25%	Increase in microscopic particles noted over 24 hr at 5 °C	349	I
	BR	1 g		TPN #1[a]	Physically compatible for 12 hr. Precipitate noted in 24 hr at 22 °C	313	I
	BR	1 g		TPN #2, #3, #5 to #9[a]	Physically incompatible with precipitate in 1 to 4 hr at 22 °C	313	I
	BR	1 g		TPN #4[a]	Physically compatible for 24 hr at 22 °C	313	C
	BR	20 mg		TPN #1[a]	Antibiotic potency retained for at least 12 hr at 22 °C	313	C
	BR	500 mg and 1 g		TPN #10[a]	Physically compatible for 24 hr and antibiotic potency retained for at least 12 hr at 22 °C	313	C
	AST	1.5 g		TPN #52[a]	69% ampicillin loss in 24 hr at 29 °C by microbiological assay	440	I
	AST	1.5 g		TPN #53[a]	22% ampicillin loss in 24 hr at 29 °C by microbiological assay	440	I
		1 and 3 g		TPN #107[a]	Physically compatible and ampicillin activity retained for 24 hr at 21 °C by microbiological assay	1326	C
Azlocillin sodium		2 g		TPN #107[a]	26% azlocillin loss in 24 hr at 21 °C by microbiological assay	1326	I
Aztreonam		2 g		TPN #107[a]	Physically compatible and aztreonam activity retained for 24 hr at 21 °C by microbiological assay	1326	C
Calcium gluconate	PR	100 mEq	CU	AA 4%, D 25%	Physically compatible for 24 hr at 22 °C	313	C
Cefamandole nafate	LI	2 g	AB	AA 3.5%	Physically compatible with 6% cefamandole loss in 48 hr at 25 °C and no loss in 10 days at 5 °C	788	C
	LI	2 g	AB	AA 7%	Physically compatible with 7% cefamandole loss in 48 hr at 25 °C and 2% loss in 10 days at 5 °C	788	C
	LI	2 g	MG	AA 8.5%	Physically compatible with 8% cefamandole loss in 48 hr at 25 °C and 4% loss in 10 days at 5 °C	788	C
	LI	2 g	TR	AA 8.5%	Physically compatible with 6% cefamandole loss in 48 hr at 25 °C and 2% loss in 10 days at 5 °C	788	C
	LI	2 g	TR	AA 8.5%, electrolytes	Physically compatible with 7% cefamandole loss in 48 hr at 25 °C and 1% loss in 10 days at 5 °C	788	C
		1.5 g		TPN #107[a]	Physically compatible and cefamandole activity retained for 24 hr at 21 °C by microbiological assay	1326	C
Cefazolin sodium	LI	1 g	MG	AA 4.25%, D 25%	No increase in particulate matter in 24 hr at 4 °C	349	C
	SKF	10 g	TR	TPN #22[a]	Physically compatible with no loss of activity by microbiological assay in 24 hr at 22 °C in the dark	837	C

Additive Compatibility (Cont.)

Amino acid injection

Drug	*Mfr*	*Conc/L*	*Mfr*	*Test Soln*	*Remarks*	*Ref*	*C/I*
		1 g		TPN #107[a]	Physically compatible with 9% cefazolin loss in 24 hr at 21 °C by microbiological assay	1326	C
Cefepime HCl	BR	1 and 4 g	AB	AA 4.25%, D 25%, electrolytes	5 to 6% cefepime loss by HPLC in 8 hr at room temperature and 3 days at 5 °C	1682	C
Cefoperazone sodium		1 g		TPN #107[a]	50% cefoperazone loss in 24 hr at 21 °C by microbiological assay	1326	I
Cefotaxime sodium		1 g		TPN #107[a]	Physically compatible and cefotaxime activity retained for 24 hr at 21 °C by microbiological assay	1326	C
Cefoxitin sodium		1 g		TPN #107[a]	Physically compatible and cefoxitin activity retained for 24 hr at 21 °C by microbiological assay	1326	C
Ceftazidime		1 g		TPN #107[a]	Physically compatible and ceftazidime activity retained for 24 hr at 21 °C by microbiological assay	1326	C
	GL[k]	6 g	AB	AA 5%, D 25%	No substantial amino acid degradation in 48 hr at 22 °C and 10 days at 4 °C. Ceftazidime stability the determining factor	1535	C
	GL[k]	1 g		TPN #141 to #143[a]	Visually compatible with 8% ceftazidime loss in 6 hr and 10% loss in 24 hr at 22 °C by HPLC. 8% ceftazidime loss in 3 days at 4 °C	1535	C
	GL[k]	6 g		TPN #141 to #143[a]	Visually compatible with 6% ceftazidime loss in 12 hr and 11 to 13% loss in 24 hr at 22 °C by HPLC. 7 to 9% ceftazidime loss in 3 days at 4 °C	1535	C
Ceftriaxone sodium		1 g		TPN #107[a]	Physically compatible and ceftriaxone activity retained for 24 hr at 21 °C by microbiological assay	1326	C
Cefuroxime sodium		1 g		TPN #107[a]	Physically compatible and cefuroxime activity retained for 24 hr at 21 °C by microbiological assay	1326	C
Cimetidine HCl	SKF	1.2 and 5 g	AB	AA 3.5%, electrolytes	Physically compatible and chemically stable for 1 week at room temperature	549	C
	SKF	1.2 and 5 g	TR	AA 5.5%	Physically compatible and chemically stable for 1 week at room temperature protected from light	550	C
	SKF	1.2 and 5 g	TR	AA 5.5%, electrolytes	Physically compatible and chemically stable for 1 week at room temperature protected from light	550	C
	SKF	1.2 and 5 g	TR	AA 8.5%	Physically compatible and chemically stable for 1 week at room temperature protected from light	550	C
	SKF	1.2 and 5 g	TR	AA 8.5%, electrolytes	Physically compatible and chemically stable for 1 week at room temperature protected from light	550	C
	SKF	300 mg	TR	TPN #34, #35, #37[a]	Physically compatible and cimetidine chemically stable for 24 hr at room temperature and 4 °C	781	C

Additive Compatibility (Cont.)

Drug	*Mfr*	*Conc/L*	Amino acid injection *Mfr*	*Test Soln*	*Remarks*	*Ref*	*C/I*
	SKF	300 mg	TR	TPN #36[a]	Physically compatible and cimetidine chemically stable for 24 hr at 4 °C. Room temperature sample gave spurious result	781	C
	SKF	400, 800, 1200 mg		TNA #72[a]	Physically compatible and no cimetidine loss in 24 hr at 25 °C. Fat emulsion particle size increased in 48 hr	998	C
	SKF	1 g		TPN #75[a]	Physically compatible and cimetidine chemically stable for 48 hr at room temperature	140	C
		600 mg		TPN #93[a]	Physically compatible and cimetidine chemically stable for 48 hr at room temperature	1320	C
		600 mg		TPN #94[a]	Physically compatible and cimetidine and copper chemically stable for 48 hr at room temperature	1320	C
	SKF	400 and 900 mg		TNA #179[a]	Visually compatible with less than 3% cimetidine loss by HPLC in 72 hr at room temperature protected from light	1622	C
	SKF	450 mg		TNA #197 to #200[a]	Physically compatible with 7% or less cimetidine loss by HPLC in 48 hr at 22 °C exposed to light	1921	C
	SKF	450 mg		TPN #196[a]	Physically compatible and no cimetidine loss by HPLC in 48 hr at 22 °C exposed to light	1921	C
	SKB	80 mg		TPN #238 to #240[a,i]	Little or no cimetidine loss by HPLC in 28 days at 5 °C	1912	C
Clindamycin phosphate	UP	250 mg	MG	TPN #21[a]	Antibiotic potency retained for 24 hr at 4 and 25 °C	87	C
	UP	600 mg	MG	AA 4.25%, D 25%	No increase in particulate matter in 24 hr at 4 °C	349	C
	UP	3 g	TR	TPN #22[a]	Physically compatible with no loss of activity by microbiological assay in 24 hr at 22 °C in the dark	837	C
		400 mg[c]		TPN #107[a]	Physically compatible and clindamycin activity retained for 24 hr at 21 °C by microbiological assay	1326	C
Cyanocobalamin	SQ	0.5 and 1 mg	CU	TPN #16 to #20[a]	Physically compatible for 24 hr at 22 °C. UV spectra of amino acids unaltered	313	C
	SQ	1 mg	CU	TPN #11 to #15[a]	Physically compatible for 24 hr at 22 °C. TLC changes of amino acids in similar solutions attributed to M.V.I. or vitamin B complex with C	313	C
Cyclophosphamide	MJ	500 mg	MG	AA 4.25%, D 25%	No increase in particulate matter in 24 hr at 4 °C	349	C
Cyclosporine	SZ	150 mg	MG	AA 5%, D 25%	Visually compatible with no cyclosporine loss by HPLC in 72 hr at 21 °C	1616	C
Cytarabine	UP	100 mg	MG	AA 4.25%, D 25%	No increase in particulate matter in 24 hr at 4 °C	349	C
	UP	50 mg		TPN #57[a]	Physically compatible with no cytarabine loss in 48 hr at 25 or 8 °C	996	C
Dopamine HCl	AS	400 mg	MG	AA 4.25%, D 25%	No increase in particulate matter in 24 hr at 4 °C	349	C

Additive Compatibility (Cont.)

Amino acid injection

Drug	*Mfr*	*Conc/L*	*Mfr*	*Test Soln*	*Remarks*	*Ref*	*C/I*
Epoetin alfa	ORT	100 units		[d]	98% of the epoetin alfa by bioassay delivered[e] over 24 hr	1878	C
Famotidine	MSD	20 and 40 mg		TPN #109 and #110[a]	Physically compatible with little or no famotidine loss and little change in amino acids in 48 hr at 21 °C and in 7 days at 4 °C	1331	C
	MSD	20 and 50 mg		TNA #111 and #112[a]	Physically compatible with little or no famotidine loss and no change in fat particle size in 48 hr at 4 and 21 °C	1332	C
	MSD	20 mg		TPN #113[a]	Physically compatible with little or no famotidine loss in 35 days at 4 °C protected from light	1334	C
	MSD	20 and 40 mg		TNA #114[a]	Physically compatible with little or no famotidine loss and no change in fat particle size in 72 hr at 21 °C under fluorescent light	1333	C
	MSD	20 mg		[f]	0 to 5% loss in 48 hr at 25 °C in light or dark and at 5 °C	1344	C
	MSD	16.7 and 33.3 mg		TPN #115 and #116[a]	No famotidine loss in 7 days at 23 and 4 °C	1352	C
	MSD	20 mg		TNA #182[a]	Visually compatible with no famotidine loss by HPLC in 24 hr at 24 °C under fluorescent light	1576	C
	MSD	20 mg		TNA #197 to #200[a]	Physically compatible with no famotidine loss by HPLC in 48 hr at 22 °C exposed to light	1921	C
	MSD	20 mg		TPN #196[a]	Physically compatible with no famotidine loss by HPLC in 48 hr at 22 °C exposed to light	1921	C
Fluorouracil	RC	500 mg	MG	AA 4.25%, D 25%	No increase in particulate matter in 24 hr at 4 °C	349	C
	RC	1 and 4 g		TPN #23[a]	Physically compatible for 42 hr at room temperature in ambient light. HPLC results erratic	562	?
	RC	1 g		TPN #23[a]	Physically compatible and fluorouracil chemically stable for 48 hr at room temperature in ambient light	826	C
Folic acid	LE	2.5 and 5 mg	CU	TPN #11 to #15[a]	Physically compatible for 24 hr at 22 °C. UV spectra of amino acids unaltered	313	C
	LE	5 mg		TPN #43 to #47[a]	Physically compatible for 24 hr at 22 °C. TLC changes of amino acids in similar solutions attributed to M.V.I. or vitamin B complex with C	313	C
		1 mg		TPN #74[a]	Folic acid stable over 8 hr at room temperature exposed to fluorescent light or sunlight	842	C
	USP	0.2 and 10 mg	MG	AA 4.25%, D 25%	Physically compatible and stable for at least 7 days at 4 °C or room temperature protected from light	895	C
	USP	0.4 mg		TPN #69[a]	Physically compatible and folic acid stable for at least 7 days at 4 and 25 °C protected from light	895	C
	LE	0.25 to 1 mg		TPN #70[a]	Folic acid stable for at least 48 hr at 6 and 21 °C in light or dark conditions	896	C

Additive Compatibility (Cont.)

Amino acid injection

Drug	*Mfr*	*Conc/L*	*Mfr*	*Test Soln*	*Remarks*	*Ref*	*C/I*
Fosphenytoin sodium	PD	1, 8, 20 mg PE/ml[j]	BA	AA 10%[h]	Visually compatible with little or no loss of fosphenytoin by HPLC in 7 days at 25 °C under fluorescent light	2083	C
Furosemide	HO	40 mg	MG	AA 4.25%, D 25%	No increase in particulate matter in 24 hr at 4 °C	349	C
Ganciclovir sodium	SY	3 and 5 g		TPN #183 to #185[a]	Precipitate forms	1744	I
	SY	2 g		TPN #183[a]	Precipitate forms	1744	I
Gentamicin sulfate	SC	80 mg	CU	AA 4%, D 25%	Physically compatible for 24 hr and antibiotic potency retained for at least 12 hr at 22 °C	313	C
	SC	80 mg	MG	AA 4.25%, D 25%	No increase in particulate matter in 24 hr at 4 °C	349	C
	SC	80 mg		TPN #1, #4, #5, #7[a]	Physically compatible for 24 hr at 22 °C	313	C
	SC	80 mg		TPN #2, #3, #6, #8, #9[a]	Physically incompatible with a precipitate in 8 to 24 hr at 22 °C	313	I
	SC	80 mg		TPN #1[a]	Antibiotic potency retained for at least 12 hr at 22 °C	313	C
	SC	80 mg		TPN #10[a]	Physically compatible for 24 hr and antibiotic potency retained for at least 12 hr at 22 °C	313	C
	SC	800 mg	TR	TPN #22[a]	Physically compatible with no loss of activity by microbiological assay in 24 hr at 22 °C in the dark	837	C
	SC	50 mg		TPN #52 and #53[a]	Physically compatible with no loss of gentamicin in 24 hr at 29 °C by microbiological assay	440	C
		75 mg		TPN #107[a]	Physically compatible and gentamicin activity retained for 24 hr at 21 °C by microbiological assay	1326	C
Heparin sodium	RI	20,000 units	MG	AA 4.25%, D 25%	No increase in particulate matter in 24 hr at 4 °C	349	C
		35,000 units		TPN #48 to #51[a]	Heparin activity retained for 24 hr at 25 °C but fell significantly after 24 hr	900	C
	LY	3000 to 20,000 units		TPN #200[a]	Heparin activity retained for 28 days at 4 °C	2025	C
Hydrochloric acid		40, 60, 100 mEq	MG	TPN #24[a]	Physically compatible and changes in amino acid concentrations considered negligible over 24 hr at 25 °C. Hydrochloric acid available from solution	582	C
Imipenem–cilastatin sodium		500 mg		TPN #107[a]	57% imipenem loss in 24 hr at 21 °C by microbiological assay	1326	I
	MSD	5 g		TPN #241, #242[a]	8 to 10% imipenem loss by HPLC within 30 min at 25 °C under fluorescent light	493	I
Insulin, regular	LI	100 units	MG	AA 4.25%, D 25%	No increase in particulate matter in 24 hr at 4 °C	349	C
Iron dextran	FI	100 mg	TR	TPN #31 to #33[a]	Physically compatible with minimal changes to iron dextran and amino acids for 18 hr at room temperature	692	C

Additive Compatibility (Cont.)

Amino acid injection

Drug	*Mfr*	*Conc/L*	*Mfr*	*Test Soln*	*Remarks*	*Ref*	*C/I*
	FI	50 mg		TNA #122[a]	Lipid oiling out in 18 to 19 hr with formation of yellow-brown layer on admixture surface	1383	I
	FI	2 mg		TNA #159 to #166[a]	Physically compatible with no change by visual and microscopic examination and no change in particle size distribution in 48 hr at 4 and 25 °C	1648	C
	SCN	10 mg		TPN #207 and #208[a]	Rust-colored precipitate forms in 12 hr at 19 °C protected from sunlight	2103	I
	SCN	10 mg		TPN #209[a]	Rust-colored precipitate forms in some samples in 18 to 24 hr at 19 °C protected from sunlight	2103	I
	SCN	10 mg		TPN #210[a]	Visually compatible for 48 hr at 19 °C protected from sunlight. Trace iron precipitation found by filtration and analysis after 48 hr	2103	?
	SCN	10 mg		TPN #211[a]	Visually compatible for 48 hr at 19 °C protected from sunlight. No iron precipitation found by filtration and analysis after 48 hr	2103	C
Isoproterenol HCl	WI	2 mg	MG	AA 4.25%, D 25%	No increase in particulate matter in 24 hr at 4 °C	349	C
Kanamycin sulfate	BR	250 mg	MG	TPN #21[a]	Antibiotic potency retained for 24 hr at 4 °C	87	C
	BR	250 mg	MG	TPN #21[a]	13% kanamycin decomposition in 24 hr at 25 °C	87	I
	BR	500 mg	MG	AA 4.25%, D 25%	No increase in particulate matter in 24 hr at 4 °C	349	C
	BR	500 mg		TPN #2, #4, #5, #7, #8[a]	Physically compatible for 24 hr at 22 °C	313	C
	BR	500 mg		TPN #1, #3, #6, #9[a]	Physically incompatible with a precipitate in 8 to 12 hr at 22 °C	313	I
	BR	400 mg		TPN #1[a]	Antibiotic potency retained for at least 12 hr at 22 °C	313	C
	BR	500 mg		TPN #10[a]	Physically compatible for 24 hr and antibiotic potency retained for at least 12 hr at 22 °C	313	C
Lidocaine HCl	AST	1 g	MG	AA 4.25%, D 25%	No increase in particulate matter in 24 hr at 4 °C	349	C
Meperidine HCl	WI	100 mg		TPN #71[a,g]	Physically compatible with no meperidine loss in 36 hr at 22 °C	1000	C
Metaraminol bitartrate	MSD	100 mg	MG	AA 4.25%, D 25%	No increase in particulate matter in 24 hr at 4 °C	349	C
Methotrexate sodium	LE	50 mg	MG	AA 4.25%, D 25%	No increase in particulate matter in 24 hr at 4 °C	349	C
Methyldopate HCl	MSD	500 mg	MG	AA 4.25%, D 25%	No increase in particulate matter in 24 hr at 4 °C	349	C
Methylprednisolone sodium succinate	UP	250 mg	MG	AA 4.25%, D 25%	No increase in particulate matter in 24 hr at 4 °C	349	C

Additive Compatibility (Cont.)

Amino acid injection

Drug	*Mfr*	*Conc/L*	*Mfr*	*Test Soln*	*Remarks*	*Ref*	*C/I*
	PHU	25, 63, 125 mg		TNA #237[a,i]	Physically compatible with no substantial change in lipid particle size. Variable assay results, but less than 10% change in drug concentration by HPLC and less than 8% change in TNA components by colorimetry after 7 days at 4 °C, followed by 24 hr at ambient temperature and light	2347	C
	PHU	25, 63, 125 mg		TPN #236[a,i]	Variable assay results, but less than 10% change in drug concentration by HPLC and less than 12% change in TPN components by colorimetry after 7 days at 4 °C, followed by 24 hr at ambient temperature and light	2347	C
Metoclopramide HCl	RB	5 and 20 mg	TR	AA 2.75%, D 25%, electrolytes	Metoclopramide chemically stable for 72 hr at room temperature	854	C
	RB	5 mg		TPN #89[a]	Physically compatible with no metoclopramide loss in 24 hr and 10% loss in 48 hr at 25 °C	1167	C
	RB	20 mg		TPN #89[a]	Physically compatible with no metoclopramide loss in 72 hr at 25 °C	1167	C
	RB	5 mg		TPN #90[a]	Physically compatible with no metoclopramide loss in 72 hr at 25 °C	1167	C
	RB	20 mg		TPN #90[a]	Physically compatible with 3% metoclopramide loss in 72 hr at 25 °C	1167	C
Metronidazole HCl with sodium bicarbonate	SE AB	5 g 50 mEq	AB	AA 10%	Initial yellow color becomes dark yellow in 24 hr	765	I
Midazolam HCl	RC	600 mg to 1 g		TPN #174 to #176[a]	Immediate precipitation	1624	I
	RC	100 and 500 mg		TPN #174 to #176[a]	Visually compatible with little or no midazolam loss and less than 10% loss of any amino acid by HPLC in 5 hr at 22 °C under fluorescent light	1624	C
Morphine sulfate	LI	100 mg		TPN #71[a,g]	Physically compatible with no morphine loss in 36 hr at 22 °C	1000	C
Multivitamins	USV	1 vial	TR	AA 10%	40% loss of thiamine HCl in 22 hr at 30 °C due to sulfite content	843	I
	USV	1 vial	TR	AA 4.25%, D 25%	No loss of thiamine HCl in 22 hr at 30 °C	843	C
(Berocca PN)	RC	4 ml	MG	AA 8.5%	97% loss of thiamine in 24 hr at 23 °C due to bisulfite content of solution. 63% loss in 24 hr at 7 °C	774	I
	RC	4 ml	TR	AA 5.5%	About 70% loss of thiamine in 24 hr at 23 °C due to bisulfite content of solution. 33% loss in 24 hr at 7 °C	774	I
(Multivitamin additive)	AB		MG	AA 8.5%	96% loss of thiamine in 24 hr at 23 °C due to bisulfite content of solution	774	I
(M.V.I.-12)	USV		MG	AA 8.5%	92% loss of thiamine in 24 hr at 23 °C due to bisulfite content of solution	774	I
(M.V.I. Pediatric)	ROR	5 ml		AA 2%, D 12.5%, electrolytes	7% phytonadione loss in 4 hr and 27% loss in 24 hr by HPLC under ambient temperature and light	1815	I

Additive Compatibility (Cont.)

Amino acid injection

Drug	*Mfr*	*Conc/L*	*Mfr*	*Test Soln*	*Remarks*	*Ref*	*C/I*
Nafcillin sodium		1 and 2 g		TPN #107[a]	Physically compatible and nafcillin activity retained for 24 hr at 21 °C by microbiological assay	1326	C
Netilmicin sulfate	SC	3 g	MG	AA 8.5%	Physically compatible and chemically stable for 7 days at 25 and 4 °C	558	C
		75 mg		TPN #107[a]	Physically compatible and netilmicin activity retained for 24 hr at 21 °C by microbiological assay	1326	C
Nizatidine	LI	0.75 and 1.5 g	TR[g]	AA 8.5%	Visually compatible and nizatidine potency by HPLC retained for 7 days at 4 and 25 °C. Amino acids not tested	1533	C
	LI	3 g	TR[g]	AA 8.5%	Visually compatible with 8% nizatidine loss in 3 days and 13% loss in 7 days at 25 °C by HPLC. 5% nizatidine loss in 7 days at 4 °C. Amino acids not tested	1533	C
	LI	150 mg		TPN #134 and TNA #135 to #138[a]	Physically compatible with no increase in fat particle size and 2 to 7% nizatidine loss by HPLC in 48 hr at 22 °C under fluorescent light	1534; 1921	C
Norepinephrine bitartrate	WI	4 mg	MG	AA 4.25%, D 25%	No increase in particulate matter in 24 hr at 4 °C	349	C
Octreotide acetate	SZ	1.5 mg		TPN #119 and #120[a,h]	Little octreotide loss over 48 hr at room temperature in ambient room light	1373	C
	SZ	450 μg		TNA #139[a,i]	Physically compatible with no change in lipid particle size in 48 hr at 22 °C under fluorescent light and 7 days at 4 °C. Octreotide activity highly variable by radioimmunoassay	1540	?
Ondansetron HCl	GL	0.03 and 0.3 g		TNA #190[a]	Physically compatible with little or no ondansetron loss by HPLC in 48 hr at 24 °C under fluorescent light	1766	C
Oxacillin sodium	BR	500 mg	MG	AA 4.25%, D 25%	No increase in particulate matter in 24 hr at 4 °C	349	C
Penicillin G potassium	SQ	5 million units	MG	TPN #21[a]	Antibiotic potency retained for 24 hr at 4 and 25 °C	87	C
	LI	1 million units	MG	AA 4.25%, D 25%	No increase in particulate matter in 24 hr at 4 °C	349	C
	AY	25 million units	TR	TPN #22[a]	Physically compatible with no loss of activity by microbiological assay in 24 hr at 22 °C in the dark	837	C
		2 g		TPN #107[a]	Physically compatible and penicillin G activity retained for 24 hr at 21 °C by microbiological assay	1326	C
Penicillin G sodium		2 g		TPN #107[a]	Physically compatible and penicillin G activity by microbiological assay retained for 24 hr at 21 °C	1326	C
Phytonadione	MSD	5 and 10 mg	CU	TPN #16 to #20[a]	Physically compatible for 24 hr at 22 °C. UV spectra of amino acids unaltered	313	C
	MSD	5 and 10 mg	CU	TPN #11 to #15[a]	Physically compatible for 24 hr at 22 °C. TLC changes of amino acids in similar solutions attributed to M.V.I. or vitamin B complex with C	313	C

Additive Compatibility (Cont.)

Amino acid injection

Drug	*Mfr*	*Conc/L*	*Mfr*	*Test Soln*	*Remarks*	*Ref*	*C/I*
	MSD	10 mg	MG	AA 4.25%, D 25%	No increase in particulate matter in 24 hr at 4 °C	349	**C**
Piperacillin sodium		2 g		TPN #107[a]	43% piperacillin loss in 24 hr at 21 °C by microbiological assay	1326	**I**
Polymyxin B sulfate	NOV	40 mg		TPN #52 and #53[a]	Physically compatible with no polymyxin loss in 24 hr at 29 °C by microbiological assay	440	**C**
Potassium phosphate	MG	100 mEq	CU	AA 4%, D 25%	Physically compatible for 24 hr at 22 °C	313	**C**
Ranitidine HCl	GL	83, 167, 250 mg		TPN #58[a]	10% ranitidine loss in 48 hr at 23 °C	997	**C**
	GL	50 and 100 mg		TPN #59 and #60[a,h]	No color change and 7 to 9% ranitidine loss in 24 hr at 24 °C under fluorescent light. Amino acids not substantially affected. Darkened color and 10 to 12% ranitidine loss in 48 hr	1010	**C**
	GL	50 and 100 mg		TNA #92[a,i]	7 to 10% ranitidine loss in 12 hr and 20 to 28% loss in 24 hr at 23 °C under fluorescent light	1183	**I**
	GL	50 and 100 mg		TPN #117[a]	Physically compatible and no more than 5% ranitidine loss in 48 hr under refrigeration and at 25 °C	1360	**C**
	GL	50 and 100 mg		TNA #118[a]	Physically compatible with no effect on emulsion stability and about 6 to 10% ranitidine loss in 36 hr under refrigeration and at 25 °C with or without light protection	1360	**C**
	GL	50 mg and 2 g	TR	AA 8.5%	Physically compatible and ranitidine chemically stable by HPLC for 24 hr at 25 °C	1515	**C**
	GL	75 mg		TNA #197 to #200[a]	Physically compatible with 7% or less ranitidine loss by HPLC in 24 hr at 22 °C exposed to light. About 15% loss in 48 hr	1921	**C**
	GL	75 mg		TPN #201[a]	Physically compatible with 7% or less ranitidine loss by HPLC in 24 hr at 22 °C exposed to light. About 12% loss in 48 hr	1921	**C**
Sodium bicarbonate		50 and 150 mEq		TPN #62 to #65 and TNA #66 to #68[a]	Physically compatible with 10% or less carbon dioxide loss and unchanged pH in 7 days at 25 °C protected from light	1011	**C**
Tacrolimus	FUJ	100 mg		TPN #201[a,g]	Visually compatible with no loss by HPLC in 24 hr at 24 °C	1922	**C**
Ticarcillin disodium	BE	10 mg		TPN #86 to #88[a]	10% ticarcillin loss in 24 hr at room temperature exposed to light	1160	**C**
	BE	20 mg		TPN #86 to #88[a]	12 to 15% ticarcillin loss in 4 hr at room temperature exposed to light	1160	**I**
		2 g		TPN #107[a]	50% ticarcillin loss in 24 hr at 21 °C by microbiological assay	1326	**I**
Tobramycin sulfate	LI	80 mg	MG	AA 4.25%, D 25%	No increase in particulate matter in 24 hr at 4 °C	349	**C**

Additive Compatibility (Cont.)

Amino acid injection

Drug	*Mfr*	*Conc/L*	*Mfr*	*Test Soln*	*Remarks*	*Ref*	*C/I*
Vancomycin HCl		400 mg		TPN #95 and #96[a]	Physically compatible and vancomycin content retained for 8 days at room temperature and under refrigeration, with and without heparin, by TDx	1321	C
		1 and 6 g		TPN #105 and #106[a]	Physically compatible with little or no vancomycin loss in 4 hr at 22 °C by HPLC	1325	C
		200 mg		TPN #107[a]	Physically compatible and vancomycin activity retained for 24 hr at 21 °C by microbiological assay	1326	C
	LI	500 mg and 1 g		TPN #202[a,h]	Visually compatible and vancomycin activity by bioassay and immunoassay retained for 35 days at 4 °C and an additional 24 hr at 22 °C	1933	C

[a]*Refer to Appendix I for the composition of parenteral nutrition solutions. TNA indicates a 3-in-1 admixture, and TPN indicates a 2-in-1 admixture.*
[b]*Tested in a pediatric parenteral nutrition solution containing 150 ml of dextrose 5% in water and 30 ml of Vamin glucose with electrolytes and vitamins.*
[c]*Expressed as clindamycin base.*
[d]*TPN composed of amino acids (TrophAmine) 0.5 or 2.25% with dextrose 12.5%, vitamins, trace elements, magnesium sulfate, calcium gluconate, sodium chloride, potassium acetate, and heparin sodium.*
[e]*Delivered from a syringe through microbore tubing, T-connector, and a Teflon neonatal 24-gauge intravenous catheter.*
[f]*Tested in Vamin 14, Vamin 18, Vamin glucose, and Vamin N.*
[g]*Tested in glass bottles.*
[h]*Tested in PVC containers.*
[i]*Tested in ethylene vinyl acetate containers.*
[j]*Concentration expressed in milligrams of phenytoin sodium equivalents (PE) per milliliter.*
[k]*Sodium carbonate–containing formulation tested.*

Y-Site Injection Compatibility (1:1 Mixture)

Amino acid injection

Drug	*Mfr*	*Conc*	*Mfr*	*Conc*	*Remarks*	*Ref*	*C/I*
Acetazolamide sodium	LE	100 mg/ml		TPN #203 and #204[g]	White precipitate forms immediately	1974	I
Acyclovir sodium	BW	7 mg/ml		TPN #203 and #204[g]	White precipitate forms immediately	1974	I
	BW	7 mg/ml[a]		TPN #212 to #215[g]	Crystalline needles form immediately, becoming a gross precipitate in 1 hr	2109	I
	GW	7 mg/ml[a]		TNA #218 to #226[g]	White precipitate forms immediately	2215	I
Amikacin sulfate		250 mg/ml		TPN #54[g]	Physically compatible and amikacin activity retained over 6 hr at 22 °C by microbiological assay	1045	C
	BR	37.5 mg/ 0.15 ml[j]		TPN #61[c,g]	Physically compatible	1012	C
	BR	225 mg/ 0.9 ml[j]		TPN #61[d,g]	Physically compatible	1012	C
	BR	15 mg[e]		TPN #91[f,g]	Physically compatible	1170	C
	BR	250 mg/ml		TNA #97 to #104[g]	Broken fat emulsion with oil floating in admixtures	1324	I
	APC	5 mg/ml		TPN #203 and #204[g]	Visually compatible for 2 hr at 23 °C	1974	C
	AB	5 mg/ml[a]		TPN #212 to #215[g]	Physically compatible with no change in measured turbidity or increase in particle content in 4 hr at 23 °C	2109	C
	AB	5 mg/ml[a]		TNA #218 to #226[g]	Visually compatible with no precipitate or emulsion damage apparent in 4 hr at 23 °C	2215	C

Y-Site Injection Compatibility (1:1 Mixture) (Cont.)

Amino acid injection

Drug	*Mfr*	*Conc*	*Mfr*	*Conc*	*Remarks*	*Ref*	*C/I*
Aminophylline	DB	1 mg/ml[b]		TPN #189[g]	Visually compatible for 24 hr at 22 °C	1767	C
	AMR	5 mg/ml		TPN #203 and #204[g]	White precipitate forms immediately	1974	I
	AB	2.5 mg/ml[a]		TPN #212 to #215[g]	Physically compatible with no change in measured turbidity or increase in particle content in 4 hr at 23 °C	2109	C
	AB	2.5 mg/ml[a]		TNA #218 to #226[g]	Visually compatible with no precipitate or emulsion damage apparent in 4 hr at 23 °C	2215	C
Amoxicillin sodium		50 mg/ml[b]		TPN #189[g]	Visually compatible for 24 hr at 22 °C	1767	C
Amphotericin B	PH	0.6 mg/ml[a]		TPN #212 to #215[g]	Gross flocculent precipitate forms immediately	2109	I
	PH	0.6 mg/ml[a]		TNA #218 to #226[g]	Yellow precipitate forms immediately	2215	I
Ampicillin sodium	BR	2 g/50 ml[b]		TNA #73[g,h]	Physically compatible for 4 hr at 25 °C by visual observation	1008	C
	WY	250 mg/ 1.3 ml[i]		TPN #61[c,g]	Heavy precipitate of calcium phosphate due to increased pH	1012	I
	WY	1.5 g/7.5 ml[i]		TPN #61[d,g]	Heavy precipitate of calcium phosphate due to increased pH	1012	I
				TPN #54[g]	Precipitate forms in 30 min at 22 °C	1045	I
	APC	100 and 250 mg/ml		TPN #203 and #204[g]	White precipitate forms immediately	1974	I
	SKB	20 mg/ml[b]		TPN #212 to #215[g]	Physically compatible with no change in measured turbidity or increase in particle content in 4 hr at 23 °C	2109	C
	SKB	20 mg/ml[b]		TNA #218 to #226[g]	Visually compatible with no precipitate or emulsion damage apparent in 4 hr at 23 °C	2215	C
Ampicillin sodium–sulbactam sodium	RR	20 + 10 mg/ ml[b]		TPN #212 to #215[g]	Physically compatible with no change in measured turbidity or increase in particle content in 4 hr at 23 °C	2109	C
	PF	20 + 10 mg/ ml[b]		TNA #218 to #226[g]	Visually compatible with no precipitate or emulsion damage apparent in 4 hr at 23 °C	2215	C
Ascorbic acid injection	DB	20 mg/ml[b]		TPN #189[g]	Visually compatible for 24 hr at 22 °C	1767	C
Atracurium besylate	WEL	10 mg/ml		TPN #189[g]	Visually compatible for 24 hr at 22 °C	1767	C
Azlocillin sodium		133 and 200 mg/ml		TPN #54[g]	Physically compatible and azlocillin activity retained over 6 hr at 22 °C by microbiological assay	1045	C
	MI	250 mg/ 2.5 ml[i]		TPN #61[c,g]	Physically compatible	1012	C
	MI	1.5 mg/15 ml[i]		TPN #61[d,g]	Physically compatible	1012	C
Aztreonam	SQ	40 mg/ml[a]		TPN #212 to #215[g]	Physically compatible with no change in measured turbidity or increase in particle content in 4 hr at 23 °C	2109	C
	SQ	40 mg/ml[a]		TNA #218 to #226[g]	Visually compatible with no precipitate or emulsion damage apparent in 4 hr at 23 °C	2215	C

Y-Site Injection Compatibility (1:1 Mixture) (Cont.)

Drug	Mfr	Conc	Mfr	Conc	Remarks	Ref	C/I
			Amino acid injection				
Bumetanide	RC	0.04 mg/ml[a]		TPN #212 to #215[g]	Physically compatible with no change in measured turbidity or increase in particle content in 4 hr at 23 °C	2109	C
	RC, BV	0.04 mg/ml[a]		TNA #218 to #226[g]	Visually compatible with no precipitate or emulsion damage apparent in 4 hr at 23 °C	2215	C
Buprenorphine HCl	RKC	0.04 mg/ml[a]		TPN #212 to #215[g]	Physically compatible with no change in measured turbidity or increase in particle content in 4 hr at 23 °C	2109	C
	RKC	0.04 mg/ml[a]		TNA #218 to #226[g]	Visually compatible with no precipitate or emulsion damage apparent in 4 hr at 23 °C	2215	C
Butorphanol tartrate	APC	0.04 mg/ml[a]		TPN #212 to #215[g]	Physically compatible with no change in measured turbidity or increase in particle content in 4 hr at 23 °C	2109	C
	APC	0.04 mg/ml[a]		TNA #218 to #226[g]	Visually compatible with no precipitate or emulsion damage apparent in 4 hr at 23 °C	2215	C
Calcium gluconate	DB	10 mg/ml[b]		TPN #189[g]	Visually compatible for 24 hr at 22 °C	1767	C
	AB	40 mg/ml[a]		TPN #212 to #215[g]	Physically compatible with no change in measured turbidity or increase in particle content in 4 hr at 23 °C	2109	C
	AB	40 mg/ml[a]		TNA #218 to #226[g]	Visually compatible with no precipitate or emulsion damage apparent in 4 hr at 23 °C	2215	C
Carboplatin	BMS	5 mg/ml[a]		TPN #212 to #215[g]	Physically compatible with no change in measured turbidity or increase in particle content in 4 hr at 23 °C	2109	C
	BMS	5 mg/ml[a]		TNA #218 to #226[g]	Visually compatible with no precipitate or emulsion damage apparent in 4 hr at 23 °C	2215	C
Cefamandole nafate		250 mg/ml		TPN #54[g]	Physically compatible and cefamandole activity retained over 6 hr at 22 °C by microbiological assay	1045	C
	LI	2 g/50 ml[a]		TNA #73[g,h]	Physically compatible for 4 hr at 25 °C by visual observation	1008	C
	LI	200 mg/ 0.7 ml[i]		TPN #61[c,g]	Physically compatible	1012	C
	LI	1.2 g/4.2 ml[i]		TPN #61[d,g]	Physically compatible	1012	C
Cefazolin sodium	SKF	1 g/50 ml[a]		TNA #73[g,h]	Physically compatible by visual observation for 4 hr at 25 °C	1008	C
	SKF	200 mg/ 0.9 ml[i]		TPN #61[c,g]	Physically compatible	1012	C
	SKF	1.2 g/5.3 ml[i]		TPN #61[d,g]	Physically compatible	1012	C
	SKB	20 mg/ml[a]		TPN #212 and #213[g]	Physically compatible with no change in measured turbidity or increase in particle content in 4 hr at 23 °C	2109	C
	SKB	20 mg/ml[a]		TPN #214 and #215[g]	Small amount of subvisual precipitate forms immediately	2109	I
	SKB	20 mg/ml[a]		TNA #218 to #226[g]	Visually compatible with no precipitate or emulsion damage apparent in 4 hr at 23 °C	2215	C

Y-Site Injection Compatibility (1:1 Mixture) (Cont.)

Amino acid injection

Drug	Mfr	Conc	Mfr	Conc	Remarks	Ref	C/I
Cefoperazone sodium	RR	250 mg/1 ml[i]		TPN #61[c,g]	Physically compatible	1012	C
	RR	1.5 g/6 ml[i]		TPN #61[d,g]	Physically compatible	1012	C
	RR	40 mg/ml[a]		TPN #212 to #215[g]	Physically compatible with no change in measured turbidity or increase in particle content in 4 hr at 23 °C	2109	C
	PF	40 mg/ml[a]		TNA #218 to #226[g]	Visually compatible with no precipitate or emulsion damage apparent in 4 hr at 23 °C	2215	C
Cefotaxime sodium	HO	200 mg/ 0.7 ml[i]		TPN #61[c,g]	Physically compatible	1012	C
	HO	1.2 g/4 ml[i]		TPN #61[d,g]	Physically compatible	1012	C
	RS	200 mg/ml[k]		TPN #189[g]	Visually compatible for 24 hr at 22 °C	1767	C
	HO	60 mg/ml		TPN #203 and #204[g]	Visually compatible for 2 hr at 23 °C	1974	C
	HO	20 mg/ml[a]		TPN #212 to #215[g]	Physically compatible with no change in measured turbidity or increase in particle content in 4 hr at 23 °C	2109	C
	HO	20 mg/ml[a]		TNA #218 to #226[g]	Visually compatible with no precipitate or emulsion damage apparent in 4 hr at 23 °C	2215	C
Cefotetan sodium	STU	20 mg/ml[a]		TPN #212 to #215[g]	Physically compatible with no change in measured turbidity or increase in particle content in 4 hr at 23 °C	2109	C
	ZEN	20 mg/ml[a]		TNA #218 to #226[g]	Visually compatible with no precipitate or emulsion damage apparent in 4 hr at 23 °C	2215	C
Cefoxitin sodium	MSD	1 g/50 ml[a]		TNA #73[g,h]	Physically compatible for 4 hr at 25 °C by visual observation	1008	C
	MSD	200 mg/ 2.1 ml[i]		TPN #61[c,g]	Physically compatible	1012	C
	MSD	1.2 g/12.6 ml[i]		TPN #61[d,g]	Physically compatible	1012	C
	MSD	200 mg/ml[k]		TPN #189[g]	Visually compatible for 24 hr at 22 °C	1767	C
	ME	20 mg/ml[a]		TPN #212 to #215[d]	Physically compatible with no change in measured turbidity or increase in particle content in 4 hr at 23 °C	2109	C
	ME	20 mg/ml[a]		TNA #218 to #226[g]	Visually compatible with no precipitate or emulsion damage apparent in 4 hr at 23 °C	2215	C
Ceftazidime	GL[v]	40 mg/ml[l]		TPN #141 to #143[g]	Visually compatible with 4% or less ceftazidime loss in 2 hr at 22 °C in 1:1 and 1:3 ratios	1535	C
	GL[v]	200 mg/ml[k]		TPN #189[g]	Visually compatible for 24 hr at 22 °C	1767	C
	LI[v]	60 mg/ml		TPN #203 and #204[g]	Visually compatible for 2 hr at 23 °C	1974	C
	SKB[v]	40 mg/ml[a]		TPN #212 to #215[g]	Physically compatible with no change in measured turbidity or increase in particle content in 4 hr at 23 °C	2109	C
	SKB[v]	40 mg/ml[a]		TNA #218 to #226[g]	Visually compatible with no precipitate or emulsion damage apparent in 4 hr at 23 °C	2215	C
	GL[w]	40 mg/ml[a]		TNA #218 to #226[g]	Visually compatible with no precipitate or emulsion damage apparent in 4 hr at 23 °C	2215	C

Y-Site Injection Compatibility (1:1 Mixture) (Cont.)

Drug	Mfr	Conc	Amino acid injection Mfr	Amino acid injection Conc	Remarks	Ref	C/I
Ceftizoxime sodium	FUJ	20 mg/ml[a]		TPN #212 to #215[g]	Physically compatible with no change in measured turbidity or increase in particle content in 4 hr at 23 °C	2109	C
	FUJ	20 mg/ml[a]		TNA #218 to #226[g]	Visually compatible with no precipitate or emulsion damage apparent in 4 hr at 23 °C	2215	C
Ceftriaxone sodium	RC	100 mg/ml[k]		TPN #189[g]	Visually compatible for 24 hr at 22 °C	1767	C
	RC	20 mg/ml[a]		TPN #212 to #215[g]	Physically compatible with no change in measured turbidity or increase in particle content in 4 hr at 23 °C	2109	C
	RC	20 mg/ml[a]		TNA #218 to #226[g]	Visually compatible with no precipitate or emulsion damage apparent in 4 hr at 23 °C	2215	C
Cefuroxime sodium	LI	30 mg/ml[a]		TPN #212 to #215[g]	Physically compatible with no change in measured turbidity or increase in particle content in 4 hr at 23 °C	2109	C
	GL	30 mg/ml[a]		TNA #218 to #226[g]	Visually compatible with no precipitate or emulsion damage apparent in 4 hr at 23 °C	2215	C
Chloramphenicol sodium succinate	PD	125 mg/ 1.25 ml[i]		TPN #61[c,g]	Physically compatible	1012	C
	PD	750 mg/ 7.5 ml[i]		TPN #61[d,g]	Physically compatible	1012	C
Chlorothiazide sodium	ME	28 mg/ml		TPN #203 and #204[g]	White precipitate forms immediately	1974	I
Chlorpromazine HCl	SCN	2 mg/ml[a]		TPN #212 to #215[g]	Physically compatible with no change in measured turbidity or increase in particle content in 4 hr at 23 °C	2109	C
	SCN	2 mg/ml[a]		TNA #218 to #226[g]	Visually compatible with no precipitate or emulsion damage apparent in 4 hr at 23 °C	2215	C
Cimetidine HCl	SKB	10 mg/ml[b]		TPN #189[g]	Visually compatible for 24 hr at 22 °C	1767	C
	SKB	12 mg/ml[a]		TPN #212 to #215[g]	Physically compatible with no change in measured turbidity or increase in particle content in 4 hr at 23 °C	2109	C
	SKB	12 mg/ml[a]		TNA #218 to #226[g]	Visually compatible with no precipitate or emulsion damage apparent in 4 hr at 23 °C	2215	C
Ciprofloxacin	MI	2 mg/ml[a]	AB	AA 5%, D 25%	Visually compatible for 2 hr at 25 °C under fluorescent light	1628	C
	MI	1 mg/ml[a]		TPN #212 to #215[g]	Amber discoloration forms in 1 to 4 hr	2109	I
	BAY	1 mg/ml[a]		TNA #218 to #226[g]	Visually compatible with no precipitate or emulsion damage apparent in 4 hr at 23 °C	2215	C
Cisplatin	BMS	1 mg/ml		TPN #212 to #215[g]	Amber discoloration forms in 1 to 4 hr	2109	I
	BMS	1 mg/ml		TNA #218 to #226[g]	Visually compatible with no precipitate or emulsion damage apparent in 4 hr at 23 °C	2215	C

Y-Site Injection Compatibility (1:1 Mixture) (Cont.)

			Amino acid injection				
Drug	*Mfr*	*Conc*	*Mfr*	*Conc*	*Remarks*	*Ref*	*C/I*
Clindamycin phosphate	UP	600 mg/ 50 ml[a]		TNA #73[g,h]	Physically compatible for 4 hr at 25 °C by visual observation	1008	C
	UP	50 mg/ 0.33 ml[m]		TPN #61[c,g]	Physically compatible	1012	C
	UP	300 mg/2 ml[m]		TPN #61[d,g]	Physically compatible	1012	C
	AB	10 mg/ml[a]		TPN #212 to #215[g]	Physically compatible with no change in measured turbidity or increase in particle content in 4 hr at 23 °C	2109	C
	AST	10 mg/ml[a]		TNA #218 to #226[g]	Visually compatible with no precipitate or emulsion damage apparent in 4 hr at 23 °C	2215	C
Clonazepam	RC	1 mg/ml[k]		TPN #189[g]	Visually compatible for 24 hr at 22 °C	1767	C
Cyclophosphamide	MJ	10 mg/ml[a]		TPN #212 to #215[g]	Physically compatible with no change in measured turbidity or increase in particle content in 4 hr at 23 °C	2109	C
	MJ	10 mg/ml[a]		TNA #218 to #226[g]	Visually compatible with no precipitate or emulsion damage apparent in 4 hr at 23 °C	2215	C
Cyclosporine	SZ	5 mg/ml[a]		TPN #212 and #213[g]	Physically compatible with no change in measured turbidity or increase in particle content in 4 hr at 23 °C	2109	C
	SZ	5 mg/ml[a]		TPN #214 and #215[g]	Small amount of subvisual precipitate forms in 4 hr	2109	I
	SZ	5 mg/ml[a]		TNA #220 and #223[g]	Small amount of precipitate forms immediately	2215	I
	SZ	5 mg/ml[a]		TNA #218, #219, #221, #222, #224 to #226[g]	Visually compatible with no precipitate or emulsion damage apparent in 4 hr at 23 °C	2215	C
Cytarabine	CHI	50 mg/ml		TPN #212 to #215[g]	Substantial loss of natural subvisual turbidity occurs immediately	2109	I
	BED	50 mg/ml		TNA #218 to #226[g]	Visually compatible with no precipitate or emulsion damage apparent in 4 hr at 23 °C	2215	C
Dexamethasone sodium phosphate	AMR	4 mg/ml		TPN #203 and #204[g]	Visually compatible for 2 hr at 23 °C	1974	C
	AMR	1 mg/ml[a]		TPN #212 to #215[g]	Physically compatible with no change in measured turbidity or increase in particle content in 4 hr at 23 °C	2109	C
	FUJ, ES	1 mg/ml[a]		TNA #218 to #226[g]	Visually compatible with no precipitate or emulsion damage apparent in 4 hr at 23 °C	2215	C
Diazepam	DB	5 mg/ml		TPN #189[g]	Visually compatible for 24 hr at 22 °C	1767	C
Digoxin	BW	0.625 mg/ 50 ml[l]		TNA #73[g]	Physically compatible for 4 hr by visual observation	1009	C
	BW	0.25 mg/ml		TPN #212 to #215[g]	Physically compatible with no change in measured turbidity or increase in particle content in 4 hr at 23 °C	2109	C
	ES, WY	0.25 mg/ml		TNA #218 to #226[g]	Visually compatible with no precipitate or emulsion damage apparent in 4 hr at 23 °C	2215	C

Y-Site Injection Compatibility (1:1 Mixture) (Cont.)

Amino acid injection

Drug	*Mfr*	*Conc*	*Mfr*	*Conc*	*Remarks*	*Ref*	*C/I*
Diphenhydramine HCl	SCN	2 mg/ml[a]		TPN #212 to #215[g]	Physically compatible with no change in measured turbidity or increase in particle content in 4 hr at 23 °C	2109	C
	SCN	50 mg/ml		TPN #212 to #215[g]	Physically compatible with no change in measured turbidity or increase in particle content in 4 hr at 23 °C	2109	C
	SCN, PD	2[a] and 50 mg/ml		TNA #218 to #226[g]	Visually compatible with no precipitate or emulsion damage apparent in 4 hr at 23 °C	2215	C
Dobutamine HCl	LI	1 mg/ml[n]		TPN #91[f,g]	Physically compatible	1170	C
	LI	50 mg/ml[b]		TPN #189[g]	Visually compatible for 24 hr at 22 °C	1767	C
	LI	5 mg/ml		TPN #203 and #204[g]	Visually compatible for 4 hr at 23 °C	1974	C
	LI	4 mg/ml[a]		TPN #212 to #215[g]	Physically compatible with no change in measured turbidity or increase in particle content in 4 hr at 23 °C	2109	C
	AST	4 mg/ml[a]		TNA #218 to #226[g]	Visually compatible with no precipitate or emulsion damage apparent in 4 hr at 23 °C	2215	C
Dopamine HCl	AB	80 mg/50 ml[l]		TNA #73[g]	Physically compatible for 4 hr by visual observation	1009	C
	DB	1.6 mg/ml[b]		TPN #189[g]	Visually compatible for 24 hr at 22 °C	1767	C
	AMR	3.2 mg/ml		TPN #203 and #204[g]	Visually compatible for 4 hr at 23 °C	1974	C
	AB	3.2 mg/ml[a]		TPN #212 to #215[g]	Physically compatible with no change in measured turbidity or increase in particle content in 4 hr at 23 °C	2109	C
	AB	3.2 mg/ml[a]		TNA #222 and #223[g]	Precipitate forms immediately	2215	I
	AB	3.2 mg/ml[a]		TNA #218 to #221 and #224 to #226[g]	Visually compatible with no precipitate or emulsion damage apparent in 4 hr at 23 °C	2215	C
Doxorubicin HCl	PH	2 mg/ml		TPN #212 to #215[g]	Substantial loss of natural subvisual turbidity occurs immediately	2109	I
	PH, GEN	2 mg/ml		TNA #218 to #226[g]	Damage to emulsion integrity occurs immediately with free oil formation possible	2215	I
Doxycycline hyclate	PF	10 mg/1 ml[j]		TPN #61[c,g]	Physically compatible	1012	C
	PF	60 mg/6 ml[j]		TPN #61[d,g]	Physically compatible	1012	C
	LY	1 mg/ml[a]		TPN #212 to #215[g]	Physically compatible with no change in measured turbidity or increase in particle content in 4 hr at 23 °C	2109	C
	FUJ	1 mg/ml[a]		TNA #218 to #226[g]	Damage to emulsion integrity occurs immediately with free oil formation possible	2215	I
Droperidol	AB	0.4 mg/ml[a]		TPN #212 to #215[g]	Physically compatible with no change in measured turbidity or increase in particle content in 4 hr at 23 °C	2109	C
	AB	0.4 mg/ml[a]		TNA #218 to #226[g]	Damage to emulsion integrity occurs in 1 to 4 hr with free oil formation possible	2215	I

Y-Site Injection Compatibility (1:1 Mixture) (Cont.)

Drug	Mfr	Conc	Amino acid injection Mfr	Amino acid injection Conc	Remarks	Ref	C/I
Enalaprilat	MSD	0.1 mg/ml[a]		TPN #212 to #215[g]	Physically compatible with no change in measured turbidity or increase in particle content in 4 hr at 23 °C	2109	C
	ME	0.1 mg/ml[a]		TNA #218 to #226[g]	Visually compatible with no precipitate or emulsion damage apparent in 4 hr at 23 °C	2215	C
Epinephrine HCl	AST	0.2 mg/ml[b]		TPN #189[g]	Visually compatible for 24 hr at 22 °C	1767	C
Erythromycin lactobionate	AB	1 g/50 ml[b]		TNA #73[g,h]	Physically compatible for 4 hr at 25 °C by visual observation	1008	C
	AB	50 mg/1 ml[j]		TPN #61[c,g]	Physically compatible	1012	C
	AB	300 mg/6 ml[j]		TPN #61[d,g]	Physically compatible	1012	C
	DB	10 mg/ml[b]		TPN #189[g]	Visually compatible for 24 hr at 22 °C	1767	C
Famotidine HCl	ME	2 mg/ml[a]		TPN #212 to #215[g]	Physically compatible with no change in measured turbidity or increase in particle content in 4 hr at 23 °C	2109	C
	ME	2 mg/ml[a]		TNA #218 to #226[g]	Visually compatible with no precipitate or emulsion damage apparent in 4 hr at 23 °C	2215	C
Fentanyl citrate	ES	0.05 mg/ml		TPN #203 and #204[g]	Visually compatible for 4 hr at 23 °C	1974	C
	ES	0.01 mg/ml[k]		TPN #216[g]	Mixed 1 ml of fentanyl with 9 ml of TPN. Visually compatible for 24 hr	2104	C
	AB	0.05 mg/ml		TPN #212 to #215[g]	Physically compatible with no change in measured turbidity or increase in particle content in 4 hr at 23 °C	2109	C
	JN	0.0125 mg/ml[a]		TPN #212 to #215[g]	Physically compatible with no change in measured turbidity or increase in particle content in 4 hr at 23 °C	2109	C
	AB	0.0125[a] and 0.05 mg/ml		TNA #218 to #226[g]	Visually compatible with no precipitate or emulsion damage apparent in 4 hr at 23 °C	2215	C
Flucloxacillin sodium	BE	50 mg/ml[b]		TPN #189[g]	Visually compatible for 24 hr at 22 °C	1767	C
Fluconazole	PF	0.5 and 1.75 mg/ml[o]		TPN #146[g,o]	Visually compatible with no fluconazole loss by HPLC in 2 hr at 24 °C under fluorescent light. Amino acid concentrations by HPLC greater than 93%	1554	C
	PF	0.5 and 1.75 mg/ml[o]		TPN #147 and #148[g,o]	Visually compatible with no fluconazole loss by HPLC in 2 hr at 24 °C under fluorescent light. Amino acids not analyzed	1554	C
	RR	2 mg/ml		TPN #212 to #215[g]	Physically compatible with no change in measured turbidity or increase in particle content in 4 hr at 23 °C	2109	C
	PF	2 mg/ml		TNA #218 to #226[g]	Visually compatible with no precipitate or emulsion damage apparent in 4 hr at 23 °C	2215	C
Fluorouracil	PH	16 mg/ml[a]		TPN #212 and #213[g]	Slight subvisual haze, crystals, and amber discoloration form in 1 to 4 hr	2109	I
	PH	16 mg/ml[a]		TPN #214 and #215[g]	Turbidity forms immediately	2109	I
	PH	16 mg/ml[a]		TNA #220 and #223[g]	Small amount of white precipitate forms immediately	2215	I

Y-Site Injection Compatibility (1:1 Mixture) (Cont.)

			Amino acid injection				
Drug	*Mfr*	*Conc*	*Mfr*	*Conc*	*Remarks*	*Ref*	*C/I*
	PH	16 mg/ml[a]		TNA #218, #219, #221, #222, #224 to #226[g]	Visually compatible with no precipitate or emulsion damage apparent in 4 hr at 23 °C	2215	C
Folic acid	AB	15 mg/ml		TPN #189[g]	Visually compatible for 24 hr at 22 °C	1767	C
Foscarnet sodium	AST	24 mg/ml		TPN #121[g]	Physically compatible for 24 hr at 25 °C under fluorescent light by visual and microscopic examination	1393	C
Furosemide	ES	165 mg/ 50 ml[l]		TNA #73[g]	Physically compatible for 4 hr by visual observation	1009	C
		10 mg/ml[b]		TPN #189[g]	Visually compatible for 24 hr at 22 °C	1767	C
	AMR	10 mg/ml		TPN #203 and #204[g]	Visually compatible for 2 hr at 23 °C	1974	C
	AB	3 mg/ml[a]		TPN #212 to #215[g]	Small amount of subvisual precipitate forms immediately	2109	I
	AB	3 mg/ml[a]		TNA #218 to #226[g]	Visually compatible with no precipitate or emulsion damage apparent in 4 hr at 23 °C	2215	C
Ganciclovir sodium	SY	1 and 5 mg/ ml[a]		TPN #144[g]	Visually compatible for 2 hr at 20 °C under fluorescent light	1522	C
	SY	10 mg/ml[a]		TPN #144[g]	Heavy precipitate forms within 30 min	1522	I
	SY	3 and 5 mg/ ml		TPN #183 to #185[g]	Precipitate forms	1744	I
	SY	2 mg/ml		TPN #183[g]	Precipitate forms	1744	I
	SY	1 mg/ml[p]		TPN #183[g]	Visually compatible with no ganciclovir loss by HPLC in 3 hr at 24 °C under fluorescent light. Less than 10% amino acids loss by HPLC in 2 hr	1744	C
	SY	2 mg/ml[q]		TPN #184 and #185[g]	Visually compatible with no ganciclovir loss by HPLC in 3 hr at 24 °C under fluorescent light. Less than 10% amino acids loss by HPLC in 3 hr	1744	C
	SY	20 mg/ml[a]		TPN #212 to #215[g]	Gross white precipitate forms immediately	2109	I
	RC	20 mg/ml[a]		TNA #218 to #226[g]	Large amount of white precipitate forms immediately	2215	I
Gentamicin sulfate	SC	80 mg/50 ml[a]		TNA #73[g,h]	Physically compatible for 4 hr at 25 °C by visual observation	1008	C
	IX	12.5 mg/ 1.25 ml[j]		TPN #61[c,g]	Physically compatible	1012	C
	IX	75 mg/1.9 ml[j]		TPN #61[d,g]	Physically compatible	1012	C
		13 and 20 mg/ml		TPN #54[g]	Physically compatible and gentamicin activity retained over 6 hr at 22 °C by microbiological assay	1045	C
	IX	5 mg[e]		TPN #91[f,g]	Physically compatible	1170	C
	ES	40 mg/ml		TNA #97 to #104[g]	Physically compatible and gentamicin content retained for 6 hr at 21 °C by TDx	1324	C
	DB	1 mg/ml[b]		TPN #189[g]	Visually compatible for 24 hr at 22 °C	1767	C
	ES	10 mg/ml		TPN #203 and #204[g]	Visually compatible for 2 hr at 23 °C	1974	C
	AB	5 mg/ml[a]		TPN #212 to #215[g]	Physically compatible with no change in measured turbidity or increase in particle content in 4 hr at 23 °C	2109	C

Y-Site Injection Compatibility (1:1 Mixture) (Cont.)

Drug	Mfr	Conc	Amino acid injection Mfr	Amino acid injection Conc	Remarks	Ref	C/I
	AB, FUJ	5 mg/ml[a]		TNA #218 to #226[g]	Visually compatible with no precipitate or emulsion damage apparent in 4 hr at 23 °C	2215	C
Granisetron HCl	SKB	0.05 mg/ml[a]		TPN #212 to #215[g]	Physically compatible with no change in measured turbidity or increase in particle content in 4 hr at 23 °C	2109	C
	SKB	0.05 mg/ml[a]		TNA #218 to #226[g]	Visually compatible with no precipitate or emulsion damage apparent in 4 hr at 23 °C	2215	C
Haloperidol lactate	SE	10 mg/ml		TPN #189[g]	Visually compatible for 24 hr at 22 °C	1767	C
	MN	0.2 mg/ml[a]		TPN #212 to #215[g]	Physically compatible with no change in measured turbidity or increase in particle content in 4 hr at 23 °C	2109	C
	MN	0.2 mg/ml[a]		TNA #218 to #226[g]	Damage to emulsion integrity occurs immediately with free oil formation possible	2215	I
Heparin sodium	DB	500 units/ml[b]		TPN #189[g]	Visually compatible for 24 hr at 22 °C	1767	C
	AB	100 units/ml		TPN #212 to #215[g]	Physically compatible with no change in measured turbidity or increase in particle content in 4 hr at 23 °C	2109	C
	AB	100 units/ml		TNA #218 to #226[g]	Damage to emulsion integrity occurs immediately with free oil formation possible	2215	I
Hydrocortisone sodium phosphate	ME	1 mg/ml[a]		TPN #212 to #215[g]	Physically compatible with no change in measured turbidity or increase in particle content in 4 hr at 23 °C	2109	C
	ME	1 mg/ml[a]		TNA #218 to #226[g]	Visually compatible with no precipitate or emulsion damage apparent in 4 hr at 23 °C	2215	C
Hydrocortisone sodium succinate	UP	50 mg/ml[b]		TPN #189[g]	Visually compatible for 24 hr at 22 °C	1767	C
	AB	1 mg/ml[a]		TPN #212 to #215[g]	Physically compatible with no change in measured turbidity or increase in particle content in 4 hr at 23 °C	2109	C
	AB	1 mg/ml[a]		TNA #218 to #226[g]	Visually compatible with no precipitate or emulsion damage apparent in 4 hr at 23 °C	2215	C
Hydromorphone HCl	ES	0.5 mg/ml[a]		TPN #212 to #215[g]	Physically compatible with no change in measured turbidity or increase in particle content in 4 hr at 23 °C	2109	C
	ES	0.5 mg/ml[a]		TNA #219, #222, #224 to #226[g]	Damage to emulsion integrity occurs immediately with free oil formation possible	2215	I
	ES	0.5 mg/ml[a]		TNA #218, #220, #221, #223[g]	Visually compatible with no precipitate or emulsion damage apparent in 4 hr at 23 °C	2215	C
Hydroxyzine HCl	ES	2 mg/ml[a]		TPN #212 to #215[g]	Physically compatible with no change in measured turbidity or increase in particle content in 4 hr at 23 °C	2109	C
	ES	2 mg/ml[a]		TNA #218 to #226[g]	Visually compatible with no precipitate or emulsion damage apparent in 4 hr at 23 °C	2215	C

Y-Site Injection Compatibility (1:1 Mixture) (Cont.)

			Amino acid injection				
Drug	*Mfr*	*Conc*	*Mfr*	*Conc*	*Remarks*	*Ref*	*C/I*
Idarubicin HCl	AD	1 mg/ml[b]		TPN #140[g]	Visually compatible for 24 hr at 25 °C under fluorescent light	1525	C
Ifosfamide	MJ	25 mg/ml[a]		TPN #212 to #215[g]	Physically compatible with no change in measured turbidity or increase in particle content in 4 hr at 23 °C	2109	C
	MJ	25 mg/ml[a]		TNA #218 to #226[g]	Visually compatible with no precipitate or emulsion damage apparent in 4 hr at 23 °C	2215	C
IL-2	RC	4800 I.U./ml[b]		TPN #145[g]	Visually compatible and IL-2 activity by bioassay retained	1552	C
Imipenem–cilastatin sodium	ME	10 mg/ml[b]		TPN #212 to #215[g]	Physically compatible with no change in measured turbidity or increase in particle content in 4 hr at 23 °C	2109	C
	ME	10 mg/ml[b]		TNA #218 to #226[g]	Visually compatible with no precipitate or emulsion damage apparent in 4 hr at 23 °C	2215	C
Indomethacin sodium trihydrate	MSD	1 mg/ml[b]	MG[r]	AA 1 and 2%, D 10%	Haze forms in 2 hr and white precipitate forms in 4 hr	1527	I
	MSD	1 mg/ml[b]	MG[r]	AA 1 and 2%, W	Haze forms in 30 min and white precipitate forms in 1 hr	1527	I
Insulin, regular	NOV	2 units/ml[s]		TPN #189[g]	Visually compatible for 24 hr at 22 °C	1767	C
	NOV	1 unit/ml[a]		TPN #212 to #215[g]	Physically compatible with no change in measured turbidity or increase in particle content in 4 hr at 23 °C	2109	C
	NOV	1 unit/ml[a]		TNA #218 to #226[g]	Visually compatible with no precipitate or emulsion damage apparent in 4 hr at 23 °C	2215	C
Isoproterenol HCl	BR	0.2 mg/50 ml[l]		TNA #73[g]	Physically compatible for 4 hr by visual observation	1009	C
Kanamycin sulfate	BR	500 mg/ 50 ml[a]		TNA #73[g]	Physically compatible for 4 hr at 25 °C by visual observation	1008	C
Leucovorin calcium	IMM	2 mg/ml[a]		TPN #212 to #215[g]	Physically compatible with no change in measured turbidity or increase in particle content in 4 hr at 23 °C	2109	C
	IMM	2 mg/ml[a]		TNA #218 to #226[g]	Visually compatible with no precipitate or emulsion damage apparent in 4 hr at 23 °C	2215	C
Levorphanol tartrate	RC	0.5 mg/ml[a]		TPN #212 to #215[g]	Physically compatible with no change in measured turbidity or increase in particle content in 4 hr at 23 °C	2109	C
	RC	0.5 mg/ml[a]		TNA #218 to #226[g]	Damage to emulsion integrity occurs immediately with free oil formation possible	2215	I
Lidocaine HCl	ES	200 mg/ 50 ml[l]		TNA #73[g]	Physically compatible for 4 hr by visual observation	1009	C
Linezolid	PHU	2 mg/ml	AB	AA 4.9%, D 20%	Physically compatible with no change in measured turbidity or increase in particle content in 4 hr at 23 °C	2264	C

Y-Site Injection Compatibility (1:1 Mixture) (Cont.)

Drug	*Mfr*	*Conc*	Amino acid injection *Mfr*	Amino acid injection *Conc*	*Remarks*	*Ref*	*C/I*
Lorazepam	WY	0.1 mg/ml[a]		TPN #212 to #215[g]	Physically compatible with no change in measured turbidity or increase in particle content in 4 hr at 23 °C	2109	C
	WY	0.1 mg/ml[a]		TNA #218 to #226[g]	Damage to emulsion integrity occurs in 1 hr	2215	I
Magnesium sulfate	AB	100 mg/ml[a]		TPN #212 to #215[g]	Physically compatible with no change in measured turbidity or increase in particle content in 4 hr at 23 °C	2109	C
	AB	100 mg/ml[a]		TNA #218 to #226[g]	Visually compatible with no precipitate or emulsion damage apparent in 4 hr at 23 °C	2215	C
Mannitol	BA	15%		TPN #212 to #215[g]	Physically compatible with no change in measured turbidity or increase in particle content in 4 hr at 23 °C	2109	C
	BA	15%		TNA #218 to #226[g]	Visually compatible with no precipitate or emulsion damage apparent in 4 hr at 23 °C	2215	C
Meperidine HCl	AB	10 mg/ml		TPN #131 and #132[g]	Physically compatible for 4 hr at 25 °C under fluorescent light	1397	C
	DB	50 mg/ml		TPN #189[g]	Visually compatible for 24 hr at 22 °C	1767	C
	AST	4 mg/ml[a]		TPN #212 to #215[g]	Physically compatible with no change in measured turbidity or increase in particle content in 4 hr at 23 °C	2109	C
	AST	4 mg/ml[a]		TNA #218 to #226[g]	Visually compatible with no precipitate or emulsion damage apparent in 4 hr at 23 °C	2215	C
Meropenem	ZEN	20 mg/ml[a]		TNA #218 to #226[g]	Visually compatible with no precipitate or emulsion damage apparent in 4 hr at 23 °C	2215	C
Mesna	MJ	10 mg/ml[a]		TPN #212 to #215[g]	Physically compatible with no change in measured turbidity or increase in particle content in 4 hr at 23 °C	2109	C
	MJ	10 mg/ml[a]		TNA #218 to #226[g]	Visually compatible with no precipitate or emulsion damage apparent in 4 hr at 23 °C	2215	C
Methotrexate sodium	LE	15 mg/ml[a]		TPN #212 to #215[g]	Substantial loss of natural subvisual turbidity with a hazy subvisual precipitate in 0 to 1 hr	2109	I
	IMM	15 mg/ml[a]		TNA #218 to #226[g]	Visually compatible with no precipitate or emulsion damage apparent in 4 hr at 23 °C	2215	C
Methyldopate HCl	MSD	250 mg/50 ml[a]		TNA #73[g]	Cracked the lipid emulsion	1009	I
	MSD	250 mg/50 ml[b]		TNA #73[g]	Physically compatible for 4 hr by visual observation	1009	C
Methylprednisolone sodium succinate	AB	5 mg/ml[a]		TPN #212 to #215[g]	Physically compatible with no change in measured turbidity or increase in particle content in 4 hr at 23 °C	2109	C
	AB	5 mg/ml[a]		TNA #218 to #226[g]	Visually compatible with no precipitate or emulsion damage apparent in 4 hr at 23 °C	2215	C

Y-Site Injection Compatibility (1:1 Mixture) (Cont.)

Drug	Mfr	Conc	Amino acid injection Mfr	Amino acid injection Conc	Remarks	Ref	C/I
Metoclopramide HCl	AB	5 mg/ml		TPN #212 to #215[g]	Substantial loss of natural subvisual turbidity occurs immediately	2109	I
	AB	5 mg/ml		TNA #218 to #226[g]	Visually compatible with no precipitate or emulsion damage apparent in 4 hr at 23 °C	2215	C
Metronidazole	DB	5 mg/ml		TPN #189[g]	Visually compatible for 24 hr at 22 °C	1767	C
	AB	5 mg/ml		TPN #203 and #204[g]	Visually compatible for 2 hr at 23 °C	1974	C
	SCS	5 mg/ml		TPN #212 to #215[g]	Physically compatible with no change in measured turbidity or increase in particle content in 4 hr at 23 °C	2109	C
	AB	5 mg/ml		TNA #218 to #226[g]	Visually compatible with no precipitate or emulsion damage apparent in 4 hr at 23 °C	2215	C
Midazolam HCl	RC	5 mg/ml		TPN #189[g]	White haze and light white precipitate form immediately. Crystals form in 24 hr	1767	I
	RC	2 mg/ml[a]		TPN #212 to #215[g]	White cloudiness forms rapidly	2109	I
	RC	2 mg/ml[a]		TNA #218 to #226[g]	Damage to emulsion integrity occurs immediately with free oil formation possible	2215	I
Milrinone lactate	SW	0.4 mg/ml[a]		TPN #217[g]	Visually compatible with no loss of milrinone by HPLC in 4 hr at 23 °C	2214	C
Minocycline HCl	LE	0.2 mg/ml[a]		TPN #212 to #215[g]	Bright yellow discoloration forms immediately	2109	I
	LE	0.2 mg/ml[a]		TNA #218 to #226[g]	Damage to emulsion integrity occurs immediately with free oil formation possible	2215	I
Mitoxantrone HCl	IMM	0.5 mg/ml[a]		TPN #212 to #215[g]	Substantial loss of natural subvisual turbidity occurs immediately	2109	I
	IMM	0.5 mg/ml[a]		TNA #218 to #226[g]	Visually compatible with no precipitate or emulsion damage apparent in 4 hr at 23 °C	2215	C
Morphine sulfate	AB	1 mg/ml		TPN #131 and #132[g]	Physically compatible for 4 hr at 25 °C under fluorescent light	1397	C
	DB	30 mg/ml		TPN #189[g]	Visually compatible for 24 hr at 22 °C	1767	C
	ES	1 mg/ml		TPN #203 and #204[g]	Visually compatible for 2 hr at 23 °C	1974	C
	AST	1 mg/ml[a]		TPN #212 to #215[g]	Physically compatible with no change in measured turbidity or increase in particle content in 4 hr at 23 °C	2109	C
	ES	1 mg/ml[a]		TNA #218 to #226[g]	Visually compatible with no precipitate or emulsion damage apparent in 4 hr at 23 °C	2215	C
	ES	15 mg/ml		TNA #218 to #226[g]	Damage to emulsion integrity occurs immediately with free oil formation possible	2215	I
Multivitamins (M.V.I-12)	RR			TPN #189[g]	Visually compatible for 24 hr at 22 °C	1767	C
Nafcillin sodium	WY	250 mg/1 ml[i]		TPN #61[c,g]	Physically compatible	1012	C

Y-Site Injection Compatibility (1:1 Mixture) (Cont.)

Amino acid injection

Drug	*Mfr*	*Conc*	*Mfr*	*Conc*	*Remarks*	*Ref*	*C/I*
	WY	1.5 g/6 ml[i]		TPN #61[d,g]	Physically compatible	1012	C
		250 mg/ml		TPN #54[g]	Physically compatible and nafcillin activity retained over 6 hr at 22 °C by microbiological assay	1045	C
	BE	20 mg/ml[a]		TPN #212 to #215[g]	Physically compatible with no change in measured turbidity or increase in particle content in 4 hr at 23 °C	2109	C
	BE, APC	20 mg/ml[a]		TNA #218 to #226[g]	Visually compatible with no precipitate or emulsion damage apparent in 4 hr at 23 °C	2215	C
Nalbuphine HCl	AB	10 mg/ml		TPN #212 to #215[g]	Physically compatible with no change in measured turbidity or increase in particle content in 4 hr at 23 °C	2109	C
	AB, AST	10 mg/ml		TNA #218 to #226[g]	Damage to emulsion integrity occurs immediately with free oil formation possible	2215	I
Netilmicin sulfate	SC	12.5 mg/ 0.13 ml[j]		TPN #61[c,g]	Physically compatible	1012	C
	SC	75 mg/ 0.75 ml[j]		TPN #61[d,g]	Physically compatible	1012	C
	SC	5 mg/ml[a]		TPN #212 to #215[g]	Physically compatible with no change in measured turbidity or increase in particle content in 4 hr at 23 °C	2109	C
	SC	5 mg/ml[a]		TNA #218 to #226[g]	Visually compatible with no precipitate or emulsion damage apparent in 4 hr at 23 °C	2215	C
Nitroglycerin	DU	0.4 mg/ml[a]		TPN #212 to #215[g]	Physically compatible with no change in measured turbidity or increase in particle content in 4 hr at 23 °C	2109	C
	DU	0.4 mg/ml[a]		TNA #218 to #226[g]	Visually compatible with no precipitate or emulsion damage apparent in 4 hr at 23 °C	2215	C
Norepinephrine bitartrate	BN	0.4 mg/50 ml[l]		TNA #73[g]	Physically compatible for 4 hr by visual observation	1009	C
	AB	0.016 mg/ml[a]		TPN #212 to #215[g]	Physically compatible with no change in measured turbidity or increase in particle content in 4 hr at 23 °C	2109	C
Octreotide acetate	SZ	0.01 mg/ml[a]		TPN #212 to #215[g]	Physically compatible with no change in measured turbidity or increase in particle content in 4 hr at 23 °C	2109	C
	SZ	0.01 mg/ml[a]		TNA #218 to #226[g]	Visually compatible with no precipitate or emulsion damage apparent in 4 hr at 23 °C	2215	C
Ofloxacin	ORT	4 mg/ml[a]		TPN #212 to #215[g]	Physically compatible with no change in measured turbidity or increase in particle content in 4 hr at 23 °C	2109	C
	ORT	4 mg/ml[a]		TNA #218 to #226[g]	Visually compatible with no precipitate or emulsion damage apparent in 4 hr at 23 °C	2215	C

Y-Site Injection Compatibility (1:1 Mixture) (Cont.)

Drug	Mfr	Conc	Amino acid injection Mfr	Amino acid injection Conc	Remarks	Ref	C/I
Ondansetron HCl	GL	1 mg/ml[a]		TPN #212 to #215[g]	Physically compatible with no change in measured turbidity or increase in particle content in 4 hr at 23 °C	2109	C
	CER	1 mg/ml[a]		TNA #218 to #226[g]	Damage to emulsion integrity occurs immediately with free oil formation possible	2215	I
Oxacillin sodium	BE	1 g/50 ml[a]		TNA #73[g,h]	Physically compatible for 4 hr at 25 °C by visual observation	1008	C
	BE	250 mg/1.5 ml[i]		TPN #61[c,g]	Physically compatible	1012	C
	BE	1.5 g/9 ml[i]		TPN #61[d,g]	Physically compatible	1012	C
		100 and 150 mg/ml		TPN #54[g]	Physically compatible and 88 to 94% oxacillin activity retained over 6 hr at 22 °C by microbiological assay	1012	C
Paclitaxel	MJ	1.2 mg/ml[a]		TPN #212 to #215[g]	Physically compatible with no change in measured turbidity or increase in particle content in 4 hr at 23 °C	2109	C
	MJ	1.2 mg/ml[a]		TNA #218 to #226[g]	Visually compatible with no precipitate or emulsion damage apparent in 4 hr at 23 °C	2215	C
Penicillin G	PF	200,000 units/2 ml[i]		TPN #61[c,g]	Physically compatible	1012	C
	PF	1.2 million units/12 ml[i]		TPN #61[d,g]	Physically compatible	1012	C
		320,000 and 500,000 units/ml		TPN #54[g]	Physically compatible and 88% penicillin activity retained over 6 hr at 22 °C by microbiological assay	1045	C
		300 mg/ml[b]		TPN #189[g]	Visually compatible for 24 hr at 22 °C	1767	C
Penicillin G potassium	SQ	2 million units/50 ml[a]		TNA #73[g,h]	Physically compatible for 4 hr at 25 °C by visual observation	1008	C
	MAR	500,000 units/ml		TPN #203 and #204[g]	Visually compatible for 2 hr at 23 °C	1974	C
Pentobarbital sodium	AB	5 mg/ml[a]		TPN #212 to #215[g]	Physically compatible with no change in measured turbidity or increase in particle content in 4 hr at 23 °C	2109	C
	AB	5 mg/ml[a]		TNA #218 to #226[g]	Damage to emulsion integrity occurs immediately with free oil formation possible	2215	I
Phenobarbital sodium	WY	5 mg/ml[a]		TPN #212 to #215[g]	Physically compatible with no change in measured turbidity or increase in particle content in 4 hr at 23 °C	2109	C
	WY	5 mg/ml[a]		TNA #218 to #226[g]	Damage to emulsion integrity occurs immediately with free oil formation possible	2215	I
Phenytoin sodium	PD	50 mg/ml		TPN #189[g]	Heavy white precipitate forms immediately	1767	I
Piperacillin sodium	LE	250 mg/1.25 ml[i]		TPN #61[c,g]	Physically compatible	1012	C
	LE	1.5 g/7.5 ml[i]		TPN #61[d,g]	Physically compatible	1012	C
		133 and 200 mg/ml		TPN #54[g]	Physically compatible and 90 to 100% piperacillin activity retained over 6 hr at 22 °C by microbiological assay	1045	C

Y-Site Injection Compatibility (1:1 Mixture) (Cont.)

Drug	*Mfr*	*Conc*	*Mfr* (Amino acid injection)	*Conc* (Amino acid injection)	*Remarks*	*Ref*	*C/I*
	LE	40 mg/ml[a]		TPN #212 to #215[g]	Physically compatible with no change in measured turbidity or increase in particle content in 4 hr at 23 °C	2109	C
	LE	40 mg/ml[a]		TNA #218 to #226[g]	Visually compatible with no precipitate or emulsion damage apparent in 4 hr at 23 °C	2215	C
Piperacillin sodium–tazobactam sodium	CY	40 + 5 mg/ml[a]		TPN #212 to #215[g]	Physically compatible with no change in measured turbidity or increase in particle content in 4 hr at 23 °C	2109	C
	LE	40 + 5 mg/ml[a]		TNA #218 to #226[g]	Visually compatible with no precipitate or emulsion damage apparent in 4 hr at 23 °C	2215	C
Potassium chloride	AST	30 mg/ml[b]		TPN #189[g]	Visually compatible for 24 hr at 22 °C	1767	C
	AB	0.1 mEq/ml[a]		TPN #212 to #215[g]	Physically compatible with no change in measured turbidity or increase in particle content in 4 hr at 23 °C	2109	C
	AB	0.1 mEq/ml[a]		TNA #218 to #226[g]	Visually compatible with no precipitate or emulsion damage apparent in 4 hr at 23 °C	2215	C
Potassium phosphates	AB	3 mmol/ml		TPN #212 to #215[g]	Increased turbidity forms immediately	2109	I
	AB	3 mmol/ml		TNA #218 to #226[g]	Damage to emulsion integrity occurs immediately with free oil formation possible	2215	I
Prochlorperazine edisylate	SCN	0.5 mg/ml[a]		TPN #212 to #215[g]	Physically compatible with no change in measured turbidity or increase in particle content in 4 hr at 23 °C	2109	C
	SCN, SO	0.5 mg/ml[a]		TNA #218 to #226[g]	Visually compatible with no precipitate or emulsion damage apparent in 4 hr at 23 °C	2215	C
Promethazine HCl	SCN	2 mg/ml[a]		TPN #212 and #214[g]	Physically compatible with no change in measured turbidity or increase in particle content in 4 hr at 23 °C	2109	C
	SCN	2 mg/ml[a]		TPN #213 and #215[g]	Amber discoloration forms in 4 hr	2109	I
	SCN	2 mg/ml[a]		TNA #218 to #226[g]	Visually compatible with no precipitate or emulsion damage apparent in 4 hr at 23 °C	2215	C
Propofol	STU	2 and 3 g		TPN #186 to #188[g]	Physically compatible with no change in particle size distribution and 6% or less propofol loss by HPLC in 5 hr at 22 °C	1805	C
	STU	500 mg		TPN #186[g]	Physically compatible with no change in particle size distribution but 28% propofol loss by HPLC in 5 hr at 22 °C	1805	I
	STU	500 mg		TPN #187 and #188[g]	Physically compatible with no change in particle size distribution and 6% or less propofol loss by HPLC in 5 hr at 22 °C	1805	C
Ranitidine HCl	GL	2.5 mg/ml[b]		TPN #189[g]	Visually compatible for 24 hr at 22 °C	1767	C
	GL	25 mg/ml		TPN #203 and #204[g]	Visually compatible for 2 hr at 23 °C	1974	C
	GL	2 mg/ml[a]		TPN #212 to #215[g]	Physically compatible with no change in measured turbidity or increase in particle content in 4 hr at 23 °C	2109	C

Y-Site Injection Compatibility (1:1 Mixture) (Cont.)

Drug	Mfr	Conc	Mfr	Conc	Remarks	Ref	C/I
				Amino acid injection			
	GL	2 mg/ml[a]		TNA #218 to #226[g]	Visually compatible with no precipitate or emulsion damage apparent in 4 hr at 23 °C	2215	C
Salbutamol	AH	0.5 mg/ml[b]		TPN #189[g]	Visually compatible for 24 hr at 22 °C	1767	C
Sargramostim	IMM	10 µg/ml[b]		TPN #133[g]	Physically compatible for 4 hr at 22 °C under fluorescent light	1436	C
	IMM	6[t] and 15 µg/ml[b]		TPN #181[g]	Visually compatible for 2 hr	1618	C
Sodium bicarbonate	AB	1 mEq/ml		TPN #212 and #214[g]	Small amount of hazy subvisual precipitate forms in 1 hr and settles	2109	I
	AB	1 mEq/ml		TPN #213 and #215[g]	Physically compatible with no change in measured turbidity or increase in particle content in 4 hr at 23 °C	2109	C
	AB	1 mEq/ml		TNA #218 to #226[g]	Visually compatible with no precipitate or emulsion damage apparent in 4 hr at 23 °C	2215	C
Sodium nitroprusside	AB	0.4 mg/ml[a]		TPN #212 to #215[g]	Physically compatible with no change in measured turbidity or increase in particle content in 4 hr at 23 °C protected from light	2109	C
	AB	0.4 mg/ml[a]		TNA #218 to #226[g]	Visually compatible with no precipitate or emulsion damage apparent in 4 hr at 23 °C protected from light	2215	C
Sodium phosphates	AB	3 mmol/ml		TPN #212 to #215[g]	Increased turbidity forms immediately	2109	I
	AB	3 mmol/ml		TNA #218 to #226[g]	Damage to emulsion integrity occurs immediately with free oil formation possible	2215	I
Tacrolimus	FUJ	1 mg/ml[a]		TPN #212 to #215[g]	Physically compatible with no change in measured turbidity or increase in particle content in 4 hr at 23 °C	2109	C
	FUJ	1 mg/ml[a]		TNA #218 to #226[g]	Visually compatible with no precipitate or emulsion damage apparent in 4 hr at 23 °C	2215	C
Thiotepa	IMM[u]	1 mg/ml[a]		TPN #193[g]	Physically compatible with no change in measured turbidity or increase in particle content in 4 hr at 23 °C	1861	C
Ticarcillin disodium	BE	3 g/50 ml[a]		TNA #73[g,h]	Physically compatible for 4 hr at 25 °C by visual observation	1008	C
	BE	250 mg/1 ml[i]		TPN #61[c,g]	Physically compatible	1012	C
	BE	1.5 g/6 ml[i]		TPN #61[d,g]	Physically compatible	1012	C
		267 and 400 mg/ml		TPN #54[g]	Physically compatible and 89 to 94% ticarcillin activity retained over 6 hr at 22 °C by microbiological assay	1045	C
	SKB	30 mg/ml[a]		TPN #212 to #215[g]	Physically compatible with no change in measured turbidity or increase in particle content in 4 hr at 23 °C	2109	C
	SKB	30 mg/ml[a]		TNA #218 to #226[g]	Visually compatible with no precipitate or emulsion damage apparent in 4 hr at 23 °C	2215	C

Y-Site Injection Compatibility (1:1 Mixture) (Cont.)

Drug	Mfr	Conc	Amino acid injection Mfr	Amino acid injection Conc	Remarks	Ref	C/I
Ticarcillin disodium–clavulanate potassium	BE	30 mg/ml[b]		TPN #189[g]	Visually compatible for 24 hr at 22 °C	1767	C
	SKB	31 mg/ml[a]		TPN #212 to #215[g]	Physically compatible with no change in measured turbidity or increase in particle content in 4 hr at 23 °C	2109	C
	SKB	31 mg/ml[a]		TNA #218 to #226[g]	Visually compatible with no precipitate or emulsion damage apparent in 4 hr at 23 °C	2215	C
Tobramycin sulfate	LI	80 mg/50 ml[a]		TNA #73[g,h]	Physically compatible for 4 hr at 25 °C by visual observation	1008	C
	DI	12.5 mg/1.25 ml[j]		TPN #61[c,g]	Physically compatible	1012	C
	DI	75 mg/1.9 ml[j]		TPN #61[d,g]	Physically compatible	1012	C
		20 mg/ml		TPN #54[g]	Physically compatible and tobramycin activity retained over 6 hr at 22 °C by microbiological assay	1045	C
	LI	5 mg[e]		TPN #91[f,g]	Physically compatible	1170	C
	LI	40 mg/ml		TNA #97 to #104[g]	Physically compatible and tobramycin content retained for 6 hr at 21 °C by TDx	1324	C
	LI	10 mg/ml		TPN #203 and #204[g]	Visually compatible for 2 hr at 23 °C	1974	C
	AB	5 mg/ml[a]		TPN #212 to #215[g]	Physically compatible with no change in measured turbidity or increase in particle content in 4 hr at 23 °C	2109	C
	AB	5 mg/ml[a]		TNA #218 to #226[g]	Visually compatible with no precipitate or emulsion damage apparent in 4 hr at 23 °C	2215	C
Trace elements	DB			TPN #189[g]	Blue discoloration forms immediately	1767	I
Trimethoprim–sulfamethoxazole	ES	0.8 + 4 mg/ml[a]		TNA #212 to #215[g]	Physically compatible with no change in measured turbidity or increase in particle content in 4 hr at 23 °C	2109	C
	ES	0.8 + 4 mg/ml[a]		TNA #218 to #226[g]	Visually compatible with no precipitate or emulsion damage apparent in 4 hr at 23 °C	2215	C
Urokinase	AB	2500 I.U./ml[b]		TPN #55 and #56[g]	No loss of urokinase activity when assayed immediately after mixing	1046	C
Vancomycin HCl	LI	50 mg/1 ml[j]		TPN #61[c,g]	Physically compatible	1012	C
	LI	300 mg/6 ml[j]		TPN #61[d,g]	Physically compatible	1012	C
	LI	30 mg[e]		TPN #91[f,g]	Physically compatible	1170	C
	DB	10 mg/ml[b]		TPN #189[g]	Visually compatible for 24 hr at 22 °C	1767	C
	LI	5 mg/ml		TPN #203 and #204[g]	Visually compatible for 2 hr at 23 °C	1974	C
	AB	10 mg/ml[a]		TPN #212 to #215[g]	Physically compatible with no change in measured turbidity or increase in particle content in 4 hr at 23 °C	2109	C
	AB	10 mg/ml[a]		TNA #218 to #226[g]	Visually compatible with no precipitate or emulsion damage apparent in 4 hr at 23 °C	2215	C
Vecuronium bromide	OR	2 mg/ml[k]		TPN #189[g]	Visually compatible for 24 hr at 22 °C	1767	C

Y-Site Injection Compatibility (1:1 Mixture) (Cont.)

			Amino acid injection				
Drug	*Mfr*	*Conc*	*Mfr*	*Conc*	*Remarks*	*Ref*	*C/I*
Zidovudine	BW	4 mg/ml		TPN #203 and #204[g]	Visually compatible for 2 hr at 23 °C	1974	C
	BW	4 mg/ml[a]		TPN #212 to #215[g]	Physically compatible with no change in measured turbidity or increase in particle content in 4 hr at 23 °C	2109	C
	GW	4 mg/ml[a]		TNA #218 to #226[g]	Visually compatible with no precipitate or emulsion damage apparent in 4 hr at 23 °C	2215	C

[a]*Tested in dextrose 5% in water.*
[b]*Tested in sodium chloride 0.9%.*
[c]*Run at 21 ml/hr.*
[d]*Run at 94 ml/hr.*
[e]*Given over one hour by syringe pump.*
[f]*Run at 10 ml/hr.*
[g]*Refer to Appendix I for the composition of parenteral nutrition solutions. TNA indicates a 3-in-1 admixture, and TPN indicates a 2-in-1 admixture.*
[h]*A 32.5-ml sample of parenteral nutrition solution and 50 ml of antibiotic in a minibottle.*
[i]*Given over five minutes by syringe pump.*
[j]*Given over 30 minutes by syringe pump.*
[k]*Tested in sterile water for injection.*
[l]*Tested in both dextrose 5% in water and sodium chloride 0.9%.*
[m]*Given over 10 minutes by syringe pump.*
[n]*Tested in dextrose 5% in water infused at 1.2 ml/hr.*
[o]*Varying volumes to simulate varying administration rates.*
[p]*Ganciclovir sodium concentration after mixing was 0.83 mg/ml.*
[q]*Ganciclovir sodium concentration after mixing was 1.4 mg/ml.*
[r]*TrophAmine.*
[s]*Tested in Haemaccel (Behring).*
[t]*With albumin human 0.1%.*
[u]*Lyophilized formulation tested.*
[v]*Sodium carbonate–containing formulation.*
[w]*L-Arginine–containing formulation.*

Additional Compatibility Information

Parenteral Nutrition Solutions — Parenteral nutrition solutions #38 through #47 (Appendix I) have been tested and found to be physically compatible for 24 hours at 22 °C. However, those solutions containing multivitamin infusion concentrate or vitamin B complex with C exhibited changes in the UV spectra of both amino acids–dextrose and the vitamins. Additionally, TLC changes were observed in similar solutions in 12 hours. (313)

Multicomponent (3-in-1; TNA) Admixtures — Because of the potential benefits in terms of simplicity, efficiency, time, and cost, the concept of mixing amino acids, carbohydrates, electrolytes, fat emulsion, and other nutritional components together in the same container has been explored. Within limits, the feasibility of preparing such 3-in-1 parenteral nutrition admixtures has been demonstrated.

However, these 3-in-1 mixtures are very complex and inherently unstable. Emulsion stability is dependent on both zeta potential and van der Waals forces, influenced by the presence of dextrose. (2029) The ultimate stability of each unique mixture depends on numerous complicated factors, making definitive stability predictions impossible. Injury and death have resulted from administration of unrecognized precipitation in 3-in-1 parenteral nutrition admixtures. (1769; 1782; 1783) See the section on Calcium and Phosphate. In addition, the use of 3-in-1 admixtures is associated with a higher rate of catheter occlusion and reduced catheter life compared with giving the fat emulsion separately from the parenteral nutrition solution. (2194)

Combining an amino acids–glucose parenteral nutrition solution containing various electrolytes with fat emulsion 20%, intravenous (Intralipid, Vitrum), resulted in a mixture which, although apparently stable for a limited time, ultimately exhibited a creaming phenomenon. Within 12 hours, a distinct 2-cm layer separated on the upper surface. Microscopic examination revealed aggregates believed to be clumps of fat droplets. Fewer and smaller aggregates were noted in the lower layer. (560; 561)

Black and Popovich reported that amino acids had no adverse effect on the emulsion stability of Intralipid 10%. In addition, the amino acids appeared to prevent the adverse impact of dextrose and to slow the flocculation and coalescence resulting from mono- and divalent cations. However, significant coalescence did result after a longer time. Therefore, it was recommended that such cations not be mixed with fat emulsion, intravenous. (656)

The compatibility and stability of parenteral nutrition solutions consisting of amino acids, dextrose, fat emulsion, and various additives, all in a single admixture, were evaluated by Cutter Laboratories. The study entailed combining, in glass bottles, various amino acid products with Intralipid 10 or 20% and dextrose 70 or 10% along with electrolytes, vitamins, and trace minerals. These parenteral nutrition solutions were stored at 5 °C for three days followed by 25 °C for two days. The compatibility and stability of the emulsion were evaluated initially and again after storage. Additive compatibility and stability were not evaluated. Cutter Laboratories concluded that most of the

Table 2. Intralipid-Containing Parenteral Nutrition Admixtures Found to be Compatible and Stable (791)

Component	Amount (ml)				
	FreAmine II 8.5%	FreAmine III 8.5%	Travasol 8.5% without Electrolytes	Travasol 10% without Electrolytes	Veinamine 8%
Amino acids	500	500	500	500	500
Dextrose 70 or 10%	500	500	500	500	500
Intralipid 20 or 10%	500 or 250	500 or 250	500 or 250	500 or 250	500 or 250
	Maximum Total Concentration				
Calcium	10 mEq	10 mEq	10 mEq	10 mEq	10 mEq
Magnesium	13 mEq	13 mEq	13 mEq	13 mEq	13 mEq
Sodium	134 mEq	134 mEq	129 mEq	129 mEq	149 mEq
Potassium	105 mEq	105 mEq	105 mEq	105 mEq	120 mEq
Chloride	244 mEq	245 mEq	261 mEq	264 mEq	279 mEq
Sulfate	13 mEq	13 mEq	13 mEq	13 mEq	13 mEq
Phosphorus	12.5 mmol	12.5 mmol	7.5 mmol	7.5 mmol	7.5 mmol
Acetate	21 mEq	37 mEq	26 mEq	44 mEq	25 mEq
Zinc	4 mg	4 mg	4 mg	4 mg	4 mg
Copper	1.5 mg	1.5 mg	1.5 mg	1.5 mg	1.5 mg
Manganese	0.8 mg	0.8 mg	0.8 mg	0.8 mg	0.8 mg
Chromium	15 μg	15 μg	15 μg	15 μg	15 μg
Multivitamin infusion concentrate (USV)	5 ml	5 ml	5 ml	5 ml	5 ml

admixtures were compatible and stable over the test period with minimal chemical and physical changes (Table 2). The exceptions were admixtures prepared with Aminosyn 7%. In the Aminosyn 7%-containing admixtures, the emulsion broke within 24 hours at room temperature and had oil globules floating on the surface. Refrigeration prevented the breaking of the emulsion, as did exclusion of the electrolytes. Presumably, the lower pH of Aminosyn 7% compared to the other amino acid products tested was associated with the disruption of the emulsion.

Although dextrose 70 and 10% were the only concentrations evaluated, Cutter Laboratories indicated that intermediate dextrose concentrations may be used as long as the amino acids–dextrose–Intralipid ratio is 1:1:1 or 1:1:½. Other ratios also have been recommended. (703; 1068)

The disruptive effects of divalent ions are not as severe in these parenteral nutrition admixtures as they are in Intralipid alone. However, they do represent complex and somewhat unpredictable interactions. Consequently, Cutter Laboratories recommends using only combinations that have been evaluated. Concentrations of additive components may be at or below the maximum amounts indicated in Table 2.

Although some admixtures were stable over longer periods, Cutter Laboratories recommends use of these combined multicomponent admixtures within 24 hours. (791)

Travenol states that 1:1:1 mixtures of amino acids 5.5, 8.5, or 10% (Travenol), fat emulsion 10 to 20% (Travenol), and dextrose 10 to 70% are physically stable but recommends administration within 24 hours. M.V.I.-12 3.3 ml/L and electrolytes may also be added to the admixtures up to the maximum amounts listed below (850):

Calcium	8.3 mEq/L
Magnesium	3.3 mEq/L
Sodium	23.3 mEq/L
Potassium	20.0 mEq/L
Chloride	23.3 mEq/L
Phosphate	20 mEq/L
Zinc	3.33 mg/L
Copper	1.33 mg/L
Manganese	0.33 mg/L
Chromium	13.33 μg/L

Knutsen et al. reported that a mixture of soybean oil emulsion 10% with amino acids 8.5%, concentrated dextrose, multivitamins, and electrolytes had good physical stability. Visual and microscopic examination of samples stored at 4 °C for one week showed the emulsion to be uniform with no flocculence. (891)

Burnham et al. evaluated the stability of mixtures of 1 L of Intralipid 20%, 1.5 L of Vamin glucose (amino acids with dextrose 10%), and 0.5 L of dextrose 10% with various electrolytes and vitamins. Initial emulsion particle size was around 1 μm. The mixture containing only monovalent cations was stable for at least nine days at 4 °C, with little change in particle size. The mixtures containing the divalent cations, such as calcium and magnesium, demonstrated much greater particle size increases, with mean diameters of around 3.3 to 3.5 μm after nine days at 4 °C. After 48 hours of storage, however, these increases were more modest, around 1.5 to 1.85 μm. After storage at 4 °C for 48 hours followed by 24 hours at room temperature, few particles exceeded 5 μm. It was found that the effect of particle aggregation caused by electrolytes demonstrates a critical concentration before the effect begins. For calcium and magnesium chlorides, the critical concentrations were 2.4 and 2.6 mmol/L, respectively. Sodium and potassium chloride had critical concentrations of 110 and 150 mmol/L, respectively. The rate of particle aggregation increased linearly with increasing electrolyte concentration. The quantity of emulsion in the mixture had a relatively small influence on stability, but higher concentrations exhibited a somewhat greater coalescence. (892)

Davis and Galloway noted that instability of the emulsion systems is manifested by (1) flocculation of oil droplets to form aggregates, producing a cream-like layer on top; or (2) coalescence of oil droplets, leading to an increase in the average droplet size and eventually a separation of free oil. The lowering of pH and the adding of electrolytes can adversely affect the mechanical and electrical properties at the oil–water interface, eventually leading to flocculation and coalescence. Amino acids act as buffering agents and provide a protective effect on emulsion stability. Adding electrolytes, especially the divalent ions Mg^{++} and Ca^{++} in excess of 2.5 mmol/L, to simple fat emulsions will cause flocculation. But in mixed parenteral nutrition solutions, the stability of the emulsion will be enhanced, depending on the quantity and nature of the amino acids present. The authors recommended a careful examination of emulsion mixtures for signs of instability prior to administration. (849)

Lawrence et al. reported good stability for an amino acid 4% (Travenol), dextrose 14%, and fat emulsion 4% (Pharmacia) parenteral nutrition solution. The solution also contained electrolytes, vitamins, and heparin sodium 4000 units/L. The aqueous solution was prepared first, with the fat emulsion added subsequently. This procedure allowed visual inspection of the aqueous phase and reduced the risk of emulsion breakdown by the divalent cations. Sample mixtures were stored at 18 to 25 and 3 to 8 °C for up to five days. They were evaluated visually and with a Coulter counter for particle size measurements. Both room temperature and refrigerated mixtures were stable for 48 hours. A marked increase in particle size was noted in the room temperature sample after 72 hours, but refrigeration delayed the changes. The authors' experience with over 1400 mixtures for administration to patients resulted in one emulsion creaming and another cracking, but the authors had no explanation for the failure of these particular emulsions. (848)

Turner reported on six parenteral nutrition solutions having various concentrations of amino acids, dextrose, soybean oil emulsion (Kabi-Vitrum), electrolytes, and multivitamins. All of the admixtures were stable for one week under refrigeration followed by 24 hours at room temperature, with no visible changes, changes in pH, or significant changes in particle size. (1013) However, other researchers questioned this interpretation of the results. (1014; 1015)

Iliano et al. reported that the addition of trace elements to a 3-in-1 parenteral nutrition solution with electrolytes had no adverse effect on the particle size of the fat emulsion after eight days of storage at 4 °C. (1017)

Harrie et al. reported on the stability of 3-in-1 parenteral nutrition solutions prepared with 500 ml of Intralipid 20% compared to Soyacal 20%, along with 500 or 1000 ml of FreAmine III 8.5% and 500 ml of dextrose 70%. Also present were relatively large amounts of electrolytes and other additives. All mixtures were similarly stable for 28 days at 4 °C followed by five days at 21 to 25 °C, with little change in the emulsion. A slight white cream layer appeared after five days at 4 °C but was easily redispersed with gentle agitation. The appearance of this cream layer did not statistically affect particle size distribution. The authors concluded that the emulsion mixture remained suitable for clinical use throughout the study period. The stability of other components was not evaluated. (1019)

Sayeed et al. reported on the stability of 3-in-1 parenteral nutrition admixtures prepared with Liposyn II 10 and 20%, Aminosyn pH 6, and dextrose along with electrolytes, trace metals, and vitamins. Thirty-one different combinations were evaluated. Samples were stored at: (1) 25 °C for one day, (2) 5 °C for two days followed by 30 °C for one day, and (3) 5 °C for nine days followed by 25 °C for one day. In all cases, there was no visual evidence of creaming, free oil droplets, and other signs of emulsion instability. Furthermore, little or no change in the particle size or zeta potential (electrostatic surface charge of lipid particles) was found, indicating emulsion stability. The dextrose and amino acids remained stable over the 10-day storage period. The greatest change of an amino acid occurred with tryptophan, which lost 6% in 10 days. Vitamin stability was not tested. (1025)

Hardy et al. reported on the stability of four parenteral nutrition admixtures, ranging from 1 L each of amino acids 5.5% (Travenol), dextrose 10%, and fat emulsion 10% (Travenol) up to a "worst case" of 1 L each of amino acids 10% with electrolytes (Travenol), dextrose 70%, and fat emulsion 10% (Travenol). The admixtures were stored for 48 hours at 5 to 9 °C followed by 24 hours at room temperature. There were no visible signs of creaming, flocculation, and free oil. The mean emulsion particle size remained within acceptable limits for all admixtures, and there were no significant changes in glucose, soybean oil, and amino acid concentrations. The authors noted that two factors were predominant in determining the stability of such admixtures: electrolyte concentrations and pH. (1065)

Hardy and Klim reported that several parenteral nutrition solutions containing amino acids (Travenol), glucose, and lipid, with and without electrolytes and trace elements, produced no visible flocculation or any significant change in mean emulsion particle size during 24 hours at room temperature. (1066)

Jeppsson and Sjoberg reported on the compatibility of 10 parenteral nutrition admixtures, evaluated over 96 hours while stored at 20 to 25 °C in both glass bottles and ethylene vinyl acetate bags. A slight creaming occurred in all admixtures, but the cream layer was easily redispersed with gentle shaking. No fat globules were visually apparent. The mean drop size was larger in the cream layer, but no globules were larger than 5 μm. Analyses of the concentrations of amino acids, dextrose, and electrolytes showed no changes over the study period. The authors concluded that such parenteral nutrition admixtures could be safely prepared as long as the component concentrations are within the following ranges (1067):

Vamin glucose or Vamin N (amino acids 7%)	1000 to 2000 ml
Dextrose 10 to 30%	100 to 550 ml
Intralipid 10 or 20%	500 to 1000 ml

Electrolyte (mmol/L)	
Sodium	20 to 70
Potassium	20 to 55
Calcium	2.3 to 2.9
Magnesium	1.1 to 3.1
Phosphorus	0 to 9.2
Chloride	27 to 71
Zinc	0.005 to 0.03

Parry et al. reported on the stability of eight parenteral nutrition admixtures with various ratios of amino acids, carbohydrates, and fat. FreAmine III 8.5%, dextrose 70%, and Soyacal 10 and 20% (mixed in ratios of 2:1:1, 1:1:1, 1:1:½, and 1:1:¼, where 1 = 500 ml) were evaluated. Additive concentrations were high to stress the admixtures and represent maximum doses likely to be encountered clinically:

Sodium acetate	150 mEq
Sodium chloride	210 mEq
Potassium acetate	45 mEq
Potassium chloride	90 mEq
Potassium phosphate	15 mM
Calcium gluconate	20 mEq
Magnesium sulfate	36 mEq
Trace elements	present
Folic acid	5 mg
M.V.I.-12	10 ml

The admixtures were stored at 4 °C for 14 days followed by four days at 22 to 25 °C. After 24 hours, all admixtures developed a thin white cream layer, which readily redispersed on gentle agitation. No free oil droplets were observed. The mean particle diameter remained near the original size of the Soyacal throughout the study. Few particles were larger than 3 μm. Osmolality and pH also remained relatively unchanged. (1068)

Bettner and Stennett had somewhat less success than others in preparing stable 3-in-1 parenteral nutrition admixtures with Aminosyn and Liposyn. Standard admixtures were prepared using Aminosyn 7% 1000 ml, dextrose 50% 1000 ml, and Liposyn 10% 500 ml. Concentrated admixtures were prepared using Aminosyn 10% 500 ml, dextrose 70% 500 ml, and Liposyn 20% 500 ml. Vitamins and trace elements were added to the admixtures along with the following electrolytes:

Electrolyte	Standard Admixture	Concentrated Admixture
Sodium	125 mEq	75 mEq
Potassium	95 mEq	74 mEq
Magnesium	25 mEq	25 mEq
Calcium	28 mEq	28 mEq
Phosphate	37 mM	36 mM
Chloride	83 mEq	50 mEq

Samples of each admixture were: (1) stored at 4 °C, (2) adjusted to pH 6.6 with sodium bicarbonate and stored at 4 °C, or (3) adjusted to pH 6.6 and stored at room temperature. The compatibility was evaluated for three weeks.

Visible signs of emulsion deterioration were evident by 96 hours in the standard admixture and by 48 hours in the concentrated admixture. Clear rings formed at the meniscus, becoming thicker, yellow, and oily over time. Free-floating oil was obvious in three weeks in the standard admixture and one week in the concentrated admixture. The samples adjusted to pH 6.6 developed visible deterioration later than the others. The authors indicated that pH may play a greater role than temperature in emulsion stability. However, precipitation (probably calcium phosphate and possibly carbonate) occurred in 36 hours in the pH 6.6 concentrated admixture but not the unadjusted (pH 5.5) samples. Mean particle counts increased for all samples over time but were greatest in the concentrated admixtures. The authors concluded that the concentrated admixtures were unsatisfactory for clinical use because of the early increase in particles and precipitation. Furthermore, they recommended that the standard admixtures be prepared immediately prior to use. (1069)

Barat et al. studied the physical stability of 10 parenteral nutrition admixtures with different amino acid sources. The admixtures contained 500 ml each of dextrose 70%, fat emulsion 20% (Alpha Therapeutic), and amino acids in various concentrations from each manufacturer. Also present were standard electrolytes, trace elements, and vitamins. The admixtures were stored for 14 days at 4 °C, followed by four days at 22 to 25 °C. Slight creaming was evident in all admixtures but redispersed easily with agitation. Emulsion particles were uniform in size, showing no tendency to aggregate. No cracked emulsions occurred. (1217)

Cripps (1218) and Davis and Galloway (1219) described the stability of parenteral nutrition solutions containing amino acids, dextrose, and fat emulsion along with electrolytes, trace elements, and vitamins. Cripps reported that the admixtures were stable for 24 hours at room temperature and for eight days at 4 °C. The visual appearance and particle size of the fat emulsion showed little change over the observation periods. (1218) Davis and Galloway reported variable stability periods, depending on electrolyte concentrations. Stability ranged from four to 25 days at room temperature. (1219)

Ang et al. studied the physical stability and clinical safety of a 3-in-1 parenteral nutrition admixture composed of amino acids (Cutter), dextrose, and fat emulsion (Cutter) plus electrolytes and vitamins. The admixture was physically stable for up to six weeks at 4 °C. Furthermore, continuous infusion to 25 adult patients did not result in any adverse reaction or abnormal laboratory parameter. (1220)

du Plesis et al. studied the effects of dilution, dextrose concentration, amino acids, and electrolytes on the physical stability of 3-in-1 parenteral nutrition admixtures prepared with Intralipid 10% or Travamulsion 10%. Travamulsion was affected by dilution up to 1:14, exhibiting an increase in mean particle size, while Intralipid remained virtually unchanged for 24 hours at 25 °C and for 72 hours at 4 °C. At dextrose concentrations above 15%, fat droplets larger than 5 μm formed during storage at either 4 °C or room temperature for 24 hours. The presence of amino acids increased the stability of the fat emulsions in the presence of dextrose. Fat droplets larger than 5 μm formed at a total electrolyte concentration above approximately 240 mmol/L (monovalent cation equivalent) for Travamulsion 10% and 156 mmol/L for Intralipid 10% in 24 hours at room temperature, although creaming or breaking of the emulsion was not observed visually. (1221)

Sayeed et al. evaluated the stability of 43 parenteral nutrition admixtures composed of various ratios of amino acid products, dextrose 10 to 70%, and four lipid emulsions 10 and 20% with electrolytes, trace elements, and vitamins. One group of admixtures included Travasol 5.5, 8.5, and 10%, FreAmine III 8.5 and 10%, Novamine 8.5 and 11.4%, Nephramine 5.4%, and RenAmine 6.5% with Liposyn II 10 and 20%. In another group, Aminosyn II 7, 8.5, and 10% was combined with Intralipid, Travamulsion, and Soyacal 10 and 20%. A third group was comprised of Aminosyn II 7, 8.5, and 10% with electrolytes combined with the latter three lipid emulsions. The admixtures were stored for 24 hours at 25 °C and for nine days at 5 °C followed by 24 hours at 25 °C. A few admixtures containing FreAmine III and Novamine with Liposyn II developed faint yellow streaks after 10 days of storage. The streaks readily dispersed with gentle shaking, as did the creaming present in most admixtures. Other properties such as pH, zeta-potential, and osmolality underwent little change in all of the admixtures. Particle size increased fourfold in one admixture (Novamine 8.5%, dextrose 50%, and Liposyn II in a 1:1:1 ratio), which the authors noted signaled the onset of particle coalescence. Nevertheless, the authors concluded that all of the admixtures were stable for the storage conditions and time periods tested. (1222)

Sayeed et al. also evaluated the stability of 24 parenteral nutrition admixtures composed of various ratios of Aminosyn II 7, 8.5, or 10%, dextrose, and Liposyn II 10 and 20% with electrolytes, trace elements, and vitamins. Four admixtures were stored for 24 hours at 25 °C, six admixtures were stored for two days at 5 °C followed by one day at 30 °C, and 14 admixtures were stored for nine days at 5 °C followed by one day at 25 °C. No visible instability was evident. Creaming was present in most admixtures but disappeared with gentle shaking. Other properties such as pH, zeta potential, particle size, and potency of the amino acids and dextrose showed little or no change during storage. (1223)

Tripp reported the emulsion stability of five parenteral nutrition formulas (TNA #126 through #130 in Appendix I) containing Liposyn II in concentrations ranging from 1.2 to 7.1%. The parenteral nutrition solutions were prepared using simultaneous pumping of the components into empty containers (as with the Nutrimix compounder) and sequential pumping of the components (as with Automix compounders). The solutions were stored for two days at 5 °C followed by 24 hours at 25 °C. Similar results were obtained for both methods of preparation using visual assessment and oil globule size distribution. (1426)

Tripp et al. evaluated the stability of 24 parenteral nutrition admixtures containing various concentrations of Aminosyn II, dextrose, and Liposyn II with a variety of electrolytes, trace elements, and multivitamins in dual-chamber, flexible, Nutrimix containers. No instability was visible in the admixtures stored at 25 °C for 24 hours or in those stored for nine days at 5 °C followed by 24 hours at 25 °C. Creaming was observed, but neither particle coalescence nor free oil was noted. The pH, particle size distribution, and amino acid and dextrose concentrations remained acceptable during the observation period. (1432)

Thomas studied two parenteral nutrition solutions composed of amino acids, dextrose 50%, fat emulsion (Intralipid) 20%, electrolytes, and vitamins. Their lipid particle sizes stayed within the manufacturer's range specifications when the solutions were stored at 23 or 4 °C and when frozen at −20 °C for 72 hours. (1488)

Bullock et al. evaluated the physical stability of 10 parenteral nutrition formulas (TNA #149 through #158 in Appendix I) containing TrophAmine and Intralipid 20%, Liposyn II 20%, and Nutrilipid 20% in varying concentrations with low and high electrolyte concentrations. All test formulas were prepared with an automatic compounder and protected from light. TNA #149 through #156 were stored for 48 hours at 4 °C followed by 24 hours at 21 °C; TNA #157 and #158 were stored for 24 hours at 4 °C followed by 24 hours at 21 °C. Although some minor creaming occurred in all formulas, it was completely reversible with agitation. No other changes were visible, and particle size analysis indicated little variation during the study period. The addition of cysteine HCl 1 g/25 g of amino acids, alone or with L-carnitine 16 mg/g fat, to TNA #157 and #158 did not adversely affect the physical stability of 3-in-1 admixtures within the study period. (1620)

Washington and Sizer evaluated the physical stability of five 3-in-1 parenteral nutrition solutions (TNA #167 through #171 in Appendix I) by visual observation, pH and osmolality determinations, and particle size distribution analysis. All five solutions were physically stable for 90 days at 4 °C. However, some irreversible flocculation occurred in all combinations after 180 days. (1651)

Tu et al. studied the stability of several parenteral nutrition formulas (TNA #159 through #166), with and without iron dextran 2 mg/L. All formulas were physically compatible both visually and microscopically for 48 hours at 4 and 25 °C, and particle size distribution remained unchanged. The order of mixing and deliberate agitation had no effect on physical compatibility. (1648)

Driscoll et al. evaluated the influence of six factors on the stability of fat emulsion in 45 different 3-in-1 parenteral nutrition mixtures. The factors evaluated were amino acid concentration (2.5 to 7%); dextrose concentration (5 to 20%); fat emulsion, intravenous, concentration (2 to 5%); monovalent cations (0 to 150 mEq/L); divalent cations (4 to 20 mEq/L); and trivalent cations from iron dextran (0 to 10 mg elemental iron/L). Although many formulations were unstable, visual examination could identify the instability in only 65% of these samples. Electronic particle size evaluation was required to identify the other unstable mixtures. Furthermore, only the concentration of trivalent ferric ions significantly and consistently affected emulsion stability during the 30-hour test. Of the parenteral nutrition mixtures containing iron dextran, 16% exhibited emulsion cracking. The authors suggested that iron dextran not be incorporated into 3-in-1 mixtures. (1814)

The drop size of 3-in-1 parenteral nutrition solutions in drip chambers is variable, being altered by the constituents of the mixture. In one study, multivitamins (Multibionta, E. Merck) caused the greatest reductions in drop size, up to 37%. This change may affect the rate of delivery if the flow is estimated from drops per minute. (1016) Similarly, flow rates delivered by infusion controllers dependent on predictable drop size may be inaccurate. Flow rates up to 29% less than expected have been reported. Therefore, variable pressure volumetric pumps, which are independent of drop size, should be used rather than infusion controllers. (1215)

Considerations and Recommendations — When multicomponent, 3-in-1, parenteral nutrition admixtures are used, the following points should be considered (490; 703; 892; 893; 1025; 1064; 1070; 1214; 1406; 1951; 2029; 2030; 2215; 2282; 2308):

1. The order of mixing is important. The amino acid solution should be added to either the fat emulsion or the dextrose before final mixing. This practice ensures the protective effect of the amino acids to emulsion disruption by changes in pH and the presence of electrolytes.
2. Electrolytes should not be added directly to the fat emulsions. Instead, they should be added to the amino acids or dextrose before the final mixing.
3. Such 3-in-1 admixtures containing electrolytes (especially divalent cations) are unstable and will eventually aggregate. The mixed systems should be carefully examined visually before use to ensure that a uniform emulsion still exists.
4. Avoid contact of 3-in-1 parenteral nutrition admixtures with heparin, which destabilizes and damages the fat emulsion upon contact. See Heparin section below.
5. The admixtures should be stored under refrigeration if not used immediately.
6. The ultimate stability of the admixtures will be the result of a complex interaction of pH, component concentrations, electrolyte concentrations, and, probably, storage temperature.

Furthermore, the use of a 1.2-μm filter to remove large lipid particles, electrolyte precipitates, and other solid particulates, aggregates, and *Candida albicans* contaminants has been recommended (1106; 1657; 1769; 2061; 2135; 2346), although others recommend a 5-μm filter to minimize the frequency of occlusion alarms. (569; 1951)

Blood Products — Amino acids injection should not be administered simultaneously with blood through the same infusion set because of possible pseudoagglutination. (341)

Calcium and Phosphate — UNRECOGNIZED CALCIUM PHOSPHATE PRECIPITATION IN A 3-IN-1 PARENTERAL NUTRITION MIXTURE RESULTED IN PATIENT DEATH.

The potential for the formation of a calcium phosphate precipitate in parenteral nutrition solutions is well studied and documented (1771; 1777), but the information is complex and difficult to apply to the clinical situation. (1770; 1772; 1777) The incorporation of fat emulsion in 3-in-1 parenteral nutrition solutions obscures any precipitate that may be present, which has led to substantial debate about the dangers associated with 3-in-1 parenteral nutrition mixtures and when or if the danger to the patient is warranted therapeutically. (1770; 1771; 1772; 2031–2036) Because such precipitation may be life threatening to patients (2037; 2291), the Food and Drug Administration issued a Safety Alert containing the following recommendations (1769):

"1. The amounts of phosphorus and of calcium added to the admixture are critical. The solubility of the added calcium should be calculated from the volume at the time the calcium is added. It should not be based upon the final volume.

Some amino acid injections for TPN admixtures contain phosphate ions (as a phosphoric acid buffer). These phosphate ions and the volume at the time the phosphate is added should be considered when calculating the concentration of phosphate additives. Also, when adding calcium and phosphate to an admixture, the phosphate should be added first.

The line should be flushed between the addition of any potentially incompatible components.

2. A lipid emulsion in a three-in-one admixture obscures the presence of a precipitate. Therefore, if a lipid emulsion is needed, either (1) use a two-in-one admixture with the lipid infused separately, or (2) if a three-in-one admixture is medically necessary, then add the calcium before the lipid emulsion and according to the recommendations in number 1 above.

If the amount of calcium or phosphate which must be added is likely to cause a precipitate, some or all of the calcium should be administered separately. Such separate infusions must be properly diluted and slowly infused to avoid serious adverse events related to the calcium.

3. When using an automated compounding device, the above steps should be considered when programming the device. In addition, automated compounders should be maintained and operated according to the manufacturer's recommendations.

Any printout should be checked against the programmed admixture and weight of components.

4. During the mixing process, pharmacists who mix parenteral nutrition admixtures should periodically agitate the admixture and check for precipitates. Medical or home care personnel who start and monitor these infusions should carefully inspect for the presence of precipitates both before and during infusion. Patients and care givers should be trained to visually inspect for signs of precipitation. They also should be advised to stop the infusion and seek medical assistance if precipitates are noted.

5. A filter should be used when infusing either central or peripheral parenteral nutrition admixtures. At this time, data have not been submitted to document which size filter is most effective in trapping precipitates.

Standards of practice vary, but the following is suggested: a 1.2-μm air-eliminating filter for lipid-containing admixtures and a 0.22-μm air-eliminating filter for non-lipid-containing admixtures.

6. Parenteral nutrition admixtures should be administered within the following time frames: if stored at room temperature, the infusion should be started within 24 hours after mixing; if stored at refrigerated temperatures, the infusion should be started within 24 hours of rewarming. Because warming parenteral nutrition admixtures may contribute to the formation of precipitates, once administration begins, care should be taken to avoid excessive warming of the admixture.

Persons administering home care parenteral nutrition admixtures may need to deviate from these time frames. Pharmacists who initially prepare these admixtures should check a reserve sample for precipitates over the duration and under the conditions of storage.

7. If symptoms of acute respiratory distress, pulmonary emboli, or interstitial pneumonitis develop, the infusion should be stopped immediately and thoroughly checked for precipitates. Appropriate medical interventions should be instituted. Home care personnel and patients should immediately seek medical assistance."

Calcium Phosphate Precipitation Fatalities—Hill et al. reported fatal cases of paroxysmal respiratory failure in two previously healthy women receiving peripheral vein parenteral nutrition. The patients experienced sudden cardiopulmonary arrest consistent with pulmonary emboli. The authors used in vitro simulations and an animal model to conclude that unrecognized calcium phosphate precipitation in a 3-in-1 total nutrition admixture caused the fatalities. The precipitation resulted during compounding by introducing calcium and phosphate near to one another in the compounding sequence and prior to complete fluid addition. This resulted in a temporarily high concentration of the drugs and precipitation of calcium phosphate. Observation of the precipitate was obscured by the incorporation of 20% fat emulsion, intravenous into the nutrition mixture. No filter was used during infusion of the fatal nutrition admixtures. (2037)

In a follow-up retrospective review, Shay et al. reported that a total of five patients were identified that had respiratory distress associated with the infusion of the 3-in-1 admixtures at around the same time. Four of these five patients died, although the cause of death could be definitively determined for only two. (2291)

Calcium and Phosphate Conditional Compatibility—Calcium salts are conditionally compatible with phosphate in parenteral nutrition solutions. The incompatibility is dependent on a solubility and concentration phenomenon and is not entirely predictable. Precipitation may occur during compounding or at some time after compounding is completed.

NOTE: Some amino acids solutions inherently contain calcium and phosphate, which must be considered in any projection of compatibility. See Table 1.

It also was noted that the order of mixing of calcium gluconate and potassium phosphate may affect compatibility at elevated concentrations. Addition of potassium phosphate should precede that of calcium gluconate. (313)

A study by Henry et al. (608) determined the maximum concentrations of calcium (as chloride and gluconate) and phosphate that can be maintained without precipitation in a parenteral nutrition solution consisting of FreAmine II 4.25% and dextrose 25% for 24 hours at 30 °C. Their results are depicted in Figure 1.

Henry et al. noted that the amino acids in parenteral nutrition solutions form soluble complexes with calcium and phosphate, reducing the available free calcium and phosphate that can form insoluble precipitates. The concentration of calcium available for precipitation is greater with the chloride salt compared to the gluconate salt, at least in part because of differences in dissociation characteristics. This can be seen in Figure 1 by the greater concentration of calcium gluconate that can be mixed with sodium phosphate. (608)

In addition to the concentrations of phosphate and calcium and the salt form of the calcium, Henry et al. noted that the concentration of amino acids and the time and temperature of storage altered the formation of calcium phosphate in parenteral nutrition solutions. As the temperature was increased, the incidence of precipitate formation also increased. This finding was attributed, at least in part, to a greater degree of dissociation of the calcium and phosphate complexes and the decreased solubility of calcium phosphate. Therefore, a solution

Figure 1. Maximum solubilities of calcium chloride (○) and calcium gluconcate (△) with sodium phosphate in an amino acid 4.25% –dextrose 25% solution at 30 °C

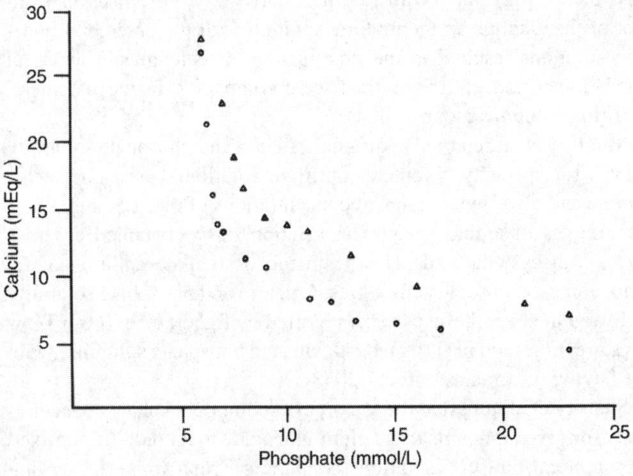

possibly may be stored at 4 °C with no precipitation, but on warming to room temperature a precipitate will form over time. (608)

Eggert et al. (609) evaluated the compatibility of calcium and phosphate in several parenteral nutrition formulas for newborn infants. Calcium gluconate 10% (Cutter) and potassium phosphate (Abbott) were used to achieve concentrations of 2.5 to 100 mEq/L of calcium and 2.5 to 100 mmol/L of phosphorus added. The parenteral nutrition solutions evaluated were as shown in Table 3. The results were reported as graphic depictions.

Eggert et al. noted the pH dependence of the phosphate–calcium precipitation. Dibasic calcium phosphate is very insoluble, while monobasic calcium phosphate is relatively soluble. At low pH, the soluble monobasic form predominates; but as the pH increases, more dibasic phosphate becomes available to bind with calcium and precipitate. Therefore, the lower the pH of the parenteral nutrition solution, the more calcium and phosphate can be solubilized. Once again, the effects of temperature were observed. As the temperature is increased, more calcium ion becomes available and more dibasic calcium phosphate is formed. Therefore, temperature increases will increase the amount of precipitate. (609)

Fitzgerald and MacKay reported similar calcium and phosphate solubility curves for neonatal parenteral nutrition solutions using TrophAmine (McGaw) 2, 1.5, and 0.8% as the sources of amino acids. The solutions also contained dextrose 10%, with cysteine and pH adjustment being used in some admixtures. Calcium and phosphate solubility followed the patterns reported by Eggert et al. (609) A slightly greater concentration of phosphate could be used in some mixtures, but this finding was not consistent. (1024)

Using a similar study design, Fitzgerald and MacKay also studied six neonatal parenteral nutrition solutions based on Aminosyn-PF

Table 3. Parenteral Nutrition Solutions Used by Eggert et al. (609)

	Solution Number			
Component	#1	#2	#3	#4
FreAmine III	4%	2%	1%	1%
Dextrose	25%	20%	10%	10%
pH	6.3	6.4	6.6	7.0[a]

[a]*Adjusted with sodium hydroxide.*

(Abbott) 2, 1.5, and 0.8%, with and without added cysteine HCl and dextrose 10%. Calcium concentrations ranged from 2.5 to 50 mEq/L, and phosphate concentrations ranged from 2.5 to 50 mmol/L. Solutions sat for 18 hours at 25 °C and then were warmed to 37 °C in a water bath to simulate the clinical situation of warming prior to infusion into a child. Solubility curves were markedly different than those for TrophAmine in the previous study. (1024) Solubilities were reported to decrease by 15 mEq/L for calcium and 15 mmol/L for phosphate. The solutions remained clear during room temperature storage, but crystals often formed on warming to 37 °C. (1211)

However, these data were questioned by Mikrut, who noted the similarities between the Aminosyn-PF and TrophAmine products and found little difference in calcium and phosphate solubilities in a preliminary report. (1212) In the full report (1213), parenteral nutrition solutions containing Aminosyn-PF or TrophAmine 1 or 2.5% with dextrose 10 or 25%, respectively, plus electrolytes and trace metals, with or without cysteine HCl, were evaluated under the same conditions used by Fitzgerald and MacKay. Calcium concentrations ranged from 2.5 to 50 mEq/L, and phosphate concentrations ranged from 5 to 50 mmol/L. In contrast to the results of Fitzgerald and MacKay, the solubility curves were very similar for the Aminosyn-PF and TrophAmine parenteral nutrition solutions but very different from those of the previous Aminosyn-PF study. (1211) The authors again showed that the solubility of calcium and phosphate is greater in solutions containing higher concentrations of amino acids and dextrose. (1213)

Dunham et al. also reported calcium and phosphate solubility curves for TrophAmine 1 and 2% with dextrose 10% and electrolytes, vitamins, heparin, and trace elements. Calcium concentrations ranged from 10 to 60 mEq/L, and phosphorus concentrations ranged from 10 to 40 mmol/L. Calcium and phosphate solubilities were assessed by analysis of the calcium concentrations and followed patterns similar to those reported by Henry et al. (608) and Eggert et al. (609) The higher percentage of amino acids (TrophAmine 2%) permitted a slightly greater solubility of calcium and phosphate, especially in the 10 to 50-mEq/L and 10 to 35-mmol/L ranges, respectively. (1614)

Knight et al. reported the maximal product of the amount of calcium (as gluconate) times phosphate (as potassium) that can be added to a parenteral nutrition solution, composed of amino acids 1% (Travenol) and dextrose 10%, for preterm infants. Turbidity was observed on initial mixing when the solubility product was around 115 to 130 $mmol^2$ or greater. After storage at 7 °C for 20 hours, visible precipitates formed at solubility products of 130 $mmol^2$ or greater. If the solution was administered through a barium-impregnated silicone rubber catheter, crystalline precipitates obstructed the catheters in 12 hours at a solubility product of 100 $mmol^2$ and in 10 days at 79 $mmol^2$, much lower than the in vitro results. (1041)

Poole et al. determined the solubility characteristics of calcium and phosphate in pediatric parenteral nutrition solutions composed of Aminosyn 0.5, 2, and 4% with dextrose 10 to 25%. Also present were electrolytes and vitamins. Sodium phosphate was added sequentially in phosphorus concentrations from 10 to 30 mmol/L. Calcium gluconate was added last in amounts ranging from 1 to 10 g/L. The solutions were stored at 25 °C for 30 hours and examined visually and microscopically for precipitation. The authors found that higher concentrations of Aminosyn increased the solubility of calcium and phosphate. Precipitation occurred at lower calcium and phosphate concentrations in the 0.5% solution compared to the 2 and 4% solutions. For example, at a phosphorus concentration of 30 mmol/L, precipitation occurred at calcium gluconate concentrations of about

1, 2, and 4 g/L in the 0.5, 2, and 4% Aminosyn mixtures, respectively. Similarly, at a calcium gluconate concentration of 8 g/L and above, precipitation occurred at phosphorus concentrations of about 13, 17, and 22 mmol/L in the 0.5, 2, and 4% solutions, respectively. The dextrose concentration did not appear to affect the calcium and phosphate solubility significantly. (1042)

Alexander and Arena evaluated the compatibility of calcium gluconate (American Quinine) and potassium phosphate (Lyphomed) in a parenteral nutrition solution, composed of dextrose 12.5% and amino acid injection (FreAmine III, McGaw) 1.33% and having a pH of 6.6, for premature infants. Potassium phosphate was added in varying amounts to samples of this solution. The samples were then titrated with calcium gluconate 10%. From the resulting data, an equation was derived to predict when precipitation would occur:

$$Y = -0.455X + 2.951$$

where Y is the Log_{10} of the calcium gluconate concentration (as mg/100 ml) and X is the phosphate concentration (as mmol/100 ml). The equation can be solved to determine the maximum concentration of calcium gluconate for a given phosphate concentration or vice versa. If either additive is sufficiently dilute, then the other can be added in high concentrations without precipitation occurring, obviating the need for the equation. These lower limits were set at 60 mg/100 ml for calcium gluconate and 0.6 mmol/100 ml for phosphate. (1004)

While the authors noted that this equation technically applies to the specific solution being tested and that other variables such as temperature can affect precipitation, in practice they found it applicable to a variety of parenteral nutrition solutions, having similar components and pH values, for premature infants. The equation is *not* applicable to parenteral nutrition solutions with amino acid and dextrose concentrations, other components, or pH values that are much different. (1004)

Venkaraman et al. evaluated the solubility of calcium and phosphorus in neonatal parenteral nutrition solutions composed of amino acids (Abbott) 1.25 and 2.5% with dextrose 5 and 10%, respectively. Also present were multivitamins and trace elements. The solutions contained calcium (as gluconate) in amounts ranging from 25 to 200 mg/100 ml. The phosphorus (as potassium phosphate) concentrations evaluated ranged from 25 to 150 mg/100 ml. If calcium gluconate was added first, cloudiness occurred immediately. If potassium phosphate was added first, substantial quantities could be added with no precipitate formation in 48 hours at 4 °C (Table 4). However, if stored at 22 °C, the solutions were stable for only 24 hours, and all contained precipitates after 48 hours. (1210)

Kirkpatrick et al. reported the physical compatibility of calcium gluconate 10 to 40 mEq/L and potassium phosphates 10 to 40 mmol/L in three neonatal parenteral nutrition solutions (TPN #123 to #125 in Appendix I), alone and with retrograde administration of aminophylline 7.5 mg diluted with 1.5 ml of sterile water for injection. Contact of the alkaline aminophylline solution with the parenteral nutrition solutions resulted in the precipitation of calcium phosphate at much lower concentrations than were compatible in the parenteral nutrition solutions alone. (1404)

MacKay et al. reported additional calcium and phosphate solubility curves for specialty parenteral nutrition solutions based on NephrAmine and also HepatAmine at concentrations of 0.8, 1.5, and 2% as the sources of amino acids. The solutions also contained dextrose 10%, with cysteine and pH adjustment to simulate addition of fat emulsion used in some admixtures. Calcium and phosphate solubility followed the hyperbolic patterns reported by Eggert et al. (609) Temperature, time, and pH affected calcium and phosphate solubility, with pH having the greatest effect. (2038)

Shatsky et al. reported the maximum sodium phosphate concentrations for given amounts of calcium gluconate that could be admixed in parenteral nutrition solutions containing TrophAmine in varying quantities (with cysteine HCl 40 mg/g of amino acid) and dextrose 10%. The solutions also contained magnesium sulfate 4 mEq/L, potassium acetate 24 mEq/L, sodium chloride 32 mEq/L, pediatric multivitamins, and trace elements. The presence of cysteine HCl reduces the solution pH and increases the amount of calcium and phosphate that can be incorporated before precipitation occurs. The results of this study cannot be safely extrapolated to TPN solutions with compositions other than the ones tested. The admixtures were compounded with the sodium phosphate added last after thorough mixing of all other components. The authors noted that this is not the preferred order of mixing (usually phosphate is added first and thoroughly mixed before adding calcium last); however, they believed this reversed order of mixing would provide a margin of error in cases in which the proper order is not followed. After compounding, the solutions were stored for 24 hours at 40 °C. The maximum calcium and phosphate amounts that could be mixed in the various solutions were reported tabularly and are shown in Table 5. (2039) However, these results are not entirely consistent with the study of Hoie and Narducci. (2196) See below.

The temperature dependence of the calcium–phosphate precipitation has resulted in the occlusion of a subclavian catheter by a solution apparently free of precipitation. The parenteral nutrition solution consisted of FreAmine III 500 ml, dextrose 70% 500 ml, sodium chloride 50 mEq, sodium phosphate 40 mmol, potassium acetate 10 mEq, potassium phosphate 40 mmol, calcium gluconate 10 mEq, magnesium sulfate 10 mEq, and Shil's trace metals solution 1 ml. Although there

Table 4. Maximum Calcium and Phosphorus Concentrations Physically Compatible for 48 Hours at 4 °C (1210)

	Phosphorus (mg/100 ml)	
Calcium (mg/100 ml)	Amino Acids 1.25% + Dextrose 5%[a]	Amino Acids 2.5% + Dextrose 10%[a]
200[b]	50	75
150	50	100
100	75	100
50	100	125
25	150[b]	150[b]

[a]*Plus multivitamins and trace elements.*
[b]*Maximum concentration tested.*

Table 5. Maximum Amount of Phosphate (as Sodium) (mmol/L) Not Resulting in Precipitation According to the Study of Shatsky et al. (2039) See CAUTION Below.[a]

	Amino Acid (as TrophAmine) plus Cysteine HCl 40 mg/g Amino Acid				
Calcium (as gluconate)	0%	0.4%	1%	2%	3%
9.8 mEq/L	0	27	42	60	66
14.7 mEq/L	0	15	18	30	36
19.6 mEq/L	0	6	15	27	30
29.4 mEq/L	0	3	6	21	24

[a]*CAUTION: The results cannot be safely extrapolated to solutions with formulas other than the ones tested. See text.*

was no evidence of precipitation in the bottle, tubing and pump cassette, and filter (all at approximately 26 °C) during administration, the occluded catheter and Vicra Loop Lock (next to the patient's body at 37 °C) had numerous crystals identified as calcium phosphate. In vitro, this parenteral nutrition solution had a precipitate in 12 hours at 37 °C but was clear for 24 hours at 26 °C. (610)

Similarly, a parenteral nutrition solution that was clear and free of particulates after two weeks under refrigeration developed a precipitate in four to six hours when stored at room temperature. When the solution was warmed in a 37 °C water bath, precipitation occurred in one hour. Administration of the solution before the precipitate was noticed led to interstitial pneumonitis due to deposition of calcium phosphate crystals. (1427)

Koorenhof and Timmer reported the maximum allowable concentrations of calcium and phosphate in a 3-in-1 parenteral nutrition mixture for children (TNA #192 in Appendix I). Added calcium was varied from 1.5 to 150 mmol/L, and added phosphate was varied from 21 to 300 mmol/L. These mixtures were stable for 48 hours at 22 and 37 °C as long as the pH was not greater than 5.7, the calcium concentration was below 16 mmol/L, the phosphate concentration was below 52 mmol/L, and the product of the calcium and phosphate concentrations was below 250 $mmol^2/L^2$. (1773)

Fausel et al. evaluated calcium phosphate precipitation phenomena in a series of parenteral nutrition admixtures composed of dextrose 22%, amino acids (FreAmine III) 2.7%, and fat emulsion (Abbott) 0, 1, and 3.2%. Incorporation of calcium gluconate 19 to 24 mEq/L and phosphate (as sodium) 22 to 28 mmol/L resulted in visible precipitation in the fat-free admixtures. New precipitate continued to form over 14 days, even after repeated filtrations of the solutions through 0.2-μm filters. The presence of the amino acids increased calcium and phosphate solubility, compared with simple aqueous solutions. However, the incorporation of the fat emulsion did not result in a statistically significant increase in calcium and phosphate solubility. The authors noted that the kinetics of calcium phosphate precipitate formation do not appear to be entirely predictable; both transient and permanent precipitation can occur either during the compounding process or at some time afterward. Because calcium phosphate precipitation can be very dangerous clinically, the use of inline filters was recommended. The authors suggested that the filters should have a porosity appropriate to the parenteral nutrition admixture—1.2 μm for fat-containing and 0.2 or 0.45 μm for fat-free nutrition mixtures. (2061)

Hoie and Narducci used laser particle analysis to evaluate the formation of calcium phosphate precipitation in pediatric TPN solutions containing TrophAmine in concentrations ranging from 0.5 to 3% with dextrose 10% and also containing L-cysteine HCl 1 g/L. The solutions also contained in each liter sodium chloride 20 mEq, sodium acetate 20 mEq, magnesium sulfate 3 mEq, trace elements 3 ml, and heparin sodium 500 units. The presence of L-cysteine HCl reduces the solution pH and increases the amount of calcium and phosphate that can be incorporated before precipitation occurs. The results of this study cannot be safely extrapolated to TPN solutions with compositions other than the ones tested. The maximum amount of phosphate that was incorporated without the appearance of a measurable increase in particulates in 24 hours at 37 °C for each of the amino acids concentrations is shown in Table 6. (2196) These results are not entirely consistent with those of Shatsky et al. See above. The use of more sensitive electronic particle measurement for the formation of subvisual particulates in this study may contribute to the differences in the results.

Zhang et al. evaluated calcium and phosphate compatibility in a series of parenteral nutrition admixtures composed of Aminosyn II in concentrations ranging from 2% up to 5% (TPN #227 to #231 in Appendix I). The solutions also contained dextrose ranging from 10% up to 25%. Also present were sodium chloride, potassium chloride, and magnesium sulfate in common amounts. Phosphates as the potassium salt and calcium as the acetate salt were added in variable quantities to determine the maximum amounts of calcium and phosphates that could be added to the representative TPN admixtures. The samples were evaluated at 23 and 37 °C over 48 hours by visual inspection in ambient light and using a Tyndall beam and electronically measured for turbidity and microparticulates. The boundaries between the compatible and incompatible concentrations were presented graphically as hyperbolic curves. (2265)

Table 6. Maximum Amount of Phosphate (as Potassium) (mmol/L) Not Resulting in Precipitation According to the Study of Hoie and Narducci. (2196) See CAUTION Below.[a]

Calcium (as Gluconate) (mEq/L)	Amino Acid (as TrophAmine) plus Cysteine HCl 1 g/L					
	0.5%	1%	1.5%	2%	2.5%	3%
10	22	28	38	38	38	43
14	18	18	18	38	38	43
19	18	18	18	33	33	38
24	12	18	18	22	28	28
28	12	18	18	18	18	18
33	12	12	12	12	12	12
37	12	12	12	12	12	12
41	9	9	9	12	12	12
45	0	9	9	12	12	12
49	0	9	9	9	12	12
53	0	9	9	9	9	9

[a]*CAUTION: The results cannot be safely extrapolated to solutions with formulas other than the ones tested. See text.*

The presence of magnesium in solutions may also influence the reaction between calcium and phosphate, including the nature and extent of precipitation. (158; 159)

The interaction of calcium and phosphate in parenteral nutrition solutions is a complex phenomenon. Various factors play a role in the solubility or precipitation of a given combination, including (608; 609; 1042; 1063; 1427; 2038; 2039; 2061):

1. Concentration of calcium
2. Salt form of calcium
3. Concentration of phosphate
4. Concentration of amino acids
5. Amino acids composition
6. Concentration of dextrose
7. Temperature of solution
8. pH of solution
9. Presence of other additives
10. Order of mixing

Enhanced precipitate formation would be expected from such factors as high concentrations of calcium and phosphate, increases in solution pH, decreased amino acid concentrations, increases in temperature, addition of calcium prior to the phosphate, lengthy standing times or slow infusion rates, and use of calcium as the chloride salt. (854)

Even if precipitation does not occur in the bottle, it has been reported that crystallization of calcium phosphate may occur in a Silastic infusion pump chamber or tubing if the rate of administration is slow, as for premature infants. Water vapor may be transmitted outward and be replaced by air rapidly enough to produce supersaturation. (202) Several other cases of catheter occlusion also have been reported. (610; 1427–1429)

The UV spectrum of an equal parts mixture of amino acids 8%–dextrose 50% solution was not altered in 24 hours at 22 °C by the addition of calcium gluconate 20 mEq and potassium phosphate 25 mEq. (313)

Vitamins — As might be expected, vitamin stability has been found to be better during nighttime when compared to daytime because of the influence of photodecomposition. (2307)

Howard et al. reported on a patient receiving 3000 I.U. of retinol daily in a parenteral nutrition solution; nevertheless, this patient experienced two episodes of night blindness. The pharmacy prepared the parenteral nutrition solution in 1-L PVC bags in weekly batches and stored them at 4 °C in the dark until use. A subsequent in vitro study showed losses of vitamin A of 23 and 77% in three- and 14-day periods, respectively, under these conditions. About 30% of the lost vitamin A could be extracted from the PVC bag. (1038)

Shenai et al. reported on losses of vitamin A from multivitamins (USV) in a neonatal parenteral nutrition solution. The solution was prepared in colorless glass bottles and run through an administration set with a burette (Travenol). The total loss of vitamin A was 75% in 24 hours, with about 16% as decomposition in the glass bottle. The decomposition was not noticeable during the first 12 hours, but then vitamin A levels fell rather precipitously to about one-third of the initial amount. The balance of the loss, averaging about 59%, occurred during transit through the administration set. Removal of the inline filter and treatment of the set with albumin human had no effect on vitamin A delivery. The authors recommended a three- to fourfold increase in the amount of vitamin A to compensate for the losses. (1039)

Kishi et al. reported on a parenteral nutrition solution in glass bottles exposed to sunlight. Vitamin A decomposed rapidly, losing more than 50% in three hours. The decomposition could be slowed by covering the bottle with a light-resistant vinyl bag, resulting in about a 25% loss in three hours. (1040)

Kishi et al. also reported that vitamin E was stable in the parenteral nutrition solution in glass bottles exposed to sunlight, with no loss occurring during six hours of exposure. (1040)

McKenna and Bieri reported that 40% retinol losses occurred in two hours and 60% in five hours from parenteral nutrition solutions pumped at 10 ml/hr through standard infusion sets at room temperature. The retinol concentration in the bottle remained constant while the retinol in the effluent decreased. Antioxidants had no effect. Much of the vitamin A was recoverable from hexane washings of the tubing. (1050)

No loss of vitamin A to PVC delivery systems of *enteral* feeding solutions, after six hours of storage without protection from light and with exposure to ambient temperature, was reported by Bryant and Neufeld. The authors attributed this result to the presence of other (undefined) substances in the enteral feeding mixtures. (1051)

Gillis et al. evaluated the delivery of vitamins A, D, and E from a parenteral nutrition solution composed of amino acids 3% solution (Pharmacia) in dextrose 10% with electrolytes, trace elements, vitamin K, folate, and vitamin B_{12}. To this solution was added 6 ml of multivitamin infusion (USV). The solution was prepared in PVC bags (Travenol), and administration was simulated through a fluid chamber (Buretrol) and infusion tubing with a 0.5-μm filter at 10 ml/hr. During the first 60 to 90 minutes, minimal delivery of the vitamins occurred. This was followed by a rise and plateau in the delivered vitamins, which were attributed to an increasing saturation of adsorptive binding sites in the tubing. Total amounts delivered over 24 hours were 31% for vitamin A, 68% for vitamin D, and 64% for vitamin E. Sorption of the vitamins was found in the PVC bag, fluid chamber, and tubing. Decomposition was not a factor. (836)

Allwood found that vitamin A was rapidly and significantly decomposed when exposed to daylight. The extent and rate of loss were dependent on the degree of exposure to daylight which, in turn, depended on various factors such as the direction of the radiation, time of day, and climatic conditions. Delivery of less than 10% of the expected amount was reported. (1047) In controlled light experiments, the decomposition initially progressed exponentially. Subsequently, the rate of decomposition slowed. This result was attributed to a protective effect of the degradation products on the remaining vitamin A. The presence of amino acids provided greater protection. Compared to degradation rates in dextrose 5% in water, decomposition was reduced by up to 50% in some amino acid mixtures. (1048)

In a parenteral nutrition solution composed of amino acids, dextrose, electrolytes, trace elements, and multivitamins in PVC bags stored at 4 and 25 °C, vitamin A rapidly deteriorated to 10% of the initial concentration in eight hours at 25 °C while exposed to light. The decomposition was slowed by light protection and refrigeration, with a loss of about 25% in four days. Folic acid concentration dropped 40% initially on admixture and then remained relatively constant for 28 days of storage. About 35% of the ascorbic acid was lost in 39 hours at 25 °C with exposure to light. The loss was reduced to a negligible amount in four days by refrigeration and light protection. Thiamine content dropped by about 50% initially but then remained unchanged over 120 hours of storage. (1063)

Riggle et al. noted a 50% loss of vitamin A from a bottle of parenteral nutrition solution prepared with multivitamin infusion (USV) after 5.5 hours of infusion. The amount delivered through an Ivex-2 filter set was only 6.3% of the added amount. Similar quantities were found after 20 hours of infusion. A reduced light exposure and use of ^{3}H-labeled vitamin A confirmed binding to the infusion bottles and tubing. (704)

Subsequently, Riggle and Brandt incubated solutions containing multivitamins (USV) spiked with ^{3}H-labeled retinol in intravenous tubing protected from light and agitated to simulate flow for five hours. About half of the vitamin A was lost in 30 minutes, and 88 to 96% was lost in five hours. Spectrophotometric assays correlated closely with the radioisotope assays. Hexane rinses and radioactivity determinations on the tubing accounted for the decrease in radioactivity. (1049)

In another experiment, neonatal parenteral nutrition solutions containing multivitamins prepared in bags were delivered at 10 ml/hr through Buretrol sets (Travenol). The bags and sets were protected from light. Spectrophotometric and radioisotope assays showed that about 26% of the vitamin A was lost before the flow was started. At 10 ml/hr, about 67% was lost from the effluent. More rapid flow reduced the extent of loss. Analysis of clinical samples of parenteral nutrition solutions showed losses of 21 to 57% after 20 hours. Because losses after five hours were of the same magnitude, the authors concluded that the loss occurs fairly rapidly and is not due to gradual decomposition. (1049)

The quantity of retinol delivered from an M.V.I.-containing 2-in-1 parenteral nutrition solution and when M.V.I. was added to Intralipid 10% was evaluated during simulated administration through a PVC administration set. The parenteral nutrition solution was composed of amino acids 2.8%, dextrose 10%, and standard electrolytes; M.V.I. was added to yield a nominal retinol concentration of 455 μg/150 ml. Retinol losses were about 80% of the admixed amount after being delivered through the PVC set. When M.V.I. was added to Intralipid 10% in a retinol concentration of 455 μg/20 ml, retinol losses were reduced to about 10% of the admixed amount. As in the study by Bluhm et al. (1607), the fat emulsion provides retinol protection from sorption to the PVC administration set. (2027)

Substantially higher amounts of retinol were found to be delivered using polyolefin administration set tubing when compared with PVC tubing during simulated neonatal intensive care administration. Retinol was added to a 2-in-1 parenteral nutrition solution (TPN #206) in concentrations of 25 and 50 I.U./ml and run at 4 and 10 ml/hr through three meter lengths of polyolefin (MiniMed) and PVC (Baxter) intravenous extension set tubing protected from light and passed through a 37 °C water bath. Using HPLC analysis, delivered quantities of retinol varied from 19 to 74% through the PVC tubing and 47 to 87% through the polyolefin tubing. The authors noted that the loss of retinol to the PVC tubing appeared to be saturable. Even so, the use of polyolefin tubing increases the amount of retinol delivered during simulated neonatal administration. (2028)

Billion-Rey et al. reported substantial loss by HPLC analysis of retinol all-*trans* palmitate and phytonadione from both TPN and TNA admixtures due to exposure to sunlight. In three hours of exposure to sunlight, essentially total loss of retinol and 50% loss of phytonadione had occurred. The presence or absence of lipids did not affect stability. In contrast, tocopherol concentrations remained essentially unchanged by exposure to sunlight through 12 hours. The container material used to store the nutrition admixtures affected the concentration of the vitamins as well. Losses were greatest (10 to 25%) in PVC containers and were slightly better in EVA and glass containers. (2049)

McGee et al. evaluated the stability of vitamin E (alpha-tocopherol acetate from M.V.I.-1000 or Soluzyme) and selenium (from Selepen) in amino acids (Abbott) and dextrose in PVC bags. Exposure to fluorescent light and room temperature (23 °C) for 24 hours and simulated infusion at 50 ml/hr for eight hours through a Medlon TPN administration set with a 0.22-μm filter did not affect the concentrations of vitamin E and selenium. (1224)

Dahl et al. reported the stability of numerous vitamins in parenteral nutrition solutions composed of amino acids (Kabi-Vitrum), dextrose 30%, and fat emulsion 20% (Kabi-Vitrum) in a 2:1:1 ratio with electrolytes, trace elements, and both fat- and water-soluble vitamins. The admixtures were stored in darkness at 2 to 8 °C for 96 hours with no significant loss of retinyl palmitate, alpha-tocopherol, thiamine mononitrate, sodium riboflavin-5′-phosphate, pyridoxine HCl, nicotinamide, folic acid, biotin, sodium pantothenate, and cyanocobalamin. Sodium ascorbate and its biologically active degradation product, dehydroascorbic acid, totaled 59 and 42% of the nominal starting concentration at 24 and 96 hours, respectively. However, the actual initial concentration was only 66% of the nominal concentration. (1225)

When the admixture was subjected to simulated infusion over 24 hours at 20 °C, either exposed to room light or light protected, or stored for six days in the dark under refrigeration and then subjected to the same simulated infusion, once again the retinyl palmitate, alpha-tocopherol, and sodium riboflavin-5′-phosphate did not undergo significant loss. However, sodium ascorbate and its degradation product, dehydroascorbic acid, had initial combined concentrations of 51 to 65% of the nominal initial concentration, with further declines during infusion. Light protection did not significantly alter the loss of total ascorbic acid. (1225)

Smith et al. reported the stability of several vitamins from M.V.I.-12 (Armour) admixed in parenteral nutrition solutions composed of different amino acid products, with or without Intralipid 10%, when stored in glass bottles and PVC bags at 25 and 5 °C for 48 hours. Riboflavin, folic acid, and vitamin E were stable in all samples. No vitamin A was lost in any formula in glass bottles, but samples in PVC containers lost as much as 35 and 60% at 5 and 25 °C, respectively, in 48 hours. Thiamine HCl was stable in the parenteral nutrition solutions prepared with amino acid products without sulfites. However, amino acid products containing sulfites (Travasol and FreAmine III) had a 25% thiamine loss in 12 hours and a 50% loss in 24 hours when the solutions were stored at 25 °C; no loss occurred when the solutions were stored at 5 °C. Ascorbic acid was lost from all samples stored at 25 °C, with the greatest losses occurring in solutions stored in plastic bags. No losses occurred in any sample stored at 5 °C. (1431)

Samples from 24 1-L and four 2-L parenteral nutrition solutions, containing one vial each of multivitamin concentrate (USV), were evaluated for thiamine HCl content at 48 to 72 hours after mixing. The parenteral nutrition solutions contained amino acids 2.75 to 5%, dextrose 15 to 25%, and electrolytes. Thiamine HCl was stable in all of the solutions tested in spite of an approximate 0.05% sulfite content. (843)

In another experiment, multivitamin concentrate (USV) was added to 500-ml glass bottles of amino acids 10% (Travenol) containing 0.1% sulfite and also to 1000-ml PVC bags containing amino acids 4.25%–dextrose 25% (Travenol) with about 0.05% sulfite. After 22 hours of storage at 30 °C, a 40% loss of thiamine HCl occurred in the amino acid 10% solution, but no loss occurred in the PVC bags of parenteral nutrition solution. The authors concluded that the thiamine HCl content is retained in usual clinical parenteral nutrition solutions, probably because of the dilution of the sulfite and buffering of pH. However, direct addition to solutions with a high sulfite content (0.1%) may result in significant decomposition. (843)

The stability of five B vitamins was studied over an eight-hour period in representative parenteral nutrition solutions exposed to fluorescent light, indirect sunlight, and direct sunlight. One 5-ml vial of multivitamin concentrate (Lyphomed) and 1 mg of folic acid (Lederle) were added to a liter of parenteral nutrition solution composed of amino acids 4.25%–dextrose 25% (Travenol) with standard electrolytes and trace elements. All five B vitamins tested were stable for eight hours at room temperature when exposed to fluorescent light. In addition, folic acid and niacinamide were stable over eight hours in direct or indirect sunlight. Exposure to indirect sunlight appeared to have little or no effect on thiamine HCl and pyridoxine HCl in eight hours, but 47% of riboflavin-5-phosphate was lost in that period. Direct sunlight caused a 26% loss of thiamine HCl and an 86% loss of pyridoxine HCl in eight hours. Four-hour exposures of riboflavin-5-phosphate to direct sunlight resulted in a 98% loss. (842)

The effects of photoirradiation on a FreAmine II–dextrose 10% parenteral nutrition solution containing 1 ml/500 ml of multivitamins (USV) were evaluated. During simulated continuous administration to an infant at 0.156 ml/min, no changes to the amino acids occurred when the bottle, infusion tubing, and collection bottle were shielded with foil. Only 20 cm of tubing in the incubator was exposed to light. However, if the flow was stopped, a marked reduction in methionine (40%), tryptophan (44%), and histidine (22%) occurred in the solution exposed to light for 24 hours. In a similar solution without vitamins, only the tryptophan concentration decreased. The difference was attributed to the presence of riboflavin, a photosensitizer. The authors recommended administering the multivitamins separately and shielding from light. (833)

In further work, the authors simulated more closely conditions occurring during phototherapy in neonatal intensive care units. Riboflavin 1 mg/100 ml was added to a solution of amino acids 2% (Abbott) with dextrose 10%. Infusion was simulated from glass bottles through PVC tubing with a Buretrol at a rate of 4 ml/hr. In addition to the fluorescent room lights, eight daylight bulbs delivered phototherapy. After a simulated 24-hour infusion, riboflavin decreased to about 50% of its initial level. Also, a 7% reduction in total amino acids was noted, including individual losses of glycine (10%), leucine (14%), methionine (24%), proline (10%), serine (9%), tryptophan (35%), and tyrosine (16%). Although the authors did not believe that these losses of amino acids were nutritionally important, they were concerned about the possibility of toxicity from photo-oxidation products. In the same solution without riboflavin, the individual amino acids decreased only slightly. (974)

Allwood reported on the extent and rapidity of ascorbic acid decomposition in parenteral nutrition solutions composed of amino acids, dextrose, electrolytes, multivitamins, and trace elements in 3-L PVC bags stored at 3 to 7 °C. About 30 to 40% was lost in 24 hours. The degradation then slowed as the oxygen supply was reduced to the diffusion through the bag. About a 55 to 65% loss occurred after seven days of storage. The oxidation was catalyzed by metal ions, especially copper. In the absence of copper from the trace elements additive, less than 10% degradation of ascorbic acid occurred in 24 hours. The author estimated that 150 to 200 mg is degraded in two to four hours at ambient temperature in the presence of copper but that only 20 to 30 mg is broken down in 24 hours without copper. To minimize ascorbic acid loss, copper must be excluded. Alternatively, inclusion of excess ascorbic acid was suggested. (1056)

Extensive decomposition of ascorbic acid and folic acid was reported in a parenteral nutrition solution composed of amino acids 3.3%, dextrose 12.5%, electrolytes, trace elements, and M.V.I.-12 (USV) in PVC bags. Half-lives were 1.1, 2.9, and 8.9 hours for ascorbic acid and 2.7, 5.4, and 24 hours for folic acid stored at 24 °C in daylight, 24 °C protected from light, and 4 °C protected from light, respectively. The decomposition was much greater than for solutions not containing catalyzing metal ions. Also, it was greater than for the vitamins singly because of interactions with the other vitamins present. (1059)

The stability of ascorbic acid in parenteral nutrition solutions, with and without fat emulsion, was studied using HPLC analysis. Both with and without fat emulsion, the total vitamin C content (ascorbic acid plus dehydroascorbic acid) remained above 90% for 12 hours when the solutions were exposed to fluorescent light and for 24 hours when they were protected from light. When stored in a cool dark place, the solutions were stable for seven days. (1227)

The influence of several factors on the rate of ascorbic acid oxidation in parenteral nutrition solutions was evaluted. Ascorbic acid is regarded as the least stable component in TPN admixtures. The type of amino acid used in the TPN was important. Some, such as FreAmine III and Vamin 14, contain antioxidant compounds (e.g., sodium metabisulfite or cysteine). Ascorbic acid stability was better in such solutions compared with those amino acid solutions having no antioxidant present. Furthermore, the pH of the solution may play a small role, with greater degradation as the pH rises from about 5 to about 7. Adding air to a compounded TPN container can also accelerate ascorbic acid decomposition. The most important factor was the type of plastic container used for the TPN. Ethylene vinyl acetate (EVA) containers (Mixieva, Miramed) allow more oxygen permeation, which results in substantial losses of ascorbic acid in relatively short time periods. In multilayer TPN bags (Ultrastab, Miramed) designed to reduce gas permeability, the rate of ascorbic acid degradation was greatly reduced. HPLC analysis of TPNs without antioxidants packaged in EVA bags found that an almost total loss of ascorbic acid activity occurred in one or two days at 5 °C. In contrast, in TPNs containing FreAmine III or Vamin 14 packaged in the multilayer bags, most of the ascorbic acid content was retained for 28 days at 5 °C. The authors concluded that TPNs made with antioxidant-containing amino acids and packaged in multilayer bags that reduce gas permeability can safely be given extended expiration dates and still retain most of the ascorbic acid activity. (2163)

Because of these interactions, recommendations to separate the administration of vitamins and trace elements have been made. (1056; 1060; 1061) Other researchers have termed such recommendations premature based on differing reports (895; 896) and the apparent absence of epidemic vitamin deficiency in parenteral nutrition patients. (1062)

Shenkin et al. evaluated the vitamin and trace element status of 22 postoperative surgical patients. Twelve patients were given parenteral nutrition with the fat emulsion containing vitamins separate from amino acids and other water-soluble nutrients; 10 patients received all nutrients in one large bag. No clinically significant differences were noted after administration periods of seven to 38 days. (1226)

Phytonadione stability in a total parenteral nutrition solution containing amino acids 2%, dextrose 12.5%, "standard" electrolytes, and multivitamins (M.V.I. Pediatric) was evaluated by HPLC over 24 hours while exposed to light. Vitamin loss, about 7% in four hours and 27% in 24 hours, was attributed partly to the light sensitivity of phytonadione. (1815)

Trace Elements — The stability of a 3-in-1 parenteral nutrition mixture (TNA #191 in Appendix I) was compared with trace elements added as gluconate salts or chloride salts. TNA #191 with copper 0.24 mg/L, iron 0.5 mg/L, and zinc 2 mg/L in either salt form was physically stable for seven days at 4 and 25 °C. (1787)

Trace elements additives, especially those containing copper ions, have the potential to be incompatible in TPN solutions, resulting in precipitation. In a TPN admixture containing 5% Synthamin 17, 25% dextrose, 1 g of ascorbic acid injection, 14 mmol of calcium chloride, and trace elements solution (David Bull), storage at 20 to 25 °C and 2 to 8 °C, protected from light, resulted in the formation of a discolored solution in three to seven days and an off-white to yellow precipitate in eight to 12 days, respectively. Electron microscopy revealed the presence of numerous bipyramidal, eight-sided crystals in sizes from 3 to 30 μm. The authors proposed that the crystals were calcium oxalate. They suggested that the ascorbic acid decomposed to oxalic acid; the oxalic acid then interacted with calcium ions to form calcium oxalate. The authors did not verify their supposition. They noted that the crystals were conformationally different from calcium phosphate crystals and that no phosphate had been added to the admixture. In addition, mixing ascorbic acid injection 500 mg/5 ml with trace elements solution 5 ml results in the formation of a transparent gel that becomes an opaque flocculent precipitate after five minutes. The authors recommended adding trace elements well away from injections that can act as ligands and with thorough mixing after each addition. Introduction of air and prolonged storage should be avoided. Incorporating trace elements and ascorbic acid on alternate days was also suggested. (2197)

Heparin — Raupp et al. reported flocculation of fat emulsion (Kabi-Vitrum) during Y-site administration into a line used to infuse a parenteral nutrition admixture containing both calcium gluconate and heparin sodium. Subsequent evaluation indicated that the combination of calcium gluconate (0.46 and 1.8 mmol/125 ml) and heparin sodium (25 and 100 units/125 ml) in amino acids plus dextrose induced flocculation of the fat emulsion within two to four minutes at concentrations that resulted in no visually apparent flocculation in 30 minutes with either agent alone. (1214)

This result was confirmed by Johnson et al. Calcium chloride quantities of 1 and 20 mmol normally result in slow flocculation of fat emulsion 20% over several hours. When heparin sodium 5 units/ml was added, the flocculation rate was accelerated greatly and a cream layer was observed visually in a few minutes. This effect was not observed when sodium ion was substituted for the divalent calcium. (1406)

Similar results were observed by Trissel et al. during simulated Y-site administration of heparin sodium into nine 3-in-1 nutrient admixtures having different compositions. Damage to the fat emulsion component was found to occur immediately, with the possible formation of free oil over time. (2215)

Silvers et al. also observed the destabilization of fat emulsion (Intralipid 20%) when administered simultaneously with a TPN admixture and heparin. The damage, detected by viscosity measurement, occurred immediately upon contact at the Y-site. The extent of the destabilization was dependent on the concentration of heparin and the presence of MVI Pediatric with its surfactant content. Additionally, phase separation was observed in two hours. The authors noted that TPN admixtures containing heparin should never be premixed with fat emulsion as a 3-in-1 total nutrient admixture because of this emulsion destabilization. The authors indicated their belief that the damage could be minimized during Y-site co-administration as long as the heparin was kept at a sufficiently low concentration (no visible separation occurred at a heparin concentration of 0.5 unit/ml) and the length of tubing between the Y-site and the patient was minimized. (2282)

However, because the damage to emulsion integrity has been found to occur immediately upon mixing with heparin in the presence of the calcium ions in TPN admixtures (1214; 2215; 2282) and no evaluation and documentation of the clinical safety of using such destabilized emulsions has been performed, use of such damaged emulsions is suspect.

Iron — Mayhew and Quick evaluated the effect of amino acid concentration on precipitation of iron from iron dextran (INFeD, Schein) 10 mg/L in neonatal parenteral nutrition mixtures (TPN #207 to #211) formulated with TrophAmine (McGaw). Rust-colored precipitate formed in the neonatal formulations having amino acids concentrations of 1.5% or less. The precipitate formed more rapidly and in greater amount at lower amino acid concentrations. Parenteral nutrition admixtures with amino acids concentrations of 2 and 2.5% were visually compatible for 48 hr at 19 °C, but trace precipitation was found upon filtration and analysis of the 2% admixture. Extrapolation of the information to other iron dextran products may not be appropriate because of possible product differences. (2103)

Bicarbonate — Due to acidity, the addition of bicarbonate ion may result in the loss of some of this ion as carbon dioxide. Also, adding bicarbonate ions to a solution containing calcium or magnesium may result in the precipitation of insoluble carbonates. (189)

While mixing potentially incompatible ions in separate bottles has been advocated by some (193; 200), it has been discouraged by others if the incompatibilities do not actually occur because potential fluctuations of ions in serum may result. (192; 201)

Insulin — Regular insulin (Lilly) in concentrations of 10 to 50 units/L was tested in parenteral nutrition solutions #38 through #47 (Appendix I). The solutions were physically compatible for 24 hours at 22 °C in all but TPN #46 at 40 and 50 units/L of insulin. In these cases, a white crystalline precipitate was noted on the surface of the solution at 24 hours. At lower concentrations of insulin in TPN #46, no precipitate was observed. (313)

It has also been stated that crystalline insulin is not inactivated by amino acids, but a physical separation may occur if not mixed thoroughly. An occasional shaking was recommended to prevent a bolus of insulin from being administered. (189)

Cimetidine — Cimetidine HCl (SKF) 13 to 19 mg/kg/24 hr was administered to patients by continuous infusion in parenteral nutrition solutions composed of essential amino acids, dextrose 50% in water with varying amounts of vitamins, electrolytes, trace elements, and albumin human. The admixtures were prepared within 24 hours prior to use. No physical incompatibilities were noted, and cimetidine blood levels were in the range achieved by long-term oral treatment. (570)

When compounding parenteral nutrition mixtures, cimetidine should be admixed in a sequence that separates it from the copper sulfate present in trace elements injections to avoid formation of a green-colored copper-cimetidine complex. (1951)

Ranitidine — The stability of ranitidine HCl has been evaluated in a number of TPN solutions with variable results. See Solutions table above. The major mechanism of ranitidine HCl decomposition is oxidation. A number of factors have been found to contribute to ranitidine HCl instability in TPN solutions, including the presence or absence of antioxidants (such as sodium metabisulfite) in the amino acids, the addition of trace elements (which can catalyze ranitidine oxidation), solution pH, and type of plastic container used. In a study of ranitidine HCl stability in several TPN solutions stored at 5 °C, the drug was most stable in FreAmine III–based (contains sodium metabisulfite) admixtures with additives when packaged in multilayer gas impermeable plastic containers (Ultrastab) with about 8% loss by HPLC in 28 days. In contrast, in ethylene vinyl acetate (EVA) bags, which are permeable to oxygen, losses of approximately 50% occurred in this time period. If Vamin 14 with no antioxidant present was used as the amino acid source, and the solution was packaged in EVA bags, ranitidine HCl losses of approximately 65% occurred in 28 days. Similarly, the addition of air to the bags during compounding increases the extent of ranitidine HCl oxidation substantially. (2195)

Gentamicin — Kern et al. evaluated the serum concentrations of gentamicin following intermittent 15 to 30-minute administration in piggyback infusions of 50 ml of dextrose 5% in water or 50 ml of TPN #177 (see Appendix I). Gentamicin serum concentrations were equivalent using both administration methods. (1573)

Other Drugs — It has been stated that antibiotics, steroids, and pressor agents should not be added to parenteral nutrition solutions. They may be administered through a Y-tube or into another vein. (193; 195; 206)

Other information indicates that hydrocortisone sodium succinate is physically and chemically compatible with amino acid injection. (189)

Other Information

Titratable Acidity — The acidity of parenteral nutrition solutions can be a factor in the development of metabolic acidosis by a patient. (577; 851) Titratable acidity is a measure of the hydrogen ion content that must be neutralized to raise the pH to a given endpoint and is often expressed as milliequivalents of titrant per liter of reactant. In a study (577) of five amino acid injections and mixtures, the titratable acidities were determined for pH 7.4 by titrating with 0.1220 N sodium hydroxide and 7.54% (0.898 M) sodium bicarbonate. The following results were observed:

	Titratable Acidity	
	NaOH (mEq/L)	$NaHCO_3$ (mEq/L)
Aminosyn 7%	37	314
FreAmine II 8.5%	16.8	176
Travasol 8.5%	34.7	354
Travasol 8.5% with electrolytes	45.2	420
Veinamine 8%	13.4	135

Corresponding (although somewhat lower) values were also obtained for 1:1 mixtures with dextrose 50%. It was concluded that use of sodium bicarbonate to adjust to pH 7.4 was not usually feasible given the large volumes of fluid and increased sodium ion required. However, smaller amounts could be used for smaller pH adjustments. (577)

AMINOCAPROIC ACID
AHFS 20:12.16

Products — Aminocaproic acid is available as a 250-mg/ml concentration in 20-ml vials containing 5 g of drug. Also present are benzyl alcohol 0.9% and hydrochloric acid and/or sodium hydroxide for pH adjustment. (1-10/99; 4)

pH — The pH is adjusted to approximately 6.8 (1-10/99) with a range of 6 to 7.6. (4)

Trade Name(s) — Amicar.

Administration — Aminocaproic acid is administered by continuous intravenous infusion after dilution in a suitable infusion solution. Rapid intravenous injection of the undiluted drug should be avoided. (1-10/99; 4)

Intravenous solutions recommended for administering aminocaproic acid are sodium chloride 0.9%, dextrose 5% in water, and Ringer's injection. (1-10/99; 4)

Stability — Intact containers of aminocaproic acid injection should be stored at controlled room temperature. Freezing should be avoided. (1-10/99; 4)

Compatibility Information

Solution Compatibility

Aminocaproic acid

Solution	*Mfr*	*Mfr*	*Conc/L*	*Remarks*	*Ref*	*C/I*
Dextrose 5% in water	BA[a]	IMM	10 and 100 g	Physically compatible with little or no loss by HPLC in 7 days at 4 and 23 °C. Yellow discoloration forms after 24 hr at 23 °C but is not associated with drug loss	2096	C
Sodium chloride 0.9%	BA[a]	IMM	10 and 100 g	Physically compatible with little or no loss by HPLC in 7 days at 4 and 23 °C	2096	C

[a]*Tested in PVC containers.*

Additive Compatibility

Aminocaproic acid

Drug	*Mfr*	*Conc/L*	*Mfr*	*Conc/L*	*Test Soln*	*Remarks*	*Ref*	*C/I*
Netilmicin sulfate	SC	3 g	LE	10 g	D5S	Physically compatible and netilmicin chemically stable for 7 days at 25 and 4 °C. Aminocaproic acid not tested	558	C

AMINOPHYLLINE
AHFS 86:16

Products — Aminophylline is available as a 25-mg/ml solution in 10-ml (250 mg) and 20-ml (500 mg) ampuls and vials for intravenous injection. Aminophylline is a 2:1 complex of theophylline and ethylenediamine. It contains excess ethylenediamine to ensure stability (6) and is approximately 79% theophylline by weight. Aminophylline 25 mg is equivalent to 19.7 mg of theophylline. (1-1/97)

pH — From 8.6 to 9. (4)

Osmolality — The calculated osmolarity of the injection is 170 mOsm/L. (1-1/97) The osmolality was determined to be 114 mOsm/kg by freezing-point depression. (1071)

The osmolality of aminophylline 250 mg was calculated for the following dilutions (1054):

	Osmolality (mOsm/kg)	
Diluent	50 ml	100 ml
Dextrose 5% in water	300	291
Sodium chloride 0.9%	327	318

Administration — Aminophylline may be administered by intravenous infusion or slow direct intravenous injection. (1-1/97; 4)

Stability — The containers should be stored at controlled room temperature and protected from freezing and light. (1-1/97) Although Searle indicated that refrigeration would not adversely affect its aminophylline, Elkins-Sinn recommended against refrigerated storage for its product because of possible reduction in solubility with crystallization. (593) Containers of aminophylline should be inspected for particulate matter and discoloration prior to use. Do not use if crystals are present. (1-1/97; 4)

Temperature Effects — The intact ampuls are stated to be stable indefinitely at room temperature. (6) Stability is reported to be maintained at pH 3.5 to 8.6 for at least 48 hours at 25 °C (6), providing aminophylline concentrations do not exceed 40 mg/ml. (4) Others have indicated that theophylline crystals may deposit below pH 8. (41)

Light Effects — Although some aminophylline products are labeled for storage with protection from light (1-1/97), one study of aminophylline (Squibb) 50 mg/ml found no change in theophylline potency after eight weeks of storage with exposure to fluorescent light. (1231)

Syringes — Aminophylline (Abbott) 5 mg/ml in bacteriostatic water for injection containing benzyl alcohol 0.9% in plastic syringes (Becton-Dickinson) exhibited 2 and 3% losses by HPLC at 4 and 22 °C, respectively, after 91 days of storage. (1586)

Sorption — Aminophylline 9 mg/L in sodium chloride 0.9% (Travenol) in PVC bags did not exhibit significant sorption to the plastic during one week of storage at room temperature (15 to 20 °C). (536)

Aminophylline (David Bull Laboratories) 9 mg/L in sodium chloride 0.9% did not exhibit any loss due to sorption during a seven-hour simulated infusion through an infusion set (Travenol) consisting of a cellulose propionate burette chamber and 170 cm of PVC tubing. (606)

The drug was also tested as a simulated infusion over at least one hour by a syringe pump system. A glass syringe on a syringe pump was fitted with 20 cm of polyethylene tubing or 50 cm of Silastic tubing. No loss of drug due to sorption was observed with either tubing. (606)

A 25-ml aliquot of aminophylline (David Bull Laboratories) 9 mg/L in sodium chloride 0.9% was stored in all-plastic syringes composed of polypropylene barrels and polyethylene plungers for 24 hours at room temperature in the dark. No loss due to sorption occurred. (606)

In another study, aminophylline, BP, 10 mg/2 ml diluted in dextrose 5% in water or sodium chloride 0.9% was stored for 18 hours at room temperature in the following plastic syringes: Brunswick (Sherwood Medical), Plastipak (Becton-Dickinson), Steriseal (Needle Industries), and Sabre (Gillette U.K.). The first three syringes have polypropylene barrels; the Sabre has a combination polypropylene–polystyrene barrel. No significant loss of aminophylline occurred due to sorption. (784)

Filtration — Aminophylline (American Quinine) 500 mg/L in dextrose 5% in water in PVC bags was passed through an Ivex-2 inline filter assembly at a rate of 2 ml/min. No decrease in the delivered aminophylline concentration or any change in the physicochemical properties occurred over the eight-hour study period. (556)

Central Venous Catheter — Aminophylline (Abbott) 2.5 mg/ml in dextrose 5% in water was found to be compatible with the ARROWg+ard Blue Plus (Arrow International) chlorhexidine-bearing triple-lumen central catheter. HPLC analysis was used to evaluate completeness of drug delivery through the catheter and the amount of chlorhexidine removed from the internal lumens. Essentially complete delivery of the drug was found with little or no drug loss occurring. Furthermore, chlorhexidine delivered from the catheter remained at trace amounts with no substantial increase due to the delivery of the drug through the catheter. (2335)

Compatibility Information

Solution Compatibility

Aminophylline

Solution	*Mfr*	*Mfr*	*Conc/L*	*Remarks*	*Ref*	*C/I*
Alcohol 5%, dextrose 5% in water	BA	SE	10 g	Physically compatible for 24 hr	315	C
Amino acids 4.25%, dextrose 25%	MG	SE	500 mg	No increase in particulate matter in 24 hr at 5 °C	349	C
Dextran 6% in dextrose 5%	AB		500 mg	Physically compatible	3	C

Solution Compatibility (Cont.)

Aminophylline

Solution	*Mfr*	*Mfr*	*Conc/L*	*Remarks*	*Ref*	*C/I*
Dextran 6% in sodium chloride 0.9%	AB		500 mg	Physically compatible	3	C
Dextrose–Ringer's injection combinations	AB		500 mg	Physically compatible	3	C
Dextrose–Ringer's injection, lactated, combinations	AB		500 mg	Physically compatible	3	C
Dextrose 5% in Ringer's injection, lactated	BA	SE	10 mg	Physically compatible for 24 hr	315	C
Dextrose–saline combinations	AB		500 mg	Physically compatible	3	C
Dextrose 4% in sodium chloride 0.18%	TR[a]		1 g	Yellow discoloration in 2 hr but theophylline content by HPLC retained for at least 24 hr	1571	C
Dextrose 5% in sodium chloride 0.2%	MG	AQ	750 mg	Physically compatible with no aminophylline decomposition in 48 hr at 25 °C. Yellow tinge at 48 hr due to slight dextrose decomposition	556	C
Dextrose 5% in sodium chloride 0.9%			250 mg	Physically compatible	74	C
	BA	SE	10 g	Physically compatible for 24 hr	315	C
	TR[a]	AQ	750 mg	Physically compatible with no aminophylline decomposition in 48 hr at 25 °C. Yellow tinge at 48 hr due to slight dextrose decomposition	556	C
Dextrose 2½% in water	AB		500 mg	Physically compatible	3	C
Dextrose 5% in water			500 mg to 2.5 g	Potency retained for 24 hr at room temperature	56	C
			250 mg	Physically compatible	74	C
	AB		500 mg	Physically compatible	3	C
	AB	SE	450 mg	Potency retained for at least 24 hr at room temperature	6	C
	BA	SE	10 g	Physically compatible for 24 hr	315	C
	AB	ES	5 and 10 g	Physically compatible with little or no decomposition in 96 hr under refrigeration	537	C
	TR[a]	AQ	750 mg	Physically compatible with no aminophylline decomposition in 48 hr at 25 °C and 7 days at 5 °C. Yellow tinge in the 25 °C admixture at 48 hr due to slight dextrose decomposition	556	C
	TR[a]	AQ	250 and 500 mg	Physically compatible with no aminophylline decomposition in 48 hr at 25 °C. Yellow tinge in the admixture at 48 hr due to slight dextrose decomposition	556	C
			250 mg	Aminophylline chemically stable for at least 24 hr at 24 to 26 °C	852	C
	TR[a]	IX	500 mg	Physically compatible with little or no loss in 48 hr at room temperature	1186	C
	AB	SE	1 g	Physically compatible with no loss in 24 hr at 24 °C under fluorescent light	1198	C
	TR[a]	LY	1 g	Physically compatible with no loss in 24 hr at room temperature under fluorescent light	1358	C
	TR[a]		1 g	Yellow discoloration in 2 hr but theophylline content by HPLC retained for at least 24 hr	1571	C
	TR[a]	ES	0.5 and 2 g	Visually compatible with little or no aminophylline loss by HPLC in 48 hr at room temperature	1802	C
Dextrose 10% in water	AB		500 mg	Physically compatible	3	C
	BA	SE	10 g	Physically compatible for 24 hr	315	C
			250 mg	Aminophylline chemically stable for at least 24 hr at 24 to 26 °C. Yellow discoloration at 2 hr and increased with time	852	C

Solution Compatibility (Cont.)

Aminophylline

Solution	*Mfr*	*Mfr*	*Conc/L*	*Remarks*	*Ref*	*C/I*
Dextrose 20% in water	BA	SE	10 g	Physically compatible for 24 hr	315	C
			250 mg	Aminophylline chemically stable for at least 24 hr at 24 to 26 °C. Yellow discoloration at 2 hr and increased with time	852	C
Fat emulsion 10%, intravenous	VT	ES	1 g	Physically compatible for 48 hr at 4 °C and room temperature	32	C
	VT	DB	500 mg	Microscopic globule coalescence in 24 hr at 25 and 8 °C	825	I
Fructose 10% in sodium chloride 0.9%	AB		500 mg	Color change	3	I
Fructose 10% in water	BA	SE	10 g	Physically compatible for 24 hr	315	C
	AB		500 mg	Color change	3	I
Invert sugar 5% in sodium chloride 0.9%	AB		500 mg	Physically compatible	3	C
Invert sugar 5% in water	AB		500 mg	Physically compatible	3	C
Invert sugar 10% in Electrolyte #1	BA	SE	10 g	Physically compatible for 24 hr	315	C
Invert sugar 10% in Electrolyte #2	BA	SE	10 g	Physically compatible for 24 hr	315	C
Invert sugar 10% in sodium chloride 0.9%	AB		500 mg	Color change	3	I
Invert sugar 10% in water	AB		500 mg	Color change	3	I
Ionosol products	AB		500 mg	Physically compatible	3	C
Polysal M with dextrose 5%	BA	SE	10 g	Physically compatible for 24 hr	315	C
Ringer's injection	AB		500 mg	Physically compatible	3	C
Ringer's injection, lactated			250 mg	Physically compatible	74	C
	AB		500 mg	Physically compatible	3	C
	BA	SE	10 g	Physically compatible for 24 hr	315	C
Sodium chloride 0.45%	AB		500 mg	Physically compatible	3	C
Sodium chloride 0.9%	AB		500 mg	Physically compatible	3	C
			250 mg	Physically compatible	74	C
	TR[a]	SE	500 mg	Potency retained for 24 hr	45	C
	BA[d]	SE	500 mg	Potency retained for 24 hr	45	C
	BA	SE	10 g	Physically compatible for 24 hr	315	C
	TR[a]	AQ	750 mg	Physically compatible with no decomposition in 48 hr at 25 °C	556	C
	TR[a]		1 g	Theophylline content by HPLC retained for at least 24 hr	1571	C
	TR[a]	ES	0.5 and 2 g	Visually compatible with little or no aminophylline loss by HPLC in 48 hr at room temperature	1802	C
Sodium lactate ⅙ M	AB		500 mg	Physically compatible	3	C
	BA	SE	10 g	Physically compatible for 24 hr	315	C
TNA #180[b]			234 and 638 mg	Little or no theophylline loss by EMIT and no substantial increase in fat particle size in 24 hr at room temperature	1617	C
TPN #25 to #27[b]		SE	250 mg, 500 mg, 1 g, 1.5 g	Physically compatible and aminophylline chemically stable for at least 24 hr at 25 °C	755	C
		SE	1 g	Physically compatible and aminophylline chemically stable for at least 24 hr at 4 °C	755	C

Solution Compatibility (Cont.)

Aminophylline

Solution	*Mfr*	*Mfr*	*Conc/L*	*Remarks*	*Ref*	*C/I*
TPN #28 to #30[b]		SE	1 g	Physically compatible and aminophylline chemically stable for at least 24 hr at 25 °C	755	C
TPN[c]			29.3 mg	No significant change in aminophylline content over 24 hr at 24 to 26 °C	852	C

[a] *Tested in PVC containers.*
[b] *Refer to Appendix I for the composition of parenteral nutrition solutions. TNA indicates a 3-in-1 admixture, and TPN indicates a 2-in-1 admixture.*
[c] *Tested in a pediatric parenteral nutrition solution containing 150 ml of dextrose 5% in water and 30 ml of Vamin glucose with electrolytes and vitamins.*
[d] *Tested in glass containers.*

Additive Compatibility

Aminophylline

Drug	*Mfr*	*Conc/L*	*Mfr*	*Conc/L*	*Test Soln*	*Remarks*	*Ref*	*C/I*
Amikacin sulfate	BR	5 g	SE	5 g	LR, NS, R, SL	Physically compatible and amikacin potency retained for 24 hr at 25 °C. Aminophylline not analyzed	294	C
	BR	5 g	SE	5 g	D5LR, D5R, D5S, D5W, D10W, IS10	Greater than 10% amikacin decomposition after 8 hr but within 24 hr at 25 °C. Aminophylline not analyzed	294	I
Amobarbital sodium	LI	500 mg	SE	500 mg		Physically compatible	6	C
Ascorbic acid injection	AB	500 mg	SE	500 mg		Physically compatible	6	C
						Physically incompatible	9	I
	UP	500 mg	SE	1 g	D5W	Physically incompatible	15	I
Atracurium besylate	BW	500 mg		1 g	D5W	Atracurium chemically unstable due to high pH	1694	I
Bleomycin sulfate	BR	20 and 30 units	ES	250 mg	NS	50% loss of bleomycin activity in 1 week at 4 °C	763	I
Bretylium tosylate	ACC	1 g	ES	1 g	D5W, NS	Physically compatible for 48 hr at 25 °C	756	C
Calcium gluconate		1 g		250 mg	D5W	Physically compatible	74	C
Cefepime HCl	BR	4 g	LY	1 g	NS	37% cefepime loss by HPLC in 18 hr at room temperature and 32% loss in 3 days at 5 °C. No aminophylline loss	1681	I
Ceftazidime	GL[a]	2 g	ES	1 g	D5W, NS	20 to 23% ceftazidime loss by HPLC in 6 hr at room temperature	1937	I
	GL[a]	6 g	ES	1 g	D5W, NS	8 to 10% ceftazidime loss and 13% theophylline loss by HPLC in 6 hr at room temperature	1937	I
	GL[a]	2 g	ES	2 g	D5W, NS	35 to 40% ceftazidime loss by HPLC in 6 hr at room temperature	1937	I
	GL[a]	6 g	ES	2 g	D5W, NS	22% ceftazidime loss by HPLC in 6 hr at room temperature	1937	I
Ceftriaxone sodium	RC	20 g	AMR	1 g	D5W, NS[b]	Yellow color forms immediately. 3 to 6% ceftriaxone loss and 8 to 12% aminophylline loss by HPLC in 24 hr	1727	I
	RC	20 g	AMR	4 g	D5W, NS[b]	Yellow color forms immediately. 15 to 20% ceftriaxone loss and 7 to 9% aminophylline loss by HPLC in 24 hr	1727	I

Additive Compatibility (Cont.)

Aminophylline

Drug	*Mfr*	*Conc/L*	*Mfr*	*Conc/L*	*Test Soln*	*Remarks*	*Ref*	*C/I*
	RC	40 g	AMR	1 g	D5W, NS[b]	Yellow color forms immediately. 15 to 18% ceftriaxone loss and 1 to 3% aminophylline loss by HPLC in 24 hr	1727	I
Chloramphenicol sodium succinate	PD	500 mg		250 mg	D5W	Physically compatible	74	C
	PD	10 g	SE	1 g	D5W	Physically compatible	15	C
Chlorpromazine HCl	BP	200 mg	BP	1 g	D5W, NS	Immediate precipitation	26	I
Cibenzoline succinate		2 g	IX	10 g	D5W, NS	Physically compatible for 24 hr at 25 °C by visual and microscopic examination	1182	C
Cimetidine HCl	SKF	1.2 g	IX	500 mg	D5W[c]	Physically compatible with about 3 to 5% cimetidine loss and little or no aminophylline loss in 48 hr at room temperature	1186	C
Ciprofloxacin	MI	1.6 g	LY	2 g	D5W, NS	Ciprofloxacin precipitate forms in 4 hr at 4 and 25 °C	1541	I
Clindamycin phosphate	UP	600 mg	SE	600 mg		Physically incompatible	101	I
Corticotropin		500 units		250 mg	D5W	Physically compatible	74	C
	AR, NA	40 units	SE	500 mg		Precipitate forms within 1 hr	6	I
Dexamethasone sodium phosphate		30 mg		625 mg	D5W	Physically compatible and chemically stable for 24 hr at 4 and 30 °C	521	C
Dimenhydrinate	SE	50 mg		250 mg	D5W	Physically compatible	74	C
	SE	500 mg	SE	1 g	D5W	Physically incompatible	15	I
Diphenhydramine HCl	PD	50 mg	SE	500 mg		Physically compatible	6	C
Dobutamine HCl	LI	1 g	SE	1 g	D5W, NS	Cloudy in 6 hr at 25 °C	789	I
	LI	1 g	ES	2.5 g	D5W, NS	White precipitate forms within 12 hr at 21 °C	812	I
Dopamine HCl	ACC	800 mg	SE	500 mg	D5W	Physically compatible. At 25 °C, 10% dopamine decomposition in 111 hr	527	C
Doxorubicin HCl	AD					Solution color darkens from red to blue-purple	524	I
Epinephrine HCl	PD	4 mg	SE	500 mg	D5W	At 25 °C, 10% epinephrine decomposition in 1.2 hr in light and 3 hr in dark	527	I
		4 mg		500 mg	D5W	Pink to brown discoloration of solution in 8 to 24 hr at room temperature	845	I
Erythromycin lactobionate	AB	1 g	SE	500 mg		Physically compatible. Erythromycin potency retained for 24 hr at 25 °C	20	C
Esmolol HCl	DU	6 g	LY	1 g	D5W	Physically compatible with no loss of either drug in 24 hr at room temperature under fluorescent light	1358	C
Floxacillin sodium	BE	20 g	ANT	1 g	NS	Physically compatible for 72 hr at 15 and 30 °C	1479	C
Flumazenil	RC	20 mg	AMR	2 g	D5W[c]	Visually compatible with no flumazenil loss by HPLC in 24 hr at 23 °C under fluorescent light. Aminophylline not tested	1710	C

Additive Compatibility (Cont.)

			Aminophylline					
Drug	*Mfr*	*Conc/L*	*Mfr*	*Conc/L*	*Test Soln*	*Remarks*	*Ref*	*C/I*
Furosemide	HO	1 g	ANT	1 g	NS	Physically compatible for 72 hr at 15 and 30 °C	1479	C
Heparin sodium		12,000 units		250 mg	D5W	Physically compatible	74	C
	UP	4000 units	SE	1 g	D5W	Physically compatible	15	C
Hydralazine HCl	BP	80 mg	BP	1 g	D5W	Yellow color produced	26	I
Hydrocortisone sodium succinate	UP	100 mg		250 mg	D5W	Physically compatible	74	C
	UP	500 mg	SE	1 g	D5W	Physically compatible	15	C
	UP	100 mg	SE	500 mg		Physically compatible	6	C
		250 mg		625 mg	D5W	Physically compatible and aminophylline chemically stable for 24 hr at 4 and 30 °C. Total hydrocortisone content changed little but substantial ester hydrolysis noted	521	C
Hydrocortisone sodium succinate with cephalothin sodium	UP LI	100 mg 1 g	SE	1 g	D5S	pH outside stability range for cephalothin. Precipitate seen in 12 hr	41	I
Hydroxyzine HCl	RR	250 mg	SE	1 g	D5W	Physically incompatible	15	I
Insulin, regular[d]	LI	20 units	SE	1 g	D5W	pH outside stability range for insulin	41	I
Isoproterenol HCl	BN	2 mg	SE	500 mg	D5W	At 25 °C, 10% isoproterenol decomposition in 2.2 to 2.5 hr in light and dark	527	I
Levorphanol bitartrate	RC					Physically incompatible	9	I
Lidocaine HCl	AST	2 g	SE	500 mg		Physically compatible	24	C
	AST	2 g	AQ	1 g	D5W, LR, NS	Physically compatible for 24 hr at 25 °C	775	C
Meperidine HCl	WI					Physically incompatible	9	I
Mephentermine sulfate		750 mg		625 mg	D5W	Physically compatible and chemically stable for 24 hr at 3 and 30 °C	520	C
Meropenem	ZEN	1 and 20 g	AMR	1 g	NS	Visually compatible for 4 hr at room temperature	1994	C
Methyldopate HCl	MSD	1 g	SE	500 mg	D, D–S, S	Physically compatible	23	C
	MSD	1 g	SE	500 mg	D5W	Physically compatible. At 25 °C, 10% methyldopate decomposition in 90 hr	527	C
Methylprednisolone sodium succinate	UP	40 to 250 mg		500 mg	D5W, NS	Clear solution for 24 hr	329	C
	UP	80 mg		1 g	D5W	Clear solution for 24 hr	329	C
	UP	125 mg	SE	500 mg		Precipitate forms after 6 hr but within 24 hr	6	I
	UP	250 mg to 1 g		1 g	D5W	Precipitate forms	329	I
	UP	10 to 20 g		~400 mg	D5S, D5W, LR	Yellow color forms	329	I
	UP	500 mg and 2 g	SE	1 g	D5W	Physically compatible with no loss of aminophylline or methylprednisolone alcohol in 3 hr at room temperature. 7 to 10% ester hydrolysis termed not clinically important	1022	C

Additive Compatibility (Cont.)

			Aminophylline					
Drug	*Mfr*	*Conc/L*	*Mfr*	*Conc/L*	*Test Soln*	*Remarks*	*Ref*	*C/I*
	UP	500 mg and 2 g	SE	1 g	NS	Physically compatible with no loss of aminophylline or methylprednisolone alcohol in 3 hr at room temperature. 12 to 18% ester hydrolysis termed not clinically important	1022	C
Metronidazole HCl with sodium bicarbonate	SE AB	5 g 50 mEq	SE	2 g	D5W, NS	Physically compatible for 48 hr	765	C
Morphine sulfate						Physically incompatible	9	I
Nafcillin sodium	WY	30 g	SE	500 mg	D5W	Nafcillin potency retained for 24 hr at 25 °C	27	C
	WY	2 g	SE	500 mg	D5W	14% nafcillin decomposition in 24 hr at 25 °C	27	I
Nitroglycerin	ACC	400 mg	IX	1 g	D5W[e]	Physically compatible with 4% nitroglycerin loss in 24 hr and 6% loss in 48 hr at 23 °C. Aminophylline not tested	929	C
	ACC	400 mg	IX	1 g	NS[e]	Physically compatible with no nitroglycerin loss in 24 hr and 5% loss in 48 hr at 23 °C. Aminophylline not tested	929	C
Norepinephrine bitartrate	WI	8 mg	SE	500 mg	D5W	At 25 °C, 10% norepinephrine decomposition in 3.6 hr	527	I
Papaverine HCl with trimecaine HCl		120 mg 600 mg		480 mg	D5W	Papaverine precipitation within 3 hr due to alkaline pH	835	I
Penicillin G potassium	SQ	1 million units	SE	500 mg	D5W	44% penicillin decomposition in 24 hr at 25 °C	47	I
	f	900,000 units	SE	500 mg	D5W	22% penicillin decomposition in 6 hr at 25 °C	48	I
Pentazocine lactate	WI	300 mg	SE	1 g	D5W	Physically incompatible	15	I
Pentobarbital sodium	AB	500 mg		500 mg		Physically compatible	3	C
	AB	1 g	SE	1 g	D5W	Physically compatible	15	C
	AB	500 mg	SE	500 mg		Physically compatible	6	C
Phenobarbital sodium	WI	200 mg	SE	1 g	D5W	Physically compatible	15	C
	AB	100 mg	SE	500 mg		Physically compatible	6	C
Potassium chloride	AB	3 g		250 mg	D5W	Physically compatible	74	C
	AB	40 mEq	SE	500 mg		Physically compatible	6	C
Procaine HCl	AB	1 g	SE	500 mg		Physically compatible	6	C
						Physically incompatible	9	I
	WI	1 g	SE	1 g	D5W	Physically incompatible	15	I
Prochlorperazine edisylate	SKF	100 mg	SE	1 g	D5W	Physically incompatible	15	I
Prochlorperazine mesylate	BP	100 mg	BP	1 g	D5W, NS	Immediate precipitate	26	I
Promazine HCl	BP	200 mg	BP	1 g	D5W, NS	Immediate precipitate	26	I
	WY	1 g	SE	1 g	D5W	Physically incompatible	15	I
Promethazine HCl	BP	100 mg	BP	1 g	D5W, NS	Immediate precipitate	26	I
	WY	250 mg	SE	1 g	D5W	Physically incompatible	15	I

Additive Compatibility (Cont.)

Aminophylline

Drug	*Mfr*	*Conc/L*	*Mfr*	*Conc/L*	*Test Soln*	*Remarks*	*Ref*	*C/I*
Ranitidine HCl	GL	50 mg and 2 g	ES	500 mg and 2 g	D5W, NS[c]	Physically compatible with 4% or less ranitidine loss in 24 hr at room temperature under fluorescent light. Aminophylline not tested	1361	C
	GL	50 mg and 2 g	ES	0.5 and 2 g	D5W, NS[c]	Visually compatible with little or no loss of either drug by HPLC in 48 hr at room temperature	1802	C
Sodium bicarbonate	AB	80 mEq	SE	1 g	D5W	Physically compatible	15	C
	AB	40 mEq	SE	500 mg		Physically compatible	6	C
	AB	2.4 mEq[g]		500 mg	D5W	Physically compatible for 24 hr	772	C
Terbutaline sulfate	CI	4 mg	SE	500 mg	D5W	Physically compatible. At 25 °C, 10% terbutaline decomposition in 44 hr exposed to light	527	C
Vancomycin HCl	LI	1 g		250 mg	D5W	Physically compatible	74	C
	LI	5 g	SE	1 g	D5W	Physically incompatible	15	I
Verapamil HCl	KN	80 mg	SE	1 g	D5W, NS	Transient precipitate clears rapidly. Solution physically compatible for 48 hr	739	C
	KN	400 mg	SE	1 g	D5W	Visible turbidity forms immediately. Filtration removes all verapamil	1198	I
	KN	100 mg	SE	1 g	D5W	Visually clear, but precipitate found by microscopic examination. Filtration removes all verapamil	1198	I
Vitamin B complex with C	RC	2 ml	SE	1 g	D5S	High pH destroys vitamin activity	41	I
Zinc (salt unspecified)		50 mg		2.5 g	D5W, NS	Precipitate forms within a few minutes	1898	I
		40 mg		2 g	D5W, NS	Precipitate forms within a few minutes	1898	I
		20 mg		1 g	D5W, NS	Precipitate forms within 24 hr at room temperature less than 25 °C	1898	I
		20 mg		1 g	AA10, D25[h]	Visually compatible for 24 hr at room temperature less than 25 °C	1898	C

[a]*Sodium carbonate–containing formulation tested.*
[b]*Tested in polyolefin containers.*
[c]*Tested in PVC containers.*
[d]*Test performed prior to the availability of neutral regular insulin.*
[e]*Tested in glass containers.*
[f]*A buffered preparation was specified.*
[g]*One vial of Neut added to a liter of admixture.*
[h]*Also contained ascorbic acid 500 mg/L and vitamin B complex with C 2 ml/L.*

Drugs in Syringe Compatibility

Aminophylline

Drug (in syringe)	*Mfr*	*Amt*	*Mfr*	*Amt*	*Remarks*	*Ref*	*C/I*
Doxapram HCl	RB	400 mg/ 20 ml		250 mg/ 10 ml	Immediate turbidity and precipitation	1177	I
Heparin sodium		2500 units/ 1 ml		0.24 g/ 10 ml	Physically compatible for at least 5 min	1053	C
Metoclopramide HCl	RB	10 mg/ 2 ml	ES	80 mg/ 3.2 ml	Physically compatible for 24 hr at room temperature	924	C
	RB	10 mg/ 2 ml	ES	500 mg/ 20 ml	Physically compatible for 24 hr at room temperature	924	C

Drugs in Syringe Compatibility (Cont.)

Aminophylline

Drug (in syringe)	*Mfr*	*Amt*	*Mfr*	*Amt*	*Remarks*	*Ref*	*C/I*
	RB	10 mg/ 2 ml	ES	80 mg/ 3.2 ml	Physically compatible for 24 hr at 25 °C	1167	**C**
	RB	10 mg/ 2 ml	ES	500 mg/ 20 ml	Physically compatible for 24 hr at 25 °C	1167	**C**
	RB	160 mg/ 32 ml	ES	500 mg/ 20 ml	Physically compatible for 24 hr at 25 °C	1167	**C**
Pentobarbital sodium	AB	500 mg/ 10 ml		500 mg/ 2 ml	Physically compatible	55	**C**
Thiopental sodium	AB	75 mg/ 3 ml	SE	500 mg/ 2 ml	Physically compatible for at least 30 min	21	**C**
	AB	75 mg/ 3 ml		500 mg/ 2 ml	Physically compatible	55	**C**

Y-Site Injection Compatibility (1:1 Mixture)

Aminophylline

Drug	*Mfr*	*Conc*	*Mfr*	*Conc*	*Remarks*	*Ref*	*C/I*
Allopurinol sodium	BW	3 mg/ml[b]	AB	2.5 mg/ml[b]	Physically compatible with no change in measured turbidity or increase in particle content in 4 hr at 22 °C	1686	**C**
Amifostine	USB	10 mg/ml[a]	AMR	2.5 mg/ml[a]	Physically compatible with no change in measured turbidity or increase in particle content in 4 hr at 23 °C	1845	**C**
Amiodarone HCl	LZ	4 mg/ml[c]	ES	5 mg/ml[c]	Haze within 15 min and white precipitate within 6 hr at 21 °C	1032	**I**
Amphotericin B cholesteryl sulfate complex	SEQ	0.83 mg/ml[a]	AB	2.5 mg/ml[a]	Physically compatible with little or no change in measured turbidity or increase in particle content in 4 hr at 23 °C under fluorescent light	2117	**C**
Aztreonam	SQ	40 mg/ml[a]	AMR	2.5 mg/ml[a]	Physically compatible with no subvisual haze or particle formation in 4 hr at 23 °C	1758	**C**
Ceftazidime	GL[d]	40 mg/ml[a]	ES	2 mg/ml[a]	Visually compatible with 4% ceftazidime loss and 9% theophylline loss by HPLC in 2 hr at room temperature	1937	**C**
	GL[d]	40 mg/ml[b]	ES	2 mg/ml[a]	Visually compatible with 5% ceftazidime loss and 4% theophylline loss by HPLC in 2 hr at room temperature	1937	**C**
	GL[e]	40 mg/ml	ES	2 mg/ml[a]	Visually compatible with no ceftazidime or theophylline loss by HPLC in 2 hr at room temperature	1937	**C**
	GL[f]	40 mg/ml[a]	ES	2 mg/ml[a]	Visually compatible with 5% ceftazidime loss and 7% theophylline loss by HPLC in 2 hr at room temperature	1937	**C**
	GL[f]	40 mg/ml[b]	ES	2 mg/ml[a]	Visually compatible with 2% ceftazidime loss and no theophylline loss by HPLC in 2 hr at room temperature	1937	**C**
Cimetidine HCl	SKF	6 mg/ml[c]	ES	4 mg/ml[c]	Physically compatible for 3 hr	1316	**C**
Ciprofloxacin	MI	2 mg/ml[c]	AB	2 mg/ml[c]	Fine white crystals form in 20 min in D5W and 2 min in NS	1655	**I**

Y-Site Injection Compatibility (1:1 Mixture) (Cont.)

			Aminophylline				
Drug	*Mfr*	*Conc*	*Mfr*	*Conc*	*Remarks*	*Ref*	*C/I*
Cisatracurium besylate	GW	0.1 and 2 mg/ml[a]	AB	2.5 mg/ml[a]	Physically compatible with no change in measured turbidity or increase in particle content in 4 hr at 23 °C	2074	C
	GW	5 mg/ml[a]	AB	2.5 mg/ml[a]	Gray subvisual haze forms in 1 hr	2074	I
Cladribine	ORT	0.015[b] and 0.5[g] mg/ml	AMR	2.5 mg/ml[b]	Physically compatible with no change in measured turbidity or increase in particle content in 4 hr at 23 °C	1969	C
Clarithromycin	AB	4 mg/ml[a]	EV	2 mg/ml[a]	Needle-like crystals form in 2 hr at 30 °C and 4 hr at 17 °C	2174	I
Diltiazem HCl	MMD	5 mg/ml	AMR	25 mg/ml[b]	Cloudiness forms	1807	I
	MMD	1 mg/ml[b]	AMR	25 mg/ml[b]	Visually compatible	1807	C
	MMD	5 mg/ml	AMR	2 mg/ml[c]	Visually compatible	1807	C
Dobutamine HCl	LI	4 mg/ml[c]	ES	4 mg/ml[c]	Slight haze or precipitate and color change in 1 hr	1316	I
Docetaxel	RPR	0.9 mg/ml[a]	AB	2.5 mg/ml[a]	Physically compatible with no change in measured turbidity or increase in particle content in 4 hr at 23 °C	2224	C
Doxorubicin HCl liposome injection	SEQ	0.4 mg/ml[a]	AB	2.5 mg/ml[a]	Physically compatible with little or no change in measured turbidity and no increase in particle content in 4 hr at 23 °C	2087	C
Enalaprilat	MSD	0.05 mg/ml[b]	ES	1 mg/ml[a]	Physically compatible for 24 hr at room temperature under fluorescent light	1355	C
Esmolol HCl	DCC	10 mg/ml[a]	ES	1 mg/ml[a]	Physically compatible for 24 hr at 22 °C	1169	C
Etoposide phosphate	BR	5 mg/ml[a]	AB	2.5 mg/ml[a]	Physically compatible with no change in measured turbidity or increase in particle content in 4 hr at 23 °C	2218	C
Famotidine	MSD	0.2 mg/ml[a]	LY	2.5 mg/ml[b]	Physically compatible for 14 hr	1196	C
	ME	2 mg/ml[a]		2.5 mg/ml[a]	Visually compatible for 4 hr at 22 °C	1936	C
Filgrastim	AMG	30 μg/ml[a]	AB	2.5 mg/ml[a]	Physically compatible with no change in measured turbidity or increase in particle content in 4 hr at 22 °C	1687	C
Fluconazole	RR	2 mg/ml	ES	25 mg/ml	Physically compatible for 24 hr at 25 °C	1407	C
	PF	0.5 and 1.5 mg/ml[c]	AMR	0.8 and 1.5 mg/ml[c]	Visually compatible with no loss of either drug by HPLC in 3 hr at 24 °C	1626	C
Fludarabine phosphate	BX	1 mg/ml[a]	ES	2.5 mg/ml[a]	Physically compatible for 4 hr at room temperature under fluorescent light	1439	C
Foscarnet sodium	AST	24 mg/ml	LY	25 mg/ml	Physically compatible for 24 hr at room temperature under fluorescent light	1335	C
Gatifloxacin	BMS	2 mg/ml[a]	AB	2.5 mg/ml[a]	Physically compatible with no change in measured haze or increase in particle content in 4 hr at 23 °C	2234	C
Gemcitabine HCl	LI	10 mg/ml[b]	AB	2.5 mg/ml[b]	Physically compatible with no change in measured turbidity or increase in particle content in 4 hr at 23 °C	2226	C
Granisetron HCl	SKB	0.05 mg/ml[a]	AB	2.5 mg/ml[a]	Physically compatible with no change in measured turbidity or increase in particle content in 4 hr at 23 °C	2000	C

Y-Site Injection Compatibility (1:1 Mixture) (Cont.)

Aminophylline

Drug	*Mfr*	*Conc*	*Mfr*	*Conc*	*Remarks*	*Ref*	*C/I*
Heparin sodium with hydrocortisone sodium succinate	RI UP	1000 units + 100 mg/L[h]	SE	25 mg/ml	Physically compatible for at least 4 hr at room temperature by visual and microscopic examination	322	C
Hetastarch in lactated electrolyte injection (Hextend)	AB	6%	AMR	2.5 mg/ml[a]	Physically compatible with no change in measured turbidity or increase in particle content in 4 hr at 23 °C	2339	C
Hydralazine HCl	SO SO	1 mg/ml[a] 1 mg/ml[b]	ES ES	4 mg/ml[a] 4 mg/ml[b]	Gross color change in 1 hr Moderate color change in 1 hr and slight haze in 3 hr	1316 1316	I I
Inamrinone lactate	WB	3 mg/ml[b]	LY	2 mg/ml[a]	Physically compatible for at least 4 hr at 25 °C under fluorescent light	992	C
Labetalol HCl	SC	1 mg/ml[a]	ES	1 mg/ml[a]	Physically compatible for 24 hr at 18 °C	1171	C
Levofloxacin	OMN	5 mg/ml[a]	AMR	25 mg/ml	Visually compatible for 4 hr at 24 °C under fluorescent light	2233	C
Linezolid	PHU	2 mg/ml	AB	2.5 mg/ml[a]	Physically compatible with no change in measured turbidity or increase in particle content in 4 hr at 23 °C	2264	C
Melphalan HCl	BW	0.1 mg/ml[b]	AB	2.5 mg/ml[b]	Physically compatible with no change in measured turbidity or increase in particle content in 3 hr at 22 °C	1557	C
Meropenem	ZEN	1 and 50 mg/ml[b]	AMR	25 mg/ml	Visually compatible for 4 hr at room temperature	1994	C
Morphine sulfate	WY	0.2 mg/ml[c]	ES	4 mg/ml[c]	Physically compatible for 3 hr	1316	C
Netilmicin sulfate	SC	5 mg/ml[i]	ES	800 μg/ml	Physically compatible and no netilmicin loss in 2 hr at 24 °C	1021	C
Ondansetron HCl	GL	1 mg/ml[b]	AMR	2.5 mg/ml[a]	Immediate turbidity and precipitation	1365	I
Paclitaxel	NCI	1.2 mg/ml[a]	AB	2.5 mg/ml[a]	Physically compatible with no change in measured turbidity in 4 hr at 22 °C	1556	C
Pancuronium bromide	ES	0.05 mg/ml[a]	AB	1 mg/ml[a]	Physically compatible for 24 hr at 28 °C	1337	C
Piperacillin sodium–tazobactam sodium	LE	40 + 5 mg/ml[a]	AB	2.5 mg/ml[a]	Physically compatible with no change in measured turbidity or increase in particle content in 4 hr at 22 °C	1688	C
Potassium chloride		40 mEq/L[h]	SE	25 mg/ml	Physically compatible for at least 4 hr at room temperature by visual and microscopic examination	322	C
Propofol	ZEN	10 mg/ml	AMR	2.5 mg/ml[a]	Physically compatible for 1 hr at 23 °C with no increase in particle content	2066	C
Ranitidine HCl	GL	0.5 mg/ml[e]	LY	4 mg/ml[a]	Physically compatible for 24 hr	1323	C
Remifentanil HCl	GW	0.025 and 0.25 mg/ml[b]	AB	2.5 mg/ml[a]	Physically compatible with no change in measured turbidity or increase in particle content in 4 hr at 23 °C	2075	C
Sargramostim	IMM	10 μg/ml[b]	ES	2.5 mg/ml[b]	Physically compatible for 4 hr at 22 °C	1436	C
Tacrolimus	FUJ	1 mg/ml[b]	ES	2 mg/ml[a]	Visually compatible for 24 hr at 25 °C	1630	C
Teniposide	BR	0.1 mg/ml[a]	AB	2.5 mg/ml[a]	Physically compatible with no subvisual haze or particle formation in 4 hr at 23 °C	1725	C

Y-Site Injection Compatibility (1:1 Mixture) (Cont.)

			Aminophylline				
Drug	*Mfr*	*Conc*	*Mfr*	*Conc*	*Remarks*	*Ref*	*C/I*
Thiotepa	IMM[j]	1 mg/ml[b]	AMR	2.5 mg/ml[b]	Physically compatible with no change in measured turbidity or increase in particle content in 4 hr at 23 °C	1861	C
TNA #218 to #226[k]			AB	2.5 mg/ml[a]	Visually compatible with no precipitate or emulsion damage apparent in 4 hr at 23 °C	2215	C
Tolazoline HCl		0.1 mg/ml[a]	AB	5[a] and 25 mg/ml	Physically compatible for 24 hr at 22 °C	1363	C
TPN #189[k]			DB	1 mg/ml[b]	Visually compatible for 24 hr at 22 °C	1767	C
TPN #203 and #204[k]			AMR	5 mg/ml	White precipitate forms immediately	1974	I
TPN #212 to #215[k]			AB	2.5 mg/ml[a]	Physically compatible with no change in measured turbidity or increase in particle content in 4 hr at 23 °C	2109	C
Vecuronium bromide	OR	0.1 mg/ml[a]	AB	1 mg/ml[a]	Physically compatible for 24 hr at 28 °C	1337	C
Vinorelbine tartrate	BW	1 mg/ml[b]	AB	2.5 mg/ml[b]	Initial light haze becomes visible in room light along with large particles in 1 hr	1558	I
Vitamin B complex with C	RC	2 ml/L[h]	SE	25 mg/ml	Physically compatible for at least 4 hr at room temperature by visual and microscopic examination	322	C
Warfarin sodium	DME	2 mg/ml[l]	ES	4 mg/ml[a]	Haze forms in 4 hr	2078	I

[a]*Tested in dextrose 5% in water.*
[b]*Tested in sodium chloride 0.9%.*
[c]*Tested in both dextrose 5% in water and sodium chloride 0.9%.*
[d]*Sodium carbonate–containing formulation tested.*
[e]*Tested in premixed infusion solution.*
[f]*Arginine formulation tested.*
[g]*Tested in bacteriostatic sodium chloride 0.9% preserved with benzyl alcohol 0.9%.*
[h]*Tested in dextrose 5% in water, sodium chloride 0.9%, and Ringer's injection, lactated.*
[i]*Tested in dextrose 5% in sodium chloride 0.2%.*
[j]*Lyophilized formulation tested.*
[k]*Refer to Appendix I for the composition of parenteral nutrition solutions. TNA indicates a 3-in-1 admixture, and TPN indicates a 2-in-1 admixture.*
[l]*Tested in sterile water for injection.*

Additional Compatibility Information

Infusion Solutions — The addition of aminophylline 750 mg/L to the dextrose-containing solutions dextrose 5% in water and dextrose 5% in sodium chloride 0.9% resulted in a yellow discoloration. The yellow color developed after 48, 24, and 6 hours of storage at 25, 35, and 55 °C, respectively. When stored in the refrigerator, these solutions remained colorless for seven days. The color intensity was increased by elevated temperatures and longer exposures. Additional peaks appeared on HPLC chromatograms as the yellow color intensified. Because the aminophylline concentration remained constant in all admixtures and the yellow color did not form in solutions lacking dextrose, it was believed that the discoloration resulted from the decomposition of dextrose. However, the dextrose decomposition products were well within compendial limits. Therefore, the authors concluded that these solutions were compatible admixtures. (556) Adams et al. reached the same conclusion in independent testing. (1571)

Storage of aminophylline 12.5 mg/50 ml of water for injection and dextrose 5, 10, and 20% in polypropylene syringes (Plastipak, Becton-Dickinson) and glass flasks for 24 hours at 24 to 26 °C resulted in no loss of aminophylline. However, a yellow discoloration of the solution began in two hours and intensified with time in the dextrose 10 and 20% mixtures. (852)

Acidic Drugs — Reports in the literature of aminophylline precipitating in acidic media do not apply to the dilute solutions found in intravenous infusions. Aminophylline should not be mixed in a syringe with other components of an admixture but should be added separately. (6)

Alkali-Labile Drugs — Because of the alkalinity of aminophylline-containing solutions, drugs known to be alkali labile should be avoided in admixtures, including epinephrine HCl, norepinephrine bitartrate, isoproterenol HCl, and penicillin G potassium. (6) Cefotaxime sodium should not be mixed in alkaline solutions such as those containing aminophylline. (792)

Calcium and Phosphate — Kirkpatrick et al. reported the physical compatibility of calcium gluconate 10 to 40 mEq/L and potassium phosphates 10 to 40 mM/L in three neonatal parenteral nutrition solutions (TPN #123 to #125 in Appendix I), alone and with retrograde administration of aminophylline 7.5 mg diluted with 1.5 ml of sterile water for injection. Contact of the alkaline aminophylline solution with the parenteral nutrition solutions resulted in the precipitation of calcium phosphate at much lower concentrations than were compatible in the parenteral nutrition solutions alone. (1404)

Methylprednisolone — Studies of the compatibility of methylprednisolone sodium succinate (Upjohn) with aminophylline added to an auxiliary medication infusion unit have been performed. Primary admixtures were prepared by adding aminophylline 500 mg/L to dextrose 5% in water, dextrose 5% in sodium chloride 0.9%, and Ringer's injection, lactated. Up to 100 ml of the primary admixture was added along with methylprednisolone sodium succinate (Upjohn) to the auxiliary medication infusion unit with the following results (329):

Methylprednisolone Sodium Succinate	Aminophylline 500 mg/L Primary Solution	Results
500 mg	D5S, D5W qs 100 ml	Clear solution for 24 hr
500 mg	LR qs 100 ml	Clear solution for 24 hr
500 mg	Added to 100 ml LR	Clear solution for 1 hr
1000 mg	D5W qs 100 ml	Yellow solution, clear for 24 hr
1000 mg	D5S qs 100 ml	Yellow solution, clear for 6 hr
1000 mg	Added to 100 ml D5S	Yellow solution, clear for 24 hr
1000 mg	LR qs 100 ml or added to 100 ml LR	Yellow solution, clear for 4 hr
2000 mg	D5S, D5W, LR qs 100 ml	Yellow solution, clear for 24 hr

Concentrated Drug Solutions — The following incompatibility determinations were performed with concentrated solutions. The drugs in dry form were reconstituted according to manufacturers' recommendations. Particulate matter was noted within two hours after adding 1 ml of aminophylline to 5 ml of sterile distilled water along with 1 ml of each of the following drugs (28):

Dimenhydrinate (Searle)
Hydroxyzine HCl (Pfizer)
Phenytoin sodium (Parke-Davis)
Prochlorperazine edisylate (SKF)
Promazine HCl (Wyeth)
Promethazine HCl (Wyeth)
Vancomycin HCl (Lilly)

AMIODARONE HCL
AHFS 24:04

Products — Amiodarone HCl is available in 3-ml ampuls. Each milliliter of the pale yellow solution contains (2):

Amiodarone HCl	50 mg
Polysorbate (Tween) 80	100 mg
Benzyl alcohol	20.2 mg
Water for injection	qs 1 ml

pH — The pH is reported to be 4.08. (1053)

Trade Name(s) — Cordarone Intravenous.

Administration — Amiodarone HCl is a concentrate that is administered by intravenous infusion after dilution in a compatible diluent. Intravenous infusion at concentrations of 1 to 6 mg/ml is performed using a volumetric pump and a dedicated central venous catheter with an inline filter when possible; concentrations greater than 2 mg/ml require a central venous catheter. (2; 4) The injection contains polysorbate 80, a surface active agent that alters drop size. The drop size reduction may lead to substantial underdosage if a drop counter infusion set is used. Consequently, the drug must be delivered with a volumetric infusion pump. (2; 1445)

Stability — Amiodarone HCl should be stored at room temperature and protected from light and excessive heat. Light protection is not necessary during administration (2), but exposure to direct sunlight should be avoided. (2258) It is recommended that amiodarone HCl be added only to dextrose 5% in water. (2) Information on the drug's compatibility in sodium chloride 0.9% has been conflicting. Amiodarone HCl 0.6 mg/ml in sodium chloride 0.9% precipitated in 24 hours at room temperature. (1443) In another study, a 1.8-mg/ml concentration in sodium chloride 0.9% was physically and chemically compatible for 24 hours at 24 °C. This difference could have been due to higher polysorbate 80 concentrations in the latter admixtures. (1031) Amiodarone HCl 0.6 mg/ml in dextrose 5% in water is stable for five days at room temperature. (1443) Solutions containing less than 0.6 mg/ml of amiodarone HCl in dextrose 5% in water are unstable and should not be used. (1442)

Amiodarone HCl (Wyeth-Ayerst) 2 mg/ml in dextrose 5% in water and also in sodium chloride 0.9% in amber glass containers was stored at 40 °C, being representative of the highest temperature to which drug solutions may be exposed. The solutions turned cloudy after 18 days of storage. HPLC analysis showed that 6 to 10% loss had occurred in sodium chloride 0.9% and dextrose 5% in water, respectively, in 18 days, with losses increasing to 11 to 14% in 24 days. (2110)

Precipitation — Amiodarone HCl may precipitate when diluted. Studies found little or no precipitation when the formulation was diluted to very small or very large concentrations. In the middle range, however, at concentrations between 45 mg/ml (90% amiodarone HCl formulation) and about 0.0025 mg/ml in phosphate buffer (pH 7.4), the drug concentration exceeds the solubility of amiodarone HCl in the mixture. Precipitation may occur immediately or on standing. Such precipitation may occur when the drug enters the bloodstream, contributing to the phlebitis associated with amiodarone HCl. (1818; 1819)

The aqueous solubility of amiodarone HCl is not substantially altered over the pH range of 1.5 to 7.5 (925), but precipitation may occur in alkaline media. (791; 1032)

Sorption—At concentrations of 1 to 6 mg/ml in dextrose 5% in water in polyolefin or glass containers, amiodarone HCl is physically compatible, with no loss in 24 hours. In PVC containers, however, the amiodarone HCl loss due to sorption occurs; acceptable potency (less than 10% loss) exists for two hours. Consequently, the manufacturer recommends that all infusions longer than two hours be made from glass or polyolefin containers only. (2) Amiodarone HCl (Labaz) 0.6 mg/ml in dextrose 5% in water did not exhibit any loss due to sorption in rigid PVC containers (PVC Container Corp.) or glass bottles (Travenol). However, losses were observed in flexible PVC bags (Travenol). The losses totaled approximately 25% in 24 hours at room temperature. (1443)

Similarly, amiodarone HCl is lost due to sorption to PVC infusion sets. (2; 1443) However, the manufacturer states that these losses are accounted for by the recommended dosage schedule. Consequently, PVC sets should be used with this drug, but the recommended infusion regimen must be followed. (2)

Filtration—Amiodarone HCl (Labaz) 0.6 mg/ml in dextrose 5% in water and sodium chloride 0.9% was filtered through a 0.22-μm cellulose ester membrane filter (Ivex-HP, Millipore) over six hours. No significant drug loss due to binding to the filter was noted. (1034) The use of an inline filter during administration is recommended. (2; 4)

Compatibility Information

Solution Compatibility

Amiodarone HCl

Solution	*Mfr*	*Mfr*	*Conc/L*	*Remarks*	*Ref*	*C/I*
Dextrose 5% in water	MG[a]	LZ	1.8 g	Physically compatible with little or no amiodarone loss in 24 hr at 24 °C under fluorescent light	1031	C
	TR[b]	LZ	0.6 g	Approximately 25% drug loss in 24 hr at room temperature	1443	I
	TR[c]	LZ	0.6 g	Physically compatible with little or no drug loss in 5 days at room temperature	1443	C
	BA[d]	WY	2 g	Visually compatible with no loss at 5 °C and 3% loss at 25 °C in 32 days	2110	C
Sodium chloride 0.9%	MG[a]	LZ	1.8 g	Physically compatible with little or no amiodarone loss in 24 hr at 24 °C under fluorescent light	1031	C
	TR[c]	LZ	0.6 g	Physically incompatible in 24 hr at room temperature	1443	I
	BA[d]	WY	2 g	Visually compatible with no loss at 5 °C and 3% loss at 25 °C in 32 days	2110	C
	MYR[c]	EBE	0.84 g	5% drug loss in 6 hr at room temperature under fluorescent light	2258	?

[a]*Tested in polyolefin containers.*
[b]*Tested in PVC containers.*
[c]*Tested in glass containers.*
[d]*Tested in amber glass containers.*

Additive Compatibility

Amiodarone HCl

Drug	*Mfr*	*Conc/L*	*Mfr*	*Conc/L*	*Test Soln*	*Remarks*	*Ref*	*C/I*
Dobutamine HCl	LI	1 g	LZ	2.5 g	D5W, NS	Physically compatible for 24 hr at 21 °C	812	C
Floxacillin sodium	BE	20 g	LZ	4 g	D5W	Immediate precipitation	1479	I
Furosemide	ES	200 mg	LZ	1.8 g	D5W, NS[a]	Physically compatible with 8% or less amiodarone loss in 24 hr at 24 °C under fluorescent light	1031	C
	HO	1 g	LZ	4 g	D5W	Haze forms in 5 hr and precipitate forms in 24 to 72 hr at 30 °C. No change at 15 °C	1479	I

Additive Compatibility (Cont.)

Amiodarone HCl

Drug	*Mfr*	*Conc/L*	*Mfr*	*Conc/L*	*Test Soln*	*Remarks*	*Ref*	*C/I*
Lidocaine HCl	AB	4 g	LZ	1.8 g	D5W, NS[a]	Physically compatible with 9% or less amiodarone loss in 24 hr at 24 °C under fluorescent light	1031	C
Potassium chloride	AB	40 mEq	LZ	1.8 g	D5W, NS[a]	Physically compatible with no amiodarone loss in 24 hr at 24 °C under fluorescent light	1031	C
Procainamide HCl	SQ	4 g	LZ	1.8 g	D5W, NS[a]	Physically compatible with 5% or less amiodarone loss in 24 hr at 24 °C under fluorescent light	1031	C
Propafenone HCl	KN	0.625 g	LZ	1.25 g[d]	D5W	Visually compatible with no propafenone loss by HPLC in 24 hr at 22 °C exposed to fluorescent light. Amiodarone not tested	412	C
Quinidine gluconate	LI	1 g	LZ	1.8 g	D5W[b]	Precipitation causes milky appearance. 13% amiodarone loss in 6 hr and 23% loss in 24 hr at 24 °C under fluorescent light	1031	I
	LI	1 g	LZ	1.8 g	D5W[c]	Precipitation causes milky appearance. No amiodarone loss in 24 hr at 24 °C under fluorescent light	1031	I
	LI	1 g	LZ	1.8 g	NS[b]	Physically compatible with 4% amiodarone loss in 6 hr and 13% loss in 24 hr at 24 °C under fluorescent light	1031	I
	LI	1 g	LZ	1.8 g	NS[c]	Physically compatible with no amiodarone loss in 24 hr at 24 °C under fluorescent light	1031	C
Verapamil HCl	KN	50 mg	LZ	1.8 g	D5W, NS[a]	Physically compatible with 8% or less amiodarone loss in 24 hr at 24 °C under fluorescent light	1031	C

[a]*Tested in both polyolefin and PVC containers.*
[b]*Tested in PVC containers.*
[c]*Tested in polyolefin containers.*
[d]*Approximate concentration.*

Drugs in Syringe Compatibility

Amiodarone HCl

Drug (in syringe)	*Mfr*	*Amt*	*Mfr*	*Amt*	*Remarks*	*Ref*	*C/I*
Heparin sodium		2500 units/ 1 ml	LZ	150 mg/ 3 ml	Turbidity or precipitate forms within 5 min	1053	I

Y-Site Injection Compatibility (1:1 Mixture)

Amiodarone HCl

Drug	*Mfr*	*Conc*	*Mfr*	*Conc*	*Remarks*	*Ref*	*C/I*
Amikacin sulfate	BR	5 mg/ml[c]	LZ	4 mg/ml[c]	Physically compatible for 4 hr at room temperature	1444	C
Aminophylline	ES	5 mg/ml[c]	LZ	4 mg/ml[c]	Haze forms within 15 min and white precipitate forms within 6 hr at 21 °C	1032	I

Y-Site Injection Compatibility (1:1 Mixture) (Cont.)

			Amiodarone HCl				
Drug	*Mfr*	*Conc*	*Mfr*	*Conc*	*Remarks*	*Ref*	*C/I*
Bretylium tosylate	ACC	8 mg/ml[c]	LZ	4 mg/ml[c]	Physically compatible for 24 hr at 21 °C	1032	C
Cefamandole nafate	LI	20 and 40 mg/ml[c]	LZ	4 mg/ml[c]	Precipitate forms	1444	I
Cefazolin sodium	LI	20 mg/ml[a]	LZ	4 mg/ml[a]	Precipitate forms	1444	I
	LI	20 mg/ml[b]	LZ	4 mg/ml[b]	Physically compatible for 4 hr at room temperature	1444	C
Clarithromycin	AB	4 mg/ml[a]	SW	3 mg/ml[a]	Visually compatible for 72 hr at both 30 and 17 °C	2174	C
Clindamycin phosphate	UP	6 mg/ml[c]	LZ	4 mg/ml[c]	Physically compatible for 4 hr at room temperature	1444	C
Dobutamine HCl	LI	2 mg/ml[c]	LZ	4 mg/ml[c]	Physically compatible for 24 hr at 21 °C	1032	C
Dopamine HCl	ES	1.6 mg/ml[c]	LZ	4 mg/ml[c]	Physically compatible for 24 hr at 21 °C	1032	C
Doxycycline hyclate	ACC	0.25 mg/ml[c]	LZ	4 mg/ml[c]	Physically compatible for 4 hr at room temperature	1444	C
Erythromycin lactobionate	AB	2 mg/ml[c]	LZ	4 mg/ml[c]	Physically compatible for 4 hr at room temperature	1444	C
Esmolol HCl	DU	40 mg/ml[a]	WY	4.8 mg/ml[a]	Visually compatible for 24 hr at 23 °C	1877	C
Gentamicin sulfate	LY	0.8 mg/ml[c]	LZ	4 mg/ml[c]	Physically compatible for 4 hr at room temperature	1444	C
Heparin sodium		50 units/ml/min[b]	LZ	150 mg/3 ml[d]	Yellow solution with opalescence	1053	I
		300 units/ml[b]		[e]	White precipitate forms upon sequential administration	791	I
Hetastarch in lactated electrolyte injection (Hextend)	AB	6%	WAY	4 mg/ml[a]	Physically compatible with no change in measured turbidity or increase in particle content in 4 hr at 23 °C	2339	C
Insulin, regular	LI	1 unit/ml[a]	WY	4.8 mg/ml[a]	Visually compatible for 24 hr at 23 °C	1877	C
Isoproterenol HCl	ES	0.004 mg/ml[c]	LZ	4 mg/ml[c]	Physically compatible for 24 hr at 21 °C	1032	C
Labetalol HCl	GL	5 mg/ml	WY	4.8 mg/ml[a]	Visually compatible for 24 hr at 23 °C	1877	C
Lidocaine HCl	AST	8 mg/ml[c]	LZ	4 mg/ml[c]	Physically compatible for 24 hr at 21 °C	1032	C
Metaraminol bitartrate	MSD	0.2 mg/ml[c]	LZ	4 mg/ml[c]	Physically compatible for 24 hr at 21 °C	1032	C
Metronidazole HCl	LY	5 mg/ml[c]	LZ	4 mg/ml[c]	Physically compatible for 4 hr at room temperature	1444	C
Midazolam HCl	RC	1 mg/ml[a]	WY	4.8 mg/ml[a]	Visually compatible for 24 hr at 23 °C	1877	C
Morphine sulfate	SX	1 mg/ml[a]	WY	4.8 mg/ml[a]	Visually compatible for 24 hr at 23 °C	1877	C
Nitroglycerin	AB	0.24 mg/ml[c]	LZ	4 mg/ml[c]	Physically compatible for 24 hr at 21 °C	1032	C
Norepinephrine bitartrate	BN	0.064 mg/ml[c]	LZ	4 mg/ml[c]	Physically compatible for 24 hr at 21 °C	1032	C
Penicillin G potassium	PF	100,000 units/ml[c]	LZ	4 mg/ml[c]	Physically compatible for 4 hr at room temperature	1444	C
Phentolamine mesylate	CI	0.04 mg/ml[c]	LZ	4 mg/ml[c]	Physically compatible for 24 hr at 21 °C	1032	C
Phenylephrine HCl	WI	0.04 mg/ml[c]	LZ	4 mg/ml[c]	Physically compatible for 24 hr at 21 °C	1032	C
Potassium chloride	AB	0.04 mEq/ml[c]	LZ	4 mg/ml[c]	Physically compatible for 24 hr at 21 °C	1032	C
Procainamide HCl	AHP	8 mg/ml[c]	LZ	4 mg/ml[c]	Physically compatible for 24 hr at 21 °C	1032	C
Sodium bicarbonate	AB	1 mEq/ml	WY	3 mg/ml[a]	Precipitate forms immediately	1851	I

Y-Site Injection Compatibility (1:1 Mixture) (Cont.)

Amiodarone HCl

Drug	*Mfr*	*Conc*	*Mfr*	*Conc*	*Remarks*	*Ref*	*C/I*
Tobramycin sulfate	LI	0.8 mg/ml[c]	LZ	4 mg/ml[c]	Physically compatible for 4 hr at room temperature	1444	C
Vancomycin HCl	LI	5 mg/ml[c]	LZ	4 mg/ml[c]	Physically compatible for 4 hr at room temperature	1444	C

[a]*Tested in dextrose 5% in water.*
[b]*Tested in sodium chloride 0.9%.*
[c]*Tested in both dextrose 5% in water and sodium chloride 0.9%.*
[d]*Given over three minutes via a Y-site into a running infusion solution of heparin sodium in sodium chloride 0.9%.*
[e]*Not specified.*

Additional Compatibility Information

Other Drugs — The manufacturer states that a precipitate forms when amiodarone HCl 4 mg/ml in dextrose 5% in water is admixed with aminophylline, cefamandole nafate, or cefazolin sodium and at 3 mg/ml with sodium bicarbonate. (2)

Evacuated Containers — Amiodarone HCl (Wyeth-Ayerst) 1.2 mg/ml in 250 ml of dextrose 5% in water has been reported to develop cloudiness upon standing when prepared in glass evacuated bottles (Abbott). The precipitation was attributed to the acetate buffers present in the small amount of residual fluid left in evacuated bottles from steam sterilization. (1982)

AMITRIPTYLINE HCL
AHFS 28:16.04

Products — Amitriptyline HCl is available as a colorless solution in 10-ml vials. Each milliliter of solution contains (2):

Amitriptyline HCl	10 mg
Dextrose	44 mg
Methylparaben	1.5 mg
Propylparaben	0.2 mg
Water for injection	qs 1 ml

pH — From 4 to 6. (4)

Trade Name(s) — Elavil.

Administration — Amitriptyline HCl is administered intramuscularly. (2; 4)

Stability — Amitriptyline HCl in intact containers should be protected from light and stored at controlled room temperature or under refrigeration. Freezing and temperatures over 30 °C should be avoided. (2; 4) Exposure to light results in the formation of ketone and, in three to four days, a precipitate. In solutions protected from light, these effects were not observed. (476)

Decomposition of amitriptyline HCl was observed when solutions in water or phosphate buffer (pH 6.8) were autoclaved at 115 °C for 30 minutes in the presence of excess oxygen. (477)

Sorption — Amitriptyline HCl (Roche) (concentration unspecified) in dextrose 5% in water in PVC containers was delivered over four hours through PVC administration sets. Little or no loss due to sorption was found by UV spectroscopy. (2045)

Compatibility Information

Sodium metabisulfite greatly increases the rate of decomposition of amitriptyline HCl. The presence of ferric or cupric ions also enhances decomposition. (478)

AMMONIUM CHLORIDE
AHFS 40:04

Products — Ammonium chloride additive solution is available in 20-ml vials containing 5.35 g of ammonium chloride, which provides 100 mEq (5 mEq/ml) of NH_4^+ and Cl^- ions. The solution also contains 2 mg/ml of disodium edetate as a stabilizer and hydrochloric acid to adjust the pH. The additive solution is intended to be used only after further dilution in a larger volume of sodium chloride 0.9% injection. (4)

One gram of ammonium chloride contains 18.7 mEq each of ammonium and chloride ions. (4)

pH — Adjusted to about pH 5 during manufacture. (4)

Osmolarity — 10 mOsm/ml (calculated). (4)

Administration — Ammonium chloride injection is a concentrate that is generally administered by slow intravenous infusion after dilution of one or two vials (100 to 200 mEq) in 500 to 1000 ml of sodium chloride 0.9% injection. The infusion rate in adults of the diluted solution should not exceed 5 ml/min. (4)

Stability — Store at controlled room temperature and protect from freezing. Highly concentrated solutions of ammonium chloride may crystallize when exposed to low temperatures. If such crystallization does occur, warming to room temperature in a water bath is recommended. (4)

Compatibility Information

Solution Compatibility

Ammonium chloride

Solution	*Mfr*	*Mfr*	*Conc/L*	*Remarks*	*Ref*	*C/I*
Dextran 6% in dextrose 5%	AB	AB	400 mEq	Physically compatible	3	C
Dextran 6% in sodium chloride 0.9%	AB	AB	400 mEq	Physically compatible	3	C
Dextrose–Ringer's injection combinations	AB	AB	400 mEq	Physically compatible	3	C
Dextrose–Ringer's injection, lactated, combinations	AB	AB	400 mEq	Physically compatible	3	C
Dextrose–saline combinations	AB	AB	400 mEq	Physically compatible	3	C
Dextrose 2½% in water	AB	AB	400 mEq	Physically compatible	3	C
Dextrose 5% in water	AB	AB	400 mEq	Physically compatible	3	C
Dextrose 10% in water	AB	AB	400 mEq	Physically compatible	3	C
Fructose 10% in sodium chloride 0.9%	AB	AB	400 mEq	Physically compatible	3	C
Fructose 10% in water	AB	AB	400 mEq	Physically compatible	3	C
Invert sugar 5 and 10% in sodium chloride 0.9%	AB	AB	400 mEq	Physically compatible	3	C
Invert sugar 5 and 10% in water	AB	AB	400 mEq	Physically compatible	3	C
Ionosol products	AB	AB	400 mEq	Physically compatible	3	C
Ringer's injection	AB	AB	400 mEq	Physically compatible	3	C
Ringer's injection, lactated	AB	AB	400 mEq	Physically compatible	3	C
Sodium chloride 0.45%	AB	AB	400 mEq	Physically compatible	3	C
Sodium chloride 0.9%	AB	AB	400 mEq	Physically compatible	3	C
Sodium lactate ⅙ M	AB	AB	400 mEq	Physically compatible	3	C

Additive Compatibility

Ammonium chloride

Drug	*Mfr*	*Conc/L*	*Mfr*	*Conc/L*	*Test Soln*	*Remarks*	*Ref*	*C/I*
Dimenhydrinate	SE					Physically incompatible	9	I
	SE	500 mg	AB	20 g	D5W	Physically compatible	15	C
Levorphanol bitartrate	RC					Physically incompatible	9	I

Y-Site Injection Compatibility (1:1 Mixture)

Ammonium chloride

Drug	*Mfr*	*Conc*	*Mfr*	*Conc*	*Remarks*	*Ref*	*C/I*
Warfarin sodium	DU	0.1 mg/ml[a]	AB	5 mEq/ml	Subvisual haze forms immediately	2011	I
	DU	0.1 mg/ml[b]	AB	5 mEq/ml	Physically compatible with no change in measured turbidity in 24 hr at 23 °C	2011	C
	DU	2 mg/ml[c]	AB	5 mEq/ml	Heavy white turbidity forms immediately and becomes flocculent precipitate in 24 hr at 23 °C	2011	I

[a]*Tested in dextrose 5% in water.*
[b]*Tested in sodium chloride 0.9%.*
[c]*Tested in sterile water for injection.*

Additional Compatibility Information

It has been stated that potassium chloride 20 and 40 mEq/L can be added to ammonium chloride injection. (128)

Ammonium chloride is stated to be incompatible with alkalies and their carbonates. (4)

AMOBARBITAL SODIUM (AMYLOBARBITONE SODIUM) AHFS 28:24.04

Products — Amobarbital sodium is available in vials containing 500 mg. Reconstitute the vials with sterile water for injection. The following table shows the amount of diluent to use to achieve various concentrations (1-3/13/98; 4):

	Concentration (mg/ml)				
Vial Size	10	25	50	100	200
500 mg	50 ml	20 ml	10 ml	5 ml	2.5 ml

Ordinarily, a 100-mg/ml concentration is used. After the addition of the sterile water for injection, rotate the vial but do not shake it. Several minutes are usually necessary to dissolve the drug, but any solution that has not become completely clear within five minutes should not be used. (1-3/13/98; 4)

pH — A 5% solution of amobarbital sodium in sterile water for injection has a pH of 9.6 to 10.4. (4)

Trade Name(s) — Amytal Sodium.

Administration — Amobarbital sodium may be administered by deep intramuscular or slow intravenous injection. No more than 5 ml of solution (regardless of concentration) should be injected intramuscularly at any one site. Subcutaneous and superficial intramuscular injections can be painful and result in tissue damage. The intravenous injection rate should not exceed 50 (1-3/13/98; 4) to 100 mg/min in adults or 60 $mg/m^2/min$ for children. (4)

Stability — Amobarbital sodium hydrolyzes in solution or when exposed to air. The contents of the vial should be injected within 30 minutes after reconstitution. (1-3/13/98; 4)

Amobarbital sodium should not be added to acidic solutions because the drug may precipitate if the resulting pH is 9.2 or less. (4)

No solution containing a precipitate should be used. (1-3/13/98; 4)

Compatibility Information

Solution Compatibility

Amobarbital sodium

Solution	*Mfr*	*Mfr*	*Conc/L*	*Remarks*	*Ref*	*C/I*
Alcohol 5%, dextrose 5%	BA	LI	10 g	Physically compatible for 24 hr	315	C
Dextrose 5% in Ringer's injection, lactated	BA	LI	10 g	Physically compatible for 24 hr	315	C
Dextrose 5% in sodium chloride 0.9%	BA	LI	10 g	Physically compatible for 24 hr	315	C

Solution Compatibility (Cont.)

Amobarbital sodium

Solution	*Mfr*	*Mfr*	*Conc/L*	*Remarks*	*Ref*	*C/I*
Dextrose 5% in water	BA	LI	10 g	Physically compatible for 24 hr	315	C
Dextrose 10% in water	BA	LI	10 g	Physically compatible for 24 hr	315	C
Dextrose 20% in water	BA	LI	10 g	Physically compatible for 24 hr	315	C
Fructose 10% in water	BA	LI	10 g	Physically compatible for 24 hr	315	C
Invert sugar 10% in Electrolyte #1	BA	LI	5 and 10 g	Precipitate forms within 24 hr	315	I
Invert sugar 10% in Electrolyte #2	BA	LI	5 and 10 g	Precipitate forms within 24 hr	315	I
Polysal M with dextrose 5%	CU	LI	10 g	Physically compatible for 24 hr	315	C
Ringer's injection, lactated	BA	LI	10 g	Physically compatible for 24 hr	315	C
Sodium chloride 0.9%	BA	LI	10 g	Physically compatible for 24 hr	315	C
Sodium lactate ⅙ M	BA	LI	10 g	Physically compatible for 24 hr	315	C

Additive Compatibility

Amobarbital sodium

Drug	*Mfr*	*Conc/L*	*Mfr*	*Conc/L*	*Test Soln*	*Remarks*	*Ref*	*C/I*
Amikacin sulfate	BR	5 g	LI	100 mg	D5LR, D5R, D5S, D5W, D10W, IS10, LR, NS, R, SL	Physically compatible. Potency of both retained for 24 hr at 25 °C	294	C
Aminophylline	SE	500 mg	LI	500 mg		Physically compatible	6	C
Dimenhydrinate	SE					Physically incompatible	9	I
	SE	500 mg	LI	1 g	D5W	Physically compatible	15	C
Diphenhydramine HCl	PD					Physically incompatible	9	I
	PD	80 mg	LI	1 g	D5W	Physically incompatible	15	I
Hydrocortisone sodium succinate						Physically incompatible	9	I
	UP	500 mg	LI	1 g	D5W	Physically compatible	15	C
Hydroxyzine HCl	PF					Physically incompatible	9	I
	RR	250 mg	LI	1 g	D5W	Physically incompatible	15	I
Insulin, regular[a]						Physically incompatible	9	I
Levorphanol bitartrate	RC					Physically incompatible	9	I
Meperidine HCl	WI					Physically incompatible	9	I
Morphine sulfate						Physically incompatible	9	I
Norepinephrine bitartrate	WI					Physically incompatible	9	I
	WI	2 mg	LI	1 g	D5W	Physically incompatible	15	I
Pentazocine lactate	WI	300 mg	LI	1 g	D5W	Physically incompatible	15	I
Procaine HCl						Physically incompatible	9	I
	WI	1 g	LI	1 g	D5W	Physically incompatible	15	I
Sodium bicarbonate	AB	2.4 mEq[b]	LI	500 mg	D5W	Physically compatible for 24 hr	772	C
Streptomycin sulfate						Physically incompatible	9	I

Additive Compatibility (Cont.)

Amobarbital sodium

Drug	*Mfr*	*Conc/L*	*Mfr*	*Conc/L*	*Test Soln*	*Remarks*	*Ref*	*C/I*
Vancomycin HCl	LI					Physically incompatible	9	I
	LI	5 g	LI	1 g	D5W	Physically incompatible	15	I

[a]*Test performed prior to availability of neutral regular insulin.*
[b]*One vial of Neut added to a liter of admixture.*

Additional Compatibility Information

Acidic Drugs — Drugs such as amobarbital sodium exhibit poor solubility in an acidic medium and may precipitate. (22) Metaraminol bitartrate is acidic and may cause precipitation, depending on the concentrations of the additives. (7) Also, the acidic methyldopate HCl imparts some buffer capacity to admixtures and may pose solubility problems with barbiturate salts. (23)

When barbiturates are mixed with succinylcholine chloride, either the free barbiturate will precipitate or the succinylcholine chloride will be hydrolyzed, depending on the final pH of the admixture. (21) Atracurium besylate may also be inactivated by alkaline solutions, such as barbiturates, and precipitation of a free acid of the admixed drug may occur, depending on the resultant pH of the admixture. (4)

Alkali-Labile Drugs — Amobarbital sodium may raise the pH of admixture solutions to the alkaline range and, therefore, should not be mixed with alkali-labile drugs such as penicillin G. (47) Significant decomposition of isoproterenol HCl and norepinephrine bitartrate may also occur. If either of these two drugs is mixed with amobarbital sodium, the admixture should be used immediately after preparation. (59; 77)

Other Drugs — Drugs stated to be incompatible with barbiturate salts include pentazocine lactate (4), clindamycin phosphate (106), cefazolin sodium (278), cimetidine HCl (360), pancuronium bromide (4), and droperidol. (4)

AMPHOTERICIN B
AHFS 8:12.04 and 84:04.08

Products — Amphotericin B is available in vials containing 50 mg of drug with sodium desoxycholate 41 mg and sodium phosphates 20.2 mg. (1-10/98) Reconstitute with 10 ml of sterile water for injection without preservatives and shake until a clear colloidal dispersion is obtained. The resultant concentration is 5 mg/ml of amphotericin B. Use only sterile water for injection without preservatives for reconstitution because other diluents, such as sodium chloride 0.9% or solutions containing a bacteriostatic agent such as benzyl alcohol, may result in the precipitation of the antibiotic. For infusion, amphotericin B must be further diluted with dextrose 5% in water with a pH above 4.2. (1-10/98; 4)

pH — The pH of amphotericin B (Squibb) 100 mg/L in dextrose 5% in water has been reported as 5.7. (149)

Osmolality — The osmolality of amphotericin B (Squibb) 0.1 mg/ml in dextrose 5% in water was determined to be 256 mOsm/kg. (1375)

Trade Name(s) — Fungizone Intravenous, Amphocin.

Administration — Amphotericin B is administered by slow intravenous infusion over approximately two to six hours. The recommended concentration of the infusion is 0.1 mg/ml. (1-10/98; 4) The drug has also been given intra-articularly, intrathecally, intrapleurally, and by irrigation. (4)

Stability — Store intact vials at 2 to 8 °C and protect from light. (1-10/98; 4) Although refrigeration is recommended, intact vials of amphotericin B (Squibb) are reported to be stable at room temperature for two weeks (853) to one month. (60) The manufacturer indicates that a 5 to 10% potency loss occurs in one month at room temperature. (1433)

Amphotericin B reconstituted with sterile water for injection without preservatives and stored in the dark is stable for 24 hours at room temperature and for one week under refrigeration at 2 to 8 °C. (1-10/98; 4; 108) One report indicates that aqueous solutions may be stable for over a week at both 5 and 28 °C. (352)

pH Effects — The pH range for optimum clarity and stability is 6 to 7. (148) At a pH of less than approximately 6, the colloidal dispersion may become turbid. (40; 148) Colloidal particles tend to coagulate rapidly at a pH of less than 5. (4)

Light Effects — Although the manufacturer recommends light protection for aqueous solutions of amphotericin B (1-10/98), several reports indicate that for short-term exposure of eight to 24 hours, little difference in potency is observed between light-protected and light-exposed solutions. (150; 335; 353) Longer exposure periods may result in unacceptable potency loss, however. (150)

Elastomeric Reservoir Pumps—Amphotericin B (Lyphomed) 0.25 mg/ml in dextrose 5% in water was evaluated for binding potential to natural rubber elastomeric reservoirs (Baxter). No binding was found after storage for two weeks at 35 °C with gentle agitation. (2014)

Amphotericin B solutions in elastomeric reservoir pumps have been stated by the pump manufacturers to be stable for the following time periods refrigerated (REF) or at room temperature (RT) (31):

Pump Reservoir(s)	Conc.	REF	RT
Homepump; Homepump Eclipse	0.2 mg/ml[a]	10 days	24 hr
Intermate; Intermate HPC; Intermate LV	0.25 to 0.5 mg/ml[a]	10 days	
Medflo	0.1 mg/ml[a]	3 days	48 hr

[a]*In dextrose 5% in water.*

Filtration—Various studies have assessed the effects of filtration on the amphotericin B colloidal dispersion with differing results. Huber and Riffkin reported that the use of a 0.22-μm membrane filter was unacceptable with colloidal solutions adjusted to pH 4.7, 5.6, and 6.5. The concentration of amphotericin B in the filtrate decreased substantially after several hours. A 0.45-μm filter was satisfactory for infusions with a pH of 6.5, but the results at pH 5.6 were inconclusive. At pH 5.6 and 6.5, 1- and 5-μm filters both proved satisfactory in that they did not reduce the concentration of amphotericin B. For the turbid mixtures resulting at pH 4.7, however, all filters sharply reduced the concentration. (148) A report by Rebagay et al. tended to support this finding for the 0.22-μm filter. At pH 5.7, fine particles of amphotericin B formed and were retained by the 0.22-μm filter. (149) Gotz and Simon, using a method similar to that of Huber and Riffkin, found no appreciable reduction in concentration with the 0.45-μm filter; but with a 0.22-μm filter, after one hour the concentration of amphotericin B delivered was about 30% of the initial concentration. (152) Tipple et al. reported that when amphotericin B 50 mg/500 ml in dextrose 5% in water was filtered through a 0.22-μm circular cellulose ester membrane (Swinnex) or a 0.22-μm cylindrical cellulose ester filter (Ivex-2), the flow rate decreased dramatically after passage of as little as 30 ml. Flow ceased altogether after 100 to 200 ml. The last sample filtered contained no drug. With a 0.45-μm circular cellulose ester membrane (Swinnex), no loss of activity was determined after filtration of 200 ml. However, the flow rate had decreased. (598) On the other hand, Piecoro et al. found no significant difference in the amount or potency of amphotericin B in dextrose 5% in water with phosphate buffer after filtration with 0.22-, 0.45-, and 5-μm filters. (151)

For amphotericin B infusions, only filters with a pore size not less than 1 μm should be used for filtration. (1-10/98; 4; 148) This would allow a margin for error that would compensate for possible variations in particle size. (148) Also, limiting the use of filtration to situations where it is believed to be necessary has been recommended. (598; 599)

Compatibility Information

Solution Compatibility

Amphotericin B

Solution	*Mfr*	*Mfr*	*Conc/L*	*Remarks*	*Ref*	*C/I*
Amino acids 4.25%, dextrose 25%	MG	SQ	100 mg	Turbidity and fine yellow particles form	349	I
Dextrose 5% in Ringer's injection, lactated	MG[a]	SQ	100 mg	Precipitate forms in 30 min. Drug concentration of about 50% of initial amount in 30 min	539	I
Dextrose 5% in sodium chloride 0.9%	MG[a]	SQ	100 mg	Precipitate forms within 2 hr. Drug concentration of 30 to 70% of initial amount in 2 hr	539	I
Dextrose 5% in water		SQ	70 and 140 mg	Bioactivity not significantly affected over 24 hr at 25 °C with or without light exposure	335	C
	MG[a]	SQ	100 mg	Physically compatible and drug concentration unchanged after 48 hr	539	C
		SQ	50 and 100 mg	No loss of bioactivity in normal light at 25 °C for 24 hr	540	C
	MG[b]	SQ	0.9, 1.2, 1.4 g	Physically compatible with little or no loss in 36 hr at 6 and 25 °C	1434	C
	MG[b]	SQ	470, 660, 750 mg	Visually compatible with no amphotericin B loss by HPLC in 24 hr at 25 °C	1537	C
	BA[c]	SQ	100 mg	Visually compatible with no amphotericin B loss by HPLC in 24 hr at 15 to 25 °C	1544	C
	BA[c]	SQ	100 and 250 mg	Visually compatible with 4% amphotericin B loss in 35 days at 4 °C in the dark	1546	C
	BA[c]	SQ	0.2, 0.5, 1 g	Visually compatible with little or no amphotericin B loss by HPLC in 5 days at 4 and 25 °C. Normal turbidity observed at 1 g/L	1728	C
	AB[c]	BMS	50 mg	Visually compatible with no loss by HPLC protected from light and 5% loss exposed to fluorescent light in 24 hr at 24 °C	2093	C

Solution Compatibility (Cont.)

Amphotericin B

Solution	Mfr	Mfr	Conc/L	Remarks	Ref	C/I
	AB[c]	BMS	500 mg	Visually compatible with no loss by HPLC protected from or exposed to fluorescent light in 24 hr at 24 °C	2093	C
Dextrose 10% in water	BA[c]	SQ	100 mg	Visually compatible with no amphotericin B loss by HPLC in 24 hr at 15 to 25 °C	1544	C
Dextrose 15% in water	BA[c]	SQ	100 mg	Visually compatible with no amphotericin B loss by HPLC in 24 hr at 15 to 25 °C	1544	C
Dextrose 20% in water	BA[c]	SQ	100 mg	Visually compatible with no amphotericin B loss by HPLC in 24 hr at 15 to 25 °C	1544	C
Fat emulsion 10 and 20%, intravenous	CL	APC, PHT	0.6 g	Precipitate forms immediately but is concealed by opaque emulsion	1808	I
Fat emulsion 20%, intravenous			90 mg	Yellow precipitate forms in 2 hr. HPLC found cumulative delivery of only 56% of the total dose	1872	I
	CL	APC	10, 50, 100, and 500 mg, 1 and 5 g	Emulsion separation occurred rapidly with visible creaming within 4 hr at 27 and 8 °C	1987	I
	KA	SQ	500 mg, 1 and 2 g	Precipitated amphotericin noted on bottom of containers within 4 hr	1988	I
	CL[d]	BMS	50 mg	Fat emulsion separates into two phases within 8 hr. No amphotericin B loss by HPLC protected from light and 4% loss exposed to fluorescent light in 24 hr at 24 °C	2093	I
	CL[d]	BMS	500 mg	Fat emulsion separates into two phases within 8 hr. No loss by HPLC protected from or exposed to fluorescent light in 24 hr at 24 °C	2093	I
Ringer's injection, lactated	MG[a]	SQ	100 mg	Precipitate forms within 2 hr. Drug concentration of 80% of initial amount in 2 hr	539	I
Sodium chloride 0.9%	AB	SQ	100 mg	Physically incompatible	15	I
	MG[a]	SQ	100 mg	Precipitate forms within 2 hr. Drug concentration of 43% of initial amount in 2 hr	539	I

[a]*Tested in both glass and polyolefin containers.*
[b]*Tested in polyolefin containers.*
[c]*Tested in PVC containers.*
[d]*Tested in glass bottles.*

Additive Compatibility

Amphotericin B

Drug	Mfr	Conc/L	Mfr	Conc/L	Test Soln	Remarks	Ref	C/I
Amikacin sulfate	BR	5 g	SQ	100 mg	D5LR, D5R, D5S, D5W, D10W, IS10, LR, NS, R, SL	Immediate precipitate	293	I
Calcium chloride	BP	4 g		200 mg	D5W	Haze develops over 3 hr	26	I
Calcium gluconate	BP	4 g		200 mg	D5W	Haze develops over 3 hr	26	I

Additive Compatibility (Cont.)

			Amphotericin B					
Drug	*Mfr*	*Conc/L*	*Mfr*	*Conc/L*	*Test Soln*	*Remarks*	*Ref*	*C/I*
Chlorpromazine HCl	BP	200 mg		200 mg	D5W	Immediate precipitate	26	I
Cimetidine HCl	SKF	600 mg	SQ	100 mg	D5W	Immediate haze formation. Precipitate observed at 24 hr at room temperature	551	I
Ciprofloxacin	MI	2 g		100 mg	D5W	Physically incompatible	888	I
Diphenhydramine HCl	PD	80 mg	SQ	100 mg	D5W	Physically incompatible	15	I
Dopamine HCl	AS	800 mg	SQ	200 mg	D5W	Immediate precipitate	78	I
Edetate calcium disodium	RI	4 g		200 mg	D5W	Haze develops over 3 hr	26	I
Fluconazole	PF	1 g	LY	50 mg	D5W	Visually compatible with no fluconazole loss by HPLC in 72 hr at 25 °C under fluorescent light. Amphotericin B not tested	1677	C
Gentamicin sulfate		320 mg		200 mg	D5W	Haze develops over 3 hr	26	I
Heparin sodium	UP	4000 units	SQ	100 mg	D5W	Physically compatible	15	C
	AB	4000 units	SQ	100 mg	D	Physically compatible	21	C
		2000 units	SQ	70 and 140 mg	D5W	Bioactivity not significantly affected over 24 hr at 25 °C with or without light exposure	335	C
Heparin sodium with hydrocortisone sodium phosphate	AB MSD	1500 units 50 and 100 mg	SQ	50 and 100 mg	D5W	Physically compatible and amphotericin B bioactivity retained in normal light at 25 °C for 24 hr. Hydrocortisone and heparin activity not tested	540	C
Hydrocortisone sodium phosphate	MSD	50 and 100 mg	SQ	50 and 100 mg	D5W	Physically compatible and amphotericin B bioactivity retained in normal light at 25 °C for 24 hr. Hydrocortisone not tested	540	C
Hydrocortisone sodium succinate	UP	500 mg	SQ	100 mg	D5W	Physically compatible	15	C
		50 mg	SQ	70 and 140 mg	D5W	Bioactivity not significantly affected over 24 hr at 25 °C with or without light exposure	335	C
Kanamycin sulfate	BPC	4 g		200 mg	D5W	Haze develops over 3 hr	26	I
Magnesium sulfate	IMS	2 and 4 g	SQ	40 and 80 mg	D5W	Physically incompatible in 3 hr at 24 °C with decreased clarity and development of supernatant. Total loss of amphotericin B in supernatant by HPLC	1578	I
Meropenem	ZEN	1 and 20 g	SQ	200 mg	NS	Precipitate forms	2068	I
Metaraminol bitartrate	BP	200 mg		200 mg	D5W	Haze develops over 3 hr	26	I
Methyldopate HCl		1 g		200 mg	D5W	Haze develops over 3 hr	26	I
Penicillin G potassium	SQ	20 million units	SQ	100 mg	D5W	Physically incompatible	15	I
	SQ	5 million units	SQ	50 mg		Precipitate forms within 1 hr	47	I

Additive Compatibility (Cont.)

Drug	Mfr	Conc/L	Amphotericin B Mfr	Amphotericin B Conc/L	Test Soln	Remarks	Ref	C/I
	BP	10 million units		200 mg	D5W	Haze develops over 3 hr	26	I
Penicillin G sodium	UP	20 million units	SQ	100 mg	D5W	Physically incompatible	15	I
	BP	10 million units		200 mg	D5W	Haze develops over 3 hr	26	I
Polymyxin B sulfate	BP	20 mg		200 mg	D5W	Haze develops over 3 hr	26	I
Potassium chloride	AB	100 mEq	SQ	100 mg	D5W	Physically incompatible	15	I
	BP	4 g		200 mg	D5W	Haze develops over 3 hr	26	I
Prochlorperazine mesylate	BP	100 mg		200 mg	D5W	Haze develops over 3 hr	26	I
Ranitidine HCl	GL	100 mg	SQ	200 mg	D5W	Color change and particle formation	1151	I
Sodium bicarbonate	AB	2.4 mEq[a]	SQ	50 mg	D5W	Physically compatible for 24 hr	772	C
Streptomycin sulfate	BP	4 g		200 mg	D5W	Haze develops over 3 hr	26	I
Verapamil HCl	KN	80 mg	SQ	100 mg	D5W	Physically incompatible after 8 hr	764	I
	KN	80 mg	SQ	100 mg	NS	Immediate physical incompatibility	764	I

[a] *One vial of Neut added to a liter of admixture.*

Drugs in Syringe Compatibility

Drug (in syringe)	Mfr	Amt	Amphotericin B Mfr	Amphotericin B Amt	Remarks	Ref	C/I
Heparin sodium		2500 units/ 1 ml		50 mg	Physically compatible for at least 5 min	1053	C

Y-Site Injection Compatibility (1:1 Mixture)

Drug	Mfr	Conc	Amphotericin B Mfr	Amphotericin B Conc	Remarks	Ref	C/I
Aldesleukin	CHI	33,800 I.U./ ml[a]	SQ	1.6 mg/ml[a]	Visually compatible for 2 hr. Bioassay not possible	1857	C
Allopurinol sodium	BW	3 mg/ml[a]	SQ	0.6 mg/ml[a]	Natural haze of amphotericin B lost immediately	1686	I
Amifostine	AD	0.6 mg/ml[a]	AMR	2.5 mg/ml[a]	Turbidity forms immediately	1845	I
Amsacrine	NCI	1 mg/ml[a]	SQ	0.6 mg/ml[a]	Immediate light yellow turbidity, becoming yellow flocculent precipitate in 15 min	1381	I
Aztreonam	SQ	40 mg/ml[a]	PHT	0.6 mg/ml[a]	Yellow turbidity forms immediately and becomes flocculent precipitate in 4 hr	1758	I
Cefepime HCl	BMS	20 mg/ml[a]	SQ	0.6 mg/ml[a]	Heavy yellow flocculent precipitate forms immediately	1689	I

Y-Site Injection Compatibility (1:1 Mixture) (Cont.)

Drug	*Mfr*	*Conc*	Amphotericin B *Mfr*	Amphotericin B *Conc*	*Remarks*	*Ref*	*C/I*
Cefpirome sulfate	HO	50 mg/ml[c]	SQ	0.1 mg/ml[c]	Little or no cefpirome loss but up to 45% amphotericin B loss by HPLC in 4 hr at 23 °C, possibly due to precipitation	2044	I
Cisatracurium besylate	GW	0.1 mg/ml[a]	PH	0.6 mg/ml[a]	Physically compatible with no change in measured turbidity or increase in particle content in 4 hr at 23 °C	2074	C
	GW	2 mg/ml[a]	PH	0.6 mg/ml[a]	Cloudiness forms immediately; gel-like precipitate forms in 1 hr	2074	I
	GW	5 mg/ml[a]	PH	0.6 mg/ml[a]	Turbidity forms immediately	2074	I
Diltiazem HCl	MMD	5 mg/ml	SQ	0.1 mg/ml[a]	Visually compatible	1807	C
Docetaxel	RPR	0.9 mg/ml[a]	PH	0.6 mg/ml[a]	Visible turbidity forms immediately	2224	I
Doxorubicin HCl liposome injection	SEQ	0.4 mg/ml[a]	APC	0.6 mg/ml[a]	Fivefold increase in measured particulates in 4 hr	2087	I
Enalaprilat	MSD	1.25 mg/ml	SQ	0.1 mg/ml[a]	Layered haze develops in 4 hr at 21 °C	1409	I
Etoposide phosphate	BR	5 mg/ml[a]	GNS	0.6 mg/ml[a]	Yellow-orange flocculent precipitate forms immediately	2218	I
Filgrastim	AMG	30 µg/ml[a]	SQ	0.6 mg/ml[a]	Yellow turbidity forms immediately and becomes flocculent precipitate	1687	I
Fluconazole	RR	2 mg/ml	SQ	5 mg/ml	Cloudiness and yellow precipitation	1407	I
Fludarabine phosphate	BX	1 mg/ml[a]	SQ	0.6 mg/ml[a]	Small amount of precipitate forms within 4 hr at room temperature	1439	I
Foscarnet sodium	AST	24 mg/ml	SQ	5 mg/ml	Delayed formation of cloudy yellow precipitate	1335	I
	AST	24 mg/ml	SQ	0.6 mg/ml[a]	Dense haze develops immediately	1397	I
Gatifloxacin	BMS	2 mg/ml[a]	PH	0.6 mg/ml[a]	Yellow flocculent precipitate forms immediately	2234	I
Gemcitabine HCl	LI	10 mg/ml[b]	PH	0.6 mg/ml[a]	Gross precipitation occurs immediately	2226	I
Granisetron HCl	SKB	0.05 mg/ml[a]	PH	0.6 mg/ml[a]	Large increase in measured turbidity occurs immediately	2000	I
Hetastarch in lactated electrolyte injection (Hextend)	AB	6%	APC	0.6 mg/ml[a]	Immediate gross precipitation	2339	I
Linezolid	PHU	2 mg/ml	AB	0.6 mg/ml[a]	Yellow flocculent precipitate forms within 5 min	2264	I
Melphalan HCl	BW	0.1 mg/ml[b]	SQ	0.6 mg/ml[a]	Immediate two- to fourfold increase in measured turbidity due to sodium chloride	1557	I
	BW	0.1 mg/ml[a]	SQ	0.6 mg/ml[a]	Physically compatible but rapid melphalan loss in D5W precludes use	1557	I
Meropenem	ZEN	1 and 50 mg/ml[b]	SQ	5 mg/ml	Precipitate forms	2068	I
Ondansetron HCl	GL	1 mg/ml[a]	SQ	0.6 mg/ml[a]	Immediate pale yellow turbidity and precipitation	1365	I
Paclitaxel	NCI	1.2 mg/ml[a]	SQ	0.6 mg/ml[a]	Immediate increase in measured turbidity followed by separation into layers in 24 hr at 22 °C	1556	I
Piperacillin sodium–tazobactam sodium	LE	40 + 5 mg/ml[a]	SQ	0.6 mg/ml[a]	Heavy yellow flocculent precipitate forms immediately	1688	I

Y-Site Injection Compatibility (1:1 Mixture) (Cont.)

Amphotericin B

Drug	*Mfr*	*Conc*	*Mfr*	*Conc*	*Remarks*	*Ref*	*C/I*
Propofol	ZEN	10 mg/ml	APC	0.6 mg/ml[a]	Gel-like precipitate forms immediately	2066	I
Remifentanil HCl	GW	0.025 mg/ml[a]	PHT	0.6 mg/ml[a]	Physically compatible with no change in measured turbidity or increase in particle content in 4 hr at 23 °C	2075	C
	GW	0.25 mg/ml[a]	PHT	0.6 mg/ml[a]	Yellow precipitate forms immediately	2075	I
Sargramostim	IMM	10 μg/ml[a]	SQ	0.6 mg/ml[a]	Physically compatible for 4 hr at 22 °C	1436	C
	IMM	10 μg/ml[b]	SQ	0.6 mg/ml[b]	Moderately heavy yellow precipitate forms immediately	1436	I
Tacrolimus	FUJ	1 mg/ml[d]	LY	5 mg/ml[a]	Visually compatible for 24 hr at 25 °C	1630	C
Teniposide	BR	0.1 mg/ml[a]	SQ	0.6 mg/ml[a]	Physically compatible with no subvisual haze or particle formation in 4 hr at 23 °C	1725	C
Thiotepa	IMM[e]	1 mg/ml[a]	APC	0.6 mg/ml[a]	Physically compatible with no change in measured turbidity or increase in particle content in 4 hr at 23 °C	1861	C
TNA #218 to #226[g]			PH	0.6 mg/ml[a]	Yellow precipitate forms immediately	2215	I
TPN #212 to #215[g]			PH	0.6 mg/ml[a]	Gross flocculent precipitate forms immediately	2109	I
Vinorelbine tartrate	BW	1 mg/ml[b]	SQ	0.6 mg/ml[f]	Heavy yellow precipitate forms immediately	1558	I
Zidovudine	BW	4 mg/ml[a]	SQ	600 μg/ml[a]	Physically compatible for 4 hr at 25 °C under fluorescent light by visual and microscopic examination	1193	C

[a]*Tested in dextrose 5% in water.*
[b]*Tested in sodium chloride 0.9%.*
[c]*Tested in dextrose 5% in water, Ringer's injection, lactated, sodium chloride 0.45%, and sodium chloride 0.9%.*
[d]*Tested in sterile water.*
[e]*Lyophilized formulation tested.*
[f]*Tested in both dextrose 5% in water and sodium chloride 0.9%.*
[g]*Refer to Appendix I for the composition of parenteral nutrition solutions. TNA indicates a 3-in-1 admixture, and TPN indicates a 2-in-1 admixture.*

Additional Compatibility Information

Fat Emulsion — In an effort to reduce toxicity, amphotericin B has been admixed in Intralipid instead of the more usual dextrose 5% in water. (1809–1811; 2178) However, amphotericin B 0.75 mg/kg/day administered using this approach in 250 ml of Intralipid 20% has been associated with acute pulmonary toxicities, including sudden onset of coughing, tachypnea, cyanosis, and deterioration of oxygen saturation following administration. The temporal relationship between the drug administration and respiratory symptoms suggested a causal relationship. Furthermore, no reduction in renal toxicity or other side effects was observed. It was concluded amphotericin B should not be administered in Intralipid. (2177)

At a concentration of 0.6 mg/ml in Intralipid 10 or 20%, amphotericin B precipitates immediately or almost immediately. The precipitate is not visible to the unaided eye because of the emulsion's dense opacity. Particle size evaluation found thousands of particles larger than 10 μm per milliliter. In dextrose 5% in water, very few particles were larger than 10 μm. Centrifuging the Intralipid admixtures resulted in rapid visualization of the precipitate as a mass at the bottom of the test tubes. (1808)

However, amphotericin B precipitation is observed in fat emulsion within two to four hours without centrifuging. In concentrations ranging from 90 mg to 2 g/L in Intralipid 20%, amphotericin B precipitate is easily seen as yellow particulate matter on the bottom of the lipid emulsion containers. (1872; 1988) Damage to the emulsion integrity with creaming has also been reported. (1987)

In other reports, the appearance of problems was observed in as little as 15 minutes, and actual amphotericin B precipitate formed within 20 minutes of mixing. Analysis of the precipitate confirmed its identity as amphotericin B. The authors hypothesized that amphotericin B precipitates as a consequence of the excipient deoxycholic acid, which is an anion, attracting oppositely charged choline groups from the egg yolk components of the fat emulsion. As a consequence, deoxycholic acid and phosphatidylcholine form a precipitate and insufficient surfactant remains to keep the amphotericin B dispersed. (2204; 2205)

Heparin Lock Flush Solution — Amphotericin B (Squibb) 0.1 mg/ml in dextrose 5% in water was combined in equal volumes with heparin lock flush solution (SoloPak) containing heparin sodium 100 units/ml in sodium chloride 0.9%, sodium chloride 0.9%, and sterile water for injection as a control. The heparin lock flush solution and sodium chloride 0.9% behaved identically. At room temperature, the mixtures were clear at 15 minutes, turbid in 30 minutes, and markedly precipitated in four hours. At 37 °C, the process was accelerated, with marked precipitation in 45 minutes. The control solutions remained clear throughout. The authors recommended flushing sodium chloride-containing solutions from venous access devices with dextrose 5% in water before and after amphotericin B administration. (1435)

Other Amphotericin B Formulations — Although various lipid complex and liposomal products of amphotericin B exist, they are sufficiently different from conventional amphotericin B formulations that extrapolating compatibility data to the other forms would be inappropriate.

Other Drugs — When 17.5 mg of amphotericin B was added to 125 ml of a 20% mannitol solution and this was further diluted to 1000 ml with dextrose 5% in water for administration by infusion, serum amphotericin B levels were satisfactory during therapy. (84; 357)

Amphotericin B in infusions appears to be compatible with limited amounts of heparin sodium (4; 356), hydrocortisone sodium succinate, and methylprednisolone sodium succinate. (4) However, amphotericin B is stated to be incompatible with antihistamines and vitamins. (40) Local anesthetics such as procaine HCl and lidocaine HCl cause precipitation of amphotericin B. (107) It also is stated to be incompatible with ranitidine HCl. (1515)

Evacuated Containers — Amphotericin B (Squibb) was reported to be physically incompatible with Abbott evacuated containers. These containers have a small residual amount of fluid composed of acetic acid and sodium acetate buffer. Preparation of amphotericin B in these containers resulted in a precipitate. Similarly, Travenol evacuated containers have a small residual amount of sodium chloride 0.9% solution, which also causes amphotericin B precipitation. McGaw uses only sterile water in its evacuated containers, and they should be satisfactory for preparing amphotericin B admixtures. (1232)

Other Information

Dilution for Infusion — Reconstituted amphotericin B may be added to dextrose 5% in water with a pH above 4.2. Buffers present in the formulation raise the pH of the admixture. If the dextrose 5% in water has a pH less than 4.2, additional buffer must be added. (1-10/98; 4) One or 2 ml of a buffer solution with the following composition should be added:

Dibasic sodium phosphate (anhydrous)	1.59 g
Monobasic sodium phosphate (anhydrous)	0.96 g
Water for injection	qs 100 ml

The buffer solution should be sterilized either by filtration or by autoclaving for 30 minutes at 121 °C at 15 pounds pressure. (1-10/98) Failure to sterilize this buffer solution coupled with prolonged storage at room temperature has resulted in severe infection. (328)

Turbidity may appear in solutions in which the final pH is less than approximately 6. (40; 148) Amphotericin B in dextrose 5% in water retained clarity for three days at pH 5.94 when stored at 5 °C. At pH 5.22, however, turbidity appeared within one day. (40) An infusion containing a precipitate or foreign matter should not be used. (4)

AMPHOTERICIN B CHOLESTERYL SULFATE COMPLEX
AHFS 8:12.04

Products — Amphotericin B cholesteryl sulfate complex is available as a lyophilized powder in 50- and 100-mg vials. The product consists of a 1:1 molar ratio complex of amphotericin B and cholesteryl sulfate along with other components. (1-10/97) The complete formulations are described in Table 1.

Amphotericin B cholesteryl sulfate complex should be reconstituted with sterile water for injection to form a colloidal dispersion of microscopic, disc-shaped particles. Add 10 ml to the 50-mg vial and 20 ml to the 100-mg vial. Shake gently and rotate the vial until all of the solid material has dissolved. Reconstitution as directed yields opalescent or clear colloidal dispersions containing amphotericin B 5 mg/ml. (1-10/97)

Amphotericin B cholesteryl sulfate complex must not be reconstituted with sodium chloride or dextrose solutions or mixed with solutions containing sodium chloride or other electrolytes. Furthermore, solutions containing a bacteriostatic agent such as benzyl alcohol should be avoided. Use of any solution other than those recommended may cause precipitate formation. (1-10/97)

Trade Name(s)— Amphotec.

Table 1. Amphotericin B Cholesteryl Sulfate Complex Products (1-10/97)

Component	50-mg vial	100-mg vial
Amphotericin B	50 mg	100 mg
Sodium cholesteryl sulfate	26.4 mg	52.8 mg
Tromethamine	5.64 mg	11.28 mg
Disodium edetate dihydrate	0.372 mg	0.744 mg
Lactose monohydrate	950 mg	1.9 g
Hydrochloric acid	to adjust pH	to adjust pH

Administration — Amphotericin B cholesteryl sulfate complex is administered intravenously only after dilution in dextrose 5% in water to a concentration of 0.16 to 0.83 mg/ml. A test dose of 10 ml of the final admixed solution containing 1.6 to 8.3 mg of drug given over 15 to 30 minutes immediately preceding each new course of treatment is recommended. The patient should be observed for the next 30 minutes. Intravenous infusion of the diluted solution is performed at a rate of 1 mg/kg/hr. The infusion time may be shortened to a minimum of two hours for patients who exhibit no evidence of intolerance or reactions. The infusion time may need to be extended for patients who experience reactions or cannot tolerate the fluid volume. (1-10/97)

The functional properties of a drug incorporated into a lipid complex like this one may differ substantially from the functional properties of the original formulation and alternative formulations, including other lipid complexes or liposome formulations. (1-10/97) CAUTION: Care should be taken to ensure that the correct drug product, dose, and administration procedure are used and that no confusion with other products occurs.

Stability — Intact vials of amphotericin B cholesteryl sulfate complex should be stored at 15 to 30 °C. After reconstitution, the colloidal dispersion should be stored at 2 to 8 °C, protected from freezing, and used within 24 hours. Partially used vials should be discarded.

The reconstituted colloidal dispersion diluted to a concentration of 0.16 to 0.83 mg/ml in dextrose 5% in water should be stored at 2 to 8 °C and used within 24 hours. (1-10/97)

Amphotericin B cholesteryl sulfate complex (Sequus) reconstituted to a concentration of 5 mg/ml with sterile water for injection was diluted to concentrations of 2 and 0.1 mg/ml with dextrose 5% in water in PVC bags and was stored at 4 and 23 °C protected from light. The drug was chemically and physically stable for at least seven days. Unacceptable visible changes to the dispersions (layering, crystalline-like precipitate formation) as well as an increase in the amount of particulates of 10 μm and larger appeared within 14 days. Frank precipitation occurred in some samples after 31 days of storage. Losses of amphotericin B content were thought to be due to precipitation rather than decomposition. (2237)

Filtration — Amphotericin B cholesteryl sulfate complex is a colloidal dispersion; filtration, including inline filtration, should not be performed. (1-10/97)

Compatibility Information

Solution Compatibility

Amphotericin B cholesteryl sulfate complex

Solution	*Mfr*	*Mfr*	*Conc/L*	*Remarks*	*Ref*	*C/I*
Dextrose 5% in water	BA	SEQ	415 mg	Physically compatible with little or no change in measured turbidity or increase in particle content in 4 hr at 23 °C under fluorescent light	2117	C
	BA[a]	SEQ	2 g and 100 mg	Physically stable for up to 7 days at 4 and 23 °C protected from light. Visible changes and unacceptable increased microparticulates formed after that time. Drug stability by HPLC retained for at least 14 days. Drug loss due to precipitation occurred thereafter	2237	C
Sodium chloride 0.9%	BA	SEQ	415 mg	Microprecipitation or aggregation occurred immediately	2117	I

[a] *Tested in PVC containers.*

Y-Site Injection Compatibility (1:1 Mixture)

Amphotericin B cholesteryl sulfate complex

Drug	*Mfr*	*Conc*	*Mfr*	*Conc*	*Remarks*	*Ref*	*C/I*
Acyclovir sodium	GW	7 mg/ml[a]	SEQ	0.83 mg/ml[a]	Physically compatible with little or no change in measured turbidity or increase in particle content in 4 hr at 23 °C under fluorescent light	2117	C
Alfentanil HCl	JN	0.5 mg/ml	SEQ	0.83 mg/ml[a]	Gross precipitate forms	2117	I
Amikacin sulfate	AB	5 mg/ml[a]	SEQ	0.83 mg/ml[a]	Gross precipitate forms	2117	I
Aminophylline	AB	2.5 mg/ml[a]	SEQ	0.83 mg/ml[a]	Physically compatible with little or no change in measured turbidity or increase in particle content in 4 hr at 23 °C under fluorescent light	2117	C
Ampicillin sodium	SKB	20 mg/ml[b]	SEQ	0.83 mg/ml[a]	Gross precipitate forms	2117	I
Ampicillin sodium–sulbactam sodium	RR	20 + 10 mg/ml[b]	SEQ	0.83 mg/ml[a]	Gross precipitate forms	2117	I
Atenolol	ZEN	0.5 mg/ml	SEQ	0.83 mg/ml[a]	Gross precipitate forms	2117	I
Aztreonam	SQ	40 mg/ml[a]	SEQ	0.83 mg/ml[a]	Gross precipitate forms	2117	I
Bretylium tosylate	AST	50 mg/ml	SEQ	0.83 mg/ml[a]	Gross precipitate forms	2117	I

Y-Site Injection Compatibility (1:1 Mixture) (Cont.)

Drug	Mfr	Conc	Amphotericin B cholesteryl sulfate complex Mfr	Conc	Remarks	Ref	C/I
Buprenorphine HCl	RKC	0.04 mg/ml[a]	SEQ	0.83 mg/ml[a]	Microprecipitate forms in 4 hr at 23 °C under fluorescent light	2117	I
Butorphanol tartrate	APC	0.04 mg/ml[a]	SEQ	0.83 mg/ml[a]	Decreased natural turbidity occurs immediately	2117	I
Calcium chloride	AST	40 mg/ml[a]	SEQ	0.83 mg/ml[a]	Gross precipitate forms	2117	I
Calcium gluconate	AB	40 mg/ml[a]	SEQ	0.83 mg/ml[a]	Gross precipitate forms	2117	I
Carboplatin	BR	5 mg/ml[a]	SEQ	0.83 mg/ml[a]	Increased turbidity forms immediately	2117	I
Cefazolin sodium	SKB	20 mg/ml[a]	SEQ	0.83 mg/ml[a]	Increased turbidity forms immediately	2117	I
Cefepime HCl	BMS	20 mg/ml[a]	SEQ	0.83 mg/ml[a]	Gross precipitate forms	2117	I
Cefoperazone sodium	RR	40 mg/ml[a]	SEQ	0.83 mg/ml[a]	Gross precipitate forms	2117	I
Cefoxitin sodium	ME	20 mg/ml[a]	SEQ	0.83 mg/ml[a]	Physically compatible with little or no change in measured turbidity or increase in particle content in 4 hr at 23 °C under fluorescent light	2117	C
Ceftazidime	SKB[c]	40 mg/ml[a]	SEQ	0.83 mg/ml[a]	Increased turbidity forms in 4 hr at 23 °C under fluorescent light	2117	I
	GW[d]	40 mg/ml[a]	SEQ	0.83 mg/ml[a]	Gross precipitate forms	2117	I
Ceftizoxime sodium	FUJ	20 mg/ml[a]	SEQ	0.83 mg/ml[a]	Physically compatible with little or no change in measured turbidity or increase in particle content in 4 hr at 23 °C under fluorescent light	2117	C
Ceftriaxone sodium	RC	20 mg/ml[a]	SEQ	0.83 mg/ml[a]	Decreased natural turbidity occurs immediately	2117	I
Chlorpromazine HCl	ES	2 mg/ml[a]	SEQ	0.83 mg/ml[a]	Gross precipitate forms	2117	I
Cimetidine HCl	AMR	12 mg/ml[a]	SEQ	0.83 mg/ml[a]	Gross precipitate forms	2117	I
Cisatracurium besylate	GW	2 mg/ml[a]	SEQ	0.83 mg/ml[a]	Gross precipitate forms	2117	I
Cisplatin	BR	1 mg/ml	SEQ	0.83 mg/ml[a]	Gross precipitate forms	2117	I
Clindamycin phosphate	UP	10 mg/ml[a]	SEQ	0.83 mg/ml[a]	Physically compatible with little or no change in measured turbidity or increase in particle content in 4 hr at 23 °C under fluorescent light	2117	C
Cyclophosphamide	MJ	10 mg/ml[a]	SEQ	0.83 mg/ml[a]	Increased turbidity forms immediately	2117	I
Cyclosporine	SZ	5 mg/ml[a]	SEQ	0.83 mg/ml[a]	Decreased natural turbidity occurs immediately	2117	I
Cytarabine	BED	50 mg/ml	SEQ	0.83 mg/ml[a]	Gross precipitate forms	2117	I
Dexamethasone sodium phosphate	ES	2 mg/ml[a]	SEQ	0.83 mg/ml[a]	Physically compatible with little or no change in measured turbidity or increase in particle content in 4 hr at 23 °C under fluorescent light	2117	C
Diazepam	SW	5 mg/ml	SEQ	0.83 mg/ml[a]	Gross precipitate forms	2117	I
Digoxin	WY	0.25 mg/ml	SEQ	0.83 mg/ml[a]	Microprecipitate forms in 4 hr at 23 °C under fluorescent light	2117	I
Diphenhydramine HCl	SCN	2 mg/ml[a]	SEQ	0.83 mg/ml[a]	Microprecipitate and increased turbidity form immediately	2117	I
Dobutamine HCl	AST	4 mg/ml[a]	SEQ	0.83 mg/ml[a]	Gross precipitate forms	2117	I

Y-Site Injection Compatibility (1:1 Mixture) (Cont.)

			Amphotericin B cholesteryl sulfate complex				
Drug	*Mfr*	*Conc*	*Mfr*	*Conc*	*Remarks*	*Ref*	*C/I*
Dopamine HCl	AB	3.2 mg/ml[a]	SEQ	0.83 mg/ml[a]	Gross precipitate forms	2117	I
Doxorubicin HCl	CHI	2 mg/ml	SEQ	0.83 mg/ml[a]	Gross precipitate forms	2117	I
Doxorubicin HCl liposome injection	SEQ	2 mg/ml	SEQ	0.83 mg/ml[a]	Gross precipitate forms	2117	I
Droperidol	AST	2.5 mg/ml	SEQ	0.83 mg/ml[a]	Gross precipitate forms	2117	I
Enalaprilat	ME	0.1 mg/ml[a]	SEQ	0.83 mg/ml[a]	Decreased natural turbidity occurs immediately	2117	I
Esmolol HCl	OHM	10 mg/ml[a]	SEQ	0.83 mg/ml[a]	Microprecipitate forms in 4 hr at 23 °C under fluorescent light	2117	I
Famotidine	ME	2 mg/ml[a]	SEQ	0.83 mg/ml[a]	Microprecipitate and increased turbidity form immediately	2117	I
Fentanyl citrate	AB	0.05 mg/ml	SEQ	0.83 mg/ml[a]	Physically compatible with little or no change in measured turbidity or increase in particle content in 4 hr at 23 °C under fluorescent light	2117	C
Fluconazole	RR	2 mg/ml	SEQ	0.83 mg/ml[a]	Gross precipitate forms	2117	I
Fluorouracil	PH	16 mg/ml[a]	SEQ	0.83 mg/ml[a]	Microprecipitate forms immediately	2117	I
Furosemide	AMR	3 mg/ml[a]	SEQ	0.83 mg/ml[a]	Physically compatible with little or no change in measured turbidity or increase in particle content in 4 hr at 23 °C under fluorescent light	2117	C
Ganciclovir sodium	RC	20 mg/ml[a]	SEQ	0.83 mg/ml[a]	Physically compatible with little or no change in measured turbidity or increase in particle content in 4 hr at 23 °C under fluorescent light	2117	C
Gatifloxacin	BMS	2 mg/ml[a]	SEQ	0.83 mg/ml[a]	Yellow flocculent precipitate forms immediately	2234	I
Gentamicin sulfate	FUJ	5 mg/ml[a]	SEQ	0.83 mg/ml[a]	Gross precipitate forms	2117	I
Granisetron HCl	SKB	0.05 mg/ml[a]	SEQ	0.83 mg/ml[a]	Physically compatible with little or no change in measured turbidity or increase in particle content in 4 hr at 23 °C under fluorescent light	2117	C
Haloperidol lactate	MN	0.2 mg/ml[a]	SEQ	0.83 mg/ml[a]	Gross precipitate forms	2117	I
Heparin sodium	WY	1000 units/ml[a]	SEQ	0.83 mg/ml[a]	Gross precipitate forms	2117	I
Hydrocortisone sodium succinate	AB	1 mg/ml[a]	SEQ	0.83 mg/ml[a]	Physically compatible with little or no change in measured turbidity or increase in particle content in 4 hr at 23 °C under fluorescent light	2117	C
Hydromorphone HCl	ES	0.5 mg/ml[a]	SEQ	0.83 mg/ml[a]	Decreased natural turbidity occurs immediately	2117	I
Hydroxyzine HCl	ES	2 mg/ml[a]	SEQ	0.83 mg/ml[a]	Gross precipitate forms	2117	I
Ifosfamide	MJ	25 mg/ml[a]	SEQ	0.83 mg/ml[a]	Physically compatible with little or no change in measured turbidity or increase in particle content in 4 hr at 23 °C under fluorescent light	2117	C

Y-Site Injection Compatibility (1:1 Mixture) (Cont.)

			Amphotericin B cholesteryl sulfate complex				
Drug	*Mfr*	*Conc*	*Mfr*	*Conc*	*Remarks*	*Ref*	*C/I*
Imipenem–cilastatin sodium	ME	10 mg/ml[b]	SEQ	0.83 mg/ml[a]	Gross precipitate forms	2117	I
Labetalol HCl	AH	5 mg/ml	SEQ	0.83 mg/ml[a]	Gross precipitate forms	2117	I
Leucovorin calcium	IMM	2 mg/ml[a]	SEQ	0.83 mg/ml[a]	Gross precipitate forms	2117	I
Lidocaine HCl	AST	10 mg/ml	SEQ	0.83 mg/ml[a]	Gross precipitate forms	2117	I
Lorazepam	WY	0.1 mg/ml[a]	SEQ	0.83 mg/ml[a]	Physically compatible with little or no change in measured turbidity or increase in particle content in 4 hr at 23 °C under fluorescent light	2117	C
Magnesium sulfate	AST	100 mg/ml[a]	SEQ	0.83 mg/ml[a]	Gross precipitate forms	2117	I
Mannitol	BA	15%	SEQ	0.83 mg/ml[a]	Physically compatible with little or no change in measured turbidity or increase in particle content in 4 hr at 23 °C under fluorescent light	2117	C
Meperidine HCl	AST	4 mg/ml[a]	SEQ	0.83 mg/ml[a]	Increased turbidity forms immediately	2117	I
Mesna	MJ	10 mg/ml[a]	SEQ	0.83 mg/ml[a]	Microprecipitate forms immediately	2117	I
Methotrexate sodium	IMM	15 mg/ml[a]	SEQ	0.83 mg/ml[a]	Physically compatible with little or no change in measured turbidity or increase in particle content in 4 hr at 23 °C under fluorescent light	2117	C
Methylprednisolone sodium succinate	PHU	5 mg/ml[a]	SEQ	0.83 mg/ml[a]	Physically compatible with little or no change in measured turbidity or increase in particle content in 4 hr at 23 °C under fluorescent light	2117	C
Metoclopramide HCl	FAU	5 mg/ml	SEQ	0.83 mg/ml[a]	Gross precipitate forms	2117	I
Metoprolol tartrate	GEM	1 mg/ml	SEQ	0.83 mg/ml[a]	Gross precipitate forms	2117	I
Metronidazole	AB	5 mg/ml	SEQ	0.83 mg/ml[a]	Gross precipitate forms	2117	I
Midazolam HCl	RC	2 mg/ml[a]	SEQ	0.83 mg/ml[a]	Gross precipitate forms	2117	I
Mitoxantrone HCl	IMM	0.5 mg/ml[a]	SEQ	0.83 mg/ml[a]	Gross precipitate forms	2117	I
Morphine sulfate	ES	1 mg/ml[a]	SEQ	0.83 mg/ml[a]	Increased turbidity forms immediately	2117	I
Nalbuphine HCl	AST	10 mg/ml	SEQ	0.83 mg/ml[a]	Gross precipitate forms	2117	I
Naloxone HCl	AST	0.4 mg/ml	SEQ	0.83 mg/ml[a]	Gross precipitate forms	2117	I
Netilmicin sulfate	SC	5 mg/ml[a]	SEQ	0.83 mg/ml[a]	Gross precipitate forms	2117	I
Nitroglycerin	AMR	0.4 mg/ml[a]	SEQ	0.83 mg/ml[a]	Physically compatible with little or no change in measured turbidity or increase in particle content in 4 hr at 23 °C under fluorescent light	2117	C
Ofloxacin	ORT	4 mg/ml[a]	SEQ	0.83 mg/ml[a]	Gross precipitate forms	2117	I
Ondansetron HCl	CER	1 mg/ml[a]	SEQ	0.83 mg/ml[a]	Gross precipitate forms	2117	I
Paclitaxel	MJ	0.6 mg/ml[a]	SEQ	0.83 mg/ml[a]	Decreased natural turbidity occurs immediately	2117	I
Pentobarbital sodium	AB	5 mg/ml[a]	SEQ	0.83 mg/ml[a]	Decreased natural turbidity occurs immediately	2117	I
Phenobarbital sodium	WY	5 mg/ml[a]	SEQ	0.83 mg/ml[a]	Increased turbidity forms immediately	2117	I
Phenytoin sodium	ES	50 mg/ml[a]	SEQ	0.83 mg/ml[a]	Gross precipitate forms	2117	I

Y-Site Injection Compatibility (1:1 Mixture) (Cont.)

			Amphotericin B cholesteryl sulfate complex				
Drug	*Mfr*	*Conc*	*Mfr*	*Conc*	*Remarks*	*Ref*	*C/I*
Piperacillin sodium	LE	40 mg/ml[a]	SEQ	0.83 mg/ml[a]	Microprecipitate forms in 4 hr at 23 °C under fluorescent light	2117	I
Piperacillin sodium–tazobactam sodium	CY	40 + 5 mg/ml[a]	SEQ	0.83 mg/ml[a]	Microprecipitate forms immediately	2117	I
Potassium chloride	AB	0.1 mEq/ml[a]	SEQ	0.83 mg/ml[a]	Gross precipitate forms	2117	I
Prochlorperazine edisylate	SKB	0.5 mg/ml[a]	SEQ	0.83 mg/ml[a]	Gross precipitate forms	2117	I
Promethazine HCl	ES	2 mg/ml[a]	SEQ	0.83 mg/ml[a]	Gross precipitate forms	2117	I
Propranolol HCl	WY	1 mg/ml	SEQ	0.83 mg/ml[a]	Gross precipitate forms	2117	I
Ranitidine HCl	GL	2 mg/ml[a]	SEQ	0.83 mg/ml[a]	Microprecipitate and increased turbidity form immediately	2117	I
Remifentanil HCl	GW	0.5 mg/ml[a]	SEQ	0.83 mg/ml[a]	Gross precipitate forms	2117	I
Sodium bicarbonate	AB	1 mEq/ml	SEQ	0.83 mg/ml[a]	Gross precipitate forms	2117	I
Sufentanil citrate	JN	0.05 mg/ml	SEQ	0.83 mg/ml[a]	Physically compatible with little or no change in measured turbidity or increase in particle content in 4 hr at 23 °C under fluorescent light	2117	C
Ticarcillin disodium	SKB	30 mg/ml[a]	SEQ	0.83 mg/ml[a]	Microprecipitate forms immediately	2117	I
Ticarcillin disodium–clavulanate potassium	SKB	31 mg/ml[a]	SEQ	0.83 mg/ml[a]	Gross precipitate forms	2117	I
Tobramycin sulfate	AB	5 mg/ml[a]	SEQ	0.83 mg/ml[a]	Gross precipitate forms	2117	I
Trimethoprim–sulfamethoxazole	ES	0.8 + 4 mg/ml[a]	SEQ	0.83 mg/ml[a]	Physically compatible with little or no change in measured turbidity or increase in particle content in 4 hr at 23 °C under fluorescent light	2117	C
Vancomycin HCl	AB	10 mg/ml[a]	SEQ	0.83 mg/ml[a]	Gross precipitate forms	2117	I
Vecuronium bromide	MAR	1 mg/ml[a]	SEQ	0.83 mg/ml[a]	Gross precipitate forms	2117	I
Verapamil HCl	AMR	2.5 mg/ml	SEQ	0.83 mg/ml[a]	Gross precipitate forms	2117	I
Vinblastine sulfate	FAU	0.12 mg/ml[a]	SEQ	0.83 mg/ml[a]	Physically compatible with little or no change in measured turbidity or increase in particle content in 4 hr at 23 °C under fluorescent light	2117	C
Vincristine sulfate	FAU	0.05 mg/ml[a]	SEQ	0.83 mg/ml[a]	Physically compatible with little or no change in measured turbidity or increase in particle content in 4 hr at 23 °C under fluorescent light	2117	C
Vinorelbine tartrate	BW	1 mg/ml[a]	SEQ	0.83 mg/ml[a]	Gross precipitate forms	2117	I
Zidovudine	BW	4 mg/ml[a]	SEQ	0.83 mg/ml[a]	Physically compatible with little or no change in measured turbidity or increase in particle content in 4 hr at 23 °C under fluorescent light	2117	C

[a] *Tested in dextrose 5% in water.*
[b] *Tested in sodium chloride 0.9%.*
[c] *Sodium carbonate–containing formulation tested.*
[d] *L-Arginine–containing formulation tested.*

Additional Compatibility Information

Infusion Solutions — Amphotericin B cholesteryl sulfate complex should be reconstituted with sterile water for injection. (See Products section above.) Sodium chloride and dextrose solutions as well as solutions containing a preservative such as benzyl alcohol must not be used, because of the potential for precipitation. The reconstituted drug should be diluted in dextrose 5% in water to a concentration of 0.16 to 0.83 mg/ml for administration. Sodium chloride or other electrolyte solutions must not be used for this dilution to avoid possible precipitate formation. (1-10/97)

Other Amphotericin B Products — Although other lipid complex and liposomal amphotericin B products exist, they are sufficiently different from amphotericin B cholesteryl sulfate complex that extrapolating compatibility data to other forms would be inappropriate.

Other Drugs — The manufacturer also recommends not mixing amphotericin B cholesteryl sulfate complex with other drug products and separating administration from other drugs given through existing intravenous lines by using a sufficient flush of the line with dextrose 5% in water to avoid contact with the other drugs. (1-10/97) Flushes both before and after administering amphotericin B cholesteryl sulfate complex would be required to avoid inadvertent mixing with other drugs in line. Given the high number of incompatibilities that have been documented with amphotericin B cholesteryl sulfate complex (2117), care should be taken to avoid inadvertent contact with incompatible drugs in administration lines.

AMPICILLIN SODIUM
AHFS 8:12.16

Products — Ampicillin sodium is available in vials containing the equivalent of ampicillin 125 mg, 250 mg, 500 mg, 1 g, or 2 g. For intramuscular injection, reconstitute the vials with sterile water for injection or bacteriostatic water for injection in the following amounts (1-8/98; 154):

Vial Size	Volume of Diluent	Withdrawable Volume	Concentration
125 mg	1.2 ml	1 ml	125 mg/ml
250 mg	1.0 ml	1 ml	250 mg/ml
500 mg	1.8 ml	2 ml	250 mg/ml
1 g	3.5 ml	4 ml	250 mg/ml
2 g	6.8 ml	8 ml	250 mg/ml

For intravenous injection, reconstitute the 125-, 250-, and 500-mg vials with 5 ml of sterile water for injection or bacteriostatic water for injection. For the 1- or 2-g vials, 10 ml of sterile water for injection or bacteriostatic water for injection is recommended. (1-8/98)

pH — Reconstituted solutions of ampicillin sodium have a pH of 8 to 10. (4) The pH values of various ampicillin sodium solutions are shown below (213):

Percent Ampicillin Sodium	Diluent	Initial pH
2	Sterile water	8.80
5	Sterile water	8.92
10	Sterile water	9.15
2	Sodium chloride 0.9%	8.7
5	Sodium chloride 0.9%	8.9
10	Sodium chloride 0.9%	9.2
2	Dextrose 5% in water	8.9
5	Dextrose 5% in water	9.3
10	Dextrose 5% in water	9.3

Osmolality — Reconstituted with sterile water for injection, ampicillin sodium (Wyeth) 100 mg/ml has an osmolality of 602 mOsm/kg. (50) At 125 mg/ml, Wyeth's product was 702 mOsm/kg and Bristol's product was 675 mOsm/kg. (1071)

In another study, the osmolality of ampicillin sodium (Bristol) diluted in sodium chloride 0.9% was determined to be 493 mOsm/kg at 50 mg/ml and 664 mOsm/kg at 100 mg/ml. (1375)

The osmolality of ampicillin sodium 1 and 2 g was calculated for the following dilutions (1054):

Diluent	Osmolality (mOsm/kg) 50 ml	100 ml
1 g		
Dextrose 5% in water	341	302
Sodium chloride 0.9%	368	328
2 g		
Dextrose 5% in water	418	346
Sodium chloride 0.9%	444	372

Robinson et al. recommended the following maximum ampicillin sodium concentrations to achieve osmolalities suitable for peripheral infusion in fluid-restricted patients (1180):

Diluent	Maximum Concentration (mg/ml)	Osmolality (mOsm/kg)
Dextrose 5% in water	62	583
Sodium chloride 0.9%	56	576
Sterile water for injection	112	588

Sodium Content — Ampicillin sodium contains approximately 2.9 to 3.1 mEq of sodium per gram of drug. (4)

Administration — Ampicillin sodium is administered by intramuscular or direct intravenous injection or intravenous infusion. Direct intravenous injection should be made slowly over 10 to 15 minutes. (4; 154)

Table 1. Suggested Storage Conditions for Ampicillin Sodium Solutions (210)

Solution	Temperature (°C)	Maximum Storage
Constituted vial	−20	48 hr
	5	4 hr
	27	1 hr
Ampicillin sodium 1% in sodium chloride 0.9%	5	5 days
	27	24 hr
Ampicillin sodium 1% in dextrose 5% in water	5	4 hr
	27	2 hr

Table 2. Recommended Maximum Concentrations and Usage Times in Intravenous Solutions (154)

Solution	Concentration	Temperature (°C)	Stability Period
Dextrose 5% in sodium chloride 0.45%	up to 2 mg/ml	25	4 hr
	up to 10 mg/ml	4	4 hr
Dextrose 5% in water	up to 20 mg/ml	25	2 hr
	up to 20 mg/ml	4	4 hr
Invert sugar 10% in water	up to 2 mg/ml	25	4 hr
	up to 20 mg/ml	4	3 hr
Ringer's injection, lactated	up to 30 mg/ml	25	8 hr
	up to 30 mg/ml	4	24 hr
Sodium chloride 0.9%	up to 30 mg/ml	25	8 hr
	up to 20 mg/ml	4	72 hr
	30 mg/ml	4	48 hr
Sodium lactate ⅙ M	up to 30 mg/ml	25	8 hr
	up to 30 mg/ml	4	8 hr
Sterile water for injection	up to 30 mg/ml	25	8 hr
	up to 20 mg/ml	4	72 hr
	30 mg/ml	4	48 hr

Stability — The stability of ampicillin sodium in solution under various conditions has been the subject of much work and numerous articles. Several characteristics of the stability of ampicillin sodium have emerged from these studies:

1. The stability is concentration dependent and decreases as the concentration increases.
2. Sodium chloride 0.9% appears to be a suitable diluent for the intravenous infusion of ampicillin sodium.
3. The stability is greatly decreased in dextrose solutions.
4. Storage temperature and the pH of solution affect the stability.

Storage and Usage Times — Savello and Shangraw offered the recommendations in Table 1 regarding storage conditions for ampicillin sodium solutions.

For ampicillin sodium (Apothecon), the manufacturer recommends using only freshly prepared solutions within one hour of reconstitution. In intravenous solutions, the maximum concentrations and stability periods in Table 2 have been recommended to ensure that not more than 10% ampicillin decomposition will result at the temperature specified.

Table 3. Percent Degradation of Ampicillin Sodium Solutions after Reconstitution with Water for Injection at 5 °C after Eight Hours (210)

Percent Concentration	Percent Degradation
1	0.8
5	3.6
10	5.8
15	10.4
20	12.3
25	13.3

Concentration Effects — The effect of concentration on ampicillin sodium stability has been attributed to a self-catalyzing effect. (210) As the concentration increases, so does the rate of decomposition. (170; 210) Savello and Shangraw reported that, even though the initial pH values of various concentrations were 9.2 to 9.3, the higher concentrations of the drug maintained their pH longer because of their greater buffer capacity. This fact, along with greater probability of collision, helps explain the higher degradation rates at higher concentrations. (210) (See Table 3.)

This concentration dependence of the stability of ampicillin sodium has been related to the polymerization of penicillins in concentrated solutions. (601; 602) Dimerization is the predominant form of degradation with high ampicillin concentrations. The extent of this effect declines as the concentration drops but still remains significant in a 2% solution. At lower concentrations, hydrolysis becomes the determining factor. (603)

In a 50% concentration, ampicillin sodium formed dimer, trimer, tetramer, and pentamer during 24 hours of storage at 24 °C in the dark. The polymer formed through a chain process by linkage of the amino group on the side chain to another molecule with a cleaved β-lactam ring. (1400)

In a 20% ampicillin sodium aqueous solution adjusted to pH 8.5 and stored at 22 °C, 90% of all decomposition products formed within 72 hours were di- and polymers. In a 5% solution, 70% of the decomposition products were di- and polymers. However, a 1% solution formed α-aminobenzylpenicilloic acid as the predominant decomposition product and a dimer concentration of 1 to 2%. The rate of dimerization was almost independent of pH in the range of 7 to 10 but increased strongly with increases in the initial ampicillin sodium concentration. (858)

However, one study showed that if the pH of the solution was held constant at 8 or 9.15, there was little dependence of the rate of decomposition on concentration in the concentration range of 2 to 10%. (213)

Infusion Diluents — Infusion diluents also affect the stability of ampicillin sodium. Although one report stated that there was no loss of ampicillin potency in a solution of ampicillin sodium 5 g/L in sodium chloride 0.9% in 14 days at 25 °C (144), the use of more accurate test methods has determined that this is not the case. For example, see the results of Savello and Shangraw in Table 4.

The work of Hiranaka et al. tends to support this result. In the concentration range of 5 to 40 g/L in sodium chloride 0.9%, approximately 1 to 6% loss of potency of ampicillin sodium was reported

Table 4. Percent Degradation of 1% Ampicillin Sodium in Sodium Chloride 0.9% According to Temperature and Time (210)

Temperature (°C)	4 hr	8 hr	24 hr
−20	1.2	1.8	3.6
0	0.4	0.8	0.9
5	1.0	2.2	3.3
27	1.8	2.6	8.3

at 5 °C in 24 hours, and 6 to 15% was found at 25 °C in 24 hours. (212)

Warren et al. reported similar results for ampicillin sodium 20 g/L in sodium chloride 0.9%. They noted approximately 3 to 4% decomposition at 5 °C and 12 to 18% at 25 °C in 24 hours. (208)

Stjernstrom et al. found that ampicillin sodium 2 to 15 g/L in sodium chloride 0.9% exhibited 10% decomposition in time periods varying from over 48 hours in the more dilute solution to 33 hours in the more concentrated solutions when stored at 25 °C. (604)

Dextrose is thought to exhibit an immense catalytic effect on the hydrolysis of ampicillin sodium (210), decreasing the stability about one-half when compared to sterile water or sodium chloride 0.9%. (213) This has been well documented and has been regarded as an incompatibility. (210; 213) (See Table 5.) This accelerated decomposition associated with dextrose extends to fructose as well, although it is not as extensive. It occurs in the alkaline pH range. Below pH 6 or 7, the decomposition rate with both dextrose and fructose appears to coincide with simple aqueous solutions. (604)

Once again, other reports support these data. Hiranaka et al. found a 35 to 44% loss of ampicillin sodium in 24 hours at 25 °C in the concentration range of 5 to 40 g/L in dextrose 5% in water. At 5 °C, the loss was reported to be 19 to 28%. (212)

Warren et al., testing a concentration of 20 g/L in dextrose 5% in water, reported approximately 40% decomposition in 24 hours at 25 °C and up to 11% decomposition at 5 °C in 24 hours. (208)

Stjernstrom et al. found that ampicillin sodium 2 to 15 g/L in dextrose 5% in water exhibited 10% decomposition at three and a half hours in the more dilute solutions and at two hours in the more concentrated solution when stored at 25 °C. (604)

Savello and Shangraw further showed that increasing the concentration of dextrose decreased the stability of ampicillin sodium. (See Table 6.)

Stjernstrom et al. found that increasing the dextrose concentration from 5 to 10% increased the rate of ampicillin decomposition by a factor of about two. (604)

pH Effects—The pH of the solution also plays a role in its stability. Hydrolysis has been shown to be catalyzed by hydroxide ions. An increase of 1 pH unit in an ampicillin sodium solution has been shown to increase the rate of decomposition 10-fold. (213)

Table 5. Percent Degradation of 1% Ampicillin Sodium in Dextrose 5% in Water According to Temperature and Time (210)

Temperature (°C)	4 hr	8 hr	24 hr
−20	13.6	22.3	45.6
0	6.2	11.6	26.3
5	10.1	15.2	29.7
27	21.3	31.1	46.5

Table 6. Percent Degradation of 1% Ampicillin Sodium at 5 °C According to Dextrose Concentration and Time (210)

Percent Dextrose	3 hr	7 hr
5	7.4	13.9
10	10.3	19.4
20	14.2	27.8

The optimum pH for ampicillin sodium stability has been variously reported as 5.8 (1072), 5.85 at 35 °C (215), approximately 5.2 at 25 °C (604), and 7.5 at room temperature. (209) The pH of ampicillin sodium solutions, however, is in the alkaline range, with higher pH values having been reported at higher concentrations. (213) (See the pH section above.)

Ampicillin sodium (Bristol) 10 g/L was tested for stability at pH 3.4 to 9.2 in various buffer additives. A 7.6% potency loss was reported in 12 hours at room temperature at pH 7.5. Significantly higher degradation rates occurred as the pH varied from 7.5, with about 70% degradation occurring in 12 hours at room temperature at pH 3.4 and 9.2. (209)

In another evaluation, rate constants for ampicillin degradation at various pH values were calculated for an aqueous solution at 25 °C. The pH providing maximum stability was 5.2. When tested in dextrose 10% in water, a minimum rate of decomposition was observed at approximately pH 5 to 5.5. The amount of ampicillin degradation was 10% or less in 24 hours at 25 °C within a pH range of about 2.75 to 6.75. At pH 8, the time to 10% decomposition was only about two hours. (604)

The stability of ampicillin sodium (Beecham) 250 mg/50 ml and 1 g/100 ml in sodium chloride 0.9% in PVC bags was compared to the stability of the same solutions buffered with potassium acid phosphate 13.6% injection. The 50- and 100-ml containers were buffered with 1 and 2 ml, respectively, lowering the pH by nearly two pH units. Larger quantities of buffer caused precipitation. When stored at 5 °C, the 250-mg/50-ml solution had a shelf life (t_{90}) of 12 days while the 1-g/100-ml solution had a shelf life of six days. This finding compares favorably to the shelf life of one to two days for the unbuffered solutions. (1820)

Temperature Effects—The storage temperature of ampicillin sodium solutions may also affect stability. It has been stated that freezing ampicillin sodium solutions at −20 °C increases the rate of decomposition over that at 5 °C. For this reason, it has been recommended that ampicillin sodium solutions not be stored in the frozen state. (123; 213)

However, Lynn noted a 20% loss of potency in six hours when 500 mg of ampicillin sodium reconstituted with 1.5 ml of water was stored at 5 °C. When stored at −20 °C, a 10% loss in 20 hours was noted. (99) Further, Savello and Shangraw reported the results in Table 7 for the temperature dependence of the stability of vials of ampicillin sodium reconstituted with sterile distilled water.

Savello and Shangraw found apparent increased ampicillin decomposition at −20 °C over that at 5 °C in two of the 1% solutions they tested (Tables 5 and 8). Warren et al. also noted this effect in their study of ampicillin sodium 2%, finding about 4 to 6% greater loss at −20 °C than at 5 °C in 24 hours in both dextrose 5% in water and sodium chloride 0.9%. (208)

An explanation of this phenomenon was proposed by Pincock and Kiovsky. Below the freezing point but above the eutectic temperature, there exists a liquid and solid phase in equilibrium. If it is assumed that −20 °C is above the eutectic temperature, then liquid regions of

Table 7. Percent Degradation of Ampicillin Sodium in the Reconstituted Vial (250 mg/ml) According to Temperature and Time (210)

Temperature (°C)	4 hr	8 hr	24 hr	48 hr
−20	2.2	2.8	5.0	8.4
−12	4.2	5.7	10.9	
0	5.8	10.4	21.9	
5	7.1	13.3	26.6	
27	11.2[a]			

[a]*Determined after two hours.*

a saturated solution of ampicillin sodium exist, which result in increased decomposition. (214) Solutions of ampicillin sodium stored at −78 °C showed no decomposition within 24 hours. (210)

In a study of long-term storage, Dinel et al. tested ampicillin sodium (Ayerst) 1 g/50 ml in dextrose 5% in water and also sodium chloride 0.9% in PVC containers frozen at −20 °C for 30 days. In sodium chloride 0.9%, they reported approximately 10% decomposition in one day and approximately 70% decomposition in 30 days. In dextrose 5% in water, even greater decomposition occurred. They reported about 50% decomposition in one day and virtually total decomposition in 30 days. (299)

Holmes et al. tested ampicillin sodium (Wyeth) 1 g/50 ml of dextrose 5% in water in PVC bags frozen at −20 °C for 30 days and then thawed by exposure to ambient temperature or microwave radiation. The admixtures showed essentially total loss of ampicillin activity determined microbiologically. (554) At −30 °C, only 18% of the ampicillin remained in 30 days. A storage temperature of −70 °C was required to retain at least 90% of the original activity for 30 days. (555)

The same concentration in sodium chloride 0.9% showed a 29% loss of ampicillin activity at −20 °C but only about a 4% loss at −30 and −70 °C after 30 days. Subsequent thawing of the −30 and −70 °C samples by exposure to microwave radiation and storage at room temperature for eight hours resulted in additional losses of activity, with the final concentration totaling about 90% of the initial amount. The authors concluded that ampicillin sodium in sodium chloride 0.9% could be stored for 30 days at −30 °C, which was presumably below the eutectic point for this admixture. However, −30 °C was believed to be above the eutectic point for the dextrose 5% in water admixture because decomposition continued to occur. (555)

Ampicillin sodium (Wyeth) 1 g/50 ml of sodium chloride 0.9% exhibited a 13% loss (by HPLC) in four days at −7 °C but only a 10% loss in the same time period at 4 °C. (1035)

Even within acceptable limits for room temperature, significant differences in the rate of ampicillin decomposition can occur. In one solution at 20 °C, a 10% ampicillin loss resulted in 44 hours. This same solution at 30 °C exhibited a 10% loss in 12 hours. Over the range of 20 to 35 °C, each 5 °C rise approximately doubled the rate of decomposition. (604)

Table 8. Percent Degradation of 1% Ampicillin Sodium in Water According to Temperature and Time (210)

Temperature (°C)	4 hr	8 hr	24 hr
−20	1.3	1.9	5.2
5	0.4	0.8	2.0

Syringes— Ampicillin sodium (Berk) 125 mg/ml in sterile water for injection was packaged as 0.25 ml in 1-ml syringes (Injekt, Braun) and sealed with blind hubs. When the syringes were stored at about 6 °C, approximately 36% of the antibiotic activity against *Micrococcus luteus* was lost in two days. (1697)

Ambulatory Pumps— Stiles et al. evaluated the stability of ampicillin sodium (Wyeth) 60 mg/ml in sterile water for injection and sodium chloride 0.9% in 100-ml portable pump reservoirs (Pharmacia Deltec) during simulated administration for 24 hours. The drug solutions were tested by HPLC analysis when administered immediately after preparation and after storage for 24 hours at 5 °C before 24-hour administration. During simulated administration, some reservoirs were kept at 30 °C; others were placed in insulated pouches with frozen (−20 °C) gel packs to keep them chilled below the ambient temperature. All ampicillin sodium solutions, whether freshly prepared or after storage, exhibited little or no potency loss. However, solutions not chilled in the insulated pouches during administration exhibited about a 10% loss in six hours and a 20 to 27% loss in 24 hours. To complete the infusions with adequate drug stability, chilling of the drug reservoirs was necessary; the insulated pouches enhanced stability substantially during the study period. (1779)

Elastomeric Reservoir Pumps— Ampicillin sodium (Apothecon) 20 mg/ml in sodium chloride 0.9% 100 ml was packaged in latex elastomeric reservoirs (Secure Medical). About 4% loss by HPLC analysis occurred in eight hours at 25 °C and 7% loss in three days at 5 °C. (1970)

Ampicillin sodium solutions in elastomeric reservoir pumps have been stated by the pump manufacturers to be stable for the following time periods refrigerated (REF) or at room temperature (RT) (31):

Pump Reservoir(s)	Conc.	REF	RT
Homepump; Homepump Eclipse	20 mg/ml[a]	3 days	8 hr
Intermate HPC	20 mg/ml[a]	3 days	8 hr
Medflo	20 mg/ml[a]	5 days	24 hr
ReadyMed	20 mg/ml[b]	3 days	
	30 mg/ml[b]	2 days	

[a]*In sodium chloride 0.9%.*
[b]*In sterile water for injection.*

Sorption— Ampicillin (as the trihydrate) 1.4 g/L in sodium chloride 0.9% (Travenol) in PVC bags did not exhibit significant sorption to the plastic during one week of storage at room temperature (15 to 20 °C). (536)

Ampicillin sodium (Beecham) 1.4 g/L in sodium chloride 0.9% did not exhibit any loss due to sorption during a seven-hour simulated infusion through an infusion set (Travenol) consisting of a cellulose propionate burette chamber and 170 cm of PVC tubing. (606)

The drug was also tested as a simulated infusion over at least one hour by a syringe pump system. A glass syringe on a syringe pump was fitted with 20 cm of polyethylene tubing or 50 cm of Silastic tubing. No loss of drug due to sorption was observed with either tubing. (606)

A 25-ml aliquot of ampicillin sodium (Beecham) 1.4 g/L in sodium chloride 0.9% was stored in all-plastic syringes composed of polypropylene barrels and polyethylene plungers for 24 hours at room temperature in the dark. No loss due to sorption occurred. (606)

Picard et al. reported little or no loss due to sorption of ampicillin sodium (Bristol) 250 mg/100 ml in dextrose 5% in water and sodium chloride 0.9% in trilayer solution bags (Bieffe Medital) composed of polyethylene, polyamide, and polypropylene. The admixtures were evaluated by HPLC analysis up to two hours after preparation. Similarly, no loss was found during one-hour simulated infusion. (1918)

Filtration — Filtration of ampicillin sodium (Wyeth) is stated to result in no adsorption, yielding solutions that maintain their potency. (829)

Ampicillin sodium (Bristol) 1.97 mg/ml in sodium chloride 0.9% was filtered through a 0.22-μm cellulose ester membrane filter (Ivex-HP, Millipore) over five hours. No significant drug loss due to binding to the filter was noted. (1034)

Central Venous Catheter — Ampicillin sodium (Apothecon) 5 mg/ml in sodium chloride 0.9% was found to be compatible with the ARROWg+ard Blue Plus (Arrow International) chlorhexidine-bearing triple-lumen central catheter. HPLC analysis was used to evaluate completeness of drug delivery through the catheter and the amount of chlorhexidine removed from the internal lumens. Essentially complete delivery of the drug was found with little or no drug loss occurring. Furthermore, chlorhexidine delivered from the catheter remained at trace amounts with no substantial increase due to the delivery of the drug through the catheter. (2335)

Compatibility Information

Solution Compatibility

Ampicillin sodium

Solution	*Mfr*	*Mfr*	*Conc/L*	*Remarks*	*Ref*	*C/I*
Amino acids 4.25%, dextrose 25%	MG	BR	1 g	Increase in microscopic particles noted in 24 hr at 5 °C	349	I
Dextran 40 10% in sodium chloride 0.9%	PH	AY	8 g	25% ampicillin decomposition in 24 hr at room temperature	99	I
	PH	BY	2 g	10% ampicillin decomposition in 2.8 hr at 25 °C	604	I
	PH	BY	5 g	10% ampicillin decomposition in 2.5 hr at 25 °C	604	I
	PH	BY	15 g	10% ampicillin decomposition in 2.3 hr at 25 °C	604	I
Dextran 40 10% in dextrose 5% in water	PH	AY	8 g	50% ampicillin decomposition in 24 hr at room temperature	99	I
	PH	BY	2 g	10% ampicillin decomposition in 3.5 hr at 25 °C	604	I
	PH	BY	5 g	10% ampicillin decomposition in 2.3 hr at 25 °C	604	I
	PH	BY	15 g	10% ampicillin decomposition in 1.5 hr at 25 °C	604	I
			4 g	46% ampicillin decomposition in 24 hr at 20 °C	834	I
Dextran 70 6% in sodium chloride 0.9%	PH	BY	2 g	10% ampicillin decomposition in 6.5 hr at 25 °C	604	I
	PH	BY	5 g	10% ampicillin decomposition in 4.3 hr at 25 °C	604	I
	PH	BY	15 g	10% ampicillin decomposition in 3.3 hr at 25 °C	604	I
Dextran 70 6% in dextrose 5% in water	PH	BY	2 g	10% ampicillin decomposition in 3.5 hr at 25 °C	604	I
	PH	BY	5 g	10% ampicillin decomposition in 2.5 hr at 25 °C	604	I
	PH	BY	15 g	10% ampicillin decomposition in 1.8 hr at 25 °C	604	I
			4 g	10% ampicillin decomposition in 6 hr and 40% decomposition in 24 hr at 20 °C	834	I
Dextrose 5% in sodium chloride 0.9%	MG	BR	1 g	19% ampicillin decomposition in 4 hr at 4 °C and 17% decomposition in 2 hr at 25 °C	105	I
Dextrose 5% in water		BE	1 g	24% ampicillin decomposition in 8 hr at 25 °C	211	I
		AY	2 and 4 g	10% ampicillin decomposition in 4 hr at room temperature	99	I
	MG	BR	1 g	11% ampicillin decomposition in 24 hr at 4 °C and 21% decomposition in 24 hr at 25 °C	105	I
	AB	AY	2 g	10% ampicillin decomposition in 24 hr at 5 °C and 20% decomposition in 24 hr at 25 °C	88	I
		BR	20 g	As much as 19% ampicillin decomposition in 4 hr at 25 °C. Approximately 40% decomposition in 24 hr at 25 °C	208	I
		BR	10 g	Approximately 46% ampicillin decomposition in 24 hr at −20 °C. Approximately 30% ampicillin decomposition in 24 hr at 5 °C. Approximately 47% ampicillin decomposition in 24 hr at 27 °C	210	I
	BA[a], TR	AY	20 g	40% decomposition in 24 hr at 22 °C and 30% decomposition in 24 hr at 5 °C	298	I

Solution Compatibility (Cont.)

Ampicillin sodium

Solution	*Mfr*	*Mfr*	*Conc/L*	*Remarks*	*Ref*	*C/I*
			2 g	5% decomposition in 2 hr and 38% decomposition in 24 hr at 20 to 25 °C	307	I
			4 g	10% decomposition in 2 hr and 45% decomposition in 24 hr at 20 to 25 °C	307	I
			10 g	12% decomposition in 2 hr and 50% decomposition in 24 hr at 20 to 25 °C	307	I
	TR[b]	WY	20 g	Ampicillin activity loss of 35% in 8 hr and 52% in 24 hr at room temperature	554	I
	PH	BY	2 g	10% ampicillin decomposition in 3.5 hr at 25 °C	604	I
	PH	BY	5 g	10% ampicillin decomposition in 2.5 hr at 25 °C	604	I
	PH	BY	15 g	10% ampicillin decomposition in 2 hr at 25 °C	604	I
			4 g	10% loss in 4 hr and 28% loss in 24 hr at room temperature	768	I
			5 g	7% loss in 2 hr and 15% loss in 4 hr at 29 °C. 8% loss in 8 hr at 4 °C	773	I
	TR[b]	WY	10 and 20 g	Approximately 60% ampicillin loss in 48 hr at 25 °C and in 7 days at 4 °C	1001	I
	TR[b]	WY	20 g	50% ampicillin loss at 24 °C and 28% at 4 °C in 1 day	1035	I
	[b]	BR	20 g	No drug loss by HPLC during 2 hr storage and 1-hr simulated infusion	1774	C
Dextrose 10% in water	MG	BR	1 g	17% ampicillin decomposition in 6 hr at 4 °C and 18% decomposition in 4 hr at 25 °C	105	I
Fat emulsion 10%, intravenous			20 g	15% ampicillin decomposition in 24 hr at 23 °C. Potency was retained through 6 hr	37	I
	VT	BE	2 g	Microscopic globule coalescence in 24 hr at 25 and 8 °C	825	I
Fructose 5.25%		BE	20 g	21% ampicillin decomposition in 6 hr at 25 °C	89	I
Hetastarch 6%			4 g	18% ampicillin decomposition in 6 hr and 35% decomposition in 24 hr at 20 °C	834	I
Invert sugar 7.5% with electrolytes		AST	1.5 g	52% ampicillin loss in 24 hr at 29 °C by microbiological assay	440	I
Invert sugar 10% in water		BY	2 g	10% ampicillin decomposition in 4 hr at 25 °C	604	I
		BY	5 g	10% ampicillin decomposition in 2.8 hr at 25 °C	604	I
		BY	15 g	10% ampicillin decomposition in 1.5 hr at 25 °C	604	I
Isolyte M with dextrose 5%	MG	BR	1 g	Potency retained for 24 hr at 4 and 25 °C	105	C
Isolyte P with dextrose 5%	MG	BR	1 g	Potency retained for 24 hr at 4 and 25 °C	105	C
Ringer's injection		AY	2 and 4 g	Less than 10% decomposition in 24 hr at room temperature	99	C
		BY	2 g	10% ampicillin decomposition in 40 hr at 25 °C	604	C
		BY	5 g	10% ampicillin decomposition in 25 hr at 25 °C	604	C
		BY	15 g	10% ampicillin decomposition in 20 hr at 25 °C	604	I
			5 g	9% loss in 8 hr and 18% loss in 24 hr at 29 °C. 3% loss in 24 hr at 4 °C	773	I
Ringer's injection, lactated		BE	1 g	17% ampicillin decomposition in 4 hr at 25 °C	211	I
		BR	1 g	11% ampicillin decomposition in 12 hr at 25 °C	87	I
	MG	BR	1 g	17% ampicillin decomposition in 6 hr at 4 °C and 25% decomposition in 6 hr at 25 °C	105	I
			5 g	20% loss in 2 hr at 29 °C and 11% loss in 4 hr at 4 °C	773	I

Solution Compatibility (Cont.)

Solution	Mfr	Ampicillin sodium Mfr	Conc/L	Remarks	Ref	C/I
Sodium bicarbonate 1.4%		AY	2 and 4 g	10% ampicillin decomposition in 6 hr at room temperature	99	I
		BY	2 g	10% ampicillin decomposition in 17 hr at 25 °C	604	I
		BY	5 g	10% ampicillin decomposition in 14 hr at 25 °C	604	I
		BY	15 g	10% ampicillin decomposition in 10 hr at 25 °C	604	I
Sodium chloride 0.9%		BY	2 g	10% ampicillin decomposition in over 48 hr at 25 °C	604	C
		BY	5 g	10% ampicillin decomposition in 38 hr at 25 °C	604	C
		BY	15 g	10% ampicillin decomposition in 33 hr at 25 °C	604	C
		BE	10 g	Less than 10% decomposition in 24 hr at 25 °C	113	C
		BR	6 g	Approximately 9% decomposition in 24 hr at room temperature. Approximately 1% decomposition in 24 hr under refrigeration	127	C
	MG	BR	1 g	Potency retained for 24 hr at 4 and 25 °C	105	C
		AY	2 to 30 g	10% decomposition in 24 hr at room temperature	99	C
		BR	20 g	Approximately 4% decomposition in 24 hr at 5 °C. Approximately 12 to 16% decomposition in 24 hr at 25 °C	208	C
		BR	10 g	Approximately 4% decomposition in 24 hr at −20 °C. Approximately 3% decomposition in 24 hr at 5 °C. Approximately 8% decomposition in 24 hr at 27 °C	210	C
		BR	5, 10, 15, 20 g	Approximately 6 to 12% decomposition in 24 hr at 25 °C	212	C
		BR	5, 10, 15, 20, 30, 40 g	Approximately 1 to 6% decomposition in 24 hr at 5 °C	212	C
	BA[a], TR	AY	20 g	Potency retained for 24 hr at 5 and 22 °C	298	C
			2, 4, 10 g	Approximately 10% decomposition in 24 hr at 20 to 25 °C	307	C
		BE	1 g	12% ampicillin decomposition in 12 hr at 25 °C and 28% decomposition in 24 hr at 25 °C	211	I
		BR	30 and 40 g	Approximately 15% ampicillin decomposition in 24 hr at 25 °C	212	I
			4 g	10% loss in 8 hr and 19% loss in 24 hr at room temperature	768	I
			5 g	10% loss in 8 hr at 29 °C and 3% loss in 24 hr at 4 °C	773	I
	TR[b]	WY	20 g	15% ampicillin loss in 1 day and 30% in 4 days at 24 °C. 6% loss in 1 day and 10% in 4 days at 4 °C.	1035	I
	[b]	BR	20 g	No drug loss by HPLC during 2 hr storage and 1-hr simulated infusion	1774	C
	AB[c]	WY	60 g	Stable by HPLC for 24 hr at 5 °C. 10% ampicillin loss in 6 hr and 20% loss in 24 hr during administration at 30 °C via portable pump	1779	C
	BA[b]	BE	10 g	Visually compatible with 10% ampicillin loss by HPLC in 2 days at 5 °C	1820	C
	BA[b]	BE	5 g	Visually compatible with 10% ampicillin loss by HPLC in 1 day at 5 °C	1820	C
	AB[d]	APC	20 g	2 to 4% loss by HPLC in 8 hr at 25 °C and 7% loss in 3 days at 5 °C	1970	C

Solution Compatibility (Cont.)

Ampicillin sodium

Solution	Mfr	Mfr	Conc/L	Remarks	Ref	C/I
Sodium lactate ⅙ M		BR	1 g	37% ampicillin decomposition in 4 hr at 25 °C	211	I
		AY	up to 30 g	10% ampicillin decomposition in 6 hr at room temperature	99	I
TPN #1[e]		BR	1 g	Physically compatible for 12 hr. Precipitate noted in 24 hr at 22 °C	313	I
		BR	20 mg	Antibiotic potency retained for at least 12 hr at 22 °C	313	C
TPN #2, #3, #5 to #9[e]		BR	1 g	Physically incompatible with a precipitate noted in 1 to 4 hr at 22 °C	313	I
TPN #4[e]		BR	1 g	Physically compatible for 24 hr at 22 °C	313	C
TPN #10[e]		BR	500 mg and 1 g	Physically compatible for 24 hr, and antibiotic potency retained for at least 12 hr at 22 °C	313	C
TPN #21[e]		BR	1 g	Antibiotic potency retained for 24 hr at 4 °C	87	C
		BR	1 g	12 to 25% ampicillin decomposition in 24 hr at 25 °C	87	I
TPN #52[e]		AST	1.5 g	69% ampicillin loss in 24 hr at 29 °C by microbiological assay	440	I
TPN #53[e]		AST	1.5 g	22% ampicillin loss in 24 hr at 29 °C by microbiological assay	440	I
TPN #107[e]			1 and 3 g	Physically compatible and ampicillin activity retained for 24 hr at 21 °C by microbiological assay	1326	C

[a]*Tested in both PVC and glass containers.*
[b]*Tested in PVC containers.*
[c]*Tested in portable pump reservoirs (Pharmacia Deltec).*
[d]*Tested in glass containers and latex elastomeric reservoirs (Secure Medical).*
[e]*Refer to Appendix I for the composition of parenteral nutrition solutions. TPN indicates a 2-in-1 admixture.*

Additive Compatibility

Ampicillin sodium

Drug	Mfr	Conc/L	Mfr	Conc/L	Test Soln	Remarks	Ref	C/I
Amikacin sulfate	BR	5 g	BR	30 g	D5LR, D5R, D5S, D5W, D10W, IS10, LR, NS, R, SL	Greater than 10% ampicillin decomposition within 4 hr at 25 C	293	I
Aztreonam	SQ	10 g	WY	20 g	D5W[a]	10% ampicillin loss in 2 hr and 10% aztreonam loss in 3 hr at 25 °C. 10% ampicillin loss in 24 hr and 10% aztreonam loss in 8 hr at 4 °C	1001	I
	SQ	10 g	WY	5 g	D5W[a]	10% ampicillin loss in 3 hr and 10% aztreonam loss in 7 hr at 25 °C. 10% loss of both drugs in 48 hr at 4 °C	1001	I
	SQ	20 g	WY	20 g	D5W[a]	10% ampicillin loss in 4 hr and 10% aztreonam loss in 5 hr at 25 °C. 10% loss of both drugs in 24 hr at 4 °C	1001	I

Additive Compatibility (Cont.)

Ampicillin sodium

Drug	*Mfr*	*Conc/L*	*Mfr*	*Conc/L*	*Test Soln*	*Remarks*	*Ref*	*C/I*
	SQ	20 g	WY	5 g	D5W[a]	10% ampicillin loss in 5 hr and 10% aztreonam loss in 8 hr at 25 °C. 10% ampicillin loss in 48 hr and 10% aztreonam loss in 72 hr at 4 °C	1001	I
	SQ	10 g	WY	20 g	NS[a]	10% ampicillin loss in 24 hr and 2% aztreonam loss in 48 hr at 25 °C. 10% ampicillin loss in 2 days and 9% aztreonam loss in 7 days at 4 °C	1001	C
	SQ	10 g	WY	5 g	NS[a]	10% ampicillin loss and no aztreonam loss in 48 hr at 25 °C. 10% ampicillin loss in 3 days and 8% aztreonam loss in 7 days at 4 °C	1001	C
	SQ	20 g	WY	20 g	NS[a]	10% ampicillin loss in 24 hr and 5% aztreonam loss in 48 hr at 25 °C. 10% ampicillin loss in 2 days and 7% loss in 7 days at 4 °C	1001	C
	SQ	20 g	WY	5 g	NS[a]	10% ampicillin loss and no aztreonam loss in 48 hr at 25 °C. 10% ampicillin loss and 5% aztreonam loss in 7 days at 4 °C	1001	C
Cefepime HCl	BR	40 g	BR	1 g	D5W	4% ampicillin loss by HPLC in 8 hr at room temperature and 5 °C. 7% cefepime loss by HPLC in 8 hr at room temperature and no loss in 8 hr at 5 °C	1682	?
	BR	40 g	BR	1 g	NS	No ampicillin loss by HPLC in 24 hr at room temperature and 9% loss in 48 hr at 5 °C. 5% cefepime loss by HPLC in 24 hr at room temperature and 2% loss in 72 hr at 5 °C	1682	C
	BR	40 g	BR	10 g	D5W	6% ampicillin loss by HPLC in 2 hr at room temperature and 2% loss in 8 hr at 5 °C. 7% cefepime loss by HPLC in 2 hr at room temperature and 8 hr at 5 °C	1682	I
	BR	40 g	BR	10 g	NS	6% ampicillin loss by HPLC in 8 hr at room temperature and 9% loss in 48 hr at 5 °C. 8% cefepime loss by HPLC in 8 hr at room temperature and 10% loss in 48 hr at 5 °C	1682	I
	BR	4 g	BR	40 g	D5W	10% ampicillin loss by HPLC in 1 hr at room temperature and 9% loss in 2 hr at 5 °C. 25% cefepime loss by HPLC in 8 hr at room temperature and 9% loss in 2 hr at 5 °C	1682	I
	BR	4 g	BR	40 g	NS	5% ampicillin loss by HPLC in 8 hr at room temperature and 4% loss in 8 hr at 5 °C. 4% cefepime loss by HPLC in 8 hr at room temperature and 6% loss in 8 hr at 5 °C	1682	?
Cefotiam HCl	TAK	20 g	GRU	20 g	W	Visually compatible with 4% or less loss of each drug by HPLC in 2 hr	1738	C
Chlorpromazine HCl	BP	200 mg	BP	2 g	D5W, NS	Immediate precipitate	26	I

Additive Compatibility (Cont.)

Ampicillin sodium

Drug	*Mfr*	*Conc/L*	*Mfr*	*Conc/L*	*Test Soln*	*Remarks*	*Ref*	*C/I*
Cimetidine HCl	SKF	1.2 and 5 g	SKF	1 g	D5W, NS	Physically compatible and cimetidine stable for 24 hr at room temperature. Ampicillin instability is determining factor	551	?
Clindamycin phosphate	UP	24 g	WY	10 and 20 g	NS	Physically compatible	1035	C
	UP	3 g	WY	3.7 g	NS	Physically compatible with 4% ampicillin loss in 1 day at 24 °C	1035	C
Dopamine HCl	AS	800 mg	BR	4 g	D5W	36% ampicillin decomposition in 6 hr at 23 to 25 °C. Apparent dopamine decomposition in 6 hr also; color change and second spot on TLC	78	I
Erythromycin lactobionate	AB	3 g	WY	3.7 g	NS	Physically compatible with 6% ampicillin loss in 1 day at 24 °C	1035	C
Floxacillin sodium	BE	20 g	BE	20 g	NS	Physically compatible for 72 hr at 15 and 30 °C	1479	C
Furosemide	HO	1 g	BE	20 g	NS	Physically compatible for 72 hr at 15 and 30 °C	1479	C
Gentamicin sulfate	RS	160 mg	BE	8 g	D5¼S, D5W, NS	50% gentamicin decomposition in 2 hr at room temperature	157	I
		100 mg		1 g	TPN #107[b]	42% gentamicin loss and 25% ampicillin loss in 24 hr at 21 °C by microbiological assay	1326	I
Heparin sodium		32,000 units		2 g	NS	Physically compatible and heparin activity retained for 24 hr	57	C
		12,000 units	BR	1 g	D10W, LR, NS	Ampicillin potency retained for 24 hr at 4 °C	87	C
	OR	20,000 units	BE	10 g	NS	Potency of both retained for 24 hr at 25 °C	113	C
		12,000 units	BR	1 g	D5S	15% ampicillin decomposition in 24 hr at 4 °C	87	I
		12,000 units	BR	1 g	D5S, D10W, LR	20 to 25% ampicillin decomposition in 24 hr at 25 °C	87	I
Hydralazine HCl	BP	80 mg	BP	2 g	D5W	Yellow color produced	26	I
Hydrocortisone sodium succinate		200 and 400 mg	BR	1 g	LR	Ampicillin potency retained for 24 hr at 25 °C	87	C
		50 and 100 mg	BR	1 g	LR	14% ampicillin decomposition in 12 hr at 25 °C	87	I
		200 mg	BE	20 g	D–S	32% ampicillin decomposition in 6 hr at 25 °C	89	I
		200 mg	BE	20 g	D5W	23% ampicillin decomposition in 6 hr at 25 °C	89	I
		200 mg	BE	20 g	NS	18% ampicillin decomposition in 6 hr at 25 °C	89	I
		1.8 g	BR	1 g	D5S, D10W, IM, IP, LR	11 to 28% ampicillin decomposition in 24 hr at 25 °C	87	I

Additive Compatibility (Cont.)

Ampicillin sodium

Drug	Mfr	Conc/L	Mfr	Conc/L	Test Soln	Remarks	Ref	C/I
		1.8 g	BR	1 g	D5S, D5W, D10W, IM, IP, LR, NS	Ampicillin potency retained for 24 hr at 4 °C	87	C
Metronidazole	RP	5 g[c]	AY	20 g		Physically compatible for at least 24 hr at 23 °C, but solution had a significant change in pH	807	?
	SE	5 g	BR	20 g		9% ampicillin loss in 22 hr at 25 °C and in 12 days at 5 °C. No metronidazole loss	993	C
Metronidazole HCl with sodium bicarbonate	SE AB	5 g 50 mEq	BR	2 g	D5W, NS	Physically compatible for 48 hr. Ampicillin instability may be determining factor	765	?
Prochlorperazine mesylate	BP	100 mg	BP	2 g	D5W, NS	Immediate precipitate	26	I
Ranitidine HCl	GL	100 mg		2 g	D5W	Physically compatible for 24 hr at ambient temperature under fluorescent light. Ampicillin instability is determining factor	1151	?
	GL	50 mg and 2 g		1 g	NS	Physically compatible and ranitidine chemically stable by HPLC for 24 hr at 25 °C. Ampicillin not tested	1515	C
Sodium bicarbonate	AB	2.4 mEq[d]	BR	500 mg	D5W	Physically compatible for 24 hr. Ampicillin instability is determining factor	772	?
Verapamil HCl	KN	80 mg	BR	4 g	D5W, NS	Physically compatible for 24 hr	764	C
	SE	[e]	WY	40 g	D5W, NS	Cloudy solution clears with agitation	1166	?

[a]*Tested in PVC containers.*
[b]*Refer to Appendix I for the composition of parenteral nutrition solutions. TPN indicates a 2-in-1 admixture.*
[c]*Minibags (100 ml) containing metronidazole 500 mg with disodium phosphate 150 mg, citric acid 44 mg, and sodium chloride 740 mg. This product differs from the Searle product.*
[d]*One vial of Neut added to a liter of admixture.*
[e]*Final concentration unspecified.*

Drugs in Syringe Compatibility

Ampicillin sodium

Drug (in syringe)	Mfr	Amt	Mfr	Amt	Remarks	Ref	C/I
Chloramphenicol sodium succinate	PD	250 and 400 mg/ml in 1.5 to 2 ml	AY	500 mg	No precipitate or color change within 1 hr at room temperature	99	C
	PD	250 mg/1 ml	AY	500 mg	Physically compatible for 1 hr at room temperature	300	C
	PD	400 mg/1 ml	AY	500 mg	Physically compatible for 1 hr at room temperature	300	C
Colistimethate sodium	PX	40 mg/2 ml	AY	500 mg	No precipitate or color change within 1 hr at room temperature	99	C
	PX	500 mg/2 ml	AY	500 mg	Physically compatible for 1 hr at room temperature	300	C
Diatrizoate meglumine 52%, diatrizoate sodium 8%	MA	5 ml	BR	30 mg/1 ml	Physically compatible for at least 2 hr	1438	C
Diatrizoate sodium 60%	WI	5 ml	BR	30 mg/1 ml	Physically compatible for at least 2 hr	1438	C

Drugs in Syringe Compatibility (Cont.)

Drug (in syringe)	*Mfr*	*Amt*	**Ampicillin sodium** *Mfr*	*Amt*	*Remarks*	*Ref*	*C/I*
Erythromycin lactobionate	AB	300 mg/ 6 ml	AY	500 mg	Precipitate forms in 1 hr at room temperature	300	I
Gentamicin sulfate		80 mg/ 2 ml	AY	500 mg	Physically incompatible within 1 hr at room temperature	99	I
Heparin sodium		2500 units/ 1 ml		2 g	Physically compatible for at least 5 min	1053	C
Hydromorphone HCl	KN	2, 10, 40 mg/ 1 ml	AY	250 mg/ 1 ml	Visually compatible but 10% loss of ampicillin by HPLC in 5 hr at room temperature	2082	I
Iohexol	WI	64.7%, 5 ml	BR	30 mg/ 1 ml	Physically compatible for at least 2 hr	1438	C
Iopamidol	SQ	61%, 5 ml	BR	30 mg/ 1 ml	Physically compatible for at least 2 hr	1438	C
Iothalamate meglumine 60%	MA	5 ml	BR	30 mg/ 1 ml	Physically compatible for at least 2 hr	1438	C
Ioxaglate meglumine 39.3%, ioxaglate sodium 19.6%	MA	5 ml	BR	30 mg/ 1 ml	Physically compatible for at least 2 hr	1438	C
Kanamycin sulfate		1 g/4 ml	AY	500 mg	Physically incompatible within 1 hr at room temperature	99	I
		1 g/2 ml	AY	500 mg	Precipitate forms in 1 hr at room temperature	300	I
Lidocaine HCl		0.5 and 2.5% in 2.5 ml	BE	500 mg	Physically compatible	89	C
		0.5 and 2.5% in 1.5 ml	BE	250 mg	Occasional turbidity	89	I
Lincomycin HCl	UP	600 mg/ 2 ml	AY	500 mg	Physically incompatible within 1 hr at room temperature	99	I
	UP	600 mg/ 2 ml	AY	500 mg	Precipitate forms in 1 hr at room temperature	300	I
Metoclopramide HCl	RB	10 mg/ 2 ml	BR	250 mg/ 2.5 ml	Incompatible. If mixed, use immediately	1167	I
	RB	10 mg/ 2 ml	BR	1 g/10 ml	Incompatible. If mixed, use immediately	1167	I
	RB	160 mg/ 32 ml	BR	1 g/10 ml	Incompatible. If mixed, use immediately	1167	I
Polymyxin B sulfate	BW	25 mg/ 1.5 ml	AY	500 mg	Physically compatible for 1 hr at room temperature	300	C
	BW	25 mg/ 1.5 ml	AY	250 mg	Precipitate forms in 1 hr at room temperature	300	I
Procaine HCl			BE		Physically compatible	89	C
Streptomycin sulfate		1 g/2 ml	AY	500 mg	No precipitate or color change within 1 hr at room temperature	99	C
	BP	1 g/2 ml	AY	500 mg	Physically compatible for 1 hr at room temperature	300	C
	BP	1 g/ 1.5 ml	AY	500 mg	Syrupy solution forms	300	I
Streptomycin sulfate stabilized	BP	0.75 g/ 1.5 ml	AY	500 mg	Precipitate forms in 1 hr at room temperature	300	I

Y-Site Injection Compatibility (1:1 Mixture)

Drug	Mfr	Conc	Mfr	Conc	Remarks	Ref	C/I
			Ampicillin sodium				
Acyclovir sodium	BW	5 mg/ml[a]	WY	20 mg/ml[b]	Physically compatible for 4 hr at 25 °C	1157	**C**
Amifostine	USB	10 mg/ml[a]	WY	20 mg/ml[b]	Physically compatible with no change in measured turbidity or increase in particle content in 4 hr at 23 °C	1845	**C**
Amphotericin B cholesteryl sulfate complex	SEQ	0.83 mg/ml[a]	SKB	20 mg/ml[b]	Gross precipitate forms	2117	**I**
Aztreonam	SQ	40 mg/ml[a]	WY	20 mg/ml[b]	Physically compatible with no subvisual haze or particle formation in 4 hr at 23 °C	1758	**C**
Calcium gluconate	AST	4 mg/ml[b]	WY	40 mg/ml[b]	Physically compatible for 3 hr	1316	**C**
	AST	4 mg/ml[a]	WY	40 mg/ml[a]	Slight color change in 1 hr	1316	**I**
Cisatracurium besylate	GW	0.1 and 2 mg/ml[a]	SKB	20 mg/ml[b]	Physically compatible with no change in measured turbidity or increase in particle content in 4 hr at 23 °C	2074	**C**
	GW	5 mg/ml[a]	SKB	20 mg/ml[b]	Gray subvisual haze forms in 1 hr	2074	**I**
Clarithromycin	AB	4 mg/ml[a]	BE	40 mg/ml[a]	Visually compatible for 72 hr at both 30 and 17 °C	2174	**C**
Cyclophosphamide	MJ	20 mg/ml[a]	BR	20 mg/ml[b]	Physically compatible for 4 hr at 25 °C	1194	**C**
Diltiazem HCl	MMD	5 mg/ml	WY	100 mg/ml[b]	Cloudiness forms	1807	**I**
	MMD	1 mg/ml[b]	WY	100 mg/ml[b]	Visually compatible	1807	**C**
	MMD	5 mg/ml	WY	10 and 20 mg/ml[b]	Visually compatible	1807	**C**
Docetaxel	RPR	0.9 mg/ml[a]	SKB	20 mg/ml[b]	Physically compatible with no change in measured turbidity or increase in particle content in 4 hr at 23 °C	2224	**C**
Doxorubicin HCl liposome injection	SEQ	0.4 mg/ml[a]	SKB	20 mg/ml[b]	Physically compatible with little or no change in measured turbidity and no increase in particle content in 4 hr at 23 °C	2087	**C**
Enalaprilat	MSD	0.05 mg/ml[b]	BR	10 mg/ml[b]	Physically compatible for 24 hr at room temperature under fluorescent light	1355	**C**
Epinephrine HCl	ES	0.032 mg/ml[c]	WY	40 mg/ml[c]	Slight color change in 3 hr	1316	**I**
Esmolol HCl	DCC	10 mg/ml[a]	WY	20 mg/ml[b]	Physically compatible for 24 hr at 22 °C	1169	**C**
Etoposide phosphate	BR	5 mg/ml[a]	APC	20 mg/ml[b]	Physically compatible with no change in measured turbidity or increase in particle content in 4 hr at 23 °C	2218	**C**
Famotidine	MSD	0.2 mg/ml[a]	ES	20 mg/ml[b]	Physically compatible for 14 hr	1196	**C**
	ME	2 mg/ml[b]		20 mg/ml[b]	Visually compatible for 4 hr at 22 °C	1936	**C**
Filgrastim	AMG	30 μg/ml[a]	WY	20 mg/ml[a]	Physically compatible with no change in measured turbidity or increase in particle content in 4 hr at 22 °C	1687	**C**
Fluconazole	RR	2 mg/ml	WY	20 mg/ml	Cloudiness	1407	**I**
Fludarabine phosphate	BX	1 mg/ml[a]	BR	20 mg/ml[b]	Physically compatible for 4 hr at room temperature under fluorescent light	1439	**C**
Foscarnet sodium	AST	24 mg/ml	WY	20 mg/ml	Physically compatible for 24 hr at room temperature under fluorescent light	1335	**C**

Y-Site Injection Compatibility (1:1 Mixture) (Cont.)

Ampicillin sodium

Drug	*Mfr*	*Conc*	*Mfr*	*Conc*	*Remarks*	*Ref*	*C/I*
Gatifloxacin	BMS	2 mg/ml[a]	APC	20 mg/ml[b]	Physically compatible with no change in measured haze or increase in particle content in 4 hr at 23 °C	2234	C
Gemcitabine HCl	LI	10 mg/ml[b]	SKB	20 mg/ml[b]	Physically compatible with no change in measured turbidity or increase in particle content in 4 hr at 23 °C	2226	C
Granisetron HCl	SKB	0.05 mg/ml[a]	MAR	20 mg/ml[b]	Physically compatible with no change in measured turbidity or increase in particle content in 4 hr at 23 °C	2000	C
Heparin sodium	TR	50 units/ml	WY	20 mg/ml[b]	Visually compatible for 4 hr at 25 °C	1793	C
Heparin sodium with hydrocortisone sodium succinate	RI UP	1000 units + 100 mg/L[d]	BR	25, 50, 100, 135 mg/ml	Physically compatible for at least 4 hr at room temperature by visual and microscopic examination	322	C
Hetastarch in lactated electrolyte injection (Hextend)	AB	6%	APC	20 mg/ml[b]	Physically compatible with no change in measured turbidity or increase in particle content in 4 hr at 23 °C	2339	C
Hetastarch in sodium chloride 0.9%	DCC	6%	BR	20 mg/ml[a]	Physically compatible for 4 hr at room temperature by visual examination	1313	C
	DCC	6%	BR	20 mg/ml[a]	One or two particles in one of five vials. Fine white strands appeared immediately during Y-site infusion	1315	I
Hydralazine HCl	SO	1 mg/ml[b]	WY	40 mg/ml[b]	Moderate color change in 3 hr	1316	I
	SO	1 mg/ml[a]	WY	40 mg/ml[a]	Moderate color change in 1 hr	1316	I
Hydromorphone HCl	WY	0.2 mg/ml[a]	BR	20 mg/ml[b]	Physically compatible for at least 4 hr at 25 °C under fluorescent light	987	C
	KN	2, 10, 40 mg/ml	AY	20[a] and 250 mg/ml	Visually compatible and hydromorphone potency by HPLC retained for 24 hr. 10% ampicillin loss by HPLC in 5 hr with or without hydromorphone	1532	I
Insulin, regular	LI	0.2 unit/ml[b]	WY	20 mg/ml[b]	Physically compatible for 2 hr at 25 °C	1395	C
Labetalol HCl	SC	1 mg/ml[a]	WY	10 mg/ml[b]	Physically compatible for 24 hr at 18 °C	1171	C
Levofloxacin	OMN	5 mg/ml[a]	MAR	50 mg/ml	Visually compatible for 4 hr at 24 °C under fluorescent light	2233	C
Linezolid	PHU	2 mg/ml	APC	20 mg/ml[b]	Physically compatible with no change in measured turbidity or increase in particle content in 4 hr at 23 °C	2264	C
Magnesium sulfate	IX	16.7, 33.3, 66.7, 100 mg/ml[a]	WY	20 mg/ml[b]	Physically compatible for at least 4 hr at 32 °C	813	C
Melphalan HCl	BW	0.1 mg/ml[b]	WY	20 mg/ml[b]	Physically compatible with no change in measured turbidity or increase in particle content in 3 hr at 22 °C	1557	C
Meperidine HCl	WY	10 mg/ml[a]	BR	20 mg/ml[b]	Physically compatible for at least 4 hr at 25 °C under fluorescent light	987	C
Midazolam HCl	RC	1 mg/ml[a]	WY	20 mg/ml[b]	Haze forms immediately	1847	I
Morphine sulfate	WI	1 mg/ml[a]	BR	20 mg/ml[b]	Physically compatible for at least 4 hr at 25 °C under fluorescent light	987	C

Y-Site Injection Compatibility (1:1 Mixture) (Cont.)

Drug	*Mfr*	*Conc*	*Mfr* (Ampicillin sodium)	*Conc* (Ampicillin sodium)	*Remarks*	*Ref*	*C/I*
Multivitamins	USV	5 ml/L[a]	AY	1 g/50 ml[c]	Physically compatible for 24 hr at room temperature	323	C
Ofloxacin	HO	2.2 mg/ml	HO	21.3 mg/ml	Visually compatible with no loss of either drug by HPLC in 2 hr at room temperature	1734	C
Ondansetron HCl	GL	1 mg/ml[b]	BR	20 mg/ml[b]	Immediate turbidity and precipitation	1365	I
Perphenazine	SC	0.02 mg/ml[a]	BR	20 mg/ml[b]	Physically compatible for 4 hr at 25 °C	1155	C
Phytonadione	MSD	0.4 mg/ml[c]	WY	40 mg/ml[b]	Physically compatible for 3 hr	1316	C
Potassium chloride		40 mEq/L[d]	BR	25, 50, 100, 135 mg/ml	Physically compatible for at least 4 hr at room temperature by visual and microscopic examination	322	C
Propofol	ZEN	10 mg/ml	WY	20 mg/ml[b]	Physically compatible for 1 hr at 23 °C with no increase in particle content	2066	C
Remifentanil HCl	GW	0.025 and 0.25 mg/ml[b]	SKB	20 mg/ml[b]	Physically compatible with no change in measured turbidity or increase in particle content in 4 hr at 23 °C	2075	C
Sargramostim	IMM	10 µg/ml[b]	BR	20 mg/ml[b]	Few small particles form in 4 hr	1436	I
Tacrolimus	FUJ	1 mg/ml[b]	WY	20 mg/ml[a]	Visually compatible for 24 hr at 25 °C	1630	C
Teniposide	BR	0.1 mg/ml[a]	WY	20 mg/ml[b]	Physically compatible with no subvisual haze or particle formation in 4 hr at 23 °C	1725	C
Theophylline	TR	4 mg/ml	WY	20 mg/ml[b]	Visually compatible for 6 hr at 25 °C	1793	C
Thiotepa	IMM[e]	1 mg/ml[a]	WY	20 mg/ml[b]	Physically compatible with no change in measured turbidity or increase in particle content in 4 hr at 23 °C	1861	C
TNA #73[f]		32.5 ml[g]	BR	2 g/50 ml[b]	Physically compatible for 4 hr at 25 °C by visual observation	1008	C
TNA #218 to #226[f]			SKB	20 mg/ml[b]	Visually compatible with no precipitate or emulsion damage apparent in 4 hr at 23 °C	2215	C
Tolazoline HCl		0.1 mg/ml[a]	WY	30 mg/ml[b]	Physically compatible for 24 hr at 22 °C	1363	C
TPN #54[f]					Precipitate forms within 30 min at 22 °C	1045	I
TPN #61[f]		[h]	WY	250 mg/1.3 ml[i]	Heavy precipitate of calcium phosphate due to increased pH	1012	I
		[j]	WY	1.5 g/7.5 ml[i]	Heavy precipitate of calcium phosphate due to increased pH	1012	I
TPN #203 and #204[f]			APC	100 and 250 mg/ml	White precipitate forms immediately	1974	I
TPN #212 to #215[f]			SKB	20 mg/ml[b]	Physically compatible with no change in measured turbidity or increase in particle content in 4 hr at 23 °C	2109	C
Vancomycin HCl	AB	20 mg/ml[a]	SKB	250 mg/ml[k]	Transient precipitate forms followed by clear solution	2189	?
	AB	20 mg/ml[a]	SKB	1, 10, and 50 mg/ml[b]	Physically compatible with no change in measured turbidity or increase in particle content in 4 hr at 23 °C	2189	C

Y-Site Injection Compatibility (1:1 Mixture) (Cont.)

Drug	Mfr	Conc	Ampicillin sodium Mfr	Ampicillin sodium Conc	Remarks	Ref	C/I
	AB	2 mg/ml[a]	SKB	1[b], 10[b], 50[b], and 250[k] mg/ml	Physically compatible with no change in measured turbidity or increase in particle content in 4 hr at 23 °C	2189	C
Verapamil HCl	SE	2.5 mg/ml	WY	40 mg/ml[c]	White milky precipitate forms immediately and persists. 91% of verapamil precipitated	1166	I
Vinorelbine tartrate	BW	1 mg/ml[b]	WY	20 mg/ml[b]	Tiny particles form immediately, becoming large white particles in cloudy solution in 1 hr	1558	I
Vitamin B complex with C	RC	2 ml/L[d]	BR	25, 50, 100, 135 mg/ml	Physically compatible for at least 4 hr at room temperature by visual and microscopic examination	322	C
	RC	4 and 20 ml/L[a]		1 g/50 ml[c]	Physically compatible for 24 hr at room temperature	323	C

[a] *Tested in dextrose 5% in water.*
[b] *Tested in sodium chloride 0.9%.*
[c] *Tested in both dextrose 5% in water and sodium chloride 0.9%.*
[d] *Tested in dextrose 5% in water, sodium chloride 0.9%, and Ringer's injection, lactated.*
[e] *Lyophilized formulation tested.*
[f] *Refer to Appendix I for the composition of parenteral nutrition solutions. TNA indicates a 3-in-1 admixture, and TPN indicates a 2-in-1 admixture.*
[g] *A 32.5-ml sample of parenteral nutrition solution mixed with 50 ml of antibiotic solution.*
[h] *Run at 21 ml/hr.*
[i] *Given over five minutes by syringe pump.*
[j] *Run at 94 ml/hr.*
[k] *Tested in sterile water for injection.*

Additional Compatibility Information

Peritoneal Dialysis Solutions — The stability of ampicillin sodium (Bristol) 50 mg/L in peritoneal dialysis solutions (Dianeal 137 and PD2) with heparin sodium 500 units/L was evaluated at 25 °C by microbiological assay. Approximately 93 ± 10% activity remained after 24 hours. (1228)

Aminoglycosides — Noone and Pattison evaluated the inactivation of gentamicin by a variety of penicillins and cephalosporins, including ampicillin sodium. They noted a 50% loss of gentamicin in two hours at room temperature when gentamicin sulfate (Roussel) 160 mg/L was combined with ampicillin sodium (Beecham) 8 g/L in several intravenous solutions. (157)

Rank et al. evaluated the inactivation of tobramycin 6 μg/ml in human serum with the sodium salts of cloxacillin and piperacillin 150 and 300 μg/ml, ampicillin 100 and 200 μg/ml, and penicillin G 75 and 150 I.U./ml at 25 and 37 °C for up to 12 hours. Piperacillin induced the greatest inactivation among the penicillins, with up to a 15% loss in 12 hours at 37 °C, in the 300-μg/ml concentration. Cloxacillin and ampicillin had an intermediate effect, causing about a 5% loss in 12 hours at 37 °C in the highest concentrations. Penicillin G did not yield significant tobramycin inactivation. (817)

The inactivation of tobramycin sulfate 8 μg/ml in human serum by ampicillin, carbenicillin disodium, and penicillin G potassium, each at 200 μg/ml, was studied at 0, 23, and 37 °C by O'Bey et al. For the tobramycin–ampicillin mixture, essentially no differences were observed at the various temperatures. The t_{90} values were 19, 16.5, and 20 hours at 0, 23, and 37 °C, respectively. Carbenicillin displayed a temperature-dependent inactivation of tobramycin. At 0 °C, the t_{90} was 36 hours; but at 23 and 37 °C, the t_{90} values were 10 and 12 hours, respectively. With penicillin G potassium, the t_{90} values for tobramycin inactivation at 0, 23, and 37 °C were 48, 44, and 16 hours, respectively. Inaccurate pharmacokinetic dosing of tobramycin may occur if serum samples are not properly handled. (832)

To determine if spurious aminoglycoside levels could result from a delay in assaying blood samples, Tindula et al. evaluated the inactivation of amikacin 35 μg/ml and gentamicin and tobramycin 10 μg/ml in human serum by 400-μg/ml concentrations of several penicillins and cephalosporins. Samples were stored for 24 hours at room temperature and frozen at −20 °C. For the room temperature samples, cefazolin and cefamandole caused relatively little inactivation. Nafcillin, cephapirin, and cefoxitin caused moderate inactivation, 20% or less. Penicillin, ampicillin, carbenicillin, and ticarcillin generally caused 25% or more inactivation of gentamicin and tobramycin. Amikacin was somewhat less affected. Freezing samples at −20 °C prevented significant inactivation of amikacin and gentamicin by any of the drugs. Freezing the tobramycin samples was satisfactory for most of the drugs except penicillin, ampicillin, and carbenicillin, which still exhibited a 15 to 20% loss in 24 hours. (824)

The comparative inactivation of five aminoglycosides by seven β-lactam antibiotics in human serum at 37 °C was reported by Riff and Thomason. Amikacin, followed by netilmicin, had the lowest degree of inactivation; tobramycin sustained the most pronounced losses. Gentamicin and kanamycin were intermediate in the extent of losses. The six penicillins that were tested all produced aminoglycoside inactivation; the greatest extent of inactivation was caused by carbenicillin followed by ticarcillin, penicillin G, oxacillin, methicillin, and ampicillin, in approximate descending order. Cephalothin produced minimal inactivation (5 to 10% in 24 hours). The rate of inactivation could be reduced by storage at 4 °C and further reduced by storage at −20 °C. The authors suggested processing blood samples rapidly to avoid inaccurate serum determinations. Storage of specimens at low temperatures until analysis may be helpful. (1052)

Townsend reported the apparent inactivation of gentamicin sulfate by ampicillin sodium in blood samples held for 12 hours prior to assay. (1382)

Vancomycin — The compatibility or incompatibility of vancomycin HCl mixed with or administered simultaneously with ampicillin sodium may be concentration dependent. (2189) See Y-Site Compatibility above. Vancomycin HCl has a low pH and is variably compatible with drugs having neutral to mildly alkaline pH, including cephalosporins and penicillins. The compatibility may depend on a number of factors, including concentration of each drug, dilution vehicle, actual pH of solutions, and completeness of mixing during administration. Combinations that are compatible when well mixed may result in precipitation if only partially mixed, presumably due to regionally different concentrations and pH values. If attempting to administer vancomycin HCl with ampicillin sodium, take care to ensure that the specific combination and the concentrations are compatible under the exact administration conditions to be used. An inline filter should be used as a final safety measure. (2189)

Other Drugs — Ampicillin sodium is stated to be physically compatible for 24 hours at room temperature with lincomycin HCl in infusion solutions. (154)

Clindamycin phosphate has been stated to be physically incompatible with ampicillin sodium. (4)

AMPICILLIN SODIUM–SULBACTAM SODIUM
AHFS 8:12.16

Products — Ampicillin sodium–sulbactam sodium is available in vials and piggyback bottles containing 1.5 g (ampicillin 1 g plus sulbactam 0.5 g) or 3 g (ampicillin 2 g plus sulbactam 1 g) as the sodium salts. (2)

For intramuscular injection, reconstitute vials with sterile water for injection or lidocaine HCl 0.5 or 2% in the following amounts (2):

Vial Size	Volume of Diluent	Withdrawable Volume	Concentration
1.5 g	3.2 ml	4 ml[a]	375 mg/ml[b]
3.0 g	6.4 ml	8 ml[a]	375 mg/ml[b]

[a]*Sufficient excess is present to permit withdrawal of the volume noted.*
[b]*Ampicillin 250 mg plus sulbactam 125 mg per milliliter.*

For intravenous use, reconstitute piggyback bottles directly with a compatible diluent to the desired concentration between 3 and 45 mg/ml (ampicillin 2 to 30 mg plus sulbactam 1 to 15 mg per milliliter). Standard vials of 1.5 and 3 g may be reconstituted with 3.2 and 6.4 ml of sterile water for injection, respectively, to yield 375-mg/ml solutions (ampicillin 250 mg plus sulbactam 125 mg per milliliter). The reconstituted solution should be diluted immediately in a compatible infusion solution to yield the desired concentration between 3 and 45 mg/ml. (2)

Allow reconstituted solutions to stand so that any foaming may dissipate before inspecting them visually to ensure complete dissolution. (2)

pH— From 8 to 10. (2)

Osmolality— Ampicillin sodium–sulbactam sodium 375 mg/ml in sterile water for injection has an osmolality exceeding 2000 mOsm/kg. (1689)

Sodium Content— Each 1.5 g (ampicillin 1 g plus sulbactam 0.5 g as the sodium salts) contains 5 mEq (115 mg) of sodium. (2)

Trade Name(s)— Unasyn.

Administration — Ampicillin sodium–sulbactam sodium may be administered by deep intramuscular injection or intravenous injection or infusion. By direct intravenous injection, the drug should be given slowly over at least 10 to 15 minutes. By infusion, it may be diluted in 50 to 100 ml of compatible diluent and infused over 15 to 30 minutes. (2; 4)

Stability — Intact vials of the white to off-white powder should be stored at or below 30 °C. Aqueous solutions are pale yellow to yellow. Dilute solutions are pale yellow to colorless. The manufacturer recommends that intramuscular solutions be used within one hour after preparation. The administration of diluted solutions for intravenous infusion should be completed within eight hours of preparation to ensure that the potency is maintained throughout the infusion. (2; 4)

Elastomeric Reservoir Pumps— Ampicillin sodium–sulbactam sodium solutions in elastomeric reservoir pumps have been stated by the pump manufacturers to be stable for the following time periods refrigerated (REF) or at room temperature (RT) (31):

Pump Reservoir(s)	Conc.	REF	RT
Homepump; Homepump Eclipse	30 + 15 mg/ml[a]	3 days	
Intermate HPC	20 + 10 mg/ml[a]	3 days	2 hr
	45 + 22.5 mg/ml[a]	3 days	2 hr

[a]*In sodium chloride 0.9%.*

Central Venous Catheter— Ampicillin sodium–sulbactam sodium (Pfizer-Roerig) 5 + 2.5 mg/ml in sodium chloride 0.9% was found to be compatible with the ARROWg+ard Blue Plus (Arrow International) chlorhexidine-bearing triple-lumen central catheter. HPLC analysis was used to evaluate completeness of drug delivery through the catheter and the amount of chlorhexidine removed from the internal lumens. Essentially complete delivery of the drug was found with little or no drug loss occurring. Furthermore, chlorhexidine delivered from the catheter remained at trace amounts with no substantial increase due to the delivery of the drug through the catheter. (2335)

Compatibility Information

Solution Compatibility

Ampicillin sodium–sulbactam sodium

Solution	Mfr	Mfr	Conc/L	Remarks	Ref	C/I
Sodium chloride 0.9%	[a]	PF	20 + 10 g	Visually compatible with 10% ampicillin loss by HPLC in 32 hr at 24 °C and 68 hr at 5 °C	1691	C

[a]*Tested in PVC containers.*

Additive Compatibility

Ampicillin sodium–sulbactam sodium

Drug	Mfr	Conc/L	Mfr	Conc/L	Test Soln	Remarks	Ref	C/I
Aztreonam	SQ	10 g	PF	20 + 10 g	NS[a]	Visually compatible with 10% ampicillin loss by HPLC in 30 hr at 24 °C and 94 hr at 5 °C. Ampicillin loss is determining factor	1691	C
Ciprofloxacin	MI	2 g		20 + 10 g	D5W	Physically incompatible	888	I

[a]*Tested in PVC containers.*

Y-Site Injection Compatibility (1:1 Mixture)

Ampicillin sodium–sulbactam sodium

Drug	Mfr	Conc	Mfr	Conc	Remarks	Ref	C/I
Amifostine	USB	10 mg/ml[a]	WY	20 + 10 mg/ml[b]	Physically compatible with no change in measured turbidity or increase in particle content in 4 hr at 23 °C	1845	C
Amphotericin B cholesteryl sulfate complex	SEQ	0.83 mg/ml[a]	RR	20 + 10 mg/ml[b]	Gross precipitate forms	2117	I
Aztreonam	SQ	40 mg/ml[a]	RR	20 + 10 mg/ml[b]	Physically compatible with no subvisual haze or particle formation in 4 hr at 23 °C	1758	C
Cefepime HCl	BMS	20 mg/ml[a]	RR	20 + 10 mg/ml[a]	Physically compatible with no change in measured turbidity or increase in particle content in 4 hr at 22 °C	1689	C
Ciprofloxacin		400 mg[c]		3 + 1.5 g[c]	Administered sequentially through a Y-site into running D5S. White crystals formed immediately	1887	I
Cisatracurium besylate	GW	0.1 and 2 mg/ml[a]	RR	20 + 10 mg/ml[b]	Physically compatible with no change in measured turbidity or increase in particle content in 4 hr at 23 °C	2074	C
	GW	5 mg/ml[a]	RR	20 + 10 mg/ml[b]	Subvisual haze develops in 15 min	2074	I
Diltiazem HCl	MMD	5 mg/ml	RR	45 + 22.5 mg/ml[b]	Cloudiness forms	1807	I
	MMD	1 mg/ml[b]	RR	45 + 22.5 mg/ml[b]	Visually compatible	1807	C
	MMD	5 mg/ml	RR	15 + 7.5 mg/ml[b]	Visually compatible	1807	C
	MMD	5 mg/ml	RR	2 + 1 mg/ml[b]	Visually compatible	1807	C

Y-Site Injection Compatibility (1:1 Mixture) (Cont.)

			Ampicillin sodium–sulbactam sodium				
Drug	*Mfr*	*Conc*	*Mfr*	*Conc*	*Remarks*	*Ref*	*C/I*
Docetaxel	RPR	0.9 mg/ml[a]	RR	20 + 10 mg/ml[b]	Physically compatible with no change in measured turbidity or increase in particle content in 4 hr at 23 °C	2224	C
Enalaprilat	MSD	0.05 mg/ml[b]	PF	10 + 5 mg/ml[b]	Physically compatible for 24 hr at room temperature under fluorescent light	1355	C
Etoposide phosphate	BR	5 mg/ml[a]	RR	20 + 10 mg/ml[b]	Physically compatible with no change in measured turbidity or increase in particle content in 4 hr at 23 °C	2218	C
Famotidine	MSD	0.2 mg/ml[a]	RR	20 + 10 mg/ml[b]	Physically compatible for 14 hr	1196	C
Filgrastim	AMG	30 μg/ml[a]	RR	20 + 10 mg/ml[a]	Physically compatible with no change in measured turbidity or increase in particle content in 4 hr at 22 °C	1687	C
Fluconazole	RR	2 mg/ml	RR	40 + 20 mg/ml	Physically compatible for 24 hr at 25 °C	1407	C
Fludarabine phosphate	BX	1 mg/ml[a]	RR	20 + 10 mg/ml[b]	Physically compatible for 4 hr at room temperature under fluorescent light	1439	C
Gatifloxacin	BMS	2 mg/ml[a]	PF	20 + 10 mg/ml[b]	Physically compatible with no change in measured haze or increase in particle content in 4 hr at 23 °C	2234	C
Gemcitabine HCl	LI	10 mg/ml[b]	RR	20 + 10 mg/ml[b]	Physically compatible with no change in measured turbidity or increase in particle content in 4 hr at 23 °C	2226	C
Granisetron HCl	SKB	0.05 mg/ml[a]	RR	20 + 10 mg/ml[b]	Physically compatible with no change in measured turbidity or increase in particle content in 4 hr at 23 °C	2000	C
Heparin sodium	TR	50 units/ml	PF	20 + 10 mg/ml[b]	Visually compatible for 4 hr at 25 °C	1793	C
Hetastarch in lactated electrolyte injection (Hextend)	AB	6 %	PF	20 + 10 mg/ml[b]	Physically compatible with no change in measured turbidity or increase in particle content in 4 hr at 23 °C	2339	C
Idarubicin HCl	AD	1 mg/ml[b]	RR	20 + 10 mg/ml[b]	Haze forms and color changes immediately. Precipitate forms within 20 min	1525	I
Insulin, regular	LI	0.2 unit/ml[b]	RR	20 + 10 mg/ml[b]	Physically compatible for 2 hr at 25 °C	1395	C
Linezolid	PHU	2 mg/ml	PF	20 + 10 mg/ml[b]	Physically compatible with no change in measured turbidity or increase in particle content in 4 hr at 23 °C	2264	C
Meperidine HCl	WY	10 mg/ml[b]	RR	20 + 10 mg/ml[b]	Physically compatible for 1 hr at 25 °C	1338	C
Morphine sulfate	ES	1 mg/ml[b]	RR	20 + 10 mg/ml[b]	Physically compatible for 1 hr at 25 °C	1338	C
Ondansetron HCl	GL	1 mg/ml[b]	RR	20 + 10 mg/ml[b]	Immediate turbidity and precipitation	1365	I

Y-Site Injection Compatibility (1:1 Mixture) (Cont.)

Drug	Mfr	Conc	Mfr	Conc	Remarks	Ref	C/I
			Ampicillin sodium–sulbactam sodium				
Paclitaxel	NCI	1.2 mg/ml[a]	RR	20 + 10 mg/ml[b]	Physically compatible with no change in measured turbidity in 4 hr at 22 °C	1556	C
Remifentanil HCl	GW	0.025 and 0.25 mg/ml[b]	RR	20 + 10 mg/ml[b]	Physically compatible with no change in measured turbidity or increase in particle content in 4 hr at 23 °C	2075	C
Sargramostim	IMM	10 μg/ml[b]	RR	20 + 10 mg/ml[b]	Few small particles in 4 hr in one of two samples	1436	I
Tacrolimus	FUJ	1 mg/ml[b]	RR	33.3 + 16.7 mg/ml[a]	Visually compatible for 24 hr at 25 °C	1630	C
Teniposide	BR	0.1 mg/ml[a]	RR	20 + 10 mg/ml[b]	Physically compatible with no subvisual haze or particle formation in 4 hr at 23 °C	1725	C
Theophylline	TR	4 mg/ml	PF	20 + 10 mg/ml[b]	Visually compatible for 6 hr at 25 °C	1793	C
Thiotepa	IMM[d]	1 mg/ml[a]	RR	20 + 10 mg/ml[b]	Physically compatible with no change in measured turbidity or increase in particle content in 4 hr at 23 °C	1861	C
TNA #218 to #226[e]			PF	20 + 10 mg/ml[b]	Visually compatible with no precipitate or emulsion damage apparent in 4 hr at 23 °C	2215	C
TPN #212 to #215[e]			RR	20 + 10 mg/ml[b]	Physically compatible with no change in measured turbidity or increase in particle content in 4 hr at 23 °C	2109	C
Vancomycin HCl	AB	20 mg/ml[a]	PF	250 + 125 mg/ml[f]	Transient precipitate forms, followed by clear solution	2189	?
	AB	20 mg/ml[a]	PF	1 + 0.5, 10 + 5, and 50 + 25 mg/ml[b]	Physically compatible with no change in measured turbidity or increase in particle content in 4 hr at 23 °C	2189	C
	AB	2 mg/ml[a]	PF	1 + 0.5[b], 10 + 5[b], 50 + 25[b], and 250 + 125[f] mg/ml	Physically compatible with no change in measured turbidity or increase in particle content in 4 hr at 23 °C	2189	C

[a]Tested in dextrose 5% in water.
[b]Tested in sodium chloride 0.9%.
[c]Concentration and volume not specified.
[d]Lyophilized formulation tested.
[e]Refer to Appendix I for the composition of parenteral nutrition solutions. TNA indicates a 3-in-1 admixture, and TPN indicates a 2-in-1 admixture.
[f]Tested in sterile water for injection.

Additional Compatibility Information

The compatibility information on ampicillin sodium should be considered. See previous monograph.

Infusion Solutions — The manufacturer recommends the following use periods for ampicillin sodium–sulbactam sodium diluted in the infusion solutions noted (2):

Infusion Solution	Maximum Concentration (mg/ml) (Ampicillin/ Sulbactam)	Storage Temperature (°C)	Use Period (hr)
Dextrose 5% in sodium chloride 0.45%	3 (2/1)	25	4
	15 (10/5)	4	4
Dextrose 5% in water	30 (20/10)	25	2
	30 (20/10)	4	4
	3 (2/1)	25	4
Invert sugar 10%	3 (2/1)	25	4
	30 (20/10)	4	3
Ringer's injection, lactated	45 (30/15)	25	8
	45 (30/15)	4	24
Sodium chloride 0.9%	45 (30/15)	25	8
	45 (30/15)	4	48
	30 (20/10)	4	72
Sodium lactate ⅙ M	45 (30/15)	25	8
	45 (30/15)	4	8
Sterile water for injection	45 (30/15)	25	8
	45 (30/15)	4	48
	30 (20/10)	4	72

Aminoglycosides — The manufacturer indicates that ampicillin sodium–sulbactam sodium should be reconstituted and administered separately from aminoglycosides because of possible in vitro inactivation. (2)

Vancomycin — The compatibility or incompatibility of vancomycin HCl mixed with or administered simultaneously with ampicillin sodium–sulbactam sodium may be concentration dependent. (2189) See Y-Site Compatibility above. Vancomycin HCl has a low pH and is variably compatible with drugs having neutral to mildly alkaline pH, including cephalosporins and penicillins. The compatibility may depend on a number of factors, including concentration of each drug, dilution vehicle, actual pH of solutions, and completeness of mixing during administration. Combinations that are compatible when well mixed may result in precipitation if only partially mixed, presumably because of regionally different concentrations and pH values. If attempting to administer vancomycin HCl with ampicillin sodium–sulbactam sodium, take care to ensure that the specific combination and the concentrations are compatible under the exact administration conditions to be used. An inline filter should be used as a final safety measure. (2189)

ASCORBIC ACID INJECTION
AHFS 88:12

Products — Ascorbic acid injection is provided as a sodium ascorbate solution equivalent to 500 mg/ml of ascorbic acid in 1- and 2-ml ampuls. The pH may be adjusted with sodium bicarbonate and ascorbic acid. Sodium hydrosulfite 0.5% is present as an antioxidant. (1-10/95)

Pressure may build up during storage of ampuls of ascorbic acid injection. At room temperature, the pressure may become excessive. When opening ascorbic acid injection, the ampuls should be wrapped in a protective covering. (1-10/95)

pH — From 5.5 to 7. (4; 17)

Osmolality — Ascorbic acid injection 500 mg/ml has an osmolality exceeding 2000 mOsm/kg. (1689)

Trade Name(s) — Cenolate.

Administration — Intramuscular injection of ascorbic acid injection is preferred, but it may also be given subcutaneously or intravenously. (1-10/95; 4) Intravenously, it should be added to a large volume of a compatible diluent and infused slowly. (1-10/95)

Stability — To avoid excessive pressure inside the ampuls, they should be stored in the refrigerator and not allowed to stand at room temperature before use. (1-10/95)

Although refrigeration is recommended, Lilly has stated that its ascorbic acid injection had a maximum room temperature stability of 96 hours. (853) Intact ampuls of commercial ascorbic acid injection (Vitarine) have been reported to be stable for four years at room temperatures not exceeding 25 °C. (60)

Ascorbic acid in solution is rapidly oxidized in air and alkaline media. (4; 2292)

The stability of ascorbic acid from a multiple vitamin product in dextrose 5% in water and sodium chloride 0.9%, in both PVC and ClearFlex containers, was evaluated. HPLC analysis showed that ascorbic acid was stable at 23 °C when protected from light, exhibiting less than a 10% loss in 24 hours. When exposed to light, however, ascorbic acid had losses of approximately 50 to 65% in 24 hours. (1509)

Light Effects — Ascorbic acid gradually darkens on exposure to light. A slight color developed during storage does not impair the therapeutic activity. (4) However, Abbott recommends protecting the intact ampuls from light by keeping them in the carton until ready for use. (1-10/95)

Sorption — Pure ascorbic acid (Merck) did not display significant sorption to a PVC plastic test strip in 24 hours. (12)

Compatibility Information

Solution Compatibility

Ascorbic acid injection

Solution	*Mfr*	*Mfr*	*Conc/L*	*Remarks*	*Ref*	*C/I*
Dextran 6% in dextrose 5%	AB	AB	1 g	Physically compatible	3	C
Dextran 6% in sodium chloride 0.9%	AB	AB	1 g	Physically compatible	3	C
Dextrose–Ringer's injection combinations	AB	AB	1 g	Physically compatible	3	C
Dextrose–Ringer's injection, lactated, combinations	AB	AB	1 g	Physically compatible	3	C
Dextrose–saline combinations	AB	AB	1 g	Physically compatible	3	C
Dextrose 5% in sodium chloride 0.45%		BTK	1.25 g	5% loss by UV spectroscopy in 24 hr at room temperature	1775	C
Dextrose 2½% in water	AB	AB	1 g	Physically compatible	3	C
Dextrose 5% in water	AB	AB	1 g	Physically compatible	3	C
		BTK	1.25 g	5% loss by UV spectroscopy in 24 hr at room temperature	1775	C
Dextrose 10% in water	AB	AB	1 g	Physically compatible	3	C
		BTK	1.25 g	4% loss by UV spectroscopy in 24 hr at room temperature	1775	C
Fat emulsion 10%, intravenous	VT	VI	1 g	Physically compatible for 48 hr at 4 °C and room temperature	32	C
	VT	DB	500 mg	Microscopic globule coalescence in 24 hr at 25 and 8 °C	825	I
	KA	KA[a]	7.2 g	Physically compatible for 24 hr at 26 °C with little loss by HPLC of most vitamins; up to 52% ascorbate loss	2050	C
Fructose 10% in sodium chloride 0.9%	AB	AB	1 g	Physically compatible	3	C
Fructose 10% in water	AB	AB	1 g	Physically compatible	3	C
Invert sugar 5 and 10% in sodium chloride 0.9%	AB	AB	1 g	Physically compatible	3	C
Invert sugar 5 and 10% in water	AB	AB	1 g	Physically compatible	3	C
Ionosol products	AB	AB	1 g	Physically compatible	3	C
Ringer's injection	AB	AB	1 g	Physically compatible	3	C
		BTK	1.25 g	6% loss by UV spectroscopy in 24 hr at room temperature	1775	C
Ringer's injection, lactated	AB	AB	1 g	Physically compatible	3	C
		BTK	1.25 g	6% loss by UV spectroscopy in 24 hr at room temperature	1775	C
Sodium chloride 0.45%	AB	AB	1 g	Physically compatible	3	C
Sodium chloride 0.9%	AB	AB	1 g	Physically compatible	3	C
		BTK	1.25 g	4% loss by UV spectroscopy in 24 hr at room temperature	1775	C
Sodium lactate ⅙ M	AB	AB	1 g	Physically compatible	3	C

[a]*From multivitamins.*

Additive Compatibility

Ascorbic acid injection

Drug	*Mfr*	*Conc/L*	*Mfr*	*Conc/L*	*Test Soln*	*Remarks*	*Ref*	*C/I*
Amikacin sulfate	BR	5 g	CO[a]	5 g	D5LR, D5R, D5S, D5W, D10W, IS10, LR, NS, R, SL	Physically compatible. Potency of both retained for 24 hr at 25 °C	294	C
Aminophylline	SE	500 mg	AB	500 mg		Physically compatible	6	C
						Physically incompatible	9	I
	SE	1 g	UP	500 mg	D5W	Physically incompatible	15	I
Bleomycin sulfate	BR	20 and 30 units	PD	2.5 and 5 g	NS	Loss of all bleomycin activity in 1 week at 4 °C	763	I
Calcium chloride	UP	1 g	UP	500 mg	D5W	Physically compatible	15	C
Calcium gluconate	UP	1 g	UP	500 mg	D5W	Physically compatible	15	C
Chloramphenicol sodium succinate	PD	1 g	AB	1 g		Physically compatible	3; 6	C
Chlorpromazine HCl	SKF	250 mg	UP	500 mg	D5W	Physically compatible	15	C
Colistimethate sodium	WC	500 mg	UP	500 mg	D5W	Physically compatible	15	C
Cyanocobalamin	AB	1000 μg	AB	1 g		Physically compatible	3	C
Diphenhydramine HCl	PD	80 mg	UP	500 mg	D5W	Physically compatible	15	C
Erythromycin lactobionate	AB	1 g	AB	1 g		Physically compatible	3	C
	AB	5 g	UP	500 mg	D5W	Physically incompatible	15	I
Heparin sodium	UP	4000 units	UP	500 mg	D5W	Physically compatible	15	C
Kanamycin sulfate	BR	4 g	UP	500 mg	D5W	Physically compatible	15	C
Methyldopate HCl	MSD	1 g	AB	1 g	D, D–S, S	Physically compatible	23	C
Nafcillin sodium	WY	5 g	UP	500 mg	D5W	Physically incompatible	15	I
Penicillin G potassium		1 million units	AB	1 g		Physically compatible	3	C
	SQ	10 million units	PD	500 mg	D5W	99% penicillin potency retained for at least 8 hr	166	C
Polymyxin B sulfate	BW	200 mg	UP	500 mg	D5W	Physically compatible	15	C
Procaine HCl	WI	1 g	UP	500 mg	D5W	Physically compatible	15	C
Prochlorperazine edisylate	SKF	100 mg	UP	500 mg	D5W	Physically compatible	15	C
Promethazine HCl	WY	250 mg	UP	500 mg	D5W	Physically compatible	15	C
Sodium bicarbonate	AB	80 mEq	UP	500 mg	D5W	Physically incompatible	15	I
Theophylline		2 g		1.9 g	D5W	Yellow discoloration with 8% ascorbic acid loss in 6 hr and 15% in 24 hr. No loss of theophylline	1909	I
Verapamil HCl	KN	80 mg	LI	1 g	D5W, NS	Physically compatible for 24 hr	764	C

[a]*As calcium ascorbate.*

Drugs in Syringe Compatibility

Drug (in syringe)	Mfr	Amt	Ascorbic acid injection Mfr	Ascorbic acid injection Amt	Remarks	Ref	C/I
Cefazolin sodium	LI	1 g/3 ml	LI	1 ml	Precipitate forms within 3 min at 32 °C	766	I
Doxapram HCl	RB	400 mg/ 20 ml		500 mg/ 2 ml	Immediate turbidity changing to precipitation in 24 hr	1177	I
Metoclopramide HCl	RB	10 mg/ 2 ml	AB	250 mg/ 0.5 ml	Physically compatible for 48 hr at room temperature	924	C
	RB	10 mg/ 2 ml	AB	250 mg/ 0.5 ml	Physically compatible for 48 hr at 25 °C	1167	C
	RB	160 mg/ 32 ml	AB	250 mg/ 0.5 ml	Physically compatible for 48 hr at 25 °C	1167	C

Y-Site Injection Compatibility (1:1 Mixture)

Drug	Mfr	Conc	Ascorbic acid injection Mfr	Ascorbic acid injection Conc	Remarks	Ref	C/I
Etomidate	AB	2 mg/ml	AB	500 mg/ml	Yellow discoloration and fine precipitate form in 24 hr	1801	I
Propofol	STU	2 mg/ml	AB	500 mg/ml	Yellow discoloration forms within 7 days at 25 °C. No visible change in 24 hr	1801	?
Thiopental sodium	AB	25 mg/ml	AB	500 mg/ml	Yellow discoloration and fine precipitate form in 24 hr	1801	I
TPN #189[c]			DB	20 mg/ml[b]	Visually compatible for 24 hr at 22 °C	1767	C
Warfarin sodium	DU	0.1[a,b] and 2[d] mg/ml	SCN	0.5 mg/ml[a,b]	Physically compatible with no change in measured turbidity or increase in particle content in 24 hr at 23 °C	2011	C

[a]*Tested in dextrose 5% in water.*
[b]*Tested in sodium chloride 0.9%.*
[c]*Refer to Appendix I for the composition of parenteral nutrition solutions. TPN indicates a 2-in-1 admixture.*
[d]*Tested in sterile water for injection.*

Additional Compatibility Information

Parenteral Nutrition Solutions — Shine and Farwell reported a 35% ascorbic acid loss from a parenteral nutrition solution, composed of amino acids, dextrose, electrolytes, trace elements, and multivitamins, in 39 hours at 25 °C with exposure to light. The loss was reduced to a negligible amount in four days by refrigeration and light protection. (1063)

Allwood reported on the extent and rapidity of ascorbic acid decomposition in parenteral nutrition solutions composed of amino acids, dextrose, electrolytes, multivitamins, and trace elements in 3-L PVC bags stored at 3 to 7 °C. About 30 to 40% was lost in 24 hours. The degradation then slowed as the oxygen supply was reduced to the diffusion through the bag. About a 55 to 65% loss occurred after seven days of storage. The oxidation was catalyzed by metal ions, especially copper. In the absence of copper from the trace elements additive, less than 10% degradation of ascorbic acid occurred in 24 hours. The author estimated that 150 to 200 mg is degraded in two to four hours at ambient temperature in the presence of copper but that only 20 to 30 mg is broken down in 24 hours without copper. To minimize ascorbic acid loss, copper must be excluded. Alternatively, inclusion of excess ascorbic acid was suggested. (1056)

Extensive decomposition of ascorbic acid and folic acid was reported in a parenteral nutrition solution composed of amino acids 3.3%, dextrose 12.5%, electrolytes, trace elements, and M.V.I.-12 (USV) in PVC bags. Half-lives were 1.1, 2.9, and 8.9 hours for ascorbic acid and 2.7, 5.4, and 24 hours for folic acid stored at 24 °C in daylight, 24 °C protected from light, and 4 °C protected from light, respectively. The decomposition was much greater than for solutions not containing catalyzing metal ions. Also, it was greater than for the vitamins singly because of interactions with the other vitamins present. (1059)

Ascorbic acid decomposition in TPN admixtures has been reported to result in the formation of precipitated calcium oxalate. Oxalic acid forms as one of the decomposition products of ascorbic acid. The oxalic acid reacts with calcium in the TPN admixture to form the precipitate. (1060)

Dahl et al. reported the stability of numerous vitamins in parenteral nutrition solutions composed of amino acids (Kabi-Vitrum), dextrose 30%, and fat emulsion 20% (Kabi-Vitrum) in a 2:1:1 ratio with electrolytes, trace elements, and both fat- and water-soluble vitamins. The admixtures were stored in darkness at 2 to 8 °C for 96 hours with no significant loss of retinyl palmitate, alpha-tocopherol, thiamine mononitrate, sodium riboflavin-5′-phosphate, pyridoxine HCl, nicotinamide, folic acid, biotin, sodium pantothenate, and cyanocobalamin.

Sodium ascorbate and its biologically active degradation product, dehydroascorbic acid, totaled 59 and 42% of the nominal starting concentration at 24 and 96 hours, respectively. However, the actual initial concentration was only 66% of the nominal concentration. (1225)

When the admixture was subjected to simulated infusion over 24 hours at 20 °C, either exposed to room light or light protected, or stored for six days in the dark under refrigeration and then subjected to the same simulated infusion, once again the retinyl palmitate, alpha-tocopherol, and sodium riboflavin-5′-phosphate did not undergo significant loss. However, sodium ascorbate and its degradation product, dehydroascorbic acid, had initial combined concentrations of 51 to 65% of the nominal initial concentration, with further declines during infusion. Light protection did not significantly alter the loss of total ascorbic acid. (1225)

The stability of ascorbic acid in parenteral nutrition solutions, with and without fat emulsion, was studied using HPLC analysis. Both with and without fat emulsion, the total vitamin C content (ascorbic acid plus dehydroascorbic acid) remained above 90% for 12 hours when the solutions were exposed to fluorescent light and for 24 hours when they were protected from light. When stored in a cool dark place, the solutions were stable for seven days. (1227)

Smith et al. reported the stability of several vitamins from M.V.I.-12 (Armour) admixed in parenteral nutrition solutions composed of different amino acid products, with or without Intralipid 10%, when stored in glass bottles and PVC bags at 25 and 5 °C for 48 hours. Ascorbic acid was lost from all samples stored at 25 °C, with the greatest losses occurring in solutions stored in plastic bags. No losses occurred in any sample stored at 5 °C. (1431)

Because of these interactions, recommendations to separate the administration of vitamins and trace elements have been made. (1056; 1060; 1061) Other researchers have termed such recommendations premature based on differing reports (895; 896) and the apparent absence of epidemic vitamin deficiency in parenteral nutrition patients. (1062)

The influence of several factors on the rate of ascorbic acid oxidation in parenteral nutrition solutions was evaluated. Ascorbic acid is regarded as the least stable component in TPN admixtures. The type of amino acid used in the TPN was important. Some, such as FreAmine III and Vamin 14, contain antioxidant compounds (e.g., sodium metabisulfite or cysteine). Ascorbic acid stability was better in such solutions compared with those amino acid solutions having no antioxidant present. Furthermore, the pH of the solution may play a small role, with greater degradation as the pH rises from about 5 to about 7. Adding air to a compounded TPN container can also accelerate ascorbic acid decomposition. The most important factor was the type of plastic container used for the TPN. Ethylene vinyl acetate (EVA) containers (Mixieva, Miramed) allow more oxygen permeation, which results in substantial losses of ascorbic acid in relatively short time periods. In multilayer TPN bags (Ultrastab, Miramed) designed to reduce gas permeability, the rate of ascorbic acid degradation was greatly reduced. HPLC analysis of TPNs without antioxidants packaged in EVA bags found that an almost total loss of ascorbic acid activity occurred in one or two days at 5 °C. In contrast, in TPNs containing FreAmine III or Vamin 14 and packaged in the multilayer bags, most of the ascorbic acid content was retained for 28 days at 5 °C. The authors concluded that TPNs made with antioxidant-containing amino acids and packaged in multilayer bags that reduce gas permeability can safely be given extended expiration dates and still retain most of the ascorbic acid activity. (2163)

Acid-Labile Drugs — Literature reports of incompatibilities between various acid-labile drugs such as penicillin G potassium (47; 165) and erythromycin lactobionate (20) with pure ascorbic acid do not pertain to ascorbic acid injection, USP. The official product has a pH of 5.5 to 7. (4; 17) and exists as a mixture of sodium ascorbate and ascorbic acid, with the sodium salt predominating. Pure ascorbic acid is quite acidic. A solution of ascorbic acid 500 mg in 2 ml of diluent had a pH of 2. The incompatibilities between pure ascorbic acid and penicillin G potassium have been attributed to the pH rather than being a characteristic of the ascorbate ion. (166)

Chloramphenicol and Hydrocortisone — Ascorbic acid injection (Upjohn) in dextrose 5% in water has been reported to be conditionally compatible with both chloramphenicol sodium succinate (Parke-Davis) and hydrocortisone sodium succinate (Upjohn). The incompatibility that may occur is concentration dependent. Therefore, if attempting to combine either chloramphenicol sodium succinate or hydrocortisone sodium succinate with ascorbic acid injection, mix the solution thoroughly and observe it closely for any sign of incompatibility. (15)

Other Drugs — Ascorbic acid with cyanocobalamin is stated to be compatible for 24 hours at room temperature protected from light without loss of activity. (52)

Ascorbic acid has been stated to be incompatible with estrogens, conjugated (204), bleomycin sulfate which is inactivated in vitro (4), and chlorothiazide sodium since the final pH may be below 7.4, resulting in precipitation. (7) However, it was not specified whether these reports refer to pure ascorbic acid or ascorbic acid injection.

In vitro testing of ascorbic acid at a concentration of 0.1% with kanamycin sulfate 0.025% in sterile distilled water showed a significant reduction in antibiotic activity in one hour at 25 °C. (314)

Stainless Steel — Ascorbic acid injection (Abbott) develops a grayish-brown color if left exposed to a stainless steel 5-μm filter needle (Monoject) for as little as one hour. (1645)

ASPARAGINASE
AHFS 10:00

Products — Asparaginase is available in vials containing 10,000 I.U. of asparaginase and 80 mg of mannitol in lyophilized form. (2)

For intravenous administration, reconstitute with 5 ml of sterile water for injection or sodium chloride 0.9% to yield a solution containing 2000 I.U./ml. For intramuscular injection, reconstitute with 2 ml of sodium chloride 0.9%. (2)

To prepare a skin test solution for intradermal administration, 0.1 ml of the 2000-I.U./ml reconstituted solution (200 I.U.) is added to 9.9 ml of diluent to yield a 20-I.U./ml solution. (2)

Units — The International Unit (I.U.) of asparaginase is defined as the quantity of enzyme that will release 1 μmol of ammonia per minute from asparagine under the assay conditions. (4) The specific activity of asparaginase (MSD) is at least 225 I.U./mg of protein. (2)

pH — Approximately 7.4. The enzyme is active over a pH range of 6.5 to 8. (4)

Osmolality — Asparaginase 2000 I.U./ml in sterile water for injection has an osmolality of 169 mOsm/kg. (1689)

Trade Name(s) — Elspar.

Administration — Asparaginase is administered intravenously, over not less than 30 minutes, through the sidearm of a running intravenous infusion of sodium chloride 0.9% or dextrose 5% in water. It may also be administered intramuscularly using a volume no greater than 2 ml; larger volumes require two injection sites. (2; 4)

Stability — It is recommended that intact vials of asparaginase be stored under refrigeration. (2) However, Merck Sharp & Dohme has indicated that asparaginase is stable for at least 48 hours at room temperature. (853)

The manufacturer indicates that the reconstituted solution should be stored under refrigeration and can be used within eight hours as long as the solution is clear. If the solution becomes turbid, it should be discarded. (2)

Ordinary shaking during reconstitution does not result in inactivation. (4) However, one source indicates that vigorous shaking may result in some loss of potency. (284) Vigorous shaking also can cause foaming, making it difficult to withdraw the entire vial contents. (4)

Filtration — Reconstituted solutions of asparaginase may occasionally develop small numbers of gelatinous fibers on standing. Filtration through a 5-μm filter will remove the fibers with no loss of potency, but filtration through a 0.2-μm filter may result in some potency loss. (2)

Compatibility Information

Y-Site Injection Compatibility (1:1 Mixture)

Asparaginase

Drug	*Mfr*	*Conc*	*Mfr*	*Conc*	*Remarks*	*Ref*	*C/I*
Methotrexate sodium		30 mg/ml	BEL	120 I.U./ml[a]	Visually compatible for 4 hr at room temperature	1788	C
Sodium bicarbonate		1.4%	BEL	120 I.U./ml[a]	Visually compatible for 4 hr at room temperature	1788	C

[a]*Tested in dextrose 5% in water.*

Additional Compatibility Information

Infusion Solutions — Dextrose 5% in water and sodium chloride 0.9% have been recommended as diluents for asparaginase. The manufacturer indicates that such solutions may be used for up to eight hours as long as they remain clear. (2)

ATENOLOL
AHFS 24:04

Products — Atenolol is available in 10-ml ampuls. Each milliliter of solution contains atenolol 0.5 mg with sodium chloride for isotonicity and citric acid and sodium hydroxide to adjust the pH. (2)

pH — From 5.5 to 6.5. (2)

Tonicity — The injection is isotonic. (2)

Trade Name(s) — Tenormin IV.

Administration — Atenolol is administered undiluted by slow intravenous injection at 1 mg/min or is diluted with dextrose 5% in water or sodium chloride 0.9%. (2; 4)

Stability — Intact ampuls should be stored at controlled room temperature and protected from light. According to the manufacturer, admixtures in dextrose- and sodium chloride-containing infusion solutions are stable for 48 hours. (2)

Compatibility Information

Y-Site Injection Compatibility (1:1 Mixture)

Drug	Mfr	Conc	Atenolol Mfr	Atenolol Conc	Remarks	Ref	C/I
Amphotericin B cholesteryl sulfate complex	SEQ	0.83 mg/ml[a]	ZEN	0.5 mg/ml	Gross precipitate forms	2117	I
Meperidine HCl	AB	10 mg/ml	ICI	0.5 mg/ml	Physically compatible for 4 hr at 25 °C	1397	C
Meropenem	ZEN	1 and 50 mg/ml[b]	ICI	0.5 mg/ml	Visually compatible for 4 hr at room temperature	1994	C
Morphine sulfate	AB	1 mg/ml	ICI	0.5 mg/ml	Physically compatible for 4 hr at 25 °C	1397	C

[a]*Tested in dextrose 5% in water.*
[b]*Tested in sodium chloride 0.9%.*

Additional Compatibility Information

Infusion Solutions — The manufacturer recommends the use of dextrose injections, sodium chloride injections, and combinations of the two for dilution of atenolol. Admixtures in these solutions are stable for 48 hours. (2)

ATRACURIUM BESYLATE
AHFS 12:20

Products — Atracurium besylate is available as a 10-mg/ml aqueous solution in 5-ml single-use vials and 10-ml multiple-dose vials with benzyl alcohol 0.9% as a preservative. The pH is adjusted with benzenesulfonic acid. (1-6/98)

pH — Adjusted to 3.25 to 3.65. (1-6/98)

Osmolality — Atracurium besylate 10 mg/ml has an osmolality of 22 mOsm/kg. (1689)

Trade Name(s) — Tracrium.

Administration — Atracurium besylate is administered by rapid intravenous injection or by intravenous infusion in concentrations of 0.2 and 0.5 mg/ml. It must not be given by intramuscular injection. Do not administer in the same syringe or through the same needle as an alkaline solution. (1-6/98; 4)

Stability — Atracurium besylate injection is a clear, colorless solution; it should be stored under refrigeration and protected from freezing. Nevertheless, the drug undergoes slow decomposition of about 6% per year. (1-6/98; 4) The estimated t_{90} at 5 °C is approximately 18 months. (859) At 25 °C, the rate of decomposition is stated to increase to about 5% per month. (1-6/98; 4) Glaxo Wellcome has indicated that intact vials of atracurium besylate may be used for 14 days when stored at room temperature. (1-6/98; 1181) Other research indicates that atracurium besylate injection in intact containers may be stable even longer at room temperature. Intact containers were found by HPLC analysis to retain 92% of the initial concentration after three months of storage at 20 °C. (777)

pH Effects — Atracurium besylate is unstable in the presence of both acids and bases. (4) Maximum stability in aqueous solution was observed at about pH 2.5. At 37 °C, aqueous solutions with pH values of 7.1 and 7.6 yielded t_{50} values of 75 and 30 minutes, respectively. (859)

Syringes — Atracurium besylate (Burroughs Wellcome) 10 mg/ml was repackaged as 10 ml of solution in 12-ml plastic syringes (Monoject) and stored at 5, 25, and 40 °C. The samples remained visually clear throughout the study. HPLC analysis found no loss in the refrigerated samples and about 4% loss in the room temperature samples after 42 days of storage. The samples stored at elevated temperature lost about 15% in 21 days, indicating that exposure of atracurium to extreme temperature conditions should be avoided. (2141)

The stability of atracurium (salt form unspecified) 10 mg/ml repackaged in polypropylene syringes was evaluated by spectrophotometric and potentiometric methods. Little or no change in concentration was found after four weeks of storage at room temperature when not exposed to direct light. (2164)

Compatibility Information

Solution Compatibility

Atracurium besylate

Solution	*Mfr*	*Mfr*	*Conc/L*	*Remarks*	*Ref*	*C/I*
Dextrose 5% in sodium chloride 0.9%		BW	200 and 500 mg	Physically compatible and chemically stable for 24 hr at 5 and 25 °C	1694	C
Dextrose 5% in water		BW	200 and 500 mg	Physically compatible and chemically stable for 24 hr at 5 and 30 °C	1694	C
		BW	1 and 5 g	Chemically stable for 48 hr	1693	C
	BA[a]	BW	0.5 g	About 50% loss by HPLC in 14 days stored at 5 and 25 °C	2141	I
Ringer's injection, lactated		BW	200 and 500 mg	Increased rate of atracurium degradation limits utility time to 8 hr at 25 °C	1694	I
	TR	BW	500 mg	About 6% loss in 12 hr at 22 °C	1692	I
			1 and 5 g	About 10 to 12% loss in 24 hr at 30 °C	1693	I
Sodium chloride 0.9%		BW	200 and 500 mg	Physically compatible and chemically stable for 24 hr at 5 and 25 °C	1694	C
		BW	1 and 5 g	Chemically stable for 24 hr	1693	C
	BA[a]	BW	0.5 g	About 60% loss by HPLC in 14 days stored at 5 and 25 °C	2141	I
	TR	BW	500 mg	About 1% loss in 12 hr at 22 °C	1692	C

[a]*Tested in glass containers.*

Additive Compatibility

Atracurium besylate

Drug	*Mfr*	*Conc/L*	*Mfr*	*Conc/L*	*Test Soln*	*Remarks*	*Ref*	*C/I*
Aminophylline		1 g	BW	500 mg	D5W	Atracurium chemically unstable due to high pH	1694	I
Bretylium tosylate		4 g	BW	500 mg	D5W	Physically compatible and atracurium chemically stable for 24 hr at 5 and 30 °C	1694	C
Cefazolin sodium		10 g	BW	500 mg	D5W	Atracurium chemically unstable and particles form	1694	I
Cimetidine HCl		5 g	BW	500 mg	D5W	Physically compatible and atracurium chemically stable for 24 hr at 5 and 30 °C	1694	C
Dobutamine HCl		1 g	BW	500 mg	D5W	Physically compatible and atracurium chemically stable for 24 hr at 5 and 30 °C	1694	C
Dopamine HCl		1.6 g	BW	500 mg	D5W	Physically compatible and atracurium chemically stable for 24 hr at 5 and 30 °C	1694	C
Esmolol HCl		10 g	BW	500 mg	D5W	Physically compatible and atracurium chemically stable for 24 hr at 5 and 30 °C	1694	C

Additive Compatibility (Cont.)

Atracurium besylate

Drug	*Mfr*	*Conc/L*	*Mfr*	*Conc/L*	*Test Soln*	*Remarks*	*Ref*	*C/I*
Gentamicin sulfate		2 g	BW	500 mg	D5W	Physically compatible and atracurium chemically stable for 24 hr at 5 and 30 °C	1694	C
Heparin sodium		40,000 units	BW	500 mg	D5W	Particles form at 5 and 30 °C	1694	I
Isoproterenol HCl		4 mg	BW	500 mg	D5W	Physically compatible and atracurium chemically stable for 24 hr at 5 and 30 °C	1694	C
Lidocaine HCl		2 g	BW	500 mg	D5W	Physically compatible and atracurium chemically stable for 24 hr at 5 and 30 °C	1694	C
Morphine sulfate		1 g	BW	500 mg	D5W	Physically compatible and atracurium chemically stable for 24 hr at 5 and 30 °C	1694	C
Potassium chloride		80 mEq	BW	500 mg	D5W	Physically compatible and atracurium chemically stable for 24 hr at 5 and 30 °C	1694	C
Procainamide HCl		4 g	BW	500 mg	D5W	Physically compatible and atracurium chemically stable for 24 hr at 5 and 30 °C	1694	C
Quinidine gluconate		8.3 g	BW	500 mg	D5W	Particles form and atracurium chemically unstable at 5 and 30 °C	1694	I
Ranitidine HCl		500 mg	BW	500 mg	D5W	Atracurium chemically unstable due to high pH	1694	I
Sodium nitroprusside		2 g	BW	500 mg	D5W	Physically incompatible. Haze, particles, and yellow color form	1694	I
Vancomycin HCl		5 g	BW	500 mg	D5W	Physically compatible and atracurium chemically stable for 24 hr at 5 and 30 °C	1694	C

Drugs in Syringe Compatibility

Atracurium besylate

Drug (in syringe)	*Mfr*	*Amt*	*Mfr*	*Amt*	*Remarks*	*Ref*	*C/I*
Alfentanil HCl		0.5 mg/ml	BW	10 mg/ml	Physically compatible and atracurium chemically stable for 24 hr at 5 and 30 °C	1694	C
Fentanyl citrate		50 µg/ml	BW	10 mg/ml	Physically compatible and atracurium chemically stable for 24 hr at 5 and 30 °C	1694	C
Midazolam HCl		5 mg/ml	BW	10 mg/ml	Physically compatible and atracurium chemically stable for 24 hr at 5 and 30 °C	1694	C
Sufentanil citrate		50 µg/ml	BW	10 mg/ml	Physically compatible and atracurium chemically stable for 24 hr at 5 and 30 °C	1694	C

Y-Site Injection Compatibility (1:1 Mixture)

Drug	Mfr	Conc	Mfr	Conc	Remarks	Ref	C/I
			Atracurium besylate				
Cefazolin sodium	LY	10 mg/ml[a]	BW	0.5 mg/ml[a]	Physically compatible for 24 hr at 28 °C	1337	C
Cefuroxime sodium	GL	7.5 mg/ml[a]	BW	0.5 mg/ml[a]	Physically compatible for 24 hr at 28 °C	1337	C
Cimetidine HCl	SKF	6 mg/ml[a]	BW	0.5 mg/ml[a]	Physically compatible for 24 hr at 28 °C	1337	C
Clarithromycin	AB	4 mg/ml[a]	GW	1 mg/ml[a]	Visually compatible for 72 hr at both 30 and 17 °C	2174	C
Diazepam	ES	5 mg/ml	BW	0.5 mg/ml[a]	Cloudy solution forms immediately	1337	I
Dobutamine HCl	LI	1 mg/ml[a]	BW	0.5 mg/ml[a]	Physically compatible for 24 hr at 28 °C	1337	C
Dopamine HCl	SO	1.6 mg/ml[a]	BW	0.5 mg/ml[a]	Physically compatible for 24 hr at 28 °C	1337	C
Epinephrine HCl	AB	4 μg/ml[a]	BW	0.5 mg/ml[a]	Physically compatible for 24 hr at 28 °C	1337	C
Esmolol HCl	DCC	10 mg/ml[a]	BW	0.5 mg/ml[a]	Physically compatible for 24 hr at 28 °C	1337	C
Etomidate	AB	2 mg/ml	BW	10 mg/ml	Visually compatible for up to 7 days at 25 °C	1801	C
Fentanyl citrate	ES	10 μg/ml[a]	BW	0.5 mg/ml[a]	Physically compatible for 24 hr at 28 °C	1337	C
Gentamicin sulfate	ES	2 mg/ml[a]	BW	0.5 mg/ml[a]	Physically compatible for 24 hr at 28 °C	1337	C
Heparin sodium	SO	40 units/ml[a]	BW	0.5 mg/ml[a]	Physically compatible for 24 hr at 28 °C	1337	C
Hetastarch in lactated electrolyte injection (Hextend)	AB	6%	GW	0.5 mg/ml[a]	Physically compatible with no change in measured turbidity or increase in particle content in 4 hr at 23 °C	2339	C
Hydrocortisone sodium succinate	AB	1 mg/ml[a]	BW	0.5 mg/ml[a]	Physically compatible for 24 hr at 28 °C	1337	C
Isoproterenol HCl	ES	4 μg/ml[a]	BW	0.5 mg/ml[a]	Physically compatible for 24 hr at 28 °C	1337	C
Lorazepam	WY	0.5 mg/ml[a]	BW	0.5 mg/ml[a]	Physically compatible for 24 hr at 28 °C	1337	C
Midazolam HCl	RC	0.05 mg/ml[a]	BW	0.5 mg/ml[a]	Physically compatible for 24 hr at 28 °C	1337	C
	RC	0.1 mg/ml[a]	GW	1 and 5 mg/ml[a]	Visually compatible with no loss of either drug by HPLC in 3 hr at 25 °C under fluorescent light	2112	C
	RC	0.5 mg/ml[a]	GW	5 mg/ml[a]	Visually compatible with no loss of either drug by HPLC in 3 hr at 25 °C under fluorescent light	2112	C
	RC	0.5 mg/ml[a]	GW	1 mg/ml[a]	Visually compatible with no loss of midazolam and 4% loss of atracurium by HPLC in 3 hr at 25 °C under fluorescent light	2112	C
Milrinone lactate	SW	0.4 mg/ml[a]	BW	1 mg/ml[a]	Visually compatible with little or no loss of either drug by HPLC in 4 hr at 23 °C	2214	C
Morphine sulfate	WY	1 mg/ml[a]	BW	0.5 mg/ml[a]	Physically compatible for 24 hr at 28 °C	1337	C
Nitroglycerin	SO	0.4 mg/ml[a]	BW	0.5 mg/ml[a]	Physically compatible for 24 hr at 28 °C	1337	C
Propofol	STU	2 mg/ml	BW	10 mg/ml	Oil droplets form within 24 hr followed by phase separation at 25 °C	1801	I
	ZEN	10 mg/ml	BW	10 mg/ml	Emulsion broke and oiled out	2066	I
	GNS, ASZ	10 mg/ml		10 mg/ml	Emulsion disruption upon mixing	2336	I
	GNS, ASZ	10 mg/ml		5 mg/ml[a]	Emulsion disruption upon mixing	2336	I
	GNS	10 mg/ml		0.5 mg/ml[a]	Emulsion disruption upon mixing	2336	I
	ASZ	10 mg/ml		0.5 mg/ml[a]	Physically compatible for at least 1 hr at room temperature	2336	C

Y-Site Injection Compatibility (1:1 Mixture) (Cont.)

			Atracurium besylate				
Drug	*Mfr*	*Conc*	*Mfr*	*Conc*	*Remarks*	*Ref*	*C/I*
Ranitidine HCl	GL	0.5 mg/ml[a]	BW	0.5 mg/ml[a]	Physically compatible for 24 hr at 28 °C	1337	C
Sodium nitroprusside	ES	0.2 mg/ml[a]	BW	0.5 mg/ml[a]	Physically compatible for 24 hr at 28 °C	1337	C
Thiopental sodium	AB	25 mg/ml	BW	10 mg/ml	White cloudiness forms immediately but clears within 24 hr at 25 °C	1801	I
TPN #189[b]			WEL	10 mg/ml	Visually compatible for 24 hr at 22 °C	1767	C
Trimethoprim–sulfamethoxazole	ES	0.64 + 3.2 mg/ml[a]	BW	0.5 mg/ml[a]	Physically compatible for 24 hr at 28 °C	1337	C
Vancomycin HCl	ES	5 mg/ml[a]	BW	0.5 mg/ml[a]	Physically compatible for 24 hr at 28 °C	1337	C

[a]*Tested in dextrose 5% in water.*
[b]*Refer to Appendix I for the composition of parenteral nutrition solutions. TPN indicates a 2-in-1 admixture.*

Additional Compatibility Information

Infusion Solutions — Atracurium besylate 0.2 and 0.5 mg/ml is physically and chemically compatible for 24 hours at 5 and 25 °C in dextrose 5% in water, sodium chloride 0.9%, and dextrose 5% in sodium chloride 0.9%. In Ringer's injection, lactated, at 0.5 mg/ml, it is stable for eight hours at 25 °C, although use of this solution is not generally recommended because of an increased rate of drug degradation. (4; 1692; 1693)

Alkaline Drugs — Atracurium besylate, which has an acid pH, should not be mixed with alkaline solutions such as barbiturates. The atracurium besylate may be inactivated and precipitation of a free acid of the admixed drug may occur, depending on the resultant pH. (1-6/98; 4)

Propofol — The incompatibility of atracurium besylate with propofol is both concentration dependent and specific to the formulation of propofol. A low atracurium besylate concentration of 0.5 mg/ml with the sulfite-containing formulation of propofol (Baxter) results in emulsion disruption whereas the edetate-containing formulation of propofol (AstraZeneca) remains compatible. However, a high atracurium besylate concentration of 5 or 10 mg/ml disrupts the emulsions of both formulations of propofol. (2336) See Y-site Injection Compatibility table above.

ATROPINE SULFATE
AHFS 12:08.08

Products — Atropine sulfate injection is available in a concentration of 0.4 mg/ml in 1-ml and 20-ml multiple-dose vials. It is also available in concentrations of 0.5 and 1 mg/ml in 1-ml multiple-dose vials. Each formulation also contains in each milliliter methylparaben 0.1% and sulfuric acid to adjust the pH (if needed) in water for injection. (1-9/98; 29)

Atropine sulfate is also available in a concentration of 0.05 mg/ml in 5-ml prefilled syringes and 0.1 mg/ml in 5- and 10-ml prefilled syringes. (29)

pH — From 3 to 6.5. (4)

Administration — Atropine sulfate injection may be administered by subcutaneous, intramuscular, or direct (usually rapid) intravenous injection. (4)

Stability — Atropine sulfate injection should be stored below 40 °C, preferably at controlled room temperature. Freezing should be avoided. (4) Minimum hydrolysis occurs at pH 3.5. (1072)

Syringes — Atropine sulfate (Wyeth) 1 mg/ml was found to retain potency for three months at room temperature when 0.5 or 1 ml of solution was repackaged in Tubex. (13)

The stability of atropine (salt form unspecified) 1 mg/ml repackaged in polypropylene syringes was evaluated by spectrophotometric and potentiometric methods. Little or no change in concentration was found after four weeks of storage at room temperature not exposed to direct light. (2164)

Compatibility Information

Additive Compatibility

Atropine sulfate

Drug	Mfr	Conc/L	Mfr	Conc/L	Test Soln	Remarks	Ref	C/I
Dobutamine HCl	LI	167 mg	AB	16.7 mg	NS	Physically compatible for 24 hr	552	C
	LI	1 g	ES	50 mg	D5W, NS	Physically compatible for 24 hr at 21 °C	812	C
Floxacillin sodium	BE	20 g	ANT	60 mg	W	Haze forms in 24 hr and precipitate forms in 48 hr at 30 °C. No change at 15 °C	1479	I
Furosemide	HO	1 g	ANT	60 mg	W	Physically compatible for 72 hr at 15 and 30 °C	1479	C
Meropenem	ZEN	1 and 20 g	ES	40 mg	NS	Visually compatible for 4 hr at room temperature	1994	C
Netilmicin sulfate	SC	3 g	BW	40 mg	D5S	Physically compatible and netilmicin chemically stable for 7 days at 4 and 25 °C. Atropine not tested	558	C
Sodium bicarbonate	AB	2.4 mEq[a]		0.4 mg	D5W	Physically compatible for 24 hr	772	C
Verapamil HCl	KN	80 mg	IX	0.8 mg	D5W, NS	Physically compatible for 24 hr	764	C

[a] *One vial of Neut added to a liter of admixture.*

Drugs in Syringe Compatibility

Atropine sulfate

Drug (in syringe)	Mfr	Amt	Mfr	Amt	Remarks	Ref	C/I
Butorphanol tartrate	BR	4 mg/ 2 ml	ST	0.4 mg/ 1 ml	Physically compatible both macroscopically and microscopically for 30 min at room temperature	566	C
Chlorpromazine HCl	SKF	50 mg/ 2 ml		0.6 mg/ 1.5 ml	Physically compatible for at least 15 min	14	C
	PO	50 mg/ 2 ml	ST	0.4 mg/ 1 ml	Physically compatible for at least 15 min	326	C
Cimetidine HCl	SKF	300 mg/ 2 ml	LI	0.6 mg/ 1.5 ml	Physically compatible and chemically stable for 90 min at room temperature	542	C
	SKF	300 mg/ 2 ml	LI	0.4 mg/ 1 ml	Physically compatible and chemically stable for 90 min at room temperature	542	C
Cimetidine HCl with pentobarbital sodium	SKF AB	300 mg/ 2 ml 100 mg/ 2 ml	LI	0.6 mg/ 1.5 ml	Immediate precipitation	542	I
Dimenhydrinate	HR	50 mg/ 1 ml	ST	0.4 mg/ 1 ml	Physically compatible for at least 15 min	326	C
Diphenhydramine HCl	PD	50 mg/ 1 ml	ST	0.4 mg/ 1 ml	Physically compatible for at least 15 min	326	C
Droperidol	MN	2.5 mg/ 1 ml	ST	0.4 mg/ 1 ml	Physically compatible for at least 15 min	326	C
Fentanyl citrate	MN	100 μg/ 1 ml		0.6 mg/ 1.5 ml	Physically compatible for at least 15 min	14	C
	MN	0.05 mg/ 1 ml	ST	0.4 mg/ 1 ml	Physically compatible for at least 15 min	326	C

Drugs in Syringe Compatibility (Cont.)

Atropine sulfate

Drug (in syringe)	*Mfr*	*Amt*	*Mfr*	*Amt*	*Remarks*	*Ref*	*C/I*
Glycopyrrolate	RB	0.2 mg/ 1 ml	ES	0.4 mg/ 1 ml	Physically compatible and pH in stability range for glycopyrrolate for 48 hr at 25 °C	331	C
	RB	0.2 mg/ 1 ml	ES	0.8 mg/ 2 ml	Physically compatible and pH in stability range for glycopyrrolate for 48 hr at 25 °C	331	C
	RB	0.4 mg/ 2 ml	ES	0.4 mg/ 1 ml	Physically compatible and pH in stability range for glycopyrrolate for 48 hr at 25 °C	331	C
Heparin sodium		2500 units/ 1 ml		0.5 mg/ 1 ml	Physically compatible for at least 5 min	1053	C
Hydromorphone HCl	KN	4 mg/ 2 ml	ES	0.4 mg/ 0.5 ml	Physically compatible for 30 min	517	C
Hydroxyzine HCl	PF	100 mg/ 4 ml		0.6 mg/ 1.5 ml	Physically compatible for at least 15 min	14	C
	NF	50 mg/ 1 ml	USP	0.4 mg/ 0.4 ml	Hydroxyzine potency retained for at least 10 days at 3 and 25 °C	49	C
	PF	50 mg/ 1 ml	ST	0.4 mg/ 1 ml	Physically compatible for at least 15 min	326	C
	PF	100 mg/ 2 ml		0.4 mg/ 1 ml	Physically compatible	771	C
	PF	50 mg/ 1 ml		0.4 mg/ 1 ml	Physically compatible	771	C
Hydroxyzine HCl with meperidine HCl[a]	PF WI	50 mg 50 mg	ES	0.4 mg/ 2.5 ml	No alteration of UV spectra in 10 days at 3 and 25 °C	301	C
Meperidine HCl	WY	100 mg/ 1 ml		0.6 mg/ 1.5 ml	Physically compatible for at least 15 min	14	C
	WI	50 mg/ 1 ml	ST	0.4 mg/ 1 ml	Physically compatible for at least 15 min	326	C
Meperidine HCl with hydroxyzine HCl[a]	WI PF	50 mg 50 mg	ES	0.4 mg/ 2.5 ml	No alteration of UV spectra in 10 days at 3 and 25 °C	301	C
Meperidine HCl with promethazine HCl	WY WY	100 mg/ 1 ml 50 mg/ 2 ml		0.6 mg/ 1.5 ml	Physically compatible	14	C
Meperidine HCl with promethazine HCl	WI WY	50 mg/ 1 ml 25 mg/ 1 ml	LI	0.4 mg/ 1 ml	No loss of any drug in 24 hr at 25 °C. Slight haze at 24 hr but not at 6 hr	991	C
Metoclopramide HCl	NO	10 mg/ 2 ml	GL	0.4 mg/ 1 ml	Physically compatible both macroscopically and microscopically for 15 min at room temperature	565	C
Midazolam HCl	RC	5 mg/ 1 ml	IX	0.4 mg/ 1 ml	Physically compatible for 4 hr at 25 °C	1145	C
Milrinone lactate	WI	5.25 mg/ 5.25 ml	IX	2 mg/ 2 ml	Physically compatible with no loss of either drug in 20 min at 23 °C	1410	C
Morphine HCl	STP, FED	5, 10, 20, 30 mg/ 1 ml	FED	1 mg/ 1 ml	Visually compatible for up to 7 days at 23 °C	2257	C

Drugs in Syringe Compatibility (Cont.)

Atropine sulfate

Drug (in syringe)	*Mfr*	*Amt*	*Mfr*	*Amt*	*Remarks*	*Ref*	*C/I*
Morphine sulfate	WY	15 mg/ 1 ml		0.6 mg/ 1.5 ml	Physically compatible for at least 15 min	14	C
	ST	15 mg/ 1 ml	ST	0.4 mg/ 1 ml	Physically compatible for at least 15 min	326	C
Nalbuphine HCl	EN	10 mg/ 1 ml	WY	0.2 mg	Physically compatible for 36 hr at 27 °C	762	C
	EN	5 mg/ 0.5 ml	WY	0.2 mg	Physically compatible for 36 hr at 27 °C	762	C
	EN	10 mg/ 1 ml	WY	0.5 mg	Physically compatible for 36 hr at 27 °C	762	C
	EN	5 mg/ 0.5 ml	WY	0.5 mg	Physically compatible for 36 hr at 27 °C	762	C
	DU	10 mg/ 1 ml		0.4 mg	Physically compatible for 48 hr	128	C
	DU	20 mg/ 1 ml		0.4 mg	Physically compatible for 48 hr	128	C
	DU	10 mg/ 1 ml		1 mg	Physically compatible for 48 hr	128	C
	DU	20 mg/ 1 ml		1 mg	Physically compatible for 48 hr	128	C
Ondansetron HCl	GW	1.33 mg/ ml[b]	GNS	0.133 mg/ ml[b]	Physically compatible with no measured increase in particulates and less than 6% ondansetron loss and less than 7% atropine loss by HPLC in 24 hr at 4 or 23 °C	2199	C
Papaveretum	RC[c]	20 mg/ 1 ml	ST	0.4 mg/ 1 ml	Visually compatible for at least 15 min	326	C
Pentazocine lactate	WI	30 mg/ 1 ml		0.6 mg/ 1.5 ml	Physically compatible for at least 15 min	14	C
	WI	30 mg/ 1 ml	ST	0.4 mg/ 1 ml	Physically compatible for at least 15 min	326	C
Pentobarbital sodium	WY	100 mg/ 2 ml		0.6 mg/ 1.5 ml	Physically compatible for at least 15 min	14	C
	AB	50 mg/ 1 ml	ST	0.4 mg/ 1 ml	Physically compatible for at least 15 min	326	C
	AB	100 mg/ 2 ml	LI	0.6 mg/ 1.5 ml	Precipitate forms within 24 hr at room temperature	542	I
Pentobarbital sodium with cimetidine HCl	AB SKF	100 mg/ 2 ml 300 mg/ 2 ml	LI	0.6 mg/ 1.5 ml	Immediate precipitation	542	I
Perphenazine	SC	5 mg/ 1 ml	ST	0.4 mg/ 1 ml	Physically compatible both macroscopically and microscopically for 30 min at room temperature	566	C
Prochlorperazine edisylate	SKF			0.6 mg/ 1.5 ml	Physically compatible for at least 15 min	14	C
	PO	5 mg/ 1 ml	ST	0.4 mg/ 1 ml	Physically compatible for at least 15 min	326	C
Promazine HCl	WY	50 mg/ 1 ml	ST	0.4 mg/ 1 ml	Physically compatible for at least 15 min	326	C

Drugs in Syringe Compatibility (Cont.)

Drug (in syringe)	Mfr	Amt	Mfr	Amt (Atropine sulfate)	Remarks	Ref	C/I
Promethazine HCl	WY	50 mg/ 2 ml		0.6 mg/ 1.5 ml	Physically compatible for at least 15 min	14	C
	PO	50 mg/ 2 ml	ST	0.4 mg/ 1 ml	Physically compatible for at least 15 min	326	C
Promethazine HCl with	WY	50 mg/ 2 ml		0.6 mg/ 1.5 ml	Physically compatible	14	C
meperidine HCl	WY	100 mg/ 1 ml					
Promethazine HCl with	WY	25 mg/ 1 ml	LI	0.4 mg/ 1 ml	No loss of any drug in 24 hr at 25 °C. Slight haze at 24 hr but not at 6 hr	991	C
meperidine HCl	WI	50 mg/ 1 ml					
Ranitidine HCl	GL	50 mg/ 2 ml	GL	0.4 mg/ 1 ml	Physically compatible for 1 hr at 25 °C by macroscopic and microscopic inspection	978	C
Scopolamine HBr	ST	0.4 mg/ 1 ml	ST	0.4 mg/ 1 ml	Physically compatible for at least 15 min	326	C
Sufentanil citrate	JN	50 μg/ml	LY	0.4 mg/ ml	Physically compatible with no subvisual haze or particle formation in 24 hr at 23 °C	1711	C

[a]Tested in both glass and plastic syringes.
[b]Tested in sodium chloride 0.9%.
[c]The former formulation was tested.

Y-Site Injection Compatibility (1:1 Mixture)

Drug	Mfr	Conc	Mfr	Conc (Atropine sulfate)	Remarks	Ref	C/I
Etomidate	AB	2 mg/ml	GNS	0.4 mg/ml	Visually compatible for up to 7 days at 25 °C	1801	C
Famotidine	MSD	0.2 mg/ml[a]	AST	0.1 mg/ml[a]	Physically compatible for at least 4 hr at 25 °C under fluorescent light	1188	C
Fentanyl citrate	JN	0.025 mg/ml[a]	LY	0.4 mg/ml	Physically compatible with no change in measured haze or increase in particle content in 48 hr at 22 °C	1706	C
Heparin sodium	UP	1000 units/L[c]	BW	0.5 mg/ml	Physically compatible for at least 4 hr at room temperature by visual and microscopic examination	534	C
Hydrocortisone sodium succinate	UP	10 mg/L[c]	BW	0.5 mg/ml	Physically compatible for at least 4 hr at room temperature by visual and microscopic examination	534	C
Hydromorphone HCl	AST	0.5 mg/ml[a]	LY	0.4 mg/ml	Physically compatible with no change in measured haze or increase in particle content in 48 hr at 22 °C	1706	C
Inamrinone lactate	WB	3 mg/ml[b]	AB	0.1 mg/ml	Physically compatible for at least 4 hr at 25 °C under fluorescent light	992	C
Meropenem	ZEN	1 and 50 mg/ ml[b]	ES	0.4 mg/ml	Visually compatible for 4 hr at room temperature	1994	C
Methadone HCl	LI	1 mg/ml[a]	LY	0.4 mg/ml	Physically compatible with no change in measured haze or increase in particle content in 48 hr at 22 °C	1706	C

Y-Site Injection Compatibility (1:1 Mixture) (Cont.)

Drug	Mfr	Conc	Mfr	Conc	Remarks	Ref	C/I
			Atropine sulfate				
Morphine sulfate	AST	1 mg/ml[a]	LY	0.4 mg/ml	Physically compatible with no change in measured haze or increase in particle content in 48 hr at 22 °C	1706	C
Nafcillin sodium	WY	33 mg/ml[b]		0.4 mg/ml	No precipitation	547	C
Potassium chloride	AB	40 mEq/L[c]	BW	0.5 mg/ml	Physically compatible for at least 4 hr at room temperature by visual and microscopic examination	534	C
Propofol	STU	2 mg/ml	GNS	0.4 mg/ml	Oil droplets form within 7 days at 25 °C. No visible change in 24 hr	1801	?
	ZEN	10 mg/ml	AST	0.1 mg/ml[a]	Physically compatible for 1 hr at 23 °C with no increase in particle content	2066	C
Sufentanil citrate	JN	12.5 μg/ml[a]	LY	0.4 mg/ml[a]	Physically compatible with no subvisual haze or particle formation in 24 hr at 23 °C	1711	C
Thiopental sodium	AB	25 mg/ml	GNS	0.4 mg/ml	White particles form immediately and yellow discoloration forms within 24 hr at 25 °C	1801	I
Vitamin B complex with C	RC	2 ml/L[c]	BW	0.5 mg/ml	Physically compatible for at least 4 hr at room temperature by visual and microscopic examination	534	C

[a]*Tested in dextrose 5% in water.*
[b]*Tested in sodium chloride 0.9%.*
[c]*Tested in dextrose 5% in water, dextrose 5% in Ringer's injection, dextrose 5% in Ringer's injection, lactated, Ringer's injection, lactated, and sodium chloride 0.9%.*
[d]*Tested in sterile water for injection.*

Additional Compatibility Information

Other Drugs — Atropine sulfate has been reported to be compatible with butorphanol tartrate (481) and buprenorphine HCl. (4) Atropine sulfate is stated to be incompatible with sodium bicarbonate, norepinephrine bitartrate, and metaraminol bitartrate. (4)

A haze or precipitate forms in 15 minutes when atropine sulfate is mixed with methohexital sodium. (4)

AZATHIOPRINE SODIUM
AHFS 92:00

Products — Azathioprine sodium is available in 20-ml vials containing the equivalent of 100 mg of azathioprine with sodium hydroxide to adjust the pH. Reconstitute by adding 10 ml of sterile water for injection and swirling until a clear solution results. (2)

pH — Approximately 9.6. (2)

Trade Name(s) — Imuran.

Administration — Azathioprine sodium is administered intravenously. Infusions are usually administered over 30 to 60 minutes but have been given over five minutes to eight hours. (2; 4)

Stability — Azathioprine sodium, a pale yellow powder, should be stored at controlled room temperature and protected from light. It is stated to be stable in neutral or acid solutions but is hydrolyzed to mercaptopurine in alkaline solutions (2; 4), especially on warming. (2) Maximum stability occurs at pH 5.5 to 6.5. (1633) Hydrolysis to mercaptopurine also occurs in the presence of sulfhydryl compounds such as cysteine. (2; 4)

Use of azathioprine sodium within 24 hours after reconstitution is recommended because the product contains no preservatives. (2; 4) Chemically, azathioprine sodium 10 mg/ml in aqueous solution is stable for about two weeks at room temperature. (4) After this time, hydrolysis of azathioprine to mercaptopurine increases.

Storage of the reconstituted solution in the original vial and in plastic syringes (Jelco) at 20 to 25 °C under fluorescent light resulted in no decomposition or precipitation in 16 days. At 4 °C in the dark, a visible precipitate formed after four days. (605)

Azathioprine sodium (Burroughs Wellcome) 100 mg/50 ml diluted in dextrose 5% in water, sodium chloride 0.9%, or sodium chloride 0.45% in PVC bags (Travenol) was stored at 20 to 25 °C under fluorescent light and at 4 °C in the dark. No decomposition occurred in the solutions over 16 days of storage. However, a precipitate formed in the dextrose 5% in water admixtures by the 16th day. No precipitate was observed after eight days of storage. (605)

Compatibility Information

Solution Compatibility

Azathioprine sodium

Solution	*Mfr*	*Mfr*	*Conc/L*	*Remarks*	*Ref*	*C/I*
Dextrose 5% in water	TR[a]	BW	2 g	Physically compatible and chemically stable for 8 days at 23 and 4 °C. Precipitate forms in 16 days	605	C
Sodium chloride 0.45%	TR[a]	BW	2 g	Physically compatible and chemically stable for 16 days at 23 and 4 °C	605	C
Sodium chloride 0.9%	TR[a]	BW	2 g	Physically compatible and chemically stable for 16 days at 23 and 4 °C	605	C

[a]*Tested in PVC containers.*

Additional Compatibility Information

Preservatives — Azathioprine sodium is stated to be incompatible with methyl and propyl parabens and phenol. (108)

Other Information

Inactivation — In the event of spills or leaks, the manufacturer recommends the use of sodium hypochlorite 5% (household bleach) and sodium hydroxide (concentration unspecified) to inactivate azathioprine. (1200)

AZTREONAM
AHFS 8:12.07

Products — Aztreonam is available in vials and 100-ml infusion bottles containing 500 mg, 1 g, or 2 g of drug. Approximately 780 mg of arginine per gram of drug is also present. Aztreonam is also available in 1- and 2-g sizes as frozen premixed solutions in dextrose 3.4 and 1.4%, respectively, for intravenous infusion. (2; 4)

For intramuscular injection, reconstitute each gram of drug in vials with at least 3 ml of one of the following diluents (2):

Sterile water for injection
Bacteriostatic water for injection
  (benzyl alcohol or parabens)
Sodium chloride 0.9%
Bacteriostatic sodium chloride 0.9%
  (benzyl alcohol)

For intravenous bolus injection, use the vials. Reconstitute with 6 to 10 ml of sterile water for injection. (2)

For intravenous infusion, the 100-ml bottle may be used. Reconstitute each gram of drug with at least 50 ml of any compatible infusion solution to yield a solution containing not more than 2% (w/v) of aztreonam. Alternatively, reconstitute a vial of aztreonam with at least 3 ml of sterile water for injection per gram and further dilute with a compatible infusion solution. (2)

On adding the diluent to the vial or bottle, shake the contents immediately and vigorously. (2)

The frozen premixed solutions may also be used for intravenous infusion after thawing and warming to room temperature. (2; 4)

pH — Aqueous solutions of aztreonam have pH values of 4.5 to 7.5. (2)

Sodium Content — Aztreonam is sodium free. (2)

Trade Name(s) — Azactam.

Administration — Aztreonam may be administered by intravenous injection or infusion or by deep intramuscular injection into a large muscle mass. By intravenous injection, the dose should be given slowly, over three to five minutes, directly into a vein or the tubing of a compatible infusion solution. Intermittent infusion at concentrations not exceeding 1 g/50 ml should be completed within 20 to 60 minutes. (2; 4)

Stability — The intact vials should be stored at controlled room temperature and protected from temperatures above 40 °C. Exposure to strong light may cause yellowing of the powder. (2; 4)

Aztreonam solutions range from colorless to light straw to yellow. They may develop a slight pink tint on standing without potency being affected. (2)

Aztreonam solutions at concentrations of 2% (w/v) or less should be used within 48 hours if stored at room temperature or seven days if refrigerated. Solutions with concentrations exceeding 2% (w/v) should be used immediately after preparation unless sterile water for injection or sodium chloride 0.9% is used. In these two excepted solutions, aztreonam at concentrations exceeding 2% (w/v) may be used up to 48 hours at room temperature or seven days under refrigeration. (2)

pH Effects—In aqueous solutions, aztreonam undergoes hydrolysis of the β-lactam ring. Specific base catalysis occurs at pH greater than 6. At pH 2 to 5, isomerization of the side chain predominates. The lowest rates of decomposition occur at pH 5 to 7, with maximum stability occurring at pH 6. (1072)

Freezing Solutions—Aztreonam in any compatible infusion solution is stable for up to three months when frozen at −20 °C. Frozen solutions should be thawed at room temperature or by overnight refrigeration and should not be refrozen. Thawed solutions should be used within 24 hours at room temperature or 72 hours under refrigeration. (4)

The commercially available frozen injection should be thawed at room temperature or under refrigeration and should not be refrozen. The manufacturer indicates that thawed solutions are stable for 48 hours at room temperature or 14 days under refrigeration. (4)

Aztreonam (Squibb) 20 mg/ml in sodium chloride 0.9% exhibited no loss by HPLC after 120 days when stored at −20 °C. Storage of the solution at 4 °C resulted in a 10% loss in a time period greater than 120 days and has the advantage of not requiring thawing. (1600)

Syringes—Aztreonam (Squibb) 2 g in sodium chloride 0.9% (volume unspecified), stored in polypropylene syringes (3M) at 25 °C under fluorescent light, exhibited a 5% loss in 48 hours. (1164)

Elastomeric Reservoir Pumps—Aztreonam solutions in elastomeric reservoir pumps have been stated by the pump manufacturers to be stable for the following time periods frozen, refrigerated (REF), or at room temperature (RT) (31):

Pump Reservoir(s)	Conc.	Frozen	REF	RT
Homepump; Homepump Eclipse	13 to 26.7 mg/ml[b]		7 days	7 days
	20 to 30 mg/ml[b]		14 days	
Intermate	5 to 20 mg/ml[a,b]	30 days	14 days	24 hr
Medflo	10 mg/ml[a,b]	12 weeks	7 days	48 hr

[a]*In dextrose 5% in water.*
[b]*In sodium chloride 0.9%.*

Central Venous Catheter—Aztreonam (Squibb) 10 mg/ml in dextrose 5% in water was found to be compatible with the ARROWg+ard Blue Plus (Arrow International) chlorhexidine-bearing triple-lumen central catheter. HPLC analysis was used to evaluate completeness of drug delivery through the catheter and the amount of chlorhexidine removed from the internal lumens. Essentially complete delivery of the drug was found with little or no drug loss occurring. Furthermore, chlorhexidine delivered from the catheter remained at trace amounts with no substantial increase due to the delivery of the drug through the catheter. (2335)

Compatibility Information

Solution Compatibility

Aztreonam

Solution	*Mfr*	*Mfr*	*Conc/L*	*Remarks*	*Ref*	*C/I*
Dextrose 5% in water	TR[a]	SQ	10 g	Physically compatible with 6% aztreonam loss in 48 hr at 25 °C and 3% in 7 days at 4 °C	1001	C
	TR[a]	SQ	20 g	Physically compatible with 2% aztreonam loss in 48 hr at 25 °C and 3% in 7 days at 4 °C	1001	C
	MG[b]	SQ	20 g	Physically compatible with no aztreonam loss in 48 hr at 25 °C under fluorescent light	1026	C
Sodium chloride 0.9%	TR[a]	SQ	10 and 20 g	Physically compatible with little or no aztreonam loss in 48 hr at 25 °C and 7 days at 4 °C	1001	C
	MG[b]	SQ	20 g	Physically compatible with no aztreonam loss in 48 hr at 25 °C under fluorescent light	1026	C
	BA	SQ	20 g	10% loss by HPLC in 37 days at 25 °C and more than 120 days at 4 °C. No loss in 120 days at −20 °C	1600	C
	[a]	SQ	10 g	Visually compatible with no aztreonam loss by HPLC in 96 hr at 5 and 24 °C	1691	C
TPN #107[c]			2 g	Physically compatible and aztreonam activity retained for 24 hr at 21 °C by microbiological assay	1326	C

[a]*Tested in PVC containers.*
[b]*Tested in glass containers.*
[c]*Refer to Appendix I for the composition of parenteral nutrition solutions. TPN indicates a 2-in-1 admixture.*

Additive Compatibility

			Aztreonam					
Drug	*Mfr*	*Conc/L*	*Mfr*	*Conc/L*	*Test Soln*	*Remarks*	*Ref*	*C/I*
Ampicillin sodium	WY	20 g	SQ	10 g	D5W[a]	10% ampicillin loss in 2 hr and 10% aztreonam loss in 3 hr at 25 °C. 10% ampicillin loss in 24 hr and 10% aztreonam loss in 8 hr at 4 °C	1001	I
	WY	5 g	SQ	10 g	D5W[a]	10% ampicillin loss in 3 hr and 10% aztreonam loss in 7 hr at 25 °C. 10% loss of both drugs in 48 hr at 4 °C	1001	I
	WY	20 g	SQ	20 g	D5W[a]	10% ampicillin loss in 4 hr and 10% aztreonam loss in 8 hr at 25 °C. 10% ampicillin loss in 48 hr and 10% aztreonam loss in 72 hr at 4 °C	1001	I
	WY	5 g	SQ	20 g	D5W[a]	10% ampicillin loss in 5 hr and 10% aztreonam loss in 48 hr at 25 °C. 10% ampicillin loss in 48 hr and 10% aztreonam loss in 72 hr at 4 °C	1001	I
	WY	20 g	SQ	10 g	NS[a]	10% ampicillin loss in 24 hr and 2% aztreonam loss in 48 hr at 25 °C. 10% ampicillin loss in 2 days and 9% aztreonam loss in 7 days at 4 °C	1001	C
	WY	5 g	SQ	10 g	NS[a]	10% ampicillin loss and no aztreonam loss in 48 hr at 25 °C. 10% ampicillin loss in 3 days and 8% aztreonam loss in 7 days at 4 °C	1001	C
	WY	20 g	SQ	20 g	NS[a]	10% ampicillin loss in 24 hr and 5% aztreonam loss in 48 hr at 25 °C. 10% ampicillin loss in 2 days and 7% aztreonam loss in 7 days at 4 °C	1001	C
	WY	20 g	SQ	5 g	NS[a]	10% ampicillin loss and no aztreonam loss in 48 hr at 25 °C. 10% ampicillin loss and 5% aztreonam loss in 7 days at 4 °C	1001	C
Ampicillin sodium–sulbactam sodium	PF	20 + 10 g	SQ	10 g	NS[a]	Visually compatible with 10% ampicillin loss by HPLC in 30 hr at 24 °C and 94 hr at 5 °C. Ampicillin loss is determining factor	1691	C
Cefazolin sodium	LI	5 and 20 g	SQ	10 and 20 g	D5W, NS[a]	Physically compatible and little or no loss of either drug in 48 hr at 25 °C and 7 days at 4 °C protected from light	1020	C
Cefoxitin sodium	MSD	10 and 20 g	SQ	10 and 20 g	NS[a]	3 to 5% aztreonam loss and no cefoxitin loss in 7 days at 4 °C	1023	C
	MSD	10 and 20 g	SQ	10 and 20 g	D5W[a]	3 to 6% cefoxitin loss and no aztreonam loss in 7 days at 4 °C	1023	C
	MSD	10 and 20 g	SQ	10 and 20 g	D5W, NS[a]	Both drugs stable for 12 hr at 25 °C. Yellow color accompanied 6 to 12% aztreonam loss and 9 to 15% cefoxitin loss in 48 hr at 25 °C	1023	I
Ciprofloxacin	MI	1 g	SQ	20 g	D5W, NS	Physically compatible for 24 hr at 22 °C under fluorescent light	1189	C
Clindamycin phosphate	UP	3 and 6 g	SQ	10 and 20 g	D5W, NS[a]	Physically compatible and little or no loss of either drug in 48 hr at 25 °C and 7 days at 4 °C	1002	C

Additive Compatibility (Cont.)

Aztreonam

Drug	*Mfr*	*Conc/L*	*Mfr*	*Conc/L*	*Test Soln*	*Remarks*	*Ref*	*C/I*
	UP	9 g	SQ	20 g	D5W[b]	Physically compatible with 3% clindamycin loss and 5% aztreonam loss in 48 hr at 25 °C under fluorescent light	1026	C
	UP	9 g	SQ	20 g	NS[b]	Physically compatible with 2% clindamycin loss and no aztreonam loss in 48 hr at 25 °C under fluorescent light	1026	C
Gentamicin sulfate	SC	200 and 800 mg	SQ	10 and 20 g	D5W, NS[a]	Little or no aztreonam loss in 48 hr at 25 °C and 7 days at 4 °C. Gentamicin potency retained for 12 hr at 25 °C and 24 hr at 4 °C with up to 10% loss in 48 hr at 25 °C and 7 days at 4 °C	1023	C
Linezolid	PHU	2 g	SQ	20 g	[c]	Physically compatible with no linezolid loss by HPLC in 7 days at 4 and 23 °C protected from light. About 9% aztreonam loss at 23 °C and less than 4% loss at 4 °C in 7 days	2263	C
Metronidazole	MG	5 g	SQ	10 and 20 g		Pink color develops in 12 hr, becoming cherry red in 48 hr at 25 °C. Pink color develops in 3 days at 4 °C. No loss of either drug detected	1023	I
Nafcillin sodium	BR	20 g	SQ	20 g	D5W, NS[a]	Cloudiness with fine precipitation forms gradually. 6 to 7% aztreonam loss and 10 to 11% nafcillin loss in 24 hr at room temperature	1028	I
Tobramycin sulfate	LI	200 and 800 mg	SQ	10 and 20 g	D5W, NS[a]	Little or no loss of either drug in 48 hr at 25 °C and 7 days at 4 °C	1023	C
Vancomycin HCl	AB	10 g	SQ	40 g	D5W, NS	Microcrystalline precipitate forms immediately. Gross turbidity and precipitate form over 24 hours	1848	I
	AB	1 g	SQ	4 g	D5W	Physically compatible with little or no loss of either drug in 31 days at 4 °C. About 8 to 10% aztreonam loss in 14 days at 23 °C and 7 days at 32 °C	1848	C
	AB	1 g	SQ	4 g	NS	Physically compatible with little or no loss of either drug in 31 days at 4 °C. About 5 to 8% aztreonam loss in 31 days at 23 °C and 7 days at 32 °C	1848	C

[a]*Tested in PVC containers.*
[b]*Tested in glass containers.*
[c]*Admixed in the linezolid infusion container.*

Drugs in Syringe Compatibility

Aztreonam

Drug (in syringe)	*Mfr*	*Amt*	*Mfr*	*Amt*	*Remarks*	*Ref*	*C/I*
Clindamycin phosphate	UP	600 mg/ 4 ml	SQ	2 g	Physically compatible with 2% clindamycin loss and 8% aztreonam loss in 48 hr at 25 °C under fluorescent light in polypropylene syringes	1164	C

Y-Site Injection Compatibility (1:1 Mixture)

Drug	Mfr	Conc	Aztreonam Mfr	Aztreonam Conc	Remarks	Ref	C/I
Acyclovir sodium	BW	7 mg/ml[a]	SQ	40 mg/ml[a]	White crystalline needles form immediately and become dense flocculent precipitate in 4 hr	1758	I
Alatrofloxacin mesylate	PF	1.43 mg/ml[a]	SQ	40 mg/ml[b]	White precipitate forms	2235	I
Allopurinol sodium	BW	3 mg/ml[b]	SQ	40 mg/ml[b]	Physically compatible with no change in measured turbidity or increase in particle content in 4 hr at 22 °C	1686	C
Amifostine	USB	10 mg/ml[a]	WY	20 mg/ml[a]	Physically compatible with no change in measured turbidity or increase in particle content in 4 hr at 23 °C	1845	C
Amikacin sulfate	BMS	5 mg/ml[a]	SQ	40 mg/ml[a]	Physically compatible with no subvisual haze or particle formation in 4 hr at 23 °C	1758	C
Aminophylline	AMR	2.5 mg/ml[a]	SQ	40 mg/ml[a]	Physically compatible with no subvisual haze or particle formation in 4 hr at 23 °C	1758	C
Amphotericin B	PHT	0.6 mg/ml[a]	SQ	40 mg/ml[a]	Yellow turbidity forms immediately and becomes flocculent precipitate in 4 hr	1758	I
Amphotericin B cholesteryl sulfate complex	SEQ	0.83 mg/ml[a]	SQ	40 mg/ml[a]	Gross precipitate forms	2117	I
Ampicillin sodium	WY	20 mg/ml[b]	SQ	40 mg/ml[a]	Physically compatible with no subvisual haze or particle formation in 4 hr at 23 °C	1758	C
Ampicillin sodium–sulbactam sodium	RR	20 + 10 mg/ml[b]	SQ	40 mg/ml[a]	Physically compatible with no subvisual haze or particle formation in 4 hr at 23 °C	1758	C
Amsacrine	NCI	1 mg/ml[a]	SQ	40 mg/ml[a]	Immediate light yellow-orange turbidity, developing into flocculent precipitate in 4 hr	1381	I
Bleomycin sulfate	MJ	1 unit/ml[b]	SQ	40 mg/ml[a]	Physically compatible with no subvisual haze or particle formation in 4 hr at 23 °C	1758	C
Bumetanide	RC	0.04 mg/ml[a]	SQ	40 mg/ml[a]	Physically compatible with no subvisual haze or particle formation in 4 hr at 23 °C	1758	C
Buprenorphine HCl	RKC	0.04 mg/ml[a]	SQ	40 mg/ml[a]	Physically compatible with no subvisual haze or particle formation in 4 hr at 23 °C	1758	C
Butorphanol tartrate	BMS	0.04 mg/ml[a]	SQ	40 mg/ml[a]	Physically compatible with no subvisual haze or particle formation in 4 hr at 23 °C	1758	C
Calcium gluconate	AMR	40 mg/ml[a]	SQ	40 mg/ml[a]	Physically compatible with no subvisual haze or particle formation in 4 hr at 23 °C	1758	C
Carboplatin	BMS	5 mg/ml[a]	SQ	40 mg/ml[a]	Physically compatible with no subvisual haze or particle formation in 4 hr at 23 °C	1758	C

Y-Site Injection Compatibility (1:1 Mixture) (Cont.)

Drug	Mfr	Conc	Aztreonam Mfr	Aztreonam Conc	Remarks	Ref	C/I
Carmustine	BMS	1.5 mg/ml[a]	SQ	40 mg/ml[a]	Physically compatible with no subvisual haze or particle formation in 4 hr at 23 °C	1758	C
Cefazolin sodium	MAR	20 mg/ml[a]	SQ	40 mg/ml[a]	Physically compatible with no subvisual haze or particle formation in 4 hr at 23 °C	1758	C
Cefepime HCl	BMS	20 mg/ml[a]	SQ	40 mg/ml[a]	Physically compatible with no change in measured turbidity or increase in particle content in 4 hr at 22 °C	1689	C
Cefoperazone sodium	RR	40 mg/ml[a]	SQ	40 mg/ml[a]	Physically compatible with no subvisual haze or particle formation in 4 hr at 23 °C	1758	C
Cefotaxime sodium	HO	20 mg/ml[a]	SQ	40 mg/ml[a]	Physically compatible with no subvisual haze or particle formation in 4 hr at 23 °C	1758	C
Cefotetan disodium	STU	20 mg/ml[a]	SQ	40 mg/ml[a]	Physically compatible with no subvisual haze or particle formation in 4 hr at 23 °C	1758	C
Cefoxitin sodium	MSD	20 mg/ml[a]	SQ	40 mg/ml[a]	Physically compatible with no subvisual haze or particle formation in 4 hr at 23 °C	1758	C
Ceftazidime	LI[f]	40 mg/ml[a]	SQ	40 mg/ml[a]	Physically compatible with no subvisual haze or particle formation in 4 hr at 23 °C	1758	C
Ceftizoxime sodium	FUJ	20 mg/ml[a]	SQ	40 mg/ml[a]	Physically compatible with no subvisual haze or particle formation in 4 hr at 23 °C	1758	C
Ceftriaxone sodium	RC	20 mg/ml[a]	SQ	40 mg/ml[a]	Physically compatible with no subvisual haze or particle formation in 4 hr at 23 °C	1758	C
Cefuroxime sodium	LI	30 mg/ml[a]	SQ	40 mg/ml[a]	Physically compatible with no subvisual haze or particle formation in 4 hr at 23 °C	1758	C
Chlorpromazine HCl	SCN	2 mg/ml[a]	SQ	40 mg/ml[a]	Dense white turbidity forms immediately	1758	I
Cimetidine HCl	SKB	12 mg/ml[a]	SQ	40 mg/ml[a]	Physically compatible with no subvisual haze or particle formation in 4 hr at 23 °C	1758	C
Ciprofloxacin	MI	1 mg/ml[a]	SQ	20 mg/ml[c]	Physically compatible for 24 hr at 22 °C	1189	C
	MI	1 mg/ml[a]	SQ	40 mg/ml[a]	Physically compatible with no subvisual haze or particle formation in 4 hr at 23 °C	1758	C
Cisatracurium besylate	GW	0.1, 2, 5 mg/ml[a]	SQ	40 mg/ml[a]	Physically compatible with no change in measured turbidity or increase in particle content in 4 hr at 23 °C	2074	C
Cisplatin	BMS	1 mg/ml	SQ	40 mg/ml[a]	Physically compatible with no subvisual haze or particle formation in 4 hr at 23 °C	1758	C

Y-Site Injection Compatibility (1:1 Mixture) (Cont.)

Aztreonam

Drug	*Mfr*	*Conc*	*Mfr*	*Conc*	*Remarks*	*Ref*	*C/I*
Clindamycin phosphate	AST	10 mg/ml[a]	SQ	40 mg/ml[a]	Physically compatible with no subvisual haze or particle formation in 4 hr at 23 °C	1758	C
Cyclophosphamide	MJ	10 mg/ml[a]	SQ	40 mg/ml[a]	Physically compatible with no subvisual haze or particle formation in 4 hr at 23 °C	1758	C
Cytarabine	CET	50 mg/ml	SQ	40 mg/ml[a]	Physically compatible with no subvisual haze or particle formation in 4 hr at 23 °C	1758	C
Dacarbazine	MI	4 mg/ml[a]	SQ	40 mg/ml[a]	Physically compatible with no subvisual haze or particle formation in 4 hr at 23 °C	1758	C
Dactinomycin	ME	0.01 mg/ml[a]	SQ	40 mg/ml[a]	Physically compatible with no subvisual haze or particle formation in 4 hr at 23 °C	1758	C
Daunorubicin HCl	WY	1 mg/ml[a]	SQ	40 mg/ml[a]	Haze forms immediately	1758	I
Dexamethasone sodium phosphate	AMR	1 mg/ml[a]	SQ	40 mg/ml[a]	Physically compatible with no subvisual haze or particle formation in 4 hr at 23 °C	1758	C
Diltiazem HCl	MMD	5 mg/ml	SQ	20 and 333 mg/ml[b]	Visually compatible	1807	C
	MMD	1 mg/ml[b]	SQ	333 mg/ml[b]	Visually compatible	1807	C
Diphenhydramine HCl	PD	2 mg/ml[a]	SQ	40 mg/ml[a]	Physically compatible with no subvisual haze or particle formation in 4 hr at 23 °C	1758	C
Dobutamine HCl	LI	4 mg/ml[a]	SQ	40 mg/ml[a]	Physically compatible with no subvisual haze or particle formation in 4 hr at 23 °C	1758	C
Docetaxel	RPR	0.9 mg/ml[a]	BMS	40 mg/ml[a]	Physically compatible with no change in measured turbidity or increase in particle content in 4 hr at 23 °C	2224	C
Dopamine HCl	AST	3.2 mg/ml[a]	SQ	40 mg/ml[a]	Physically compatible with no subvisual haze or particle formation in 4 hr at 23 °C	1758	C
Doxorubicin HCl	CET	2 mg/ml	SQ	40 mg/ml[a]	Physically compatible with no subvisual haze or particle formation in 4 hr at 23 °C	1758	C
Doxorubicin HCl liposome injection	SEQ	0.4 mg/ml[a]	SQ	40 mg/ml[a]	Physically compatible with little or no change in measured turbidity and no increase in particle content in 4 hr at 23 °C	2087	C
Doxycycline hyclate	ES	1 mg/ml[a]	SQ	40 mg/ml[a]	Physically compatible with no subvisual haze or particle formation in 4 hr at 23 °C	1758	C
Droperidol	JN	0.4 mg/ml[a]	SQ	40 mg/ml[a]	Physically compatible with no subvisual haze or particle formation in 4 hr at 23 °C	1758	C

Y-Site Injection Compatibility (1:1 Mixture) (Cont.)

			Aztreonam				
Drug	*Mfr*	*Conc*	*Mfr*	*Conc*	*Remarks*	*Ref*	*C/I*
Enalaprilat	MSD	0.05 mg/ml[b]	SQ	10 mg/ml[a]	Physically compatible for 24 hr at room temperature under fluorescent light	1355	C
	MSD	0.1 mg/ml[a]	SQ	40 mg/ml[a]	Physically compatible with no subvisual haze or particle formation in 4 hr at 23 °C	1758	C
Etoposide	BMS	0.4 mg/ml[a]	SQ	40 mg/ml[a]	Physically compatible with no subvisual haze or particle formation in 4 hr at 23 °C	1758	C
Etoposide phosphate	BR	5 mg/ml[a]	SQ	40 mg/ml[a]	Physically compatible with no change in measured turbidity or increase in particle content in 4 hr at 23 °C	2218	C
Famotidine	ME	2 mg/ml[a]	SQ	40 mg/ml[a]	Physically compatible with no subvisual haze or particle formation in 4 hr at 23 °C	1758	C
Filgrastim	AMG	30 μg/ml[a]	SQ	40 mg/ml[a]	Physically compatible with no change in measured turbidity or increase in particle content in 4 hr at 22 °C	1687	C
	AMG	30 μg/ml[a]	SQ	40 mg/ml[a]	Physically compatible with no subvisual haze or particle formation in 4 hr at 23 °C	1758	C
Floxuridine	RC	3 mg/ml[a]	SQ	40 mg/ml[a]	Physically compatible with no subvisual haze or particle formation in 4 hr at 23 °C	1758	C
Fluconazole	RR	2 mg/ml	SQ	40 mg/ml	Visually compatible for 24 hr at 25 °C	1407	C
	RR	2 mg/ml	SQ	40 mg/ml[a]	Physically compatible with no subvisual haze or particle formation in 4 hr at 23 °C	1758	C
Fludarabine phosphate	BX	1 mg/ml[a]	SQ	40 mg/ml[a]	Physically compatible for 4 hr at room temperature under fluorescent light	1439	C
	BX	1 mg/ml[a]	SQ	40 mg/ml[a]	Physically compatible with no subvisual haze or particle formation in 4 hr at 23 °C	1758	C
Fluorouracil	AD	16 mg/ml[a]	SQ	40 mg/ml[a]	Physically compatible with no subvisual haze or particle formation in 4 hr at 23 °C	1758	C
Foscarnet sodium	AST	24 mg/ml	SQ	40 mg/ml	Physically compatible for 24 hr at room temperature under fluorescent light	1335	C
	AST	24 mg/ml	SQ	40 mg/ml[c]	Physically compatible for 24 hr at 25 °C under fluorescent light by visual and microscopic examination	1393	C
Furosemide	AB	3 mg/ml[a]	SQ	40 mg/ml[a]	Physically compatible with no subvisual haze or particle formation in 4 hr at 23 °C	1758	C
Ganciclovir sodium	SY	20 mg/ml[a]	SQ	40 mg/ml[a]	White crystalline needles form immediately and become dense flocculent precipitate in 1 hr	1758	I

Y-Site Injection Compatibility (1:1 Mixture) (Cont.)

			Aztreonam				
Drug	*Mfr*	*Conc*	*Mfr*	*Conc*	*Remarks*	*Ref*	*C/I*
Gatifloxacin	BMS	2 mg/ml[a]	SQ	40 mg/ml[a]	Physically compatible with no change in measured haze or increase in particle content in 4 hr at 23 °C	2234	C
Gemcitabine HCl	LI	10 mg/ml[b]	SQ	40 mg/ml[b]	Physically compatible with no change in measured turbidity or increase in particle content in 4 hr at 23 °C	2226	C
Gentamicin sulfate	ES	5 mg/ml[a]	SQ	40 mg/ml[a]	Physically compatible with no subvisual haze or particle formation in 4 hr at 23 °C	1758	C
Granisetron HCl	SKB	0.05 mg/ml[a]	SQ	40 mg/ml[a]	Physically compatible with no change in measured turbidity or increase in particle content in 4 hr at 23 °C	2000	C
Haloperidol lactate	MN	0.2 mg/ml[a]	SQ	40 mg/ml[a]	Physically compatible with no subvisual haze or particle formation in 4 hr at 23 °C	1758	C
Heparin sodium	ES	100 units/ml[a]	SQ	40 mg/ml[a]	Physically compatible with no subvisual haze or particle formation in 4 hr at 23 °C	1758	C
	TR	50 units/ml	BV	20 mg/ml[a]	Visually compatible for 4 hr at 25 °C	1793	C
Hydrocortisone sodium phosphate	MSD	1 mg/ml[a]	SQ	40 mg/ml[a]	Physically compatible with no subvisual haze or particle formation in 4 hr at 23 °C	1758	C
Hydrocortisone sodium succinate	UP	1 mg/ml[a]	SQ	40 mg/ml[a]	Physically compatible with no subvisual haze or particle formation in 4 hr at 23 °C	1758	C
Hydromorphone HCl	KN	0.5 mg/ml[a]	SQ	40 mg/ml[a]	Physically compatible with no subvisual haze or particle formation in 4 hr at 23 °C	1758	C
Hydroxyzine HCl	WI	4 mg/ml[a]	SQ	40 mg/ml[a]	Physically compatible with no subvisual haze or particle formation in 4 hr at 23 °C	1758	C
Idarubicin HCl	AD	0.5 mg/ml[a]	SQ	40 mg/ml[a]	Increase in measured turbidity no greater than dilution of idarubicin with NS. No increase in particle content in 4 hr at 23 °C	1758	C
Ifosfamide	MJ	25 mg/ml[a]	SQ	40 mg/ml[a]	Physically compatible with no subvisual haze or particle formation in 4 hr at 23 °C	1758	C
Imipenem–cilastatin sodium	MSD	10 mg/ml[a]	SQ	40 mg/ml[a]	Physically compatible with no subvisual haze or particle formation in 4 hr at 23 °C	1758	C
Insulin, regular	LI	0.2 unit/ml[b]	SQ	20 mg/ml	Physically compatible for 2 hr at 25 °C	1395	C
Leucovorin calcium	LE	2 mg/ml[a]	SQ	40 mg/ml[a]	Physically compatible with no subvisual haze or particle formation in 4 hr at 23 °C	1758	C
Linezolid	PHU	2 mg/ml	SQ	40 mg/ml[a]	Physically compatible with no change in measured turbidity or increase in particle content in 4 hr at 23 °C	2264	C

Y-Site Injection Compatibility (1:1 Mixture) (Cont.)

			Aztreonam				
Drug	*Mfr*	*Conc*	*Mfr*	*Conc*	*Remarks*	*Ref*	*C/I*
Lorazepam	WY	0.1 mg/ml[a]	SQ	40 mg/ml[a]	Haze forms within 1 hr	1758	I
Magnesium sulfate	AST	100 mg/ml[a]	SQ	40 mg/ml[a]	Physically compatible with no subvisual haze or particle formation in 4 hr at 23 °C	1758	C
Mannitol	BA	15%	SQ	40 mg/ml[a]	Physically compatible with no subvisual haze or particle formation in 4 hr at 23 °C	1758	C
Mechlorethamine HCl	MSD	1 mg/ml	SQ	40 mg/ml[a]	Physically compatible with no subvisual haze or particle formation in 4 hr at 23 °C	1758	C
Melphalan HCl	BW	0.1 mg/ml[b]	SQ	40 mg/ml[b]	Physically compatible with no change in measured turbidity or increase in particle content in 3 hr at 22 °C	1557	C
Meperidine HCl	AB	10 mg/ml	SQ	20 mg/ml[a]	Physically compatible for 4 hr at 25 °C	1397	C
	WY	4 mg/ml[a]	SQ	40 mg/ml[a]	Physically compatible with no subvisual haze or particle formation in 4 hr at 23 °C	1758	C
Mesna	MJ	10 mg/ml[a]	SQ	40 mg/ml[a]	Physically compatible with no subvisual haze or particle formation in 4 hr at 23 °C	1758	C
Methotrexate sodium	LE	15 mg/ml[a]	SQ	40 mg/ml[a]	Physically compatible with no subvisual haze or particle formation in 4 hr at 23 °C	1758	C
Methylprednisolone sodium succinate	AB	5 mg/ml[a]	SQ	40 mg/ml[a]	Physically compatible with no subvisual haze or particle formation in 4 hr at 23 °C	1758	C
Metoclopramide HCl	ES	5 mg/ml	SQ	40 mg/ml[a]	Physically compatible with no subvisual haze or particle formation in 4 hr at 23 °C	1758	C
Metronidazole	BA	5 mg/ml	SQ	40 mg/ml[a]	Color changes from colorless to orange in 4 hr	1758	I
Minocycline HCl	LE	0.2 mg/ml[a]	SQ	40 mg/ml[a]	Physically compatible with no subvisual haze or particle formation in 4 hr at 23 °C	1758	C
Mitomycin	BMS	0.5 mg/ml	SQ	40 mg/ml[a]	Color changes from pale blue to reddish purple in 4 hr	1758	I
Mitoxantrone HCl	LE	0.5 mg/ml[a]	SQ	40 mg/ml[a]	Heavy precipitate forms in 1 hr	1758	I
Morphine sulfate	AB	1 mg/ml	SQ	20 mg/ml[a]	Physically compatible for 4 hr at 25 °C	1397	C
	AST	1 mg/ml[a]	SQ	40 mg/ml[a]	Physically compatible with no subvisual haze or particle formation in 4 hr at 23 °C	1758	C
Nalbuphine HCl	AST	10 mg/ml	SQ	40 mg/ml[a]	Physically compatible with no subvisual haze or particle formation in 4 hr at 23 °C	1758	C
Netilmicin sulfate	SC	5 mg/ml[a]	SQ	40 mg/ml[a]	Physically compatible with no subvisual haze or particle formation in 4 hr at 23 °C	1758	C

Y-Site Injection Compatibility (1:1 Mixture) (Cont.)

			Aztreonam				
Drug	*Mfr*	*Conc*	*Mfr*	*Conc*	*Remarks*	*Ref*	*C/I*
Ondansetron HCl	GL	1 mg/ml[b]	SQ	40 mg/ml[a]	Physically compatible for 4 hr at 22 °C	1365	C
	GL	0.03 and 0.3 mg/ml[a]	SQ	40 mg/ml[a]	Visually compatible with little or no loss of either drug by HPLC in 4 hr at 25 °C under fluorescent light	1732	C
	GL	1 mg/ml[a]	SQ	40 mg/ml[a]	Physically compatible with no subvisual haze or particle formation in 4 hr at 23 °C	1758	C
Piperacillin sodium	LE	40 mg/ml[a]	SQ	40 mg/ml[a]	Physically compatible with no subvisual haze or particle formation in 4 hr at 23 °C	1758	C
Piperacillin sodium–tazobactam sodium	LE	40 + 5 mg/ml[a]	SQ	40 mg/ml[a]	Physically compatible with no change in measured turbidity or increase in particle content in 4 hr at 22 °C	1688	C
Plicamycin	MI	0.01 mg/ml[a]	SQ	40 mg/ml[a]	Physically compatible with no subvisual haze or particle formation in 4 hr at 23 °C	1758	C
Potassium chloride	AB	0.1 mEq/ml[a]	SQ	40 mg/ml[a]	Physically compatible with no subvisual haze or particle formation in 4 hr at 23 °C	1758	C
Prochlorperazine edisylate	ES	0.5 mg/ml[a]	SQ	40 mg/ml[a]	Haze and tiny particles form within 4 hr	1758	I
Promethazine HCl	SCN	2 mg/ml[a]	SQ	40 mg/ml[a]	Physically compatible with no subvisual haze or particle formation in 4 hr at 23 °C	1758	C
Propofol	ZEN	10 mg/ml	SQ	40 mg/ml[a]	Physically compatible for 1 hr at 23 °C with no increase in particle content	2066	C
Ranitidine HCl	GL	1 mg/ml[b]	SQ	16.7 mg/ml[b]	No loss of either drug by HPLC in 4 hr at 22 °C under fluorescent light	1632	C
	GL	2 mg/ml[a]	SQ	40 mg/ml[a]	Physically compatible with no subvisual haze or particle formation in 4 hr at 23 °C	1758	C
Remifentanil HCl	GW	0.025 and 0.25 mg/ml[b]	SQ	40 mg/ml[a]	Physically compatible with no change in measured turbidity or increase in particle content in 4 hr at 23 °C	2075	C
Sargramostim	IMM	10 μg/ml[b]	SQ	40 mg/ml[b]	Physically compatible for 4 hr at 22 °C	1436	C
	IMM	10 μg/ml[b]	SQ	40 mg/ml[a]	Physically compatible with no subvisual haze or particle formation in 4 hr at 23 °C	1758	C
Sodium bicarbonate	AB	1 mEq/ml	SQ	40 mg/ml[a]	Physically compatible with no subvisual haze or particle formation in 4 hr at 23 °C	1758	C
Streptozocin	UP	40 mg/ml[a]	SQ	40 mg/ml[a]	Color changes from pale gold to red in 1 hr	1758	I
Teniposide	BR	0.1 mg/ml[a]	SQ	40 mg/ml[a]	Physically compatible with no subvisual haze or particle formation in 4 hr at 23 °C	1725; 1758	C
Theophylline	TR	4 mg/ml	BV	20 mg/ml[a]	Visually compatible for 6 hr at 25 °C	1793	C

Y-Site Injection Compatibility (1:1 Mixture) (Cont.)

Drug	*Mfr*	*Conc*	Aztreonam *Mfr*	Aztreonam *Conc*	*Remarks*	*Ref*	*C/I*
Thiotepa	LE	1 mg/ml[a]	SQ	40 mg/ml[a]	Physically compatible with no subvisual haze or particle formation in 4 hr at 23 °C	1758	C
	IMM[d]	1 mg/ml[a]	SQ	40 mg/ml[a]	Physically compatible with no change in measured turbidity or increase in particle content in 4 hr at 23 °C	1861	C
Ticarcillin disodium	BE	30 mg/ml[a]	SQ	40 mg/ml[a]	Physically compatible with no subvisual haze or particle formation in 4 hr at 23 °C	1758	C
Ticarcillin disodium–clavulanate potassium	SKB	31 mg/ml[a]	SQ	40 mg/ml[a]	Physically compatible with no subvisual haze or particle formation in 4 hr at 23 °C	1758	C
TNA #218 to #226[e]			SQ	40 mg/ml[a]	Visually compatible with no precipitate or emulsion damage apparent in 4 hr at 23 °C	2215	C
Tobramycin sulfate	LI	5 mg/ml[a]	SQ	40 mg/ml[a]	Physically compatible with no subvisual haze or particle formation in 4 hr at 23 °C	1758	C
TPN #212 to #215[e]			SQ	40 mg/ml[a]	Physically compatible with no change in measured turbidity or increase in particle content in 4 hr at 23 °C	2109	C
Trimethoprim–sulfamethoxazole	ES	0.8 + 4 mg/ml[a]	SQ	40 mg/ml[a]	Physically compatible with no subvisual haze or particle formation in 4 hr at 23 °C	1758	C
Vancomycin HCl	LI	67 mg/ml[b]	SQ	200 mg/ml[b]	White granular precipitate forms immediately in tubing when given sequentially	1364	I
	AB	10 mg/ml[a]	SQ	40 mg/ml[a]	Physically compatible with no subvisual haze or particle formation in 4 hr at 23 °C	1758	C
Vinblastine sulfate	LI	0.12 mg/ml[a]	SQ	40 mg/ml[a]	Physically compatible with no subvisual haze or particle formation in 4 hr at 23 °C	1758	C
Vincristine sulfate	LI	0.05 mg/ml[a]	SQ	40 mg/ml[a]	Physically compatible with no subvisual haze or particle formation in 4 hr at 23 °C	1758	C
Vinorelbine tartrate	BW	1 mg/ml[b]	SQ	40 mg/ml[b]	Physically compatible with no change in measured turbidity or increase in particle content in 4 hr at 22 °C	1558	C
Zidovudine	BW	4 mg/ml[a]	SQ	40 mg/ml[a]	Physically compatible for 4 hr at 25 °C under fluorescent light by visual and microscopic examination	1193	C
	BW	4 mg/ml[a]	SQ	40 mg/ml[a]	Physically compatible with no subvisual haze or particle formation in 4 hr at 23 °C	1758	C

[a] *Tested in dextrose 5% in water.*
[b] *Tested in sodium chloride 0.9%.*
[c] *Tested in both dextrose 5% in water and sodium chloride 0.9%.*
[d] *Lyophilized formulation tested.*
[e] *Refer to Appendix I for the composition of parenteral nutrition solutions. TNA indicates a 3-in-1 admixture, and TPN indicates a 2-in-1 admixture.*
[f] *Sodium carbonate–containing formulation tested.*

Additional Compatibility Information

Infusion Solutions — For intravenous infusion, the manufacturer recommends dilution of aztreonam in the following infusion solutions (2):

Dextrose 5% in Ringer's injection, lactated
Dextrose 5% in sodium chloride 0.2, 0.45, and 0.9%
Dextrose 5 and 10% in water
Invert sugar 10% in water
Invert sugar 10% in Electrolyte #1, #2, and #3
Ionosol B in dextrose 5%
Isolyte E
Isolyte E with dextrose 5%
Isolyte M with dextrose 5%
Mannitol 5 and 10%
Normosol M in dextrose 5%
Normosol R
Normosol R in dextrose 5%
Plasma-Lyte M in dextrose 5%
Ringer's injection
Ringer's injection, lactated
Sodium chloride 0.9%
Sodium lactate ⅙ M

Peritoneal Dialysis Solutions — Aztreonam with cloxacillin sodium and aztreonam with vancomycin HCl admixtures are stable in Dianeal 137 with dextrose 4.25% for 24 hours at room temperature. (2)

Other Drugs — The manufacturer states that solutions of aztreonam in sodium chloride 0.9% or dextrose 5% in water with clindamycin phosphate, gentamicin sulfate, tobramycin sulfate, or cefazolin sodium are stable for up to 48 hours at room temperature or seven days under refrigeration. (2)

Aztreonam is incompatible with nafcillin sodium and metronidazole. (2)

The manufacturer also states that ampicillin sodium admixtures with aztreonam in sodium chloride 0.9% are stable for 24 hours at room temperature or 48 hours under refrigeration. However, in dextrose 5% in water, the stability is reduced to two hours at room temperature or eight hours under refrigeration. (2)

BACLOFEN
AHFS 12:20

Products — Baclofen injection is available as a preservative-free injection in intrathecal refill kits at a concentration of 0.5 mg/ml in 20-ml ampuls and at a concentration of 2 mg/ml in 5-ml ampuls. Each milliliter of solution contains baclofen 0.5 or 2 mg (500 or 2000 μg, respectively) with sodium chloride 9 mg in water for injection. (1-4/97)

Baclofen preservative-free intrathecal injection is also available in intrathecal screening kits at a concentration of 0.05 mg/ml in 1-ml ampuls. Each milliliter of solution contains baclofen 0.05 mg (50 μg) with sodium chloride 9 mg in water for injection. (1-4/97)

pH — From 5 to 7. (1-4/97)

Tonicity — Baclofen injection is an isotonic solution. (1-4/97; 4)

Sodium Content — Baclofen injection contains 0.15 mEq of sodium per milliliter. (4)

Trade Name(s) — Lioresal Intrathecal.

Administration — For screening, baclofen injection must be diluted with sterile, preservative-free sodium chloride 0.9% injection to a concentration of 50 μg/ml. The dilution is administered by direct intrathecal injection via lumbar puncture or catheter over at least one minute using barbotage. In maintenance treatment, baclofen injection is also given by intrathecal infusion using an implantable infusion control device; concentration and rate of delivery must be carefully titrated to each patient's needs. (1-4/97; 4)

Stability — Baclofen injection may be stored at controlled room temperatures not exceeding 30 °C. It should be protected from freezing. (1-4/97; 4) The product is stable in implantable infusion pumps at a temperature of 37 °C. (4) It should not be autoclaved. The product contains no preservatives and is intended for single-use only; unused portions must be discarded. (1-4/97; 4)

Baclofen injection must be diluted only with sterile, preservative-free sodium chloride 0.9%. It is compatible with cerebrospinal fluid. (1-4/97; 4)

Implantable Pumps — Baclofen 0.5 mg/ml was filled into an implantable pump (Fresenius model VIP 30) and associated capillary tubing and stored at 37 °C. Samples were analyzed using an HPLC assay. No baclofen loss and no contamination from components of pump materials occurred during eight weeks of storage. (1903)

Baclofen (Ciba) 0.2 mg/ml with morphine sulfate (David Bull) 1 mg/ml in an implantable pump (Infusaid) was physically compatible and exhibited little or no loss of either drug within 30 days at 37 °C. (1911)

In a follow-up study at higher concentrations, baclofen (Ciba) 1 mg/ml with morphine sulfate (David Bull) 15 mg/ml in an implantable pump (Infusaid) was physically compatible, with only a slight yellowing of the solution observed. HPLC analysis found no substantial loss of either baclofen or morphine. Statistical analysis showed no significant time-dependent change in the baclofen concentration. However, a small decrease in morphine concentration of less than 4% may occur during a 30-day course of infusion at 37 °C. (2170)

Baclofen 0.5 and 2 mg/ml in the Synchromed implantable pump is stated to be stable at body temperature for 90 days. (31)

Compatibility Information

Additive Compatibility

Drug	Baclofen Mfr	Conc/L	Mfr	Conc/L	Test Soln	Remarks	Ref	C/I
Morphine sulfate	DB	1 and 1.5 g	CI	200 mg	NS[a]	Physically compatible with little or no loss of either drug by HPLC in 30 days at 37 °C	1911	C
	DB	1 g	CI	800 mg	NS[a]	Physically compatible with little or no baclofen loss and less than 7% morphine loss by HPLC in 29 days at 37 °C	1911	C
	DB	1.5 g	CI	800 mg	NS[a]	Physically compatible with little or no loss of either drug by HPLC in 30 days at 37 °C	1911	C
	DB	7.5 g	CI	1.5 g	NS[a]	Physically compatible with little or no loss of either drug by HPLC in 30 days at 37 °C	2170	C
	DB	15 g	CI	1 g	NS[a]	Physically compatible with little or no loss of either drug by HPLC in 30 days at 37 °C	2170	C
	DB	21 g	CI	200 mg	NS[a]	Physically compatible with about 7% baclofen loss and little or no morphine loss by HPLC in 30 days at 37 °C	2170	C

[a]*Tested in glass containers.*

BENZTROPINE MESYLATE
AHFS 12:08.04

Products — Benztropine mesylate is available in 2-ml ampuls containing 2 mg of drug. Each milliliter of solution contains (2):

Benztropine mesylate	1 mg
Sodium chloride	9 mg
Water for injection	qs 1 ml

pH — From 5 to 8. (4)

Osmolality — Benztropine mesylate 1 mg/ml has an osmolality of 282 mOsm/kg. (1689)

Trade Name(s) — Cogentin.

Administration — Benztropine mesylate may be administered by intramuscular or, rarely, intravenous injection. (2; 4)

Stability — Store the ampuls at controlled room temperature. Avoid freezing and storing at temperatures over 40 °C. (4)

Compatibility Information

Drugs in Syringe Compatibility

Drug (in syringe)	Mfr	Amt	Benztropine mesylate Mfr	Amt	Remarks	Ref	C/I
Chlorpromazine HCl	STS	50 mg/ 2 ml	MSD	2 mg/ 2 ml	Visually compatible for 60 min	1784	C
Fluphenazine HCl	LY	5 mg/ 2 ml	MSD	2 mg/ 2 ml	Visually compatible for 60 min	1784	C
Haloperidol lactate	MN	0.25, 0.5, 1 mg	MSD	2 mg	Visually compatible for 24 hr at 21 °C	1781	C
	MN	2 mg	MSD	2 mg	Precipitate forms within 4 hr at 21 °C	1781	I

Drugs in Syringe Compatibility (Cont.)

Benztropine mesylate

Drug (in syringe)	*Mfr*	*Amt*	*Mfr*	*Amt*	*Remarks*	*Ref*	*C/I*
	MN	3, 4, 5 mg	MSD	2 mg	Precipitate forms within 15 min at 21 °C	1781	I
	MN	0.25 and 0.5 mg	MSD	1 mg	Visually compatible for 24 hr at 21 °C	1781	C
	MN	1 to 5 mg	MSD	1 mg	Precipitate forms within 15 min at 21 °C	1781	I
	MN	0.25 to 5 mg	MSD	0.5 mg	Precipitate forms within 15 min at 21 °C	1781	I
	MN	10 mg/ 2 ml	MSD	2 mg/ 2 ml	White precipitate forms within 5 min	1784	I
Metoclopramide HCl	RB	10 mg/ 2 ml	MSD	2 mg/ 2 ml	Physically compatible for 48 hr at room temperature	924	C
	RB	10 mg/ 2 ml	MSD	2 mg/ 2 ml	Physically compatible for 48 hr at 25 °C	1167	C
	RB	160 mg/ 32 ml	MSD	2 mg/ 2 ml	Physically compatible for 48 hr at 25 °C	1167	C
Perphenazine	SC	10 mg/ 2 ml	MSD	2 mg/ 2 ml	Visually compatible for 60 min	1784	C

Y-Site Injection Compatibility (1:1 Mixture)

Benztropine mesylate

Drug	*Mfr*	*Conc*	*Mfr*	*Conc*	*Remarks*	*Ref*	*C/I*
Fluconazole	RR	2 mg/ml	MSD	1 mg/ml	Physically compatible for 24 hr at 25 °C	1407	C
Tacrolimus	FUJ	1 mg/ml[a]	MSD	1 mg/ml	Visually compatible for 24 hr at 25 °C	1630	C

[a]*Tested in sodium chloride 0.9%.*

BETAMETHASONE SODIUM PHOSPHATE AHFS 68:04

Products — Betamethasone sodium phosphate is available in 5-ml multiple-dose vials. Each milliliter of solution contains (4; 29; 154):

Betamethasone (present as betamethasone sodium phosphate 4 mg)	3 mg
Dibasic sodium phosphate	10 mg
Edetate disodium	0.1 mg
Phenol	5 mg
Sodium bisulfite	3.2 mg
Sodium hydroxide	to adjust pH

pH — Approximately 8.5. (4)

Trade Name(s) — Celestone Phosphate.

Administration — Betamethasone sodium phosphate may be administered intravenously or intramuscularly. Intra-articular, intrasynovial, intralesional, and soft tissue injections are also recommended. (4)

Stability — Betamethasone sodium phosphate should be protected from light and stored at a temperature below 40 °C, preferably between 15 and 30 °C. The injection should not be frozen. (4)

Compatibility Information

Y-Site Injection Compatibility (1:1 Mixture)

Drug	Mfr	Conc	Mfr	Conc	Remarks	Ref	C/I
			Betamethasone sodium phosphate				
Heparin sodium	UP	1000 units/L[a]	SC	3 mg/ml	Physically compatible for at least 4 hr at room temperature by visual and microscopic examination	534	C
Hydrocortisone sodium succinate	UP	10 mg/L[a]	SC	3 mg/ml	Physically compatible for at least 4 hr at room temperature by visual and microscopic examination	534	C
Potassium chloride	AB	40 mEq/L[a]	SC	3 mg/ml	Physically compatible for at least 4 hr at room temperature by visual and microscopic examination	534	C
Vitamin B complex with C	RC	2 ml/L[a]	SC	3 mg/ml	Physically compatible for at least 4 hr at room temperature by visual and microscopic examination	534	C

[a]*Tested in dextrose 5% in water, dextrose 5% in Ringer's injection, dextrose 5% in Ringer's injection, lactated, Ringer's injection, lactated, and sodium chloride 0.9%.*

BLEOMYCIN SULFATE
AHFS 10:00

Products — Bleomycin sulfate is available in vials containing 15 and 30 units of bleomycin as the sulfate. For intramuscular or subcutaneous administration, reconstitute the 15-unit vial with 1 to 5 ml and the 30-unit vial with 2 to 10 ml of sterile water for injection, sodium chloride 0.9%, or bacteriostatic water for injection, yielding a solution containing 3 to 15 units/ml. For intravenous injection, reconstitute the 15-unit vial with a minimum of 5 ml and the 30-unit vial with a minimum of 10 ml of sodium chloride 0.9%, resulting in a solution of not more than 3 units/ml. For intrapleural administration, 60 units is dissolved in 50 to 100 ml of sodium chloride 0.9%. (2; 4)

Units — Bleomycin sulfate is a mixture of cytotoxic glycopeptide antibiotics. A unit of bleomycin is equal to the term milligram activity, which was formerly used. (2) One unit of bleomycin is equivalent in activity to 1 mg of bleomycin A_2 reference standard. (4)

pH — The pH of the reconstituted solution varies from 4.5 to 6, depending on the diluent. (4)

Osmolality — Bleomycin sulfate 15 units/ml in sterile water for injection has an osmolality of 89 mOsm/kg. (1689)

Density — Bleomycin sulfate (Mead Johnson) reconstituted with sterile water for injection to a concentration of 3 units/ml has a solution density of 0.99 g/ml. (2041; 2248)

Trade Name(s) — Blenoxane.

Administration — Bleomycin sulfate may be administered by intramuscular, subcutaneous, intravenous, or intrapleural injection. Intravenous injections should be given slowly over a 10-minute period. (2; 4)

Stability — Intact vials are stable under refrigeration and bear an expiration date. (2) They are stated to be stable for 28 days at room temperature. (1181; 1433) Bristol-Myers Squibb states that bleomycin sulfate is stable in sodium chloride 0.9% for 24 hours at room temperature. (2) Other information indicates that solutions reconstituted with dextrose 5% in water may be less stable, with losses exceeding 10% in 24 hours at room temperature. (1441) Bleomycin sulfate solutions reconstituted with sodium chloride 0.9% are reported to be stable for four weeks when stored at 2 to 8 °C (4; 1369), for two weeks (4) or longer (860; 1369) at room temperature, and for 10 days at 37 °C. (1073) However, because of the risk of microbial contamination in products without preservatives, it is recommended that the solutions be used within 24 hours of reconstitution. (2; 4; 860)

pH Effects — Bleomycin sulfate (Bristol) is stable in solution over a pH range of 4 to 10. (763)

Elastomeric Reservoir Pumps — Bleomycin sulfate 0.4 unit/ml in dextrose 5% in water in Infusor elastomeric reservoir pumps has been stated by the pump manufacturer to be stable for 30 days at room temperature and under refrigeration. (31)

Sorption — Koberda et al. studied the stability of bleomycin sulfate 0.3 to 3 units/ml in sodium chloride 0.9% and dextrose 5% in water in both glass and PVC containers. Contrary to a previous report (519), no loss due to sorption to PVC containers occurred. Storage for 24 hours at 23 °C resulted in similar losses in the dextrose 5% in water admixtures in both containers, while little or no loss occurred in the sodium chloride 0.9% admixtures in both containers. The authors speculated that the losses previously attributed to container sorption actually resulted from adduct formation with dextrose. (1441)

DeVroe et al. confirmed this result. They compared the delivery of bleomycin sulfate 7.5 units/500 ml in dextrose 5% in water and sodium chloride 0.9% in glass, PVC, and high-density polyethylene containers and in PVC, polyethylene, and polybutadiene infusion sets. The bleomycin delivered from all of these container/set configurations was equivalent, with no evidence of sorption. (1577)

Filtration—Bleomycin sulfate (Bristol) 15 units/50 ml in dextrose 5% in water and sodium chloride 0.9% filtered at a rate of about 3 ml/min through a 0.22-μm cellulose ester membrane filter (Ivex-2) showed no significant reduction in potency due to binding to the filter. (533)

Bleomycin sulfate 10 to 300 μg/ml exhibited no loss due to sorption to either cellulose nitrate/cellulose acetate ester (Millex OR) or Teflon (Millex FG) filters. (1415; 1416)

Bleomycin sulfate 7.5 units/500 ml in dextrose 5% in water and sodium chloride 0.9% lost potency initially when infused over 24 hours through cellulose ester and nylon filters. However, the concentration returned to expected levels within minutes, and the total amount of drug lost was negligible. (1577)

Compatibility Information

Solution Compatibility

Bleomycin sulfate

Solution	*Mfr*	*Mfr*	*Conc/L*	*Remarks*	*Ref*	*C/I*
Dextrose 5% in water	[a]		150 units	About 54% loss in 28 days at room temperature in the dark	1369	I
	BA[b]	BR	300 and 3000 units	About 10% loss in 8 to 10 hr and 11 to 16% loss in 24 hr at 23 °C in glass and PVC	1441	I
	[c]	BEL	15 units	No loss by UV spectroscopy in 24 hr at room temperature exposed to light	1577	C
Sodium chloride 0.9%	[a]		150 units	About 4% loss in 28 days at room temperature in the dark	1369	C
	BA[b]	BR	300 and 3000 units	Little or no loss in 24 hr at 23 °C in glass and PVC	1441	C
	[c]	BEL	15 units	No loss by UV spectroscopy in 48 hr at room temperature exposed to light	1577	C

[a]*Tested in PVC containers.*
[b]*Tested in both glass and PVC containers.*
[c]*Tested in glass, PVC, and high-density polyethylene containers.*

Additive Compatibility

Bleomycin sulfate

Drug	*Mfr*	*Conc/L*	*Mfr*	*Conc/L*	*Test Soln*	*Remarks*	*Ref*	*C/I*
Amikacin sulfate	BR	1.25 g	BR	20 and 30 units	NS	Physically compatible and bleomycin activity retained for 1 week at 4 °C. Amikacin not tested	763	C
Aminophylline	ES	250 mg	BR	20 and 30 units	NS	50% loss of bleomycin activity in 1 week at 4 °C	763	I
Ascorbic acid injection	PD	2.5 and 5 g	BR	20 and 30 units	NS	Loss of all bleomycin activity in 1 week at 4 °C	763	I
Cefazolin sodium	LI	1 g	BR	20 and 30 units	NS	43% loss of bleomycin activity in 1 week at 4 °C	763	I
Dexamethasone sodium phosphate	MSD	50 mg	BR	20 and 30 units	NS	Physically compatible and bleomycin activity retained for 1 week at 4 °C. Dexamethasone not tested	763	C
Diazepam	RC	50 and 100 mg	BR	20 and 30 units	NS	Physically incompatible	763	I

Additive Compatibility (Cont.)

			Bleomycin sulfate					
Drug	*Mfr*	*Conc/L*	*Mfr*	*Conc/L*	*Test Soln*	*Remarks*	*Ref*	*C/I*
Diphenhydramine HCl	PD	100 mg	BR	20 and 30 units	NS	Physically compatible and bleomycin activity retained for 1 week at 4 °C. Diphenhydramine not tested	763	C
Fluorouracil	RC	1 g	BR	20 and 30 units	NS	Physically compatible and bleomycin activity retained for 1 week at 4 °C. Fluorouracil not tested	763	C
Gentamicin sulfate	SC	50, 100, 300, 600 mg	BR	20 and 30 units	NS	Physically compatible and bleomycin activity retained for 1 week at 4 °C. Gentamicin not tested	763	C
Heparin sodium	RI	10,000 to 200,000 units	BR	20 and 30 units	NS	Physically compatible and bleomycin activity retained for 1 week at 4 °C. Heparin not tested	763	C
Hydrocortisone sodium phosphate	MSD	100 mg, 500 mg, 1 g, 2 g	BR	20 and 30 units	NS	Physically compatible and bleomycin activity retained for 1 week at 4 °C. Hydrocortisone not tested	763	C
Hydrocortisone sodium succinate	AB	300 mg, 750 mg, 1 g, 2.5 g	BR	20 and 30 units	NS	60 to 100% loss of bleomycin activity in 1 week at 4 °C	763	I
Methotrexate	LE	250 and 500 mg	BR	20 and 30 units	NS	About 60% loss of bleomycin activity in 1 week at 4 °C	763	I
Mitomycin	BR	10 mg	BR	20 and 30 units	NS	20% loss of bleomycin activity in 1 week at 4 °C	763	I
	BR	50 mg	BR	20 and 30 units	NS	52% loss of bleomycin activity in 1 week at 4 °C	763	I
Nafcillin sodium	BR	2.5 g	BR	20 and 30 units	NS	Substantial loss of bleomycin activity in 1 week at 4 °C	763	I
Penicillin G sodium	SQ	2 million units	BR	20 and 30 units	NS	77% loss of bleomycin activity in 1 week at 4 °C	763	I
	SQ	5 million units	BR	20 and 30 units	NS	41% loss of bleomycin activity in 1 week at 4 °C	763	I
Phenytoin sodium	PD	500 mg	BR	20 and 30 units	NS	Physically compatible and bleomycin activity retained for 1 week at 4 °C. Phenytoin not tested	763	C
Streptomycin sulfate	PF	4 g	BR	20 and 30 units	NS	Physically compatible and bleomycin activity retained for 1 week at 4 °C. Streptomycin not tested	763	C
Terbutaline sulfate	GG	7.5 mg	BR	20 and 30 units	NS	36% loss of bleomycin activity in 1 week at 4 °C	763	I
Tobramycin sulfate	LI	500 mg	BR	20 and 30 units	NS	Physically compatible and bleomycin activity retained for 1 week at 4 °C	763	C
Vinblastine sulfate	LI	10 and 100 mg	BR	20 and 30 units	NS	Physically compatible and bleomycin activity retained for 1 week at 4 °C. Vinblastine not tested	763	C

Additive Compatibility (Cont.)

Drug	Mfr	Conc/L	Mfr (Bleomycin sulfate)	Conc/L (Bleomycin sulfate)	Test Soln	Remarks	Ref	C/I
Vincristine sulfate	LI	50 and 100 mg	BR	20 and 30 units	NS	Physically compatible and bleomycin activity retained for 1 week at 4 °C. Vincristine not tested	763	C

Drugs in Syringe Compatibility

Drug (in syringe)	Mfr	Amt	Mfr (Bleomycin sulfate)	Amt (Bleomycin sulfate)	Remarks	Ref	C/I
Cisplatin		0.5 mg/ 0.5 ml		1.5 units/ 0.5 ml	Physically compatible for 5 min at room temperature followed by 8 min of centrifugation	980	C
Cyclophosphamide		10 mg/ 0.5 ml		1.5 units/ 0.5 ml	Physically compatible for 5 min at room temperature followed by 8 min of centrifugation	980	C
Doxorubicin HCl		1 mg/ 0.5 ml		1.5 units/ 0.5 ml	Physically compatible for 5 min at room temperature followed by 8 min of centrifugation	980	C
Droperidol		1.25 mg/ 0.5 ml		1.5 units/ 0.5 ml	Physically compatible for 5 min at room temperature followed by 8 min of centrifugation	980	C
Fluorouracil		25 mg/ 0.5 ml		1.5 units/ 0.5 ml	Physically compatible for 5 min at room temperature followed by 8 min of centrifugation	980	C
Furosemide		5 mg/ 0.5 ml		1.5 units/ 0.5 ml	Physically compatible for 5 min at room temperature followed by 8 min of centrifugation	980	C
Heparin sodium		500 units/ 0.5 ml		1.5 units/ 0.5 ml	Physically compatible for 5 min at room temperature followed by 8 min of centrifugation	980	C
Leucovorin calcium		5 mg/ 0.5 ml		1.5 units/ 0.5 ml	Physically compatible for 5 min at room temperature followed by 8 min of centrifugation	980	C
Methotrexate sodium		12.5 mg/ 0.5 ml		1.5 units/ 0.5 ml	Physically compatible for 5 min at room temperature followed by 8 min of centrifugation	980	C
Metoclopramide HCl		2.5 mg/ 0.5 ml		1.5 units/ 0.5 ml	Physically compatible for 5 min at room temperature followed by 8 min of centrifugation	980	C
Mitomycin		0.25 mg/ 0.5 ml		1.5 units/ 0.5 ml	Physically compatible for 5 min at room temperature followed by 8 min of centrifugation	980	C
Vinblastine sulfate		0.5 mg/ 0.5 ml		1.5 units/ 0.5 ml	Physically compatible for 5 min at room temperature followed by 8 min of centrifugation	980	C
Vincristine sulfate		0.5 mg/ 0.5 ml		1.5 units/ 0.5 ml	Physically compatible for 5 min at room temperature followed by 8 min of centrifugation	980	C

Y-Site Injection Compatibility (1:1 Mixture)

Drug	Mfr	Conc	Mfr (Bleomycin sulfate)	Conc (Bleomycin sulfate)	Remarks	Ref	C/I
Allopurinol sodium	BW	3 mg/ml[b]	BR	1 unit/ml[b]	Physically compatible with no change in measured turbidity or increase in particle content in 4 hr at 22 °C	1686	C
Amifostine	USB	10 mg/ml[a]	MJ	1 unit/ml[b]	Physically compatible with no change in measured turbidity or increase in particle content in 4 hr at 23 °C	1845	C

Y-Site Injection Compatibility (1:1 Mixture) (Cont.)

Bleomycin sulfate

Drug	*Mfr*	*Conc*	*Mfr*	*Conc*	*Remarks*	*Ref*	*C/I*
Aztreonam	SQ	40 mg/ml[a]	MJ	1 unit/ml[b]	Physically compatible with no subvisual haze or particle formation in 4 hr at 23 °C	1758	C
Cefepime HCl	BMS	20 mg/ml[a]	BR	1 unit/ml[b]	Physically compatible with no change in measured turbidity or increase in particle content in 4 hr at 22 °C	1689	C
Cisplatin		1 mg/ml		3 units/ml	Drugs injected sequentially into Y-site with no flush between. No visually apparent precipitate forms	980	C
Cyclophosphamide		20 mg/ml		3 units/ml	Drugs injected sequentially into Y-site with no flush between. No visually apparent precipitate forms	980	C
Doxorubicin HCl		2 mg/ml		3 units/ml	Drugs injected sequentially into Y-site with no flush between. No visually apparent precipitate forms	980	C
Doxorubicin HCl liposome injection	SEQ	0.4 mg/ml[a]	MJ	1 unit/ml[b]	Physically compatible with little or no change in measured turbidity and no increase in particle content in 4 hr at 23 °C	2087	C
Droperidol		2.5 mg/ml		3 units/ml	Drugs injected sequentially into Y-site with no flush between. No visually apparent precipitate forms	980	C
Etoposide phosphate	BR	5 mg/ml[a]	MJ	1 unit/ml[b]	Physically compatible with no change in measured turbidity or increase in particle content in 4 hr at 23 °C	2218	C
Filgrastim	AMG	30 μg/ml[a]	BR	1 unit/ml[a]	Physically compatible with no change in measured turbidity or increase in particle content in 4 hr at 22 °C under fluorescent light	1687	C
Fludarabine phosphate	BX	1 mg/ml[a]	BR	1 unit/ml[b]	Physically compatible for 4 hr at room temperature under fluorescent light	1439	C
Fluorouracil		50 mg/ml		3 units/ml	Drugs injected sequentially into Y-site with no flush between. No visually apparent precipitate forms	980	C
Gemcitabine HCl	LI	10 mg/ml[b]	MJ	1 unit/ml[b]	Physically compatible with no change in measured turbidity or increase in particle content in 4 hr at 23 °C	2226	C
Granisetron HCl	SKB	0.05 mg/ml[a]	MJ	1 unit/ml[b]	Physically compatible with no change in measured turbidity or increase in particle content in 4 hr at 23 °C	2000	C
Heparin sodium		1000 units/ml		3 units/ml	Drugs injected sequentially into Y-site with no flush between. No visually apparent precipitate forms	980	C
Leucovorin calcium		10 mg/ml		3 units/ml	Drugs injected sequentially into Y-site with no flush between. No visually apparent precipitate forms	980	C
Melphalan HCl	BW	0.1 mg/ml[b]	BR	1 unit/ml[b]	Physically compatible with no change in measured turbidity or increase in particle content in 3 hr at 22 °C	1557	C

Y-Site Injection Compatibility (1:1 Mixture) (Cont.)

			Bleomycin sulfate				
Drug	*Mfr*	*Conc*	*Mfr*	*Conc*	*Remarks*	*Ref*	*C/I*
Methotrexate sodium		25 mg/ml		3 units/ml	Drugs injected sequentially into Y-site with no flush between. No visually apparent precipitate forms	980	C
Metoclopramide HCl		5 mg/ml		3 units/ml	Drugs injected sequentially into Y-site with no flush between. No visually apparent precipitate forms	980	C
Mitomycin		0.5 mg/ml		3 units/ml	Drugs injected sequentially into Y-site with no flush between. No visually apparent precipitate forms	980	C
Ondansetron HCl	GL	1 mg/ml[b]	BR	1 unit/ml[b]	Physically compatible for 4 hr at 22 °C	1365	C
Paclitaxel	NCI	1.2 mg/ml[a]	MJ	1 unit/ml[a]	Physically compatible with no change in measured turbidity in 4 hr at 22 °C	1556	C
Piperacillin sodium–tazobactam sodium	LE	40 + 5 mg/ml[a]	BR	1 unit/ml[b]	Physically compatible with no change in measured turbidity or increase in particle content in 4 hr at 22 °C	1688	C
Sargramostim	IMM	10 μg/ml[b]	MJ	1 unit/ml[b]	Physically compatible for 4 hr at 22 °C	1436	C
Teniposide	BR	0.1 mg/ml[a]	BR	1 unit/ml[b]	Physically compatible with no subvisual haze or particle formation in 4 hr at 23 °C	1725	C
Thiotepa	IMM[c]	1 mg/ml[a]	MJ	1 unit/ml[b]	Physically compatible with no change in measured turbidity or increase in particle content in 4 hr at 23 °C	1861	C
Vinblastine sulfate		1 mg/ml		3 units/ml	Drugs injected sequentially into Y-site with no flush between. No visually apparent precipitate forms	980	C
Vincristine sulfate		1 mg/ml		3 units/ml	Drugs injected sequentially into Y-site with no flush between. No visually apparent precipitate forms	980	C
Vinorelbine tartrate	BW	1 mg/ml[b]	BR	1 unit/ml[b]	Physically compatible with no change in measured turbidity or increase in particle content in 4 hr at 22 °C	1558	C

[a]*Tested in dextrose 5% in water.*
[b]*Tested in sodium chloride 0.9%.*
[c]*Lyophilized formulation tested.*

Additional Compatibility Information

Infusion Solutions — The manufacturer states that bleomycin sulfate is stable for 24 hours in sodium chloride 0.9% at room temperature. (See Stability.) Diluted in sodium chloride 0.9% to concentrations of 15 units/100 ml in PVC bags and 60 units/100 ml in polypropylene syringes, bleomycin sulfate lost 4 and 6%, respectively, in 28 days at room temperature in the dark. However, at a concentration of 15 units/100 ml in dextrose 5% in water, a 54% loss occurred in PVC bags in 28 days at room temperature in the dark. (1369)

Other Drugs — Bleomycin sulfate is inactivated in vitro by agents containing sulfhydryl groups, hydrogen peroxide, and ascorbic acid. (4)

No alteration in the ultraviolet/visible spectra was observed when dacarbazine was combined in solution with bleomycin sulfate. (492)

Aluminum — Ogawa et al. reported that immersion of a needle with an aluminum component in bleomycin sulfate (Bristol) 3 units/ml resulted in no visually apparent reaction after seven days at 24 °C. (988)

Other Information

Inactivation — In the event of spills or leaks, Bristol-Myers recommends the use of sodium hypochlorite 5% (household bleach) or potassium permanganate 1% to inactivate bleomycin sulfate. (1200)

BRETYLIUM TOSYLATE
AHFS 24:04

Products — Bretylium tosylate is available at a concentration of 50 mg/ml in 10-ml single-use vials and prefilled syringes. Hydrochloric acid or sodium hydroxide may be present to adjust the pH. (1-4/00; 29)

Bretylium tosylate is available premixed in dextrose 5% in water in concentrations of 2 and 4 mg/ml. (4)

pH — Injection: 3.5 to 7. (1-4/00) Premixed infusion: from 3 to 6.5. (4)

Osmolarity — Injection: approximately 241 mOsm/L. Premixed infusion: 2 mg/ml, 262 mOsm/L; and 4 mg/ml, 272 mOsm/L. (4)

Administration — Bretylium tosylate may be administered intramuscularly or intravenously. Bretylium tosylate injection should not be diluted for intramuscular injection, and no more than 5 ml should be administered at each site. Intramuscular injection sites should be rotated to avoid tissue damage. Bretylium tosylate is administered intravenously by direct injection or intermittent or continuous infusion after dilution to at least 50 ml in dextrose 5% in water or sodium chloride 0.9%. Infusion using a precision volume-control delivery device is preferred. The patient should be recumbent or closely observed for postural hypotension during administration. (1-4/00; 4)

Stability — The injection should be stored at controlled room temperature. The premixed infusion should be stored at room temperature and protected from freezing. Brief exposure to temperatures up to 40 °C does not adversely affect the products. Slight discoloration does not indicate potency loss. (4) Solutions of bretylium tosylate are stable over a pH range of 2 to 12. (607)

Compatibility Information

Solution Compatibility

Bretylium tosylate

Solution	*Mfr*	*Mfr*	*Conc/L*	*Remarks*	*Ref*	*C/I*
Dextrose 5% in Ringer's injection, lactated	MG[a], TR[b]	ACC	10 g	Physically compatible and chemically stable for 48 hr at room temperature and 7 days at 4 °C	541	C
Dextrose 5% in sodium chloride 0.45%	MG[a], TR[b]	ACC	10 g	Physically compatible and chemically stable for 48 hr at room temperature and 7 days at 4 °C	541	C
Dextrose 5% in sodium chloride 0.9%	MG[a], TR[b]	ACC	10 g	Physically compatible and chemically stable for 48 hr at room temperature and 7 days at 4 °C	541	C
Dextrose 5% in water	MG[a], TR[b]	ACC	10 g	Physically compatible and chemically stable for 48 hr at room temperature and 7 days at 4 °C	541	C
	AB[a]	ACC	1 g	Physically compatible and chemically stable for at least 48 hr (total study duration) at 25 °C	756	C
	AB[b]	ACC	1 g	Physically compatible and chemically stable for 30 days at 25 °C	756	C
	TR[b]	ES	1 g	Physically compatible with no loss in 24 hr at room temperature under fluorescent light	1358	C
Mannitol 20%	MG[a]	ACC	10 g	Physically compatible and chemically stable for 48 hr at room temperature. Mannitol crystallizes when refrigerated	541	C
Ringer's injection, lactated	MG[a], TR[b]	ACC	10 g	Physically compatible and chemically stable for 48 hr at room temperature and 7 days at 4 °C	541	C
	AB[a,b]	ACC	1 g	Physically compatible and chemically stable for 30 days at 25 °C	756	C
Sodium bicarbonate 5%	MG[a]	ACC	10 g	Physically compatible and chemically stable for 48 hr at room temperature and 7 days at 4 °C	541	C
Sodium chloride 0.9%	MG[a], TR[b]	ACC	10 g	Physically compatible and chemically stable for 48 hr at room temperature and 7 days at 4 °C	541	C
	CU[a], AB[b]	ACC	1 g	Physically compatible and chemically stable for 30 days at 25 °C	756	C
Sodium lactate ⅙ M	MG[a], TR[b]	ACC	10 g	Physically compatible and chemically stable for 48 hr at room temperature and 7 days at 4 °C	541	C

[a]*Tested in glass containers.*
[b]*Tested in PVC containers.*

Additive Compatibility

			Bretylium tosylate					
Drug	*Mfr*	*Conc/L*	*Mfr*	*Conc/L*	*Test Soln*	*Remarks*	*Ref*	*C/I*
Aminophylline	ES	1 g	ACC	1 g	D5W, NS	Physically compatible for 48 hr at 25 °C	756	C
Atracurium besylate	BW	500 mg		4 g	D5W	Physically compatible and atracurium chemically stable for 24 hr at 5 and 30 °C	1694	C
Calcium chloride	ES	54.4 mEq	ACC	10 g	D5W[a]	Physically compatible and bretylium chemically stable for 48 hr at room temperature and 7 days at 4 °C	541	C
Calcium gluconate	ES	2 g	ACC	1 g	D5W, NS	Physically compatible for 48 hr at 25 °C	756	C
Cibenzoline succinate		2 g	ACC	10 g	D5W, NS	Physically compatible for 24 hr at 25 °C by visual and microscopic examination	1182	C
Digoxin	BW	2 mg	ACC	1 g	D5W, NS	Physically compatible for 48 hr at 25 °C	756	C
Dobutamine HCl	LI	1 g	ACC	2 g	D5W, NS	Slightly pink in 24 hr at 25 °C	789	I
	LI	1 g	ACC	4 and 25 g	D5W, NS	Physically compatible for 24 hr at 21 °C	812	C
Dopamine HCl	ACC	800 mg	ACC	10 g	D5S[a]	Physically compatible and both drugs chemically stable for 48 hr at room temperature and 7 days at 4 °C	522	C
Esmolol HCl	DU	6 g	ES	1 g	D5W	Physically compatible with no loss of either drug in 24 hr at room temperature	1358	C
Insulin, regular	SQ	1000 units	ACC	1 g	D5W, NS	Physically compatible for 48 hr at 25 °C	756	C
Lidocaine HCl	AST	1 g	ACC	10 g	D5S[a]	Physically compatible and both drugs chemically stable for 48 hr at room temperature and 7 days at 4 °C	522	C
	AST	2 g	ACC	1 g	D5W, NS	Physically compatible for 48 hr at 25 °C	756	C
	AST	2 g	AS	1 g	D5W, LR, NS	Physically compatible for 24 hr at 25 °C	775	C
Nitroglycerin	ACC	100 mg	ACC	10 g	D5S[b]	Physically compatible and bretylium chemically stable for 48 hr at room temperature and 7 days at 4 °C. 40% loss of nitroglycerin at room temperature and 10% at 4 °C in 24 hr due to sorption to PVC	522	I
	ACC	100 mg	ACC	10 g	D5S[c]	Physically compatible and both drugs chemically stable for 48 hr at room temperature and 7 days at 4 °C	522	C
	ACC	400 mg	ACC	10 g	D5W, NS[c]	Physically compatible with little or no nitroglycerin loss in 48 hr at 23 °C. Bretylium not tested	929	C
Phenytoin sodium	PD	2 g	ACC	1 g	D5W, NS	Immediate precipitation	756	I
Potassium chloride	AB	40 mEq	ACC	10 g	D5W[a]	Physically compatible and bretylium chemically stable for 48 hr at room temperature and 7 days at 4 °C	541	C
Procainamide HCl	SQ	4 g	ACC	10 g	D5S[a]	Physically compatible and bretylium chemically stable for 48 hr at room temperature. Approximately 14% procainamide loss in 24 hr at room temperature	522	I

Additive Compatibility (Cont.)

Bretylium tosylate

Drug	*Mfr*	*Conc/L*	*Mfr*	*Conc/L*	*Test Soln*	*Remarks*	*Ref*	*C/I*
	SQ	4 g	ACC	10 g	D5S[a]	Physically compatible and bretylium chemically stable for 7 days at 4 °C. Approximately 7% procainamide loss in 24 hr at 4 °C	522	C
	SQ	1 g	ACC	1 g	D5W, NS	Physically compatible for 48 hr at 25 °C	756	C
Quinidine gluconate	LI	800 mg	ACC	1 g	D5W, NS	Physically compatible for 48 hr at 25 °C	756	C
Verapamil HCl	KN	80 mg	ACC	2 g	D5W, NS	Physically compatible for 48 hr	739	C

[a]*Tested in both glass and PVC containers.*
[b]*Tested in PVC containers.*
[c]*Tested in glass containers.*

Y-Site Injection Compatibility (1:1 Mixture)

Bretylium tosylate

Drug	*Mfr*	*Conc*	*Mfr*	*Conc*	*Remarks*	*Ref*	*C/I*
Amiodarone HCl	LZ	4 mg/ml[c]	ACC	8 mg/ml[c]	Physically compatible for 24 hr at 21 °C	1032	C
Amphotericin B cholesteryl sulfate complex	SEQ	0.83 mg/ml[a]	AST	50 mg/ml	Gross precipitate forms	2117	I
Cisatracurium besylate	GW	0.1, 2, 5 mg/ml[a]	AST	4 mg/ml[a]	Physically compatible with no change in measured turbidity or increase in particle content in 4 hr at 23 °C	2074	C
Diltiazem HCl	MMD	5 mg/ml	DU	10[b] and 50 mg/ml	Visually compatible	1807	C
	MMD	1 mg/ml[b]	DU	50 mg/ml	Visually compatible	1807	C
Dobutamine HCl	LI	4 mg/ml[c]	LY	4 mg/ml[c]	Physically compatible for 3 hr	1316	C
Famotidine	MSD	0.2 mg/ml[a]	AB	4 mg/ml[a]	Physically compatible for 4 hr at 25 °C	1188	C
Gatifloxacin	BMS	2 mg/ml[a]	AST	50 mg/ml	Physically compatible with no change in measured haze or increase in particle content in 4 hr at 23 °C	2234	C
Inamrinone lactate	WB	3 mg/ml[b]	ACC	10 mg/ml[a]	Physically compatible for at least 4 hr at 25 °C under fluorescent light	992	C
Isoproterenol HCl	ES	0.032 mg/ml[c]	LY	4 mg/ml[c]	Physically compatible for 3 hr	1316	C
Linezolid	PHU	2 mg/ml	AST	50 mg/ml	Physically compatible with no change in measured turbidity or increase in particle content in 4 hr at 23 °C	2264	C
Propofol	ZEN	10 mg/ml	AST	50 mg/ml	Emulsion broke and oiled out	2066	I
Ranitidine HCl	GL	0.5 mg/ml[d]	LY	4 mg/ml[a]	Physically compatible for 24 hr	1323	C
Remifentanil HCl	GW	0.025 and 0.25 mg/ml[b]	AST	4 mg/ml[a]	Physically compatible with no change in measured turbidity or increase in particle content in 4 hr at 23 °C	2075	C
Warfarin sodium	DU	2 mg/ml[e]	FAU	10 mg/ml[a]	Haze forms immediately	2010	I
	DME	2 mg/ml[e]	DU	10 mg/ml[a]	Haze forms immediately	2078	I

[a]*Tested in dextrose 5% in water.*
[b]*Tested in sodium chloride 0.9%.*
[c]*Tested in dextrose 5% in water and sodium chloride 0.9%.*
[d]*Premixed infusion solution.*
[e]*Tested in sterile water for injection.*

BUMETANIDE
AHFS 40:28

Products — Bumetanide is available as a 0.25-mg/ml solution in 2-, 4-, and 10-ml vials. The solution also contains sodium chloride 0.85%, ammonium acetate 0.4%, disodium edetate 0.01%, and benzyl alcohol 1% with sodium hydroxide to adjust the pH. (1-12/98; 4)

pH — Adjusted to 6.8 to 7.8. (4)

Osmolality — Bumetanide 0.25 mg/ml has an osmolality of 453 mOsm/kg. (1689)

Trade Name(s) — Bumex.

Administration — Bumetanide is administered by intramuscular injection, direct intravenous injection over one to two minutes, and by intravenous infusion. (1-12/98; 4)

Stability — Bumetanide discolors when exposed to light. The injection should be stored at controlled room temperature and protected from light. Bumetanide is reported to be stable at pH 4 to 10. (4) Precipitation may occur at pH values less than 4. (1644)

Sorption — Substantial sorption to glass and PVC containers does not occur. (1-12/98; 4)

Bumetanide (Roche) at a low concentration of 0.02 mg/ml in PVC containers of dextrose 5% in water exhibited 4 to 5% loss by HPLC analysis within three hours of mixing. No further loss of drug occurred during storage for 72 hours at 24 °C under fluorescent light. A 10-fold higher concentration exhibited little or no loss under the same conditions. The authors postulated that a small amount of bumetanide loss due to sorption to the PVC might be occurring, although this was not confirmed. (2090)

Central Venous Catheter — Bumetanide (Ohmeda) 0.04 mg/ml in dextrose 5% in water was found to be compatible with the ARROWg+ard Blue Plus (Arrow International) chlorhexidine-bearing triple-lumen central catheter. HPLC analysis was used to evaluate completeness of drug delivery through the catheter and the amount of chlorhexidine removed from the internal lumens. Essentially complete delivery of the drug was found with little or no drug loss occurring. Furthermore, chlorhexidine delivered from the catheter remained at trace amounts with no substantial increase due to the delivery of the drug through the catheter. (2335)

Compatibility Information

Solution Compatibility

Bumetanide

Solution	*Mfr*	*Mfr*	*Conc/L*	*Remarks*	*Ref*	*C/I*
Dextrose 5% in water	AB[a]	RC	20 mg	4 to 5% loss by HPLC occurs within 3 hr with no further loss throughout 72 hr at 24 °C under fluorescent light	2090	C
	AB[a]	RC	200 mg	Little or no loss by HPLC occurs within 72 hr at 24 °C under fluorescent light	2090	C

[a]*Tested in PVC containers.*

Additive Compatibility

Bumetanide

Drug	*Mfr*	*Conc/L*	*Mfr*	*Conc/L*	*Test Soln*	*Remarks*	*Ref*	*C/I*
Dobutamine HCl	LI	1 g	RC	125 mg	D5W, NS	Immediate yellow discoloration with yellow precipitate within 6 hr at 21 °C	812	I
Floxacillin sodium	BE	20 g	LEO	6 mg	NS	Physically compatible for 72 hr at 15 and 30 °C	1479	C
Furosemide	HO	1 g	LEO	6 mg	NS	Physically compatible for 72 hr at 15 and 30 °C	1479	C

Drugs in Syringe Compatibility

Bumetanide

Drug (in syringe)	*Mfr*	*Amt*	*Mfr*	*Amt*	*Remarks*	*Ref*	*C/I*
Doxapram HCl	RB	400 mg/ 20 ml		0.5 mg/ 1 ml	Physically compatible with 3% doxapram loss in 24 hr	1177	C

Y-Site Injection Compatibility (1:1 Mixture)

			Bumetanide				
Drug	*Mfr*	*Conc*	*Mfr*	*Conc*	*Remarks*	*Ref*	*C/I*
Allopurinol sodium	BW	3 mg/ml[b]	RC	0.04 mg/ml[b]	Physically compatible with no change in measured turbidity or increase in particle content in 4 hr at 22 °C	1686	C
Amifostine	USB	10 mg/ml[a]	RC	0.04 mg/ml[a]	Physically compatible with no change in measured turbidity or increase in particle content in 4 hr at 23 °C	1845	C
Aztreonam	SQ	40 mg/ml[a]	RC	0.04 mg/ml[a]	Physically compatible with no subvisual haze or particle formation in 4 hr at 23 °C	1758	C
Cefepime HCl	BMS	20 mg/ml[a]	RC	0.04 mg/ml[a]	Physically compatible with no change in measured turbidity or increase in particle content in 4 hr at 22 °C	1689	C
Cisatracurium besylate	GW	0.1, 2, 5 mg/ml[a]	BV	0.04 mg/ml[a]	Physically compatible with no change in measured turbidity or increase in particle content in 4 hr at 23 °C	2074	C
Cladribine	ORT	0.015[b] and 0.5[c] mg/ml	RC	0.04 mg/ml[b]	Physically compatible with no change in measured turbidity or increase in particle content in 4 hr at 23 °C	1969	C
Clarithromycin	AB	4 mg/ml[a]	LEO	0.5 mg/ml	Visually compatible for 72 hr at both 30 and 17 °C	2174	C
Diltiazem HCl	MMD	1[b] and 5 mg/ml	RC	0.25 mg/ml	Visually compatible	1807	C
Docetaxel	RPR	0.9 mg/ml[a]	RC	0.04 mg/ml[a]	Physically compatible with no change in measured turbidity or increase in particle content in 4 hr at 23 °C	2224	C
Etoposide phosphate	BR	5 mg/ml[a]	RC	0.04 mg/ml[a]	Physically compatible with no change in measured turbidity or increase in particle content in 4 hr at 23 °C	2218	C
Filgrastim	AMG	30 μg/ml[a]	RC	0.04 mg/ml[a]	Physically compatible with no change in measured turbidity or increase in particle content in 4 hr at 22 °C	1687	C
Gemcitabine HCl	LI	10 mg/ml[b]	RC	0.04 mg/ml[b]	Physically compatible with no change in measured turbidity or increase in particle content in 4 hr at 23 °C	2226	C
Granisetron HCl	SKB	0.05 mg/ml[a]	RC	0.04 mg/ml[a]	Physically compatible with no change in measured turbidity or increase in particle content in 4 hr at 23 °C	2000	C
Hetastarch in lactated electrolyte injection (Hextend)	AB	6%	OH	0.04 mg/ml[a]	Physically compatible with no change in measured turbidity or increase in particle content in 4 hr at 23 °C	2339	C
Lorazepam	WY	0.33 mg/ml[b]	LEO	0.5 mg/ml	Visually compatible for 24 hr at 22 °C	1855	C
Melphalan HCl	BW	0.1 mg/ml[b]	RC	0.04 mg/ml[b]	Physically compatible with no change in measured turbidity or increase in particle content in 3 hr at 22 °C	1557	C
Meperidine HCl	AB	10 mg/ml	RC	0.25 mg/ml	Physically compatible for 4 hr at 25 °C	1397	C
Midazolam HCl	RC	5 mg/ml	LEO	0.5 mg/ml	White precipitate forms immediately	1855	I
Milrinone lactate	SW	0.4 mg/ml[a]	RC	0.25 mg/ml	Visually compatible with little or no loss of either drug by HPLC in 4 hr at 23 °C	2214	C

Y-Site Injection Compatibility (1:1 Mixture) (Cont.)

Bumetanide

Drug	*Mfr*	*Conc*	*Mfr*	*Conc*	*Remarks*	*Ref*	*C/I*
Morphine sulfate	AB	1 mg/ml	RC	0.25 mg/ml	Physically compatible for 4 hr at 25 °C	1397	C
Piperacillin sodium–tazobactam sodium	LE	40 + 5 mg/ml[a]	RC	0.04 mg/ml[a]	Physically compatible with no change in measured turbidity or increase in particle content in 4 hr at 22 °C	1688	C
Propofol	ZEN	10 mg/ml	RC	0.04 mg/ml[a]	Physically compatible for 1 hr at 23 °C with no increase in particle content	2066	C
Remifentanil HCl	GW	0.025 and 0.25 mg/ml[b]	RC	0.04 mg/ml[a]	Physically compatible with no change in measured turbidity or increase in particle content in 4 hr at 23 °C	2075	C
Teniposide	BR	0.1 mg/ml[a]	RC	0.04 mg/ml[a]	Physically compatible with no subvisual haze or particle formation in 4 hr at 23 °C	1725	C
Thiotepa	IMM[d]	1 mg/ml[a]	RC	0.04 mg/ml[a]	Physically compatible with no change in measured turbidity or increase in particle content in 4 hr at 23 °C	1861	C
TNA #218 to #226[e]			RC, BV	0.04 mg/ml[a]	Visually compatible with no precipitate or emulsion damage apparent in 4 hr at 23 °C	2215	C
TPN #212 to #215[e]			RC	0.04 mg/ml[a]	Physically compatible with no change in measured turbidity or increase in particle content in 4 hr at 23 °C	2109	C
Vinorelbine tartrate	BW	1 mg/ml[b]	RC	0.04 mg/ml[b]	Physically compatible with no change in measured turbidity or increase in particle content in 4 hr at 22 °C	1558	C

[a]Tested in dextrose 5% in water.
[b]Tested in sodium chloride 0.9%.
[c]Tested in bacteriostatic sodium chloride 0.9% preserved with benzyl alcohol 0.9%.
[d]Lyophilized formulation tested.
[e]Refer to Appendix I for the composition of parenteral nutrition solutions. TNA indicates a 3-in-1 admixture, and TPN indicates a 2-in-1 admixture.

Additional Compatibility Information

Infusion Solutions — Bumetanide is stated to be physically and chemically compatible in glass or PVC containers of dextrose 5% in water, sodium chloride 0.9%, and Ringer's injection, lactated, for at least 24 hours. (2; 4)

Milrinone — Bumetanide may precipitate if mixed with milrinone lactate infusions. (1442)

BUPIVACAINE HCL
AHFS 72:00

Products — Bupivacaine HCl is available in concentrations of 0.25, 0.5, and 0.75% (2.5, 5, and 7.5 mg/ml, respectively) in single-dose containers. The 0.25 and 0.5% concentrations also come in 50-ml multiple-dose vials with methylparaben 1 mg/ml as a preservative. Sodium hydroxide or hydrochloric acid is used to adjust the pH. (2)

Bupivacaine HCl is also available in concentrations of 0.25, 0.5, and 0.75% with epinephrine 1:200,000 as the bitartrate. In addition to bupivacaine HCl, each milliliter contains epinephrine bitartrate 0.005 mg, sodium metabisulfite 0.5 mg, and citric acid 0.2 mg. Multiple-dose vials contain methylparaben 1 mg/ml as a preservative while single-dose containers are preservative free. Sodium hydroxide or hydrochloric acid is used to adjust the pH. (2)

A hyperbaric solution of bupivacaine HCl is available in 2-ml ampuls. Each milliliter contains bupivacaine HCl 7.5 mg and dextrose 82.5 mg (8.25%) with sodium hydroxide or hydrochloric acid to adjust the pH. (4; 29)

pH — Bupivacaine HCl injection and the hyperbaric solution have a pH of 4 to 6.5. Bupivacaine HCl with epinephrine 1:200,000 has a pH of 3.3 to 5.5. (2; 4)

Specific Gravity — The hyperbaric solution has a specific gravity of 1.030 to 1.035 at 25 °C and 1.03 at 37 °C. (4)

Trade Name(s)—Marcaine, Sensorcaine, Sensorcaine-MPF.

Administration— Bupivacaine HCl may be administered by infiltration or by epidural, spinal, or peripheral or sympathetic nerve block as a single injection or repeat injections. Injections should be made slowly, with frequent aspirations, to guard against intravascular injection. Products containing preservatives should not be used for epidural or caudal block. (2; 4)

Stability— Bupivacaine HCl injections should be stored at controlled room temperature; freezing should be avoided. (2; 4) Products containing epinephrine should be protected from light during storage. Partially used containers that do not contain antibacterial preservatives should be discarded after entry. (4)

Bupivacaine HCl without epinephrine and the hyperbaric solution may be autoclaved at 121 °C and 15 psi for 15 minutes. Products containing epinephrine should not be autoclaved. (4)

Bupivacaine HCl with epinephrine should not be used if a pinkish color, a color darker than "slightly" yellow, or a precipitate develops. (4)

Syringes—The stability of bupivacaine (salt form unspecified) 5 mg/ml repackaged in polypropylene syringes was evaluated by spectrophotometric and potentiometric methods. Little or no change in concentration was found after four weeks of storage at room temperature not exposed to direct light. (2164)

Ambulatory Pumps—Bupivacaine HCl (Astra) 7.5 mg/ml was filled into 50-ml ambulatory pump cassette reservoirs (Pharmacia Deltec) and stored at room temperature protected from light for 90 days. HPLC analysis found no loss of the drug. Instead, the drug concentration increased 12% during the observation period, possibly because of loss of water from the solutions. (1850)

Bupivacaine HCl 5 mg/ml in sodium chloride 0.9% in CADD cassettes (Sims Deltec) has been stated by the pump manufacturer to be stable for seven days at room temperature and under refrigeration. Bupivacaine HCl 1.25 mg/ml in sodium chloride 0.9% has been stated to be stable for seven days under refrigeration but four days at room temperature. (31)

Elastomeric Reservoir Pumps—Bupivacaine HCl 0.6 mg/ml solutions in dextrose 5% in water or sodium chloride 0.9% in an Infusor elastomeric reservoir pump has been stated by the pump manufacturer to be stable for 30 days at room temperature. At a concentration of 7.5 mg/ml, the drug solution is stated to be stable for 14 days at room temperature and 180 days under refrigeration. (31)

Compatibility Information

Solution Compatibility

Bupivacaine HCl

Solution	*Mfr*	*Mfr*	*Conc/L*	*Remarks*	*Ref*	*C/I*
Sodium chloride 0.9%	AB	AST	1.25 g	Visually compatible with no bupivacaine loss by HPLC in 32 days at 3 °C in the dark and 23 °C exposed to light when stored in polypropylene syringes	1718	C
	AB[a]	AB	625 mg and 1.25 g	Visually compatible with little or no bupivacaine loss by HPLC in 72 hr at 24 °C under fluorescent light	1870; 2058	C
	GRI[a]		850 mg	No change in concentration by UV spectroscopy in 28 days at 4 °C and room temperature	1910	C

[a]*Tested in PVC containers.*

Additive Compatibility

Bupivacaine HCl

Drug	*Mfr*	*Conc/L*	*Mfr*	*Conc/L*	*Test Soln*	*Remarks*	*Ref*	*C/I*
Buprenorphine HCl	RC	180 mg	AST	3 g	[a]	Little or no loss of either drug by HPLC in 30 days at 18 °C	1932	C
Diamorphine HCl		0.125 g	GL	1.25 g	NS	Visually compatible with 8% diamorphine loss and no bupivacaine loss by HPLC in 28 days at room temperature	1791	C
	NAP	20 mg	AST	150 mg	NS[c]	5% diamorphine and no bupivacaine loss by HPLC in 14 days at 7 °C. Both drugs were stable for 6 months at −20 °C	2070	C
Fentanyl citrate	JN	20 mg	WI	1.25 g	NS[a]	Physically compatible with little or no loss of either drug in 30 days at 3 and 23 °C	1396	C

Additive Compatibility (Cont.)

Bupivacaine HCl

Drug	Mfr	Conc/L	Mfr	Conc/L	Test Soln	Remarks	Ref	C/I
		2 mg		1.25 g	NS[a]	Physically compatible with no bupivacaine loss and about 6 to 7% fentanyl loss by HPLC in 30 days at both 4 and 23 °C	2305	C
		2 mg		600 mg	NS[a]	Physically compatible with no bupivacaine loss and about 2 to 4% fentanyl loss by HPLC in 30 days at both 4 and 23 °C	2305	C
Hydromorphone HCl	KN	20 mg	AB	625 mg and 1.25 g	NS[a]	Visually compatible with little or no loss of either drug by HPLC in 72 hr at 24 °C under fluorescent light	1870	C
	KN	100 mg	AB	625 mg and 1.25 g	NS[a]	Visually compatible with little or no loss of either drug by HPLC in 72 hr at 24 °C under fluorescent light	1870	C
Morphine HCl		140 and 190 mg		850 mg	NS[a]	No change in concentration by UV spectroscopy in 28 days at 4 °C and room temperature	1910	C
Morphine sulfate		1 g	AST	3 g	[a]	Little or no loss of either drug by HPLC in 30 days at 18 °C	1932	C
	SCN	100 mg	AB	625 mg and 1.25 g	NS[a]	Visually compatible with no loss of either drug by HPLC in 72 hr at 24 °C under fluorescent light	2058	C
	SCN	500 mg	AB	625 mg and 1.25 g	NS[a]	Visually compatible with no loss of either drug by HPLC in 72 hr at 24 °C under fluorescent light	2058	C
Sufentanil citrate	JN	5 mg	AST	2 g	D5W[b]	9% sufentanil loss and 5% bupivacaine loss by HPLC in 30 days at 32 °C. Little or no loss of either drug in 30 days at 4 °C	1756	C
	JN	20 mg		3 g	NS[b]	5% sufentanil loss and no bupivacaine loss by HPLC in 10 days at 5, 26, and 37 °C	1751	C

[a]Tested in PVC containers.
[b]Tested in PVC/Kalex 3000 (phthalate ester) CADD pump reservoirs.
[c]Tested in PVC containers.

Drugs in Syringe Compatibility

Bupivacaine HCl

Drug (in syringe)	Mfr	Amt	Mfr	Amt	Remarks	Ref	C/I
Clonidine HCl with morphine sulfate	BI ES	0.03 mg/ml 0.2 mg/ml	SW	1.5 mg/ml	Diluted to 5 ml with NS. Visually compatible with no new GC/MS peaks appearing in 1 hr at room temperature	1956	C
Diamorphine HCl	EV	1 and 10 mg/ml	AST	0.5%	10 to 11% diamorphine loss by HPLC in 5 weeks at 20 °C and 3 to 7% loss in 8 weeks at 6 °C. Little or no bupivacaine loss at 6 or 20 °C in 8 weeks	1952	C
Fentanyl citrate with ketamine HCl	JN PD	0.01 mg/ml 2 mg/ml	SW	1.5 mg/ml	Diluted to 5 ml with NS. Visually compatible with no new GC/MS peaks appearing in 1 hr at room temperature	1956	C
Hydromorphone HCl	KN	65 mg/ml	AST	7.5 mg/ml	Visually compatible for 30 days at 25 °C	1660	C

Drugs in Syringe Compatibility (Cont.)

Bupivacaine HCl

Drug (in syringe)	*Mfr*	*Amt*	*Mfr*	*Amt*	*Remarks*	*Ref*	*C/I*
Iohexol		1 ml	AST	0.25 and 0.125%[a]/ 4 ml	Visually compatible with no bupivacaine loss by HPLC in 24 hr at room temperature. Iohexol not tested	1611	C
Morphine sulfate		1 mg/ml	AST	3 mg/ml	Little or no loss of either drug in 30 days at 18 °C	1932	C
Sodium bicarbonate	AB	4%, 0.05 to 0.6 ml	AST, WI	0.25, 0.5[b], 0.75%[b], 20 ml	Precipitate forms in 1 to 2 min up to 2 hr at lowest amount of bicarbonate	1724	I
		1.4%, 1.5 ml	BEL	0.5%[c], 20 ml	Little or no epinephrine loss by HPLC in 7 days at room temperature. Bupivacaine not tested	1743	C
		4.2 and 8.4%, 1.5 ml	BEL	0.5%[c], 20 ml	5 to 7% epinephrine loss by HPLC in 7 days at room temperature. Bupivacaine not tested	1743	C

[a]*Diluted 1:1 in sodium chloride 0.9%.*
[b]*Tested with and without epinephrine HCl 1:200,000 added.*
[c]*Tested with epinephrine HCl 1:200,000 added.*

Additional Compatibility Information

Epinephrine and Fentanyl — A solution composed of bupivacaine HCl (Winthrop) 0.44 mg/ml, fentanyl citrate (Janssen) 1.25 μg/ml, and epinephrine HCl (Abbott) 0.69 μg/ml was stored in 100-ml portable infusion pump reservoirs (Pharmacia Deltec) for 30 days at 3 and 23 °C. The samples were then delivered through the infusion pumps over 48 hours at near-body temperature (30 °C). The samples were visually compatible throughout, and bupivacaine HCl and fentanyl citrate exhibited no loss by HPLC analysis. Epinephrine HCl sustained about a 5 to 6% loss by HPLC analysis after 20 days of storage at both temperatures and about a 9 to 10% loss after 30 days of storage and subsequent pump delivery. The authors recommended restricting storage before administration to only 20 days. (1627)

Clonidine HCl — Clonidine HCl (Fujisawa) 100 μg/ml and bupivacaine HCl (Sanofi Winthrop) 7.5 mg/ml were mixed in ratios of 1:1 and 1:8 to provide final concentrations of (1:1) clonidine HCl 50 μg/ml and bupivacaine HCl 3.75 mg/ml and (1:8) clonidine HCl 11.11 μg/ml and bupivacaine HCl 6.67 mg/ml. The combinations were transferred to flint glass vials with rubber stoppers and stored for 14 days at controlled room temperature protected from light. The solutions remained clear and colorless with no increase in particulate content. HPLC analysis found little or no change in concentration for either drug during the study period. (2069)

Multiple Drugs — A seven-drug combination consisting of bupivacaine HCl (Sanofi Winthrop) 1.5 mg/ml, clonidine HCl (Boehringer Ingelheim) 0.03 mg/ml, fentanyl citrate (Janssen) 0.01 mg/ml, ketamine HCl (Parke-Davis) 2 mg/ml, lidocaine HCl (Astra) 2 mg/ml, morphine sulfate (Elkins-Sinn) 0.2 mg/ml, and tetracaine HCl (Sanofi Winthrop) 2 mg/ml mixed together in equal volumes was found to be visually compatible with no new GC/MS peaks appearing in one hour at room temperature. (1956)

Clonidine HCl (Boehringer) 30 μg/ml, bupivacaine HCl (Astra) 3 mg/ml, and morphine HCl (Merck) 6.66 mg/ml were combined in 50-ml ambulatory pump cassette reservoirs (Pharmacia Deltec). The reservoirs were stored at room temperature and protected from light for 90 days. HPLC analysis found no loss of any of the drugs. Instead, drug concentrations increased 12 to 16% during the observation period, possibly because of loss of water from the solutions. (1850)

BUPRENORPHINE HCL
AHFS 28:08.12

Products — Buprenorphine HCl is available in 1-ml ampuls. Each milliliter contains buprenorphine 0.3 mg (as the hydrochloride) with anhydrous dextrose 50 mg in water for injection. The pH is adjusted with hydrochloric acid. (2)

pH — From 3.5 to 5.5. (4)

Osmolality — The osmolality of buprenorphine HCl was determined to be 297 mOsm/kg by osmometer. (1233)

Trade Name(s) — Buprenex.

Administration — Buprenorphine HCl is administered by deep intramuscular injection or by intravenous injection slowly over at least two minutes. (2; 4) It has also been given by continuous intravenous infusion at a concentration of 15 μg/ml in sodium chloride 0.9% and by epidural injection at a concentration of 6 to 30 μg/ml. (4)

Stability — The clear solution should be stored at 15 to 30 °C and protected from prolonged exposure to light and exposure to temperatures in excess of 40 °C and freezing. (2; 4) Buprenorphine HCl may undergo substantial decomposition when autoclaved. (4)

Central Venous Catheter — Buprenorphine HCl (Reckitt & Colman) 0.04 mg/ml in dextrose 5% in water was found to be compatible with the ARROWg+ard Blue Plus (Arrow International) chlorhexidine-bearing triple-lumen central catheter. HPLC analysis was used to evaluate completeness of drug delivery through the catheter and the amount of chlorhexidine removed from the internal lumens. Essentially complete delivery of the drug was found with little or no drug loss occurring. Furthermore, chlorhexidine delivered from the catheter remained at trace amounts with no substantial increase due to the delivery of the drug through the catheter. (2335)

Compatibility Information

Additive Compatibility

			Buprenorphine HCl					
Drug	*Mfr*	*Conc/L*	*Mfr*	*Conc/L*	*Test Soln*	*Remarks*	*Ref*	*C/I*
Bupivacaine HCl	AST	3 g	RC	180 mg	[a]	Little or no loss of either drug by HPLC in 30 days at 18 °C	1932	C
Floxacillin sodium	BE	20 g		75 mg	W	Thick haze forms in 24 hr and precipitate forms in 47 hr at 30 °C. No change at 15 °C	1479	I
Furosemide	HO	1 g		75 mg	W	Haze for 6 hr at 30 °C. No change at 15 °C	1479	I

[a]*Tested in PVC containers.*

Drugs in Syringe Compatibility

			Buprenorphine HCl				
Drug (in syringe)	*Mfr*	*Amt*	*Mfr*	*Amt*	*Remarks*	*Ref*	*C/I*
Heparin sodium		2500 units/ 1 ml	BM	300 mg/ 1 ml	Visually compatible for at least 5 min	1053	C
Midazolam HCl	RC	5 mg/ 1 ml	NE	0.3 mg/ 1 ml	Physically compatible for 4 hr at 25 °C	1145	C

Y-Site Injection Compatibility (1:1 Mixture)

			Buprenorphine HCl				
Drug	*Mfr*	*Conc*	*Mfr*	*Conc*	*Remarks*	*Ref*	*C/I*
Allopurinol sodium	BW	3 mg/ml[b]	RKC	0.04 mg/ml[b]	Physically compatible with no change in measured turbidity or increase in particle content in 4 hr at 22 °C	1686	C
Amifostine	USB	10 mg/ml[a]	RKC	0.04 mg/ml[a]	Physically compatible with no change in measured turbidity or increase in particle content in 4 hr at 23 °C	1845	C
Amphotericin B cholesteryl sulfate complex	SEQ	0.83 mg/ml[a]	RKC	0.04 mg/ml[a]	Microprecipitate forms in 4 hr	2117	I
Aztreonam	SQ	40 mg/ml[a]	RKC	0.04 mg/ml[a]	Physically compatible with no subvisual haze or particle formation in 4 hr at 23 °C	1758	C
Cefepime HCl	BMS	20 mg/ml[a]	RKC	0.04 mg/ml[a]	Physically compatible with no change in measured turbidity or increase in particle content in 4 hr at 22 °C	1689	C

Y-Site Injection Compatibility (1:1 Mixture) (Cont.)

			Buprenorphine HCl				
Drug	*Mfr*	*Conc*	*Mfr*	*Conc*	*Remarks*	*Ref*	*C/I*
Cisatracurium besylate	GW	0.1, 2, 5 mg/ml[a]	RKC	0.04 mg/ml[a]	Physically compatible with no change in measured turbidity or increase in particle content in 4 hr at 23 °C	2074	C
Cladribine	ORT	0.015[b] and 0.5[c] mg/ml	RKC	0.04 mg/ml[b]	Physically compatible with no change in measured turbidity or increase in particle content in 4 hr at 23 °C	1969	C
Docetaxel	RPR	0.9 mg/ml[a]	RKC	0.04 mg/ml[a]	Physically compatible with no change in measured turbidity or increase in particle content in 4 hr at 23 °C	2224	C
Doxorubicin HCl liposome injection	SEQ	0.4 mg/ml[a]	RKC	0.04 mg/ml[a]	Partial loss of measured natural turbidity	2087	I
Etoposide phosphate	BR	5 mg/ml[a]	RKC	0.04 mg/ml[a]	Physically compatible with no change in measured turbidity or increase in particle content in 4 hr at 23 °C	2218	C
Filgrastim	AMG	30 μg/ml[a]	RKC	0.04 mg/ml[a]	Physically compatible with no change in measured turbidity or increase in particle content in 4 hr at 22 °C	1687	C
Gatifloxacin	BMS	2 mg/ml[a]	RKC	0.04 mg/ml[a]	Physically compatible with no change in measured haze or increase in particle content in 4 hr at 23 °C	2234	C
Gemcitabine HCl	LI	10 mg/ml[b]	RKC	0.04 mg/ml[b]	Physically compatible with no change in measured turbidity or increase in particle content in 4 hr at 23 °C	2226	C
Granisetron HCl	SKB	0.05 mg/ml[a]	RKC	0.04 mg/ml[a]	Physically compatible with no change in measured turbidity or increase in particle content in 4 hr at 23 °C	2000	C
Linezolid	PHU	2 mg/ml	RKC	0.04 mg/ml[a]	Physically compatible with no change in measured turbidity or increase in particle content in 4 hr at 23 °C	2264	C
Melphalan HCl	BW	0.1 mg/ml[b]	RKC	0.04 mg/ml[b]	Physically compatible with no change in measured turbidity or increase in particle content in 3 hr at 22 °C	1557	C
Piperacillin sodium–tazobactam sodium	LE	40 + 5 mg/ml[a]	RKC	0.04 mg/ml[a]	Physically compatible with no change in measured turbidity or increase in particle content in 4 hr at 22 °C	1688	C
Propofol	ZEN	10 mg/ml	RKC	0.04 mg/ml[a]	Physically compatible for 1 hr at 23 °C with no increase in particle content	2066	C
Remifentanil HCl	GW	0.025 and 0.25 mg/ml[b]	RKC	0.04 mg/ml[a]	Physically compatible with no change in measured turbidity or increase in particle content in 4 hr at 23 °C	2075	C
Teniposide	BR	0.1 mg/ml[a]	RKC	0.04 mg/ml[a]	Physically compatible with no subvisual haze or particle formation in 4 hr at 23 °C	1725	C
Thiotepa	IMM[d]	1 mg/ml[a]	RKC	0.04 mg/ml[a]	Physically compatible with no change in measured turbidity or increase in particle content in 4 hr at 23 °C	1861	C

Y-Site Injection Compatibility (1:1 Mixture) (Cont.)

Buprenorphine HCl

Drug	Mfr	Conc	Mfr	Conc	Remarks	Ref	C/I
TNA #218 to #226[e]			RKC	0.04 mg/ml[a]	Visually compatible with no precipitate or emulsion damage apparent in 4 hr at 23 °C	2215	C
TPN #212 to #215[e]			RKC	0.04 mg/ml[a]	Physically compatible with no change in measured turbidity or increase in particle content in 4 hr at 23 °C	2109	C
Vinorelbine tartrate	BW	1 mg/ml[b]	RKC	0.04 mg/ml[b]	Physically compatible with no change in measured turbidity or increase in particle content in 4 hr at 22 °C	1558	C

[a]*Tested in dextrose 5% in water.*
[b]*Tested in sodium chloride 0.9%.*
[c]*Tested in bacteriostatic sodium chloride 0.9% preserved with benzyl alcohol 0.9%.*
[d]*Lyophilized formulation tested.*
[e]*Refer to Appendix I for the composition of parenteral nutrition solutions. TNA indicates a 3-in-1 admixture, and TPN indicates a 2-in-1 admixture.*

Additional Compatibility Information

Infusion Solutions — Buprenorphine HCl is stated to be physically and chemically compatible in a 1:1 volume ratio with dextrose 5% in sodium chloride 0.9%, dextrose 5% in water, Ringer's injection, lactated, and sodium chloride 0.9%. (4)

Other Drugs — Buprenorphine HCl is stated to be physically and chemically compatible in a 1:1 volume ratio with atropine sulfate, diphenhydramine HCl, droperidol, glycopyrrolate, haloperidol lactate, hydroxyzine HCl, promethazine HCl, and scopolamine hydrobromide. (4)

The drug is stated to be incompatible with diazepam and lorazepam. (4)

BUSULFAN
AHFS 10:00

Products — Busulfan is available as a 6-mg/ml concentrated solution dissolved in a vehicle composed of 33% w/w *N,N*-dimethylacetamide and 67% w/w polyethylene glycol 400. The product is packaged in 10-ml colorless single-use ampuls along with 25-mm 5-µm nylon membrane filters. The concentrated injection must be diluted for administration. (1-2/00)

pH — An infusion admixture of busulfan diluted for infusion in sodium chloride 0.9% or dextrose 5% in water to a concentration greater than 0.5 mg/ml has a pH of 3.4 to 3.9. (1-2/00)

Trade Name(s) — Busulfex.

Administration — Busulfan must be diluted for administration. Sodium chloride 0.9% and dextrose 5% in water are both recommended diluents for busulfan infusion. The quantity of infusion solution should be ten times the volume of the busulfan concentrate dose to ensure that the final concentration is equal to or greater than 0.5 mg/ml. As an example, if 9.3 ml of busulfan injection provides the needed dose, then that amount should be added to 93 ml of sodium chloride 0.9% or dextrose 5% in water to yield the final admixture suitable for administration. (1-2/00)

Appropriate gloves should be worn during preparation; accidental skin exposure may result in skin reactions. To prepare the infusion admixture, break open the ampul top and withdraw the contents through the 5-µm nylon filter. The filter and needle are removed and a new needle is attached. The busulfan is added into an intravenous solution bag that already contains the appropriate amount of sodium chloride 0.9% or dextrose 5% in water, making sure that the drug flows into and throughout the solution. The drug should always be added to the diluent. The solution should be mixed thoroughly by inverting several times. Other diluents should not be used. Similarly, other medications of unknown compatibility should not be infused simultaneously. (1-2/00)

Busulfan admixtures should be administered intravenously through a central venous catheter as a two-hour infusion every six hours for four consecutive days (a total of 16 doses). More rapid infusion has not been tested and is not recommended. An infusion pump should be used to control the flow rate. The central venous catheter should be flushed before and after busulfan administration with about 5 ml of sodium chloride 0.9% or dextrose 5% in water. (1-2/00)

Stability — Busulfan injection in intact ampuls is a clear colorless solution and should be stored under refrigeration at 2 to 8 °C. Busulfan diluted for infusion in sodium chloride 0.9% or dextrose 5% in water is stable for up to eight hours at 25 °C; administration should be completed within that time. Admixed in sodium chloride

0.9%, the drug is stable for up to 12 hours under refrigeration at 2 to 8 °C; administration should be completed within that time. (1-2/00)

Filtration— Busulfan injection is packaged with 25-mm 5-μm nylon filters for use in withdrawing the injection from the opened ampuls. The use of filters other than this type is not recommended. (1-2/00)

Compatibility Information

Solution Compatibility

Busulfan

Solution	*Mfr*	*Mfr*	*Conc/L*	*Remarks*	*Ref*	*C/I*
Dextrose 5% in water	BA[a], MG[b]		0.5 g	Physically compatible with no change in measured turbidity or particulates. Less than 10% loss by HPLC in 8 hr at 23 °C but 20% or more loss in 24 hr	2183	I[c]
	BA[a], MG[b]		0.1 g	Physically compatible with no change in measured turbidity or particulates. Less than 10% loss by HPLC in 4 hr at 23 °C but up to 19% loss in 8 hr	2183	I[c]
Sodium chloride 0.9%	BA[a], MG[b]		0.5 g	Physically compatible with no change in measured turbidity or particulates. Less than 10% loss by HPLC in 8 hr at 23 °C but more than 20% loss in 24 hr	2183	I[c]
	BA[a], MG[b]		0.1 g	Physically compatible with no change in measured turbidity or particulates. Less than 10% loss by HPLC in 4 hr at 23 °C but up to 13% loss in 8 hr	2183	I[c]

[a]*Tested in PVC containers.*
[b]*Tested in polyolefin containers.*
[c]*Incompatible by conventional standards but may be used in shorter periods of time.*

BUTORPHANOL TARTRATE
AHFS 28:08.12

Products — Butorphanol tartrate is available in concentrations of 1 mg/ml in 1-ml vials and also 2 mg/ml in 1- and 2-ml single-use vials and 10-ml multiple-dose vials. (1-4/99)

Each milliliter of solution also contains citric acid 3.3 mg, sodium citrate 6.4 mg, and sodium chloride 6.4 mg. Benzethonium chloride 0.1 mg/ml is used as a preservative in the multiple-dose vials only. (1-4/99)

pH— From 3 to 5.5. (4)

Osmolality— Butorphanol tartrate 2 mg/ml has an osmolality of 284 mOsm/kg. (1689)

Trade Name(s)— Stadol.

Administration — Butorphanol tartrate may be administered by intramuscular or intravenous injection. (1-4/99; 4)

Stability — Butorphanol tartrate injection should be stored at controlled room temperature and protected from light. Freezing should be avoided. (4)

Central Venous Catheter— Butorphanol tartrate (Apothecon) 0.04 mg/ml in dextrose 5% in water was found to be compatible with the ARROWg+ard Blue Plus (Arrow International) chlorhexidine-bearing triple-lumen central catheter. HPLC analysis was used to evaluate completeness of drug delivery through the catheter and the amount of chlorhexidine removed from the internal lumens. Essentially complete delivery of the drug was found with little or no drug loss occurring. Furthermore, chlorhexidine delivered from the catheter remained at trace amounts with no substantial increase due to the delivery of the drug through the catheter. (2335)

Compatibility Information

Drugs in Syringe Compatibility

Butorphanol tartrate

Drug (in syringe)	Mfr	Amt	Mfr	Amt	Remarks	Ref	C/I
Atropine sulfate	ST	0.4 mg/ 1 ml	BR	4 mg/ 2 ml	Physically compatible both macroscopically and microscopically for 30 min at room temperature	566	C
Chlorpromazine HCl	MB	25 mg/ 1 ml	BR	4 mg/ 2 ml	Physically compatible both macroscopically and microscopically for 30 min at room temperature	566	C
Cimetidine HCl	SKF	300 mg/ 2 ml	BR	2 mg/ 1 ml	Physically compatible for 4 hr at 25 °C	25	C
Dimenhydrinate	HR	50 mg/ 1 ml	BR	4 mg/ 2 ml	Gas evolves	761	I
Diphenhydramine HCl	PD	50 mg/ 1 ml	BR	4 mg/ 2 ml	Physically compatible both macroscopically and microscopically for 30 min at room temperature	566	C
Droperidol	MN	5 mg/ 2 ml	BR	4 mg/ 2 ml	Physically compatible both macroscopically and microscopically for 30 min at room temperature	566	C
Fentanyl citrate	MN	0.1 mg/ 2 ml	BR	4 mg/ 2 ml	Physically compatible both macroscopically and microscopically for 30 min at room temperature	566	C
Hydroxyzine HCl	PF	50 mg/ 1 ml	BR	2 mg/ 1 ml	Physically compatible	771	C
	PF	100 mg/ 2 ml	BR	1 mg/ 1 ml	Physically compatible	771	C
Meperidine HCl	WI	50 mg/ 1 ml	BR	4 mg/ 2 ml	Physically compatible both macroscopically and microscopically for 30 min at room temperature	566	C
Methotrimeprazine		25 mg/ 1 ml	BR	4 mg/ 2 ml	Physically compatible for 30 min at room temperature both macroscopically and microscopically	566	C
Metoclopramide HCl	NO	10 mg/ 2 ml	BR	4 mg/ 2 ml	Physically compatible for 30 min at room temperature both macroscopically and microscopically	566	C
Midazolam HCl	RC	5 mg/ 1 ml	BR	2 mg/ 1 ml	Physically compatible for 4 hr at 25 °C under fluorescent light	1145	C
Morphine sulfate	AH	15 mg/ 1 ml	BR	4 mg/ 2 ml	Physically compatible both macroscopically and microscopically for 30 min at room temperature	566	C
Papaveretum	RC[a]	20 mg/ 1 ml	BR	4 mg/ 2 ml	Physically compatible both macroscopically and microscopically for 30 min at room temperature	761	C
Pentazocine lactate	WI	30 mg/ 1 ml	BR	4 mg/ 2 ml	Physically compatible both macroscopically and microscopically for 30 min at room temperature	566	C
Pentobarbital sodium	AB	50 mg/ 1 ml	BR	4 mg/ 2 ml	Immediate precipitation	761	I

Drugs in Syringe Compatibility (Cont.)

Drug (in syringe)	Mfr	Amt	Mfr	Amt	Remarks	Ref	C/I
			Butorphanol tartrate				
Perphenazine	SC	5 mg/ 1 ml	BR	4 mg/ 2 ml	Physically compatible both macroscopically and microscopically for 30 min at room temperature	761	C
Prochlorperazine edisylate	MB	5 mg/ 1 ml	BR	4 mg/ 2 ml	Physically compatible both macroscopically and microscopically for 30 min at room temperature	566	C
Promethazine HCl	WY	25 mg/ 1 ml	BR	4 mg/ 2 ml	Physically compatible both macroscopically and microscopically for 30 min at room temperature	566	C
Scopolamine HBr	ST	0.4 mg/ 1 ml	BR	4 mg/ 2 ml	Physically compatible both macroscopically and microscopically for 30 min at room temperature	566	C
Thiethylperazine malate	BI	10 mg/ 1 ml	BR	4 mg/ 2 ml	Physically compatible both macroscopically and microscopically for 30 min at room temperature	761	C

[a]*The former formulation was tested.*

Y-Site Injection Compatibility (1:1 Mixture)

Drug	Mfr	Conc	Mfr	Conc	Remarks	Ref	C/I
			Butorphanol tartrate				
Allopurinol sodium	BW	3 mg/ml[b]	BR	0.04 mg/ml[b]	Physically compatible with no change in measured turbidity or increase in particle content in 4 hr at 22 °C	1686	C
Amifostine	USB	10 mg/ml[a]	BR	0.04 mg/ml[a]	Physically compatible with no change in measured turbidity or increase in particle content in 4 hr at 23 °C	1845	C
Amphotericin B cholesteryl sulfate complex	SEQ	0.83 mg/ml[a]	APC	0.04 mg/ml[a]	Decreased natural turbidity occurs immediately	2117	I
Aztreonam	SQ	40 mg/ml[a]	BMS	0.04 mg/ml[a]	Physically compatible with no subvisual haze or particle formation in 4 hr at 23 °C	1758	C
Cefepime HCl	BMS	20 mg/ml[a]	BR	0.04 mg/ml[a]	Physically compatible with no change in measured turbidity or increase in particle content in 4 hr at 22 °C	1689	C
Cisatracurium besylate	GW	0.1, 2, 5 mg/ ml[a]	APC	0.04 mg/ml[a]	Physically compatible with no change in measured turbidity or increase in particle content in 4 hr at 23 °C	2074	C
Cladribine	ORT	0.015[b] and 0.5[c] mg/ml	APC	0.04 mg/ml[b]	Physically compatible with no change in measured turbidity or increase in particle content in 4 hr at 23 °C	1969	C
Docetaxel	RPR	0.9 mg/ml[a]	APC	0.04 mg/ml[a]	Physically compatible with no change in measured turbidity or increase in particle content in 4 hr at 23 °C	2224	C
Doxorubicin HCl liposome injection	SEQ	0.4 mg/ml[a]	APC	0.04 mg/ml[a]	Physically compatible with little or no change in measured turbidity and no increase in particle content in 4 hr at 23 °C	2087	C

Y-Site Injection Compatibility (1:1 Mixture) (Cont.)

			Butorphanol tartrate				
Drug	*Mfr*	*Conc*	*Mfr*	*Conc*	*Remarks*	*Ref*	*C/I*
Enalaprilat	MSD	0.05 mg/ml[b]	BR	0.4 mg/ml[a]	Physically compatible for 24 hr at room temperature under fluorescent light	1355	C
Esmolol HCl	DCC	10 mg/ml[a]	BR	0.04 mg/ml[a]	Physically compatible for 24 hr at 22 °C	1169	C
Etoposide phosphate	BR	5 mg/ml[a]	APC	0.04 mg/ml[a]	Physically compatible with no change in measured turbidity or increase in particle content in 4 hr at 23 °C	2218	C
Filgrastim	AMG	30 μg/ml[a]	BR	0.04 mg/ml[a]	Physically compatible with no change in measured turbidity or increase in particle content in 4 hr at 22 °C	1687	C
Fludarabine phosphate	BX	1 mg/ml[a]	BR	0.04 mg/ml[a]	Physically compatible for 4 hr at room temperature under fluorescent light	1439	C
Gatifloxacin	BMS	2 mg/ml[a]	BMS	0.04 mg/ml[a]	Physically compatible with no change in measured haze or increase in particle content in 4 hr at 23 °C	2234	C
Gemcitabine HCl	LI	10 mg/ml[b]	APC	0.04 mg/ml[b]	Physically compatible with no change in measured turbidity or increase in particle content in 4 hr at 23 °C	2226	C
Granisetron HCl	SKB	0.05 mg/ml[a]	APC	0.04 mg/ml[a]	Physically compatible with no change in measured turbidity or increase in particle content in 4 hr at 23 °C	2000	C
Hetastarch in lactated electrolyte injection (Hextend)	AB	6%	APC	0.04 mg/ml[a]	Physically compatible with no change in measured turbidity or increase in particle content in 4 hr at 23 °C	2339	C
Labetalol HCl	SC	1 mg/ml[a]	BR	0.04 mg/ml[a]	Physically compatible for 24 hr at 18 °C	1171	C
Linezolid	PHU	2 mg/ml	APC	0.04 mg/ml[a]	Physically compatible with no change in measured turbidity or increase in particle content in 4 hr at 23 °C	2264	C
Melphalan HCl	BW	0.1 mg/ml[b]	BR	0.04 mg/ml[b]	Physically compatible with no change in measured turbidity or increase in particle content in 3 hr at 22 °C	1557	C
Midazolam HCl	RC	[f]	BR	[f]	Crystalline precipitate identified as midazolam by HPLC formed in infusion line several hours after administration was completed	2144	I
Paclitaxel	NCI	1.2 mg/ml[a]	BR	0.04 mg/ml[a]	Physically compatible with no change in measured turbidity in 4 hr at 22 °C	1556	C
Piperacillin sodium–tazobactam sodium	LE	40 + 5 mg/ml[a]	BR	0.04 mg/ml[a]	Physically compatible with no change in measured turbidity or increase in particle content in 4 hr at 22 °C	1688	C
Propofol	ZEN	10 mg/ml	APC	0.04 mg/ml[a]	Physically compatible for 1 hr at 23 °C with no increase in particle content	2066	C
Remifentanil HCl	GW	0.025 and 0.25 mg/ml[b]	APC	0.04 mg/ml[a]	Physically compatible with no change in measured turbidity or increase in particle content in 4 hr at 23 °C	2075	C
Sargramostim	IMM	10 μg/ml[b]	BR	0.04 mg/ml[b]	Physically compatible for 4 hr at 22 °C	1436	C
Teniposide	BR	0.1 mg/ml[a]	BR	0.04 mg/ml[a]	Physically compatible with no subvisual haze or particle formation in 4 hr at 23 °C	1725	C

Y-Site Injection Compatibility (1:1 Mixture) (Cont.)

			Butorphanol tartrate				
Drug	*Mfr*	*Conc*	*Mfr*	*Conc*	*Remarks*	*Ref*	*C/I*
Thiotepa	IMM[d]	1 mg/ml[a]	APC	0.04 mg/ml[a]	Physically compatible with no change in measured turbidity or increase in particle content in 4 hr at 23 °C	1861	C
TNA #218 to #226[e]			APC	0.04 mg/ml[a]	Visually compatible with no precipitate or emulsion damage apparent in 4 hr at 23 °C	2215	C
TPN #212 to #215[e]			APC	0.04 mg/ml[a]	Physically compatible with no change in measured turbidity or increase in particle content in 4 hr at 23 °C	2109	C
Vinorelbine tartrate	BW	1 mg/ml[b]	BR	0.04 mg/ml[b]	Physically compatible with no change in measured turbidity or increase in particle content in 4 hr at 22 °C	1558	C

[a] *Tested in dextrose 5% in water.*
[b] *Tested in sodium chloride 0.9%.*
[c] *Tested in bacteriostatic sodium chloride 0.9% preserved with benzyl alcohol 0.9%.*
[d] *Lyophilized formulation tested.*
[e] *Refer to Appendix I for the composition of parenteral nutrition solutions. TNA indicates a 3-in-1 admixture, and TPN indicates a 2-in-1 admixture.*
[f] *Concentration unspecified.*

Additional Compatibility Information

Other Drugs — Butorphanol tartrate is stated to be physically and chemically compatible with atropine sulfate, hydroxyzine HCl, and promethazine HCl for at least 24 hours. (481)

Other Information

One milligram of the tartrate is equal to 0.68 mg of butorphanol base. (1-4/99)

CALCITRIOL
AHFS 88:16

Products — Calcitriol is available in 1-ml ampuls in two strengths. Each milliliter of the aqueous solution contains (2):

Calcitriol	1 or 2 μg
Polysorbate 20	4 mg
Sodium ascorbate	2.5 mg
Hydrochloric acid and/or sodium hydroxide	to adjust pH

pH — The injection has a target pH of 6.5 with a range of 5.9 to 7.0. (2)

Tonicity — The injection is an isotonic solution. (2)

Trade Name(s) — Calcijex.

Administration — Calcitriol is given by intravenous injection. For patients undergoing hemodialysis, it may be administered by rapid intravenous injection through the catheter after a period of hemodialysis. (4)

Stability — Calcitriol injection is a clear, colorless to yellow solution. It should be stored at controlled room temperature and protected from light. (2; 4) Freezing and excessive heat should be avoided, although brief exposure to temperatures up to 40 °C does not adversely affect the injection. (4)

The product does not contain a preservative, and the manufacturer recommends discarding any unused solution. (2; 4)

Syringes — Calcitriol (Abbott) 1 and 2 μg/ml undiluted and 0.5 μg/ml diluted in dextrose 5% in water, sodium chloride 0.9%, and water for injection was evaluated for stability. It was stored in 1-ml polypropylene tuberculin syringes (Becton-Dickinson) for eight hours at room temperature while exposed to normal room light. HPLC analysis showed little or no loss during the study period. (1662)

Sorption — Pecosky et al. evaluated the sorption potential of calcitriol (Abbott) to PVC bags and administration sets and to polypropylene syringes by determining the apparent calcitriol polymer–water partition coefficients. The mean apparent partition coefficient was 66 times greater for PVC than polypropylene. In this test, 50% of the calcitriol was lost to PVC within two hours while approximately 4% was lost to polypropylene in 20 days. (1662)

CALCIUM ACETATE
AHFS 40:12

Products — Calcium acetate injection is available in 10-ml vials and pharmacy bulk packages of 50 and 100 ml. Each milliliter of solution contains 39.55 mg of calcium acetate, anhydrous and provides 0.5 mEq (10 mg) of calcium in water for injection. Acetic acid may have been used to adjust pH during manufacturing. (1-1/91; 1-5/95)

pH — About 6.3 with a range from 5.5 to 7. (1-1/91; 1-5/95; 4)

Osmolarity — 600 mOsm/L or 0.6 mOsm/ml. (1-1/91; 1-5/95)

Specific Gravity — 1.020. (1-1/91; 1-5/95)

Administration — Calcium acetate is administered by direct intravenous injection or by continuous or intermittent intravenous infusion. Direct intravenous administration should be performed slowly at a rate not exceeding 0.7 to 1.8 mEq/min. (4) In central venous total parenteral nutrition, calcium is administered at an approximate concentration of 5 mEq/L. (1-5/95)

Stability — Intact vials of calcium acetate should be stored at controlled room temperature. The single-use vials do not contain a preservative; the manufacturer recommends discarding any unused solution within four hours of initial entry. (1-1/91; 1-5/95)

Compatibility Information

Calcium and Phosphate — UNRECOGNIZED CALCIUM PHOSPHATE PRECIPITATION IN A 3-IN-1 PARENTERAL NUTRITION MIXTURE RESULTED IN PATIENT DEATH.

The potential for the formation of a calcium phosphate precipitate in parenteral nutrition solutions is well studied and documented (1771; 1777), but the information is complex and difficult to apply to the clinical situation. (1770; 1772; 1777) The incorporation of fat emulsion in 3-in-1 parenteral nutrition solutions obscures any precipitate that may be present, which has led to substantial debate about the dangers associated with 3-in-1 parenteral nutrition mixtures and when or if the danger to the patient is warranted therapeutically. (1770–1772; 2031–2036) Because such precipitation may be life threatening to patients (2037; 2291), the Food and Drug Administration issued a Safety Alert containing the following recommendations (1769):

"1. The amounts of phosphorus and of calcium added to the admixture are critical. The solubility of the added calcium should be calculated from the volume at the time the calcium is added. It should not be based upon the final volume.

Some amino acid injections for TPN admixtures contain phosphate ions (as a phosphoric acid buffer). These phosphate ions and the volume at the time the phosphate is added should be considered when calculating the concentration of phosphate additives. Also, when adding calcium and phosphate to an admixture, the phosphate should be added first.

The line should be flushed between the addition of any potentially incompatible components.

2. A lipid emulsion in a three-in-one admixture obscures the presence of a precipitate. Therefore, if a lipid emulsion is needed, either (1) use a two-in-one admixture with the lipid infused separately, or (2) if a three-in-one admixture is medically necessary, then add the calcium before the lipid emulsion and according to the recommendations in number 1 above.

If the amount of calcium or phosphate which must be added is likely to cause a precipitate, some or all of the calcium should be administered separately. Such separate infusions must be properly diluted and slowly infused to avoid serious adverse events related to the calcium.

3. When using an automated compounding device, the above steps should be considered when programming the device. In addition, automated compounders should be maintained and operated according to the manufacturer's recommendations.

Any printout should be checked against the programmed admixture and weight of components.

4. During the mixing process, pharmacists who mix parenteral nutrition admixtures should periodically agitate the admixture and check for precipitates. Medical or home care personnel who start and monitor these infusions should carefully inspect for the presence of precipitates both before and during infusion. Patients and care givers should be trained to visually inspect for signs of precipitation. They also should be advised to stop the infusion and seek medical assistance if precipitates are noted.

5. A filter should be used when infusing either central or peripheral parenteral nutrition admixtures. At this time, data have not been submitted to document which size filter is most effective in trapping precipitates.

Standards of practice vary, but the following is suggested: a 1.2-μm air-eliminating filter for lipid-containing admixtures and a 0.22-μm air-eliminating filter for non-lipid-containing admixtures.

6. Parenteral nutrition admixtures should be administered within the following time frames: if stored at room temperature, the infusion should be started within 24 hours after mixing; if stored at refrigerated temperatures, the infusion should be started within 24 hours of rewarming. Because warming parenteral nutrition admixtures may contribute to the formation of precipitates, once administration begins, care should be taken to avoid excessive warming of the admixture.

Persons administering home care parenteral nutrition admixtures may need to deviate from these time frames. Pharmacists who initially prepare these admixtures should check a reserve sample for precipitates over the duration and under the conditions of storage.

7. If symptoms of acute respiratory distress, pulmonary emboli, or interstitial pneumonitis develop, the infusion should be stopped immediately and thoroughly checked for precipitates. Appropriate medical interventions should be instituted. Home care personnel and patients should immediately seek medical assistance."

Calcium Phosphate Precipitation Fatalities — Hill et al. reported fatal cases of paroxysmal respiratory failure in two previously healthy women receiving peripheral vein parenteral nutrition. The patients experienced sudden cardiopulmonary arrest consistent with pulmonary emboli. The authors used in vitro simulations and an animal model to conclude that unrecognized calcium phosphate precipitation in a 3-in-1 total nutrition admixture caused the fatalities. The precipitation resulted during compounding by introducing calcium and phosphate near to one another in the compounding sequence and prior to complete fluid addition. This resulted in a temporarily high concentration of the drugs and precipitation of calcium phosphate. Observation of the precipitate was obscured by the incorporation of 20% fat emulsion, intravenous into the nutrition mixture. No filter was used during infusion of the fatal nutrition admixtures. (2037)

In a follow-up retrospective review, Shay et al. reported that five patients were identified that had respiratory distress associated with the infusion of the 3-in-1 admixtures at around the same time. Four of these five patients died, although the cause of death could be definitively determined for only two. (2291)

Calcium and Phosphate Conditional Compatibility—Calcium salts are conditionally compatible with phosphate in parenteral nutrition solutions. The incompatibility is dependent on a solubility and concentration phenomenon and is not entirely predictable. Precipitation may occur during compounding or at some time after compounding is completed.

NOTE: Some amino acid solutions inherently contain calcium and phosphate, which must be considered in any projection of compatibility. See the Amino Acid Injection monograph, Table 1.

Zhang et al. evaluated calcium and phosphate compatibility in a series of parenteral nutrition admixtures composed of Aminosyn II in concentrations ranging from 2% up to 5% (TPN #227 to #231 in Appendix I). The solutions also contained dextrose ranging from 10% up to 25%. Also present were sodium chloride, potassium chloride, and magnesium sulfate in common amounts. Phosphates as the potassium salt and calcium as the acetate salt were added in variable quantities to determine the maximum amounts of calcium and phosphates that could be added to the representative TPN admixtures. The samples were evaluated at 23 and 37 °C over 48 hours by visual inspection in ambient light and using a Tyndall beam and electronically measured for turbidity and microparticulates. The boundaries between the compatible and incompatible concentrations were presented graphically as hyperbolic curves. (2265)

The presence of magnesium in solutions may also influence the reaction between calcium and phosphate, including the nature and extent of precipitation. (158; 159)

The interaction of calcium and phosphate in parenteral nutrition solutions is a complex phenomenon. Various factors play a role in the solubility or precipitation of a given combination, including (608; 609; 1042; 1063; 1210; 1234; 2265):

1. Concentration of calcium
2. Salt form of calcium
3. Concentration of phosphate
4. Concentration of amino acids
5. Amino acids composition
6. Concentration of dextrose
7. Temperature of solution
8. pH of solution
9. Presence of other additives
10. Order of mixing

Enhanced precipitate formation would be expected from such factors as high concentrations of calcium and phosphate, increases in solution pH, decreased amino acid concentrations, increases in temperature, addition of calcium prior to the phosphate, lengthy standing times or slow infusion rates, and use of calcium as the chloride salt. (854)

Also see the Calcium Gluconate monograph.

Even if precipitation does not occur in the container, it has been reported that crystallization of calcium phosphate may occur in a Silastic infusion pump chamber or tubing if the rate of administration is slow, as for premature infants. Water vapor may be transmitted outward and be replaced by air rapidly enough to produce supersaturation. (202) Several other cases of catheter occlusion also have been reported. (610; 1427–1429)

CALCIUM CHLORIDE
AHFS 40:12

Products — Calcium chloride is available in 10-ml single-dose vials and prefilled syringes containing 1 g of calcium chloride (dihydrate), providing 13.6 mEq (270 mg) of calcium and 13.6 mEq of chloride in water for injection. The pH may have been adjusted with hydrochloric acid and/or calcium hydroxide. (1-5/99; 4; 29)

pH—From 5.5 to 7.5. (1-5/99; 4)

Osmolarity—The 10% injection is labeled as having an osmolarity of 2.04 mOsm/ml. (1-5/99)

The osmolality of a calcium chloride 10% solution was determined by osmometer to be 1765 mOsm/kg. (1233)

Administration — Calcium chloride is administered by direct intravenous injection or by continuous or intermittent intravenous infusion. (1-5/99; 4) Intravenous administration should be performed slowly at a rate not exceeding 0.7 to 1.8 mEq/min. The drug may also be injected into the ventricular cavity in cardiac resuscitation. It must not be injected into the myocardium. Severe necrosis and sloughing may result if calcium chloride is injected intramuscularly or subcutaneously or leaks into the perivascular tissue. (1-5/99; 4)

Stability — The injection is clear and colorless. Intact vials should be stored at controlled room temperature. The single-use vials do not contain a preservative; the manufacturer recommends discarding any unused solution. (1-5/99)

Compatibility Information

Solution Compatibility

Calcium chloride

Solution	Mfr	Mfr	Conc/L	Remarks	Ref	C/I
Fat emulsion 10%, intravenous	CU		13.6 mEq (1 g)	Immediate flocculation with visually apparent layer in 2 hr at room temperature	656	I
	CU		6.8 mEq (500 mg)	Flocculation within 4 hr at room temperature	656	I
	VT	DB	1 g	Globule coalescence and creaming within 8 hr at 8 and 25 °C	825	I
	KV		10 and 20 mEq	Immediate flocculation, aggregation, and creaming	1018	I

Additive Compatibility

Calcium chloride

Drug	Mfr	Conc/L	Mfr	Conc/L	Test Soln	Remarks	Ref	C/I
Amikacin sulfate	BR	5 g	UP	1 g	D5LR, D5R, D5S, D5W, D10W, IS10, LR, NS, R, SL	Physically compatible and potency of both drugs retained for 24 hr at 25 °C	294	C
Amphotericin B		200 mg	BP	4 g	D5W	Haze develops over 3 hr	26	I
Ascorbic acid injection	UP	500 mg	UP	1 g	D5W	Physically compatible	15	C
Bretylium tosylate	ACC	10 g	ES	54.4 mEq	D5W[a]	Physically compatible and bretylium chemically stable for 48 hr at room temperature and 7 days at 4 °C	541	C
Chloramphenicol sodium succinate	PD	10 g	UP	1 g	D5W	Physically compatible	15	C
Chlorpheniramine maleate						Physically incompatible	9	I
	SC	100 mg	UP	1 g	D5W	Physically incompatible	15	I
Dobutamine HCl	LI	182 mg	UP	9 g	NS	Physically compatible for 20 hr. Haze forms at 24 hr	552	I
	LI	1 g	ES	2 g	D5W, NS	Deeply pink in 24 hr at 25 °C	789	I
	LI	1 g	ES	50 g	D5W, NS	Physically compatible for 24 hr at 21 °C	812	C
Dopamine HCl	AS	800 mg	UP		D5W	No dopamine decomposition in 24 hr at 25 °C	312	C
Hydrocortisone sodium succinate	UP	500 mg	UP	1 g	D5W	Physically compatible	15	C
Isoproterenol HCl	WI	4 mg	UP	1 g		Physically compatible	59	C
Lidocaine HCl	AST	2 g	UP	1 g		Physically compatible	24	C
Norepinephrine bitartrate	WI	8 mg	UP	1 g	D, D–S, S	Physically compatible	77	C
Penicillin G potassium	SQ	20 million units	UP	1 g	D5W	Physically compatible	15	C
	SQ	5 million units	UP	1 g	D	Physically compatible	47	C

Additive Compatibility (Cont.)

Calcium chloride

Drug	*Mfr*	*Conc/L*	*Mfr*	*Conc/L*	*Test Soln*	*Remarks*	*Ref*	*C/I*
Penicillin G sodium	UP	20 million units	UP	1 g	D5W	Physically compatible	15	C
Pentobarbital sodium	AB	1 g	UP	1 g	D5W	Physically compatible	15	C
Phenobarbital sodium	WI	200 mg	UP	1 g	D5W	Physically compatible	15	C
Sodium bicarbonate	AB	2.4 mEq[b]		1 g	D5W	Physically compatible for 24 hr	772	C
Verapamil HCl	KN	80 mg	ES	2 g	D5W, NS	Physically compatible for 24 hr	764	C
Vitamin B complex with C	AB	5 ml	UP	1 g	D5W	Physically compatible	15	C

[a]*Tested in both glass and PVC containers.*
[b]*One vial of Neut added to a liter of admixture.*

Drugs in Syringe Compatibility

Calcium chloride

Drug (in syringe)	*Mfr*	*Amt*	*Mfr*	*Amt*	*Remarks*	*Ref*	*C/I*
Milrinone lactate	WI	5.25 mg/ 5.25 ml	AB	3 g/30 ml	Physically compatible with no milrinone loss in 20 min at 23 °C under fluorescent light	1410	C

Y-Site Injection Compatibility (1:1 Mixture)

Calcium chloride

Drug	*Mfr*	*Conc*	*Mfr*	*Conc*	*Remarks*	*Ref*	*C/I*
Amphotericin B cholesteryl sulfate complex	SEQ	0.83 mg/ml[a]	AST	40 mg/ml[a]	Gross precipitate forms	2117	I
Dobutamine HCl	LI	4 mg/ml[c]	AB	4 mg/ml[c]	Physically compatible for 3 hr	1316	C
Epinephrine HCl	ES	0.032 mg/ml[c]	AB	4 mg/ml[c]	Physically compatible for 3 hr	1316	C
Esmolol HCl	DCC	10 mg/ml[a]	AB	20 mg/ml[a]	Physically compatible for 24 hr at 22 °C	1169	C
Gatifloxacin	BMS	2 mg/ml[a]	FUJ	40 mg/ml[a]	Physically compatible with no change in measured haze or increase in particle content in 4 hr at 23 °C	2234	C
Inamrinone lactate	WB	3 mg/ml[b]	AB	100 mg/ml	Physically compatible for at least 4 hr at 25 °C under fluorescent light	992	C
Morphine sulfate	WY	0.2 mg/ml[c]	AB	4 mg/ml[c]	Physically compatible for 3 hr	1316	C
Paclitaxel	NCI	1.2 mg/ml[a]	AST	20 mg/ml[a]	Physically compatible with no change in measured turbidity in 4 hr at 22 °C	1556	C
Propofol	ZEN	10 mg/ml	AST	40 mg/ml[a]	White precipitate forms in 1 hr	2066	I
Sodium bicarbonate	AB	1 mEq/ml	AB	4 mg/ml[c]	Slight haze or precipitate in 1 hr	1316	I

[a]*Tested in dextrose 5% in water.*
[b]*Tested in sodium chloride 0.9%.*
[c]*Tested in both dextrose 5% in water and sodium chloride 0.9%.*

Additional Compatibility Information

Infusion Solutions — Calcium chloride is compatible in most common intravenous infusion solutions.

Calcium and Phosphate — UNRECOGNIZED CALCIUM PHOSPHATE PRECIPITATION IN A 3-IN-1 PARENTERAL NUTRITION MIXTURE RESULTED IN PATIENT DEATH.

The potential for the formation of a calcium phosphate precipitate in parenteral nutrition solutions is well studied and documented (1771; 1777), but the information is complex and difficult to apply to the clinical situation. (1770; 1772; 1777) The incorporation of fat emulsion in 3-in-1 parenteral nutrition solutions obscures any precipitate that is present, which has led to substantial debate on the dangers associated with 3-in-1 parenteral nutrition mixtures and when or if the danger to the patient is warranted therapeutically. (1770–1772; 2031–2036) Because such precipitation may be life-threatening to patients (2037; 2291), the Food and Drug Administration issued a Safety Alert containing the following recommendations (1769):

"1. The amounts of phosphorus and of calcium added to the admixture are critical. The solubility of the added calcium should be calculated from the volume at the time the calcium is added. It should not be based upon the final volume.

   Some amino acid injections for TPN admixtures contain phosphate ions (as a phosphoric acid buffer). These phosphate ions and the volume at the time the phosphate is added should be considered when calculating the concentration of phosphate additives. Also, when adding calcium and phosphate to an admixture, the phosphate should be added first.

   The line should be flushed between the addition of any potentially incompatible components.

2. A lipid emulsion in a three-in-one admixture obscures the presence of a precipitate. Therefore, if a lipid emulsion is needed, either (1) use a two-in-one admixture with the lipid infused separately, or (2) if a three-in-one admixture is medically necessary, then add the calcium before the lipid emulsion and according to the recommendations in number 1 above.

   If the amount of calcium or phosphate which must be added is likely to cause a precipitate, some or all of the calcium should be administered separately. Such separate infusions must be properly diluted and slowly infused to avoid serious adverse events related to the calcium.

3. When using an automated compounding device, the above steps should be considered when programming the device. In addition, automated compounders should be maintained and operated according to the manufacturer's recommendations.

   Any printout should be checked against the programmed admixture and weight of components.

4. During the mixing process, pharmacists who mix parenteral nutrition admixtures should periodically agitate the admixture and check for precipitates. Medical or home care personnel who start and monitor these infusions should carefully inspect for the presence of precipitates both before and during infusion. Patients and care givers should be trained to visually inspect for signs of precipitation. They also should be advised to stop the infusion and seek medical assistance if precipitates are noted.

5. A filter should be used when infusing either central or peripheral parenteral nutrition admixtures. At this time, data have not been submitted to document which size filter is most effective in trapping precipitates.

   Standards of practice vary, but the following is suggested: a 1.2-μm air-eliminating filter for lipid-containing admixtures and a 0.22-μm air-eliminating filter for non-lipid-containing admixtures.

6. Parenteral nutrition admixtures should be administered within the following time frames: if stored at room temperature, the infusion should be started within 24 hours after mixing; if stored at refrigerated temperatures, the infusion should be started within 24 hours of rewarming. Because warming parenteral nutrition admixtures may contribute to the formation of precipitates, once administration begins, care should be taken to avoid excessive warming of the admixture.

   Persons administering home care parenteral nutrition admixtures may need to deviate from these time frames. Pharmacists who initially prepare these admixtures should check a reserve sample for precipitates over the duration and under the conditions of storage.

7. If symptoms of acute respiratory distress, pulmonary emboli, or interstitial pneumonitis develop, the infusion should be stopped immediately and thoroughly checked for precipitates. Appropriate medical interventions should be instituted. Home care personnel and patients should immediately seek medical assistance."

Calcium Phosphate Precipitation Fatalities — Hill et al. reported fatal cases of paroxysmal respiratory failure in two previously healthy women receiving peripheral vein parenteral nutrition. The patients experienced sudden cardiopulmonary arrest consistent with pulmonary emboli. The authors used in vitro simulations and an animal model to conclude that unrecognized calcium phosphate precipitation in a 3-in-1 total nutrition admixture caused the fatalities. The precipitation resulted during compounding by introducing calcium and phosphate near to one another in the compounding sequence and prior to complete fluid addition. This resulted in a temporarily high concentration of the drugs and precipitation of calcium phosphate. Observation of the precipitate was obscured by the incorporation of 20% fat emulsion, intravenous into the nutrition mixture. No filter was used during infusion of the fatal nutrition admixtures. (2037)

In a follow-up retrospective review, Shay et al. reported that five patients were identified that had respiratory distress associated with the infusion of the 3-in-1 admixtures at around the same time. Four of these five patients died, although the cause of death could be definitively determined for only two of them from the available information. (2291)

Calcium and Phosphate Conditional Compatibility — Calcium salts are conditionally compatible with phosphate in parenteral nutrition solutions. The incompatibility is dependent on a solubility and concentration phenomenon and is not entirely predictable. Precipitation may occur during compounding or at some time after compounding is completed.

NOTE: Some amino acid solutions inherently contain calcium and phosphate, which must be considered in any projection of compatibility. See the amino acid injection monograph, Table 1.

A study by Henry et al. (608) determined the maximum concentrations of calcium (as chloride and gluconate) and phosphate that can be maintained without precipitation in a parenteral nutrition solution consisting of FreAmine II 4.25% and dextrose 25% for 24 hours at 30 °C. Their results are depicted in Figure 1.

Figure 1. Maximum solubilities of calcium chloride (○) and calcium gluconcate (△) with sodium phosphate in an amino acid 4.25% -dextrose 25% solution at 30 °C

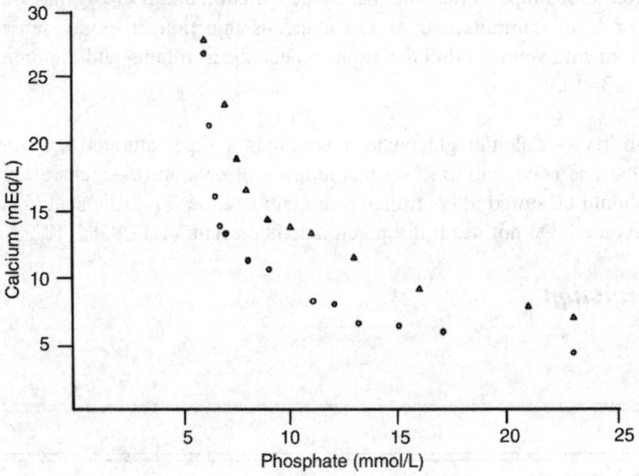

Henry et al. noted that the amino acids in parenteral nutrition solutions form soluble complexes with calcium and phosphate, reducing the available free calcium and phosphate that can form insoluble precipitates. The concentration of calcium available for precipitation is greater with the chloride salt compared to the gluconate salt, at least in part because of differences in dissociation characteristics. This can be seen in Figure 1 by the greater concentration of calcium gluconate that can be mixed with sodium phosphate. (608)

In addition to the concentrations of phosphate and calcium and the salt form of the calcium, Henry et al. noted that the concentration of amino acids and the time and temperature of storage altered the formation of calcium phosphate in parenteral nutrition solutions. As the temperature was increased, the incidence of precipitate formation also increased. This finding was attributed, at least in part, to a greater degree of dissociation of the calcium and phosphate complexes and the decreased solubility of calcium phosphate. Therefore, it is possible for a solution to be stored at 4 °C with no precipitation, but on warming to room temperature a precipitate will form over time. (608)

Koorenhof and Timmer reported the maximum allowable concentrations of calcium and phosphate in a 3-in-1 parenteral nutrition mixture for children (TNA #192 in Appendix I). Added calcium was varied from 1.5 to 150 mmol/L, while added phosphate was varied from 21 to 300 mmol/L. The mixtures were stable for 48 hours at 22 and 37 °C as long as the pH was not greater than 5.7, the calcium concentration was below 16 mmol/L, the phosphate concentration was below 52 mmol/L, and the product of the calcium and phosphate concentrations was below 250 $mmol^2/L^2$. (1773)

The presence of magnesium in solutions may also influence the reaction between calcium and phosphate, including the nature and extent of precipitation. (158; 159)

The interaction of calcium and phosphate in parenteral nutrition solutions is a complex phenomenon. Various factors play a role in the solubility or precipitation of a given combination, including (608; 609; 1042; 1063; 1210; 1234; 1427):

1. Concentration of calcium
2. Salt form of calcium
3. Concentration of phosphate
4. Concentration of amino acids
5. Amino acids composition
6. Concentration of dextrose
7. Temperature of solution
8. pH of solution
9. Presence of other additives
10. Order of mixing

Enhanced precipitate formation would be expected from such factors as high concentrations of calcium and phosphate, increases in solution pH, decreases in amino acid concentrations, increases in temperature, addition of calcium before phosphate, lengthy standing times or slow infusion rates, and use of calcium as the chloride salt. (854)

Also see the monograph on calcium gluconate.

Even if precipitation does not occur in the container, it has been reported that crystallization of calcium phosphate may occur in a Silastic infusion pump chamber or tubing if the rate of administration is slow, as for premature infants. Water vapor may be transmitted outward and be replaced by air rapidly enough to produce supersaturation. (202) Several other cases of catheter occlusion have been reported. (610; 1427–1429)

Tobramycin — Calcium ions are stated to inhibit the activity of tobramycin sulfate. (145)

Other Drugs — Calcium chloride (Upjohn) in dextrose 5% in water has been reported to be conditionally compatible with sodium bicarbonate (Abbott). The incompatibility is dependent on the concentration of the additives. Therefore, if attempting to combine calcium chloride with sodium bicarbonate, mix the solution thoroughly and observe it closely for any sign of incompatibility. (15)

Calcium chloride is stated to be incompatible with soluble carbonates, phosphates, sulfates, and tartrates. Because of the presence of sodium carbonate in the cefamandole nafate (Lilly) formulation, it is incompatible with calcium ions. (4; 376)

CALCIUM GLUCONATE
AHFS 40:12

Products — Calcium gluconate is available from various manufacturers in 10-ml ampuls and 10-, 50-, and 100-ml vials as a 10% solution. Each milliliter contains 94 (American Pharmaceutical Partners) or 98 (American Regent) mg of calcium gluconate with calcium D-saccharate tetrahydrate 4.5 to 4.6 mg in water for injection, providing 9.3 mg (0.465 mEq) of elementary calcium. The pH may be adjusted with sodium hydroxide and/or hydrochloric acid. (1-11/95; 1-12/98)

pH — From 6 to 8.2. (1-12/98; 4)

Osmolarity—The osmolarity is stated to be 0.68 mOsm/ml. (1-12/98)

The osmolality of a calcium gluconate 10% solution was determined by osmometer to be 276 mOsm/kg. (1233)

Administration—Calcium gluconate is usually administered intravenously as a 10% solution (4), slowly by direct intravenous injection, or by continuous or intermittent intravenous infusion. A maximum administration rate of 1.5 ml/min has been recommended for direct intravenous injection. (1-12/98) By intermittent infusion, a maximum of 200 mg/min has been suggested. (1-11/95) Calcium gluconate has been given by intramuscular or, rarely, subcutaneous injection to adults (4), but these routes are not recommended because of possible tissue necrosis, sloughing, and abscess formation. (1-11/95; 1-12/98) Numerous reports indicate that tissue irritation and necrosis may occur from intramuscular or subcutaneous injection or extravasation from intravenous administration, especially in infants and children. (183–185; 359)

Stability—Calcium gluconate injection is a supersaturated solution that has been stabilized by the addition of calcium D-saccharate. It should be stored at controlled room temperature. Freezing should be avoided. Do not use it if a precipitate is present. (1-11/95; 1-12/98)

Compatibility Information

Solution Compatibility

Calcium gluconate

Solution	*Mfr*	*Mfr*	*Conc/L*	*Remarks*	*Ref*	*C/I*
Alcohol 5%, dextrose 5%	BA	PD	2 g	Physically compatible for 24 hr	315	C
Amino acids 4%, dextrose 25%	CU	PR	100 mEq	Physically compatible for 24 hr at 22 °C	313	C
Dextrose 5% in Ringer's injection, lactated	BA	PD	2 g	Physically compatible for 24 hr	315	C
Dextrose 5% in sodium chloride 0.9%			1 g	Physically compatible	74	C
	BA	PD	2 g	Physically compatible for 24 hr	315	C
Dextrose 5% in water			1 g	Physically compatible	74	C
	BA	PD	2 g	Physically compatible for 24 hr	315	C
Dextrose 10% in sodium chloride 0.18%		BP	18 g	Physically compatible for 30 hr at room temperature under fluorescent light	1347	C
Dextrose 10% in water	BA	PD	2 g	Physically compatible for 24 hr	315	C
		BP	18 g	Physically compatible for 30 hr at room temperature under fluorescent light	1347	C
Dextrose 20% in water	BA	PD	2 g	Physically compatible for 24 hr	315	C
Fat emulsion 10%, intravenous	VT	PR	2 g	Produced cracked emulsion	32	I
	KV		7.2 and 9.6 mEq	Immediate flocculation, aggregation, and creaming	1018	I
Fructose 10% in water	BA	PD	2 g	Physically compatible for 24 hr	315	C
Invert sugar 10% in Electrolyte #1	BA	PD	2 g	Physically compatible for 24 hr	315	C
Invert sugar 10% in Electrolyte #2	BA	PD	2 g	Physically compatible for 24 hr	315	C
Polysal M with dextrose 5%	CU	PD	2 g	Physically compatible for 24 hr	315	C
Ringer's injection, lactated			1 g	Physically compatible	74	C
	BA	PD	2 g	Physically compatible for 24 hr	315	C
Sodium chloride 0.9%			1 g	Physically compatible	74	C
	BA	PD	2 g	Physically compatible for 24 hr	315	C
Sodium lactate ⅙ M	BA	PD	2 g	Physically compatible for 24 hr	315	C
TPN #38 to #42[a]		PR		Physically compatible for 24 hr at 22 °C. Alterations in UV spectra in solutions containing MVI or vitamin B complex with C and TLC changes in similar solutions attributed to the vitamins	313	C
TPN #43 to #47[a]		PR		Physically compatible for 24 hr at 22 °C. TLC changes of amino acids in similar solutions attributed to MVI or vitamin B complex with C	313	C

[a]*Refer to Appendix I for the composition of parenteral nutrition solutions. TPN indicates a 2-in-1 admixture.*

Additive Compatibility

Drug	Mfr	Conc/L	Calcium gluconate Mfr	Calcium gluconate Conc/L	Test Soln	Remarks	Ref	C/I
Amikacin sulfate	BR	5 g	UP	500 mg	D5LR, D5R, D5S, D5W, D10W, IS10, LR, NS, R, SL	Physically compatible and potency of both retained for 24 hr at 25 °C	294	C
Aminophylline		250 mg		1 g	D5W	Physically compatible	74	C
Amphotericin B		200 mg	BP	4 g	D5W	Haze develops over 3 hr	26	I
Ascorbic acid injection	UP	500 mg	UP	1 g	D5W	Physically compatible	15	C
Bretylium tosylate	ACC	1 g	ES	2 g	D5W, NS	Physically compatible for 48 hr at 25 °C	756	C
Cefamandole nafate	LI	2 g		200 mg	D5W, NS, W	Haze or precipitate forms	788	I
	LI	20 g		2 g	D5W, NS, W	Haze or precipitate forms	788	I
Chloramphenicol sodium succinate	PD	500 mg		1 g	D5W	Physically compatible	74	C
	PD	10 g	UP	1 g	D5W	Physically compatible	15	C
	PD	10 g	UP	1 g		Physically compatible	6	C
Corticotropin		500 units		1 g	D5W	Physically compatible	74	C
Dimenhydrinate	SE	50 mg		1 g	D5W	Physically compatible	74	C
Dobutamine HCl	LI	182 mg	VI	9 g	NS	Small particles form within 4 hr. White precipitate and haze after 15 hr	522	I
	LI	1 g	ES	2 g	D5W, NS	Deeply pink in 24 hr at 25 °C	789	I
	LI	1 g	IX	50 g	D5W, NS	Small white particles form within 24 hr at 21 °C	812	I
Floxacillin sodium	BE	20 g	ANT	2 g	NS	Thick white precipitate forms immediately	1479	I
Furosemide	HO	1 g	ANT	2 g	NS	Physically compatible for 72 hr at 15 and 30 °C	1479	C
Heparin sodium		12,000 units		1 g	D5W	Physically compatible	74	C
	UP	4000 units	UP	1 g	D5W	Physically compatible	15	C
	AB	20,000 units	UP	1 g		Physically compatible	21	C
Hydrocortisone sodium succinate	UP	100 mg		1 g	D5W	Physically compatible	74	C
	UP	500 mg	UP	1 g	D5W	Physically compatible	15	C
Lidocaine HCl	AST	2 g	ES	2 g	D5W, LR, NS	Physically compatible for 24 hr at 25 °C	775	C
Magnesium sulfate	LI	1, 2, 3, 4 mEq	PR	10, 20, 30, 40 mEq	AA 4%, D 25%	Physically compatible for 24 hr at 22 °C	313	C
	LI	4 to 100 mEq	PR	4 to 100 mEq	PH 4%, D 20%	Physically compatible for 24 hr at room temperature	464	C
Methylprednisolone sodium succinate	UP	40 mg		1 g	D5S	Physically incompatible	329	I
Norepinephrine bitartrate	WI	8 mg		1 g	D5W	Physically compatible	74	C

Additive Compatibility (Cont.)

Calcium gluconate

Drug	*Mfr*	*Conc/L*	*Mfr*	*Conc/L*	*Test Soln*	*Remarks*	*Ref*	*C/I*
Penicillin G potassium		1 million units		1 g	D5W	Physically compatible	74	C
	SQ	20 million units	UP	1 g	D5W	Physically compatible	15	C
Penicillin G sodium	UP	20 million units	UP	1 g	D5W	Physically compatible	15	C
Phenobarbital sodium	WI	200 mg	UP	1 g	D5W	Physically compatible	15	C
Potassium chloride		3 g		1 g	D5W	Physically compatible	74	C
Prochlorperazine edisylate	SKF	100 mg	UP	1 g	D5W	Physically compatible	15	C
	SKF					Physically incompatible	9	I
Tobramycin sulfate	LI	5 g		16 g	D5W	Physically compatible with no loss of tobramycin activity in 60 min at room temperature	984	C
	LI	1 g		33 g	D5W	Physically compatible with no loss of tobramycin activity in 60 min at room temperature	984	C
Vancomycin HCl	LI	1 g		1 g	D5W	Physically compatible	74	C
Verapamil HCl	KN	80 mg	IX	2 g	D5W, NS	Physically compatible for 48 hr	739	C
Vitamin B complex with C		1 vial		1 g	D5W	Physically compatible	74	C
	AB	5 ml	UP	1 g	D5W	Physically compatible	15	C

Drugs in Syringe Compatibility

Calcium gluconate

Drug (in syringe)	*Mfr*	*Amt*	*Mfr*	*Amt*	*Remarks*	*Ref*	*C/I*
Metoclopramide HCl	RB	10 mg/2 ml	ES	1 g/10 ml	Possible precipitate formation	924	I
	RB	10 mg/2 ml	ES	1 g/10 ml	Incompatible. If mixed, use immediately	1167	I
	RB	160 mg/32 ml	ES	1 g/10 ml	Incompatible. If mixed, use immediately	1167	I

Y-Site Injection Compatibility (1:1 Mixture)

Calcium gluconate

Drug	*Mfr*	*Conc*	*Mfr*	*Conc*	*Remarks*	*Ref*	*C/I*
Aldesleukin	CHI	33,800 I.U./ml[a]	LY	100 mg/ml	Visually compatible with little or no loss of aldesleukin activity by bioassay	1857	C
Allopurinol sodium	BW	3 mg/ml[b]	AMR	40 mg/ml[b]	Physically compatible with no change in measured turbidity or increase in particle content in 4 hr at 22 °C	1686	C
Amifostine	USB	10 mg/ml[a]	AMR	40 mg/ml[a]	Physically compatible with no change in measured turbidity or increase in particle content in 4 hr at 23 °C	1845	C

Y-Site Injection Compatibility (1:1 Mixture) (Cont.)

Calcium gluconate

Drug	*Mfr*	*Conc*	*Mfr*	*Conc*	*Remarks*	*Ref*	*C/I*
Amphotericin B cholesteryl sulfate complex	SEQ	0.83 mg/ml[a]	AB	40 mg/ml[a]	Gross precipitate forms	2117	I
Ampicillin sodium	WY	40 mg/ml[b]	AST	4 mg/ml[b]	Physically compatible for 3 hr	1316	C
	WY	40 mg/ml[a]	AST	4 mg/ml[a]	Slight color change in 1 hr	1316	I
Aztreonam	SQ	40 mg/ml[a]	AMR	40 mg/ml[a]	Physically compatible with no subvisual haze or particle formation in 4 hr at 23 °C	1758	C
Cefazolin sodium	LI	40 mg/ml[c]	AST	4 mg/ml[c]	Physically compatible for 3 hr	1316	C
Cefepime HCl	BMS	20 mg/ml[a]	AMR	40 mg/ml[a]	Physically compatible with no change in measured turbidity or increase in particle content in 4 hr at 22 °C	1689	C
Ciprofloxacin	MI	2 mg/ml[a]	LY	10%	Visually compatible for 2 hr at 25 °C	1628	C
Cisatracurium besylate	GW	0.1, 2, 5 mg/ml[a]	AB	40 mg/ml[a]	Physically compatible with no change in measured turbidity or increase in particle content in 4 hr at 23 °C	2074	C
Cladribine	ORT	0.015[b] and 0.5[d] mg/ml	AMR	40 mg/ml[b]	Physically compatible with no change in measured turbidity or increase in particle content in 4 hr at 23 °C	1969	C
Dobutamine HCl	LI	4 mg/ml[c]	AST	4 mg/ml[c]	Physically compatible for 3 hr	1316	C
Docetaxel	RPR	0.9 mg/ml[a]	FUJ	40 mg/ml[a]	Physically compatible with little or no change in measured turbidity and no increase in particle content in 4 hr at 23 °C	2224	C
Doxorubicin HCl liposome injection	SEQ	0.4 mg/ml[a]	AB	40 mg/ml[a]	Physically compatible with no change in measured turbidity or increase in particle content in 4 hr at 23 °C	2087	C
Enalaprilat	MSD	0.05 mg/ml[b]	ES	0.092 mEq/ml[a]	Physically compatible for 24 hr at room temperature under fluorescent light	1355	C
Epinephrine HCl	ES	0.032 mg/ml[c]	AST	4 mg/ml[c]	Physically compatible for 3 hr	1316	C
Etoposide phosphate	BR	5 mg/ml[a]	FUJ	40 mg/ml[a]	Physically compatible with no change in measured turbidity or increase in particle content in 4 hr at 23 °C	2218	C
Famotidine	MSD	0.2 mg/ml[a]	LY	0.00465 mEq/ml[b]	Physically compatible for 14 hr	1196	C
Filgrastim	AMG	30 μg/ml[a]	AST	40 mg/ml[a]	Physically compatible with no change in measured turbidity or increase in particle content in 4 hr at 22 °C	1687	C
Fluconazole	RR	2 mg/ml	ES	100 mg/ml	Cloudiness	1407	I
Gatifloxacin	BMS	2 mg/ml[a]	FUJ	40 mg/ml[a]	Physically compatible with no change in measured haze or increase in particle content in 4 hr at 23 °C	2234	C
Gemcitabine HCl	LI	10 mg/ml[b]	FUJ	40 mg/ml[b]	Physically compatible with no change in measured turbidity or increase in particle content in 4 hr at 23 °C	2226	C
Granisetron HCl	SKB	0.05 mg/ml[a]	AB	40 mg/ml[a]	Physically compatible with no change in measured turbidity or increase in particle content in 4 hr at 23 °C	2000	C

Y-Site Injection Compatibility (1:1 Mixture) (Cont.)

			Calcium gluconate				
Drug	*Mfr*	*Conc*	*Mfr*	*Conc*	*Remarks*	*Ref*	*C/I*
Heparin sodium with hydrocortisone sodium succinate	RI UP	1000 units + 100 mg/L[e]	ES	100 mg/ml	Physically compatible for at least 4 hr at room temperature by visual and microscopic examination	322	C
Hetastarch in lactated electrolyte injection (Hextend)	AB	6%	FUJ	40 mg/ml[a]	Physically compatible with no change in measured turbidity or increase in particle content in 4 hr at 23 °C	2339	C
Indomethacin sodium trihydrate	MSD	1 mg/ml[b]	AMR	100 mg/ml	Fine yellow precipitate forms within 1 hr	1527	I
Labetalol HCl	SC	1 mg/ml[a]	AMR	0.23 mEq/ml[a]	Physically compatible for 24 hr at 18 °C	1171	C
Linezolid	PHU	2 mg/ml	AMR	40 mg/ml[a]	Physically compatible with no change in measured turbidity or increase in particle content in 4 hr at 23 °C	2264	C
Melphalan HCl	BW	0.1 mg/ml[b]	AST	40 mg/ml[b]	Physically compatible with no change in measured turbidity or increase in particle content in 3 hr at 22 °C	1557	C
Meropenem	ZEN	1 mg/ml[b]	AMR	4 mg/ml[f]	Visually compatible for 4 hr at room temperature	1994	C
	ZEN	50 mg/ml[b]	AMR	4 mg/ml[f]	Yellow discoloration forms in 4 hr at room temperature	1994	I
Midazolam HCl	RC	1 mg/ml[a]	FUJ	100 mg/ml	Visually compatible for 24 hr at 23 °C	1847	C
Milrinone lactate	SW	0.4 mg/ml[a]	LY	0.465 mEq/ml	Visually compatible with no loss of milrinone by HPLC in 4 hr at 23 °C	2214	C
Netilmicin sulfate	SC	5 mg/ml[g]	LY	40 mg/ml[g]	Physically compatible and no netilmicin loss in 2 hr at 24 °C	1021	C
Piperacillin sodium–tazobactam sodium	LE	40 + 5 mg/ml[a]	AMR	40 mg/ml[a]	Physically compatible with no change in measured turbidity or increase in particle content in 4 hr at 22 °C	1688	C
Potassium chloride		40 mEq/L[e]	ES	100 mg/ml	Physically compatible for at least 4 hr at room temperature by visual and microscopic examination	322	C
Prochlorperazine edisylate	SCN	5 mg/ml	AMR	10 mg/ml[b]	Visually compatible for 24 hr at room temperature in test tubes. No precipitate found on filter from Y-site delivery	2063	C
Propofol	ZEN	10 mg/ml	AMR	40 mg/ml[a]	Physically compatible for 1 hr at 23 °C with no increase in particle content	2066	C
Remifentanil HCl	GW	0.025 and 0.25 mg/ml[b]	AB	40 mg/ml[a]	Physically compatible with no change in measured turbidity or increase in particle content in 4 hr at 23 °C	2075	C
Sargramostim	IMM	10 μg/ml[b]	AMR	40 mg/ml[b]	Physically compatible for 4 hr at 22 °C	1436	C
Tacrolimus	FUJ	1 mg/ml[b]	ES	100 mg/ml	Visually compatible for 24 hr at 25 °C	1630	C
Teniposide	BR	0.1 mg/ml[a]	AMR	40 mg/ml[a]	Physically compatible with no subvisual haze or particle formation in 4 hr at 23 °C	1725	C
Thiotepa	IMM[h]	1 mg/ml[a]	AMR	40 mg/ml[a]	Physically compatible with no change in measured turbidity or increase in particle content in 4 hr at 23 °C	1861	C

Y-Site Injection Compatibility (1:1 Mixture) (Cont.)

			Calcium gluconate				
Drug	*Mfr*	*Conc*	*Mfr*	*Conc*	*Remarks*	*Ref*	*C/I*
TNA #218 to #226[i]			AB	40 mg/ml[a]	Visually compatible with no precipitate or emulsion damage apparent in 4 hr at 23 °C	2215	C
Tolazoline HCl		0.1 mg/ml[a]	AMR	100 mg/ml	Physically compatible for 24 hr at 22 °C	1363	C
TPN #189[i]			DB	10 mg/ml[b]	Visually compatible for 24 hr at 22 °C	1767	C
TPN #212 to #215[i]			AB	40 mg/ml[a]	Physically compatible with no change in measured turbidity or increase in particle content in 4 hr at 23 °C	2109	C
Vinorelbine tartrate	BW	1 mg/ml[b]	AMR	40 mg/ml[b]	Physically compatible with no change in measured turbidity or increase in particle content in 4 hr at 22 °C	1558	C
Vitamin B complex with C	RC	2 ml/L[e]	ES	100 mg/ml	Physically compatible for at least 4 hr at room temperature by visual and microscopic examination	322	C

[a]*Tested in dextrose 5% in water.*
[b]*Tested in sodium chloride 0.9%.*
[c]*Tested in both dextrose 5% in water and sodium chloride 0.9%.*
[d]*Tested in bacteriostatic sodium chloride 0.9% preserved with benzyl alcohol 0.9%.*
[e]*Tested in dextrose 5% in water, Ringer's injection, lactated, and sodium chloride 0.9%.*
[f]*Tested in sterile water for injection.*
[g]*Tested in dextrose 5% in sodium chloride 0.9%.*
[h]*Lyophilized formulation tested.*
[i]*Refer to Appendix I for the composition of parenteral nutrition solutions. TNA indicates a 3-in-1 admixture, and TPN indicates a 2-in-1 admixture.*

Additional Compatibility Information

Calcium and Phosphate — UNRECOGNIZED CALCIUM PHOSPHATE PRECIPITATION IN A 3-IN-1 PARENTERAL NUTRITION MIXTURE RESULTED IN PATIENT DEATH. The potential for the formation of a calcium phosphate precipitate in parenteral nutrition solutions is well studied and documented (1771; 1777), but the information is complex and difficult to apply to the clinical situation. (1770; 1772; 1777) The incorporation of fat emulsion in 3-in-1 parenteral nutrition solutions obscures any precipitate that is present, which has led to substantial debate on the dangers associated with 3-in-1 parenteral nutrition mixtures and when or if the danger to the patient is warranted therapeutically. (1770–1772; 2031–2036) Because such precipitation may be life-threatening to patients (2037; 2291), the Food and Drug Administration issued a Safety Alert containing the following recommendations (1769):

"1. The amounts of phosphorus and of calcium added to the admixture are critical. The solubility of the added calcium should be calculated from the volume at the time the calcium is added. It should not be based upon the final volume.

   Some amino acid injections for TPN admixtures contain phosphate ions (as a phosphoric acid buffer). These phosphate ions and the volume at the time the phosphate is added should be considered when calculating the concentration of phosphate additives. Also, when adding calcium and phosphate to an admixture, the phosphate should be added first.

   The line should be flushed between the addition of any potentially incompatible components.

2. A lipid emulsion in a three-in-one admixture obscures the presence of a precipitate. Therefore, if a lipid emulsion is needed, either (1) use a two-in-one admixture with the lipid infused separately, or (2) if a three-in-one admixture is medically necessary, then add the calcium before the lipid emulsion and according to the recommendations in number 1 above.

   If the amount of calcium or phosphate which must be added is likely to cause a precipitate, some or all of the calcium should be administered separately. Such separate infusions must be properly diluted and slowly infused to avoid serious adverse events related to the calcium.

3. When using an automated compounding device, the above steps should be considered when programming the device. In addition, automated compounders should be maintained and operated according to the manufacturer's recommendations.

   Any printout should be checked against the programmed admixture and weight of components.

4. During the mixing process, pharmacists who mix parenteral nutrition admixtures should periodically agitate the admixture and check for precipitates. Medical or home care personnel who start and monitor these infusions should carefully inspect for the presence of precipitates both before and during infusion. Patients and care givers should be trained to visually inspect for signs of precipitation. They also should be advised to stop the infusion and seek medical assistance if precipitates are noted.

5. A filter should be used when infusing either central or peripheral parenteral nutrition admixtures. At this time, data have not been submitted to document which size filter is most effective in trapping precipitates.

Standards of practice vary, but the following is suggested: a 1.2-μm air-eliminating filter for lipid-containing admixtures and a 0.22-μm air-eliminating filter for non-lipid-containing admixtures.

6. Parenteral nutrition admixtures should be administered within the following time frames: if stored at room temperature, the infusion should be started within 24 hours after mixing; if stored at refrigerated temperatures, the infusion should be started within 24 hours of rewarming. Because warming parenteral nutrition admixtures may contribute to the formation of precipitates, once administration begins, care should be taken to avoid excessive warming of the admixture.

   Persons administering home care parenteral nutrition admixtures may need to deviate from these time frames. Pharmacists who initially prepare these admixtures should check a reserve sample for precipitates over the duration and under the conditions of storage.

7. If symptoms of acute respiratory distress, pulmonary emboli, or interstitial pneumonitis develop, the infusion should be stopped immediately and thoroughly checked for precipitates. Appropriate medical interventions should be instituted. Home care personnel and patients should immediately seek medical assistance."

Calcium Phosphate Precipitation Fatalities—Hill et al. reported fatal cases of paroxysmal respiratory failure in two previously healthy women receiving peripheral vein parenteral nutrition. The patients experienced sudden cardiopulmonary arrest consistent with pulmonary emboli. The authors used in vitro simulations and an animal model to conclude that unrecognized calcium phosphate precipitation in a 3-in-1 total nutrition admixture caused the fatalities. The precipitation resulted during compounding by introducing calcium and phosphate near to one another in the compounding sequence and prior to complete fluid addition. This resulted in a temporarily high concentration of the drugs and precipitation of calcium phosphate. Observation of the precipitate was obscured by the incorporation of a 20% fat emulsion, intravenous into the nutrition mixture. No filter was used during infusion of the fatal nutrition admixtures. (2037)

In a follow-up retrospective review, Shay et al. reported that five patients were identified that had respiratory distress associated with the infusion of the 3-in-1 admixtures at around the same time. Four of these five patients died, although the cause of death could be definitively determined for only two of them from the available information. (2291)

Calcium and Phosphate Conditional Compatibility—Calcium salts are conditionally compatible with phosphate in parenteral nutrition solutions. The incompatibility is dependent on a solubility and concentration phenomenon and is not entirely predictable. Precipitation may occur during compounding or at some time after compounding is completed.

NOTE: Some amino acid solutions inherently contain both calcium and phosphate, which must be considered in any projection of compatibility. See the amino acid injection monograph, Table 1.

The order of mixing of calcium gluconate and potassium phosphate may affect compatibility at elevated concentrations. Addition of potassium phosphate should precede that of calcium gluconate. (313; 1210)

A study by Henry et al. (608) determined the maximum concentrations of calcium (as chloride and gluconate) and phosphate that can be maintained without precipitation in a parenteral nutrition solution

Figure 1. *Maximum solubilities of calcium chloride (○) and calcium gluconcate (△) with sodium phosphate in an amino acid 4.25% -dextrose 25% solution at 30 °C*

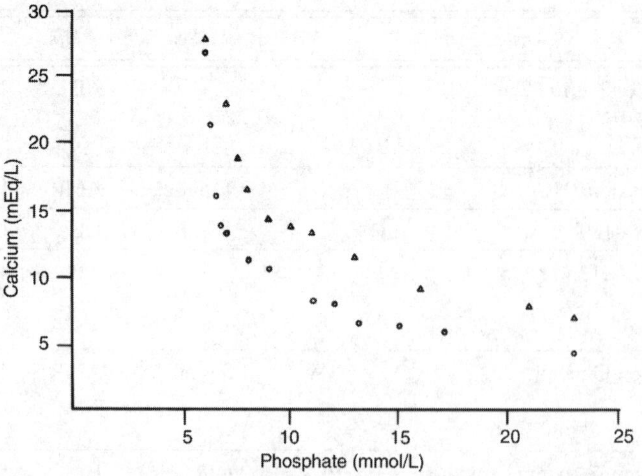

consisting of FreAmine II 4.25% and dextrose 25% for 24 hours at 30 °C. Their results are depicted in Figure 1.

Henry et al. noted that the amino acids in parenteral nutrition solutions form soluble complexes with calcium and phosphate, reducing the available free calcium and phosphate that can form insoluble precipitates. The concentration of calcium available for precipitation is greater with the chloride salt compared to the gluconate salt, at least in part because of differences in dissociation characteristics. This can be seen in Figure 1 by the greater concentration of calcium gluconate that can be mixed with sodium phosphate. (608)

In addition to the concentrations of phosphate and calcium and the salt form of the calcium, Henry et al. noted that the concentration of amino acids and the time and temperature of storage altered the formation of calcium phosphate in parenteral nutrition solutions. As the temperature was increased, the incidence of precipitate formation also increased. This finding was attributed, at least in part, to a greater degree of dissociation of the calcium and phosphate complexes and the decreased solubility of calcium phosphate. Therefore, a solution possibly may be stored at 4 °C with no precipitation, but on warming to room temperature a precipitate will form over time. (608)

Eggert et al. (609) evaluated the compatibility of calcium and phosphate in several parenteral nutrition formulas for newborn infants. Calcium gluconate 10% (Cutter) and potassium phosphate (Abbott) were used to achieve concentrations of 2.5 to 100 mEq/L of calcium and 2.5 to 100 mmol/L of phosphorus added. The parenteral nutrition solutions evaluated were as shown in Table 1. The results were reported as graphic depictions.

Eggert et al. noted the pH dependence of the phosphate–calcium precipitation. Dibasic calcium phosphate is very insoluble, while monobasic calcium phosphate is relatively soluble. At low pH, the

Table 1. Parenteral Nutrition Solutions Used by Eggert et al. (609)

	Solution Number			
Component	#1	#2	#3	#4
FreAmine III	4%	2%	1%	1%
Dextrose	25%	20%	10%	10%
pH	6.3	6.4	6.6	7.0[a]

[a]*Adjusted with sodium hydroxide.*

soluble monobasic form predominates; but as the pH increases, more dibasic phosphate becomes available to bind with calcium and precipitates. Therefore, the lower the pH of the parenteral nutrition solution, the more calcium and phosphate can be solubilized. Once again, the effects of temperature were observed. As the temperature is increased, more calcium ion becomes available and more dibasic calcium phosphate is formed. Therefore, temperature increases will increase the amount of precipitate. (609)

Fitzgerald and MacKay reported similar calcium and phosphate solubility curves for neonatal parenteral nutrition solutions using TrophAmine (McGaw) 2, 1.5, and 0.8% as the sources of amino acids. The solutions also contained dextrose 10%, with cysteine and pH adjustment being used in some admixtures. Calcium and phosphate solubility followed the patterns reported by Eggert et al. (609) A slightly greater concentration of phosphate could be used in some mixtures, but this finding was not consistent. (1024)

Using a similar study design, Fitzgerald and MacKay also studied six neonatal parenteral nutrition solutions based on Aminosyn-PF (Abbott) 2, 1.5, and 0.8%, with and without added cysteine HCl and dextrose 10%. Calcium concentrations ranged from 2.5 to 50 mEq/L, and phosphate concentrations ranged from 2.5 to 50 mmol/L. Solutions sat for 18 hours at 25 °C and then were warmed to 37 °C in a water bath to simulate the clinical situation of warming prior to infusion into a child. Solubility curves were markedly different than those for TrophAmine in the previous study. (1024) Solubilities were reported to decrease by 15 mEq/L for calcium and 15 mmol/L for phosphate. The solutions remained clear during room temperature storage, but crystals often formed on warming to 37 °C. (1211)

However, these data were questioned by Mikrut, who noted the similarities between the Aminosyn-PF and TrophAmine products and found little difference in calcium and phosphate solubilities in a preliminary report. (1212) In the full report (1213), parenteral nutrition solutions containing Aminosyn-PF or TrophAmine 1 or 2.5% with dextrose 10 or 25%, respectively, plus electrolytes and trace metals, with or without cysteine HCl, were evaluated under the same conditions used by Fitzgerald and MacKay. Calcium concentrations ranged from 2.5 to 50 mEq/L, and phosphate concentrations ranged from 5 to 50 mmol/L. In contrast to the results of Fitzgerald and MacKay, the solubility curves were very similar for the Aminosyn-PF and TrophAmine parenteral nutrition solutions but very different from those of the previous Aminosyn-PF study. (1211) The authors again showed that the solubility of calcium and phosphate is greater in solutions containing higher concentrations of amino acids and dextrose. (1213)

Dunham et al. also reported calcium and phosphate solubility curves for TrophAmine 1 and 2% with dextrose 10% and electrolytes, vitamins, heparin, and trace elements. Calcium concentrations ranged from 10 to 60 mEq/L, and phosphorus concentrations ranged from 10 to 40 mmol/L. Calcium and phosphate solubilities were assessed by analysis of the calcium concentrations and followed patterns similar to those reported by Henry et al. (608) The higher percentage of amino acids (TrophAmine 2%) permitted a slightly greater solubility of calcium and phosphate, especially in the 10- to 50-mEq/L and 10- to 35-mmol/L ranges, respectively. (1614)

Knight et al. reported the maximal product of the amount of calcium (as gluconate) times phosphate (as potassium) that can be added to a parenteral nutrition solution, composed of amino acids 1% (Travenol) and dextrose 10%, for preterm infants. Turbidity was observed on initial mixing when the solubility product was around 115 to 130 mM^2 or greater. After storage at 7 °C for 20 hours, visible precipitates formed at solubility products of 130 mM^2 or greater. If the solution was administered through a barium-impregnated silicone rubber catheter, crystalline precipitates obstructed the catheters in 12 hours at a solubility product of 100 mM^2 and in 10 days at 79 mM^2, much lower than the in vitro results. (1041)

Poole et al. determined the solubility characteristics of calcium and phosphate in pediatric parenteral nutrition solutions composed of Aminosyn 0.5, 2, and 4% with dextrose 10 to 25%. Also present were electrolytes and vitamins. Sodium phosphate was added sequentially in phosphorus concentrations from 10 to 30 mmol/L. Calcium gluconate was added last in amounts ranging from 1 to 10 g/L. The solutions were stored at 25 °C for 30 hours and examined visually and microscopically for precipitation. The authors found that higher concentrations of Aminosyn increased the solubility of calcium and phosphate. Precipitation occurred at lower calcium and phosphate concentrations in the 0.5% solution compared to the 2 and 4% solutions. For example, at a phosphorus concentration of 30 mmol/L, precipitation occurred at calcium gluconate concentrations of about 1, 2, and 4 g/L in the 0.5, 2, and 4% Aminosyn mixtures, respectively. Similarly, at a calcium gluconate concentration of 8 g/L and above, precipitation occurred at phosphorus concentrations of about 13, 17, and 22 mmol/L in the 0.5, 2, and 4% solutions, respectively. The dextrose concentration did not appear to affect the calcium and phosphate solubility significantly. (1042)

Alexander and Arena evaluated the compatibility of calcium gluconate (American Quinine) and potassium phosphate (Lyphomed) in a parenteral nutrition solution, composed of dextrose 12.5% and amino acid injection (FreAmine III, McGaw) 1.33% and having a pH of 6.6, for premature infants. Potassium phosphate was added in varying amounts to samples of this solution. The samples were then titrated with calcium gluconate 10%. From the resulting data, an equation was derived to predict when precipitation would occur:

$$Y = -0.455X + 2.951$$

where Y is the Log_{10} of the calcium gluconate concentration (as mg/100 ml) and X is the phosphate concentration (as mmol/100 ml). The equation can be solved to determine the maximum concentration of calcium gluconate for a given phosphate concentration or vice versa. If either additive is sufficiently dilute, then the other can be added in high concentrations without precipitation occurring, obviating the need for the equation. These lower limits were set at 60 mg/100 ml for calcium gluconate and 0.6 mmol/100 ml for phosphate. (1004)

While the authors noted that this equation technically applies to the specific solution being tested and that other variables such as temperature can affect precipitation, in practice they found it applicable to a variety of parenteral nutrition solutions, having similar components and pH values, for premature infants. The equation is *not* applicable to parenteral nutrition solutions with amino acid and dextrose concentrations, other components, or pH values that are much different. (1004)

Venkataraman et al. evaluated the solubility of calcium and phosphorus in neonatal parenteral nutrition solutions composed of amino acids (Abbott) 1.25 and 2.5% with dextrose 5 and 10%, respectively. Also present were multivitamins and trace elements. The solutions contained calcium (as gluconate) in amounts ranging from 25 to 200 mg/100 ml. The phosphorus (as potassium phosphate) concentrations evaluated ranged from 25 to 150 mg/100 ml. If calcium gluconate was added first, cloudiness occurred immediately. If potassium phosphate was added first, substantial quantities could be added with no precipitate formation in 48 hours at 4 °C (Table 2). However, if stored at 22 °C, the solutions were stable for only 24 hours, and all contained precipitates after 48 hours. (1210)

Table 2. Maximum Calcium and Phosphorus Concentrations Physically Compatible for 48 Hours at 4 °C (1210)

	Phosphorus (mg/100 ml)	
Calcium (mg/100 ml)	Amino Acids 1.25% + Dextrose 5%[a]	Amino Acids 2.5% + Dextrose 10%[a]
200[b]	50	75
150	50	100
100	75	100
50	100	125
25	150[b]	150[b]

[a]*Plus multivitamins and trace elements.*
[b]*Maximum concentration tested.*

Kirkpatrick et al. reported the physical compatibility of calcium gluconate 10 to 40 mEq/L and potassium phosphates 10 to 40 mmol/L in three neonatal parenteral nutrition solutions (TPN #123 to #125 in Appendix I), alone and with retrograde administration of aminophylline 7.5 mg diluted with 1.5 ml of sterile water for injection. Contact of the alkaline aminophylline solution with the parenteral nutrition solutions resulted in the precipitation of calcium phosphate at much lower concentrations than were compatible in the parenteral nutrition solutions alone. (1404)

Koorenhof and Timmer reported the maximum allowable concentrations of calcium and phosphate in a 3-in-1 parenteral nutrition mixture for children (TNA #192 in Appendix I). Added calcium was varied from 1.5 to 150 mmol/L, while added phosphate was varied from 21 to 300 mmol/L. The mixtures were stable for 48 hours at 22 and 37 °C as long as the pH was not greater than 5.7, the calcium concentration was below 16 mmol/L, the phosphate concentration was below 52 mmol/L, and the product of the calcium and phosphate concentrations was below 250 $mmol^2/L^2$. (1773)

MacKay et al. reported additional calcium and phosphate solubility curves for specialty parenteral nutrition solutions based on NephrAmine and also HepatAmine at concentrations of 0.8, 1.5, and 2% as the sources of amino acids. The solutions also contained dextrose 10%, with cysteine and pH adjustment to simulate addition of fat emulsion used in some admixtures. Calcium and phosphate solubility followed the hyperbolic patterns reported by Eggert et al. (609) Temperature, time, and pH affected calcium and phosphate solubility, with pH having the greatest effect. (2038)

Shatsky et al. reported the maximum sodium phosphate concentrations for given amounts of calcium gluconate that could be admixed in parenteral nutrition solutions containing TrophAmine in varying quantities (with cysteine HCl 40 mg/g of amino acid) and dextrose 10%. The solutions also contained magnesium sulfate 4 mEq/L, potassium acetate 24 mEq/L, sodium chloride 32 mEq/L, pediatric multivitamins, and trace elements. The presence of cysteine HCl reduces the solution pH and increases the amount of calcium and phosphate that can be incorporated before precipitation occurs. The results of this study cannot be safely extrapolated to TPN solutions with compositions other than the ones tested. The admixtures were compounded with the sodium phosphate added last after thorough mixing of all other components. The authors noted this is not the preferred order of mixing (usually phosphate is added first and thoroughly mixed before adding calcium last); however, they believed this reversed order of mixing would provide a margin of error in cases where the proper order is not followed. After compounding, the solutions were stored for 24 hours at 40 °C. The maximum calcium and phosphate amounts that could be mixed in the various solutions were reported tabularly and are shown in Table 3. (2039) However, these results are not entirely consistent with the study of Hoie and Narducci. (2196) See below.

The temperature dependence of the calcium–phosphate precipitation has resulted in the occlusion of a subclavian catheter by a solution apparently free of precipitation. The parenteral nutrition solution consisted of FreAmine III 500 ml, dextrose 70% 500 ml, sodium chloride 50 mEq, sodium phosphate 40 mmol, potassium acetate 10 mEq, potassium phosphate 40 mmol, calcium gluconate 10 mEq, magnesium sulfate 10 mEq, and Shil's trace metals solution 1 ml. Although there was no evidence of precipitation in the bottle, tubing and pump cassette, and filter (all at approximately 26 °C) during administration, the occluded catheter and Vicra Loop Lock (next to the patient's body at 37 °C) had numerous crystals identified as calcium phosphate. In vitro, this parenteral nutrition solution had a precipitate in 12 hours at 37 °C but was clear for 24 hours at 26 °C. (610)

Similarly, a parenteral nutrition solution that was clear and free of particulates after two weeks under refrigeration developed a precipitate in four to six hours when stored at room temperature. When the solution was warmed in a 37 °C water bath, precipitation occurred in one hour. Administration of the solution before the precipitate was noticed led to interstitial pneumonitis due to deposition of calcium phosphate crystals. (1427)

A 2-ml fluid barrier of dextrose 5% in water in a microbore retrograde infusion set failed to prevent precipitation when used between calcium gluconate 200 mg/2 ml and sodium phosphate 0.3 mmol/0.1 ml. (1385)

Fausel et al. evaluated calcium phosphate precipitation phenomena in a series of parenteral nutrition admixtures composed of dextrose 22%, amino acids (FreAmine III) 2.7%, and fat emulsion (Abbott) 0, 1, and 3.2%. Incorporation of calcium gluconate 19 to 24 mEq/L and phosphate (as sodium) 22 to 28 mmol/L resulted in visible precipitation in the fat-free admixtures. New precipitate continued to form over 14 days, even after repeated filtrations of the solutions through 0.2-μm filters. The presence of the amino acids increased calcium and phosphate solubility compared with simple aqueous solutions. However, the incorporation of the fat emulsion did not result in a statistically significant increase in calcium and phosphate solubility. The authors noted that the kinetics of calcium phosphate precipitate formation do not appear to be entirely predictable; both transient and permanent precipitation can occur either during the compounding process or at some time afterward. Because calcium phosphate precipitation can be clinically very dangerous, the use of inline filters was recommended. The filters should have a porosity appropriate to the

Table 3. Maximum Amount of Phosphate (as Sodium) (mmol/L) Not Resulting in Precipitation According to the Study of Shatsky et al. (2039) See CAUTION Below.[a]

	Amino Acid (as TrophAmine) with Cysteine HCl 40 mg/g of Amino Acid				
Calcium (as gluconate)	0%	0.4%	1%	2%	3%
9.8 mEq/L	0	27	42	60	66
14.7 mEq/L	0	15	18	30	36
19.6 mEq/L	0	6	15	27	30
29.4 mEq/L	0	3	6	21	24

[a]*CAUTION: The results cannot be safely extrapolated to solutions with formulas other than the ones tested. See text.*

parenteral nutrition admixture—1.2 μm for fat-containing and 0.2 or 0.45 μm for fat-free nutrition mixtures. (2061)

Hoie and Narducci used laser particle analysis to evaluate the formation of calcium phosphate precipitation in pediatric TPN solutions containing TrophAmine in concentrations ranging from 0.5 to 3% with dextrose 10% and also containing L-cysteine HCl 1 g/L. The solutions also contained in each liter sodium chloride 20 mEq, sodium acetate 20 mEq, magnesium sulfate 3 mEq, trace elements 3 ml, and heparin sodium 500 units. The presence of L-cysteine HCl reduces the solution pH and increases the amount of calcium and phosphate that can be incorporated before precipitation occurs. The results of this study cannot be safely extrapolated to TPN solutions with compositions other than the ones tested. The maximum amounts of phosphate that were incorporated without the appearance of a measurable increase in particulates in 24 hours at 37 °C for each of the amino acid concentrations is shown in Table 4. (2196) These results are not entirely consistent with those of Shatsky et al. See above. The use of more sensitive electronic particle measurement for the formation of subvisual particulates in this study may contribute to the differences in the results.

The presence of magnesium in solutions may also influence the reaction between calcium and phosphate, including the nature and extent of precipitation. (158; 159)

The interaction of calcium and phosphate in parenteral nutrition solutions is a complex phenomenon. Various factors play a role in the solubility or precipitation of a given combination, including (608; 609; 1042; 1063; 1210; 1234; 1427):

1. Concentration of calcium
2. Salt form of calcium
3. Concentration of phosphate
4. Concentration of amino acids
5. Amino acids composition
6. Concentration of dextrose
7. Temperature of solution
8. pH of solution
9. Presence of other additives
10. Order of mixing

Enhanced precipitate formation would be expected from such factors as high concentrations of calcium and phosphate, increases in solution pH, decreases in amino acid concentrations, increases in temperature, addition of calcium before phosphate, lengthy standing times or slow infusion rates, and use of calcium as the chloride salt. (854)

Even if precipitation does not occur in the container, it has been reported that crystallization of calcium phosphate may occur in a Silastic infusion pump chamber or tubing if the rate of administration is slow, as for premature infants. Water vapor may be transmitted outward and be replaced by air rapidly enough to produce supersaturation. (202) Several other cases of catheter occlusion also have been reported. (610; 1427–1429)

The UV spectrum of an equal parts mixture of amino acids 8%–dextrose 50% solution was not altered in 24 hours at 22 °C by the addition of calcium gluconate 20 mEq and potassium phosphate 25 mEq. (313)

Table 4. Maximum Amount of Phosphate (as Potassium) (mmol/L) Not Resulting in Precipitation According to the Study of Hoie and Narducci. (2196) See CAUTION Below.[a]

	Amino Acid (as TrophAmine) plus Cysteine HCl 1 g/L					
Calcium (as Gluconate) (mEq/L)	0.5%	1%	1.5%	2%	2.5%	3%
10	22	28	38	38	38	43
14	18	18	18	38	38	43
19	18	18	18	33	33	38
24	12	18	18	22	28	28
28	12	18	18	18	18	18
33	12	12	12	12	12	12
37	12	12	12	12	12	12
41	9	9	9	12	12	12
45	0	9	9	12	12	12
49	0	9	9	9	12	12
53	0	9	9	9	9	9

[a]*CAUTION: The results cannot be safely extrapolated to solutions with formulas other than the ones tested. See text.*

Folic Acid — Calcium gluconate (Parke-Davis) and folic acid injection (Lederle) have been shown to interact even though a precipitate is not present. The recoverable amount of folic acid from a 10-μg/ml solution declined with increasing concentrations (0.5 to 10 μg/ml) of calcium gluconate. This interaction was reversed by the addition of edetic acid. (538)

Other Drugs — Calcium ions are stated to inhibit the activity of tobramycin sulfate. (145) Clindamycin phosphate (Upjohn) is reported to be physically incompatible with calcium gluconate. (2) In addition, cefazolin sodium appears to be incompatible with calcium gluconate. (143; 278)

Calcium gluconate (Upjohn) in dextrose 5% in water has been reported as conditionally compatible with sodium bicarbonate (Abbott). The incompatibility is dependent on the concentration of the additives. Therefore, if attempting to combine calcium gluconate with sodium bicarbonate, mix the solution thoroughly and observe it for any sign of incompatibility. (15) A white precipitate and turbidity were reported in concentrated solutions. (845)

Calcium gluconate is stated to be incompatible with citrates, soluble carbonates, phosphates, and sulfates. Because of the presence of sodium carbonate in the cefamandole nafate (Lilly) formulation, it is incompatible with calcium ions. (4; 376)

Aluminum — Calcium gluconate injection in glass vials is a significant source of aluminum, which has been associated with neurological impairment in premature neonates. Aluminum is leached from the glass vial during the autoclaving of the vials for sterilization. The use of calcium gluconate injection in polyethylene plastic vials in countries where it is available has been recommended to reduce the aluminum burden for neonates. (2322)

CARBOPLATIN
AHFS 10:00

Products — Carboplatin is available as a lyophilized powder in vials containing 50, 150, or 450 mg with an equal amount of mannitol. Reconstitute the vials with dextrose 5% in water, sodium chloride 0.9%, or sterile water for injection in the following amounts (2):

Vial Size	Volume of Diluent
50 mg	5 ml
150 mg	15 ml
450 mg	45 ml

The reconstituted solutions have a carboplatin concentration of 10 mg/ml.

pH — A 1% solution has a pH of 5 to 7. (2)

Osmolality — Carboplatin 10 mg/ml in sterile water for injection has an osmolality of 94 mOsm/kg. (1689)

Density — Carboplatin (Bristol) reconstituted with sterile water for injection to a concentration of 10 mg/ml has a solution density of 1.01 g/ml. (2041; 2248)

Trade Name(s) — Paraplatin.

Administration — Carboplatin is administered by intravenous infusion over a period of at least 15 minutes or longer. It has also been administered as a continuous intravenous infusion over 24 hours. It may be diluted with compatible diluents to a concentration as low as 0.5 mg/ml for administration. (2; 4)

Stability — Intact vials should be stored at controlled room temperature and protected from light. (2; 4)

The manufacturer states that reconstituted solutions are stable for eight hours at a room temperature not exceeding 25 °C. Because no antibacterial preservative is present, the manufacturer recommends that carboplatin solutions should be discarded eight hours after dilution. (2) However, other information indicates that the drug may be stable for a much longer time. At a concentration of 15 mg/ml in sterile water for injection or at concentrations of 2 and 0.5 mg/ml in dextrose 5% in water, no decomposition occurs in 24 hours at 22 to 25 °C. (234) Aqueous solutions of 10 mg/ml prefilled into plastic syringes exhibited no decomposition in five days at 4 °C and only a 3% loss in 24 hours at 37 °C. (1238)

Carboplatin 1 mg/ml in sterile water for injection was reported to exhibit less than a 10% loss in 14 days at room temperature. (1379)

Carboplatin 7 mg/ml in sterile water for injection exhibited a 4% loss in seven days at 27 °C. At this concentration in sodium chloride 0.9%, an 8% loss occurred in 24 hours at 27 °C. In a sodium bicarbonate 200 mM solution, the carboplatin loss increased to 13% in 24 hours at 27 °C. (1379)

Carboplatin (Bristol-Myers Oncology) 1 mg/ml in sterile water for injection was stable in PVC reservoirs (Parker Micropump) for 14 days at 4 and 37 °C, exhibiting no loss by HPLC analysis. (1696)

pH Effects — The pH range of maximum stability has been reported to be pH 4 to 6 (1919) to 6.5. (1369) The degradation rate increases above pH 6.5. (1369)

Ambulatory Pumps — The stability of carboplatin (Bristol-Myers Oncology) 1 mg/ml in dextrose 5% in water in drug reservoirs of three portable pumps was evaluated and compared to the stability in glass bottles and PVC bags. A PVC reservoir (Pharmacia Deltec pump), an ethylene vinyl acetate reservoir (Celsa Celinject CO1), and an elastomeric balloon (Baxter Infusor) were stored at 4, 22, and 35 °C for 28 days. HPLC analyses for carboplatin content were performed periodically. No color changes or precipitation was observed in any sample at any time. Furthermore, little or no drug loss was found. The largest losses in 28 days were with the glass bottles (5 to 6% loss) and PVC reservoir (2 to 4% loss). However, the ethylene vinyl acetate reservoir and the elastomeric balloon showed carboplatin concentration increases of 4 and 14%, respectively, in 28 days at 35 °C due to moisture transfer through the container material. (1823)

Carboplatin 10 mg/ml (Bristol-Myers Squibb) was repackaged into 30-ml polypropylene syringes for use in the Intelliject portable syringe pump. The carboplatin solution exhibited no visual changes, and HPLC analysis found no loss of carboplatin content when stored at 25 °C for eight days. No evidence of interaction between carboplatin and the syringe plastic was identified, and no impact on the functioning of the syringe pump was observed. (2147)

Carboplatin (Bristol-Myers) 10-mg/ml reconstituted solution and 6 mg/ml in dextrose 5% in water was packaged in 100-ml Pharmacia Deltec medication cassette reservoirs and stored at 37 °C for 14 days protected from light. HPLC analysis found little or no loss of carboplatin under these conditions. Loss of moisture (about 3.7%) due to evaporation was observed by the end of the study period. (2321)

Elastomeric Reservoir Pumps — Carboplatin 0.5 to 10 mg/ml in dextrose 5% in water in Infusor elastomeric reservoir pumps has been stated by the pump manufacturer to be stable for 91 days under refrigeration followed by seven days at 37 °C. (31)

Sorption — Comparison of the stability of carboplatin 1 mg/ml in dextrose 5% in sodium chloride 0.45% in both glass and PVC containers showed no difference, with each sustaining less than a 2% loss in 24 hours at 25 °C. (1087) Simulated infusion of carboplatin 10 mg/ml through a Silastic catheter over 24 hours at 37 °C did not affect the delivered drug concentration. (1238)

Compatibility Information

Solution Compatibility

Carboplatin

Solution	*Mfr*	*Mfr*	*Conc/L*	*Remarks*	*Ref*	*C/I*
Dextrose 5% in sodium chloride 0.2%	AB[a]	NCI	1 g	Physically compatible with less than 2% loss in 24 hr at 25 °C	1087	C

Solution Compatibility (Cont.)

Carboplatin

Solution	*Mfr*	*Mfr*	*Conc/L*	*Remarks*	*Ref*	*C/I*
Dextrose 5% in sodium chloride 0.45%	AB[b]	NCI	1 g	Physically compatible with less than 2% loss in 24 hr at 25 °C	1087	C
Dextrose 5% in sodium chloride 0.9%	AB[a]	NCI	1 g	Physically compatible with 4% loss in 24 hr at 25 °C	1087	C
Dextrose 5% in water	[a]	NCI	500 mg and 2 g	Physically compatible with no decomposition for at least 24 hr at 25 °C	234	C
	AB[a]	NCI	100 mg and 1 g	Physically compatible with 1.5% or less decomposition in 6 hr at 25 °C	1087	C
	[c]	BR	2.4 g	No carboplatin loss by HPLC in 9 days at 23 °C when protected from light	1757	C
	[c]	BR	1 g	Visually compatible and little or no carboplatin loss by HPLC in 28 days at 4, 22, and 35 °C	1823	C
	[a]	BR	1 g	Visually compatible with 5 to 6% carboplatin loss by HPLC in 28 days at 4, 22, and 35 °C	1823	C
	[d]	BR	1 g	Visually compatible with no carboplatin loss by HPLC in 28 days at 4, 22, and 35 °C	1823	C
	[e]	BR	1 g	Visually compatible with little or no carboplatin loss by HPLC in 28 days at 4 and 22 °C. Drug concentration increased by 14% in 28 days at 35 °C due to moisture transfer through container	1823	C
	BA[a]	BMS	500 mg and 4 g	Visually compatible with 3 to 5% loss by HPLC at 25 °C and no loss at 4 °C protected from light in 21 days	2099	C
	BA[a]	BMS	750 mg and 2 g	Visually compatible with no loss by HPLC at 25 and 4 °C protected from light in 7 days	2099	C
	[f]	BR	6 g	Little or no loss by HPLC within 14 days at 37 °C protected from light	2321	C
Sodium bicarbonate 200 mM			1 g	13% loss in 24 hr at 27 °C	1379	I
Sodium chloride 0.9%	AB[a]	NCI	1 g	Physically compatible with 5% loss in 24 hr at 25 °C	1087	C
			7 g	8% loss in 24 hr at 27 °C	1379	C

[a]*Tested in glass containers.*
[b]*Tested in both glass and PVC containers.*
[c]*Tested in PVC containers.*
[d]*Tested in ethylene vinyl acetate containers.*
[e]*Tested in elastomeric balloon reservoirs (Baxter Infusor).*
[f]*Tested in Pharmacia Deltec medication cassette reservoirs.*

Additive Compatibility

Carboplatin

Drug	*Mfr*	*Conc/L*	*Mfr*	*Conc/L*	*Test Soln*	*Remarks*	*Ref*	*C/I*
Cisplatin		200 mg		1 g	NS	Less than 10% loss of both drugs in 24 hr at 23 °C protected from light	1954	C
Etoposide		200 mg		1 g	W	Less than 10% loss of both drugs in 7 days at 23 °C protected from light	1954	C
Floxuridine		10 g		1 g	W	Less than 10% loss of both drugs in 7 days at 23 °C protected from light	1954	C
Fluorouracil		10 g		1 g	W	Greater than 20% carboplatin loss in 24 hr at room temperature	1379	I

Additive Compatibility (Cont.)

Carboplatin

Drug	*Mfr*	*Conc/L*	*Mfr*	*Conc/L*	*Test Soln*	*Remarks*	*Ref*	*C/I*
Ifosfamide		1 g		1 g	W	Both drugs stable for 5 days at room temperature	1379	C
Ifosfamide with etoposide		2 g 200 mg		1 g	W	All drugs stable for 7 days at room temperature	1379	C
Mesna		1 g		1 g	W	Greater than 10% carboplatin loss in 24 hr at room temperature	1379	I
Paclitaxel	BMS	300 mg and 1.2 g	BMS	2 g	NS	No paclitaxel loss but carboplatin losses of less than 2, 5, and 6 to 7% at 4, 24, and 32 °C, respectively, in 24 hr by HPLC. Physically compatible for 24 hr but subvisual particulates of paclitaxel form after 3 to 5 days	2094	C
	BMS	300 mg and 1.2 g	BMS	2 g	D5W	No paclitaxel and carboplatin loss by HPLC at 4, 24, and 32 °C in 24 hr. Physically compatible for 24 hr but subvisual particulates of paclitaxel form after 3 to 5 days	2094	C

Y-Site Injection Compatibility (1:1 Mixture)

Carboplatin

Drug	*Mfr*	*Conc*	*Mfr*	*Conc*	*Remarks*	*Ref*	*C/I*
Allopurinol sodium	BW	3 mg/ml[b]	BR	5 mg/ml[b]	Physically compatible with no change in measured turbidity or increase in particle content in 4 hr at 22 °C	1686	C
Amifostine	USB	10 mg/ml[a]	BR	5 mg/ml[a]	Physically compatible with no change in measured turbidity or increase in particle content in 4 hr at 23 °C	1845	C
Amphotericin B cholesteryl sulfate complex	SEQ	0.83 mg/ml[a]	BR	5 mg/ml[a]	Increased turbidity forms immediately	2117	I
Aztreonam	SQ	40 mg/ml[a]	BMS	5 mg/ml[a]	Physically compatible with no subvisual haze or particle formation in 4 hr at 23 °C	1758	C
Cefepime HCl	BMS	20 mg/ml[a]	BR	5 mg/ml[a]	Physically compatible with no change in measured turbidity or increase in particle content in 4 hr at 22 °C	1689	C
Cladribine	ORT	0.015[b] and 0.5[c] mg/ml	BR	5 mg/ml[b]	Physically compatible with no change in measured turbidity or increase in particle content in 4 hr at 23 °C	1969	C
Doxorubicin HCl liposome injection	SEQ	0.4 mg/ml[a]	BR	5 mg/ml[a]	Physically compatible with little or no change in measured turbidity and no increase in particle content in 4 hr at 23 °C	2087	C
Etoposide phosphate	BR	5 mg/ml[a]	BR	5 mg/ml[a]	Physically compatible with no change in measured turbidity or increase in particle content in 4 hr at 23 °C	2218	C

Y-Site Injection Compatibility (1:1 Mixture) (Cont.)

Drug	*Mfr*	*Conc*	Carboplatin *Mfr*	Carboplatin *Conc*	*Remarks*	*Ref*	*C/I*
Filgrastim	AMG	30 μg/ml[a]	BR	5 mg/ml[a]	Physically compatible with no change in measured turbidity or increase in particle content in 4 hr at 22 °C	1687	C
Fludarabine phosphate	BX	1 mg/ml[a]	BR	5 mg/ml[a]	Physically compatible for 4 hr at room temperature under fluorescent light	1439	C
Gatifloxacin	BMS	2 mg/ml[a]	BR	5 mg/ml[a]	Physically compatible with no change in measured haze or increase in particle content in 4 hr at 23 °C	2234	C
Gemcitabine HCl	LI	10 mg/ml[b]	BR	5 mg/ml[b]	Physically compatible with no change in measured turbidity or increase in particle content in 4 hr at 23 °C	2226	C
Granisetron HCl	SKB	1 mg/ml	BR	1 mg/ml[b]	Physically compatible with little or no loss of either drug by HPLC in 4 hr at 22 °C	1883	C
Linezolid	PHU	2 mg/ml	BR	5 mg/ml[a]	Physically compatible with no change in measured turbidity or increase in particle content in 4 hr at 23 °C	2264	C
Melphalan HCl	BW	0.1 mg/ml[b]	BR	5 mg/ml[b]	Physically compatible with no change in measured turbidity or increase in particle content in 3 hr at 22 °C	1557	C
Ondansetron HCl	GL	1 mg/ml[b]	BR	5 mg/ml[a]	Physically compatible for 4 hr at 22 °C under fluorescent light	1365	C
	GL	16 to 160 μg/ml		0.18 to 9.9 mg/ml	Physically compatible when carboplatin given over 10 to 60 min via Y-site	1366	C
Paclitaxel	NCI	1.2 mg/ml[a]		5 mg/ml[a]	Physically compatible with no change in measured turbidity in 4 hr at 22 °C	1528	C
Piperacillin sodium–tazobactam sodium	LE	40 + 5 mg/ml[a]	BR	5 mg/ml[a]	Physically compatible with no change in measured turbidity or increase in particle content in 4 hr at 22 °C	1688	C
Propofol	ZEN	10 mg/ml	BR	5 mg/ml[a]	Physically compatible for 1 hr at 23 °C with no increase in particle content	2066	C
Sargramostim	IMM	10 μg/ml[b]	BR	5 mg/ml[b]	Physically compatible for 4 hr at 22 °C	1436	C
Teniposide	BR	0.1 mg/ml[a]	BR	5 mg/ml[a]	Physically compatible with no subvisual haze or particle formation in 4 hr at 23 °C	1725	C
Thiotepa	IMM[d]	1 mg/ml[a]	BMS	5 mg/ml[a]	Physically compatible with no change in measured turbidity or increase in particle content in 4 hr at 23 °C	1861	C
TNA #218 to #226[e]			BMS	5 mg/ml[a]	Visually compatible with no precipitate or emulsion damage apparent in 4 hr at 23 °C	2215	C
Topotecan HCl	SKB	56 μg/ml[a,b]	BR	0.9 mg/ml[a,b]	Visually compatible with little or no loss of either drug by HPLC in 4 hr at 22 °C under fluorescent light	2245	C
TPN #212 to #215[e]			BMS	5 mg/ml[a]	Physically compatible with no change in measured turbidity or increase in particle content in 4 hr at 23 °C	2109	C

Y-Site Injection Compatibility (1:1 Mixture) (Cont.)

Carboplatin

Drug	*Mfr*	*Conc*	*Mfr*	*Conc*	*Remarks*	*Ref*	*C/I*
Vinorelbine tartrate	BW	1 mg/ml[b]	BR	5 mg/ml[b]	Physically compatible with no change in measured turbidity or increase in particle content in 4 hr at 22 °C	1558	C

[a]*Tested in dextrose 5% in water.*
[b]*Tested in sodium chloride 0.9%.*
[c]*Tested in bacteriostatic sodium chloride 0.9% preserved with benzyl alcohol 0.9%.*
[d]*Lyophilized formulation tested.*
[e]*Refer to Appendix I for the composition of parenteral nutrition solutions. TNA indicates a 3-in-1 admixture, and TPN indicates a 2-in-1 admixture.*

Additional Compatibility Information

Infusion Solutions — The manufacturer states that carboplatin may be reconstituted and further diluted with sodium chloride 0.9%, along with other diluents, and used within eight hours. (2) Cheung et al. noted an increased rate of carboplatin loss in sodium chloride 0.9% and dextrose 5% in sodium chloride 0.9% compared to other diluents, although they still qualify as compatible solutions. About 4 to 5% was lost in 24 hours at 25 °C. (1087)

However, Perrone et al. found little conversion of carboplatin to cisplatin in sodium chloride solutions. Cisplatin formation was evaluated by HPLC analysis of carboplatin 1 mg/ml in sodium chloride 0.9% at 25 °C with exposure to fluorescent light. Less than 0.1% of the carboplatin had converted to cisplatin in two hours, and 0.7% had converted in 24 hours. These authors do not believe that the formation of cisplatin from carboplatin is a justifiable concern. (1695)

Aluminum — Because of an interaction occurring between carboplatin and the metal aluminum, resulting in precipitate formation and loss of potency, only administration equipment such as needles, syringes, catheters, and sets that contain no aluminum should be used for this drug. (2)

CARMUSTINE (BCNU)
AHFS 10:00

Products — Carmustine is available in vials containing 100 mg of drug, packaged with a vial containing 3 ml of dehydrated alcohol injection, USP, for use as a diluent. (2)

Dissolve the contents of the vial of carmustine with 3 ml of dehydrated alcohol injection, USP. Further dilute with 27 ml of sterile water for injection. The resultant solution will contain 3.3 mg/ml of carmustine in 10% ethanol. (2)

Avoid accidental contact of the reconstituted solution with the skin. Transient hyperpigmentation in the affected areas has occurred. (2; 4)

pH — From 5.6 to 6. (8)

Osmolality — Carmustine (Bristol) 3.3 mg/ml, reconstituted as directed in ethanol and water, has an apparent osmolality that exceeds 2000 mOsm/kg. (2043)

Density — Carmustine (Bristol-Myers Squibb) reconstituted according to the manufacturer's instructions to a concentration of 3.3 mg/ml has a solution density of 0.98 g/ml. (2041; 2248)

Trade Name(s) — BiCNU.

Administration — Carmustine is administered as an intravenous infusion over one to two hours. Shorter durations may result in pain and burning at the injection site and flushing. (2; 4)

Stability — The product consists of vacuum-dried pale yellow flakes or is a congealed mass. Intact vials are stored under refrigeration and are stable for at least two years. (2) The manufacturer states that intact vials are stable for seven days at room temperatures not exceeding 25 °C. (1181; 1236; 1433) Room temperature storage of intact vials results in slow decomposition, with approximately 3% degradation occurring in 36 days. (285)

Reconstitution as directed results in a colorless to pale yellow solution. This solution is stable for eight hours at room temperature protected from light. (2; 4) Decomposition of the reconstituted solution at room temperature is linear with time. About a 6% loss occurs in three hours and about an 8% loss occurs in six hours. (285) A loss of 20% in 21 hours was also reported. (484)

Refrigeration of the solution significantly increases its stability. In 24 hours at 2 to 8 °C with protection from light, approximately 4% decomposition occurs. (285)

Carmustine has a melting point of approximately 30.5 to 32 °C. At this temperature, the drug liquifies, becoming an oily film on the bottom of the vial. Should this occur, the manufacturer recommends that the vials be discarded, because the melting is a sign of decomposition. (2) However, one study showed that storage of the vials at 37 °C for 15 minutes followed by storage at 22 to 25 °C resulted in no decomposition in eight days and about an 8% loss in 37 days. Storage of the vials at 37 °C for seven days resulted in about 10% decomposition. (862)

In 95% ethanol, carmustine 2 mg/ml is reported to be stable for at least 24 hours at 22 to 25 and 37 °C. (862) Under refrigeration, carmustine 0.5 to 0.6 mg/ml in 95% ethanol or absolute ethanol is stable at 0 to 5 °C for up to three months. (863)

Carmustine, reconstituted according to the manufacturer's instructions, was cultured with human lymphoblasts to determine whether its cytotoxic activity was retained. The solution retained cytotoxicity for 24 hours when stored at 4 °C. (1575)

pH Effects—The degradation rate for carmustine in aqueous solution was reported to be at a minimum between pH 5.2 and 5.5 (619) and 3.3 and 4.8. (1237) Above pH 6, the degradation rate increases greatly. (619) Decomposition of 10% occurred in less than two hours at pH 6.5 but in 5.5 hours at optimum pH. (1237)

Light Effects—Increased decomposition rates were reported when carmustine, in solution, was exposed to increasing intensities of light. The observed reaction rate increased sixfold when illumination rose from 500 to 4000 luxes. In this report, light protection for the infusion container was recommended. (1237) However, the reconstituted drug remains stable for eight hours at 25 °C when exposed to normal fluorescent light. (4)

The stability of carmustine (Bristol-Myers Squibb) 0.1, 0.5, and 1 mg/ml in dextrose 5% in water was evaluated at 25 °C both exposed to and protected from light. No clear effect on rate of carmustine loss from exposure to light was demonstrated. Some samples seemed to demonstrate increased rate of loss due to light exposure while others did not. The inherent rapid decomposition of carmustine coupled with container sorption may have masked some light effects. (2337)

Sorption—The manufacturer recommends the use of glass containers for carmustine administration. (2; 4) The rate of loss of carmustine from infusion admixtures in dextrose 5% in water in PVC containers is substantially greater than the rate of loss in glass (519; 1658) or polyolefin (1658) containers. That observation also was confirmed in a study where the rate of loss of carmustine in dextrose 5% in water in glass containers was no more than the usual chemical degradation. A much greater loss occurred when the solution was prepared in a PVC container. (1237)

Substantial loss to PVC infusion sets was also noted. In static tests, 10% of the carmustine was lost in five minutes and only 35% remained after two hours. An ethylene vinyl acetate set resulted in similar sorption; a polyurethane set was substantially worse, with only 20% remaining after two hours. Only a set lined with polyethylene proved resistant to carmustine sorption, resulting in little loss in two hours. (1237)

During simulated infusion, the greatest quantity of carmustine was lost during the first few minutes, with the concentration delivered increasing with time. The drug concentration in the effluent was the lowest from the slowest flow rate because of the longer contact time. For a nominal 500-ml infusion at a flow rate of 530 ml/hr, 4.6% of the drug was lost during the first hour. At 265 ml/hr, the loss increased to 8.1% in the first hour; at a flow rate of 88 ml/hr, the loss soared to 23% in the first hour. (1237)

Carmustine (Bristol-Myers Squibb) 0.1, 0.5, and 1 mg/ml in dextrose 5% in water exhibited more rapid rates of loss in PVC containers than in glass or polyethylene-lined trilayer plastic bags (Bieffe Medital). The increased rate of loss was attributed to sorption to the PVC containers. (2337)

Compatibility Information

Solution Compatibility

Carmustine

Solution	Mfr	Mfr	Conc/L	Remarks	Ref	C/I
Dextrose 5% in water	TR[a]	BR	1.25 g	10% loss in 7.7 hr at room temperature	519	I
	TR[b]	BR	1.25 g	18.5% loss in 1 hr at room temperature	519	I
	CU	BR	100 mg	No decomposition over 90-min study period	523	C
	MG, TR[a]		1.25 g	10% loss by HPLC in 7.7 to 8.3 hr at room temperature exposed to light	1658	I
	MG[c]		1.25 g	10% loss by HPLC in 7 hr at room temperature exposed to light	1658	I
	TR[b]		1.25 g	10% loss by HPLC in 0.6 hr at room temperature exposed to light	1658	I
	FAN[a]	BMS	100 mg	6 to 7% loss in 2 hr and 11 to 12% loss in 4 hr at 25 °C protected from or exposed to light. 7% loss in 48 hr at 4 °C	2337	I[e]
	MAC[b]	BMS	100 mg	10% loss in 1 hr at 25 °C protected from or exposed to light. 5% loss in 12 hr and 12% loss in 24 hr at 4 °C	2337	I
	BFE[d]	BMS	100 mg	5 to 8% loss in 4 hr and 11 to 14% loss in 6 hr at 25 °C protected from or exposed to light. 5% loss in 48 hr and 15% loss in 7 days at 4 °C	2337	I[e]
	FAN[a]	BMS	500 mg	9% loss in 4 hr and 17% loss in 6 hr at 25 °C protected from or exposed to light. 9% loss in 48 hr at 4 °C	2337	I[e]
	MAC[b]	BMS	500 mg	7% loss in 1 hr and 10 to 13% loss in 2 hr at 25 °C protected from or exposed to light. 7% loss in 12 hr and 18% loss in 24 hr at 4 °C	2337	I

Solution Compatibility (Cont.)

Carmustine

Solution	*Mfr*	*Mfr*	*Conc/L*	*Remarks*	*Ref*	*C/I*
	BFE[d]	BMS	500 mg	9% loss in 6 hr and 13 to 15% loss in 8 hr at 25 °C protected from or exposed to light. 5% loss in 48 hr and 15% loss in 7 days at 4 °C	2337	I[e]
	FAN[a]	BMS	1 g	4% loss in 4 hr and 9% loss in 6 hr protected from light and 9% loss in 4 hr exposed to fluorescent light at 25 °C. 4% loss in 48 hr and 13% loss in 7 days at 4 °C	2337	I[e]
	MAC[b]	BMS	1 g	4 to 7% loss in 1 hr and 9 to 10% loss in 2 hr at 25 °C protected from or exposed to light. 7% loss in 6 hr and 12% loss in 24 hr at 4 °C	2337	I
	BFE[d]	BMS	1 g	7 to 10% loss in 6 hr and 10 to 14% loss in 8 hr at 25 °C protected from or exposed to light. 9% loss in 48 hr and 14% loss in 7 days at 4 °C	2337	I[e]
Sodium chloride 0.9%	CU	BR	100 mg	No decomposition over 90-min study period	523	C

[a] *Tested in glass containers.*
[b] *Tested in PVC containers.*
[c] *Tested in polyolefin containers.*
[d] *Polyethylene-lined trilayer containers.*
[e] *Incompatible by conventional standards but may be used in lesser time periods.*

Additive Compatibility

Carmustine

Drug	*Mfr*	*Conc/L*	*Mfr*	*Conc/L*	*Test Soln*	*Remarks*	*Ref*	*C/I*
Sodium bicarbonate	AB	100 mEq	BR	100 mg	D5W, NS	10% carmustine decomposition in 15 min, 27% in 90 min	523	I

Y-Site Injection Compatibility (1:1 Mixture)

Carmustine

Drug	*Mfr*	*Conc*	*Mfr*	*Conc*	*Remarks*	*Ref*	*C/I*
Allopurinol sodium	BW	3 mg/ml[b]	BR	1.5 mg/ml[b]	Gas evolves immediately	1686	I
Amifostine	USB	10 mg/ml[a]	BR	1.5 mg/ml[a]	Physically compatible with no change in measured turbidity or increase in particle content in 4 hr at 23 °C	1845	C
Aztreonam	SQ	40 mg/ml[a]	BMS	1.5 mg/ml[a]	Physically compatible with no subvisual haze or particle formation in 4 hr at 23 °C	1758	C
Cefepime HCl	BMS	20 mg/ml[a]	BR	1.5 mg/ml[a]	Physically compatible with no change in measured turbidity or increase in particle content in 4 hr at 22 °C	1689	C
Etoposide phosphate	BR	5 mg/ml[a]	BR	1.5 mg/ml[a]	Physically compatible with no change in measured turbidity or increase in particle content in 4 hr at 23 °C	2218	C
Filgrastim	AMG	30 µg/ml[a]	BR	1.5 mg/ml[a]	Physically compatible with no change in measured turbidity or increase in particle content in 4 hr at 22 °C	1687	C
Fludarabine phosphate	BX	1 mg/ml[a]	BR	1.5 mg/ml[a]	Physically compatible for 4 hr at room temperature under fluorescent light	1439	C

Y-Site Injection Compatibility (1:1 Mixture) (Cont.)

Carmustine

Drug	*Mfr*	*Conc*	*Mfr*	*Conc*	*Remarks*	*Ref*	*C/I*
Gemcitabine HCl	LI	10 mg/ml[b]	BR	1.5 mg/ml[b]	Physically compatible with no change in measured turbidity or increase in particle content in 4 hr at 23 °C	2226	C
Granisetron HCl	SKB	0.05 mg/ml[a]	BMS	1.5 mg/ml[a]	Physically compatible with no change in measured turbidity or increase in particle content in 4 hr at 23 °C	2000	C
Melphalan HCl	BW	0.1 mg/ml[b]	BR	1.5 mg/ml[b]	Physically compatible with no change in measured turbidity or increase in particle content in 3 hr at 22 °C	1557	C
Ondansetron HCl	GL	1 mg/ml[b]	BR	1.5 mg/ml[a]	Physically compatible for 4 hr at 22 °C	1365	C
Piperacillin sodium–tazobactam sodium	LE	40 +5 mg/ml[a]	BR	1.5 mg/ml[a]	Physically compatible with no change in measured turbidity or increase in particle content in 4 hr at 22 °C	1688	C
Sargramostim	IMM	10 µg/ml[b]	BR	1.5 mg/ml[b]	Physically compatible for 4 hr at room temperature under fluorescent light	1436	C
Teniposide	BR	0.1 mg/ml[a]	BR	1.5 mg/ml[a]	Physically compatible with no subvisual haze or particle formation in 4 hr at 23 °C	1725	C
Thiotepa	IMM[c]	1 mg/ml[a]	BMS	1.5 mg/ml[a]	Physically compatible with no change in measured turbidity or increase in particle content in 4 hr at 23 °C	1861	C
Vinorelbine tartrate	BW	1 mg/ml[b]	BR	1.5 mg/ml[b]	Physically compatible with no change in measured turbidity or increase in particle content in 4 hr at 22 °C	1558	C

[a]*Tested in dextrose 5% in water.*
[b]*Tested in sodium chloride 0.9%.*
[c]*Lyophilized formulation tested.*

Additional Compatibility Information

Infusion Solutions — The manufacturer states that dilution of the reconstituted solution to a 0.2-mg/ml concentration in dextrose 5% in water results in a solution that is stable for eight hours at room temperature protected from light. (2)

Dacarbazine — No alteration in the ultraviolet/visible spectra was observed when dacarbazine was combined in solution with carmustine. (492)

CEFAMANDOLE NAFATE
AHFS 8:12.06

Products — Cefamandole nafate is available in 1- and 2-g vials. The product contains 63 mg of sodium carbonate per gram of cefamandole activity. (2)

For intramuscular administration, each gram of cefamandole should be reconstituted with 3 ml of sterile water for injection, bacteriostatic water for injection, sodium chloride 0.9%, or bacteriostatic sodium chloride 0.9%. (2) The final concentration is approximately 285 mg/ml with a withdrawable volume of about 3.5 ml. The drug dissolves in as little as 1.2 ml of these diluents, but 3 ml yields the most acceptable solution for intramuscular administration. (788) Lidocaine HCl 1% has been used to reconstitute the drug for intramuscular administration, reducing the pain upon injection. Serum concentrations and urine outputs were similar to dosing in sodium chloride 0.9%. (625)

For direct intravenous administration, each gram of cefamandole should be reconstituted with 10 ml of sterile water for injection, dextrose 5% in water, or sodium chloride 0.9%. (2)

For administration as a continuous intravenous infusion, each gram of cefamandole should be reconstituted with 10 ml of sterile water for injection. This solution may then be further diluted in an appropriate amount of a compatible infusion solution. (2) (See Compatibility Information.)

Cefamandole nafate is difficult to dissolve and requires vigorous shaking. Dissolution is reportedly facilitated by keeping the powder at the stopper end of the vial while adding the diluent to the other end of the vial. Subsequent shaking tends to disperse the powder before the diluent wets the surface of a larger powder mass. (620)

Because the cefamandole nafate (Lilly) formulation contains sodium carbonate, carbon dioxide gas is formed after reconstitution. The pressure may be dissipated prior to withdrawal; or it may be utilized to aid in withdrawal of the solution from the vial by inverting the vial over the syringe needle, allowing the solution to flow into the syringe. (2)

pH—Freshly reconstituted solutions have a pH of 6 to 8.5. (2) Immediately after reconstitution, the pH may be near 8.5 but equilibrates near neutrality within a few minutes. (376)

Storage of cefamandole nafate 2 g/100 ml in dextrose 5% in water and sodium chloride 0.9% resulted in dramatic decreases in pH from approximately 7 initially to about 4 after four days at 24 °C. The decline was less rapid at 5 °C. (525)

Osmolality—A solution of cefamandole nafate 1 g/22 ml of sterile water for injection is isotonic. (2)

The osmolality of cefamandole nafate 1 and 2 g was calculated for the following dilutions (1054):

Diluent	Osmolality (mOsm/kg) 50 ml	100 ml
1 g		
Dextrose 5% in water	314	287
Sodium chloride 0.9%	341	314
2 g		
Dextrose 5% in water	357	316
Sodium chloride 0.9%	383	343

Robinson et al. recommended the following maximum cefamandole concentrations to achieve osmolalities suitable for peripheral infusion in fluid-restricted patients (1180):

Diluent	Maximum Concentration (mg/ml)	Osmolality (mOsm/kg)
Dextrose 5% in water	54	530
Sodium chloride 0.9%	49	519
Sterile water for injection	98	466

Sodium Content—The total sodium content per gram of cefamandole activity is 3.3 mEq (77 mg). (2)

Trade Name(s)—Mandol.

Administration—Cefamandole nafate may be administered by deep intramuscular injection, by direct intravenous injection over three to five minutes, by intermittent infusion over 15 to 30 minutes, or by continuous infusion. (2; 4) The manufacturer recommends temporarily discontinuing other solutions being administered at the same site. (2)

Stability—Store intact containers of cefamandole nafate at controlled room temperature. (4) Solutions of cefamandole nafate range from light yellow to amber, depending on the concentration of the drug and the diluent used. (2; 471) The reconstituted solution need not be protected from light. However, light protection is recommended during storage of the vials because the powder discolors upon prolonged exposure to light. (624)

Sodium carbonate is present in the formulation to prevent turbidity or precipitation when reconstituted with some intravenous solutions. (471; 474; 621) This results from the precipitation of cefamandole nafate and cefamandole free acids as the pH of the solution drops from aqueous ester hydrolysis. (472)

Any solutions having an unusual color or containing turbidity or a precipitate should not be used. (471)

The sodium carbonate also enhances in vitro hydrolysis from the nafate to the sodium form. (471; 622; 788) This occurs partially in vitro but proceeds very rapidly in vivo with a $t½$ of about 13 minutes. (622) The rate of in vitro hydrolysis is greater in dextrose 5% in water than in sodium chloride 0.9% due to attack by the dextrose on the formyl ester moiety. However, this is of no clinical significance. (626) The antibacterial activity of both the nafate and sodium salts is essentially the same in normal clinical situations. (471; 621) In vivo, cefamandole is the major circulating species, representing 85 to 89% of the total plasma concentration. (622)

After reconstitution, room temperature storage results in carbon dioxide evolution from the solution because of the sodium carbonate present in the formulation. This gas production has been reported to result in an "explosive like" reaction when cefamandole nafate is repackaged in syringes. (473) The observed phenomenon was not an actual shattering of the syringe (623) but rather the separation of the plunger from the barrel of the syringe. (620; 623) This phenomenon has been described, perhaps more accurately, as "rifling." (620) The manufacturer has indicated that reconstituted solutions should be left in the original containers and should be withdrawn into syringes just prior to use. (474) This carbon dioxide production is apparently of little consequence on addition to an intravenous solution (473), nor does it preclude storage of the reconstituted product for appropriate time periods in the original vial. (474)

The manufacturer states that reconstituted solutions are stable for 24 hours at 25 °C or 96 hours at 5 °C. (2) These time limits appear to reflect concern over possible microbiological contamination rather than drug instability. (788) The drug actually appears to be stable for longer periods. At the concentrations used for intramuscular injection (approximately 285 mg/ml), the drug is stable (less than 10% decomposition) for 72 hours at 25 °C or 10 days at 5 °C in the following vehicles (788):

Bacteriostatic sodium chloride 0.9% (parabens or benzyl alcohol)
Bacteriostatic water for injection (parabens or benzyl alcohol)
Lidocaine 0.5, 1, or 2%
Sodium chloride 0.9%
Water for injection

Freezing Solutions—Cefamandole nafate (Lilly) solutions are stable in the frozen state. At the intramuscular concentration of 1 g/3 ml in the original vials using water for injection, dextrose 5% in water, or sodium chloride 0.9% as diluents, the drug exhibited 1 to 6% decomposition in 52 weeks at −20 °C. At −10 °C, the solution did not completely freeze and a transient turbidity developed when thawed to room temperature. (475)

Further diluted in dextrose 5% in water or sodium chloride 0.9% to a concentration of 1 g/50 ml in glass bottles or PVC containers or a concentration of 1 g/100 ml in glass bottles, cefamandole nafate maintained stability for at least 26 weeks at −20 °C, exhibiting 7% or less decomposition. At −10 °C in sodium chloride 0.9%, the solution was acceptable after 26 weeks; but in dextrose 5% in water at −10 °C, a transient haze developed. (475) At either concentration, the pH of the frozen solutions declined as a function of age. (475)

In another study, cefamandole nafate (Lilly) 1 g/50 ml of dextrose 5% in water in PVC bags was frozen at −20 °C for 30 days. The bags were then thawed by exposure to ambient temperature or microwave radiation. There was no evidence of precipitation or color change and no loss of potency as determined microbiologically in the solutions thawed by either technique. Subsequent storage of the admixture at room temperature for 24 hours also yielded physically compatible solutions exhibiting little or no loss of potency. (554)

Cefamandole nafate (Lilly) 1 g/3.5 ml frozen at −20 °C in glass syringes (Hy-Pod) retained potency for nine months. No gas formation was seen in the frozen syringes. It was recommended that the syringes be used in a "reasonable" time after thawing and warming to room temperature to avoid gas formation and expulsion of the plunger. (532)

Minibags of cefamandole nafate in dextrose 5% in water or sodium chloride 0.9%, frozen at −20 °C for up to 35 days, were thawed at room temperature and in a microwave oven; the thawed solution temperature never exceeded 25 °C. No significant differences in cefamandole nafate concentrations occurred between the two thawing methods. (1192)

If the frozen solution is to be warmed for thawing, a maximum of 37 °C should be observed. Heating after the frozen solution has thawed should be avoided. Thawed solutions should not be refrozen. (2)

Elastomeric Reservoir Pumps—Cefamandole nafate 5 to 40 mg/ml in dextrose 5% in water or sodium chloride 0.9% in Intermate elastomeric reservoir pumps has been stated by the pump manufacturer to be stable for 24 hours at room temperature, 10 days under refrigeration, and 30 days frozen. (31)

Compatibility Information

Solution Compatibility

Cefamandole nafate

Solution	*Mfr*	*Mfr*	*Conc/L*	*Remarks*	*Ref*	*C/I*
Acetated Ringer's injection		LI	2 g	Physically incompatible due to haze formation	788	I
Amino acids 3.5%	AB	LI	2 g	Physically compatible with 6% cefamandole loss in 48 hr at 25 °C and no loss in 10 days at 5 °C	788	C
Amino acids 7%	AB	LI	2 g	Physically compatible with 7% cefamandole loss in 48 hr at 25 °C and 2% loss in 10 days at 5 °C	788	C
Amino acids 8.5% (FreAmine II)	MG	LI	2 g	Physically compatible with 8% cefamandole loss in 48 hr at 25 °C and 4% loss in 10 days at 5 °C	788	C
Amino acids 8.5% with electrolytes	TR	LI	2 g	Physically compatible with 7% cefamandole loss in 48 hr at 25 °C and 1% loss in 10 days at 5 °C	788	C
Amino acids 8.5% without electrolytes	TR	LI	2 g	Physically compatible with 6% cefamandole loss in 48 hr at 25 °C and 2% loss in 10 days at 5 °C	788	C
Dextran 40 and dextrose			2 g	Physically compatible and chemically stable for 24 hr at 25 °C	596	C
Dextran 40 and sodium chloride 0.9%			2 g	Physically compatible and chemically stable for 24 hr at 25 °C	596	C
Dextran 70 and dextrose			2 g	Physically compatible with 6% cefamandole loss in 24 hr at 25 °C	596	C
Dextrose 70 and sodium chloride 0.9%			2 g	Physically compatible with 6% cefamandole loss in 24 hr at 25 °C	596	C
Dextrose 5% and potassium chloride 0.15%		LI	2 g	Physically compatible for 24 hr at 5 and 25 °C with haze formation after that time. 4% loss in 24 hr at 25 °C	788	C
Dextrose 5% in Ringer's injection, lactated		LI	2 g	Physically compatible with 6% loss in 72 hr at 25 °C and no loss in 10 days at 5 °C	788	C
Dextrose 5% in sodium chloride 0.2%		LI	2 g	Physically compatible with 5% loss in 48 hr at 25 °C and no loss in 7 days at 5 °C	376; 788	C

Solution Compatibility (Cont.)

Cefamandole nafate

Solution	*Mfr*	*Mfr*	*Conc/L*	*Remarks*	*Ref*	*C/I*
Dextrose 5% in sodium chloride 0.45%		LI	2 g	Physically compatible with 8% loss in 48 hr at 25 °C and 3% loss in 10 days at 5 °C	788	C
Dextrose 5% in sodium chloride 0.9%		LI	20 g	Physically compatible with 5% loss in 72 hr at 25 °C and 2% loss in 10 days at 5 °C	788	C
		LI	2 g	Physically compatible with 10% loss in 72 hr at 25 °C and no loss in 10 days at 5 °C	788	C
Dextrose 5% in water	[a]	LI	20 g	Physically compatible with 3 to 5% loss in 72 hr at 25 °C and 1 to 3% loss in 10 days at 5 °C	788	C
		LI	2 g	Physically compatible with 5% loss in 48 hr (14% loss in 72 hr) at 25 °C and no loss in 10 days at 5 °C	788	C
	TR[b]	LI	20 g	4% decomposition in 1 day and 10% in 5 days at 24 °C. 2% loss in 4 days and 5% in 44 days at 5 °C	525	C
	TR[b]	LI	20 g	Physically compatible with little or no loss of potency in 24 hr at room temperature	554	C
			2 g	Physically compatible and chemically stable for 24 hr at 25 °C	596	C
	MG[c]	LI	10 g	Physically compatible with 4% loss in 48 hr at room temperature under fluorescent light	983	C
Dextrose 10% in water		LI	20 g	Physically compatible with 6% loss in 72 hr at 25 °C and no loss in 7 days at 5 °C	788	C
		LI	2 g	Physically compatible with 3 to 5% loss in 48 hr at 25 °C and no loss in 7 days at 5 °C	376; 788	C
			2 g	Physically compatible and chemically stable for 24 hr at 25 °C	596	C
Fat emulsion, intravenous			2 g	Physically compatible and chemically stable for 24 hr at 25 °C	596	C
Ionosol B in dextrose 5% in water	AB	LI	2 g	Physically compatible for 24 hr at 5 and 25 °C with haze formation after that time. 4% loss in 24 hr at 25 °C	788	C
Isolyte E with dextrose 5%	MG	LI	2 g	Physically compatible for 24 hr at 5 and 25 °C with haze formation after that time. 5% loss in 24 hr at 25 °C	788	C
Isolyte M with dextrose 5%	MG	LI	2 g	Physically incompatible due to haze formation	788	I
Mannitol 10% in water			2 g	Physically compatible and chemically stable for 24 hr at 25 °C	596	C
Mannitol 15% in water	TR	LI	20 g	9% cefamandole loss in 72 hr at 25 °C and 2% loss in 7 days at 5 °C	376	C
	TR	LI	20 g	Physically compatible with 9% loss in 72 hr at 25 °C and 5% loss in 10 days at 5 °C	788	C
Mannitol 20% in water			2 g	Physically compatible and chemically stable for 24 hr at 25 °C	596	C
Normosol M in dextrose 5% in water	AB	LI	2 g	Physically compatible with 6% loss in 72 hr at 25 °C and 1% loss in 10 days at 5 °C	788	C
Plasma-Lyte	TR	LI	2 g	Physically incompatible due to haze formation	788	I
Plasma-Lyte M in dextrose 5%	TR	LI	2 g	Physically compatible with 5% loss in 72 hr at 25 °C and 2% loss in 10 days at 5 °C	788	C

Solution Compatibility (Cont.)

Cefamandole nafate

Solution	*Mfr*	*Mfr*	*Conc/L*	*Remarks*	*Ref*	*C/I*
Ringer's injection		LI	2 g	Physically incompatible due to haze formation	788	I
Ringer's injection, lactated		LI	2 g	Physically incompatible due to haze formation	788	I
Sodium chloride 0.9%	[a]	LI	20 g	Physically compatible with 3 to 4% loss in 72 hr at 25 °C and 0 to 3% loss in 10 days at 5 °C	788	C
		LI	2 g	Physically compatible with 1% loss in 48 hr (13% loss in 72 hr) at 25 °C and no loss in 10 days at 5 °C	788	C
	TR[b]	LI	20 g	3% decomposition in 1 day and 6% in 5 days at 24 °C. 1% loss in 4 days and 6% in 44 days at 5 °C	525	C
			2 g	Physically compatible and chemically stable for 24 hr at 25 °C	596	C
	MG[c]	LI	10 g	Physically compatible with 4% loss in 12 hr at room temperature under fluorescent light. No further loss occurred through 48 hr	983	C
Sodium lactate ⅙ M		LI	2 g	Physically compatible with 9% loss in 48 hr at 25 °C and no loss in 10 days at 5 °C	788	C
TPN #107[d]			1.5 g	Physically compatible and cefamandole activity retained for 24 hr at 21 °C by microbiological assay	1326	C

[a]*Tested in glass and PVC containers.*
[b]*Tested in PVC containers.*
[c]*Tested in glass bottles.*
[d]*Refer to Appendix I for the composition of parenteral nutrition solutions. TPN indicates a 2-in-1 admixture.*

Additive Compatibility

Cefamandole nafate

Drug	*Mfr*	*Conc/L*	*Mfr*	*Conc/L*	*Test Soln*	*Remarks*	*Ref*	*C/I*
Calcium gluconate		200 mg	LI	2 g	D5W, NS, W	Haze or precipitate forms	788	I
		2 g	LI	20 g	D5W, NS, W	Haze or precipitate forms	788	I
Cimetidine HCl	SKF	3 g		10 g	D5W, NS	Cloudiness forms after 4 to 5 hr, increasing to dense precipitate in 24 hr at room temperature	516	I
	SKF	6 g		20 g	D5W, NS	Cloudiness forms after 4 to 5 hr, increasing to dense precipitate in 24 hr at room temperature	516	I
	SKF	6 g	LI	20 g	D5W	Immediate haze formation, and gelatinous precipitate observed at 24 hr at room temperature. Cimetidine loss of 7% attributed to precipitate	551	I
	SKF	300 mg	LI	1 g	D5W	Physically compatible and cimetidine chemically stable for 24 hr at room temperature. Cefamandole not tested	551	C
Clindamycin phosphate	UP	9 g	LI	10 g	D5W, NS[a]	Physically compatible with no clindamycin loss and 4 to 7% cefamandole loss in 48 hr at room temperature under fluorescent light	983	C

Additive Compatibility (Cont.)

Cefamandole nafate

Drug	*Mfr*	*Conc/L*	*Mfr*	*Conc/L*	*Test Soln*	*Remarks*	*Ref*	*C/I*
Floxacillin sodium	BE	20 g	DI	20 g	W	Physically compatible for 24 hr at 15 and 30 °C. Haze forms in 48 hr and precipitate forms in 72 hr at 30 °C. No change at 15 °C	1479	C
Furosemide	HO	1 g	DI	20 g	W	Physically compatible for 72 hr at 15 and 30 °C	1479	C
Gentamicin sulfate		80 mg	LI	2 and 20 g	D5W, NS, W	Haze or precipitate forms within 4 hr	376; 788	I
		100 mg		1 g	TPN #107[b]	14% gentamicin loss in 24 hr at 21 °C by microbiological assay	1326	I
Metronidazole	RP	5 g[c]	LI	20 g		Physically compatible with little or no pH change for at least 72 hr at 4 °C	807	C
	RP	5 g[c]	LI	20 g		Physically compatible for at least 24 hr at 23 °C, but pH changed significantly	807	?
	SE	5 g	LI	20 g		10% metronidazole loss in 2 hr at 25 °C and in 6 hr at 5 °C, with no further loss occurring up to 3 days. No cefamandole loss noted	979	I
	SE	200 mg	LI	800 mg	W	No immediate loss of potency of either drug	979	C
	BAY	4.2 g	LI	16.7 g	[d]	Visually compatible with little cefamandole loss and 8% or less metronidazole loss in 4 hr at room temperature by HPLC	1888	C
Metronidazole HCl with sodium bicarbonate	SE AB	5 g 50 mEq	LI	2 g	D5W, NS	Physically compatible for 48 hr. Gradual darkening attributed to normal cephalosporin color change with time	765	C
Ranitidine HCl	GL	50 mg and 2 g		1 g	D5W	Ranitidine chemically stable by HPLC for only 6 hr at 25 °C. Cefamandole not tested	1515	I
Tobramycin sulfate	LI	80 mg	LI	2 and 20 g	D5W, NS, W	Haze or precipitate forms within 4 hr	376; 788	I
Verapamil HCl	KN	80 mg	LI	4 g	D5W, NS	Physically compatible for 24 hr	764	C

[a]*Tested in glass bottles.*
[b]*Refer to Appendix I for the composition of parenteral nutrition solutions. TPN indicates a 2-in-1 admixture.*
[c]*Minibags (100 ml) containing metronidazole 500 mg with disodium phosphate 150 mg, citric acid 44 mg, and sodium chloride 740 mg. This product differs from the Searle product.*
[d]*Cefamandole reconstituted with water and added to metronidazole infusion.*

Drugs in Syringe Compatibility

Cefamandole nafate

Drug (in syringe)	*Mfr*	*Amt*	*Mfr*	*Amt*	*Remarks*	*Ref*	*C/I*
Cimetidine HCl	SKF	300 mg/ 2 ml		1 g/5 ml	Immediate precipitation	516	I
Gentamicin sulfate		80 mg/ 2 ml	LI	1 g/10 ml	Haze or precipitate forms within 4 hr	376; 788	I
		80 mg/ 2 ml	LI	1 g/3 ml	Haze or precipitate forms within 4 hr	376	I

Drugs in Syringe Compatibility (Cont.)

Cefamandole nafate

Drug (in syringe)	*Mfr*	*Amt*	*Mfr*	*Amt*	*Remarks*	*Ref*	*C/I*
Heparin sodium		2500 units/ 1 ml	LI	2 g	Physically compatible for at least 5 min	1053	C
Tobramycin sulfate	LI	80 mg/ 2 ml	LI	1 g/10 ml	Haze or precipitate forms within 4 hr	376; 788	I
	LI	80 mg/ 2 ml	LI	1 g/3 ml	Haze or precipitate forms within 4 hr	376	I

Y-Site Injection Compatibility (1:1 Mixture)

Cefamandole nafate

Drug	*Mfr*	*Conc*	*Mfr*	*Conc*	*Remarks*	*Ref*	*C/I*
Acyclovir sodium	BW	5 mg/ml[a]	LI	20 mg/ml[a]	Physically compatible for 4 hr at 25 °C	1157	C
Amiodarone HCl	LZ	4 mg/ml[c]	LI	20 and 40 mg/ml[c]	Precipitate forms	1444	I
Cyclophosphamide	MJ	20 mg/ml[a]	LI	20 mg/ml[a]	Physically compatible for 4 hr at 25 °C	1194	C
Diltiazem HCl	MMD	5 mg/ml	LI	200 mg/ml[b]	Cloudiness forms but clears with swirling	1807	?
	MMD	5 mg/ml	LI	10[b] and 20[a] mg/ml	Cloudiness forms and persists	1807	I
	MMD	1 mg/ml[c]	LI	10[b], 20[a], 200[b] mg/ml	Visually compatible	1807	C
Hetastarch in sodium chloride 0.9%	DCC	6%	LI	20 mg/ml[a]	Small crystals formed immediately after mixing and persisted for 4 hr	1313	I
Hydromorphone HCl	WY	0.2 mg/ml[a]	LI	20 mg/ml[a]	Physically compatible for at least 4 hr at 25 °C under fluorescent light	987	C
Magnesium sulfate	IX	16.7, 33.3, 66.7, 100 mg/ ml[a]	LI	20 mg/ml[a]	Physically compatible for at least 4 hr at 32 °C	813	C
Meperidine HCl	WY	10 mg/ml[a]	LI	20 mg/ml[a]	Physically compatible for at least 4 hr at 25 °C under fluorescent light	987	C
	WY	10 mg/ml[b]	LI	40 mg/ml[a]	Physically compatible for 1 hr at 25 °C	1338	C
Morphine sulfate	WI	1 mg/ml[a]	LI	20 mg/ml[a]	Physically compatible for at least 4 hr at 25 °C under fluorescent light	987	C
	ES	1 mg/ml[b]	LI	40 mg/ml[a]	Physically compatible for 1 hr at 25 °C	1338	C
Perphenazine	SC	0.02 mg/ml[a]	LI	20 mg/ml[a]	Physically compatible for 4 hr at 25 °C	1155	C
TNA #73[d]		32.5 ml[e]	LI	2 g/50 ml[a]	Physically compatible for 4 hr at 25 °C by visual observation	1008	C
TPN #54[d]				250 mg/ml	Physically compatible and cefamandole activity retained over 6 hr at 22 °C by microbiological assay	1045	C
TPN #61[d]		[f]	LI	200 mg/ 0.7 ml[g]	Physically compatible	1012	C
		[h]	LI	1.2 g/4.2 ml[g]	Physically compatible	1012	C

[a]*Tested in dextrose 5% in water.*
[b]*Tested in sodium chloride 0.9%.*
[c]*Tested in both dextrose 5% in water and sodium chloride 0.9%.*
[d]*Refer to Appendix I for the composition of parenteral nutrition solutions. TNA indicates a 3-in-1 admixture, and TPN indicates a 2-in-1 admixture.*
[e]*A 32.5-ml sample of parenteral nutrition solution combined with 50 ml of piggyback solution.*
[f]*Run at 21 ml/hr.*
[g]*Given over five minutes by syringe pump.*
[h]*Run at 94 ml/hr.*

Additional Compatibility Information

Peritoneal Dialysis Solutions — Cefamandole nafate (Lilly) 2 and 5 mg/ml in peritoneal dialysis fluid concentrates (American McGaw) with dextrose 30 and 50% was evaluated for compatibility. The 2-mg/ml concentration was physically compatible for 24 hours at 25 °C with no loss of cefamandole, but a haze formed at 5 °C. The 5-mg/ml concentration developed a haze at both 5 and 25 °C with a 5 to 6% cefamandole loss at 25 °C in 24 hours. (788)

Cefamandole nafate 2 mg/ml in peritoneal dialysis solution (McGaw) containing dextrose 2.5% and electrolytes was physically compatible for three hours at room temperature. Furthermore, no significant loss of antibacterial activity was apparent by microbiological determination. (142)

Aminoglycosides — The manufacturer recommends that no aminoglycoside be mixed with cefamandole nafate. If combination therapy is indicated, aminoglycosides should be administered at a different site than the cefamandole. (2)

However, Teil et al. studied the stability of gentamicin 3.8 μg/ml and cefamandole 11 μg/ml in serum stored at 24, 6, and −17 °C for 24 hours. No substantial differences in the concentrations of either drug occurred, indicating that gentamicin is not inactivated in the presence of cefamandole. (864)

To determine if spurious aminoglycoside levels could result from a delay in assaying blood samples, Tindula et al. evaluated the inactivation of amikacin 35 μg/ml and gentamicin and tobramycin 10 μg/ml in human serum by 400-μg/ml concentrations of several penicillins and cephalosporins. Samples were stored for 24 hours at room temperature and frozen at −20 °C. For samples at both temperatures, cefamandole caused relatively little inactivation of the aminoglycosides. (824)

Spruill et al. evaluated the effect of various cephalosporins on tobramycin sulfate 7.7 μg/ml in human serum. At concentrations of 250 and 1000 μg/ml, cefazolin, cefoxitin, cefamandole, cefoperazone, and cefotaxime caused about a 10 to 15% loss of tobramycin over 48 hours at 0 and 21 °C. Moxalactam caused about a 15% loss at 0 °C and a 20 to 30% loss at 21 °C over 48 hours. (1005)

Cefamandole nafate (Lilly) 125 μg/ml combined separately with the aminoglycosides amikacin sulfate (Bristol), gentamicin sulfate (Schering), and tobramycin sulfate (Lilly) at a concentration of 25 μg/ml in peritoneal dialysis solution (Dianeal 1.5%) exhibited enhanced rates of lethality to *Staphylococcus aureus, Escherichia coli,* and *Pseudomonas aeruginosa* compared to any of the drugs alone. (1623)

Other Drugs — Cefamandole is compatible with lidocaine HCl 0.5, 1, and 2%. If the concentration of cefamandole nafate is less than 10%, however, turbidity, a precipitate, or both develop. (376)

Because of its sodium carbonate content, cefamandole nafate has been stated to be incompatible with calcium ions (4; 788), forming a viscous gel. (596) It may also be incompatible with solutions containing magnesium ions. (4; 471) It is reported to be incompatible with tromethamine-containing solutions that have a high pH. (596)

CEFAZOLIN SODIUM
AHFS 8:12.06

Products — Cefazolin as the sodium salt is available in 500-mg and 1-, 10-, and 20-g vials; 500-mg and 1-g piggyback units; and 1-g flexible plastic bags. For intramuscular administration, reconstitute the vials with the volumes indicated in the table below and shake well until dissolved. Sterile water for injection, bacteriostatic water for injection, or sodium chloride 0.9% may be used for reconstitution (2; 4; 29):

Vial Size	Volume of Diluent	Approximate Solution Volume	Approximate Concentration
500 mg	2 ml	2.2 ml	225 mg/ml
1 g	2.5 ml	3 ml	330 mg/ml

For direct intravenous injection, further dilute the reconstituted cefazolin sodium with approximately 5 ml of sterile water for injection. (2; 4)

For intermittent intravenous infusion, reconstituted cefazolin sodium should be diluted further in 50 to 100 ml of compatible infusion solution. (2; 4) (See Compatibility Information.)

The 10-g bulk vials may be reconstituted with sterile water for injection, bacteriostatic water for injection, or sodium chloride 0.9%. The 10-g vial should be reconstituted with 45 or 96 ml to yield concentrations of 1 g/5 ml or 1 g/10 ml, respectively. (2)

Cefazolin sodium is also available frozen in PVC bags in concentrations of 500 mg and 1 g in 50 ml of dextrose 5% in water. (4)

pH — From 4.5 to 6. The frozen premixed solutions have a pH of 4.5 to 7. (4)

Osmolality — The osmolality of a 225-mg/ml concentration in sterile water for injection was determined to be 636 mOsm/kg by freezing-point depression. (1071)

The osmolality of cefazolin sodium 1 and 2 g was calculated for the following dilutions (1054):

Diluent	Osmolality (mOsm/kg) 50 ml	100 ml
1 g		
Dextrose 5% in water	321	291
Sodium chloride 0.9%	344	317
2 g		
Dextrose 5% in water	379	324
Sodium chloride 0.9%	406	351

The osmolality of cefazolin sodium (Lyphomed) 20 mg/ml was determined to be 325 mOsm/kg in dextrose 5% in water and 347 mOsm/kg in sodium chloride 0.9%. At a 50-mg/ml concentration, the osmolality was determined to be 412 mOsm/kg in dextrose 5% in water and 426 mOsm/kg in sodium chloride 0.9%. (1375)

The frozen premixed solutions have osmolalities of 260 to 320 mOsm/kg for the 500 mg/50-ml concentration and 310 to 380 mOsm/kg for the 1 g/50-ml concentration. (4)

Robinson et al. recommended the following maximum cefazolin sodium concentrations to achieve osmolalities suitable for peripheral infusion in fluid-restricted patients (1180):

Diluent	Maximum Concentration (mg/ml)	Osmolality (mOsm/kg)
Dextrose 5% in water	77	507
Sodium chloride 0.9%	69	494
Sterile water for injection	138	404

Sodium Content—Each gram of cefazolin sodium contains 48 mg or approximately 2 mEq of sodium. (2; 4)

Trade Name(s)—Ancef, Kefzol.

Administration — Cefazolin sodium may be administered by deep intramuscular injection or by intravenous injection. By direct intravenous injection, it is given over three to five minutes directly into the vein or tubing of a running infusion solution. It may also be given by intermittent infusion in 50 to 100 ml of compatible diluent or by continuous infusion. (2; 4; 338)

Stability — Intact containers of the sterile powder should be stored at controlled room temperature. Reconstituted solutions of cefazolin sodium are light yellow to yellow. Protection from light is recommended for both the powder and its solutions. (2; 4)

A test of cefazolin sodium 250 mg/ml in water for injection showed that the drug lost less than 3% potency in 14 days at 5 °C. A potency loss of 8 to 10% was noted in four days at 25 °C. (276) Borst et al. reported that cefazolin sodium (SKF) 1 and 2 g/10 ml in sterile water for injection, packaged in plastic syringes (Monoject), exhibited a 10% cefazolin loss in 13 days at 24 °C as determined by UV spectroscopy. At 4 °C, the drug exhibited less than a 10% loss during the 28-day study period. (1178) The manufacturer recommends that solutions of cefazolin sodium be discarded after 24 hours at room temperature or 10 days under refrigeration. (2) This recommendation is made to reduce the potential for the growth of microorganisms and to minimize an increase in color and a change in pH. (276) Refrigeration of reconstituted solutions of cefazolin sodium may result in crystal formation. (875)

Crystallization—Crystal formation has also been observed in reconstituted cefazolin sodium 330 mg/ml stored at room temperature after complete dissolution when sodium chloride 0.9% is the diluent. The crystals formed initially are fine and may be easily overlooked. At 330 mg/ml, cefazolin sodium is near its saturation point, and the room temperature and ionic content of the diluent are important for maintaining the drug in solution. In an evaluation of the 1-g Kefzol and Ancef products reconstituted with 2.5 ml of either sodium chloride 0.9% or sterile water for injection and stored at 24 or 26 °C, none of the vials reconstituted with sterile water for injection formed crystals within 24 hours. However, when sodium chloride 0.9% was the diluent, all Kefzol vials had crystals within 20 to 30 minutes, and two Ancef vials had crystals within 150 minutes at 24 °C. All Ancef vials had crystals within 24 hours at 24 °C. At 26 °C, all Kefzol vials had crystals within 45 minutes, but none of the Ancef vials had crystals after 24 hours. Consequently, sterile water for injection was recommended as the diluent for intramuscular doses when possible. (875) The crystals of cefazolin sodium can be redissolved by hand-warming the vials or by immersion in a 35 °C water bath for two minutes. The clear solution will then be suitable for use. However, the use of sodium chloride 0.9% as a diluent for the 1-g vials was deleted from the current labeling. (1075)

pH Effects—Cefazolin sodium solutions are relatively stable at pH 4.5 to 8.5. Above pH 8.5, rapid hydrolysis of the drug occurs. Below pH 4.5, precipitation of the insoluble free acid may occur. (4; 284)

Cefazolin sodium in solutions containing dextrose, fructose, sucrose, dextran 40 or 70, mannitol, sorbitol, or glycerol in concentrations up to 15% was most stable at pH 5 to 6.5. At neutral and alkaline pH, the rate of degradation was accelerated by the carbohydrates and alcohols. (820)

Cefazolin sodium 3.33 mg/ml was evaluated in several aqueous buffer solutions. The drug was most stable in pH 4.5 acetate buffer, exhibiting 10% decomposition in three days at 35 °C and in five days at 25 °C. In pH 5.7 acetate buffer, a 13% loss occurred in three days at 35 °C and a 10% loss occurred in five days at 25 °C. No loss occurred in either acetate buffer in seven days at 4 °C. (1147)

In pH 7.5 phosphate buffer, a yellow color and particulate matter developed after three to four days at 35 °C. This change was accompanied by a 6% cefazolin loss in one day and an 18% loss in three days. At 25 and 4 °C, 10 and 5% cefazolin losses occurred, respectively, in five days. (1147)

Freezing Solutions—Solutions of cefazolin sodium 125, 225, and 330 mg/ml frozen in the original containers at −20 °C immediately after reconstitution with sterile water for injection, bacteriostatic water for injection, or sodium chloride 0.9% are stated to be stable for 12 weeks. Thawed solutions are stable for 24 hours at room temperature or 10 days under refrigeration; they should not be refrozen. (2; 4)

When reconstituted with water for injection, dextrose 5% in water, or sodium chloride 0.9% in concentrations of 1 g/2.5 ml, 500 mg/100 ml, and 10 g/45 ml, cefazolin sodium retained more than 90% potency for up to 26 weeks when frozen within one hour after reconstitution at −10 and −20 °C. In a concentration of 500 mg/100 ml in dextrose 5% in Ringer's injection, lactated, Ionosol B in dextrose 5% in water, Normosol M in dextrose 5% in water, Plasma-Lyte in dextrose 5% in water, or Ringer's injection, lactated, cefazolin sodium was stable for up to four weeks when frozen within one hour after reconstitution at −10 °C. (277)

In another study, cefazolin sodium (SKF) 1 g/50 ml of dextrose 5% in water and also sodium chloride 0.9% in PVC containers was frozen at −20 °C for 30 days. The results indicate that potency was retained for the duration of the study. (299)

Cefazolin sodium (Lilly) 1 g/100 ml in dextrose 5% in water in PVC bags was frozen at −20 °C for 30 days and then thawed by exposure to ambient temperature or microwave radiation. The solutions showed no evidence of precipitation or color change and showed no loss of potency as determined microbiologically. Subsequent storage of the admixture at room temperature for 24 hours also yielded a physically compatible solution which exhibited a 3 to 6% loss of potency. (554)

In an additional study, cefazolin sodium (Lilly and SKF) 10 mg/ml in 50, 100, and 250 ml of dextrose 5% in water and sodium chloride 0.9% in PVC bags was frozen at −20 °C for 48 hours. Thawing was then performed by exposure to microwave radiation carefully applied so that the solution temperature did not exceed 20 °C and so that a small amount of ice remained at the endpoint. This procedure avoids accelerated decomposition due to inadvertent excessive temperature increases. The solutions were stored for four hours at room temperature. Both brands of cefazolin sodium retained at least 90% of the initial activity as determined by microbiological assay. In addition, the solutions did not exhibit color changes or significant pH changes. (627)

Miller and Pesko reported an approximate fourfold increase in particles of 2 to 60 μm produced by freezing and thawing cefazolin sodium (Lilly) 2 g/100 ml of dextrose 5% in water (Travenol). The reconstituted drug was filtered through a 0.45-μm filter into PVC bags of solution and frozen for seven days at −20 °C. Thawing was performed at room temperature (29 °C) for 12 hours. Although the total number of particles increased significantly, no particles greater than 60 μm were observed; the solution complied with USP standards for particle sizes and numbers in large volume parenteral solutions. (822)

Cefazolin sodium (SKF) reconstituted with sterile water for injection to a concentration of 1 g/3 ml frozen at −20 °C in glass syringes (Hy-Pod) retained potency for nine months. However, when 0.5% lidocaine HCl (Astra) was used to constitute the cefazolin sodium, a clear solution did not result upon thawing. The solution was unsuitable for injection. (532)

Borst et al. reported that cefazolin sodium (SKF) 1 and 2 g/10 ml in sterile water for injection, packaged in plastic syringes (Monoject) and frozen at −15 °C, was stable for the three-month study period, exhibiting less than a 10% loss as determined by UV spectroscopy. (1178)

Stiles et al. reported no loss of cefazolin sodium (SKF) from a solution containing 73.2 mg/ml in sterile water for injection in PVC and glass containers after 30 days at −20 °C. Subsequent thawing and storage for four days at 5 °C, followed by 24 hours at 37 °C to simulate the use of a portable infusion pump, also did not result in a cefazolin loss. (1391)

Cefazolin sodium (Schein) 20 mg/ml in dextrose 5% in water and sodium chloride 0.9% frozen at −20 °C for 12 weeks exhibited little or no loss of potency by HPLC analysis in latex elastomeric reservoirs (Secure Medical) and in glass containers. (1970)

The manufacturer warns against continued heating of a completely thawed solution (2), which can result in accelerated drug decomposition and possibly dangerous pressure increases in the container. (627)

Ambulatory Pumps—Exposure of cefazolin sodium (SKF) 73.2 mg/ml in sterile water for injection to 37 °C for 24 hours, to simulate the use of a portable infusion pump, did not result in a loss of cefazolin sodium. (1391)

Elastomeric Reservoir Pumps—Cefazolin sodium (Schein) 20 mg/ml in dextrose 5% in water and sodium chloride 0.9% 50 ml was packaged in elastomeric latex reservoirs (Secure Medical). Little or no loss of potency by HPLC analysis occurred in 24 hours at 25 °C and in three days at 5 °C. (1970)

Cefazolin sodium solutions in elastomeric reservoir pumps have been stated by the pump manufacturers to be stable for the following time periods frozen, refrigerated (REF), or at room temperature (RT) (31):

Pump Reservoir(s)	Conc.	Frozen	REF	RT
Homepump; Homepump Eclipse	20 mg/ml[b]		7 days	24 hr
Intermate	5 to 40 mg/ml[a,b]	30 days	10 days	24 hr
Intermate HPC	10 to 40 mg/ml[a]		14 days	96 hr
Medflo	20 mg/ml[a,b]	12 weeks	10 days	24 hr
ReadyMed	20 mg/ml[b]	4 weeks	14 days	48 hr
	5 mg/ml[a]		14 days	4 days

[a] *In dextrose 5% in water.*
[b] *In sodium chloride 0.9%.*

Filtration—Cefazolin sodium (SKF) 10 g/L in dextrose 5% in water and also in sodium chloride 0.9% was filtered through 0.45- and 0.22-μm Millipore membrane filters at time zero and at 4, 8, and 24 hours after mixing. HPLC analysis showed no significant difference in concentration between any of the filtered samples compared to unfiltered solutions at these time intervals. It was concluded that filtration of cefazolin sodium solutions through these membrane filters could be performed without adversely affecting the drug concentration. (375)

Central Venous Catheter—Cefazolin sodium (SmithKline Beecham) 5 mg/ml in dextrose 5% in water was found to be compatible with the ARROWg+ard Blue Plus (Arrow International) chlorhexidine-bearing triple-lumen central catheter. HPLC analysis was used to evaluate completeness of drug delivery through the catheter and the amount of chlorhexidine removed from the internal lumens. Essentially complete delivery of the drug was found with little or no drug loss occurring. Furthermore, chlorhexidine delivered from the catheter remained at trace amounts with no substantial increase due to the delivery of the drug through the catheter. (2335)

Compatibility Information

Solution Compatibility

Cefazolin sodium

Solution	*Mfr*	*Mfr*	*Conc/L*	*Remarks*	*Ref*	*C/I*
Amino acids 4.25%, dextrose 25%	MG	LI	1 g	No increase in particulate matter in 24 hr at 5 °C	349	C
Dextrose 5% in Ringer's injection, lactated		LI	5 g	Potency retained for 14 days at 5 °C. 8% potency loss in 4 days at 25 °C	276	C
Dextrose 5% in water		LI	5 g	4% potency loss in 14 days at 5 °C, 6% loss in 4 days at 25 °C	276	C

Solution Compatibility (Cont.)

Cefazolin sodium

Solution	*Mfr*	*Mfr*	*Conc/L*	*Remarks*	*Ref*	*C/I*
	BA[a], TR	SKF	20 g	Potency retained for 24 hr at 5 and 22 °C	298	C
	TR[b]	LI	10 g	Physically compatible with approximately 3% potency loss in 24 hr at room temperature	554	C
	MG[c]	SKF	10 g	Physically compatible with no loss in 48 hr at room temperature under fluorescent light	983	C
	AB[d]	SCN	20 g	Little or no cefazolin loss by HPLC in 24 hr at 25 °C and in 7 days at 5 °C	1970	C
	BA[a]	BR	10 g	Visually compatible with about 7% loss by HPLC in 30 days at 4 °C	2142	C
Ionosol B in dextrose 5% in water		LI	5 g	2% potency loss in 14 days at 5 °C, 1 to 4% loss in 4 days at 25 °C	276	C
Normosol M in dextrose 5% in water		LI	5 g	3% potency loss in 14 days at 5 °C, 1 to 4% loss in 4 days at 25 °C	276	C
Plasma-Lyte in dextrose 5% in water		LI	5 g	Potency retained for 14 days at 5 °C. 6% potency loss in 7 days at 25 °C	276	C
Ringer's injection, lactated		LI	5 g	Potency retained for 14 days at 5 °C. 9% potency loss in 7 days at 25 °C	276	C
Sodium chloride 0.9%		LI	5 g	4% potency loss in 7 days at 5 °C, 8% loss in 4 days at 25 °C	276	C
	BA[a], TR	SKF	20 g	Potency retained for 24 hr at 5 and 22 °C	298	C
	MG[c]	SKF	10 g	Physically compatible with no loss in 48 hr at room temperature under fluorescent light	983	C
		LI	3.33 g	Physically compatible with 10% loss at 35 °C and 5% loss at 25 °C in 3 days. No loss in 7 days at 4 °C	1147	C
	AB[d]	SCN	20 g	4% or less cefazolin loss by HPLC in 24 hr at 25 °C and in 7 days at 5 °C	1970	C
TPN #22[e]		SKF	10 g	Physically compatible with no loss of activity by microbiological assay in 24 hr at 22 °C in the dark	837	C
TPN #107[e]			1 g	9% cefazolin loss in 24 hr at 21 °C by microbiological assay	1326	C

[a]Tested in both glass and PVC containers.
[b]Tested in PVC containers.
[c]Tested in glass bottles.
[d]Tested in glass containers and latex elastomeric reservoirs (Secure Medical).
[e]Refer to Appendix I for the composition of parenteral nutrition solutions. TPN indicates a 2-in-1 admixture.

Additive Compatibility

Cefazolin sodium

Drug	*Mfr*	*Conc/L*	*Mfr*	*Conc/L*	*Test Soln*	*Remarks*	*Ref*	*C/I*
Amikacin sulfate	BR	5 g	LI	20 g	D5LR, D5R, D5S, D5W, D10W, IS10, LR, NS, R, SL	Potency of both retained for at least 8 hr at 25 °C. Turbidity observed at 24 hr	293	I
Atracurium besylate	BW	500 mg		10 g	D5W	Atracurium chemically unstable and particles form	1694	I

Additive Compatibility (Cont.)

			Cefazolin sodium					
Drug	*Mfr*	*Conc/L*	*Mfr*	*Conc/L*	*Test Soln*	*Remarks*	*Ref*	*C/I*
Aztreonam	SQ	10 and 20 g	LI	5 and 20 g	D5W, NS[a]	Physically compatible with little or no loss of either drug in 48 hr at 25 °C and 7 days at 4 °C protected from light	1020	C
Bleomycin sulfate	BR	20 and 30 units	LI	1 g	NS	43% loss of bleomycin activity in 1 week at 4 °C	763	I
Cimetidine HCl	SKF	3 g		10 g	D5W, NS	Physically compatible for 48 hr at room temperature. Precipitate forms upon freezing	516	C
	SKF	6 g		20 g	D5W, NS	Physically compatible for 48 hr at room temperature. Precipitate forms upon freezing	516	C
	SKF	3 g	SKF	10 g	D5W	Haze observed at 24 hr at room temperature. Cimetidine chemically stable. Cefazolin not tested	551	I
	SKF	1.2 and 5 g	SKF	1 g	D5W, NS	Physically compatible and cimetidine chemically stable for 24 hr at room temperature. Cefazolin not tested	551	C
Clindamycin phosphate	UP	9 g	SKF	10 g	D5W[b]	Physically compatible with no clindamycin loss and 8% cefazolin loss in 48 hr at room temperature under fluorescent light	983	C
	UP	9 g	SKF	10 g	NS[b]	Physically compatible with no clindamycin loss and 3% cefazolin loss in 48 hr at room temperature under fluorescent light	983	C
Clindamycin phosphate with gentamicin sulfate	UP ES	9 g 800 mg	SKF	10 g	D5W[b]	10% cefazolin loss in 4 hr at 25 °C. Clindamycin and gentamicin potency retained for 24 hr	1328	I
Clindamycin phosphate with gentamicin sulfate	UP ES	9 g 800 mg	SKF	10 g	NS[b]	10% cefazolin loss after 12 hr at 25 °C. Clindamycin and gentamicin potency retained for 24 hr	1328	I
Famotidine	YAM	200 mg	FUJ	10 g	D5W	Visually compatible with 10% cefazolin loss and 5% famotidine loss by HPLC in 24 hr at 25 °C. 9% cefazolin loss and 5% famotidine loss in 48 hr at 4 °C	1762	C
Fluconazole	PF	1 g	SM	10 g	D5W	Visually compatible with no fluconazole loss by HPLC in 72 hr at 25 °C under fluorescent light. Cefazolin not tested	1677	C
Linezolid	PHU	2 g	APC	10 g	[d]	Physically compatible with 5% or less loss of either drug by HPLC in 3 days at 23 °C and in 7 days at 4 °C protected from light	2262	C
Meperidine HCl		0.5 g	FUJ	10 g	D5W	Visually compatible with about 5% loss by HPLC of each drug in 5 days at 25 °C. 5% cefazolin loss and 7% meperidine loss in 20 days at 4 °C.	1966	C
Metronidazole	RP	5 g[c]	LI	10 g		Physically compatible with little or no pH change for at least 24 hr at 23 °C and 72 hr at 4 °C	807	C
	SE	5 g	LI	10 g		5% cefazolin loss and no metronidazole loss in 7 days at 25 °C. No loss of either drug in 12 days at 5 °C	993	C

Additive Compatibility (Cont.)

Drug	Mfr	Conc/L	Mfr	Conc/L	Test Soln	Remarks	Ref	C/I
			Cefazolin sodium					
	AB	5 g	LI	10 g		Visually compatible with no loss of either drug by HPLC in 72 hr at 8 °C	1649	C
Metronidazole HCl with sodium bicarbonate	SE AB	5 g 50 mEq	SKF	5 g	D5W, NS	Physically compatible for 48 hr. Gradual darkening attributed to normal cephalosporin color change with time	765	C
Ranitidine HCl	GL	100 mg		2 g	D5W	Color change within 24 hr at ambient temperature under fluorescent light	1151	?
	GL	50 mg and 2 g		1 g	D5W	Ranitidine chemically stable by HPLC for only 6 hr at 25 °C. Cefazolin not tested	1515	I
Verapamil HCl	KN	80 mg	SKF	2 g	D5W, NS	Physically compatible for 24 hr	764	C

[a]Tested in PVC bags.
[b]Tested in glass bottles.
[c]Minibags (100 ml) containing metronidazole 500 mg with disodium phosphate 150 mg, citric acid 44 mg, and sodium chloride 740 mg. This product differs from the Searle product.
[d]Admixed in the linezolid infusion container.

Drugs in Syringe Compatibility

Drug (in syringe)	Mfr	Amt	Mfr	Amt	Remarks	Ref	C/I
			Cefazolin sodium				
Ascorbic acid injection	LI	1 ml	LI	1 g/3 ml	Precipitate forms within 3 min at 32 °C	766	I
Cimetidine HCl	SKF	300 mg/ 2 ml		1 g/5 ml	Immediate precipitation	516	I
Heparin sodium		2500 units/ 1 ml		2 g	Physically compatible for at least 5 min	1053	C
Hydromorphone HCl	KN	2, 10, 40 mg/ 1 ml	SKF	>200 mg/ 1 ml	Precipitate forms	2082	I
	KN	2, 10, 40 mg/ 1 ml	SKF	150 mg/ 1 ml	Visually compatible with less than 10% loss of either drug by HPLC in 24 hr at room temperature	2082	C
Lidocaine HCl	AST	0.5%/ 3 ml	SKF	1 g	Precipitate forms over 3 to 4 hr at 4 °C	532	I
Vitamin B complex (Betalin complex)	LI	1 ml	LI	1 g/3 ml	Physically compatible for 24 hr at 32 °C	766	C
Vitamin B complex with C (Berocca-C)	RC	1 ml	LI	1 g/3 ml	Crystals form below 32 °C but redissolve when warmed above 32 °C. Antibiotic activity retained for 24 hr at 4 and 32 °C	766	I
(Berocca-C)	RC	0.1 ml	LI	1 g/ 3.9 ml	Physically compatible and antibiotic activity retained for 24 hr at 4 and 32 °C	766	C
(Solu-B with ascorbic acid)	UP	1 ml	LI	1 g/3 ml	Precipitate forms within 1.5 hr at 32 °C	766	I

Y-Site Injection Compatibility (1:1 Mixture)

Drug	Mfr	Conc	Mfr	Conc	Remarks	Ref	C/I
			Cefazolin sodium				
Acyclovir sodium	BW	5 mg/ml[a]	SKF	20 mg/ml[a]	Physically compatible for 4 hr at 25 °C	1157	C

Y-Site Injection Compatibility (1:1 Mixture) (Cont.)

Drug	Mfr	Conc	Mfr	Conc	Remarks	Ref	C/I
			Cefazolin sodium				
Allopurinol sodium	BW	3 mg/ml[b]	GEM	20 mg/ml[b]	Physically compatible with no change in measured turbidity or increase in particle content in 4 hr at 22 °C	1686	C
Amifostine	USB	10 mg/ml[a]	MAR	20 mg/ml[a]	Physically compatible with no change in measured turbidity or increase in particle content in 4 hr at 23 °C	1845	C
Amiodarone HCl	LZ	4 mg/ml[a]	LI	20 mg/ml[a]	Precipitate forms	1444	I
	LZ	4 mg/ml[b]	LI	20 mg/ml[b]	Physically compatible for 4 hr at room temperature	1444	C
Amphotericin B cholesteryl sulfate complex	SEQ	0.83 mg/ml[a]	SKB	20 mg/ml[a]	Increased turbidity forms immediately	2117	I
Atracurium besylate	BW	0.5 mg/ml[a]	LY	10 mg/ml[a]	Physically compatible for 24 hr at 28 °C	1337	C
Aztreonam	SQ	40 mg/ml[a]	MAR	20 mg/ml[a]	Physically compatible with no subvisual haze or particle formation in 4 hr at 23 °C	1758	C
Calcium gluconate	AST	4 mg/ml[c]	LI	40 mg/ml[c]	Physically compatible for 3 hr	1316	C
Cefpirome sulfate	HO	50 mg/ml[d]	LI	10 mg/ml[d]	Visually and microscopically compatible with 7% or less cefpirome loss and little or no cefazolin loss by HPLC in 8 hr at 23 °C	2044	C
Cisatracurium besylate	GW	0.1 mg/ml[a]	SKB	20 mg/ml[a]	Physically compatible with no change in measured turbidity or increase in particle content in 4 hr at 23 °C	2074	C
	GW	2 mg/ml[a]	SKB	20 mg/ml[a]	Gray subvisual haze forms immediately	2074	I
	GW	5 mg/ml[a]	SKB	20 mg/ml[a]	Gray haze forms immediately	2074	I
Cyclophosphamide	MJ	20 mg/ml[a]	SKF	20 mg/ml[a]	Physically compatible for 4 hr at 25 °C	1194	C
Diltiazem HCl	MMD	5 mg/ml	LI	20 and 200 mg/ml[b]	Visually compatible	1807	C
	MMD	1 mg/ml[b]	LI	200 mg/ml[b]	Visually compatible	1807	C
Docetaxel	RPR	0.9 mg/ml[a]	APC	20 mg/ml[a]	Physically compatible with no change in measured turbidity or increase in particle content in 4 hr at 23 °C	2224	C
Doxorubicin HCl liposome injection	SEQ	0.4 mg/ml[a]	SKB	20 mg/ml[a]	Physically compatible with little or no change in measured turbidity and no increase in particle content in 4 hr at 23 °C	2087	C
Enalaprilat	MSD	0.05 mg/ml[b]	SKF	20 mg/ml[e]	Physically compatible for 24 hr at room temperature under fluorescent light	1355	C
Esmolol HCl	DCC	10 mg/ml[a]	LI	10 mg/ml[a]	Physically compatible for 24 hr at 22 °C	1169	C
Etoposide phosphate	BR	5 mg/ml[a]	APC	20 mg/ml[a]	Physically compatible with no change in measured turbidity or increase in particle content in 4 hr at 23 °C	2218	C
Famotidine	MSD	0.2 mg/ml[a]	LY	20 mg/ml[b]	Physically compatible for 14 hr	1196	C
	ME	2 mg/ml[b]		20 mg/ml[a]	Visually compatible for 4 hr at 22 °C	1936	C
Filgrastim	AMG	30 μg/ml[a]	LI	20 mg/ml[a]	Physically compatible with no change in measured turbidity or increase in particle content in 4 hr at 22 °C	1687	C
Fluconazole	RR	2 mg/ml	LY	40 mg/ml	Physically compatible for 24 hr at 25 °C	1407	C

Y-Site Injection Compatibility (1:1 Mixture) (Cont.)

Cefazolin sodium

Drug	*Mfr*	*Conc*	*Mfr*	*Conc*	*Remarks*	*Ref*	*C/I*
Fludarabine phosphate	BX	1 mg/ml[a]	LEM	20 mg/ml[a]	Physically compatible for 4 hr at room temperature under fluorescent light	1439	C
Foscarnet sodium	AST	24 mg/ml	SKF	40 mg/ml	Physically compatible for 24 hr at room temperature under fluorescent light	1335	C
Gatifloxacin	BMS	2 mg/ml[a]	SKB	20 mg/ml[a]	Physically compatible with no change in measured haze or increase in particle content in 4 hr at 23 °C	2234	C
Gemcitabine HCl	LI	10 mg/ml[b]	APC	20 mg/ml[b]	Physically compatible with no change in measured turbidity or increase in particle content in 4 hr at 23 °C	2226	C
Granisetron HCl	SKB	0.05 mg/ml[a]	SKB	20 mg/ml[a]	Physically compatible with no change in measured turbidity or increase in particle content in 4 hr at 23 °C	2000	C
Heparin sodium	TR	50 units/ml	SKB	20 mg/ml[a]	Visually compatible for 4 hr at 25 °C	1793	C
Hetastarch in lactated electrolyte injection (Hextend)	AB	6%	LI	20 mg/ml[a]	Physically compatible with no change in measured turbidity or increase in particle content in 4 hr at 23 °C	2339	C
Hetastarch in sodium chloride 0.9%	DCC	6%	SKF	20 mg/ml[a]	Physically compatible for 4 hr at room temperature by visual examination	1313	C
	DCC	6%	SKF	20 mg/ml[a]	Simulation in vials showed no incompatibility, but white precipitate formed in Y-site during infusion	1315	I
Hydromorphone HCl	WY	0.2 mg/ml[a]	SKF	20 mg/ml[a]	Physically compatible for at least 4 hr at 25 °C under fluorescent light	987	C
	KN	2, 10, 40 mg/ml	SKF	20[a] and 150 mg/ml	Visually compatible and potency of both drugs by HPLC retained for 24 hr	1532	C
	KN	2, 10, 40 mg/ml	SKF	>200 mg/ml	Precipitate forms immediately	1532	I
Idarubicin HCl	AD	1 mg/ml[b]	LI	20 mg/ml[a]	Precipitate forms in 1 hr	1525	I
Insulin, regular	LI	0.2 unit/ml[b]	LI	20 mg/ml[a]	Physically compatible for 2 hr at 25 °C	1395	C
Labetalol HCl	SC	1 mg/ml[a]	LI	10 mg/ml[a]	Physically compatible for 24 hr at 18 °C	1171	C
Lidocaine HCl	AB	8 mg/ml[c]	LI	40 mg/ml[c]	Physically compatible for 3 hr	1316	C
Linezolid	PHU	2 mg/ml	SKB	20 mg/ml[a]	Physically compatible with no change in measured turbidity or increase in particle content in 4 hr at 23 °C	2264	C
Magnesium sulfate	IX	16.7, 33.3, 66.7, 100 mg/ml[a]	LI	20 mg/ml[a]	Physically compatible for at least 4 hr at 32 °C	813	C
Melphalan HCl	BW	0.1 mg/ml[b]	GEM	20 mg/ml[b]	Physically compatible with no change in measured turbidity or increase in particle content in 3 hr at 22 °C	1557	C
Meperidine HCl	WY	10 mg/ml[a]	SKF	20 mg/ml[a]	Physically compatible for at least 4 hr at 25 °C under fluorescent light	987	C
Midazolam HCl	RC	1 mg/ml[a]	MAR	20 mg/ml[a]	Visually compatible for 24 hr at 23 °C	1847	C
Morphine sulfate	WI	1 mg/ml[a]	SKF	20 mg/ml[a]	Physically compatible for at least 4 hr at 25 °C under fluorescent light	987	C

Y-Site Injection Compatibility (1:1 Mixture) (Cont.)

Drug	*Mfr*	*Conc*	*Mfr*	*Conc*	*Remarks*	*Ref*	*C/I*
			Cefazolin sodium				
Multivitamins	USV	5 ml/L[a]	SKF	1 g/50 ml[a]	Physically compatible for 24 hr at room temperature	323	C
Ondansetron HCl	GL	1 mg/ml[b]	LEM	20 mg/ml[a]	Physically compatible for 4 hr at 22 °C	1365	C
	GL	0.03 and 0.3 mg/ml[a]	LI	20 mg/ml[a]	Visually compatible with little or no loss of either drug by HPLC in 4 hr at 25 °C	1732	C
Pancuronium bromide	ES	0.05 mg/ml[a]	LY	10 mg/ml[a]	Physically compatible for 24 hr at 28 °C	1337	C
Pentamidine isethionate	FUJ	3 mg/ml[a]	SKB	20 mg/ml[a]	Cloudiness and gelatin-like precipitate form immediately	1880	I
Perphenazine	SC	0.02 mg/ml[a]	SKF	20 mg/ml[e]	Physically compatible for 4 hr at 25 °C	1155	C
Promethazine HCl	ES	25 mg	LI	10 mg/ml[a]	Fine cloudy precipitate forms immediately and dissolves in seconds	1753	?
Propofol	ZEN	10 mg/ml	MAR	20 mg/ml[a]	Physically compatible for 1 hr at 23 °C with no increase in particle content	2066	C
Ranitidine HCl	GL	1 mg/ml[b]	FUJ	20 mg/ml[b]	Visually compatible with little or no loss of either drug by HPLC in 4 hr at 25 °C exposed to fluorescent light	2259	C
Remifentanil HCl	GW	0.025 and 0.25 mg/ml[b]	SKB	20 mg/ml[a]	Physically compatible with no change in measured turbidity or increase in particle content in 4 hr at 23 °C	2075	C
Sargramostim	IMM	10 μg/ml[b]	LEM	20 mg/ml[b]	Physically compatible for 4 hr at 22 °C	1436	C
Tacrolimus	FUJ	1 mg/ml[b]	BR	40 mg/ml[a]	Visually compatible for 24 hr at 25 °C	1630	C
Teniposide	BR	0.1 mg/ml[a]	MAR	20 mg/ml[a]	Physically compatible with no subvisual haze or particle formation in 4 hr at 23 °C	1725	C
Theophylline	TR	4 mg/ml	SKB	20 mg/ml	Visually compatible for 6 hr at 25 °C	1793	C
Thiotepa	IMM[f]	1 mg/ml[a]	MAR	20 mg/ml[a]	Physically compatible with no change in measured turbidity or increase in particle content in 4 hr at 23 °C	1861	C
TNA #73[g]		32.5 ml[h]	SKF	1 g/50 ml[a]	Physically compatible for 4 hr at 25 °C by visual observation	1008	C
TNA #218 to #226[g]			SKB	20 mg/ml[a]	Visually compatible with no precipitate or emulsion damage apparent in 4 hr at 23 °C	2215	C
TPN #61[g]		[i]	SKF	200 mg/ 0.9 ml[j]	Physically compatible	1012	C
		[k]	SKF	1.2 g/5.3 ml[j]	Physically compatible	1012	C
TPN #212 and #213[g]			SKB	20 mg/ml[a]	Physically compatible with no change in measured turbidity or increase in particle content in 4 hr at 23 °C	2109	C
TPN #214 and #215[g]			SKB	20 mg/ml[a]	Small amount of subvisual precipitate forms immediately	2109	I
Vancomycin HCl	AB	20 mg/ml[a]	SKB	200 mg/ml[l]	Transient precipitate forms followed by clear solution	2189	?
	AB	20 mg/ml[a]	SKB	10 and 50 mg/ml[a]	Gross white precipitate forms immediately	2189	I
	AB	20 mg/ml[a]	SKB	1 mg/ml[a]	Physically compatible with no change in measured turbidity or increase in particle content in 4 hr at 23 °C	2189	C

Y-Site Injection Compatibility (1:1 Mixture) (Cont.)

Drug	Mfr	Conc	Mfr	Conc	Remarks	Ref	C/I
				Cefazolin sodium			
	AB	2 mg/ml[a]	SKB	200 mg/ml[l]	Physically compatible with no change in measured turbidity or increase in particle content in 4 hr at 23 °C	2189	C
	AB	2 mg/ml[a]	SKB	50 mg/ml[a]	Subvisual measured haze forms immediately	2189	I
	AB	2 mg/ml[a]	SKB	1 and 10 mg/ml[a]	Physically compatible with no change in measured turbidity or increase in particle content in 4 hr at 23 °C	2189	C
Vecuronium bromide	OR	0.1 mg/ml[a]	LY	10 mg/ml[a]	Physically compatible for 24 hr at 28 °C	1337	C
Vinorelbine tartrate	BW	1 mg/ml[b]	GEM	20 mg/ml[b]	Large increase in measured turbidity occurs immediately and grows over 4 hr at 22 °C	1558	I
Vitamin B complex with C (Berocca-C 500)	RC	4 ml/L[a]	SKF	1 g/50 ml[a]	Physically compatible for at least 4 hr at 25 °C under fluorescent light	323	C
Vitamin B complex with C (Berocca-C)	RC	20 ml/L[a]	SKF	1 g/50 ml[a]	Physically compatible for at least 4 hr at 25 °C under fluorescent light	323	C
Warfarin sodium	DU	2 mg/ml[l]	SKB	20 mg/ml[a]	Visually compatible with no warfarin loss by HPLC in 30 min	2010	C
	DME	2 mg/ml[l]	SKB	20 mg/ml[a]	Visually compatible for 24 hr at 24 °C	2078	C

[a]*Tested in dextrose 5% in water.*
[b]*Tested in sodium chloride 0.9%.*
[c]*Tested in both dextrose 5% in water and sodium chloride 0.9%.*
[d]*Tested in dextrose 5% in water, Ringer's injection, lactated, sodium chloride 0.45%, and sodium chloride 0.9%.*
[e]*Manufacturer's premixed solution.*
[f]*Lyophilized formulation tested.*
[g]*Refer to Appendix I for the composition of parenteral nutrition solutions. TNA indicates a 3-in-1 admixture, and TPN indicates a 2-in-1 admixture.*
[h]*A 32.5-ml sample of parenteral nutrition solution combined with 50 ml of antibiotic solution.*
[i]*Run at 21 ml/hr.*
[j]*Given over five minutes by syringe pump.*
[k]*Run at 94 ml/hr.*
[l]*Tested in sterile water for injection.*

Additional Compatibility Information

Infusion Solutions — The manufacturer indicates that reconstituted cefazolin sodium may be diluted in or administered into lines running the following infusion solutions (2; 4):

- Dextrose 5% in Ringer's injection, lactated
- Dextrose 5% in sodium chloride 0.2%
- Dextrose 5% in sodium chloride 0.45%
- Dextrose 5% in sodium chloride 0.9%
- Dextrose 5% in water
- Dextrose 10% in water
- Invert sugar 5% in water
- Invert sugar 10% in water
- Ionosol B with dextrose 5%
- Normosol M in dextrose 5% in water
- Plasma-Lyte with dextrose 5%
- Ringer's injection
- Ringer's injection, lactated
- Sodium bicarbonate 5%
- Sodium chloride 0.9%

Peritoneal Dialysis Solutions — Cefazolin sodium 2 mg/ml in peritoneal dialysis solution (McGaw) containing dextrose 2.5% and electrolytes was physically compatible for three hours at room temperature. Furthermore, no significant loss of antibacterial activity was apparent by microbiological determination. (142)

The stability of cefazolin sodium 75 and 150 mg/L, alone and with gentamicin sulfate 8 mg/L, was evaluated in a peritoneal dialysis solution of dextrose 1.5% with heparin sodium 1000 units/L. Cefazolin activity was retained for 48 hours at both 4 and 26 °C at both concentrations, alone and with gentamicin. Gentamicin activity was also retained over the study period. At 37 °C, however, cefazolin losses were greater, with about a 10 to 12% loss occurring in 48 hours. Gentamicin losses ranged from 4 to 8% in this time period. (1029)

Halstead et al. evaluated gentamicin 4 μg/ml in Dianeal PDS with dextrose 1.5 and 4.25% (Travenol) with cefazolin sodium 125 μg/ml, heparin 500 units, and albumin 80 mg in 2-L bags. The gentamicin content, determined by EMIT assay, was retained for 72 hours. (1413)

Nahata and Ahalt studied the stability of cefazolin sodium (Lilly) 0.5 mg/ml in Dianeal PD-1 with dextrose 1.5 and 4.25% (Travenol). The drug was stable, exhibiting losses of 10.5% or less in 14 days at 4 °C, eight days at 25 °C, and 24 hours at 37 °C. However, losses of

11.7 and 14.6% occurred in the solutions containing dextrose 1.5% and dextrose 4.25%, respectively, in 11 days at 25 °C. (1480)

Vancomycin — The compatibility or incompatibility of vancomycin HCl mixed with or administered simultaneously with cefazolin sodium is concentration dependent. (2189) See Y-Site Compatibility above. Vancomycin HCl has a low pH and is variably compatible with drugs having neutral to mildly alkaline pH, including cephalosporins and penicillins. The compatibility may depend on a number of factors, including concentration of each drug, dilution vehicle, actual pH of solutions, and completeness of mixing during administration. Combinations that are compatible when well mixed may result in precipitation if only partially mixed, presumably because of regionally different concentrations and pH values. If attempting to administer vancomycin HCl with cefazolin sodium, take care to ensure that the specific combination and the concentrations are compatible under the exact administration conditions to be used. An inline filter should be used as a final safety measure. (2189)

Other Drugs — Cefazolin sodium is stated to be incompatible with the following drugs (278):

Amobarbital sodium
Calcium gluconate
Colistimethate sodium
Kanamycin sulfate
Pentobarbital sodium
Polymyxin B sulfate

To determine if spurious aminoglycoside levels could result from a delay in assaying blood samples, Tindula et al. evaluated the inactivation of amikacin 36 μg/ml and gentamicin and tobramycin 10 μg/ml in human serum by 400-μg/ml concentrations of several penicillins and cephalosporins. Samples were stored for 24 hours at room temperature and frozen at −20 °C. For samples at both temperatures, cefazolin caused relatively little inactivation of the aminoglycosides. (824)

Spruill et al. evaluated the effect of various cephalosporins on tobramycin sulfate 7.7 μg/ml in human serum. At concentrations of 250 and 100 μg/ml, cefazolin, cefoxitin, cefamandole, cefoperazone, and cefotaxime caused about a 10 to 15% loss of tobramycin over 48 hours at 0 and 21 °C. Moxalactam caused about a 15% loss at 0 °C and a 20 to 30% loss at 21 °C over 48 hours. (1005)

The inactivation of gentamicin, tobramycin, and amikacin, each 5 μg/ml, by seven β-lactam antibiotics, 250 and 500 μg/ml, in serum at 25 °C over 24 hours was studied using bioassay, enzyme-mediated immunoassay technique (EMIT), fluorescence polarization immunoassay (TDx), and radioimmunoassay. No inactivation of any aminoglycoside by the cephalosporins moxalactam, cefotaxime, and cefazolin occurred within the study period. (654)

Cefazolin sodium (Lilly) 125 μg/ml combined separately with the aminoglycosides amikacin sulfate (Bristol), gentamicin sulfate (Schering), and tobramycin sulfate (Lilly) at a concentration of 25 μg/ml in peritoneal dialysis solution (Dianeal 1.5%) exhibited enhanced rates of lethality to *Staphylococcus aureus*, *Escherichia coli*, and *Pseudomonas aeruginosa* compared to any of the drugs alone. (1623)

Other Information

A study was conducted to compare Kefzol with Ancef with regard to dissolution rate, color, clarity, and particulate matter content. The only significant difference noted was a faster dissolution rate for Kefzol. (373)

In contrast, a study by Janousek and Minisci reported more extensive differences. They too noted a difference in dissolution rate. Interestingly, they reported Ancef to dissolve more rapidly. Further, differences in color, clarity, and rate at which the drugs passed through a 0.45-μm filter were also noted. The authors concluded that while Kefzol took longer to dissolve, it did so more completely as reflected in less color, lower optical density (clarity), and a much greater rate of flow through a 0.45-μm filter, indicative of less particulate matter. (628)

CEFEPIME HCL
AHFS 8:12.06

Products — Cefepime HCl is available as 500 mg, 1 g, and 2 g of cefepime in vials and 1 and 2 g of cefepime in piggyback bottles. The products contain L-arginine in an approximate concentration of 725 mg/g of cefepime. (2)

For intramuscular administration, reconstitute the vials with sterile water for injection, sodium chloride 0.9%, dextrose 5% in water, lidocaine HCl 0.5 or 1%, or bacteriostatic water for injection preserved with parabens or benzyl alcohol with the volumes indicated in Table 1. (2)

For intravenous injection, reconstitute the containers with compatible diluent in the volumes indicated in Table 1. The reconstituted solutions should be added to compatible intravenous solutions for intermittent infusion. (2)

Table 1. Recommended Reconstitution of Cefepime HCl (2)

Container Size	Volume of Diluent (ml)	Approximate Solution Volume (ml)	Approximate Concentration (mg/ml)
Intramuscular			
500-mg vial	1.3	1.8	280
1-g vial	2.4	3.6	280
Intravenous			
500-mg vial	5	5.6	100
1-g vial	10	11.3	100
1-g piggyback	50 to 100	50 to 100	20 to 10
2-g vial	10	12.5	160
2-g piggyback	50 to 100	50 to 100	40 to 20

pH—From 4 to 6. (2)

Trade Name(s)—Maxipime.

Administration — Cefepime HCl is administered by deep intramuscular injection and by intermittent intravenous infusion over approximately 30 minutes. (2; 4)

Stability — The intact vials should be stored between 2 and 25 °C and protected from light. Reconstituted solutions may vary from colorless to amber. Both the powder and reconstituted solutions may darken during storage like other cephalosporins. When stored as recommended, potency is not adversely affected. Reconstituted solutions of cefepime HCl in compatible diluents are stable for 24 hours at room temperatures of 20 to 25 °C and for seven days under refrigeration. (2)

Cefepime HCl (Bristol-Myers Squibb) 280 mg/ml reconstituted in the following diluents is physically compatible and chemically stable by HPLC analysis for 24 hours at room temperature exposed to light and for seven days at 5 °C (1680):

Bacteriostatic water for injection (parabens or benzyl alcohol)
Dextrose 5% in water
Lidocaine HCl 0.5 and 1%
Sodium chloride 0.9%
Sterile water for injection

At concentrations of 100 and 160 mg/ml in dextrose 5% in water, sodium chloride 0.9%, and sterile water for injection, cefepime HCl is also physically compatible and chemically stable for 24 hours at room temperature and for seven days at 5 °C. (1681)

Freezing Solutions—Cefepime HCl (Bristol-Myers Squibb) 100 and 200 mg/ml in dextrose 5% in water, sodium chloride 0.9%, and sterile water for injection was packaged as 10 ml of solution in 10-ml polypropylene syringes and capped (Becton-Dickinson). The samples were stored frozen at −20 °C for 90 days. Cefepime HCl samples at both concentrations in all three diluents remained clear and had no apparent color change. HPLC analysis found little or no cefepime loss in any of the samples. (2220)

Cefepime HCl (Bristol-Myers Squibb) 100 and 200 mg/ml in dextrose 5% in water, sodium chloride 0.9%, and sterile water for injection was packaged as 10 ml of solution in 10-ml polypropylene syringes and capped (Becton-Dickinson). After frozen storage for up to 90 days, the samples were thawed and stored at 4 °C for seven days. The solutions remained visually clear but exhibited a gradual darkening of color. HPLC analysis found cefepime losses of 7% or less. (2220)

Samples that had been frozen for 90 days and refrigerated for three to seven days were stored for an additional one or two days at room temperature (about 23 °C). Room temperature storage for one day in the thawed samples stored under refrigeration for three or five days exhibited cefepime losses of 10% or less; cefepime losses had increased up to 11 to 19% after two days at room temperature. However, thawed samples stored under refrigeration for seven days exhibited up to 12 to 15% loss after one day at room temperature. (2220)

Syringes—Cefepime HCl (Bristol-Myers Squibb) 100 and 200 mg/ml in dextrose 5% in water, sodium chloride 0.9%, and sterile water for injection packaged as 10 ml of solution in 10-ml polypropylene syringes and capped (Becton-Dickinson) was also tested without having been frozen. The solutions remained stable by HPLC analysis for up to 14 days refrigerated at 4 °C, losing 10% or less of the cefepime. In samples stored at room temperature of about 23 °C, less than 10% loss occurred in one day in most cases, but losses as high as 13% occurred in two days in some (but not all) samples that were evaluated. (2220; 2221) Samples refrigerated up to five days followed by room temperature storage exhibited similar stability, exhibiting less than 10% loss in one day but higher losses after two days. (2220)

Cefepime HCl (Bristol-Myers Squibb) 20 mg/ml in sodium chloride 0.9% was packaged in 10-ml polypropylene syringes (Becton-Dickinson) and stored at 25 and 5 °C. The drug solutions remained clear, but the color deepened to a darker yellow during storage at room temperature. HPLC analysis found about 5% loss in two days and 11% loss in four days at 25 °C. About 3% loss was found after 21 days at 5 °C. The losses were comparable to the drug solution stored in a glass flask, indicating sorption to syringe components did not occur. (2341)

Elastomeric Reservoir Pumps—Cefepime HCl solutions in elastomeric reservoir pumps have been stated by the pump manufacturers to be stable for the following time periods frozen, refrigerated (REF), or at room temperature (RT) (31):

Pump Reservoir(s)	Conc.	Frozen	REF	RT
Homepump; Homepump Eclipse	20 mg/ml[b]		14 days	24 hr
Intermate HPC	> 5 to 60 mg/ml[a,b]	63 days		24 hr
	1 to 5 mg/ml[a,b]	63 days	14 days	2 days

[a]*In dextrose 5% in water.*
[b]*In sodium chloride 0.9%.*

Central Venous Catheter—Cefepime HCl (Bristol-Myers Squibb) 5 mg/ml in dextrose 5% in water was found to be compatible with the ARROWg+ard Blue Plus (Arrow International) chlorhexidine-bearing triple-lumen central catheter. HPLC analysis was used to evaluate completeness of drug delivery through the catheter and the amount of chlorhexidine removed from the internal lumens. Delivery of the cefepime HCl ranged from 92 to 95% of the initial concentration among the three lumens. Furthermore, chlorhexidine delivered from the catheter remained at trace amounts with no substantial increase due to the delivery of the drug through the catheter. (2335)

Compatibility Information

Solution Compatibility

Cefepime HCl

Solution	*Mfr*	*Mfr*	*Conc/L*	*Remarks*	*Ref*	*C/I*
Amino acids 4.25%, dextrose 25% with electrolytes	AB	BR	1 and 4 g	5 to 6% cefepime loss by HPLC in 8 hr at room temperature and 3 days at 5 °C	1682	C

Solution Compatibility (Cont.)

Solution	Mfr	Cefepime HCl Mfr	Conc/L	Remarks	Ref	C/I
Dextrose 5% in Ringer's injection, lactated	[a]	BR	1 g	Visually compatible with 2 to 4% cefepime loss by HPLC in 24 hr at room temperature exposed to light and about 2% loss in 7 days at 5 °C	1680	C
	[a]	BR	40 g	Visually compatible with 6% cefepime loss by HPLC in 24 hr at room temperature exposed to light and about 3% loss in 7 days at 5 °C	1680	C
Dextrose 5% in sodium chloride 0.9%	[a]	BR	1 g	Visually compatible with 3 to 4% cefepime loss by HPLC in 24 hr at room temperature exposed to light and 1% loss in 7 days at 5 °C	1680	C
	[a]	BR	40 g	Visually compatible with 5% cefepime loss by HPLC in 24 hr at room temperature exposed to light and 3% loss in 7 days at 5 °C	1680	C
Dextrose 5% in water	[b]	BR	1 g	Visually compatible with 2 to 4% cefepime loss by HPLC in 24 hr at room temperature exposed to light and 1 to 2% loss in 7 days at 5 °C	1680	C
	[b]	BR	40 g	Visually compatible with 4 to 7% cefepime loss by HPLC in 24 hr at room temperature exposed to light and about 2% loss in 7 days at 5 °C	1680	C
	BA[a]	BMS	20 g	6% loss by HPLC in 2 days at 25 °C and in 23 days at 5 °C. Slight increase in yellow color observed	2102	C
	BFM[c]	BMS	8 g	8 to 9% loss by HPLC in 48 hr at 24 °C and in 15 days at 4 °C. Amber discoloration observed	2150	C
Dextrose 10% in water	[a]	BR	1 g	Visually compatible with 3 to 5% cefepime loss by HPLC in 24 hr at room temperature exposed to light and 1% loss in 7 days at 5 °C	1680	C
	[a]	BR	40 g	Visually compatible with 4 to 5% cefepime loss by HPLC in 24 hr at room temperature exposed to light and 3% loss in 7 days at 5 °C	1680	C
Normosol M in dextrose 5%	AB[a]	BR	1 g	Visually compatible with 2 to 3% cefepime loss by HPLC in 24 hr at room temperature exposed to light and 2% loss in 7 days at 5 °C	1680	C
	AB[a]	BR	40 g	Visually compatible with 5% cefepime loss by HPLC in 24 hr at room temperature exposed to light and 2% loss in 7 days at 5 °C	1680	C
Normosol R	AB[a]	BR	1 g	Visually compatible with 2% cefepime loss by HPLC in 24 hr at room temperature exposed to light and 1% loss in 7 days at 5 °C	1680	C
	AB[a]	BR	40 g	Visually compatible with 5% cefepime loss by HPLC in 24 hr at room temperature exposed to light and 2% loss in 7 days at 5 °C	1680	C
Normosol R in dextrose 5%	AB[a]	BR	1 g	Visually compatible with 2% cefepime loss by HPLC in 24 hr at room temperature exposed to light	1680	C
Sodium chloride 0.9%	[b]	BR	1 g	Visually compatible with 2 to 5% cefepime loss by HPLC in 24 hr at room temperature exposed to light and about 1% loss in 7 days at 5 °C	1680	C
	[a]	BR	40 g	Visually compatible with 4 to 5% cefepime loss by HPLC in 24 hr at room temperature exposed to light and 2 to 3% loss in 7 days at 5 °C	1680	C
	BA[a]	BMS	20 g	6% loss by HPLC in 2 days at 25 °C and in 23 days at 5 °C. Slight increase in yellow color observed	2102	C

Solution Compatibility (Cont.)

Cefepime HCl

Solution	Mfr	Mfr	Conc/L	Remarks	Ref	C/I
	BFM[c]	BMS	8 g	8% loss by HPLC in 72 hr at 24 °C and in 15 days at 4 °C. Amber discoloration observed	2150	C

[a]Tested in PVC containers.
[b]Tested in both glass and PVC containers.
[c]Tested in polyethylene-lined trilayer (Clear-Flex) containers.

Additive Compatibility

Cefepime HCl

Drug	Mfr	Conc/L	Mfr	Conc/L	Test Soln	Remarks	Ref	C/I
Amikacin sulfate	BR	6 g	BR	40 g	D5W, NS	Visually compatible with 6% cefepime loss by HPLC in 24 hr at room temperature and 4% loss in 7 days at 5 °C. No amikacin loss by bioassay	1681	C
Aminophylline	LY	1 g	BR	4 g	NS	37% cefepime loss by HPLC in 18 hr at room temperature and 32% loss in 3 days at 5 °C. No aminophylline loss	1681	I
Ampicillin sodium	BR	1 g	BR	40 g	D5W	4% ampicillin loss by HPLC in 8 hr at room temperature and 5 °C. 7% cefepime loss by HPLC in 8 hr at room temperature and no loss in 8 hr at 5 °C	1682	?
	BR	1 g	BR	40 g	NS	No ampicillin loss by HPLC in 24 hr at room temperature and 9% loss in 48 hr at 5 °C. 5% cefepime loss by HPLC in 24 hr at room temperature and 2% loss in 72 hr at 5 °C	1682	C
	BR	10 g	BR	40 g	D5W	6% ampicillin loss by HPLC in 2 hr at room temperature and 2% loss in 8 hr at 5 °C. 7% cefepime loss by HPLC in 2 hr at room temperature and 8 hr at 5 °C	1682	I
	BR	10 g	BR	40 g	NS	6% ampicillin loss by HPLC in 8 hr at room temperature and 9% loss in 48 hr at 5 °C. 8% cefepime loss by HPLC in 8 hr at room temperature and 10% loss in 48 hr at 5 °C	1682	I
	BR	40 g	BR	4 g	D5W	10% ampicillin loss by HPLC in 1 hr at room temperature and 9% loss in 2 hr at 5 °C. 25% cefepime loss by HPLC in 1 hr at room temperature and 9% loss in 2 hr at 5 °C	1682	I
	BR	40 g	BR	4 g	NS	5% ampicillin loss by HPLC in 8 hr at room temperature and 4% loss in 8 hr at 5 °C. 4% cefepime loss by HPLC in 8 hr at room temperature and 6% loss in 8 hr at 5 °C	1682	?
Clindamycin phosphate	UP	0.25 g	BR	40 g	D5W, NS	7% or less cefepime loss by HPLC in 24 hr at room temperature and 10% or less loss in 7 days at 5 °C. No clindamycin loss by HPLC in 24 hr at room temperature and 8% or less loss in 7 days at 5 °C	1682	C

Additive Compatibility (Cont.)

Drug	Mfr	Conc/L	Cefepime HCl Mfr	Cefepime HCl Conc/L	Test Soln	Remarks	Ref	C/I
	UP	6 g	BR	4 g	D5W, NS	7% or less cefepime loss by HPLC in 24 hr at room temperature and 10% or less loss in 7 days at 5 °C. No clindamycin loss by HPLC in 24 hr at room temperature and 8% or less loss in 7 days at 5 °C	1682	C
Gentamicin sulfate	ES	1.2 g	BR	40 g	D5W, NS	Cloudiness forms in 18 hr at room temperature	1681	I
Heparin sodium	MG	10,000 and 50,000 units	BR	4 g	D5W, NS	Visually compatible with 4% cefepime loss by HPLC in 24 hr at room temperature and 3% in 7 days at 5 °C. Little or no heparin loss	1681	C
Metronidazole	AB, ES, SE	5 g	BR	40 g		7% cefepime loss by HPLC in 24 hr at room temperature exposed to light and 8% loss in 5 days at 5 °C. Little or no metronidazole loss by HPLC. However, orange color develops in 18 hr at room temperature and 24 hr at 5 °C	1682	?
	AB, ES, SE	5 g	BR	4 g		6% cefepime loss by HPLC in 24 hr at room temperature exposed to light and 3% loss in 5 days at 5 °C. Little or no metronidazole loss by HPLC. However, orange color develops in 18 hr at room temperature and 24 hr at 5 °C.	1682	?
	SCS	5 g	BMS	20 g	[b]	Visually compatible. 7% cefepime loss by HPLC in 48 hr and 11% loss in 72 hr at 23 °C; 8% cefepime loss in 7 days at 4 °C. No metronidazole loss by HPLC in 7 days at 4 and 23 °C	2324	C
	SCS	5 g	BMS	10 g	[b]	Visually compatible. 9% cefepime loss by HPLC in 72 hr at 23 °C and 4% or less loss in 7 days at 4 °C. 7% or less metronidazole loss by HPLC in 7 days at 4 and 23 °C	2324	C
	SCS	5 g	BMS	5 g	[b]	Visually compatible. 9% cefepime loss by HPLC in 48 hr at 23 °C and 2% or less loss in 7 days at 4 °C. Little or no metronidazole loss by HPLC in 7 days at 4 and 23 °C	2324	C
	SCS	5 g	BMS	2.5 g	[b]	Visually compatible. 8% cefepime loss by HPLC in 48 hr and 12% loss in 72 hr at 23 °C; 7% cefepime loss in 7 days at 4 °C. 5% or less metronidazole loss by HPLC in 7 days at 4 and 23 °C	2324	C
Metronidazole HCl	SE	5 g[a]	BR	40 g	D5W, NS	7% cefepime loss by HPLC in 24 hr at room temperature exposed to light and 8% loss in 5 days at 5 °C. Little or no metronidazole loss by HPLC. However, orange color develops in 18 hr at room temperature and 24 hr at 5 °C	1682	?

Additive Compatibility (Cont.)

Cefepime HCl

Drug	*Mfr*	*Conc/L*	*Mfr*	*Conc/L*	*Test Soln*	*Remarks*	*Ref*	*C/I*
	SE	8 g[a]	BR	4 g	D5W, NS	6% cefepime loss by HPLC in 24 hr at room temperature exposed to light and 3% loss in 5 days at 5 °C. Little or no metronidazole loss by HPLC. However, orange color develops in 18 hr at room temperature and 24 hr at 5 °C. A precipitate forms in 48 hr at 5 °C	1682	?
	SCS	5 g	BMS	20 g	NS[b]	Visually compatible. 7% cefepime loss by HPLC in 24 hr and 17% loss in 48 hr at 23 °C; 4% cefepime loss in 7 days at 4 °C. No metronidazole loss by HPLC in 7 days at 4 and 23 °C	2324	C
	SCS	5 g	BMS	10 g	NS[b]	Visually compatible. 9% cefepime loss by HPLC in 48 hr and 15% loss in 72 hr at 23 °C; 6% cefepime loss in 7 days at 4 °C. 8% or less metronidazole loss by HPLC in 7 days at 4 and 23 °C	2324	C
	SCS	5 g	BMS	5 g	NS[b]	Visually compatible. 8% cefepime loss by HPLC in 48 hr and 11% loss in 72 hr at 23 °C; 7% cefepime loss in 7 days at 4 °C. 5% or less metronidazole loss by HPLC in 7 days at 4 and 23 °C	2324	C
	SCS	5 g	BMS	2.5 g	NS[b]	Visually compatible. 12% cefepime loss by HPLC in 48 hr at 23 °C; 7% cefepime loss in 7 days at 4 °C. 6% metronidazole loss by HPLC in 7 days at 4 and 23 °C	2324	C
	SCS	5 g	BMS	20 g	D5W[b]	Visually compatible. 9% cefepime loss by HPLC in 24 hr and 15% loss in 48 hr at 23 °C; 9% cefepime loss in 7 days at 4 °C. Little or no metronidazole loss by HPLC in 7 days at 4 and 23 °C	2324	C
	SCS	5 g	BMS	10 g	D5W[b]	Visually compatible. 9% cefepime loss by HPLC in 12 hr and 20% loss in 24 hr at 23 °C; 10% cefepime loss in 72 hr at 4 °C. No metronidazole loss by HPLC in 7 days at 4 and 23 °C	2324	I
	SCS	5 g	BMS	5 g	D5W[b]	Visually compatible. 7% cefepime loss by HPLC in 12 hr and 13% loss in 24 hr at 23 °C; 9% cefepime loss in 5 days at 4 °C. No metronidazole loss by HPLC in 7 days at 4 and 23 °C	2324	I
	SCS	5 g	BMS	2.5 g	D5W[b]	Visually compatible. 4% cefepime loss by HPLC in 8 hr and 11% loss in 12 hr at 23 °C; 10% cefepime loss in 6 days at 4 °C. No metronidazole loss by HPLC in 7 days at 4 and 23 °C	2324	I
Netilmicin sulfate	SC	1 g	BR	40 g	D5W, NS	Cloudiness forms immediately	1682	I
	SC	5 g	BR	2.5 g	D5W, NS	Cloudiness forms immediately	1682	I
Potassium chloride	AB	40 mEq	BR	4 g	D5W, NS	Visually compatible with 2% cefepime loss by HPLC in 24 hr at room temperature and 7 days at 5 °C	1682	C

Additive Compatibility (Cont.)

Cefepime HCl

Drug	Mfr	Conc/L	Mfr	Conc/L	Test Soln	Remarks	Ref	C/I
	AB	10 mEq	BR	4 g	D5W	Visually compatible with 2% cefepime loss by HPLC in 24 hr at room temperature and 7 days at 5 °C	1682	C
Theophylline	BA	800 mg	BR	4 g	D5W	Visually compatible with 3% cefepime loss by HPLC in 24 hr at room temperature and in 7 days at 5 °C. No theophylline loss	1681	C
Tobramycin sulfate	AB	0.4 g	BR	40 g	D5W, NS	Cloudiness forms immediately	1682	I
	AB	2 g	BR	2.5 g	D5W, NS, W	Cloudiness forms immediately	1682	I
Vancomycin HCl	LI	5 g	BR	4 g	D5W, NS	4% cefepime loss by HPLC in 24 hr at room temperature exposed to light and 2% loss in 7 days at 5 °C. No vancomycin loss by HPLC, but cloudiness develops in 5 days at 5 °C	1682	C
	LI	1 g	BR	40 g	D5W, NS	4% cefepime loss by HPLC in 24 hr at room temperature exposed to light and 2% loss in 7 days at 5 °C. No vancomycin loss by HPLC and no cloudiness	1682	C

[a]*Neutralized with sodium bicarbonate.*
[b]*Tested in PVC containers.*

Y-Site Injection Compatibility (1:1 Mixture)

Cefepime HCl

Drug	Mfr	Conc	Mfr	Conc	Remarks	Ref	C/I
Acyclovir sodium	BW	7 mg/ml[a]	BMS	20 mg/ml[a]	Tiny crystals form in 4 hr	1689	I
Amphotericin B	SQ	0.6 mg/ml[a]	BMS	20 mg/ml[a]	Heavy yellow flocculent precipitate forms immediately	1689	I
Amphotericin B cholesteryl sulfate complex	SEQ	0.83 mg/ml[a]	BMS	20 mg/ml[a]	Gross precipitate forms	2117	I
Ampicillin sodium–sulbactam sodium	RR	20 + 10 mg/ml[a]	BMS	20 mg/ml[a]	Physically compatible with no change in measured turbidity or increase in particle content in 4 hr at 22 °C	1689	C
Aztreonam	SQ	40 mg/ml[a]	BMS	20 mg/ml[a]	Physically compatible with no change in measured turbidity or increase in particle content in 4 hr at 22 °C	1689	C
Bleomycin sulfate	BR	1 unit/ml[b]	BMS	20 mg/ml[a]	Physically compatible with no change in measured turbidity or increase in particle content in 4 hr at 22 °C	1689	C
Bumetanide	RC	0.04 mg/ml[a]	BMS	20 mg/ml[a]	Physically compatible with no change in measured turbidity or increase in particle content in 4 hr at 22 °C	1689	C
Buprenorphine HCl	RKC	0.04 mg/ml[a]	BMS	20 mg/ml[a]	Physically compatible with no change in measured turbidity or increase in particle content in 4 hr at 22 °C	1689	C
Butorphanol tartrate	BR	0.04 mg/ml[a]	BMS	20 mg/ml[a]	Physically compatible with no change in measured turbidity or increase in particle content in 4 hr at 22 °C	1689	C

Y-Site Injection Compatibility (1:1 Mixture) (Cont.)

Drug	*Mfr*	*Conc*	Cefepime HCl *Mfr*	*Conc*	*Remarks*	*Ref*	*C/I*
Calcium gluconate	AMR	40 mg/ml[a]	BMS	20 mg/ml[a]	Physically compatible with no change in measured turbidity or increase in particle content in 4 hr at 22 °C	1689	C
Carboplatin	BR	5 mg/ml[a]	BMS	20 mg/ml[a]	Physically compatible with no change in measured turbidity or increase in particle content in 4 hr at 22 °C	1689	C
Carmustine	BR	1.5 mg/ml[a]	BMS	20 mg/ml[a]	Physically compatible with no change in measured turbidity or increase in particle content in 4 hr at 22 °C	1689	C
Chlordiazepoxide HCl	RC	20 mg/ml	BMS	20 mg/ml[a]	Haze forms immediately. Flocculent precipitate forms in 4 hr	1689	I
Chlorpromazine HCl	SCN	2 mg/ml[a]	BMS	20 mg/ml[a]	Cloudiness forms immediately. Flocculent precipitate forms in 4 hr	1689	I
Cimetidine HCl	SKB	12 mg/ml[a]	BMS	20 mg/ml[a]	Cloudiness forms immediately	1689	I
Ciprofloxacin	MI	1 mg/ml[a]	BMS	20 mg/ml[a]	Cloudiness forms immediately. Flocculent precipitate forms in 4 hr	1689	I
Cisplatin	BR	1 mg/ml	BMS	20 mg/ml[a]	Haze forms in 1 hr. Cloudiness and particulates form in 4 hr	1689	I
Cyclophosphamide	MJ	10 mg/ml[a]	BMS	20 mg/ml[a]	Physically compatible with no change in measured turbidity or increase in particle content in 4 hr at 22 °C	1689	C
Cytarabine	CET	50 mg/ml	BMS	20 mg/ml[a]	Physically compatible with no change in measured turbidity or increase in particle content in 4 hr at 22 °C	1689	C
Dacarbazine	MI	4 mg/ml[a]	BMS	20 mg/ml[a]	Cloudiness forms immediately. Flocculent precipitate forms in 4 hr	1689	I
Dactinomycin	MSD	0.01 mg/ml[a]	BMS	20 mg/ml[a]	Physically compatible with no change in measured turbidity or increase in particle content in 4 hr at 22 °C	1689	C
Daunorubicin HCl	WY	1 mg/ml[a]	BMS	20 mg/ml[a]	Haze forms immediately. Flocculent precipitate forms in 4 hr	1689	I
Dexamethasone sodium phosphate	AMR	1 mg/ml[a]	BMS	20 mg/ml[a]	Physically compatible with no change in measured turbidity or increase in particle content in 4 hr at 22 °C	1689	C
Diazepam	ES	5 mg/ml	BMS	20 mg/ml[a]	Cloudiness forms immediately	1689	I
Diphenhydramine HCl	WY	2 mg/ml[a]	BMS	20 mg/ml[a]	Cloudy solution with precipitate forms immediately	1689	I
Dobutamine HCl	LI	4 mg/ml[a]	BMS	20 mg/ml[a]	Cloudiness forms immediately. Precipitate forms in 4 hr	1689	I
Docetaxel	RPR	0.9 mg/ml[a]	BMS	20 mg/ml[a]	Physically compatible with no change in measured turbidity or increase in particle content in 4 hr at 23 °C	2224	C
Dopamine HCl	AST	3.2 mg/ml[a]	BMS	20 mg/ml[a]	Haze and precipitate form in 1 hr	1689	I
Doxorubicin HCl	CET	2 mg/ml[a]	BMS	20 mg/ml[a]	Haze forms immediately. Flocculent precipitate forms in 4 hr	1689	I
Doxorubicin HCl liposome injection	SEQ	0.4 mg/ml[a]	BMS	20 mg/ml[a]	Physically compatible with little or no change in measured turbidity and no increase in particle content in 4 hr at 23 °C	2087	C

Y-Site Injection Compatibility (1:1 Mixture) (Cont.)

Cefepime HCl

Drug	*Mfr*	*Conc*	*Mfr*	*Conc*	*Remarks*	*Ref*	*C/I*
Droperidol	JN	0.4 mg/ml[a]	BMS	20 mg/ml[a]	Haze forms immediately. Flocculent precipitate forms in 4 hr	1689	I
Enalaprilat	MSD	0.1 mg/ml[a]	BMS	20 mg/ml[a]	Tiny particles form in 4 hr	1689	I
Etoposide	BR	0.4 mg/ml[a]	BMS	20 mg/ml[a]	Haze increases and tiny particles form in 1 hr	1689	I
Etoposide phosphate	BR	5 mg/ml[a]	BMS	20 mg/ml[a]	Increased haze and particulates form within 1 hr	2218	I
Famotidine	ME	2 mg/ml[a]	BMS	20 mg/ml[a]	Haze forms immediately. Flocculent precipitate forms in 4 hr	1689	I
Filgrastim	AMG	30 μg/ml[a]	BMS	20 mg/ml[a]	Hazy turbid solution forms immediately	1689	I
Floxuridine	RC	3 mg/ml[a]	BMS	20 mg/ml[a]	Haze and tiny particles form immediately	1689	I
Fluconazole	RR	2 mg/ml	BMS	20 mg/ml[a]	Physically compatible with no change in measured turbidity or increase in particle content in 4 hr at 22 °C	1689	C
Fludarabine phosphate	BX	1 mg/ml[a]	BMS	20 mg/ml[a]	Physically compatible with no change in measured turbidity or increase in particle content in 4 hr at 22 °C	1689	C
Fluorouracil	AD	16 mg/ml[a]	BMS	20 mg/ml[a]	Physically compatible with no change in measured turbidity or increase in particle content in 4 hr at 22 °C	1689	C
Furosemide	AB	3 mg/ml[a]	BMS	20 mg/ml[a]	Physically compatible with no change in measured turbidity or increase in particle content in 4 hr at 22 °C	1689	C
Ganciclovir sodium	SY	20 mg/ml[a]	BMS	20 mg/ml[a]	Flocculent precipitate forms immediately	1689	I
Granisetron HCl	SKB	0.05 mg/ml[a]	BMS	20 mg/ml[a]	Physically compatible with no change in measured turbidity or increase in particle content in 4 hr at 23 °C	2000	C
Haloperidol lactate	MN	0.2 mg/ml[a]	BMS	20 mg/ml[a]	Haze forms immediately	1689	I
Hetastarch in lactated electrolyte injection (Hextend)	AB	6%	BMS	20 mg/ml[a]	Physically compatible with no change in measured turbidity or increase in particle content in 4 hr at 23 °C	2339	C
Hydrocortisone sodium phosphate	MSD	1 mg/ml[a]	BMS	20 mg/ml[a]	Physically compatible with no change in measured turbidity or increase in particle content in 4 hr at 22 °C	1689	C
Hydrocortisone sodium succinate	UP	1 mg/ml[a]	BMS	20 mg/ml[a]	Physically compatible with no change in measured turbidity or increase in particle content in 4 hr at 22 °C	1689	C
Hydromorphone HCl	ES	0.5 mg/ml[a]	BMS	20 mg/ml[a]	Physically compatible with no change in measured turbidity or increase in particle content in 4 hr at 22 °C	1689	C
Hydroxyzine HCl	WI	4 mg/ml[a]	BMS	20 mg/ml[a]	Haze forms immediately. Flocculent precipitate forms in 4 hr	1689	I
Idarubicin HCl	AD	0.5 mg/ml[a]	BMS	20 mg/ml[a]	Flocculent precipitate forms in 4 hr	1689	I
Ifosfamide	MJ	25 mg/ml[a]	BMS	20 mg/ml[a]	Haze and precipitate form in 1 hr	1689	I
Imipenem–cilastatin sodium	MSD	10 mg/ml[a]	BMS	20 mg/ml[a]	Physically compatible with no change in measured turbidity or increase in particle content in 4 hr at 22 °C	1689	C

Y-Site Injection Compatibility (1:1 Mixture) (Cont.)

			Cefepime HCl				
Drug	*Mfr*	*Conc*	*Mfr*	*Conc*	*Remarks*	*Ref*	*C/I*
Leucovorin calcium	LE	2 mg/ml[a]	BMS	20 mg/ml[a]	Physically compatible with no change in measured turbidity or increase in particle content in 4 hr at 22 °C	1689	C
Lorazepam	WY	0.1 mg/ml[a]	BMS	20 mg/ml[a]	Physically compatible with no change in measured turbidity or increase in particle content in 4 hr at 22 °C	1689	C
Magnesium sulfate	AST	100 mg/ml[a]	BMS	20 mg/ml[a]	Haze forms immediately	1689	I
Mannitol	BA	15%	BMS	20 mg/ml[a]	Slight haze with particles forms immediately	1689	I
Mechlorethamine HCl	MSD	1 mg/ml	BMS	20 mg/ml[a]	Slight haze with particles forms immediately	1689	I
Melphalan	BW	0.1 mg/ml[a]	BMS	20 mg/ml[a]	Physically compatible with no change in measured turbidity or increase in particle content in 4 hr at 22 °C	1689	C
Meperidine HCl	WY	4 mg/ml[a]	BMS	20 mg/ml[a]	Haze forms immediately with particles in 1 hr	1689	I
Mesna	MJ	10 mg/ml[a]	BMS	20 mg/ml[a]	Physically compatible with no change in measured turbidity or increase in particle content in 4 hr at 22 °C	1689	C
Methotrexate sodium	LE	15 mg/ml[a]	BMS	20 mg/ml[a]	Physically compatible with no change in measured turbidity or increase in particle content in 4 hr at 22 °C	1689	C
Methylprednisolone sodium succinate	AB	5 mg/ml[a]	BMS	20 mg/ml[a]	Physically compatible with no change in measured turbidity or increase in particle content in 4 hr at 22 °C	1689	C
Metoclopramide HCl	RB	5 mg/ml	BMS	20 mg/ml[a]	Haze forms immediately	1689	I
Metronidazole	BA	5 mg/ml	BMS	20 mg/ml[a]	Physically compatible with no change in measured turbidity or increase in particle content in 4 hr at 22 °C	1689	C
Mitomycin	BR	0.5 mg/ml[a]	BMS	20 mg/ml[a]	Color changes to pinkish purple in 1 hr	1689	I
Mitoxantrone HCl	LE	0.5 mg/ml[a]	BMS	20 mg/ml[a]	Haze forms immediately. Flocculent precipitate forms in 4 hr	1689	I
Morphine sulfate	AST	1 mg/ml[a]	BMS	20 mg/ml[a]	Haze forms immediately with particles in 1 hr	1689	I
Nalbuphine HCl	DU	10 mg/ml	BMS	20 mg/ml[a]	Haze forms immediately. Flocculent precipitate forms in 4 hr	1689	I
Ofloxacin	ORT	4 mg/ml[a]	BMS	20 mg/ml[a]	Haze forms immediately. Flocculent precipitate forms in 4 hr	1689	I
Ondansetron HCl	GL	1 mg/ml[a]	BMS	20 mg/ml[a]	Haze forms immediately	1689	I
Paclitaxel	BR	0.6 mg/ml[a]	BMS	20 mg/ml[a]	Physically compatible with no change in measured turbidity or increase in particle content in 4 hr at 22 °C	1689	C
Piperacillin sodium–tazobactam sodium	LE	40 + 5 mg/ml[a]	BMS	20 mg/ml[a]	Physically compatible with no change in measured turbidity or increase in particle content in 4 hr at 22 °C	1689	C
Plicamycin	MI	0.01 mg/ml[a]	BMS	20 mg/ml[a]	Haze forms immediately. Particles form in 1 hr	1689	I

Y-Site Injection Compatibility (1:1 Mixture) (Cont.)

Cefepime HCl

Drug	*Mfr*	*Conc*	*Mfr*	*Conc*	*Remarks*	*Ref*	*C/I*
Prochlorperazine edisylate	SN	0.5 mg/ml[a]	BMS	20 mg/ml[a]	Haze forms immediately. Flocculent precipitate forms in 4 hr	1689	I
Promethazine HCl	WY	2 mg/ml[a]	BMS	20 mg/ml[a]	Haze forms immediately. Flocculent precipitate forms in 4 hr	1689	I
Propofol	ASZ	10 mg/ml	BMS	20 mg/ml[a]	Physically compatible for 1 hr at 23 °C with no increase in particle content	1916	C
Ranitidine HCl	GL	2 mg/ml[a]	BMS	20 mg/ml[a]	Physically compatible with no change in measured turbidity or increase in particle content in 4 hr at 22 °C	1689	C
Sargramostim	IMM	10 μg/ml[b]	BMS	20 mg/ml[a]	Physically compatible with no change in measured turbidity or increase in particle content in 4 hr at 22 °C	1689	C
Sodium bicarbonate	AB	1 mEq/ml	BMS	20 mg/ml[a]	Physically compatible with no change in measured turbidity or increase in particle content in 4 hr at 22 °C	1689	C
Streptozocin	UP	40 mg/ml[a]	BMS	20 mg/ml[a]	Haze forms immediately. Particles form in 1 hr. Deep red color forms in 4 hr	1689	I
Thiotepa	LE	1 mg/ml[a]	BMS	20 mg/ml[a]	Physically compatible with no change in measured turbidity or increase in particle content in 4 hr at 22 °C	1689	C
Ticarcillin disodium–clavulanate potassium	SKB	31 mg/ml[a]	BMS	20 mg/ml[a]	Physically compatible with no change in measured turbidity or increase in particle content in 4 hr at 22 °C	1689	C
Trimethoprim–sulfamethoxazole	ES	0.8 + 4 mg/ml[a]	BMS	20 mg/ml[a]	Physically compatible with no change in measured turbidity or increase in particle content in 4 hr at 22 °C	1689	C
Vancomycin HCl	AB	10 mg/ml[a]	BMS	20 mg/ml[a]	Haze forms immediately. Flocculent precipitate forms in 4 hr	1689	I
Vinblastine sulfate	LI	0.12 mg/ml[a]	BMS	20 mg/ml[a]	Haze with particles forms immediately	1689	I
Vincristine sulfate	LI	0.05 mg/ml[a]	BMS	20 mg/ml[a]	Small particles form immediately	1689	I
Zidovudine	BW	4 mg/ml[a]	BMS	20 mg/ml[a]	Physically compatible with no change in measured turbidity or increase in particle content in 4 hr at 22 °C	1689	C

[a]*Tested in dextrose 5% in water.*
[b]*Tested in sodium chloride 0.9%.*

Additional Compatibility Information

Infusion Solutions — The manufacturer states that cefepime HCl 1 to 40 mg/ml is stable for 24 hours at room temperatures between 20 and 25 °C and for seven days under refrigeration at 2 to 8 °C in the following infusion solutions (2):

Dextrose 5% in Ringer's injection, lactated
Dextrose 5% in sodium chloride 0.9%
Dextrose 5% in water
Dextrose 10% in water
Normosol M in 5% dextrose
Normosol R
Sodium chloride 0.9%
Sodium lactate ⅙ M

Peritoneal Dialysis Solutions — Cefepime HCl (Bristol-Myers Squibb) 0.125 and 0.25 mg/ml in Inpersol (Abbott) peritoneal dialysis solution with dextrose 4.25% is stable, exhibiting 2 to 3% loss by HPLC analysis in seven days at 5 °C, 2% loss in 24 hours at room temperature, and 7 to 8% loss in 24 hours at 37 °C. (1682)

Cefepime HCl (Bristol-Myers Squibb) 0.1 mg/ml in Delflex solution with dextrose 1.5% (Fresenius) stored at various temperatures was evaluated for physical and chemical stability. No visible particulates or changes in color or clarity were observed in any sample. HPLC analysis found that cefepime exhibited no loss in 14 days at

4 °C, about 7% loss in seven days at 25 °C, and about 4% loss in 24 hours and 9% loss in 48 hours at body temperature of 37 °C. (2283)

Other Drugs — The manufacturer states that cefepime HCl should not be mixed with aminophylline, gentamicin sulfate, metronidazole, netilmicin sulfate, tobramycin sulfate, and vancomycin HCl because of the potential for interaction. These medications should be administered separately from cefepime HCl. (2)

CEFOPERAZONE
AHFS 8:12.06

Products — Cefoperazone is available in vials and piggyback units containing 1 and 2 g of drug. In addition, 10-g pharmacy bulk vials are available. The vials may be reconstituted with a compatible diluent and should be allowed to stand so that any foaming may dissipate; the vials should then be inspected visually to assure complete solubilization. At concentrations above 333 mg/ml, vigorous and prolonged shaking is required to solubilize the drug. The maximum solubility is 475 mg/ml. (2)

For intramuscular injection, sterile water for injection, bacteriostatic water for injection (benzyl alcohol or parabens), or another compatible solution may be used as the diluent in the dilutions listed in Table 1. (2; 4)

For concentrations above 250 mg/ml, the manufacturer recommends that a lidocaine HCl solution be used for reconstitution. (2) To prepare intramuscular injections with lidocaine HCl 2%, a two-step procedure can be followed. Initially, sterile water for injection is added in the amounts indicated in Table 2. After complete dissolution of the drug, the specified volume of lidocaine HCl 2% is added. The final lidocaine HCl concentration will be about 0.5%. (2)

For intravenous administration, each gram of cefoperazone is reconstituted with 5 ml of any compatible diluent except Ringer's injection, lactated, with or without dextrose 5%. (See Additional Compatibility Information.) The minimum volume of diluent is 2.8 ml per gram of cefoperazone. After dissolution is complete, the entire content of the vial is withdrawn and further diluted for intravenous administration. For intermittent infusion, further dilution in 20 to 40 ml of diluent per gram of drug is recommended. For continuous infusion, a concentration of 2 to 25 mg/ml can be used. (2)

The 1- and 2-g piggyback units should be reconstituted with 20 to 40 ml of any compatible diluent per gram of drug. (See Additional Compatibility Information.) If Ringer's injection, lactated, with or without dextrose 5% is used as the vehicle, the manufacturer recommends an initial reconstitution with 2.8 to 5 ml of another compatible diluent per gram of drug prior to final dilution. (2)

Cefoperazone is available frozen as a premixed solution of 1 or 2 g per 50 ml of dextrose 4.6 or 3.6%, respectively. (2; 4)

The 10-g pharmacy bulk vial may be reconstituted with 95 ml of sterile water for injection in two separate, approximately equal aliquots. The resulting solution contains 100 mg/ml. (2)

Table 1. Recommended Intramuscular Dilutions of Cefoperazone (2)

Vial Size	Volume of Diluent	Withdrawable Volume	Concentration
1 g	2.6 ml	3 ml	333 mg/ml
	3.8 ml	4 ml	250 mg/ml
2 g	5.0 ml	6 ml	333 mg/ml
	7.2 ml	8 ml	250 mg/ml

Table 2. Preparing Cefoperazone with Lidocaine HCl 2%

Vial Size	Step 1, Sterile Water Volume	Step 2, Lidocaine HCl 2% Volume	Cefoperazone Concentration
1 g	2.0 ml	0.6 ml	333 mg/ml
	2.8 ml	1.0 ml	250 mg/ml
2 g	3.8 ml	1.2 ml	333 mg/ml
	5.4 ml	1.8 ml	250 mg/ml

pH — From 4.5 to 6.5. (2; 4)

Osmolality — The osmolality of cefoperazone 1 and 2 g was calculated for the following dilutions (1054):

Diluent	Osmolality (mOsm/kg) 50 ml	100 ml
1 g		
Dextrose 5% in water	302	280
Sodium chloride 0.9%	328	307
2 g		
Dextrose 5% in water	343	304
Sodium chloride 0.9%	370	330

The frozen premixed solutions have osmolalities of approximately 300 mOsm/kg. (4)

Robinson et al. recommended the following maximum cefoperazone concentrations to achieve osmolalities suitable for peripheral infusion in fluid-restricted patients (1180):

Diluent	Maximum Concentration (mg/ml)	Osmolality (mOsm/kg)
Dextrose 5% in water	113	461
Sodium chloride 0.9%	102	439
Sterile water for injection	202	312

Sodium Content — Cefoperazone contains 1.5 mEq (34 mg) of sodium per gram. (2)

Trade Name(s) — Cefobid.

Administration — Cefoperazone is administered by deep intramuscular injection or by continuous intravenous infusion at a concentration of 2 to 25 mg/ml or intermittent intravenous infusion diluted in 20 to 40 ml of compatible diluent per gram of cefoperazone administered over 15 to 30 minutes. (2; 4) Although not recommended by the manufacturer, cefoperazone has also been given by direct intravenous injection over three to five minutes. (4)

Stability — Intact vials of cefoperazone should be stored at room temperatures not exceeding 25 °C and protected from light. Reconstituted solutions are colorless to straw yellow and do not need light protection. Solutions of cefoperazone in compatible diluents are stable for 24 hours at room temperature and five days under refrigeration. (See Additional Compatibility Information.) Cefoperazone solutions may be stored in glass or plastic syringes or in glass or PVC infusion solution containers. (2; 4)

Cefoperazone (Roerig) 1 g/10 ml reconstituted with sterile water for injection or 1 g/50 ml in dextrose 5% in water in PVC bags exhibited no visible changes and no significant increases in particulate matter in 24 hours at 5 and 25 °C. (986)

Freezing Solutions — Reconstitution to a concentration of 300 mg/ml with sodium chloride 0.9% or sterile water for injection yields solutions that are stable for five weeks at −20 to −10 °C. Solutions containing 50 mg/ml in dextrose 5% in water or 2 mg/ml in dextrose 5% in sodium chloride 0.2 or 0.9% are stable for three weeks at −20 to −10 °C. Frozen solutions should be thawed at room temperature; microwave techniques and heating are not recommended. Thawed solutions should not be refrozen. (2; 4)

Cefoperazone 40 mg/ml in both dextrose 5% in water and sodium chloride 0.9% exhibited no decomposition after 96 days at −10 °C. Thawing in a microwave oven did not affect stability. (1341)

Elastomeric Reservoir Pumps — Cefoperazone solutions in elastomeric reservoir pumps have been stated by the pump manufacturers to be stable for the following time periods frozen, refrigerated (REF), or at room temperature (RT) (31):

Pump Reservoir(s)	Conc.	Frozen	REF	RT
Homepump; Homepump Eclipse	2 to 50 mg/ml[a,b]	3 weeks	5 days	24 hr
Intermate	2 to 50 mg/ml[a]	30 days	10 days	24 hr
Medflo	10 to 20 mg/ml[a,b]	3 weeks	21 days	48 hr
ReadyMed	25 mg/ml[b]	4 weeks	14 days	48 hr

[a]*In dextrose 5% in water.*
[b]*In sodium chloride 0.9%.*

Central Venous Catheter — Cefoperazone (Roerig) 10 mg/ml in dextrose 5% in water was found to be compatible with the ARROWg+ard Blue Plus (Arrow International) chlorhexidine-bearing triple-lumen central catheter. HPLC analysis was used to evaluate completeness of drug delivery through the catheter and the amount of chlorhexidine removed from the internal lumens. Delivery of the cefoperazone ranged from 94 to 95% of the initial concentration among the three lumens. Furthermore, chlorhexidine delivered from the catheter remained at trace amounts with no substantial increase due to the delivery of the drug through the catheter. (2335)

Compatibility Information

Solution Compatibility

Cefoperazone

Solution	*Mfr*	*Mfr*	*Conc/L*	*Remarks*	*Ref*	*C/I*
Dextrose 5% in water	MG[a]	RR	20 g	2% loss in 48 hr at 25 °C under fluorescent light	1164	C
	TR		40 g	Physically compatible with 8% loss in 8 days at 25 °C and no loss in 80 days at 5 °C	1341	C
Sodium chloride 0.9%	MG[a]	RR	20 g	3% loss in 48 hr at 25 °C under fluorescent light	1164	C
	TR		40 g	Physically compatible with 8% loss in 8 days at 25 °C and no loss in 80 days at 5 °C	1341	C
TPN #107[b]			1 g	50% cefoperazone loss in 24 hr at 21 °C by microbiological assay	1326	I

[a]*Tested in glass bottles.*
[b]*Refer to Appendix I for the composition of parenteral nutrition solutions. TPN indicates a 2-in-1 admixture.*

Additive Compatibility

Cefoperazone

Drug	*Mfr*	*Conc/L*	*Mfr*	*Conc/L*	*Test Soln*	*Remarks*	*Ref*	*C/I*
Cimetidine HCl	SKF	2 g	RR	5 g	D5W	Physically compatible. 5% cefoperazone loss at 25 °C and 3% loss at 4 °C in 48 hr. 2% or less cimetidine loss in 48 hr at 25 and 4 °C	1403	C

Additive Compatibility (Cont.)

Drug	Mfr	Conc/L	Cefoperazone Mfr	Cefoperazone Conc/L	Test Soln	Remarks	Ref	C/I
Clindamycin phosphate	UP	12 g	RR	20 g	D5W, NS[a]	Physically compatible with no clindamycin loss and 5% cefoperazone loss in 48 hr at 25 °C under fluorescent light	174; 1164	C
Furosemide	HO	200 mg	RR	10 g	D5W	Physically compatible. 10% loss of both drugs in 15 days at 25 °C and 20 days at 4 °C in the dark	1402	C

[a]*Tested in both glass and PVC containers.*

Drugs in Syringe Compatibility

Drug (in syringe)	Mfr	Amt	Cefoperazone Mfr	Cefoperazone Amt	Remarks	Ref	C/I
Doxapram HCl	RB	400 mg/ 20 ml		500 mg/ 4 ml	Immediate precipitation	1177	I
Heparin sodium		2500 units/ 1 ml	RR	2 g	Physically compatible for at least 5 min	1053	C

Y-Site Injection Compatibility (1:1 Mixture)

Drug	Mfr	Conc	Cefoperazone Mfr	Cefoperazone Conc	Remarks	Ref	C/I
Acyclovir sodium	BW	5 mg/ml[a]	RR	20 mg/ml[a]	Physically compatible for 4 hr at 25 °C	1157	C
Allopurinol sodium	BW	3 mg/ml[b]	RR	40 mg/ml[b]	Physically compatible with no change in measured turbidity or increase in particle content in 4 hr at 22 °C	1686	C
Amifostine	USB	10 mg/ml[a]	RR	40 mg/ml[a]	Haze forms immediately, becoming cloudy with microprecipitation in 4 hr	1845	I
Amphotericin B cholesteryl sulfate complex	SEQ	0.83 mg/ml[a]	RR	40 mg/ml[a]	Gross precipitate forms	2117	I
Aztreonam	SQ	40 mg/ml[a]	RR	40 mg/ml[a]	Physically compatible with no subvisual haze or particle formation in 4 hr at 23 °C	1758	C
Cisatracurium besylate	GW	0.1, 2, 5 mg/ ml[a]	RR	40 mg/ml[a]	White cloudiness forms immediately	2074	I
Cyclophosphamide	MJ	20 mg/ml[a]	RR	20 mg/ml[a]	Physically compatible for 4 hr at 25 °C	1194	C
Diltiazem HCl	MMD	1[b] and 5 mg/ ml	RR	20[a], 25[b], 50[b] mg/ml	Cloudiness and precipitate form	1807	I
	MMD	5 mg/ml	RR	10 mg/ml[b]	Precipitate forms	1807	I
	MMD	1 mg/ml[b]	RR	10 mg/ml[b]	Visually compatible	1807	C
	MMD	1[b] and 5 mg/ ml	RR	2 and 5 mg/ ml[b]	Visually compatible	1807	C
Docetaxel	RPR	0.9 mg/ml[a]	RR	40 mg/ml[a]	Physically compatible with no change in measured turbidity or increase in particle content in 4 hr at 23 °C	2224	C

Y-Site Injection Compatibility (1:1 Mixture) (Cont.)

Cefoperazone

Drug	*Mfr*	*Conc*	*Mfr*	*Conc*	*Remarks*	*Ref*	*C/I*
Doxorubicin HCl liposome injection	SEQ	0.4 mg/ml[a]	RR	40 mg/ml[a]	Partial loss of measured natural turbidity	2087	I
Enalaprilat	MSD	0.05 mg/ml[b]	RR	10 mg/ml[a]	Physically compatible for 24 hr at room temperature under fluorescent light	1355	C
Esmolol HCl	DCC	10 mg/ml[a]	RR	10 mg/ml[a]	Physically compatible for 24 hr at 22 °C	1169	C
Etoposide phosphate	BR	5 mg/ml[a]	RR	40 mg/ml[a]	Physically compatible with no change in measured turbidity or increase in particle content in 4 hr at 23 °C	2218	C
Famotidine	MSD	0.2 mg/ml[a]	RR	40 mg/ml[b]	Physically compatible for 14 hr	1196	C
Filgrastim	AMG	30 μg/ml[a]	RR	40 mg/ml[a]	Haze and particles form immediately	1687	I
Fludarabine phosphate	BX	1 mg/ml[a]	RR	40 mg/ml[a]	Physically compatible for 4 hr at room temperature under fluorescent light	1439	C
Foscarnet sodium	AST	24 mg/ml	RR	40 mg/ml	Physically compatible for 24 hr at room temperature under fluorescent light	1335	C
Gatifloxacin	BMS	2 mg/ml[a]	RR	40 mg/ml[a]	White precipitate forms immediately	2234	I
Gemcitabine HCl	LI	10 mg/ml[b]	RR	40 mg/ml[b]	Gross precipitation occurs immediately	2226	I
Granisetron HCl	SKB	0.05 mg/ml[a]	RR	40 mg/ml[a]	Physically compatible with no change in measured turbidity or increase in particle content in 4 hr at 23 °C	2000	C
Hetastarch in lactated electrolyte injection (Hextend)	AB	6%	RR	40 mg/ml[a]	Physically compatible with no change in measured turbidity or increase in particle content in 4 hr at 23 °C	2339	C
Hetastarch in sodium chloride 0.9%	DCC	6%	RR	20 mg/ml[a]	Small crystals formed immediately after mixing and persisted for 4 hr	1313	I
Hydromorphone HCl	WY	0.2 mg/ml[a]	RR	20 mg/ml[a]	Physically compatible for at least 4 hr at 25 °C under fluorescent light	987	C
Labetalol HCl	SC	1 mg/ml[a]	RR	10 mg/ml[a]	Cloudiness and fine precipitate form immediately	1171	I
Linezolid	PHU	2 mg/ml	RR	40 mg/ml[a]	Physically compatible with no change in measured turbidity or increase in particle content in 4 hr at 23 °C	2264	C
Magnesium sulfate	IX	16.7, 33.3, 66.7, 100 mg/ml[a]	RR	20 mg/ml[a]	Physically compatible for at least 4 hr at 32 °C	813	C
Melphalan HCl	BW	0.1 mg/ml[b]	RR	40 mg/ml[b]	Physically compatible with no change in measured turbidity or increase in particle content in 3 hr at 22 °C	1557	C
Meperidine HCl	WY	10 mg/ml[a]	RR	20 mg/ml[a]	Immediate precipitation	987	I
Morphine sulfate	WI	1 mg/ml[a]	RR	20 mg/ml[a]	Physically compatible for at least 4 hr at 25 °C under fluorescent light	987	C
Ondansetron HCl	GL	1 mg/ml[b]	RR	40 mg/ml[a]	Immediate turbidity and precipitation	1365	I
Pentamidine isethionate	FUJ	3 mg/ml[a]	RR	20 mg/ml[c]	Heavy white precipitate forms immediately	1880	I

Y-Site Injection Compatibility (1:1 Mixture) (Cont.)

Cefoperazone

Drug	*Mfr*	*Conc*	*Mfr*	*Conc*	*Remarks*	*Ref*	*C/I*
Perphenazine	SC	0.02 mg/ml[a]	RR	20 mg/ml[a]	Cloudy solution forms immediately with fine precipitate persisting for 4 hr at 25 °C	1155	I
Promethazine HCl		6.25 mg	RR	[d]	White precipitate forms due to ionic complex formation	1336	I
Propofol	ZEN	10 mg/ml	RR	40 mg/ml[a]	Physically compatible for 1 hr at 23 °C with no increase in particle content	2066	C
Ranitidine HCl	GL	1 mg/ml[b]	TAK	20 mg/ml[b]	Visually compatible with no loss of either drug by HPLC in 4 hr at 25 °C	2209	C
Remifentanil HCl	GW	0.025 mg/ml[b]	RR	40 mg/ml[a]	Physically compatible with no change in measured turbidity or increase in particle content in 4 hr at 23 °C	2075	C
	GW	0.25 mg/ml[b]	RR	40 mg/ml[a]	Subvisual haze forms in 1 hr	2075	I
Sargramostim	IMM	10 μg/ml[b]	RR	40 mg/ml[b]	Slight haze, visible with high intensity light, forms immediately	1436	I
Teniposide	BR	0.1 mg/ml[a]	RR	40 mg/ml[a]	Physically compatible with no subvisual haze or particle formation in 4 hr at 23 °C	1725	C
Thiotepa	IMM[e]	1 mg/ml[a]	RR	40 mg/ml[a]	Physically compatible with no change in measured turbidity or increase in particle content in 4 hr at 23 °C	1861	C
TNA #218 to #226[f]			RR	40 mg/ml[a]	Visually compatible with no precipitate or emulsion damage apparent in 4 hr at 23 °C	2215	C
TPN #61[f]		[g]	RR	250 mg/1 ml[h]	Physically compatible	1012	C
		[i]	RR	1.5 g/6 ml[h]	Physically compatible	1012	C
TPN #212 to #215[f]			RR	40 mg/ml[a]	Physically compatible with no change in measured turbidity or increase in particle content in 4 hr at 23 °C	2109	C
Vinorelbine tartrate	BW	1 mg/ml[b]	RR	40 mg/ml[b]	Heavy white flocculent precipitate forms immediately	1558	I

[a]*Tested in dextrose 5% in water.*
[b]*Tested in sodium chloride 0.9%.*
[c]*Tested in dextrose 4.6% in water.*
[d]*Tested in dextrose 5% in water; concentration unspecified.*
[e]*Lyophilized formulation tested.*
[f]*Refer to Appendix I for the composition of parenteral nutrition solutions. TNA indicates a 3-in-1 admixture, and TPN indicates a 2-in-1 admixture.*
[g]*Run at 21 ml/hr.*
[h]*Given over five minutes by syringe pump.*
[i]*Run at 94 ml/hr.*

Additional Compatibility Information

Infusion Solutions — The stability of cefoperazone in various solutions, as stated by the manufacturer, is shown in Table 3. (2)

When frozen at −20 to −10 °C, cefoperazone is stated to be stable as indicated in Table 4. (2)

Table 3. Stability of Cefoperazone in Various Solutions (2)

Solution	Cefoperazone Concentration	Stability Period 15 to 25 °C	Stability Period 2 to 8 °C
Bacteriostatic water for injection (benzyl alcohol or parabens)	300 mg/ml	24 hr	5 days
Dextrose 5% in Ringer's injection, lactated	2 to 50 mg/ml	24 hr	
Dextrose 5% in sodium chloride 0.2 or 0.9%	2 to 50 mg/ml	24 hr	5 days
Dextrose 5% in water	2 to 50 mg/ml	24 hr	5 days
Dextrose 10% in water	2 to 50 mg/ml	24 hr	
Lidocaine HCl 0.5%	300 mg/ml	24 hr	5 days
Normosol M and dextrose 5%	2 to 50 mg/ml	24 hr	5 days
Normosol R	2 to 50 mg/ml	24 hr	5 days
Ringer's injection, lactated	2 mg/ml	24 hr	5 days
Sodium chloride 0.9%	2 to 300 mg/ml	24 hr	5 days
Sterile water for injection	300 mg/ml	24 hr	5 days

Table 4. Stability of Cefoperazone Solutions Frozen at −20 to −10 °C (2)

Solution	Cefoperazone Concentration	Stability Period
Dextrose 5% in sodium chloride 0.2 or 0.9%	2 mg/ml	3 weeks
Dextrose 5% in water	50 mg/ml	3 weeks
Sodium chloride 0.9%	300 mg/ml	5 weeks
Sterile water for injection	300 mg/ml	5 weeks

Aminoglycosides — The manufacturer recommends that aminoglycosides not be mixed in the same solution because of physical incompatibility. (2) When tobramycin sulfate (Lilly) 80 mg/100 ml in dextrose 5% in water was run through an administration set previously used to administer cefoperazone (Roerig) 4 g/100 ml in dextrose 5% in water, a precipitate formed immediately in the infusion tubing where the two solutions mixed. A retest, using cefoperazone 1 g/100 ml, produced the same result. Substituting gentamicin sulfate (Schering) 80 mg/100 ml for the tobramycin also yielded a precipitate immediately. (831)

Spruill et al. evaluated the effect of various cephalosporins on tobramycin sulfate 7.7 μg/ml in human serum. At concentrations of 250 and 1000 μg/ml, cefazolin, cefoxitin, cefamandole, cefoperazone, and cefotaxime caused about a 10 to 15% loss of tobramycin over 48 hours at 0 and 21 °C. Moxalactam caused about a 15% loss at 0 °C and a 20 to 30% loss at 21 °C over 48 hours. (1005)

Pennell et al. evaluated the potential for inactivation of tobramycin sulfate (Lilly) 9 μg/ml with 100- and 200-μg/ml concentrations of cefoperazone (Roerig) in human serum. No loss of tobramycin sulfate was determined by TDx fluorescence polarization immunoassay over 48 hours when stored at 4, 24, and 37 °C. (1420)

CEFOTAXIME SODIUM
AHFS 8:12.06

Products — Cefotaxime sodium is available in vials containing the equivalent of 500 mg and 1 and 2 g of cefotaxime and in infusion bottles containing the equivalent of 1 and 2 g of cefotaxime. It is also available in 10-g pharmacy bulk packages. (2)

For intravenous administration, the contents of any size vial may be reconstituted with 10 ml of sterile water for injection. (See Table 1.) The 1- and 2-g infusion bottles may be reconstituted with 50 or 100 ml of dextrose 5% in water or sodium chloride 0.9%. For intramuscular injection, reconstitute with sterile water for injection or bacteriostatic water for injection in the amounts shown in Table 1. (2)

The 10-g pharmacy bulk package may be reconstituted with 47 or 97 ml of compatible diluent to yield a 200- or 100-mg/ml concentration, respectively. Doses from this bulk package must be diluted further for administration. (2; 4)

After addition of the diluent, shake to dissolve the contents and inspect for particulate matter or discoloration. (2)

Table 1. Recommended Reconstitution of Cefotaxime Sodium (2)

Vial Size	Volume of Diluent	Withdrawable Volume	Approximate Concentration
Intravenous			
500 mg	10 ml	10.2 ml	50 mg/ml
1 g	10 ml	10.4 ml	95 mg/ml
2 g	10 ml	11.0 ml	180 mg/ml
Intramuscular			
500 mg	2 ml	2.2 ml	230 mg/ml
1 g	3 ml	3.4 ml	300 mg/ml
2 g	5 ml	6.0 ml	330 mg/ml

For intravenous infusion, the primary solution may be diluted further to 50 to 1000 ml in a compatible diluent. (2) (See Additional Compatibility Information.)

Cefotaxime sodium is also available as a frozen premixed iso-osmotic infusion solution of 1 or 2 g in dextrose 3.4 or 1.4%, respectively, buffered with sodium citrate. Hydrochloric acid and sodium hydroxide, if needed, are used to adjust the pH during manufacturing. (2; 4)

pH—Injectable solutions of the drug have pH values ranging from 5 to 7.5. (2)

Osmolality—A solution of cefotaxime sodium 1 g/14 ml of sterile water for injection is isotonic. (2)

The osmolality of cefotaxime sodium 1, 2, and 3 g was calculated for the following dilutions (1054):

Diluent	Osmolality (mOsm/kg) 50 ml	100 ml
1 g		
Dextrose 5% in water	350	319
Sodium chloride 0.9%	375	344
2 g		
Dextrose 5% in water	343	327
Sodium chloride 0.9%	406	351
3 g		
Dextrose 5% in water	433	344
Sodium chloride 0.9%	458	382

The frozen premixed solutions have osmolalities of 340 to 420 mOsm/kg for the 1-g/50 ml concentration and 450 to 540 mOsm/kg for the 2-g/50 ml concentration. (4)

The osmolality of cefotaxime sodium (Hoechst) 50 mg/ml was determined to be 326 mOsm/kg in dextrose 5% in water and 333 mOsm/kg in sodium chloride 0.9%. (1375)

Robinson et al. recommended the following maximum cefotaxime sodium concentrations to achieve osmolalities suitable for peripheral infusion in fluid-restricted patients (1180):

Diluent	Maximum Concentration (mg/ml)	Osmolality (mOsm/kg)
Dextrose 5% in water	86	577
Sodium chloride 0.9%	73	555
Sterile water for injection	147	525

Sodium Content—Cefotaxime sodium contains approximately 2.2 mEq (50.5 mg) of sodium per gram of cefotaxime activity. (2)

Trade Name(s)—Claforan.

Administration—Cefotaxime sodium may be administered by deep intramuscular injection; doses of 2 g should be divided between different injection sites. It may also be administered by direct intravenous injection over three to five minutes directly into the vein or into the tubing of a running compatible infusion solution. In addition, cefotaxime sodium may be administered in 50 to 100 ml of compatible diluent over 20 to 30 minutes by intermittent intravenous infusion or by continuous intravenous infusion. (2; 4; 8)

Stability—Intact vials of cefotaxime sodium (Aventis) should be stored below 30 °C. The dry powder is off-white to pale yellow in color. Solutions may range from light yellow to amber, depending on the diluent, concentration, and storage conditions. Both the dry material and solutions may darken and should be protected from elevated temperatures and excessive light. Discoloration of the powder or solution may indicate a loss of potency. (2; 4)

Table 2. Manufacturer's Recommended Storage Times of Reconstituted Cefotaxime Sodium (2)

Vial Size	Concentration	Storage Temperature 22 °C	5 °C
500 mg	200 mg/ml	12 hr	7 days
	50 mg/ml	24 hr	7 days
	50 mg/ml	24 hr	7 days
1 g	300 mg/ml	12 hr	7 days
	95 mg/ml	24 hr	7 days
(Infusion bottle)	10 to 20 mg/ml	24 hr	10 days
2 g	330 mg/ml	12 hr	7 days
	180 mg/ml	12 hr	7 days
(Infusion bottle)	20 to 40 mg/ml	24 hr	10 days

Store the frozen premixed cefotaxime sodium infusions at −20 °C or below. Thaw at room temperature or under refrigeration. Accelerated thawing using water bath immersion or microwave irradiation should not be used. Thawed solutions should not be refrozen. (2; 4)

When reconstituted as described in the Products section, cefotaxime sodium (Aventis) is stable in the original containers as indicated in Table 2. Storage of reconstituted solutions in disposable glass or plastic syringes for five days under refrigeration is also recommended. Dilutions of cefotaxime sodium in dextrose 5% in water or sodium chloride 0.9% in PVC bags are also stable for 24 hours at room temperature or five days under refrigeration. (2)

Cefotaxime sodium (Hoechst-Roussel) 1 g/10 ml reconstituted with sterile water for injection or 1 g/50 ml in dextrose 5% in water in PVC bags exhibited no visible changes in 24 hours at 5 and 25 °C. Although increased levels of particulate matter were observed in most solutions, the increases were significant only in solutions stored at 25 °C. (986)

pH Effects—The primary factor in the stability of cefotaxime sodium is solution pH. (792) Cefotaxime sodium in aqueous solutions is stable at pH 5 to 7 (2) or 4.3 to 6.2. (1077) The theoretical pH of minimum decomposition is 5.13. (793) However, between pH 3 and 7, the hydrolysis rate is virtually independent of pH. (1072) Determination of decomposition kinetics in various aqueous buffer systems at 25 °C showed 10% decomposition occurring in 24 hours or longer over a pH range of 3.9 to 7.6. At pH 2.2 and 8.4, 10% decomposition occurred in about 13 hours. (793)

The manufacturer recommends that cefotaxime sodium not be diluted in solutions with a pH greater than 7.5. (2; 4)

Freezing Solutions—When reconstituted as recommended, cefotaxime sodium may be stored frozen in the vial or in disposable glass or plastic syringes for 13 weeks. Similarly, dilutions of cefotaxime sodium in dextrose 5% in water or sodium chloride 0.9% in PVC bags may be stored frozen for 13 weeks. Thawing at room temperature is recommended; frozen solutions should not be heated. Once thawed, the solutions are stable for 24 hours at room temperature or five days at less than 5 °C. Thawed solutions should not be refrozen. (2; 4)

In one study, cefotaxime sodium (Hoechst-Roussel) 10 g/L in PVC bags of dextrose 5% in water and sodium chloride 0.9% (Travenol) exhibited no decomposition after 63 days of storage at −10 °C. (751)

Syringes — Cefotaxime sodium (Roussel) 250 mg/ml in sterile water for injection, packaged as 0.18 ml in 1-ml Injekt syringes (Braun) sealed with blind hubs and stored at about 6 °C, retained antibiotic activity against *Pseudomonas aeruginosa* for seven days. However, the yellow color of the solution became much darker over this period. (1697)

Elastomeric Reservoir Pumps — Cefotaxime sodium solutions in elastomeric reservoir pumps have been stated by the pump manufacturers to be stable for the following time periods frozen, refrigerated (REF), or at room temperature (RT) (31):

Pump Reservoir(s)	Conc.	Frozen	REF	RT
Homepump; Homepump Eclipse	10 to 20 mg/ml[a,b]	13 weeks	5 days	
	16.66 mg/ml[b]			24 hr
Intermate	40 mg/ml[b]	30 days	10 days	24 hr
Medflo	20 mg/ml[a]	13 weeks	22 days	48 hr
ReadyMed	10 mg/ml[a]		22 days	24 hr
	20 mg/ml[b]	4 weeks	14 days	48 hr

[a]*In dextrose 5% in water.*
[b]*In sodium chloride 0.9%.*

Central Venous Catheter — Cefotaxime sodium (Hoechst-Roussel) 5 mg/ml in dextrose 5% in water was found to be compatible with the ARROWg+ard Blue Plus (Arrow International) chlorhexidine-bearing triple-lumen central catheter. HPLC analysis was used to evaluate completeness of drug delivery through the catheter and the amount of chlorhexidine removed from the internal lumens. Delivery of the cefotaxime sodium ranged from 93 to 95% of the initial concentration among the three lumens. Furthermore, chlorhexidine delivered from the catheter remained at trace amounts with no substantial increase due to the delivery of the drug through the catheter. (2335)

Compatibility Information

Solution Compatibility

Cefotaxime sodium

Solution	*Mfr*	*Mfr*	*Conc/L*	*Remarks*	*Ref*	*C/I*
Dextrose 5% in water	TR[a]	HO	10 g	Physically compatible with 3% decomposition in 24 hr at 24 °C. No decomposition in 22 days at 4 °C	751; 1077	C
	AB[b]	HO	20 g	Physically compatible with little or no cefotaxime loss in 24 hr at 25 °C	994	C
Sodium chloride 0.9%	TR[a]	HO	10 g	Physically compatible with 2% decomposition in 24 hr at 24 °C. No decomposition in 22 days at 4 °C	751; 1077	C
	AB[b]	HO	20 g	Physically compatible with little or no cefotaxime loss in 24 hr at 25 °C	994	C
TPN #107[c]			1 g	Physically compatible and cefotaxime activity retained for 24 hr at 21 °C by microbiological assay	1326	C

[a]*Tested in PVC containers.*
[b]*Tested in both glass bottles and PVC bags.*
[c]*Refer to Appendix I for the composition of parenteral nutrition solutions. TPN indicates a 2-in-1 admixture.*

Additive Compatibility

			Cefotaxime sodium					
Drug	*Mfr*	*Conc/L*	*Mfr*	*Conc/L*	*Test Soln*	*Remarks*	*Ref*	*C/I*
Clindamycin phosphate	UP	9 g	HO	20 g	D5W, NS[a]	Physically compatible with no clindamycin loss and 3% cefotaxime loss in 24 hr at 25 °C	994	C
Metronidazole	RP	5 g[b]	RS	20 g		Physically compatible with little or no pH change for at least 24 hr at 4 °C	807	C
	AB	5 g	HO	10 g		Potency of both drugs by HPLC retained for 72 hr at 8 °C	1547	C
	AB	5 g	HO	10 g		Visually compatible with 10% cefotaxime loss by HPLC in 19 hr at 28 °C and 8% loss in 96 hr at 5 °C. No metronidazole loss in 96 hr at 5 or 28 °C	1754	C
Metronidazole HCl	SE	5 g	HO	10 g	NS	Visually compatible with 10% cefotaxime loss by HPLC in 24 hr at 28 °C and no loss in 96 hr at 5 °C. No metronidazole loss in 96 hr at 5 or 28 °C	1754	C
Verapamil HCl	KN	80 mg	HO	4 g	D5W, NS	Physically compatible for 24 hr	764	C

[a]*Tested in both glass and PVC containers.*
[b]*Minibags (100 ml) containing metronidazole 500 mg with disodium phosphate 150 mg, citric acid 44 mg, and sodium chloride 740 mg. This product differs from the Searle product.*

Drugs in Syringe Compatibility

			Cefotaxime sodium				
Drug (in syringe)	*Mfr*	*Amt*	*Mfr*	*Amt*	*Remarks*	*Ref*	*C/I*
Doxapram HCl	RB	400 mg/ 20 ml		500 mg/ 4 ml	Immediate precipitation	1171	I
Heparin sodium		2500 units/ 1 ml	HO	2 g	Physically compatible for at least 5 min	1053	C
Ofloxacin	HO	200 mg	HO	2 g	Visually compatible with no loss of either drug by HPLC in 4 hr at room temperature	1735	C

Y-Site Injection Compatibility (1:1 Mixture)

			Cefotaxime sodium				
Drug	*Mfr*	*Conc*	*Mfr*	*Conc*	*Remarks*	*Ref*	*C/I*
Acyclovir sodium	BW	5 mg/ml[a]	HO	20 mg/ml[a]	Physically compatible for 4 hr at 25 °C	1157	C
Allopurinol sodium	BW	3 mg/ml[b]	HO	20 mg/ml[b]	Tiny particles form immediately	1668	I
Amifostine	USB	10 mg/ml[a]	HO	20 mg/ml[a]	Physically compatible with no change in measured turbidity or increase in particle content in 4 hr at 23 °C	1845	C
Aztreonam	SQ	40 mg/ml[a]	HO	20 mg/ml[a]	Physically compatible with no subvisual haze or particle formation in 4 hr at 23 °C	1758	C

Y-Site Injection Compatibility (1:1 Mixture) (Cont.)

Cefotaxime sodium

Drug	*Mfr*	*Conc*	*Mfr*	*Conc*	*Remarks*	*Ref*	*C/I*
Cisatracurium besylate	GW	0.1 mg/ml[a]	HO	20 mg/ml[a]	Physically compatible with no change in measured turbidity or increase in particle content in 4 hr at 23 °C	2074	**C**
	GW	2 mg/ml[a]	HO	20 mg/ml[a]	Subvisual haze forms in 4 hr	2074	**I**
	GW	5 mg/ml[a]	HO	20 mg/ml[a]	Subvisual haze forms immediately	2074	**I**
Cyclophosphamide	MJ	20 mg/ml[a]	HO	20 mg/ml[a]	Physically compatible for 4 hr at 25 °C	1194	**C**
Diltiazem HCl	MMD	5 mg/ml	HO	10 and 180 mg/ml[b]	Visually compatible	1807	**C**
	MMD	1 mg/ml[b]	HO	180 mg/ml[b]	Visually compatible	1807	**C**
Docetaxel	RPR	0.9 mg/ml[a]	HO	20 mg/ml[a]	Physically compatible with no change in measured turbidity or increase in particle content in 4 hr at 23 °C	2224	**C**
Etoposide phosphate	BR	5 mg/ml[a]	HO	20 mg/ml[a]	Physically compatible with no change in measured turbidity or increase in particle content in 4 hr at 23 °C	2218	**C**
Famotidine	MSD	0.2 mg/ml[a]	HO	20 mg/ml[b]	Physically compatible for 14 hr	1196	**C**
	ME	2 mg/ml[b]		20 mg/ml[a]	Visually compatible for 4 hr at 22 °C	1936	**C**
Filgrastim	AMG	30 μg/ml[a]	HO	20 mg/ml[a]	Particles form in 4 hr	1687	**I**
Fluconazole	RR	2 mg/ml	HO	20 mg/ml	Cloudiness and amber color develop	1407	**I**
Fludarabine phosphate	BX	1 mg/ml[a]	HO	20 mg/ml[a]	Physically compatible for 4 hr at room temperature under fluorescent light	1439	**C**
Gemcitabine HCl	LI	10 mg/ml[b]	HO	20 mg/ml[b]	Slight subvisual haze forms in 1 hr with increased haze and a subvisual precipitate in 4 hr	2226	**I**
Granisetron HCl	SKB	0.05 mg/ml[a]	HO	20 mg/ml[a]	Physically compatible with no change in measured turbidity or increase in particle content in 4 hr at 23 °C	2000	**C**
Hetastarch in lactated electrolyte injection (Hextend)	AB	6%	HO	20 mg/ml[a]	Physically compatible with no change in measured turbidity or increase in particle content in 4 hr at 23 °C	2339	**C**
Hetastarch in sodium chloride 0.9%	DCC	6%	HO	20 mg/ml[a]	Small crystals formed immediately after mixing and persisted for 4 hr	1313	**I**
Hydromorphone HCl	WY	0.2 mg/ml[a]	HO	20 mg/ml[a]	Physically compatible for at least 4 hr at 25 °C under fluorescent light	987	**C**
Levofloxacin	OMN	5 mg/ml[a]	HO	200 mg/ml	Visually compatible for 4 hr at 24 °C under fluorescent light	2233	**C**
Lorazepam	WY	0.33 mg/ml[b]	RS	10 mg/ml	Visually compatible for 24 hr at 22 °C	1855	**C**
Magnesium sulfate	IX	16.7, 33.3, 66.7, 100 mg/ml[a]	HO	20 mg/ml[a]	Physically compatible for at least 4 hr at 32 °C	813	**C**
Melphalan HCl	BW	0.1 mg/ml[b]	HO	20 mg/ml[b]	Physically compatible with no change in measured turbidity or increase in particle content in 3 hr at 22 °C	1557	**C**
Meperidine HCl	WY	10 mg/ml[a]	HO	20 mg/ml[a]	Physically compatible for at least 4 hr at 25 °C under fluorescent light	987	**C**

Y-Site Injection Compatibility (1:1 Mixture) (Cont.)

			Cefotaxime sodium				
Drug	*Mfr*	*Conc*	*Mfr*	*Conc*	*Remarks*	*Ref*	*C/I*
Midazolam HCl	RC	1 mg/ml[a]	HO	20 mg/ml[a]	Visually compatible for 24 hr at 23 °C	1847	C
	RC	5 mg/ml	RS	10 mg/ml	Visually compatible for 24 hr at 22 °C	1855	C
Morphine sulfate	WI	1 mg/ml[a]	HO	20 mg/ml[a]	Physically compatible for at least 4 hr at 25 °C under fluorescent light	987	C
Ondansetron HCl	GL	1 mg/ml[b]	HO	20 mg/ml[a]	Physically compatible for 4 hr at 22 °C	1365	C
Pentamidine isethionate	FUJ	3 mg/ml[a]	HO	20 mg/ml[a]	Fine precipitate, difficult to see, forms immediately	1880	I
Perphenazine	SC	0.02 mg/ml[a]	HO	20 mg/ml[a]	Physically compatible for 4 hr at 25 °C	1155	C
Propofol	ZEN	10 mg/ml	HO	20 mg/ml[a]	Physically compatible for 1 hr at 23 °C with no increase in particle content	2066	C
Remifentanil HCl	GW	0.025 and 0.25 mg/ml[b]	HO	20 mg/ml[a]	Physically compatible with no change in measured turbidity or increase in particle content in 4 hr at 23 °C	2075	C
Sargramostim	IMM	10 μg/ml[b]	HO	20 mg/ml[b]	Physically compatible for 4 hr at 22 °C	1436	C
Teniposide	BR	0.1 mg/ml[a]	HO	20 mg/ml[a]	Physically compatible with no subvisual haze or particle formation in 4 hr at 23 °C	1725	C
Thiotepa	IMM[c]	1 mg/ml[a]	HO	20 mg/ml[a]	Physically compatible with no change in measured turbidity or increase in particle content in 4 hr at 23 °C	1861	C
TNA #218 to #226[d]			HO	20 mg/ml[a]	Visually compatible with no precipitate or emulsion damage apparent in 4 hr at 23 °C	2215	C
Tolazoline HCl		0.1 mg/ml[a]	HO	60 mg/ml[a]	Physically compatible for 24 hr at 22 °C	1363	C
TPN #61[d]		[e]	HO	200 mg/ 0.7 ml[f]	Physically compatible	1012	C
		[g]	HO	1.2 g/4 ml[f]	Physically compatible	1012	C
TPN #189[d]			RS	200 mg/ml[e]	Visually compatible for 24 hr at 22 °C	1767	C
TPN #203 and #204[d]			HO	60 mg/ml	Visually compatible for 2 hr at 23 °C	1974	C
TPN #212 to #215[d]			HO	20 mg/ml[a]	Physically compatible with no change in measured turbidity or increase in particle content in 4 hr at 23 °C	2109	C
Vancomycin HCl		12.5, 25, 30, 50 mg/ml[h]		100 mg/ml[h]	White precipitate forms immediately	1721	I
		5 mg/ml[h]		100 mg/ml[h]	No precipitate visually observed over 7 days at room temperature, but nonvisual incompatibility cannot be ruled out	1721	?
	AB	20 mg/ml[a]	HO	200 mg/ml[h]	Transient precipitate forms, followed by clear solution	2189	?
	AB	20 mg/ml[a]	HO	50 mg/ml[a]	White cloudiness forms immediately	2189	I
	AB	20 mg/ml[a]	HO	1 and 10 mg/ ml[a]	Physically compatible with no change in measured turbidity or increase in particle content in 4 hr at 23 °C	2189	C
	AB	2 mg/ml[a]	HO	1[a], 10[a], 50[a], and 200[h] mg/ ml	Physically compatible with no change in measured turbidity or increase in particle content in 4 hr at 23 °C	2189	C

Y-Site Injection Compatibility (1:1 Mixture) (Cont.)

Drug	Mfr	Conc	Cefotaxime sodium Mfr	Cefotaxime sodium Conc	Remarks	Ref	C/I
Vinorelbine tartrate	BW	1 mg/ml[b]	HO	20 mg/ml[b]	Physically compatible with little change in measured turbidity or increase in particle content in 4 hr at 22 °C	1558	C

[a]*Tested in dextrose 5% in water.*
[b]*Tested in sodium chloride 0.9%.*
[c]*Lyophilized formulation tested.*
[d]*Refer to Appendix I for the composition of parenteral nutrition solutions. TNA indicates a 3-in-1 admixture, and TPN indicates a 2-in-1 admixture.*
[e]*Run at 21 ml/hr.*
[f]*Given over five minutes by syringe pump.*
[g]*Run at 94 ml/hr.*
[h]*Tested in sterile water for injection.*

Additional Compatibility Information

Infusion Solutions — Cefotaxime sodium maintains potency for 24 hours at room temperature and at least five days under refrigeration diluted in 50 to 1000 ml of the following infusion solutions (2):

Amino acid injection 8.5%
Dextrose 5% in sodium chloride 0.2, 0.45, and 0.9%
Dextrose 5 and 10% in water
Invert sugar 10% in water
Ringer's injection, lactated
Sodium chloride 0.9%
Sodium lactate ⅙ M

The manufacturer recommends that additives not be introduced into the premixed cefotaxime sodium in dextrose infusion. (2)

Peritoneal Dialysis Solutions — Cefotaxime sodium 2 mg/ml in peritoneal dialysis solution (McGaw) containing dextrose 2.5% and electrolytes was physically compatible for three hours at room temperature. Furthermore, no significant loss of antibacterial activity was apparent by microbiological determination. (142)

The stability of cefotaxime sodium (Hoechst-Roussel) 125 mg/L in peritoneal dialysis solutions (Dianeal 137 and PD2) with heparin sodium 500 units/L was evaluated at 25 °C by microbiological assay. Approximately 95 ± 6% activity remained after 24 hours. (1228)

Paap and Nahata studied the stability of cefotaxime sodium (Hoechst-Roussel) 1 mg/ml in Dianeal PD-1 with dextrose 1.5 and 4.25% (Travenol). At 25 °C, the drug exhibited an 8% loss in 24 hours and a 16% loss in 48 hours in both solutions. Storage at 37 °C for 12 hours resulted in 11 and 14% losses in the solutions containing dextrose 1.5% and dextrose 4.25%, respectively. (1481)

Alkaline Drugs — Cefotaxime sodium should not be mixed in alkaline solutions such as sodium bicarbonate injection (2) or solutions containing aminophylline. (792)

Aminoglycosides — The manufacturer states that cefotaxime sodium should not be admixed with aminoglycosides. (2) However, they may be administered separately to the same patient. (2; 792)

No inactivation of tobramycin, gentamicin, and amikacin 10 μg/ml was caused by cefotaxime 100 and 500 μg/ml when the mixtures were stored at 37 °C for six hours. Further, no loss of cefotaxime activity was detected in any combination. (973)

The inactivation of gentamicin, tobramycin, and amikacin, each 5 μg/ml, by seven β-lactam antibiotics, 250 and 500 μg/ml, in serum at 25 °C over 24 hours was studied using bioassay, enzyme-mediated immunoassay technique (EMIT), fluorescence polarization immunoassay (TDx), and radioimmunoassay. No inactivation of any aminoglycosides by the cephalosporins moxalactam, cefotaxime, and cefazolin occurred within the study period. (654)

Spruill et al. evaluated the effect of various cephalosporins on tobramycin sulfate 7.7 μg/ml in human serum. At concentrations of 250 and 1000 μg/ml, cefazolin, cefoxitin, cefamandole, cefoperazone, and cefotaxime caused about a 10 to 15% loss of tobramycin over 48 hours at 0 and 21 °C. Moxalactam caused about a 15% loss at 0 °C and a 20 to 30% loss at 21 °C over 48 hours. (1005)

Pennell et al. evaluated the potential for inactivation of tobramycin sulfate (Lilly) 9 μg/ml with 100- and 200-μg/ml concentrations of cefotaxime sodium (Hoechst-Roussel) in human serum. No loss of tobramycin sulfate was determined by TDx fluorescence polarization immunoassay over 48 hours when stored at 4, 24, and 37 °C. (1420)

Vancomycin — The compatibility or incompatibility of vancomycin HCl mixed with or administered simultaneously with cefotaxime sodium is concentration dependent. (2189) See Y-Site Compatibility above. Vancomycin HCl has a low pH and is variably compatible with drugs having neutral to mildly alkaline pH, including cephalosporins and penicillins. The compatibility may depend on a number of factors, including concentration of each drug, dilution vehicle, actual pH of solutions, and completeness of mixing during administration. Combinations that are compatible when well mixed may result in precipitation if only partially mixed, presumably because of regionally different concentrations and pH values. If attempting to administer vancomycin HCl with cefotaxime sodium, take care to ensure that the specific combination and the concentrations are compatible under the exact administration conditions to be used. An inline filter should be used as a final safety measure. (2189)

CEFOTETAN DISODIUM
AHFS 8:12.07

Products — Cefotetan disodium is available in 1- and 2-g vials and infusion bottles and 10-g pharmacy bulk packages. (2)

For intramuscular injection, reconstitute the vials with sterile water for injection, bacteriostatic water for injection, sodium chloride 0.9%, or lidocaine HCl 0.5 or 1%. Then shake well to dissolve and let stand until clear. Recommended volumes for reconstitution are shown in Table 1. (2)

For intravenous use, reconstitute the vials with sterile water for injection in the amounts noted in Table 1, shake well to dissolve, and let stand until clear. Piggyback infusion vials may be reconstituted with 50 to 100 ml of dextrose 5% in water or sodium chloride 0.9%. (2)

Reconstitute the 10-g pharmacy bulk package with sterile water for injection, dextrose 5% in water, or sodium chloride 0.9% according to the instructions on the package label. Then shake it well to dissolve and let stand until clear. (2)

Cefotetan is also available as a frozen premixed infusion solution of 1 or 2 g in 50 ml of dextrose 5% in water. For use, they may be thawed at room temperature or under refrigeration. (2; 4)

pH — Reconstituted solutions have a pH of 4.5 to 6.5. (2)

Osmolarity — Concentrations of 100 to 200 mg/ml in sterile water for injection have osmolarities of 400 to 800 mOsm/L, respectively. The 1- and 2-g infusion bottles reconstituted with 50 to 100 ml of dextrose 5% in water or sodium chloride 0.9%, having concentrations of 10 to 39 mg/ml, have osmolarities of 340 to 480 mOsm/L. Intramuscular concentrations of 375 to 471.5 mg/ml are extremely hypertonic, with osmolarities greater than 1500 mOsm/L. (4)

Sodium Content — Each gram of cefotetan disodium contains approximately 3.5 mEq (80 mg) of sodium. (2)

Trade Name(s) — Cefotan.

Administration — Cefotetan disodium may be administered by deep intramuscular injection, direct intravenous injection over three to five minutes, and intermittent intravenous infusion in 50 to 100 ml of dextrose 5% in water or sodium chloride 0.9%. (2; 4) infused over 20 to 60 minutes. (2; 4) The manufacturer recommends temporarily discontinuing other solutions being administered at the same site. (2; 4)

Table 1. Recommended Dilutions of Cefotetan Disodium Vials (2; 4)

Vial Size	Volume of Diluent	Withdrawable Volume	Approximate Concentration
Intramuscular			
1 g	2 ml	2.5 ml	400 mg/ml
2 g	3 ml	4.0 ml	500 mg/ml
Intravenous			
1 g	10 ml	10.5 ml	95 mg/ml
2 g	10 to 20 ml	11 to 21 ml	182 to 95 mg/ml
Piggyback			
1 g	50 ml		20 mg/ml
	100 ml		10 mg/ml
2 g	50 ml		39 mg/ml
	100 ml		20 mg/ml

Stability — Intact vials should be stored at 22 °C or less and protected from light. The frozen premixed infusion solutions should be stored at −20 °C. (2) Cefotetan disodium powder is white to pale yellow. Solutions may vary from colorless to yellow, depending on the concentration. (2)

When reconstituted as recommended, cefotetan disodium solutions are stable for 24 hours at room temperature (25 °C) and 96 hours under refrigeration (5 °C). In disposable glass or plastic syringes, the drug also is stable for 24 hours at room temperature and 96 hours under refrigeration. (2; 4)

Thawed solutions of the commercially available frozen injections are stable for 48 hours at a room temperature of 25 °C and 21 days when refrigerated at 5 °C. (4)

Freezing Solutions — The manufacturer states that solutions reconstituted as recommended are stable for at least one week when frozen at −20 °C. (2) The manufacturer also has stated that cefotetan disodium as the reconstituted solution in vials is stable for one year at −20 °C; in a large volume parenteral solution, it is stable for 30 weeks at −20 °C. (283) Thawing should be performed at room temperature, and thawed solutions should not be refrozen. (2; 4)

In one study, cefotetan disodium (Stuart) 20 mg/ml in dextrose 5% in water (Travenol) in PVC containers showed a potency loss of about 2% after two weeks at −20 °C by antimicrobial assay. (966)

In another study, cefotetan disodium (Stuart) 20 mg/ml in dextrose 5% in water and sodium chloride 0.9% in PVC bags was visually clear and exhibited little or no loss by HPLC after 60 days when frozen at −10 °C. (1598)

Elastomeric Reservoir Pumps — Cefotetan disodium solutions in elastomeric reservoir pumps have been stated by the pump manufacturers to be stable for the following time periods frozen, refrigerated (REF), or at room temperature (RT) (31):

Pump Reservoir(s)	Conc.	Frozen	REF	RT
Homepump; Homepump Eclipse	100 to 200 mg/ml[a,b]	7 days	4 days	24 hr
Intermate	60 mg/ml[a,b]	30 days	10 days	24 hr
Medflo	20 mg/ml[a]	7 days	14 days	24 hr
ReadyMed	20 mg/ml[a]	7 days	4 days	24 hr

[a] *In dextrose 5% in water.*
[b] *In sodium chloride 0.9%.*

Central Venous Catheter — Cefotetan disodium (Zeneca) 5 mg/ml in dextrose 5% in water was found to be compatible with the ARROWg+ard Blue Plus (Arrow International) chlorhexidine-bearing triple-lumen central catheter. HPLC analysis was used to evaluate completeness of drug delivery through the catheter and the amount of chlorhexidine removed from the internal lumens. Essentially complete delivery of the drug was found with little or no drug loss occurring. Furthermore, chlorhexidine delivered from the catheter remained at trace amounts with no substantial increase due to the delivery of the drug through the catheter. (2335)

Compatibility Information

Solution Compatibility

Cefotetan disodium

Solution	Mfr	Mfr	Conc/L	Remarks	Ref	C/I
Dextrose 5% in water	TR[a]	STU	2 g	4% loss in 14 days at 20 °C and no loss at 4 °C by antimicrobial assay	966	C
	[a]	AY	20 and 40 g	Visually compatible with 10% loss in 3.5 days at 23 °C and 13 days at 4 °C	1591	C
	TR[a]	STU	20 g	8% loss by HPLC in 2 days and 11% loss in 3 days at 25 °C. 6% loss in 41 days at 5 °C	1598	C
Sodium chloride 0.9%	[a]	AY	20 and 40 g	Visually compatible with 10% loss in 3.5 days at 23 °C and 14 days at 4 °C	1591	C
	TR[a]	STU	20 g	8% loss by HPLC in 2 days and 11% loss in 3 days at 25 °C. 5% loss in 41 days at 5 °C	1598	C

[a]*Tested in PVC containers.*

Drugs in Syringe Compatibility

Cefotetan disodium

Drug (in syringe)	Mfr	Amt	Mfr	Amt	Remarks	Ref	C/I
Doxapram HCl	RB	400 mg/20 ml		1 g/10 ml	Immediate turbidity	1177	I
Promethazine HCl	ES	25 mg/1 ml	ZE	10 mg/ml[a]	White precipitate, resembling cottage cheese, forms immediately	1753	I

[a]*Tested in dextrose 5% in water.*

Y-Site Injection Compatibility (1:1 Mixture)

Cefotetan disodium

Drug	Mfr	Conc	Mfr	Conc	Remarks	Ref	C/I
Allopurinol sodium	BW	3 mg/ml[b]	STU	20 mg/ml[b]	Physically compatible with no change in measured turbidity or increase in particle content in 4 hr at 22 °C	1686	C
Amifostine	USB	10 mg/ml[a]	STU	20 mg/ml[a]	Physically compatible with no change in measured turbidity or increase in particle content in 4 hr at 23 °C	1845	C
Aztreonam	SQ	40 mg/ml[b]	STU	20 mg/ml[b]	Physically compatible with no subvisual haze or particle formation in 4 hr at 23 °C	1758	C
Cisatracurium besylate	GW	0.1 and 2 mg/ml[a]	STU	20 mg/ml[a]	Physically compatible with no change in measured turbidity or increase in particle content in 4 hr at 23 °C	2074	C
	GW	5 mg/ml[a]	STU	20 mg/ml[a]	Dense turbidity forms immediately	2074	I
Diltiazem HCl	MMD	5 mg/ml	STU	10 and 200 mg/ml[b]	Visually compatible	1807	C
	MMD	1 mg/ml[b]	STU	200 mg/ml[b]	Visually compatible	1807	C
Docetaxel	RPR	0.9 mg/ml[a]	ZEN	20 mg/ml[a]	Physically compatible with no change in measured turbidity or increase in particle content in 4 hr at 23 °C	2224	C
Etoposide phosphate	BR	5 mg/ml[a]	ZEN	20 mg/ml[a]	Physically compatible with no change in measured turbidity or increase in particle content in 4 hr at 23 °C	2218	C

Y-Site Injection Compatibility (1:1 Mixture) (Cont.)

Cefotetan disodium

Drug	*Mfr*	*Conc*	*Mfr*	*Conc*	*Remarks*	*Ref*	*C/I*
Famotidine	MSD	0.2 mg/ml[a]	STU	20 mg/ml[b]	Physically compatible for 14 hr	1196	C
Filgrastim	AMG	30 μg/ml[a]	STU	20 mg/ml[a]	Physically compatible with no change in measured turbidity or increase in particle content in 4 hr at 22 °C	1687	C
Fluconazole	RR	2 mg/ml	STU	40 mg/ml	Physically compatible for 24 hr at 25 °C	1407	C
Fludarabine phosphate	BX	1 mg/ml[a]	STU	20 mg/ml[a]	Physically compatible for 4 hr at room temperature under fluorescent light	1439	C
Gatifloxacin	BMS	2 mg/ml[a]	ZEN	20 mg/ml[a]	Physically compatible with no change in measured haze or increase in particle content in 4 hr at 23 °C	2234	C
Gemcitabine HCl	LI	10 mg/ml[b]	ZEN	20 mg/ml[b]	Physically compatible with no change in measured turbidity or increase in particle content in 4 hr at 23 °C	2226	C
Granisetron HCl	SKB	0.05 mg/ml[a]	STU	20 mg/ml[a]	Physically compatible with no change in measured turbidity or increase in particle content in 4 hr at 23 °C	2000	C
Heparin sodium	TR	50 units/ml	STU	40 mg/ml[a]	Visually compatible for 4 hr at 25 °C	1793	C
Hetastarch in lactated electrolyte injection (Hextend)	AB	6%	ZEN	20 mg/ml[a]	Physically compatible with no change in measured turbidity or increase in particle content in 4 hr at 23 °C	2339	C
Insulin, regular	LI	0.2 unit/ml[b]	STU	20 and 40 mg/ml[a]	Physically compatible for 2 hr at 25 °C	1395	C
Linezolid	PHU	2 mg/ml	ZEN	20 mg/ml[a]	Physically compatible with no change in measured turbidity or increase in particle content in 4 hr at 23 °C	2264	C
Melphalan HCl	BW	0.1 mg/ml[b]	STU	20 mg/ml[b]	Physically compatible with no change in measured turbidity or increase in particle content in 3 hr at 22 °C	1557	C
Meperidine HCl	WY	10 mg/ml[b]	STU	20 and 40 mg/ml[a]	Physically compatible for 1 hr at 25 °C	1338	C
Morphine sulfate	ES	1 mg/ml[b]	STU	20 and 40 mg/ml[a]	Physically compatible for 1 hr at 25 °C	1338	C
Paclitaxel	NCI	1.2 mg/ml[a]	STU	20 mg/ml[a]	Physically compatible with no change in measured turbidity in 4 hr at 22 °C	1556	C
Promethazine HCl	ES	25 mg	ZE	10 mg/ml[a]	White precipitate forms immediately	1753	I
Propofol	ZEN	10 mg/ml	STU	20 mg/ml[a]	Physically compatible for 1 hr at 23 °C with no increase in particle content	2066	C
Remifentanil HCl	GW	0.025 and 0.25 mg/ml[b]	ZEN	20 mg/ml[a]	Physically compatible with no change in measured turbidity or increase in particle content in 4 hr at 23 °C	2075	C
Sargramostim	IMM	10 μg/ml[b]	STU	20 mg/ml[b]	Physically compatible for 4 hr at 22 °C	1436	C
Tacrolimus	FUJ	1 mg/ml[b]	STU	40 mg/ml[a]	Visually compatible for 24 hr at 25 °C	1630	C
Teniposide	BR	0.1 mg/ml[a]	STU	20 mg/ml[a]	Physically compatible with no subvisual haze or particle formation in 4 hr at 23 °C	1725	C
Theophylline	TR	4 mg/ml	STU	40 mg/ml[a]	Visually compatible for 6 hr at 25 °C	1793	C

Y-Site Injection Compatibility (1:1 Mixture) (Cont.)

			Cefotetan disodium				
Drug	*Mfr*	*Conc*	*Mfr*	*Conc*	*Remarks*	*Ref*	*C/I*
Thiotepa	IMM[c]	1 mg/ml[a]	STU	20 mg/ml[a]	Physically compatible with no change in measured turbidity or increase in particle content in 4 hr at 23 °C	1861	C
TNA #218 to #226[d]			ZEN	20 mg/ml[a]	Visually compatible with no precipitate or emulsion damage apparent in 4 hr at 23 °C	2215	C
TPN #212 to #215[d]			STU	20 mg/ml[a]	Physically compatible with no change in measured turbidity or increase in particle content in 4 hr at 23 °C	2109	C
Vancomycin HCl	AB	20 mg/ml[a]	ZEN	200 mg/ml[e]	Transient precipitate forms, followed by clear solution. White precipitate forms in 4 hr	2189	I
	AB	20 mg/ml[a]	ZEN	10 and 50 mg/ml[a]	Gross white precipitate forms immediately	2189	I
	AB	20 mg/ml[a]	ZEN	1 mg/ml[a]	Subvisual measured haze forms immediately, followed by white precipitate in 4 hr	2189	I
	AB	2 mg/ml[a]	ZEN	1[a], 10[a], 50[a], 200[e] mg/ml	Physically compatible with no change in measured turbidity or increase in particle content in 4 hr at 23 °C	2189	C
Vinorelbine tartrate	BW	1 mg/ml[b]	STU	20 mg/ml[b]	Tiny particles form immediately, becoming numerous in cloudy solution in 4 hr at 22 °C	1558	I

[a]*Tested in dextrose 5% in water.*
[b]*Tested in sodium chloride 0.9%.*
[c]*Lyophilized formulation tested.*
[d]*Refer to Appendix I for the composition of parenteral nutrition solutions. TNA indicates a 3-in-1 admixture, and TPN indicates a 2-in-1 admixture.*
[e]*Tested in sterile water for injection.*

Additional Compatibility Information

Infusion Solutions — Cefotetan disodium retains its potency for 24 hours at room temperature and 96 hours under refrigeration in concentrations of 10 to 40 mg/ml in dextrose 5% in water and sodium chloride 0.9%. (4)

Vancomycin — The compatibility or incompatibility of vancomycin HCl mixed with or administered simultaneously with cefotetan disodium is concentration dependent. (2189) See Y-Site Compatibility above. Vancomycin HCl has a low pH and is variably compatible with drugs having neutral to mildly alkaline pH, including cephalosporins and penicillins. The compatibility may depend on a number of factors, including concentration of each drug, dilution vehicle, actual pH of solutions, and completeness of mixing during administration. Combinations that are compatible when well mixed may result in precipitation if only partially mixed, presumably because of regionally different concentrations and pH values. If attempting to administer vancomycin HCl with cefotetan disodium, take care to ensure that the specific combination and the concentrations are compatible under the exact administration conditions to be used. An inline filter should be used as a final safety measure. (2189)

Other Drugs — Cefotetan disodium is stated to be physically incompatible with tetracyclines and heparin, possibly resulting in cloudiness and precipitation. (4) The manufacturer recommends that cefotetan disodium not be mixed with aminoglycoside antibiotics. (2)

However, the manufacturer has stated that cefotetan disodium is compatible with the following drugs (283):

Amikacin sulfate	Mezlocillin disodium
Aminophylline	Multivitamins
Ampicillin sodium	Oxytocin
Atropine sulfate	Penicillin G potassium
Azlocillin sodium	Piperacillin sodium
Cimetidine HCl	Ticarcillin disodium
Digoxin	Tobramycin sulfate
Dopamine HCl	Vitamin B complex with C
Doxycycline hyclate	
Epinephrine HCl	
Erythromycin lactobionate	
Furosemide	
Kanamycin sulfate	

The manufacturer has also stated that cefotetan disodium is incompatible with gentamicin sulfate, heparin sodium, and netilmicin sulfate. (283)

CEFOXITIN SODIUM
AHFS 8:12.07

Products — Cefoxitin sodium is available in vials and infusion bottles containing the equivalent of 1 and 2 g of cefoxitin. It is also available in 10-g bulk bottles. (2)

Cefoxitin sodium is also available as a frozen premixed infusion solution of 1 or 2 g in dextrose 4 or 2.2 %, respectively. Sodium bicarbonate or hydrochloric acid or both may have been added to adjust the pH. (2; 4)

For intravenous administration, the vial contents may be reconstituted with sterile water for injection. The 1- and 2-g infusion bottles may be reconstituted with sodium chloride 0.9%, dextrose 5% in water, dextrose 10% in water, or other compatible diluent. (2; 4) (See Table 1.)

After addition of the diluent, shake the vial and allow the solution to stand until it becomes clear. (2)

For intravenous infusion, the primary solution may be diluted further in 50 to 1000 ml of compatible diluent. (2) (See Compatibility Information.)

The frozen premixed infusion should be thawed at room temperature and checked for leaks by squeezing the bag. It should not be thawed by immersion in a warm water bath or exposure to microwave radiation. (2; 4)

pH—Reconstituted solutions have a pH of 4.2 to 7. The frozen premixed infusion has a pH of about 6.5. (2; 4)

Osmolality—The osmolality of cefoxitin sodium 1 and 2 g was calculated for the following dilutions (1054):

Diluent	Osmolality (mOsm/kg) 50 ml	100 ml
1 g		
Dextrose 5% in water	326	293
Sodium chloride 0.9%	352	319
2 g		
Dextrose 5% in water	388	329
Sodium chloride 0.9%	415	355

The osmolality of cefoxitin sodium (MSD) 50 mg/ml was determined to be 348 mOsm/kg in dextrose 5% in water and 361 mOsm/kg in sodium chloride 0.9%. (1375) At 100 mg/ml in sterile water for injection, the osmolality is 468 mOsm/kg. (1689)

Robinson et al. recommended the following maximum cefoxitin sodium concentrations to achieve osmolalities suitable for peripheral infusion in fluid-restricted patients (1180):

Diluent	Maximum Concentration (mg/ml)	Osmolality (mOsm/kg)
Dextrose 5% in water	62	531
Sodium chloride 0.9%	56	508
Sterile water for injection	112	437

Sodium Content—Each gram of cefoxitin sodium contains 2.3 mEq (53.8 mg) of sodium. (2)

Displacement Volume—Each gram of cefoxitin sodium displaces about 0.7 ml. (865)

Trade Name(s)—Mefoxin.

Administration — Cefoxitin sodium may be administered by direct intravenous injection over three to five minutes directly into the vein or slowly into the tubing of a running compatible infusion solution, or by continuous or intermittent intravenous infusion. The manufacturer recommends temporarily discontinuing other solutions being administered at the site. (2; 4)

Table 1. Recommended Dilutions of Cefoxitin Sodium (2)

Vial Size	Route	Volume of Diluent	Withdrawable Volume	Approximate Concentration
1 g	Intravenous	10 ml	10.5 ml	95 mg/ml
(Infusion bottle)	Intravenous	50 or 100 ml	50 or 100 ml	20 or 10 mg/ml
2 g	Intravenous	10 ml	11.1 ml	180 mg/ml
2 g	Intravenous	20 ml	21 ml	95 mg/ml
(Infusion bottle)	Intravenous	50 or 100 ml	50 or 100 ml	40 or 20 mg/ml
10-g bulk	Intravenous	43 or	49 or	200 or
10-g bulk		93 ml	98.5 ml	100 mg/ml

Stability — Intact vials of cefoxitin sodium should be stored between 2 and 25 °C. Exposure to temperatures above 50 °C should be avoided. The powder is white to off-white in color. Solutions may range from colorless to light amber. (2) Both the dry material and solutions may darken, depending on storage conditions. Although moisture plays a role in the rate and intensity of the darkening, exposure to oxygen is the most significant factor. However, this discoloration is stated not to affect potency or relate to any significant chemical change. The concern over color is purely aesthetic. (865)

Exposure of cefoxitin sodium (MSD) 40 mg/ml in sterile water for injection to 37 °C for 24 hours, to simulate the use of a portable infusion pump, resulted in about a 3 to 4% cefoxitin loss. (1391)

Cefoxitin sodium solutions reconstituted as indicated in Table 2 are stable for 48 hours at 25 °C and at least seven days and, in some cases, up to one month at 5 °C. (308)

Borst et al. reported that cefoxitin sodium (MSD) 1 and 2 g/10 ml in sterile water for injection, packaged in plastic syringes (Monoject), exhibited a 10% cefoxitin loss in two days at 24 °C and 23 days at 4 °C as determined by UV spectroscopy. (1178)

pH Effects—Cefoxitin sodium at 1 and 10 mg/ml in aqueous solution is stable over pH 4 to 8. The time to 10% decomposition when stored at 25 °C was essentially independent of pH, ranging from 40 to 44 hours at pH 4 to 5 to 33 hours at pH 8. Under refrigeration, a pH 7 (unbuffered) aqueous solution showed 10% decomposition in 26 days. At pH less than 4, precipitation of the free acid may occur. Above pH 8, hydrolysis of the β-lactam group may result. (308)

In another study, cefoxitin sodium in aqueous solution at 25 °C exhibited minimum rates of decomposition at pH 5 to 7. The solutions in this pH range showed 10% decomposition in about two days. At pH 3, about 40 hours elapsed before 10% decomposition occurred.

Table 2. Stability of Reconstituted Cefoxitin Sodium 1 g (308)

Diluent	Volume	Remarks
Bacteriostatic water for injection (benzyl alcohol)	2 ml	9% decomposition in 48 hr at 25 °C. 4% in 7 days and 10% in 1 month at 5 °C
Bacteriostatic water for injection (parabens)	2 ml	9% decomposition in 48 hr at 25 °C. 5% in 7 days and 12% in 1 month at 5 °C
Dextrose 5% in water	10 ml	9% decomposition in 48 hr at 25 °C, 2% in 7 days at 5 °C
Lidocaine HCl 0.5% (with parabens)	2 ml	8% decomposition in 48 hr at 25 °C. 5% in 7 days and 10% in 1 month at 5 °C
Lidocaine HCl 1% (with parabens)	2 ml	7% decomposition in 48 hr at 25 °C. 2% in 7 days and 10% in 1 month at 5 °C
Sodium chloride 0.9%	10 ml	8% decomposition in 48 hr at 25 °C
Water for injection	10 ml	10% decomposition in 48 hr at 25 °C, 1% in 7 days at 5 °C
Water for injection	4 ml	7% decomposition in 48 hr at 25 °C, 2% in 7 days at 5 °C
Water for injection	2 ml	8% decomposition in 48 hr at 25 °C. 2% in 7 days and 10% in 1 month at 5 °C
(In plastic syringe)	10 ml	6% decomposition in 24 hr and 11% in 48 hr at 25 °C

However, at pH 9, only 14 hours was required to incur a 10% loss. (630)

Freezing Solutions—The stability of cefoxitin sodium reconstituted with the diluents as shown in Table 3 was evaluated in the frozen state at −20 °C. The solutions retained adequate potency for at least 30 weeks. (308) Thawed solutions should not be refrozen. (2)

In another study, cefoxitin sodium (MSD) 1 g/50 ml of dextrose 5% in water in PVC bags frozen at −20 °C for 30 days and then thawed by exposure to ambient temperature or microwave radiation showed no evidence of precipitation or color change and showed no loss of potency as determined microbiologically. Subsequent storage of the admixture at room temperature for 24 hours yielded a physically compatible solution which exhibited a 3 to 5% loss of potency. (554)

A further evaluation using an HPLC procedure was performed on frozen cefoxitin sodium solutions thawed by microwave radiation. At concentrations of 1 g/50 ml and 1 g/100 ml in both dextrose 5% in water and sodium chloride 0.9% in PVC bags, the cefoxitin sodium solutions were frozen at −20 °C for 72 hours. They were then thawed by exposure to microwave radiation and allowed to stand at room temperature for six hours. No changes were noted in the visual appearance or pH. Also, no significant differences in concentration occurred, with all solutions being at least within 97% of the initial concentration. (629)

Borst et al. reported that cefoxitin sodium (MSD) 1 and 2 g/10 ml in sterile water for injection, packaged in plastic syringes (Monoject) and frozen at −15 °C, was stable for the three-month study period, exhibiting less than a 10% loss as determined by UV spectroscopy. (1178)

Table 3. Stability of Reconstituted Cefoxitin Sodium 1 g Frozen at −20 °C (308)

Diluent	Volume	Remarks
Bacteriostatic water for injection (benzyl alcohol)	10 ml	2% decomposition in 30 weeks. Thawed solutions showed 6% decomposition in 24 hr at 25 °C and 1% in 7 days at 5 °C
Bacteriostatic water for injection (parabens)	10 ml	2% decomposition in 30 weeks. Thawed solutions showed no decomposition in 24 hr at 25 °C and 1% in 7 days at 5 °C
Dextrose 5% in water	10 ml	3% decomposition in 30 weeks. Thawed solutions showed 8% decomposition in 24 hr at 25 °C and 6% in 7 days at 5 °C
Lidocaine HCl 0.5%	2 ml	2% cefoxitin decomposition in 26 weeks. Thawed solutions showed 6% decomposition in 24 hr at 25 °C. HPLC demonstrated lidocaine potency
Sodium chloride 0.9%	10 ml	5% decomposition in 30 weeks. Thawed solutions showed 3% decomposition in 24 hr at 25 °C and 6% in 7 days at 5 °C
Water for injection	10 ml	1% decomposition in 30 weeks. Thawed solutions showed 3% decomposition in 24 hr at 25 °C and 5% in 7 days at 5 °C
Water for injection	4 ml	No decomposition in 13 weeks

Miller and Pesko reported an approximate twofold increase in particles of 2 to 60 μm produced by freezing and thawing cefoxitin sodium (MSD) 2 g/100 ml of dextrose 5% in water (Travenol). The reconstituted drug was filtered through a 0.45-μm filter into PVC bags of solution and frozen for seven days at −20 °C. Thawing was performed at room temperature (29 °C) for 12 hours. Although the total number of particles increased significantly, no particles greater than 60 μm were observed; the solutions complied with USP standards for particle sizes and numbers in large volume parenteral solutions. (822)

Stiles et al. reported a 3% or less cefoxitin sodium (MSD) loss from a solution containing 40 mg/ml in sterile water for injection in PVC and glass containers after 30 days at −20 °C. Subsequent thawing and storage for four days at 5 °C, followed by 24 hours at 37 °C to simulate the use of a portable infusion pump, resulted in an additional 3 to 4% cefoxitin loss. (1391)

Cefoxitin sodium in sodium chloride 0.9%, Ringer's injection, lactated, and dextrose 5% in water in PVC bags is stable for 26 weeks if kept frozen. (4)

Elastomeric Reservoir Pumps—Cefoxitin sodium solutions in elastomeric reservoir pumps have been stated by the pump manufacturers to be stable for the following time periods frozen, refrigerated (REF), or at room temperature (RT) (31):

Additive Compatibility (Cont.)

Cefoxitin sodium

Drug	*Mfr*	*Conc/L*	*Mfr*	*Conc/L*	*Test Soln*	*Remarks*	*Ref*	*C/I*
Cimetidine HCl	SKF	3 g	MSD	10 g	D5W	Physically compatible and cimetidine chemically stable for 24 hr at room temperature. Cefoxitin not tested	551	C
Clindamycin phosphate	UP	9 g	MSD	20 g	D5W[b]	Physically compatible with no loss of either drug in 48 hr at room temperature under fluorescent light	983	C
	UP	9 g	MSD	20 g	NS[b]	Physically compatible with no clindamycin loss and 7% cefoxitin loss in 48 hr at room temperature under fluorescent light	983	C
Gentamicin sulfate	SC	400 mg	MSD	5 g	D5S	4% cefoxitin decomposition in 24 hr and 11% in 48 hr at 25 °C. 2% in 48 hr at 5 °C. 9% gentamicin decomposition in 24 hr and 23% in 48 hr at 25 °C. 2% in 48 hr at 5 °C	308	C
Kanamycin sulfate	BR	5 g	MSD	5 g	D5S	9% cefoxitin decomposition at 25 °C and 1% at 5 °C in 48 hr. 6% kanamycin decomposition at 25 °C and none at 5 °C in 48 hr	308	C
Metronidazole	RP	5 g[c]	FC	30 g		Physically compatible with little or no pH change for at least 24 hr at 4 °C	807	C
	RP	5 g[c]	FC	30 g		Physically compatible but with a significant change in pH in 6 to 12 hr at 23 °C	807	?
	SE	5 g	MSD	30 g		9% cefoxitin loss in 48 hr at 25 °C and 3% loss in 12 days at 5 °C. No metronidazole loss occurred	993	C
Metronidazole HCl with sodium bicarbonate	SE AB	5 g 50 mEq	MSD	2 g	D5W, NS	Physically compatible for 48 hr	765	C
Multivitamins	USV	50 ml	MSD	10 g	W	5% cefoxitin decomposition in 24 hr and 10% in 48 hr at 25 °C. 3% in 48 hr at 5 °C. TLC showed no other transformation products	308	C
Ranitidine HCl	GL	50 mg and 2 g		10 g	D5W	Ranitidine chemically stable by HPLC for only 4 hr at 25 °C. Cefoxitin not tested	1515	I
Sodium bicarbonate (Neut)	AB	200 mg/g cefoxitin	MSD	1, 2, 10, 20 g	W	5 to 6% cefoxitin decomposition in 24 hr and 11 to 12% in 48 hr at 25 °C. 2 to 3% in 7 days at 5 °C	308	C
Tobramycin sulfate	LI	400 mg	MSD	5 g	D5S	5% cefoxitin decomposition in 24 hr and 13% in 48 hr at 25 °C. 3% in 48 hr at 5 °C. 8% tobramycin decomposition in 24 hr and 37% in 48 hr at 25 °C. 3% in 48 hr at 5 °C	308	C
Verapamil HCl	KN	80 mg	MSD	4 g	D5W, NS	Physically compatible for 24 hr	764	C
Vitamin B complex with C	RC	50 ml	MSD	10 g	W	No cefoxitin decomposition in 24 hr and 8% in 48 hr at 25 °C. 6% in 48 hr at 5 °C. TLC showed no other transformation products	308	C

[a] *Tested in PVC containers.*
[b] *Tested in glass bottles.*
[c] *Minibags (100 ml) containing metronidazole 500 mg with disodium phosphate 150 mg, citric acid 44 mg, and sodium chloride 740 mg. This product differs from the Searle product.*

Drugs in Syringe Compatibility

Drug (in syringe)	Mfr	Amt	Cefoxitin sodium Mfr	Amt	Remarks	Ref	C/I
Heparin sodium		2500 units/ 1 ml	MSD	2 g	Physically compatible for at least 5 min	1053	C

Y-Site Injection Compatibility (1:1 Mixture)

Drug	Mfr	Conc	Cefoxitin sodium Mfr	Conc	Remarks	Ref	C/I
Acyclovir sodium	BW	5 mg/ml[a]	MSD	20 mg/ml[a]	Physically compatible for 4 hr at 25 °C	1157	C
Amifostine	USB	10 mg/ml[a]	MSD	20 mg/ml[a]	Physically compatible with no change in measured turbidity or increase in particle content in 4 hr at 23 °C	1845	C
Amphotericin B cholesteryl sulfate complex	SEQ	0.83 mg/ml[a]	ME	20 mg/ml[a]	Physically compatible with little or no change in measured turbidity or increase in particle content in 4 hr at 23 °C under fluorescent light	2117	C
Aztreonam	SQ	40 mg/ml[a]	MSD	20 mg/ml[a]	Physically compatible with no subvisual haze or particle formation in 4 hr at 23 °C	1758	C
Cisatracurium besylate	GW	0.1 mg/ml[a]	ME	20 mg/ml[a]	Physically compatible with no change in measured turbidity or increase in particle content in 4 hr 23 °C	2074	C
	GW	2 and 5 mg/ ml[a]	ME	20 mg/ml[a]	Subvisual haze forms immediately	2074	I
Cyclophosphamide	MJ	20 mg/ml[a]	MSD	20 mg/ml[a]	Physically compatible for 4 hr at 25 °C	1194	C
Diltiazem HCl	MMD	5 mg/ml	MSD	10 and 200 mg/ml[b]	Visually compatible	1807	C
	MMD	1 mg/ml[b]	MSD	200 mg/ml[b]	Visually compatible	1807	C
Docetaxel	RPR	0.9 mg/ml[a]	ME	20 mg/ml[a]	Physically compatible with no change in measured turbidity or increase in particle content in 4 hr at 23 °C	2224	C
Doxorubicin HCl liposome injection	SEQ	0.4 mg/ml[a]	ME	20 mg/ml[a]	Physically compatible with little or no change in measured turbidity and no increase in particle content in 4 hr at 23 °C	2087	C
Etoposide phosphate	BR	5 mg/ml[a]	ME	20 mg/ml[a]	Physically compatible with no change in measured turbidity or increase in particle content in 4 hr at 23 °C	2218	C
Famotidine	MSD	0.2 mg/ml[a]	MSD	20 mg/ml[b]	Physically compatible for 14 hr	1196	C
	ME	2 mg/ml[b]		20 mg/ml[a]	Visually compatible for 4 hr at 22 °C	1936	C
Filgrastim	AMG	30 μg/ml[a]	MSD	20 mg/ml[a]	Haze, particles, and filaments form immediately	1687	I
Fluconazole	RR	2 mg/ml	MSD	40 mg/ml	Physically compatible for 24 hr at 25 °C	1407	C
Foscarnet sodium	AST	24 mg/ml	MSD	40 mg/ml	Physically compatible for 24 hr at room temperature under fluorescent light	1335	C
Gatifloxacin	BMS	2 mg/ml[a]	ME	20 mg/ml[a]	Measured haze increases immediately	2234	I
Gemcitabine HCl	LI	10 mg/ml[b]	ME	20 mg/ml[b]	Physically compatible with no change in measured turbidity or increase in particle content in 4 hr at 23 °C	2226	C

Y-Site Injection Compatibility (1:1 Mixture) (Cont.)

Drug	*Mfr*	*Conc*	*Mfr*	*Conc*	*Remarks*	*Ref*	*C/I*
			Cefoxitin sodium				
Granisetron HCl	SKB	0.05 mg/ml[a]	ME	20 mg/ml[a]	Physically compatible with no change in measured turbidity or increase in particle content in 4 hr at 23 °C	2000	C
Hetastarch in lactated electrolyte injection (Hextend)	AB	6%	ME	20 mg/ml[a]	Physically compatible with no change in measured turbidity or increase in particle content in 4 hr at 23 °C	2339	C
Hetastarch in sodium chloride 0.9%	DCC	6%	MSD	20 mg/ml[a]	Precipitate forms after 1 hr at room temperature	1313	I
Hydromorphone HCl	WY	0.2 mg/ml[a]	MSD	20 mg/ml[a]	Physically compatible for at least 4 hr at 25 °C under fluorescent light	987	C
Linezolid	PHU	2 mg/ml	ME	20 mg/ml[a]	Physically compatible with no change in measured turbidity or increase in particle content in 4 hr at 23 °C	2264	C
Magnesium sulfate	IX	16.7, 33.3, 66.7, 100 mg/ml[a]	MSD	20 mg/ml[a]	Physically compatible for at least 4 hr at 32 °C	813	C
Meperidine HCl	WY	10 mg/ml[a]	MSD	20 mg/ml[a]	Physically compatible for at least 4 hr at 25 °C under fluorescent light	987	C
	WY	10 mg/ml[b]	MSD	40 mg/ml[a]	Physically compatible for 1 hr at 25 °C	1338	C
Morphine sulfate	WI	1 mg/ml[a]	MSD	20 mg/ml[a]	Physically compatible for at least 4 hr at 25 °C under fluorescent light	987	C
	ES	1 mg/ml[b]	MSD	40 mg/ml[a]	Physically compatible for 1 hr at 25 °C	1338	C
Ondansetron HCl	GL	1 mg/ml[b]	MSD	20 mg/ml[a]	Physically compatible for 4 hr at 22 °C	1365	C
Pentamidine isethionate	FUJ	3 mg/ml[a]	ME	20 mg/ml[c]	Cloudiness and powder-like precipitate form immediately	1880	I
Perphenazine	SC	0.02 mg/ml[a]	MSD	20 mg/ml[d]	Physically compatible for 4 hr at 25 °C	1155	C
Propofol	ZEN	10 mg/ml	ME	20 mg/ml[a]	Physically compatible for 1 hr at 23 °C with no increase in particle content	2066	C
Ranitidine HCl	GL	1 mg/ml[b]	BAN	20 mg/ml[b]	Visually compatible with no cefoxitin loss and less than 8% ranitidine loss by HPLC in 4 hr at 25 °C exposed to fluorescent light	2259	C
Remifentanil HCl	GW	0.025 and 0.25 mg/ml[b]	ME	20 mg/ml[a]	Physically compatible with no change in measured turbidity or increase in particle content in 4 hr at 23 °C	2075	C
Teniposide	BR	0.1 mg/ml[a]	MSD	20 mg/ml[a]	Physically compatible with no subvisual haze or particle formation in 4 hr at 23 °C	1725	C
Thiotepa	IMM[e]	1 mg/ml[a]	ME	20 mg/ml[a]	Physically compatible with no change in measured turbidity or increase in particle content in 4 hr at 23 °C	1861	C
TNA #73[f]		32.5 ml[g]	MSD	1 g/50 ml[a]	Physically compatible for 4 hr at 25 °C by visual observation	1008	C
TNA #218 to #226[f]			ME	20 mg/ml[a]	Visually compatible with no precipitate or emulsion damage apparent in 4 hr at 23 °C	2215	C
TPN #61[f]		[h]	MSD	200 mg/2.1 ml[i]	Physically compatible	1012	C
		[j]	MSD	1.2 g/12.6 ml[i]	Physically compatible	1012	C

Y-Site Injection Compatibility (1:1 Mixture) (Cont.)

			Cefoxitin sodium				
Drug	*Mfr*	*Conc*	*Mfr*	*Conc*	*Remarks*	*Ref*	*C/I*
TPN #189[f]			MSD	200 mg/ml[k]	Visually compatible for 24 hr at 22 °C	1767	C
TPN #212 to #215[f]			ME	20 mg/ml[a]	Physically compatible with no change in measured turbidity or increase in particle content in 4 hr at 23 °C	2109	C
Vancomycin HCl	AB	20 mg/ml[a]	ME	180 mg/ml[k]	Transient precipitate forms, followed by clear solution	2189	?
	AB	20 mg/ml[a]	ME	50 mg/ml[a]	Gross white precipitate forms immediately	2189	I
	AB	20 mg/ml[a]	ME	10 mg/ml[a]	Visible haze forms in 4 hr at 23 °C	2189	I
	AB	20 mg/ml[a]	ME	1 mg/ml[a]	Physically compatible with no change in measured turbidity or increase in particle content in 4 hr at 23 °C	2189	C
	AB	2 mg/ml[a]	ME	1[a], 10[a], 50[a], 180[k] mg/ml	Physically compatible with no change in measured turbidity or increase in particle content in 4 hr at 23 °C	2189	C

[a]*Tested in dextrose 5% in water.*
[b]*Tested in sodium chloride 0.9%.*
[c]*Tested in dextrose 4% in water.*
[d]*Manufacturer's premixed solution.*
[e]*Lyophilized formulation tested.*
[f]*Refer to Appendix I for the composition of parenteral nutrition solutions. TNA indicates a 3-in-1 admixture, and TPN indicates a 2-in-1 admixture.*
[g]*A 32.5-ml sample of parenteral nutrition solution combined with 50 ml of antibiotic solution.*
[h]*Run at 21 ml/hr.*
[i]*Given over five minutes by syringe pump.*
[j]*Run at 94 ml/hr.*
[k]*Tested in sterile water for injection.*

Additional Compatibility Information

Peritoneal Dialysis Solutions — Cefoxitin sodium 2 mg/ml in peritoneal dialysis solution (McGaw) containing dextrose 2.5% and electrolytes was physically compatible for three hours at room temperature. Furthermore, no significant loss of antibacterial activity was apparent by microbiological determination. (142)

Aminoglycosides — The manufacturer recommends that cefoxitin sodium not be mixed with aminoglycoside antibiotics such as amikacin sulfate, gentamicin sulfate, and tobramycin sulfate. (2) However, compatibility studies show that such admixtures may indeed be sufficiently stable to allow combined mixture in the same solution.

To determine if spurious aminoglycoside levels could result from a delay in assaying blood samples, Tindula et al. evaluated the inactivation of amikacin 35 μg/ml and gentamicin and tobramycin 10 μg/ml in human serum by 400-μg/ml concentrations of several penicillins and cephalosporins. Samples were stored for 24 hours at room temperature and frozen at −20 °C. In the room temperature samples, cefoxitin caused moderate inactivation, 20% or less. Freezing the samples at −20 °C prevented significant inactivation of the aminoglycosides. (824)

Spruill et al. evaluated the effect of various cephalosporins on tobramycin sulfate 7.7 μg/ml in human serum. At concentrations of 250 and 1000 μg/ml, cefazolin, cefoxitin, cefamandole, cefoperazone, and cefotaxime caused about a 10 to 15% loss of tobramycin over 48 hours at 0 and 21 °C. Moxalactam caused about a 15% loss at 0 °C and a 20 to 30% loss at 21 °C over 48 hours. (1005)

Cefoxitin sodium (MSD) 125 μg/ml separately combined with the aminoglycosides amikacin sulfate (Bristol), gentamicin sulfate (Schering), and tobramycin sulfate (Lilly) at a concentration of 25 μg/ml in peritoneal dialysis solution (Dianeal 1.5%) exhibited enhanced rates of lethality to *Staphylococcus aureus, Escherichia coli,* and *Pseudomonas aeruginosa* compared to any of the drugs alone. (1623)

Vancomycin — The compatibility or incompatibility of vancomycin HCl mixed with or administered simultaneously with cefoxitin sodium is concentration dependent. (2189) See Y-Site Compatibility above. Vancomycin HCl has a low pH and is variably compatible with drugs having neutral to mildly alkaline pH, including cephalosporins and penicillins. The compatibility may depend on a number of factors, including concentration of each drug, dilution vehicle, actual pH of solutions, and completeness of mixing during administration. Combinations that are compatible when well mixed may result in precipitation if only partially mixed, presumably because of regionally different concentrations and pH values. If attempting to administer vancomycin HCl with cefoxitin sodium, take care to ensure that the specific combination and the concentrations are compatible under the exact administration conditions to be used. An inline filter should be used as a final safety measure. (2189)

Plastics — Cefoxitin sodium (MSD) at a concentration of 1 g/L in sodium chloride 0.9% exhibited a 4 to 7% loss of potency in 24 hours and an 8 to 9% loss of potency in 48 hours at 25 °C in Saftiset, Soluset, and Viaflex chambers and tubing. (308)

CEFTAZIDIME
AHFS 8:12.06

Products — Ceftazidime is available as a sodium carbonate-containing formulation (Fortaz; Tazidime; Tazicef) and an L-arginine-containing formulation (Ceptaz). (2)

Fortaz is supplied in vials containing 500 mg, 1 g, and 2 g of drug (under reduced pressure), infusion packs containing 1 and 2 g of drug, and 6-g pharmacy bulk packages. The Fortaz dosage forms contain sodium carbonate 118 mg per gram of ceftazidime. The sodium salt of ceftazidime and carbon dioxide are formed during reconstitution. (2; 4) The use of a venting needle has been suggested for ease of use. (1136) Spraying or leaking of the solution after needle withdrawal has been reported, especially with smaller vials. (1137) The use of larger vials reduces the occurrence of such leakage. (1137; 1138) Care must be taken if a multiple-additive set with a two-way valve is used for reconstitution. The negative pressure in the Glaxo Wellcome product may cause inaccuracies in the volume of diluent added to the vial. In one test, almost 3 ml extra entered the vial during reconstitution. (1240) Vials have been vented prior to reconstitution, but Glaxo Wellcome recommends clamping the tubing from the supply bottle prior to adding the diluent to the vial when multiple-additive sets are used. (1241)

Fortaz is also supplied in frozen solutions containing 1 and 2 g/50 ml of dextrose 4.4 and 3.2%, respectively. (2; 4)

Ceptaz is available in vials containing 1 and 2 g of drug (under slightly reduced pressure), infusion packs containing 1 and 2 g of drug, and 10-g pharmacy bulk packages. The dosage forms contain L-arginine 349 mg per gram of ceftazidime. Ceptaz dissolves without gas evolution. (2; 1699)

For intramuscular injection, Fortaz and Ceptaz should be reconstituted with sterile water for injection, bacteriostatic water for injection, or lidocaine HCl 0.5 or 1% in the amounts shown in Table 1. For the sodium carbonate-containing formulations, any carbon dioxide bubbles that are withdrawn into the syringe should be expelled prior to injection. (2; 4)

For direct intravenous injection, Fortaz should be reconstituted with sterile water for injection. Carbon dioxide will form during dissolution, but the solution will clear in about one to two minutes. Ceptaz should be reconstituted with sterile water for injection, dextrose 5% in water, or sodium chloride 0.9% as shown in Table 2. (2; 4)

For intravenous infusion, the reconstituted solution can be added to a compatible infusion solution (after expelling any carbon dioxide bubbles that have entered the syringe). Alternatively, the 1- or 2-g infusion packs can be reconstituted with 100 ml of compatible infusion solution, yielding a 10- or 20-mg/ml solution, respectively. (2; 4) To reconstitute the Fortaz infusion packs, add the diluent in two increments. Initially, add 10 ml with shaking to dissolve the drug. To release the carbon dioxide pressure, insert a venting needle through the closure only after the drug has dissolved and become clear (about one to two minutes). Then add the remaining 90 ml and remove the venting needle. Additional pressure may develop, especially during storage, and should be released prior to use. (4)

Table 1. Reconstitution for Intramuscular Injection (2)

Product	Volume of Diluent	Withdrawable Volume	Concentration
Fortaz			
500 mg	1.5 ml	1.8 ml	280 mg/ml
1 g	3.0 ml	3.6 ml	280 mg/ml
Ceptaz			
1 g	3.0 ml		250 mg/ml

Table 2. Reconstitution for Intravenous Injection (2)

Product	Volume of Diluent	Withdrawable Volume	Concentration
Fortaz			
500 mg	5 ml	5.3 ml	100 mg/ml
1 g	10 ml	10.6 ml	100 mg/ml
2 g	10 ml	11.5 ml	170 mg/ml
Ceptaz			
1 g	10 ml		90 mg/ml
2 g	10 ml		170 mg/ml

The Fortaz 6-g pharmacy bulk package should be reconstituted with 26 ml of a compatible diluent to yield 30 ml of solution containing 200 mg/ml of ceftazidime. The carbon dioxide pressure that develops should be released using a venting needle. The 200-mg/ml concentrated solution must be diluted further for intravenous use. (2)

The Ceptaz 10-g pharmacy bulk package should be reconstituted with 40 ml of a compatible diluent to yield a solution containing 200 mg/ml of ceftazidime. The 200-mg/ml concentrated solution must be diluted further for intravenous use. (2)

pH — Fortaz, from 5 to 8 (2; 4); Ceptaz, from 5 to 7.5. (2)

Osmolality — The osmolality of ceftazidime (Glaxo) 50 mg/ml was determined to be 321 mOsm/kg in dextrose 5% in water and 330 mOsm/kg in sodium chloride 0.9%. (1375)

Robinson et al. recommended the following maximum ceftazidime concentrations to achieve osmolalities suitable for peripheral infusion in fluid-restricted patients (1180):

Diluent	Maximum Concentration (mg/ml)	Osmolality (mOsm/kg)
Dextrose 5% in water	70	503
Sodium chloride 0.9%	63	486
Sterile water for injection	126	302

Sodium Content — Each gram of ceftazidime activity in Fortaz provides 2.3 mEq (54 mg) of sodium from the sodium carbonate present in the formulation. (2; 4) Ceptaz is sodium free. (2)

Trade Name(s) — Ceptaz, Fortaz, Tazicef, Tazidime.

Administration — Ceftazidime may be administered by deep intramuscular injection, by direct intravenous injection over three to five minutes directly into a vein or through the tubing of a running compatible infusion solution, or by intermittent intravenous infusion over 15 to 30 minutes. (2; 4) The manufacturer recommends temporarily discontinuing other solutions being administered at the same site during ceftazidime infusion. The sodium carbonate-containing formulation may be instilled intraperitoneally in a concentration of 250 mg/2 L of compatible dialysis solution. (2; 4)

Stability — Intact vials should be stored at controlled room temperature and protected from light. (2) Approximately 2% decomposition has been reported after 12 months of storage at 37 °C with protection from light. (1136)

Reconstituted ceftazidime solutions are light yellow to amber, depending on the diluent and concentration, and may darken on storage. Color changes do not necessarily indicate a potency loss. (2; 4)

Solutions of Fortaz in sterile water for injection at 95 to 280 mg/ml, in lidocaine HCl 0.5 or 1% or bacteriostatic water for injection at 280 mg/ml, and in sodium chloride 0.9% or dextrose 5% in water at 10 or 20 mg/ml in piggyback infusion packs are stable for 24 hours at room temperature and seven days under refrigeration. Tazicef and Tazidime in sterile water for injection at 95 to 280 mg/ml or in sodium chloride 0.9% at 10 to 20 mg/ml is stable for 24 hours at room temperature and seven days under refrigeration. (2)

One report of ceftazidime in concentrations of 1, 40, and 333 mg/ml in water indicated no loss after 24 hours at 4 °C and six hours at 25 °C. About a 4 to 6% loss was reported after 24 hours at 25 °C. (1136)

Ceftazidime vials reconstituted with sterile water for injection to a concentration of 270 mg/ml were evaluated for stability at four temperatures. HPLC and capillary electrophoresis analyses were in good agreement for the samples. About 8 to 9% ceftazidime loss occurred in 7 days under refrigeration at 4 °C and in 4 days at 10 °C. At 20 °C about 7 to 8% loss occurred in 24 hours, but at a higher room temperature of 30 °C about 5% loss occurred in six hours and 12% loss occurred in 18 hours. (2285)

Solutions of Ceptaz 250 mg/ml in sterile water for injection, bacteriostatic water for injection, or lidocaine HCl 0.5 or 1% for intramuscular injection are stable for 18 hours at room temperature or seven days under refrigeration. (2)

According to the manufacturer, the stability of Ceptaz for intravenous injection in sterile water for injection, dextrose 5% in water, and sodium chloride 0.9% depends on the solution concentration. Concentrations greater than 100 mg/ml are stable for 18 hours at room temperature and seven days under refrigeration. Concentrations of 100 mg/ml or less are stable for 24 hours at room temperature and seven days under refrigeration. (2)

Freezing Solutions — The various sodium carbonate-containing ceftazidime products differ in their reported stabilities, both during frozen storage of their solutions and after thawing. Table 3 summarizes the reported stabilities. (4)

The commercially available frozen ceftazidime sodium solutions (Fortaz) of 1 and 2 g/50 ml of sodium chloride 0.9%, when thawed, are stable for 24 hours at room temperature or seven days under refrigeration. (4)

At concentrations ranging from 10 to 250 mg/ml in the recommended diluents, Ceptaz is stable for six months when frozen at −20 °C. A precipitate may form during frozen storage, but it dissolves on warming to room temperature. Once thawed, concentrations greater than 100 mg/ml are stable for up to 12 hours at room temperature or seven days under refrigeration. Concentrations of 100 mg/ml or less are stable for up to 18 hours at room temperature or seven days under refrigeration. (2; 4)

Minibags of ceftazidime in dextrose 5% in water or sodium chloride 0.9%, frozen at −20 °C for up to 35 days, were thawed at room temperature and in a microwave oven, with care taken that the thawed solution temperature never exceeded 25 °C. No significant differences in ceftazidime concentrations occurred between the two thawing methods. (1192)

Table 3. Reported Stabilities of Frozen and Thawed Solutions of Ceftazidime Sodium Carbonate-Containing Products (2; 4)

Concentration	Fortaz	Tazidime	Tazicef
280 mg/ml	3 months[a]	3 months[a]	3 months[a]
Thawed/RT[b]	8 hr	8 hr	8 hr
Thawed/4 °C[c]	4 days	4 days	4 days
100 to 180 mg/ml	6 months[a,d]	3 months[e]	3 months[e]
Thawed/RT	24 hr	8 hr	8 hr
Thawed/4 °C	7 days	4 days	4 days
10 to 20 mg/ml[f]	9 months[a]		
Thawed/RT	24 hr		
Thawed/4 °C	7 days		

[a]*In sterile water for injection.*
[b]*Thawed and stored at room temperature.*
[c]*Thawed and stored at 4 to 5 °C.*
[d]*In sodium chloride 0.9%.*
[e]*In sodium chloride 0.9% and dextrose 5% in water.*
[f]*In infusion packs.*

Ceftazidime (Lilly) 40 mg/ml in both dextrose 5% in water and sodium chloride 0.9% exhibited approximately a 4 to 6% loss after storage at −10 °C for 90 days. Thawing in a microwave oven did not affect stability. (1341)

Stiles et al. reported less than a 2% ceftazidime (Glaxo) loss from a solution containing 36.6 mg/ml in sterile water for injection in PVC and glass containers after 30 days at −20 °C. Subsequent thawing and storage for four days at 5 °C, followed by 24 hours at 37 °C to simulate the use of a portable infusion pump, resulted in little additional ceftazidime loss. (1391)

Ceftazidime (Ceptaz) 100 mg/ml in sterile water for injection in polypropylene syringes (Becton-Dickinson) exhibited about a 2% loss by HPLC after 91 days at −20 °C. Subsequent storage at 22 °C for 24 hours resulted in a cumulative loss of 7%; subsequent storage at 4 °C for five days resulted in a cumulative loss of 6%. (1584)

Ceftazidime (Ceptaz) 30 and 60 mg/ml in sterile water for injection in PVC portable infusion pump reservoirs (Pharmacia Deltec) and glass vials exhibited no loss by HPLC after 30 days at −20 °C. Subsequent storage for four days at 3 °C resulted in about a 10% loss in the PVC bags and no loss in the glass vials. (1581)

Ceftazidime (Fortaz) 100 and 200 mg/ml in sterile water for injection in glass vials and polypropylene syringes (Becton-Dickinson) was stored frozen at −20 °C for 91 days followed by eight hours at 22 °C. Losses of about 5 and 10% by HPLC occurred in the 100- and 200-mg/ml concentrations, respectively. Freezing at −20 °C for 91 days followed by refrigeration at 4 °C for four days resulted in losses of about 10 and 6% in the 100- and 200-mg/ml concentrations, respectively. Particle counts remained within USP limits throughout the study. (1580)

Ceftazidime (sodium carbonate formulation) (Glaxo) 20 mg/ml in dextrose 5% in water and sodium chloride 0.9% frozen at −20 °C for 12 weeks exhibited 5% or less loss of potency by HPLC analysis in latex elastomeric reservoirs (Secure Medical) and in glass containers. (1970)

Usually, frozen solutions should be thawed at room temperature. Other techniques are not recommended. Thawed solutions should not be refrozen. (2; 4)

Light Effects — Ceftazidime reconstituted with sterile water for injection to a concentration of 270 mg/ml exhibited no substantial difference in stability when stored protected from light or exposed to daylight. (2285)

Syringes — Ceftazidime (Ceptaz) 100 mg/ml in sterile water for injection in polypropylene syringes (Becton-Dickinson) exhibited a 7 to 8% loss by HPLC after 24 hours at 22 °C and little or no loss after 10 days at 4 °C. (1584)

Ceftazidime (Fortaz) 100 and 200 mg/ml in sterile water for injection in polypropylene syringes (Becton-Dickinson) and glass vials exhibited a 5% or less loss by HPLC in eight hours at 22 °C and 96 hours at 4 °C. (1580)

Ceftazidime (Fortaz) 100 mg/ml in sterile water for injection, packaged as 0.4 ml in 1-ml Injekt syringes (Braun) sealed with blind hubs and stored at about 6 °C, retained antibiotic activity against *Pseudomonas aeruginosa* for seven days. However, the yellow color of the solution became much darker over this period. (1697)

Ambulatory Pumps — Ceftazidime (Ceptaz) 30 and 60 mg/ml in sterile water for injection in PVC portable infusion pump reservoirs (Pharmacia Deltec) exhibited a 7 to 10% loss by HPLC after 10 days at 3 °C followed by 24 hours at 30 °C. (1581)

Exposure of ceftazidime (Glaxo) 36.6 mg/ml in sterile water for injection to 37 °C for 24 hours, to simulate the use of a portable infusion pump, resulted in little or no ceftazidime loss. (1391)

Ceftazidime (Glaxo) (sodium carbonate formulation) at a concentration of 60 mg/ml in water for injection was filled into PVC portable infusion pump reservoirs (Pharmacia Deltec). Storage at −20 °C resulted in less than 3% loss in 14 days. The thawed reservoirs were then stored under refrigeration at 6 °C. Losses totaled 10% after five days of refrigerated storage. Under simulated use conditions at 30 °C, ceftazidime decomposes at a rate of about 10% in 18 hours. The authors concluded prefilling of reservoirs with ceftazidime (sodium carbonate) solutions for home use was not advisable. (2008)

Elastomeric Reservoir Pumps — Ceftazidime containing L-arginine (Glaxo) 3 g/50-ml and 6 g/50-ml solutions in sodium chloride 0.9% were packaged in Singleday Infusors made of polyisoprene. The infusors were stored at 27 °C to simulate use with no prior storage and also at 4 °C for up to 144 hours followed by 24 hours at 27 °C to simulate storage followed by use. The 3 g/50-ml concentration exhibited 9% ceftazidime loss in 24 hours at 27 °C and in 20 hours at 27 °C if stored under refrigeration prior to use. The 6 g/50-ml concentration was slightly less stable. Ceftazidime losses of 9 to 11% were found in all samples after 16 hours at 27 °C. (1860)

Ceftazidime (sodium carbonate formulation) (Glaxo) 20 mg/ml in dextrose 5% in water and sodium chloride 0.9% 100 ml was packaged in latex elastomeric reservoirs (Secure Medical). A 5% loss by HPLC analysis occurred in seven days at 5 °C. Stored at 25 °C, a 9% loss in dextrose 5% in water and a 4% loss in sodium chloride 0.9% occurred in 18 hours. (1970)

Ceftazidime (Glaxo) (sodium carbonate formulation) was prepared as a 60-mg/ml solution in sodium chloride 0.9% and packaged in elastomeric ambulatory pumps (Homepump, Block Medical). The solutions were visually compatible and exhibited 9% loss stored at 4 °C and no loss at −20 °C in 14 days protected from light. However, potentially toxic pyridine 0.53 mg/ml was found in the refrigerated solutions. Frozen solutions had much less pyridine. The authors recommended freezing such solutions if long-term storage is needed. (2113)

Ceftazidime containing L-arginine (Glaxo Wellcome) 24 mg/ml in sodium chloride 0.9% in Homepump (Block Medical) elastomeric infusion devices was evaluated for stability of the drug by HPLC analysis. The test solutions were packaged in the elastomeric infusion devices with ice packs placed next to the infuser shells that were changed every four hours to extend drug stability. Ceftazidime concentration remaining after 24 hours in five of six samples ranged from no loss to about 4% loss. The sixth sample exhibited about 18% loss. The authors offered no explanation for the low concentration in the sixth sample. (2273)

Solutions of ceftazidime containing sodium carbonate (except as noted below) in elastomeric reservoir pumps have been stated by the pump manufacturers to be stable for the following time periods frozen, refrigerated (REF), or at room temperature (RT) (31):

Pump Reservoir(s)	Conc.	Frozen	REF	RT
Homepump; Homepump Eclipse	20 mg/ml[b]	84 days	7 days	18 hr
	5 to 40 mg/ml[b,c]		14 days	24 hr
Intermate	5 to 40 mg/ml[a,b]		7 days	24 hr
	5 to 60 mg/ml[b]	8 weeks		
Medflo	20 mg/ml[a,b]	12 weeks	10 days	24 hr
ReadyMed	20 mg/ml[b]	4 weeks	14 days	48 hr

[a]*In dextrose 5% in water.*
[b]*In sodium chloride 0.9%.*
[c]*Ceptaz (containing L-arginine)*

Sorption — Ceftazidime 4 mg/ml in dextrose 5% in water and sodium chloride 0.9% exhibited no loss due to sorption to PVC containers over 24 hours and to administration sets during one-hour simulated infusions. (1953)

Ceftazidime (Glaxo Wellcome) 10 mg/ml in dextrose 5% in water and sodium chloride 0.9% packaged in PVC, polyethylene, and glass containers exhibited little or no loss due to sorption to any of the container types when stored at 4 and 22 °C for 24 hours protected from light. (2289)

Central Venous Catheter — Ceftazidime (Glaxo Wellcome) (sodium carbonate–containing formulation) 10 mg/ml in dextrose 5% in water was found to be compatible with the ARROWg+ard Blue Plus (Arrow International) chlorhexidine-bearing triple-lumen central catheter. HPLC analysis was used to evaluate completeness of drug delivery through the catheter and the amount of chlorhexidine removed from the internal lumens. Essentially complete delivery of the drug was found with little or no drug loss occurring. Furthermore, chlorhexidine delivered from the catheter remained at trace amounts with no substantial increase due to the delivery of the drug through the catheter. (2335)

Compatibility Information

Solution Compatibility

Ceftazidime

Solution	Mfr	Mfr	Conc/L	Remarks	Ref	C/I
Amino acids 5%, dextrose 25%	AB	GL[c]	6 g	No substantial amino acid degradation in 48 hr at 22 °C and 10 days at 4 °C. Ceftazidime stability the determining factor	1535	C
Dextrose 5% in sodium chloride 0.9%		GL[c]	20 g	5% loss in 24 hr at 25 °C and no loss in 48 hr at 4 °C	1136	C
Dextrose 5% in water	MG[a]	GL[c]	20 g	Physically compatible with 5% drug loss in 24 hr and 9% in 48 hr at 25 °C under fluorescent light	1026	C
		GL[c]	20 g	6% loss in 24 hr at 25 °C. No loss in 24 hr and 3% loss in 48 hr at 4 °C	1136	C
	TR[a]		40 g	Physically compatible with 8% loss in 2 days at 25 °C and 6% loss in 21 days at 5 °C	1341	C
	[b]	GL[c]	40 g	Physically compatible with 7% loss in 1 day and 19% loss in 3 days at 23 °C; 8% loss in 10 days at 4 °C	1353	C
	BA[b]	GL[c]	2 and 6 g	Visually compatible with 7 to 9% loss by HPLC in 24 hr at room temperature	1937	C
	[b]		4 g	Visually compatible with little or no loss by HPLC in 24 hr at room temperature and 4 °C	1953	C
	AB[d]	GL[c]	20 g	6 to 9% loss by HPLC in 18 hr at 25 °C and in 7 days at 5 °C	1970	C
	BA[b], BRN[a,j]	GW	10 g	Visually compatible with little or no loss by HPLC in 24 hr at 4 and 22 °C	2289	C
Ringer's injection, lactated		GL[c]	20 g	6% loss in 24 hr at 25 °C and 1% loss in 48 hr at 4 °C	1136	C
Sodium bicarbonate 4.2%		GL[c]	20 g	3% loss in 6 hr and 11% in 24 hr at 25 °C. 1% loss in 24 hr and 3% in 48 hr at 4 °C	1136	C
Sodium chloride 0.9%	MG[a]	GL[c]	20 g	Physically compatible with 2% drug loss in 24 hr and 5% in 48 hr at 25 °C under fluorescent light	1026	C
		GL[c]	20 g	7% loss in 24 hr at 25 °C and no loss in 48 hr at 4 °C	1136	C
	TR[a]		40 g	Physically compatible with 5% loss in 2 days and 12% loss in 3 days at 25 °C; 7% loss in 28 days at 5 °C	1341	C
	[b]	GL[c]	40 g	Physically compatible with 3% loss in 1 day and 14% loss in 3 days at 25 °C; 10% loss in 14 days at 5 °C	1353	C
	BA[e]	GL[f]	60 g	9% loss by HPLC in 24 hr stored at 27 °C	1860	C
	BA[e]	GL[f]	60 g	Stored for up to 144 hr at 4 °C followed by 27 °C; 9% loss by HPLC in 20 hr at 27 °C	1860	C
	BA[e]	GL[f]	120 g	9% loss by HPLC in 16 hr stored at 27 °C	1860	C
	BA[e]	GL[f]	120 g	Stored for up to 144 hr at 4 °C followed by 27 °C; 9 to 11% loss by HPLC in 16 hr at 27 °C	1860	C
	BA[b]	GL[c]	2 and 6 g	Visually compatible with 4 to 6% loss by HPLC in 24 hr at room temperature	1937	C
	[b]		4 g	Visually compatible with little or no loss by HPLC in 24 hr at room temperature and 4 °C	1953	C
	AB[d]	GL[c]	20 g	3 to 5% loss of drug by HPLC in 18 hr at 25 °C and 7 days at 5 °C	1970	C
	KA[h]	GL[c]	60 g	Visually compatible with little or no loss of ceftazidime by HPLC and little formation of pyridine in 14 days frozen at −20 °C protected from light	2113	C

Solution Compatibility (Cont.)

Ceftazidime

Solution	*Mfr*	*Mfr*	*Conc/L*	*Remarks*	*Ref*	*C/I*
	KA[h]	GL[c]	60 g	Visually compatible with 9% loss of ceftazidime by HPLC but formation of potentially toxic pyridine 0.53 mg/ml in 14 days at 4 °C protected from light	2113	?
	BA[i]	GW[f]	24 g	Losses of 0 to 4% by HPLC in 24 hr in samples cooled by ice packs. One sample exhibited 18% loss	2273	?
	BA[b], BRN[a,j]	GW	10 g	Visually compatible with little or no loss by HPLC in 24 hr at 4 and 22 °C	2289	C
TPN #107[g]			1 g	Physically compatible and ceftazidime activity retained for 24 hr at 21 °C by microbiological assay	1326	C
TPN #141 to #143[g]		GL[c]	1 g	Visually compatible with 8% ceftazidime loss in 6 hr and 10% loss in 24 hr by HPLC at 22 °C. 8% ceftazidime loss in 3 days at 4 °C	1535	C
		GL[c]	6 g	Visually compatible with 6% ceftazidime loss in 12 hr and 11 to 13% loss in 24 hr by HPLC at 22 °C. 7 to 9% ceftazidime loss in 3 days at 4 °C	1535	C

[a]Tested in glass containers.
[b]Tested in PVC containers.
[c]Sodium carbonate–containing formulation.
[d]Tested in glass containers and latex elastomeric reservoirs (Secure Medical).
[e]Tested in Singleday Infusors (Baxter).
[f]Arginine-containing formulation.
[g]Refer to Appendix I for the composition of parenteral nutrition solutions. TPN indicates a 2-in-1 admixture.
[h]Tested in elastomeric ambulatory pumps (Homepump, Block Medical).
[i]Tested in Homepump (Block Medical) elastomeric infusion devices.
[j]Tested in polyethylene plastic containers.

Additive Compatibility

Ceftazidime

Drug	*Mfr*	*Conc/L*	*Mfr*	*Conc/L*	*Test Soln*	*Remarks*	*Ref*	*C/I*
Aminophylline	ES	1 g	GL[a]	2 g	D5W, NS	20 to 23% ceftazidime loss by HPLC in 6 hr at room temperature	1937	I
	ES	1 g	GL[a]	6 g	D5W, NS	8 to 10% ceftazidime loss and 13% theophylline loss by HPLC in 6 hr at room temperature	1937	I
	ES	2 g	GL[a]	2 g	D5W, NS	35 to 40% ceftazidime loss by HPLC in 6 hr at room temperature	1937	I
	ES	2 g	GL[a]	6 g	D5W, NS	22% ceftazidime loss by HPLC in 6 hr at room temperature	1937	I
Ciprofloxacin	MI	1 g	SKF[a]	20 g	D5W, NS	Physically compatible for 24 hr at 22 °C	1189	C
	MI	2 g		20 g	D5W	Physically incompatible	888	I
Clindamycin phosphate	UP	9 g	GL[a]	20 g	D5W[b]	Physically compatible with 9% clindamycin loss and 11% ceftazidime loss in 48 hr at 25 °C under fluorescent light	1026	C
	UP	9 g	GL[a]	20 g	NS[b]	Physically compatible with 5% clindamycin loss and 7% ceftazidime loss in 48 hr at 25 °C under fluorescent light	1026	C

Additive Compatibility (Cont.)

Ceftazidime

Drug	*Mfr*	*Conc/L*	*Mfr*	*Conc/L*	*Test Soln*	*Remarks*	*Ref*	*C/I*
Fluconazole	PF	1 g	GL	20 g	D5W	Visually compatible with no fluconazole loss by HPLC in 72 hr at 25 °C under fluorescent light. Ceftazidime not tested	1677	C
Linezolid	PHU	2 g	GW[a]	20 g	[c]	Physically compatible with no linezolid loss by HPLC in 7 days at 4 and 23 °C protected from light. Ceftazidime losses of 5% in 24 hr and 12% in 3 days at 23 °C and about 3% in 7 days at 4 °C	2262	C
Metronidazole		5 g	GL[a]	20 g		No loss of either drug in 4 hr	1345	C
	AB	5 g	LI[a]	10 g		Visually compatible with little or no loss of either drug by HPLC in 72 hr at 8 °C	1849	C
Ofloxacin	HO	1.67 g	GL[a]	8.3 g	W	Visually compatible with little or no loss of either drug by HPLC in 48 hr	1613	C
Ranitidine HCl	GL	500 mg	GL[a]	10 g	D2.5½S	8% ranitidine loss in 4 hr and 39% loss in 24 hr by HPLC at 22 °C	1632	I

[a]*Sodium carbonate–containing formulation tested.*
[b]*Tested in glass containers.*
[c]*Admixed in the linezolid infusion container.*

Drugs in Syringe Compatibility

Ceftazidime

Drug (in syringe)	*Mfr*	*Amt*	*Mfr*	*Amt*	*Remarks*	*Ref*	*C/I*
Hydromorphone HCl	KN	2, 10, 40 mg/ 1 ml	GL[a]	180 mg/ 1 ml	Visually compatible with less than 10% loss of either drug by HPLC in 24 hr at room temperature	2082	C

[a]*Sodium carbonate–containing formulation tested.*

Y-Site Injection Compatibility (1:1 Mixture)

Ceftazidime

Drug	*Mfr*	*Conc*	*Mfr*	*Conc*	*Remarks*	*Ref*	*C/I*
Acyclovir sodium	BW	5 mg/ml[a]	SKF[c]	20 mg/ml[a]	Physically compatible for 4 hr at 25 °C	1157	C
Alatrofloxacin mesylate	PF	1.43 mg/ml[a]	GW[c]	40 mg/ml[b]	White precipitate forms	2235	I
Allopurinol sodium	BW	3 mg/ml[b]	LI[c]	40 mg/ml[a]	Physically compatible with no change in measured turbidity or increase in particle content in 4 hr at 22 °C	1686	C
Amifostine	USB	10 mg/ml[a]	LI[c]	40 mg/ml[a]	Physically compatible with no change in measured turbidity or increase in particle content in 4 hr at 23 °C	1845	C
Aminophylline	ES	2 mg/ml[a]	GL[c]	40 mg/ml[a]	Visually compatible with 4% ceftazidime loss and 9% theophylline loss by HPLC in 2 hr at room temperature	1937	C
	ES	2 mg/ml[a]	GL[c]	40 mg/ml[b]	Visually compatible with 5% ceftazidime loss and 4% theophylline loss by HPLC in 2 hr at room temperature	1937	C
	ES	2 mg/ml[a]	GL[d]	40 mg/ml	Visually compatible with no ceftazidime or theophylline loss by HPLC in 2 hr at room temperature	1937	C

Y-Site Injection Compatibility (1:1 Mixture) (Cont.)

			Ceftazidime				
Drug	*Mfr*	*Conc*	*Mfr*	*Conc*	*Remarks*	*Ref*	*C/I*
	ES	2 mg/ml[a]	GL[e]	40 mg/ml[a]	Visually compatible with 5% ceftazidime loss and 7% theophylline loss by HPLC in 2 hr at room temperature	1937	C
	ES	2 mg/ml[a]	GL[e]	40 mg/ml[b]	Visually compatible with 2% ceftazidime loss and no theophylline loss by HPLC in 2 hr at room temperature	1937	C
Amphotericin B cholesteryl sulfate complex	SEQ	0.83 mg/ml[a]	SKB[c]	40 mg/ml[a]	Increased turbidity forms in 4 hr at 23 °C under fluorescent light	2117	I
	SEQ	0.83 mg/ml[a]	GW[e]	40 mg/ml[a]	Gross precipitate forms	2117	I
Amsacrine	NCI	1 mg/ml[a]	GL[c]	40 mg/ml[a]	Light flocculent orange precipitate forms immediately, becoming heavier with time	1381	I
Aztreonam	SQ	40 mg/ml[a]	LI[c]	40 mg/ml[a]	Physically compatible with no subvisual haze or particle formation in 4 hr at 23 °C	1758	C
Ciprofloxacin	MI	1 mg/ml[a]	SKF[c]	20 mg/ml[f]	Physically compatible for 24 hr at 22 °C	1189	C
Cisatracurium besylate	GW	0.1 and 2 mg/ml[a]	SKB[c]	40 mg/ml[a]	Physically compatible with no change in measured turbidity or increase in particle content in 4 hr at 23 °C	2074	C
	GW	5 mg/ml[a]	SKB[c]	40 mg/ml[a]	Subvisual haze forms immediately	2074	I
	GW	0.1, 2, 5 mg/ml[a]	GW[e]	40 mg/ml[a]	Physically compatible with no change in measured turbidity or increase in particle content in 4 hr at 23 °C	2074	C
Diltiazem HCl	MMD	5 mg/ml	GL[c]	10 and 170 mg/ml[b]	Visually compatible	1807	C
	MMD	1 mg/ml[b]	GL[c]	170 mg/ml[b]	Visually compatible	1807	C
Docetaxel	RPR	0.9 mg/ml[a]	SKB[c]	40 mg/ml[a]	Physically compatible with no change in measured turbidity or increase in particle content in 4 hr at 23 °C	2224	C
Doxorubicin HCl liposome injection	SEQ	0.4 mg/ml[a]	SKB[c]	40 mg/ml[a]	Partial loss of measured natural turbidity	2087	I
Enalaprilat	MSD	0.05 mg/ml[b]	GL[c]	10 mg/ml[a]	Physically compatible for 24 hr at room temperature under fluorescent light	1355	C
Esmolol HCl	DCC	10 mg/ml[a]	GL[c]	10 mg/ml[a]	Physically compatible for 24 hr at 22 °C	1169	C
Etoposide phosphate	BR	5 mg/ml[a]	SKB[c]	40 mg/ml[a]	Physically compatible with no change in measured turbidity or increase in particle content in 4 hr at 23 °C	2218	C
Famotidine	MSD	0.2 mg/ml[a]	GL[c]	20 mg/ml[b]	Physically compatible for 14 hr	1196	C
	ME	2 mg/ml[b]	[c]	20 mg/ml[a]	Visually compatible for 4 hr at 22 °C	1936	C
Filgrastim	AMG	30 µg/ml[a]	LI[c]	40 mg/ml[a]	Physically compatible with no change in measured turbidity or increase in particle content in 4 hr at 22 °C	1687	C
	AMG	10[g] and 40[a] µg/ml	LI[c]	10 mg/ml[a]	Visually compatible with little or no loss of filgrastim activity by bioassay and ceftazidime by HPLC in 4 hr at 25 °C	2060	C
Fluconazole	RR	2 mg/ml	GL	20 mg/ml	Immediate precipitation	1407	I
Fludarabine phosphate	BX	1 mg/ml[a]	GL[c]	40 mg/ml[a]	Physically compatible for 4 hr at room temperature under fluorescent light	1439	C

Y-Site Injection Compatibility (1:1 Mixture) (Cont.)

			Ceftazidime				
Drug	*Mfr*	*Conc*	*Mfr*	*Conc*	*Remarks*	*Ref*	*C/I*
Foscarnet sodium	AST	24 mg/ml	GL	20 mg/ml	Physically compatible for 24 hr at room temperature under fluorescent light	1335	C
	AST	24 mg/ml	GL	20 mg/ml[f]	Physically compatible for 24 hr at 25 °C under fluorescent light by visual and microscopic examination	1393	C
Gatifloxacin	BMS	2 mg/ml[a]	SKB[c]	40 mg/ml[a]	Physically compatible with no change in measured haze or increase in particle content in 4 hr at 23 °C	2234	C
Gemcitabine HCl	LI	10 mg/ml[b]	SKB[c]	40 mg/ml[b]	Physically compatible with no change in measured turbidity or increase in particle content in 4 hr at 23 °C	2226	C
Granisetron HCl	SKB	1 mg/ml	SKB[c]	16.7 mg/ml[b]	Physically compatible with little or no loss of either drug by HPLC in 4 hr at 22 °C	1883	C
Heparin sodium	TR	50 units/ml	LI[c]	20 mg/ml	Visually compatible for 4 hr at 25 °C	1793	C
Hetastarch in lactated electrolyte injection (Hextend)	AB	6%	GW[c]	40 mg/ml[a]	Physically compatible with no change in measured turbidity or increase in particle content in 4 hr at 23 °C	2339	C
Hydromorphone HCl	KN	2, 10, 40 mg/ml	GL[c]	40[a] and 180 mg/ml	Visually compatible and potency of both drugs by HPLC retained for 24 hr	1532	C
Idarubicin HCl	AD	1 mg/ml[b]	LI[c]	20 mg/ml[a]	Haze forms in 1 hr	1525	I
Labetalol HCl	SC	1 mg/ml[a]	GL[c]	10 mg/ml[a]	Physically compatible for 24 hr at 18 °C	1171	C
Linezolid	PHU	2 mg/ml	SKB[c]	40 mg/ml[a]	Physically compatible with no change in measured turbidity or increase in particle content in 4 hr at 23 °C	2264	C
	PHU	2 mg/ml	GW[e]	40 mg/ml[a]	Physically compatible with no change in measured turbidity or increase in particle content in 4 hr at 23 °C	2264	C
Melphalan HCl	BW	0.1 mg/ml[b]	LI[c]	40 mg/ml[b]	Physically compatible with no change in measured turbidity or increase in particle content in 3 hr at 22 °C	1557	C
Meperidine HCl	AB	10 mg/ml	LI[c]	20 and 40 mg/ml[a]	Physically compatible for 4 hr at 25 °C	1397	C
Midazolam HCl	RC	1 mg/ml[a]	LI[c]	20 mg/ml[a]	Haze forms in 1 hr	1847	I
Morphine sulfate	AB	1 mg/ml	LI[c]	20 and 40 mg/ml[a]	Physically compatible for 4 hr at 25 °C	1397	C
Ondansetron HCl	GL	1 mg/ml[b]	GL[c]	40 mg/ml[a]	Physically compatible for 4 hr at 22 °C	1365	C
	GL	16 to 160 μg/ml		100 to 200 mg/ml	Physically compatible when ceftazidime given as 5-min bolus via Y-site	1366	C
	GL	1 mg/ml[b]	GL[e]	40 mg/ml[a]	Physically compatible for 4 hr at 22 °C	1365	C
	GL	0.03 and 0.3 mg/ml[a]	LI[c]	40 mg/ml[a]	Visually compatible with less than 10% loss of either drug by HPLC in 4 hr at 25 °C	1732	C
Paclitaxel	NCI	1.2 mg/ml[a]	LI[c]	40 mg/ml[a]	Physically compatible with no change in measured turbidity in 4 hr at 22 °C	1556	C
Pentamidine isethionate	FUJ	3 mg/ml[a]	LI[c]	20 mg/ml[a]	Fine precipitate, difficult to see, forms immediately	1880	I
Propofol	ZEN	10 mg/ml	SKB[c]	40 mg/ml[a]	Physically compatible for 1 hr at 23 °C with no increase in particle content	2066	C

Y-Site Injection Compatibility (1:1 Mixture) (Cont.)

Ceftazidime

Drug	*Mfr*	*Conc*	*Mfr*	*Conc*	*Remarks*	*Ref*	*C/I*
Ranitidine HCl	GL	1 mg/ml[b]	GL[c]	20 mg/ml[a]	8% ranitidine loss and no ceftazidime loss by HPLC in 4 hr at 22 °C	1632	C
Remifentanil HCl	GW	0.025 and 0.25 mg/ml[b]	GW[e]	40 mg/ml[a]	Physically compatible with no change in measured turbidity or increase in particle content in 4 hr at 23 °C	2075	C
Sargramostim	IMM	10 μg/ml[b]	GL[c]	40 mg/ml[b]	Particles and filaments form in 4 hr	1436	I
	IMM	6[h] and 15 μg/ml[b]	LI[c]	40 mg/ml[f]	Visually compatible for 2 hr	1618	C
Tacrolimus	FUJ	1 mg/ml[b]	GL[c]	20 mg/ml[a]	Visually compatible for 24 hr at 25 °C	1630	C
	FUJ	10 and 40 μg/ml[a]	GW[c]	40 mg/ml[a]	Visually compatible with no loss of either drug by HPLC in 4 hr at 24 °C under fluorescent light	2216	C
	FUJ	10 and 40 μg/ml[a]	GW[c]	200 mg/ml[a]	Visually compatible with no loss of either drug by HPLC in 4 hr at 24 °C under fluorescent light	2216	C
Teniposide	BR	0.1 mg/ml[a]	LI[c]	40 mg/ml[a]	Physically compatible with no subvisual haze or particle formation in 4 hr at 23 °C	1725	C
Theophylline	TR	4 mg/ml	LI[c]	20 mg/ml	Visually compatible for 6 hr at 25 °C	1793	C
Thiotepa	IMM[i]	1 mg/ml[a]	LI[c]	40 mg/ml[a]	Physically compatible with no change in measured turbidity or increase in particle content in 4 hr at 23 °C	1861	C
TNA #218 to #226[j]			SKB[c]	40 mg/ml[a]	Visually compatible with no precipitate or emulsion damage apparent in 4 hr at 23 °C	2215	C
			GL[e]	40 mg/ml[a]	Visually compatible with no precipitate or emulsion damage apparent in 4 hr at 23 °C	2215	C
TPN #141 to #143[j]			GL[c]	40 mg/ml[f]	Visually compatible with 4% or less ceftazidime loss in 2 hr at 22 °C in 1:1 and 1:3 ratios	1535	C
TPN #189[j]			GL[c]	200 mg/ml[k]	Visually compatible for 24 hr at 22 °C	1767	C
TPN #203 and #204[j]			LI[c]	60 mg/ml	Visually compatible for 2 hr at 23 °C	1974	C
TPN #212 to #215[j]			SKB[c]	40 mg/ml[a]	Physically compatible with no change in measured turbidity or increase in particle content in 4 hr at 23 °C	2109	C
Vancomycin HCl	AB	3 mg/ml[a]	GL[c]	25 and 60 mg/ml[a]	Physically compatible with no subvisual haze or particle formation in 4 hr at 23 °C	1563	C
	AB	10 mg/ml[a]	GL[c]	25 mg/ml[a]	Subvisual haze forms immediately	1563	I
	AB	10 mg/ml[a]	GL[c]	60 mg/ml[a]	Dense turbidity and white particles form immediately and become gross precipitate in 1 hr	1563	I
	AB	20 mg/ml[a]	SKB[c]	10[a], 50[a], 200[k] mg/ml	Gross white precipitate forms immediately	2189	I
	AB	20 mg/ml[a]	SKB[c]	1 mg/ml[a]	Physically compatible with no change in measured turbidity or increase in particle content in 4 hr at 23 °C	2189	C

Y-Site Injection Compatibility (1:1 Mixture) (Cont.)

Ceftazidime

Drug	*Mfr*	*Conc*	*Mfr*	*Conc*	*Remarks*	*Ref*	*C/I*
	AB	2 mg/ml[a]	SKB[c]	1[a], 10[a], 50[a], 200[k] mg/ml	Physically compatible with no change in measured turbidity or increase in particle content in 4 hr at 23 °C	2189	C
Vinorelbine tartrate	BW	1 mg/ml[b]	LI[c]	40 mg/ml[b]	Physically compatible with no change in measured turbidity or increase in particle content in 4 hr at 22 °C	1558	C
Warfarin sodium	DME	2 mg/ml[k]	SKB[c]	20 mg/ml[a]	Haze forms in 24 hr at 24 °C	2078	I
Zidovudine	BW	4 mg/ml[a]	GL[c]	20 mg/ml[a]	Physically compatible for 4 hr at 25 °C under fluorescent light by visual and microscopic examination	1193	C

[a]Tested in dextrose 5% in water.
[b]Tested in sodium chloride 0.9%.
[c]Sodium carbonate-containing formulation tested.
[d]Tested in the ceftazidime premixed infusion.
[e]Arginine formulation tested.
[f]Tested in both dextrose 5% in water and sodium chloride 0.9%.
[g]Tested in dextrose 5% in water with human albumin 2 mg/ml.
[h]With human albumin 0.1%.
[i]Lyophilized formulation tested.
[j]Refer to Appendix I for the composition of parenteral nutrition solutions. TNA indicates a 3-in-1 admixture, and TPN indicates a 2-in-1 admixture.
[k]Tested in sterile water for injection.

Additional Compatibility Information

Infusion Solutions — Ceftazidime, at the concentrations and in the infusion solutions noted in Table 4, is stated to be physically compatible and chemically stable for 24 hours at room temperature and for seven days under refrigeration. (2; 4)

Infusions in sodium chloride 0.9% or dextrose 5% in water are stated to be stable for six hours at room temperature in plastic tubing, drip chambers, and volume-control devices of administration sets. (2; 4)

Table 4. Infusion Solutions and Concentrations for Ceftazidime Dilution

Infusion Solution	Concentration (mg/ml) Ceptaz and Fortaz	Tazidime	Tazicef
Dextrose 5% in sodium chloride 0.2, 0.45, or 0.9%	1 to 40	1 to 40	1 to 40
Dextrose 5% in water	1 to 40	1 to 40	1 to 40
Dextrose 10% in water	1 to 40	1 to 40	1 to 40
Invert sugar 10%	1 to 20		
Normosol M in dextrose 5%	1 to 20		
Ringer's injection	1 to 20	1 to 40	1 to 40
Ringer's injection, lactated	1 to 20	1 to 40	1 to 40
Sodium chloride 0.9%	1 to 40	1 to 40	1 to 40
Sodium lactate ⅙ M	1 to 40		

The drug is stated to be less stable in sodium bicarbonate injection, and its use as a diluent is not recommended. (2; 4)

Peritoneal Dialysis Solutions — Ceftazidime 2 mg/ml in Dianeal with dextrose 1.5% is stated to be stable for 10 days under refrigeration, 24 hours at room temperature, and at least four hours at 37 °C. (4)

Ceftazidime (Fortaz) 125 mg/L and tobramycin sulfate (Lilly) 8 mg/L in Dianeal PD-2 with dextrose 2.5% (Baxter) were visually compatible and chemically stable by HPLC (ceftazidime) and fluorescence polarization immunoassay (tobramycin). After 16 hours of storage at 25 °C under fluorescent light, the loss of both drugs was less than 3%. Additional storage for eight hours at 37 °C, to simulate the maximum peritoneal dwell time, showed tobramycin sulfate concentrations of 96% and ceftazidime concentrations of 92 to 96%. (1652)

Ceftazidime (sodium carbonate formulation) (Glaxo) 0.1 mg/ml in Dianeal PD-2 with dextrose 1.5% in PVC containers was physically and chemically stable by HPLC analysis for 24 hours at 25 °C exposed to light, exhibiting about 9% loss; additional storage for eight hours at 37 °C resulted in additional loss of about 6%. Under refrigeration at 4 °C protected from light, no loss occurred in seven days. Additional storage for 16 hours at 25 °C followed by eight hours at 37 °C resulted in about 6% loss. (1989)

Ceftazidime (sodium carbonate formulation) (Glaxo) 0.1 mg/ml admixed with teicoplanin (Marion Merrell Dow) 0.025 mg/ml in Dianeal PD-2 with dextrose 1.5% in PVC containers did not result in a stable mixture. Using HPLC analysis, large (but variable) teicoplanin losses generally in the 20% range were noted in as little as two hours at 25 °C exposed to light. Ceftazidime losses of about 9% occurred in 16 hours. Refrigeration and protection from light of the peritoneal dialysis admixture reduced losses of both drugs to negligible levels. Even so, the authors did not recommend admixing these two drugs because of the high levels of teicoplanin loss at room temperature. (1989)

Ceftazidime (sodium carbonate formulation) (Glaxo) 0.1 mg/ml in Dianeal PD-2 with dextrose 1.5% with or without heparin sodium 1 unit/ml in PVC bags was chemically stable by HPLC analysis for up to six days at 4 °C (about 3 to 4% loss), four days at 25 °C (about 9 to 10% loss), and less than 12 hours at body temperature of 37 °C. (866)

The addition of vancomycin HCl (Lederle) 0.05 mg/ml to this peritoneal dialysis solution demonstrated similar stability with the ceftazidime being the defining component. Ceftazidime was chemically stable by HPLC analysis for up to six days at 4 °C (about 3% loss), three days at 25 °C (about 9 to 10% loss), and 12 hours at body temperature of 37 °C with the vancomycin exhibiting less loss throughout. (866)

Vancomycin HCl (Lilly) 1 mg/ml admixed with ceftazidime (sodium carbonate–containing formulation) (Lilly) 0.5 mg/ml in Dianeal PD-2 (Baxter) with 1.5% and also 4.25% dextrose were evaluated for compatibility and stability. Samples were stored under fluorescent light at 4 and 24 °C for 24 hours and at 37 °C for 12 hours. No precipitation or other change was observed by visual inspection in any sample. HPLC analysis found no loss of either drug in the samples stored at 4 °C and no loss of vancomycin HCl and about 4 to 5% ceftazidime loss in the samples stored at 24 °C in 24 hours. Vancomycin HCl losses of 3% or less and ceftazidime loss of about 6% were found in the samples stored at 37 °C for 12 hours. No difference in stability was found between samples at either dextrose concentration. (2217) Also see Vancomycin below.

Aminoglycosides — The manufacturers recommend that ceftazidime not be admixed with aminoglycosides because of the potential for interactions. (2; 4)

Pennell et al. evaluated the potential for inactivation of tobramycin sulfate (Lilly) 9 µg/ml with 100- and 200-µg/ml concentrations of ceftazidime (Lilly) in human serum. No loss of tobramycin sulfate was determined by TDx fluorescence polarization immunoassay over 48 hours when stored at 4, 24, and 37 °C. (1420)

Vancomycin — The compatibility or incompatibility of vancomycin HCl mixed with or administered simultaneously with ceftazidime is concentration dependent. (2189) See Y-Site Compatibility above. Vancomycin HCl has a low pH and is variably compatible with drugs having neutral to mildly alkaline pH, including cephalosporins and penicillins. The compatibility may depend on a number of factors, including concentration of each drug, dilution vehicle, actual pH of solutions, and completeness of mixing during administration. Combinations that are compatible when well mixed may result in precipitation if only partially mixed, presumably because of regionally different concentrations and pH values. If attempting to administer vancomycin HCl with ceftazidime, take care to ensure that the specific combination and the concentrations are compatible under the exact administration conditions to be used. An inline filter should be used as a final safety measure. (2189)

A precipitate formed instantaneously when ceftazidime 2 g/50 ml of sterile water for injection was added to a burette previously used to administer vancomycin HCl 1 g/100 ml of dextrose 5% in water. The authors suggested that vancomycin may have precipitated because of the alkaline pH due to the sodium carbonate in the ceftazidime formulation. (873) However, the manufacturer of Ceptaz also notes precipitation with vancomycin HCl, even though no sodium carbonate is present. (2)

Other Drugs — Ceftazidime 4 mg/ml in sodium chloride 0.9% and dextrose 5% in water is stated to be stable for 24 hours at room temperature or seven (Ceptaz and Fortaz) or 10 (Tazidime) days under refrigeration when admixed with heparin 10 or 50 units/ml, potassium chloride 10 or 40 mEq/L, or cefuroxime 3 mg/ml. (4)

Tazicef 20 mg/ml in sterile water for injection is stated to be stable for 18 hours at room temperature or seven days under refrigeration when admixed with cefazolin sodium 330 mg/ml, cimetidine 150 mg/ml, or heparin 1000 units/ml. At 20 mg/ml in dextrose 5% in water, Tazicef is stated to be stable for 24 hours at room temperature or seven days refrigerated when admixed with potassium chloride 40 mEq/L. (4)

Ceptaz 20 mg/ml is stated to be stable for 24 hours at room temperature or seven days under refrigeration with metronidazole 5 mg/ml or clindamycin phosphate 6 mg/ml in sodium chloride 0.9% or dextrose 5% in water. (2; 4)

CEFTIZOXIME SODIUM
AHFS 8:12.06

Products — Ceftizoxime sodium is available in vials and piggyback bottles containing the equivalent of 500 mg and 1 and 2 g of ceftizoxime and in 10-g pharmacy bulk vials. Reconstitute the contents of the vials with sterile water for injection in the amounts shown in Table 1 and shake well. Reconstitute the pharmacy bulk vials according to the manufacturer's label directions. Piggyback bottles should be reconstituted with sodium chloride 0.9% or any compatible solution. (2) (See Additional Compatibility Information.)

Ceftizoxime sodium is also available as a frozen premixed infusion solution of 1 or 2 g in dextrose 3.8 or 1.9%, respectively. It should be thawed at room temperature and checked for leaks by squeezing the bag. (2; 4)

Table 1. Recommended Dilutions of Ceftizoxime Sodium (2)

Vial Size	Route	Volume of Diluent	Withdrawable Volume	Approximate Concentration
500 mg	Intramuscular	1.5 ml	1.8 ml	280 mg/ml
	Intravenous	5 ml	5.3 ml	95 mg/ml
1 g	Intramuscular	3 ml	3.7 ml	270 mg/ml
	Intravenous	10 ml	10.7 ml	95 mg/ml
(Piggyback)	Intravenous	50 to 100 ml	50 to 100 ml	20 to 10 mg/ml
2 g	Intramuscular	6 ml	7.4 ml	270 mg/ml
	Intravenous	20 ml	21.4 ml	95 mg/ml
(Piggyback)	Intravenous	50 to 100 ml	50 to 100 ml	40 to 20 mg/ml

pH—The reconstituted solution has a pH of 6 to 8, and the frozen premixed infusion solutions have a pH of 5.5 to 8. (4)

Osmolality—Ceftizoxime 1 g as the sodium salt in 13 ml of sterile water for injection is isotonic. (2)

The frozen premixed infusion solutions have osmolalities of 330 to 405 mOsm/kg for the 1 g/50-ml concentration and 410 to 505 mOsm/kg for the 2 g/50-ml concentration. (4)

Robinson et al. recommended the following maximum ceftizoxime sodium concentrations to achieve osmolalities suitable for peripheral infusion in fluid-restricted patients (1180):

Diluent	Maximum Concentration (mg/ml)	Osmolality (mOsm/kg)
Dextrose 5% in water	69	530
Sodium chloride 0.9%	62	517
Sterile water for injection	125	437

Sodium Content—Each gram of ceftizoxime sodium contains 2.6 mEq (60 mg) of sodium. (2)

Trade Name(s)—Cefizox.

Administration — Ceftizoxime sodium is administered by deep intramuscular injection, by direct intravenous injection over three to five minutes directly into the vein or into the tubing of a running compatible infusion solution, as an intermittent intravenous infusion in 50 to 100 ml of diluent over 15 to 30 minutes, and as a continuous intravenous infusion. Intramuscular doses of 2 g should be divided between different large muscles. (2; 4)

Stability — Intact containers should be stored at controlled room temperature and protected from light. The freshly reconstituted solution is colorless to pale yellow but may darken on storage. Solutions may change to a yellow to amber color without a loss of potency. If a precipitate forms, the solution should be discarded. Reconstituted solutions of 95 mg/ml for intravenous use are stable for 24 hours at 25 °C and for 96 hours refrigerated at 4 °C. Concentrations of 270 or 280 mg/ml for intramuscular use are stable for 16 hours at 25 °C. (2; 4)

The frozen premixed infusions should be stored at or below −20 °C. After thawing, the solutions are stable for 48 hours at room temperature or 21 days at 5 °C. Thawed solutions should not be refrozen. (4)

Precipitation—An evaluation of ceftizoxime sodium (SKF) solutions showed significantly increased particulate levels in four and a half hours at 25 °C, with gross precipitation in eight hours at 25 °C or 24 hours at 5 °C. (986) The manufacturer subsequently reformulated the product, adding sodium bicarbonate. An evaluation of the new ceftizoxime sodium formulation 1 g/10 ml in sterile water for injection or 1 g/50 ml in dextrose 5% in water in PVC bags showed that the particulate levels were not significantly different from some other cephalosporins and were acceptable for 24 hours at 5 and 25 °C. (1078)

In another evaluation, the original formulation and the new formulation containing sodium bicarbonate were compared for compatibility in solution. Samples of each were reconstituted with sterile water for injection. An aliquot of 1.07 g/10.7 ml was diluted further with 9.3 ml of Ionosol MB, Ionosol T, Isolyte P, or Isolyte M and run at 40 ml/hr for 30 minutes through PVC administration sets. With the original formulation, a granular, white precipitate formed in the reservoir and tubing of all Ionosol T samples. Flushing the tubing of the Ionosol MB samples with drug-free solution failed to prevent precipitate formation in most samples within two to four hours. Precipitation did not occur with the original formulation in Isolyte P or Isolyte M. Furthermore, precipitation did not occur in any solution with the new formulation. (1079)

The development of a precipitate in ceftizoxime sodium solutions seems to correlate with the solution pH; at pH values greater than 6, a precipitate did not develop. Precipitation appears to occur more readily at high concentrations, at low pH values, and when dextrose 5% in water is the vehicle. (1318)

Freezing Solutions—Ceftizoxime sodium 1 and 2 g/50 ml in sodium chloride 0.9% in both PVC bags and glass bottles was stable for 90 days when frozen at −10 °C. However, these concentrations in dextrose 5% in water in PVC bags and glass bottles were stable for only 27 days when frozen at −10 °C due to precipitate formation. A 2-g/30 ml concentration in water frozen at −10 °C in plastic syringes was stable for 90 days. (1319)

Syringes—Ceftizoxime sodium 2 g/30 ml in water stored in plastic syringes exhibited a 9% loss in 24 hours at 25 °C and in five days at 5 °C. (1318)

Elastomeric Reservoir Pumps—Ceftizoxime sodium solutions in elastomeric reservoir pumps have been stated by the pump manufacturers to be stable for the following time periods frozen, refrigerated (REF), or at room temperature (RT) (31):

Pump Reservoir(s)	Conc.	Frozen	REF	RT
Homepump; Homepump Eclipse	20 to 40 mg/ml[a,b]	60 days	7 days	48 hr
Intermate	5 to 80 mg/ml[a,b]	30 days	10 days	24 hr
Medflo	20 mg/ml[a,b]	12 weeks	7 days	48 hr
ReadyMed	20 mg/ml[a]		2 days	24 hr

[a]*In dextrose 5% in water.*
[b]*In sodium chloride 0.9%.*

Central Venous Catheter—Ceftizoxime sodium (Fujisawa) 5 mg/ml in dextrose 5% in water was found to be compatible with the ARROWg+ard Blue Plus (Arrow International) chlorhexidine-bearing triple-lumen central catheter. HPLC analysis was used to evaluate completeness of drug delivery through the catheter and the amount of chlorhexidine removed from the internal lumens. Essentially complete delivery of the drug was found with little or no drug loss occurring. Furthermore, chlorhexidine delivered from the catheter remained at trace amounts with no substantial increase due to the delivery of the drug through the catheter. (2335)

Compatibility Information

Solution Compatibility

Ceftizoxime sodium

Solution	Mfr	Mfr	Conc/L	Remarks	Ref	C/I
Dextrose 5% in water	MG[a]	SKF	20 g	Physically compatible with no loss in 24 hr and 3% in 48 hr at room temperature under fluorescent light	983	C
	[b]		20 and 40 g	Physically compatible and chemically stable for 48 hr at 25 °C and for 7 days at 5 °C	1319	C
	[a]		40 g	Physically compatible and chemically stable for 48 hr at 25 °C and for 7 days at 5 °C	1319	C
Sodium chloride 0.9%	MG[a]	SKF	20 g	Physically compatible with 3% loss in 24 hr and 10% in 48 hr at room temperature under fluorescent light	983	C
	[c]		20 and 40 g	Physically compatible and chemically stable for 48 hr at 25 °C and for 7 days at 5 °C	1319	C

[a]Tested in glass bottles.
[b]Tested in PVC containers.
[c]Tested in both PVC containers and glass bottles.

Additive Compatibility

Ceftizoxime sodium

Drug	Mfr	Conc/L	Mfr	Conc/L	Test Soln	Remarks	Ref	C/I
Clindamycin phosphate	UP	9 g	SKF	20 g	D5W[a]	Physically compatible with 3% clindamycin loss and 4% ceftizoxime loss in 48 hr at room temperature under fluorescent light	983	C
	UP	9 g	SKF	20 g	NS[a]	Physically compatible with 7% ceftizoxime loss in 48 hr at room temperature under fluorescent light. 10% clindamycin loss in 8 hr but no further loss through 48 hr	983	C
Metronidazole	AB	5 g	FUJ	10 g		Visually compatible with little or no loss of either drug by HPLC in 72 hr at 8 °C	1849	C
	AB	5 g	SKB	10 g		Visually compatible with 8 to 9% loss of both drugs by HPLC in 14 days at 4 °C followed by 48 hr at 25 °C. 3 to 4% loss of both drugs in 3 days and 10 to 13% in 5 days at 25 °C	1879	C

[a]Tested in glass bottles.

Y-Site Injection Compatibility (1:1 Mixture)

Ceftizoxime sodium

Drug	Mfr	Conc	Mfr	Conc	Remarks	Ref	C/I
Acyclovir sodium	BW	5 mg/ml[a]	SKF	20 mg/ml[a]	Physically compatible for 4 hr at 25 °C	1157	C
Allopurinol sodium	BW	3 mg/ml[b]	FUJ	20 mg/ml[b]	Physically compatible with no change in measured turbidity or increase in particle content in 4 hr at 22 °C	1686	C
Amifostine	USB	10 mg/ml[a]	FUJ	20 mg/ml[a]	Physically compatible with no change in measured turbidity or increase in particle content in 4 hr at 23 °C	1845	C

Y-Site Injection Compatibility (1:1 Mixture) (Cont.)

Drug	Mfr	Conc	Mfr	Conc	Remarks	Ref	C/I
			Ceftizoxime sodium				
Amphotericin B cholesteryl sulfate complex	SEQ	0.83 mg/ml[a]	FUJ	20 mg/ml[a]	Physically compatible with little or no change in measured turbidity or increase in particle content in 4 hr at 23 °C under fluorescent light	2117	C
Aztreonam	SQ	40 mg/ml[a]	FUJ	20 mg/ml[a]	Physically compatible with no subvisual haze or particle formation in 4 hr at 23 °C	1758	C
Cisatracurium besylate	GW	0.1 and 2 mg/ml[a]	FUJ	20 mg/ml[a]	Physically compatible with no change in measured turbidity or increase in particle content in 4 hr at 23 °C	2074	C
	GW	5 mg/ml[a]	FUJ	20 mg/ml[a]	Subvisual haze forms in 1 hr	2074	I
Docetaxel	RPR	0.9 mg/ml[a]	FUJ	20 mg/ml[a]	Physically compatible with no change in measured turbidity or increase in particle content in 4 hr at 23 °C	2224	C
Doxorubicin HCl liposome injection	SEQ	0.4 mg/ml[a]	FUJ	20 mg/ml[a]	Physically compatible with little or no change in measured turbidity and no increase in particle content in 4 hr at 23 °C	2087	C
Enalaprilat	MSD	0.05 mg/ml[b]	SKF	10 mg/ml[a]	Physically compatible for 24 hr at room temperature under fluorescent light	1355	C
Esmolol HCl	DCC	10 mg/ml[a]	SKF	10 mg/ml[a]	Physically compatible for 24 hr at 22 °C	1169	C
Etoposide phosphate	BR	5 mg/ml[a]	FUJ	20 mg/ml[a]	Physically compatible with no change in measured turbidity or increase in particle content in 4 hr at 23 °C	2218	C
Famotidine	MSD	0.2 mg/ml[a]	SKF	20 mg/ml[b]	Physically compatible for 14 hr	1196	C
Filgrastim	AMG	30 µg/ml[a]	FUJ	20 mg/ml[a]	Particles and filaments form immediately	1687	I
Fludarabine phosphate	BX	1 mg/ml[a]	SKF	20 mg/ml[a]	Physically compatible for 4 hr at room temperature under fluorescent light	1439	C
Foscarnet sodium	AST	24 mg/ml	SKF	40 mg/ml	Physically compatible for 24 hr at room temperature under fluorescent light	1335	C
Gatifloxacin	BMS	2 mg/ml[a]	FUJ	20 mg/ml[a]	Physically compatible with no change in measured haze or increase in particle content in 4 hr at 23 °C	2234	C
Gemcitabine HCl	LI	10 mg/ml[b]	FUJ	20 mg/ml[b]	Physically compatible with no change in measured turbidity or increase in particle content in 4 hr at 23 °C	2226	C
Granisetron HCl	SKB	0.05 mg/ml[a]	FUJ	20 mg/ml[a]	Physically compatible with no change in measured turbidity or increase in particle content in 4 hr at 23 °C	2000	C
Hetastarch in lactated electrolyte injection (Hextend)	AB	6%	FUJ	20 mg/ml[a]	Physically compatible with no change in measured turbidity or increase in particle content in 4 hr at 23 °C	2339	C
Hydromorphone HCl	WY	0.2 mg/ml[a]	SKF	20 mg/ml[a]	Physically compatible for at least 4 hr at 25 °C under fluorescent light	987	C
Labetalol HCl	SC	1 mg/ml[a]	SKF	10 mg/ml[a]	Physically compatible for 24 hr at 18 °C	1171	C
Linezolid	PHU	2 mg/ml	FUJ	20 mg/ml[a]	Physically compatible with no change in measured turbidity or increase in particle content in 4 hr at 23 °C	2264	C

Y-Site Injection Compatibility (1:1 Mixture) (Cont.)

Ceftizoxime sodium

Drug	*Mfr*	*Conc*	*Mfr*	*Conc*	*Remarks*	*Ref*	*C/I*
Melphalan HCl	BW	0.1 mg/ml[b]	FUJ	20 mg/ml[b]	Physically compatible with no change in measured turbidity or increase in particle content in 3 hr at 22 °C	1557	C
Meperidine HCl	WY	10 mg/ml[a]	SKF	20 mg/ml[a]	Physically compatible for at least 4 hr at 25 °C under fluorescent light	987	C
Morphine sulfate	WI	1 mg/ml[a]	SKF	20 mg/ml[a]	Physically compatible for at least 4 hr at 25 °C under fluorescent light	987	C
Ondansetron HCl	GL	1 mg/ml[b]	FUJ	20 mg/ml[a]	Physically compatible for 4 hr at 22 °C	1365	C
Promethazine HCl	ES	25 mg	FUJ	10 mg/ml[a]	Fine cloudy precipitate forms immediately and dissolves in seconds	1753	?
Propofol	ZEN	10 mg/ml	FUJ	20 mg/ml[a]	Physically compatible for 1 hr at 23 °C with no increase in particle content	2066	C
Ranitidine HCl	GL	1 mg/ml[b]	FUJ	20 mg/ml[b]	Visually compatible with no loss of either drug by HPLC in 4 hr at 25 °C	2209	C
Remifentanil HCl	GW	0.025 and 0.25 mg/ml[b]	FUJ	20 mg/ml[a]	Physically compatible with no change in measured turbidity or increase in particle content in 4 hr at 23 °C	2075	C
Sargramostim	IMM	10 µg/ml[b]	FUJ	20 mg/ml[b]	Physically compatible for 4 hr at room temperature under fluorescent light	1436	C
Teniposide	BR	0.1 mg/ml[a]	FUJ	20 mg/ml[a]	Physically compatible with no subvisual haze or particle formation in 4 hr at 23 °C	1725	C
Thiotepa	IMM[c]	1 mg/ml[a]	FUJ	20 mg/ml[a]	Physically compatible with no change in measured turbidity or increase in particle content in 4 hr at 23 °C	1861	C
TNA #218 to #226[d]			FUJ	20 mg/ml[a]	Visually compatible with no precipitate or emulsion damage apparent in 4 hr at 23 °C	2215	C
TPN #212 to #215[d]			FUJ	20 mg/ml[a]	Physically compatible with no change in measured turbidity or increase in particle content in 4 hr at 23 °C	2109	C
Vancomycin HCl	AB	20 mg/ml[a]	FUJ	280 mg/ml[e]	Transient precipitate forms, followed by clear solution	2189	?
	AB	20 mg/ml[a]	FUJ	1, 10, and 50 mg/ml[a]	Physically compatible with no change in measured turbidity or increase in particle content in 4 hr at 23 °C	2189	C
	AB	2 mg/ml[a]	FUJ	1[a], 10[a], 50[a], and 280[e] mg/ml	Physically compatible with no change in measured turbidity or increase in particle content in 4 hr at 23 °C	2189	C
Vinorelbine tartrate	BW	1 mg/ml[b]	FUJ	20 mg/ml[b]	Physically compatible with no change in measured turbidity or increase in particle content in 4 hr at 22 °C	1558	C

[a] *Tested in dextrose 5% in water.*
[b] *Tested in sodium chloride 0.9%.*
[c] *Lyophilized formulation tested.*
[d] *Refer to Appendix I for the composition of parenteral nutrition solutions. TNA indicates a 3-in-1 admixture, and TPN indicates a 2-in-1 admixture.*
[e] *Tested in sterile water for injection.*

Additional Compatibility Information

Infusion Solutions — Ceftizoxime sodium is stable for 24 hours at room temperature and 96 hours when refrigerated at 5 °C in the following infusion solutions (2; 4):

Dextrose 5% in sodium chloride 0.2, 0.45, and 0.9%
Dextrose 5 and 10% in water
Invert sugar 10%
Ringer's injection
Ringer's injection, lactated
Sodium bicarbonate 5%
Sodium chloride 0.9%

The drug is similarly stable in dextrose 5% in Ringer's injection, lactated, if initially reconstituted with sodium bicarbonate 4%. (2; 4)

Vancomycin — The compatibility or incompatibility of vancomycin HCl mixed with or administered simultaneously with ceftizoxime sodium may be concentration dependent. (2189) See Y-Site Compatibility above. Vancomycin HCl has a low pH and is variably compatible with drugs having neutral to mildly alkaline pH, including cephalosporins and penicillins. The compatibility may depend on a number of factors, including concentration of each drug, dilution vehicle, actual pH of solutions, and completeness of mixing during administration. Combinations that are compatible when well mixed may result in precipitation if only partially mixed, presumably because of regionally different concentrations and pH values. If attempting to administer vancomycin HCl with ceftizoxime sodium, take care to ensure that the specific combination and the concentrations are compatible under the exact administration conditions to be used. An inline filter should be used as a final safety measure. (2189)

CEFTRIAXONE SODIUM
AHFS 8:12.06

Products — Ceftriaxone sodium is available in vials containing the equivalent of 250 mg, 500 mg, 1 g, and 2 g of ceftriaxone. It is also available in 1- and 2-g piggyback bottles and 10-g bulk pharmacy containers. (2)

For intramuscular use, reconstitute the vials with a compatible diluent in the amounts indicated (2):

Vial Size	Volume of Diluent for 250 mg/ml	Volume of Diluent for 350 mg/ml
250 mg	0.9 ml	[a]
500 mg	1.8 ml	1.0 ml
1 g	3.6 ml	2.1 ml
2 g	7.2 ml	4.2 ml

[a]*This vial size not recommended for 350-mg/ml concentration because withdrawal of the entire contents may not be possible.*

More dilute solutions for intramuscular injection may be prepared if required. (2)

For intermittent intravenous infusion, reconstitute the vials with a compatible diluent in the amounts indicated to yield a 100-mg/ml solution (2):

Vial Size	Volume of Diluent
250 mg	2.4 ml
500 mg	4.8 ml
1 g	9.6 ml
2 g	19.2 ml

After reconstitution, withdraw the entire vial contents and further dilute in a compatible infusion solution to the desired concentration. Concentrations between 10 and 40 mg/ml are recommended, but lower concentrations may be used. (2)

The piggyback bottles should be reconstituted with 10 or 20 ml of compatible diluent for the 1- or 2-g size, respectively. After reconstitution, further dilution to 50 to 100 ml with a compatible infusion solution is recommended. (2)

The bulk pharmacy container should be reconstituted with 95 ml of a compatible diluent. The solution is not for direct administration and must be diluted further before use. (4)

Ceftriaxone sodium is also available as a frozen premixed infusion solution of 1 or 2 g in 50 ml of dextrose 3.8 or 2.4%, respectively, in water. It should be thawed at room temperature. (2; 4)

pH — The pH of a 1% aqueous solution is approximately 6.7. (2), and the frozen premixed infusion solutions have a pH of approximately 6.6 (range 6 to 8). (4)

Osmolality — The frozen premixed infusion solutions have osmolalities of 276 to 324 mOsm/kg. (4)

The osmolality of ceftriaxone sodium (Roche) 50 mg/ml was determined to be 351 mOsm/kg in dextrose 5% in water and 364 mOsm/kg in sodium chloride 0.9%. (1375)

Sodium Content — Ceftriaxone sodium contains approximately 3.6 mEq (83 mg) of sodium per gram of ceftriaxone activity. (2)

Trade Name(s) — Rocephin.

Administration — Ceftriaxone sodium is administered by deep intramuscular injection or intermittent intravenous infusion over 15 to 30 minutes in adults or over 10 to 30 minutes in pediatric patients. (2; 4)

Stability — Intact vials of ceftriaxone sodium should be stored at room temperature of 25 °C or below and protected from light. After reconstitution, normal exposure to light is permitted. Solutions may vary from light yellow to amber, depending on length of storage, diluent, and concentration. (2)

Reconstituted solutions of ceftriaxone sodium are stable, exhibiting less than a 10% potency loss for the time periods indicated (2):

Diluent	Ceftriaxone Concentration (mg/ml)	25 °C	4 °C
Sterile water for injection	100	3 days	10 days
	250, 350	24 hr	3 days
Sodium chloride 0.9%	100	3 days	10 days
	250, 350	24 hr	3 days
Dextrose 5% in water	100	3 days	10 days
	250, 350	24 hr	3 days
Bacteriostatic water for injection (benzyl alcohol 0.9%)	100	24 hr	10 days
Bacteriostatic water for injection (benzyl alcohol 0.9%)	250, 350	24 hr	3 days
Lidocaine HCl 1% (without epinephrine)	100	24 hr	10 days
	250, 350	24 hr	3 days

pH Effects—The pH of maximum stability for ceftriaxone sodium has been variously reported as 2.5 to 4.5 (1080) and 7.2. (1244)

Freezing Solutions—The manufacturer indicates that ceftriaxone sodium 10 to 40 mg/ml in dextrose 5% in water or sodium chloride 0.9%, when frozen at −20 °C in PVC or polyolefin containers, is stable for 26 weeks. Thawing should be performed at room temperature; thawed solutions should not be refrozen. (2)

The frozen premixed infusion solutions are stable for at least 90 days at −20 °C. Thawed solutions are stable for 72 hours at room temperature or 21 days at 5 °C. (4)

In one study, ceftriaxone sodium (Roche) 20 mg/ml in dextrose 5% in water (Travenol) in PVC containers was evaluated by antimicrobial assay after two weeks of storage at −20 °C. The potency loss was less than 3%. (966)

Ceftriaxone sodium (Roche) 10 and 50 mg/ml in dextrose 5% in water and sodium chloride 0.9% frozen at −22 °C was stable for at least 26 weeks, exhibiting no more than a 7% loss. Microwave thawing did not adversely affect stability. (1245)

Ceftriaxone sodium (Roche) solutions containing 250 and 450 mg/ml in dextrose 5% in water, 250 mg/ml in bacteriostatic water for injection, and 450 mg/ml in lidocaine HCl 1% (Lyphomed) were evaluated for stability and pharmaceutical integrity during frozen storage at −15 °C. The solutions were packaged in 10-ml polypropylene syringes with attached needles (Becton-Dickinson) and frozen for eight weeks. Some syringes were stored further at 4 °C for 10 days or at 20 °C for three days. Ceftriaxone sodium losses of 5% or less were found by HPLC analysis after eight weeks of frozen storage. However, particulate matter levels were unacceptable in most samples. Only the 250-mg/ml solution in dextrose 5% in water met USP limits for the particulate matter test. While additional storage at 4 °C for 10 days did not cause an unacceptable drug loss, storage at 20 °C for three days resulted in an 11 to 12% drug loss. (1824)

Ceftriaxone sodium (Roche) 20 mg/ml in dextrose 5% in water and sodium chloride 0.9% frozen at −20 °C for 12 weeks exhibited 3 to 7% loss of potency by HPLC analysis in latex elastomeric reservoirs (Secure Medical) and in glass containers. (1970)

Two studies reported little or no loss of ceftriaxone by HPLC analysis during frozen storage in syringes. At concentrations of 10 and 40 mg/ml in dextrose 5% in water and sodium chloride 0.9%, less than 5% loss was found in 10 days at −10 °C. (1720) At 100 mg/ml in sterile water for injection, less than 3% loss occurred in 180 days at −20 °C. (1990) Furthermore, freezing the ceftriaxone sodium solutions for 60 days at −20 °C had little adverse effect on stability when stored subsequently at 4 and 20 °C. Stability periods after thawing of 30 days at 4 °C and three days at 20 °C were recommended. (1990)

Reconstituted with lidocaine HCl 1% to 250 and 450 mg/ml, ceftriaxone sodium (Roche) losses were 4 to 6% in 168 days at −20 °C. (1991)

Syringes—Bailey et al. reported the stability of ceftriaxone sodium (Roche) 10 and 40 mg/ml in dextrose 5% in water and sodium chloride 0.9% packaged in polypropylene syringes. The solutions were visually compatible and lost 5% or less ceftriaxone in 48 hours at 4 and 20 °C and ten days stored frozen at −10 °C. (1720)

Plumridge et al. reported on the stability of ceftriaxone sodium (Roche) 100 mg/ml in sterile water for injection packaged in polypropylene syringes (Terumo). About 9 to 10% loss of ceftriaxone by HPLC analysis occurred in five days at 20 °C and 40 days at 4 °C. However, the room temperature samples underwent color intensification that the authors found unacceptable after about 72 hours. Little or no loss occurred during 180 days of frozen storage at −20 °C. (1990)

O'Connell et al. evaluated the stability of reconstituted ceftriaxone sodium 100 mg/ml packaged in 10-ml polypropylene syringes. Stored under refrigeration at 8 °C, about 5% loss occurred in 10 days and 8% in 13 days. (1999)

Elastomeric Reservoir Pumps—Ceftriaxone sodium (Roche) 20 mg/ml in dextrose 5% in water and sodium chloride 0.9% was packaged in 100-ml latex elastomeric reservoirs (Secure Medical). About 3 to 5% loss by HPLC analysis occurred in 72 hours at 25 °C and in 10 days at 5 °C. (1970)

Ceftriaxone sodium (Roche) 10 mg/ml in both dextrose 5% in water and sodium chloride 0.9% was evaluated for binding potential to natural rubber elastomeric reservoirs (Baxter). No binding was found after storage for two weeks at 35 °C with gentle agitation. (2014)

Ceftriaxone sodium solutions in elastomeric reservoir pumps have been stated by the pump manufacturers to be stable for the following time periods frozen, refrigerated (REF), or at room temperature (RT) (31):

Pump Reservoir(s)	Conc.	Frozen	REF	RT
Homepump; Homepump Eclipse	20 mg/ml[b]			72 hr
	10 to 100 mg/ml[b]		10 days	72 hr
Intermate	5 to 40 mg/ml[a,b]	30 days	10 days	
Intermate HPC	5 to 40 mg/ml[a,b]		14 days	48 hr
Medflo	20 mg/ml[a,b]	26 weeks	10 days	72 hr
ReadyMed	20 mg/ml[a]		10 days	72 hr
	20 mg/ml[b]	4 weeks	14 days	48 hr

[a]*In dextrose 5% in water.*
[b]*In sodium chloride 0.9%.*

Central Venous Catheter—Ceftriaxone sodium (Roche) 5 mg/ml in dextrose 5% in water was found to be compatible with the ARROWg+ard Blue Plus (Arrow International) chlorhexidine-bearing triple-lumen central catheter. HPLC analysis was used to evaluate completeness of drug delivery through the catheter and the amount of chlorhexidine removed from the internal lumens. Essentially complete delivery of the drug was found with little or no drug loss occurring. Furthermore, chlorhexidine delivered from the catheter remained at trace amounts with no substantial increase due to the delivery of the drug through the catheter. (2335)

Compatibility Information

Solution Compatibility

Ceftriaxone sodium

Solution	*Mfr*	*Mfr*	*Conc/L*	*Remarks*	*Ref*	*C/I*
Dextrose 3.4% in sodium chloride 0.3%	[a]	RC	1 g	10% loss calculated to occur in 48 hr at 20 °C	1244	C
Dextrose 5% with potassium chloride 10 mEq/L		RC	10 g	5% loss in 24 hr and 8% in 48 hr at 20 °C. 2% loss in 48 hr and 7% in 72 hr at 4 °C	965	C
Dextrose 5% in sodium chloride 0.2% with potassium chloride 20 mEq/L		RC	10 g	3% loss in 24 hr and 4% in 48 hr at 20 °C. 4% loss in 72 hr and 5% in 96 hr at 4 °C	965	C
Dextrose 5% in sodium chloride 0.45%		RC	10 g	3% loss in 48 hr at 20 °C. 5% loss in 72 hr and 9% in 96 hr at 4 °C	965	C
Dextrose 5% in water		RC	10 g	No loss in 48 hr and 8% in 72 hr at 20 °C. 4% loss in 72 hr and 9% in 96 hr at 4 °C	965	C
	TR[b]	RC	2 g	Little or no loss in 14 days at 20 and 4 °C	966	C
	MG[c]	RC	20 g	Physically compatible with 5% drug loss in 24 hr and 9% in 48 hr at 25 °C under fluorescent light	1026	C
	[b]	RC	40 g	Physically compatible with 12% loss in 3 days at 23 °C and 10% loss in 14 days at 4 °C	1243	C
	[a]	RC	1 g	10% loss calculated to occur in 48 hr at 20 °C	1244	C
		RC	10 g	Physically compatible with 8% loss in 7 days at room temperature. 5 to 8% loss in 12 weeks at 5 °C	1245	C
		RC	50 g	Physically compatible with no loss in 24 hr but 12 to 17% loss in 7 days at room temperature. 5% loss in 8 weeks at 5 °C	1245	C
	MG	RC	10 and 40 g	Visually compatible with 5% or less ceftriaxone loss in 48 hr at 4 and 20 °C after 10 days storage at −15 °C in polypropylene syringes	1720	C
	AB[d]	RC	20 g	3 to 6% loss by HPLC in 72 hr at 25 °C and in 10 days at 5 °C	1970	C
Dextrose 10% in water		RC	10 g	No loss in 48 hr and 8% in 72 hr at 20 °C. 2% loss in 72 hr and 8% in 96 hr at 4 °C	965	C
Ringer's injection, lactated	[a]	RC	1 g	10% loss calculated to occur in about 3 days at 20 °C	1244	C
		RC	10 and 13 g	Precipitate forms relatively rapidly	2222	I
Sodium chloride 0.9%		RC	10 g	4% loss in 48 hr and 14% in 72 hr at 20 °C. 3% loss in 48 hr and 9% in 72 hr at 4 °C	965	C
	MG[c]	RC	20 g	Physically compatible with 10% drug loss in 24 hr and 16% in 48 hr at 25 °C under fluorescent light	1026	C
	[b]	RC	40 g	Physically compatible with 5% loss in 3 days at 23 °C and 9% loss in 30 days at 4 °C	1243	C
	[a]	RC	1 g	10% loss calculated to occur in 10 days at 20 °C	1244	C
		RC	10 g	Physically compatible with 9% loss in 7 days at room temperature. 11 to 12% loss in 6 weeks at 5 °C	1245	C
		RC	50 g	Physically compatible with 8 to 9% loss in 7 days at room temperature. 5% loss in 5 weeks and 15% in 8 weeks at 5 °C	1245	C

Solution Compatibility (Cont.)

Ceftriaxone sodium

Solution	*Mfr*	*Mfr*	*Conc/L*	*Remarks*	*Ref*	*C/I*
	BA	RC	10 and 40 g	Visually compatible with 5% or less ceftriaxone loss in 48 hr at 4 and 20 °C after 10 days storage at −15 °C in polypropylene syringes	1720	C
	AB[d]	RC	20 g	3 to 5% or less loss by HPLC in 72 hr at 25 °C and in 10 days at 5 °C	1970	C
TPN[e]		RC	10 g	7% loss in 48 hr and 12% in 72 hr at 20 °C. 2% loss in 48 hr and 10% in 72 hr at 4 °C	965	C
TPN #107[f]			1 g	Physically compatible and ceftriaxone activity retained for 24 hr at 21 °C by microbiological assay	1326	C

[a]Tested in glass, PVC, and polyethylene containers.
[b]Tested in PVC containers.
[c]Tested in glass containers.
[d]Tested in glass containers and latex elastomeric reservoirs (Secure Medical).
[e]Tested in a parenteral nutrition solution composed of amino acids 2.2%, dextrose 20%, multivitamins 10 ml, and standard electrolytes and trace elements.
[f]Refer to Appendix I for the composition of parenteral nutrition solutions. TPN indicates a 2-in-1 admixture.

Additive Compatibility

Ceftriaxone sodium

Drug	*Mfr*	*Conc/L*	*Mfr*	*Conc/L*	*Test Soln*	*Remarks*	*Ref*	*C/I*
Aminophylline	AMR	1 g	RC	20 g	D5W, NS[a]	Yellow color forms immediately. 3 to 6% ceftriaxone loss and 8 to 12% aminophylline loss by HPLC in 24 hr	1727	I
	AMR	4 g	RC	20 g	D5W, NS[a]	Yellow color forms immediately, 15 to 20% ceftriaxone loss and 7 to 9% aminophylline loss by HPLC in 24 hr	1727	I
	AMR	1 g	RC	40 g	D5W, NS[a]	Yellow color forms immediately, 15 to 18% ceftriaxone loss and 1 to 3% aminophylline loss by HPLC in 24 hr	1727	I
Clindamycin phosphate	UP	12 g	RC	20 g	D5W[b]	10% ceftriaxone loss in 4 hr and 17% in 24 hr at 25 °C under fluorescent light. No clindamycin loss in 48 hr	1026	I
	UP	12 g	RC	20 g	NS[b]	10% ceftriaxone loss in 1 hr and 12% in 24 hr at 25 °C under fluorescent light. 6% clindamycin loss in 48 hr	1026	I
Linezolid	PHU	2 g	RC	10 g	[d]	Physically compatible, but up to 37% ceftriaxone loss by HPLC in 24 hr at 23 °C and 10% loss in 3 days at 4 °C	2262	I
Metronidazole	AB	5 g	RC	10 g		Visually compatible with little or no loss of either drug by HPLC in 72 hr at 8 °C	1849	C
	BA	5 g	RC	10 g		Visually compatible with no metronidazole loss by HPLC and with 6% ceftriaxone loss in 3 days and 8% in 4 days at 25 °C	2101	C
Metronidazole HCl	SCS	15 g	RC	20 g	D5W, NS	Metronidazole begins to precipitate immediately and increases with time stored at 4 and 24 °C. 22 to 50% of the metronidazole precipitates in 4 hr	2091	I
	SCS	7.5 g	RC	10 g	D5W, NS	Visually compatible with little or no loss of either drug by HPLC at 24 °C in 72 hr	2091	C

Additive Compatibility (Cont.)

		Ceftriaxone sodium						
Drug	*Mfr*	*Conc/L*	*Mfr*	*Conc/L*	*Test Soln*	*Remarks*	*Ref*	*C/I*
	SCS	7.5 g	RC	10 g	D5W, NS	Visually compatible with little or no loss of either drug by HPLC at 4 °C through 24 hr. Slight precipitation occurred in 48 hr	2091	C
Theophylline	BA[c]	4 g	RC	40 g		Yellow color forms immediately. 14% ceftriaxone loss and no theophylline loss by HPLC in 24 hr	1727	I

[a]*Tested in polyolefin containers.*
[b]*Tested in glass containers.*
[c]*Tested in PVC containers.*
[d]*Admixed in the linezolid infusion container.*

Drugs in Syringe Compatibility

			Ceftriaxone sodium				
Drug (in syringe)	*Mfr*	*Amt*	*Mfr*	*Amt*	*Remarks*	*Ref*	*C/I*
Lidocaine HCl	LY	1%	RC	450 mg/ml	5% or less ceftriaxone loss by HPLC in 8 weeks at −15 °C but solution failed the particulate matter test	1824	I
	DW	1%	RC	250 and 450 mg/ml	10% ceftriaxone loss in 3 days at 20 °C, 7 to 8% loss in 35 days at 4 °C, and 4 to 6% loss in 168 days at −20 °C. Lidocaine not tested	1991	C

Y-Site Injection Compatibility (1:1 Mixture)

			Ceftriaxone sodium				
Drug	*Mfr*	*Conc*	*Mfr*	*Conc*	*Remarks*	*Ref*	*C/I*
Acyclovir sodium	BW	5 mg/ml[a]	RC	20 mg/ml[a]	Physically compatible for 4 hr at 25 °C	1157	C
Alatrofloxacin mesylate	PF	1.43 mg/ml[a]	RC	66.7 mg/ml[g]	White precipitate forms	2235	I
Allopurinol sodium	BW	3 mg/ml[b]	RC	20 mg/ml[b]	Physically compatible with no change in measured turbidity or increase in particle content in 4 hr at 22 °C	1686	C
Amifostine	USB	10 mg/ml[a]	RC	20 mg/ml[a]	Physically compatible with no change in measured turbidity or increase in particle content in 4 hr at 23 °C	1845	C
Amphotericin B cholesteryl sulfate complex	SEQ	0.83 mg/ml[a]	RC	20 mg/ml[a]	Decreased natural turbidity occurs immediately	2117	I
Amsacrine	NCI	1 mg/ml[a]	RC	40 mg/ml[a]	Immediate orange turbidity, developing into flocculent precipitate in 4 hr	1381	I
Aztreonam	SQ	40 mg/ml[a]	RC	20 mg/ml[a]	Physically compatible with no subvisual haze or particle formation in 4 hr at 23 °C	1758	C
Cisatracurium besylate	GW	0.1, 2, 5 mg/ml[a]	RC	20 mg/ml[a]	Physically compatible with no change in measured turbidity or increase in particle content in 4 hr at 23 °C	2074	C
Diltiazem HCl	MMD	5 mg/ml	RC	40 mg/ml[b]	Visually compatible	1807	C
Docetaxel	RPR	0.9 mg/ml[a]	RC	20 mg/ml[a]	Physically compatible with no change in measured turbidity or increase in particle content in 4 hr at 23 °C	2224	C

Y-Site Injection Compatibility (1:1 Mixture) (Cont.)

			Ceftriaxone sodium				
Drug	*Mfr*	*Conc*	*Mfr*	*Conc*	*Remarks*	*Ref*	*C/I*
Doxorubicin HCl liposome injection	SEQ	0.4 mg/ml[a]	RC	20 mg/ml[a]	Physically compatible with little or no change in measured turbidity and no increase in particle content in 4 hr at 23 °C	2087	C
Etoposide phosphate	BR	5 mg/ml[a]	RC	20 mg/ml[a]	Physically compatible with no change in measured turbidity or increase in particle content in 4 hr at 23 °C	2218	C
Famotidine	ME	2 mg/ml[b]		20 mg/ml[a]	Visually compatible for 4 hr at 22 °C	1936	C
Filgrastim	AMG	30 μg/ml[a]	RC	20 mg/ml[a]	Particles and filaments form in 1 hr	1687	I
Fluconazole	RR	2 mg/ml	RC	40 mg/ml	Immediate precipitation	1407	I
Fludarabine phosphate	BX	1 mg/ml[a]	RC	20 mg/ml[a]	Physically compatible for 4 hr at room temperature under fluorescent light	1439	C
Foscarnet sodium	AST	24 mg/ml	RC	20 mg/ml[c]	Physically compatible for 24 hr at 25 °C under fluorescent light by visual and microscopic examination	1393	C
Gatifloxacin	BMS	2 mg/ml[a]	RC	20 mg/ml[a]	Physically compatible with no change in measured haze or increase in particle content in 4 hr at 23 °C	2234	C
Gemcitabine HCl	LI	10 mg/ml[b]	RC	20 mg/ml[b]	Physically compatible with no change in measured turbidity or increase in particle content in 4 hr at 23 °C	2226	C
Granisetron HCl	SKB	0.05 mg/ml[a]	RC	20 mg/ml[a]	Physically compatible with no change in measured turbidity or increase in particle content in 4 hr at 23 °C	2000	C
Heparin sodium	TR	50 units/ml	RC	20 mg/ml	Visually compatible for 4 hr at 25 °C	1793	C
Hetastarch in lactated electrolyte injection (Hextend)	AB	6%	RC	20 mg/ml[a]	Physically compatible with no change in measured turbidity or increase in particle content in 4 hr at 23 °C	2339	C
Labetalol HCl	GL	2.5[d] and 5 mg/ml	RC	20[a,b] and 100[d] mg/ml	Fluffy white precipitate forms immediately	1964	I
Linezolid	PHU	2 mg/ml	RC	20 mg/ml[a]	Physically compatible with no change in measured turbidity or increase in particle content in 4 hr at 23 °C	2264	C
Melphalan HCl	BW	0.1 mg/ml[b]	RC	20 mg/ml[b]	Physically compatible with no change in measured turbidity or increase in particle content in 3 hr at 22 °C	1557	C
Meperidine HCl	AB	10 mg/ml	RC	20 and 40 mg/ml[a]	Physically compatible for 4 hr at 25 °C	1397	C
Methotrexate sodium		30 mg/ml	RC	100 mg/ml	Visually compatible for 4 hr at room temperature	1788	C
Morphine sulfate	AB	1 mg/ml	RC	20 and 40 mg/ml[a]	Physically compatible for 4 hr at 25 °C	1397	C
Paclitaxel	NCI	1.2 mg/ml[a]	RC	20 mg/ml[a]	Physically compatible with no change in measured turbidity in 4 hr at 22 °C	1556	C
Pentamidine isethionate	FUJ	3 mg/ml[a]	RC	20 mg/ml[a]	Heavy white precipitate forms immediately	1880	I

Y-Site Injection Compatibility (1:1 Mixture) (Cont.)

			Ceftriaxone sodium				
Drug	*Mfr*	*Conc*	*Mfr*	*Conc*	*Remarks*	*Ref*	*C/I*
Propofol	ZEN	10 mg/ml	RC	20 mg/ml[a]	Physically compatible for 1 hr at 23 °C with no increase in particle content	2066	C
Remifentanil HCl	GW	0.025 and 0.25 mg/ml[b]	RC	20 mg/ml[a]	Physically compatible with no change in measured turbidity or increase in particle content in 4 hr at 23 °C	2075	C
Sargramostim	IMM	10 μg/ml[b]	RC	20 mg/ml[b]	Physically compatible for 4 hr at 22 °C	1436	C
Sodium bicarbonate		1.4%	RC	100 mg/ml	Visually compatible for 4 hr at room temperature	1788	C
Tacrolimus	FUJ	1 mg/ml[b]	RC	40 mg/ml[a]	Visually compatible for 24 hr at 25 °C	1630	C
Teniposide	BR	0.1 mg/ml[a]	RC	20 mg/ml[a]	Physically compatible with no subvisual haze or particle formation in 4 hr at 23 °C	1725	C
Theophylline	TR	4 mg/ml	RC	20 mg/ml	Visually compatible for 6 hr at 25 °C	1793	C
Thiotepa	IMM[e]	1 mg/ml[a]	RC	20 mg/ml[a]	Physically compatible with no change in measured turbidity or increase in particle content in 4 hr at 23 °C	1861	C
TNA #218 to #226[f]			RC	20 mg/ml[a]	Visually compatible with no precipitate or emulsion damage apparent in 4 hr at 23 °C	2215	C
TPN #189[f]			RC	100 mg/ml[d]	Visually compatible for 24 hr at 22 °C	1767	C
TPN #212 to #215[f]			RC	20 mg/ml[a]	Physically compatible with no change in measured turbidity or increase in particle content in 4 hr at 23 °C	2109	C
Vancomycin HCl	LI	20 mg/ml	RC	100 mg/ml	White precipitate forms immediately	1398	I
	AB	20 mg/ml[a]	RC	250 mg/ml[d]	Transient precipitate forms, followed by clear solution	2189	?
	AB	20 mg/ml[a]	RC	10 and 50 mg/ml[a]	Gross white precipitate forms immediately	2189	I
	AB	20 mg/ml[a]	RC	1 mg/ml[a]	Subvisual measured haze forms immediately	2189	I
	AB	2 mg/ml[a]	RC	1[a], 10[a], 50[a], 250[d] mg/ml	Physically compatible with no change in measured turbidity or increase in particle content in 4 hr at 23 °C	2189	C
Vinorelbine tartrate	BW	1 mg/ml[b]	RC	20 mg/ml[b]	Tiny particles form immediately, becoming more numerous in 4 hr	1558	I
Warfarin sodium	DME	2 mg/ml[d]	RC	20 mg/ml[a]	Visually compatible for 24 hr at 24 °C	2078	C
Zidovudine	BW	4 mg/ml[a]	RC	20 mg/ml[a]	Physically compatible for 4 hr at 25 °C under fluorescent light by visual and microscopic examination	1193	C

[a]*Tested in dextrose 5% in water.*
[b]*Tested in sodium chloride 0.9%.*
[c]*Tested in both dextrose 5% in water and sodium chloride 0.9%.*
[d]*Tested in sterile water for injection.*
[e]*Lyophilized formulation tested.*
[f]*Refer to Appendix I for the composition of parenteral nutrition solutions. TNA indicates a 3-in-1 admixture, and TPN indicates a 2-in-1 admixture.*
[g]*Tested in sodium chloride 0.45%.*

Additional Compatibility Information

Infusion Solutions — Ceftriaxone sodium is stable, exhibiting less than a 10% potency loss in the following solutions in the time periods indicated (2):

Diluent	Concentrations (mg/ml)	25 °C	4 °C
Amino acid injection 8.5% (FreAmine III)	10 to 40[a]	24 hr	
Dextrose 5% in sodium chloride 0.45%	10[b], 20[b], 40[b], 100[a]	3 days	Incompatible
Dextrose 5% in sodium chloride 0.9%	10[c], 20[c], 40[c], 100[a]	3 days	Incompatible
Dextrose 5% in water	10[b], 20[b], 40[b], 100[a]	3 days	10 days
Dextrose 10% in water	10[b], 20[b], 40[b], 100[a]	3 days	10 days
Ionosol B in dextrose 5%	10 to 40[a]	24 hr	
Invert sugar 10% in water	10 to 40[a]	24 hr	
Mannitol 5% in water	10 to 40[a]	24 hr	
Mannitol 10% in water	10 to 40[a]	24 hr	
Normosol M in dextrose 5%	10 to 40[b]	24 hr	
Sodium bicarbonate 5%	10 to 40[a]	24 hr	
Sodium chloride 0.9%	10[b], 20[b], 40[b], 100[a]	3 days	10 days
Sodium lactate injection	10 to 40[c]	24 hr	
Sterile water for injection	10[b], 20[b], 40[b], 100[a]	3 days	10 days

[a] *Tested in glass containers.*
[b] *Tested in both glass and PVC containers.*
[c] *Tested in PVC containers.*

Ceftriaxone sodium at concentrations of 10 to 40 mg/ml is incompatible with calcium-containing solutions, including Ringer's injection and Ringer's injection, lactated. Precipitation has been observed to form rapidly. (2222)

Peritoneal Dialysis Solutions — Ceftriaxone sodium (Roche) 1 mg/ml in Dianeal PD-1 with dextrose 1.5 and 4.25% was stable, retaining at least 90% potency by HPLC for 14 days at 4 °C, 24 hours at 23 °C, or six hours at 37 °C. (1592)

Vancomycin — The compatibility or incompatibility of vancomycin HCl mixed with or administered simultaneously with ceftriaxone sodium is concentration dependent. (2189) See Y-Site Compatibility above. Vancomycin HCl has a low pH and is variably compatible with drugs having neutral to mildly alkaline pH, including cephalosporins and penicillins. The compatibility may depend on a number of factors, including concentration of each drug, dilution vehicle, actual pH of solutions, and completeness of mixing during administration. Combinations that are compatible when well mixed may result in precipitation if only partially mixed, presumably due to regionally different concentrations and pH values. If attempting to administer vancomycin HCl with ceftriaxone sodium, take care to ensure that the specific combination and the concentrations are compatible under the exact administration conditions to be used. An inline filter should be used as a final safety measure. (2189)

Other Drugs — The manufacturer recommends that ceftriaxone sodium not be physically combined with other drugs. (2)

CEFUROXIME SODIUM
AHFS 8:12.06

Products — Cefuroxime sodium is available in vials and infusion packs containing 750 mg and 1.5 g of drug. The drug is also available in a 7.5-g pharmacy bulk package. (2)

The vials should be reconstituted with sterile water for injection. Infusion packs may be reconstituted with sterile water for injection or any compatible infusion solution. (See Additional Compatibility Information.) Recommended volumes for reconstitution are shown in Table 1. (2)

The intramuscular concentration of 220 mg/ml is a suspension. The suspension should be dispersed with shaking before the dose is withdrawn. (2)

The 7.5-g pharmacy bulk package should be reconstituted with 77 ml of sterile water for injection to yield a 95-mg/ml concentration. (2)

Previously, a significant overfill was present in the 750-mg vials of cefuroxime sodium (Glaxo). (1081) However, the manufacturer has changed the product, greatly reducing the overfill. (1082)

Table 1. Recommended Dilutions of Cefuroxime Sodium (2)

Vial Size	Route	Volume of Diluent	Approximate Concentration
750 mg	Intramuscular (suspension)	3 ml	220 mg/ml
	Intravenous	8 ml	90 mg/ml
(Infusion pack)	Intravenous	100 ml	7.5 mg/ml
1.5 g	Intravenous	16 ml	90 mg/ml
(Infusion pack)	Intravenous	100 ml	15 mg/ml

Cefuroxime sodium is also available as a frozen premixed solution containing 750 mg or 1.5 g in 50-ml PVC bags. Approximately 1.4 g of dextrose hydrous has been added to the 750-mg bags to adjust the osmolality. Both the 750-mg and 1.5-g bags also contain sodium citrate hydrous 300 and 600 mg, respectively. The pH is adjusted with hydrochloric acid and may have been adjusted with sodium hydroxide. (2)

pH—The reconstituted vials have a pH of 6 to 8.5. The frozen premixed solutions have a pH of 5 to 7.5. (2)

Osmolality—The osmolality of the frozen premixed cefuroxime sodium solutions is approximately 300 mOsm/kg. (2)

The osmolality of cefuroxime sodium (Glaxo) 30 mg/ml was determined to be 315 mOsm/kg in dextrose 5% in water and 314 mOsm/kg in sodium chloride 0.9%. At a concentration of 50 mg/ml, the osmolality was determined to be 329 mOsm/kg in dextrose 5% in water and 335 mOsm/kg in sodium chloride 0.9%. (1375)

Robinson et al. recommended the following maximum cefuroxime sodium concentrations to achieve osmolalities suitable for peripheral infusion in fluid-restricted patients (1180):

Diluent	Maximum Concentration (mg/ml)	Osmolality (mOsm/kg)
Dextrose 5% in water	76	568
Sodium chloride 0.9%	68	541
Sterile water for injection	137	489

Sodium Content—Cefuroxime sodium vials contain 2.4 mEq (54.2 mg) per gram of cefuroxime activity. The frozen premixed 750-mg and 1.5-g solutions contain 4.8 mEq (111 mg) and 9.7 mEq (222 mg), respectively. (2)

Trade Name(s)—Zinacef.

Administration — Cefuroxime sodium is administered by deep intramuscular injection, by direct intravenous injection over three to five minutes directly into the vein or into the tubing of a running infusion solution, by intermittent intravenous infusion over 15 to 60 minutes, or by continuous intravenous infusion. The manufacturer recommends temporarily discontinuing the primary solution when giving the drug by Y-site infusion. (2; 4)

Stability — Intact vials should be stored at controlled room temperature and protected from light. The drug is present as a white to off-white powder. Solutions may range in color from light yellow to amber. Both the powder and solutions of cefuroxime sodium darken, depending on storage conditions, without affecting their potency. (2; 4)

The reconstituted suspension for intramuscular injection and the 90 to 100-mg/ml intravenous solution concentrations are stable for 24 hours at room temperature and 48 hours when refrigerated at 5 °C. The bulk pharmacy vial reconstituted to a concentration of 95 mg/ml is stable for 24 hours at room temperature or seven days under refrigeration. Dilution to concentrations of 1 to 30 mg/ml in compatible diluents results in solutions that are stable for 24 hours at room temperature or seven days under refrigeration. (2; 4)

pH Effects—The pH of maximum stability is in the range of 4.5 to 7.3. (712)

Freezing Solutions—Commercial, frozen, premixed cefuroxime sodium injections are stable for at least 90 days after shipment when stored at −20 °C. Frozen solutions should be thawed at room temperature or under refrigeration. Some solution components may precipitate in the frozen state, but the precipitate redissolves upon thawing and reaching room temperature. Thawed solutions are stable for 24 hours at room temperature or 28 days at 5 °C. (2; 4)

Extemporaneously prepared solutions of cefuroxime sodium 750 mg or 1.5 g added to 50- to 100-ml PVC bags of dextrose 5% in water or sodium chloride 0.9% are stable for six months at −20 °C. The manufacturer does not recommend the use of water baths or microwaves for thawing. Following thawing at room temperature, the solutions are stable for 24 hours at room temperature or seven days under refrigeration. The thawed solutions should not be refrozen. (2; 4)

Minibags of cefuroxime sodium in dextrose 5% in water or sodium chloride 0.9%, frozen at −20 °C for up to 35 days, were thawed at room temperature and in a microwave oven, with care taken that the thawed solution temperature never exceeded 25 °C. No significant differences in cefuroxime sodium concentrations occurred between the two thawing methods. (1192)

Cefuroxime sodium (Glaxo) 30 and 60 mg/ml in sterile water for injection in PVC portable infusion pump reservoirs (Pharmacia Deltec) and glass vials exhibited a 4% loss by HPLC after 30 days at −20 °C. Subsequent storage for four days at 3 °C resulted in about a 10% loss in the PVC bags and a 4% loss in the glass vials. (1581)

Cefuroxime sodium (Glaxo) 5 and 10 mg/ml in both dextrose 5% in water and in sodium chloride 0.9% in glass containers and PVC bags was stored frozen at −10 °C for 30 days. The drug solutions remained clear and exhibited no loss determined by stability-indicating HPLC analysis. (712)

Syringes—Cefuroxime sodium (Glaxo) 125 mg/ml in sterile water for injection, packaged as 0.24 ml in 1-ml Injekt syringes (Braun) sealed with blind hubs and stored at about 6 °C, retained antibiotic activity against *Escherichia coli* for seven days. However, the yellow color of the solution became much darker over this period. About 14% loss occurred in 14 days. (1697)

Ambulatory Pumps—Cefuroxime sodium (Glaxo) 22.5 and 45 mg/ml in sterile water for injection in PVC portable infusion pump reservoirs (Pharmacia Deltec) exhibited a 4 to 6% loss by HPLC in eight hours and an 11 to 12% loss in 16 hours at 30 °C. No loss occurred in 7 days at 3 °C. (1581)

Elastomeric Reservoir Pumps—Cefuroxime sodium solutions in elastomeric reservoir pumps have been stated by the pump manufacturers to be stable for the following time periods frozen, refrigerated (REF), or at room temperature (RT) (31):

Pump Reservoir(s)	Conc.	Frozen	REF	RT
Homepump; Homepump Eclipse	1 to 30 mg/ml[a,b]	6 months	7 days	24 hr
Intermate	15 to 30 mg/ml[a]		7 days	15 hr
Intermate HPC	5 to 30 mg/ml[a,b]	30 days	10 days	
ReadyMed	15 mg/ml[b]	4 weeks	14 days	48 hr

[a]*In dextrose 5% in water.*
[b]*In sodium chloride 0.9%.*

Sorption—Cefuroxime sodium 6 mg/ml in dextrose 5% in water and sodium chloride 0.9% exhibited no loss due to sorption to PVC containers over 24 hours and to administration sets during one-hour simulated infusions. (1953)

Central Venous Catheter—Cefuroxime sodium (Glaxo Wellcome) 10 mg/ml in dextrose 5% in water was found to be compatible with the ARROWg+ard Blue Plus (Arrow International) chlorhexidine-bearing triple-lumen central catheter. HPLC analysis was used to evaluate completeness of drug delivery through the catheter and the amount of chlorhexidine removed from the internal lumens. Essentially complete delivery of the drug was found with little or no drug loss occurring. Furthermore, chlorhexidine delivered from the catheter remained at trace amounts with no substantial increase due to the delivery of the drug through the catheter. (2335)

Compatibility Information

Solution Compatibility

Cefuroxime sodium

Solution	*Mfr*	*Mfr*	*Conc/L*	*Remarks*	*Ref*	*C/I*
Dextrose 5% in water	MG[a]	GL	15 g	5% loss in 48 hr at 25 °C under fluorescent light	1164	C
	[b]		6 g	Visually compatible with little or no loss by HPLC in 24 hr at room temperature and 4 °C	1953	C
	BA[a]	GL	15 g	Visually compatible with 7% loss by HPLC in 11 days at 4 °C	2142	C
	BA[a,b]	GL	5 and 10 g	Physically compatible with about 7% cefuroxime loss in 24 hr and 13% loss in 48 hr at 25 °C. About 4% loss at 5 °C and no loss at −10 °C in 30 days	712	C
Sodium chloride 0.9%	MG[a]	GL	15 g	5% loss in 48 hr at 25 °C under fluorescent light	1164	C
	[b]		6 g	Visually compatible with little or no loss by HPLC in 24 hr at room temperature and 4 °C	1953	C
	BA[a,b]	GL	5 and 10 g	Physically compatible with about 7% cefuroxime loss in 24 hr and 13% loss in 48 hr at 25 °C. About 4% loss at 5 °C and no loss at −10 °C in 30 days	712	C
TPN #107[c]			1 g	Physically compatible and cefuroxime activity retained for 24 hr at 21 °C by microbiological assay	1326	C

[a]*Tested in glass bottles.*
[b]*Tested in PVC containers.*
[c]*Refer to Appendix I for the composition of parenteral nutrition solutions. TPN indicates a 2-in-1 admixture.*

Additive Compatibility

Cefuroxime sodium

Drug	*Mfr*	*Conc/L*	*Mfr*	*Conc/L*	*Test Soln*	*Remarks*	*Ref*	*C/I*
Ciprofloxacin	MI	2 g		30 g	D5W	Physically incompatible	888	I
Clindamycin phosphate	UP	9 g	GL	15 g	D5W	Physically compatible with 4% clindamycin loss and 6 to 8% cefuroxime loss in 48 hr at 25 °C under fluorescent light	1164	C
	UP	9 g	GL	15 g	NS	Physically compatible with 9% clindamycin and cefuroxime loss in 48 hr at 25 °C under fluorescent light	1164	C
	UP	9 g	GL	15 g	D5W[a]	Physically compatible with 6% cefuroxime loss and 4% clindamycin loss in 48 hr at room temperature	174	C
	UP	9 g	GL	15 g	NS[a]	Physically compatible with 9% cefuroxime and clindamycin loss in 48 hr at room temperature	174	C
Floxacillin sodium	BE	20 g	GL	37.5 g	W	Physically compatible for 72 hr at 15 and 30 °C	1479	C
	BE	10 g	GL	7.5 g	D5W, NS	Physically compatible for 48 hr. Potency of both drugs retained when assayed after 1 hr at room temperature	1036	C

Additive Compatibility (Cont.)

Cefuroxime sodium

Drug	*Mfr*	*Conc/L*	*Mfr*	*Conc/L*	*Test Soln*	*Remarks*	*Ref*	*C/I*
Furosemide	HO	1 g	GL	37.5 g	W	Physically compatible for 72 hr at 15 and 30 °C	1479	C
Gentamicin sulfate	EX	800 mg	GL	7.5 g	D5W, NS[b]	Physically compatible with no loss of either drug in 1 hr	1036	C
		100 mg		1 g	TPN #107[c]	32% gentamicin loss in 24 hr at 21 °C by microbiological assay	1326	I
Metronidazole		5 g	GL	7.5 g	[b]	Physically compatible with no loss of either drug in 1 hr	1036	C
		5 g	GL	15 g		No loss of either drug in 4 hr at 24 °C	1376	C
		5 g	GL	7.5 g		10% cefuroxime loss by HPLC in 16 days at 4 °C and 35 hr at 25 °C. No metronidazole loss by HPLC in 15 days at 4 and 25 °C	1565	C
	IVX	5 g	GL	7.5 and 15 g		Physically compatible with no visible precipitation or increase in measured particulates. No loss of metronidazole and about 6% cefuroxime loss in 49 days at 5 °C	2192	C
Netilmicin sulfate	EX	1 g	GL	7.5 g	D5W, NS[b]	Physically compatible with no loss of either drug in 1 hr	1036	C
Ranitidine HCl	GL	100 mg	GL	1.5 g	D5W	Color change within 24 hr at ambient temperature under fluorescent light	1151	?
	GL	50 mg and 2 g		6 g	D5W	Ranitidine chemically stable by HPLC for only 6 hr at 25 °C. Cefuroxime not tested	1515	I

[a]*Tested in both glass and PVC containers.*
[b]*Tested in PVC containers.*
[c]*Refer to Appendix I for the composition of parenteral nutrition solutions. TPN indicates a 2-in-1 admixture.*

Drugs in Syringe Compatibility

Cefuroxime sodium

Drug (in syringe)	*Mfr*	*Amt*	*Mfr*	*Amt*	*Remarks*	*Ref*	*C/I*
Doxapram HCl	RB	400 mg/ 20 ml	GL	750 mg/ 7 ml	Immediate turbidity	1177	I

Y-Site Injection Compatibility (1:1 Mixture)

Cefuroxime sodium

Drug	*Mfr*	*Conc*	*Mfr*	*Conc*	*Remarks*	*Ref*	*C/I*
Acyclovir sodium	BW	5 mg/ml[a]	GL	15 mg/ml[a]	Physically compatible for 4 hr at 25 °C	1157	C
Allopurinol sodium	BW	3 mg/ml[b]	GL	20 mg/ml[b]	Physically compatible with no change in measured turbidity or increase in particle content in 4 hr at 22 °C	1686	C
Amifostine	USB	10 mg/ml[a]	GL	30 mg/ml[a]	Physically compatible with no change in measured turbidity or increase in particle content in 4 hr at 23 °C	1845	C
Atracurium besylate	BW	0.5 mg/ml[a]	GL	7.5 mg/ml[a]	Physically compatible for 24 hr at 28 °C	1337	C

Y-Site Injection Compatibility (1:1 Mixture) (Cont.)

Cefuroxime sodium

Drug	*Mfr*	*Conc*	*Mfr*	*Conc*	*Remarks*	*Ref*	*C/I*
Aztreonam	SQ	40 mg/ml[a]	LI	30 mg/ml[a]	Physically compatible with no subvisual haze or particle formation in 4 hr at 23 °C	1758	C
Cisatracurium besylate	GW	0.1 mg/ml[a]	LI	30 mg/ml[a]	Physically compatible with no change in measured turbidity or increase in particle content in 4 hr at 23 °C	2074	C
	GW	2 mg/ml[a]	LI	30 mg/ml[a]	White cloudiness forms immediately	2074	I
	GW	5 mg/ml[a]	LI	30 mg/ml[a]	Turbidity formed immediately	2074	I
Clarithromycin	AB	4 mg/ml[a]	GW	60 mg/ml[a]	White precipitate forms in 3 hr at 30 °C and 24 hr at 17 °C	2174	I
Cyclophosphamide	MJ	20 mg/ml[a]	GL	30 mg/ml[a]	Physically compatible for 4 hr at 25 °C	1194	C
Diltiazem HCl	MMD	5 mg/ml	LI	15 and 100 mg/ml[b]	Visually compatible	1807	C
	MMD	1 mg/ml[b]	LI	100 mg/ml[b]	Visually compatible	1807	C
Docetaxel	RPR	0.9 mg/ml[a]	LI	30 mg/ml[a]	Physically compatible with no change in measured turbidity or increase in particle content in 4 hr at 23 °C	2224	C
Etoposide phosphate	BR	5 mg/ml[a]	GW	30 mg/ml[a]	Physically compatible with no change in measured turbidity or increase in particle content in 4 hr at 23 °C	2218	C
Famotidine	MSD	0.2 mg/ml[a]	GL	15 mg/ml[b]	Physically compatible for 14 hr	1196	C
	ME	2 mg/ml[b]		20 mg/ml[a]	Visually compatible for 4 hr at 22 °C	1936	C
Filgrastim	AMG	30 μg/ml[a]	GL	20 mg/ml[a]	Haze, particles, and filaments form immediately	1687	I
Fluconazole	RR	2 mg/ml	GL	30 mg/ml	Immediate precipitation	1407	I
Fludarabine phosphate	BX	1 mg/ml[a]	GL	30 mg/ml[a]	Physically compatible for 4 hr at room temperature under fluorescent light	1439	C
Foscarnet sodium	AST	24 mg/ml	GL	30 mg/ml	Physically compatible for 24 hr at room temperature under fluorescent light	1335	C
Gemcitabine HCl	LI	10 mg/ml[b]	GW	30 mg/ml[b]	Physically compatible with no change in measured turbidity or increase in particle content in 4 hr at 23 °C	2226	C
Granisetron HCl	SKB	0.05 mg/ml[a]	LI	30 mg/ml[a]	Physically compatible with no change in measured turbidity or increase in particle content in 4 hr at 23 °C	2000	C
Hetastarch in lactated electrolyte injection (Hextend)	AB	6%	LI	30 mg/ml[a]	Physically compatible with no change in measured turbidity or increase in particle content in 4 hr at 23 °C	2339	C
Hydromorphone HCl	WY	0.2 mg/ml[a]	GL	30 mg/ml[a]	Physically compatible for at least 4 hr at 25 °C under fluorescent light	987	C
Linezolid	PHU	2 mg/ml	GL	30 mg/ml[a]	Physically compatible with no change in measured turbidity or increase in particle content in 4 hr at 23 °C	2264	C
Melphalan HCl	BW	0.1 mg/ml[b]	GL	20 mg/ml[b]	Physically compatible with no change in measured turbidity or increase in particle content in 3 hr at 22 °C	1557	C

Y-Site Injection Compatibility (1:1 Mixture) (Cont.)

			Cefuroxime sodium				
Drug	*Mfr*	*Conc*	*Mfr*	*Conc*	*Remarks*	*Ref*	*C/I*
Meperidine HCl	WY	10 mg/ml[a]	GL	30 mg/ml[a]	Physically compatible for at least 4 hr at 25 °C under fluorescent light	987	C
Midazolam HCl	RC	1 mg/ml[a]	LI	15 mg/ml[a]	Particles form in 8 hr	1847	I
Morphine sulfate	WI	1 mg/ml[a]	GL	30 mg/ml[a]	Physically compatible for at least 4 hr at 25 °C under fluorescent light	987	C
Ondansetron HCl	GL	1 mg/ml[b]	LI	30 mg/ml[a]	Physically compatible for 4 hr at 22 °C	1365	C
Pancuronium bromide	ES	0.05 mg/ml[a]	GL	7.5 mg/ml[a]	Physically compatible for 24 hr at 28 °C	1337	C
Perphenazine	SC	0.02 mg/ml[a]	GL	30 mg/ml[a]	Physically compatible for 4 hr at 25 °C	1155	C
Propofol	ZEN	10 mg/ml	LI	30 mg/ml[a]	Physically compatible for 1 hr at 23 °C with no increase in particle content	2066	C
Remifentanil HCl	GW	0.025 and 0.25 mg/ml[b]	LI	30 mg/ml[a]	Physically compatible with no change in measured turbidity or increase in particle content in 4 hr at 23 °C	2075	C
Sargramostim	IMM	10 μg/ml[b]	GL	30 mg/ml[b]	Physically compatible for 4 hr at 22 °C	1436	C
Tacrolimus	FUJ	1 mg/ml[b]	LI	30 mg/ml[a]	Visually compatible for 24 hr at 25 °C	1630	C
Teniposide	BR	0.1 mg/ml[a]	GL	20 mg/ml[a]	Physically compatible with no subvisual haze or particle formation in 4 hr at 23 °C	1725	C
Thiotepa	IMM[c]	1 mg/ml[a]	LI	30 mg/ml[a]	Physically compatible with no change in measured turbidity or increase in particle content in 4 hr at 23 °C	1861	C
TNA #218 to #226[d]			GL	30 mg/ml[a]	Visually compatible with no precipitate or emulsion damage apparent in 4 hr at 23 °C	2215	C
TPN #212 to #215[d]			LI	30 mg/ml[a]	Physically compatible with no change in measured turbidity or increase in particle content in 4 hr at 23 °C	2109	C
Vancomycin HCl	AB	20 mg/ml[a]	GW	150 mg/ml[e]	Transient precipitate forms, followed by a subvisual measured haze	2189	I
	AB	20 mg/ml[a]	GW	50 mg/ml[a]	Gross white precipitate forms immediately	2189	I
	AB	20 mg/ml[a]	GW	10 mg/ml[a]	Subvisual measured haze forms immediately	2189	I
	AB	20 mg/ml[a]	GW	1 mg/ml[a]	Physically compatible with no change in measured turbidity or increase in particle content in 4 hr at 23 °C	2189	C
	AB	2 mg/ml[a]	GW	1[a], 10[a], 50[a], 150[e] mg/ml	Physically compatible with no change in measured turbidity or increase in particle content in 4 hr at 23 °C	2189	C
Vecuronium bromide	OR	0.1 mg/ml[a]	GL	7.5 mg/ml[a]	Physically compatible for 24 hr at 28 °C	1337	C
Vinorelbine tartrate	BW	1 mg/ml[b]	GL	20 mg/ml[b]	Large increase in measured turbidity occurs immediately and grows over 4 hr at 22 °C	1558	I

[a]*Tested in dextrose 5% in water.*
[b]*Tested in sodium chloride 0.9%.*
[c]*Lyophilized formulation tested.*
[d]*Refer to Appendix I for the composition of parenteral nutrition solutions. TNA indicates a 3-in-1 admixture, and TPN indicates a 2-in-1 admixture.*
[e]*Tested in sterile water for injection.*

Additional Compatibility Information

Infusion Solutions — The manufacturer states that cefuroxime sodium 1 to 30 mg/ml is stable in the following infusion solutions for 24 hours at room temperature or at least seven days under refrigeration, losing not more than 10% activity (2):

Dextrose 5% in sodium chloride 0.2, 0.45, and 0.9%
Dextrose 5 and 10% in water
Invert sugar 10%
Ringer's injection
Ringer's injection, lactated
Sodium chloride 0.9%
Sodium lactate ⅙ M

Vancomycin — The compatibility or incompatibility of vancomycin HCl mixed with or administered simultaneously with cefuroxime sodium is concentration dependent. (2189) See Y-Site Compatibility above. Vancomycin HCl has a low pH and is variably compatible with drugs having neutral to mildly alkaline pH, including cephalosporins and penicillins. The compatibility may depend on a number of factors, including concentration of each drug, dilution vehicle, actual pH of solutions, and completeness of mixing during administration. Combinations that are compatible when well mixed may result in precipitation if only partially mixed, presumably because of regionally different concentrations and pH values. If attempting to administer vancomycin HCl with cefuroxime sodium, take care to ensure that the specific combination and the concentrations are compatible under the exact administration conditions to be used. An inline filter should be used as a final safety measure. (2189)

Other Drugs — The manufacturer states that cefuroxime sodium is compatible admixed with heparin sodium 10 and 50 units/ml and potassium chloride 10 and 40 mEq/L in sodium chloride 0.9%. (2)

The manufacturer recommends that cefuroxime sodium not be mixed with sodium bicarbonate injection or aminoglycosides. (2)

CHLORAMPHENICOL SODIUM SUCCINATE
AHFS 8:12.08

Products — Chloramphenicol sodium succinate is available in vials containing the equivalent of chloramphenicol 1 g as the sodium succinate salt. The manufacturer recommends reconstitution with 10 ml of an aqueous diluent such as water for injection or dextrose 5% in water to yield a solution containing 100 mg/ml (10%) of chloramphenicol. (1-3/99; 4)

pH — From 6.4 to 7. (4; 6)

Osmolality — Chloramphenicol sodium succinate 100 mg/ml in sterile water for injection has an osmolality of 533 mOsm/kg as determined by freezing-point depression. (1071)

The osmolality of chloramphenicol sodium succinate 1 g was calculated for the following dilutions (1054):

	Osmolality (mOsm/kg)	
Diluent	50 ml	100 ml
Dextrose 5% in water	341	303
Sodium chloride 0.9%	368	330

The osmolality of chloramphenicol sodium succinate (Parke-Davis) 20 mg/ml was determined to be 330 mOsm/kg in dextrose 5% in water and 344 mOsm/kg in sodium chloride 0.9%. At 50 mg/ml, the osmolality was determined to be 417 and 422 mOsm/kg, respectively. (1375)

Robinson et al. recommended the following maximum chloramphenicol sodium succinate concentrations to achieve osmolalities suitable for peripheral infusion in fluid-restricted patients (1180):

Diluent	Maximum Concentration (mg/ml)	Osmolality (mOsm/kg)
Dextrose 5% in water	71	554
Sodium chloride 0.9%	64	538
Sterile water for injection	128	473

Sodium Content — Chloramphenicol sodium succinate contains 2.25 mEq (52 mg) of sodium per gram of drug. (1-3/99; 4)

Trade Name(s) — Chloromycetin Sodium Succinate.

Administration — Chloramphenicol sodium succinate injection at a concentration not exceeding 100 mg/ml may be administered by direct intravenous injection over at least one minute. (1-3/99; 4)

Stability — Intact vials should be stored at controlled room temperature. The reconstituted solution is stable for 30 days at room temperature. (4; 6; 108) Cloudy solutions should not be used. (4) The stability of frozen solutions of chloramphenicol sodium succinate has been stated to be six months. (108)

pH Effects — Chloramphenicol is stable over a pH range of 2 to 7, with maximum stability at pH 6. (1072) Chloramphenicol activity was retained for 24 hours at pH 3.6 to 7.5 in dextrose 5% in water. (6)

Sorption — Chloramphenicol sodium succinate (Parke-Davis) 12 mg/L in sodium chloride 0.9% (Travenol) in PVC bags did not exhibit significant sorption to the plastic during one week of storage at room temperature (15 to 20 °C). (536)

In another study, chloramphenicol sodium succinate (Parke-Davis) 12 mg/L in sodium chloride 0.9% did not exhibit any loss due to sorption during a seven-hour simulated infusion through an infusion set (Travenol) consisting of a cellulose propionate burette chamber and 170 cm of PVC tubing. (606)

The drug was also tested as a simulated infusion over at least one hour by a syringe pump system. A glass syringe on a syringe pump was fitted with 20 cm of polyethylene tubing or 50 cm of Silastic tubing. No loss of drug due to sorption was observed with either tubing. (606)

A 25-ml aliquot of chloramphenicol sodium succinate (Parke-Davis) 12 mg/L in sodium chloride 0.9% stored in all-plastic syringes composed of polypropylene barrels and polyethylene plungers for 24 hours at room temperature in the dark did not exhibit any loss due to sorption. (606)

Compatibility Information

Solution Compatibility

Chloramphenicol sodium succinate

Solution	*Mfr*	*Mfr*	*Conc/L*	*Remarks*	*Ref*	*C/I*
Dextran 40,000	PH			Physically compatible	44	C
Dextran 6% in dextrose 5%	AB	PD	1 g	Physically compatible	3	C
Dextran 6% in sodium chloride 0.9%	AB	PD	1 g	Physically compatible	3	C
Dextrose–Ringer's injection combinations	AB	PD	1 g	Physically compatible	3	C
Dextrose–Ringer's injection, lactated, combinations	AB	PD	1 g	Physically compatible	3	C
Dextrose 5% in Ringer's injection, lactated	AB			Potency retained for 24 hr	6	C
Dextrose–saline combinations	AB	PD	1 g	Physically compatible	3	C
Dextrose 5% in sodium chloride 0.9%		PD	500 mg	Physically compatible	74	C
	AB			Potency retained for 24 hr	6	C
		PD	2 g	Potency retained for 24 hr	109	C
Dextrose 2½% in water	AB	PD	1 g	Physically compatible	3	C
Dextrose 5% in water	AB	PD	1 g	Physically compatible	3	C
		PD	500 mg	Physically compatible	74	C
	AB			Potency retained for 24 hr	6	C
		PD	2 g	Potency retained for 24 hr	109	C
			10 g	4% loss in 24 hr at room temperature	768	C
Dextrose 10% in water	AB	PD	1 g	Physically compatible	3	C
	AB			Potency retained for 24 hr	6	C
		PD	2 g	Potency retained for 24 hr	109	C
Fat emulsion 10%, intravenous	VT	PD	2 g	Physically compatible for 48 hr at 4 °C and room temperature	32	C
	VT	PD	2 g	Physically compatible for 24 hr at 25 and 8 °C	825	C
Fructose 10% in sodium chloride 0.9%	AB	PD	1 g	Physically compatible	3	C
Fructose 10% in water	AB	PD	1 g	Physically compatible	3	C
Invert sugar 5 and 10% in sodium chloride 0.9%	AB	PD	1 g	Physically compatible	3	C
Invert sugar 5 and 10% in water	AB	PD	1 g	Physically compatible	3	C
Ionosol products	AB	PD	1 g	Physically compatible	3	C
Normosol M in dextrose 5% in water	AB			Potency retained for 24 hr	6	C
Normosol R	AB			Potency retained for 24 hr	6	C
Ringer's injection	AB	PD	1 g	Physically compatible	3	C
	AB			Potency retained for 24 hr	6	C
Ringer's injection, lactated	AB	PD	1 g	Physically compatible	3	C
		PD	500 mg	Physically compatible	74	C
	AB			Potency retained for 24 hr	6	C

Solution Compatibility (Cont.)

Chloramphenicol sodium succinate

Solution	*Mfr*	*Mfr*	*Conc/L*	*Remarks*	*Ref*	*C/I*
Sodium chloride 0.45%	AB	PD	1 g	Physically compatible	3	C
Sodium chloride 0.9%	AB	PD	1 g	Physically compatible	3	C
		PD	500 mg	Physically compatible	74	C
	AB			Potency retained for 24 hr	6	C
		PD	2 g	Potency retained for 24 hr	109	C
			10 g	4% loss in 24 hr at room temperature	768	C
Sodium lactate ⅙ M	AB	PD	1 g	Physically compatible	3	C

Additive Compatibility

Chloramphenicol sodium succinate

Drug	*Mfr*	*Conc/L*	*Mfr*	*Conc/L*	*Test Soln*	*Remarks*	*Ref*	*C/I*
Amikacin sulfate	BR	5 g	PD	10 g	D5LR, D5R, D5S, D5W, D10W, IS10, LR, NS, R, SL	Physically compatible and potency of both retained for 24 hr at 25 °C	293	C
Aminophylline	SE	1 g	PD	10 g	D5W	Physically compatible	15	C
		250 mg	PD	500 mg	D5W	Physically compatible	74	C
Ascorbic acid injection	AB	1 g	PD	1 g		Physically compatible	3	C
	AB	1 g	PD	1 g		Physically compatible	6	C
Calcium chloride	UP	1 g	PD	10 g	D5W	Physically compatible	15	C
Calcium gluconate		1 g	PD	500 mg	D5W	Physically compatible	74	C
	UP	1 g	PD	10 g	D5W	Physically compatible	15	C
	UP	1 g	PD	10 g		Physically compatible	6	C
Chlorpromazine HCl	BP	200 mg	BP	4 g	D5W	Immediate precipitation	26	I
	BP	200 mg	BP	4 g	NS	Haze develops over 3 hr	26	I
Colistimethate sodium	WC	500 mg	PD	10 g	D5W	Physically compatible	15	C
	WC	500 mg	PD	10 g		Physically compatible	6	C
Corticotropin		500 units	PD	500 mg	D5W	Physically compatible	74	C
Cyanocobalamin	AB	1000 µg	PD	1 g		Physically compatible	6	C
Dimenhydrinate	SE	50 mg	PD	500 mg	D5W	Physically compatible	74	C
Dopamine HCl	AS	800 mg	PD	4 g	D5W	Chloramphenicol and dopamine potency retained for 24 hr at 23 to 25 °C	78	C
Ephedrine sulfate	AB	50 mg	PD	1 g		Physically compatible	6	C
Heparin sodium	UP	4000 units	PD	10 g	D5W	Physically compatible	15	C
	AB	20,000 units	PD	1 g		Physically compatible	6; 21	C
		12,000 units	PD	500 mg	D5W	Physically compatible	74	C
Hydrocortisone sodium succinate	UP	500 mg	PD	10 g	D5W	Physically compatible	15	C
	UP	500 mg	PD	1 g		Physically compatible	6	C
	UP	100 mg	PD	500 mg	D5W	Physically compatible	74	C

Additive Compatibility (Cont.)

Drug	Mfr	Conc/L	Chloramphenicol sodium succinate Mfr	Conc/L	Test Soln	Remarks	Ref	C/I
Hydroxyzine HCl	RR	250 mg	PD	10 g	D5W	Physically incompatible	15	I
Kanamycin sulfate	BR	4 g	PD	10 g	D5W	Physically compatible	15	C
	BR	4 g	PD	10 g		Physically compatible	6	C
Lidocaine HCl	AST	2 g	PD	1 g		Physically compatible	24	C
Magnesium sulfate	LI	16 mEq	PD	10 g	D5W	Physically compatible	15	C
Metaraminol bitartrate	MSD	100 mg	PD	1 g		Physically compatible	7	C
	MSD	200 mg	PD	1 g		Physically compatible	6	C
Methyldopate HCl	MSD	1 g	PD	1 g	D, D–S, S	Physically compatible	23	C
Methylprednisolone sodium succinate	UP	40 mg	PD	1 g	D5W	Clear solution for 20 hr	329	C
	UP	80 mg	PD	2 g	D5W	Clear solution for 20 hr	329	C
Metronidazole	RP	5 g[a]	PD	10 g		Physically compatible with little or no pH change for at least 72 hr at 23 °C	807	C
Metronidazole HCl with sodium bicarbonate	SE AB	5 g 50 mEq	PD	2 g	D5W, NS	Physically compatible for 48 hr	765	C
Nafcillin sodium	WY	500 mg	PD	1 g		Physically compatible	27	C
Oxacillin sodium	BR	2 g	PD	1 g		Physically compatible	6	C
	BR	500 mg	PD	500 mg	D5S, D5W	Therapeutic availability maintained	110	C
	BR	2 g	PD	1 g	D5S, D5W	Therapeutic availability maintained	110	C
Oxytocin	PD	5 units	PD	1 g		Physically compatible	6	C
Penicillin G potassium		1 million units	PD	1 g		Physically compatible	3	C
	SQ	1 million units	PD	500 mg	D5S, D5W	Therapeutic availability maintained	110	C
	SQ	5 million units	PD	1 g		Physically compatible	47	C
	SQ	5 million units	PD	1 g	D5S, D5W	Therapeutic availability maintained	110	C
	SQ	10 million units	PD	1 g		Physically compatible	6	C
	SQ	10 million units	PD	1 g	D5S, D5W	Therapeutic availability maintained	110	C
	SQ	20 million units	PD	10 g	D5W	Physically compatible	15	C
Penicillin G sodium	UP	20 million units	PD	10 g	D5W	Physically compatible	15	C
Pentobarbital sodium	AB	200 mg	PD	1 g		Physically compatible	6	C

Additive Compatibility (Cont.)

Chloramphenicol sodium succinate

Drug	*Mfr*	*Conc/L*	*Mfr*	*Conc/L*	*Test Soln*	*Remarks*	*Ref*	*C/I*
Phenylephrine HCl	WI	2.5 g	PD	500 mg	D5W, NS	Phenylephrine potency retained for over 24 hr at 22 °C	132	C
Phenylephrine HCl with sodium bicarbonate	WI AB	2.5 g 7.5 g	PD	500 mg	D5W	Phenylephrine potency retained for over 24 hr at 22 °C	132	C
Phytonadione	MSD	50 mg	PD	1 g		Physically compatible	6	C
Plasma protein fraction	CU	5 g	PD	1 g		Physically compatible	6	C
Polymyxin B sulfate	BW	200 mg	PD	10 g	D5W	Physically incompatible	15	I
	BW	200 mg	PD	10 g		Precipitate forms within 1 hr	6	I
Potassium chloride		20 and 40 mEq	PD	500 mg	D5W, D2.5½S	Therapeutic availability maintained	110	C
		20 and 40 mEq	PD	1 g	D5W, D2.5½S	Therapeutic availability maintained	110	C
	AB	40 mEq	PD	1 g		Physically compatible	6	C
		3 g	PD	500 mg	D5W	Physically compatible	74	C
Prochlorperazine edisylate	SKF	100 mg	PD	10 g	D5W	Physically incompatible	15	I
Prochlorperazine mesylate	BP	100 mg	BP	4 g	NS	Haze develops over 3 hr	26	I
Promazine HCl	WY	100 mg	PD	1 g		Physically compatible	6	C
Promethazine HCl	WY	250 mg	PD	10 g	D5W	Physically incompatible	15	I
Ranitidine HCl	GL	100 mg		2 g	D5W	Physically compatible for 24 hr at ambient temperature	1151	C
Sodium bicarbonate		80 mEq	PD	1 g		Physically compatible	6	C
	AB	80 mEq	PD	1 g	D5W	Physically compatible	15	C
Sodium bicarbonate with phenylephrine HCl	AB WI	7.5 g 2.5 g	PD	500 mg	D5W	Phenylephrine potency retained for over 24 hr at 22 °C	132	C
Thiopental sodium	AB	2.5 g	PD	1 g	D5W	Physically compatible	21	C
Vancomycin HCl	LI	5 g	PD	10 g	D5W	Physically incompatible	15	I
Verapamil HCl	KN	80 mg	PD	2 g	D5W, NS	Physically compatible for 24 hr	764	C
Vitamin B complex with C	AB	10 ml	PD	1 g		Physically compatible	6	C
	AB	2 ml	PD	1 g		Physically compatible	3	C
		1 vial	PD	500 mg	D5W	Physically compatible	74	C

[a]*Minibags (100 ml) containing metronidazole 500 mg with disodium phosphate 150 mg, citric acid 44 mg, and sodium chloride 740 mg. This product differs from the Searle product.*

Drugs in Syringe Compatibility

Chloramphenicol sodium succinate

Drug (in syringe)	*Mfr*	*Amt*	*Mfr*	*Amt*	*Remarks*	*Ref*	*C/I*
Ampicillin sodium	AY	500 mg	PD	250 and 400 mg/ ml in 1.5 to 2 ml	No precipitate or color change within 1 hr at room temperature	99	C
	AY	500 mg	PD	250 and 400 mg/ 1 ml	Physically compatible for 1 hr at room temperature	300	C
Diatrizoate meglumine and diatrizoate sodium	MA	52% + 8%, 5 ml	PD	33 mg/ 1 ml	Physically compatible for at least 2 hr	1438	C

Drugs in Syringe Compatibility (Cont.)

Chloramphenicol sodium succinate

Drug (in syringe)	*Mfr*	*Amt*	*Mfr*	*Amt*	*Remarks*	*Ref*	*C/I*
Diatrizoate sodium	WI	60%, 5 ml	PD	33 mg/ 1 ml	Physically compatible for at least 2 hr	1438	C
Glycopyrrolate	RB	0.2 mg/ 1 ml	PD	100 mg/ 1 ml	Gas evolves	331	I
	RB	0.2 mg/ 1 ml	PD	200 mg/ 2 ml	Gas evolves	331	I
	RB	0.4 mg/ 2 ml	PD	100 mg/ 1 ml	Gas evolves	331	I
Heparin sodium	AB	20,000 units/ 1 ml	PD	1 g	Physically compatible for at least 30 min	21	C
		2500 units/ 1 ml		1 g	Physically compatible for at least 5 min	1053	C
Iohexol	WI	64.7%, 5 ml	PD	33 mg/ 1 ml	Physically compatible for at least 2 hr	1438	C
Iopamidol	SQ	61%, 5 ml	PD	33 mg/ 1 ml	Physically compatible for at least 2 hr	1438	C
Iothalamate meglumine	MA	60%, 5 ml	PD	33 mg/ 1 ml	Physically compatible for at least 2 hr	1438	C
Ioxaglate meglumine and ioxaglate sodium	MA	39.3% + 19.6%, 5 ml	PD	33 mg/ 1 ml	Physically compatible for at least 2 hr	1438	C
Metoclopramide HCl	RB	10 mg/ 2 ml	PD	250 mg/ 2.5 ml	Incompatible. Do not mix	924	I
	RB	10 mg/ 2 ml	PD	2 g/20 ml	Incompatible. Do not mix	924	I
	RB	10 mg/ 2 ml	PD	250 mg/ 2.5 ml	White precipitate forms within 1 hr at 25 °C	1167	I
	RB	10 mg/ 2 ml	PD	2 g/20 ml	White precipitate forms within 1 hr at 25 °C	1167	I
	RB	160 mg/ 32 ml	PD	2 g/20 ml	White precipitate forms within 1 hr at 25 °C	1167	I
Penicillin G sodium		1 million units	PD	250 and 400 mg/ ml in 1.5 to 2 ml	No precipitate or color change within 1 hr at room temperature	99	C

Y-Site Injection Compatibility (1:1 Mixture)

Chloramphenicol sodium succinate

Drug	*Mfr*	*Conc*	*Mfr*	*Conc*	*Remarks*	*Ref*	*C/I*
Acyclovir sodium	BW	5 mg/ml[a]	ES	20 mg/ml[a]	Physically compatible for 4 hr at 25 °C	1157	C
Cyclophosphamide	MJ	20 mg/ml[a]	ES	20 mg/ml[a]	Physically compatible for 4 hr at 25 °C	1194	C
Enalaprilat	MSD	0.05 mg/ml[b]	PD	10 mg/ml[a]	Physically compatible for 24 hr at room temperature under fluorescent light	1355	C
Esmolol HCl	DCC	10 mg/ml[a]	PD	10 mg/ml[a]	Physically compatible for 24 hr at 22 °C	1169	C

Y-Site Injection Compatibility (1:1 Mixture) (Cont.)

Chloramphenicol sodium succinate

Drug	*Mfr*	*Conc*	*Mfr*	*Conc*	*Remarks*	*Ref*	*C/I*
Fluconazole	RR	2 mg/ml	PD	20 mg/ml	Gas production	1407	**I**
Foscarnet sodium	AST	24 mg/ml	PD	20 mg/ml	Physically compatible for 24 hr at room temperature under fluorescent light	1335	C
Hydromorphone HCl	WY	0.2 mg/ml[a]	LY	20 mg/ml[a]	Physically compatible for at least 4 hr at 25 °C under fluorescent light	987	C
Labetalol HCl	SC	1 mg/ml[a]	PD	10 mg/ml[a]	Physically compatible for 24 hr at 18 °C	1171	C
Magnesium sulfate	IX	16.7, 33.3, 66.7, 100 mg/ml[a]	PD	20 mg/ml[a]	Physically compatible for at least 4 hr at 32 °C	813	C
Meperidine HCl	WY	10 mg/ml[a]	LY	20 mg/ml[a]	Physically compatible for at least 4 hr at 25 °C under fluorescent light	987	C
Morphine sulfate	WI	1 mg/ml[a]	LY	20 mg/ml[a]	Physically compatible for at least 4 hr at 25 °C under fluorescent light	987	C
Perphenazine	SC	0.02 mg/ml[a]	ES	20 mg/ml[a]	Physically compatible for 4 hr at 25 °C	1155	C
Tacrolimus	FUJ	1 mg/ml[b]	PD	20 mg/ml[a]	Visually compatible for 24 hr at 25 °C	1630	C
TPN #61[c]		[d]	PD	125 mg/1.25 ml[e]	Physically compatible	1012	C
		[f]	PD	750 mg/7.5 ml[e]	Physically compatible	1012	C

[a]*Tested in dextrose 5% in water.*
[b]*Tested in sodium chloride 0.9%.*
[c]*Refer to Appendix I for the composition of parenteral nutrition solutions. TPN indicates a 2-in-1 admixture.*
[d]*Run at 21 ml/hr.*
[e]*Given over five minutes by syringe pump.*
[f]*Run at 94 ml/hr.*

Additional Compatibility Information

Infusion Solutions — Chloramphenicol sodium succinate (Parke-Davis) 1 g/L is physically compatible with all Abbott infusion solutions. It is also compatible with benzyl alcohol–preserved bacteriostatic water for injection. (6)

Concentrated Drug Solutions — The following incompatibility determinations were performed with concentrated solutions. The drugs in dry form were reconstituted according to the manufacturers' recommendations. One milliliter of chloramphenicol sodium succinate (Parke-Davis) was added to 5 ml of sterile distilled water along with 1 ml of each of the following drugs. Particulate matter was noted within two hours (28):

Hydroxyzine HCl (Pfizer)
Phenytoin sodium (Parke-Davis)
Prochlorperazine edisylate (SKF)
Promazine HCl (Wyeth)
Promethazine HCl (Wyeth)
Vancomycin HCl (Lilly)

Other Drugs — Chloramphenicol sodium succinate is stated to be physically compatible for 24 hours at room temperature with lincomycin HCl in infusion solutions. (154)

Concentrations of chloramphenicol sodium succinate higher than 1 g/L should be used cautiously with other macromolecules. (6)

Chloramphenicol sodium succinate (Parke-Davis) in dextrose 5% in water has been reported to be conditionally compatible with ascorbic acid injection (Upjohn), erythromycin lactobionate (Abbott), and vitamin B complex with C (Abbott). The incompatibility is concentration dependent. Therefore, if attempting to combine chloramphenicol sodium succinate with any of these drugs, mix the solution thoroughly and observe it closely for any sign of incompatibility. (15)

CHLORDIAZEPOXIDE HCL
AHFS 28:24.08

Products — Chlordiazepoxide HCl is available in 5-ml dry-filled ampuls containing 100 mg of drug. Accompanying the ampul of drug is a 2-ml ampul of diluent for intramuscular administration. The diluent contains (2):

Benzyl alcohol	1.5%
Polysorbate 80	4%
Propylene glycol	20%
Maleic acid	1.6%
Sodium hydroxide	to adjust pH

For intramuscular injection, the 2 ml of special intramuscular diluent should be added to the 100-mg ampul of the drug. Avoid excessive pressure in adding the diluent to preclude bubble formation. Agitate gently until a clear solution is obtained. The resultant solution has a concentration of 50 mg/ml. Do not use other diluents for intramuscular injection because of pain on injection. (2; 4)

For intravenous injection, 5 ml of sterile water for injection or sodium chloride 0.9% should be added to the 100-mg ampul of chlordiazepoxide HCl. Agitate gently until dissolved. The resultant solution has a concentration of 20 mg/ml. The special intramuscular diluent should not be used to reconstitute chlordiazepoxide HCl for intravenous use because air bubbles may form during reconstitution. (2; 4)

pH — The special intramuscular diluent has a pH of 2.5 to 3.5. After reconstitution of 100 mg of chlordiazepoxide HCl with 2 ml of this special diluent or 5 ml of sterile water for injection or sodium chloride 0.9%, the pH is approximately 3. (2; 4)

Trade Name(s) — Librium.

Administration — Chlordiazepoxide HCl is usually administered by slow direct intravenous injection over one minute. It may also be given by deep intramuscular injection slowly into the upper outer quadrant of the gluteus muscle (2; 4), but this route is rarely justified because of slow and erratic absorption. (4)

Stability — Chlordiazepoxide HCl for injection is unstable in solution, and the manufacturer recommends that the solution be prepared immediately before use. Also, it is recommended that any unused solution be discarded. Heat sterilization of the solution should not be attempted. (2; 4)

Hydrolysis of the polysorbate 80 in the special intramuscular diluent may occur, resulting in opalescence. Consequently, refrigerated storage is recommended. However, the diluent is stated to be stable for at least 48 hours at temperatures not exceeding 25 °C. (4) Previously, Roche indicated the diluent was stable for up to one month stored at 15 to 30 °C if haziness or turbidity does not develop. (853) The special intramuscular diluent should not be used if it is opalescent or hazy. (2; 4)

The manufacturer recommends that the powder be protected from light. (4)

Sorption — Chlordiazepoxide HCl (Roche) 1 and 2 g/L in sodium chloride 0.9% (Baxter), when transferred to PVC bags, showed about a 10 to 20% loss of drug over two hours at 22 °C in normal light. In Ringer's injection at the same concentrations and conditions, losses of about 10% occurred in four hours. Because decomposition products were well within normal USP limits and because similar losses were not observed when the admixtures were tested in glass bottles, the losses were attributed to sorption to the PVC bag. When dextrose 5% in water was the vehicle, little or no drug loss (5% or less) due to sorption to the PVC bag occurred. (745)

Plasticizer Leaching — Chlordiazepoxide HCl (Roche) 2 mg/ml in dextrose 5% in water leached relatively minor amounts of diethylhexyl phthalate (DEHP) plasticizer from PVC bags. This leaching was due to the surfactant polysorbate 80 (Tween 80) in the formulation. After 24 hours at 24 °C, the DEHP concentration in 50-ml bags of infusion solution was 3.2 μg/ml. This finding is consistent with the low surfactant concentration (0.16%) in the final admixture solution. The actual amount of DEHP leached from PVC containers and administration sets may vary in clinical situations, depending on surfactant concentration, bag size, and contact time. (1683)

Compatibility Information

Solution Compatibility

Chlordiazepoxide HCl

Solution	*Mfr*	*Mfr*	*Conc/L*	*Remarks*	*Ref*	*C/I*
Dextrose 5% in water	BA[a]	RC	1 and 2 g	Physically compatible and chemically stable at 22 °C for 4-hr study period	745	C
	BA[b]	RC	1 and 2 g	Physically compatible and chemically stable at 22 °C with little or no loss due to sorption during 4-hr study period	745	C
Ringer's injection	BA[a]	RC	1 and 2 g	Physically compatible and chemically stable at 22 °C for 4-hr study period	745	C
	BA[b]	RC	1 and 2 g	Physically compatible but with approximately 10% loss in 4 hr at 22 °C apparently due to sorption	745	I
Sodium chloride 0.9%	BA[a]	RC	1 and 2 g	Physically compatible and chemically stable at 22 °C for 4-hr study period	745	C

Solution Compatibility (Cont.)

Chlordiazepoxide HCl

Solution	*Mfr*	*Mfr*	*Conc/L*	*Remarks*	*Ref*	*C/I*
	BA[b]	RC	1 g	Approximately 10% loss in 2 hr and 20% loss in 4 hr at 22 °C apparently due to sorption	745	I
	BA[b]	RC	2 g	Approximately 20% loss in 2 hr at 22 °C apparently due to sorption	745	I

[a]*Tested in glass containers.*
[b]*Tested in PVC containers.*

Y-Site Injection Compatibility (1:1 Mixture)

Chlordiazepoxide HCl

Drug	*Mfr*	*Conc*	*Mfr*	*Conc*	*Remarks*	*Ref*	*C/I*
Cefepime HCl	BMS	20 mg/ml[a]	RC	20 mg/ml	Haze forms immediately and becomes flocculent precipitate in 4 hr	1689	I
Heparin sodium	UP	1000 units/L[b]	RC	10 mg/ml	Physically compatible for at least 4 hr at room temperature by visual and microscopic examination	534	C
Hydrocortisone sodium succinate	UP	10 mg/L[b]	RC	10 mg/ml	Physically compatible for at least 4 hr at room temperature by visual and microscopic examination	534	C
Potassium chloride	AB	40 mEq/L[b]	RC	10 mg/ml	Physically compatible for at least 4 hr at room temperature by visual and microscopic examination	534	C
Vitamin B complex with C	RC	2 ml/L[b]	RC	10 mg/ml	Physically compatible for at least 4 hr at room temperature by visual and microscopic examination	534	C

[a]*Tested in dextrose 5% in water.*
[b]*Tested in dextrose 5% in Ringer's injection, dextrose 5% in Ringer's injection, lactated, dextrose 5% in water, Ringer's injection, lactated, and sodium chloride 0.9%.*

CHLOROQUINE HCL (CHLOROQUINE PHOSPHATE; CHLOROQUINE SULFATE) AHFS 8:20

Products — Chloroquine HCl is available in 5-ml ampuls. Each milliliter contains 40 mg of the base as the dihydrochloride salt. (2; 4)

pH—From 5.5 to 6.6. (4)

Trade Name(s)—Aralen.

Administration — Chloroquine HCl is administered by intramuscular injection. (2; 4) It has also been administered by subcutaneous or intravenous infusion. (4)

Stability — Intact ampuls should be stored at controlled room temperature and protected from freezing. (2; 4)

Sorption—Chloroquine HCl has been stated to bind to glass. (877; 878) In one study, 30 or 40% of a solution of chloroquine 1×10^{-6} M or 0.32 mg/ml in various aqueous media bound to the glass of test tubes. Most of the binding took place during the first hour of contact and seemed to be independent of temperature. This binding did not occur with polycarbonate, polystyrene, or polypropylene plastic containers. (877) Although concern has been expressed as to the impact of such binding on drug availability (879), the relevance of these results using a highly dilute (1×10^{-6} M) concentration compared to the clinical concentration is problematic. Of more concern is that binding to glass may lead to inaccurate conclusions of resistance during laboratory studies of chloroquine sensitivity in *Plasmodium falciparum* or to inaccurate results during pharmacokinetic studies. (879)

However, Martens et al. could not confirm this result. Chloroquine sulfate 500 µg/ml in sodium chloride 0.9% in PVC bags, glass bottles, and polyethylene-lined laminated bags showed little or no loss due to sorption during storage for 24 hours at 21 °C when protected from light. (1392)

Filtration— Chloroquine was also found to bind to cellulose acetate filter media. Ten milliliters of a 1 × 10^{-6} M solution (approximately 0.32 mg/ml) was passed through 0.45-μm cellulose acetate filters (Millipore and Nalgene). Up to 60 or 70% of the drug was removed. No drug was lost when a similar solution was filtered through a polycarbonate filter. (877) Once again, the relevance of this binding phenomenon at the much greater concentrations found in clinical dosing is problematic.

Compatibility Information

Solution Compatibility

Chloroquine sulfate

Solution	*Mfr*	*Mfr*	*Conc/L*	*Remarks*	*Ref*	*C/I*
Sodium chloride 0.9%	[a]	RP	500 mg	Physically compatible with little or no drug loss in 24 hr at 21 °C in the dark	1392	C

[a]*Tested in PVC bags, glass bottles, and polyethylene-lined laminated bags.*

Additive Compatibility

Chloroquine phosphate

Drug	*Mfr*	*Conc/L*	*Mfr*	*Conc/L*	*Test Soln*	*Remarks*	*Ref*	*C/I*
Promethazine HCl		5 mg		5 mg	W	Visually compatible with no change in UV spectra	1745	C
		5 mg		25 mg	W	Visually compatible with no change in UV spectra	1745	C
		25 mg		5 mg	W	Visually compatible with no change in UV spectra	1745	C

Drugs in Syringe Compatibility

Chloroquine phosphate

Drug (in syringe)	*Mfr*	*Amt*	*Mfr*	*Amt*	*Remarks*	*Ref*	*C/I*
Promethazine HCl		50 mg/ 2 ml		250 mg/ 5 ml	Greenish-yellow discoloration becomes precipitate in 22 hr	1745	I
		50 mg/ 2 ml		50 mg/ 1 ml	Greenish-yellow discoloration becomes precipitate in 17 hr	1745	I

CHLOROTHIAZIDE SODIUM
AHFS 40:28

Products — Chlorothiazide sodium is supplied in vials containing lyophilized drug equivalent to 500 mg of chlorothiazide with mannitol 250 mg and sodium hydroxide to adjust the pH. Reconstitute with 18 ml of sterile water for injection to obtain an isotonic solution yielding a concentration of 28 mg/ml of drug. (2; 4; 7) No less than 18 ml should be used for reconstitution. (2; 4)

pH— From 9.2 to 10. (4; 7)

Osmolality— Chlorothiazide sodium 28 mg/ml in sterile water for injection has an osmolality of 344 mOsm/kg. (1689)

Sodium Content— Each 500-mg vial of chlorothiazide sodium contains approximately 2.5 mEq of sodium. (4)

Trade Name(s)— Sodium Diuril.

Administration — Chlorothiazide sodium is administered intravenously by direct injection or infusion. It must not be administered intramuscularly or subcutaneously, and extravasation must be avoided. (2; 4)

Stability — Intact vials should be stored between 2 and 25 °C. (2) The reconstituted solution is intended for single use and unused solution should be discarded. (2; 4) However, the reconstituted solution has been stated to be stable for 24 hours. (7) Depending on concentration, precipitation of chlorothiazide will occur in less than 24 hours if the pH of the reconstituted solution is less than approximately 7.4. (4; 7)

pH Effects— Chlorothiazide sodium appears to be stable at pH 7.5 to 9.5 in dextrose 5% in water. No loss of potency was noted over a 24-hour study period. (7)

The solubility of chlorothiazide sodium is very pH sensitive. Depending on concentration, precipitation occurs at approximately pH 7.4 and below. Additives that result in a final pH in this range, such as vitamins, should not be mixed. Chlorothiazide sodium is sufficiently alkaline to raise the pH of unbuffered solutions such as dextrose, saline, and their combinations. But if an acidic buffer is present, such as lactate or acetate buffers, the resultant pH may fall below pH 7.4, causing precipitation. (7)

Chlorothiazide sodium possesses some alkalizing power. Therefore, it should not be combined with drugs known to be unstable in alkaline media. (7)

Compatibility Information

Solution Compatibility

Chlorothiazide sodium

Solution	*Mfr*	*Mfr*	*Conc/L*	*Remarks*	*Ref*	*C/I*
Dextran 6% in dextrose 5%	AB	MSD	2 g	Physically compatible	3	C
Dextran 6% in sodium chloride 0.9%	AB	MSD	1 g	Potency retained for 24 hr	7	C
	AB	MSD	2 g	Physically compatible	3	C
Dextrose–Ringer's injection combinations	AB	MSD	2 g	Physically compatible	3	C
Dextrose–Ringer's injection, lactated, combinations	AB	MSD	2 g	Physically compatible	3	C
Dextrose–saline combinations	AB	MSD	2 g	Physically compatible	3	C
Dextrose 5% in sodium chloride 0.9%	AB	MSD	1 g	Potency retained for 24 hr	7	C
Dextrose 2½% in water	AB	MSD	2 g	Physically compatible	3	C
Dextrose 5% in water	AB	MSD	1 g	Potency retained for 24 hr	7	C
	AB	MSD	2 g	Physically compatible	3	C
Dextrose 10% in water	AB	MSD	2 g	Physically compatible	3	C
Fructose 10% in sodium chloride 0.9%	AB	MSD	2 g	Physically compatible	3	C
Fructose 10% in water	AB	MSD	2 g	Physically compatible	3	C
Invert sugar 5 and 10% in sodium chloride 0.9%	AB	MSD	2 g	Physically compatible	3	C
Invert sugar 5 and 10% in water	AB	MSD	2 g	Physically compatible	3	C
Ionosol B with dextrose 5%	AB	MSD	500 mg	Physically incompatible	15	I
	AB	MSD	2 g	Precipitate forms after 6 hr	7	I
	AB	MSD	2 g	Haze or precipitate forms within 24 hr	3	I
Ionosol MB with dextrose 5%	AB	MSD	2 g	Physically compatible	3	C
Ionosol T with dextrose 5%	AB	MSD	2 g	Physically compatible	3	C
Normosol M in dextrose 5%	AB	MSD	2 g	Precipitate forms after 6 hr	7	I
Normosol M, 900 cal	AB	MSD	2 g	Precipitate forms after 1 hr	7	I
Normosol R in dextrose 5%	AB	MSD	2 g	Precipitate forms after 6 hr	7	I
Ringer's injection	AB	MSD	1 g	Potency retained for 24 hr	7	C
	AB	MSD	2 g	Physically compatible	3	C
Ringer's injection, lactated	AB	MSD	1 g	Potency retained for 24 hr	7	C
	AB	MSD	2 g	Physically compatible	3	C
Sodium chloride 0.45%	AB	MSD	2 g	Physically compatible	3	C
Sodium chloride 0.9%	AB	MSD	1 g	Potency retained for 24 hr	7	C
	AB	MSD	2 g	Physically compatible	3	C
Sodium lactate ⅙ M	AB	MSD	2 g	Physically compatible	3	C

Additive Compatibility

Chlorothiazide sodium

Drug	Mfr	Conc/L	Mfr	Conc/L	Test Soln	Remarks	Ref	C/I
Amikacin sulfate	BR	5 g	MSD	10 mg	D5LR, D5R, D5S, D5W, D10W, IS10, LR, NS, R, SL	Precipitate forms within 4 hr at 25 °C	294	I
Chlorpromazine HCl	BP	200 mg	BP	2 g	D5W, NS	Immediate precipitation	26	I
Cimetidine HCl	SKF	3 g	MSD	5 g	D5W	Physically compatible and cimetidine chemically stable for 24 hr at room temperature. Chlorothiazide not tested	551	C
Hydralazine HCl	BP	80 mg	BP	2 g	D5W, NS	Yellow color with precipitate in 3 hr	26	I
Insulin, regular[a]			MSD			Physically incompatible	9	I
Levorphanol bitartrate	RC		MSD			Physically incompatible	9	I
Lidocaine HCl	AST	2 g	MSD	500 mg		Physically compatible	24	C
Morphine sulfate			MSD			Physically incompatible	9	I
Nafcillin sodium	WY	500 mg	MSD	500 mg		Physically compatible	27	C
Norepinephrine bitartrate	WI		MSD			Physically incompatible	9	I
Polymyxin B sulfate	BP	20 mg	BP	2 g	D5W	Yellow color	26	I
Procaine HCl			MSD			Physically incompatible	9	I
Prochlorperazine edisylate	SKF		MSD			Physically incompatible	9	I
Prochlorperazine mesylate	BP BP	100 mg 100 mg	BP BP	2 g 2 g	D5W NS	Immediate precipitation Haze develops over 3 hr	26 26	I I
Promazine HCl	BP WY	200 mg	BP MSD	2 g	D5W, NS	Immediate precipitation Physically incompatible	26 9	I I
Promethazine HCl	BP WY	100 mg	BP MSD	2 g	D5W, NS	Immediate precipitation Physically incompatible	26 9	I I
Ranitidine HCl	GL	50 mg and 2 g		5 g	D5W	Physically compatible and ranitidine chemically stable by HPLC for 24 hr at 25 °C. Chlorothiazide not tested	1515	C
Sodium bicarbonate	AB	2.4 mEq[b]	MSD	500 mg	D5W	Physically compatible for 24 hr	772	C
Streptomycin sulfate			MSD			Physically incompatible	9	I
Triflupromazine HCl	SQ					Precipitate forms	40	I
Vancomycin HCl	LI		MSD			Physically incompatible	9	I

[a]*Test performed prior to availability of neutral regular insulin.*
[b]*One vial of Neut added to a liter of admixture.*

Y-Site Injection Compatibility (1:1 Mixture)

Chlorothiazide sodium

Drug	Mfr	Conc	Mfr	Conc	Remarks	Ref	C/I
TPN #203 and #204[a]			ME	28 mg/ml	White precipitate forms immediately	1974	I

[a]*Refer to Appendix I for the composition of the parenteral nutrition solutions. TPN indicates a 2-in-1 admixture.*

Additional Compatibility Information

Blood Products — Simultaneous administration of chlorothiazide sodium with blood or its derivatives should be avoided. (2)

Multivitamins — Chlorothiazide sodium (MSD) is stated to be physically incompatible with multivitamins (Astra). (1-7/99)

CHLORPROMAZINE HCL
AHFS 28:16.08

Products — Chlorpromazine HCl is available in 1- and 2-ml ampuls and 10-ml multiple-dose vials. Each milliliter of solution contains (2):

Component	Ampul	Vial
Chlorpromazine HCl	25 mg	25 mg
Ascorbic acid	2 mg	2 mg
Sodium bisulfite	1 mg	1 mg
Sodium sulfite	1 mg	1 mg
Sodium chloride	6 mg	1 mg
Benzyl alcohol		2%

pH — From 3 to 5. (4) A 10% solution in water has a pH of 3.5 to 4.5. (5)

Osmolality — Chlorpromazine HCl 25 mg/ml has an osmolality of 262 mOsm/kg. (1689)

Trade Name(s) — Thorazine.

Administration — Chlorpromazine HCl may be administered slowly by deep intramuscular injection into the upper outer quadrant of the buttock. Dilution with sodium chloride 0.9% or procaine HCl 2% has been recommended for intramuscular injection if local irritation is a problem. Subcutaneous injection is not recommended. The drug may be diluted to 1 mg/ml with sodium chloride 0.9% and administered by direct intravenous injection at a rate of 1 mg/min to adults and 0.5 mg/min to children. For infusion, it may be diluted in 500 to 1000 ml of sodium chloride 0.9%. (2; 4)

Care should be taken to avoid contact of chlorpromazine hydrochloride with skin and clothing when handling the products. Rare cases of contact dermatitis have occurred. (2; 4)

Stability — Intact containers should be stored at controlled room temperature. Freezing should be avoided. Protect the solution from light during storage or it may discolor. A slightly yellowed solution does not indicate potency loss. However, a markedly discolored solution should be discarded. (2)

Diluted to a 1-mg/ml concentration with sodium chloride 0.9% and stored in 5-ml vials at 18 to 23 °C in the dark, chlorpromazine HCl (SKF) remained relatively stable for 30 days. The HPLC assay results were variable during the study, with the peak-height ratio to the internal standard being 86% on day 30. However, the authors attributed the variable results to the inherent variability of their assay method because no shifts in retention times or extra peaks on the chromatogram were observed. They concluded that the chlorpromazine HCl dilution had not undergone a significant loss of potency. (1083)

pH Effects — The pH of maximum stability is 6. (67) Oxidation of chlorpromazine HCl occurs in alkaline media. (4) The titration of chlorpromazine HCl in sodium chloride 0.9% with alkali resulted in precipitation of chlorpromazine base at pH 6.7 to 6.8. (138) Precipitation may occur if chlorpromazine HCl is admixed with alkaline drugs or solutions.

Light Effects — Chlorpromazine HCl ampuls and vials should be protected from light during storage. (2; 4) However, chlorpromazine HCl infusion solutions in PVC bags exposed to light during administration lost less than 2% of the drug over a six-hour administration period. Light protection of infusion sets during administration was found not to be necessary. (2280)

Sorption — Chlorpromazine HCl (May & Baker) 9 mg/L in sodium chloride 0.9% (Travenol) in PVC bags exhibited only about 5% sorption to the plastic bag during one week of storage at room temperature (15 to 20 °C). However, when the solution was buffered from its initial pH of 5 to pH 7.4, approximately 86% of the drug was lost in one week due to sorption. (536)

Chlorpromazine HCl (May & Baker) 9 mg/L in sodium chloride 0.9% exhibited a cumulative 41% loss due to sorption during a seven-hour simulated infusion through an infusion set (Travenol) consisting of a cellulose propionate burette chamber and 170 cm of PVC tubing. Both the burette chamber and the tubing contributed to the loss. The extent of sorption was found to be independent of concentration. (606)

The drug was also tested as a simulated infusion over at least one hour by a syringe pump system. A glass syringe on a syringe pump was fitted with 20 cm of polyethylene tubing or 50 cm of Silastic tubing. A negligible amount of drug was lost with the polyethylene tubing, but a cumulative loss of 79% occurred during the one-hour infusion through the Silastic tubing. (606)

A 25-ml aliquot of chlorpromazine HCl 9 mg/L in sodium chloride 0.9% was stored in all-plastic syringes composed of polypropylene barrels and polyethylene plungers for 24 hours at room temperature in the dark. The solution did not exhibit any loss due to sorption. (606)

In a continuation of this work, chlorpromazine HCl (May & Baker) 90 mg/L in sodium chloride 0.9% in a glass bottle was delivered through a polyethylene administration set (Tridilset) over eight hours at 15 to 20 °C. The flow rate was set at 1 ml/min. No appreciable loss due to sorption occurred. (769) This finding is in contrast to a 41% loss using a conventional administration set. (606)

Central Venous Catheter—Chlorpromazine HCl (Elkin-Sinn) 2 mg/ml in dextrose 5% in water was found to be compatible with the ARROWg+ard Blue Plus (Arrow International) chlorhexidine-bearing triple-lumen central catheter. HPLC analysis was used to evaluate completeness of drug delivery through the catheter and the amount of chlorhexidine removed from the internal lumens. Essentially complete delivery of the drug was found with little or no drug loss occurring. Furthermore, chlorhexidine delivered from the catheter remained at trace amounts with no substantial increase due to the delivery of the drug through the catheter. (2335)

Compatibility Information

Solution Compatibility

Chlorpromazine HCl

Solution	*Mfr*	*Mfr*	*Conc/L*	*Remarks*	*Ref*	*C/I*
Dextran 6% in dextrose 5%	AB	SKF	50 mg	Physically compatible	3	C
Dextran 6% in sodium chloride 0.9%	AB	SKF	50 mg	Physically compatible	3	C
Dextrose–Ringer's injection combinations	AB	SKF	50 mg	Physically compatible	3	C
Dextrose–Ringer's injection, lactated, combinations	AB	SKF	50 mg	Physically compatible	3	C
Dextrose–saline combinations	AB	SKF	50 mg	Physically compatible	3	C
Dextrose 2½% in water	AB	SKF	50 mg	Physically compatible	3	C
Dextrose 5% in water	AB	SKF	50 mg	Physically compatible	3	C
Dextrose 10% in water	AB	SKF	50 mg	Physically compatible	3	C
Fructose 10% in sodium chloride 0.9%	AB	SKF	50 mg	Physically compatible	3	C
Fructose 10% in water	AB	SKF	50 mg	Physically compatible	3	C
Invert sugar 5 and 10% in sodium chloride 0.9%	AB	SKF	50 mg	Physically compatible	3	C
Invert sugar 5 and 10% in water	AB	SKF	50 mg	Physically compatible	3	C
Ionosol products	AB	SKF	50 mg	Physically compatible	3	C
Ringer's injection	AB	SKF	50 mg	Physically compatible	3	C
Ringer's injection, lactated	AB	SKF	50 mg	Physically compatible	3	C
Sodium chloride 0.45%	AB	SKF	50 mg	Physically compatible	3	C
Sodium chloride 0.9%	AB	SKF	50 mg	Physically compatible	3	C
Sodium lactate ⅙ M	AB	SKF	50 mg	Physically compatible	3	C

Additive Compatibility

Chlorpromazine HCl

Drug	*Mfr*	*Conc/L*	*Mfr*	*Conc/L*	*Test Soln*	*Remarks*	*Ref*	*C/I*
Aminophylline	BP	1 g	BP	200 mg	D5W, NS	Immediate precipitation	26	I
Amphotericin B		200 mg	BP	200 mg	D5W	Immediate precipitation	26	I
Ampicillin sodium	BP	2 g	BP	200 mg	D5W, NS	Immediate precipitation	26	I
Ascorbic acid injection	UP	500 mg	SKF	250 mg	D5W	Physically compatible	15	C
Chloramphenicol sodium succinate	BP	4 g	BP	200 mg	D5W	Immediate precipitation	26	I
	BP	4 g	BP	200 mg	NS	Haze develops over 3 hr	26	I
Chlorothiazide sodium	BP	2 g	BP	200 mg	D5W, NS	Immediate precipitation	26	I

Additive Compatibility (Cont.)

Chlorpromazine HCl

Drug	*Mfr*	*Conc/L*	*Mfr*	*Conc/L*	*Test Soln*	*Remarks*	*Ref*	*C/I*
Ethacrynate sodium	MSD	50 mg	SKF	50 mg	NS	Little alteration of UV spectra within 8 hr at room temperature	16	C
Floxacillin sodium	BE	20 g	ANT	5 g	W	Sticky yellow precipitate forms immediately	1479	I
Furosemide	HO	1 g	ANT	5 g	W	Immediate precipitation	1479	I
Methohexital sodium	BP	2 g	BP	200 mg	D5W, NS	Immediate precipitation	26	I
Netilmicin sulfate	SC	3 g	SKF	100 mg	D5S	Physically compatible and netilmicin chemically stable for 7 days at 25 and 4 °C. Chlorpromazine not tested	558	C
Penicillin G potassium or sodium	BP	10 million units	BP	200 mg	NS	Haze develops over 3 hr	26	I
Phenobarbital sodium	BP	800 mg	BP	200 mg	D5W, NS	Immediate precipitation	26	I
Theophylline		2 g		200 mg	D5W	Visually compatible with little or no theophylline loss and 7% chlorpromazine loss in 48 hr	1909	C
Vitamin B complex with C	AB	2 ml	SKF	50 mg		Physically compatible	3	C
	AB	5 ml	SKF	250 mg	D5W	Physically compatible	15	C

Drugs in Syringe Compatibility

Chlorpromazine HCl

Drug (in syringe)	*Mfr*	*Amt*	*Mfr*	*Amt*	*Remarks*	*Ref*	*C/I*
Atropine sulfate		0.6 mg/ 1.5 ml	SKF	50 mg/ 2 ml	Physically compatible for at least 15 min	14	C
	ST	0.4 mg/ 1 ml	PO	50 mg/ 2 ml	Physically compatible for at least 15 min	326	C
Benztropine mesylate	MSD	2 mg/ 2 ml	STS	50 mg/ 2 ml	Visually compatible for 60 min	1784	C
Butorphanol tartrate	BR	4 mg/ 2 ml	MB	25 mg/ 1 ml	Physically compatible for 30 min at room temperature both macroscopically and microscopically	566	C
Cimetidine HCl	SKF	300 mg/ 2 ml	WY	25 mg/ 1 ml	Haze develops immediately	25	I
Dimenhydrinate	HR	50 mg/ 1 ml	PO	50 mg/ 2 ml	Physically incompatible within 15 min	326	I
Diphenhydramine HCl	PD	50 mg/ 1 ml	PO	50 mg/ 2 ml	Physically compatible for at least 15 min	326	C
	ES	100 mg/ 2 ml	STS	50 mg/ 2 ml	Visually compatible for 60 min	1784	C
Doxapram HCl	RB	400 mg/ 20 ml		250 mg/ 5 ml	Physically compatible with no doxapram loss in 24 hr	1177	C
Droperidol	MN	2.5 mg/ 1 ml	PO	50 mg/ 2 ml	Physically compatible for at least 15 min	326	C
Fentanyl citrate	MN	0.05 mg/ 1 ml	PO	50 mg/ 2 ml	Physically compatible for at least 15 min	326	C

Drugs in Syringe Compatibility (Cont.)

Drug (in syringe)	Mfr	Amt	Chlorpromazine HCl Mfr	Chlorpromazine HCl Amt	Remarks	Ref	C/I
Glycopyrrolate	RB	0.2 mg/ 1 ml	SKF	25 mg/ 1 ml	Physically compatible and pH in stability range for glycopyrrolate for 48 hr at 25 °C	331	C
	RB	0.2 mg/ 1 ml	SKF	50 mg/ 2 ml	Physically compatible and pH in stability range for glycopyrrolate for 48 hr at 25 °C	331	C
	RB	0.4 mg/ 2 ml	SKF	25 mg/ 1 ml	Physically compatible and pH in stability range for glycopyrrolate for 48 hr at 25 °C	331	C
Heparin sodium		2500 units/ 1 ml		50 mg/ 2 ml	Turbidity or precipitate forms within 5 min	1053	I
Hydromorphone HCl	KN	4 mg/ 2 ml	ES	25 mg/ 1 ml	Physically compatible for 30 min	517	C
Hydroxyzine HCl	PF	50 mg/ 1 ml	PO	50 mg/ 2 ml	Physically compatible for at least 15 min	326	C
	ES	100 mg/ 2 ml	STS	50 mg/ 2 ml	Visually compatible for 60 min	1784	C
Meperidine HCl	WY	100 mg/ 1 ml	SKF	50 mg/ 2 ml	Physically compatible for at least 15 min	14	C
	WI	50 mg/ 1 ml	PO	50 mg/ 2 ml	Physically compatible for at least 15 min	326	C
Metoclopramide HCl	NO	10 mg/ 2 ml	MB	25 mg/ 1 ml	Physically compatible for 15 min at room temperature both macroscopically and microscopically	565	C
Midazolam HCl	RC	5 mg/ 1 ml	SKF	50 mg/ 2 ml	Physically compatible for 4 hr at 25 °C under fluorescent light	1145	C
Morphine sulfate	WY	15 mg/ 1 ml	SKF	50 mg/ 2 ml	Physically compatible for at least 15 min	14	C
	ST	15 mg/ 1 ml	PO	50 mg/ 2 ml	Physically compatible for at least 15 min	326	C
Morphine tartrate	DB	[a]	DB	10 mg/ 2 ml	Discoloration develops, although no morphine loss by HPLC in 48 hr at room temperature exposed to light. Chlorpromazine not tested	1599	?
Papaveretum	RC[b]	20 mg/ 1 ml	PO	50 mg/ 2 ml	Visually compatible for at least 15 min	326	C
Pentazocine lactate	WI	30 mg/ 1 ml	SKF	50 mg/ 2 ml	Physically compatible for at least 15 min	14	C
	WI	30 mg/ 1 ml	PO	50 mg/ 2 ml	Physically compatible for at least 15 min	326	C
Pentobarbital sodium	WY	100 mg/ 2 ml	SKF	50 mg/ 2 ml	Precipitate forms within 15 min	14	I
	AB	500 mg/ 10 ml	SKF	50 mg/ 2 ml	Physically incompatible	55	I
	AB	50 mg/ 1 ml	PO	50 mg/ 2 ml	Physically incompatible within 15 min	326	I
Perphenazine	SC	5 mg/ 1 ml	MB	25 mg/ 1 ml	Physically compatible for 30 min at room temperature both macroscopically and microscopically	566	C
Prochlorperazine edisylate	SKF		SKF	50 mg/ 2 ml	Physically compatible for at least 15 min	14	C
	PO	5 mg/ 1 ml	PO	50 mg/ 2 ml	Physically compatible for at least 15 min	326	C

Drugs in Syringe Compatibility (Cont.)

Chlorpromazine HCl

Drug (in syringe)	*Mfr*	*Amt*	*Mfr*	*Amt*	*Remarks*	*Ref*	*C/I*
Promazine HCl	WY	50 mg/ 1 ml	PO	50 mg/ 2 ml	Physically compatible for at least 15 min	326	C
Promethazine HCl	PO	50 mg/ 2 ml	PO	50 mg/ 2 ml	Physically compatible for at least 15 min	326	C
Ranitidine HCl	GL	50 mg/ 2 ml	RP	25 mg/ 1 ml	Physically compatible for 1 hr at 25 °C both macroscopically and microscopically	978	C
	GL	50 mg/ 5 ml	RP	25 mg	Gas formation	1151	I
Scopolamine HBr		0.6 mg/ 1.5 ml	SKF	50 mg/ 2 ml	Physically compatible for at least 15 min	14	C
	ST	0.4 mg/ 1 ml	PO	50 mg/ 2 ml	Physically compatible for at least 15 min	326	C
Thiopental sodium	AB	50 mg/ 2 ml	SKF	75 mg/ 3 ml	Physically incompatible	21	I
	AB	75 mg/ 3 ml	SKF	50 mg/ 2 ml	Physically incompatible	55	I

[a]*Amount unspecified.*
[b]*The former formulation was tested.*

Y-Site Injection Compatibility (1:1 Mixture)

Chlorpromazine HCl

Drug	*Mfr*	*Conc*	*Mfr*	*Conc*	*Remarks*	*Ref*	*C/I*
Allopurinol sodium	BW	3 mg/ml[b]	RU	2 mg/ml[b]	Heavy white turbidity and precipitate form immediately	1686	I
Amifostine	USB	10 mg/ml[a]	SCN	2 mg/ml[a]	Subvisual haze forms immediately	1845	I
Amphotericin B cholesteryl sulfate complex	SEQ	0.83 mg/ml[a]	ES	2 mg/ml[a]	Gross precipitate forms	2117	I
Amsacrine	NCI	1 mg/ml[a]	ES	2 mg/ml[a]	Physically compatible for 4 hr at room temperature under fluorescent light	1381	C
Aztreonam	SQ	40 mg/ml[a]	SCN	2 mg/ml[a]	Dense white turbidity forms immediately	1758	I
Cefepime HCl	BMS	20 mg/ml[a]	SCN	2 mg/ml[a]	Cloudy solution forms immediately. Flocculent precipitate forms in 4 hr	1689	I
Cisatracurium besylate	GW	0.1, 2, 5 mg/ ml[a]	SCN	2 mg/ml[a]	Physically compatible with no change in measured turbidity or increase in particle content in 4 hr at 23 °C	2074	C
Cisplatin	BR	1 mg/ml	SKF	2 mg/ml[a]	Visually compatible for 4 hr at room temperature under fluorescent light	1685	C
Cladribine	ORT	0.015[b] and 0.5[c] mg/ml	SCN	2 mg/ml[b]	Physically compatible with no change in measured turbidity or increase in particle content in 4 hr at 23 °C	1969	C
Cyclophosphamide	MJ	10 mg/ml[a]	SKF	2 mg/ml[a]	Visually compatible for 4 hr at room temperature under fluorescent light	1685	C
Cytarabine	UP	50 mg/ml	SKF	2 mg/ml[a]	Visually compatible for 4 hr at room temperature under fluorescent light	1685	C
Docetaxel	RPR	0.9 mg/ml[a]	SCN	2 mg/ml[a]	Physically compatible with no change in measured turbidity or increase in particle content in 4 hr at 23 °C	2224	C

Y-Site Injection Compatibility (1:1 Mixture) (Cont.)

			Chlorpromazine HCl				
Drug	*Mfr*	*Conc*	*Mfr*	*Conc*	*Remarks*	*Ref*	*C/I*
Doxorubicin HCl	AD	0.2 mg/ml[a]	SKF	2 mg/ml[a]	Visually compatible for 4 hr at room temperature under fluorescent light	1685	C
Doxorubicin HCl liposome injection	SEQ	0.4 mg/ml[a]	ES	2 mg/ml[a]	Physically compatible with little or no change in measured turbidity and no increase in particle content in 4 hr at 23 °C	2087	C
Etoposide phosphate	BR	5 mg/ml[a]	ES	2 mg/ml[a]	White cloudy solution with brown undertones forms immediately with particulates in 4 hr	2218	I
Famotidine	ME	2 mg/ml[b]		2 mg/ml[a]	Visually compatible for 4 hr at 22 °C	1936	C
Filgrastim	AMG	30 μg/ml[a]	RU	2 mg/ml[a]	Physically compatible with no change in measured turbidity or increase in particle content in 4 hr at 22 °C	1687	C
Fluconazole	RR	2 mg/ml	ES	25 mg/ml	Physically compatible for 24 hr at 25 °C	1407	C
Fludarabine phosphate	BX	1 mg/ml[a]	ES	2 mg/ml[a]	Initial light haze intensifies within 30 min	1439	I
Furosemide	HMR	2.6 mg/ml[a]	RPR	0.13 mg/ml[a]	Precipitate forms immediately	2244	I
Gatifloxacin	BMS	2 mg/ml[a]	ES	2 mg/ml[a]	Physically compatible with no change in measured haze or increase in particle content in 4 hr at 23 °C	2234	C
Gemcitabine HCl	LI	10 mg/ml[b]	ES	2 mg/ml[b]	Physically compatible with no change in measured turbidity or increase in particle content in 4 hr at 23 °C	2226	C
Granisetron HCl	SKB	0.05 mg/ml[a]	SCN	2 mg/ml[a]	Physically compatible with no change in measured turbidity or increase in particle content in 4 hr at 23 °C	2000	C
Heparin sodium	UP	1000 units/L[d]	SKF	25 mg/ml	Physically compatible for at least 4 hr at room temperature by visual and microscopic examination	534	C
	NOV	29.2 units/ml[a]	RPR	0.13 mg/ml[a]	Visually compatible for 150 min	2244	C
Hetastarch in lactated electrolyte injection (Hextend)	AB	6%	ES	2 mg/ml[a]	Physically compatible with no change in measured turbidity or increase in particle content in 4 hr at 23 °C	2339	C
Hydrocortisone sodium succinate	UP	10 mg/L[d]	SKF	25 mg/ml	Physically compatible for at least 4 hr at room temperature by visual and microscopic examination	534	C
Linezolid	PHU	2 mg/ml	ES	2 mg/ml[a]	Measured haze level increases immediately	2264	I
Melphalan HCl	BW	0.1 mg/ml[b]	ES	2 mg/ml[b]	Large increase in measured turbidity occurs within 1 hr and grows over 3 hr	1557	I
Methotrexate sodium	AD	15 mg/ml[e]	SKF	2 mg/ml[a]	Turbidity and yellow precipitate form immediately	1685	I
Ondansetron HCl	GL	1 mg/ml[b]	ES	2 mg/ml[a]	Physically compatible for 4 hr at 22 °C	1365	C
Paclitaxel	NCI	1.2 mg/ml[a]	ES	2 mg/ml[a]	Normal inherent haze from paclitaxel decreases immediately	1556	I
Piperacillin sodium–tazobactam sodium	LE	40 + 5 mg/ml[a]	RU	2 mg/ml[a]	Heavy white turbidity forms immediately. White precipitate forms in 4 hr	1688	I

Y-Site Injection Compatibility (1:1 Mixture) (Cont.)

Drug	Mfr	Conc	Chlorpromazine HCl Mfr	Chlorpromazine HCl Conc	Remarks	Ref	C/I
Potassium chloride	AB	40 mEq/L[d]	SKF	25 mg/ml	Physically compatible for at least 4 hr at room temperature by visual and microscopic examination	534	C
	BRN	0.625 mEq/ml[a]	RPR	0.13 mg/ml[a]	Visually compatible for 150 min	2244	C
Propofol	ZEN	10 mg/ml	SCN	2 mg/ml[a]	Physically compatible for 1 hr at 23 °C with no increase in particle content	2066	C
Remifentanil HCl	GW	0.025 mg/ml[b]	SCN	2 mg/ml[a]	Slight subvisual haze forms in 1 hr	2075	I
	GW	0.25 mg/ml[b]	SCN	2 mg/ml[a]	Physically compatible with no change in measured turbidity or increase in particle content in 4 hr at 23 °C	2075	C
Sargramostim	IMM	10 μg/ml[b]	ES	2 mg/ml[b]	Slight haze, visible with high intensity light, forms immediately	1436	I
Teniposide	BR	0.1 mg/ml[a]	SCN	2 mg/ml[a]	Physically compatible with no subvisual haze or particle formation in 4 hr at 23 °C	1725	C
Thiotepa	IMM[f]	1 mg/ml[a]	SCN	2 mg/ml[a]	Physically compatible with no change in measured turbidity or increase in particle content in 4 hr at 23 °C	1861	C
TNA #218 to #226[g]			SCN	2 mg/ml[a]	Visually compatible with no precipitate or emulsion damage apparent in 4 hr at 23 °C	2215	C
TPN #212 to #215[g]			SCN	2 mg/ml[a]	Physically compatible with no change in measured turbidity or increase in particle content in 4 hr at 23 °C	2109	C
Vinorelbine tartrate	BW	1 mg/ml[b]	RU	2 mg/ml[b]	Physically compatible with little change in measured turbidity or increase in particle content in 4 hr at 22 °C	1558	C
Vitamin B complex with C	RC	2 ml/L[d]	SKF	25 mg/ml	Physically compatible for at least 4 hr at room temperature by visual and microscopic examination	534	C

[a]*Tested in dextrose 5% in water.*
[b]*Tested in sodium chloride 0.9%.*
[c]*Tested in bacteriostatic sodium chloride 0.9% preserved with benzyl alcohol 0.9%.*
[d]*Tested in dextrose 5% in Ringer's injection, dextrose 5% in Ringer's injection, lactated, dextrose 5% in water, Ringer's injection, lactated, and sodium chloride 0.9%.*
[e]*Tested in dextrose 5% in water with sodium bicarbonate 0.05 mEq/ml.*
[f]*Lyophilized formulation tested.*
[g]*Refer to Appendix I for the composition of parenteral nutrition solutions. TNA indicates a 3-in-1 admixture, and TPN indicates a 2-in-1 admixture.*

Additional Compatibility Information

Hydroxyzine and Meperidine — Chlorpromazine HCl (Elkins-Sinn) 6.25 mg/ml, hydroxyzine HCl (Pfizer) 12.5 mg/ml, and meperidine HCl (Winthrop) 25 mg/ml, in both glass and plastic syringes, have been reported to be physically compatible and chemically stable for at least one year at 4 and 25 °C when protected from light. Significant discoloration, ranging from yellow to brownish yellow, occurred on storage at 44 °C. (989)

Meperidine and Promethazine — Chlorpromazine HCl (Elkins-Sinn), meperidine HCl (Winthrop), and promethazine HCl (Elkins-Sinn), combined as an extemporaneous mixture for preoperative sedation, developed a brownish-yellow color after two weeks of storage with protection from light. The discoloration was attributed to the metacresol preservative content of Winthrop's meperidine HCl. Use of meperidine HCl (Wyeth) instead, which contains a different preservative, resulted in a solution that remained clear and colorless for at least three months when protected from light. (1148)

Pentobarbital — Chlorpromazine HCl (SKF) 50 mg/L has been reported to be conditionally compatible with pentobarbital sodium (Abbott) 500 mg/L. The mixture is physically incompatible in most Abbott infusion solutions except as noted below (3):

Ionosol MB with dextrose 5%	Physically compatible
Ionosol T with dextrose 5%	Physically compatible

Other Drugs — The formation of a precipitate was noted when chlorpromazine was mixed in a syringe with a morphine product preserved with chlorocresol 0.2%. The precipitate results from a chlorpromazine interaction with the chlorocresol rather than the morphine. (467; 468)

Chlorpromazine HCl is stated to be compatible with diamorphine HCl. (1442)

CIDOFOVIR
AHFS 8:18

Products — Cidofovir is available in 5-ml vials. Each milliliter contains cidofovir 75 mg with sodium hydroxide and/or hydrochloric acid to adjust pH. (2) The product must be diluted in sodium chloride 0.9% for administration. (2; 4)

pH — Cidofovir has a pH adjusted to 7.4. (2)

The pH values of cidofovir admixtures in three infusion solutions were (1963):

Solution	Concentration	pH
Dextrose 5% in sodium chloride 0.45%	0.085 and 3.51 mg/ml	6.7 to 7.0
Dextrose 5% in water	0.21 and 8.12 mg/ml	7.2 to 7.6
Sodium chloride 0.9%	0.21 and 8.12 mg/ml	7.1 to 7.5

Osmolality — Cidofovir is hypertonic and is diluted for administration. The osmolalities of cidofovir admixtures in three infusion solutions were (1963):

Solution	Concentration	Osmolality (mOsm/kg)
Dextrose 5% in sodium chloride 0.45%	0.085 and 3.51 mg/ml	382 and 392
Dextrose 5% in water	0.21 and 8.12 mg/ml	241 and 286
Sodium chloride 0.9%	0.21 and 8.12 mg/ml	275 and 315

Trade Name(s) — Vistide.

Administration — Cidofovir is administered by intravenous infusion in 100 ml of sodium chloride 0.9% at a constant rate over a one-hour period using an infusion-control pump. Shorter periods must not be used. Patients must be prehydrated with sodium chloride 0.9% and treated with probenecid. Intraocular administration is contraindicated. (2; 4)

Stability — Cidofovir should be stored at controlled room temperature between 20 and 25 °C. The manufacturer states that, diluted in 100 ml of sodium chloride 0.9% for administration, cidofovir should be used within 24 hours of preparation. Admixtures not used immediately should be stored under refrigeration at 2 to 8 °C but should still be used within 24 hours of preparation. Refrigeration or freezing should not be used to extend beyond the 24-hour limit. (2; 4)

Freezing Solutions — Cidofovir (Gilead Sciences) 0.2 and 8.1 mg/ml in sodium chloride 0.9% was physically and chemically stable for five days when stored frozen at –20 °C in PVC or polyethylene-polypropylene containers. (2076)

Sorption — Cidofovir is stated to be compatible with glass, PVC, and ethylene/propylene copolymer infusion solution containers. (2)

Cidofovir (Gilead Sciences) 0.21 and 8.12 mg/ml in dextrose 5% in water and sodium chloride 0.9% as well as 0.085 and 3.51 mg/ml in dextrose 5% in sodium chloride 0.45% exhibited no loss due to sorption to PVC or polyolefin containers for 24 hours at 4 and 30 °C and when run through PVC administration sets. (1963) Similarly, cidofovir exhibited no losses due to sorption to PVC or polyolefin (ethylene and propylene copolymer) containers determined by HPLC analysis of 0.2 and 8.1 mg/ml solutions in sodium chloride 0.9% when stored under refrigeration at 2 to 8 °C or frozen at –20 °C over a period of five days. (2076)

Compatibility Information

Solution Compatibility

Cidofovir

Solution	*Mfr*	*Mfr*	*Conc/L*	*Remarks*	*Ref*	*C/I*
Dextrose 5% in sodium chloride 0.45%	AB[a], BA[a], MG[b]	GIL	85 mg and 3.51 g	Physically compatible with no increase in subvisual particulates in 24 hr at 4 and 30 °C	1963	C
Dextrose 5% in water	AB[a], BA[a], MG[b]	GIL	210 mg and 8.12 g	Physically compatible with no increase in subvisual particulates and no loss by HPLC in 24 hr at 4 and 30 °C	1963	C

Solution Compatibility (Cont.)

Cidofovir

Solution	*Mfr*	*Mfr*	*Conc/L*	*Remarks*	*Ref*	*C/I*
Sodium chloride 0.9%	AB[a], BA[a], MG[b]	GIL	210 mg and 8.12 g	Physically compatible with no increase in subvisual particulates and no loss by HPLC in 24 hr at 4 and 30 °C	1963	C
	AB[a], BA[a], MG[b]	GIL	200 mg and 8.1 g	Physically compatible with no increase in subvisual particulates and no loss by HPLC in 5 days at 4 and −20 °C	2076	C

[a]*Tested in PVC containers.*
[b]*Tested in polyolefin containers.*

Additional Compatibility Information

Miscellaneous — The manufacturer states that cidofovir compatibility with Ringer's injection, lactated Ringer's injection, and solutions containing bacteriostatic agents has not been established. (2; 4) Similarly, there are no data for compatibility with other drugs or supplements. (2)

Other Information

Disposal — Partially used vials, diluted solutions, and materials used in admixture preparation and administration should be sealed in leak- and puncture-proof containers and incinerated at high temperature. (2; 4)

Skin Contact — Appropriate safety precautions for handling mutagenic substances should be taken; preparation in a biological safety cabinet and wearing of suitable gloves and gowns with knit cuffs are recommended. If cidofovir solution contacts skin or mucosa, wash the affected area immediately with soap and water. (2; 4)

CIMETIDINE HCL
AHFS 56:40

Products — Cimetidine HCl is available in 2-ml vials and 8-ml multiple-dose vials. Each milliliter contains cimetidine HCl equivalent to cimetidine 150 mg and phenol 5 mg with sodium hydroxide to adjust pH. (2)

Cimetidine HCl is also available as a premixed infusion solution of 300 mg/50 ml in sodium chloride 0.9%. (2)

pH — The injection has a pH range of 3.8 to 6. The premixed infusion has a pH range of 5 to 7. (2; 4)

Osmolality — The osmolality of cimetidine HCl (SKF) 6 mg/ml was determined to be 291 mOsm/kg in dextrose 5% in water and 314 mOsm/kg in sodium chloride 0.9%. At 15 mg/ml, the osmolality was determined to be 338 and 359 mOsm/kg, respectively. (1375)

The osmolality of cimetidine HCl 300 mg was calculated for the following dilutions (1054):

	Osmolality (mOsm/kg)	
Diluent	50 ml	100 ml
Dextrose 5% in water	286	274
Sodium chloride 0.9%	313	301

The premixed infusion solution of 300 mg/50 ml of sodium chloride 0.9% has an osmolality of about 336 mOsm/kg. (4)

Sodium Content — The premixed infusion contains about 7.7 mEq of sodium in 50 ml. (4)

Trade Name(s) — Tagamet.

Administration — Cimetidine HCl is administered intramuscularly with no dilution necessary, by slow direct intravenous injection over five minutes or more after dilution to a total of 20 ml with a compatible diluent such as sodium chloride 0.9%, by intermittent intravenous infusion over 15 to 20 minutes in at least 50 ml of compatible diluent, or by continuous intravenous infusion in 100 to 1000 ml of compatible diluent over 24 hours. (2; 4)

Stability — Intact containers of cimetidine HCl should be stored at controlled room temperature and protected from light. The products should be protected from excessive heat, but brief exposure of the premixed solution to temperatures up to 40 °C does not adversely affect stability. (2; 4) Cimetidine HCl may precipitate from solution on exposure to cold but reportedly can be redissolved by warming without degradation. (140; 854) In aqueous solution, cimetidine HCl exhibits maximum stability at pH 6. (549)

Cimetidine HCl (SmithKline Beecham) injection was diluted with sterile water for injection to a concentration of 15 mg/ml for use in minimizing measurement errors in pediatric dosing. The dilution was packaged in glass vials, and samples were stored at 22 °C in a closed cabinet and at 4 °C. The dilution remained visually free of particulate matter at both storage conditions throughout the study. HPLC analysis of the samples stored at 22 °C found cimetidine losses of 6% in 14 days and 10% in 28 days. Samples stored at 4 °C exhibited 5% loss in 28 days and 14% loss in 56 days. (1714)

Freezing Solutions—Cimetidine HCl (SKF) 300 mg/50 ml of dextrose 5% in water in PVC bags (Travenol) was frozen at −20 °C for up to 30 days. The bags were then thawed for two to three hours at room temperature and subsequently stored for eight days at 4 °C in a refrigerator. The cimetidine concentration, determined by an HPLC technique, was constant over the entire study period at about 100% of the initial amount. No significant deviation from the initial concentration occurred. In addition, the admixtures remained sterile throughout the study. (632)

In another study, microwave thawing of frozen cimetidine HCl admixtures was compared to room temperature thawing. Cimetidine HCl (SKF) 300 mg in 50-ml PVC bags of dextrose 5% in water and 100-ml PVC bags of sodium chloride 0.9% was frozen at −10 °C for 28 days. Samples were then thawed by microwave radiation or by standing at 27 °C. No visual changes and no loss of cimetidine occurred between the initial admixtures and the frozen solutions thawed by either means. Even overheating the 100-ml bags of sodium chloride 0.9% to allow boiling to occur for five seconds did not result in a significant loss of cimetidine. (780)

Elastomeric Reservoir Pumps—Cimetidine HCl solutions in elastomeric reservoir pumps have been stated by the pump manufacturers to be stable for the following time periods frozen, refrigerated (REF), or at room temperature (RT) (31):

Pump Reservoir(s)	Conc.	Frozen	REF	RT
Medflo	6 mg/ml[a,b]	4 weeks	8 days	8 days
ReadyMed	6 mg/ml[a,b]	4 weeks	8 days	48 hr

[a] *In dextrose 5% in water.*
[b] *In sodium chloride 0.9%.*

Sorption—Cimetidine (SKF) 6 mg/L in sodium chloride 0.9% (Travenol) in PVC bags did not exhibit significant sorption to the plastic during one week of storage at room temperature (15 to 20 °C). (536)

In addition, a 6-mg/L admixture in sodium chloride 0.9% did not exhibit any loss due to sorption during a seven-hour simulated infusion through an infusion set (Travenol) consisting of a cellulose propionate burette chamber and 170 cm of PVC tubing. (606)

The cimetidine solution was also tested as a simulated infusion over at least one hour by a syringe pump system. A glass syringe on a syringe pump was fitted with 20 cm of polyethylene tubing or 50 cm of Silastic tubing. No loss of drug due to sorption was observed with either tubing. (606)

Finally, a 25-ml aliquot of the cimetidine (SKF) 6 mg/L in sodium chloride 0.9% admixture was stored in all-plastic syringes composed of polypropylene barrels and polyethylene plungers for 24 hours at room temperature in the dark. The solution did not exhibit any loss due to sorption. (606)

Central Venous Catheter—Cimetidine HCl (SmithKline Beecham) 2 mg/ml in dextrose 5% in water was found to be compatible with the ARROWg+ard Blue Plus (Arrow International) chlorhexidine-bearing triple-lumen central catheter. HPLC analysis was used to evaluate completeness of drug delivery through the catheter and the amount of chlorhexidine removed from the internal lumens. Essentially complete delivery of the drug was found with little or no drug loss occurring. Furthermore, chlorhexidine delivered from the catheter remained at trace amounts with no substantial increase due to the delivery of the drug through the catheter. (2335)

Compatibility Information

Solution Compatibility

Cimetidine HCl

Solution	*Mfr*	*Mfr*	*Conc/L*	*Remarks*	*Ref*	*C/I*
Amino acids 3.5% with electrolytes	AB	SKF	1.2 and 5 g	Physically compatible and chemically stable for 1 week at room temperature	549	C
Amino acids 5.5%	TR	SKF	1.2 and 5 g	Physically compatible and chemically stable for 1 week at room temperature protected from light	550	C
Amino acids 5.5% with electrolytes	TR	SKF	1.2 and 5 g	Physically compatible and chemically stable for 1 week at room temperature protected from light	550	C
Amino acids 8.5%	TR	SKF	1.2 and 5 g	Physically compatible and chemically stable for 1 week at room temperature protected from light	550	C
Amino acids 8.5% with electrolytes	TR	SKF	1.2 and 5 g	Physically compatible and chemically stable for 1 week at room temperature protected from light	550	C
Dextrose 5% with Ascor-B-Sol	TR	SKF	1.2 and 5 g	Physically compatible and chemically stable for 1 week at room temperature protected from light	549	C
Dextrose 5% and Electrolyte #48	TR	SKF	1.2 and 5 g	Physically compatible and chemically stable for 1 week at room temperature	550	C

Solution Compatibility (Cont.)

Cimetidine HCl

Solution	*Mfr*	*Mfr*	*Conc/L*	*Remarks*	*Ref*	*C/I*
Dextrose 5% and Electrolyte #75	TR	SKF	1.2 and 5 g	Physically compatible and chemically stable for 1 week at room temperature	550	C
Dextrose 5% in Ringer's injection, lactated	TR	SKF	1.2 and 5 g	Physically compatible and chemically stable for 1 week at room temperature	549	C
Dextrose 5% in sodium chloride 0.2%	TR	SKF	1.2 and 5 g	Physically compatible and chemically stable for 1 week at room temperature	549	C
Dextrose 5% in sodium chloride 0.45%	TR	SKF	1.2 and 5 g	Physically compatible and chemically stable for 1 week at room temperature	549	C
Dextrose 5% in sodium chloride 0.9%	TR	SKF	1.2 and 5 g	Physically compatible and chemically stable for 1 week at room temperature	549	C
Dextrose 10% in sodium chloride 0.9%	TR	SKF	1.2 and 5 g	Physically compatible and chemically stable for 1 week at room temperature	549	C
Dextrose 5% in water	TR[a]	SKF	1.2 and 5 g	Physically compatible and chemically stable for 1 week at room temperature	549	C
	TR[b]	SKF	1.2 g	Physically compatible with about 3% cimetidine loss in 48 hr at room temperature	1186	C
	TR[b]	SKF	3 g	Physically compatible with little or no drug loss in 24 hr at 24 °C	1418	C
Dextrose 10% in water	TR[a]	SKF	1.2 and 5 g	Physically compatible and chemically stable for 1 week at room temperature	549	C
Dextrose 5% in water with vitamins	TR	SKF	1.2 and 5 g	Physically compatible and chemically stable for 1 week at room temperature	550	C
Fructose 5% and Electrolyte #48	TR	SKF	1.2 and 5 g	Physically compatible and chemically stable for 1 week at room temperature	550	C
Fructose 5% and Electrolyte #75	TR	SKF	1.2 and 5 g	Physically compatible with 4 to 7% decomposition in 1 week at room temperature	550	C
Invert sugar 5% in water	TR	SKF	1.2 and 5 g	Physically compatible and chemically stable for 1 week at room temperature	549	C
Invert sugar 10% in water	TR	SKF	1.2 and 5 g	Physically compatible and chemically stable for 1 week at room temperature	549	C
Ionosol B in dextrose 5% in water	AB	SKF	1.2 and 5 g	Physically compatible and chemically stable for 1 week at room temperature	549	C
Ionosol MB in dextrose 5% in water	AB	SKF	1.2 and 5 g	Physically compatible with 2 to 4% decomposition in 1 week at room temperature	550	C
Ionosol T in dextrose 5% in water	AB	SKF	1.2 and 5 g	Physically compatible with 4 to 6% decomposition in 1 week at room temperature	550	C
Mannitol 10% in water	TR	SKF	1.2 and 5 g	Physically compatible and chemically stable for 1 week at room temperature	549	C
Normosol M, 900 cal	AB	SKF	1.2 and 5 g	Physically compatible with 2 to 5% decomposition in 1 week at room temperature	550	C
Normosol M in dextrose 5% in water	AB	SKF	1.2 and 5 g	Physically compatible and chemically stable for 1 week at room temperature	549	C
Normosol M and Surbex T in dextrose 5% in water	AB	SKF	1.2 and 5 g	Physically compatible with 5 to 8% decomposition in 1 week at room temperature	550	C
Normosol R	AB	SKF	1.2 and 5 g	Physically compatible and chemically stable for 1 week at room temperature	550	C

Solution Compatibility (Cont.)

Cimetidine HCl

Solution	*Mfr*	*Mfr*	*Conc/L*	*Remarks*	*Ref*	*C/I*
Normosol R, pH 7.4	AB	SKF	1.2 and 5 g	Physically compatible and chemically stable for 1 week at room temperature	550	C
Normosol R in dextrose 5% in water	AB	SKF	1.2 and 5 g	Physically compatible and chemically stable for 1 week at room temperature	550	C
Plasma-Lyte 56 in dextrose 5% in water	TR	SKF	1.2 and 5 g	Physically compatible and chemically stable for 1 week at room temperature	549	C
Plasma-Lyte M in dextrose 5% in water	TR	SKF	1.2 and 5 g	Physically compatible and chemically stable for 1 week at room temperature	549	C
Ringer's injection	TR	SKF	1.2 and 5 g	Physically compatible and chemically stable for 1 week at room temperature	549	C
Ringer's injection, lactated	TR	SKF	1.2 and 5 g	Physically compatible and chemically stable for 1 week at room temperature	549	C
Sodium bicarbonate 5%	TR	SKF	1.2 and 5 g	Physically compatible and chemically stable for 1 week at room temperature	549	C
Sodium chloride 0.9%	AB	SKF	1.2 and 5 g	Physically compatible and chemically stable for 1 week at room temperature	549	C
	BA[c]	SKB	600 mg	Visually compatible with no loss by HPLC in 48 hr at 24 °C	1854	C
TNA #72[d]		SKF	400, 800, 1200 mg	Physically compatible and no cimetidine loss in 24 hr at 25 °C. Fat emulsion particle size increased in 48 hr	998	C
TNA #75[d]		SKF	1 g	Physically compatible and cimetidine chemically stable for 48 hr at room temperature	140	C
TNA #179[d]		SKF	400 and 900 mg	Visually compatible with less than 3% cimetidine loss by HPLC in 72 hr at room temperature protected from light	1622	C
TNA #197 to #200[d]		SKF	450 mg	Physically compatible with 7% or less loss by HPLC in 48 hr at 22 °C exposed to light	1921	C
TPN #34, #35, #37[d]		SKF	300 mg	Physically compatible and cimetidine chemically stable for 24 hr at room temperature and 4 °C	781	C
TPN #36[d]		SKF	300 mg	Physically compatible and cimetidine chemically stable for 24 hr at 4 °C. Room temperature sample gave spurious result	781	C
TPN #93[d]			600 mg	Physically compatible and cimetidine chemically stable for 48 hr at room temperature	1320	C
TPN #94[d]			600 mg	Physically compatible and cimetidine and copper chemically stable for 48 hr at room temperature	1320	C
TPN #196[d]		SKF	450 mg	Physically compatible with no loss by HPLC in 48 hr at 22 °C exposed to light	1921	C
TPN #238, #239, #240[d,e]		SKB	80 mg	Little or no cimetidine loss by HPLC in 28 days at 5 °C	1912	C

[a]*Tested in both glass and PVC containers.*
[b]*Tested in PVC containers.*
[c]*Tested in glass containers.*
[d]*Refer to Appendix I for the composition of parenteral nutrition solutions. TNA indicates a 3-in-1 admixture, and TPN indicates a 2-in-1 admixture.*
[e]*Tested in EVA containers.*

Additive Compatibility

Cimetidine HCl

Drug	*Mfr*	*Conc/L*	*Mfr*	*Conc/L*	*Test Soln*	*Remarks*	*Ref*	*C/I*
Acetazolamide sodium	LE	5 g	SKF	3 g	D5W	Physically compatible and cimetidine chemically stable for 24 hr at room temperature. Acetazolamide not tested	551	C
Amikacin sulfate	BR	2.5 g	SKF	1.5 g	D5W	Physically compatible and cimetidine chemically stable for 24 hr at room temperature. Amikacin not tested	551	C
Aminophylline	IX	500 mg	SKF	1.2 g	D5W[a]	Physically compatible with about 3 to 5% cimetidine loss and little or no aminophylline loss in 48 hr at room temperature	1186	C
Amphotericin B	SQ	100 mg	SKF	600 mg	D5W	Immediate haze formation. Precipitate observed at 24 hr at room temperature	551	I
Ampicillin sodium	SKF	1 g	SKF	1.2 and 5 g	D5W, NS	Physically compatible and cimetidine chemically stable for 24 hr at room temperature. Ampicillin stability is determining factor	551	?
Atracurium besylate	BW	500 mg		5 g	D5W	Physically compatible and atracurium chemically stable for 24 hr at 5 and 30 °C	1694	C
Cefamandole nafate	LI	20 g	SKF	6 g	D5W	Immediate haze formation. Gelatinous precipitate observed at 24 hr at room temperature. Cimetidine loss of 7% attributed to precipitation	551	I
	LI	1 g	SKF	300 mg	D5W	Physically compatible and cimetidine chemically stable for 24 hr at room temperature. Cefamandole not tested	551	C
		10 g	SKF	3 g	D5W, NS	Cloudiness forms after 4 to 5 hr, increasing to a dense precipitate in 24 hr at room temperature	516	I
		20 g	SKF	6 g	D5W, NS	Cloudiness forms after 4 to 5 hr, increasing to a dense precipitate in 24 hr at room temperature	516	I
Cefazolin sodium	SKF	10 g	SKF	3 g	D5W	Haze observed at 24 hr at room temperature. Cimetidine chemically stable but cefazolin not tested	551	I
		10 g	SKF	3 g	D5W, NS	Physically compatible for 48 hr at room temperature. Precipitate forms on freezing	516	C
		20 g	SKF	6 g	D5W, NS	Physically compatible for 48 hr at room temperature. Precipitate forms on freezing	516	C
	SKF	1 g	SKF	1.2 and 5 g	D5W, NS	Physically compatible and cimetidine chemically stable for 24 hr at room temperature. Cefazolin not tested	551	C
Cefoperazone sodium	RR	5 g	SKF	2 g	D5W	Physically compatible. 5% cefoperazone loss at 25 °C and 3% at 4 °C in 48 hr. 2% or less cimetidine loss in 48 hr at 25 and 4 °C	1403	C
Cefoxitin sodium	MSD	10 g	SKF	3 g	D5W	Physically compatible and cimetidine chemically stable for 24 hr at room temperature. Cefoxitin not tested	551	C

Additive Compatibility (Cont.)

			Cimetidine HCl					
Drug	*Mfr*	*Conc/L*	*Mfr*	*Conc/L*	*Test Soln*	*Remarks*	*Ref*	*C/I*
Chlorothiazide sodium	MSD	5 g	SKF	3 g	D5W	Physically compatible and cimetidine chemically stable for 24 hr at room temperature. Chlorothiazide not tested	551	C
Clindamycin phosphate	UP	1.2 g	SKF	1.2 and 5 g	D5W, NS	Physically compatible and cimetidine chemically stable for 24 hr at room temperature. Clindamycin not tested	551	C
Colistimethate sodium	WC	1.5 g	SKF	3 g	D5W	Physically compatible and cimetidine chemically stable for 24 hr at room temperature. Colistimethate not tested	551	C
Cryptenamine acetate	MA	1.3 g	SKF	3 g	D5W	Physically compatible and cimetidine chemically stable for 24 hr at room temperature. Cryptenamine not tested	551	C
Dexamethasone sodium phosphate	MSD	40 mg	SKF	3 g	D5W	Physically compatible and cimetidine chemically stable for 24 hr at room temperature. Dexamethasone not tested	551	C
Digoxin	BW	2.5 mg	SKF	3 g	D5W	Physically compatible and cimetidine chemically stable for 24 hr at room temperature. Digoxin not tested	551	C
Epinephrine HCl	PD	100 mg	SKF	3 g	D5W	Physically compatible and cimetidine chemically stable for 24 hr at room temperature. Epinephrine not tested	551	C
Erythromycin lactobionate	AB	5 g	SKF	3 g	D5W	Physically compatible and cimetidine chemically stable for 24 hr at room temperature. Erythromycin not tested	551	C
Ethacrynate sodium	MSD	500 mg	SKF	3 g	D5W	Physically compatible and cimetidine chemically stable for 24 hr at room temperature. Ethacrynate not tested	551	C
Floxacillin sodium	BE	20 g	SKF	4 g	NS	Physically compatible for 72 hr at 15 and 30 °C	1479	C
Flumazenil	RC	20 mg	SKB	2.4 g	D5W[a]	Visually compatible with no flumazenil loss by HPLC in 24 hr at 23 °C under fluorescent light. Cimetidine not tested	1710	C
Furosemide	HO	400 mg	SKF	3 g	D5W	Physically compatible and cimetidine chemically stable for 24 hr at room temperature. Furosemide not tested	551	C
	HO	1 g	SKF	4 g	NS	Physically compatible for 72 hr at 15 and 30 °C	1479	C
Gentamicin sulfate	SC	800 mg	SKF	3 g	D5W	Physically compatible and cimetidine chemically stable for 24 hr at room temperature. Gentamicin not tested	551	C
	SC	800 mg	SKF	1.2 and 5 g	D5W, NS	Physically compatible and cimetidine chemically stable for 24 hr at room temperature. Gentamicin not tested	551	C
Insulin, regular	LI	100 units	SKF	1.2 and 5 g	D5W, NS	Physically compatible and cimetidine chemically stable for 24 hr at room temperature. Insulin not tested	551	C
Isoproterenol HCl	WI	20 mg	SKF	3 g	D5W	Physically compatible and cimetidine chemically stable for 24 hr at room temperature. Isoproterenol not tested	551	C

Additive Compatibility (Cont.)

Cimetidine HCl

Drug	*Mfr*	*Conc/L*	*Mfr*	*Conc/L*	*Test Soln*	*Remarks*	*Ref*	*C/I*
Lidocaine HCl	AST	2.5 g	SKF	3 g	D5W	Physically compatible and cimetidine chemically stable for 24 hr at room temperature. Lidocaine not tested	551	C
Lincomycin HCl	UP	6 g	SKF	3 g	D5W	Physically compatible and cimetidine chemically stable for 24 hr at room temperature. Lincomycin not tested	551	C
Meropenem	ZEN	1 and 20 g	SKB	3 g	NS	Visually compatible for 4 hr at room temperature	1994	C
Metaraminol bitartrate	MSD	1 g	SKF	3 g	D5W	Physically compatible and cimetidine chemically stable for 24 hr at room temperature. Metaraminol not tested	551	C
Methylprednisolone sodium succinate	UP	400 mg	SKF	3 g	D5W	Physically compatible and cimetidine chemically stable for 24 hr at room temperature. Methylprednisolone not tested	551	C
	UP	400 mg	SKF	3 g	D5W[a]	Physically compatible with no cimetidine loss and 3% methylprednisolone 21-succinate ester loss in 24 hr at 24 °C	1418	C
	UP	1.25 g	SKF	3 g	D5W[a]	Physically compatible with no cimetidine loss and 8% methylprednisolone 21-succinate ester loss in 24 hr at 24 °C	1418	C
Metoclopramide HCl	RB	100 mg	SKF	3 g	NS	Physically compatible for 48 hr at room temperature, but bioavailability of cimetidine may be reduced	924	?
	RB	100 mg and 1.6 g	SKF	3 g		Physically compatible for 48 hr at 25 °C	1167	C
Norepinephrine bitartrate	WI	40 mg	SKF	3 g	D5W	Physically compatible and cimetidine chemically stable for 24 hr at room temperature. Norepinephrine not tested	551	C
Penicillin G potassium	LI	2.4 million units	SKF	1.2 and 5 g	D5W, NS	Physically compatible and cimetidine chemically stable for 24 hr at room temperature. Penicillin not tested	551	C
Phytonadione	MSD	100 mg	SKF	3 g	D5W	Physically compatible and cimetidine chemically stable for 24 hr at room temperature. Phytonadione not tested	551	C
Polymyxin B sulfate	BW	10 million units	SKF	1.2 g	D5W	Physically compatible and cimetidine chemically stable for 24 hr at room temperature. Polymyxin B not tested	551	C
Potassium chloride	SKF	20 mEq	SKF	1.2 and 5 g	D5S, D5W, NS	Physically compatible and cimetidine chemically stable for 24 hr at room temperature. Potassium chloride not tested	551	C
	SKF	80 mEq	SKF	1.2 and 5 g	D5S, D5W, NS	Physically compatible and cimetidine chemically stable for 24 hr at room temperature. Potassium chloride not tested	551	C
Protamine sulfate	LI	500 mg	SKF	3 g	D5W	Physically compatible and cimetidine chemically stable for 24 hr at room temperature. Protamine not tested	551	C
Quinidine gluconate	LI	3.2 g	SKF	3 g	D5W	Physically compatible and cimetidine chemically stable for 24 hr at room temperature. Quinidine not tested	551	C

Additive Compatibility (Cont.)

Cimetidine HCl

Drug	*Mfr*	*Conc/L*	*Mfr*	*Conc/L*	*Test Soln*	*Remarks*	*Ref*	*C/I*
Sodium nitroprusside	RC	500 mg	SKF	3 g	D5W	Physically compatible and cimetidine chemically stable for 24 hr at room temperature. Sodium nitroprusside not tested	551	C
Tacrolimus	FUJ	10 mg	SKB	600 mg	NS[b]	Visually compatible with no cimetidine loss and 3% tacrolimus loss by HPLC in 48 hr at 24 °C	1854	C
Vancomycin HCl	LI	5 g	SKF	3 g	D5W	Physically compatible and cimetidine chemically stable for 24 hr at room temperature. Vancomycin not tested	551	C
Verapamil HCl	KN	80 mg	SKF	2.4 g	D5W, NS	Physically compatible for 24 hr	764	C
Vitamin B complex	UP	1 vial	SKF	1.2 and 5 g	D5W, NS	Physically compatible and cimetidine chemically stable for 24 hr at room temperature. Vitamins not tested	551	C
Vitamin B complex with C	TR		SKF	1.2 and 5 g	D5W	Physically compatible and stable for 48 hr	360	C

[a]*Tested in PVC containers.*
[b]*Tested in glass containers.*

Drugs in Syringe Compatibility

Cimetidine HCl

Drug (in syringe)	*Mfr*	*Amt*	*Mfr*	*Amt*	*Remarks*	*Ref*	*C/I*
Atropine sulfate	LI	0.6 mg/ 1.5 ml	SKF	300 mg/ 2 ml	Physically compatible and cimetidine chemically stable for 90 min at room temperature	542	C
	LI	0.4 mg/ 1 ml	SKF	300 mg/ 2 ml	Physically compatible and cimetidine chemically stable for 90 min at room temperature	542	C
Atropine sulfate with pentobarbital sodium	LI AB	0.6 mg/ 1.5 ml 100 mg/ 2 ml	SKF	300 mg/ 2 ml	Immediate precipitation	542	I
Butorphanol tartrate	BR	2 mg/ 1 ml	SKF	300 mg/ 2 ml	Physically compatible for 4 hr at 25 °C	25	C
Cefamandole nafate		1 g/5 ml	SKF	300 mg/ 2 ml	Immediate precipitation	516	I
Cefazolin sodium		1 g/5 ml	SKF	300 mg/ 2 ml	Immediate precipitation	516	I
Chlorpromazine HCl	WY	25 mg/ 1 ml	SKF	300 mg/ 2 ml	Immediate haze formation	25	I
Diatrizoate meglumine and diatrizoate sodium	MA	52 + 8%, 5 ml	SKF	150 mg/ 1 ml	Physically compatible for at least 2 hr	1438	C
Diatrizoate sodium	WI	60%, 5 ml	SKF	150 mg/ 1 ml	Physically compatible for at least 2 hr	1438	C
Diazepam	RC	10 mg/ 2 ml	SKF	300 mg/ 2 ml	Physically compatible for 4 hr at 25 °C	25	C
Diphenhydramine HCl	PD	50 mg/ 1 ml	SKF	300 mg/ 2 ml	Physically compatible for 4 hr at 25 °C	25	C

Drugs in Syringe Compatibility (Cont.)

Drug (in syringe)	*Mfr*	*Amt*	Cimetidine HCl *Mfr*	*Amt*	*Remarks*	*Ref*	*C/I*
Doxapram HCl	RB	400 mg/ 20 ml	SKF	50 mg/ 2 ml	Physically compatible with no doxapram loss in 24 hr	1177	C
Droperidol	JN	5 mg/ 2 ml	SKF	300 mg/ 2 ml	Physically compatible for 4 hr at 25 °C	25	C
Fentanyl citrate	JN	0.1 mg/ 2 ml	SKF	300 mg/ 2 ml	Physically compatible for 4 hr at 25 °C	25	C
Glycopyrrolate	ES	0.2 mg/ 1 ml	SKF	300 mg/ 2 ml	Physically compatible for 4 hr at 25 °C	25	C
Heparin sodium		5000 units/ 5 ml	SKF	300 mg/ 2 ml	Physically compatible for 48 hr at room temperature	516	C
		2500 units/ 1 ml		200 mg/ 2 ml	Turbidity or precipitate forms within 5 min	1053	I
Hydromorphone HCl	WI	2 mg/ 1 ml	SKF	300 mg/ 2 ml	Physically compatible for 4 hr at 25 °C	25	C
Hydroxyzine HCl	ES	100 mg/ 2 ml	SKF	300 mg/ 2 ml	Physically compatible for 4 hr at 25 °C	25	C
Iohexol	WI	64.7%, 5 ml	SKF	150 mg/ 1 ml	Physically compatible for at least 2 hr	1438	C
Iopamidol	SQ	61%, 5 ml	SKF	150 mg/ 1 ml	Physically compatible for at least 2 hr	1438	C
Iothalamate meglumine	MA	60%, 5 ml	SKF	150 mg/ 1 ml	Physically compatible for at least 2 hr	1438	C
Ioxaglate meglumine and ioxaglate sodium	MA	39.3% + 19.6%, 5 ml	SKF	150 mg/ 1 ml	Precipitate forms immediately and persists for at least 2 hr	1438	I
Lorazepam	WY	2 mg/ 1 ml	SKF	300 mg/ 2 ml	Physically compatible for 4 hr at 25 °C	25	C
Meperidine HCl	WI	100 mg/ 2 ml	SKF	300 mg/ 2 ml	Physically compatible for 4 hr at 25 °C	25	C
Midazolam HCl	RC	5 mg/ 1 ml	SKF	300 mg/ 2 ml	Physically compatible for 4 hr at 25 °C under fluorescent light	1145	C
Morphine sulfate	WI	10 mg/ 1 ml	SKF	300 mg/ 2 ml	Physically compatible for 4 hr at 25 °C	25	C
Nafcillin sodium		1 g/5 ml	SKF	300 mg/ 2 ml	Physically compatible for 48 hr at room temperature	516	C
Nalbuphine HCl	EN	10 mg/ 1 ml	SKF	300 mg/ 2 ml	Physically compatible for 4 hr at 25 °C	25	C
	DU	10 mg/ 1 ml		300 mg/ 2 ml	Physically compatible for 48 hr	128	C
	DU	20 mg/ 1 ml		300 mg/ 2 ml	Physically compatible for 48 hr	128	C
Papaveretum	RC[a]	20 mg/ 1 ml	SKF	300 mg/ 2 ml	Visually compatible for 4 hr at 25 °C	25	C
Penicillin G sodium		1 million units/ 5 ml	SKF	300 mg/ 2 ml	Precipitate forms between 36 and 48 hr at room temperature	516	C

Drugs in Syringe Compatibility (Cont.)

Cimetidine HCl

Drug (in syringe)	*Mfr*	*Amt*	*Mfr*	*Amt*	*Remarks*	*Ref*	*C/I*
Pentazocine lactate	WI	60 mg/ 2 ml	SKF	300 mg/ 2 ml	Physically compatible for 4 hr at 25 °C	25	C
Pentobarbital sodium	AB	100 mg/ 2 ml	SKF	300 mg/ 2 ml	Immediate precipitation	542	I
Pentobarbital sodium with atropine sulfate	AB LI	100 mg/ 2 ml 0.6 mg/ 1.5 ml	SKF	300 mg/ 2 ml	Immediate precipitation	542	I
Perphenazine	SC	5 mg/ 1 ml	SKF	300 mg/ 2 ml	Physically compatible for 4 hr at 25 °C	25	C
Prochlorperazine edisylate	SKF	10 mg/ 2 ml	SKF	300 mg/ 2 ml	Physically compatible for 4 hr at 25 °C	25	C
Promazine HCl	WY	25 mg/ 1 ml	SKF	300 mg/ 2 ml	Physically compatible for 4 hr at 25 °C	25	C
Promethazine HCl	WY	25 mg/ 1 ml	SKF	300 mg/ 2 ml	Physically compatible for 4 hr at 25 °C	25	C
Scopolamine HBr	BW	0.43 mg/ 0.5 ml	SKF	300 mg/ 2 ml	Physically compatible for 4 hr at 25 °C	25	C
Secobarbital sodium	WY	100 mg/ 2 ml	SKF	300 mg/ 2 ml	Immediate precipitation	25	I
Sodium acetate		10 mEq/ 5 ml	SKF	300 mg/ 2 ml	Physically compatible for 48 hr at room temperature	516	C
Sodium chloride		12.5 mEq/ 5 ml	SKF	300 mg/ 2 ml	Precipitate forms between 36 and 48 hr at room temperature	516	C
Sodium lactate		25 mEq/ 5 ml	SKF	300 mg/ 2 ml	Physically compatible for 48 hr at room temperature	516	C

[a]The former formulation was tested.

Y-Site Injection Compatibility (1:1 Mixture)

Cimetidine HCl

Drug	*Mfr*	*Conc*	*Mfr*	*Conc*	*Remarks*	*Ref*	*C/I*
Acyclovir sodium	BW	5 mg/ml[a]	SKF	6 mg/ml[a]	Physically compatible for 4 hr at 25 °C	1157	C
Allopurinol sodium	BW	3 mg/ml[b]	SKB	12 mg/ml[b]	Tiny crystals form in 1 hr and become large crystals in 4 hr	1686	I
Amifostine	USB	10 mg/ml[a]	SKB	12 mg/ml[a]	Physically compatible with no change in measured turbidity or increase in particle content in 4 hr at 23 °C	1845	C
Aminophylline	ES	4 mg/ml[c]	SKF	6 mg/ml[c]	Physically compatible for 3 hr	1316	C
Amphotericin B cholesteryl sulfate complex	SEQ	0.83 mg/ml[a]	AMR	12 mg/ml[a]	Gross precipitate forms	2117	I
Amsacrine	NCI	1 mg/ml[a]	SKF	12 mg/ml[a]	Initially clear, but yellow-orange turbidity develops in 1 hr, becoming flocculent precipitate in 4 hr	1381	I
Atracurium besylate	BW	0.5 mg/ml[a]	SKF	6 mg/ml[a]	Physically compatible for 24 hr at 28 °C	1337	C

Y-Site Injection Compatibility (1:1 Mixture) (Cont.)

Cimetidine HCl

Drug	*Mfr*	*Conc*	*Mfr*	*Conc*	*Remarks*	*Ref*	*C/I*
Aztreonam	SQ	40 mg/ml[a]	SKB	12 mg/ml[a]	Physically compatible with no subvisual haze or particle formation in 4 hr at 23 °C	1758	C
Cefepime HCl	BMS	20 mg/ml[a]	SKB	12 mg/ml[a]	Cloudy solution forms immediately	1689	I
Cisatracurium besylate	GW	0.1, 2, 5 mg/ml[a]	SKB	12 mg/ml[a]	Physically compatible with no change in measured turbidity or increase in particle content in 4 hr at 23 °C	2074	C
Cisplatin	BR	1 mg/ml	SKF	12 mg/ml[a]	Visually compatible for 4 hr at room temperature under fluorescent light	1685	C
Cladribine	ORT	0.015[b] and 0.5[d] mg/ml	SKB	12 mg/ml[b]	Physically compatible with no change in measured turbidity or increase in particle content in 4 hr at 23 °C	1969	C
Clarithromycin	AB	4 mg/ml[a]	SKB	8 mg/ml[a]	Visually compatible for 72 hr at both 30 and 17 °C	2174	C
Cyclophosphamide	MJ	10 mg/ml[a]	SKF	12 mg/ml[a]	Visually compatible for 4 hr at room temperature under fluorescent light	1685	C
Cytarabine	UP	50 mg/ml	SKF	12 mg/ml[a]	Visually compatible for 4 hr at room temperature under fluorescent light	1685	C
Diltiazem HCl	MMD	5 mg/ml	SKF	6[c] and 150 mg/ml	Visually compatible	1807	C
	MMD	1 mg/ml[b]	SKF	150 mg/ml	Visually compatible	1807	C
Docetaxel	RPR	0.9 mg/ml[a]	AMR	12 mg/ml[a]	Physically compatible with no change in measured turbidity or increase in particle content in 4 hr at 23 °C	2224	C
Doxorubicin HCl	AD	0.2 mg/ml[a]	SKF	12 mg/ml[a]	Visually compatible for 4 hr at room temperature under fluorescent light	1685	C
Doxorubicin HCl liposome injection	SEQ	0.4 mg/ml[a]	SKB	12 mg/ml[a]	Physically compatible with little or no change in measured turbidity and no increase in particle content in 4 hr at 23 °C	2087	C
Enalaprilat	MSD	0.05 mg/ml[b]	SKF	3 mg/ml[a]	Physically compatible for 24 hr at room temperature under fluorescent light	1355	C
Esmolol HCl	DCC	10 mg/ml[a]	SKF	6 mg/ml[a]	Physically compatible for 24 hr at 22 °C	1169	C
Etoposide phosphate	BR	5 mg/ml[a]	AMR	12 mg/ml[a]	Physically compatible with no change in measured turbidity or increase in particle content in 4 hr at 23 °C	2218	C
Filgrastim	AMG	30 µg/ml[a]	SKB	12 mg/ml[a]	Physically compatible with no change in measured turbidity or increase in particle content in 4 hr at 22 °C	1687	C
Fluconazole	RR	2 mg/ml	SKF	150 mg/ml	Physically compatible for 24 hr at 25 °C	1407	C
	RR	2 mg/ml	SKB	1 and 2 mg/ml[c]	Visually compatible for 24 hr at 28 °C	1760	C
Fludarabine phosphate	BX	1 mg/ml[a]	SKF	12 mg/ml	Physically compatible for 4 hr at room temperature under fluorescent light	1439	C
Foscarnet sodium	AST	24 mg/ml	SKF	150 mg/ml	Physically compatible for 24 hr at room temperature under fluorescent light	1335	C

Y-Site Injection Compatibility (1:1 Mixture) (Cont.)

Cimetidine HCl

Drug	*Mfr*	*Conc*	*Mfr*	*Conc*	*Remarks*	*Ref*	*C/I*
Gatifloxacin	BMS	2 mg/ml[a]	SKB	12 mg/ml[a]	Physically compatible with no change in measured haze or increase in particle content in 4 hr at 23 °C	2234	C
Gemcitabine HCl	LI	10 mg/ml[b]	AMR	12 mg/ml[b]	Physically compatible with no change in measured turbidity or increase in particle content in 4 hr at 23 °C	2226	C
Granisetron HCl	SKB	1 mg/ml	SKB	3 mg/ml[b]	Physically compatible with little or no loss of either drug by HPLC in 4 hr at 22 °C	1883	C
Haloperidol lactate	MN	0.5[a] and 5 mg/ml	SKF	6 mg/ml[a]	Visually compatible for 24 hr at 21 °C	1523	C
Heparin sodium		50 units/ml/min[b]		200 mg/2 ml[e]	Clear solution	1053	C
	TR	50 units/ml	SKB	6 mg/ml[a]	Visually compatible for 4 hr at 25 °C	1793	C
Hetastarch in lactated electrolyte injection (Hextend)	AB	6%	SKB	12 mg/ml[a]	Physically compatible with no change in measured turbidity or increase in particle content in 4 hr at 23 °C	2339	C
Hetastarch in sodium chloride 0.9%	DCC	6%	SKF	6 mg/ml[a]	Physically compatible for 4 hr at room temperature by visual examination	1313; 1315	C
Idarubicin HCl	AD	1 mg/ml[b]	SKF	6 mg/ml[a]	Visually compatible for 24 hr at 25 °C	1525	C
Inamrinone lactate	WB	3 mg/ml[b]	SKF	15 mg/ml[a]	Physically compatible for at least 4 hr at 25 °C under fluorescent light	992	C
Indomethacin sodium trihydrate	MSD	1 mg/ml[b]	SKB	6 mg/ml[a]	Haze and fine precipitate form immediately	1527	I
Labetalol HCl	SC	1 mg/ml[a]	SKF	3 mg/ml[a]	Physically compatible for 24 hr at 18 °C	1171	C
Levofloxacin	OMN	5 mg/ml[a]	AMR	150 mg/ml	Visually compatible for 4 hr at 24 °C under fluorescent light	2233	C
Linezolid	PHU	2 mg/ml	AMR	12 mg/ml[a]	Physically compatible with no change in measured turbidity or increase in particle content in 4 hr at 23 °C	2264	C
Melphalan HCl	BW	0.1 mg/ml[b]	SKB	12 mg/ml[b]	Physically compatible with no change in measured turbidity or increase in particle content in 3 hr at 22 °C	1557	C
Meropenem	ZEN	1 and 50 mg/ml[b]	SKB	150 mg/ml	Visually compatible for 4 hr at room temperature	1994	C
Methotrexate sodium	AD	15 mg/ml[f]	SKF	12 mg/ml[a]	Visually compatible for 4 hr at room temperature under fluorescent light	1685	C
Midazolam HCl	RC	1 mg/ml[a]	SKB	15 mg/ml[a]	Visually compatible for 24 hr at 23 °C	1847	C
Milrinone lactate	SW	0.4 mg/ml[a]	SKB	6 mg/ml[a]	Visually compatible with little or no loss of either drug by HPLC in 4 hr at 23 °C	2214	C
Ondansetron HCl	GL	1 mg/ml[b]	SKF	12 mg/ml[a]	Physically compatible for 4 hr at 22 °C	1365	C
Paclitaxel	NCI	1.2 mg/ml[a]		12 mg/ml[a]	Physically compatible with no change in measured turbidity in 4 hr at 22 °C	1528	C
Pancuronium bromide	ES	0.05 mg/ml[a]	SKF	6 mg/ml[a]	Physically compatible for 24 hr at 28 °C	1337	C

Y-Site Injection Compatibility (1:1 Mixture) (Cont.)

Cimetidine HCl

Drug	*Mfr*	*Conc*	*Mfr*	*Conc*	*Remarks*	*Ref*	*C/I*
Piperacillin sodium–tazobactam sodium	LE	40 + 5 mg/ml[a]	SKB	12 mg/ml[a]	Physically compatible with no change in measured turbidity or increase in particle content in 4 hr at 22 °C	1688	C
Propofol	ZEN	10 mg/ml	SKB	12 mg/ml[a]	Physically compatible for 1 hr at 23 °C with no increase in particle content	2066	C
Remifentanil HCl	GW	0.025 and 0.25 mg/ml[b]	SKB	12 mg/ml[a]	Physically compatible with no change in measured turbidity or increase in particle content in 4 hr at 23 °C	2075	C
Sargramostim	IMM	10 μg/ml[b]	SKF	12 mg/ml[b]	Physically compatible for 4 hr at 22 °C	1436	C
Tacrolimus	FUJ	1 mg/ml[b]	SKB	150 mg/ml	Visually compatible for 24 hr at 25 °C	1630	C
Teniposide	BR	0.1 mg/ml[a]	SKB	12 mg/ml[a]	Physically compatible with no subvisual haze or particle formation in 4 hr at 23 °C	1725	C
Theophylline	TR	4 mg/ml	SKB	6 mg/ml[a]	Visually compatible for 6 hr at 25 °C	1793	C
Thiotepa	IMM[g]	1 mg/ml[a]	SKB	12 mg/ml[a]	Physically compatible with no change in measured turbidity or increase in particle content in 4 hr at 23 °C	1861	C
TNA #218 to #226[h]			SKB	12 mg/ml[a]	Visually compatible with no precipitate or emulsion damage apparent in 4 hr at 23 °C	2215	C
Tolazoline HCl		0.1 mg/ml[a]	SKF	15 mg/ml[a]	Physically compatible for 24 hr at 22 °C	1363	C
Topotecan HC1	SKB	56 μg/ml[a,b]	SKB	5.76 mg/ml[a,b]	Visually compatible with little or no loss of either drug by HPLC in 4 hr at 22 °C under fluorescent light	2245	C
TPN #189[h]			SKB	10 mg/ml[b]	Visually compatible for 24 hr at 22 °C	1767	C
TPN #212 to #215[h]			SKB	12 mg/ml[a]	Physically compatible with no change in measured turbidity or increase in particle content in 4 hr at 23 °C	2109	C
Vecuronium bromide	OR	0.1 mg/ml[a]	SKF	6 mg/ml[a]	Physically compatible for 24 hr at 28 °C	1337	C
Vinorelbine tartrate	BW	1 mg/ml[b]	SKB	12 mg/ml[b]	Physically compatible with no change in measured turbidity or increase in particle content in 4 hr at 22 °C	1558	C
Warfarin sodium	DU	2 mg/ml[i]	SKB	3.6 mg/ml[a]	Haze forms in 1 hr	2010	I
	DU	2 mg/ml[i]	EN	3.6 mg/ml[a]	Haze forms immediately	2010	I
	DME	2 mg/ml[i]	SKB	3.6 mg/ml[a]	Haze forms in 1 hr	2078	I
Zidovudine	BW	4 mg/ml[a]	SKF	6 mg/ml[a]	Physically compatible for 4 hr at 25 °C under fluorescent light by visual and microscopic examination	1193	C

[a]Tested in dextrose 5% in water.
[b]Tested in sodium chloride 0.9%.
[c]Tested in both dextrose 5% in water and sodium chloride 0.9%.
[d]Tested in bacteriostatic sodium chloride 0.9% preserved with benzyl alcohol 0.9%.
[e]Given over three minutes via a Y-site into a running infusion solution.
[f]Tested in dextrose 5% in water with sodium bicarbonate 0.05 mEq/ml.
[g]Lyophilized formulation tested.
[h]Refer to Appendix I for the composition of parenteral nutrition solutions. TNA indicates a 3-in-1 admixture, and TPN indicates a 2-in-1 admixture.
[i]Tested in sterile water for injection.

Additional Compatibility Information

Infusion Solutions — The manufacturer states that cimetidine HCl may be admixed in most common intravenous solutions, including sodium chloride 0.9%, dextrose 5 and 10% in water, lactated Ringer's injection, and sodium bicarbonate 5%, and used for 48 hours at room temperature. (2) Other information indicates that cimetidine HCl may be stable for longer than 48 hours. (549; 550) See Compatibility Information.

Parenteral Nutrition Solutions — Cimetidine HCl (SKF) 13 to 19 mg/kg every 24 hours was administered to patients by continuous infusion in parenteral nutrition solutions composed of essential amino acids, dextrose 50% in water with varying amounts of vitamins, electrolytes, trace elements, and albumin human. The admixtures were prepared within 24 hours prior to use. No physical incompatibilities were noted, and cimetidine blood levels were in the range achieved by long-term oral treatment. (570) In fact, the dose required to maintain therapeutic levels may be lower than with an intermittent infusion. (1084)

When compounding parenteral nutrition mixtures, cimetidine should be admixed in a sequence that separates it from the copper sulfate present in trace elements injections to avoid formation of a green-colored copper-cimetidine complex. (1951)

Other Drugs — Cimetidine HCl is stated to be physically incompatible with barbiturates (360) as well as with amphotericin B and cephalosporins. (868)

Complex formation between cimetidine and theophylline has been noted in pH 7.4 phosphate buffer solution and human plasma. (1043)

Ceftazidime (Tazicef) 20 mg/ml in sterile water for injection is stated to be stable for 18 hours at room temperature or seven days under refrigeration when admixed with cimetidine HCl 150 mg/ml. (4)

CIPROFLOXACIN
AHFS 8:22

Products — Ciprofloxacin is available as a concentrate in 20- and 40-ml vials and 120-ml pharmacy bulk packages. Each milliliter of solution contains 10 mg of ciprofloxacin, with lactic acid as a solubilizer and hydrochloric acid to adjust the pH. (2)

Ciprofloxacin (Bayer) is also available as a premixed, ready-to-use solution in 100- and 200-ml PVC containers. Each milliliter contains 2 mg of ciprofloxacin with dextrose 5%, lactic acid as a solubilizer, and hydrochloric acid to adjust the pH. (2)

pH — Vials: from 3.3 to 3.9. PVC bags: from 3.5 to 4.6. (2)

Trade Name(s) — Cipro I.V.

Administration — Ciprofloxacin is administered at a concentration of 1 to 2 mg/ml by intravenous infusion into a large vein slowly over 60 minutes. When given intermittently through a Y-site, the primary solution should be discontinued temporarily. (2; 4)

Stability — Ciprofloxacin is a clear, colorless to slightly yellow solution. It should be stored between 5 and 25 °C (bags) or 30 °C (vials) and protected from light, temperatures over 40 °C, and freezing. (2; 4)

pH Effects — Ciprofloxacin in aqueous solution is stated to be stable for up to 14 days at room temperature in the pH range of 1.5 to 7.5. (4) However, Teraoka et al. reported substantial loss of ciprofloxacin content in admixtures with a pH over 6. (1924)

Elastomeric Reservoir Pumps — Ciprofloxacin solutions in elastomeric reservoir pumps have been stated by the pump manufacturers to be stable for the following time periods refrigerated (REF) or at room temperature (RT) (31):

Pump Reservoir(s)	Conc.	REF	RT
Homepump; Homepump Eclipse	0.5 to 2 mg/ml[a,b]	14 days	14 days
Intermate	0.5 to 6 mg/ml[a,b]	90 days	30 days
Medflo	2 to 4 mg/ml[a,b]	14 days	14 days
ReadyMed	10 mg/ml[a,b]	14 days	14 days

[a]*In dextrose 5% in water.*
[b]*In sodium chloride 0.9%.*

Sorption — Ciprofloxacin (Bayer) 200 mg/250 ml in dextrose 5% in water and sodium chloride 0.9% in PVC bags was infused through infusion sets at about 4 ml/min. No drug loss due to sorption was detected by HPLC. (1698)

Ciprofloxacin (Bayer) 2 mg/ml in sodium chloride 0.9% exhibited no loss due to sorption to PVC administration sets including Venoset (Abbott), Ivex HP filter set (Abbott), and 9200 Accuset (IMED) during simulated administration and static studies. (1934)

Central Venous Catheter — Ciprofloxacin (Bayer) 1 mg/ml in dextrose 5% in water was found to be compatible with the ARROWg+ard Blue Plus (Arrow International) chlorhexidine-bearing triple-lumen central catheter. HPLC analysis was used to evaluate completeness of drug delivery through the catheter and the amount of chlorhexidine removed from the internal lumens. Essentially complete delivery of the drug was found with little or no drug loss occurring. Furthermore, chlorhexidine delivered from the catheter remained at trace amounts with no substantial increase due to the delivery of the drug through the catheter. (2335)

Compatibility Information

Solution Compatibility

Ciprofloxacin

Solution	*Mfr*	*Mfr*	*Conc/L*	*Remarks*	*Ref*	*C/I*
Dextrose 5% in Electrolyte #75		MI	0.5 and 1 g	Stable for 14 days at 5 and 25 °C	888	C
Dextrose 5% in sodium chloride 0.225%		MI	0.5 and 2 g	Stable for 14 days at 5 and 25 °C	888	C
Dextrose 5% in sodium chloride 0.45%		MI	0.5 and 2 g	Stable for 14 days at 5 and 25 °C	888	C
Dextrose 5% in water	AB[a]	MI	1.5 g	Visually compatible with no loss by HPLC in 48 hr at 25 °C under fluorescent light	1541	C
	[a]	BAY	800 mg	Visually compatible with no significant loss by HPLC in 6 hr at 22 °C exposed to light	1698	C
		MI	0.5 and 2 g	Stable for 14 days at 5 and 25 °C	888	C
	BA[a]	MI	2.86 g	Visually compatible with no loss by HPLC in 90 days at room temperature and 5 °C	1891	C
Dextrose 10% in water		MI	0.5 and 2 g	Stable for 14 days at 5 and 25 °C	888	C
Fructose 10% in water		MI	0.5 and 1 g	Stable for 14 days at 5 and 25 °C	888	C
Ringer's injection		MI	0.5 and 1 g	Stable for 14 days at 5 and 25 °C	888	C
Ringer's injection, lactated		MI	0.5 and 2 g	Stable for 14 days at 5 and 25 °C	888	C
Sodium chloride 0.9%	AB[a]	MI	1.5 g	Visually compatible with no loss by HPLC in 48 hr at 25 °C under fluorescent light	1541	C
	[a]	BAY	800 mg	Visually compatible with no significant loss by HPLC in 6 hr at 22 °C exposed to light	1698	C
		MI	0.5 and 2 g	Stable for 14 days at 5 and 25 °C	888	C
	BA[a]	MI	2.86 g	Visually compatible with no loss by HPLC in 90 days at room temperature and 5 °C	1891	C
	AB	BAY	2 g	Visually compatible with no loss by HPLC in 24 hr at 25 °C	1934	C

[a]*Tested in PVC containers.*

Additive Compatibility

Ciprofloxacin

Drug	*Mfr*	*Conc/L*	*Mfr*	*Conc/L*	*Test Soln*	*Remarks*	*Ref*	*C/I*
Amikacin sulfate	BR	4.1 g	MI	1.6 g	D5W, NS	Visually compatible and ciprofloxacin potency by HPLC and amikacin potency by immunoassay retained for 48 hr at 25 °C under fluorescent light	1541	C
Aminophylline	LY	2 g	MI	1.6 g	D5W, NS	Ciprofloxacin precipitate forms in 4 hr at 4 and 25 °C	1541	I
Amoxicillin sodium		10 g		2 g	[a]	Immediate precipitation	1473	I
Amoxicillin sodium–clavulanate potassium		10 + 2 g		2 g	[a]	Immediate precipitation	1473	I

Additive Compatibility (Cont.)

Ciprofloxacin

Drug	*Mfr*	*Conc/L*	*Mfr*	*Conc/L*	*Test Soln*	*Remarks*	*Ref*	*C/I*
Amphotericin B		100 mg	MI	2 g	D5W	Physically incompatible	888	I
Ampicillin sodium–sulbactam sodium		20+10 g	MI	2 g	D5W	Physically incompatible	888	I
Aztreonam	SQ	20 g	MI	1 g	D5W, NS	Physically compatible for 24 hr at 22 °C	1189	C
Ceftazidime	SKF	20 g	MI	1 g	D5W, NS	Physically compatible for 24 hr at 22 °C	1189	C
		20 g	MI	2 g	D5W	Physically incompatible	888	I
Cefuroxime sodium		30 g	MI	2 g	D5W	Physically incompatible	888	I
Clindamycin phosphate	LY	7.1 g	MI	1.6 g	D5W, NS	Precipitate forms immediately. HPLC showed no intact clindamycin	1541	I
Cyclosporine	SZ	500 mg	BAY	2 g	NS	Visually compatible with about 8% ciprofloxacin loss by HPLC in 24 hr at 25 °C. Cyclosporine not tested	1934	C
Dopamine HCl		400 mg	MI	2 g	NS	Compatible for 24 hr at 25 °C	888	C
		1.04 g	MI	2 g	NS	Compatible for 24 hr at 25 °C	888	C
Floxacillin sodium		10 g		2 g	[a]	Immediate precipitation	1473	I
Gentamicin sulfate	LY	1 g	MI	1.6 g	D5W, NS	Visually compatible and ciprofloxacin potency by HPLC and gentamicin potency by immunoassay retained for 48 hr at 25 °C under fluorescent light and 4 °C in the dark	1541	C
	SC	10 g	BAY	2 g	NS	Visually compatible with little or no ciprofloxacin loss by HPLC in 24 hr at 25 °C. Gentamicin not tested	1934	C
Heparin sodium	CP	10,000, 100,000, and 1 million units	BAY	2 g	NS	White precipitate forms immediately	1934	I
		4100 units	MI	2 g	NS	Physically incompatible	888	I
		8300 units	MI	2 g	NS	Physically incompatible	888	I
Lidocaine HCl		1 g	MI	2 g	NS	Compatible for 24 hr at 25 °C	888	C
		1.5 g	MI	2 g	NS	Compatible for 24 hr at 25 °C	888	C
Linezolid	PHU	2 g	BAY	4 g	[b]	Physically compatible with little or no loss of either drug by HPLC in 7 days at 23 °C protected from light. Refrigeration results in precipitation after 1 day	2334	C
Metronidazole		5 g		2 g		No loss of either drug in 4 hr at 24 °C	1346	C
	SE	4.2 g	MI	1.6 g		Visually compatible and potency of both drugs by HPLC retained for 48 hr at 25 °C under fluorescent light and 4 °C in the dark	1541	C
Metronidazole HCl		1 g	MI	1 g	D5W	Physically incompatible	888	I
Netilmicin sulfate	SC	2.5 g	BAY	2 g	NS	Visually compatible with little or no ciprofloxacin loss by HPLC in 24 hr at 25 °C. Netilmicin not tested	1934	C
Piperacillin sodium	LE	40 g	MI	1 g	D5W, NS	Physically compatible for 24 hr at 22 °C	1189	C
		40 g	MI	2 g	D5W	Physically incompatible	888	I

Additive Compatibility (Cont.)

Ciprofloxacin

Drug	Mfr	Conc/L	Mfr	Conc/L	Test Soln	Remarks	Ref	C/I
Potassium chloride	AB	40 mEq	BAY	2 g	NS	Visually compatible with little or no ciprofloxacin loss by HPLC in 24 hr at 25 °C	1934	C
		40 mEq	MI	2 g	NS	Compatible for 24 hr at 25 °C	888	C
Ranitidine HCl	GL	500 mg and 1 g	BAY	2 g	NS	Visually compatible with little or no ciprofloxacin loss by HPLC in 24 hr at 25 °C. Ranitidine not tested	1934	C
Sodium bicarbonate		[c]	MI	2 g	D5W	Physically incompatible	888	I
Ticarcillin disodium		30 g	MI	2 g	D5W	Physically incompatible	888	I
Tobramycin sulfate	LI	1.6 g	MI	1 g	D5W, NS	Physically compatible for 24 hr at 22 °C	1189	C
	LI	1 g	MI	1.6 g	D5W, NS	Visually compatible and ciprofloxacin potency by HPLC and tobramycin potency by immunoassay retained for 48 hr at 25 °C under fluorescent light and 4 °C in the dark	1541	C
Vitamin B complex	BC	2 ml	BAY	2 g	NS	Visually compatible with 8% ciprofloxacin loss by HPLC in 24 hr at 25 °C. Vitamins not tested	1934	C

[a]Drug added to ciprofloxacin solution.
[b]Admixed in the linezolid infusion container.
[c]Final sodium bicarbonate concentration not specified.

Y-Site Injection Compatibility (1:1 Mixture)

Ciprofloxacin

Drug	Mfr	Conc	Mfr	Conc	Remarks	Ref	C/I
Amifostine	USB	10 mg/ml[a]	MI	1 mg/ml[a]	Physically compatible with no change in measured turbidity or increase in particle content in 4 hr at 23 °C	1845	C
Amino acids, dextrose	AB	AA 5%, D 25%	MI	2 mg/ml[a]	Visually compatible for 2 hr at 25 °C	1628	C
Aminophylline	AB	2 mg/ml[a,b]	MI	2 mg/ml[a,b]	Fine white crystals form in 20 min in D5W and 2 min in NS	1655	I
Ampicillin sodium–sulbactam sodium		3 g[c]		400 mg[c]	When administered sequentially through a Y-site into running D5S, white crystals form immediately	1887	I
Aztreonam	SQ	20 mg/ml[a,b]	MI	1 mg/ml[a]	Physically compatible for 24 hr at 22 °C	1189	C
	SQ	40 mg/ml[a]	MI	1 mg/ml[a]	Physically compatible with no subvisual haze or particle formation in 4 hr at 23 °C	1758	C
Calcium gluconate	LY	10%	MI	2 mg/ml[a]	Visually compatible for 2 hr at 25 °C	1628	C
Cefepime HCl	BMS	20 mg/ml[a]	MI	1 mg/ml[b]	Cloudy solution forms immediately. Flocculent precipitate forms in 4 hr	1689	I
Ceftazidime	SKF[d]	20 mg/ml[a,b]	MI	1 mg/ml[a]	Physically compatible for 24 hr at 22 °C	1189	C
Cisatracurium besylate	GW	0.1, 2, 5 mg/ml[a]	BAY	1 mg/ml[a]	Physically compatible with no change in measured turbidity or increase in particle content in 4 hr at 23 °C	2074	C
Clarithromycin	AB	4 mg/ml[a]	BAY	2 mg/ml[a]	Visually compatible for 72 hr at both 30 and 17 °C	2174	C

Y-Site Injection Compatibility (1:1 Mixture) (Cont.)

			Ciprofloxacin				
Drug	*Mfr*	*Conc*	*Mfr*	*Conc*	*Remarks*	*Ref*	*C/I*
Dexamethasone sodium phosphate	LY	4 mg/ml	MI	2 mg/ml[a,b]	Transient white cloudiness rapidly dissipates. White crystals and flocculence form in 1 hr at 24 °C	1655	I
Digoxin	ES	0.25 mg/ml	MI	2 mg/ml[a,b]	Visually compatible for 24 hr at 24 °C	1655	C
	BW	0.25 mg/ml	BAY	2 mg/ml[b]	Visually compatible with no ciprofloxacin loss by HPLC in 15 min. Digoxin not tested	1934	C
Diltiazem HCl	MMD	5 mg/ml	MI	2 and 10 mg/ml[b]	Visually compatible	1807	C
Diphenhydramine HCl	ES	50 mg/ml	MI	2 mg/ml[a,b]	Visually compatible for 24 hr at 24 °C	1655	C
Dobutamine HCl	LI	250 µg/ml[a,b]	MI	2 mg/ml[a,b]	Visually compatible for 24 hr at 24 °C	1655	C
Docetaxel	RPR	0.9 mg/ml[a]	BAY	1 mg/ml[a]	Physically compatible with no change in measured turbidity or increase in particle content in 4 hr at 23 °C	2224	C
Dopamine HCl	AB	1.6 mg/ml[a,b]	MI	2 mg/ml[a,b]	Visually compatible for 24 hr at 24 °C	1655	C
Doxorubicin HCl liposome injection	SEQ	0.4 mg/ml[a]	BAY	1 mg/ml[a]	Physically compatible with little or no change in measured turbidity and no increase in particle content in 4 hr at 23 °C	2087	C
Etoposide phosphate	BR	5 mg/ml[a]	BAY	1 mg/ml[a]	Physically compatible with no change in measured turbidity or increase in particle content in 4 hr at 23 °C	2218	C
Furosemide	AB	10 mg/ml	MI	2 mg/ml[a,b]	Immediate precipitation	1655	I
	DMX	5 mg/ml	BAY	2 mg/ml[b]	White precipitate forms immediately	1934	I
Gemcitabine HCl	LI	10 mg/ml[b]	BAY	1 mg/ml[b]	Physically compatible with no change in measured turbidity or increase in particle content in 4 hr at 23 °C	2226	C
Gentamicin sulfate	LY	1.6 mg/ml[a,b]	MI	2 mg/ml[a,b]	Visually compatible for 24 hr at 24 °C	1655	C
Granisetron HCl	SKB	0.05 mg/ml[a]	MI	1 mg/ml[a]	Physically compatible with no change in measured turbidity or increase in particle content in 4 hr at 23 °C	2000	C
Heparin sodium		10 units/ml		2 mg/ml	Turbidity forms rapidly with subsequent white precipitate	1483	I
	LY	100 units/ml[a,b]	MI	2 mg/ml[a,b]	Immediate crystal formation	1655	I
	CP	10, 100, and 1000 units/ml[b]	BAY	2 mg/ml[b]	White precipitate forms immediately	1934	I
Hetastarch in lactated electrolyte injection (Hextend)	AB	6%	BAY	2 mg/ml[a]	Physically compatible with no change in measured turbidity or increase in particle content in 4 hr at 23 °C	2339	C
Hydrocortisone sodium succinate	UP	50 mg/ml	MI	2 mg/ml[a,b]	Transient white cloudiness rapidly dissipates. White crystals form in 1 hr at 24 °C	1655	I
Hydroxyzine HCl	ES	50 mg/ml	MI	2 mg/ml[a,b]	Visually compatible for 24 hr at 24 °C	1655	C
Lidocaine HCl	AB	4[a] and 20 mg/ml	MI	2 mg/ml[a,b]	Visually compatible for 24 hr at 24 °C	1655	C

Y-Site Injection Compatibility (1:1 Mixture) (Cont.)

			Ciprofloxacin				
Drug	*Mfr*	*Conc*	*Mfr*	*Conc*	*Remarks*	*Ref*	*C/I*
Linezolid	PHU	2 mg/ml	BAY	1 mg/ml[a]	Physically compatible with no change in measured turbidity or increase in particle content in 4 hr at 23 °C	2264	C
Lorazepam	WY	0.33 mg/ml[b]	BAY	2 mg/ml	Visually compatible for 24 hr at 22 °C	1855	C
Magnesium sulfate	AB	4 mEq/ml	MI	2 mg/ml[a,b]	Precipitate forms in 4 hr in D5W and 1 hr in NS at 24 °C	1655	I
	LY	50%	MI	2 mg/ml[a]	Visually compatible for 2 hr at 25 °C	1628	C
Methylprednisolone sodium succinate	UP	62.5 mg/ml	MI	2 mg/ml[a,b]	Transient white cloudiness rapidly dissipates. White crystals form in 2 hr at 24 °C	1655	I
Metoclopramide HCl	DU	5 mg/ml	MI	2 mg/ml[a,b]	Visually compatible for 24 hr at 24 °C	1655	C
		5 mg/ml	BAY	2 mg/ml[b]	Visually compatible with no ciprofloxacin loss by HPLC in 15 min. Metoclopramide not tested	1934	C
Midazolam HCl	RC	5 mg/ml	BAY	2 mg/ml	Visually compatible for 24 hr at 22 °C	1855	C
Midodrine HCl	CP	5 mg/ml	BAY	2 mg/ml[b]	Visually compatible with no ciprofloxacin loss by HPLC in 15 min. Midodrine not tested	1934	C
Phenytoin sodium	PD	50 mg/ml	MI	2 mg/ml[a,b]	Immediate crystal formation	1655	I
Piperacillin sodium	LE	40 mg/ml[a,b]	MI	1 mg/ml[a]	Physically compatible for 24 hr at 22 °C	1189	C
Potassium acetate	LY	2 mEq/ml	MI	2 mg/ml[a]	Visually compatible for 2 hr at 25 °C	1628	C
Potassium chloride	LY	0.04 mEq/ml	MI	2 mg/ml[a,b]	Visually compatible for 24 hr at 24 °C	1655	C
	AMR	2 mEq/ml	MI	2 mg/ml[a]	Visually compatible for 2 hr at 25 °C	1628	C
Potassium phosphates	APP	3 mmol/ml	BAY	2 mg/ml[a,b]	Transient precipitate forms on first contact, becoming crystalline precipitate within 1 hr	2290	I
	APP	0.06 mmol/ml[a,b]	BAY	2 mg/ml[a,j]	Transient precipitate forms on first contact, becoming crystalline precipitate within 1 hr	2290	I
Promethazine HCl	ES	25 mg/ml	MI	2 mg/ml[a,b]	Visually compatible for 24 hr at 24 °C	1655	C
Propofol	ZEN	10 mg/ml	MI	1 mg/ml[a]	Emulsion broke and oiled out	1916	I
Ranitidine HCl	GL	0.5 mg/ml[a,b]	MI	2 mg/ml[a,b]	Visually compatible for 24 hr at 24 °C	1655	C
Remifentanil HCl	GW	0.025 and 0.25 mg/ml[b]	BAY	1 mg/ml[a]	Physically compatible with no change in measured turbidity or increase in particle content in 4 hr at 23 °C	2075	C
Ringer's injection, lactated	AB		MI	2 mg/ml[a,b]	Visually compatible for 24 hr at 24 °C	1655	C
Sodium bicarbonate	AB	1 mEq/ml	MI	2 mg/ml[a]	Visually compatible for 24 hr at 24 °C	1655	C
	AB	1 mEq/ml	MI	2 mg/ml[b]	Very fine crystals form in 20 min in NS	1655	I
	AB	1 mEq/ml	MI	2 mg/ml[a]	Physically compatible with no change in measured turbidity or increase in particle content in 4 hr at 23 °C	1869	C
	AB	0.1 mEq/ml[a]	MI	2 mg/ml[a]	Subvisual haze forms immediately, becoming a white crystalline precipitate in 4 hr at 23 °C	1869	I
	AB	1 and 0.75[a] mEq/ml	BAY	1 and 2 mg/ml[a]	Physically compatible with no change in measured turbidity or increase in particle content in 4 hr at 23 °C	2065	C

Y-Site Injection Compatibility (1:1 Mixture) (Cont.)

Drug	Mfr	Conc	Ciprofloxacin Mfr	Ciprofloxacin Conc	Remarks	Ref	C/I
	AB	1 and 0.75[b] mEq/ml	BAY	1 mg/ml[b]	Physically compatible with no change in measured turbidity or increase in particle content in 4 hr at 23 °C	2065	C
	AB	1 and 0.75[b] mEq/ml	BAY	2 mg/ml[b]	Small amount of particles forms immediately, becoming more numerous over 4 hr at 23 °C	2065	I
	AB	0.5, 0.25, and 0.1 mEq/ml[a]	BAY	1 and 2 mg/ml[a]	Small amount of particles forms immediately, becoming more numerous over 4 hr at 23 °C	2065	I
	AB	0.5, 0.25, and 0.1 mEq/ml[b]	BAY	1 mg/ml[b]	Small amount of particles forms in 1 hr, becoming more numerous over 4 hr at 23 °C	2065	I
	AB	0.5, 0.25, and 0.1 mEq/ml[b]	BAY	2 mg/ml[b]	Precipitate forms immediately	2065	I
Sodium chloride	AMR	4 mEq/ml	MI	2 mg/ml[a]	Visually compatible for 2 hr at 25 °C	1628	C
Sodium phosphates	AB	3 mmol/ml	BAY	2 mg/ml[a]	Subvisual microcrystals form in 1 hr at 23 °C	1972	I
	AB	3 mmol/ml	BAY	2 mg/ml[f]	White crystalline precipitate forms immediately	1971; 1972	I
Tacrolimus	FUJ	1 mg/ml[b]	MI	1 mg/ml[a]	Visually compatible for 24 hr at 25 °C	1630	C
Teicoplanin	GRP	60 mg/ml	BAY	2 mg/ml[b]	White precipitate forms immediately but disappears with shaking	1934	?
Teniposide	BR	0.1 mg/ml[a]	MI	2 mg/ml[a]	Physically compatible with no subvisual haze or particle formation in 4 hr at 23 °C	1725	C
Thiotepa	IMM[g]	1 mg/ml[a]	MI	1 mg/ml[a]	Physically compatible with no change in measured turbidity or increase in particle content in 4 hr at 23 °C	1861	C
TNA #218 to #226[i]			BAY	1 mg/ml[a]	Visually compatible with no precipitate or emulsion damage apparent in 4 hr at 23 °C	2215	C
Tobramycin sulfate	LI	1.6 mg/ml[a,b]	MI	1 mg/ml[a]	Physically compatible for 24 hr at 22 °C	1189	C
TPN #212 to #215[i]			MI	1 mg/ml[a]	Amber discoloration forms in 1 to 4 hr	2109	I
Verapamil HCl	KN	2.5 mg/ml	MI	2 mg/ml[a,b]	Visually compatible for 24 hr at 24 °C	1655	C
Warfarin sodium	DU	2 mg/ml[a]	MI	2 mg/ml[h]	Haze forms immediately; crystals form in 1 hr	2010	I
	DME	2 mg/ml[h]	MI	2 mg/ml[a]	Haze forms immediately; crystals form in 1 hr	2078	I

[a] *Tested in dextrose 5% in water.*
[b] *Tested in sodium chloride 0.9%.*
[c] *Concentration and volume not specified.*
[d] *Sodium carbonate–containing formulation tested.*
[e] *Form unspecified.*
[f] *Tested in both sodium chloride 0.9% and 0.45%.*
[g] *Lyophilized formulation tested.*
[h] *Tested in sterile water for injection.*
[i] *Refer to Appendix I for the composition of parenteral nutrition solutions. TNA indicates a 3-in-1 admixture, and TPN indicates a 2-in-1 admixture.*
[j] *Manufacturer's premixed solution.*

Additional Compatibility Information

Infusion Solutions — Ciprofloxacin in concentrations between 0.5 and 2 mg/ml in dextrose 5% in water or sodium chloride 0.9% is stable for 14 days at room temperature or under refrigeration. (2; 4)

Peritoneal Dialysis Solutions — Ciprofloxacin (Bayer) 25 mg/L in peritoneal dialysis solution (Dianeal 137, Baxter) exhibited little or no loss by HPLC and bioassay after 42 days at 4, 22, and 37 °C when protected from light. (1585)

The stability of ciprofloxacin (Miles) 25 mg/L in Dianeal PD-1 (Baxter) with dextrose 1.5 and 4.5% in PVC bags was evaluated by HPLC analysis during storage at 4, 25, and 37 °C. Drug losses of about 10 to 12% and 5 to 6% occurred during the first 12 hours at 4 and at 25 °C, respectively; however, concentrations were steady thereafter for two weeks at 4 °C and one week at 25 °C. Because no decomposition products were detected, the losses were attributed to sorption to the PVC containers. At 37 °C over 48 hours, losses of up to 10% occurred in the Dianeal PD-1 with dextrose 1.5%; losses of up to 7% occurred in the Dianeal PD-1 with dextrose 4.5%. (1826)

Phosphates — Although ciprofloxacin was reported to be compatible with potassium phosphates (1628), subsequent testing has found that crystalline precipitation forms during simultaneous administration with either potassium or sodium phosphates. (671; 1971; 1972; 2290) See Y-Site Injection Compatibility table above.

Ciprofloxacin (Bayer) 2 mg/ml in sodium chloride 0.9% or dextrose 5% in water was evaluated for compatibility with potassium phosphates 3 mmol/ml (undiluted) and diluted to 0.06 mg/ml in sodium chloride 0.9% or dextrose 5% in water in simulated simultaneous administration. All samples exhibited transient white precipitate upon first contact that became a crystalline precipitate within an hour. (2290) Precipitation was also reported during clinical administration of a premixed solution of ciprofloxacin 2 mg/ml in dextrose 5% in water (Bayer) with potassium phosphates 0.06 mg/ml in dextrose 5% in water. (671) In addition, the manufacturer has had reports of precipitation of these drugs. (2009) Sodium phosphates 3 mmol/ml was similarly incompatible with ciprofloxacin (Bayer) 2 mg/ml in dextrose 5% in water or sodium chloride 0.9%, resulting in crystalline precipitation. (1971; 1972)

Consequently, ciprofloxacin and phosphates should be considered incompatible across a broad range of phosphate concentrations.

Sodium Bicarbonate — Ciprofloxacin mixed with sodium bicarbonate in lower concentrations has resulted in the formation of a haze and precipitate, while 10-fold higher concentrations of sodium bicarbonate appear to be physically compatible with the same amount of ciprofloxacin. (1869) Although not unprecedented, it is less common for high concentrations of drugs to be compatible while lower concentrations are incompatible. The differing compatibility results have been ascribed to pH-dependency of ciprofloxacin solubility. (2012) However, a thorough evaluation of the compatibility of ciprofloxacin with a wide range of sodium bicarbonate concentrations found that incompatibility cannot be predicted by pH of the solutions alone; the solutions were generally in a very narrow pH range (8.0 to 8.3). Because the interaction between ciprofloxacin and sodium bicarbonate appears to be complex and variable, simultaneous administration of these drugs should be avoided. (2065)

CISATRACURIUM BESYLATE
AHFS 12:20

Products — Cisatracurium besylate is available as a 2-mg/ml solution in 5- and 10-ml vials. The drug is also available as a 10-mg/ml solution in 20-ml vials intended for use in intensive care units only. The pH is adjusted with benzenesulfonic acid. The 2-mg/ml concentration in 10-ml vials also contains benzyl alcohol 0.9%. The other dosage forms have no preservative and are for single use only. (1-1/00)

pH — From 3.25 to 3.65. (1-1/00)

Trade Name(s) — Nimbex.

Administration — Cisatracurium besylate is administered intravenously only. Both initial bolus doses and continuous intravenous infusion have been used. Rates of administration depend on the drug concentration in the solution, desired dose, and patient weight. Avoid contact with alkaline drugs during administration. (1-1/00)

Stability — Cisatracurium besylate injection is a colorless to slightly yellow or greenish-yellow solution. Intact vials of cisatracurium besylate should be stored under refrigeration at 2 to 8 °C protected from light and freezing. Potency losses of 5% per year occur under refrigeration. However, at 25 °C, potency losses increase to about 5% per month. The manufacturer recommends that vials that have been warmed to room temperature be used within 21 days even if rerefrigerated. (1-1/00)

In an independent study, cisatracurium besylate (Glaxo Wellcome) 2 mg/ml in the original 5- and 10-ml vials and the 10-mg/ml solution in original 20-ml vials was stored at 4 and 23 °C both protected from light and exposed to fluorescent light. All the samples remained physically stable throughout the 90-day study period. HPLC analysis found that samples stored under refrigeration exhibited little or no drug loss in 90 days whether exposed to or protected from light. At 23 °C, samples were stable through 45 days of storage with losses near 5 to 7% in most samples. However, most samples became unacceptable after 90 days of storage at 23 °C, exhibiting losses of 9 to 14%. (2116)

pH Effects — The manufacturer indicates that cisatracurium besylate may not be compatible with barbiturates and other alkaline solutions having a pH greater than 8.5. (1-1/00)

Syringes — Cisatracurium besylate 2 mg/ml was repackaged in 3-ml plastic syringes (Becton-Dickinson) and sealed with tip caps (Red

Cap, Burron). The syringes were stored at 4 and 23 °C both protected from light and exposed to fluorescent light. All of the samples remained physically stable throughout the 30-day study period. HPLC analysis found little or no loss in the samples stored under refrigeration, whereas the samples stored at 23 °C exhibited 4 to 7% loss in 30 days. (2116)

Compatibility Information

Solution Compatibility

Cisatracurium besylate

Solution	*Mfr*	*Mfr*	*Conc/L*	*Remarks*	*Ref*	*C/I*
Dextrose 5% in water	BA[a]	GW	100 mg	Physically compatible with 8% loss by HPLC in 7 days and 15% loss in 14 days at 23 °C under fluorescent light. Little or no loss in 30 days at 4 °C	2116	C
	BA[a]	GW	2 g	Physically compatible with 10% loss by HPLC in 14 days and 14% loss in 30 days at 23 °C under fluorescent light. Little or no loss in 30 days at 4 °C	2116	C
	BA[a]	GW	5 g	Physically compatible with 4% loss by HPLC in 30 days at 23 °C under fluorescent light. Little or no loss in 30 days at 4 °C	2116	C
Sodium chloride 0.9%	BA[a]	GW	100 mg	Physically compatible with 8% loss by HPLC in 14 days and 14% loss in 30 days at 23 °C under fluorescent light. Little or no loss in 30 days at 4 °C	2116	C
	BA[a]	GW	2 g	Physically compatible with 6% loss by HPLC in 30 days at 23 °C under fluorescent light. Little or no loss in 30 days at 4 °C	2116	C
	BA[a]	GW	5 g	Physically compatible with 3% loss by HPLC in 30 days at 23 °C under fluorescent light. Little or no loss in 30 days at 4 °C	2116	C

[a]*Tested in PVC containers.*

Y-Site Injection Compatibility (1:1 Mixture)

Cisatracurium besylate

Drug	*Mfr*	*Conc*	*Mfr*	*Conc*	*Remarks*	*Ref*	*C/I*
Acyclovir sodium	BW	7 mg/ml[a]	GW	0.1 and 2 mg/ml[a]	Physically compatible with no change in measured turbidity or increase in particle content in 4 hr at 23 °C	2074	C
	BW	7 mg/ml[a]	GW	5 mg/ml[a]	White cloudiness forms immediately	2074	I
Alfentanil HCl	JN	0.125 mg/ml[a]	GW	0.1, 2, 5 mg/ml[a]	Physically compatible with no change in measured turbidity or increase in particle content in 4 hr at 23 °C	2074	C
Amikacin sulfate	AB	5 mg/ml[a]	GW	0.1, 2, 5 mg/ml[a]	Physically compatible with no change in measured turbidity or increase in particle content in 4 hr at 23 °C	2074	C
Aminophylline	AB	2.5 mg/ml[a]	GW	0.1 and 2 mg/ml[a]	Physically compatible with no change in measured turbidity or increase in particle content in 4 hr at 23 °C	2074	C
	AB	2.5 mg/ml[a]	GW	5 mg/ml[a]	Gray subvisual haze forms in 1 hr	2074	I
Amphotericin B	PH	0.6 mg/ml[a]	GW	0.1 mg/ml[a]	Physically compatible with no change in measured turbidity or increase in particle content in 4 hr at 23 °C	2074	C

Y-Site Injection Compatibility (1:1 Mixture) (Cont.)

Cisatracurium besylate

Drug	*Mfr*	*Conc*	*Mfr*	*Conc*	*Remarks*	*Ref*	*C/I*
	PH	0.6 mg/ml[a]	GW	2 mg/ml[a]	Cloudiness forms immediately; gel-like precipitate forms in 1 hr	2074	I
	PH	0.6 mg/ml[a]	GW	5 mg/ml[a]	Turbidity forms immediately	2074	I
Amphotericin B cholesteryl sulfate complex	SEQ	0.83 mg/ml[a]	GW	2 mg/ml[a]	Gross precipitate forms	2117	I
Ampicillin sodium	SKB	20 mg/ml[b]	GW	0.1 and 2 mg/ml[a]	Physically compatible with no change in measured turbidity or increase in particle content in 4 hr at 23 °C	2074	C
	SKB	20 mg/ml[b]	GW	5 mg/ml[a]	Gray subvisual haze forms in 1 hr	2074	I
Ampicillin sodium–sulbactam sodium	RR	20 + 10 mg/ml[b]	GW	0.1 and 2 mg/ml[a]	Physically compatible with no change in measured turbidity or increase in particle content in 4 hr at 23 °C	2074	C
	RR	20 + 10 mg/ml[b]	GW	5 mg/ml[a]	Subvisual haze develops in 15 min	2074	I
Aztreonam	SQ	40 mg/ml[a]	GW	0.1, 2, 5 mg/ml[a]	Physically compatible with no change in measured turbidity or increase in particle content in 4 hr at 23 °C	2074	C
Bretylium tosylate	AST	4 mg/ml[a]	GW	0.1, 2, 5 mg/ml[a]	Physically compatible with no change in measured turbidity or increase in particle content in 4 hr at 23 °C	2074	C
Bumetanide	BV	0.04 mg/ml[a]	GW	0.1, 2, 5 mg/ml[a]	Physically compatible with no change in measured turbidity or increase in particle content in 4 hr at 23 °C	2074	C
Buprenorphine HCl	RKC	0.04 mg/ml[a]	GW	0.1, 2, 5 mg/ml[a]	Physically compatible with no change in measured turbidity or increase in particle content in 4 hr at 23 °C	2074	C
Butorphanol tartrate	APC	0.04 mg/ml[a]	GW	0.1, 2, 5 mg/ml[a]	Physically compatible with no change in measured turbidity or increase in particle content in 4 hr at 23 °C	2074	C
Calcium gluconate	AB	40 mg/ml[a]	GW	0.1, 2, 5 mg/ml[a]	Physically compatible with no change in measured turbidity or increase in particle content in 4 hr at 23 °C	2074	C
Cefazolin sodium	SKB	20 mg/ml[a]	GW	0.1 mg/ml[a]	Physically compatible with no change in measured turbidity or increase in particle content in 4 hr at 23 °C	2074	C
	SKB	20 mg/ml[a]	GW	2 mg/ml[a]	Gray subvisual haze forms immediately	2074	I
	SKB	20 mg/ml[a]	GW	5 mg/ml[a]	Gray haze forms immediately	2074	I
Cefoperazone sodium	RR	40 mg/ml[a]	GW	0.1, 2, 5 mg/ml[a]	White cloudiness forms immediately	2074	I
Cefotaxime sodium	HO	20 mg/ml[a]	GW	0.1 mg/ml[a]	Physically compatible with no change in measured turbidity or increase in particle content in 4 hr at 23 °C	2074	C
	HO	20 mg/ml[a]	GW	2 mg/ml[a]	Subvisual haze forms in 4 hr	2074	I
	HO	20 mg/ml[a]	GW	5 mg/ml[a]	Subvisual haze forms immediately	2074	I
Cefotetan sodium	STU	20 mg/ml[a]	GW	0.1 and 2 mg/ml[a]	Physically compatible with no change in measured turbidity or increase in particle content in 4 hr at 23 °C	2074	C
	STU	20 mg/ml[a]	GW	5 mg/ml[a]	Dense turbidity forms immediately	2074	I

Y-Site Injection Compatibility (1:1 Mixture) (Cont.)

Drug	Mfr	Conc	Mfr	Conc	Remarks	Ref	C/I
			Cisatracurium besylate				
Cefoxitin sodium	ME	20 mg/ml[a]	GW	0.1 mg/ml[a]	Physically compatible with no change in measured turbidity or increase in particle content in 4 hr at 23 °C	2074	C
	ME	20 mg/ml[a]	GW	2 and 5 mg/ml[a]	Subvisual haze forms immediately	2074	I
Ceftazidime	SKB[c]	40 mg/ml[a]	GW	0.1 and 2 mg/ml[a]	Physically compatible with no change in measured turbidity or increase in particle content in 4 hr at 23 °C	2074	C
	SKB[c]	40 mg/ml[a]	GW	5 mg/ml[a]	Subvisual haze forms immediately	2074	I
	GW[d]	40 mg/ml[a]	GW	0.1, 2, 5 mg/ml[a]	Physically compatible with no change in measured turbidity or increase in particle content in 4 hr at 23 °C	2074	C
Ceftizoxime sodium	FUJ	20 mg/ml[a]	GW	0.1 and 2 mg/ml[a]	Physically compatible with no change in measured turbidity or increase in particle content in 4 hr at 23 °C	2074	C
	FUJ	20 mg/ml[a]	GW	5 mg/ml[a]	Subvisual haze forms in 1 hr	2074	I
Ceftriaxone sodium	RC	20 mg/ml[a]	GW	0.1, 2, 5 mg/ml[a]	Physically compatible with no change in measured turbidity or increase in particle content in 4 hr at 23 °C	2074	C
Cefuroxime sodium	LI	30 mg/ml[a]	GW	0.1 mg/ml[a]	Physically compatible with no change in measured turbidity or increase in particle content in 4 hr at 23 °C	2074	C
	LI	30 mg/ml[a]	GW	2 mg/ml[a]	White cloudiness forms immediately	2074	I
	LI	30 mg/ml[a]	GW	5 mg/ml[a]	Turbidity forms immediately	2074	I
Chlorpromazine HCl	SCN	2 mg/ml[a]	GW	0.1, 2, 5 mg/ml[a]	Physically compatible with no change in measured turbidity or increase in particle content in 4 hr at 23 °C	2074	C
Cimetidine HCl	SKB	12 mg/ml[a]	GW	0.1, 2, 5 mg/ml[a]	Physically compatible with no change in measured turbidity or increase in particle content in 4 hr at 23 °C	2074	C
Ciprofloxacin	BAY	1 mg/ml[a]	GW	0.1, 2, 5 mg/ml[a]	Physically compatible with no change in measured turbidity or increase in particle content in 4 hr at 23 °C	2074	C
Clindamycin phosphate	AST	10 mg/ml[a]	GW	0.1, 2, 5 mg/ml[a]	Physically compatible with no change in measured turbidity or increase in particle content in 4 hr at 23 °C	2074	C
Dexamethasone sodium phosphate	FUJ	2 mg/ml[a]	GW	0.1, 2, 5 mg/ml[a]	Physically compatible with no change in measured turbidity or increase in particle content in 4 hr at 23 °C	2074	C
Diazepam	ES	5 mg/ml	GW	0.1, 2, 5 mg/ml[a]	White turbidity forms immediately	2074	I
	ES	0.25 mg/ml[a]	GW	0.1, 2, 5 mg/ml[a]	Physically compatible with no change in measured turbidity or increase in particle content in 4 hr at 23 °C	2074	C
Digoxin	ES	0.25 mg/ml	GW	0.1, 2, 5 mg/ml[a]	Physically compatible with no change in measured turbidity or increase in particle content in 4 hr at 23 °C	2074	C
Diphenhydramine HCl	SCN	2 mg/ml[a]	GW	0.1, 2, 5 mg/ml[a]	Physically compatible with no change in measured turbidity or increase in particle content in 4 hr at 23 °C	2074	C

Y-Site Injection Compatibility (1:1 Mixture) (Cont.)

			Cisatracurium besylate				
Drug	*Mfr*	*Conc*	*Mfr*	*Conc*	*Remarks*	*Ref*	*C/I*
Dobutamine HCl	LI	4 mg/ml[a]	GW	0.1, 2, 5 mg/ml[a]	Physically compatible with no change in measured turbidity or increase in particle content in 4 hr at 23 °C	2074	C
Dopamine HCl	AB	3.2 mg/ml[a]	GW	0.1, 2, 5 mg/ml[a]	Physically compatible with no change in measured turbidity or increase in particle content in 4 hr at 23 °C	2074	C
Doxycycline hyclate	FUJ	1 mg/ml[a]	GW	0.1, 2, 5 mg/ml[a]	Physically compatible with no change in measured turbidity or increase in particle content in 4 hr at 23 °C	2074	C
Droperidol	AB	2.5 mg/ml	GW	0.1, 2, 5 mg/ml[a]	Physically compatible with no change in measured turbidity or increase in particle content in 4 hr at 23 °C	2074	C
Enalaprilat	ME	0.1 mg/ml[a]	GW	0.1, 2, 5 mg/ml[a]	Physically compatible with no change in measured turbidity or increase in particle content in 4 hr at 23 °C	2074	C
Epinephrine HCl	AMR	0.05 mg/ml[a]	GW	0.1, 2, 5 mg/ml[a]	Physically compatible with no change in measured turbidity or increase in particle content in 4 hr at 23 °C	2074	C
Esmolol HCl	OHM	10 mg/ml[a]	GW	0.1, 2, 5 mg/ml[a]	Physically compatible with no change in measured turbidity or increase in particle content in 4 hr at 23 °C	2074	C
Famotidine	ME	2 mg/ml[a]	GW	0.1, 2, 5 mg/ml[a]	Physically compatible with no change in measured turbidity or increase in particle content in 4 hr at 23 °C	2074	C
Fentanyl citrate	AB	0.0125 mg/ml[a]	GW	0.1, 2, 5 mg/ml[a]	Physically compatible with no change in measured turbidity or increase in particle content in 4 hr at 23 °C	2074	C
Fluconazole	RR	2 mg/ml	GW	0.1, 2, 5 mg/ml[a]	Physically compatible with no change in measured turbidity or increase in particle content in 4 hr at 23 °C	2074	C
Furosemide	AB	3 mg/ml[a]	GW	0.1 mg/ml[a]	Physically compatible with no change in measured turbidity or increase in particle content in 4 hr at 23 °C	2074	C
	AB	3 mg/ml[a]	GW	2 and 5 mg/ml[a]	White cloudiness forms immediately	2074	I
Ganciclovir sodium	SY	20 mg/ml[a]	GW	0.1 and 2 mg/ml[a]	Physically compatible with no change in measured turbidity or increase in particle content in 4 hr at 23 °C	2074	C
	SY	20 mg/ml[a]	GW	5 mg/ml[a]	White cloudiness forms immediately	2074	I
Gatifloxacin	BMS	2 mg/ml[a]	GW	2 mg/ml	Physically compatible with no change in measured haze or increase in particle content in 4 hr at 23 °C	2234	C
Gentamicin sulfate	ES	5 mg/ml[a]	GW	0.1, 2, 5 mg/ml[a]	Physically compatible with no change in measured turbidity or increase in particle content in 4 hr at 23 °C	2074	C
Haloperidol lactate	MN	0.2 mg/ml[a]	GW	0.1, 2, 5 mg/ml[a]	Physically compatible with no change in measured turbidity or increase in particle content in 4 hr at 23 °C	2074	C

Y-Site Injection Compatibility (1:1 Mixture) (Cont.)

			Cisatracurium besylate				
Drug	*Mfr*	*Conc*	*Mfr*	*Conc*	*Remarks*	*Ref*	*C/I*
Heparin sodium	AB	100 units/ml	GW	0.1 and 2 mg/ml[a]	Physically compatible with no change in measured turbidity or increase in particle content in 4 hr at 23 °C	2074	C
	AB	100 units/ml	GW	5 mg/ml[a]	White cloudiness forms immediately	2074	I
Hetastarch in lactated electrolyte injection (Hextend)	AB	6%	GW	0.5 mg/ml[a]	Physically compatible with no change in measured turbidity or increase in particle content in 4 hr at 23 °C	2339	C
Hydrocortisone sodium succinate	AB	1 mg/ml[a]	GW	0.1, 2, 5 mg/ml[a]	Physically compatible with no change in measured turbidity or increase in particle content in 4 hr at 23 °C	2074	C
Hydromorphone HCl	ES	0.5 mg/ml[a]	GW	0.1, 2, 5 mg/ml[a]	Physically compatible with no change in measured turbidity or increase in particle content in 4 hr at 23 °C	2074	C
Hydroxyzine HCl	ES	2 mg/ml[a]	GW	0.1, 2, 5 mg/ml[a]	Physically compatible with no change in measured turbidity or increase in particle content in 4 hr at 23 °C	2074	C
Imipenem–cilastatin sodium	ME	10 mg/ml[b]	GW	0.1, 2, 5 mg/ml[a]	Physically compatible with no change in measured turbidity or increase in particle content in 4 hr at 23 °C	2074	C
Inamrinone lactate	SW	2.5 mg/ml[b]	GW	0.1, 2, 5 mg/ml[a]	Physically compatible with no change in measured turbidity or increase in particle content in 4 hr at 23 °C	2074	C
Isoproterenol HCl	AB	0.02 mg/ml[a]	GW	0.1, 2, 5 mg/ml[a]	Physically compatible with no change in measured turbidity or increase in particle content in 4 hr at 23 °C	2074	C
Ketorolac tromethamine	RC	15 mg/ml[a]	GW	0.1, 2, 5 mg/ml[a]	Physically compatible with no change in measured turbidity or increase in particle content in 4 hr at 23 °C	2074	C
Lidocaine HCl	AST	8 mg/ml[a]	GW	0.1, 2, 5 mg/ml[a]	Physically compatible with no change in measured turbidity or increase in particle content in 4 hr at 23 °C	2074	C
Linezolid	PHU	2 mg/ml	GW	2 mg/ml	Physically compatible with no change in measured turbidity or increase in particle content in 4 hr at 23 °C	2264	C
Lorazepam	WY	0.5 mg/ml[a]	GW	0.1, 2, 5 mg/ml[a]	Physically compatible with no change in measured turbidity or increase in particle content in 4 hr at 23 °C	2074	C
Magnesium sulfate	AB	100 mg/ml[a]	GW	0.1, 2, 5 mg/ml[a]	Physically compatible with no change in measured turbidity or increase in particle content in 4 hr at 23 °C	2074	C
Mannitol	BA	15%	GW	0.1, 2, 5 mg/ml[a]	Physically compatible with no change in measured turbidity or increase in particle content in 4 hr at 23 °C	2074	C
Meperidine HCl	AST	4 mg/ml[a]	GW	0.1, 2, 5 mg/ml[a]	Physically compatible with no change in measured turbidity or increase in particle content in 4 hr at 23 °C	2074	C

Y-Site Injection Compatibility (1:1 Mixture) (Cont.)

			Cisatracurium besylate				
Drug	*Mfr*	*Conc*	*Mfr*	*Conc*	*Remarks*	*Ref*	*C/I*
Methylprednisolone sodium succinate	AB	5 mg/ml[a]	GW	0.1 mg/ml[a]	Physically compatible with no change in measured turbidity or increase in particle content in 4 hr at 23 °C	2074	C
	AB	5 mg/ml[a]	GW	2 mg/ml[a]	Subvisual haze forms immediately	2074	I
	AB	5 mg/ml[a]	GW	5 mg/ml[a]	Haze forms immediately	2074	I
Metoclopramide HCl	AB	5 mg/ml	GW	0.1, 2, 5 mg/ml[a]	Physically compatible with no change in measured turbidity or increase in particle content in 4 hr at 23 °C	2074	C
Metronidazole	AB	5 mg/ml	GW	0.1, 2, 5 mg/ml[a]	Physically compatible with no change in measured turbidity or increase in particle content in 4 hr at 23 °C	2074	C
Midazolam HCl	RC	1 mg/ml[a]	GW	0.1, 2, 5 mg/ml[a]	Physically compatible with no change in measured turbidity or increase in particle content in 4 hr at 23 °C	2074	C
Minocycline HCl	LE	0.2 mg/ml[a]	GW	0.1, 2, 5 mg/ml[a]	Physically compatible with no change in measured turbidity or increase in particle content in 4 hr at 23 °C	2074	C
Morphine sulfate	AST	1 mg/ml[a]	GW	0.1, 2, 5 mg/ml[a]	Physically compatible with no change in measured turbidity or increase in particle content in 4 hr at 23 °C	2074	C
Nalbuphine HCl	AST	10 mg/ml	GW	0.1, 2, 5 mg/ml[a]	Physically compatible with no change in measured turbidity or increase in particle content in 4 hr at 23 °C	2074	C
Netilmicin sulfate	SC	5 mg/ml[a]	GW	0.1, 2, 5 mg/ml[a]	Physically compatible with no change in measured turbidity or increase in particle content in 4 hr at 23 °C	2074	C
Nitroglycerin	DU	0.4 mg/ml[a]	GW	0.1, 2, 5 mg/ml[a]	Physically compatible with no change in measured turbidity or increase in particle content in 4 hr at 23 °C	2074	C
Norepinephrine bitartrate	SW	0.12 mg/ml[a]	GW	0.1, 2, 5 mg/ml[a]	Physically compatible with no change in measured turbidity or increase in particle content in 4 hr at 23 °C	2074	C
Ofloxacin	ORT	4 mg/ml[a]	GW	0.1, 2, 5 mg/ml[a]	Physically compatible with no change in measured turbidity or increase in particle content in 4 hr at 23 °C	2074	C
Ondansetron HCl	CER	1 mg/ml[a]	GW	0.1, 2, 5 mg/ml[a]	Physically compatible with no change in measured turbidity or increase in particle content in 4 hr at 23 °C	2074	C
Phenylephrine HCl	GNS	1 mg/ml[a]	GW	0.1, 2, 5 mg/ml[a]	Physically compatible with no change in measured turbidity or increase in particle content in 4 hr at 23 °C	2074	C
Piperacillin sodium	LE	40 mg/ml[a]	GW	0.1 mg/ml[a]	Physically compatible with no change in measured turbidity or increase in particle content in 4 hr at 23 °C	2074	C
	LE	40 mg/ml[a]	GW	2 mg/ml[a]	Subvisual haze forms immediately	2074	I
	LE	40 mg/ml[a]	GW	5 mg/ml[a]	Haze forms immediately	2074	I

Y-Site Injection Compatibility (1:1 Mixture) (Cont.)

			Cisatracurium besylate				
Drug	*Mfr*	*Conc*	*Mfr*	*Conc*	*Remarks*	*Ref*	*C/I*
Piperacillin sodium–tazobactam sodium	CY	40 + 5 mg/ml[a]	GW	0.1 and 2 mg/ml[a]	Physically compatible with no change in measured turbidity or increase in particle content in 4 hr at 23 °C	2074	C
	CY	40 + 5 mg/ml[a]	GW	5 mg/ml[a]	Tiny particles and subvisual haze within 4 hr	2074	I
Potassium chloride	AB	0.1 mEq/ml[a]	GW	0.1, 2, 5 mg/ml[a]	Physically compatible with no change in measured turbidity or increase in particle content in 4 hr at 23 °C	2074	C
Procainamide HCl	ES	10 mg/ml[a]	GW	0.1, 2, 5 mg/ml[a]	Physically compatible with no change in measured turbidity or increase in particle content in 4 hr at 23 °C	2074	C
Prochlorperazine edisylate	SO	0.5 mg/ml[a]	GW	0.1, 2, 5 mg/ml[a]	Physically compatible with no change in measured turbidity or increase in particle content in 4 hr at 23 °C	2074	C
Promethazine HCl	ES	2 mg/ml[a]	GW	0.1, 2, 5 mg/ml[a]	Physically compatible with no change in measured turbidity or increase in particle content in 4 hr at 23 °C	2074	C
Propofol	GNS, ASZ	10 mg/ml	GW	5 mg/ml[a]	Emulsion disruption upon mixing	2336	I
	GNS	10 mg/ml	GW	0.5 mg/ml[a]	Emulsion disruption upon mixing	2336	I
	ASZ	10 mg/ml	GW	0.5 mg/ml[a]	Physically compatible for at least 1 hr at room temperature	2336	C
Ranitidine HCl	GL	2 mg/ml[a]	GW	0.1, 2, 5 mg/ml[a]	Physically compatible with no change in measured turbidity or increase in particle content in 4 hr at 23 °C	2074	C
Remifentanil HCl	GW	0.025 and 0.25 mg/ml[b]	GW	2 mg/ml[a]	Physically compatible with no change in measured turbidity or increase in particle content in 4 hr at 23 °C	2075	C
Sodium bicarbonate	AB	1 mEq/ml	GW	0.1 mg/ml[a]	Physically compatible with no change in measured turbidity or increase in particle content in 4 hr at 23 °C	2074	C
	AB	1 mEq/ml	GW	2 mg/ml[a]	Subvisual light brown discoloration with subvisual haze in 1 hr	2074	I
	AB	1 mEq/ml	GW	5 mg/ml[a]	Subvisual haze forms immediately; subvisual light brown discoloration with turbidity forms in 4 hr	2074	I
Sodium nitroprusside	AB	2 mg/ml[a]	GW	0.1 mg/ml[a]	Physically compatible with no change in measured turbidity or increase in particle content in 4 hr at 23 °C protected from light	2074	C
	AB	2 mg/ml[a]	GW	2 and 5 mg/ml[a]	White cloudiness forms immediately	2074	I
Sufentanil citrate	ES	0.0125 mg/ml[a]	GW	0.1, 2, 5 mg/ml[a]	Physically compatible with no change in measured turbidity or increase in particle content in 4 hr at 23 °C	2074	C
Theophylline	AB	3.2 mg/ml	GW	0.1, 2, 5 mg/ml[a]	Physically compatible with no change in measured turbidity or increase in particle content in 4 hr at 23 °C	2074	C

Y-Site Injection Compatibility (1:1 Mixture) (Cont.)

Drug	Mfr	Conc	Mfr	Conc	Remarks	Ref	C/I
			Cisatracurium besylate				
Thiopental sodium	AB	25 mg/ml[a]	GW	0.1 mg/ml[a]	Physically compatible with no change in measured turbidity or increase in particle content in 4 hr at 23 °C	2074	C
	AB	25 mg/ml[a]	GW	2 mg/ml[a]	White turbidity forms immediately but dissipates within 1 min; subvisual haze remains	2074	I
	AB	25 mg/ml[a]	GW	5 mg/ml[a]	White cloudiness forms immediately	2074	I
Ticarcillin disodium	SKB	30 mg/ml[a]	GW	0.1, 2, 5 mg/ml[a]	Physically compatible with no change in measured turbidity or increase in particle content in 4 hr at 23 °C	2074	C
Ticarcillin disodium–clavulanate potassium	SKB	31 mg/ml[a]	GW	0.1 and 2 mg/ml[a]	Physically compatible with no change in measured turbidity or increase in particle content in 4 hr at 23 °C	2074	C
	SKB	31 mg/ml[a]	GW	5 mg/ml[a]	Subvisual haze forms immediately	2074	I
Tobramycin sulfate	AB	5 mg/ml[a]	GW	0.1, 2, 5 mg/ml[a]	Physically compatible with no change in measured turbidity or increase in particle content in 4 hr at 23 °C	2074	C
Trimethoprim–sulfamethoxazole	ES	0.8 + 4 mg/ml[a]	GW	0.1 mg/ml[a]	Physically compatible with no change in measured turbidity or increase in particle content in 4 hr at 23 °C	2074	C
	ES	0.8 + 4 mg/ml[a]	GW	2 mg/ml[a]	Subvisual haze forms in 1 hr	2074	I
	ES	0.8 + 4 mg/ml[a]	GW	5 mg/ml[a]	Subvisual haze forms immediately	2074	I
Vancomycin HCl	AB	10 mg/ml[a]	GW	0.1, 2, 5 mg/ml[a]	Physically compatible with no change in measured turbidity or increase in particle content in 4 hr at 23 °C	2074	C
Zidovudine	BW	4 mg/ml[a]	GW	0.1, 2, 5 mg/ml[a]	Physically compatible with no change in measured turbidity or increase in particle content in 4 hr at 23 °C	2074	C

[a]*Tested in dextrose 5% in water.*
[b]*Tested in sodium chloride 0.9%.*
[c]*Sodium carbonate–containing formulation tested.*
[d]*L-Arginine–containing formulation tested.*

Additional Compatibility Information

Infusion Solutions — Cisatracurium besylate is compatible with dextrose 5% in water, sodium chloride 0.9%, and dextrose 5% in sodium chloride 0.9%. The manufacturer indicates that dilutions to concentrations down to 0.1 mg/ml may be stored under refrigeration or at room temperature for 24 hours without significant potency loss. At concentrations between 0.1 and 0.2 mg/ml, the drug may be diluted in dextrose 5% in lactated Ringer's injection and used within 24 hours if stored under refrigeration. (1-1/00) Cisatracurium besylate should not be diluted in lactated Ringer's injection due to instability. (1-1/00)

Propofol — The incompatibility of cisatracurium besylate with propofol is both concentration dependent and specific to the formulation of propofol. A low cisatracurium besylate concentration of 0.5 mg/ml with the sulfite-containing formulation of propofol (Baxter) results in emulsion disruption whereas the edetate-containing formulation of propofol (AstraZeneca) remains compatible. However, a high cisatracurium besylate concentration of 5 mg/ml disrupts the emulsions of both formulations of propofol. (2336) See Y-site Injection Compatibility table above.

Other Drugs — The manufacturer indicates that cisatracurium besylate is compatible with alfentanil HCl, droperidol, fentanyl citrate, midazolam HCl, and sufentanil citrate. (1-1/00)

Cisatracurium besylate is stated to be incompatible with propofol and ketorolac tromethamine. (1-1/00)

CISPLATIN
AHFS 10:00

Products — Cisplatin is available as a sterile aqueous injection containing cisplatin 1 mg/ml and sodium chloride 9 mg/ml, with hydrochloric acid and/or sodium hydroxide to adjust the pH. This aqueous solution is available in 50-ml (50-mg), 100-ml (100-mg), and 200-ml (200-mg) vials. (2; 4; 29)

pH — From 3.7 to 6. (4)

Osmolality — The aqueous injection has an osmolality of about 285 mOsm/kg. (4)

Density — Cisplatin (Bristol) 1 mg/ml undiluted aqueous injection has a solution density of 1.00 g/ml. (2041; 2248)

Sodium Content — Each 10 mg of cisplatin contains 1.54 mEq of sodium. (846; 869)

Trade Name(s) — Platinol-AQ.

Administration — Cisplatin is administered by intravenous infusion with a regimen of hydration (with or without mannitol and/or furosemide) prior to therapy. One regimen consists of 1 to 2 L of fluid given over eight to 12 hours prior to cisplatin administration. In addition, adequate hydration and urinary output must be maintained for 24 hours after therapy. The manufacturer recommends diluting the cisplatin dose in 2 L of compatible infusion solution containing mannitol 37.5 g and infusing over six to eight hours. (2; 4) Other dilutions and rates of administration have been used, including intravenous infusions over periods from 15 to 120 minutes and continuous infusion over one to five days. Intra-arterial infusion and intraperitoneal instillation have been used. (4)

Stability — Intact vials of the clear, colorless aqueous injection should be stored between 15 and 25 °C and protected from light; they should not be refrigerated. (2; 4)

After initial vial entry, the aqueous cisplatin injection in amber vials is stable for 28 days if it is protected from light or for seven days if it is exposed to fluorescent room light. (2)

Concern has been expressed that storage of cisplatin solutions for several weeks might result in substantial amounts of the toxic mono- and di-aquo species. (1199) However, the solution's chloride content, rather than extended storage time periods, appears to determine the extent of aquated product formation. (See Effect of Chloride Ion below.)

Kristjansson et al. evaluated the long-term stability of cisplatin 1 mg/ml in an aqueous solution containing sodium chloride 9 mg/ml and mannitol 10 mg/ml in glass vials. After 22 months at 5 °C, the 4% loss of cisplatin could be explained as the expected equilibrium between cisplatin and its aquated products. Furthermore, a precipitate formed and required sonication at 40 °C for about 20 to 30 minutes to redissolve. Storage of the cisplatin solution at 40 °C for 10 months resulted in no physical change. After an additional one year at 5 °C, these samples exhibited an average 15% loss, which the authors concluded was not the result of the formation of aquated species or the toxic and inactive oligomeric species. These proposed degradation products were not present in the 40 °C sample. (1246)

Cisplatin was cultured with human lymphoblasts to determine whether its cytotoxic activity was retained. The solution retained cytotoxicity for 24 hours when stored at either 4 °C or room temperature. (1575)

Theuer et al. reported little or no loss of cisplatin potency by HPLC, after 27 days at room temperature with protection from light, from a solution of cisplatin 500 μg/ml in sodium chloride 0.9% at pH 4.75 and 3.25. (1605)

pH Effects — The pH of maximum stability is 3.5 to 5.5. Alkaline media should be avoided because of increased hydrolysis. (1379)

In the dark at pH 6.3, cisplatin (Bristol) 1 mg/ml in sodium chloride 0.9% reached the maximum amount of decomposition product permitted in the *USP* in 34 days. Half of that amount was formed in 96 days at pH 4.3. (1647)

Cisplatin degradation results in ammonia formation, which increases the solution pH. Thus, the initial cisplatin degradation rate may be slow but increases with time. (1647)

Temperature Effects — It is recommended that cisplatin not be refrigerated because of the formation of a crystalline precipitate. (2; 4; 633; 636; 1246) In a study of cisplatin at concentrations of 0.4 to 1 mg/ml in sodium chloride 0.9%, it was found that at 0.6 mg/ml or greater a precipitate formed on refrigeration at 2 to 6 °C. At 1 mg/ml the precipitation was noted in one hour. However, the 0.6-mg/ml solution did not have a precipitate until after 48 hours under refrigeration. The 0.5-mg/ml and lower solutions did not precipitate for up to 72 hours at 2 to 6 °C. In solutions where precipitate did form, redissolution occurred very slowly with warming back to room temperature. (317) Sonication at 40 °C has been used to redissolve the precipitate in about 20 to 30 minutes. (1246) The warming of precipitated cisplatin solutions to effect redissolution is not recommended, however. Solutions containing a precipitate should not be used. (4; 633)

Freezing Solutions — If the solution is frozen, it should be thawed at room temperature until the precipitate dissolves. The manufacturer states that this thawing will not adversely affect the chemical or physical stability of the product. (4)

Cisplatin (Bristol) 50 and 200 mg/L in dextrose 5% in sodium chloride 0.45% in PVC bags and admixed with either mannitol 18.75 g/L or magnesium sulfate 1 or 2 g/L is reportedly stable for 30 days when frozen at −15 °C followed by an additional 48 hours at 25 °C. (1088)

Light Effects — Although changes in the UV spectra of cisplatin solutions on exposure to intense light have long been recognized (317), their significance was questioned. (483; 635) It was reported that exposure to normal laboratory light for 72 hours had no significant effect on cisplatin's stability by HPLC. (635)

More recently, however, Zieske et al. reported substantial cisplatin decomposition after exposure to typical laboratory light, a mixture of incandescent and fluorescent illumination. As much as 12% degraded to trichloroammineplatinate (II) after 25 hours. Cisplatin was most sensitive to light in the UV to blue region and had little sensitivity to yellow or red light. It was protected from light-induced degradation by low-actinic amber glass flasks but not by PVC bags, clear glass vials, or polyethylene syringes. The authors concluded that exposure to moderately intense white light for more than one hour should be avoided. (1647)

The manufacturer recommends that a cisplatin solution removed from its amber vial be protected from light if it is not used within six hours. Even in the amber vial, the cisplatin solution should be discarded after seven days if exposed to fluorescent room light. (2)

Chloride Ion Effects— The stability of cisplatin in solution is dependent on the chloride ion concentration present. Cisplatin is stable in solutions containing an adequate amount of chloride ion but is incompatible in solutions having a low chloride content. (4; 316; 317; 634; 635; 637) In solutions with an inadequate chloride content, one or both chloride ions in the cisplatin molecule are displaced by water, forming mono- and diaquo species. The minimum acceptable chloride ion concentration is about 0.040 mol/L, the equivalent of about 0.2% sodium chloride. (317; 634; 635)

At a cisplatin concentration of 200 mg/L in sodium chloride 0.9% with the pH adjusted to 4, about 3% decomposition occurs in less than one hour at room temperature. An equilibrium is then reached, with the cisplatin remaining stable thereafter. At lesser concentrations of chloride ion, greater decomposition of cisplatin occurs. In sodium chloride 0.45 and 0.2%, approximately 4 and 7% decomposition occurred at equilibrium, respectively. In very low chloride-containing solutions, most of the drug may be decomposed. The decomposition appears to be reversible, with cisplatin being reformed in the presence of high chloride concentrations. (317)

In another study, the stability of cisplatin 50 and 500 mg/L was evaluated in aqueous solutions containing sodium chloride 0.9, 0.45, and 0.1% and also in water over 24 hours at 25 °C exposed to light. Approximately 2 and 4% of the cisplatin were lost in the sodium chloride 0.9 and 0.45% solutions, respectively. In the 0.1% solution, about 4 to 10% decomposition occurred in four to six hours, increasing to approximately 11 to 15% at both 12 and 24 hours. In aqueous solution with no chloride content, cisplatin decomposed rapidly, with about a 30 to 35% loss in four hours increasing to a 70 to 80% loss in 24 hours. (635)

Cisplatin 0.2 mg/ml in sodium chloride 0.9% has been stated to exhibit less than a 10% loss in 14 days at room temperature. (1379)

Ambulatory Pumps— The stability of cisplatin (R. Bellon) 0.5 and 0.9 mg/ml in sodium chloride 0.9% was evaluated in ethylene vinyl acetate bags for use with a portable infusion pump (Celsa Celinject CO1). The bags were stored at 22 and 35 °C and protected from light for 28 days. HPLC analysis found little or no cisplatin loss and no degradation peaks at either concentration or temperature. However, about a 3% moisture loss due to permeation through the container was found in the 35 °C samples. (1827)

Cisplatin (David Bull) reconstituted to concentrations of 1 and 1.6 mg/ml with sterile water for injection was evaluated for stability for 14 days protected from light in Pharmacia Deltec medication cassettes at 24 and 37 °C. The 1.6-mg/ml concentration developed a yellow crystalline precipitate rendering it unfit for use. For the 1-mg/ml concentration, little change in cisplatin concentration by HPLC analysis was found, but water loss due to evaporation was found to be about 1% at 24 °C and 3% at 37 °C in 14 days. (2319)

Elastomeric Reservoir Pumps— Cisplatin 0.2 mg/ml in sodium chloride 0.9% in Homepump and Homepump Eclipse elastomeric reservoir pumps has been stated by the pump manufacturer to be stable for 14 days at room temperature. Cisplatin 1.25 mg/ml in sodium chloride 0.9% in Intermate pumps is stated by the pump manufacturer to be stable for 96 hours at body temperature. (31)

Filtration— Cisplatin 10 to 300 μg/ml exhibited no loss due to sorption to cellulose nitrate/cellulose acetate ester (Millex OR) or Teflon (Millex FG) filters. (1415; 1416)

Compatibility Information

Solution Compatibility

Cisplatin

Solution	*Mfr*	*Mfr*	*Conc/L*	*Remarks*	*Ref*	*C/I*
Dextrose 5% in sodium chloride 0.225%	AB[a]	NCI	300 mg/L	3% loss in 23 hr at 25 °C under fluorescent light	1087	C
Dextrose 5% in sodium chloride 0.45%		BV	50 and 500 mg	Less than 10% decomposition in 24 hr at room temperature	234	C
	AB[b]	NCI	300 mg/L	Less than 2% loss in 23 hr at 25 °C under fluorescent light	1087	C
Dextrose 5% in sodium chloride 0.9%		BV	50 and 500 mg	Less than 10% decomposition in 24 hr at room temperature	234	C
			500 mg	Approximately 2% decomposition in 24 hr at 25 °C	635	C
	AB[a]	NCI	300 mg/L	1% loss in 23 hr at 25 °C under fluorescent light	1087	C
Dextrose 5% in sodium chloride 0.45% with mannitol 1.875%		BR	50, 100, 200 mg	Physically compatible and cisplatin chemically stable for 72 hr at 25 and 4 °C with 2 to 10% decomposition observed after a subsequent 8-hr infusion	636	C
Dextrose 5% in sodium chloride 0.33% with mannitol 1.875%		BR	50, 100, 200 mg	Physically compatible and cisplatin chemically stable for 72 hr at 25 and 4 °C with 0 to 8% decomposition observed after a subsequent 8-hr infusion	636	C

Solution Compatibility (Cont.)

Cisplatin

Solution	*Mfr*	*Mfr*	*Conc/L*	*Remarks*	*Ref*	*C/I*
Dextrose 5% in sodium chloride 0.33% with potassium chloride 20 mEq and mannitol 1.875%		BR	50, 100, 200 mg	Physically compatible and cisplatin chemically stable for 72 hr at 25 and 4 °C	636	C
Dextrose 5% in water	TR	BV	100 mg	TLC indicates decomposition occurs in less than 2 hr at room temperature	316	I
	AB[a]	NCI	300 mg/L	4% loss in 2 hr and 6% in 23 hr at 25 °C under fluorescent light	1087	C
	AB[a]	NCI	75 mg/L	10% loss in 2 hr and 16% in 6 hr at 25 °C under fluorescent light	1087	I
Sodium bicarbonate 5%			50 and 500 mg	Bright gold precipitate forms within 8 to 24 hr at 25 °C	635	I
Sodium chloride 0.9%			50 and 500 mg	Approximately 2% decomposition in 24 hr at 25 °C	635	C
	TR	BV	100 mg	TLC indicates no decomposition in 24 hr at room temperature	316	C
		BV	200 mg	2 to 3% decomposition in 1 hr and no further decomposition for at least 24 hr at room temperature and pH adjusted to 4	317	C
	AB[a]	NCI	300 mg/L	1% loss in 23 hr at 25 °C under fluorescent light	1087	C
	[c]	BEL	600 mg	Little or no loss by HPLC in 9 days at 23 °C protected from light	1757	C
	[d]	BEL	500 and 900 mg	Little or no loss by HPLC in 28 days at 22 and 35 °C protected from light	1827	C
	[e]	WAS	167 mg	Little or no loss by HPLC in 14 days at 30 °C protected from light	1828	C
		EBE	100 mg	About 9% loss by HPLC in 5 days and 13% loss in 6 days at 22 °C protected from light. Less than 3% loss in 7 days at 4 °C protected from light	2293	C
Sodium chloride 0.45%			50 and 500 mg	Approximately 4% decomposition in 24 hr at 25 °C	635	C
		BV	200 mg	4 to 5% decomposition in 1 hr and no further decomposition for at least 24 hr at room temperature and pH adjusted to 4	317	C
Sodium chloride 0.3%		BR	50, 100, 200 mg	Physically compatible and 2 to 3% cisplatin loss over 72 hr at 25 and 4 °C	636	C
Sodium chloride 0.225%		BR	50, 100, 200 mg	Physically compatible and 2 to 5% cisplatin loss over 72 hr at 25 and 4 °C	636	C

[a] *Tested in glass bottles.*
[b] *Tested in both glass and PVC containers.*
[c] *Tested in PVC containers.*
[d] *Tested in ethylene vinyl acetate containers.*
[e] *Tested in glass, PVC, polyethylene, and polypropylene containers.*

Additive Compatibility

Cisplatin

Drug	*Mfr*	*Conc/L*	*Mfr*	*Conc/L*	*Test Soln*	*Remarks*	*Ref*	*C/I*
Carboplatin		1 g		200 mg	NS	Less than 10% loss of both drugs in 24 hr at 23 °C protected from light	1954	C

Additive Compatibility (Cont.)

			Cisplatin					
Drug	*Mfr*	*Conc/L*	*Mfr*	*Conc/L*	*Test Soln*	*Remarks*	*Ref*	*C/I*
Cyclophosphamide with etoposide		2 g 200 mg		200 mg	NS	All drugs stable for 7 days at room temperature	1379	C
Etoposide	BR	400 mg	BR	200 mg	NS[a]	Physically compatible with less than 10% loss of both drugs in 48 hr at 22 °C in light and dark	1329	C
	BR	200 mg	BR	200 mg	NS[a]	Physically compatible with less than 10% loss of both drugs in 24 hr at 22 °C. Possible excess cisplatin loss in 48 hr exposed to light	1329	C
	BR	200 and 400 mg	BR	200 mg	D5½S[a]	Physically compatible with less than 10% loss of both drugs in 24 hr at 22 °C in light and dark	1329	C
		400 mg		200 mg	NS	10% etoposide loss and no cisplatin loss in 7 days at room temperature	1388	C
		200 mg		200 mg	NS	Both drugs stable for 15 days at room temperature protected from light	1379	C
Etoposide with floxuridine		300 mg 700 mg		200 mg	NS	All drugs stable for 7 days at room temperature	1379	C
Etoposide with mannitol and potassium chloride	BR LY LY	400 mg 1.875% 20 mEq	BR	200 mg	NS[a]	Physically compatible and etoposide and cisplatin chemically stable for 8 hr at 22 °C. Precipitate forms within 24 hr	1329	I
Etoposide with mannitol and potassium chloride	BR LY LY	400 mg 1.875% 20 mEq	BR	200 mg	D5½S[a]	Physically compatible and etoposide and cisplatin chemically stable for 24 hr at 22 °C. Precipitate forms within 48 hr	1329	C
Floxuridine	RC	10 g	BR	500 mg	NS	13% FUdR loss in 7 days and 18% in 14 days at room temperature protected from light	1386	C
Floxuridine with leucovorin calcium		700 mg 140 mg		200 mg	NS	All drugs stable for 7 days at room temperature	1379	C
Fluorouracil	SO	1 g	BR	200 mg	NS[b]	10% cisplatin loss in 1.5 hr and 25% loss in 4 hr at 25 °C under fluorescent light or in the dark	1339	I
	SO	10 g	BR	500 mg	NS[b]	10% cisplatin loss in 1.2 hr and 25% loss in 3 hr at 25 °C under fluorescent light or in the dark	1339	I
	AD	10 g	BR	500 mg	NS	80% cisplatin loss in 24 hr at room temperature due to low pH	1386	I
Hydroxyzine HCl	LY	500 mg	BR	200 mg	NS[c]	Physically compatible for 48 hr	1190	C
Ifosfamide		2 g		200 mg	NS	Both drugs stable for 7 days at room temperature	1379	C
Ifosfamide with etoposide		2 g 200 mg		200 mg	NS	All drugs stable for 5 days at room temperature	1379	C
Leucovorin calcium		140 mg		200 mg	NS	Both drugs stable for 15 days at room temperature protected from light	1379	C
Magnesium sulfate		1 and 2 g	BR	50 and 200 mg	D5½S[b]	Compatible for 48 hr at 25 °C and 96 hr at 4 °C followed by 48 hr at 25 °C	1088	C
Mannitol		18.75 g	BR	50 and 200 mg	D5½S[b]	Compatible for 48 hr at 25 °C and 96 hr at 4 °C followed by 48 hr at 25 °C	1088	C

Additive Compatibility (Cont.)

Cisplatin

Drug	Mfr	Conc/L	Mfr	Conc/L	Test Soln	Remarks	Ref	C/I
Mesna		3.33 g		67 mg	NS	Cisplatin not detectable after 1 hr	1291	I
		110 mg		67 mg	NS	Cisplatin weakly detected after 1 hr	1291	I
Ondansetron HCl	GL	1.031 g	BR	485 mg	NS[b]	Physically compatible with little or no loss of either drug by HPLC in 24 hr at 4 °C followed by 7 days at 30 °C	1846	C
	GL	479 mg	BR	219 mg	NS[d]	Physically compatible with little or no loss of either drug by HPLC in 24 hr at 4 °C followed by 7 days at 30 °C	1846	C
Paclitaxel	BMS	300 mg	BMS	200 mg	NS	No paclitaxel loss and cisplatin losses of 1, 4, and 5% at 4, 24, and 32 °C, respectively, in 24 hr by HPLC. Physically compatible for 24 hr but subvisual particulates of paclitaxel form after 3 to 5 days	2094	C
	BMS	1.2 g	BMS	200 mg	NS	No paclitaxel loss but cisplatin losses of 10, 19, and 22% at 4, 24, and 32 °C, respectively, in 24 hr by HPLC. Physically compatible for 24 hr but subvisual particulates of paclitaxel form after 3 to 5 days	2094	I
Thiotepa		1 g		200 mg	NS	Yellow precipitation	1379	I

[a]*Tested in both glass and PVC containers.*
[b]*Tested in PVC containers.*
[c]*Tested in glass containers.*
[d]*Tested in polyisoprene reservoirs (Travenol Infusors).*

Drugs in Syringe Compatibility

Cisplatin

Drug (in syringe)	Mfr	Amt	Mfr	Amt	Remarks	Ref	C/I
Bleomycin sulfate		1.5 units/ 0.5 ml		0.5 mg/ 0.5 ml	Physically compatible for 5 min at room temperature followed by 8 min of centrifugation	980	C
Cyclophosphamide		10 mg/ 0.5 ml		0.5 mg/ 0.5 ml	Physically compatible for 5 min at room temperature followed by 8 min of centrifugation	980	C
Doxapram HCl	RB	400 mg/ 20 ml		10 mg/ 20 ml	Physically compatible with no doxapram loss in 24 hr	1177	C
Doxorubicin HCl		1 mg/ 0.5 ml		0.5 mg/ 0.5 ml	Physically compatible for 5 min at room temperature followed by 8 min of centrifugation	980	C
Droperidol		1.25 mg/ 0.5 ml		0.5 mg/ 0.5 ml	Physically compatible for 5 min at room temperature followed by 8 min of centrifugation	980	C
Fluorouracil		25 mg/ 0.5 ml		0.5 mg/ 0.5 ml	Physically compatible for 5 min at room temperature followed by 8 min of centrifugation	980	C
Furosemide		5 mg/ 0.5 ml		0.5 mg/ 0.5 ml	Physically compatible for 5 min at room temperature followed by 8 min of centrifugation	980	C
Heparin sodium		500 units/ 0.5 ml		0.5 mg/ 0.5 ml	Physically compatible for 5 min at room temperature followed by 8 min of centrifugation	980	C
Leucovorin calcium		5 mg/ 0.5 ml		0.5 mg/ 0.5 ml	Physically compatible for 5 min at room temperature followed by 8 min of centrifugation	980	C

Drugs in Syringe Compatibility (Cont.)

		Cisplatin					
Drug (in syringe)	*Mfr*	*Amt*	*Mfr*	*Amt*	*Remarks*	*Ref*	*C/I*
Methotrexate sodium		12.5 mg/ 0.5 ml		0.5 mg/ 0.5 ml	Physically compatible for 5 min at room temperature followed by 8 min of centrifugation	980	C
Metoclopramide HCl		2.5 mg/ 0.5 ml		0.5 mg/ 0.5 ml	Physically compatible for 5 min at room temperature followed by 8 min of centrifugation	980	C
Mitomycin		0.25 mg/ 0.5 ml		0.5 mg/ 0.5 ml	Physically compatible for 5 min at room temperature followed by 8 min of centrifugation	980	C
Vinblastine sulfate		0.5 mg/ 0.5 ml		0.5 mg/ 0.5 ml	Physically compatible for 5 min at room temperature followed by 8 min of centrifugation	980	C
Vincristine sulfate		0.5 mg/ 0.5 ml		0.5 mg/ 0.5 ml	Physically compatible for 5 min at room temperature followed by 8 min of centrifugation	980	C

Y-Site Injection Compatibility (1:1 Mixture)

			Cisplatin				
Drug	*Mfr*	*Conc*	*Mfr*	*Conc*	*Remarks*	*Ref*	*C/I*
Allopurinol sodium	BW	3 mg/ml[b]	BR	1 mg/ml	Physically compatible with no change in measured turbidity or increase in particle content in 4 hr at 22 °C	1686	C
Amifostine	USB	10 mg/ml[a]	BR	1 mg/ml	Subvisual haze forms in 4 hr	1845	I
Amphotericin B cholesteryl sulfate complex	SEQ	0.83 mg/ml[a]	BR	1 mg/ml	Gross precipitate forms	2117	I
Aztreonam	SQ	40 mg/ml[a]	BMS	1 mg/ml	Physically compatible with no subvisual haze or particle formation in 4 hr at 23 °C	1758	C
Bleomycin sulfate		3 units/ml		1 mg/ml	Drugs injected sequentially into Y-site with no flush between. No visually apparent precipitate	980	C
Cefepime HCl	BMS	20 mg/ml[a]	BR	1 mg/ml	Haze forms in 1 hr. Cloudiness and particulates form in 4 hr	1689	I
Chlorpromazine HCl	SKF	2 mg/ml[a]	BR	1 mg/ml	Visually compatible for 4 hr at room temperature under fluorescent light	1685	C
Cimetidine HCl	SKF	12 mg/ml[a]	BR	1 mg/ml	Visually compatible for 4 hr at room temperature under fluorescent light	1685	C
Cladribine	ORT	0.015[b] and 0.5[c] mg/ml	BR	1 mg/ml	Physically compatible with no change in measured turbidity or increase in particle content in 4 hr at 23 °C	1969	C
Cyclophosphamide		20 mg/ml		1 mg/ml	Drugs injected sequentially into Y-site with no flush between. No visually apparent precipitate	980	C
Dexamethasone sodium phosphate	QU	1 mg/ml[a]	BR	1 mg/ml	Visually compatible for 4 hr at room temperature under fluorescent light	1685	C
Diphenhydramine HCl	PD	2 mg/ml[a]	BR	1 mg/ml	Visually compatible for 4 hr at room temperature under fluorescent light	1685	C
Doxorubicin HCl		2 mg/ml		1 mg/ml	Drugs injected sequentially into Y-site with no flush between. No visually apparent precipitate	980	C

Y-Site Injection Compatibility (1:1 Mixture) (Cont.)

Cisplatin

Drug	*Mfr*	*Conc*	*Mfr*	*Conc*	*Remarks*	*Ref*	*C/I*
Doxorubicin HCl liposome injection	SEQ	0.4 mg/ml[a]	BR	1 mg/ml	Physically compatible with little or no change in measured turbidity and no increase in particle content in 4 hr at 23 °C	2087	C
Droperidol		2.5 mg/ml		1 mg/ml	Drugs injected sequentially into Y-site with no flush between. No visually apparent precipitate	980	C
	JN	20 μg/ml[a]	BR	1 mg/ml	Visually compatible for 4 hr at room temperature under fluorescent light	1685	C
Etoposide phosphate	BR	5 mg/ml[a]	BR	1 mg/ml	Physically compatible with no change in measured turbidity or increase in particle content in 4 hr at 23 °C	2218	C
Famotidine	MSD	2 mg/ml[a]	BR	1 mg/ml	Visually compatible for 4 hr at room temperature under fluorescent light	1685	C
Filgrastim	AMG	30 μg/ml[a]	BR	1 mg/ml	Physically compatible with no change in measured turbidity or increase in particle content in 4 hr at 22 °C	1687	C
Fludarabine phosphate	BX	1 mg/ml[a]	BR	1 mg/ml	Physically compatible for 4 hr at room temperature under fluorescent light	1439	C
Fluorouracil		50 mg/ml		1 mg/ml	Drugs injected sequentially into Y-site with no flush between. No visually apparent precipitate	980	C
Furosemide		10 mg/ml		1 mg/ml	Drugs injected sequentially into Y-site with no flush between. No visually apparent precipitate	980	C
	ES	3 mg/ml[a]	BR	1 mg/ml	Visually compatible for 4 hr at room temperature under fluorescent light	1685	C
Ganciclovir sodium	SY	20 mg/ml[a]	BR	1 mg/ml	Visually compatible for 4 hr at room temperature under fluorescent light	1685	C
Gatifloxacin	BMS	2 mg/ml[a]	BR	1 mg/ml	Physically compatible with no change in measured haze or increase in particle content in 4 hr at 23 °C	2234	C
Gemcitabine HCl	LI	10 mg/ml[b]	BR	1 mg/ml	Physically compatible with no change in measured turbidity or increase in particle content in 4 hr at 23 °C	2226	C
Granisetron HCl	SKB	1 mg/ml	BR	1 mg/ml	Physically compatible with little or no loss of either drug by HPLC in 4 hr at 22 °C	1883	C
	SKB	1 mg/ml	BR	0.05 mg/ml[b]	Physically compatible with little or no granisetron loss by HPLC in 4 hr at 22 °C	1883	C
Heparin sodium		1000 units/ml		1 mg/ml	Drugs injected sequentially into Y-site with no flush between. No visually apparent precipitate	980	C
	SO	40 units/ml[a]	BR	1 mg/ml	Visually compatible for 4 hr at room temperature under fluorescent light	1685	C
Hydromorphone HCl	ES	0.04 mg/ml[a]	BR	1 mg/ml	Visually compatible for 4 hr at room temperature under fluorescent light	1685	C
Leucovorin calcium		10 mg/ml		1 mg/ml	Drugs injected sequentially into Y-site with no flush between. No visually apparent precipitate	980	C

Y-Site Injection Compatibility (1:1 Mixture) (Cont.)

Cisplatin

Drug	*Mfr*	*Conc*	*Mfr*	*Conc*	*Remarks*	*Ref*	*C/I*
Linezolid	PHU	2 mg/ml	BR	1 mg/ml	Physically compatible with no change in measured turbidity or increase in particle content in 4 hr at 23 °C	2264	C
Lorazepam	WY	0.1 mg/ml[a]	BR	1 mg/ml	Visually compatible for 4 hr at room temperature under fluorescent light	1685	C
Melphalan HCl	BW	0.1 mg/ml[b]	BR	1 mg/ml	Physically compatible with no change in measured turbidity or increase in particle content in 3 hr at 22 °C	1557	C
Methotrexate sodium		25 mg/ml		1 mg/ml	Drugs injected sequentially into Y-site with no flush between. No visually apparent precipitate	980	C
Methylprednisolone sodium succinate	UP	0.5 mg/ml[a]	BR	1 mg/ml	Visually compatible for 4 hr at room temperature under fluorescent light	1685	C
Metoclopramide HCl		5 mg/ml		1 mg/ml	Drugs injected sequentially into Y-site with no flush between. No visually apparent precipitate	980	C
	RB	2.5 mg/ml[a]	BR	1 mg/ml	Visually compatible for 4 hr at room temperature under fluorescent light	1685	C
Mitomycin		0.5 mg/ml		1 mg/ml	Drugs injected sequentially into Y-site with no flush between. No visually apparent precipitate	980	C
Morphine sulfate	ES	0.12 mg/ml[a]	BR	1 mg/ml	Visually compatible for 4 hr at room temperature under fluorescent light	1685	C
Ondansetron HCl	GL	1 mg/ml[b]	BR	1 mg/ml	Physically compatible for 4 hr at 22 °C under fluorescent light	1365	C
	GL	16 to 160 μg/ml		0.48 mg/ml	Physically compatible when cisplatin given over 1 to 8 hr via Y-site	1366	C
Paclitaxel	NCI	1.2 mg/ml[a]		1 mg/ml	Physically compatible with no change in measured turbidity in 4 hr at 22 °C	1528	C
Piperacillin sodium–tazobactam sodium	LE	40 + 5 mg/ml[a]	BR	1 mg/ml	Haze and particles form in 1 hr	1688	I
Prochlorperazine edisylate	SKF	0.5 mg/ml[a]	BR	1 mg/ml	Visually compatible for 4 hr at room temperature under fluorescent light	1685	C
Promethazine HCl	WY	2 mg/ml[a]	BR	1 mg/ml	Visually compatible for 4 hr at room temperature under fluorescent light	1685	C
Propofol	ZEN	10 mg/ml	BR	1 mg/ml	Physically compatible for 1 hr at 23 °C with no increase in particle content	2066	C
Ranitidine HCl	GL	1 mg/ml[a]	BR	1 mg/ml	Visually compatible for 4 hr at room temperature under fluorescent light	1685	C
Sargramostim	IMM	10 μg/ml[b]	BR	1 mg/ml	Physically compatible for 4 hr at 22 °C	1436	C
Teniposide	BR	0.1 mg/ml[a]	BR	1 mg/ml	Physically compatible with no subvisual haze or particle formation in 4 hr at 23 °C	1725	C
Thiotepa	IMM[d]	1 mg/ml[a]	BMS	1 mg/ml	White cloudiness appears in 4 hr at 23 °C	1861	I
TNA #218 to #226[e]			BMS	1 mg/ml	Visually compatible with no precipitate or emulsion damage apparent in 4 hr at 23 °C	2215	C

Y-Site Injection Compatibility (1:1 Mixture) (Cont.)

Cisplatin

Drug	*Mfr*	*Conc*	*Mfr*	*Conc*	*Remarks*	*Ref*	*C/I*
Topotecan HCl	SKB	56 µg/ml[b]	BR	0.168 mg/ml[b]	Visually compatible with little or no loss of either drug by HPLC in 4 hr at 22 °C under fluorescent light	2245	C
TPN #212 to #215[e]			BMS	1 mg/ml	Amber discoloration formed in 1 to 4 hr	2109	I
Vinblastine sulfate		1 mg/ml		1 mg/ml	Drugs injected sequentially into Y-site with no flush between. No visually apparent precipitate	980	C
Vincristine sulfate		1 mg/ml		1 mg/ml	Drugs injected sequentially into Y-site with no flush between. No visually apparent precipitate	980	C
Vinorelbine tartrate	BW	1 mg/ml[b]	BR	1 mg/ml	Physically compatible with no change in measured turbidity or increase in particle content in 4 hr at 22 °C	1558	C

[a]*Tested in dextrose 5% in water.*
[b]*Tested in sodium chloride 0.9%.*
[c]*Tested in bacteriostatic sodium chloride 0.9% preserved with benzyl alcohol 0.9%.*
[d]*Lyophilized formulation tested.*
[e]*Refer to Appendix I for the composition of parenteral nutrition solutions. TNA indicates a 3-in-1 admixture, and TPN indicates a 2-in-1 admixture.*

Additional Compatibility Information

Other Drugs — In solutions containing sodium chloride 0.45 or 0.9%, the presence of mannitol 5% did not adversely affect solution stability. (635) Such solutions have been reported to be compatible for 48 hours at 25 °C. (1088) However, some authors believe that advanced mixing of mannitol and cisplatin should be avoided because of the formation of a mannitol–cisplatin complex over several days. (524; 870)

The combination of cisplatin with bicarbonate solutions, and perhaps any alkaline solution, should be avoided because of enhanced decomposition of cisplatin. In addition, the formation of a bright gold precipitate may occur in some cases. (635)

Cisplatin may react with sodium thiosulfate, sodium metabisulfite, and sodium bisulfite in solution, rapidly and completely inactivating the cisplatin. (4; 1089; 1175)

The sodium metabisulfite antioxidant in the former metoclopramide HCl formulation reacted rapidly and extensively with cisplatin, displacing chloride ligands. At clinically relevant concentrations, a 10% cisplatin loss occurred in less than five minutes. A total loss of cisplatin occurred in about 30 minutes. (1175) The current Reglan and Maxolon formulations contain no sulfites (4; 1247), but sulfites in other drug formulations may pose a similar stability risk.

Aluminum — Because of an interaction occurring between cisplatin and the metal aluminum, only administration equipment such as needles, syringes, catheters, and sets that contain no aluminum should be used for this drug. Aluminum in contact with cisplatin solution will result in a replacement oxidation–reduction reaction, forcing platinum from the cisplatin molecule out of solution and appearing as a black or brown precipitate. Other metal components such as stainless steel needles and plated brass hubs do not elicit an observable reaction within 24 hours. (2; 203; 204; 512; 988)

Bohart and Ogawa noted this reaction after piggybacking a 1-mg/ml cisplatin solution through an infusion line at a rate of 1 mg/min. A brownish precipitate accumulated about the inner hub of the aluminum needle. Further tests, exposing metallic aluminum, copper, and stainless steel to 1-mg/ml cisplatin solutions, showed that a brownish precipitate formed on the aluminum within a few minutes. The other two metals showed no evidence of a reaction. (203)

Prestayko et al. investigated this reaction further. When metallic aluminum was placed in contact with a 1-mg/ml solution of cisplatin, microscopic examination revealed a black precipitate, accompanied by the evolution of gas bubbles, in five to 10 minutes. The black precipitate became visually apparent within 30 to 60 minutes. This precipitate contained platinum, aluminum, and oxygen. (204)

When commercially marketed intravenous administration equipment such as needles, indwelling intravenous catheters, and intravenous administration sets were tested, only units containing needles with aluminum hubs were found to react. A visible black precipitate appeared in 60 to 90 minutes and increased over the 24-hour study. The extent of cisplatin loss was also determined in 1-mg/ml solutions in contact with aluminum-hubbed needles. The loss of cisplatin was approximately 29% in three hours and 50% in six hours at room temperature. (204)

Other Information

Microbial Growth — Cisplatin (Bristol-Myers Oncology) 20 mg/20 ml did not support the growth of several microorganisms and may impart an antimicrobial effect at this concentration. Loss of viability was observed for *Staphylococcus aureus, Escherichia coli, Pseudomonas aeruginosa, Pseudomonas cepacia, Candida albicans,* and *Aspergillus niger.* (1187)

CLADRIBINE
AHFS 10:00

Products — Cladribine is available as a solution in 10-ml single-use vials. Each milliliter of the solution contains cladribine 1 mg, sodium chloride 9 mg, and phosphoric acid and/or dibasic sodium phosphate to adjust the pH. (2) The injection is a concentrate that must be diluted for administration. (2; 4)

pH — From 5.5 to 8. (2)

Tonicity — Cladribine injection is isotonic. (2)

Sodium Content — Each milliliter of cladribine injection contains 0.15 mEq of sodium. (2)

Trade Name(s) — Leustatin.

Administration — Cladribine is administered by continuous intravenous infusion after dilution in 500 ml of sodium chloride 0.9% for repeated single daily doses. Alternatively, cladribine may be diluted in bacteriostatic sodium chloride 0.9% containing benzyl alcohol 0.9% for a seven-day continuous infusion. The seven-day solution should be prepared by adding both the drug and solution to the pump reservoir through 0.22-μm filters, bringing the final volume to 100 ml. Remove air in the reservoirs by aspiration using a syringe and filter or vent-filter assembly. The finished preserved solution is then administered continuously over seven days. (2; 4)

The use of dextrose 5% in water as a diluent is not recommended because of an increased rate of cladribine degradation. (2)

Stability — Intact cladribine vials should be stored under refrigeration and protected from light. The solution is clear and colorless. A precipitate may develop upon low-temperature storage; the precipitate may be redissolved by allowing the solution to warm to room temperature with vigorous shaking. (2) Heating the solution is not recommended. However, less than 5% loss is reported to occur in seven days when the solution is stored at 37 °C. (1369) Freezing does not adversely affect stability of the product. Thawing should be allowed to occur naturally by exposure to room temperature. The vials should not be heated or exposed to microwaves. After thawing, the vial contents are stable under refrigeration until expiration. Thawed vials should not be refrozen. (2)

Ambulatory Pumps — Prepared in bacteriostatic sodium chloride 0.9% preserved with benzyl alcohol 0.9%, cladribine exhibits both chemical and physical stability for at least seven days in Sims Deltec ambulatory infusion pump reservoirs. Preservative effectiveness may be reduced in solutions prepared for patients weighing more than 85 kg due to greater benzyl alcohol dilution. (2)

Compatibility Information

Solution Compatibility

Cladribine

Solution	*Mfr*	*Mfr*	*Conc/L*	*Remarks*	*Ref*	*C/I*
Sodium chloride 0.9%	[a,b]	JC	16 mg	Visually compatible and little or no loss by HPLC in 30 days at 4 and 18 °C exposed to or protected from light	2154	C

[a]*Tested in PVC containers.*
[b]*Tested in polyethylene-lined trilayer (Clearflex) containers.*

Y-Site Injection Compatibility (1:1 Mixture)

Cladribine

Drug	*Mfr*	*Conc*	*Mfr*	*Conc*	*Remarks*	*Ref*	*C/I*
Aminophylline	AMR	2.5 mg/ml[a]	ORT	0.015[a] and 0.5[b] mg/ml	Physically compatible with no change in measured turbidity or increase in particle content in 4 hr at 23 °C	1969	C
Bumetanide	RC	0.04 mg/ml[a]	ORT	0.015[a] and 0.5[b] mg/ml	Physically compatible with no change in measured turbidity or increase in particle content in 4 hr at 23 °C	1969	C
Buprenorphine HCl	RKC	0.04 mg/ml[a]	ORT	0.015[a] and 0.5[b] mg/ml	Physically compatible with no change in measured turbidity or increase in particle content in 4 hr at 23 °C	1969	C
Butorphanol tartrate	APC	0.04 mg/ml[a]	ORT	0.015[a] and 0.5[b] mg/ml	Physically compatible with no change in measured turbidity or increase in particle content in 4 hr at 23 °C	1969	C
Calcium gluconate	AMR	40 mg/ml[a]	ORT	0.015[a] and 0.5[b] mg/ml	Physically compatible with no change in measured turbidity or increase in particle content in 4 hr at 23 °C	1969	C

Y-Site Injection Compatibility (1:1 Mixture) (Cont.)

			Cladribine				
Drug	*Mfr*	*Conc*	*Mfr*	*Conc*	*Remarks*	*Ref*	*C/I*
Carboplatin	BR	5 mg/ml[a]	ORT	0.015[a] and 0.5[b] mg/ml	Physically compatible with no change in measured turbidity or increase in particle content in 4 hr at 23 °C	1969	C
Chlorpromazine HCl	SCN	2 mg/ml[a]	ORT	0.015[a] and 0.5[b] mg/ml	Physically compatible with no change in measured turbidity or increase in particle content in 4 hr at 23 °C	1969	C
Cimetidine HCl	SKB	12 mg/ml[a]	ORT	0.015[a] and 0.5[b] mg/ml	Physically compatible with no change in measured turbidity or increase in particle content in 4 hr at 23 °C	1969	C
Cisplatin	BR	1 mg/ml	ORT	0.015[a] and 0.5[b] mg/ml	Physically compatible with no change in measured turbidity or increase in particle content in 4 hr at 23 °C	1969	C
Cyclophosphamide	MJ	10 mg/ml[a]	ORT	0.015[a] and 0.5[b] mg/ml	Physically compatible with no change in measured turbidity or increase in particle content in 4 hr at 23 °C	1969	C
Cytarabine	CHI	50 mg/ml	ORT	0.015[a] and 0.5[b] mg/ml	Physically compatible with no change in measured turbidity or increase in particle content in 4 hr at 23 °C	1969	C
Dexamethasone sodium phosphate	AMR	1 mg/ml[a]	ORT	0.015[a] and 0.5[b] mg/ml	Physically compatible with no change in measured turbidity or increase in particle content in 4 hr at 23 °C	1969	C
Diphenhydramine HCl	SCN	2 mg/ml[a]	ORT	0.015[a] and 0.5[b] mg/ml	Physically compatible with no change in measured turbidity or increase in particle content in 4 hr at 23 °C	1969	C
Dobutamine HCl	LI	4 mg/ml[a]	ORT	0.015[a] and 0.5[b] mg/ml	Physically compatible with no change in measured turbidity or increase in particle content in 4 hr at 23 °C	1969	C
Dopamine HCl	AST	3.2 mg/ml[a]	ORT	0.015[a] and 0.5[b] mg/ml	Physically compatible with no change in measured turbidity or increase in particle content in 4 hr at 23 °C	1969	C
Doxorubicin HCl	CHI	2 mg/ml	ORT	0.015[a] and 0.5[b] mg/ml	Physically compatible with no change in measured turbidity or increase in particle content in 4 hr at 23 °C	1969	C
Droperidol	JN	0.4 mg/ml[a]	ORT	0.015[a] and 0.5[b] mg/ml	Physically compatible with no change in measured turbidity or increase in particle content in 4 hr at 23 °C	1969	C
Enalaprilat	MSD	0.1 mg/ml[a]	ORT	0.015[a] and 0.5[b] mg/ml	Physically compatible with no change in measured turbidity or increase in particle content in 4 hr at 23 °C	1969	C
Etoposide	BR	0.4 mg/ml[a]	ORT	0.015[a] and 0.5[b] mg/ml	Physically compatible with no change in measured turbidity or increase in particle content in 4 hr at 23 °C	1969	C
Famotidine	ME	2 mg/ml[a]	ORT	0.015[a] and 0.5[b] mg/ml	Physically compatible with no change in measured turbidity or increase in particle content in 4 hr at 23 °C	1969	C
Furosemide	AB	3 mg/ml[a]	ORT	0.015[a] and 0.5[b] mg/ml	Physically compatible with no change in measured turbidity or increase in particle content in 4 hr at 23 °C	1969	C

Y-Site Injection Compatibility (1:1 Mixture) (Cont.)

Cladribine

Drug	*Mfr*	*Conc*	*Mfr*	*Conc*	*Remarks*	*Ref*	*C/I*
Granisetron HCl	SKB	0.05 mg/ml[a]	ORT	0.015[a] and 0.5[b] mg/ml	Physically compatible with no change in measured turbidity or increase in particle content in 4 hr at 23 °C	1969	C
Haloperidol lactate	MN	0.2 mg/ml[a]	ORT	0.015[a] and 0.5[b] mg/ml	Physically compatible with no change in measured turbidity or increase in particle content in 4 hr at 23 °C	1969	C
Heparin sodium	WY	100 units/ml[a]	ORT	0.015[a] and 0.5[b] mg/ml	Physically compatible with no change in measured turbidity or increase in particle content in 4 hr at 23 °C	1969	C
Hydrocortisone sodium phosphate	MSD	1 mg/ml[a]	ORT	0.015[a] and 0.5[b] mg/ml	Physically compatible with no change in measured turbidity or increase in particle content in 4 hr at 23 °C	1969	C
Hydrocortisone sodium succinate	UP	1 mg/ml[a]	ORT	0.015[a] and 0.5[b] mg/ml	Physically compatible with no change in measured turbidity or increase in particle content in 4 hr at 23 °C	1969	C
Hydromorphone HCl	KN	0.5 mg/ml[a]	ORT	0.015[a] and 0.5[b] mg/ml	Physically compatible with no change in measured turbidity or increase in particle content in 4 hr at 23 °C	1969	C
Hydroxyzine HCl	ES	4 mg/ml[a]	ORT	0.015[a] and 0.5[b] mg/ml	Physically compatible with no change in measured turbidity or increase in particle content in 4 hr at 23 °C	1969	C
Idarubicin HCl	AD	0.5 mg/ml[a]	ORT	0.015[a] and 0.5[b] mg/ml	Increase in measured turbidity no greater than simple dilution alone. No increase in particle content in 4 hr at 23 °C	1969	C
Leucovorin calcium	IMM	2 mg/ml[a]	ORT	0.015[a] and 0.5[b] mg/ml	Physically compatible with no change in measured turbidity or increase in particle content in 4 hr at 23 °C	1969	C
Lorazepam	WY	0.1 mg/ml[a]	ORT	0.015[a] and 0.5[b] mg/ml	Physically compatible with no change in measured turbidity or increase in particle content in 4 hr at 23 °C	1969	C
Mannitol	BA	15%	ORT	0.015[a] and 0.5[b] mg/ml	Physically compatible with no change in measured turbidity or increase in particle content in 4 hr at 23 °C	1969	C
Meperidine HCl	WY	4 mg/ml[a]	ORT	0.015[a] and 0.5[b] mg/ml	Physically compatible with no change in measured turbidity or increase in particle content in 4 hr at 23 °C	1969	C
Mesna	MJ	10 mg/ml[a]	ORT	0.015[a] and 0.5[b] mg/ml	Physically compatible with no change in measured turbidity or increase in particle content in 4 hr at 23 °C	1969	C
Methylprednisolone sodium succinate	AB	5 mg/ml[a]	ORT	0.015[a] and 0.5[b] mg/ml	Physically compatible with no change in measured turbidity or increase in particle content in 4 hr at 23 °C	1969	C
Metoclopramide HCl	RB	5 mg/ml	ORT	0.015[a] and 0.5[b] mg/ml	Physically compatible with no change in measured turbidity or increase in particle content in 4 hr at 23 °C	1969	C
Mitoxantrone HCl	LE	0.5 mg/ml[a]	ORT	0.015[a] and 0.5[b] mg/ml	Physically compatible with no change in measured turbidity or increase in particle content in 4 hr at 23 °C	1969	C

Y-Site Injection Compatibility (1:1 Mixture) (Cont.)

			Cladribine				
Drug	*Mfr*	*Conc*	*Mfr*	*Conc*	*Remarks*	*Ref*	*C/I*
Morphine sulfate	AST	1 mg/ml[a]	ORT	0.015[a] and 0.5[b] mg/ml	Physically compatible with no change in measured turbidity or increase in particle content in 4 hr at 23 °C	1969	C
Nalbuphine HCl	AST	10 mg/ml	ORT	0.015[a] and 0.5[b] mg/ml	Physically compatible with no change in measured turbidity or increase in particle content in 4 hr at 23 °C	1969	C
Ondansetron HCl	CER	1 mg/ml[a]	ORT	0.015[a] and 0.5[b] mg/ml	Physically compatible with no change in measured turbidity or increase in particle content in 4 hr at 23 °C	1969	C
Paclitaxel	BR	0.6 mg/ml[a]	ORT	0.015[a] and 0.5[b] mg/ml	Physically compatible with no change in measured turbidity or increase in particle content in 4 hr at 23 °C	1969	C
Potassium chloride	AB	0.1 mEq/ml[a]	ORT	0.015[a] and 0.5[b] mg/ml	Physically compatible with no change in measured turbidity or increase in particle content in 4 hr at 23 °C	1969	C
Prochlorperazine edisylate	SCN	0.5 mg/ml[a]	ORT	0.015[a] and 0.5[b] mg/ml	Physically compatible with no change in measured turbidity or increase in particle content in 4 hr at 23 °C	1969	C
Promethazine HCl	SCN	2 mg/ml[a]	ORT	0.015[a] and 0.5[b] mg/ml	Physically compatible with no change in measured turbidity or increase in particle content in 4 hr at 23 °C	1969	C
Ranitidine HCl	GL	2 mg/ml[a]	ORT	0.015[a] and 0.5[b] mg/ml	Physically compatible with no change in measured turbidity or increase in particle content in 4 hr at 23 °C	1969	C
Sodium bicarbonate	AB	1 mEq/ml	ORT	0.015[a] and 0.5[b] mg/ml	Physically compatible with no change in measured turbidity or increase in particle content in 4 hr at 23 °C	1969	C
Teniposide	BR	0.1 mg/ml[a]	ORT	0.015[a] and 0.5[b] mg/ml	Physically compatible with no change in measured turbidity or increase in particle content in 4 hr at 23 °C	1969	C
Vincristine sulfate	LI	0.05 mg/ml[a]	ORT	0.015[a] and 0.5[b] mg/ml	Physically compatible with no change in measured turbidity or increase in particle content in 4 hr at 23 °C	1969	C

[a]*Tested in sodium chloride 0.9%.*
[b]*Tested in bacteriostatic sodium chloride 0.9% preserved with benzyl alcohol 0.9%.*

Additional Compatibility Information

Infusion Solutions — The manufacturer states that admixtures of the drug in sodium chloride 0.9% are chemically and physically stable for at least 24 hours at room temperature exposed to normal fluorescent light. Dextrose 5% in water should not be used due to increased rates of drug degradation. Cladribine diluted for administration should be used promptly; storage should be limited to no more than eight hours under refrigeration prior to administration. (2) In concentrations of 0.15 to 0.3 mg/ml in bacteriostatic sodium chloride 0.9% containing benzyl alcohol, the drug is stated to be stable for at least 14 days. (1369)

Other Information

Microbial Growth — Cladribine (Ortho Biotech) 0.025 mg/ml diluted in sodium chloride 0.9% did not exhibit an antimicrobial effect on the growth of four organisms (*Enterococcus faecium, Staphylococcus aureus, Pseudomonas aeruginosa,* and *Candida albicans*) inoculated into the solution. Diluted solutions should be stored under refrigeration whenever possible, and the potential for microbiological growth should be considered when assigning expiration periods. (2160)

CLINDAMYCIN PHOSPHATE
AHFS 8:12.28

Products — Clindamycin phosphate is available in 2-, 4-, and 6-ml vials and a 60-ml pharmacy bulk container. Each milliliter of solution contains (2; 4):

Component	Amount
Clindamycin (as phosphate)	150 mg
Benzyl alcohol	9.45 mg
Disodium edetate	0.5 mg
Sodium hydroxide and/or hydrochloric acid	to adjust pH
Water for injection	qs 1 ml

Clindamycin phosphate also is available in 50-ml bags containing 300, 600, or 900 mg of drug in dextrose 5% in water. Disodium edetate 0.04 mg/ml and sodium hydroxide and/or hydrochloric acid are also present to adjust the pH. (2)

pH — The product pH may range from 5.5 to 7 (4) but is usually about 6 to 6.3. (102; 103)

Osmolality — Clindamycin phosphate (Upjohn) 150 mg/ml has been reported to have an osmolality of 795 mOsm/kg (50) or 835 mOsm/kg (1071) as determined by freezing-point depression. However, the manufacturer has stated that the osmolality is usually 825 to 880 mOsm/kg. (1705)

The osmolality of clindamycin phosphate (Upjohn) 12 mg/ml was determined to be 293 mOsm/kg in dextrose 5% in water and 309 mOsm/kg in sodium chloride 0.9%. (1375)

The osmolalities of the 300-, 600-, and 900-mg premixed infusion solutions in dextrose 5% in water are 296, 322, and 339 mOsm/kg, respectively. (4)

The osmolality of clindamycin phosphate 600 mg was calculated for the following dilutions (1054):

	Osmolality (mOsm/kg)	
Diluent	50 ml	100 ml
Dextrose 5% in water	279	268
Sodium chloride 0.9%	306	294

Trade Name(s) — Cleocin Phosphate.

Administration — Clindamycin phosphate is administered by intramuscular injection; single injections greater than 600 mg are not recommended. It may also be administered by intermittent intravenous infusion in concentrations not exceeding 18 mg/ml. Intermittent infusions should be infused over 10 to 60 minutes at a rate not exceeding 30 mg/min. Intravenous doses under 900 mg may be diluted in 50 ml of a compatible diluent; doses of 900 mg or more should be diluted in 100 ml of diluent. Not more than 1200 mg of clindamycin phosphate should be given in a one-hour period. The drug should not be given undiluted as a bolus. (2; 4)

Alternatively, following an initial single rapid infusion, continuous intravenous infusion at rates of 0.75 to 1.25 mg/min have been suggested. (2; 4)

Stability — Intact containers of clindamycin phosphate should be stored at controlled room temperature; temperatures above 30 °C should be avoided. (2) Less than 10% decomposition occurs in two years at 25 °C at pH 3.5 to 6.5. (102; 103) Crystallization may occur on refrigeration; the crystals resolubilize on warming to room temperature, but care should be exercised to ensure that all crystals have redissolved. This would also apply if the product is frozen. (102)

pH Effects — Maximum stability occurs at pH 4, but an acceptable long-term shelf life is attained at pH 1 to 6.5. (1072)

Freezing Solutions — Clindamycin phosphate 6, 9, and 12 mg/ml in dextrose 5% in water, sodium chloride 0.9%, or Ringer's injection, lactated, is physically and chemically stable for eight weeks when frozen at −10 °C. Solutions should be thawed at room temperature and should not be refrozen. (4)

Clindamycin phosphate (Upjohn) 6, 9, and 12 g/L, in both PVC and glass containers of dextrose 5% in water, sodium chloride 0.9%, or Ringer's injection, lactated, was stored frozen at −10 °C. The drug was stable for the eight weeks of the study with only minor changes in concentration. (753)

One study of clindamycin phosphate 600 mg in 100-ml PVC containers of dextrose 5% in water frozen at −20 °C showed approximately a 13% loss of potency after 23 days of storage. (155)

However, in another study, clindamycin phosphate (Upjohn) 300 mg/50 ml of dextrose 5% in water in PVC bags frozen at −20 °C for 30 days and then thawed by exposure to ambient temperature or microwave radiation showed no evidence of precipitation or color change and showed little or no loss of potency determined microbiologically. Subsequent storage of the admixture at room temperature for 24 hours also yielded a physically compatible solution, which exhibited a 7 to 8% loss of activity. (555; 871; 872)

Marble et al. reported that clindamycin phosphate (Upjohn) 900 mg/50 ml in dextrose 5% in water and sodium chloride 0.9% in PVC bags frozen at −20 °C lost 3 to 4% potency in 28 days. (981)

Minibags of clindamycin phosphate in dextrose 5% in water or sodium chloride 0.9%, frozen at −20 °C for up to 35 days, were thawed at room temperature and in a microwave oven, with care taken that the thawed solution temperature never exceeded 25 °C. No significant differences in clindamycin phosphate concentrations occurred between the two thawing methods. (1192)

At a concentration of 6 mg/ml dextrose 5% in water, clindamycin phosphate retained 97% of the initial concentration after 79 days of storage at −10 °C. (174)

Clindamycin phosphate diluted with sterile water for injection to concentrations of 20, 40, 60, and 120 mg/ml was stored frozen at −15 °C in Monoject plastic syringes or glass vials. After 60 days of storage, the changes from the original concentrations ranged from −5 to +2.5%. Visual examination showed no particulate matter. (173)

Clindamycin phosphate (Quad) 6 and 12 mg/ml in dextrose 5% in water and sodium chloride 0.9% exhibited no loss after 68 days when frozen at −10 °C. (1351)

Clindamycin phosphate (Upjohn) 7.6 mg/ml in dextrose 5% in water was visually compatible and had no potency loss by HPLC after frozen storage (−20 °C) for 30 days followed by 14 days of refrigeration at 4 °C. (1539)

Syringes — Clindamycin phosphate 900 mg/6 ml in polypropylene syringes (Becton-Dickinson) retained more than 95% of the initial concentration over at least 48 hours at room temperature. (172) Diluted with sterile water for injection to concentrations of 20, 40, 60, and 120 mg/ml and stored in Monoject plastic syringes or glass vials, clindamycin phosphate exhibited little or no change in concentration and was free of visually apparent particulate matter over 30 days of storage at 25 °C. (173)

Clindamycin phosphate (Upjohn) 900 mg/6 ml showed no more than a 4 to 5% loss when stored in polypropylene syringes (Becton-Dickinson) for 48 hours at 25 °C under fluorescent light. (1159)

Clindamycin phosphate (Upjohn) 600 mg stored in polypropylene syringes (3M) at 25 °C under fluorescent light exhibited no loss in 48 hours. (1164)

Vials—Dilution of clindamycin phosphate 300 and 900 mg in glass vials containing 20 ml of dextrose 10% in water resulted in no visual changes and less than a 10% loss by HPLC after 30 days of refrigeration at 10 °C. (1604)

Clindamycin phosphate (Abbott) injection was diluted with sterile water for injection to a concentration of 15 mg/ml for use in minimizing measurement errors in pediatric dosing. The dilution was packaged in glass vials, and samples were stored at 22 and 4 °C. The dilution remained visually free of particulate matter at both storage conditions throughout the study. HPLC analysis of the samples found no clindamycin loss after 91 days at either 4 or 22 °C. (1714)

Clindamycin phosphate is incompatible with natural rubber closures because of the extraction of crystalline particulate matter, primarily β-sitosterol and stigmasterol. Simple cleaning procedures for the closures do not effectively remove the source of contamination. It is recommended that if clindamycin phosphate is repackaged in vials or disposable syringes, storage at room temperature should be limited to a few days. (102)

Elastomeric Reservoir Pumps—Clindamycin phosphate solutions in elastomeric reservoir pumps have been stated by the pump manufacturers to be stable for the following time periods frozen, refrigerated (REF), or at room temperature (RT) (31):

Pump Reservoir(s)	Conc.	Frozen	REF	RT
Homepump; Homepump Eclipse	10 mg/ml[b]		10 days	24 hr
Intermate	12 mg/ml[a]	30 days	10 days	24 hr
	2 to 12 mg/ml[b]	30 days	10 days	24 hr
Medflo	>3 mg/ml[a,b]	8 weeks	32 days	16 days
ReadyMed	6 mg/ml[a]		32 days	16 days
	6 mg/ml[b]	4 weeks	14 days	48 hr

[a]*In dextrose 5% in water.*
[b]*In sodium chloride 0.9%.*

Sorption—Clindamycin phosphate (Upjohn) 3 mg/ml in dextrose 5% in water and sodium chloride 0.9% packaged in PVC, polyethylene, and glass containers exhibited little or no loss due to sorption to any of the container types when stored at 4 and 22 °C for 24 hours protected from light. (2289)

Central Venous Catheter—Clindamycin phosphate (Upjohn) 2 mg/ml in dextrose 5% in water was found to be compatible with the ARROWg+ard Blue Plus (Arrow International) chlorhexidine-bearing triple-lumen central catheter. HPLC analysis was used to evaluate completeness of drug delivery through the catheter and the amount of chlorhexidine removed from the internal lumens. Essentially complete delivery of the drug was found with little or no drug loss occurring. Furthermore, chlorhexidine delivered from the catheter remained at trace amounts with no substantial increase due to the delivery of the drug through the catheter. (2335)

Compatibility Information

Solution Compatibility

Clindamycin phosphate

Solution	*Mfr*	*Mfr*	*Conc/L*	*Remarks*	*Ref*	*C/I*
Amino acids 4.25%, dextrose 25%	MG	UP	600 mg	No increase in particulate matter in 24 hr at 5 °C	349	C
Dextrose 2.5% in Ringer's injection, lactated		UP	600 mg	Physically compatible and clindamycin potency retained for 24 hr at room temperature	104	C
Dextrose 5% in Ringer's injection		UP	600 mg	Physically compatible and clindamycin potency retained for 24 hr at room temperature	104	C
Dextrose 5% in sodium chloride 0.45%		UP	600 mg	Clindamycin stability maintained for 24 hr	101	C
Dextrose 5% in sodium chloride 0.9%	MG	UP	250 mg	Clindamycin potency retained for 24 hr at 4 and 25 °C	105	C
		UP	600 mg	Physically compatible and clindamycin potency retained for 24 hr at room temperature	104	C
Dextrose 5% in water	MG	UP	250 mg	Clindamycin potency retained for 24 hr at 4 and 25 °C	105	C
		UP	600 mg	Physically compatible and clindamycin potency retained for 24 hr at room temperature	104	C
		UP	6, 9, 12 g	Clindamycin stability maintained for 24 hr	101	C
	TR[a]	UP	6 g	Physically compatible and approximately 9% loss of potency in 24 hr at room temperature	555	C
	TR[a,b]	UP	6, 9, 12 g	Physically compatible and chemically stable for at least 16 days at 25 °C and 32 days at 4 °C	753	C

Solution Compatibility (Cont.)

Clindamycin phosphate

Solution	*Mfr*	*Mfr*	*Conc/L*	*Remarks*	*Ref*	*C/I*
	AB[a,b]	UP	9 g	Physically compatible and no clindamycin loss in 24 hr at 25 °C	994	C
	AB[a]	UP	18 g	3% loss in 28 days frozen at −20 °C	981	C
	TR[a]	QU	6 and 12 g	Physically compatible with no loss in 22 days at 25 °C, 54 days at 5 °C, and 68 days at −10 °C	1351	C
	MG[c]	UP	7.6 g	Visually compatible with no clindamycin loss by HPLC after 30 days at −20 °C followed by 14 days at 4 °C	1539	C
	BA[a], BRN[b,c]	GW	3 g	Visually compatible with little or no loss by HPLC in 24 hr at 4 and 22 °C	2289	C
Dextrose 10% in water	MG	UP	250 mg	Clindamycin potency retained for 24 hr at 4 and 25 °C	105	C
Isolyte H	MG	UP	1.2 g	Physically compatible and clindamycin potency retained for 24 hr	101	C
Isolyte M with dextrose 5%	MG	UP	250 mg	Clindamycin potency retained for 24 hr at 4 and 25 °C	105	C
Isolyte P with dextrose 5%	MG	UP	250 mg	Clindamycin potency retained for 24 hr at 4 and 25 °C	105	C
Normosol R	AB	UP	1.2 g	Clindamycin stability maintained for 24 hr	101	C
Ringer's injection, lactated	MG	UP	250 mg	Clindamycin potency retained for 24 hr at 4 and 25 °C	105	C
	TR[a,b]	UP	6, 9, 12 g	Physically compatible and chemically stable for at least 16 days at 25 °C and 32 days at 4 °C	753	C
Sodium chloride 0.9%		UP	600 mg	Physically compatible and clindamycin potency retained for 24 hr at room temperature	104	C
		UP	6 g	Clindamycin stability maintained for 24 hr	101	C
	MG	UP	250 mg	Clindamycin potency retained for 24 hr at 4 and 25 °C	105	C
	TR[a,b]	UP	6, 9, 12 g	Physically compatible and chemically stable for at least 16 days at 25 °C and 32 days at 4 °C	753	C
	AB[a,b]	UP	9 g	Physically compatible and no clindamycin loss in 24 hr at 25 °C	994	C
	AB[a]	UP	18 g	4% loss in 28 days frozen at −20 °C	981	C
	TR[a]	QU	6 and 12 g	Physically compatible with no loss in 22 days at 25 °C, 54 days at 5 °C, and 68 days at −10 °C	1351	C
	BR[a], BRN[b,c]	GW	3 g	Visually compatible with little or no loss by HPLC in 24 hr at 4 and 22 °C	2289	C
TPN #21[d]		UP	250 mg	Clindamycin potency retained for 24 hr at 4 and 25 °C	87	C
TPN #22[d]		UP	3 g	Physically compatible with no loss of activity by microbiological assay in 24 hr at 22 °C in the dark	837	C
TPN #107[d]			400 mg[e]	Physically compatible and clindamycin activity retained for 24 hr at 21 °C by microbiological assay	1326	C

[a] *Tested in PVC containers.*
[b] *Tested in glass bottles.*
[c] *Tested in polyolefin containers.*
[d] *Refer to Appendix I for the composition of parenteral nutrition solutions. TPN indicates a 2-in-1 admixture.*
[e] *Present as clindamycin base.*

Additive Compatibility

Clindamycin phosphate

Drug	*Mfr*	*Conc/L*	*Mfr*	*Conc/L*	*Test Soln*	*Remarks*	*Ref*	*C/I*
Amikacin sulfate	BR	5 g	UP	6 g	D5LR, D5R, D5S, D5W, D10W, IS10, LR, NS, R, SL	Physically compatible and amikacin potency retained for 24 hr at 25 °C. Clindamycin not analyzed	293	C
	BR	4 g	UP	9 g	D5W, NS[a]	Potency of both drugs retained for 48 hr at 25 °C under fluorescent light	981	C
Aminophylline	SE	600 mg	UP	600 mg		Physically incompatible	101	I
Ampicillin sodium	WY	10 and 20 g	UP	24 g	NS	Physically compatible	1035	C
	WY	3.7 g	UP	3 g	NS	Physically compatible with 4% ampicillin loss in 1 day at 24 °C	1035	C
Aztreonam	SQ	10 and 20 g	UP	3 and 6 g	D5W, NS[b]	Physically compatible with little or no loss of either drug in 48 hr at 25 °C and 7 days at 4 °C	1002	C
	SQ	20 g	UP	9 g	D5W[a]	Physically compatible with 3% clindamycin loss and 5% aztreonam loss in 48 hr at 25 °C under fluorescent light	1026	C
	SQ	20 g	UP	9 g	NS[a]	Physically compatible with 2% clindamycin loss and no aztreonam loss in 48 hr at 25 °C under fluorescent light	1026	C
Cefamandole nafate	LI	10 g	UP	9 g	D5W, NS[a]	Physically compatible with no clindamycin loss and 4 to 7% cefamandole loss in 48 hr at room temperature under fluorescent light	983	C
Cefazolin sodium	SKF	10 g	UP	9 g	D5W[a]	Physically compatible with no clindamycin loss and 8% cefazolin loss in 48 hr at room temperature under fluorescent light	983	C
	SKF	10 g	UP	9 g	NS[a]	Physically compatible with no clindamycin loss and 3% cefazolin loss in 48 hr at room temperature under fluorescent light	983	C
Cefepime HCl	BR	40 g	UP	0.25 g	D5W, NS	7% or less cefepime loss by HPLC in 24 hr at room temperature and 10% or less loss in 7 days at 5 °C. No clindamycin loss by HPLC in 24 hr at room temperature and 8% or less loss in 7 days at 5 °C	1682	C
	BR	4 g	UP	6 g	D5W, NS	7% or less cefepime loss by HPLC in 24 hr at room temperature and 10% or less loss in 7 days at 5 °C. No clindamycin loss by HPLC in 24 hr at room temperature and 8% or less loss in 7 days at 5 °C	1682	C
Cefoperazone sodium	RR	20 g	UP	12 g	D5W, NS[c]	Physically compatible with no clindamycin loss and 5% cefoperazone loss in 48 hr at 25 °C under fluorescent light	174; 1164	C
Cefotaxime sodium	HO	20 g	UP	9 g	D5W, NS[c]	Physically compatible with no clindamycin loss and 3% cefotaxime loss in 24 hr at 25 °C	994	C

Additive Compatibility (Cont.)

			Clindamycin phosphate					
Drug	*Mfr*	*Conc/L*	*Mfr*	*Conc/L*	*Test Soln*	*Remarks*	*Ref*	*C/I*
Cefoxitin sodium	MSD	20 g	UP	9 g	D5W[a]	Physically compatible with no loss of either drug in 48 hr at room temperature under fluorescent light	983	C
	MSD	20 g	UP	9 g	NS[a]	Physically compatible with no clindamycin loss and 7% cefoxitin loss in 48 hr at room temperature under fluorescent light	983	C
Ceftazidime sodium	GL[g]	20 g	UP	9 g	D5W[a]	Physically compatible with 9% clindamycin loss and 11% ceftazidime loss in 48 hr at 25 °C under fluorescent light	1026	C
	GL[g]	20 g	UP	9 g	NS[a]	Physically compatible with 5% clindamycin loss and 7% ceftazidime loss in 48 hr at 25 °C under fluorescent light	1026	C
Ceftizoxime sodium	SKF	20 g	UP	9 g	D5W[a]	Physically compatible with 3% clindamycin loss and 4% ceftizoxime loss in 48 hr at room temperature under fluorescent light	983	C
	SKF	20 g	UP	9 g	NS[a]	Physically compatible with 7% ceftizoxime loss in 48 hr at room temperature under fluorescent light. 10% clindamycin loss in 8 hr with no further loss through 48 hr	983	C
Ceftriaxone sodium	RC	20 g	UP	12 g	D5W[a]	10% ceftriaxone loss in 4 hr and 17% in 24 hr at 25 °C under fluorescent light. No clindamycin loss in 48 hr	1026	I
	RC	20 g	UP	12 g	NS[a]	10% ceftriaxone loss in 1 hr and 12% in 24 hr at 25 °C under fluorescent light. 6% clindamycin loss in 48 hr	1026	I
Cefuroxime sodium	GL	15 g	UP	9 g	D5W[c]	Physically compatible with 4% clindamycin loss and 6 to 8% cefuroxime loss in 48 hr at 25 °C under fluorescent light	174	C
	GL	15 g	UP	9 g	NS[c]	Physically compatible with 9% clindamycin and cefuroxime losses in 48 hr at 25 °C under fluorescent light	174	C
	GL	15 g	UP	9 g	D5W	Physically compatible with 4% clindamycin loss and 6 to 8% cefuroxime loss in 48 hr at 25 °C under fluorescent light	1164	C
	GL	15 g	UP	9 g	NS	Physically compatible with 9% clindamycin and cefuroxime losses in 48 hr at 25 °C under fluorescent light	1164	C
Cimetidine HCl	SKF	1.2 and 5 g	UP	1.2 g	D5W, NS	Physically compatible and cimetidine chemically stable for 24 hr at room temperature. Clindamycin not tested	551	C
Ciprofloxacin	MI	1.6 g	LY	7.1 g	D5W, NS	Precipitate forms immediately. HPLC showed no intact clindamycin	1541	I
Fluconazole	PF	1 g	AST	6 g	D5W	Visually compatible with no fluconazole loss by HPLC in 72 hr at 25 °C under fluorescent light. Clindamycin not tested	1677	C
Gentamicin sulfate		120 mg	UP	2.4 g	D5W	Physically compatible and clindamycin potency retained for 24 hr at room temperature	104	C
		60 mg	UP	1.2 g	D5W	Physically compatible and clindamycin potency retained for 24 hr at room temperature	104	C

Additive Compatibility (Cont.)

			Clindamycin phosphate					
Drug	*Mfr*	*Conc/L*	*Mfr*	*Conc/L*	*Test Soln*	*Remarks*	*Ref*	*C/I*
		600 mg	UP	12 g	D5W	Physically compatible	101	C
		800 mg	UP	9 g	D5W	Clindamycin stability maintained for 24 hr	101	C
	AB	1 g	UP	9 g	D5W, NS[c]	Physically compatible and potency of both drugs retained for 48 hr at room temperature exposed to light and 1 week frozen	174	C
	LY	1.2 g	UP	9 g	D5W[a]	Physically compatible and potency of both drugs retained for 7 days at 4 and 25 °C	174	C
	LY	1.2 g	UP	9 g	NS[a]	Physically compatible and potency of both drugs retained for 14 days at 4 and 25 °C	174	C
	LY	2.4 g	UP	18 g	D5W, NS[c]	Physically compatible and potency of both drugs retained for 14 days at 4 and 25 °C	174	C
	ES	1.2 g	UP	9 g	D5W, NS[a]	Physically compatible and potency of both drugs retained for 28 days frozen at −20 °C	174	C
	ES	2.4 g	UP	18 g	D5W, NS[b]	Potency of both drugs retained for 28 days frozen at −20 °C	981	C
	ES	667 mg	UP	6 g	D5W[b]	Physically compatible with no clindamycin loss and 9% gentamicin loss in 24 hr at room temperature	995	C
		75 mg		400 mg[d]	TPN #107[e]	19% gentamicin loss and 15% clindamycin loss in 24 hr at 21 °C by microbiological assay	1326	I
Gentamicin sulfate with cefazolin sodium	ES SKF	800 mg 10 g	UP	9 g	D5W[a]	10% cefazolin loss in 4 hr at 25 °C. Clindamycin and gentamicin potency retained for 24 hr	1328	I
Gentamicin sulfate with cefazolin sodium	ES SKF	800 mg 10 g	UP	9 g	NS[a]	10% cefazolin loss after 12 hr at 25 °C. Clindamycin and gentamicin potency retained for 24 hr	1328	I
Heparin sodium		100,000 units	UP	9 g	D5W	Clindamycin stability maintained for 24 hr	101	C
Hydrocortisone sodium succinate	UP	1 g	UP	1.2 g	W	Clindamycin stability maintained for 24 hr	101	C
Kanamycin sulfate		1 g	UP	2.4 g	D5W	Physically compatible and clindamycin potency retained for 24 hr at room temperature	104	C
		500 mg	UP	1.2 g	D5W	Physically compatible and clindamycin potency retained for 24 hr at room temperature	104	C
Methylprednisolone sodium succinate	UP	500 mg	UP	1.2 g	D5W, W	Clindamycin stability maintained for 24 hr	101	C
Metoclopramide HCl	RB	100 and 200 mg	UP	600 mg	NS	Physically compatible for 24 hr at room temperature	924	C
	RB	100 and 200 mg	UP	6 g		Physically compatible for 24 hr at 25 °C	1167	C
	RB	1.9 g	UP	3.5 g		Physically compatible for 24 hr at 25 °C	1167	C
	RB	1.2 g	UP	4.4 g		Physically compatible for 24 hr at 25 °C	1167	C
Metronidazole	RP	5 g[f]	UP	10 g		Physically compatible with little or no pH change for at least 24 hr at 23 °C	807	C
Metronidazole HCl with sodium bicarbonate	SE AB	5 g 50 mEq	UP	2.4 g	D5W, NS	Physically compatible for 48 hr	765	C

Additive Compatibility (Cont.)

Clindamycin phosphate

Drug	*Mfr*	*Conc/L*	*Mfr*	*Conc/L*	*Test Soln*	*Remarks*	*Ref*	*C/I*
Netilmicin sulfate	SC	3 g	UP	9 g	D5W, NS[c]	Physically compatible with no clindamycin loss and 2 to 5% netilmicin loss in 24 hr at 25 °C	994	C
Ofloxacin	HO	2 g	UP	6 g	W	Visually compatible with little or no loss of either drug by HPLC in 48 hr	1613	C
Penicillin G		20 million units	UP	2.4 g	D5W	Physically compatible and clindamycin potency retained for 24 hr at room temperature	104	C
		10 million units	UP	1.2 g	D5W	Physically compatible and clindamycin potency retained for 24 hr at room temperature	104	C
Piperacillin sodium	LE	40 g	UP	9 g	D5W, NS	Physically compatible with 2% clindamycin loss and 3 to 5% piperacillin loss in 48 hr at 25 °C under fluorescent light	1026	C
Potassium chloride		40 mEq	UP	600 mg	D5½S	Physically compatible and clindamycin potency retained for 24 hr at room temperature	104	C
		100 mEq	UP	600 mg	D5W, NS	Physically compatible	101	C
		400 mEq	UP	6 g	D5½S	Clindamycin stability maintained for 24 hr	101	C
Ranitidine HCl	GL	100 mg	UP	1.2 g	D5W	Color change and gas formation	1151	I
	GL	50 mg and 2 g		1.2 g	D5W, NS	Physically compatible and ranitidine chemically stable by HPLC for 24 hr at 25 °C. Clindamycin not tested	1515	C
Sodium bicarbonate		44 mEq	UP	1.2 g	D5S, D5W	Clindamycin stability maintained for 24 hr	101	C
Tobramycin sulfate	DI	1 g	UP	9 g	D5W, NS[c]	Physically compatible and potency of both drugs retained for 48 hr at room temperature exposed to light and 1 week frozen	174	C
	DI	1.2 g	UP	9 g	D5W[a]	Physically compatible and clindamycin potency retained for 28 days frozen. About 8% tobramycin loss in 14 days and 17% in 28 days	174	C
	DI	1.2 g	UP	9 g	NS[a]	Physically compatible and potency of both drugs retained for 28 days frozen	174	C
	DI	2.4 g	UP	18 g	D5W[b]	8% tobramycin activity loss in 14 days and 17% in 28 days frozen at −20 °C. Clindamycin potency retained	981	C
	DI	2.4 g	UP	18 g	NS[b]	Potency of both drugs retained for 28 days frozen at −20 °C	981	C
Verapamil HCl	KN	80 mg	UP	1.2 g	D5W, NS	Physically compatible for 24 hr	764	C
Vitamin B complex with C	UP	10 ml	UP	600 mg	D5W	Clindamycin potency retained for 24 hr	102	C

[a]*Tested in glass bottles.*
[b]*Tested in PVC containers.*
[c]*Tested in both glass and PVC containers.*
[d]*Present as clindamycin base.*
[e]*Refer to Appendix I for the composition of parenteral nutrition solutions. TPN indicates a 2-in-1 admixture.*
[f]*Minibags (100 ml) containing metronidazole 500 mg with disodium phosphate 150 mg, citric acid 44 mg, and sodium chloride 740 mg. This product differs from the Searle product.*
[g]*Sodium carbonate–containing formulation tested.*

Drugs in Syringe Compatibility

Drug (in syringe)	Mfr	Amt	Mfr	Amt	Remarks	Ref	C/I
			Clindamycin phosphate				
Amikacin sulfate	BR	750 mg/ 4 ml[a]	UP	900 mg/ 6 ml	Physically compatible with little or no loss of either drug in 48 hr at 25 °C in polypropylene syringes	1159	C
Aztreonam	SQ	2 g	UP	600 mg/ 4 ml	Physically compatible with 2% clindamycin loss and 8% aztreonam loss in 48 hr at 25 °C under fluorescent light in polypropylene syringes	1164	C
Gentamicin sulfate	ES	120 mg/ 4 ml[a]	UP	900 mg/ 6 ml	Physically compatible with little or no loss of either drug in 48 hr at 25 °C in polypropylene syringes	1159	C
Heparin sodium		2500 units/ 1 ml	UP	300 mg	Physically compatible for at least 5 min	1053	C
Tobramycin sulfate	DI	120 mg/ 4 ml[a]	UP	900 mg/ 6 ml	Cloudy white precipitate forms immediately and changes to gel-like precipitate	1159	I

[a]*Diluted to 4 ml with 1 ml of sodium chloride 0.9%.*

Y-Site Injection Compatibility (1:1 Mixture)

Drug	Mfr	Conc	Mfr	Conc	Remarks	Ref	C/I
			Clindamycin phosphate				
Allopurinol sodium	BW	3 mg/ml[b]	AB	10 mg/ml[b]	Tiny particles form immediately and become more numerous over 4 hr	1686	I
Amifostine	USB	10 mg/ml[a]	AST	10 mg/ml[a]	Physically compatible with no change in measured turbidity or increase in particle content in 4 hr at 23 °C	1845	C
Amiodarone HCl	LZ	4 mg/ml[c]	UP	6 mg/ml[c]	Physically compatible for 4 hr at room temperature	1444	C
Amphotericin B cholesteryl sulfate complex	SEQ	0.83 mg/ml[a]	UP	10 mg/ml[a]	Physically compatible with little or no change in measured turbidity or increase in particle content in 4 hr at 23 °C under fluorescent light	2117	C
Amsacrine	NCI	1 mg/ml[a]	UP	10 mg/ml[a]	Physically compatible for 4 hr at room temperature under fluorescent light	1381	C
Aztreonam	SQ	40 mg/ml[a]	AST	10 mg/ml[a]	Physically compatible with no subvisual haze or particle formation in 4 hr at 23 °C	1758	C
Cefpirome sulfate	HO	50 mg/ml[d]	AB	12 mg/ml[d]	Visually and microscopically compatible with 5% or less cefpirome loss and 4% or less clindamycin loss by HPLC in 8 hr at 23 °C	2044	C
Cisatracurium besylate	GW	0.1, 2, 5 mg/ ml[a]	AST	10 mg/ml[a]	Physically compatible with no change in measured turbidity or increase in particle content in 4 hr at 23 °C	2074	C
Cyclophosphamide	MJ	20 mg/ml[a]	UP	12 mg/ml[a]	Physically compatible for 4 hr at 25 °C	1194	C
Diltiazem HCl	MMD	5 mg/ml	UP	12[b] and 150 mg/ml	Visually compatible	1807	C

Y-Site Injection Compatibility (1:1 Mixture) (Cont.)

Clindamycin phosphate

Drug	*Mfr*	*Conc*	*Mfr*	*Conc*	*Remarks*	*Ref*	*C/I*
Docetaxel	RPR	0.9 mg/ml[a]	AST	10 mg/ml[a]	Physically compatible with no change in measured turbidity or increase in particle content in 4 hr at 23 °C	2224	C
Doxorubicin HCl liposome injection	SEQ	0.4 mg/ml[a]	AST	10 mg/ml[a]	Physically compatible with little or no change in measured turbidity and no increase in particle content in 4 hr at 23 °C	2087	C
Enalaprilat	MSD	0.05 mg/ml[b]	UP	9 mg/ml[a]	Physically compatible for 24 hr at room temperature under fluorescent light	1355	C
Esmolol HCl	DCC	10 mg/ml[a]	UP	9 mg/ml[a]	Physically compatible for 24 hr at 22 °C	1169	C
Etoposide phosphate	BR	5 mg/ml[a]	AST	10 mg/ml[a]	Physically compatible with no change in measured turbidity or increase in particle content in 4 hr at 23 °C	2218	C
Filgrastim	AMG	30 μg/ml[a]	AB	10 mg/ml[a]	Particles and filaments form immediately	1687	I
Fluconazole	RR	2 mg/ml	AB	24 mg/ml	Immediate precipitation	1407	I
Fludarabine phosphate	BX	1 mg/ml[a]	LY	10 mg/ml[a]	Physically compatible for 4 hr at room temperature under fluorescent light	1439	C
Foscarnet sodium	AST	24 mg/ml	AB	24 mg/ml	Physically compatible for 24 hr at room temperature under fluorescent light	1335	C
	AST	24 mg/ml	UP	12 mg/ml[c]	Physically compatible for 24 hr at 25 °C under fluorescent light by visual and microscopic examination	1393	C
Gatifloxacin	BMS	2 mg/ml[a]	UP	10 mg/ml[a]	Physically compatible with no change in measured haze or increase in particle content in 4 hr at 23 °C	2234	C
Gemcitabine HCl	LI	10 mg/ml[b]	AST	10 mg/ml[b]	Physically compatible with no change in measured turbidity or increase in particle content in 4 hr at 23 °C	2226	C
Granisetron HCl	SKB	0.05 mg/ml[a]	AB	10 mg/ml[a]	Physically compatible with no change in measured turbidity or increase in particle content in 4 hr at 23 °C	2000	C
Heparin sodium	TR	50 units/ml	UP	12 mg/ml[a]	Visually compatible for 4 hr at 25 °C	1793	C
Hetastarch in lactated electrolyte injection (Hextend)	AB	6%	PHU	10 mg/ml[a]	Physically compatible with no change in measured turbidity or increase in particle content in 4 hr at 23 °C	2339	C
Hydromorphone HCl	WY	0.2 mg/ml[a]	UP	12 mg/ml[a]	Physically compatible for at least 4 hr at 25 °C under fluorescent light	987	C
Idarubicin HCl	AD	1 mg/ml[b]	AST	12 mg/ml[a]	Haze and precipitate form immediately	1525	I
Labetalol HCl	SC	1 mg/ml[a]	UP	9 mg/ml[a]	Physically compatible for 24 hr at 18 °C	1171	C
Levofloxacin	OMN	5 mg/ml[a]	UP	150 mg/ml	Visually compatible for 4 hr at 24 °C under fluorescent light	2233	C
Linezolid	PHU	2 mg/ml	UP	10 mg/ml[a]	Physically compatible with no change in measured turbidity or increase in particle content in 4 hr at 23 °C	2264	C
Magnesium sulfate	IX	16.7, 33.3, 66.7, 100 mg/ml[a]	UP	12 mg/ml[a]	Physically compatible for at least 4 hr at 32 °C	813	C

Y-Site Injection Compatibility (1:1 Mixture) (Cont.)

Drug	*Mfr*	*Conc*	Clindamycin phosphate *Mfr*	Clindamycin phosphate *Conc*	*Remarks*	*Ref*	*C/I*
Melphalan HCl	BW	0.1 mg/ml[b]	AB	10 mg/ml[b]	Physically compatible with no change in measured turbidity or increase in particle content in 3 hr at 22 °C	1557	C
Meperidine HCl	WY	10 mg/ml[a]	UP	12 mg/ml[a]	Physically compatible for at least 4 hr at 25 °C under fluorescent light	987	C
Midazolam HCl	RC	1 mg/ml[a]	UP	9 mg/ml[a]	Visually compatible for 24 hr at 23 °C	1847	C
Morphine sulfate	WI	1 mg/ml[a]	UP	12 mg/ml[a]	Physically compatible for at least 4 hr at 25 °C under fluorescent light	987	C
Multivitamins	USV	5 ml/L[a]	UP	600 mg/ 100 ml[a]	Physically compatible for 24 hr at room temperature	323	C
Ondansetron HCl	GL	1 mg/ml[b]	LY	10 mg/ml[a]	Physically compatible for 4 hr at 22 °C	1365	C
Perphenazine	SC	0.02 mg/ml[a]	UP	12 mg/ml[a]	Physically compatible for 4 hr at 25 °C	1155	C
Piperacillin sodium–tazobactam sodium	LE	40 + 5 mg/ ml[a]	AB	10 mg/ml[a]	Physically compatible with no change in measured turbidity or increase in particle content in 4 hr at 22 °C	1688	C
Propofol	ZEN	10 mg/ml	AST	10 mg/ml[a]	Physically compatible for 1 hr at 23 °C with no increase in particle content	2066	C
Remifentanil HCl	GW	0.025 and 0.25 mg/ml[b]	AST	10 mg/ml[a]	Physically compatible with no change in measured turbidity or increase in particle content in 4 hr at 23 °C	2075	C
Sargramostim	IMM	10 μg/ml[b]	LY	10 mg/ml[b]	Physically compatible for 4 hr at 22 °C	1436	C
Tacrolimus	FUJ	1 mg/ml[b]	ES	12 mg/ml[a]	Visually compatible for 24 hr at 25 °C	1630	C
Teniposide	BR	0.1 mg/ml[a]	AST	10 mg/ml[a]	Physically compatible with no subvisual haze or particle formation in 4 hr at 23 °C	1725	C
Theophylline	TR	4 mg/ml	UP	12 mg/ml[a]	Visually compatible for 6 hr at 25 °C	1793	C
Thiotepa	IMM[e]	1 mg/ml[a]	AST	10 mg/ml[a]	Physically compatible with no change in measured turbidity or increase in particle content in 4 hr at 23 °C	1861	C
TNA #73[f]		32.5 ml[g]	UP	600 mg/ 50 ml[a]	Physically compatible for 4 hr at 25 °C by visual assessment	1008	C
TNA #218 to #226[f]			AST	10 mg/ml[a]	Visually compatible with no precipitate or emulsion damage apparent in 4 hr at 23 °C	2215	C
TPN #61[f]		[h]	UP	50 mg/ 0.33 ml[i]	Physically compatible	1012	C
		[j]	UP	300 mg/2 ml[i]	Physically compatible	1012	C
TPN #212 to #215[f]			AB	10 mg/ml[a]	Physically compatible with no change in measured turbidity or increase in particle content in 4 hr at 23 °C	2109	C
Vinorelbine tartrate	BW	1 mg/ml[b]	AB	10 mg/ml[b]	Physically compatible with no change in measured turbidity or increase in particle content in 4 hr at 22 °C	1558	C
Vitamin B complex with C (Berocca-C 500)	RC	4 ml/L[a]	UP	600 mg/ 100 ml[a]	Physically compatible for 24 hr at room temperature	323	C
(Berocca-C)	RC	20 ml/L[a]	UP	600 mg/ 100 ml[a]	Physically compatible for 24 hr at room temperature	323	C

Y-Site Injection Compatibility (1:1 Mixture) (Cont.)

Clindamycin phosphate

Drug	*Mfr*	*Conc*	*Mfr*	*Conc*	*Remarks*	*Ref*	*C/I*
Zidovudine	BW	4 mg/ml[a]	UP	12 mg/ml[a]	Physically compatible for 4 hr at 25 °C under fluorescent light by visual and microscopic examination	1193	C

[a]*Tested in dextrose 5% in water.*
[b]*Tested in sodium chloride 0.9%.*
[c]*Tested in both dextrose 5% in water and sodium chloride 0.9%.*
[d]*Tested in dextrose 5% in water, Ringer's injection, lactated, sodium chloride 0.45%, and sodium chloride 0.9%.*
[e]*Lyophilized formulation tested.*
[f]*Refer to Appendix I for the composition of parenteral nutrition solutions. TNA indicates a 3-in-1 admixture, and TPN indicates a 2-in-1 admixture.*
[g]*A 32.5-ml sample of parenteral nutrition solution mixed with 50 ml of antibiotic solution.*
[h]*Run at 21 ml/hr.*
[i]*Given over 10 minutes by syringe pump.*
[j]*Run at 94 ml/hr.*

Additional Compatibility Information

Infusion Solutions — Clindamycin phosphate (Upjohn) 6, 9, and 12 mg/ml is physically and chemically stable for 16 days at 25 °C and 32 days at 4 °C in dextrose 5% in water, sodium chloride 0.9%, or Ringer's injection, lactated. When frozen at −10 °C, the solutions are stable for at least eight weeks. (4)

Dilution of clindamycin phosphate, using the ADD-Vantage system, to concentrations of 6, 9, and 12 mg/ml in dextrose 5% in water or sodium chloride 0.9% results in solutions that are stable for 24 hours at room temperature or 14 days at 5 °C. (4)

Peritoneal Dialysis Solutions — The stability of clindamycin phosphate (Upjohn) 10 mg/L in peritoneal dialysis solutions (Dianeal 137 and PD2) with heparin sodium 500 units/L was evaluated by microbiological assay. Approximately 102 ± 9% activity remained after 24 hours at 25 °C. (1228)

Other Drugs — Clindamycin phosphate (Upjohn) is stated to be physically compatible and stable for 24 hours at room temperature in intravenous infusion solutions containing potassium or vitamin B complex. Additionally, no incompatibility has been demonstrated with cephalothin, gentamicin, kanamycin, or penicillin. (2)

Clindamycin phosphate (Upjohn) has been stated to be physically incompatible with aminophylline, ampicillin, barbiturates, calcium gluconate, magnesium sulfate, and phenytoin sodium. (2)

Clindamycin phosphate will form a precipitate with various metals. Although it has been stated that there is no incompatibility or inactivation of clindamycin phosphate in intravenous solutions containing calcium, sufficient concentrations of this ion will result in physical instability. (102)

Tobramycin sulfate 80 mg/L has been reported to be conditionally compatible with clindamycin phosphate (Upjohn) 600 mg/L. Clindamycin stability is maintained for 24 hours in sodium chloride 0.9%, but an unstable mixture results in dextrose 5% in water. (101)

Ceftazidime (Ceptaz) 20 mg/ml is stated to be stable for 24 hours at room temperature or for seven days under refrigeration with clindamycin phosphate 6 mg/ml. (4)

CLONIDINE HCL
AHFS 24:08

Products — Clonidine HCl is available in concentrations of 0.1 mg/ml (100 μg/ml) and 0.5 mg/ml (500 μg/ml) in 10-ml vials. Each milliliter of the preservative-free solution also contains sodium chloride 9 mg in water for injection. Hydrochloric acid and/or sodium hydroxide may have been added to adjust the pH. (2)

pH — From 5 to 7. (2)

Trade Name(s) — Duraclon.

Administration — Clonidine HCl injection is administered by continuous epidural infusion using an appropriate epidural infusion device. Clonidine HCl injection must not be used with a preservative. (2)

Stability — Intact vials containing the clear, colorless solution should be stored at controlled room temperature. (2) They are stable for at least six months stored at an elevated temperature of 40 °C, remaining clear and colorless and exhibiting no loss of clonidine HCl by HPLC analysis. (2069)

Clonidine HCl (Roxane) 100 μg/ml was filled into plastic syringes (Becton-Dickinson), pump medication reservoirs (Bard), and empty glass vials (Abbott) and stored at 22 to 27 °C for seven days. The solution was also filled into intravenous administration set tubing (Kendall McGaw) and stored under the same conditions. In all cases, the solution remained clear and colorless and little or no loss of potency was found by HPLC analysis. (2069)

Clonidine HCl 100 μg/ml was delivered at a rate of 0.1 ml/hr for seven days through two epidural catheter sets, Epi-Cath (Abbott) and Port-A-Cath (Pharmacia Deltec). The temperature was maintained at 37 °C with a water bath to simulate internal use of the set. The delivered clonidine HCl solution remained clear and colorless throughout the study. Furthermore, the solution delivered through the Epi-Cath resulted in little or no loss by HPLC analysis. With the Port-A-Cath, a concentrating effect due to a loss of water was countered by a small clonidine HCl loss of drug (about 5%). The net effect was delivery of about 95% of the clonidine HCl dose. (2069)

Compatibility Information

Drugs in Syringe Compatibility

Clonidine HCl

Drug (in syringe)	*Mfr*	*Amt*	*Mfr*	*Amt*	*Remarks*	*Ref*	*C/I*
Bupivacaine HCl with morphine sulfate	SW ES	1.5 mg/ml 0.2 mg/ml	BI	0.03 mg/ml	Diluted to 5 ml with NS. Visually compatible with no new GC/MS peaks in 1 hr at room temperature	1956	C
Fentanyl citrate with lidocaine HCl	JN AST	0.01 mg/ml 2 mg/ml	BI	0.03 mg/ml	Diluted to 5 ml with NS. Visually compatible with no new GC/MS peaks in 1 hr at room temperature	1956	C
Heparin sodium		2500 units/ 1 ml	BI	0.15 mg/ 1 ml	Visually compatible for at least 5 min	1053	C
Ketamine HCl with tetracaine HCl	PD SW	2 mg/ml 2 mg/ml	BI	0.03 mg/ml	Diluted to 5 ml with NS. Visually compatible with no new GC/MS peaks in 1 hr at room temperature	1956	C

Y-Site Injection Compatibility (1:1 Mixture)

Clonidine HCl

Drug	*Mfr*	*Conc*	*Mfr*	*Conc*	*Remarks*	*Ref*	*C/I*
Lorazepam	WY	0.33 mg/ml[a]	BI	0.015 mg/ml	Visually compatible for 24 hr at 22 °C	1855	C

[a]*Tested in sodium chloride 0.9%.*

Additional Compatibility Information

Bupivacaine HCl — Clonidine HCl (Fujisawa) 100 μg/ml and bupivacaine HCl (Sanofi Winthrop) 7.5 mg/ml were mixed in ratios of 1:1 and 1:8 to provide final concentrations of (1:1) clonidine HCl 50 μg/ml and bupivacaine HCl 3.75 mg/ml and (1:8) clonidine HCl 11.11 μg/ml and bupivacaine HCl 6.67 mg/ml. The combinations were transferred to flint glass vials with rubber stoppers and stored for 14 days at controlled room temperature protected from light. The solutions remained clear and colorless with no increase in particulate content. HPLC analysis found little or no change in concentration for either drug during the study period. (2069)

Morphine Sulfate — Clonidine HCl (Fujisawa) 100 μg/ml and morphine sulfate (Elkins-Sinn) 10 mg/ml were mixed in equal quantities and were transferred to flint glass vials with rubber stoppers and stored for 14 days at controlled room temperature protected from light. The solutions remained clear and colorless with no increase in particulate content. HPLC analysis found little or no change in concentration for either drug during the study period. (2069)

Multiple Drugs — A seven-drug combination consisting of bupivacaine HCl (Sanofi Winthrop) 1.5 mg/ml, clonidine HCl (Boehringer Ingelheim) 0.03 mg/ml, fentanyl citrate (Janssen) 0.01 mg/ml, ketamine HCl (Parke-Davis) 2 mg/ml, lidocaine HCl (Astra) 2 mg/ml, morphine sulfate (Elkins-Sinn) 0.2 mg/ml, and tetracaine HCl (Sanofi Winthrop) 2 mg/ml mixed together in equal quantities was found to be visually compatible with no new GC/MS peaks appearing in one hour at room temperature. (1956)

Clonidine HCl (Boehringer) 30 μg/ml, bupivacaine HCl (Astra) 3 mg/ml, and morphine HCl (Merck) 6.66 mg/ml were combined in 50-ml ambulatory pump cassette reservoirs (Pharmacia Deltec). The reservoirs were stored at room temperature and protected from light for 90 days. HPLC analysis found no loss of any of the drugs. Instead, drug concentrations increased 12 to 16% during the observation period, possibly due to loss of water from the solutions. (1850)

CODEINE PHOSPHATE
AHFS 28:08.08

Products — Codeine phosphate is available in concentrations of 15, 30, and 60 mg/ml in 2-ml cartridge units. (29) The solution also contains sodium lactate and sulfites. (4)

pH — From 3 to 6. (4)

Administration — Codeine phosphate is usually administered by intramuscular or subcutaneous injection, but intravenous injection has also been used. (4; 154)

Stability — Store codeine phosphate injection between 15 and 30 °C and protected from light. Freezing should be avoided. Do not use the injection if it is discolored or contains a precipitate. (4)

Compatibility Information

Drugs in Syringe Compatibility

Codeine phosphate

Drug (in syringe)	*Mfr*	*Amt*	*Mfr*	*Amt*	*Remarks*	*Ref*	*C/I*
Dimenhydrinate	HR	50 mg/ 1 ml		30 mg/ 1 ml	Physically compatible	711	C
	HR	50 mg/ 1 ml		60 mg/ 1 ml	Physically compatible	711	C
Glycopyrrolate	RB	0.2 mg/ 1 ml	LI	30 mg/ 1 ml	Physically compatible and pH in stability range for glycopyrrolate for 48 hr at 25 °C	331	C
	RB	0.2 mg/ 1 ml	LI	60 mg/ 2 ml	Physically compatible and pH in stability range for glycopyrrolate for 48 hr at 25 °C	331	C
	RB	0.4 mg/ 2 ml	LI	30 mg/ 1 ml	Physically compatible and pH in stability range for glycopyrrolate for 48 hr at 25 °C	331	C
Hydroxyzine HCl	PF	50 mg/ 1 ml		120 mg/ 4 ml	Physically compatible	771	C
	PF	100 mg/ 2 ml		60 mg/ 2 ml	Physically compatible	771	C

COLISTIMETHATE SODIUM
AHFS 8:12.28

Products — Colistimethate sodium parenteral is available in vials containing the equivalent of 150 mg of colistin base. The 150-mg vial should be reconstituted with 2 ml of sterile water for injection to yield a solution containing 75 mg/ml of colistin base activity. During reconstitution, the contents of the vials should be gently swirled to avoid frothing. (2; 4)

pH — The pH of the reconstituted solution is 7 to 8. (4)

Trade Name(s) — Coly-Mycin M Parenteral.

Administration — Colistimethate sodium parenteral may be administered by intramuscular injection, by direct intravenous injection injected slowly over three to five minutes, or by continuous intravenous infusion of half the daily dose at a rate of 5 to 6 mg/hr begun one to two hours after an initial half-daily dose by direct intravenous injection. (4)

Stability — Intact vials should be stored at controlled room temperature. Reconstituted solutions are stable for seven days when stored under refrigeration at 2 to 8 °C or at controlled room temperature. (2; 4)

Filtration — Colistimethate sodium (R. Bellon) 0.16 mg/ml in dextrose 5% in water and sodium chloride 0.9% was filtered through a 0.22-μm cellulose ester membrane filter (Ivex-HP, Millipore) over six hours. No significant drug loss due to binding to the filter was noted. (1034)

Compatibility Information

Additive Compatibility

Colistimethate sodium

Drug	Mfr	Conc/L	Mfr	Conc/L	Test Soln	Remarks	Ref	C/I
Amikacin sulfate	BR	5 g	WC	500 mg	D5LR, D5R, D5S, D5W, D10W, IS10, LR, NS, R, SL	Physically compatible and amikacin potency retained for 24 hr at 25 °C. Colistimethate not analyzed	293	C
Ascorbic acid injection	UP	500 mg	WC	500 mg	D5W	Physically compatible	15	C
Chloramphenicol sodium succinate	PD	10 g	WC	500 mg	D5W	Physically compatible	15	C
	PD	10 g	WC	500 mg		Physically compatible	6	C
Cimetidine HCl	SKF	3 g	WC	1.5 g	D5W	Physically compatible and cimetidine chemically stable for 24 hr at room temperature. Colistimethate not tested	551	C
Diphenhydramine HCl	PD	80 mg	WC	500 mg	D5W	Physically compatible	15	C
Erythromycin lactobionate	AB	5 g	WC	500 mg	D5W	Physically incompatible	15	I
	AB	1 g	WC	500 mg	D	Precipitate forms within 1 hr	20	I
Heparin sodium	UP	4000 units	WC	500 mg	D5W	Physically compatible	15	C
	AB	20,000 units	WC	500 mg	D	Physically compatible	21	C
Hydrocortisone sodium succinate	UP	500 mg	WC	500 mg	D5W	Physically incompatible	15	I
Kanamycin sulfate	BR	4 g	WC	500 mg	D5W	Physically incompatible	15	I
Penicillin G potassium	SQ	20 million units	WC	500 mg	D5W	Physically compatible	15	C
	SQ	5 million units	WC	500 mg	D	Physically compatible	47	C
Penicillin G sodium	UP	20 million units	WC	500 mg	D5W	Physically compatible	15	C
Phenobarbital sodium	WI	200 mg	WC	500 mg	D5W	Physically compatible	15	C
Polymyxin B sulfate	BW	200 mg	WC	500 mg	D5W	Physically compatible	15	C
Ranitidine HCl	GL	50 mg and 2 g		1.5 g	D5W	Physically compatible and ranitidine chemically stable by HPLC for 24 hr at 25 °C. Colistimethate not tested	1515	C
Vitamin B complex with C	AB	5 ml	WC	500 mg	D5W	Physically compatible	15	C

Drugs in Syringe Compatibility

Colistimethate sodium

Drug (in syringe)	*Mfr*	*Amt*	*Mfr*	*Amt*	*Remarks*	*Ref*	*C/I*
Ampicillin sodium	AY	500 mg	PX	40 mg/ 2 ml	No precipitate or color change within 1 hr at room temperature	99	C
	AY	500 mg	PX	500 mg/ 2 ml	Physically compatible for 1 hr at room temperature	300	C
Penicillin G sodium		1 million units	PX	40 mg/ 2 ml	No precipitate or color change within 1 hr at room temperature	99	C

Additional Compatibility Information

Infusion Solutions — Colistimethate sodium is physically and chemically compatible with the following infusion solutions and should be used within 24 hours (2; 4):

Dextrose 5% in sodium chloride 0.225%
Dextrose 5% in sodium chloride 0.45%
Dextrose 5% in sodium chloride 0.9%
Dextrose 5% in water
Invert sugar 10%
Ringer's injection, lactated
Sodium chloride 0.9%

Other Drugs — Colistimethate sodium is stated to be physically compatible for only four hours at room temperature with lincomycin HCl in infusion solutions. (154)

Cefazolin sodium is stated to be incompatible with colistimethate sodium. (278)

CORTICOTROPIN (ACTH) AHFS 36:04 and 68:28

Products — Corticotropin is available in vials containing 25 or 40 units of drug with 9 or 14 mg, respectively, of hydrolyzed gelatin. It should be reconstituted with a sufficient quantity of sterile water for injection or sodium chloride 0.9% to yield a solution containing an individual dose in 1 to 2 ml of solution. (4)

Repository corticotropin is available in 5-ml vials. Each milliliter of solution contains 80 units of corticotropin and 16% gelatin to provide prolonged release. Also present in the formulation are phenol 0.5%, not more than 0.1% cysteine, and sodium hydroxide and/or acetic acid to adjust the pH in water for injection. (1-4/96; 29)

Units — One USP unit of corticotropin is equivalent to 1 mg of the international standard. (4)

pH — Reconstituted solutions of corticotropin have a pH of 2.5 to 6. Repository corticotropin has a pH of 3 to 7. (4)

Osmolality — Corticotropin 25 units/ml has an osmolality of 89 mOsm/kg. (1689)

Trade Name(s) — Acthar (corticotropin), H.P. Acthar Gel (repository corticotropin).

Administration — Corticotropin may be administered intramuscularly or subcutaneously. It may also be given by direct intravenous injection or by intravenous infusion if the label states that the specific product may be given intravenously. (1-4/96; 4)

Repository corticotropin is administered by intramuscular and subcutaneous injection only. (4)

Stability — Corticotropin is stable for the period noted on the label when stored at room temperature (15 to 30 °C). The reconstituted solution should be refrigerated and used within 24 hours (4) or within eight hours if at room temperature. (108)

Repository corticotropin is a colorless or light straw-colored solution. It is stable for the period noted on the label when stored under refrigeration (2 to 8 °C). The solution may be quite viscous even at room temperature. (1-4/96; 4) Repository corticotropin is reported to be stable for less than 72 hours at room temperature in intact vials. (1181)

Compatibility Information

Solution Compatibility

Corticotropin

Solution	Mfr	Mfr	Conc/L	Remarks	Ref	C/I
Dextrose 5% in sodium chloride 0.9%			500 units	Physically compatible	74	C
Dextrose 5% in water			500 units	Physically compatible	74	C
Ringer's injection, lactated			500 units	Physically compatible	74	C
Sodium chloride 0.9%			500 units	Physically compatible	74	C

Additive Compatibility

Corticotropin

Drug	Mfr	Conc/L	Mfr	Conc/L	Test Soln	Remarks	Ref	C/I
Aminophylline		250 mg		500 units	D5W	Physically compatible	74	C
	SE	500 mg	AR, NA	40 units		Precipitate forms within 1 hr	6	I
Calcium gluconate		1 g		500 units	D5W	Physically compatible	74	C
Chloramphenicol sodium succinate	PD	500 mg		500 units	D5W	Physically compatible	74	C
Cytarabine	UP	100 mg	AR	25 units	D5W	Physically compatible for 8 hr	174	C
Dimenhydrinate	SE	50 mg		500 units	D5W	Physically compatible	74	C
Heparin sodium		12,000 units		500 units	D5W	Physically compatible	74	C
Hydrocortisone sodium succinate	UP	100 mg		500 units	D5W	Physically compatible	74	C
Norepinephrine bitartrate	WI	8 mg		500 units	D5W	Physically compatible	74	C
Oxytetracycline HCl	PF	250 mg		500 units	D5W	Physically compatible	74	C
Penicillin G potassium		1 million units		500 units	D5W	Physically compatible	74	C
Potassium chloride		3 g		500 units	D5W	Physically compatible	74	C
Sodium bicarbonate						Physically incompatible	9	I
	AB	80 mEq	AR	250 units	D5W	Physically incompatible	15	I
	AB	2.4 mEq[a]	AR	40 units	D5W	Physically compatible for 24 hr	772	C
Vancomycin HCl	LI	1 g		500 units	D5W	Physically compatible	74	C
Vitamin B complex with C		1 vial		500 units	D5W	Physically compatible	74	C

[a]*One vial of Neut added to a liter of admixture.*

Additional Compatibility Information

Infusion Solutions — Dextrose 5% in water (1-4/96; 4), Ringer's injection, lactated, and sodium chloride 0.9% (4) have been recommended as diluents for corticotropin administered by intravenous infusion.

CYANOCOBALAMIN
AHFS 88:08

Products — Cyanocobalamin is available in various strengths ranging from 100 μg/ml to 1 mg/ml in ampuls and vials. Benzyl alcohol, sodium chloride, and either sodium hydroxide or hydrochloric acid for pH adjustment may also be present. (4; 29; 154)

pH — From 4.5 to 7. (4)

Osmolality — Cyanocobalamin 100 μg/ml has an osmolality of 446 mOsm/kg. (1689)

Administration — Cyanocobalamin is administered by intramuscular or deep subcutaneous injection. The intravenous route is not recommended. (4)

Stability — The clear pink to red solutions are stable at room temperature and may be autoclaved at 121 °C for short periods such as 15 to 20 minutes. Cyanocobalamin is light sensitive, so protection from light is recommended. (4) Exposure to light results in the organometallic bond being cleaved, with the extent of degradation generally increasing with increasing light intensity. (1072)

pH Effects — Cyanocobalamin is stable at pH 3 to 7 but is most stable at pH 4.5 to 5. (1072) It is stated to be incompatible with alkaline and strongly acidic solutions. (4)

Sorption — Cyanocobalamin (Organon) 30 mg/L did not display significant sorption to a PVC plastic test strip in 24 hours. (12)

Filtration — Cyanocobalamin (Wyeth) 1 mg/L in dextrose 5% in water and in sodium chloride 0.9% was filtered at a rate of 120 ml/hr for six hours through a 0.22-μm cellulose ester membrane filter (Ivex-2). No significant reduction in potency due to binding to the filter was noted. (533)

Compatibility Information

Solution Compatibility

Cyanocobalamin

Solution	*Mfr*	*Mfr*	*Conc/L*	*Remarks*	*Ref*	*C/I*
Dextran 6% in dextrose 5%	AB	AB	1000 μg	Physically compatible	3	C
Dextran 6% in sodium chloride 0.9%	AB	AB	1000 μg	Physically compatible	3	C
Dextrose–Ringer's injection combinations	AB	AB	1000 μg	Physically compatible	3	C
Dextrose–Ringer's injection, lactated, combinations	AB	AB	1000 μg	Physically compatible	3	C
Dextrose–saline combinations	AB	AB	1000 μg	Physically compatible	3	C
Dextrose 2½% in water	AB	AB	1000 μg	Physically compatible	3	C
Dextrose 5% in water	AB	AB	1000 μg	Physically compatible	3	C
Dextrose 10% in water	AB	AB	1000 μg	Physically compatible	3	C
Fructose 10% in sodium chloride 0.9%	AB	AB	1000 μg	Physically compatible	3	C
Fructose 10% in water	AB	AB	1000 μg	Physically compatible	3	C
Invert sugar 5 and 10% in sodium chloride 0.9%	AB	AB	1000 μg	Physically compatible	3	C
Invert sugar 5 and 10% in water	AB	AB	1000 μg	Physically compatible	3	C
Ionosol products	AB	AB	1000 μg	Physically compatible	3	C
Ringer's injection	AB	AB	1000 μg	Physically compatible	3	C
Ringer's injection, lactated	AB	AB	1000 μg	Physically compatible	3	C
Sodium chloride 0.45%	AB	AB	1000 μg	Physically compatible	3	C
Sodium chloride 0.9%	AB	AB	1000 μg	Physically compatible	3	C
Sodium lactate ⅙ M	AB	AB	1000 μg	Physically compatible	3	C
TPN #11 to #15[a]		SQ	1 mg	Physically compatible for 24 hr at 22 °C. TLC changes of amino acids in similar solutions attributed to M.V.I. or vitamin B complex with C were observed	313	C
TPN #16 to #20[a]		SQ	0.5 and 1 mg	Physically compatible for 24 hr at 22 °C. UV spectra of amino acids solution unaltered	313	C

[a] *Refer to Appendix I for the composition of parenteral nutrition solutions. TPN indicates a 2-in-1 admixture.*

Additive Compatibility

			Cyanocobalamin					
Drug	*Mfr*	*Conc/L*	*Mfr*	*Conc/L*	*Test Soln*	*Remarks*	*Ref*	*C/I*
Ascorbic acid injection	AB	1 g	AB	1000 μg		Physically compatible	3	C
Chloramphenicol sodium succinate	PD	1 g	AB	1000 μg		Physically compatible	6	C
Metaraminol bitartrate	MSD	100 mg	AB	1000 μg		Physically compatible	7	C
Vitamin B complex with C	AB	2 ml	AB	1000 μg		Physically compatible	3	C

Y-Site Injection Compatibility (1:1 Mixture)

			Cyanocobalamin				
Drug	*Mfr*	*Conc*	*Mfr*	*Conc*	*Remarks*	*Ref*	*C/I*
Heparin sodium	UP	1000 units/L[a]	PD	0.1 mg/ml	Physically compatible for at least 4 hr at room temperature by visual and microscopic examination	534	C
Hydrocortisone sodium succinate	UP	10 mg/L[a]	PD	0.1 mg/ml	Physically compatible for at least 4 hr at room temperature by visual and microscopic examination	534	C
Potassium chloride	AB	40 mEq/L[a]	PD	0.1 mg/ml	Physically compatible for at least 4 hr at room temperature by visual and microscopic examination	534	C
Vitamin B complex with C	RC	2 ml/L[a]	PD	0.1 mg/ml	Physically compatible for at least 4 hr at room temperature by visual and microscopic examination	534	C

[a]*Tested in dextrose 5% in Ringer's injection, dextrose 5% in Ringer's injection, lactated, dextrose 5% in water, Ringer's injection, lactated, and sodium chloride 0.9%.*

Additional Compatibility Information

Other Drugs — It has been stated that cyanocobalamin with ascorbic acid can be stored for 24 hours at room temperature protected from light without loss of activity. It also has been stated that the drug is compatible with other vitamins of the B complex and with iron–dextran complex. (52)

Some incompatibilities of cyanocobalamin reported in the literature were actually due to hydroxocobalamin, which was formerly present as a contaminant. (52)

Cyanocobalamin (Abbott) 1000 μg/L has been reported to be conditionally compatible with hydrocortisone sodium succinate (Upjohn) 250 mg/L. The mixture is physically compatible in most Abbott infusion solutions except Ionosol D-CM with dextrose 5% with which a haze or precipitate is noted within 24 hours. (3)

Cyanocobalamin injection has been reported to be incompatible with ascorbic acid, chlorpromazine HCl, dextrose, phytonadione, prochlorperazine edisylate, and warfarin sodium. It is also stated to be incompatible with heavy metals, oxidizing agents, and reducing agents. (4)

CYCLOPHOSPHAMIDE
AHFS 10:00

Products — Cyclophosphamide is available as a lyophilized product in vials containing cyclophosphamide 100, 200, and 500 mg and 1 and 2 g with 75 mg of mannitol per 100 mg of drug. Reconstitute the vials with sterile water for injection (2; 4) or bacteriostatic water for injection (paraben preserved only) in the following amounts (4):

Vial Size	Volume of Diluent
100 mg	5 ml
200 mg	10 ml
500 mg	20 to 25 ml
1 g	50 ml
2 g	80 to 100 ml

Shake the vials to dissolve the powder. (2) The lyophilized products yield solutions with concentrations of 20 to 25 mg/ml. (4)

pH — Reconstituted solutions have a pH of 3 to 9. (17) A 22-mg/ml solution was found to have a pH of 6.87. (126)

Osmolarity — The lyophilized product, reconstituted to 20 or 25 mg/ml, has an osmolarity of 172 or 219 mOsm/L, respectively. (2; 4)

Density — Cyclophosphamide (Mead Johnson) reconstituted with sterile water for injection to a concentration of 20 mg/ml has a solution density of 1.00 g/ml. (2041; 2248)

Trade Name(s) — Cytoxan, Neosar.

Administration — Cyclophosphamide may be administered intramuscularly, intraperitoneally, intrapleurally, by direct intravenous injection, or by continuous or intermittent intravenous infusion. (2; 4; 8; 338)

Stability — Cyclophosphamide products should not be stored at temperatures above 25 °C, although they will withstand brief exposures to temperatures up to 30 °C. Reconstituted solutions should be used within 24 hours if stored at room temperature or within six days if stored under refrigeration. (2; 4) When reconstituted with sterile water for injection or paraben-preserved bacteriostatic water for injection to a concentration of 21 mg/ml, less than 1.5% cyclophosphamide decomposition will occur within eight hours at 24 to 27 °C and within six days at 5 °C. The rate constant for decomposition of cyclophosphamide when reconstituted with benzyl alcohol-preserved bacteriostatic water for injection is significantly higher than with sterile water for injection. It was suggested that benzyl alcohol may catalyze somewhat the decomposition of cyclophosphamide. (125) The rate of decomposition is independent of pH over the range of 2 to 10. (1369)

Heating cyclophosphamide solutions at a concentration of 21 mg/ml to 50 and 60 °C for 15 minutes resulted in a negligible loss of potency. However, heating to 70 and 80 °C for 15 minutes resulted in approximately 10 and 23% decomposition, respectively. The use of heat to speed dissolution is, therefore, not recommended since decomposition of cyclophosphamide may result in poorly controlled situations. (126)

Kirk et al. evaluated the stability of cyclophosphamide 20 mg/ml, reconstituted with sterile water for injection and stored in various containers at several temperatures. In glass ampuls at 20 to 23 °C, approximately 13 and 35% were lost in one and four weeks, respectively. Under refrigeration at 4 °C or frozen at −20 °C, the solution lost not more than 3% over four weeks. (1090)

Cyclophosphamide (Bristol-Myers Squibb) reconstituted with sterile water for injection to a concentration of 20 mg/ml was found by HPLC analysis to undergo about 10% degradation in 4 days at 25 °C. When the solutions were stored under refrigeration at 5 °C, approximately 6% loss occurred in 52 days and 10 to 12% loss occurred in 119 days. (2255)

Further diluted to a concentration of 2 g/500 ml of sodium chloride 0.9% in PVC bags, cyclophosphamide remained relatively stable at 4 °C and frozen at −20 °C (with microwave thawing), with no loss in four weeks and about an 8% loss in 19 weeks. (1090)

pH Effects — Cyclophosphamide exhibits maximum solution stability over the range of 2 to 11; the rate of decomposition is essentially the same over this broad pH range. At pH values less than 2 and above 11, increased rates of decomposition have been observed. (2002)

Syringes — In polypropylene syringes (Plastipak, Becton-Dickinson) sealed with blind Luer locking hubs, the 20-mg/ml cyclophosphamide solution similarly lost about 3% in four weeks at 4 °C and about 10% in 11 to 14 weeks. When frozen at −20 °C (with microwave thawing), the solution lost about 4% in 19 weeks. However, the syringe plungers contracted markedly during freezing, resulting in drug solution seeping past the plunger onto the inner surface of the barrel. This seeping poses the risk of bacterial contamination. Furthermore, cyclophosphamide precipitated during microwave thawing and required vigorous shaking for five minutes to redissolve. This precipitation during thawing appears not to occur at concentrations less than 8 mg/ml. (1090)

Elastomeric Reservoir Pumps — Cyclophosphamide solutions in elastomeric reservoir pumps have been stated by the pump manufacturers to be stable for the following time periods refrigerated (REF) or at room temperature (RT) (31):

Pump Reservoir(s)	Conc.	REF	RT
Homepump; Homepump Eclipse	4.5 mg/ml[a]	7 days	7 days
Infusor	2 to 20 mg/ml[a]	48 days	2 days

[a] *In sodium chloride 0.9%.*

Central Venous Catheter — Cyclophosphamide (Mead Johnson) 2 mg/ml in dextrose 5% in water was found to be compatible with the ARROWg+ard Blue Plus (Arrow International) chlorhexidine-bearing triple-lumen central catheter. HPLC analysis was used to evaluate completeness of drug delivery through the catheter and the amount of chlorhexidine removed from the internal lumens. Essentially complete delivery of the drug was found with little or no drug loss occurring. Furthermore, chlorhexidine delivered from the catheter remained at trace amounts with no substantial increase due to the delivery of the drug through the catheter. (2335)

Compatibility Information

Solution Compatibility

Cyclophosphamide

Solution	*Mfr*	*Mfr*	*Conc/L*	*Remarks*	*Ref*	*C/I*
Amino acids 4.25%, dextrose 25%	MG	MJ	500 mg	No increase in particulate matter in 24 hr at 5 °C	349	C
Dextrose 5% in sodium chloride 0.9%	CU	MJ	100 mg	1.5% decomposition or less in 8 hr at 24 to 27 °C and 6 days at 5 °C	125	C
	CU	MJ	3.1 g	1.5% decomposition or less in 8 hr at 24 to 27 °C and 6 days at 5 °C	125	C
Dextrose 5% in water	CU	MJ	100 mg	1.5% decomposition or less in 8 hr at 24 to 27 °C and 6 days at 5 °C	125	C
	CU	MJ	3.1 g	1.5% decomposition or less in 8 hr at 24 to 27 °C and 6 days at 5 °C	125	C
	TR[a]	MJ	6.6 g	Less than 10% decrease in 24 hr at room temperature	519	C
	MG, TR[b]		6.7 g	Less than 10% cyclophosphamide loss by HPLC in 24 hr at room temperature exposed to light	1658	C
Sodium chloride 0.9%		MJ	4 g	3.5% decomposition in 24 hr at room temperature	127	C
		MJ	4 g	1% decomposition in 4 weeks under refrigeration	127	C
	TR	CE	4 g[c]	Physically compatible with no cyclophosphamide loss in 4 weeks and 8% in 19 weeks at 4 and −20 °C	1090	C
		BMS	400 mg	8% loss in 6 days at 23 °C and less than 2% loss in 14 days at 4 °C by HPLC	2255	C

[a]*Tested in both glass and PVC containers.*
[b]*Tested in glass, PVC, and polyolefin containers.*
[c]*Tested in PVC containers.*

Additive Compatibility

Cyclophosphamide

Drug	*Mfr*	*Conc/L*	*Mfr*	*Conc/L*	*Test Soln*	*Remarks*	*Ref*	*C/I*
Cisplatin with etoposide		200 mg 200 mg		2 g	NS	All drugs stable for 7 days at room temperature	1379	C
Fluorouracil		8.3 g		1.67 g	NS	Both drugs stable for 15 days at room temperature	1389	C
Hydroxyzine HCl	LY	500 mg	AD	1 g	D5W[a]	Physically compatible for 48 hr	1190	C
Methotrexate sodium		25 mg		1.67 g	NS	6.6% cyclophosphamide loss in 14 days at room temperature	1379; 1389	C
Methotrexate sodium with fluorouracil		25 mg 8.3 g		1.67 g	NS	9.3% cyclophosphamide loss in 7 days at room temperature. No loss of other drugs observed	1389	C
Mitoxantrone HCl	LE	500 mg	AD	10 g	D5W	Visually compatible and mitoxantrone potency by HPLC retained for 24 hr at room temperature. Cyclophosphamide not tested	1531	C
Ondansetron HCl	GL	50 mg	MJ	300 mg	D5W[b], NS[b]	Visually compatible with 9 to 10% cyclophosphamide loss and no ondansetron loss by HPLC in 5 days at 24 °C. No loss of either drug in 8 days at 4 °C	1812	C

Additive Compatibility (Cont.)

Cyclophosphamide

Drug	Mfr	Conc/L	Mfr	Conc/L	Test Soln	Remarks	Ref	C/I
	GL	400 mg	MJ	2 g	D5W[b], NS[b]	Visually compatible with 10% cyclophosphamide loss and no ondansetron loss by HPLC in 5 days at 24 °C. No loss of either drug in 8 days at 4 °C	1812	C

[a]*Tested in glass containers.*
[b]*Tested in PVC containers.*

Drugs in Syringe Compatibility

Cyclophosphamide

Drug (in syringe)	Mfr	Amt	Mfr	Amt	Remarks	Ref	C/I
Bleomycin sulfate		1.5 units/ 0.5 ml		10 mg/ 0.5 ml	Physically compatible for 5 min at room temperature followed by 8 min of centrifugation	980	C
Cisplatin		0.5 mg/ 0.5 ml		10 mg/ 0.5 ml	Physically compatible for 5 min at room temperature followed by 8 min of centrifugation	980	C
Doxapram HCl	RB	400 mg/ 20 ml		100 mg/ 5 ml	Physically compatible with 2% doxapram loss in 24 hr	1177	C
Doxorubicin HCl		1 mg/ 0.5 ml		10 mg/ 0.5 ml	Physically compatible for 5 min at room temperature followed by 8 min of centrifugation	980	C
Droperidol		1.25 mg/ 0.5 ml		10 mg/ 0.5 ml	Physically compatible for 5 min at room temperature followed by 8 min of centrifugation	980	C
Fluorouracil		25 mg/ 0.5 ml		10 mg/ 0.5 ml	Physically compatible for 5 min at room temperature followed by 8 min of centrifugation	980	C
Furosemide		5 mg/ 0.5 ml		10 mg/ 0.5 ml	Physically compatible for 5 min at room temperature followed by 8 min of centrifugation	980	C
Heparin sodium		500 units/ 0.5 ml		10 mg/ 0.5 ml	Physically compatible for 5 min at room temperature followed by 8 min of centrifugation	980	C
Leucovorin calcium		5 mg/ 0.5 ml		10 mg/ 0.5 ml	Physically compatible for 5 min at room temperature followed by 8 min of centrifugation	980	C
Methotrexate sodium		12.5 mg/ 0.5 ml		10 mg/ 0.5 ml	Physically compatible for 5 min at room temperature followed by 8 min of centrifugation	980	C
Metoclopramide HCl		2.5 mg/ 0.5 ml		10 mg/ 0.5 ml	Physically compatible for 5 min at room temperature followed by 8 min of centrifugation	980	C
	RB	10 mg/ 2 ml	MJ	40 mg/ 2 ml	Physically compatible for 24 hr at room temperature	924	C
	RB	10 mg/ 2 ml	MJ	40 mg/ 2 ml	Physically compatible for 24 hr at 25 °C	1167	C
	RB	10 mg/ 2 ml	MJ	1 g/50 ml	Physically compatible for 24 hr at 25 °C	1167	C
	RB	160 mg/ 32 ml	MJ	1 g/50 ml	Physically compatible for 24 hr at 25 °C	1167	C
Mitomycin		0.25 mg/ 0.5 ml		10 mg/ 0.5 ml	Physically compatible for 5 min at room temperature followed by 8 min of centrifugation	980	C
Vinblastine sulfate		0.5 mg/ 0.5 ml		10 mg/ 0.5 ml	Physically compatible for 5 min at room temperature followed by 8 min of centrifugation	980	C
Vincristine sulfate		0.5 mg/ 0.5 ml		10 mg/ 0.5 ml	Physically compatible for 5 min at room temperature followed by 8 min of centrifugation	980	C

Y-Site Injection Compatibility (1:1 Mixture)

Drug	*Mfr*	*Conc*	Cyclophosphamide *Mfr*	Cyclophosphamide *Conc*	*Remarks*	*Ref*	*C/I*
Allopurinol sodium	BW	3 mg/ml[b]	MJ	10 mg/ml[b]	Physically compatible with no change in measured turbidity or increase in particle content in 4 hr at 22 °C	1686	C
Amifostine	USB	10 mg/ml[a]	MJ	10 mg/ml[a]	Physically compatible with no change in measured turbidity or increase in particle content in 4 hr at 23 °C	1845	C
Amikacin sulfate	BR	5 mg/ml[a]	MJ	20 mg/ml[a]	Physically compatible for 4 hr at 25 °C	1194	C
Amphotericin B cholesteryl sulfate complex	SEQ	0.83 mg/ml[a]	MJ	10 mg/ml[a]	Increased turbidity forms immediately	2117	I
Ampicillin sodium	BR	20 mg/ml[b]	MJ	20 mg/ml[a]	Physically compatible for 4 hr at 25 °C	1194	C
Azlocillin sodium	MI	20 mg/ml[a]	MJ	20 mg/ml[a]	Physically compatible for 4 hr at 25 °C	1194	C
Aztreonam	SQ	40 mg/ml[a]	MJ	10 mg/ml[a]	Physically compatible with no subvisual haze or particle formation in 4 hr at 23 °C	1758	C
Bleomycin sulfate		3 units/ml		20 mg/ml	Drugs injected sequentially into Y-site with no flush between. No visually apparent precipitate	980	C
Cefamandole nafate	LI	20 mg/ml[a]	MJ	20 mg/ml[a]	Physically compatible for 4 hr at 25 °C	1194	C
Cefazolin sodium	SKF	20 mg/ml[a]	MJ	20 mg/ml[a]	Physically compatible for 4 hr at 25 °C	1194	C
Cefepime HCl	BMS	20 mg/ml[a]	MJ	10 mg/ml[a]	Physically compatible with no change in measured turbidity or increase in particle content in 4 hr at 22 °C	1689	C
Cefoperazone sodium	RR	20 mg/ml[a]	MJ	20 mg/ml[a]	Physically compatible for 4 hr at 25 °C	1194	C
Cefotaxime sodium	HO	20 mg/ml[a]	MJ	20 mg/ml[a]	Physically compatible for 4 hr at 25 °C	1194	C
Cefoxitin sodium	MSD	20 mg/ml[a]	MJ	20 mg/ml[a]	Physically compatible for 4 hr at 25 °C	1194	C
Cefuroxime sodium	GL	30 mg/ml[a]	MJ	20 mg/ml[a]	Physically compatible for 4 hr at 25 °C	1194	C
Chloramphenicol sodium succinate	ES	20 mg/ml[a]	MJ	20 mg/ml[a]	Physically compatible for 4 hr at 25 °C	1194	C
Chlorpromazine HCl	SKF	2 mg/ml[a]	MJ	10 mg/ml[a]	Visually compatible for 4 hr at room temperature under fluorescent light	1685	C
Cimetidine HCl	SKF	12 mg/ml[a]	MJ	10 mg/ml[a]	Visually compatible for 4 hr at room temperature under fluorescent light	1685	C
Cisplatin		1 mg/ml		20 mg/ml	Drugs injected sequentially into Y-site with no flush between. No visually apparent precipitate	980	C
Cladribine	ORT	0.015[b] and 0.5[c] mg/ml	MJ	10 mg/ml[b]	Physically compatible with no change in measured turbidity or increase in particle content in 4 hr at 23 °C	1969	C
Clindamycin phosphate	UP	12 mg/ml[a]	MJ	20 mg/ml[a]	Physically compatible for 4 hr at 25 °C	1194	C
Dexamethasone sodium phosphate	QU	1 mg/ml[a]	MJ	10 mg/ml[a]	Visually compatible for 4 hr at room temperature under fluorescent light	1685	C
Diphenhydramine HCl	PD	2 mg/ml[a]	MJ	10 mg/ml[a]	Visually compatible for 4 hr at room temperature under fluorescent light	1685	C
Doxorubicin HCl		2 mg/ml		20 mg/ml	Drugs injected sequentially into Y-site with no flush between. No visually apparent precipitate	980	C

Y-Site Injection Compatibility (1:1 Mixture) (Cont.)

			Cyclophosphamide				
Drug	*Mfr*	*Conc*	*Mfr*	*Conc*	*Remarks*	*Ref*	*C/I*
Doxorubicin HCl liposome injection	SEQ	0.4 mg/ml[a]	MJ	10 mg/ml[a]	Physically compatible with little or no change in measured turbidity and no increase in particle content in 4 hr at 23 °C	2087	C
Doxycycline hyclate	ES	1 mg/ml[a]	MJ	20 mg/ml[a]	Physically compatible for 4 hr at 25 °C	1194	C
Droperidol		2.5 mg/ml		20 mg/ml	Drugs injected sequentially into Y-site with no flush between. No visually apparent precipitate	980	C
	JN	20 μg/ml[a]	MJ	10 mg/ml[a]	Visually compatible for 4 hr at room temperature under fluorescent light	1685	C
Erythromycin lactobionate	AB	5 mg/ml[a]	MJ	20 mg/ml[a]	Physically compatible for 4 hr at 25 °C	1194	C
Etoposide phosphate	BR	5 mg/ml[a]	MJ	10 mg/ml[a]	Physically compatible with no change in measured turbidity or increase in particle content in 4 hr at 23 °C	2218	C
Famotidine	MSD	2 mg/ml[a]	MJ	10 mg/ml[a]	Visually compatible for 4 hr at room temperature under fluorescent light	1685	C
Filgrastim	AMG	30 μg/ml[a]	MJ	10 mg/ml[a]	Physically compatible with no change in measured turbidity or increase in particle content in 4 hr at 22 °C	1687	C
Fludarabine phosphate	BX	1 mg/ml[a]	MJ	10 mg/ml[a]	Physically compatible for 4 hr at room temperature under fluorescent light	1439	C
Fluorouracil		50 mg/ml		20 mg/ml	Drugs injected sequentially into Y-site with no flush between. No visually apparent precipitate	980	C
Furosemide		10 mg/ml		20 mg/ml	Drugs injected sequentially into Y-site with no flush between. No visually apparent precipitate	980	C
	ES	3 mg/ml[a]	MJ	10 mg/ml[a]	Visually compatible for 4 hr at room temperature under fluorescent light	1685	C
Ganciclovir sodium	SY	20 mg/ml[a]	MJ	10 mg/ml[a]	Visually compatible for 4 hr at room temperature under fluorescent light	1685	C
Gatifloxacin	BMS	2 mg/ml[a]	MJ	10 mg/ml[a]	Physically compatible with no change in measured haze or increase in particle content in 4 hr at 23 °C	2234	C
Gemcitabine HCl	LI	10 mg/ml[b]	BR	10 mg/ml[b]	Physically compatible with no change in measured turbidity or increase in particle content in 4 hr at 23 °C	2226	C
Gentamicin sulfate	TR	1.6 mg/ml[a]	MJ	20 mg/ml[a]	Physically compatible for 4 hr at 25 °C	1194	C
Granisetron HCl	SKB	1 mg/ml	MJ	2 mg/ml[b]	Physically compatible with little or no loss of either drug by HPLC in 4 hr at 22 °C	1883	C
Heparin sodium		1000 units/ml		20 mg/ml	Drugs injected sequentially into Y-site with no flush between. No visually apparent precipitate	980	C
	SO	40 units/ml[a]	MJ	10 mg/ml[a]	Visually compatible for 4 hr at room temperature under fluorescent light	1685	C
Hydromorphone HCl	ES	0.04 mg/ml[a]	MJ	10 mg/ml[a]	Visually compatible for 4 hr at room temperature under fluorescent light	1685	C
Idarubicin HCl	AD	1 mg/ml[b]	CET	4 mg/ml[a]	Visually compatible for 24 hr at 25 °C	1525	C

Y-Site Injection Compatibility (1:1 Mixture) (Cont.)

Drug	*Mfr*	*Conc*	*Mfr* (Cyclophosphamide)	*Conc* (Cyclophosphamide)	*Remarks*	*Ref*	*C/I*
Kanamycin sulfate	BR	2.5 mg/ml[a]	MJ	20 mg/ml[a]	Physically compatible for 4 hr at 25 °C	1194	C
Leucovorin calcium		10 mg/ml		20 mg/ml	Drugs injected sequentially into Y-site with no flush between. No visually apparent precipitate	980	C
Linezolid	PHU	2 mg/ml	MJ	10 mg/ml[a]	Physically compatible with no change in measured turbidity or increase in particle content in 4 hr at 23 °C	2264	C
Lorazepam	WY	0.1 mg/ml[a]	MJ	10 mg/ml[a]	Visually compatible for 4 hr at room temperature under fluorescent light	1685	C
Melphalan HCl	BW	0.1 mg/ml[b]	BR	10 mg/ml[b]	Physically compatible with no change in measured turbidity or increase in particle content in 3 hr at 22 °C	1557	C
Methotrexate sodium		25 mg/ml		20 mg/ml	Drugs injected sequentially into Y-site with no flush between. No visually apparent precipitate	980	C
		30 mg/ml		20 mg/ml[a]	Visually compatible for 4 hr at room temperature	1788	C
Methylprednisolone sodium succinate	UP	0.5 mg/ml[a]	MJ	10 mg/ml[a]	Visually compatible for 4 hr at room temperature under fluorescent light	1685	C
Metoclopramide HCl		5 mg/ml		20 mg/ml	Drugs injected sequentially into Y-site with no flush between. No visually apparent precipitate	980	C
	RB	2.5 mg/ml[a]	MJ	10 mg/ml[a]	Visually compatible for 4 hr at room temperature under fluorescent light	1685	C
Metronidazole	SE	5 mg/ml	MJ	20 mg/ml[a]	Physically compatible for 4 hr at 25 °C	1194	C
Minocycline HCl	LE	0.2 mg/ml[a]	MJ	20 mg/ml[a]	Physically compatible for 4 hr at 25 °C	1194	C
Mitomycin		0.5 mg/ml		20 mg/ml	Drugs injected sequentially into Y-site with no flush between. No visually apparent precipitate	980	C
Morphine sulfate	ES	0.12 mg/ml[a]	MJ	10 mg/ml[a]	Visually compatible for 4 hr at room temperature under fluorescent light	1685	C
Nafcillin sodium	WY	20 mg/ml[a]	MJ	20 mg/ml[a]	Physically compatible for 4 hr at 25 °C	1194	C
Ondansetron HCl	GL	1 mg/ml[b]	MJ	10 mg/ml[a]	Physically compatible for 4 hr at 22 °C	1365	C
	GL	16 to 160 μg/ml		20 mg/ml	Physically compatible when cyclophosphamide given as 5-min bolus via Y-site	1366	C
Oxacillin sodium	BE	20 mg/ml[a]	MJ	20 mg/ml[a]	Physically compatible for 4 hr at 25 °C	1194	C
Paclitaxel	NCI	1.2 mg/ml[a]		10 mg/ml[a]	Physically compatible with no change in measured turbidity in 4 hr at 22 °C	1528	C
Penicillin G potassium	PF	100,000 units/ml[a]	MJ	20 mg/ml[a]	Physically compatible for 4 hr at 25 °C	1194	C
Piperacillin sodium	LE	60 mg/ml[a]	MJ	20 mg/ml[a]	Physically compatible for 4 hr at 25 °C	1194	C
Piperacillin sodium–tazobactam sodium	LE	40 + 5 mg/ml[a]	MJ	10 mg/ml[a]	Physically compatible with no change in measured turbidity or increase in particle content in 4 hr at 22 °C	1688	C
Prochlorperazine edisylate	SKF	0.5 mg/ml[a]	MJ	10 mg/ml[a]	Visually compatible for 4 hr at room temperature under fluorescent light	1685	C

Y-Site Injection Compatibility (1:1 Mixture) (Cont.)

Cyclophosphamide

Drug	*Mfr*	*Conc*	*Mfr*	*Conc*	*Remarks*	*Ref*	*C/I*
Promethazine HCl	WY	2 mg/ml[a]	MJ	10 mg/ml[a]	Visually compatible for 4 hr at room temperature under fluorescent light	1685	C
Propofol	ZEN	10 mg/ml	MJ	10 mg/ml[a]	Physically compatible for 1 hr at 23 °C with no increase in particle content	2066	C
Ranitidine HCl	GL	1 mg/ml[a]	MJ	10 mg/ml[a]	Visually compatible for 4 hr at room temperature under fluorescent light	1685	C
Sargramostim	IMM	10 μg/ml[b]	MJ	10 mg/ml[b]	Physically compatible for 4 hr at 22 °C	1436	C
Sodium bicarbonate		1.4%		20 mg/ml[a]	Visually compatible for 4 hr at room temperature	1788	C
Teniposide	BR	0.1 mg/ml[a]	MJ	10 mg/ml[a]	Physically compatible with no subvisual haze or particle formation in 4 hr at 23 °C	1725	C
Thiotepa	IMM[d]	1 mg/ml[a]	MJ	10 mg/ml[a]	Physically compatible with no change in measured turbidity or increase in particle content in 4 hr at 23 °C	1861	C
Ticarcillin disodium	BE	30 mg/ml[a]	MJ	20 mg/ml[a]	Physically compatible for 4 hr at 25 °C	1194	C
Ticarcillin disodium–clavulanate potassium	BE	31 mg/ml[a]	MJ	20 mg/ml[a]	Physically compatible for 4 hr at 25 °C	1194	C
TNA #218 to #226[e]			MJ	10 mg/ml[a]	Visually compatible with no precipitate or emulsion damage apparent in 4 hr at 23 °C	2215	C
Tobramycin sulfate	DI	0.8 mg/ml[a]	MJ	20 mg/ml[a]	Physically compatible for 4 hr at 25 °C	1194	C
Topotecan HCl	SKB	56 μg/ml[a,b]	MJ	20 mg/ml	Visually compatible with little or no loss of either drug by HPLC in 4 hr at 22 °C under fluorescent light	2245	C
TPN #212 to #215[e]			MJ	10 mg/ml[a]	Physically compatible with no change in measured turbidity or increase in particle content in 4 hr at 23 °C	2109	C
Trimethoprim–sulfamethoxazole	BW	0.8 + 4 mg/ml[a]	MJ	20 mg/ml[a]	Physically compatible for 4 hr at 25 °C	1194	C
Vancomycin HCl	LI	5 mg/ml[a]	MJ	20 mg/ml[a]	Physically compatible for 4 hr at 25 °C	1194	C
Vinblastine sulfate		1 mg/ml		20 mg/ml	Drugs injected sequentially into Y-site with no flush between. No visually apparent precipitate	980	C
Vincristine sulfate		1 mg/ml		20 mg/ml	Drugs injected sequentially into Y-site with no flush between. No visually apparent precipitate	980	C
Vinorelbine tartrate	BW	1 mg/ml[b]	MJ	10 mg/ml[b]	Physically compatible with no change in measured turbidity or increase in particle content in 4 hr at 22 °C	1558	C

[a]*Tested in dextrose 5% in water.*
[b]*Tested in sodium chloride 0.9%.*
[c]*Tested in bacteriostatic sodium chloride 0.9% preserved with benzyl alcohol 0.9%.*
[d]*Lyophilized formulation tested.*
[e]*Refer to Appendix I for the composition of parenteral nutrition solutions. TNA indicates a 3-in-1 admixture, and TPN indicates a 2-in-1 admixture.*

Additional Compatibility Information

Infusion Solutions — The following solutions have been recommended as diluents for intravenous infusion (2):

Dextrose 5% in Ringer's injection
Dextrose 5% in sodium chloride 0.9%
Dextrose 5% in water
Ringer's injection, lactated
Sodium chloride 0.45%
Sodium lactate ⅙ M

Dacarbazine — No alteration in the ultraviolet/visible spectra was observed when dacarbazine was combined in solution with cyclophosphamide. (492)

Mesna — Cyclophosphamide is stated to be stable for 24 hours in dextrose 5% in water or Ringer's injection, lactated, when admixed with mesna. (4; 1292)

Aluminum — Ogawa et al. reported that immersion of a needle with an aluminum component in cyclophosphamide (Adria) 20 mg/ml resulted in a slight darkening of the aluminum and gas production after a few days at 24 °C with protection from light. (988)

CYCLOSPORINE
AHFS 92:00

Products — Cyclosporine is available as a concentrate in 5-ml ampuls. Each milliliter of the sterile solution contains cyclosporine 50 mg, polyoxyethylated castor oil (Cremophor EL) 650 mg, and alcohol 278 mg (32.9%). (2; 874)

Nitrogen is utilized as the atmosphere in the sealed ampuls. Cyclosporine concentrate must be diluted before administration. (2; 874)

Trade Name(s) — Sandimmune.

Administration — Cyclosporine concentrate for injection is administered over two to six hours by intravenous infusion after dilution. Each milliliter of concentrate should be diluted in 20 to 100 ml of dextrose 5% in water or sodium chloride 0.9%. (2; 4)

Stability — Cyclosporine injection is a clear, faintly brown-yellow solution. It should be stored below 30 °C and protected from light and freezing. (2; 4; 874) Light protection is not required for intravenous admixtures of cyclosporine. (4; 1091)

Sorption — Simulated infusion studies of cyclosporine (Sandoz) 2 mg/ml in dextrose 5% in water and sodium chloride 0.9% were performed at a rate of 0.67 mg/ml over 75 minutes through 70-inch microdrip administration sets (Abbott). Significant amounts of cyclosporine were lost, presumably as a result of sorption to the tubing. Approximately 7% of the dose was lost from the dextrose 5% in water admixture, and about 13% was lost from the sodium chloride 0.9% admixture. The authors noted that as much as 30% of a pediatric dose could be lost. (1091)

In contrast, Parr et al. did not find any significant cyclosporine loss when 2.38 and 0.495 mg/ml in dextrose 5% in water and sodium chloride 0.9%, in either glass or PVC containers, were delivered over six hours by an electronic infusion pump. (1154)

Plasticizer Leaching — Polyoxyethylated castor oil (Cremophor EL), a nonionic surfactant, may leach phthalate from PVC containers such as bags of infusion solutions. (2; 4) An acceptability limit of no more than 5 parts per million (5 μg/ml) for diethylhexyl phthalate (DEHP) plasticizer leached from PVC containers, etc. has been proposed. The limit was proposed based on a review of metabolic and toxicologic considerations. (2185)

Cyclosporine (Sandoz) 3 mg/ml in dextrose 5% in water leached relatively large amounts of DEHP plasticizer from PVC bags. This leaching was due to the surfactant Cremophor EL in the formulation. After four hours at 24 °C, the DEHP concentration in 50-ml bags of infusion solution was as much as 13 μg/ml and it increased through 24 hours to 104 μg/ml. This finding is consistent with the high surfactant concentration (3.9%) in the final admixture solution. The actual amount of DEHP leached from PVC containers and administration sets may vary in clinical situations, depending on surfactant concentration, bag size, and contact time. Non-PVC containers and administration sets should be used to administer cyclosporine solutions. (1683)

Storage of cyclosporine (Sandoz) 3 mg/ml in dextrose 5% in water in PVC bags at 24 °C was shown to cause leaching of significant amounts of DEHP due to the vehicle containing Cremophor EL and alcohol. Use of glass containers and tubing that does not contain DEHP to administer cyclosporine was recommended. (1092)

Filtration — Parr et al. reported that the use of either a 0.22- or 0.45-μm filter reduced the delivered cyclosporine concentration from 2.38- and 0.495-mg/ml solutions in dextrose 5% in water and sodium chloride 0.9%. They found a significant (but unspecified) decrease in the first sample, taken at one minute. At the six-hour time point, the concentration had returned to the original concentration. The total amount of drug delivered over six hours was not quantified. (1154)

Compatibility Information

Solution Compatibility

Cyclosporine

Solution	*Mfr*	*Mfr*	*Conc/L*	*Remarks*	*Ref*	*C/I*
Amino acids 5%, dextrose 25%	MG	SZ	150 mg	Visually compatible with no cyclosporine loss by HPLC in 72 hr at 21 °C	1616	C
Dextrose 5% in water	AB[a]	SZ	2 g	Physically compatible with no cyclosporine loss in 24 hr at 24 °C in the dark or light	1091	C
	AB[b]	SZ	2 g	Physically compatible with 5% cyclosporine loss in 48 hr at 24 °C under fluorescent light and refrigerated at 6 °C	1330	C
	BA	SZ	1 g	Visually compatible with no cyclosporine loss by HPLC in 72 hr at 21 °C	1616	C
Fat emulsion 10%, intravenous	AB	SZ	400 mg	No cyclosporine loss by HPLC in 72 hr at 21 °C	1616	C
Fat emulsion 10 and 20%, intravenous	KA	SZ	500 mg and 2 g	Physically compatible by visual examination and particle size assessment with no cyclosporine loss by HPLC in 48 hr at 24 °C under fluorescent light	1625	C
Sodium chloride 0.9%	AB[a]	SZ	2 g	Physically compatible with 7 to 8% cyclosporine loss in 24 hr at 24 °C in the dark or light	1091	C

[a]*Tested in both glass and PVC containers.*
[b]*Tested in glass bottles.*

Additive Compatibility

Cyclosporine

Drug	*Mfr*	*Conc/L*	*Mfr*	*Conc/L*	*Test Soln*	*Remarks*	*Ref*	*C/I*
Ciprofloxacin	BAY	2 g	SZ	500 mg	NS	Visually compatible with about 8% ciprofloxacin loss by HPLC in 24 hr at 25 °C. Cyclosporine not tested	1934	C
Magnesium sulfate	LY	30 g	SZ	2 g	D5W	Transient turbidity appears upon preparation but dissipates in 30 sec and remains clear for 36 hr at 24 °C. 5% cyclosporine loss in 6 hr and 10% loss in 12 hr by HPLC at 24 °C under fluorescent light	1629	I

Y-Site Injection Compatibility (1:1 Mixture)

Cyclosporine

Drug	*Mfr*	*Conc*	*Mfr*	*Conc*	*Remarks*	*Ref*	*C/I*
Alatrofloxacin mesylate	PF	1.43 mg/ml[a]	SZ	4.2 mg/ml[a]	Visually and microscopically compatible run through a Y-site over at least 60 min	2235	C
Amphotericin B cholesteryl sulfate complex	SEQ	0.83 mg/ml[a]	SZ	5 mg/ml[a]	Decreased natural turbidity occurs immediately	2117	I
Gatifloxacin	BMS	2 mg/ml[a]	SZ	5 mg/ml[a]	Physically compatible with no change in measured haze or increase in particle content in 4 hr at 23 °C	2234	C
Linezolid	PHU	2 mg/ml	SZ	5 mg/ml[a]	Physically compatible with no change in measured turbidity or increase in particle content in 4 hr at 23 °C	2264	C

Y-Site Injection Compatibility (1:1 Mixture) (Cont.)

			Cyclosporine				
Drug	*Mfr*	*Conc*	*Mfr*	*Conc*	*Remarks*	*Ref*	*C/I*
Propofol	ZEN	10 mg/ml	SZ	5 mg/ml[a]	Physically compatible for 1 hr at 23 °C with no increase in particle content	2066	C
Sargramostim	IMM	6[c] and 15[b] μg/ml	SZ	5 mg/ml[b]	Visually compatible for 2 hr	1618	C
TNA #220 and #223[d]			SZ	5 mg/ml[a]	Small amount of precipitate forms immediately	2215	I
TNA #218, #219, #221, #222, #224 to #226[d]			SZ	5 mg/ml[a]	Visually compatible with no precipitate or emulsion damage apparent in 4 hr at 23 °C	2215	C
TPN #212 and #213[d]			SZ	5 mg/ml[a]	Physically compatible with no change in measured turbidity or increase in particle content in 4 hr at 23 °C	2109	C
TPN #214 and #215[d]			SZ	5 mg/ml[a]	Small amount of subvisual precipitate forms in 4 hr	2109	I

[a]*Tested in dextrose 5% in water.*
[b]*Tested in sodium chloride 0.9%.*
[c]*Tested in sodium chloride 0.9% with albumin human 0.1%.*
[d]*Refer to Appendix I for the composition of parenteral nutrition solutions. TNA indicates a 3-in-1 admixture, and TPN indicates a 2-in-1 admixture.*

Additional Compatibility Information

Infusion Solutions — Dextrose 5% in water and sodium chloride 0.9% are recommended for dilution of cyclosporine concentrate. (2; 4) Although the drug is stable for 24 hours in these solutions (1091), it has been suggested that admixtures in sodium chloride 0.9% be considered usable for six hours in PVC containers and 12 hours in glass containers because of the combined losses from storage and sorption through PVC tubing. (4) However, see Plasticizer Leaching above.

CYTARABINE (CYTOSINE ARABINOSIDE) AHFS 10:00

Products — Cytarabine for injection is available as lyophilized products in 100-mg, 500-mg, 1-g, and 2-g vials. For intravenous or subcutaneous use, reconstitute the vials with bacteriostatic water for injection containing benzyl alcohol in the following amounts (1-8/00):

Vial Size	Volume of Diluent	Concentration
100 mg	5 ml	20 mg/ml
500 mg	10 ml	50 mg/ml
1 g	10 ml	100 mg/ml
2 g	20 ml	100 mg/ml

For intrathecal injection, *only* a preservative-free diluent should be used. (1-8/00; 4)

Hydrochloric acid and/or sodium hydroxide may have been added to adjust the pH. (1-8/00; 4)

Cytarabine injection is available at a 20-mg/ml concentration in 25-ml (500-mg) vials with benzyl alcohol 0.9% in water for injection. Hydrochloric acid and/or sodium hydroxide may have been added during manufacturing to adjust pH. (1-2/98)

pH — After reconstitution of the lyophilized products, the USP specifies a pH range of 4 to 6. (17) Cytarabine injection has a pH of about 7.4, with a range of 7 to 9. (4)

Osmolality — Cytarabine 20 mg/ml in sterile water for injection has an osmolality of 150 mOsm/kg. (1689)

Density — Cytarabine (Schein) powder reconstituted with sterile water for injection to a concentration of 20 mg/ml and also the undiluted 20-mg/ml injection have a solution density of 1.00 g/ml. Cytarabine (Chiron) reconstituted with sterile water for injection to a concentration of 50 mg/ml has a solution density of 1.01 g/ml. (2041; 2248)

Sodium Content — Cytarabine injection contains 0.12 mEq of sodium per milliliter. (4)

Trade Name(s) — Cytosar-U.

Administration — Cytarabine may be administered by subcutaneous, intrathecal (prepared in preservative-free diluent), or direct intravenous injection and by continuous or intermittent intravenous infusion. (1-8/00; 4) It has been administered by intramuscular injection and continuous subcutaneous infusion as well. (4)

Stability — Intact vials of lyophilized cytarabine for injection and cytarabine injection should be stored at controlled room temperature. (1-2/98; 1-8/00)

Cytarabine reconstituted with bacteriostatic water for injection containing benzyl alcohol may be stored at a controlled room temperature for up to 48 hours. Solutions with a slight haze should be discarded. (4) However, a stability study of cytarabine in aqueous solution showed maximum stability in the neutral pH range. It was calculated to retain 90% potency for six and a half months at pH 6.9 at 25 °C. The rate of decomposition of cytarabine in alkaline solutions is about 10 times as great as in acid solutions. (82)

The manufacturer indicates that for concentrations of 20 and 250 mg/ml in bacteriostatic water for injection, greater than 99% potency is retained after five days of storage at room temperature. (174) However, cytarabine has an aqueous solubility of 100 mg/ml (4; 1369), and precipitation from more highly concentrated solutions has been observed in varying time frames. In another test, concentrations of 40 and 80 mg/ml in bacteriostatic water for injection were stored in plastic syringes (Becton-Dickinson) at 37, 25, 4, and −20 °C. Cytarabine remained stable for at least 15 days at 25 and 4 °C and for seven days at 37 °C. However, storage at −20 °C resulted in a precipitate. (174)

Cytarabine (Upjohn) 50 mg/ml in polypropylene syringes containing 5, 10, and 20 ml was stable by HPLC for 29 days at 8 and 21 °C in the dark, exhibiting losses of 8.5% or less. (1566)

In another report, reconstituted 100- and 500-mg vials retained between 89.2 and 92% potency at 17 days after reconstitution when stored at 25 °C. (226)

Cytarabine, reconstituted according to the manufacturer's instructions, was cultured with human lymphoblasts to determine whether its cytotoxic activity was retained. The solution retained cytotoxicity for 24 hours at 4 °C and room temperature. (1575)

Intrathecal Injections — Reconstituted solutions containing 20 and 50 mg/ml of cytarabine (Upjohn) were stored in plastic syringes (Pharmaseal) at 22, 8, and −10 °C. No decomposition occurred during one week of storage at these temperatures. (748)

In another study, cytarabine (Upjohn) 50 mg/2.5 ml was stored at 5 and 25 °C in 5-ml plastic syringes (Becton-Dickinson) with rubber tip caps and in glass flasks covered with parafilm. After seven days, samples in the plastic syringes showed a 2 to 3% loss of cytarabine at both temperatures. The 25 °C sample in glass also showed a 2% loss, but the 5 °C sample in glass showed no loss after seven days. (759)

In a study of solutions for intrathecal injection, cytarabine (Upjohn) was reconstituted to a concentration of 5 mg/ml with Elliott's B solution (artificial cerebrospinal fluid), sodium chloride 0.9%, and Ringer's injection, lactated. In Elliott's B solution and Ringer's injection, lactated, cytarabine exhibited no change in concentration by UV spectroscopy over seven days at room temperature under fluorescent light and at 30 °C. In sodium chloride 0.9%, no decomposition was noted in 24 hours, but a 3% loss was observed at room temperature and 6% at 30 °C over seven days. (327)

Bacterially contaminated intrathecal solutions could pose very grave risks; consequently, such solutions should be administered as soon as possible after preparation. (328)

The osmolarity and pH of cytarabine in these three solutions at a concentration of 2.5 mg/ml were as follows (327):

In Elliott's B solution	299 mOsm/kg, pH 7.3
In Ringer's injection, lactated	262 mOsm/kg, pH 5.6
In sodium chloride 0.9%	299 mOsm/kg, pH 5.3

In another study, the stability and compatibility of cytarabine (Upjohn), methotrexate (NCI), and hydrocortisone (Upjohn), mixed together in intrathecal injections, were evaluated. Two combinations were tested: (1) cytarabine 50 mg, methotrexate 12 mg (as the sodium salt), and hydrocortisone 25 mg (as the sodium succinate salt); and (2) cytarabine 30 mg, methotrexate 12 mg (as the sodium salt), and hydrocortisone 15 mg (as the sodium succinate salt). Each drug combination was added to 12 ml of Elliott's B solution (NCI), sodium chloride 0.9% (Abbott), dextrose 5% in water (Abbott), and Ringer's injection, lactated (Abbott), and stored for 24 hours at 25 °C. Cytarabine and methotrexate were both chemically stable, with no drug loss after the full 24 hours in all solutions. Hydrocortisone was also stable in the sodium chloride 0.9%, dextrose 5% in water, and Ringer's injection, lactated, with about a 2% drug loss. However, in Elliott's B solution, hydrocortisone was significantly less stable, with a 6% loss in the 25-mg concentration over 24 hours. The 15-mg concentration was worse, with a 5% loss in 10 hours and a 13% loss in 24 hours. The higher pH of Elliott's B solution and the lower concentration of hydrocortisone may have been factors in this increased decomposition. All mixtures were physically compatible during this study, but a precipitate formed after several days of storage. (819)

Elliott's B solution has been recommended as a diluent for cytosine arabinoside for intrathecal administration because it is more nearly physiologic. (435) The patient's own spinal fluid has been recommended also. (830)

Cytarabine (Upjohn) 3 mg/ml diluted in Elliott's B solution (Orphan Medical) was packaged as 20 ml in 30-ml glass vials and 20-ml plastic syringes (Becton-Dickinson) with Red Cap (Burron) Luer-Lok syringe tip caps. The solution was physically compatible, with no change in measured turbidity or increase in particulate content and was chemically stable, exhibiting little or no loss by HPLC analysis during storage for 48 hours at 4 and 23 °C. (1976)

Elastomeric Reservoir Pumps — Cytarabine 5-mg/ml solutions in dextrose 5% in water in an Infusor elastomeric reservoir pump have been stated by the pump manufacturer to be stable for 30 days frozen, refrigerated, or at room temperature. (31)

Implantable Pumps — Cytarabine (Upjohn) 1 mg/ml in Elliott's B solution was evaluated for stability in an implantable infusion pump (Infusaid model 400). In this in vitro assessment, no cytarabine loss occurred in 15 days at 37 °C with mild agitation. (767)

Sorption — In an admixture composed of cytarabine (Upjohn) 0.157 mg/ml, daunorubicin HCl (Bellon) 15.7 μg/ml, and etoposide (Sandoz) 0.157 mg/ml in dextrose 5% in water, little or no loss of the drugs due to sorption occurred when delivered through PVC and polyethylene-lined sets and silicone central catheters. (1955)

Filtration — Cytarabine 100 mg/15 ml was injected as a bolus through a 0.2-μm nylon, air-eliminating filter (Ultipor, Pall) to evaluate the effect of filtration on simulated intravenous push delivery. Spectrophotometric evaluation showed that about 96% of the drug was delivered through the filter after flushing with 10 ml of sodium chloride 0.9%. (809)

Cytarabine 10 to 100 μg/ml exhibited no loss due to sorption to either cellulose nitrate/cellulose acetate ester (Millex OR) or polytetrafluoroethylene (Millex FG) filters. (1416)

Central Venous Catheter—Cytarabine (Fujisawa) 5 mg/ml in dextrose 5% in water was found to be compatible with the ARROWg+ard Blue Plus (Arrow International) chlorhexidine-bearing triple-lumen central catheter. HPLC analysis was used to evaluate completeness of drug delivery through the catheter and the amount of chlorhexidine removed from the internal lumens. Essentially complete delivery of the drug was found with little or no drug loss occurring. Furthermore, chlorhexidine delivered from the catheter remained at trace amounts with no substantial increase due to the delivery of the drug through the catheter. (2335)

Compatibility Information

Solution Compatibility

Cytarabine

Solution	*Mfr*	*Mfr*	*Conc/L*	*Remarks*	*Ref*	*C/I*
Amino acids 4.25%, dextrose 25%	MG	UP	100 mg	No increase in particulate matter in 24 hr at 5 °C	349	C
Dextrose 5% in Ringer's injection, lactated	TR[a]	UP	500 mg	Potency retained for 24 hr at 5 °C	282	C
Dextrose 5% in sodium chloride 0.2%	[a]	UP	8, 24, 32 g	No cytarabine loss in 7 days at room temperature or 4 or −20 °C	174	C
Dextrose 5% in sodium chloride 0.9%	TR[a]	UP	500 mg	Potency retained for 24 hr at 5 °C	282	C
		UP	3.6 g	Physically compatible	174	C
Dextrose 10% in sodium chloride 0.9%		UP	3.6 g	Physically compatible	174	C
Dextrose 5% in water	TR[a]	UP	500 mg	Potency retained for 24 hr at 5 °C	282	C
	TR[a]	UP	1.87 g	Less than 10% decrease in 24 hr at room temperature	519	C
		UP	500 mg	Chemically stable for 7 days at room temperature	174	C
	[a]	UP	8, 24, 32 g	No cytarabine loss in 7 days at room temperature or 4 or −20 °C	174	C
	[b]	UP	1.25 and 25 g	Visually compatible with less than 6% cytarabine loss by HPLC in 28 days at 4 and 22 °C and 7 days at 35 °C protected from light. Excessive decomposition products in 14 days at 35 °C	1548	C
	MG, TR[a]		1.83 g	Less than 10% cytarabine loss by HPLC in 24 hr at room temperature exposed to light	1658	C
		UP	157 mg	Less than 2% loss in 48 hr by HPLC at room temperature, exposed to light and in the dark, and at 4 °C	1955	C
Invert sugar 10% in Electrolyte #1	TR	UP	3.6 g	Physically compatible	174	C
Ringer's injection		UP	3.6 g	Physically compatible	174	C
Ringer's injection, lactated	TR[a]	UP	500 mg	Potency retained for 24 hr at 5 °C	282	C
Sodium chloride 0.9%	TR[a]	UP	500 mg	Potency retained for 24 hr at 5 °C	282	C
		UP	500 mg	Chemically stable for 7 days at room temperature	174	C
	[a]	UP	8, 24, 32 g	No cytarabine loss in 7 days at room temperature or 4 or −20 °C	174	C
		UP	3.6 g	Physically compatible	174	C
	[b]	UP	1.25 and 25 g	Visually compatible with less than 6% cytarabine loss by HPLC in 28 days at 4 and 22 °C and 7 days at 35 °C protected from light. Excessive decomposition products in 14 days at 35 °C	1548	C
Sodium lactate ⅙ M		UP	3.6 g	Physically compatible	174	C
TPN #57[c]		UP	50 mg	Physically compatible with no cytarabine loss in 48 hr at 25 or 8 °C	996	C

[a]*Tested in both glass and PVC containers.*
[b]*Tested in ethylene vinyl acetate (EVA) containers.*
[c]*Refer to Appendix I for the composition of parenteral nutrition solutions. TPN indicates a 2-in-1 admixture.*

Additive Compatibility

			Cytarabine					
Drug	*Mfr*	*Conc/L*	*Mfr*	*Conc/L*	*Test Soln*	*Remarks*	*Ref*	*C/I*
Corticotropin	AR	25 units	UP	100 mg	D5W	Physically compatible for over 8 hr	174	C
Daunorubicin HCl with etoposide	RP BR	33 mg 400 mg	UP	267 mg	D5½S	Physically compatible with about 6% cytarabine loss and no loss of other drugs in 72 hr at 20 °C	1162	C
Daunorubicin HCl with etoposide	BEL SZ	15.7 mg 157 mg	UP	157 mg	D5W	Less than 10% loss of any drug in 48 hr at room temperature, exposed to light and in the dark, and at 4 °C	1955	C
Etoposide	BR	660 mg	CHI	1.2 g	D5W	Physically compatible with no subvisual haze or particle formation in 4 hr at 23 °C	1736	C
Fluorouracil	RC	250 mg	UP	400 mg	D5W	Altered UV spectra for cytarabine within 1 hr at room temperature	207	I
Gentamicin sulfate		80 mg	UP	100 mg	D5W	Physically compatible for 24 hr	174	C
		240 mg	UP	300 mg	D5W	Physically incompatible	174	I
Heparin sodium		10,000 units	UP	500 mg	NS	Haze formation	174	I
		20,000 units	UP	500 mg	D5W	Haze formation	174	I
Hydrocortisone sodium succinate	UP	500 mg	UP	360 mg	D5S, D10S	Physically compatible for 40 hr	174	C
	UP	500 mg	UP	360 mg	R, SL	Physically incompatible	174	I
Hydroxyzine HCl	LY	500 mg	UP	1 g	D5W[a]	Physically compatible for 48 hr	1198	C
Insulin, regular		40 units	UP	100 and 500 mg	D5W	Fine precipitate forms	174	I
Lincomycin HCl		1, 1.5, 2, 2.4, 3 g	UP	500 mg		Physically compatible for 48 hr	174	C
Methotrexate sodium	LE	200 mg	UP	400 mg	D5W	Physically compatible. Very little change in UV spectra in 8 hr at room temperature	207	C
Methylprednisolone sodium succinate	UP	250 mg	UP	360 mg	D5S, D10S, NS	Clear solution for 24 hr	329	C
	UP	250 mg	UP	360 mg	R, SL	Physically incompatible	329	I
Mitoxantrone HCl	LE	500 mg	UP	500 mg	D5W	Visually compatible and mitoxantrone potency by HPLC retained for 24 hr at room temperature. Cytarabine not tested	1531	C
Nafcillin sodium		4 g	UP	100 mg	D5W	Heavy crystalline precipitate forms	174	I
Ondansetron HCl	GL	30 and 300 mg	UP	200 mg	D5W[b]	Physically compatible with little or no loss of either drug by HPLC in 48 hr at 23 °C	1876	C
	GL	30 and 300 mg	UP	40 g	D5W[b]	Physically compatible with little or no loss of either drug by HPLC in 48 hr at 23 °C	1876	C
Oxacillin sodium		2 g	UP	100 mg	D5W	pH outside stability range for oxacillin	174	I
Penicillin G sodium		2 million units	UP	200 mg	D5W	pH outside stability range for penicillin	174	I

Additive Compatibility (Cont.)

Cytarabine

Drug	*Mfr*	*Conc/L*	*Mfr*	*Conc/L*	*Test Soln*	*Remarks*	*Ref*	*C/I*
Potassium chloride		80 mEq	UP	170 mg	D5S	Physically compatible for 24 hr	174	C
		100 mEq	UP	2 g	D5S	Physically compatible and chemically stable for 8 days	174	C
Sodium bicarbonate	AB	50 mEq	UP	200 mg and 1 g	D5W[c]	Physically compatible and no loss of cytarabine in 7 days at 8 and 22 °C	748	C
	AB	50 mEq	UP	200 mg	D5¼ S[c]	Physically compatible and no loss of cytarabine in 7 days at 8 and 22 °C	748	C
Vincristine sulfate	LI	4 mg	UP	16 mg	D5W	Physically compatible. No alteration of UV spectra in 8 hr at room temperature	207	C

[a]*Tested in glass containers.*
[b]*Tested in PVC containers.*
[c]*Tested in both glass and PVC containers.*

Drugs in Syringe Compatibility

Cytarabine

Drug (in syringe)	*Mfr*	*Amt*	*Mfr*	*Amt*	*Remarks*	*Ref*	*C/I*
Metoclopramide HCl	RB	10 mg/ 2 ml	UP	50 mg/ 1 ml	Physically compatible for 48 hr at room temperature	924	C
	RB	10 mg/ 2 ml	UP	50 mg/ 1 ml	Physically compatible for 48 hr at 25 °C	1167	C
	RB	160 mg/ 32 ml	UP	500 mg/ 10 ml	Physically compatible for 48 hr at 25 °C	1167	C

Y-Site Injection Compatibility (1:1 Mixture)

Cytarabine

Drug	*Mfr*	*Conc*	*Mfr*	*Conc*	*Remarks*	*Ref*	*C/I*
Allopurinol sodium	BW	3 mg/ml[b]	SCN	50 mg/ml	Tiny particles form within 4 hr	1686	I
Amifostine	USB	10 mg/ml[a]	CET	50 mg/ml	Physically compatible with no change in measured turbidity or increase in particle content in 4 hr at 23 °C	1845	C
Amphotericin B cholesteryl sulfate complex	SEQ	0.83 mg/ml[a]	BED	50 mg/ml	Gross precipitate forms	2117	I
Amsacrine	NCI	1 mg/ml[a]	QU	50 mg/ml	Physically compatible for 4 hr at room temperature under fluorescent light	1381	C
Aztreonam	SQ	40 mg/ml[a]	CET	50 mg/ml	Physically compatible with no subvisual haze or particle formation in 4 hr at 23 °C	1758	C
Cefepime HCl	BMS	20 mg/ml[a]	CET	50 mg/ml	Physically compatible with no change in measured turbidity or increase in particle content in 4 hr at 22 °C	1689	C
Chlorpromazine HCl	SKF	2 mg/ml[a]	UP	50 mg/ml	Visually compatible for 4 hr at room temperature under fluorescent light	1685	C
Cimetidine HCl	SKF	12 mg/ml[a]	UP	50 mg/ml	Visually compatible for 4 hr at room temperature under fluorescent light	1685	C

Y-Site Injection Compatibility (1:1 Mixture) (Cont.)

Cytarabine

Drug	*Mfr*	*Conc*	*Mfr*	*Conc*	*Remarks*	*Ref*	*C/I*
Cladribine	ORT	0.015[b] and 0.5[c] mg/ml	CHI	50 mg/ml	Physically compatible with no change in measured turbidity or increase in particle content in 4 hr at 23 °C	1969	C
Dexamethasone sodium phosphate	QU	1 mg/ml[a]	UP	50 mg/ml	Visually compatible for 4 hr at room temperature under fluorescent light	1685	C
Diphenhydramine HCl	PD	2 mg/ml[a]	UP	50 mg/ml	Visually compatible for 4 hr at room temperature under fluorescent light	1685	C
Doxorubicin HCl liposome injection	SEQ	0.4 mg/ml[a]	CHI	50 mg/ml	Physically compatible with little or no change in measured turbidity and no increase in particle content in 4 hr at 23 °C	2087	C
Droperidol	JN	20 μg/ml[a]	UP	50 mg/ml	Visually compatible for 4 hr at room temperature under fluorescent light	1685	C
Etoposide phosphate	BR	5 mg/ml[a]	BED	50 mg/ml	Physically compatible with no change in measured turbidity or increase in particle content in 4 hr at 23 °C	2218	C
Famotidine	MSD	2 mg/ml[a]	UP	50 mg/ml	Visually compatible for 4 hr at room temperature under fluorescent light	1685	C
Filgrastim	AMG	30 μg/ml[a]	CET	50 mg/ml	Physically compatible with no change in measured turbidity or increase in particle content in 4 hr at 22 °C	1687	C
Fludarabine phosphate	BX	1 mg/ml[a]	UP	50 mg/ml	Physically compatible for 4 hr at room temperature under fluorescent light	1439	C
Furosemide	ES	3 mg/ml[a]	UP	50 mg/ml	Visually compatible for 4 hr at room temperature under fluorescent light	1685	C
Ganciclovir sodium	SY	20 mg/ml[a]	UP	50 mg/ml	Turbidity and particles form in 30 min and become gel-like in 4 hr	1685	I
Gatifloxacin	BMS	2 mg/ml[a]	BV	50 mg/ml	Physically compatible with no change in measured haze or increase in particle content in 4 hr at 23 °C	2234	C
Gemcitabine HCl	LI	10 mg/ml[b]	BED	50 mg/ml	Physically compatible with no change in measured turbidity or increase in particle content in 4 hr at 23 °C	2226	C
Gentamicin sulfate	GNS	15 mg/ml[d]	UP	16 mg/ml[b]	Visually compatible for 24 hr at room temperature in test tubes. No precipitate found on filter from Y-site delivery	2063	C
Granisetron HCl	SKB	1 mg/ml	UP	2 mg/ml[b]	Physically compatible with little or no loss of either drug by HPLC in 4 hr at 22 °C	1883	C
	SKB	0.05 mg/ml[a]	UP	50 mg/ml	Physically compatible with no change in measured turbidity or increase in particle content in 4 hr at 23 °C	2000	C
Heparin sodium	SO	40 units/ml[a]	UP	50 mg/ml	Visually compatible for 4 hr at room temperature under fluorescent light	1685	C
Hydrocortisone sodium succinate	UP	125 mg/ml	UP	16 mg/ml[b]	Visually compatible for 24 hr at room temperature in test tubes. No precipitate found on filter from Y-site delivery	2063	C
Hydromorphone HCl	ES	0.04 mg/ml[a]	UP	50 mg/ml	Visually compatible for 4 hr at room temperature under fluorescent light	1685	C

Y-Site Injection Compatibility (1:1 Mixture) (Cont.)

			Cytarabine				
Drug	*Mfr*	*Conc*	*Mfr*	*Conc*	*Remarks*	*Ref*	*C/I*
Idarubicin HCl	AD	1 mg/ml[b]	CET	6 mg/ml[a]	Visually compatible for 24 hr at 25 °C	1525	C
Linezolid	PHU	2 mg/ml	BED	50 mg/ml	Physically compatible with no change in measured turbidity or increase in particle content in 4 hr at 23 °C	2264	C
Lorazepam	WY	0.1 mg/ml[a]	UP	50 mg/ml	Visually compatible for 4 hr at room temperature under fluorescent light	1685	C
Melphalan HCl	BW	0.1 mg/ml[b]	UP	50 mg/ml	Physically compatible with no change in measured turbidity or increase in particle content in 3 hr at 22 °C	1557	C
Methotrexate sodium		30 mg/ml	UP	0.6 mg/ml[a]	Visually compatible for 4 hr at room temperature	1788	C
Methylprednisolone sodium succinate	UP	0.5 mg/ml[a]	UP	50 mg/ml	Visually compatible for 4 hr at room temperature under fluorescent light	1685	C
	UP	5 mg/ml[a]	UP	16 mg/ml[b]	Visually compatible for 24 hr at room temperature in test tubes. No precipitate found on filter from Y-site delivery	2063	C
Metoclopramide HCl	RB	2.5 mg/ml[a]	UP	50 mg/ml	Visually compatible for 4 hr at room temperature under fluorescent light	1685	C
Morphine sulfate	ES	0.12 mg/ml[a]	UP	50 mg/ml	Visually compatible for 4 hr at room temperature under fluorescent light	1685	C
Ondansetron HCl	GL	1 mg/ml[b]	UP	50 mg/ml	Physically compatible for 4 hr at 22 °C	1365	C
Paclitaxel	NCI	1.2 mg/ml[a]		50 mg/ml	Physically compatible with no change in measured turbidity in 4 hr at 22 °C	1528	C
Piperacillin sodium–tazobactam sodium	LE	40 + 5 mg/ml[a]	SCN	50 mg/ml	Physically compatible with no change in measured turbidity or increase in particle content in 4 hr at 22 °C	1688	C
Prochlorperazine edisylate	SKF	0.5 mg/ml[a]	UP	50 mg/ml	Visually compatible for 4 hr at room temperature under fluorescent light	1685	C
Promethazine HCl	WY	2 mg/ml[a]	UP	50 mg/ml	Visually compatible for 4 hr at room temperature under fluorescent light	1685	C
Propofol	ZEN	10 mg/ml	CHI	50 mg/ml	Physically compatible for 1 hr at 23 °C with no increase in particle content	2066	C
Ranitidine HCl	GL	1 mg/ml[a]	UP	50 mg/ml	Visually compatible for 4 hr at room temperature under fluorescent light	1685	C
Sargramostim	IMM	10 µg/ml[b]	SCN	50 mg/ml	Physically compatible for 4 hr at 22 °C	1436	C
Sodium bicarbonate		1.4%	UP	0.6 mg/ml[a]	Visually compatible for 4 hr at room temperature	1788	C
Teniposide	BR	0.1 mg/ml[a]	CET	50 mg/ml	Physically compatible with no subvisual haze or particle formation in 4 hr at 23 °C	1725	C
Thiotepa	IMM[e]	1 mg/ml[a]	CET	50 mg/ml	Physically compatible with no change in measured turbidity or increase in particle content in 4 hr at 23 °C	1861	C
TNA #218 to #226[f]			BED	50 mg/ml	Visually compatible with no precipitate or emulsion damage apparent in 4 hr at 23 °C	2215	C

Y-Site Injection Compatibility (1:1 Mixture) (Cont.)

Cytarabine

Drug	*Mfr*	*Conc*	*Mfr*	*Conc*	*Remarks*	*Ref*	*C/I*
TPN #212 to #215[f]			CHI	50 mg/ml	Substantial loss of natural subvisual turbidity occurs immediately	2109	I
Vinorelbine tartrate	BW	1 mg/ml[b]	CET	50 mg/ml	Physically compatible with no change in measured turbidity or increase in particle content in 4 hr at 22 °C	1558	C

[a]*Tested in dextrose 5% in water.*
[b]*Tested in sodium chloride 0.9%.*
[c]*Tested in bacteriostatic sodium chloride 0.9% preserved with benzyl alcohol 0.9%.*
[d]*Tested in sodium chloride 0.45%.*
[e]*Lyophilized formulation tested.*
[f]*Refer to Appendix I for the composition of parenteral nutrition solutions. TNA indicates a 3-in-1 admixture, and TPN indicates a 2-in-1 admixture.*

Additional Compatibility Information

Infusion Solutions — At a concentration of 500 mg/L, cytarabine is stable for eight days at room temperature in dextrose 5% in water, sodium chloride 0.9%, and water for injection. (1-8/00; 1-2/98; 4)

Another report stated that cytarabine 0.5 to 5 mg/ml in dextrose 5% in water, sodium chloride 0.9%, Ringer's injection, and sterile water for injection exhibited less than a 10% loss in 14 days at room temperature. (1379)

Dacarbazine — No alteration in the ultraviolet/visible spectra was observed when dacarbazine was combined in solution with cytarabine. (492)

Aluminum — Ogawa et al. reported that immersion of a needle with an aluminum component in cytarabine (Upjohn) 20 mg/ml resulted in no visually apparent reaction after seven days at 24 °C. (988)

Other Information

Microbial Growth — Cytarabine (Quad) 12.5 mg/ml in sodium chloride 0.9% did not inhibit the growth of deliberately inoculated *Staphylococcus epidermidis* (10^6 to 10^7 CFU/ml) during 21 days at 35 °C (representing near body temperature). At a concentration of 50 mg/ml in sodium chloride 0.9%, however, viable *S. epidermidis* was reduced over the 21 days but not eliminated. (1659)

DACARBAZINE
AHFS 10:00

Products — Dacarbazine is available in vials containing 100 and 200 mg of drug along with anhydrous citric acid and mannitol. Reconstitute the 100- and 200-mg vials with 9.9 and 19.7 ml of sterile water for injection, respectively, to yield solutions containing 10 mg/ml of dacarbazine. (2)

pH — From 3 to 4. (2)

Osmolality — Dacarbazine 10 mg/ml in sterile water for injection has an osmolality of 109 mOsm/kg. (1689)

Density — Dacarbazine (Miles) reconstituted with sterile water for injection to a concentration of 10 mg/ml has a solution density of 1.00 g/ml. (2041; 2248)

Trade Name(s) — DTIC-Dome.

Administration — Dacarbazine is administered as a direct intravenous injection over one minute and as an intravenous infusion in up to 250 ml of dextrose 5% in water or sodium chloride 0.9% over 15 to 30 minutes. (4) Extravasation may result in severe pain and tissue damage. (2; 4; 377)

Stability — Intact vials of dacarbazine should be stored at 2 to 8 °C and protected from light. (2; 4) However, dacarbazine in intact vials stored at controlled room temperature has been stated to be stable for periods of four weeks (1239; 1433) to three months. (1433) Bayer also recommends storage of reconstituted solutions for up to eight hours at normal room temperatures and light or up to 72 hours at 4 °C. (2) However, it has been reported that solutions are stable for at least 24 hours at room temperature (1% decomposition) and at least 96 hours under refrigeration (less than 1% decomposition) when protected from light. (285) A change in color from pale yellow or ivory to pink or red is a sign of decomposition. (4; 285; 1093)

Dacarbazine, reconstituted according to the manufacturer's instructions, was cultured with human lymphoblasts to determine whether its cytotoxic activity was retained. The solution retained cytotoxicity for 24 hours at room temperature. (1575)

Light Effects — Administration of dacarbazine in a room illuminated only with a red photographic light apparently reduced the incidence of disagreeable side effects. The authors attributed this result to a reduced amount of photodegradation of dacarbazine. (469)

Kirk reported the effects of daylight and fluorescent light on dacarbazine (Bayer) 4 mg/ml in sodium chloride 0.9%. Exposure to direct sunlight resulted in up to a 12% loss in 30 minutes, and a pink color formed in 35 to 40 minutes. Exposure to indirect daylight resulted in less than a 2% loss in 30 minutes. Solutions protected from light or exposed to fluorescent light lost about 4% of their dacarbazine in 24 hours. (1248)

The photostability of dacarbazine has been shown to increase with the addition of reduced glutathione at about 5 mg/100 ml. (1829)

Elastomeric Reservoir Pumps— Dacarbazine 7.3 mg/ml in combination with doxorubicin HCl 0.63 mg/ml in dextrose 5% in water in Infusor elastomeric reservoir pumps has been stated by the pump manufacturer to be stable for five days frozen and refrigerated. (31)

Compatibility Information

Solution Compatibility

Dacarbazine

Solution	*Mfr*	*Mfr*	*Conc/L*	*Remarks*	*Ref*	*C/I*
Dextrose 5% in water	[a]		1.7 g	Less than 10% loss in 24 hr at room temperature	519	C
	MG, TR[b]		1.7 g	Less than 10% loss by HPLC in 24 hr at room temperature exposed to light	1658	C
	BA[c]	MI	1 and 3 g	Physically compatible with 4% loss by HPLC in 8 hr and 10 to 15% loss in 24 hr at 23 °C	1876	I

[a]*Tested in both glass and PVC containers.*
[b]*Tested in glass, PVC, and polyolefin containers.*
[c]*Tested in PVC containers.*

Additive Compatibility

Dacarbazine

Drug	*Mfr*	*Conc/L*	*Mfr*	*Conc/L*	*Test Soln*	*Remarks*	*Ref*	*C/I*
Ondansetron HCl	GL	30 and 300 mg	MI	1 g	D5W[a]	Physically compatible with little or no loss of ondansetron by HPLC in 48 hr at 23 °C. 8 to 12% dacarbazine loss in 24 hr and 20% loss in 48 hr at 23 °C	1876	C
	GL	30 and 300 mg	MI	3 g	D5W[a]	Physically compatible with little or no loss of ondansetron by HPLC in 48 hr at 23 °C. 8% dacarbazine loss in 24 hr and 15% loss in 48 hr at 23 °C	1876	C
Ondansetron HCl with doxorubicin HCl	GL AD	640 mg 800 mg	LY	8 g	D5W[a]	Visually compatible with >90% ondansetron and doxorubicin potency by HPLC over 24 hr at 30 °C and after 7 days at 4 °C followed by 24 hr at 30 °C. Dacarbazine stable for 8 hr but up to 13% loss in 24 hr	2092	I
Ondansetron HCl with doxorubicin HCl	GL AD	640 mg 1.5 g	LY	20 g	D5W[a]	Visually compatible with >90% potency of all drugs by HPLC over 24 hr at 30 °C and after 7 days at 4 °C followed by 24 hr at 30 °C	2092	C
Ondansetron HCl with doxorubicin HCl	GL AD	640 mg 800 mg	LY	8 g	D5W[b]	Visually compatible with >90% potency of all drugs by HPLC over 24 hr at 30 °C and after 7 days at 4 °C followed by 24 hr at 30 °C	2092	C
Ondansetron HCl with doxorubicin HCl	GL AD	640 mg 1.5 g	LY	20 g	D5W[b]	Visually compatible with >90% potency of all drugs by HPLC over 24 hr at 30 °C and after 7 days at 4 °C followed by 24 hr at 30 °C	2092	C

[a]*Tested in PVC containers.*
[b]*Tested in polyisoprene infusion pump reservoirs.*

Y-Site Injection Compatibility (1:1 Mixture)

			Dacarbazine				
Drug	*Mfr*	*Conc*	*Mfr*	*Conc*	*Remarks*	*Ref*	*C/I*
Allopurinol sodium	BW	3 mg/ml[b]	MI	4 mg/ml[b]	Small particles form within 1 hr and become large pink pellets in 24 hr	1686	I
Amifostine	USB	10 mg/ml[a]	MI	4 mg/ml[a]	Physically compatible with no change in measured turbidity or increase in particle content in 4 hr at 23 °C	1845	C
Aztreonam	SQ	40 mg/ml[a]	MI	4 mg/ml[a]	Physically compatible with no subvisual haze or particle formation in 4 hr at 23 °C	1758	C
Cefepime HCl	BMS	20 mg/ml[a]	MI	4 mg/ml[a]	Cloudy solution forms immediately and develops flocculent precipitate in 4 hr	1689	I
Doxorubicin HCl liposome injection	SEQ	0.4 mg/ml[a]	MI	4 mg/ml[a]	Physically compatible with little or no change in measured turbidity or increase in particle content in 4 hr at 23 °C	2087	C
Etoposide phosphate	BR	5 mg/ml[a]	MI	4 mg/ml[a]	Physically compatible with no change in measured turbidity or increase in particle content in 4 hr at 23 °C	2218	C
Filgrastim	AMG	30 μg/ml[a]	MI	4 mg/ml[a]	Physically compatible with no change in measured turbidity or increase in particle content in 4 hr at 22 °C	1687	C
Fludarabine phosphate	BX	1 mg/ml[a]	MI	4 mg/ml[a]	Physically compatible for 4 hr at room temperature under fluorescent light	1439	C
Granisetron HCl	SKB	1 mg/ml	MI	1.7 mg/ml[b]	Physically compatible with little or no loss of either drug by HPLC in 4 hr at 22 °C	1883	C
Heparin sodium	WY	100 units/ml	MI	25 mg/ml[b]	White flocculent precipitate forms immediately[c]	1158	I
	WY	100 units/ml	MI	10 mg/ml[b]	No observable precipitation[c]	1158	C
Melphalan HCl	BW	0.1 mg/ml[b]	MI	4 mg/ml[b]	Physically compatible with no change in measured turbidity or increase in particle content in 3 hr at 22 °C	1557	C
Ondansetron HCl	GL	1 mg/ml[b]	MI	4 mg/ml[a]	Physically compatible for 4 hr at 22 °C	1365	C
Paclitaxel	NCI	1.2 mg/ml[a]	MI	4 mg/ml[a]	Physically compatible with no change in measured turbidity in 4 hr at 22 °C	1556	C
Piperacillin sodium–tazobactam sodium	LE	40 + 5 mg/ml[a]	MI	4 mg/ml[a]	Turbidity and particles form immediately and increase over 4 hr	1688	I
Sargramostim	IMM	10 μg/ml[b]	MI	4 mg/ml[b]	Physically compatible for 4 hr at 22 °C	1436	C
Teniposide	BR	0.1 mg/ml[a]	MI	4 mg/ml[a]	Physically compatible with no subvisual haze or particle formation in 4 hr at 23 °C	1725	C
Thiotepa	IMM[d]	1 mg/ml[a]	MI	4 mg/ml[a]	Physically compatible with no change in measured turbidity or increase in particle content in 4 hr at 23 °C	1861	C
Vinorelbine tartrate	BW	1 mg/ml[b]	MI	4 mg/ml[b]	Physically compatible with no change in measured turbidity or increase in particle content in 4 hr at 22 °C	1558	C

[a] *Tested in dextrose 5% in water.*
[b] *Tested in sodium chloride 0.9%.*
[c] *Dacarbazine in intravenous tubing flushed with heparin sodium.*
[d] *Lyophilized formulation tested.*

Additional Compatibility Information

Infusion Solutions — Dextrose 5% in water and sodium chloride 0.9% have been recommended as diluents for dacarbazine intravenous infusions. (2; 4; 285) The manufacturer indicates that dacarbazine is stable in intravenous infusion solutions for eight hours under normal room conditions and 24 hours when refrigerated at 4 °C. (2) However, other reports indicated that the drug is stable for 24 hours. (285; 519; 1658) One report noted that if the solutions stored at room temperature were not protected from light, they exhibited 5% decomposition in 24 hours. (285) Also see Compatibility Information.

Cytotoxic Agents — No alteration in the ultraviolet/visible spectra was observed when dacarbazine was combined in solution with the following cytotoxic agents (492):

Bleomycin sulfate
Carmustine
Cyclophosphamide
Cytarabine
Dactinomycin
Doxorubicin HCl
Fluorouracil
Mercaptopurine sodium
Methotrexate sodium
Vinblastine sulfate

Hydrocortisone — Dacarbazine is stated to form a pink precipitate immediately when mixed with hydrocortisone sodium succinate (Upjohn). However, a similar precipitate was not noted when mixed with hydrocortisone sodium phosphate or lidocaine HCl 1 or 2%. (524)

Cysteine — Dacarbazine has been stated to couple with the thiol group of L-cysteine in the presence of light to yield an unstable azothioether. (492)

Aluminum — Ogawa et al. reported that immersion of a needle with an aluminum component in dacarbazine (Miles) 10 mg/ml resulted in no visually apparent unexpected reaction after seven days at 24 °C. (988)

Other Information

Inactivation — In the event of spills or leaks, the manufacturer recommends the use of sulfuric acid 10% in contact for 24 hours to inactivate dacarbazine. (1200)

DACTINOMYCIN (ACTINOMYCIN D) AHFS 10:00

Products — Dactinomycin is available in vials containing 0.5 mg of drug with mannitol 20 mg. Reconstitute with 1.1 ml of sterile water for injection *without* preservatives to yield a gold-colored solution containing 0.5 mg/ml of dactinomycin. (2) Other solvents, especially those containing preservatives such as bacteriostatic water for injection (benzyl alcohol or parabens), may cause precipitation. (2; 4)

pH — The pH of the reconstituted solution is 5.5 to 7. (4)

Osmolality — Dactinomycin 0.5 mg/ml in sterile water for injection has an osmolality of 189 mOsm/kg. (1689)

Density — Dactinomycin (Merck) reconstituted with sterile water for injection to a concentration of 0.5 mg/ml has a solution density of 1.00 g/ml. (2041; 2248)

Trade Name(s) — Cosmegen.

Administration — Dactinomycin may be administered by direct intravenous injection, intravenous infusion, and isolation perfusion technique. It must *not* be given intramuscularly or subcutaneously. (2; 4) Extravasation should be avoided because of possible corrosion of soft tissue. (2; 4; 377) An inline cellulose ester membrane filter should not be used for administration of dactinomycin. See Filtration below.

Stability — Intact vials of dactinomycin should be stored at controlled room temperature and protected from excessive heat and humidity. (2) The clear, gold-colored, reconstituted solution is stable at room temperature; however, this solution contains no preservative so it has been suggested that unused portions of the injection be discarded. (2; 4) The drug is reported to be most stable at pH 5 to 7. (1369) A 30-μg/ml concentration at this pH range exhibits about a 2 to 3% loss in six hours at 25 °C; at pH 9, an 80% loss occurs under these conditions. (51)

Dactinomycin, reconstituted according to the manufacturer's instructions, was cultured with human lymphoblasts to determine whether its cytotoxic activity was retained. The solution retained cytotoxicity for 24 hours at 4 °C and room temperature. (1575)

Filtration — Dactinomycin may exhibit considerable binding to cellulose acetate/nitrate (Millex OR) and polytetrafluoroethylene (Millex GV) filters. (1249)

Dactinomycin (MSD) 0.5 mg/L in dextrose 5% in water, sodium chloride 0.9%, and Ringer's injection, lactated, was filtered over 12 hours through a 5-μm stainless steel depth filter (Argyle Filter Connector), a 0.22-μm cellulose ester membrane filter (Ivex-2 Filter Set), and a 0.22-μm polycarbonate membrane filter (In-Sure Filter Set). No significant reduction in potency due to binding was observed with the stainless steel filter. Approximately 25% of the drug delivered through the polycarbonate filter in the first 10 ml of solution was bound, but binding decreased rapidly thereafter, resulting in only 0.3% of the total delivered dose in 12 hours being bound. (320)

In contrast, filtration through the cellulose ester filter resulted in the binding of about 95 to 99% of the drug in the first 10 ml, with the total cumulative amount of drug bound in 12 hours being 13%. Approximately half of the bound drug was released by rinsing three times with 100 ml of the same intravenous solutions used in the admixtures. (320)

A filter material specially treated with a proprietary agent was evaluated for a reduction in dactinomycin binding. Dactinomycin (MSD) 0.5 mg/L in dextrose 5% in water and sodium chloride 0.9% was run at a rate of 2 ml/min through an administration set with a treated 0.22-µm cellulose ester inline filter. Cumulative dactinomycin losses of less than 3% occurred from both solutions, compared to much higher losses previously reported for untreated cellulose ester filter material. Furthermore, equilibrium binding studies showed a sixfold reduction in binding from both solutions. (904) All Abbott Ivex integral filter and extension sets currently use this treated filter material. (1074)

In another study, dactinomycin 0.5 mg/1 ml was injected as a bolus through a 0.2-µm nylon, air-eliminating, filter (Ultipor, Pall) to evaluate the effect of filtration on simulated intravenous push delivery. Spectrophotometric evaluation showed that about 87% of the drug was delivered through the filter after flushing with 10 ml of sodium chloride 0.9%. (809)

Dactinomycin 4 to 50 µg/ml exhibited a greater than 95% loss due to sorption to cellulose nitrate/cellulose acetate ester filters (Millex OR) and a 50 to 60% loss with polytetrafluoroethylene filters (Millex FG). (1415; 1416)

Compatibility Information

Solution Compatibility

Dactinomycin

Solution	*Mfr*	*Mfr*	*Conc/L*	*Remarks*	*Ref*	*C/I*
Dextrose 5% in water	[a]	MSD	9.8 mg	Less than 10% loss in 24 hr at room temperature	519	C
	MG, TR[a]	MSD	9.8 mg	Less than 10% loss by HPLC in 24 hr at room temperature exposed to light	1658	C
	MG, TR[b]	MSD	7.5 mg	Less than 10% loss by HPLC in 24 hr at room temperature exposed to light	1658	C

[a]*Tested in both glass and PVC containers.*
[b]*Tested in both glass and polyolefin containers.*

Y-Site Injection Compatibility (1:1 Mixture)

Dactinomycin

Drug	*Mfr*	*Conc*	*Mfr*	*Conc*	*Remarks*	*Ref*	*C/I*
Allopurinol sodium	BW	3 mg/ml[b]	MSD	0.01 mg/ml[b]	Physically compatible with no change in measured turbidity or increase in particle content in 4 hr at 22 °C	1686	C
Amifostine	USB	10 mg/ml[a]	ME	0.01 mg/ml[a]	Physically compatible with no change in measured turbidity or increase in particle content in 4 hr at 23 °C	1845	C
Aztreonam	SQ	40 mg/ml[a]	ME	0.01 mg/ml[a]	Physically compatible with no subvisual haze or particle formation in 4 hr at 23 °C	1758	C
Cefepime HCl	BMS	20 mg/ml[a]	MSD	0.01 mg/ml[a]	Physically compatible with no change in measured turbidity or increase in particle content in 4 hr at 22 °C	1689	C
Etoposide phosphate	BR	5 mg/ml[a]	ME	0.01 mg/ml[a]	Physically compatible with no change in measured turbidity or increase in particle content in 4 hr at 23 °C	2218	C
Filgrastim	AMG	30 µg/ml[a]	MSD	0.01 mg/ml[a]	Particles and filaments form immediately	1687	I
Fludarabine phosphate	BX	1 mg/ml[a]	MSD	0.01 mg/ml[a]	Physically compatible for 4 hr at room temperature under fluorescent light	1439	C
Gemcitabine HCl	LI	10 mg/ml[b]	ME	0.01 mg/ml[b]	Physically compatible with no change in measured turbidity or increase in particle content in 4 hr at 23 °C	2226	C
Granisetron HCl	SKB	0.05 mg/ml[a]	ME	0.01 mg/ml[a]	Physically compatible with no change in measured turbidity or increase in particle content in 4 hr at 23 °C	2000	C

Y-Site Injection Compatibility (1:1 Mixture) (Cont.)

Drug	Mfr	Conc	Dactinomycin Mfr	Dactinomycin Conc	Remarks	Ref	C/I
Melphalan HCl	BW	0.1 mg/ml[b]	MSD	0.01 mg/ml[b]	Physically compatible with no change in measured turbidity or increase in particle content in 3 hr at 22 °C	1557	C
Ondansetron HCl	GL	1 mg/ml[b]	MSD	0.01 mg/ml[a]	Physically compatible for 4 hr at 22 °C	1365	C
Sargramostim	IMM	10 μg/ml[b]	MSD	0.01 mg/ml[b]	Physically compatible for 4 hr at 22 °C	1436	C
Teniposide	BR	0.1 mg/ml[a]	MSD	0.01 mg/ml[a]	Physically compatible with no subvisual haze or particle formation in 4 hr at 23 °C	1725	C
Thiotepa	IMM[c]	1 mg/ml[a]	ME	0.01 mg/ml[a]	Physically compatible with no change in measured turbidity or increase in particle content in 4 hr at 23 °C	1861	C
Vinorelbine tartrate	BW	1 mg/ml[b]	MSD	0.01 mg/ml[b]	Physically compatible with no change in measured turbidity or increase in particle content in 4 hr at 22 °C	1558	C

[a]*Tested in dextrose 5% in water.*
[b]*Tested in sodium chloride 0.9%.*
[c]*Lyophilized formulation tested.*

Additional Compatibility Information

Infusion Solutions — Dextrose 5% in water and sodium chloride 0.9% have been suggested as diluents for the reconstituted drug. It also may be injected into the tubing of a running infusion of these solutions. (2; 4)

Dacarbazine — No alteration in the ultraviolet/visible spectra was observed when dacarbazine was combined in solution with dactinomycin. (492)

Other Information

Inactivation — In the event of spills or leaks, MSD recommends the use of trisodium phosphate 5% to inactivate dactinomycin. (1200)

DALTEPARIN SODIUM
AHFS 20:12.04

Products — Dalteparin is available in 9.5-ml multiple-dose vials, providing 10,000 anti-Factor Xa units/ml (64 mg/ml). It is also available in 0.2-ml prefilled syringes, providing 2500 anti-Factor Xa units per syringe (16 mg/syringe) and 5000 anti-Factor Xa units per syringe (32 mg/syringe). Also present in the products are sodium chloride and water for injection. The multiple-dose vials contain benzyl alcohol 14 mg/ml as a preservative. (2)

pH — From 5 to 7.5. (2)

Units — Each milligram of dalteparin sodium is equivalent to 156.25 anti-Factor Xa units. (4)

Trade Name(s) — Fragmin.

Administration — Dalteparin is administered by deep subcutaneous injection to patients who are seated or lying down. It must not be administered by intramuscular injection.

Stability — Intact containers of dalteparin sodium should be stored at controlled room temperature. (2)

Syringes — Dalteparin sodium (Pharmacia & Upjohn) 10,000 units/ml was packaged in 1-ml tuberculin syringes (Becton-Dickinson), apparently with the needles left attached, and stored at room temperature of about 25 °C exposed to fluorescent light and under refrigeration at about 4 °C for 15 days. Chromogenic assays of the dalteparin activity were variable, but there was no indication of substantial loss of activity. Dalteparin activity remained at 95% or above of the initial level throughout. HPLC analysis of the benzyl alcohol preservative demonstrated an 8% loss in 10 days and a 10% loss in 15 days in the room temperature samples. Benzyl alcohol losses from refrigerated samples were minimal. Unfortunately, many syringes became nonfunctional during the study with the fluid unable to be expressed through the attached needles, thus necessitating removal of the needles. The cause of this needle blockage was not addressed. (2323) However, evaporation from the needle tip opening, leaving dried material that blocked the fluid flow, is a possibility.

DAUNORUBICIN HCL
AHFS 10:00

Products — Daunorubicin HCl is available in vials containing daunorubicin base 20 mg (21.4 mg as the hydrochloride salt) with mannitol 100 mg. Reconstitute with 4 ml of sterile water for injection to yield a solution containing 5 mg/ml of daunorubicin. (2)

pH — From 4.5 to 6.5. (2; 4)

Osmolality — Daunorubicin HCl 5 mg/ml in sterile water for injection has an osmolality of 141 mOsm/kg. (1689)

Trade Name(s) — Cerubidine.

Administration — Daunorubicin HCl is administered intravenously *only*. Extravasation will result in severe tissue damage. The dose may be diluted with 10 to 15 ml of sodium chloride 0.9% and injected over two or three minutes into the sidearm or tubing of a rapidly flowing intravenous infusion of dextrose 5% in water or sodium chloride 0.9%. (2; 4) Alternatively, the dose has been diluted in 100 ml and infused over 30 to 45 minutes. (4)

Stability — Intact vials of daunorubicin HCl should be stored at controlled room temperature protected from light. The manufacturer states that the reconstituted solution is stable for 24 hours at controlled room temperature and 48 hours under refrigeration. (2; 4)

Daunorubicin HCl, reconstituted according to the manufacturer's instructions, was cultured with human lymphoblasts to determine whether its cytotoxic activity was retained. The solution retained cytotoxicity for 24 hours at 4 °C and room temperature. (1575)

pH Effects — Daunorubicin HCl appears to have pH-dependent stability in solution. (526; 1250) Solutions of daunorubicin HCl are less stable at pH values above 8. Decomposition occurs, as indicated by a color change from red to blue-purple. The drug becomes progressively more stable as the pH of drug–infusion solution admixtures becomes more acidic from 7.4 down to 4.5. (526) The pH range of maximum stability was reported to be approximately 4.5 to 5.5. Below pH 4, decomposition increases substantially. (1207)

Freezing Solutions — Wood et al. reported that daunorubicin HCl (Rhone-Poulenc) 100 mg/L in sodium chloride 0.9% and dextrose 5% in water in PVC bags (Travenol) was stable, exhibiting little or no loss by HPLC analysis after 43 days stored at −20 °C, even when subjected to 11 freeze-thaw repetitions. (1460)

Light Effects — Protection of the reconstituted solution from sunlight has been recommended. (2) Photoinactivation of daunorubicin HCl exposed to radiation of 366 nm and fluorescent light has been reported. (1094) One source indicates that significant losses due to light exposure for a sufficient time may occur in concentrations below 100 μg/ml. However, in clinical concentrations at or above 500 μg/ml, no special light protection is required. (1369)

Syringes — Daunorubicin HCl (Rhone-Poulenc) 2 mg/ml repackaged in polypropylene syringes exhibited little or no loss by HPLC analysis after storage for 43 days at 4 °C. (1460)

Sorption — Daunorubicin HCl (Roger Bellon) 16 μg/ml in dextrose 5% in water and sodium chloride 0.9% in PVC containers was infused through PVC administration sets at 21 ml/hr over 24 hours at 22 °C while exposed to light. Fluctuations in the delivered concentration by HPLC were relatively minor, with no evidence of sorption. (1700)

Wood et al. reported that daunorubicin HCl was minimally adsorbed to PVC bags. After eight days of storage, HPLC analysis of solutions containing daunorubicin HCl 100 μg/ml in sodium chloride 0.9% and dextrose 5% in water stored at 4 and 25 °C indicated losses of up to 5%. At concentrations used in clinical practice, sorptive losses during storage and delivery are negligible. (1460)

In an admixture composed of cytarabine (Upjohn) 0.157 mg/ml, daunorubicin HCl (Bellon) 15.7 μg/ml, and etoposide (Sandoz) 0.157 mg/ml in dextrose 5% in water, little or no loss of the drugs due to sorption occurred when delivered through PVC, PVC with polyethylene-lined sets, and a silicone central catheter. (1955)

Filtration — Daunorubicin HCl (May & Baker) 10 mg/100 ml in sodium chloride 0.9% in a burette was filtered through a nylon 0.2-μm filter (ELD96LL, Pall). Little drug loss due to sorption was found spectrophotometrically. (1568)

Daunorubicin HCl binds only slightly to cellulose acetate/nitrate (Millex OR) and polytetrafluoroethylene (Millex FG) filters. (1249; 1415; 1416)

Compatibility Information

Solution Compatibility

Daunorubicin HCl

Solution	*Mfr*	*Mfr*	*Conc/L*	*Remarks*	*Ref*	*C/I*
Dextrose 3.3% in sodium chloride 0.3%		RP	100 mg	Drug loss of 5% or less in 4 weeks at 25 °C in the dark	1007	C
Dextrose 5% in water	AB	NCI	20 mg	Physically compatible with 2% decomposition in 24 hr at 21 °C	526	C
		RP	100 mg	Drug loss of 5% or less in 4 weeks at 25 °C in the dark	1007	C
	[a]	BEL	16 mg	No loss by HPLC in 7 days at 4 °C protected from light	1700	C
	TR[a]	RP	100 mg	7% or less loss by HPLC in 43 days at 4 and 25 °C in the dark	1460	C

Solution Compatibility (Cont.)

Daunorubicin HCl

Solution	*Mfr*	*Mfr*	*Conc/L*	*Remarks*	*Ref*	*C/I*
		BEL	15.7 mg	5 to 8% loss by spectroscopy in 48 hr at room temperature, exposed to light and in the dark, and at 4 °C	1955	C
Normosol R, pH 7.4	AB	NCI	20 mg	Physically compatible with 5% decomposition in 24 hr at 21 °C	526	C
Ringer's injection, lactated	AB	NCI	20 mg	Physically compatible with 5% decomposition in 24 hr at 21 °C	526	C
		RP	100 mg	Drug loss of 5% or less in 4 weeks at 25 °C in the dark	1007	C
Sodium chloride 0.9%	AB	NCI	20 mg	Physically compatible with 3% decomposition in 24 hr at 21 °C	526	C
		RP	100 mg	Drug loss of 5% or less in 4 weeks at 25 °C in the dark	1007	C
	[a]	BEL	16 mg	No loss by HPLC in 7 days at 4 °C protected from light	1700	C
	TR[a]	RP	100 mg	10% or less loss by HPLC in 43 days at 4 and 25 °C in the dark	1460	C

[a]*Tested in PVC containers.*

Additive Compatibility

Daunorubicin HCl

Drug	*Mfr*	*Conc/L*	*Mfr*	*Conc/L*	*Test Soln*	*Remarks*	*Ref*	*C/I*
Cytarabine with etoposide	UP BR	267 mg 400 mg	RP	33 mg	D5½S	Physically compatible with about 6% cytarabine loss and no loss of other drugs in 72 hr at 20 °C	1162	C
Cytarabine with etoposide	UP SZ	157 mg 157 mg	BEL	15.7 mg	D5W	Less than 10% loss of any drug in 48 hr at room temperature, exposed to light and in the dark, and at 4 °C	1955	C
Dexamethasone sodium phosphate						Immediate milky precipitate	524	I
Heparin sodium	UP	4000 units	FA	200 mg	D5W	Physically incompatible	15	I
Hydrocortisone sodium succinate	UP	500 mg	FA	200 mg	D5W	Physically compatible	15	C

Y-Site Injection Compatibility (1:1 Mixture)

Daunorubicin HCl

Drug	*Mfr*	*Conc*	*Mfr*	*Conc*	*Remarks*	*Ref*	*C/I*
Allopurinol sodium	BW	3 mg/ml[b]	WY	1 mg/ml[b]	Reddish-purple color and haze form immediately. Reddish-brown particles form within 1 hr	1686	I
Amifostine	USB	10 mg/ml[a]	WY	1 mg/ml[a]	Physically compatible with no change in measured turbidity or increase in particle content in 4 hr at 23 °C	1845	C
Aztreonam	SQ	40 mg/ml[a]	WY	1 mg/ml[a]	Haze forms immediately	1758	I
Cefepime HCl	BMS	20 mg/ml[a]	WY	1 mg/ml[a]	Haze forms immediately and becomes flocculent precipitate in 4 hr	1689	I

Y-Site Injection Compatibility (1:1 Mixture) (Cont.)

Drug	Mfr	Conc	Daunorubicin HCl Mfr	Daunorubicin HCl Conc	Remarks	Ref	C/I
Etoposide phosphate	BR	5 mg/ml[a]	BED	1 mg/ml[a]	Physically compatible with no change in measured turbidity or increase in particle content in 4 hr at 23 °C	2218	C
Filgrastim	AMG	30 µg/ml[a]	WY	1 mg/ml[a]	Physically compatible with no change in measured turbidity or increase in particle content in 4 hr at 22 °C	1687	C
Fludarabine phosphate	BX	1 mg/ml[a]	WY	2 mg/ml[a]	Slight haze, visible under high intensity light, forms in 4 hr at room temperature	1439	I
Gemcitabine HCl	LI	10 mg/ml[b]	BED	1 mg/ml[b]	Physically compatible with no change in measured turbidity or increase in particle content in 4 hr at 23 °C	2226	C
Granisetron HCl	SKB	0.05 mg/ml[a]	CHI	1 mg/ml[a]	Physically compatible with no change in measured turbidity or increase in particle content in 4 hr at 23 °C	2000	C
Melphalan HCl	BW	0.1 mg/ml[b]	WY	1 mg/ml[b]	Physically compatible with little change in measured turbidity or increase in particle content in 3 hr at 22 °C	1557	C
Methotrexate sodium		30 mg/ml	BEL	0.52 mg/ml[a]	Visually compatible for 4 hr at room temperature	1788	C
Ondansetron HCl	GL	1 mg/ml[b]	WY	2 mg/ml[a]	Physically compatible for 4 hr at 22 °C	1365	C
Piperacillin sodium–tazobactam sodium	LE	40 + 5 mg/ml[a]	WY	1 mg/ml[a]	Turbidity increases immediately	1688	I
Sodium bicarbonate		1.4%	BEL	0.52 mg/ml[a]	Visually compatible for 4 hr at room temperature	1788	C
Teniposide	BR	0.1 mg/ml[a]	WY	1 mg/ml[a]	Physically compatible with no subvisual haze or particle formation in 4 hr at 23 °C	1725	C
Thiotepa	IMM[c]	1 mg/ml[a]	WY	1 mg/ml[a]	Physically compatible with no change in measured turbidity or increase in particle content in 4 hr at 23 °C	1861	C
Vinorelbine tartrate	BW	1 mg/ml[b]	WY	1 mg/ml[b]	Physically compatible with little change in measured turbidity or increase in particle content in 4 hr at 22 °C	1558	C

[a]*Tested in dextrose 5% in water.*
[b]*Tested in sodium chloride 0.9%.*
[c]*Lyophilized formulation tested.*

Additional Compatibility Information

Other Drugs — The manufacturer recommends that no other drugs be mixed with daunorubicin HCl. (2)

Aluminum — Ogawa et al. reported that immersion of a needle with an aluminum component in daunorubicin HCl (Ives) 5 mg/ml resulted in a darkening of the solution, with black patches forming on the aluminum in 12 to 24 hours at 24 °C with protection from light. (988)

Other Information

Inactivation — In the event of spills or leaks, Wyeth-Ayerst recommends the use of sodium hypochlorite 5% (household bleach) until a colorless liquid results to inactivate daunorubicin HCl. (1200)

DEFEROXAMINE MESYLATE
AHFS 64:00

Products — Deferoxamine mesylate is available in vials containing 500 mg and 2 g of sterile drug in dry form. Reconstitute the 500-mg vial with 5 or 2 ml of sterile water for injection to yield a 100- or 250-mg/ml solution, respectively. Reconstitute the 2-g vial with 20 or 8 ml of sterile water for injection to yield a 100- or 250-mg/ml solution, respectively. (2)

Tonicity — Reconstituted deferoxamine 100 mg/ml is isotonic. (2)

Trade Name(s) — Desferal.

Administration — Deferoxamine mesylate is administered by intramuscular injection, by slow intravenous infusion after dilution at a rate not exceeding 15 mg/kg/hr, and by subcutaneous infusion using a portable infusion control device. (2)

Stability — Store the intact vials at temperatures not exceeding 25 °C. Deferoxamine mesylate is a white to off-white powder that forms a clear colorless to yellow solution when reconstituted with sterile water for injection. The manufacturer states that reconstitution with other diluents may result in precipitation. Turbid solutions should not be used. The reconstituted solution is stable for one week at room temperature when protected from light. The solution should not be refrigerated. (2; 4)

For intravenous infusion, sodium chloride 0.9%, dextrose 5% in water, or lactated Ringer's injection are recommended for use as diluents. (2)

Syringes — Deferoxamine mesylate (Ciba-Geigy) 250 mg/ml in sterile water for injection was packaged as 3 ml in 10-ml polypropylene infusion pump syringes (Pharmacia Deltec). Little or no loss by HPLC analysis occurred during 14 days of storage at 30 °C. (1967)

Ambulatory Pumps — Deferoxamine mesylate stability was evaluated at concentrations of 210, 285, and 370 mg/ml in sterile water for injection in PVC infusion cassette reservoirs (Pharmacia Deltec) stored at 20 to 23 °C. HPLC analysis of the drug content was inconclusive because of an inordinate degree of assay variation. However, a white precipitate formed in varying time periods, depending on the concentration. Higher concentrations precipitated more rapidly than lower concentrations. In the 370-mg/ml concentration, precipitation was observed in as little as one day while the 285- and 210-mg/ml concentrations developed precipitation in 9 and 17 days, respectively. This study's inordinate degree of assay variability coupled with the propensity for precipitation preclude a reasonable determination of stability for these high concentrations of deferoxamine mesylate. (672)

Elastomeric Reservoir Pumps — Deferoxamine mesylate (Ciba-Geigy) 5 mg/ml in both dextrose 5% in water and sodium chloride 0.9% was evaluated for binding potential to natural rubber elastomeric reservoirs (Baxter). No binding was found after storage for two weeks at 35 °C with gentle agitation. (2014)

Deferoxamine mesylate 5 mg/ml solutions in elastomeric reservoir pumps have been stated by the pump manufacturers to be stable for 12 days at room temperature in sodium chloride 0.9% in the Homepump and Homepump Eclipse and in both dextrose 5% in water and sodium chloride 0.9% in the Infusor and Intermate HPC. (31)

DEXAMETHASONE SODIUM PHOSPHATE
AHFS 68:04

Products — Dexamethasone sodium phosphate is available in 4- and 24-mg/ml strengths. The 4-mg/ml solution is available in 1-, 5-, 25-, and 30-ml vials. The 24-mg/ml solution is available in 5-ml vials. Each milliliter of these solutions contains (2; 29):

Component	4 mg/ml	24 mg/ml
Dexamethasone sodium phosphate (equivalent to dexamethasone phosphate)	4 mg	24 mg
Creatinine	8 mg	8 mg
Sodium citrate	10 mg	10 mg
Sodium bisulfite	1 mg	1 mg
Methylparaben	1.5 mg	1.5 mg
Propylparaben	0.2 mg	0.2 mg
Disodium edetate		0.5 mg
Sodium hydroxide	to adjust pH	to adjust pH
Water for injection	qs	qs

Each milliliter of solution containing the equivalent of 24 mg of dexamethasone phosphate is equal to 20 mg of dexamethasone. (2)

Each milliliter of solution containing the equivalent of 4 mg of dexamethasone phosphate is equal to 3.33 mg of dexamethasone. (2)

Dexamethasone sodium phosphate is also available as a 10-mg/ml concentration in vials. (2; 4)

pH — From 7 to 8.5. (2; 4) Dexamethasone sodium phosphate (David Bull) 0.5, 1, and 2 mg/ml in sodium chloride 0.9% for continuous subcutaneous infusion had pH values of 7.3, 7.3, and 7.5, respectively. (2161)

Osmolality — The osmolality of the 4-mg/ml concentration of dexamethasone sodium phosphate (Elkins-Sinn) was determined by freezing-point depression to be 356 mOsm/kg. (1071) Another study reported the osmolality of a dexamethasone injection (manufacturer not noted) to be 255 mOsm/kg. (1233)

Dexamethasone sodium phosphate (David Bull) 0.5, 1, and 2 mg/ml in sodium chloride 0.9% for continuous subcutaneous infusion had osmolalities of 269, 260, and 238 mOsm/kg, respectively. (2161)

Trade Name(s) — Decadron, Dexasone, Primethasone, Solurex.

Administration — Dexamethasone sodium phosphate 4- and 24-mg/ml concentrations may be administered intravenously by direct injection slowly over one to several minutes or by continuous or intermittent intravenous infusion. The 4-mg/ml concentration may be administered by intramuscular, intra-articular, intrasynovial, intralesional, or soft-tissue injection. (2; 4)

Stability — The 4-mg/ml solution is clear and colorless while the 24-mg/ml solution is clear and colorless to light yellow. The solutions should be protected from light and freezing. In addition, dexamethasone sodium phosphate is heat labile and should not be autoclaved to sterilize the vial's exterior. (2; 4)

Dexamethasone sodium phosphate (Lyphomed) was diluted to a concentration of 1 mg/ml with bacteriostatic sodium chloride 0.9% and packaged in 10-ml sterile glass vials. The dilutions remained clear and colorless, and little or no loss of dexamethasone was found by HPLC analysis after 28 days of storage at 4 and 22 °C. (1940)

Syringes — Lau et al. reported the stability of dexamethasone sodium phosphate (Organon Teknica) 10 mg/ml repackaged into 1- and 2.5-ml Glaspak (Becton-Dickinson) and 1- and 3-ml plastic (Monoject, Sherwood) syringes. Samples in the Glaspak syringes were stored at 4 and 23 °C, unprotected from light and both shaken and unshaken during storage. Samples in plastic syringes were stored only at 23 °C. HPLC analysis for drug content showed not more than 5% loss in the Glaspak syringes after 91 days of storage at either temperature. Similarly, losses in the 3-ml plastic syringes were 7% or less after 55 days while losses in the 1-ml plastic syringes were 3% or less in 35 days; these time periods were the maximum that the plastic syringes were evaluated in this study. Furthermore, no contamination by the rubber components was found to leach into the drug solution during this time frame. (1897)

These results are very different from those reported by Speaker et al. (1562) In that study, dexamethasone sodium phosphate 4 mg/ml was filled into 3-ml plastic syringes (Becton-Dickinson, Sherwood Monoject, and Terumo) and stored at −20, 4, and 25 °C in the dark. Substantial losses of UV absorbance were attributed to dexamethasone losses calculated to range from 5 to 20% in one day at all temperatures. Long-term storage for seven days at 4 °C and 30 days at −20 °C resulted in losses of 11 to 28%. The authors concluded that dexamethasone should not be prefilled and stored in plastic syringes. (1562)

Speaker et al. presumed the losses in UV absorbance they observed were due to sorption to syringe surfaces and/or elastomeric plunger seals. However, the UV assay Speaker et al. used is nonspecific, and loss of absorbance could be due to loss of components other than dexamethasone. Using a more specific HPLC technique, Lau et al. did not observe this dexamethasone loss. (1896)

Dexamethasone sodium phosphate (MSD) 4 mg/ml was found to retain potency for three months at room temperature when 1 ml of solution was packaged in Tubex cartridges. (13) Furthermore, dexamethasone sodium phosphate exhibited no significant changes in 196 days at room temperature in glass disposable syringes. (108)

Elastomeric Reservoir Pumps — Dexamethasone sodium phosphate 0.8 mg/ml solutions in dextrose 5% in water and sodium chloride 0.9% in Medflo and ReadyMed elastomeric reservoir pumps have been stated by the pump manufacturers to be stable 24 hours at room temperature. (31)

Sorption — Dexamethasone sodium phosphate (MSD) 9 mg/L in sodium chloride 0.9% (Travenol) in PVC bags did not exhibit significant sorption to the plastic during one week of storage at room temperature (15 to 20 °C). (536)

In another study, dexamethasone sodium phosphate (MSD) 9 mg/L in sodium chloride 0.9% did not exhibit any loss due to sorption during a seven-hour simulated infusion through an infusion set (Travenol) consisting of a cellulose propionate burette chamber and 170 cm of PVC tubing. (606)

The drug was also tested as a simulated infusion over at least one hour by a syringe pump system. A glass syringe on a syringe pump was fitted with 20 cm of polyethylene tubing or 50 cm of Silastic tubing. No loss of drug due to sorption was observed with either tubing. (606)

A 25-ml aliquot of dexamethasone sodium phosphate (MSD) 9 mg/L in sodium chloride 0.9% was stored in an all-plastic syringe composed of a polypropylene barrel and a polyethylene plunger for 24 hours at room temperature in the dark. The solution did not exhibit any loss due to sorption. (606)

Filtration — Dexamethasone sodium phosphate (MSD) 4 mg/L in dextrose 5% in water, sodium chloride 0.9%, and Ringer's injection, lactated, filtered over 12 hours through a 5-μm stainless steel depth filter (Argyle Filter Connector), a 0.22-μm cellulose ester membrane filter (Ivex-2 Filter Set), and a 0.22-μm polycarbonate membrane filter (In-Sure Filter Set), showed no significant reduction in potency due to binding to the filters. (320)

In another study, dexamethasone sodium phosphate (MSD) 4 mg/L in dextrose 5% in water and sodium chloride 0.9% did not display significant sorption to a 0.45-μm cellulose membrane filter (Abbott S-A-I-F) during an eight-hour simulated infusion. (567)

Central Venous Catheter — Dexamethasone sodium phosphate (American Regent) 0.5 mg/ml in dextrose 5% in water was found to be compatible with the ARROWg+ard Blue Plus (Arrow International) chlorhexidine-bearing triple-lumen central catheter. HPLC analysis was used to evaluate completeness of drug delivery through the catheter and the amount of chlorhexidine removed from the internal lumens. Essentially complete delivery of the drug was found with little or no drug loss occurring. Furthermore, chlorhexidine delivered from the catheter remained at trace amounts with no substantial increase due to the delivery of the drug through the catheter. (2335)

Compatibility Information

Solution Compatibility

Dexamethasone sodium phosphate

Solution	*Mfr*	*Mfr*	*Conc/L*	*Remarks*	*Ref*	*C/I*
Dextrose 5% in water	[a]	AMR	94 and 658 mg	Visually compatible with no loss by HPLC in 14 days stored at 24 °C protected from light	1875	C
Sodium chloride 0.9%	[a]	AMR	92 and 660 mg	Visually compatible with no loss by HPLC in 14 days stored at 24 °C protected from light	1875	C
	BA[a]	ES	200 and 400 mg	Visually compatible with no loss by HPLC in 30 days at 4 °C followed by 2 days at 23 °C	1882	C

[a]*Tested in PVC containers.*

Additive Compatibility

			Dexamethasone sodium phosphate					
Drug	*Mfr*	*Conc/L*	*Mfr*	*Conc/L*	*Test Soln*	*Remarks*	*Ref*	*C/I*
Amikacin sulfate	BR	5 g	MSD	40 mg	D5LR, D5R, D5S, D5W, D10W, IS10, LR, NS, R, SL	Physically compatible and potency of both retained for 24 hr at 25 °C	294	C
	BR	5 g	MSD	40 mg	D2.5S	16% dexamethasone decomposition in 4 hr at 25 °C	294	I
Aminophylline		625 mg		30 mg	D5W	Physically compatible and chemically stable for 24 hr at 4 and 30 °C	521	C
Bleomycin sulfate	BR	20 and 30 units	MSD	50 mg	NS	Physically compatible and bleomycin activity retained for 1 week at 4 °C. Dexamethasone not tested	763	C
Cimetidine HCl	SKF	3 g	MSD	40 mg	D5W	Physically compatible and cimetidine chemically stable for 24 hr at room temperature. Dexamethasone not tested	551	C
Daunorubicin HCl						Immediate milky precipitation	524	I
Diphenhydramine HCl with lorazepam and metoclopramide HCl	ES WY DU	2 g 40 mg 4 g	AMR	400 mg	NS[a]	Rapid lorazepam losses of 8, 10, and 15% at 3, 23, and 30 °C, respectively, in 24 hr by HPLC. Other drugs stable for 14 days by HPLC at all three storage temperatures	1733	I
Floxacillin sodium	BE	20 g	MSD	4 g	NS	Physically compatible for 72 hr at 15 and 30 °C	1479	C
Furosemide	HO	1 g	MSD	4 g	NS	Physically compatible for 72 hr at 15 and 30 °C	1479	C
Granisetron HCl	SKB	10 and 40 mg	AMR	92 mg	D5W, NS[b]	Visually compatible with little or no loss of either drug by HPLC in 14 days at 4 and 24 °C protected from light	1875	C
	SKB	10 and 40 mg	AMR	660 mg	D5W, NS[b]	Visually compatible with little or no dexamethasone loss and up to 8% granisetron loss by HPLC in 14 days at 4 and 24 °C protected from light	1875	C
	BE	55 and 51 mg	MSD	75 and 345 mg	D5W, NS[b]	Visually compatible with little or no loss of either drug by HPLC in 72 hr at room temperature	1884	C
Lidocaine HCl	AST	2 g	MSD	4 mg		Physically compatible	24	C
Meropenem	ZEN	1 and 20 g	MSD	4 g	NS	Visually compatible for 4 hr at room temperature	1994	C
Metaraminol bitartrate	MSD	100 mg	MSD	20 mg	D5W, NS	Altered UV spectra for dexamethasone within 1 hr at room temperature	42	I
	MSD	500 mg	MSD	100 mg	D5W	Altered UV spectra for dexamethasone within 1 hr at room temperature	42	I
Mitomycin	BR	100 mg	LY	5 g	NS[c]	Visually compatible with 10% mitomycin loss calculated in 68 hr and 10% dexamethasone loss calculated in 250 hr at 25 °C	1866	C
	BR	100 mg	LY	5 g	NS[b]	Visually compatible with 10% mitomycin loss calculated in 91 hr and 10% dexamethasone loss calculated in 154 hr at 25 °C	1866	C

Additive Compatibility (Cont.)

Dexamethasone sodium phosphate

Drug	*Mfr*	*Conc/L*	*Mfr*	*Conc/L*	*Test Soln*	*Remarks*	*Ref*	*C/I*
	BR	100 mg	LY	5 g	NS[c]	Visually compatible with 10% mitomycin loss calculated in 211 hr and 10% dexamethasone loss calculated in 98 hr at 4 °C	1866	C
	BR	100 mg	LY	5 g	NS[b]	Visually compatible with 10% mitomycin loss calculated in 238 hr and 10% dexamethasone loss calculated in 355 hr at 25 °C	1866	C
Nafcillin sodium	WY	500 mg	MSD	4 mg		Physically compatible	27	C
Netilmicin sulfate	SC	3 g	MSD	80 mg	D5S	Physically compatible and netilmicin chemically stable for 7 days at 25 and 4 °C. Dexamethasone not tested	558	C
Ondansetron HCl	GL	48 mg		20 and 40 mg	D5W, NS	Visually compatible for 24 hr at 22 °C	1608	C
	GL	160 mg		200 and 400 mg	NS	Visually compatible for 24 hr at 22 °C	1608	C
	CER	100 mg	ES	200 mg	NS[b]	Visually compatible with no dexamethasone loss and 8% ondansetron loss by HPLC after 30 days at 4 °C followed by 2 days at 23 °C	1882	C
	CER	100 and 200 mg	ES	400 mg	NS[b]	Visually compatible with no dexamethasone loss and 7 to 10% ondansetron loss by HPLC after 30 days at 4 °C followed by 2 days at 23 °C	1882	C
	CER	200, 400, and 640 mg	ES	200 mg	NS[b]	Visually compatible with no dexamethasone loss and not more than 5% ondansetron loss by HPLC after 30 days at 4 °C followed by 2 days at 23 °C	1882	C
	CER	400 and 640 mg	ES	400 mg	NS[b]	Visually compatible with no dexamethasone loss and not more than 3% ondansetron loss by HPLC after 30 days at 4 °C followed by 2 days at 23 °C	1882	C
	CER	640 mg	ES	200 and 400 mg	D5W[d]	Visually compatible with 7% dexamethasone loss and no ondansetron loss by HPLC after 30 days at 4 °C followed by 2 days at 23 °C	1882	C
	GL	150 mg	MSD	400 mg	NS[a]	Visually compatible with 4% or less loss of either drug by HPLC in 28 days at 4 and 22 °C	2084	C
	GL	150 mg	MSD	400 mg	D5W[a]	Visually compatible with 4% or less loss of either drug by HPLC in 28 days at 4 °C. Up to 10% ondansetron loss in 3 days at 22 °C	2084	C
	GL	750 mg	MSD	230 mg	NS[a]	Visually compatible with 4% or less loss of either drug by HPLC in 28 days at 4 °C. Up to 10% ondansetron loss in 7 days at 22 °C	2084	C
	GL	750 mg	MSD	230 mg	D5W[a]	Visually compatible with up to 13% ondansetron loss by HPLC in 3 days at 4 and 22 °C	2084	?
Prochlorperazine edisylate	SKF	100 mg	MSD	20 mg	D5W	Physically compatible	15	C

Additive Compatibility (Cont.)

Dexamethasone sodium phosphate

Drug	*Mfr*	*Conc/L*	*Mfr*	*Conc/L*	*Test Soln*	*Remarks*	*Ref*	*C/I*
Ranitidine HCl	GL	50 mg and 2 g		40 mg	D5W	Physically compatible and ranitidine chemically stable by HPLC for 24 hr at 25 °C. Dexamethasone not tested	1515	C
Vancomycin HCl	LI					Physically incompatible	9	I
Verapamil HCl	KN	80 mg	MSD	40 mg	D5W, NS	Physically compatible for 24 hr	764	C

[a]Tested in Pharmacia-Deltec PVC pump reservoirs.
[b]Tested in PVC containers.
[c]Tested in glass containers.
[d]Tested in ondansetron HCl ready-to-use CR3 polyester bags.

Drugs in Syringe Compatibility

Dexamethasone sodium phosphate

Drug (in syringe)	*Mfr*	*Amt*	*Mfr*	*Amt*	*Remarks*	*Ref*	*C/I*
Diphenhydramine HCl	PD	50 mg/ml[a]	DB, SX	4 and 10 mg/ml[a]	White turbidity and precipitate form immediately	1542	I
	PD	4.54 mg/ml[b]	DB	9.52 mg/ml[b]	Visually compatible for 24 hr at 24 °C	1542	C
	PD	4.54 to 15 mg/ml[b]	DB	5 to 9.02 mg/ml[b]	Precipitate forms	1542	I
	PD	34.8 to 40 mg/ml[b]	SX	2 mg/ml[b]	Visually compatible for 24 hr at 24 °C	1542	C
	PD	25 mg/ml[b]	SX	1 mg/ml[b]	Precipitate forms	1542	I
Doxapram HCl	RB	400 mg/20 ml	MSD	3.3 mg/1 ml	Immediate turbidity and precipitation	1177	I
Glycopyrrolate	RB	0.2 mg/1 ml	MSD	4 mg/1 ml	Physically compatible for 48 hr at 25 °C. But the pH>6. Approximately 5% glycopyrrolate decomposition may occur in 4 to 7 hr	331	I
	RB	0.2 mg/1 ml	MSD	8 mg/2 ml	Physically compatible for 48 hr at 25 °C. But the pH>6. Approximately 5% glycopyrrolate decomposition may occur in 4 to 7 hr	331	I
	RB	0.4 mg/2 ml	MSD	4 mg/1 ml	Physically compatible for 48 hr at 25 °C. But the pH>6. Approximately 5% glycopyrrolate decomposition may occur in 4 to 7 hr	331	I
	RB	0.2 mg/1 ml	MSD	24 mg/1 ml	Physically compatible for 48 hr at 25 °C. But the pH>6. Approximately 5% glycopyrrolate decomposition may occur in 4 to 7 hr	331	I
	RB	0.2 mg/1 ml	MSD	48 mg/2 ml	Physically compatible for 48 hr at 25 °C. But the pH>6. Approximately 5% glycopyrrolate decomposition may occur in 4 to 7 hr	331	I
	RB	0.4 mg/2 ml	MSD	24 mg/1 ml	Physically compatible for 48 hr at 25 °C. But the pH>6. Approximately 5% glycopyrrolate decomposition may occur in 4 to 7 hr	331	I
Granisetron HCl	BE	0.15 mg/ml[c]	MSD	0.2 and 1 mg/ml[c]	Visually compatible with little or no loss of either drug by HPLC in 72 hr at room temperature	1884	C

Drugs in Syringe Compatibility (Cont.)

			Dexamethasone sodium phosphate				
Drug (in syringe)	*Mfr*	*Amt*	*Mfr*	*Amt*	*Remarks*	*Ref*	*C/I*
Hydromorphone HCl	KN	2, 10, 40 mg/ ml[a]	SX	4 mg/ml[a]	Visually compatible and potency of both drugs by HPLC retained for 24 hr at 24 °C	1542	C
	KN	2 and 10 mg/ ml[a]	DB	10 mg/ ml[a]	Visually compatible and potency of both drugs by HPLC retained for 24 hr at 24 °C	1542	C
	KN	40 mg/ ml[a]	DB	10 mg/ ml[a]	White turbidity forms immediately	1542	I
	KN	11.6 mg/ ml[b]	DB	7.1 mg/ ml[b]	Visually compatible for 24 hr at 24 °C	1542	C
	KN	13.3 to 17.5 mg/ ml[b]	DB	5.5 to 6.6 mg/ ml[b]	Precipitate forms	1542	I
	KN	10.5 mg/ ml[b]	DB	4.75 mg/ ml[b]	Visually compatible for 24 hr at 24 °C	1542	C
	KN	14.75 to 25 mg/ ml[b]	DB	3 to 4.1 mg/ ml[b]	Precipitate forms	1542	I
	KN	26.66 mg/ ml[b]	SX	3.34 mg/ ml[b]	Visually compatible for 24 hr at 24 °C	1542	C
Metoclopramide HCl	RB	10 mg/ 2 ml	ES, MSD	8 mg/ 2 ml	Physically compatible for 48 hr at room temperature	924	C
	RB	10 mg/ 2 ml	ES, MSD	8 mg/ 2 ml	Physically compatible for 48 hr at 25 °C	1167	C
	RB	160 mg/ 32 ml	ES, MSD	8 mg/ 2 ml	Physically compatible for 48 hr at 25 °C	1167	C
Ondansetron HCl	CER	0.17 mg/ ml[d]	ES	0.33 and 0.67 mg/ ml[d]	Visually compatible with no loss of either drug by HPLC after 30 days at 4 °C followed by 2 days at 23 °C	1882	C
	CER	0.25 mg/ ml[d]	ES	0.5 mg/ ml[d]	Visually compatible with no loss of either drug by HPLC after 30 days at 4 °C followed by 2 days at 23 °C	1882	C
	CER	0.25 mg/ ml[d]	ES	1 mg/ml[d]	Visually compatible for 3 days at 4 °C. Precipitation of ondansetron observed at 7 days as opaque white ring	1882	C
	CER	0.33 mg/ ml[d]	ES	0.33 and 0.67 mg/ ml[d]	Visually compatible with no loss of either drug by HPLC after 30 days at 4 °C followed by 2 days at 23 °C	1882	C
	CER	0.5 mg/ ml[d]	ES	0.5 mg/ ml[d]	Visually compatible with no loss of either drug by HPLC after 30 days at 4 °C followed by 2 days at 23 °C	1882	C
	CER	0.5 mg/ ml[d]	ES	1 mg/ml[d]	Visually compatible for 3 days at 4 °C. Precipitation of ondansetron observed at 5 days as opaque white ring	1882	C
	CER	0.67 mg/ ml[d]	ES	0.33 and 0.67 mg/ ml[d]	Visually compatible with no loss of either drug by HPLC after 30 days at 4 °C followed by 2 days at 23 °C	1882	C
	CER	1.07 mg/ ml[d]	ES	0.33 mg/ ml[d]	Visually compatible with no loss of either drug by HPLC after 30 days at 4 °C followed by 2 days at 23 °C	1882	C
	CER	1.07 mg/ ml[d]	ES	0.67 mg/ ml[d]	Heavy white flocculent precipitate appears within 72 hr at 4 °C with 25 to 30% loss of both drugs by HPLC from solution	1882	I

Drugs in Syringe Compatibility (Cont.)

Drug (in syringe)	Mfr	Amt	Dexamethasone sodium phosphate Mfr	Amt	Remarks	Ref	C/I
Ranitidine HCl	GL	50 mg/ 5 ml	ME	4 mg	Physically compatible for 4 hr at ambient temperature under fluorescent light	1151	C
Sufentanil citrate	JN	50 μg/ml	AMR	4 mg/ml	Physically compatible with no subvisual haze or particle formation in 24 hr at 23 °C	1711	C

[a]Mixed in equal quantities. Final concentration is one-half the indicated concentration.
[b]Mixed in varying quantities to yield the final concentrations noted.
[c]Diluted with water.
[d]Diluted with sodium chloride 0.9% drawn into a syringe prior to drugs to yield the concentrations cited.

Y-Site Injection Compatibility (1:1 Mixture)

Drug	Mfr	Conc	Dexamethasone sodium phosphate Mfr	Conc	Remarks	Ref	C/I
Acyclovir sodium	BW	5 mg/ml[a]	ES	0.2 mg/ml[a]	Physically compatible for 4 hr at 25 °C	1157	C
Allopurinol sodium	BW	3 mg/ml[b]	LY	1 mg/ml[b]	Physically compatible with no change in measured turbidity or increase in particle content in 4 hr at 22 °C	1686	C
Amifostine	USB	10 mg/ml[a]	AMR	1 mg/ml[a]	Physically compatible with no change in measured turbidity or increase in particle content in 4 hr at 23 °C	1845	C
Amikacin sulfate	SQ	50 mg/ml[c]	AMR	4 mg/ml	Visually compatible for 24 hr at room temperature in test tubes. No precipitate found on filter from Y-site delivery	2063	C
Amphotericin B cholesteryl sulfate complex	SEQ	0.83 mg/ml[a]	ES	2 mg/ml[a]	Physically compatible with little or no change in measured turbidity or increase in particle content in 4 hr at 23 °C under fluorescent light	2117	C
Amsacrine	NCI	1 mg/ml[a]	QU	1 mg/ml[a]	Physically compatible for 4 hr at room temperature under fluorescent light	1381	C
Aztreonam	SQ	40 mg/ml[a]	AMR	1 mg/ml[a]	Physically compatible with no subvisual haze or particle formation in 4 hr at 23 °C	1758	C
Cefepime HCl	BMS	20 mg/ml[a]	AMR	1 mg/ml[a]	Physically compatible with no change in measured turbidity or increase in particle content in 4 hr at 22 °C	1689	C
Cefpirome sulfate	HO	50 mg/ml[d]	LY	4 mg/ml[d]	Visually and microscopically compatible with 5% or less cefpirome loss and little or no dexamethasone loss by HPLC in 8 hr at 23 °C	2044	C
Ciprofloxacin	MI	2 mg/ml[e]	LY	4 mg/ml	Transient white cloudiness rapidly dissipates. White crystals and flocculation form in 1 hr at 24 °C	1655	I
Cisatracurium besylate	GW	0.1, 2, 5 mg/ml[a]	FUJ	2 mg/ml[a]	Physically compatible with no change in measured turbidity or increase in particle content in 4 hr at 23 °C	2074	C
Cisplatin	BR	1 mg/ml	QU	1 mg/ml[a]	Visually compatible for 4 hr at room temperature under fluorescent light	1685	C

Y-Site Injection Compatibility (1:1 Mixture) (Cont.)

			Dexamethasone sodium phosphate				
Drug	*Mfr*	*Conc*	*Mfr*	*Conc*	*Remarks*	*Ref*	*C/I*
Cladribine	ORT	0.015[b] and 0.5[f] mg/ml	AMR	1 mg/ml[b]	Physically compatible with no change in measured turbidity or increase in particle content in 4 hr at 23 °C	1969	C
Cyclophosphamide	MJ	10 mg/ml[a]	QU	1 mg/ml[a]	Visually compatible for 4 hr at room temperature under fluorescent light	1685	C
Cytarabine	UP	50 mg/ml	QU	1 mg/ml[a]	Visually compatible for 4 hr at room temperature under fluorescent light	1685	C
Docetaxel	RPR	0.9 mg/ml[a]	ES	2 mg/ml[a]	Physically compatible with no change in measured turbidity or increase in particle content in 4 hr at 23 °C	2224	C
Doxorubicin HCl	AD	0.2 mg/ml[a]	QU	1 mg/ml[a]	Visually compatible for 4 hr at room temperature under fluorescent light	1685	C
Doxorubicin HCl liposome injection	SEQ	0.4 mg/ml[a]	ES	2 mg/ml[a]	Physically compatible with little or no change in measured turbidity and no increase in particle content in 4 hr at 23 °C	2087	C
Etoposide phosphate	BR	5 mg/ml[a]	ES	1 mg/ml[a]	Physically compatible with no change in measured turbidity or increase in particle content in 4 hr at 23 °C	2218	C
Famotidine	MSD	0.2 mg/ml[a]	ES	10 mg/ml	Physically compatible for 14 hr	1196	C
	ME	2 mg/ml[b]		1 mg/ml[a]	Visually compatible for 4 hr at 22 °C	1936	C
Fentanyl citrate	JN	0.025 mg/ml[a]	AMR	1 mg/ml[a]	Physically compatible with no change in measured haze or increase in particle content in 48 hr at 22 °C	1706	C
Filgrastim	AMG	30 μg/ml[a]	LY	1 mg/ml[a]	Physically compatible with no change in measured turbidity or increase in particle content in 4 hr at 22 °C	1687	C
Fluconazole	RR	2 mg/ml	ES	4 mg/ml	Physically compatible for 24 hr at 25 °C	1407	C
Fludarabine phosphate	BX	1 mg/ml[a]	MSD	1 mg/ml[a]	Physically compatible for 4 hr at room temperature under fluorescent light	1439	C
Foscarnet sodium	AST	24 mg/ml	OR	10 mg/ml	Physically compatible for 24 hr at room temperature under fluorescent light	1335	C
Gatifloxacin	BMS	2 mg/ml[a]	FUJ	1 mg/ml[a]	Physically compatible with no change in measured haze or increase in particle content in 4 hr at 23 °C	2234	C
Gemcitabine HCl	LI	10 mg/ml[b]	ES	1 mg/ml[b]	Physically compatible with no change in measured turbidity or increase in particle content in 4 hr at 23 °C	2226	C
Granisetron HCl	SKB	1 mg/ml	ME	0.24 mg/ml[b]	Physically compatible with little or no loss of either drug by HPLC in 4 hr at 22 °C	1883	C
Heparin sodium	TR	50 units/ml	ES	1 mg/ml[a]	Visually compatible for 4 hr at 25 °C	1793	C
Heparin sodium with hydrocortisone sodium succinate	RI UP	1000 units + 100 mg/L[g]	MSD	4 mg/ml	Physically compatible for at least 4 hr at room temperature by visual and microscopic examination	322	C
Hetastarch in lactated electrolyte injection (Hextend)	AB	6%	APP	1 mg/ml[a]	Physically compatible with no change in measured turbidity or increase in particle content in 4 hr at 23 °C	2339	C

Y-Site Injection Compatibility (1:1 Mixture) (Cont.)

			Dexamethasone sodium phosphate				
Drug	*Mfr*	*Conc*	*Mfr*	*Conc*	*Remarks*	*Ref*	*C/I*
Hydromorphone HCl	AST	0.5 mg/ml[a]	AMR	1 mg/ml[a]	Physically compatible with no change in measured haze or increase in particle content in 48 hr at 22 °C	1706	C
Idarubicin HCl	AD	1 mg/ml[b]	OR	10 mg/ml	Haze forms immediately and precipitate forms in 20 min	1525	I
	AD	1 mg/ml[b]	AMR	0.2 mg/ml[b]	Haze forms in 20 min	1525	I
Levofloxacin	OMN	5 mg/ml[a]	ES	4 mg/ml	Visually compatible for 4 hr at 24 °C under fluorescent light	2233	C
Linezolid	PHU	2 mg/ml	FUJ	1 mg/ml[a]	Physically compatible with no change in measured turbidity or increase in particle content in 4 hr at 23 °C	2264	C
Lorazepam	WY	0.33 mg/ml[b]		4 mg/ml	Visually compatible for 24 hr at 22 °C	1855	C
Melphalan HCl	BW	0.1 mg/ml[b]	LY	1 mg/ml[b]	Physically compatible with no change in measured turbidity or increase in particle content in 3 hr at 22 °C	1557	C
Meperidine HCl	AB	10 mg/ml	LY	0.2 mg/ml[a]	Physically compatible for 4 hr at 25 °C	1397	C
Meropenem	ZEN	1 and 50 mg/ml[b]	MSD	10 mg/ml[h]	Visually compatible for 4 hr at room temperature	1994	C
Methadone HCl	LI	1 mg/ml[a]	AMR	1 mg/ml[a]	Physically compatible with no change in measured haze or increase in particle content in 48 hr at 22 °C	1706	C
Methotrexate sodium	AD	15 mg/ml[i]	QU	1 mg/ml[a]	Visually compatible for 4 hr at room temperature under fluorescent light	1685	C
		30 mg/ml	MSD	4 mg/ml	Visually compatible for 2 hr at room temperature. Dark yellow precipitate forms in 4 hr	1788	I
Midazolam HCl	RC	1 mg/ml[a]	ES	4 mg/ml	Haze forms immediately. Precipitate forms in 8 hr	1847	I
	RC	5 mg/ml		4 mg/ml	White precipitate forms immediately	1855	I
Morphine sulfate	AB	1 mg/ml	LY	0.2 mg/ml[a]	Physically compatible for 4 hr at 25 °C	1397	C
	AST	1 mg/ml[a]	AMR	1 mg/ml[a]	Physically compatible with no change in measured haze or increase in particle content in 48 hr at 22 °C	1706	C
Ondansetron HCl	GL	1 mg/ml[b]	MSD	1 mg/ml[a]	Physically compatible for 4 hr at 22 °C	1365	C
Paclitaxel	NCI	1.2 mg/ml[a]		1 mg/ml[a]	Physically compatible with no change in measured turbidity in 4 hr at 22 °C	1528	C
Piperacillin sodium–tazobactam sodium	LE	40 + 5 mg/ml[a]	LY	1 mg/ml[a]	Physically compatible with no change in measured turbidity or increase in particle content in 4 hr at 22 °C	1688	C
Potassium chloride		40 mEq/L[g]	MSD	4 mg/ml	Physically compatible for at least 4 hr at room temperature by visual and microscopic examination	322	C
Propofol	ZEN	10 mg/ml	AMR	1 mg/ml[a]	Physically compatible for 1 hr at 23 °C with no increase in particle content	2066	C
Remifentanil HCl	GW	0.025 and 0.25 mg/ml[b]	FUJ	2 mg/ml[a]	Physically compatible with no change in measured turbidity or increase in particle content in 4 hr at 23 °C	2075	C
Sargramostim	IMM	10 μg/ml[b]	ES	1 mg/ml[b]	Physically compatible for 4 hr at 22 °C	1436	C

Y-Site Injection Compatibility (1:1 Mixture) (Cont.)

			Dexamethasone sodium phosphate				
Drug	*Mfr*	*Conc*	*Mfr*	*Conc*	*Remarks*	*Ref*	*C/I*
Sodium bicarbonate		1.4%	MSD	4 mg/ml	Visually compatible for 4 hr at room temperature	1788	C
Sufentanil citrate	JN	12.5 μg/ml[a]	AMR	1 mg/ml[a]	Physically compatible with no subvisual haze or particle formation in 24 hr at 23 °C	1711	C
Tacrolimus	FUJ	1 mg/ml[b]	ES	4 mg/ml[a]	Visually compatible for 24 hr at 25 °C	1630	C
Teniposide	BR	0.1 mg/ml[a]	LY	1 mg/ml[a]	Physically compatible with no subvisual haze or particle formation in 4 hr at 23 °C	1725	C
Theophylline	TR	4 mg/ml	ES	0.08 mg/ml[a]	Visually compatible for 6 hr at 25 °C	1793	C
Thiotepa	IMM[j]	1 mg/ml[a]	AMR	1 mg/ml[a]	Physically compatible with no change in measured turbidity or increase in particle content in 4 hr at 23 °C	1861	C
TNA #218 to #226[k]			FUJ, ES	1 mg/ml[a]	Visually compatible with no precipitate or emulsion damage apparent in 4 hr at 23 °C	2215	C
Topotecan HCl	SKB	56 μg/ml[b]	RU	4 mg/ml	Haze and color change to intense yellow occur immediately	2245	I
TPN #203 and #204[k]			AMR	4 mg/ml	Visually compatible for 2 hr at 23 °C	1974	C
TPN #212 to #215[k]			AMR	1 mg/ml[a]	Physically compatible with no change in measured turbidity or increase in particle content in 4 hr at 23 °C	2109	C
Vinorelbine tartrate	BW	1 mg/ml[b]	LY	1 mg/ml[b]	Physically compatible with no change in measured turbidity or increase in particle content in 4 hr at 22 °C	1558	C
Vitamin B complex with C	RC	2 ml/L[g]	MSD	4 mg/ml	Physically compatible for at least 4 hr at room temperature by visual and microscopic examination	322	C
Zidovudine	BW	4 mg/ml[a]	ES	0.16 mg/ml[a]	Physically compatible for 4 hr at 25 °C under fluorescent light by visual and microscopic examination	1193	C

[a] *Tested in dextrose 5% in water.*
[b] *Tested in sodium chloride 0.9%.*
[c] *Tested in sodium chloride 0.45%.*
[d] *Tested in dextrose 5% in water, Ringer's injection, lactated, sodium chloride 0.45%, and sodium chloride 0.9%.*
[e] *Tested in both dextrose 5% in water and sodium chloride 0.9%.*
[f] *Tested in bacteriostatic sodium chloride 0.9% preserved with benzyl alcohol 0.9%.*
[g] *Tested in dextrose 5% in water, Ringer's injection, lactated, and sodium chloride 0.9%.*
[h] *Tested in sterile water for injection.*
[i] *Tested in dextrose 5% in water with sodium bicarbonate 0.05 mEq/ml.*
[j] *Lyophilized formulation tested.*
[k] *Refer to Appendix I for the composition of the parenteral nutrition solutions. TNA indicates a 3-in-1 admixture, and TPN indicates a 2-in-1 admixture.*

Additional Compatibility Information

Infusion Solutions — Dextrose 5% in water and sodium chloride 0.9% have been recommended as diluents for intravenous infusions. (2; 4)

Concentrated Drug Solutions — The following incompatibility determinations were performed with concentrated solutions. One milliliter of dexamethasone sodium phosphate (MSD) was added to 5 ml of sterile distilled water along with 1 ml of prochlorperazine edisylate (SKF) or vancomycin HCl (Lilly). Particulate matter was noted within two hours. (28)

DEXTRAN 40
AHFS 40:12

Products — Dextran 40 products are available as 10% (10 g/100 ml) injections in dextrose 5% or sodium chloride 0.9% in 500-ml containers. The colloidal dextran products are prepared from low molecular weight dextran (average molecular weight of 40,000) with either dextrose, hydrous, 5 g/100 ml or sodium chloride 0.9 g/100 ml in water for injection. (4; 154)

pH — The pH of dextran 40 10% in dextrose 5% ranges from 3 to 7. The pH of dextran 40 10% in sodium chloride 0.9% ranges from 3.5 to 7. (4)

Sodium Content — Dextran 40 10% in sodium chloride 0.9% provides 77 mEq of sodium per 500-ml bottle. (4)

Trade Name(s) — Gentran, LMD, Rheomacrodex.

Administration — Dextran 40 10% injection is administered by intravenous infusion. (4)

Stability — Dextran 40 products should not be administered unless they are clear. Long periods of storage or exposure to temperature fluctuations may cause the formation of dextran flakes. Therefore, solutions should be stored at a constant temperature, preferably 25 °C, and protected from freezing and extreme heat. If flakes do appear, they can be dissolved by heating in a water bath at 100 °C or autoclaving at 110 °C for 15 minutes. (4; 1484; 1485) Because no antibacterial preservative is present, partially used containers should be discarded. (4)

Compatibility Information

Additive Compatibility

Dextran 40

Drug	Mfr	Conc/L	Mfr	Conc/L	Test Soln	Remarks	Ref	C/I
Amoxicillin sodium		10, 20, 50 g		10%	D5W	9, 12, and 12% amoxicillin loss at 10, 20, and 50 g/L, respectively, in 1 hr at 25 °C	1469	I
		10, 20, 50 g		10%	NS	12, 14, and 20% amoxicillin loss at 10, 20, and 50 g/L, respectively, in 3 hr at 25 °C	1469	I

Y-Site Injection Compatibility (1:1 Mixture)

Dextran 40

Drug	Mfr	Conc	Mfr	Conc	Remarks	Ref	C/I
Enalaprilat	MSD	0.05 mg/ml[b]	TR	100 mg/ml[a]	Physically compatible for 24 hr at room temperature under fluorescent light	1355	C
Famotidine	MSD	0.2 mg/ml[a]	PH	100 mg/ml[a]	Physically compatible for 4 hr at 25 °C under fluorescent light	1188	C

[a]*Tested in dextrose 5% in water.*
[b]*Tested in sodium chloride 0.9%.*

DIATRIZOATE MEGLUMINE
AHFS 36:68

Products — Diatrizoate meglumine is available in concentrations ranging from 18 to 76%. It is also available in combination with other radiopaque contrast agents. The formulations may also contain edetate and parabens. Hydrochloric acid, diatrizoic acid, or meglumine may have been used during manufacturing to adjust pH. Some examples of single-agent products are listed in Table 1. (4; 154)

pH — From 6.5 to 7.7. (4)

Osmolarity — Osmolarities of the various concentrations range from 640 to 1761 mOsm/L. (4)

Trade Name(s) — See Table 1.

Administration — Appropriate dosage forms and concentrations of diatrizoate meglumine may be administered intravenously, intramuscularly, intra-arterially, or intra-articularly. Some products may be injected or instilled directly into selected areas to be visualized. (4)

Stability — Diatrizoate meglumine solutions are colorless to pale yellow. On standing, a crystalline precipitate may form. To redissolve the crystals, place the container in hot water and shake gently. Allow the solution to cool to body temperature before administration. (4)

Diatrizoate meglumine in combination with diatrizoate sodium as Renografin products is sensitive to low pH values. At about pH 3 to 4, turbidity or frank precipitation may appear. (479)

Table 1. Some Representative Diatrizoate Meglumine Products

Diatrizoate Meglumine Content (%)	Bound Iodine (mg/ml)	Representative Trade Names
Urogenital solutions (not for intravascular use)		
18	85	Cystografin Dilute
30	141	Cystografin, Reno-30, Hypaque Cysto, Hypaque Cysto Pediatric
Parenteral solutions		
30	141	Hypaque Meglumine 30%, Reno-DIP
60	282	Hypaque Meglumine 60%, Reno-60

Diatrizoate meglumine solutions should be protected from strong light. (4)

Syringes—Plastic syringes have been stated to be unsuitable for accommodating radiopaque solutions for any length of time. The plastic is attacked, and the plunger tends to freeze on prolonged storage. (40)

An increased incidence of adverse reactions to diatrizoate meglumine in combination with diatrizoate sodium in intravenous pyelography was attributed to extraction of phenolic compounds from the rubber plunger-stoppers when Plastipak (Becton-Dickinson) disposable syringes were used to administer the radiopaque contrast media. The use of glass syringes only was recommended. (821)

Compatibility Information

Drugs in Syringe Compatibility

Diatrizoate meglumine

Drug (in syringe)	*Mfr*	*Amt*	*Mfr*	*Amt*	*Remarks*	*Ref*	*C/I*
Diphenhydramine HCl	PD	50 mg/ 1 ml	SQ	5 ml[a]	No precipitate observed	309	C

[a]*Percentage unspecified.*

Additional Compatibility Information

Other Drugs— Diatrizoate meglumine products (Squibb) have been generally found to be compatible with chlorpheniramine maleate (Schering) and hyaluronidase (Wyeth). (40)

Diphenhydramine HCl (Parke-Davis) has been stated to be compatible for short periods with diatrizoate meglumine products (Squibb). (40)

Diatrizoate meglumine products (Squibb) were found to be physically incompatible with promethazine HCl (Wyeth). (40)

Diatrizoate meglumine in combination with diatrizoate sodium as Renografin products may be physically incompatible with additives that lower the pH to 4 or below. (479)

DIATRIZOATE MEGLUMINE AND DIATRIZOATE SODIUM AHFS 36:68

Products— Diatrizoate meglumine–diatrizoate sodium is available in combined concentrations of 60 and 76%. The formulations may also contain edetate and citrate. Hydrochloric acid, sodium hydroxide, or sodium carbonate may have been used during manufacturing to adjust pH. Some examples of representative products are listed in Table 1. (4; 29; 154)

pH—From 6.5 to 7.7. (4)

Osmolarity—Osmolarities of the various concentrations range from 1510 to 2175 mOsm/L. (4)

Trade Name(s)—See Table 1.

Administration— Appropriate dosage forms and concentrations of diatrizoate meglumine–diatrizoate sodium may be administered intravenously, intramuscularly, intra-arterially, or intra-articularly. Some products may be injected or instilled directly into selected areas to be visualized. (4)

Stability— Diatrizoate meglumine–diatrizoate sodium solutions are colorless to pale yellow. They should be protected from strong light. On standing, a crystalline precipitate may form. To redissolve the crystals, place the container in hot water and shake gently. Allow the solution to cool to body temperature before administration. (4)

Diatrizoate meglumine–diatrizoate sodium (Renografin) products are sensitive to low pH values. At about pH 3 to 4, turbidity or frank precipitation may appear. (479)

Table 1. Some Representative Diatrizoate Meglumine–Diatrizoate Sodium Products

Diatrizoate Meglumine Content (%)	Diatrizoate Sodium Content (%)	Bound Iodine (mg/ml)	Representative Trade Names
52	8	290	Renografin-60
66	10	370	Hypaque-76, MD-76, Reno-Cal

Syringes—Plastic syringes have been stated to be unsuitable for accommodating radiopaque solutions for any length of time. The plastic is attacked, and the plunger tends to freeze on prolonged storage. (40) However, when diatrizoate meglumine 52%–diatrizoate sodium 8% (Renografin-60, Squibb) and diatrizoate meglumine 34.3%–diatrizoate sodium 35% (Renovist, Squibb) were stored in polystyrene syringes (Pharmaseal) at 25 and 37 °C, no apparent changes were noted visually or spectrophotometrically over five days. (530)

An increased incidence of adverse reactions to diatrizoate meglumine–diatrizoate sodium (Hypaque-M, 75%) in intravenous pyelography was attributed to extraction of phenolic compounds from the rubber plunger-stoppers when Plastipak (Becton-Dickinson) disposable syringes were used to administer the radiopaque contrast media. The use of glass syringes only was recommended. (821)

Sorption—Diatrizoate meglumine–diatrizoate sodium (Squibb Diagnostics) (concentration unspecified) was filled into 3-ml plastic syringes (Becton-Dickinson, Sherwood Monoject, and Terumo) and stored at −20, 4, and 25 °C in the dark. Little or no loss occurred in one day at 25 °C, seven days at 4 °C, and 30 days at −20 °C. (1562)

Compatibility Information

Drugs in Syringe Compatibility

Diatrizoate meglumine + Diatrizoate sodium

Drug (in syringe)	*Mfr*	*Amt*	*Mfr*	*Amt*	*Remarks*	*Ref*	*C/I*
Ampicillin sodium	BR	30 mg/ 1 ml	MA	52% + 8%, 5 ml	Physically compatible for at least 2 hr	1438	C
Chloramphenicol sodium succinate	PD	33 mg/ 1 ml	MA	52% + 8%, 5 ml	Physically compatible for at least 2 hr	1438	C
Chlorpheniramine maleate	SC	1 ml[a]	SQ	52% + 8%, 40 to 1 ml	Physically compatible for 48 hr	530	C
	SC	1 ml[a]	SQ	34% + 35%, 40 to 1 ml	Physically compatible for 48 hr	530	C
Cimetidine HCl	SKF	150 mg/ 1 ml	MA	52% + 8%, 5 ml	Physically compatible for at least 2 hr	1438	C
Dimenhydrinate	SE	50 mg/ 1 ml	SQ	52% + 8%, 40 to 1 ml	Physically compatible for 48 hr	530	C
	SE	50 mg/ 1 ml	SQ	34% + 35%, 40 to 1 ml	Physically compatible for 48 hr	530	C
Diphenhydramine HCl	PD	1 ml[a]	SQ	52% + 8%, 40 to 5 ml	Physically compatible for 48 hr	530	C
	PD	1 ml[a]	SQ	52% + 8%, 2 and 1 ml	Physically compatible for 1 hr, but precipitate forms within 48 hr	530	I
	PD	1 ml[a]	SQ	34% + 35%, 40 to 1 ml	Physically compatible for 48 hr	530	C
	PD	12.5 mg/ 0.25 ml	MA	52% + 8%, 5 ml	Transient precipitate clears and then reforms within 1 hr	1438	I
Epinephrine HCl	PD	1 mg/ 1 ml	MA	52% + 8%, 5 ml	Physically compatible for at least 2 hr	1438	C
Gentamicin sulfate	SC	0.8 mg/ 1 ml	MA	52% + 8%, 5 ml	Physically compatible for at least 2 hr	1438	C
Heparin sodium	OR	5000 units/ 0.5 ml	MA	52% + 8%, 5 ml	Physically compatible for at least 2 hr	1438	C
Hyaluronidase	WY	150 units/ 1 ml	SQ	52% + 8%, 40 to 5 ml	Physically compatible for 48 hr	530	C

Drugs in Syringe Compatibility (Cont.)

Diatrizoate meglumine + Diatrizoate sodium

Drug (in syringe)	*Mfr*	*Amt*	*Mfr*	*Amt*	*Remarks*	*Ref*	*C/I*
	WY	150 units/ 1 ml	SQ	52% + 8%, 2 and 1 ml	Physically compatible for 1 hr, but precipitate forms within 48 hr	530	I
	WY	150 units/ 1 ml	SQ	34% + 35%, 40 to 1 ml	Physically compatible for 48 hr	530	C
Hydrocortisone sodium succinate	UP	10 mg/ 1 ml	MA	52% + 8%, 5 ml	Physically compatible for at least 2 hr	1438	C
Methylprednisolone sodium succinate	UP	10 mg/ 1 ml	MA	52% + 8%, 5 ml	Physically compatible for at least 2 hr	1438	C
Papaverine HCl	LI	30 mg/ 1 ml	SQ	66% + 10%, 3 ml	White precipitate disappears after 1 to 2 min	1437	?
	ME	32 mg/ 1 ml	MA	52% + 8%, 5 ml	Transient precipitate clears and then reforms after 2 hr	1438	I
Promethazine HCl	WY	1 ml[a]	SQ	52% + 8%, 40 to 1 ml	Immediate precipitation	530	I
	WY	1 ml[a]	SQ	34% + 35%, 40 to 1 ml	Immediate precipitation	530	I
Protamine sulfate	LI	10 mg/ 1 ml	MA	52% + 8%, 5 ml	Precipitate forms immediately and persists for at least 2 hr	1438	I

[a] *Concentration unspecified.*

Additional Compatibility Information

Other Drugs — Diatrizoate meglumine–diatrizoate sodium (Renografin) products may be physically incompatible with additives that lower the pH to 4 or below. (479)

Protamine sulfate has been found to be physically incompatible with diatrizoate meglumine 66%–diatrizoate sodium 10% (Renografin-76). A thick whitish gel formed upon administration of 40 mg of protamine sulfate directly into a catheter filled with the contrast medium. The precipitate would not dissolve after heating to body temperature but dissolved slowly when further diluted 10-fold with water. Even flushing the catheter filled with contrast medium with 50 ml of sodium chloride 0.9% first did not eliminate the appearance of a precipitate upon administration of protamine sulfate through the catheter. However, the precipitate was much less dense than that formed without a saline flush. (651)

DIATRIZOATE SODIUM
AHFS 36:68

Products — Diatrizoate sodium is available in concentrations ranging from 20 to 50%. It is also available in combination with other radiopaque contrast agents. The formulations may also contain edetate and benzyl alcohol. Sodium carbonate, hydrochloric acid, and/or sodium hydroxide may have been used during manufacturing to adjust pH. Some examples of single-agent products are listed in Table 1. (4; 29; 154)

pH — From 6.5 to 7.7. (4)

Table 1. Some Representative Diatrizoate Sodium Products

Diatrizoate Sodium Content (%)	Bound Iodine (mg/ml)	Representative Trade Names
Urogenital solution (not for intravascular use)		
20	120	Hypaque Sodium 20%
Parenteral solutions		
25	150	Hypaque Sodium 25%
50	300	Hypaque Sodium 50%

Osmolarity—The 25 and 50% concentrations have osmolarities of 660 and 1270 mOsm/L, respectively. (4)

Sodium Content—Diatrizoate sodium contains about 1.57 mEq of sodium per gram of drug. (4)

Trade Name(s)—See Table 1.

Administration — Appropriate dosage forms and concentrations of diatrizoate sodium may be administered intravenously, intramuscularly, subcutaneously, intra-arterially, or by intraosseous injection. Some products may be injected or instilled directly into selected areas to be visualized. (4)

Stability — Diatrizoate sodium solutions are colorless to pale yellow. Precipitates that may form in the solutions may be redissolved by placing the container in hot water. Allow the solution to cool to body temperature before administration. The solutions should be protected from strong light. (4)

Diatrizoate sodium products, singly and in combinations, are sensitive to low pH values. At about pH 3 to 4, turbidity or frank precipitation may appear. (479)

Syringes—Plastic syringes have been stated to be unsuitable for accommodating radiopaque solutions for any length of time. The plastic is attacked, and the plunger tends to freeze on prolonged storage. (40) However, when diatrizoate sodium (Winthrop) 75% was stored in polystyrene syringes (Pharmaseal) at 25 and 37 °C, no apparent changes were noted visually or spectrophotometrically over five days. (530)

An increased incidence of adverse reactions to diatrizoate sodium in combination with diatrizoate meglumine in intravenous pyelography was attributed to extraction of phenolic compounds from the rubber plunger-stopper when Plastipak (Becton-Dickinson) disposable syringes were used to administer the radiopaque contrast media. The use of glass syringes only was recommended. (821)

Compatibility Information

Drugs in Syringe Compatibility

Diatrizoate sodium

Drug (in syringe)	*Mfr*	*Amt*	*Mfr*	*Amt*	*Remarks*	*Ref*	*C/I*
Ampicillin sodium	BR	30 mg/ 1 ml	WI	60%, 5 ml	Physically compatible for at least 2 hr	1438	C
Chloramphenicol sodium succinate	PD	33 mg/ 1 ml	WI	60%, 5 ml	Physically compatible for at least 2 hr	1438	C
Chlorpheniramine maleate	RB	1 ml[a]	WI	75%, 1 to 40 ml	Physically compatible for 48 hr	530	C
Cimetidine HCl	SKF	150 mg/ 1 ml	WI	60%, 5 ml	Physically compatible for at least 2 hr	1438	C
Dimenhydrinate	SE	50 mg/ 1 ml	WI	75%, 1 to 40 ml	Physically compatible for 48 hr	530	C
Diphenhydramine HCl	PD	50 mg/ 1 ml	WI	5 ml[a]	No precipitate observed	309	C
	PD	1 ml[a]	WI	75%, 1 to 40 ml	Physically compatible for 48 hr	530	C
	PD	12.5 mg/ 0.25 ml	WI	60%, 5 ml	Transient precipitate clears and then reforms after 1 hr	1438	I
Epinephrine HCl	PD	1 mg/ 1 ml	WI	60%, 5 ml	Physically compatible for at least 2 hr	1438	C
Gentamicin sulfate	SC	0.8 mg/ 1 ml	WI	60%, 5 ml	Physically compatible for at least 2 hr	1438	C
Heparin sodium	OR	5000 units/ 0.5 ml	WI	60%, 5 ml	Physically compatible for at least 2 hr	1438	C
Hyaluronidase	WY	150 units/ 1 ml	WI	75%, 5 to 40 ml	Physically compatible for 48 hr	530	C
	WY	150 units/ 1 ml	WI	75%, 2 and 1 ml	Physically compatible for at least 1 hr, but precipitate forms within 48 hr	530	I

Drugs in Syringe Compatibility (Cont.)

Diatrizoate sodium

Drug (in syringe)	*Mfr*	*Amt*	*Mfr*	*Amt*	*Remarks*	*Ref*	*C/I*
Hydrocortisone sodium succinate	UP	10 mg/ 1 ml	WI	60%, 5 ml	Physically compatible for at least 2 hr	1438	C
Methylprednisolone sodium succinate	UP	10 mg/ 1 ml	WI	60%, 5 ml	Physically compatible for at least 2 hr	1438	C
Papaverine HCl	ME	32 mg/ 1 ml	WI	60%, 5 ml	Transient precipitate clears within 5 min	1438	?
Promethazine HCl	WY	1 ml[a]	WI	75%, 1 to 40 ml	Immediate precipitation	530	I
Protamine sulfate	LI	10 mg/ 1 ml	WI	60%, 5 ml	Precipitate forms immediately and persists for at least 2 hr	1438	I

[a]*Concentration unspecified.*

Additional Compatibility Information

Other Drugs — Diatrizoate sodium, singly or in combination, may be physically incompatible with additives that lower the pH to 4 or below. (479)

DIAZEPAM
AHFS 28:24.08

Products — Diazepam is available in 1- and 2-ml ampuls and vials, 10-ml vials, and 2-ml disposable syringes and syringe cartridges. Each milliliter of solution contains (2):

Diazepam	5 mg
Propylene glycol	40%
Ethyl alcohol	10%
Sodium benzoate and benzoic acid	5%
Benzyl alcohol	1.5%

pH — From 6.2 to 6.9. (4)

Osmolality — The osmolality of diazepam (Roche) was determined to be 7775 mOsm/kg. Diazemuls (Kabi) has an osmolality of 349 mOsm/kg. (1233)

Trade Name(s) — Valium.

Administration — Diazepam is administered by direct intravenous injection into a large vein (2; 4) or, if necessary, into the tubing of a running infusion solution. (4) Extravasation should be avoided. It is recommended that the rate of administration in adults not exceed 5 mg/min; for children, it is recommended that the dose be administered over not less than three minutes. Diazepam can be given by deep intramuscular injection (2; 4), but this route may yield low or erratic plasma levels. (4; 121; 638) Intravenous infusion of diazepam diluted in infusion solutions has been performed but is not recommended. (2; 4) See Dilution under Additional Compatibility Information.

Stability — The commercial product should be stored at controlled room temperature and protected from light. (4) Diazepam (Roche) 5 mg/ml was found to retain potency for three months at room temperature when 2 ml of solution was repackaged in Tubex cartridges. (13)

The drug is most stable at pH 4 to 8 and is subject to acid-catalyzed hydrolysis below pH 3. (643)

In tropical climates, diazepam injection is subject to discoloration from degradation by an oxidative hydrolytic mechanism. The rate of degradation leading to discoloration is dependent on various factors including the polarity/dielectric constant of the vehicle, pH, oxygen and electrolyte content, access to light, and storage temperature. (1749)

Syringes — Diazepam 5 mg/ml was filled into 3-ml plastic syringes (Becton-Dickinson, Sherwood Monoject, and Terumo) and stored at −20, 4, and 25 °C in the dark. Diazepam concentration losses, presumably due to sorption to surfaces and/or the elastomeric plunger seal, ranged from 6% at 25 °C to 2 or 3% at 4 °C to 1% or less at −20 °C in one day. Long-term storage for seven days at 4 °C and 30 days at −20 °C resulted in losses of 4 to 8% and 5 to 13%, respectively. (1562)

Diazepam (Roche) 10 mg/2 ml was stored in plastic syringes composed of polypropylene and polyethylene. No loss of diazepam was detected by UV spectroscopy after four hours of storage. (351)

Diazepam (Roche) 5 mg/ml was stored in 1.5-ml disposable glass syringes with slit rubber plunger-stoppers (Hy-Pod) for 90 days at 30 and 4 °C in light-resistant bags. Diazepam was gradually lost from the solution, with the disappearance being essentially complete in 60 days. At 4 °C, about 5% was lost at the 60- and 90-day intervals; about 9 to 10% was lost at 30 °C in this period. The loss was attributed to sorption to the rubber plunger-stoppers. (794)

Sorption — The apparent stability of diazepam in several infusion fluids in glass containers (321) does not extend to the solutions in PVC bags in which substantial sorption occurs. At concentrations of 10 mg in 100 and 200 ml, a greater than 24% loss of potency occurred in 30 minutes. The potency loss appears to be a function of drug concentration and time, with approximately 80 to 90% loss occurring in 24 hours. (330) (See table.)

In another test, diazepam (David Bull Laboratories) 8 mg/L in sodium chloride 0.9% (Travenol) in PVC bags exhibited approximately 20% loss in 24 hours and 32% loss in one week at room temperature (15 to 20 °C) due to sorption. (536)

Cloyd et al. also evaluated the sorption of diazepam to PVC infusion bags. At concentrations of 5 and 20 mg/100 ml in dextrose 5% in water and sodium chloride 0.9%, the diazepam content of the solutions was less than 45% in two hours and further declined to about 20 to 25% in eight hours. (647)

In addition, Cloyd et al. tested the diazepam sorption that results from administration through plastic infusion sets. Dilutions of 7.5 and 30 mg in 150 ml of dextrose 5% in water and sodium chloride 0.9% were prepared in the burette chamber of a Buretrol. The solutions flowed through the tubing at 30 ml/hr for two hours. A relatively small (less than 10%) but significant decrease in diazepam content occurred in the burette chamber. However, running the solution through the tubing resulted in steep declines in potency to about 43% of the initial amount. When diazepam solutions of 25 and 100 mg/500 ml of dextrose 5% in water and sodium chloride 0.9% were prepared in glass bottles and 100-ml aliquots were run through the Buretrol over one hour, only about 60 to 70% of the diazepam was delivered. The presence of a 0.5-μm inline filter did not affect the diazepam concentration delivered. (647)

MacKichan et al. reported over a 90% loss due to sorption to the administration set (Abbott) and the extension tubing (Extracorporeal) both with and without a 0.22-μm inline filter (Abbott). Solutions containing 0.02 to 0.04 mg/ml of diazepam in dextrose 5% in water had no evidence of precipitation, and solutions in glass bottles retained their initial potency over 24 hours. However, the amount delivered through the tubing was only 40 to 55% at time zero, and this amount dropped to 2 to 7% at 24 hours. No difference was noted from the inline filter. (645)

Parker and MacCara also evaluated the sorption of diazepam to administration sets from solutions of diazepam 25 and 50 mg/500 ml in glass bottles of dextrose 5% in water and Ringer's injection, lactated, or 12.5 and 25 mg/250 ml of these same solutions in Soluset burette chambers. The admixtures showed no evidence of physical incompatibility by macroscopic or microscopic examination over four hours of storage at room temperature. The solutions in glass bottles were run through Venosets composed of PVC drip chambers and tubing at 2.5 and 5 mg/hr. The solutions stored in the cellulose propionate burette chambers of the Solusets were also run through their PVC tubing at the same rates. The solution delivered through the Venosets contained about 91 to 97% of the initial concentration, with the more dilute solution having slightly more drug remaining. However, the Soluset delivered only about 50 to 60% in two hours and about 35 to 45% of the initial concentration after four hours. The authors believed that most of the loss was due to sorption to the cellulose propionate burette chamber. This result was attributed to the larger surface area of the burette compared with the tubing and/or the difference in plastic composition. Almost all of the lost diazepam could be recovered through desorption from the burettes. (646) This result is in striking contrast to the results of Cloyd et al. reported above. (647) The use of 0.45-μm inline filters had no effect on the drug concentration. The authors recommended that diazepam infusions be prepared only in glass bottles and be administered only through sets not having burette chambers. (646)

Dasta et al. assessed a 50-mg/500 ml solution in dextrose 5% in water prepared in glass bottles and run through an administration set (Travenol) at 100 ml/hr. Only 63% of the predicted diazepam concentration was initially delivered, but this amount gradually climbed to a maximum concentration of 81% at the end of five hours. (649)

Boatman and Johnson noted a 27 to 33% diazepam loss from admixtures in both dextrose 5% in water and sodium chloride 0.9% in PVC bags. The diazepam concentrations evaluated ranged from 0.05 to 0.2 mg/ml. No drug decomposition could be detected, and nearly quantitative recovery of the drug could be obtained from the PVC bags. Diazepam solutions in dextrose 5% in water were also run through a 70-inch Travenol set. A steep decline to less than 70% of the expected amount of diazepam was delivered during the first 15 minutes, after which the delivered amount increased to between 80 and 90% of the expected amount over the next 85 minutes as saturation of the tubing occurred. A quantitatively smaller, but qualitatively similar, effect was observed when diazepam was administered by intravenous push through an intravenous catheter (Abbott Venocath-18) of 11.5-inch total length. The decline in delivered diazepam reached a nadir of approximately 95% in about eight minutes before returning to 100% at 10 minutes. The smaller effect of the intravenous catheter relates to its relatively shorter length. (650)

Kowaluk et al. found that diazepam (David Bull Laboratories) 8 mg/L in sodium chloride 0.9% in glass bottles exhibited a cumulative 7% loss due to sorption during a seven-hour simulated infusion through an infusion set (Travenol). The set consisted of a cellulose propionate burette chamber and 170 cm of PVC tubing. Diazepam sorption was attributed mainly to the tubing. The extent of sorption was found to be independent of concentration. (606)

Diazepam was also tested as a simulated infusion over at least one hour by a syringe pump system. A glass syringe on a syringe pump was fitted with 20 cm of polyethylene tubing or 50 cm of Silastic tubing. A negligible amount of drug was lost with the polyethylene tubing, but a cumulative loss of 21% occurred during the one-hour infusion through the Silastic tubing. (606)

Storage of a 25-ml aliquot of the 8-mg/L diazepam solution in all-plastic syringes composed of polypropylene barrels and polyethylene plungers for 24 hours at room temperature in the dark did not result in any drug loss due to sorption. (606)

Winsnes et al. prepared a diazepam (Roche) infusion of 20 mg/500 ml in dextrose 5% in water and delivered it at 4 ml/hr through PVC tubing by means of an infusion pump. Less than 20% of this diazepam concentration was delivered at any time point over the 24-hour observation period. Increasing the concentration to 50 mg/500 ml in dextrose 5% in water and increasing the infusion rate to 20 ml/hr decreased the amount of diazepam lost from the solution. After 30 minutes of solution delivery, the diazepam in the tubing effluent was about 30% of the initial concentration. Subsequently, the delivered diazepam concentration climbed to about 60% over 24 hours, presumably due to saturation of the tubing. (351)

Mason et al. determined the partition coefficients of diazepam with various plastics from intravenous containers and administration sets. It was found that PVC bags and tubings from a variety of suppliers were all similar in partitioning and hundreds of times greater than McGaw polyolefin semirigid containers. Volume-control chambers made from cellulose propionate were determined to have partition coefficients much smaller than those of PVC but still sufficient to cause serious depletion of diazepam from the chambers. Because these volume-control chambers are not essential, the authors recommended against their use. (644)

It was further determined that the uptake of diazepam into PVC is absorption into the plastic matrix rather than adsorption to the surface. The absorption is independent of concentration but clearly related to contact time with the plastic. Decreasing the flow rate or increasing the tubing length increases the amount of diazepam absorbed. (644)

Mason et al. found that increasing the flow rate from 10 to 264 ml/hr through 198 cm of PVC tubing decreased the amount of diazepam absorbed from a 90-ml delivered volume from 88 down to 28%. Increasing the tubing length from 100 to 350 cm increased the amount absorbed after 55 minutes at 121 ml/hr from 17 to 59%. However, it was noted that absorption is not markedly affected by tubing length within the range of lengths commercially available. (644)

In a continuation of this work, diazepam (David Bull Laboratories) 50 mg/L in sodium chloride 0.9% in a glass bottle was delivered through a polyethylene administration set (Tridilset) over eight hours at 15 to 20 °C. The flow rate was set at 1 ml/min. No appreciable loss due to sorption occurred. This finding is in contrast to a 20% loss using a conventional administration set. (769)

The sorption of diazepam 40 and 120 mg/L in sodium chloride 0.9% was evaluated in 100- and 500-ml PVC infusion bags (Travenol). After eight hours at 20 to 24 °C, 58 to 60% of the diazepam was lost in the 100-ml bag and 31% was lost in the 500-ml bag. The extent of sorption was independent of concentration but was greatly influenced by the size of the PVC container. This difference results from the ratio of the surface area of plastic to the volume of solution. As the volume of solution in the bag decreases, the ratio and, therefore, the extent of sorption increase. (770)

Diazepam showed negligible (<3%) loss when aqueous solutions were stored in polypropylene bags. (770)

Smith and Bird found extensive sorption of diazepam from dextrose 5% in water and sodium chloride 0.9% to PVC containers (Travenol and Boots). Solutions of 10 to 80 mg/L showed a 12 to 20% diazepam loss in one hour. In six hours, the potency loss was about 30% at 5 °C and about 40% at room temperature. Over 30% of the missing diazepam could be recovered by washing the PVC with methanol. This result did not extend to glass or polyethylene (Polyfusor, Boots) containers, which showed drug losses of about 6 to 8% in 24 hours. (796)

Similarly, Yliruusi et al. found no loss of diazepam to glass or polyethylene containers in 200-mg/L concentrations in dextrose 5% in water or sodium chloride 0.9%. However, in PVC containers, drug losses of around 37 to 43% occurred in 24 hours at 25 °C. (797)

Cossum and Roberts also investigated the administration of diazepam (Roche) with a glass syringe on an infusion pump connected with high-density polyethylene tubing, and they found negligible drug loss. (795)

In another report, plastic syringes having polypropylene barrels and polyethylene plungers (Pharma-Plast, AHS Australia) and all-glass containers were compared for the possible sorption of diazepam. After 24 hours of storage of aqueous solutions of diazepam (concentration unspecified), no drug loss was found in either container. The authors indicated that these plastic syringes could be substituted for glass syringes for use with syringe pumps. (782)

Kowaluk et al. evaluated the effect of several factors on the rate and extent of sorption of diazepam by PVC. The sorption proved to be independent of changes in ethanol–propylene glycol concentrations in the vehicle, pH changes in the admixtures over 4.2 to 7.5, and the initial diazepam concentration. However, the rate and extent of sorption could be minimized by decreasing the storage temperature, minimizing the storage time, and increasing the surface area to volume ratio by storing the largest possible fluid volume in a given PVC bag and using short lengths of small diameter infusion tubing. Use of glass or polyolefin solution bottles and polyolefin infusion tubing avoids the loss of diazepam. (880)

The comparative sorption of diazepam (Roche) 20 mg/500 ml in sodium chloride 0.9%, run at 1 ml/min through PVC and polybutadiene (PBD) administration sets (Avon Medicals, U.K.), was reported. The delivered concentration through the PVC set was about 80% of the expected amount initially and then climbed to about 90% after four hours. For a concentration of 10 mg/120 ml prepared in a cellulose propionate burette, 10 to 15% sorption occurred in the burette. Conversely, use of the PBD set, with or without a methacrylate butadiene styrene burette chamber, resulted in no detectable loss of diazepam potency. (1027)

Hancock and Black compared the delivery of diazepam (Roche) 50 and 100 mg/500 ml of dextrose 5% in water and sodium chloride 0.9% through a PVC administration set (Accuset 9210, IMED) and a set composed of ethylene–vinyl acetate with a polyethylene inner wall (Accuset 9630, IMED). The solutions were run through the sets at 50 and 100 ml/hr. The delivered diazepam concentration varied between 44 and 71% at 50 ml/hr and between 62 and 89% at 100 ml/hr, increasing from the lower to the higher percentage over the five-hour study period. The non-PVC set exhibited no sorption of diazepam, delivering essentially 100% of the diazepam at each time point measured. (1096)

Yliruusi et al. found that the percentage of diazepam delivered through PVC administration sets varied with the length of the tubing; the longer the tubing, the smaller was the percentage delivered. For a 25-mg/500 ml admixture in sodium chloride 0.9%, delivery through PVC tubing in lengths from 23 to 185 cm varied from 88% of the theoretical amount for the shortest length to 53% for the 185-cm length. (1097)

Yliruusi et al. also evaluated the effect of container type and flow rate on the sorption of diazepam. Glass and polyethylene containers showed 0 and 5% sorption, respectively, of the diazepam content of a 25-mg/500 ml admixture in sodium chloride 0.9% in seven days at 25 °C. However, PVC containers showed a 75% loss in this time period. Simulated infusion of this solution from glass bottles through PVC sets at flow rates of 30 to 120 ml/hr showed that a greater percentage of diazepam was lost at the slower infusion rates. At 30 ml/hr, 63% was lost after four hours, while only 23% was lost after four hours at 120 ml/hr. (1098)

Martens et al. reported a rapid diazepam loss from a 40-µg/ml solution in sodium chloride 0.9% in a PVC container at 21 °C protected from light. A 15% loss occurred in two hours, and a 55% loss occurred in 24 hours. Little or no diazepam loss occurred in 24 hours in glass bottles or polyethylene-lined laminated bags. (1392)

Diazepam (Orion) 100 µg/ml in sodium chloride 0.9% exhibited no loss due to sorption by UV spectroscopy and HPLC analysis in 24 hours at 21 °C in glass bottles and polypropylene trilayer bags (Softbag, Orion). However, about a 70% loss occurred due to sorption under these conditions in PVC bags. (1796)

Diazepam (Takeda) 40 µg/ml in 0.9% sodium chloride and in pH 7 buffer also underwent sorption to ethylene vinyl acetate (EVA) plastic bags (Terumo). Losses exceeding 25% occurred within 24 hours stored at 30 °C in dim light. The solutions appeared to reach equilibrium after 96 hours of storage. The authors speculated that both absorption and adsorption of the diazepam to the EVA bags were occurring. (1917)

Diazepam (B. Braun) 0.04 mg/ml in dextrose 5% in water and sodium chloride 0.9% packaged in PVC, polyethylene, and glass containers exhibited only 4 to 5% loss in glass and polyethylene containers but 66% loss due to sorption in PVC containers when stored at 4 and 22 °C for 24 hours protected from light. (2289)

Other reports support and confirm these findings. (1251; 1252)

In summary, the delivery of diazepam by intravenous infusion is problematic. To minimize the sorption of diazepam, glass or polyolefin containers should be used. Alternatively, a syringe pump has been recommended since sorption to plastic syringes has not been found. (1033) If PVC bags are used, the lowest possible surface-to-volume ratio should be selected and storage time should be minimized. The use of non-PVC administration sets will reduce loss. If PVC tubing is used, it should be the shortest possible length with a small diameter, and the set should not contain a burette chamber. More rapid flow rates (consistent with safe clinical use) will also reduce the loss of diazepam.

Also see Dilution under Additional Compatibility Information.

Filtration—Diazepam (Roche) 50 µg/ml in dextrose 5% in water and sodium chloride 0.9% was delivered over seven hours through four kinds of 0.2-µm membrane filters varying in size and composition. Diazepam concentration losses of 7 to 17% were found during the first 60 minutes; subsequent diazepam levels returned to the original concentration when the binding sites became saturated. (1399)

Compatibility Information

Solution Compatibility

Diazepam

Solution	*Mfr*	*Mfr*	*Conc/L*	*Remarks*	*Ref*	*C/I*
Dextrose 5% in water	BA[a]	RC	>250 mg	Immediate white precipitation	321	I
	BA[a]	RC	250 mg	No precipitate in 24 hr. 6% potency loss in 4 hr	321	I
	BA[a]	RC	100 and 125 mg	No precipitate and 8 to 10% potency loss in 24 hr	321	C
	BA[a]	RC	50 and 67 mg	No precipitate and 0 to 1% potency loss in 24 hr	321	C
	BA[b]	RC	100 mg	35% potency loss in 30 min. 90% potency loss in 24 hr at room temperature	330	I
	BA[b]	RC	50 mg	35% potency loss in 30 min. 77% potency loss in 24 hr at room temperature	330	I
		RC	370 mg	Precipitate formed. Diazepam concentration unchanged after filtration	640	I
	TR[b]	RC	50 and 200 mg	Solution initially cloudy but clears by completion of admixture. 55 to 60% potency loss within 2 hr	647	I
	BT[b]	RC	40 mg	No precipitate but 12 to 14% potency loss in 1 hr at room temperature and 5 °C	796	I
	BT[c]	RC	40 mg	No precipitate and about 10% potency loss in 24 hr at room temperature	796	C
	ON[a,c]	ON	200 mg	No precipitate and negligible potency loss in 24 hr at 25 °C	797	C
	[b]	ON	200 mg	No precipitate but about 10% potency loss in 3.5 hr and about 37% in 24 hr at 25 °C	797	I
	BA[b]	BRN	40 mg	Visually compatible but 66% loss due to sorption to the PVC container in 24 hr at 4 and 22 °C	2289	I
	BRN[a,c]	BRN	40 mg	Visually compatible with 4 to 5% loss by HPLC in 24 hr at 4 and 22 °C	2289	C
Ringer's injection	BA[a]	RC	>250 mg	Immediate white precipitation	321	I
	BA[a]	RC	250 mg	White precipitate formed in 6 to 8 hr. 8% potency loss in 4 hr	321	I
	BA[a]	RC	100 and 125 mg	No precipitate and 7 to 12% potency loss in 24 hr	321	C
	BA[a]	RC	50 and 67 mg	No precipitate and 0 to 3% potency loss in 24 hr	321	C
	BA[b]	RC	100 mg	38% potency loss in 30 min. 89% potency loss in 24 hr at room temperature	330	I

Solution Compatibility (Cont.)

Diazepam

Solution	*Mfr*	*Mfr*	*Conc/L*	*Remarks*	*Ref*	*C/I*
	BA[b]	RC	50 mg	29% potency loss in 30 min. 78% potency loss in 24 hr at room temperature	330	I
Ringer's injection, lactated	BA[a]	RC	>250 mg	Immediate white precipitation	321	I
	BA[a]	RC	250 mg	White precipitate formed in 8 to 12 hr. 5% potency loss in 4 hr	321	I
		RC	200 mg	Transient cloudiness followed by clear solution	392	C
	BA[a]	RC	100 and 125 mg	No precipitate and 8 to 10% potency loss in 24 hr	321	C
	BA[a]	RC	50 and 67 mg	No precipitate and 6% potency loss in 24 hr	321	C
	BA[b]	RC	100 mg	35% potency loss in 30 min. 89% potency loss in 24 hr at room temperature	330	I
	BA[b]	RC	50 mg	40% potency loss in 30 min. 78% potency loss in 24 hr at room temperature	330	I
Sodium chloride 0.9%	BA[a]	RC	>250 mg	Immediate white precipitation	321	I
	BA[a]	RC	250 mg	No precipitate in 24 hr. 6% potency loss in 4 hr	321	I
	BA[a]	RC	125 mg	No precipitate and 6% potency loss in 24 hr	321	C
	BA[a]	RC	100 mg	No precipitate and 4 to 5% potency loss in 24 hr	321; 330	C
	BA[a]	RC	67 mg	No precipitate and 6% potency loss in 24 hr	321	C
	BA[a]	RC	50 mg	No precipitate and 1 to 3% potency loss in 24 hr	321; 330	C
	BA[b]	RC	100 mg	29% potency loss in 30 min. 89% potency loss in 24 hr at room temperature	330	I
	BA[b]	RC	50 mg	24% potency loss in 30 min. 80% potency loss in 24 hr at room temperature	330	I
	TR[b]	RC	50 and 200 mg	Solution initially cloudy but clears by completion of admixture. 55 to 60% potency loss within 2 hr	647	I
	[a]	RC	40 mg	No precipitate and about 6% potency loss in 24 hr at room temperature	796	C
	BT, TR[b]	RC	10 to 80 mg	No precipitate but about 12 to 20% potency loss in 1 hr at room temperature and 5 °C	796	I
	BT[c]	RC	10 to 80 mg	No precipitate and about 2 to 8% potency loss in 24 hr at room temperature and 5 °C	796	C
	ON[a,c]	ON	200 mg	No precipitate and negligible potency loss in 24 hr at 25 °C	797	C
	[b]	ON	200 mg	No precipitate but about 10% potency loss in 1 hr and about 43% in 24 hr at 25 °C	797	I
	[a]		400 mg	Precipitate forms immediately or within 1 min	1095	I
	[a]		333 mg	Precipitate forms after 30 min	1095	I
	[a]		100 and 200 mg	Remained clear for 10 days	1095	C
	[a]		50 mg	No diazepam loss in 7 days at 25 °C	1098	C
	[b]		50 mg	More than 40% loss in 1 day and 75% in 7 days at 25 °C	1098	I
	[c]		50 mg	About 5% loss in 7 days at 25 °C	1098	C
	[b]		40 mg	15% diazepam loss in 2 hr and 55% loss in 24 hr at 21 °C in the dark	1392	I
	[a,c]		40 mg	Little or no diazepam loss in 24 hr at 21 °C in the dark	1392	C
	ON[d]	ON	100 mg	Visually compatible with no loss by UV and HPLC in 24 hr at 21 °C	1796	C

Solution Compatibility (Cont.)

Diazepam

Solution	Mfr	Mfr	Conc/L	Remarks	Ref	C/I
	ON[b]	ON	100 mg	Visually compatible but 70% loss due to sorption by UV and HPLC in 24 hr at 21 °C	1796	I
	BA[b]	BRN	40 mg	Visually compatible but 66% loss due to sorption to the PVC container in 24 hr at 4 and 22 °C	2289	I
	BRN[a,c]	BRN	40 mg	Visually compatible with 4 to 5% loss by HPLC in 24 hr at 4 and 22 °C	2289	C

[a]Tested in glass containers.
[b]Tested in PVC containers.
[c]Tested in polyethylene containers.
[d]Tested in glass containers and polypropylene trilayer containers.

Additive Compatibility

Diazepam

Drug	Mfr	Conc/L	Mfr	Conc/L	Test Soln	Remarks	Ref	C/I
Bleomycin sulfate	BR	20 and 30 units	RC	50 and 100 mg	NS	Physically incompatible	763	I
Dobutamine HCl	LI	1 g	RC	2.5 g	D5W, NS	Rapid clouding of solution with yellow precipitate in 24 hr at 21 °C	812	I
Doxorubicin HCl	AD		RC			Immediate precipitation	524	I
Floxacillin sodium	BE	20 g	PHX	1 g	D5W	Haze forms in 7 hr at 30 °C and 48 hr at 15 °C	1479	I
Fluorouracil			RC			Immediate precipitation	524	I
Furosemide	HO	20 g	PHX	1 g	D5W	Immediate precipitation	1479	I
Netilmicin sulfate	SC	3 g	RC	40 mg	D5S	Physically compatible and netilmicin chemically stable for 7 days at 25 and 4 °C. Diazepam not tested	558	C
Verapamil HCl	KN	80 mg	RC	20 mg	D5W, NS	Physically compatible for 24 hr	764	C

Drugs in Syringe Compatibility

Diazepam

Drug (in syringe)	Mfr	Amt	Mfr	Amt	Remarks	Ref	C/I
Cimetidine HCl	SKF	300 mg/ 2 ml	RC	10 mg/ 2 ml	Physically compatible for 4 hr at 25 °C	25	C
Doxapram HCl	RB	400 mg/ 20 ml		10 mg/ 2 ml	Immediate turbidity and precipitation	1177	I
Glycopyrrolate	RB	0.2 mg/ 1 ml	RC	5 mg/ 1 ml	Immediate precipitation	331	I
	RB	0.2 mg/ 1 ml	RC	10 mg/ 2 ml	Immediate precipitation	331	I
	RB	0.4 mg/ 2 ml	RC	5 mg/ 1 ml	Immediate precipitation	331	I
Heparin sodium		2500 units/ 1 ml		10 mg/ 2 ml	Turbidity or precipitate forms within 5 min	1053	I

Drugs in Syringe Compatibility (Cont.)

Diazepam

Drug (in syringe)	*Mfr*	*Amt*	*Mfr*	*Amt*	*Remarks*	*Ref*	*C/I*
Hydromorphone HCl	KN	2, 10, 40 mg/ 1 ml	SX	5 mg/ 1 ml	Diazepam precipitate forms immediately due to aqueous dilution	2082	I
Ketorolac tromethamine	SY	180 mg/ 6 ml	ES	15 mg/ 3 ml	Visually compatible for 4 hr at 24 °C under ambient light. Increase in spectrophotometric absorbance occurs immediately, persists for 30 min, and dissipates by 1 hr	1703	?
Nalbuphine HCl	EN	10 mg/ 1 ml	RC	5 mg/ 1 ml	Immediate white milky precipitate that persisted for 36 hr at 27 °C	762	I
	EN	5 mg/ 0.5 ml	RC	5 mg/ 1 ml	Immediate white milky precipitate that cleared upon vigorous shaking; remained clear for 36 hr at 27 °C	762	I
	EN	2.5 mg/ 0.25 ml	RC	5 mg/ 1 ml	Immediate white milky precipitate that cleared upon vigorous shaking; remained clear for 36 hr at 27 °C	762	I
	DU	10 mg/ 1 ml	RC	10 mg/ 2 ml	Physically incompatible	128	I
	DU	20 mg/ 1 ml	RC	10 mg/ 2 ml	Physically incompatible	128	I
Ranitidine HCl	GL	50 mg/ 2 ml	RC	10 mg/ 2 ml	Immediate white haze that disappeared following vortex mixing	978	I
	GL	50 mg/ 5 ml		10 mg	Physically compatible for 4 hr at ambient temperature under fluorescent light	1151	C
Sufentanil citrate	JN	50 μg/ml	ES	5 mg/ml	White turbidity forms immediately. Precipitate forms in 24 hr at 23 °C	1711	I

Y-Site Injection Compatibility (1:1 Mixture)

Diazepam

Drug	*Mfr*	*Conc*	*Mfr*	*Conc*	*Remarks*	*Ref*	*C/I*
Amphotericin B cholesteryl sulfate complex	SEQ	0.83 mg/ml[a]	SW	5 mg/ml	Gross precipitate forms	2117	I
Atracurium besylate	BW	0.5 mg/ml[a]	ES	5 mg/ml	Cloudy solution forms immediately	1337	I
Cefepime HCl	BMS	20 mg/ml[a]	ES	5 mg/ml	Cloudy solution forms immediately	1689	I
Cisatracurium besylate	GW	0.1, 2, and 5 mg/ml[a]	ES	5 mg/ml	White turbidity forms immediately	2074	I
	GW	0.1, 2, and 5 mg/ml[a]	ES	0.25 mg/ml[a]	Physically compatible with no change in measured turbidity or increase in particle content in 4 hr at 23 °C	2074	C
Diltiazem HCl	MMD	1[b] and 5 mg/ ml	ES	5 mg/ml	Cloudiness and precipitate form	1807	I
Dobutamine HCl	LI	4 mg/ml[a,b]	ES	0.2 mg/ml[a,b]	Physically compatible for 3 hr	1316	C
Fentanyl citrate	JN	0.025 mg/ml[a]	ES	0.5 mg/ml[a]	Physically compatible with no change in measured haze or increase in particle content in 48 hr at 22 °C	1706	C
Fluconazole	RR	2 mg/ml	ES	5 mg/ml	Immediate precipitation	1407	I
Foscarnet sodium	AST	24 mg/ml	ES	5 mg/ml	Gas production	1335	I
Gatifloxacin	BMS	2 mg/ml[a]	AB	5 mg/ml	White turbid precipitate forms immediately	2234	I

Y-Site Injection Compatibility (1:1 Mixture) (Cont.)

Diazepam

Drug	*Mfr*	*Conc*	*Mfr*	*Conc*	*Remarks*	*Ref*	*C/I*
Heparin sodium		50 units/ml/min[b]		10 mg/2 ml[c]	Turbidity	1053	I
Heparin sodium with hydrocortisone sodium succinate	RI UP	1000 units + 100 mg/L[a,b,d]	RC	5 mg/ml	Immediate haziness and globule formation	322	I
Hetastarch in lactated electrolyte injection (Hextend)	AB	6%	AB	5 mg/ml	Dense white turbid precipitate forms immediately	2339	I
Hydromorphone HCl	KN	2, 10, 40 mg/ml	SX	5 mg/ml	Turbidity forms immediately and diazepam precipitate develops	1532	I
	AST	0.5 mg/ml[a]	ES	0.5 mg/ml[a]	Physically compatible with no change in measured haze or increase in particle content in 48 hr at 22 °C	1706	C
Linezolid	PHU	2 mg/ml	AB	5 mg/ml	Turbid precipitate forms immediately	2264	I
Meropenem	ZEN	1 and 50 mg/ml[b]	RC	5 mg/ml	White precipitate forms immediately	1994	I
Methadone HCl	LI	1 mg/ml[a]	ES	0.5 mg/ml[a]	Physically compatible with no change in measured haze or increase in particle content in 48 hr at 22 °C	1706	C
Morphine sulfate	AST	1 mg/ml[a]	ES	0.5 mg/ml[a]	Physically compatible with no change in measured haze or increase in particle content in 48 hr at 22 °C	1706	C
Nafcillin sodium	WY	33 mg/ml[b]		5 mg/ml	No precipitation	547	C
Pancuronium bromide	ES	0.05 mg/ml[a]	ES	5 mg/ml	Cloudy solution forms immediately	1337	I
Potassium chloride		40 mEq/L[a,b,d]	RC	5 mg/ml	Immediate haziness and globule formation	322	I
Propofol	ZEN	10 mg/ml	ES	5 mg/ml	Emulsion broke and oiled out	2066	I
Quinidine gluconate	LI	6 mg/ml[a,b]	ES	0.2 mg/ml[a,b]	Physically compatible for 3 hr	1316	C
Remifentanil HCl	GW	0.025 and 0.25 mg/ml[b]	ES	5 mg/ml	White turbidity forms immediately	2075	I
	GW	0.025 and 0.25 mg/ml[b]	ES	0.25 mg/ml[a]	Physically compatible with no change in measured turbidity or increase in particle content in 4 hr at 23 °C	2075	C
Sufentanil citrate	JN	12.5 µg/ml[a]	ES	0.5 mg/ml[a]	Physically compatible with no subvisual haze or particle formation in 24 hr at 23 °C	1711	C
TPN #189[e]			DB	5 mg/ml	Visually compatible for 24 hr at 22 °C	1767	C
Vecuronium bromide	OR	0.1 mg/ml[a]	ES	5 mg/ml	Cloudy solution forms immediately	1337	I
Vitamin B complex with C	RC	2 ml/L[a,b,d]		5 mg/ml	Immediate haziness and globule formation	322	I

[a]*Tested in dextrose 5% in water.*
[b]*Tested in sodium chloride 0.9%.*
[c]*Given over three minutes via a Y-site into the running heparin admixture.*
[d]*Tested in Ringer's injection, lactated.*
[e]*Refer to Appendix I for the composition of parenteral nutrition solutions. TPN indicates a 2-in-1 admixture.*

Additional Compatibility Information

Infusion Solutions — Although the package insert for diazepam contains a caveat against dilution of the product before intravenous administration (2), interest in the intravenous administration of diluted diazepam has been expressed repeatedly in the literature.

Sillers noted that dilution of diazepam to a concentration of 1 mg/ml (diluent unspecified) decreased thrombophlebitis occurring from extravasation. (378) In a reply, Roche indicated that an ampul of diazepam should be diluted in no more than 5 ml or, alternatively, all the way to 20 ml to avoid precipitation. Between these concentrations, a fine white precipitate may occur. (379)

Aqueous dilution of diazepam injection in a volume of 25% or more of the diazepam volume is stated to result in the immediate precipitation of diazepam. However, no precipitation was observed if aqueous dilution was made with a volume of less than 25% of the diazepam volume. (2082)

Friedenberg and Barker indicated that the dilution of diazepam may be a predisposing factor to thrombophlebitis. In contacting Roche, they were told that because diazepam has a very low solubility in aqueous systems, sodium benzoate was incorporated in the formula as a buffer. Dilution of the product, it was stated, would cause precipitation of diazepam. If the solution were then acidified, benzoic acid would precipitate and could coprecipitate with the drug. (380)

Jusko et al. tried adding diazepam injection to sodium chloride 0.9% and noted the immediate formation of a light yellow to white precipitate. The maximum dilution that produced such a precipitate was 15-fold, representing a mixture of about 0.3 to 0.4 mg/ml. They noted that a precipitate also formed in human plasma. To try to identify the precipitate, they prepared a solution composed of all ingredients of diazepam injection except diazepam. Dilution yielded no precipitate. UV spectrophotometric analysis of the diazepam injection–sodium chloride 0.9% precipitate showed that the composition was almost entirely diazepam. They further estimated that injection of 5 mg/min into the tubing of an intravenous infusion of sodium chloride 0.9% would result in a precipitate unless the administration rate exceeded 17 ml/min. (381)

Dam and Christiansen reported the formation of cloudiness or a precipitate upon the admixture of diazepam 370 mg/L in dextrose 5% injection, BP. A difference in the nature of the incompatibility among different manufacturers of diazepam injection was noted. The products from Roche and Dumex exhibited a precipitate. The product supplied by Apotekernes Laboratorium produced a slight cloudiness. Filtration of these solutions retained the precipitate. However, the concentration of diazepam in the filtrate was determined by a TLC method to be nearly the same in all samples and corresponded well with the calculated initial concentration. In contrast to Jusko et al., the authors concluded that the precipitate was not diazepam but was probably due to the benzoates. (640)

However, this conclusion was apparently in error. Huber and Raymond, using gas chromatography–mass spectrometry, determined that the precipitate induced by adding 2 ml of sterile water for injection to 1 ml of diazepam injection is, in fact, only diazepam. No benzoate is present. The precipitate appeared to be oily and adhered to the walls of the container, leaving a clear solution. The authors postulated that this phenomenon may explain the reports of the clearing of cloudy solutions with time. (641; 642)

Kortilla et al. found a similar result to that of Jusko et al. for diazepam injection in dextrose 5% in water. As little as 10 mg of diazepam in 100 ml of dextrose 5% in water resulted in a precipitate. They also found that an infusion rate of greater than 15 to 20 ml/min was required to prevent precipitation of diazepam being injected at a rate of 5 mg/min in running infusions of dextrose 5% in water and sodium chloride 0.9%. (382)

Nevertheless, interest in infusing diazepam has persisted because of bioavailability problems associated with intramuscular injection (121; 383; 384; 638) and a growing belief in the utility of diazepam infusions. (386–392; 1099)

Baxter et al. stated that 10 mg of diazepam in 250 ml of sodium chloride 0.9% resulted in no observable precipitate. They also tried 5 mg in 50 ml of sodium chloride 0.9% with no apparent precipitate in one hour. It was noted that diazepam has a solubility of 10 mg/4 ml of water, which should permit dilution in intravenous fluids. (385)

Tehrani and Cavanaugh reported observing a transient cloudiness when 100 mg of diazepam was added to 500 ml of Ringer's injection, lactated. The solution thereafter remained clear, and the clinical response to the diazepam infusion was good. (392)

More recently, a study was conducted by Morris on the compatibility and stability of diazepam in a variety of intravenous infusion solutions. Results indicate that a visible precipitate is produced in dilutions of 1:1 to 1:10. Haziness was reported at 1:15, and delayed precipitates forming after six to eight hours were seen in some solutions at 1:20. Dilutions of 1:40 to 1:100 remained clear for 24 hours. Further, the potency of the 1:40 to 1:100 dilutions was retained for 24 hours. (See table.) The author stopped short of recommending the use of diazepam infusions in clinical practice, noting that additional studies were necessary. For example, the possibility of microcrystal formation had not been evaluated. (321)

Just such a possibility was raised by McLean in decrying the use of diazepam by infusion. (393)

Newton et al. (643) determined the equilibrium solubilities of diazepam in water for injection, sodium chloride 0.9%, dextrose 5% in water, and Ringer's injection, lactated. The equilibrium solubilities were found to be about 0.04 to 0.05 mg/ml in all of the solutions at 25 °C. This finding corroborated the work of others which indicated the solubility to be about 0.05 to 0.06 mg/ml. It also was in general agreement with the work of Morris, which found 0.12 mg/ml (1:40) to be the lowest volume dilution to remain clear for 24 hours. Newton et al. concluded that a more conservative 1:100 dilution should be used for diazepam infusion to guarantee complete solubility for up to 24 hours. (643)

Mason et al. also determined the aqueous solubility of diazepam over a pH range of approximately 3 to 8 in phosphate buffer adjusted with hydrochloric acid or sodium hydroxide as well as dextrose 5% in water, sodium chloride 0.9%, and Ringer's injection, lactated. In the pH range of 4 to 8, which included all three infusion solutions, the solubility was approximately 0.05 to 0.06 mg/ml at 25 °C. Mason et al. recommended dilution to at least 0.04 mg/ml to ensure rapid and complete re-solution upon addition to the infusion solution. (644)

Maloney investigated various dilutions of diazepam in water for injection and sodium chloride 0.9%. The observations are tabulated here (1095):

Diazepam Concentration	Diluent	Observation
10 mg/5 ml	W, NS	Clear for 1 min but then precipitate forms
10 mg/10 ml	W, NS	Immediate precipitation
10 mg/20 ml	NS	Immediate precipitation
10 mg/25 ml	NS	Immediate precipitation
10 mg/30 ml	NS	Clear for 30 min but then precipitate forms
10 mg/50 ml	NS	Clear for 10 days
10 mg/100 ml	NS	Clear for 10 days

Order of Mixing — It has been reported that addition of diazepam to dextrose 5% in water and sodium chloride 0.9% to form concentrations of 50 and 200 mg/L results in an immediate and persistent yellow precipitate. However, addition of the diluent to the diazepam injection to these same concentrations results initially in a cloudy solution which clears before the completion of admixture. It was recommended that admixtures of diazepam be prepared by adding the infusion solution to the diazepam injection. (647; 648)

Buprenorphine — Diazepam is stated to be incompatible with buprenorphine HCl. (4)

DIAZOXIDE
AHFS 24:08

Products — Diazoxide is available in 20-ml ampuls containing 300 mg (15 mg/ml) of drug and sodium hydroxide to adjust the pH in aqueous solution. (2)

pH — The pH is adjusted to approximately 11.6. (2; 4)

Osmolality — The osmolality of diazoxide was determined to be 130 mOsm/kg. (1233)

Trade Name(s) — Hyperstat.

Administration — Diazoxide should be administered intravenously undiluted and rapidly, over 30 seconds or less, into a peripheral vein via an established intravenous line. Extravasation should be avoided. It should not be injected by other routes. (2; 4)

Stability — Diazoxide can be stored at controlled room temperature or in the refrigerator. The clear, colorless solution darkens on exposure to light and should be protected from light, heat, and freezing. (2; 4) Darkened solutions may be subpotent and should not be administered. (4)

Compatibility Information

Y-Site Injection Compatibility (1:1 Mixture)

			Diazoxide				
Drug	*Mfr*	*Conc*	*Mfr*	*Conc*	*Remarks*	*Ref*	*C/I*
Hydralazine HCl	SO	1 mg/ml[a,b]	SC	15 mg/ml[a,b]	Moderate precipitate and color change in 1 hr	1316	I
Propranolol HCl	AY	0.08 mg/ml[a]	SC	15 mg/ml[a]	Moderate precipitate and slight color change in 1 hr	1316	I
	AY	0.08 mg/ml[b]	SC	15 mg/ml[b]	Moderate precipitate in 3 hr	1316	I

[a]*Tested in dextrose 5% in water.*
[b]*Tested in sodium chloride 0.9%.*

Additional Compatibility Information

Heparin — Diazoxide 300 mg/20 ml mixed in a syringe with heparin sodium 2500 units/1 ml has been reported to be physically compatible for at least five minutes. (1053)

DIGOXIN
AHFS 24:04

Products — Digoxin is available in 1- and 2-ml ampuls and vials containing 0.25 mg/ml in propylene glycol 40% and alcohol 10%, along with sodium phosphate 0.17% and citric acid 0.08%. (2; 29)

Digoxin pediatric injection is available in 1-ml ampuls containing 0.1 mg/ml in propylene glycol 40% and alcohol 10%, along with sodium phosphate 0.17% and citric acid 0.08%. (2)

pH — From 6.8 to 7.2. (2)

Osmolality—The osmolality of digoxin pediatric injection (Burroughs Wellcome) was determined to be 9105 mOsm/kg by freezing-point depression and 5885 mOsm/kg by vapor pressure. (1071)

Trade Name(s)—Lanoxin.

Administration — Digoxin is administered by direct intravenous injection slowly over a minimum of five minutes or longer given undiluted or diluted with a fourfold or greater volume of sterile water for injection, dextrose 5% in water, or sodium chloride 0.9%. If a tuberculin syringe is used for very small doses, the possibility of inadvertent overdosage exists. Following intravenous administration, the syringe should not be flushed with parenteral solution. (2; 4) Deep intramuscular injection of not more than 2 ml at a single site followed by massage has been performed. However, it is painful and causes severe local irritation. (4)

Stability — Intact containers of digoxin should be stored at controlled room temperature and protected from light. (2)

pH Effects—Digoxin is hydrolyzed in acidic solutions with a pH less than 3. At pH 5 to 8, however, digoxin is not hydrolyzed in aqueous solutions. (798; 799; 800; 801)

Syringes—Digoxin (Burroughs Wellcome) 0.25 mg/ml was found to retain potency for three months at room temperature when 1 ml of solution was repackaged in Tubex cartridges. (13)

Plasticizer Leaching—Digoxin (Elkins-Sinn) 0.04 mg/ml in dextrose 5% in water did not leach diethylhexyl phthalate (DEHP) plasticizer from 50-ml PVC bags in 24 hours at 24 °C. (1683)

Filtration—Digoxin (Burroughs Wellcome) 1 mg/L in dextrose 5% in water, sodium chloride 0.9%, and Ringer's injection, lactated, filtered over 12 hours through a 5-μm stainless steel depth filter (Argyle Filter Connector), a 0.22-μm cellulose ester membrane filter (Ivex-2 Filter Set), and a 0.22-μm polycarbonate membrane filter (In-Sure Filter Set), showed no significant reduction in potency due to binding to the filters. (320)

In another evaluation, digoxin (Burroughs Wellcome) 3 mg/L in dextrose 5% in water and sodium chloride 0.9% did not display significant sorption to a 0.45-μm cellulose membrane filter (Abbott S-A-I-F) during an eight-hour simulated infusion. (567)

Digoxin (Wellcome) 1 μg/ml in dextrose 5% in water and sodium chloride 0.9% was delivered over eight hours through four kinds of 0.2-μm membrane filters varying in size and composition. In the first 20 minutes, digoxin concentration losses were 10 to 23% through the Sterifix filter and 24 to 32% through the Pall ELD-96LL filter. However, losses of 63 to 73% occurred in the first 20 minutes with the Ivex-HP and Pall FAE-020LL filters. Subsequent digoxin levels returned to the original concentration when the binding sites became saturated. (1399)

Compatibility Information

Solution Compatibility

Digoxin

Solution	*Mfr*	*Mfr*	*Conc/L*	*Remarks*	*Ref*	*C/I*
Dextrose 5% in sodium chloride 0.45% with potassium chloride 20 mEq	AB	BW	2.5 mg	Physically compatible with no loss of digoxin in 6-hr study period at 23 °C	778	C
Dextrose 5% in water	AB	BW	2.5 mg	Physically compatible with no loss of digoxin in 48 hr at 4 and 23 °C	778	C
Ringer's injection, lactated	AB	BW	2.5 mg	Physically compatible with no loss of digoxin in 6-hr study period at 23 °C	778	C
Sodium chloride 0.45%		ES	125 mg	Physically compatible with no loss of digoxin in 4 hr at 22 °C	1419	C
Sodium chloride 0.9%	AB	BW	2.5 mg	Physically compatible with no loss of digoxin in 48 hr at 4 and 23 °C	778	C

Additive Compatibility

Digoxin

Drug	*Mfr*	*Conc/L*	*Mfr*	*Conc/L*	*Test Soln*	*Remarks*	*Ref*	*C/I*
Bretylium tosylate	ACC	1 g	BW	2 mg	D5W, NS	Physically compatible for 48 hr at 25 °C	756	C
Cimetidine HCl	SKF	3 g	BW	2.5 mg	D5W	Physically compatible and cimetidine chemically stable for 24 hr at room temperature. Digoxin not tested	551	C
Dobutamine HCl	LI	1 g	BW	4 mg	D5W, NS	Slightly pink in 24 hr at 25 °C	789	I

Additive Compatibility (Cont.)

			Digoxin					
Drug	*Mfr*	*Conc/L*	*Mfr*	*Conc/L*	*Test Soln*	*Remarks*	*Ref*	*C/I*
Floxacillin sodium	BE	20 g	BW	25 mg	NS	Physically compatible for 72 hr at 15 and 30 °C	1479	C
Furosemide	HO	20 g	BW	25 mg	NS	Physically compatible for 72 hr at 15 and 30 °C	1479	C
Lidocaine HCl	AST	2 g	ES	1 mg	D5W, LR, NS	Physically compatible for 24 hr at 25 °C	775	C
Ranitidine HCl	GL	50 mg and 2 g		2.5 mg	D5W	Physically compatible and ranitidine chemically stable by HPLC for 24 hr at 25 °C. Digoxin not tested	1515	C
Verapamil HCl	KN	80 mg	BW	2 mg	D5W, NS	Physically compatible for 48 hr	739	C

Drugs in Syringe Compatibility

			Digoxin				
Drug (in syringe)	*Mfr*	*Amt*	*Mfr*	*Amt*	*Remarks*	*Ref*	*C/I*
Doxapram HCl	RB	400 mg/ 20 ml		0.25 mg/ 1 ml	10% doxapram loss in 9 hr and 17% in 24 hr	1177	I
Heparin sodium		2500 units/ 1 ml		0.25 mg/ 1 ml	Physically compatible for at least 5 min	1053	C
Milrinone	WI	3.5 mg/ 3.5 ml		0.5 mg/ 2 ml	Brought to 10 ml total volume with D5W. Physically compatible with no loss of either drug in 4 hr at 23 °C	1191	C

Y-Site Injection Compatibility (1:1 Mixture)

			Digoxin				
Drug	*Mfr*	*Conc*	*Mfr*	*Conc*	*Remarks*	*Ref*	*C/I*
Amphotericin B cholesteryl sulfate complex	SEQ	0.83 mg/ml[a]	WY	0.25 mg/ml	Microprecipitate forms in 4 hr at 23 °C under fluorescent light	2117	I
Ciprofloxacin	MI	2 mg/ml[c]	ES	0.25 mg/ml	Visually compatible for 24 hr at 24 °C	1655	C
	BAY	2 mg/ml[b]	BW	0.25 mg/ml	Visually compatible with no ciprofloxacin loss by HPLC in 15 min. Digoxin not tested	1934	C
Cisatracurium besylate	GW	0.1, 2, 5 mg/ ml[a]	ES	0.25 mg/ml	Physically compatible with no change in measured turbidity or increase in particle content in 4 hr at 23 °C	2074	C
Diltiazem HCl	MMD	1[b] and 5 mg/ ml	ES	0.5 mg/ml	Visually compatible	1807	C
Famotidine	MSD	0.2 mg/ml[a]	ES	0.25 mg/ml	Physically compatible for 14 hr	1196	C
Fluconazole	RR	2 mg/ml	BW	0.25 mg/ml	Gas production	1407	I
Foscarnet sodium	AST	24 mg/ml	WY	0.25 mg/ml	Gas production	1335	I
Gatifloxacin	BMS	2 mg/ml[a]	ES	0.25 mg/ml	Physically compatible with no change in measured haze or increase in particle content in 4 hr at 23 °C	2234	C

Y-Site Injection Compatibility (1:1 Mixture) (Cont.)

			Digoxin				
Drug	*Mfr*	*Conc*	*Mfr*	*Conc*	*Remarks*	*Ref*	*C/I*
Heparin sodium with hydrocortisone sodium succinate	RI UP	1000 units + 100 mg/L[d]	BW	0.25 mg/ml	Physically compatible for at least 4 hr at room temperature by visual and microscopic examination	322	C
Hetastarch in lactated electrolyte injection (Hextend)	AB	6%	ES	0.25 mg/ml	Physically compatible with no change in measured turbidity or increase in particle content in 4 hr at 23 °C	2339	C
Inamrinone lactate	WI	2.5 mg/ml[a]	ES	0.25 mg/ml	Physically compatible with little or no loss of either drug in 4 hr at 22 °C	1419	C
Insulin, regular (beef pork)	LI	1 unit/ml[b]	ES	0.005 mg/ml[b]	Physically compatible for 3 hr	1316	C
(beef pork)	LI	1 unit/ml[a]	ES	0.005 mg/ml[a]	Slight haze in 1 hr	1316	I
(Humulin R)	LI	1 unit/ml[b]	ES	0.005 mg/ml[b]	Physically compatible for 3 hr	1316	C
(Humulin R)	LI	1 unit/ml[a]	ES	0.005 mg/ml[a]	Slight haze in 1 hr	1316	I
Linezolid	PHU	2 mg/ml	ES	0.25 mg/ml	Physically compatible with no change in measured turbidity or increase in particle content in 4 hr at 23 °C	2264	C
Meperidine HCl	AB	10 mg/ml	BW	0.25 mg/ml	Physically compatible for 4 hr at 25 °C	1397	C
Meropenem	ZEN	1 and 50 mg/ml[b]	BW	0.25 mg/ml	Visually compatible for 4 hr at room temperature	1994	C
Midazolam HCl	RC	1 mg/ml[a]	BW	0.1 mg/ml	Visually compatible for 24 hr at 23 °C	1847	C
Milrinone lactate	WI	200 μg/ml[a]	BW	0.25 mg/ml	Physically compatible with no loss of either drug in 4 hr at 23 °C	1191	C
Morphine sulfate	AB	1 mg/ml	BW	0.25 mg/ml	Physically compatible for 4 hr at 25 °C	1397	C
Potassium chloride		40 mEq/L[d]	BW	0.25 mg/ml	Physically compatible for at least 4 hr at room temperature by visual and microscopic examination	322	C
Propofol	ZEN	10 mg/ml	ES	0.25 mg/ml	Emulsion broke and oiled out	1916	I
Remifentanil HCl	GW	0.025 and 0.25 mg/ml[b]	ES	0.25 mg/ml	Physically compatible with no change in measured turbidity or increase in particle content in 4 hr at 23 °C	2075	C
Tacrolimus	FUJ	1 mg/ml[b]	WY	0.25 mg/ml	Visually compatible for 24 hr at 25 °C	1630	C
TNA #73[e]			BW	0.625 mg/50 ml[c]	Physically compatible for 4 hr by visual observation	1009	C
TNA #218 to #226[e]			ES, WY	0.25 mg/ml	Visually compatible with no precipitate or emulsion damage apparent in 4 hr at 23 °C	2215	C
TPN #212 to #215[e]			BW	0.25 mg/ml	Physically compatible with no change in measured turbidity or increase in particle content in 4 hr at 23 °C	2109	C
Vitamin B complex with C	RC	2 ml/L[e]	BW	0.25 mg/ml	Physically compatible for at least 4 hr at room temperature by visual and microscopic examination	322	C

[a] *Tested in dextrose 5% in water.*
[b] *Tested in sodium chloride 0.9%.*
[c] *Tested in both dextrose 5% in water and sodium chloride 0.9%.*
[d] *Tested in dextrose 5% in water, Ringer's injection, lactated, and sodium chloride 0.9%.*
[e] *Refer to Appendix I for the composition of parenteral nutrition solutions. TNA indicates a 3-in-1 admixture, and TPN indicates a 2-in-1 admixture.*

Additional Compatibility Information

Infusion Solutions — The manufacturer recommends dilution with at least a fourfold volume of sterile water for injection, dextrose 5% in water, or sodium chloride 0.9%. Dilution to a more concentrated solution than this fourfold volume of diluent may lead to precipitation of the digoxin. (2; 4)

Parenteral Nutrition Solutions — Digoxin (Burroughs Wellcome) in doses of 0.25 and 0.125 mg/L in a parenteral nutrition solution composed of 500 ml of amino acids 5.5% with electrolytes (Travenol) and 500 ml of dextrose 50% was reported to be therapeutically available to a patient on home total parenteral nutrition, providing digoxin serum levels in the normal range. (802)

In another report, digoxin 0.25 to 1 mg/L in parenteral nutrition solutions in PVC bags was reported to be stable for up to 96 hours at 4 °C when evaluated by a radioimmunoassay. Furthermore, adequate serum levels and therapeutic response were obtained in two patients. Nevertheless, the routine addition of digoxin to parenteral nutrition solutions was not recommended until additional stability testing has been conducted and pharmacologic efficacy has been documented. (854)

Other Drugs — The manufacturer recommends that digoxin not be mixed with other drugs. (2)

DILTIAZEM HCL
AHFS 24:04

Products — Diltiazem HCl is available as a 5-mg/ml solution in 5-ml (25 mg) and 10-ml (50 mg) vials. Also present in each milliliter of solution are citric acid 0.75 mg, sodium citrate dihydrate 0.65 mg, sorbitol solution 71.4 mg, and water for injection. Sodium hydroxide or hydrochloric acid may be used to adjust the pH. (2)

Diltiazem HCl is also available as a lyophilized powder in a 25-mg dual-chamber, single-use syringe and a 100-mg single-dose vial (called "Monovial"). The first chamber of the dual-chamber syringe contains lyophilized diltiazem HCl 25 mg and mannitol 37.5 mg. The second chamber contains 5 ml of sterile water for injection with 0.5% benzyl alcohol and sodium chloride 0.6%. The single-dose vials contain diltiazem HCl 100 mg and mannitol 75 mg. They are packaged with a transfer needle set. (2; 4)

pH — From 3.7 to 4.1. The pH of the solution in the dual-chamber syringe after reconstitution is in the range of 4 to 7. (2; 4)

Trade Name(s) — Cardizem.

Administration — Diltiazem HCl is administered by direct intravenous injection over two minutes and by continuous intravenous infusion after dilution in dextrose 5% in water, sodium chloride 0.9%, or dextrose 5% in sodium chloride 0.45%. (2)

The dry powder in single-dose vials is prepared for continuous administration by diluting the contents of one vial (100 mg) in 100 ml of compatible diluent to yield a 1-mg/ml solution or diluting two vials (200 mg) in 250 ml or 500 ml of compatible diluent to yield 0.8- or 0.4-mg/ml solutions, respectively. (2)

The manufacturer recommends not using the product in the dual-chamber syringe on newborns because of the benzyl alcohol content. (2)

See Table 1 for recommended dilutions for infusion.

Stability — Intact vials of the liquid injection should be stored under refrigeration and protected from freezing. Diltiazem HCl may be stored for up to one month at room temperature but should then be destroyed. (2)

Table 1. Recommended Diltiazem HCl Dilutions for Intravenous Infusion Admixtures (2)

Diluent Volume (ml)	Quantity of Diltiazem HCl Added	Final Admixture Concentration (mg/ml)	Final Admixture Volume (ml)
Liquid Dosage Forms			
100	125 mg (25 ml)	1	125
250	250 mg (50 ml)	0.83	300
500	250 mg (50 ml)	0.45	550
Lyophilized Vials			
100	100 mg (1 vial)	1	
250	200 mg (2 vials)	0.8	
500	200 mg (2 vials)	0.4	

Diltiazem HCl powder for injection in single-dose vials or in dual-chamber syringes should be stored at controlled room temperature. Freezing should be avoided. The reconstituted solutions are stable for 24 hours at controlled room temperature. (2; 4)

pH Effects — Kawano et al. reported an increased rate of diltiazem HCl hydrolysis with increasing pH. Within the pH range tested, hydrolysis was lowest at pH 5 and 6 but increased substantially at pH 7 and 8. Diltiazem HCl 100 μg/ml in sodium chloride 0.9% with a pH between 5 and 6 exhibited no loss using HPLC analysis in 24 hours. Buffered to pH 7, losses of 3 to 4% in 24 hours were found. (1915)

Sorption — Kawano et al. reported a pH-dependent loss of diltiazem HCl due to sorption to PVC containers and administration sets. Diltiazem HCl 100 μg/ml in sodium chloride 0.9% buffered to neutrality exhibited a loss of 11% in 24 hours in PVC containers but only 3 to 4% in glass and polypropylene containers. (1915)

Similar results were found with PVC administration sets. Buffered to pH 8, diltiazem HCl concentration was initially reduced to about 83% when delivered at 0.52 ml/min through a 100-cm PVC administration set. At pH 6 and 7, initial losses were much less, about 1 and 5%, respectively. Delivered diltiazem HCl returned to full concentration in less than one hour at pH 6 and 7 but at pH 8 was only about 93% in two hours. The authors postulated the increased rate of hydrolysis at higher pH leads to increased sorption to PVC. (1915)

Diltiazem HCl 0.05 mg/ml in dextrose 5% in water and sodium chloride 0.9% packaged in PVC, polyethylene, and glass containers exhibited little or no loss due to sorption to any of the container types when stored at 4 and 22 °C for 24 hours protected from light. (2289)

Compatibility Information

Solution Compatibility

Diltiazem HCl

Solution	*Mfr*	*Mfr*	*Conc/L*	*Remarks*	*Ref*	*C/I*
Dextrose 5% in water	BA[a]	GO	50 mg	Visually compatible with about 4% loss by HPLC in 24 hr at 22 °C and little or no loss at 4 °C	2289	C
	BRN[b]	GO	50 mg	Visually compatible with little or no loss by HPLC in 24 hr at 4 and 22 °C	2289	C
Sodium chloride 0.9%	BA[a]	GO	50 mg	Visually compatible with about 4% loss by HPLC in 24 hr at 22 °C and little or no loss at 4 °C	2289	C
	BRN[b]	GO	50 mg	Visually compatible with little or no loss by HPLC in 24 hr at 4 and 22 °C	2289	C

[a]*Tested in PVC containers.*
[b]*Tested in polyethylene and glass containers.*

Y-Site Injection Compatibility (1:1 Mixture)

Diltiazem HCl

Drug	*Mfr*	*Conc*	*Mfr*	*Conc*	*Remarks*	*Ref*	*C/I*
Acetazolamide sodium	LE	100 mg/ml	MMD	5 mg/ml	Precipitate forms	1807	I
	LE	100 mg/ml	MMD	1 mg/ml[b]	Visually compatible	1807	C
Acyclovir sodium	BW	5[a] and 7[b] mg/ml	MMD	5 mg/ml	Cloudiness and precipitate form	1807	I
	BW	5[a] and 7[b] mg/ml	MMD	1 mg/ml[b]	Visually compatible	1807	C
Albumin human	AR, AT	5 and 25%	MMD	5 mg/ml	Visually compatible	1807	C
Amikacin sulfate	BR	5[b] and 250 mg/ml	MMD	5 mg/ml	Visually compatible	1807	C
Aminophylline	AMR	25 mg/ml[b]	MMD	5 mg/ml	Cloudiness forms	1807	I
	AMR	25 mg/ml[b]	MMD	1 mg/ml[b]	Visually compatible	1807	C
	AMR	2 mg/ml[a,b]	MMD	5 mg/ml	Visually compatible	1807	C
Amphotericin B	SQ	0.1 mg/ml[a]	MMD	5 mg/ml	Visually compatible	1807	C
Ampicillin sodium	WY	100 mg/ml[b]	MMD	5 mg/ml	Cloudiness forms	1807	I
	WY	100 mg/ml[b]	MMD	1 mg/ml[b]	Visually compatible	1807	C
	WY	10 and 20 mg/ml[b]	MMD	5 mg/ml	Visually compatible	1807	C
Ampicillin sodium–sulbactam sodium	RR	45 + 22.5 mg/ml[b]	MMD	5 mg/ml	Cloudiness forms	1807	I
	RR	45 + 22.5 mg/ml[b]	MMD	1 mg/ml[b]	Visually compatible	1807	C
	RR	2 + 1 and 15 + 7.5 mg/ml[b]	MMD	5 mg/ml	Visually compatible	1807	C
Aztreonam	SQ	20 and 333 mg/ml[b]	MMD	5 mg/ml	Visually compatible	1807	C
	SQ	333 mg/ml[b]	MMD	1 mg/ml[b]	Visually compatible	1807	C

Y-Site Injection Compatibility (1:1 Mixture) (Cont.)

			Diltiazem HCl				
Drug	*Mfr*	*Conc*	*Mfr*	*Conc*	*Remarks*	*Ref*	*C/I*
Bretylium tosylate	DU	10[b] and 50 mg/ml	MMD	5 mg/ml	Visually compatible	1807	C
	DU	50 mg/ml	MMD	1 mg/ml[b]	Visually compatible	1807	C
Bumetanide	RC	0.25 mg/ml	MMD	1[b] and 5 mg/ml	Visually compatible	1807	C
Cefamandole nafate	LI	200 mg/ml[b]	MMD	5 mg/ml	Cloudiness forms but clears with swirling	1807	?
	LI	10[b] and 20[a] mg/ml	MMD	5 mg/ml	Cloudiness forms and persists	1807	I
	LI	10[b], 20[a], 200[b] mg/ml	MMD	1 mg/ml[b]	Visually compatible	1807	C
Cefazolin sodium	LI	20 and 200 mg/ml[b]	MMD	5 mg/ml	Visually compatible	1807	C
	LI	200 mg/ml[b]	MMD	1 mg/ml[b]	Visually compatible	1807	C
Cefoperazone sodium	RR	20[a], 25[b], 50[b] mg/ml	MMD	1[b] and 5 mg/ml	Cloudiness and precipitate form	1807	I
	RR	10 mg/ml[b]	MMD	5 mg/ml	Precipitate forms	1807	I
	RR	10 mg/ml[b]	MMD	1 mg/ml[b]	Visually compatible	1807	C
	RR	2 and 5 mg/ml[b]	MMD	1[b] and 5 mg/ml	Visually compatible	1807	C
Cefotaxime sodium	HO	10 and 180 mg/ml[b]	MMD	5 mg/ml	Visually compatible	1807	C
	HO	180 mg/ml[b]	MMD	1 mg/ml[b]	Visually compatible	1807	C
Cefotetan disodium	STU	10 and 200 mg/ml[b]	MMD	5 mg/ml	Visually compatible	1807	C
	STU	200 mg/ml[b]	MMD	1 mg/ml[b]	Visually compatible	1807	C
Cefoxitin sodium	MSD	10 and 200 mg/ml[b]	MMD	5 mg/ml	Visually compatible	1807	C
	MSD	200 mg/ml[b]	MMD	1 mg/ml[b]	Visually compatible	1807	C
Ceftazidime	GL[f]	10 and 170 mg/ml[b]	MMD	5 mg/ml	Visually compatible	1807	C
	GL[f]	170 mg/ml[b]	MMD	1 mg/ml[b]	Visually compatible	1807	C
Ceftriaxone sodium	RC	40 mg/ml[b]	MMD	5 mg/ml	Visually compatible	1807	C
Cefuroxime sodium	LI	15 and 100 mg/ml[b]	MMD	5 mg/ml	Visually compatible	1807	C
	LI	100 mg/ml[b]	MMD	1 mg/ml[b]	Visually compatible	1807	C
Cimetidine HCl	SKF	6[c] and 150 mg/ml	MMD	5 mg/ml	Visually compatible	1807	C
	SKF	150 mg/ml	MMD	1 mg/ml[b]	Visually compatible	1807	C
Ciprofloxacin	MI	2 and 10 mg/ml[b]	MMD	5 mg/ml	Visually compatible	1807	C
Clindamycin phosphate	UP	12[b] and 150 mg/ml	MMD	5 mg/ml	Visually compatible	1807	C
Diazepam	ES	5 mg/ml	MMD	1[b] and 5 mg/ml	Cloudiness and precipitate form	1807	I
Digoxin	ES	0.5 mg/ml	MMD	1[b] and 5 mg/ml	Visually compatible	1807	C
Dobutamine HCl	LI	2 mg/ml[a]	MMD	1 mg/ml[a]	Visually compatible for 24 hr at 25 °C	1530	C
	LI	1 mg/ml[c]	MMD	5 mg/ml	Visually compatible	1807	C
	LI	4 mg/ml[a]	MMD	1 mg/ml[a]	Visually compatible for 4 hr at 27 °C	2062	C

Y-Site Injection Compatibility (1:1 Mixture) (Cont.)

Diltiazem HCl

Drug	*Mfr*	*Conc*	*Mfr*	*Conc*	*Remarks*	*Ref*	*C/I*
Dopamine HCl	AB	1.6 mg/ml[a]	MMD	1 mg/ml[a]	Visually compatible for 24 hr at 25 °C	1530	C
	AB, SO	0.8 mg/ml[c]	MMD	5 mg/ml	Visually compatible	1807	C
	AB	3.2 mg/ml[a]	MMD	1 mg/ml[a]	Visually compatible for 4 hr at 27 °C	2062	C
Doxycycline hyclate	RR	1 and 10 mg/ml[b]	MMD	5 mg/ml	Visually compatible	1807	C
Epinephrine HCl	PD	0.004 and 0.05 mg/ml[b]	MMD	5 mg/ml	Visually compatible	1807	C
	PD	0.05 mg/ml[b]	MMD	1 mg/ml[b]	Visually compatible	1807	C
	AB	0.02 mg/ml[a]	MMD	1 mg/ml[a]	Visually compatible for 4 hr at 27 °C	2062	C
Erythromycin lactobionate	ES	5 and 50 mg/ml[b]	MMD	5 mg/ml	Visually compatible	1807	C
Esmolol HCl	DU	10 mg/ml[a]	MMD	1 mg/ml[a]	Visually compatible for 24 hr at 25 °C	1530	C
Fentanyl citrate	ES	0.05 mg/ml	MMD	1 mg/ml[a]	Visually compatible for 4 hr at 27 °C	2062	C
Fluconazole	RR	2 mg/ml	MMD	5 mg/ml	Visually compatible	1807	C
Furosemide	AMR	10 mg/ml	MMD	1[b] and 5 mg/ml	Heavy precipitate forms	1807	I
	AMR	10 mg/ml	MMD	1 mg/ml[a]	Precipitate forms immediately	2062	I
Gentamicin sulfate	SC	2.4[b] and 40 mg/ml	MMD	1[b] and 5 mg/ml	Visually compatible	1807	C
Heparin sodium	LY	20,000 units/ml	MMD	5 mg/ml	Precipitate forms	1807	I
	LY	20,000 units/ml	MMD	1 mg/ml[b]	Visually compatible	1807	C
	SCN	5000 and 10,000 units/ml	MMD	1[b] and 5 mg/ml	Visually compatible	1807	C
	LY, SCN	80 units/ml[c]	MMD	5 mg/ml	Visually compatible	1807	C
	ES	100 units/ml[a]	MMD	1 mg/ml[a]	Visually compatible for 4 hr at 27 °C	2062	C
Hetastarch in lactated electrolyte injection (Hextend)	AB	6%	BA	5 mg/ml	Physically compatible with no change in measured turbidity or increase in particle content in 4 hr at 23 °C	2339	C
Hetastarch in sodium chloride 0.9%	DU	6%	MMD	5 mg/ml	Visually compatible	1807	C
Hydrocortisone sodium succinate	UP	50 and 125 mg/ml	MMD	5 mg/ml	Precipitate forms but clears with swirling	1807	?
	UP	50 and 125 mg/ml	MMD	1 mg/ml[b]	Visually compatible	1807	C
	UP	1[b] and 2[a] mg/ml	MMD	5 mg/ml	Visually compatible	1807	C
Hydromorphone HCl	KN	1 mg/ml	MMD	1 mg/ml[a]	Visually compatible for 4 hr at 27 °C	2062	C
Imipenem–cilastatin sodium	MSD	5 mg/ml[c]	MMD	5 mg/ml	Visually compatible	1807	C
Insulin, regular	NOV	100 units/ml	MMD	1[b] and 5 mg/ml	Precipitate forms and persists	1807	I
	NOV	0.4 unit/ml	MMD	5 mg/ml	Visually compatible	1807	C
Labetalol HCl	AH	2 mg/ml[a]	MMD	1 mg/ml[a]	Visually compatible for 4 hr at 27 °C	2062	C
Lidocaine HCl	AST	8 mg/ml[a]	MMD	1 mg/ml[a]	Visually compatible for 24 hr at 25 °C	1530	C
	AB	10 mg/ml[b]	MMD	1[b] and 5 mg/ml	Visually compatible	1807	C

Y-Site Injection Compatibility (1:1 Mixture) (Cont.)

			Diltiazem HCl				
Drug	*Mfr*	*Conc*	*Mfr*	*Conc*	*Remarks*	*Ref*	*C/I*
	AB, SCN	4 and 8 mg/ml[a]	MMD	5 mg/ml	Visually compatible	1807	C
Lorazepam	WY	4 mg/ml	MMD	5 mg/ml	Visually compatible	1807	C
	WY	2 mg/ml[b]	MMD	1 mg/ml[b]	Visually compatible	1807	C
	WY	0.5 mg/ml[a]	MMD	1 mg/ml[a]	Visually compatible for 4 hr at 27 °C	2062	C
Meperidine HCl	WY	100 mg/ml	MMD	1[b] and 5 mg/ml	Visually compatible	1807	C
	WY	10 mg/ml[b]	MMD	5 mg/ml	Visually compatible	1807	C
Methylprednisolone sodium succinate	UP	2.5[a], 20[b], 62.5 mg/ml	MMD	1 mg/ml[b]	Visually compatible	1807	C
	UP	2.5 mg/ml[a]	MMD	5 mg/ml	Cloudiness forms	1807	I
	UP	20 mg/ml[b]	MMD	5 mg/ml	Precipitate forms	1807	I
	UP	62.5 mg/ml	MMD	5 mg/ml	Cloudiness forms but clears with swirling	1807	?
Metoclopramide HCl	RB	5 mg/ml	MMD	1[b] and 5 mg/ml	Visually compatible	1807	C
	RB	0.2 mg/ml[b]	MMD	5 mg/ml	Visually compatible	1807	C
Metronidazole	SE	5 mg/ml	MMD	5 mg/ml	Visually compatible	1807	C
Metronidazole HCl	SE	8 mg/ml[b]	MMD	5 mg/ml	Visually compatible	1807	C
Midazolam HCl	RC	2 mg/ml[a]	MMD	1 mg/ml[a]	Visually compatible for 4 hr at 27 °C	2062	C
Milrinone lactate	SW	0.2 mg/ml[a]	MMD	1 mg/ml[a]	Visually compatible for 4 hr at 27 °C	2062	C
	SW	0.4 mg/ml[a]	MMD	1 mg/ml[a]	Visually compatible with little or no loss of either drug by HPLC in 4 hr at 23 °C	2214	C
Morphine sulfate	SCN	15 mg/ml	MMD	1[b] and 5 mg/ml	Visually compatible	1807	C
	SCN	0.4 mg/ml[b]	MMD	5 mg/ml	Visually compatible	1807	C
	SCN	2 mg/ml[a]	MMD	1 mg/ml[a]	Visually compatible for 4 hr at 27 °C	2062	C
Multivitamins (M.V.I.-12)		[d]	MMD	5 mg/ml	Visually compatible	1807	C
Nafcillin sodium	WY	10 mg/ml[b]	MMD	5 mg/ml	Cloudiness forms and persists	1807	I
	WY	200 mg/ml[b]	MMD	5 mg/ml	Cloudiness forms but clears with swirling	1807	?
	WY	10 and 200 mg/ml[b]	MMD	1 mg/ml[b]	Visually compatible	1807	C
Nicardipine HCl	WY	1 mg/ml[a]	MMD	1 mg/ml[a]	Visually compatible for 4 hr at 27 °C	2062	C
Nitroglycerin	DU	0.032 mg/ml[a]	MMD	1 mg/ml[a]	Visually compatible for 24 hr at 25 °C	1530	C
	DU	400 μg/ml[b]	MMD	1[b] and 5 mg/ml	Visually compatible	1807	C
	DU	400 μg/ml[a]	MMD	5 mg/ml	Visually compatible	1807	C
	AB	0.4 mg/ml[a]	MMD	1 mg/ml[a]	Visually compatible for 4 hr at 27 °C	2062	C
Norepinephrine bitartrate	WI	0.12 mg/ml[a]	MMD	1 mg/ml[a]	Visually compatible for 24 hr at 25 °C	1530	C
	AB	0.128 mg/ml[a]	MMD	1 mg/ml[a]	Visually compatible for 4 hr at 27 °C	2062	C
Oxacillin sodium		100 mg/ml[b]	MMD	1[b] and 5 mg/ml	Visually compatible	1807	C
		10 mg/ml[b]	MMD	5 mg/ml	Visually compatible	1807	C
Penicillin G potassium	RR	1 million units/ml	MMD	1[b] and 5 mg/ml	Visually compatible	1807	C
	RR	100,000 units/ml[b]	MMD	5 mg/ml	Visually compatible	1807	C
Pentamidine isethionate	LY	6 and 30 mg/ml[a]	MMD	5 mg/ml	Visually compatible	1807	C

Y-Site Injection Compatibility (1:1 Mixture) (Cont.)

Diltiazem HCl

Drug	*Mfr*	*Conc*	*Mfr*	*Conc*	*Remarks*	*Ref*	*C/I*
Phenytoin sodium	PD	50 mg/ml	MMD	1 mg/ml[b]	Precipitate forms	1807	I
Piperacillin sodium	LE	200 mg/ml[b]	MMD	1[b] and 5 mg/ml	Visually compatible	1807	C
	LE	20 mg/ml[b]	MMD	5 mg/ml	Visually compatible	1807	C
Potassium chloride	LY	0.08[a] and 2 mEq/ml	MMD	5 mg/ml	Visually compatible	1807	C
Potassium phosphates	AMR	0.015 mmol/ml	MMD	5 mg/ml	Visually compatible	1807	C
Procainamide HCl	ES	500 mg/ml	MMD	5 mg/ml	Cloudiness forms but clears in 2 min	1807	?
	ES	50 mg/ml[a]	MMD	1 mg/ml[b]	Visually compatible	1807	C
	ES	2 mg/ml[a]	MMD	5 mg/ml	Visually compatible	1807	C
Ranitidine HCl	GL	25 mg/ml	MMD	1[b] and 5 mg/ml	Visually compatible	1807	C
	GL	1[b] and 0.5[e] mg/ml	MMD	5 mg/ml	Visually compatible	1807	C
	GL	1 mg/ml[a]	MMD	1 mg/ml[a]	Visually compatible for 4 hr at 27 °C	2062	C
Rifampin	MMD	6 mg/ml[b]	MMD	1[b] and 5 mg/ml	Precipitate forms	1807	I
Sodium bicarbonate	LY	1 mEq/ml	MMD	5 mg/ml	Precipitate forms	1807	I
	LY	1 mEq/ml	MMD	1 mg/ml[b]	Visually compatible	1807	C
	AMR	0.05 mEq/ml[a]	MMD	5 mg/ml	Visually compatible	1807	C
Sodium nitroprusside	AB	0.2 mg/ml[a]	MMD	5 mg/ml	Visually compatible	1807	C
Theophylline	AB	0.8 mg/ml[a]	MMD	5 mg/ml	Visually compatible	1807	C
Thiopental sodium	AB	25 mg/ml[g]	MMD	1 mg/ml[a]	Precipitate forms immediately	2062	I
Ticarcillin disodium	BE	200 mg/ml[b]	MMD	1[b] and 5 mg/ml	Visually compatible	1807	C
	BE	10 mg/ml[b]	MMD	5 mg/ml	Visually compatible	1807	C
Ticarcillin disodium–clavulanate potassium	BE	200 mg/ml[b]	MMD	1[b] and 5 mg/ml	Visually compatible	1807	C
	BE	10 mg/ml[b]	MMD	5 mg/ml	Visually compatible	1807	C
Tobramycin sulfate	LI	2.4[b] and 40 mg/ml	MMD	5 mg/ml	Visually compatible	1807	C
Trimethoprim–sulfamethoxazole	BW, RC	0.21 + 1 and 0.63 + 3.2 mg/ml[a]	MMD	5 mg/ml	Visually compatible	1807	C
Vancomycin HCl	LI	5 and 50 mg/ml[b]	MMD	5 mg/ml	Visually compatible	1807	C
Vecuronium bromide	OR	1 mg/ml	MMD	1 mg/ml[a]	Visually compatible for 4 hr at 27 °C	2062	C

[a]*Tested in dextrose 5% in water.*
[b]*Tested in sodium chloride 0.9%.*
[c]*Tested in both dextrose 5% in water and sodium chloride 0.9%.*
[d]*Concentration not specified.*
[e]*Tested in sodium chloride 0.45%.*
[f]*Sodium carbonate–containing formulation tested.*
[g]*Reconstituted with sterile water for injection.*

Additional Compatibility Information

Infusion Solutions — Dextrose 5% in water, sodium chloride 0.9%, and dextrose 5% in sodium chloride 0.45% are the recommended infusion vehicles. At concentrations up to 1 mg/ml, diltiazem HCl is physically compatible and chemically stable in these solutions in glass or PVC containers for at least 24 hours at room temperature or under refrigeration. The manufacturer recommends refrigeration storage and use within 24 hours. (2)

DIMENHYDRINATE
AHFS 56:22

Products — Dimenhydrinate is available in 1-ml syringe cartridge units and 10-ml vials containing dimenhydrinate 50 mg/ml in propylene glycol 50% and water. Sodium hydroxide and/or hydrochloric acid may be used to adjust the pH and benzyl alcohol is present in multiple-dose vials as a preservative. Dimenhydrinate contains 53 to 55.5% of diphenhydramine and 44 to 47% of 8-chlorotheophylline. (4; 29; 154)

pH — From 6.4 to 7.2. (4)

Administration — Dimenhydrinate is administered by intramuscular injection or by intravenous injection over two minutes after dilution with 10 ml of sodium chloride 0.9%. (4)

Stability — Intact containers should be stored at controlled room temperature and protected from freezing. (4) Dimenhydrinate (Searle) 50 mg/ml was found to retain potency for three months at room temperature when 1 ml of solution was repackaged in Tubex cartridges. (13)

Dilution with water for injection, sodium chloride 0.9%, or dextrose 5% in water results in a solution that is stable for at least 10 days at room temperature. (279)

pH Effects — A test of dimenhydrinate solutions at pH 2 to 10 showed no separation or precipitation at pH 5.4 to 8.6 on extended room temperature storage. Below pH 5.4, a white powdery precipitate of 8-chlorotheophylline formed within 24 hours. Above pH 8.6, an oily liquid separated within 30 minutes. (279)

Compatibility Information

Solution Compatibility

Dimenhydrinate

Solution	*Mfr*	*Mfr*	*Conc/L*	*Remarks*	*Ref*	*C/I*
Dextran 6% in dextrose 5%	AB	SE	50 mg	Physically compatible	3	C
Dextran 6% in sodium chloride 0.9%	AB	SE	50 mg	Physically compatible	3	C
Dextrose–Ringer's injection combinations	AB	SE	50 mg	Physically compatible	3	C
Dextrose–Ringer's injection, lactated, combinations	AB	SE	50 mg	Physically compatible	3	C
Dextrose–saline combinations	AB	SE	50 mg	Physically compatible	3	C
Dextrose 5% in sodium chloride 0.9%		SE	50 mg	Physically compatible	74	C
Dextrose 2½% in water	AB	SE	50 mg	Physically compatible	3	C
Dextrose 5% in water	AB	SE SE	50 mg 50 mg	Physically compatible Physically compatible	3 74	C C
Dextrose 10% in water	AB	SE	50 mg	Physically compatible	3	C
Fructose 10% in sodium chloride 0.9%	AB	SE	50 mg	Physically compatible	3	C
Fructose 10% in water	AB	SE	50 mg	Physically compatible	3	C
Invert sugar 5 and 10% in sodium chloride 0.9%	AB	SE	50 mg	Physically compatible	3	C
Invert sugar 5 and 10% in water	AB	SE	50 mg	Physically compatible	3	C
Ionosol products	AB	SE	50 mg	Physically compatible	3	C
Ringer's injection	AB	SE	50 mg	Physically compatible	3	C

Solution Compatibility (Cont.)

Dimenhydrinate

Solution	*Mfr*	*Mfr*	*Conc/L*	*Remarks*	*Ref*	*C/I*
Ringer's injection, lactated	AB	SE	50 mg	Physically compatible	3	C
		SE	50 mg	Physically compatible	74	C
Sodium chloride 0.45%	AB	SE	50 mg	Physically compatible	3	C
Sodium chloride 0.9%	AB	SE	50 mg	Physically compatible	3	C
		SE	50 mg	Physically compatible	74	C
Sodium lactate ⅙ M	AB	SE	50 mg	Physically compatible	3	C

Additive Compatibility

Dimenhydrinate

Drug	*Mfr*	*Conc/L*	*Mfr*	*Conc/L*	*Test Soln*	*Remarks*	*Ref*	*C/I*
Amikacin sulfate	BR	5 g	SE	100 mg	D5LR, D5R, D5S, D5W, D10W, IS10, LR, NS, R, SL	Physically compatible and potency of both retained for 24 hr at 25 °C	294	C
Aminophylline		250 mg	SE	50 mg	D5W	Physically compatible	74	C
	SE	1 g	SE	500 mg	D5W	Physically incompatible	15	I
Ammonium chloride	AB	20 g	SE	500 mg	D5W	Physically compatible	15	C
			SE			Physically incompatible	9	I
Amobarbital sodium	LI	1 g	SE	500 mg	D5W	Physically compatible	15	C
			SE			Physically incompatible	9	I
Calcium gluconate		1 g	SE	50 mg	D5W	Physically compatible	74	C
Chloramphenicol sodium succinate	PD	500 mg	SE	50 mg	D5W	Physically compatible	74	C
Corticotropin		500 units	SE	50 mg	D5W	Physically compatible	74	C
Heparin sodium		12,000 units	SE	50 mg	D5W	Physically compatible	74	C
	UP	4000 units	SE	500 mg	D5W	Physically compatible	15	C
	AB	20,000 units	SE	50 mg	D	Physically compatible	21	C
Hydrocortisone sodium succinate	UP	100 mg	SE	50 mg	D5W	Physically compatible	74	C
	UP	500 mg	SE	500 mg	D5W	Physically incompatible	15	I
Hydroxyzine HCl	RR	250 mg	SE	500 mg	D5W	Physically compatible	15	C
Norepinephrine bitartrate	WI	8 mg	SE	50 mg	D5W	Physically compatible	74	C
Penicillin G potassium		1 million units	SE	50 mg	D5W	Physically compatible	74	C
Pentobarbital sodium	AB	1 g	SE	500 mg	D5W	Physically compatible	15	C
Phenobarbital sodium	WI	200 mg	SE	500 mg	D5W	Physically compatible	15	C
Potassium chloride		3 g	SE	50 mg	D5W	Physically compatible	74	C
Prochlorperazine edisylate	SKF	100 mg	SE	500 mg	D5W	Physically compatible	15	C

Additive Compatibility (Cont.)

Dimenhydrinate

Drug	Mfr	Conc/L	Mfr	Conc/L	Test Soln	Remarks	Ref	C/I
Thiopental sodium	AB		SE			Physically incompatible	9	I
Vancomycin HCl	LI	1 g	SE	50 mg	D5W	Physically compatible	74	C
Vitamin B complex with C		1 vial	SE	50 mg	D5W	Physically compatible	74	C

Drugs in Syringe Compatibility

Dimenhydrinate

Drug (in syringe)	Mfr	Amt	Mfr	Amt	Remarks	Ref	C/I
Atropine sulfate	ST	0.4 mg/ 1 ml	HR	50 mg/ 1 ml	Physically compatible for at least 15 min	326	C
Butorphanol tartrate	BR	4 mg/ 2 ml	HR	50 mg/ 1 ml	Gas evolves	761	I
Chlorpromazine HCl	PO	50 mg/ 2 ml	HR	50 mg/ 1 ml	Physically incompatible within 15 min	326	I
Codeine phosphate		30 mg/ 1 ml	HR	50 mg/ 1 ml	Physically compatible	711	C
		60 mg/ 1 ml	HR	50 mg/ 1 ml	Physically compatible	711	C
Diatrizoate meglumine 34.3%, diatrizoate sodium 35% (Renovist)	SQ	40 to 1 ml	SE	50 mg/ 1 ml	Physically compatible for 48 hr	530	C
Diatrizoate meglumine 52%, diatrizoate sodium 8% (Renografin-60)	SQ	40 to 1 ml	SE	50 mg/ 1 ml	Physically compatible for 48 hr	530	C
Diatrizoate sodium 75% (Hypaque)	WI	40 to 1 ml	SE	50 mg/ 1 ml	Physically compatible for 48 hr	530	C
Diphenhydramine HCl	PD	50 mg/ 1 ml	HR	50 mg/ 1 ml	Physically compatible for at least 15 min	326	C
Droperidol	MN	2.5 mg/ 1 ml	HR	50 mg/ 1 ml	Physically compatible for at least 15 min	326	C
Fentanyl citrate	MN	0.05 mg/ 1 ml	HR	50 mg/ 1 ml	Physically compatible for at least 15 min	326	C
Glycopyrrolate	RB	0.2 mg/ 1 ml	SE	50 mg/ 1 ml	Immediate precipitation	331	I
	RB	0.2 mg/ 1 ml	SE	100 mg/ 2 ml	Immediate precipitation	331	I
	RB	0.4 mg/ 2 ml	SE	50 mg/ 1 ml	Immediate precipitation	331	I
Heparin sodium		2500 units/ 1 ml		65 mg/ 10 ml	Physically compatible for at least 5 min	1053	C
Hydromorphone HCl	KN	2, 10, 40 mg/ 1 ml	SQ	50 mg/ 1 ml	Visually compatible with both drugs stable by HPLC for 24 hr at 4, 23, and 37 °C. Precipitate forms after 24 hr	1776	C
Hydroxyzine HCl	PF	50 mg/ 1 ml	HR	50 mg/ 1 ml	Physically incompatible within 15 min	326	I

Drugs in Syringe Compatibility (Cont.)

Dimenhydrinate

Drug (in syringe)	*Mfr*	*Amt*	*Mfr*	*Amt*	*Remarks*	*Ref*	*C/I*
Hyoscine butylbromide	BI	20 mg/ 1 ml	HR	50 mg/ 1 ml	Physically compatible	711	C
	BI	20 mg/ 1 ml	HR	10 mg/ 1 ml	Physically compatible	711	C
Iodipamide meglumine 52% (Cholografin)	SQ	40 ml	SE	50 mg/ 1 ml	Forms a precipitate initially but clears within 1 hr and remains clear for 48 hr	530	I
	SQ	20 to 1 ml	SE	50 mg/ 1 ml	Forms a precipitate initially but clears within 1 hr. Precipitate reforms upon standing	530	I
Iothalamate meglumine 60% (Conray)	MA	40 to 1 ml	SE	50 mg/ 1 ml	Physically compatible for 48 hr	530	C
Iothalamate sodium 80% (Angio-Conray)	MA	40 to 1 ml	SE	50 mg/ 1 ml	Physically compatible for 48 hr	530	C
Meperidine HCl	WI	50 mg/ 1 ml	HR	50 mg/ 1 ml	Physically compatible for at least 15 min	326	C
	WI	50 mg/ 1 ml	HR	10 mg/ 1 ml	Physically compatible	711	C
Metoclopramide HCl	NO	10 mg/ 2 ml	HR	50 mg/ 1 ml	Physically compatible both macroscopically and microscopically for 15 min at room temperature	565	C
Midazolam HCl	RC	5 mg/ 1 ml	SE	50 mg/ 1 ml	White precipitate forms immediately	1145	I
Morphine sulfate	ST	15 mg/ 1 ml	HR	50 mg/ 1 ml	Physically compatible for at least 15 min	326	C
Nalbuphine HCl	EN	10 mg/ 1 ml	HR	50 mg/ 1 ml	Physically incompatible	711	I
	EN	20 mg/ 1 ml	HR	50 mg/ 1 ml	Physically incompatible	711	I
Papaveretum	RC[a]	20 mg/ 1 ml	HR	50 mg/ 1 ml	Incompatible within 15 min	326	I
Pentazocine lactate	WI	30 mg/ 1 ml	HR	50 mg/ 1 ml	Physically compatible for at least 15 min	326	C
Pentobarbital sodium	AB	500 mg/ 10 ml	SE	50 mg/ 1 ml	Physically incompatible	55	I
	AB	50 mg/ 1 ml	HR	50 mg/ 1 ml	Physically incompatible within 15 min	326	I
Perphenazine	SC	5 mg/ 1 ml	HR	50 mg/ 1 ml	Physically compatible both macroscopically and microscopically for 30 min at room temperature	761	C
Prochlorperazine edisylate	PO	5 mg/ 1 ml	HR	50 mg/ 1 ml	Physically incompatible within 15 min	326	I
Promazine HCl	WY	50 mg/ 1 ml	HR	50 mg/ 1 ml	Physically incompatible within 15 min	326	I
Promethazine HCl	PO	50 mg/ 2 ml	HR	50 mg/ 1 ml	Physically incompatible within 15 min	326	I
	WY	25 mg/ 1 ml	HR	50 mg/ 1 ml	Physically incompatible	711	I
Ranitidine HCl	GL	50 mg/ 2 ml	HR	50 mg/ 1 ml	Physically compatible for 1 hr at 25 °C both macroscopically and microscopically	978	C

Drugs in Syringe Compatibility (Cont.)

Dimenhydrinate

Drug (in syringe)	*Mfr*	*Amt*	*Mfr*	*Amt*	*Remarks*	*Ref*	*C/I*
Scopolamine HBr	ST	0.4 mg/ 1 ml	HR	50 mg/ 1 ml	Physically compatible for at least 15 min	326	C
		0.6 mg/ 1 ml	HR	50 mg/ 1 ml	Physically compatible	711	C
Thiopental sodium	AB	75 mg/ 3 ml	SE	50 mg/ 1 ml	Physically incompatible	21	I

[a]*The former formulation was tested.*

Y-Site Injection Compatibility (1:1 Mixture)

Dimenhydrinate

Drug	*Mfr*	*Conc*	*Mfr*	*Conc*	*Remarks*	*Ref*	*C/I*
Acyclovir sodium	BW	5 mg/ml[a]	SE	1 mg/ml[a]	Physically compatible for 4 hr at 25 °C under fluorescent light	1157	C

[a]*Tested in dextrose 5% in water.*

Additional Compatibility Information

Concentrated Drug Solutions — The following incompatibility determinations were performed with concentrated solutions. The drugs in dry form were reconstituted according to manufacturers' recommendations. One milliliter of dimenhydrinate (Searle) was added to 5 ml of sterile distilled water along with 1 ml of each of the following drugs. Particulate matter was noted within two hours (28):

Aminophylline
Heparin sodium
Hydrocortisone sodium succinate (Upjohn)
Hydroxyzine HCl (Pfizer)
Phenobarbital sodium (Winthrop)
Phenytoin sodium (Parke-Davis)
Prochlorperazine edisylate (SKF)
Promazine HCl (Wyeth)
Promethazine HCl (Wyeth)

DIPHENHYDRAMINE HCL
AHFS 4:00

Products — Diphenhydramine HCl is available as a 50-mg/ml solution in 1-ml ampuls, vials, and disposable syringes and in 10-ml vials. Also present in the 10-ml vials is 0.1 mg/ml of benzethonium chloride. The pH may have been adjusted with sodium hydroxide or hydrochloric acid. (2)

pH — From 5 to 6. (2; 4)

Osmolality — Diphenhydramine HCl 50 mg/ml has an osmolality of 240 mOsm/kg, and the osmolality of the 10-mg/ml concentration is 65 mOsm/kg. (1689)

Trade Name(s) — Banaril, Benadryl.

Administration — Diphenhydramine HCl is administered by deep intramuscular injection, slow direct intravenous injection, or continuous or intermittent intravenous infusion. (2; 4) Subcutaneous or perivascular injection should be avoided due to irritation. (4)

Stability — Diphenhydramine HCl in intact containers should be stored in light-resistant containers at controlled room temperature. Freezing should be avoided. (2; 4)

Central Venous Catheter — Diphenhydramine HCl (Schein) 2 mg/ml in dextrose 5% in water was found to be compatible with the ARROWg+ard Blue Plus (Arrow International) chlorhexidine-bearing triple-lumen central catheter. HPLC analysis was used to evaluate completeness of drug delivery through the catheter and the amount of chlorhexidine removed from the internal lumens. Essentially complete delivery of the drug was found with little or no drug loss occurring. Furthermore, chlorhexidine delivered from the catheter remained at trace amounts with no substantial increase due to the delivery of the drug through the catheter. (2335)

Compatibility Information

Solution Compatibility

Diphenhydramine HCl

Solution	*Mfr*	*Mfr*	*Conc/L*	*Remarks*	*Ref*	*C/I*
Dextran 6% in dextrose 5%	AB	PD	100 mg	Physically compatible	3	C
Dextran 6% in sodium chloride 0.9%	AB	PD	100 mg	Physically compatible	3	C
Dextrose–Ringer's injection combinations	AB	PD	100 mg	Physically compatible	3	C
Dextrose–Ringer's injection, lactated, combinations	AB	PD	100 mg	Physically compatible	3	C
Dextrose–saline combinations	AB	PD	100 mg	Physically compatible	3	C
Dextrose 2½% in water	AB	PD	100 mg	Physically compatible	3	C
Dextrose 5% in water	AB	PD	100 mg	Physically compatible	3	C
Dextrose 10% in water	AB	PD	100 mg	Physically compatible	3	C
Fat emulsion 10%, intravenous	VT	PD	200 mg	Physically compatible for 48 hr at 4 °C and room temperature	32	C
Fructose 10% in sodium chloride 0.9%	AB	PD	100 mg	Physically compatible	3	C
Fructose 10% in water	AB	PD	100 mg	Physically compatible	3	C
Invert sugar 5 and 10% in sodium chloride 0.9%	AB	PD	100 mg	Physically compatible	3	C
Invert sugar 5 and 10% in water	AB	PD	100 mg	Physically compatible	3	C
Ionosol products	AB	PD	100 mg	Physically compatible	3	C
Ringer's injection	AB	PD	100 mg	Physically compatible	3	C
Ringer's injection, lactated	AB	PD	100 mg	Physically compatible	3	C
Sodium chloride 0.45%	AB	PD	100 mg	Physically compatible	3	C
Sodium chloride 0.9%	AB	PD	100 mg	Physically compatible	3	C
Sodium lactate ⅙ M	AB	PD	100 mg	Physically compatible	3	C

Additive Compatibility

Diphenhydramine HCl

Drug	*Mfr*	*Conc/L*	*Mfr*	*Conc/L*	*Test Soln*	*Remarks*	*Ref*	*C/I*
Amikacin sulfate	BR	5 g	PD	100 mg	D5LR, D5R, D5S, D5W, IS10, LR, NS, R, SL	Physically compatible and potency of both retained for 24 hr at 25 °C	294	C
Aminophylline	SE	500 mg	PD	50 mg		Physically compatible	6	C
Amobarbital sodium			PD			Physically incompatible	9	I
	LI	1 g	PD	80 mg	D5W	Physically incompatible	15	I
Amphotericin B	SQ	100 mg	PD	80 mg	D5W	Physically incompatible	15	I
Ascorbic acid injection	UP	500 mg	PD	80 mg	D5W	Physically compatible	15	C
Bleomycin sulfate	BR	20 and 30 units	PD	100 mg	NS	Physically compatible and bleomycin activity retained for 1 week at 4 °C. Diphenhydramine not tested	763	C
Colistimethate sodium	WC	500 mg	PD	80 mg	D5W	Physically compatible	15	C

Additive Compatibility (Cont.)

Diphenhydramine HCl

Drug	*Mfr*	*Conc/L*	*Mfr*	*Conc/L*	*Test Soln*	*Remarks*	*Ref*	*C/I*
Dexamethasone sodium phosphate with lorazepam and metoclopramide HCl	AMR WY DU	400 mg 40 mg 4 g	ES	2 g	NS[a]	Rapid lorazepam losses of 8, 10, and 15% at 3, 23, and 30 °C, respectively, in 24 hr by HPLC. Other drugs stable for 14 days by HPLC at all three storage temperatures	1733	I
Erythromycin lactobionate	AB	1 g	PD	50 mg		Physically compatible. Erythromycin potency retained for 24 hr at 25 °C	20	C
	AB	1 g	PD	50 mg	D5W	Erythromycin potency retained for 24 hr at 25 °C	48	C
Hydrocortisone sodium succinate	UP	500 mg	SCN	80 mg	D5W[b]	Physically compatible with no subvisual haze or particle formation in 24 hr at 23 °C	1729	C
	UP	1 g	SCN	500 mg	D5W[b]	Physically compatible with no subvisual haze or particle formation in 24 hr at 23 °C	1729	C
Iodipamide meglumine (% unspecified)	SQ		PD	20 to 200 mg	NS	Dense putty-like white precipitate immediately forms	309	I
Lidocaine HCl	AST	2 g	PD	50 mg		Physically compatible	24	C
Methyldopate HCl	MSD	1 g	PD	50 mg	D, D–S, S	Physically compatible	23	C
Nafcillin sodium	WY	500 mg	PD	50 mg		Physically compatible	27	C
Netilmicin sulfate	SC	3 g	PD	400 mg	D5S	Physically compatible and netilmicin chemically stable for 3 days at 25 and 4 °C. 17% loss noted after 7 days at 25 °C. Diphenhydramine not tested	558	C
Penicillin G potassium	SQ	20 million units	PD	80 mg	D5W	Physically compatible	15	C
	SQ	1 million units	PD	50 mg	D5W	Physically compatible. Penicillin potency retained for 24 hr at 25 °C	47	C
Penicillin G sodium	UP	20 million units	PD	80 mg	D5W	Physically compatible	15	C
Polymyxin B sulfate	BW	200 mg	PD	80 mg	D5W	Physically compatible	15	C
Thiopental sodium	AB		PD			Physically incompatible	9	I
Vitamin B complex with C	AB	5 ml	PD	80 mg	D5W	Physically compatible	15	C

[a]Tested in Pharmacia-Deltec PVC pump reservoirs.
[b]Tested in PVC containers.

Drugs in Syringe Compatibility

Diphenhydramine HCl

Drug (in syringe)	*Mfr*	*Amt*	*Mfr*	*Amt*	*Remarks*	*Ref*	*C/I*
Atropine sulfate	ST	0.4 mg/ 1 ml	PD	50 mg/ 1 ml	Physically compatible for at least 15 min	326	C
Butorphanol tartrate	BR	4 mg/ 2 ml	PD	50 mg/ 1 ml	Physically compatible both macroscopically and microscopically for 30 min at room temperature	566	C

Drugs in Syringe Compatibility (Cont.)

Diphenhydramine HCl

Drug (in syringe)	*Mfr*	*Amt*	*Mfr*	*Amt*	*Remarks*	*Ref*	*C/I*
Chlorpromazine HCl	PO	50 mg/ 2 ml	PD	50 mg/ 1 ml	Physically compatible for at least 15 min	326	**C**
	STS	50 mg/ 2 ml	ES	100 mg/ 2 ml	Visually compatible for 60 min	1784	**C**
Cimetidine HCl	SKF	300 mg/ 2 ml	PD	50 mg/ 1 ml	Physically compatible for 4 hr at 25 °C	25	**C**
Dexamethasone sodium phosphate	DB, SX	4 and 10 mg/ ml[a]	PD	50 mg/ ml[a]	White turbidity and precipitate form immediately	1542	**I**
	DB	9.52 mg/ ml[b]	PD	4.54 mg/ ml[b]	Visually compatible for 24 hr at 24 °C	1542	**C**
	DB	5 to 9.02 mg/ ml[b]	PD	4.54 to 15 mg/ ml[b]	Precipitate forms	1542	**I**
	SX	2 mg/ml[b]	PD	34.8 to 40 mg/ ml[b]	Visually compatible for 24 hr at 24 °C	1542	**C**
	SX	1 mg/ml[b]	PD	25 mg/ ml[b]	Precipitate forms	1542	**I**
Diatrizoate meglumine (% unspecified)	SQ	5 ml	PD	50 mg/ 1 ml	No precipitate observed	309	**C**
Diatrizoate meglumine 34.3%, diatrizoate sodium 35% (Renovist)	SQ	40 to 1 ml	PD	1 ml[c]	Physically compatible for 48 hr	530	**C**
Diatrizoate meglumine 52%, diatrizoate sodium 8% (Renografin-60)	SQ	2 and 1 ml	PD	1 ml[c]	Physically compatible for at least 1 hr but a precipitate observed at 48 hr	530	**I**
	SQ	40 to 5 ml	PD	1 ml[c]	Physically compatible for 48 hr	530	**C**
Diatrizoate meglumine 52%, diatrizoate sodium 8%	MA	5 ml	PD	12.5 mg/ 0.25 ml	Transient precipitate clears and then reforms within 1 hr	1438	**I**
Diatrizoate sodium (% unspecified)	WI	5 ml	PD	50 mg/ 1 ml	No precipitate observed	309	**C**
Diatrizoate sodium 60%	WI	5 ml	PD	12.5 mg/ 0.25 ml	Transient precipitate clears and then reforms within 1 hr	1438	**I**
Diatrizoate sodium 75% (Hypaque)	WI	40 to 1 ml	PD	1 ml[c]	Physically compatible for 48 hr	530	**C**
Dimenhydrinate	HR	50 mg/ 1 ml	PD	50 mg/ 1 ml	Physically compatible for at least 15 min	326	**C**
Droperidol	MN	2.5 mg/ 1 ml	PD	50 mg/ 1 ml	Physically compatible for at least 15 min	326	**C**
Fentanyl citrate	MN	0.05 mg/ 1 ml	PD	50 mg/ 1 ml	Physically compatible for at least 15 min	326	**C**
Fluphenazine HCl	LY	5 mg/ 2 ml	ES	100 mg/ 2 ml	Visually compatible for 60 min	1784	**C**
Glycopyrrolate	RB	0.2 mg/ 1 ml	PD	10 mg/ 1 ml	Physically compatible and pH in stability range for glycopyrrolate for 48 hr at 25 °C	331	**C**
	RB	0.2 mg/ 1 ml	PD	20 mg/ 2 ml	Physically compatible and pH in stability range for glycopyrrolate for 48 hr at 25 °C	331	**C**
	RB	0.4 mg/ 2 ml	PD	10 mg/ 1 ml	Physically compatible and pH in stability range for glycopyrrolate for 48 hr at 25 °C	331	**C**

Drugs in Syringe Compatibility (Cont.)

Diphenhydramine HCl

Drug (in syringe)	*Mfr*	*Amt*	*Mfr*	*Amt*	*Remarks*	*Ref*	*C/I*
	RB	0.2 mg/ 1 ml	PD	50 mg/ 1 ml	Physically compatible and pH in stability range for glycopyrrolate for 48 hr at 25 °C	331	C
	RB	0.2 mg/ 1 ml	PD	100 mg/ 2 ml	Physically compatible and pH in stability range for glycopyrrolate for 48 hr at 25 °C	331	C
	RB	0.4 mg/ 2 ml	PD	50 mg/ 1 ml	Physically compatible and pH in stability range for glycopyrrolate for 48 hr at 25 °C	331	C
Haloperidol lactate	MN	10 mg/ 2 ml	ES	100 mg/ 2 ml	White precipitate forms within 5 min	1784	I
	MN	5 mg/ 1 ml	ES	50 mg/ 1 ml	White cloudy precipitate forms in 2 hr at room temperature	1886	I
Hydromorphone HCl	KN	4 mg/ 2 ml	PD	50 mg/ 1 ml	Physically compatible for 30 min	517	C
Hydroxyzine HCl	PF	50 mg/ 1 ml	PD	50 mg/ 1 ml	Physically compatible for at least 15 min	326	C
Iodipamide meglumine (% unspecified)	SQ		PD	5 mg/ 0.1 ml to 50 mg/ 1 ml	Dense putty-like white precipitate immediately forms	309	I
Iodipamide meglumine 52% (Cholografin)	SQ	40 to 1 ml	PD	1 ml[c]	Forms a precipitate initially but clears within 1 hr and remains clear for 48 hr	530	I
Iohexol	WI	64.7%, 5 ml	PD	12.5 mg/ 0.25 ml	Physically compatible for at least 2 hr	1438	C
Iopamidol	SQ	61%, 5 ml	PD	12.5 mg/ 0.25 ml	Physically compatible for at least 2 hr	1438	C
Iothalamate meglumine (% unspecified)	MA	5 ml	PD	50 mg/ 1 ml	No precipitate observed	309	C
Iothalamate meglumine 60% (Conray)	MA	40 to 1 ml	PD	1 ml[c]	Physically compatible for 48 hr	530	C
Iothalamate meglumine 60%	MA	5 ml	PD	12.5 mg/ 0.25 ml	Physically compatible for at least 2 hr	1438	C
Iothalamate sodium 80% (Angio-Conray)	MA	40 to 1 ml	PD	1 ml[c]	Physically compatible for 48 hr	530	C
Ioxaglate meglumine 39.3%, ioxaglate sodium 19.6%	MA	5 ml	PD	12.5 mg/ 0.25 ml	Precipitate forms immediately and persists for at least 2 hr	1438	I
Meperidine HCl	WY	100 mg/ 1 ml	PD	50 mg/ 1 ml	Physically compatible for at least 15 min	14	C
	WI	50 mg/ 1 ml	PD	50 mg/ 1 ml	Physically compatible for at least 15 min	309	C
Metoclopramide HCl	NO	10 mg/ 2 ml	PD	50 mg/ 1 ml	Physically compatible both macroscopically and microscopically for 15 min at room temperature	565	C
	RB	10 mg/ 2 ml	PD	50 mg/ 5 ml	Physically compatible for 48 hr at room temperature	924	C
	RB	10 mg/ 2 ml	PD	250 mg/ 25 ml	Physically compatible for 48 hr at room temperature	924	C
	RB	10 mg/ 2 ml	PD	50 mg/ 5 ml	Physically compatible for 48 hr at 25 °C	1167	C
	RB	10 mg/ 2 ml	PD	250 mg/ 25 ml	Physically compatible for 48 hr at 25 °C	1167	C

Drugs in Syringe Compatibility (Cont.)

Diphenhydramine HCl

Drug (in syringe)	*Mfr*	*Amt*	*Mfr*	*Amt*	*Remarks*	*Ref*	*C/I*
	RB	160 mg/ 32 ml	PD	40 mg/ 4 ml	Physically compatible for 48 hr at 25 °C	1167	C
	RB	160 mg/ 32 ml	PD	200 mg/ 20 ml	Physically compatible for 48 hr at 25 °C	1167	C
Midazolam HCl	RC	5 mg/ 1 ml	ES	50 mg/ 1 ml	Physically compatible for 4 hr at 25 °C under fluorescent light	1145	C
Morphine sulfate	WY	15 mg/ 1 ml	PD	50 mg/ 1 ml	Physically compatible for at least 15 min	14	C
	ST	15 mg/ 1 ml	PD	50 mg/ 1 ml	Physically compatible for at least 15 min	326	C
Nalbuphine HCl	DU	10 mg/ 1 ml	PD	50 mg/ 1 ml	Physically compatible for 48 hr	128	C
	DU	20 mg/ 1 ml	PD	50 mg/ 1 ml	Physically compatible for 48 hr	128	C
Papaveretum	RC[d]	20 mg/ 1 ml	PD	50 mg/ 1 ml	Visually compatible for at least 15 min	326	C
Pentazocine lactate	WI	30 mg/ 1 ml	PD	50 mg/ 1 ml	Physically compatible for at least 15 min	326	C
Pentobarbital sodium	WY	100 mg/ 2 ml	PD	50 mg/ 1 ml	Precipitate observed within 15 min	14	I
	AB	500 mg/ 10 ml	PD	50 mg/ 1 ml	Physically incompatible	55	I
	AB	50 mg/ 1 ml	PD	50 mg/ 1 ml	Physically incompatible within 15 min	326	I
Perphenazine	SC	5 mg/ 1 ml	PD	50 mg/ 1 ml	Physically compatible both macroscopically and microscopically for 30 min at room temperature	566	C
	SC	10 mg/ 2 ml	ES	100 mg/ 2 ml	Visually compatible for 60 min	1784	C
Prochlorperazine edisylate	PO	5 mg/ 1 ml	PD	50 mg/ 1 ml	Physically compatible for at least 15 min	326	C
Promazine HCl	WY	50 mg/ 1 ml	PD	50 mg/ 1 ml	Physically compatible for at least 15 min	326	C
Promethazine HCl	WY	50 mg/ 2 ml	PD	50 mg/ 1 ml	Physically compatible for at least 15 min	14	C
	PO	50 mg/ 2 ml	PD	50 mg/ 1 ml	Physically compatible for at least 15 min	326	C
Ranitidine HCl	GL	50 mg/ 2 ml	PD	50 mg/ 1 ml	Physically compatible for 1 hr at 25 °C both macroscopically and microscopically	978	C
Scopolamine HBr	ST	0.4 mg/ 1 ml	PD	50 mg/ 1 ml	Physically compatible for at least 15 min	326	C
Sufentanil citrate	JN	50 μg/ml	SCN	50 mg/ml	Physically compatible with no subvisual haze or particle formation in 24 hr at 23 °C	1711	C
Thiopental sodium	AB	75 mg/ 3 ml	PD	50 mg/ 1 ml	Physically incompatible	21	I

[a] *Mixed in equal quantities. Final concentration is one-half the indicated concentration.*
[b] *Mixed in varying quantities to yield the final concentrations noted.*
[c] *Diphenhydramine HCl concentration unspecified.*
[d] *The former formulation was tested.*

Y-Site Injection Compatibility (1:1 Mixture)

			Diphenhydramine HCl				
Drug	*Mfr*	*Conc*	*Mfr*	*Conc*	*Remarks*	*Ref*	*C/I*
Acyclovir sodium	BW	5 mg/ml[a]	ES	1 mg/ml[a]	Physically compatible for 4 hr at 25 °C	1157	C
Aldesleukin	CHI	33,800 I.U./ml[a]	SCN	50 mg/ml	Visually compatible for 2 hr. Bioassay not possible	1857	C
Allopurinol sodium	BW	3 mg/ml[b]	PD	2 mg/ml[b]	Heavy white turbidity and precipitate form immediately	1686	I
Amifostine	USB	10 mg/ml[a]	PD	2 mg/ml[a]	Physically compatible with no change in measured turbidity or increase in particle content in 4 hr at 23 °C	1845	C
Amphotericin B cholesteryl sulfate complex	SEQ	0.83 mg/ml[a]	SCN	2 mg/ml[a]	Microprecipitate and increased turbidity form immediately	2117	I
Amsacrine	NCI	1 mg/ml[a]	PD	2 mg/ml[a]	Physically compatible for 4 hr at room temperature under fluorescent light	1381	C
Aztreonam	SQ	40 mg/ml[a]	PD	2 mg/ml[a]	Physically compatible with no subvisual haze or particle formation in 4 hr at 23 °C	1758	C
Cefepime HCl	BMS	20 mg/ml[a]	WY	2 mg/ml[a]	Cloudy solution with precipitate forms immediately	1689	I
Ciprofloxacin	MI	2 mg/ml[c]	ES	50 mg/ml	Visually compatible for 24 hr at 24 °C	1655	C
Cisatracurium besylate	GW	0.1, 2, 5 mg/ml[a]	SCN	2 mg/ml[a]	Physically compatible with no change in measured turbidity or increase in particle content in 4 hr at 23 °C	2074	C
Cisplatin	BR	1 mg/ml	PD	2 mg/ml[a]	Visually compatible for 4 hr at room temperature under fluorescent light	1685	C
Cladribine	ORT	0.015[b] and 0.5[d] mg/ml	SCN	2 mg/ml[b]	Physically compatible with no change in measured turbidity or increase in particle content in 4 hr at 23 °C	1969	C
Cyclophosphamide	MJ	10 mg/ml	PD	2 mg/ml[a]	Visually compatible for 4 hr at room temperature under fluorescent light	1685	C
Cytarabine	UP	50 mg/ml	PD	2 mg/ml[a]	Visually compatible for 4 hr at room temperature under fluorescent light	1685	C
Docetaxel	RPR	0.9 mg/ml[a]	ES	2 mg/ml[a]	Physically compatible with no change in measured turbidity or increase in particle content in 4 hr at 23 °C	2224	C
Doxorubicin HCl	AD	0.2 mg/ml[a]	PD	2 mg/ml[a]	Visually compatible for 4 hr at room temperature under fluorescent light	1685	C
Doxorubicin HCl liposome injection	SEQ	0.4 mg/ml[a]	SCN	2 mg/ml[a]	Physically compatible with little or no change in measured turbidity and no increase in particle content in 4 hr at 23 °C	2087	C
Etoposide phosphate	BR	5 mg/ml[a]	ES	2 mg/ml[a]	Physically compatible with no change in measured turbidity or increase in particle content in 4 hr at 23 °C	2218	C
Famotidine	ME	2 mg/ml[b]		2 mg/ml[a]	Visually compatible for 4 hr at 22 °C	1936	C
Fentanyl citrate	JN	0.025 mg/ml[a]	SCN	2 mg/ml[a]	Physically compatible with no change in measured haze or increase in particle content in 48 hr at 22 °C	1706	C

Y-Site Injection Compatibility (1:1 Mixture) (Cont.)

Diphenhydramine HCl

Drug	*Mfr*	*Conc*	*Mfr*	*Conc*	*Remarks*	*Ref*	*C/I*
Filgrastim	AMG	30 μg/ml[a]	ES	2 mg/ml[a]	Physically compatible with no change in measured turbidity or increase in particle content in 4 hr at 22 °C	1687	C
Fluconazole	RR	2 mg/ml	ES	50 mg/ml	Physically compatible for 24 hr at 25 °C	1407	C
Fludarabine phosphate	BX	1 mg/ml[a]	WY	2 mg/ml[a]	Physically compatible for 4 hr at room temperature under fluorescent light	1439	C
Foscarnet sodium	AST	24 mg/ml	PD	50 mg/ml	Cloudy solution	1335	I
Gatifloxacin	BMS	2 mg/ml[a]	ES	2 mg/ml[a]	Physically compatible with no change in measured haze or increase in particle content in 4 hr at 23 °C	2234	C
Gemcitabine HCl	LI	10 mg/ml[b]	SCN	2 mg/ml[b]	Physically compatible with no change in measured turbidity or increase in particle content in 4 hr at 23 °C	2226	C
Granisetron HCl	SKB	1 mg/ml	PD	1 mg/ml[b]	Physically compatible with little or no loss of either drug by HPLC in 4 hr at 22 °C	1883	C
	SKB	0.05 mg/ml[a]	SCN	2 mg/ml[a]	Physically compatible with no change in measured turbidity or increase in particle content in 4 hr at 23 °C	2000	C
Heparin sodium	UP	1000 units/L[e]	PD	50 mg/ml	Physically compatible for at least 4 hr at room temperature by visual and microscopic examination	534	C
Hetastarch in lactated electrolyte injection (Hextend)	AB	6%	SCN	2 mg/ml[a]	Physically compatible with no change in measured turbidity or increase in particle content in 4 hr at 23 °C	2339	C
Hydrocortisone sodium succinate	UP	10 mg/L[e]	PD	50 mg/ml	Physically compatible for at least 4 hr at room temperature by visual and microscopic examination	534	C
	UP	1 mg/ml[a]	SCN	0.16 mg/ml[a]	Physically compatible with no subvisual haze or particle formation in 24 hr at 23 °C	1729	C
	UP	2 mg/ml[a]	SCN	1 mg/ml[a]	Physically compatible with no subvisual haze or particle formation in 24 hr at 23 °C	1729	C
Hydromorphone HCl	AST	0.5 mg/ml[a]	SCN	2 mg/ml[a]	Physically compatible with no change in measured haze or increase in particle content in 48 hr at 22 °C	1706	C
Idarubicin HCl	AD	1 mg/ml[b]	ES	1[a] and 50 mg/ml	Visually compatible for 24 hr at 25 °C	1525	C
Linezolid	PHU	2 mg/ml	ES	2 mg/ml[a]	Physically compatible with no change in measured turbidity or increase in particle content in 4 hr at 23 °C	2264	C
Melphalan HCl	BW	0.1 mg/ml[b]	WY	2 mg/ml[b]	Physically compatible with no change in measured turbidity or increase in particle content in 3 hr at 22 °C	1557	C
Meperidine HCl	AB	10 mg/ml	ES	1[a] and 50 mg/ml	Physically compatible for 4 hr at 25 °C	1397	C
Meropenem	ZEN	1 and 50 mg/ml[b]	PD	50 mg/ml	Visually compatible for 4 hr at room temperature	1994	C

Y-Site Injection Compatibility (1:1 Mixture) (Cont.)

Diphenhydramine HCl

Drug	*Mfr*	*Conc*	*Mfr*	*Conc*	*Remarks*	*Ref*	*C/I*
Methadone HCl	LI	1 mg/ml[a]	SCN	2 mg/ml[a]	Physically compatible with no change in measured haze or increase in particle content in 48 hr at 22 °C	1706	C
Methotrexate sodium	AD	15 mg/ml[f]	PD	2 mg/ml[a]	Visually compatible for 4 hr at room temperature under fluorescent light	1685	C
Morphine sulfate	AST	1 mg/ml[a]	SCN	2 mg/ml[a]	Physically compatible with no change in measured haze or increase in particle content in 48 hr at 22 °C	1706	C
Ondansetron HCl	GL	1 mg/ml[b]	PD	2 mg/ml[a]	Physically compatible for 4 hr at 22 °C	1365	C
Paclitaxel	NCI	1.2 mg/ml[a]		2 mg/ml[a]	Physically compatible with no change in measured turbidity in 4 hr at 22 °C	1528	C
Piperacillin sodium–tazobactam sodium	LE	40 + 5 mg/ml[a]	WY	2 mg/ml[a]	Physically compatible with no change in measured turbidity or increase in particle content in 4 hr at 22 °C	1688	C
Potassium chloride	AB	40 mEq/L[e]	PD	50 mg/ml	Physically compatible for at least 4 hr at room temperature by visual and microscopic examination	534	C
Propofol	ZEN	10 mg/ml	SCN	2 mg/ml[a]	Physically compatible for 1 hr at 23 °C with no increase in particle content	2066	C
Remifentanil HCl	GW	0.025 and 0.25 mg/ml[b]	SCN	2 mg/ml[a]	Physically compatible with no change in measured turbidity or increase in particle content in 4 hr at 23 °C	2075	C
Sargramostim	IMM	10 μg/ml[b]	RU	1 mg/ml[b]	Physically compatible for 4 hr at 22 °C	1436	C
Sufentanil citrate	JN	12.5 μg/ml[a]	SCN	2 mg/ml[a]	Physically compatible with no subvisual haze or particle formation in 24 hr at 23 °C	1711	C
Tacrolimus	FUJ	1 mg/ml[b]	ES	1 mg/ml[a]	Visually compatible for 24 hr at 25 °C	1630	C
Teniposide	BR	0.1 mg/ml[a]	ES	2 mg/ml[a]	Physically compatible with no subvisual haze or particle formation in 4 hr at 23 °C	1725	C
Thiotepa	IMM[g]	1 mg/ml[a]	WY	2 mg/ml[a]	Physically compatible with no change in measured turbidity or increase in particle content in 4 hr at 23 °C	1861	C
TNA #218 to #226[h]			SCN, PD	2[a] and 50 mg/ml	Visually compatible with no precipitate or emulsion damage apparent in 4 hr at 23 °C	2215	C
TPN #212 to #215[h]			SCN	2 mg/ml[a]	Physically compatible with no change in measured turbidity or increase in particle content in 4 hr at 23 °C	2109	C
			SCN	50 mg/ml	Physically compatible with no change in measured turbidity or increase in particle content in 4 hr at 23 °C	2109	C
Vinorelbine tartrate	BW	1 mg/ml[b]	ES	2 mg/ml[b]	Physically compatible with no change in measured turbidity or increase in particle content in 4 hr at 22 °C	1558	C

Y-Site Injection Compatibility (1:1 Mixture) (Cont.)

Diphenhydramine HCl

Drug	*Mfr*	*Conc*	*Mfr*	*Conc*	*Remarks*	*Ref*	*C/I*
Vitamin B complex with C	RC	2 ml/L[e]	PD	50 mg/ml	Physically compatible for at least 4 hr at room temperature by visual and microscopic examination	534	C

[a]*Tested in dextrose 5% in water.*
[b]*Tested in sodium chloride 0.9%.*
[c]*Tested in both dextrose 5% in water and sodium chloride 0.9%.*
[d]*Tested in bacteriostatic sodium chloride 0.9% preserved with benzyl alcohol 0.9%.*
[e]*Tested in dextrose 5% in Ringer's injection, dextrose 5% in Ringer's injection, lactated, dextrose 5% in water, Ringer's injection, lactated, and sodium chloride 0.9%.*
[f]*Tested in dextrose 5% in water with sodium bicarbonate 0.05 mEq/ml.*
[g]*Lyophilized formulation tested.*
[h]*Refer to Appendix I for the composition of parenteral nutrition solutions. TNA indicates a 3-in-1 admixture, and TPN indicates a 2-in-1 admixture.*

Additional Compatibility Information

Other Drugs — Diphenhydramine HCl (Parke-Davis) has been found to be compatible with diatrizoate meglumine products (Squibb) for at least short periods. (40) It is also stated to be physically and chemically compatible with buprenorphine HCl. (4)

Diphenhydramine HCl has been found to be incompatible with iodipamide meglumine (Squibb). (40)

The following incompatibility determinations were performed with concentrated solutions: 1 ml of diphenhydramine HCl (Parke-Davis) was added to 5 ml of sterile distilled water along with 1 ml of either phenytoin sodium (Parke-Davis) or phenobarbital sodium (Winthrop). Particulate matter was noted within two hours. (28)

DOBUTAMINE HCL
AHFS 12:12

Products — Dobutamine HCl is available in 1-, 20-, 40-, and 100-ml single-dose vials as a concentrate for injection. Each milliliter contains 12.5 mg of dobutamine (as the hydrochloride), sodium bisulfite 0.24 mg, and hydrochloric acid and/or sodium hydroxide to adjust the pH. Dobutamine HCl concentrate for injection must be diluted further to a concentration not greater than 5 mg/ml before administration. (2; 4; 29)

A concentration of 250 μg/ml may be prepared by diluting 250 mg of drug in 1000 ml of compatible infusion solution. Concentrations of 500 and 1000 μg/ml (1 mg/ml) may be prepared by diluting 250 mg of drug in 500 ml and 250 ml of compatible infusion solution, respectively. (2; 4)

Dobutamine HCl is also available in plastic bags as premixed solutions in concentrations of 0.5, 1, 2, and 4 mg/ml in dextrose 5% in water. Sodium metabisulfite and edetate disodium dihydrate may also be present. (2; 29)

pH — From 2.5 to 5.5. (4; 17) The premixed infusion solutions in dextrose 5% in water have a pH range of 2.5 to 5.5. (2)

Osmolality — The osmolality of dobutamine HCl injection (Lilly) was determined to be 273 mOsm/kg by freezing-point depression and vapor pressure. (1071) At a concentration of 5 mg/ml (manufacturer and diluent unstated), the osmolality was determined to be 361 mOsm/kg by freezing-point depression. (1233)

The premixed infusion solutions in dextrose 5% in water (Abbott) have osmolalities ranging from 260 to 284 mOsm/kg for the four concentrations available. (4)

Trade Name(s) — Dobutrex.

Administration — Dobutamine HCl is administered by intravenous infusion after dilution to a concentration no greater than 5 mg/ml. The concentration used is dependent on the patient's dosage and fluid requirements. An infusion pump or other infusion control device should be used to control the flow rate. (2; 4)

Stability — Intact containers should be stored at controlled room temperature and protected from excessive heat and freezing. Brief exposure to temperatures up to 40 °C does not adversely affect the products. Solutions that are further diluted for intravenous infusion should be used within 24 hours. (2; 4)

Dobutamine HCl concentrate for injection is a clear, colorless to pale straw-colored solution. (4) Solutions of dobutamine HCl may have a pink discoloration. This discoloration, which will increase with time, results from a slight oxidation of the drug. However, there is no significant loss of drug potency within the recommended storage times for solutions of the drug. (2; 4)

Syringes — Dobutamine HCl (Lilly) 250 mg/50 ml in dextrose 5% in water exhibited no change in appearance and no loss in potency by HPLC when stored in 60-ml plastic syringes (Becton-Dickinson) for 24 hours at 25 °C. (1579)

Dobutamine HCl (Lilly) 5 mg/ml in dextrose 5% in water was packaged in 50-ml polypropylene syringes (Becton-Dickinson) and stored at 4 and 24 °C in the dark and exposed to room light for 48 hours. Dobutamine concentration losses determined by HPLC analysis were less than 10% throughout the study. (1961)

Sorption— Delivering dobutamine HCl (Lilly) 5 mg/ml in dextrose 5% in water by syringe pump over 12 hours at 24 °C through PVC and polyethylene administration tubing did not result in substantial dobutamine losses determined by HPLC analysis. (1961)

Dobutamine HCl (Giulini) 0.5 mg/ml in dextrose 5% in water and sodium chloride 0.9% packaged in PVC, polyethylene, and glass containers exhibited no loss due to sorption to any of the container types when stored at 4 and 22 °C for 24 hours protected from light. (2289)

Filtration— Dobutamine HCl (Lilly) 0.5 mg/ml in dextrose 5% in water and sodium chloride 0.9% was filtered through a 0.22-μm cellulose ester membrane filter (Ivex-HP, Millipore) over six hours. No significant drug loss due to binding to the filter was noted. (1034)

Central Venous Catheter— Dobutamine HCl (Astra) 4 mg/ml in dextrose 5% in water was found to be compatible with the ARROWg+ard Blue Plus (Arrow International) chlorhexidine-bearing triple-lumen central catheter. HPLC analysis was used to evaluate completeness of drug delivery through the catheter and the amount of chlorhexidine removed from the internal lumens. Essentially complete delivery of the drug was found with little or no drug loss occurring. Furthermore, chlorhexidine delivered from the catheter remained at trace amounts with no substantial increase due to the delivery of the drug through the catheter. (2335)

Compatibility Information

Solution Compatibility

Dobutamine HCl

Solution	*Mfr*	*Mfr*	*Conc/L*	*Remarks*	*Ref*	*C/I*
Dextrose 2.5% in half-strength Ringer's injection, lactated	MG[a]	LI	1 g	No decomposition in 48 hr at 25 °C. Slight pink color at 8 hr becoming slightly brown at 24 hr without affecting potency	789	C
Dextrose 5% in Ringer's injection, lactated	MG[a]	LI	1 g	No decomposition in 48 hr at 25 °C. Slight pink color at 24 hr becoming slightly brown at 48 hr without affecting potency	789	C
Dextrose 2.5% in sodium chloride 0.45%	MG[a]	LI	1 g	No decomposition in 48 hr at 25 °C. Slight pink color at 24 hr becoming slightly brown at 48 hr without affecting potency	789	C
Dextrose 5% in sodium chloride 0.45%	AB[b], CU[a]	LI	1 g	No decomposition in 48 hr at 25 °C. Slight pink color at 24 hr becoming slightly brown at 48 hr without affecting potency	749	C
Dextrose 5% in sodium chloride 0.9%	MG[b]	LI	1 g	No decomposition in 48 hr at 25 °C. Slight pink color at 24 hr becoming slightly brown at 48 hr without affecting potency	789	C
Dextrose 5% in water	CU[a], TR[b]	LI	1 g	No decomposition in 48 hr at 25 °C. Slight pink color at 24 hr becoming slightly brown in 48 hr without affecting potency	749	C
	TR[b]	LI	250 mg	Physically compatible with no loss in 48 hr at 24 °C. Transient light pink color. No decomposition after 7 days at 5 °C	811	C
	[a]		2 to 8 g	Pale pink discoloration with 4% or less dobutamine loss in 24 hr exposed to light	1412	C
	BA[b]	LI	5 g	5% loss by HPLC in 100 days at 5 °C protected from light	1610	C
	BA[b]	LI	1 g	5% loss by HPLC in 234.7 days at 5 °C protected from light	1610	C
	TR[b]	LI	0.25 and 1 g	Visually compatible with no dobutamine loss by HPLC in 48 hr at room temperature	1802	C
	AB[b]	AB	4 g	Visually compatible with no loss by HPLC in 30 days at 4 and 23 °C protected from light	2241	C
	BA[b], BRN[a,c]	GIU	0.5 g	Visually compatible with little or no loss by HPLC in 24 hr at 4 and 22 °C	2289	C
Ringer's injection, lactated	CU[a], TR[b]	LI	1 g	No decomposition in 48 hr at 25 °C. Slight pink color at 3 hr becoming slightly brown at 48 hr without affecting potency	749	C

Solution Compatibility (Cont.)

Dobutamine HCl

Solution	*Mfr*	*Mfr*	*Conc/L*	*Remarks*	*Ref*	*C/I*
Sodium bicarbonate 5%	MG[a]	LI	1 g	Cloudy brownish solution with precipitate in 3 hr at 25 °C. 18% dobutamine loss with dense precipitate in 24 hr	789	I
Sodium chloride 0.45%	MG[a]	LI	1 g	No decomposition in 48 hr at 25 °C. Slight pink color at 24 hr becoming slightly brown at 48 hr without affecting potency	789	C
Sodium chloride 0.9%	CU[a], TR[b]	LI	1 g	No decomposition in 48 hr at 25 °C. Slight pink color at 24 hr becoming slightly brown at 48 hr without affecting potency	749	C
		LI	200 mg	Physically compatible for 24 hr	552	C
	TR[b]	LI	250 mg	About 3% dobutamine loss in 48 hr at 24 °C. Initially colorless solution becomes pink with time. No decomposition after 7 days at 5 °C	811	C
	[a]		2 to 8 g	Pale pink discoloration with 3% or less dobutamine loss in 24 hr exposed to light	1412	C
	TR[a]	LI	0.25 and 1 g	Visually compatible with no dobutamine loss by HPLC in 48 hr at room temperature	1802	C
	BA[b], BRN[a,c]	GIU	0.5 g	Visually compatible with little or no loss by HPLC in 24 hr at 4 and 22 °C	2289	C

[a]*Tested in glass containers.*
[b]*Tested in PVC containers.*
[c]*Tested in polyethylene containers.*

Additive Compatibility

Dobutamine HCl

Drug	*Mfr*	*Conc/L*	*Mfr*	*Conc/L*	*Test Soln*	*Remarks*	*Ref*	*C/I*
Acyclovir sodium	BW	5 g	LI	1 g	D5W	Discoloration developed in 25 min and cloudiness and brown color developed in 2 hr due to dobutamine oxidation. No acyclovir loss found	1343	I
Alteplase	GEN	0.5 g	LI	5 g	D5W, NS	Yellow discoloration and precipitate form	1856	I
Aminophylline	SE	1 g	LI	1 g	D5W, NS	Cloudy in 6 hr at 25 °C	789	I
	ES	2.5 g	LI	1 g	D5W, NS	White precipitate forms within 12 hr at 21 °C	812	I
Amiodarone HCl	LZ	2.5 g	LI	1 g	D5W, NS	Physically compatible for 24 hr at 21 °C	812	C
Atracurium besylate	BW	500 mg		1 g	D5W	Physically compatible and atracurium chemically stable for 24 hr at 5 and 30 °C	1694	C
Atropine sulfate	AB	16.7 mg	LI	167 mg	NS	Physically compatible for 24 hr	552	C
	ES	50 mg	LI	1 g	D5W, NS	Physically compatible for 24 hr at 21 °C	812	C
Bretylium tosylate	ACC	2 g	LI	1 g	D5W, NS	Slightly pink in 24 hr at 25 °C	789	I
	ACC	4 and 25 g	LI	1 g	D5W, NS	Physically compatible for 24 hr at 21 °C	812	C
Bumetanide	RC	125 mg	LI	1 g	D5W, NS	Immediate yellow discoloration with yellow precipitate within 6 hr at 21 °C	812	I
Calcium chloride	UP	9 g	LI	182 mg	NS	Physically compatible for 20 hr. Haze formation at 24 hr	552	I
	ES	2 g	LI	1 g	D5W, NS	Deeply pink in 24 hr at 25 °C	789	I
	ES	50 g	LI	1 g	D5W, NS	Physically compatible for 24 hr at 21 °C	812	C

Additive Compatibility (Cont.)

Dobutamine HCl

Drug	*Mfr*	*Conc/L*	*Mfr*	*Conc/L*	*Test Soln*	*Remarks*	*Ref*	*C/I*
Calcium gluconate	VI	9 g	LI	182 mg	NS	Small particles form within 4 hr. White precipitate and haze after 15 hr	552	I
	ES	2 g	LI	1 g	D5W, NS	Deeply pink in 24 hr at 25 °C	789	I
	IX	50 g	LI	1 g	D5W, NS	Small white particles form within 24 hr at 21 °C	812	I
Cibenzoline succinate		2 g	LI	4 g	D5W, NS	Physically compatible for 24 hr at 25 °C by visual and microscopic examination	1182	C
Diazepam	RC	2.5 g	LI	1 g	D5W, NS	Rapid clouding of solution with yellow precipitate within 24 hr at 21 °C	812	I
Digoxin	BW	4 mg	LI	1 g	D5W, NS	Slightly pink in 24 hr at 25 °C	789	I
Dopamine HCl	AS	5.5 g	LI	172 mg	NS	Physically compatible for 24 hr	552	C
	ACC	1.6 g	LI	1 g	D5W, NS	Physically compatible with no color change in 24 hr at 25 °C	789	C
	ES	800 mg	LI	1 g	D5W, NS	Physically compatible for 24 hr at 21 °C	812	C
Enalaprilat	MSD	12 mg	LI	1 g	D5W[a]	Visually compatible with little or no enalaprilat loss by HPLC in 24 hr at room temperature under fluorescent light. Dobutamine not tested	1572	C
Epinephrine HCl	BR	50 mg	LI	1 g	D5W, NS	Physically compatible for 24 hr at 21 °C	812	C
Floxacillin sodium	BE	20 g	LI	500 mg	NS	Haze forms immediately and precipitate forms in 24 to 48 hr at 15 and 30 °C	1479	I
Flumazenil	RC	20 mg	LI	2 g	D5W[a]	Visually compatible with no flumazenil loss by HPLC in 24 hr at 23 °C under fluorescent light. Dobutamine not tested	1710	C
Furosemide	HO	1 g	LI	1 g	D5W, NS	Cloudy in 1 hr at 25 °C	789	I
	WY	5 g	LI	1 g	D5W, NS	Immediate white precipitate	812	I
	HO	1 g	LI	500 mg	NS	Haze forms immediately	1479	I
Heparin sodium	ES	40,000 units	LI	1 g	D5W, NS	Physically compatible with no color change in 24 hr at 25 °C	789	C
	LY	50,000 units	LI	1 g	D5W, NS	Physically compatible for 24 hr at 21 °C	812	C
	ES	5 million units	LI	1 g	D5W, NS	Pink discoloration within 6 hr at 21 °C	812	I
	ES	50,000 units	LI	1 g	D5W	Precipitate forms within 3 min when heparin is added to D5W and then mixed with an equal volume of dobutamine in D5W	841	I
	LY	50,000 units	LI	1.5 g	D5W, NS	Obvious precipitation	1318	I
	LY	50,000 units	LI	900 mg	D5W, W	Physically compatible for 4 hr, but heat of reaction detected by microcalorimetry	1318	I
	LY	50,000 units	LI	900 mg	NS	Physically compatible for 4 hr with no heat of reaction detected by microcalorimetry	1318	C
Hydralazine HCl	CI	200 mg	LI	200 mg	NS	Physically compatible for 24 hr	552	C
Insulin, regular	LI	1,000 units	LI	1 g	D5W, NS	Slightly pink in 24 hr at 25 °C	789	I
	LI	50,000 units	LI	1 g	D5W, NS	White precipitate forms rapidly	812	I
Isoproterenol HCl	ES	2 mg	LI	1 g	D5W, NS	Physically compatible for 24 hr at 21 °C	812	C

Additive Compatibility (Cont.)

Dobutamine HCl

Drug	*Mfr*	*Conc/L*	*Mfr*	*Conc/L*	*Test Soln*	*Remarks*	*Ref*	*C/I*
Lidocaine HCl	ES	4 g	LI	1 g	D5W, NS	Physically compatible with no color change in 24 hr at 25 °C	789	C
	AST	4 and 10 g	LI	1 g	D5W, NS	Physically compatible for 24 hr at 21 °C	812	C
Magnesium sulfate	TO	2 g	LI	1 g	D5W, NS	Slightly pink in 24 hr at 25 °C	789	I
	ES	83 g[b]	LI	167 mg	NS	Physically compatible for 20 hr. Haze formation at 24 hr	552	I
Meperidine HCl	ES	50 g	LI	1 g	D5W, NS	Physically compatible for 24 hr at 21 °C	812	C
Meropenem	ZEN	1 and 20 g	LI	1 g	NS	Visually compatible for 4 hr at room temperature	1994	C
Metaraminol bitartrate	MSD	100 mg	LI	1 g	D5W, NS	Physically compatible for 24 hr at 21 °C	812	C
Morphine sulfate	ES	5 g	LI	1 g	D5W, NS	Physically compatible for 24 hr at 21 °C	812	C
Nitroglycerin	AB	120 mg	LI	1 g	D5W, NS	Physically compatible for 24 hr at 21 °C	812	C
	ACC	100 mg	LI	500 mg	D5S	Chemically stable with no loss of either drug after 24 hr at 25 °C. Pale pink color after 4 hr	990	C
Nitroglycerin with sodium nitroprusside		200 to 800 mg 200 to 800 mg		2 to 8 g	D5W[c]	Pale pink discoloration with small amount of dark brown precipitate and 11 to 19% sodium nitroprusside loss in 24 hr exposed to light	1412	I
Nitroglycerin with sodium nitroprusside		200 to 800 mg 200 to 800 mg		2 to 8 g	NS[c]	Pale pink discoloration with all drugs stable for 24 hr exposed to light. 8% or less loss for any drug in any combination	1412	C
Norepinephrine bitartrate	BN	32 mg	LI	1 g	D5W, NS	Physically compatible for 24 hr at 21 °C	812	C
Phentolamine mesylate	CI	20 mg	LI	1 g	D5W, NS	Physically compatible for 24 hr at 21 °C	812	C
Phenylephrine HCl	WI	20 mg	LI	1 g	D5W, NS	Physically compatible for 24 hr at 21 °C	812	C
Phenytoin sodium	AHP	25 g	LI	1 g	D5W, NS	White precipitate forms rapidly with brown solution within 6 hr at 21 °C	812	I
	ES	1 g	LI	1 g	D5W, NS	White precipitate forms in 5 to 10 min	789	I
Potassium chloride	ES	160 mEq	LI	1 g	D5W, NS	Slightly pink in 24 hr at 25 °C	789	I
	AB	20 mEq	LI	1 g	D5W, NS	Physically compatible for 24 hr at 21 °C	812	C
Potassium phosphates	AB	100 mM	LI	200 mg	NS	Small particles form after 1 hr. White precipitate noted after 15 hr	552	I
Procainamide HCl	SQ	1 g	LI	1 g	D5W, NS	Physically compatible with no color change in 24 hr at 25 °C	789	C
	AHP	4 and 50 g	LI	1 g	D5W, NS	Physically compatible for 24 hr at 21 °C	812	C
Propranolol HCl	AY	50 mg	LI	1 g	D5W, NS	Physically compatible for 24 hr at 21 °C	812	C
Ranitidine HCl	GL	2 g	LI	250 mg and 1 g	D5W, NS[a]	Physically compatible with no ranitidine loss in 48 hr at room temperature under fluorescent light. Dobutamine not tested	1361	C
	GL	50 mg	LI	250 mg and 1 g	D5W[a]	Physically compatible with 5 to 7% ranitidine loss in 48 hr at room temperature under fluorescent light. Dobutamine not tested	1361	C
	GL	50 mg	LI	250 mg and 1 g	NS[a]	Physically compatible with no ranitidine loss in 48 hr at room temperature under fluorescent light. Dobutamine not tested	1361	C

Additive Compatibility (Cont.)

Dobutamine HCl

Drug	*Mfr*	*Conc/L*	*Mfr*	*Conc/L*	*Test Soln*	*Remarks*	*Ref*	*C/I*
	GL	50 mg and 2 g	LI	0.25 and 1 g	D5W, NS[a]	Visually compatible with little or no loss of either drug by HPLC in 48 hr at room temperature	1802	C
Sodium bicarbonate	IX	500 mEq	LI	1 g	D5W, NS	White precipitate forms within 6 hr at 21 °C	812	I
Verapamil HCl	KN	1.25 g	LI	1 g	D5W, NS	Physically compatible for 24 hr at 21 °C	812	C
	KN	160 mg	LI	250 mg	D5W	No decomposition of either drug in 48 hr at 24 °C or 7 days at 5 °C. Transient light pink color	811	C
	KN	160 mg	LI	250 mg	NS	No verapamil decomposition and 3% dobutamine loss in 48 hr at 24 °C. Initially colorless solution becomes pink with time. At 5 °C, no loss of either drug for 7 days	811	C
	KN	80 mg	LI	500 mg	D5W, NS	Slight pink color after 24 hr due to dobutamine oxidation	764	I

[a]*Tested in PVC containers.*
[b]*Tested as 1 g/12 ml final concentration.*
[c]*Tested in glass containers.*

Drugs in Syringe Compatibility

Dobutamine HCl

Drug (in syringe)	*Mfr*	*Amt*	*Mfr*	*Amt*	*Remarks*	*Ref*	*C/I*
Doxapram HCl	RB	400 mg/ 20 ml	LI	100 mg/ 10 ml	5% doxapram loss in 3 hr and 11% in 24 hr	1177	I
Heparin sodium		2500 units/ 1 ml	LI	250 mg/ 10 ml	Physically compatible for at least 5 min	1053	C
Ranitidine HCl	GL	50 mg/ 5 ml	LI	25 mg	Physically compatible for 4 hr at ambient temperature under fluorescent light	1151	C

Y-Site Injection Compatibility (1:1 Mixture)

Dobutamine HCl

Drug	*Mfr*	*Conc*	*Mfr*	*Conc*	*Remarks*	*Ref*	*C/I*
Acyclovir sodium	BW	5 mg/ml[a]	LI	1 mg/ml[a]	Solution turns cloudy and brown in 1 hr at 25 °C under fluorescent light	1157	I
Alatrofloxacin mesylate	PF	1.43 mg/ml[a]	ES	4.2 mg/ml[a]	Microscopic particles form	2235	I
Alteplase	GEN	1 mg/ml	LI	2 mg/ml[a]	Haze noted in 20 min by spectrophotometric examination and in 2 hr by visual examination	1340	I
Amifostine	USB	10 mg/ml[a]	LI	4 mg/ml[a]	Physically compatible with no change in measured turbidity or increase in particle content in 4 hr at 23 °C	1845	C
Aminophylline	ES	4 mg/ml[c]	LI	4 mg/ml[c]	Slight haze or precipitate and color change in 1 hr	1316	I
Amiodarone HCl	LZ	4 mg/ml[c]	LI	2 mg/ml[c]	Physically compatible for 24 hr at 21 °C	1032	C
Amphotericin B cholesteryl sulfate complex	SEQ	0.83 mg/ml[a]	AST	4 mg/ml[a]	Gross precipitate forms	2117	I

Y-Site Injection Compatibility (1:1 Mixture) (Cont.)

Dobutamine HCl

Drug	*Mfr*	*Conc*	*Mfr*	*Conc*	*Remarks*	*Ref*	*C/I*
Atracurium besylate	BW	0.5 mg/ml[a]	LI	1 mg/ml[a]	Physically compatible for 24 hr at 28 °C	1337	C
Aztreonam	SQ	40 mg/ml[a]	LI	4 mg/ml[a]	Physically compatible with no subvisual haze or particle formation in 4 hr at 23 °C	1758	C
Bretylium tosylate	LY	4 mg/ml[c]	LI	4 mg/ml[c]	Physically compatible for 3 hr	1316	C
Calcium chloride	AB	4 mg/ml[c]	LI	4 mg/ml[c]	Physically compatible for 3 hr	1316	C
Calcium gluconate	AST	4 mg/ml[c]	LI	4 mg/ml[c]	Physically compatible for 3 hr	1316	C
Cefepime HCl	BMS	20 mg/ml[a]	LI	4 mg/ml[a]	Cloudy solution forms immediately. Precipitate forms in 4 hr	1689	I
Ciprofloxacin	MI	2 mg/ml[c]	LI	250 μg/ml[c]	Visually compatible for 24 hr at 24 °C	1655	C
Cisatracurium besylate	GW	0.1, 2, 5 mg/ml[a]	LI	4 mg/ml[a]	Physically compatible with no change in measured turbidity or increase in particle content in 4 hr at 23 °C	2074	C
Cladribine	ORT	0.015[b] and 0.5[e] mg/ml	LI	4 mg/ml[b]	Physically compatible with no change in measured turbidity or increase in particle content in 4 hr at 23 °C	1969	C
Clarithromycin	AB	4 mg/ml[a]	BI	2 mg/ml[a]	Visually compatible for 72 hr at both 30 and 17 °C	2174	C
Diazepam	ES	0.2 mg/ml[c]	LI	4 mg/ml[c]	Physically compatible for 3 hr	1316	C
Diltiazem HCl	MMD	1 mg/ml[a]	LI	2 mg/ml[a]	Visually compatible for 24 hr at 25 °C	1530	C
	MMD	5 mg/ml	LI	1 mg/ml[c]	Visually compatible	1807	C
	MMD	1 mg/ml[a]	LI	4 mg/ml[a]	Visually compatible for 4 hr at 27 °C	2062	C
Docetaxel	RPR	0.9 mg/ml[a]	AST	4 mg/ml[a]	Physically compatible with no change in measured turbidity or increase in particle content in 4 hr at 23 °C	2224	C
Dopamine HCl	DCC	3.2 mg/ml[c]	LI	4 mg/ml[c]	Physically compatible for 3 hr	1316	C
	AB	3.2 mg/ml[a]	LI	4 mg/ml[a]	Visually compatible for 4 hr at 27 °C	2062	C
Dopamine HCl with lidocaine HCl	DCC AB	3.2 mg/ml[c] 8 mg/ml[c]	LI	4 mg/ml[c]	Physically compatible for 3 hr	1316	C
Dopamine HCl with nitroglycerin	DCC LY	3.2 mg/ml[c] 0.4 mg/ml[c]	LI	4 mg/ml[c]	Physically compatible for 3 hr	1316	C
Dopamine HCl with sodium nitroprusside	DCC ES	3.2 mg/ml[c] 0.4 mg/ml[c]	LI	4 mg/ml[c]	Physically compatible for 3 hr	1316	C
Doxorubicin HCl liposome injection	SEQ	0.4 mg/ml[a]	BA	4 mg/ml[a]	Physically compatible with little or no change in measured turbidity and no increase in particle content in 4 hr at 23 °C	2087	C
Enalaprilat	MSD	0.05 mg/ml[b]	LI	1 mg/ml[a]	Physically compatible for 24 hr at room temperature under fluorescent light	1355	C
Epinephrine HCl	AB	0.02 mg/ml[a]	LI	4 mg/ml[a]	Visually compatible for 4 hr at 27 °C	2062	C
Etoposide phosphate	BR	5 mg/ml[a]	AST	4 mg/ml[a]	Physically compatible with no change in measured turbidity or increase in particle content in 4 hr at 23 °C	2218	C
Famotidine	MSD	0.2 mg/ml[a]	LI	1 mg/ml[a]	Physically compatible for 4 hr at 25 °C	1188	C
	ME	2 mg/ml[b]		4 mg/ml[a]	Visually compatible for 4 hr at 22 °C	1936	C
Fentanyl citrate	ES	0.05 mg/ml	LI	4 mg/ml[a]	Visually compatible for 4 hr at 27 °C	2062	C
Fluconazole	RR	2 mg/ml	LI	2 mg/ml[a]	Visually compatible for 24 hr at 28 °C	1760	C

Y-Site Injection Compatibility (1:1 Mixture) (Cont.)

Drug	Mfr	Conc	Dobutamine HCl Mfr	Dobutamine HCl Conc	Remarks	Ref	C/I
Foscarnet sodium	AST	24 mg/ml	LI	12.5 mg/ml	Delayed formation of muddy precipitate	1335	I
Furosemide	ES	1 mg/ml[b]	LI	4 mg/ml[b]	Physically compatible for 3 hr	1316	C
	ES	1 mg/ml[a]	LI	4 mg/ml[a]	Slight precipitate in 1 hr	1316	I
	AMR	10 mg/ml	LI	4 mg/ml[a]	Precipitate forms immediately	2062	I
Gatifloxacin	BMS	2 mg/ml[a]	AST	4 mg/ml[a]	Physically compatible with no change in measured haze or increase in particle content in 4 hr at 23 °C	2234	C
Gemcitabine HCl	LI	10 mg/ml[b]	AST	4 mg/ml[b]	Physically compatible with no change in measured turbidity or increase in particle content in 4 hr at 23 °C	2226	C
Granisetron HCl	SKB	0.05 mg/ml[a]	BA	4 mg/ml[a]	Physically compatible with no change in measured turbidity or increase in particle content in 4 hr	2000	C
Haloperidol lactate	MN	0.5[a] and 5 mg/ml	DU	4 mg/ml[a]	Visually compatible for 24 hr at 21 °C	1523	C
Heparin sodium	ES	50 units/ml[b]	LI	4 mg/ml[b]	Physically compatible for 3 hr	1316	C
	ES	50 units/ml[a]	LI	4 mg/ml[a]	Immediate gross precipitation	1316	I
	LI	1 mg/ml[a]	TR	50 units/ml	Visually compatible for 4 hr at 25 °C	1793	C
	OR	100 units/ml[a]	LI	4 mg/ml[a]	Haze and white precipitate form	1877	I
	ES	100 units/ml[a]	LI	4 mg/ml[a]	Precipitate forms in 4 hr at 27 °C	2062	I
Hetastarch in lactated electrolyte injection (Hextend)	AB	6%	AST	4 mg/ml[a]	Physically compatible with no change in measured turbidity or increase in particle content in 4 hr at 23 °C	2339	C
Hydromorphone HCl	KN	1 mg/ml	LI	4 mg/ml[a]	Visually compatible for 4 hr at 27 °C	2062	C
Inamrinone lactate	WB	3 mg/ml[b]	LI	4 mg/ml[a]	Physically compatible for at least 4 hr at 25 °C under fluorescent light	992	C
Indomethacin sodium trihydrate	MSD	1 mg/ml[b]	AB	1.2 mg/ml[a]	Haze and fine precipitate form immediately	1527	I
Insulin, regular (beef pork)	LI	1 unit/ml[c]	LI	4 mg/ml[c]	Physically compatible for 3 hr	1316	C
(Humulin R)	LI	1 unit/ml[c]	LI	4 mg/ml[c]	Physically compatible for 3 hr	1316	C
Labetalol HCl	GL	1 mg/ml[a]	LI	2.5 mg/ml[a]	Visually compatible with little or no loss of either drug by HPLC in 4 hr at room temperature	1762	C
	GL	5 mg/ml	LI	4 mg/ml[a]	Visually compatible for 24 hr at 23 °C	1877	C
	AH	2 mg/ml[a]	LI	4 mg/ml[a]	Visually compatible for 4 hr at 27 °C	2062	C
Levofloxacin	OMN	5 mg/ml[a]	AB	12.5 mg/ml	Visually compatible for 4 hr at 24 °C under fluorescent light	2233	C
Lidocaine HCl	AB	8 mg/ml[c]	LI	4 mg/ml[c]	Physically compatible for 3 hr	1316	C
Lidocaine HCl with dopamine HCl	AB DCC	8 mg/ml[c] 3.2 mg/ml[c]	LI	4 mg/ml[c]	Physically compatible for 3 hr	1316	C
Lidocaine HCl with nitroglycerin	AB LY	8 mg/ml[c] 0.4 mg/ml[c]	LI	4 mg/ml[c]	Physically compatible for 3 hr	1316	C
Lidocaine HCl with sodium nitroprusside	AB ES	8 mg/ml[c] 0.4 mg/ml[c]	LI	4 mg/ml[c]	Physically compatible for 3 hr	1316	C
Linezolid	PHU	2 mg/ml	AST	4 mg/ml[a]	Physically compatible with no change in measured turbidity or increase in particle content in 4 hr at 23 °C	2264	C
Lorazepam	WY	0.5 mg/ml[a]	LI	4 mg/ml[a]	Visually compatible for 4 hr at 27 °C	2062	C

Y-Site Injection Compatibility (1:1 Mixture) (Cont.)

			Dobutamine HCl				
Drug	*Mfr*	*Conc*	*Mfr*	*Conc*	*Remarks*	*Ref*	*C/I*
Magnesium sulfate	LY	40 mg/ml[c]	LI	4 mg/ml[c]	Physically compatible for 3 hr	1316	C
Meperidine HCl	AB	10 mg/ml	LI	1 mg/ml[a]	Physically compatible for 4 hr at 25 °C	1397	C
Midazolam HCl	RC	1 mg/ml[a]	GNS	2 mg/ml[a]	Particles form in 8 hr	1847	I
	RC	1 mg/ml[a]	LI	4 mg/ml[a]	Visually compatible for 24 hr at 23 °C	1877	C
	RC	2 mg/ml[a]	LI	4 mg/ml[a]	Visually compatible for 4 hr at 27 °C	2062	C
Milrinone lactate	SW	0.2 mg/ml[a]	LI	4 mg/ml[a]	Visually compatible for 4 hr at 27 °C	2062	C
	SW	0.4 mg/ml[a]	GEN	8 mg/ml[a]	Visually compatible with little or no loss of either drug by HPLC in 4 hr at 23 °C	2214	C
Morphine sulfate	SCN	2 mg/ml[a]	LI	4 mg/ml[a]	Visually compatible for 4 hr at 27 °C	2062	C
Nicardipine HCl	WY	1 mg/ml[a]	LI	4 mg/ml[a]	Visually compatible for 4 hr at 27 °C	2062	C
Nitroglycerin	LY	0.4 mg/ml[c]	LI	4 mg/ml[c]	Physically compatible for 3 hr	1316	C
	AB	0.4 mg/ml[a]	LI	4 mg/ml[a]	Visually compatible for 4 hr at 27 °C	2062	C
Nitroglycerin with dopamine HCl	LY DCC	0.4 mg/ml[c] 3.2 mg/ml[c]	LI	4 mg/ml[c]	Physically compatible for 3 hr	1316	C
Nitroglycerin with lidocaine HCl	LY AB	0.4 mg/ml[c] 8 mg/ml[c]	LI	4 mg/ml[c]	Physically compatible for 3 hr	1316	C
Nitroglycerin with sodium nitroprusside	LY ES	0.4 mg/ml[c] 0.4 mg/ml[c]	LI	4 mg/ml[c]	Physically compatible for 3 hr	1316	C
Norepinephrine bitartrate	AB	0.128 mg/ml[a]	LI	4 mg/ml[a]	Visually compatible for 4 hr at 27 °C	2062	C
Pancuronium bromide	ES	0.05 mg/ml[a]	LI	1 mg/ml[a]	Physically compatible for 24 hr at 28 °C	1337	C
Phytonadione	MSD	0.4 mg/ml[c]	LI	4 mg/ml[c]	Slight haze in 3 hr	1316	I
Piperacillin sodium–tazobactam sodium	LE	40 + 5 mg/ml[a]	LI	4 mg/ml[a]	Heavy white turbidity forms immediately	1688	I
Potassium chloride	AB	0.06 mEq/ml[c]	LI	4 mg/ml[c]	Physically compatible for 3 hr	1316	C
Propofol	ZEN	10 mg/ml	LI	4 mg/ml[a]	Physically compatible for 1 hr at 23 °C with no increase in particle content	2066	C
Ranitidine HCl	GL	0.5 mg/ml[f]	LI	1 mg/ml[a]	Physically compatible for 24 hr	1323	C
	GL	1 mg/ml[a]	LI	4 mg/ml[a]	Visually compatible for 4 hr at 27 °C	2062	C
Remifentanil HCl	GW	0.025 and 0.25 mg/ml[b]	LI	4 mg/ml[a]	Physically compatible with no change in measured turbidity or increase in particle content in 4 hr at 23 °C	2075	C
Sodium nitroprusside	ES	0.4 mg/ml[c]	LI	4 mg/ml[c]	Physically compatible for 3 hr	1316	C
Sodium nitroprusside with dopamine HCl	ES DCC	0.4 mg/ml[c] 3.2 mg/ml[c]	LI	4 mg/ml[c]	Physically compatible for 3 hr	1316	C
Sodium nitroprusside with lidocaine HCl	ES AB	0.4 mg/ml[c] 8 mg/ml[c]	LI	4 mg/ml[c]	Physically compatible for 3 hr	1316	C
Sodium nitroprusside with nitroglycerin	ES LY	0.4 mg/ml[c] 0.4 mg/ml[c]	LI	4 mg/ml[c]	Physically compatible for 3 hr	1316	C
Streptokinase	HO	30,000 units/ml[a]	LI	2 mg/ml[a]	Physically compatible for at least 48 hr by spectrophotometric and visual examination	1340	C
Tacrolimus	FUJ	1 mg/ml[b]	LI	1 mg/ml[a]	Visually compatible for 24 hr at 25 °C	1630	C
Theophylline	TR	4 mg/ml	LI	1 mg/ml[a]	Visually compatible for 6 hr at 25 °C	1793	C
Thiopental sodium	AB	25 mg/ml[d]	LI	4 mg/ml[a]	Precipitate forms immediately	2062	I

Y-Site Injection Compatibility (1:1 Mixture) (Cont.)

			Dobutamine HCl				
Drug	*Mfr*	*Conc*	*Mfr*	*Conc*	*Remarks*	*Ref*	*C/I*
Thiotepa	IMM[g]	1 mg/ml[a]	LI	4 mg/ml[a]	Physically compatible with no change in measured turbidity or increase in particle content in 4 hr at 23 °C	1861	C
TNA #91[h]		[i]	LI	1 mg/ml[j]	Physically compatible	1170	C
TNA #218 to #226[h]			AST	4 mg/ml[a]	Visually compatible with no precipitate or emulsion damage apparent in 4 hr at 23 °C	2215	C
Tolazoline HCl		0.1 mg/ml[a]	LI	1.2 mg/ml[a]	Physically compatible for 24 hr at 22 °C	1363	C
TPN #189[h]			LI	50 mg/ml[b]	Visually compatible for 24 hr at 22 °C	1767	C
TPN #203 and #204[h]			LI	5 mg/ml	Visually compatible for 4 hr at 23 °C	1974	C
TPN #212 to #215[h]			LI	4 mg/ml[a]	Physically compatible with no change in measured turbidity or increase in particle content in 4 hr at 23 °C	2109	C
Vecuronium bromide	OR	0.1 mg/ml[a]	LI	1 mg/ml[a]	Physically compatible for 24 hr at 28 °C	1337	C
	OR	1 mg/ml	LI	4 mg/ml[a]	Visually compatible for 4 hr at 27 °C	2062	C
Verapamil HCl	LY	0.2 mg/ml[c]	LI	4 mg/ml[c]	Physically compatible for 3 hr	1316	C
Warfarin sodium	DU	2 mg/ml[d]	LI	1 mg/ml[a]	Haze and precipitate form immediately	2010	I
	DME	2 mg/ml[d]	LI	1 mg/ml[a]	Haze and precipitate form immediately	2078	I
Zidovudine	BW	4 mg/ml[a]	LI	5 mg/ml[a]	Physically compatible for 4 hr at 25 °C under fluorescent light by visual and microscopic examination	1193	C

[a]*Tested in dextrose 5% in water.*
[b]*Tested in sodium chloride 0.9%.*
[c]*Tested in both dextrose 5% in water and sodium chloride 0.9%.*
[d]*Tested in sterile water for injection.*
[e]*Tested in bacteriostatic sodium chloride 0.9% preserved with benzyl alcohol 0.9%.*
[f]*Premixed infusion solution.*
[g]*Lyophilized formulation tested.*
[h]*Refer to Appendix I for the composition of parenteral nutrition solutions. TNA indicates a 3-in-1 admixture, and TPN indicates a 2-in-1 admixture.*
[i]*Run at 10 ml/hr.*
[j]*In dextrose 5% in water infused at 1.2 ml/hr.*

Additional Compatibility Information

Infusion Solutions — The manufacturer recommends that admixtures in the following infusion solutions be used within 24 hours (2):

Dextrose 5% in Ringer's injection, lactated
Dextrose 5% in sodium chloride 0.45 and 0.9%
Dextrose 5% in water
Dextrose 10% in water
Isolyte M with dextrose 5%
Mannitol 20%
Normosol M in dextrose 5%
Ringer's injection, lactated
Sodium chloride 0.9%
Sodium lactate ⅙ M

Dobutamine HCl has been stated to be incompatible with alkaline solutions and should not be mixed with sodium bicarbonate 5%, other alkaline solutions, or other drugs or diluents containing both bisulfite and ethanol. (2; 4)

Peritoneal Dialysis Solutions — Dobutamine HCl (Lilly) 2.5, 5, and 7.5 μg/ml in Dianeal PD-1 (Baxter) with dextrose 1.5 and 4.25% retained at least 90% of its potency when stored for 24 hours at 4, 26, and 37 °C. (1417; 1702)

Dopamine, Lidocaine, Nitroglycerin, and Nitroprusside — Dobutamine HCl (Lilly) 4 mg/ml, dopamine HCl (Dupont Critical Care) 3.2 mg/ml, lidocaine HCl (Abbott) 8 mg/ml, nitroglycerin (Lyphomed) 0.4 mg/ml, and sodium nitroprusside (Elkins-Sinn) 0.4 mg/ml, prepared in dextrose 5% in water and sodium chloride 0.9%, were combined in equal quantities in all possible combinations of two, three, four, and five drugs and then evaluated for physical compatibility. No physical incompatibility was observed in any combination within the three-hour study period. (1316)

DOCETAXEL
AHFS 10:00

Products — Docetaxel is available as a concentrate in polysorbate 80 in single-use vials containing 20 mg (0.5 ml) and 80 mg (2 ml). Each size vial is packaged with a vial of special diluent composed of ethanol 13% in water for injection. Both the docetaxel vials and the accompanying diluent contain an overfill. Table 1 cites the vial sizes and actual fill amounts for docetaxel products and diluents. (2)

The preparation of the product is a two-step procedure. The first step is the preparation of the premix solution. The premix solution is then further diluted prior to administration (step 2).

To prepare the premix, allow the proper number of vials of docetaxel concentrate to stand at room temperature for about five minutes after taking them from the refrigerator. Then withdraw the entire contents of each of the accompanying vials of special diluent and add to each vial of docetaxel concentrate. Gently rotate each vial of premix solution for about 15 seconds to ensure thorough mixing. This final premix solution is a clear solution having a docetaxel concentration of 10 mg/ml. If foam appears from the surfactant in the formulation, allow the vials to stand until most of the foam has dissipated; it is not necessary for all of the foam to have dissipated before proceeding with the rest of the preparation steps. (2)

Withdraw the necessary amount of the docetaxel 10-mg/ml premix solution using a syringe and add it into a 250-ml glass or polyolefin (polyethylene or polypropylene) container of dextrose 5% in water or sodium chloride 0.9% to produce a final concentration between 0.3 and 0.74 mg/ml. It is necessary to use a larger volume of infusion solution if the docetaxel dose exceeds 240 mg so that the concentration does not exceed 0.74 mg/ml. The infusion admixture should be mixed thoroughly by rotation. (2)

The use of gloves during preparation of docetaxel doses is recommended. If the docetaxel concentrate, premix solution, or admixture comes in contact with skin, the affected area should be washed thoroughly with soap and water. Contact with mucosa requires thorough flushing with water. (2)

Trade Name(s) — Taxotere.

Administration — Docetaxel is administered as a one-hour intravenous infusion at ambient temperature and light to patients adequately premedicated to control adverse effects. (2)

Table 1. Docetaxel Sizes and Diluent Volumes (2)

Vial Size	Actual Vial Fill	Actual Diluent Fill
20 mg/0.5 ml	23.6 mg/0.59 ml	1.83 ml
80 mg/2 ml	94.4 mg/2.36 ml	7.33 ml

Stability — Docetaxel concentrate is a clear, viscous yellow to yellow-brown liquid. (1310) Intact containers of docetaxel with the accompanying special diluent should be stored under refrigeration or at controlled room temperature. Freezing of the concentrate does not adversely affect docetaxel. The vials should be left in the original packages to protect the drug from bright light. (2)

The manufacturer recommends that the premix solution and the fully diluted admixture in dextrose 5% in water or sodium chloride 0.9% be used as soon as possible after preparation. The premix solution is stable for at least eight hours after preparation under refrigeration or at room temperatures up to 25 °C according to the labeling. (2) Thiesen and Kramer evaluated the stability of docetaxel (Rhone-Poulenc Rorer) 10-mg/ml mixed concentrate over 28 days at 25 and 4 °C. The mixed concentrate remained visually clear with no color change, and HPLC analysis found no docetaxel loss at either temperature. (2242)

The drug diluted in infusion solutions for administration has been stated to be stable for four hours at room temperature and is not light sensitive. (1310) The manufacturer recommends use of the dilution for infusion within four hours, including the one-hour period needed for infusion. (2)

Plasticizer Leaching — The surfactant (polysorbate 80) contained in the docetaxel formulation can leach plasticizer from diethylhexyl phthalate (DEHP)-plasticized PVC containers and administration sets. The amount leached is time and concentration dependent. (1683) The manufacturer recommends that docetaxel concentrate not be allowed to contact such containers and equipment. To minimize the amount of plasticizer exposure to the patient, the use of glass or polyolefin (such as polyethylene, polypropylene, etc.) containers and polyethylene-lined administration sets is recommended for the administration of docetaxel admixtures. (2)

Mazzo et al. evaluated the leaching of DEHP plasticizer by docetaxel 0.56 and 0.96 mg/ml in dextrose 5% in water and in sodium chloride 0.9%. PVC bags of the solutions were used to prepare the admixtures. The leaching of the plasticizer was found to be time and concentration dependent; however, there was little difference between the two infusion solutions. After storage for eight hours at 21 °C, HPLC analysis found leached DEHP in the range of 30 to 51 μg/ml for the 0.96-mg/ml concentration and 25 to 36 μg/ml for the 0.56-mg/ml concentration. During a simulated one-hour infusion, the amount of leached DEHP did not exceed 14 μg/ml. (1825)

An acceptability limit of no more than 5 parts per million (5 μg/ml) for DEHP plasticizer leached from PVC containers, etc. has been proposed. The limit was proposed based on a review of metabolic and toxicologic considerations. (2185)

Filtration — The use of inline filters for docetaxel administration is not required by the manufacturer. (4)

Compatibility Information

Solution Compatibility

Docetaxel

Solution	*Mfr*	*Mfr*	*Conc/L*	*Remarks*	*Ref*	*C/I*
Dextrose 5% in water	BRN[a]	RPR	0.3 and 0.9 g	Visually compatible with little or no loss by HPLC in 28 days at 25 °C protected from light	2242	C
	BRN[b]	RPR	0.3 and 0.9 g	Visually compatible with little or no loss by HPLC in 28 days at 25 °C protected from light	2242	C

Solution Compatibility (Cont.)

Docetaxel

Solution	*Mfr*	*Mfr*	*Conc/L*	*Remarks*	*Ref*	*C/I*
	BR[c]	RPR	0.3 and 0.9 g	Visually compatible with little or no loss by HPLC in 5 days at 25 °C protected from light. Precipitation and accompanying loss of drug occurred after 5 days in some samples	2242	C
Sodium chloride 0.9%	BRN[a]	RPR	0.3 and 0.9 g	Visually compatible with little or no loss by HPLC in 28 days at 25 °C protected from light	2242	C
	BRN[d]	RPR	0.3 and 0.9 g	Visually compatible with little or no loss by HPLC in 28 days at 25 °C protected from light	2242	C
	BR[c]	RPR	0.3 and 0.9 g	Visually compatible with little or no loss by HPLC in 3 days at 25 °C protected from light. Precipitation and accompanying loss of drug occurred after 3 days in some samples	2242	C

[a]*Tested in glass containers.*
[b]*Tested in polypropylene containers.*
[c]*Tested in PVC containers.*
[d]*Tested in polyethylene containers.*

Y-Site Injection Compatibility (1:1 Mixture)

Docetaxel

Drug	*Mfr*	*Conc*	*Mfr*	*Conc*	*Remarks*	*Ref*	*C/I*
Acyclovir sodium	GW	7 mg/ml[a]	RPR	0.9 mg/ml[a]	Physically compatible with no change in measured turbidity or increase in particle content in 4 hr at 23 °C	2224	C
Amifostine	ALZ	10 mg/ml[b]	RPR	0.9 mg/ml[a]	Physically compatible with no change in measured turbidity or increase in particle content in 4 hr at 23 °C	2224	C
Amikacin sulfate	AB	5 mg/ml[a]	RPR	0.9 mg/ml[a]	Physically compatible with no change in measured turbidity or increase in particle content in 4 hr at 23 °C	2224	C
Aminophylline	AB	2.5 mg/ml[a]	RPR	0.9 mg/ml[a]	Physically compatible with no change in measured turbidity or increase in particle content in 4 hr at 23 °C	2224	C
Amphotericin B	PH	0.6 mg/ml[a]	RPR	0.9 mg/ml[a]	Visible turbidity forms immediately	2224	I
Ampicillin sodium	SKB	20 mg/ml[b]	RPR	0.9 mg/ml[a]	Physically compatible with no change in measured turbidity or increase in particle content in 4 hr at 23 °C	2224	C
Ampicillin sodium–sulbactam sodium	RR	20 + 10 mg/ml[b]	RPR	0.9 mg/ml[a]	Physically compatible with no change in measured turbidity or increase in particle content in 4 hr at 23 °C	2224	C
Aztreonam	BMS	40 mg/ml[a]	RPR	0.9 mg/ml[a]	Physically compatible with no change in measured turbidity or increase in particle content in 4 hr at 23 °C	2224	C
Bumetanide	RC	0.04 mg/ml[a]	RPR	0.9 mg/ml[a]	Physically compatible with no change in measured turbidity or increase in particle content in 4 hr at 23 °C	2224	C
Buprenorphine HCl	RKC	0.04 mg/ml[a]	RPR	0.9 mg/ml[a]	Physically compatible with no change in measured turbidity or increase in particle content in 4 hr at 23 °C	2224	C

Y-Site Injection Compatibility (1:1 Mixture) (Cont.)

			Docetaxel				
Drug	*Mfr*	*Conc*	*Mfr*	*Conc*	*Remarks*	*Ref*	*C/I*
Butorphanol tartrate	APC	0.04 mg/ml[a]	RPR	0.9 mg/ml[a]	Physically compatible with no change in measured turbidity or increase in particle content in 4 hr at 23 °C	2224	C
Calcium gluconate	FUJ	40 mg/ml[a]	RPR	0.9 mg/ml[a]	Physically compatible with no change in measured turbidity or increase in particle content in 4 hr at 23 °C	2224	C
Cefazolin sodium	APC	20 mg/ml[a]	RPR	0.9 mg/ml[a]	Physically compatible with no change in measured turbidity or increase in particle content in 4 hr at 23 °C	2224	C
Cefepime HCl	BMS	20 mg/ml[a]	RPR	0.9 mg/ml[a]	Physically compatible with no change in measured turbidity or increase in particle content in 4 hr at 23 °C	2224	C
Cefoperazone sodium	PF	40 mg/ml[a]	RPR	0.9 mg/ml[a]	Physically compatible with no change in measured turbidity or increase in particle content in 4 hr at 23 °C	2224	C
Cefotaxime sodium	HO	20 mg/ml[a]	RPR	0.9 mg/ml[a]	Physically compatible with no change in measured turbidity or increase in particle content in 4 hr at 23 °C	2224	C
Cefotetan sodium	ZEN	20 mg/ml[a]	RPR	0.9 mg/ml[a]	Physically compatible with no change in measured turbidity or increase in particle content in 4 hr at 23 °C	2224	C
Cefoxitin sodium	ME	20 mg/ml[a]	RPR	0.9 mg/ml[a]	Physically compatible with no change in measured turbidity or increase in particle content in 4 hr at 23 °C	2224	C
Ceftazidime	SKB[c]	40 mg/ml[a]	RPR	0.9 mg/ml[a]	Physically compatible with no change in measured turbidity or increase in particle content in 4 hr at 23 °C	2224	C
Ceftizoxime sodium	FUJ	20 mg/ml[a]	RPR	0.9 mg/ml[a]	Physically compatible with no change in measured turbidity or increase in particle content in 4 hr at 23 °C	2224	C
Ceftriaxone sodium	RC	20 mg/ml[a]	RPR	0.9 mg/ml[a]	Physically compatible with no change in measured turbidity or increase in particle content in 4 hr at 23 °C	2224	C
Cefuroxime sodium	LI	30 mg/ml[a]	RPR	0.9 mg/ml[a]	Physically compatible with no change in measured turbidity or increase in particle content in 4 hr at 23 °C	2224	C
Chlorpromazine HCl	SCN	2 mg/ml[a]	RPR	0.9 mg/ml[a]	Physically compatible with no change in measured turbidity or increase in particle content in 4 hr at 23 °C	2224	C
Cimetidine HCl	AMR	12 mg/ml[a]	RPR	0.9 mg/ml[a]	Physically compatible with no change in measured turbidity or increase in particle content in 4 hr at 23 °C	2224	C
Ciprofloxacin	BAY	1 mg/ml[a]	RPR	0.9 mg/ml[a]	Physically compatible with no change in measured turbidity or increase in particle content in 4 hr at 23 °C	2224	C
Clindamycin phosphate	AST	10 mg/ml[a]	RPR	0.9 mg/ml[a]	Physically compatible with no change in measured turbidity or increase in particle content in 4 hr at 23 °C	2224	C

Y-Site Injection Compatibility (1:1 Mixture) (Cont.)

Drug	*Mfr*	*Conc*	Docetaxel *Mfr*	Docetaxel *Conc*	*Remarks*	*Ref*	*C/I*
Dexamethasone sodium phosphate	ES	2 mg/ml[a]	RPR	0.9 mg/ml[a]	Physically compatible with no change in measured turbidity or increase in particle content in 4 hr at 23 °C	2224	C
Diphenhydramine HCl	ES	2 mg/ml[a]	RPR	0.9 mg/ml[a]	Physically compatible with no change in measured turbidity or increase in particle content in 4 hr at 23 °C	2224	C
Dobutamine HCl	AST	4 mg/ml[a]	RPR	0.9 mg/ml[a]	Physically compatible with no change in measured turbidity or increase in particle content in 4 hr at 23 °C	2224	C
Dopamine HCl	AB	3.2 mg/ml[a]	RPR	0.9 mg/ml[a]	Physically compatible with no change in measured turbidity or increase in particle content in 4 hr at 23 °C	2224	C
Doxorubicin HCl liposome injection	SEQ	0.4 mg/ml[a]	RPR	2 mg/ml[a]	Partial loss of measured natural turbidity	2087	I
Doxycycline hyclate	FUJ	1 mg/ml[a]	RPR	0.9 mg/ml[a]	Physically compatible with no change in measured turbidity or increase in particle content in 4 hr at 23 °C	2224	C
Droperidol	AST	0.4 mg/ml[a]	RPR	0.9 mg/ml[a]	Physically compatible with no change in measured turbidity or increase in particle content in 4 hr at 23 °C	2224	C
Enalaprilat	ME	0.1 mg/ml[a]	RPR	0.9 mg/ml[a]	Physically compatible with no change in measured turbidity or increase in particle content in 4 hr at 23 °C	2224	C
Famotidine	ME	2 mg/ml[a]	RPR	0.9 mg/ml[a]	Physically compatible with no change in measured turbidity or increase in particle content in 4 hr at 23 °C	2224	C
Fluconazole	RR	2 mg/ml	RPR	0.9 mg/ml[a]	Physically compatible with no change in measured turbidity or increase in particle content in 4 hr at 23 °C	2224	C
Furosemide	AMR	3 mg/ml[a]	RPR	0.9 mg/ml[a]	Physically compatible with no change in measured turbidity or increase in particle content in 4 hr at 23 °C	2224	C
Ganciclovir sodium	RC	20 mg/ml[a]	RPR	0.9 mg/ml[a]	Physically compatible with no change in measured turbidity or increase in particle content in 4 hr at 23 °C	2224	C
Gemcitabine HCl	LI	10 mg/ml[b]	RPR	2 mg/ml[a]	Physically compatible with no change in measured turbidity or increase in particle content in 4 hr at 23 °C	2226	C
Gentamicin sulfate	AB	5 mg/ml[a]	RPR	0.9 mg/ml[a]	Physically compatible with no change in measured turbidity or increase in particle content in 4 hr at 23 °C	2224	C
Granisetron HCl	SKB	0.05 mg/ml[a]	RPR	0.9 mg/ml[a]	Physically compatible with no change in measured turbidity or increase in particle content in 4 hr at 23 °C	2224	C
Haloperidol lactate	MN	0.2 mg/ml[a]	RPR	0.9 mg/ml[a]	Physically compatible with no change in measured turbidity or increase in particle content in 4 hr at 23 °C	2224	C
Heparin sodium	ES	100 units/ml	RPR	0.9 mg/ml[a]	Physically compatible with no change in measured turbidity or increase in particle content in 4 hr at 23 °C	2224	C

Y-Site Injection Compatibility (1:1 Mixture) (Cont.)

Drug	*Mfr*	*Conc*	Docetaxel *Mfr*	Docetaxel *Conc*	*Remarks*	*Ref*	*C/I*
Hydrocortisone sodium phosphate	ME	1 mg/ml[a]	RPR	0.9 mg/ml[a]	Physically compatible with no change in measured turbidity or increase in particle content in 4 hr at 23 °C	2224	C
Hydrocortisone sodium succinate	AB	1 mg/ml[a]	RPR	0.9 mg/ml[a]	Physically compatible with no change in measured turbidity or increase in particle content in 4 hr at 23 °C	2224	C
Hydromorphone HCl	AST	0.5 mg/ml[a]	RPR	0.9 mg/ml[a]	Physically compatible with no change in measured turbidity or increase in particle content in 4 hr at 23 °C	2224	C
Hydroxyzine HCl	ES	2 mg/ml[a]	RPR	0.9 mg/ml[a]	Physically compatible with no change in measured turbidity or increase in particle content in 4 hr at 23 °C	2224	C
Imipenem–cilastatin sodium	ME	10 mg/ml[b]	RPR	0.9 mg/ml[a]	Physically compatible with no change in measured turbidity or increase in particle content in 4 hr at 23 °C	2224	C
Leucovorin calcium	ES	2 mg/ml[a]	RPR	0.9 mg/ml[a]	Physically compatible with no change in measured turbidity or increase in particle content in 4 hr at 23 °C	2224	C
Lorazepam	WY	0.5 mg/ml[a]	RPR	0.9 mg/ml[a]	Physically compatible with no change in measured turbidity or increase in particle content in 4 hr at 23 °C	2224	C
Magnesium sulfate	AST	100 mg/ml[a]	RPR	0.9 mg/ml[a]	Physically compatible with no change in measured turbidity or increase in particle content in 4 hr at 23 °C	2224	C
Mannitol	BA	15%	RPR	0.9 mg/ml[a]	Physically compatible with no change in measured turbidity or increase in particle content in 4 hr at 23 °C	2224	C
Meperidine HCl	AST	4 mg/ml[a]	RPR	0.9 mg/ml[a]	Physically compatible with no change in measured turbidity or increase in particle content in 4 hr at 23 °C	2224	C
Meropenem	ZEN	20 mg/ml[b]	RPR	0.9 mg/ml[a]	Physically compatible with no change in measured turbidity or increase in particle content in 4 hr at 23 °C	2224	C
Mesna	MJ	10 mg/ml[a]	RPR	0.9 mg/ml[a]	Physically compatible with no change in measured turbidity or increase in particle content in 4 hr at 23 °C	2224	C
Methylprednisolone sodium succinate	PHU	5 mg/ml[a]	RPR	0.9 mg/ml[a]	Partial loss of measured natural turbidity occurs immediately	2224	I
Metoclopramide HCl	AB	5 mg/ml	RPR	0.9 mg/ml[a]	Physically compatible with no change in measured turbidity or increase in particle content in 4 hr at 23 °C	2224	C
Metronidazole	BA	5 mg/ml	RPR	0.9 mg/ml[a]	Physically compatible with no change in measured turbidity or increase in particle content in 4 hr at 23 °C	2224	C
Minocycline HCl	LE	0.2 mg/ml[a]	RPR	0.9 mg/ml[a]	Physically compatible with no change in measured turbidity or increase in particle content in 4 hr at 23 °C	2224	C
Morphine sulfate	ES	1 mg/ml[a]	RPR	0.9 mg/ml[a]	Physically compatible with no change in measured turbidity or increase in particle content in 4 hr at 23 °C	2224	C

Y-Site Injection Compatibility (1:1 Mixture) (Cont.)

Drug	*Mfr*	*Conc*	Docetaxel *Mfr*	Docetaxel *Conc*	*Remarks*	*Ref*	*C/I*
Nalbuphine HCl	AST	10 mg/ml	RPR	0.9 mg/ml[a]	Increase in measured subvisual turbidity occurs immediately	2224	I
Netilmicin sulfate	SC	5 mg/ml[a]	RPR	0.9 mg/ml[a]	Physically compatible with no change in measured turbidity or increase in particle content in 4 hr at 23 °C	2224	C
Ofloxacin	MN	4 mg/ml[a]	RPR	0.9 mg/ml[a]	Physically compatible with no change in measured turbidity or increase in particle content in 4 hr at 23 °C	2224	C
Ondansetron HCl	GW	1 mg/ml[a]	RPR	0.9 mg/ml[a]	Physically compatible with no change in measured turbidity or increase in particle content in 4 hr at 23 °C	2224	C
Piperacillin sodium	LE	40 mg/ml[a]	RPR	0.9 mg/ml[a]	Physically compatible with no change in measured turbidity or increase in particle content in 4 hr at 23 °C	2224	C
Piperacillin sodium–tazobactam sodium	CY	40 + 5 mg/ml[a]	RPR	0.9 mg/ml[a]	Physically compatible with no change in measured turbidity or increase in particle content in 4 hr at 23 °C	2224	C
Potassium chloride	AB	0.1 mEq/ml[a]	RPR	0.9 mg/ml[a]	Physically compatible with no change in measured turbidity or increase in particle content in 4 hr at 23 °C	2224	C
Prochlorperazine edisylate	SO	0.5 mg/ml[a]	RPR	0.9 mg/ml[a]	Physically compatible with no change in measured turbidity or increase in particle content in 4 hr at 23 °C	2224	C
Promethazine HCl	SCN	2 mg/ml[a]	RPR	0.9 mg/ml[a]	Physically compatible with no change in measured turbidity or increase in particle content in 4 hr at 23 °C	2224	C
Ranitidine HCl	GL	2 mg/ml[a]	RPR	0.9 mg/ml[a]	Physically compatible with no change in measured turbidity or increase in particle content in 4 hr at 23 °C	2224	C
Ringer's injection, lactated	BA		RPR	0.9 mg/ml[a]	Physically compatible with no change in measured turbidity or increase in particle content in 4 hr at 23 °C	2224	C
Sodium bicarbonate	AB	1 mEq/ml	RPR	0.9 mg/ml[a]	Physically compatible with no change in measured turbidity or increase in particle content in 4 hr at 23 °C	2224	C
Ticarcillin disodium	SKB	30 mg/ml[a]	RPR	0.9 mg/ml[a]	Physically compatible with no change in measured turbidity or increase in particle content in 4 hr at 23 °C	2224	C
Ticarcillin disodium–clavulanate potassium	SKB	31 mg/ml[a]	RPR	0.9 mg/ml[a]	Physically compatible with no change in measured turbidity or increase in particle content in 4 hr at 23 °C	2224	C
Tobramycin sulfate	LI	5 mg/ml[a]	RPR	0.9 mg/ml[a]	Physically compatible with no change in measured turbidity or increase in particle content in 4 hr at 23 °C	2224	C
Trimethoprim–sulfamethoxazole	ES	0.8 + 4 mg/ml[a]	RPR	0.9 mg/ml[a]	Physically compatible with no change in measured turbidity or increase in particle content in 4 hr at 23 °C	2224	C

Y-Site Injection Compatibility (1:1 Mixture) (Cont.)

Docetaxel

Drug	*Mfr*	*Conc*	*Mfr*	*Conc*	*Remarks*	*Ref*	*C/I*
Vancomycin HCl	LI	10 mg/ml[a]	RPR	0.9 mg/ml[a]	Physically compatible with no change in measured turbidity or increase in particle content in 4 hr at 23 °C	2224	C
Zidovudine	GW	4 mg/ml[a]	RPR	0.9 mg/ml[a]	Physically compatible with no change in measured turbidity or increase in particle content in 4 hr at 23 °C	2224	C

[a]*Tested in dextrose 5% in water.*
[b]*Tested in sodium chloride 0.9%.*
[c]*Sodium carbonate–containing formulation tested.*

Other Information

Microbial Growth — Docetaxel (Rhone-Poulenc) 0.8 mg/ml diluted in sodium chloride 0.9% did not exhibit an antimicrobial effect on the growth of four organisms (*Enterococcus faecium, Staphylococcus aureus, Pseudomonas aeruginosa,* and *Candida albicans*) inoculated into the solution. Diluted solutions should be stored under refrigeration whenever possible, and the potential for microbiological growth should be considered when assigning expiration periods. (2160)

DOLASETRON MESYLATE
AHFS 56:22

Products — Dolasetron mesylate is available in 0.625-ml (12.5-mg) single-use ampuls and 5-ml (100-mg) single-use vials. Each milliliter of solution contains 20 mg of dolasetron mesylate and 38.2 mg of mannitol with acetate buffer in water for injection. (2)

pH — From 3.2 to 3.8. (2)

Trade Name(s) — Anzemet.

Administration — Dolasetron mesylate is administered intravenously undiluted up to a rate of 100 mg/30 seconds or diluted in a compatible infusion solution to a volume of 50 ml for infusion over 15 minutes. The administration line should be flushed both before and after dolasetron mesylate administration. (2)

Stability — Dolasetron mesylate injection is a clear, colorless solution. Intact containers should be stored at controlled room temperature and protected from light. (2)

Compatibility Information

Y-Site Injection Compatibility (1:1 Mixture)

Dolasetron mesylate

Drug	*Mfr*	*Conc*	*Mfr*	*Conc*	*Remarks*	*Ref*	*C/I*
Hetastarch in lactated electrolyte injection (Hextend)	AB	6%	HO	2 mg/ml[a]	Physically compatible with no change in measured turbidity or increase in particle content in 4 hr at 23 °C	2339	C

[a]*Tested in dextrose 5% in water.*

Additional Compatibility Information

Infusion Solutions — Dolasetron mesylate diluted for infusion is stated by the manufacturer to be stable for 24 hours at room temperature exposed to normal light and 48 hours under refrigeration in the following infusion solutions (2):

Dextrose 5% in lactated Ringer's injection
Dextrose 5% in sodium chloride 0.45%
Dextrose 5% in water
Lactated Ringer's injection
Mannitol 10%
Sodium chloride 0.9%

DOPAMINE HCL
AHFS 12:12

Products — Dopamine HCl is available in 200-mg (40 mg/ml), 400-mg (40 mg/ml), 400-mg (80 mg/ml), 800-mg (80 mg/ml), and 800-mg (160 mg/ml) vials and prefilled syringes. The solutions also contain sodium metabisulfite 0.9% as an antioxidant, citric acid and sodium citrate buffer, and hydrochloric acid or sodium hydroxide to adjust the pH in water for injection. (1-3/97; 4; 29)

Dopamine HCl is available premixed for infusion in concentrations of 0.8, 1.6, and 3.2 mg/ml in dextrose 5% in water. Also present are sodium metabisulfite 0.5 mg/ml and hydrochloric acid and/or sodium hydroxide for pH adjustment. (4)

pH — Dopamine HCl injection has a pH of about 3.3 (range 2.5 to 5). (1-3/97; 4) The premixed dopamine HCl infusions have a pH of about 3.3 to 3.8 (range 2.5 to 4.5). (4)

Osmotic Values — The osmolality of dopamine HCl 40 mg/ml was determined to be 619 mOsm/kg by freezing-point depression and 581 mOsm/kg by vapor pressure. (1071) At a concentration of 10 mg/ml (manufacturer and diluent unspecified), the osmolality was determined to be 277 mOsm/kg. (1233) The osmolarity of Abbott's premixed dopamine HCl in dextrose 5% in water is 270, 275, and 295 mOsm/L for the 0.8-, 1.6-, and 3.2-mg/ml concentrations, respectively. (4)

Administration — Dopamine HCl is administered by intravenous infusion into a large vein using an infusion pump or other infusion control device. The premixed infusion solutions are suitable for administration without dilution, but the concentrated injection must be diluted for use. Often the dose of concentrate is added to 250 or 500 ml of compatible solution. The concentration used depends on the patient's requirements. Concentrations as high as 3200 μg/ml have been used. (1-3/97; 4)

Stability — Intact containers of dopamine HCl should be stored at controlled room temperature. (1-3/97; 4) The injections should be protected from excessive heat and from freezing. (4) The commercial preparation is stable for five years from manufacture if protected from light. (79)

pH Effects — The pH of the solution is one of the most critical factors determining dopamine HCl stability. While dopamine HCl has been found to be stable over a pH range of 4 to 6.4 when mixed with other drugs in dextrose 5% in water (312), it is most stable at pH 5 or below. (79) In alkaline solutions, the catechol moieties are oxidized, cyclized, and polymerized to colored materials (312), forming a pink to violet color. (78) Decomposition may also be indicated by the formation of a yellow or brown discoloration of the solution. (4) Discolored solutions should not be used. (4; 312)

Light Effects — Exposure of dopamine HCl (American Critical Care) 100 mg/100 ml in dextrose 5% in water to fluorescent and blue phototherapy light for 36 hours at 25 °C, while static or flowing through tubing at 2 ml/hr, resulted in no significant difference in drug concentration compared to controls stored in the dark. Because no unacceptable potency loss occurs, protection of dopamine HCl infusions from blue phototherapy lights is not necessary. (1100)

Syringes — Dopamine HCl (Abbott) 200 mg/50 ml in dextrose 5% in water exhibited no change in appearance and no loss in potency by HPLC when stored in 60-ml plastic syringes (Becton-Dickinson) for 24 hours at 25 °C. (1579)

Dopamine HCl (Therabel Lucien Pharma) 4 mg/ml in dextrose 5% in water was packaged in 50-ml polypropylene syringes (Becton-Dickinson) and stored at 4 and 24 °C in the dark and exposed to room light for 48 hours. Dopamine concentration losses determined by HPLC analysis were less than 10% throughout the study. (1961)

Sorption — Dopamine HCl (Sigma) 72 mg/L was added to sodium chloride 0.9% (Travenol) in PVC bags and stored for one week at room temperature (15 to 20 °C). No significant sorption of the dopamine HCl to the plastic was exhibited. (536)

Dopamine HCl (Arnar-Stone) 20 mg/2 ml diluted in dextrose 5% in water or sodium chloride 0.9% was stored for 18 hours at room temperature in the following plastic syringes: Brunswick (Sherwood Medical), Plastipak (Becton-Dickinson), Steriseal (Needle Industries), and Sabre (Gillette U.K.). The first three syringes have polypropylene barrels; the Sabre has a combination polypropylene–polystyrene barrel. No significant loss of dopamine occurred due to sorption. (784)

Delivering dopamine HCl (Therabel Lucien Pharma) 4 mg/ml in dextrose 5% in water by syringe pump over 12 hours at 24 °C through PVC and polyethylene administration tubing did not result in substantial dopamine concentration losses determined by HPLC analysis. (1961)

Filtration — Dopamine HCl 100 μg/ml in dextrose 5% in water or sodium chloride 0.9% was delivered over five hours through four kinds of 0.2-μm membrane filters varying in size and composition. Dopamine concentration losses of 3 to 5% were found during the first 60 minutes; subsequent dopamine levels returned to the original concentration when the binding sites became saturated. (1399)

Central Venous Catheter — Dopamine HCl (Abbott) 3.2 mg/ml in dextrose 5% in water was found to be compatible with the ARROWg+ard Blue Plus (Arrow International) chlorhexidine-bearing triple-lumen central catheter. HPLC analysis was used to evaluate completeness of drug delivery through the catheter and the amount of chlorhexidine removed from the internal lumens. Essentially complete delivery of the drug was found with little or no drug loss occurring. Furthermore, chlorhexidine delivered from the catheter remained at trace amounts with no substantial increase due to the delivery of the drug through the catheter. (2335)

Compatibility Information

Solution Compatibility

Dopamine HCl

Solution	*Mfr*	*Mfr*	*Conc/L*	*Remarks*	*Ref*	*C/I*
Amino acids 4.25%, dextrose 25%	MG	AS	400 mg	No increase in particulate matter in 24 hr at 4 °C	349	C
Dextrose 5% in Ringer's injection, lactated	MG	AS	800 mg	Less than 5% decomposition in 48 hr at 23 to 25 °C	79	C
Dextrose 5% in sodium chloride 0.45%	MG	AS	800 mg	Less than 5% decomposition in 48 hr at 23 to 25 °C	79	C
Dextrose 5% in sodium chloride 0.9%	MG	AS	800 mg	Less than 5% decomposition in 48 hr at 23 to 25 °C	79	C
Dextrose 10% in sodium chloride 0.18%	TR[a]		300 mg	Visually compatible with no loss colorimetrically in 96 hr at room temperature under fluorescent light	1569	C
Dextrose 5% in water	MG	AS	800 mg	Less than 5% decomposition in 48 hr at 23 to 25 °C	79	C
	TR[a]	AS	800 mg	Potency retained for 24 hr at 25 °C	79	C
		AS	800 mg	Potency retained for 7 days at 5 °C	79	C
	AB	ACC	800 mg	Physically compatible and chemically stable. 10% decomposition calculated to occur after 142 hr at 25 °C	527	C
	BA[a]	DB	3.2 g	5% loss by HPLC in 14.75 days at 5 °C protected from light	1610	C
	TR[a]	ES	0.4 and 3.2 g	Visually compatible with no dopamine loss by HPLC in 48 hr at room temperature	1802	C
	BA[a]	SO	6.1 g	3% dopamine loss by HPLC in 24 hr at 23 °C	2085	C
Dextrose 10% in water	TR[a]		300 mg	Visually compatible with no loss colorimetrically in 96 hr at room temperature under fluorescent light	1569	C
Mannitol 20% in water	MG	AS	800 mg	Less than 5% decomposition in 48 hr at 23 to 25 °C	79	C
Ringer's injection, lactated	MG	AS	800 mg	Less than 5% decomposition in 48 hr at 23 to 25 °C	79	C
Sodium bicarbonate 5%	MG	AS	800 mg	Color change 5 min after mixing. Also second spot appeared on TLC	79	I
Sodium chloride 0.9%	MG	AS	800 mg	Less than 5% decomposition in 48 hr at 23 to 25 °C	79	C
	TR[a]	ES	0.4 and 3.2 g	Visually compatible with 5% or less dopamine loss by HPLC in 48 hr at room temperature	1802	C
Sodium lactate ⅙ M	MG	AS	800 mg	Less than 5% decomposition in 48 hr at 23 to 25 °C	79	C

[a]*Tested in PVC containers.*

Additive Compatibility

Dopamine HCl

Drug	*Mfr*	*Conc/L*	*Mfr*	*Conc/L*	*Test Soln*	*Remarks*	*Ref*	*C/I*
Acyclovir sodium	BW	5 g	SO	1.6 g	D5W	Yellow color developed in 1.5 hr due to dopamine oxidation. No acyclovir loss	1343	I
Alteplase	GEN	0.5 g	ACC	5 g	D5W, NS	About 30% alteplase clot-lysis activity loss in 24 hr at 25 °C	1856	I

Additive Compatibility (Cont.)

			Dopamine HCl					
Drug	*Mfr*	*Conc/L*	*Mfr*	*Conc/L*	*Test Soln*	*Remarks*	*Ref*	*C/I*
Aminophylline	SE	500 mg	ACC	800 mg	D5W	Physically compatible. 10% dopamine decomposition occurs in 111 hr at 25 °C	527	C
Amphotericin B	SQ	200 mg	AS	800 mg	D5W	Immediate precipitation	78	I
Ampicillin sodium	BR	4 g	AS	800 mg	D5W	36% ampicillin decomposition in 6 hr at 23 to 25 °C. Apparent dopamine decomposition also. Color change and second spot on TLC	78	I
Atracurium besylate	BW	500 mg		1.6 g	D5W	Physically compatible and atracurium chemically stable for 24 hr at 5 and 30 °C	1694	C
Bretylium tosylate	ACC	10 g	ACC	800 mg	D5S[a]	Physically compatible and both drugs chemically stable for 48 hr at room temperature and 7 days at 4 °C	522	C
Calcium chloride	UP		AS	800 mg	D5W	No dopamine decomposition in 24 hr at 25 °C	312	C
Chloramphenicol sodium succinate	PD	4 g	AS	800 mg	D5W	Chloramphenicol and dopamine potency retained for 24 hr at 23 to 25 °C	78	C
Cibenzoline succinate		2 g	ACC	3.2 g	D5W, NS	Physically compatible for 24 hr at 25 °C by visual and microscopic examination	1182	C
Ciprofloxacin	MI	2 g		400 mg	NS	Compatible for 24 hr at 25 °C	888	C
	MI	2 g		1.04 g	NS	Compatible for 24 hr at 25 °C	888	C
Dobutamine HCl	LI	172 mg	AS	5.5 g	NS	Physically compatible for 24 hr	552	C
	LI	1 g	ACC	1.6 g	D5W, NS	Physically compatible with no color change in 24 hr at 25 °C	789	C
	LI	1 g	ES	800 mg	D5W, NS	Physically compatible for 24 hr at 21 °C	812	C
Enalaprilat	MSD	12 mg	AMR	1.6 g	D5W[b]	Visually compatible with about 5% enalaprilat loss by HPLC in 24 hr at room temperature under fluorescent light. Dopamine not tested	1572	C
Flumazenil	RC	20 mg	AB	3.2 g	D5W[b]	Visually compatible with 7% flumazenil loss by HPLC in 24 hr at 23 °C under fluorescent light. Dopamine not tested	1710	C
Gentamicin sulfate	SC	2 g	AS	800 mg	D5W	No dopamine decomposition and 7% gentamicin decomposition in 24 hr at 25 °C	312	C
	SC	320 mg	AS	800 mg	D5W	Gentamicin potency retained only through 6 hr. 80% gentamicin decomposition in 24 hr at 23 to 25 °C. Dopamine potency retained for 24 hr	78	I
Heparin sodium	AB	200,000 units	AS	800 mg	D5W	No dopamine or heparin decomposition in 24 hr at 25 °C	312	C
Hydrocortisone sodium succinate	UP	1 g	AS	800 mg	D5W	No dopamine decomposition in 18 hr at 25 °C	312	C
Kanamycin sulfate	BR	2 g	AS	800 mg	D5W	Kanamycin and dopamine potency retained for 24 hr at 23 to 25 °C	78	C
Lidocaine HCl	AST	4 g	AS	800 mg	D5W	No dopamine or lidocaine decomposition in 24 hr at 25 °C	312	C
	AST	4 g	AS	800 mg	D5W[b]	No dopamine or lidocaine decomposition in 24 hr at 25 °C	312	C

Additive Compatibility (Cont.)

Dopamine HCl

Drug	*Mfr*	*Conc/L*	*Mfr*	*Conc/L*	*Test Soln*	*Remarks*	*Ref*	*C/I*
	AST	2 g	ACC	800 mg	D5W, LR, NS	Physically compatible for 24 hr at 25 °C	775	C
Meropenem	ZEN	1 and 20 g	DU	800 mg	NS	Visually compatible for 4 hr at room temperature	1994	C
Methylprednisolone sodium succinate	UP	500 mg	AS	800 mg	D5W	No dopamine decomposition in 18 hr at 25 °C	312	C
	UP	500 mg	AS	800 mg	D5W	Clear solution for 24 hr	329	C
Metronidazole HCl with sodium bicarbonate	SE AB	5 g 50 mEq	ACC	1 g	D5W, NS	Markedly discolored, turning yellow and then brown	765	I
Nitroglycerin	ACC	400 mg	ACC	800 mg	D5W, NS[c]	Physically compatible with little or no nitroglycerin loss in 48 hr at 23 °C. Dopamine not tested	929	C
Oxacillin sodium	BR	2 g	AS	800 mg	D5W	No dopamine and 2% oxacillin decomposition in 24 hr at 25 °C	312	C
Penicillin G potassium	LI	20 million units	AS	800 mg	D5W	14% penicillin decomposition in 24 hr at 23 to 25 °C. Dopamine potency retained for 24 hr	78	I
Potassium chloride	MG		AS	800 mg	D5W	No dopamine decomposition in 24 hr at 25 °C	312	C
Propafenone HCl	KN	0.54 g	DU	0.9 and 2.3 g[d]	D5W	Visually compatible with little or no propafenone loss by HPLC in 24 hr at 22 °C exposed to fluorescent light. Dopamine not tested	412	C
Ranitidine HCl	GL	50 mg and 2 g	ES	400 mg and 3.2 g	D5W, NS[b]	Physically compatible with 6% or less ranitidine loss in 48 hr at room temperature under fluorescent light. Dopamine not tested	1361	C
	GL	50 mg and 2 g	ES	0.4 and 3.2 g	D5W, NS[a]	Visually compatible with 5 to 7% ranitidine loss and little or no dopamine loss by HPLC in 48 hr at room temperature	1802	C
Verapamil HCl	KN	80 mg	ES	400 mg	D5W, NS	Physically compatible for 24 hr	764	C

[a] *Tested in both glass and PVC containers.*
[b] *Tested in PVC containers.*
[c] *Tested in glass containers.*
[d] *Approximate concentration.*

Drugs in Syringe Compatibility

Dopamine HCl

Drug (in syringe)	*Mfr*	*Amt*	*Mfr*	*Amt*	*Remarks*	*Ref*	*C/I*
Doxapram HCl	RB	400 mg/ 20 ml		100 mg/ 5 ml	Physically compatible with 3% doxapram loss in 24 hr	1177	C
Heparin sodium		2500 units/ 1 ml		50 mg/ 5 ml	Physically compatible for at least 5 min	1053	C
Ranitidine HCl	GL	50 mg/ 5 ml		40 mg	Physically compatible for 4 hr at ambient temperature under fluorescent light	1151	C

Y-Site Injection Compatibility (1:1 Mixture)

Dopamine HCl

Drug	*Mfr*	*Conc*	*Mfr*	*Conc*	*Remarks*	*Ref*	*C/I*
Acyclovir sodium	BW	5 mg/ml[a]	AB	1.6 mg/ml[a]	Solution turns dark brown in 2 hr at 25 °C under fluorescent light	1157	I
Alatrofloxacin mesylate	PF	1.43 mg/ml[a]	AB	4.2 mg/ml[a]	Visually and microscopically compatible run through a Y-site over at least 60 min	2235	C
Aldesleukin	CHI	33,800 I.U./ml[a]	ES	1.6 mg/ml[a]	Visually compatible with little or no loss of aldesleukin activity by bioassay	1857	C
Alteplase	GEN	1 mg/ml	DU	8 mg/ml[a]	Haze noted in 4 hr by visual examination	1340	I
Amifostine	USB	10 mg/ml[a]	AST	3.2 mg/ml[a]	Physically compatible with no change in measured turbidity or increase in particle content in 4 hr at 23 °C	1845	C
Amiodarone HCl	LZ	4 mg/ml[c]	ES	1.6 mg/ml[c]	Physically compatible for 24 hr at 21 °C	1032	C
Amphotericin B cholesteryl sulfate complex	SEQ	0.83 mg/ml[a]	AB	3.2 mg/ml[a]	Gross precipitate forms	2117	I
Atracurium besylate	BW	0.5 mg/ml[a]	SO	1.6 mg/ml[a]	Physically compatible for 24 hr at 28 °C	1337	C
Aztreonam	SQ	40 mg/ml[a]	AST	3.2 mg/ml[a]	Physically compatible with no subvisual haze or particle formation in 4 hr at 23 °C	1758	C
Cefepime HCl	BMS	20 mg/ml[a]	AST	3.2 mg/ml[a]	Haze and precipitate form in 1 hr	1689	I
Cefpirome sulfate	HO	50 mg/ml[e]	AB	0.8 mg/ml[e]	Visually and microscopically compatible with 7% or less cefpirome loss and 6% or less dopamine loss by HPLC in 8 hr at 23 °C	2044	C
Ciprofloxacin	MI	2 mg/ml[c]	AB	1.6 mg/ml[c]	Visually compatible for 24 hr at 24 °C	1655	C
Cisatracurium besylate	GW	0.1, 2, 5 mg/ml[a]	AB	3.2 mg/ml[a]	Physically compatible with no change in measured turbidity or increase in particle content in 4 hr at 23 °C	2074	C
Cladribine	ORT	0.015[b] and 0.5[f] mg/ml	AST	3.2 mg/ml[b]	Physically compatible with no change in measured turbidity or increase in particle content in 4 hr at 23 °C	1969	C
Clarithromycin	AB	4 mg/ml[a]	DB	3.2 mg/ml[a]	Visually compatible for 72 hr at both 30 and 17 °C	2174	C
Diltiazem HCl	MMD	1 mg/ml[a]	AB	1.6 mg/ml[a]	Visually compatible for 24 hr at 25 °C	1530	C
	MMD	5 mg/ml	AB, SO	0.8 mg/ml[c]	Visually compatible	1807	C
	MMD	1 mg/ml[a]	AB	3.2 mg/ml[a]	Visually compatible for 4 hr at 27 °C	2062	C
Dobutamine HCl	LI	4 mg/ml[b]	DCC	3.2 mg/ml[c]	Physically compatible for 3 hr	1316	C
	LI	4 mg/ml[a]	AB	3.2 mg/ml[a]	Visually compatible for 4 hr at 27 °C	2062	C
Dobutamine HCl with lidocaine HCl	LI AB	4 mg/ml[c] 8 mg/ml[c]	DCC	3.2 mg/ml[c]	Physically compatible for 3 hr	1316	C
Dobutamine HCl with nitroglycerin	LI LY	4 mg/ml[c] 0.4 mg/ml[c]	DCC	3.2 mg/ml[c]	Physically compatible for 3 hr	1316	C
Dobutamine HCl with sodium nitroprusside	LI ES	4 mg/ml[c] 0.4 mg/ml[c]	DCC	3.2 mg/ml[c]	Physically compatible for 3 hr	1316	C
Docetaxel	RPR	0.9 mg/ml[a]	AB	3.2 mg/ml[a]	Physically compatible with no change in measured turbidity or increase in particle content in 4 hr at 23 °C	2224	C

Y-Site Injection Compatibility (1:1 Mixture) (Cont.)

Dopamine HCl

Drug	*Mfr*	*Conc*	*Mfr*	*Conc*	*Remarks*	*Ref*	*C/I*
Doxorubicin HCl liposome injection	SEQ	0.4 mg/ml[a]	AB	3.2 mg/ml[a]	Physically compatible with little or no change in measured turbidity and no increase in particle content in 4 hr at 23 °C	2087	C
Enalaprilat	MSD	0.05 mg/ml[b]	IMS	1.6 mg/ml[a]	Physically compatible for 24 hr at room temperature under fluorescent light	1355	C
Epinephrine HCl	AB	0.02 mg/ml[a]	AB	3.2 mg/ml[a]	Visually compatible for 4 hr at 27 °C	2062	C
Esmolol HCl	DCC	10 mg/ml[a]	IMS	1.6 mg/ml[a]	Physically compatible for 24 hr at 22 °C	1169	C
Etoposide phosphate	BR	5 mg/ml[a]	AST	3.2 mg/ml[a]	Physically compatible with no change in measured turbidity or increase in particle content in 4 hr at 23 °C	2218	C
Famotidine	MSD	0.2 mg/ml[a]	TR	1.6 mg/ml[a]	Physically compatible for at least 4 hr at 25 °C under fluorescent light	1188	C
	ME	2 mg/ml[b]		1.6 mg/ml[a]	Visually compatible for 4 hr at 22 °C	1936	C
Fentanyl citrate	ES	0.05 mg/ml	AB	3.2 mg/ml[a]	Visually compatible for 4 hr at 27 °C	2062	C
Fluconazole	RR	2 mg/ml	AMR	1.6 mg/ml[a]	Visually compatible for 24 hr at 28 °C	1760	C
Foscarnet sodium	AST	24 mg/ml	DU	80 mg/ml	Physically compatible for 24 hr at room temperature under fluorescent light	1335	C
Furosemide	AB, AMR	5 mg/ml	AST, DU	12.8 mg/ml	Physically compatible for 3 hr at room temperature	1978	C
	AB, AMR	5 mg/ml	AB, AMR	12.8 mg/ml	White precipitate forms immediately	1978	I
	AMR	10 mg/ml	AB	3.2 mg/ml[a]	Precipitate forms in 4 hr at 27 °C	2062	I
Gatifloxacin	BMS	2 mg/ml[a]	AB	3.2 mg/ml[a]	Physically compatible with no change in measured haze or increase in particle content in 4 hr at 23 °C	2234	C
Gemcitabine HCl	LI	10 mg/ml[b]	AB	3.2 mg/ml[b]	Physically compatible with no change in measured turbidity or increase in particle content in 4 hr at 23 °C	2226	C
Granisetron HCl	SKB	0.05 mg/ml[a]	AB	3.2 mg/ml[a]	Physically compatible with no change in measured turbidity or increase in particle content in 4 hr at 23 °C	2000	C
Haloperidol lactate	MN	0.5[a] and 5 mg/ml	DU	1.6 mg/ml[a]	Visually compatible for 24 hr at 21 °C	1523	C
Heparin sodium	UP	1000 units/L[g]	ACC	40 mg/ml	Physically compatible for at least 4 hr at room temperature by visual and microscopic examination	534	C
	ES	100 units/ml[a]	AB	3.2 mg/ml[a]	Visually compatible for 4 hr at 27 °C	2062	C
	TR	50 units/ml	BA	1.6 mg/ml	Visually compatible for 4 hr at 25 °C	1793	C
Hetastarch in lactated electrolyte injection (Hextend)	AB	6%	AB	3.2 mg/ml[a]	Physically compatible with no change in measured turbidity or increase in particle content in 4 hr at 23 °C	2339	C
Hydrocortisone sodium succinate	UP	10 mg/L[g]	ACC	40 mg/ml	Physically compatible for at least 4 hr at room temperature by visual and microscopic examination	534	C
Hydromorphone HCl	KN	1 mg/ml	AB	3.2 mg/ml[a]	Visually compatible for 4 hr at 27 °C	2062	C
Inamrinone lactate	WB	3 mg/ml[b]	ACC	1.6 mg/ml[a]	Physically compatible for at least 4 hr at 25 °C under fluorescent light	992	C

Y-Site Injection Compatibility (1:1 Mixture) (Cont.)

			Dopamine HCl				
Drug	*Mfr*	*Conc*	*Mfr*	*Conc*	*Remarks*	*Ref*	*C/I*
Indomethacin sodium trihydrate	MSD	1 mg/ml[b]	AB	1.2 mg/ml[a]	Haze and fine precipitate form immediately	1527	I
Insulin, regular	LI	1 unit/ml[a]	DU	3.2 mg/ml[a]	White precipitate forms immediately, dissolves quickly, and reforms in 24 hr at 23 °C	1877	I
Labetalol HCl	SC	1 mg/ml[a]	IMS	1.6 mg/ml[a]	Physically compatible for 24 hr at 18 °C	1171	C
	GL	1 mg/ml[a]	ES	1.6 mg/ml[a]	Visually compatible with little or no loss of either drug by HPLC in 4 hr at room temperature	1762	C
	AH	2 mg/ml[a]	AB	3.2 mg/ml[a]	Visually compatible for 4 hr at 27 °C	2062	C
Levofloxacin	OMN	5 mg/ml[a]	AMR	80 mg/ml	Visually compatible for 4 hr at 24 °C under fluorescent light	2233	C
Lidocaine HCl	AB	8 mg/ml[c]	DCC	3.2 mg/ml[c]	Physically compatible for 3 hr	1316	C
Lidocaine HCl with dobutamine HCl	AB LI	8 mg/ml[c] 4 mg/ml[c]	DCC	3.2 mg/ml[c]	Physically compatible for 3 hr	1316	C
Lidocaine HCl with nitroglycerin	AB LY	8 mg/ml[c] 0.4 mg/ml[c]	DCC	3.2 mg/ml[c]	Physically compatible for 3 hr	1316	C
Lidocaine HCl with sodium nitroprusside	AB ES	8 mg/ml[c] 0.4 mg/ml[c]	DCC	3.2 mg/ml[c]	Physically compatible for 3 hr	1316	C
Linezolid	PHU	2 mg/ml	AB	3.2 mg/ml[a]	Physically compatible with no change in measured turbidity or increase in particle content in 4 hr at 23 °C	2264	C
Lorazepam	WY	0.5 mg/ml[a]	AB	3.2 mg/ml[a]	Visually compatible for 4 hr at 27 °C	2062	C
Meperidine HCl	AB	10 mg/ml	AB	1.6 mg/ml[a]	Physically compatible for 4 hr at 25 °C	1397	C
Methylprednisolone sodium succinate	UP	5 mg/ml[a]	AB	0.8 mg/ml[a]	Visually compatible for 24 hr at room temperature in test tubes. No precipitate found on filter from Y-site delivery	2063	C
Metronidazole	MG	5 mg/ml	AB	0.8 mg/ml[a]	Visually compatible for 24 hr at room temperature in test tubes. No precipitate found on filter from Y-site delivery	2063	C
Midazolam HCl	RC	1 mg/ml[a]	AB	1.6 mg/ml[a]	Visually compatible for 24 hr at 23 °C	1847	C
	RC	1 mg/ml[a]	DU	3.2 mg/ml[a]	Visually compatible for 24 hr at 23 °C	1877	C
	RC	2 mg/ml[a]	AB	3.2 mg/ml[a]	Visually compatible for 4 hr at 27 °C	2062	C
Milrinone lactate	SW	0.2 mg/ml[a]	AB	3.2 mg/ml[a]	Visually compatible for 4 hr at 27 °C	2062	C
	SW	0.4 mg/ml[a]	SO	6.4 mg/ml[a]	Visually compatible with little or no loss of either drug by HPLC in 4 hr at 23 °C	2214	C
Morphine sulfate	AB	1 mg/ml	AB	1.6 mg/ml[a]	Physically compatible for 4 hr at 25 °C	1397	C
	SCN	2 mg/ml[a]	AB	3.2 mg/ml[a]	Visually compatible for 4 hr at 27 °C	2062	C
Nicardipine HCl	WY	1 mg/ml[a]	AB	3.2 mg/ml[a]	Visually compatible for 4 hr at 27 °C	2062	C
Nitroglycerin	LY	0.4 mg/ml[c]	DCC	3.2 mg/ml[c]	Physically compatible for 3 hr	1316	C
	AB	0.4 mg/ml[a]	AB	3.2 mg/ml[a]	Visually compatible for 4 hr at 27 °C	2062	C
Nitroglycerin with dobutamine HCl	LY LI	0.4 mg/ml[c] 4 mg/ml[c]	DCC	3.2 mg/ml[c]	Physically compatible for 3 hr	1316	C
Nitroglycerin with lidocaine HCl	LY AB	0.4 mg/ml[c] 8 mg/ml[c]	DCC	3.2 mg/ml[c]	Physically compatible for 3 hr	1316	C
Nitroglycerin with sodium nitroprusside	LY ES	0.4 mg/ml[c] 0.4 mg/ml[c]	DCC	3.2 mg/ml[c]	Physically compatible for 3 hr	1316	C

Y-Site Injection Compatibility (1:1 Mixture) (Cont.)

			Dopamine HCl				
Drug	*Mfr*	*Conc*	*Mfr*	*Conc*	*Remarks*	*Ref*	*C/I*
Norepinephrine bitartrate	STR	0.064 mg/ml[a]	DU	3.2 mg/ml[a]	Visually compatible for 24 hr at 23 °C	1877	C
	AB	0.128 mg/ml[a]	AB	3.2 mg/ml[a]	Visually compatible for 4 hr at 27 °C	2062	C
Ondansetron HCl	GL	0.32 mg/ml[b]	AB	0.8 mg/ml[a]	Visually compatible for 24 hr at room temperature in test tubes. No precipitate found on filter from Y-site delivery	2063	C
Pancuronium bromide	ES	0.05 mg/ml[a]	SO	1.6 mg/ml[a]	Physically compatible for 24 hr at 28 °C	1337	C
Piperacillin sodium–tazobactam sodium	LE	40 + 5 mg/ml[a]	AST	3.2 mg/ml[a]	Physically compatible with no change in measured turbidity or increase in particle content in 4 hr at 22 °C	1688	C
Potassium chloride	AB	40 mEq/L[g]	ACC	40 mg/ml	Physically compatible for at least 4 hr at room temperature by visual and microscopic examination	534	C
Propofol	ZEN	10 mg/ml	AST	3.2 mg/ml[a]	Physically compatible for 1 hr at 23 °C with no increase in particle content	2066	C
Ranitidine HCl	GL	0.5 mg/ml[h]	ES	1.6 mg/ml[a]	Physically compatible for 24 hr	1323	C
	GL	1 mg/ml[a]	AB	3.2 mg/ml[a]	Visually compatible for 4 hr at 27 °C	2062	C
Remifentanil HCl	GW	0.025 and 0.25 mg/ml[b]	AB	3.2 mg/ml[a]	Physically compatible with no change in measured turbidity or increase in particle content in 4 hr at 23 °C	2075	C
Sargramostim	IMM	6[b,i] and 15[b] μg/ml	DU	1.6 mg/ml[c]	Visually compatible for 2 hr	1618	C
Sodium nitroprusside	ES	0.4 mg/ml[c]	DCC	3.2 mg/ml[c]	Physically compatible for 3 hr	1316	C
Sodium nitroprusside with dobutamine HCl	ES LI	0.4 mg/ml[c] 4 mg/ml[c]	DCC	3.2 mg/ml[c]	Physically compatible for 3 hr	1316	C
Sodium nitroprusside with lidocaine HCl	ES AB	0.4 mg/ml[c] 8 mg/ml[c]	DCC	3.2 mg/ml[c]	Physically compatible for 3 hr	1316	C
Sodium nitroprusside with nitroglycerin	ES LY	0.4 mg/ml[c] 0.4 mg/ml[c]	DCC	3.2 mg/ml[c]	Physically compatible for 3 hr	1316	C
Streptokinase	HO	30,000 units/ml[a]	DU	8 mg/ml[a]	Physically compatible for at least 4 days by visual examination	1340	C
Tacrolimus	FUJ	1 mg/ml[b]	ES	1.6 mg/ml[a]	Visually compatible for 24 hr at 25 °C	1630	C
Theophylline	TR	4 mg/ml	BA	1.6 mg/ml	Visually compatible for 6 hr at 25 °C	1793	C
Thiopental sodium	AB	25 mg/ml[d]	AB	3.2 mg/ml[a]	Precipitate forms immediately	2062	I
Thiotepa	IMM[j]	1 mg/ml[a]	AST	3.2 mg/ml[a]	Physically compatible with no change in measured turbidity or increase in particle content in 4 hr at 23 °C	1861	C
Tirofiban HCl	ME	0.05 mg/ml[b]	AMR	0.2 and 3.2 mg/ml[a]	Physically compatible with little or no loss of either drug by HPLC in 4 hr at room temperature under fluorescent light	2250	C
	ME	0.05 mg/ml[a]	AMR	0.2 and 3.2 mg/ml[b]	Physically compatible with little or no loss of either drug by HPLC in 4 hr at room temperature under fluorescent light	2250	C
TNA #73[k]			AB	80 mg/50 ml[c]	Physically compatible for 4 hr by visual observation	1009	C
TNA #222 and #223[k]			AB	3.2 mg/ml[a]	Precipitate forms immediately	2215	I

Y-Site Injection Compatibility (1:1 Mixture) (Cont.)

Dopamine HCl

Drug	*Mfr*	*Conc*	*Mfr*	*Conc*	*Remarks*	*Ref*	*C/I*
TNA #218 to #221 and #224 to #226[k]			AB	3.2 mg/ml[a]	Visually compatible with no precipitate or emulsion damage apparent in 4 hr at 23 °C	2215	C
Tolazoline HCl		0.1 mg/ml[a]	AB	1.2 mg/ml[a]	Physically compatible for 24 hr at 22 °C	1363	C
TPN #189[k]			DB	1.6 mg/ml[b]	Visually compatible for 24 hr at 22 °C	1767	C
TPN #203 and #204[k]			AMR	3.2 mg/ml	Visually compatible for 4 hr at 23 °C	1974	C
TPN #212 to #215[k]			AB	3.2 mg/ml[a]	Physically compatible with no change in measured turbidity or increase in particle content in 4 hr at 23 °C	2109	C
Vecuronium bromide	OR	0.1 mg/ml[a]	SO	1.6 mg/ml[a]	Physically compatible for 24 hr at 28 °C	1337	C
	OR	1 mg/ml	AB	3.2 mg/ml[a]	Visually compatible for 4 hr at 27 °C	2062	C
Verapamil HCl		[l]			Physically compatible	840	C
Vitamin B complex with C	RC	2 ml/L[g]	ACC	40 mg/ml	Physically compatible for at least 4 hr at room temperature by visual and microscopic examination	534	C
Warfarin sodium	DU	2 mg/ml[d]	FAU	1.6 mg/ml[a]	Visually compatible with no warfarin loss by HPLC in 30 min	2010	C
	DME	2 mg/ml[d]	DU	1.6 mg/ml[a]	Visually compatible for 24 hr at 24 °C	2078	C
Zidovudine	BW	4 mg/ml[a]	AB	1.6 mg/ml[a]	Physically compatible for 4 hr at 25 °C under fluorescent light by visual and microscopic examination	1193	C

[a]*Tested in dextrose 5% in water.*
[b]*Tested in sodium chloride 0.9%.*
[c]*Tested in both dextrose 5% in water and sodium chloride 0.9%.*
[d]*Tested in sterile water for injection.*
[e]*Tested in dextrose 5% in water, Ringer's injection, lactated, sodium chloride 0.45%, and sodium chloride 0.9%.*
[f]*Tested in bacteriostatic sodium chloride 0.9% preserved with benzyl alcohol 0.9%.*
[g]*Tested in dextrose 5% in Ringer's injection, dextrose 5% in Ringer's injection, lactated, dextrose 5% in water, Ringer's injection, lactated, and sodium chloride 0.9%.*
[h]*Premixed infusion solution.*
[i]*Tested with albumin human 0.1%.*
[j]*Lyophilized formulation tested.*
[k]*Refer to Appendix I for the composition of parenteral nutrition solutions. TNA indicates a 3-in-1 admixture, and TPN indicates a 2-in-1 admixture.*
[l]*Injected into a line being used to infuse dopamine HCl in dextrose 5% in sodium chloride 0.3% with potassium chloride 20 mEq.*

Additional Compatibility Information

Dopamine HCl is stated to be incompatible with iron salts, oxidizing agents, sodium bicarbonate, and other alkaline solutions. The drug is inactivated in alkaline solutions. (1-3/97; 4; 312)

Furosemide — Furosemide has been demonstrated to be compatible or incompatible with dopamine HCl during simultaneous Y-site administration, depending on the formulation of dopamine HCl tested. Dopamine formulations supplied by Astra and DuPont have the pH adjusted with sodium hydroxide and/or hydrochloric acid and are compatible with furosemide. Formulations supplied by Abbott and American Regent contain citrate buffer and are incompatible with furosemide, forming a white precipitate immediately. (1978)

Heparin — The interaction between dopamine HCl and heparin sodium in aqueous solution was evaluated by microcalorimetry. An exothermic reaction occurred in dextrose 5% in water but not sodium chloride 0.9%. Consequently, sodium chloride 0.9% was recommended as a vehicle to minimize the interaction between these two drugs. (1185)

Dobutamine, Lidocaine, Nitroglycerin, and Nitroprusside — Dobutamine HCl (Lilly) 4 mg/ml, dopamine HCl (Dupont Critical Care) 3.2 mg/ml, lidocaine HCl (Abbott) 8 mg/ml, nitroglycerin (Lyphomed) 0.4 mg/ml, and sodium nitroprusside (Elkins-Sinn) 0.4 mg/ml, prepared in dextrose 5% in water and sodium chloride 0.9%, were combined in equal quantities in all possible combinations of two, three, four, and five drugs and then evaluated for physical compatibility. No physical incompatibility was observed in any combination within the three-hour study period. (1316)

DOXACURIUM CHLORIDE
AHFS 12:20

Products — Doxacurium chloride is available in 5-ml multiple-dose vials. Each milliliter of solution contains doxacurium (as the chloride) 1 mg, benzyl alcohol 0.9%, and hydrochloric acid to adjust the pH in water for injection. (1-12/97)

pH — From 3.9 to 5. (1-12/97)

Trade Name(s) — Nuromax.

Administration — Doxacurium chloride is administered intravenously, undiluted or diluted up to 1:10 in dextrose 5% in water or sodium chloride 0.9%. (1-12/97; 4)

Stability — Doxacurium chloride should be stored at controlled room temperature and protected from freezing. The drug may not be compatible with alkaline solutions having a pH greater than 8.5. (1-12/97)

Diluted 1:10 with dextrose 5% in water or sodium chloride 0.9%, doxacurium chloride is physically and chemically stable for up to 24 hours when stored in polypropylene syringes at 5 to 25 °C. Because the benzyl alcohol preservative is diluted, its effectiveness is diminished. Consequently, aseptic procedures should be followed to prepare the dilutions and they should be used within eight hours. (1-12/97)

Compatibility Information

Y-Site Injection Compatibility (1:1 Mixture)

Doxacurium chloride

Drug	*Mfr*	*Conc*	*Mfr*	*Conc*	*Remarks*	*Ref*	*C/I*
Etomidate	AB	2 mg/ml	BW	1 mg/ml	Visually compatible for up to 7 days at 25 °C	1801	C
Propofol	STU	2 mg/ml	BW	1 mg/ml	Separates into layers within 7 days at 25 °C. No visible change in 24 hr	1801	?
Thiopental sodium	AB	25 mg/ml	BW	1 mg/ml	Visually compatible for up to 7 days at 25 °C	1801	C

Additional Compatibility Information

Infusion Solutions — Doxacurium chloride is stated to be compatible with dextrose 5% in lactated Ringer's injection, dextrose 5% in sodium chloride 0.9%, dextrose 5% in water, lactated Ringer's injection, and sodium chloride 0.9%. (1-12/97)

Other Drugs — Doxacurium chloride is also stated to be compatible with alfentanil HCl, fentanyl citrate, and sufentanil citrate diluted as directed. (1-12/97)

DOXAPRAM HCL
AHFS 28:20

Products — Doxapram HCl is available in 20-ml multiple-dose vials. Each milliliter of solution contains doxapram HCl 20 mg and benzyl alcohol 0.9% in water for injection. (2)

pH — From 3.5 to 5. (2)

Osmolality — Doxapram HCl 20 mg/ml has an osmolality of 159 mOsm/kg. (1689)

Trade Name(s) — Dopram.

Administration — Doxapram HCl is administered by intravenous injection or infusion of a solution diluted to 1 or 2 mg/ml with a compatible diluent. (2; 4)

Stability — Doxapram HCl injection should be stored at controlled room temperature and protected from freezing. (2; 4)

pH Effects — Doxapram HCl in solution became turbid when the pH was adjusted from 3.8 to 5.7 with 0.1 *N* sodium hydroxide. When the pH was adjusted down to 1.9 with 0.1 *N* HCl, no visible change occurred to the clear solution. (1177)

At pH 2.5 to 6.5, doxapram HCl remained chemically stable for 24 hours. At pH 7.5 and above, a 10 to 15% doxapram HCl loss occurred in about six hours. (1177)

Compatibility Information

Drugs in Syringe Compatibility

Doxapram HCl

Drug (in syringe)	*Mfr*	*Amt*	*Mfr*	*Amt*	*Remarks*	*Ref*	*C/I*
Amikacin sulfate		100 mg/ 2 ml	RB	400 mg/ 20 ml	Physically compatible with no doxapram loss in 24 hr	1177	C
Aminophylline		250 mg/ 10 ml	RB	400 mg/ 20 ml	Immediate turbidity and precipitation	1177	I
Ascorbic acid injection		500 mg/ 2 ml	RB	400 mg/ 20 ml	Immediate turbidity changing to precipitation in 24 hr	1177	I
Bumetanide		0.5 mg/ 1 ml	RB	400 mg/ 20 ml	Physically compatible with 3% doxapram loss in 24 hr	1177	C
Cefoperazone sodium		500 mg/ 4 ml	RB	400 mg/ 20 ml	Immediate precipitation	1177	I
Cefotaxime sodium		500 mg/ 4 ml	RB	400 mg/ 20 ml	Immediate precipitation	1177	I
Cefotetan disodium		1 g/10 ml	RB	400 mg/ 20 ml	Immediate turbidity	1177	I
Cefuroxime sodium	GL	750 mg/ 7 ml	RB	400 mg/ 20 ml	Immediate turbidity	1177	I
Chlorpromazine HCl		250 mg/ 5 ml	RB	400 mg/ 20 ml	Physically compatible with no doxapram loss in 24 hr	1177	C
Cimetidine HCl	SKF	50 mg/ 2 ml	RB	400 mg/ 20 ml	Physically compatible with no doxapram loss in 24 hr	1177	C
Cisplatin		10 mg/ 20 ml	RB	400 mg/ 20 ml	Physically compatible with no doxapram loss in 24 hr	1177	C
Cyclophosphamide		100 mg/ 5 ml	RB	400 mg/ 20 ml	Physically compatible with 2% doxapram loss in 24 hr	1177	C
Dexamethasone sodium phosphate	MSD	3.3 mg/ 1 ml	RB	400 mg/ 20 ml	Immediate turbidity and precipitation	1177	I
Diazepam		10 mg/ 2 ml	RB	400 mg/ 20 ml	Immediate turbidity and precipitation	1177	I
Digoxin		0.25 mg/ 1 ml	RB	400 mg/ 20 ml	10% doxapram loss in 9 hr and 17% in 24 hr	1177	I
Dobutamine HCl	LI	100 mg/ 10 ml	RB	400 mg/ 20 ml	5% doxapram loss in 3 hr and 11% in 24 hr	1177	I
Dopamine HCl		100 mg/ 5 ml	RB	400 mg/ 20 ml	Physically compatible with 3% doxapram loss in 24 hr	1177	C
Doxycycline hyclate		100 mg/ 5 ml	RB	400 mg/ 20 ml	Physically compatible with 3% doxapram loss in 24 hr	1177	C
Epinephrine HCl		1 mg/ 1 ml	RB	400 mg/ 20 ml	Physically compatible with no doxapram loss in 24 hr	1177	C
Folic acid		15 mg/ 1 ml	RB	400 mg/ 20 ml	Immediate turbidity	1177	I
Furosemide	HO	100 mg/ 10 ml	RB	400 mg/ 20 ml	Immediate turbidity	1177	I
Hydrocortisone sodium phosphate	MSD	100 mg/ 2 ml	RB	400 mg/ 20 ml	Immediate turbidity and precipitation	1177	I

Drugs in Syringe Compatibility (Cont.)

Doxapram HCl

Drug (in syringe)	*Mfr*	*Amt*	*Mfr*	*Amt*	*Remarks*	*Ref*	*C/I*
Hydrocortisone sodium succinate	UP	500 mg/ 2 ml	RB	400 mg/ 20 ml	Immediate turbidity and precipitation	1177	I
Hydroxyzine HCl		25 mg/ 1 ml	RB	400 mg/ 20 ml	Physically compatible with no doxapram loss in 24 hr	1177	C
Isoniazid		100 mg/ 2 ml	RB	400 mg/ 20 ml	Physically compatible with 2% doxapram loss in 24 hr	1177	C
Ketamine HCl	PD	200 mg/ 20 ml	RB	400 mg/ 20 ml	Physically compatible with no doxapram loss in 9 hr and 12% loss in 24 hr	1177	I
Lincomycin HCl		300 mg/ 1 ml	RB	400 mg/ 20 ml	Physically compatible with no doxapram loss in 24 hr	1177	C
Methotrexate sodium		50 mg/ 20 ml	RB	400 mg/ 20 ml	Physically compatible with 4% doxapram loss in 24 hr	1177	C
Methylprednisolone sodium succinate	UP	40 mg/ 2 ml	RB	400 mg/ 20 ml	Immediate turbidity and precipitation	1177	I
Minocycline HCl		100 mg/ 5 ml	RB	400 mg/ 20 ml	8% doxapram loss in 3 hr and 13% loss in 6 hr	1177	I
Netilmicin sulfate		100 mg/ 2 ml	RB	400 mg/ 20 ml	Physically compatible with 2% doxapram loss in 24 hr	1177	C
Phytonadione		10 mg/ 1 ml	RB	400 mg/ 20 ml	Physically compatible with no doxapram loss in 24 hr	1177	C
Pyridoxine HCl		10 mg/ 1 ml	RB	400 mg/ 20 ml	Physically compatible with 6% doxapram loss in 24 hr	1177	C
Terbutaline sulfate		0.2 mg/ 1 ml	RB	400 mg/ 20 ml	Physically compatible with 6% doxapram loss in 24 hr	1177	C
Thiamine HCl		10 mg/ 2 ml	RB	400 mg/ 20 ml	Physically compatible with 6% doxapram loss in 24 hr	1177	C
Thiopental sodium		300 mg/ 12 ml	RB	400 mg/ 20 ml	Immediate precipitation	1177	I
Ticarcillin disodium		1 g/20 ml	RB	400 mg/ 20 ml	18% doxapram loss in 3 hr	1177	I
Tobramycin sulfate		60 mg/ 1.5 ml	RB	400 mg/ 20 ml	Physically compatible with no doxapram loss in 24 hr	1177	C
Vincristine sulfate		1 mg/ 10 ml	RB	400 mg/ 20 ml	Physically compatible with 7% doxapram loss in 24 hr	1177	C

Additional Compatibility Information

Infusion Solutions — Doxapram HCl is stated to be physically compatible with most intravenous infusion solutions (4), but sodium chloride 0.9% and dextrose 5 and 10% are recommended. (2; 4)

Alkaline Drugs — The drug is stated to be incompatible with alkaline drugs such as aminophylline, thiopental sodium, and sodium bicarbonate. (4) (See pH Effects.)

DOXORUBICIN HCL
AHFS 10:00

Products — Doxorubicin HCl (Adriamycin RDF) is available as a lyophilized product in a rapid dissolution formula in 10-, 20-, and 50-mg single-dose glass vials and 150-mg multiple-dose glass vials. Also present are 50 mg of lactose and 1 mg of methylparaben for each 10 mg of doxorubicin HCl. (2) The methylparaben enhances the dissolution rate by disrupting bonding between doxorubicin and other components. (1253; 1254)

Reconstitution of the lyophilized products should be performed with sodium chloride 0.9%. Bacteriostatic diluents are not recommended. Add 5, 10, or 25 ml sodium chloride 0.9% to the 10-, 20-, or 50-mg vial, respectively. The 150-mg multiple-dose vials should be reconstituted with 75 ml of sodium chloride 0.9%. After the diluent is added, the vial should be shaken and the drug allowed to dissolve, forming a 2-mg/ml solution. (2)

Additionally, doxorubicin HCl is available in 5-, 10-, 25-, and 100-ml vials as a 2-mg/ml solution without preservatives. The solution also contains sodium chloride 0.9% and hydrochloric acid to adjust the pH in water for injection. (2)

pH — The pH of lyophilized doxorubicin HCl reconstituted with sodium chloride 0.9% is 3.8 to 6.5. (4) The pH of the solution products is adjusted to 2.5 to 3.5. (4)

Osmolality — Doxorubicin HCl 2 mg/ml in sterile water for injection has an osmolality of 280 mOsm/kg. (1689)

Density — Doxorubicin HCl (Chiron) powder reconstituted with sterile water for injection to a concentration of 2 mg/ml and the undiluted liquid injection at 2 mg/ml have a solution density of 1.00 g/ml. (2041; 2248)

Trade Name(s) — Adriamycin PFS, Adriamycin RDF, Rubex.

Administration — Doxorubicin HCl is administered intravenously, preferably into the tubing of a running intravenous infusion of sodium chloride 0.9% or dextrose 5% in water over not less than three to five minutes. (2; 4) The drug should not be administered intramuscularly or subcutaneously, and extravasation should be avoided because of local tissue necrosis. (2)

Stability — Doxorubicin HCl liquid injections should be stored under refrigeration and protected from light. Intact vials should be kept in their cartons until use. (2; 4)

The lyophilized products in intact vials should be stored at room temperature and protected from sunlight. The solution products, in their original cartons, should be refrigerated and protected from sunlight until ready for use. (2; 4) The manufacturer states that its reconstituted lyophilized products are stable for seven days at room temperature and 15 days under refrigeration. (2)

Wood et al. assessed the stability of doxorubicin HCl (Farmitalia) 100 mg/L in sodium chloride 0.9% (pH 6.47 and pH 5.20) and in dextrose 5% in water (pH 4.36) when stored in PVC bags at 4 and 25 °C in the dark. The drug was stable for at least 43 days at both temperatures, exhibiting not more than 10 or 11% loss by HPLC analysis. (1460)

For 50-µg/ml and 0.5-mg/ml doxorubicin HCl solutions, Janssen et al. reported that a greater rate of decomposition occurred in the more concentrated solution. (1206) However, most other studies found no concentration dependence for the degradation rate. (489; 526; 1208; 1255)

Incorporation of doxorubicin HCl into liposomes did not affect the drug decomposition rate. (1206)

Steam heating a doxorubicin HCl 1-mg/ml solution for one hour at 100 °C resulted in about a 26% drug loss. (1256)

pH Effects — Doxorubicin HCl appears to have pH-dependent stability in solution. (526; 1007; 1037) It becomes progressively more stable as the pH of drug–infusion solution admixtures becomes more acidic at 7.4 to 4.5. (526) The pH range of maximum stability has been variously stated to be about 4 to 5 (1007; 1460), 3 to 4 (1037), and about 4. (1208) At a concentration of 0.1 mg/ml in buffer solutions stored at 4 °C, no significant doxorubicin loss occurred in 60 days at pH 4, but substantial decomposition occurred at pH 7.4. (1206) Doxorubicin HCl is unstable at pH values less than 3 or greater than 7. (4) In acidic media, splitting of the glycosidic bond results in a red-colored, water-insoluble aglycone and a water-soluble amino sugar. (4) In alkaline media, a color change to deep purple is indicative of decomposition. This color change also occurs with other anthracyclines. (394) It is thought to reflect cleavage of the amino sugar, resulting in an ineffective moiety. (524)

Freezing Solutions — The manufacturer does not recommend freezing the solutions. (108)

However, Hoffman et al. found that doxorubicin HCl, reconstituted to 2 mg/ml with sterile water for injection and stored under refrigeration (4 °C), exhibited about a 1.5% loss in one month and about a 10.5% loss in six months. Freezing the solutions at −20 °C resulted in no loss of potency over 30 days. It was indicated that filtration of stored solutions through a 0.22-µm filter was appropriate to ensure sterility. (652)

Karlsen et al. found that doxorubicin HCl (Farmitalia) 70 mg/50 ml in PVC bags of sodium chloride 0.9% (Travenol) could be frozen at −20 °C for at least 30 days and thawed by exposure to microwave radiation for two minutes with no significant change in concentration. However, the doxorubicin HCl concentration apparently began declining after the fourth repetition of the freeze–thaw treatment, with a loss of about 5%. (818)

Keusters et al. studied the stability of doxorubicin HCl 1 mg/ml in sodium chloride 0.9% in PVC containers frozen at −20 °C. No drug loss occurred after two weeks of storage and thawing for 150 minutes at room temperature or 180 seconds in a 700-watt microwave oven. Refreezing the solutions and rethawing at room temperature or in a microwave oven three weeks later (total of five weeks of frozen storage) resulted in about a 3% doxorubicin loss. (1256)

Although the thawing of frozen doxorubicin HCl solutions in microwave ovens has been suggested (818; 1256), Adria recommends only room temperature thawing because of the risks of drug decomposition from overheating and exposure if the bags burst. (1257)

Wood et al. reported that doxorubicin HCl (Farmitalia) 100 mg/L in sodium chloride 0.9% and dextrose 5% in water in PVC bags (Travenol) was stable, exhibiting little or no loss by HPLC analysis after 43 days stored at −20 °C, even when subjected to 11 freeze-thaw repetitions. (1460)

Light Effects — Doxorubicin HCl is sensitive to light, especially in very dilute solutions. (489; 1073; 1094) However, the photolability of dilute solutions is not observed with more concentrated solutions. A 10-fold difference in photolability half-life was found between concentrations of 0.01 and 0.1 mg/ml. (1594) The manufacturers recommend protecting the solutions from exposure to sunlight and that any unused solution be discarded. (2; 4)

Syringes—Doxorubicin HCl (Farmitalia) 2 mg/ml repackaged in polypropylene syringes exhibited little or no loss by HPLC analysis after storage for 43 days at 4 °C. (1460)

Doxorubicin HCl (Adria) 2 mg/ml in sodium chloride 0.9% in glass vials and plastic syringes (Monoject and Terumo) and also 1 mg/ml in sodium chloride 0.9% in plastic syringes (Monoject) exhibited no visual changes and little or no loss by HPLC analysis when stored at 4 and 23 °C while exposed to light for 142 days. Potential extractable materials from the syringes were not detected during the study period. (1594)

Ambulatory Pumps—Doxorubicin HCl (Cetus), reconstituted with sodium chloride 0.9% to a 2-mg/ml concentration or as the 2-mg/ml commercial solution, in portable pump reservoirs (Pharmacia Deltec) was chemically stable by HPLC analysis for 14 days at 3 and 23 °C and for an additional 28 days at 30 °C. (1538)

Elastomeric Reservoir Pumps—Doxorubicin HCl (Astra) 2 mg/ml in sodium chloride 0.9% 25ml was packaged in latex elastomeric reservoirs (Secure Medical). Little or no loss by HPLC analysis occurred in 24 hours at 25 °C and in two days at 5 °C. (1970)

Doxorubicin HCl solutions in elastomeric reservoir pumps have been stated by the pump manufacturers to be stable for the following time periods frozen, refrigerated (REF), or at room temperature (RT) (31):

Pump Reservoir(s)	Conc.	Frozen	REF	RT
Homepump; Homepump Eclipse	2 mg/ml[b]		2 days	
Infusor	3 mg/ml[a]	30 days	30 days	30 days
	0.2 to 5 mg/ml[b]		34 days	9 days

[a]*In dextrose 5% in water.*
[b]*In sodium chloride 0.9%.*

Doxorubicin HCl 0.63 mg/ml in combination with dacarbazine 7.3 mg/ml in dextrose 5% in water in Infusor elastomeric reservoir pumps has been stated by the pump manufacturer to be stable for five days frozen and under refrigeration. (31)

Implantable Pumps—Vogelzang et al. reported the stability of 3- and 5-mg/ml concentrations in sodium chloride 0.9% in the reservoir of a Medtronic DAD implantable pump at 37 °C. HPLC analysis found losses of about 5 to 6% in one week and 9 to 11% in two weeks. Analyses after longer periods continued to show about a 5 to 6% loss per week at 37 °C. (1255)

Sorption—Doxorubicin HCl (Farmitalia) 16 μg/ml in dextrose 5% in water and sodium chloride 0.9% in PVC containers was infused through PVC infusion sets at 21 ml/hr over 24 hours at 22 °C while exposed to light. Fluctuations in the delivered concentration by HPLC analysis were relatively minor, with no evidence of sorption. (1700)

Doxorubicin HCl (Farmitalia) 1 mg/ml in sodium chloride 0.9% exhibited no loss by UV spectroscopy due to sorption to PVC and polyethylene administration lines during simulated infusions at 0.875 ml/hr for 2.5 hours via a syringe pump. (1795)

Wood et al. reported that doxorubicin HCl was adsorbed to PVC bags. Losses depended on temperature, concentration, and vehicle. Losses were greatest in sodium chloride 0.9% (pH 6.47), compared with dextrose 5% in water at pH 4.36. After eight days of storage, HPLC analysis of solutions containing doxorubicin HCl 100 μg/ml stored at 4 and 25 °C indicated losses of up to 7 to 8%. At concentrations used in clinical practice, sorptive losses during storage and delivery are negligible. (1460)

Filtration—Although doxorubicin HCl was reported to undergo considerable binding to cellulose ester and polytetrafluoroethylene filters (1249; 1415; 1416), other studies did not confirm unacceptable losses at clinical concentrations. Doxorubicin HCl 2 mg/ml in sterile water for injection showed no loss of potency due to filtration when filtered through a 0.22-μm Millex filter. (652)

In another study, doxorubicin HCl (Adria) 30 mg/15 ml was injected as a bolus through a 0.2-μm nylon, air-eliminating filter (Ultipor, Pall) to evaluate the effect of filtration on simulated intravenous push delivery. Spectrophotometric evaluation showed that about 92% of the drug was delivered through the filter after flushing with 10 ml of sodium chloride 0.9%. (809)

Doxorubicin HCl (Farmitalia) 5 mg/100 ml in sodium chloride 0.9% in a burette was filtered through a nylon 0.2-μm filter (Pall, ELD96LL). No drug loss due to sorption was found spectrophotometrically. (1568)

Doxorubicin HCl (Farmitalia) 1 mg/ml in sodium chloride 0.9% exhibited little or no loss by UV spectroscopy due to sorption to cellulose acetate (Minisart 45, Sartorius), polysulfone (Acrodisc 45, Gelman), and nylon (Nylaflo, Gelman) filters. However, a 20 to 25% loss due to sorption occurred during the first 60 minutes of infusion through nylon filters (Utipore, Pall). About a 35% loss was found during the first 15 min using a nylon filter (Posidyne ELD96, Pall). The delivered concentrations gradually returned to the full concentrations within 1.5 to 2.5 hours. (1795)

Central Venous Catheter—Doxorubicin HCl (Pharmacia) 0.25 mg/ml in dextrose 5% in water was found to be compatible with the ARROWg+ard Blue Plus (Arrow International) chlorhexidine-bearing triple-lumen central catheter. HPLC analysis was used to evaluate completeness of drug delivery through the catheter and the amount of chlorhexidine removed from the internal lumens. Essentially complete delivery of the drug was found with little or no drug loss occurring. Furthermore, chlorhexidine delivered from the catheter remained at trace amounts with no substantial increase due to the delivery of the drug through the catheter. (2335)

Compatibility Information

Solution Compatibility

Doxorubicin HCl

Solution	*Mfr*	*Mfr*	*Conc/L*	*Remarks*	*Ref*	*C/I*
Dextrose 3.3% in sodium chloride 0.3%			100 mg	5% or less drug loss in 4 weeks at 25 °C in the dark	1007	C
Dextrose 5% in water	TR[a]	AD	180 mg	10% loss of doxorubicin in 40 hr at room temperature along with a color change and an increase in pH	519	C
	TR[b]	AD	180 mg	No decrease in doxorubicin in 48 hr at room temperature	519	C
	AB[a]	AD	10 and 20 mg	Physically compatible. 2% decomposition in 24 hr at 21 °C under fluorescent light	526	C
			100 mg	5% or less drug loss in 4 weeks at 25 °C in the dark	1007	C
	[c]	BEL	0.5 g	Visually compatible with 5% or less doxorubicin loss by HPLC in 28 days at 4 °C and 14 days at 22 and 35 °C protected from light	1548	C
	[c]	BEL	1.25 g	Visually compatible with 5% or less doxorubicin loss by HPLC in 28 days at 4 and 22 °C and 7 days at 35 °C protected from light	1548	C
	MG[d], TR[b]		180 mg	Less than 10% loss by HPLC in 48 hr at room temperature exposed to light	1658	C
	[b]		40 mg	10% loss by HPLC in 7 days at 4 °C protected from light	1700	C
	TR[b]	FA	100 mg	10% or less loss by HPLC in 43 days at 4 and 25 °C in the dark	1460	C
Normosol R, pH 7.4	AB[a]	AD	10 and 20 mg	Physically compatible. 10% decomposition in 24 hr at 21 °C under fluorescent light	526	C
Ringer's injection, lactated	AB[a]	AD	10 and 20 mg	Physically compatible. 8% decomposition in 24 hr at 21 °C under fluorescent light	526	C
			100 mg	10% doxorubicin loss in 1.7 days at 25 °C in the dark	1007	C
Sodium chloride 0.9%	AB[a]	AD	10 and 20 mg	Physically compatible. 5% decomposition in 24 hr at 21 °C under fluorescent light	526	C
			100 mg	10% doxorubicin loss in 6 days at 25 °C in the dark	1007	C
	[c]	BEL	0.5 g	Visually compatible with 5% or less doxorubicin loss by HPLC in 14 days at 4 and 22 °C and 7 days at 35 °C protected from light	1548	C
	[c]	BEL	1.25 g	Visually compatible with 5% or less doxorubicin loss by HPLC in 28 days at 4 and 22 °C and 7 days at 35 °C protected from light	1548	C
	BA[e]	CET	2 g	Chemically stable by HPLC in 14 days at 3 and 23 °C and an additional 28 days at 30 °C	1538	C
	[b]		40 mg	6% loss by HPLC in 7 days at 4 °C protected from light	1700	C
	TR[b]	FA	100 mg	10% or less loss by HPLC in 43 days at 4 and 25 °C in the dark	1460	C
	AB[f]	AST	2 g	Little or no loss by HPLC in 24 hr at 25 °C and in 2 days at 5 °C	1970	C

[a] *Tested in glass containers.*
[b] *Tested in PVC containers.*
[c] *Tested in ethylene vinyl acetate (EVA) containers.*
[d] *Tested in both glass and polyolefin containers.*
[e] *Tested in Pharmacia Deltec reservoirs.*
[f] *Tested in glass containers and latex elastomeric reservoirs (Secure Medical).*

Additive Compatibility

Drug	Mfr	Conc/L	Doxorubicin HCl Mfr	Doxorubicin HCl Conc/L	*Test Soln*	*Remarks*	*Ref*	*C/I*
Aminophylline			AD			Solution color darkens from red to blue-purple	524	I
Dacarbazine with ondansetron HCl	LY GL	8 g 640 mg	AD	800 mg	D5W[a]	Visually compatible with >90% ondansetron and doxorubicin potency by HPLC over 24 hr at 30 °C and after 7 days at 4 °C followed by 24 hr at 30 °C. Dacarbazine stable for 8 hr but up to 13% loss in 24 hr	2092	I
Dacarbazine with ondansetron HCl	LY GL	20 g 640 mg	AD	1.5 g	D5W[a]	Visually compatible with >90% potency of all drugs by HPLC over 24 hr at 30 °C and after 7 days at 4 °C followed by 24 hr at 30 °C	2092	C
Dacarbazine with ondansetron HCl	LY GL	8 g 640 mg	AD	800 mg	D5W[b]	Visually compatible with >90% potency of all drugs by HPLC over 24 hr at 30 °C and after 7 days at 4 °C followed by 24 hr at 30 °C	2092	C
Dacarbazine with ondansetron HCl	LY GL	20 g 640 mg	AD	1.5 g	D5W[b]	Visually compatible with >90% potency of all drugs by HPLC over 24 hr at 30 °C and after 7 days at 4 °C followed by 24 hr at 30 °C	2092	C
Diazepam	RC		AD			Immediate precipitation	524	I
Etoposide with vincristine sulfate	BMS LI	200 mg 1.6 mg	PHU	40 mg	NS[c]	Visually compatible with all drugs chemically stable by HPLC for up to 72 hr at 30 °C protected from light	2239	C
Etoposide with vincristine sulfate	BMS LI	125 mg 1 mg	PHU	25 mg	NS[c]	Visually compatible with all drugs chemically stable by HPLC for up to 96 hr at 24 °C protected from or exposed to light	2239	C
Etoposide with vincristine sulfate	BMS LI	175 mg 1.4 mg	PHU	35 mg	NS[c]	Visually compatible with all drugs chemically stable by HPLC for up to 96 hr at 24 °C protected from or exposed to light	2239	C
Etoposide with vincristine sulfate	BMS LI	250 mg 2 mg	PHU	50 mg	NS[c]	Visually compatible with all drugs chemically stable by HPLC for up to 48 hr at 24 °C protected from or exposed to light. Etoposide precipitate formed in 72 hr	2239	C
Etoposide with vincristine sulfate	BMS LI	350 mg 2.8 mg	PHU	70 mg	NS[c]	Visually compatible with all drugs chemically stable by HPLC for up to 24 hr at 24 °C protected from or exposed to light. Etoposide precipitate formed in 36 hr	2239	C
Etoposide with vincristine sulfate	BMS LI	500 mg 4 mg	PHU	100 mg	NS[c]	Etoposide precipitate formed in 12 hr at 24 °C protected from or exposed to light	2239	I
Etoposide phosphate with vincristine sulfate	BMS LI	600 mg 5 mg	PHU	120 mg	NS[c]	Physically compatible with little or no loss of any drug by HPLC in 124 hr under refrigeration or at 35 to 40 °C	2343	C
Etoposide phosphate with vincristine sulfate	BMS LI	1.2 g 10 mg	PHU	240 mg	NS[c]	Physically compatible with little or no loss of any drug by HPLC in 124 hr under refrigeration or at 35 to 40 °C	2343	C
Etoposide phosphate with vincristine sulfate	BMS LI	2 g 16 mg	PHU	400 mg	NS[c]	Physically compatible with not more than 4% loss of any drug by HPLC in 124 hr under refrigeration or at 35 to 40 °C	2343	C
Fluorouracil	RC		AD			Solution color darkens from red to blue-purple	524	I
	RC	250 mg	AD	10 mg	D5W	Color changes to deep purple	296	I

Additive Compatibility (Cont.)

Doxorubicin HCl

Drug	*Mfr*	*Conc/L*	*Mfr*	*Conc/L*	*Test Soln*	*Remarks*	*Ref*	*C/I*
Ondansetron HCl	GL	30 and 300 mg	MJ	100 mg	D5W[a]	Physically compatible with little or no loss of either drug by HPLC in 48 hr at 23 °C	1876	C
	GL	30 and 300 mg	MJ	2 g	D5W[a]	Physically compatible with little or no loss of either drug by HPLC in 48 hr at 23 °C	1876	C
Ondansetron HCl with vincristine sulfate	GL LI	480 mg 14 mg	AD	400 mg	D5W[b]	Visually compatible with >90% potency of all drugs by HPLC after 5 days at 4 °C followed by 24 hr at 30 °C	2092	C
Ondansetron HCl with vincristine sulfate	GL LI	960 mg 28 mg	AD	800 mg	D5W[a]	Visually compatible with >90% potency of all drugs by HPLC after 120 hr at 30 °C	2092	C
Paclitaxel	BMS	300 mg	PH	200 mg	D5W, NS	Visually compatible for at least 1 day with microprecipitation appearing in 3 to 5 days and gross precipitation in 7 days at 4, 23, and 32 °C protected from light. No paclitaxel loss and less than 8% doxorubicin loss in 7 days	2247	C
	BMS	1.2 g	PH	200 mg	D5W, NS	Visually compatible for at least 1 day with microprecipitation appearing in 3 to 5 days and gross precipitation in 7 days at 4, 23, and 32 °C protected from light. No paclitaxel loss and less than 7% doxorubicin loss in 7 days	2247	C
Vinblastine sulfate	LI	75 mg	AD	500 mg	NS[a]	Physically compatible for at least 10 days at 8, 25, and 32 °C. HPLC assays highly erratic	838	?
	LI	150 mg	AD	1.5 g	NS[a]	Physically compatible for at least 10 days at 8, 25, and 32 °C. HPLC assays highly erratic	838	?
Vincristine sulfate	FAU	200 mg	PHU	2 g	W[d]	Physically compatible with no loss of either drug by HPLC in 7 days at 37 °C. About 4% loss of both drugs in 14 days at 4 °C	2288	C

[a]*Tested in PVC containers.*
[b]*Tested in polyisoprene infusion pump reservoirs.*
[c]*Tested in polyolefin-lined plastic bags.*
[d]*Tested in PVC reservoirs for the Graseby 9000 ambulatory pumps.*

Drugs in Syringe Compatibility

Doxorubicin HCl

Drug (in syringe)	*Mfr*	*Amt*	*Mfr*	*Amt*	*Remarks*	*Ref*	*C/I*
Bleomycin sulfate		1.5 units/ 0.5 ml		1 mg/ 0.5 ml	Physically compatible for 5 min at room temperature followed by 8 min of centrifugation	980	C
Cisplatin		0.5 mg/ 0.5 ml		1 mg/ 0.5 ml	Physically compatible for 5 min at room temperature followed by 8 min of centrifugation	980	C
Cyclophosphamide		10 mg/ 0.5 ml		1 mg/ 0.5 ml	Physically compatible for 5 min at room temperature followed by 8 min of centrifugation	980	C
Droperidol		1.25 mg/ 0.5 ml		1 mg/ 0.5 ml	Physically compatible for 5 min at room temperature followed by 8 min of centrifugation	980	C

Drugs in Syringe Compatibility (Cont.)

Doxorubicin HCl

Drug (in syringe)	*Mfr*	*Amt*	*Mfr*	*Amt*	*Remarks*	*Ref*	*C/I*
Fluorouracil		25 mg/ 0.5 ml		1 mg/ 0.5 ml	Physically compatible for 5 min at room temperature followed by 8 min of centrifugation	980	C
		500 mg/ 10 ml		5 and 10 mg/ 10 ml[a]	Precipitate forms within several hours of mixing	1564	I
Furosemide		5 mg/ 0.5 ml		1 mg/ 0.5 ml	Immediate precipitation	980	I
Heparin sodium		500 units/ 0.5 ml		1 mg/ 0.5 ml	Immediate precipitation	980	I
Leucovorin calcium		5 mg/ 0.5 ml		1 mg/ 0.5 ml	Physically compatible for 5 min at room temperature followed by 8 min of centrifugation	980	C
Methotrexate sodium		12.5 mg/ 0.5 ml		1 mg/ 0.5 ml	Physically compatible for 5 min at room temperature followed by 8 min of centrifugation	980	C
Metoclopramide HCl		2.5 mg/ 0.5 ml		1 mg/ 0.5 ml	Physically compatible for 5 min at room temperature followed by 8 min of centrifugation	980	C
	RB	10 mg/ 2 ml	AD	40 mg/ 20 ml	Physically compatible for 48 hr at room temperature	924	C
	RB	10 mg/ 2 ml	AD	40 mg/ 20 ml	Physically compatible for 48 hr at 25 °C	1167	C
	RB	160 mg/ 32 ml	AD	90 mg/ 45 ml	Physically compatible for 48 hr at 25 °C	1167	C
Mitomycin		0.25 mg/ 0.5 ml		1 mg/ 0.5 ml	Physically compatible for 5 min at room temperature followed by 8 min of centrifugation	980	C
Vinblastine sulfate	LI	4.5 mg/ 4.5 ml	AD	45 mg/ 22.5 ml	(Brought to 30 ml total volume with NS) Physically compatible for at least 10 days at 8, 25, and 32 °C. HPLC assays highly erratic	838	?
	LI	2.25 mg/ 2.25 ml	AD	15 mg/ 7.5 ml	(Brought to 30 ml total volume with NS) Physically compatible for at least 10 days at 8, 25, and 32 °C. HPLC assays highly erratic	838	?
		0.5 mg/ 0.5 ml		1 mg/ 0.5 ml	Physically compatible for 5 min at room temperature followed by 8 min of centrifugation	980	C
Vincristine sulfate		0.5 mg/ 0.5 ml		1 mg/ 0.5 ml	Physically compatible for 5 min at room temperature followed by 8 min of centrifugation	980	C

[a]*Diluted in sodium chloride 0.9%.*

Y-Site Injection Compatibility (1:1 Mixture)

Doxorubicin HCl

Drug	*Mfr*	*Conc*	*Mfr*	*Conc*	*Remarks*	*Ref*	*C/I*
Allopurinol sodium	BW	3 mg/ml[b]	CET	2 mg/ml	Dark red color and haze form immediately. Reddish-brown particles form within 1 hr	1686	I
Amifostine	USB	10 mg/ml[a]	CET	2 mg/ml	Physically compatible with no change in measured turbidity or increase in particle content in 4 hr at 23 °C	1845	C
Amphotericin B cholesteryl sulfate complex	SEQ	0.83 mg/ml[a]	CHI	2 mg/ml	Gross precipitate forms	2117	I

Y-Site Injection Compatibility (1:1 Mixture) (Cont.)

			Doxorubicin HCl				
Drug	*Mfr*	*Conc*	*Mfr*	*Conc*	*Remarks*	*Ref*	*C/I*
Aztreonam	SQ	40 mg/ml[a]	CET	2 mg/ml	Physically compatible with no subvisual haze or particle formation in 4 hr at 23 °C	1758	C
Bleomycin sulfate		3 units/ml		2 mg/ml	Drugs injected sequentially into Y-site with no flush between. No visually apparent precipitate	980	C
Cefepime HCl	BMS	20 mg/ml[a]	CET	2 mg/ml	Haze forms immediately and becomes flocculent precipitate in 4 hr	1689	I
Chlorpromazine HCl	SKF	2 mg/ml[a]	AD	0.2 mg/ml[a]	Visually compatible for 4 hr at room temperature under fluorescent light	1685	C
Cimetidine HCl	SKF	12 mg/ml[a]	AD	0.2 mg/ml[a]	Visually compatible for 4 hr at room temperature under fluorescent light	1685	C
Cisplatin		1 mg/ml		2 mg/ml	Drugs injected sequentially into Y-site with no flush between. No visually apparent precipitate	980	C
Cladribine	ORT	0.015[b] and 0.5[c] mg/ml	CHI	2 mg/ml	Physically compatible with no change in measured turbidity or increase in particle content in 4 hr at 23 °C	1969	C
Cyclophosphamide		20 mg/ml		2 mg/ml	Drugs injected sequentially into Y-site with no flush between. No visually apparent precipitate	980	C
Dexamethasone sodium phosphate	QU	1 mg/ml[a]	AD	0.2 mg/ml[a]	Visually compatible for 4 hr at room temperature under fluorescent light	1685	C
Diphenhydramine HCl	PD	2 mg/ml[a]	AD	0.2 mg/ml[a]	Visually compatible for 4 hr at room temperature under fluorescent light	1685	C
Droperidol		2.5 mg/ml		2 mg/ml	Drugs injected sequentially into Y-site with no flush between. No visually apparent precipitate	980	C
	JN	20 μg/ml[a]	AD	0.2 mg/ml[a]	Visually compatible for 4 hr at room temperature under fluorescent light	1685	C
Etoposide phosphate	BR	5 mg/ml[a]	GEN	2 mg/ml	Physically compatible with no change in measured turbidity or increase in particle content in 4 hr at 23 °C	2218	C
Famotidine	MSD	2 mg/ml[a]	AD	0.2 mg/ml[a]	Visually compatible for 4 hr at room temperature under fluorescent light	1685	C
Filgrastim	AMG	30 μg/ml[a]	CET	2 mg/ml	Physically compatible with no change in measured turbidity or increase in particle content in 4 hr at 22 °C	1687	C
Fludarabine phosphate	BX	1 mg/ml[a]	CET	2 mg/ml	Physically compatible for 4 hr at room temperature under fluorescent light	1439	C
Fluorouracil		50 mg/ml		2 mg/ml	Drugs injected sequentially into Y-site with no flush between. No visually apparent precipitate	980	C
Furosemide		10 mg/ml		2 mg/ml	Drugs injected sequentially into Y-site with no flush between. Immediate precipitation	980	I
	ES	3 mg/ml[a]	AD	0.2 mg/ml[a]	Visually compatible for 4 hr at room temperature under fluorescent light	1685	C

Y-Site Injection Compatibility (1:1 Mixture) (Cont.)

Doxorubicin HCl

Drug	*Mfr*	*Conc*	*Mfr*	*Conc*	*Remarks*	*Ref*	*C/I*
Ganciclovir sodium	SY	20 mg/ml[a]	AD	0.2 mg/ml[a]	Color changes to deep purple immediately	1685	I
Gatifloxacin	BMS	2 mg/ml[a]	PH	2 mg/ml	Physically compatible with no change in measured haze or increase in particle content in 4 hr at 23 °C	2234	C
Gemcitabine HCl	LI	10 mg/ml[b]	PH	2 mg/ml	Physically compatible with no change in measured turbidity or increase in particle content in 4 hr at 23 °C	2226	C
Granisetron HCl	SKB	1 mg/ml	AD	0.2 mg/ml[b]	Physically compatible with little or no loss of either drug by HPLC in 4 hr at 22 °C	1883	C
Heparin sodium		1000 units/ml		2 mg/ml	Drugs injected sequentially into Y-site with no flush between. Immediate precipitation	980	I
	SO	40 units/ml[a]	AD	0.2 mg/ml[a]	Visually compatible for 4 hr at room temperature under fluorescent light	1685	C
Hydromorphone HCl	ES	0.04 mg/ml[a]	AD	0.2 mg/ml[a]	Visually compatible for 4 hr at room temperature under fluorescent light	1685	C
Leucovorin calcium		10 mg/ml		2 mg/ml	Drugs injected sequentially into Y-site with no flush between. No visually apparent precipitate	980	C
Linezolid	PHU	2 mg/ml	FUJ	2 mg/ml	Physically compatible with no change in measured turbidity or increase in particle content in 4 hr at 23 °C	2264	C
Lorazepam	WY	0.1 mg/ml[a]	AD	0.2 mg/ml[a]	Visually compatible for 4 hr at room temperature under fluorescent light	1685	C
Melphalan HCl	BW	0.1 mg/ml[b]	AD	2 mg/ml	Physically compatible with no change in measured turbidity or increase in particle content in 3 hr at 22 °C	1557	C
Methotrexate sodium		25 mg/ml		2 mg/ml	Drugs injected sequentially into Y-site with no flush between. No visually apparent precipitate	980	C
		30 mg/ml	FA	0.4 mg/ml[a]	Visually compatible for 4 hr at room temperature	1788	C
Methylprednisolone sodium succinate	UP	0.5 mg/ml[a]	AD	0.2 mg/ml[a]	Visually compatible for 4 hr at room temperature under fluorescent light	1685	C
Metoclopramide HCl		5 mg/ml		2 mg/ml	Drugs injected sequentially into Y-site with no flush between. No visually apparent precipitate	980	C
	RB	2.5 mg/ml[a]	AD	0.2 mg/ml[a]	Visually compatible for 4 hr at room temperature under fluorescent light	1685	C
Mitomycin		0.5 mg/ml		2 mg/ml	Drugs injected sequentially into Y-site with no flush between. No visually apparent precipitate	980	C
Morphine sulfate	ES	0.12 mg/ml[a]	AD	0.2 mg/ml[a]	Visually compatible for 4 hr at room temperature under fluorescent light	1685	C
Ondansetron HCl	GL	1 mg/ml[b]	CET	2 mg/ml	Physically compatible for 4 hr at 22 °C	1365	C
	GL	16 to 160 μg/ml		2 mg/ml	Physically compatible when doxorubicin given as 5-min bolus via Y-site	1366	C
Paclitaxel	NCI	1.2 mg/ml[a]		2 mg/ml	Physically compatible with no change in measured turbidity in 4 hr at 22 °C	1528	C

Y-Site Injection Compatibility (1:1 Mixture) (Cont.)

Drug	Mfr	Conc	Doxorubicin HCl Mfr	Doxorubicin HCl Conc	Remarks	Ref	C/I
Piperacillin sodium–tazobactam sodium	LE	40 + 5 mg/ml[a]	CET	2 mg/ml	Turbidity forms immediately	1688	I
Prochlorperazine edisylate	SKF	0.5 mg/ml[a]	AD	0.2 mg/ml[a]	Visually compatible for 4 hr at room temperature under fluorescent light	1685	C
Promethazine HCl	WY	2 mg/ml[a]	AD	0.2 mg/ml[a]	Visually compatible for 4 hr at room temperature under fluorescent light	1685	C
Propofol	ZEN	10 mg/ml	CHI	2 mg/ml	Emulsion broke and oiled out	1916	I
Ranitidine HCl	GL	1 mg/ml[a]	AD	0.2 mg/ml[a]	Visually compatible for 4 hr at room temperature under fluorescent light	1685	C
Sargramostim	IMM	10 μg/ml[b]	CET	2 mg/ml	Physically compatible for 4 hr at 22 °C	1436	C
Sodium bicarbonate		1.4%	FA	0.4 mg/ml[a]	Visually compatible for 2 hr at room temperature	1788	C
Teniposide	BR	0.1 mg/ml[a]	CET	2 mg/ml	Physically compatible with no subvisual haze or particle formation in 4 hr at 23 °C	1725	C
Thiotepa	IMM[d]	1 mg/ml[a]	CHI	2 mg/ml	Physically compatible with no change in measured turbidity or increase in particle content in 4 hr at 23 °C	1861	C
TNA #218 to #226[e]			PH, GEN	2 mg/ml	Damage to emulsion integrity occurs immediately with free oil formation possible	2215	I
Topotecan HCl	SKB	56 μg/ml[a,b]	PH	2 mg/ml	Visually compatible with little or no loss of either drug by HPLC in 4 hr at 22 °C under fluorescent light	2245	C
TPN #212 to #215[e]			PH	2 mg/ml	Substantial loss of natural subvisual turbidity occurs immediately	2109	I
Vinblastine sulfate		1 mg/ml		2 mg/ml	Drugs injected sequentially into Y-site with no flush between. No visually apparent precipitate	980	C
Vincristine sulfate		1 mg/ml		2 mg/ml	Drugs injected sequentially into Y-site with no flush between. No visually apparent precipitate	980	C
Vinorelbine tartrate	BW	1 mg/ml[b]	CET	2 mg/ml	Physically compatible with no change in measured turbidity or increase in particle content in 4 hr at 22 °C	1558	C

[a]*Tested in dextrose 5% in water.*
[b]*Tested in sodium chloride 0.9%.*
[c]*Tested in bacteriostatic sodium chloride 0.9% preserved with benzyl alcohol 0.9%.*
[d]*Lyophilized formulation tested.*
[e]*Refer to Appendix I for the composition of parenteral nutrition solutions. TNA indicates a 3-in-1 admixture, and TPN indicates a 2-in-1 admixture.*

Additional Compatibility Information

Dacarbazine — No alteration in the ultraviolet/visible spectra was observed when dacarbazine was combined in solution with doxorubicin HCl. (492)

Fluorouracil and Heparin — Doxorubicin HCl has been stated to be incompatible with fluorouracil and heparin sodium because of possible precipitate formation. (2; 4)

Vincristine — The compatibility of doxorubicin HCl (Farmitalia) 1.4 mg/ml with vincristine sulfate (Lilly) 0.033 mg/ml in three infusion solutions was reported for conditions simulating prolonged infusion of the solution via an implanted device (37 °C) or a pump kept under the clothing (30 °C) as well as at 25 °C. In sodium chloride 0.9% and in dextrose 2.5% in sodium chloride 0.45%, there was no precipitate or color change; the concentrations of both drugs showed a 10% or less loss after 14 days of storage at any of the temperatures. The greatest losses of doxorubicin HCl and vincristine sulfate were about 10 and 6 to 8%, respectively, in the 37 °C samples. (1030)

However, when sodium chloride 0.45% with Ringer's acetate was used as the infusion solution, the stability of both drugs was much worse, probably because of the substantially higher solution pH. At 37 °C, a red-pink precipitate formed after two to three days, with about 40% doxorubicin HCl and 14% vincristine sulfate losses occurring in four days. The lower temperature samples showed 17 to 27% doxorubicin HCl losses in four days, followed by the eventual formation of opalescence in the solutions. Also, the degradation products of doxorubicin adsorbed extensively to the walls of the low density polyethylene–polysiloxane bags. (1030)

Increasing the concentration of doxorubicin HCl from 1.4 to 1.88 and 2.37 mg/ml increased the extent of decomposition at 37 °C from 10% at the lowest concentration to 12 and 16%, respectively, after 14 days. Increasing the vincristine sulfate concentration to 0.05 mg/ml did not alter the stability of either drug. (1030)

Doxorubicin HCl (Nycomed) was combined with vincristine sulfate (Lilly) in both PVC (Pharmacia-Deltec) and polyisoprene (Infusor, Baxter) infusion reservoirs. The drug solution concentrates were diluted slightly with sodium chloride 0.9% to yield a doxorubicin HCl concentration of 1.67 mg/ml and a vincristine sulfate concentration of 0.036 mg/ml. The reservoirs were stored at 4 °C for seven days. This was followed by incubation for four days at 35 °C to simulate near-body temperature during use. No visible changes occurred, and neither drug sustained any loss by HPLC analysis throughout the course of the study in either reservoir. (1874)

Doxorubicin HCl (Pharmacia & Upjohn) 2 mg/ml and vincristine sulfate (Faulding) 0.2 mg/ml in water for injection were evaluated for stability and compatibility in PVC reservoirs for the Graseby 9000 ambulatory pumps. The solutions were physically compatible and no loss of either drug was found by HPLC analysis in 7 days at 37 °C. About 4% loss of both drugs was found after 14 days at 4 °C. Furthermore, weight losses due to moisture transmission were minimal. (2288)

Aluminum — A darkening of doxorubicin HCl color has been noted when solutions of the drug contact aluminum metal. This change was initially noticed in the first small amount of drug to be injected through a needle with an aluminum hub. When solutions of doxorubicin HCl containing aluminum are allowed to stand, the color becomes much darker than the control. Precipitation may also occur. As a precautionary measure, the author recommended not using any aluminum-containing apparatus for preparing or administering doxorubicin HCl. (653)

In another evaluation, stainless steel needles with steel or plastic hubs and pieces of aluminum were immersed in doxorubicin HCl 2 mg/ml in sterile water for injection or sodium chloride 0.9%. After 24 hours, the solutions containing the needles were unchanged in appearance and pH. The solution containing the aluminum was darker in color, and the pH had changed from 4.8 to 5.2. The potency of all solutions remained the same after six hours; but after three days, the solution containing aluminum was down to 91.9% while the others were only down to 94.4%. The authors concluded that doxorubicin HCl does react with aluminum but at a slow rate and without major loss of potency. They recommended not storing the drug in syringes capped with aluminum-hubbed needles but thought that doxorubicin could be injected safely through aluminum-hubbed needles. (887)

Ogawa et al. reported that immersion of a needle with an aluminum component in doxorubicin HCl (Adria) 2 mg/ml resulted in a darkening of the solution, with black patches forming on the aluminum in 12 to 24 hours at 24 °C with protection from light. (988)

Other Information

Microbial Growth — At a concentration of 0.5 mg/ml in sodium chloride 0.9%, doxorubicin HCl supported the growth of several microorganisms commonly implicated in nosocomial infections, including *Escherichia coli, Klebsiella pneumoniae, Pseudomonas aeruginosa,* and *Candida albicans*. Therefore, the arbitrary application of an extended expiration date to doxorubicin HCl solutions used in ambulatory pump systems is highly questionable. (827)

Admixtures containing doxorubicin HCl, etoposide phosphate, and vincristine sulfate in a variety of concentration combinations were unable to pass the USP test for antimicrobial growth effectiveness. Mixtures of these drugs are not "self-preserving" and will permit microbial growth. (2343)

Inactivation — In the event of spills or leaks, Adria recommends the use of sodium hypochlorite 5% (household bleach) to inactivate doxorubicin HCl. (1200)

DOXORUBICIN HCL LIPOSOME INJECTION AHFS 10:00

Products — Doxorubicin HCl liposome injection is available as a red translucent liposomal dispersion providing 2 mg/ml of doxorubicin HCl packaged in 10- and 25-ml vials. (2)

Over 90% of the doxorubicin HCl is provided inside liposome carriers composed of *N*-(carbonyl-methoxypolyethylene glycol 2000)-1,2-distearoyl-*sn*-glycero-3-phosphoethanolamine sodium, 3.19 mg/ml; fully hydrogenated soy phosphatidylcholine, 9.58 mg/ml; and cholesterol, 3.19 mg/ml. The product also contains about 2 mg/ml of ammonium sulfate, histidine as a buffer, hydrochloric acid and/or sodium hydroxide to adjust pH, and sucrose to adjust tonicity. (2)

pH — Approximately 6.5. (2)

Trade Name(s) — Doxil.

Administration — Doxorubicin HCl liposome injection is administered intravenously after dilution in 250 ml of dextrose 5% in water. The product should not be administered as a bolus injection, as the undiluted dispersion, as a rapid infusion, or by other routes. Extravasation should be avoided; the drug is extremely irritating to tissues. The manufacturer recommends the use of protective gloves during dose preparation. (2)

The functional properties of a drug incorporated into a liposomal dispersion like this one may differ substantially from the functional properties of the conventional aqueous formulation. (2) CAUTION: Care should be taken to ensure that the correct drug product, dose, and administration procedures are used and that no confusion with other products occurs.

Stability — Intact vials of doxorubicin HCl liposome injection should be stored under refrigeration at 2 to 8 °C. Freezing should be avoided because prolonged freezing may adversely affect liposomal products. However, short-term freezing (one month) did not adversely affect this product. (2)

Filtration — Doxorubicin HCl liposome injection is a liposomal dispersion; filtration, including inline filtration, should not be performed. (2)

Compatibility Information

Y-Site Injection Compatibility (1:1 Mixture)

			Doxorubicin HCl liposome injection				
Drug	*Mfr*	*Conc*	*Mfr*	*Conc*	*Remarks*	*Ref*	*C/I*
Acyclovir sodium	GW	7 mg/ml[a]	SEQ	0.4 mg/ml[a]	Physically compatible with little or no change in measured turbidity and no increase in particle content in 4 hr at 23 °C	2087	C
Allopurinol sodium	BW	3 mg/ml[a]	SEQ	0.4 mg/ml[a]	Physically compatible with little or no change in measured turbidity and no increase in particle content in 4 hr at 23 °C	2087	C
Aminophylline	AB	2.5 mg/ml[a]	SEQ	0.4 mg/ml[a]	Physically compatible with little or no change in measured turbidity and no increase in particle content in 4 hr at 23 °C	2087	C
Amphotericin B	APC	0.6 mg/ml[a]	SEQ	0.4 mg/ml[a]	Fivefold increase in measured particulates in 4 hours	2087	I
Amphotericin B cholesteryl sulfate complex	SEQ	0.83 mg/ml[a]	SEQ	2 mg/ml[a]	Gross precipitate forms	2117	I
Ampicillin sodium	SKB	20 mg/ml[b]	SEQ	0.4 mg/ml[a]	Physically compatible with little or no change in measured turbidity and no increase in particle content in 4 hr at 23 °C	2087	C
Aztreonam	SQ	40 mg/ml[a]	SEQ	0.4 mg/ml[a]	Physically compatible with little or no change in measured turbidity and no increase in particle content in 4 hr at 23 °C	2087	C
Bleomycin sulfate	MJ	1 unit/ml[b]	SEQ	0.4 mg/ml[a]	Physically compatible with little or no change in measured turbidity and no increase in particle content in 4 hr at 23 °C	2087	C
Buprenorphine HCl	RKC	0.04 mg/ml[a]	SEQ	0.4 mg/ml[a]	Partial loss of measured natural turbidity	2087	I
Butorphanol tartrate	APC	0.04 mg/ml[a]	SEQ	0.4 mg/ml[a]	Physically compatible with little or no change in measured turbidity and no increase in particle content in 4 hr at 23 °C	2087	C
Calcium gluconate	AB	40 mg/ml[a]	SEQ	0.4 mg/ml[a]	Physically compatible with little or no change in measured turbidity and no increase in particle content in 4 hr at 23 °C	2087	C
Carboplatin	BR	5 mg/ml[a]	SEQ	0.4 mg/ml[a]	Physically compatible with little or no change in measured turbidity and no increase in particle content in 4 hr at 23 °C	2087	C

Y-Site Injection Compatibility (1:1 Mixture) (Cont.)

Doxorubicin HCl liposome injection

Drug	*Mfr*	*Conc*	*Mfr*	*Conc*	*Remarks*	*Ref*	*C/I*
Cefazolin sodium	SKB	20 mg/ml[a]	SEQ	0.4 mg/ml[a]	Physically compatible with little or no change in measured turbidity and no increase in particle content in 4 hr at 23 °C	2087	C
Cefepime HCl	BMS	20 mg/ml[a]	SEQ	0.4 mg/ml[a]	Physically compatible with little or no change in measured turbidity and no increase in particle content in 4 hr at 23 °C	2087	C
Cefoperazone sodium	RR	40 mg/ml[a]	SEQ	0.4 mg/ml[a]	Partial loss of measured natural turbidity	2087	I
Cefoxitin sodium	ME	20 mg/ml[a]	SEQ	0.4 mg/ml[a]	Physically compatible with little or no change in measured turbidity and no increase in particle content in 4 hr at 23 °C	2087	C
Ceftazidime	SKB[c]	40 mg/ml[a]	SEQ	0.4 mg/ml[a]	Partial loss of measured natural turbidity	2087	I
Ceftizoxime sodium	FUJ	20 mg/ml[a]	SEQ	0.4 mg/ml[a]	Physically compatible with little or no change in measured turbidity and no increase in particle content in 4 hr at 23 °C	2087	C
Ceftriaxone sodium	RC	20 mg/ml[a]	SEQ	0.4 mg/ml[a]	Physically compatible with little or no change in measured turbidity and no increase in particle content in 4 hr at 23 °C	2087	C
Chlorpromazine HCl	ES	2 mg/ml[a]	SEQ	0.4 mg/ml[a]	Physically compatible with little or no change in measured turbidity and no increase in particle content in 4 hr at 23 °C	2087	C
Cimetidine HCl	SKB	12 mg/ml[a]	SEQ	0.4 mg/ml[a]	Physically compatible with little or no change in measured turbidity and no increase in particle content in 4 hr at 23 °C	2087	C
Ciprofloxacin	BAY	1 mg/ml[a]	SEQ	0.4 mg/ml[a]	Physically compatible with little or no change in measured turbidity and no increase in particle content in 4 hr at 23 °C	2087	C
Cisplatin	BR	1 mg/ml	SEQ	0.4 mg/ml[a]	Physically compatible with little or no change in measured turbidity and no increase in particle content in 4 hr at 23 °C	2087	C
Clindamycin phosphate	AST	10 mg/ml[a]	SEQ	0.4 mg/ml[a]	Physically compatible with little or no change in measured turbidity and no increase in particle content in 4 hr at 23 °C	2087	C
Cyclophosphamide	MJ	10 mg/ml[a]	SEQ	0.4 mg/ml[a]	Physically compatible with little or no change in measured turbidity and no increase in particle content in 4 hr at 23 °C	2087	C
Cytarabine	CHI	50 mg/ml	SEQ	0.4 mg/ml[a]	Physically compatible with little or no change in measured turbidity and no increase in particle content in 4 hr at 23 °C	2087	C

Y-Site Injection Compatibility (1:1 Mixture) (Cont.)

			Doxorubicin HCl liposome injection				
Drug	*Mfr*	*Conc*	*Mfr*	*Conc*	*Remarks*	*Ref*	*C/I*
Dacarbazine	MI	4 mg/ml[a]	SEQ	0.4 mg/ml[a]	Physically compatible with little or no change in measured turbidity and no increase in particle content in 4 hr at 23 °C	2087	C
Dexamethasone sodium phosphate	ES	2 mg/ml[a]	SEQ	0.4 mg/ml[a]	Physically compatible with little or no change in measured turbidity and no increase in particle content in 4 hr at 23 °C	2087	C
Diphenhydramine HCl	SCN	2 mg/ml[a]	SEQ	0.4 mg/ml[a]	Physically compatible with little or no change in measured turbidity and no increase in particle content in 4 hr at 23 °C	2087	C
Dobutamine HCl	BA	4 mg/ml[a]	SEQ	0.4 mg/ml[a]	Physically compatible with little or no change in measured turbidity and no increase in particle content in 4 hr at 23 °C	2087	C
Docetaxel	RP	2 mg/ml[a]	SEQ	0.4 mg/ml[a]	Partial loss of measured natural turbidity	2087	I
Dopamine HCl	AB	3.2 mg/ml[a]	SEQ	0.4 mg/ml[a]	Physically compatible with little or no change in measured turbidity and no increase in particle content in 4 hr at 23 °C	2087	C
Droperidol	AST	0.4 mg/ml[a]	SEQ	0.4 mg/ml[a]	Physically compatible with little or no change in measured turbidity and no increase in particle content in 4 hr at 23 °C	2087	C
Enalaprilat	MSD	0.1 mg/ml[a]	SEQ	0.4 mg/ml[a]	Physically compatible with little or no change in measured turbidity and no increase in particle content in 4 hr at 23 °C	2087	C
Etoposide	BR	0.4 mg/ml[a]	SEQ	0.4 mg/ml[a]	Physically compatible with little or no change in measured turbidity and no increase in particle content in 4 hr at 23 °C	2087	C
Famotidine	ME	2 mg/ml[a]	SEQ	0.4 mg/ml[a]	Physically compatible with little or no change in measured turbidity and no increase in particle content in 4 hr at 23 °C	2087	C
Fluconazole	RR	2 mg/ml	SEQ	0.4 mg/ml[a]	Physically compatible with little or no change in measured turbidity and no increase in particle content in 4 hr at 23 °C	2087	C
Fluorouracil	PH	16 mg/ml[a]	SEQ	0.4 mg/ml[a]	Physically compatible with little or no change in measured turbidity and no increase in particle content in 4 hr at 23 °C	2087	C
Furosemide	AMR	3 mg/ml[a]	SEQ	0.4 mg/ml[a]	Physically compatible with little or no change in measured turbidity and no increase in particle content in 4 hr at 23 °C	2087	C

Y-Site Injection Compatibility (1:1 Mixture) (Cont.)

			Doxorubicin HCl liposome injection				
Drug	*Mfr*	*Conc*	*Mfr*	*Conc*	*Remarks*	*Ref*	*C/I*
Ganciclovir sodium	RC	20 mg/ml[a]	SEQ	0.4 mg/ml[a]	Physically compatible with little or no change in measured turbidity and no increase in particle content in 4 hr at 23 °C	2087	**C**
Gentamicin sulfate	ES	5 mg/ml[a]	SEQ	0.4 mg/ml[a]	Physically compatible with little or no change in measured turbidity and no increase in particle content in 4 hr at 23 °C	2087	**C**
Granisetron HCl	SKB	0.05 mg/ml[a]	SEQ	0.4 mg/ml[a]	Physically compatible with little or no change in measured turbidity and no increase in particle content in 4 hr at 23 °C	2087	**C**
Haloperidol lactate	MN	0.2 mg/ml[a]	SEQ	0.4 mg/ml[a]	Physically compatible with little or no change in measured turbidity and no increase in particle content in 4 hr at 23 °C	2087	**C**
Heparin sodium	ES	1000 units/ml[a]	SEQ	0.4 mg/ml[a]	Physically compatible with little or no change in measured turbidity and no increase in particle content in 4 hr at 23 °C	2087	**C**
Hydrocortisone sodium succinate	AB	1 mg/ml[a]	SEQ	0.4 mg/ml[a]	Physically compatible with little or no change in measured turbidity and no increase in particle content in 4 hr at 23 °C	2087	**C**
Hydromorphone HCl	ES	0.5 mg/ml[a]	SEQ	0.4 mg/ml[a]	Physically compatible with little or no change in measured turbidity and no increase in particle content in 4 hr at 23 °C	2087	**C**
Hydroxyzine HCl	ES	2 mg/ml[a]	SEQ	0.4 mg/ml[a]	10-fold increase in particles ≥10 μm in 4 hr	2087	**I**
Ifosfamide	MJ	25 mg/ml[a]	SEQ	0.4 mg/ml[a]	Physically compatible with little or no change in measured turbidity and no increase in particle content in 4 hr at 23 °C	2087	**C**
Leucovorin calcium	IMM	2 mg/ml[a]	SEQ	0.4 mg/ml[a]	Physically compatible with little or no change in measured turbidity and no increase in particle content in 4 hr at 23 °C	2087	**C**
Lorazepam	WY	0.1 mg/ml[a]	SEQ	0.4 mg/ml[a]	Physically compatible with little or no change in measured turbidity and no increase in particle content in 4 hr at 23 °C	2087	**C**
Magnesium sulfate	AST	100 mg/ml[a]	SEQ	0.4 mg/ml[a]	Physically compatible with little or no change in measured turbidity and no increase in particle content in 4 hr at 23 °C	2087	**C**
Mannitol	BA	15%	SEQ	0.4 mg/ml[a]	Partial loss of measured natural turbidity	2087	**I**
Meperidine HCl	AST	4 mg/ml[a]	SEQ	0.4 mg/ml[a]	Increase in measured turbidity	2087	**I**

Y-Site Injection Compatibility (1:1 Mixture) (Cont.)

			Doxorubicin HCl liposome injection				
Drug	*Mfr*	*Conc*	*Mfr*	*Conc*	*Remarks*	*Ref*	*C/I*
Mesna	MJ	10 mg/ml[a]	SEQ	0.4 mg/ml[a]	Physically compatible with little or no change in measured turbidity and no increase in particle content in 4 hr at 23 °C	2087	C
Methotrexate sodium	IMM	15 mg/ml[a]	SEQ	0.4 mg/ml[a]	Physically compatible with little or no change in measured turbidity and no increase in particle content in 4 hr at 23 °C	2087	C
Methylprednisolone sodium succinate	UP	5 mg/ml[a]	SEQ	0.4 mg/ml[a]	Physically compatible with little or no change in measured turbidity and no increase in particle content in 4 hr at 23 °C	2087	C
Metoclopramide HCl	GNS	5 mg/ml	SEQ	0.4 mg/ml[a]	Increase in measured turbidity	2087	I
Metronidazole	AB	5 mg/ml	SEQ	0.4 mg/ml[a]	Physically compatible with little or no change in measured turbidity and no increase in particle content in 4 hr at 23 °C	2087	C
Mitoxantrone HCl	IMM	0.5 mg/ml[a]	SEQ	0.4 mg/ml[a]	Partial loss of measured natural turbidity	2087	I
Morphine sulfate	ES	1 mg/ml[a]	SEQ	0.4 mg/ml[a]	Partial loss of measured natural turbidity	2087	I
Netilmicin sulfate	SC	5 mg/ml[a]	SEQ	0.4 mg/ml[a]	Physically compatible with little or no change in measured turbidity and no increase in particle content in 4 hr at 23 °C	2087	C
Ofloxacin	ORT	4 mg/ml[a]	SEQ	0.4 mg/ml[a]	Increase in measured turbidity	2087	I
Ondansetron HCl	CER	1 mg/ml[a]	SEQ	0.4 mg/ml[a]	Physically compatible with little or no change in measured turbidity and no increase in particle content in 4 hr at 23 °C	2087	C
Paclitaxel	MJ	0.6 mg/ml[a]	SEQ	0.4 mg/ml[a]	Partial loss of measured natural turbidity	2087	I
Piperacillin disodium	LE	40 mg/ml[a]	SEQ	0.4 mg/ml[a]	Physically compatible with little or no change in measured turbidity and no increase in particle content in 4 hr at 23 °C	2087	C
Piperacillin sodium–tazobactam sodium	CY	40 + 5 mg/ml[a]	SEQ	0.4 mg/ml[a]	Partial loss of measured natural turbidity	2087	I
Potassium chloride	AB	0.1 mEq/ml[a]	SEQ	0.4 mg/ml[a]	Physically compatible with little or no change in measured turbidity and no increase in particle content in 4 hr at 23 °C	2087	C
Prochlorperazine edisylate	SO	0.5 mg/ml[a]	SEQ	0.4 mg/ml[a]	Physically compatible with little or no change in measured turbidity and no increase in particle content in 4 hr at 23 °C	2087	C
Promethazine HCl	ES	2 mg/ml[a]	SEQ	0.4 mg/ml[a]	Increase in measured turbidity	2087	I
Ranitidine HCl	GL	2 mg/ml[a]	SEQ	0.4 mg/ml[a]	Physically compatible with little or no change in measured turbidity and no increase in particle content in 4 hr at 23 °C	2087	C

Y-Site Injection Compatibility (1:1 Mixture) (Cont.)

			Doxorubicin HCl liposome injection				
Drug	*Mfr*	*Conc*	*Mfr*	*Conc*	*Remarks*	*Ref*	*C/I*
Sodium bicarbonate	AB	1 mEq/ml	SEQ	0.4 mg/ml[a]	Partial loss of measured natural turbidity	2087	I
Ticarcillin disodium	SKB	30 mg/ml[a]	SEQ	0.4 mg/ml[a]	Physically compatible with little or no change in measured turbidity and no increase in particle content in 4 hr at 23 °C	2087	C
Ticarcillin disodium–clavulanate potassium	SKB	31 mg/ml[a]	SEQ	0.4 mg/ml[a]	Physically compatible with little or no change in measured turbidity and no increase in particle content in 4 hr at 23 °C	2087	C
Tobramycin sulfate	AB	5 mg/ml[a]	SEQ	0.4 mg/ml[a]	Physically compatible with little or no change in measured turbidity and no increase in particle content in 4 hr at 23 °C	2087	C
Trimethoprim–sulfamethoxazole	ES	0.8 + 4 mg/ml[a]	SEQ	0.4 mg/ml[a]	Physically compatible with little or no change in measured turbidity and no increase in particle content in 4 hr at 23 °C	2087	C
Vancomycin HCl	AB	10 mg/ml[a]	SEQ	0.4 mg/ml[a]	Physically compatible with little or no change in measured turbidity and no increase in particle content in 4 hr at 23 °C	2087	C
Vinblastine sulfate	FAU	0.12 mg/ml[a]	SEQ	0.4 mg/ml[a]	Physically compatible with little or no change in measured turbidity and no increase in particle content in 4 hr at 23 °C	2087	C
Vincristine sulfate	FAU	0.05 mg/ml[a]	SEQ	0.4 mg/ml[a]	Physically compatible with little or no change in measured turbidity and no increase in particle content in 4 hr at 23 °C	2087	C
Vinorelbine tartrate	BW	1 mg/ml[a]	SEQ	0.4 mg/ml[a]	Physically compatible with little or no change in measured turbidity and no increase in particle content in 4 hr at 23 °C	2087	C
Zidovudine	BW	4 mg/ml[a]	SEQ	0.4 mg/ml[a]	Physically compatible with little or no change in measured turbidity and no increase in particle content in 4 hr at 23 °C	2087	C

[a]*Tested in dextrose 5% in water.*
[b]*Tested in sodium chloride 0.9%.*
[c]*Sodium carbonate–containing formulation tested.*

Additional Compatibility Information

Infusion Solutions — Doxorubicin HCl liposome injection should be diluted for infusion only with dextrose 5% in water. Other diluents, including those containing a bacteriostatic agent such as benzyl alcohol, should not be used. After dilution in dextrose 5% in water, the admixture should be stored under refrigeration at 2 to 8 °C and administered within 24 hours. (2)

Other Drugs — The manufacturer recommends not mixing doxorubicin HCl liposome injection with other drugs. (2)

DOXYCYCLINE HYCLATE
AHFS 8:12.24

Products — Doxycycline hyclate (doxycycline HCl hemiethanolate hemihydrate) is available in vials containing the equivalent of 100 and 200 mg of doxycycline with 480 and 960 mg of ascorbic acid, respectively. Mannitol is also present in products from some manufacturers. (2; 4)

Reconstitute the 100-mg vial with 10 ml and the 200-mg vial with 20 ml of sterile water for injection or other compatible diluent. The resultant solution contains the equivalent of 10 mg/ml of doxycycline. This solution must be further diluted to a concentration of 0.1 to 1 mg/ml with a compatible infusion solution prior to use. (2; 4) (See Stability and Additional Compatibility Information.)

pH — The pH range for reconstituted solutions is 1.8 to 3.3. (4)

Osmolality — Doxycycline hyclate 10 mg/ml in sterile water for injection has an osmolality of 507 mOsm/kg. (1689) The osmolality of doxycycline hyclate (Elkins-Sinn) 1 mg/ml was determined to be 292 mOsm/kg in dextrose 5% in water and 310 mOsm/kg in sodium chloride 0.9%. (1375)

Trade Name(s) — Vibramycin Intravenous.

Administration — Doxycycline hyclate is administered by slow intravenous infusion, usually over one to four hours; rapid administration should be avoided. The reconstituted solution should be diluted further with a compatible infusion solution to a concentration of approximately 0.1 to 1 mg/ml. Other parenteral routes are not recommended, and extravasation should be avoided. (2; 4)

Stability — Solutions of doxycycline hyclate diluted for infusion must be protected from direct sunlight. (2)

Doxycycline hyclate 0.1- to 1-mg/ml solutions may be stored for up to 72 hours prior to starting the infusion when kept in the refrigerator and protected from both direct sunlight and artificial light and when diluted in the following infusion solutions:

Dextrose 5% in water
Invert sugar 10% in water
Normosol M in dextrose 5% in water
Normosol R in dextrose 5% in water
Plasma-Lyte 56 in dextrose 5%
Plasma-Lyte 148 in dextrose 5%
Ringer's injection
Sodium chloride 0.9%

Infusion must then be completed within 12 hours. (2)

Doxycycline hyclate is stable for 48 hours at 25 °C when diluted to 0.1 to 1 mg/ml in dextrose 5% in water or sodium chloride 0.9%. (2)

Freezing Solutions — The manufacturers state that at a concentration of 10 mg/ml in sterile water for injection, doxycycline hyclate is stable for eight weeks when frozen at −20 °C. Frozen solutions that have been completely thawed should not be heated. Thawed solutions should not be refrozen. (2; 4)

Doxycycline hyclate (Pfizer) 10 mg/ml in sterile water for injection retained potency for eight weeks when frozen at −20 °C, as determined by both microbiological and spectrophotometric assays. At a concentration of 1 mg/ml in dextrose 5% in water, doxycycline hyclate also showed no significant decomposition over eight weeks at −20 °C when assayed by either method. (310)

Ambulatory Pumps — Stiles et al. evaluated the stability of doxycycline hyclate (Elkins-Sinn) 2 mg/ml in sterile water for injection and sodium chloride 0.9% in 100-ml portable pump reservoirs (Pharmacia Deltec) during simulated administration for 24 hours. The drug solutions were tested by HPLC analysis when administered immediately after preparation and after storage for 24 hours at 5 °C before 24-hour administration. During simulated administration, some reservoirs were kept at 30 °C; others were placed in insulated pouches with frozen (−20 °C) gel packs to keep them chilled below the ambient temperature. Freshly prepared doxycycline hyclate solutions exhibited a 5% or less loss by HPLC with or without the insulated pouch. However, solutions stored for 24 hours at 5 °C maintained adequate stability through six hours only; the presence or absence of the insulated pouch had no consistent effect on drug stability. (1779)

Elastomeric Reservoir Pumps — Doxycycline hyclate solutions in elastomeric reservoir pumps have been stated by the pump manufacturers to be stable for the following time periods frozen, refrigerated (REF), or at room temperature (RT) (31):

Pump Reservoir(s)	Conc.	Frozen	REF	RT
Medflo	1.5 mg/ml[a,b]	8 weeks	3 days	2 days
ReadyMed	1 mg/ml	8 weeks[a]	3 days[a,b]	12 hr[a,b]

[a] *In dextrose 5% in water.*
[b] *In sodium chloride 0.9%.*

Sorption — Doxycycline (Pfizer) 15 mg/L in sodium chloride 0.9% (Travenol) in PVC bags did not exhibit significant sorption to the plastic during one week of storage at room temperature (15 to 20 °C). (536)

In another evaluation, doxycycline (Pfizer) 15 mg/L in sodium chloride 0.9% did not exhibit any loss due to sorption during a seven-hour simulated infusion through an infusion set (Travenol) consisting of a cellulose propionate burette chamber and 170 cm of PVC tubing. (606)

The drug was also tested as a simulated infusion over at least one hour by a syringe pump system. A glass syringe on a syringe pump was fitted with 20 cm of polyethylene tubing or 50 cm of Silastic tubing. No loss of drug due to sorption was observed with either tubing. (606)

A 25-ml aliquot of the doxycycline (Pfizer) 15 mg/L in sodium chloride 0.9% solution was stored in all-plastic syringes composed of polypropylene barrels and polyethylene plungers for 24 hours at room temperature in the dark. No loss of drug due to sorption was observed. (606)

Central Venous Catheter — Doxycycline hyclate (Fujisawa) 0.5 mg/ml in dextrose 5% in water was found to be compatible with the ARROWg+ard Blue Plus (Arrow International) chlorhexidine-bearing triple-lumen central catheter. HPLC analysis was used to evaluate completeness of drug delivery through the catheter and the amount of chlorhexidine removed from the internal lumens. Essentially complete delivery of the drug was found with little or no drug loss occurring. Furthermore, chlorhexidine delivered from the catheter remained at trace amounts with no substantial increase due to the delivery of the drug through the catheter. (2335)

Compatibility Information

Solution Compatibility

Doxycycline hyclate

Solution	*Mfr*	*Mfr*	*Conc/L*	*Remarks*	*Ref*	*C/I*
Dextrose 5% in water	BA[a]	PF	800 mg and 1 g	Visually compatible with 5 to 8% loss by HPLC in 96 hr at 23 °C. 2% loss in 7 days at 4 °C	1928	C
Sodium chloride 0.9%	AB[b]	ES	2 g	5% loss by HPLC for freshly prepared solutions during 24-hr simulated administration at 30 °C via portable pump	1779	C
	BA[a]	PF	800 mg and 1 g	Visually compatible with 8% loss by HPLC in 96 hr at 23 °C. 4% or less loss in 7 days at 4 °C	1928	C

[a] *Tested in PVC containers.*
[b] *Tested in portable pump reservoirs (Pharmacia Deltec).*

Additive Compatibility

Doxycycline hyclate

Drug	*Mfr*	*Conc/L*	*Mfr*	*Conc/L*	*Test Soln*	*Remarks*	*Ref*	*C/I*
Meropenem	ZEN	1 g	RR	200 mg	NS	Visually compatible for 4 hr at room temperature	1994	C
	ZEN	20 g	RR	200 mg	NS	Brown discoloration forms in 1 hr at room temperature	1994	I
Ranitidine HCl	GL	100 mg	PF	200 mg	D5W	Physically compatible for 24 hr at ambient temperature under fluorescent light	1151	C

[a] *Tested in PVC containers.*

Drugs in Syringe Compatibility

Doxycycline hyclate

Drug (in syringe)	*Mfr*	*Amt*	*Mfr*	*Amt*	*Remarks*	*Ref*	*C/I*
Doxapram HCl	RB	400 mg/ 20 ml		100 mg/ 5 ml	Physically compatible with 3% doxapram loss in 24 hr	1177	C

Y-Site Injection Compatibility (1:1 Mixture)

Doxycycline hyclate

Drug	*Mfr*	*Conc*	*Mfr*	*Conc*	*Remarks*	*Ref*	*C/I*
Acyclovir sodium	BW	5 mg/ml[a]	PF	1 mg/ml[a]	Physically compatible for 4 hr at 25 °C	1157	C
Allopurinol sodium	BW	3 mg/ml[b]	ES	1 mg/ml[b]	Small particles form immediately. Hazy brown solution with precipitate develops in 4 hr	1686	I
Amifostine	USB	10 mg/ml[a]	LY	1 mg/ml[a]	Physically compatible with no change in measured turbidity or increase in particle content in 4 hr at 23 °C	1845	C
Amiodarone HCl	LZ	4 mg/ml[c]	ACC	0.25 mg/ml[c]	Physically compatible for 4 hr at room temperature	1444	C
Aztreonam	SQ	40 mg/ml[a]	ES	1 mg/ml[a]	Physically compatible with no subvisual haze or particle formation in 4 hr at 23 °C	1758	C

Y-Site Injection Compatibility (1:1 Mixture) (Cont.)

Drug	*Mfr*	*Conc*	Doxycycline hyclate *Mfr*	Doxycycline hyclate *Conc*	*Remarks*	*Ref*	*C/I*
Cisatracurium besylate	GW	0.1, 2, 5 mg/ml[a]	FUJ	1 mg/ml[a]	Physically compatible with no change in measured turbidity or increase in particle content in 4 hr at 23 °C	2074	C
Cyclophosphamide	MJ	20 mg/ml[a]	ES	1 mg/ml[a]	Physically compatible for 4 hr at 25 °C	1194	C
Diltiazem HCl	MMD	5 mg/ml	RR	1 and 10 mg/ml[b]	Visually compatible	1807	C
Docetaxel	RPR	0.9 mg/ml[a]	FUJ	1 mg/ml[a]	Physically compatible with no change in measured turbidity or increase in particle content in 4 hr at 23 °C	2224	C
Etoposide phosphate	BR	5 mg/ml[a]	FUJ	1 mg/ml[a]	Physically compatible with no change in measured turbidity or increase in particle content in 4 hr at 23 °C	2218	C
Filgrastim	AMG	30 μg/ml[a]	ES	1 mg/ml[a]	Physically compatible with no change in measured turbidity or increase in particle content in 4 hr at 22 °C	1687	C
Fludarabine phosphate	BX	1 mg/ml[a]	ES	1 mg/ml[a]	Physically compatible for 4 hr at room temperature under fluorescent light	1439	C
Gemcitabine HCl	LI	10 mg/ml[b]	FUJ	1 mg/ml[b]	Physically compatible with no change in measured turbidity or increase in particle content in 4 hr at 23 °C	2226	C
Granisetron HCl	SKB	0.05 mg/ml[a]	LY	1 mg/ml[a]	Physically compatible with no change in measured turbidity or increase in particle content in 4 hr at 23 °C	2000	C
Heparin sodium	TR	50 units/ml	ES	1 mg/ml[a]	Visually incompatible within 4 hr at 25 °C	1793	I
Hetastarch in lactated electrolyte injection (Hextend)	AB	6%	APP	1 mg/ml[a]	Physically compatible with no change in measured turbidity or increase in particle content in 4 hr at 23 °C	2339	C
Hetastarch in 0.9% sodium chloride	DCC	6%	LY	1 mg/ml[a]	Physically compatible for 4 hr at room temperature by visual examination	1313	C
	DCC	6%	LY	1 mg/ml[a]	White particle in one of five vials. No evidence of incompatibility during Y-site infusion	1315	?
Hydromorphone HCl	WY	0.2 mg/ml[a]	ES	1 mg/ml[a]	Physically compatible for at least 4 hr at 25 °C under fluorescent light	987	C
Linezolid	PHU	2 mg/ml	FUJ	1 mg/ml[a]	Physically compatible with no change in measured turbidity or increase in particle content in 4 hr at 23 °C	2264	C
Magnesium sulfate	IX	16.7, 33.3, 66.7, 100 mg/ml[a]	PF	1 mg/ml[a]	Physically compatible for at least 4 hr at 32 °C	813	C
Melphalan HCl	BW	0.1 mg/ml[b]	LY	1 mg/ml[b]	Physically compatible with no change in measured turbidity or increase in particle content in 3 hr at 22 °C	1557	C
Meperidine HCl	WY	10 mg/ml[a]	ES	1 mg/ml[a]	Physically compatible for at least 4 hr at 25 °C under fluorescent light	987	C
Meropenem	ZEN	1 mg/ml[b]	RR	1 mg/ml[d]	Visually compatible for 4 hr at room temperature	1994	C
	ZEN	50 mg/ml[b]	RR	1 mg/ml[d]	Amber discoloration forms within 30 min	1994	I

Y-Site Injection Compatibility (1:1 Mixture) (Cont.)

Doxycycline hyclate

Drug	*Mfr*	*Conc*	*Mfr*	*Conc*	*Remarks*	*Ref*	*C/I*
Morphine sulfate	WI	1 mg/ml[a]	ES	1 mg/ml[a]	Physically compatible for at least 4 hr at 25 °C under fluorescent light	987	C
Ondansetron HCl	GL	1 mg/ml[b]	ES	1 mg/ml[a]	Physically compatible for 4 hr at 22 °C	1365	C
Perphenazine	SC	0.02 mg/ml[a]	ES	1 mg/ml[a]	Physically compatible for 4 hr at 25 °C	1155	C
Piperacillin sodium–tazobactam sodium	LE	40 + 5 mg/ml[a]	ES	1 mg/ml[a]	Heavy white turbidity forms immediately	1688	I
Propofol	ZEN	10 mg/ml	LY	1 mg/ml[a]	Physically compatible for 1 hr at 23 °C with no increase in particle content	2066	C
Remifentanil HCl	GW	0.025 and 0.25 mg/ml[b]	FUJ	1 mg/ml[a]	Physically compatible with no change in measured turbidity or increase in particle content in 4 hr at 23 °C	2075	C
Sargramostim	IMM	10 μg/ml[b]	LY	1 mg/ml[b]	Physically compatible for 4 hr at 22 °C	1436	C
Tacrolimus	FUJ	1 mg/ml[b]	RR	5 mg/ml[a]	Visually compatible for 24 hr at 25 °C	1630	C
Teniposide	BR	0.1 mg/ml[a]	LY	1 mg/ml[a]	Physically compatible with no subvisual haze or particle formation in 4 hr at 23 °C	1725	C
Theophylline	TR	4 mg/ml	ES	1 mg/ml[a]	Visually compatible for 6 hr at 25 °C	1793	C
Thiotepa	IMM[e]	1 mg/ml[a]	LY	1 mg/ml[a]	Physically compatible with no change in measured turbidity or increase in particle content in 4 hr at 23 °C	1861	C
TNA #218 to #226[f]			FUJ	1 mg/ml[a]	Damage to emulsion integrity occurs immediately with free oil formation possible	2215	I
TPN #61[f]		[g]	PF	10 mg/ml[h]	Physically compatible	987	C
		[i]	PF	60 mg/6 ml[h]	Physically compatible	987	C
TPN #212 to #215[f]			LY	1 mg/ml[a]	Physically compatible with no change in measured turbidity or increase in particle content in 4 hr at 23 °C	2109	C
Vinorelbine tartrate	BW	1 mg/ml[b]	ES	1 mg/ml[b]	Physically compatible with no change in measured turbidity or increase in particle content in 4 hr at 22 °C	1558	C

[a] *Tested in dextrose 5% in water.*
[b] *Tested in sodium chloride 0.9%.*
[c] *Tested in both dextrose 5% in water and sodium chloride 0.9%.*
[d] *Tested in sterile water for injection.*
[e] *Lyophilized formulation tested.*
[f] *Refer to Appendix I for the composition of parenteral nutrition solutions. TNA indicates a 3-in-1 admixture, and TPN indicates a 2-in-1 admixture.*
[g] *Run at 21 ml/hr.*
[h] *Given over 30 minutes by syringe pump.*
[i] *Run at 94 ml/hr.*

Additional Compatibility Information

Infusion Solutions — When protected from direct sunlight, the Elkins-Sinn product of doxycycline hyclate at concentrations of 0.1 to 1 mg/ml must be completely infused within 24 hours of reconstitution to ensure adequate stability in the following infusion solutions (4):

Dextrose 5% in water
Invert sugar 10% in water
Normosol M in dextrose 5% in water
Normosol R in dextrose 5% in water
Plasma-Lyte 56 in dextrose 5%
Plasma-Lyte 148 in dextrose 5%
Ringer's injection
Sodium chloride 0.9%

Vibramycin is stable at these concentrations for 48 hours at 25 °C in dextrose 5% in water and sodium chloride 0.9%. However, to ensure stability of admixtures in the other infusion solutions listed above, infusion must be completed within 12 hours. (2) When stored under refrigeration and protected from light, doxycycline hyclate is stable in these same solutions for 72 hours. (2; 4)

At a concentration of 0.1 to 1.0 mg/ml in Ringer's injection, lactated, or dextrose 5% in Ringer's injection, lactated, and with protection from direct sunlight, infusion of doxycycline hyclate (Roerig and Elkins-Sinn) must be completed within six hours after constitution to ensure adequate stability. (2; 4)

Riboflavin — In vitro testing of riboflavin-5′-phosphate at a concentration of 0.1% with doxycycline HCl 0.025% in sterile distilled water showed significant reduction in antibiotic activity in one hour at 25 °C. (314)

Acid-Sensitive Additives — Because of the acidity of the solution, doxycycline hyclate may precipitate the free acids of barbiturate salts and sulfonamide derivatives. It may also adversely affect the stability of acid-labile additives such as erythromycin lactobionate, penicillin G potassium, oxacillin sodium, methicillin sodium, and nafcillin sodium. (6; 20; 22; 27)

DROPERIDOL
AHFS 28:24.92

Products — Droperidol is available from various manufacturers in 1- and 2-ml ampuls, 2-ml syringe cartridges, and 1- and 2-ml vials. (29; 154) Each milliliter of solution contains droperidol 2.5 mg with lactic acid to adjust the pH. (4)

pH — From 3 to 3.8. (4)

Osmolality — The osmolality of droperidol 2.5 mg/ml was determined to be 16 mOsm/kg. (1233)

Trade Name(s) — Inapsine.

Administration — Droperidol may be administered intramuscularly or slowly intravenously. Intravenous infusion has been used in high-risk patients. (4)

Stability — Intact ampuls and vials of droperidol should be stored at controlled room temperature and protected from light. (4)

Syringes — The stability of droperidol 2.5 mg/ml repackaged in polypropylene syringes was evaluated by spectrophotometric and potentiometric methods. Little or no change in concentration was found after four weeks of storage at room temperature not exposed to direct light. (2164)

Droperidol (American Regent) 1.25 mg/ml in sodium chloride injection 0.9% packaged in polypropylene syringes (Sherwood) was physically stable and exhibited little or no loss by stability-indicating HPLC analysis in 24 hours stored at 23 °C. Under refrigeration at 4 °C, droperidol precipitated within four hours. (2199)

Sorption — Storage of droperidol (Janssen) 20 mg/L in PVC containers of dextrose 5% in water and sodium chloride 0.9% for seven days at 27 °C resulted in no apparent drug loss due to sorption. In fact, small increases in the droperidol concentration occurred due to permeation and evaporation of water. (750)

When Ringer's injection, lactated, in PVC containers was the diluent for the 20-mg/L dilution, however, the droperidol concentration only remained constant for 24 hours at 27 °C. By 48 hours, a 15% drug loss had occurred; in seven days, a 25% loss was observed. The authors attributed the drug loss to sorption to the PVC bags. The 24-hour delay was believed to result from the use of new evacuated PVC bags that were subsequently filled for the tests, causing a delayed initial hydration of the plastic. Presumably, this sorption phenomenon can occur more rapidly if commercially prepared PVC bags of Ringer's injection, lactated, with well-hydrated plastic are used to prepare the admixture. (750)

Central Venous Catheter — Droperidol (Abbott) 0.4 mg/ml in dextrose 5% in water was found to be compatible with the ARROWg+ard Blue Plus (Arrow International) chlorhexidine-bearing triple-lumen central catheter. HPLC analysis was used to evaluate completeness of drug delivery through the catheter and the amount of chlorhexidine removed from the internal lumens. Essentially complete delivery of the drug was found with little or no drug loss occurring. Furthermore, chlorhexidine delivered from the catheter remained at trace amounts with no substantial increase due to the delivery of the drug through the catheter. (2335)

Compatibility Information

Solution Compatibility

Droperidol

Solution	*Mfr*	*Mfr*	*Conc/L*	*Remarks*	*Ref*	*C/I*
Dextrose 5% in water	AB[a], TR[b]	JN	20 mg	Physically compatible and chemically stable with no drug loss for 7 days at 27 °C	750	C
Ringer's injection, lactated	TR[a]	JN	20 mg	Physically compatible and chemically stable with no drug loss for 7 days at 27 °C	750	C

Solution Compatibility (Cont.)

Droperidol

Solution	*Mfr*	*Mfr*	*Conc/L*	*Remarks*	*Ref*	*C/I*
	TR[b]	JN	20 mg	Physically compatible and chemically stable with no drug loss for 24 hr at 27 °C. 15% loss in 48 hr attributed to sorption. See Sorption section	750	C
Sodium chloride 0.9%	AB[a]	JN	20 mg	Physically compatible with about 5% drug loss in 7 days at 27 °C	750	C
	TR[b]	JN	20 mg	Physically compatible and chemically stable with no drug loss for 7 days at 27 °C	750	C

[a]*Tested in glass containers.*
[b]*Tested in PVC containers.*

Drugs in Syringe Compatibility

Droperidol

Drug (in syringe)	*Mfr*	*Amt*	*Mfr*	*Amt*	*Remarks*	*Ref*	*C/I*
Atropine sulfate	ST	0.4 mg/ 1 ml	MN	2.5 mg/ 1 ml	Physically compatible for at least 15 min	326	C
Bleomycin sulfate		1.5 units/ 0.5 ml		1.25 mg/ 0.5 ml	Physically compatible for 5 min at room temperature followed by 8 min of centrifugation	980	C
Butorphanol tartrate	BR	4 mg/ 2 ml	MN	5 mg/ 2 ml	Physically compatible both macroscopically and microscopically for 30 min at room temperature	566	C
Chlorpromazine HCl	PO	50 mg/ 2 ml	MN	2.5 mg/ 1 ml	Physically compatible for at least 15 min	326	C
Cimetidine HCl	SKF	300 mg/ 2 ml	JN	5 mg/ 2 ml	Physically compatible for 4 hr at 25 °C	25	C
Cisplatin		0.5 mg/ 0.5 ml		1.25 mg/ 0.5 ml	Physically compatible for 5 min at room temperature followed by 8 min of centrifugation	980	C
Cyclophosphamide		10 mg/ 0.5 ml		1.25 mg/ 0.5 ml	Physically compatible for 5 min at room temperature followed by 8 min of centrifugation	980	C
Dimenhydrinate	HR	50 mg/ 1 ml	MN	2.5 mg/ 1 ml	Physically compatible for at least 15 min	326	C
Diphenhydramine HCl	PD	50 mg/ 1 ml	MN	2.5 mg/ 1 ml	Physically compatible for at least 15 min	326	C
Doxorubicin HCl		1 mg/ 0.5 ml		1.25 mg/ 0.5 ml	Physically compatible for 5 min at room temperature followed by 8 min of centrifugation	980	C
Fentanyl citrate	MN	0.05 mg/ 1 ml	MN	2.5 mg/ 1 ml	Physically compatible for at least 15 min	326	C
Fluorouracil		25 mg/ 0.5 ml		1.25 mg/ 0.5 ml	Immediate precipitation	980	I
Furosemide		5 mg/ 0.5 ml		1.25 mg/ 0.5 ml	Immediate precipitation	980	I
Glycopyrrolate	RB	0.2 mg/ 1 ml	MN	2.5 mg/ 1 ml	Physically compatible and pH in stability range for glycopyrrolate for 48 hr at 25 °C	331	C
	RB	0.2 mg/ 1 ml	MN	5 mg/ 2 ml	Physically compatible and pH in stability range for glycopyrrolate for 48 hr at 25 °C	331	C
	RB	0.4 mg/ 2 ml	MN	2.5 mg/ 1 ml	Physically compatible and pH in stability range for glycopyrrolate for 48 hr at 25 °C	331	C

Drugs in Syringe Compatibility (Cont.)

			Droperidol				
Drug (in syringe)	*Mfr*	*Amt*	*Mfr*	*Amt*	*Remarks*	*Ref*	*C/I*
Heparin sodium		500 units/ 0.5 ml		1.25 mg/ 0.5 ml	Immediate precipitation	980	I
		2500 units/ 1 ml		5 mg/ 2 ml	Turbidity or precipitate forms within 5 min	1053	I
Hydroxyzine HCl	PF	50 mg/ 1 ml	MN	2.5 mg/ 1 ml	Physically compatible for at least 15 min	326	C
Leucovorin calcium		5 mg/ 0.5 ml		1.25 mg/ 0.5 ml	Immediate precipitation	980	I
Meperidine HCl	WI	50 mg/ 1 ml	MN	2.5 mg/ 1 ml	Physically compatible for at least 15 min	326	C
Methotrexate sodium		12.5 mg/ 0.5 ml		1.25 mg/ 0.5 ml	Immediate precipitation	980	I
Metoclopramide HCl	NO	10 mg/ 2 ml	MN	2.5 mg/ 1 ml	Physically compatible both macroscopically and microscopically for 15 min at room temperature	565	C
		2.5 mg/ 0.5 ml		1.25 mg/ 0.5 ml	Physically compatible for 5 min at room temperature followed by 8 min of centrifugation	980	C
Midazolam HCl	RC	5 mg/ 1 ml	JN	2.5 mg/ 1 ml	Physically compatible for 4 hr at 25 °C under fluorescent light	1145	C
Mitomycin		0.25 mg/ 0.5 ml		1.25 mg/ 0.5 ml	Physically compatible for 5 min at room temperature followed by 8 min of centrifugation	980	C
Morphine sulfate	ST	15 mg/ 1 ml	MN	2.5 mg/ 1 ml	Physically compatible for at least 15 min	326	C
Nalbuphine HCl	EN	5 mg/ 0.5 ml	JN	5 mg/ 2 ml	Physically compatible for 36 hr at 27 °C	762	C
	EN	10 mg/ 1 ml	JN	2.5 mg/ 1 ml	Physically compatible for 36 hr at 27 °C	762	C
	EN	5 mg/ 0.5 ml	JN	2.5 mg/ 1 ml	Physically compatible for 36 hr at 27 °C	762	C
	DU	10 mg/ 1 ml	JN	5 mg/ 2 ml	Physically compatible for 48 hr	128	C
	DU	20 mg/ 1 ml	JN	5 mg/ 2 ml	Physically compatible for 48 hr	128	C
Ondansetron HCl	GW	1 mg/ml[a]	AMR	1.25 mg/ ml[a]	Droperidol precipitates in less than 4 hr at 4 °C. At 23 °C, little or no loss of either drug occurs by HPLC in 8 hr, but droperidol precipitates after that time	2199	I
Papaveretum	RC[b]	20 mg/ 1 ml	MN	2.5 mg/ 1 ml	Visually compatible for at least 15 min	326	C
Pentazocine lactate	WI	30 mg/ 1 ml	MN	2.5 mg/ 1 ml	Physically compatible for at least 15 min	326	C
Pentobarbital sodium	AB	50 mg/ 1 ml	MN	2.5 mg/ 1 ml	Physically incompatible within 15 min	326	I
Perphenazine	SC	5 mg/ 1 ml	MN	5 mg/ 2 ml	Physically compatible both macroscopically and microscopically for 30 min at room temperature	566	C

Drugs in Syringe Compatibility (Cont.)

			Droperidol				
Drug (in syringe)	*Mfr*	*Amt*	*Mfr*	*Amt*	*Remarks*	*Ref*	*C/I*
Prochlorperazine edisylate	PO	5 mg/ 1 ml	MN	2.5 mg/ 1 ml	Physically compatible for at least 15 min	326	C
Promazine HCl	WY	50 mg/ 1 ml	MN	2.5 mg/ 1 ml	Physically compatible for at least 15 min	326	C
Promethazine HCl	PO	50 mg/ 2 ml	MN	2.5 mg/ 1 ml	Physically compatible for at least 15 min	326	C
Scopolamine HBr	ST	0.4 mg/ 1 ml	MN	2.5 mg/ 1 ml	Physically compatible for at least 15 min	326	C
Vinblastine sulfate		0.5 mg/ 0.5 ml		1.25 mg/ 0.5 ml	Physically compatible for 5 min at room temperature followed by 8 min of centrifugation	980	C
Vincristine sulfate		0.5 mg/ 0.5 ml		1.25 mg/ 0.5 ml	Physically compatible for 5 min at room temperature followed by 8 min of centrifugation	980	C

[a]Tested in sodium chloride 0.9%.
[b]The former formulation was tested.

Y-Site Injection Compatibility (1:1 Mixture)

			Droperidol				
Drug	*Mfr*	*Conc*	*Mfr*	*Conc*	*Remarks*	*Ref*	*C/I*
Alatrofloxacin mesylate	PF	1.43 mg/ml[a]	AMR	2.5 mg/ml	Visually and microscopically compatible with the droperidol pushed through a Y-site over 2 min	2235	C
Allopurinol sodium	BW	3 mg/ml[b]	JN	0.4 mg/ml[b]	Heavy turbidity with particles forms immediately	1686	I
Amifostine	USB	10 mg/ml[a]	JN	0.4 mg/ml[a]	Physically compatible with no change in measured turbidity or increase in particle content in 4 hr at 23 °C	1845	C
Amphotericin B cholesteryl sulfate complex	SEQ	0.83 mg/ml[a]	AST	2.5 mg/ml	Gross precipitate forms	2117	I
Aztreonam	SQ	40 mg/ml[a]	JN	0.4 mg/ml[a]	Physically compatible with no subvisual haze or particle formation in 4 hr at 23 °C	1758	C
Bleomycin sulfate		3 units/ml		2.5 mg/ml	Drugs injected sequentially into Y-site with no flush between. No visually apparent precipitate	980	C
Cefepime HCl	BMS	20 mg/ml[a]	JN	0.4 mg/ml[a]	Haze forms immediately and becomes flocculent precipitate in 4 hr	1689	I
Cisatracurium besylate	GW	0.1, 2, 5 mg/ ml[a]	AB	2.5 mg/ml	Physically compatible with no change in measured turbidity or increase in particle content in 4 hr at 23 °C	2074	C
Cladribine	ORT	0.015[b] and 0.5[c] mg/ml	JN	0.4 mg/ml[b]	Physically compatible with no change in measured turbidity or increase in particle content in 4 hr at 23 °C	1969	C
Cisplatin		1 mg/ml		2.5 mg/ml	Drugs injected sequentially into Y-site with no flush between. No visually apparent precipitate	980	C
	BR	1 mg/ml	JN	20 μg/ml[a]	Visually compatible for 4 hr at room temperature under fluorescent light	1685	C

Y-Site Injection Compatibility (1:1 Mixture) (Cont.)

			Droperidol				
Drug	*Mfr*	*Conc*	*Mfr*	*Conc*	*Remarks*	*Ref*	*C/I*
Cyclophosphamide		20 mg/ml		2.5 mg/ml	Drugs injected sequentially into Y-site with no flush between. No visually apparent precipitate	980	C
	MJ	10 mg/ml[a]	JN	20 μg/ml[a]	Visually compatible for 4 hr at room temperature under fluorescent light	1685	C
Cytarabine	UP	50 mg/ml	JN	20 μg/ml[a]	Visually compatible for 4 hr at room temperature under fluorescent light	1685	C
Docetaxel	RPR	0.9 mg/ml[a]	AST	0.4 mg/ml[a]	Physically compatible with no change in measured turbidity or increase in particle content in 4 hr at 23 °C	2224	C
Doxorubicin HCl		2 mg/ml		2.5 mg/ml	Drugs injected sequentially into Y-site with no flush between. No visually apparent precipitate	980	C
	AD	0.2 mg/ml[a]	JN	20 μg/ml[a]	Visually compatible for 4 hr at room temperature under fluorescent light	1685	C
Doxorubicin HCl liposome injection	SEQ	0.4 mg/ml[a]	AST	0.4 mg/ml[a]	Physically compatible with little or no change in measured turbidity and no increase in particle content in 4 hr at 23 °C	2087	C
Etoposide phosphate	BR	5 mg/ml[a]	AST	0.4 mg/ml[a]	Physically compatible with no change in measured turbidity or increase in particle content in 4 hr at 23 °C	2218	C
Famotidine	ME	2 mg/ml[b]		0.4 mg/ml[a]	Visually compatible for 4 hr at 22 °C	1936	C
Filgrastim	AMG	30 μg/ml[a]	JN	0.4 mg/ml[a]	Physically compatible with no change in measured turbidity or increase in particle content in 4 hr at 22 °C	1687	C
Fluconazole	RR	2 mg/ml	DU	2.5 mg/ml	Physically compatible for 24 hr at 25 °C	1407	C
Fludarabine phosphate	BX	1 mg/ml[a]	JN	0.4 mg/ml[a]	Physically compatible for 4 hr at room temperature under fluorescent light	1439	C
Fluorouracil		50 mg/ml		2.5 mg/ml	Drugs injected sequentially into Y-site with no flush between. Immediate precipitation	980	I
Foscarnet sodium	AST	24 mg/ml	QU	2.5 mg/ml	Delayed formation of fine yellow precipitate	1335	I
Furosemide		10 mg/ml		2.5 mg/ml	Drugs injected sequentially into Y-site with no flush between. Immediate precipitation	980	I
		10 mg/ml		2.5 mg/ml	Precipitate forms	977	I
Gatifloxacin	BMS	2 mg/ml[a]	AMR	0.4 mg/ml[a]	Physically compatible with no change in measured haze or increase in particle content in 4 hr at 23 °C	2234	C
Gemcitabine HCl	LI	10 mg/ml[b]	AST	0.4 mg/ml[b]	Physically compatible with no change in measured turbidity or increase in particle content in 4 hr at 23 °C	2226	C
Granisetron HCl	SKB	0.05 mg/ml[a]	AB	0.4 mg/ml[a]	Physically compatible with no change in measured turbidity or increase in particle content in 4 hr at 23 °C	2000	C

Y-Site Injection Compatibility (1:1 Mixture) (Cont.)

			Droperidol				
Drug	*Mfr*	*Conc*	*Mfr*	*Conc*	*Remarks*	*Ref*	*C/I*
Heparin sodium		1000 units/ml		2.5 mg/ml	Drugs injected sequentially into Y-site with no flush between. Immediate precipitation	980	I
		50 units/ml/min[b]	JN	5 mg/2 ml[d]	White turbidity	1053	I
	UP	1000 units/L[e]	CR	1.25 mg/ml	Physically compatible for at least 4 hr at room temperature by visual and microscopic examination	534	C
Hetastarch in lactated electrolyte injection (Hextend)	AB	6%	AMR	2.5 mg/ml	Physically compatible with no change in measured turbidity or increase in particle content in 4 hr at 23 °C	2339	C
Hydrocortisone sodium succinate	UP	10 mg/L[e]	CR	1.25 mg/ml	Physically compatible for at least 4 hr at room temperature by visual and microscopic examination	534	C
Idarubicin HCl	AD	1 mg/ml[b]	AMR	0.04[a] and 2.5 mg/ml	Visually compatible for 24 hr at 25 °C	1525	C
Leucovorin calcium		10 mg/ml		2.5 mg/ml	Drugs injected sequentially into Y-site with no flush between. Immediate precipitation	980	I
Linezolid	PHU	2 mg/ml	AMR	0.4 mg/ml[a]	Physically compatible with no change in measured turbidity or increase in particle content in 4 hr at 23 °C	2264	C
Melphalan HCl	BW	0.1 mg/ml[b]	JN	0.4 mg/ml[b]	Physically compatible with no change in measured turbidity or increase in particle content in 3 hr at 22 °C	1557	C
Meperidine HCl	AB	10 mg/ml	AMR	2.5 mg/ml	Physically compatible for 4 hr at 25 °C	1397	C
Methotrexate sodium		25 mg/ml		2.5 mg/ml	Precipitate forms	977	I
		25 mg/ml		2.5 mg/ml	Drugs injected sequentially into Y-site with no flush between. Immediate precipitation	980	I
	AD	15 mg/ml[f]	JN	20 μg/ml[a]	Visually compatible for 4 hr at room temperature under fluorescent light	1685	C
Metoclopramide HCl		5 mg/ml		2.5 mg/ml	Drugs injected sequentially into Y-site with no flush between. No visually apparent precipitate	980	C
Mitomycin		0.5 mg/ml		2.5 mg/ml	Drugs injected sequentially into Y-site with no flush between. No visually apparent precipitate	980	C
Nafcillin sodium	WY	33 mg/ml[b]		2.5 mg/ml	Precipitate forms, probably free nafcillin	547	I
Ondansetron HCl	GL	1 mg/ml[b]	JN	0.4 mg/ml[a]	Physically compatible for 4 hr at 22 °C	1365	C
Paclitaxel	NCI	1.2 mg/ml[a]	JN	0.4 mg/ml[a]	Physically compatible with no change in measured turbidity in 4 hr at 22 °C	1556	C
Piperacillin sodium–tazobactam sodium	LE	40 + 5 mg/ml[a]	JN	0.4 mg/ml[a]	Heavy white turbidity with white precipitate forms immediately	1688	I
Potassium chloride	AB	40 mEq/L[e]	CR	1.25 mg/ml	Physically compatible for at least 4 hr at room temperature by visual and microscopic examination	534	C

Y-Site Injection Compatibility (1:1 Mixture) (Cont.)

Drug	Mfr	Conc	Droperidol Mfr	Droperidol Conc	Remarks	Ref	C/I
Propofol	ZEN	10 mg/ml	JN	0.4 mg/ml[a]	Physically compatible for 1 hr at 23 °C with no increase in particle content	2066	C
Remifentanil HCl	GW	0.025 and 0.25 mg/ml[b]	AST	2.5 mg/ml	Physically compatible with no change in measured turbidity or increase in particle content in 4 hr at 23 °C	2075	C
Sargramostim	IMM	10 μg/ml[b]	DU	0.4 mg/ml[b]	Physically compatible for 4 hr at 22 °C	1436	C
Teniposide	BR	0.1 mg/ml[a]	JN	0.4 mg/ml[a]	Physically compatible with no subvisual haze or particle formation in 4 hr at 23 °C	1725	C
Thiotepa	IMM[g]	1 mg/ml[a]	JN	0.4 mg/ml[a]	Physically compatible with no change in measured turbidity or increase in particle content in 4 hr at 23 °C	1861	C
TNA #218 to #226[h]			AB	0.4 mg/ml[a]	Damage to emulsion integrity occurs in 1 to 4 hr with free oil formation possible	2215	I
TPN #212 to #215[h]			AB	0.4 mg/ml[a]	Physically compatible with no change in measured turbidity or increase in particle content in 4 hr at 23 °C	2109	C
Vinblastine sulfate		1 mg/ml		2.5 mg/ml	Drugs injected sequentially into Y-site with no flush between. No visually apparent precipitate	980	C
Vincristine sulfate		1 mg/ml		2.5 mg/ml	Drugs injected sequentially into Y-site with no flush between. No visually apparent precipitate	980	C
Vinorelbine tartrate	BW	1 mg/ml[b]	JN	0.4 mg/ml[b]	Physically compatible with no change in measured turbidity or increase in particle content in 4 hr at 22 °C	1558	C
Vitamin B complex with C	RC	2 ml/L[e]	CR	1.25 mg/ml	Physically compatible for at least 4 hr at room temperature by visual and microscopic examination	534	C

[a] *Tested in dextrose 5% in water.*
[b] *Tested in sodium chloride 0.9%.*
[c] *Tested in bacteriostatic sodium chloride 0.9% preserved with benzyl alcohol 0.9%.*
[d] *Given over three minutes via a Y-site into a running infusion solution of heparin sodium in sodium chloride 0.9%.*
[e] *Tested in dextrose 5% in Ringer's injection, dextrose 5% in Ringer's injection, lactated, dextrose 5% in water, Ringer's injection, lactated, and sodium chloride 0.9%.*
[f] *Tested in dextrose 5% in water with sodium bicarbonate 0.05 mEq/ml.*
[g] *Lyophilized formulation tested.*
[h] *Refer to Appendix I for the composition of parenteral nutrition solutions. TNA indicates a 3-in-1 admixture, and TPN indicates a 2-in-1 admixture.*

Additional Compatibility Information

Infusion Solutions — Dextrose 5% in water and Ringer's injection, lactated, have been recommended as diluents for intravenous infusion of droperidol. (4)

Buprenorphine HCl — Droperidol has been stated to be physically and chemically compatible with buprenorphine HCl. (4)

Barbiturates — Precipitation occurs if droperidol is mixed with barbiturates. (4)

EDETATE CALCIUM DISODIUM
AHFS 64:00

Products — Edetate calcium disodium is available in 5-ml ampuls containing 200 mg/ml of drug. (2)

pH — From 6.5 to 8. (4)

Osmolality — Edetate calcium disodium 200 mg/ml has an osmolality of 1514 mOsm/kg. (1689)

Sodium Content — Edetate calcium disodium contains approximately 5.3 mEq of sodium per gram of calcium EDTA. (4)

Trade Name(s) — Calcium Disodium Versenate.

Administration — Edetate calcium disodium may be administered by slow intermittent or continuous intravenous infusion after dilution with sodium chloride 0.9% or dextrose 5% in water to a concentration of 2 to 4 mg/ml. Infusions are made over eight to 12 (2; 4) or up to 24 hours. (4) Although a single, prolonged daily infusion is recommended by the manufacturer (2), the drug has been given in divided daily doses by intermittent intravenous infusions of 15 to 60 minutes in low-risk patients. (4)

The total daily drug dose may also be given by intramuscular injection in equally divided doses at eight- or 12-hour intervals. To minimize pain from intramuscular injection, it should be mixed in equal quantities with procaine HCl 1% or lidocaine HCl 1% (e.g., 1 ml of local anesthetic for each milliliter of edetate calcium disodium) or 0.25 ml of lidocaine HCl 10% can be added to 5 ml of edetate calcium disodium to yield a final local anesthetic concentration of 0.5%. (2; 4)

Stability — Edetate calcium disodium in intact ampuls should be stored at controlled room temperature. (2; 4)

Compatibility Information

Additive Compatibility

Edetate calcium disodium

Drug	*Mfr*	*Conc/L*	*Mfr*	*Conc/L*	*Test Soln*	*Remarks*	*Ref*	*C/I*
Amphotericin B		200 mg	RI	4 g	D5W	Haze develops over 3 hr	26	I
Hydralazine HCl	BP	80 mg	RI	4 g	D5W	Yellow color produced	26	I
Netilmicin sulfate	SC	3 mg	RI	4 g	D5S	Physically compatible and netilmicin chemically stable for 7 days at 25 and 4 °C. Edetate not tested	558	C

Additional Compatibility Information

Infusion Solutions — The manufacturer recommends that dextrose 5% in water or sodium chloride 0.9% be used as a diluent for intravenous infusion. (2)

Edetate calcium disodium is stated to be physically incompatible with dextrose 10% in water, invert sugar 10% in water, invert sugar 10% in sodium chloride 0.9%, Ringer's injection, lactated, Ringer's injection, and sodium lactate ⅙ M. (4)

EDETATE DISODIUM
AHFS 64:00

Products — Edetate disodium is available in 20-ml ampuls containing 150 mg/ml of drug. The pH is adjusted with sodium hydroxide. (4; 29)

pH — From 6.5 to 7.5. (4)

Sodium Content — Edetate disodium contains approximately 5.4 mEq of sodium per gram of drug. (4)

Trade Name(s) — Endrate.

Administration — Edetate disodium is administered by slow intravenous infusion over at least three hours. It must be diluted prior to administration, usually in 500 ml of sodium chloride 0.9% or dextrose 5% in water. Extravasation should be avoided because of tissue irritation. (4)

Compatibility Information

Solution Compatibility

Edetate disodium

Solution	*Mfr*	*Mfr*	*Conc/L*	*Remarks*	*Ref*	*C/I*
Alcohol 5%, dextrose 5%	AB	AB	6 g	Color change	3	I
Dextran 6% in dextrose 5%	AB	AB	6 g	Physically compatible	3	C
Dextran 6% in sodium chloride 0.9%	AB	AB	6 g	Physically compatible	3	C
Dextrose–saline combinations	AB	AB	6 g	Physically compatible	3	C
Dextrose 2½% in water	AB	AB	6 g	Physically compatible	3	C
Dextrose 5% in water	AB	AB	6 g	Physically compatible	3	C
Dextrose 10% in water	AB	AB	6 g	Physically compatible	3	C
Fructose 10% in sodium chloride 0.9%	AB	AB	6 g	Physically compatible	3	C
Fructose 10% in water	AB	AB	6 g	Physically compatible	3	C
Invert sugar 5 and 10% in sodium chloride 0.9%	AB	AB	6 g	Physically compatible	3	C
Invert sugar 5 and 10% in water	AB	AB	6 g	Physically compatible	3	C
Sodium chloride 0.45%	AB	AB	6 g	Physically compatible	3	C
Sodium chloride 0.9%	AB	AB	6 g	Physically compatible	3	C
Sodium lactate ⅙ M	AB	AB	6 g	Physically compatible	3	C

Additional Compatibility Information

Infusion Solutions — Dextrose 5% in water and sodium chloride 0.9% have been recommended as diluents for intravenous infusion. (4)

EDROPHONIUM CHLORIDE
AHFS 36:56

Products — Edrophonium chloride is available in 1-ml ampuls and 10- and 15-ml multiple-dose vials. Each milliliter of solution contains edrophonium chloride 10 mg with sodium sulfite 0.2% and sodium citrate and citric acid as buffers. The multiple-dose vials also contain phenol 0.45%. (2)

pH — Approximately 5.4. (2)

Osmolality — Edrophonium chloride 10 mg/ml has an osmolality of 329 mOsm/kg. (1689)

Trade Name(s) — Enlon, Reversol, Tensilon.

Administration — Edrophonium chloride may be given intramuscularly or subcutaneously but is usually given intravenously. (2; 4)

Stability — Intact containers should be stored at controlled room temperature. (4)

Compatibility Information

Y-Site Injection Compatibility (1:1 Mixture)

Edrophonium chloride

Drug	*Mfr*	*Conc*	*Mfr*	*Conc*	*Remarks*	*Ref*	*C/I*
Heparin sodium	UP	1000 units/L[a]	RC	10 mg/ml	Physically compatible for at least 4 hr at room temperature by visual and microscopic examination	534	C

Y-Site Injection Compatibility (1:1 Mixture) (Cont.)

Edrophonium chloride

Drug	*Mfr*	*Conc*	*Mfr*	*Conc*	*Remarks*	*Ref*	*C/I*
Hydrocortisone sodium succinate	UP	10 mg/L[a]	RC	10 mg/ml	Physically compatible for at least 4 hr at room temperature by visual and microscopic examination	534	C
Potassium chloride	AB	40 mEq/L[a]	RC	10 mg/ml	Physically compatible for at least 4 hr at room temperature by visual and microscopic examination	534	C
Vitamin B complex with C	RC	2 ml/L[a]	RC	10 mg/ml	Physically compatible for at least 4 hr at room temperature by visual and microscopic examination	534	C

[a]Tested in dextrose 5% in Ringer's injection, dextrose 5% in Ringer's injection, lactated, dextrose 5% in water, Ringer's injection, lactated, and sodium chloride 0.9%.

ENALAPRILAT
AHFS 24:04

Products — Enalaprilat is available in 1- and 2-ml vials. Each milliliter of solution contains enalaprilat 1.25 mg with sodium chloride to adjust tonicity, sodium hydroxide to adjust pH, and benzyl alcohol 9 mg in water for injection. (2)

pH — About 7. (1689)

Trade Name(s) — Vasotec I.V.

Administration — Enalaprilat is slowly injected intravenously over at least five minutes if undiluted or infused in up to 50 ml of compatible intravenous infusion solution. (2; 4)

Stability — Enalaprilat is a clear, colorless solution. The product should be stored below 30 °C. (2; 4)

Central Venous Catheter — Enalaprilat (Merck) 0.1 mg/ml in dextrose 5% in water was found to be compatible with the ARROWg+ard Blue Plus (Arrow International) chlorhexidine-bearing triple-lumen central catheter. HPLC analysis was used to evaluate completeness of drug delivery through the catheter and the amount of chlorhexidine removed from the internal lumens. Essentially complete delivery of the drug was found with little or no drug loss occurring. Furthermore, chlorhexidine delivered from the catheter remained at trace amounts with no substantial increase due to the delivery of the drug through the catheter. (2335)

Compatibility Information

Solution Compatibility

Enalaprilat

Solution	*Mfr*	*Mfr*	*Conc/L*	*Remarks*	*Ref*	*C/I*
Dextran 40 10% in dextrose 5%	TR	MSD	25 mg	Physically compatible for 24 hr at room temperature under fluorescent light	1355	C
Dextrose 5% in water	TR[a]	MSD	12 mg	Visually compatible with no loss by HPLC in 24 hr at room temperature under fluorescent light	1572	C
Hetastarch 6%	DU	MSD	25 mg	Physically compatible for 24 hr at room temperature under fluorescent light	1355	C
Normosol R	AB	MSD	25 mg	Physically compatible for 24 hr at room temperature under fluorescent light	1355	C
Plasma-Lyte A	TR	MSD	25 mg	Physically compatible for 24 hr at room temperature under fluorescent light	1355	C

[a]Tested in PVC containers.

Additive Compatibility

Enalaprilat

Drug	Mfr	Conc/L	Mfr	Conc/L	Test Soln	Remarks	Ref	C/I
Dobutamine HCl	LI	1 g	MSD	12 mg	D5W[a]	Visually compatible with little or no enalaprilat loss by HPLC in 24 hr at room temperature under fluorescent light. Dobutamine not tested	1572	C
Dopamine HCl	AMR	1.6 g	MSD	12 mg	D5W[a]	Visually compatible with about 5% enalaprilat loss by HPLC in 24 hr at room temperature under fluorescent light. Dopamine not tested	1572	C
Heparin sodium	ES	50,000 units	MSD	12 mg	D5W[a]	Visually compatible with little or no enalaprilat loss by HPLC in 24 hr at room temperature under fluorescent light. Heparin not tested	1572	C
Meropenem	ZEN	1 and 20 g	MSD	50 mg	NS	Visually compatible for 4 hr at room temperature	1994	C
Nitroglycerin	DU	200 mg	MSD	12 mg	D5W[b]	Visually compatible with about 4% enalaprilat loss by HPLC in 24 hr at room temperature under fluorescent light. Nitroglycerin not tested	1572	C
Potassium chloride	AB	3 g	MSD	12 mg	D5W[a]	Visually compatible with little or no enalaprilat loss by HPLC in 24 hr at room temperature under fluorescent light. Potassium chloride not tested	1572	C
Sodium nitroprusside	ES	1 g	MSD	12 mg	D5W[a]	Visually compatible with little or no enalaprilat loss by HPLC in 24 hr at room temperature under fluorescent light. Nitroprusside not tested	1572	C

[a]*Tested in PVC containers.*
[b]*Tested in glass containers.*

Y-Site Injection Compatibility (1:1 Mixture)

Enalaprilat

Drug	Mfr	Conc	Mfr	Conc	Remarks	Ref	C/I
Allopurinol sodium	BW	3 mg/ml[b]	MSD	0.1 mg/ml[b]	Physically compatible with no change in measured turbidity or increase in particle content in 4 hr at 22 °C	1686	C
Amifostine	USB	10 mg/ml[a]	MSD	0.1 mg/ml[a]	Physically compatible with no change in measured turbidity or increase in particle content in 4 hr at 23 °C	1845	C
Amikacin sulfate	BR	2 mg/ml[a]	MSD	0.05 mg/ml[b]	Physically compatible for 24 hr at room temperature under fluorescent light	1355	C
Aminophylline	ES	1 mg/ml[a]	MSD	0.05 mg/ml[b]	Physically compatible for 24 hr at room temperature under fluorescent light	1355	C
Amphotericin B	SQ	0.1 mg/ml[a]	MSD	1.25 mg/ml	Layered haze develops in 4 hr at 21 °C	1409	I
Amphotericin B cholesteryl sulfate complex	SEQ	0.83 mg/ml[a]	ME	0.1 mg/ml[a]	Decreased natural turbidity occurs immediately	2117	I
Ampicillin sodium	PF	15 mg/ml[b]	MSD	0.05 mg/ml[b]	Physically compatible for 24 hr at room temperature under fluorescent light	1355	C

Y-Site Injection Compatibility (1:1 Mixture) (Cont.)

Enalaprilat

Drug	*Mfr*	*Conc*	*Mfr*	*Conc*	*Remarks*	*Ref*	*C/I*
Ampicillin sodium–sulbactam sodium	PF	10 + 5 mg/ml[b]	MSD	0.05 mg/ml[b]	Physically compatible for 24 hr at room temperature under fluorescent light	1355	C
Aztreonam	SQ	10 mg/ml[a]	MSD	0.05 mg/ml[b]	Physically compatible for 24 hr at room temperature under fluorescent light	1355	C
	SQ	40 mg/ml[a]	MSD	0.1 mg/ml[a]	Physically compatible with no subvisual haze or particle formation in 4 hr at 23 °C	1758	C
Butorphanol tartrate	BR	0.4 mg/ml[a]	MSD	0.05 mg/ml[b]	Physically compatible for 24 hr at room temperature under fluorescent light	1355	C
Calcium gluconate	ES	0.092 mEq/ml[a]	MSD	0.05 mg/ml[b]	Physically compatible for 24 hr at room temperature under fluorescent light	1355	C
Cefazolin sodium	SKF	20 mg/ml[c]	MSD	0.05 mg/ml[b]	Physically compatible for 24 hr at room temperature under fluorescent light	1355	C
Cefepime HCl	BMS	20 mg/ml[a]	MSD	0.1 mg/ml[a]	Tiny particles form in 4 hr	1689	I
Cefoperazone sodium	RR	10 mg/ml[a]	MSD	0.05 mg/ml[b]	Physically compatible for 24 hr at room temperature under fluorescent light	1355	C
Ceftazidime	GL[i]	10 mg/ml[a]	MSD	0.05 mg/ml[b]	Physically compatible for 24 hr at room temperature under fluorescent light	1355	C
Ceftizoxime sodium	SKF	10 mg/ml[a]	MSD	0.05 mg/ml[b]	Physically compatible for 24 hr at room temperature under fluorescent light	1355	C
Chloramphenicol sodium succinate	PD	10 mg/ml[a]	MSD	0.05 mg/ml[b]	Physically compatible for 24 hr at room temperature under fluorescent light	1355	C
Cimetidine HCl	SKF	3 mg/ml[a]	MSD	0.05 mg/ml[b]	Physically compatible for 24 hr at room temperature under fluorescent light	1355	C
Cisatracurium besylate	GW	0.1, 2, 5 mg/ml[a]	ME	0.1 mg/ml[a]	Physically compatible with no change in measured turbidity or increase in particle content in 4 hr at 23 °C	2074	C
Cladribine	ORT	0.015[b] and 0.5[d] mg/ml	MSD	0.1 mg/ml[b]	Physically compatible with no change in measured turbidity or increase in particle content in 4 hr at 23 °C	1969	C
Clindamycin phosphate	UP	9 mg/ml[a]	MSD	0.05 mg/ml[b]	Physically compatible for 24 hr at room temperature under fluorescent light	1355	C
Dextran 40	TR	100 mg/ml[a]	MSD	0.05 mg/ml[b]	Physically compatible for 24 hr at room temperature under fluorescent light	1355	C
Dobutamine HCl	LI	1 mg/ml[a]	MSD	0.05 mg/ml[b]	Physically compatible for 24 hr at room temperature under fluorescent light	1355	C
Docetaxel	RPR	0.9 mg/ml[a]	ME	0.1 mg/ml[a]	Physically compatible with no change in measured turbidity or increase in particle content in 4 hr at 23 °C	2224	C
Dopamine HCl	IMS	1.6 mg/ml[a]	MSD	0.05 mg/ml[b]	Physically compatible for 24 hr at room temperature under fluorescent light	1355	C
Doxorubicin HCl liposome injection	SEQ	0.4 mg/ml[a]	MSD	0.1 mg/ml[a]	Physically compatible with little or no change in measured turbidity and no increase in particle content in 4 hr at 23 °C	2087	C
Erythromycin lactobionate	AB	5 mg/ml[a]	MSD	0.05 mg/ml[b]	Physically compatible for 24 hr at room temperature under fluorescent light	1355	C

Y-Site Injection Compatibility (1:1 Mixture) (Cont.)

			Enalaprilat				
Drug	*Mfr*	*Conc*	*Mfr*	*Conc*	*Remarks*	*Ref*	*C/I*
Esmolol HCl	DU	10 mg/ml[a]	MSD	0.05 mg/ml[b]	Physically compatible for 24 hr at room temperature under fluorescent light	1355	C
Etoposide phosphate	BR	5 mg/ml[a]	ME	0.1 mg/ml[a]	Physically compatible with no change in measured turbidity or increase in particle content in 4 hr at 23 °C	2218	C
Famotidine	MSD	0.2 mg/ml[a]	MSD	0.05 mg/ml[b]	Physically compatible for 24 hr at room temperature under fluorescent light	1355	C
Fentanyl citrate	ES	2 µg/ml[a]	MSD	0.05 mg/ml[b]	Physically compatible for 24 hr at room temperature under fluorescent light	1355	C
Filgrastim	AMG	30 µg/ml[a]	MSD	0.1 mg/ml[a]	Physically compatible with no change in measured turbidity or increase in particle content in 4 hr at 22 °C	1687	C
Ganciclovir sodium	SY	5 mg/ml[e]	MSD	1.25 mg/ml	Physically compatible for 4 hr at 21 °C under fluorescent light by macroscopic and microscopic examination	1409	C
Gatifloxacin	BMS	2 mg/ml[a]	ME	0.1 mg/ml[a]	Physically compatible with no change in measured haze or increase in particle content in 4 hr at 23 °C	2234	C
Gemcitabine HCl	LI	10 mg/ml[b]	ME	0.1 mg/ml[b]	Physically compatible with no change in measured turbidity or increase in particle content in 4 hr at 23 °C	2226	C
Gentamicin sulfate	ES	0.8 mg/ml[a]	MSD	0.05 mg/ml[b]	Physically compatible for 24 hr at room temperature under fluorescent light	1355	C
Granisetron HCl	SKB	0.05 mg/ml[a]	MSD	0.1 mg/ml[a]	Physically compatible with no change in measured turbidity or increase in particle content in 4 hr at 23 °C	2000	C
Heparin sodium	IX	40 units/ml[a]	MSD	0.05 mg/ml[b]	Physically compatible for 24 hr at room temperature under fluorescent light	1355	C
Hetastarch in lactated electrolyte injection (Hextend)	AB	6%	ME	0.1 mg/ml[a]	Physically compatible with no change in measured turbidity or increase in particle content in 4 hr at 23 °C	2339	C
Hetastarch in sodium chloride 0.9%	DCC	6%	MSD	0.05 mg/ml[b]	Physically compatible for 24 hr at room temperature under fluorescent light	1355	C
Hydrocortisone sodium succinate	UP	2 mg/ml[a]	MSD	0.05 mg/ml[b]	Physically compatible for 24 hr at room temperature under fluorescent light	1355	C
Labetalol HCl	GL	1 mg/ml[a]	MSD	0.05 mg/ml[b]	Physically compatible for 24 hr at room temperature under fluorescent light	1355	C
Lidocaine HCl	AST	4 mg/ml[a]	MSD	0.05 mg/ml[b]	Physically compatible for 24 hr at room temperature under fluorescent light	1355	C
Linezolid	PHU	2 mg/ml	ME	0.1 mg/ml[a]	Physically compatible with no change in measured turbidity or increase in particle content in 4 hr at 23 °C	2264	C
Magnesium sulfate	LY	10 mEq/ml[a]	MSD	0.05 mg/ml[b]	Physically compatible for 24 hr at room temperature under fluorescent light	1355	C
Melphalan HCl	BW	0.1 mg/ml[b]	MSD	0.1 mg/ml[b]	Physically compatible with no change in measured turbidity or increase in particle content in 3 hr at 22 °C	1557	C

Y-Site Injection Compatibility (1:1 Mixture) (Cont.)

			Enalaprilat				
Drug	*Mfr*	*Conc*	*Mfr*	*Conc*	*Remarks*	*Ref*	*C/I*
Meropenem	ZEN	1 and 50 mg/ml[b]	MSD	0.05 mg/ml[f]	Visually compatible for 4 hr at room temperature	1994	C
Methylprednisolone sodium succinate	UP	0.8 mg/ml[a]	MSD	0.05 mg/ml[b]	Physically compatible for 24 hr at room temperature under fluorescent light	1355	C
Metronidazole	SE	5 mg/ml	MSD	0.05 mg/ml[b]	Physically compatible for 24 hr at room temperature under fluorescent light	1355	C
Morphine sulfate	WY	0.2 mg/ml[a]	MSD	0.05 mg/ml[b]	Physically compatible for 24 hr at room temperature under fluorescent light	1355	C
Nafcillin sodium	BR	10 mg/ml[a]	MSD	0.05 mg/ml[b]	Physically compatible for 24 hr at room temperature under fluorescent light	1355	C
Nicardipine HCl	DU	0.1 mg/ml[a]	MSD	0.05 mg/ml[b]	Physically compatible for 24 hr at room temperature under fluorescent light	1355	C
Penicillin G potassium	PF	50,000 units/ml[a]	MSD	0.05 mg/ml[b]	Physically compatible for 24 hr at room temperature under fluorescent light	1355	C
Phenobarbital sodium	WY	0.32 mg/ml[e]	MSD	1.25 mg/ml	Physically compatible for 4 hr at 21 °C under fluorescent light by macroscopic and microscopic examination	1409	C
Phenytoin sodium	PD	1 mg/ml[b]	MSD	1.25 mg/ml	Crystalline precipitate forms immediately	1409	I
Piperacillin sodium	LE	12 mg/ml[a]	MSD	0.05 mg/ml[b]	Physically compatible for 24 hr at room temperature under fluorescent light	1355	C
Piperacillin sodium–tazobactam sodium	LE	40 + 5 mg/ml[a]	MSD	0.1 mg/ml[a]	Physically compatible with no change in measured turbidity or increase in particle content in 4 hr at 22 °C	1688	C
Potassium chloride	LY	0.4 mEq/ml[a]	MSD	0.05 mg/ml[b]	Physically compatible for 24 hr at room temperature under fluorescent light	1355	C
Potassium phosphates	LY	0.44 mEq/ml[a]	MSD	0.05 mg/ml[b]	Physically compatible for 24 hr at room temperature under fluorescent light	1355	C
Propofol	ZEN	10 mg/ml	MSD	0.1 mg/ml[a]	Physically compatible for 1 hr at 23 °C with no increase in particle content	2066	C
Ranitidine HCl	GL	0.5 mg/ml[a]	MSD	0.05 mg/ml[b]	Physically compatible for 24 hr at room temperature under fluorescent light	1355	C
Remifentanil HCl	GW	0.025 and 0.25 mg/ml[b]	ME	0.1 mg/ml[a]	Physically compatible with no change in measured turbidity or increase in particle content in 4 hr at 23 °C	2075	C
Sodium acetate	LY	0.4 mEq/ml[a]	MSD	0.05 mg/ml[b]	Physically compatible for 24 hr at room temperature under fluorescent light	1355	C
Sodium nitroprusside	LY	0.2 mg/ml[a]	MSD	0.05 mg/ml[b]	Physically compatible for 24 hr at room temperature under fluorescent light	1355	C
Teniposide	BR	0.1 mg/ml[a]	MSD	0.1 mg/ml[a]	Physically compatible with no subvisual haze or particle formation in 4 hr at 23 °C	1725	C
Thiotepa	IMM[g]	1 mg/ml[a]	ME	0.1 mg/ml[a]	Physically compatible with no change in measured turbidity or increase in particle content in 4 hr at 23 °C	1861	C
TNA #218 to #226[h]			ME	0.1 mg/ml[a]	Visually compatible with no precipitate or emulsion damage apparent in 4 hr at 23 °C	2215	C

Y-Site Injection Compatibility (1:1 Mixture) (Cont.)

			Enalaprilat				
Drug	*Mfr*	*Conc*	*Mfr*	*Conc*	*Remarks*	*Ref*	*C/I*
Tobramycin sulfate	LI	0.8 mg/ml[a]	MSD	0.05 mg/ml[b]	Physically compatible for 24 hr at room temperature under fluorescent light	1355	C
TPN #212 to #215[h]			MSD	0.1 mg/ml[a]	Physically compatible with no change in measured turbidity or increase in particle content in 4 hr at 23 °C	2109	C
Trimethoprim–sulfamethoxazole	QU	0.16 + 0.8 mg/ml[a]	MSD	0.05 mg/ml[b]	Physically compatible for 24 hr at room temperature under fluorescent light	1355	C
Vancomycin HCl	LE	5 mg/ml[a]	MSD	0.05 mg/ml[b]	Physically compatible for 24 hr at room temperature under fluorescent light	1355	C
Vinorelbine tartrate	BW	1 mg/ml[b]	MSD	0.1 mg/ml[b]	Physically compatible with no change in measured turbidity or increase in particle content in 4 hr at 22 °C	1558	C

[a]*Tested in dextrose 5% in water.*
[b]*Tested in sodium chloride 0.9%.*
[c]*Premixed solution.*
[d]*Tested in bacteriostatic sodium chloride 0.9% preserved with benzyl alcohol 0.9%.*
[e]*Tested in both dextrose 5% in water and sodium chloride 0.9%.*
[f]*Tested in sterile water for injection.*
[g]*Lyophilized formulation tested.*
[h]*Refer to Appendix I for the composition of parenteral nutrition solutions. TNA indicates a 3-in-1 admixture, and TPN indicates a 2-in-1 admixture.*
[i]*Sodium carbonate–containing formulation tested.*

Additional Compatibility Information

Infusion Solutions — The manufacturer states that enalaprilat is stable for 24 hours at room temperature in the following infusion solutions (2):

Dextrose 5% in Ringer's injection, lactated
Dextrose 5% in sodium chloride 0.9%
Dextrose 5% in water
Isolyte E
Sodium chloride 0.9%

ENOXAPARIN SODIUM
AHFS 20:12.04

Products — Enoxaparin sodium is available in ampuls containing 30 mg/0.3 ml and prefilled syringes containing 30 mg/0.3 ml, 40 mg/0.4 ml, 60 mg/0.6 ml, 80 mg/0.8 ml, and 100 mg/1 ml in water for injection. The solution is preservative-free and is intended for use as a single-dose injection. (2)

pH — From 5.5 to 7.5. (2)

Units — The approximate anti-factor Xa activity is 1000 I.U. for every 10 mg of enoxaparin sodium. (2; 4)

Trade Name(s) — Lovenox.

Administration — Enoxaparin sodium is administered by deep subcutaneous injection, alternating administration sites between the left and right anterolateral and left and right posterolateral abdominal wall. It must not be given intramuscularly. (2; 4)

Stability — Enoxaparin sodium injection is a clear, colorless to pale yellow solution. Intact containers should be stored at controlled room temperature of 15 to 25 °C. (2)

Syringes — Enoxaparin (Rhone-Poulenc Rorer) 100 mg/1 ml was packaged in 1-ml tuberculin syringes fitted with 27-gauge, ½-inch needles. The syringes were stored at 22 and 3 °C for 10 days. Chromogenic assay of anticoagulant activity found about a 7 to 8% loss in 10 days under refrigeration but 15 to 25% losses in as little as two days at room temperature. (2272)

However, the manufacturer of enoxaparin sodium has indicated that the undiluted injection at a concentration of 100 mg/1 ml repackaged in plastic syringes is stable for five days at room temperature. (31)

Compatibility Information

Solution Compatibility

Enoxaparin sodium

Solution	Mfr	Mfr	Conc/L	Remarks	Ref	C/I
Sodium chloride 0.9%	AB[a]	RP	1.2 g	No loss of activity by bioassay in 48 hr at 21 °C under fluorescent light	1871	C

[a]*Tested in PVC containers.*

EPHEDRINE SULFATE
AHFS 12:12

Products — Ephedrine sulfate is available in 1-ml ampuls and vials containing 50 mg of drug in water for injection. (1-7/98; 29)

pH — From 4.5 to 7. (4)

Osmolarity — The current product labeling does not specify an osmotic value for the injection, but a previous package insert indicated that the osmolarity of the 50-mg/ml concentration was calculated to be 0.35 mOsm/ml. (1-10/91)

Administration — Ephedrine sulfate may be administered subcutaneously, intramuscularly, or slowly intravenously. (1-7/98; 4)

Stability — Intact containers of ephedrine sulfate should be stored at controlled room temperature and protected from light. (1-7/98; 4)

Syringes — The stability of ephedrine (salt form unspecified) 10 mg/ml repackaged in polypropylene syringes was evaluated by spectrophotometric and potentiometric methods. Little or no change in concentration was found after four weeks of storage at room temperature not exposed to direct light. (2164)

Compatibility Information

Solution Compatibility

Ephedrine sulfate

Solution	Mfr	Mfr	Conc/L	Remarks	Ref	C/I
Dextran 6% in dextrose 5%	AB		50 mg	Physically compatible	3	C
Dextran 6% in sodium chloride 0.9%	AB		50 mg	Physically compatible	3	C
Dextrose–Ringer's injection combinations	AB		50 mg	Physically compatible	3	C
Dextrose–Ringer's injection, lactated, combinations	AB		50 mg	Physically compatible	3	C
Dextrose–saline combinations	AB		50 mg	Physically compatible	3	C
Dextrose 2½% in water	AB		50 mg	Physically compatible	3	C
Dextrose 5% in water	AB		50 mg	Physically compatible	3	C
Dextrose 10% in water	AB		50 mg	Physically compatible	3	C
Fructose 10% in sodium chloride 0.9%	AB		50 mg	Physically compatible	3	C
Fructose 10% in water	AB		50 mg	Physically compatible	3	C
Invert sugar 5 and 10% in sodium chloride 0.9%	AB		50 mg	Physically compatible	3	C
Invert sugar 5 and 10% in water	AB		50 mg	Physically compatible	3	C
Ionosol products	AB		50 mg	Physically compatible	3	C
Ringer's injection	AB		50 mg	Physically compatible	3	C
Ringer's injection, lactated	AB		50 mg	Physically compatible	3	C
Sodium chloride 0.45%	AB		50 mg	Physically compatible	3	C
Sodium chloride 0.9%	AB		50 mg	Physically compatible	3	C
Sodium lactate ⅙ M	AB		50 mg	Physically compatible	3	C

Additive Compatibility

Drug	Mfr	Conc/L	Mfr	Conc/L	Test Soln	Remarks	Ref	C/I
			Ephedrine sulfate					
Chloramphenicol sodium succinate	PD	1 g	AB	50 mg		Physically compatible	6	C
Hydrocortisone sodium succinate						Physically incompatible	9	I
Lidocaine HCl	AST	2 g		50 mg		Physically compatible	24	C
Metaraminol bitartrate	MSD	100 mg	AB	50 mg		Physically compatible	7	C
Nafcillin sodium	WY	500 mg		50 mg		Physically compatible	27	C
Penicillin G potassium		1 million units		50 mg		Physically compatible	3	C
	SQ	5 million units	AB	50 mg		Physically compatible	47	C
Pentobarbital sodium						Physically incompatible	9	I
	AB	1 g	LI	250 mg	D5W	Physically incompatible	15	I
Phenobarbital sodium	WI					Physically incompatible	9	I
	WI	200 mg	LI	250 mg	D5W	Physically incompatible	15	I
Thiopental sodium	AB	2.5 g	AB	50 mg	D5W	Physically compatible	21	C
	AB					Physically incompatible	9	I

Drugs in Syringe Compatibility

Drug (in syringe)	Mfr	Amt	Mfr	Amt	Remarks	Ref	C/I
			Ephedrine sulfate				
Pentobarbital sodium	AB	500 mg/ 10 ml		50 mg/ 1 ml	Physically compatible	55	C
Thiopental sodium	AB	75 mg/ 3 ml	AB	50 mg/ 1 ml	Physically incompatible	21	I

Y-Site Injection Compatibility (1:1 Mixture)

Drug	Mfr	Conc	Mfr	Conc	Remarks	Ref	C/I
			Ephedrine sulfate				
Etomidate	AB	2 mg/ml	AB	50 mg/ml	Visually compatible for up to 7 days at 25 °C	1801	C
Hetastarch in lactated electrolyte injection (Hextend)	AB	6%	TAY	5 mg/ml[a]	Physically compatible with no change in measured turbidity or increase in particle content in 4 hr at 23 °C	2339	C
Propofol	ZEN	10 mg/ml	AB	5 mg/ml[a]	Physically compatible for 1 hr at 23 °C with no increase in particle content	2066	C
Thiopental sodium	AB	25 mg/ml	AB	50 mg/ml	White cloudiness forms immediately, followed by fine crystalline particles	1801	I

[a]*Tested in dextrose 5% in water.*

Additional Compatibility Information

Hydrocortisone Sodium Succinate — Ephedrine sulfate 50 mg/L has been reported to be conditionally compatible with hydrocortisone sodium succinate (Upjohn) 250 mg/L. Although occasional precipitation has been observed when unusual and/or discontinued infusion solutions were used as vehicles, the combination is physically compatible in most common currently available intravenous infusion solutions. (3)

Phenobarbital Sodium — Titration of 50 ml of a 0.5 M aqueous solution of ephedrine HCl (BP) with 30.8 ml or more of a 0.5 M aqueous solution of phenobarbital sodium (BP) resulted in precipitation of an ephedrine–phenobarbital complex. The point at which precipitation began corresponded to the point at which the pH of the ephedrine HCl solution had been increased from its initial pH of 7 to 8.5. Further additions of the phenobarbital sodium solution resulted in additional precipitation but did not alter the pH. (332)

EPINEPHRINE HCL
AHFS 12:12

Products — Epinephrine HCl at a concentration of 1 mg/ml is available in 1-ml ampuls, 30-ml vials, and 0.3-ml auto-injector syringes. (2; 29) Epinephrine HCl is also available at a concentration of 0.5 mg/ml in auto-injector syringes and at a concentration of 0.1 mg/ml (1:10,000) in vials and prefilled syringes. (4; 29) Some products also contain sodium chloride, a bisulfite antioxidant, and an antibacterial preservative such as chlorobutanol. (2; 4; 154)

pH — From 2.2 to 5.0. (4; 17)

Osmolality — The osmolality of epinephrine HCl (Abbott) 0.1 mg/ml was determined to be 273 mOsm/kg by freezing-point depression. (1071) A 1-mg/ml solution was determined to have an osmolality of 348 mOsm/kg. (1233)

Trade Name(s) — Adrenalin Chloride, Epipen.

Administration — Epinephrine HCl may be administered by subcutaneous, intramuscular, intravenous, or intracardiac injection. Intramuscular injection into the buttocks should be avoided. (2; 4) Intravenous infusion at a rate of 1 to 10 μg/min has also been described. (4)

Stability — Epinephrine HCl is sensitive to light and air. (4; 1259) Protection from light is recommended. Withdrawal of doses from multiple-dose vials introduces air, which results in oxidation. As epinephrine oxidizes, it changes from colorless to pink, as adrenochrome forms, to brown, as melanin forms. (4; 1072) Discolored solutions or solutions containing a precipitate should not be used. (4) The various epinephrine preparations have varying stabilities, depending on the form and the preservatives present. The manufacturer's recommendations should be followed with regard to storage. (4)

The stability of epinephrine HCl in intact ampuls subjected to resterilization to provide a sterile outer surface was evaluated. Epinephrine HCl (adrenalin injection, BP) ampuls were resterilized by the following methods:

1. Autoclaved at 121 °C for 15 minutes.
2. Autoclaved at 115 °C for 30 minutes.
3. Exposed to ethylene oxide–freon (12:88) at 55 °C for four hours followed by aeration at 50 °C for 12 hours.

No differences in epinephrine HCl concentration were detected by HPLC analysis of samples from any of these methods. However, if ampuls were resterilized twice by autoclaving two times at 121 °C for 15 minutes, approximately 8% of the drug was lost. (803)

pH Effects — The primary determinant of catecholamine stability in intravenous admixtures is the pH of the solution. (527) Epinephrine HCl is unstable in dextrose 5% in water at a pH above 5.5. (48) The pH of optimum stability is 3 to 4. (1072) In one study, the decomposition rate increased twofold (from 5 to 10% in 200 days at 30 °C) when the pH was increased from 2.5 to 4.5. (1259)

Syringes — Epinephrine HCl (Parke-Davis) was diluted to concentrations of 1 and 7 mg/10 ml with sterile water for injection and repackaged into 10-ml glass vials and plastic syringes with 18-gauge needles (Becton-Dickinson). The diluted injections were stored at room temperature protected from light. Epinephrine stability was evaluated by HPLC analysis over 56 days of storage. The 1-mg/10 ml samples had an epinephrine loss of 4 to 6% in seven days and about 13% in 14 days. The 7-mg/10 ml samples lost 2% in the glass vials and 5% in the syringes in 56 days. (1902)

Central Venous Catheter — Epinephrine HCl (American Regent) 0.1 mg/ml in dextrose 5% in water was found to be compatible with the ARROWg+ard Blue Plus (Arrow International) chlorhexidine-bearing triple-lumen central catheter. HPLC analysis was used to evaluate completeness of drug delivery through the catheter and the amount of chlorhexidine removed from the internal lumens. Essentially complete delivery of the drug was found with little or no drug loss occurring. Furthermore, chlorhexidine delivered from the catheter remained at trace amounts with no substantial increase due to the delivery of the drug through the catheter. (2335)

Compatibility Information

Solution Compatibility

Epinephrine HCl

Solution	Mfr	Mfr	Conc/L	Remarks	Ref	C/I
Dextran 40,000	PH	PD		Physically compatible	44	C
Dextran 6% in dextrose 5%	AB	PD	4 mg	Physically compatible	3	C
Dextran 6% in sodium chloride 0.9%	AB	PD	4 mg	Physically compatible	3	C
Dextrose–Ringer's injection combinations	AB	PD	4 mg	Physically compatible	3	C
Dextrose–Ringer's injection, lactated, combinations	AB	PD	4 mg	Physically compatible	3	C
Dextrose 5% in Ringer's injection, lactated	TR[a]	PD	1 mg	Potency retained for 24 hr at 5 °C	282	C
Dextrose–saline combinations	AB	PD	4 mg	Physically compatible	3	C
Dextrose 5% in sodium chloride 0.9%	TR[a]	PD	1 mg	Potency retained for 24 hr at 5 °C	282	C
Dextrose 2½% in water	AB	PD	4 mg	Physically compatible	3	C
Dextrose 5% in water	AB	PD	4 mg	Physically compatible	3	C
	TR[a]	PD	1 mg	Potency retained for 24 hr at 5 °C	282	C
	AB	PD	4 mg	Physically compatible and chemically stable. At 25 °C, 10% decomposition is calculated to occur in 50 hr in light and in 1000 hr in the dark	527	C
	BA[b]	ANT	16 mg	5% loss by HPLC in 20.75 days at 5 °C protected from light	1610	C
	BA[a]	AMR	87 mg	No epinephrine loss by HPLC in 24 hr at 23 °C protected from light	2085	C
Dextrose 10% in water	AB	PD	4 mg	Physically compatible	3	C
Fructose 10% in sodium chloride 0.9%	AB	PD	4 mg	Physically compatible	3	C
Fructose 10% in water	AB	PD	4 mg	Physically compatible	3	C
Invert sugar 5 and 10% in sodium chloride 0.9%	AB	PD	4 mg	Physically compatible	3	C
Invert sugar 5 and 10% in water	AB	PD	4 mg	Physically compatible	3	C
Ionosol products (except as noted below)	AB	PD	4 mg	Physically compatible	3	C
Ionosol PSL (Darrow's)	AB	PD	4 mg	Color change	3	I
Ionosol T with dextrose 5%	AB	PD	4 mg	Haze or precipitate within 6 to 24 hr	3	I
Ringer's injection	AB	PD	4 mg	Physically compatible	3	C
Ringer's injection, lactated	AB	PD	4 mg	Physically compatible	3	C
	TR[a]	PD	1 mg	Potency retained for 24 hr at 5 °C	282	C
Sodium bicarbonate 5%			4 mg	Epinephrine rapidly decomposes. 58% loss immediately after mixing	48	I
Sodium chloride 0.9%	TR[a]	PD	1 mg	Potency retained for 24 hr at 5 °C	282	C
Sodium lactate ⅙ M	AB	PD	4 mg	Physically compatible	3	C

[a]*Tested in both glass and PVC containers.*
[b]*Tested in PVC containers.*

Additive Compatibility

Epinephrine HCl

Drug	*Mfr*	*Conc/L*	*Mfr*	*Conc/L*	*Test Soln*	*Remarks*	*Ref*	*C/I*
Amikacin sulfate	BR	5 g	PD	2.5 mg	D5LR, D5R, D5S, D5W, D10W, IS10, LR, NS, R, SL	Physically compatible and potency of both retained for 24 hr at 25 °C	294	C
Aminophylline	SE	500 mg	PD	4 mg	D5W	At 25 °C, 10% epinephrine decomposition in 1.2 hr in the light and 3 hr in the dark	527	I
		500 mg		4 mg	D5W	Pink to brown discoloration in 8 to 24 hr at room temperature	845	I
Cimetidine HCl	SKF	3 g	PD	100 mg	D5W	Physically compatible and cimetidine chemically stable for 24 hr at room temperature. Epinephrine not tested	551	C
Dobutamine HCl	LI	1 g	BR	50 mg	D5W, NS	Physically compatible for 24 hr at 21 °C	812	C
Floxacillin sodium	BE	20 g	ANT	8 mg	W	Physically compatible for 72 hr at 15 and 30 °C	1479	C
Furosemide	HO	1 g	ANT	8 mg	W	Physically compatible for 72 hr at 15 and 30 °C	1479	C
Hyaluronidase			PD			Physically incompatible	10	I
	WY		PD			Physically incompatible	9	I
Mephentermine sulfate	WY		PD			Physically incompatible	10	I
Metaraminol bitartrate	MSD	100 mg	PD	4 mg		Physically compatible	7	C
Ranitidine HCl	GL	50 mg and 2 g		50 mg	D5W	Physically compatible and ranitidine chemically stable by HPLC for 24 hr at 25 °C. Epinephrine not tested	1515	C
Sodium bicarbonate	AB	2.4 mEq[a]		4 mg	D5W	Epinephrine inactivated	772	I
Verapamil HCl	KN	80 mg	PD	2 mg	D5W, NS	Physically compatible for 24 hr	764	C

[a] *One vial of Neut added to a liter of admixture.*

Drugs in Syringe Compatibility

Epinephrine HCl

Drug (in syringe)	*Mfr*	*Amt*	*Mfr*	*Amt*	*Remarks*	*Ref*	*C/I*
Diatrizoate meglumine 52%, diatrizoate sodium 8%	MA	5 ml	PD	1 mg/ml	Physically compatible for at least 2 hr	1438	C
Diatrizoate sodium 60%	WI	5 ml	PD	1 mg/ml	Physically compatible for at least 2 hr	1438	C
Doxapram HCl	RB	400 mg/ 20 ml		1 mg/ 1 ml	Physically compatible with no doxapram loss in 24 hr	1177	C
Heparin sodium		2500 units/ 1 ml		1 mg/ 1 ml	Physically compatible for at least 5 min	1053	C
Iohexol	WI	64.7%, 5 ml	PD	1 mg/ 1 ml	Physically compatible for at least 2 hr	1438	C
Iopamidol	SQ	61%, 5 ml	PD	1 mg/ 1 ml	Physically compatible for at least 2 hr	1438	C
Iothalamate meglumine 60%	MA	5 ml	PD	1 mg/ml	Physically compatible for at least 2 hr	1438	C

Drugs in Syringe Compatibility (Cont.)

Epinephrine HCl

Drug (in syringe)	*Mfr*	*Amt*	*Mfr*	*Amt*	*Remarks*	*Ref*	*C/I*
Ioxaglate meglumine 39.3%, ioxaglate sodium 19.6%	MA	5 ml	PD	1 mg/ml	Physically compatible for at least 2 hr	1438	C
Milrinone lactate	WI	5.25 mg/ 5.25 ml	AB	0.5 mg/ 0.5 ml	Physically compatible with no loss of either drug in 20 min at 23 °C under fluorescent light	1410	C
Sodium bicarbonate	AB	3 mEq/ 3 ml	ES	1: 100,000[a], 30 ml	11% lidocaine loss in 1 week and 22% loss in 2 weeks at 25 °C by GC. 28% epinephrine loss by HPLC in 1 week at 25 °C	1712	I
	AB	3 mEq/ 3 ml	ES	1: 100,000[a], 30 ml	6% lidocaine loss by GC in 4 weeks at 4 °C. 2% epinephrine loss in 1 week and 12% loss in 3 weeks at 4 °C by HPLC	1712	C
	LY	0.1 mEq/ ml	AST	1: 100,000[b]	25% epinephrine loss by HPLC in 1 week at room temperature. Lidocaine not tested	1713	I
	AST	8.4%, 2 ml	AST	1: 200,000[c], 20 ml	Visually compatible for up to 5 hr at room temperature	1724	C
	AST	8.4%, 2 ml	AST	1: 200,000[d], 20 ml	Haze clarifies with gentle agitation	1724	?
	AB	4%, 4 ml	AST	1: 200,000[c], 20 ml	Visually compatible for up to 5 hr at room temperature	1724	C
	AB	4%, 4 ml	AST	1: 200,000[d], 20 ml	Haze clarifies with gentle agitation	1724	?
	AB	4%, 0.05 to 0.6 ml	AST, WI	1: 200,000[e], 20 ml	Precipitate forms in 1 to 2 min up to 2 hr at lowest amount of bicarbonate	1724	I
		1.4 and 8.4%, 1.5 ml	BEL	1:80,000[f], 20 ml	8% epinephrine loss by HPLC in 7 days at room temperature. Lidocaine not tested	1743	C
		4.2 and 8.4%, 1.5 ml	BEL	1: 200,000[g], 20 ml	5 to 7% epinephrine loss by HPLC in 7 days at room temperature. Bupivacaine not tested	1743	C
		1.4%, 1.5 ml	BEL	1: 200,000[g], 20 ml	Little or no epinephrine loss by HPLC in 7 days at room temperature. Bupivacaine not tested	1743	C

[a]Lidocaine HCl 2% with epinephrine HCl 1:100,000.
[b]Lidocaine HCl 1% with epinephrine HCl 1:100,000.
[c]Lidocaine HCl 1 and 1.5% with epinephrine HCl 1:200,000.
[d]Lidocaine HCl 2% with epinephrine HCl 1:200,000.
[e]Bupivacaine HCl 0.5 and 0.75% with epinephrine HCl 1:200,000.
[f]Lidocaine HCl 2% with epinephrine HCl 1:80,000.
[g]Bupivacaine HCl 0.5% with epinephrine HCl 1:200,000.

Y-Site Injection Compatibility (1:1 Mixture)

Epinephrine HCl

Drug	*Mfr*	*Conc*	*Mfr*	*Conc*	*Remarks*	*Ref*	*C/I*
Ampicillin sodium	WY	40 mg/ml[c]	ES	0.032 mg/ml[c]	Slight color change in 3 hr	1316	I
Atracurium besylate	BW	0.5 mg/ml[a]	AB	4 µg/ml[a]	Physically compatible for 24 hr at 28 °C	1337	C
Calcium chloride	AB	4 mg/ml[c]	ES	0.032 mg/ml[c]	Physically compatible for 3 hr	1316	C
Calcium gluconate	AST	4 mg/ml[c]	ES	0.032 mg/ml[c]	Physically compatible for 3 hr	1316	C

Y-Site Injection Compatibility (1:1 Mixture) (Cont.)

Epinephrine HCl

Drug	*Mfr*	*Conc*	*Mfr*	*Conc*	*Remarks*	*Ref*	*C/I*
Cefpirome sulfate	HO	50 mg/ml[g]	AB	0.1 mg/ml[g]	Visually and microscopically compatible with 6% or less cefpirome loss and 5% or less epinephrine loss by HPLC in 8 hr at 23 °C	2044	C
Cisatracurium besylate	GW	0.1, 2, 5 mg/ml[a]	AMR	0.05 mg/ml[a]	Physically compatible with no change in measured turbidity or increase in particle content in 4 hr at 23 °C	2074	C
Diltiazem HCl	MMD	5 mg/ml	PD	0.004 and 0.05 mg/ml[b]	Visually compatible	1807	C
	MMD	1 mg/ml[b]	PD	0.05 mg/ml[b]	Visually compatible	1807	C
	MMD	1 mg/ml[a]	AB	0.02 mg/ml[a]	Visually compatible for 4 hr at 27 °C	2062	C
Dobutamine HCl	LI	4 mg/ml[a]	AB	0.02 mg/ml[a]	Visually compatible for 4 hr at 27 °C	2062	C
Dopamine HCl	AB	3.2 mg/ml[a]	AB	0.02 mg/ml[a]	Visually compatible for 4 hr at 27 °C	2062	C
Famotidine	MSD	0.2 mg/ml[a]	ES	0.004 mg/ml[a]	Physically compatible for 4 hr at 25 °C	1188	C
Fentanyl citrate	ES	0.05 mg/ml	AB	0.02 mg/ml[a]	Visually compatible for 4 hr at 27 °C	2062	C
Furosemide	AMR	10 mg/ml	AB	0.02 mg/ml[a]	Visually compatible for 4 hr at 27 °C	2062	C
Heparin sodium	UP	1000 units/L[d]	AB	0.1 mg/ml	Physically compatible for at least 4 hr at room temperature by visual and microscopic examination	534	C
	ES	100 units/ml[a]	AB	0.02 mg/ml[a]	Visually compatible for 4 hr at 27 °C	2062	C
Hetastarch in lactated electrolyte injection (Hextend)	AB	6%	AB	0.05 mg/ml[a]	Physically compatible with no change in measured turbidity or increase in particle content in 4 hr at 23 °C	2339	C
Hydrocortisone sodium succinate	UP	10 mg/L[d]	AB	0.1 mg/ml	Physically compatible for at least 4 hr at room temperature by visual and microscopic examination	534	C
Hydromorphone HCl	KN	1 mg/ml	AB	0.02 mg/ml[a]	Visually compatible for 4 hr at 27 °C	2062	C
Inamrinone lactate	WB	3 mg/ml[b]	AB	0.1 mg/ml	Physically compatible for at least 4 hr at 25 °C under fluorescent light	992	C
Labetalol HCl	AH	2 mg/ml[a]	AB	0.02 mg/ml[a]	Visually compatible for 4 hr at 27 °C	2062	C
Levofloxacin	OMN	5 mg/ml[a]	AB	1 mg/ml	Visually compatible for 4 hr at 24 °C under fluorescent light	2233	C
Lorazepam	WY	0.5 mg/ml[a]	AB	0.02 mg/ml[a]	Visually compatible for 4 hr at 27 °C	2062	C
Midazolam HCl	RC	2 mg/ml[a]	AB	0.02 mg/ml[a]	Visually compatible for 4 hr at 27 °C	2062	C
Milrinone lactate	SW	0.2 mg/ml[a]	AB	0.02 mg/ml[a]	Visually compatible for 4 hr at 27 °C	2062	C
	SW	0.4 mg/ml[a]	AB	0.064 mg/ml[a]	Visually compatible with little or no loss of either drug by HPLC in 4 hr at 23 °C	2214	C
Morphine sulfate	SCN	2 mg/ml[a]	AB	0.02 mg/ml[a]	Visually compatible for 4 hr at 27 °C	2062	C
Nicardipine HCl	WY	1 mg/ml[a]	AB	0.02 mg/ml[a]	Visually compatible for 4 hr at 27 °C	2062	C
Nitroglycerin	AB	0.4 mg/ml[a]	AB	0.02 mg/ml[a]	Visually compatible for 4 hr at 27 °C	2062	C
Norepinephrine bitartrate	AB	0.128 mg/ml[a]	AB	0.02 mg/ml[a]	Visually compatible for 4 hr at 27 °C	2062	C
Pancuronium bromide	ES	0.05 mg/ml[a]	AB	4 µg/ml[a]	Physically compatible for 24 hr at 28 °C	1337	C
Phytonadione	MSD	0.4 mg/ml[c]	ES	0.032 mg/ml[c]	Physically compatible for 3 hr	1316	C

Y-Site Injection Compatibility (1:1 Mixture) (Cont.)

			Epinephrine HCl				
Drug	*Mfr*	*Conc*	*Mfr*	*Conc*	*Remarks*	*Ref*	*C/I*
Potassium chloride	AB	40 mEq/L[d]	AB	0.1 mg/ml	Physically compatible for at least 4 hr at room temperature by visual and microscopic examination	534	C
Propofol	ZEN	10 mg/ml	AMR	0.1 mg/ml	Physically compatible for 1 hr at 23 °C with no increase in particle content	2066	C
Ranitidine HCl	GL	1 mg/ml[a]	AB	0.02 mg/ml[a]	Visually compatible for 4 hr at 27 °C	2062	C
Remifentanil HCl	GW	0.025 and 0.25 mg/ml[b]	AMR	0.05 mg/ml[a]	Physically compatible with no change in measured turbidity or increase in particle content in 4 hr at 23 °C	2075	C
Thiopental sodium	AB	25 mg/ml[e]	AB	0.02 mg/ml[a]	Yellow color forms in 4 hr at 27 °C	2062	I
TPN #189[f]			AST	0.2 mg/ml[b]	Visually compatible for 24 hr at 22 °C	1767	C
Vecuronium bromide	OR	0.1 mg/ml[a]	AB	4 μg/ml[a]	Physically compatible for 24 hr at 28 °C	1337	C
	OR	1 mg/ml	AB	0.02 mg/ml[a]	Visually compatible for 4 hr at 27 °C	2062	C
Vitamin B complex with C	RC	2 ml/L[d]	AB	0.1 mg/ml	Physically compatible for at least 4 hr at room temperature by visual and microscopic examination	534	C
Warfarin sodium	DU	0.1[c] and 2[e] mg/ml	AMR	0.1 mg/ml[c]	Physically compatible with no change in measured turbidity or increase in particle content in 24 hr at 23 °C	2011	C

[a]*Tested in dextrose 5% in water.*
[b]*Tested in sodium chloride 0.9%.*
[c]*Tested in both dextrose 5% in water and sodium chloride 0.9%.*
[d]*Tested in dextrose 5% in Ringer's injection, dextrose 5% in Ringer's injection, lactated, dextrose 5% in water, Ringer's injection, lactated, and sodium chloride 0.9%.*
[e]*Tested in sterile water for injection.*
[f]*Refer to Appendix I for the composition of parenteral nutrition solutions. TPN indicates a 2-in-1 admixture.*
[g]*Tested in dextrose 5% in water, Ringer's injection, lactated, sodium chloride 0.45%, and sodium chloride 0.9%.*

Additional Compatibility Information

Alkalies and Oxidizing Agents — Epinephrine HCl is rapidly destroyed by alkalies or oxidizing agents including sodium bicarbonate, halogens, permanganates, chromates, nitrates, nitrites, and salts of easily reducible metals such as iron, copper, and zinc. (4)

Drugs known to be alkali labile such as epinephrine should not be mixed in aminophylline-containing solutions because of the alkalinity of these solutions. (6)

Color Changes — Visual inspection for color changes may be inadequate to assess compatibility of admixtures. In one evaluation with aminophylline stored at 25 °C, a color change was not noted until eight hours had elapsed. However, only 40% of the initial epinephrine HCl was still present in the admixture at 24 hours. (527)

Bupivacaine and Fentanyl — A solution composed of bupivacaine HCl (Winthrop) 0.44 mg/ml, fentanyl citrate (Janssen) 1.25 μg/ml, and epinephrine HCl (Abbott) 0.69 μg/ml was stored in 100-ml portable infusion pump reservoirs (Pharmacia Deltec) for 30 days at 3 and 23 °C. The samples were then delivered through the infusion pumps over 48 hours at near-body temperature (30 °C). The samples were visually compatible throughout, and bupivacaine HCl and fentanyl citrate exhibited no loss by HPLC analysis. Epinephrine HCl sustained about a 5 to 6% loss by HPLC analysis after 20 days of storage at both temperatures and about a 9 to 10% loss after 30 days of storage and subsequent pump delivery. The authors recommended restricting storage before administration to only 20 days. (1627)

Lidocaine HCl — When lidocaine HCl is mixed with epinephrine HCl, the buffering capacity of the lidocaine HCl may raise the pH of intravenous admixtures above 5.5, the maximum necessary for stability of epinephrine HCl. The final pH is usually about 6. Epinephrine HCl will begin to deteriorate within several hours. Therefore, admixtures should be used promptly after preparation or the separate administration of the epinephrine HCl should be considered. This restriction does not apply to commercial lidocaine–epinephrine combinations that have had the pH adjusted to retain the maximum epinephrine potency. (24)

EPIRUBICIN HCL
AHFS 10:00

Products — Epirubicin HCl is available as a 2-mg/ml, preservative-free, ready-to-use solution in single-use polypropylene vials of 25 and 100 ml containing 50 and 200 mg of drug, respectively. The solution also contains sodium chloride and water for injection. The pH has been adjusted with hydrochloric acid. (2)

pH — The solution pH has been adjusted to 3. (2)

Trade Name(s) — Ellence.

Administration — Epirubicin HCl is administered by intravenous infusion over three to five minutes; infusion into the tubing of a freely running intravenous infusion of sodium chloride 0.9% or dextrose 5% in water is recommended. Administration by direct push is not recommended because of the risk of extravasation. Extravasation may cause pain, severe tissue lesions, and necrosis and should be avoided. Burning or stinging may indicate extravasation, requiring immediate termination of the infusion and restarting in another vein. Epirubicin HCl must *not* be given by intramuscular or subcutaneous injection. (2)

Personnel preparing and administering this drug should take protective measures to avoid contact with the solution, including use of disposable gloves, gowns, masks, and eye goggles. Dose preparation should be performed in a suitable laminar airflow device on a work surface protected by plastic-backed absorbent paper. All equipment and materials used in preparing and administering doses should be disposed of safely using high-temperature incineration. (2) See Inactivation below.

Stability — Epirubicin HCl in intact vials should be stored under refrigeration at 2 to 8 °C and protected from freezing and exposure to light. The manufacturer recommends discarding any unused solution from the single-dose vials within 24 hours after initial puncture of the vial stopper. (2)

Beijnen et al. examined the stability of epirubicin HCl infusions. In solutions containing 100 mg/L in dextrose 5% in water (pH 4.35), the drug was stable for 28 days at 25 °C when protected from light. Epirubicin HCl was less stable in sodium chloride 0.9% or Ringer's injection, lactated, with a 10% loss in eight days under the same conditions. (1007)

Wood et al. assessed the stability of epirubicin HCl 100 mg/L in sodium chloride 0.9% (pH 6.47) when stored in PVC bags at 4 and 25 °C in the dark. Epirubicin HCl was stable for at least 43 and 20 days at 4 and 25 °C, respectively. The drug admixed in dextrose 5% in water (pH 4.36) also was stable for at least 43 days at 4 °C. (1460)

Epirubicin HCl was cultured with human lymphoblasts to determine whether its cytotoxic activity was retained. The solution retained cytotoxicity for 24 hours at 4 °C and room temperature. (1575)

pH Effects — Epirubicin HCl stability is pH dependent. It becomes progressively more stable at acid pH. Maximum stability is obtained at pH 4 to 5. (1007; 1460) Prolonged contact of epirubicin HCl with any solution having an alkaline pH should be avoided because of the resulting hydrolysis of the drug. (2)

Freezing Solutions — Epirubicin HCl was stable for at least 43 days when stored at −20 °C at a concentration of 100 mg/L in sodium chloride 0.9% or dextrose 5% in water in PVC bags (Travenol). (1460)

Keusters et al. also reported that epirubicin HCl 1 g/L in sodium chloride 0.9% in PVC bags (Urotainer, Roussel) was stable when stored for four weeks at −20 °C and thawed by microwave or natural warming, exhibiting less than 5% degradation. (1462)

Light Effects — Although epirubicin HCl is photosensitive, no special precautions are necessary to protect solutions containing epirubicin HCl 500 μg/ml or greater during intravenous administration (1463) even over periods extending to 14 days in room light. (2081)

Syringes — Epirubicin HCl 2 mg/ml in sterile water for injection was stable for at least 43 days at 4 °C in Plastipak (Becton-Dickinson) plastic syringes. (1460)

Adams et al. reported that epirubicin HCl 0.5 mg/ml in sodium chloride 0.9% was stable for at least 28 days at 4 and 20 °C when stored in plastic syringes. (1564)

Pujol et al. reported that epirubicin HCl 2 mg/ml in sodium chloride 0.9% was packaged in 50-ml polypropylene syringes with blind luer hubs and stored at 25 °C both exposed to and protected from light and at 4 °C protected from light. HPLC analysis found about a 2 to 4% loss in 14 days at 25 °C whether exposed to or protected from room light. No loss was found after 180 days of refrigerated storage. (2081)

Sorption — Wood et al. reported that epirubicin HCl was adsorbed to PVC bags. Losses depended on temperature, concentration, and vehicle. Losses were greatest in sodium chloride 0.9% at pH 6.47, compared with dextrose 5% in water at pH 4.36. After eight days of storage, examination of solutions containing epirubicin HCl 100 mg/L indicated combined losses of 4% at 4 °C and 8% at 25 °C. In clinical practice, epirubicin HCl at concentrations of at least 500 μg/ml exhibits negligible adsorptive losses during storage and delivery. Sorption to Plastipak (Becton-Dickinson) polypropylene syringes is also insignificant. (1460)

DeVroe et al. compared the delivery of epirubicin HCl from 50-mg/1000 ml solutions in dextrose 5% in water and sodium chloride 0.9% in glass, PVC, and high density polyethylene containers and PVC, polyethylene, and polybutadiene infusion sets. The epirubicin HCl delivered from the container/set configurations was equivalent, with no evidence of sorption. (1577)

Epirubicin HCl (Farmitalia) 20 μg/ml in dextrose 5% in water and sodium chloride 0.9% in PVC containers was infused through PVC infusion sets at 21 ml/hr over 24 hours at 22 °C while exposed to light. HPLC showed relatively minor fluctuations in delivered concentrations, with no evidence of sorption. (1700)

Filtration — Epirubicin HCl 50 mg/1000 ml in dextrose 5% in water and sodium chloride 0.9% was infused over 24 hours and exhibited a potency loss during the initial period of filtration through cellulose ester and nylon filters. However, the concentrations returned to expected levels within minutes, and the total amount of drug lost was deemed negligible. (1577)

Compatibility Information

Solution Compatibility

Epirubicin HCl

Solution	Mfr	Mfr	Conc/L	Remarks	Ref	C/I
Dextrose 3.3% in sodium chloride 0.3%		FA	100 mg	5% or less loss in 4 weeks at 25 °C in the dark	1007	C
Dextrose 5% in water		FA	100 mg	5% or less loss in 4 weeks at 25 °C in the dark	1007	C
	TR[a]	FA	100 mg	10% or less loss in 43 days at 4 and 25 °C in the dark	1460	C
	[b]	FA	50 mg	8 to 9% loss by HPLC in 30 days at 4 °C protected from light	1577	C
	[a]	FA	40 mg	Potency retained for 7 days at 4 °C protected from light	1700	C
Ringer's injection, lactated		FA	100 mg	5% or less loss in 4 weeks at 25 °C in the dark	1007	C
Sodium chloride 0.9%		FA	100 mg	5% or less loss in 4 weeks at 25 °C in the dark	1007	C
	TR[a]	FA	100 mg	10% or less loss in 43 days at 4 and 25 °C in the dark	1460	C
	[b]	FA	50 mg	6% or less loss by HPLC in 25 days at 4 °C protected from light	1577	C
	[a]	FA	40 mg	Potency retained for 7 days at 4 °C protected from light	1700	C

[a]*Tested in PVC containers.*
[b]*Tested in glass, PVC, and high density polyethylene containers.*

Drugs in Syringe Compatibility

Epirubicin HCl

Drug (in syringe)	Mfr	Amt	Mfr	Amt	Remarks	Ref	C/I
Fluorouracil		500 mg/ 10 ml		5 and 10 mg/ ml[a]	Precipitate forms within several hours	1564	I
Ifosfamide		50 mg/ ml[a]		1 mg/ml[a]	Little or no loss of either drug by HPLC in 28 days at 4 and 20 °C	1564	C
Ifosfamide with mesna		50 mg/ ml[a] 40 mg/ ml[a]		1 mg/ml[a]	50% epirubicin loss by HPLC in 7 days at 4 and 20 °C. No loss of other drugs in 7 days	1564	I

[a]*Tested in sodium chloride 0.9%.*

Additional Compatibility Information

Other Drugs — The manufacturer recommends that other drugs not be mixed with epirubicin HCl. Heparin sodium and fluorouracil are incompatible with epirubicin HCl because of the potential for precipitation. Contact with any alkaline solution should be avoided because of the resulting hydrolysis of epirubicin HCl. (2) See pH Effects above.

Other Information

Inactivation — Spills or leakage of epirubicin HCl solutions should be diluted with sodium hypochlorite having 1% available chlorine, preferably by soaking, and then diluted further with water. (2)

Methylparaben — The methylparaben present in the lyophilized epirubicin HCl formulations available in some countries enhances the dissolution rate by disrupting bonding between epirubicin and other components. (1442)

EPOETIN ALFA
AHFS 20:16

Products — Epoetin alfa is available in 1-ml single-use (unpreserved) vials containing 2000, 3000, 4000, and 10,000 units/ml. The solution also contains in each milliliter albumin human 2.5 mg, sodium citrate 5.8 mg, sodium chloride 5.8 mg, and citric acid 0.06 mg in water for injection. (2)

Preservative-free single-dose epoetin alfa is also available in 1-ml vials containing 40,000 units along with albumin human 2.5 mg, sodium phosphate monobasic monohydrate 1.2 mg, sodium phosphate dibasic anhydrate 1.8 mg, sodium citrate 0.7 mg, sodium chloride 5.8 mg, and citric acid 6.8 mg in water for injection. (2)

Epoetin alfa is also available in 2-ml multidose (preserved) vials containing 10,000 units/ml and 1-ml multidose (preserved) vials containing 20,000 units/ml. The solution also contains in each milliliter albumin human 2.5 mg, sodium citrate 1.3 mg, sodium chloride 8.2 mg, citric acid 0.11 mg, and benzyl alcohol 1% in water for injection. (2)

pH — Single-use vials: from 6.6 to 7.2. Multidose vials: from 5.8 to 6.4. (2)

Tonicity — The injection is isotonic. (2)

Trade Name(s) — Epogen, Procrit.

Administration — Epoetin alfa is administered by intravenous or subcutaneous injection. For subcutaneous injection, epoetin alfa (single-dose) may be diluted at the time of administration with an equal quantity of bacteriostatic sodium chloride 0.9% containing benzyl alcohol 0.9% to help ameliorate local discomfort at the subcutaneous injection site. (2; 4)

Stability — Epoetin alfa is a colorless solution. It should not be used if it contains particulate matter or is discolored. Intact vials should be stored under refrigeration and protected from freezing. To prevent foaming and inactivation, the product should not be shaken; vigorous prolonged shaking may denature the protein, inactivating it. (2; 4) However, a small amount of flocculated protein in the solution does not affect potency. In addition, exposure to light for less than 24 hours does not adversely affect the product. (4)

The single-dose vials have no preservative. After a single dose has been removed from this product, the vial should not be re-entered and should be discarded. (2) Drawn into plastic tuberculin syringes, the preservative-free products at 2000 or 10,000 units/ml are reported to be stable for two weeks at room temperature or under refrigeration. However, use shortly after drawing up in syringes is recommended because of the absence of preservative. (4)

Usually, epoetin alfa should not be diluted and transferred to new containers or admixed with other drugs and solutions because of possible protein loss from adsorption to PVC containers and tubing. However, when 10,000-unit/ml single-use product is diluted in the original vial with benzyl alcohol-preserved sodium chloride 0.9% injection to a concentration of 4000 units/ml for subcutaneous use, it is stated to be stable for at least 12 weeks stored at 5 and 30 °C. Furthermore, the final benzyl alcohol concentration of 0.54% enabled the dilution to pass the USP preservative effectiveness test. (1905) Restriction of this dilution to 28 days used as a multiple-dose vial has been recommended. (1906) Higher concentrations of epoetin alfa (e.g., 5000 units/ml), which would have lower benzyl alcohol concentrations, were found to fail the preservative effectiveness test. (1905)

The multidose vials contain a preservative and may be stored under refrigeration after initial dose removal. The vials should be discarded 21 days after initial entry. (2)

Compatibility Information

Solution Compatibility

Epoetin alfa

Solution	*Mfr*	*Mfr*	*Conc/L*	*Remarks*	*Ref*	*C/I*
Dextrose 10% in water	[a]	ORT	100 units	Up to 40% of epoetin alfa lost by bioassay over 24-hr delivery	1878	I
Dextrose 10% in water with albumin human 0.01%	[a]	ORT	100 units	Up to 40% of epoetin alfa lost by bioassay over 24-hr delivery	1878	I
Dextrose 10% in water with albumin human 0.05%	[a]	ORT	100 units	98% of the epoetin alfa by bioassay delivered over 24 hr	1878	C
Dextrose 10% in water with albumin human 0.1%	[a]	ORT	100 units	98% of the epoetin alfa by bioassay delivered over 24 hr	1878	C
Sodium chloride 0.9%	[a]	ORT	100 units	15% of epoetin alfa lost by bioassay over 24-hr delivery	1878	I
TPN[b]	[a]	ORT	100 units	98% of the epoetin alfa by bioassay delivered over 24 hr	1878	C

[a] *Delivered from a syringe through microbore tubing, T-connector, and a Teflon neonatal 24-gauge intravenous catheter.*
[b] *TPN composed of amino acids (TrophAmine) 0.5% or 2.25% with dextrose 12.5%, vitamins, trace elements, magnesium sulfate, calcium gluconate, sodium chloride, potassium acetate, and heparin sodium.*

ERGONOVINE MALEATE
AHFS 76:00

Products — Ergonovine maleate is available in 1-ml vials. Each milliliter of solution contains (1-3/95):

Ergonovine maleate	0.2 mg
Ethyl lactate	0.1%
Lactic acid	0.1%
Phenol	0.25%
Water for injection	qs 1 ml

pH — From 2.7 to 3.5. (4)

Trade Name(s) — Ergotrate Maleate.

Administration — Ergonovine maleate may be administered by intramuscular injection or intravenous injection over at least one minute. Dilution of intravenous doses to 5 ml with sodium chloride 0.9% has been recommended. (4)

Stability — Although storage of ergonovine maleate below 8 °C is recommended, intact ampuls are stable for 60 to 90 days at controlled room temperature. (4; 60; 853; 1433) If discoloration occurs, the drug should not be used. (4)

Filtration — Ergonovine maleate (Lilly) 0.2 mg/25 ml in dextrose 5% in water and sodium chloride 0.9%, filtered at a rate of about 3 ml/min through a 0.22-μm cellulose ester membrane filter (Ivex-2), showed no significant reduction in potency due to binding to the filter. (533)

Compatibility Information

Additive Compatibility

Ergonovine maleate

Drug	*Mfr*	*Conc/L*	*Mfr*	*Conc/L*	*Test Soln*	*Remarks*	*Ref*	*C/I*
Amikacin sulfate	BR	5 g	LI	0.2 mg	D5LR, D5R, D5S, D5W, D10W, IS10, LR, NS, R, SL	Physically compatible and amikacin potency retained for 24 hr at 25 °C. Ergonovine not analyzed	294	C
Sodium bicarbonate	AB	2.4 mEq[a]		0.2 mg	D5W	Physically compatible for 24 hr	772	C

[a]*One vial of Neut added to a liter of admixture.*

ERYTHROMYCIN LACTOBIONATE
AHFS 8:12.12

Products — Erythromycin lactobionate is available in vials containing the equivalent of 1 g of erythromycin with benzyl alcohol 180 mg and in vials containing the equivalent of 500 mg of erythromycin with benzyl alcohol 90 mg. (1-10/96) Reconstitute the 1-g vials with at least 20 ml and the 500-mg vials with at least 10 ml of sterile water for injection without preservatives. (1-10/96; 4; 20) The resultant concentration is 5% (50 mg/ml). (1-10/96; 20)

Erythromycin lactobionate is also available in piggyback containers containing the equivalent of 500 mg of erythromycin with benzyl alcohol 90 mg. Reconstitute the 500-mg piggyback vial by adding 100 ml of sodium chloride 0.9%, Ringer's injection, lactated, or Normosol R. Alternatively, reconstitution may be made with 100 ml of the following solutions that have been buffered with 1 ml of sodium bicarbonate 4% additive solution (Neut, Abbott) (4):

Dextrose 5% in water
Dextrose 5% in Ringer's injection, lactated
Dextrose 5% in sodium chloride 0.9%
Normosol M and dextrose 5%
Normosol R and dextrose 5%

Immediately after adding the diluent, shake the product well to decrease the time required to effect dissolution. (4)

pH — Reconstitution with sterile water for injection to a 50-mg/ml concentration results in a solution with a pH of 6.5 to 7.5. (20)

One report indicated that the addition of 4% sodium bicarbonate buffer may not be necessary, even in dextrose-containing solutions. The pH of erythromycin lactobionate 500 mg/100 ml was determined to be 6.8 when dextrose 5% in water was the diluent and 7.15 when sodium chloride 0.9% was the diluent. The sodium bicarbonate buffer raised the solution pH about 0.5 to 0.7 pH unit above these values. (1260)

Osmolality — Erythromycin lactobionate (Abbott) 50 mg/ml in sterile water for injection has an osmolality of 223 mOsm/kg. (50)

The osmolality of erythromycin lactobionate was calculated for the following dilutions (1054):

Diluent	Osmolality (mOsm/kg) 50 ml	100 ml
500 mg		
Dextrose 5% in water	273	265
Sodium chloride 0.9%	299	291
1 g		
Dextrose 5% in water	287	273
Sodium chloride 0.9%	313	300

Trade Name(s)—Erythrocin Lactobionate-I.V., Erythrocin Piggyback.

Administration — Erythromycin lactobionate may be administered by continuous or intermittent intravenous infusion; it must not be given by direct intravenous injection. (1-10/96; 4) To minimize venous irritation, slow continuous infusion of a 1-mg/ml concentration is recommended. By intermittent infusion, one-fourth of the daily dose at a concentration of 1 to 5 mg/ml in at least 100 ml of infusion solution may be given over 20 to 60 minutes every six hours. (1-10/96; 4)

Stability — Do not use sodium chloride 0.9% or other solutions containing inorganic ions in the initial reconstitution of the regular vials. Such solutions result in the formation of a precipitate. (1-10/96; 4; 20) (Note: This restriction does not apply to the drug in piggyback containers.)

The commercial vials are stable at room temperature (20) and have an expiration date four years from manufacture. (4) Reconstituted (5%) solutions are stable for 14 days when stored under refrigeration at 2 to 15 °C (1-10/96; 20) or for 24 hours when kept at room temperature. (1-10/96; 4)

The manufacturer indicates that the reconstituted erythromycin lactobionate in piggyback containers should be used within eight hours at room temperature or 24 hours under refrigeration. (4)

pH Effects—The stability of erythromycin lactobionate is extremely pH dependent. It is most stable at pH 6 to 8 (20; 1935) or 9. (1101) Erythromycin lactobionate is unstable in acidic solutions. Decomposition occurs at an increasingly more rapid rate as the pH approaches 4. (20) A pH of at least 5.5 is recommended for the final diluted solution. (1-10/96) At pH 5.5 or below and at pH 10 or above, erythromycin (both gluceptate and lactobionate) is particularly unstable, with 10% decomposition occurring in about eight or nine hours. Pluta and Morgan determined the following pH profile for erythromycin in solution (1101):

Solution pH	Approximate Time for 10% Decomposition (t_{90})
5.0	2.5 hr
5.5	8.8 hr
6.0	1 day
7.0	4.6 days
8.0	7.3 days
9.0	2.6 days
10.0	8.8 hr
11.0	53 min

The effect of buffering erythromycin lactobionate (Abbott) solutions was evaluated by Allwood. Erythromycin lactobionate 2 mg/ml in sodium chloride 0.9% (pH 7.15 to 7.25) exhibited 5% losses by HPLC analysis in about 20 days at 5 °C. However, buffering with sodium bicarbonate to pH 7.5 to 8 extended stability, with 5% losses occurring in about 85 days at 5 °C. (1587)

Freezing Solutions—Although the freezing of erythromycin lactobionate solutions was not previously recommended (108), the manufacturers indicate that freezing is acceptable for the piggyback containers and vials. The reconstituted solution should be frozen within four hours of preparation. The solution is stable for 30 days when stored frozen at −10 to −20 °C. Thawing should be performed in the refrigerator, and use of the thawed solution within eight hours is recommended. The thawed solution should not be refrozen. (4)

Erythromycin lactobionate (Abbott) 500 mg/110 ml in sodium chloride 0.9% in PVC bags was frozen at −20 °C; HPLC analysis found no loss after 12 months of storage followed by microwave thawing. Furthermore, the solution was physically compatible, with no increase in subvisual particles. In addition, no erythromycin loss was found by HPLC analysis after six months at −20 °C followed by three freeze–thaw cycles. (1612)

Ambulatory Pumps—Stiles et al. evaluated the stability of erythromycin lactobionate (Elkins-Sinn) 20 mg/ml in sterile water for injection and sodium chloride 0.9% in 100-ml portable pump reservoirs (Pharmacia Deltec) during simulated administration for 24 hours. The drug solutions were tested by HPLC analysis when administered immediately after preparation and after storage for 24 hours at 5 °C before 24-hour administration. During simulated administration, some reservoirs were kept at 30 °C; others were placed in insulated pouches with frozen (−20 °C) gel packs to keep them chilled below the ambient temperature. The erythromycin lactobionate solutions exhibited little or no loss by HPLC under all study conditions. Chilling of the drug reservoirs was not necessary to complete the infusions, nor did it enhance stability substantially during the study period. (1779)

Compatibility Information

Solution Compatibility

Erythromycin lactobionate

Solution	*Mfr*	*Mfr*	*Conc/L*	*Remarks*	*Ref*	*C/I*
Dextrose 2½% in half-strength Ringer's injection, lactated	AB	AB	1 g	10% decomposition in 4 hr at 25 °C	20	I
Dextrose 5% in Ringer's injection, lactated	AB	AB	1 g	10% decomposition in 3 hr at 25 °C	20	I
	TR[a]	AB	1 g	10 to 24% decomposition in 24 hr at 5 °C	282	I

Solution Compatibility (Cont.)

Erythromycin lactobionate

Solution	*Mfr*	*Mfr*	*Conc/L*	*Remarks*	*Ref*	*C/I*
Dextrose 5% in sodium chloride 0.9%	TR[a]	AB	1 g	Potency retained for 24 hr at 5 °C	282	C
	AB	AB	1 g	33% decomposition in 24 hr	46	I
		AB	1 g	12% decomposition in 6 hr at 25 °C	48	I
		AB	2 g	15% decomposition in 6 hr	109	I
Dextrose 5% in water	TR[a]	AB	1 g	Potency retained for 24 hr at 5 °C	282	C
	AB	AB	1 g	15% decomposition in 24 hr	46	I
	AB	AB	1 g	10% decomposition in 10 hr at 25 °C	20	I
		AB	1 g	15% decomposition in 24 hr at 25 °C	48	I
		AB	2 g	14% decomposition in 6 hr	109	I
	TR[b]	AB	4 g	21% reduction in microbiologic inhibition in 24 hr at room temperature	518	I
	TR[b]	AB	4 g	Buffered[c]—physically compatible and potency retained for 24 hr at room temperature	518	C
Dextrose 10% in water		AB	2 g	14% decomposition in 6 hr	109	I
Multielectrolyte solution	AB	AB	1 g	14% decomposition in 24 hr	46	I
Normosol M in dextrose 5%	AB	AB	1 g	10% decomposition in 6 hr at 25 °C	20	I
Normosol R		AB	1 g	14% decomposition in 24 hr at 25 °C	48	I
Ringer's injection	AB	AB	1 g	10% decomposition in 11 hr at 25 °C	20	I
Ringer's injection, lactated	TR[a]	AB	1 g	Potency retained for 24 hr at 5 °C	282	C
	AB	AB	1 g	10% decomposition in 18 hr at 25 °C	20	I
Sodium chloride 0.9%		AB	1 g	Potency retained for 24 hr at 25 °C	48	C
		AB	2 g	Potency retained for 24 hr	109	C
	AB	AB	1 g	Potency retained for 24 hr	46	C
	AB	AB	1 g	10% decomposition in 22 hr at 25 °C	20	C
	TR[a]	AB	1 g	Potency retained for 24 hr at 5 °C	282	C
	TR[b]	AB	4 g	Physically compatible and potency retained for 24 hr at room temperature	518	C
	TR[b]	AB	4 g	Buffered[c]—physically compatible and potency retained for 24 hr at room temperature	518	C
		AB	2 g	5% loss by HPLC in about 20 days at 5 °C	1587	C
	BA[b]	AB	8.3 g	No more than 5% loss by HPLC after 60 days at 5 °C	1597	C
	AB[d]	ES	20 g	Little or no loss by HPLC with 24-hr storage at 5 °C followed by 24-hr simulated administration at 30 °C via portable pump	1779	C

[a]*Tested in both glass and PVC containers.*
[b]*Tested in PVC containers.*
[c]*Buffered with sodium bicarbonate 4% (Neut, Abbott).*
[d]*Tested in portable pump reservoirs (Pharmacia Deltec).*

Additive Compatibility

Erythromycin lactobionate

Drug	*Mfr*	*Conc/L*	*Mfr*	*Conc/L*	*Test Soln*	*Remarks*	*Ref*	*C/I*
Aminophylline	SE	500 mg	AB	1 g		Physically compatible. Erythromycin potency retained for 24 hr at 25 °C	20	C
Ampicillin sodium	WY	3.7 g	AB	3 g	NS	Physically compatible with 6% ampicillin loss in 1 day at 24 °C	1035	C
Ascorbic acid injection	AB	1 g	AB	1 g		Physically compatible	3	C
	UP	500 mg	AB	5 g	D5W	Physically incompatible	15	I

Additive Compatibility (Cont.)

			Erythromycin lactobionate					
Drug	*Mfr*	*Conc/L*	*Mfr*	*Conc/L*	*Test Soln*	*Remarks*	*Ref*	*C/I*
Cimetidine HCl	SKF	3 g	AB	5 g	D5W	Physically compatible and cimetidine chemically stable for 24 hr at room temperature. Erythromycin not tested	551	C
Colistimethate sodium	WC	500 mg	AB	5 g	D5W	Physically incompatible	15	I
	WC	500 mg	AB	1 g	D	Precipitate forms within 1 hr	20	I
Diphenhydramine HCl	PD	50 mg	AB	1 g		Physically compatible. Erythromycin potency retained for 24 hr at 25 °C	20	C
	PD	50 mg	AB	1 g	D5W	Erythromycin potency retained for 24 hr at 25 °C	48	C
Floxacillin sodium	BE	20 g	AB	5 g	NS	Immediate precipitation. Crystals form in 5 hr at 15 °C	1479	I
Furosemide	HO	1 g	AB	5 g	NS	Immediate precipitation. Crystals form in 12 to 24 hr at 15 and 30 °C	1479	I
Heparin sodium	UP	4000 units	AB	5 g	D5W	Physically incompatible	15	I
	AB	1500 units	AB	1 g		Precipitate forms within 1 hr	20	I
	AB	20,000 units	AB	1 g		Precipitate forms within 1 hr	21	I
	OR	20,000 units	AB	1.5 g	D5W, NS	Precipitate forms	113	I
Hydrocortisone sodium succinate	UP	500 mg	AB	5 g	D5W	Physically compatible	15	C
	UP	250 mg	AB	1 g		Physically compatible	3; 20	C
Lidocaine HCl	AST	2 g	AB	1 g		Physically compatible	24	C
Linezolid	PHU	2 g	AB	5 g	[b]	Very rapid erythromycin decomposition; loss by HPLC of 15% in 1 hr and 30% in 4 hr at 23 °C. Losses of about 45% in 1 day at 4 °C	2333	I
Metaraminol bitartrate	MSD	100 mg	AB	750 mg	D5W	92% erythromycin decomposition in 24 hr at 25 °C	20	I
	MSD	100 mg	AB	1 g	D5W	44% erythromycin decomposition in 6 hr at 25 °C	48	I
Metoclopramide HCl	RB	400 mg	AB	4 g	NS	Incompatible. If mixed, use immediately	924	I
	RB	100 mg	AB	5 g	NS	Incompatible. If mixed, use immediately	924	I
	RB	416 mg	AB	4.1 g		Incompatible. If mixed, use immediately	1167	I
	RB	100 mg	AB	5 g		Incompatible. If mixed, use immediately	1167	I
	RB	1.1 g	AB	3.5 g		Incompatible. If mixed, use immediately	1167	I
Penicillin G potassium		1 million units	AB	1 g		Physically compatible	3	C
	SQ	20 million units	AB	5 g	D5W	Physically compatible	15	C
	SQ	5 million units	AB	1 g		Physically compatible	20; 47	C
Penicillin G sodium	UP	20 million units	AB	5 g	D5W	Physically compatible	15	C

Additive Compatibility (Cont.)

Erythromycin lactobionate

Drug	*Mfr*	*Conc/L*	*Mfr*	*Conc/L*	*Test Soln*	*Remarks*	*Ref*	*C/I*
Pentobarbital sodium	AB	500 mg	AB	1 g		Physically compatible. Erythromycin potency retained for 24 hr at 25 °C	20	C
Polymyxin B sulfate	BW	200 mg	AB	5 g	D5W	Physically compatible	15	C
Potassium chloride	AB	40 mEq	AB	1 g		Physically compatible	20	C
Prochlorperazine edisylate	SKF	10 mg	AB	1 g		Physically compatible. Erythromycin potency retained for 24 hr at 25 °C	20	C
Promazine HCl	WY	100 mg	AB	1 g		Physically compatible	20	C
Ranitidine HCl	GL	50 mg and 2 g		5 g	NS	Physically compatible and ranitidine chemically stable by HPLC for 24 hr at 25 °C. Erythromycin not tested	1515	C
Sodium bicarbonate	AB	3.75 g	AB	1 g		Physically compatible. Erythromycin potency retained for 24 hr at 25 °C	20	C
	AB	2.4 mEq[a]	AB	1 g	D5W	Physically compatible for 24 hr	772	C
Verapamil HCl	KN	80 mg	AB	2 g	D5W, NS	Physically compatible for 24 hr	764	C
Vitamin B complex with C	AB	5 ml		5 g	D5W	pH outside stability range	100	I
	AB	10 ml	AB	500 mg	D5W	90% erythromycin decomposition in 24 hr at 25 °C	20	I
		10 ml	AB	1 g	D5W	74% erythromycin decomposition in 6 hr at 25 °C	48	I

[a] *One vial of Neut added to a liter of admixture.*
[b] *Admixed in the linezolid infusion container.*

Drugs in Syringe Compatibility

Erythromycin lactobionate

Drug (in syringe)	*Mfr*	*Amt*	*Mfr*	*Amt*	*Remarks*	*Ref*	*C/I*
Ampicillin sodium	AY	500 mg	AB	300 mg/ 6 ml	Precipitate forms in 1 hr at room temperature	300	I
Heparin sodium	AB	20,000 units/ 1 ml	AB	1 g	Physically incompatible	21	I
		2500 units/ 1 ml	SC	250 mg	Turbidity or precipitate forms within 5 min	1053	I

Y-Site Injection Compatibility (1:1 Mixture)

Erythromycin lactobionate

Drug	*Mfr*	*Conc*	*Mfr*	*Conc*	*Remarks*	*Ref*	*C/I*
Acyclovir sodium	BW	5 mg/ml[a]	AB	4 mg/ml[a]	Physically compatible for 4 hr at 25 °C	1157	C
Amiodarone HCl	LZ	4 mg/ml[c]	AB	2 mg/ml[c]	Physically compatible for 4 hr at room temperature	1444	C
Cyclophosphamide	MJ	20 mg/ml[a]	AB	5 mg/ml[a]	Physically compatible for 4 hr at 25 °C	1194	C
Diltiazem HCl	MMD	5 mg/ml	ES	5 and 50 mg/ ml[b]	Visually compatible	1807	C

Y-Site Injection Compatibility (1:1 Mixture) (Cont.)

Drug	*Mfr*	*Conc*	*Mfr*	*Conc*	*Remarks*	*Ref*	*C/I*
			Erythromycin lactobionate				
Enalaprilat	MSD	0.05 mg/ml[b]	AB	5 mg/ml[a]	Physically compatible for 24 hr at room temperature under fluorescent light	1355	C
Esmolol HCl	DCC	10 mg/ml[a]	AB	5 mg/ml[a]	Physically compatible for 24 hr at 22 °C	1169	C
Famotidine	MSD	0.2 mg/ml[a]	ES	2 mg/ml[b]	Physically compatible for 14 hr	1196	C
Fluconazole	RR	2 mg/ml	LY	20 mg/ml	Immediate precipitation	1407	I
Foscarnet sodium	AST	24 mg/ml	AB	20 mg/ml	Physically compatible for 24 hr at room temperature under fluorescent light	1335	C
	AST	24 mg/ml	ES	20 mg/ml[c]	Physically compatible for 24 hr at 25 °C under fluorescent light by visual and microscopic examination	1393	C
Heparin sodium	TR	50 units/ml	AB	3.3 mg/ml[b]	Visually compatible for 4 hr at 25 °C	1793	C
Hetastarch in lactated electrolyte injection (Hextend)	AB	6%	AB	5 mg/ml[b]	Physically compatible with no change in measured turbidity or increase in particle content in 4 hr at 23 °C	2339	C
Hydromorphone HCl	WY	0.2 mg/ml[a]	AB	5 mg/ml[a]	Physically compatible for at least 4 hr at 25 °C under fluorescent light	987	C
Idarubicin HCl	AD	1 mg/ml[b]	ES	2 mg/ml[b]	Visually compatible for 24 hr at 25 °C	1525	C
Labetalol HCl	SC	1 mg/ml[a]	AB	5 mg/ml[a]	Physically compatible for 24 hr at 18 °C	1171	C
Lorazepam	WY	0.33 mg/ml[b]	AB	5 mg/ml	Visually compatible for 24 hr at 22 °C	1855	C
Magnesium sulfate	IX	16.7, 33.3, 66.7, 100 mg/ml[a]	AB	5 mg/ml[a]	Physically compatible for at least 4 hr at 32 °C	813	C
Meperidine HCl	WY	10 mg/ml[a]	AB	5 mg/ml[a]	Physically compatible for at least 4 hr at 25 °C under fluorescent light	987	C
Midazolam HCl	RC	5 mg/ml	AB	5 mg/ml	Visually compatible for 24 hr at 22 °C	1855	C
Morphine sulfate	WI	1 mg/ml[a]	AB	5 mg/ml[a]	Physically compatible for at least 4 hr at 25 °C under fluorescent light	987	C
Multivitamins	USV	5 ml/L[a]	AB	500 mg/250 ml[b]	Physically compatible for 24 hr at room temperature	323	C
Perphenazine	SC	0.02 mg/ml[a]	AB	5 mg/ml[a]	Physically compatible for 4 hr at 25 °C	1155	C
Tacrolimus	FUJ	1 mg/ml[b]	AB	20 mg/ml[a]	Visually compatible for 24 hr at 25 °C	1630	C
Theophylline	TR	4 mg/ml	AB	3.3 mg/ml[b]	Visually compatible for 6 hr at 25 °C	1793	C
TNA #73[d]		32.5 ml[e]	AB	1 g/50 ml[b]	Physically compatible for 4 hr at 25 °C by visual assessment	1008	C
TPN #61[d]		[f]	AB	50 mg/1 ml[g]	Physically compatible	1012	C
		[h]	AB	300 mg/6 ml[g]	Physically compatible	1012	C
TPN #189[d]			DB	10 mg/ml[a]	Visually compatible for 24 hr at 22 °C	1767	C
Vitamin B complex with C (Berocca-C 500)	RC	4 ml/L[a]	AB	500 mg/250 ml[b]	Physically compatible for 24 hr at room temperature	323	C
(Berocca-C)	RC	20 ml/L[a]	AB	500 mg/250 ml[b]	Physically compatible for 24 hr at room temperature	323	C

Y-Site Injection Compatibility (1:1 Mixture) (Cont.)

Drug	Mfr	Conc	Erythromycin lactobionate Mfr	Erythromycin lactobionate Conc	Remarks	Ref	C/I
Zidovudine	BW	4 mg/ml[a]	AB	20 mg/ml[a,i]	Physically compatible for 4 hr at 25 °C under fluorescent light by visual and microscopic examination	1193	C

[a]*Tested in dextrose 5% in water.*
[b]*Tested in sodium chloride 0.9%.*
[c]*Tested in both dextrose 5% in water and sodium chloride 0.9%.*
[d]*Refer to Appendix I for the composition of parenteral nutrition solutions. TNA indicates a 3-in-1 admixture, and TPN indicates a 2-in-1 admixture.*
[e]*A 32.5-ml sample of parenteral nutrition solution mixed with 50 ml of antibiotic solution.*
[f]*Run at 21 ml/hr.*
[g]*Given over 30 minutes by syringe pump.*
[h]*Run at 94 ml/hr.*
[i]*Sodium bicarbonate 2.5 mEq added to adjust pH.*

Additional Compatibility Information

Infusion Solutions — Erythromycin lactobionate can alter the pH of solutions and give itself some protection against decomposition for varying periods. The length of time is dependent on the initial pH and the buffer capacity of the solution. (48) The pH of unbuffered dextrose 5% in water is raised one pH unit by the addition of erythromycin lactobionate. (20) The use of admixtures with a pH of less than 5 is not recommended. If the admixture pH is 5 to 6, it should be used immediately. (48) (See pH Effects.)

Erythromycin lactobionate (Abbott) 1 g/L is physically compatible with all Abbott infusion solutions. (20) The reconstituted drug may be added to sodium chloride 0.9%, Ringer's injection, lactated, or Normosol R for infusion. It can also be infused in dextrose 5% in water, dextrose 5% in sodium chloride 0.9%, and dextrose 5% in Ringer's injection, lactated, providing the solutions are first buffered with sodium bicarbonate 4% additive solution (Neut, Abbott). The manufacturers recommend the use of 1 ml of Neut for each 100 ml of these solutions. (1-10/96)

Chloramphenicol — Erythromycin lactobionate (Abbott) in dextrose 5% in water has been reported to be conditionally compatible with chloramphenicol sodium succinate (Parke-Davis). The incompatibility is dependent on the concentration of the additives. Therefore, if attempting to combine erythromycin with chloramphenicol sodium succinate, mix the solution thoroughly and observe it closely for any sign of incompatibility. (15)

Riboflavin — Erythromycin 5 mg/ml as the lactobionate in pH 8 buffer was combined with riboflavin in concentrations varying from 1 mg/ml to 20 μg/ml. On exposure to light for four hours, almost total decomposition of the erythromycin occurred, with only 4 to 12% remaining. Protection from light resulted in 12 to 25% decomposition. When no riboflavin was present, 10% or less decomposition of the erythromycin occurred. It was concluded that a photodynamic decomposition reaction was taking place. (564)

Other Drugs — Erythromycin lactobionate may exhibit physical incompatibility with sodium salts of several biologically derived macromolecules such as antibiotics. (20)

In addition, additives that may result in a final admixture pH below 5.5 should not be mixed with erythromycin lactobionate. These additives include metaraminol bitartrate, ascorbic acid (but not sodium ascorbate), and vitamin B complex with C. (20)

ESMOLOL HCL
AHFS 24:04

Products — Esmolol HCl is available as a concentrate containing 250 mg/ml in 10-ml ampuls with propylene glycol 25% and ethanol 25% in water for injection. The product is buffered with sodium acetate 17 mg and glacial acetic acid 0.00715 ml in each milliliter and may contain sodium hydroxide and/or hydrochloric acid to adjust the pH if necessary. (2; 4)

Esmolol HCl concentrate must be diluted before use. The manufacturer recommends adding the contents of two 2.5-g ampuls to 500 ml or one 2.5-g ampul to 250 ml (with prior removal of solution overage as necessary) to yield a 10-mg/ml solution. (2; 4)

A ready-to-use formulation containing esmolol HCl 10 mg/ml in 10-ml single-dose vials also is available. Each milliliter of this ready-to-use product is buffered with sodium acetate 2.8 mg and glacial acetic acid 0.546 mg and may contain sodium hydroxide and/or hydrochloric acid for pH adjustment. (2; 4)

pH — Concentrate: from 3.5 to 5.5. Ready-to-use: from 4.5 to 5.5. (4)

Osmolarity — Dilution of the esmolol HCl concentrate to 25 mg/ml in water results in a solution with an osmolarity of 1063 mOsm/L. (4)

Trade Name(s) — Brevibloc.

Administration — Esmolol HCl is administered by intravenous infusion at a concentration of 10 mg/ml, usually with an infusion control device. Concentrations exceeding 10 mg/ml are not recommended. (2; 4)

Stability — Esmolol HCl is a clear, colorless to light yellow solution. It should be stored at controlled room temperature and protected from elevated temperatures. Freezing does not affect the product adversely. (2; 4) When stored appropriately, the product has an expiration date three years from manufacture. (4)

pH Effects — Esmolol HCl is relatively stable at neutral pH; the optimal pH is 4.5 to 5.5. However, ester hydrolysis occurs rapidly in strongly acidic or basic solutions. (1358; 1359)

Compatibility Information

Solution Compatibility

Esmolol HCl

Solution	*Mfr*	*Mfr*	*Conc/L*	*Remarks*	*Ref*	*C/I*
Dextrose 5% in Ringer's injection, lactated	BA[a], MG[b]	ACC	10 g	Visually compatible with little or no drug loss by HPLC in 7 days at 5 or 27 °C, 48 hr at 40 °C, and 24 hr under intense light	1831	C
Dextrose 5% in sodium chloride 0.45%	BA[a], MG[b]	ACC	10 g	Visually compatible with little or no drug loss by HPLC in 7 days at 5 or 27 °C, 48 hr at 40 °C, and 24 hr under intense light	1831	C
Dextrose 5% in sodium chloride 0.9%	BA[a], MG[b]	ACC	10 g	Visually compatible with little or no drug loss by HPLC in 7 days at 5 or 27 °C, 48 hr at 40 °C, and 24 hr under intense light	1831	C
Dextrose 5% in water	TR[a]	DU	6 g	Physically compatible with no loss in 24 hr at room temperature under fluorescent light	1358	C
	BA[a]	DU	10, 20, 30 g	Visually compatible with little or no drug loss by HPLC in 48 hr at 23 °C	1830	C
	BA[a], MG[b]	ACC	10 g	Visually compatible with little or no drug loss by HPLC in 7 days at 5 or 27 °C, 48 hr at 40 °C, and 24 hr under intense light	1831	C
Dextrose 5% in water with potassium chloride 40 mEq/L	BA[a], MG[b]	ACC	10 g	Visually compatible with little or no drug loss by HPLC in 7 days at 5 or 27 °C, 48 hr at 40 °C, and 24 hr under intense light	1831	C
Ringer's injection, lactated	BA[a], MG[b]	ACC	10 g	Visually compatible with little or no drug loss by HPLC in 7 days at 5 or 27 °C, 48 hr at 40 °C, and 24 hr under intense light	1831	C
Sodium bicarbonate 5%	MG[b]	ACC	10 g	Visually compatible with 5 and 8% esmolol losses by HPLC in 7 days at 5 and 27 °C, respectively. 9 and 4% losses in 24 hr at 40 °C and under intense light, respectively	1831	C
Sodium chloride 0.45%	BA[a], MG[b]	ACC	10 g	Visually compatible with little or no drug loss by HPLC in 7 days at 5 or 27 °C, 48 hr at 40 °C, and 24 hr under intense light	1831	C
Sodium chloride 0.9%	BA[a], MG[b]	ACC	10 g	Visually compatible with little or no drug loss by HPLC in 7 days at 5 or 27 °C, 48 hr at 40 °C, and 24 hr under intense light	1831	C

[a]Tested in PVC containers.
[b]Tested in glass containers.

Additive Compatibility

Esmolol HCl

Drug	*Mfr*	*Conc/L*	*Mfr*	*Conc/L*	*Test Soln*	*Remarks*	*Ref*	*C/I*
Aminophylline	LY	1 g	DU	6 g	D5W	Physically compatible with no loss of either drug in 24 hr at room temperature under fluorescent light	1358	C

Additive Compatibility (Cont.)

Esmolol HCl

Drug	Mfr	Conc/L	Mfr	Conc/L	Test Soln	Remarks	Ref	C/I
Atracurium besylate	BW	500 mg		10 g	D5W	Physically compatible and atracurium chemically stable for 24 hr at 5 and 30 °C	1694	C
Bretylium tosylate	ES	1 g	DU	6 g	D5W	Physically compatible with no loss of either drug in 24 hr at room temperature under fluorescent light	1358	C
Heparin sodium	LY	50,000 units	DU	6 g	D5W	Physically compatible with no esmolol loss in 24 hr at room temperature under fluorescent light. Heparin not tested	1358	C
Procainamide HCl	ES	4 g	DU	6 g	D5W	43% procainamide loss in 24 hr at room temperature under fluorescent light	1358	I

Y-Site Injection Compatibility (1:1 Mixture)

Esmolol HCl

Drug	Mfr	Conc	Mfr	Conc	Remarks	Ref	C/I
Amikacin sulfate	BR	5 mg/ml[a]	DCC	10 mg/ml[a]	Physically compatible for 24 hr at 22 °C	1169	C
Aminophylline	ES	1 mg/ml[a]	DCC	10 mg/ml[a]	Physically compatible for 24 hr at 22 °C	1169	C
Amiodarone HCl	WY	4.8 mg/ml[a]	DU	40 mg/ml[a]	Visually compatible for 24 hr at 23 °C	1877	C
Amphotericin B cholesteryl sulfate complex	SEQ	0.83 mg/ml[a]	OHM	10 mg/ml[a]	Microprecipitate forms in 4 hr at 23 °C under fluorescent light	2117	I
Ampicillin sodium	WY	20 mg/ml[b]	DCC	10 mg/ml[a]	Physically compatible for 24 hr at 22 °C	1169	C
Atracurium besylate	BW	0.5 mg/ml[a]	DCC	10 mg/ml[a]	Physically compatible for 24 hr at 28 °C	1337	C
Butorphanol tartrate	BR	0.04 mg/ml[a]	DCC	10 mg/ml[a]	Physically compatible for 24 hr at 22 °C	1169	C
Calcium chloride	AB	20 mg/ml[a]	DCC	10 mg/ml[a]	Physically compatible for 24 hr at 22 °C	1169	C
Cefazolin sodium	LI	10 mg/ml[a]	DCC	10 mg/ml[a]	Physically compatible for 24 hr at 22 °C	1169	C
Cefoperazone sodium	RR	10 mg/ml[a]	DCC	10 mg/ml[a]	Physically compatible for 24 hr at 22 °C	1169	C
Ceftazidime	GL[g]	10 mg/ml[a]	DCC	10 mg/ml[a]	Physically compatible for 24 hr at 22 °C	1169	C
Ceftizoxime sodium	SKF	10 mg/ml[a]	DCC	10 mg/ml[a]	Physically compatible for 24 hr at 22 °C	1169	C
Chloramphenicol sodium succinate	PD	10 mg/ml[a]	DCC	10 mg/ml[a]	Physically compatible for 24 hr at 22 °C	1169	C
Cimetidine HCl	SKF	6 mg/ml[a]	DCC	10 mg/ml[a]	Physically compatible for 24 hr at 22 °C	1169	C
Cisatracurium besylate	GW	0.1, 2, 5 mg/ml[a]	OHM	10 mg/ml[a]	Physically compatible with no change in measured turbidity or increase in particle content in 4 hr at 23 °C	2074	C
Clindamycin phosphate	UP	9 mg/ml[a]	DCC	10 mg/ml[a]	Physically compatible for 24 hr at 22 °C	1169	C
Diltiazem HCl	MMD	1 mg/ml[a]	DU	10 mg/ml[a]	Visually compatible for 24 hr at 25 °C	1530	C
Dopamine HCl	IMS	1.6 mg/ml[a]	DCC	10 mg/ml[a]	Physically compatible for 24 hr at 22 °C	1169	C
Enalaprilat	MSD	0.05 mg/ml[b]	DU	10 mg/ml[a]	Physically compatible for 24 hr at room temperature under fluorescent light	1355	C
Erythromycin lactobionate	AB	5 mg/ml[a]	DCC	10 mg/ml[a]	Physically compatible for 24 hr at 22 °C	1169	C
Famotidine	MSD	0.2 mg/ml[a]	DU	10 mg/ml[b]	Physically compatible for 4 hr at 25 °C	1188	C
Fentanyl citrate	JN	0.05 mg/1 ml	DCC	1 g/100 ml[d]	Physically compatible when fentanyl is injected into Y-site of flowing admixture[e]	1168	C

Y-Site Injection Compatibility (1:1 Mixture) (Cont.)

Esmolol HCl

Drug	*Mfr*	*Conc*	*Mfr*	*Conc*	*Remarks*	*Ref*	*C/I*
	JN	0.05 mg/ml	DCC	10 mg/ml[d]	Physically compatible with no loss of either drug in 8 hr at ambient temperature exposed to light	1168	C
Furosemide	HO	10 mg/ml	ACC	10 mg/ml[f]	Cloudy white precipitate forms immediately	1146	I
Gatifloxacin	BMS	2 mg/ml[a]	OHM	10 mg/ml	Physically compatible with no change in measured haze or increase in particle content in 4 hr at 23 °C	2234	C
Gentamicin sulfate	ES	0.8 mg/ml[a]	DCC	10 mg/ml[a]	Physically compatible for 24 hr at 22 °C	1169	C
Heparin sodium	IX	40 units/ml[a]	DCC	10 mg/ml[a]	Physically compatible for 24 hr at 22 °C	1169	C
Hetastarch in lactated electrolyte injection (Hextend)	AB	6%	OH	10 mg/ml	Physically compatible with no change in measured turbidity or increase in particle content in 4 hr at 23 °C	2339	C
Hydrocortisone sodium succinate	LY	1 mg/ml[a]	DCC	10 mg/ml[a]	Physically compatible for 24 hr at 22 °C	1169	C
Insulin, regular	LI	1 unit/ml[a]	DU	40 mg/ml[a]	Visually compatible for 24 hr at 23 °C	1877	C
Labetalol HCl	GL	5 mg/ml	DU	40 mg/ml[a]	Visually compatible for 24 hr at 23 °C	1877	C
Linezolid	PHU	2 mg/ml	OHM	10 mg/ml	Physically compatible with no change in measured turbidity or increase in particle content in 4 hr at 23 °C	2264	C
Magnesium sulfate	LY	10 mg/ml[a]	DCC	10 mg/ml[a]	Physically compatible for 24 hr at 22 °C	1169	C
Methyldopate HCl	MSD	5 mg/ml[a]	DCC	10 mg/ml[a]	Physically compatible for 24 hr at 22 °C	1169	C
Metronidazole	SE	5 mg/ml	DCC	10 mg/ml[a]	Physically compatible for 24 hr at 22 °C	1169	C
Midazolam HCl	RC	1 mg/ml[a]	DU	40 mg/ml[a]	Visually compatible for 24 hr at 23 °C	1877	C
Morphine sulfate	ES	15 mg/1 ml	DCC	1 g/100 ml[d]	Physically compatible when morphine is injected into Y-site of flowing admixture[d]	1168	C
	ES	15 mg/ml	DCC	10 mg/ml[d]	Physically compatible with no loss of either drug in 8 hr at ambient temperature exposed to light	1168	C
Nafcillin sodium	BR	10 mg/ml[a]	DCC	10 mg/ml[a]	Physically compatible for 24 hr at 22 °C	1169	C
Nitroglycerin	OM	0.2 mg/ml[a]	DU	40 mg/ml[a]	Visually compatible for 24 hr at 23 °C	1877	C
Norepinephrine HCl	STR	0.064 mg/ml[a]	DU	40 mg/ml[a]	Visually compatible for 24 hr at 23 °C	1877	C
Pancuronium bromide	ES	0.05 mg/ml[a]	DCC	10 mg/ml[a]	Physically compatible for 24 hr at 28 °C	1337	C
Penicillin G potassium	PF	50,000 units/ml[a]	DCC	10 mg/ml[a]	Physically compatible for 24 hr at 22 °C	1169	C
Phenytoin sodium	IX	1 mg/ml[a]	DCC	10 mg/ml[a]	Physically compatible for 24 hr at 22 °C	1169	C
Piperacillin sodium	LE	30 mg/ml[a]	DCC	10 mg/ml[a]	Physically compatible for 24 hr at 22 °C	1169	C
Polymyxin B sulfate	PF	0.005 unit/ml[a]	DCC	10 mg/ml[a]	Physically compatible for 24 hr at 22 °C	1169	C
Potassium chloride	IX	0.4 mEq/ml[a]	DCC	10 mg/ml[a]	Physically compatible for 24 hr at 22 °C	1169	C
Potassium phosphates	LY	0.44 mEq/ml[a]	DCC	10 mg/ml[a]	Physically compatible for 24 hr at 22 °C	1169	C
Propofol	ZEN	10 mg/ml	OHM	10 mg/ml	Physically compatible for 1 hr at 23 °C with no increase in particle content	2066	C
Ranitidine HCl	GL	0.5 mg/ml[a]	DCC	10 mg/ml[a]	Physically compatible for 24 hr at 22 °C	1169	C

Y-Site Injection Compatibility (1:1 Mixture) (Cont.)

Esmolol HCl

Drug	*Mfr*	*Conc*	*Mfr*	*Conc*	*Remarks*	*Ref*	*C/I*
Remifentanil HCl	GW	0.025 and 0.25 mg/ml[b]	OHM	10 mg/ml[a]	Physically compatible with no change in measured turbidity or increase in particle content in 4 hr at 23 °C	2075	C
Sodium acetate	LY	0.4 mEq/ml[a]	DCC	10 mg/ml[a]	Physically compatible for 24 hr at 22 °C	1169	C
Sodium nitroprusside	RC	0.2 mg/ml[a]	DU	40 mg/ml[a]	Visually compatible for 24 hr at 23 °C	1877	C
Streptomycin sulfate	PF	10 mg/ml[a]	DCC	10 mg/ml[a]	Physically compatible for 24 hr at 22 °C	1169	C
Tacrolimus	FUJ	1 mg/ml[b]	DU	10 mg/ml[a]	Visually compatible for 24 hr at 25 °C	1630	C
Tobramycin sulfate	LI	0.8 mg/ml[a]	DCC	10 mg/ml[a]	Physically compatible for 24 hr at 22 °C	1169	C
Trimethoprim–sulfamethoxazole	BW	0.64 + 3.2 mg/ml[a]	DCC	10 mg/ml[a]	Physically compatible for 24 hr at 22 °C	1169	C
Vancomycin HCl	LE	5 mg/ml[a]	DCC	10 mg/ml[a]	Physically compatible for 24 hr at 22 °C	1169	C
Vecuronium bromide	OR	0.1 mg/ml[a]	DCC	10 mg/ml[a]	Physically compatible for 24 hr at 28 °C	1337	C
Warfarin sodium	DU	2 mg/ml[c]	OHM	10 mg/ml[a]	Haze forms immediately	2010	I
	DME	2 mg/ml[c]	OHM	10 mg/ml[a]	Haze forms immediately	2078	I

[a]*Tested in dextrose 5% in water.*
[b]*Tested in sodium chloride 0.9%.*
[c]*Tested in sterile water for injection.*
[d]*Tested in dextrose 5% in sodium chloride 0.9%.*
[e]*Flowing at 1.6 ml/min.*
[f]*Tested in both dextrose 5% in water and sodium chloride 0.9%.*
[g]*Sodium carbonate–containing formulation tested.*

Additional Compatibility Information

Infusion Solutions — Esmolol HCl (Baxter) is physically compatible and chemically stable at a concentration of 10 mg/ml for 24 hours at room temperature or under refrigeration in the following infusion solutions (2; 4):

- Dextrose 5% in Ringer's injection
- Dextrose 5% in Ringer's injection, lactated
- Dextrose 5% in sodium chloride 0.45 and 0.9%
- Dextrose 5% in water
- Ringer's injection, lactated
- Sodium chloride 0.45 and 0.9%

Other Drugs — Although it has been stated that esmolol HCl is incompatible with sodium bicarbonate 5% and should not be admixed with it (2; 4), Baaske et al. reported little loss in an esmolol HCl 10-mg/ml solution in sodium bicarbonate 5%. By HPLC, esmolol losses were 5 and 8% in seven days at 4 and 27 °C, respectively. When the solution was stored at 40 °C, 9% esmolol loss occurred in 24 hours. (1831) Esmolol HCl also is stated to be incompatible with diazepam and thiopental sodium. (4)

Esmolol HCl is physically compatible and stable for at least 24 hours at room temperature or under refrigeration with potassium chloride 40 mEq/L in dextrose 5% in water (2) and is stated to be compatible with digoxin, dopamine HCl, and lidocaine HCl. (4)

ESTROGENS, CONJUGATED
AHFS 68:16

Products — Estrogens, conjugated is available in packages containing a vial with lyophilized estrogens, conjugated, 25 mg; lactose 200 mg; sodium citrate 12.2 mg; simethicone 0.2 mg; and sodium hydroxide or hydrochloric acid for pH adjustment. Also in the package is a 5-ml ampul of sterile diluent composed of water for injection and benzyl alcohol 2%. To reconstitute, withdraw the air from the vial of estrogens, conjugated; flow the sterile diluent slowly against the side of the vial, and agitate gently—not violently. (2)

Osmolality — Estrogens, conjugated, 1 mg/ml in its sterile diluent has an osmolality exceeding 2000 mOsm/kg. (1689)

Trade Name(s) — Premarin Intravenous.

Administration — Estrogens, conjugated may be administered by deep intramuscular injection or slow direct intravenous injection. Intravenous infusion is not recommended, but injection into the tubing of a running infusion may be performed. (2; 4)

Stability — The manufacturer recommends refrigeration of the intact containers at 2 to 8 °C. (2) Such storage provides a shelflife of up to 60 months. At room temperature, the product in intact vials is stable for 24 months. (853) The reconstituted solution should be stored at 2 to 8 °C. (2) The reconstituted drug is stable for 60 days. Do not use it, however, if precipitation or discoloration occurs. (2)

Compatibility Information

Y-Site Injection Compatibility (1:1 Mixture)

Estrogens, conjugated

Drug	*Mfr*	*Conc*	*Mfr*	*Conc*	*Remarks*	*Ref*	*C/I*
Heparin sodium with hydrocortisone sodium succinate	RI UP	1000 units + 100 mg/L[a]	AY	5 mg/ml	Physically compatible for at least 4 hr at room temperature by visual and microscopic examination	322	C
Potassium chloride		40 mEq/L[a]	AY	5 mg/ml	Physically compatible for at least 4 hr at room temperature by visual and microscopic examination	322	C
Vitamin B complex with C	RC	2 ml/L[a]	AY	5 mg/ml	Physically compatible for at least 4 hr at room temperature by visual and microscopic examination	322	C

[a]*Tested in dextrose 5% in water, sodium chloride 0.9%, and Ringer's injection, lactated.*

Additional Compatibility Information

Infusion Solutions — Dextrose, saline, and invert sugar solutions have been stated to be compatible with estrogens, conjugated. (2)

Other Drugs — Estrogens, conjugated, has been stated to be incompatible with ascorbic acid or any solution with an acid pH. (2; 4)

ETHACRYNATE SODIUM
AHFS 40:28

Products — Each 50-ml vial has ethacrynate sodium equivalent to ethacrynic acid 50 mg and mannitol 62.5 mg. Reconstitute with 50 ml of dextrose 5% in water or sodium chloride 0.9% to yield a 1-mg/ml solution. Some dextrose 5% in water has a pH below 5 and results in a hazy or opalescent solution, which is not recommended for use. (2; 4)

pH — Reconstitution with dextrose 5% in water or sodium chloride 0.9% results in a solution having a pH of 6.3 to 7.7. (4)

Osmolality — Ethacrynate sodium 1 mg/ml in dextrose 5% in water has an osmolality of 268 mOsm/kg. (1689)

Sodium Content — Ethacrynate sodium contains 0.165 mEq of sodium per 50 mg of ethacrynic acid equivalent. (846)

Trade Name(s) — Sodium Edecrin.

Administration — Ethacrynate sodium may be given slowly through the tubing of a running intravenous infusion solution or directly into a vein over several minutes. (2; 4) Intravenous infusion over 20 to 30 minutes has also been recommended. (4) Subcutaneous or intramuscular injection should not be used because of local pain and irritation. (2; 4)

Stability — Solutions of ethacrynate sodium are relatively stable for short periods at pH 7 at room temperature; but as the pH or temperature or both increase, the solutions are less stable. It is recommended that the reconstituted solution be discarded after 24 hours. (2; 4)

Compatibility Information

Additive Compatibility

Ethacrynate sodium

Drug	*Mfr*	*Conc/L*	*Mfr*	*Conc/L*	*Test Soln*	*Remarks*	*Ref*	*C/I*
Chlorpromazine HCl	SKF	50 mg	MSD	50 mg	NS	Little alteration of UV spectra within 8 hr at room temperature	16	C

Additive Compatibility (Cont.)

			Ethacrynate sodium					
Drug	*Mfr*	*Conc/L*	*Mfr*	*Conc/L*	*Test Soln*	*Remarks*	*Ref*	*C/I*
Cimetidine HCl	SKF	3 g	MSD	500 mg	D5W	Physically compatible and cimetidine chemically stable for 24 hr at room temperature. Ethacrynate sodium not tested	551	C
Hydralazine HCl	CI	20 mg	MSD	50 mg	NS	Altered UV spectra for both at room temperature	16	I
Procainamide HCl	SQ	1 g	MSD	50 mg	NS	Altered UV spectra for both at room temperature	16	I
Prochlorperazine edisylate	SKF	20 mg	MSD	80 mg	NS	Little alteration of UV spectra within 8 hr at room temperature	16	C
Promazine HCl	WY	50 mg	MSD	50 mg	NS	Little alteration of UV spectra within 8 hr at room temperature	16	C
Ranitidine HCl	GL	50 mg and 2 g		500 mg	D5W	Ranitidine chemically stable by HPLC for only 6 hr at 25 °C. Ethacrynate not tested	1515	I
Tolazoline HCl	CI	400 mg	MSD	50 mg	NS	Altered UV spectra for both at room temperature	16	I
Triflupromazine HCl	SQ		MSD		NS	Occasional gas bubble formation	16	I

Y-Site Injection Compatibility (1:1 Mixture)

			Ethacrynate sodium				
Drug	*Mfr*	*Conc*	*Mfr*	*Conc*	*Remarks*	*Ref*	*C/I*
Heparin sodium with hydrocortisone sodium succinate	RI UP	1000 units + 100 mg/L[a]	MSD	1 mg/ml	Physically compatible for at least 4 hr at room temperature by visual and microscopic examination	322	C
Potassium chloride		40 mEq/L[a]	MSD	1 mg/ml	Physically compatible for at least 4 hr at room temperature by visual and microscopic examination	322	C
Vitamin B complex with C	RC	2 ml/L[a]	MSD	1 mg/ml	Physically compatible for at least 4 hr at room temperature by visual and microscopic examination	322	C

[a]*Tested in dextrose 5% in water, sodium chloride 0.9%, and Ringer's injection, lactated.*

Additional Compatibility Information

Infusion Solutions — Ethacrynate sodium is reported to be compatible with the following Abbott infusion solutions (4):

Dextran 75 6% in sodium chloride 0.9%
Dextrose 5% in sodium chloride 0.9%
Dextrose 5% in water
Normosol R, pH 7.4
Ringer's injection
Ringer's injection, lactated
Sodium chloride 0.9%

Ethacrynate sodium is incompatible with solutions or drugs with a final pH below 5 and with whole blood and its derivatives. (2) It is also stated to be incompatible with Normosol M. (4)

ETOMIDATE
AHFS 28:24.04

Products — Etomidate is available at a concentration of 2 mg/ml in 10- and 20-ml single-dose vials. Each milliliter also contains propylene glycol 35% (v/v). (1-10/98)

Administration — Etomidate is administered by intravenous injection over 30 to 60 seconds. (1-10/98)

Stability — Intact containers should be stored at controlled room temperature. Unused portions remaining in vials should be discarded. (1-10/98)

Compatibility Information

Drugs in Syringe Compatibility

Drug (in syringe)	*Mfr*	*Amt*	Etomidate *Mfr*	Etomidate *Amt*	*Remarks*	*Ref*	*C/I*
Heparin sodium		2500 units/ 1 ml	JN	20 mg/ 10 ml	Visually compatible for at least 5 min	1053	C

Y-Site Injection Compatibility (1:1 Mixture)

Drug	*Mfr*	*Conc*	Etomidate *Mfr*	Etomidate *Conc*	*Remarks*	*Ref*	*C/I*
Alfentanil HCl	JN	0.5 mg/ml	AB	2 mg/ml	Visually compatible for up to 7 days at 25 °C	1801	C
Ascorbic acid	AB	500 mg/ml	AB	2 mg/ml	Yellow discoloration and fine precipitate form in 24 hr	1801	I
Atracurium besylate	BW	10 mg/ml	AB	2 mg/ml	Visually compatible for up to 7 days at 25 °C	1801	C
Atropine sulfate	GNS	0.4 mg/ml	AB	2 mg/ml	Visually compatible for up to 7 days at 25 °C	1801	C
Doxacurium chloride	BW	1 mg/ml	AB	2 mg/ml	Visually compatible for up to 7 days at 25 °C	1801	C
Ephedrine sulfate	AB	50 mg/ml	AB	2 mg/ml	Visually compatible for up to 7 days at 25 °C	1801	C
Fentanyl citrate	ES	0.05 mg/ml	AB	2 mg/ml	Visually compatible for up to 7 days at 25 °C	1801	C
Lidocaine HCl	AST	20 mg/ml	AB	2 mg/ml	Visually compatible for up to 7 days at 25 °C	1801	C
Lorazepam	WY	2 mg/ml	AB	2 mg/ml	Visually compatible for up to 7 days at 25 °C	1801	C
Midazolam HCl	RC	5 mg/ml	AB	2 mg/ml	Visually compatible for up to 7 days at 25 °C	1801	C
Mivacurium chloride	BW	2 mg/ml	AB	2 mg/ml	Visually compatible for up to 7 days at 25 °C	1801	C
Morphine sulfate	ES	10 mg/ml	AB	2 mg/ml	Visually compatible for up to 7 days at 25 °C	1801	C
Pancuronium bromide	GNS	2 mg/ml	AB	2 mg/ml	Visually compatible for up to 7 days at 25 °C	1801	C
Phenylephrine HCl	ES	10 mg/ml	AB	2 mg/ml	Visually compatible for up to 7 days at 25 °C	1801	C
Succinylcholine chloride	AB	20 mg/ml	AB	2 mg/ml	Visually compatible for up to 7 days at 25 °C	1801	C

Y-Site Injection Compatibility (1:1 Mixture) (Cont.)

			Etomidate				
Drug	*Mfr*	*Conc*	*Mfr*	*Conc*	*Remarks*	*Ref*	*C/I*
Sufentanil citrate	JN	0.05 mg/ml	AB	2 mg/ml	Visually compatible for up to 7 days at 25 °C	1801	C
Vecuronium bromide	OR	1 mg/ml	AB	2 mg/ml	Slight turbidity and white particles form	1801	I

ETOPOSIDE
AHFS 10:00

Products — Etoposide is available in 5-, 7.5-, 25-, and 50-ml multiple-dose vials. Each milliliter contains (2):

Etoposide	20 mg
Polyethylene glycol 300	650 mg
Ethyl alcohol	30.5% (v/v)
Polysorbate 80 (Tween 80)	80 mg
Benzyl alcohol	30 mg
Citric acid	2 mg

pH — From 3 to 4. (2)

Osmolality — Etoposide 20 mg/ml has an osmolality exceeding 2000 mOsm/kg. (1689)

Density — Etoposide (Bristol) 20-mg/ml undiluted injection has a solution density of 1.02 g/ml. (2041; 2248)

Trade Name(s) — VePesid, Toposar.

Administration — Etoposide should be diluted for administration and given by slow intravenous infusion; concentrations of 0.2 to 0.4 mg/ml should be given over at least 30 to 60 minutes. (2; 4; 915) Continuous intravenous infusion has also been used. The drug should not be given by rapid intravenous injection. (4)

The surfactant content of the etoposide formulation decreases surface tension and has been found to produce a 30% reduction in drop size compared to simple aqueous solutions. The altered drop size may interfere with accurate infusion rates if infusion devices that rely on drop counting are used. The use of infusion devices that operate independently of drop size has been recommended. (181)

Stability — The clear, yellow solution is stable for 24 months in intact vials at 25 °C. (2) Stability is not affected by exposure to normal room fluorescent light. (1374) Also see Solutions under Additional Compatibility Information below.

Etoposide was cultured with human lymphoblasts to determine whether its cytotoxic activity was retained. The solution retained cytotoxicity for 24 hours at room temperature. (1575)

Precipitation — Etoposide has a very low aqueous solubility (about 0.03 mg/ml). Therefore, organic solvents and a surfactant (polysorbate 80) are used in the formulation to aid in dispersing the drug in aqueous media. However, aqueous dispersion is temporary, and precipitation is inevitable, even if irregular and unpredictable in terms of time. At concentrations above 0.4 mg/ml, precipitation may occur rapidly.

The rate of precipitation of a supersaturated etoposide solution depends on the presence of crystalline nuclei, agitation, contact with incompatible surfaces, and possibly other factors. (1374)

Etoposide 1 mg/ml in sodium chloride 0.9% in polypropylene syringes (Braun Omnifix) developed a pure etoposide precipitate in about 10% of the prefilled syringes. It also precipitated at various locations in subclavian lines. (1564)

Precipitation of etoposide from infusion solutions is reportedly exacerbated by the use of peristaltic pumps, especially at concentrations of 0.4 mg/ml or above. Use of volumetric pumps has been recommended to reduce this problem. (1832; 1949) Also see Solutions under Additional Compatibility Information below.

pH Effects — Etoposide is most stable at a pH of about 3.5 to 6, with a calculated minimum degradation rate occurring at pH 4.8. (1262) Epimerization to the less active *cis*-etoposide may occur at pH values above 6. Hydrolysis may occur in alkaline solutions. (1379)

Syringes — When etoposide 1 mg/ml in sodium chloride 0.9% was stored in plastic syringes (Gillette), seizing of the syringes occurred. (1564)

Ambulatory Pumps — Etoposide (Bristol-Myers Squibb) 0.5 mg/ml in sterile water for injection was evaluated for stability and compatibility in PVC reservoirs of Graseby 9000 ambulatory pumps. Etoposide was chemically stable at 37 °C for seven days with no loss of drug by HPLC analysis. However, refrigerated storage at 4 °C resulted in precipitation of the etoposide in some samples. In addition, substantial amounts of diethylhexyl phthalate (DEHP) plasticizer (up to 90 μg/ml) were leached from the PVC reservoirs. The authors concluded that etoposide was unsuitable for use in this pump reservoir and recommended consideration of etoposide phosphate, which should not be subject to precipitation and leaching of plasticizer. (2288)

Elastomeric Reservoir Pumps — Etoposide 0.1 to 0.4 mg/ml in sodium chloride 0.9% in Homepump and Homepump Eclipse elastomeric reservoir pumps has been stated by the pump manufacturer to be stable for nine days at room temperature. (31) However, etoposide is subject to irregular precipitation, particularly over periods as long as nine days. See the Precipitation section above and Solutions under Additional Compatibility Information below.

Sorption — No loss of etoposide because of sorption to PVC containers has been observed. (1374) At a concentration of 0.2 mg/ml in dextrose

5% in water or sodium chloride 0.9% in PVC containers, no etoposide loss due to sorption was found during 72 hours at 5 and 25 °C. (1369)

In an admixture composed of cytarabine (Upjohn) 0.157 mg/ml, daunorubicin HCl (Bellon) 15.7 μg/ml, and etoposide (Sandoz) 0.157 mg/ml in dextrose 5% in water, little or no loss of the drugs due to sorption occurred when delivered through PVC, PVC with polyethylene-lined sets, and silicone central catheter. (1955)

Plasticizer Leaching—Etoposide (Bristol) 0.4 mg/ml in PVC bags of dextrose 5% in water leached relatively minor amounts of DEHP plasticizer from PVC bags. This leaching was due to the surfactant polysorbate 80 (Tween 80) in the formulation. After 24 hours at 24 °C, the DEHP concentration in 50-ml bags of infusion solution was 2.6 μg/ml. This finding is consistent with the low surfactant concentration (0.16%) in the final admixture solution. The actual amount of DEHP leached from PVC containers and administration sets may vary in clinical situations, depending on surfactant concentration, bag size, and contact time. (1683)

Etoposide (Sandoz) 0.4 mg/ml in sodium chloride 0.9% in PVC containers leached DEHP plasticizer from the container material. This leaching increased with storage time from about 12 μg/ml in eight hours to over 50 μg/ml in 96 hours at 24 °C. Refrigeration reduced, but did not eliminate, DEHP leaching. (1833)

Filtration—Etoposide 0.1 to 0.4 mg/ml in dextrose 5% in water or sodium chloride 0.9% has been filtered through several commercially available filters (such as the 0.22-μm Millex-GS or Millex GV) without filter decomposition. (4)

Etoposide (Sandoz) 0.2 mg/ml in dextrose 5% in water and sodium chloride 0.9% was filtered through a 0.22-μm cellulose ester membrane filter (Ivex-HP, Millipore) over six hours. No significant drug loss due to binding to the filter was noted. (1034)

Central Venous Catheter—Etoposide infused undiluted at a rate of 30 ml/hr for 24 hours through a polyurethane central catheter caused substantial damage to the catheter. In addition to cracking the catheter, a 36% decrease in elasticity, a 3.7% increase in catheter length, and damage similar to melting on the internal catheter wall were found. The damage also occurred with the etoposide vehicle and ethanol alone. Consequently, the damage was attributed to the ethanol component of the formulation. (2286)

The damage to polyurethane catheters caused by the etoposide formulation did not extend to silicone central catheters. The authors stated that administration of undiluted etoposide could be performed using the silicone catheters. (2286)

Compatibility Information

Solution Compatibility

Etoposide

Solution	Mfr	Mfr	Conc/L	Remarks	Ref	C/I
Dextrose 5% in water	[a]	BR	400 mg	Physically compatible with 3 to 4% etoposide loss in 4 days at 21 °C in the dark or exposed to fluorescent light	1374	C
		SZ	157 mg	2% or less loss in 48 hr by HPLC at room temperature, exposed to light and in the dark, and at 4 °C	1955	C
Ringer's injection, lactated	[a]	BR	400 mg	Physically compatible with 5% etoposide loss in 4 days at 21 °C exposed to fluorescent light	1374	C
Sodium chloride 0.9%	[b]	BR	400 mg	Physically compatible with 1 to 5% etoposide loss in 4 days at 21 °C in the dark or exposed to fluorescent light	1374	C
	[a]	BR	50 to 400 mg	Physically compatible for at least 4 days	1374	C
	[a]	BR	500 mg	Precipitate forms after 48 hr at 21 °C exposed to fluorescent light	1374	C
	[a]	BR	600 and 700 mg	Precipitate forms within 24 hr at 21 °C exposed to fluorescent light	1374	I
	[c]		400 mg	Chemically stable by HPLC for 24 hr at 4 and 24 °C. Precipitation occurs at varying times after 24 hr	1833	C

[a]*Tested in glass containers.*
[b]*Tested in both glass and PVC containers.*
[c]*Tested in glass, PVC, and polyethylene containers.*

Additive Compatibility

Etoposide

Drug	Mfr	Conc/L	Mfr	Conc/L	Test Soln	Remarks	Ref	C/I
Carboplatin		1 g		200 mg	W	Less than 10% loss of both drugs in 7 days at 23 °C	1954	C
Cisplatin	BR	200 mg	BR	400 mg	NS[a]	Physically compatible with less than 10% loss of both drugs in 48 hr at 22 °C in light and dark	1329	C
	BR	200 mg	BR	200 mg	NS[a]	Physically compatible with less than 10% loss of both drugs in 24 hr at 22 °C. Possible excess cisplatin loss in 48 hr exposed to light	1329	C
	BR	200 mg	BR	200 and 400 mg	D5½S[a]	Physically compatible with less than 10% loss of both drugs in 24 hr at 22 °C in light and dark	1329	C
		200 mg		200 mg	NS	Both drugs stable for 15 days at room temperature protected from light	1379	C
		200 mg		400 mg	NS	10% etoposide loss and no cisplatin loss in 7 days at room temperature	1388	C
Cisplatin with cyclophosphamide		200 mg 2 g		200 mg	NS	All drugs stable for 7 days at room temperature	1379	C
Cisplatin with floxuridine		200 mg 700 mg		300 mg	NS	All drugs stable for 7 days at room temperature	1379	C
Cisplatin with mannitol and potassium chloride	BR LY LY	200 mg 1.875% 20 mEq	BR	400 mg	NS[a]	Physically compatible and etoposide and cisplatin chemically stable for 8 hr at 22 °C. Precipitate forms within 24 hr	1329	I
Cisplatin with mannitol and potassium chloride	BR LY LY	200 mg 1.875% 20 mEq	BR	400 mg	D5½S[a]	Physically compatible and etoposide and cisplatin chemically stable for 24 hr at 22 °C. Precipitate forms within 48 hr	1329	C
Cytarabine	CHI	1.2 g	BR	660 mg	D5W	Physically compatible with no subvisual haze or particle formation in 4 hr at 23 °C	1736	C
Cytarabine with daunorubicin HCl	UP RP	267 mg 33 mg	BR	400 mg	D5½S	Physically compatible with about 6% cytarabine loss and no loss of other drugs in 72 hr at 20 °C	1162	C
Cytarabine with daunorubicin HCl	UP BEL	157 mg 15.7 mg	SZ	157 mg	D5W[b]	Less than 10% loss of any drug in 48 hr at room temperature, exposed to light and in the dark, and at 4 °C	1955	C
Doxorubicin HCl with vincristine sulfate	PHU LI	40 mg 1.6 mg	BMS	200 mg	NS	Visually compatible and all drugs chemically stable by HPLC for up to 72 hr at 30 °C protected from light	2239	C
Doxorubicin HCl with vincristine sulfate	PHU LI	25 mg 1 mg	BMS	125 mg	NS	Visually compatible and all drugs chemically stable by HPLC for up to 96 hr at 24 °C protected from or exposed to light	2239	C
Doxorubicin HCl with vincristine sulfate	PHU LI	35 mg 1.4 mg	BMS	175 mg	NS	Visually compatible and all drugs chemically stable by HPLC for up to 96 hr at 24 °C protected from or exposed to light	2239	C
Doxorubicin HCl with vincristine sulfate	PHU LI	50 mg 2 mg	BMS	250 mg	NS	Visually compatible and all drugs chemically stable by HPLC for up to 48 hr at 24 °C protected from or exposed to light. Etoposide precipitate formed in 72 hr	2239	C
Doxorubicin HCl with vincristine sulfate	PHU LI	70 mg 2.8 mg	BMS	350 mg	NS	Visually compatible and all drugs chemically stable by HPLC for up to 24 hr at 24 °C protected from or exposed to light. Etoposide precipitate formed in 36 hr	2239	C

Additive Compatibility (Cont.)

Drug	Mfr	Conc/L	Mfr (Etoposide)	Conc/L (Etoposide)	Test Soln	Remarks	Ref	C/I
Doxorubicin HCl with vincristine sulfate	PHU LI	100 mg 4 mg	BMS	500 mg	NS	Etoposide precipitate formed in 12 hr at 24 °C protected from or exposed to light	2239	I
Floxuridine		10 g		200 mg	NS	Both drugs stable for 15 days at room temperature	1379	C
Fluorouracil		10 g		200 mg	NS	Both drugs stable for 7 days at room temperature and 1 day at 35 °C	1379	C
Hydroxyzine HCl	LY	500 mg	BR	1 g	D5W[c]	Physically compatible for 48 hr	1190	C
Ifosfamide		2 g		200 mg	NS	Both drugs stable for 5 days at room temperature	1379	C
Ifosfamide with carboplatin		2 g 1 g		200 mg	W	All drugs stable for 7 days at room temperature	1379	C
Ifosfamide with cisplatin		2 g 200 mg		200 mg	NS	All drugs stable for 5 days at room temperature	1379	C
Mitoxantrone HCl	LE	50 mg	BR	500 mg	NS	Visually compatible with no loss of either drug by HPLC in 22 hr at room temperature	2271	C
Ondansetron HCl	GL	30 and 300 mg	BR	100 mg	D5W[b]	Physically compatible with little or no loss of ondansetron by HPLC in 48 hr at 23 °C. 4% etoposide loss in 24 hr and 6% loss in 48 hr at 23 °C	1876	C
	GL	30 and 300 mg	BR	400 mg	D5W[b]	Physically compatible with little or no loss of either drug by HPLC in 48 hr at 23 °C	1876	C

[a]*Tested in both glass and PVC containers.*
[b]*Tested in PVC containers.*
[c]*Tested in glass containers.*

Y-Site Injection Compatibility (1:1 Mixture)

Drug	Mfr	Conc	Mfr (Etoposide)	Conc (Etoposide)	Remarks	Ref	C/I
Allopurinol sodium	BW	3 mg/ml[b]	BR	0.4 mg/ml[b]	Physically compatible with no change in measured turbidity or increase in particle content in 4 hr at 22 °C	1686	C
Amifostine	USB	10 mg/ml[a]	BR	0.4 mg/ml[a]	Physically compatible with no change in measured turbidity or increase in particle content in 4 hr at 23 °C	1845	C
Aztreonam	SQ	40 mg/ml[a]	BMS	0.4 mg/ml[a]	Physically compatible with no subvisual haze or particle formation in 4 hr at 23 °C	1758	C
Cefepime HCl	BMS	20 mg/ml[a]	BR	0.4 mg/ml[a]	Haze increases and tiny particles form in 1 hr	1689	I
Cladribine	ORT	0.015[b] and 0.5[c] mg/ml	BR	0.4 mg/ml[b]	Physically compatible with no change in measured turbidity or increase in particle content in 4 hr at 23 °C	1969	C
Doxorubicin HCl liposome injection	SEQ	0.4 mg/ml[a]	BR	0.4 mg/ml[a]	Physically compatible with little or no change in measured turbidity and no increase in particle content in 4 hr at 23 °C	2087	C

Y-Site Injection Compatibility (1:1 Mixture) (Cont.)

Etoposide

Drug	*Mfr*	*Conc*	*Mfr*	*Conc*	*Remarks*	*Ref*	*C/I*
Filgrastim	AMG	30 µg/ml[a]	BR	0.4 mg/ml[a]	Particles form immediately. Filaments form in 1 hr	1687	I
Fludarabine phosphate	BX	1 mg/ml[a]	BR	0.4 mg/ml[a]	Physically compatible for 4 hr at room temperature under fluorescent light	1439	C
Gemcitabine HCl	LI	10 mg/ml[b]	BR	0.4 mg/ml[b]	Physically compatible with no change in measured turbidity or increase in particle content in 4 hr at 23 °C	2226	C
Granisetron HCl	SKB	1 mg/ml	BMS	0.4 mg/ml[b]	Physically compatible with little or no loss of either drug by HPLC in 4 hr at 22 °C	1883	C
	SKB	0.05 mg/ml[a]	BR	0.4 mg/ml[a]	Physically compatible with no change in measured turbidity or increase in particle content in 4 hr at 23 °C	2000	C
Idarubicin HCl	AD	1 mg/ml[b]	BR	0.4 mg/ml[a]	Gas forms immediately	1525	I
Melphalan HCl	BW	0.1 mg/ml[b]	BR	0.4 mg/ml[b]	Physically compatible with no change in measured turbidity or increase in particle content in 3 hr at 22 °C	1557	C
Methotrexate sodium		30 mg/ml	BR	0.6 mg/ml[b]	Visually compatible for 4 hr at room temperature	1788	C
Mitoxantrone HCl	LE	2 mg/ml	BR	20 mg/ml	Visually compatible with no loss of either drug by HPLC in 22 hr at room temperature	2271	C
Ondansetron HCl	GL	1 mg/ml[b]	BR	0.4 mg/ml[a]	Physically compatible for 4 hr at 22 °C	1365	C
	GL	16 to 160 µg/ml		0.144 to 0.25 mg/ml	Physically compatible when etoposide given over 30 to 60 min via Y-site	1366	C
Paclitaxel	NCI	1.2 mg/ml[a]		0.4 mg/ml[a]	Physically compatible with no change in measured turbidity in 4 hr at 22 °C	1528	C
Piperacillin sodium–tazobactam sodium	LE	40 + 5 mg/ml[a]	BR	0.4 mg/ml[a]	Physically compatible with no change in measured turbidity or increase in particle content in 4 hr at 22 °C	1688	C
Sargramostim	IMM	10 µg/ml[b]	BR	0.4 mg/ml[b]	Physically compatible for 4 hr at 22 °C	1436	C
Sodium bicarbonate		30 mg/ml	BR	0.6 mg/ml[b]	Visually compatible for 4 hr at room temperature	1788	C
		1.4%	BR	0.6 mg/ml[b]	Visually compatible for 4 hr at room temperature	1788	C
Teniposide	BR	0.1 mg/ml[a]	BR	0.4 mg/ml[a]	Physically compatible with no subvisual haze or particle formation in 4 hr at 23 °C	1725	C
Thiotepa	IMM[d]	1 mg/ml[a]	BR	0.4 mg/ml[a]	Physically compatible with no change in measured turbidity or increase in particle content in 4 hr at 23 °C	1861	C
Topotecan HCl	SKB	56 µg/ml[a,b]	BR	0.4 mg/ml[a,b]	Visually compatible with little or no loss of either drug by HPLC in 4 hr at 22 °C under fluorescent light	2245	C
Vinorelbine tartrate	BW	1 mg/ml[b]	BR	0.4 mg/ml[b]	Physically compatible with no change in measured turbidity or increase in particle content in 4 hr at 22 °C	1558	C

[a]*Tested in dextrose 5% in water.*
[b]*Tested in sodium chloride 0.9%.*
[c]*Tested in bacteriostatic sodium chloride 0.9% preserved with benzyl alcohol 0.9%.*
[d]*Lyophilized formulation tested.*

Additional Compatibility Information

Infusion Solutions — Dextrose 5% in water and sodium chloride 0.9% have been recommended as diluents for the infusion of etoposide. The aqueous solubility of etoposide is poor (0.03 mg/ml), but the formulation temporarily increases its miscibility in an aqueous medium. Nevertheless, the drug will eventually crystallize in varying time periods, and the crystallization is reported to be exacerbated by peristaltic pumps. (1949) At concentrations of 0.2 and 0.4 mg/ml in dextrose 5% in water and sodium chloride 0.9%, the solutions are stable for 96 and 24 hours, respectively, at 25 °C under normal fluorescent light in either glass or plastic containers. However, precipitation in shorter time periods has been observed. At concentrations of 0.2 and 0.4 mg/ml in Ringer's injection, lactated, or mannitol 10% in glass containers under the same conditions, the solutions are stable for eight hours. Seargent et al. reported no precipitate formation in 72 hours at 20 °C in solutions of etoposide 0.4 mg/ml in dextrose 5% in water or sodium chloride 0.9%. (1162) However, at 1 mg/ml, crystallization may occur in 30 minutes in a standing solution or five minutes if the solution is stirred. Occasionally, 1-mg/ml concentrations may remain in solution for extended periods. (1374) Nevertheless, concentrations greater than 0.4 mg/ml are not recommended by the manufacturer. Because of the poor solubility of etoposide in aqueous media, monitor closely for precipitation before and during administration. (2; 4; 915; 916)

Aluminum — Ogawa et al. reported that immersion of a needle with an aluminum component in etoposide (Bristol) 20 mg/ml resulted in no visually apparent reaction after seven days at 24 °C. (988)

Plastics — Devices composed of hard ABS plastic may be incompatible with undiluted etoposide. In one study, a multiport disposable infusion cassette (Omni-Flow) developed cracks within five minutes after infusion was started and leakage was evident within 15 minutes. This phenomenon did not occur when etoposide was diluted to concentrations up to 1 mg/ml. In addition, a venting pin and a connector on an extension set reportedly cracked. Exposure to the polyethylene glycol 300 content of the etoposide formulation can cause cracks in minutes. However, dehydrated alcohol did not cause any cracks within one hour. (1261)

Other Information

Skin Reactions — The manufacturer notes that accidental exposure to this potentially toxic agent may cause skin reactions. Therefore, protective gloves and syringes with Luer-Lok fittings should be used during preparation of solutions. A soap and water wash should be employed after accidental contact with the skin or mucosa. (2; 4)

Inactivation — In the event of spills or leaks, Bristol-Myers Oncology recommends the use of sodium hypochlorite 5% (household bleach) or potassium permanganate 1% to inactivate etoposide. (1200)

ETOPOSIDE PHOSPHATE
AHFS 10:00

Products — Etoposide phosphate is available in single-dose lyophilized vials containing the equivalent of 100 mg of etoposide as the phosphate along with sodium citrate 32.7 mg and 300 mg of dextran 40. Reconstitute with 5 or 10 ml of compatible diluent to yield solutions of 20 or 10 mg/ml, respectively. Sterile water for injection, dextrose 5% in water, sodium chloride 0.9%, bacteriostatic water for injection preserved with benzyl alcohol, or bacteriostatic sodium chloride 0.9% preserved with benzyl alcohol may be used for reconstitution. (2)

pH — Reconstitution with sterile water for injection to a concentration of 1 mg/ml results in a pH of approximately 2.9. (4)

Osmolality — Etoposide phosphate (Bristol-Myers Squibb) 10 mg/ml in sterile water for injection has an osmolality of 62 mOsm/kg. (2043)

Trade Name(s) — Etopophos.

Administration — Etoposide phosphate is administered by intravenous infusion over periods from 5 to 210 minutes. The reconstituted drug may be given without further dilution or may be diluted to a concentration as low as 0.1 mg/ml with dextrose 5% in water or sodium chloride 0.9%. (2; 4)

Stability — Etoposide phosphate is a white to off-white powder. (4) Intact vials should be stored under refrigeration at 2 to 8 °C and protected from light. (2)

The manufacturer states that etoposide phosphate reconstituted with an unpreserved diluent (such as sterile water for injection, dextrose 5% in water, or sodium chloride 0.9%) is stable for 24 hours at room temperatures of 20 to 25 °C and under refrigeration at 2 to 8 °C. (2; 4) Previously, the manufacturer's labeling indicated that if a diluent containing benzyl alcohol as a preservative (such as bacteriostatic water for injection or bacteriostatic sodium chloride 0.9%) is used to reconstitute etoposide phosphate, the solution is stable for 48 hours at room temperatures of 20 to 25 °C and for seven days under refrigeration at 2 to 8 °C. (1-4/98)

Unlike etoposide, the phosphate ester is highly water soluble, having a solubility over 100 mg/ml. (4) Consequently, the potential for precipitation when diluted in aqueous media is reduced greatly compared with the older surfactant- and organic solvent-based formulation. (2219)

Etoposide production by hydrolysis from infusion admixtures of etoposide phosphate (Bristol-Myers Squibb) was measured using HPLC. The admixtures, equivalent to etoposide 1.5 mg/ml in 66.7 ml and 1.5 mg/ml in 20 ml, were filled into PVC ambulatory infusion pump reservoirs (Pharmacia Deltec) and stored at 20 and 37 °C protected from light. Etoposide levels in the etoposide phosphate admixtures increased at both temperatures; in seven days the increase in concentration was about 2% at 20 °C and about 7% at 37 °C. The authors concluded that etoposide phosphate is suitable for multiple-day ambulatory infusion. (2024)

Light Effects—An evaluation of etoposide phosphate (Bristol-Myers Squibb) 2 mg/ml, doxorubicin HCl 0.4 mg/ml, and vincristine sulfate 0.016 mg/ml (16 μg/ml) in sodium chloride 0.9% in polyolefin plastic bags (McGaw) found little or no effect of constant exposure to normal fluorescent room light for 124 hours. The admixtures were physically compatible, and all three drugs in the admixture remained stable throughout the time stored at an elevated temperature of 35 to 40 °C. (2343)

Syringes—Etoposide phosphate (Bristol Laboratories Oncology Products) 10 and 20 mg/ml was prepared with bacteriostatic water for injection preserved with benzyl alcohol 0.9% (Abbott). The solutions were packaged as 4 ml of solution in 5-ml polypropylene syringes (Becton-Dickinson) and sealed with tip caps (Red Cap, Burron Medical). The syringes were stored at 32 °C for seven days, 23 °C for 31 days, and 4 °C for 31 days. All samples were physically stable, with no visual change and no increase in measured haze or particle content. HPLC analysis found little loss of drug. At 32 °C, 2 to 4% loss occurred in seven days. At 23 °C, about 6 to 7% loss occurred in 31 days. Losses under refrigeration were 4% or less in 31 days. (2219)

Compatibility Information

Solution Compatibility

Etoposide phosphate

Solution	*Mfr*	*Mfr*	*Conc/L*	*Remarks*	*Ref*	*C/I*
Dextrose 5% in water	BA[a]	BR	0.1 and 10 g	Physically compatible with no increase in measured haze or particles and little or no loss by HPLC in 7 days at 32 °C and in 31 days at 23 and 4 °C	2219	C
Sodium chloride 0.9%	BA[a]	BR	0.1 and 10 g	Physically compatible with no increase in measured haze or particles and little or no loss by HPLC in 7 days at 32 °C and in 31 days at 23 and 4 °C	2219	C

[a]*Tested in PVC containers.*

Additive Compatibility

Etoposide phosphate

Drug	*Mfr*	*Conc/L*	*Mfr*	*Conc/L*	*Test Soln*	*Remarks*	*Ref*	*C/I*
Doxorubicin HCl with vincristine sulfate	PHU LI	120 mg 5 mg	BMS	600 mg	NS[a]	Physically compatible with little or no loss of any drug by HPLC in 124 hr under refrigeration or at 35 to 40 °C	2343	C
Doxorubicin HCl with vincristine sulfate	PHU LI	240 mg 10 mg	BMS	1.2 g	NS[a]	Physically compatible with little or no loss of any drug by HPLC in 124 hr under refrigeration or at 35 to 40 °C	2343	C
Doxorubicin HCl with vincristine sulfate	PHU LI	400 mg 16 mg	BMS	2 g	NS[a]	Physically compatible with not more than 4% loss of any drug by HPLC in 124 hr under refrigeration or at 35 to 40 °C	2343	C

[a]*Tested in polyolefin-lined plastic bags.*

Y-Site Injection Compatibility (1:1 Mixture)

Etoposide phosphate

Drug	*Mfr*	*Conc*	*Mfr*	*Conc*	*Remarks*	*Ref*	*C/I*
Acyclovir sodium	GW	7 mg/ml[a]	BR	5 mg/ml[a]	Physically compatible with no change in measured turbidity or increase in particle content in 4 hr at 23 °C	2218	C
Amikacin sulfate	APC	5 mg/ml[a]	BR	5 mg/ml[a]	Physically compatible with no change in measured turbidity or increase in particle content in 4 hr at 23 °C	2218	C

Y-Site Injection Compatibility (1:1 Mixture) (Cont.)

Etoposide phosphate

Drug	*Mfr*	*Conc*	*Mfr*	*Conc*	*Remarks*	*Ref*	*C/I*
Aminophylline	AB	2.5 mg/ml[a]	BR	5 mg/ml[a]	Physically compatible with no change in measured turbidity or increase in particle content in 4 hr at 23 °C	2218	C
Amphotericin B	GNS	0.6 mg/ml[a]	BR	5 mg/ml[a]	Yellow-orange flocculent precipitate forms immediately	2218	I
Ampicillin sodium	APC	20 mg/ml[b]	BR	5 mg/ml[a]	Physically compatible with no change in measured turbidity or increase in particle content in 4 hr at 23 °C	2218	C
Ampicillin sodium–sulbactam sodium	RR	20 + 10 mg/ml[b]	BR	5 mg/ml[a]	Physically compatible with no change in measured turbidity or increase in particle content in 4 hr at 23 °C	2218	C
Aztreonam	SQ	40 mg/ml[a]	BR	5 mg/ml[a]	Physically compatible with no change in measured turbidity or increase in particle content in 4 hr at 23 °C	2218	C
Bleomycin sulfate	MJ	1 unit/ml[b]	BR	5 mg/ml[a]	Physically compatible with no change in measured turbidity or increase in particle content in 4 hr at 23 °C	2218	C
Bumetanide	RC	0.04 mg/ml[a]	BR	5 mg/ml[a]	Physically compatible with no change in measured turbidity or increase in particle content in 4 hr at 23 °C	2218	C
Buprenorphine HCl	RKC	0.04 mg/ml[a]	BR	5 mg/ml[a]	Physically compatible with no change in measured turbidity or increase in particle content in 4 hr at 23 °C	2218	C
Butorphanol tartrate	APC	0.04 mg/ml[a]	BR	5 mg/ml[a]	Physically compatible with no change in measured turbidity or increase in particle content in 4 hr at 23 °C	2218	C
Calcium gluconate	FUJ	40 mg/ml[a]	BR	5 mg/ml[a]	Physically compatible with no change in measured turbidity or increase in particle content in 4 hr at 23 °C	2218	C
Carboplatin	BR	5 mg/ml[a]	BR	5 mg/ml[a]	Physically compatible with no change in measured turbidity or increase in particle content in 4 hr at 23 °C	2218	C
Carmustine	BR	1.5 mg/ml[a]	BR	5 mg/ml[a]	Physically compatible with no change in measured turbidity or increase in particle content in 4 hr at 23 °C	2218	C
Cefazolin sodium	APC	20 mg/ml[a]	BR	5 mg/ml[a]	Physically compatible with no change in measured turbidity or increase in particle content in 4 hr at 23 °C	2218	C
Cefepime HCl	BMS	20 mg/ml[a]	BR	5 mg/ml[a]	Increased haze and particulates form within 1 hr	2218	I
Cefoperazone sodium	PF	40 mg/ml[a]	BR	5 mg/ml[a]	Physically compatible with no change in measured turbidity or increase in particle content in 4 hr at 23 °C	2218	C
Cefotaxime sodium	HO	20 mg/ml[a]	BR	5 mg/ml[a]	Physically compatible with no change in measured turbidity or increase in particle content in 4 hr at 23 °C	2218	C

Y-Site Injection Compatibility (1:1 Mixture) (Cont.)

			Etoposide phosphate				
Drug	*Mfr*	*Conc*	*Mfr*	*Conc*	*Remarks*	*Ref*	*C/I*
Cefotetan disodium	ZEN	20 mg/ml[a]	BR	5 mg/ml[a]	Physically compatible with no change in measured turbidity or increase in particle content in 4 hr at 23 °C	2218	C
Cefoxitin sodium	ME	20 mg/ml[a]	BR	5 mg/ml[a]	Physically compatible with no change in measured turbidity or increase in particle content in 4 hr at 23 °C	2218	C
Ceftazidime	SKB[c]	40 mg/ml[a]	BR	5 mg/ml[a]	Physically compatible with no change in measured turbidity or increase in particle content in 4 hr at 23 °C	2218	C
Ceftizoxime sodium	FUJ	20 mg/ml[a]	BR	5 mg/ml[a]	Physically compatible with no change in measured turbidity or increase in particle content in 4 hr at 23 °C	2218	C
Ceftriaxone sodium	RC	20 mg/ml[a]	BR	5 mg/ml[a]	Physically compatible with no change in measured turbidity or increase in particle content in 4 hr at 23 °C	2218	C
Cefuroxime sodium	GW	30 mg/ml[a]	BR	5 mg/ml[a]	Physically compatible with no change in measured turbidity or increase in particle content in 4 hr at 23 °C	2218	C
Chlorpromazine HCl	ES	2 mg/ml[a]	BR	5 mg/ml[a]	White cloudy solution with brown undertones forms immediately with particulates in 4 hr	2218	I
Cimetidine HCl	AMR	12 mg/ml[a]	BR	5 mg/ml[a]	Physically compatible with no change in measured turbidity or increase in particle content in 4 hr at 23 °C	2218	C
Ciprofloxacin	BAY	1 mg/ml[a]	BR	5 mg/ml[a]	Physically compatible with no change in measured turbidity or increase in particle content in 4 hr at 23 °C	2218	C
Cisplatin	BR	1 mg/ml	BR	5 mg/ml[a]	Physically compatible with no change in measured turbidity or increase in particle content in 4 hr at 23 °C	2218	C
Clindamycin phosphate	AST	10 mg/ml[a]	BR	5 mg/ml[a]	Physically compatible with no change in measured turbidity or increase in particle content in 4 hr at 23 °C	2218	C
Cyclophosphamide	MJ	10 mg/ml[a]	BR	5 mg/ml[a]	Physically compatible with no change in measured turbidity or increase in particle content in 4 hr at 23 °C	2218	C
Cytarabine	BED	50 mg/ml	BR	5 mg/ml[a]	Physically compatible with no change in measured turbidity or increase in particle content in 4 hr at 23 °C	2218	C
Dacarbazine	MI	4 mg/ml[a]	BR	5 mg/ml[a]	Physically compatible with no change in measured turbidity or increase in particle content in 4 hr at 23 °C	2218	C
Dactinomycin	ME	0.01 mg/ml[a]	BR	5 mg/ml[a]	Physically compatible with no change in measured turbidity or increase in particle content in 4 hr at 23 °C	2218	C
Daunorubicin HCl	BED	1 mg/ml[a]	BR	5 mg/ml[a]	Physically compatible with no change in measured turbidity or increase in particle content in 4 hr at 23 °C	2218	C

Y-Site Injection Compatibility (1:1 Mixture) (Cont.)

			Etoposide phosphate				
Drug	*Mfr*	*Conc*	*Mfr*	*Conc*	*Remarks*	*Ref*	*C/I*
Dexamethasone sodium phosphate	ES	1 mg/ml[a]	BR	5 mg/ml[a]	Physically compatible with no change in measured turbidity or increase in particle content in 4 hr at 23 °C	2218	C
Diphenhydramine HCl	ES	2 mg/ml[a]	BR	5 mg/ml[a]	Physically compatible with no change in measured turbidity or increase in particle content in 4 hr at 23 °C	2218	C
Dobutamine HCl	AST	4 mg/ml[a]	BR	5 mg/ml[a]	Physically compatible with no change in measured turbidity or increase in particle content in 4 hr at 23 °C	2218	C
Dopamine HCl	AST	3.2 mg/ml[a]	BR	5 mg/ml[a]	Physically compatible with no change in measured turbidity or increase in particle content in 4 hr at 23 °C	2218	C
Doxorubicin HCl	GEN	2 mg/ml	BR	5 mg/ml[a]	Physically compatible with no change in measured turbidity or increase in particle content in 4 hr at 23 °C	2218	C
Doxycycline hyclate	FUJ	1 mg/ml[a]	BR	5 mg/ml[a]	Physically compatible with no change in measured turbidity or increase in particle content in 4 hr at 23 °C	2218	C
Droperidol	AST	0.4 mg/ml[a]	BR	5 mg/ml[a]	Physically compatible with no change in measured turbidity or increase in particle content in 4 hr at 23 °C	2218	C
Enalaprilat	ME	0.1 mg/ml[a]	BR	5 mg/ml[a]	Physically compatible with no change in measured turbidity or increase in particle content in 4 hr at 23 °C	2218	C
Famotidine	ME	2 mg/ml[a]	BR	5 mg/ml[a]	Physically compatible with no change in measured turbidity or increase in particle content in 4 hr at 23 °C	2218	C
Floxuridine	RC	3 mg/ml[a]	BR	5 mg/ml[a]	Physically compatible with no change in measured turbidity or increase in particle content in 4 hr at 23 °C	2218	C
Fluconazole	RR	2 mg/ml	BR	5 mg/ml[a]	Physically compatible with no change in measured turbidity or increase in particle content in 4 hr at 23 °C	2218	C
Fludarabine phosphate	BX	1 mg/ml[a]	BR	5 mg/ml[a]	Physically compatible with no change in measured turbidity or increase in particle content in 4 hr at 23 °C	2218	C
Fluorouracil	PH	16 mg/ml[a]	BR	5 mg/ml[a]	Physically compatible with no change in measured turbidity or increase in particle content in 4 hr at 23 °C	2218	C
Furosemide	AMR	3 mg/ml[a]	BR	5 mg/ml[a]	Physically compatible with no change in measured turbidity or increase in particle content in 4 hr at 23 °C	2218	C
Ganciclovir sodium	RC	20 mg/ml[a]	BR	5 mg/ml[a]	Physically compatible with no change in measured turbidity or increase in particle content in 4 hr at 23 °C	2218	C
Gatifloxacin	BMS	2 mg/ml[a]	BR	5 mg/ml[a]	Physically compatible with no change in measured haze or increase in particle content in 4 hr at 23 °C	2234	C

Y-Site Injection Compatibility (1:1 Mixture) (Cont.)

Drug	Mfr	Conc	Etoposide phosphate Mfr	Etoposide phosphate Conc	Remarks	Ref	C/I
Gemcitabine HCl	LI	10 mg/ml[b]	BR	5 mg/ml[b]	Physically compatible with no change in measured turbidity or increase in particle content in 4 hr at 23 °C	2226	C
Gentamicin sulfate	AB	5 mg/ml[a]	BR	5 mg/ml[a]	Physically compatible with no change in measured turbidity or increase in particle content in 4 hr at 23 °C	2218	C
Granisetron HCl	SKB	0.05 mg/ml[a]	BR	5 mg/ml[a]	Physically compatible with no change in measured turbidity or increase in particle content in 4 hr at 23 °C	2218	C
Haloperidol lactate	MN	0.2 mg/ml[a]	BR	5 mg/ml[a]	Physically compatible with no change in measured turbidity or increase in particle content in 4 hr at 23 °C	2218	C
Heparin sodium	ES	100 units/ml[a]	BR	5 mg/ml[a]	Physically compatible with no change in measured turbidity or increase in particle content in 4 hr at 23 °C	2218	C
Hydrocortisone sodium phosphate	ME	0.5 mg/ml[a]	BR	5 mg/ml[a]	Physically compatible with no change in measured turbidity or increase in particle content in 4 hr at 23 °C	2218	C
Hydrocortisone sodium succinate	UP	1 mg/ml[a]	BR	5 mg/ml[a]	Physically compatible with no change in measured turbidity or increase in particle content in 4 hr at 23 °C	2218	C
Hydromorphone HCl	ES	0.5 mg/ml[a]	BR	5 mg/ml[a]	Physically compatible with no change in measured turbidity or increase in particle content in 4 hr at 23 °C	2218	C
Hydroxyzine HCl	ES	4 mg/ml[a]	BR	5 mg/ml[a]	Physically compatible with no change in measured turbidity or increase in particle content in 4 hr at 23 °C	2218	C
Idarubicin HCl	AD	0.5 mg/ml[a]	BR	5 mg/ml[a]	Physically compatible with no change in measured turbidity or increase in particle content in 4 hr at 23 °C	2218	C
Ifosfamide	MJ	25 mg/ml[a]	BR	5 mg/ml[a]	Physically compatible with no change in measured turbidity or increase in particle content in 4 hr at 23 °C	2218	C
Imipenem–cilastatin sodium	ME	10 mg/ml[b]	BR	5 mg/ml[a]	Yellow discoloration forms in 4 hr at 23 °C	2218	I
Leucovorin calcium	IMM	2 mg/ml[a]	BR	5 mg/ml[a]	Physically compatible with no change in measured turbidity or increase in particle content in 4 hr at 23 °C	2218	C
Linezolid	PHU	2 mg/ml	BR	5 mg/ml[a]	Physically compatible with no change in measured turbidity or increase in particle content in 4 hr at 23 °C	2264	C
Lorazepam	WY	0.5 mg/ml[a]	BR	5 mg/ml[a]	Physically compatible with no change in measured turbidity or increase in particle content in 4 hr at 23 °C	2218	C
Magnesium sulfate	AST	100 mg/ml[a]	BR	5 mg/ml[a]	Physically compatible with no change in measured turbidity or increase in particle content in 4 hr at 23 °C	2218	C

Y-Site Injection Compatibility (1:1 Mixture) (Cont.)

Etoposide phosphate

Drug	*Mfr*	*Conc*	*Mfr*	*Conc*	*Remarks*	*Ref*	*C/I*
Mannitol	BA	15%	BR	5 mg/ml[a]	Physically compatible with no change in measured turbidity or increase in particle content in 4 hr at 23 °C	2218	**C**
Meperidine HCl	AST	4 mg/ml[a]	BR	5 mg/ml[a]	Physically compatible with no change in measured turbidity or increase in particle content in 4 hr at 23 °C	2218	**C**
Mesna	MJ	10 mg/ml[a]	BR	5 mg/ml[a]	Physically compatible with no change in measured turbidity or increase in particle content in 4 hr at 23 °C	2218	**C**
Methotrexate sodium	IMM	15 mg/ml[a]	BR	5 mg/ml[a]	Physically compatible with no change in measured turbidity or increase in particle content in 4 hr at 23 °C	2218	**C**
Methylprednisolone sodium succinate	AB	5 mg/ml[a]	BR	5 mg/ml[a]	Haze with small subvisual particles forms immediately. Particle content increases fivefold over 4 hr at 23 °C	2218	**I**
Metoclopramide HCl	FAU	5 mg/ml	BR	5 mg/ml[a]	Physically compatible with no change in measured turbidity or increase in particle content in 4 hr at 23 °C	2218	**C**
Metronidazole	AB	5 mg/ml	BR	5 mg/ml[a]	Physically compatible with no change in measured turbidity or increase in particle content in 4 hr at 23 °C	2218	**C**
Minocycline HCl	LE	0.2 mg/ml[a]	BR	5 mg/ml[a]	Physically compatible with no change in measured turbidity or increase in particle content in 4 hr at 23 °C	2218	**C**
Mitomycin	BR	0.5 mg/ml	BR	5 mg/ml[a]	Color changed from light blue to reddish-purple in 4 hr at 23 °C	2218	**I**
Mitoxantrone HCl	IMM	0.5 mg/ml[a]	BR	5 mg/ml[a]	Physically compatible with no change in measured turbidity or increase in particle content in 4 hr at 23 °C	2218	**C**
Morphine sulfate	ES	1 mg/ml[a]	BR	5 mg/ml[a]	Physically compatible with no change in measured turbidity or increase in particle content in 4 hr at 23 °C	2218	**C**
Nalbuphine HCl	AST	10 mg/ml	BR	5 mg/ml[a]	Physically compatible with no change in measured turbidity or increase in particle content in 4 hr at 23 °C	2218	**C**
Netilmicin sulfate	SC	5 mg/ml[a]	BR	5 mg/ml[a]	Physically compatible with no change in measured turbidity or increase in particle content in 4 hr at 23 °C	2218	**C**
Ofloxacin	MN	4 mg/ml[a]	BR	5 mg/ml[a]	Physically compatible with no change in measured turbidity or increase in particle content in 4 hr at 23 °C	2218	**C**
Ondansetron HCl	GW	1 mg/ml[a]	BR	5 mg/ml[a]	Physically compatible with no change in measured turbidity or increase in particle content in 4 hr at 23 °C	2218	**C**
Paclitaxel	MJ	1.2 mg/ml[a]	BR	5 mg/ml[a]	Physically compatible with no change in measured turbidity or increase in particle content in 4 hr at 23 °C	2218	**C**

Y-Site Injection Compatibility (1:1 Mixture) (Cont.)

Drug	Mfr	Conc	Etoposide phosphate Mfr	Etoposide phosphate Conc	Remarks	Ref	C/I
Piperacillin sodium	LE	40 mg/ml[a]	BR	5 mg/ml[a]	Physically compatible with no change in measured turbidity or increase in particle content in 4 hr at 23 °C	2218	C
Piperacillin sodium–tazobactam sodium	LE	40 + 5 mg/ml[b]	BR	5 mg/ml[a]	Physically compatible with no change in measured turbidity or increase in particle content in 4 hr at 23 °C	2218	C
Plicamycin	MI	0.01 mg/ml[a]	BR	5 mg/ml[a]	Physically compatible with no change in measured turbidity or increase in particle content in 4 hr at 23 °C	2218	C
Potassium chloride	AB	0.1 mEq/ml[a]	BR	5 mg/ml[a]	Physically compatible with no change in measured turbidity or increase in particle content in 4 hr at 23 °C	2218	C
Prochlorperazine edisylate	ES	0.5 mg/ml[a]	BR	5 mg/ml[a]	White cloudy solution forms immediately with precipitate in 4 hr	2218	I
Promethazine HCl	SCN	2 mg/ml[a]	BR	5 mg/ml[a]	Physically compatible with no change in measured turbidity or increase in particle content in 4 hr at 23 °C	2218	C
Ranitidine HCl	GL	2 mg/ml[a]	BR	5 mg/ml[a]	Physically compatible with no change in measured turbidity or increase in particle content in 4 hr at 23 °C	2218	C
Sodium bicarbonate	AB	1 mEq/ml	BR	5 mg/ml[a]	Physically compatible with no change in measured turbidity or increase in particle content in 4 hr at 23 °C	2218	C
Streptozocin	UP	40 mg/ml[a]	BR	5 mg/ml[a]	Physically compatible with no change in measured turbidity or increase in particle content in 4 hr at 23 °C	2218	C
Teniposide	BR	0.1 mg/ml[a]	BR	5 mg/ml[a]	Physically compatible with no change in measured turbidity or increase in particle content in 4 hr at 23 °C	2218	C
Thiotepa	IMM	1 mg/ml[a]	BR	5 mg/ml[a]	Physically compatible with no change in measured turbidity or increase in particle content in 4 hr at 23 °C	2218	C
Ticarcillin disodium	SKB	30 mg/ml[a]	BR	5 mg/ml[a]	Physically compatible with no change in measured turbidity or increase in particle content in 4 hr at 23 °C	2218	C
Ticarcillin disodium–clavulanate potassium	SKB	31 mg/ml[a]	BR	5 mg/ml[a]	Physically compatible with no change in measured turbidity or increase in particle content in 4 hr at 23 °C	2218	C
Tobramycin sulfate	LI	5 mg/ml[a]	BR	5 mg/ml[a]	Physically compatible with no change in measured turbidity or increase in particle content in 4 hr at 23 °C	2218	C
Trimethoprim–sulfamethoxazole	ES	0.8 + 4 mg/ml[a]	BR	5 mg/ml[a]	Physically compatible with no change in measured turbidity or increase in particle content in 4 hr at 23 °C	2218	C
Vancomycin HCl	LI	10 mg/ml[a]	BR	5 mg/ml[a]	Physically compatible with no change in measured turbidity or increase in particle content in 4 hr at 23 °C	2218	C

Y-Site Injection Compatibility (1:1 Mixture) (Cont.)

Etoposide phosphate

Drug	*Mfr*	*Conc*	*Mfr*	*Conc*	*Remarks*	*Ref*	*C/I*
Vinblastine sulfate	FAU	0.12 mg/ml[a]	BR	5 mg/ml[a]	Physically compatible with no change in measured turbidity or increase in particle content in 4 hr at 23 °C	2218	C
Vincristine sulfate	FAU	0.05 mg/ml[a]	BR	5 mg/ml[a]	Physically compatible with no change in measured turbidity or increase in particle content in 4 hr at 23 °C	2218	C
Zidovudine	BW	4 mg/ml[a]	BR	5 mg/ml[a]	Physically compatible with no change in measured turbidity or increase in particle content in 4 hr at 23 °C	2218	C

[a]*Tested in dextrose 5% in water.*
[b]*Tested in sodium chloride 0.9%.*
[c]*Sodium carbonate–containing formulation tested.*

Additional Compatibility Information

Infusion Solutions — Etoposide phosphate reconstituted as directed may be diluted further to concentrations as low as 0.1 mg/ml in dextrose 5% in water or sodium chloride 0.9%. The drug is stated to be stable in either glass or plastic containers for 24 hours at both room temperatures of 20 to 25 °C and under refrigeration at 2 to 8 °C. (2; 4)

Other Information

Etoposide 100 mg is provided in approximately 113.6 mg of etoposide phosphate. (4)

Microbial Growth — Admixtures containing doxorubicin HCl, etoposide phosphate, and vincristine sulfate in a variety of concentration combinations were unable to pass the USP test for antimicrobial growth effectiveness. Mixtures of these drugs are not "self-preserving" and will permit microbial growth. (2343)

FAMOTIDINE
AHFS 56:40

Products — Famotidine is available as a 10-mg/ml injection in 2-ml single-dose vials and 4- and 20-ml multiple-dose vials. Each milliliter of the solution also contains L-aspartic acid 4 mg and mannitol 20 mg. Benzyl alcohol 0.9% is present as a preservative in the multiple-dose product. (2)

Famotidine is also available premixed at a concentration of 20 mg/50 ml. Each 50 ml of solution also contains L-aspartic acid 6.8 mg and sodium chloride 450 mg in water for injection. Additional L-aspartic acid or sodium hydroxide may be added to adjust the pH. (2)

pH — The injection has a pH from 5 to 5.6. (4) The premixed solution has a pH from 5.7 to 6.4. (2)

Osmolarity — The osmolarities of the single- and multiple-dose products are 217 and 290 mOsm/L, respectively. (4)

Trade Name(s) — Pepcid.

Administration — Famotidine is administered by slow intravenous injection or infusion. For injection, 20 mg should be diluted to 5 to 10 ml with a compatible diluent and injected no faster than 10 mg/min. For infusion, 20 mg should be diluted in 100 ml of dextrose 5% in water or another compatible diluent and infused over 15 to 30 minutes. Alternatively, famotidine premixed solution may be administered by intravenous infusion over 15 to 30 minutes. (2; 4)

Stability — Famotidine injection is a clear, colorless solution. The vials should be stored under refrigeration and protected from freezing. If freezing occurs, thaw at room temperature or by warming in a water bath or under a warm tap; make sure that all components have resolubilized. (2; 4) Use of a microwave oven for thawing is not recommended because of the potential hazard of vapor pressure increases in the vials. (4)

Although refrigeration is recommended, the manufacturer indicates that famotidine vials may be stored for up to 26 weeks at controlled room temperature not exceeding 25 °C. (1239)

Famotidine premixed infusion solution should be stored at controlled room temperature (25 °C) and protected from excessive heat. Brief exposure to temperatures up to 35 °C does not affect the stability of the product adversely. (2)

Freezing Solutions — Famotidine (MSD) 200 μg/ml in dextrose 5% in water or sodium chloride 0.9% in PVC bags showed no loss of potency when frozen at −20 °C for 28 days followed by storage at 4 °C for 14 days. (1271)

Famotidine (MSD) 2 mg/ml in dextrose 5% in water, sodium chloride 0.9%, or sterile water for injection stored in polypropylene syringes (Becton-Dickinson) exhibited a 5 to 8% loss in eight weeks when frozen at −20 °C. (1486)

Syringes— Bullock et al. reported that famotidine (MSD) 2 mg/ml in dextrose 5% in water, sodium chloride 0.9%, or sterile water for injection stored in plastic syringes (Becton-Dickinson) exhibited no loss in 14 days at 4 °C. (1487)

Keyi et al. evaluated the stability of famotidine (Merck) 0.2 mg/ml in dextrose 5% in water and in sodium chloride 0.9% packaged in PVC minibags (Abbott) and polypropylene syringes (Becton-Dickinson) and stored for 15 days at 22 °C both exposed to and protected from light. All samples were visually clear and colorless throughout the study, and famotidine concentrations remained within 95% percent of the initial values by HPLC analysis. (1936)

Central Venous Catheter— Famotidine (Merck) 2 mg/ml in dextrose 5% in water was found to be compatible with the ARROWg+ard Blue Plus (Arrow International) chlorhexidine-bearing triple-lumen central catheter. HPLC analysis was used to evaluate completeness of drug delivery through the catheter and the amount of chlorhexidine removed from the internal lumens. Essentially complete delivery of the drug was found with little or no drug loss occurring. Furthermore, chlorhexidine delivered from the catheter remained at trace amounts with no substantial increase due to the delivery of the drug through the catheter. (2335)

Compatibility Information

Solution Compatibility

Famotidine

Solution	*Mfr*	*Mfr*	*Conc/L*	*Remarks*	*Ref*	*C/I*
Amino acids	[a]	MSD	20 mg	0 to 5% loss in 48 hr at 25 °C in light or dark and at 5 °C	1344	C
Dextrose 5% in water	AB[b]	MSD	200 mg	Physically compatible with no potency loss in 14 days at 4 °C	1271	C
	TR[b]		200 mg	Physically compatible with 6% loss in 15 days at 25 °C and no loss in 63 days at 5 °C	1342	C
		MSD	20 mg	No loss in 48 hr at 25 °C in light or dark and at 5 °C	1344	C
	AB[b]	ME	200 mg	Visually compatible with less than 5% loss by HPLC in 15 days at 22 °C both with and without light protection	1936	C
Fat emulsion 10%, intravenous		MSD	20 mg	Little or no loss in 48 hr at 25 °C in light or dark and at 5 °C	1344	C
Sodium chloride 0.9%	AB[b]	MSD	200 mg	Physically compatible with no potency loss in 14 days at 4 °C	1271	C
	TR[b]		200 mg	Physically compatible with little or no loss in 15 days at 25 °C and in 63 days at 5 °C	1342	C
		MSD	20 mg	No loss in 48 hr at 25 °C in light or dark and at 5 °C	1344	C
	AB[b]	ME	200 mg	Visually compatible with less than 5% loss by HPLC in 15 days at 22 °C both with and without light protection	1936	C
TNA #111 and #112[c]		MSD	20 and 50 mg	Physically compatible with little or no famotidine loss and no change in fat particle size in 48 hr at 4 and 21 °C	1332	C
TNA #114[c]		MSD	20 and 40 mg	Physically compatible with little or no famotidine loss and no change in fat particle size in 72 hr at 21 °C under fluorescent light	1333	C
TNA #182[c]		MSD	20 mg	Visually compatible with no famotidine loss by HPLC in 24 hr at 24 °C under fluorescent light	1576	C
TNA #197 to #200[c]		MSD	20 mg	Physically compatible with no famotidine loss by HPLC in 48 hr at 22 °C exposed to light	1921	C
TPN #109 and #110[c]		MSD	20 and 40 mg	Physically compatible with little or no famotidine loss and little change in amino acids in 48 hr at 21 °C and in 7 days at 4 °C	1331	C

Solution Compatibility (Cont.)

Famotidine

Solution	*Mfr*	*Mfr*	*Conc/L*	*Remarks*	*Ref*	*C/I*
TPN #113[c]		MSD	20 mg	Physically compatible with little or no famotidine loss in 35 days at 4 °C protected from light	1334	C
TPN #115 and #116[c]		MSD	16.7 and 33.3 mg	No famotidine loss in 7 days at 23 and 4 °C	1352	C
TPN #196[c]		MSD	20 mg	Physically compatible with no famotidine loss by HPLC in 48 hr at 22 °C exposed to light	1921	C

[a]*Tested in Vamin 14, Vamin 18, Vamin glucose, and Vamin N.*
[b]*Tested in PVC containers.*
[c]*Refer to Appendix I for the composition of parenteral nutrition solutions. TNA indicates a 3-in-1 admixture, and TPN indicates a 2-in-1 admixture.*

Additive Compatibility

Famotidine

Drug	*Mfr*	*Conc/L*	*Mfr*	*Conc/L*	*Test Soln*	*Remarks*	*Ref*	*C/I*
Cefazolin sodium	FUJ	10 g	YAM	200 mg	D5W	Visually compatible with 10% cefazolin loss and 5% famotidine loss by HPLC in 24 hr at 25 °C. 9% cefazolin loss and 5% famotidine loss in 48 hr at 4 °C	1763	C
Flumazenil	RC	20 mg	MSD	80 mg	D5W[a]	Visually compatible with 3% flumazenil loss by HPLC in 24 hr at 23 °C under fluorescent light. Famotidine not tested	1710	C
Vancomycin HCl	AB	5 g	YAM	200 mg	D5W[b]	Visually compatible with 9% vancomycin loss and 6% famotidine loss by HPLC in 14 days at 25 °C. At 4 °C, losses of 3 to 4% occurred in 14 days	2111	C

[a]*Tested in PVC containers.*
[b]*Tested in methyl-methacrylate-butadiene-styrene plastic containers.*

Y-Site Injection Compatibility (1:1 Mixture)

Famotidine

Drug	*Mfr*	*Conc*	*Mfr*	*Conc*	*Remarks*	*Ref*	*C/I*
Acyclovir sodium		7 mg/ml[a]	ME	2 mg/ml[b]	Visually compatible for 4 hr at 22 °C	1936	C
Alatrofloxacin mesylate	PF	1.43 mg/ml[a]	ME	2 mg/ml[i]	Microscopic particles form	2235	I
Allopurinol sodium	BW	3 mg/ml[b]	MSD	2 mg/ml[b]	Physically compatible with no change in measured turbidity or increase in particle content in 4 hr at 22 °C	1686	C
Amifostine	USB	10 mg/ml[a]	ME	2 mg/ml[a]	Physically compatible with no change in measured turbidity or increase in particle content in 4 hr at 23 °C	1845	C
Aminophylline	LY	2.5 mg/ml[b] 2.5 mg/ml[a]	MSD ME	0.2 mg/ml[a] 2 mg/ml	Physically compatible for 14 hr Visually compatible for 4 hr at 22 °C	1196 1936	C C
Amphotericin B cholesteryl sulfate complex	SEQ	0.83 mg/ml[a]	ME	2 mg/ml[a]	Microprecipitate and increased turbidity form immediately	2117	I
Ampicillin sodium	ES	20 mg/ml[b] 20 mg/ml[b]	MSD ME	0.2 mg/ml[a] 2 mg/ml[b]	Physically compatible for 14 hr Visually compatible for 4 hr at 22 °C	1196 1936	C C
Ampicillin sodium–sulbactam sodium	RR	20 + 10 mg/ml[b]	MSD	0.2 mg/ml[a]	Physically compatible for 14 hr	1196	C

Y-Site Injection Compatibility (1:1 Mixture) (Cont.)

			Famotidine				
Drug	*Mfr*	*Conc*	*Mfr*	*Conc*	*Remarks*	*Ref*	*C/I*
Amsacrine	NCI	1 mg/ml[a]	MSD	2 mg/ml[a]	Physically compatible for 4 hr at room temperature under fluorescent light	1381	C
Atropine sulfate	AST	0.1 mg/ml[a]	MSD	0.2 mg/ml[a]	Physically compatible for 4 hr at 25 °C	1188	C
Aztreonam	SQ	40 mg/ml[a]	ME	2 mg/ml[a]	Physically compatible with no subvisual haze or particle formation in 4 hr at 23 °C	1758	C
Bretylium tosylate	AB	4 mg/ml[a]	MSD	0.2 mg/ml[a]	Physically compatible for 4 hr at 25 °C	1188	C
Calcium gluconate	LY	0.00465 mEq/ml[b]	MSD	0.2 mg/ml[a]	Physically compatible for 14 hr	1196	C
Cefazolin sodium	LY	20 mg/ml[b] 20 mg/ml[a]	MSD ME	0.2 mg/ml[a] 2 mg/ml[b]	Physically compatible for 14 hr Visually compatible for 4 hr at 22 °C	1196 1936	C C
Cefepime HCl	BMS	20 mg/ml[a]	ME	2 mg/ml[a]	Haze forms immediately. Flocculent precipitate forms in 4 hr	1689	I
Cefoperazone sodium	RR	40 mg/ml[b]	MSD	0.2 mg/ml[a]	Physically compatible for 14 hr	1196	C
Cefotaxime sodium	HO	20 mg/ml[b] 20 mg/ml[a]	MSD ME	0.2 mg/ml[a] 2 mg/ml[b]	Physically compatible for 14 hr Visually compatible for 4 hr at 22 °C	1196 1936	C C
Cefotetan disodium	STU	20 mg/ml[b]	MSD	0.2 mg/ml[a]	Physically compatible for 14 hr	1196	C
Cefoxitin sodium	MSD	20 mg/ml[b] 20 mg/ml[a]	MSD ME	0.2 mg/ml[a] 2 mg/ml[b]	Physically compatible for 14 hr Visually compatible for 4 hr at 22 °C	1196 1936	C C
Ceftazidime	GL[c] [c]	20 mg/ml[b] 20 mg/ml[a]	MSD ME	0.2 mg/ml[a] 2 mg/ml[b]	Physically compatible for 14 hr Visually compatible for 4 hr at 22 °C	1196 1936	C C
Ceftizoxime sodium	FUJ	20 mg/ml[b]	MSD	0.2 mg/ml[a]	Physically compatible for 14 hr	1196	C
Ceftriaxone sodium		20 mg/ml[a]	ME	2 mg/ml[b]	Visually compatible for 4 hr at 22 °C	1936	C
Cefuroxime sodium	GL	15 mg/ml[b] 20 mg/ml[a]	MSD ME	0.2 mg/ml[a] 2 mg/ml[b]	Physically compatible for 14 hr Visually compatible for 4 hr at 22 °C	1196 1936	C C
Chlorpromazine HCl		2 mg/ml[a]	ME	2 mg/ml[b]	Visually compatible for 4 hr at 22 °C	1936	C
Cisatracurium besylate	GW	0.1, 2, 5 mg/ml[a]	ME	2 mg/ml[a]	Physically compatible with no change in measured turbidity or increase in particle content in 4 hr at 23 °C	2074	C
Cisplatin	BR	1 mg/ml	MSD	2 mg/ml[a]	Visually compatible for 4 hr at room temperature under fluorescent light	1685	C
Cladribine	ORT	0.015[b] and 0.5[d] mg/ml	ME	2 mg/ml[b]	Physically compatible with no change in measured turbidity or increase in particle content in 4 hr at 23 °C	1969	C
Cyclophosphamide	MJ	10 mg/ml[a]	MSD	2 mg/ml[a]	Visually compatible for 4 hr at room temperature under fluorescent light	1685	C
Cytarabine	UP	50 mg/ml	MSD	2 mg/ml[a]	Visually compatible for 4 hr at room temperature under fluorescent light	1685	C
Dexamethasone sodium phosphate	ES	10 mg/ml 1 mg/ml[a]	MSD ME	0.2 mg/ml[a] 2 mg/ml[b]	Physically compatible for 14 hr Visually compatible for 4 hr at 22 °C	1196 1936	C C
Dextran 40	PH	100 mg/ml[a]	MSD	0.2 mg/ml[a]	Physically compatible for 4 hr at 25 °C	1188	C
Digoxin	ES	0.25 mg/ml	MSD	0.2 mg/ml[a]	Physically compatible for 14 hr	1196	C
Diphenhydramine HCl		2 mg/ml[a]	ME	2 mg/ml[b]	Visually compatible for 4 hr at 22 °C	1936	C
Dobutamine HCl	LI	1 mg/ml[a] 4 mg/ml[a]	MSD ME	0.2 mg/ml[a] 2 mg/ml[b]	Physically compatible for 4 hr at 25 °C Visually compatible for 4 hr at 22 °C	1188 1936	C C

Y-Site Injection Compatibility (1:1 Mixture) (Cont.)

			Famotidine				
Drug	*Mfr*	*Conc*	*Mfr*	*Conc*	*Remarks*	*Ref*	*C/I*
Docetaxel	RPR	0.9 mg/ml[a]	ME	2 mg/ml[a]	Physically compatible with no change in measured turbidity or increase in particle content in 4 hr at 23 °C	2224	C
Dopamine HCl	TR	1.6 mg/ml[a]	MSD	0.2 mg/ml[a]	Physically compatible for 4 hr at 25 °C	1188	C
		1.6 mg/ml[a]	ME	2 mg/ml[b]	Visually compatible for 4 hr at 22 °C	1936	C
Doxorubicin HCl	AD	0.2 mg/ml[a]	MSD	2 mg/ml[a]	Visually compatible for 4 hr at room temperature under fluorescent light	1685	C
Doxorubicin HCl liposome injection	SEQ	0.4 mg/ml[a]	ME	2 mg/ml[a]	Physically compatible with little or no change in measured turbidity and no increase in particle content in 4 hr at 23 °C	2087	C
Droperidol		0.4 mg/ml[a]	ME	2 mg/ml[b]	Visually compatible for 4 hr at 22 °C	1936	C
Enalaprilat	MSD	0.05 mg/ml[b]	MSD	0.2 mg/ml[a]	Physically compatible for 24 hr at room temperature under fluorescent light	1355	C
Epinephrine HCl	ES	0.004 mg/ml[a]	MSD	0.2 mg/ml[a]	Physically compatible for 4 hr at 25 °C	1188	C
Erythromycin lactobionate	ES	2 mg/ml[b]	MSD	0.2 mg/ml[a]	Physically compatible for 14 hr	1196	C
Esmolol HCl	DU	10 mg/ml[b]	MSD	0.2 mg/ml[a]	Physically compatible for 4 hr at 25 °C	1188	C
Etoposide phosphate	BR	5 mg/ml[a]	ME	2 mg/ml[a]	Physically compatible with no change in measured turbidity or increase in particle content in 4 hr at 23 °C	2218	C
Filgrastim	AMG	30 μg/ml[a]	MSD	2 mg/ml[a]	Physically compatible with no change in measured turbidity or increase in particle content in 4 hr at 22 °C	1687	C
Fluconazole	RR	2 mg/ml	MSD	10 mg/ml	Physically compatible for 24 hr at 25 °C	1407	C
		2 mg/ml[a]	ME	2 mg/ml[b]	Visually compatible for 4 hr at 22 °C	1936	C
Fludarabine phosphate	BX	1 mg/ml[a]	MSD	2 mg/ml[a]	Physically compatible for 4 hr at room temperature under fluorescent light	1439	C
Folic acid	LE	5 mg/ml	MSD	0.2 mg/ml[a]	Physically compatible for 14 hr	1196	C
Furosemide	ES	10 mg/ml	MSD	0.2 mg/ml[a]	Physically compatible for 14 hr	1196	C
	IMS	0.8 mg/ml[a]	MSD	0.2 mg/ml[a]	Physically compatible for 4 hr at 25 °C	1188	C
		3 mg/ml[a]	ME	2 mg/ml[b]	White precipitate forms immediately	1936	I
Gatifloxacin	BMS	2 mg/ml[a]	ME	2 mg/ml[a]	Physically compatible with no change in measured haze or increase in particle content in 4 hr at 23 °C	2234	C
Gemcitabine HCl	LI	10 mg/ml[b]	ME	2 mg/ml[b]	Physically compatible with no change in measured turbidity or increase in particle content in 4 hr at 23 °C	2226	C
Gentamicin sulfate	ES	0.8 mg/ml[b]	MSD	0.2 mg/ml[a]	Physically compatible for 14 hr	1196	C
		5 mg/ml[a]	ME	2 mg/ml[b]	Visually compatible for 4 hr at 22 °C	1936	C
Granisetron HCl	SKB	0.05 mg/ml[a]	ME	2 mg/ml[a]	Physically compatible with no change in measured turbidity or increase in particle content in 4 hr at 23 °C	2000	C
Haloperidol lactate	MN	0.5[a] and 5 mg/ml	MSD	0.267 mg/ml[a]	Visually compatible for 24 hr at 21 °C	1523	C
		0.2 mg/ml[a]	ME	2 mg/ml[b]	Visually compatible for 4 hr at 22 °C	1936	C
Heparin sodium	ES	40 units/ml[b]	MSD	0.2 mg/ml[a]	Physically compatible for 14 hr	1196	C
	TR	50 units/ml[a]	MSD	0.2 mg/ml[a]	Physically compatible for 4 hr at 25 °C	1188	C
		40 units/ml[a]	ME	2 mg/ml[b]	Visually compatible for 4 hr at 22 °C	1936	C

Y-Site Injection Compatibility (1:1 Mixture) (Cont.)

Drug	Mfr	Conc	Famotidine Mfr	Famotidine Conc	Remarks	Ref	C/I
Hetastarch in lactated electrolyte injection (Hextend)	AB	6%	ME	2 mg/ml[a]	Physically compatible with no change in measured turbidity or increase in particle content in 4 hr at 23 °C	2339	C
Hydrocortisone[e]		1 mg/ml[a]	ME	2 mg/ml[b]	Visually compatible for 4 hr at 22 °C	1936	C
Hydrocortisone sodium succinate	AB	1 mg/ml[a]	MSD	0.2 mg/ml[a]	Physically compatible for 4 hr at 25 °C	1188	C
	AB	125 mg/ml	MSD	0.2 mg/ml[a]	Physically compatible for 14 hr	1196	C
Hydromorphone HCl		0.5 mg/ml[a]	ME	2 mg/ml[b]	Visually compatible for 4 hr at 22 °C	1936	C
Hydroxyzine HCl		4 mg/ml[a]	ME	2 mg/ml[b]	Visually compatible for 4 hr at 22 °C	1936	C
Imipenem–cilastatin sodium	MSD	10 mg/ml[b]	MSD	0.2 mg/ml[a]	Physically compatible for 14 hr	1196	C
		5 mg/ml[b]	ME	2 mg/ml[b]	Visually compatible for 4 hr at 22 °C	1936	C
Inamrinone lactate	WI	2 mg/ml[b]	MSD	0.2 mg/ml[a]	Physically compatible for 4 hr at 25 °C	1188	C
Insulin, regular	LI	0.03 unit/ml[a]	MSD	0.2 mg/ml[a]	Physically compatible for 4 hr at 25 °C	1188	C
Isoproterenol HCl	ES	0.004 mg/ml[a]	MSD	0.2 mg/ml[a]	Physically compatible for 4 hr at 25 °C	1188	C
Labetalol HCl	SC	1 mg/ml[a]	MSD	0.2 mg/ml[a]	Physically compatible for 4 hr at 25 °C	1188	C
Lidocaine HCl	LY	1 mg/ml[a]	MSD	0.2 mg/ml[a]	Physically compatible for 14 hr	1196	C
	TR	4 mg/ml[a]	MSD	0.2 mg/ml[a]	Physically compatible for 4 hr at 25 °C	1188	C
Linezolid	PHU	2 mg/ml	ME	2 mg/ml[a]	Physically compatible with no change in measured turbidity or increase in particle content in 4 hr at 23 °C	2264	C
Lorazepam		0.1 mg/ml[a]	ME	2 mg/ml[b]	Visually compatible for 4 hr at 22 °C	1936	C
Magnesium sulfate	SO	100 mg/ml[b]	MSD	0.2 mg/ml[a]	Physically compatible for 14 hr	1196	C
		100 mg/ml[a]	ME	2 mg/ml[b]	Visually compatible for 4 hr at 22 °C	1936	C
Melphalan HCl	BW	0.1 mg/ml[b]	MSD	2 mg/ml[b]	Physically compatible with no change in measured turbidity or increase in particle content in 3 hr at 22 °C	1557	C
Meperidine HCl	AB	10 mg/ml	MSD	0.2 mg/ml[a]	Physically compatible for 4 hr at 25 °C	1397	C
		4 mg/ml[a]	ME	2 mg/ml[b]	Visually compatible for 4 hr at 22 °C	1936	C
Methotrexate sodium	AD	15 mg/ml[f]	MSD	2 mg/ml[a]	Visually compatible for 4 hr at room temperature under fluorescent light	1685	C
Methylprednisolone sodium succinate	QU	40 mg/ml	MSD	0.2 mg/ml[a]	Physically compatible for 14 hr	1196	C
	AB	1 mg/ml[a]	MSD	0.2 mg/ml[a]	Physically compatible for 4 hr at 25 °C	1188	C
		5 mg/ml[a]	ME	2 mg/ml[b]	Visually compatible for 4 hr at 22 °C	1936	C
Metoclopramide HCl	RB	5 mg/ml	MSD	0.2 mg/ml[a]	Physically compatible for 14 hr	1196	C
		5 mg/ml	ME	2 mg/ml[b]	Visually compatible for 4 hr at 22 °C	1936	C
Midazolam HCl	RC	0.15 mg/ml[a]	MSD	0.2 mg/ml[a]	Physically compatible for 4 hr at 25 °C	1188	C
		1.5 mg/ml[a]	ME	2 mg/ml[b]	Visually compatible for 4 hr at 22 °C	1936	C
Morphine sulfate	ES	0.2 mg/ml[a]	MSD	0.2 mg/ml[a]	Physically compatible for 4 hr at 25 °C	1188	C
	AB	1 mg/ml	MSD	0.2 mg/ml[a]	Physically compatible for 4 hr at 25 °C	1397	C
		1 mg/ml[a]	ME	2 mg/ml[b]	Visually compatible for 4 hr at 22 °C	1936	C
Nafcillin sodium	WY	15 mg/ml[b]	MSD	0.2 mg/ml[a]	Physically compatible for 14 hr	1196	C
Nitroglycerin	PD	85 μg/ml[b]	MSD	0.2 mg/ml[a]	Physically compatible for 14 hr	1196	C
	IMS	0.8 mg/ml[a]	MSD	0.2 mg/ml[a]	Physically compatible for 4 hr at 25 °C	1188	C
Norepinephrine bitartrate	WI	0.004 mg/ml[a]	MSD	0.2 mg/ml[a]	Physically compatible for 4 hr at 25 °C	1188	C
Ondansetron HCl	GL	1 mg/ml[b]	MSD	2 mg/ml[a]	Physically compatible for 4 hr at 22 °C	1365	C
Oxacillin sodium	BE	20 mg/ml[b]	MSD	0.2 mg/ml[a]	Physically compatible for 14 hr	1196	C

Y-Site Injection Compatibility (1:1 Mixture) (Cont.)

Famotidine

Drug	*Mfr*	*Conc*	*Mfr*	*Conc*	*Remarks*	*Ref*	*C/I*
Paclitaxel	NCI	1.2 mg/ml[a]	MSD	2 mg/ml[a]	Physically compatible with no change in measured turbidity in 4 hr at 22 °C	1556	C
Perphenazine	SC	0.04 mg/ml[a]	MSD	0.2 mg/ml[a]	Physically compatible for 4 hr at 25 °C	1188	C
Phenylephrine HCl	WI	0.02 mg/ml[a]	MSD	0.2 mg/ml[a]	Physically compatible for 4 hr at 25 °C	1188	C
Phenytoin sodium	PD	50 mg/ml	MSD	0.2 mg/ml[a]	Physically compatible for 14 hr	1196	C
Phytonadione	MSD	2 mg/ml	MSD	0.2 mg/ml[a]	Physically compatible for 14 hr	1196	C
Piperacillin sodium	LE	40 mg/ml[b]	MSD	0.2 mg/ml[a]	Physically compatible for 14 hr	1196	C
		40 mg/ml[a]	ME	2 mg/ml[b]	Visually compatible for 4 hr at 22 °C	1936	C
Piperacillin sodium–tazobactam sodium	LE	40 + 5 mg/ml[a]	MSD	2 mg/ml[a]	Particles form immediately	1688	I
Potassium chloride	AB	0.04 mEq/ml[a]	MSD	0.2 mg/ml[a]	Physically compatible for 4 hr at 25 °C	1188	C
		0.1 mEq/ml[a]	ME	2 mg/ml[b]	Visually compatible for 4 hr at 22 °C	1936	C
Potassium phosphates	LY	3 mmol/ml	MSD	0.2 mg/ml[a]	Physically compatible for 14 hr	1196	C
Procainamide HCl	ASC	5 mg/ml[a]	MSD	0.2 mg/ml[a]	Physically compatible for 4 hr at 25 °C	1188	C
Propofol	ZEN	10 mg/ml	ME	2 mg/ml[a]	Physically compatible with no increase in particle content in 1 hr at 23 °C	2066	C
Remifentanil HCl	GW	0.025 and 0.25 mg/ml[b]	MSD	2 mg/ml[a]	Physically compatible with no change in measured turbidity or increase in particle content in 4 hr at 23 °C	2075	C
Sargramostim	IMM	10 μg/ml[b]	MSD	2 mg/ml[b]	Physically compatible for 4 hr at 22 °C	1436	C
Sodium bicarbonate	AB	1 mEq/ml	MSD	0.2 mg/ml[a]	Physically compatible for 4 hr at 25 °C	1188	C
Sodium nitroprusside	ES	0.2 mg/ml[a]	MSD	0.2 mg/ml[a]	Physically compatible for 4 hr at 25 °C protected from light	1188	C
Teniposide	BR	0.1 mg/ml[a]	MSD	2 mg/ml[a]	Physically compatible with no subvisual haze or particle formation in 4 hr at 23 °C	1725	C
Theophylline	TR	1.6 mg/ml[a]	MSD	0.2 mg/ml[a]	Physically compatible for 4 hr at 25 °C	1188	C
Thiamine HCl	ES	100 mg/ml	MSD	0.2 mg/ml[a]	Physically compatible for 14 hr	1196	C
Thiotepa	IMM[g]	1 mg/ml[a]	ME	2 mg/ml[a]	Physically compatible with no change in measured turbidity or increase in particle content in 4 hr at 23 °C	1861	C
Ticarcillin disodium	BE	30 mg/ml[b]	MSD	0.2 mg/ml[a]	Physically compatible for 14 hr	1196	C
Ticarcillin disodium–clavulanate potassium	BE	31 mg/ml[b]	MSD	0.2 mg/ml[a]	Physically compatible for 14 hr	1196	C
Tirofiban HCl	ME	0.05 mg/ml[b]	ME	2 and 4 mg/ml[a]	Physically compatible with little or no loss of either drug by HPLC in 4 hr at room temperature under fluorescent light	2250	C
	ME	0.05 mg/ml[a]	ME	2 and 4 mg/ml[b]	Physically compatible with little or no loss of either drug by HPLC in 4 hr at room temperature under fluorescent light	2250	C
TNA #218 to #226[h]			ME	2 mg/ml[a]	Visually compatible with no precipitate or emulsion damage apparent in 4 hr at 23 °C	2215	C
TPN #212 to #215[h]			ME	2 mg/ml[a]	Physically compatible with no change in measured turbidity or increase in particle content in 4 hr at 23 °C	2109	C

Y-Site Injection Compatibility (1:1 Mixture) (Cont.)

Famotidine

Drug	*Mfr*	*Conc*	*Mfr*	*Conc*	*Remarks*	*Ref*	*C/I*
Verapamil HCl	KN	0.1 mg/ml[a]	MSD	0.2 mg/ml[a]	Physically compatible for 4 hr at 25 °C	1188	C
Vinorelbine tartrate	BW	1 mg/ml[b]	MSD	2 mg/ml[b]	Physically compatible with no change in measured turbidity or increase in particle content in 4 hr at 22 °C	1558	C

[a]Tested in dextrose 5% in water.
[b]Tested in sodium chloride 0.9%.
[c]Sodium carbonate-containing formulation.
[d]Tested in bacteriostatic sodium chloride 0.9% preserved with benzyl alcohol 0.9%.
[e]Form not specified.
[f] Tested in dextrose 5% in water with sodium bicarbonate 0.05 mEq/ml.
[g]Lyophilized formulation tested.
[h]Refer to Appendix I for the composition of parenteral nutrition solutions. TNA indicates a 3-in-1 admixture, and TPN indicates a 2-in-1 admixture.
[i]Diluent not specified.

Additional Compatibility Information

Infusion Solutions — The manufacturer states that famotidine 0.2 to 4 mg/ml is stable for 48 hours at room temperature in common infusion solutions, including (2; 4):

Dextrose 5 and 10% in water
Ringer's injection, lactated
Sodium bicarbonate 5%
Sodium chloride 0.9%

FAT EMULSION, INTRAVENOUS
AHFS 40:20

Products — The compositions and characteristics of the fat emulsion products are listed in Table 1.

The pH of fat emulsion, intravenous, products is adjusted with sodium hydroxide.

Trade Name(s) — See Table 1.

Administration — Fat emulsion, intravenous, may be administered intravenously via a peripheral vein or by central venous infusion. The particle size of the emulsions may exceed the porosity of some inline filters. (658; 1106) However, the use of a 1.2-μm or 5-μm inline filter to remove particulates, aggregates, precipitates, and large fat

Table 1. Composition and Characteristics of Various Intravenous Fat Emulsions (4; 29)

Component or Characteristic	Intralipid (Clinitec)			Liposyn II (Abbott)		Liposyn III (Abbott)		
Soybean oil	10%	20%	30%[a]	5%	10%	10%	20%	30%[a]
Safflower oil	—	—	—	5%	10%	—	—	—
Egg yolk phospholipids	1.2%	1.2%	1.2%	up to 1.2%	1.2%	up to 1.2%	1.2%	1.8%
Glycerin	2.25%	2.25%	1.7%	2.5%	2.5%	2.5%	2.5%	2.5%
Water for injection	qs	qs	qs	qs	qs	qs	qs	qs
Fatty acids:								
Linoleic acid	50%	50%	44–62%	65.8%		54.5%		
Oleic acid	26%	26%	19–30%	17.7%		22.4%		
Palmitic acid	10%	10%	7–14%	8.8%		10.5%		
Linolenic acid	9%	9%	4–11%	4.2%		8.3%		
Stearic acid	3.5%	3.5%	1.4–5.5%	3.4%		4.2%		
Osmolarity (mOsm/L)	260	260	310	276	258	284	292	293
Approximate pH	6–8.9	6–8.9	6–8.9	6–9	6–9	6–9	6–9	6–9
Fat particle size (μm)	0.5	0.5	0.5	0.4	0.4	0.4	0.4	0.4
Caloric value (cal/ml)	1.1	2	3	1.1	2	1.1	2	2.9
Size (ml)	50, 100, 250, 500	100, 250, 500, 1000	500	100, 200 500	50, 200, 500	100, 200, 500	200, 500	500

[a]Not for direct infusion. Must be diluted to 20% or less for administration.

globules has been suggested to protect patients during parenteral nutrition administration. (569; 1106; 2135; 2346)

Fat emulsion, intravenous, may also be administered intravenously in total nutrient admixtures (TNA, 3-in-1) in combination with amino acids, dextrose, and other nutrients. (4; 154)

It has been recommended that administration sets used to administer lipid emulsions be changed within 24 hours of initiating infusion because of the potential for bacterial and fungal contamination. (2342)

Stability — Fat emulsion, intravenous, products may be stored in the intact containers at controlled room temperature of 25 °C (Intralipid products) to 30 °C (Liposyn products) or below. They should be protected from freezing. (154)

Several factors can influence the stability of fat emulsions. A two-year study of Intralipid 10% found an increase in free fatty acids and a decrease of pH on storage. Gross particles formed and toxicity to rabbits increased with time. These changes were greatest during storage at 40 °C but were measurable at 20 and even 4 °C. The toxicity of the emulsions to rabbits could be correlated to the extent of free fatty acid formation in the emulsions. The formation of free fatty acids, with a consequent lowering of pH, is the major route of degradation of fat emulsions. The rate of degradation is minimized at pH 6 to 7. (889)

The container-closure system is important for long-term stability. Plastic containers are generally permeable to oxygen, which can readily oxidize the lipid emulsions, so glass bottles are used. Furthermore, the stoppers must not be permeable to oxygen and must not soften on contact with the emulsions. Teflon-coated stoppers have been recommended. Finally, the emulsions are packed under an atmosphere of nitrogen. (889)

The long-term room temperature stability of the emulsions is lost when the intact containers are entered. The integrity of the nitrogen layer in the sealed container is essential for room temperature stability. Exposure of Intralipid 10% to the atmosphere results in gradual changes in the emulsion system. No changes in the particle size distribution occurred during the first 36 hours of room temperature storage. After 48 hours at room temperature, globule coalescence was noticeable. By 72 hours, the changes had become significant. However, the visual appearance after 72 hours was unchanged. Long-term storage for 15 months at room temperature resulted in formation of a nonhomogeneous cream layer with oil globules on top. (656; 657) If the pH of the emulsion is optimal and the emulsion is stored under nitrogen and not exposed to direct sunlight, oxidative degradation is not likely to be significant. (889)

The manufacturers recommend that a partly used bottle should not be stored for later use, and no bottle should be used if the emulsion appears to be oiling out. (513; 514; 655)

As mentioned previously, storage temperature may be a factor in the shelflife of fat emulsion products. Because of the increase in free fatty acid content associated with temperature increases, and because of the imprecision of shelflife stability determinations of this type of product, refrigeration was originally required for long-term storage. (889) Currently, however, the restriction has been lifted to approve storage at 25 °C (Intralipid products) to 30 °C (Liposyn products) or below. (154)

The emulsions should not be frozen. (154) Freezing may cause physical damage. The emulsions may become coarse and coalesce, and they can undergo irreversible phase separation. If accidental freezing occurs, the products should be discarded. (559)

Oscillatory movement may cause separation of some phosphatide-stabilized emulsions but does not appear to be a problem with fat emulsion, intravenous, products. (889)

Plasticizer Leaching — Fat emulsion extracts diethylhexyl phthalate (DEHP) plasticizer from PVC in amounts exceeding comparable volumes of whole blood. The amount of plasticizer leached from PVC sets by fat emulsion is directly related to the length of administration time and inversely related to the flow rate; these two factors influence the amount of contact time between the fat emulsion and the PVC tubing. Longer administration times and slower administration rates increase the amount of leached plasticizer. Non-PVC plastic containers, such as an ethylene vinyl acetate bag, may be used to avoid plasticizer exposure. If PVC tubing is used, phthalate leaching can be minimized by not storing primed sets. (658; 661; 673; 893; 1105)

Storage of Intralipid 10 and 20% for 24 hours in PVC sets resulted in phthalate contents of 64 to 70 μg/ml at 5 °C and 144 to 160 μg/ml at ambient temperature. When the fat emulsions were simply infused through PVC sets, phthalate content dropped to 3.6 to 8.5 μg/ml. A patient being administered 500 ml of fat emulsion per day would receive about 1.5 to 2.75 mg/day. Negligible levels of phthalate were delivered from a parenteral nutrition admixture containing fat emulsion. (1264)

Mazur et al. reported that a parenteral nutrition solution containing an amino acid solution, dextrose, and electrolytes in a PVC bag did not leach measurable quantities of DEHP plasticizer during 21 days of storage at 4 and 25 °C. However, addition of fat emulsion 10 or 20% to the formula caused detectable leaching of DEHP from the PVC containers stored for 48 hours. Higher DEHP levels were found in the 25 °C samples than in the 4 °C samples. The authors recommended limiting the use of lipid-containing parenteral nutrition admixtures to 24 to 36 hours. Use of non-PVC containers and tubing is another option. (1430)

Filtration — The use of a 1.2- or 5-μm inline filter to remove particulates, aggregates, precipitates, and large fat globules has been suggested to protect patients during parenteral nutrition administration. (569; 1106; 2135; 2346) The particle size of the fat emulsion products may exceed the porosity of some inline filters. Such small porosity filters should not be used with fat emulsion products. (658; 1106)

Compatibility Information

Solution Compatibility

Fat emulsion, intravenous

Solution	*Mfr*	*Mfr*	*Conc/L*	*Remarks*	*Ref*	*C/I*
Amino acids injection 8.5%	MG	VT	10%	Mixed in equal parts. Physically compatible for 48 hr at 4 °C and room temperature	32	C

Solution Compatibility (Cont.)

Fat emulsion, intravenous

Solution	*Mfr*	*Mfr*	*Conc/L*	*Remarks*	*Ref*	*C/I*
	MG	CU	10%	Mixed in equal parts. Physically compatible for 72 hr at room temperature	656	C
	TR	CU	10%	Mixed in equal parts. Physically compatible for 72 hr at room temperature	656	C
Amino acids injection 7%	AB	CU	10%	Mixed in equal parts. Physically compatible for 72 hr at room temperature	656	C
Amino acids injection 10%		VT	10%	Mixed in equal parts. Changes observed in 20 min. Globule coalescence and creaming in 8 hr at 8 and 25 °C	825	I
Dextrose 5% in Ringer's injection, lactated	CU	VT	10%	Mixed in equal parts. Physically compatible for 48 hr at 4 °C and room temperature	32	C
Dextrose 10% in water	MG	CU		Mixed in equal parts. Increased globule association in 8 hr at room temperature, considered significant at 48 hr. Formation of a top cream layer by 72 hr	656	I
Dextrose 25% in water	MG	CU	10%	Mixed in equal parts. Increased globule association in 8 hr, progressing to globule coalescence at 48 hr at room temperature. Formation of a top cream layer by 72 hr	656	I
Dextrose 50% in water		VT	10%	Mixed in equal parts. Physically compatible for 48 hr at 4 °C and room temperature	32	C
	AB	VT	10%	Mixed in equal parts. Physically compatible for 24 hr at 8 and 25 °C	825	C
Ringer's injection, lactated	CU	VT	10%	Mixed in equal parts. Physically compatible for 48 hr at 4 °C and room temperature	32	C
Sodium chloride 0.9%	CU	VT	10%	Mixed in equal parts. Physically compatible for 48 hr at 4 °C and room temperature	32	C

Additive Compatibility

Fat emulsion, intravenous

Drug	*Mfr*	*Conc/L*	*Mfr*	*Conc/L*	*Test Soln*	*Remarks*	*Ref*	*C/I*
Albumin human		9.5 g			TNA #232[a,b]	Microscopically observed emulsion disruption found with increased fat globule size in 48 hr at room temperature	2267	?
		9.5 g			TNA #233[a,b]	Visually apparent emulsion disruption with creaming in as little as 4 hr at room temperature. Increased disruption attributed to the added effect of calcium and magnesium ions	2267	I
		18.2 g			TNA #234[a,b]	Creaming and free oil formation visually observed in 24 hr at room temperature	2267	I
		18.2 g			TNA #235[a,b]	Visually apparent emulsion disruption with creaming and free oil in as little as 4 hr at room temperature. Increased disruption attributed to the added effect of calcium and magnesium ions	2267	I
Aminophylline	ES	1 g	VT	10%		Physically compatible for 48 hr at 4 °C and room temperature	32	C

Additive Compatibility (Cont.)

Fat emulsion, intravenous

Drug	*Mfr*	*Conc/L*	*Mfr*	*Conc/L*	*Test Soln*	*Remarks*	*Ref*	*C/I*
	DB	500 mg	VT	10%		Microscopic globule coalescence in 24 hr at 8 and 25 °C	825	I
		234 and 638 mg			TNA #180[a]	Little or no theophylline loss by EMIT and no substantial increase in fat particle size in 24 hr at room temperature	1617	C
Amphotericin B	APC, PHT	0.6 g	CL	10 and 20%		Precipitate forms immediately but is concealed by opaque emulsion	1808	I
		90 mg		20%		Yellow precipitate forms in 2 hr. Cumulative delivery of only 56% of total amphotericin B dose by HPLC	1872	I
	APC	10, 50, 100, and 500 mg, 1 and 5 g	CL	20%		Emulsion separation occurred rapidly, with visible creaming within 4 hr at 27 and 8 °C	1987	I
	SQ	500 mg, 1 and 2 g	KA	20%		Precipitated amphotericin noted on bottom of containers within 4 hr	1988	I
	BMS	50 mg	CL[c]	20%		Fat emulsion separates into two phases within 8 hr. No amphotericin B loss by HPLC protected from light and 4% loss exposed to fluorescent light in 24 hr at 24 °C	2093	I
	BMS	500 mg	CL[c]	20%		Fat emulsion separates into two phases within 8 hr. No amphotericin B loss by HPLC protected from or exposed to fluorescent light in 24 hr at 24 °C	2093	I
Ampicillin sodium		20 g		10%		15% ampicillin decomposition in 24 hr. Potency retained through 6 hr at 23 °C	37	I
	BE	2 g	VT	10%		Microscopic globule coalescence in 24 hr at 8 and 25 °C	825	I
Ascorbic acid injection	VI	1 g	VT	10%		Physically compatible for 48 hr at 4 °C and room temperature	32	C
	DB	500 mg	VT	10%		Microscopic globule coalescence in 24 hr at 8 and 25 °C	825	I
Calcium chloride		13.6 mEq (1 g)	CU	10%		Immediate flocculation with visually apparent layer in 2 hr at room temperature	656	I
		6.8 mEq (500 mg)	CU	10%		Flocculation within 4 hr at room temperature	656	I
	DB	1 g	VT	10%		Globule coalescence and creaming in 8 hr at 8 and 25 °C	825	I
		10 and 20 mEq	KV	10%		Immediate flocculation, aggregation, and creaming	1018	I
Calcium gluconate	PR	2 g	CU	10%		Produced cracked emulsion	32	I
		7.2 and 9.6 mEq	KV	10%		Immediate flocculation, aggregation, and creaming	1018	I
Cefamandole nafate		2 g				Physically compatible and chemically stable for 24 hr at 25 °C	596	C
Cephalothin sodium	LI	4 g	VT	10%		Physically compatible for 48 hr at 4 °C and room temperature	32	C
	GL	2 g	VT	10%		Microscopic globule coalescence in 24 hr at 8 and 25 °C	825	I

Additive Compatibility (Cont.)

Fat emulsion, intravenous

Drug	*Mfr*	*Conc/L*	*Mfr*	*Conc/L*	*Test Soln*	*Remarks*	*Ref*	*C/I*
Chloramphenicol sodium succinate	PD	2 g	VT	10%		Physically compatible for 48 hr at 4 °C and room temperature	32	C
	PD	2 g	VT	10%		Physically compatible for 24 hr at 8 and 25 °C	825	C
Cimetidine HCl	SKF	400, 800, 1200 mg	TR		TNA #72[a,b]	Physically compatible with no cimetidine loss in 24 hr at 25 °C. In 48 hr, fat emulsion particle size increases noted	998	C
	SKF	450 mg	AB, KV		TNA #197 to #200[a]	Physically compatible with 7% or less cimetidine loss by HPLC in 48 hr at 22 °C exposed to light	1921	C
Cyclosporine	SZ	400 mg	AB	10%		No cyclosporine loss by HPLC in 72 hr at 21 °C	1616	C
	SZ	500 mg and 2 g	KA	10 and 20%		Physically compatible by visual examination and particle size assessment with no cyclosporine loss by HPLC in 48 hr at 24 °C under fluorescent light	1625	C
Diphenhydramine HCl	PD	200 mg	VT	10%		Physically compatible for 48 hr at 4 °C and room temperature	32	C
Famotidine	MSD	20 and 50 mg			TNA #111 and #112[a]	Physically compatible with little or no famotidine loss and no change in fat particle size in 48 hr at 4 and 21 °C	1332	C
	MSD	20 and 40 mg			TNA #114[a]	Physically compatible with little or no famotidine loss and no change in fat particle size in 72 hr at 21 °C under fluorescent light	1333	C
	MSD	20 mg	KV		TNA #182[a]	Visually compatible with no famotidine loss by HPLC in 24 hr at 24 °C under fluorescent light	1576	C
	MSD	20 mg	AB, KV		TNA #197 to #200[a]	Physically compatible with no famotidine loss by HPLC in 48 hr at 22 °C exposed to light	1921	C
Folic acid	USP	20 and 0.2 mg	KV	10%		Physically compatible for up to 2 weeks at 4 °C and room temperature when protected from light but highly erratic radioimmunoassays	895	?
Gentamicin sulfate	RS	160 mg	VT	10%		Microscopic globule coalescence in 24 hr at 8 and 25 °C	825	I
Hydrocortisone sodium phosphate	MSD	200 mg	VT	10%		Physically compatible for 48 hr at 4 °C and room temperature	32	C
Hydrocortisone sodium succinate	GL	200 mg	VT	10%		Physically compatible for 24 hr at 8 and 25 °C	825	C
Iron dextran	FI	50 mg			TNA #122[a]	Lipid oiling out in 18 to 19 hr with formation of yellow-brown layer on admixture surface	1383	I
	FI	2 mg			TNA #159 to #166[a]	Physically compatible with no change visually, microscopically, and in particle size distribution in 48 hr at 4 and 25 °C	1648	C
Magnesium chloride		13.6 mEq	CU	10%		Immediate flocculation with visually apparent layer in 2 hr at room temperature	656	I

Additive Compatibility (Cont.)

Fat emulsion, intravenous

Drug	*Mfr*	*Conc/L*	*Mfr*	*Conc/L*	*Test Soln*	*Remarks*	*Ref*	*C/I*
Methylprednisolone sodium succinate	PHU	25, 63 125 mg			TNA #237[a,b]	Physically compatible with no substantial change in lipid particle size. Variable assay results, but less than 10% change in drug concentration by HPLC and less than 8% change in TNA components by colorimetry after 7 days at 4 °C followed by 24 hr at ambient temperature and light	2347	C
Multivitamins	USV	4 ml	VT	10%		Physically compatible for 48 hr at 4 °C and room temperature	32	C
	KA		KA	10%		Physically compatible for 24 hr at 26 °C with little loss by HPLC of most vitamins; up to 52% ascorbate loss	2050	C
Nizatidine	LI	150 mg			TNA #135 to #138[a]	Physically compatible with no increase in fat particle size and 2 to 7% nizatidine loss by HPLC in 48 hr at 22 °C under fluorescent light	1534	C
Octreotide acetate	SZ	450 μg	KV		TNA #139[a,b]	Physically compatible with no change in lipid particle size in 48 hr at 22 °C under fluorescent light and 7 days at 4 °C. Octreotide activity highly variable by radioimmunoassay	1540	?
Penicillin G		2 million units	VT	10%		Microscopic globule coalescence in 24 hr at 8 and 25 °C	825	I
Penicillin G potassium	SQ	10 million units	VT	10%		Physically compatible for 48 hr at 4 °C and room temperature	32	C
Phenytoin sodium	PD	1 g	VT	10%		Phenytoin crystal precipitation	32	I
Potassium chloride		7.5 g (100 mEq)	VT	10%		Physically compatible for 48 hr at 4 °C and room temperature	32	C
		100 mEq	CU	10%		No significant change in emulsion for 24 hr at room temperature, but significant emulsion globule coalescence in 48 hr	656	C
		200 mEq	CU	10%		Globule coalescence with noticeable surface creaming in 4 hr at room temperature. Oil globules on surface at 48 hr	656	I
	DB	4 g	VT	10%		Microscopic globule coalescence in 24 hr at 8 and 25 °C	825	I
Ranitidine HCl	GL	50 and 100 mg	KA		TNA #92[a,b]	7 to 10% ranitidine loss in 12 hr and 20 to 28% loss in 24 hr at 23 °C under fluorescent light	1183	I
	GL	50 and 100 mg			TNA #118[a]	Physically compatible with no effect on emulsion stability and about 6 to 10% ranitidine loss in 36 hr under refrigeration and at 25 °C with or without light protection	1360	C
	GL	50 mg	KV	10%		Physically compatible with no effect on emulsion stability and 2 to 4% ranitidine loss in 48 hr at 25 °C with or without light protection	1360	C

Additive Compatibility (Cont.)

Fat emulsion, intravenous

Drug	*Mfr*	*Conc/L*	*Mfr*	*Conc/L*	*Test Soln*	*Remarks*	*Ref*	*C/I*
	GL	100 mg	KV	10%		Physically compatible with no effect on emulsion stability and no ranitidine loss in 48 hr under refrigeration and at 25 °C with or without light protection	1360	C
	GL	75 mg	AB, KV		TNA #197 to #200[a]	Physically compatible with 7% or less ranitidine loss by HPLC in 24 hr at 22 °C exposed to light. About 15% loss in 48 hr	1921	C
Sodium bicarbonate	BR	7.5 g	VT	10%		Physically compatible for 48 hr at 4 °C and room temperature	32	C
		3.4 g	VT	10%		Microscopic globule coalescence in 24 hr at 8 and 25 °C	825	I
		50 and 150 mEq			TNA #66 to #68[a]	Physically compatible with 10% or less carbon dioxide loss and unchanged pH in 7 days at 25 °C protected from light	1011	C
Sodium chloride		100 mEq	CU	10%		No significant change in emulsion for 24 hr at room temperature, but significant emulsion globule coalescence in 48 hr	656	C
		200 mEq	CU	10%		Globule coalescence with noticeable surface creaming in 4 hr at room temperature. Oil globules on surface at 48 hr	656	I
Vitamin B complex	DB	10 ml	VT	10%		Microscopic globule coalescence in 24 hr at 8 and 25 °C	825	I

[a]Refer to Appendix I for the composition of parenteral nutrition solutions. TNA indicates a 3-in-1 admixture.
[b]Tested in ethylene vinyl acetate (EVA) containers.
[c]Tested in glass bottles.

Y-Site Injection Compatibility (1:1 Mixture)

Fat emulsion, intravenous

Drug	*Mfr*	*Conc*	*Mfr*	*Conc*	*Remarks*	*Ref*	*C/I*
Acyclovir sodium	GW	7 mg/ml[a]		TNA #218 to #226[c]	White precipitate forms immediately	2215	I
Albumin human		20%		20%	Emulsion destabilization was evident immediately	2267	I
Amikacin sulfate	BR	250 mg/ml		TNA #97 to #104[c]	Broken fat emulsion with oil floating in admixtures	1324	I
	AB	5 mg/ml[a]		TNA #218 to #226[c]	Visually compatible with no precipitate or emulsion damage apparent in 4 hr at 23 °C	2215	C
Aminophylline	AB	2.5 mg/ml[a]		TNA #218 to #226[c]	Visually compatible with no precipitate or emulsion damage apparent in 4 hr at 23 °C	2215	C
Amphotericin B	PH	0.6 mg/ml[a]		TNA #218 to #226[c]	Yellow precipitate forms immediately	2215	I
Ampicillin sodium	BR	2 g/50 ml[b]		TNA #73[c]	Physically compatible for 4 hr at 25 °C by visual observation	1008	C
	SKB	20 mg/ml[b]		TNA #218 to #226[c]	Visually compatible with no precipitate or emulsion damage apparent in 4 hr at 23 °C	2215	C

Y-Site Injection Compatibility (1:1 Mixture) (Cont.)

Fat emulsion, intravenous

Drug	*Mfr*	*Conc*	*Mfr*	*Conc*	*Remarks*	*Ref*	*C/I*
Ampicillin sodium–sulbactam sodium	PF	20 + 10 mg/ml[b]		TNA #218 to #226[c]	Visually compatible with no precipitate or emulsion damage apparent in 4 hr at 23 °C	2215	C
Aztreonam	SQ	40 mg/ml[a]		TNA #218 to #226[c]	Visually compatible with no precipitate or emulsion damage apparent in 4 hr at 23 °C	2215	C
Bumetanide	RC, BV	0.04 mg/ml[a]		TNA #218 to #226[c]	Visually compatible with no precipitate or emulsion damage apparent in 4 hr at 23 °C	2215	C
Buprenorphine HCl	RKC	0.04 mg/ml[a]		TNA #218 to #226[c]	Visually compatible with no precipitate or emulsion damage apparent in 4 hr at 23 °C	2215	C
Butorphanol tartrate	APC	0.04 mg/ml[a]		TNA #218 to #226[c]	Visually compatible with no precipitate or emulsion damage apparent in 4 hr at 23 °C	2215	C
Calcium gluconate	AB	40 mg/ml[a]		TNA #218 to #226[c]	Visually compatible with no precipitate or emulsion damage apparent in 4 hr at 23 °C	2215	C
Carboplatin	BMS	5 mg/ml[a]		TNA #218 to #226[c]	Visually compatible with no precipitate or emulsion damage apparent in 4 hr at 23 °C	2215	C
Cefamandole nafate	LI	2 g/50 ml[a]		TNA #73[c]	Physically compatible for 4 hr at 25 °C by visual observation	1008	C
Cefazolin sodium	SKF	1 g/50 ml[a]		TNA #73[c]	Physically compatible for 4 hr at 25 °C by visual observation	1008	C
	SKB	20 mg/ml[a]		TNA #218 to #226[c]	Visually compatible with no precipitate or emulsion damage apparent in 4 hr at 23 °C	2215	C
Cefoperazone sodium	PF	40 mg/ml[a]		TNA #218 to #226[c]	Visually compatible with no precipitate or emulsion damage apparent in 4 hr at 23 °C	2215	C
Cefotaxime sodium	HO	20 mg/ml[a]		TNA #218 to #226[c]	Visually compatible with no precipitate or emulsion damage apparent in 4 hr at 23 °C	2215	C
Cefotetan sodium	ZEN	20 mg/ml[a]		TNA #218 to #226[c]	Visually compatible with no precipitate or emulsion damage apparent in 4 hr at 23 °C	2215	C
Cefoxitin sodium	MSD	1 g/50 ml[a]		TNA #73[c]	Physically compatible for 4 hr at 25 °C by visual observation	1008	C
	ME	20 mg/ml[a]		TNA #218 to #226[c]	Visually compatible with no precipitate or emulsion damage apparent in 4 hr at 23 °C	2215	C
Ceftazidime	SKB[d]	40 mg/ml[a]		TNA #218 to #226[c]	Visually compatible with no precipitate or emulsion damage apparent in 4 hr at 23 °C	2215	C
	GL[e]	40 mg/ml[a]		TNA #218 to #226[c]	Visually compatible with no precipitate or emulsion damage apparent in 4 hr at 23 °C	2215	C

Y-Site Injection Compatibility (1:1 Mixture) (Cont.)

Drug	Mfr	Conc	Fat emulsion, intravenous Mfr	Conc	Remarks	Ref	C/I
Ceftizoxime sodium	FUJ	20 mg/ml[a]		TNA #218 to #226[c]	Visually compatible with no precipitate or emulsion damage apparent in 4 hr at 23 °C	2215	C
Ceftriaxone sodium	RC	20 mg/ml[a]		TNA #218 to #226[c]	Visually compatible with no precipitate or emulsion damage apparent in 4 hr at 23 °C	2215	C
Cefuroxime sodium	GL	30 mg/ml[a]		TNA #218 to #226[c]	Visually compatible with no precipitate or emulsion damage apparent in 4 hr at 23 °C	2215	C
Chlorpromazine HCl	SCN	2 mg/ml[a]		TNA #218 to #226[c]	Visually compatible with no precipitate or emulsion damage apparent in 4 hr at 23 °C	2215	C
Cimetidine HCl	SKB	12 mg/ml[a]		TNA #218 to #226[c]	Visually compatible with no precipitate or emulsion damage apparent in 4 hr at 23 °C	2215	C
Ciprofloxacin	BAY	1 mg/ml[a]		TNA #218 to #226[c]	Visually compatible with no precipitate or emulsion damage apparent in 4 hr at 23 °C	2215	C
Cisplatin	BMS	1 mg/ml		TNA #218 to #226[c]	Visually compatible with no precipitate or emulsion damage apparent in 4 hr at 23 °C	2215	C
Clindamycin phosphate	UP	600 mg/ 50 ml[a]		TNA #73[c]	Physically compatible for 4 hr at 25 °C by visual observation	1008	C
	AST	10 mg/ml[a]		TNA #218 to #226[c]	Visually compatible with no precipitate or emulsion damage apparent in 4 hr at 23 °C	2215	C
Cyclophosphamide	MJ	10 mg/ml[a]		TNA #218 to #226[c]	Visually compatible with no precipitate or emulsion damage apparent in 4 hr at 23 °C	2215	C
Cyclosporine	SZ	5 mg/ml[a]		TNA #220 and #223[c]	Small amount of precipitate forms immediately	2215	I
	SZ	5 mg/ml[a]		TNA #218, #219, #221, #222, #224 to #226[c]	Visually compatible with no precipitate or emulsion damage apparent in 4 hr at 23 °C	2215	C
Cytarabine	BED	50 mg/ml		TNA #218 to #226[c]	Visually compatible with no precipitate or emulsion damage apparent in 4 hr at 23 °C	2215	C
Dexamethasone sodium phosphate	FUJ, ES	1 mg/ml[a]		TNA #218 to #226[c]	Visually compatible with no precipitate or emulsion damage apparent in 4 hr at 23 °C	2215	C
Digoxin	BW	0.625 mg/ 50 ml[a,b]		TNA #73[c]	Physically compatible for 4 hr by visual observation	1009	C
	ES, WY	0.25 mg/ml		TNA #218 to #226[c]	Visually compatible with no precipitate or emulsion damage apparent in 4 hr at 23 °C	2215	C
Diphenhydramine HCl	SCN, PD	2[a] and 50 mg/ ml		TNA #218 to #226[c]	Visually compatible with no precipitate or emulsion damage apparent in 4 hr at 23 °C	2215	C

Y-Site Injection Compatibility (1:1 Mixture) (Cont.)

Fat emulsion, intravenous

Drug	*Mfr*	*Conc*	*Mfr*	*Conc*	*Remarks*	*Ref*	*C/I*
Dobutamine HCl	AST	4 mg/ml[a]		TNA #218 to #226[c]	Visually compatible with no precipitate or emulsion damage apparent in 4 hr at 23 °C	2215	C
Dopamine HCl	AB	80 mg/ 50 ml[a,b]		TNA #73[c]	Physically compatible for 4 hr by visual observation	1009	C
	AB	3.2 mg/ml[a]		TNA #222 and #223[c]	Precipitate forms immediately	2215	I
	AB	3.2 mg/ml[a]		TNA #218 to #221 and #224 to #226[c]	Visually compatible with no precipitate or emulsion damage apparent in 4 hr at 23 °C	2215	C
Doxorubicin HCl	PH, GEN	2 mg/ml		TNA #218 to #226[c]	Damage to emulsion integrity occurs immediately with free oil formation possible	2215	I
Doxycycline hyclate	FUJ	1 mg/ml[a]		TNA #218 to #226[c]	Damage to emulsion integrity occurs immediately with free oil formation possible	2215	I
Droperidol	AB	0.4 mg/ml[a]		TNA #218 to #226[c]	Damage to emulsion integrity occurs in 1 to 4 hr with free oil formation possible	2215	I
Enalaprilat	ME	0.1 mg/ml[a]		TNA #218 to #226[c]	Visually compatible with no precipitate or emulsion damage apparent in 4 hr at 23 °C	2215	C
Erythromycin lactobionate	AB	1 g/50 ml[b]		TNA #73[c]	Physically compatible for 4 hr at 25 °C by visual observation	1008	C
Famotidine HCl	ME	2 mg/ml[a]		TNA #218 to #226[c]	Visually compatible with no precipitate or emulsion damage apparent in 4 hr at 23 °C	2215	C
Fentanyl citrate	AB	0.0125[a] and 0.05 mg/ml		TNA #218 to #226[c]	Visually compatible with no precipitate or emulsion damage apparent in 4 hr at 23 °C	2215	C
Fluconazole	PF	2 mg/ml		TNA #218 to #226[c]	Visually compatible with no precipitate or emulsion damage apparent in 4 hr at 23 °C	2215	C
Fluorouracil	PH	16 mg/ml[a]		TNA #220 and #223[c]	Small amount of white precipitate forms immediately	2215	I
	PH	16 mg/ml[a]		TNA #218, #219, #221, #222, #224 to #226[c]	Visually compatible with no precipitate or emulsion damage apparent in 4 hr at 23 °C	2215	C
Furosemide	ES	165 mg/ 50 ml[a,b]		TNA #73[c]	Physically compatible for 4 hr by visual observation	1009	C
	AB	3 mg/ml[a]		TNA #218 to #226[c]	Visually compatible with no precipitate or emulsion damage apparent in 4 hr at 23 °C	2215	C
Ganciclovir sodium	RC	20 mg/ml[a]		TNA #218 to #226[c]	Large amount of white precipitate forms immediately	2215	I
Gentamicin sulfate	SC	80 mg/50 ml[a]		TNA #73[c]	Physically compatible for 4 hr at 25 °C by visual observation	1008	C
	ES	40 mg/ml		TNA #97 to #104[c]	Physically compatible and gentamicin content retained for 6 hr at 21 °C by TDx	1324	C

Y-Site Injection Compatibility (1:1 Mixture) (Cont.)

Fat emulsion, intravenous

Drug	*Mfr*	*Conc*	*Mfr*	*Conc*	*Remarks*	*Ref*	*C/I*
	AB, FUJ	5 mg/ml[a]		TNA #218 to #226[c]	Visually compatible with no precipitate or emulsion damage apparent in 4 hr at 23 °C	2215	C
Granisetron HCl	SKB	0.05 mg/ml[a]		TNA #218 to #226[c]	Visually compatible with no precipitate or emulsion damage apparent in 4 hr at 23 °C	2215	C
Haloperidol lactate	MN	0.2 mg/ml[a]		TNA #218 to #226[c]	Damage to emulsion integrity occurs immediately with free oil formation possible	2215	I
Heparin sodium	AB	100 units/ml		TNA #218 to #226[c]	Damage to emulsion integrity occurs immediately with free oil formation possible	2215	I
Hydrocortisone sodium phosphate	ME	1 mg/ml[a]		TNA #218 to #226[c]	Visually compatible with no precipitate or emulsion damage apparent in 4 hr at 23 °C	2215	C
Hydrocortisone sodium succinate	AB	1 mg/ml[a]		TNA #218 to #226[c]	Visually compatible with no precipitate or emulsion damage apparent in 4 hr at 23 °C	2215	C
Hydromorphone HCl	ES	0.5 mg/ml[a]		TNA #219, #222, #224 to #226[c]	Damage to emulsion integrity occurs immediately with free oil formation possible	2215	I
	ES	0.5 mg/ml[a]		TNA #218, #220, #221, #223[c]	Visually compatible with no precipitate or emulsion damage apparent in 4 hr at 23 °C	2215	C
Hydroxyzine HCl	ES	2 mg/ml[a]		TNA #218 to #226[c]	Visually compatible with no precipitate or emulsion damage apparent in 4 hr at 23 °C	2215	C
Ifosfamide	MJ	25 mg/ml[a]		TNA #218 to #226[c]	Visually compatible with no precipitate or emulsion damage apparent in 4 hr at 23 °C	2215	C
IL-2	RC	4800 I.U./ml[b]	KA	20%	Visually compatible and IL-2 activity by bioassay retained. Fat emulsion not tested	1552	C
Imipenem–cilastatin sodium	ME	10 mg/ml[b]		TNA #218 to #226[c]	Visually compatible with no precipitate or emulsion damage apparent in 4 hr at 23 °C	2215	C
Insulin, regular	NOV	1 unit/ml[a]		TNA #218 to #226[c]	Visually compatible with no precipitate or emulsion damage apparent in 4 hr at 23 °C	2215	C
Isoproterenol HCl	BR	0.2 mg/ 50 ml[a,b]		TNA #73[c]	Physically compatible for 4 hr by visual observation	1009	C
Kanamycin sulfate	BR	500 mg/ 50 ml[a]		TNA #73[c]	Physically compatible for 4 hr at 25 °C by visual observation	1008	C
Leucovorin calcium	IMM	2 mg/ml[a]		TNA #218 to #226[c]	Visually compatible with no precipitate or emulsion damage apparent in 4 hr at 23 °C	2215	C
Levorphanol tartrate	RC	0.5 mg/ml[a]		TNA #218 to #226[c]	Damage to emulsion integrity occurs immediately with free oil formation possible	2215	I

Y-Site Injection Compatibility (1:1 Mixture) (Cont.)

Fat emulsion, intravenous

Drug	*Mfr*	*Conc*	*Mfr*	*Conc*	*Remarks*	*Ref*	*C/I*
Lidocaine HCl	ES	200 mg/ 50 ml[a,b]		TNA #73[c]	Physically compatible for 4 hr by visual observation	1009	C
Lorazepam	WY	0.1 mg/ml[a]		TNA #218 to #226[c]	Damage to emulsion integrity occurs in 1 hr	2215	I
Magnesium sulfate	AB	100 mg/ml[a]		TNA #218 to #226[c]	Visually compatible with no precipitate or emulsion damage apparent in 4 hr at 23 °C	2215	C
Mannitol	BA	15%		TNA #218 to #226[c]	Visually compatible with no precipitate or emulsion damage apparent in 4 hr at 23 °C	2215	C
Meperidine HCl	AST	4 mg/ml[a]		TNA #218 to #226[c]	Visually compatible with no precipitate or emulsion damage apparent in 4 hr at 23 °C	2215	C
Meropenem	ZEN	20 mg/ml[a]		TNA #218 to #226[c]	Visually compatible with no precipitate or emulsion damage apparent in 4 hr at 23 °C	2215	C
Mesna	MJ	10 mg/ml[a]		TNA #218 to #226[c]	Visually compatible with no precipitate or emulsion damage apparent in 4 hr at 23 °C	2215	C
Methotrexate sodium	IMM	15 mg/ml[a]		TNA #218 to #226[c]	Visually compatible with no precipitate or emulsion damage apparent in 4 hr at 23 °C	2215	C
Methyldopate HCl	MSD	250 mg/ 50 ml[b]		TNA #73[c]	Physically compatible for 4 hr by visual observation	1009	C
	MSD	250 mg/ 50 ml[a]		TNA #73[c]	Cracked the lipid emulsion	1009	I
Methylprednisolone sodium succinate	AB	5 mg/ml[a]		TNA #218 to #226[c]	Visually compatible with no precipitate or emulsion damage apparent in 4 hr at 23 °C	2215	C
Metoclopramide	AB	5 mg/ml		TNA #218 to #226[c]	Visually compatible with no precipitate or emulsion damage apparent in 4 hr at 23 °C	2215	C
Metronidazole	AB	5 mg/ml		TNA #218 to #226[c]	Visually compatible with no precipitate or emulsion damage apparent in 4 hr at 23 °C	2215	C
Midazolam HCl	RC	2 mg/ml[a]		TNA #218 to #226[c]	Damage to emulsion integrity occurs immediately with free oil formation possible	2215	I
Minocycline HCl	LE	0.2 mg/ml[a]		TNA #218 to #226[c]	Damage to emulsion integrity occurs immediately with free oil formation possible	2215	I
Mitoxantrone HCl	IMM	0.5 mg/ml[a]		TNA #218 to #226[c]	Visually compatible with no precipitate or emulsion damage apparent in 4 hr at 23 °C	2215	C
Morphine sulfate	ES	1 mg/ml[a]		TNA #218 to #226[c]	Visually compatible with no precipitate or emulsion damage apparent in 4 hr at 23 °C	2215	C

Y-Site Injection Compatibility (1:1 Mixture) (Cont.)

Fat emulsion, intravenous

Drug	*Mfr*	*Conc*	*Mfr*	*Conc*	*Remarks*	*Ref*	*C/I*
	ES	15 mg/ml		TNA #218 to #226[c]	Damage to emulsion integrity occurs immediately with free oil formation possible	2215	I
Nafcillin sodium	BE, APC	20 mg/ml[a]		TNA #218 to #226[c]	Visually compatible with no precipitate or emulsion damage apparent in 4 hr at 23 °C	2215	C
Nalbuphine HCl	AB, AST	10 mg/ml		TNA #218 to #226[c]	Damage to emulsion integrity occurs immediately with free oil formation possible	2215	I
Netilmicin sulfate	SC	5 mg/ml[a]		TNA #218 to #226[c]	Visually compatible with no precipitate or emulsion damage apparent in 4 hr at 23 °C	2215	C
Nitroglycerin	DU	0.4 mg/ml[a]		TNA #218 to #226[c]	Visually compatible with no precipitate or emulsion damage apparent in 4 hr at 23 °C	2215	C
Norepinephrine bitartrate	BN	0.4 mg/ 50 ml[a,b]		TNA #73[c]	Physically compatible for 4 hr by visual observation	1009	C
Octreotide acetate	SZ	0.01 mg/ml[a]		TNA #218 to #226[c]	Visually compatible with no precipitate or emulsion damage apparent in 4 hr at 23 °C	2215	C
Ofloxacin	ORT	4 mg/ml[a]		TNA #218 to #226[c]	Visually compatible with no precipitate or emulsion damage apparent in 4 hr at 23 °C	2215	C
Ondansetron HCl	CER	1 mg/ml[a]		TNA #218 to #226[c]	Damage to emulsion integrity occurs immediately with free oil formation possible	2215	I
Oxacillin sodium	BE	1 g/50 ml[a]		TNA #73[c]	Physically compatible for 4 hr at 25 °C by visual observation	1008	C
Paclitaxel	MJ	1.2 mg/ml[a]		TNA #218 to #226[c]	Visually compatible with no precipitate or emulsion damage apparent in 4 hr at 23 °C	2215	C
Penicillin G potassium	SQ	2 million units/50 ml[a]		TNA #73[c]	Physically compatible for 4 hr at 25 °C by visual observation	1008	C
Pentobarbital sodium	AB	5 mg/ml[a]		TNA #218 to #226[c]	Damage to emulsion integrity occurs immediately with free oil formation possible	2215	I
Phenobarbital sodium	WY	5 mg/ml[a]		TNA #218 to #226[c]	Damage to emulsion integrity occurs immediately with free oil formation possible	2215	I
Piperacillin sodium	LE	40 mg/ml[a]		TNA #218 to #226[c]	Visually compatible with no precipitate or emulsion damage apparent in 4 hr at 23 °C	2215	C
Piperacillin sodium–tazobactam sodium	LE	40 + 5 mg/ ml[a]		TNA #218 to #226[c]	Visually compatible with no precipitate or emulsion damage apparent in 4 hr at 23 °C	2215	C

Y-Site Injection Compatibility (1:1 Mixture) (Cont.)

Fat emulsion, intravenous

Drug	*Mfr*	*Conc*	*Mfr*	*Conc*	*Remarks*	*Ref*	*C/I*
Potassium chloride	AB	0.1 mEq/ml[a]		TNA #218 to #226[c]	Visually compatible with no precipitate or emulsion damage apparent in 4 hr at 23 °C	2215	C
Potassium phosphates	AB	3 mmol/ml		TNA #218 to #226[c]	Damage to emulsion integrity occurs immediately with free oil formation possible	2215	I
Prochlorperazine edisylate	SCN, SO	0.5 mg/ml[a]		TNA #218 to #226[c]	Visually compatible with no precipitate or emulsion damage apparent in 4 hr at 23 °C	2215	C
Promethazine HCl	SCN	2 mg/ml[a]		TNA #218 to #226[c]	Visually compatible with no precipitate or emulsion damage apparent in 4 hr at 23 °C	2215	C
Ranitidine HCl	GL	2 mg/ml[a]		TNA #218 to #226[c]	Visually compatible with no precipitate or emulsion damage apparent in 4 hr at 23 °C	2215	C
Sodium bicarbonate	AB	1 mEq/ml		TNA #218 to #226[c]	Visually compatible with no precipitate or emulsion damage apparent in 4 hr at 23 °C	2215	C
Sodium nitroprusside	AB	0.4 mg/ml[a]		TNA #218 to #226[c]	Visually compatible with no precipitate or emulsion damage apparent in 4 hr at 23 °C protected from light	2215	C
Sodium phosphates	AB	3 mmol/ml		TNA #218 to #226[c]	Damage to emulsion integrity occurs immediately with free oil formation possible	2215	I
Tacrolimus	FUJ	1 mg/ml[a]		TNA #218 to #226[c]	Visually compatible with no precipitate or emulsion damage apparent in 4 hr at 23 °C	2215	C
Ticarcillin disodium	BE	3 g/50 ml[a]		TNA #73[c]	Physically compatible for 4 hr at 25 °C by visual observation	1008	C
	SKB	30 mg/ml[a]		TNA #218 to #226[c]	Visually compatible with no precipitate or emulsion damage apparent in 4 hr at 23 °C	2215	C
Ticarcillin disodium–clavulanate potassium	SKB	31 mg/ml[a]		TNA #218 to #226[c]	Visually compatible with no precipitate or emulsion damage apparent in 4 hr at 23 °C	2215	C
Tobramycin sulfate	LI	80 mg/50 ml[a]		TNA #73[c]	Physically compatible for 4 hr at 25 °C by visual observation	1008	C
	LI	40 mg/ml		TNA #97 to #104[c]	Physically compatible and tobramycin content retained for 6 hr at 21 °C by TDx	1324	C
	AB	5 mg/ml[a]		TNA #218 to #226[c]	Visually compatible with no precipitate or emulsion damage apparent in 4 hr at 23 °C	2215	C
Trimethoprim–sulfamethoxazole	ES	0.8 + 4 mg/ml[a]		TNA #218 to #226[c]	Visually compatible with no precipitate or emulsion damage apparent in 4 hr at 23 °C	2215	C
Vancomycin HCl	AB	10 mg/ml[a]		TNA #218 to #226[c]	Visually compatible with no precipitate or emulsion damage apparent in 4 hr at 23 °C	2215	C

Y-Site Injection Compatibility (1:1 Mixture) (Cont.)

			Fat emulsion, intravenous				
Drug	*Mfr*	*Conc*	*Mfr*	*Conc*	*Remarks*	*Ref*	*C/I*
Zidovudine	GW	4 mg/ml[a]		TNA #218 to #226[c]	Visually compatible with no precipitate or emulsion damage apparent in 4 hr at 23 °C	2215	C

[a]*Tested in dextrose 5% in water.*
[b]*Tested in sodium chloride 0.9%.*
[c]*Refer to Appendix I for the composition of parenteral nutrition solutions. TNA indicates a 3-in-1 admixture.*
[d]*Sodium carbonate–containing formulation tested.*
[e]*Arginine-containing formulation tested.*

Additional Compatibility Information

It has been recommended that no other drugs or solutions be added to fat emulsion, intravenous, because the stability of the emulsion may be disturbed. (32; 37) Further, the bioavailability of a drug from an emulsion system is uncertain. (32)

More recently, however, the combining of fat emulsions with amino acids, dextrose, and certain other additives in parenteral nutrition multicomponent admixtures has been evaluated. See Multicomponent ("3-in-1") Admixtures below.

Calcium and Phosphate — UNRECOGNIZED CALCIUM PHOSPHATE PRECIPITATION IN A 3-IN-1 PARENTERAL NUTRITION MIXTURE RESULTED IN PATIENT DEATH. The potential for the formation of a calcium phosphate precipitate in parenteral nutrition solutions is well studied and documented (1771; 1777), but the information is complex and difficult to apply to the clinical situation. (1770; 1772; 1777) The incorporation of fat emulsion in 3-in-1 parenteral nutrition solutions obscures any precipitate that is present, which has led to substantial debate on the dangers associated with 3-in-1 parenteral nutrition mixtures and when or if the danger to the patient is warranted therapeutically. (1770–1772; 2031–2036) Because such precipitation may be life-threatening to patients (2037; 2291), the Food and Drug Administration issued a Safety Alert containing the following recommendations (1769):

"1. The amounts of phosphorus and of calcium added to the admixture are critical. The solubility of the added calcium should be calculated from the volume at the time the calcium is added. It should not be based upon the final volume.

   Some amino acid injections for TPN admixtures contain phosphate ions (as a phosphoric acid buffer). These phosphate ions and the volume at the time the phosphate is added should be considered when calculating the concentration of phosphate additives. Also, when adding calcium and phosphate to an admixture, the phosphate should be added first.

   The line should be flushed between the addition of any potentially incompatible components.

2. A lipid emulsion in a three-in-one admixture obscures the presence of a precipitate. Therefore, if a lipid emulsion is needed, either (1) use a two-in-one admixture with the lipid infused separately, or (2) if a three-in-one admixture is medically necessary, then add the calcium before the lipid emulsion and according to the recommendations in number 1 above.

   If the amount of calcium or phosphate which must be added is likely to cause a precipitate, some or all of the calcium should be administered separately. Such separate infusions must be properly diluted and slowly infused to avoid serious adverse events related to the calcium.

3. When using an automated compounding device, the above steps should be considered when programming the device. In addition, automated compounders should be maintained and operated according to the manufacturer's recommendations.

   Any printout should be checked against the programmed admixture and weight of components.

4. During the mixing process, pharmacists who mix parenteral nutrition admixtures should periodically agitate the admixture and check for precipitates. Medical or home care personnel who start and monitor these infusions should carefully inspect for the presence of precipitates both before and during infusion. Patients and care givers should be trained to visually inspect for signs of precipitation. They also should be advised to stop the infusion and seek medical assistance if precipitates are noted.

5. A filter should be used when infusing either central or peripheral parenteral nutrition admixtures. At this time, data have not been submitted to document which size filter is most effective in trapping precipitates.

   Standards of practice vary, but the following is suggested: a 1.2-μm air-eliminating filter for lipid-containing admixtures and a 0.22-μm air-eliminating filter for non-lipid-containing admixtures.

6. Parenteral nutrition admixtures should be administered within the following time frames: if stored at room temperature, the infusion should be started within 24 hours after mixing; if stored at refrigerated temperatures, the infusion should be started within 24 hours of rewarming. Because warming parenteral nutrition admixtures may contribute to the formation of precipitates, once administration begins, care should be taken to avoid excessive warming of the admixture.

   Persons administering home care parenteral nutrition admixtures may need to deviate from these time frames. Pharmacists who initially prepare these admixtures should check a reserve sample for precipitates over the duration and under the conditions of storage.

7. If symptoms of acute respiratory distress, pulmonary emboli, or interstitial pneumonitis develop, the infusion should be stopped immediately and thoroughly checked for precipitates. Appropriate medical interventions should be instituted. Home care personnel and patients should immediately seek medical assistance."

Calcium Phosphate Precipitation Fatalities — Hill et al. reported fatal cases of paroxysmal respiratory failure in two previously healthy women receiving peripheral vein parenteral nutrition. The patients experienced sudden cardiopulmonary arrest consistent with pulmonary emboli. The authors used in vitro simulations and an animal model to conclude that unrecognized calcium phosphate precipitation in a 3-in-1 total nutrition admixture caused the fatalities. The precipitation resulted during compounding by introducing calcium and phosphate near to one another in the compounding sequence and prior to complete fluid addition. This resulted in a temporarily high concentration of the drugs and precipitation of calcium phosphate. Observation of the precipitate was obscured by the incorporation of 20% fat emulsion, intravenous, into the nutrition mixture. No filter was used during infusion of the fatal nutrition admixtures. (2037)

In a follow-up retrospective review, Shay et al. reported that five patients were identified who had respiratory distress associated with the infusion of the 3-in-1 admixtures at around the same time. Four of these five patients died, although the cause of death could be definitively determined for only two. (2291)

Calcium and Phosphate Conditional Compatibility — Calcium salts are conditionally compatible with phosphates in parenteral nutrition mixtures. The incompatibility is dependent on a solubility and concentration phenomenon and is not entirely predictable. Precipitation may occur during compounding or at some time after compounding is completed. See the Calcium Gluconate monograph.

NOTE: Some amino acid solutions inherently contain calcium and phosphate, which must be considered in any projection of compatibility. See Table 1 in the Amino Acid Injection monograph.

Dextrose — Dextrose in final concentrations of 5 to 12.5% has been shown to cause a progressive coalescence of the globules in Intralipid 10% due to its alteration of pH from about 7 down to about 3.5 in 48 hours. (656)

Monovalent Cations — Monovalent cations such as potassium and sodium also cause progressive globule coalescence in Intralipid 10 and 20%, leading to surface creaming. (480; 490; 656; 890) The degree and rate of this effect are dependent on the concentration of the ions. A decreasing degree and rate of coalescence were noted as concentrations of sodium chloride or potassium chloride decreased. At 200 mEq/L, the rate is rapid and the effect is severe. In the range of 100 mEq/L or less, significant effects may not occur for over 24 hours. (490; 656)

Divalent Cations — Divalent cations such as calcium and magnesium cause immediate flocculation, with a nonhomogeneous white granular layer forming at the surface of the Intralipid 10%. This is followed by a substantial, visibly distinct layer, which does not redisperse on shaking. (480; 490; 656)

The creaming of Intralipid 20% when calcium chloride was admixed in concentrations from 0.25 to 5% was found to be concentration dependent, with maximum creaming occurring with the 5% additive in 30 minutes. (890)

Multicomponent ("3-in-1") Admixtures — Because of the potential benefits in terms of simplicity, efficiency, time, and cost savings, the concept of mixing amino acids, carbohydrates, electrolytes, fat emulsion, and other nutritional components together in the same container has been explored. Within limits, the feasibility of preparing such "3-in-1" parenteral nutrition admixtures has been demonstrated. (1813)

However, these 3-in-1 mixtures are very complex and inherently unstable. Emulsion stability is dependent on both zeta potential and van der Waals forces, influenced by the presence of dextrose. (2029) Because the ultimate stability of each mixture is the result of various complicated factors, a definitive prediction of stability is impossible. Death and injury resulted from administration of unrecognized precipitation in 3-in-1 parenteral nutrition admixtures. In addition, the use of 3-in-1 admixtures is associated with a higher rate of catheter occlusion and reduced catheter life compared with giving the fat emulsion separately from the parenteral nutrition solution. (2194)

Combining an amino acids–dextrose parenteral nutrition solution containing various electrolytes with fat emulsion 20%, intravenous (Intralipid, Vitrum), resulted in a mixture that was apparently stable for a limited time. However, it ultimately exhibited a creaming phenomenon. Within 12 hours, a distinct 2-cm layer separated on the upper surface. Microscopic examination revealed aggregates believed to be clumps of fat droplets. Fewer and smaller aggregates were noted in the lower layer. (560; 561)

Amino acids have been reported to have no adverse effect on the emulsion stability of Intralipid 10%. In addition, the amino acids appeared to prevent the adverse impact of dextrose and to slow the coalescence and flocculation resulting from mono- and divalent cations. However, significant coalescence did result after a somewhat longer time. Therefore, it was recommended that such cations not be mixed with fat emulsion, intravenous. (656)

The compatibility and stability of parenteral nutrition solutions consisting of amino acids, dextrose, fat emulsion, and various additives, all in a single admixture, were evaluated by Cutter Laboratories. (791) The study entailed combining, in glass bottles, various amino acid products with Intralipid 10 or 20% and dextrose 10 or 70% along with electrolytes, vitamins, and trace minerals. These parenteral nutrition solutions were stored at 5 °C for three days followed by 25 °C for two days. Compatibility and stability of the emulsion were evaluated initially and again after storage. Additive compatibility and stability were not evaluated. Cutter Laboratories concluded that most of the admixtures tested were compatible and stable over the test period, with minimal chemical and physical changes. (See Table 2.) The exceptions were admixtures prepared with Aminosyn 7%. In the Aminosyn 7%-containing admixtures, the emulsion broke within 24 hours at room temperature and oil globules floated on the surface. Refrigeration prevented the breaking of the emulsion, as did exclusion of the electrolytes. Presumably, the lower pH of Aminosyn 7% compared to the other amino acid products tested was associated with the disruption of the emulsion.

Although dextrose 10 and 70% were the only concentrations evaluated, Cutter Laboratories indicated that intermediate dextrose concentrations may be used as long as the amino acids–dextrose–Intralipid ratio is 1:1:1 or 1:1:0.5. Other ratios also have been recommended. (703; 1068)

The disruptive effects of divalent ions are not as severe in these parenteral nutrition admixtures as they are in Intralipid alone. However, they do represent complex and somewhat unpredictable interactions. Consequently, Cutter Laboratories recommended using only combinations that have been evaluated. Concentrations of additive components may be at or below the maximum amounts indicated in Table 2.

Although some admixtures were stable over longer periods, Cutter Laboratories recommended use of these combined multicomponent admixtures within 24 hours. (791)

Travenol has stated that 1:1:1 mixtures of amino acids 5.5, 8.5, or 10% (Travenol), fat emulsion 10 or 20% (Travenol), and dextrose 10 to 70% are physically stable but recommends administration within

Table 2. Intralipid-Containing Parenteral Nutrition Admixtures Found to be Compatible and Stable (791)

Component	Amount (ml)				
	FreAmine II 8.5%	FreAmine III 8.5%	Travasol 8.5% without Electrolytes	Travasol 10% without Electrolytes	Veinamine 8%
Amino acids	500	500	500	500	500
Dextrose 70 or 10%	500	500	500	500	500
Intralipid 20 or 10%	500 or 250	500 or 250	500 or 250	500 or 250	500 or 250
	Maximum Total Concentration				
Calcium	10 mEq	10 mEq	10 mEq	10 mEq	10 mEq
Magnesium	13 mEq	13 mEq	13 mEq	13 mEq	13 mEq
Sodium	134 mEq	134 mEq	129 mEq	129 mEq	149 mEq
Potassium	105 mEq	105 mEq	105 mEq	105 mEq	120 mEq
Chloride	244 mEq	245 mEq	261 mEq	264 mEq	279 mEq
Sulfate	13 mEq	13 mEq	13 mEq	13 mEq	13 mEq
Phosphorus	12.5 mmol	12.5 mmol	7.5 mmol	7.5 mmol	7.5 mmol
Acetate	21 mEq	37 mEq	26 mEq	44 mEq	25 mEq
Zinc	4 mg	4 mg	4 mg	4 mg	4 mg
Copper	1.5 mg	1.5 mg	1.5 mg	1.5 mg	1.5 mg
Manganese	0.8 mg	0.8 mg	0.8 mg	0.8 mg	0.8 mg
Chromium	15 μg	15 μg	15 μg	15 μg	15 μg
Multivitamin infusion concentrate (USV)	5 ml	5 ml	5 ml	5 ml	5 ml

24 hours. M.V.I.-12 3.3 ml/L and electrolytes may also be added to the admixtures up to the maximum amounts listed below (850):

Calcium	8.3 mEq/L
Magnesium	3.3 mEq/L
Sodium	23.3 mEq/L
Potassium	20 mEq/L
Chloride	23.3 mEq/L
Phosphate	20 mEq/L
Zinc	3.33 mg/L
Copper	1.33 mg/L
Manganese	0.33 mg/L
Chromium	13.33 μg/L

Knutsen et al. reported that a mixture of soybean oil emulsion 10% with amino acids 8.5%, concentrated dextrose, multivitamins, and electrolytes had good physical stability. Visual and microscopic examination of samples stored at 4 °C for one week showed the emulsion to be uniform with no flocculence. (891)

Burnham et al. evaluated the stability of mixtures of Intralipid 20% 1 L, Vamin glucose (amino acids with dextrose 10%) 1.5 L, and dextrose 10% 0.5 L with various electrolytes and vitamins. Initial emulsion particle size was around 1 μm. The mixture containing only monovalent cations was stable for at least nine days at 4 °C, with little change in particle size. The mixtures containing the divalent cations, such as calcium and magnesium, demonstrated much greater particle size increases, with mean diameters of around 3.3 to 3.5 μm after nine days at 4 °C. After 48 hours of storage, however, these increases were more modest, around 1.5 to 1.85 μm. After storage at 4 °C for 48 hours followed by 24 hours at room temperature, very few particles exceeded 5 μm. It was found that the effect of particle aggregation caused by electrolytes demonstrates a critical concentration before the effect begins. For calcium and magnesium chlorides, the critical concentrations were 2.4 and 2.6 mmol/L, respectively. Sodium and potassium chloride had critical concentrations of 110 and 150 mmol/L, respectively. The rate of particle aggregation increased linearly with increasing electrolyte concentration. Heparin 667 units/L had no effect on emulsion stability. The quantity of emulsion in the mixture had a relatively small influence on stability, but higher concentrations exhibited a somewhat greater coalescence. (892)

Davis and Galloway noted that instability of the emulsion systems is manifested by (1) flocculation of oil droplets to form aggregates that produce a cream-like layer on top or (2) coalescence of oil droplets leading to an increase in the average droplet size and eventually to a separation of free oil. The lowering of pH and adding of electrolytes can adversely affect the mechanical and electrical properties at the oil–water interface, eventually leading to flocculation and coalescence. Amino acids act as buffering agents and provide a protective effect on emulsion stability. Addition of electrolytes, especially the divalent ions Mg^{++} and Ca^{++} in excess of 2.5 mmol/L, to simple fat emulsions causes flocculation. But in mixed parenteral nutrition solutions, the stability of the emulsion is enhanced, depending on the quantity and nature of the amino acids present. The authors recommended a careful examination of emulsion mixtures for instability prior to administration. (849)

Lawrence et al. reported the stability of an amino acid 4% (Travenol), dextrose 14%, fat emulsion 4% (Pharmacia) parenteral nutrition solution to be quite good. The solution also contained electrolytes, vitamins, and heparin sodium 4000 units/L. The aqueous solution was prepared first, with the fat emulsion added subsequently. This procedure allowed visual inspection of the aqueous phase and reduced the risk of emulsion breakdown by the divalent cations. Sample mixtures were stored at 18 to 25 and 3 to 8 °C for up to five days. They were evaluated visually and with a Coulter counter for particle size measurements. Both room temperature and refrigerated mixtures were stable for 48 hours. A marked increase in particle size was noted in the room temperature sample after 72 hours, but refrigeration delayed the changes. The authors' experience with over 1400 mixtures for administration to patients resulted in one emulsion creaming and another cracking. The authors had no explanation for the failure of these particular emulsions. (848)

Turner reported on six parenteral nutrition solutions having various concentrations of amino acids, dextrose, soybean oil emulsion (Kabi-Vitrum), electrolytes, and multivitamins. All of the admixtures were stable for one week under refrigeration followed by 24 hours at room temperature, with no visible changes, pH changes, or significant particle size changes. (1013) However, other researchers questioned this interpretation of the results. (1014; 1015)

Iliano et al. reported that the addition of trace elements to a 3-in-1 parenteral nutrition solution with electrolytes had no adverse effect on the particle size of the fat emulsion after eight days of storage at 4 °C. (1017)

Harrie et al. reported on the stability of 3-in-1 parenteral nutrition solutions prepared with 500 ml of Intralipid 20% compared to Soyacal 20%, along with 500 or 1000 ml of FreAmine III 8.5% and 500 ml of dextrose 70%. Also present were relatively large amounts of electrolytes and other additives. All mixtures were similarly stable for 28 days at 4 °C followed by five days at 21 to 25 °C, with little change in the emulsion. A slight white cream layer appeared after five days at 4 °C, but it was easily dispersed with gentle agitation. The appearance of this cream layer did not statistically affect particle size distribution. The authors concluded that the emulsion mixture remained suitable for clinical use throughout the study period. The stability of other components was not evaluated. (1019)

Sayeed et al. reported on the stability of 3-in-1 parenteral nutrition admixtures prepared with Liposyn II 10 and 20%, Aminosyn pH 6, and dextrose along with electrolytes, trace metals, and vitamins. Thirty-one different combinations were evaluated. Samples were stored under the following conditions: (1) 25 °C for one day, (2) 5 °C for two days followed by 30 °C for one day, or (3) 5 °C for nine days followed by 25 °C for one day. In all cases, there was no visual evidence of creaming, free oil droplets, and other signs of emulsion instability. Furthermore, little or no change in the particle size or zeta potential (electrostatic surface charge of lipid particles) was found, indicating emulsion stability. The dextrose and amino acids remained stable over the 10-day storage period. The greatest change of an amino acid occurred with tryptophan, which lost 6% in 10 days. Vitamin stability was not tested. (1025)

Hardy et al. reported on the stability of four parenteral nutrition admixtures, ranging from 1 L each of amino acids 5.5% (Travenol), dextrose 10%, and fat emulsion 10% (Travenol) up to a "worst case" of 1 L each of amino acids 10% with electrolytes (Travenol), dextrose 70%, and fat emulsion 10% (Travenol). The admixtures were stored for 48 hours at 5 to 9 °C followed by 24 hours at room temperature. There were no visible signs of creaming, flocculation, or free oil. The mean emulsion particle size remained within acceptable limits for all admixtures, and there were no significant changes in glucose, soybean oil, and amino acid concentrations. The authors noted that two factors were predominant in determining the stability of such admixtures: electrolyte concentrations and pH. (1065)

Hardy and Klim reported that several parenteral nutrition solutions containing amino acids (Travenol), glucose, and lipid, with and without electrolytes and trace elements, produced no visible flocculation or any significant change in mean emulsion particle size during 24 hours at room temperature. (1066)

Jeppsson and Sjoberg reported on the compatibility of 10 parenteral nutrition admixtures, evaluated over 96 hours while stored at 20 to 25 °C in both glass bottles and ethylene vinylacetate bags. A slight creaming occurred in all admixtures, but this cream layer was easily dispersed by gentle shaking. No fat globules were visually apparent. The mean drop size was larger in the cream layer, but no globules were larger than 5 μm. Analyses of the concentrations of amino acids, dextrose, and electrolytes showed no changes over the study period. The authors concluded that such parenteral nutrition admixtures can be prepared safely as long as the component concentrations are within the following ranges (1067):

Vamin glucose or Vamin N (amino acids 7%)	1000 to 2000 ml
Dextrose 10 to 30%	100 to 550 ml
Intralipid 10 or 20%	500 to 1000 ml
Electrolytes (mmol/L)	
Sodium	20 to 70
Potassium	20 to 55
Calcium	2.3 to 2.9
Magnesium	1.1 to 3.1
Phosphorus	0 to 9.2
Chloride	27 to 71
Zinc	0.005 to 0.03

Parry et al. reported on the stability of eight parenteral nutrition admixtures with various ratios of amino acids, carbohydrates, and fat. FreAmine III 8.5%, dextrose 70%, and Soyacal 10 and 20% (mixed in ratios of 2:1:1, 1:1:1, 1:1:½, and 1:1:¼, where 1 = 500 ml) were evaluated. Additive concentrations were high to stress the admixtures and represent maximum doses likely to be encountered clinically:

Sodium acetate	150 mEq
Sodium chloride	210 mEq
Potassium acetate	45 mEq
Potassium chloride	90 mEq
Potassium phosphate	15 mM
Calcium gluconate	20 mEq
Magnesium sulfate	36 mEq
Trace elements	present
Folic acid	5 mg
M.V.I.-12	10 ml

The admixtures were stored at 4 °C for 14 days followed by four days at 22 to 25 °C. After 24 hours, all admixtures developed a thin white cream layer, which was readily dispersed by gentle agitation. No free oil droplets were observed. The mean particle diameter remained near the original size of the Soyacal throughout the study. Few particles were larger than 3 μm. Osmolality and pH also remained relatively unchanged. (1068)

Bettner and Stennett had somewhat less success than others in preparing stable 3-in-1 parenteral nutrition admixtures with Aminosyn and Liposyn. Standard admixtures were prepared using Aminosyn 7% 1000 ml, dextrose 50% 1000 ml, and Liposyn 10% 500 ml. Concentrated admixtures were prepared using Aminosyn 10% 500 ml, dextrose 70% 500 ml, and Liposyn 20% 500 ml. Vitamins and trace elements were added to the admixtures along with the following electrolytes:

Electrolyte	Standard Admixture	Concentrated Admixture
Sodium	125 mEq	75 mEq
Potassium	95 mEq	74 mEq
Magnesium	25 mEq	25 mEq
Calcium	28 mEq	28 mEq
Phosphate	37 mmol	36 mmol
Chloride	83 mEq	50 mEq

Samples of each admixture were (1) stored at 4 °C, (2) adjusted to pH 6.6 with sodium bicarbonate and stored at 4 °C, or (3) adjusted to pH 6.6 and stored at room temperature. Compatibility was evaluated for three weeks.

Signs of emulsion deterioration were visible by 96 hours in the standard admixture and by 48 hours in the concentrated admixture. Clear rings formed at the meniscus, becoming thicker, yellow, and oily over time. Free-floating oil was obvious in three weeks in the standard admixture and in one week in the concentrated admixture. The samples adjusted to pH 6.6 developed visible deterioration later than the others. The authors indicated that pH may play a greater role than temperature in emulsion stability. However, precipitation (probably calcium phosphate and possibly carbonate) occurred in 36 hours in the pH 6.6 concentrated admixture but not the unadjusted (pH 5.5) samples. Mean particle counts increased for all samples over time but were greatest in the concentrated admixtures. The authors concluded that the concentrated admixtures were unsatisfactory for clinical use because of the early increase in particles and precipitation. Furthermore, they recommended that the standard admixtures be prepared immediately prior to use. (1069) These results do not extend to Aminosyn II as a component of 3-in-1 admixtures, as reported by Sayeed et al. below.

Barat et al. studied the physical stability of 10 parenteral nutrition admixtures with different amino acid sources. The admixtures contained 500 ml each of dextrose 70%, fat emulsion 20% (Alpha Therapeutics), and amino acids in various concentrations from each manufacturer. Also present were standard electrolytes, trace elements, and vitamins. The admixtures were stored for 14 days at 4 °C, followed by four days at 22 to 25 °C. Slight creaming was evident in all admixtures but redispersed easily with agitation. Emulsion particles were uniform in size, showing no tendency to aggregate. No cracked emulsions occurred. (1217)

Cripps (1218) and Davis and Galloway (1219) described the stability of parenteral nutrition solutions containing amino acids, dextrose, and fat emulsion along with electrolytes, trace elements, and vitamins. Cripps reported that the admixtures were stable for 24 hours at room temperature and for eight days at 4 °C. The visual appearance and particle size of the fat emulsion showed little change over the observation periods. (1218) Davis and Galloway reported variable stability periods, depending on electrolyte concentrations. Stability ranged from four to 25 days at room temperature. (1219)

Ang et al. studied the physical stability and clinical safety of a 3-in-1 parenteral nutrition admixture composed of amino acids (Cutter), dextrose, and fat emulsion (Cutter) plus electrolytes and vitamins. The admixture was physically stable for up to six weeks at 4 °C. Furthermore, continuous infusion to 25 adult patients did not result in any adverse reaction or abnormal laboratory parameter. (1220)

du Plesis et al. studied the effects of dilution, dextrose concentration, amino acids, and electrolytes on the physical stability of 3-in-1 parenteral nutrition admixtures prepared with Intralipid 10% or Travamulsion 10%. Travamulsion was affected by dilution up to 1:14, exhibiting an increase in mean particle size, while Intralipid remained virtually unchanged for 24 hours at 25 °C and for 72 hours at 4 °C. At dextrose concentrations above 15%, fat droplets larger than 5 μm formed during storage for 24 hours at either 4 °C or room temperature. The presence of amino acids increased the stability of the fat emulsions in the presence of dextrose. Fat droplets larger than 5 μm formed at a total electrolyte concentration above approximately 240 mmol/L (monovalent cation equivalent) for Travamulsion 10% and 156 mmol/L for Intralipid 10% in 24 hours at room temperature, although creaming or breaking of the emulsion was not observed visually. (1221)

Sayeed et al. evaluated the stability of 43 parenteral nutrition admixtures composed of various ratios of amino acid products, dextrose 10 to 70%, and four lipid emulsions 10 and 20% with electrolytes, trace elements, and vitamins. One group of admixtures included Travasol 5.5, 8.5, and 10%, FreAmine III 8.5 and 10%, Novamine 8.5 and 11.4%, Nephramine 5.4%, and RenAmine 6.5% with Liposyn II 10 and 20%. In another group, Aminosyn II 7, 8.5, and 10% was combined with Intralipid, Travamulsion, and Soyacal 10 and 20%. A third group was comprised of Aminosyn II 7, 8.5, and 10% with electrolytes combined with the latter three lipid emulsions. The admixtures were stored for 24 hours at 25 °C and for nine days at 5 °C followed by 24 hours at 25 °C. A few admixtures containing FreAmine III and Novamine with Liposyn II developed faint yellow streaks after 10 days of storage. The streaks readily dispersed with gentle shaking, as did the creaming present in most admixtures. Other properties such as pH, zeta-potential, and osmolality underwent little change in all of the admixtures. Particle size increased fourfold in one admixture (Novamine 8.5%, dextrose 50%, and Liposyn II in a 1:1:1 ratio), which the authors noted signaled the onset of particle coalescence. Nevertheless, the authors concluded that all of the admixtures were stable for the storage conditions and time periods tested. (1222)

Sayeed et al. also evaluated the stability of 24 parenteral nutrition admixtures composed of various ratios of Aminosyn II 7, 8.5, or 10%, dextrose, and Liposyn II 10 and 20% with electrolytes, trace elements, and vitamins. Four admixtures were stored for 24 hours at 25 °C, six admixtures were stored for two days at 5 °C followed by one day at 30 °C, and 14 admixtures were stored for nine days at 5 °C followed by one day at 25 °C. No visible instability was evident. Creaming was present in most admixtures but disappeared with gentle shaking. Other properties such as pH, zeta-potential, particle size, and potency of the amino acids and dextrose showed little or no change during storage. (1223)

Tripp reported the emulsion stability of five parenteral nutrition formulas (TNA #126 through #130 in Appendix I) containing Liposyn II in concentrations ranging from 1.2 to 7.1%. The parenteral nutrition solutions were prepared using simultaneous pumping of the components into empty containers (as with the Nutrimix compounder) and sequential pumping of the components (as with Automix compounders). The solutions were stored for two days at 5 °C followed by 24 hours at 25 °C. Similar results were obtained for both methods of preparation using visual assessment and oil globule size distribution. (1426)

Tripp et al. evaluated the stability of 24 parenteral nutrition admixtures containing various concentrations of Aminosyn II, dextrose, and Liposyn II with a variety of electrolytes, trace elements, and multivitamins in dual-chamber, flexible, Nutrimix containers. No instability was visible in the admixtures stored at 25 °C for 24 hours or in those stored for nine days at 5 °C followed by 24 hours at 25 °C. Creaming was observed, but neither particle coalescence nor free oil was noted. The pH, particle size distribution, and amino acid and dextrose concentrations remained acceptable during the observation period. (1432)

Thomas reported that the lipid particle size in two parenteral nutrition solutions composed of amino acids, dextrose 50%, fat emulsion 20% (Intralipid), electrolytes, and vitamins stayed within the manufacturer's size range specifications when stored at 23 and 4 °C and when frozen at −20 °C for 72 hours. (1488)

Bullock et al. evaluated the physical stability of 10 parenteral nutrition formulas (TNA #149 through #158 in Appendix I) containing TrophAmine and Intralipid 20%, Liposyn II 20%, and Nutrilipid 20% in varying concentrations with low and high electrolyte concentrations. All test formulas were prepared with an automatic compounder and protected from light. TNA #149 through #156 were stored for 48 hours at 4 °C followed by 24 hours at 21 °C; TNA #157 and #158 were stored for 24 hours at 4 °C followed by 24 hours at 21 °C. Although some minor creaming occurred in all formulas, it was completely reversible with agitation. No other changes were visible, and particle size analysis indicated little variation during the study period. The addition of cysteine HCl 1 g/25 g of amino acids, alone or with L-carnitine 16 mg/g fat, to TNA #157 and #158 did not adversely affect the physical stability of 3-in-1 admixtures within the study period. (1620)

Washington and Sizer evaluated the physical stability of five 3-in-1 parenteral nutrition solutions (TNA #167 through #171 in Appendix I) by visual observation, pH and osmolality determinations, and particle size distribution analysis. All five solutions were physically stable for 90 days at 4 °C. However, some irreversible flocculation occurred in all combinations after 180 days. (1651)

Tu et al. studied the stability of several parenteral nutrition formulas (TNA #159 through #166 in Appendix I), with and without iron dextran 2 mg/L. All formulas were physically compatible both visually and microscopically for 48 hours at 4 and 25 °C, and particle size distribution remained unchanged. The order of mixing and deliberate agitation had no effect on physical compatibility. (1648)

Koorenhof and Timmer reported the maximum allowable concentrations of calcium and phosphate in a 3-in-1 parenteral nutrition mixture for children (TNA #192 in Appendix I). Added calcium varied from 1.5 to 150 mmol/L, while added phosphate varied from 21 to 300 mmol/L. The mixtures were stable for 48 hours at 22 and 37 °C as long as the pH was not greater than 5.7, the calcium concentration was below 16 mmol/L, the phosphate concentration was below 52 mM/L, and the product of the calcium and phosphate concentrations was below 250 $mmol^2/L^2$. (1773)

Driscoll et al. evaluated the influence of six factors on the stability of fat emulsion in 45 different 3-in-1 parenteral nutrition mixtures. The factors were amino acid concentration (2.5 to 7%); dextrose (5 to 20%); fat emulsion, intravenous (2 to 5%); monovalent cations (0 to 150 mEq/L); divalent cations (4 to 20 mEq/L); and trivalent cations from iron dextran (0 to 10 mg elemental iron/L). Although many formulations were unstable, visual examination could identify instability in only 65% of the samples. Electronic evaluation of particle size identified the remaining unstable mixtures. Furthermore, only the concentration of trivalent ferric ions significantly and consistently affected the emulsion stability during the 30-hour test period. Of the parenteral nutrition mixtures containing iron dextran, 16% were unstable, exhibiting emulsion cracking. The authors suggested that iron dextran should not be incorporated into 3-in-1 mixtures. (1814)

Shenkin et al. evaluated the vitamin and trace element status of 22 postoperative surgical patients. Twelve patients were given parenteral nutrition with the fat emulsion containing vitamins separate from amino acids and other water-soluble nutrients; 10 patients received all nutrients in one large bag. No clinically significant differences were noted after administration periods of seven to 38 days. (1226)

The drop size of 3-in-1 parenteral nutrition solutions in drip chambers is variable, being altered by the constituents of the mixture. In one study, multivitamins (Multibionta, E. Merck) caused the greatest reductions in drop size, up to 37%. This change may affect the rate of delivery if flow is estimated from drops per minute. (1016) Similarly, flow rates delivered by infusion controllers dependent on predictable drop size may be inaccurate. Flow rates up to 29% less than expected have been reported. Therefore, variable-pressure volumetric pumps, which are independent of drop size, should be used rather than infusion controllers. (1215)

When using multicomponent, 3-in-1, parenteral nutrition admixtures, the following points should be considered (490; 703; 892; 893; 1025; 1064; 1070; 1214; 1324; 1406; 1670; 2215; 2282; 2308):

1. The order of mixing is important. The amino acid solution should be added to either the fat emulsion or the dextrose before final mixing. This practice ensures that the protective effect of the amino acids to emulsion disruption by changes in pH and the presence of electrolytes is realized.
2. Electrolytes should not be added directly to the fat emulsion. Instead, they should be added to the amino acids or dextrose before the final mixing.
3. Such 3-in-1 admixtures containing electrolytes (especially divalent cations) are unstable and will eventually aggregate. The mixed systems should be carefully examined visually before use to ensure that a uniform emulsion still exists.
4. Avoid contact of 3-in-1 parenteral nutrition admixtures with heparin, which destabilizes and damages the fat emulsion upon contact.
5. The admixtures should be stored under refrigeration if not used immediately.
6. The ultimate stability of the admixtures will be the result of a complex interaction of pH, component concentrations, electrolyte concentrations, and, probably, storage temperature.

Furthermore, the use of a 1.2-μm filter to remove large lipid particles, electrolyte precipitates, other solid particulates, aggregates, and *Candida albicans* contaminants has been recommended (1106; 1657; 1769; 2061; 2135; 2346), although others recommend a 5-μm filter to minimize the frequency of occlusion alarms. (569; 1951)

Separate Y-Type Infusion — The simultaneous administration of fat emulsion and amino acids by a Y-type infusion set so that mixture occurs just before entering the peripheral vein has been recommended. The fat emulsion may be administered through separate lines into the same central or peripheral vein as the carbohydrate–amino acids solutions by using a Y-connector located near the infusion site. (1-12/98; 35; 61) The flow rates of each solution should be controlled by infusion pumps. (1-12/98) The fat emulsion line should be kept higher than the carbohydrate–amino acids line because the lower specific gravity of the fat emulsion would otherwise cause it to run up the carbohydrate–amino acids line. (35) If a syringe pump is used to administer fat emulsion, intravenous, into a Y-site of a carbohydrate–amino acids line, the syringe tip should be positioned above the mixture point to avoid entry of the carbohydrate–amino acids solution into the syringe. (1107)

Heparin — Heparin sodium has been stated to be compatible in fat emulsion. (480; 660) The addition of heparin sodium (Abbott) 1 and 2 units/ml to Liposyn 10% and Intralipid 10% did not break the emulsion and effectively reversed the blood hypercoagulability associated with intravenous fat emulsion administration. (568)

However, Raupp et al. reported flocculation of fat emulsion (KabiVitrum) during Y-site administration into a line used to infuse a parenteral nutrition solution containing both calcium gluconate and heparin sodium. Subsequent evaluation indicated that the combination of calcium gluconate (0.46 and 1.8 mmol/125 ml) and heparin sodium (25 and 100 units/125 ml) in amino acids plus dextrose induced flocculation of the fat emulsion within two to four minutes at concentrations that resulted in no visually apparent flocculation in 30 minutes with either agent alone. (1214)

This result was confirmed by Johnson et al. Calcium chloride quantities of 1 to 20 mmol normally result in slow flocculation of fat emulsion 20% over several hours. When heparin sodium 5 units/ml was added, the flocculation rate was accelerated greatly and a cream layer was observed visually in a few minutes. This effect was not observed when sodium ion was substituted for the divalent calcium. (1406)

Similar results were observed by Trissel et al. during simulated Y-site administration of heparin sodium into nine 3-in-1 nutrient admixtures having different compositions. Damage to the fat emulsion component was found to occur immediately, with the possible formation of free oil over time. (2215)

Silvers et al. also observed the destabilization of fat emulsion (Intralipid 20%) when administered simultaneously with a TPN admixture and heparin. The damage, detected by viscosity measurement, occurred immediately upon contact at the Y-site. The extent of the destabilization was dependent on the concentration of heparin and the presence of MVI Pediatric with its surfactant content. Additionally, phase separation was observed in two hours. The authors noted that TPN admixtures containing heparin should never be premixed with fat emulsion as a 3-in-1 total nutrient admixture because of this emulsion destabilization. The authors indicated their belief that the damage could be minimized during Y-site co-administration as long as the heparin was kept at a sufficiently low concentration (no visible separation occurred at a heparin concentration of 0.5 unit/ml) and the length of tubing between the Y-site and the patient was minimized. (2282)

However, because the damage to emulsion integrity has been found to occur immediately upon mixing with heparin in the presence of the calcium ions in TPN admixtures (1214; 2215; 2282) and no evaluation and documentation of the clinical safety of using such destabilized emulsions has been performed, use of such damaged emulsions in patients is suspect.

Trace Elements — The stability of a 3-in-1 parenteral nutrition mixture (TNA #191 in Appendix I) was compared when trace elements were added as gluconate or chloride salts. TNA #191 with copper 0.24 mg/L, iron 0.5 mg/L, and zinc 2 mg/L in either salt form was physically stable for seven days at both 4 and 25 °C. (1787)

Amphotericin B — In an effort to reduce toxicity, amphotericin B has been admixed in Intralipid instead of the more usual dextrose 5% in water. (1809–1811; 2178) However, amphotericin B 0.75 mg/kg/day administered using this approach in 250 ml of Intralipid 20% has been associated with acute pulmonary toxicities, including sudden onset of coughing, tachypnea, agitation, cyanosis, and deterioration of oxygen saturation. The temporal relationship between the drug administration and respiratory symptoms suggested a causal relationship. Furthermore, no reduction in renal toxicity or other side effects associated with amphotericin B was observed. The authors concluded amphotericin B should not be administered to patients in Intralipid. (2177)

At a concentration of 0.6 mg/ml in Intralipid 10 or 20%, amphotericin B precipitated immediately or almost immediately. The precipitate was not visible to the unaided eye because of the emulsion's dense opacity. Particle size evaluation found thousands of particles larger than 10 μm per milliliter. In dextrose 5% in water, very few particles were larger than 10 μm. Centrifuging the Intralipid admixtures resulted in rapid visualization of the precipitate as a mass at the bottom of the test tubes. (1808)

However, amphotericin B precipitation is observed in fat emulsion within two to four hours without centrifuging. In concentrations ranging from 90 mg/L to 2 g/L in Intralipid 20%, amphotericin precipitate is easily seen as yellow particulate matter on the bottom of the lipid emulsion containers. (1872; 1987) Damage to the emulsion integrity with creaming has also been reported. (1986)

In other reports, the appearance of problems was observed in as little as 15 minutes, and actual amphotericin B precipitate formed within 20 minutes of mixing. Analysis of the precipitate confirmed its identity as amphotericin B. The authors hypothesized that amphotericin B precipitates because the excipient deoxycholic acid, an anion, attracts oppositely charged choline groups from the egg yolk components of the fat emulsion and forms a precipitate with phosphatidylcholine, leaving insufficient surfactant to keep the amphotericin B dispersed. (2204; 2205)

Gentamicin — Kern et al. evaluated serum concentrations of gentamicin following intermittent 15 to 30-minute administration in piggyback infusions of 50 ml of dextrose 5% in water or 50 ml of TNA #177 (Appendix I). Gentamicin serum concentrations were equivalent using both administration methods. (1573)

Plasma Expanders — Fat emulsion (Abbott) 10 and 20% were combined with the plasma expanders Macrodex 6% in sodium chloride 0.9% (Schiwa), Gelafundin (Braun), Haes Steril 10% (Fresenius), and Expafusin Sine (Pfrimmer); fat particles exceeding 5 μm resulted, as observed by microscopic examination. These combinations were incompatible. (1668)

Other Information

Microbial Growth — Fat emulsion, intravenous, based on either soybean oil or safflower oil, has been shown to support the growth of various microbes, including both bacterial and fungal species. No visual changes occurred in the emulsions to suggest contamination. (1102–1104; 1216)

The 3-in-1 parenteral nutrition solutions that have a lower pH and higher osmolality due to the presence of amino acids and dextrose do not support microbial growth as well as fat emulsion alone. (1216)

FENTANYL CITRATE
AHFS 28:08.08

Products — Fentanyl citrate is available in 2-, 5-, 10-, and 20-ml ampuls, 2- and 5-ml syringe cartridges, and 30- and 50-ml vials. (29; 154) Each milliliter contains fentanyl (as the citrate) 50 μg (0.05 mg) with hydrochloric acid and/or sodium hydroxide for pH adjustment. (1-4/99; 4)

pH — From 4 to 7.5. (1-4/99; 4)

Osmolality — The product osmolality was determined to be essentially 0 mOsm/kg. (1233)

Trade Name(s) — Sublimaze.

Administration — Fentanyl citrate is administered by intramuscular or intravenous injection. (4)

Stability — Intact containers should be stored at controlled room temperature and protected from light. Brief exposure to temperatures up to 40 °C does not affect potency. (4)

pH Effects — Fentanyl citrate is most stable at pH 3.5 to 7.5. (1638) Fentanyl is hydrolyzed in acidic solutions. (4)

Syringes — Fentanyl citrate (Elkins Sinn) 0.0167 mg/ml in sodium chloride 0.9% packaged in polypropylene syringes (Sherwood) was physically stable and exhibited little or no loss by stability-indicating HPLC analysis in 24 hours stored at 4 and 23 °C in the dark. (2199)

Fentanyl citrate (David Bull) at a concentration of 12.5 μg/ml in sodium chloride 0.9% was packaged as 8 ml in 10-ml polypropylene syringes (Terumo) with 19-gauge needles attached (Becton-Dickinson). Fentanyl citrate (David Bull) at a concentration of 33.3 μg/ml in sodium chloride 0.9% was packaged as 18 ml in 20-ml polypropylene syringes (Terumo) with 19-gauge needles attached (Becton-Dickinson). The syringes were stored refrigerated at 5 °C, at 22 °C exposed to light, and at 38 °C for seven days. The solutions were visually unchanged, and HPLC analysis found no loss at 5 and 22 °C. At 38 °C, the 12.5-μg/ml solution exhibited less than 7% loss, whereas the 33.3-μg/ml solution had no loss in seven days. (2202)

Ambulatory Pumps — Fentanyl citrate (Janssen) 20 μg/ml in sodium chloride 0.9% in PVC portable infusion pump reservoirs exhibited little or no loss after 30 days at 23 and 3 °C. Wrapping the reservoirs to prevent possible moisture loss was not necessary for storage of 30 days. (1356)

Elastomeric Reservoir Pumps — Fentanyl citrate 1 to 5 μg/ml in dextrose 5% in water or in sodium chloride 0.9% in Infusor elastomeric reservoir pumps has been stated by the pump manufacturer to be stable for 90 days under refrigeration followed by 14 days at room temperature and then followed by seven additional days at 37 °C. The manufacturer also has indicated that these fentanyl citrate solutions are stable for 30 days at room temperature followed by seven days at 37 °C. (31)

Sorption — Fentanyl citrate (Janssen) 5 μg/ml in dextrose 5% in water or sodium chloride 0.9% exhibited no loss due to sorption to PVC infusion solution containers when compared to glass containers. Furthermore, use of a PCA infusion pump to deliver fentanyl citrate 4.5 μg/ml in dextrose 5% in water in a PVC bag did not result in concentration losses associated with sorption. Delivered concentrations were relatively consistent during the 30-hour evaluation period. (1357)

Xu et al. reported extensive and rapid loss of fentanyl citrate due to sorption to PVC containers when the solution pH was adjusted to the alkaline range. Fentanyl citrate 12.5 μg/ml in both dextrose 5% in water and sodium chloride 0.9% at pH 9 (with added sodium hydroxide) or combined with fluorouracil with nearly the same pH lost 25% of the fentanyl content in 15 minutes and 50% in one hour by HPLC analysis. Loss of fentanyl citrate did not occur in polyethylene containers under these conditions. Sorptive loss of fentanyl citrate to PVC containers is expected to occur from any alkaline solution. (2064)

Fentanyl citrate 2 μg/ml in various buffer solutions ranging from pH 5.5 to pH 6.7 packaged in PVC containers (Baxter) was shown to undergo slow sorption to the PVC in amounts dependent on the pH of the solution. The lower pH solutions exhibited less loss with increasing loss as the pH increased. At the highest pH tested of 6.7, 17% fentanyl loss occurred in one day. Refrigeration decreased the extent of loss but did not eliminate it. See Table 1. Little or no fentanyl loss was found in identical fentanyl citrate 2-μg/ml solutions packaged in glass containers. (2305)

Filtration — Fentanyl citrate (Janssen) 2.5 μg/ml in dextrose 5% in water or sodium chloride 0.9% was delivered over four hours through three kinds of 0.2-μm membrane filters varying in size and composition. HPLC analysis of the delivered solution showed no fentanyl loss due to sorption to the filter. (1399)

Central Venous Catheter — Fentanyl citrate (Abbott) 10 μg/ml in dextrose 5% in water was found to be compatible with the ARROWg+ard Blue Plus (Arrow International) chlorhexidine-bearing triple-lumen central catheter. HPLC analysis was used to evaluate completeness of drug delivery through the catheter and the amount of chlorhexidine removed from the internal lumens. Essentially complete delivery of the drug was found with little or no drug loss occurring. Furthermore, chlorhexidine delivered from the catheter remained at trace amounts with no substantial increase due to the delivery of the drug through the catheter. (2335)

Table 1. Percentage of Fentanyl Citrate 2 μg/ml Remaining After Storage for 30 Days at 23 °C in PVC Containers at Room Temperature (2305)

Buffer pH	Fentanyl Remaining (%)
5.5	85
5.8	77
6.3	56
6.7	27

Compatibility Information

Solution Compatibility

Fentanyl citrate

Solution	Mfr	Mfr	Conc/L	Remarks	Ref	C/I
Dextrose 5% in water	DB,[a] TR[b]	JN	5 mg	Physically compatible with no fentanyl loss in 48 hr at 22 °C in normal room light	1357	C
	AB	JN	20 and 40 mg	Visually compatible with 3% or less loss by HPLC in 3 hr at 24 °C	1852	C
Sodium chloride 0.9%	TR[b]	JN	20 mg	Physically compatible with little or no fentanyl loss in 30 days at 3 and 23 °C	1356	C
	DB,[a] TR[b]	JN	5 mg	Physically compatible with no fentanyl loss in 48 hr at 22 °C in normal room light	1357	C

[a]*Tested in glass containers.*
[b]*Tested in PVC containers.*

Additive Compatibility

Fentanyl citrate

Drug	Mfr	Conc/L	Mfr	Conc/L	Test Soln	Remarks	Ref	C/I
Bupivacaine HCl	WI	1.25 g	JN	20 mg	NS[a]	Physically compatible with little or no loss of either drug in 30 days at 3 and 23 °C	1396	C
		1.25 g		2 mg	NS[a]	Physically compatible with no bupivacaine loss and about 6 to 7% fentanyl loss by HPLC in 30 days at 4 and 23 °C	2305	C
		600 mg		2 mg	NS[a]	Physically compatible with no bupivacaine loss and about 2 to 4% fentanyl loss by HPLC in 30 days at 4 and 23 °C	2305	C
Fluorouracil	AB	1 and 16 g	AB	12.5 mg	D5W, NS[a]	25% fentanyl loss in 15 min due to sorption to PVC	2064	I
Lidocaine HCl	AST	2.5 g		2 mg	NS[a]	Physically compatible with no loss of either drug by HPLC in 30 days at 4 and 23 °C	2305	C
	BRN	2.5 g		2 mg	NS[a]	Physically compatible with little lidocaine loss but 18% fentanyl loss by HPLC at 23 °C and 10% loss at 4 °C in 2 days due to sorption at pH 6.7 from higher pH lidocaine product	2305	I

[a]*Tested in PVC containers.*

Drugs in Syringe Compatibility

Fentanyl citrate

Drug (in syringe)	Mfr	Amt	Mfr	Amt	Remarks	Ref	C/I
Atracurium besylate	BW	10 mg/ml		50 μg/ml	Physically compatible and atracurium chemically stable for 24 hr at 5 and 25 °C	1694	C
Atropine sulfate		0.6 mg/ 1.5 ml	MN	100 μg/ 1 ml	Physically compatible for at least 15 min	14	C
	ST	0.4 mg/ 1 ml	MN	0.05 mg/ 1 ml	Physically compatible for at least 15 min	326	C
Bupivacaine HCl with ketamine HCl	SW PD	1.5 mg/ ml 2 mg/ml	JN	0.01 mg/ ml	Diluted to 5 ml with NS. Visually compatible with no new GC/MS peaks in 1 hr at room temperature	1956	C

Drugs in Syringe Compatibility (Cont.)

Fentanyl citrate

Drug (in syringe)	*Mfr*	*Amt*	*Mfr*	*Amt*	*Remarks*	*Ref*	*C/I*
Butorphanol tartrate	BR	4 mg/ 2 ml	MN	0.1 mg/ 2 ml	Physically compatible both macroscopically and microscopically for 30 min at room temperature	566	C
Chlorpromazine HCl	PO	50 mg/ 2 ml	MN	0.05 mg/ 1 ml	Physically compatible for at least 15 min	326	C
Cimetidine HCl	SKF	300 mg/ 2 ml	JN	0.1 mg/ 2 ml	Physically compatible for 4 hr at 25 °C	25	C
Clonidine HCl with lidocaine HCl	BI AST	0.03 mg/ ml 2 mg/ml	JN	0.01 mg/ ml	Diluted to 5 ml with NS. Visually compatible with no new GC/MS peaks in 1 hr at room temperature	1956	C
Dimenhydrinate	HR	50 mg/ 1 ml	MN	0.05 mg/ 1 ml	Physically compatible for at least 15 min	326	C
Diphenhydramine HCl	PD	50 mg/ 1 ml	MN	0.05 mg/ 1 ml	Physically compatible for at least 15 min	326	C
Droperidol	MN	2.5 mg/ 1 ml	MN	0.05 mg/ 1 ml	Physically compatible for at least 15 min	326	C
Heparin sodium		2500 units/ 1 ml	JN	0.1 mg/ 2 ml	Physically compatible for at least 5 min	1053	C
Hydromorphone HCl	KN	4 mg/ 2 ml	MN	0.05 mg/ 1 ml	Physically compatible for 30 min	517	C
Hydroxyzine HCl	PF	50 mg/ 1 ml	MN	0.05 mg/ 1 ml	Physically compatible for at least 15 min	326	C
	PF	50 mg/ 1 ml	CR	0.05 mg/ 1 ml	Physically compatible	771	C
	PF	100 mg/ 2 ml	CR	0.05 mg/ 1 ml	Physically compatible	771	C
Hyoscine butylbromide with midazolam HCl	BI RC	30 mg/ 1.5 ml 15 mg/ 3 ml	DB	1 mg/ 20 ml	Visually compatible with 9% or less loss of each drug in 7 days at 32 °C	2268	C
Meperidine HCl	WI	50 mg/ 1 ml	MN	0.05 mg/ 1 ml	Physically compatible for at least 15 min	326	C
Metoclopramide HCl	NO	10 mg/ 2 ml	MN	0.05 mg/ 1 ml	Physically compatible both macroscopically and microscopically for 15 min at room temperature	565	C
Metoclopramide HCl with midazolam HCl	AST RC	20 mg/ 4 ml 15 mg/ 3 ml	DB	1 mg/ 20 ml	Visually compatible with 7% or less loss of each drug in 10 days at 32 °C	2268	C
Midazolam HCl	RC	5 mg/ 1 ml	ES	0.1 mg/ 2 ml	Physically compatible for 4 hr at 25 °C under fluorescent light	1145	C
	RC	0.625 and 0.938 mg/ ml[a]	DB	12.5 µg/ ml[a]	Visually compatible with little fentanyl loss and 7 to 9% midazolam loss by HPLC in 7 days at 5 and 22 °C, respectively	2202	C
	RC	0.625 mg/ ml[a]	DB	37.5 µg/ ml[a]	Visually compatible with no fentanyl loss and 5 to 8% midazolam loss by HPLC in 7 days at 5 and 22 °C, respectively	2202	C

Drugs in Syringe Compatibility (Cont.)

Drug (in syringe)	Mfr	Amt	Mfr	Amt	Remarks	Ref	C/I
				Fentanyl citrate			
	RC	0.938 mg/ ml[a]	DB	37.5 μg/ ml[a]	Visually compatible with little fentanyl loss and 7 to 9% midazolam loss by HPLC in 7 days at 5 and 22 °C, respectively	2202	C
	RC	0.278 and 0.833 mg/ ml[a]	DB	33.3 μg/ ml[a]	Visually compatible with no fentanyl loss and not more than 5 to 7% midazolam loss by HPLC in 7 days at 5 and 22 °C, respectively	2202	C
Morphine sulfate	ST	15 mg/ 1 ml	MN	0.05 mg/ 1 ml	Physically compatible for at least 15 min	326	C
Ondansetron HCl	GW	1.33 mg/ ml[a]	ES	0.0167 mg/ml[a]	Physically compatible with no measured increase in particulates and little or no loss of either drug by HPLC in 24 hr at 4 or 23 °C	2199	C
Papaveretum	RC[b]	20 mg/ 1 ml	MN	0.05 mg/ 1 ml	Visually compatible for at least 15 min	326	C
Pentazocine lactate	WI	30 mg/ 1 ml	MN	0.05 mg/ 1 ml	Physically compatible for at least 15 min	326	C
Pentobarbital sodium	AB	50 mg/ 1 ml	MN	0.05 mg/ 1 ml	Physically incompatible within 15 min	326	I
Perphenazine	SC	5 mg/ 1 ml	MN	0.1 mg/ 2 ml	Physically compatible both macroscopically and microscopically for 30 min at room temperature	566	C
Prochlorperazine edisylate	PO	5 mg/ 1 ml	MN	0.05 mg/ 1 ml	Physically compatible for at least 15 min	326	C
Promazine HCl	WY	50 mg/ 1 ml	MN	0.05 mg/ 1 ml	Physically compatible for at least 15 min	326	C
Promethazine HCl	PO	50 mg/ 2 ml	MN	0.05 mg/ 1 ml	Physically compatible for at least 15 min	326	C
Ranitidine HCl	GL	50 mg/ 2 ml	JN	0.1 mg/ 2 ml	Physically compatible for 1 hr at 25 °C both macroscopically and microscopically	978	C
Scopolamine HBr		0.6 mg/ 1.5 ml	MN	100 μg/ 1 ml	Physically compatible for at least 15 min	14	C
	ST	0.4 mg/ 1 ml	MN	0.05 mg/ 1 ml	Physically compatible for at least 15 min	326	C

[a]Tested in sodium chloride 0.9%.
[b]The former formulation was tested.

Y-Site Injection Compatibility (1:1 Mixture)

Drug	Mfr	Conc	Mfr	Conc	Remarks	Ref	C/I
				Fentanyl citrate			
Alatrofloxacin mesylate	PF	1.43 mg/ml[a]	ES	0.05 mg/ml	Visually and microscopically compatible with the fentanyl citrate pushed through a Y-site over 2 min	2235	C
Amphotericin B cholesteryl sulfate complex	SEQ	0.83 mg/ml[a]	AB	0.05 mg/ml	Physically compatible with little or no change in measured turbidity or increase in particle content in 4 hr at 23 °C under fluorescent light	2117	C
Atracurium besylate	BW	0.5 mg/ml[a]	ES	10 μg/ml[a]	Physically compatible for 24 hr at 28 °C	1337	C

Y-Site Injection Compatibility (1:1 Mixture) (Cont.)

			Fentanyl citrate				
Drug	*Mfr*	*Conc*	*Mfr*	*Conc*	*Remarks*	*Ref*	*C/I*
Atropine sulfate	LY	0.4 mg/ml	JN	0.025 mg/ml[a]	Physically compatible with no change in measured haze or increase in particle content in 48 hr at 22 °C	1706	C
Cisatracurium besylate	GW	0.1, 2, 5 mg/ml[a]	AB	0.0125 mg/ml[a]	Physically compatible with no change in measured turbidity or increase in particle content in 4 hr at 23 °C	2074	C
Dexamethasone sodium phosphate	AMR	1 mg/ml[a]	JN	0.025 mg/ml[a]	Physically compatible with no change in measured haze or increase in particle content in 48 hr at 22 °C	1706	C
Diazepam	ES	0.5 mg/ml[a]	JN	0.025 mg/ml[a]	Physically compatible with no change in measured haze or increase in particle content in 48 hr at 22 °C	1706	C
Diltiazem HCl	MMD	1 mg/ml[a]	ES	0.05 mg/ml	Visually compatible for 4 hr at 27 °C	2062	C
Diphenhydramine HCl	SCN	2 mg/ml[a]	JN	0.025 mg/ml[a]	Physically compatible with no change in measured haze or increase in particle content in 48 hr at 22 °C	1706	C
Dobutamine HCl	LI	4 mg/ml[a]	ES	0.05 mg/ml	Visually compatible for 4 hr at 27 °C	2062	C
Dopamine HCl	AB	3.2 mg/ml[a]	ES	0.05 mg/ml	Visually compatible for 4 hr at 27 °C	2062	C
Enalaprilat	MSD	0.05 mg/ml[b]	ES	2 μg/ml[a]	Physically compatible for 24 hr at room temperature under fluorescent light	1355	C
Epinephrine HCl	AB	0.02 mg/ml[a]	ES	0.05 mg/ml	Visually compatible for 4 hr at 27 °C	2062	C
Esmolol HCl	DCC	1 g/100 ml[c]	JN	0.05 mg/1 ml	Physically compatible when fentanyl is injected into Y-site of flowing admixture[d]	1168	C
	DCC	10 mg/ml[c]	JN	0.05 mg/ml	Physically compatible with no loss of either drug in 8 hr at ambient temperature exposed to light	1168	C
Etomidate	AB	2 mg/ml	ES	0.05 mg/ml	Visually compatible for up to 7 days at 25 °C	1801	C
Furosemide	AMR	10 mg/ml	ES	0.05 mg/ml	Visually compatible for 4 hr at 27 °C	2062	C
Gatifloxacin	BMS	2 mg/ml[a]	AB	0.05 mg/ml	Physically compatible with no change in measured haze or increase in particle content in 4 hr at 23 °C	2234	C
Haloperidol lactate	MN	0.2 mg/ml[a]	JN	0.025 mg/ml[a]	Physically compatible with no change in measured haze or increase in particle content in 48 hr at 22 °C	1706	C
Heparin sodium	UP	1000 units/L[e]	MN	0.05 mg/ml	Physically compatible for at least 4 hr at room temperature by visual and microscopic examination	534	C
	ES	100 units/ml[a]	ES	0.05 mg/ml	Visually compatible for 4 hr at 27 °C	2062	C
Hetastarch in lactated electrolyte injection (Hextend)	AB	6%	ES	12.5 μg/ml[a]	Physically compatible with no change in measured turbidity or increase in particle content in 4 hr at 23 °C	2339	C
Hydrocortisone sodium succinate	UP	10 mg/L[e]	MN	0.05 mg/ml	Physically compatible for at least 4 hr at room temperature by visual and microscopic examination	534	C
Hydromorphone HCl	KN	1 mg/ml	ES	0.05 mg/ml	Visually compatible for 4 hr at 27 °C	2062	C

Y-Site Injection Compatibility (1:1 Mixture) (Cont.)

			Fentanyl citrate				
Drug	*Mfr*	*Conc*	*Mfr*	*Conc*	*Remarks*	*Ref*	*C/I*
Hydroxyzine HCl	WI	4 mg/ml[a]	JN	0.025 mg/ml[a]	Physically compatible with no change in measured haze or increase in particle content in 48 hr at 22 °C	1706	C
Ketorolac tromethamine	WY	1 mg/ml[a]	JN	0.025 mg/ml[a]	Physically compatible with no change in measured haze or increase in particle content in 48 hr at 22 °C	1706	C
Labetalol HCl	SC	1 mg/ml[a]	JN	10 µg/ml[a]	Physically compatible for 24 hr at 18 °C	1171	C
	AH	2 mg/ml[a]	ES	0.05 mg/ml	Visually compatible for 4 hr at 27 °C	2062	C
Levofloxacin	OMN	5 mg/ml[a]	AB	0.05 mg/ml	Visually compatible for 4 hr at 24 °C under fluorescent light	2233	C
Linezolid	PHU	2 mg/ml	AB	0.05 mg/ml	Physically compatible with no change in measured turbidity or increase in particle content in 4 hr at 23 °C	2264	C
Lorazepam	WY	0.33 mg/ml[b]		0.05 mg/ml	Visually compatible for 24 hr at 22 °C	1855	C
	WY	0.5 mg/ml[a]	ES	0.05 mg/ml	Visually compatible for 4 hr at 27 °C	2062	C
	WY	0.1 mg/ml[a]	JN	0.025 mg/ml[a]	Physically compatible with no change in measured haze or increase in particle content in 48 hr at 22 °C	1706	C
Methotrimeprazine	LE	0.2 mg/ml[a]	JN	0.025 mg/ml[a]	Physically compatible with no change in measured haze or increase in particle content in 48 hr at 22 °C	1706	C
Metoclopramide HCl	DU	5 mg/ml	JN	0.025 mg/ml[a]	Physically compatible with no change in measured haze or increase in particle content in 48 hr at 22 °C	1706	C
Midazolam HCl	RC	1 mg/ml[a]	ES	0.05 mg/ml	Visually compatible for 24 hr at 23 °C	1847	C
	RC	0.1 and 0.5 mg/ml[a]	JN	0.02 mg/ml[a]	Visually compatible with no midazolam loss and 3 to 4% fentanyl loss by HPLC in 3 hr at 24 °C	1852	C
	RC	0.1 and 0.5 mg/ml[a]	JN	0.04 mg/ml[a]	Visually compatible with no loss of either drug by HPLC in 3 hr at 24 °C	1852	C
	RC	5 mg/ml		0.05 mg/ml	Visually compatible for 24 hr at 22 °C	1855	C
	RC	2 mg/ml[a]	ES	0.05 mg/ml	Visually compatible for 4 hr at 27 °C	2062	C
	RC	0.2 mg/ml[a]	JN	0.025 mg/ml[a]	Physically compatible with no change in measured haze or increase in particle content in 48 hr at 22 °C	1706	C
Milrinone lactate	SW	0.2 mg/ml[a]	ES	0.05 mg/ml	Visually compatible for 4 hr at 27 °C	2062	C
	SW	0.4 mg/ml[a]	ES	50 µg/ml	Visually compatible with little or no loss of either drug by HPLC in 4 hr at 23 °C	2214	C
Morphine sulfate	SCN	2 mg/ml[a]	ES	0.05 mg/ml	Visually compatible for 4 hr at 27 °C	2062	C
Nafcillin sodium	WY	33 mg/ml[b]		0.05 mg/ml	No precipitation	547	C
Nicardipine HCl	WY	1 mg/ml[a]	ES	0.05 mg/ml	Visually compatible for 4 hr at 27 °C	2062	C
Nitroglycerin	AB	0.4 mg/ml[a]	ES	0.05 mg/ml	Visually compatible for 4 hr at 27 °C	2062	C
Norepinephrine bitartrate	AB	0.128 mg/ml[a]	ES	0.05 mg/ml	Visually compatible for 4 hr at 27 °C	2062	C
Pancuronium bromide	ES	0.05 mg/ml[a]	ES	10 µg/ml[a]	Physically compatible for 24 hr at 28 °C	1337	C
Phenobarbital sodium	WY	2 mg/ml[a]	JN	0.025 mg/ml[a]	Physically compatible with no change in measured haze or increase in particle content in 48 hr at 22 °C	1706	C
Phenytoin sodium	ES	2 mg/ml[a,b]	JN	0.025 mg/ml[a]	Precipitate forms within 1 hr	1706	I

Y-Site Injection Compatibility (1:1 Mixture) (Cont.)

Fentanyl citrate

Drug	*Mfr*	*Conc*	*Mfr*	*Conc*	*Remarks*	*Ref*	*C/I*
Potassium chloride	AB	40 mEq/L[e]	MN	0.05 mg/ml	Physically compatible for at least 4 hr at room temperature by visual and microscopic examination	534	C
Propofol	ZEN	10 mg/ml	AB	0.05 mg/ml	Physically compatible for 1 hr at 23 °C with no increase in particle content	2066	C
Ranitidine HCl	GL	1 mg/ml[a]	ES	0.05 mg/ml	Visually compatible for 4 hr at 27 °C	2062	C
Remifentanil HCl	GW	0.025 and 0.25 mg/ml[b]	ES	0.0125 mg/ml[a]	Physically compatible with no change in measured turbidity or increase in particle content in 4 hr at 23 °C	2075	C
Sargramostim	IMM	6[f] and 15 μg/ml[b]	ES	50 μg/ml	Visually compatible for 2 hr	1618	C
Scopolamine HBr	LY	0.05 mg/ml[a]	JN	0.025 mg/ml[a]	Physically compatible with no change in measured haze or increase in particle content in 48 hr at 22 °C	1706	C
Thiopental sodium	AB	25 mg/ml	ES	0.05 mg/ml	Visually compatible for up to 7 days at 25 °C	1801	C
	AB	25 mg/ml[g]	ES	0.05 mg/ml	Visually compatible for 4 hr at 27 °C	2062	C
TNA #218 to #226[h]			AB	0.0125[a] and 0.05 mg/ml	Visually compatible with no precipitate or emulsion damage apparent in 4 hr at 23 °C	2215	C
TPN #203 and #204[h]			ES	0.05 mg/ml	Visually compatible for 4 hr at 23 °C	1974	C
TPN #212 to #215[h]			AB	0.05 mg/ml	Physically compatible with no change in measured turbidity or increase in particle content in 4 hr at 23 °C	2109	C
			JN	0.0125 mg/ml[a]	Physically compatible with no change in measured turbidity or increase in particle content in 4 hr at 23 °C	2109	C
TPN #216[h]			ES	0.01 mg/ml[g]	Mixed 1 ml of fentanyl with 9 ml of TPN. Visually compatible for 24 hr	2104	C
Vecuronium bromide	OR	0.1 mg/ml[a]	ES	10 μg/ml[a]	Physically compatible for 24 hr at 28 °C	1337	C
	OR	1 mg/ml	ES	0.05 mg/ml	Visually compatible for 4 hr at 27 °C	2062	C
Vitamin B complex with C	RC	2 ml/L[e]	MN	0.05 mg/ml	Physically compatible for at least 4 hr at room temperature by visual and microscopic examination	534	C

[a]*Tested in dextrose 5% in water.*
[b]*Tested in sodium chloride 0.9%.*
[c]*Tested in dextrose 5% in sodium chloride 0.9%.*
[d]*Flowing at 1.6 ml/min.*
[e]*Tested in dextrose 5% in Ringer's injection, dextrose 5% in Ringer's injection, lactated, dextrose 5% in water, Ringer's injection, lactated, and sodium chloride 0.9%.*
[f]*Tested with albumin human 0.1%.*
[g]*Tested in sterile water for injection.*
[h]*Refer to Appendix I for the composition of parenteral nutrition solutions. TNA indicates a 3-in-1 admixture, and TPN indicates a 2-in-1 admixture.*

Additional Compatibility Information

Bupivacaine and Epinephrine — A solution composed of bupivacaine HCl (Winthrop) 0.44 mg/ml, fentanyl citrate (Janssen) 1.25 μg/ml, and epinephrine HCl (Abbott) 0.69 μg/ml was stored in 100-ml portable infusion pump reservoirs (Pharmacia Deltec) for 30 days at 3 and 23 °C. The samples were then delivered through the infusion pumps over 48 hours at near-body temperature (30 °C). The samples were visually compatible throughout, and bupivacaine HCl and fentanyl citrate exhibited no loss by HPLC analysis. Epinephrine HCl sustained about a 5 to 6% loss by HPLC analysis after 20 days of storage at both temperatures and about a 9 to 10% loss after 30 days of storage and subsequent pump delivery. The authors recommended restricting storage before administration to only 20 days. (1627)

Multiple Drugs — A seven-drug combination consisting of bupivacaine HCl (Sanofi Winthrop) 1.5 mg/ml, clonidine HCl (Boehringer Ingelheim) 0.03 mg/ml, fentanyl citrate (Janssen) 0.01 mg/ml, ketamine (Parke-Davis) 2 mg/ml, lidocaine HCl (Astra) 2 mg/ml, morphine sulfate (Elkins-Sinn) 0.2 mg/ml, and tetracaine HCl (Sanofi Winthrop) 2 mg/ml mixed together in equal quantities was found to be visually compatible with no new GC/MS peaks appearing in one hour at room temperature. (1956)

Other Drugs — Fentanyl citrate is stated to be physically incompatible with methohexital, pentobarbital, and thiopental. (4)

FILGRASTIM
AHFS 20:16

Products — Filgrastim is available in 300-μg and 480-μg sizes with the product compositions and package configurations shown in Table 1. (2)

pH—4. (4)

Trade Name(s)—Neupogen.

Administration — Filgrastim is administered by subcutaneous injection undiluted or by intravenous or subcutaneous infusion. For intravenous infusion, it is diluted in 50 to 100 ml of dextrose 5% in water and given over 15 to 30 (2; 4) or 60 minutes (4) or over 24 hours by continuous infusion. It may also be given over 24 hours by continuous subcutaneous infusion after diluting the dose in 10 to 50 ml of dextrose 5% in water and infusing at a rate not exceeding 10 ml/24 hours. For extended infusions by either route, a controlled-infusion device is used. For filgrastim concentrations of 5 to 15 μg/ml albumin human should be added to the solution at a final concentration of 0.2% (2 mg/ml) before the filgrastim is added. The drug should not be diluted to concentrations less than 5 μg/ml. (2; 4)

Stability — Filgrastim injection is a clear, colorless solution. Intact containers should be refrigerated at 2 to 8 °C and protected from direct sunlight. The product also should be protected from freezing and temperatures above 30 °C to avoid aggregation. The solution should not be shaken since bubbles and/or foam may form. If foaming occurs, the solution should be left undisturbed for a few minutes until bubbles dissipate. (2; 4)

Filgrastim is stable for 24 hours at 9 to 30 °C as long as it is clear and contains no precipitate; the manufacturer recommends discarding it after 24 hours. (2; 4) The product is packaged in single-use containers with no antibacterial preservative. The manufacturer recommends that vials not be reentered and that unused portions be discarded. (2)

Because filgrastim contains no antibacterial preservatives, dilutions prepared for infusion should be stored under refrigeration and used within 24 hours of preparation because of concern about possible bacterial contamination. (4)

Table 1. Filgrastim Products and Compositions (2)

	300 μg/1-ml Vial	480 μg/1.6-ml Vial	300 μg/0.5-ml Syringe	480 μg/0.8-ml Syringe
Filgrastim	300 μg	480 μg	300 μg	480 μg
Acetate	0.59 mg	0.94 mg	0.295 mg	0.472 mg
Sorbitol	50 mg	80 mg	25 mg	40 mg
Polysorbate 80	0.004%	0.004%	0.004%	0.004%
Sodium	0.035 mg	0.056 mg	0.0175 mg	0.028 mg
Water for injection	1 ml	1.6 ml	0.5 ml	0.8 ml

pH Effects—Filgrastim is stable at pH 3.8 to 4.2, but stability is limited at neutral pH. (4)

Syringes—Undiluted filgrastim is stable for 24 hours at 15 to 30 °C and for seven days refrigerated at 2 to 8 °C repackaged in tuberculin syringes (Becton-Dickinson). However, refrigeration and use within 24 hours are recommended because of concern about bacterial contamination. (4)

Sorption—For filgrastim concentrations between 5 and 15 μg/ml, albumin human should be added before adding the filgrastim to make a final albumin human concentration of 0.2% (2 mg/ml) to minimize filgrastim adsorption to infusion containers and equipment. At filgrastim concentrations above 15 μg/ml, albumin human is unnecessary. The product should not be diluted to a final concentration of less than 5 μg/ml. (2; 4)

The amount of loss of filgrastim (Amgen) from the undiluted injection at a concentration of 300 μg/ml when delivered through 6.6-French, single-lumen, silicone rubber, Broviac catheters (Bard) was evaluated. The catheters were filled with dextrose 5% in water (about 0.45 ml) and flushed before and after introduction of the filgrastim. Injected amounts of filgrastim 300 μg/ml ranged from 0.17 to 1 ml. The delivered flush solution was collected and analyzed by immunoassay for filgrastim content and bioassay for maintenance of activity. The lowest volume (0.17 ml) incurred about 32% loss of filgrastim upon delivery. The other volumes incurred lower losses, ranging from 12% to none. A second repeat filgrastim injection incurred similar losses. The filgrastim that was delivered through the catheters remained active according to bioassay. (2017)

Compatibility Information

Y-Site Injection Compatibility (1:1 Mixture)

Drug	Mfr	Conc	Filgrastim Mfr	Filgrastim Conc	Remarks	Ref	C/I
Acyclovir sodium	BW	7 mg/ml[a]	AMG	30 μg/ml[a]	Physically compatible with no change in measured turbidity or increase in particle content in 4 hr at 22 °C	1687	C
Allopurinol sodium	BW	3 mg/ml[a]	AMG	30 μg/ml[a]	Physically compatible with no change in measured turbidity or increase in particle content in 4 hr at 22 °C	1687	C
Amikacin sulfate	ES	5 mg/ml[a]	AMG	30 μg/ml[a]	Physically compatible with no change in measured turbidity or increase in particle content in 4 hr at 22 °C	1687	C
	BMS	5 mg/ml[a]	AMG	10[b] and 40[a] μg/ml	Visually compatible with little or no loss of filgrastim activity by bioassay and amikacin by immunoassay in 4 hr at 25 °C	2060	C
Aminophylline	AB	2.5 mg/ml[a]	AMG	30 μg/ml[a]	Physically compatible with no change in measured turbidity or increase in particle content in 4 hr at 22 °C	1687	C
Amphotericin B	SQ	0.6 mg/ml[a]	AMG	30 μg/ml[a]	Yellow turbidity forms immediately and becomes flocculent precipitate	1687	I
Ampicillin sodium	WY	20 mg/ml[a]	AMG	30 μg/ml[a]	Physically compatible with no change in measured turbidity or increase in particle content in 4 hr at 22 °C	1687	C
Ampicillin sodium–sulbactam sodium	RR	20 + 10 mg/ml[a]	AMG	30 μg/ml[a]	Physically compatible with no change in measured turbidity or increase in particle content in 4 hr at 22 °C	1687	C
Aztreonam	SQ	40 mg/ml[a]	AMG	30 μg/ml[a]	Physically compatible with no change in measured turbidity or increase in particle content in 4 hr at 22 °C	1687	C
	SQ	40 mg/ml[a]	AMG	30 μg/ml[a]	Physically compatible with no subvisual haze or particle formation in 4 hr at 23 °C	1758	C
Bleomycin sulfate	BR	1 unit/ml[a]	AMG	30 μg/ml[a]	Physically compatible with no change in measured turbidity or increase in particle content in 4 hr at 22 °C	1687	C
Bumetanide	RC	0.04 mg/ml[a]	AMG	30 μg/ml[a]	Physically compatible with no change in measured turbidity or increase in particle content in 4 hr at 22 °C	1687	C
Buprenorphine HCl	RKC	0.04 mg/ml[a]	AMG	30 μg/ml[a]	Physically compatible with no change in measured turbidity or increase in particle content in 4 hr at 22 °C	1687	C
Butorphanol tartrate	BR	0.04 mg/ml[a]	AMG	30 μg/ml[a]	Physically compatible with no change in measured turbidity or increase in particle content in 4 hr at 22 °C	1687	C
Calcium gluconate	AST	40 mg/ml[a]	AMG	30 μg/ml[a]	Physically compatible with no change in measured turbidity or increase in particle content in 4 hr at 22 °C	1687	C
Carboplatin	BR	5 mg/ml[a]	AMG	30 μg/ml[a]	Physically compatible with no change in measured turbidity or increase in particle content in 4 hr at 22 °C	1687	C

Y-Site Injection Compatibility (1:1 Mixture) (Cont.)

			Filgrastim				
Drug	*Mfr*	*Conc*	*Mfr*	*Conc*	*Remarks*	*Ref*	*C/I*
Carmustine	BR	1.5 mg/ml[a]	AMG	30 μg/ml[a]	Physically compatible with no change in measured turbidity or increase in particle content in 4 hr at 22 °C	1687	C
Cefazolin sodium	LI	20 mg/ml[a]	AMG	30 μg/ml[a]	Physically compatible with no change in measured turbidity or increase in particle content in 4 hr at 22 °C	1687	C
Cefepime HCl	BMS	20 mg/ml[a]	AMG	30 μg/ml[a]	Hazy turbid solution forms immediately	1689	I
Cefoperazone sodium	RR	40 mg/ml[a]	AMG	30 μg/ml[a]	Haze and particles form immediately	1687	I
Cefotaxime sodium	HO	20 mg/ml[a]	AMG	30 μg/ml[a]	Particles form in 4 hr	1687	I
Cefotetan disodium	STU	20 mg/ml[a]	AMG	30 μg/ml[a]	Physically compatible with no change in measured turbidity or increase in particle content in 4 hr at 22 °C	1687	C
Cefoxitin sodium	MSD	20 mg/ml[a]	AMG	30 μg/ml[a]	Haze, particles, and filaments form immediately	1687	I
Ceftazidime	LI[c]	40 mg/ml[a]	AMG	30 μg/ml[a]	Physically compatible with no change in measured turbidity or increase in particle content in 4 hr at 22 °C	1687	C
	LI[c]	10 mg/ml[a]	AMG	10[b] and 40[a] μg/ml	Visually compatible with little or no loss of filgrastim activity by bioassay and ceftazidime by HPLC in 4 hr at 25 °C	2060	C
Ceftizoxime sodium	FUJ	20 mg/ml[a]	AMG	30 μg/ml[a]	Particles and filaments form immediately	1687	I
Ceftriaxone sodium	RC	20 mg/ml[a]	AMG	30 μg/ml[a]	Particles and filaments form in 1 hr	1687	I
Cefuroxime sodium	GL	20 mg/ml[a]	AMG	30 μg/ml[a]	Haze, particles, and filaments form immediately	1687	I
Chlorpromazine HCl	RU	2 mg/ml[a]	AMG	30 μg/ml[a]	Physically compatible with no change in measured turbidity or increase in particle content in 4 hr at 22 °C	1687	C
Cimetidine HCl	SKB	12 mg/ml[a]	AMG	30 μg/ml[a]	Physically compatible with no change in measured turbidity or increase in particle content in 4 hr at 22 °C	1687	C
Cisplatin	BR	1 mg/ml	AMG	30 μg/ml[a]	Physically compatible with no change in measured turbidity or increase in particle content in 4 hr at 22 °C	1687	C
Clindamycin phosphate	AB	10 mg/ml[a]	AMG	30 μg/ml[a]	Particles and filaments form immediately	1687	I
Cyclophosphamide	MJ	10 mg/ml[a]	AMG	30 μg/ml[a]	Physically compatible with no change in measured turbidity or increase in particle content in 4 hr at 22 °C	1687	C
Cytarabine	CET	50 mg/ml	AMG	30 μg/ml[a]	Physically compatible with no change in measured turbidity or increase in particle content in 4 hr at 22 °C	1687	C
Dacarbazine	MI	4 mg/ml[a]	AMG	30 μg/ml[a]	Physically compatible with no change in measured turbidity or increase in particle content in 4 hr at 22 °C	1687	C
Dactinomycin	MSD	0.01 mg/ml[a]	AMG	30 μg/ml[a]	Particles and filaments form immediately	1687	I
Daunorubicin HCl	WY	1 mg/ml[a]	AMG	30 μg/ml[a]	Physically compatible with no change in measured turbidity or increase in particle content in 4 hr at 22 °C	1687	C

Y-Site Injection Compatibility (1:1 Mixture) (Cont.)

			Filgrastim				
Drug	*Mfr*	*Conc*	*Mfr*	*Conc*	*Remarks*	*Ref*	*C/I*
Dexamethasone sodium phosphate	LY	1 mg/ml[a]	AMG	30 μg/ml[a]	Physically compatible with no change in measured turbidity or increase in particle content in 4 hr at 22 °C	1687	C
Diphenhydramine HCl	ES	2 mg/ml[a]	AMG	30 μg/ml[a]	Physically compatible with no change in measured turbidity or increase in particle content in 4 hr at 22 °C	1687	C
Doxorubicin HCl	CET	2 mg/ml	AMG	30 μg/ml[a]	Physically compatible with no change in measured turbidity or increase in particle content in 4 hr at 22 °C	1687	C
Doxycycline hyclate	ES	1 mg/ml[a]	AMG	30 μg/ml[a]	Physically compatible with no change in measured turbidity or increase in particle content in 4 hr at 22 °C	1687	C
Droperidol	JN	0.4 mg/ml[a]	AMG	30 μg/ml[a]	Physically compatible with no change in measured turbidity or increase in particle content in 4 hr at 22 °C	1687	C
Enalaprilat	MSD	0.1 mg/ml[a]	AMG	30 μg/ml[a]	Physically compatible with no change in measured turbidity or increase in particle content in 4 hr at 22 °C	1687	C
Etoposide	BR	0.4 mg/ml[a]	AMG	30 μg/ml[a]	Particles form immediately. Filaments form in 1 hr	1687	I
Famotidine	MSD	2 mg/ml[a]	AMG	30 μg/ml[a]	Physically compatible with no change in measured turbidity or increase in particle content in 4 hr at 22 °C	1687	C
Floxuridine	RC	3 mg/ml[a]	AMG	30 μg/ml[a]	Physically compatible with no change in measured turbidity or increase in particle content in 4 hr at 22 °C	1687	C
Fluconazole	RR	2 mg/ml	AMG	30 μg/ml[a]	Physically compatible with no change in measured turbidity or increase in particle content in 4 hr at 22 °C	1687	C
	RR	2 mg/ml[a]	AMG	10[b] and 40[a] μg/ml	Visually compatible with little or no loss of filgrastim activity by bioassay and fluconazole by HPLC in 4 hr at 25 °C	2060	C
Fludarabine phosphate	BX	1 mg/ml[a]	AMG	30 μg/ml[a]	Physically compatible with no change in measured turbidity or increase in particle content in 4 hr at 22 °C	1687	C
Fluorouracil	RC	16 mg/ml[a]	AMG	30 μg/ml[a]	Particles and long filaments form in 1 hr	1687	I
Furosemide	AB	3 mg/ml[a]	AMG	30 μg/ml[a]	Turbidity forms immediately. Filaments and particles form in 1 hr	1687	I
Ganciclovir sodium	SY	20 mg/ml[a]	AMG	30 μg/ml[a]	Physically compatible with no change in measured turbidity or increase in particle content in 4 hr at 22 °C	1687	C
Gentamicin sulfate	LY	5 mg/ml[a]	AMG	30 μg/ml[a]	Physically compatible with no change in measured turbidity or increase in particle content in 4 hr at 22 °C	1687	C
	GES	1.6 mg/ml[a]	AMG	40 μg/ml[a]	Visually compatible with little or no loss of filgrastim activity by bioassay and gentamicin by immunoassay in 4 hr at 25 °C	2060	C

Y-Site Injection Compatibility (1:1 Mixture) (Cont.)

			Filgrastim				
Drug	*Mfr*	*Conc*	*Mfr*	*Conc*	*Remarks*	*Ref*	*C/I*
	GES	1.6 mg/ml[a]	AMG	10 μg/ml[b]	23% loss of filgrastim activity by bioassay in 4 hr at 25 °C. Little or no gentamicin loss by immunoassay	2060	I
Granisetron HCl	SKB	0.05 mg/ml[a]	AMG	30 μg/ml[a]	Physically compatible with no change in measured turbidity or increase in particle content in 4 hr at 23 °C	2000	C
Haloperidol lactate	MN	0.2 mg/ml[a]	AMG	30 μg/ml[a]	Physically compatible with no change in measured turbidity or increase in particle content in 4 hr at 22 °C	1687	C
Heparin sodium	ES	100 units/ml[a]	AMG	30 μg/ml[a]	Particles and filaments form immediately	1687	I
Hydrocortisone sodium phosphate	MSD	1 mg/ml[a]	AMG	30 μg/ml[a]	Physically compatible with no change in measured turbidity or increase in particle content in 4 hr at 22 °C	1687	C
Hydrocortisone sodium succinate	UP	1 mg/ml[a]	AMG	30 μg/ml[a]	Physically compatible with no change in measured turbidity or increase in particle content in 4 hr at 22 °C	1687	C
Hydromorphone HCl	KN	0.5 mg/ml[a]	AMG	30 μg/ml[a]	Physically compatible with no change in measured turbidity or increase in particle content in 4 hr at 22 °C	1687	C
Hydroxyzine HCl	ES	4 mg/ml[a]	AMG	30 μg/ml[a]	Physically compatible with no change in measured turbidity or increase in particle content in 4 hr at 22 °C	1687	C
Idarubicin HCl	AD	0.5 mg/ml[a]	AMG	30 μg/ml[a]	Physically compatible with no change in measured turbidity or increase in particle content in 4 hr at 22 °C	1687	C
Ifosfamide	MJ	25 mg/ml[a]	AMG	30 μg/ml[a]	Physically compatible with no change in measured turbidity or increase in particle content in 4 hr at 22 °C	1687	C
Imipenem–cilastatin sodium	MSD	10 mg/ml[a]	AMG	30 μg/ml[a]	Physically compatible with no change in measured turbidity or increase in particle content in 4 hr at 22 °C	1687	C
	ME	5 mg/ml[a]	AMG	40 μg/ml[a]	16% loss of filgrastim activity by bioassay in 4 hr at 25 °C. Little or no imipenem and cilastatin loss by HPLC	2060	I
	ME	5 mg/ml[a]	AMG	10 μg/ml[b]	Visually compatible with little or no loss of filgrastim activity by bioassay and imipenem and cilastatin by HPLC in 4 hr at 25 °C	2060	C
Leucovorin calcium	LE	2 mg/ml[a]	AMG	30 μg/ml[a]	Physically compatible with no change in measured turbidity or increase in particle content in 4 hr at 22 °C	1687	C
Lorazepam	WY	0.1 mg/ml[a]	AMG	30 μg/ml[a]	Physically compatible with no change in measured turbidity or increase in particle content in 4 hr at 22 °C	1687	C
Mannitol	BA	15%	AMG	30 μg/ml[a]	Filaments form immediately	1687	I
Mechlorethamine HCl	MSD	1 mg/ml	AMG	30 μg/ml[a]	Physically compatible with no change in measured turbidity or increase in particle content in 4 hr at 22 °C	1687	C

Y-Site Injection Compatibility (1:1 Mixture) (Cont.)

			Filgrastim				
Drug	*Mfr*	*Conc*	*Mfr*	*Conc*	*Remarks*	*Ref*	*C/I*
Melphalan HCl	BW	0.1 mg/ml[a]	AMG	30 μg/ml[a]	Physically compatible with no change in measured turbidity or increase in particle content in 4 hr at 22 °C	1687	C
Meperidine HCl	WY	4 mg/ml[a]	AMG	30 μg/ml[a]	Physically compatible with no change in measured turbidity or increase in particle content in 4 hr at 22 °C	1687	C
Mesna	MJ	10 mg/ml[a]	AMG	30 μg/ml[a]	Physically compatible with no change in measured turbidity or increase in particle content in 4 hr at 22 °C	1687	C
Methotrexate sodium	LE	15 mg/ml[a]	AMG	30 μg/ml[a]	Physically compatible with no change in measured turbidity or increase in particle content in 4 hr at 22 °C	1687	C
Methylprednisolone sodium succinate	AB	5 mg/ml[a]	AMG	30 μg/ml[a]	Haze, particles, and filaments form immediately	1687	I
Metoclopramide HCl	ES	5 mg/ml	AMG	30 μg/ml[a]	Physically compatible with no change in measured turbidity or increase in particle content in 4 hr at 22 °C	1687	C
Metronidazole	BA	5 mg/ml	AMG	30 μg/ml[a]	Particles form immediately. Filaments form in 1 hr	1687	I
Minocycline HCl	LE	0.2 mg/ml[a]	AMG	30 μg/ml[a]	Physically compatible with no change in measured turbidity or increase in particle content in 4 hr at 22 °C	1687	C
Mitomycin	BR	0.5 mg/ml	AMG	30 μg/ml[a]	Color changes to reddish purple in 1 hr	1687	I
Mitoxantrone HCl	LE	0.5 mg/ml[a]	AMG	30 μg/ml[a]	Physically compatible with no change in measured turbidity or increase in particle content in 4 hr at 22 °C	1687	C
Morphine sulfate	WY	1 mg/ml[a]	AMG	30 μg/ml[a]	Physically compatible with no change in measured turbidity or increase in particle content in 4 hr at 22 °C	1687	C
Nalbuphine HCl	DU	10 mg/ml	AMG	30 μg/ml[a]	Physically compatible with no change in measured turbidity or increase in particle content in 4 hr at 22 °C	1687	C
Netilmicin sulfate	SC	5 mg/ml[a]	AMG	30 μg/ml[a]	Physically compatible with no change in measured turbidity or increase in particle content in 4 hr at 22 °C	1687	C
Ondansetron HCl	GL	1 mg/ml[a]	AMG	30 μg/ml[a]	Physically compatible with no change in measured turbidity or increase in particle content in 4 hr at 22 °C	1687	C
Piperacillin sodium	LE	40 mg/ml[a]	AMG	30 μg/ml[a]	Particles and filaments form immediately	1687	I
Plicamycin	MI	0.01 mg/ml[a]	AMG	30 μg/ml[a]	Physically compatible with no change in measured turbidity or increase in particle content in 4 hr at 22 °C	1687	C
Potassium chloride	AB	0.1 mEq/ml[a]	AMG	30 μg/ml[a]	Physically compatible with no change in measured turbidity or increase in particle content in 4 hr at 22 °C	1687	C
Prochlorperazine edisylate	SCN	0.5 mg/ml[a]	AMG	30 μg/ml[a]	Particles form immediately. Filaments form in 1 hr	1687	I

Y-Site Injection Compatibility (1:1 Mixture) (Cont.)

Filgrastim

Drug	*Mfr*	*Conc*	*Mfr*	*Conc*	*Remarks*	*Ref*	*C/I*
Promethazine HCl	SCN	2 mg/ml[a]	AMG	30 μg/ml[a]	Physically compatible with no change in measured turbidity or increase in particle content in 4 hr at 22 °C	1687	C
Ranitidine HCl	GL	2 mg/ml[a]	AMG	30 μg/ml[a]	Physically compatible with no change in measured turbidity or increase in particle content in 4 hr at 22 °C	1687	C
Sodium bicarbonate	AB	1 mEq/ml	AMG	30 μg/ml[a]	Physically compatible with no change in measured turbidity or increase in particle content in 4 hr at 22 °C	1687	C
Streptozocin	UP	40 mg/ml[a]	AMG	30 μg/ml[a]	Physically compatible with no change in measured turbidity or increase in particle content in 4 hr at 22 °C	1687	C
Thiotepa	LE	1 mg/ml[a]	AMG	30 μg/ml[a]	Particles and filaments form immediately	1687	I
Ticarcillin disodium	BE	30 mg/ml[a]	AMG	30 μg/ml[a]	Physically compatible with no change in measured turbidity or increase in particle content in 4 hr at 22 °C	1687	C
Ticarcillin disodium–clavulanate potassium	SKB	31 mg/ml[a]	AMG	30 μg/ml[a]	Physically compatible with no change in measured turbidity or increase in particle content in 4 hr at 22 °C	1687	C
Tobramycin sulfate	LI	5 mg/ml[a]	AMG	30 μg/ml[a]	Physically compatible with no change in measured turbidity or increase in particle content in 4 hr at 22 °C	1687	C
	LI	1.6 mg/ml[a]	AMG	10[b] and 40[a] μg/ml	Visually compatible with little or no loss of filgrastim activity by bioassay and tobramycin by immunoassay in 4 hr at 25 °C	2060	C
Trimethoprim–sulfamethoxazole	ES	0.8 + 4 mg/ml[a]	AMG	30 μg/ml[a]	Physically compatible with no change in measured turbidity or increase in particle content in 4 hr at 22 °C	1687	C
Vancomycin HCl	AB	10 mg/ml[a]	AMG	30 μg/ml[a]	Physically compatible with no change in measured turbidity or increase in particle content in 4 hr at 22 °C	1687	C
Vinblastine sulfate	LI	0.12 mg/ml[a]	AMG	30 μg/ml[a]	Physically compatible with no change in measured turbidity or increase in particle content in 4 hr at 22 °C	1687	C
Vincristine sulfate	LI	0.05 mg/ml[a]	AMG	30 μg/ml[a]	Physically compatible with no change in measured turbidity or increase in particle content in 4 hr at 22 °C	1687	C
Vinorelbine tartrate	BW	1 mg/ml[a]	AMG	30 μg/ml[a]	Physically compatible with no change in measured turbidity or increase in particle content in 4 hr at 22 °C	1687	C
Zidovudine	BW	4 mg/ml[a]	AMG	30 μg/ml[a]	Physically compatible with no change in measured turbidity or increase in particle content in 4 hr at 22 °C	1687	C

[a]*Tested in dextrose 5% in water.*
[b]*Tested in dextrose 5% in water with albumin human 2 mg/ml.*
[c]*Sodium carbonate–containing formulation.*

Additional Compatibility Information

Infusion Solutions — Although dilution to concentrations below 5 μg/ml is not recommended by the manufacturer, filgrastim has been stated to be stable for seven days under refrigeration when diluted with dextrose 5% in water to a concentration of at least 2 μg/ml. The manufacturer recommends use within 24 hours because of bacterial contamination concerns. (4)

Filgrastim is incompatible with sodium chloride 0.9%; this solution should not be used as a diluent. (4)

Plastics — Filgrastim in dextrose 5% in water at concentrations above 15 μg/ml and between 2 and 15 μg/ml with added albumin human 0.2% is compatible with common plastics used in syringes, administration sets, solution containers, and pump cassettes including PVC, polyolefin, and polypropylene. (4)

Other Information

Microbial Growth — In one study, filgrastim injection repackaged in 1-ml tuberculin syringes remained sterile for seven days under refrigeration. (1764) In another study, the sterility of filgrastim 300 μg/ml packaged aseptically as 0.25 ml in tuberculin syringes (Becton-Dickinson) closed with Luer Lock tip caps was evaluated. Sterility testing found no growth after seven days of storage at 4 °C. (2186) However, the sterility of repackaged solutions is a function of the quality of the specific aseptic process of packaging and the quality of the environment in which the sterile product is packaged rather than a property of this unpreserved solution. Consequently, these results are valid only for the specific facilities and operators evaluated in the studies. The adequacy and safety of repackaging in another location and with other individuals should be validated independently for each institution that repackages filgrastim injection. Each institution needs to establish specific validation testing results for its own aseptic processing facilities, equipment, procedures, and personnel. (1765; 2187)

Carleton et al. evaluated the sterility of filgrastim 0.2 ml (60 μg) extemporaneously drawn aseptically into tuberculin syringes and kept under "patient use" storage conditions. The syringes were sent home with patients to be stored in their home refrigerators for seven days and then were returned for sterility testing. A contamination rate as high as 1.25% was reported. The authors expressed the opinion and hope that the high rate of contamination was an artifact of the sterility testing itself. However, contamination during storage in the patients' refrigerators may have occurred. (2294)

FLOXURIDINE
AHFS 10:00

Products — Floxuridine is supplied in 5-ml vials containing 500 mg of drug. Reconstitute with 5 ml of sterile water for injection to yield a 100-mg/ml concentration. (2; 4)

pH — From 4 to 5.5. (2; 4)

Osmolality — Floxuridine 100 mg/ml in sterile water for injection has an osmolality of 353 mOsm/kg. (1689)

Trade Name(s) — FUDR.

Administration — Floxuridine is administered by continuous arterial infusion using an appropriate infusion device after dilution in dextrose 5% in water or sodium chloride 0.9%. (2; 4) Floxuridine has also been administered investigationally by intravenous injection or infusion. (4)

Stability — The reconstituted solution should be stored under refrigeration at 2 to 8 °C and used within two weeks. (2; 4)

The pH of optimum stability is 4 to 7. Extreme acidity or alkalinity may result in hydrolysis. (1379)

Syringes — Floxuridine (Roche) 50 mg/ml and 1 mg/ml in sodium chloride 0.9% was packaged as 3 ml in 10-ml polypropylene infusion pump syringes (Pharmacia Deltec). Little or no loss by HPLC analysis occurred during 21 days of storage at 30 °C. (1967)

Implantable Pumps — Floxuridine 10 mg/ml was filled into an implantable infusion pump (Fresenius VIP 30) and associated capillary tubing and stored at 37 °C. Samples were analyzed using HPLC assay. No floxuridine loss and no contamination from components of pump materials occurred during six weeks of storage. However, an unidentified additional peak on the chromatogram appeared in seven weeks, and 22% loss of floxuridine occurred by eight weeks. (1903)

Floxuridine (Roche), at concentrations ranging from about 2.5 to 12 mg/ml with heparin sodium 200 units/ml in bacteriostatic sodium chloride 0.9%, was evaluated for stability in an implantable infusion pump (Infusaid model 400). In this in vivo assessment, the floxuridine concentrations were determined prior to implantation in patients and again at the time of pump refills. No appreciable floxuridine loss occurred during eight courses of therapy, from 4 to 12 days in duration, in five patients. (767)

At a concentration of 5 mg/ml in sodium chloride 0.9%, floxuridine supported the growth of several microorganisms commonly implicated in nosocomial infections, including *Escherichia coli, Pseudomonas aeruginosa*, and *Candida albicans*. The arbitrary application of an extended expiration date to floxuridine solutions used in ambulatory pump systems is, therefore, highly questionable. (827)

Compatibility Information

Additive Compatibility

Drug	Mfr	Conc/L	Floxuridine Mfr	Floxuridine Conc/L	Test Soln	Remarks	Ref	C/I
Carboplatin		1 g		10 g	W	Less than 10% loss of both drugs in 7 days at 23 °C	1954	C
Cisplatin	BR	500 mg	RC	10 g	NS	13% floxuridine loss in 7 days and 18% loss in 14 days at room temperature protected from light	1386	C
Cisplatin with etoposide		200 mg 300 mg		700 mg	NS	All drugs stable for 7 days at room temperature	1379	C
Cisplatin with leucovorin calcium		200 mg 140 mg		700 mg	NS	All drugs stable for 7 days at room temperature	1379	C
Etoposide		200 mg		10 g	NS	Both drugs stable for 15 days at room temperature	1379	C
Fluorouracil		10 g		10 g	NS	Both drugs stable for 15 days at room temperature	1390	C
Leucovorin calcium	QU	30 mg	QU	1 g	NS	Physically compatible and chemically stable for 48 hr at 4 and 20 °C. No floxuridine loss and 10% leucovorin loss in 48 hr at 40 °C	1317	C
	QU	240 mg	QU	2 g	NS	Physically compatible and chemically stable for 48 hr at 4 and 20 °C. No floxuridine loss and 7% leucovorin loss in 48 hr at 40 °C	1317	C
	QU	960 mg	QU	4 g	NS	Physically compatible and chemically stable for 48 hr at 4, 20, and 40 °C	1317	C
		200 mg		10 g	NS	Both drugs stable for 15 days at room temperature protected from light	1387	C

Y-Site Injection Compatibility (1:1 Mixture)

Drug	Mfr	Conc	Floxuridine Mfr	Floxuridine Conc	Remarks	Ref	C/I
Allopurinol sodium	BW	3 mg/ml[b]	RC	3 mg/ml[b]	Tiny particles form in 1 to 4 hr	1686	I
Amifostine	USB	10 mg/ml[a]	RC	3 mg/ml[a]	Physically compatible with no change in measured turbidity or increase in particle content in 4 hr at 23 °C	1845	C
Aztreonam	SQ	40 mg/ml[a]	RC	3 mg/ml[a]	Physically compatible with no subvisual haze or particle formation in 4 hr at 23 °C	1758	C
Cefepime HCl	BMS	20 mg/ml[a]	RC	3 mg/ml[a]	Haze and tiny particles form immediately	1689	I
Etoposide phosphate	BR	5 mg/ml[a]	RC	3 mg/ml[a]	Physically compatible with no change in measured turbidity or increase in particle content in 4 hr at 23 °C	2218	C
Filgrastim	AMG	30 μg/ml[a]	RC	3 mg/ml[a]	Physically compatible with no change in measured turbidity or increase in particle content in 4 hr at 22 °C	1687	C

Y-Site Injection Compatibility (1:1 Mixture) (Cont.)

			Floxuridine				
Drug	*Mfr*	*Conc*	*Mfr*	*Conc*	*Remarks*	*Ref*	*C/I*
Fludarabine phosphate	BX	1 mg/ml[a]	RC	3 mg/ml[a]	Physically compatible for 4 hr at room temperature under fluorescent light	1439	C
Gemcitabine HCl	LI	10 mg/ml[b]	RC	3 mg/ml[b]	Physically compatible with no change in measured turbidity or increase in particle content in 4 hr at 23 °C	2226	C
Granisetron HCl	SKB	0.05 mg/ml[a]	RC	3 mg/ml[a]	Physically compatible with no change in measured turbidity or increase in particle content in 4 hr at 23 °C	2000	C
Melphalan HCl	BW	0.1 mg/ml[b]	RC	3 mg/ml[b]	Physically compatible with no change in measured turbidity or increase in particle content in 3 hr at 22 °C	1557	C
Ondansetron HCl	GL	1 mg/ml[b]	RC	3 mg/ml[a]	Physically compatible for 4 hr at 22 °C	1365	C
Paclitaxel	NCI	1.2 mg/ml[a]	RC	3 mg/ml[a]	Physically compatible with no change in measured turbidity in 4 hr at 22 °C	1556	C
Piperacillin sodium–tazobactam sodium	LE	40 + 5 mg/ml[a]	RC	3 mg/ml[a]	Physically compatible with no change in measured turbidity or increase in particle content in 4 hr at 22 °C	1688	C
Sargramostim	IMM	10 μg/ml[b]	RC	3 mg/ml[b]	Physically compatible for 4 hr at 22 °C	1436	C
Teniposide	BR	0.1 mg/ml[a]	RC	3 mg/ml[a]	Physically compatible with no subvisual haze or particle formation in 4 hr at 23 °C	1725	C
Thiotepa	IMM[c]	1 mg/ml[a]	RC	3 mg/ml[a]	Physically compatible with no change in measured turbidity or increase in particle content in 4 hr at 23 °C	1861	C
Vinorelbine tartrate	BW	1 mg/ml[b]	RC	3 mg/ml[b]	Physically compatible with no change in measured turbidity or increase in particle content in 4 hr at 22 °C	1558	C

[a]*Tested in dextrose 5% in water.*
[b]*Tested in sodium chloride 0.9%.*
[c]*Lyophilized formulation tested.*

Additional Compatibility Information

Infusion Solutions — Floxuridine is usually diluted in dextrose 5% in water or sodium chloride 0.9% for infusion. (4) At a concentration of 0.5 mg/ml in dextrose 5% in water or sodium chloride 0.9% in glass and PVC containers, floxuridine remained stable during seven days of storage at 20 and 37 °C. (108)

Floxuridine 5 to 10 mg/ml in dextrose 5% in water, sodium chloride 0.9%, or sterile water for injection has been reported to exhibit less than a 10% loss in 14 days at room temperature. (1379)

Leucovorin — The stability of leucovorin calcium (Quad) 30 to 960 mg/L admixed with floxuridine (Quad) 1 to 4 g/L in sodium chloride 0.9% was evaluated under a sequence of temperatures to simulate use conditions as intraperitoneal chemotherapy solutions. The admixtures were stored for 48 hours at 4 °C, followed by 12 hours at 20 °C, and finally followed by 12 hours at 40 °C (near-physiologic temperature). No floxuridine loss and about a 3 to 6% leucovorin calcium loss occurred during the study period. (1317)

FLUCONAZOLE
AHFS 8:12.04

Products — Fluconazole is available for intravenous infusion in 100- and 200-ml glass bottles and PVC bags in sodium chloride or dextrose diluents. Each milliliter of solution contains fluconazole 2 mg and either sodium chloride 9 mg or dextrose 56 mg. (2)

pH — From 4 to 8 in the sodium chloride diluent and from 3.5 to 6.5 in the dextrose diluent. (2)

Osmolarity — The infusion solution is iso-osmotic (2), having an osmolarity of 300 to 315 mOsm/L. (4)

Trade Name(s) — Diflucan.

Administration — Fluconazole is administered by intravenous infusion at a rate not exceeding 200 mg/hr. (2; 4)

Stability — Fluconazole injection in glass bottles or PVC bags should be stored between 5 and 30 °C or between 5 and 25 °C, respectively, and protected from freezing. Brief exposure to temperatures up to 40 °C does not adversely affect the product in PVC bags. The overwrap moisture barrier should not be removed from the PVC bags until ready for use. The solution should not be used if it is cloudy or precipitated. (2; 4)

Elastomeric Reservoir Pumps — Fluconazole (Pfizer) 2 mg/ml in sodium chloride 0.9% was evaluated for binding potential to natural rubber elastomeric reservoirs (Baxter). Less than 2% binding was found after storage for two weeks at 35 °C with gentle agitation. (2014)

Fluconazole solutions in elastomeric reservoir pumps have been stated by the pump manufacturers to be stable for the following time periods refrigerated (REF) or at room temperature (RT) (31):

Pump Reservoir(s)	Conc.	REF	RT
Homepump; Homepump Eclipse	2 mg/ml[a]	14 days	24 hr
Intermate HPC	2 mg/ml[b]	15 days	
ReadyMed	2 mg/ml[b]		7 days

[a] *Solution not specified.*
[b] *In sodium chloride 0.9%.*

Central Venous Catheter — Fluconazole (Roerig) 2 mg/ml in dextrose 5% in water was found to be compatible with the ARROWg+ard Blue Plus (Arrow International) chlorhexidine-bearing triple-lumen central catheter. HPLC analysis was used to evaluate completeness of drug delivery through the catheter and the amount of chlorhexidine removed from the internal lumens. Essentially complete delivery of the drug was found with little or no drug loss occurring. Furthermore, chlorhexidine delivered from the catheter remained at trace amounts with no substantial increase due to the delivery of the drug through the catheter. (2335)

Compatibility Information

Solution Compatibility

Fluconazole

Solution	*Mfr*	*Mfr*	*Conc/L*	*Remarks*	*Ref*	*C/I*
Dextrose 5% in water	BA[a]	PF	1 g	Fluconazole chemically stable by gas chromatography for at least 24 hr at 25 °C under fluorescent light	1676	C
Ringer's injection, lactated	BA[a]	PF	1 g	Fluconazole chemically stable by gas chromatography for at least 24 hr at 25 °C under fluorescent light	1676	C

[a] *Tested in PVC containers.*

Additive Compatibility

Fluconazole

Drug	*Mfr*	*Conc/L*	*Mfr*	*Conc/L*	*Test Soln*	*Remarks*	*Ref*	*C/I*
Acyclovir sodium	BW	5 g	PF	1 g	D5W	Visually compatible with no fluconazole loss by HPLC in 72 hr at 25 °C under fluorescent light. Acyclovir not tested	1677	C
Amikacin sulfate	BR	2.5 g	PF	1 g	D5W	Visually compatible with no fluconazole loss by HPLC in 72 hr at 25 °C under fluorescent light. Amikacin not tested	1677	C
Amphotericin B	LY	50 mg	PF	1 g	D5W	Visually compatible with no fluconazole loss by HPLC in 72 hr at 25 °C under fluorescent light. Amphotericin B not tested	1677	C

Additive Compatibility (Cont.)

Fluconazole

Drug	*Mfr*	*Conc/L*	*Mfr*	*Conc/L*	*Test Soln*	*Remarks*	*Ref*	*C/I*
Cefazolin sodium	SM	10 g	PF	1 g	D5W	Visually compatible with no fluconazole loss by HPLC in 72 hr at 25 °C under fluorescent light. Cefazolin not tested	1677	C
Ceftazidime	GL	20 g	PF	1 g	D5W	Visually compatible with no fluconazole loss by HPLC in 72 hr at 25 °C under fluorescent light. Ceftazidime not tested	1677	C
Clindamycin phosphate	AST	6 g	PF	1 g	D5W	Visually compatible with no fluconazole loss by HPLC in 72 hr at 25 °C under fluorescent light. Clindamycin not tested	1677	C
Gentamicin sulfate	SO	0.5 g	PF	1 g	D5W	Visually compatible with no fluconazole loss by HPLC in 72 hr at 25 °C under fluorescent light. Gentamicin not tested	1677	C
Heparin sodium	BA	50,000 units	PF	1 g	D5W[a]	Fluconazole chemically stable by gas chromatography for at least 24 hr at 25 °C under fluorescent light. Heparin not tested	1676	C
Meropenem	ZEN	1 and 20 g	RR	2 g	NS	Visually compatible for 4 hr at room temperature	1994	C
Metronidazole	AB	2.5 g	PF	1 g	D5W	Visually compatible with no fluconazole loss by HPLC in 72 hr at 25 °C under fluorescent light. Metronidazole not tested	1677	C
Morphine sulfate	ES	0.25 g	PF	1 g	D5W[a]	Fluconazole chemically stable by gas chromatography for at least 24 hr at 25 °C under fluorescent light. Morphine not tested	1676	C
Piperacillin sodium	LE	40 g	PF	1 g	D5W	Visually compatible with no fluconazole loss by HPLC in 72 hr at 25 °C under fluorescent light. Piperacillin not tested	1677	C
Potassium chloride	AB	10 mEq	PF	1 g	D5W[a]	Fluconazole chemically stable by gas chromatography for at least 24 hr at 25 °C under fluorescent light	1676	C
Ranitidine HCl with ondansetron HCl	GL GL	500 mg 100 mg	RR	2 g	[a]	Visually compatible with no loss of any drug by HPLC in 4 hr	1730	C
Theophylline	BA	0.4 g	PF	1 g	D5W[a]	Fluconazole chemically stable by gas chromatography for at least 72 hr at 25 °C under fluorescent light. Theophylline not tested	1676	C
Trimethoprim–sulfamethoxazole	ES	0.4 + 2 g	PF	1 g	D5W	Delayed cloudiness and precipitation. No fluconazole loss by HPLC in 72 hr at 25 °C under fluorescent light	1677	I

[a]*Tested in PVC containers.*

Y-Site Injection Compatibility (1:1 Mixture)

Fluconazole

Drug	*Mfr*	*Conc*	*Mfr*	*Conc*	*Remarks*	*Ref*	*C/I*
Acyclovir sodium	BW	10 mg/ml	RR	2 mg/ml	Physically compatible for 24 hr at 25 °C	1407	C

Y-Site Injection Compatibility (1:1 Mixture) (Cont.)

Drug	*Mfr*	*Conc*	Fluconazole *Mfr*	Fluconazole *Conc*	*Remarks*	*Ref*	*C/I*
Aldesleukin	CHI	33,800 I.U./ml[a]	RR	2 mg/ml[a]	Visually compatible with little or no loss of aldesleukin activity by bioassay	1857	C
Allopurinol sodium	BW	3 mg/ml[b]	RR	2 mg/ml	Physically compatible with no change in measured turbidity or increase in particle content in 4 hr at 22 °C	1686	C
Amifostine	USB	10 mg/ml[a]	RR	2 mg/ml	Physically compatible with no change in measured turbidity or increase in particle content in 4 hr at 23 °C	1845	C
Amikacin sulfate	BR	20 mg/ml	RR	2 mg/ml	Physically compatible for 24 hr at 25 °C	1407	C
Aminophylline	ES	25 mg/ml	RR	2 mg/ml	Physically compatible for 24 hr at 25 °C	1407	C
	AMR	0.8 and 1.5 mg/ml[c]	PF	0.5 and 1.5 mg/ml[c]	Visually compatible with no loss of either drug by HPLC in 3 hr at 24 °C	1626	C
Amphotericin B	SQ	5 mg/ml	RR	2 mg/ml	Cloudiness and yellow precipitate develop	1407	I
Amphotericin B cholesteryl sulfate complex	SEQ	0.83 mg/ml[a]	RR	2 mg/ml	Gross precipitate forms	2117	I
Ampicillin sodium	WY	20 mg/ml	RR	2 mg/ml	Cloudiness develops	1407	I
Ampicillin sodium–sulbactam sodium	PF	40 + 20 mg/ml	RR	2 mg/ml	Physically compatible for 24 hr at 25 °C	1407	C
Aztreonam	SQ	40 mg/ml	RR	2 mg/ml	Physically compatible for 24 hr at 25 °C	1407	C
	SQ	40 mg/ml[a]	RR	2 mg/ml	Physically compatible with no subvisual haze or particle formation in 4 hr at 23 °C	1758	C
Benztropine mesylate	MSD	1 mg/ml	RR	2 mg/ml	Physically compatible for 24 hr at 25 °C	1407	C
Calcium gluconate	ES	100 mg/ml	RR	2 mg/ml	Cloudiness develops	1407	I
Cefazolin sodium	LY	40 mg/ml	RR	2 mg/ml	Physically compatible for 24 hr at 25 °C	1407	C
Cefepime HCl	BMS	20 mg/ml[a]	RR	2 mg/ml	Physically compatible with no change in measured turbidity or increase in particle content in 4 hr at 22 °C	1689	C
Cefotaxime sodium	HO	20 mg/ml	RR	2 mg/ml	Cloudiness and amber color develop	1407	I
Cefotetan disodium	STU	40 mg/ml	RR	2 mg/ml	Physically compatible for 24 hr at 25 °C	1407	C
Cefoxitin sodium	MSD	40 mg/ml	RR	2 mg/ml	Physically compatible for 24 hr at 25 °C	1407	C
Cefpirome sulfate	HO	50 mg/ml[d]	RR	2 mg/ml	Visually and microscopically compatible with little or no cefpirome loss and 8% or less fluconazole loss by HPLC in 8 hr at 23 °C	2044	C
Ceftazidime	GL	20 mg/ml	RR	2 mg/ml	Immediate precipitation	1407	I
Ceftriaxone sodium	RC	40 mg/ml	RR	2 mg/ml	Immediate precipitation	1407	I
Cefuroxime sodium	GL	30 mg/ml	RR	2 mg/ml	Immediate precipitation	1407	I
Chloramphenicol sodium succinate	PD	20 mg/ml	RR	2 mg/ml	Gas production	1407	I
Chlorpromazine HCl	ES	25 mg/ml	RR	2 mg/ml	Physically compatible for 24 hr at 25 °C	1407	C
Cimetidine HCl	SKF	150 mg/ml	RR	2 mg/ml	Physically compatible for 24 hr at 25 °C	1407	C
	SKB	1 and 2 mg/ml[c]	RR	2 mg/ml	Visually compatible for 24 hr at 28 °C	1760	C

Y-Site Injection Compatibility (1:1 Mixture) (Cont.)

			Fluconazole				
Drug	*Mfr*	*Conc*	*Mfr*	*Conc*	*Remarks*	*Ref*	*C/I*
Cisatracurium besylate	GW	0.1, 2, 5 mg/ml[a]	RR	2 mg/ml	Physically compatible with no change in measured turbidity or increase in particle content in 4 hr at 23 °C	2074	C
Clindamycin phosphate	AB	24 mg/ml	RR	2 mg/ml	Immediate precipitation	1407	I
Dexamethasone sodium phosphate	ES	4 mg/ml	RR	2 mg/ml	Physically compatible for 24 hr at 25 °C	1407	C
Diazepam	ES	5 mg/ml	RR	2 mg/ml	Immediate precipitation	1407	I
Digoxin	BW	0.25 mg/ml	RR	2 mg/ml	Gas production	1407	I
Diltiazem HCl	MMD	5 mg/ml	RR	2 mg/ml	Visually compatible	1807	C
Diphenhydramine HCl	ES	50 mg/ml	RR	2 mg/ml	Physically compatible for 24 hr at 25 °C	1407	C
Dobutamine HCl	LI	2 mg/ml[a]	RR	2 mg/ml	Visually compatible for 24 hr at 28 °C under fluorescent light	1760	C
Docetaxel	RPR	0.9 mg/ml[a]	RR	2 mg/ml	Physically compatible with no change in measured turbidity or increase in particle content in 4 hr at 23 °C	2224	C
Dopamine HCl	AMR	1.6 mg/ml[a]	RR	2 mg/ml	Visually compatible for 24 hr at 28 °C under fluorescent light	1760	C
Doxorubicin HCl liposome injection	SEQ	0.4 mg/ml[a]	RR	2 mg/ml	Physically compatible with little or no change in measured turbidity and no increase in particle content in 4 hr at 23 °C	2087	C
Droperidol	DU	2.5 mg/ml	RR	2 mg/ml	Physically compatible for 24 hr at 25 °C	1407	C
Erythromycin lactobionate	LY	20 mg/ml	RR	2 mg/ml	Immediate precipitation	1407	I
Etoposide phosphate	BR	5 mg/ml[a]	RR	2 mg/ml	Physically compatible with no change in measured turbidity or increase in particle content in 4 hr at 23 °C	2218	C
Famotidine	MSD	10 mg/ml	RR	2 mg/ml	Physically compatible for 24 hr at 25 °C	1407	C
	ME	2 mg/ml[b]		2 mg/ml[a]	Visually compatible for 4 hr at 22 °C	1936	C
Filgrastim	AMG	30 μg/ml[a]	RR	2 mg/ml	Physically compatible with no change in measured turbidity or increase in particle content in 4 hr at 22 °C	1687	C
	AMG	10[e] and 40[a] μg/ml	RR	2 mg/ml[a]	Visually compatible with little or no loss of filgrastim activity by bioassay and fluconazole by HPLC in 4 hr at 25 °C	2060	C
Fludarabine phosphate	BX	1 mg/ml[a]	RR	2 mg/ml	Physically compatible for 4 hr at room temperature under fluorescent light	1439	C
Foscarnet sodium	AST	24 mg/ml	RR	2 mg/ml	Physically compatible for 24 hr at 25 °C	1407	C
Furosemide	ES	10 mg/ml	RR	2 mg/ml	Precipitate forms	1407	I
Ganciclovir sodium	SY	50 mg/ml	RR	2 mg/ml	Physically compatible for 24 hr at 25 °C	1407	C
Gatifloxacin	BMS	2 mg/ml[a]	RR	2 mg/ml[a]	Physically compatible with no change in measured haze or increase in particle content in 4 hr at 23 °C	2234	C
Gemcitabine HCl	LI	10 mg/ml[b]	RR	2 mg/ml	Physically compatible with no change in measured turbidity or increase in particle content in 4 hr at 23 °C	2226	C
Gentamicin sulfate	ES	4 mg/ml	RR	2 mg/ml	Physically compatible for 24 hr at 25 °C	1407	C

Y-Site Injection Compatibility (1:1 Mixture) (Cont.)

Drug	Mfr	Conc	Fluconazole Mfr	Fluconazole Conc	Remarks	Ref	C/I
Granisetron HCl	SKB	0.05 mg/ml[a]	PF	2 mg/ml	Physically compatible with no change in measured turbidity or increase in particle content in 4 hr at 23 °C	2000	C
Haloperidol lactate	MN	5 mg/ml	RR	2 mg/ml	Precipitate forms	1407	I
Heparin sodium	LY	1000 units/ml	RR	2 mg/ml	Physically compatible for 24 hr at 25 °C	1407	C
	TR	50 units/ml	PF	2 mg/ml	Visually compatible for 4 hr at 25 °C	1793	C
Hetastarch in lactated electrolyte injection (Hextend)	AB	6%	PF	2 mg/ml	Physically compatible with no change in measured turbidity or increase in particle content in 4 hr at 23 °C	2339	C
Hydrocortisone sodium phosphate	MSD	50 mg/ml	RR	2 mg/ml	Physically compatible for 24 hr at 25 °C	1407	C
Hydroxyzine HCl	ES	50 mg/ml	RR	2 mg/ml	Cloudiness develops	1407	I
Imipenem–cilastatin sodium	MSD	10 mg/ml	RR	2 mg/ml	Immediate precipitation	1407	I
Immune globulin intravenous	CU	50 mg/ml	RR	2 mg/ml	Physically compatible for 24 hr at 25 °C	1407	C
Leucovorin calcium	LE	10 mg/ml	RR	2 mg/ml	Physically compatible for 24 hr at 25 °C	1407	C
Linezolid	PHU	2 mg/ml	RR	2 mg/ml	Physically compatible with no change in measured turbidity or increase in particle content in 4 hr at 23 °C	2264	C
Lorazepam	WY	0.33 mg/ml[b]	PF	2 mg/ml	Visually compatible for 24 hr at 22 °C	1855	C
Melphalan HCl	BW	0.1 mg/ml[b]	RR	2 mg/ml	Physically compatible with no change in measured turbidity or increase in particle content in 3 hr at 22 °C	1557	C
Meperidine HCl	AB	10 mg/ml	RR	2 mg/ml	Physically compatible for 4 hr at 25 °C	1397	C
Meropenem	ZEN	1 and 50 mg/ml[b]	RR	2 mg/ml	Visually compatible for 4 hr at room temperature	1994	C
Metoclopramide HCl	RB	5 mg/ml	RR	2 mg/ml	Physically compatible for 24 hr at 25 °C	1407	C
Metronidazole	AB	5 mg/ml	RR	2 mg/ml	Physically compatible for 24 hr at 25 °C	1407	C
Midazolam HCl	RC	5 mg/ml	RR	2 mg/ml	Physically compatible for 24 hr at 25 °C	1407	C
	RC	5 mg/ml	PF	2 mg/ml	Visually compatible for 24 hr at 22 °C	1855	C
Morphine sulfate	IMS	25 mg/ml	RR	2 mg/ml	Physically compatible for 24 hr at 25 °C	1407	C
	AB	1 mg/ml	RR	2 mg/ml	Physically compatible for 4 hr at 25 °C	1397	C
Nafcillin sodium	BR	20 mg/ml	RR	2 mg/ml	Physically compatible for 24 hr at 25 °C	1407	C
Nitroglycerin	AMR	0.2 mg/ml[a]	RR	2 mg/ml	Visually compatible for 24 hr at 28 °C under fluorescent light	1760	C
Ondansetron HCl	GL	1 mg/ml[b]	PF	2 mg/ml	Physically compatible for 4 hr at 22 °C	1365	C
	GL	0.03 and 0.3 mg/ml[a]	RR	2 mg/ml[b]	Visually compatible with little or no loss of either drug by HPLC in 4 hr at 25 °C under fluorescent light	1732	C
	GL	0.03, 0.1, and 0.3 mg/ml[a,b]	RR	2 mg/ml	Visually compatible with little or no ondansetron or fluconazole loss by HPLC in 4 hr and 5% or less loss of both drugs in 12 hr at room temperature	2168	C
Oxacillin sodium	BE	40 mg/ml	RR	2 mg/ml	Physically compatible for 24 hr at 25 °C	1407	C
Paclitaxel	NCI	1.2 mg/ml[a]	RR	2 mg/ml	Physically compatible with no change in measured turbidity in 4 hr at 22 °C	1556	C
	BR	0.3 and 1.2 mg/ml[a]	PF	2 mg/ml	Visually compatible with no loss of either drug by HPLC in 4 hr at 23 °C	1790	C

Y-Site Injection Compatibility (1:1 Mixture) (Cont.)

Fluconazole

Drug	*Mfr*	*Conc*	*Mfr*	*Conc*	*Remarks*	*Ref*	*C/I*
Pancuronium bromide	GNS	0.5 mg/ml[b]	RR	2 mg/ml	Visually compatible for 24 hr at 28 °C under fluorescent light	1760	**C**
Penicillin G potassium	RR	100,000 units/ml	RR	2 mg/ml	Physically compatible for 24 hr at 25 °C	1407	**C**
Pentamidine isethionate	LY	6 mg/ml	RR	2 mg/ml	Cloudiness develops	1407	**I**
Phenytoin sodium	PD	50 mg/ml	RR	2 mg/ml	Physically compatible for 24 hr at 25 °C	1407	**C**
Piperacillin sodium	LE	80 mg/ml	RR	2 mg/ml	Viscous gel-like substance forms	1407	**I**
Piperacillin sodium–tazobactam sodium	LE	40 + 5 mg/ml[a]	RR	2 mg/ml	Physically compatible with no change in measured turbidity or increase in particle content in 4 hr at 22 °C	1688	**C**
Prochlorperazine edisylate	SKF	5 mg/ml	RR	2 mg/ml	Physically compatible for 24 hr at 25 °C	1407	**C**
Promethazine HCl	ES	50 mg/ml	RR	2 mg/ml	Physically compatible for 24 hr at 25 °C	1407	**C**
Propofol	ZEN	10 mg/ml	PF	2 mg/ml[a]	Physically compatible for 1 hr at 23 °C with no increase in particle content	2066	**C**
Ranitidine HCl	GL	0.5 and 2 mg/ml[a]	RR	2 mg/ml[b]	Visually compatible with no loss of either drug by HPLC in 4 hr	1730	**C**
Remifentanil HCl	GW	0.025 and 0.25 mg/ml[b]	RR	2 mg/ml	Physically compatible with no change in measured turbidity or increase in particle content in 4 hr at 23 °C	2075	**C**
Sargramostim	IMM	10 μg/ml[b]	RR	2 mg/ml	Physically compatible for 4 hr at 22 °C	1436	**C**
Tacrolimus	FUJ	1 mg/ml[b]	RR	2 mg/ml[a]	Visually compatible for 24 hr at 25 °C	1630	**C**
	FUJ	10 and 40 μg/ml[b]	PF	1 mg/ml[b]	Visually compatible with no loss of either drug by HPLC in 3 hr at 24 °C under fluorescent light	2225	**C**
	FUJ	50 and 200 μg/2.5 ml[b]	PF	15 mg/7.5 ml[b]	Mixed in the amounts indicated.[i] Visually compatible with no loss of either drug by HPLC in 3 hr at 24 °C under fluorescent light	2225	**C**
	FUJ	5 μg/ml[b]	PF	0.5 mg/ml ml[b]	Visually compatible with no loss of either drug in 3 hr at 24 °C under fluorescent light	2236	**C**
	FUJ	5 μg/ml[b]	PF	1.5 mg/ml ml[b]	Visually compatible with no loss of either drug in 3 hr at 24 °C under fluorescent light	2236	**C**
	FUJ	20 μg/ml[b]	PF	0.5 mg/ml ml[b]	Visually compatible with no loss of either drug in 3 hr at 24 °C under fluorescent light	2236	**C**
	FUJ	20 μg/ml[b]	PF	1.5 mg/ml ml[b]	Visually compatible with no loss of either drug in 3 hr at 24 °C under fluorescent light	2236	**C**
Teniposide	BR	0.1 mg/ml[a]	RR	2 mg/ml	Physically compatible with no subvisual haze or particle formation in 4 hr at 23 °C	1725	**C**
Theophylline	AMR	1.6 mg/ml[a]	RR	2 mg/ml	Visually compatible for 24 hr at 28 °C under fluorescent light	1760	**C**
	TR	4 mg/ml	PF	2 mg/ml	Visually compatible for 6 hr at 25 °C	1793	**C**
Thiotepa	IMM[f]	1 mg/ml[a]	RR	2 mg/ml	Physically compatible with no change in measured turbidity or increase in particle content in 4 hr at 23 °C	1861	**C**

Y-Site Injection Compatibility (1:1 Mixture) (Cont.)

Fluconazole

Drug	*Mfr*	*Conc*	*Mfr*	*Conc*	*Remarks*	*Ref*	*C/I*
Ticarcillin disodium	BE	15 mg/ml	RR	2 mg/ml	Viscous gel-like substance forms	1407	I
Ticarcillin disodium–clavulanate potassium	BE	60 mg/ml	RR	2 mg/ml	Physically compatible for 24 hr at 25 °C	1407	C
Tobramycin sulfate	LI	40 mg/ml	RR	2 mg/ml	Physically compatible for 24 hr at 25 °C	1407	C
TNA #218 to #226[g]			PF	2 mg/ml	Visually compatible with no precipitate or emulsion damage apparent in 4 hr at 23 °C	2215	C
TPN #146[g]		[h]	PF	0.5 and 1.75 mg/ml[h]	Visually compatible with no fluconazole loss by HPLC in 2 hr at 24 °C under fluorescent light. Amino acid concentrations by HPLC greater than 93%	1554	C
TPN #147 and #148[g]		[h]	PF	0.5 and 1.75 mg/ml[h]	Visually compatible with no fluconazole loss by HPLC in 2 hr at 24 °C under fluorescent light. Amino acids not tested	1554	C
TPN #212 to #215[g]			RR	2 mg/ml	Physically compatible with no change in measured turbidity or increase in particle content in 4 hr at 23 °C	2109	C
Trimethoprim–sulfamethoxazole	BW	16 + 80 mg/ml	RR	2 mg/ml	Viscous gel-like substance forms	1407	I
Vancomycin HCl	LY	20 mg/ml	RR	2 mg/ml	Physically compatible for 24 hr at 25 °C	1407	C
Vecuronium bromide	OR	1 mg/ml[a]	RR	2 mg/ml	Visually compatible for 24 hr at 28 °C under fluorescent light	1760	C
Vinorelbine tartrate	BW	1 mg/ml[b]	RR	2 mg/ml	Physically compatible with no change in measured turbidity or increase in particle content in 4 hr at 22 °C	1558	C
Zidovudine	BW	10 mg/ml	RR	2 mg/ml	Physically compatible for 24 hr at 25 °C	1407	C

[a]*Tested in dextrose 5% in water.*
[b]*Tested in sodium chloride 0.9%.*
[c]*Tested in both dextrose 5% in water and sodium chloride 0.9%.*
[d]*Tested in dextrose 5% in water, Ringer's injection, lactated, sodium chloride 0.45%, and sodium chloride 0.9%.*
[e]*Tested in dextrose 5% in water with albumin human 2 mg/ml.*
[f]*Lyophilized formulation tested.*
[g]*Refer to Appendix I for the composition of parenteral nutrition solutions. TNA indicates a 3-in-1 admixture, and TPN indicates a 2-in-1 admixture.*
[h]*Varying volumes to simulate varying administration rates.*
[i]*Final concentrations were 1.5 mg/ml of fluconazole and 5 and 20 μg/ml of tacrolimus.*

Additional Compatibility Information

The manufacturer recommends that no supplementary medications be added to fluconazole injection. (2)

FLUDARABINE PHOSPHATE
AHFS 10:00

Products — Fludarabine phosphate is supplied as a lyophilized product in 6-ml vials containing 50 mg of drug with mannitol 50 mg and sodium hydroxide for pH adjustment. Reconstitute with 2 ml of sterile water for injection to yield a 25-mg/ml concentration. (2)

pH — From 7.2 to 8.2. (2)

Osmolality — Fludarabine phosphate 25 mg/ml in sterile water for injection has an osmolality of 352 mOsm/kg. (1689)

Density — Fludarabine phosphate reconstituted with sterile water for injection to a concentration of 25 mg/ml has a solution density of 1.01 g/ml. (2041; 2248)

Trade Name(s) — Fludara.

Administration — Fludarabine phosphate is administered by intravenous infusion over 30 minutes in 100 or 125 ml of dextrose 5% in water or sodium chloride 0.9%. (2; 4) The drug also has been administered by rapid intravenous injection and continuous infusion, although the risk of toxicity may be increased. (4)

Stability — Intact vials should be stored under refrigeration. The manufacturer recommends use of the reconstituted solution within eight hours because it does not contain an antibacterial preservative. (2) Nevertheless, the drug is chemically stable in solution, exhibiting less than 2% decomposition in 16 days when stored at room temperature and exposed to normal laboratory light. (234)

pH Effects — Fludarabine phosphate is chemically stable in aqueous solution at pH 4.5 to 8. The pH of optimum stability is approximately 7.6. (234)

Sorption — Fludarabine phosphate 0.04 mg/ml in dextrose 5% in water or sodium chloride 0.9% was equally stable in either glass or PVC containers, exhibiting no loss due to sorption during 48 hours at room temperature or under refrigeration. (234)

Compatibility Information

Y-Site Injection Compatibility (1:1 Mixture)

			Fludarabine phosphate				
Drug	*Mfr*	*Conc*	*Mfr*	*Conc*	*Remarks*	*Ref*	*C/I*
Acyclovir sodium	BW	7 mg/ml[a]	BX	1 mg/ml[a]	Darker color visible with high-intensity light within 4 hr	1439	I
Allopurinol sodium	BW	3 mg/ml[b]	BX	1 mg/ml[b]	Physically compatible with no change in measured turbidity or increase in particle content in 4 hr at 22 °C	1686	C
Amifostine	USB	10 mg/ml[a]	BX	1 mg/ml[a]	Physically compatible with no change in measured turbidity or increase in particle content in 4 hr at 23 °C	1845	C
Amikacin sulfate	BR	5 mg/ml[a]	BX	1 mg/ml[a]	Physically compatible for 4 hr at room temperature under fluorescent light	1439	C
Aminophylline	ES	2.5 mg/ml[a]	BX	1 mg/ml[a]	Physically compatible for 4 hr at room temperature under fluorescent light	1439	C
Amphotericin B	SQ	0.6 mg/ml[a]	BX	1 mg/ml[a]	Small amount of particulate matter develops in 4 hr at room temperature	1439	I
Ampicillin sodium	BR	20 mg/ml[b]	BX	1 mg/ml[a]	Physically compatible for 4 hr at room temperature under fluorescent light	1439	C
Ampicillin sodium–sulbactam sodium	RR	20 + 10 mg/ml[b]	BX	1 mg/ml[a]	Physically compatible for 4 hr at room temperature under fluorescent light	1439	C
Amsacrine	NCI	1 mg/ml[a]	BX	1 mg/ml[a]	Physically compatible for 4 hr at room temperature under fluorescent light	1439	C
Aztreonam	SQ	40 mg/ml[a]	BX	1 mg/ml[a]	Physically compatible for 4 hr at room temperature under fluorescent light	1439	C
	SQ	40 mg/ml[a]	BX	1 mg/ml[a]	Physically compatible with no subvisual haze or particle formation in 4 hr at 23 °C	1758	C
Bleomycin sulfate	BR	1 unit/ml[b]	BX	1 mg/ml[a]	Physically compatible for 4 hr at room temperature under fluorescent light	1439	C

Y-Site Injection Compatibility (1:1 Mixture) (Cont.)

Drug	Mfr	Conc	Mfr	Conc	Remarks	Ref	C/I
			Fludarabine phosphate				
Butorphanol tartrate	BR	0.04 mg/ml[a]	BX	1 mg/ml[a]	Physically compatible for 4 hr at room temperature under fluorescent light	1439	C
Carboplatin	BR	5 mg/ml[a]	BX	1 mg/ml[a]	Physically compatible for 4 hr at room temperature under fluorescent light	1439	C
Carmustine	BR	1.5 mg/ml[a]	BX	1 mg/ml[a]	Physically compatible for 4 hr at room temperature under fluorescent light	1439	C
Cefazolin sodium	LEM	20 mg/ml[a]	BX	1 mg/ml[a]	Physically compatible for 4 hr at room temperature under fluorescent light	1439	C
Cefepime HCl	BMS	20 mg/ml[a]	BX	1 mg/ml[a]	Physically compatible with no change in measured turbidity or increase in particle content in 4 hr at 22 °C	1689	C
Cefoperazone sodium	RR	40 mg/ml[a]	BX	1 mg/ml[a]	Physically compatible for 4 hr at room temperature under fluorescent light	1439	C
Cefotaxime sodium	HO	20 mg/ml[a]	BX	1 mg/ml[a]	Physically compatible for 4 hr at room temperature under fluorescent light	1439	C
Cefotetan disodium	STU	20 mg/ml[a]	BX	1 mg/ml[a]	Physically compatible for 4 hr at room temperature under fluorescent light	1439	C
Ceftazidime	GL[d]	40 mg/ml[a]	BX	1 mg/ml[a]	Physically compatible for 4 hr at room temperature under fluorescent light	1439	C
Ceftizoxime sodium	SKF	20 mg/ml[a]	BX	1 mg/ml[a]	Physically compatible for 4 hr at room temperature under fluorescent light	1439	C
Ceftriaxone sodium	RC	20 mg/ml[a]	BX	1 mg/ml[a]	Physically compatible for 4 hr at room temperature under fluorescent light	1439	C
Cefuroxime sodium	GL	30 mg/ml[a]	BX	1 mg/ml[a]	Physically compatible for 4 hr at room temperature under fluorescent light	1439	C
Chlorpromazine HCl	ES	2 mg/ml[a]	BX	1 mg/ml[a]	Initial light haze intensifies within 30 min	1439	I
Cimetidine HCl	SKF	12 mg/ml[a]	BX	1 mg/ml[a]	Physically compatible for 4 hr at room temperature under fluorescent light	1439	C
Cisplatin	BR	1 mg/ml	BX	1 mg/ml[a]	Physically compatible for 4 hr at room temperature under fluorescent light	1439	C
Clindamycin phosphate	LY	10 mg/ml[a]	BX	1 mg/ml[a]	Physically compatible for 4 hr at room temperature under fluorescent light	1439	C
Cyclophosphamide	MJ	10 mg/ml[a]	BX	1 mg/ml[a]	Physically compatible for 4 hr at room temperature under fluorescent light	1439	C
Cytarabine	UP	50 mg/ml	BX	1 mg/ml[a]	Physically compatible for 4 hr at room temperature under fluorescent light	1439	C
Dacarbazine	MI	4 mg/ml[a]	BX	1 mg/ml[a]	Physically compatible for 4 hr at room temperature under fluorescent light	1439	C
Dactinomycin	MSD	0.01 mg/ml[a]	BX	1 mg/ml[a]	Physically compatible for 4 hr at room temperature under fluorescent light	1439	C
Daunorubicin HCl	WY	2 mg/ml[a]	BX	1 mg/ml[a]	Slight haze, visible with high-intensity light, forms within 4 hr at room temperature	1439	I
Dexamethasone sodium phosphate	MSD	1 mg/ml[a]	BX	1 mg/ml[a]	Physically compatible for 4 hr at room temperature under fluorescent light	1439	C

Y-Site Injection Compatibility (1:1 Mixture) (Cont.)

Drug	Mfr	Conc	Fludarabine phosphate Mfr	Fludarabine phosphate Conc	Remarks	Ref	C/I
Diphenhydramine HCl	WY	2 mg/ml[a]	BX	1 mg/ml[a]	Physically compatible for 4 hr at room temperature under fluorescent light	1439	C
Doxorubicin HCl	CET	2 mg/ml	BX	1 mg/ml[a]	Physically compatible for 4 hr at room temperature under fluorescent light	1439	C
Doxycycline hyclate	ES	1 mg/ml[a]	BX	1 mg/ml[a]	Physically compatible for 4 hr at room temperature under fluorescent light	1439	C
Droperidol	JA	0.4 mg/ml[a]	BX	1 mg/ml[a]	Physically compatible for 4 hr at room temperature under fluorescent light	1439	C
Etoposide	BR	0.4 mg/ml[a]	BX	1 mg/ml[a]	Physically compatible for 4 hr at room temperature under fluorescent light	1439	C
Etoposide phosphate	BR	5 mg/ml[a]	BX	1 mg/ml[a]	Physically compatible with no change in measured turbidity or increase in particle content in 4 hr at 23 °C	2218	C
Famotidine	MSD	2 mg/ml[a]	BX	1 mg/ml[a]	Physically compatible for 4 hr at room temperature under fluorescent light	1439	C
Filgrastim	AMG	30 μg/ml[a]	BX	1 mg/ml[a]	Physically compatible with no change in measured turbidity or increase in particle content in 4 hr at 22 °C	1687	C
Floxuridine	RC	3 mg/ml[a]	BX	1 mg/ml[a]	Physically compatible for 4 hr at room temperature under fluorescent light	1439	C
Fluconazole	RR	2 mg/ml	BX	1 mg/ml[a]	Physically compatible for 4 hr at room temperature under fluorescent light	1439	C
Fluorouracil	LY	16 mg/ml[a]	BX	1 mg/ml[a]	Physically compatible for 4 hr at room temperature under fluorescent light	1439	C
Furosemide	AB	3 mg/ml[a]	BX	1 mg/ml[a]	Physically compatible for 4 hr at room temperature under fluorescent light	1439	C
Ganciclovir sodium	SY	20 mg/ml[a]	BX	1 mg/ml[a]	Darker color forms within 4 hr	1439	I
Gemcitabine HCl	LI	10 mg/ml[b]	BX	1 mg/ml[b]	Physically compatible with no change in measured turbidity or increase in particle content in 4 hr at 23 °C	2226	C
Gentamicin sulfate	ES	5 mg/ml[a]	BX	1 mg/ml[a]	Physically compatible for 4 hr at room temperature under fluorescent light	1439	C
Granisetron HCl	SKB	0.05 mg/ml[a]	BX	1 mg/ml[a]	Physically compatible with no change in measured turbidity or increase in particle content in 4 hr at 23 °C	2000	C
Haloperidol lactate	MN	0.2 mg/ml[a]	BX	1 mg/ml[a]	Physically compatible for 4 hr at room temperature under fluorescent light	1439	C
Heparin sodium	SO, WY	40[a], 100, 1000 units/ml	BX	1 mg/ml[a]	Physically compatible for 4 hr at room temperature under fluorescent light	1439	C
Hydrocortisone sodium phosphate	MSD	1 mg/ml[a]	BX	1 mg/ml[a]	Physically compatible for 4 hr at room temperature under fluorescent light	1439	C
Hydrocortisone sodium succinate	UP	1 mg/ml[a]	BX	1 mg/ml[a]	Physically compatible for 4 hr at room temperature under fluorescent light	1439	C
Hydromorphone HCl	KN	0.5 mg/ml[a]	BX	1 mg/ml[a]	Physically compatible for 4 hr at room temperature under fluorescent light	1439	C

Y-Site Injection Compatibility (1:1 Mixture) (Cont.)

Drug	Mfr	Conc	Fludarabine phosphate Mfr	Fludarabine phosphate Conc	Remarks	Ref	C/I
Hydroxyzine HCl	WI	4 mg/ml[a]	BX	1 mg/ml[a]	Slight haze, visible with high-intensity light, forms immediately	1439	I
Ifosfamide	MJ	25 mg/ml[a]	BX	1 mg/ml[a]	Physically compatible for 4 hr at room temperature under fluorescent light	1439	C
Imipenem–cilastatin sodium	MSD	5 mg/ml[b]	BX	1 mg/ml[a]	Physically compatible for 4 hr at room temperature under fluorescent light	1439	C
Lorazepam	WY	0.1 mg/ml[a]	BX	1 mg/ml[a]	Physically compatible for 4 hr at room temperature under fluorescent light	1439	C
Magnesium sulfate	SO	100 mg/ml[a]	BX	1 mg/ml[a]	Physically compatible for 4 hr at room temperature under fluorescent light	1439	C
Mannitol	BA	150 mg/ml	BX	1 mg/ml[a]	Physically compatible for 4 hr at room temperature under fluorescent light	1439	C
Mechlorethamine HCl	MSD	1 mg/ml	BX	1 mg/ml[a]	Physically compatible for 4 hr at room temperature under fluorescent light	1439	C
Melphalan HCl	BW	0.1 mg/ml[b]	BX	1 mg/ml[b]	Physically compatible with no change in measured turbidity or increase in particle content in 3 hr at 22 °C	1557	C
Meperidine HCl	WI	4 mg/ml[a]	BX	1 mg/ml[a]	Physically compatible for 4 hr at room temperature under fluorescent light	1439	C
Mesna	BR	10 mg/ml[a]	BX	1 mg/ml[a]	Physically compatible for 4 hr at room temperature under fluorescent light	1439	C
Methotrexate sodium	CET	15 mg/ml[a]	BX	1 mg/ml[a]	Physically compatible for 4 hr at room temperature under fluorescent light	1439	C
Methylprednisolone sodium succinate	UP	5 mg/ml[a]	BX	1 mg/ml[a]	Physically compatible for 4 hr at room temperature under fluorescent light	1439	C
Metoclopramide HCl	DU	5 mg/ml	BX	1 mg/ml[a]	Physically compatible for 4 hr at room temperature under fluorescent light	1439	C
Minocycline HCl	LE	0.2 mg/ml[a]	BX	1 mg/ml[a]	Physically compatible for 4 hr at room temperature under fluorescent light	1439	C
Mitoxantrone HCl	LE	0.5 mg/ml[a]	BX	1 mg/ml[a]	Physically compatible for 4 hr at room temperature under fluorescent light	1439	C
Morphine sulfate	WI	1 mg/ml[a]	BX	1 mg/ml[a]	Physically compatible for 4 hr at room temperature under fluorescent light	1439	C
Multivitamins	ROR	0.01 ml/ml[a]	BX	1 mg/ml[a]	Physically compatible for 4 hr at room temperature under fluorescent light	1439	C
Nalbuphine HCl	DU	10 mg/ml	BX	1 mg/ml[a]	Physically compatible for 4 hr at room temperature under fluorescent light	1439	C
Netilmicin sulfate	SC	5 mg/ml[a]	BX	1 mg/ml[a]	Physically compatible for 4 hr at room temperature under fluorescent light	1439	C
Ondansetron HCl	GL	0.5 mg/ml[a]	BX	1 mg/ml[a]	Physically compatible for 4 hr at room temperature under fluorescent light	1439	C
Pentostatin	NCI	0.4 mg/ml[b]	BX	1 mg/ml[a]	Physically compatible for 4 hr at room temperature under fluorescent light	1439	C
Piperacillin sodium	LE	40 mg/ml[a]	BX	1 mg/ml[a]	Physically compatible for 4 hr at room temperature under fluorescent light	1439	C

Y-Site Injection Compatibility (1:1 Mixture) (Cont.)

Fludarabine phosphate

Drug	*Mfr*	*Conc*	*Mfr*	*Conc*	*Remarks*	*Ref*	*C/I*
Piperacillin sodium–tazobactam sodium	LE	40 + 5 mg/ml[a]	BX	1 mg/ml[a]	Physically compatible with no change in measured turbidity or increase in particle content in 4 hr at 22 °C	1688	C
Potassium chloride	AB	0.1 mEq/ml[a]	BX	1 mg/ml[a]	Physically compatible for 4 hr at room temperature under fluorescent light	1439	C
Prochlorperazine edisylate	WY	0.5 mg/ml[a]	BX	1 mg/ml[a]	Slight haze forms within 30 min	1439	I
Promethazine HCl	WY	2 mg/ml[a]	BX	1 mg/ml[a]	Physically compatible for 4 hr at room temperature under fluorescent light	1439	C
Ranitidine HCl	GL	2 mg/ml[a]	BX	1 mg/ml[a]	Physically compatible for 4 hr at room temperature under fluorescent light	1439	C
Sodium bicarbonate	AB	1 mEq/ml	BX	1 mg/ml[a]	Physically compatible for 4 hr at room temperature under fluorescent light	1439	C
Teniposide	BR	0.1 mg/ml[a]	BX	1 mg/ml[a]	Physically compatible with no subvisual haze or particle formation in 4 hr at 23 °C	1725	C
Thiotepa	IMM[c]	1 mg/ml[a]	BX	1 mg/ml[a]	Physically compatible with no change in measured turbidity or increase in particle content in 4 hr at 23 °C	1861	C
Ticarcillin disodium	BE	30 mg/ml[a]	BX	1 mg/ml[a]	Physically compatible for 4 hr at room temperature under fluorescent light	1439	C
Ticarcillin disodium–clavulanate potassium	BE	31 mg/ml[a]	BX	1 mg/ml[a]	Physically compatible for 4 hr at room temperature under fluorescent light	1439	C
Tobramycin sulfate	LI	5 mg/ml[a]	BX	1 mg/ml[a]	Physically compatible for 4 hr at room temperature under fluorescent light	1439	C
Trimethoprim–sulfamethoxazole	ES	0.8 + 4 mg/ml[a]	BX	1 mg/ml[a]	Physically compatible for 4 hr at room temperature under fluorescent light	1439	C
Vancomycin HCl	LI	10 mg/ml[a]	BX	1 mg/ml[a]	Physically compatible for 4 hr at room temperature under fluorescent light	1439	C
Vinblastine sulfate	LY	0.12 mg/ml[a]	BX	1 mg/ml[a]	Physically compatible for 4 hr at room temperature under fluorescent light	1439	C
Vincristine sulfate	LY	1 mg/ml	BX	1 mg/ml[a]	Physically compatible for 4 hr at room temperature under fluorescent light	1439	C
Vinorelbine tartrate	BW	1 mg/ml[b]	BX	1 mg/ml[b]	Physically compatible with no change in measured turbidity or increase in particle content in 4 hr at 22 °C	1558	C
Zidovudine	BW	4 mg/ml[a]	BX	1 mg/ml[a]	Physically compatible for 4 hr at room temperature under fluorescent light	1439	C

[a] *Tested in dextrose 5% in water.*
[b] *Tested in sodium chloride 0.9%.*
[c] *Lyophilized formulation tested.*
[d] *Sodium carbonate–containing formulation tested.*

Additional Compatibility Information

Infusion Solutions — The manufacturer recommends diluting the dose in 100 to 125 ml of dextrose 5% in water or sodium chloride 0.9%. (2) At a concentration of 1 mg/ml in these solutions, less than 3% decomposition occurred in 16 days at room temperature with exposure to normal laboratory light. At a concentration of 0.04 mg/ml in dextrose 5% in water or sodium chloride 0.9%, little or no loss occurred in 48 hours at room temperature or under refrigeration. (234)

Other Information

Microbial Growth — Fludarabine phosphate (Berlex) 0.2 mg/ml diluted in sodium chloride 0.9% and stored at 22 °C did not exhibit an antimicrobial effect on the growth of four organisms (*Enterococcus faecium, Staphylococcus aureus, Pseudomonas aeruginosa,* and *Candida albicans*) inoculated into the solution. Diluted solutions should be stored under refrigeration whenever possible, and the potential for microbiological growth should be considered when assigning expiration dates. (2160)

FLUMAZENIL
AHFS 28:92

Products — Flumazenil is available as a 0.1-mg/ml solution in 5- and 10-ml multiple-dose vials. In addition to flumazenil, each milliliter also contains methylparaben 1.8 mg, propylparaben 0.2 mg, sodium chloride 0.9%, edetate disodium 0.01%, and acetic acid 0.01%. The pH is adjusted with hydrochloric acid and, if necessary, sodium hydroxide. (2)

pH — The injection has a pH of approximately 4. (2)

Trade Name(s) — Romazicon.

Administration — Flumazenil is administered intravenously over 15 to 30 seconds. To minimize pain at the injection site, flumazenil should be administered through a freely running intravenous infusion line into a large vein. Extravasation should be avoided. (2; 4)

Stability — Flumazenil injection is a stable aqueous solution; it should be stored at controlled room temperature. The manufacturer recommends discarding the product 24 hours after removal from its original vial, whether admixed in an infusion solution or simply drawn into a syringe. (2)

Compatibility Information

Solution Compatibility

Flumazenil

Solution	*Mfr*	*Mfr*	*Conc/L*	*Remarks*	*Ref*	*C/I*
Dextrose 5% in water	BA[a]	RC	20 mg	Visually compatible with no flumazenil loss by HPLC in 24 hr at 23 °C under fluorescent light	1710	C

[a]*Tested in PVC containers.*

Additive Compatibility

Flumazenil

Drug	*Mfr*	*Conc/L*	*Mfr*	*Conc/L*	*Test Soln*	*Remarks*	*Ref*	*C/I*
Aminophylline	AMR	2 g	RC	20 mg	D5W[a]	Visually compatible with no flumazenil loss by HPLC in 24 hr at 23 °C under fluorescent light. Aminophylline not tested	1710	C
Cimetidine HCl	SKB	2.4 g	RC	20 mg	D5W[a]	Visually compatible with no flumazenil loss by HPLC in 24 hr at 23 °C under fluorescent light. Cimetidine not tested	1710	C
Dobutamine HCl	LI	2 g	RC	20 mg	D5W[a]	Visually compatible with no flumazenil loss by HPLC in 24 hr at 23 °C under fluorescent light. Dobutamine not tested	1710	C

Additive Compatibility (Cont.)

Flumazenil

Drug	*Mfr*	*Conc/L*	*Mfr*	*Conc/L*	*Test Soln*	*Remarks*	*Ref*	*C/I*
Dopamine HCl	AB	3.2 g	RC	20 mg	D5W[a]	Visually compatible with 7% flumazenil loss by HPLC in 24 hr at 23 °C under fluorescent light. Dopamine not tested	1710	C
Famotidine	MSD	80 mg	RC	20 mg	D5W[a]	Visually compatible with 3% flumazenil loss by HPLC in 24 hr at 23 °C under fluorescent light. Famotidine not tested	1710	C
Heparin sodium	ES	50,000 units	RC	20 mg	D5W[a]	Visually compatible with 4% flumazenil loss by HPLC in 24 hr at 23 °C under fluorescent light. Heparin not tested	1710	C
Lidocaine HCl	AB	4 g	RC	20 mg	D5W[a]	Visually compatible with 4% flumazenil loss by HPLC in 24 hr at 23 °C under fluorescent light. Lidocaine not tested	1710	C
Procainamide HCl	ES	4 g	RC	20 mg	D5W[a]	Visually compatible with no flumazenil loss by HPLC in 24 hr at 23 °C under fluorescent light. Procainamide not tested	1710	C
Ranitidine HCl	GL	300 mg	RC	20 mg	D5W[a]	Visually compatible with 3% flumazenil loss by HPLC in 24 hr at 23 °C under fluorescent light. Ranitidine not tested	1710	C

[a]*Tested in PVC containers.*

Additional Compatibility Information

Infusion Solutions — The manufacturer states that flumazenil is compatible with dextrose 5% in water, sodium chloride 0.9%, and Ringer's injection, lactated. (2)

FLUOROURACIL (5-FLUOROURACIL) AHFS 10:00

Products — Fluorouracil injection is available in 10- and 20-ml single-use vials and in 50- and 100-ml bulk pharmacy vials for preparation of individual doses. (4; 29) Each milliliter contains fluorouracil 50 mg with sodium hydroxide and/or hydrochloric acid for pH adjustment. (1-12/98; 4)

pH — The pH is adjusted to approximately 9.2 with a range of 8.6 to 9.4. (1-12/98; 4)

Osmolality — Fluorouracil 50 mg/ml has an osmolality of 650 mOsm/kg. (1689)

Density — Fluorouracil (Adria) 50-mg/ml undiluted injection has a solution density of 1.03 g/ml. (2041; 2248)

Trade Name(s) — Adrucil.

Administration — Fluorouracil is administered intravenously. Care should be taken to avoid extravasation. Dilution of the injection is not required for administration. (2; 4) Fluorouracil has also been given by portal vein or hepatic artery infusion. (4)

Stability — The solution is normally colorless to faint yellow. Its potency and safety are not affected by slight discoloration during storage. It should be stored at controlled room temperature and protected from light (1-12/98; 4) and freezing (4). Storing the vials in the original cartons until the time of use is recommended. (1-12/98) The color of the solution results from the presence of free fluorine. A dark yellow indicates greater decomposition. Such decomposition may result from storage for several months at temperatures above room temperature. It is suggested that solutions having a darker yellow color be discarded. (398) Exposure to sunlight or intense incandescent light has also caused degradation. The solutions changed in color to dark amber to brown. (760) A precipitate may form from exposure to low temperatures and may be resolubilized by heating to 60 °C with vigorous shaking. (1-12/98; 4) (Note: Allow the solution to cool to body temperature before administration.)

Microwave radiation also has been used to resolubilize the precipitate. Ampuls of fluorouracil (Adria) containing a precipitate were exposed to microwave radiation and shaken until clear. These ampuls were then compared to ampuls that were heated to 60 °C in a water bath and shaken until clear and also to unheated controls. The precipitate was redissolved by microwave radiation without significantly affecting the drug. No significant decrease in drug potency was observed. There was a slight change in pH. The authors concluded that microwave radiation was a suitable method for solubilizing the precipitate that may form in fluorouracil ampuls. However, they warned that extreme care should be taken to avoid overheating and the resulting explosions from excessive pressure in the ampuls. (662)

Fluorouracil (Roche) 1 mg/ml in dextrose 5% in water was evaluated for stability in translucent containers (Perfupack Y, Baxter) and five opaque containers [green PVC Opafuseur (Bruneau), white EVA Perfu-opaque (Baxter), orange PVC PF170 (Cair), white PVC V86 (Codan), and white EVA Perfecran (Fandre)] when exposed to sunlight for 28 days. No photodegradation or sorption was found by HPLC analysis. However, an increase in concentration due to moisture permeation was detected after two weeks. (1750)

pH Effects—At a pH greater than 11, slow hydrolysis of fluorouracil occurs. At a pH less than 8, solubility is reduced and precipitation may or may not occur, depending on the concentration. (1369; 1379)

Stiles et al. found that fluorouracil 50 mg/ml (Lyphomed, Roche, and SoloPak) exhibited precipitation in two to four hours at pH 8.6 to 8.68; precipitation occurred immediately at pH 8.52 or less. The precipitate consisted of needle-shaped crystals at pH 8.26 to 8.68. Cluster-shaped crystals formed at pH 8.18 and below. (1489)

Freezing Solutions—Fluorouracil (Abic) 5 mg/0.5 ml in sodium chloride 0.9% in polypropylene syringes (Plastipak, Becton-Dickinson) was stored frozen at −20 °C. HPLC analysis showed no fluorouracil loss after eight weeks. Refreezing and further storage at −20 °C for another two weeks (total of 10 weeks) also did not result in a fluorouracil loss. (1666)

Syringes—Fluorouracil 25 mg/ml in polypropylene syringes (Braun Omnifix) was stable by HPLC analysis for 28 days at 4 and 20 °C. (1564)

Fluorouracil (Roche) 50 mg/ml was packaged as 3 ml in 10-ml polypropylene infusion pump syringes (Pharmacia Deltec). Little or no loss by HPLC analysis occurred during 21 days of storage at 30 °C. (1967)

Fluorouracil (Roche) 12 and 40 mg/ml diluted with sodium chloride 0.9% and dextrose 5% in water was packaged in 60-ml polypropylene syringes and stored at 25 °C protected from light. Losses of 5% or less were determined by HPLC analysis of the solutions after storage for 72 hours. Furthermore, the solutions had no visually apparent precipitate or discoloration. (1983)

Ambulatory Pumps—The stability of fluorouracil (Roche) diluted in dextrose 5% in water was determined for use with an ambulatory infusion system for home therapy. Fluorouracil 500 mg/50 ml was evaluated in the PVC drug reservoir used in the PL 146 MVP ambulatory pump (Travenol) at 5 and 25 °C. No significant change occurred in samples stored at 5 °C in the PVC bags during 16 weeks of storage. However, at 25 °C, the PVC bag samples demonstrated a progressive increase in fluorouracil content over 16 weeks, presumably caused by water evaporation through the bag. During the first seven days of 25 °C storage, there appeared to be little change in fluorouracil content. (894)

Stiles et al. reported the stability of undiluted fluorouracil 50 mg/ml from three manufacturers (Lyphomed, Roche, and SoloPak) in the reservoirs of four portable infusion pumps (Pharmacia Deltec CADD-1, Model 5100; Cormed II, Model 10500; Medfusion Infumed 200; and Pancretec Provider I.V., Model 2000). The fluorouracil was delivered by the pumps at a rate of 10 ml/day over a seven-day cycle at 25 and 37 °C. All fluorouracil samples in all pump reservoirs were stable over the seven-day study period, exhibiting little or no drug loss and only minimal leached plasticizer (DEHP) at either temperature. (1489)

However, precipitation of the Roche fluorouracil was observed with all pumps; a fine white precipitate originated close to the connection junction and migrated in both directions until it occupied most of the tubing and was in the drug reservoir. In some cases, the pumps stopped due to the extent of precipitation. The authors noted that various factors, including solution pH, temperature, drug concentration and solubility, and the manipulative techniques used could contribute to precipitate formation. (1489)

Rochard et al. reported that undiluted fluorouracil (Roche) 50 mg/ml in ethylene vinyl acetate (EVA) bags for use with portable infusion pumps remained stable, with little or no potency loss by HPLC analysis after 28 days at 4, 22, and 35 °C. The containers at 35 °C did sustain approximately a 3% water loss due to evaporation during storage, increasing the fluorouracil concentration slightly. (1548)

Fluorouracil (David Bull Laboratories) 25 mg/ml was stable in PVC reservoirs (Parker Micropump) for 14 days at 4 and 37 °C, exhibiting no loss by HPLC analysis. (1696)

Baud-Camus et al. packaged fluorouracil 15 and 45 mg/ml diluted in sodium chloride 0.9% in 100-ml ethylene vinyl acetate (EVA) infusion pump reservoirs and stored them at 25 °C protected from light. Little or no loss was found by HPLC analysis of the solutions after storage for 72 hours. Furthermore, the solutions had no visually apparent precipitate or discoloration. (1983)

Martel et al. evaluated the stability of undiluted fluorouracil injection (Roche) 50 mg/ml in EVA reservoirs (Celsa) and PVC reservoirs (Pharmacia) for use with ambulatory infusion pumps. The filled reservoirs were stored for 14 days at 4 °C and at 33 °C to simulate the conditions of prolonged infusion from the reservoirs kept under patients' clothing. No loss of fluorouracil due to decomposition was found by HPLC analysis. However, the refrigerated samples exhibited substantial (up to 15%) loss of drug content from solution due to gross precipitation. Flocculent precipitation was observed in as little as three days. (Subvisual precipitation may occur earlier.) At the elevated temperature, substantial increases in concentration of fluorouracil occurred in the EVA reservoirs due to water loss from permeation through the plastic reservoir. Approximately 5% increase in drug concentration occurred in 14 days. No change in concentration occurred in the PVC reservoirs during this time frame. (2004)

Elastomeric Reservoir Pumps—Fluorouracil (Roche) 500 mg/60 ml in dextrose 5% in water was tested for stability at 5 °C in the elastomeric reservoir of the Infusor (Travenol) disposable pump. Changes in drug concentration of less than 10% occurred in 16 weeks. (894)

Fluorouracil (SoloPak) 5 mg/ml in sodium chloride 0.9% 100 ml was packaged in latex elastomeric reservoirs (Secure Medical). Little or no loss by HPLC analysis occurred in 24 hours at 25 °C. (1970)

Fluorouracil solutions in elastomeric reservoir pumps have been stated by the pump manufacturers to be stable for the following time periods refrigerated (REF), at room temperature (RT), and at 37 °C (31):

Pump Reservoir(s)	Conc.	REF	RT	37 °C
Homepump; Homepump Eclipse	50 mg/ml		8 weeks	
Infusor	5 to 42 mg/ml[b]	14 days	10 days	7 days
	10 mg/ml[a]		30 days	
	8.3 mg/ml[a]	16 weeks		
Intermate LV2	5 to 42 mg/ml[b]	14 days	10 days	5 days
Medflo	5 mg/ml[a]	16 weeks	7 days	

[a]*In dextrose 5% in water.*
[b]*In sodium chloride 0.9%.*

Implantable Pumps— Fluorouracil 50 mg/ml was filled into an implantable infusion pump (Fresenius VIP 30) and associated capillary tubing and stored at 37 °C. Samples were analyzed using an HPLC assay. No fluorouracil loss and no contamination from components of pump materials occurred during eight weeks of storage. (1903)

Sorption— Fluorouracil (Sigma) 10 mg/L in sodium chloride 0.9% (Travenol) in PVC bags did not exhibit significant sorption to the plastic during one week of storage at room temperature (15 to 20 °C). (536)

In another study, fluorouracil (Sigma) 10 mg/L in sodium chloride 0.9% did not exhibit any loss due to sorption during a seven-hour simulated infusion through an infusion set (Travenol) consisting of a cellulose propionate burette chamber and 170 cm of PVC tubing. (606)

The drug was also tested as a simulated infusion over at least one hour by a syringe pump system. A glass syringe on a syringe pump was fitted with 20 cm of polyethylene tubing or 50 cm of Silastic tubing. No loss of drug due to sorption was observed with either tubing. (606)

A 25-ml aliquot of fluorouracil (Sigma) 10 mg/L in sodium chloride 0.9% was stored in all-plastic syringes composed of polypropylene barrels and polyethylene plungers for 24 hours at room temperature in the dark. No loss of drug due to sorption occurred. (606)

Undiluted fluorouracil (Roche) 50 mg/ml was stored for seven days at room temperature in plastic syringes (Monoject) and glass vials (Elkins-Sinn). Little or no loss of potency occurred over this period in either container. (760)

Fluorouracil may be more extensively adsorbed to glass surfaces than to plastic. In one report, significant loss occurred from solutions in glass vials, but almost quantitative recovery was obtained from polyethylene and polypropylene plastic vials. The loss was ascribed to adsorption to the glass surface. (663) This difference was also observed in dextrose 5% in water in glass and PVC infusion containers. A 10% loss of fluorouracil occurred in 43 hours in the PVC containers but in only seven hours in the glass containers. (519)

Filtration— Fluorouracil 10 to 75 µg/ml exhibited little or no loss due to sorption to either cellulose nitrate/cellulose acetate ester (Millex OR) or Teflon (Millex FG) filters. (1415; 1416)

Central Venous Catheter— Fluorouracil (Roche) 5 mg/ml in dextrose 5% in water was found to be compatible with the ARROWg+ard Blue Plus (Arrow International) chlorhexidine-bearing triple-lumen central catheter. HPLC analysis was used to evaluate completeness of drug delivery through the catheter and the amount of chlorhexidine removed from the internal lumens. Essentially complete delivery of the drug was found with little or no drug loss occurring. Furthermore, chlorhexidine delivered from the catheter remained at trace amounts with no substantial increase due to the delivery of the drug through the catheter. (2335)

Compatibility Information

Solution Compatibility

Fluorouracil

Solution	*Mfr*	*Mfr*	*Conc/L*	*Remarks*	*Ref*	*C/I*
Amino acids 4.25%, dextrose 25%	MG	RC	500 mg	No increase in particulate matter in 24 hr at 5 °C	349	C
Dextrose 5% in Ringer's injection, lactated	MG[a]		500 mg	No decomposition in 24 hr	399	C
Dextrose 3.3% in sodium chloride 0.3%	TR[b]	RC	1.5 g	Physically compatible and chemically stable for 8 weeks at ambient temperature both in the dark and exposed to fluorescent light	1153	C
Dextrose 5% in water		RC	10 g	No loss of fluorouracil by HPLC during 16 weeks at 5 °C. Little or no change in fluorouracil by HPLC during 7 days at 25 °C	894	C
	TR[b]	RC	1.5 g	Physically compatible and chemically stable for 8 weeks at ambient temperature both in the dark and exposed to fluorescent light	1153	C
			1 and 2 g	Physically compatible and no fluorouracil loss in 48 hr at room temperature and 7 °C by UV and TLC	1152	C
	[c]	RC	10 g	Visually compatible with little or no fluorouracil loss by HPLC in 28 days at 4, 22, and 35 °C protected from light. At 35 °C, concentration increased due to water evaporation	1548	C

Solution Compatibility (Cont.)

Fluorouracil

Solution	Mfr	Mfr	Conc/L	Remarks	Ref	C/I
	MG[a]		8.3 g	Less than 10% loss by HPLC in 48 hr at room temperature exposed to light	1658	C
	BA[d]	RC	1 and 10 g	Visually compatible with less than 3% loss by HPLC in 14 days at 4 and 21 °C	2004	C
	BA[d]	RC[g]	0.5 and 5 g	Little or no loss by HPLC in 13 days at 4 and 25 °C	2175	C
Plasmalyte 3G5	BA[d]	RC[g]	0.5 and 5 g	Little or no loss by HPLC in 13 days at 4 and 25 °C	2175	C
Sodium chloride 0.9%	TR[b]	RC	1.5 g	Physically compatible and chemically stable for 8 weeks at ambient temperature both in the dark and exposed to fluorescent light	1153	C
			1 and 2 g	Physically compatible and no fluorouracil loss in 48 hr at room temperature and 7 °C by UV and TLC	1152	C
	[c]	RC	10 g	Visually compatible with little or no fluorouracil loss by HPLC in 28 days at 4, 22, and 35 °C protected from light. At 35 °C, concentration increased due to water evaporation	1548	C
	[b]	FA, RC	5 and 50 g	Visually compatible with little or no loss by HPLC in 91 days at 4 °C followed by 7 days at 25 °C in the dark	1567	C
	AB[e]	RC	5 g	Little or no loss of drug by HPLC in 24 hr at 25 °C	1970	C
	[c]	RC	15 and 45 g	Visually compatible with little or no loss of drug by HPLC in 72 hr at 25 °C protected from light	1983	C
	BA[d]	RC	1 and 10 g	Visually compatible with less than 3% loss by HPLC in 14 days at 4 and 21 °C	2004	C
	BA[d]	RC[g]	0.5 and 5 g	Little or no loss by HPLC in 13 days at 4 and 25 °C	2175	C
TPN #23[f]		RC	1 and 4 g	Physically compatible for 42 hr at room temperature in ambient light. Results of HPLC analysis were erratic	562	?
		RC	1 g	Physically compatible and fluorouracil chemically stable for 48 hr at room temperature in ambient light	826	C

[a]*Tested in both glass and polyolefin containers.*
[b]*Tested in both glass and PVC containers.*
[c]*Tested in ethylene vinyl acetate (EVA) containers.*
[d]*Tested in PVC containers.*
[e]*Tested in glass containers and latex elastomeric reservoirs (Secure Medical).*
[f]*Refer to Appendix I for the composition of parenteral nutrition solutions. TPN indicates a 2-in-1 admixture.*
[g]*A modified fluorouracil formulation containing tromethamine (TRIS, THAM, trometamol) instead of sodium hydroxide.*

Additive Compatibility

Fluorouracil

Drug	Mfr	Conc/L	Mfr	Conc/L	Test Soln	Remarks	Ref	C/I
Bleomycin sulfate	BR	20 and 30 units	RC	1 g	NS	Physically compatible and bleomycin activity retained for 1 week at 4 °C. Fluorouracil not tested	763	C
Carboplatin		1 g		10 g	W	Greater than 20% carboplatin loss in 24 hr at room temperature	1379	I

Additive Compatibility (Cont.)

Fluorouracil

Drug	*Mfr*	*Conc/L*	*Mfr*	*Conc/L*	*Test Soln*	*Remarks*	*Ref*	*C/I*
Cisplatin	BR	200 mg	SO	1 g	NS[a]	10% cisplatin loss in 1.5 hr and 25% loss in 4 hr at 25 °C under fluorescent light or in the dark	1339	I
	BR	500 mg	SO	10 g	NS[a]	10% cisplatin loss in 1.2 hr and 25% loss in 3 hr at 25 °C under fluorescent light or in the dark	1339	I
	BR	500 mg	AD	10 g	NS	80% cisplatin loss in 24 hr at room temperature due to low pH	1386	I
Cyclophosphamide		1.67 g		8.3 g	NS	Both drugs stable for 15 days at room temperature	1389	C
Cyclophosphamide with methotrexate sodium		1.67 g 25 mg		8.3 g	NS	9.3% cyclophosphamide loss in 7 days at room temperature. No loss of other drugs observed	1389	C
Cytarabine	UP	400 mg	RC	250 mg	D5W	Altered UV spectrum for cytarabine within 1 hr at room temperature	207	I
Diazepam	RC					Immediate precipitation	524	I
Doxorubicin HCl	AD					Solution color darkens from red to blue-purple	524	I
	AD	10 mg	RC	250 mg	D5W	Color change to deep purple	296	I
Etoposide		200 mg		10 g	NS	Both drugs stable for 7 days at room temperature and 1 day at 35 °C	1379	C
Fentanyl citrate	AB	12.5 mg	AB	1 and 16 g	D5W, NS[a]	25% fentanyl loss in 15 min due to sorption to PVC	2064	I
Floxuridine		10 g		10 g	NS	Both drugs stable for 15 days at room temperature	1390	C
Hydromorphone HCl	AST	500 mg	AB	1 g	D5W, NS[a]	Physically compatible with no increase in measured turbidity or particulates and little or no loss by HPLC of either drug in 7 days at 32 °C and 35 days at 23, 4, and −20 °C	1977	C
	AST	500 mg	AB	16 g	D5W, NS[a]	Physically compatible with no increase in measured turbidity or particulates and little or no loss by HPLC of either drug in 3 days at 32 °C, 7 days at 23 °C, and 35 days at 4 and −20 °C	1977	C
Ifosfamide		2 g		10 g	NS	Both drugs stable for 5 days at room temperature	1379	C
Leucovorin calcium	LE	1.5 to 13.3 g	AD	16.7 to 46.2 g	[b]	Subvisual particulate matter forms in all combinations in variable periods from 1 to 4 days at 4, 23, and 32 °C	1816	I
Methotrexate sodium		30 mg		10 g	NS	Both drugs stable for 15 days at room temperature	1379	C
Metoclopramide HCl	FUJ	100 mg	RC	2.5 g	D5W	10% metoclopramide loss in 6 hr and 27% loss in 24 hr at 25 °C. 5% metoclopramide loss in 120 hr at 4 °C. 5 and 7% fluorouracil losses in 120 hr at 4 and 25 °C, respectively	1780	I

Additive Compatibility (Cont.)

Fluorouracil

Drug	*Mfr*	*Conc/L*	*Mfr*	*Conc/L*	*Test Soln*	*Remarks*	*Ref*	*C/I*
Mitoxantrone HCl	LE	500 mg		25 g	D5W	Visually compatible and mitoxantrone potency by HPLC retained for 24 hr at room temperature. Fluorouracil not tested	1531	C
Morphine sulfate	AST	1 g	AB	1 and 16 g	D5W, NS[a]	Subvisual morphine precipitate forms immediately, becoming grossly visible within 24 hr. Morphine losses by HPLC of 60 to 80% occur within 1 day	1977	I
Vincristine sulfate	LI	4 mg	RC	10 mg	D5W	Physically compatible. No alteration of UV spectra in 8 hr at room temperature	207	C

[a]*Tested in PVC containers.*
[b]*Tested with both drugs undiluted and diluted by 25% with dextrose 5% in water.*

Drugs in Syringe Compatibility

Fluorouracil

Drug (in syringe)	*Mfr*	*Amt*	*Mfr*	*Amt*	*Remarks*	*Ref*	*C/I*
Bleomycin sulfate		1.5 units/ 0.5 ml		25 mg/ 0.5 ml	Physically compatible for 5 min at room temperature followed by 8 min of centrifugation	980	C
Cisplatin		0.5 mg/ 0.5 ml		25 mg/ 0.5 ml	Physically compatible for 5 min at room temperature followed by 8 min of centrifugation	980	C
Cyclophosphamide		10 mg/ 0.5 ml		25 mg/ 0.5 ml	Physically compatible for 5 min at room temperature followed by 8 min of centrifugation	980	C
Doxorubicin HCl		1 mg/ 0.5 ml		25 mg/ 0.5 ml	Physically compatible for 5 min at room temperature followed by 8 min of centrifugation	980	C
		5 and 10 mg/ 10 ml[a]		500 mg/ 10 ml	Precipitate forms within several hours of mixing	1564	I
Droperidol		1.25 mg/ 0.5 ml		25 mg/ 0.5 ml	Immediate precipitation	980	I
Epirubicin HCl		5 and 10 mg/ 10 ml[a]		500 mg/ 10 ml	Precipitate forms within several hours of mixing	1564	I
Furosemide		5 mg/ 0.5 ml		25 mg/ 0.5 ml	Physically compatible for 5 min at room temperature followed by 8 min of centrifugation	980	C
Heparin sodium		500 units/ 0.5 ml		25 mg/ 0.5 ml	Physically compatible for 5 min at room temperature followed by 8 min of centrifugation	980	C
Leucovorin calcium		5 mg/ 0.5 ml		25 mg/ 0.5 ml	Physically compatible for 5 min at room temperature followed by 8 min of centrifugation	980	C
Methotrexate sodium		12.5 mg/ 0.5 ml		25 mg/ 0.5 ml	Physically compatible for 5 min at room temperature followed by 8 min of centrifugation	980	C
Metoclopramide HCl		2.5 mg/ 0.5 ml		25 mg/ 0.5 ml	Physically compatible for 5 min at room temperature followed by 8 min of centrifugation	980	C
Mitomycin		0.25 mg/ 0.5 ml		25 mg/ 0.5 ml	Physically compatible for 5 min at room temperature followed by 8 min of centrifugation	980	C
Vinblastine sulfate		0.5 mg/ 0.5 ml		25 mg/ 0.5 ml	Physically compatible for 5 min at room temperature followed by 8 min of centrifugation	980	C

Drugs in Syringe Compatibility (Cont.)

Fluorouracil

Drug (in syringe)	*Mfr*	*Amt*	*Mfr*	*Amt*	*Remarks*	*Ref*	*C/I*
Vincristine sulfate		0.5 mg/ 0.5 ml		25 mg/ 0.5 ml	Physically compatible for 5 min at room temperature followed by 8 min of centrifugation	980	C

[a]*Diluted in sodium chloride 0.9%.*

Y-Site Injection Compatibility (1:1 Mixture)

Fluorouracil

Drug	*Mfr*	*Conc*	*Mfr*	*Conc*	*Remarks*	*Ref*	*C/I*
Allopurinol sodium	BW	3 mg/ml[b]	RC	16 mg/ml[b]	Physically compatible with no change in measured turbidity or increase in particle content in 4 hr at 22 °C	1686	C
Amifostine	USB	10 mg/ml[a]	AD	16 mg/ml[b]	Physically compatible with no change in measured turbidity or increase in particle content in 4 hr at 23 °C	1845	C
Amphotericin B cholesteryl sulfate complex	SEQ	0.83 mg/ml[a]	PH	16 mg/ml[a]	Microprecipitate forms immediately	2117	I
Aztreonam	SQ	40 mg/ml[a]	AD	16 mg/ml[a]	Physically compatible with no subvisual haze or particle formation in 4 hr at 23 °C	1758	C
Bleomycin sulfate		3 units/ml		50 mg/ml	Drugs injected sequentially into Y-site with no flush between. No visually apparent precipitate	980	C
Cefepime HCl	BMS	20 mg/ml[a]	AD	16 mg/ml[a]	Physically compatible with no change in measured turbidity or increase in particle content in 4 hr at 22 °C	1689	C
Cisplatin		1 mg/ml		50 mg/ml	Drugs injected sequentially into Y-site with no flush between. No visually apparent precipitate	980	C
Cyclophosphamide		20 mg/ml		50 mg/ml	Drugs injected sequentially into Y-site with no flush between. No visually apparent precipitate	980	C
Doxorubicin HCl		2 mg/ml		50 mg/ml	Drugs injected sequentially into Y-site with no flush between. No visually apparent precipitate	980	C
Doxorubicin HCl liposome injection	SEQ	0.4 mg/ml[a]	PH	16 mg/ml[a]	Physically compatible with little or no change in measured turbidity and no increase in particle content in 4 hr at 23 °C	2087	C
Droperidol		2.5 mg/ml		50 mg/ml	Drugs injected sequentially into Y-site with no flush between. Immediate precipitation	980	I
Etoposide phosphate	BR	5 mg/ml[a]	PH	16 mg/ml[a]	Physically compatible with no change in measured turbidity or increase in particle content in 4 hr at 23 °C	2218	C
Filgrastim	AMG	30 μg/ml[a]	RC	16 mg/ml[a]	Particles and long filaments form in 1 hr	1687	I
Fludarabine phosphate	BX	1 mg/ml[a]	LY	16 mg/ml[a]	Physically compatible for 4 hr at room temperature under fluorescent light	1439	C

Y-Site Injection Compatibility (1:1 Mixture) (Cont.)

Fluorouracil

Drug	*Mfr*	*Conc*	*Mfr*	*Conc*	*Remarks*	*Ref*	*C/I*
Furosemide		10 mg/ml		50 mg/ml	Drugs injected sequentially into Y-site with no flush between. No visually apparent precipitate	980	C
Gatifloxacin	BMS	2 mg/ml[a]	PH	16 mg/ml[a]	Physically compatible with no change in measured haze or increase in particle content in 4 hr at 23 °C	2234	C
Gemcitabine HCl	LI	10 mg/ml[b]	PH	16 mg/ml[b]	Physically compatible with no change in measured turbidity or increase in particle content in 4 hr at 23 °C	2226	C
Granisetron HCl	SKB	0.05 mg/ml[b]	AD	16 mg/ml[b]	Physically compatible with no subvisual haze or particle formation in 4 hr at 23 °C	1804	C
	SKB	1 mg/ml	RC	2 mg/ml[b]	Physically compatible with little or no loss of either drug by HPLC in 4 hr at 22 °C	1883	C
	SKB	0.05 mg/ml[a]	AD	16 mg/ml[a]	Physically compatible with no change in measured turbidity or increase in particle content in 4 hr at 23 °C	2000	C
Heparin sodium		1000 units/ml		50 mg/ml	Drugs injected sequentially into Y-site with no flush between. No visually apparent precipitate	980	C
	UP	1000 units/L[c]	RC	50 mg/ml	Physically compatible for at least 4 hr at room temperature by visual and microscopic examination	534	C
Hydrocortisone sodium succinate	UP	10 mg/L[c]	RC	50 mg/ml	Physically compatible for at least 4 hr at room temperature by visual and microscopic examination	534	C
Leucovorin calcium		10 mg/ml		50 mg/ml	Drugs injected sequentially into Y-site with no flush between. No visually apparent precipitate	980	C
Linezolid	PHU	2 mg/ml	PH	16 mg/ml[a]	Physically compatible with no change in measured turbidity or increase in particle content in 4 hr at 23 °C	2264	C
Mannitol		20%	SO	1 and 2 mg/ml[d]	Physically compatible both visually and microscopically and fluorouracil chemically stable by HPLC for 24 hr. Mannitol not tested	1526	C
Melphalan HCl	BW	0.1 mg/ml[b]	LY	16 mg/ml[b]	Physically compatible with no change in measured turbidity or increase in particle content in 3 hr at 22 °C	1557	C
Methotrexate sodium		25 mg/ml		50 mg/ml	Drugs injected sequentially into Y-site with no flush between. No visually apparent precipitate	980	C
Metoclopramide HCl		5 mg/ml		50 mg/ml	Drugs injected sequentially into Y-site with no flush between. No visually apparent precipitate	980	C
Mitomycin		0.5 mg/ml		50 mg/ml	Drugs injected sequentially into Y-site with no flush between. No visually apparent precipitate	980	C

Y-Site Injection Compatibility (1:1 Mixture) (Cont.)

Fluorouracil

Drug	*Mfr*	*Conc*	*Mfr*	*Conc*	*Remarks*	*Ref*	*C/I*
Ondansetron HCl	GL	1 mg/ml[b]	SO	16 mg/ml[a]	Immediate precipitation	1365	I
	GL	16 to 160 μg/ml		0.8 mg/ml	Physically compatible when fluorouracil given at 20 ml/hr via Y-site	1366	C
Paclitaxel	NCI	1.2 mg/ml[a]		16 mg/ml[a]	Physically compatible with no change in measured turbidity in 4 hr at 22 °C	1528	C
Piperacillin sodium–tazobactam sodium	LE	40 + 5 mg/ml[a]	LY	16 mg/ml[a]	Physically compatible with no change in measured turbidity or increase in particle content in 4 hr at 22 °C	1688	C
Potassium chloride	AB	40 mEq/L[c]	RC	50 mg/ml	Physically compatible for at least 4 hr at room temperature by visual and microscopic examination	534	C
Propofol	ZEN	10 mg/ml	AD	16 mg/ml[a]	Physically compatible for 1 hr at 23 °C with no increase in particle content	2066	C
Sargramostim	IMM	10 μg/ml[b]	SO	16 mg/ml[b]	Physically compatible for 4 hr at 22 °C	1436	C
Teniposide	BR	0.1 mg/ml[a]	AD	16 mg/ml[a]	Physically compatible with no subvisual haze or particle formation in 4 hr at 23 °C	1725	C
Thiotepa	IMM[e]	1 mg/ml[a]	AD	16 mg/ml[a]	Physically compatible with no change in measured turbidity or increase in particle content in 4 hr at 23 °C	1861	C
TNA #218, #219, #221, #222, #224 to #226[f]			PH	16 mg/ml[a]	Visually compatible with no precipitate or emulsion damage apparent in 4 hr at 23 °C	2215	C
TNA #220 and #223[f]			PH	16 mg/ml[a]	Small amount of white precipitate forms immediately	2215	I
Topotecan HCl	SKB	56 μg/ml[b]	RC	50 mg/ml	Haze and color change to intense yellow occur immediately	2245	I
TPN #212 and #213[f]			PH	16 mg/ml[a]	Slight subvisual haze and crystals and amber discoloration form in 1 to 4 hr	2109	I
TPN #214 and #215[f]			PH	16 mg/ml[a]	Turbidity forms immediately	2109	I
Vinblastine sulfate		1 mg/ml		50 mg/ml	Drugs injected sequentially into Y-site with no flush between. No visually apparent precipitate	980	C
Vincristine sulfate		1 mg/ml		50 mg/ml	Drugs injected sequentially into Y-site with no flush between. No visually apparent precipitate	980	C
Vinorelbine tartrate	BW	1 mg/ml[b]	RC	16 mg/ml[b]	Heavy white precipitate forms immediately	1558	I
Vitamin B complex with C	RC	2 ml/L[c]	RC	50 mg/ml	Physically compatible for at least 4 hr at room temperature by visual and microscopic examination	534	C

[a]*Tested in dextrose 5% in water.*
[b]*Tested in sodium chloride 0.9%.*
[c]*Tested in dextrose 5% in Ringer's injection, dextrose 5% in Ringer's injection, lactated, dextrose 5% in water, Ringer's injection, lactated, and sodium chloride 0.9%.*
[d]*Tested in dextrose 5% in sodium chloride 0.45%, dextrose 5% in water, and sodium chloride 0.9%.*
[e]*Lyophilized formulation tested.*
[f]*Refer to Appendix I for the composition of parenteral nutrition solutions. TNA indicates a 3-in-1 admixture, and TPN indicates a 2-in-1 admixture.*

Additional Compatibility Information

Infusion Solutions — Fluorouracil 5 to 10 mg/ml in dextrose 5% in water, sodium chloride 0.9%, or sterile water for injection exhibited less than a 10% loss in 14 days at room temperature. (1379)

Leucovorin Calcium — Several articles reported the chemical stability and physical compatibility of fluorouracil with leucovorin calcium. (980; 1387; 1817) However, more recent work found substantial subvisual particles in this drug combination over numerous concentrations when stored at 4, 23, and 32 °C. Particulate formation sometimes clogged filters and disrupted multiple-day treatment. Particulate formation began in about 24 hours in most samples, and particles were found in all samples within seven days. Fluorouracil and leucovorin calcium in the same container can no longer be considered a compatible combination. (1816)

Methotrexate — The reported incompatibility of fluorouracil (Roche) 250 mg/L with methotrexate sodium (Lederle) 200 mg/L in dextrose 5% in water (207) has been questioned on the grounds that the observed alteration in UV spectra for both drugs might be an artifact of the experiment, merely being a result of methotrexate's altered UV spectra at varying pH values. It was observed that the altered methotrexate spectrum could contribute to an altered spectrum for fluorouracil. (318)

In reply, King noted that the pH of fluorouracil, rather than the drug itself, might be responsible for changes in methotrexate's UV spectrum. However, use of a buffered aqueous solution to simulate the admixture with a pH of approximately 8 and decrease of the pH with 0.2 M HCl back to the range of methotrexate sodium in dextrose 5% in water (pH 6.5) failed to return the UV spectrum to that of the pH 6.5 solution; in fact, it was not significantly different from the pH 8 scan. King concluded that irreversible changes were occurring that make the compatibility of the admixture suspect. (319)

It is interesting to note, however, that the commercial methotrexate sodium (Lederle) used in the study is formulated in solution at a pH of approximately 8.5, not significantly different from that of the admixture suspected of incompatibility, and yet is stable for an extended period until its expiration date.

Other Drugs — Admixture with acidic drugs or drugs that decompose in an alkaline environment should be avoided. (524)

A color change to deep purple was reported for the mixtures of doxorubicin HCl (Adria) 10 mg/L with fluorouracil (Roche) 250 mg/L in dextrose 5% in water. (296) This color change is indicative of decomposition occurring in solutions with an alkaline pH. It also occurs with other anthracyclines. (394)

No alteration in the ultraviolet/visible spectra was observed when dacarbazine was combined in solution with fluorouracil. (492)

Aluminum — Ogawa et al. reported that immersion of a needle with an aluminum component in fluorouracil (Adria) 50 mg/ml resulted in no visually apparent reaction after seven days at 24 °C. (988)

Other Information

Microbial Growth — Fluorouracil (Adria) 500 mg/10 ml did not support the growth of several microorganisms commonly implicated in nosocomial infections. The bacteriostatic properties were observed against *Escherichia coli, Klebsiella pneumoniae, Staphylococcus epidermidis, Pseudomonas aeruginosa, Candida albicans,* and *Clostridium perfringens.* (828)

In another study, fluorouracil (Adria) 1 g/20 ml transferred to PVC containers did not support the growth of several microorganisms and may have imparted an antimicrobial effect at this concentration. Loss of viability was observed for *Staphylococcus aureus, Escherichia coli, Pseudomonas aeruginosa, Pseudomonas cepacia, Candida albicans,* and *Aspergillus niger.* (1187)

Fluorouracil (Lyphomed) eliminated the viability of *Staphylococcus epidermidis* (10^6 to 10^7 CFU/ml) in varying time periods, depending on concentration and diluent, when stored at near-body temperature (35 °C). At 50 mg/ml, no viability was found after five days of incubation. At 10 mg/ml in sodium chloride 0.9% and dextrose 5% in water, no viability was found after seven and five days, respectively. Following dilution to 10 mg/ml with bacteriostatic sodium chloride 0.9%, no viability was found after two days. (1659)

Inactivation — In the event of spills or leaks, Adria recommends the use of sodium hypochlorite 5% (household bleach) to inactivate fluorouracil. (1200)

FLUPHENAZINE HCL
AHFS 28:16.08

Products — Fluphenazine HCl is available in 10-ml multiple-dose vials. Each milliliter contains fluphenazine HCl 2.5 mg with sodium chloride for isotonicity, sodium hydroxide or hydrochloric acid to adjust the pH, and methylparaben 0.1% and propylparaben 0.01% as preservatives. (4; 29)

pH — From 4.8 to 5.2. (4)

Administration — Fluphenazine HCl is administered by intramuscular injection. (4)

Stability — Intact vials should be stored at controlled room temperature and protected from freezing and light. Parenteral solutions of fluphenazine HCl vary from colorless to light amber. Solutions that are darker than light amber, are discolored in some other way, or contain a precipitate should not be used. (4)

Compatibility Information

Drugs in Syringe Compatibility

Fluphenazine HCl

Drug (in syringe)	*Mfr*	*Amt*	*Mfr*	*Amt*	*Remarks*	*Ref*	*C/I*
Benztropine mesylate	MSD	2 mg/ 2 ml	LY	5 mg/ 2 ml	Visually compatible for 60 min	1784	C
Diphenhydramine HCl	ES	100 mg/ 2 ml	LY	5 mg/ 2 ml	Visually compatible for 60 min	1784	C
Hydroxyzine HCl	ES	100 mg/ 2 ml	LY	5 mg/ 2 ml	Visually compatible for 60 min	1784	C

FOLIC ACID
AHFS 88:08

Products — Folic acid injection is available in 10-ml vials. Each milliliter of solution contains (1-3/99):

Folic acid (as sodium salt)	5 mg
Edetate sodium	2 mg
Benzyl alcohol	15 mg
Hydrochloric acid and/or sodium hydroxide	to adjust pH
Water for injection	qs

pH — From 8 to 11. (1-3/99; 4)

Osmolality — Folic acid 5 mg/ml has an osmolality of 186 mOsm/kg. (1689)

Administration — Folic acid injection is administered by deep intramuscular, intravenous, or subcutaneous injection. (1-3/99; 4)

Stability — Intact vials should be stored at controlled room temperature and protected from light. (1-3/99)The yellow to orange-yellow solutions are heat sensitive and should be protected from light (4) for long-term storage. However, exposure of folic acid in parenteral nutrition solutions to fluorescent light for 48 hours did not cause any significant loss of folic acid. (896)

pH Effects — Folic acid is soluble in solutions of pH 5.6 or above at room temperature to a concentration of 1 g/L. However, below about pH 4.5 to 5, folic acid may precipitate in varying time periods, depending on the acidity of the solution. In the small concentrations used for parenteral nutrition, a pH of above 5 ensures that folic acid will remain in solution. Most parenteral nutrition solutions are buffered by the amino acids to pH 5 to 6. (895)

Sorption — A parenteral nutrition solution containing 13 μg/L of folic acid injection in a 3-L PVC bag and run through an administration set delivered the full amount of folic acid, with no loss detected by radioimmunoassay. (895)

Filtration — Folic acid (Lederle) 0.5 mg/L in dextrose 5% in water and sodium chloride 0.9% was filtered at 120 ml/hr for six hours through a 0.22-μm cellulose ester membrane filter (Ivex-2). No significant reduction in potency due to binding to the filter was noted. (533)

Compatibility Information

Solution Compatibility

Folic acid

Solution	*Mfr*	*Mfr*	*Conc/L*	*Remarks*	*Ref*	*C/I*
Amino acids 4.25%, dextrose 25%	MG	USP	0.2 and 10 mg	Physically compatible and stable for at least 7 days at 4 °C and room temperature protected from light	895	C
Dextrose 20% in water		USP	0.2 and 20 mg	Physically compatible and stable for at least 7 days at 4 °C and room temperature protected from light	895	C
Dextrose 40% in water		USP	0.2 and 20 mg	Approximately 17 to 25% loss in 24 hr at 4 °C and room temperature protected from light, with precipitation at the higher concentration after 48 hr	895	I

Solution Compatibility (Cont.)

Solution	Mfr	Folic acid Mfr	Conc/L	Remarks	Ref	C/I
Dextrose 50% in water		USP	20 mg	Precipitate forms within 24 hr at 4 °C and room temperature protected from light	895	I
Fat emulsion 10%, intravenous	KV	USP	0.2 and 20 mg	Physically compatible for up to 2 weeks at 4 °C and room temperature protected from light, but highly erratic assays	895	?
	KA	KA[a]	11 mg	Physically compatible for 24 hr at 26 °C with little loss of folic acid and of most other vitamins by HPLC; up to 52% ascorbate loss	2050	C
TPN #11 to #15[b]		LE	2.5 and 5 mg	Physically compatible for 24 hr at 22 °C. UV spectra of amino acids unaltered	313	C
TPN #43 to #47[b]		LE	5 mg	Physically compatible for 24 hr at 22 °C. TLC changes of amino acids in similar solutions attributed to MVI or vitamin B complex with C	313	C
TPN #69[b]		USP	0.4 mg	Physically compatible and folic acid stable for at least 7 days at 4 and 25 °C protected from light	895	C
TPN #70[b]		LE	0.25 to 1 mg	Folic acid stable for at least 48 hr at 6 and 21 °C in the light or dark	896	C
TPN #74[b]			1 mg	Folic acid stable over 8 hr at room temperature exposed to fluorescent light or sunlight	842	C
TPN #189[b]		AB	15 mg/ml	Visually compatible for 24 hr at 22 °C	1767	C

[a]*From multivitamins.*
[b]*Refer to Appendix I for the composition of parenteral nutrition solutions. TPN indicates a 2-in-1 admixture.*

Drugs in Syringe Compatibility

Drug (in syringe)	Mfr	Amt	Folic acid Mfr	Amt	Remarks	Ref	C/I
Doxapram HCl	RB	400 mg/20 ml		15 mg/1 ml	Immediate turbidity	1177	I

Y-Site Injection Compatibility (1:1 Mixture)

Drug	Mfr	Conc	Folic acid Mfr	Conc	Remarks	Ref	C/I
Famotidine	MSD	0.2 mg/ml[a]	LE	5 mg/ml	Physically compatible for 14 hr	1196	C

[a]*Tested in dextrose 5% in water.*

Additional Compatibility Information

Infusion Solutions — The stability of folic acid from a multiple vitamin product in dextrose 5% in water and sodium chloride 0.9%, in both PVC and ClearFlex containers, was evaluated. HPLC analysis showed that folic acid was stable at 23 °C when either protected from or exposed to light, exhibiting little or no loss. (1509)

Parenteral Nutrition Solutions — Shine and Farwell reported a 40% drop in folic acid concentration immediately after admixture in a parenteral nutrition solution composed of amino acids, dextrose, electrolytes, trace elements, and multivitamins in PVC bags. The folic acid concentration then remained relatively constant for 28 days when stored at both 4 and 25 °C. (1063)

Extensive decomposition of ascorbic acid and folic acid was reported in a parenteral nutrition solution composed of amino acids 3.3%, dextrose 12.5%, electrolytes, trace elements, and M.V.I.-12 (USV) in PVC bags. Half-lives were 1.1, 2.9, and 8.9 hours for ascorbic acid and 2.7, 5.4, and 24 hours for folic acid stored at 24 °C in daylight, 24 °C protected from light, and 4 °C protected from light, respectively. The decomposition was much greater than for solutions not containing catalyzing metal ions. Also, it was greater than for the vitamins singly because of interactions with the other vitamins present. (1059)

Because of these interactions, recommendations to separate the administration of vitamins and trace elements have been made. (1056; 1060; 1061) Other researchers have termed such recommendations premature based on differing reports (895; 896) and the apparent absence of epidemic vitamin deficiency in parenteral nutrition patients. (1062)

Smith et al. reported the stability of several vitamins from M.V.I.-12 (Armour) admixed in parenteral nutrition solutions composed of different amino acid products, with or without Intralipid 10%, in glass bottles and PVC bags at 25 and 5 °C for 48 hours. Folic acid was stable in all samples. (1431)

Calcium — Calcium gluconate (Parke-Davis) and folic acid injection (Lederle) have been shown to interact even though a precipitate is not present. The recoverable amount of folic acid from a 10-µg/ml solution declined with increasing concentrations (0.5 to 10 µg/ml) of calcium gluconate. This interaction was reversed by the addition of edetic acid. (538)

Other Drugs — Folic acid injection is stated to be incompatible with oxidizing and reducing agents and heavy metal ions. (4)

FOSCARNET SODIUM
AHFS 8:18

Products — Foscarnet sodium is available as a 24-mg/ml infusion solution in water for injection in 250- and 500-ml glass bottles. Hydrochloric acid and/or sodium hydroxide may have been added to adjust the pH. (2)

pH—Adjusted to pH 7.4. (2)

Osmolality—Foscarnet sodium 24 mg/ml has an osmolality of 271 mOsm/kg. (1689)

Trade Name(s)—Foscavir.

Administration — Foscarnet sodium is administered by intravenous infusion, using an infusion pump. It should not be given by rapid injection. Recommended rates of infusion are a minimum of one hour for doses of 60 mg/kg and up to two hours for doses of 120 mg/kg. Recommended dosage, frequency, and administration rates should not be exceeded. For peripheral administration, foscarnet sodium solution must be diluted to 12 mg/ml with dextrose 5% in water or sodium chloride 0.9%. The drug may be infused without dilution through a central catheter. (2; 4)

Stability — Foscarnet sodium injection is a clear, colorless solution. It should be stored at controlled room temperature and protected from temperatures above 40 °C and from freezing. The product should be used only if the seal is intact and a vacuum is present. (2)

The manufacturer has stated that foscarnet sodium diluted in dextrose 5% in water or sodium chloride 0.9% and transferred to PVC containers is stable for 24 hours at room temperature or under refrigeration. (71)

Autoclaving—The concentration of foscarnet sodium (Astra), diluted in sodium chloride 0.9% to 12 mg/ml and packaged in glass infusion bottles with rubber bungs, was compared before and after autoclaving at 30 psi for 15 minutes at 121 °C. HPLC analysis determined that the foscarnet sodium concentration did not change after autoclaving. Therefore, the dilution may be autoclaved to avoid limiting its shelf life due to sterility concerns. (1835)

Elastomeric Reservoir Pumps—Foscarnet sodium (Astra) 24 mg/ml was evaluated for binding potential to natural rubber elastomeric reservoirs (Baxter). No binding was found after storage for two weeks at 35 °C with gentle agitation. (2014)

Foscarnet sodium solutions in elastomeric reservoir pumps have been stated by the pump manufacturers to be stable for the following time periods refrigerated (REF) or at room temperature (RT) (31):

Pump Reservoir(s)	Conc.	REF	RT
Homepump; Homepump Eclipse	24 mg/ml	14 days	7 days
	12 mg/ml[b]	14 days	7 days
Intermate	2 to 10 mg/ml[a,b]	14 days	4 days
Intermate HPC and LV	24 mg/ml	14 days	2 days
Medflo	24 mg/ml	72 days	72 days
ReadyMed	24 mg/ml	28 days	28 days

[a] *In dextrose 5% in water.*
[b] *In sodium chloride 0.9%.*

Compatibility Information

Solution Compatibility

Foscarnet sodium

Solution	*Mfr*	*Mfr*	*Conc/L*	*Remarks*	*Ref*	*C/I*
Dextrose 5% in water	BA[a]	AST	12 g	Visually compatible and chemically stable by UV spectroscopy for 35 days at 5 and 25 °C	1834	C

Solution Compatibility (Cont.)

Solution	Mfr	Foscarnet sodium Mfr	Conc/L	Remarks	Ref	C/I
Sodium chloride 0.9%	MG[a]	AST	12 g	Visually compatible and chemically stable by HPLC for 30 days at 25 °C in light or dark and at 5 °C in the dark	1726	C
	BA[a]	AST	12 g	Visually compatible and chemically stable by UV spectroscopy for 35 days at 5 and 25 °C	1834	C

[a]*Tested in PVC containers.*

Additive Compatibility

Drug	Mfr	Conc/L	Foscarnet sodium Mfr	Conc/L	Test Soln	Remarks	Ref	C/I
Potassium chloride		20, 40, 60, 80, 120 mmol	AST	12 g	NS	Foscarnet stability was maintained for at least 65 hr. UV analysis found concentrations of 93 to 99% throughout	2156	C

Y-Site Injection Compatibility (1:1 Mixture)

Drug	Mfr	Conc	Foscarnet sodium Mfr	Conc	Remarks	Ref	C/I
Acyclovir sodium	BW	10 mg/ml	AST	24 mg/ml	Immediate precipitation	1335	I
	BW	7 mg/ml[a,b]	AST	24 mg/ml	Acyclovir crystals form immediately	1393	I
Aldesleukin	CHI	33,800 I.U./ml[a]	AST	24 mg/ml	Visually compatible with little or no loss of aldesleukin activity by bioassay	1857	C
Amikacin sulfate	BR	20 mg/ml	AST	24 mg/ml	Physically compatible for 24 hr at room temperature under fluorescent light	1335	C
Aminophylline	LY	25 mg/ml	AST	24 mg/ml	Physically compatible for 24 hr at room temperature under fluorescent light	1335	C
Amphotericin B	SQ	5 mg/ml	AST	24 mg/ml	Delayed formation of cloudy yellow precipitate	1335	I
	SQ	0.6 mg/ml[a]	AST	24 mg/ml	Dense haze forms immediately	1393	I
Ampicillin sodium	WY	20 mg/ml	AST	24 mg/ml	Physically compatible for 24 hr at room temperature under fluorescent light	1335	C
Aztreonam	SQ	40 mg/ml	AST	24 mg/ml	Physically compatible for 24 hr at room temperature under fluorescent light	1335	C
	SQ	40 mg/ml[a,b]	AST	24 mg/ml	Physically compatible for 24 hr at 25 °C under fluorescent light by visual and microscopic examination	1393	C
Cefazolin sodium	SKF	40 mg/ml	AST	24 mg/ml	Physically compatible for 24 hr at room temperature under fluorescent light	1335	C
Cefoperazone sodium	RR	40 mg/ml	AST	24 mg/ml	Physically compatible for 24 hr at room temperature under fluorescent light	1335	C
Cefoxitin sodium	MSD	40 mg/ml	AST	24 mg/ml	Physically compatible for 24 hr at room temperature under fluorescent light	1335	C
Ceftazidime	GL	20 mg/ml	AST	24 mg/ml	Physically compatible for 24 hr at room temperature under fluorescent light	1335	C
	GL	20 mg/ml[a,b]	AST	24 mg/ml	Physically compatible for 24 hr at 25 °C under fluorescent light by visual and microscopic examination	1393	C

Y-Site Injection Compatibility (1:1 Mixture) (Cont.)

			Foscarnet sodium				
Drug	*Mfr*	*Conc*	*Mfr*	*Conc*	*Remarks*	*Ref*	*C/I*
Ceftizoxime sodium	SKF	40 mg/ml	AST	24 mg/ml	Physically compatible for 24 hr at room temperature under fluorescent light	1335	C
Ceftriaxone sodium	RC	20 mg/ml[a,b]	AST	24 mg/ml	Physically compatible for 24 hr at 25 °C under fluorescent light by visual and microscopic examination	1393	C
Cefuroxime sodium	GL	30 mg/ml	AST	24 mg/ml	Physically compatible for 24 hr at room temperature under fluorescent light	1335	C
Chloramphenicol sodium succinate	PD	20 mg/ml	AST	24 mg/ml	Physically compatible for 24 hr at room temperature under fluorescent light	1335	C
Cimetidine HCl	SKF	150 mg/ml	AST	24 mg/ml	Physically compatible for 24 hr at room temperature under fluorescent light	1335	C
Clindamycin phosphate	AB	24 mg/ml	AST	24 mg/ml	Physically compatible for 24 hr at room temperature under fluorescent light	1335	C
	UP	12 mg/ml[a,b]	AST	24 mg/ml	Physically compatible for 24 hr at 25 °C under fluorescent light by visual and microscopic examination	1393	C
Dexamethasone sodium phosphate	OR	10 mg/ml	AST	24 mg/ml	Physically compatible for 24 hr at room temperature under fluorescent light	1335	C
Diazepam	ES	5 mg/ml	AST	24 mg/ml	Gas production	1335	I
Digoxin	WY	0.25 mg/ml	AST	24 mg/ml	Gas production	1335	I
Diphenhydramine HCl	PD	50 mg/ml	AST	24 mg/ml	Cloudy solution	1335	I
Dobutamine HCl	LI	12.5 mg/ml	AST	24 mg/ml	Delayed formation of muddy precipitate	1335	I
Dopamine HCl	DU	80 mg/ml	AST	24 mg/ml	Physically compatible for 24 hr at room temperature under fluorescent light	1335	C
Droperidol	QU	2.5 mg/ml	AST	24 mg/ml	Delayed formation of fine yellow precipitate	1335	I
Erythromycin lactobionate	AB	20 mg/ml	AST	24 mg/ml	Physically compatible for 24 hr at room temperature under fluorescent light	1335	C
	ES	20 mg/ml[a,b]	AST	24 mg/ml	Physically compatible for 24 hr at 25 °C under fluorescent light by visual and microscopic examination	1393	C
Fluconazole	RR	2 mg/ml	AST	24 mg/ml	Physically compatible for 24 hr at 25 °C	1407	C
Flucytosine	RC	10 mg/ml[b]	AST	24 mg/ml	Physically compatible for 24 hr at 25 °C under fluorescent light by visual and microscopic examination	1393	C
Furosemide	AB	10 mg/ml	AST	24 mg/ml	Physically compatible for 24 hr at room temperature under fluorescent light	1335	C
Ganciclovir sodium		50 mg/ml	AST	24 mg/ml	Immediate precipitation	1335	I
Gentamicin sulfate	ES	4 mg/ml	AST	24 mg/ml	Physically compatible for 24 hr at room temperature under fluorescent light	1335	C
	ES	2 mg/ml[a,b]	AST	24 mg/ml	Physically compatible for 24 hr at 25 °C under fluorescent light by visual and microscopic examination	1393	C
Haloperidol lactate	LY	5 mg/ml	AST	24 mg/ml	Delayed formation of fine white precipitate	1335	I
Heparin sodium	ES	1000 units/ml	AST	24 mg/ml	Physically compatible for 24 hr at room temperature under fluorescent light	1335	C

Y-Site Injection Compatibility (1:1 Mixture) (Cont.)

Drug	Mfr	Conc	Foscarnet sodium Mfr	Foscarnet sodium Conc	Remarks	Ref	C/I
	LY	100 units/ml[a,b]	AST	24 mg/ml	Physically compatible for 24 hr at 25 °C under fluorescent light by visual and microscopic examination	1393	C
Hydrocortisone sodium succinate	UP	50 mg/ml	AST	24 mg/ml	Physically compatible for 24 hr at room temperature under fluorescent light	1335	C
Hydromorphone HCl	KN	10 mg/ml	AST	24 mg/ml	Physically compatible for 24 hr at room temperature under fluorescent light	1335	C
Hydroxyzine HCl	LY	50 mg/ml	AST	24 mg/ml	Physically compatible for 24 hr at room temperature under fluorescent light	1335	C
Imipenem–cilastatin sodium	MSD	10 mg/ml	AST	24 mg/ml	Physically compatible for 24 hr at room temperature under fluorescent light	1335	C
	MSD	5 mg/ml[a]	AST	24 mg/ml	Physically compatible for 24 hr at 25 °C under fluorescent light by visual and microscopic examination	1393	C
Leucovorin calcium	QU	10 mg/ml	AST	24 mg/ml	Cloudy yellow solution	1335	I
Lorazepam	WY	4 mg/ml	AST	24 mg/ml	Gas production	1335	I
	WY	0.08 mg/ml[a,b]	AST	24 mg/ml	Physically compatible for 24 hr at 25 °C under fluorescent light by visual and microscopic examination	1393	C
Metoclopramide HCl	RB	4 mg/ml	AST	24 mg/ml	Physically compatible for 24 hr at room temperature under fluorescent light	1335	C
	RB	2 mg/ml[a,b]	AST	24 mg/ml	Physically compatible for 24 hr at 25 °C under fluorescent light by visual and microscopic examination	1393	C
Metronidazole	AB	5 mg/ml	AST	24 mg/ml	Physically compatible for 24 hr at room temperature under fluorescent light	1335	C
	SE	5 mg/ml	AST	24 mg/ml	Physically compatible for 24 hr at 25 °C under fluorescent light by visual and microscopic examination	1393	C
Midazolam HCl	RC	5 mg/ml	AST	24 mg/ml	Gas production	1335	I
Morphine sulfate	IMS	1 mg/ml	AST	24 mg/ml	Physically compatible for 24 hr at room temperature under fluorescent light	1335	C
	ES	1 mg/ml[a,b]	AST	24 mg/ml	Physically compatible for 24 hr at 25 °C under fluorescent light by visual and microscopic examination	1393	C
	ES	5[b] and 15 mg/ml	AST	24 mg/ml	Visually compatible for 24 hr at 23 °C under fluorescent light	1529	C
Nafcillin sodium	BR	20 mg/ml[a,b]	AST	24 mg/ml	Physically compatible for 24 hr at 25 °C under fluorescent light by visual and microscopic examination	1393	C
Oxacillin sodium	BR	40 mg/ml	AST	24 mg/ml	Physically compatible for 24 hr at room temperature under fluorescent light	1335	C
	BE	20 mg/ml[a,b]	AST	24 mg/ml	Physically compatible for 24 hr at 25 °C under fluorescent light by visual and microscopic examination	1393	C
Penicillin G potassium	SQ	100,000 units/ml	AST	24 mg/ml	Physically compatible for 24 hr at room temperature under fluorescent light	1335	C
Pentamidine isethionate	LY	6 mg/ml	AST	24 mg/ml	Immediate precipitation	1335	I
	LY	6 mg/ml[a,b]	AST	24 mg/ml	Pentamidine crystals form immediately	1393	I

Y-Site Injection Compatibility (1:1 Mixture) (Cont.)

			Foscarnet sodium				
Drug	*Mfr*	*Conc*	*Mfr*	*Conc*	*Remarks*	*Ref*	*C/I*
Phenytoin sodium	PD	50 mg/ml	AST	24 mg/ml	Physically compatible for 24 hr at room temperature under fluorescent light	1335	C
Piperacillin sodium	LE	80 mg/ml	AST	24 mg/ml	Physically compatible for 24 hr at room temperature under fluorescent light	1335	C
Prochlorperazine edisylate	SKF	5 mg/ml	AST	24 mg/ml	Cloudy brown solution	1335	I
Promethazine HCl	ES	50 mg/ml	AST	24 mg/ml	Gas production	1335	I
Ranitidine HCl	GL	2 mg/ml[a,b]	AST	24 mg/ml	Physically compatible for 24 hr at 25 °C under fluorescent light by visual and microscopic examination	1393	C
Ticarcillin disodium–clavulanate potassium	BE	100 mg/ml[a,b]	AST	24 mg/ml	Physically compatible for 24 hr at 25 °C under fluorescent light by visual and microscopic examination	1393	C
Tobramycin sulfate	LI	40 mg/ml	AST	24 mg/ml	Physically compatible for 24 hr at room temperature under fluorescent light	1335	C
Trimethoprim–sulfamethoxazole	RC	16 + 80 mg/ml	AST	24 mg/ml	Immediate precipitation and gas production	1335	I
	BW	0.53 + 2.6 mg/ml[a]	AST	24 mg/ml	Physically compatible for 24 hr at 25 °C under fluorescent light by visual and microscopic examination	1393	C
Trimetrexate	WL	1 mg/ml[a]	AST	24 mg/ml	Trimetrexate crystals form immediately	1393	I
Vancomycin HCl	LE	20 mg/ml	AST	24 mg/ml	Immediate precipitation	1335	I
	LE	15 mg/ml[a,b]	AST	24 mg/ml	Physically compatible for 24 hr at 25 °C under fluorescent light by visual and microscopic examination	1393	C
	LE	10 mg/ml[b]	AST	24 mg/ml	Visually compatible for 24 hr at room temperature in test tubes. No precipitate found on filter from Y-site delivery	2063	C
TPN #121[d]		[c]	AST	24 mg/ml	Physically compatible for 24 hr at 25 °C under fluorescent light by visual and microscopic examination	1393	C

[a] *Tested in dextrose 5% in water.*
[b] *Tested in sodium chloride 0.9%.*
[c] *Tested in equal quantities.*
[d] *Refer to Appendix I for the composition of parenteral nutrition solutions. TPN indicates a 2-in-1 admixture.*

Additional Compatibility Information

Infusion Solutions — The manufacturer recommends dextrose 5% in water or sodium chloride 0.9% for diluting foscarnet sodium for peripheral administration and the use of such dilutions within 24 hours of first opening the sealed bottle. (2)

Other Drugs — The manufacturer also recommends that no other drug or solution be administered concurrently through the same catheter as foscarnet sodium. Dextrose 30% and numerous drugs have been reported to cause physical incompatibilities with foscarnet sodium. (See Compatibility Information.) Additionally, foscarnet sodium may chelate divalent metal ions and is chemically incompatible with solutions containing calcium such as Ringer's injection, lactated, and parenteral nutrition solutions. (2)

Other Information

Microbial Growth — Foscarnet sodium (Astra) 13 mg/ml diluted in sodium chloride 0.9% at 22 °C did not exhibit an antibacterial effect on the growth of three organisms (*Enterococcus faecium, Staphylococcus aureus,* and *Pseudomonas aeruginosa*) inoculated into the solution. Foscarnet sodium did exhibit moderate antifungal activity against *Candida albicans*. The authors recommended that ready-to-use solutions be stored under refrigeration whenever possible and that the potential for microbiological growth should be considered when assigning expiration periods. (2160)

FOSPHENYTOIN SODIUM
AHFS 28:12.12

Products — Fosphenytoin is the prodrug for its metabolite, phenytoin. Fosphenytoin sodium is available in 2- and 10-ml vials as a 75-mg/ml solution, which is the equivalent of phenytoin sodium 50 mg/ml after administration. Each milliliter also contains tromethamine (TRIS) buffer along with hydrochloric acid or sodium hydroxide to adjust pH in water for injection. (2) CAUTION: Care should be taken to avoid confusion between the two different forms fosphenytoin sodium and phenytoin sodium to prevent dosing errors.

Units — Each 75 mg of fosphenytoin sodium is metabolically converted to 50 mg of phenytoin after administration. NOTE: The amount and concentration of fosphenytoin sodium are expressed in terms of the equivalent mass of phenytoin sodium, called phenytoin sodium equivalents (PE). The manufacturer indicates that this avoids the need to perform conversions based on molecular weight between the two forms. (2) However, it creates the need to express all prescribing, dispensing, and dosing consistently in PE to avoid dosing errors that could result from confusion between the two forms.

pH — From 8.6 to 9.0. (2)

Trade Name(s) — Cerebyx.

Administration — Fosphenytoin sodium is dosed in terms of phenytoin sodium equivalents (PE). (See Units section above.) CAUTION: Care should be taken to ensure that all prescribing, preparation, and dosing is performed using the correct units and that any confusion between the two forms (fosphenytoin sodium and phenytoin sodium) is avoided.

Fosphenytoin sodium is administered intravenously at a rate no greater than 150 mg PE/min. The drug may be diluted in dextrose 5% in water or sodium chloride 0.9% to a concentration of 1.5 to 25 mg PE/ml. It has also been given intramuscularly. (2)

Stability — Fosphenytoin sodium injection is a clear, colorless to pale yellow solution. Intact vials should be stored under refrigeration at 2 to 8 °C. Storage at controlled room temperature should not exceed 48 hours. Any vials that develop particulate matter should not be used. (2)

Freezing Solutions — Fosphenytoin sodium (Parke-Davis) 1, 8, and 20 mg PE (phenytoin sodium equivalents) per milliliter in dextrose 5% in water (Baxter) and sodium chloride 0.9% (Baxter) in PVC containers and undiluted fosphenytoin sodium 50 mg PE per milliliter were packaged in 3-ml polypropylene syringes sealed with tip caps (Becton-Dickinson). The samples were frozen at −20 °C. Little or no loss of fosphenytoin sodium occurred after 30 days of frozen storage followed by seven days at 4 or 25 °C. Stability was also maintained if the thawed samples that had been stored at 25 °C were returned to the freezer for an additional seven days. (2083)

Syringes — Fosphenytoin sodium (Parke-Davis) 50 mg PE (phenytoin sodium equivalents) per milliliter was packaged in 3-ml polypropylene syringes with syringe caps (Becton-Dickinson) and stored at −20, 4, and 25 °C. The samples stored at 4 and 25 °C exhibited little or no loss of fosphenytoin sodium by HPLC analysis in 30 days. The samples stored at −20 °C also showed little or no loss of fosphenytoin sodium after 30 days' storage followed by seven days at 4 °C or at 25 °C. Also, stability was maintained if the thawed samples that had been stored at 25 °C were returned to the freezer for an additional seven days. (2083)

Sorption — No loss of fosphenytoin sodium (Parke-Davis) due to sorption to PVC containers was observed when compared to glass bottles. (2083)

Compatibility Information

Solution Compatibility

Fosphenytoin sodium[a]

Solution	*Mfr*	*Mfr*	*Conc/L*	*Remarks*	*Ref*	*C/I*
Amino acid injection 10%	BA[b]	PD	1, 8, 20 mg PE/ml	Visually compatible with little or no loss of fosphenytoin by HPLC in 7 days at 25 °C under fluorescent light	2083	C
Dextrose 5% in Ringer's injection, lactated	BA[b]	PD	1, 8, 20 mg PE/ml	Visually compatible with little or no loss of fosphenytoin by HPLC in 7 days at 25 °C under fluorescent light	2083	C
Dextrose 5% in sodium chloride 0.45%	BA[b]	PD	1, 8, 20 mg PE/ml	Visually compatible with little or no loss of fosphenytoin by HPLC in 7 days at 25 °C under fluorescent light	2083	C
Dextrose 5% in water	BA[b,c]	PD	1, 8, 20 mg PE/ml	Visually compatible with little or no loss of fosphenytoin by HPLC in 30 days at 25 °C under fluorescent light	2083	C
	BA[b]	PD	1, 8, 20 mg PE/ml	Visually compatible with little or no loss of fosphenytoin by HPLC in 30 days at 4 °C under fluorescent light	2083	C

Solution Compatibility (Cont.)

Fosphenytoin sodium[a]

Solution	*Mfr*	*Mfr*	*Conc/L*	*Remarks*	*Ref*	*C/I*
Dextrose 10% in water	BA[b]	PD	1, 8, 20 mg PE/ml	Visually compatible with little or no loss of fosphenytoin by HPLC in 7 days at 25 °C under fluorescent light	2083	C
Hetastarch 6% in sodium chloride 0.9%	MG	PD	1, 8, 20 mg PE/ml	Visually compatible with little or no loss of fosphenytoin by HPLC in 7 days at 25 °C under fluorescent light	2083	C
Mannitol 20%	BA[b]	PD	1, 8, 20 mg PE/ml	Visually compatible with little or no loss of fosphenytoin by HPLC in 7 days at 25 °C under fluorescent light	2083	C
Plasma-Lyte A, pH 7.4	BA[b]	PD	1, 8, 20 mg PE/ml	Visually compatible with little or no loss of fosphenytoin by HPLC in 7 days at 25 °C under fluorescent light	2083	C
Ringer's injection, lactated	BA[b]	PD	1, 8, 20 mg PE/ml	Visually compatible with little or no loss of fosphenytoin by HPLC in 7 days at 25 °C under fluorescent light	2083	C
Sodium chloride 0.9%	BA[b,c]	PD	1, 8, 20 mg PE/ml	Visually compatible with little or no loss of fosphenytoin by HPLC in 30 days at 25 °C under fluorescent light	2083	C
	BA[b]	PD	1, 8, 20 mg PE/ml	Visually compatible with little or no loss of fosphenytoin by HPLC in 30 days at 4 °C under fluorescent light	2083	C

[a]Concentration expressed in milligrams of phenytoin sodium equivalents (PE) per milliliter.
[b]Tested in PVC containers.
[c]Tested in glass bottles.

Additive Compatibility

Fosphenytoin sodium[a]

Drug	*Mfr*	*Conc/L*	*Mfr*	*Conc/L*	*Test Soln*	*Remarks*	*Ref*	*C/I*
Potassium chloride	BA	20 and 40 mEq	PD	1, 8, 20 mg PE/ml	D5½S[b]	Visually compatible with little or no loss of fosphenytoin by HPLC in 7 days at 25 °C under fluorescent light	2083	C

[a]Concentration expressed in milligrams of phenytoin sodium equivalents (PE) per milliliter.
[b]Tested in PVC containers.

Y-Site Injection Compatibility (1:1 Mixture)

Fosphenytoin sodium[a]

Drug	*Mfr*	*Conc*	*Mfr*	*Conc*	*Remarks*	*Ref*	*C/I*
Lorazepam	WY	2 mg/ml	PD	1 mg PE/ml[b]	Samples remained clear with no loss of either drug by HPLC in 8 hr	2223	C
Midazolam HCl	RC	2 mg/ml[b]	PD	1 mg PE/ml[b]	Midazolam base precipitates immediately	2223	I
Phenobarbital sodium		130 mg/ml	PD	10 mg PE/ml[b]	Visually compatible with no loss of either drug by HPLC in 8 hr at room temperature	2212	C

[a]Concentration expressed in milligrams of phenytoin sodium equivalents (PE) per milliliter.
[b]Tested in sodium chloride 0.9%.

FUROSEMIDE (FRUSEMIDE) AHFS 40:28

Products — Furosemide is available in 2-, 4-, and 10-ml amber ampuls, single-use vials, prefilled syringes, and syringe cartridges. (4; 29) Each milliliter of solution contains furosemide 10 mg, water for injection, with sodium chloride for isotonicity, sodium hydroxide, and, if necessary, hydrochloric acid to adjust pH. (1-5/97; 4)

pH — From 8 to 9.3. (4)

Osmolality — Furosemide (Hoechst-Roussel) 10 mg/ml has an osmolality of 287 mOsm/kg. (50) The osmolality of the Elkins-Sinn product has been determined to be 289 mOsm/kg by freezing-point depression. (1071)

In another study, the osmolality of furosemide injection (manufacturer unspecified) was determined to be 291 mOsm/kg. (1233)

Sodium Content — The injection contains 0.162 mEq of sodium per milliliter. (4)

Administration — Furosemide may be administered by intramuscular injection, by direct intravenous injection over one to two minutes, and by intravenous infusion at a rate not exceeding 4 mg/min. (1-5/97; 4)

Stability — Exposure to light may cause discoloration; protection from light for the syringes once they are removed from the package is recommended. Do not use furosemide solutions if they have a yellow color. Furosemide products should be stored at controlled room temperature. (1-5/97; 4) Refrigeration may result in precipitation or crystallization. However, resolubilization at room temperature or on warming may be performed without affecting the drug's stability. (593)

pH Effects — Furosemide is soluble in alkaline solutions and is prepared as a mildly buffered alkaline product. (1-5/97; 4) It can usually be mixed with infusion solutions that are neutral or weakly basic (pH 7 to 10) and with some weakly acidic solutions that have a low buffer capacity. (4) It should not be mixed with acidic solutions having a pH below 5.5. Solutions such as sodium chloride 0.9%, Ringer's injection, lactated, and dextrose 5% in water have been recommended. If the solution pH is below 5.5, pH adjustment has been recommended. (1-5/97; 4) In addition, furosemide has been found to be unstable in acidic media but very stable in basic media. (664) Also see Acidic Additives under Additional Compatibility Information below.

Autoclaving — Autoclaving of furosemide 1 mg/ml in sodium chloride 0.9% in glass bottles at 115 °C for 34 minutes resulted in no loss of furosemide. Storage of the solution for 70 days at room temperature with protection from light also showed no detectable change in furosemide content. However, storage at room temperature with exposure to light for 70 days resulted in about a 60% loss of furosemide and the formation of a yellow-orange precipitate. (1108)

Light Effects — Furosemide is subject to photodegradation by several mechanisms. Photodegradation is minimized at pH 7; rates of decomposition increase as the pH becomes more acidic or basic. Photodegradation is unaffected by ionic strength and initial concentration (in the range of 10 μg/ml to 1 mg/ml), but the rate of loss may decrease at the higher concentration due to a light-filtering effect of the yellow discoloration. In pH 7 phosphate buffer, more than 60% furosemide loss occurred in transparent glass vials exposed to fluorescent light for 90 hours; little or no loss occurred if the transparent vials were covered with aluminum foil or if amber glass containers were used. (2067)

Syringes — Furosemide (Hoechst-Roussel) 10 mg/ml retained potency for three months at room temperature when 2 ml of solution was packaged in Tubex cartridges. (13)

Furosemide (Hoechst) 10 mg/ml was filled into 25-ml polypropylene syringes (Becton-Dickinson) and stored at 25 °C while exposed to normal room light or in the dark for 24 hours. There was no detectable change in furosemide content in either light-exposed or light-protected syringes. (1108)

Filtration — Furosemide (Hoechst) 0.04 mg/ml in dextrose 5% in water and sodium chloride 0.9% was filtered through a 0.22-μm cellulose ester membrane filter (Ivex-HP, Millipore) over six hours. No significant drug loss due to binding to the filter was noted. (1034)

Central Venous Catheter — Furosemide (American Regent) 1 mg/ml in dextrose 5% in water was found to be compatible with the ARROWg+ard Blue Plus (Arrow International) chlorhexidine-bearing triple-lumen central catheter. HPLC analysis was used to evaluate completeness of drug delivery through the catheter and the amount of chlorhexidine removed from the internal lumens. Essentially complete delivery of the drug was found with little or no drug loss occurring. Furthermore, chlorhexidine delivered from the catheter remained at trace amounts with no substantial increase due to the delivery of the drug through the catheter. (2335)

Compatibility Information

Solution Compatibility

Furosemide

Solution	*Mfr*	*Mfr*	*Conc/L*	*Remarks*	*Ref*	*C/I*
Alcohol 5% and dextrose 5%	BA	HO	600 mg	Physically compatible for 24 hr	315	C
Amino acids 4.25%, dextrose 25%	MG	HO	40 mg	No increase in particulate matter in 24 hr at 25 °C	349	C
Dextrose 5% in Ringer's injection, lactated	BA	HO	600 mg	Physically compatible for 24 hr	315	C
Dextrose 5% in sodium chloride 0.9%	BA	HO	600 mg	Physically compatible for 24 hr	315	C

Solution Compatibility (Cont.)

Furosemide

Solution	*Mfr*	*Mfr*	*Conc/L*	*Remarks*	*Ref*	*C/I*
Dextrose 5% in water	BA	HO	600 mg	Physically compatible for 24 hr	315	C
			200 and 400 mg	4 to 5% loss in 24 hr at 25 °C	1348	C
Dextrose 10% in water	BA	HO	600 mg	Physically compatible for 24 hr	315	C
Dextrose 20% in water	BA	HO	600 mg	Physically compatible for 24 hr	315	C
Fructose 10% in water	BA	HO	300 and 600 mg	Precipitate forms within 24 hr	315	I
Invert sugar 10% in Electrolyte #1	BA	HO	600 mg	Physically compatible for 24 hr	315	C
Invert sugar 10% in Electrolyte #2	BA	HO	300 and 600 mg	Precipitate forms within 24 hr	315	I
Mannitol 20%	BA[a]	AB	200, 400, 800 mg	Visually compatible for 72 hr at 22 °C	1803	C
Ringer's injection, lactated	BA	HO	600 mg	Physically compatible for 24 hr	315	C
	TR[a]	HO	1 g	No furosemide loss in 24 hr at 25 °C exposed to light or in the dark	1108	C
Sodium chloride 0.9%	BA	HO	600 mg	Physically compatible for 24 hr	315	C
	TR[a]	HO	1 g	No furosemide loss in 24 hr at 25 °C exposed to light or in the dark. 10% loss in 26 days at 6 °C	1108	C
			200 and 400 mg	5 to 7% loss in 24 hr at 25 °C	1348	C
Sodium lactate ⅙ M	BA	HO	600 mg	Physically compatible for 24 hr	315	C

[a]*Tested in PVC containers.*

Additive Compatibility

Furosemide

Drug	*Mfr*	*Conc/L*	*Mfr*	*Conc/L*	*Test Soln*	*Remarks*	*Ref*	*C/I*
Amikacin sulfate	BR	2 g	HO	160 mg	D5W, NS	Transient cloudiness during admixture but then physically compatible for 24 hr at 21 °C	876	C
Aminophylline	ANT	1 g	HO	1 g	NS	Physically compatible for 72 hr at 15 and 30 °C	1479	C
Amiodarone HCl	LZ	1.8 g	ES	200 mg	D5W, NS[a]	Physically compatible with 8% or less amiodarone loss in 24 hr at 24 °C under fluorescent light	1031	C
	LZ	4 g	HO	1 g	D5W	Haze forms in 5 hr and precipitate forms in 24 to 72 hr at 30 °C. No change at 15 °C	1479	I
Ampicillin sodium	BE	20 g	HO	1 g	NS	Physically compatible for 72 hr at 15 and 30 °C	1479	C
Atropine sulfate	ANT	60 mg	HO	1 g	W	Physically compatible for 72 hr at 15 and 30 °C	1479	C
Bumetanide	LEO	6 mg	HO	1 g	NS	Physically compatible for 72 hr at 15 and 30 °C	1479	C
Buprenorphine HCl		75 mg	HO	1 g	W	Haze for 6 hr at 30 °C. No change at 15 °C	1479	I
Calcium gluconate	ANT	2 g	HO	1 g	NS	Physically compatible for 72 hr at 15 and 30 °C	1479	C

Additive Compatibility (Cont.)

Drug	*Mfr*	*Conc/L*	*Mfr*	*Conc/L*	*Test Soln*	*Remarks*	*Ref*	*C/I*
			Furosemide					
Cefamandole nafate	DI	20 g	HO	1 g	W	Physically compatible for 72 hr at 15 and 30 °C	1479	C
Cefoperazone sodium	RR	10 g	HO	200 mg	D5W	Physically compatible with 10% loss of both drugs in 15 days at 25 °C and in 20 days at 4 °C in the dark	1402	C
Cefuroxime sodium	GL	37.5 g	HO	1 g	W	Physically compatible for 72 hr at 15 and 30 °C	1479	C
Chlorpromazine HCl	ANT	5 g	HO	1 g	W	Immediate precipitation	1479	I
Cimetidine HCl	SKF	3 g	HO	400 mg	D5W	Physically compatible and cimetidine chemically stable for 24 hr at room temperature. Furosemide not tested	551	C
	SKF	4 g	HO	1 g	NS	Physically compatible for 72 hr at 15 and 30 °C	1479	C
Dexamethasone sodium phosphate	MSD	4 g	HO	1 g	NS	Physically compatible for 72 hr at 15 and 30 °C	1479	C
Diamorphine HCl	EV	500 mg	HO	1 g	W	Physically compatible for 72 hr at 15 and 30 °C	1479	C
Diazepam	PHX	1 g	HO	1 g	D5W	Immediate precipitation	1479	I
Digoxin	BW	25 mg	HO	1 g	NS	Physically compatible for 72 hr at 15 and 30 °C	1479	C
Dobutamine HCl	LI	1 g	HO	1 g	D5W, NS	Cloudy in 1 hr at 25 °C	789	I
	LI	1 g	WY	5 g	D5W, NS	Immediate white precipitate	812	I
	LI	500 mg	HO	1 g	NS	Haze forms immediately	1479	I
Epinephrine HCl	ANT	8 mg	HO	1 g	W	Physically compatible for 72 hr at 15 and 30 °C	1479	C
Erythromycin lactobionate	AB	5 g	HO	1 g	NS	Immediate precipitation. Crystals form in 12 to 24 hr at 15 and 30 °C	1479	I
Gentamicin sulfate	SC	1.6 g	HO	800 mg	D5W, NS	Immediate precipitation of furosemide	876	I
	RS	8 g	HO	1 g	NS	Physically compatible for 24 hr at 15 and 30 °C. Slight precipitate forms in 48 to 72 hr	1479	C
Heparin sodium	WED	20,000 units	HO	1 g	NS	Physically compatible for 72 hr at 15 and 30 °C	1479	C
Hydrocortisone sodium succinate		1 g		200 and 400 mg	D5W, NS	6 to 8% hydrocortisone loss and 5 to 6% furosemide loss in 24 hr at 25 °C	1348	C
		300 mg		200 and 400 mg	D5W, NS	6 to 8% hydrocortisone loss in 6 hr and 10 to 14% loss in 24 hr at 25 °C. 5 to 6% furosemide loss in 24 hr	1348	I
	UP	50 g	HO	1 g	NS	Physically compatible for 72 hr at 15 and 30 °C	1479	C
Isoproterenol HCl	PX	4 mg	HO	1 g	D5W	Immediate precipitation	1479	I
Isosorbide dinitrate		1 g	HO	1 g		Physically compatible for 72 hr at 15 and 30 °C	1479	C
Kanamycin sulfate	BE	2 g	HO	160 mg	D5W, NS	Transient cloudiness during admixture, but then physically compatible for 24 hr at 21 °C	876	C
Lidocaine HCl	ANT	2 g	HO	1 g	NS	Physically compatible for 72 hr at 15 and 30 °C	1479	C

Additive Compatibility (Cont.)

			Furosemide					
Drug	*Mfr*	*Conc/L*	*Mfr*	*Conc/L*	*Test Soln*	*Remarks*	*Ref*	*C/I*
Meperidine HCl	RC	5 g	HO	1 g	W	Fine precipitate forms immediately	1479	I
Meropenem	ZEN	1 and 20 g	HO	1 g	NS	Visually compatible for 4 hr at room temperature	1994	C
Metoclopramide HCl	ANT	1 g	HO	1 g	NS	Immediate precipitation	1479	I
Morphine sulfate	EV	1 g	HO	1 g	W	Physically compatible for 72 hr at 15 and 30 °C	1479	C
Netilmicin sulfate	SC	1.5 g	HO	400 mg	D5W, NS	Immediate precipitation of furosemide	876	I
Nitroglycerin	ACC	400 mg	HO	1 g	D5W[b]	Physically compatible with no nitroglycerin loss in 48 hr at 23 °C. Furosemide not tested	929	C
	ACC	400 mg	HO	1 g	NS[b]	Physically compatible with 3% nitroglycerin loss in 48 hr at 23 °C. Furosemide not tested	929	C
Papaveretum	RC[c]	2 g	HO	1 g	W	Thick white precipitate forms	1479	I
Penicillin G	GL	12 g	HO	1 g	NS	Physically compatible for 24 hr at 15 and 30 °C. Precipitate forms in 48 to 72 hr at 30 °C. No change at 15 °C	1479	C
Potassium chloride	ANT	40 mM	HO	1 g	W	Physically compatible for 72 hr at 15 and 30 °C	1479	C
Prochlorperazine edisylate	MB	1.25 g	HO	1 g	W	Yellow globular precipitate forms immediately	1479	I
Promethazine HCl	MB	5 g	HO	1 g	W	White precipitate forms immediately	1479	I
Ranitidine HCl	GL	500 mg	HO	1 g	NS	Physically compatible for 72 hr at 15 and 30 °C	1479	C
	GL	50 mg and 2 g		400 mg	D5W	Physically compatible and ranitidine chemically stable by HPLC for 24 hr at 25 °C. Furosemide not tested	1515	C
Scopolamine butylbromide	BI	2 g	HO	1 g	W	Physically compatible for 72 hr at 15 and 30 °C	1479	C
Sodium bicarbonate	IMS	84 g	HO	1 g	W	Physically compatible for 72 hr at 15 and 30 °C	1479	C
Sulphadimidine	ICI	100 g	HO	1 g	W	Physically compatible for 72 hr at 15 and 30 °C	1479	C
Theophylline		2 g		330 mg	D5W	Visually compatible with little or no theophylline loss and 10% furosemide loss in 48 hr	1909	C
Tobramycin sulfate	DI	1.6 g	HO	800 mg	D5W, NS	Transient cloudiness during admixture but then physically compatible for 24 hr at 21 °C	876	C
	LI	8 g	HO	1 g	NS	Physically compatible for 72 hr at 15 and 30 °C	1479	C
Verapamil HCl	KN	80 mg	HO	200 mg	D5W, NS	Physically compatible for 24 hr	764	C
	AB	500 mg	HO	1 g	NS	Slight precipitate forms but dissipates	1479	?

[a]*Tested in both polyolefin and PVC containers.*
[b]*Tested in glass containers.*
[c]*The former formulation was tested.*

Drugs in Syringe Compatibility

			Furosemide				
Drug (in syringe)	*Mfr*	*Amt*	*Mfr*	*Amt*	*Remarks*	*Ref*	*C/I*
Bleomycin sulfate		1.5 units/ 0.5 ml		5 mg/ 0.5 ml	Physically compatible for 5 min at room temperature followed by 8 min of centrifugation	980	C
Cisplatin		0.5 mg/ 0.5 ml		5 mg/ 0.5 ml	Physically compatible for 5 min at room temperature followed by 8 min of centrifugation	980	C
Cyclophosphamide		10 mg/ 0.5 ml		5 mg/ 0.5 ml	Physically compatible for 5 min at room temperature followed by 8 min of centrifugation	980	C
Doxapram HCl	RB	400 mg/ 20 ml	HO	100 mg/ 10 ml	Immediate turbidity	1177	I
Doxorubicin HCl		1 mg/ 0.5 ml		5 mg/ 0.5 ml	Immediate precipitation	980	I
Droperidol		1.25 mg/ 0.5 ml		5 mg/ 0.5 ml	Immediate precipitation	980	I
Fluorouracil		25 mg/ 0.5 ml		5 mg/ 0.5 ml	Physically compatible for 5 min at room temperature followed by 8 min of centrifugation	980	C
Heparin sodium		500 units/ 0.5 ml		5 mg/ 0.5 ml	Physically compatible for 5 min at room temperature followed by 8 min of centrifugation	980	C
		2500 units/ 1 ml		20 mg/ 2 ml	Physically compatible for at least 5 min	1053	C
Leucovorin calcium		5 mg/ 0.5 ml		5 mg/ 0.5 ml	Physically compatible for 5 min at room temperature followed by 8 min of centrifugation	980	C
Methotrexate sodium		12.5 mg/ 0.5 ml		5 mg/ 0.5 ml	Physically compatible for 5 min at room temperature followed by 8 min of centrifugation	980	C
Metoclopramide HCl		2.5 mg/ 0.5 ml		5 mg/ 0.5 ml	Immediate precipitation	980	I
Milrinone lactate	WI	3.5 mg/ 3.5 ml	LY	40 mg/ 4 ml	(Brought to 10-ml total volume with D5W) Immediate precipitation	1191	I
Mitomycin		0.25 mg/ 0.5 ml		5 mg/ 0.5 ml	Physically compatible for 5 min at room temperature followed by 8 min of centrifugation	980	C
Vinblastine sulfate		0.5 mg/ 0.5 ml		5 mg/ 0.5 ml	Immediate precipitation	980	I
Vincristine sulfate		0.5 mg/ 0.5 ml		5 mg/ 0.5 ml	Immediate precipitation	980	I

Y-Site Injection Compatibility (1:1 Mixture)

			Furosemide				
Drug	*Mfr*	*Conc*	*Mfr*	*Conc*	*Remarks*	*Ref*	*C/I*
Alatrofloxacin mesylate	PF	1.43 mg/ml[a]	AMR	10 mg/ml	White precipitate forms	2235	I
Allopurinol sodium	BW	3 mg/ml[b]	ES	3 mg/ml[b]	Physically compatible with no change in measured turbidity or increase in particle content in 4 hr at 22 °C	1686	C
Amifostine	USB	10 mg/ml[a]	AB	3 mg/ml[a]	Physically compatible with no change in measured turbidity or increase in particle content in 4 hr at 23 °C	1845	C
Amikacin sulfate	BR	2 mg/ml[c]	HO	10 mg/ml	Physically compatible for 24 hr at 21 °C	876	C

Y-Site Injection Compatibility (1:1 Mixture) (Cont.)

Drug	Mfr	Conc	Mfr	Conc	Remarks	Ref	C/I
			Furosemide				
Amphotericin B cholesteryl sulfate complex	SEQ	0.83 mg/ml[a]	AMR	3 mg/ml[a]	Physically compatible with little or no change in measured turbidity or increase in particle content in 4 hr at 23 °C under fluorescent light	2117	C
Amsacrine	NCI	1 mg/ml[a]	ES	3 mg/ml[a]	Heavy yellow-orange turbidity forms initially, becoming colorless liquid with yellow precipitate	1381	I
Aztreonam	SQ	40 mg/ml[a]	AB	3 mg/ml[a]	Physically compatible with no subvisual haze or particle formation in 4 hr at 23 °C	1758	C
Bleomycin sulfate		3 units/ml		10 mg/ml	Drugs injected sequentially into Y-site with no flush between. No visually apparent precipitate	980	C
Cefepime HCl	BMS	20 mg/ml[a]	AB	3 mg/ml[a]	Physically compatible with no change in measured turbidity or increase in particle content in 4 hr at 22 °C	1689	C
Chlorpromazine HCl	RPR	0.13 mg/ml[a]	HMR	2.6 mg/ml[a]	Precipitate forms immediately	2244	I
Ciprofloxacin	MI	2 mg/ml[c]	AB	10 mg/ml	Immediate precipitation	1655	I
	BAY	2 mg/ml[b]	DMX	5 mg/ml	White precipitate forms immediately	1934	I
Cisatracurium besylate	GW	0.1 mg/ml[a]	AB	3 mg/ml[a]	Physically compatible with no change in measured turbidity or increase in particle content in 4 hr at 23 °C	2074	C
	GW	2 and 5 mg/ml[a]	AB	3 mg/ml[a]	White cloudiness forms immediately	2074	I
Cisplatin		1 mg/ml		10 mg/ml	Drugs injected sequentially into Y-site with no flush between. No visually apparent precipitate	980	C
	BR	1 mg/ml	ES	3 mg/ml[a]	Visually compatible for 4 hr at room temperature under fluorescent light	1685	C
Cladribine	ORT	0.015[b] and 0.5[e] mg/ml	AB	3 mg/ml[b]	Physically compatible with no change in measured turbidity or increase in particle content in 4 hr at 23 °C	1969	C
Clarithromycin	AB	4 mg/ml[a]	ANT	10 mg/ml	White cloudiness forms immediately, becoming an obvious precipitate in 15 min	2174	I
Cyclophosphamide		20 mg/ml		10 mg/ml	Drugs injected sequentially into Y-site with no flush between. No visually apparent precipitate	980	C
	MJ	10 mg/ml[a]	ES	3 mg/ml[a]	Visually compatible for 4 hr at room temperature under fluorescent light	1685	C
Cytarabine	UP	50 mg/ml	ES	3 mg/ml[a]	Visually compatible for 4 hr at room temperature under fluorescent light	1685	C
Diltiazem HCl	MMD	1[b] and 5 mg/ml	AMR	10 mg/ml	Heavy precipitate forms	1807	I
	MMD	1 mg/ml[a]	AMR	10 mg/ml	Precipitate forms immediately	2062	I
Dobutamine HCl	LI	4 mg/ml[b]	ES	1 mg/ml[b]	Physically compatible for 3 hr	1316	C
	LI	4 mg/ml[a]	ES	1 mg/ml[a]	Slight precipitate in 1 hr	1316	I
	LI	4 mg/ml[a]	AMR	10 mg/ml	Precipitate forms immediately	2062	I

Y-Site Injection Compatibility (1:1 Mixture) (Cont.)

			Furosemide				
Drug	*Mfr*	*Conc*	*Mfr*	*Conc*	*Remarks*	*Ref*	*C/I*
Docetaxel	RPR	0.9 mg/ml[a]	AMR	3 mg/ml[a]	Physically compatible with no change in measured turbidity or increase in particle content in 4 hr at 23 °C	2224	C
Dopamine HCl	AST, DU	12.8 mg/ml	AB, AMR	5 mg/ml	Physically compatible for 3 hr at room temperature	1978	C
	AB, AMR	12.8 mg/ml	AB, AMR	5 mg/ml	White precipitate forms immediately	1978	I
	AB	3.2 mg/ml[a]	AMR	10 mg/ml	Precipitate forms in 4 hr at 27 °C	2062	I
Doxorubicin HCl		2 mg/ml		10 mg/ml	Drugs injected sequentially into Y-site with no flush between. Immediate precipitation	980	I
	AD	0.2 mg/ml[a]	ES	3 mg/ml[a]	Visually compatible for 4 hr at room temperature under fluorescent light	1685	C
Doxorubicin HCl liposome injection	SEQ	0.4 mg/ml[a]	AMR	3 mg/ml[a]	Physically compatible with little or no change in measured turbidity and no increase in particle content in 4 hr at 23 °C	2087	C
Droperidol		2.5 mg/ml		10 mg/ml	Drugs injected sequentially into Y-site with no flush between. Immediate precipitation	980	I
		2.5 mg/ml		10 mg/ml	Precipitate forms	977	I
Epinephrine HCl	AB	0.02 mg/ml[a]	AMR	10 mg/ml	Visually compatible for 4 hr at 27 °C	2062	C
Esmolol HCl	ACC	10 mg/ml[c]	HO	10 mg/ml	Cloudy white precipitate forms immediately	1146	I
Etoposide phosphate	BR	5 mg/ml[a]	AMR	3 mg/ml[a]	Physically compatible with no change in measured turbidity or increase in particle content in 4 hr at 23 °C	2218	C
Famotidine	MSD	0.2 mg/ml[a]	IMS	0.8 mg/ml[a]	Physically compatible for 4 hr at 25 °C	1188	C
	MSD	0.2 mg/ml[a]	ES	10 mg/ml	Physically compatible for 14 hr	1196	C
	ME	2 mg/ml[b]		3 mg/ml[a]	White precipitate forms immediately	1936	I
Fentanyl citrate	ES	0.05 mg/ml	AMR	10 mg/ml	Visually compatible for 4 hr at 27 °C	2062	C
Filgrastim	AMG	30 μg/ml[a]	AB	3 mg/ml[a]	Turbidity forms immediately. Filaments and particles form in 1 hr	1687	I
Fluconazole	RR	2 mg/ml	ES	10 mg/ml	Precipitate forms	1407	I
Fludarabine phosphate	BX	1 mg/ml[a]	AB	3 mg/ml[a]	Physically compatible for 4 hr at room temperature under fluorescent light	1439	C
Fluorouracil		50 mg/ml		10 mg/ml	Drugs injected sequentially into Y-site with no flush between. No visually apparent precipitate	980	C
Foscarnet sodium	AST	24 mg/ml	AB	10 mg/ml	Physically compatible for 24 hr at room temperature under fluorescent light	1335	C
Gatifloxacin	BMS	2 mg/ml[a]	AMR	3 mg/ml[a]	White turbid precipitate forms immediately	2234	I
Gemcitabine HCl	LI	10 mg/ml[b]	AMR	3 mg/ml[b]	Gross precipitation occurs immediately	2226	I
Gentamicin sulfate	SC	1.6 mg/ml[c]	HO	10 mg/ml	White precipitate of furosemide forms immediately	876	I
Granisetron HCl	SKB	0.05 mg/ml[a]	AB	3 mg/ml[a]	Physically compatible with no subvisual haze or particle formation in 4 hr at 23 °C	1804	C

Y-Site Injection Compatibility (1:1 Mixture) (Cont.)

			Furosemide					
Drug	*Mfr*	*Conc*	*Mfr*	*Conc*	*Remarks*	*Ref*	*C/I*
	SKB	1 mg/ml	HO	0.4 mg/ml[b]	Physically compatible with little or no loss of either drug by HPLC in 4 hr at 22 °C	1883	C
Heparin sodium		1000 units/ml		10 mg/ml	Drugs injected sequentially into Y-site with no flush between. No visually apparent precipitate	980	C
	UP	1000 units/L[f]	HO	10 mg/ml	Physically compatible for at least 4 hr at room temperature by visual and microscopic examination	534	C
	ES	100 units/ml[a]	AMR	10 mg/ml	Visually compatible for 4 hr at 27 °C	2062	C
	NOV	29.2 units/ml[a]	HMR	2.6 mg/ml[a]	Visually compatible for 150 min	2244	C
Hetastarch in lactated electrolyte injection (Hextend)	AB	6%	AMR	3 mg/ml[a]	Physically compatible with no change in measured turbidity or increase in particle content in 4 hr at 23 °C	2339	C
Hydralazine HCl	SO	1 mg/ml[c]	ES	1 mg/ml[c]	Slight color change in 3 hr	1316	I
Hydrocortisone sodium succinate	UP	10 mg/L[f]	HO	10 mg/ml	Physically compatible for at least 4 hr at room temperature by visual and microscopic examination	534	C
Hydromorphone HCl	KN	1 mg/ml	AMR	10 mg/ml	Visually compatible for 4 hr at 27 °C	2062	C
Idarubicin HCl	AD	1 mg/ml[b]	AB	10 mg/ml	Precipitate forms immediately	1525	I
	AD	1 mg/ml[b]	AB	0.8 mg/ml[b]	Haze forms immediately	1525	I
Indomethacin sodium trihydrate	MSD	1 mg/ml[b]	AB	10 mg/ml	Visually compatible for 24 hr at 28 °C	1527	C
Kanamycin sulfate	BE	2 mg/ml[c]	HO	10 mg/ml	Physically compatible for 24 hr at 21 °C	876	C
Labetalol HCl	AB	2.5 mg/ml[a]	AB	10 mg/ml	White turbidity forms immediately. Flocculent precipitate forms in 4 hr	1704	I
	AB	2.5 mg/ml[a]	AB	0.5 mg/ml[a]	Physically compatible with no change in measured turbidity or increase in particle content in 4 hr at 22 °C	1704	C
	AB	0.25 mg/ml[a]	AB	0.5[a] and 10 mg/ml	Physically compatible with no change in measured turbidity or increase in particle content in 4 hr at 22 °C	1704	C
	SC	1.6 mg/ml[g]	ES	10 mg/ml[g]	White precipitate forms immediately	1715	I
	AH	2 mg/ml[a]	AMR	10 mg/ml	Precipitate forms immediately	2062	I
Leucovorin calcium		10 mg/ml		10 mg/ml	Drugs injected sequentially into Y-site with no flush between. No visually apparent precipitate	980	C
Levofloxacin	OMN	5 mg/ml[a]	AST	10 mg/ml	Cloudy precipitate forms	2233	I
Linezolid	PHU	2 mg/ml	AMR	3 mg/ml[a]	Physically compatible with no change in measured turbidity or increase in particle content in 4 hr at 23 °C	2264	C
Lorazepam	WY	0.33 mg/ml[b]	CNF	10 mg/ml	Visually compatible for 24 hr at 22 °C	1855	C
	WY	0.5 mg/ml[a]	AMR	10 mg/ml	Visually compatible for 4 hr at 27 °C	2062	C
Melphalan HCl	BW	0.1 mg/ml[b]	AB	3 mg/ml[b]	Physically compatible with no change in measured turbidity or increase in particle content in 3 hr at 22 °C	1557	C
Meperidine HCl	AB	10 mg/ml	ES	0.8 mg/ml[a]	Physically compatible for 4 hr at 25 °C under fluorescent light	1397	C
	AB	10 mg/ml	ES	2.4 mg/ml[a]	White cloudiness forms immediately	1397	I
	AB	10 mg/ml	ES	10 mg/ml	White flocculent precipitate forms immediately	1397	I

Y-Site Injection Compatibility (1:1 Mixture) (Cont.)

			Furosemide				
Drug	*Mfr*	*Conc*	*Mfr*	*Conc*	*Remarks*	*Ref*	*C/I*
Meropenem	ZEN	1 and 50 mg/ml[b]	HO	10 mg/ml	Visually compatible for 4 hr at room temperature	1994	C
Methotrexate sodium		25 mg/ml		10 mg/ml	Drugs injected sequentially into Y-site with no flush between. No visually apparent precipitate	980	C
	AD	15 mg/ml[h]	ES	3 mg/ml[c]	Visually compatible for 4 hr at room temperature under fluorescent light	1685	C
Metoclopramide HCl		5 mg/ml		10 mg/ml	Drugs injected sequentially into Y-site with no flush between. Immediate precipitation	980	I
Midazolam HCl	RC	1 mg/ml[a]	AST	10 mg/ml	Haze forms immediately. Precipitate forms in 2 hr	1847	I
	RC	5 mg/ml	CNF	10 mg/ml	White precipitate forms immediately	1855	I
	RC	2 mg/ml[a]	AMR	10 mg/ml	Precipitate forms immediately	2062	I
Milrinone lactate	WI	200 μg/ml[a]	LY	10 mg/ml	Immediate precipitation	1191	I
	SW	0.2 mg/ml[a]	AMR	10 mg/ml	Precipitate forms in 4 hr at 27 °C	2062	I
Mitomycin		0.5 mg/ml		10 mg/ml	Drugs injected sequentially into Y-site with no flush between. No visually apparent precipitate	980	C
Morphine sulfate	AB	1 mg/ml	ES	0.8[a], 2.4[a], 10 mg/ml	White precipitate forms within 1 hr at 25 °C under fluorescent light	1397	I
	SCN	2 mg/ml[a]	AMR	10 mg/ml	Visually compatible for 4 hr at 27 °C	2062	C
Netilmicin sulfate	SC	1.5 mg/ml[c]		10 mg/ml	White precipitate of furosemide forms immediately	876	I
Nicardipine HCl	WY	1 mg/ml[a]	AMR	10 mg/ml	Precipitate forms immediately	2062	I
Nitroglycerin	AB	0.4 mg/ml[a]	AMR	10 mg/ml	Visually compatible for 4 hr at 27 °C	2062	C
Norepinephrine bitartrate	AB	0.128 mg/ml[a]	AMR	10 mg/ml	Visually compatible for 4 hr at 27 °C	2062	C
Ondansetron HCl	GL	1 mg/ml[b]	AB	3 mg/ml[a]	Immediate turbidity and precipitation	1365	I
Paclitaxel	NCI	1.2 mg/ml[a]	AST	3 mg/ml[a]	Physically compatible with no change in measured turbidity in 4 hr at 22 °C	1556	C
Piperacillin sodium–tazobactam sodium	LE	40 + 5 mg/ml[a]	AB	3 mg/ml[a]	Physically compatible with no change in measured turbidity or increase in particle content in 4 hr at 22 °C	1688	C
Potassium chloride	AB	40 mEq/L[f]	HO	10 mg/ml	Physically compatible for at least 4 hr at room temperature by visual and microscopic examination	534	C
	BRN	0.625 mEq/ml[a]	HMR	2.6 mg/ml[a]	Visually compatible for 150 min	2244	C
Propofol	ZEN	10 mg/ml	AB	3 mg/ml[a]	Physically compatible with no increase in particle content in 1 hr at 23 °C	2066	C
Ranitidine HCl	GL	1 mg/ml[a]	AMR	10 mg/ml	Visually compatible for 4 hr at 27 °C	2062	C
Remifentanil HCl	GW	0.025 and 0.25 mg/ml[b]	AMR	3 mg/ml[a]	Physically compatible with no change in measured turbidity or increase in particle content in 4 hr at 23 °C	2075	C
Quinidine gluconate	LI	6 mg/ml[c]	ES	4 mg/ml[c]	Immediate gross precipitation	1316	I
Sargramostim	IMM	10 μg/ml[b]	AB	3 mg/ml[b]	Physically compatible for 4 hr at 22 °C	1436	C
Tacrolimus	FUJ	1 mg/ml[b]	ES	10 mg/ml	Visually compatible for 24 hr at 25 °C	1630	C

Y-Site Injection Compatibility (1:1 Mixture) (Cont.)

			Furosemide				
Drug	*Mfr*	*Conc*	*Mfr*	*Conc*	*Remarks*	*Ref*	*C/I*
Teniposide	BR	0.1 mg/ml[a]	AB	3 mg/ml[a]	Physically compatible with no subvisual haze or particle formation in 4 hr at 23 °C	1725	C
Thiopental sodium	AB	25 mg/ml[d]	AMR	10 mg/ml	Precipitate forms immediately	2062	I
Thiotepa	IMM[i]	1 mg/ml[a]	AMR	3 mg/ml[a]	Physically compatible with no change in measured turbidity or increase in particle content in 4 hr at 23 °C	1861	C
TNA #73[j]			ES	165 mg/ 50 ml[c]	Physically compatible for 4 hr by visual observation	1009	C
TNA #218 to #226[j]			AB	3 mg/ml[a]	Visually compatible with no precipitate or emulsion damage apparent in 4 hr at 23 °C	2215	C
Tobramycin sulfate	DI	1.6 mg/ml	HO	10 mg/ml	Physically compatible for 24 hr at 21 °C	876	C
Tolazoline HCl		0.1 mg/ml[a]	AB	10 mg/ml	Physically compatible for 24 hr at 22 °C	1363	C
TPN #189[j]				10 mg/ml[b]	Visually compatible for 24 hr at 22 °C	1767	C
TPN #203 and #204[j]			AMR	10 mg/ml	Visually compatible for 2 hr at 23 °C	1974	C
TPN #212 to #215[j]			AB	3 mg/ml[a]	Small amount of subvisual precipitate forms immediately	2109	I
Vecuronium bromide	OR	1 mg/ml	AMR	10 mg/ml	Precipitate forms immediately	2062	I
Vinblastine sulfate		1 mg/ml		10 mg/ml	Drugs injected sequentially into Y-site with no flush between. Immediate precipitation	980	I
Vincristine sulfate		1 mg/ml		10 mg/ml	Drugs injected sequentially into Y-site with no flush between. Immediate precipitation	980	I
Vinorelbine tartrate	BW	1 mg/ml[b]	ES	3 mg/ml[b]	Heavy white precipitate forms immediately	1558	I
Vitamin B complex with C	RC	2 ml/L[f]	HO	10 mg/ml	Physically compatible for at least 4 hr at room temperature by visual and microscopic examination	534	C

[a]*Tested in dextrose 5% in water.*
[b]*Tested in sodium chloride 0.9%.*
[c]*Tested in both dextrose 5% in water and sodium chloride 0.9%.*
[d]*Tested in sterile water for injection.*
[e]*Tested in bacteriostatic sodium chloride 0.9% preserved with benzyl alcohol 0.9%.*
[f]*Tested in dextrose 5% in Ringer's injection, dextrose 5% in Ringer's injection, lactated, dextrose 5% in water, Ringer's injection, lactated, and sodium chloride 0.9%.*
[g]*Furosemide 0.5 ml injected in the Y-site port of a running infusion of labetalol HCl in dextrose 5% in water.*
[h]*Tested in dextrose 5% in water with sodium bicarbonate 0.05 mEq/ml.*
[i]*Lyophilized formulation tested.*
[j]*Refer to Appendix I for the composition of parenteral nutrition solutions. TNA indicates a 3-in-1 admixture, and TPN indicates a 2-in-1 admixture.*

Additional Compatibility Information

Acidic Drugs — Furosemide may precipitate if combined with ascorbic acid, epinephrine, or norepinephrine. (4)

The acidic pH of aminoglycoside admixtures may cause transient cloudiness or frank precipitation if furosemide is added, depending on which aminoglycoside is used and the concentration of the additives. Avoiding the admixture of furosemide and aminoglycosides has been recommended. (876)

A 2-ml fluid barrier of dextrose 5% in water in a microbore retrograde infusion set failed to prevent precipitation when used between gentamicin sulfate 5 mg/0.5 ml and furosemide 2 mg/0.2 ml. (1385)

Furosemide may precipitate if mixed with milrinone lactate infusions. (1442)

Dopamine HCl — Furosemide has demonstrated compatibility or incompatibility with dopamine HCl during simultaneous Y-site administration, depending on the formulation of dopamine HCl tested. Dopamine formulations supplied by Astra and DuPont have the pH adjusted with sodium hydroxide and/or hydrochloric acid and are compatible with furosemide. Formulations supplied by Abbott and American Regent contain citrate buffer and are incompatible with furosemide, forming a white precipitate immediately upon contact. (1978)

GANCICLOVIR SODIUM
AHFS 8:18

Products — Ganciclovir sodium is available in vials containing, in dry form, the equivalent of ganciclovir 500 mg. Reconstitute with 10 ml of sterile water for injection and shake to dissolve the drug to yield a solution containing ganciclovir 50 mg/ml. Do not use paraben-containing diluents to reconstitute ganciclovir sodium because precipitation may result. (2)

pH — Approximately 11. (2)

Osmolality — Ganciclovir sodium 50 mg/ml in sterile water for injection has an osmolality of 320 mOsm/kg. (1689)

Sodium Content — Each 500-mg vial contains 46 mg of sodium. (2)

Trade Name(s) — Cytovene-IV.

Administration — Ganciclovir sodium is administered by intravenous infusion. After reconstitution, the required dose may be diluted in 50 to 250 ml (usually 100 ml) of compatible infusion solution and given over one hour. Concentrations greater than 10 mg/ml are not recommended. Ganciclovir sodium should not be administered by intramuscular, subcutaneous, or rapid intravenous injection or infusion. (2; 4)

Stability — According to the manufacturer, intact vials should be stored at controlled room temperature and protected from temperatures above 40 °C. The reconstituted solution is stable for 12 hours at room temperature. Refrigeration of the reconstituted solution is not recommended because of the possibility of precipitation. (2; 4) However, Heni reported that ganciclovir sodium 500 mg/10 ml in sterile water for injection was stable, with no significant loss by HPLC analysis, for 60 days when stored at 4 °C. (1637)

Freezing Solutions — The manufacturer does not recommend freezing ganciclovir sodium solutions. (2) However, ganciclovir sodium (Syntex) 1.4, 4, and 7 mg/ml in sodium chloride 0.9% packaged in polypropylene syringes and 0.28 and 1.4 mg/ml in sodium chloride 0.9% packaged in PVC containers was evaluated. All samples exhibited 4% or less drug loss by HPLC analysis after 364 days at −20 °C. (1836)

Syringes — Ganciclovir sodium (Syntex) 5.8 mg/ml in sodium chloride 0.9%, packaged in polypropylene infusion-pump syringes (Health-tek), exhibited 3% or less drug loss in 10 days at 4 °C and no loss in 12 hours at 25 °C by HPLC analysis. (1742)

Ganciclovir sodium (Syntex) 1.4, 4, and 7 mg/ml in sodium chloride 0.9% was packaged in polypropylene syringes and stored at 20, 4, and −20 °C. HPLC analysis found 4% or less drug loss in seven days at 20 °C, in 80 days at 4 °C, and in 364 days at −20 °C. (1836)

Ambulatory Pumps — Ganciclovir sodium (Roche) 1 and 5 mg/ml in sodium chloride 0.9% was stored in latex pump reservoirs (Baxter Intermate) and PVC pump reservoirs (I-Flow Sidekick) as well as PVC minibags for comparison. No loss of ganciclovir by HPLC analysis occurred in any of the containers over 35 days stored at 4 °C protected from light. The particulate burdens of each container system did vary however. The PVC minibag and PVC Sidekick pump reservoir developed 20-fold increases in microparticulates, mostly of 10 μm or less, while the solution latex reservoir did not develop a substantial increase in particulates. The authors attributed this increase in particle burden in PVC to an interaction of the high pH of the ganciclovir solution with PVC. (2251)

Elastomeric Reservoir Pumps — Ganciclovir sodium (Syntex) 5 mg/ml in sodium chloride 0.9% 100 ml was packaged in latex elastomeric reservoirs (Secure Medical). About 4 to 6% loss by HPLC analysis occurred in 24 hours at 25 °C and in five days at 5 °C. (1970)

Ganciclovir sodium solutions in elastomeric reservoir pumps have been stated by the pump manufacturers to be stable for the following time periods refrigerated (REF) or at room temperature (RT) (31):

Pump Reservoir(s)	Conc.	REF	RT
Homepump; Homepump Eclipse	5 mg/ml[b]	15 days	24 hr
	2 to 5 mg/ml[b]		7 days
Intermate HPC	1 to 6 mg/ml[a,b]	15 days	24 hr
Medflo	5 mg/ml[b]	35 days	35 days
ReadyMed	5 mg/ml[b]	15 days	48 hr

[a]*In dextrose 5% in water.*
[b]*In sodium chloride 0.9%.*

Also see Ambulatory Pumps section above.

Sorption — During a solution stability study, no sorption to PVC containers was noted. (1288)

Central Venous Catheter — Ganciclovir sodium (Roche) 5 mg/ml in dextrose 5% in water was found to be compatible with the ARROWg+ard Blue Plus (Arrow International) chlorhexidine-bearing triple-lumen central catheter. HPLC analysis was used to evaluate completeness of drug delivery through the catheter and the amount of chlorhexidine removed from the internal lumens. Essentially complete delivery of the drug was found with little or no drug loss occurring. Furthermore, chlorhexidine delivered from the catheter remained at trace amounts with no substantial increase due to the delivery of the drug through the catheter. (2335)

Compatibility Information

Solution Compatibility

Ganciclovir sodium

Solution	Mfr	Mfr	Conc/L	Remarks	Ref	C/I
Dextrose 5% in water	TR[a]	SY	2.44 g	Physically compatible and chemically stable with no drug loss in 5 days at 25 °C exposed to light or in the dark and at 4 °C	1288	C
	BA[a]	SY	1, 5, 10 g	Visually compatible with 3 to 7% ganciclovir loss by HPLC in 35 days at 4 to 8 °C in the dark	1545	C
	AB[a]	SY	1 and 5 g	Visually compatible with 1% or less ganciclovir loss by HPLC in 35 days at 5 and 25 °C	1643	C
Sodium chloride 0.9%	TR[a]	SY	2.59 g	Physically compatible and chemically stable with no drug loss in 5 days at 25 °C exposed to light or in the dark and at 4 °C	1288	C
	AB[a]	SY	1 and 5 g	Visually compatible with 1% or less ganciclovir loss by HPLC in 35 days at 5 and 25 °C	1643	C
		SY	2.2 g	Little or no ganciclovir loss by HPLC in 14 days at 4 °C	1637	C
	[a]	SY	0.28 and 1.4 g	4% or less drug loss by HPLC in 7 days at 20 °C, 80 days at 4 °C, and 364 days at −20 °C	1836	C
	AB[b]	SY	5 g	4 to 6% loss of drug by HPLC in 24 hr at 25 °C and in 5 days at 5 °C	1970	C
	BA[a]	RC	1 and 5 g	No ganciclovir loss in 35 days at 4 °C protected from light. No visible particulates but a substantial increase in microparticulates less than 10 μm in size developed	2251	C
	BA[d]	RC	1 and 5 g	Physically compatible with no ganciclovir loss in 35 days at 4 °C protected from light	2251	C
TPN #183[c]		SY	2 g	Precipitate forms	1744	I
TPN #183 to #185[c]		SY	3 and 5 g	Precipitate forms	1744	I

[a]*Tested in PVC containers.*
[b]*Tested in glass containers and latex elastomeric reservoirs (Secure Medical).*
[c]*Refer to Appendix I for the composition of parenteral nutrition solutions. TPN indicates a 2-in-1 admixture.*
[d]*Tested in latex elastomeric pump reservoirs (Baxter Intermate).*

Y-Site Injection Compatibility (1:1 Mixture)

Ganciclovir sodium

Drug	Mfr	Conc	Mfr	Conc	Remarks	Ref	C/I
Aldesleukin	CHI	33,800 I.U./ml[a]	SY	10 mg/ml[a]	Aldesleukin bioactivity inhibited	1857	I
Allopurinol sodium	BW	3 mg/ml[b]	SY	20 mg/ml[b]	Physically compatible with no change in measured turbidity or increase in particle content in 4 hr at 22 °C	1686	C
Amifostine	USB	10 mg/ml[a]	SY	20 mg/ml[a]	Crystalline needles form immediately, becoming a dense flocculent precipitate in 1 hr	1845	I
Amphotericin B cholesteryl sulfate complex	SEQ	0.83 mg/ml[a]	RC	20 mg/ml[a]	Physically compatible with little or no change in measured turbidity or increase in particle content in 4 hr at 23 °C under fluorescent light	2117	C
Amsacrine	NCI	1 mg/ml[a]	SY	20 mg/ml[a]	Immediate dark orange turbidity	1381	I

Y-Site Injection Compatibility (1:1 Mixture) (Cont.)

Drug	Mfr	Conc	Mfr	Conc	Remarks	Ref	C/I
			Ganciclovir sodium				
Aztreonam	SQ	40 mg/ml[a]	SY	20 mg/ml[a]	White crystalline needles form immediately and become dense flocculent precipitate in 1 hr	1758	I
Cefepime HCl	BMS	20 mg/ml[a]	SY	20 mg/ml[a]	Flocculent precipitate forms immediately	1689	I
Cisatracurium besylate	GW	0.1 and 2 mg/ml[a]	SY	20 mg/ml[a]	Physically compatible with no change in measured turbidity or increase in particle content in 4 hr at 23 °C	2074	C
	GW	5 mg/ml[a]	SY	20 mg/ml[a]	White cloudiness forms immediately	2074	I
Cisplatin	BR	1 mg/ml	SY	20 mg/ml[a]	Visually compatible for 4 hr at room temperature under fluorescent light	1685	C
Cyclophosphamide	MJ	10 mg/ml[a]	SY	20 mg/ml[a]	Visually compatible for 4 hr at room temperature under fluorescent light	1685	C
Cytarabine	UP	50 mg/ml	SY	20 mg/ml[a]	Turbidity and particles form in 30 min, becoming gel-like in 4 hr	1685	I
Docetaxel	RPR	0.9 mg/ml[a]	RC	20 mg/ml[a]	Physically compatible with no change in measured turbidity or increase in particle content in 4 hr at 23 °C	2224	C
Doxorubicin HCl	AD	0.2 mg/ml[a]	SY	20 mg/ml[a]	Color changes to deep purple immediately	1685	I
Doxorubicin HCl liposome injection	SEQ	0.4 mg/ml[a]	RC	20 mg/ml[a]	Physically compatible with little or no change in measured turbidity and no increase in particle content in 4 hr at 23 °C	2087	C
Enalaprilat	MSD	1.25 mg/ml	SY	5 mg/ml[c]	Physically compatible for 4 hr at 21 °C under fluorescent light by macroscopic and microscopic examination	1409	C
Etoposide phosphate	BR	5 mg/ml[a]	RC	20 mg/ml[a]	Physically compatible with no change in measured turbidity or increase in particle content in 4 hr at 23 °C	2218	C
Filgrastim	AMG	30 μg/ml[a]	SY	20 mg/ml[a]	Physically compatible with no change in measured turbidity or increase in particle content in 4 hr at 22 °C	1687	C
Fluconazole	RR	2 mg/ml	SY	50 mg/ml	Physically compatible for 24 hr at 25 °C	1407	C
Fludarabine phosphate	BX	1 mg/ml[a]	SY	20 mg/ml[a]	Darker color visible under high intensity light within 4 hr	1439	I
Foscarnet sodium	AST	24 mg/ml		50 mg/ml	Immediate precipitation	1335	I
Gatifloxacin	BMS	2 mg/ml[a]	RC	20 mg/ml[a]	Physically compatible with no change in measured haze or increase in particle content in 4 hr at 23 °C	2234	C
Gemcitabine HCl	LI	10 mg/ml[b]	RC	20 mg/ml[b]	Subvisual crystals form immediately, becoming a gross precipitate in 1 hr	2226	I
Granisetron HCl	SKB	0.05 mg/ml[a]	SY	20 mg/ml[a]	Physically compatible with no change in measured turbidity or increase in particle content in 4 hr at 23 °C	2000	C
Linezolid	PHU	2 mg/ml	RC	20 mg/ml[a]	Physically compatible with no change in measured turbidity or increase in particle content in 4 hr at 23 °C	2264	C
Melphalan HCl	BW	0.1 mg/ml[b]	SY	20 mg/ml[b]	Physically compatible with no change in measured turbidity or increase in particle content in 3 hr at 22 °C	1557	C

Y-Site Injection Compatibility (1:1 Mixture) (Cont.)

			Ganciclovir sodium				
Drug	*Mfr*	*Conc*	*Mfr*	*Conc*	*Remarks*	*Ref*	*C/I*
Methotrexate sodium	AD	15 mg/ml[d]	SY	20 mg/ml[a]	Visually compatible for 4 hr at room temperature under fluorescent light	1685	C
Ondansetron HCl	GL	1 mg/ml[b]	SY	20 mg/ml[a]	Immediate turbidity and precipitation	1365	I
Paclitaxel	NCI	1.2 mg/ml[a]	SY	20 mg/ml[a]	Physically compatible with no change in measured turbidity in 4 hr at 22 °C	1556	C
Piperacillin sodium–tazobactam sodium	LE	40 + 5 mg/ml[a]	SY	20 mg/ml[a]	Large crystals form in 1 hr and become heavy white precipitate in 4 hr	1688	I
Propofol	ZEN	10 mg/ml	SY	20 mg/ml[a]	Physically compatible for 1 hr at 23 °C with no increase in particle content	2066	C
Remifentanil HCl	GW	0.025 and 0.25 mg/ml[b]	SY	20 mg/ml[a]	Physically compatible with no change in measured turbidity or increase in particle content in 4 hr at 23 °C	2075	C
Sargramostim	IMM	10 µg/ml[b]	SY	20 mg/ml[b]	Few small particles formed in 4 hr in one of two samples	1436	I
Tacrolimus	FUJ	1 mg/ml[b]	SY	50 mg/ml[a]	Visually compatible for 24 hr at 25 °C	1630	C
Teniposide	BR	0.1 mg/ml[a]	SY	20 mg/ml[a]	Physically compatible with no subvisual haze or particle formation in 4 hr at 23 °C	1725	C
Thiotepa	IMM[e]	1 mg/ml[a]	SY	20 mg/ml[a]	Physically compatible with no change in measured turbidity or increase in particle content in 4 hr at 23 °C	1861	C
TNA #218 to #226[f]			RC	20 mg/ml[a]	Large amount of white precipitate forms immediately	2215	I
TPN #144[f]			SY	1 and 5 mg/ml[a]	Visually compatible for 2 hr at 20 °C	1522	C
			SY	10 mg/ml[a]	Heavy precipitate forms within 30 min	1522	I
TPN #183[f]			SY	2 mg/ml	Precipitate forms	1744	I
			SY	1 mg/ml[g]	Visually compatible with no ganciclovir loss by HPLC in 3 hr at 24 °C under fluorescent light. Less than 10% amino acid loss by HPLC in 2 hr	1744	C
TPN #183 to #185[f]			SY	3 and 5 mg/ml	Precipitate forms	1744	I
TPN #184 and #185[f]			SY	2 mg/ml[h]	Visually compatible with no ganciclovir loss by HPLC in 3 hr at 24 °C under fluorescent light. Less than 10% amino acid loss by HPLC in 3 hr	1744	C
TPN #212 to #215[f]			SY	20 mg/ml[a]	Gross white precipitate forms immediately	2109	I
Vinorelbine tartrate	BW	1 mg/ml[b]	SY	20 mg/ml[b]	White turbid solution with precipitate forms immediately	1558	I

[a] *Tested in dextrose 5% in water.*
[b] *Tested in sodium chloride 0.9%.*
[c] *Tested in both dextrose 5% in water and sodium chloride 0.9%.*
[d] *Tested in dextrose 5% in water with sodium bicarbonate 0.05 mEq/ml.*
[e] *Lyophilized formulation tested.*
[f] *Refer to Appendix I for the composition of parenteral nutrition solutions. TNA indicates a 3-in-1 admixture, and TPN indicates a 2-in-1 admixture.*
[g] *Ganciclovir sodium concentration after mixing was 0.83 mg/ml.*
[h] *Ganciclovir sodium concentration after mixing was 1.4 mg/ml.*

Additional Compatibility Information

Infusion Solutions — The manufacturer states that ganciclovir sodium is chemically and physically compatible when diluted for intravenous infusion in the following solutions (2):

Dextrose 5% in water
Ringer's injection
Ringer's injection, lactated
Sodium chloride 0.9%

The manufacturer recommends that admixtures of ganciclovir sodium in compatible infusion solutions be stored under refrigeration but not frozen. Ganciclovir reconstituted with sterile water for injection and diluted further in sodium chloride 0.9% in PVC bags is physically and chemically stable for up to 14 days when stored under refrigeration at 5 °C. However, because of the absence of an antibacterial preservative, use within 24 hours is recommended. (2)

Parabens — Ganciclovir sodium is stated to be incompatible with paraben-containing solutions. Reconstitution with bacteriostatic water for injection containing parabens may cause precipitation. (2)

Other Information

Microbial Growth — Ganciclovir sodium (Syntex) 0.35 mg/ml diluted in sodium chloride 0.9% and stored at 22 °C did not exhibit a substantial antimicrobial effect on the growth of four organisms (*Enterococcus faecium, Staphylococcus aureus, Pseudomonas aeruginosa,* and *Candida albicans*) inoculated into the solution. *S. aureus* and *C. albicans* remained viable for 24 hours, and the others remained viable to the end of the study at 120 hours. The author recommended that diluted solutions of ganciclovir sodium be stored under refrigeration whenever possible and that the potential for microbiological growth should be considered when assigning expiration periods. (2160)

GATIFLOXACIN
AHFS 8:22

Products — Gatifloxacin is available as a concentrated solution in 20- and 40-ml single-use vials. Each milliliter of concentrated solution provides gatifloxacin 10 mg in 5% dextrose with sodium hydroxide or hydrochloric acid to adjust pH in water for injection. The concentrated solution must be diluted prior to intravenous administration. (2)

Gatifloxacin is also available premixed as a ready-to-use solution for infusion in 100- and 200-ml flexible plastic bags. Each milliliter of the ready-to-use infusion provides gatifloxacin 2 mg in 5% dextrose with sodium hydroxide or hydrochloric acid to adjust pH in water for injection. (2)

pH — From 3.5 to 5.5. (2)

Trade Name(s) — Tequin.

Administration — Gatifloxacin for injection is administered only by intravenous infusion. It should not be given by other routes of administration or by rapid or bolus intravenous administration. The concentrated solution should be diluted to a final concentration of 2 mg/ml using a compatible infusion solution. Gatifloxacin is infused over 60 minutes. (2)

Stability — Gatifloxacin concentrated solution and ready-to-use infusion are clear and light yellow to greenish-yellow solutions. Intact vials should be stored at controlled room temperature at 25 °C with temperature excursions in the range of 15 to 30 °C permitted. The manufacturer recommends that the ready-to-use solution in plastic bags be protected from freezing, although freezing of the diluted concentrate is permitted. (2) See Freezing Solutions below.

Dilution of the concentrated solution to a concentration of 2 mg/ml in a compatible intravenous fluid results in a solution that is stable for at least 14 days at room temperature of 20 to 26 °C and under refrigeration at 2 to 8 °C. (2) See Additional Compatibility Information below.

Freezing Solutions — Dilution of the concentrated solution in a compatible intravenous fluid, except sodium bicarbonate 5%, results in a solution that is stable for at least six months frozen at –25 to –20 °C. Frozen solutions thawed at room temperature are stable for 14 days stored at room temperature or under refrigeration. Thawed solutions should not be refrozen. (2)

Compatibility Information

Y-Site Injection Compatibility (1:1 Mixture)

			Gatifloxacin				
Drug	*Mfr*	*Conc*	*Mfr*	*Conc*	*Remarks*	*Ref*	*C/I*
Acyclovir sodium	APP	7 mg/ml[a]	BMS	2 mg/ml[a]	Physically compatible with no change in measured haze or increase in particle content in 4 hr at 23 °C	2234	C

Y-Site Injection Compatibility (1:1 Mixture) (Cont.)

Drug	*Mfr*	*Conc*	Gatifloxacin *Mfr*	Gatifloxacin *Conc*	*Remarks*	*Ref*	*C/I*
Alfentanil HCl	TAY	0.5 mg/ml	BMS	2 mg/ml[a]	Physically compatible with no change in measured haze or increase in particle content in 4 hr at 23 °C	2234	C
Amikacin sulfate	AB	5 mg/ml[a]	BMS	2 mg/ml[a]	Physically compatible with no change in measured haze or increase in particle content in 4 hr at 23 °C	2234	C
Aminophylline	AB	2.5 mg/ml[a]	BMS	2 mg/ml[a]	Physically compatible with no change in measured haze or increase in particle content in 4 hr at 23 °C	2234	C
Amphotericin B	PH	0.6 mg/ml[a]	BMS	2 mg/ml[a]	Yellow flocculent precipitate forms immediately	2234	I
Amphotericin B cholesteryl sulfate complex	SEQ	0.83 mg/ml[a]	BMS	2 mg/ml[a]	Yellow flocculent precipitate forms immediately	2234	I
Ampicillin sodium	APC	20 mg/ml[b]	BMS	2 mg/ml[a]	Physically compatible with no change in measured haze or increase in particle content in 4 hr at 23 °C	2234	C
Ampicillin sodium–sulbactam sodium	PF	20 + 10 mg/ml[b]	BMS	2 mg/ml[a]	Physically compatible with no change in measured haze or increase in particle content in 4 hr at 23 °C	2234	C
Aztreonam	SQ	40 mg/ml[a]	BMS	2 mg/ml[a]	Physically compatible with no change in measured haze or increase in particle content in 4 hr at 23 °C	2234	C
Bretylium tosylate	AST	50 mg/ml	BMS	2 mg/ml[a]	Physically compatible with no change in measured haze or increase in particle content in 4 hr at 23 °C	2234	C
Buprenorphine HCl	RKC	0.04 mg/ml[a]	BMS	2 mg/ml[a]	Physically compatible with no change in measured haze or increase in particle content in 4 hr at 23 °C	2234	C
Butorphanol tartrate	BMS	0.04 mg/ml[a]	BMS	2 mg/ml[a]	Physically compatible with no change in measured haze or increase in particle content in 4 hr at 23 °C	2234	C
Calcium chloride	FUJ	40 mg/ml[a]	BMS	2 mg/ml[a]	Physically compatible with no change in measured haze or increase in particle content in 4 hr at 23 °C	2234	C
Calcium gluconate	FUJ	40 mg/ml[a]	BMS	2 mg/ml[a]	Physically compatible with no change in measured haze or increase in particle content in 4 hr at 23 °C	2234	C
Carboplatin	BR	5 mg/ml[a]	BMS	2 mg/ml[a]	Physically compatible with no change in measured haze or increase in particle content in 4 hr at 23 °C	2234	C
Cefazolin sodium	SKB	20 mg/ml[a]	BMS	2 mg/ml[a]	Physically compatible with no change in measured haze or increase in particle content in 4 hr at 23 °C	2234	C
Cefoperazone sodium	RR	40 mg/ml[a]	BMS	2 mg/ml[a]	White precipitate forms immediately	2234	I
Cefotetan disodium	ZEN	20 mg/ml[a]	BMS	2 mg/ml[a]	Physically compatible with no change in measured haze or increase in particle content in 4 hr at 23 °C	2234	C
Cefoxitin sodium	ME	20 mg/ml[a]	BMS	2 mg/ml[a]	Measured haze increases immediately	2234	I

Y-Site Injection Compatibility (1:1 Mixture) (Cont.)

Drug	Mfr	Conc	Gatifloxacin Mfr	Gatifloxacin Conc	Remarks	Ref	C/I
Ceftazidime[c]	SKB	40 mg/ml[a]	BMS	2 mg/ml[a]	Physically compatible with no change in measured haze or increase in particle content in 4 hr at 23 °C	2234	C
Ceftizoxime sodium	FUJ	20 mg/ml[a]	BMS	2 mg/ml[a]	Physically compatible with no change in measured haze or increase in particle content in 4 hr at 23 °C	2234	C
Ceftriaxone sodium	RC	20 mg/ml[a]	BMS	2 mg/ml[a]	Physically compatible with no change in measured haze or increase in particle content in 4 hr at 23 °C	2234	C
Chlorpromazine HCl	ES	2 mg/ml[a]	BMS	2 mg/ml[a]	Physically compatible with no change in measured haze or increase in particle content in 4 hr at 23 °C	2234	C
Cimetidine HCl	SKB	12 mg/ml[a]	BMS	2 mg/ml[a]	Physically compatible with no change in measured haze or increase in particle content in 4 hr at 23 °C	2234	C
Cisatracurium besylate	GW	2 mg/ml	BMS	2 mg/ml[a]	Physically compatible with no change in measured haze or increase in particle content in 4 hr at 23 °C	2234	C
Cisplatin	BR	1 mg/ml	BMS	2 mg/ml[a]	Physically compatible with no change in measured haze or increase in particle content in 4 hr at 23 °C	2234	C
Clindamycin phosphate	UP	10 mg/ml[a]	BMS	2 mg/ml[a]	Physically compatible with no change in measured haze or increase in particle content in 4 hr at 23 °C	2234	C
Cyclophosphamide	MJ	10 mg/ml[a]	BMS	2 mg/ml[a]	Physically compatible with no change in measured haze or increase in particle content in 4 hr at 23 °C	2234	C
Cyclosporine	SZ	5 mg/ml[a]	BMS	2 mg/ml[a]	Physically compatible with no change in measured haze or increase in particle content in 4 hr at 23 °C	2234	C
Cytarabine	BV	50 mg/ml	BMS	2 mg/ml[a]	Physically compatible with no change in measured haze or increase in particle content in 4 hr at 23 °C	2234	C
Dexamethasone sodium phosphate	FUJ	1 mg/ml[a]	BMS	2 mg/ml[a]	Physically compatible with no change in measured haze or increase in particle content in 4 hr at 23 °C	2234	C
Diazepam	AB	5 mg/ml	BMS	2 mg/ml[a]	White turbid precipitate forms immediately	2234	I
Digoxin	ES	0.25 mg/ml	BMS	2 mg/ml[a]	Physically compatible with no change in measured haze or increase in particle content in 4 hr at 23 °C	2234	C
Diphenhydramine HCl	ES	2 mg/ml[a]	BMS	2 mg/ml[a]	Physically compatible with no change in measured haze or increase in particle content in 4 hr at 23 °C	2234	C
Dobutamine HCl	AST	4 mg/ml[a]	BMS	2 mg/ml[a]	Physically compatible with no change in measured haze or increase in particle content in 4 hr at 23 °C	2234	C
Dopamine HCl	AB	3.2 mg/ml[a]	BMS	2 mg/ml[a]	Physically compatible with no change in measured haze or increase in particle content in 4 hr at 23 °C	2234	C

Y-Site Injection Compatibility (1:1 Mixture) (Cont.)

			Gatifloxacin				
Drug	*Mfr*	*Conc*	*Mfr*	*Conc*	*Remarks*	*Ref*	*C/I*
Doxorubicin HCl	PH	2 mg/ml	BMS	2 mg/ml[a]	Physically compatible with no change in measured haze or increase in particle content in 4 hr at 23 °C	2234	C
Droperidol	AMR	0.4 mg/ml[a]	BMS	2 mg/ml[a]	Physically compatible with no change in measured haze or increase in particle content in 4 hr at 23 °C	2234	C
Enalaprilat	ME	0.1 mg/ml[a]	BMS	2 mg/ml[a]	Physically compatible with no change in measured haze or increase in particle content in 4 hr at 23 °C	2234	C
Esmolol HCl	OHM	10 mg/ml	BMS	2 mg/ml[a]	Physically compatible with no change in measured haze or increase in particle content in 4 hr at 23 °C	2234	C
Etoposide phosphate	BR	5 mg/ml[a]	BMS	2 mg/ml[a]	Physically compatible with no change in measured haze or increase in particle content in 4 hr at 23 °C	2234	C
Famotidine	ME	2 mg/ml[a]	BMS	2 mg/ml[a]	Physically compatible with no change in measured haze or increase in particle content in 4 hr at 23 °C	2234	C
Fentanyl citrate	AB	0.05 mg/ml	BMS	2 mg/ml[a]	Physically compatible with no change in measured haze or increase in particle content in 4 hr at 23 °C	2234	C
Fluconazole	RR	2 mg/ml[a]	BMS	2 mg/ml[a]	Physically compatible with no change in measured haze or increase in particle content in 4 hr at 23 °C	2234	C
Fluorouracil	PH	16 mg/ml[a]	BMS	2 mg/ml[a]	Physically compatible with no change in measured haze or increase in particle content in 4 hr at 23 °C	2234	C
Furosemide	AMR	3 mg/ml[a]	BMS	2 mg/ml[a]	White turbid precipitate forms immediately	2234	I
Ganciclovir sodium	RC	20 mg/ml[a]	BMS	2 mg/ml[a]	Physically compatible with no change in measured haze or increase in particle content in 4 hr at 23 °C	2234	C
Gemcitabine HCl	LI	10 mg/ml[b]	BMS	2 mg/ml[a]	Physically compatible with no change in measured haze or increase in particle content in 4 hr at 23 °C	2234	C
Gentamicin sulfate	FUJ	5 mg/ml[a]	BMS	2 mg/ml[a]	Physically compatible with no change in measured haze or increase in particle content in 4 hr at 23 °C	2234	C
Granisetron HCl	SKB	0.05 mg/ml[a]	BMS	2 mg/ml[a]	Physically compatible with no change in measured haze or increase in particle content in 4 hr at 23 °C	2234	C
Haloperidol lactate	MN	0.2 mg/ml[a]	BMS	2 mg/ml[a]	Physically compatible with no change in measured haze or increase in particle content in 4 hr at 23 °C	2234	C
Heparin sodium	ES	1000 units/ml[a]	BMS	2 mg/ml[a]	White cloudy precipitate forms immediately	2234	I
Hydrocortisone sodium succinate	AB	1 mg/ml[a]	BMS	2 mg/ml[a]	Physically compatible with no change in measured haze or increase in particle content in 4 hr at 23 °C	2234	C

Y-Site Injection Compatibility (1:1 Mixture) (Cont.)

			Gatifloxacin				
Drug	*Mfr*	*Conc*	*Mfr*	*Conc*	*Remarks*	*Ref*	*C/I*
Hydromorphone HCl	AST	0.5 mg/ml[a]	BMS	2 mg/ml[a]	Physically compatible with no change in measured haze or increase in particle content in 4 hr at 23 °C	2234	C
Hydroxyzine HCl	ES	2 mg/ml[a]	BMS	2 mg/ml[a]	Physically compatible with no change in measured haze or increase in particle content in 4 hr at 23 °C	2234	C
Ifosfamide	MJ	25 mg/ml[a]	BMS	2 mg/ml[a]	Physically compatible with no change in measured haze or increase in particle content in 4 hr at 23 °C	2234	C
Imipenem–cilastatin sodium	ME	10 mg/ml[b]	BMS	2 mg/ml[a]	Physically compatible with no change in measured haze or increase in particle content in 4 hr at 23 °C	2234	C
Labetalol HCl	GW	5 mg/ml	BMS	2 mg/ml[a]	Physically compatible with no change in measured haze or increase in particle content in 4 hr at 23 °C	2234	C
Leucovorin calcium	GNS	2 mg/ml[a]	BMS	2 mg/ml[a]	Physically compatible with no change in measured haze or increase in particle content in 4 hr at 23 °C	2234	C
Lidocaine HCl	AST	10 mg/ml[a]	BMS	2 mg/ml[a]	Physically compatible with no change in measured haze or increase in particle content in 4 hr at 23 °C	2234	C
Lorazepam	WY	0.1 mg/ml[a]	BMS	2 mg/ml[a]	Physically compatible with no change in measured haze or increase in particle content in 4 hr at 23 °C	2234	C
Magnesium sulfate	AST	100 mg/ml[a]	BMS	2 mg/ml[a]	Physically compatible with no change in measured haze or increase in particle content in 4 hr at 23 °C	2234	C
Mannitol	BA	15%	BMS	2 mg/ml[a]	Physically compatible with no change in measured haze or increase in particle content in 4 hr at 23 °C	2234	C
Meperidine HCl	AST	4 mg/ml[a]	BMS	2 mg/ml[a]	Physically compatible with no change in measured haze or increase in particle content in 4 hr at 23 °C	2234	C
Mesna	MJ	10 mg/ml[a]	BMS	2 mg/ml[a]	Physically compatible with no change in measured haze or increase in particle content in 4 hr at 23 °C	2234	C
Methotrexate sodium	BV	15 mg/ml[a]	BMS	2 mg/ml[a]	Physically compatible with no change in measured haze or increase in particle content in 4 hr at 23 °C	2234	C
Methylprednisolone sodium succinate	PHU	5 mg/ml[a]	BMS	2 mg/ml[a]	Physically compatible with no change in measured haze or increase in particle content in 4 hr at 23 °C	2234	C
Metoclopramide HCl	AB	5 mg/ml	BMS	2 mg/ml[a]	Physically compatible with no change in measured haze or increase in particle content in 4 hr at 23 °C	2234	C
Metronidazole	BA	5 mg/ml	BMS	2 mg/ml[a]	Physically compatible with no change in measured haze or increase in particle content in 4 hr at 23 °C	2234	C

Y-Site Injection Compatibility (1:1 Mixture) (Cont.)

Gatifloxacin

Drug	*Mfr*	*Conc*	*Mfr*	*Conc*	*Remarks*	*Ref*	*C/I*
Midazolam HCl	RC	2 mg/ml[a]	BMS	2 mg/ml[a]	Physically compatible with no change in measured haze or increase in particle content in 4 hr at 23 °C	2234	C
Mitoxantrone HCl	IMM	0.5 mg/ml[a]	BMS	2 mg/ml[a]	Physically compatible with no change in measured haze or increase in particle content in 4 hr at 23 °C	2234	C
Morphine sulfate	WY	1 mg/ml[a]	BMS	2 mg/ml[a]	Physically compatible with no change in measured haze or increase in particle content in 4 hr at 23 °C	2234	C
Nalbuphine HCl	AST	10 mg/ml	BMS	2 mg/ml[a]	Physically compatible with no change in measured haze or increase in particle content in 4 hr at 23 °C	2234	C
Naloxone HCl	AST	0.4 mg/ml	BMS	2 mg/ml[a]	Physically compatible with no change in measured haze or increase in particle content in 4 hr at 23 °C	2234	C
Nicardipine HCl	WY	1 mg/ml[a]	BMS	2 mg/ml[a]	Physically compatible with no change in measured haze or increase in particle content in 4 hr at 23 °C	2234	C
Nitroglycerin	FAU	0.4 mg/ml[a]	BMS	2 mg/ml[a]	Physically compatible with no change in measured haze or increase in particle content in 4 hr at 23 °C	2234	C
Ondansetron HCl	GW	1 mg/ml[a]	BMS	2 mg/ml[a]	Physically compatible with no change in measured haze or increase in particle content in 4 hr at 23 °C	2234	C
Paclitaxel	MJ	0.6 mg/ml[a]	BMS	2 mg/ml[a]	Physically compatible with no change in measured haze or increase in particle content in 4 hr at 23 °C	2234	C
Pentamidine isethionate	FUJ	6 mg/ml[a]	BMS	2 mg/ml[a]	Physically compatible with no change in measured haze or increase in particle content in 4 hr at 23 °C	2234	C
Pentobarbital sodium	WY	5 mg/ml[a]	BMS	2 mg/ml[a]	Physically compatible with no change in measured haze or increase in particle content in 4 hr at 23 °C	2234	C
Phenobarbital sodium	WY	5 mg/ml[a]	BMS	2 mg/ml[a]	Physically compatible with no change in measured haze or increase in particle content in 4 hr at 23 °C	2234	C
Phenytoin sodium	ESI	50 mg/ml	BMS	2 mg/ml[a]	Large amount of crystalline precipitate forms immediately	2234	I
Piperacillin sodium	LE	40 mg/ml[a]	BMS	2 mg/ml[a]	Haze increases immediately, becoming a microprecipitate in 4 hr	2234	I
Piperacillin sodium–tazobactam sodium	LE	40 + 5 mg/ml[a]	BMS	2 mg/ml[a]	Haze increases and microprecipitate forms immediately	2234	I
Potassium chloride	AB	0.1 mEq/ml[a]	BMS	2 mg/ml[a]	Physically compatible with no change in measured haze or increase in particle content in 4 hr at 23 °C	2234	C
Potassium phosphates	AB	3 mmol/ml	BMS	2 mg/ml[a]	Microprecipitate formed in 1 of 6 replicates	2234	I

Y-Site Injection Compatibility (1:1 Mixture) (Cont.)

Drug	*Mfr*	*Conc*	Gatifloxacin *Mfr*	Gatifloxacin *Conc*	*Remarks*	*Ref*	*C/I*
Prochlorperazine edisylate	SO	0.5 mg/ml[a]	BMS	2 mg/ml[a]	Physically compatible with no change in measured haze or increase in particle content in 4 hr at 23 °C	2234	C
Promethazine HCl	SCN	2 mg/ml[a]	BMS	2 mg/ml[a]	Physically compatible with no change in measured haze or increase in particle content in 4 hr at 23 °C	2234	C
Propranolol HCl	WAY	1 mg/ml	BMS	2 mg/ml[a]	Physically compatible with no change in measured haze or increase in particle content in 4 hr at 23 °C	2234	C
Ranitidine HCl	GW	2 mg/ml[a]	BMS	2 mg/ml[a]	Physically compatible with no change in measured haze or increase in particle content in 4 hr at 23 °C	2234	C
Remifentanil HCl	GW	0.5 mg/ml[a]	BMS	2 mg/ml[a]	Physically compatible with no change in measured haze or increase in particle content in 4 hr at 23 °C	2234	C
Sodium bicarbonate	AB	1 mEq/ml	BMS	2 mg/ml[a]	Physically compatible with no change in measured haze or increase in particle content in 4 hr at 23 °C	2234	C
	AB	0.25 mEq/ml[a]	BMS	2 mg/ml[a]	Physically compatible with no change in measured haze or increase in particle content in 4 hr at 23 °C	2234	C
Sodium phosphates	AB	3 mmol/ml	BMS	2 mg/ml[a]	Physically compatible with no change in measured haze or increase in particle content in 4 hr at 23 °C	2234	C
Sufentanil citrate	ES	0.05 mg/ml	BMS	2 mg/ml[a]	Physically compatible with no change in measured haze or increase in particle content in 4 hr at 23 °C	2234	C
Theophylline	BA	4 mg/ml[a]	BMS	2 mg/ml[a]	Physically compatible with no change in measured haze or increase in particle content in 4 hr at 23 °C	2234	C
Ticarcillin disodium	SKB	30 mg/ml[a]	BMS	2 mg/ml[a]	Physically compatible with no change in measured haze or increase in particle content in 4 hr at 23 °C	2234	C
Ticarcillin disodium–clavulanate potassium	SKB	31 mg/ml[a]	BMS	2 mg/ml[a]	Physically compatible with no change in measured haze or increase in particle content in 4 hr at 23 °C	2234	C
Tobramycin sulfate	GNS	5 mg/ml[a]	BMS	2 mg/ml[a]	Physically compatible with no change in measured haze or increase in particle content in 4 hr at 23 °C	2234	C
Trimethoprim–sulfamethoxazole	ES	0.8 + 4 mg/ml[a]	BMS	2 mg/ml[a]	Physically compatible with no change in measured haze or increase in particle content in 4 hr at 23 °C	2234	C
Vancomycin HCl	LI	10 mg/ml[a]	BMS	2 mg/ml[a]	Measured haze increases and microprecipitate forms immediately	2234	I
Vecuronium bromide	MAR	1 mg/ml	BMS	2 mg/ml[a]	Physically compatible with no change in measured haze or increase in particle content in 4 hr at 23 °C	2234	C
Verapamil HCl	AB	2.5 mg/ml	BMS	2 mg/ml[a]	Physically compatible with no change in measured haze or increase in particle content in 4 hr at 23 °C	2234	C

Y-Site Injection Compatibility (1:1 Mixture) (Cont.)

Drug	Mfr	Conc	Gatifloxacin Mfr	Gatifloxacin Conc	Remarks	Ref	C/I
Vinblastine sulfate	LI	0.12 mg/ml[b]	BMS	2 mg/ml[a]	Physically compatible with no change in measured haze or increase in particle content in 4 hr at 23 °C	2234	C
Vincristine sulfate	LI	0.05 mg/ml[a]	BMS	2 mg/ml[a]	Physically compatible with no change in measured haze or increase in particle content in 4 hr at 23 °C	2234	C
Vinorelbine tartrate	GW	1 mg/ml[a]	BMS	2 mg/ml[a]	Physically compatible with no change in measured haze or increase in particle content in 4 hr at 23 °C	2234	C
Zidovudine	GW	4 mg/ml[a]	BMS	2 mg/ml[a]	Physically compatible with no change in measured haze or increase in particle content in 4 hr at 23 °C	2234	C

[a]*Tested in dextrose 5% in water.*
[b]*Tested in sodium chloride 0.9%.*
[c]*Sodium carbonate–containing formulation tested.*

Additional Compatibility Information

Infusion Solutions — Gatifloxacin concentrated solution diluted to a concentration of 2 mg/ml is physically compatible and chemically stable for 14 days at room temperature and under refrigeration in the following infusion solutions (2):

Dextrose 5% in Ringer's injection, lactated
Dextrose 5% in sodium chloride 0.45% with potassium chloride 20 mEq/L
Dextrose 5% in sodium chloride 0.9%
Dextrose 5% in water
Plasma-Lyte 56 and 5% dextrose
Sodium bicarbonate 5%
Sodium chloride 0.9%
Sodium lactate ⅙ M

Other Drugs — The manufacturer indicates that gatifloxacin should not be mixed with or administered simultaneously through the same line with other drugs. If gatifloxacin is to be infused sequentially before or after other drugs through a common line, it is recommended that the line be flushed both before and after the gatifloxacin is infused using a solution compatible with gatifloxacin and the other drugs. (2)

GEMCITABINE HCL
AHFS 10:00

Products — Gemcitabine HCl is available as a lyophilized powder in vials containing 200 mg of drug (as the base) with mannitol 200 mg and sodium acetate 12.5 mg. Reconstitute the 200-mg vial with 5 ml of sodium chloride 0.9% (without preservatives) and shake to dissolve the powder. (2)

Gemcitabine HCl is also available as a lyophilized powder in vials containing 1 g of drug (as the base) with mannitol 1 g and sodium acetate 62.5 mg. Reconstitute the 1-g vial with 25 ml of sodium chloride 0.9% (without preservatives) and shake to dissolve the powder. (2)

When reconstituted as directed, the resulting solution from either size vial has a gemcitabine concentration of 38 mg/ml, which accounts for the displacement volume of the powder. The total volumes after reconstitution will be 5.26 ml for the 200-mg vial and 26.3 ml for the 1-g vial. (2)

Because of the drug's aqueous solubility, reconstitution to concentrations higher than 40 mg/ml may result in incomplete dissolution and should be avoided. (2)

The pH of the products may have been adjusted by the manufacturer with sodium hydroxide and/or hydrochloric acid. (2)

pH — The reconstituted solution has a pH in the range of 2.7 to 3.3. (2)

Displacement Volume — The displacement volume of the powder in the 200-mg vial is 0.26 ml and in the 1-g vial is 1.3 ml. (2)

Trade Name(s) — Gemzar.

Administration — Gemcitabine HCl is administered weekly by intravenous infusion over 30 minutes. It may be administered as reconstituted or diluted further in additional sodium chloride 0.9% to a concentration as low as 0.1 mg/ml. (2)

Stability — Gemcitabine HCl in intact vials should be stored at controlled room temperature. The white lyophilized powder becomes a colorless to light straw-colored solution on reconstitution. The manufacturer states that the reconstituted solution is stable for 24 hours at controlled room temperature. Unused solution should be discarded. (2) However, other information indicates the reconstituted solution may be stable for longer periods. (2227) See Reconstituted Solutions below. The reconstituted solution should not be refrigerated because crystallization may occur. (2)

Reconstituted Solutions—Gemcitabine HCl (Lilly) 200-mg and 1-g vials reconstituted to 38 mg/ml with sterile water for injection and also sodium chloride 0.9% were evaluated over periods of 35 days at 23 °C exposed to and protected from fluorescent light and at 4 °C protected from light. The samples stored at 23 °C were physically stable with no visible particulates and no increase in electronically measured particulates throughout the study period. HPLC analysis found less than 4% gemcitabine loss after 35 days of storage at 23 °C. Under refrigeration, the solutions remained physically and chemically stable for at least seven days, but large colorless crystals formed in some samples after that time. The crystals did not redissolve on warming to room temperature. HPLC analysis found little or no gemcitabine loss in the refrigerated solutions unless crystals formed; gemcitabine losses of 20 to 35% were determined in samples containing crystals. Exposure to or protection from fluorescent light did not affect gemcitabine stability. (2227)

Syringes—Gemcitabine HCl (Lilly) 38 mg/ml in sodium chloride 0.9% was repackaged as 10 ml of solution in 20-ml polypropylene plastic syringes (Becton-Dickinson) and sealed with tip caps (Red Cap, Burron). Sample syringes were stored at 23 °C both exposed to and protected from fluorescent light and at 4 °C protected from light for 35 days. All samples were physically stable with no visible particulates and no increase in electronically measured particulates throughout the study period. Although not observed in these solutions packaged in plastic syringes, reconstituted solutions stored under refrigeration are subject to possible crystal formation. See Reconstituted Solutions above. HPLC analysis found little or no gemcitabine loss after 35 days of storage under any of the conditions. (2227)

Ambulatory Pumps—Gemcitabine HCl (Lilly) 0.1, 10, and 38 mg/ml in dextrose 5% in water and in sodium chloride 0.9% in 50-ml PVC bags were evaluated over seven days for physical and chemical stability at 32 °C in the dark to simulate conditions during ambulatory infusion from a solution reservoir worn under clothes next to the body. All samples were physically stable with no visible particulates and no increase in electronically measured particulates throughout the study period. HPLC analysis found no loss of gemcitabine in any of the samples. (2227)

Sorption—Gemcitabine HCl has not exhibited any incompatibilities with infusion bottles or PVC bags and administration sets. (2)

Compatibility Information

Solution Compatibility

Gemcitabine HCl

Solution	*Mfr*	*Mfr*	*Conc/L*	*Remarks*	*Ref*	*C/I*
Dextrose 5% in water	BA[a]	LI	0.1 and 10 g	Physically compatible with no increase in particle content and chemically stable with no loss by HPLC in 35 days at 23 °C exposed to or protected from fluorescent light and at 4 °C in the dark	2227	C
Sodium chloride 0.9%	BA[a]	LI	0.1 and 10 g	Physically compatible with no increase in particle content and chemically stable with no loss by HPLC in 35 days at 23 °C exposed to or protected from fluorescent light and at 4 °C in the dark	2227	C

[a]*Tested in PVC containers.*

Y-Site Injection Compatibility (1:1 Mixture)

Gemcitabine HCl

Drug	*Mfr*	*Conc*	*Mfr*	*Conc*	*Remarks*	*Ref*	*C/I*
Acyclovir sodium	GW	7 mg/ml[b]	LI	10 mg/ml[b]	Gross precipitation occurs immediately	2226	I
Amifostine	USB	10 mg/ml[b]	LI	10 mg/ml[b]	Physically compatible with no change in measured turbidity or increase in particle content in 4 hr at 23 °C	2226	C
Amikacin sulfate	APC	5 mg/ml[b]	LI	10 mg/ml[b]	Physically compatible with no change in measured turbidity or increase in particle content in 4 hr at 23 °C	2226	C

Y-Site Injection Compatibility (1:1 Mixture) (Cont.)

Gemcitabine HCl

Drug	*Mfr*	*Conc*	*Mfr*	*Conc*	*Remarks*	*Ref*	*C/I*
Aminophylline	AB	2.5 mg/ml[b]	LI	10 mg/ml[b]	Physically compatible with no change in measured turbidity or increase in particle content in 4 hr at 23 °C	2226	C
Amphotericin B	PH	0.6 mg/ml[a]	LI	10 mg/ml[b]	Gross precipitation occurs immediately	2226	I
Ampicillin sodium	SKB	20 mg/ml[b]	LI	10 mg/ml[b]	Physically compatible with no change in measured turbidity or increase in particle content in 4 hr at 23 °C	2226	C
Ampicillin sodium–sulbactam sodium	RR	20 + 10 mg/ml[b]	LI	10 mg/ml[b]	Physically compatible with no change in measured turbidity or increase in particle content in 4 hr at 23 °C	2226	C
Aztreonam	SQ	40 mg/ml[b]	LI	10 mg/ml[b]	Physically compatible with no change in measured turbidity or increase in particle content in 4 hr at 23 °C	2226	C
Bleomycin sulfate	MJ	1 unit/ml[b]	LI	10 mg/ml[b]	Physically compatible with no change in measured turbidity or increase in particle content in 4 hr at 23 °C	2226	C
Bumetanide	RC	0.04 mg/ml[b]	LI	10 mg/ml[b]	Physically compatible with no change in measured turbidity or increase in particle content in 4 hr at 23 °C	2226	C
Buprenorphine HCl	RKC	0.04 mg/ml[b]	LI	10 mg/ml[b]	Physically compatible with no change in measured turbidity or increase in particle content in 4 hr at 23 °C	2226	C
Butorphanol tartrate	APC	0.04 mg/ml[b]	LI	10 mg/ml[b]	Physically compatible with no change in measured turbidity or increase in particle content in 4 hr at 23 °C	2226	C
Calcium gluconate	FUJ	40 mg/ml[b]	LI	10 mg/ml[b]	Physically compatible with no change in measured turbidity or increase in particle content in 4 hr at 23 °C	2226	C
Carboplatin	BR	5 mg/ml[b]	LI	10 mg/ml[b]	Physically compatible with no change in measured turbidity or increase in particle content in 4 hr at 23 °C	2226	C
Carmustine	BR	1.5 mg/ml[b]	LI	10 mg/ml[b]	Physically compatible with no change in measured turbidity or increase in particle content in 4 hr at 23 °C	2226	C
Cefazolin sodium	APC	20 mg/ml[b]	LI	10 mg/ml[b]	Physically compatible with no change in measured turbidity or increase in particle content in 4 hr at 23 °C	2226	C
Cefoperazone sodium	PF	40 mg/ml[b]	LI	10 mg/ml[b]	Gross precipitation occurs immediately	2226	I
Cefotaxime sodium	HO	20 mg/ml[b]	LI	10 mg/ml[b]	Slight subvisual haze forms in 1 hr with increased haze and a subvisual precipitate in 4 hr	2226	I
Cefotetan sodium	ZEN	20 mg/ml[b]	LI	10 mg/ml[b]	Physically compatible with no change in measured turbidity or increase in particle content in 4 hr at 23 °C	2226	C
Cefoxitin sodium	ME	20 mg/ml[b]	LI	10 mg/ml[b]	Physically compatible with no change in measured turbidity or increase in particle content in 4 hr at 23 °C	2226	C

Y-Site Injection Compatibility (1:1 Mixture) (Cont.)

Drug	Mfr	Conc	Gemcitabine HCl Mfr	Gemcitabine HCl Conc	Remarks	Ref	C/I
Ceftazidime	SKB[c]	40 mg/ml[b]	LI	10 mg/ml[b]	Physically compatible with no change in measured turbidity or increase in particle content in 4 hr at 23 °C	2226	C
Ceftizoxime sodium	FUJ	20 mg/ml[b]	LI	10 mg/ml[b]	Physically compatible with no change in measured turbidity or increase in particle content in 4 hr at 23 °C	2226	C
Ceftriaxone sodium	RC	20 mg/ml[b]	LI	10 mg/ml[b]	Physically compatible with no change in measured turbidity or increase in particle content in 4 hr at 23 °C	2226	C
Cefuroxime sodium	GW	30 mg/ml[b]	LI	10 mg/ml[b]	Physically compatible with no change in measured turbidity or increase in particle content in 4 hr at 23 °C	2226	C
Chlorpromazine HCl	ES	2 mg/ml[b]	LI	10 mg/ml[b]	Physically compatible with no change in measured turbidity or increase in particle content in 4 hr at 23 °C	2226	C
Cimetidine HCl	AMR	12 mg/ml[b]	LI	10 mg/ml[b]	Physically compatible with no change in measured turbidity or increase in particle content in 4 hr at 23 °C	2226	C
Ciprofloxacin	BAY	1 mg/ml[b]	LI	10 mg/ml[b]	Physically compatible with no change in measured turbidity or increase in particle content in 4 hr at 23 °C	2226	C
Cisplatin	BR	1 mg/ml	LI	10 mg/ml[b]	Physically compatible with no change in measured turbidity or increase in particle content in 4 hr at 23 °C	2226	C
Clindamycin phosphate	AST	10 mg/ml[b]	LI	10 mg/ml[b]	Physically compatible with no change in measured turbidity or increase in particle content in 4 hr at 23 °C	2226	C
Cyclophosphamide	BR	10 mg/ml[b]	LI	10 mg/ml[b]	Physically compatible with no change in measured turbidity or increase in particle content in 4 hr at 23 °C	2226	C
Cytarabine	BED	50 mg/ml	LI	10 mg/ml[b]	Physically compatible with no change in measured turbidity or increase in particle content in 4 hr at 23 °C	2226	C
Dactinomycin	ME	0.01 mg/ml[b]	LI	10 mg/ml[b]	Physically compatible with no change in measured turbidity or increase in particle content in 4 hr at 23 °C	2226	C
Daunorubicin HCl	BED	1 mg/ml[b]	LI	10 mg/ml[b]	Physically compatible with no change in measured turbidity or increase in particle content in 4 hr at 23 °C	2226	C
Dexamethasone sodium phosphate	ES	1 mg/ml[b]	LI	10 mg/ml[b]	Physically compatible with no change in measured turbidity or increase in particle content in 4 hr at 23 °C	2226	C
Dexrazoxane	PH	5 mg/ml[b]	LI	10 mg/ml[b]	Physically compatible with no change in measured turbidity or increase in particle content in 4 hr at 23 °C	2226	C
Diphenhydramine HCl	SCN	2 mg/ml[b]	LI	10 mg/ml[b]	Physically compatible with no change in measured turbidity or increase in particle content in 4 hr at 23 °C	2226	C

Y-Site Injection Compatibility (1:1 Mixture) (Cont.)

Gemcitabine HCl

Drug	*Mfr*	*Conc*	*Mfr*	*Conc*	*Remarks*	*Ref*	*C/I*
Dobutamine HCl	AST	4 mg/ml[b]	LI	10 mg/ml[b]	Physically compatible with no change in measured turbidity or increase in particle content in 4 hr at 23 °C	2226	C
Docetaxel	RPR	2 mg/ml[a]	LI	10 mg/ml[b]	Physically compatible with no change in measured turbidity or increase in particle content in 4 hr at 23 °C	2226	C
Dopamine HCl	AB	3.2 mg/ml[b]	LI	10 mg/ml[b]	Physically compatible with no change in measured turbidity or increase in particle content in 4 hr at 23 °C	2226	C
Doxorubicin HCl	PH	2 mg/ml	LI	10 mg/ml[b]	Physically compatible with no change in measured turbidity or increase in particle content in 4 hr at 23 °C	2226	C
Doxycycline hyclate	FUJ	1 mg/ml[b]	LI	10 mg/ml[b]	Physically compatible with no change in measured turbidity or increase in particle content in 4 hr at 23 °C	2226	C
Droperidol	AST	0.4 mg/ml[b]	LI	10 mg/ml[b]	Physically compatible with no change in measured turbidity or increase in particle content in 4 hr at 23 °C	2226	C
Enalaprilat	ME	0.1 mg/ml[b]	LI	10 mg/ml[b]	Physically compatible with no change in measured turbidity or increase in particle content in 4 hr at 23 °C	2226	C
Etoposide	BR	0.4 mg/ml[b]	LI	10 mg/ml[b]	Physically compatible with no change in measured turbidity or increase in particle content in 4 hr at 23 °C	2226	C
Etoposide phosphate	BR	5 mg/ml[b]	LI	10 mg/ml[b]	Physically compatible with no change in measured turbidity or increase in particle content in 4 hr at 23 °C	2226	C
Famotidine	ME	2 mg/ml[b]	LI	10 mg/ml[b]	Physically compatible with no change in measured turbidity or increase in particle content in 4 hr at 23 °C	2226	C
Floxuridine	RC	3 mg/ml[b]	LI	10 mg/ml[b]	Physically compatible with no change in measured turbidity or increase in particle content in 4 hr at 23 °C	2226	C
Fluconazole	RR	2 mg/ml	LI	10 mg/ml[b]	Physically compatible with no change in measured turbidity or increase in particle content in 4 hr at 23 °C	2226	C
Fludarabine phosphate	BX	1 mg/ml[b]	LI	10 mg/ml[b]	Physically compatible with no change in measured turbidity or increase in particle content in 4 hr at 23 °C	2226	C
Fluorouracil	PH	16 mg/ml[b]	LI	10 mg/ml[b]	Physically compatible with no change in measured turbidity or increase in particle content in 4 hr at 23 °C	2226	C
Furosemide	AMR	3 mg/ml[b]	LI	10 mg/ml[b]	Gross precipitation occurs immediately	2226	I
Ganciclovir sodium	RC	20 mg/ml[b]	LI	10 mg/ml[b]	Subvisual crystals form immediately, becoming a gross precipitate in 1 hr	2226	I
Gatifloxacin	BMS	2 mg/ml[a]	LI	10 mg/ml[b]	Physically compatible with no change in measured haze or increase in particle content in 4 hr at 23 °C	2234	C

Y-Site Injection Compatibility (1:1 Mixture) (Cont.)

Drug	Mfr	Conc	Mfr	Conc	Remarks	Ref	C/I
			Gemcitabine HCl				
Gentamicin sulfate	AB	5 mg/ml[b]	LI	10 mg/ml[b]	Physically compatible with no change in measured turbidity or increase in particle content in 4 hr at 23 °C	2226	C
Granisetron HCl	SKB	0.05 mg/ml[b]	LI	10 mg/ml[b]	Physically compatible with no change in measured turbidity or increase in particle content in 4 hr at 23 °C	2226	C
Haloperidol lactate	MN	0.2 mg/ml[b]	LI	10 mg/ml[b]	Physically compatible with no change in measured turbidity or increase in particle content in 4 hr at 23 °C	2226	C
Heparin sodium	ES	100 units/ml[b]	LI	10 mg/ml[b]	Physically compatible with no change in measured turbidity or increase in particle content in 4 hr at 23 °C	2226	C
Hydrocortisone sodium phosphate	ME	1 mg/ml[b]	LI	10 mg/ml[b]	Physically compatible with no change in measured turbidity or increase in particle content in 4 hr at 23 °C	2226	C
Hydrocortisone sodium succinate	UP	1 mg/ml[b]	LI	10 mg/ml[b]	Physically compatible with no change in measured turbidity or increase in particle content in 4 hr at 23 °C	2226	C
Hydromorphone HCl	AST	0.5 mg/ml[b]	LI	10 mg/ml[b]	Physically compatible with no change in measured turbidity or increase in particle content in 4 hr at 23 °C	2226	C
Hydroxyzine HCl	ES	2 mg/ml[b]	LI	10 mg/ml[b]	Physically compatible with no change in measured turbidity or increase in particle content in 4 hr at 23 °C	2226	C
Idarubicin HCl	AD	0.5 mg/ml[b]	LI	10 mg/ml[b]	Physically compatible with no change in measured turbidity or increase in particle content in 4 hr at 23 °C	2226	C
Ifosfamide	MJ	25 mg/ml[b]	LI	10 mg/ml[b]	Physically compatible with no change in measured turbidity or increase in particle content in 4 hr at 23 °C	2226	C
Imipenem–cilastatin sodium	ME	10 mg/ml[b]	LI	10 mg/ml[b]	Yellow-green discoloration forms in 1 hr	2226	I
Irinotecan	PHU	5 mg/ml[b]	LI	10 mg/ml[b]	Subvisual haze with green discoloration forms immediately	2226	I
Leucovorin calcium	IMM	2 mg/ml[b]	LI	10 mg/ml[b]	Physically compatible with no change in measured turbidity or increase in particle content in 4 hr at 23 °C	2226	C
Linezolid	PHU	2 mg/ml	LI	10 mg/ml[a]	Physically compatible with no change in measured turbidity or increase in particle content in 4 hr at 23 °C	2264	C
Lorazepam	WY	0.5 mg/ml[a]	LI	10 mg/ml[b]	Physically compatible with no change in measured turbidity or increase in particle content in 4 hr at 23 °C	2226	C
Mannitol	BA	15%	LI	10 mg/ml[b]	Physically compatible with no change in measured turbidity or increase in particle content in 4 hr at 23 °C	2226	C
Meperidine HCl	AST	4 mg/ml[b]	LI	10 mg/ml[b]	Physically compatible with no change in measured turbidity or increase in particle content in 4 hr at 23 °C	2226	C

Y-Site Injection Compatibility (1:1 Mixture) (Cont.)

Gemcitabine HCl

Drug	*Mfr*	*Conc*	*Mfr*	*Conc*	*Remarks*	*Ref*	*C/I*
Mesna	MJ	10 mg/ml[b]	LI	10 mg/ml[b]	Physically compatible with no change in measured turbidity or increase in particle content in 4 hr at 23 °C	2226	C
Methotrexate sodium	IMM	15 mg/ml[b]	LI	10 mg/ml[b]	Gross precipitate forms immediately, redissolves, but reprecipitates within 15 to 20 min	2226	I
Methylprednisolone sodium succinate	AB	5 mg/ml[b]	LI	10 mg/ml[b]	Gross precipitation occurs immediately	2226	I
Metoclopramide HCl	FAU	5 mg/ml	LI	10 mg/ml[b]	Physically compatible with no change in measured turbidity or increase in particle content in 4 hr at 23 °C	2226	C
Metronidazole	AB	5 mg/ml	LI	10 mg/ml[b]	Physically compatible with no change in measured turbidity or increase in particle content in 4 hr at 23 °C	2226	C
Minocycline HCl	LE	0.2 mg/ml[b]	LI	10 mg/ml[b]	Physically compatible with no change in measured turbidity or increase in particle content in 4 hr at 23 °C	2226	C
Mitomycin	BR	0.5 mg/ml	LI	10 mg/ml[b]	Reddish-purple discoloration forms in 1 hr	2226	I
Mitoxantrone HCl	IMM	0.5 mg/ml[b]	LI	10 mg/ml[b]	Physically compatible with no change in measured turbidity or increase in particle content in 4 hr at 23 °C	2226	C
Morphine sulfate	ES	1 mg/ml[b]	LI	10 mg/ml[b]	Physically compatible with no change in measured turbidity or increase in particle content in 4 hr at 23 °C	2226	C
Nalbuphine HCl	AST	10 mg/ml	LI	10 mg/ml[b]	Physically compatible with no change in measured turbidity or increase in particle content in 4 hr at 23 °C	2226	C
Netilmicin sulfate	SC	5 mg/ml[b]	LI	10 mg/ml[b]	Physically compatible with no change in measured turbidity or increase in particle content in 4 hr at 23 °C	2226	C
Ofloxacin	MN	4 mg/ml[b]	LI	10 mg/ml[b]	Physically compatible with no change in measured turbidity or increase in particle content in 4 hr at 23 °C	2226	C
Ondansetron HCl	GW	1 mg/ml[b]	LI	10 mg/ml[b]	Physically compatible with no change in measured turbidity or increase in particle content in 4 hr at 23 °C	2226	C
Paclitaxel	MJ	1.2 mg/ml[a]	LI	10 mg/ml[b]	Physically compatible with no change in measured turbidity or increase in particle content in 4 hr at 23 °C	2226	C
Piperacillin sodium	LE	40 mg/ml[b]	LI	10 mg/ml[b]	Cloudiness forms immediately, becoming precipitated clumps in 4 hr	2226	I
Piperacillin sodium–tazobactam sodium	LE	40 + 5 mg/ml[b]	LI	10 mg/ml[b]	Cloudiness forms immediately, becoming flocculent precipitate in 1 hr	2226	I
Plicamycin	BAY	0.01 mg/ml[b]	LI	10 mg/ml[b]	Physically compatible with no change in measured turbidity or increase in particle content in 4 hr at 23 °C	2226	C
Potassium chloride	AB	0.1 mEq/ml[b]	LI	10 mg/ml[b]	Physically compatible with no change in measured turbidity or increase in particle content in 4 hr at 23 °C	2226	C

Y-Site Injection Compatibility (1:1 Mixture) (Cont.)

Drug	Mfr	Conc	Gemcitabine HCl Mfr	Gemcitabine HCl Conc	Remarks	Ref	C/I
Prochlorperazine edisylate	SCN	0.5 mg/ml[b]	LI	10 mg/ml[b]	Subvisual haze forms immediately and increases over 4 hr	2226	I
Promethazine HCl	SCN	2 mg/ml[b]	LI	10 mg/ml[b]	Physically compatible with no change in measured turbidity or increase in particle content in 4 hr at 23 °C	2226	C
Ranitidine HCl	GL	2 mg/ml[b]	LI	10 mg/ml[b]	Physically compatible with no change in measured turbidity or increase in particle content in 4 hr at 23 °C	2226	C
Sodium bicarbonate	AB	1 mEq/ml	LI	10 mg/ml[b]	Physically compatible with no change in measured turbidity or increase in particle content in 4 hr at 23 °C	2226	C
Streptozocin	UP	40 mg/ml[b]	LI	10 mg/ml[b]	Physically compatible with no change in measured turbidity or increase in particle content in 4 hr at 23 °C	2226	C
Teniposide	BR	0.1 mg/ml[a]	LI	10 mg/ml[b]	Physically compatible with no change in measured turbidity or increase in particle content in 4 hr at 23 °C	2226	C
Thiotepa	IMM	1 mg/ml[b]	LI	10 mg/ml[b]	Physically compatible with no change in measured turbidity or increase in particle content in 4 hr at 23 °C	2226	C
Ticarcillin disodium	SKB	30 mg/ml[b]	LI	10 mg/ml[b]	Physically compatible with no change in measured turbidity or increase in particle content in 4 hr at 23 °C	2226	C
Ticarcillin disodium–clavulanate potassium	SKB	31 mg/ml[b]	LI	10 mg/ml[b]	Physically compatible with no change in measured turbidity or increase in particle content in 4 hr at 23 °C	2226	C
Tobramycin sulfate	LI	5 mg/ml[b]	LI	10 mg/ml[b]	Physically compatible with no change in measured turbidity or increase in particle content in 4 hr at 23 °C	2226	C
Topotecan HCl	SKB	0.1 mg/ml[b]	LI	10 mg/ml[b]	Physically compatible with no change in measured turbidity or increase in particle content in 4 hr at 23 °C	2226	C
Trimethoprim–sulfamethoxazole	ES	0.8 + 4 mg/ml[b]	LI	10 mg/ml[b]	Physically compatible with no change in measured turbidity or increase in particle content in 4 hr at 23 °C	2226	C
Vancomycin HCl	LI	10 mg/ml[b]	LI	10 mg/ml[b]	Physically compatible with no change in measured turbidity or increase in particle content in 4 hr at 23 °C	2226	C
Vinblastine sulfate	FAU	0.12 mg/ml[b]	LI	10 mg/ml[b]	Physically compatible with no change in measured turbidity or increase in particle content in 4 hr at 23 °C	2226	C
Vincristine sulfate	FAU	0.05 mg/ml[b]	LI	10 mg/ml[b]	Physically compatible with no change in measured turbidity or increase in particle content in 4 hr at 23 °C	2226	C
Vinorelbine tartrate	GW	1 mg/ml[b]	LI	10 mg/ml[b]	Physically compatible with no change in measured turbidity or increase in particle content in 4 hr at 23 °C	2226	C

Y-Site Injection Compatibility (1:1 Mixture) (Cont.)

Gemcitabine HCl

Drug	*Mfr*	*Conc*	*Mfr*	*Conc*	*Remarks*	*Ref*	*C/I*
Zidovudine	GW	4 mg/ml[b]	LI	10 mg/ml[b]	Physically compatible with no change in measured turbidity or increase in particle content in 4 hr at 23 °C	2226	C

[a]*Tested in dextrose 5% in water.*
[b]*Tested in sodium chloride 0.9%.*
[c]*Sodium carbonate–containing formulation tested.*

Other Information

Microbial Growth — Gemcitabine HCl (Lilly) 2.4 mg/ml diluted in sodium chloride 0.9% and stored at 22 °C did not exhibit a substantial antimicrobial effect on the growth of four organisms (*Enterococcus faecium, Staphylococcus aureus, Pseudomonas aeruginosa,* and *Candida albicans*) inoculated into the solution. *C. albicans* maintained viability for 120 hours, and the others were viable for 24 hours. The author recommended that diluted solutions of gemcitabine HCl be stored under refrigeration whenever possible and that the potential for microbiological growth should be considered when assigning expiration periods. (2160)

GENTAMICIN SULFATE
AHFS 8:12.02

Products — Gentamicin (as the sulfate) is available at a concentration of 40 mg/ml in 2- and 20-ml vials and 1.5- and 2-ml syringe cartridges. The drug is also available at a concentration of 10 mg/ml in 2-ml vials for pediatric use. The products may also contain edetate disodium, sodium bisulfite, and parabens. (4; 29; 154)

Gentamicin sulfate is also available from several manufacturers premixed in various concentrations in sodium chloride 0.9% for intravenous infusion. (4)

pH — The injection for intravenous or intramuscular administration has a pH of 3 to 5.5. Premixed infusions of gentamicin sulfate in sodium chloride 0.9% have a pH of around 4 to 4.5. (4)

Osmolality — Gentamicin sulfate (Wyeth) 40 mg/ml has a reported osmolality of 160 mOsm/kg. (50) Gentamicin sulfate pediatric injection (Elkins-Sinn) 10 mg/ml has a reported osmolality of 116 mOsm/kg by freezing-point depression or 212 mOsm/kg by vapor pressure. (1071)

The osmolality of gentamicin sulfate (SoloPak) 1 mg/ml was determined to be 262 mOsm/kg in dextrose 5% in water and 278 mOsm/kg in sodium chloride 0.9%. At a 2.5-mg/ml concentration, the osmolality was determined to be 278 mOsm/kg in dextrose 5% in water and 293 mOsm/kg in sodium chloride 0.9%. (1375)

The osmolality of gentamicin sulfate 80 mg was calculated for the following dilutions (1054):

	Osmolality (mOsm/kg)	
Diluent	50 ml	100 ml
Dextrose 5% in water	293	285
Sodium chloride 0.9%	320	315

The osmolarity of the premixed infusions in sodium chloride 0.9% is approximately 284 to 308 mOsm/L. (4)

Administration — Gentamicin sulfate is administered by intramuscular injection or intermittent intravenous infusion over 0.5 to two hours. For adults, intravenous administration after dilution in 50 to 200 ml of sodium chloride 0.9% or dextrose 5% in water is recommended, while the volume for pediatric patients should be reduced consistent with the patient's needs. (1-6/97; 4)

Stability — Gentamicin sulfate injection is colorless to slightly yellow. (4) Intact containers should be stored at controlled room temperature and protected from freezing. (1-6/97; 4) Potency loss has been determined to be unrelated to color intensity of gentamicin sulfate solutions. (2139)

Freezing Solutions — Gentamicin sulfate (Schering) 50 mg in 50 ml of dextrose 5% in water and also sodium chloride 0.9% in PVC containers was frozen at −20 °C for 30 days. Potency was retained for the duration of the study. (299)

In another study, gentamicin sulfate (Schering) 80 mg/100 ml of dextrose 5% in water in PVC bags was frozen at −20 °C for 30 days and then thawed by exposure to ambient temperature or microwave radiation. No evidence of precipitation or color change was observed, and no loss of potency was determined microbiologically. Subsequent storage of the admixture at room temperature for 24 hours also yielded a physically compatible solution, exhibiting little or no loss of potency. (554)

Marble et al. reported that gentamicin sulfate (Elkins-Sinn) 120 mg/50 ml lost 6% activity in dextrose 5% in water and 2% activity in sodium chloride 0.9% in 28 days when frozen at −20 °C. (981)

Syringes — Gentamicin sulfate (Schering) 40 mg/ml was found to retain potency for three months at room temperature when 1 and 2 ml of solution were packaged in Tubex cartridges. (13)

In another report, the stability of gentamicin sulfate (Schering) repackaged in plastic syringes (Monoject) was significantly less than in glass syringes (Glaspak, Becton-Dickinson) at both 4 and 25 °C. The commercial concentrations were tested in the following amounts: 40 mg/ml—1, 0.75, 0.5, and 0.25 ml; and 10 mg/ml—1.5, 1, and 0.5 ml. Storage in plastic syringes resulted in an average potency loss of 16% in 30 days and in the formation of a brown precipitate. In glass syringes, the average potency loss was 7% at 30 days. The brown precipitate did not appear after 30 days but was present at 60 days. It appeared in the cannula of the needle in both glass and plastic syringes. For the 40-mg/ml concentration, the volume of the sample also affected stability. Significantly less potency loss was noted in the smaller volumes (0.25 and 0.5 ml) than in the larger volumes (0.5 and 1 ml). This volume-related phenomenon was not demonstrated in the 10-mg/ml pediatric concentration. Storage temperature had no effect on potency during the 90-day study period. The authors recommended that only glass disposable syringes be used for long-term unit dose storage of gentamicin sulfate and that storage not exceed 30 days. (297)

The appearance of this report stimulated the interest of Kresel et al. They packaged gentamicin sulfate 40 mg/1 ml in polypropylene syringes (Plastipak, Becton-Dickinson) and found no significant change in potency by enzymatic assay over 30 days at 4 or 25 °C. (401)

In reply, McNealy et al. noted that a different brand of polypropylene syringes had been used in the study and that plastic composition can vary considerably. Further, they disputed the applicability of the enzymatic assay to long-term plastic-stored samples. (402)

The manufacturer also expressed concern about plastic packaging of gentamicin, noting a possibly inadequate oxygen and moisture barrier both through the tip and the walls of the syringe. It was indicated that gentamicin is oxygen sensitive and that depletion of the antioxidant present could result in instability. Further, loss of moisture at the tip could result in occlusion by the dried product. It was noted that disposable syringes are manufactured by Schering with a two-year expiration date. (403)

Zbrozek et al. found that gentamicin sulfate (Elkins-Sinn) 120 mg, diluted with 1 ml of sodium chloride 0.9% to a final volume of 4 ml, was stable (less than 10% loss) when stored in polypropylene syringes (Becton-Dickinson) for 48 hours at 25 °C under fluorescent light. (1159)

Nahata et al. studied the stability of gentamicin sulfate (Elkins-Sinn) diluted to 10 mg/ml with sodium chloride 0.9% and stored in glass syringes (Becton-Dickinson) at 4 °C. No loss of gentamicin sulfate was found by enzyme-mediated immunoassay during 12 weeks of storage. (1265)

Ambulatory Pumps—Tu et al. studied the stability of gentamicin sulfate (Schering) 5.45 mg/ml in dextrose 5% in water in an ambulatory pump reservoir. The drug-filled reservoirs were stored at −20 °C for 30 days and then thawed at 5 °C for four days. This thawing was then followed by two days of drug delivery through the pump at 37 °C. No visible changes and no gentamicin loss occurred during the entire storage and delivery sequence. Furthermore, plasticizer (DEHP) levels were insignificant. (1490)

Elastomeric Reservoir Pumps—Gentamicin sulfate (Lyphomed) 0.8 mg/ml in sodium chloride 0.9% 100 ml was packaged in latex elastomeric reservoirs (Secure Medical). Little or no loss by HPLC analysis occurred in 24 hours at 25 °C. (1970)

Gentamicin sulfate 0.6 mg/ml in both dextrose 5% in water and sodium chloride 0.9% was evaluated for binding potential to natural rubber elastomeric reservoirs (Baxter). No binding was found after storage for two weeks at 35 °C with gentle agitation. (2014)

Gentamicin sulfate solutions in elastomeric reservoir pumps have been stated by the pump manufacturers to be stable for the following time periods frozen, refrigerated (REF), or at room temperature (RT) (31):

Pump Reservoir(s)	Conc.	Frozen	REF	RT
Intermate	0.5 to 5 mg/ml[a,b]	30 days	10 days	24 hr
Intermate HPC	0.8 to 2.4 mg/ml[a,b]		14 days	14 days
Medflo	0.8 mg/ml[a,b]	4 weeks	4 days	48 hr
ReadyMed	1 mg/ml[b]	4 weeks	14 days	48 hr

[a]*In dextrose 5% in water.*
[b]*In sodium chloride 0.9%.*

Sorption—Gentamicin sulfate (Schering) 40 mg/L in sodium chloride 0.9% (Travenol) in PVC bags did not exhibit significant sorption to the plastic during one week of storage at room temperature (15 to 20 °C). (536)

In another study, gentamicin sulfate (Schering) 40 mg/L in sodium chloride 0.9% did not exhibit any loss due to sorption during a seven-hour simulated infusion through an infusion set (Travenol) consisting of a cellulose propionate burette chamber and 170 cm of PVC tubing. (606)

The drug was also tested as a simulated infusion over at least one hour by a syringe pump system. A glass syringe on a syringe pump was fitted with 20 cm of polyethylene tubing or 50 cm of Silastic tubing. No drug loss due to sorption was observed with either tubing. (606)

A 25-ml aliquot of gentamicin sulfate (Schering) 40 mg/L in sodium chloride 0.9% was stored in all-plastic syringes composed of polypropylene barrels and polyethylene plungers for 24 hours at room temperature in the dark. No loss of drug due to sorption occurred. (606)

Gentamicin sulfate (Dakota) 1.6 mg/ml in dextrose 5% in water and in sodium chloride 0.9% was packaged in PVC bags (Macropharma) and in multilayer bags composed of polyethylene, polyamide, and polypropylene (Bieffe Medital). The solutions were delivered through PVC administration sets (Abbott) over one hour and evaluated for drug loss by HPLC analysis. No loss due to sorption to any of the plastic materials was found. (2269)

Filtration—The effect of several filters on the delivered concentration of gentamicin sulfate (Roussel) from simulated pediatric infusions was studied by Nazeravich and Otten. A syringe containing dextrose 10% in water on a syringe pump set at 8.26 ml/hr was connected by intravenous tubing to a 0.5-μm air-blocking filter set (Travenol), a 0.22-μm air-eliminating filter set (Travenol), and a 0.2-μm air-eliminating filter set (Pall). Gentamicin doses of 2.5 and 7.5 mg were injected antegrade to the filter. The effluents were sampled at 1, 1.5, 2, and 4 hours and tested using an enzyme-mediated immunoassay technique (EMIT) assay. No significant drug sorption to the plastic tubing or inline filters occurred. However, because of the difference in specific gravity of the drug (1.010) and intravenous solution (1.032), variations in delivered gentamicin did occur due to filter design and position. With the Travenol filters, gentamicin delivery was more rapid with ascending flow in both horizontal and vertical positions. Drug delivery was significantly delayed with descending flow in both positions. The Pall filter delivered gentamicin more rapidly in the horizontal position with either ascending or descending flow. The vertical filter position significantly delayed drug delivery in both flow directions. (804)

However, in another study, gentamicin sulfate 60 mg/15 ml was injected as a bolus through a 0.2-µm nylon air-eliminating filter (Ultipor, Pall) to evaluate the effect of filtration on simulated intravenous push delivery. Enzyme-mediated assays showed that only about 38% of the drug was delivered through the filter after flushing with 10 ml of sodium chloride 0.9%. (809)

Filtration of 30 ml of a solution of gentamicin 500 µg/ml (as the sulfate) (Schering) through Seitz sterilizing filters resulted in substantial binding of the drug to the filters. Losses ranged from 31 to 66%, depending on the filter size. (823) However, this filter medium does not resemble current clinical filters. Subsequent reassay using membrane filters indicated little or no loss of activity. (829)

Thompson et al. evaluated gentamicin sulfate 5 and 10 mg/55 ml of dextrose 5% in water and sodium chloride 0.9% filtered over 20 minutes through a 0.22-µm cellulose ester filter set (Ivex-2, Millipore). EMIT showed that virtually all of the drug was delivered through the filter. (1003)

Kane et al. evaluated the binding of gentamicin sulfate to the filter of a set used for continuous ambulatory peritoneal dialysis (CAPD). Gentamicin sulfate (Schering) 60 mg/2 L in Dianeal 137 with dextrose 4.25 and 1.5% was filtered through a Peridex CAPD filter set (Millipore); this set has a surface area 27 times larger than an inline intravenous filter. About 25% binding occurred from the solution containing dextrose 4.25%, but only 7.5% was bound with the 1.5% solution. (1112)

Gentamicin sulfate (Unicet-Unilabo) 0.32 mg/ml in dextrose 5% in water and sodium chloride 0.9% was filtered through a 0.22-µm cellulose ester membrane filter (Ivex-HP, Millipore) over six hours. No significant drug loss due to binding to the filter was noted. (1034)

Central Venous Catheter—Gentamicin sulfate (Fujisawa) 1 mg/ml in dextrose 5% in water was found to be compatible with the ARROWg+ard Blue Plus (Arrow International) chlorhexidine-bearing triple-lumen central catheter. HPLC analysis was used to evaluate completeness of drug delivery through the catheter and the amount of chlorhexidine removed from the internal lumens. Essentially complete delivery of the drug was found with little or no drug loss occurring. Furthermore, chlorhexidine delivered from the catheter remained at trace amounts with no substantial increase due to the delivery of the drug through the catheter. (2335)

Compatibility Information

Solution Compatibility

Gentamicin sulfate

Solution	*Mfr*	*Mfr*	*Conc/L*	*Remarks*	*Ref*	*C/I*
Amino acids 4.25%, dextrose 25%	MG	SC	80 mg	No increase in particulate matter in 24 hr at 5 °C	349	C
Dextrose 4.3% in sodium chloride 0.18%		RS	160 mg	Potency retained for up to 48 hr at room temperature	157	C
Dextrose 5% in water		RS	160 mg	Potency retained for up to 48 hr at room temperature	157	C
	AB	SC	160 mg	Potency retained for 24 hr at 5 and 25 °C	88	C
	BA[a], TR	SC	1 g	Potency retained for 24 hr at 5 and 22 °C	298	C
	BA[b]	SC	1 g	Potency retained for 30 days at −20 °C	299	C
	TR[b]	SC	800 mg	Physically compatible with little or no loss of potency in 24 hr at room temperature	554	C
			120 mg	Physically compatible and gentamicin stable by microbiological assay for 24 hr at 25 °C	897	C
	AB[b]	LY	1.2 g	Visually compatible and potency by immunoassay retained for 48 hr at 25 °C under fluorescent light and 4 °C in the dark	1541	C
			600 mg	Formation of decomposition products found by HPLC in 48 hr at room temperature. Gentamicin not quantified	2139	?
Dextrose 10% in water	SO	SC	60 mg/21.5 ml[c]	Visually compatible with no gentamicin loss by TDx in 30 days at 5 °C in the dark	1731	C
	SO	SC	120 mg/23 ml[c]	Visually compatible with no gentamicin loss by TDx in 30 days at 5 °C in the dark	1731	C
Fat emulsion 10%, intravenous	VT	RS	160 mg	Microscopic globule coalescence within 24 hr at 8 and 25 °C	825	I
Fructose 5% in water			120 mg	Physically compatible and gentamicin stable by microbiological assay for 24 hr at 25 °C	897	C
Invert sugar 7.5% with electrolytes		SC	50 mg	Physically compatible with no gentamicin loss in 24 hr at 29 °C by microbiological assay	440	C

Solution Compatibility (Cont.)

Gentamicin sulfate

Solution	Mfr	Mfr	Conc/L	Remarks	Ref	C/I
Mannitol 20%			120 mg	Physically compatible and gentamicin stable by microbiological assay for 24 hr at 25 °C	897	C
Ringer's injection			120 mg	Physically compatible and gentamicin stable by microbiological assay for 24 hr at 25 °C	897	C
Sodium chloride 0.9%			120 mg	Physically compatible and gentamicin stable by microbiological assay for 24 hr at 25 °C	897	C
		RS	160 mg	Potency retained for up to 48 hr at room temperature	157	C
	BA[a], TR	SC	1 g	Potency retained for 24 hr at 5 and 22 °C	298	C
	BA[b]	SC	1 g	Potency retained for 30 days at −20 °C	299	C
	AB[b]	LY	1.2 g	Visually compatible and potency by immunoassay retained for 48 hr at 25 °C under fluorescent light and 4 °C in the dark	1541	C
	AB[d]	LY	800 mg	Little or no loss of drug by HPLC in 24 hr at 25 °C	1970	C
TPN #1, #4, #5, #7[e]		SC	80 mg	Physically compatible for 24 hr at 22 °C	313	C
TPN #2, #3, #6, #8, #9[e]		SC	80 mg	Physically incompatible with precipitate noted in 8 to 24 hr at 22 °C	313	I
TPN #1[e]		SC	80 mg	Antibiotic potency retained for at least 12 hr at 22 °C	313	C
TPN #10[e]		SC	80 mg	Physically compatible for 24 hr and antibiotic potency retained for at least 12 hr at 22 °C	313	C
TPN #22[e]		SC	800 mg	Physically compatible with no loss of activity by microbiological assay in 24 hr at 22 °C in the dark	837	C
TPN #52 and #53[e]		SC	50 mg	Physically compatible with no gentamicin loss in 24 hr at 29 °C by microbiological assay	440	C
TPN #107[e]			75 mg	Physically compatible and gentamicin activity retained for 24 hr at 21 °C by microbiological assay	1326	C

[a]Tested in both glass and PVC containers.
[b]Tested in PVC containers.
[c]Tested in glass vials as a concentrate.
[d]Tested in glass containers and latex elastomeric reservoirs (Secure Medical).
[e]Refer to Appendix I for the composition of parenteral nutrition solutions. TPN indicates a 2-in-1 admixture.

Additive Compatibility

Gentamicin sulfate

Drug	Mfr	Conc/L	Mfr	Conc/L	Test Soln	Remarks	Ref	C/I
Amphotericin B		200 mg		320 mg	D5W	Haze develops over 3 hr	26	I
Ampicillin sodium	BE	8 g	RS	160 mg	D5¼S, D5W, NS	50% gentamicin decomposition in 2 hr at room temperature	157	I
		1 g		100 mg	TPN #107[a]	42% gentamicin loss and 25% ampicillin loss in 24 hr at 21 °C by microbiological assay	1326	I
Atracurium besylate	BW	500 mg		2 g	D5W	Physically compatible and atracurium chemically stable for 24 hr at 5 and 30 °C	1694	C

Additive Compatibility (Cont.)

Gentamicin sulfate

Drug	*Mfr*	*Conc/L*	*Mfr*	*Conc/L*	*Test Soln*	*Remarks*	*Ref*	*C/I*
Aztreonam	SQ	10 and 20 g	SC	200 and 800 mg	D5W, NS[b]	Little or no aztreonam loss in 48 hr at 25 °C and 7 days at 4 °C. Gentamicin potency retained for 12 hr at 25 °C and 24 hr at 4 °C, with up to 10% loss in 48 hr at 25 °C and 7 days at 4 °C	1023	C
Bleomycin sulfate	BR	20 and 30 units	SC	50, 100, 300, 600 mg	NS	Physically compatible and bleomycin activity retained for 1 week at 4 °C. Gentamicin not tested	763	C
Cefamandole nafate	LI	2 and 20 g		80 mg	D5W, NS, W	Haze or precipitate forms within 4 hr	376; 788	I
		1 g		100 mg	TPN #107[a]	14% gentamicin loss in 24 hr at 21 °C by microbiological assay	1326	I
Cefazolin sodium with clindamycin phosphate	SKF UP	10 g 9 g	ES	800 mg	D5W[c]	10% cefazolin loss in 4 hr at 25 °C. Clindamycin and gentamicin potency retained for 24 hr	1328	I
Cefazolin sodium with clindamycin phosphate	SKF UP	10 g 9 g	ES	800 mg	NS[c]	10% cefazolin loss in 12 hr at 25 °C. Clindamycin and gentamicin potency retained for 24 hr	1328	I
Cefepime HCl	BR	40 g	ES	1.2 g	D5W, NS	Cloudiness forms in 18 hr at room temperature	1681	I
Cefoxitin sodium	MSD	5 g	SC	400 mg	D5S	4% cefoxitin decomposition in 24 hr and 11% in 48 hr at 25 °C. 2% in 48 hr at 5 °C. 9% gentamicin decomposition in 24 hr and 23% in 48 hr at 25 °C. 2% in 48 hr at 5 °C	308	C
Cefuroxime sodium	GL	7.5 g	EX	800 mg	D5W, NS[b]	Physically compatible with no loss of either drug in 1 hr	1036	C
		1 g		100 mg	TPN #107[a]	32% gentamicin loss in 24 hr at 21 °C by microbiological assay	1326	I
Cimetidine HCl	SKF	3 g	SC	800 mg	D5W	Physically compatible and cimetidine chemically stable for 24 hr at room temperature. Gentamicin not tested	551	C
	SKF	1.2 and 5 g	SC	80 mg	D5W, NS	Physically compatible and cimetidine chemically stable for 24 hr at room temperature. Gentamicin not tested	551	C
Ciprofloxacin	MI	1.6 g	LY	1 g	D5W, NS	Visually compatible and ciprofloxacin potency by HPLC and gentamicin potency by immunoassay retained for 48 hr at 25 °C under fluorescent light and 4 °C in the dark	1541	C
	BAY	2 g	SC	10 g	NS	Visually compatible with little or no ciprofloxacin loss by HPLC in 24 hr at 25 °C. Gentamicin not tested	1934	C
Clindamycin phosphate	UP	1.2 g		60 mg	D5W	Physically compatible. Clindamycin potency retained for 24 hr at room temperature	104	C
	UP	2.4 g		120 mg	D5W	Physically compatible. Clindamycin potency retained for 24 hr at room temperature	104	C
	UP	9 g		800 mg	D5W	Clindamycin stability maintained for 24 hr	101	C

Additive Compatibility (Cont.)

Gentamicin sulfate

Drug	*Mfr*	*Conc/L*	*Mfr*	*Conc/L*	*Test Soln*	*Remarks*	*Ref*	*C/I*
	UP	12 g		600 mg	D5W	Physically compatible	101	C
	UP	9 g	AB	1 g	D5W, NS[d]	Physically compatible and potency of both drugs retained for 48 hr at room temperature exposed to light and 1 week frozen	174	C
	UP	9 g	ES	1.2 g	D5W, NS[c]	Physically compatible and potency of both drugs retained for 28 days frozen	174	C
	UP	9 g	LY	1.2 g	D5W[c]	Physically compatible and potency of both drugs retained for 7 days at 4 and 25 °C	174	C
	UP	18 g	LY	2.4 g	D5W[b]	Physically compatible and potency of both drugs retained for 14 days at 4 and 25 °C	174	C
	UP	9 g	LY	1.2 g	NS[c]	Physically compatible and potency of both drugs retained for 14 days at 4 and 25 °C	174	C
	UP	18 g	LY	2.4 g	NS[b]	Physically compatible and potency of both drugs retained for 14 days at 4 and 25 °C	174	C
	UP	18 g	ES	2.4 g	D5W, NS[b]	Potency of both drugs retained for 28 days frozen at −20 °C	981	C
	UP	6 g	ES	667 mg	D5W[b]	Physically compatible with no clindamycin loss and 9% gentamicin loss in 24 hr at room temperature	995	C
		400 mg		75 mg	TPN #107[a]	19% gentamicin loss and 15% clindamycin loss in 24 hr at 21 °C by microbiological assay	1326	I
Cytarabine	UP	100 mg		80 mg	D5W	Physically compatible for 24 hr	174	C
	UP	300 mg		240 mg	D5W	Physically incompatible	174	I
Dopamine HCl	AS	800 mg	SC	2 g	D5W	No dopamine decomposition and 7% gentamicin decomposition in 24 hr at 25 °C	312	C
	AS	800 mg	SC	320 mg	D5W	80% gentamicin decomposition in 24 hr at 23 to 25 °C. Gentamicin potency retained for 6 hr. Dopamine potency retained for 24 hr	78	I
Floxacillin sodium	BE	20 g	RS	8 g	NS	Haze forms immediately and precipitate forms in 2 hr	1479	I
	BE	10 g	EX	8 g	NS	Physically compatible for 48 hr. Potency of both drugs retained when assayed after 1 hr at room temperature	1036	C
	BE	10 g	EX	8 g	D5W	Immediate precipitation	1036	I
Fluconazole	PF	1 g	SO	0.5 g	D5W	Visually compatible with no fluconazole loss by HPLC in 72 hr at 25 °C under fluorescent light. Gentamicin not tested	1677	C
Furosemide	HO	800 mg	SC	1.6 g	D5W, NS	Immediate precipitation of furosemide	876	I
	HO	1 g	RS	8 g	NS	Physically compatible for 24 hr at 15 to 30 °C. Slight precipitate forms in 48 to 72 hr	1479	C
Heparin sodium	BP	20,000 units		320 mg	D5W, NS	Immediate precipitation	26	I
	OR	20,000 units	SC	1 g	D5W, NS	Opalescence	113	I

Additive Compatibility (Cont.)

Gentamicin sulfate

Drug	*Mfr*	*Conc/L*	*Mfr*	*Conc/L*	*Test Soln*	*Remarks*	*Ref*	*C/I*
	BRN	1000 to 6000 units	ME	88 mg	D10W, NS	Activity of both drugs by biological assays greatly reduced	1570	I
Linezolid	PHU	2 g	AB	800 mg	[f]	Physically compatible with little or no linezolid loss by HPLC in 7 days at 4 and 23 °C protected from light. Gentamicin losses of about 5 to 7% occurred in 7 days at 4 °C and losses of about 8% occurred in 5 days at 23 °C	2332	C
Meropenem	ZEN	1 and 20 g	SCH	800 mg	NS	Visually compatible for 4 hr at room temperature	1994	C
Metronidazole	RP	5 g[e]	RS	800 mg		Physically compatible with little or no pH change for at least 72 hr at 23 °C	807	C
		5 g	EX	800 mg	D5W, NS[b]	Physically compatible with no loss of either drug in 1 hr	1036	C
	SE	5 g	SC	800 mg and 1.2 g		Physically compatible with no loss of either drug in 2 days at 18 °C. At 4 °C, no metronidazole loss but up to 10% gentamicin loss in 7 days	1242	C
	RP	5 g		800 mg		Visually compatible with no loss of metronidazole by HPLC in 15 days at 5 and 25 °C. 10% gentamicin loss by immunoassay in 63 hr at 25 °C and 10.6 days at 5 °C	1931	C
Metronidazole HCl with sodium bicarbonate	SE AB	5 g 50 mEq	SC	320 mg	D5W, NS	Physically compatible for 48 hr	765	C
Nafcillin sodium		1 g		75 mg	TPN #107[a]	10% gentamicin loss in 24 hr at 21 °C by microbiological assay	1326	I
Ofloxacin	HO	2 g	ESX	800 mg	W	Visually compatible with little or no loss of either drug by HPLC in 48 hr	1613	C
Penicillin G sodium	GL	13 and 40 million units	RS	160 mg	D5¼S, D5W, NS	Gentamicin potency retained for 24 hr at room temperature	157	C
Ranitidine HCl	GL	100 mg		160 mg	D5W	Physically compatible for 24 hr at ambient temperature under fluorescent light	1151	C
	GL	50 mg and 2 g		80 mg	D5W, NS	Physically compatible and ranitidine chemically stable by HPLC for 24 hr at 25 °C. Gentamicin not tested	1515	C
Ticarcillin disodium		2 g		100 mg	TPN #107[a]	Over 98% gentamicin loss in 24 hr at 21 °C by microbiological assay	1326	I
Verapamil HCl	KN	80 mg	SC	160 mg	D5W, NS	Physically compatible for 24 hr	764	C

[a] *Refer to Appendix I for the composition of parenteral nutrition solutions. TPN indicates a 2-in-1 admixture.*
[b] *Tested in PVC containers.*
[c] *Tested in glass containers.*
[d] *Tested in both glass and PVC containers.*
[e] *Minibags (100 ml) containing metronidazole 500 mg with disodium phosphate 150 mg, citric acid 44 mg, and sodium chloride 740 mg. This product differs from the Searle product.*
[f] *Admixed in the linezolid infusion container.*

Drugs in Syringe Compatibility

			Gentamicin sulfate				
Drug (in syringe)	*Mfr*	*Amt*	*Mfr*	*Amt*	*Remarks*	*Ref*	*C/I*
Ampicillin sodium	AY	500 mg		80 mg/ 2 ml	Physically incompatible within 1 hr at room temperature	99	I
Cefamandole nafate	LI	1 g/10 ml		80 mg/ 2 ml	Haze or precipitate forms within 4 hr	376; 788	I
	LI	1 g/3 ml		80 mg/ 2 ml	Haze or precipitate forms within 4 hr	376; 788	I
Clindamycin phosphate	UP	900 mg/ 6 ml	ES	120 mg/ 4 ml[a]	Physically compatible with little or no loss of either drug for 48 hr at 25 °C in polypropylene syringes	1159	C
Diatrizoate meglumine 52%, diatrizoate sodium 8%	MA	5 ml	SC	0.8 mg/ 1 ml	Physically compatible for at least 2 hr	1438	C
Diatrizoate sodium 60%	MA	5 ml	SC	0.8 mg/ 1 ml	Physically compatible for at least 2 hr	1438	C
Heparin sodium		2500 units/ 1 ml		40 mg	Turbidity or precipitate forms within 5 min	1053	I
Iohexol	WI	64.7%, 5 ml	SC	0.8 mg/ 1 ml	Physically compatible for at least 2 hr	1438	C
Iopamidol	SQ	61%, 5 ml	SC	0.8 mg/ 1 ml	Physically compatible for at least 2 hr	1438	C
Iothalamate meglumine 60%	MA	5 ml	SC	0.8 mg/ 1 ml	Physically compatible for at least 2 hr	1438	C
Ioxaglate meglumine 39.3%, ioxaglate sodium 19.6%	MA	5 ml	SC	0.8 mg/ 1 ml	Transient precipitate clears within 5 min	1438	?
Penicillin G sodium		1 million units		80 mg/ 2 ml	No precipitate or color change within 1 hr at room temperature	99	C

[a]Diluted to 4 ml with 1 ml of sodium chloride 0.9%.

Y-Site Injection Compatibility (1:1 Mixture)

			Gentamicin sulfate				
Drug	*Mfr*	*Conc*	*Mfr*	*Conc*	*Remarks*	*Ref*	*C/I*
Acyclovir sodium	BW	5 mg/ml[a]	TR	1.6 mg/ml[a]	Physically compatible for 4 hr at 25 °C under fluorescent light	1157	C
Alatrofloxacin mesylate	PF	1.43 mg/ml[a]	FUJ	21 mg/ml[e]	Visually and microscopically compatible run through a Y-site over 25 min	2235	C
Allopurinol sodium	BW	3 mg/ml[b]	ES	5 mg/ml[b]	Hazy solution with crystals forms in 1 hr	1686	I
Amifostine	USB	10 mg/ml[a]	ES	5 mg/ml[a]	Physically compatible with no change in measured turbidity or increase in particle content in 4 hr at 23 °C	1845	C
Amiodarone HCl	LZ	4 mg/ml[c]	LY	0.8 mg/ml[c]	Physically compatible for 4 hr at room temperature	1444	C
Amphotericin B cholesteryl sulfate complex	SEQ	0.83 mg/ml[a]	FUJ	5 mg/ml[a]	Gross precipitate forms	2117	I
Amsacrine	NCI	1 mg/ml[a]	SO	5 mg/ml[a]	Physically compatible for 4 hr at room temperature under fluorescent light	1381	C
Atracurium besylate	BW	0.5 mg/ml[a]	ES	2 mg/ml[a]	Physically compatible for 24 hr at 28 °C	1337	C

Y-Site Injection Compatibility (1:1 Mixture) (Cont.)

Drug	Mfr	Conc	Mfr	Conc	Remarks	Ref	C/I
			Gentamicin sulfate				
Aztreonam	SQ	40 mg/ml[a]	ES	5 mg/ml[a]	Physically compatible with no subvisual haze or particle formation in 4 hr at 23 °C	1758	C
Cefpirome sulfate	HO	50 mg/ml[d]	LY	1 mg/ml[d]	Visually and microscopically compatible with little or no cefpirome and cefazolin loss by HPLC in 8 hr at 23 °C	2044	C
Ciprofloxacin	MI	2 mg/ml[c]	LY	1.6 mg/ml[c]	Visually compatible for 24 hr at 24 °C	1655	C
Cisatracurium besylate	GW	0.1, 2, 5 mg/ml[a]	ES	5 mg/ml[a]	Physically compatible with no change in measured turbidity or increase in particle content in 4 hr at 23 °C	2074	C
Clarithromycin	AB	4 mg/ml[a]	RS	40 mg/ml	Visually compatible for 72 hr at both 30 and 17 °C	2174	C
Cyclophosphamide	MJ	20 mg/ml[a]	TR	1.6 mg/ml[a]	Physically compatible for 4 hr at 25 °C	1194	C
Cytarabine	UP	16 mg/ml[b]	GNS	15 mg/ml[e]	Visually compatible for 24 hr at room temperature in test tubes. No precipitate found on filter from Y-site delivery	2063	C
Diltiazem HCl	MMD	1[b] and 5 mg/ml	SCH	2.4[b] and 40 mg/ml	Visually compatible	1807	C
Docetaxel	RPR	0.9 mg/ml[a]	AB	5 mg/ml[a]	Physically compatible with no change in measured turbidity or increase in particle content in 4 hr at 23 °C	2224	C
Doxorubicin HCl liposome injection	SEQ	0.4 mg/ml[a]	ES	5 mg/ml[a]	Physically compatible with little or no change in measured turbidity and no increase in particle content in 4 hr at 23 °C	2087	C
Enalaprilat	MSD	0.05 mg/ml[b]	ES	0.8 mg/ml[a]	Physically compatible for 24 hr at room temperature under fluorescent light	1355	C
Esmolol HCl	DCC	10 mg/ml[a]	ES	0.8 mg/ml[a]	Physically compatible for 24 hr at 22 °C	1169	C
Etoposide phosphate	BR	5 mg/ml[a]	AB	5 mg/ml[a]	Physically compatible with no change in measured turbidity or increase in particle content in 4 hr at 23 °C	2218	C
Famotidine	MSD	0.2 mg/ml[a]	ES	0.8 mg/ml[b]	Physically compatible for 14 hr	1196	C
	ME	2 mg/ml[b]		5 mg/ml[a]	Visually compatible for 4 hr at 22 °C	1936	C
Filgrastim	AMG	30 µg/ml[a]	LY	5 mg/ml[a]	Physically compatible with no change in measured turbidity or increase in particle content in 4 hr at 22 °C	1687	C
	AMG	40 µg/ml[a]	GNS	1.6 mg/ml[a]	Visually compatible with little or no loss of filgrastim activity by bioassay and gentamicin by immunoassay in 4 hr at 25 °C	2060	C
	AMG	10 µg/ml[f]	GNS	1.6 mg/ml[a]	23% loss of filgrastim activity by bioassay in 4 hr at 25 °C. Little or no gentamicin loss by immunoassay	2060	I
Fluconazole	RR	2 mg/ml	ES	4 mg/ml	Physically compatible for 24 hr at 25 °C	1407	C
Fludarabine phosphate	BX	1 mg/ml[a]	ES	5 mg/ml[a]	Physically compatible for 4 hr at room temperature under fluorescent light	1439	C
Foscarnet sodium	AST	24 mg/ml	ES	4 mg/ml	Physically compatible for 24 hr at room temperature under fluorescent light	1335	C

Y-Site Injection Compatibility (1:1 Mixture) (Cont.)

Drug	*Mfr*	*Conc*	Gentamicin sulfate *Mfr*	Gentamicin sulfate *Conc*	*Remarks*	*Ref*	*C/I*
	AST	24 mg/ml	ES	2 mg/ml[c]	Physically compatible for 24 hr at 25 °C under fluorescent light by visual and microscopic examination	1393	C
Furosemide	HO	10 mg/ml	SC	1.6 mg/ml[c]	White precipitate of furosemide forms immediately	876	I
Gatifloxacin	BMS	2 mg/ml[a]	FUJ	5 mg/ml[a]	Physically compatible with no change in measured haze or increase in particle content in 4 hr at 23 °C	2234	C
Gemcitabine HCl	LI	10 mg/ml[b]	AB	5 mg/ml[b]	Physically compatible with no change in measured turbidity or increase in particle content in 4 hr at 23 °C	2226	C
Granisetron HCl	SKB	1 mg/ml	ES	1.5 mg/ml[b]	Physically compatible with little or no loss of either drug by HPLC in 4 hr at 22 °C	1883	C
Heparin sodium	ES	50 units/ml[c]	ES	3.2 mg/ml[c]	Immediate gross haze	1316	I
	TR	50 units/ml	TR	2 mg/ml	Visually incompatible within 4 hr at 25 °C	1793	I
Hetastarch in lactated electrolyte injection (Hextend)	AB	6%	SC	5 mg/ml[a]	Physically compatible with no change in measured turbidity or increase in particle content in 4 hr at 23 °C	2339	C
Hetastarch in sodium chloride 0.9%	DCC	6%	TR	0.8 mg/ml[b]	Immediate precipitation which disappeared after 1 hr at room temperature	1313	I
Hydromorphone HCl	WY	0.2 mg/ml[a]	TR	0.8 mg/ml[a]	Physically compatible for at least 4 hr at 25 °C under fluorescent light	987	C
Idarubicin HCl	AD	1 mg/ml[b]	ES	3 mg/ml[a]	Color changes immediately	1525	I
IL-2	RC	4800 I.U./ml[b]	ES	40 mg/ml	Visually compatible and IL-2 activity by bioassay retained. Gentamicin not tested	1552	C
Indomethacin sodium trihydrate	MSD	0.5 and 1 mg/ml[a]		1 mg/ml[a]	White turbidity forms immediately and becomes white flakes in 1 hr	1550	I
Insulin	LI	0.2 unit/ml[b]	TR	1.2 mg/ml[b]	Physically compatible for 2 hr at 25 °C	1395	C
Iodipamide meglumine	SQ				White precipitate forms immediately downstream to Y-site when given into a set through which gentamicin was administered previously	324	I
Labetalol HCl	SC	1 mg/ml[a]	ES	0.8 mg/ml[a]	Physically compatible for 24 hr at 18 °C	1171	C
Levofloxacin	OMN	5 mg/ml[a]	ES	10 mg/ml	Visually compatible for 4 hr at 24 °C under fluorescent light	2233	C
Linezolid	PHU	2 mg/ml	FUJ	5 mg/ml[a]	Physically compatible with no change in measured turbidity or increase in particle content in 4 hr at 23 °C	2264	C
Lorazepam	WY	0.33 mg/ml[b]	CNF	3 mg/ml	Visually compatible for 24 hr at 22 °C	1855	C
Magnesium sulfate	IX	16.7, 33.3, 66.7, 100 mg/ml[a]	SC	0.8 mg/ml[a]	Physically compatible for at least 4 hr at 32 °C	813	C
Melphalan HCl	BW	0.1 mg/ml[b]	LY	5 mg/ml[b]	Physically compatible with no change in measured turbidity or increase in particle content in 3 hr at 22 °C	1557	C
Meperidine HCl	WY	10 mg/ml[a]	TR	0.8 mg/ml[a]	Physically compatible for at least 4 hr at 25 °C under fluorescent light	987	C

Y-Site Injection Compatibility (1:1 Mixture) (Cont.)

Gentamicin sulfate

Drug	*Mfr*	*Conc*	*Mfr*	*Conc*	*Remarks*	*Ref*	*C/I*
	WY	10 mg/ml[b]	ES	1.2 and 2 mg/ml[b]	Physically compatible for 1 hr at 25 °C	1338	C
Meropenem	ZEN	1 and 50 mg/ml[b]	SC	4 mg/ml[g]	Visually compatible for 4 hr at room temperature	1994	C
Midazolam HCl	RC	1 mg/ml[a]	ES	10 mg/ml	Visually compatible for 24 hr at 23 °C	1847	C
	RC	5 mg/ml	CNF	3 mg/ml	Visually compatible for 24 hr at 22 °C	1855	C
Morphine sulfate	WI	1 mg/ml[a]	TR	0.8 mg/ml[a]	Physically compatible for at least 4 hr at 25 °C under fluorescent light	987	C
	ES	1 mg/ml[b]	ES	1.2 and 2 mg/ml[b]	Physically compatible for 1 hr at 25 °C	1338	C
Multivitamins	USV	5 ml/L[a]	SC	80 mg/100 ml[a]	Physically compatible for 24 hr at room temperature	323	C
Ondansetron HCl	GL	1 mg/ml[b]	ES	5 mg/ml[a]	Physically compatible for 4 hr at 22 °C	1365	C
Paclitaxel	NCI	1.2 mg/ml[a]	ES	5 mg/ml[a]	Physically compatible with no change in measured turbidity in 4 hr at 22 °C	1556	C
Pancuronium bromide	ES	0.05 mg/ml[a]	ES	2 mg/ml[a]	Physically compatible for 24 hr at 28 °C	1337	C
Perphenazine	SC	0.02 mg/ml[a]	TR	1.6 mg/ml[a]	Physically compatible for 4 hr at 25 °C	1155	C
Propofol	ZEN	10 mg/ml	ES	5 mg/ml[a]	White precipitate forms immediately	2066	I
Remifentanil HCl	GW	0.025 and 0.25 mg/ml[b]	ES	5 mg/ml[a]	Physically compatible with no change in measured turbidity or increase in particle content in 4 hr at 23 °C	2075	C
Sargramostim	IMM	10 µg/ml[b]	SO	5 mg/ml[a]	Physically compatible for 4 hr at 22 °C	1436	C
Tacrolimus	FUJ	1 mg/ml[b]	SCN	4 mg/ml[a]	Visually compatible for 24 hr at 25 °C	1630	C
Teniposide	BR	0.1 mg/ml[a]	LY	5 mg/ml[a]	Physically compatible with no subvisual haze or particle formation in 4 hr at 23 °C	1725	C
Theophylline	TR	4 mg/ml	TR	2 mg/ml	Visually compatible for 6 hr at 25 °C	1793	C
Thiotepa	IMM[h]	1 mg/ml[a]	ES	5 mg/ml[a]	Physically compatible with no change in measured turbidity or increase in particle content in 4 hr at 23 °C	1861	C
TNA #73[i]		32.5 ml[j]	SC	80 mg/50 ml[a]	Physically compatible for 4 hr at 25 °C by visual observation	1008	C
TNA #97 to #104[i]			ES	40 mg/ml	Physically compatible and gentamicin content retained for 6 hr at 21 °C by TDx	1324	C
TNA #218 to #226[i]			AB, FUJ	5 mg/ml[a]	Visually compatible with no precipitate or emulsion damage apparent in 4 hr at 23 °C	2215	C
Tolazoline HCl		0.1 mg/ml[a]	ES	10 mg/ml[a]	Physically compatible for 24 hr at 22 °C	1363	C
TPN #54[i]				13 and 20 mg/ml	Physically compatible and gentamicin activity retained over 6 hr at 22 °C by microbiological assay	1045	C
TPN #61[i]		[k]	IX	12.5 mg/1.25 ml[l]	Physically compatible	1012	C
		[m]	IX	75 mg/1.9 ml[l]	Physically compatible	1012	C
TPN #91[i]		[n]	IX	5 mg[o]	Physically compatible	1170	C
TPN #189[i]			DB	1 mg/ml[b]	Visually compatible for 24 hr at 22 °C	1767	C

Y-Site Injection Compatibility (1:1 Mixture) (Cont.)

			Gentamicin sulfate				
Drug	*Mfr*	*Conc*	*Mfr*	*Conc*	*Remarks*	*Ref*	*C/I*
TPN #203 and #204[i]			ES	10 mg/ml	Visually compatible for 2 hr at 23 °C	1974	C
TPN #212 to #215[i]			AB	5 mg/ml[a]	Physically compatible with no change in measured turbidity or increase in particle content in 4 hr at 23 °C	2109	C
Vecuronium bromide	OR	0.1 mg/ml[a]	ES	2 mg/ml[a]	Physically compatible for 24 hr at 28 °C	1337	C
Vinorelbine tartrate	BW	1 mg/ml[b]	ES	5 mg/ml[b]	Physically compatible with no change in measured turbidity or increase in particle content in 4 hr at 22 °C	1558	C
Vitamin B complex with C (Berocca-C 500)	RC	4 ml/L[a]	SC	80 mg/ 100 ml[a]	Physically compatible for 24 hr at room temperature	323	C
Vitamin B complex with C (Berocca-C)	RC	20 ml/L[a]	SC	80 mg/ 100 ml[a]	Physically compatible for 24 hr at room temperature	323	C
Warfarin sodium	DU	2 mg/ml[g]	SC	1.6 mg/ml[a]	Haze forms immediately	2010	I
	DME	2 mg/ml[g]	SC	1.6 mg/ml[a]	Haze forms immediately	2078	I
Zidovudine	BW	4 mg/ml[a]	IMS	2 mg/ml[a]	Physically compatible for 4 hr at 25 °C under fluorescent light by visual and microscopic examination	1193	C

[a]*Tested in dextrose 5% in water.*
[b]*Tested in sodium chloride 0.9%.*
[c]*Tested in both dextrose 5% in water and sodium chloride 0.9%.*
[d]*Tested in dextrose 5% in water, Ringer's injection, lactated, sodium chloride 0.45%, and sodium chloride 0.9%.*
[e]*Tested in sodium chloride 0.45%.*
[f]*Tested in dextrose 5% in water with albumin human 2 mg/ml.*
[g]*Tested in sterile water for injection.*
[h]*Lyophilized formulation tested.*
[i]*Refer to Appendix I for the composition of parenteral nutrition solutions. TNA indicates a 3-in-1 admixture, and TPN indicates a 2-in-1 admixture.*
[j]*A 32.5-ml sample of parenteral nutrition solution mixed with 50 ml of antibiotic solution.*
[k]*Run at 21 ml/hr.*
[l]*Given over 30 minutes by syringe pump.*
[m]*Run at 94 ml/hr.*
[n]*Run at 10 ml/hr.*
[o]*Given over one hour by syringe pump.*

Additional Compatibility Information

Infusion Solutions — Gentamicin sulfate maintains potency for 24 hours at room temperature in the following solutions (227):

- Dextran 40 (Dextran 10% in dextrose 5%)
- Dextrose 5% in Polysal
- Dextrose 5% in Polysal M
- Dextrose 5% in water
- Dextrose 10% in water
- Isolyte E with dextrose 5%
- Isolyte M with dextrose 5%
- Isolyte P with dextrose 5%
- Normosol M in dextrose 5% in water
- Normosol R
- Normosol R in dextrose 5% in water
- Normosol R, pH 7.4
- Ringer's injection
- Ringer's injection, lactated
- Sodium chloride 0.9%
- Travert 5% with Electrolyte #2
- Travert 10% with Electrolyte #3

Kern et al. evaluated serum concentrations of gentamicin sulfate following intermittent 15 to 30-minute administration as piggyback infusions in 50 ml of dextrose 5% in water or 50 ml of TPN #177 (see Appendix I). Gentamicin serum concentrations were equivalent using both administration methods. (1573)

Peritoneal Dialysis Solutions — The activity of gentamicin 10 mg/L was evaluated in peritoneal dialysis fluids containing 1.5 or 4.25% dextrose (Dianeal 137, Travenol). Storage at 25 °C resulted in no loss of antimicrobial activity in 24 hours. (515)

Gentamicin sulfate (Schering) 3 and 10 mg/L in peritoneal dialysis concentrate with 50% dextrose (McGaw) retained about 90% of initial activity in seven hours and about 50 to 70% in 24 hours at room temperature as determined by microbiological assay. (1044)

The stability of gentamicin sulfate 8 mg/L, alone and with cefazolin sodium 75 and 150 mg/L, was evaluated in a peritoneal dialysis solution of dextrose 1.5% with heparin sodium 1000 units/L. Gentamicin activity was retained for 48 hours at both 4 and 26 °C, alone and with both concentrations of cefazolin. Cefazolin activity was also retained over the study period. At 37 °C, gentamicin losses ranged from 4 to 8% and cefazolin losses ranged from 10 to 12% in 48 hours. (1029)

In another study, the stability of gentamicin sulfate (Schering) was evaluated in peritoneal dialysate concentrates containing dextrose 30 and 50% (Dianeal) as well as in a diluted solution containing dextrose 2.5%. The gentamicin sulfate concentrations were 100 and 160 mg/L in the peritoneal dialysate concentrates and 5 and 8 mg/L in the diluted solutions. By immunoassay techniques, gentamicin sulfate was found to be stable in all of these solutions for at least 24 hours at 23 °C. (1229)

Halstead et al. evaluated gentamicin 4 μg/ml in Dianeal PDS with dextrose 1.5 and 4.25% (Travenol) with cefazolin 125 μg/ml, heparin 500 units, and albumin human 80 mg in 2-L bags. The gentamicin content, determined by EMIT assay, was retained for 72 hours. (1413)

Drake et al. evaluated the retention of antimicrobial activity, using a disc diffusion bioassay, of gentamicin sulfate (SoloPak) 120 mg/L alone and with vancomycin HCl (Lilly) 1 g/L in Dianeal PD-2 (Travenol) with dextrose 1.5%. Little or no loss of either antibiotic occurred in eight hours at 37 °C. Gentamicin sulfate alone retained activity for at least 48 hours at 4 and 25 °C. In combination with vancomycin HCl, antimicrobial activity of both antibiotics was retained for up to 48 hours. However, the authors recommended refrigeration at 4 °C for storage periods greater than 24 hours. (1414)

β-Lactam Antibiotics — In common with other aminoglycoside antibiotics, gentamicin activity may be impaired by β-lactam antibiotics. The inactivation is dependent on concentration, temperature, and time of exposure.

In 1971, McLaughlin and Reeves first reported the inactivation of gentamicin sulfate by carbenicillin disodium. They cited two cases in which gentamicin serum levels fell when carbenicillin was subsequently added to the regimen. They further noted a decrease in gentamicin half-life in serum, distilled water, and phosphate buffer to 40 hours at 35 °C and 70 hours at 20 °C. Gentamicin alone showed no loss of activity in 140 hours under these conditions. (219) Because the combined use of carbenicillin disodium and gentamicin sulfate has been reported to be additive or synergistic in its antibacterial effect against Pseudomonas and the combination has been used extensively in the clinical treatment of Pseudomonas infections, this article provoked quite a response in the literature.

Klastersky was not convinced of the result, citing the possibility that the antibacterial properties of gentamicin might have been inhibited by some other substance. It was further stated that given the success of combination therapy, even if such inhibition did occur, its clinical significance was not great. (220)

Levison and Kaye were not convinced either. Their tests of carbenicillin and gentamicin in serum and trypticase soy broth did not show loss of gentamicin in 18 hours at 37 °C. (221)

Eykyn et al., however, did note slow inactivation of gentamicin by carbenicillin in vitro after several hours at 37 °C. (222)

Furthermore, Riff and Jackson reported that gentamicin was biologically not detectable after prolonged mixture in solution with carbenicillin. They stated that gentamicin loses potency in proportion to time, temperature, and the concentration of carbenicillin. (223)

McLaughlin and Reeves combined, in vitro, 5 μg/ml of gentamicin with carbenicillin concentrations of 250, 500, and 1000 μg/ml. With incubation at 35 °C, they detected no change in gentamicin at 250 μg/ml of carbenicillin in eight hours; but in the 500-μg/ml combination, a 44% loss of gentamicin was detected at eight hours. At 1000 μg/ml of carbenicillin, 42 and 66% losses of gentamicin occurred in four and eight hours, respectively. (665)

Noone and Pattison evaluated the inactivation of gentamicin by various penicillins (and cephalosporins), including carbenicillin disodium. They noted a significant loss of gentamicin activity after 30 minutes and a 50% loss of potency after eight to 12 hours when gentamicin sulfate (Roussel) 160 mg/L was combined with carbenicillin disodium (Beecham) 20 g/L in various intravenous solutions at room temperature. (157)

Winters et al. confirmed that significant loss of gentamicin activity occurred in vitro when mixed with carbenicillin. Gentamicin in concentrations of 5 to 10 μg/ml was mixed with a high concentration of carbenicillin, 500 μg/ml. Within four to six hours at room temperature, significant loss of gentamicin activity had occurred. At lower concentrations, 50 to 100 μg/ml, the loss of activity was much slower. Further experiments in dogs and humans showed that gentamicin serum levels were not significantly altered by concomitant carbenicillin therapy provided the two drugs were not mixed and allowed to stand before administration. (361)

In a similar in vitro experiment, Waitz et al. found the same result. Gentamicin activity dropped from 4.3 μg/ml to 2.2 μg/ml in 24 hours and to 1.4 μg/ml in 72 hours at 20 °C in the presence of carbenicillin 100 μg/ml in distilled water. The amount of inactivation was dependent on temperature and time and was slowed by the addition of pH 7.0 buffers. Tests in mice and dogs failed to reveal any effect of carbenicillin on gentamicin serum levels. (362)

Zost and Yanchick failed to elucidate the situation further in their report since only the stability of carbenicillin disodium was reported (88), although they later said that the two antibiotics were stable for 24 hours. (224)

Riff and Jackson, however, found a 50% inactivation of gentamicin in four to six hours at room temperature when 24 g of carbenicillin disodium was added to 240 mg of gentamicin sulfate in sodium chloride 0.9%. They also noted that the half-life of gentamicin sulfate decreased as the ratio of carbenicillin disodium increased with respect to gentamicin sulfate in distilled water at 37 °C. The authors stated that the inactivation of gentamicin by carbenicillin is dependent on the integrity of the β-lactam ring, with carbenicillin and gentamicin interacting to form a conjugate inactivating both. The higher the concentration of carbenicillin, the faster is the inactivation of gentamicin. Further, the rate of gentamicin inactivation is decreased by the presence of other solutes, especially proteins. (218)

Young et al. determined the degree of gentamicin loss in vitro for combinations of gentamicin plus carbenicillin of 400 μg/ml plus 12.8 mg/ml, 40 μg/ml plus 1.28 mg/ml, and 4 μg/ml plus 0.128 mg/ml in distilled water. The solutions were incubated at 35 and 39 °C. Gentamicin levels fell to 35 to 47% of initial amounts in eight hours at 35 °C while the carbenicillin concentration was about 84 to 91% of the initial amount. At 39 °C after eight hours, gentamicin levels of 12 to 24% and carbenicillin levels of 65 to 68% were determined. (666)

In vitro studies by Ervin et al. showed extensive decomposition of gentamicin by carbenicillin at 37 °C in human serum. (363)

Similar inactivation effects on gentamicin sulfate occur in combination with ticarcillin (363; 365; 614), although the extent of inactivation appears to be less than with carbenicillin. (574; 575)

Holt et al. found that incubation of gentamicin sulfate 10 mg/L in sodium chloride 0.9% with 500 mg/L of carbenicillin or ticarcillin at 37 °C for 24 hours resulted in about 60 to 70% reduction of gentamicin activity. When serum was substituted for the sodium chloride solution, 30 to 50% reduction in activity was reported. However, when buffered to pH 7.4 in aqueous solution, essentially all of the gentamicin activity was lost. (574)

Pickering and Gearhart reported that gentamicin sulfate 5 and 10 μg/ml, dissolved in human serum and incubated with carbenicillin and ticarcillin 100 to 600 μg/ml at 37 °C, demonstrated greater rates of decomposition at the higher concentrations of the penicillins. In 24 hours, about a 9% loss of gentamicin activity occurred at 100 μg/ml and about a 60% loss occurred at 600 μg/ml of carbenicillin. Approximately a 20% loss at 100 μg/ml and an 85% loss at 600 μg/ml occurred in 72 hours with carbenicillin. Ticarcillin affected gentamicin less under these conditions. Little or no loss of gentamicin activity occurred at 100 μg/ml of ticarcillin in 72 hours. However, the gentamicin loss increased to 20% at 300 μg/ml and to 70% at 600 μg/ml of ticarcillin in 72 hours. (575)

Murillo et al. determined that lower serum levels of gentamicin occurred in patients with normal renal function when concomitant ticarcillin disodium was administered compared to concomitant cephalothin sodium. The dose of ticarcillin disodium was 12 g/m²/day while cephalothin sodium was given at 7 g/m²/day. The gentamicin sulfate dose was 180 mg/m²/day. In one hour, gentamicin serum levels of 3.1 μg/ml resulted in patients receiving the cephalothin while only 2.0 μg/ml was achieved in patients on ticarcillin. Ticarcillin levels also were substantially reduced. (667)

Several aminoglycosides in combination with several penicillins were evaluated. Gentamicin sulfate, netilmicin sulfate, and tobramycin sulfate 5 μg/ml were combined with carbenicillin disodium, azlocillin sodium, and mezlocillin sodium 50, 250, and 500 μg/ml in human plasma. Samples were evaluated over nine days at 27 and 37 °C. All of the aminoglycosides underwent significant inactivation during the evaluation. Aminoglycoside decomposition of 17 to 61% in 24 hours occurred at the higher two concentrations of penicillins—the highest inactivation was sustained by tobramycin and the lowest by netilmicin. Little if any aminoglycoside inactivation occurred at 50 μg/ml of penicillin. Carbenicillin caused greater aminoglycoside decomposition than did azlocillin or mezlocillin. (616)

Flournoy noted the relative degree of inactivation of tobramycin, gentamicin, netilmicin, and amikacin 10 mg/L in serum when combined with carbenicillin 125 to 1000 mg/L at −20 to 42 °C. Tobramycin was more susceptible to inactivation than the others. Amikacin was the least susceptible, and gentamicin and netilmicin were similar in intermediate susceptibility to inactivation. (617)

Although piperacillin sodium and aminoglycosides act synergistically and have been used successfully clinically when recommended doses of each drug have been administered, mixing piperacillin sodium directly in a syringe or infusion bottle with an aminoglycoside can substantially inactivate the aminoglycoside. (740)

Hale et al. evaluated piperacillin and carbenicillin at concentrations of 62.5 to 1000 μg/ml in human serum in combination with amikacin, gentamicin, or tobramycin 10 μg/ml at 37 °C for up to 24 hours by bioassay and radioimmunoassay. Penicillin concentrations of 62.5 and 125 μg/ml had relatively little effect on the aminoglycoside concentration, even after 24 hours. However, increasing the penicillin concentration to 250 or 500 μg/ml greatly increased decomposition. After 24 hours with carbenicillin 500 μg/ml, the amounts of aminoglycosides remaining were amikacin, 82%; gentamicin, 43%; and tobramycin, 27%. After 24 hours with piperacillin 500 μg/ml, the remaining concentrations were 95, 45, and 52%, respectively. Even greater inactivation occurred at 1000 μg/ml of the penicillins, including the essentially complete loss of tobramycin in 24 hours. The authors concluded that amikacin is much more resistant to inactivation than the other aminoglycosides tested and that carbenicillin is apparently more aggressive in its inactivation than piperacillin. (816)

To determine if spurious aminoglycoside levels could result from a delay in assaying blood samples, Tindula et al. evaluated the inactivation of amikacin 35 μg/ml and gentamicin and tobramycin 10 μg/ml in human serum by 400-μg/ml concentrations of several penicillins and cephalosporins. Samples were stored for 24 hours at room temperature and frozen at −20 °C. For the room temperature samples, cefazolin and cefamandole caused relatively little inactivation. Nafcillin, cephapirin, and cefoxitin caused moderate inactivation, 20% or less. Penicillin, ampicillin, carbenicillin, and ticarcillin generally caused 25% or more inactivation of gentamicin and tobramycin. Amikacin was somewhat less affected. Freezing samples at −20 °C prevented significant inactivation of amikacin and gentamicin by any of the drugs. Freezing the tobramycin samples was satisfactory for most of the drugs except penicillin, ampicillin, and carbenicillin, which still exhibited a 15 to 20% tobramycin loss in 24 hours. (824)

Pickering and Rutherford evaluated several aminoglycosides combined with a number of penicillins. Gentamicin sulfate, netilmicin sulfate, and tobramycin sulfate 5 and 10 μg/ml and amikacin 10 and 20 μg/ml were combined in human serum with 125, 250, and 500 μg/ml of azlocillin, carbenicillin disodium, amdinocillin, mezlocillin, and piperacillin individually. Tobramycin and gentamicin sustained greater losses than netilmicin and amikacin at each of the penicillin concentrations. Significant decomposition of all aminoglycosides occurred in 24 hours at 37 °C at a penicillin concentration of 500 μg/ml. Tobramycin and gentamicin had losses of 40 to 60%, while 15 to 30% losses occurred for netilmicin. Amikacin sustained the least inactivation with losses of about 10 to 20%. At penicillin concentrations of 125 to 250 μg/ml, smaller losses of aminoglycosides were observed. (68)

The inactivation of gentamicin 10 μg/ml in sterile distilled water by several β-lactam antibiotics stored at 37 °C was reported by Jorgensen and Crawford. Ticarcillin and carbenicillin 500 μg/ml caused 34 and 44% gentamicin losses, respectively, in six hours, but only ticarcillin caused a significant loss (about 15%) at 100 μg/ml. Cephalothin 500 μg/ml caused a 17% gentamicin loss in four hours but no significant loss at 100 μg/ml. Gentamicin was not inactivated by 500- or 100-μg/ml concentrations of penicillin G, cefotaxime, or moxalactam. No loss of β-lactam antibiotic activity was detected in any concentration. (973)

The comparative inactivation of five aminoglycosides by seven β-lactam antibiotics in human serum at 37 °C was reported by Riff and Thomason. Amikacin, followed by netilmicin, had the lowest degree of inactivation; tobramycin sustained the most pronounced losses. Gentamicin and kanamycin were intermediate in the extent of losses. The six penicillins that were tested all produced aminoglycoside inactivation; the greatest extent of inactivation was caused by carbenicillin, ticarcillin, penicillin G, oxacillin, methicillin, and ampicillin, in approximate descending order. Cephalothin produced minimal inactivation (5 to 10% in 24 hours). The rate of inactivation could be reduced by storage at 4 °C and further reduced by storage at −20 °C. The authors suggested processing blood samples rapidly to avoid inaccurate serum determinations. Storage of specimens at low temperature until analysis may be helpful. (1052)

Townsend reported the apparent inactivation of gentamicin sulfate by ampicillin sodium in blood samples held for 12 hours prior to assay. (1382)

Roberts et al. studied the stability of azlocillin sodium 500 mg/L combined with the aminoglycosides amikacin sulfate 20 mg/L, gentamicin sulfate 8 mg/L, and netilmicin sulfate 7.5 mg/L in peritoneal dialysis solution (Dianeal 1.36%) stored at 37 °C. No azlocillin sodium loss occurred by HPLC during the eight-hour study period. However, the aminoglycosides tested by the enzyme-multiplied immunoassay technique (EMIT) showed 10% losses in about six hours for gentamicin sulfate and netilmicin sulfate and in about 30 minutes for amikacin sulfate. (1179)

Gentamicin sulfate (Schering) 25 μg/ml combined separately with the cephalosporins cefazolin sodium (Lilly), cefamandole nafate (Lilly), and cefoxitin sodium (MSD) at a concentration of 125 μg/ml in peritoneal dialysis solution (Dianeal 1.5%) exhibited enhanced rates of lethality to *Staphylococcus aureus, Escherichia coli,* and *Pseudomonas aeruginosa* compared to any of the drugs alone. (1623)

The inactivation of gentamicin, tobramycin, and amikacin, each 5 μg/ml, by seven β-lactam antibiotics, 250 and 500 μg/ml, in serum at 25 °C over 24 hours was studied using bioassay, EMIT, fluorescence polarization immunoassay (TDx), and radioimmunoassay. No inactivation of any aminoglycoside by the cephalosporins moxalactam, cefotaxime, and cefazolin occurred within the study period. Results with the penicillins varied, depending on the assay technique used. The bioassay was the most sensitive to loss, TDx and radioimmunoassay were intermediate, and EMIT was the least sensitive. Azlocillin, carbenicillin, mezlocillin, and piperacillin all caused variable but extensive inactivation (up to 70%) of gentamicin and tobramycin in 24 hours. Amikacin, however, had only minor losses compared to the other aminoglycosides. (654)

The clinical significance of these interactions in patients appears to be primarily confined to those with renal failure. (218; 334; 361; 364; 616; 737; 816; 847) Literature reports of greatly reduced aminoglycoside levels in such patients have appeared frequently. (363; 365–367; 614; 615; 962) In addition, the interaction may be clinically important if assays for aminoglycoside levels in serum are sufficiently delayed. (576; 618; 735; 832; 847; 1052; 1382)

Most authors believe that in vitro mixing of penicillins such as ticarcillin disodium with aminoglycoside antibiotics should be avoided but that clinical use of the drugs in combination can be of great value. It is generally recommended that the drugs be given separately in such combined therapy. (157; 218; 222; 224; 361; 364; 368–370)

Cephalosporins — Cefotaxime sodium (Hoechst-Roussel) should not be mixed with aminoglycosides in the same solution, but they may be administered to the same patient separately. (2; 792)

Cefotetan disodium is stated to be physically incompatible with aminoglycosides. (4; 283)

When gentamicin sulfate (Schering) 80 mg/100 ml in dextrose 5% in water was run through an administration set previously used to administer cefoperazone (Roerig) 1 g/100 ml in dextrose 5% in water, an immediate precipitate formed in the infusion tubing where the two solutions mixed. (831)

Teil et al. studied the stability of gentamicin 3.8 μg/ml and cefamandole 11 μg/ml in serum stored at 24, 6, and −17 °C for 24 hours. No substantial differences in the concentration of either drug occurred, indicating that gentamicin is not inactivated in the presence of cefamandole. (864) (Also see the section on β-Lactam Antibiotics.)

Local Anesthetics — Gentamicin sulfate 80 mg (2 ml) was physically compatible with 1 ml of each of the following local anesthetics and did not show significant loss of potency in 24 hours at room temperature or under refrigeration (227):

Chloroprocaine HCl 1 and 2% (Pennwalt)
Hexylcaine HCl 1% (MSD)
Lidocaine HCl 1 and 2% (Astra)
Lidocaine HCl 1 and 2% with epinephrine 1:100,000 (Astra)
Mepivacaine HCl 1 and 2% (Winthrop)
Piperocaine HCl 2% (Lilly)
Procaine HCl 1 and 2% (Winthrop)

Heparin — Addition of gentamicin sulfate (Roussel) 80 mg to the tubing of an infusion solution of sodium chloride 0.9% containing heparin resulted in immediate precipitation. (528)

Gentamicin sulfate 10 mg/L with heparin sodium 1000 units/L in Dianeal with dextrose 5% peritoneal dialysis solution was reported to be conditionally compatible. Koup and Gerbracht reported no significant reduction in gentamicin sulfate concentration or in the UV absorbance of heparin sodium in four to six hours. (228) However, a clarifying communication noted a marked reduction in the anticoagulant activity of heparin sodium if opalescence or a precipitate formed (which results if the undiluted drugs are combined), even if the precipitate redissolved. Heparin activity was retained if one drug was added to a dilute solution of the other and no precipitate formed. (295)

The incompatibility of heparin sodium with gentamicin sulfate is said to result from coprecipitation. (230)

A white precipitate may result from the administration of gentamicin sulfate through a heparinized intravenous cannula. (976) Flushing heparin locks with sodium chloride 0.9% before and after administering drugs incompatible with heparin has been recommended. (4)

Phenytoin and Furosemide — A 2-ml fluid barrier of dextrose 5% in water in a microbore retrograde infusion set failed to prevent precipitation when used between gentamicin sulfate 5 mg/0.5 ml and phenytoin sodium 5 mg/0.1 ml or furosemide 2 mg/0.2 ml. (1385)

Other Information

Heating Plasma — Heating plasma samples to 56 °C for one hour to inactivate potential HIV content resulted in no gentamicin loss as determined by TDx. (1615)

GLYCOPYRROLATE
AHFS 12:08.08

Products — Glycopyrrolate is available in 1- and 2-ml single-dose vials and 5- and 20-ml multiple-dose vials. Each milliliter of solution contains glycopyrrolate 0.2 mg, sodium hydroxide and/or hydrochloric acid to adjust the pH, and benzyl alcohol 0.9% in water for injection. (2)

pH — From 2 to 3. (2)

Osmolality — Glycopyrrolate 0.2 mg/ml has an osmolality of 91 mOsm/kg. (1689)

Trade Name(s) — Robinul.

Administration — Glycopyrrolate may be administered by intravenous or intramuscular injection without dilution. The drug may also be given via the tubing of a running intravenous infusion. (2; 4)

Stability — Glycopyrrolate (Robins) is a clear, colorless solution; intact vials should be stored at controlled room temperature. (2)

pH Effects — The stability of glycopyrrolate in solution is pH dependent. At pH 2 to 3, the drug is very stable. Above pH 6, the stability becomes questionable because of ester hydrolysis. The speed of this hydrolysis is increased with increasing pH. (331)

The effect of increasing pH on stability can be seen in Table 1. Ingallinera et al. showed a significant decline in stability as the pH was increased above 6. (331)

Also see Alkaline Drugs in Additional Compatibility Information below.

Syringes — Glycopyrrolate (American Regent) 0.1 mg/ml in sodium chloride 0.9% packaged in polypropylene syringes (Sherwood) was physically stable and exhibited little or no loss by stability-indicating HPLC analysis in 24 hours stored at 4 and 23 °C. (2199)

Table 1. Stability of Glycopyrrolate 0.8 mg/L in Dextrose 5% in Water Adjusted to Various pH Values (25 °C)

Admixture pH	Approximate Time for 5% Decomposition (hr)
4.0	>48
5.0	>48
6.0	30
6.5	7
7.0	4
8.0	2

Compatibility Information

Solution Compatibility

Glycopyrrolate

Solution	*Mfr*	*Mfr*	*Conc/L*	*Remarks*	*Ref*	*C/I*
Dextrose 5% in sodium chloride 0.45%	MG	RB	0.8 mg	Physically compatible and pH in stability range for glycopyrrolate for 48 hr at 25 °C	331	C
Dextrose 5% in water	AB	RB	0.8 mg	Physically compatible and pH in stability range for glycopyrrolate for 48 hr at 25 °C	331	C
Ringer's injection	AB	RB	0.8 mg	Physically compatible and pH in stability range for glycopyrrolate for 48 hr at 25 °C	331	C
Sodium chloride 0.9%	CU	RB	0.8 mg	Physically compatible and pH in stability range for glycopyrrolate for 48 hr at 25 °C	331	C

Additive Compatibility

Glycopyrrolate

Drug	*Mfr*	*Conc/L*	*Mfr*	*Conc/L*	*Test Soln*	*Remarks*	*Ref*	*C/I*
Methylprednisolone sodium succinate	UP	250 mg	RB	Up to 1.33 mg	D5½S	Physically incompatible	329	I

Drugs in Syringe Compatibility

Glycopyrrolate

Drug (in syringe)	*Mfr*	*Amt*	*Mfr*	*Amt*	*Remarks*	*Ref*	*C/I*
Atropine sulfate	ES	0.4 mg/ 1 ml	RB	0.2 mg/ 1 ml	[a]	331	C
	ES	0.8 mg/ 2 ml	RB	0.2 mg/ 1 ml	[a]	331	C

Drugs in Syringe Compatibility (Cont.)

Glycopyrrolate

Drug (in syringe)	*Mfr*	*Amt*	*Mfr*	*Amt*	*Remarks*	*Ref*	*C/I*
	ES	0.4 mg/ 1 ml	RB	0.4 mg/ 2 ml	[a]	331	C
Chloramphenicol sodium succinate	PD	100 mg/ 1 ml	RB	0.2 mg/ 1 ml	Gas evolves	331	I
	PD	200 mg/ 2 ml	RB	0.2 mg/ 1 ml	Gas evolves	331	I
	PD	100 mg/ 1 ml	RB	0.4 mg/ 2 ml	Gas evolves	331	I
Chlorpromazine HCl	SKF	25 mg/ 1 ml	RB	0.2 mg/ 1 ml	[a]	331	C
	SKF	50 mg/ 2 ml	RB	0.2 mg/ 1 ml	[a]	331	C
	SKF	25 mg/ 1 ml	RB	0.4 mg/ 2 ml	[a]	331	C
Cimetidine HCl	SKF	300 mg/ 2 ml	ES	0.2 mg/ 1 ml	Physically compatible for 4 hr at 25 °C	25	C
Codeine phosphate	LI	30 mg/ 1 ml	RB	0.2 mg/ 1 ml	[a]	331	C
	LI	60 mg/ 2 ml	RB	0.2 mg/ 1 ml	[a]	331	C
	LI	30 mg/ 1 ml	RB	0.4 mg/ 2 ml	[a]	331	C
Dexamethasone sodium phosphate	MSD	4 mg/ 1 ml	RB	0.2 mg/ 1 ml	Physically compatible for 48 hr at 25 °C but pH >6.0. 5% glycopyrrolate decomposition may occur in 4 to 7 hr	331	I
	MSD	8 mg/ 2 ml	RB	0.2 mg/ 1 ml	Physically compatible for 48 hr at 25 °C but pH >6.0. 5% glycopyrrolate decomposition may occur in 4 to 7 hr	331	I
	MSD	4 mg/ 1 ml	RB	0.4 mg/ 2 ml	Physically compatible for 48 hr at 25 °C but pH >6.0. 5% glycopyrrolate decomposition may occur in 4 to 7 hr	331	I
	MSD	24 mg/ 1 ml	RB	0.2 mg/ 1 ml	Physically compatible for 48 hr at 25 °C but pH >6.0. 5% glycopyrrolate decomposition may occur in 4 to 7 hr	331	I
	MSD	48 mg/ 2 ml	RB	0.2 mg/ 1 ml	Physically compatible for 48 hr at 25 °C but pH >6.0. 5% glycopyrrolate decomposition may occur in 4 to 7 hr	331	I
	MSD	24 mg/ 1 ml	RB	0.4 mg/ 2 ml	Physically compatible for 48 hr at 25 °C but pH >6.0. 5% glycopyrrolate decomposition may occur in 4 to 7 hr	331	I
Diazepam	RC	5 mg/ 1 ml	RB	0.2 mg/ 1 ml	Immediate precipitation	331	I
	RC	10 mg/ 2 ml	RB	0.2 mg/ 1 ml	Immediate precipitation	331	I
	RC	5 mg/ 1 ml	RB	0.4 mg/ 2 ml	Immediate precipitation	331	I
Dimenhydrinate	SE	50 mg/ 1 ml	RB	0.2 mg/ 1 ml	Immediate precipitation	331	I
	SE	100 mg/ 2 ml	RB	0.2 mg/ 1 ml	Immediate precipitation	331	I
	SE	50 mg/ 1 ml	RB	0.4 mg/ 2 ml	Immediate precipitation	331	I

Drugs in Syringe Compatibility (Cont.)

Drug (in syringe)	*Mfr*	*Amt*	*Mfr*	*Amt*	*Remarks*	*Ref*	*C/I*
			Glycopyrrolate				
Diphenhydramine HCl	PD	10 mg/ 1 ml	RB	0.2 mg/ 1 ml	[a]	331	C
	PD	20 mg/ 2 ml	RB	0.2 mg/ 1 ml	[a]	331	C
	PD	10 mg/ 1 ml	RB	0.4 mg/ 2 ml	[a]	331	C
	PD	50 mg/ 1 ml	RB	0.2 mg/ 1 ml	[a]	331	C
	PD	100 mg/ 2 ml	RB	0.2 mg/ 1 ml	[a]	331	C
	PD	50 mg/ 1 ml	RB	0.4 mg/ 2 ml	[a]	331	C
Droperidol	MN	2.5 mg/ 1 ml	RB	0.2 mg/ 1 ml	[a]	331	C
	MN	5 mg/ 2 ml	RB	0.2 mg/ 1 ml	[a]	331	C
	MN	2.5 mg/ 1 ml	RB	0.4 mg/ 2 ml	[a]	331	C
Hydromorphone HCl	KN	2 mg/ 1 ml	RB	0.2 mg/ 1 ml	[a]	331	C
	KN	4 mg/ 2 ml	RB	0.2 mg/ 1 ml	[a]	331	C
	KN	2 mg/ 1 ml	RB	0.4 mg/ 2 ml	[a]	331	C
Hydroxyzine HCl	PF	25 mg/ 1 ml	RB	0.2 mg/ 1 ml	[a]	331	C
	PF	50 mg/ 2 ml	RB	0.2 mg/ 1 ml	[a]	331	C
	PF	25 mg/ 1 ml	RB	0.4 mg/ 2 ml	[a]	331	C
Levorphanol tartrate	RC	2 mg/ 1 ml	RB	0.2 mg/ 1 ml	[a]	331	C
	RC	4 mg/ 2 ml	RB	0.2 mg/ 1 ml	[a]	331	C
	RC	2 mg/ 1 ml	RB	0.4 mg/ 2 ml	[a]	331	C
Lidocaine HCl	ES	10 mg/ 1 ml	RB	0.2 mg/ 1 ml	[a]	331	C
	ES	20 mg/ 2 ml	RB	0.2 mg/ 1 ml	[a]	331	C
	ES	10 mg/ 1 ml	RB	0.4 mg/ 2 ml	[a]	331	C
	ES	20 mg/ 1 ml	RB	0.2 mg/ 1 ml	[a]	331	C
	ES	40 mg/ 2 ml	RB	0.2 mg/ 1 ml	[a]	331	C
	ES	20 mg/ 1 ml	RB	0.4 mg/ 2 ml	[a]	331	C
Meperidine HCl	WI	50 mg/ 1 ml	RB	0.2 mg/ 1 ml	[a]	331	C
	WI	100 mg/ 2 ml	RB	0.2 mg/ 1 ml	[a]	331	C
	WI	50 mg/ 1 ml	RB	0.4 mg/ 2 ml	[a]	331	C

Drugs in Syringe Compatibility (Cont.)

Drug (in syringe)	*Mfr*	*Amt*	Glycopyrrolate *Mfr*	Glycopyrrolate *Amt*	*Remarks*	*Ref*	*C/I*
Meperidine HCl and promethazine HCl (Mepergan)	WY	25 mg + 25 mg/ 1 ml	RB	0.2 mg/ 1 ml	[a]	331	C
	WY	50 mg + 50 mg/ 2 ml	RB	0.2 mg/ 1 ml	[a]	331	C
	WY	25 mg + 25 mg/ 1 ml	RB	0.4 mg/ 2 ml	[a]	331	C
Methohexital sodium	LI	10 mg/ 1 ml	RB	0.2 mg/ 1 ml	Immediate precipitation	331	I
	LI	20 mg/ 2 ml	RB	0.2 mg/ 1 ml	Immediate precipitation	331	I
	LI	10 mg/ 1 ml	RB	0.4 mg/ 2 ml	Immediate precipitation	331	I
Midazolam HCl	RC	5 mg/ 1 ml	RB	0.2 mg/ 1 ml	Physically compatible for 4 hr at 25 °C under fluorescent light	1145	C
Morphine sulfate	LI	15 mg/ 1 ml	RB	0.2 mg/ 1 ml	[a]	331	C
	LI	30 mg/ 2 ml	RB	0.2 mg/ 1 ml	[a]	331	C
	LI	15 mg/ 1 ml	RB	0.4 mg/ 2 ml	[a]	331	C
Nalbuphine HCl	DU	10 mg/ 1 ml	RB	0.2 mg/ 1 ml	Physically compatible for 48 hr	128	C
	DU	20 mg/ 1 ml	RB	0.2 mg/ 1 ml	Physically compatible for 48 hr	128	C
Neostigmine methylsulfate	RC	0.5 mg/ 1 ml	RB	0.2 mg/ 1 ml	[a]	331	C
	RC	1 mg/ 2 ml	RB	0.2 mg/ 1 ml	[a]	331	C
	RC	0.5 mg/ 1 ml	RB	0.4 mg/ 2 ml	[a]	331	C
Ondansetron HCl	GW	1 mg/ml[b]	AMR	0.1 mg/ ml[b]	Physically compatible with no measured increase in particulates and little or no loss of either drug by HPLC in 24 hr at 4 or 23 °C	2199	C
Oxymorphone HCl	EN	1 mg/ 1 ml	RB	0.2 mg/ 1 ml	[a]	331	C
	EN	2 mg/ 2 ml	RB	0.2 mg/ 1 ml	[a]	331	C
	EN	1 mg/ 1 ml	RB	0.4 mg/ 2 ml	[a]	331	C
	EN	1.5 mg/ 1 ml	RB	0.2 mg/ 1 ml	[a]	331	C
	EN	3 mg/ 2 ml	RB	0.2 mg/ 1 ml	[a]	331	C
	EN	1.5 mg/ 1 ml	RB	0.4 mg/ 2 ml	[a]	331	C
Papaveretum	RC[c]	20 mg/ 1 ml	RB	0.2 mg/ 1 ml	[a]	331	C
	RC[c]	40 mg/ 2 ml	RB	0.2 mg/ 1 ml	[a]	331	C

Drugs in Syringe Compatibility (Cont.)

Glycopyrrolate

Drug (in syringe)	*Mfr*	*Amt*	*Mfr*	*Amt*	*Remarks*	*Ref*	*C/I*
	RC[c]	20 mg/ 1 ml	RB	0.4 mg/ 2 ml	[a]	331	**C**
Pentazocine lactate	WI	30 mg/ 1 ml	RB	0.2 mg/ 1 ml	Immediate precipitation	331	**I**
	WI	60 mg/ 2 ml	RB	0.2 mg/ 1 ml	Immediate precipitation	331	**I**
	WI	30 mg/ 1 ml	RB	0.4 mg/ 2 ml	Immediate precipitation	331	**I**
Pentobarbital sodium	AB	50 mg/ 1 ml	RB	0.2 mg/ 1 ml	Immediate precipitation	331	**I**
	AB	100 mg/ 2 ml	RB	0.2 mg/ 1 ml	Immediate precipitation	331	**I**
	AB	50 mg/ 1 ml	RB	0.4 mg/ 2 ml	Immediate precipitation	331	**I**
Procaine HCl	ES	10 mg/ 1 ml	RB	0.2 mg/ 1 ml	[a]	331	**C**
	ES	20 mg/ 2 ml	RB	0.2 mg/ 1 ml	[a]	331	**C**
	ES	10 mg/ 1 ml	RB	0.4 mg/ 2 ml	[a]	331	**C**
	ES	20 mg/ 1 ml	RB	0.2 mg/ 1 ml	[a]	331	**C**
	ES	40 mg/ 2 ml	RB	0.2 mg/ 1 ml	[a]	331	**C**
	ES	20 mg/ 1 ml	RB	0.4 mg/ 2 ml	[a]	331	**C**
Prochlorperazine edisylate	SKF	5 mg/ 1 ml	RB	0.2 mg/ 1 ml	[a]	331	**C**
	SKF	10 mg/ 2 ml	RB	0.2 mg/ 1 ml	[a]	331	**C**
	SKF	5 mg/ 1 ml	RB	0.4 mg/ 2 ml	[a]	331	**C**
Promazine HCl	WY	50 mg/ 1 ml	RB	0.2 mg/ 1 ml	[a]	331	**C**
	WY	100 mg/ 2 ml	RB	0.2 mg/ 1 ml	[a]	331	**C**
	WY	50 mg/ 1 ml	RB	0.4 mg/ 2 ml	[a]	331	**C**
Promethazine HCl	WY	25 mg/ 1 ml	RB	0.2 mg/ 1 ml	[a]	331	**C**
	WY	50 mg/ 2 ml	RB	0.2 mg/ 1 ml	[a]	331	**C**
	WY	25 mg/ 1 ml	RB	0.4 mg/ 2 ml	[a]	331	**C**
Promethazine HCl and meperidine HCl (Mepergan)	WY	25 mg + 25 mg/ 1 ml	RB	0.2 mg/ 1 ml	[a]	331	**C**
	WY	50 mg + 50 mg/ 2 ml	RB	0.2 mg/ 1 ml	[a]	331	**C**

Drugs in Syringe Compatibility (Cont.)

			Glycopyrrolate				
Drug (in syringe)	*Mfr*	*Amt*	*Mfr*	*Amt*	*Remarks*	*Ref*	*C/I*
	WY	25 mg + 25 mg/ 1 ml	RB	0.4 mg/ 2 ml	[a]	331	C
Pyridostigmine bromide	RC	5 mg/ 1 ml	RB	0.2 mg/ 1 ml	[a]	331	C
	RC	10 mg/ 2 ml	RB	0.2 mg/ 1 ml	[a]	331	C
	RC	5 mg/ 1 ml	RB	0.4 mg/ 2 ml	[a]	331	C
Ranitidine HCl	GL	50 mg/ 2 ml	RB	0.2 mg/ 1 ml	Physically compatible for 1 hr at 25 °C both macroscopically and microscopically	978	C
Scopolamine HBr	ES	0.4 mg/ 1 ml	RB	0.2 mg/ 1 ml	[a]	331	C
	ES	0.8 mg/ 2 ml	RB	0.2 mg/ 1 ml	[a]	331	C
	ES	0.4 mg/ 1 ml	RB	0.4 mg/ 2 ml	[a]	331	C
Secobarbital sodium	LI	50 mg/ 1 ml	RB	0.2 mg/ 1 ml	Immediate precipitation	331	I
	LI	100 mg/ 2 ml	RB	0.2 mg/ 1 ml	Immediate precipitation	331	I
	LI	50 mg/ 1 ml	RB	0.4 mg/ 2 ml	Immediate precipitation	331	I
Sodium bicarbonate	AB	75 mg/ 1 ml	RB	0.2 mg/ 1 ml	Gas evolves	331	I
	AB	150 mg/ 2 ml	RB	0.2 mg/ 1 ml	Gas evolves	331	I
	AB	75 mg/ 1 ml	RB	0.4 mg/ 2 ml	Gas evolves	331	I
Thiopental sodium	AB	25 mg/ 1 ml	RB	0.2 mg/ 1 ml	Immediate precipitation	331	I
	AB	50 mg/ 2 ml	RB	0.2 mg/ 1 ml	Immediate precipitation	331	I
	AB	25 mg/ 1 ml	RB	0.4 mg/ 2 ml	Immediate precipitation	331	I
Triflupromazine HCl	SQ	10 mg/ 1 ml	RB	0.2 mg/ 1 ml	[a]	331	C
	SQ	20 mg/ 2 ml	RB	0.2 mg/ 1 ml	[a]	331	C
	SQ	10 mg/ 1 ml	RB	0.4 mg/ 2 ml	[a]	331	C
	SQ	20 mg/ 1 ml	RB	0.2 mg/ 1 ml	[a]	331	C
	SQ	40 mg/ 2 ml	RB	0.2 mg/ 1 ml	[a]	331	C
	SQ	20 mg/ 1 ml	RB	0.4 mg/ 2 ml	[a]	331	C
Trimethobenzamide HCl	BE	100 mg/ 1 ml	RB	0.2 mg/ 1 ml	[a]	331	C
	BE	200 mg/ 2 ml	RB	0.2 mg/ 1 ml	[a]	331	C

Drugs in Syringe Compatibility (Cont.)

Drug (in syringe)	Mfr	Amt	Mfr	Amt	Remarks	Ref	C/I
		Glycopyrrolate					
	BE	100 mg/ 1 ml	RB	0.4 mg/ 2 ml	[a]	331	C

[a]*Physically compatible for 48 hours at 25 °C. The pH of the mixture was within the stability range of glycopyrrolate (2 to 6) for 48 hours at 25 °C.*
[b]*Tested in sodium chloride 0.9%.*
[c]*The former formulation was tested.*

Y-Site Injection Compatibility (1:1 Mixture)

Drug	Mfr	Conc	Mfr	Conc	Remarks	Ref	C/I
			Glycopyrrolate				
Propofol	ZEN	10 mg/ml	RB	0.2 mg/ml	Physically compatible for 1 hr at 23 °C with no increase in particle content	2066	C

Additional Compatibility Information

Infusion Solutions — Glycopyrrolate (Robins) is stated to be physically compatible with dextrose 5% in water, dextrose 10% in water, and sodium chloride 0.9%. (2) Glycopyrrolate 0.8 mg/L in Ringer's injection, lactated, is physically compatible for 48 hours at 25 °C. The pH of the solution (6.1) is slightly higher than the pH range yielding acceptable glycopyrrolate stability (2 to 6). In dextrose 5% in water with the pH adjusted to 6, less than 5% decomposition occurred in 30 hours at 25 °C. With the pH adjusted to 6.5, 5% decomposition resulted in only seven hours. (331) However, the drug can be administered via the tubing of a running intravenous infusion of lactated Ringer's injection. (2; 4)

Alkaline Drugs — Because of the low pH of glycopyrrolate (Robins), mixtures with alkaline drugs such as barbiturates result in precipitation of the free acid. If the pH of the admixture is increased above 6 by an alkaline additive or solution, rapid ester hydrolysis of the glycopyrrolate results. (331)

Buprenorphine HCl — Glycopyrrolate is stated to be physically and chemically compatible with buprenorphine HCl. (4)

GRANISETRON HCL
AHFS 56:22

Products — Granisetron HCl is available in 1-ml single-use vials containing granisetron 1 mg and sodium chloride 9 mg. Granisetron HCl is also available in 4-ml multiple-dose vials providing in each milliliter granisetron 1 mg, sodium chloride 9 mg, citric acid 2 mg, and benzyl alcohol 10 mg as a preservative. (1-12/00)

pH — Single-use vials: from 4.7 to 7.3. Multiple-dose vials: from 4 to 6. (1-12/00)

Equivalency — Granisetron HCl 1.12 mg provides 1 mg of granisetron. (1-12/00)

Osmolality — Granisetron HCl (SmithKline Beecham) 1 mg/ml has an osmolality of 290 mOsm/kg. (2043)

Trade Name(s) — Kytril.

Administration — Granisetron HCl may be administered intravenously undiluted over 30 seconds or by intravenous infusion over five minutes after dilution to 20 to 50 ml with dextrose 5% in water or sodium chloride 0.9%. (1-12/00; 4)

Stability — Granisetron HCl is a clear, colorless injection. Intact vials should be stored at controlled room temperature and protected from freezing and light. The drug is stable for at least 24 hours when diluted as directed in dextrose 5% in water or sodium chloride 0.9% and stored at room temperature under normal lighting conditions. (1-12/00)

Syringes — Granisetron HCl (SmithKline Beecham) 0.05, 0.07, and 0.1 mg/ml (as granisetron) in sodium chloride 0.9% and in dextrose 5% in water was repackaged in polypropylene syringes (Sherwood Medical) (closure used not cited). Little or no granisetron HCl loss occurred by HPLC analysis after 14 days at 5 and 24 °C. (1968)

Granisetron HCl (SmithKline Beecham) 1 mg/ml was repackaged into Plastipak (Becton-Dickinson) polypropylene syringes and stored at room temperature exposed to or protected from light and refrigerated at 4 °C. HPLC analysis found little or no granisetron HCl loss in 15 days under any of these storage conditions. (2149)

Granisetron HCl (Beecham) 0.15 mg/ml in water packaged in polypropylene syringes (Becton-Dickinson) was stored for three days at

20 °C, for seven days at 4 °C followed by three days at 20 °C, and frozen at –20 °C for 30 days, followed by seven days at 4 °C and then three more days at 20 °C. All the solutions remained visually clear and without color change, and HPLC analysis found little or no loss of granisetron HCl. (1884)

Elastomeric Reservoir Pumps—The stability of granisetron HCl (SmithKline Beecham) 0.02 mg/ml in dextrose 5% in water and sodium chloride 0.9% in elastomeric balloons, composed of the polymer Krayton (Shell), for a portable pump (Homepump, 100 ml/hr, Block Medical) was evaluated. The disposable balloons were stored at 4 °C for 14 days and assayed periodically by HPLC analysis. Granisetron losses of 5% or less were found during seven days in sodium chloride 0.9% and during 14 days in dextrose 5% in water. However, after 14 days, a granisetron sample in sodium chloride 0.9% exhibited a 13% loss and could not be considered stable for this time period. (1837)

Central Venous Catheter—Granisetron HCl (SmithKline Beecham) 10 µg/ml in dextrose 5% in water was found to be compatible with the ARROWg+ard Blue Plus (Arrow International) chlorhexidine-bearing triple-lumen central catheter. HPLC analysis was used to evaluate completeness of drug delivery through the catheter and the amount of chlorhexidine removed from the internal lumens. Essentially complete delivery of the drug was found with little or no drug loss occurring. Furthermore, chlorhexidine delivered from the catheter remained at trace amounts with no substantial increase due to the delivery of the drug through the catheter. (2335)

Compatibility Information

Solution Compatibility

Granisetron HCl

Solution	*Mfr*	*Mfr*	*Conc/L*	*Remarks*	*Ref*	*C/I*
Dextrose 5% in sodium chloride 0.45%	BA[b]	SKB	20 mg	Physically compatible with little or no loss by HPLC in 24 hr at 20 °C under fluorescent light	1883	C
Dextrose 5% in sodium chloride 0.9%	BA[b]	SKB	20 mg	Physically compatible with little or no loss by HPLC in 24 hr at 20 °C under fluorescent light	1883	C
Dextrose 5% in water	BA[b]	SKB	20 mg	Physically compatible with little or no loss by HPLC in 24 hr at 20 °C under fluorescent light	1883	C
	BA[a]	SKB	200 mg	Physically compatible with little or no loss by HPLC in 24 hr at 20 °C under fluorescent light	1883	C
		BE	56[b] and 150[a] mg	Visually compatible with little or no loss by HPLC in 30 days at −20 °C followed by 7 days at 4 °C followed by 3 days at 20 °C	1884	C
	MG[c]	SKB	20 mg	5% or less drug loss by HPLC in 14 days at 4 °C	1837	C
Sodium chloride 0.9%	BA[b]	SKB	20 mg	Physically compatible with little or no loss by HPLC in 24 hr at 20 °C under fluorescent light	1883	C
	BA[a]	SKB	200 mg	Physically compatible with little or no loss by HPLC in 24 hr at 20 °C under fluorescent light	1883	C
		BE	56[b] and 150[a] mg	Visually compatible with little or no loss by HPLC in 30 days at −20 °C followed by 7 days at 4 °C followed by 3 days at 20 °C	1884	C
	MG[c]	SKB	20 mg	5% or less drug loss by HPLC in 7 days at 4 °C, but 13% loss in 14 days	1837	C

[a]*Tested in polypropylene syringes.*
[b]*Tested in PVC containers.*
[c]*Tested in Homepump (Block Medical) elastomeric reservoir pumps.*

Additive Compatibility

Granisetron HCl

Drug	*Mfr*	*Conc/L*	*Mfr*	*Conc/L*	*Test Soln*	*Remarks*	*Ref*	*C/I*
Dexamethasone sodium phosphate	AMR	92 mg	SKB	10 and 40 mg	D5W, NS[a]	Visually compatible with little or no loss of either drug by HPLC in 14 days at 4 and 24 °C protected from light	1875	C
	AMR	660 mg	SKB	10 and 40 mg	D5W, NS[a]	Visually compatible with little or no dexamethasone loss and up to 8% granisetron loss by HPLC in 14 days at 4 and 24 °C protected from light	1875	C

Additive Compatibility (Cont.)

Drug	Mfr	Conc/L	Mfr	Conc/L	Test Soln	Remarks	Ref	C/I
			Granisetron HCl					
	MSD	75 and 345 mg	BE	55 and 51 mg	D5W, NS[a]	Visually compatible with little or no loss of either drug by HPLC in 72 hr at room temperature	1884	C
Methylprednisolone sodium succinate	DAK	2.26 g	BE	56 mg	D5W, NS[a]	Visually compatible with little or no loss of either drug by HPLC in 72 hr at room temperature	1884	C

[a]*Tested in PVC containers.*

Drugs in Syringe Compatibility

Drug (in syringe)	Mfr	Amt	Mfr	Amt	Remarks	Ref	C/I
			Granisetron HCl				
Dexamethasone sodium phosphate	MSD	0.2 and 1 mg/ml[a]	BE	0.15 mg/ml[a]	Visually compatible with little or no loss of either drug by HPLC in 72 hr at room temperature	1884	C
Methylprednisolone sodium succinate	DAK	6 mg/ml[a]	BE	0.15 mg/ml[a]	Visually compatible with little or no loss of either drug by HPLC in 72 hr at room temperature	1884	C

[a]*Diluted with water.*

Y-Site Injection Compatibility (1:1 Mixture)

Drug	Mfr	Conc	Mfr	Conc	Remarks	Ref	C/I
			Granisetron HCl				
Acyclovir sodium	BW	7 mg/ml[a]	SKB	0.05 mg/ml[a]	Physically compatible with no change in measured turbidity or increase in particle content in 4 hr at 23 °C	2000	C
Allopurinol sodium	BW	3 mg/ml[a]	SKB	0.05 mg/ml[a]	Physically compatible with no change in measured turbidity or increase in particle content in 4 hr at 23 °C	2000	C
Amifostine	USB	10 mg/ml[a]	SKB	0.05 mg/ml[a]	Physically compatible with no change in measured turbidity or increase in particle content in 4 hr at 23 °C	2000	C
Amikacin sulfate	AB	5 mg/ml[a]	SKB	0.05 mg/ml[a]	Physically compatible with no change in measured turbidity or increase in particle content in 4 hr at 23 °C	2000	C
Aminophylline	AB	2.5 mg/ml[a]	SKB	0.05 mg/ml[a]	Physically compatible with no change in measured turbidity or increase in particle content in 4 hr at 23 °C	2000	C
Amphotericin B	PH	0.6 mg/ml[a]	SKB	0.05 mg/ml[a]	Large increase in measured turbidity occurs immediately	2000	I
Amphotericin B cholesteryl sulfate complex	SEQ	0.83 mg/ml[a]	SKB	0.05 mg/ml[a]	Physically compatible with little or no change in measured turbidity or increase in particle content in 4 hr at 23 °C under fluorescent light	2117	C
Ampicillin sodium	MAR	20 mg/ml[b]	SKB	0.05 mg/ml[a]	Physically compatible with no change in measured turbidity or increase in particle content in 4 hr at 23 °C	2000	C

Y-Site Injection Compatibility (1:1 Mixture) (Cont.)

Granisetron HCl

Drug	*Mfr*	*Conc*	*Mfr*	*Conc*	*Remarks*	*Ref*	*C/I*
Ampicillin sodium–sulbactam sodium	RR	20 + 10 mg/ml[b]	SKB	0.05 mg/ml[a]	Physically compatible with no change in measured turbidity or increase in particle content in 4 hr at 23 °C	2000	C
Amsacrine	NCI	1 mg/ml[a]	SKB	0.05 mg/ml[a]	Physically compatible with no change in measured turbidity or increase in particle content in 4 hr at 23 °C. Precipitate forms in 24 hr	2000	C
Aztreonam	SQ	40 mg/ml[a]	SKB	0.05 mg/ml[a]	Physically compatible with no change in measured turbidity or increase in particle content in 4 hr at 23 °C	2000	C
Bleomycin	MJ	1 unit/ml[b]	SKB	0.05 mg/ml[a]	Physically compatible with no change in measured turbidity or increase in particle content in 4 hr at 23 °C	2000	C
Bumetanide	RC	0.04 mg/ml[a]	SKB	0.05 mg/ml[a]	Physically compatible with no change in measured turbidity or increase in particle content in 4 hr at 23 °C	2000	C
Buprenorphine HCl	RKC	0.04 mg/ml[a]	SKB	0.05 mg/ml[a]	Physically compatible with no change in measured turbidity or increase in particle content in 4 hr at 23 °C	2000	C
Butorphanol tartrate	APC	0.04 mg/ml[a]	SKB	0.05 mg/ml[a]	Physically compatible with no change in measured turbidity or increase in particle content in 4 hr at 23 °C	2000	C
Calcium gluconate	AB	40 mg/ml[a]	SKB	0.05 mg/ml[a]	Physically compatible with no change in measured turbidity or increase in particle content in 4 hr at 23 °C	2000	C
Carboplatin	BR	1 mg/ml[b]	SKB	1 mg/ml	Physically compatible with little or no loss of either drug by HPLC in 4 hr at 22 °C	1883	C
Carmustine	BMS	1.5 mg/ml[a]	SKB	0.05 mg/ml[a]	Physically compatible with no change in measured turbidity or increase in particle content in 4 hr at 23 °C	2000	C
Cefazolin sodium	SKB	20 mg/ml[a]	SKB	0.05 mg/ml[a]	Physically compatible with no change in measured turbidity or increase in particle content in 4 hr at 23 °C	2000	C
Cefepime HCl	BMS	20 mg/ml[a]	SKB	0.05 mg/ml[a]	Physically compatible with no change in measured turbidity or increase in particle content in 4 hr at 23 °C	2000	C
Cefoperazone sodium	RR	40 mg/ml[a]	SKB	0.05 mg/ml[a]	Physically compatible with no change in measured turbidity or increase in particle content in 4 hr at 23 °C	2000	C
Cefotaxime sodium	HO	20 mg/ml[a]	SKB	0.05 mg/ml[a]	Physically compatible with no change in measured turbidity or increase in particle content in 4 hr at 23 °C	2000	C
Cefotetan sodium	STU	20 mg/ml[a]	SKB	0.05 mg/ml[a]	Physically compatible with no change in measured turbidity or increase in particle content in 4 hr at 23 °C	2000	C
Cefoxitin sodium	ME	20 mg/ml[a]	SKB	0.05 mg/ml[a]	Physically compatible with no change in measured turbidity or increase in particle content in 4 hr at 23 °C	2000	C

Y-Site Injection Compatibility (1:1 Mixture) (Cont.)

Drug	*Mfr*	*Conc*	*Mfr*	*Conc*	*Remarks*	*Ref*	*C/I*
			Granisetron HCl				
Ceftazidime[c]	SKB	16.7 mg/ml[b]	SKB	1 mg/ml	Physically compatible with little or no loss of either drug by HPLC in 4 hr at 22 °C	1883	C
Ceftizoxime sodium	FUJ	20 mg/ml[a]	SKB	0.05 mg/ml[a]	Physically compatible with no change in measured turbidity or increase in particle content in 4 hr at 23 °C	2000	C
Ceftriaxone sodium	RC	20 mg/ml[a]	SKB	0.05 mg/ml[a]	Physically compatible with no change in measured turbidity or increase in particle content in 4 hr at 23 °C	2000	C
Cefuroxime sodium	LI	30 mg/ml[a]	SKB	0.05 mg/ml[a]	Physically compatible with no change in measured turbidity or increase in particle content in 4 hr at 23 °C	2000	C
Chlorpromazine HCl	SCN	2 mg/ml[a]	SKB	0.05 mg/ml[a]	Physically compatible with no change in measured turbidity or increase in particle content in 4 hr at 23 °C	2000	C
Cimetidine HCl	SKB	3 mg/ml[b]	SKB	1 mg/ml	Physically compatible with little or no loss of either drug by HPLC in 4 hr at 22 °C	1883	C
Ciprofloxacin	MI	1 mg/ml[a]	SKB	0.05 mg/ml[a]	Physically compatible with no change in measured turbidity or increase in particle content in 4 hr at 23 °C	2000	C
Cisplatin	BR	1 mg/ml	SKB	1 mg/ml	Physically compatible with little or no loss of either drug by HPLC in 4 hr at 22 °C	1883	C
	BR	0.05 mg/ml[b]	SKB	1 mg/ml	Physically compatible with little or no granisetron loss by HPLC in 4 hr at 22 °C	1883	C
Cladribine	ORT	0.015[b] and 0.5[d] mg/ml	SKB	0.05 mg/ml[b]	Physically compatible with no change in measured turbidity or increase in particle content in 4 hr at 23 °C	1969	C
Clindamycin phosphate	AB	10 mg/ml[a]	SKB	0.05 mg/ml[a]	Physically compatible with no change in measured turbidity or increase in particle content in 4 hr at 23 °C	2000	C
Cyclophosphamide	MJ	2 mg/ml[b]	SKB	1 mg/ml	Physically compatible with little or no loss of either drug by HPLC in 4 hr at 22 °C	1883	C
Cytarabine	UP	2 mg/ml[b]	SKB	1 mg/ml	Physically compatible with little or no loss of either drug by HPLC in 4 hr at 22 °C	1883	C
	UP	50 mg/ml	SKB	0.05 mg/ml[a]	Physically compatible with no change in measured turbidity or increase in particle content in 4 hr at 23 °C	2000	C
Dacarbazine	MI	1.7 mg/ml[b]	SKB	1 mg/ml	Physically compatible with little or no loss of either drug by HPLC in 4 hr at 22 °C	1883	C
Dactinomycin	ME	0.01 mg/ml[a]	SKB	0.05 mg/ml[a]	Physically compatible with no change in measured turbidity or increase in particle content in 4 hr at 23 °C	2000	C
Daunorubicin HCl	CHI	1 mg/ml[a]	SKB	0.05 mg/ml[a]	Physically compatible with no change in measured turbidity or increase in particle content in 4 hr at 23 °C	2000	C
Dexamethasone sodium phosphate	ME	0.24 mg/ml[b]	SKB	1 mg/ml	Physically compatible with little or no loss of either drug by HPLC in 4 hr at 22 °C	1883	C

Y-Site Injection Compatibility (1:1 Mixture) (Cont.)

			Granisetron HCl				
Drug	*Mfr*	*Conc*	*Mfr*	*Conc*	*Remarks*	*Ref*	*C/I*
Diphenhydramine HCl	PD	1 mg/ml[b]	SKB	1 mg/ml	Physically compatible with little or no loss of either drug by HPLC in 4 hr at 22 °C	1883	C
	SCN	2 mg/ml[a]	SKB	0.05 mg/ml[a]	Physically compatible with no change in measured turbidity or increase in particle content in 4 hr at 23 °	2000	C
Dobutamine HCl	BA	4 mg/ml[a]	SKB	0.05 mg/ml[a]	Physically compatible with no change in measured turbidity or increase in particle content in 4 hr at 23 °C	2000	C
Docetaxel	RPR	0.9 mg/ml[a]	SKB	0.05 mg/ml[a]	Physically compatible with no change in measured turbidity or increase in particle content in 4 hr at 23 °C	2224	C
Dopamine HCl	AB	3.2 mg/ml[a]	SKB	0.05 mg/ml[a]	Physically compatible with no change in measured turbidity or increase in particle content in 4 hr at 23 °C	2000	C
Doxorubicin HCl	AD	0.2 mg/ml[b]	SKB	1 mg/ml	Physically compatible with little or no loss of either drug by HPLC in 4 hr at 22 °C	1883	C
Doxorubicin HCl liposome injection	SEQ	0.4 mg/ml[a]	SKB	0.05 mg/ml[a]	Physically compatible with little or no change in measured turbidity and no increase in particle content in 4 hr at 23 °C	2087	C
Doxycycline hyclate	LY	1 mg/ml[a]	SKB	0.05 mg/ml[a]	Physically compatible with no change in measured turbidity or increase in particle content in 4 hr at 23 °C	2000	C
Droperidol	AB	0.4 mg/ml[a]	SKB	0.05 mg/ml[a]	Physically compatible with no change in measured turbidity or increase in particle content in 4 hr at 23 °C	2000	C
Enalaprilat	MSD	0.1 mg/ml[a]	SKB	0.05 mg/ml[a]	Physically compatible with no change in measured turbidity or increase in particle content in 4 hr at 23 °C	2000	C
Etoposide	BMS	0.4 mg/ml[b]	SKB	1 mg/ml	Physically compatible with little or no loss of either drug by HPLC in 4 hr at 22 °C	1883	C
	BR	0.4 mg/ml[a]	SKB	0.05 mg/ml[a]	Physically compatible with no change in measured turbidity or increase in particle content in 4 hr at 23 °C	2000	C
Etoposide phosphate	BR	5 mg/ml[a]	SKB	0.05 mg/ml[a]	Physically compatible with no change in measured turbidity or increase in particle content in 4 hr at 23 °C	2218	C
Famotidine	ME	2 mg/ml[a]	SKB	0.05 mg/ml[a]	Physically compatible with no change in measured turbidity or increase in particle content in 4 hr at 23 °C	2000	C
Filgrastim	AMG	30 μg/ml[a]	SKB	0.05 mg/ml[a]	Physically compatible with no change in measured turbidity or increase in particle content in 4 hr at 23 °C	2000	C
Floxuridine	RC	3 mg/ml[a]	SKB	0.05 mg/ml[a]	Physically compatible with no change in measured turbidity or increase in particle content in 4 hr at 23 °C	2000	C
Fluconazole	PF	2 mg/ml	SKB	0.05 mg/ml[a]	Physically compatible with no change in measured turbidity or increase in particle content in 4 hr at 23 °C	2000	C

Y-Site Injection Compatibility (1:1 Mixture) (Cont.)

Drug	Mfr	Conc	Granisetron HCl Mfr	Granisetron HCl Conc	Remarks	Ref	C/I
Fludarabine phosphate	BX	1 mg/ml[a]	SKB	0.05 mg/ml[a]	Physically compatible with no change in measured turbidity or increase in particle content in 4 hr at 23 °C	2000	C
Fluorouracil	AD	16 mg/ml[a]	SKB	0.05 mg/ml[a]	Physically compatible with no subvisual haze or particle formation in 4 hr at 23 °C	1804	C
	RC	2 mg/ml[b]	SKB	1 mg/ml	Physically compatible with little or no loss of either drug by HPLC in 4 hr at 22 °C	1883	C
	AD	16 mg/ml[a]	SKB	0.05 mg/ml[a]	Physically compatible with no change in measured turbidity or increase in particle content in 4 hr at 23 °C	2000	C
Furosemide	AB	3 mg/ml[a]	SKB	0.05 mg/ml[a]	Physically compatible with no subvisual haze or particle formation in 4 hr at 23 °C	1804	C
	HO	0.4 mg/ml[b]	SKB	1 mg/ml	Physically compatible with little or no loss of either drug by HPLC in 4 hr at 22 °C	1883	C
Ganciclovir sodium	SY	20 mg/ml[a]	SKB	0.05 mg/ml[a]	Physically compatible with no change in measured turbidity or increase in particle content in 4 hr at 23 °C	2000	C
Gatifloxacin	BMS	2 mg/ml[a]	SKB	0.05 mg/ml[a]	Physically compatible with no change in measured haze or increase in particle content in 4 hr at 23 °C	2234	C
Gemcitabine HCl	LI	10 mg/ml[b]	SKB	0.05 mg/ml[b]	Physically compatible with no change in measured turbidity or increase in particle content in 4 hr at 23 °C	2226	C
Gentamicin sulfate	ES	1.5 mg/ml[b]	SKB	1 mg/ml	Physically compatible with little or no loss of either drug by HPLC in 4 hr at 22 °C	1883	C
Haloperidol lactate	MN	0.2 mg/ml[a]	SKB	0.05 mg/ml[a]	Physically compatible with no change in measured turbidity or increase in particle content in 4 hr at 23 °C	2000	C
Heparin sodium	AB	100 units/ml[a]	SKB	0.05 mg/ml[a]	Physically compatible with no change in measured turbidity or increase in particle content in 4 hr at 23 °C	2000	C
Hetastarch in lactated electrolyte injection (Hextend)	AB	6%	SKB	0.05 mg/ml[a]	Physically compatible with no change in measured turbidity or increase in particle content in 4 hr at 23 °C	2339	C
Hydrocortisone sodium phosphate	MSD	1 mg/ml[a]	SKB	0.05 mg/ml[a]	Physically compatible with no change in measured turbidity or increase in particle content in 4 hr at 23 °C	2000	C
Hydrocortisone sodium succinate	AB	1 mg/ml[a]	SKB	0.05 mg/ml[a]	Physically compatible with no change in measured turbidity or increase in particle content in 4 hr at 23 °C	2000	C
Hydromorphone HCl	KN	0.5 mg/ml[b]	SKB	1 mg/ml	Physically compatible with little or no loss of either drug by HPLC in 4 hr at 22 °C	1883	C
	ES	0.5 mg/ml[a]	SKB	0.05 mg/ml[a]	Physically compatible with no change in measured turbidity or increase in particle content in 4 hr at 23 °C	2000	C
Hydroxyzine HCl	ES	2 mg/ml[a]	SKB	0.05 mg/ml[a]	Physically compatible with no change in measured turbidity or increase in particle content in 4 hr at 23 °C	2000	C

Y-Site Injection Compatibility (1:1 Mixture) (Cont.)

Granisetron HCl

Drug	*Mfr*	*Conc*	*Mfr*	*Conc*	*Remarks*	*Ref*	*C/I*
Idarubicin HCl	AD	0.5 mg/ml[a]	SKB	0.05 mg/ml[a]	Increase in turbidity no greater than dilution with D5W alone. No increase in particle content in 4 hr at 23 °C	2000	C
Ifosfamide	MJ	4 mg/ml[b]	SKB	1 mg/ml	Physically compatible with little or no loss of either drug by HPLC in 4 hr at 22 °C	1883	C
Imipenem–cilastatin sodium	ME	10 mg/ml[a]	SKB	0.05 mg/ml[a]	Physically compatible with no change in measured turbidity or increase in particle content in 4 hr at 23 °C	2000	C
Leucovorin calcium	IMM	2 mg/ml[a]	SKB	0.05 mg/ml[a]	Physically compatible with no change in measured turbidity or increase in particle content in 4 hr at 23 °C	2000	C
Levoleucovorin calcium	LE	2 mg/ml[a]	SKB	0.05 mg/ml[a]	Physically compatible with no change in measured turbidity or increase in particle content in 4 hr at 23 °C	2000	C
Linezolid	PHU	2 mg/ml	SKB	0.05 mg/ml[a]	Physically compatible with no change in measured turbidity or increase in particle content in 4 hr at 23 °C	2264	C
Lorazepam	WY	0.1 mg/ml[b]	SKB	1 mg/ml	Physically compatible with little or no loss of either drug by HPLC in 4 hr at 22 °C	1883	C
	WY	0.1 mg/ml[a]	SKB	0.05 mg/ml[a]	Physically compatible with no change in measured turbidity or increase in particle content in 4 hr at 23 °C	2000	C
Magnesium sulfate	AB	16 mg/ml[b]	SKB	1 mg/ml	Physically compatible with little or no loss of granisetron by HPLC in 4 hr at 22 °C	1883	C
	AB	100 mg/ml[a]	SKB	0.05 mg/ml[a]	Physically compatible with no change in measured turbidity or increase in particle content in 4 hr at 23 °C	2000	C
Mechlorethamine HCl	MSD	0.5 mg/ml[b]	SKB	1 mg/ml	Physically compatible with little or no loss of either drug by HPLC in 4 hr at 22 °C	1883	C
Melphalan	BW	0.1 mg/ml[b]	SKB	0.05 mg/ml[a]	Physically compatible with no change in measured turbidity or increase in particle content in 4 hr at 23 °C	2000	C
Meperidine HCl	WY	4 mg/ml[a]	SKB	0.05 mg/ml[a]	Physically compatible with no change in measured turbidity or increase in particle content in 4 hr at 23 °C	2000	C
Mesna	MJ	4 mg/ml[b]	SKB	1 mg/ml	Physically compatible with little or no loss of either drug by HPLC in 4 hr at 22 °C	1883	C
Methotrexate sodium	CET	12.5 mg/ml[b]	SKB	1 mg/ml	Physically compatible with little or no loss of either drug by HPLC in 4 hr at 22 °C	1883	C
Methylprednisolone sodium succinate	WY	5 mg/ml[a]	SKB	0.05 mg/ml[a]	Physically compatible with no change in measured turbidity or increase in particle content in 4 hr at 23 °C	2000	C
Metoclopramide HCl	AB	5 mg/ml	SKB	0.05 mg/ml[a]	Physically compatible with no change in measured turbidity or increase in particle content in 4 hr at 23 °C	2000	C
Metronidazole	BA	5 mg/ml	SKB	0.05 mg/ml[a]	Physically compatible with no change in measured turbidity or increase in particle content in 4 hr at 23 °C	2000	C

Y-Site Injection Compatibility (1:1 Mixture) (Cont.)

Drug	*Mfr*	*Conc*	*Mfr*	*Conc*	*Remarks*	*Ref*	*C/I*
			Granisetron HCl				
Minocycline HCl	LE	0.2 mg/ml[a]	SKB	0.05 mg/ml[a]	Physically compatible with no change in measured turbidity or increase in particle content in 4 hr at 23 °C	2000	C
Mitomycin	BMS	0.5 mg/ml	SKB	0.05 mg/ml[a]	Physically compatible with no change in measured turbidity or increase in particle content in 4 hr at 23 °C	2000	C
Mitoxantrone HCl	IMM	0.5 mg/ml[a]	SKB	0.05 mg/ml[a]	Physically compatible with no change in measured turbidity or increase in particle content in 4 hr at 23 °C	2000	C
Morphine sulfate	AST	1 mg/ml[b]	SKB	1 mg/ml	Physically compatible with little or no loss of either drug by HPLC in 4 hr at 22 °C	1883	C
	AST	1 mg/ml[a]	SKB	0.05 mg/ml[a]	Physically compatible with no change in measured turbidity or increase in particle content in 4 hr at 23 °C	2000	C
Nalbuphine HCl	AB	10 mg/ml	SKB	0.05 mg/ml[a]	Physically compatible with no change in measured turbidity or increase in particle content in 4 hr at 23 °C	2000	C
Netilmicin sulfate	SC	5 mg/ml[a]	SKB	0.05 mg/ml[a]	Physically compatible with no change in measured turbidity or increase in particle content in 4 hr at 23 °C	2000	C
Ofloxacin	ORT	4 mg/ml[a]	SKB	0.05 mg/ml[a]	Physically compatible with no change in measured turbidity or increase in particle content in 4 hr at 23 °C	2000	C
Paclitaxel	MJ	0.3 mg/ml[b]	SKB	1 mg/ml	Physically compatible with little or no loss of either drug by HPLC in 4 hr at 22 °C	1883	C
	MJ	1.2 mg/ml[a]	SKB	0.05 mg/ml[a]	Physically compatible with no change in measured turbidity or increase in particle content in 4 hr at 23 °C	2000	C
Piperacillin sodium	LE	40 mg/ml[a]	SKB	0.05 mg/ml[a]	Physically compatible with no change in measured turbidity or increase in particle content in 4 hr at 23 °C	2000	C
Piperacillin sodium–tazobactam sodium	CY	40 + 5 mg/ml[a]	SKB	0.05 mg/ml[a]	Physically compatible with no change in measured turbidity or increase in particle content in 4 hr at 23 °C	2000	C
Plicamycin	BAY	0.01 mg/ml[a]	SKB	0.05 mg/ml[a]	Physically compatible with no change in measured turbidity or increase in particle content in 4 hr at 23 °C	2000	C
Potassium chloride	LY	0.04 mEq/ml[b]	SKB	1 mg/ml	Physically compatible with little or no loss of granisetron by HPLC in 4 hr at 22 °C	1883	C
Prochlorperazine edisylate	SCN	0.5 mg/ml[a]	SKB	0.05 mg/ml[a]	Physically compatible with no change in measured turbidity or increase in particle content in 4 hr at 23 °C	2000	C
Promethazine HCl	WY	2 mg/ml[a]	SKB	0.05 mg/ml[a]	Physically compatible with no change in measured turbidity or increase in particle content in 4 hr at 23 °C	2000	C
Propofol	ZEN	10 mg/ml	SKB	0.05 mg/ml[a]	Physically compatible for 1 hr at 23 °C with no increase in particle content	2066	C

Y-Site Injection Compatibility (1:1 Mixture) (Cont.)

Granisetron HCl

Drug	*Mfr*	*Conc*	*Mfr*	*Conc*	*Remarks*	*Ref*	*C/I*
Ranitidine HCl	GL	2 mg/ml[a]	SKB	0.05 mg/ml[a]	Physically compatible with no change in measured turbidity or increase in particle content in 4 hr at 23 °C	2000	C
Sargramostim	IMM	10 μg/ml[b]	SKB	0.05 mg/ml[a]	Physically compatible with no change in measured turbidity or increase in particle content in 4 hr at 23 °C	2000	C
Sodium bicarbonate	AB	1 mEq/ml	SKB	0.05 mg/ml[a]	Physically compatible with no subvisual haze or particle formation in 4 hr at 23 °C	1804	C
	AB	0.33 mEq/ml[b]	SKB	1 mg/ml	Physically compatible with 8% loss of granisetron by HPLC in 4 hr at 22 °C	1883	C
	AB	1 mEq/ml	SKB	0.05 mg/ml[a]	Physically compatible with no change in measured turbidity or increase in particle content in 4 hr at 23 °C	2000	C
Streptozocin	UP	9.1 mg/ml[b]	SKB	1 mg/ml	Physically compatible with little or no loss of either drug by HPLC in 4 hr at 22 °C	1883	C
Teniposide	BMS	0.1 mg/ml[a]	SKB	0.05 mg/ml[a]	Physically compatible with no change in measured turbidity or increase in particle content in 4 hr at 23 °C	2000	C
Thiotepa	IMM[f]	1 mg/ml[a]	SKB	0.05 mg/ml[a]	Physically compatible with no change in measured turbidity or increase in particle content in 4 hr at 23 °C	1861; 2000	C
Ticarcillin disodium	SKB	30 mg/ml[a]	SKB	0.05 mg/ml[a]	Physically compatible with no change in measured turbidity or increase in particle content in 4 hr at 23 °C	2000	C
Ticarcillin disodium–clavulanate potassium	SKB	27 mg/ml[b]	SKB	1 mg/ml	Physically compatible with little or no loss of either drug by HPLC in 4 hr at 22 °C	1883	C
	SKB	31 mg/ml[a]	SKB	0.05 mg/ml[a]	Physically compatible with no change in measured turbidity or increase in particle content in 4 hr at 23 °C	2000	C
TNA #218 to #226[g]			SKB	0.05 mg/ml[a]	Visually compatible with no precipitate or emulsion damage apparent in 4 hr at 23 °C	2215	C
Tobramycin sulfate	AB	5 mg/ml[a]	SKB	0.05 mg/ml[a]	Physically compatible with no change in measured turbidity or increase in particle content in 4 hr at 23 °C	2000	C
Topotecan HCl	SKB	56 μg/ ml[a,b]	SKB	20 μg/ml[a,b]	Visually compatible with little or no loss of either drug by HPLC in 4 hr at 22 °C under fluorescent light	2245	C
TPN #212 to #215[g]			SKB	0.05 mg/ml[a]	Physically compatible with no change in measured turbidity or increase in particle content in 4 hr at 23 °C	2109	C
Trimethoprim–sulfamethoxazole	ES	0.8 + 4 mg/ ml[a]	SKB	0.05 mg/ml[a]	Physically compatible with no change in measured turbidity or increase in particle content in 4 hr at 23 °C	2000	C
Vancomycin HCl	AB	10 mg/ml[a]	SKB	0.05 mg/ml[a]	Physically compatible with no change in measured turbidity or increase in particle content in 4 hr at 23 °C	2000	C

Y-Site Injection Compatibility (1:1 Mixture) (Cont.)

			Granisetron HCl				
Drug	*Mfr*	*Conc*	*Mfr*	*Conc*	*Remarks*	*Ref*	*C/I*
Vinblastine sulfate	LI	0.12 mg/ml[a]	SKB	0.05 mg/ml[a]	Physically compatible with no change in measured turbidity or increase in particle content in 4 hr at 23 °C	2000	C
Vincristine sulfate	LI	0.34 mg/ml[b]	SKB	1 mg/ml	Physically compatible with little or no loss of either drug by HPLC in 4 hr at 22 °C	1883	C
	LI	0.01 mg/ml[b]	SKB	1 mg/ml	Physically compatible with little or no loss of granisetron by HPLC in 4 hr at 22 °C	1883	C
Vinorelbine tartrate	BW	1 mg/ml[a]	SKB	0.05 mg/ml[a]	Physically compatible with no change in measured turbidity or increase in particle content in 4 hr at 23 °C	2000	C
Zidovudine	BW	4 mg/ml[a]	SKB	0.05 mg/ml[a]	Physically compatible with no change in measured turbidity or increase in particle content in 4 hr at 23 °C	2000	C

[a]*Tested in dextrose 5% in water.*
[b]*Tested in sodium chloride 0.9%.*
[c]*Sodium carbonate–containing formulation tested.*
[d]*Tested in bacteriostatic sodium chloride 0.9% preserved with benzyl alcohol 0.9%.*
[e]*Granisetron HCl tested in both sodium chloride 0.9% and dextrose 5% in water.*
[f]*Lyophilized formulation tested.*
[g]*Refer to Appendix I for the composition of parenteral nutrition solutions. TNA indicates a 3-in-1 admixture, and TPN indicates a 2-in-1 admixture.*

Additional Compatibility Information

Infusion Solutions — Dextrose 5% in water and sodium chloride 0.9% are recommended for dilution of granisetron HCl. (2)

HALOPERIDOL LACTATE
AHFS 28:16.08

Products — Haloperidol lactate is available in 1-ml ampuls and vials and 10-ml multiple-dose vials. Each milliliter of solution contains haloperidol 5 mg (as the lactate), methylparaben 1.8 mg, propylparaben 0.2 mg, and lactic acid for pH adjustment. (2; 29)

pH — From 3 to 3.6. (2)

Trade Name(s) — Haldol.

Administration — Haloperidol lactate should be administered intramuscularly (2; 4), although intravenous administration has been performed. (4; 571; 1258)

Stability — Haloperidol lactate should be stored at controlled room temperature and protected from light; freezing and temperatures above 40 °C should be avoided. (2; 4)

Central Venous Catheter — Haloperidol lactate (McNeil) 0.2 mg/ml in dextrose 5% in water was found to be compatible with the ARROWg+ard Blue Plus (Arrow International) chlorhexidine-bearing triple-lumen central catheter. HPLC analysis was used to evaluate completeness of drug delivery through the catheter and the amount of chlorhexidine removed from the internal lumens. Essentially complete delivery of the drug was found with little or no drug loss occurring. Furthermore, chlorhexidine delivered from the catheter remained at trace amounts with no substantial increase due to the delivery of the drug through the catheter. (2335)

Compatibility Information

Solution Compatibility

Haloperidol lactate

Solution	*Mfr*	*Mfr*	*Conc/L*	*Remarks*	*Ref*	*C/I*
Dextrose 5% in sodium chloride 0.2%	AB	MN	0.1 to 1 g	Visually compatible for 7 days at 21 °C	1740	C
	AB	MN	2 and 3 g	Precipitate forms in 30 to 60 min	1740	I
Dextrose 5% in water	TR[a]	MN	100 mg	Physically compatible and potency retained for 38 days at 24 °C	571	C
	AB	MN	0.1 to 3 g	Visually compatible for 7 days at 21 °C	1740	C
Ringer's injection, lactated	AB	MN	0.1 to 1 g	Visually compatible for 7 days at 21 °C	1740	C
	AB	MN	2 g	Precipitate forms within 15 min	1740	I
	AB	MN	3 g	Precipitate forms immediately	1740	I
Sodium chloride 0.45%	AB	MN	0.1 to 1 g	Visually compatible for 7 days at 21 °C	1740	C
	AB	MN	2 g	Precipitate forms within 15 min	1740	I
	AB	MN	3 g	Precipitate forms immediately	1740	I
Sodium chloride 0.9%	AB[b]	MN	2 and 3 g	Slight precipitate forms immediately and becomes much heavier within 15 to 30 min	1523	I
	AB[b]	MN	1 g	Slight precipitate forms immediately and persists through 8 hr of observation	1523	I
	AB[b]	MN	100 and 500 mg	Visually compatible for 8 hr at 21 °C under fluorescent light	1523	C
	AB	MN	0.1 to 0.75 g	Visually compatible for 7 days at 21 °C	1740	C
	AB	MN	1 to 3 g	Precipitate forms immediately	1740	I

[a] *Tested in both glass and PVC containers.*
[b] *Tested in glass containers.*

Drugs in Syringe Compatibility

Haloperidol lactate

Drug (in syringe)	*Mfr*	*Amt*	*Mfr*	*Amt*	*Remarks*	*Ref*	*C/I*
Benztropine mesylate	MSD	2 mg	MN	0.25, 0.5, 1 mg	Visually compatible for 24 hr at 21 °C	1781	C
	MSD	2 mg	MN	2 mg	Precipitate forms within 4 hr at 21 °C	1781	I
	MSD	2 mg	MN	3, 4, 5 mg	Precipitate forms within 15 min at 21 °C	1781	I
	MSD	1 mg	MN	0.25 and 0.5 mg	Visually compatible for 24 hr at 21 °C	1781	C
	MSD	1 mg	MN	1 to 5 mg	Precipitate forms within 15 min at 21 °C	1781	I
	MSD	0.5 mg	MN	0.25 to 5 mg	Precipitate forms within 15 min at 21 °C	1781	I
	MSD	2 mg/ 2 ml	MN	10 mg/ 2 ml	White precipitate forms within 5 min	1784	I
Cyclizine lactate	WEL	150 mg/ 3 ml	SE	1.5 mg/ 0.3 ml	Diluted with 17 ml of NS. Crystals of cyclizine form within 24 hr at 25 °C	1761	I
	WEL	150 mg/ 3 ml	SE	1.5 mg/ 0.3 ml	Diluted with 17 ml of D5W or W. Visually compatible for 24 hr at 25 °C	1761	C

Drugs in Syringe Compatibility (Cont.)

Haloperidol lactate

Drug (in syringe)	*Mfr*	*Amt*	*Mfr*	*Amt*	*Remarks*	*Ref*	*C/I*
Cyclizine lactate with diamorphine HCl	WEL BP	16 mg/ml 11 mg/ml	JC	2.2 mg/ ml	Physically compatible with less than 10% loss of any drug by HPLC in 7 days at 23 °C	2071	C
Cyclizine lactate with diamorphine HCl	WEL BP	16 mg/ml 25 mg/ml	JC	2.2 mg/ ml	Physically compatible with less than 10% loss of any drug by HPLC in 7 days at 23 °C	2071	C
Cyclizine lactate with diamorphine HCl	WEL BP	11 mg/ml 40 mg/ml	JC	2.2 mg/ ml	Physically compatible with less than 10% loss of any drug by HPLC in 7 days at 23 °C	2071	C
Cyclizine lactate with diamorphine HCl	WEL BP	13 mg/ml 42 mg/ml	JC	2.1 mg/ ml	Physically compatible with less than 10% loss of any drug by HPLC in 7 days at 23 °C	2071	C
Cyclizine lactate with diamorphine HCl	WEL BP	9 mg/ml 55 mg/ml	JC	2.1 mg/ ml	Physically compatible with less than 10% loss of any drug by HPLC in 7 days at 23 °C	2071	C
Cyclizine lactate with diamorphine HCl	WEL BP	13 mg/ml 56 mg/ml	JC	2.1 mg/ ml	Physically compatible with less than 10% loss of any drug by HPLC in 7 days at 23 °C	2071	C
Diamorphine HCl	MB	10, 25, 50 mg/ 1 ml	SE	1.5 mg/ 1 ml[a]	Physically compatible and diamorphine content retained for 24 hr at room temperature	1454	C
	EV	20 mg/ 1 ml	SE	2 mg/ 1 ml	Crystallization with 58% haloperidol loss in 7 days at room temperature	1455	I
	EV	50 and 150 mg/ 1 ml	SE	5 mg/ 1 ml	Immediate precipitation	1455	I
	EV	100 mg/ 8 ml	SE	2.5 mg/ 8 ml	Physically compatible for 24 hr at room temperature and 7 days at 6 °C	1456	C
	HC	20 to 100 mg/ ml	SE	0.75 mg/ ml	Visually compatible for 48 hr at 5 and 20 °C	1672	C
	HC	2 mg/ml	SE	0.75 mg/ ml	5% diamorphine loss by HPLC in 14.8 days at 20 °C. Haloperidol potency by HPLC retained for at least 45 days	1672	C
	HC	20 mg/ml	SE	0.75 mg/ ml	5% diamorphine loss by HPLC in 20.7 days at 20 °C. Haloperidol potency by HPLC retained for at least 45 days	1672	C
	BP	20, 50, 100 mg/ ml	JC	2 mg/ml	Physically compatible with no loss of either drug in 7 days at 23 °C	2071	C
	BP	20, 50, 100 mg/ ml	JC	3 mg/ml	Physically compatible with no loss of either drug in 7 days at 23 °C	2071	C
	BP	20, 50, 100 mg/ ml	JC	4 mg/ml	Physically compatible with no loss of either drug in 7 days at 23 °C	2071	C
Diphenhydramine HCl	ES	100 mg/ 2 ml	MN	10 mg/ 2 ml	White precipitate forms within 5 min	1784	I
	ES	50 mg/ 1 ml	MN	5 mg/ 1 ml	White cloudy precipitate forms in 2 hr at room temperature	1886	I
Heparin sodium		2500 units/ 1 ml	JN	5 mg/ 1 ml	Turbidity or precipitate forms within 5 min	1053	I
Hydromorphone HCl	KN	1[a] and 10 mg/ 1 ml	MN	1[a], 2[a], 5 mg/ 1 ml	Visually compatible for 24 hr at 25 °C under fluorescent light	1785	C
Hydroxyzine HCl	ES	100 mg/ 2 ml	MN	10 mg/ 2 ml	White precipitate forms within 5 min	1784	I

Drugs in Syringe Compatibility (Cont.)

Haloperidol lactate

Drug (in syringe)	*Mfr*	*Amt*	*Mfr*	*Amt*	*Remarks*	*Ref*	*C/I*
Ketorolac tromethamine	SY	30 mg/ 1 ml	SO	5 mg/ 1 ml	White crystalline precipitate forms immediately	1786	I
Lorazepam	WY	2 mg/ 1 ml	MN	5 mg/ 1 ml	Physically compatible and chemically stable for 16 hr at room temperature	1838	C
Morphine HCl	STP, FED	5, 10, 20, 30 mg/ 1 ml	JC	5 mg/ 1 ml	Visually compatible for up to 7 days at 23 °C	2257	C
Morphine sulfate		5 and 10 mg/ 1 ml[b,c]	MN	5 mg/ 1 ml	Cloudiness forms immediately, becoming a crystalline precipitate of haloperidol and parabens	1901	I
Sufentanil citrate	JN	50 µg/ml	MN	5 mg/ml	Physically compatible with no subvisual haze or particle formation in 24 hr at 23 °C	1711	C

[a] *Diluted with sterile water for injection.*
[b] *Morphine sulfate powder dissolved in dextrose 5% in water.*
[c] *Morphine sulfate powder dissolved in water and sodium chloride 0.9%.*

Y-Site Injection Compatibility (1:1 Mixture)

Haloperidol lactate

Drug	*Mfr*	*Conc*	*Mfr*	*Conc*	*Remarks*	*Ref*	*C/I*
Allopurinol sodium	BW	3 mg/ml[b]	MN	0.2 mg/ml[b]	Heavy turbidity forms immediately. Crystals form within 1 hr	1686	I
Amifostine	USB	10 mg/ml[a]	MN	0.2 mg/ml[a]	Physically compatible with no change in measured turbidity or increase in particle content in 4 hr at 23 °C	1845	C
Amphotericin B cholesteryl sulfate complex	SEQ	0.83 mg/ml[a]	MN	0.2 mg/ml[a]	Gross precipitate forms	2117	I
Amsacrine	NCI	1 mg/ml[a]	MN	0.2 mg/ml[a]	Physically compatible for 4 hr at room temperature under fluorescent light	1381	C
Aztreonam	SQ	40 mg/ml[a]	MN	0.2 mg/ml[a]	Physically compatible with no subvisual haze or particle formation in 4 hr at 23 °C	1758	C
Cefepime HCl	BMS	20 mg/ml[a]	MN	0.2 mg/ml[a]	Haze forms immediately	1689	I
Cimetidine HCl	SKF	6 mg/ml[a]	MN	0.5[a] and 5 mg/ml	Visually compatible for 24 hr at 21 °C	1523	C
Cisatracurium besylate	GW	0.1, 2, and 5 mg/ml[a]	MN	0.2 mg/ml[a]	Physically compatible with no change in measured turbidity or increase in particle content in 4 hr at 23 °C	2074	C
Cladribine	ORT	0.015[b] and 0.5[c] mg/ml	MN	0.2 mg/ml[b]	Physically compatible with no change in measured turbidity or increase in particle content in 4 hr at 23 °C	1969	C
Dobutamine HCl	LI	4 mg/ml[a]	MN	0.5[a] and 5 mg/ml	Visually compatible for 24 hr at 21 °C	1523	C
Docetaxel	RPR	0.9 mg/ml[a]	MN	0.2 mg/ml[a]	Physically compatible with no change in measured turbidity or increase in particle content in 4 hr at 23 °C	2224	C
Dopamine HCl	DU	1.6 mg/ml[a]	MN	0.5[a] and 5 mg/ml	Visually compatible for 24 hr at 21 °C	1523	C

Y-Site Injection Compatibility (1:1 Mixture) (Cont.)

			Haloperidol lactate				
Drug	*Mfr*	*Conc*	*Mfr*	*Conc*	*Remarks*	*Ref*	*C/I*
Doxorubicin HCl liposome injection	SEQ	0.4 mg/ml[a]	MN	0.2 mg/ml[a]	Physically compatible with little or no change in measured turbidity and no increase in particle content in 4 hr at 23 °C	2087	C
Etoposide phosphate	BR	5 mg/ml[a]	MN	0.2 mg/ml[a]	Physically compatible with no change in measured turbidity or increase in particle content in 4 hr at 23 °C	2218	C
Famotidine	MSD	0.267 mg/ml[a]	MN	0.5[a] and 5 mg/ml	Visually compatible for 24 hr at 21 °C	1523	C
	ME	2 mg/ml[b]		0.2 mg/ml[a]	Visually compatible for 4 hr at 22 °C	1936	C
Fentanyl citrate	JN	0.025 mg/ml[a]	MN	0.2 mg/ml[a]	Physically compatible with no change in measured haze or increase in particle content in 48 hr at 22 °C	1706	C
Filgrastim	AMG	30 μg/ml[a]	MN	0.2 mg/ml[a]	Physically compatible with no change in measured turbidity or increase in particle content in 4 hr at 22 °C	1687	C
Fluconazole	RR	2 mg/ml	MN	5 mg/ml	Precipitate forms	1407	I
Fludarabine phosphate	BX	1 mg/ml[a]	MN	0.2 mg/ml[a]	Physically compatible for 4 hr at room temperature under fluorescent light	1439	C
Foscarnet sodium	AST	24 mg/ml	LY	5 mg/ml	Delayed formation of fine white precipitate	1335	I
Gatifloxacin	BMS	2 mg/ml[a]	MN	0.2 mg/ml[a]	Physically compatible with no change in measured haze or increase in particle content in 4 hr at 23 °C	2234	C
Gemcitabine HCl	LI	10 mg/ml[b]	MN	0.2 mg/ml[b]	Physically compatible with no change in measured turbidity or increase in particle content in 4 hr at 23 °C	2226	C
Granisetron HCl	SKB	0.05 mg/ml[a]	MN	0.2 mg/ml[a]	Physically compatible with no change in measured turbidity or increase in particle content in 4 hr at 23 °C	2000	C
Heparin sodium	OR	25,000 and 50,000 units/ 250 ml[e]	MN	5 mg/1 ml[d]	White precipitate forms immediately	779	I
		50 units/ml[b,f]	JN	5 mg/1 ml[g]	White turbidity	1053	I
Hetastarch in lactated electrolyte injection (Hextend)	AB	6%	MN	0.2 mg/ml[a]	Physically compatible with no change in measured turbidity or increase in particle content in 4 hr at 23 °C	2339	C
Hydromorphone HCl	AST	0.5 mg/ml[a]	MN	0.2 mg/ml[a]	Physically compatible with no change in measured haze or increase in particle content in 48 hr at 22 °C	1706	C
Lidocaine HCl	AB	4 mg/ml[a]	MN	0.5[a] and 5 mg/ml	Visually compatible for 24 hr at 21 °C	1523	C
Linezolid	PHU	2 mg/ml	MN	0.2 mg/ml[a]	Physically compatible with no change in measured turbidity or increase in particle content in 4 hr at 23 °C	2264	C
Lorazepam	WY	0.33 mg/ml[b]	JN	0.5 and 5 mg/ ml	Visually compatible for 24 hr at 22 °C	1855	C
Melphalan HCl	BW	0.1 mg/ml[b]	MN	0.2 mg/ml[b]	Physically compatible with no change in measured turbidity or increase in particle content in 3 hr at 22 °C	1557	C

Y-Site Injection Compatibility (1:1 Mixture) (Cont.)

Drug	Mfr	Conc	Mfr	Conc	Remarks	Ref	C/I
			Haloperidol lactate				
Methadone HCl	LI	1 mg/ml[a]	MN	0.2 mg/ml[a]	Physically compatible with no change in measured haze or increase in particle content in 48 hr at 22 °C	1706	C
Midazolam HCl	RC	5 mg/ml	JN	0.5 and 5 mg/ml	Visually compatible for 24 hr at 22 °C	1855	C
Morphine sulfate	AST	1 mg/ml[a]	MN	0.2 mg/ml[a]	Physically compatible with no change in measured haze or increase in particle content in 48 hr at 22 °C	1706	C
Nitroglycerin	DU	0.4 mg/ml[a]	MN	0.5[a] and 5 mg/ml	Visually compatible for 24 hr at 21 °C	1523	C
Norepinephrine bitartrate	WI	0.032 mg/ml[a]	MN	0.5[a] and 5 mg/ml	Visually compatible for 24 hr at 21 °C	1523	C
Ondansetron HCl	GL	1 mg/ml[b]	LY	0.2 mg/ml[a]	Physically compatible for 4 hr at 22 °C	1365	C
Paclitaxel	NCI	1.2 mg/ml[a]		0.2 mg/ml[a]	Physically compatible with no change in measured turbidity in 4 hr at 22 °C	1528	C
Phenylephrine HCl	WB	0.02 mg/ml[a]	MN	0.5[a] and 5 mg/ml	Visually compatible for 24 hr at 21 °C	1523	C
Piperacillin sodium–tazobactam sodium	LE	40 + 5 mg/ml[a]	MN	0.2 mg/ml[a]	White turbidity and particles form immediately	1688	I
Propofol	ZEN	10 mg/ml	MN	0.2 mg/ml[a]	Physically compatible for 1 hr at 23 °C with no increase in particle content	2066	C
Remifentanil HCl	GW	0.025 and 0.25 mg/ml[b]	MN	0.2 mg/ml[a]	Physically compatible with no change in measured turbidity or increase in particle content in 4 hr at 23 °C	2075	C
Sargramostim	IMM	10 μg/ml[b]	LY	0.2 mg/ml[b]	Small particles formed in 4 hr in one of two samples	1436	I
Sodium nitroprusside	AB	0.2 mg/ml[h]	MN	5 mg/ml	Turbidity forms immediately and persists, developing fine precipitate in 24 hr at 21 °C under fluorescent light	1523	I
	AB	0.2 mg/ml[h]	MN	0.5 mg/ml[a]	Visually compatible for 24 hr at 21 °C	1523	C
Sufentanil citrate	JN	12.5 μg/ml[a]	MN	0.2 mg/ml[a]	Physically compatible with no subvisual haze or particle formation in 24 hr at 23 °C	1711	C
Tacrolimus	FUJ	1 mg/ml[b]	SO	2.5 mg/ml[a]	Visually compatible for 24 hr at 25 °C	1630	C
Teniposide	BR	0.1 mg/ml[a]	MN	0.2 mg/ml[a]	Physically compatible with no subvisual haze or particle formation in 4 hr at 23 °C	1725	C
Theophylline	TR	1.6 mg/ml[a]	MN	0.5[a] and 5 mg/ml	Visually compatible for 24 hr at 21 °C	1523	C
Thiotepa	IMM[i]	1 mg/ml[b]	MN	0.2 mg/ml[b]	Physically compatible with no change in measured turbidity or increase in particle content in 4 hr at 23 °C	1861	C
TNA #218 to #226[j]			MN	0.2 mg/ml[a]	Damage to emulsion integrity occurs immediately with free oil formation possible	2215	I
TPN #189[j]			SE	10 mg/ml	Visually compatible for 24 hr at 22 °C	1767	C

Y-Site Injection Compatibility (1:1 Mixture) (Cont.)

			Haloperidol lactate				
Drug	*Mfr*	*Conc*	*Mfr*	*Conc*	*Remarks*	*Ref*	*C/I*
TPN #212 to #215[j]			MN	0.2 mg/ml[a]	Physically compatible with no change in measured turbidity or increase in particle content in 4 hr at 23 °C	2109	C
Vinorelbine tartrate	BW	1 mg/ml[b]	MN	0.2 mg/ml[b]	Physically compatible with no change in measured turbidity or increase in particle content in 4 hr at 22 °C	1558	C

[a]*Tested in dextrose 5% in water.*
[b]*Tested in sodium chloride 0.9%.*
[c]*Tested in bacteriostatic sodium chloride 0.9% preserved with benzyl alcohol 0.9%.*
[d]*Injected over one minute.*
[e]*Tested in both dextrose 5% in water and sodium chloride 0.9%. Run at 1000 units/hr.*
[f]*Run at 1 ml/min.*
[g]*Given over three minutes.*
[h]*Tested in sterile water for injection.*
[i]*Lyophilized formulation tested.*
[j]*Refer to Appendix I for the composition of parenteral nutrition solutions. TNA indicates a 3-in-1 admixture, and TPN indicates a 2-in-1 admixture.*

Additional Compatibility Information

Buprenorphine HCl — Haloperidol lactate is stated to be physically and chemically compatible with buprenorphine HCl. (4)

Heparin — Heparin sodium forms a precipitate when combined with haloperidol lactate. (779; 1053) It has been recommended that heparin infusions be stopped and that lines be flushed with sodium chloride 0.9% or dextrose 5% in water before and after injecting haloperidol lactate into an injection port. Administration of haloperidol lactate through a heparin lock would require a similar flushing procedure. (779)

HEPARIN SODIUM
AHFS 20:12.04

Products — Heparin sodium derived from beef lung or porcine intestinal mucosa is available from various manufacturers in concentrations ranging from 1000 to 20,000 units/ml, packaged in sizes ranging from 0.5- to 1-ml ampuls, vials, or prefilled syringes to 30-ml multiple-dose vials. Benzyl alcohol or parabens may also be present as preservatives, and hydrochloric acid and/or sodium hydroxide may have been added to adjust pH. Sodium chloride may have been added to some products for isotonicity. In addition, dilute solutions of 10 and 100 units/ml in 1- to 5-ml disposable syringes and 1- to 30-ml vials are available for use in flushing heparin locks. (4; 29)

Heparin sodium is also available premixed in various concentrations in sodium chloride 0.45 and 0.9% and dextrose 5% in water. (4; 154)

pH — Heparin sodium injection has a pH of 5 to 8. Heparin lock flush solution is adjusted to pH 5 to 7.5. (4)

Osmolality — The osmolality of heparin sodium (Elkins-Sinn) 1000 units/ml was determined to be 384 mOsm/kg by freezing-point depression and 283 mOsm/kg by vapor pressure. (1071)

One heparin lock flush solution is reported to have an osmolarity of 392 mOsm/L. (4)

Commercial heparin sodium infusion solutions in sodium chloride 0.9% and dextrose 5% in water have osmolalities of 322 and 270 mOsm/kg, respectively. (4)

Administration — Heparin sodium may be administered by deep subcutaneous injection, by intermittent intravenous injection undiluted or diluted in 50 to 100 ml of dextrose 5% in water or sodium chloride 0.9%, or by continuous intravenous infusion in a liter of compatible solution, preferably using an electronic rate-control device. The container should be inverted at least six times after heparin sodium addition to prevent pooling of the heparin. Intramuscular injection should not be used because of pain and hematoma formation. (2; 4)

Stability — Heparin sodium solutions are colorless to slightly yellow. (4) Heparin sodium solution should not be used if it is discolored or contains a precipitate. (2) Heparin sodium should be stored at controlled room temperature (2; 4) and protected from freezing and temperatures exceeding 40 °C. (2; 4; 21) Heparin sodium retains its activity during autoclaving. (1492) In a study of hospital-manufactured heparin sodium 1 unit/ml in sodium chloride 0.9%, full anticoagulant activity was retained for at least 12 months after sterilization by autoclaving and subsequent storage at room temperature exposed to daylight. (675)

In another study, heparin sodium solutions of 10 to 35,000 units/

ml in distilled water at pH 7 to 8 were stable for 15 years at 4 °C and for seven years at 18 °C. (243)

pH Effects—A pH profile of heparin sodium (Abbott) 20,000 units/L in dextrose 5% in water over a pH range of 3.8 to 7.6 did not reveal a potency loss during the 24-hour study. (21) In another report, heparin sodium in sodium chloride 0.9% was tested at pH 3.2 (adjusted with hydrochloric acid) and 9.2 (adjusted with sodium hydroxide). No loss of potency was noted in 24 hours. (57) However, a pH profile of heparin sodium 660 units/ml, when autoclaved for 10 minutes at 10 pounds/inch^2 at 115 °C, showed loss of activity at pH values above 8.5 and especially below 5. (243)

Syringes—The stability of 50 ml of a 500-unit/ml heparin sodium solution in sodium chloride 0.9% packaged in 50-ml polypropylene syringes was studied. Storage both at room temperature and at 0 to 4 °C showed an overall trend to lower activity by about 8% after three weeks.

When glass containers were compared to plastic syringes, the glass containers consistently showed lower retained activity in as little as two hours after preparation. The possibility of adsorption to glass surfaces was noted (676) but has not been demonstrated. (See Sorption below.)

Heparin sodium 1 unit/ml, prefilled into Injekt (Braun) all-plastic syringes having polyethylene barrels and polypropylene plungers, showed no significant activity loss over 52 weeks at 37 °C due to decomposition or sorption. However, plastic syringes with rubber-tipped plungers, such as Plastipak (Becton-Dickinson) and Perfusor (Braun), exhibited extra ultraviolet peaks, presumably due to leaching of rubber components. (1491)

Heparin sodium (Leo) 300 units/ml in dextrose 5% in water or water for injection was drawn into 50-ml polypropylene syringes (Plastipak, Becton-Dickinson) and stored for eight hours at room temperature and 4 °C. HPLC analysis found no loss in either solvent. (1799)

The stability of heparin sodium repackaged in 10-ml polypropylene syringes for use in CADD-Micro syringe pumps was evaluated. Ten milliliters of heparin sodium 1000 units/ml (Elkins-Sinn) and 40,000 units/ml (Schein) were packaged in the test syringes and capped. Syringes were stored at a near-body temperature of 30 °C for 30 days. HPLC analysis found little or no loss of heparin sodium content; actual activity in prolonging blood clotting was not evaluated. (2275)

Elastomeric Reservoir Pumps—Heparin sodium 3250 units/ml in sodium chloride 0.9% in Infusor elastomeric reservoir pumps has been stated by the pump manufacturer to be stable for seven days at room temperature and 14 days under refrigeration. (31)

Sorption—No measurable adsorption of heparin sodium to the surface of glass containers occurred during a study of admixture compatibility. (407)

Heparin sodium, BP, 2000 units/2 ml was stored for 18 hours at room temperature in the following plastic syringes: Brunswick (Sherwood Medical), Plastipak (Becton-Dickinson), Steriseal (Needle Industries), and Sabre (Gillette U.K.). The first three syringes have polypropylene barrels; the Sabre has a combination polypropylene–polystyrene barrel. No significant loss of heparin occurred due to sorption. (784)

Heparin sodium (Leo) 300 units/ml in dextrose 5% in water or water for injection was delivered at 4 ml/hr by syringe pump through PVC and polyethylene-lined PVC infusion tubing for 12 hours at room temperature. HPLC analysis found no loss due to sorption to the polyethylene-lined tubing. However, losses of about 15 to 25% occurred with the PVC tubing and were especially high during the first 15 minutes of infusion. (1799)

Heparin sodium (B. Braun) 7 units/ml in dextrose 5% in water and sodium chloride 0.9% packaged in PVC, polyethylene, and glass containers exhibited little or no loss due to sorption to any of the container types when stored at 4 and 22 °C for 24 hours protected from light. (2289)

Filtration—Heparin sodium (Abbott) 10,000 units/L in dextrose 5% in water and sodium chloride 0.9% was filtered at 120 ml/hr for six hours through a 0.22-μm cellulose ester membrane filter (Ivex-2). No significant reduction in potency due to binding to the filter was noted. (533)

Central Venous Catheter—Heparin sodium (Elkins-Sinn) 100 units/ml in dextrose 5% in water was found to be compatible with the ARROWg+ard Blue Plus (Arrow International) chlorhexidine-bearing triple-lumen central catheter. HPLC analysis was used to evaluate completeness of drug delivery through the catheter and the amount of chlorhexidine removed from the internal lumens. Essentially complete delivery of the drug was found with little or no drug loss occurring. Furthermore, chlorhexidine delivered from the catheter remained at trace amounts with no substantial increase due to the delivery of the drug through the catheter. (2335)

Compatibility Information

Solution Compatibility

Heparin sodium

Solution	*Mfr*	*Mfr*	*Conc/L*	*Remarks*	*Ref*	*C/I*
Amino acids 4.25%, dextrose 25%	MG	RI	20,000 units	No increase in particulate matter in 24 hr at 5 °C	349	C
Dextran 40,000	PH			Physically compatible	44	C
Dextran 6% in dextrose 5%	AB	AB	1000 and 4000 units	Physically compatible	3	C

Solution Compatibility (Cont.)

Solution	Mfr	Heparin sodium Mfr	Conc/L	Remarks	Ref	C/I
Dextran 6% in sodium chloride 0.9%	AB	AB	1000 and 4000 units	Physically compatible	3	C
Dextrose–Ringer's injection combinations	AB	AB	1000 and 4000 units	Physically compatible	3	C
Dextrose–Ringer's injection, lactated, combinations	AB	AB	1000 and 4000 units	Physically compatible	3	C
Dextrose 5% in Ringer's injection, lactated	TR[a]	UP	10,000 units	Potency retained for 24 hr at 5 °C	282	C
Dextrose–saline combinations	AB	AB	1000 and 4000 units	Physically compatible	3	C
Dextrose 2.5% in sodium chloride 0.45%	BA	DB	1000 units	Heparin activity retained for 12 months at 4 °C	1914	C
Dextrose 3.75% in sodium chloride 0.2%	BA	DB	1000 units	Heparin activity retained for 12 months at 4 and 22 °C	1914	C
Dextrose 4.3% in sodium chloride 0.18%		OR	20,000 units	40% potency loss within 1 hr at 23 °C	113	I
		AH	35,000 units	Apparent temporary 50% loss of heparin activity in 4 to 6 hr with recovery in 8 hr at 25 °C. Heparin activity then maintained for 14 days at 4 °C	900	?
Dextrose 5% in sodium chloride 0.45%	TR	AB	20,000 units	No decrease in activity in 24 hr at room temperature	407	C
Dextrose 5% in sodium chloride 0.9%			12,000 units	Physically compatible	74	C
			32,000 units	Potency retained for 24 hr	57	C
	AB	AB	20,000 units	Potency retained for 24 hr	21	C
	AB		20,000 units	Potency retained for 72 hr	46	C
	TR[a]	UP	10,000 units	Potency retained for 24 hr at 5 °C	282	C
	BA		30,000 units	40% potency loss in 5 hr at 15, 25, and 35 °C. Activity recovered 5 to 7 hr later	674	I
Dextrose 2½% in water	AB	AB	1000 and 4000 units	Physically compatible	3	C
Dextrose 5% in water			12,000 units	Physically compatible	74	C
	AB	AB	1000 and 4000 units	Physically compatible	3	C

Solution Compatibility (Cont.)

Heparin sodium

Solution	*Mfr*	*Mfr*	*Conc/L*	*Remarks*	*Ref*	*C/I*
	BP		40,000 units	Potency retained for 24 hr at 23 °C	252	C
			32,000 units	Potency retained for 24 hr	57	C
	AB	AB	20,000 units	Potency retained for 24 hr	21	C
	AB		20,000 units	Potency retained for 72 hr	46	C
	TR[b]	OR	20,000 and 40,000 units	Potency retained for 48 hr at 27 °C	254	C
	TR[a]	UP	10,000 units	Potency retained for 24 hr at 5 °C	282	C
	TR	AS	20,000 units	No decrease in activity in 24 hr at room temperature	407	C
		OR	20,000 units	50% potency loss within 1 hr at 23 °C	113	I
	MG	UP	10,000 units	30 to 50% activity loss in 6 hr at room temperature. Partial rebound in 24 hr	406	I
	BA		30,000 units	65% potency loss in 5 hr at 15, 25, and 35 °C. Activity recovered in 24 to 48 hr	674	I
		AH	35,000 units	Apparent temporary 50% loss of heparin activity in 4 hr with recovery in 6 hr at 25 °C. Heparin activity then maintained for 14 days at 4 °C	900	?
	BA	DB	1000 units	Heparin activity retained for 7 days at 22 °C	1914	C
	BA	DB	10,000 units	Heparin activity retained for 12 months at 22 °C	1914	C
	BA[b]	BRN	7000 units	Visually compatible with about 5% loss by HPLC in 24 hr at 22 °C but little or no loss at 4 °C	2289	C
	BRN[d]	BRN	7000 units	Visually compatible with little or no loss by HPLC in 24 hr at 4 and 22 °C	2289	C
Dextrose 10% in water	AB	AB	1000 and 4000 units	Physically compatible	3	C
	MG	UP	10,000 units	40% activity loss in 6 hr at room temperature. Partial rebound at 24 hr	406	I
Dextrose 25% in water		LY	5000 units	About 6% heparin activity loss in 21 days and 11% loss in 28 days at 4 °C	2025	C
Fructose 10% in sodium chloride 0.9%	AB	AB	1000 and 4000 units	Physically compatible	3	C
Fructose 10% in water	AB	AB	1000 and 4000 units	Physically compatible	3	C
Invert sugar 5 and 10% in sodium chloride 0.9%	AB	AB	1000 and 4000 units	Physically compatible	3	C

Solution Compatibility (Cont.)

Heparin sodium

Solution	*Mfr*	*Mfr*	*Conc/L*	*Remarks*	*Ref*	*C/I*
Invert sugar 5 and 10% in water	AB	AB	1000 and 4000 units	Physically compatible	3	C
Ionosol products	AB	AB	1000 and 4000 units	Physically compatible	3	C
Normosol R	AB	AB	20,000 units	Potency retained for 24 hr	21	C
Ringer's injection	AB	AB	1000 and 4000 units	Physically compatible	3	C
Ringer's injection, lactated	AB	AB	1000 and 4000 units	Physically compatible	3	C
			12,000 units	Physically compatible	74	C
	TR[a]	UP	10,000 units	Potency retained for 24 hr at 5 °C	282	C
		OR	20,000 units	40% potency loss within 1 hr at 23 °C	113	I
	MG	UP	10,000 units	50 to 60% activity loss in 6 hr at room temperature. Partial rebound at 24 hr	406	I
		AH	35,000 units	Apparent temporary 50% loss of heparin activity in 4 hr with recovery in 6 hr at 25 °C. Heparin activity gradually lost over 14 days	900	?
Sodium chloride 0.45%	AB	AB	1000 and 4000 units	Physically compatible	3	C
Sodium chloride 0.9%			12,000 units	Physically compatible	74	C
	AB	AB	1000 and 4000 units	Physically compatible	3	C
			32,000 units	Potency retained for 24 hr	57	C
	AB	AB	20,000 units	Potency retained for 24 hr	21	C
	AB		20,000 units	Potency retained for 72 hr	46	C
	TR[a]	UP	10,000 units	Potency retained for 24 hr at 5 °C	282	C
	TR[b]	OR	20,000 and 40,000 units	Potency retained for 48 hr at 27 °C	254	C
		AH	35,000 units	Heparin activity stable for 24 hr at 25 °C followed by 14 days at 4 °C	900	C

Solution Compatibility (Cont.)

Heparin sodium

Solution	*Mfr*	*Mfr*	*Conc/L*	*Remarks*	*Ref*	*C/I*
	MG	UP	10,000 units	30 to 50% activity loss in 6 hr at room temperature. Partial rebound at 24 hr	406	I
	BA	DB	1000 units	Heparin activity retained for 12 months at 22 °C	1914	C
	BA	DB	10,000 units	Heparin activity retained for 12 months at 4 and 22 °C	1914	C
		LY	5000 units	Heparin activity retained for 28 days at 4 °C	2025	C
	BA[b]	BRN	7000 units	Visually compatible with about 5% loss by HPLC in 24 hr at 22 °C but little or no loss at 4 °C	2289	C
	BRN[d]	BRN	7000 units	Visually compatible with little or no loss by HPLC in 24 hr at 4 and 22 °C	2289	C
Sodium lactate ⅙ M		OR	20,000 units	50% potency loss within 1 hr at 23 °C	113	I
TPN #48 to #51[c]		AH	35,000 units	Heparin activity retained for 24 hr at 25 °C but significantly decreased after 24 hr	900	C
TPN #205[c]		LY	3000 to 20,000 units	Heparin activity retained for 28 days at 4 °C	2025	C

[a]*Tested in both glass and PVC containers.*
[b]*Tested in PVC containers.*
[c]*Refer to Appendix I for the composition of parenteral nutrition solutions. TPN indicates a 2-in-1 admixture.*
[d]*Tested in polyethylene and glass containers.*

Additive Compatibility

Heparin sodium

Drug	*Mfr*	*Conc/L*	*Mfr*	*Conc/L*	*Test Soln*	*Remarks*	*Ref*	*C/I*
Alteplase	GEN	0.5 g	ES	40,000 units	NS	Heparin interacts with alteplase. Opalescence forms within 5 min with peak intensity at 4 hr at 25 °C. Alteplase activity reduced slightly	1856	I
Amikacin sulfate	BR	5 g	AB	30,000 units	D5LR, D5R, D5S, D5W, D10W, IS10, LR, NS, R, SL	Immediate precipitation	294	I
Aminophylline		250 mg		12,000 units	D5W	Physically compatible	74	C
	SE	1 g	UP	4000 units	D5W	Physically compatible	15	C
Amphotericin B	SQ	100 mg	AB	4000 units	D	Physically compatible	21	C
	SQ	100 mg	AB	4000 units	D5W	Physically compatible	15	C
Amphotericin B with hydrocortisone sodium phosphate	SQ MSD	50 mg 50 and 100 mg	AB	1500 units	D5W	Physically compatible and amphotericin B bioactivity retained in normal light at 25 °C for 24 hr. Hydrocortisone and heparin activity not tested	540	C

Additive Compatibility (Cont.)

Heparin sodium

Drug	*Mfr*	*Conc/L*	*Mfr*	*Conc/L*	*Test Soln*	*Remarks*	*Ref*	*C/I*
Amphotericin B with hydrocortisone sodium phosphate	SQ MSD	100 mg 50 and 100 mg	AB	1500 units	D5W	Physically compatible and amphotericin B bioactivity retained in normal light at 25 °C for 24 hr. Hydrocortisone and heparin activity not tested	540	C
Ampicillin sodium		2 g		32,000 units	NS	Physically compatible and heparin activity retained for 24 hr	57	C
	BE	10 g	OR	20,000 units	NS	Potency of both retained for 24 hr at 25 °C	113	C
	BR	1 g		12,000 units	D10W, LR, NS	Ampicillin potency retained for 24 hr at 4 °C	87	C
	BR	1 g		12,000 units	D5S	15% ampicillin decomposition in 24 hr at 4 °C	87	I
	BR	1 g		12,000 units	D5S, D10W, LR	20 to 25% ampicillin decomposition in 24 hr at 25 °C	87	I
Ascorbic acid injection	UP	500 mg	UP	4000 units	D5W	Physically compatible	15	C
Atracurium besylate	BW	500 mg		40,000 units	D5W	Particles form at 5 and 30 °C	1694	I
Bleomycin sulfate	BR	20 and 30 units	RI	10,000 to 200,000 units	NS	Physically compatible and bleomycin activity retained for 1 week at 4 °C. Heparin not tested	763	C
Calcium gluconate		1 g		12,000 units	D5W	Physically compatible	74	C
	UP	1 g	UP	4000 units	D5W	Physically compatible	15	C
	UP	1 g	AB	20,000 units		Physically compatible	21	C
Cefepime HCl	BR	4 g	MG	10,000 and 50,000 units	D5W, NS	Visually compatible with 4% cefepime loss by HPLC in 24 hr at room temperature and 3% loss in 7 days at 5 °C. Little or no heparin loss	1681	C
Chloramphenicol sodium succinate	PD	500 mg		12,000 units	D5W	Physically compatible	74	C
	PD	10 g	UP	4000 units	D5W	Physically compatible	15	C
	PD	1 g	AB	20,000 units		Physically compatible	6; 21	C
Cibenzoline succinate		2 g	ES	40,000 units	D5W, NS	Physically compatible for 24 hr at 25 °C by visual and microscopic examination	1182	C
Ciprofloxacin	BAY	2 g	CP	10,000, 100,000, and 1 million units	NS	White precipitate forms immediately	1934	I
	MI	2 g		4100 units	NS	Physically incompatible	888	I

Additive Compatibility (Cont.)

Heparin sodium

Drug	*Mfr*	*Conc/L*	*Mfr*	*Conc/L*	*Test Soln*	*Remarks*	*Ref*	*C/I*
	MI	2 g		8300 units	NS	Physically incompatible	888	I
Clindamycin phosphate	UP	9 g		100,000 units	D5W	Clindamycin stability maintained for 24 hr	101	C
Colistimethate sodium	WC	500 mg	AB	20,000 units	D	Physically compatible	21	C
	WC	500 mg	UP	4000 units	D5W	Physically compatible	15	C
Cytarabine	UP	500 mg		10,000 units	NS	Haze formation	174	I
	UP	500 mg		20,000 units	D5W	Haze formation	174	I
Daunorubicin HCl	FA	200 mg	UP	4000 units	D5W	Physically incompatible	15	I
Dimenhydrinate	SE	50 mg		12,000 units	D5W	Physically compatible	74	C
	SE	500 mg	UP	4000 units	D5W	Physically compatible	15	C
	SE	50 mg	AB	20,000 units	D	Physically compatible	21	C
Dobutamine HCl	LI	1 g	ES	40,000 units	D5W, NS	Physically compatible with no color change in 24 hr at 25 °C	789	C
	LI	1 g	LY	50,000 units	D5W, NS	Physically compatible for 24 hr at 21 °C	812	C
	LI	1 g	ES	5 million units	D5W, NS	Pink discoloration within 6 hr at 21 °C	812	I
	LI	1 g	ES	50,000 units	D5W	Heparin added to D5W and then mixed with an equal volume of dobutamine in D5W. Precipitate forms within 3 min	841	I
	LI	1.5 g	LY	50,000 units	D5W, NS	Obvious precipitation	1318	I
	LI	900 mg	LY	50,000 units	D5W, W	Physically compatible for 4 hr, but heat of reaction detected by microcalorimetry	1318	I
	LI	900 mg	LY	50,000 units	NS	Physically compatible for 4 hr with no heat of reaction detected by microcalorimetry	1318	C
Dopamine HCl	AS	800 mg	AB	200,000 units	D5W	No dopamine or heparin decomposition in 24 hr at 25 °C	312	C
Enalaprilat	MSD	12 mg	ES	50,000 units	D5W[a]	Visually compatible with little or no enalaprilat loss by HPLC in 24 hr at room temperature under fluorescent light. Heparin not tested	1572	C
Erythromycin lactobionate	AB	1 g	AB	1500 units		Precipitate forms within 1 hr	20	I
	AB	5 g	UP	4000 units	D5W	Physically incompatible	15	I
	AB	1.5 g	OR	20,000 units	D5W, NS	Precipitate forms	113	I
	AB	1 g	AB	20,000 units		Precipitate forms within 1 hr	21	I

Additive Compatibility (Cont.)

Heparin sodium

Drug	*Mfr*	*Conc/L*	*Mfr*	*Conc/L*	*Test Soln*	*Remarks*	*Ref*	*C/I*
Esmolol HCl	DU	6 g	LY	50,000 units	D5W	Physically compatible with no esmolol loss in 24 hr at room temperature under fluorescent light. Heparin not tested	1358	C
Floxacillin sodium	BE	20 g	WED	20,000 units	NS	Physically compatible for 24 hr at 15 and 30 °C. Haze forms in 48 hr at 30 °C. No change at 15 °C	1479	C
Fluconazole	PF	1 g	BA	50,000 units	D5W	Fluconazole chemically stable by gas chromatography for at least 24 hr at 25 °C under fluorescent light. Heparin not tested	1676	C
Flumazenil	RC	20 mg	ES	50,000 units	D5W[a]	Visually compatible with 4% flumazenil loss by HPLC in 24 hr at 23 °C under fluorescent light. Heparin not tested	1710	C
Furosemide	HO	1 g	WED	20,000 units	NS	Physically compatible for 72 hr at 15 and 30 °C	1479	C
Gentamicin sulfate		320 mg	BP	20,000 units	D5W, NS	Immediate precipitation	26	I
	SC	1 g	OR	20,000 units	D5W, NS	Opalescence	113	I
	ME	88 mg	BRN	1000 to 6000 units	D10W, NS	Activity of both drugs by biological assays greatly reduced	1570	I
Hyaluronidase						Physically incompatible	10	I
	WY					Physically incompatible	9	I
Hydrocortisone sodium phosphate with amphotericin B	MSD SQ	50 and 100 mg 50 mg	AB	1500 units	D5W	Physically compatible and amphotericin B bioactivity retained in normal light at 25 °C for 24 hr. Hydrocortisone and heparin activity not tested	540	C
Hydrocortisone sodium phosphate with amphotericin B	MSD SQ	50 and 100 mg 100 mg	AB	1500 units	D5W	Physically compatible and amphotericin B bioactivity retained in normal light at 25 °C for 24 hr. Hydrocortisone and heparin activity not tested	540	C
Hydrocortisone sodium succinate		800 mg		32,000 units	NS	Physically compatible and heparin activity retained for 24 hr	57	C
						Physically incompatible	9	I
	UP	500 mg	UP	4000 units	D5W	Physically incompatible	15	I
Isoproterenol HCl		2 mg		32,000 units	NS	Physically compatible and heparin activity retained for 24 hr	57	C
	WI	4 mg	AB	20,000 units		Physically compatible	59	C
Kanamycin sulfate	BR	4 g	UP	4000 units	D5W	Physically incompatible	15	I
	BR	500 mg	AB	20,000 units		Precipitate forms within 1 hr	21	I
	TE	2 g	OR	20,000 units	D5W, NS	Precipitate forms	113	I

Additive Compatibility (Cont.)

Heparin sodium

Drug	*Mfr*	*Conc/L*	*Mfr*	*Conc/L*	*Test Soln*	*Remarks*	*Ref*	*C/I*
	BR	250 mg		12,000 units	D5S, D5W, D10W, IM, IP, LR, NS	Immediate precipitation	87	**I**
	BPC	4 g	BP	20,000 units	D5W, NS	Immediate precipitation	26	**I**
Levorphanol bitartrate	RC					Physically incompatible	9	**I**
Lidocaine HCl		4 g		32,000 units	NS	Physically compatible and heparin activity retained for 24 hr	57	**C**
	AST	2 g	AB	20,000 units		Physically compatible	24	**C**
Lincomycin HCl	UP	600 mg	AB	20,000 units		Physically compatible	21	**C**
Magnesium sulfate		130 mEq		50,000 units	NS[b]	Visually compatible with heparin activity retained for 14 days at 24 °C under fluorescent light	1908	**C**
Meperidine HCl	WI					Physically incompatible	9	**I**
Meropenem	ZEN	1 and 20 g	ES	20,000 units	NS	Visually compatible for 4 hr at room temperature	1994	**C**
Methyldopate HCl	MSD	1 g	AB	20,000 units	D, D–S, S	Physically compatible	23	**C**
Methylprednisolone sodium succinate	UP	40 mg		10,000 units	D5S	Clear solution for 24 hr	329	**C**
	UP	125 mg		5000 units	D5S, D5W, LR, R	Clear solution for 24 hr	329	**C**
	UP	25 g		40,000 units	NS	Clear solution for 24 hr	329	**C**
Metronidazole HCl with sodium bicarbonate	SE AB	5 g 50 mEq	UP	30,000 units	D5W, NS	Physically compatible for 48 hr	765	**C**
Mitomycin	BR	167 mg	ES	33,300 units	NS[b]	Visually compatible with 10% mitomycin loss calculated in 21 hr and no decrease in heparin bioactivity at 25 °C	1866	**I**
	BR	167 mg	ES	33,300 units	NS[a]	Visually compatible with 10% mitomycin loss calculated in 25 hr and no decrease in heparin bioactivity at 25 °C	1866	**C**
	BR	500 mg	ES	33,300 units	NS[b]	Visually compatible with 10% mitomycin loss calculated in 42 hr and no decrease in heparin bioactivity at 25 °C	1866	**C**
	BR	500 mg	ES	33,300 units	NS[a]	Visually compatible with 10% mitomycin loss calculated in 61 hr and no decrease in heparin bioactivity at 25 °C	1866	**C**
Morphine sulfate						Physically incompatible	9	**I**
Nafcillin sodium	WY	500 mg	AB, WY	20,000 units		Physically compatible	27	**C**
	WY	500 mg	AB	20,000 units		Physically compatible	21	**C**

Additive Compatibility (Cont.)

Heparin sodium

Drug	*Mfr*	*Conc/L*	*Mfr*	*Conc/L*	*Test Soln*	*Remarks*	*Ref*	*C/I*
Norepinephrine bitartrate	WI	8 mg		12,000 units	D5W	Physically compatible	74	C
	WI	8 mg	AB	20,000 units	D, D–S, S	Physically compatible	77	C
Octreotide acetate	SZ	1.5 mg	ES	1000 units	TPN #120[c]	Little octreotide loss over 48 hr at room temperature in ambient light	1373	C
Penicillin G[d]		20 million units		32,000 units	NS	Physically compatible and heparin activity retained for 24 hr	57	C
Penicillin G potassium		1 million units		12,000 units	D5W	Physically compatible	74	C
	SQ	1 million units	AB	20,000 units	D5W	Penicillin potency retained for 24 hr at 25 °C	47	C
		20 million units		32,000 units	NS	Physically compatible and heparin activity retained for 24 hr	57	C
	SQ	20 million units		4000 units	D5W	Physically incompatible	15	I
Penicillin G sodium	BE	20 million units	OR	20,000 units	NS	Potency of both retained for 24 hr at 25 °C	113	C
	UP	20 million units	UP	4000 units	D5W	Physically incompatible	15	I
Polymyxin B sulfate	BP	20 mg	BP	20,000 units	D5W	Immediate precipitation	26	I
	BP	20 mg	BP	20,000 units	NS	Haze develops over 3 hr	26	I
Potassium chloride		3 g		12,000 units	D5W	Physically compatible	74	C
	AB	40 mEq	AB	20,000 units		Physically compatible	21	C
		80 mEq		32,000 units	NS	Physically compatible and heparin activity retained for 24 hr	57	C
Promazine HCl	WY	100 mg	AB	20,000 units		Physically compatible	21	C
Promethazine HCl	WY	250 mg	UP	4000 units	D5W	Physically incompatible	15	I
Ranitidine HCl	GL	2 g	ES	10,000 and 40,000 units	D5W, NS[a]	Physically compatible with 2% or less ranitidine loss in 48 hr at room temperature under fluorescent light. Heparin not tested	1361	C
	GL	50 mg	ES	10,000 and 40,000 units	NS[a]	Physically compatible with no ranitidine loss in 48 hr at room temperature under fluorescent light. Heparin not tested	1361	C

Additive Compatibility (Cont.)

Heparin sodium

Drug	*Mfr*	*Conc/L*	*Mfr*	*Conc/L*	*Test Soln*	*Remarks*	*Ref*	*C/I*
	GL	50 mg	ES	10,000 and 40,000 units	D5W[a]	Physically compatible with 7% ranitidine loss in 24 hr and about 12% loss in 48 hr at room temperature under fluorescent light. Heparin not tested	1361	C
Sodium bicarbonate	AB	2.4 mEq[e]	AB	20,000 units	D5W	Physically compatible for 24 hr	772	C
Streptomycin sulfate						Physically incompatible	9	I
		1 g	AB	20,000 units		Precipitate forms within 1 hr	21	I
	BP	4 g	BP	20,000 units	D5W, NS	Immediate precipitation	26	I
Teicoplanin	HO	2 g	CPP	20,000 and 40,000 units	D5W, NS	Visually compatible with no loss of teicoplanin by HPLC and microbiological assay and no loss of heparin activity in 24 hr at 25 °C	2165	C
Vancomycin HCl	LI	1 g		12,000 units	D5W	Immediate precipitation	74	I
	LE	400 mg	IX	1000 units	TPN #95[c]	Physically compatible and vancomycin content retained for 8 days at room temperature and under refrigeration by TDx	1321	C
	LI	15 mg to 5.3 g	OR	500 to 14,300 units	[f]	Physically compatible for 24 hr at 25 °C	1322	C
	LI	6.9 to 14.3 g	OR	500 to 14,300 units	[f]	Immediate white precipitation	1322	I
Verapamil HCl	KN	80 mg	ES	20,000 units	D5W, NS	Physically compatible for 24 hr	764	C
Vitamin B complex	WY	20 ml		32,000 units	NS	Physically compatible and heparin activity retained for 24 hr	57	C
Vitamin B complex with C		1 vial		12,000 units	D5W	Physically compatible	74	C
	AB	5 ml	UP	4000 units	D5W	Physically compatible	15	C
	AB	10 ml	AB	20,000 units		Physically compatible	21	C
	WY	4 ampuls		32,000 units	NS	Physically compatible and heparin activity retained for 24 hr	57	C

[a] *Tested in PVC containers.*
[b] *Tested in glass containers.*
[c] *Refer to Appendix I for the composition of parenteral nutrition solutions. TPN indicates a 2-in-1 admixture.*
[d] *Salt form unspecified.*
[e] *One vial of Neut added to a liter of admixture.*
[f] *Tested in Dianeal with dextrose 2.5 and 4.25%.*

Drugs in Syringe Compatibility

Heparin sodium

Drug (in syringe)	*Mfr*	*Amt*	*Mfr*	*Amt*	*Remarks*	*Ref*	*C/I*
Amikacin sulfate		100 mg		2500 units/ 1 ml	Turbidity or precipitate forms within 5 min	1053	I
Aminophylline		240 mg/ 10 ml		2500 units/ 1 ml	Physically compatible for at least 5 min	1053	C
Amiodarone HCl	LZ	150 mg/ 3 ml		2500 units/ 1 ml	Turbidity or precipitate forms within 5 min	1053	I
Amphotericin B		50 mg		2500 units/ 1 ml	Physically compatible for at least 5 min	1053	C
Ampicillin sodium		2 g		2500 units/ 1 ml	Physically compatible for at least 5 min	1053	C
Atropine sulfate		0.5 mg/ 1 ml		2500 units/ 1 ml	Physically compatible for at least 5 min	1053	C
Azlocillin sodium		2 g		2500 units/ 1 ml	Physically compatible for at least 5 min	1053	C
Bleomycin sulfate		1.5 units/ 0.5 ml		500 units/ 0.5 ml	Physically compatible for 5 min at room temperature followed by 8 min of centrifugation	980	C
Buprenorphine HCl	BM	300 mg/ 1 ml		2500 units/ 1 ml	Visually compatible for at least 5 min	1053	C
Cefamandole nafate	LI	2 g		2500 units/ 1 ml	Physically compatible for at least 5 min	1053	C
Cefazolin sodium		2 g		2500 units/ 1 ml	Physically compatible for at least 5 min	1053	C
Cefoperazone sodium	RR	2 g		2500 units/ 1 ml	Physically compatible for at least 5 min	1053	C
Cefotaxime sodium	HO	2 g		2500 units/ 1 ml	Physically compatible for at least 5 min	1053	C
Cefoxitin sodium	MSD	2 g		2500 units/ 1 ml	Physically compatible for at least 5 min	1053	C
Chloramphenicol sodium succinate	PD	1 g	AB	20,000 units/ 1 ml	Physically compatible for at least 30 min	21	C
		1 g		2500 units/ 1 ml	Physically compatible for at least 5 min	1053	C

Drugs in Syringe Compatibility (Cont.)

Heparin sodium

Drug (in syringe)	*Mfr*	*Amt*	*Mfr*	*Amt*	*Remarks*	*Ref*	*C/I*
Chlorpromazine HCl		50 mg/ 2 ml		2500 units/ 1 ml	Turbidity or precipitate forms within 5 min	1053	I
Cimetidine HCl	SKF	300 mg/ 2 ml		5000 units/ 5 ml	Physically compatible for 48 hr at room temperature	516	C
		200 mg/ 2 ml		2500 units/ 1 ml	Turbidity or precipitate forms within 5 min	1053	I
Cisplatin		0.5 mg/ 0.5 ml		500 units/ 0.5 ml	Physically compatible for 5 min at room temperature followed by 8 min of centrifugation	980	C
Clindamycin phosphate	UP	300 mg		2500 units/ 1 ml	Physically compatible for at least 5 min	1053	C
Clonazepam	RC	1 mg/ 2 ml		2500 units/ 1 ml	Visually compatible for at least 5 min	1053	C
Clonidine HCl	BI	0.15 mg/ 1 ml		2500 units/ 1 ml	Visually compatible for at least 5 min	1053	C
Cyclophosphamide		10 mg/ 0.5 ml		500 units/ 0.5 ml	Physically compatible for 5 min at room temperature followed by 8 min of centrifugation	980	C
Diatrizoate meglumine 52%, diatrizoate sodium 8%	MA	5 ml	OR	5000 units/ 0.5 ml	Physically compatible for at least 2 hr	1438	C
Diatrizoate sodium 60%	WI	5 ml	OR	5000 units/ 0.5 ml	Physically compatible for at least 2 hr	1438	C
Diazepam		10 mg/ 2 ml		2500 units/ 1 ml	Turbidity or precipitate forms within 5 min	1053	I
Diazoxide		300 mg/ 20 ml		2500 units/ 1 ml	Physically compatible for at least 5 min	1053	C
Digoxin		0.25 mg/ 1 ml		2500 units/ 1 ml	Physically compatible for at least 5 min	1053	C
Dimenhydrinate		65 mg/ 10 ml		2500 units/ 1 ml	Physically compatible for at least 5 min	1053	C
Dobutamine HCl	LI	250 mg/ 10 ml		2500 units/ 1 ml	Physically compatible for at least 5 min	1053	C
Dopamine HCl		50 mg/ 5 ml		2500 units/ 1 ml	Physically compatible for at least 5 min	1053	C

Drugs in Syringe Compatibility (Cont.)

Heparin sodium

Drug (in syringe)	*Mfr*	*Amt*	*Mfr*	*Amt*	*Remarks*	*Ref*	*C/I*
Doxorubicin HCl		1 mg/ 0.5 ml		500 units/ 0.5 ml	Immediate precipitation	980	I
Droperidol		1.25 mg/ 0.5 ml		500 units/ 0.5 ml	Immediate precipitation	980	I
	JN	5 mg/ 2 ml		2500 units/ 1 ml	Turbidity or precipitate forms within 5 min	1053	I
Epinephrine HCl		1 mg/ 1 ml		2500 units/ 1 ml	Physically compatible for at least 5 min	1053	C
Erythromycin lactobionate	AB	1 g	AB	20,000 units/ 1 ml	Physically incompatible	21	I
Erythromycin (form unspecified)	SC	250 mg		2500 units/ 1 ml	Turbidity or precipitate forms within 5 min	1053	I
Etomidate	JN	20 mg/ 10 ml		2500 units/ 1 ml	Visually compatible for at least 5 min	1053	C
Fentanyl citrate	JN	0.1 mg/ 2 ml		2500 units/ 1 ml	Physically compatible for at least 5 min	1053	C
Flecainide acetate		10 mg/ 5 ml		2500 units/ 1 ml	Turbidity or precipitate forms within 5 min	1053	I
Flucloxacillin sodium	BE	1 g		2500 units/ 1 ml	Visually compatible for at least 5 min	1053	C
Fluorouracil		25 mg/ 0.5 ml		500 units/ 0.5 ml	Physically compatible for 5 min at room temperature followed by 8 min of centrifugation	980	C
Fosfomycin	BM	3 g		2500 units/ 1 ml	Visually compatible for at least 5 min	1053	C
Furosemide		5 mg/ 0.5 ml		500 units/ 0.5 ml	Physically compatible for 5 min at room temperature followed by 8 min of centrifugation	980	C
		20 mg/ 2 ml		2500 units/ 1 ml	Physically compatible for at least 5 min	1053	C
Gentamicin sulfate		40 mg		2500 units/ 1 ml	Turbidity or precipitate forms within 5 min	1053	I
Haloperidol lactate	JN	5 mg/ 1 ml		2500 units/ 1 ml	Turbidity or precipitate forms within 5 min	1053	I

Drugs in Syringe Compatibility (Cont.)

Heparin sodium

Drug (in syringe)	*Mfr*	*Amt*	*Mfr*	*Amt*	*Remarks*	*Ref*	*C/I*
Iohexol	WI	64.7%, 5 ml	OR	5000 units/ 0.5 ml	Physically compatible for at least 2 hr	1438	C
Iopamidol	SQ	61%, 5 ml	OR	5000 units/ 0.5 ml	Physically compatible for at least 2 hr	1438	C
Iothalamate meglumine 60%	MA	5 ml	OR	5000 units/ 0.5 ml	Physically compatible for at least 2 hr	1438	C
Ioxaglate meglumine 39.3%, ioxaglate sodium 19.6%	MA	5 ml	OR	5000 units/ 0.5 ml	Physically compatible for at least 2 hr	1438	C
Kanamycin sulfate	BR	500 mg	AB	20,000 units/ 1 ml	Physically incompatible	21	I
Leucovorin calcium		5 mg/ 0.5 ml		500 units/ 0.5 ml	Physically compatible for 5 min at room temperature followed by 8 min of centrifugation	980	C
Lidocaine HCl	AST	100 mg/ 5 ml		2500 units/ 1 ml	Physically compatible for at least 5 min	1053	C
Lincomycin HCl	UP	600 mg	AB	20,000 units/ 1 ml	Physically compatible for at least 30 min	21	C
Meperidine HCl	HO	100 mg/ 2 ml		2500 units/ 1 ml	Turbidity or precipitate forms within 5 min	1053	I
Methotrexate sodium		12.5 mg/ 0.5 ml		500 units/ 0.5 ml	Physically compatible for 5 min at room temperature followed by 8 min of centrifugation	980	C
Methotrimeprazine		25 mg/ 1 ml		2500 units/ 1 ml	Turbidity or precipitate forms within 5 min	1053	I
Metoclopramide HCl		2.5 mg/ 0.5 ml		500 units/ 0.5 ml	Physically compatible for 5 min at room temperature followed by 8 min of centrifugation	980	C
		10 mg/ 2 ml		2500 units/ 1 ml	Physically compatible for at least 5 min	1053	C
	RB	10 mg/ 2 ml	ES	2000 units/ 2 ml	Physically compatible for 48 hr at room temperature	924	C
	RB	10 mg/ 2 ml	ES	4000 units/ 4 ml	Physically compatible for 48 hr at room temperature	924	C
	RB	10 mg/ 2 ml	ES	2000 units/ 2 ml	Physically compatible for 48 hr at 25 °C	1167	C
	RB	10 mg/ 2 ml	ES	4000 units/ 4 ml	Physically compatible for 48 hr at 25 °C	1167	C

Drugs in Syringe Compatibility (Cont.)

			Heparin sodium				
Drug (in syringe)	*Mfr*	*Amt*	*Mfr*	*Amt*	*Remarks*	*Ref*	*C/I*
	RB	160 mg/ 32 ml	ES	16,000 units/ 16 ml	Physically compatible for 48 hr at 25 °C	1167	C
Mexilitene HCl	BI	250 mg/ 10 ml		2500 units/ 1 ml	Turbidity or precipitate forms within 5 min	1053	I
Midazolam HCl	RC	15 mg/ 3 ml		2500 units/ 1 ml	Turbidity or precipitate forms within 5 min	1053	I
Mitomycin		0.25 mg/ 0.5 ml		500 units/ 0.5 ml	Physically compatible for 5 min at room temperature followed by 8 min of centrifugation	980	C
Morphine sulfate		1, 2, 5, 10 mg	WY	100 and 200 units	Brought to 5 ml with NS. Physically compatible with no morphine loss in 24 hr at 23 °C	985	C
		1, 2, 5 mg	WY	100 and 200 units	Brought to 5 ml with W. Physically compatible with no morphine loss in 24 hr at 23 °C	985	C
		10 mg	WY	100 and 200 units	Brought to 5 ml with W. Immediate haze with white precipitate and 5 to 7% loss of morphine potency	985	I
Nafcillin sodium	WY	500 mg	AB	20,000 units/ 1 ml	Physically compatible for at least 30 min	21	C
Naloxone HCl	DU	0.4 mg/ 1 ml		2500 units/ 1 ml	Physically compatible for at least 5 min	1053	C
Neostigmine methylsulfate	RC	0.5 mg/ 1 ml		2500 units/ 1 ml	Physically compatible for at least 5 min	1053	C
Netilmicin sulfate		150 mg		2500 units/ 1 ml	Turbidity or precipitate forms within 5 min	1053	I
Nitroglycerin		25 mg/ 25 ml		2500 units/ 1 ml	Physically compatible for at least 5 min	1053	C
Norepinephrine HCl	HO	1 mg/ 1 ml		2500 units/ 1 ml	Physically compatible for at least 5 min	1053	C
Pancuronium bromide		4 mg/ 2 ml		2500 units/ 1 ml	Physically compatible for at least 5 min	1053	C
Penicillin G		10 million units		2500 units/ 1 ml	Physically compatible for at least 5 min	1053	C
Pentazocine lactate	WI	30 mg/ 1 ml		2500 units/ 1 ml	Turbidity or precipitate forms within 5 min	1053	I
Pentoxifylline	RS	300 mg/ 15 ml		2500 units/ 1 ml	Visually compatible for at least 5 min	1053	C

Drugs in Syringe Compatibility (Cont.)

Heparin sodium

Drug (in syringe)	*Mfr*	*Amt*	*Mfr*	*Amt*	*Remarks*	*Ref*	*C/I*
Phenobarbital sodium		200 mg/ 1 ml		2500 units/ 1 ml	Physically compatible for at least 5 min	1053	C
Piperacillin sodium	LE	2 g		2500 units/ 1 ml	Physically compatible for at least 5 min	1053	C
Promethazine HCl		50 mg/ 2 ml		2500 units/ 1 ml	Turbidity or precipitate forms within 5 min	1053	I
Propafenone HCl	KN	70 mg/ 20 ml		2500 units/ 1 ml	Turbidity or precipitate forms within 5 min	1053	I
Ranitidine HCl	GL	50 mg/ 5 ml		2500 units/ 1 ml	Visually compatible for at least 5 min	1053	C
Sodium nitroprusside		60 mg/ 5 ml		2500 units/ 1 ml	Physically compatible for at least 5 min	1053	C
Streptomycin sulfate		1 g	AB	20,000 units/ 1 ml	Physically incompatible	21	I
Succinylcholine chloride		100 mg/ 5 ml		2500 units/ 1 ml	Physically compatible for at least 5 min	1053	C
Tobramycin sulfate		80 mg/ 2 ml		10 units/ 1 ml	Turbidity or fine white precipitate due to formation of insoluble salt	845	I
	LI	40 mg		2500 units/ 1 ml	Turbidity or precipitate forms within 5 min	1053	I
Tramadol HCl	GRU	100 mg/ 2 ml		2500 units/ 1 ml	Visually compatible for at least 5 min	1053	C
Triflupromazine HCl		10 mg/ 1 ml		2500 units/ 1 ml	Turbidity or precipitate forms within 5 min	1053	I
Trimethoprim–sulfamethoxazole		80 + 400 mg/ 5 ml		2500 units/ 1 ml	Physically compatible for at least 5 min	1053	C
Vancomycin HCl	LI	500 mg		2500 units/ 1 ml	Turbidity or precipitate forms within 5 min	1053	I
Verapamil HCl	KN	5 mg/ 2 ml		2500 units/ 1 ml	Physically compatible for at least 5 min	1053	C
Vinblastine sulfate		0.5 mg/ 0.5 ml		500 units/ 0.5 ml	Physically compatible for 5 min at room temperature followed by 8 min of centrifugation	980	C
	LI	1 mg/ml		200 units/ml[a]	Turbidity appears in 2 to 3 min	767	I

Drugs in Syringe Compatibility (Cont.)

Heparin sodium

Drug (in syringe)	*Mfr*	*Amt*	*Mfr*	*Amt*	*Remarks*	*Ref*	*C/I*
Vincristine sulfate		0.5 mg/ 0.5 ml		500 units/ 0.5 ml	Physically compatible for 5 min at room temperature followed by 8 min of centrifugation	980	C
Warfarin sodium	DU	2 mg/ 1 ml[b]	ES	5000 units/ 1 ml	Low-level haze forms immediately and becomes visible in ambient light in 1 hr	2010	I

[a]*Tested in bacteriostatic sodium chloride 0.9%.*
[b]*Tested in sterile water for injection.*

Y-Site Injection Compatibility (1:1 Mixture)

Heparin sodium

Drug	*Mfr*	*Conc*	*Mfr*	*Conc*	*Remarks*	*Ref*	*C/I*
Acyclovir sodium	BW	5 mg/ml[a]	ES	50 units/ml[a]	Physically compatible for 4 hr at 25 °C	1157	C
Alatrofloxacin mesylate	PF	1.43 mg/ml[a]	BA	100 units/ml[a]	Yellow precipitate forms	2235	I
Aldesleukin	CHI	33,800 I.U./ ml[a]	BA	100 units/ml	Visually compatible with little or no loss of aldesleukin activity by bioassay	1857	C
Allopurinol sodium	BW	3 mg/ml[b]	ES	100 units/ml[b]	Physically compatible with no change in measured turbidity or increase in particle content in 4 hr at 22 °C	1686	C
Alteplase	GEN	1 mg/ml	ES	100 units/ml[a]	Haze noted in 24 hr by visual examination. Erratic spectrophotometer readings	1340	I
Amifostine	USB	10 mg/ml[a]	ES	100 units/ml[a]	Physically compatible with no change in measured turbidity or increase in particle content in 4 hr at 23 °C	1845	C
Aminophylline	SE	25 mg/ml	RI	1000 units/L[c]	Physically compatible for at least 4 hr at room temperature by visual and microscopic examination	322	C
Amiodarone HCl	LZ	150 mg/3 ml[d]		50 units/ml/ min[b]	Yellow solution with opalescence	1053	I
	q			300 units/ml[b]	White precipitate forms upon sequential administration	791	I
Amphotericin B cholesteryl sulfate complex	SEQ	0.83 mg/ml[a]	WY	1000 units/ ml[a]	Gross precipitate forms	2117	I
Ampicillin sodium	BR	25, 50, 100, 135 mg/ml	RI	1000 units/L[c]	Physically compatible for at least 4 hr at room temperature by visual and microscopic examination	322	C
	WY	20 mg/ml[b]	TR	50 units/ml	Visually compatible for 4 hr at 25 °C	1793	C
Ampicillin sodium–sulbactam sodium	PF	20 + 10 mg/ ml[b]	TR	50 units/ml	Visually compatible for 4 hr at 25 °C	1793	C
Amsacrine	NCI	1 mg/ml[a]	SO	40 units/ml[a]	Light flocculent orange precipitate forms immediately	1381	I
Atracurium besylate	BW	0.5 mg/ml[a]	SO	40 units/ml[a]	Physically compatible for 24 hr at 28 °C	1337	C
Atropine sulfate	BW	0.5 mg/ml	UP	1000 units/L[e]	Physically compatible for at least 4 hr at room temperature by visual and microscopic examination	534	C

Y-Site Injection Compatibility (1:1 Mixture) (Cont.)

			Heparin sodium				
Drug	*Mfr*	*Conc*	*Mfr*	*Conc*	*Remarks*	*Ref*	*C/I*
Aztreonam	SQ	40 mg/ml[a]	ES	100 units/ml[a]	Physically compatible with no subvisual haze or particle formation in 4 hr at 23 °C	1758	C
	BV	20 mg/ml[a]	TR	50 units/ml	Visually compatible for 4 hr at 25 °C	1793	C
Betamethasone sodium phosphate	SC	3 mg/ml	UP	1000 units/L[e]	Physically compatible for at least 4 hr at room temperature by visual and microscopic examination	534	C
Bleomycin sulfate		3 units/ml		1000 units/ml	Drugs injected sequentially into Y-site with no flush between. No visually apparent precipitate	980	C
Calcium gluconate	ES	100 mg/ml	RI	1000 units/L[c]	Physically compatible for at least 4 hr at room temperature by visual and microscopic examination	322	C
Cefazolin sodium	SKB	20 mg/ml	TR	50 units/ml	Visually compatible for 4 hr at 25 °C	1793	C
Cefotetan disodium	STU	40 mg/ml[a]	TR	50 units/ml	Visually compatible for 4 hr at 25 °C	1793	C
Cefotiam	GRU	8 mg/ml	RC	333 and 666 units/ml	Little cefotiam loss in 1 hr by HPLC	1889	C
Ceftazidime	LI[p]	20 mg/ml	TR	50 units/ml	Visually compatible for 4 hr at 25 °C	1793	C
Ceftriaxone sodium	RC	20 mg/ml	TR	50 units/ml	Visually compatible for 4 hr at 25 °C	1793	C
Chlordiazepoxide HCl	RC	10 mg/ml	UP	1000 units/L[e]	Physically compatible for at least 4 hr at room temperature by visual and microscopic examination	534	C
Chlorpromazine HCl	SKF	25 mg/ml	UP	1000 units/L[e]	Physically compatible for at least 4 hr at room temperature by visual and microscopic examination	534	C
	RPR	0.13 mg/ml[a]	NOV	29.2 units/ml[a]	Visually compatible for 150 min	2244	C
Cimetidine HCl		200 mg/2 ml[d]		50 units/ml/min[b]	Clear solution	1053	C
	SKB	6 mg/ml[a]	TR	50 units/ml	Visually compatible for 4 hr at 25 °C	1793	C
Ciprofloxacin		2 mg/ml		10 units/ml	Turbidity forms rapidly with subsequent white precipitate	1483	I
	MI	2 mg/ml[f]	LY	100 units/ml	Crystals form immediately	1655	I
	BAY	2 mg/ml[b]	CP	10, 100, and 1000 units/ml[b]	White precipitate forms immediately	1934	I
Cisatracurium besylate	GW	0.1 and 2 mg/ml[a]	AB	100 units/ml	Physically compatible with no change in measured turbidity or increase in particle content in 4 hr at 23 °C	2074	C
	GW	5 mg/ml[a]	AB	100 units/ml	White cloudiness forms immediately	2074	I
Cisplatin		1 mg/ml		1000 units/ml	Drugs injected sequentially into Y-site with no flush between. No visually apparent precipitate	980	C
	BR	1 mg/ml	SO	40 units/ml[a]	Visually compatible for 4 hr at room temperature under fluorescent light	1685	C
Cladribine	ORT	0.015[b] and 0.5[g] mg/ml	WY	100 units/ml[b]	Physically compatible with no change in measured turbidity or increase in particle content in 4 hr at 23 °C	1969	C

Y-Site Injection Compatibility (1:1 Mixture) (Cont.)

Heparin sodium

Drug	*Mfr*	*Conc*	*Mfr*	*Conc*	*Remarks*	*Ref*	*C/I*
Clarithromycin	AB	4 mg/ml[a]	CPP	1000 units/ml[a]	White cloudiness forms immediately	2174	I
Clindamycin phosphate	UP	12 mg/ml[a]	TR	50 units/ml	Visually compatible for 4 hr at 25 °C	1793	C
Cyanocobalamin	PD	0.1 mg/ml	UP	1000 units/L[e]	Physically compatible for at least 4 hr at room temperature by visual and microscopic examination	534	C
Cyclophosphamide		20 mg/ml		1000 units/ml	Drugs injected sequentially into Y-site with no flush between. No visually apparent precipitate	980	C
	MJ	10 mg/ml[a]	SO	40 units/ml[a]	Visually compatible for 4 hr at room temperature under fluorescent light	1685	C
Cytarabine	UP	50 mg/ml	SO	40 units/ml[a]	Visually compatible for 4 hr at room temperature under fluorescent light	1685	C
Dacarbazine	MI	25 mg/ml[b]	WY	100 units/ml	White flocculent precipitate forms immediately[h]	1158	I
	MI	10 mg/ml[b]	WY	100 units/ml	No observable precipitation[g]	1158	C
Dexamethasone sodium phosphate	MSD	4 mg/ml	RI	1000 units/L[c]	Physically compatible for at least 4 hr at room temperature by visual and microscopic examination	322	C
	ES	0.08 mg/ml[a]	TR	50 units/ml	Visually compatible for 4 hr at 25 °C	1793	C
Diazepam		10 mg/2 ml[d]		50 units/ml/min[b]	Turbidity	1053	I
	RC	5 mg/ml	RI	1000 units/L[c]	Immediate haziness and globule formation	322	I
Digoxin	BW	0.25 mg/ml	RI	1000 units/L[c]	Physically compatible for at least 4 hr at room temperature by visual and microscopic examination	322	C
Diltiazem HCl	MMD	5 mg/ml	LY	20,000 units/ml	Precipitate forms	1807	I
	MMD	1 mg/ml[b]	LY	20,000 units/ml	Visually compatible	1807	C
	MMD	1[b] and 5 mg/ml	SCN	5000 and 10,000 units/ml	Visually compatible	1807	C
	MMD	5 mg/ml	LY, SCN	80 units/ml[f]	Visually compatible	1807	C
	MMD	1 mg/ml[a]	ES	100 units/ml[a]	Visually compatible for 4 hr at 27 °C	2062	C
Diphenhydramine HCl	PD	50 mg/ml	UP	1000 units/L[e]	Physically compatible for at least 4 hr at room temperature by visual and microscopic examination	534	C
Dobutamine HCl	LI	4 mg/ml[b]	ES	50 units/ml[b]	Physically compatible for 3 hr	1316	C
	LI	4 mg/ml[a]	ES	50 units/ml[a]	Immediate gross precipitation	1316	I
	LI	1 mg/ml[a]	TR	50 units/ml	Visually compatible for 4 hr at 25 °C	1793	C
	LI	4 mg/ml[a]	OR	100 units/ml[a]	Haze and white precipitate form	1877	I
	LI	4 mg/ml[a]	ES	100 units/ml[a]	Precipitate forms in 4 hr at 27 °C	2062	I
Docetaxel	RPR	0.9 mg/ml[a]	ES	100 units/ml	Physically compatible with no change in measured turbidity or increase in particle content in 4 hr at 23 °C	2224	C

Y-Site Injection Compatibility (1:1 Mixture) (Cont.)

Heparin sodium

Drug	*Mfr*	*Conc*	*Mfr*	*Conc*	*Remarks*	*Ref*	*C/I*
Dopamine HCl	ACC	40 mg/ml	UP	1000 units/L[e]	Physically compatible for at least 4 hr at room temperature by visual and microscopic examination	534	C
	BA	1.6 mg/ml	TR	50 units/ml	Visually compatible for 4 hr at 25 °C	1793	C
	AB	3.2 mg/ml[a]	ES	100 units/ml[a]	Visually compatible for 4 hr at 27 °C	2062	C
Doxorubicin HCl		2 mg/ml		1000 units/ml	Drugs injected sequentially into Y-site with no flush between. Immediate precipitation	980	I
	AD	0.2 mg/ml[a]	SO	40 units/ml[a]	Visually compatible for 4 hr at room temperature under fluorescent light	1685	C
Doxorubicin HCl liposome injection	SEQ	0.4 mg/ml[a]	ES	1000 units/ml[a]	Physically compatible with little or no change in measured turbidity and no increase in particle content in 4 hr at 23 °C	2087	C
Doxycycline hyclate	ES	1 mg/ml[a]	TR	50 units/ml	Visually incompatible within 4 hr at 25 °C	1793	I
Droperidol		2.5 mg/ml		1000 units/ml	Drugs injected sequentially into Y-site with no flush between. Immediate precipitation	980	I
	CR	1.25 mg/ml	UP	1000 units/L[e]	Physically compatible for at least 4 hr at room temperature by visual and microscopic examination	534	C
	JN	5 mg/2 ml[d]		50 units/ml/min[b]	White turbidity	1053	I
Edrophonium chloride	RC	10 mg/ml	UP	1000 units/L[e]	Physically compatible for at least 4 hr at room temperature by visual and microscopic examination	534	C
Enalaprilat	MSD	0.05 mg/ml[c]	IX	40 units/ml[a]	Physically compatible for 24 hr at room temperature under fluorescent light	1355	C
Epinephrine HCl	AB	0.1 mg/ml	UP	1000 units/L[e]	Physically compatible for at least 4 hr at room temperature by visual and microscopic examination	534	C
	AB	0.02 mg/ml[a]	ES	100 units/ml[a]	Visually compatible for 4 hr at 27 °C	2062	C
Ergotamine tartrate	SZ	0.5 mg/ml	UP	1000 units/L[e]	Crystal formation and brown discoloration in 4 hr at room temperature	534	I
Erythromycin lactobionate	AB	3.3 mg/ml[b]	TR	50 units/ml	Visually compatible for 4 hr at 25 °C	1793	C
Esmolol HCl	DCC	10 mg/ml[a]	IX	40 units/ml[a]	Physically compatible for 24 hr at 22 °C	1169	C
Estrogens, conjugated	AY	5 mg/ml	RI	1000 units/L[c]	Physically compatible for at least 4 hr at room temperature by visual and microscopic examination	322	C
Ethacrynate sodium	MSD	1 mg/ml	RI	1000 units/L[c]	Physically compatible for at least 4 hr at room temperature by visual and microscopic examination	322	C
Etoposide phosphate	BR	5 mg/ml[a]	ES	100 units/ml[a]	Physically compatible with no change in measured turbidity or increase in particle content in 4 hr at 23 °C	2218	C
Famotidine	MSD	0.2 mg/ml[a]	ES	40 units/ml[b]	Physically compatible for 14 hr	1196	C
	MSD	0.2 mg/ml[a]	TR	50 units/ml[a]	Physically compatible for 4 hr at 25 °C	1188	C
	ME	2 mg/ml[b]		40 units/ml[a]	Visually compatible for 4 hr at 22 °C	1936	C

Y-Site Injection Compatibility (1:1 Mixture) (Cont.)

Heparin sodium

Drug	*Mfr*	*Conc*	*Mfr*	*Conc*	*Remarks*	*Ref*	*C/I*
Fentanyl citrate	MN	0.05 mg/ml	UP	1000 units/L[e]	Physically compatible for at least 4 hr at room temperature by visual and microscopic examination	534	C
	ES	0.05 mg/ml	ES	100 units/ml[a]	Visually compatible for 4 hr at 27 °C	2062	C
Filgrastim	AMG	30 μg/ml[a]	ES	100 units/ml[a]	Particles and filaments form immediately	1687	I
Flecainide acetate		10 mg/5 ml[d]		50 units/ml/min[b]	Clear solution	1053	C
Fluconazole	RR	2 mg/ml	LY	1000 units/ml	Physically compatible for 24 hr at 25 °C	1407	C
	PF	2 mg/ml	TR	50 units/ml	Visually compatible for 4 hr at 25 °C	1793	C
Fludarabine phosphate	BX	1 mg/ml[a]	SO, WY	40[a], 100, 1000 units/ml	Physically compatible for 4 hr at room temperature under fluorescent light	1439	C
Fluorouracil	RC	50 mg/ml	UP	1000 units/L[e]	Physically compatible for at least 4 hr at room temperature by visual and microscopic examination	534	C
		50 mg/ml		1000 units/ml	Drugs injected sequentially into Y-site with no flush between. No visually apparent precipitate	980	C
Foscarnet sodium	AST	24 mg/ml	ES	1000 units/ml	Physically compatible for 24 hr at room temperature under fluorescent light	1335	C
	AST	24 mg/ml	LY	100 units/ml[f]	Physically compatible for 24 hr at 25 °C under fluorescent light by visual and microscopic examination	1393	C
Furosemide		10 mg/ml		1000 units/ml	Drugs injected sequentially into Y-site with no flush between. No visually apparent precipitate	980	C
	HO	10 mg/ml	UP	1000 units/L[e]	Physically compatible for at least 4 hr at room temperature by visual and microscopic examination	534	C
	AMR	10 mg/ml	ES	100 units/ml[a]	Visually compatible for 4 hr at 27 °C	2062	C
	HMR	2.6 mg/ml[a]	NOV	29.2 units/ml[a]	Visually compatible for 150 min	2244	C
Gatifloxacin	BMS	2 mg/ml[a]	ES	1000 units/ml[a]	White cloudy precipitate forms immediately	2234	I
Gemcitabine HCl	LI	10 mg/ml[b]	ES	100 units/ml[b]	Physically compatible with no change in measured turbidity or increase in particle content in 4 hr at 23 °C	2226	C
Gentamicin sulfate	ES	3.2 mg/ml[f]	ES	50 units/ml[f]	Immediate gross haze	1316	I
	TR	2 mg/ml	TR	50 units/ml	Visually incompatible within 4 hr at 25 °C	1793	I
Granisetron HCl	SKB	0.05 mg/ml[a]	AB	100 units/ml[a]	Physically compatible with no change in measured turbidity or increase in particle content in 4 hr at 23 °C	2000	C
Haloperidol lactate	JN	5 mg/1 ml[d]		50 units/ml/min[b]	White turbidity	1053	I
	MN	5 mg/1 ml[i]	OR	25,000 and 50,000 units/250 ml[f]	White precipitate forms immediately	1436	I
Hetastarch in lactated electrolyte injection (Hextend)	AB	6%	ES	100 units/ml	Physically compatible with no change in measured turbidity or increase in particle content in 4 hr at 23 °C	2339	C

Y-Site Injection Compatibility (1:1 Mixture) (Cont.)

Heparin sodium

Drug	Mfr	Conc	Mfr	Conc	Remarks	Ref	C/I
Hydralazine HCl	CI	20 mg/ml	UP	1000 units/L[e]	Physically compatible for at least 4 hr at room temperature by visual and microscopic examination	534	C
Hydrocortisone sodium succinate	UP	2 mg/ml[a]	TR	50 units/ml	Visually compatible for 4 hr at 25 °C	1793	C
	UP	125 mg/ml	ES	100 units/ml[f]	Visually compatible for 24 hr at room temperature in test tubes. No precipitate found on filter from Y-site delivery	2063	C
Hydromorphone HCl	KN	1 mg/ml	ES	100 units/ml[a]	Visually compatible for 4 hr at 27 °C	2062	C
Idarubicin HCl	AD	1 mg/ml[b]	ES	1000 units/ml	Haze forms immediately and precipitate forms in 20 min	1525	I
	AD	1 mg/ml[b]	SO	100 units/ml	Haze forms immediately and precipitate forms in 12 min	1525	I
Insulin, regular	LI	40 units/ml	RI	1000 units/L[c]	Physically compatible for at least 4 hr at room temperature by visual and microscopic examination	322	C
	LI	0.2 unit/ml[b]	ES	60 units/ml[a]	Physically compatible for 2 hr at 25 °C	1395	C
Isoproterenol HCl	WI	0.2 mg/ml	UP	1000 units/L[e]	Physically compatible for at least 4 hr at room temperature by visual and microscopic examination	534	C
Isosorbide dinitrate	RP	10 mg/ml	LEO	300 units/ml[a]	Erratic availability of both drugs delivered through PVC tubing	1799	I
Kanamycin sulfate	BR	250 mg/ml	RI	1000 units/L[c]	Physically compatible for at least 4 hr at room temperature by visual and microscopic examination	322	C
Labetalol HCl	SC	1 mg/ml[a]	IX	40 units/ml[a]	Physically compatible for 24 hr at 18 °C	1171	C
	GL	5 mg/ml	OR	100 units/ml[a]	Cloudiness with particles forms immediately	1877	I
	AH	2 mg/ml[a]	ES	100 units/ml[a]	Visually compatible for 4 hr at 27 °C	2062	C
Leucovorin calcium		10 mg/ml		1000 units/ml	Drugs injected sequentially into Y-site with no flush between. No visually apparent precipitate	980	C
Levofloxacin	OMN	5 mg/ml[a]	ES	10 units/ml	Cloudy precipitate forms	2233	I
Lidocaine HCl	AST	20 mg/ml	RI	1000 units/L[c]	Physically compatible for at least 4 hr at room temperature by visual and microscopic examination	322	C
	TR	4 mg/ml	TR	50 units/ml	Visually compatible for 4 hr at 25 °C	1793	C
Linezolid	PHU	2 mg/ml	ES	1000 units/ml[a]	Physically compatible with no change in measured turbidity or increase in particle content in 4 hr at 23 °C	2264	C
Lorazepam	WY	0.33 mg/ml[b]		417 units/ml	Visually compatible for 24 hr at 22 °C	1855	C
	WY	0.5 mg/ml[a]	ES	100 units/ml[a]	Visually compatible for 4 hr at 27 °C	2062	C
Magnesium sulfate	AB	500 mg/ml	UP	1000 units/L	Physically compatible for at least 4 hr at room temperature by visual and microscopic examination	534	C
Melphalan HCl	BW	0.1 mg/ml[b]	WY	100 units/ml[b]	Physically compatible with no change in measured turbidity or increase in particle content in 3 hr at 22 °C	1557	C

Y-Site Injection Compatibility (1:1 Mixture) (Cont.)

			Heparin sodium				
Drug	*Mfr*	*Conc*	*Mfr*	*Conc*	*Remarks*	*Ref*	*C/I*
Meperidine HCl	HO	100 mg/2 ml[d]		50 units/ml/min[b]	Clear solution	1053	C
	WY	10 mg/ml[b]	ES	60 units/ml[a]	Physically compatible for 1 hr at 25 °C	1338	C
Meropenem	ZEN	1 and 50 mg/ml[b]	ES	1 unit/ml[j]	Visually compatible for 4 hr at room temperature	1994	C
Methotrexate sodium		25 mg/ml		1000 units/ml	Drugs injected sequentially into Y-site with no flush between. No visually apparent precipitate	980	C
	AD	15 mg/ml[k]	SO	40 units/ml[a]	Visually compatible for 4 hr at room temperature under fluorescent light	1685	C
		30 mg/ml	CH	500 units/ml[b]	Visually compatible for 4 hr at room temperature	1788	C
Methotrimeprazine		25 mg/ml[d]		50 units/ml/min[b]	White precipitate	1053	I
Methoxamine HCl	BW	10 mg/ml	UP	1000 units/L[e]	Physically compatible for at least 4 hr at room temperature by visual and microscopic examination	534	C
Methyldopate HCl	ES	5 mg/ml[a]	TR	50 units/ml	Visually compatible for 4 hr at 25 °C	1793	C
Methylergonovine maleate	SZ	0.2 mg/ml	UP	1000 units/L[e]	Physically compatible for at least 4 hr at room temperature by visual and microscopic examination	534	C
Methylprednisolone sodium succinate	UP	40 mg/ml	RI	1000 units/L[l]	In D5W. Physically compatible for at least 4 hr at room temperature by visual and microscopic examination	322	C
	UP	40 mg/ml	RI	1000 units/L[l]	In RL and NS. Physically compatible initially but haziness in 4 hr at room temperature	322	I
	UP	2.5 mg/ml[a]	TR	50 units/ml	Visually compatible for 4 hr at 25 °C	1793	C
	UP	5 mg/ml[b]	ES	100 units/ml[f]	Visually compatible for 24 hr at room temperature in test tubes. No precipitate found on filter from Y-site delivery	2063	C
Metoclopramide HCl		5 mg/ml		1000 units/ml	Drugs injected sequentially into Y-site with no flush between. No visually apparent precipitate	980	C
Metronidazole	MG	5 mg/ml	TR	50 units/ml	Visually compatible for 4 hr at 25 °C	1793	C
Mexilitene HCl	BI	250 mg/10 ml[d]		50 units/ml/min[b]	Opalescent solution	1053	I
Midazolam HCl	RC	5 mg/ml		417 units/ml	Visually compatible for 24 hr at 22 °C	1855	C
	RC	2 mg/ml[a]	ES	100 units/ml[a]	Visually compatible for 4 hr at 27 °C	2062	C
	RC	15 mg/3 ml[d]		50 units/ml/min[b]	Clear solution	1053	C
Milrinone lactate	SW	0.2 mg/ml[a]	ES	100 units/ml[a]	Visually compatible for 4 hr at 27 °C	2062	C
	SW	0.4 mg/ml[a]	ES	100 units/ml[a]	Visually compatible with little or no loss of milrinone by HPLC and heparin by immunoassay in 4 hr at 23 °C	2214	C
Minocycline HCl	LE	50 mg/ml	UP	1000 units/L[e]	Physically compatible for at least 4 hr at room temperature by visual and microscopic examination	534	C

Y-Site Injection Compatibility (1:1 Mixture) (Cont.)

Heparin sodium

Drug	*Mfr*	*Conc*	*Mfr*	*Conc*	*Remarks*	*Ref*	*C/I*
Mitomycin		0.5 mg/ml		1000 units/ml	Drugs injected sequentially into Y-site with no flush between. No visually apparent precipitate	980	C
Morphine sulfate	WY	15 mg/ml	UP	1000 units/L[e]	Physically compatible for at least 4 hr at room temperature by visual and microscopic examination	534	C
	WY	0.2 mg/ml[f]	ES	50 units/ml[f]	Physically compatible for 3 hr	1316	C
	ES	1 mg/ml[b]	ES	60 units/ml[a]	Physically compatible for 1 hr at 25 °C	1338	C
	SCN	2 mg/ml[a]	ES	100 units/ml[a]	Visually compatible for 4 hr at 27 °C	2062	C
Nafcillin sodium	WY	20 mg/ml[a]	TR	50 units/ml	Visually compatible for 4 hr at 25 °C	1793	C
Neostigmine methylsulfate	RC	0.5 mg/ml	UP	1000 units/L[e]	Physically compatible for at least 4 hr at room temperature by visual and microscopic examination	534	C
Nicardipine HCl	WY	1 mg/ml[a]	ES	100 units/ml[a]	Precipitate forms immediately	2062	I
Nitroglycerin	BA	0.2 mg/ml	ES	50 units/ml	Visually compatible for 24 hr at 23 °C	1794	C
	OM	0.2 mg/ml[a]	OR	100 units/ml[a]	Visually compatible for 24 hr at 23 °C	1877	C
	AB	0.4 mg/ml[a]	ES	100 units/ml[a]	Visually compatible for 4 hr at 27 °C	2062	C
Norepinephrine bitartrate	WI	1 mg/ml	UP	1000 units/L[e]	Physically compatible for at least 4 hr at room temperature by visual and microscopic examination	534	C
	AB	0.128 mg/ml[a]	ES	100 units/ml[a]	Visually compatible for 4 hr at 27 °C	2062	C
Ondansetron HCl	GL	1 mg/ml[b]	SO	40 units/ml[a]	Physically compatible for 4 hr at 22 °C	1365	C
Oxacillin sodium	BR	100 mg/ml	UP	1000 units/L[e]	Physically compatible for at least 4 hr at room temperature by visual and microscopic examination	534	C
Oxytocin	SZ	1 mg/ml	UP	1000 units/L[e]	Physically compatible for at least 4 hr at room temperature by visual and microscopic examination	534	C
Paclitaxel	NCI	1.2 mg/ml[a]	WY	100 units/ml[a]	Physically compatible with no change in measured turbidity in 4 hr at 22 °C	1556	C
Pancuronium bromide	ES	0.05 mg/ml[a]	SO	40 units/ml[a]	Physically compatible for 24 hr at 28 °C	1337	C
Penicillin G potassium	LI	200,000 units/ml	RI	1000 units/L[c]	Physically compatible for at least 4 hr at room temperature by visual and microscopic examination	322	C
	RR	40,000 units/ml[a]	TR	50 units/ml	Visually compatible for 4 hr at 25 °C	1793	C
Pentazocine lactate	WI	30 mg/ml	UP	1000 units/L[e]	Physically compatible for at least 4 hr at room temperature by visual and microscopic examination	534	C
Phenytoin sodium	PD	50 mg/ml	RI	1000 units/L[c]	Immediate crystal formation	322	I
	ES	2 mg/ml[b]	TR	50 units/ml	Cloudiness forms immediately and becomes dense, white, flocculent precipitate in 4 hr at 25 °C	1793	I
Phytonadione	RC	10 mg/ml	UP	1000 units/L[e]	Physically compatible for at least 4 hr at room temperature by visual and microscopic examination	534	C
Piperacillin sodium	LE	60 mg/ml[a]	TR	50 units/ml	Visually compatible for 4 hr at 25 °C	1793	C

Y-Site Injection Compatibility (1:1 Mixture) (Cont.)

Heparin sodium

Drug	*Mfr*	*Conc*	*Mfr*	*Conc*	*Remarks*	*Ref*	*C/I*
Piperacillin sodium–tazobactam sodium	LE	40 + 5 mg/ml[a]	ES	100 units/ml[a]	Physically compatible with no change in measured turbidity or increase in particle content in 4 hr at 22 °C	1688	C
Potassium chloride	AB	0.2 mEq/ml[a]	TR	50 units/ml	Visually compatible for 4 hr at 25 °C	1793	C
	BRN	0.625 mEq/ml[a]	NOV	29.2 units/ml[a]	Visually compatible for 150 min	2244	C
Procainamide HCl	SQ	100 mg/ml	UP	1000 units/L[e]	Physically compatible for at least 4 hr at room temperature by visual and microscopic examination	534	C
Prochlorperazine edisylate	SKF	5 mg/ml	UP	1000 units/L[e]	Physically compatible for at least 4 hr at room temperature by visual and microscopic examination	534	C
Promethazine HCl	SV	50 mg/ml	UP	1000 units/L	In D5LR, D5W, LR, and NS. Physically compatible for at least 4 hr at room temperature by visual and microscopic examination	534	C
	SV	50 mg/ml	UP	1000 units/L	In D5R. Physically compatible initially but cloudiness in 4 hr at room temperature	534	I
		50 mg/2 ml[d]		50 units/ml/min[b]	Distinctly turbid	1053	I
Propafenone HCl	KN	70 mg/20 ml[d]		50 units/ml/min[b]	White opalescence forms	1053	I
Propofol	ZEN	10 mg/ml	ES	100 units/ml[a]	Physically compatible for 1 hr at 23 °C with no increase in particle content	2066	C
Propranolol HCl	AY	1 mg/ml	UP	1000 units/L[e]	Physically compatible for at least 4 hr at room temperature by visual and microscopic examination	534	C
Pyridostigmine bromide	RC	5 mg/ml	UP	1000 units/L[e]	Physically compatible for at least 4 hr at room temperature by visual and microscopic examination	534	C
Quinidine gluconate	LI	6 mg/ml[b]	ES	50 units/ml[b]	Physically compatible for 3 hr	1316	C
	LI	6 mg/ml[a]	ES	50 units/ml[a]	Immediate gross haze	1316	I
Ranitidine HCl	GL	0.5 mg/ml[m]	LY	50 units/ml[a]	Physically compatible for 24 hr	1323	C
	GL	1 mg/ml	TR	50 units/ml	Visually compatible for 4 hr at 25 °C	1793	C
	GL	1 mg/ml[a]	ES	100 units/ml[a]	Visually compatible for 4 hr at 27 °C	2062	C
Remifentanil HCl	GW	0.025 and 0.25 mg/ml[b]	AB	100 units/ml	Physically compatible with no change in measured turbidity or increase in particle content in 4 hr at 23 °C	2075	C
Sargramostim	IMM	10 μg/ml[b]	WY	100 units/ml	Physically compatible for 4 hr at 22 °C	1436	C
Scopolamine HBr	BW	0.86 mg/ml	UP	1000 units/L[e]	Physically compatible for at least 4 hr at room temperature by visual and microscopic examination	534	C
Sodium bicarbonate	BR	75 mg/ml	RI	1000 units/L[c]	Physically compatible for at least 4 hr at room temperature by visual and microscopic examination	322	C
		1.4%	CH	500 units/ml[b]	Visually compatible for 4 hr at room temperature	1788	C

Y-Site Injection Compatibility (1:1 Mixture) (Cont.)

Heparin sodium

Drug	*Mfr*	*Conc*	*Mfr*	*Conc*	*Remarks*	*Ref*	*C/I*
Sodium nitroprusside	ES	0.2 mg/ml[a]	TR	50 units/ml	Visually compatible for 4 hr at 25 °C protected from light	1793	C
	RC	0.2 mg/ml[a]	OR	100 units/ml[a]	Visually compatible for 24 hr at 23 °C	1877	C
Streptokinase	HO	30,000 units/ml[a]	ES	100 units/ml[a]	Physically compatible for at least 5 days by visual examination	1340	C
Succinylcholine chloride	BW	20 mg/ml	RI	1000 units/L[c]	Physically compatible for at least 4 hr at room temperature by visual and microscopic examination	322	C
Tacrolimus	FUJ	1 mg/ml[b]	ES	10 units/ml[a]	Visually compatible for 24 hr at 25 °C	1630	C
Theophylline	TR	4 mg/ml	TR	50 units/ml	Visually compatible for 4 hr at 25 °C	1793	C
Thiopental sodium	AB	25 mg/ml[j]	ES	100 units/ml[a]	Visually compatible for 4 hr at 27 °C	2062	C
Thiotepa	IMM[n]	1 mg/ml[a]	ES	100 units/ml[a]	Physically compatible with no change in measured turbidity or increase in particle content in 4 hr at 23 °C	1861	C
Ticarcillin disodium	BE	20 mg/ml[a]	TR	50 units/ml	Visually compatible for 4 hr at 25 °C	1793	C
Ticarcillin disodium–clavulanate potassium	BE	31 mg/ml[a]	TR	50 units/ml	Visually compatible for 4 hr at 25 °C	1793	C
Tirofiban HCl	ME	0.05 mg/ml[a,b]	AB	40 units/ml[a]	Physically compatible with no tirofiban loss by HPLC or loss of heparin activity in 4 hr at room temperature under fluorescent light	2250	C
	ME	0.05 mg/ml[b]	AB	50 units/ml[b]	Physically compatible with no tirofiban loss by HPLC or loss of heparin activity in 4 hr at room temperature under fluorescent light	2250	C
	ME	0.05 mg/ml[a,b]	AB	100 units/ml[a,b]	Physically compatible with no tirofiban loss by HPLC or loss of heparin activity in 4 hr at room temperature under fluorescent light	2250	C
TNA #218 to #226[o]			AB	100 units/ml	Damage to emulsion integrity occurs immediately with free oil formation possible	2215	I
Tobramycin sulfate	LI	3.2 mg/ml[f]	ES	50 units/ml[f]	Immediate gross haze	1316	I
	LI	0.8 mg/ml[a]	TR	50 units/ml	Visually incompatible within 4 hr at 25 °C	1793	I
TPN #189[o]			DB	500 units/ml[b]	Visually compatible for 24 hr at 22 °C	1767	C
TPN #212 to #215[o]			AB	100 units/ml	Physically compatible with no change in measured turbidity or increase in particle content in 4 hr at 23 °C	2109	C
Tramadol HCl	GRU	100 mg/2 ml[d]		50 units/ml/min[b]	Turbidity forms	1053	I
Triflupromazine HCl	SQ	10 mg/1 ml[d]		50 units/ml/min[b]	White precipitate forms	1053	I
Trimethobenzamide HCl	RC	100 mg/ml	UP	1000 units/L[e]	Physically compatible for at least 4 hr at room temperature by visual and microscopic examination	534	C
Vancomycin HCl	LI	6.6 mg/ml[a]	TR	50 units/ml	Visually incompatible within 4 hr at 25 °C	1793	I
	LE	10 mg/ml[b]	ES	100 units/ml[f]	Precipitate forms	2063	I

Y-Site Injection Compatibility (1:1 Mixture) (Cont.)

			Heparin sodium				
Drug	*Mfr*	*Conc*	*Mfr*	*Conc*	*Remarks*	*Ref*	*C/I*
Vecuronium bromide	OR	0.1 mg/ml[a]	SO	40 units/ml[a]	Physically compatible for 24 hr at 28 °C	1337	C
	OR	1 mg/ml	ES	100 units/ml[a]	Visually compatible for 4 hr at 27 °C	2062	C
Vinblastine sulfate		1 mg/ml		1000 units/ml	Drugs injected sequentially into Y-site with no flush between. No visually apparent precipitate	980	C
Vincristine sulfate		1 mg/ml		1000 units/ml	Drugs injected sequentially into Y-site with no flush between. No visually apparent precipitate	980	C
Vinorelbine tartrate	BW	1 mg/ml[b]	ES	100 units/ml[b]	Physically compatible with no change in measured turbidity or increase in particle content in 4 hr at 22 °C	1558	C
	GW	3 mg/ml[b]		100 units/ml[b]	A fine haze forms immediately, becoming cloudy in 15 min	2238	I
	GW	2 mg/ml[b]		100 units/ml[b]	Visually compatible for at least 15 min	2238	C
	GW	1 mg/ml[b]		100 units/ml[b]	Visually compatible for at least 15 min	2238	C
	GW	4 mg/4 ml[b]		100 units/ 1 ml[b]	Volumes mixed as cited. Visually compatible for at least 15 min	2238	C
	GW	8 mg/4 ml[b]		100 units/ 1 ml[b]	Volumes mixed as cited. Precipitate forms	2238	I
	GW	12 mg/4 ml[b]		100 units/ 1 ml[b]	Volumes mixed as cited. Precipitate forms	2238	I
Warfarin sodium	DU	2 mg/ml[j]	AB	100 units/ml[a]	Visually compatible with no warfarin loss by HPLC in 30 min	2010	C
	DME	2 mg/ml[j]	AB	100 units/ml[a]	Visually compatible for 24 hr at 24 °C	2078	C
Zidovudine	BW	4 mg/ml[a]	LY	100 units/ml[a]	Physically compatible for 4 hr at 25 °C under fluorescent light by visual and microscopic examination	1193	C

[a]*Tested in dextrose 5% in water.*
[b]*Tested in sodium chloride 0.9%.*
[c]*Tested in combination with hydrocortisone sodium succinate (Upjohn) 100 mg/L in dextrose 5% in water, sodium chloride 0.9%, and Ringer's injection, lactated.*
[d]*Given over three minutes into a heparin infusion run at 1 ml/min.*
[e]*Tested in dextrose 5% in Ringer's injection, dextrose 5% in Ringer's injection, lactated, dextrose 5% in water, Ringer's injection, lactated, and sodium chloride 0.9%.*
[f]*Tested in both dextrose 5% in water and sodium chloride 0.9%.*
[g]*Tested in bacteriostatic sodium chloride 0.9% preserved with benzyl alcohol 0.9%.*
[h]*Dacarbazine in intravenous tubing flushed with heparin sodium.*
[i]*Injected over one minute.*
[j]*Tested in sterile water for injection.*
[k]*Tested in dextrose 5% in water with sodium bicarbonate 0.05 mEq/ml.*
[l]*Also contained hydrocortisone sodium succinate (Upjohn) 100 mg/ml.*
[m]*Premixed infusion solution.*
[n]*Lyophilized formulation tested.*
[o]*Refer to Appendix I for the composition of parenteral nutrition solutions. TNA indicates a 3-in-1 admixture, and TPN indicates a 2-in-1 admixture.*
[p]*Sodium carbonate–containing formulation.*
[q]*Not specified.*

Additional Compatibility Information

Dextrose Solutions — Evaluations of the stability of heparin sodium in dextrose-containing solutions have appeared frequently in the literature, but the results are conflicting.

Pritchard found that heparin sodium solutions, autoclaved for 10 minutes at 10 pounds/inch^2 at 115 °C, exhibited rapid loss of activity at pH values less than 5. It was speculated that a 50% loss of activity could occur if heparin sodium in dextrose 5% in water was autoclaved. The author suggested that heparin sodium should be added to the dextrose solution immediately before use. (243)

Jacobs et al. noted a 50% reduction of activity within one hour at 23 °C when heparin sodium 10,000 units was added to 500 ml of dextrose 5% in water. A 40% reduction of activity occurred when dextrose 4.3% in sodium chloride 0.18% was used as the diluent. The pH of both solutions initially was 3.9, but the addition of heparin sodium raised the pH to approximately 6. After the initial fall in activity, the levels remained constant for the duration of the 24-hour test. The authors had no explanation for this phenomenon. (113)

Okuno and Nelson, using two different assay methods, noted a similar result. A 25 to 60% reduction in heparin activity was observed when heparin sodium was added to several intravenous infusion solutions, including dextrose 5 and 10% in water, at a concentration of 10,000 units/L at room temperature. The nadir of activity was reached at six hours, although substantial loss occurred as early as two hours after mixing. This loss of activity extended to the non-dextrose-containing solutions sodium chloride 0.9% and Ringer's injection, lactated. Surprisingly, a partial rebound in activity was noted at the 24-hour observation period by one method. As an explanation of the rebound of activity, the authors speculated that heparin might transiently undergo molecular alteration in fluids or that the fluids could interfere in the coagulation process. (406)

Anderson et al. reported a 65% loss of activity in five hours in a heparin sodium solution of 30 units/ml in dextrose 5% in water stored at 15, 25, and 35 °C. A total recovery of activity occurred in 24 to 48 hours, however. In dextrose 5% in sodium chloride 0.9%, 40% of the activity was lost in five hours, but only five to seven hours elapsed before complete recovery of activity was noted. If the sodium chloride content of the solution was increased up to 2% or if the dextrose concentration was decreased, no fall in activity was observed. Because of the eventual recovery of full activity and the lack of temperature effect, the authors concluded that degradation was not occurring. They speculated that a molecular rearrangement or interaction might be occurring. (674)

Matthews noted a 50% loss of heparin activity in four hours at 25 °C in a concentration of 35,000 units/L in dextrose 5% in water and dextrose 4.3% in sodium chloride 0.9%. The activity recovered to initial levels by six hours after mixing and remained stable through 24 hours. Subsequent storage at 4 °C for 14 days resulted in no further loss in potency. (900)

Parker's work did not support these results. No loss of potency was found in 24 hours when heparin sodium 20,000 units/L in dextrose 5% in water was tested at pH 3.8 to 7.6. (21) In another study, he found that heparin sodium 20,000 units/L was stable for 72 hours in several solutions, including dextrose 5% in water and dextrose 5% in sodium chloride 0.9%. (46)

Hadgraft noted that both dextrose 5% in water and fructose 5% in water have little buffer capacity. A sample of dextrose 5% in water with a pH of 4.1 was mixed with 10,000 units of heparin sodium. The pH of the resultant solution was 5.95. Use of fructose 5% in water with a pH of 3.67 resulted in a final pH of 4.14 with the addition of heparin sodium 10,000 units. The author stated that at either of these pH values, heparin sodium would remain stable at room temperature. (251)

Stock and Warner added heparin sodium to dextrose 5% in water having a pH of 4.4. The concentrations tested were 40, 200, and 964 units/ml having pH values of 6.6, 6.8, and 7, respectively, after addition of heparin sodium. No loss of potency was observed within 24 hours at 23 °C. The authors observed deterioration only after 60 hours at a minimum concentration of 1000 units/ml. (252)

Hodby et al. found no significant loss of heparin activity in 24 hours when heparin sodium 8000 units was added to dextrose 5% in water or dextrose 5% in sodium chloride 0.9%. Additionally, they found no loss of activity in 24 hours of heparin sodium in sodium chloride 0.9% adjusted to pH 3.2 with hydrochloric acid or to pH 9.2 with sodium hydroxide. (57)

Chessels et al. found that, in 10 male patients, the effectiveness of heparin sodium 20,000 units in 500 ml of dextrose 5% administered as a 12-hour infusion was not impaired. (253)

Mitchell et al. reported on heparin sodium 10,000 and 20,000 units in PVC containers of dextrose 5% in water and sodium chloride 0.9%. They found that the heparin activity remained stable for 48 hours at 27 °C. Additionally, they found that the mean pH was 6.17 for the dextrose admixtures and 5.97 for the sodium chloride admixtures. They did note a decrease in pH at four hours, which rose again at eight hours. (254)

Turco reported the results of two tests of heparin stability, obtained as personal communications from a second party. In the first, heparin was stable for 24 hours in dextrose solutions containing heparin sodium 40,000 units/L. The second indicated that heparin stability was maintained for 48 hours at concentrations of 10,000 units/L in dextrose–saline solutions. (244)

Joy et al. studied heparin sodium 20,000 units/L in dextrose 5% in water at pH 2, 5.4, and 9 at room temperature. No decrease in anticoagulant effectiveness was observed at any point over the 24-hour test period at any of the pH values. In an analogous manner, heparin activity was evaluated in dextrose 5% in sodium chloride 0.45%. Again, no change in anticoagulant effectiveness was observed in 24 hours. (407)

Anderson and Harthill described a fluctuating effect of dextrose-containing solutions on heparin activity, which they termed the "dextrose effect." They noted that no evidence supports the degradation of heparin; the reversible nature of the activity reduction rules it out. In fact, they observed both decreased and increased heparin activity, presumably fluctuating in response to certain variables. Although pH may be a factor, it is not the determining one. Other factors may include heparin concentration, salt concentration, dextrose degradation products from autoclaving, heparin molecular weight distribution in the product, differences in proprietary dextrose products, and container effects. The authors attributed the variable activity results to reversible conformational changes in the heparin molecule itself, such as chain extension or, possibly, folding. (905)

Wright and Hecker evaluated the activity of heparin sodium by activated partial thromboplastin time and by thrombin time in several dextrose-containing infusion solutions over periods up to one year. At a concentration of 1 unit/ml in dextrose 5% in water, heparin activity was retained for up to seven days at room temperature but fell substantially after that time. At 10 units/ml in dextrose 5% in water, no loss of activity was observed after 12 months of storage at either 4 °C or room temperature. At both 1 and 10 units/ml in several dextrose-containing solutions that also contained sodium chloride, no loss of heparin activity was found after 12 months of storage at either 4 °C or room temperature. (1914)

Although conflicting information exists (113; 243; 406; 674; 900), most authors believe that heparin sodium may be administered in dextrose-containing solutions. (21; 46; 57; 244; 251–254; 407; 1914)

Parenteral Nutrition Solutions — It has been stated that heparin sodium is physically and chemically compatible in amino acid injection (McGaw). (189)

The addition of heparin sodium (Abbott) 1 and 2 units/ml to fat emulsion 10%, intravenous, from both Abbott (Liposyn) and Cutter (Intralipid) did not break the emulsion and effectively reversed the blood hypercoagulability associated with intravenous fat emulsion administration. (568)

In solutions of amino acids 5% and dextrose 5 or 25% with vitamins or trace elements, heparin activity was retained for 24 hours at 25 °C. However, the activity fell significantly after 24 hours. (900)

However, Raupp et al. reported flocculation of fat emulsion (KabiVitrum) during Y-site administration into a line being used to infuse a parenteral nutrition solution containing both calcium gluconate and heparin sodium. Subsequent evaluation indicated that the combination of calcium gluconate (0.46 and 1.8 mM/125 ml) plus heparin sodium (25 and 100 units/125 ml) in amino acids plus dextrose would induce flocculation of the fat emulsion within two to four minutes at concentrations that resulted in no visually apparent flocculation in 30 minutes with either agent alone. (1214)

This result was confirmed by Johnson et al. Calcium chloride concentrations of 1 to 20 mM normally result in slow flocculation of fat emulsion 20%, intravenous, over a period of hours. When heparin sodium 5 units/ml was added, the flocculation rate accelerated greatly; a cream layer was observed visually in a few minutes. This effect was not observed when sodium ion was substituted for the divalent calcium. (1406)

Fat Emulsion — Silvers et al. observed the destabilization of fat emulsion (Intralipid 20%) when administered simultaneously with a TPN admixture. The damage, detected by viscosity measurement, occurred immediately upon contact at the Y-site. The extent of the destabilization was dependent on the concentration of the heparin and the presence of MVI Pediatric with its surfactant content. In addition to the viscosity changes, phase separation was observed in two hours. The authors noted that TPN admixtures containing heparin should never be premixed with fat emulsion as a 3-in-1 total nutrient admixture because of this emulsion destabilization. The authors indicated their belief that the damage could be minimized during Y-site coadministration as long as the heparin was kept at a sufficiently low concentration (no visible separation occurred at a heparin concentration of 0.5 unit/ml) and the length of tubing between the Y-site and the patient was minimized. (2282)

However, because the damage to emulsion integrity has been found to occur immediately upon mixing with heparin in the presence of the calcium ions in TPN admixtures (1214; 2215; 2282) and no evaluation and documentation of the clinical safety of using such destabilized emulsions has been performed, use of such damaged emulsions in patients is suspect.

Peritoneal Dialysis Solutions — The activity of heparin 35,000 units/L was evaluated in peritoneal dialysis fluids containing 1.5 and 2.5% dextrose (Dianeal, Travenol). Storage at 25 °C resulted in an apparent temporary 50% loss of heparin activity in four hours with recovery in six hours. Heparin activity was then retained for 14 days at 4 °C. (900)

Aminoglycosides — Gentamicin sulfate 10 mg/L with heparin sodium 1000 units/L in Dianeal with dextrose 5% peritoneal dialysis solution has been reported conditionally compatible. Koup and Gerbracht reported no significant reduction in gentamicin sulfate concentration or in the UV absorbance of heparin sodium in four to six hours. (228) However, a clarifying communication noted a marked reduction in the anticoagulant activity of heparin sodium if opalescence or a precipitate is formed (which results if the undiluted drugs are combined), even if the precipitate redissolves. Heparin activity was retained if one drug was added to a dilute solution of the other and no precipitate formed. (295)

Addition of gentamicin sulfate (Roussel) 80 mg to the tubing of an infusion solution of sodium chloride 0.9% containing heparin resulted in immediate precipitation. (528)

The incompatibility of heparin sodium with gentamicin sulfate is said to result from coprecipitation. (230) Similar precipitation may result from the administration of tobramycin sulfate (4; 147; 976), netilmicin sulfate, and amikacin sulfate through heparinized intravenous cannulas. (976)

Dobutamine — Several studies (789; 812; 841) have concerned the physical compatibility of dobutamine HCl in admixture with heparin sodium. The results have not been entirely consistent. Most reports indicate that the combinations tested were physically compatible. However, Hasegawa and Eder reported the formation of a precipitate with this combination. Heparin sodium (Elkins-Sinn) was diluted to a concentration of 100 units/ml with dextrose 5% in water and added to an equal volume of dobutamine HCl (Lilly), which had been diluted to 2 mg/ml with dextrose 5% in water. The precipitate formed within three minutes of combining the two drug dilutions. However, if the same heparin sodium lot or other lots (Elkins-Sinn and Invenex) were added undiluted to the dobutamine HCl in dextrose 5% in water, no visible precipitate resulted in 24 hours. Furthermore, no precipitate formed using either dilution method or any lot of heparin sodium tested when sodium chloride 0.9% was the diluent. The authors thought that precipitation may occur unpredictably. Because of this possibility plus Eli Lilly's consideration that the drugs are incompatible, the authors recommended not mixing the two drugs or infusing them through the same line. (841)

Dopamine — The interaction between dopamine HCl and heparin sodium in aqueous solution was evaluated by microcalorimetry. An exothermic reaction occurred in dextrose 5% in water but not sodium chloride 0.9%. Consequently, sodium chloride 0.9% was recommended as a vehicle to minimize the interaction between the two drugs. (1185)

Haloperidol — Heparin sodium (Organon) 25,000 and 50,000 units/250 ml of dextrose 5% in water and sodium chloride 0.9% was delivered through an administration set at a rate of 1000 units/hr. Haloperidol lactate (McNeil) 5 mg/1 ml was injected undiluted over one minute through an injection site on the set. In all cases, a precipitate formed immediately. The sodium chloride 0.9% admixtures developed a hazy milky white precipitate, while the dextrose 5% in water admixtures formed an opaque milky white precipitate with solid white particles of varying size. Injecting haloperidol lactate through sets with the infusion solutions and no heparin sodium did not yield a precipitate, ruling out incompatibility with the sets or solutions. The haloperidol lactate lowered the pH of the heparin sodium admixtures by 2 to 3 pH units, resulting in the unidentified precipitate. It was recommended that heparin infusions be stopped and that lines be flushed with sodium chloride 0.9% or dextrose 5% in water before and after injecting haloperidol lactate into the injection port. Administration of haloperidol lactate through a heparin lock would require a similar flushing procedure. (779)

Heparin Locks — Heparin locks, weak heparin solutions instilled or "locked" into infusion ports or sets through a resealing latex diaphragm, are useful in providing an established intravenous route for intermittent intravenous injections. To maintain patency, a weak heparin solution is left in the tubing. Concentrations of heparin sodium used have varied from about 10 to 1000 units/ml of sodium chloride 0.9%, with 10 and 100 units/ml being the most common. The volume of dilute heparin sodium in sodium chloride 0.9% usually used to flush the set is 0.2 to 1 ml. (255–258; 405; 677; 678; 901; 2119)

However, the use of sodium chloride 0.9% instead of a solution containing heparin has been suggested to maintain patency. Studies have found sodium chloride 0.9% to be as effective in maintaining patency as 10- and 100-unit/ml solutions of heparin. (902; 903; 1109; 1266–1269; 1639–1641; 1656; 1839; 1959; 2003; 2119) Other investigators reported that even small amounts of heparin solution are more effective than sodium chloride 0.9% alone. (678; 1270; 2120; 2121)

Evaluations of the use of heparinized solutions as locks or continuous flow solutions to help maintain patency in central venous catheters and arterial catheters have resulted in similarly variable results and recommendations. (2122–2126) Although use of such heparinized solutions has been generally considered a benign technique causing minimal problems, a number of adverse effects have been reported, especially from solutions with a high heparin concentration and/or numerous heparin flushes. (2127–2132)

It has been noted that if drugs such as meperidine HCl, promethazine HCl, and hydroxyzine HCl are injected into a heparinized scalp vein infusion set, a precipitate forms. (97) It has been suggested that the venipuncture device be flushed with sterile water for injection or sodium chloride 0.9% prior to and immediately after drug administration. Heparin lock flush solution may then be reinjected into the device. (4; 97)

Precipitation during the administration of aminoglycosides, such as gentamicin sulfate, tobramycin sulfate, netilmicin sulfate, and amikacin sulfate, through heparinized intravenous cannulas also may occur. (976)

Methylprednisolone — The compatibility of methylprednisolone sodium succinate (Upjohn) with heparin sodium added to an auxiliary medication infusion unit has been studied. Primary admixtures were prepared by adding heparin sodium 10,000 units/L to dextrose 5% in water, dextrose 5% in sodium chloride 0.9%, and Ringer's injection, lactated. Up to 100 ml of the primary admixture was added along with methylprednisolone sodium succinate (Upjohn) to the auxiliary medication infusion unit with the following results (329):

Methylprednisolone Sodium Succinate	Heparin Sodium 10,000 units/L of Primary Solution	Results
500 mg	D5S, D5W qs 100 ml	Clear solution for 24 hr
	LR qs 100 ml or added to 100 ml LR	Clear solution for 6 hr
1000 mg	D5S, D5W qs 100 ml	Clear solution for 6 hr
	Added to 100 ml D5W	Clear solution for 24 hr
	LR qs 100 ml or added to 100 ml LR	Clear solution for 4 to 6 hr
2000 mg	D5W qs 100 ml	Clear solution for 6 hr
	D5S, LR qs 100 ml	Clear solution for 24 hr

Urokinase — To simulate an admixture used to maintain patency in implantable vascular-access devices, heparin (Burgess) 100 units/ml was used to constitute urokinase (Leo) to a concentration of 6250 units/ml. The mixture was stored for 21 days at 37 °C. No visible precipitation and no loss of anticoagulant activity occurred. An apparent decline in urokinase thrombolytic activity was noted, however. Nevertheless, marked fibrinolytic activity still remained after 24 days of incubation. The authors concluded that the mixture could be used in implantable vascular-access devices for up to three weeks. (1174)

Vancomycin — Heparin sodium 5000 units/L (approximately) has been reported to be conditionally compatible with vancomycin HCl 2 g/L. A satisfactory solution is obtained if the infusion solution used is sodium chloride 0.9%. However, if dextrose 5% in water is used, a precipitate may form. (143)

Vancomycin HCl (Lilly) 25 µg/ml and heparin sodium (Elkins-Sinn) 100 units/ml in 0.9% sodium chloride injection as a catheter flush solution was evaluated for stability when stored at 4 °C for 14 days. The flush solution was visually clear, and vancomycin activity (by bioassay and immunoassay) and heparin activity (by colorimetric assay) were retained throughout the storage period. However, an additional 24 hours at 37 °C to simulate use conditions resulted in losses of both agents ranging from 20 to 37%. (1933)

Concentrated Drug Solutions — The following incompatibility determinations were performed with concentrated solutions. The drugs in dry form were reconstituted according to manufacturers' recommendations. One milliliter of heparin sodium was added to 5 ml of sterile distilled water along with 1 ml of each of the following drugs. Particulate matter was noted within two hours (28):

Dimenhydrinate (Searle)
Hydroxyzine HCl (Pfizer)
Kanamycin sulfate (Bristol)
Prochlorperazine edisylate (SKF)
Promazine HCl (Wyeth)
Promethazine HCl (Wyeth)
Vancomycin HCl (Lilly)

Other Drugs — Amphotericin B infusions appear to be compatible with limited amounts of heparin sodium. (4) Also, epirubicin HCl (1442), ceftazidime (4), and cefotetan disodium (283) have been stated to be compatible with heparin sodium.

Heparin is strongly acidic, reacting with certain basic compounds and losing activity. (4) Solutions containing heparin sodium have been reported to be incompatible with tobramycin sulfate and gentamicin sulfate. (4; 147; 230) A precipitate resulted when heparin sodium was added to an infusion solution containing antihuman lymphocyte globulin (Pressimmune, Hoechst). (408) Heparin is reported to decrease the antibacterial activity of neomycin. (409) Ciprofloxacin, doxorubicin HCl, droperidol, mitoxantrone (4), and idarubicin HCl (2) have been reported to be incompatible with heparin sodium because of possible precipitate formation. Immunex also recommends not combining heparin sodium with mitoxantrone HCl in the same admixture because of possible precipitate formation. (2; 1293)

Other Information

Care is required when adding heparin sodium to infusion solutions, especially in flexible containers. When heparin sodium was added to a flexible PVC container of sodium chloride 0.9% hanging in the use position, pooling of the heparin resulted; 97% of the heparin was delivered in the first 30% of the solution. Repeated inversion and agitation of the containers to effect thorough mixing eliminates this pooling (and the danger of overdosage), yielding an even distribution and a constant delivery concentration. (85)

HETASTARCH IN LACTATED ELECTROLYTE INJECTION
AHFS 40:12

Products — Hetastarch 6% in lactated electrolyte injection is available in 500- and 1000-ml flexible plastic infusion containers. Each 100 milliliters of solution contains (1-9/99):

Component	Amount
Hetastarch	6 g
Sodium chloride	672 mg
Sodium lactate anhydrous	317 mg
Dextrose hydrous	99 mg
Calcium chloride dihydrate	37 mg
Potassium chloride	22 mg
Magnesium chloride hexahydrate	9 mg
Water for injection	qs 100 ml

pH— Approximately 5.9 with negligible buffering capacity. (1-9/99)

Osmolarity— Approximately 307 mOsm/L. (1-9/99)

Electrolyte Content— The concentrations of electrolytes are shown in Table 1.

Trade Name(s)— Hextend.

Administration — Hetastarch 6% in lactated electrolyte injection is administered by intravenous infusion. The amount of solution and rate of administration depend on the clinical condition and needs of the patient. The product should be inspected for cloudiness, haze, and particulate matter prior to use. Solutions such as this product that contain calcium should not be administered simultaneously with blood through the same set because of the likelihood of coagulation. (1-9/99)

Stability — Intact containers of hetastarch 6% in lactated electrolyte injection should be stored at controlled room temperature and protected from freezing and excessive heat. Brief exposure at temperatures up to 40 °C does not adversely affect the product. (1-9/99)

The product is a clear, pale yellow to amber solution. Prolonged exposure to adverse conditions may result in the formation of a turbid deep brown appearance or crystalline precipitate; such solutions should not be used. (1-9/99)

Table 1. Electrolyte Composition (1-9/99)

Electrolyte	mEq/L
Sodium	143
Calcium	5
Potassium	3
Magnesium	0.9
Chloride	124
Lactate	28

Compatibility Information

Y-Site Injection Compatibility (1:1 Mixture)

Hetastarch in lactated electrolyte injection

Drug	*Mfr*	*Conc*	*Mfr*	*Conc*	*Remarks*	*Ref*	*C/I*
Alatrofloxacin mesylate	PF	2 mg/ml[a]	AB	6%	Physically compatible with no change in measured turbidity or increase in particle content in 4 hr at 23 °C	2339	C
Alfentanil HCl	TAY	0.125 mg/ml[a]	AB	6%	Physically compatible with no change in measured turbidity or increase in particle content in 4 hr at 23 °C	2339	C
Amikacin sulfate	APC	5 mg/ml[a]	AB	6%	Physically compatible with no change in measured turbidity or increase in particle content in 4 hr at 23 °C	2339	C
Aminophylline	AMR	2.5 mg/ml[a]	AB	6%	Physically compatible with no change in measured turbidity or increase in particle content in 4 hr at 23 °C	2339	C
Amiodarone HCl	WAY	4 mg/ml[a]	AB	6%	Physically compatible with no change in measured turbidity or increase in particle content in 4 hr at 23 °C	2339	C
Amphotericin B	APC	0.6 mg/ml[a]	AB	6%	Immediate gross precipitation	2339	I
Ampicillin sodium	APC	20 mg/ml[b]	AB	6%	Physically compatible with no change in measured turbidity or increase in particle content in 4 hr at 23 °C	2339	C
Ampicillin sodium–sulbactam sodium	PF	20+10 mg/ml[b]	AB	6%	Physically compatible with no change in measured turbidity or increase in particle content in 4 hr at 23 °C	2339	C

Y-Site Injection Compatibility (1:1 Mixture) (Cont.)

Drug	*Mfr*	*Conc*	Hetastarch in lactated electrolyte injection *Mfr*	*Conc*	*Remarks*	*Ref*	*C/I*
Atracurium besylate	GW	0.5 mg/ml[a]	AB	6%	Physically compatible with no change in measured turbidity or increase in particle content in 4 hr at 23 °C	2339	C
Azithromycin	PF	2 mg/ml[a]	AB	6%	Physically compatible with no change in measured turbidity or increase in particle content in 4 hr at 23 °C	2339	C
Bumetanide	OH	0.04 mg/ml[a]	AB	6%	Physically compatible with no change in measured turbidity or increase in particle content in 4 hr at 23 °C	2339	C
Butorphanol tartrate	APC	0.04 mg/ml[a]	AB	6%	Physically compatible with no change in measured turbidity or increase in particle content in 4 hr at 23 °C	2339	C
Calcium gluconate	FUJ	40 mg/ml[a]	AB	6%	Physically compatible with no change in measured turbidity or increase in particle content in 4 hr at 23 °C	2339	C
Cefazolin sodium	LI	20 mg/ml[a]	AB	6%	Physically compatible with no change in measured turbidity or increase in particle content in 4 hr at 23 °C	2339	C
Cefepime HCl	BMS	20 mg/ml[a]	AB	6%	Physically compatible with no change in measured turbidity or increase in particle content in 4 hr at 23 °C	2339	C
Cefoperazone sodium	RR	40 mg/ml[a]	AB	6%	Physically compatible with no change in measured turbidity or increase in particle content in 4 hr at 23 °C	2339	C
Cefotaxime sodium	HO	20 mg/ml[a]	AB	6%	Physically compatible with no change in measured turbidity or increase in particle content in 4 hr at 23 °C	2339	C
Cefotetan sodium	ZEN	20 mg/ml[a]	AB	6%	Physically compatible with no change in measured turbidity or increase in particle content in 4 hr at 23 °C	2339	C
Cefoxitin sodium	ME	20 mg/ml[a]	AB	6%	Physically compatible with no change in measured turbidity or increase in particle content in 4 hr at 23 °C	2339	C
Ceftazidime[c]	GW	40 mg/ml[a]	AB	6%	Physically compatible with no change in measured turbidity or increase in particle content in 4 hr at 23 °C	2339	C
Ceftizoxime sodium	FUJ	20 mg/ml[a]	AB	6%	Physically compatible with no change in measured turbidity or increase in particle content in 4 hr at 23 °C	2339	C
Ceftriaxone sodium	RC	20 mg/ml[a]	AB	6%	Physically compatible with no change in measured turbidity or increase in particle content in 4 hr at 23 °C	2339	C
Cefuroxime sodium	LI	30 mg/ml[a]	AB	6%	Physically compatible with no change in measured turbidity or increase in particle content in 4 hr at 23 °C	2339	C
Chlorpromazine HCl	ES	2 mg/ml[a]	AB	6%	Physically compatible with no change in measured turbidity or increase in particle content in 4 hr at 23 °C	2339	C

Y-Site Injection Compatibility (1:1 Mixture) (Cont.)

			Hetastarch in lactated electrolyte injection				
Drug	*Mfr*	*Conc*	*Mfr*	*Conc*	*Remarks*	*Ref*	*C/I*
Cimetidine HCl	SKB	12 mg/ml[a]	AB	6%	Physically compatible with no change in measured turbidity or increase in particle content in 4 hr at 23 °C	2339	C
Ciprofloxacin	BAY	2 mg/ml[a]	AB	6%	Physically compatible with no change in measured turbidity or increase in particle content in 4 hr at 23 °C	2339	C
Cisatracurium besylate	GW	0.5 mg/ml[a]	AB	6%	Physically compatible with no change in measured turbidity or increase in particle content in 4 hr at 23 °C	2339	C
Clindamycin phosphate	PHU	10 mg/ml[a]	AB	6%	Physically compatible with no change in measured turbidity or increase in particle content in 4 hr at 23 °C	2339	C
Dexamethasone sodium phosphate	APP	1 mg/ml[a]	AB	6%	Physically compatible with no change in measured turbidity or increase in particle content in 4 hr at 23 °C	2339	C
Diazepam	AB	5 mg/ml	AB	6%	Dense white turbid precipitate forms immediately	2339	I
Digoxin	ES	0.25 mg/ml	AB	6%	Physically compatible with no change in measured turbidity or increase in particle content in 4 hr at 23 °C	2339	C
Diltiazem HCl	BA	5 mg/ml	AB	6%	Physically compatible with no change in measured turbidity or increase in particle content in 4 hr at 23 °C	2339	C
Diphenhydramine HCl	SCN	2 mg/ml[a]	AB	6%	Physically compatible with no change in measured turbidity or increase in particle content in 4 hr at 23 °C	2339	C
Dobutamine HCl	AST	4 mg/ml[a]	AB	6%	Physically compatible with no change in measured turbidity or increase in particle content in 4 hr at 23 °C	2339	C
Dolasetron HCl	HO	2 mg/ml[a]	AB	6%	Physically compatible with no change in measured turbidity or increase in particle content in 4 hr at 23 °C	2339	C
Dopamine HCl	AB	3.2 mg/ml[a]	AB	6%	Physically compatible with no change in measured turbidity or increase in particle content in 4 hr at 23 °C	2339	C
Doxycycline hyclate	APP	1 mg/ml[a]	AB	6%	Physically compatible with no change in measured turbidity or increase in particle content in 4 hr at 23 °C	2339	C
Droperidol	AMR	2.5 mg/ml	AB	6%	Physically compatible with no change in measured turbidity or increase in particle content in 4 hr at 23 °C	2339	C
Enalaprilat	ME	0.1 mg/ml[a]	AB	6%	Physically compatible with no change in measured turbidity or increase in particle content in 4 hr at 23 °C	2339	C
Ephedrine sulfate	TAY	5 mg/ml[a]	AB	6%	Physically compatible with no change in measured turbidity or increase in particle content in 4 hr at 23 °C	2339	C

Y-Site Injection Compatibility (1:1 Mixture) (Cont.)

Hetastarch in lactated electrolyte injection

Drug	*Mfr*	*Conc*	*Mfr*	*Conc*	*Remarks*	*Ref*	*C/I*
Epinephrine HCl	AB	0.05 mg/ml[a]	AB	6%	Physically compatible with no change in measured turbidity or increase in particle content in 4 hr at 23 °C	2339	C
Erythromycin lactobionate	AB	5 mg/ml[b]	AB	6%	Physically compatible with no change in measured turbidity or increase in particle content in 4 hr at 23 °C	2339	C
Esmolol	OH	10 mg/ml	AB	6%	Physically compatible with no change in measured turbidity or increase in particle content in 4 hr at 23 °C	2339	C
Famotidine	ME	2 mg/ml[a]	AB	6%	Physically compatible with no change in measured turbidity or increase in particle content in 4 hr at 23 °C	2339	C
Fentanyl citrate	ES	12.5 μg/ml[a]	AB	6%	Physically compatible with no change in measured turbidity or increase in particle content in 4 hr at 23 °C	2339	C
Fluconazole	PF	2 mg/ml	AB	6%	Physically compatible with no change in measured turbidity or increase in particle content in 4 hr at 23 °C	2339	C
Furosemide	AMR	3 mg/ml[a]	AB	6%	Physically compatible with no change in measured turbidity or increase in particle content in 4 hr at 23 °C	2339	C
Gentamicin sulfate	SC	5 mg/ml[a]	AB	6%	Physically compatible with no change in measured turbidity or increase in particle content in 4 hr at 23 °C	2339	C
Granisetron HCl	SKB	0.05 mg/ml[a]	AB	6%	Physically compatible with no change in measured turbidity or increase in particle content in 4 hr at 23 °C	2339	C
Haloperidol lactate	MN	0.2 mg/ml[a]	AB	6%	Physically compatible with no change in measured turbidity or increase in particle content in 4 hr at 23 °C	2339	C
Heparin sodium	ES	100 units/ml	AB	6%	Physically compatible with no change in measured turbidity or increase in particle content in 4 hr at 23 °C	2339	C
Hydrocortisone sodium succinate	PHU	1 mg/ml[a]	AB	6%	Physically compatible with no change in measured turbidity or increase in particle content in 4 hr at 23 °C	2339	C
Hydromorphone HCl	AST	0.5 mg/ml[a]	AB	6%	Physically compatible with no change in measured turbidity or increase in particle content in 4 hr at 23 °C	2339	C
Hydroxyzine HCl	ES	2 mg/ml[a]	AB	6%	Physically compatible with no change in measured turbidity or increase in particle content in 4 hr at 23 °C	2339	C
Inamrinone lactate	AB	2.5 mg/ml[b]	AB	6%	Physically compatible with no change in measured turbidity or increase in particle content in 4 hr at 23 °C	2339	C
Isoproterenol HCl	AB	0.02 mg/ml[a]	AB	6%	Physically compatible with no change in measured turbidity or increase in particle content in 4 hr at 23 °C	2339	C

Y-Site Injection Compatibility (1:1 Mixture) (Cont.)

Drug	Mfr	Conc	Hetastarch in lactated electrolyte injection Mfr	Conc	Remarks	Ref	C/I
Ketorolac tromethamine	AB	15 mg/ml	AB	6%	Physically compatible with no change in measured turbidity or increase in particle content in 4 hr at 23 °C	2339	C
Labetalol HCl	GW	2 mg/ml[a]	AB	6%	Physically compatible with no change in measured turbidity or increase in particle content in 4 hr at 23 °C	2339	C
Levofloxacin	OMN	5 mg/ml[a]	AB	6%	Physically compatible with no change in measured turbidity or increase in particle content in 4 hr at 23 °C	2339	C
Lidocaine HCl	AB	8 mg/ml[a]	AB	6%	Physically compatible with no change in measured turbidity or increase in particle content in 4 hr at 23 °C	2339	C
Lorazepam	OH	0.5 mg/ml[a]	AB	6%	Physically compatible with no change in measured turbidity or increase in particle content in 4 hr at 23 °C	2339	C
Magnesium sulfate	AST	100 mg/ml[a]	AB	6%	Physically compatible with no change in measured turbidity or increase in particle content in 4 hr at 23 °C	2339	C
Mannitol	BA	15%	AB	6%	Physically compatible with no change in measured turbidity or increase in particle content in 4 hr at 23 °C	2339	C
Meperidine HCl	OH	4 mg/ml[a]	AB	6%	Physically compatible with no change in measured turbidity or increase in particle content in 4 hr at 23 °C	2339	C
Methylprednisolone sodium succinate	PHU	5 mg/ml[a]	AB	6%	Physically compatible with no change in measured turbidity or increase in particle content in 4 hr at 23 °C	2339	C
Metoclopramide HCl	FAU	5 mg/ml	AB	6%	Physically compatible with no change in measured turbidity or increase in particle content in 4 hr at 23 °C	2339	C
Metronidazole	AB	5 mg/ml	AB	6%	Physically compatible with no change in measured turbidity or increase in particle content in 4 hr at 23 °C	2339	C
Midazolam HCl	RC	1 mg/ml[a]	AB	6%	Physically compatible with no change in measured turbidity or increase in particle content in 4 hr at 23 °C	2339	C
Milrinone lactate	SAN	0.2 mg/ml[a]	AB	6%	Physically compatible with no change in measured turbidity or increase in particle content in 4 hr at 23 °C	2339	C
Mivacurium chloride	GW	0.5 mg/ml[a]	AB	6%	Physically compatible with no change in measured turbidity or increase in particle content in 4 hr at 23 °C	2339	C
Morphine sulfate	AST	1 mg/ml[a]	AB	6%	Physically compatible with no change in measured turbidity or increase in particle content in 4 hr at 23 °C	2339	C
Nalbuphine HCl	AST	10 mg/ml	AB	6%	Physically compatible with no change in measured turbidity or increase in particle content in 4 hr at 23 °C	2339	C

Y-Site Injection Compatibility (1:1 Mixture) (Cont.)

			Hetastarch in lactated electrolyte injection				
Drug	*Mfr*	*Conc*	*Mfr*	*Conc*	*Remarks*	*Ref*	*C/I*
Nitroglycerin	AMR	0.4 mg/ml[a]	AB	6%	Physically compatible with no change in measured turbidity or increase in particle content in 4 hr at 23 °C	2339	C
Norepinephrine bitartrate	AB	0.12 mg/ml[a]	AB	6%	Physically compatible with no change in measured turbidity or increase in particle content in 4 hr at 23 °C	2339	C
Ofloxacin	OMN	4 mg/ml[a]	AB	6%	Physically compatible with no change in measured turbidity or increase in particle content in 4 hr at 23 °C	2339	C
Ondansetron HCl	GW	1 mg/ml[a]	AB	6%	Physically compatible with no change in measured turbidity or increase in particle content in 4 hr at 23 °C	2339	C
Pancuronium bromide	ES	0.1 mg/ml[a]	AB	6%	Physically compatible with no change in measured turbidity or increase in particle content in 4 hr at 23 °C	2339	C
Phenylephrine HCl	OH	1 mg/ml[a]	AB	6%	Physically compatible with no change in measured turbidity or increase in particle content in 4 hr at 23 °C	2339	C
Piperacillin sodium	LE	40 mg/ml[a]	AB	6%	Physically compatible with no change in measured turbidity or increase in particle content in 4 hr at 23 °C	2339	C
Piperacillin sodium–tazobactam sodium	LE	40 +5 mg/ml[a]	AB	6%	Physically compatible with no change in measured turbidity or increase in particle content in 4 hr at 23 °C	2339	C
Potassium chloride	AB	0.1 mEq/ml[a]	AB	6%	Physically compatible with no change in measured turbidity or increase in particle content in 4 hr at 23 °C	2339	C
Procainamide HCl	ES	10 mg/ml[a]	AB	6%	Physically compatible with no change in measured turbidity or increase in particle content in 4 hr at 23 °C	2339	C
Prochlorperazine edisylate	SO	0.5 mg/ml[a]	AB	6%	Physically compatible with no change in measured turbidity or increase in particle content in 4 hr at 23 °C	2339	C
Promethazine HCl	SCN	2 mg/ml[a]	AB	6%	Physically compatible with no change in measured turbidity or increase in particle content in 4 hr at 23 °C	2339	C
Ranitidine HCl	GW	2 mg/ml[a]	AB	6%	Physically compatible with no change in measured turbidity or increase in particle content in 4 hr at 23 °C	2339	C
Rocuronium bromide	OR	1 mg/ml[a]	AB	6%	Physically compatible with no change in measured turbidity or increase in particle content in 4 hr at 23 °C	2339	C
Sodium bicarbonate	AB	1 mEq/ml	AB	6%	Microprecipitate develops rapidly	2339	I
Sodium nitroprusside	OH	2 mg/ml[a]	AB	6%	Physically compatible with no change in measured turbidity or increase in particle content in 4 hr at 23 °C protected from light	2339	C

Y-Site Injection Compatibility (1:1 Mixture) (Cont.)

Drug	Mfr	Conc	Hetastarch in lactated electrolyte injection Mfr	Conc	Remarks	Ref	C/I
Succinylcholine chloride	AB	2 mg/ml[a]	AB	6%	Physically compatible with no change in measured turbidity or increase in particle content in 4 hr at 23 °C	2339	C
Sufentanil citrate	BA	12.5 µg/ml[a]	AB	6%	Physically compatible with no change in measured turbidity or increase in particle content in 4 hr at 23 °C	2339	C
Theophylline	BA	4 mg/ml[a]	AB	6%	Physically compatible with no change in measured turbidity or increase in particle content in 4 hr at 23 °C	2339	C
Thiopental sodium	OH	25 mg/ml	AB	6%	Physically compatible with no change in measured turbidity or increase in particle content in 4 hr at 23 °C	2339	C
Ticarcillin disodium	SKB	30 mg/ml[a]	AB	6%	Physically compatible with no change in measured turbidity or increase in particle content in 4 hr at 23 °C	2339	C
Ticarcillin disodium–clavulanate potassium	SKB	31 mg/ml[a]	AB	6%	Physically compatible with no change in measured turbidity or increase in particle content in 4 hr at 23 °C	2339	C
Tobramycin sulfate	GNS	5 mg/ml[a]	AB	6%	Physically compatible with no change in measured turbidity or increase in particle content in 4 hr at 23 °C	2339	C
Trimethoprim–sulfamethoxazole	ES	0.8+4 mg/ml[a]	AB	6%	Physically compatible with no change in measured turbidity or increase in particle content in 4 hr at 23 °C	2339	C
Vancomycin HCl	LI	10 mg/ml[a]	AB	6%	Physically compatible with no change in measured turbidity or increase in particle content in 4 hr at 23 °C	2339	C
Vecuronium bromide	OR	0.2 mg/ml[a]	AB	6%	Physically compatible with no change in measured turbidity or increase in particle content in 4 hr at 23 °C	2339	C
Verapamil HCl	AMR	1.25 mg/ml[a]	AB	6%	Physically compatible with no change in measured turbidity or increase in particle content in 4 hr at 23 °C	2339	C

[a]*Tested in dextrose 5% in water.*
[b]*Tested in sodium chloride 0.9%.*
[c]*Sodium carbonate–containing formulation was tested.*

HETASTARCH IN SODIUM CHLORIDE 0.9% AHFS 40:12

Products — Hetastarch is available as a 6% (6 g/100 ml) injection in sodium chloride 0.9% in 500-ml plastic containers. The solution also contains sodium hydroxide for pH adjustment. (1-3/99)

pH — Approximately 5.5; range: 3.5 to 7. (1-3/99; 4)

Osmolarity — The product has an osmolarity of 310 mOsm/L. (1-3/99; 4)

Sodium Content — Hetastarch 6% in sodium chloride 0.9% provides 77 mEq of sodium per 500-ml container. (4)

Trade Name(s) — Hespan.

Administration — Hetastarch is given only by intravenous infusion; discard any remaining solution in partially used containers. The dosage and rate of infusion must be individualized to the patient's condition and response. (1-3/99; 4)

Stability — Hetastarch injection is a clear, pale yellow to amber colloidal solution. The product should be stored at controlled room temperature and protected from freezing and excessive heat. Brief exposure to temperatures up to 40 °C does not affect potency. However, prolonged storage under adverse conditions may result in a crystalline precipitate or a deep brown turbid appearance. Such solutions should not be administered. (1-3/99; 4)

Amylose starch has been shown to associate and precipitate over time in solution. (2296) Before hetastarch is used, the colloidal solution should be checked for clarity and particulates and the flexible plastic containers should be squeezed to check for small leaks. (1-3/99)

Compatibility Information

Additive Compatibility

Hetastarch in sodium chloride 0.9%

Drug	*Mfr*	*Conc/L*	*Mfr*	*Conc/L*	*Test Soln*	*Remarks*	*Ref*	*C/I*
Fosphenytoin sodium	PD	1, 8, 20 mg PE/ml[a]	MG	6%[b]		Visually compatible with little or no loss of fosphenytoin by HPLC in 7 days at 25 °C under fluorescent light	2083	C

[a]Concentration expressed in milligrams of phenytoin sodium equivalents (PE) per milliliter.
[b]In sodium chloride 0.9%.

Y-Site Injection Compatibility (1:1 Mixture)

Hetastarch in sodium chloride 0.9%

Drug	*Mfr*	*Conc*	*Mfr*	*Conc*	*Remarks*	*Ref*	*C/I*
Amikacin sulfate	BR	5 mg/ml[a]	DCC	6%	Small crystals formed immediately after mixing and persisted for 4 hr	1313	I
Ampicillin sodium	BR	20 mg/ml[a]	DCC	6%	Physically compatible for 4 hr at room temperature by visual examination	1313	C
	BR	20 mg/ml[a]	DCC	6%	One or two particles in one of five vials. Fine white strands appeared immediately during Y-site infusion	1315	I
Cefamandole nafate	LI	20 mg/ml[a]	DCC	6%	Small crystals formed immediately after mixing and persisted for 4 hr	1313	I
Cefazolin sodium	SKF	20 mg/ml[a]	DCC	6%	Physically compatible for 4 hr at room temperature by visual examination	1313	C
	SKF	20 mg/ml[a]	DCC	6%	Simulation in vials showed no incompatibility, but white precipitate formed in Y-site during infusion	1315	I
Cefoperazone sodium	RR	20 mg/ml[a]	DCC	6%	Small crystals formed immediately after mixing and persisted for 4 hr	1313	I
Cefotaxime sodium	HO	20 mg/ml[a]	DCC	6%	Small crystals formed immediately after mixing and persisted for 4 hr	1313	I
Cefoxitin sodium	MSD	20 mg/ml[a]	DCC	6%	Precipitate forms after 1 hr at room temperature	1313	I
Cimetidine HCl	SKF	6 mg/ml[a]	DCC	6%	Physically compatible for 4 hr at room temperature by visual examination	1313; 1315	C
Diltiazem HCl	MMD	5 mg/ml	DU	6%	Visually compatible	1807	C
Doxycycline hyclate	LY	1 mg/ml[a]	DCC	6%	Physically compatible for 4 hr at room temperature by visual examination	1313	C
	LY	1 mg/ml[a]	DCC	6%	White particle in one of five vials. No evidence of incompatibility during Y-site infusion	1315	?

Y-Site Injection Compatibility (1:1 Mixture) (Cont.)

			Hetastarch in sodium chloride 0.9%				
Drug	*Mfr*	*Conc*	*Mfr*	*Conc*	*Remarks*	*Ref*	*C/I*
Enalaprilat	MSD	0.05 mg/ml[b]	DCC	6%	Physically compatible for 24 hr at room temperature under fluorescent light	1355	C
Gentamicin sulfate	TR	0.8 mg/ml[c]	DCC	6%	Immediate precipitation which disappeared after 1 hr at room temperature	1313	I
Ranitidine HCl	GL	0.5 mg/ml[c]	DCC	6%	Barely visible single particle appeared after 1 hr but disappeared when vial was rotated	1313	?
	GL	0.5 mg/ml[c]	DCC	6%	Barely visible particles appeared and disappeared in three of five vials	1314	I
	GL	0.5 mg/ml[c]	DCC	6%	Small white particle in two of five vials. Small white fiber formed on needle during Y-site infusion	1315	I
Theophylline	TR	4 mg/ml[c]	DCC	6%	Precipitation after 2 hr at room temperature	1313	I
Tobramycin sulfate	LI	0.8 mg/ml[c]	DCC	6%	Small crystals formed immediately after mixing and persisted for 4 hr	1313	I

[a]*Tested in dextrose 5% in water.*
[b]*Tested in sodium chloride 0.9%.*
[c]*Premixed infusion solution.*

HYDRALAZINE HCL
AHFS 24:08

Products — Hydralazine HCl is available in 1-ml vials. Each milliliter of solution contains hydralazine HCl 20 mg and propylene glycol 103.6 mg in water for injection. (1-5/99) The pH may have been adjusted with hydrochloric acid and/or sodium hydroxide. (1-5/99)

pH — From 3.4 to 4.4. (1-5/99)

Administration — Hydralazine HCl may be administered intramuscularly or as a rapid intravenous injection directly into the vein; the manufacturer does not recommend adding the drug to infusion solutions. (1-5/99; 4)

Stability — Hydralazine HCl in intact vials should be stored at controlled room temperature and protected from freezing. (1-5/99; 4) Refrigeration of the intact containers may result in precipitation or crystallization. (593)

Hydralazine HCl undergoes color changes in most infusion solutions. However, it has been stated that color changes within eight to 12 hours of admixture preparation in solutions stored at 30 °C are not indicative of potency losses. (4) The manufacturer does not recommend admixture in infusion solutions. (1-5/99)

Hydralazine HCl (Ciba) at a concentration of 40 mg/L in dextrose 5% in water, with the pH varied by the addition of hydrochloric acid, was stable at pH 3 to 5 by UV spectroscopy. (466)

Light Effects — Exposure to light increases the rate of hydralazine HCl decomposition during long-term storage. At a hydralazine HCl concentration of 0.35 mg/ml in sodium chloride 0.9% in glass bottles, 10% decomposition was calculated to occur in 14.4 weeks in the dark and 12.3 weeks under fluorescent light. In PVC containers, decomposition occurs more rapidly; a 10% loss was calculated to occur in 12.8 weeks in the dark and 9.9 weeks under fluorescent light. (1561)

Sorption — Hydralazine HCl (Sigma) 27 mg/L in sodium chloride 0.9% (Travenol) in PVC bags exhibited approximately 10% loss in one week at room temperature (15 to 20 °C) due to sorption. (536)

However, hydralazine HCl (Sigma) 27 mg/L in sodium chloride 0.9% did not exhibit any loss due to sorption during a seven-hour simulated infusion through an infusion set (Travenol) consisting of a cellulose propionate burette chamber and 170 cm of PVC tubing. (606)

The drug also was tested as a simulated infusion over at least one hour by a syringe pump system. A glass syringe on a syringe pump was fitted with 20 cm of polyethylene tubing or 50 cm of Silastic tubing. No loss of drug due to sorption was observed with either tubing. (606)

In addition, a 25-ml aliquot of hydralazine HCl (Sigma) 27 mg/L in sodium chloride 0.9% was stored in all-plastic syringes composed of polypropylene barrels and polyethylene plungers for 24 hours at room temperature in the dark. No loss due to sorption occurred. (606)

Compatibility Information

Solution Compatibility

Hydralazine HCl

Solution	*Mfr*	*Mfr*	*Conc/L*	*Remarks*	*Ref*	*C/I*
Dextran 6% in dextrose 5%	AB	CI	400 mg	Physically compatible	3	C
Dextran 6% in sodium chloride 0.9%	AB	CI	400 mg	Physically compatible	3	C
Dextrose–Ringer's injection combinations	AB	CI	400 mg	Physically compatible	3	C
Dextrose 5% in Ringer's injection, lactated	AB	CI	400 mg	Physically compatible	3	C
Dextrose 2½% in half-strength Ringer's injection, lactated	AB	CI	400 mg	Physically compatible	3	C
Dextrose–saline combinations	AB	CI	400 mg	Physically compatible	3	C
Dextrose 2½% in water	AB	CI	400 mg	Physically compatible	3	C
Dextrose 5% in water		CI	40 mg	Yellow color within 1 hr. 4% decomposition in 2 hr and 8% in 3.5 hr by UV	466	I
			200 to 400 mg	Progressive yellow discoloration due to hydralazine reaction with dextrose	845	I
	TR[a]		350 mg	10% loss by HPLC in 1 hr at 21 °C under fluorescent light. Approximately 11 to 12% loss in 1.5 hr at 21 °C in the dark	1561	I
Dextrose 10% in water	AB	CI	400 mg	Physically compatible	3	C
Dextrose 10% in Ringer's injection, lactated	AB	CI	400 mg	Color change	3	I
Fructose 10% in sodium chloride 0.9%	AB	CI	400 mg	Color change	3	I
Fructose 10% in water	AB	CI	400 mg	Color change	3	I
Invert sugar 5 and 10% in sodium chloride 0.9%	AB	CI	400 mg	Physically compatible	3	C
Invert sugar 5 and 10% in water	AB	CI	400 mg	Physically compatible	3	C
Ionosol products	AB	CI	400 mg	Physically compatible	3	C
Ringer's injection	AB	CI	400 mg	Physically compatible	3	C
Ringer's injection, lactated	AB	CI	400 mg	Physically compatible	3	C
		CI	40 mg	No decomposition in 2.5 hr	466	C
Sodium chloride 0.45%	AB	CI	400 mg	Physically compatible	3	C
Sodium chloride 0.9%	AB	CI	400 mg	Physically compatible	3	C
		CI	40 mg	No decomposition in 4 days by UV	466	C
			200 to 400 mg	Physically compatible	845	C
	TR[a]		350 mg	6 to 8% loss by HPLC in 52 days at 21 °C under fluorescent light	1561	C
Sodium lactate ⅙ M	AB	CI	400 mg	Physically compatible	3	C

[a] *Tested in both glass and PVC containers.*

Additive Compatibility

Hydralazine HCl

Drug	*Mfr*	*Conc/L*	*Mfr*	*Conc/L*	*Test Soln*	*Remarks*	*Ref*	*C/I*
Aminophylline	BP	1 g	BP	80 mg	D5W	Yellow color produced	26	I
Ampicillin sodium	BP	2 g	BP	80 mg	D5W	Yellow color produced	26	I

Additive Compatibility (Cont.)

Hydralazine HCl

Drug	Mfr	Conc/L	Mfr	Conc/L	Test Soln	Remarks	Ref	C/I
Chlorothiazide sodium	BP	2 g	BP	80 mg	D5W, NS	Yellow color produced with precipitate in 3 hr	26	I
Dobutamine HCl	LI	200 mg	CI	200 mg	NS	Physically compatible for 24 hr	552	C
Edetate calcium disodium	RI	4 g	BP	80 mg	D5W	Yellow color produced	26	I
Ethacrynate sodium	MSD	50 mg	CI	20 mg	NS	Altered UV spectra for both at room temperature	16	I
Hydrocortisone sodium succinate	BP	400 mg	BP	80 mg	D5W	Yellow color produced	26	I
Mephentermine sulfate	BP	120 mg	BP	80 mg	D5W	Yellow color produced	26	I
Methohexital sodium	BP	2 g	BP	80 mg	D5W, NS	Yellow color produced with precipitate in 3 hr	26	I
Nitroglycerin	ACC	400 mg	CI	1 g	D5W[a]	Deep yellow color produced. 4% nitroglycerin loss in 48 hr at 23 °C. Hydralazine not tested	929	I
	ACC	400 mg	CI	1 g	NS[a]	Pale yellow color produced. No nitroglycerin loss in 48 hr at 23 °C. Hydralazine not tested	929	I
Phenobarbital sodium	BP	800 mg	BP	80 mg	D5W	Yellow color produced with precipitate in 3 hr	26	I
Verapamil HCl	KN	80 mg	CI	40 mg	D5W, NS	Yellow color produced	764	I

[a]*Tested in glass containers.*

Y-Site Injection Compatibility (1:1 Mixture)

Hydralazine HCl

Drug	Mfr	Conc	Mfr	Conc	Remarks	Ref	C/I
Aminophylline	ES	4 mg/ml[a]	SO	1 mg/ml[a]	Gross color change in 1 hr	1316	I
	ES	4 mg/ml[b]	SO	1 mg/ml[b]	Moderate color change in 1 hr and slight haze in 3 hr	1316	I
Ampicillin sodium	WY	40 mg/ml[a]	SO	1 mg/ml[a]	Moderate color change in 1 hr	1316	I
	WY	40 mg/ml[b]	SO	1 mg/ml[b]	Moderate color change in 3 hr	1316	I
Diazoxide	SC	15 mg/ml[c]	SO	1 mg/ml[c]	Moderate precipitate and color change in 1 hr	1316	I
Furosemide	ES	1 mg/ml[c]	SO	1 mg/ml[c]	Slight color change in 3 hr	1316	I
Heparin sodium	UP	1000 units/L[d]	CI	20 mg/ml	Physically compatible for at least 4 hr at room temperature by visual and microscopic examination	534	C
Hydrocortisone sodium succinate	UP	10 mg/L[d]	CI	20 mg/ml	Physically compatible for at least 4 hr at room temperature by visual and microscopic examination	534	C
Nitroglycerin	LY	0.4 mg/ml[a]	SO	1 mg/ml[a]	Physically compatible for 3 hr	1316	C
	LY	0.4 mg/ml[b]	SO	1 mg/ml[b]	Slight precipitate in 3 hr	1316	I
Potassium chloride	AB	40 mEq/L[d]	CI	20 mg/ml	Physically compatible for at least 4 hr at room temperature by visual and microscopic examination	534	C

Y-Site Injection Compatibility (1:1 Mixture) (Cont.)

Hydralazine HCl

Drug	*Mfr*	*Conc*	*Mfr*	*Conc*	*Remarks*	*Ref*	*C/I*
Verapamil HCl	LY	0.2 mg/ml[c]	SO	1 mg/ml[c]	Physically compatible for 3 hr	1316	C
Vitamin B complex with C	RC	2 ml/L[d]	CI	20 mg/ml	Physically compatible for at least 4 hr at room temperature by visual and microscopic examination	534	C

[a] *Tested in dextrose 5% in water.*
[b] *Tested in sodium chloride 0.9%.*
[c] *Tested in both dextrose 5% in water and sodium chloride 0.9%.*
[d] *Tested in dextrose 5% in Ringer's injection, dextrose 5% in Ringer's injection, lactated, dextrose 5% in water, Ringer's injection, lactated, and sodium chloride 0.9%.*

Additional Compatibility Information

Metals — Hydralazine HCl may react with various metals (1-5/99) to yield discolored solutions, often yellow or pink. One report indicated a pink discoloration in prefilled syringes when the hydralazine HCl had been drawn up through filter needles (Monoject) with a stainless steel filter and stored for up to 12 hours. The reaction is not specific to any one metal. Consequently, contact with metal parts should be minimized, and hydralazine HCl should be prepared just prior to use. (906)

HYDROCORTISONE SODIUM PHOSPHATE
AHFS 68:04

Products — Hydrocortisone sodium phosphate is available in 2-ml single-dose vials. Each milliliter of solution contains (2):

Hydrocortisone (as sodium phosphate)	50 mg
Creatinine	8 mg
Sodium citrate	10 mg
Sodium bisulfite	3.2 mg
Methylparaben	1.5 mg
Propylparaben	0.2 mg
Sodium hydroxide	to adjust pH
Water for injection	qs 1 ml

pH — From 7.5 to 8.5. (2)

Osmolality — Hydrocortisone sodium phosphate 50 mg/ml has an osmolality of 533 mOsm/kg. (1689)

Trade Name(s) — Hydrocortone Phosphate.

Administration — Hydrocortisone sodium phosphate may be administered by subcutaneous, intramuscular, or direct intravenous injection or by continuous or intermittent intravenous infusion after addition to dextrose or sodium chloride injections. It is usually given at 12-hour intervals. (2; 4)

Stability — Hydrocortisone sodium phosphate in intact vials should be stored at controlled room temperature and protected from freezing and temperatures above 40 °C. (4) The drug is a clear, light yellow solution which is heat labile and should not be autoclaved to sterilize the outside of the vial. (2; 4)

Solutions of hydrocortisone buffered to pH 9.1 showed oxidation to 21-dehydrocortisone at rates of 1.6 to 2.8%/hr at 26 °C. This rate is four or five times greater than that observed at pH 6.9 to 7.9. (531)

Sorption — Hydrocortisone sodium phosphate (Glaxo) 16 mg/2 ml diluted in dextrose 5% in water or sodium chloride 0.9% was stored for 18 hours at room temperature in the following plastic syringes: Brunswick (Sherwood Medical), Plastipak (Becton-Dickinson), Steriseal (Needle Industries), and Sabre (Gillette U.K.). The first three syringes have polypropylene barrels; the Sabre has a combination polypropylene–polystyrene barrel. No significant loss of hydrocortisone occurred due to sorption. (784)

Central Venous Catheter — Hydrocortisone sodium phosphate (Merck) 1 mg/ml in dextrose 5% in water was found to be compatible with the ARROWg+ard Blue Plus (Arrow International) chlorhexidine-bearing triple-lumen central catheter. HPLC analysis was used to evaluate completeness of drug delivery through the catheter and the amount of chlorhexidine removed from the internal lumens. Essentially complete delivery of the drug was found with little or no drug loss occurring. Furthermore, chlorhexidine delivered from the catheter remained at trace amounts with no substantial increase due to the delivery of the drug through the catheter. (2335)

Compatibility Information

Solution Compatibility

Hydrocortisone sodium phosphate

Solution	*Mfr*	*Mfr*	*Conc/L*	*Remarks*	*Ref*	*C/I*
Fat emulsion 10%, intravenous	VT		200 mg	Physically compatible for 48 hr at 4 °C and room temperature	32	C

Additive Compatibility

Hydrocortisone sodium phosphate

Drug	*Mfr*	*Conc/L*	*Mfr*	*Conc/L*	*Test Soln*	*Remarks*	*Ref*	*C/I*
Amikacin sulfate	BR	5 g	MSD	250 mg	D5LR, D5R, D5S, D5W, D10W, IS10, LR, NS, R, SL	Physically compatible and potency of both retained for 24 hr at 25 °C	294	C
Amphotericin B	SQ	50 mg	MSD	50 and 100 mg	D5W	Physically compatible and amphotericin B bioactivity retained in normal light at 25 °C for 24 hr. Hydrocortisone activity not tested	540	C
	SQ	100 mg	MSD	50 and 100 mg	D5W	Physically compatible and amphotericin B bioactivity retained in normal light at 25 °C for 24 hr. Hydrocortisone activity not tested	540	C
Amphotericin B with heparin sodium	SQ AB	50 mg 1500 units	MSD	50 and 100 mg	D5W	Physically compatible and amphotericin B bioactivity retained in normal light at 25 °C for 24 hr. Heparin and hydrocortisone activity not tested	540	C
Amphotericin B with heparin sodium	SQ AB	100 mg 1500 units	MSD	50 and 100 mg	D5W	Physically compatible and amphotericin B bioactivity retained in normal light at 25 °C for 24 hr. Heparin and hydrocortisone activity not tested	540	C
Bleomycin sulfate	BR	20 and 30 units	MSD	100 mg, 500 mg, 1 g, 2 g	NS	Physically compatible and bleomycin activity retained for 1 week at 4 °C. Hydrocortisone not tested	763	C
Metaraminol bitartrate	MSD	500 mg	MSD	250 mg	D5W, NS	UV spectra of both not altered in 8 hr at room temperature	42	C
Mitoxantrone HCl	LE	50 to 200 mg		100 mg to 2 g	NS[a]	Physically compatible and potency of both drugs retained for 24 hr at room temperature	1293	C
	LE	50 to 200 mg		100 mg to 2 g	D5W[a]	Small blue particles on inner surface of bag	1293	I
	LE	50 to 200 mg		100 mg to 2 g	D5W[b]	Physically compatible	1293	C
Sodium bicarbonate	AB	2.4 mEq[c]	MSD	100 mg	D5W	Physically compatible for 24 hr	772	C
Verapamil HCl	KN	80 mg	MSD	200 mg	D5W, NS	Physically compatible for 24 hr	764	C

[a]*Tested in PVC containers.*
[b]*Tested in glass containers.*
[c]*One vial of Neut added to a liter of admixture.*

Drugs in Syringe Compatibility

			Hydrocortisone sodium phosphate				
Drug (in syringe)	*Mfr*	*Amt*	*Mfr*	*Amt*	*Remarks*	*Ref*	*C/I*
Doxapram HCl	RB	400 mg/ 20 ml	MSD	100 mg/ 2 ml	Immediate turbidity and precipitation	1177	I
Metoclopramide HCl	RB	10 mg/ 2 ml	MSD	10 mg/ 2 ml	Physically compatible for 48 hr at 25 °C	1167	C
	RB	10 mg/ 2 ml	MSD	20 mg/ 4 ml	Physically compatible for 48 hr at 25 °C	1167	C
	RB	160 mg/ 32 ml	MSD	80 mg/ 16 ml	Physically compatible for 48 hr at 25 °C	1167	C

Y-Site Injection Compatibility (1:1 Mixture)

			Hydrocortisone sodium phosphate				
Drug	*Mfr*	*Conc*	*Mfr*	*Conc*	*Remarks*	*Ref*	*C/I*
Allopurinol sodium	BW	3 mg/ml[b]	MSD	1 mg/ml[b]	Physically compatible with no change in measured turbidity or increase in particle content in 4 hr at 22 °C	1686	C
Amifostine	USB	10 mg/ml[a]	MSD	1 mg/ml[a]	Physically compatible with no change in measured turbidity or increase in particle content in 4 hr at 23 °C	1845	C
Aztreonam	SQ	40 mg/ml[a]	MSD	1 mg/ml[a]	Physically compatible with no subvisual haze or particle formation in 4 hr at 23 °C	1758	C
Cefepime HCl	BMS	20 mg/ml[a]	MSD	1 mg/ml[a]	Physically compatible with no change in measured turbidity or increase in particle content in 4 hr at 22 °C	1689	C
Cladribine	ORT	0.015[b] and 0.5[c] mg/ml	MSD	1 mg/ml[b]	Physically compatible with no change in measured turbidity or increase in particle content in 4 hr at 23 °C	1969	C
Clarithromycin	AB	4 mg/ml[a]	GL	100 mg/ml	Visually compatible for 72 hr at both 30 and 17 °C	2174	C
Docetaxel	RPR	0.9 mg/ml[a]	ME	1 mg/ml[a]	Physically compatible with no change in measured turbidity or increase in particle content in 4 hr at 23 °C	2224	C
Etoposide phosphate	BR	5 mg/ml[a]	ME	0.5 mg/ml[a]	Physically compatible with no change in measured turbidity or increase in particle content in 4 hr at 23 °C	2218	C
Famotidine	ME	2 mg/ml[b]	[d]	1 mg/ml[a]	Visually compatible for 4 hr at 22 °C	1936	C
Filgrastim	AMG	30 µg/ml[a]	MSD	1 mg/ml[a]	Physically compatible with no change in measured turbidity or increase in particle content in 4 hr at 22 °C	1687	C
Fluconazole	RR	2 mg/ml	MSD	50 mg/ml	Physically compatible for 24 hr at 25 °C	1407	C
Fludarabine phosphate	BX	1 mg/ml[a]	MSD	1 mg/ml[a]	Physically compatible for 4 hr at room temperature under fluorescent light	1439	C
Gemcitabine HCl	LI	10 mg/ml[b]	ME	1 mg/ml[b]	Physically compatible with no change in measured turbidity or increase in particle content in 4 hr at 23 °C	2226	C

Y-Site Injection Compatibility (1:1 Mixture) (Cont.)

			Hydrocortisone sodium phosphate				
Drug	*Mfr*	*Conc*	*Mfr*	*Conc*	*Remarks*	*Ref*	*C/I*
Granisetron HCl	SKB	0.05 mg/ml[a]	MSD	1 mg/ml[a]	Physically compatible with no change in measured turbidity or increase in particle content in 4 hr at 23 °C	2000	C
Melphalan HCl	BW	0.1 mg/ml[b]	MSD	1 mg/ml[b]	Physically compatible with no change in measured turbidity or increase in particle content in 3 hr at 22 °C	1557	C
Ondansetron HCl	GL	1 mg/ml[b]	MSD	1 mg/ml[a]	Physically compatible for 4 hr at 22 °C	1365	C
Paclitaxel	NCI	1.2 mg/ml[a]	MSD	1 mg/ml[a]	Physically compatible with no change in measured turbidity in 4 hr at 22 °C	1556	C
Piperacillin sodium–tazobactam sodium	LE	40 + 5 mg/ml[a]	MSD	1 mg/ml[a]	Physically compatible with no change in measured turbidity or increase in particle content in 4 hr at 22 °C	1688	C
Sargramostim	IMM	10 μg/ml[b]	MSD	1 mg/ml[b]	Filament formation in 4 hr in one of two samples	1436	I
Teniposide	BR	0.1 mg/ml[a]	MSD	1 mg/ml[a]	Physically compatible with no subvisual haze or particle formation in 4 hr at 23 °C	1725	C
Thiotepa	IMM[e]	1 mg/ml[a]	MSD	1 mg/ml[a]	Physically compatible with no change in measured turbidity or increase in particle content in 4 hr at 23 °C	1861	C
TNA #218 to #226[f]			ME	1 mg/ml[a]	Visually compatible with no precipitate or emulsion damage apparent in 4 hr at 23 °C	2215	C
TPN #212 to #215[f]			ME	1 mg/ml[a]	Physically compatible with no change in measured turbidity or increase in particle content in 4 hr at 23 °C	2109	C
Vinorelbine tartrate	BW	1 mg/ml[b]	MSD	1 mg/ml[b]	Physically compatible with no change in measured turbidity or increase in particle content in 4 hr at 22 °C	1558	C

[a]*Tested in dextrose 5% in water.*
[b]*Tested in sodium chloride 0.9%.*
[c]*Tested in bacteriostatic sodium chloride 0.9% preserved with benzyl alcohol 0.9%.*
[d]*Form not specified.*
[e]*Lyophilized formulation tested.*
[f]*Refer to Appendix I for the composition of parenteral nutrition solutions. TNA indicates a 3-in-1 admixture, and TPN indicates a 2-in-1 admixture.*

Additional Compatibility Information

Infusion Solutions — Dextrose injections and sodium chloride injections have been recommended as diluents for the intravenous infusion of hydrocortisone sodium phosphate. (2; 4)

Dacarbazine — Dacarbazine is stated to be physically compatible when mixed with hydrocortisone sodium phosphate. (524)

HYDROCORTISONE SODIUM SUCCINATE
AHFS 68:04

Products — Hydrocortisone sodium succinate is available in a variety of sizes and containers (4; 154), including 100-mg conventional vials containing hydrocortisone sodium succinate equivalent to hydrocortisone 100 mg with monobasic sodium phosphate anhydrous 0.8 mg and dibasic sodium phosphate dried 8.73 mg. Reconstitute the vial by adding not more than 2 ml of bacteriostatic water for injection or bacteriostatic sodium chloride injection. (1-6/99)

Hydrocortisone sodium succinate is also supplied in "Act-O-Vial" containers of 100, 250, 500, and 1000 mg. For the "Act-O-Vial" containers, press the plastic activator down to force the diluent into the lower chamber. Agitate gently to dissolve the drug. When reconstituted, each milliliter of solution contains (1-6/99):

Component	100 mg	250, 500, 1000 mg
Hydrocortisone equivalent (as sodium succinate)	50 mg	125 mg
Monobasic sodium phosphate anhydrous	0.4 mg	1 mg
Dibasic sodium phosphate dried	4.38 mg	11 mg
Benzyl alcohol	~9 mg	~8.3 mg
Water for injection	qs	qs

The pH has been adjusted when necessary with sodium hydroxide.

pH — From 7 to 8. (4)

Osmolality — The osmolality of hydrocortisone sodium succinate (Abbott) 50 mg/ml was determined to be 292 mOsm/kg by freezing-point depression and 260 mOsm/kg by vapor pressure. (1071)

Sodium Content — Hydrocortisone sodium succinate contains 2.066 mEq of sodium per gram of drug. (846)

Trade Name(s) — A-Hydrocort, Solu-Cortef.

Administration — Hydrocortisone sodium succinate may be administered by intramuscular injection, direct intravenous injection over 30 seconds to several minutes, or continuous or intermittent intravenous infusion at a concentration of 0.1 to 1 mg/ml in a compatible infusion solution. (1-6/99; 4)

Stability — Hydrocortisone sodium succinate in intact containers should be stored at controlled room temperatures of 20 to 25 °C. (1-6/99) After reconstitution, solutions are stable at controlled room temperature or below if protected from light. The solution should only be used if it is clear. Unused solutions should be discarded after three days. Hydrocortisone sodium succinate is heat labile and must not be autoclaved. (1-6/99; 4)

pH Effects — Hydrocortisone sodium succinate is optimally stable at pH 7 to 8. It is stable for 72 hours at pH 6 and for 12 hours at pH 5. More acidic solutions cause precipitation. (41)

Solutions of hydrocortisone buffered to pH 9.1 showed oxidation to 21-dehydrocortisone at rates of 1.6 to 2.8%/hr at 26 °C. This rate is four or five times greater than that observed at pH 6.9 to 7.9. (531)

Freezing Solutions — Hydrocortisone sodium succinate (Upjohn) 500-mg/4 ml reconstituted solution exhibited no loss of potency over four weeks when stored frozen. (69)

Intrathecal Injections — In a study of solutions for intrathecal injection, hydrocortisone sodium succinate (Upjohn) was reconstituted to a concentration of 1 mg/ml with Elliott's B solution (295 mOsm/kg, pH 7.3), sodium chloride 0.9% injection (296 mOsm/kg, pH 7), and Ringer's injection, lactated (258 mOsm/kg, pH 7). In Ringer's injection, lactated, and sodium chloride 0.9% injection, no decomposition was observed by UV spectroscopy in 24 hours at room temperature under fluorescent light or at 30 °C. However, in seven days, approximately 10% decomposition occurred at room temperature and about 15% was noted at 30 °C. In Elliott's B solution, hydrocortisone sodium succinate is much less stable. In 24 hours, a 7% loss occurred at room temperature and a 12% loss occurred at 30 °C, increasing to 21 and 32%, respectively, at 72 hours. The authors noted that less than 10% decomposition of this combination occurred in four to eight hours. (327)

In another study, the stability and compatibility of cytarabine (Upjohn), methotrexate (NCI), and hydrocortisone (Upjohn), mixed together in intrathecal injections, were evaluated. Two combinations were tested: (1) cytarabine 50 mg, methotrexate 12 mg (as the sodium salt), and hydrocortisone 25 mg (as the sodium succinate salt); and (2) cytarabine 30 mg, methotrexate 12 mg (as the sodium salt), and hydrocortisone 15 mg (as the sodium succinate salt). Each drug combination was added to 12 ml of Elliott's B solution (NCI), sodium chloride 0.9% (Abbott), dextrose 5% in water (Abbott), and Ringer's injection, lactated (Abbott), and stored for 24 hours at 25 °C. Cytarabine and methotrexate were both chemically stable, with no drug loss after the full 24 hours in all solutions. Hydrocortisone was also stable in the sodium chloride 0.9%, dextrose 5% in water, and Ringer's injection, lactated, with about a 2% drug loss. However, in Elliott's B solution, hydrocortisone was significantly less stable, with a 6% loss in the 25-mg concentration over 24 hours. The 15-mg concentration was worse, with a 5% loss in 10 hours and a 13% loss in 24 hours. The higher pH of Elliott's B solution and the lower concentration of hydrocortisone may have been factors in this increased decomposition. All mixtures were physically compatible during this study, but a precipitate formed after several days of storage. (819)

Hydrocortisone sodium succinate (Upjohn) 2 mg/ml diluted in Elliott's B solution (Orphan Medical) was packaged as 20 ml in 30-ml glass vials and 20-ml plastic syringes (Becton-Dickinson) with Red Cap (Burron) Luer-lok syringe tip caps. The solution was physically compatible with no increase in measured turbidity or particulates and was chemically stable exhibiting about 9% or less loss by HPLC analysis during storage for 24 hours at 23 °C and 7% or less loss in 48 hours at 4 °C. (1976)

Bacterially contaminated intrathecal solutions could pose grave risks and, consequently, such solutions should be administered as soon as possible after preparation. (328)

Syringes — Hydrocortisone sodium succinate (Upjohn) 10 mg/ml in sodium chloride 0.9% was packaged in polypropylene syringes (Becton-Dickinson) and stored under refrigeration at 5 °C and at room temperature of 25 °C. The drug solution remained clear throughout the study, and HPLC analysis found about 2% hydrocortisone loss after 21 days under refrigeration. At room temperature, about 5% loss occurred in three days and 10% loss occurred in seven days. Stability in glass containers was found to be comparable. (2331)

Sorption — Hydrocortisone sodium succinate (Upjohn) 25 mg/L did not display significant sorption to a PVC plastic test strip in 24 hours. (12)

Hydrocortisone sodium succinate (Upjohn) 9 mg/L in sodium chloride 0.9% (Travenol) in PVC bags did not exhibit significant sorption to the plastic during one week of storage at room temperature (15 to 20 °C). (536)

In another study, hydrocortisone sodium succinate (Upjohn) 9 mg/L in sodium chloride 0.9% did not exhibit any loss due to sorption during a seven-hour simulated infusion through an infusion set (Travenol) consisting of a cellulose propionate burette chamber and 170 cm of PVC tubing. (606)

The drug also was tested as a simulated infusion over at least one hour by a syringe pump system. A glass syringe on a syringe pump was fitted with 20 cm of polyethylene tubing or 50 cm of Silastic tubing. No loss of drug due to sorption was observed with either tubing. (606)

A 25-ml aliquot of hydrocortisone sodium succinate (Upjohn) 9 mg/L in sodium chloride 0.9% was stored in all-plastic syringes composed of polypropylene barrels and polyethylene plungers for 24 hours at room temperature in the dark. No loss due to sorption occurred. (606)

Filtration — Hydrocortisone sodium succinate (Upjohn) 10 mg/L in dextrose 5% in water and sodium chloride 0.9% did not display significant sorption to a 0.45-μm cellulose membrane filter (Abbott S-A-I-F) during an eight-hour simulated infusion. (567)

Central Venous Catheter — Hydrocortisone sodium succinate (Abbott) 1 mg/ml in dextrose 5% in water was found to be compatible with the ARROWg+ard Blue Plus (Arrow International) chlorhexidine-bearing triple-lumen central catheter. HPLC analysis was used to evaluate completeness of drug delivery through the catheter and the amount of chlorhexidine removed from the internal lumens. Essentially complete delivery of the drug was found with little or no drug loss occurring. Furthermore, chlorhexidine delivered from the catheter remained at trace amounts with no substantial increase due to the delivery of the drug through the catheter. (2335)

Compatibility Information

Solution Compatibility

Hydrocortisone sodium succinate

Solution	*Mfr*	*Mfr*	*Conc/L*	*Remarks*	*Ref*	*C/I*
Alcohol 5%, dextrose 5%	BA	UP	600 mg	Physically compatible for 24 hr	315	C
Dextran 40,000	PH			Physically compatible	44	C
Dextran 6% in dextrose 5%	AB	UP	250 mg	Physically compatible	3	C
Dextran 6% in sodium chloride 0.9%	AB	UP	250 mg	Physically compatible	3	C
Dextrose–Ringer's injection combinations	AB	UP	250 mg	Physically compatible	3	C
Dextrose–Ringer's injection, lactated, combinations	AB	UP	250 mg	Physically compatible	3	C
Dextrose 5% in Ringer's injection, lactated	TR[a]	UP	500 mg	Potency retained for 24 hr at 5 °C	282	C
	BA	UP	600 mg	Physically compatible for 24 hr	315	C
Dextrose–saline combinations	AB	UP	250 mg	Physically compatible	3	C
Dextrose 5% in sodium chloride 0.9%		UP	100, 200, 300 mg	Potency retained for 48 hr	43	C
	AB	UP	250 mg	Potency retained for 48 hr	46	C
		UP	100 mg	Physically compatible	74	C
	TR[a]	UP	500 mg	Potency retained for 24 hr at 5 °C	282	C
	BA	UP	600 mg	Physically compatible for 24 hr	315	C
Dextrose 2½% in water	AB	UP	250 mg	Physically compatible	3	C
Dextrose 5% in water	AB	UP	250 mg	Physically compatible	3	C
	AB	UP	250 mg	Potency retained for 48 hr	46	C
		UP	100 mg	Physically compatible	74	C
	TR[a]	UP	500 mg	Potency retained for 24 hr at 5 °C	282	C
	BA	UP	600 mg	Physically compatible for 24 hr	315	C
Dextrose 10% in water	AB	UP	250 mg	Physically compatible	3	C
	BA	UP	600 mg	Physically compatible for 24 hr	315	C
Dextrose 20% in water	BA	UP	600 mg	Physically compatible for 24 hr	315	C
Fat emulsion 10%, intravenous	VT	GL	200 mg	Physically compatible for 24 hr at 8 and 25 °C	825	C
Fructose 10% in sodium chloride 0.9%	AB	UP	250 mg	Physically compatible	3	C

Solution Compatibility (Cont.)

Hydrocortisone sodium succinate

Solution	Mfr	Mfr	Conc/L	Remarks	Ref	C/I
Fructose 10% in water	AB	UP	250 mg	Physically compatible	3	C
	BA	UP	600 mg	Physically compatible for 24 hr	315	C
Invert sugar 10% in Electrolyte #1	BA	UP	600 mg	Physically compatible for 24 hr	315	C
Invert sugar 10% in Electrolyte #2	BA	UP	600 mg	Physically compatible for 24 hr	315	C
Invert sugar 5 and 10% in sodium chloride 0.9%	AB	UP	250 mg	Physically compatible	3	C
Invert sugar 5 and 10% in water	AB	UP	250 mg	Physically compatible	3	C
Ionosol products (except as noted below)	AB	UP	250 mg	Physically compatible	3	C
Ionosol B with invert sugar 10%	AB	UP	250 mg	Haze or precipitate forms within 24 hr	3	I
Polysal M with dextrose 5%	CU	UP	600 mg	Physically compatible for 24 hr	315	C
Ringer's injection	AB	UP	250 mg	Physically compatible	3	C
Ringer's injection, lactated	AB	UP	250 mg	Physically compatible	3	C
		UP	100 mg	Physically compatible	74	C
	TR[a]	UP	500 mg	Potency retained for 24 hr at 5 °C	282	C
	BA	UP	600 mg	Physically compatible for 24 hr	315	C
Sodium chloride 0.45%	AB	UP	250 mg	Physically compatible	74	C
Sodium chloride 0.9%	AB	UP	250 mg	Physically compatible	3	C
	AB	UP	250 mg	Potency retained for 48 hr	46	C
		UP	100 mg	Physically compatible	74	C
	TR[a]	UP	500 mg	Potency retained for 24 hr at 5 °C	282	C
	BA	UP	600 mg	Physically compatible for 24 hr	315	C
Sodium lactate ⅙ M	AB	UP	250 mg	Physically compatible	3	C
	BA	UP	600 mg	Physically compatible for 24 hr	315	C

[a]*Tested in both glass and PVC containers.*

Additive Compatibility

Hydrocortisone sodium succinate

Drug	Mfr	Conc/L	Mfr	Conc/L	Test Soln	Remarks	Ref	C/I
Amikacin sulfate	BR	5 g	UP	200 mg	D5LR, D5R, D5S, D5W, D10W, IS10, LR, NS, R, SL	Physically compatible and potency of both retained for 24 hr at 25 °C	294	C
Aminophylline		250 mg	UP	100 mg	D5W	Physically compatible	74	C
	SE	1 g	UP	500 mg	D5W	Physically compatible	15	C
	SE	500 mg	UP	100 mg		Physically compatible	6	C
		625 mg		250 mg	D5W	Physically compatible and aminophylline chemically stable for 24 hr at 4 and 30 °C. Total hydrocortisone content changed little but substantial ester hydrolysis noted	521	C
Aminophylline with cephalothin sodium	SE LI	1 g 1 g	UP	100 mg	D5S	pH outside stability range for cephalothin. Precipitate forms within 12 hr	41	I
Amobarbital sodium						Physically incompatible	9	I
	LI	1 g	UP	500 mg	D5W	Physically compatible	15	C

Additive Compatibility (Cont.)

Hydrocortisone sodium succinate

Drug	*Mfr*	*Conc/L*	*Mfr*	*Conc/L*	*Test Soln*	*Remarks*	*Ref*	*C/I*
Amphotericin B	SQ	100 mg	UP	500 mg	D5W	Physically compatible	15	C
Ampicillin sodium	BR	1 g		200 and 400 mg	LR	Ampicillin potency retained for 24 hr at 25 °C	87	C
	BR	1 g		1.8 g	D5S, D5W, D10W, IM, IP, LR, NS	Ampicillin potency retained for 24 hr at 4 °C	87	C
	BR	1 g		100 mg	LR	14% ampicillin decomposition in 12 hr at 25 °C	87	I
	BR	1 g		50 mg	LR	14% ampicillin decomposition in 12 hr at 25 °C	87	I
	BR	1 g		1.8 g	D5S, D10W, IP, IM, LR	11 to 28% ampicillin decomposition in 24 hr at 25 °C	87	I
	BE	20 g		200 mg	NS	18% ampicillin decomposition in 6 hr at 25 °C	89	I
	BE	20 g		200 mg	D5W	23% ampicillin decomposition in 6 hr at 25 °C	89	I
	BE	20 g		200 mg	D–S	32% ampicillin decomposition in 6 hr at 25 °C	89	I
Bleomycin sulfate	BR	20 and 30 units	AB	300 mg, 750 mg, 1 g, 2.5 g	NS	60 to 100% bleomycin activity lost in 1 week at 4 °C	763	I
Calcium chloride	UP	1 g	UP	500 mg	D5W	Physically compatible	15	C
Calcium gluconate		1 g	UP	100 mg	D5W	Physically compatible	74	C
	UP	1 g	UP	500 mg	D5W	Physically compatible	15	C
Chloramphenicol sodium succinate	PD	500 mg	UP	100 mg	D5W	Physically compatible	74	C
	PD	10 g	UP	500 mg	D5W	Physically compatible	15	C
	PD	1 g	UP	500 mg		Physically compatible	6	C
Clindamycin phosphate	UP	1.2 g	UP	1 g	W	Clindamycin stability maintained for 24 hr	101	C
Colistimethate sodium	WC	500 mg	UP	500 mg	D5W	Physically incompatible	15	I
Corticotropin		500 units	UP	100 mg	D5W	Physically compatible	74	C
Cytarabine	UP	360 mg	UP	500 mg	D5S, D10S	Physically compatible for 40 hr	174	C
	UP	360 mg	UP	500 mg	R, SL	Physically incompatible	174	I
Daunorubicin HCl	FA	200 mg	UP	500 mg	D5W	Physically compatible	15	C
Dimenhydrinate	SE	50 mg	UP	100 mg	D5W	Physically compatible	74	C
	SE	500 mg	UP	500 mg	D5W	Physically incompatible	15	I
Diphenhydramine HCl	SCN	80 mg	UP	500 mg	D5W[a]	Physically compatible with no subvisual haze or particle formation in 24 hr at 23 °C	1729	C
	SCN	500 mg	UP	1 g	D5W[a]	Physically compatible with no subvisual haze or particle formation in 24 hr at 23 °C	1729	C

Additive Compatibility (Cont.)

Hydrocortisone sodium succinate

Drug	*Mfr*	*Conc/L*	*Mfr*	*Conc/L*	*Test Soln*	*Remarks*	*Ref*	*C/I*
Dopamine HCl	AS	800 mg	UP	1 g	D5W	No dopamine decomposition in 18 hr at 25 °C	312	C
Ephedrine sulfate						Physically incompatible	9	I
Erythromycin lactobionate	AB	5 g	UP	500 mg	D5W	Physically compatible	15	C
	AB	1 g	UP	250 mg		Physically compatible	3; 20	C
Floxacillin sodium	BE	20 g	UP	50 g	NS	Physically compatible for 72 hr at 15 and 30 °C	1479	C
Furosemide		200 and 400 mg		1 g	D5W, NS	6 to 8% hydrocortisone loss and 5 to 6% furosemide loss in 24 hr at 25 °C	1348	C
		200 and 400 mg		300 mg	D5W, NS	6 to 8% hydrocortisone loss in 6 hr and 10 to 14% loss in 24 hr at 25 °C. 5 to 6% furosemide loss in 24 hr	1348	I
	HO	1 g	UP	50 g	NS	Physically compatible for 72 hr at 15 and 30 °C	1479	C
Heparin sodium		32,000 units		800 mg	NS	Physically compatible and heparin activity retained for 24 hr	57	C
						Physically incompatible	9	I
	UP	4000 units	UP	500 mg	D5W	Physically incompatible	15	I
		12,000 units	UP	100 mg	D5W	Immediate precipitation	74	I
Hydralazine HCl	BP	80 mg	BP	400 mg	D5W	Yellow color produced	26	I
Kanamycin sulfate	BR	250 mg		1.8 g	D5S, D5W, D10W, IM, IP, LR, NS	Kanamycin potency retained for 24 hr at 4 and 25 °C	87	C
	BR	4 g	UP	500 mg	D5W	Physically incompatible	15	I
Lidocaine HCl	AST	2 g	UP	250 mg		Physically compatible	24	C
Magnesium sulfate	ES	750 mg	UP	100 g	AA 3.5%, D 25%	Physically compatible	302	C
Mephentermine sulfate		750 mg		250 mg	D5W	Physically compatible and chemically stable for 24 hr at 3 and 30 °C	520	C
Metaraminol bitartrate	MSD	100 mg	UP	100 mg	D5S	Potency of both retained for 24 hr	43	C
	MSD					Physically incompatible	9	I
	MSD	100, 200, 300 mg	UP	200 and 300 mg	D5S	Precipitate forms and chemical decomposition of hydrocortisone occurs	43	I
	MSD	500 mg		250 mg	D5W, NS	Precipitate forms within 1 hr	42	I
	MSD	100 mg	UP	250 mg		Precipitate forms within 1 hr	7	I
Metronidazole	RP	5 g[b]	UP	10 g		Physically compatible for at least 72 hr at 23 °C, but a significant change in pH	807	?
	SE	5 g	UP	10 g		No loss of either drug in 7 days at 25 °C and 12 days at 5 °C	993	C
Metronidazole HCl with sodium bicarbonate	SE AB	5 g 50 mEq	UP	1 g	D5W, NS	Physically compatible for 48 hr	765	C

Additive Compatibility (Cont.)

Hydrocortisone sodium succinate

Drug	*Mfr*	*Conc/L*	*Mfr*	*Conc/L*	*Test Soln*	*Remarks*	*Ref*	*C/I*
Mitomycin	BR	1 g	AB	33.3 g	W[c]	Visually compatible with 10% mitomycin loss calculated in 172 hr and 10% hydrocortisone loss calculated in 212 hr at 25 °C	1866	C
	BR	1 g	AB	33.3 g	W[a]	Visually compatible with 10% mitomycin loss calculated in 206 hr and 10% hydrocortisone loss calculated in 218 hr at 25 °C	1866	C
	BR	1 g	AB	33.3 g	W[c]	Visually compatible with 10% mitomycin loss calculated in 1423 hr and 10% hydrocortisone loss calculated in 176 hr at 4 °C	1866	C
	BR	1 g	AB	33.3 g	W[a]	Visually compatible with 10% mitomycin loss calculated in 820 hr and 10% hydrocortisone loss calculated in 807 hr at 4 °C	1866	C
Mitoxantrone HCl	LE	50 to 200 mg		100 mg to 2 g	D5W, NS[a]	Physically compatible and potency of both drugs retained for 24 hr at room temperature	1293	C
Nafcillin sodium	WY	500 mg	UP	250 mg		Precipitate forms within 1 hr	27	I
Netilmicin sulfate	SC	3 g	UP	400 mg	D5S	Physically compatible and netilmicin chemically stable for 7 days at 4 and 25 °C. Hydrocortisone not tested	558	C
Netilmicin sulfate with potassium chloride	SC AB	3 g 160 mEq	UP	400 mg	D5S	Physically compatible and netilmicin chemically stable for 7 days at 4 and 25 °C. Other drugs not tested	558	C
Norepinephrine bitartrate	WI	8 mg	UP	100 mg	D5W	Physically compatible	74	C
Penicillin G potassium		1 million units	UP	100 mg	D5W	Physically compatible	74	C
	SQ	20 million units	UP	500 mg	D5W	Physically compatible	15	C
	SQ	5 million units	UP	250 mg	D	Physically compatible	47	C
Penicillin G sodium	UP	20 million units	UP	500 mg	D5W	Physically compatible	15	C
Pentobarbital sodium						Physically incompatible	9	I
	AB	1 g	UP	500 mg	D5W	Physically incompatible	15	I
Phenobarbital sodium	WI					Physically incompatible	9	I
	WI	200 mg	UP	500 mg	D5W	Physically incompatible	15	I
Piperacillin sodium	LE	40 g	UP	40 mg	D5S[a]	Physically compatible and piperacillin chemically stable for 24 hr at room temperature and 1 week under refrigeration. Hydrocortisone not tested	740	C
Polymyxin B sulfate	BW	200 mg	UP	500 mg	D5W	Physically compatible	15	C
Potassium chloride		3 g	UP	100 mg	D5W	Physically compatible	74	C

Additive Compatibility (Cont.)

Hydrocortisone sodium succinate

Drug	*Mfr*	*Conc/L*	*Mfr*	*Conc/L*	*Test Soln*	*Remarks*	*Ref*	*C/I*
Potassium chloride with netilmicin sulfate	AB SC	160 mEq 3 g	UP	400 mg	D5S	Physically compatible and netilmicin chemically stable for 7 days at 4 and 25 °C. Other drugs not tested	558	C
Procaine HCl	WI	1 g	UP	500 mg	D5W	Physically compatible	15	C
Prochlorperazine edisylate	SKF					Physically incompatible	9	I
Promethazine HCl	WY	250 mg	UP	500 mg	D5W	Physically incompatible	15	I
Sodium bicarbonate	AB	2.4 mEq[d]	UP	250 mg	D5W	Physically compatible for 24 hr	772	C
Theophylline		2 g		390 mg[e]	D5W	Visually compatible with little or no loss of either drug in 48 hr	1909	C
Thiopental sodium	AB	2.5 g	UP	100 mg	D5W	Physically compatible	21	C
Vancomycin HCl	LI	1 g	UP	100 mg	D5W	Physically compatible	74	C
Verapamil HCl	KN	80 mg	UP	200 mg	D5W, NS	Physically compatible for 24 hr	764	C
Vitamin B complex with C	 RC	1 vial 2 ml	UP UP	100 mg 100 mg	D5W D5W, LR	Physically compatible pH within stability range for both	74 41	C C

[a]Tested in PVC containers.
[b]Minibags (100 ml) containing metronidazole 500 mg with disodium phosphate 150 mg, citric acid 44 mg, and sodium chloride 740 mg. This product differs from the Searle product.
[c]Tested in glass containers.
[d]One vial of Neut added to a liter of admixture.
[e]Tested as the hemisuccinate.

Drugs in Syringe Compatibility

Hydrocortisone sodium succinate

Drug (in syringe)	*Mfr*	*Amt*	*Mfr*	*Amt*	*Remarks*	*Ref*	*C/I*
Diatrizoate meglumine 52%, diatrizoate sodium 8%	MA	5 ml	UP	10 mg/ 1 ml	Physically compatible for at least 2 hr	1438	C
Diatrizoate sodium 60%	MA	5 ml	UP	10 mg/ 1 ml	Physically compatible for at least 2 hr	1438	C
Doxapram HCl	RB	400 mg/ 20 ml	UP	500 mg/ 2 ml	Immediate turbidity and precipitation	1177	I
Iohexol	WI	64.7%, 5 ml	UP	10 mg/ 1 ml	Physically compatible for at least 2 hr	1438	C
Iopamidol	SQ	61%, 5 ml	UP	10 mg/ 1 ml	Physically compatible for at least 2 hr	1438	C
Iothalamate meglumine 60%	MA	5 ml	UP	10 mg/ 1 ml	Physically compatible for at least 2 hr	1438	C
Ioxaglate meglumine 39.3%, ioxaglate sodium 19.6%	MA	5 ml	UP	10 mg/ 1 ml	Physically compatible for at least 2 hr	1438	C
Metoclopramide HCl	RB RB	10 mg/ 2 ml 10 mg/ 2 ml	MSD MSD	10 mg/ 2 ml[a] 20 mg/ 4 ml[a]	Physically compatible for 48 hr at room temperature Physically compatible for 48 hr at room temperature	924 924	C C
Thiopental sodium	AB	75 mg/ 3 ml	UP	250 mg/ 2 ml	Physically compatible for at least 30 min	21	C

[a]Brought to volume with distilled water.

Y-Site Injection Compatibility (1:1 Mixture)

			Hydrocortisone sodium succinate				
Drug	*Mfr*	*Conc*	*Mfr*	*Conc*	*Remarks*	*Ref*	*C/I*
Acyclovir sodium	BW	5 mg/ml[a]	LY	1 mg/ml[a]	Physically compatible for 4 hr at 25 °C	1157	C
Allopurinol sodium	BW	3 mg/ml[b]	UP	1 mg/ml[b]	Physically compatible with no change in measured turbidity or increase in particle content in 4 hr at 22 °C	1686	C
Amifostine	USB	10 mg/ml[a]	UP	1 mg/ml[a]	Physically compatible with no change in measured turbidity or increase in particle content in 4 hr at 23 °C	1845	C
Aminophylline	SE	25 mg/ml	UP	100 mg/L[c]	Physically compatible for at least 4 hr at room temperature by visual and microscopic examination	322	C
Amphotericin B cholesteryl sulfate complex	SEQ	0.83 mg/ml[a]	AB	1 mg/ml[a]	Physically compatible with little or no change in measured turbidity or increase in particle content in 4 hr at 23 °C under fluorescent light	2117	C
Ampicillin sodium	BR	25, 50, 100, 135 mg/ml	UP	100 mg/L[c]	Physically compatible for at least 4 hr at room temperature by visual and microscopic examination	322	C
Amsacrine	NCI	1 mg/ml[a]	UP	1 mg/ml[a]	Physically compatible for 4 hr at room temperature under fluorescent light	1381	C
Atracurium besylate	BW	0.5 mg/ml[a]	AB	1 mg/ml[a]	Physically compatible for 24 hr at 28 °C	1337	C
Atropine sulfate	BW	0.5 mg/ml	UP	10 mg/L[d]	Physically compatible for at least 4 hr at room temperature by visual and microscopic examination	534	C
Aztreonam	SQ	40 mg/ml[a]	UP	1 mg/ml[a]	Physically compatible with no subvisual haze or particle formation in 4 hr at 23 °C	1758	C
Betamethasone sodium phosphate	SC	3 mg/ml	UP	10 mg/L[d]	Physically compatible for at least 4 hr at room temperature by visual and microscopic examination	534	C
Calcium gluconate	ES	100 mg/ml	UP	100 mg/L[c]	Physically compatible for at least 4 hr at room temperature by visual and microscopic examination	322	C
Cefepime HCl	BMS	20 mg/ml[a]	UP	1 mg/ml[a]	Physically compatible with no change in measured turbidity or increase in particle content in 4 hr at 22 °C	1689	C
Chlordiazepoxide HCl	RC	10 mg/ml	UP	10 mg/L[d]	Physically compatible for at least 4 hr at room temperature by visual and microscopic examination	534	C
Chlorpromazine HCl	SKF	25 mg/ml	UP	10 mg/L[d]	Physically compatible for at least 4 hr at room temperature by visual and microscopic examination	534	C
Ciprofloxacin	MI	2 mg/ml[e]	UP	50 mg/ml	Transient white cloudiness rapidly dissipates. White crystals form in 1 hr at 24 °C	1655	I
Cisatracurium besylate	GW	0.1, 2, 5 mg/ml[a]	AB	1 mg/ml[a]	Physically compatible with no change in measured turbidity or increase in particle content in 4 hr at 23 °C	2074	C

Y-Site Injection Compatibility (1:1 Mixture) (Cont.)

			Hydrocortisone sodium succinate				
Drug	*Mfr*	*Conc*	*Mfr*	*Conc*	*Remarks*	*Ref*	*C/I*
Cladribine	ORT	0.015[b] and 0.5[f] mg/ml	UP	1 mg/ml[b]	Physically compatible with no change in measured turbidity or increase in particle content in 4 hr at 23 °C	1969	C
Cyanocobalamin	PD	0.1 mg/ml	UP	10 mg/L[d]	Physically compatible for at least 4 hr at room temperature by visual and microscopic examination	534	C
Cytarabine	UP	16 mg/ml[b]	UP	125 mg/ml	Visually compatible for 24 hr at room temperature in test tubes. No precipitate found on filter from Y-site delivery	2063	C
Dexamethasone sodium phosphate	MSD	4 mg/ml	UP	100 mg/L[c]	Physically compatible for at least 4 hr at room temperature by visual and microscopic examination	322	C
Diazepam	RC	5 mg/ml	UP	100 mg/L[c]	Immediate haziness with globule formation	322	I
Digoxin	BW	0.25 mg/ml	UP	100 mg/L[c]	Physically compatible for at least 4 hr at room temperature by visual and microscopic examination	322	C
Diltiazem HCl	MMD	5 mg/ml	UP	50 and 125 mg/ml	Precipitate forms but clears with swirling	1807	?
	MMD	1 mg/ml[b]	UP	50 and 125 mg/ml	Visually compatible	1807	C
	MMD	5 mg/ml	UP	1[b] and 2[a] mg/ml	Visually compatible	1807	C
Diphenhydramine HCl	PD	50 mg/ml	UP	10 mg/L[d]	Physically compatible for at least 4 hr at room temperature by visual and microscopic examination	534	C
	SCN	0.16 mg/ml[a]	UP	1 mg/ml[a]	Physically compatible with no subvisual haze or particle formation in 4 hr at 23 °C	1729	C
	SCN	1 mg/ml[a]	UP	2 mg/ml[a]	Physically compatible with no subvisual haze or particle formation in 4 hr at 23 °C	1729	C
Docetaxel	RPR	0.9 mg/ml[a]	AB	1 mg/ml[a]	Physically compatible with no change in measured turbidity or increase in particle content in 4 hr at 23 °C	2224	C
Dopamine HCl	ACC	40 mg/ml	UP	10 mg/L[d]	Physically compatible for at least 4 hr at room temperature by visual and microscopic examination	534	C
Doxorubicin HCl liposome injection	SEQ	0.4 mg/ml[a]	AB	1 mg/ml[a]	Physically compatible with little or no change in measured turbidity and no increase in particle content in 4 hr at 23 °C	2087	C
Droperidol	CR	1.25 mg/ml	UP	10 mg/L[d]	Physically compatible for at least 4 hr at room temperature by visual and microscopic examination	534	C
Edrophonium chloride	RC	10 mg/ml	UP	10 mg/L[d]	Physically compatible for at least 4 hr at room temperature by visual and microscopic examination	534	C
Enalaprilat	MSD	0.05 mg/ml[b]	UP	2 mg/ml[a]	Physically compatible for 24 hr at room temperature under fluorescent light	1355	C

Y-Site Injection Compatibility (1:1 Mixture) (Cont.)

Hydrocortisone sodium succinate

Drug	*Mfr*	*Conc*	*Mfr*	*Conc*	*Remarks*	*Ref*	*C/I*
Epinephrine HCl	AB	0.1 mg/ml	UP	10 mg/L[d]	Physically compatible for at least 4 hr at room temperature by visual and microscopic examination	534	C
Esmolol HCl	DCC	10 mg/ml[a]	LY	1 mg/ml[a]	Physically compatible for 24 hr at 22 °C	1169	C
Estrogens, conjugated	AY	5 mg/ml	UP	100 mg/L[c]	Physically compatible for at least 4 hr at room temperature by visual and microscopic examination	322	C
Ethacrynate sodium	MSD	1 mg/ml	UP	100 mg/L[c]	Physically compatible for at least 4 hr at room temperature by visual and microscopic examination	322	C
Etoposide phosphate	BR	5 mg/ml[a]	UP	1 mg/ml[a]	Physically compatible with no change in measured turbidity or increase in particle content in 4 hr at 23 °C	2218	C
Famotidine	MSD	0.2 mg/ml[a]	AB	1 mg/ml[a]	Physically compatible for 4 hr at 25 °C under fluorescent light	1188	C
	MSD	0.2 mg/ml[a]	AB	125 mg/ml	Physically compatible for 14 hr	1196	C
	ME	2 mg/ml[b]	[g]	1 mg/ml[a]	Visually compatible for 4 hr at 22 °C	1936	C
Fentanyl citrate	MN	0.05 mg/ml	UP	10 mg/L[d]	Physically compatible for at least 4 hr at room temperature by visual and microscopic examination	322	C
Filgrastim	AMG	30 μg/ml[a]	UP	1 mg/ml[a]	Physically compatible with no change in measured turbidity or increase in particle content in 4 hr at 22 °C	1687	C
Fludarabine phosphate	UP	1 mg/ml[a]	UP	1 mg/ml[a]	Physically compatible for 4 hr at room temperature under fluorescent light	1439	C
Fluorouracil	RC	50 mg/ml	UP	10 mg/L[d]	Physically compatible for at least 4 hr at room temperature by visual and microscopic examination	534	C
Foscarnet sodium	AST	24 mg/ml	UP	50 mg/ml	Physically compatible for 24 hr at room temperature under fluorescent light	1335	C
Furosemide	HO	10 mg/ml	UP	10 mg/L[d]	Physically compatible for at least 4 hr at room temperature by visual and microscopic examination	534	C
Gatifloxacin	BMS	2 mg/ml[a]	AB	1 mg/ml[a]	Physically compatible with no change in measured haze or increase in particle content in 4 hr at 23 °C	2234	C
Gemcitabine HCl	LI	10 mg/ml[b]	UP	1 mg/ml[b]	Physically compatible with no change in measured turbidity or increase in particle content in 4 hr at 23 °C	2226	C
Granisetron HCl	SKB	0.05 mg/ml[a]	AB	1 mg/ml[a]	Physically compatible with no change in measured turbidity or increase in particle content in 4 hr at 23 °C	2000	C
Heparin sodium	TR	50 units/ml	UP	2 mg/ml[b]	Visually compatible for 4 hr at 25 °C	1793	C
	ES	100 units/ml[e]	UP	125 mg/ml	Visually compatible for 24 hr at room temperature in test tubes. No precipitate found on filter from Y-site delivery	2063	C
Hetastarch in lactated electrolyte injection (Hextend)	AB	6%	PHU	1 mg/ml[a]	Physically compatible with no change in measured turbidity or increase in particle content in 4 hr at 23 °C	2339	C

Y-Site Injection Compatibility (1:1 Mixture) (Cont.)

Hydrocortisone sodium succinate

Drug	*Mfr*	*Conc*	*Mfr*	*Conc*	*Remarks*	*Ref*	*C/I*
Hydralazine HCl	CI	20 mg/ml	UP	10 mg/L[d]	Physically compatible for at least 4 hr at room temperature by visual and microscopic examination	534	C
Idarubicin HCl	AD	1 mg/ml[b]	UP	2[a] and 50 mg/ml	Haze forms immediately and precipitate forms in 20 min	1525	I
Inamrinone lactate	WB	3 mg/ml[b]	ES	1 mg/ml[a]	Physically compatible for at least 4 hr at 25 °C under fluorescent light	992	C
Insulin, regular	LI	40 units/ml	UP	100 mg/L[c]	Physically compatible for at least 4 hr at room temperature by visual and microscopic examination	322	C
Isoproterenol HCl	WI	0.2 mg/ml	UP	10 mg/L[d]	Physically compatible for at least 4 hr at room temperature by visual and microscopic examination	534	C
Kanamycin sulfate	BR	250 mg/ml	UP	100 mg/L[c]	Physically compatible for at least 4 hr at room temperature by visual and microscopic examination	322	C
Lidocaine HCl	AST	20 mg/ml	UP	100 mg/L[c]	Physically compatible for at least 4 hr at room temperature by visual and microscopic examination	322	C
Linezolid	PHU	2 mg/ml	UP	1 mg/ml[a]	Physically compatible with no change in measured turbidity or increase in particle content in 4 hr at 23 °C	2264	C
Lorazepam	WY	0.33 mg/ml[b]	UP	50 mg/ml	Visually compatible for 24 hr at 22 °C	1855	C
Magnesium sulfate	AB	500 mg/ml	UP	10 mg/L[d]	Physically compatible for at least 4 hr at room temperature by visual and microscopic examination	534	C
Melphalan HCl	BW	0.1 mg/ml[b]	UP	1 mg/ml[b]	Physically compatible with no change in measured turbidity or increase in particle content in 3 hr at 22 °C	1557	C
Meperidine HCl	AB	10 mg/ml	AB	2 mg/ml[a]	Physically compatible for 4 hr at 25 °C	1397	C
Methoxamine HCl	BW	10 mg/ml	UP	10 mg/L[d]	Physically compatible for at least 4 hr at room temperature by visual and microscopic examination	534	C
Methylergonovine maleate	SZ	0.2 mg/ml	UP	10 mg/L[d]	Physically compatible for at least 4 hr at room temperature by visual and microscopic examination	534	C
Methylprednisolone sodium succinate	UP	40 mg/ml	UP	100 mg/L[h]	In D5W. Physically compatible for at least 4 hr at room temperature by visual and microscopic examination	322	C
	UP	40 mg/ml	UP	100 mg/L[h]	In NS and RL. Physically compatible initially but haziness in 4 hr at room temperature	322	I
Midazolam HCl	RC	5 mg/ml	UP	50 mg/ml	White precipitate forms immediately	1855	I
Minocycline HCl	LE	50 mg/ml	UP	10 mg/L[d]	Physically compatible for at least 4 hr at room temperature by visual and microscopic examination	534	C
Morphine sulfate	WY	15 mg/ml	UP	10 mg/L[d]	Physically compatible for at least 4 hr at room temperature by visual and microscopic examination	534	C

Y-Site Injection Compatibility (1:1 Mixture) (Cont.)

			Hydrocortisone sodium succinate				
Drug	*Mfr*	*Conc*	*Mfr*	*Conc*	*Remarks*	*Ref*	*C/I*
Neostigmine methylsulfate	RC	0.5 mg/ml	UP	10 mg/L[d]	Physically compatible for at least 4 hr at room temperature by visual and microscopic examination	534	C
Norepinephrine bitartrate	WI	1 mg/ml	UP	10 mg/L[d]	Physically compatible for at least 4 hr at room temperature by visual and microscopic examination	534	C
Ondansetron HCl	GL	1 mg/ml[b]	UP	1 mg/ml[a]	Physically compatible for 4 hr at 22 °C	1365	C
Oxacillin sodium	BR	100 mg/ml	UP	10 mg/L[d]	Physically compatible for at least 4 hr at room temperature by visual and microscopic examination	534	C
Oxytocin	SZ	1 mg/ml	UP	10 mg/L[d]	Physically compatible for at least 4 hr at room temperature by visual and microscopic examination	534	C
Paclitaxel	NCI	1.2 mg/ml[a]	AB	1 mg/ml[a]	Physically compatible with no change in measured turbidity in 4 hr at 22 °C	1556	C
Pancuronium bromide	ES	0.05 mg/ml[a]	AB	1 mg/ml[a]	Physically compatible for 24 hr at 28 °C	1337	C
Penicillin G potassium	LI	200,000 units/ml	UP	100 mg/L[c]	Physically compatible for at least 4 hr at room temperature by visual and microscopic examination	322	C
Pentazocine lactate	WI	30 mg/ml	UP	10 mg/L[d]	Physically compatible for at least 4 hr at room temperature by visual and microscopic examination	534	C
Phenytoin sodium	PD	50 mg/ml	UP	100 mg/L[c]	Immediate crystal formation	322	I
Phytonadione	RC	10 mg/ml	UP	10 mg/L[d]	Physically compatible for at least 4 hr at room temperature by visual and microscopic examination	534	C
Piperacillin sodium–tazobactam sodium	LE	40 + 5 mg/ml[a]	UP	1 mg/ml[a]	Physically compatible with no change in measured turbidity or increase in particle content in 4 hr at 22 °C	1688	C
Procainamide HCl	SQ	100 mg/ml	UP	10 mg/L[d]	Physically compatible for at least 4 hr at room temperature by visual and microscopic examination	534	C
Prochlorperazine edisylate	SKF	5 mg/ml	UP	10 mg/L[d]	Physically compatible for at least 4 hr at room temperature by visual and microscopic examination	534	C
Promethazine HCl	SV	50 mg/ml	UP	10 mg/L	In D5LR, D5W, NS, and LR. Physically compatible for at least 4 hr at room temperature by visual and microscopic examination	534	C
	SV	50 mg/ml	UP	10 mg/L	In D5R. Physically compatible initially but cloudiness in 4 hr at room temperature	534	I
Propofol	ZEN	10 mg/ml	UP	1 mg/ml[a]	Physically compatible for 1 hr at 23 °C with no increase in particle content	2066	C
Propranolol HCl	AY	1 mg/ml	UP	10 mg/L[d]	Physically compatible for at least 4 hr at room temperature by visual and microscopic examination	534	C

Y-Site Injection Compatibility (1:1 Mixture) (Cont.)

			Hydrocortisone sodium succinate				
Drug	*Mfr*	*Conc*	*Mfr*	*Conc*	*Remarks*	*Ref*	*C/I*
Pyridostigmine bromide	RC	5 mg/ml	UP	10 mg/L[d]	Physically compatible for at least 4 hr at room temperature by visual and microscopic examination	534	C
Remifentanil HCl	GW	0.025 and 0.25 mg/ml[b]	AB	1 mg/ml[a]	Physically compatible with no change in measured turbidity or increase in particle content in 4 hr at 23 °C	2075	C
Sargramostim	IMM	10 μg/ml[b]	UP	1 mg/ml[b]	Few small particles form in 1 hr	1436	I
Scopolamine HBr	BW	0.86 mg/ml	UP	10 mg/L[d]	Physically compatible for at least 4 hr at room temperature by visual and microscopic examination	534	C
Sodium bicarbonate	BR	75 mg/ml	UP	100 mg/L[c]	Physically compatible for at least 4 hr at room temperature by visual and microscopic examination	322	C
Succinylcholine chloride	BW	20 mg/ml	UP	100 mg/L[c]	Physically compatible for at least 4 hr at room temperature by visual and microscopic examination	322	C
Tacrolimus	FUJ	1 mg/ml[b]	AB	50 mg/ml[a]	Visually compatible for 24 hr at 25 °C	1630	C
Teniposide	BR	0.1 mg/ml[a]	UP	1 mg/ml[a]	Physically compatible with no subvisual haze or particle formation in 4 hr at 23 °C	1725	C
Theophylline	TR	4 mg/ml	UP	2 mg/ml[a]	Visually compatible for 6 hr at 25 °C	1793	C
Thiotepa	IMM[i]	1 mg/ml[a]	UP	1 mg/ml[a]	Physically compatible with no change in measured turbidity or increase in particle content in 4 hr at 23 °C	1861	C
TNA #218 to #226[j]			AB	1 mg/ml[a]	Visually compatible with no precipitate or emulsion damage apparent in 4 hr at 23 °C	2215	C
TPN #189[j]			UP	50 mg/ml[b]	Visually compatible for 24 hr at 22 °C	1767	C
TPN #212 to #215[j]			AB	1 mg/ml[a]	Physically compatible with no change in measured turbidity or increase in particle content in 4 hr at 23 °C	2109	C
Trimethobenzamide HCl	RC	100 mg/ml	UP	10 mg/L[d]	Physically compatible for at least 4 hr at room temperature by visual and microscopic examination	534	C
Vecuronium bromide	OR	0.1 mg/ml[a]	AB	1 mg/ml[a]	Physically compatible for 24 hr at 28 °C	1337	C
Vinorelbine tartrate	BW	1 mg/ml[b]	UP	1 mg/ml[b]	Physically compatible with no change in measured turbidity or increase in particle content in 4 hr at 22 °C	1558	C

[a]*Tested in dextrose 5% in water.*
[b]*Tested in sodium chloride 0.9%.*
[c]*Tested in combination with heparin sodium (Riker) 1000 units/L in dextrose 5% in water, sodium chloride 0.9%, and Ringer's injection, lactated.*
[d]*Tested in dextrose 5% in Ringer's injection, dextrose 5% in Ringer's injection, lactated, dextrose 5% in water, Ringer's injection, lactated, and sodium chloride 0.9%.*
[e]*Tested in both dextrose 5% in water and sodium chloride 0.9%.*
[f]*Tested in bacteriostatic sodium chloride 0.9% preserved with benzyl alcohol 0.9%.*
[g]*Form not specified.*
[h]*Also contained heparin sodium (Riker) 1000 units/L.*
[i]*Lyophilized formulation tested.*
[j]*Refer to Appendix I for the composition of parenteral nutrition solutions. TNA indicates a 3-in-1 admixture, and TPN indicates a 2-in-1 admixture.*

Additional Compatibility Information

Infusion Solutions — Dextrose 5% in water, sodium chloride 0.9%, and dextrose 5% in sodium chloride 0.9% have been recommended as diluents for the administration of hydrocortisone sodium succinate as an intravenous infusion. In concentrations of 100 mg to 3 g/50 ml of these diluents for piggyback administration, the drug is stated by the manufacturer to be stable for at least four hours. (1-6/99) In addition, hydrocortisone sodium succinate is stated to be physically and chemically compatible in amino acid injection (McGaw). (189)

Amphotericin B — Amphotericin B in infusions appears to be compatible with limited amounts of hydrocortisone sodium succinate. (4)

Dacarbazine — Dacarbazine forms a pink precipitate immediately when mixed with hydrocortisone sodium succinate (Upjohn). (524)

Ephedrine Sulfate — Hydrocortisone sodium succinate (Upjohn) 250 mg/L with ephedrine sulfate 50 mg/L; the mixture is physically compatible in most Abbott infusion solutions except as noted below (3):

Fructose 10% in sodium chloride 0.9%	Haze or precipitate forms within 24 hr
Ionosol B with invert sugar 10%	Haze or precipitate forms within 24 hr
Ionosol D-CM with dextrose 5%	Haze or precipitate forms within 24 hr
Ionosol D with invert sugar 10%	Haze or precipitate forms within 6 hr
Ionosol D modified with invert sugar 10%	Haze or precipitate forms within 24 hr

Magnesium Sulfate — A white flocculent precipitate was observed when hydrocortisone sodium succinate (Upjohn) 100 mg in 2 ml was drawn up into a syringe previously used to add magnesium sulfate 50% (Elkins-Sinn) 1.5 ml to a parenteral nutrition solution. Hydrocortisone sodium succinate (Upjohn) contains phosphate buffers, and it was postulated that insoluble magnesium phosphate was formed. This finding indicates that magnesium sulfate and hydrocortisone sodium succinate should not be admixed as concentrated solutions and should be added separately to large volume parenteral solutions, with thorough mixing after each addition. (302)

Penicillin G — Hydrocortisone sodium succinate (Upjohn) 250 mg/L with penicillin G potassium 1 million units/L; the mixture is physically compatible in most Abbott infusion solutions except as noted below (3):

Ionosol B with invert sugar 10%	Haze or precipitate forms within 24 hr
Ionosol D-CM with dextrose 5%	Haze or precipitate forms within 24 hr
Ionosol D with invert sugar 10%	Haze or precipitate forms within 24 hr

Pentobarbital — Hydrocortisone sodium succinate (Upjohn) 250 mg/L with pentobarbital sodium (Abbott) 500 mg/L; the mixture is physically compatible in most Abbott infusion solutions except Ionosol G with invert sugar 10%. A haze or precipitate forms within six hours. (3)

Procaine HCl — Hydrocortisone sodium succinate (Upjohn) 250 mg/L with procaine HCl 1 g/L; the mixture is physically compatible in most Abbott infusion solutions except as noted below (3):

Ionosol B with invert sugar 10%	Haze or precipitate forms within 24 hr

Vitamins — The following conditional compatibilities have been reported:

Hydrocortisone sodium succinate (Upjohn) in dextrose 5% in water with ascorbic acid injection (Upjohn) and vitamin B complex with C (Abbott); the compatibility is dependent on the concentration of the additives. Therefore, if attempting to combine hydrocortisone sodium succinate with either of these drugs, mix the solution thoroughly and observe it closely for any sign of incompatibility. (15)

Hydrocortisone sodium succinate (Upjohn) 250 mg/L with vitamin B complex with C (Abbott) 2 ml/L; the mixture is physically compatible in most Abbott infusion solutions except Beclysyl 5 and 10%. (3)

Hydrocortisone sodium succinate (Upjohn) 250 mg/L with cyanocobalamin (Abbott) 1000 μg/L; the mixture is physically compatible in most Abbott infusion solutions except Ionosol D-CM with dextrose 5%. A haze or precipitate forms within 24 hours. (3)

Concentrated Drug Solutions — The following incompatibility determinations were performed with concentrated solutions. The drugs in dry form were reconstituted according to manufacturers' recommendations. One milliliter of hydrocortisone sodium succinate (Upjohn) was added to 5 ml of sterile distilled water along with 1 ml of each of the following drugs. Particulate matter was noted within two hours (28):

Dimenhydrinate (Searle)
Kanamycin sulfate (Bristol)
Promazine HCl (Wyeth)
Promethazine HCl (Wyeth)
Vancomycin HCl (Lilly)
Vitamin B complex with C (Lederle)

HYDROMORPHONE HCL
AHFS 28:08.08

Products — Hydromorphone HCl is available in 1-ml ampuls and 20-ml multiple-dose vials. Each milliliter of the solution contains (2):

Component	Ampul	Vial
Hydromorphone HCl	1, 2, or 4 mg	2 mg
Sodium citrate	0.2%	
Citric acid	0.2%	
Edetate disodium		0.5 mg
Methylparaben		1.8 mg
Propylparaben		0.2 mg

Sodium hydroxide or hydrochloric acid may have been used to adjust the pH of the solutions in vials. (2)

Hydromorphone HCl is also available in 1- and 5-ml amber ampuls and 50-ml single-dose vials as a high potency form (Dilaudid-HP). Each milliliter of the solution contains 10 mg of hydromorphone HCl with citric acid 0.2% and sodium citrate 0.2%. (2)

In addition to the liquid dosage forms, high potency hydromorphone HCl (Dilaudid-HP, Knoll) is available as a 250-mg single-dose vial as a lyophilized powder. Reconstitute with 25 ml of sterile water for injection to yield a 10-mg/ml solution. (2)

pH — From 4 to 5.5. (4)

Trade Name(s) — Dilaudid, Dilaudid-HP.

Administration — Hydromorphone HCl may be administered by subcutaneous, intramuscular, or slow direct intravenous injection over at least two to three minutes. (2; 4)

Stability — Hydromorphone HCl products should be stored at controlled room temperature and protected from light. (2) The liquid dosage forms in intact ampuls or vials should not be stored under refrigeration because of possible precipitation or crystallization. Resolubilization at room temperature or on warming may be performed without affecting the stability of the drug. (593) The manufacturer recommends inspecting for particulate matter or discoloration. A slight yellowish discoloration may develop in both the ampuls and vials, but it has not been associated with a loss of potency. (2; 4)

Extemporaneously prepared hydromorphone HCl 10 and 50 mg/ml, stored in 100-ml glass vials or PVC bags, exhibited no loss in 42 days at 4 and 23 °C. (1394)

Syringes — Hydromorphone HCl (Knoll) 10 mg/ml undiluted and diluted to 0.1 mg/ml in sodium chloride 0.9% was packaged as 3 ml in 10-ml polypropylene infusion pump syringes (Pharmacia Deltec). No loss by HPLC analysis occurred during 30 days storage at 30 °C. (1967)

Elastomeric Reservoir Pumps — Hydromorphone HCl 1 mg/ml in dextrose 5% in water and 1 to 10 mg/ml in sodium chloride 0.9% in Infusor elastomeric reservoir pumps has been stated by the pump manufacturer to be stable for seven days at room temperature and 32 days under refrigeration followed by three days at room temperature. (31)

Central Venous Catheter — Hydromorphone HCl (Knoll) 0.5 mg/ml in dextrose 5% in water was found to be compatible with the ARROWg+ard Blue Plus (Arrow International) chlorhexidine-bearing triple-lumen central catheter. HPLC analysis was used to evaluate completeness of drug delivery through the catheter and the amount of chlorhexidine removed from the internal lumens. Essentially complete delivery of the drug was found with little or no drug loss occurring. Furthermore, chlorhexidine delivered from the catheter remained at trace amounts with no substantial increase due to the delivery of the drug through the catheter. (2335)

Compatibility Information

Solution Compatibility

Hydromorphone HCl

Solution	*Mfr*	*Mfr*	*Conc/L*	*Remarks*	*Ref*	*C/I*
Amino acids 7%	AB	KN[a]	80 mg	Physically compatible and TLC indicates no decomposition in 24 hr at 25 °C	572	C
Amino acids 8%	CU	KN[a]	80 mg	Physically compatible and TLC indicates no decomposition in 24 hr at 25 °C	572	C
Amino acids 8.5%	MG	KN[a]	80 mg	Physically compatible and TLC indicates no decomposition in 24 hr at 25 °C	572	C
	TR	KN[a]	80 mg	Physically compatible and TLC indicates no decomposition in 24 hr at 25 °C	572	C
Amino acids 8.5% with electrolytes	TR	KN[a]	80 mg	Physically compatible and TLC indicates no decomposition in 24 hr at 25 °C	572	C
Amino acids, essential, 5.4%	MG	KN[a]	80 mg	Physically compatible and TLC indicates no decomposition in 24 hr at 25 °C	572	C
Dextrose 5% in Ringer's injection	CU	KN[a]	80 mg	Physically compatible and TLC indicates no decomposition in 24 hr at 25 °C	572	C

Solution Compatibility (Cont.)

Hydromorphone HCl

Solution	*Mfr*	*Mfr*	*Conc/L*	*Remarks*	*Ref*	*C/I*
Dextrose 5% in Ringer's injection, lactated	MG	KN[a]	80 mg	Physically compatible and TLC indicates no decomposition in 24 hr at 25 °C	572	C
Dextrose 5% in water	CU	KN[a]	80 mg	Physically compatible and TLC indicates no decomposition in 24 hr at 25 °C	572	C
	TR[b]	KN[a]	80 mg	Physically compatible and TLC indicates no decomposition in 24 hr at 25 °C	572	C
	MG[c]	KN[a]	80 mg	Physically compatible and TLC indicates no decomposition in 24 hr at 25 °C	572	C
	[b]	KN	1 and 5 g	No hydromorphone loss in 42 days at 4 and 23 °C	1394	C
Dextrose 5% in sodium chloride 0.45%	MG	KN[a]	80 mg	Physically compatible and TLC indicates no decomposition in 24 hr at 25 °C	572	C
Dextrose 5% in sodium chloride 0.9%	MG	KN[a]	80 mg	Physically compatible and TLC indicates no decomposition in 24 hr at 25 °C	572	C
Fructose 10% in water	CU	KN[a]	80 mg	Physically compatible and TLC indicates no decomposition in 24 hr at 25 °C	572	C
Ringer's injection	MG	KN[a]	80 mg	Physically compatible and TLC indicates no decomposition in 24 hr at 25 °C	572	C
Ringer's injection, lactated	MG	KN[a]	80 mg	Physically compatible and TLC indicates no decomposition in 24 hr at 25 °C	572	C
Sodium chloride 0.45%	MG	KN[a]	80 mg	Physically compatible and TLC indicates no decomposition in 24 hr at 25 °C	572	C
Sodium chloride 0.9%	CU	KN[a]	80 mg	Physically compatible and TLC indicates no decomposition in 24 hr at 25 °C	572	C
	TR[b]	KN[a]	80 mg	Physically compatible and TLC indicates no decomposition in 24 hr at 25 °C	572	C
	MG[c]	KN[a]	80 mg	Physically compatible and TLC indicates no decomposition in 24 hr at 25 °C	572	C
	[b]	KN	1 and 5 g	No hydromorphone loss in 42 days at 4 and 23 °C	1394	C
	AB[b]	KN	20 and 100 mg	Visually compatible with little or no loss by HPLC in 72 hr at 24 °C under fluorescent light	1870	C
Sodium lactate ⅙ M	CU	KN[a]	80 mg	Physically compatible and TLC indicates no decomposition in 24 hr at 25 °C	572	C

[a]Both ampul and vial formulations tested.
[b]Tested in PVC containers.
[c]Tested in polyolefin containers.

Additive Compatibility

Hydromorphone HCl

Drug	*Mfr*	*Conc/L*	*Mfr*	*Conc/L*	*Test Soln*	*Remarks*	*Ref*	*C/I*
Bupivacaine HCl	AB	625 mg and 1.25 g	KN	20 mg	NS[a]	Visually compatible with little or no loss of either drug by HPLC in 72 hr at 24 °C under fluorescent light	1870	C
	AB	625 mg and 1.25 g	KN	100 mg	NS[a]	Visually compatible with little or no loss of either drug by HPLC in 72 hr at 24 °C under fluorescent light	1870	C

Additive Compatibility (Cont.)

Hydromorphone HCl

Drug	*Mfr*	*Conc/L*	*Mfr*	*Conc/L*	*Test Soln*	*Remarks*	*Ref*	*C/I*
Fluorouracil	AB	1 g	AST	500 mg	D5W, NS[a]	Physically compatible with no increase in measured turbidity or particulates and little or no loss of either drug by HPLC in 7 days at 32 °C and 35 days at 23, 4, and −20 °C	1977	C
	AB	16 g	AST	500 mg	D5W, NS[a]	Physically compatible with no increase in measured turbidity or particulates and little or no loss of either drug by HPLC in 3 days at 32 °C, 7 days at 23 °C, and 35 days at 4 and −20 °C	1977	C
Midazolam HCl	RC	0.1 to 4.5 g	KN	0.5 to 45 g	D5W, NS	Visually compatible for 24 hr at room temperature	2086	C
	RC	100 mg	KN	2 and 20 g	D5W, NS	Visually compatible with less than 7% hydromorphone loss and less than 3% midazolam loss by HPLC in 23 days at 4 and 23 °C	2086	C
	RC	500 mg	KN	2 and 20 g	D5W, NS	Visually compatible with less than 6% hydromorphone loss and less than 7% midazolam loss by HPLC in 23 days at 4 and 23 °C	2086	C
Ondansetron HCl	GL	100 mg and 1 g	ES	500 mg	NS	Physically compatible with no loss of either drug by HPLC in 7 days at 32 °C or 31 days at 4 and 22 °C protected from light	1690	C
Promethazine HCl	ES	300 mg	KN	1 g	NS[a]	Visually compatible for 21 days at 4 and 25 °C	1992	C
Sodium bicarbonate						Physically incompatible	9	I
Thiopental sodium	AB					Physically incompatible	9	I
Verapamil HCl	KN	80 mg	KN	16 mg	D5W, NS	Physically compatible for 24 hr	764	C

[a]*Tested in PVC containers.*

Drugs in Syringe Compatibility

Hydromorphone HCl

Drug (in syringe)	*Mfr*	*Amt*	*Mfr*	*Amt*	*Remarks*	*Ref*	*C/I*
Ampicillin sodium	AY	250 mg/1 ml	KN	2, 10, 40 mg/1 ml	Visually compatible but 10% loss of ampicillin by HPLC in 5 hr at room temperature	2082	I
Atropine sulfate	ES	0.4 mg/0.5 ml	KN	4 mg/2 ml[a]	Physically compatible for 30 min	517	C
Bupivacaine HCl	AST	7.5 mg/ml	KN	65 mg/ml	Visually compatible for 30 days at 25 °C	1660	C
Cefazolin sodium	SKF	>200 mg/1 ml	KN	2, 10, 40 mg/1 ml	Precipitate forms	2082	I
	SKF	150 mg/1 ml	KN	2, 10, 40 mg/1 ml	Visually compatible with less than 10% loss of either drug by HPLC in 24 hr at room temperature	2082	C

Drugs in Syringe Compatibility (Cont.)

Hydromorphone HCl

Drug (in syringe)	*Mfr*	*Amt*	*Mfr*	*Amt*	*Remarks*	*Ref*	*C/I*
Ceftazidime	GL[i]	180 mg/ 1 ml	KN	2, 10, 40 mg/ 1 ml	Visually compatible with less than 10% loss of either drug by HPLC in 24 hr at room temperature	2082	C
Chlorpromazine HCl	ES	25 mg/ 1 ml	KN	4 mg/ 2 ml[a]	Physically compatible for 30 min	517	C
Cimetidine HCl	SKF	300 mg/ 2 ml	WI	2 mg/ 1 ml	Physically compatible for 4 hr at 25 °C	25	C
Dexamethasone sodium phosphate	SX	4 mg/ml[b]	KN	2, 10, 40 mg/ ml[b]	Visually compatible and potency of both drugs by HPLC retained for 24 hr at 24 °C	1542	C
	DB	10 mg/ ml[b]	KN	2 and 10 mg/ ml[b]	Visually compatible and potency of both drugs by HPLC retained for 24 hr at 24 °C	1542	C
	DB	10 mg/ ml[b]	KN	40 mg/ ml[b]	White turbidity forms immediately	1542	I
	DB	7.1 mg/ ml[c]	KN	11.6 mg/ ml[c]	Visually compatible for 24 hr at 24 °C	1542	C
	DB	5.5 to 6.6 mg/ ml[c]	KN	13.3 to 17.5 mg/ ml[c]	Precipitate forms	1542	I
	DB	4.75 mg/ ml[c]	KN	10.5 mg/ ml[c]	Visually compatible for 24 hr at 24 °C	1542	C
	DB	3 to 4.1 mg/ ml[c]	KN	14.75 to 25 mg/ ml[c]	Precipitate forms	1542	I
	SX	3.34 mg/ ml[c]	KN	26.66 mg/ ml[c]	Visually compatible for 24 hr at 24 °C	1542	C
Diazepam	SX	5 mg/ 1 ml	KN	2, 10, 40 mg/ 1 ml	Diazepam precipitate forms immediately due to aqueous dilution	2082	I
Dimenhydrinate	SQ	50 mg/ 1 ml	KN	2, 10, 40 mg/ 1 ml	Visually compatible with both drugs stable by HPLC for 24 hr at 4, 23, and 37 °C. Precipitate forms after 24 hr	1776	C
Diphenhydramine HCl	PD	50 mg/ 1 ml	KN	4 mg/ 2 ml[a]	Physically compatible for 30 min	517	C
Fentanyl citrate	MN	0.05 mg/ 1 ml	KN	4 mg/ 2 ml[a]	Physically compatible for 30 min	517	C
Glycopyrrolate	RB	0.2 mg/ 1 ml	KN	2 mg/ 1 ml	Physically compatible and pH in stability range for glycopyrrolate for 48 hr at 25 °C	331	C
	RB	0.2 mg/ 1 ml	KN	4 mg/ 2 ml	Physically compatible and pH in stability range for glycopyrrolate for 48 hr at 25 °C	331	C
	RB	0.4 mg/ 2 ml	KN	2 mg/ 1 ml	Physically compatible and pH in stability range for glycopyrrolate for 48 hr at 25 °C	331	C
Haloperidol lactate	MN	1[d], 2[d], 5 mg/ 1 ml	KN	1[d] and 10 mg/ 1 ml	Visually compatible for 24 hr at 25 °C under fluorescent light	1785	C
Hyaluronidase	WY	150 units/ml[e]	KN	2 mg/ml[e]	43 and 56% hyaluronidase loss in 24 hr at 4 and 23 °C, respectively	1907	I
	WY	150 units/ml[e]	KN	10 and 40 mg/ ml[e]	70 to 82% hyaluronidase loss in 24 hr at 4 and 23 °C	1907	I

Drugs in Syringe Compatibility (Cont.)

Hydromorphone HCl

Drug (in syringe)	*Mfr*	*Amt*	*Mfr*	*Amt*	*Remarks*	*Ref*	*C/I*
Hydroxyzine HCl	PF	50 mg/ 1 ml	KN	4 mg/ 2 ml[a]	Physically compatible for 30 min	517	**C**
	PF	100 mg/ 2 ml	KN	0.75 mg/ 0.8 ml	Physically compatible	771	**C**
Ketorolac tromethamine	SY	30 mg/ 1 ml	KN	10 mg/ 1 ml	Cloudiness forms immediately but clears with swirling	1785	**?**
	SY	30 mg/ 1 ml	KN	1 mg/ 1 ml[d]	Visually compatible for 24 hr at 25 °C under fluorescent light	1785	**C**
	SY	15 mg/ 1 ml[d]	KN	1[d] and 10 mg/ 1 ml	Visually compatible for 24 hr at 25 °C under fluorescent light	1785	**C**
Lorazepam	WY	4 mg/ 1 ml	KN	2, 10, 40 mg/ 1 ml	Visually compatible with 10% lorazepam loss by HPLC in 6 days at 4 °C, 4 days at 23 °C, and 24 hr at 37 °C. Little or no hydromorphone loss in 7 days at all three temperatures	1776	**C**
Midazolam HCl	RC	5 mg/ 1 ml	WB	2 mg/ 0.5 ml	Physically compatible for 4 hr at 25 °C under fluorescent light	1145	**C**
Pentazocine lactate	WI	30 mg/ 1 ml	KN	4 mg/ 2 ml[a]	Physically compatible for 30 min	517	**C**
Pentobarbital sodium	AB	50 mg/ 1 ml	KN	4 mg/ 2 ml[f]	Physically compatible for 30 min	517	**C**
	AB	50 mg/ 1 ml	KN	4 mg/ 2 ml[g]	Transient precipitate that dissipates after mixing. Physically compatible for 30 min	517	**C**
Phenobarbital sodium	AB	120 mg/ 1 ml	KN	2, 10, 40 mg/ 1 ml	Precipitate forms immediately but dissipates with shaking. A white precipitate of phenobarbital reforms after 6 hr at room temperature	2082	**I**
Phenytoin sodium	AB	50 mg/ 1 ml	KN	2, 10, 40 mg/ 1 ml	White precipitate of phenytoin forms immediately	2082	**I**
Prochlorperazine edisylate	SKF	5 mg/ 1 ml	KN	4 mg/ 2 ml[f]	Immediate precipitation	517	**I**
	SKF	5 mg/ 1 ml	KN	4 mg/ 2 ml[g]	Physically compatible for 30 min	517	**C**
Prochlorperazine mesylate	RP	5 mg/ 1 ml	KN	2, 10, 40 mg/ 1 ml	Visually compatible with little or no loss of either drug by HPLC in 7 days at 4, 23, and 37 °C	1776	**C**
	RP	1.5 mg/ ml[j]	SX	0.5 mg/ ml[j]	Visually and microscopically compatible for 96 hr at room temperature exposed to light	2171	**C**
Promethazine HCl	WY	50 mg/ 1 ml	KN	4 mg/ 2 ml[a]	Physically compatible for 30 min	517	**C**
	WY	25 mg/ 1 ml	KN	4 mg/ 2 ml[a]	Physically compatible for 30 min	517	**C**
Ranitidine HCl	GL	50 mg/ 2 ml	PE	2 mg/ 1 ml	Physically compatible for 1 hr at 25 °C both macroscopically and microscopically	978	**C**
Salbutamol	GL	2.5 mg/ 2.5 ml[h]	KN	1 mg/ 0.5 ml	Visually compatible for one hour both macroscopically and microscopically	1904	**C**
Scopolamine HBr	BW	0.43 mg/ 0.5 ml	KN	4 mg/ 2 ml[a]	Physically compatible for 30 min	517	**C**

Drugs in Syringe Compatibility (Cont.)

			Hydromorphone HCl				
Drug (in syringe)	*Mfr*	*Amt*	*Mfr*	*Amt*	*Remarks*	*Ref*	*C/I*
Thiethylperazine malate	SZ	5 mg/ 1 ml	KN	4 mg/ 2 ml[a]	Physically compatible for 30 min	517	C
Trimethobenzamide HCl	BE	100 mg/ 1 ml	KN	4 mg/ 2 ml[a]	Physically compatible for 30 min	517	C

[a]*Both ampul and vial formulations tested.*
[b]*Mixed in equal quantities. Final concentration is one-half the indicated concentration.*
[c]*Mixed in varying quantities to yield the final concentrations noted.*
[d]*Dilution prepared in sterile water for injection.*
[e]*Mixed in equal quantities for testing.*
[f]*Vial formulation tested.*
[g]*Ampul formulation tested.*
[h]*Both preserved (benzyl alcohol 0.9%; benzalkonium chloride 0.01%) and unpreserved sodium chloride 0.9% were used as a diluent.*
[i]*Sodium carbonate–containing formulation.*
[j]*Diluted in sodium chloride 0.9%.*

Y-Site Injection Compatibility (1:1 Mixture)

			Hydromorphone HCl				
Drug	*Mfr*	*Conc*	*Mfr*	*Conc*	*Remarks*	*Ref*	*C/I*
Acyclovir sodium	BW	5 mg/ml[a]	WB	0.04 mg/ml[a]	Physically compatible for 4 hr at 25 °C	1157	C
Allopurinol sodium	BW	3 mg/ml[b]	KN	0.5 mg/ml[b]	Physically compatible with no change in measured turbidity or increase in particle content in 4 hr at 22 °C	1686	C
Amifostine	USB	10 mg/ml[a]	AST	0.5 mg/ml[a]	Physically compatible with no change in measured turbidity or increase in particle content in 4 hr at 23 °C	1845	C
Amikacin sulfate	BR	5 mg/ml[a]	WY	0.2 mg/ml[a]	Physically compatible for at least 4 hr at 25 °C under fluorescent light	987	C
Amphotericin B cholesteryl sulfate complex	SEQ	0.83 mg/ml[a]	ES	0.5 mg/ml[a]	Decreased natural turbidity occurs immediately	2117	I
Ampicillin sodium	BR	20 mg/ml[b]	WY	0.2 mg/ml[a]	Physically compatible for at least 4 hr at 25 °C under fluorescent light	987	C
	AY	20[a] and 250 mg/ml	KN	2, 10, 40 mg/ ml	Visually compatible and hydromorphone potency by HPLC retained for 24 hr. 10% ampicillin loss by HPLC in 5 hr with or without hydromorphone	1532	I
Amsacrine	NCI	1 mg/ml[a]	AST	0.5 mg/ml[a]	Physically compatible for 4 hr at room temperature under fluorescent light	1381	C
Atropine sulfate	LY	0.4 mg/ml	AST	0.5 mg/ml[a]	Physically compatible with no change in measured haze or increase in particle content in 48 hr at 22 °C	1706	C
Aztreonam	SQ	40 mg/ml[a]	KN	0.5 mg/ml[a]	Physically compatible with no subvisual haze or particle formation in 4 hr at 23 °C	1758	C
Cefamandole nafate	LI	20 mg/ml[a]	WY	0.2 mg/ml[a]	Physically compatible for at least 4 hr at 25 °C under fluorescent light	987	C
Cefazolin sodium	SKF	20 mg/ml[a]	WY	0.2 mg/ml[a]	Physically compatible for at least 4 hr at 25 °C under fluorescent light	987	C
	SKF	20[a] and 150 mg/ml	KN	2, 10, 40 mg/ ml	Visually compatible and potency of both drugs by HPLC retained for 24 hr	1532	C

Y-Site Injection Compatibility (1:1 Mixture) (Cont.)

Hydromorphone HCl

Drug	*Mfr*	*Conc*	*Mfr*	*Conc*	*Remarks*	*Ref*	*C/I*
	SKF	>200 mg/ml	KN	2, 10, 40 mg/ml	Precipitate forms immediately	1532	I
Cefepime HCl	BMS	20 mg/ml[a]	ES	0.5 mg/ml[a]	Physically compatible with no change in measured turbidity or increase in particle content in 4 hr at 22 °C	1689	C
Cefoperazone sodium	RR	20 mg/ml[a]	WY	0.2 mg/ml[a]	Physically compatible for at least 4 hr at 25 °C under fluorescent light	987	C
Cefotaxime sodium	HO	20 mg/ml[a]	WY	0.2 mg/ml[a]	Physically compatible for at least 4 hr at 25 °C under fluorescent light	987	C
Cefoxitin sodium	MSD	20 mg/ml[a]	WY	0.2 mg/ml[a]	Physically compatible for at least 4 hr at 25 °C under fluorescent light	987	C
Ceftazidime	GL[f]	40[a] and 180 mg/ml	KN	2, 10, 40 mg/ml	Visually compatible and potency of both drugs by HPLC retained for 24 hr	1532	C
Ceftizoxime sodium	SKF	20 mg/ml[a]	WY	0.2 mg/ml[a]	Physically compatible for at least 4 hr at 25 °C under fluorescent light	987	C
Cefuroxime sodium	GL	30 mg/ml[a]	WY	0.2 mg/ml[a]	Physically compatible for at least 4 hr at 25 °C under fluorescent light	987	C
Chloramphenicol sodium succinate	LY	20 mg/ml[a]	WY	0.2 mg/ml[a]	Physically compatible for at least 4 hr at 25 °C under fluorescent light	987	C
Cisatracurium besylate	GW	0.1, 2, 5 mg/ml[a]	ES	0.5 mg/ml[a]	Physically compatible with no change in measured turbidity or increase in particle content in 4 hr at 23 °C	2074	C
Cisplatin	BR	1 mg/ml	ES	0.04 mg/ml[a]	Visually compatible for 4 hr at room temperature under fluorescent light	1685	C
Cladribine	ORT	0.015[b] and 0.5[d] mg/ml	KN	0.5 mg/ml[b]	Physically compatible with no change in measured turbidity or increase in particle content in 4 hr at 23 °C	1969	C
Clindamycin phosphate	UP	12 mg/ml[a]	WY	0.2 mg/ml[a]	Physically compatible for at least 4 hr at 25 °C under fluorescent light	987	C
Cyclophosphamide	MJ	10 mg/ml	ES	0.04 mg/ml[a]	Visually compatible for 4 hr at room temperature under fluorescent light	1685	C
Cytarabine	UP	50 mg/ml	ES	0.04 mg/ml[a]	Visually compatible for 4 hr at room temperature under fluorescent light	1685	C
Dexamethasone sodium phosphate	AMR	1 mg/ml[a]	AST	0.5 mg/ml[a]	Physically compatible with no change in measured haze or increase in particle content in 48 hr at 22 °C	1706	C
Diazepam	SX	5 mg/ml	KN	2, 10, 40 mg/ml	Turbidity forms immediately and diazepam precipitate develops	1532	I
	ES	0.5 mg/ml[a]	AST	0.5 mg/ml[a]	Physically compatible with no change in measured haze or increase in particle content in 48 hr at 22 °C	1706	C
Diltiazem HCl	MMD	1 mg/ml[a]	KN	1 mg/ml	Visually compatible for 4 hr at 27 °C	2062	C
Diphenhydramine HCl	SCN	2 mg/ml[a]	AST	0.5 mg/ml[a]	Physically compatible with no change in measured haze or increase in particle content in 48 hr at 22 °C	1706	C
Dobutamine HCl	LI	4 mg/ml[a]	KN	1 mg/ml	Visually compatible for 4 hr at 27 °C	2062	C

Y-Site Injection Compatibility (1:1 Mixture) (Cont.)

Hydromorphone HCl

Drug	*Mfr*	*Conc*	*Mfr*	*Conc*	*Remarks*	*Ref*	*C/I*
Docetaxel	RPR	0.9 mg/ml[a]	AST	0.5 mg/ml[a]	Physically compatible with no change in measured turbidity or increase in particle content in 4 hr at 23 °C	2224	C
Dopamine HCl	AB	3.2 mg/ml[a]	KN	1 mg/ml	Visually compatible for 4 hr at 27 °C	2062	C
Doxorubicin HCl	AD	0.2 mg/ml[a]	ES	0.04 mg/ml[a]	Visually compatible for 4 hr at room temperature under fluorescent light	1685	C
Doxorubicin HCl liposome injection	SEQ	0.4 mg/ml[a]	ES	0.5 mg/ml[a]	Physically compatible with little or no change in measured turbidity and no increase in particle content in 4 hr at 23 °C	2087	C
Doxycycline hyclate	ES	1 mg/ml[a]	WY	0.2 mg/ml[a]	Physically compatible for at least 4 hr at 25 °C under fluorescent light	987	C
Epinephrine HCl	AB	0.02 mg/ml[a]	KN	1 mg/ml	Visually compatible for 4 hr at 27 °C	2062	C
Erythromycin lactobionate	AB	5 mg/ml[a]	WY	0.2 mg/ml[a]	Physically compatible for at least 4 hr at 25 °C under fluorescent light	987	C
Etoposide phosphate	BR	5 mg/ml[a]	ES	0.5 mg/ml[a]	Physically compatible with no change in measured turbidity or increase in particle content in 4 hr at 23 °C	2218	C
Famotidine	ME	2 mg/ml[b]		0.5 mg/ml[a]	Visually compatible for 4 hr at 22 °C	1936	C
Fentanyl citrate	ES	0.05 mg/ml	KN	1 mg/ml	Visually compatible for 4 hr at 27 °C	2062	C
Filgrastim	AMG	30 μg/ml[a]	KN	0.5 mg/ml[a]	Physically compatible with no change in measured turbidity or increase in particle content in 4 hr at 22 °C	1687	C
Fludarabine phosphate	BX	1 mg/ml[a]	KN	0.5 mg/ml[a]	Physically compatible for 4 hr at room temperature under fluorescent light	1439	C
Foscarnet sodium	AST	24 mg/ml	KN	10 mg/ml	Physically compatible for 24 hr at room temperature under fluorescent light	1335	C
Furosemide	AMR	10 mg/ml	KN	1 mg/ml	Visually compatible for 4 hr at 27 °C	2062	C
Gatifloxacin	BMS	2 mg/ml[a]	AST	0.5 mg/ml[a]	Physically compatible with no change in measured haze or increase in particle content in 4 hr at 23 °C	2234	C
Gemcitabine HCl	LI	10 mg/ml[b]	AST	0.5 mg/ml[b]	Physically compatible with no change in measured turbidity or increase in particle content in 4 hr at 23 °C	2226	C
Gentamicin sulfate	TR	0.8 mg/ml[a]	WY	0.2 mg/ml[a]	Physically compatible for at least 4 hr at 25 °C under fluorescent light	987	C
Granisetron HCl	SKB	1 mg/ml	KN	0.5 mg/ml[b]	Physically compatible with little or no loss of either drug by HPLC in 4 hr at 22 °C	1883	C
	SKB	0.05 mg/ml[a]	ES	0.5 mg/ml[a]	Physically compatible with no change in measured turbidity or increase in particle content in 4 hr at 23 °C	2000	C
Haloperidol lactate	MN	0.2 mg/ml[a]	AST	0.5 mg/ml[a]	Physically compatible with no change in measured haze or increase in particle content in 48 hr at 22 °C	1706	C
Heparin sodium	ES	100 units/ml[a]	KN	1 mg/ml	Visually compatible for 4 hr at 27 °C	2062	C

Y-Site Injection Compatibility (1:1 Mixture) (Cont.)

Hydromorphone HCl

Drug	*Mfr*	*Conc*	*Mfr*	*Conc*	*Remarks*	*Ref*	*C/I*
Hetastarch in lactated electrolyte injection (Hextend)	AB	6%	AST	0.5 mg/ml[a]	Physically compatible with no change in measured turbidity or increase in particle content in 4 hr at 23 °C	2339	C
Hydroxyzine HCl	WI	4 mg/ml[a]	AST	0.5 mg/ml[a]	Physically compatible with no change in measured haze or increase in particle content in 48 hr at 22 °C	1706	C
Kanamycin sulfate	BR	2.5 mg/ml[a]	WY	0.2 mg/ml[a]	Physically compatible for at least 4 hr at 25 °C under fluorescent light	987	C
Ketorolac tromethamine	WY	1 mg/ml[a]	AST	0.5 mg/ml[a]	Physically compatible with no change in measured haze or increase in particle content in 48 hr at 22 °C	1706	C
Labetalol HCl	AH	2 mg/ml[a]	KN	1 mg/ml	Visually compatible for 4 hr at 27 °C	2062	C
Linezolid	PHU	2 mg/ml	AST	0.5 mg/ml[a]	Physically compatible with no change in measured turbidity or increase in particle content in 4 hr at 23 °C	2264	C
Lorazepam	WY	0.5 mg/ml[a]	KN	1 mg/ml	Visually compatible for 4 hr at 27 °C	2062	C
	WY	0.1 mg/ml[a]	AST	0.5 mg/ml[a]	Physically compatible with no change in measured haze or increase in particle content in 48 hr at 22 °C	1706	C
Magnesium sulfate	LY	16.7, 33.3, 50, 100 mg/ml[a]	KN	2 mg/ml[a]	Visually compatible for 4 hr at 25 °C under fluorescent light	1549	C
Melphalan HCl	BW	0.1 mg/ml[b]	KN	0.5 mg/ml[b]	Physically compatible with no change in measured turbidity or increase in particle content in 3 hr at 22 °C	1557	C
Methotrexate sodium	AD	15 mg/ml[e]	ES	0.04 mg/ml[a]	Visually compatible for 4 hr at room temperature under fluorescent light	1685	C
Methotrimeprazine	LE	0.2 mg/ml[a]	AST	0.5 mg/ml[a]	Physically compatible with no change in measured haze or increase in particle content in 48 hr at 22 °C	1706	C
Metoclopramide HCl	DU	5 mg/ml	AST	0.5 mg/ml[a]	Physically compatible with no change in measured haze or increase in particle content in 48 hr at 22 °C	1706	C
Metronidazole	SE	5 mg/ml	WY	0.2 mg/ml[a]	Physically compatible for at least 4 hr at 25 °C under fluorescent light	987	C
Midazolam HCl	RC	2 mg/ml[a]	KN	1 mg/ml	Visually compatible for 4 hr at 27 °C	2062	C
	RC	0.2 mg/ml[a]	AST	0.5 mg/ml[a]	Physically compatible with no change in measured haze or increase in particle content in 48 hr at 22 °C	1706	C
Milrinone lactate	SW	0.2 mg/ml[a]	KN	1 mg/ml	Visually compatible for 4 hr at 27 °C	2062	C
Minocycline HCl	LE	0.2 mg/ml[a]	WY	0.2 mg/ml[a]	Color changed from pale yellow to light green within 1 hr at 25 °C	987	I
Morphine sulfate	SCN	2 mg/ml[a]	KN	1 mg/ml	Visually compatible for 4 hr at 27 °C	2062	C
Nafcillin sodium	WY	20 mg/ml[a]	WY	0.2 mg/ml[a]	Physically compatible for at least 4 hr at 25 °C under fluorescent light	987	C
Nicardipine HCl	WY	1 mg/ml[a]	KN	1 mg/ml	Visually compatible for 4 hr at 27 °C	2062	C
Nitroglycerin	AB	0.4 mg/ml[a]	KN	1 mg/ml	Visually compatible for 4 hr at 27 °C	2062	C

Y-Site Injection Compatibility (1:1 Mixture) (Cont.)

			Hydromorphone HCl				
Drug	*Mfr*	*Conc*	*Mfr*	*Conc*	*Remarks*	*Ref*	*C/I*
Norepinephrine bitartrate	AB	0.128 mg/ml[a]	KN	1 mg/ml	Visually compatible for 4 hr at 27 °C	2062	C
Ondansetron HCl	GL	1 mg/ml[b]	KN	0.5 mg/ml[a]	Physically compatible for 4 hr at 22 °C	1365	C
Oxacillin sodium	BE	20 mg/ml[a]	WY	0.2 mg/ml[a]	Physically compatible for at least 4 hr at 25 °C under fluorescent light	987	C
Paclitaxel	NCI	1.2 mg/ml[a]	KN	0.5 mg/ml[a]	Physically compatible with no change in measured turbidity in 4 hr at 22 °C	1556	C
Penicillin G potassium	PF	100,000 units/ml[a]	WY	0.2 mg/ml[a]	Physically compatible for at least 4 hr at 25 °C under fluorescent light	987	C
Phenobarbital sodium	AB	120 mg/ml	KN	2, 10, 40 mg/ml	Turbidity forms immediately but dissipates; phenobarbital precipitate develops in 6 hr	1532	I
	WY	2 mg/ml[a]	AST	0.5 mg/ml[a]	Physically compatible with no change in measured haze or increase in particle content in 48 hr at 22 °C	1706	C
Phenytoin sodium	AB	50 mg/ml	KN	2, 10, 40 mg/ml	Turbidity forms immediately and phenytoin precipitate develops	1532	I
	ES	2 mg/ml[a,b]	AST	0.5 mg/ml[a]	Precipitate forms within 1 hr	1706	I
Piperacillin sodium	LE	60 mg/ml[a]	WY	0.2 mg/ml[a]	Physically compatible for at least 4 hr at 25 °C under fluorescent light	987	C
Piperacillin sodium–tazobactam sodium	LE	40 + 5 mg/ml[a]	KN	0.5 mg/ml[a]	Physically compatible with no change in measured turbidity or increase in particle content in 4 hr at 22 °C	1688	C
Propofol	ZEN	10 mg/ml	AST	0.5 mg/ml[a]	Physically compatible for 1 hr at 23 °C with no increase in particle content	2066	C
Ranitidine HCl	GL	1 mg/ml[a]	KN	1 mg/ml	Visually compatible for 4 hr at 27 °C	2062	C
Remifentanil HCl	GW	0.025 and 0.25 mg/ml[b]	ES	0.5 mg/ml[a]	Physically compatible with no change in measured turbidity or increase in particle content in 4 hr at 23 °C	2075	C
Sargramostim	IMM	10 μg/ml[b]	KN	0.5 mg/ml[b]	Few small particles form in 30 min	1436	I
Scopolamine HBr	LY	0.05 mg/ml[a]	AST	0.5 mg/ml[a]	Physically compatible with no change in measured haze or increase in particle content in 48 hr at 22 °C	1706	C
Tacrolimus	FUJ	10 and 40 μg/ml[a]	KN	200 μg/ml[a]	Visually compatible with no loss of either drug by HPLC in 4 hr at 24 °C under fluorescent light	2216	C
	FUJ	10 and 40 μg/ml[a]	KN	2 mg/ml[a]	Visually compatible with no loss of either drug by HPLC in 4 hr at 24 °C under fluorescent light	2216	C
Teniposide	BR	0.1 mg/ml[a]	KN	0.5 mg/ml[a]	Physically compatible with no subvisual haze or particle formation in 4 hr at 23 °C	1725	C
Thiopental sodium	AB	25 mg/ml[c]	KN	1 mg/ml	Precipitate forms in 4 hr at 27 °C	2062	I
Thiotepa	IMM[g]	1 mg/ml[a]	AST	0.5 mg/ml[a]	Physically compatible with no change in measured turbidity or increase in particle content in 4 hr at 23 °C	1861	C
Ticarcillin disodium	BE	60 mg/ml[a]	WY	0.2 mg/ml[a]	Physically compatible for at least 4 hr at 25 °C under fluorescent light	987	C

Y-Site Injection Compatibility (1:1 Mixture) (Cont.)

			Hydromorphone HCl				
Drug	*Mfr*	*Conc*	*Mfr*	*Conc*	*Remarks*	*Ref*	*C/I*
TNA #218, #220, #221, #223[h]			ES	0.5 mg/ml[a]	Visually compatible with no precipitate or emulsion damage apparent in 4 hr at 23 °C	2215	C
TNA #219, #222, #224 to #226[h]			ES	0.5 mg/ml[a]	Damage to emulsion integrity occurs immediately with free oil formation possible	2215	I
Tobramycin sulfate	DI	0.8 mg/ml[a]	WY	0.2 mg/ml[a]	Physically compatible for at least 4 hr at 25 °C under fluorescent light	987	C
TPN #212 to #215[h]			ES	0.5 mg/ml[a]	Physically compatible with no change in measured turbidity or increase in particle content in 4 hr at 23 °C	2109	C
Trimethoprim–sulfamethoxazole	BW	0.8 + 4 mg/ml[a]	WY	0.2 mg/ml[a]	Physically compatible for at least 4 hr at 25 °C under fluorescent light	987	C
Vancomycin HCl	LI	5 mg/ml[a]	WY	0.2 mg/ml[a]	Physically compatible for at least 4 hr at 25 °C under fluorescent light	987	C
Vecuronium bromide	OR	1 mg/ml	KN	1 mg/ml	Visually compatible for 4 hr at 27 °C	2062	C
Vinorelbine tartrate	BW	1 mg/ml[b]	KN	0.5 mg/ml[b]	Physically compatible with no change in measured turbidity or increase in particle content in 4 hr at 22 °C	1558	C

[a] *Tested in dextrose 5% in water.*
[b] *Tested in sodium chloride 0.9%.*
[c] *Tested in sterile water for injection.*
[d] *Tested in bacteriostatic sodium chloride 0.9% preserved with benzyl alcohol 0.9%.*
[e] *Tested in dextrose 5% in water with sodium bicarbonate 0.05 mEq/ml.*
[f] *Sodium carbonate–containing formulation.*
[g] *Lyophilized formulation tested.*
[h] *Refer to Appendix I for the composition of parenteral nutrition solutions. TNA indicates a 3-in-1 admixture, and TPN indicates a 2-in-1 admixture.*

Additional Compatibility Information

Infusion Solutions — Hydromorphone HCl reportedly is physically and chemically stable for at least 24 hours in most common intravenous infusion solutions when stored protected from light at 25 °C. However, it is reported to be physically or chemically incompatible with sodium bicarbonate–containing solutions. (4)

Tetracaine HCl — Hydromorphone HCl (Winthrop) 4.38 mg/ml with tetracaine HCl (Winthrop) 1.25 mg/ml in sodium chloride 0.9% in an implantable pump controlled pain through 18 days of use. After that time, supplementary medication was needed. The authors speculated that a potency loss after 18 days at 37 °C caused the inadequate pain control, but this speculation was not verified. (1524)

HYDROXYZINE HCL
AHFS 28:24.92

Products — Hydroxyzine HCl is available as a 25-mg/ml solution in 1-ml vials, 1-ml syringe cartridges, and 10-ml multiple-dose vials. It is also available as a 50-mg/ml solution in 1- and 2-ml single-dose vials and 10-ml multiple-dose vials. Also present in the solutions are benzyl alcohol 0.9% and sodium hydroxide to adjust the pH. (2; 4; 29)

pH — From 3.5 to 6. (4)

Osmolality — Hydroxyzine HCl (Elkins-Sinn) 50 mg/ml has an osmolality of 345 mOsm/kg. (2043)

Trade Name(s) — Vistaril.

Administration — Hydroxyzine HCl may be administered undiluted by intramuscular injection only, preferably into the upper outer quadrant of the buttock or the midlateral muscles of the thigh in adults. In children, the midlateral muscles of the thigh are preferred. (2; 4)

Stability — Hydroxyzine injection should be stored at controlled room temperature and protected from freezing and excessive temperatures. (2; 4) Hydroxyzine HCl (Pfizer) 50 mg/ml retained its potency for three months at room temperature when 1 and 2 ml of solution were packaged in Tubex cartridges. (13)

Compatibility Information

Additive Compatibility

Hydroxyzine HCl

Drug	*Mfr*	*Conc/L*	*Mfr*	*Conc/L*	*Test Soln*	*Remarks*	*Ref*	*C/I*
Aminophylline	SE	1 g	RR	250 mg	D5W	Physically incompatible	15	I
Amobarbital sodium			PF			Physically incompatible	9	I
	LI	1 g	RR	250 mg	D5W	Physically incompatible	15	I
Chloramphenicol sodium succinate	PD	10 g	RR	250 mg	D5W	Physically incompatible	15	I
Cisplatin	BR	200 mg	LY	500 mg	NS[a]	Physically compatible for 48 hr	1190	C
Cyclophosphamide	AD	1 g	LY	500 mg	D5W[a]	Physically compatible for 48 hr	1190	C
Cytarabine	UP	1 g	LY	500 mg	D5W[a]	Physically compatible for 48 hr	1190	C
Dimenhydrinate	SE	500 mg	RR	250 mg	D5W	Physically compatible	15	C
Etoposide	BR	1 g	LY	500 mg	D5W[a]	Physically compatible for 48 hr	1190	C
Lidocaine HCl	AST	2 g	PF	100 mg		Physically compatible	24	C
Mesna	AW	3 g	LY	500 mg	D5W[a]	Physically compatible for 48 hr	1190	C
Methotrexate sodium	BV	1 and 3 g	LY	500 mg	D5W[a]	Physically compatible for 48 hr	1190	C
Nafcillin sodium	WY	500 mg	PF	100 mg		Physically compatible	27	C
Penicillin G potassium	SQ	20 million units	RR	250 mg	D5W	Physically incompatible	15	I
Penicillin G sodium	UP	20 million units	RR	250 mg	D5W	Physically incompatible	15	I
Pentobarbital sodium			PF			Physically incompatible	9	I
	AB	1 g	RR	250 mg	D5W	Physically incompatible	15	I
Phenobarbital sodium	WI	200 mg	RR	250 mg	D5W	Physically incompatible	15	I

[a]*Tested in glass containers.*

Drugs in Syringe Compatibility

Hydroxyzine HCl

Drug (in syringe)	*Mfr*	*Amt*	*Mfr*	*Amt*	*Remarks*	*Ref*	*C/I*
Atropine sulfate		0.4 mg/ 1 ml	PF	100 mg/ 2 ml	Physically compatible	771	C
		0.4 mg/ 1 ml	PF	50 mg/ 1 ml	Physically compatible	771	C
		0.6 mg/ 1.5 ml	PF	100 mg/ 4 ml	Physically compatible for at least 15 min	14	C
	USP	0.4 mg/ 0.4 ml	NF	50 mg/ 1 ml	Hydroxyzine potency retained for at least 10 days at 3 and 25 °C	49	C
	ST	0.4 mg/ 1 ml	PF	50 mg/ 1 ml	Physically compatible for at least 15 min	326	C

Drugs in Syringe Compatibility (Cont.)

Hydroxyzine HCl

Drug (in syringe)	*Mfr*	*Amt*	*Mfr*	*Amt*	*Remarks*	*Ref*	*C/I*
Atropine sulfate with meperidine HCl[a]	ES WI	0.4 mg 50 mg	PF	50 mg/ 2.5 ml	No alteration of UV spectra in 10 days at 3 and 25 °C	301	**C**
Butorphanol tartrate	BR	2 mg/ 1 ml	PF	50 mg/ 1 ml	Physically compatible	771	**C**
	BR	1 mg/ 1 ml	PF	100 mg/ 2 ml	Physically compatible	771	**C**
Chlorpromazine HCl	PO	50 mg/ 2 ml	PF	50 mg/ 1 ml	Physically compatible for at least 15 min	326	**C**
	STS	50 mg/ 2 ml	ES	100 mg/ 2 ml	Visually compatible for 60 min	1784	**C**
Cimetidine HCl	SKF	300 mg/ 2 ml	ES	100 mg/ 2 ml	Physically compatible for 4 hr at 25 °C	25	**C**
Codeine phosphate		120 mg/ 4 ml	PF	50 mg/ 1 ml	Physically compatible	771	**C**
		60 mg/ 2 ml	PF	100 mg/ 2 ml	Physically compatible	771	**C**
Dimenhydrinate	HR	50 mg/ 1 ml	PF	50 mg/ 1 ml	Physically incompatible within 15 min	326	**I**
Diphenhydramine HCl	PD	50 mg/ 1 ml	PF	50 mg/ 1 ml	Physically compatible for at least 15 min	326	**C**
Doxapram HCl	RB	400 mg/ 20 ml		25 mg/ 1 ml	Physically compatible with no doxapram loss in 24 hr	1177	**C**
Droperidol	MN	2.5 mg/ 1 ml	PF	50 mg/ 1 ml	Physically compatible for at least 15 min	326	**C**
Fentanyl citrate	MN	0.05 mg/ 1 ml	PF	50 mg/ 1 ml	Physically compatible for at least 15 min	326	**C**
	CR	0.05 mg/ 1 ml	PF	50 mg/ 1 ml	Physically compatible	771	**C**
	CR	0.05 mg/ 1 ml	PF	100 mg/ 2 ml	Physically compatible	771	**C**
Fluphenazine HCl	LY	5 mg/ 2 ml	ES	100 mg/ 2 ml	Visually compatible for 60 min	1784	**C**
Glycopyrrolate	RB	0.2 mg/ 1 ml	PF	25 mg/ 1 ml	Physically compatible and pH in stability range for glycopyrrolate for 48 hr at 25 °C	331	**C**
	RB	0.2 mg/ 1 ml	PF	50 mg/ 2 ml	Physically compatible and pH in stability range for glycopyrrolate for 48 hr at 25 °C	331	**C**
	RB	0.4 mg/ 2 ml	PF	25 mg/ 1 ml	Physically compatible and pH in stability range for glycopyrrolate for 48 hr at 25 °C	331	**C**
Haloperidol lactate	MN	10 mg/ 2 ml	ES	100 mg/ 2 ml	White precipitate forms within 5 min	1784	**I**
Hydromorphone HCl	KN	4 mg/ 2 ml	PF	50 mg/ 1 ml	Physically compatible for 30 min	517	**C**
	KN	0.75 mg/ 0.8 ml	PF	100 mg/ 2 ml	Physically compatible	771	**C**
Ketorolac tromethamine	SY	180 mg/ 6 ml	SO	150 mg/ 3 ml	Heavy white precipitate forms immediately, separating into two layers over time	1703	**I**
Lidocaine HCl	AST	2%/2 ml	PF	50 mg/ 2 ml	Physically compatible	771	**C**

Drugs in Syringe Compatibility (Cont.)

Hydroxyzine HCl

Drug (in syringe)	*Mfr*	*Amt*	*Mfr*	*Amt*	*Remarks*	*Ref*	*C/I*
	AST	2%/2 ml	PF	100 mg/ 2 ml	Physically compatible	771	C
Meperidine HCl	WI	100 mg/ 2 ml	PF	50 mg/ 1 ml	Physically compatible	771	C
	WI	50 mg/ 1 ml	PF	100 mg/ 2 ml	Physically compatible	771	C
	WY	100 mg/ 1 ml	PF	100 mg/ 4 ml	Physically compatible for at least 15 min	14	C
	WI	50 mg/ 1 ml	PF	50 mg/ 1 ml	Physically compatible for at least 15 min	326	C
Meperidine HCl with atropine sulfate[a]	WI ES	50 mg 0.4 mg	PF	50 mg/ 2.5 ml	No alteration of UV spectra in 10 days at 3 and 25 °C	301	C
Methotrimeprazine	LE	20 mg/ 1 ml	PF	50 mg/ 1 ml	Physically compatible	771	C
	LE	10 mg/ 0.5 ml	PF	100 mg/ 2 ml	Physically compatible	771	C
Metoclopramide HCl	NO	10 mg/ 2 ml	PF	50 mg/ 1 ml	Physically compatible both macroscopically and microscopically for 15 min at room temperature	565	C
Midazolam HCl	RC	5 mg/ 1 ml	ES	100 mg/ 2 ml	Physically compatible for 4 hr at 25 °C under fluorescent light	1145	C
Morphine sulfate	WY	15 mg/ 1 ml	PF	100 mg/ 4 ml	Physically compatible for at least 15 min	14	C
	ST	15 mg/ 1 ml	PF	50 mg/ 1 ml	Physically compatible for at least 15 min	326	C
		10 mg/ 0.7 ml	PF	50 mg/ 1 ml	Physically compatible	771	C
		5 mg/ 0.3 ml	PF	100 mg/ 2 ml	Physically compatible	771	C
Nalbuphine HCl	EN	10 mg/ 1 ml	PF	50 mg	Physically compatible for 36 hr at 27 °C	762	C
	EN	5 mg/ 0.5 ml	PF	50 mg	Physically compatible for 36 hr at 27 °C	762	C
	EN	2.5 mg/ 0.25 ml	PF	50 mg	Physically compatible for 36 hr at 27 °C	762	C
	DU	10 mg/ 1 ml	PF	25 mg/ 1 ml	Physically compatible for 48 hr	128	C
	DU	20 mg/ 1 ml	PF	25 mg/ 1 ml	Physically compatible for 48 hr	128	C
Oxymorphone HCl	EN	0.75 mg/ 0.5 ml	PF	100 mg/ 2 ml	Physically compatible	771	C
Papaveretum	RC[b]	20 mg/ 1 ml	PF	50 mg/ 1 ml	Visually compatible for at least 15 min	326	C
Pentazocine lactate	WI	60 mg/ 2 ml	PF	50 mg/ 1 ml	Physically compatible	771	C
	WI	30 mg/ 1 ml	PF	100 mg/ 2 ml	Physically compatible	771	C
	WI	30 mg/ 1 ml	PF	100 mg/ 4 ml	Physically compatible for at least 15 min	14	C
	WI	30 mg/ 1 ml	PF	50 mg/ 1 ml	Physically compatible for at least 15 min	326	C

Drugs in Syringe Compatibility (Cont.)

Hydroxyzine HCl

Drug (in syringe)	*Mfr*	*Amt*	*Mfr*	*Amt*	*Remarks*	*Ref*	*C/I*
Pentobarbital sodium	WY	100 mg/ 2 ml	PF	100 mg/ 4 ml	Precipitate forms within 15 min	14	I
	AB	50 mg/ 1 ml	PF	50 mg/ 1 ml	Physically incompatible within 15 min	326	I
Perphenazine	SC	10 mg/ 2 ml	ES	100 mg/ 2 ml	Visually compatible for 60 min	1784	C
Procaine HCl	WI	2%/2 ml	PF	50 mg/ 2 ml	Physically compatible	771	C
	WI	2%/2 ml	PF	100 mg/ 2 ml	Physically compatible	771	C
Prochlorperazine edisylate	PO	5 mg/ 1 ml	PF	50 mg/ 1 ml	Physically compatible for at least 15 min	326	C
Promazine HCl	WY	50 mg/ 1 ml	PF	50 mg/ 1 ml	Physically compatible for at least 15 min	326	C
Promethazine HCl	WY	50 mg/ 2 ml	PF	100 mg/ 4 ml	Physically compatible for at least 15 min	14	C
	PO	50 mg/ 2 ml	PF	50 mg/ 1 ml	Physically compatible for at least 15 min	326	C
Ranitidine HCl	GL	50 mg/ 2 ml	PF	50 mg/ 1 ml	Immediate white haze that disappeared following vortex mixing	978	I
Scopolamine HBr		0.6 mg/ 1.5 ml	PF	100 mg/ 4 ml	Physically compatible for at least 15 min	14	C
	ST	0.4 mg/ 1 ml	PF	50 mg/ 1 ml	Physically compatible for at least 15 min	326	C
		0.65 mg/ 1 ml	PF	100 mg/ 2 ml	Physically compatible	771	C
		0.65 mg/ 1 ml	PF	50 mg/ 1 ml	Physically compatible	771	C
Sufentanil citrate	JN	50 µg/ml	ES	50 mg/ml	Physically compatible with no subvisual haze or particle formation in 24 hr at 23 °C	1711	C

[a]*Tested in both glass and plastic syringes.*
[b]*The former formulation was tested.*

Y-Site Injection Compatibility (1:1 Mixture)

Hydroxyzine HCl

Drug	*Mfr*	*Conc*	*Mfr*	*Conc*	*Remarks*	*Ref*	*C/I*
Allopurinol sodium	BW	3 mg/ml[b]	ES	4 mg/ml[b]	Heavy white turbidity and precipitate form immediately	1686	I
Amifostine	USB	10 mg/ml[a]	WI	4 mg/ml[a]	Subvisual haze forms immediately	1845	I
Amphotericin B cholesteryl sulfate complex	SEQ	0.83 mg/ml[a]	ES	2 mg/ml[a]	Gross precipitate forms	2117	I
Aztreonam	SQ	40 mg/ml[a]	WI	4 mg/ml[a]	Physically compatible with no subvisual haze or particle formation in 4 hr at 23 °C	1758	C
Cefepime HCl	BMS	20 mg/ml[a]	WI	4 mg/ml[a]	Haze forms immediately and becomes flocculent precipitate in 4 hr	1689	I
Ciprofloxacin	MI	2 mg/ml[c]	ES	50 mg/ml	Visually compatible for 24 hr at 24 °C	1655	C

Y-Site Injection Compatibility (1:1 Mixture) (Cont.)

Drug	*Mfr*	*Conc*	Hydroxyzine HCl *Mfr*	Hydroxyzine HCl *Conc*	*Remarks*	*Ref*	*C/I*
Cisatracurium besylate	GW	0.1, 2, 5 mg/ml[a]	ES	2 mg/ml[a]	Physically compatible with no change in measured turbidity or increase in particle content in 4 hr at 23 °C	2074	C
Cladribine	ORT	0.015[b] and 0.5[d] mg/ml	ES	4 mg/ml[b]	Physically compatible with no change in measured turbidity or increase in particle content in 4 hr at 23 °C	1969	C
Docetaxel	RPR	0.9 mg/ml[a]	ES	2 mg/ml[a]	Physically compatible with no change in measured turbidity or increase in particle content in 4 hr at 23 °C	2224	C
Doxorubicin HCl liposome injection	SEQ	0.4 mg/ml[a]	ES	2 mg/ml[a]	10-fold increase in particles ≥10 μm in 4 hr	2087	I
Etoposide phosphate	BR	5 mg/ml[a]	ES	4 mg/ml[a]	Physically compatible with no change in measured turbidity or increase in particle content in 4 hr at 23 °C	2218	C
Famotidine	ME	2 mg/ml[b]		4 mg/ml[a]	Visually compatible for 4 hr at 22 °C	1936	C
Fentanyl citrate	JN	0.025 mg/ml[a]	WI	4 mg/ml[a]	Physically compatible with no change in measured haze or increase in particle content in 48 hr at 22 °C	1706	C
Filgrastim	AMG	30 μg/ml[a]	ES	4 mg/ml[a]	Physically compatible with no change in measured turbidity or increase in particle content in 4 hr at 22 °C	1687	C
Fluconazole	RR	2 mg/ml	ES	50 mg/ml	Cloudiness develops	1407	I
Fludarabine phosphate	BX	1 mg/ml[a]	WI	4 mg/ml[a]	Slight haze, visible with high intensity light, forms immediately	1439	I
Foscarnet sodium	AST	24 mg/ml	LY	50 mg/ml	Physically compatible for 24 hr at room temperature under fluorescent light	1335	C
Gatifloxacin	BMS	2 mg/ml[a]	ES	2 mg/ml[a]	Physically compatible with no change in measured haze or increase in particle content in 4 hr at 23 °C	2234	C
Gemcitabine HCl	LI	10 mg/ml[b]	ES	2 mg/ml[b]	Physically compatible with no change in measured turbidity or increase in particle content in 4 hr at 23 °C	2226	C
Granisetron HCl	SKB	0.05 mg/ml[a]	ES	2 mg/ml[a]	Physically compatible with no change in measured turbidity or increase in particle content in 4 hr at 23 °C	2000	C
Hetastarch in lactated electrolyte injection (Hextend)	AB	6%	ES	2 mg/ml[a]	Physically compatible with no change in measured turbidity or increase in particle content in 4 hr at 23 °C	2339	C
Hydromorphone HCl	AST	0.5 mg/ml[a]	WI	4 mg/ml[a]	Physically compatible with no change in measured haze or increase in particle content in 48 hr at 22 °C	1706	C
Linezolid	PHU	2 mg/ml	ES	2 mg/ml[a]	Physically compatible with no change in measured turbidity or increase in particle content in 4 hr at 23 °C	2264	C
Melphalan HCl	BW	0.1 mg/ml[b]	WI	4 mg/ml[b]	Physically compatible with no change in measured turbidity or increase in particle content in 3 hr at 22 °C	1557	C

Y-Site Injection Compatibility (1:1 Mixture) (Cont.)

Drug	Mfr	Conc	Hydroxyzine HCl Mfr	Hydroxyzine HCl Conc	Remarks	Ref	C/I
Methadone HCl	LI	1 mg/ml[a]	WI	4 mg/ml[a]	Physically compatible with no change in measured haze or increase in particle content in 48 hr at 22 °C	1706	C
Morphine sulfate	AST	1 mg/ml[a]	WI	4 mg/ml[a]	Physically compatible with no change in measured haze or increase in particle content in 48 hr at 22 °C	1706	C
Ondansetron HCl	GL	1 mg/ml[b]	WI	4 mg/ml[a]	Physically compatible for 4 hr at 22 °C	1365	C
Paclitaxel	NCI	1.2 mg/ml[a]	ES	4 mg/ml[a]	Normal inherent haze from paclitaxel decreases immediately	1556	I
Piperacillin sodium–tazobactam sodium	LE	40 + 5 mg/ml[a]	WI	4 mg/ml[a]	Haze and particles form immediately	1688	I
Propofol	ZEN	10 mg/ml	ES	2 mg/ml[a]	Physically compatible for 1 hr at 23 °C with no increase in particle content	2066	C
Remifentanil HCl	GW	0.025 and 0.25 mg/ml[b]	ES	2 mg/ml[a]	Physically compatible with no change in measured turbidity or increase in particle content in 4 hr at 23 °C	2075	C
Sargramostim	IMM	10 μg/ml[b]	ES	4 mg/ml[b]	Slight haze, visible with high intensity light, and small flake-like particles formed in 4 hr in one of two samples	1436	I
Sufentanil citrate	JN	12.5 μg/ml[a]	ES	4 mg/ml[a]	Physically compatible with little subvisual haze or particle formation in 24 hr at 23 °C	1711	C
Teniposide	BR	0.1 mg/ml[a]	WI	4 mg/ml[a]	Physically compatible with no subvisual haze or particle formation in 4 hr at 23 °C	1725	C
Thiotepa	IMM[e]	1 mg/ml[a]	ES	4 mg/ml[a]	Physically compatible with no change in measured turbidity or increase in particle content in 4 hr at 23 °C	1861	C
TNA #218 to #226[f]			ES	2 mg/ml[a]	Visually compatible with no precipitate or emulsion damage apparent in 4 hr at 23 °C	2215	C
TPN #212 to #215[f]			ES	2 mg/ml[a]	Physically compatible with no change in measured turbidity or increase in particle content in 4 hr at 23 °C	2109	C
Vinorelbine tartrate	BW	1 mg/ml[b]	ES	4 mg/ml[b]	Physically compatible with no change in measured turbidity or increase in particle content in 4 hr at 22 °C	1558	C

[a] *Tested in dextrose 5% in water.*
[b] *Tested in sodium chloride 0.9%.*
[c] *Tested in both dextrose 5% in water and sodium chloride 0.9%.*
[d] *Tested in bacteriostatic sodium chloride 0.9% preserved with benzyl alcohol 0.9%.*
[e] *Lyophilized formulation tested.*
[f] *Refer to Appendix I for the composition of parenteral nutrition solutions. TNA indicates a 3-in-1 admixture, and TPN indicates a 2-in-1 admixture.*

Additional Compatibility Information

Chlorpromazine and Meperidine — Chlorpromazine HCl (Elkins-Sinn) 6.25 mg/ml, hydroxyzine HCl (Pfizer) 12.5 mg/ml, and meperidine HCl (Winthrop) 25 mg/ml, in both glass and plastic syringes, were reported to be physically compatible and chemically stable for at least one year at 4 and 25 °C when protected from light. Significant discoloration, ranging from yellow to brownish yellow, occurred on storage at 44 °C. (989)

Heparin — It has been stated that if hydroxyzine HCl is injected into a heparinized scalp vein infusion set, a precipitate will form. It has been suggested that these heparinized sets be flushed with sterile water for injection or sodium chloride 0.9% before and after administering a drug. Heparin lock flush solution may then be reinjected into the device. (97)

Concentrated Drug Solutions — The following incompatibility determinations were performed with concentrated solutions. The drugs in dry form were constituted according to the manufacturers' recommendations. One milliliter of hydroxyzine HCl (Pfizer) was added to 5 ml of sterile distilled water along with 1 ml of each of the following drugs. Particulate matter was noted within two hours (28):

Aminophylline
Chloramphenicol sodium succinate (Parke-Davis)
Dimenhydrinate (Searle)
Heparin sodium
Penicillin G potassium
Phenobarbital sodium (Winthrop)
Phenytoin sodium (Parke-Davis)
Vitamin B complex with C (Lederle)

Other Drugs — Hydroxyzine HCl is stated to be physically and chemically compatible with butorphanol tartrate (Bristol) (481) and buprenorphine HCl. (4)

IDARUBICIN HCL
AHFS 10:00

Products — Idarubicin HCl (Idamycin) is available as an orange-red lyophilized powder in single-use vials containing 20 mg. Also present is lactose NF (hydrous) 200 mg. (1-8/98; 29)

The 20-mg vials should be reconstituted with 20 ml of water for injection to yield a 1-mg/ml concentration. Bacteriostatic diluents are not recommended by the manufacturer. The vial contents are under negative pressure to minimize aerosolization. (1-8/98)

Idarubicin HCl (Idamycin PFS) is also available as a 1-mg/ml orange-red solution in single-use vials containing 5, 10, and 20 ml. In addition to the drug, each milliliter also contains glycerin 25 mg and hydrochloric acid to adjust pH in water for injection. (2)

pH — The reconstituted lyophilized idarubicin HCl (Idamycin) has a pH in the range of 5 to 7. (1368) The idarubicin HCl solution (Idamycin PFS) has been adjusted with hydrochloric acid to a target pH of 3.5. (2)

Density — Idarubicin HCl (Idamycin) reconstituted with sterile water for injection to a concentration of 1 mg/ml has a solution density of 1.00 g/ml. (2041; 2248)

Trade Name(s) — Idamycin, Idamycin PFS.

Administration — Idarubicin HCl should be administered by slow intravenous injection over 10 to 15 minutes into the tubing of a running infusion of sodium chloride 0.9% or dextrose 5% in water. The drug should not be given subcutaneously or intramuscularly, and extravasation should be avoided to prevent severe tissue necrosis. Care should be exercised during dose preparation to avoid inadvertent skin contact with the drug. (1-8/98; 2)

Stability — Idarubicin HCl (Idamycin) in intact lyophilized vials should be stored at room temperature and protected from light. The reconstituted solution is physically and chemically stable for at least 72 hours under refrigeration or at room temperature. (1-8/98)

Idarubicin HCl solution (Idamycin PFS) in intact vials should be stored under refrigeration at 2 to 8 °C and protected from light. Leaving the vials in the carton until the time of use is recommended. (2)

pH Effects — Idarubicin HCl in prolonged contact with alkaline solutions will undergo decomposition. (1-8/98; 2; 1368)

Light Effects — Dilute solutions (0.01 mg/ml) of idarubicin HCl are light sensitive, undergoing some degradation with exposure to light over periods greater than six hours. (1368) However, the manufacturer indicates that no special precautions are necessary to protect freshly prepared solutions for administration. (1369)

Sorption — Idarubicin HCl is compatible with PVC, glass, and polypropylene. (1369)

Haze Formation — Idarubicin HCl solutions in sodium chloride 0.9% exhibit a low level haze that is visible under high intensity light and measurable with a turbidimeter. Dilution of the drug from a concentration of 1 mg/ml increases this haze until a maximum is reached at about 0.05 mg/ml. This haze increase appears to be normal for idarubicin HCl in solution and is not an incompatibility. (1675)

Compatibility Information

Solution Compatibility

Idarubicin HCl

Solution	*Mfr*	*Mfr*	*Conc/L*	*Remarks*	*Ref*	*C/I*
Dextrose 3.3% in sodium chloride 0.3%		FA	100 mg	5% or less drug loss in 4 weeks at 25 °C in the dark	1007	C

Solution Compatibility (Cont.)

Idarubicin HCl

Solution	*Mfr*	*Mfr*	*Conc/L*	*Remarks*	*Ref*	*C/I*
Dextrose 5% in sodium chloride 0.9%		FA	10 mg	No drug loss in 72 hr at room temperature protected from light. Less than 10% loss in 6 hr at room temperature exposed to light	1493	C
Dextrose 5% in water		FA	100 mg	5% or less drug loss in 4 weeks at 25 °C in the dark	1007	C
		FA	10 mg	No drug loss in 72 hr at room temperature protected from light. Less than 10% loss in 6 hr at room temperature exposed to light	1493	C
Ringer's injection, lactated		FA	100 mg	5% or less drug loss in 4 weeks at 25 °C in the dark	1007	C
Sodium chloride 0.9%		FA	100 mg	5% or less drug loss in 4 weeks at 25 °C in the dark	1007	C
		FA	10 mg	No drug loss in 72 hr at room temperature protected from light. Less than 10% loss in 6 hr at room temperature exposed to light	1493	C

Y-Site Injection Compatibility (1:1 Mixture)

Idarubicin HCl

Drug	*Mfr*	*Conc*	*Mfr*	*Conc*	*Remarks*	*Ref*	*C/I*
Acyclovir sodium	BW	5 mg/ml[b]	AD	1 mg/ml[b]	Haze forms and color changes immediately. Precipitate forms in 12 min	1525	I
Allopurinol sodium	BW	3 mg/ml[b]	AD	0.5 mg/ml[b]	Reddish-purple color forms immediately. Particles form within 1 hr. Complete color loss in 24 hr	1686	I
Amifostine	USB	10 mg/ml[a]	AD	0.5 mg/ml[a]	Increase in turbidity no greater than dilution with D5W alone. No increase in particle content in 4 hr at 23 °C	1845	C
Amikacin sulfate	BR	5 mg/ml[a]	AD	1 mg/ml[b]	Visually compatible for 24 hr at 25 °C	1525	C
Ampicillin sodium–sulbactam sodium	RR	20 + 10 mg/ml[b]	AD	1 mg/ml[b]	Haze forms and color changes immediately. Precipitate forms in 20 min	1525	I
Aztreonam	SQ	40 mg/ml[a]	AD	0.5 mg/ml[a]	Increase in measured turbidity no greater than dilution of idarubicin with NS. No increase in particle content in 4 hr at 23 °C	1758	C
Cefazolin sodium	LI	20 mg/ml[a]	AD	1 mg/ml[b]	Precipitate forms in 1 hr	1525	I
Cefepime HCl	BMS	20 mg/ml[a]	AD	0.5 mg/ml[a]	Flocculent precipitate forms in 4 hr	1689	I
Ceftazidime	LI[f]	20 mg/ml[a]	AD	1 mg/ml[b]	Haze forms in 1 hr	1525	I
Cimetidine HCl	SKF	6 mg/ml[a]	AD	1 mg/ml[b]	Visually compatible for 24 hr at 25 °C	1525	C
Cladribine	ORT	0.015[b] and 0.5[c] mg/ml	AD	0.5 mg/ml[b]	Increase in measured turbidity no greater than simple dilution alone. No increase in particle content in 4 hr at 23 °C	1969	C
Clindamycin phosphate	AST	12 mg/ml[a]	AD	1 mg/ml[b]	Haze and precipitate form immediately	1525	I
Cyclophosphamide	AD	4 mg/ml[a]	AD	1 mg/ml[b]	Visually compatible for 24 hr at 25 °C	1525	C
Cytarabine	CET	6 mg/ml[a]	AD	1 mg/ml[b]	Visually compatible for 24 hr at 25 °C	1525	C

Y-Site Injection Compatibility (1:1 Mixture) (Cont.)

			Idarubicin HCl				
Drug	*Mfr*	*Conc*	*Mfr*	*Conc*	*Remarks*	*Ref*	*C/I*
Dexamethasone sodium phosphate	OR	10 mg/ml	AD	1 mg/ml[b]	Haze forms immediately and precipitate forms in 20 min	1525	I
	AMR	0.2 mg/ml[b]	AD	1 mg/ml[b]	Haze forms in 20 min	1525	I
Diphenhydramine HCl	ES	1[a] and 50 mg/ml	AD	1 mg/ml[b]	Visually compatible for 24 hr at 25 °C	1525	C
Droperidol	AMR	0.04[a] and 2.5 mg/ml	AD	1 mg/ml[b]	Visually compatible for 24 hr at 25 °C	1525	C
Erythromycin lactobionate	ES	2 mg/ml[b]	AD	1 mg/ml[b]	Visually compatible for 24 hr at 25 °C	1525	C
Etoposide	BR	0.4 mg/ml[a]	AD	1 mg/ml[b]	Gas forms immediately	1525	I
Etoposide phosphate	BR	5 mg/ml[a]	AD	0.5 mg/ml[a]	Physically compatible with no change in measured turbidity or increase in particle content in 4 hr at 23 °C	2218	C
Filgrastim	AMG	30 μg/ml[a]	AD	0.5 mg/ml[a]	Physically compatible with no change in measured turbidity or increase in particle content in 4 hr at 22 °C	1687	C
Furosemide	AB	10 mg/ml	AD	1 mg/ml[b]	Precipitate forms immediately	1525	I
	AB	0.8 mg/ml[b]	AD	1 mg/ml[b]	Haze forms immediately	1525	I
Gemcitabine HCl	LI	10 mg/ml[b]	AD	0.5 mg/ml[b]	Physically compatible with no change in measured turbidity or increase in particle content in 4 hr at 23 °C	2226	C
Gentamicin sulfate	ES	3 mg/ml[a]	AD	1 mg/ml[b]	Color changes immediately	1525	I
Granisetron HCl	SKB	0.05 mg/ml[a]	AD	0.5 mg/ml[a]	Increase in turbidity no greater than dilution with D5W alone. No increase in particle content in 4 hr at 23 °C	2000	C
Heparin sodium	ES	1000 units/ml	AD	1 mg/ml[b]	Haze forms immediately and precipitate forms in 20 min	1525	I
	SO	100 units/ml	AD	1 mg/ml[b]	Haze forms immediately and precipitate forms in 12 min	1525	I
Hydrocortisone sodium succinate	UP	2[a] and 50 mg/ml	AD	1 mg/ml[b]	Haze forms immediately and precipitate forms in 20 min	1525	I
Imipenem–cilastatin sodium	MSD	5 mg/ml[b]	AD	1 mg/ml[b]	Visually compatible for 12 hr at 25 °C under fluorescent light. Precipitate forms in 24 hr	1525	C
Lorazepam	WY	2 mg/ml	AD	1 mg/ml[b]	Color changes immediately	1525	I
Magnesium sulfate	SO	2 mg/ml[b]	AD	1 mg/ml[b]	Visually compatible for 24 hr at 25 °C	1525	C
Mannitol	AB	12.5 mg/ml[a]	AD	1 mg/ml[b]	Visually compatible for 24 hr at 25 °C	1525	C
Melphalan HCl	BW	0.1 mg/ml[b]	AD	0.5 mg/ml[b]	Increase in measured turbidity no greater than dilution of idarubicin with sodium chloride 0.9%. No increase in particle content in 3 hr at 22 °C	1557; 1675	C
Meperidine HCl	WY	1[a] and 50 mg/ml	AD	1 mg/ml[b]	Color changes immediately	1525	I
Methotrexate sodium	LE	25 mg/ml	AD	1 mg/ml[b]	Color changes immediately	1525	I
Metoclopramide HCl	SO	5 mg/ml	AD	1 mg/ml[b]	Visually compatible for 24 hr at 25 °C	1525	C
Piperacillin sodium–tazobactam sodium	LE	40 + 5 mg/ml[a]	AD	0.5 mg/ml[a]	Immediate increase in haze much larger than from simple dilution alone	1688	I

Y-Site Injection Compatibility (1:1 Mixture) (Cont.)

Idarubicin HCl

Drug	*Mfr*	*Conc*	*Mfr*	*Conc*	*Remarks*	*Ref*	*C/I*
Potassium chloride	AB	0.03 mEq/ml[b]	AD	1 mg/ml[b]	Visually compatible for 24 hr at 25 °C	1525	C
Ranitidine HCl	GL	1 mg/ml[a]	AD	1 mg/ml[b]	Visually compatible for 24 hr at 25 °C	1525	C
Sargramostim	IMM	10 μg/ml[b]	AD	0.5 mg/ml[b]	Increase in measured turbidity no greater than dilution of idarubicin with sodium chloride 0.9%	1675	C
Sodium bicarbonate	AB	0.09 mEq/ml[a]	AD	1 mg/ml[b]	Haze forms and color changes immediately. Precipitate forms in 20 min	1525	I
Teniposide	BR	0.1 mg/ml[a]	AD	0.5 mg/ml[a]	Unacceptable increase in turbidity occurs immediately	1725	I
Thiotepa	IMM[d]	1 mg/ml[a]	AD	0.5 mg/ml[a]	Increase in measured turbidity no greater than simple dilution alone. No increase in particle content in 4 hr at 23 °C	1861	C
TPN #140[e]			AD	1 mg/ml[b]	Visually compatible for 24 hr at 25 °C	1525	C
Vancomycin HCl	AD	4 mg/ml[a]	AD	1 mg/ml[b]	Color changes immediately	1525	I
Vincristine sulfate	AD	1 mg/ml	AD	1 mg/ml[b]	Color changes immediately	1525	I
Vinorelbine tartrate	BW	1 mg/ml[b]	AD	0.5 mg/ml[b]	Increase in measured turbidity no greater than dilution of idarubicin with sodium chloride 0.9%. No increase in particle content in 4 hr at 22 °C	1558; 1675	C

[a] *Tested in dextrose 5% in water.*
[b] *Tested in sodium chloride 0.9%.*
[c] *Tested in bacteriostatic sodium chloride 0.9% preserved with benzyl alcohol 0.9%.*
[d] *Lyophilized formulation tested.*
[e] *Refer to Appendix I for the composition of parenteral nutrition solutions. TPN indicates a 2-in-1 admixture.*
[f] *Sodium carbonate–containing formulation tested.*

Additional Compatibility Information

Heparin — According to the manufacturer, idarubicin HCl is physically incompatible with heparin due to precipitate formation. (1-8/98; 2; 1368)

Other Information

Microbial Growth — Idarubicin HCl (Farmitalia) 0.07 mg/ml diluted in sodium chloride 0.9% and stored at 22 °C did not exhibit an antimicrobial effect on the growth of four organisms (*Enterococcus faecium, Staphylococcus aureus, Pseudomonas aeruginosa,* and *Candida albicans*) inoculated into the solution. Viability was maintained for periods of 48 to 120 hours. The author recommended that diluted solutions of idarubicin HCl be stored under refrigeration whenever possible and that the potential for microbiological growth should be considered when assigning expiration periods. (2160)

IFOSFAMIDE
AHFS 10:00

Products — Ifosfamide is available in vials containing 1 or 3 g of drug in combination packages with mesna injection. Reconstitute the ifosfamide with 20 or 60 ml of sterile water for injection or bacteriostatic water for injection (parabens or benzyl alcohol), respectively, to yield a 50-mg/ml solution. (2)

pH — Approximately 6. (72)

Density — Ifosfamide (Mead Johnson) reconstituted with sterile water for injection to a concentration of 50 mg/ml has a solution density of 1.01 g/ml. (2041; 2248)

Trade Name(s) — Ifex.

Administration — Ifosfamide is administered by slow intravenous infusion over a minimum of 30 minutes diluted to a concentration between 0.6 and 20 mg/ml. (2; 4) Ifosfamide has also been administered by continuous intravenous infusion. (4) To prevent bladder toxicity, mesna and at least 2 L/day of fluid should also be given. (2; 4)

Stability — Intact vials of ifosfamide should be stored at controlled room temperature and protected from temperatures above 30 °C. (2) Ifosfamide may liquify at temperatures above 35 °C. (72)

The reconstituted solution is stated to be chemically and physically stable for seven days at 30 °C and for up to six weeks under refrigeration. (4; 72) Because of microbiological concerns, the manufacturer recommends storage under refrigeration and use in 24 hours for reconstituted or diluted ifosfamide solutions. (2)

Radford et al. reported that ifosfamide (Boehringer-Ingelheim) 80 mg/ml in sodium chloride 0.9% is chemically stable, exhibiting about a 7% loss in nine days at 37 °C in the dark. (1494)

Reconstitution to an ifosfamide concentration of 100 mg/ml with benzyl alcohol-preserved bacteriostatic water for injection resulted in a turbid mixture, separating into two distinct liquid phases. The separate phases dissolved completely, with no loss of drug or preservative, when diluted to about 60 mg/ml or less. (1289)

Ifosfamide, reconstituted according to the manufacturer's instructions, was cultured with human lymphoblasts to determine whether its cytotoxic activity was retained. The solution retained cytotoxicity for 24 hours at 4 °C and room temperature. (1575)

pH Effects — Ifosfamide exhibits maximum solution stability in the pH range of 4 to 10; the rate of decomposition is essentially the same over this pH range. At pH values less than 4 and above 10, increased rates of decomposition have been observed. (2002)

Syringes — Ifosfamide 0.6 and 20 mg/ml in dextrose 5% in water, lactated Ringer's injection, sodium chloride 0.9%, and sterile water for injection in polypropylene syringes (Becton-Dickinson) is physically and chemically stable for at least 24 hours at 30 °C. (1496)

Ambulatory Pumps — Ifosfamide (Asta Medica) 20 mg/ml and mesna (Asta Medica) 20 mg/ml in water for injection were evaluated for stability and compatibility in PVC reservoirs for Graseby 9000 ambulatory pumps. The solutions were physically compatible and HPLC analysis found about 3% ifosfamide loss and 9% mesna loss in 7 days at 37 °C. About 2% or less loss of both drugs was found after 14 days at 4 °C. Furthermore, weight losses due to moisture transmission were minimal. (2288)

Compatibility Information

Solution Compatibility

Ifosfamide

Solution	*Mfr*	*Mfr*	*Conc/L*	*Remarks*	*Ref*	*C/I*
Dextrose 5% in Ringer's injection			600 mg and 16 g	Physically compatible with less than 5% loss in 7 days at room temperature and no loss in 6 weeks under refrigeration	72	C
Dextrose 5% in sodium chloride 0.9%			600 mg and 16 g	Physically compatible with less than 5% loss in 7 days at room temperature and no loss in 6 weeks under refrigeration	72	C
Dextrose 5% in water			600 mg and 16 g	Physically compatible with less than 5% loss in 7 days at room temperature and no loss in 6 weeks under refrigeration	72	C
Ringer's injection, lactated			600 mg and 16 g	Physically compatible with less than 5% loss in 7 days at room temperature and no loss in 6 weeks under refrigeration	72	C
Sodium chloride 0.45%			600 mg and 16 g	Physically compatible with less than 5% loss in 7 days at room temperature and no loss in 6 weeks under refrigeration	72	C
Sodium chloride 0.9%			600 mg and 16 g	Physically compatible with less than 5% loss in 7 days at room temperature and no loss in 6 weeks under refrigeration	72	C
	[a]		10 g	No ifosfamide loss by HPLC in 8 days at 4 and 25 °C protected from light and at 25 °C exposed to light	1551	C
	[a]		20, 40, 80 g	No ifosfamide loss by HPLC in 8 days at 35 °C	1551	C
Sodium lactate ⅙ M			600 mg and 16 g	Physically compatible with less than 5% loss in 7 days at room temperature and no loss in 6 weeks under refrigeration	72	C

[a]*Tested in PVC containers.*

Additive Compatibility

Ifosfamide

Drug	*Mfr*	*Conc/L*	*Mfr*	*Conc/L*	*Test Soln*	*Remarks*	*Ref*	*C/I*
Carboplatin		1 g		1 g	W	Both drugs stable for 5 days at room temperature	1379	C
Carboplatin with etoposide		1 g 200 mg		2 g	W	Both drugs stable for 7 days at room temperature	1379	C
Cisplatin		200 mg		2 g	NS	Both drugs stable for 7 days at room temperature	1379	C
Cisplatin with etoposide		200 mg 200 mg		2 g	NS	All drugs stable for 5 days at room temperature	1379	C
Epirubicin HCl		1 g		50 g	NS	Both drugs stable for 14 days at room temperature	1380	C
Etoposide		200 mg		2 g	NS	Both drugs stable for 5 days at room temperature	1379	C
Fluorouracil		10 g		2 g	NS	Both drugs stable for 5 days at room temperature	1379	C
Mesna	AW	3.3 g	MJ	3.3 g	D5W, LR	Physically compatible with no ifosfamide loss and about 5% mesna loss in 24 hr at 21 °C exposed to light	72	C
	AW	5 g	MJ	5 g	D5W, LR	Physically compatible with no ifosfamide loss and about 5% mesna loss in 24 hr at 21 °C exposed to light	72	C
		40 g		50 g	NS	Both drugs stable for 14 days at room temperature	1380	C
	BI	79 g	BI	83.3 g	NS	Little or no ifosfamide loss in 9 days at room temperature and 7% ifosfamide loss in 9 days at 37 °C. Mesna not tested	1494	C
		1.6 g		2.6 g	D5S[a]	No increase in decomposition products in 8 hr at room temperature	1495	C
	BR	600 mg	BR	600 mg	D5½S, D5W, LR, NS[b]	Both drugs chemically stable for at least 24 hr at room temperature	1496	C
	AM	20 g	AM	20 g	W[c]	Physically compatible with about 3% ifosfamide loss and 9% mesna loss in 7 days at 37 °C. About 2% or less loss of both drugs in 14 days at 4 °C	2288	C
Mesna with epirubicin HCl		80 g 500 mg		50 g	NS	Over 50% epirubicin loss in 7 days at room temperature	1380	I

[a]*Tested in polyethylene containers.*
[b]*Tested in PVC containers.*
[c]*Tested in PVC reservoirs for Graseby 9000 ambulatory pumps.*

Drugs in Syringe Compatibility

Ifosfamide

Drug (in syringe)	*Mfr*	*Amt*	*Mfr*	*Amt*	*Remarks*	*Ref*	*C/I*
Epirubicin HCl		1 mg/ml[a]		50 mg/ml[a]	Little or no loss of either drug by HPLC in 28 days at 4 and 20 °C	1564	C
Mesna		200 mg/5 ml		250 mg/5 ml	3% ifosfamide loss in 7 days and 12% in 4 weeks at 4 °C and room temperature. No mesna loss	1290	C

Drugs in Syringe Compatibility (Cont.)

Ifosfamide

Drug (in syringe)	*Mfr*	*Amt*	*Mfr*	*Amt*	*Remarks*	*Ref*	*C/I*
		40 mg/ml[a]		50 mg/ml[a]	Little or no loss of either drug by HPLC in 28 days at 4 and 20 °C	1564	C
Mesna with epirubicin HCl		40 mg/ml[a] 1 mg/ml		50 mg/ml[a]	50% epirubicin loss by HPLC in 7 days at 4 and 20 °C. No loss of other drugs in 7 days	1564	I

[a]*Diluted in sodium chloride 0.9%.*

Y-Site Injection Compatibility (1:1 Mixture)

Ifosfamide

Drug	*Mfr*	*Conc*	*Mfr*	*Conc*	*Remarks*	*Ref*	*C/I*
Allopurinol sodium	BW	3 mg/ml[b]	MJ	25 mg/ml[b]	Physically compatible with no change in measured turbidity or increase in particle content in 4 hr at 22 °C	1686	C
Amifostine	USB	10 mg/ml[a]	MJ	25 mg/ml[a]	Physically compatible with no change in measured turbidity or increase in particle content in 4 hr at 23 °C	1845	C
Amphotericin B cholesteryl sulfate complex	SEQ	0.83 mg/ml[a]	MJ	25 mg/ml[a]	Physically compatible with little or no change in measured turbidity or increase in particle content in 4 hr at 23 °C under fluorescent light	2117	C
Aztreonam	SQ	40 mg/ml[a]	MJ	25 mg/ml[a]	Physically compatible with no subvisual haze or particle formation in 4 hr at 23 °C	1758	C
Cefepime HCl	BMS	20 mg/ml[a]	MJ	25 mg/ml[a]	Haze and precipitate form in 1 hr	1689	I
Doxorubicin HCl liposome injection	SEQ	0.4 mg/ml[a]	MJ	25 mg/ml[a]	Physically compatible with little or no change in measured turbidity and no increase in particle content in 4 hr at 23 °C	2087	C
Etoposide phosphate	BR	5 mg/ml[a]	MJ	25 mg/ml[a]	Physically compatible with no change in measured turbidity or increase in particle content in 4 hr at 23 °C	2118	C
Filgrastim	AMG	30 μg/ml[a]	MJ	25 mg/ml[a]	Physically compatible with no change in measured turbidity or increase in particle content in 4 hr at 22 °C	1687	C
Fludarabine phosphate	BX	1 mg/ml[a]	MJ	25 mg/ml[a]	Physically compatible for 4 hr at room temperature under fluorescent light	1439	C
Gatifloxacin	BMS	2 mg/ml[a]	MJ	25 mg/ml[a]	Physically compatible with no change in measured haze or increase in particle content in 4 hr at 23 °C	2234	C
Gemcitabine HCl	LI	10 mg/ml[b]	MJ	25 mg/ml[b]	Physically compatible with no change in measured turbidity or increase in particle content in 4 hr at 23 °C	2226	C
Granisetron HCl	SKB	1 mg/ml	MJ	4 mg/ml[b]	Physically compatible with little or no loss of either drug by HPLC in 4 hr at 22 °C	1883	C
Linezolid	PHU	2 mg/ml	MJ	25 mg/ml[a]	Physically compatible with no change in measured turbidity or increase in particle content in 4 hr at 23 °C	2264	C
Melphalan HCl	BW	0.1 mg/ml[b]	BR	25 mg/ml[b]	Physically compatible with no change in measured turbidity or increase in particle content in 3 hr at 22 °C	1557	C

Y-Site Injection Compatibility (1:1 Mixture) (Cont.)

			Ifosfamide				
Drug	*Mfr*	*Conc*	*Mfr*	*Conc*	*Remarks*	*Ref*	*C/I*
Methotrexate sodium		30 mg/ml		36 mg/ml[a]	Visually compatible for 2 hr at room temperature. Dark yellow precipitate forms in 4 hr	1788	I
Ondansetron HCl	GL	1 mg/ml[b]	MJ	25 mg/ml[a]	Physically compatible for 4 hr at 22 °C	1365	C
Paclitaxel	NCI	1.2 mg/ml[a]	BR	25 mg/ml[a]	Physically compatible with no change in measured turbidity in 4 hr at 22 °C	1556	C
Piperacillin sodium–tazobactam sodium	LE	40 + 5 mg/ml[a]	MJ	25 mg/ml[a]	Physically compatible with no change in measured turbidity or increase in particle content in 4 hr at 22 °C	1688	C
Propofol	ZEN	10 mg/ml	MJ	25 mg/ml[a]	Physically compatible for 1 hr at 23 °C with no increase in particle content	2066	C
Sargramostim	IMM	10 μg/ml[b]	MJ	25 mg/ml[b]	Physically compatible for 4 hr at 22 °C	1436	C
Sodium bicarbonate		1.4%		36 mg/ml[a]	Visually compatible for 4 hr at room temperature	1788	C
Teniposide	BR	0.1 mg/ml[a]	MJ	25 mg/ml[a]	Physically compatible with no subvisual haze or particle formation in 4 hr at 23 °C	1725	C
Thiotepa	IMM[c]	1 mg/ml[a]	MJ	25 mg/ml[a]	Physically compatible with no change in measured turbidity or increase in particle content in 4 hr at 23 °C	1861	C
TNA #218 to #226[d]			MJ	25 mg/ml[a]	Visually compatible with no precipitate or emulsion damage apparent in 4 hr at 23 °C	2215	C
Topotecan HCl	SKB	56 μg/ml[a,b]	MJ	14.28 mg/ml[a,b]	Visually compatible with little or no loss of either drug by HPLC in 4 hr at 22 °C under fluorescent light	2245	C
TPN #212 to #215[d]			MJ	25 mg/ml[a]	Physically compatible with no change in measured turbidity or increase in particle content in 4 hr at 23 °C	2109	C
Vinorelbine tartrate	BW	1 mg/ml[b]	MJ	25 mg/ml[b]	Physically compatible with no change in measured turbidity or increase in particle content in 4 hr at 22 °C	1558	C

[a]Tested in dextrose 5% in water.
[b]Tested in sodium chloride 0.9%.
[c]Lyophilized formulation tested.
[d]Refer to Appendix I for the composition of parenteral nutrition solutions. TNA indicates a 3-in-1 admixture, and TPN indicates a 2-in-1 admixture.

Additional Compatibility Information

Infusion Solutions — The manufacturer states that ifosfamide may be diluted to concentrations between 0.6 and 20 mg/ml in the following solutions (2):

Dextrose 5% in water
Ringer's injection, lactated
Sodium chloride 0.9%

Intermediate concentrations and mixtures of these diluents (e.g., dextrose 2.5% in water, dextrose 5% in sodium chloride 0.9%, etc.) are also acceptable as infusion solutions for the dilution of ifosfamide. (2)

Reconstituted solutions of ifosfamide that are diluted for administration in one of the compatible infusion solutions are stated to be physically and chemically stable in glass, polyolefin, or PVC containers for at least a week at 30 °C and six weeks at 5 °C. (4)

Mesna — Ifosfamide is stated to be physically and chemically stable for 24 hours in dextrose 5% in water or Ringer's injection, lactated, when admixed with mesna. (4)

Mesna and ifosfamide have been found to be stable in combined admixtures. (72; 1380; 1494–1496) See Additive Compatibility table above. However, mesna has been found to undergo more extensive decomposition when mixed with ifosfamide in an infusion solution made alkaline with sodium bicarbonate. At pH 8, mesna retained adequate potency by HPLC analysis for six hours but lost about 13% in 24 hours and 23% in 48 hours. Ifosfamide underwent only 6% loss in 24 hours but 14% loss in 24 hours by HPLC. (2281)

IMIPENEM–CILASTATIN SODIUM
AHFS 8:12.07

Products — Imipenem–cilastatin sodium for intravenous use is available as a fixed combination of equal quantities of both drugs. The combination is provided in vials and infusion bottles containing 250 and 500 mg of each drug with sodium bicarbonate 10 and 20 mg, respectively. (2)

The vials should be reconstituted with about 10 ml of a compatible diluent from a 100-ml infusion container and shaken well to form a suspension. Diluents containing benzyl alcohol should not be used to reconstitute the drug for use in neonates and small pediatric patients. The suspension must be transferred to the remaining solution in the infusion container for dilution. The suspension is *not* for direct injection. The procedure is then repeated: a 10-ml aliquot from the admixture is added to the vial and, once again, returned to the infusion admixture. This procedure ensures that all of the vial contents are transferred. The admixture should be agitated until it is clear to yield either a 2.5- or 5-mg/ml concentration, depending on the vial content. The admixture should *not* be heated to aid dissolution. (2; 4)

ADD-Vantage vials of imipenem–cilastatin sodium should be prepared with 100 ml of dextrose 5% in water or sodium chloride 0.9% in ADD-Vantage diluent bags. (2; 4)

The 250- and 500-mg piggyback infusion bottles should be reconstituted with 100 ml of compatible diluent and shaken until clear to yield 2.5- and 5-mg/ml concentrations, respectively. (2; 4)

Imipenem–cilastatin sodium for intramuscular use is available in vials containing 500 or 750 mg of each component. The vials should be reconstituted with 2 or 3 ml, respectively, of lidocaine HCl 1% (without epinephrine) and agitated to form a suspension. This intramuscular formulation is not for intravenous use. (2; 4)

pH — The intravenous product is buffered to pH 6.5 to 8.5. (2)

Osmolarity — When reconstituted and diluted as directed by the manufacturer, the osmolarity of the intravenous admixture approximates that of the diluent. (4)

Sodium Content — The 250- and 500-mg intravenous vials contain 0.8 mEq (18.8 mg) and 1.6 mEq (37.5 mg) of sodium, respectively. The 500- and 750-mg intramuscular vials contain 1.4 mEq (32 mg) and 2.1 mEq (48 mg) of sodium, respectively. (2; 4)

Trade Name(s) — Primaxin I.V., Primaxin I.M.

Administration — Imipenem–cilastatin sodium for intravenous use is given by intermittent intravenous infusion, usually in sodium chloride 0.9%, at a concentration not exceeding 5 mg/ml. Infusion periods vary from 20 to 30 minutes up to 40 to 60 minutes, depending on the dose. The intramuscular formulation reconstituted as directed should be injected deeply into a large muscle mass. Suspensions of either formulation should not be given intravenously. (2; 4)

Stability — The sterile powder for injection should be stored below 25 °C. (2; 4)

Reconstituted as directed, intravenous solutions are colorless to yellow but may become a deeper yellow over time. Intramuscular suspensions are white to light tan. The manufacturer indicates that potency is not affected by color variations within this range (2), but the solutions should be discarded if they darken to brown. (4) Intramuscular suspensions prepared with lidocaine HCl (without epinephrine) should be used within one hour of preparation. (2; 4)

In solution, imipenem is substantially less stable than cilastatin and is the determining factor in the overall stability of the combination product. Reconstitution with most recommended infusion solutions (see Additional Compatibility Information) results in solutions that are stable for four hours at room temperature or 24 hours under refrigeration at 4 °C. (2)

Imipenem degradation kinetics were determined for a 2.5-mg/ml solution in sodium chloride 0.9%. The degradation rates were temperature dependent, with a half-life of over 44 hours at 2 °C dropping to six hours at 25 °C and to two hours at 37 °C. The decomposition was consistent with hydrolysis, and the loss of antimicrobial activity suggests cleavage of the β-lactam ring. (1272)

The decomposition of imipenem as a 5-mg/ml solution in dextrose 5% in water in the presence of cilastatin was estimated to occur at a rate of about 1.4% per hour at room temperature. At this rate, the time to 10% decomposition will be reached in 6 to 7 hours. (2166)

pH Effects — Imipenem is inactivated at acidic or alkaline pH but is more stable at neutral pH. (4) The pH range of maximum stability appears to be 6.5 to 7.5, with increasing rates of decomposition occurring as the pH moves away from this range. (1273) At a pH of about 4, the half-life of imipenem is about 35 minutes. (2166)

Freezing Solutions — The manufacturer recommends that imipenem–cilastatin solutions not be frozen. (2) At concentrations of 250 and 500 mg/100 ml in sodium chloride 0.9%, imipenem losses of around 15% occurred in one week when frozen at −20 and −10 °C. (1141) Freezing solutions at temperatures above −70 °C offers no stability advantage over refrigerated storage (1141) and results in decomposition of imipenem in a manner similar to ampicillin. (4)

Effects of Solution Components — Dextrose exerts an adverse effect on the stability of imipenem. Dextrose 5 and 10% reduced the time to 10% decomposition by about one-half compared to sterile water. Similarly, increasing mannitol concentrations reduce imipenem stability. Sodium chloride content increases imipenem stability because of a positive kinetic salt effect similar to other β-lactam antibiotics. Both lactate and bicarbonate anions attack the β-lactam ring and decrease imipenem stability. (1141) (See Additional Compatibility Information.)

Elastomeric Reservoir Pumps — Imipenem–cilastatin sodium (Merck) 5 mg/ml in dextrose 5% in water and sodium chloride 0.9% 100 ml was packaged in latex elastomeric reservoirs (Secure Medical). Little or no loss by HPLC analysis occurred in 4 hours at 25 °C and in 24 hr at 5 °C. (1970)

Imipenem–cilastatin sodium (Merck) 5 mg/ml in both dextrose 5% in water and sodium chloride 0.9% was evaluated for binding potential to natural rubber elastomeric reservoirs (Baxter). Less than 1% binding was found after storage for two weeks at 35 °C with gentle agitation. (2014)

Imipenem–cilastatin solutions in elastomeric reservoir pumps have been stated by the pump manufacturers to be stable for the following time periods refrigerated (REF) and at room temperature (RT) (31):

Pump Reservoir(s)	Conc.	REF	RT
Homepump; Homepump Eclipse	5 mg/ml[b]	48 hr	10 hr
Medflo	5 mg/ml[a]	24 hr	4 hr
	5 mg/ml[b]	48 hr	10 hr
ReadyMed	5 mg/ml[b]	72 hr	24 hr

[a] *In dextrose 5% in water.*
[b] *In sodium chloride 0.9%.*

Sorption— Imipenem–cilastatin (MSD) 2.5 mg/ml in dextrose 5% in water and sodium chloride 0.9% packaged in PVC, polyethylene, and glass containers exhibited no loss due to sorption to any of the container types when stored at 4 and 22 °C for 24 hours protected from light. (2289)

Central Venous Catheter— Imipenem–cilastatin (MSD) 2 mg/ml in sodium chloride 0.9% was found to be compatible with the ARROWg+ard Blue Plus (Arrow International) chlorhexidine-bearing triple-lumen central catheter. HPLC analysis was used to evaluate completeness of drug delivery through the catheter and the amount of chlorhexidine removed from the internal lumens. Essentially complete delivery of the drug was found with little or no drug loss occurring. Furthermore, chlorhexidine delivered from the catheter remained at trace amounts with no substantial increase due to the delivery of the drug through the catheter. (2335)

Compatibility Information

Solution Compatibility

Imipenem–cilastatin sodium

Solution	*Mfr*	*Mfr*	*Conc/L*	*Remarks*	*Ref*	*C/I*
Dextrose 5% with potassium chloride 0.15%	AB[a]	MSD	2.5 g	9% imipenem loss in 6 hr and 15% in 9 hr at 25 °C. 8% loss in 48 hr and 14% in 72 hr at 4 °C	1141	I[b]
	AB[a]	MSD	5 g	8% imipenem loss in 3 hr and 15% in 6 hr at 25 °C. 8% loss in 24 hr and 13% in 48 hr at 4 °C	1141	I[b]
Dextrose 5% in Ringer's injection, lactated	AB[a]	MSD	2.5 g	8% imipenem loss in 3 hr and 15% in 6 hr at 25 °C. 9% loss in 24 hr and 15% in 48 hr at 4 °C	1141	I
	AB[a]	MSD	5 g	14% imipenem loss in 3 hr at 25 °C and 13% in 24 hr at 4 °C	1141	I
Dextrose 5% with sodium bicarbonate 0.02%	AB[a]	MSD	2.5 g	7% imipenem loss in 3 hr and 13% in 6 hr at 25 °C. 9% loss in 24 hr and 13% in 48 hr at 4 °C	1141	I[b]
	AB[a]	MSD	5 g	5% imipenem loss in 3 hr and 11% in 6 hr at 25 °C. 9% loss in 24 hr and 15% in 48 hr at 4 °C	1141	I[b]
Dextrose 5% in sodium chloride 0.225%	AB[a]	MSD	2.5 g	8% imipenem loss in 6 hr and 12% in 9 hr at 25 °C. 10% loss in 48 hr at 4 °C	1141	I[b]
	AB[a]	MSD	5 g	5% imipenem loss in 3 hr and 13% in 6 hr at 25 °C. 7% loss in 24 hr and 13% in 48 hr at 4 °C	1141	I[b]
Dextrose 5% in sodium chloride 0.45%	AB[a]	MSD	2.5 g	8% imipenem loss in 6 hr and 11% in 9 hr at 25 °C. 9% loss in 48 hr and 13% in 72 hr at 4 °C	1141	I[b]
	AB[a]	MSD	5 g	5% imipenem loss in 3 hr and 11% in 6 hr at 25 °C. 6% loss in 24 hr and 13% in 48 hr at 4 °C	1141	I[b]
Dextrose 5% in sodium chloride 0.9%	AB[a]	MSD	2.5 g	6% imipenem loss in 6 hr and 10% in 9 hr at 25 °C. 6% loss in 24 hr and 11% in 48 hr at 4 °C	1141	I[b]
	AB[a]	MSD	5 g	6% imipenem loss in 3 hr and 11% in 6 hr at 25 °C. 6% loss in 24 hr and 13% in 48 hr at 4 °C	1141	I[b]
Dextrose 5% in water	AB[a]	MSD	2.5 g	5% imipenem loss in 3 hr and 10% in 6 hr at 25 °C. 8% loss in 24 hr and 14% in 48 hr at 4 °C	1141	I[b]
	AB[a]	MSD	5 g	6% imipenem loss in 3 hr and 15% in 6 hr at 25 °C. 8% loss in 24 hr and 14% in 48 hr at 4 °C	1141	I[b]
	AB[c]	ME	5 g	Little or no loss of drug by HPLC in 4 hr at 25 °C and in 24 hr at 5 °C	1970	C

Solution Compatibility (Cont.)

Imipenem–cilastatin sodium

Solution	*Mfr*	*Mfr*	*Conc/L*	*Remarks*	*Ref*	*C/I*
	BA	MSD	5 g	Visually compatible with 10% imipenem loss by HPLC in about 6 hr at 23 °C and in 48 hr at 4 °C	2166	I[b]
	BA[e], BRN[f]	MSD	2.5 g	Visually compatible with little or no loss by HPLC in 24 hr at 4 and 22 °C	2289	C
Dextrose 10% in water	AB[a]	MSD	2.5 g	6% imipenem loss in 3 hr and 10% in 6 hr at 25 °C. 8% loss in 24 hr and 13% in 48 hr at 4 °C	1141	I[b]
	AB[a]	MSD	5 g	8% imipenem loss in 3 hr and 13% in 6 hr at 25 °C. 10% loss in 24 hr at 4 °C	1141	I[b]
Mannitol 2.5% in water	AB[a]	MSD	2.5 g	9% imipenem loss in 9 hr at 25 °C. 7% loss in 48 hr and 11% in 72 hr at 4 °C	1141	I[b]
	AB[a]	MSD	5 g	6% imipenem loss in 3 hr and 12% in 6 hr at 25 °C. 7% loss in 24 hr and 10% in 48 hr at 4 °C	1141	I[b]
Mannitol 5% in water	AB[a]	MSD	2.5 g	6% imipenem loss in 3 hr and 10% in 6 hr at 25 °C. 9% loss in 48 hr and 13% in 72 hr at 4 °C	1141	I[b]
	AB[a]	MSD	5 g	7% imipenem loss in 3 hr and 12% in 6 hr at 25 °C. 12% loss in 48 hr at 4 °C	1141	I[b]
Mannitol 10% in water	AB[a]	MSD	2.5 g	6% imipenem loss in 3 hr and 10% in 6 hr at 25 °C. 7% loss in 24 hr and 12% in 48 hr at 4 °C	1141	I[b]
	AB[a]	MSD	5 g	12% imipenem loss in 3 hr at 25 °C. 13% loss in 48 hr at 4 °C	1141	I[b]
Normosol M in dextrose 5%	AB[a]	MSD	2.5 g	7% imipenem loss in 3 hr and 11% in 6 hr at 25 °C. 9% loss in 24 hr and 19% in 48 hr at 4 °C	1141	I[b]
	AB[a]	MSD	5 g	8% imipenem loss in 3 hr and 14% in 6 hr at 25 °C. 10% loss in 24 hr at 4 °C	1141	I[b]
Ringer's injection, lactated	AB[a]	MSD	2.5 g	9% imipenem loss in 6 hr and 12% in 9 hr at 25 °C. 4% loss in 24 hr and 10% in 48 hr at 4 °C	1141	I
	AB[a]	MSD	5 g	6% imipenem loss in 3 hr and 12% in 6 hr at 25 °C. 7% loss in 24 hr and 12% in 48 hr at 4 °C	1141	I
Sodium bicarbonate 5%	AB[a]	MSD	2.5 g	43% imipenem loss in 3 hr at 25 °C. 52% loss in 24 hr at 4 °C	1141	I
	AB[a]	MSD	5 g	45% imipenem loss in 3 hr at 25 °C. 50% loss in 24 hr at 4 °C	1141	I
Sodium chloride 0.9%	AB[a]	MSD	2.5 g	6% imipenem loss in 9 hr at 25 °C. 7% loss in 72 hr at 4 °C	1141	I[b]
	AB[a]	MSD	5 g	8% imipenem loss in 9 hr at 25 °C. 7% loss in 48 hr and 11% in 72 hr at 4 °C	1141	I[b]
	AB[c]	ME	5 g	Little or no loss of drug by HPLC in 4 hr at 25 °C and in 24 hr at 5 °C	1970	C
	BA[e], BRN[f]	MSD	2.5 g	Visually compatible with little or no loss by HPLC in 24 hr at 4 and 22 °C	2289	C
Sodium lactate ⅙ M	AB[a]	MSD	2.5 g	13% imipenem loss in 3 hr at 25 °C. 8% loss in 24 hr and 15% in 48 hr at 4 °C	1141	I
	AB[a]	MSD	5 g	18% imipenem loss in 3 hr at 25 °C. 14% loss in 24 hr at 4 °C	1141	I

Solution Compatibility (Cont.)

Imipenem–cilastatin sodium

Solution	*Mfr*	*Mfr*	*Conc/L*	*Remarks*	*Ref*	*C/I*
TPN #107[d]			500 mg	57% imipenem loss in 24 hr at 21 °C by microbiological assay	1326	I
TPN #241, #242[d]		MSD	5 g	8 to 10% imipenem loss by HPLC within 30 min at 25 °C under fluorescent light	493	I

[a]*Tested in glass containers.*
[b]*Incompatible by conventional standards but recommended for dilution of imipenem–cilastatin with use in shorter periods of time.*
[c]*Tested in glass containers and latex elastomeric reservoirs (Secure Medical).*
[d]*Refer to Appendix I for the composition of parenteral nutrition solutions. TPN indicates a 2-in-1 admixture.*
[e]*Tested in PVC containers.*
[f]*Tested in polyethylene and glass containers.*

Y-Site Injection Compatibility (1:1 Mixture)

Imipenem–cilastatin sodium

Drug	*Mfr*	*Conc*	*Mfr*	*Conc*	*Remarks*	*Ref*	*C/I*
Acyclovir sodium	BW	5 mg/ml[a]	MSD	5 mg/ml[b]	Physically compatible for 4 hr at 25 °C	1157	C
Allopurinol sodium	BW	3 mg/ml[b]	MSD	10 mg/ml[b]	Haze and particles form in 1 hr	1686	I
Amifostine	USB	10 mg/ml[a]	MSD	10 mg/ml[a]	Physically compatible with no change in measured turbidity or increase in particle content in 4 hr at 23 °C	1845	C
Amphotericin B cholesteryl sulfate complex	SEQ	0.83 mg/ml[a]	ME	10 mg/ml[b]	Gross precipitate forms	2117	I
Aztreonam	SQ	40 mg/ml[a]	MSD	10 mg/ml[a]	Physically compatible with no subvisual haze or particle formation in 4 hr at 23 °C	1758	C
Cefepime HCl	BMS	20 mg/ml[a]	MSD	10 mg/ml[a]	Physically compatible with no change in measured turbidity or increase in particle content in 4 hr at 22 °C	1689	C
Cisatracurium besylate	GW	0.1, 2, 5 mg/ml[a]	ME	10 mg/ml[b]	Physically compatible with no change in measured turbidity or increase in particle content in 4 hr at 23 °C	2074	C
Diltiazem HCl	MMD	5 mg/ml	MSD	5 mg/ml[c]	Visually compatible	1807	C
Docetaxel	RPR	0.9 mg/ml[a]	ME	10 mg/ml[b]	Physically compatible with no change in measured turbidity or increase in particle content in 4 hr at 23 °C	2224	C
Etoposide phosphate	BR	5 mg/ml[a]	ME	10 mg/ml[b]	Yellow discoloration forms in 4 hr at 23 °C	2218	I
Famotidine	MSD	0.2 mg/ml[a]	MSD	10 mg/ml[b]	Physically compatible for 14 hr	1196	C
	ME	2 mg/ml[b]		5 mg/ml[b]	Visually compatible for 4 hr at 22 °C	1936	C
Filgrastim	AMG	30 μg/ml[a]	MSD	10 mg/ml[a]	Physically compatible with no change in measured turbidity or increase in particle content in 4 hr at 22 °C	1687	C
	AMG	40 μg/ml[a]	ME	5 mg/ml[a]	16% loss of filgrastim activity by bioassay in 4 hr at 25 °C. Little or no imipenem and cilastatin loss by HPLC	2060	I
	AMG	10 μg/ml[d]	ME	5 mg/ml[a]	Visually compatible with little or no loss of filgrastim activity by bioassay and imipenem and cilastatin by HPLC in 4 hr at 25 °C	2060	C

Y-Site Injection Compatibility (1:1 Mixture) (Cont.)

			Imipenem–cilastatin sodium				
Drug	*Mfr*	*Conc*	*Mfr*	*Conc*	*Remarks*	*Ref*	*C/I*
Fluconazole	RR	2 mg/ml	MSD	10 mg/ml	Immediate precipitation	1407	I
Fludarabine phosphate	BX	1 mg/ml[a]	MSD	5 mg/ml[a]	Physically compatible for 4 hr at room temperature under fluorescent light	1439	C
Foscarnet sodium	AST	24 mg/ml	MSD	10 mg/ml	Physically compatible for 24 hr at room temperature under fluorescent light	1335	C
	AST	24 mg/ml	MSD	5 mg/ml[a]	Physically compatible for 24 hr at 25 °C under fluorescent light by visual and microscopic examination	1393	C
Gatifloxacin	BMS	2 mg/ml[a]	ME	10 mg/ml[b]	Physically compatible with no change in measured haze or increase in particle content in 4 hr at 23 °C	2234	C
Gemcitabine HCl	LI	10 mg/ml[b]	ME	10 mg/ml[b]	Yellow-green discoloration forms in 1 hr	2226	I
Granisetron HCl	SKB	0.05 mg/ml[a]	ME	10 mg/ml[a]	Physically compatible with no change in measured turbidity or increase in particle content in 4 hr at 23 °C	2000	C
Idarubicin HCl	AD	1 mg/ml[b]	MSD	5 mg/ml[b]	Visually compatible for 12 hr at 25 °C under fluorescent light. Precipitate forms in 24 hr	1525	C
Insulin, regular	LI	0.2 unit/ml[b]	MSD	4 and 5 mg/ml[b]	Physically compatible for 2 hr at 25 °C	1395	C
Linezolid	PHU	2 mg/ml	ME	10 mg/ml[b]	Physically compatible with no change in measured turbidity or increase in particle content in 4 hr at 23 °C	2264	C
Lorazepam	WY	0.33 mg/ml[b]	MSD	5 mg/ml	Yellow precipitate forms in 24 hr	1855	I
Melphalan HCl	BW	0.1 mg/ml[b]	MSD	10 mg/ml[b]	Physically compatible with no change in measured turbidity or increase in particle content in 3 hr at 22 °C	1557	C
Meperidine HCl	AB	10 mg/ml	MSD	5 mg/ml[a]	Yellow discoloration forms within 2 hr at 25 °C under fluorescent light	1397	I
Methotrexate sodium		30 mg/ml	MSD	5 mg/ml	Visually compatible for 4 hr at room temperature	1788	C
Midazolam HCl	RC	5 mg/ml	MSD	5 mg/ml	Haze forms in 24 hr	1855	I
Ondansetron HCl	GL	1 mg/ml[b]	MSD	5 mg/ml[b]	Physically compatible for 4 hr at 22 °C	1365	C
Propofol	ZEN	10 mg/ml	ME	10 mg/ml[b]	Physically compatible for 1 hr at 23 °C with no increase in particle content	2066	C
Remifentanil HCl	GW	0.025 and 0.25 mg/ml[b]	ME	10 mg/ml[a]	Physically compatible with no change in measured turbidity or increase in particle content in 4 hr at 23 °C	2075	C
Sargramostim	IMM	10 µg/ml[b]	MSD	5 mg/ml[b]	Large particle and fibrous clump form in 4 hr	1436	I
Sodium bicarbonate		1.4%		5 mg/ml[a]	Pale yellow precipitate forms in 1 hr at room temperature	1788	I
Tacrolimus	FUJ	1 mg/ml[b]	MSD	10 mg/ml[b]	Visually compatible for 24 hr at 25 °C	1630	C
Teniposide	BR	0.1 mg/ml[a]	MSD	10 mg/ml[b]	Physically compatible with no subvisual haze or particle formation in 4 hr at 23 °C	1725	C

Y-Site Injection Compatibility (1:1 Mixture) (Cont.)

			Imipenem–cilastatin sodium				
Drug	*Mfr*	*Conc*	*Mfr*	*Conc*	*Remarks*	*Ref*	*C/I*
Thiotepa	IMM[e]	1 mg/ml[a]	ME	10 mg/ml[a]	Physically compatible with no change in measured turbidity or increase in particle content in 4 hr at 23 °C	1861	C
TNA #218 to #226[f]			ME	10 mg/ml[b]	Visually compatible with no precipitate or emulsion damage apparent in 4 hr at 23 °C	2215	C
TPN #212 to #215[f]			ME	10 mg/ml[b]	Physically compatible with no change in measured turbidity or increase in particle content in 4 hr at 23 °C	2109	C
Vinorelbine tartrate	BW	1 mg/ml[b]	MSD	10 mg/ml[b]	Physically compatible with no change in measured turbidity or increase in particle content in 4 hr at 22 °C	1558	C
Zidovudine	BW	4 mg/ml[a]	MSD	5 mg/ml[a]	Physically compatible for 4 hr at 25 °C under fluorescent light by visual and microscopic examination	1193	C

[a]*Tested in dextrose 5% in water.*
[b]*Tested in sodium chloride 0.9%.*
[c]*Tested in both dextrose 5% in water and sodium chloride 0.9%.*
[d]*Tested in dextrose 5% in water with albumin human 2 mg/ml.*
[e]*Lyophilized formulation tested.*
[f]*Refer to Appendix I for the composition of parenteral nutrition solutions. TNA indicates a 3-in-1 admixture, and TPN indicates a 2-in-1 admixture.*

Additional Compatibility Information

Infusion Solutions — The manufacturer recommends the following infusion solutions for the dilution of imipenem–cilastatin (2):

Dextrose 5% with potassium chloride 0.15%
Dextrose 5% in sodium chloride 0.225, 0.45, and 0.9%
Dextrose 5 and 10% in water
Mannitol 5 and 10% in water
Sodium chloride 0.9%

Imipenem–cilastatin is stated to be stable in these infusion solutions for four hours at room temperature or 24 hours when refrigerated at 5 °C. (4)

The utility time, or time to 10% decomposition (t_{90}), for imipenem–cilastatin in various infusion solutions has been determined. (1141) The results are presented in Table 1.

Aminoglycosides — The manufacturer recommends not physically combining imipenem–cilastatin with other anti-infectives such as aminoglycosides. However, the drugs may be administered from separate containers through the same tubing. (2; 4)

Tobramycin — The potential for inactivation of tobramycin sulfate by the carbapenem antibiotic imipenem–cilastatin sodium was investigated by Ariano et al. Tobramycin sulfate 10 μg/ml was incubated at 37 °C for five days with imipenem–cilastatin sodium at concentrations ranging from 10 to 40 μg/ml in human serum. Degradation rates of tobramycin sulfate determined by fluorescence polarization immunoassay were not enhanced by the presence of imipenem–cilastatin sodium. (2013)

Table 1. Utility Time (t_{90}) of Imipenem–Cilastatin in Infusion Solutions. (1141)

	Time (hr) to 10% Decomposition			
	25 °C		4 °C	
Infusion Solution	250 mg/100 ml	500 mg/100 ml	250 mg/100 ml	500 mg/100 ml
Dextrose 5% with potassium chloride 0.15%	6.3	4.2	51.4	35.4
Dextrose 5% in Ringer's injection, lactated	4.1	2.5	30.9	24.7
Dextrose 5% with sodium bicarbonate 0.02%	5.5	5.4	37.1	34.6
Dextrose 5% in sodium chloride 0.225%	7.3	5.4	52.9	36.7
Dextrose 5% in sodium chloride 0.45%	7.8	5.8	53.0	37.7
Dextrose 5% in sodium chloride 0.9%	9.0	5.5	46.6	39.7
Dextrose 5% in water	6.6	4.7	37.0	36.4
Dextrose 10% in water	5.9	4.3	39.0	31.3
Mannitol 2.5% in water	10.1	6.3	65.0	43.6
Mannitol 5% in water	6.4	5.9	54.9	44.7
Mannitol 10% in water	5.9	3.9	43.6	41.7
Normosol M in dextrose 5%	5.2	4.6	26.8	33.4
Ringer's injection, lactated	6.8	5.4	47.4	41.9
Sodium bicarbonate 5%	0.5	0.4	2.6	2.9
Sodium chloride 0.9%	15.0	11.1	103.0	67.3
Sodium lactate ⅙ M	2.2	1.9	33.6	19.3

IMMUNE GLOBULIN INTRAVENOUS
AHFS 80:04

Products — Immune globulin intravenous 5% (Gamimune N) is available in 10-, 50-, 100-, 200-, and 250-ml sizes. Each milliliter of sterile solution contains approximately 4.5 to 5.5% protein stabilized with 9 to 11% maltose. It also is available in 10-, 50-, 100-, and 200-ml sizes as a 10% solution. Each milliliter of sterile solution contains approximately 9 to 11% protein in 0.16 to 0.24 M glycine. A minimum of 98% of the protein is gamma globulin (immunoglobulin G, IgG). (2; 4)

Immune globulin intravenous (Sandoglobulin) is available as a lyophilized product in vials containing 1, 3, 6, or 12 g with 1.67 g of sucrose per gram of protein along with small amounts of sodium chloride. The vials may be reconstituted with dextrose 5% in water, sodium chloride 0.9% injection, or sterile water for injection, using a syringe, in the following amounts to yield a 3 to 12% (30 to 120 mg/ml) solution (2; 4):

Vial Size	3%	6%	9%	12%
1 g	33 ml	16.5 ml	11 ml	8.3 ml
3 g	100 ml	50 ml	33 ml	25 ml
6 g	200 ml	100 ml	66 ml	50 ml
12 g	[a]	200 ml	132 ml	100 ml

[a] *Container size precludes this concentration.*

Do not shake the product. Rotate or swirl the vial to dissolve particles. Foaming results from shaking and should be avoided (2) because it may impede dissolution. (1499)

Reconstitution of Sandoglobulin with dextrose 5% in water has resulted in extended dissolution times of 75 and 135 minutes for the 3 and 6% solutions, respectively. With sodium chloride 0.9%, dissolution occurs over a few minutes; exceptional cases take up to 20 minutes. (1498)

pH — Gamimune N: 4 to 4.5. Sandoglobulin: 6.4 to 6.8. (2; 4)

Osmotic Values — Gamimune N 5% has an osmolality of 309 mOsm/kg. (2; 4) The 10% product has an osmolality of 274 mOsm/kg. (2)

Sandoglobulin in various concentrations has the following osmolarities (mOsm/L) (2):

	Sandoglobulin Concentration			
Diluent	3%	6%	9%	12%
Dextrose 5% in water	444	636	828	1020
Sodium chloride 0.9%	498	690	882	1074
Sterile water for injection	192	384	576	768

Trade Name(s) — Gamimune N, Gammagard S/D, Gammar-P IV, Iveegam EN, Panglobulin, Polygam S/D, Sandoglobulin, Venoglobulin-S.

Administration — Immune globulin intravenous is administered initially by slow intravenous infusion; the rate is gradually increased after 15 to 30 minutes according to patient tolerance. (2; 4)

Stability — Gamimune N should be stored under refrigeration at 2 to 8 °C and protected from freezing. Solutions that have been frozen should not be used. (2; 4)

Sandoglobulin should be stored at controlled room temperature not exceeding 30 °C. The reconstituted solution should be used only if it is clear. (2; 4) Administration may be initiated within 24 hours of reconstitution if the solution is stored under refrigeration and prepared using aseptic technique in a laminar airflow hood. Sandoglobulin solutions should not be frozen. (2; 34)

Partially used immune globulin containers should be discarded. (4)

Compatibility Information

Solution Compatibility

Immune globulin intravenous

Solution	*Mfr*	*Mfr*	*Conc/L*	*Remarks*	*Ref*	*C/I*
Dextrose 5% in water	[a]	HY	2.5%	Visually compatible with no alteration of IgG concentration or functional activity by bioassay	1885	C
Dextrose 15% in water	[a]	HY	2.5%	Visually compatible with no alteration of IgG concentration or functional activity by bioassay	1885	C
Dextrose 5% in sodium chloride 0.225%	[a]	HY	2.5%	Visually compatible with no alteration of IgG concentration or functional activity by bioassay	1885	C
TPN #194 and #195[b]	[a]	HY	2.5%	Visually compatible with no alteration of IgG concentration or functional activity by bioassay	1885	C

[a]*Tested in PVC containers.*
[b]*Refer to Appendix I for the composition of parenteral nutrition solutions. TPN indicates a 2-in-1 admixture.*

Y-Site Injection Compatibility (1:1 Mixture)

Immune globulin intravenous

Drug	*Mfr*	*Conc*	*Mfr*	*Conc*	*Remarks*	*Ref*	*C/I*
Fluconazole	RR	2 mg/ml	CU	50 mg/ml	Physically compatible for 24 hr at 25 °C under fluorescent light	1407	C
Sargramostim	IMM	6[a,b] and 15 μg/ml[b]	CU	50 mg/ml	Visually compatible for 2 hr	1618	C

[a]*With albumin human 0.1%.*
[b]*Tested in sodium chloride 0.9%.*

Additional Compatibility Information

Immune globulin products may be manufactured using differing procedures and may exhibit differing compatibility characteristics. All manufacturers recommend not mixing other drugs with the immune globulin. In addition, different brands of immune globulin cannot be safely mixed because of possible aggregate formation. The manufacturers make the recommendations cited in Table 1 regarding compatibility with infusion solutions. (2; 1135)

Table 1. Immune Globulin Products: Compatibility with Infusion Solutions

Product	Remarks
Gamimune N	Incompatible with sodium chloride 0.9%. Dextrose 5% in water is recommended for dilution if needed.
Gammagard S/D	Packaged with sterile water for injection for use as a diluent. No other diluents or solutions are recommended.
Gammar-P	Reconstitute with sterile water for injection. May be administered sequentially with dextrose 5% or sodium chloride 0.9%.
Iveegam EN	Reconstitute with sterile water for injection. May be diluted in dextrose 5% or sodium chloride 0.9%.
Panglobulin	May be reconstituted with sodium chloride 0.9%, dextrose 5% in water, or sterile water for injection.
Sandoglobulin	May be reconstituted with sodium chloride 0.9%, dextrose 5% in water, or sterile water for injection.
Venoglobulin-S	May be administered sequentially or flushed with dextrose 5% or sodium chloride 0.9%. Do not add infusion solutions to the immune globulin container.

INAMRINONE LACTATE
AHFS 24:04

Products — Inamrinone lactate is available as an aqueous solution in 20-ml ampuls. Each milliliter of solution contains 5 mg of inamrinone base (as the lactate), 0.25 mg of sodium metabisulfite, and lactic acid or sodium hydroxide to adjust the pH. The total lactic acid concentration may range from 5 to 7.5 mg/ml. (1-3/00; 4)

pH — From 3.2 to 4. (1-3/00; 4)

Osmolality — 101 mOsm/kg. (4)

Administration — Inamrinone lactate may be administered by slow direct intravenous injection or continuous intravenous infusion. Direct intravenous injection should be performed slowly over two or three minutes directly into a vein or the tubing of a running infusion solution. (4)

Stability — Inamrinone lactate injection is a clear, yellow solution. Intact ampuls should be stored at controlled room temperature and should be protected from light. (1-3/00; 4)

Inamrinone lactate decomposes when mixed in dextrose-containing solutions and should not be diluted in such solutions prior to use. Sodium chloride 0.9 or 0.45% are recommended for dilution of inamrinone lactate. (1-3/00; 4) See Additional Compatibility Information below.

pH Effects — The solubilities of inamrinone at pH 4.1, 6, and 8 are 25, 0.9, and 0.7 mg/ml, respectively. (1-3/00; 4)

Central Venous Catheter — Inamrinone lactate (Abbott) 0.5 mg/ml in dextrose 5% in water was found to be compatible with the ARROWg+ard Blue Plus (Arrow International) chlorhexidine-bearing triple-lumen central catheter. HPLC analysis was used to evaluate completeness of drug delivery through the catheter and the amount of chlorhexidine removed from the internal lumens. Essentially complete delivery of the drug was found with little or no drug loss occurring. Furthermore, chlorhexidine delivered from the catheter remained at trace amounts with no substantial increase due to the delivery of the drug through the catheter. (2335)

Compatibility Information

Solution Compatibility

Inamrinone lactate

Solution	*Mfr*	*Mfr*	*Conc/L*	*Remarks*	*Ref*	*C/I*
Dextrose 5% in water		WI	1.25 g	Physically compatible with 5 to 6% loss in 4 hr at 22 °C	1419	I[a]
		WI	2.5 g	Physically compatible with 8% loss in 4 hr at 22 °C	1419	I[a]
Sodium chloride 0.45%		WI	1.25 and 2.5 g	Physically compatible with no loss in 4 hr at 22 °C	1419	C

[a] *Unacceptable losses occur in 24 hours.*

Additive Compatibility

Inamrinone lactate

Drug	*Mfr*	*Conc/L*	*Mfr*	*Conc/L*	*Test Soln*	*Remarks*	*Ref*	*C/I*
Propafenone HCl	KN	0.5 g	SW	1 and 2.5 g[a]	NS	Visually compatible with little or no propafenone loss by HPLC in 24 hr at 22 °C exposed to fluorescent light. Inamrinone not tested	412	C

[a] *Approximate concentration.*

Drugs in Syringe Compatibility

Inamrinone lactate

Drug (in syringe)	*Mfr*	*Amt*	*Mfr*	*Amt*	*Remarks*	*Ref*	*C/I*
Propranolol HCl	LY	1 mg/ 1 ml	WI	5 mg/ 1 ml	Physically compatible with little or no loss of either drug in 4 hr at 22 °C	1419	C
Verapamil HCl	LY	10 mg/ 4 ml	WI	5 mg/ 1 ml	Physically compatible with little or no loss of either drug in 4 hr at 22 °C	1419	C

Y-Site Injection Compatibility (1:1 Mixture)

Drug	Mfr	Conc	Inamrinone lactate Mfr	Conc	Remarks	Ref	C/I
Aminophylline	LY	2 mg/ml[a]	WB	3 mg/ml[b]	Physically compatible for at least 4 hr at 25 °C under fluorescent light	992	C
Atropine sulfate	AB	0.1 mg/ml[a]	WB	3 mg/ml[b]	Physically compatible for at least 4 hr at 25 °C under fluorescent light	992	C
Bretylium tosylate	ACC	10 mg/ml[a]	WB	3 mg/ml[b]	Physically compatible for at least 4 hr at 25 °C under fluorescent light	992	C
Calcium chloride	AB	100 mg/ml	WB	3 mg/ml[b]	Physically compatible for at least 4 hr at 25 °C under fluorescent light	992	C
Cimetidine HCl	SKF	15 mg/ml[a]	WB	3 mg/ml[b]	Physically compatible for at least 4 hr at 25 °C under fluorescent light	992	C
Cisatracurium besylate	GW	0.1, 2, 5 mg/ml[a]	SW	2.5 mg/ml[b]	Physically compatible with no change in measured turbidity or increase in particle content in 4 hr at 23 °C	2074	C
Digoxin	ES	0.25 mg/ml	WI	2.5 mg/ml[c]	Physically compatible with little or no loss of either drug in 4 hr at 22 °C	1419	C
Dobutamine HCl	LI	4 mg/ml[a]	WB	3 mg/ml[b]	Physically compatible for at least 4 hr at 25 °C under fluorescent light	992	C
Dopamine HCl	ACC	1.6 mg/ml[a]	WB	3 mg/ml[b]	Physically compatible for at least 4 hr at 25 °C under fluorescent light	992	C
Epinephrine HCl	AB	0.1 mg/ml[a]	WB	3 mg/ml[b]	Physically compatible for at least 4 hr at 25 °C under fluorescent light	992	C
Famotidine	MSD	0.2 mg/ml[a]	WI	2 mg/ml[a]	Physically compatible for 4 hr at 25 °C	1188	C
Hetastarch in lactated electrolyte injection (Hextend)	AB	6%	AB	2.5 mg/ml[b]	Physically compatible with no change in measured turbidity or increase in particle content in 4 hr at 23 °C	2339	C
Hydrocortisone sodium succinate	ES	1 mg/ml[a]	WB	3 mg/ml[b]	Physically compatible for at least 4 hr at 25 °C under fluorescent light	992	C
Isoproterenol HCl	BR	0.004 mg/ml[a]	WB	3 mg/ml[b]	Physically compatible for at least 4 hr at 25 °C under fluorescent light	992	C
Lidocaine HCl	ES	8 mg/ml[a]	WB	3 mg/ml[b]	Physically compatible for at least 4 hr at 25 °C under fluorescent light	992	C
Metaraminol bitartrate	MSD	0.2 mg/ml[a]	WB	3 mg/ml[b]	Physically compatible for at least 4 hr at 25 °C under fluorescent light	992	C
Methylprednisolone sodium succinate	ES	1 mg/ml[a]	WB	3 mg/ml[b]	Physically compatible for at least 4 hr at 25 °C under fluorescent light	992	C
Nitroglycerin		0.8 mg/ml[a]	WB	3 mg/ml[b]	Physically compatible for at least 4 hr at 25 °C under fluorescent light	992	C
Norepinephrine bitartrate	BR	0.004 mg/ml[a]	WB	3 mg/ml[b]	Physically compatible for at least 4 hr at 25 °C under fluorescent light	992	C
Phenylephrine HCl	WI	0.02 mg/ml[a]	WB	3 mg/ml[b]	Physically compatible for at least 4 hr at 25 °C under fluorescent light	992	C
Potassium chloride	IX	0.04 mEq/ml[a]	WB	3 mg/ml[b]	Physically compatible for at least 4 hr at 25 °C under fluorescent light	992	C
	LY	80 mEq/L[c]	WI	5 mg/ml	Physically compatible with little or no loss of either drug in 4 hr at 22 °C	1419	C
	LY	80 mEq/L[c]	WI	2.5 mg/ml[c]	Physically compatible with little or no loss of either drug in 4 hr at 22 °C	1419	C

Y-Site Injection Compatibility (1:1 Mixture) (Cont.)

Inamrinone lactate

Drug	*Mfr*	*Conc*	*Mfr*	*Conc*	*Remarks*	*Ref*	*C/I*
Procainamide HCl	SQ	4 mg/ml[a]	WB	3 mg/ml[b]	Physically compatible for at least 4 hr at 25 °C under fluorescent light	992	C
	LY	20 mg/ml[c]	WI	2.5 mg/ml[c]	Physically compatible with little or no loss of either drug in 4 hr at 22 °C	1419	C
	LY	20 mg/ml[a]	WI	2.5 mg/ml[a]	18% procainamide loss and 10% inamrinone loss in 4 hr at 22 °C due to dextrose diluent	1419	I
	LY	4 mg/ml[c]	WI	5 mg/ml	Physically compatible with little or no loss of either drug in 4 hr at 22 °C	1419	C
	LY	4 mg/ml[a]	WI	5 mg/ml	20% procainamide loss and 8% inamrinone loss in 4 hr at 22 °C due to dextrose diluent	1419	I
	LY	4 mg/ml[c]	WI	2.5 mg/ml[c]	Physically compatible with little or no loss of either drug in 4 hr at 22 °C	1419	C
	LY	4 mg/ml[a]	WI	2.5 mg/ml[a]	17% procainamide loss in 4 hr at 22 °C due to dextrose diluent	1419	I
Propofol	ZEN	10 mg/ml	WI	1 mg/ml[a]	Physically compatible for 1 hr at 23 °C with no increase in particle content	2066	C
Propranolol HCl	LY	1 mg/ml	WI	2.5 mg/ml[c]	Physically compatible with little or no loss of either drug in 4 hr at 22 °C	1419	C
Remifentanil HCl	GW	0.025 and 0.25 mg/ml[b]	SW	2.5 mg/ml[a]	Physically compatible with no change in measured turbidity or increase in particle content in 4 hr at 23 °C	2075	C
Sodium bicarbonate	AB	1 mEq/ml	WB	3 mg/ml[b]	Immediate color change from yellow to colorless	992	I
	AST	75 mg/ml	WI	5 mg/ml	Immediate precipitation	1419	I
	AST	75 mg/ml	WI	2.5 mg/ml[c]	Precipitate forms within 10 min	1419	I
Sodium nitroprusside	AB	0.2 mg/ml[a]	WB	3 mg/ml[b]	Physically compatible for at least 4 hr at 25 °C under fluorescent light	992	C
Verapamil HCl	SE	0.1 mg/ml[a]	WB	3 mg/ml[b]	Physically compatible for at least 4 hr at 25 °C under fluorescent light	992	C
	LY	2.5 mg/ml	WI	2.5 mg/ml[c]	Physically compatible with little or no loss of either drug in 4 hr at 22 °C	1419	C

[a]*Tested in dextrose 5% in water.*
[b]*Tested in sodium chloride 0.9%.*
[c]*Tested in sodium chloride 0.45%.*

Additional Compatibility Information

Infusion Solutions — For intravenous infusions, dilution of inamrinone lactate in sodium chloride 0.45 or 0.9% to a concentration of 1 to 3 mg/ml is recommended. These solutions are stable for 24 hours at room temperature or under refrigeration in normal lighting conditions. (4)

Inamrinone lactate undergoes a slow chemical interaction with dextrose. (4) At a concentration of 2.5 mg/ml in dextrose 5% in water, an 11 to 13% loss of potency occurs in 24 hours at room temperature. Therefore, the manufacturer states that the drug should not be diluted with dextrose-containing solutions prior to administration. However, inamrinone lactate may be injected into running dextrose infusions through a Y-site or directly into the tubing. (4)

Furosemide — A precipitate forms immediately when furosemide is injected into the tubing of a running inamrinone lactate infusion. (4)

INDOMETHACIN SODIUM TRIHYDRATE
AHFS 28:08.04

Products — Indomethacin sodium trihydrate is supplied as a lyophilized product in vials containing the equivalent of 1 mg of indomethacin. Reconstitute with 1 or 2 ml of preservative-free sterile water for injection or sodium chloride 0.9% to yield a 1- or 0.5-mg/ml solution, respectively. (2)

pH — From 6 to 7.5. (4)

Trade Name(s) — Indocin I.V.

Administration — Indomethacin sodium trihydrate is usually administered by intravenous injection over 20 to 30 minutes, although dilution after reconstitution is not recommended. Extravasation should be avoided. (2; 4)

Stability — Indomethacin sodium trihydrate is supplied as a white to yellow powder. Color variations have no relationship to indomethacin content. The vials should be stored below 30 °C and protected from light. (2)

The manufacturer recommends discarding any unused solution because of the absence of an antibacterial preservative. (2) However, at 1 mg/ml in sodium chloride 0.9%, the drug is stated to be chemically stable for 16 days at room temperature. (4)

Solutions of indomethacin sodium trihydrate (Abbott and Fujisawa) diluted in sodium chloride 0.9% to a concentration of 0.1 mg/ml were evaluated for visual and chemical stability stored in the original vials. Little or no loss was found by HPLC analysis after storage for 10 days at 25 °C. (2105)

Walker et al. reported on the stability of indomethacin sodium trihydrate (Merck Sharp & Dohme) 0.5 mg/ml reconstituted with sterile water for injection in the original vials. The reconstituted solutions were stored at room temperature (about 23 °C) exposed to fluorescent light for 12 hours daily and under refrigeration (about 4 °C) in the dark. Stability-indicating HPLC analysis found little or no loss of indomethacin in the refrigerated solutions after 14 days of storage. The solutions stored at room temperature exhibited 9% loss in 10 days. The solutions at both temperatures remained visually clear and colorless throughout the study. (2228)

pH Effects — Reconstitution of indomethacin sodium trihydrate with solutions having pH values below 6 may result in precipitation of free indomethacin. (2; 4)

Syringes — Walker et al. also evaluated the stability of indomethacin sodium trihydrate 0.5 mg/ml reconstituted with sterile water for injection and repackaged into 1-ml polypropylene syringes (Sherwood). The syringes were stored at room temperature (about 23 °C) exposed to fluorescent light for 12 hours daily and under refrigeration (about 4 °C) in the dark. Stability-indicating HPLC analysis found little or no loss of indomethacin in samples stored at either temperature after 14 days of storage. The solutions stored at both temperatures remained visually clear and colorless throughout the study. (2228)

Compatibility Information

Y-Site Injection Compatibility (1:1 Mixture)

Indomethacin sodium trihydrate

Drug	*Mfr*	*Conc*	*Mfr*	*Conc*	*Remarks*	*Ref*	*C/I*
Amino acid injection (TrophAmine)	MG	1 and 2%[c]	MSD	1 mg/ml[b]	Haze forms in 2 hr and white precipitate forms in 4 hr	1527	I
	MG	1 and 2%[d]	MSD	1 mg/ml[b]	Haze forms in 30 min and white precipitate forms in 1 hr	1527	I
Calcium gluconate	AMR	100 mg/ml	MSD	1 mg/ml[b]	Fine yellow precipitate forms within 1 hr	1527	I
Cimetidine HCl	SKB	6 mg/ml[a]	MSD	1 mg/ml[b]	Haze and fine precipitate form immediately	1527	I
Dextrose injection	BA	2.5%	MSD	1 mg/ml[b]	Visually compatible for 24 hr at 28 °C	1527	C
	BA	5%	MSD	1 mg/ml[b]	Visually compatible for 24 hr at 28 °C	1527	C
	BA	7.5%	MSD	1 mg/ml[b]	Haze forms in 2 hr and precipitate forms in 4 hr	1527	I
	BA	10%	MSD	1 mg/ml[b]	Haze forms in 2 hr and precipitate forms in 4 hr	1527	I
Dobutamine HCl	LI	1.2 mg/ml[a]	MSD	1 mg/ml[b]	Haze and fine precipitate form immediately	1527	I
Dopamine HCl	AB	1.2 mg/ml[a]	MSD	1 mg/ml[b]	Haze and fine precipitate form immediately	1527	I
Furosemide	AB	10 mg/ml	MSD	1 mg/ml[b]	Visually compatible for 24 hr at 28 °C	1527	C
Gentamicin sulfate		1 mg/ml[a]	MSD	0.5 and 1 mg/ml[a]	White turbidity forms immediately and becomes white flakes in 1 hr	1550	I
Insulin, regular	NOV	1 unit/ml[b]	MSD	1 mg/ml[b]	Visually compatible for 24 hr at 28 °C	1527	C

Y-Site Injection Compatibility (1:1 Mixture) (Cont.)

			Indomethacin sodium trihydrate				
Drug	*Mfr*	*Conc*	*Mfr*	*Conc*	*Remarks*	*Ref*	*C/I*
Levofloxacin	OMN	5 mg/ml[a]	ME	1 mg/ml	Cloudy precipitate forms	2233	I
Potassium chloride	AB	0.2 mEq/ml[a]	MSD	1 mg/ml[b]	Visually compatible for 24 hr at 28 °C	1527	C
Sodium bicarbonate	AB	0.5 mEq/ml[a]	MSD	1 mg/ml[b]	Visually compatible for 24 hr at 28 °C	1527	C
Sodium nitroprusside	AB	0.2 mg/ml[a]	MSD	1 mg/ml[b]	Visually compatible for 24 hr at 28 °C	1527	C
Tobramycin sulfate		1 mg/ml[a]	MSD	0.5 and 1 mg/ml[a]	White turbidity forms immediately and becomes white flakes in 1 hr	1550	I
Tolazoline HCl		0.1 mg/ml[a]	MSD	1 mg/ml	White precipitate forms within 30 min	1363	I

[a]*Tested in dextrose 5% in water.*
[b]*Tested in sodium chloride 0.9%.*
[c]*TrophAmine in dextrose 10% in water.*
[d]*TrophAmine in sterile water for injection.*

INSULIN
AHFS 68:20.08

Products — Regular insulin is available from several manufacturers in 10-ml vials and 1.5-ml prefilled syringes and syringe cartridges at a concentration of 100 units/ml. The insulin may be derived from pork sources or may be human insulin produced using recombinant DNA technology. Regular concentrated insulin (Lilly) also is available in 20-ml vials containing 500 units/ml. Glycerin 1.4 to 1.8% and phenol or cresol 0.1 to 0.25% may also be present. (2; 4)

Several modified forms of insulin (Isophane, Lente, etc.) are available, each having a characteristic onset of action, time to peak effect, and duration of action. (4)

Adequately mixing these products is necessary prior to use, but vigorous shaking may entrain air bubbles that could interfere with accurate dosing. Gentle shaking of the vial combined with end-over-end inversion and rolling in the palms has been suggested. (2270)

pH — All regular insulin products have a neutral pH of approximately 7 to 7.8. (4; 261) Prior to 1973, the older acidic form having a pH of 2.5 to 3.5 was available. (4; 263)

Trade Name(s) — Humulin R, Iletin II Regular, Novolin R, Velosulin BR.

Administration — Regular insulin is usually administered by subcutaneous injection into the thighs, arms, buttocks, or abdomen, with sites rotated. Syringes calibrated for the particular concentration of insulin to be given must be used. Regular insulin may also be administered intramuscularly or by intravenous infusion, usually diluted in sodium chloride 0.9%. Regular insulin is the only form of insulin that can be given intravenously. (4)

Stability — Regular insulin should be stored under refrigeration and protected from freezing. (2; 4) Freezing of insulin products may alter the protein structure, decreasing potency. (559) In one study of several insulin products, one cycle of freezing for 45 hours followed by slow thawing at 21 °C or rapid thawing in a water bath at 37 °C did not result in a loss of bioactivity. However, microscopic examination revealed particle aggregation, and some crystal damage had occurred. (680)

The currently available regular insulin formulations having a neutral pH are more stable than the older acidic forms used to be. (413; 907) At 25 °C, regular insulin has been found to be stable for 24 to 30 months (414), although Lilly has recommended a maximum of 30 days. (1433) One study found approximately 5% loss of biological potency after about 36 months at 25 °C. At 37 °C, a 5% loss occurred in about five months. (907)

As with other protein and peptide products, insulin aggregation with possible reduced bioactivity can be a problem. Aggregates have been found to form in a variety of infusion devices and under various storage conditions, including static storage and continuous rotational or reciprocating motion. (1948; 1995) Aggregation may occur at air-water interfaces. Such interfaces have been generated by turbulence, such as shaking and repeatedly passing insulin through a syringe and needle. With sufficient vigor, both actions can turn the insulin turbid from insoluble aggregates. (1948) In addition, contact with silicone rubber appears to promote insulin aggregation. (1995)

Gregory et al. evaluated factors that increase the formation rate of insulin transformation products (such as deamidated insulin, covalent dimers, and higher oligamers) in beef and human insulin products during six months of storage. HPLC analysis showed a low rate of transformation product appearance at 4 °C. Higher temperatures, as might occur when insulin is carried in a shirt pocket or car glove compartment, accelerated this production (especially for human insulin) and also fibril formation. Exposure to light increased the dimer and higher oligamer content. According to these authors, insulin should not be exposed to direct sunlight or subjected to vibration or extremes of temperature. (1663)

Regular insulin, containing 100 units/ml, is clear and colorless or almost colorless. The concentrated injection containing 500 units/ml may be straw colored. Discoloration, turbidity, or unusual viscosity indicates deterioration or contamination. (4)

Syringes — It has been stated that neutral regular insulin (and also NPH and Lente insulin) can be stored for five to seven days under refrigeration in either glass or plastic syringes. Mixtures of these insulins can also be stored similarly. (679)

In a study by Simmons and Allwood, insulin soluble, BP, 1.6 units/2 ml diluted in sodium chloride 0.9% was stored for 18 hours at room temperature in the following plastic syringes: Brunswick (Sherwood Medical), Plastipak (Becton-Dickinson), and Sabre (Gillette U.K.). The first two syringes have polypropylene barrels; the Sabre has a combination polypropylene–polystyrene barrel. No significant loss of insulin occurred due to sorption. Significant (but unspecified) losses did occur when the concentration was reduced to 0.2 unit/ml, but the make of syringe did not influence this adsorption. (784)

Zell and Paone, using a radioimmunoassay, found no apparent degradation or binding for at least 14 days when insulin, USP (Lilly), 100 units/ml was stored under refrigeration in 1-ml polypropylene syringes (Becton-Dickinson). (805)

Adams et al. reported that the soluble insulins Velosulin (Nordisk), Actrapid and Human Actrapid (Novo), Humulin S (Lilly), Neusulin (Wellcome), and Quicksol (Boots) in 1-ml 100-unit Plastipak syringes (Becton-Dickinson) exhibited no loss of potency by HPLC in 29 days when stored at 4 and 20 °C. (1275)

Regular insulin human (Humulin R, 100 units/ml, Lilly), isophane insulin human (Humulin N, 100 units/ml, Lilly), and the combination product (Humulin N/R 70/30, Lilly) were evaluated for stability packaged in plastic syringes. Test samples of 0.4 ml of each insulin product were drawn into 1-ml polypropylene syringes (Plastipak, Becton-Dickinson) and 1-ml polypropylene–ethylene copolymer syringes (Terumo) and stored for 28 days at 4 and 23 °C. HPLC analysis found no loss of insulin from any insulin product in either syringe type. However, the antibacterial preservatives present in the insulin formulations were lost, especially in the polypropylene syringes at room temperature. The authors recommended storage under refrigeration to slow the loss of preservative as much as possible. (1124)

Infusion Pumps — Insulin solutions may form highly insoluble polymers. In areas having high shear rates such as the tubing, cannula, and needle, aggregation can lead to blockage. In low shear areas such as the insulin reservoir of implantable pumps, gentle agitation can lead to the formation of a cross-linked gel. (1112)

Sorption — The adsorption of insulin to the surfaces of intravenous infusion solution containers, glass and plastic (including PVC, ethylene vinyl acetate, polyethylene, and other polyolefins), tubing, and filters has been demonstrated. Estimates of the potency loss range up to about 80% for the entire infusion apparatus, although varying results using differing test methods, equipment, and procedures have been reported. Estimates of adsorption of around 20 to 30% are common. The percent adsorbed is inversely proportional to the concentration of insulin. Other important factors are the amount of container surface area and the fill volume of the solution. The amount of insulin adsorbed varies directly with the available surface area and indirectly with the ratio of fluid volume to container capacity. The container material is a factor, with glass possibly adsorbing insulin more extensively than some plastics. Other factors influencing the extent of insulin adsorption include the type of solution, type and length of administration set, rate of infusion, temperature, previous exposure of tubing to insulin, and presence of albumin human, whole blood, electrolytes, and other drugs. (266–269; 420; 422–426; 428; 533; 681–690; 854; 908–913; 1111; 1112; 1274; 1282; 1408; 1497; 1664; 1665; 2079; 2301)

The adsorption of insulin to container surfaces is an instantaneous process. (267; 425; 911–913) However, the effect of adsorption on the deliverable amount of insulin appears to vary with time. Several investigators reported a dramatic initial drop in delivered insulin followed by a return to higher (although variable) levels. The bulk of the insulin adsorption apparently occurs in the first 30 to 60 minutes. Although flow rate does not influence total insulin binding, the plateau phase of delivered insulin may be reached more quickly at faster infusion rates. (422; 424–426; 428; 687–689; 854; 2301)

In a study of insulin loss during simulated delivery to low-birth-weight infants, insulin 0.2 unit/ml was delivered at rates of 0.05 and 0.2 ml/hr through microbore PVC tubing and polyethylene-lined PVC tubing. During the early hours, the amount of insulin delivered through both types of tubing was much reduced, especially at the slower delivery rate. The authors indicated that this loss might contribute to the 14- to 24-hour delays in blood glucose normalization in these infants. The priming of microbore tubing with 5 units/ml of insulin for 20 minutes was suggested to accelerate the achievement of steady-state insulin delivery. The time courses of insulin delivery observed for representative unprimed and primed sets are presented in Table 1. (2301)

The addition of albumin human to infusion solutions helps to reduce the adsorption of insulin. The degree to which albumin human prevents adsorption is uncertain. Reported losses of insulin in albumin-containing solutions have varied from about zero to approximately 30%. However, most work indicates a substantial reduction in insulin adsorption. (266–269; 418; 428; 683–685; 908; 909) Other additives such as vitamins, electrolytes, and drugs may also have a similar effect. (425; 909; 914)

Other recommended approaches to avoiding or minimizing adsorption include adding a small amount of the patient's blood to the insulin solution (689–691) and storing or flushing the administration apparatus with the insulin solution to saturate the set prior to administration. (428; 1111; 2301) Addition of extra insulin to compensate for the losses has also been suggested. (1112) As an alternative, administration of insulin using a syringe pump with a short cannula has been recommended. This procedure will reduce the surface area in relation to the amount of insulin present. (1033)

The clinical significance of this adsorption is uncertain. Some clinical studies indicated no relevant effect on the success of therapy. (415; 427; 685) Some investigators felt that the importance of insulin adsorption to the surfaces of the infusion container and tubing may be a moot point since the dosage is individualized on the basis of blood and urine glucose determinations. Simply adding more insulin may saturate binding sites and yield the desired response. (270; 271; 854; 909)

Still others indicated that the adsorption may indeed be relevant for solutions with an insulin content of less than 100 or 200 units/L. (424; 426; 428; 908; 2301)

If the apparent dose of intravenous insulin is used as the basis for determining the subsequent dose upon discontinuing the intravenous one, then a potential for dosing error exists. The actual amount of

Table 1. Approximate Amount of Insulin Delivered through Unprimed and Primed[a] Administration Sets (2301)

	Delivered Insulin (%)				
Set Type	1 hr	2 hr	4 hr	8 hr	24 hr
Unprimed	17	11	27	55	≈100
Primed	70	70	70	≈100	≈100

[a] *Primed with insulin 5 units/ml for 20 minutes.*

insulin being administered could be substantially less than the apparent amount. (533)

Whether one attempts to prevent insulin adsorption or not, it does not appear to be possible to add an amount of insulin to an infusion solution and know precisely what portion of that amount will actually be given to the patient. Monitoring the patient's response to therapy and making the appropriate adjustments on the basis of that response are, therefore, of prime importance. (690; 854; 1664)

Filtration—A filter material specially treated with a proprietary agent was evaluated for a reduction in insulin binding. Insulin, regular (Lilly), 40 units/L in dextrose 5% in water and sodium chloride 0.9% was run through an administration set with a treated 0.22-μm cellulose ester inline filter at a rate of 2 ml/min. Cumulative insulin losses from the first 150 ml of solution were about 12% from dextrose 5% in water and 4% from sodium chloride 0.9%, compared to much higher losses previously reported for untreated cellulose ester filter material. Furthermore, equilibrium binding studies showed a reduction to 5% of the binding to untreated filter material from either solution. (904) All Abbott Ivex integral filter and extension sets currently use this treated filter material. (1074)

Compatibility Information

Solution Compatibility

Insulin, regular

Solution	*Mfr*	*Mfr*	*Conc/L*	*Remarks*	*Ref*	*C/I*
Amino acids 4.25%, dextrose 25%	MG	LI	100 units	No increase in particulate matter in 24 hr at 5 °C	349	C
Sodium chloride 0.9%	BA[a]	LI[b]	1000 units	10% insulin loss by HPLC in 1 hr in 50-ml bag and in 4 hr in 250-ml bag	2079	I
TPN #38 to #45 and #47[c]		LI	10 to 50 units	Physically compatible for 24 hr at 22 °C	313	C
TPN #46[c]		LI	10 to 30 units	Physically compatible for 24 hr at 22 °C	313	C
		LI	40 and 50 units	White crystalline precipitate forms in 24 hr at 22 °C	313	I

[a]Tested in PVC containers.
[b]Regular human insulin.
[c]Refer to Appendix I for the composition of parenteral nutrition solutions. TPN indicates a 2-in-1 admixture.

Additive Compatibility

Insulin, regular

Drug	*Mfr*	*Conc/L*	*Mfr*	*Conc/L*	*Test Soln*	*Remarks*	*Ref*	*C/I*
Aminophylline	SE	1 g	LI[a]	20 units	D5W	pH outside stability range for insulin	41	I
Amobarbital sodium			[a]			Physically incompatible	9	I
Bretylium tosylate	ACC	1 g	SQ	1000 units	D5W, NS	Physically compatible for 48 hr at 25 °C	756	C
Chlorothiazide sodium	MSD		[a]			Physically incompatible	9	I
Cimetidine HCl	SKF	1.2 and 5 g	LI	100 units	D5W, NS	Physically compatible and cimetidine chemically stable for 24 hr at room temperature. Insulin not tested	551	C
Cytarabine	UP	100 and 500 mg		40 units	D5W	Fine precipitate forms	174	I
Dobutamine HCl	LI	1 g	LI	1000 units	D5W, NS	Slightly pink in 24 hr at 25 °C	789	I
	LI	1 g	LI	50,000 units	D5W, NS	White precipitate forms rapidly	812	I
Lidocaine HCl	AST	2 g	SQ	1000 units	D5W, LR, NS	Physically compatible for 24 hr at 25 °C	775	C
Meropenem	ZEN	1 and 20 g	LI	1000 units	NS	Visually compatible for 4 hr at room temperature	1994	C

Additive Compatibility (Cont.)

Insulin, regular

Drug	*Mfr*	*Conc/L*	*Mfr*	*Conc/L*	*Test Soln*	*Remarks*	*Ref*	*C/I*
Pentobarbital sodium			[a]			Physically incompatible	9	I
Phenobarbital sodium	WI		[a]			Physically incompatible	9	I
Phenytoin sodium	PD		[a]			Physically incompatible	9	I
Ranitidine HCl	GL	50 mg and 2 g		100 units	NS	Physically compatible and ranitidine chemically stable by HPLC for 24 hr at 25 °C. Insulin not tested	1515	C
	GL	600 mg	LI	1000 units[c]	NS[b]	Visually compatible with little or no loss by HPLC of ranitidine in 24 hr at ambient temperature but insulin losses of 9% in 4 hr and 14% in 24 hr, presumably due to sorption	2079	I
Thiopental sodium	AB		[a]			Physically incompatible	9	I
Verapamil HCl	KN	80 mg	SQ	200 units	D5W, NS	Physically compatible for 48 hr	739	C

[a]Test performed prior to availability of neutral regular insulin.
[b]Tested in PVC containers.
[c]Regular human insulin.

Drugs in Syringe Compatibility

Insulin, regular

Drug (in syringe)	*Mfr*	*Amt*	*Mfr*	*Amt*	*Remarks*	*Ref*	*C/I*
Metoclopramide HCl	RB	10 mg/ 2 ml	LI	10 units/ 2 ml[a]	Physically compatible for 24 hr at room temperature	924	C
	RB	10 mg/ 2 ml	LI	20 units/ 4 ml[a]	Physically compatible for 24 hr at room temperature	924	C
	RB	10 mg/ 2 ml	LI	10 units/ 2 ml	Physically compatible for 24 hr at 25 °C	1167	C
	RB	10 mg/ 2 ml	LI	20 units/ 4 ml	Physically compatible for 24 hr at 25 °C	1167	C
	RB	160 mg/ 32 ml	LI	80 units/ 16 ml	Physically compatible for 24 hr at 25 °C	1167	C

[a]Brought to volume with distilled water.

Y-Site Injection Compatibility (1:1 Mixture)

Insulin, regular

Drug	*Mfr*	*Conc*	*Mfr*	*Conc*	*Remarks*	*Ref*	*C/I*
Alatrofloxacin mesylate	PF	1.43 mg/ml[a]	LI	1 unit/ml[b]	Microscopic particles form	2235	I
Amiodarone HCl	WY	4.8 mg/ml[a]	LI	1 unit/ml[a]	Visually compatible for 24 hr at 23 °C	1877	C
Ampicillin sodium	WY	20 mg/ml[b]	LI	0.2 unit/ml[b]	Physically compatible for 2 hr at 25 °C	1395	C
Ampicillin sodium–sulbactam sodium	RR	20 + 10 mg/ ml[b]	LI	0.2 unit/ml[b]	Physically compatible for 2 hr at 25 °C	1395	C
Aztreonam	SQ	20 mg/ml	LI	0.2 unit/ml[b]	Physically compatible for 2 hr at 25 °C	1395	C
Cefazolin sodium	LI	20 mg/ml[a]	LI	0.2 unit/ml[b]	Physically compatible for 2 hr at 25 °C	1395	C
Cefotetan disodium	STU	20 and 40 mg/ml[a]	LI	0.2 unit/ml[b]	Physically compatible for 2 hr at 25 °C	1395	C

Y-Site Injection Compatibility (1:1 Mixture) (Cont.)

			Insulin, regular				
Drug	*Mfr*	*Conc*	*Mfr*	*Conc*	*Remarks*	*Ref*	*C/I*
Clarithromycin	AB	4 mg/ml[a]	NOV[l]	4 units/ml[a]	Visually compatible for 72 hr at both 30 and 17 °C	2174	C
Digoxin	ES	0.005 mg/ml[b]	LI[c]	1 unit/ml[b]	Physically compatible for 3 hr	1316	C
	ES	0.005 mg/ml[b]	LI[d]	1 unit/ml[b]	Physically compatible for 3 hr	1316	C
	ES	0.005 mg/ml[a]	LI[c]	1 unit/ml[a]	Slight haze in 1 hr	1316	I
	ES	0.005 mg/ml[a]	LI[d]	1 unit/ml[a]	Slight haze in 1 hr	1316	I
Diltiazem HCl	MMD	1[b] and 5 mg/ml	NOV	100 units/ml	Precipitate forms and persists	1807	I
	MMD	5 mg/ml	NOV	0.4 unit/ml	Visually compatible	1807	C
Dobutamine HCl	LI	4 mg/ml[e]	LI[c]	1 unit/ml[e]	Physically compatible for 3 hr	1316	C
	LI	4 mg/ml[e]	LI[d]	1 unit/ml[e]	Physically compatible for 3 hr	1316	C
Dopamine HCl	DU	3.2 mg/ml[a]	LI	1 unit/ml[a]	White precipitate forms immediately, dissolves quickly, and reforms in 24 hr at 23 °C	1877	I
Esmolol HCl	DU	40 mg/ml[a]	LI	1 unit/ml[a]	Visually compatible for 24 hr at 23 °C	1877	C
Famotidine	MSD	0.2 mg/ml[a]	LI	0.03 unit/ml[a]	Physically compatible for 4 hr at 25 °C	1188	C
Gentamicin sulfate	TR	1.2 mg/ml[b]	LI	0.2 unit/ml[b]	Physically compatible for 2 hr at 25 °C	1395	C
Heparin sodium	ES	60 units/ml[a]	LI	0.2 unit/ml[b]	Physically compatible for 2 hr at 25 °C	1395	C
Heparin sodium with hydrocortisone sodium succinate	RI UP	1000 units + 100 mg/L[f]	LI	40 units/ml	Physically compatible for at least 4 hr at room temperature by visual and microscopic examination	322	C
Imipenem–cilastatin sodium	MSD	4 and 5 mg/ml[b]	LI	0.2 unit/ml[b]	Physically compatible for 2 hr at 25 °C	1395	C
Indomethacin sodium trihydrate	MSD	1 mg/ml[b]	NOV	1 unit/ml[b]	Visually compatible for 24 hr at 28 °C	1527	C
Labetalol HCl	GL	5 mg/ml	LI	1 unit/ml[a]	Visually compatible for 4 hr. White precipitate forms in 24 hr 23 °C	1877	?
Levofloxacin	OMN	5 mg/ml[a]	LI[l]	100 units/ml	Cloudy precipitate forms	2233	I
	OMN	5 mg/ml[a]	LI[l]	1 unit/ml	Visually compatible for 4 hr at 24 °C under fluorescent light	2233	C
Magnesium sulfate	LY	40 mg/ml[g]	LI	0.2 unit/ml[b]	Physically compatible for 2 hr at 25 °C	1395	C
Meperidine HCl	WY	10 mg/ml[b]	LI	0.2 unit/ml[b]	Physically compatible for 1 hr at 25 °C	1338	C
	AST	50 mg/ml[a]	LI	0.2 unit/ml[b]	Physically compatible for 2 hr at 25 °C	1395	C
Meropenem	ZEN	1 and 50 mg/ml[b]	LI	0.2 unit/ml[h]	Visually compatible for 4 hr at room temperature	1994	C
Midazolam HCl	RC	1 mg/ml[a]	LI	1 unit/ml[a]	Visually compatible for 24 hr at 23 °C	1877	C
Milrinone lactate	SW	0.4 mg/ml[a]	NOV[l]	1 unit/ml[b]	Visually compatible with little or no loss of either drug by HPLC in 4 hr at 23 °C	2214	C
Morphine sulfate	ES	1 mg/ml[b]	LI	0.2 unit/ml[b]	Physically compatible for 1 hr at 25 °C	1338	C
	ES	5 mg/ml[a]	LI	0.2 unit/ml[b]	Physically compatible for 2 hr at 25 °C	1395	C
	SX	1 mg/ml[a]	LI	1 unit/ml[a]	Visually compatible for 24 hr at 23 °C	1877	C
Nafcillin sodium	BA	20 and 40 mg/ml[a]	LI	0.2 unit/ml[b]	Immediate precipitation	1395	I
Nitroglycerin	OM	0.2 mg/ml[a]	LI	1 unit/ml[a]	Visually compatible for 24 hr at 23 °C	1877	C
Norepinephrine bitartrate	STR	0.064 mg/ml[a]	LI	1 unit/ml[a]	White precipitate forms immediately	1877	I

Y-Site Injection Compatibility (1:1 Mixture) (Cont.)

Insulin, regular

Drug	*Mfr*	*Conc*	*Mfr*	*Conc*	*Remarks*	*Ref*	*C/I*
Oxytocin	PD	0.02 unit/ml[l]	LI	0.2 unit/ml[b]	Physically compatible for 2 hr at 25 °C	1395	C
Pentobarbital sodium	WY	2 mg/ml[e]	LI[c]	1 unit/ml[e]	Physically compatible for 3 hr	1316	C
	WY	2 mg/ml[e]	LI[d]	1 unit/ml[e]	Physically compatible for 3 hr	1316	C
Potassium chloride		40 mEq/L[f]	LI	40 units/ml	Physically compatible for at least 4 hr at room temperature by visual and microscopic examination	322	C
Propofol	ZEN	10 mg/ml	NOV	1 unit/ml[a]	Physically compatible for 1 hr at 23 °C with no increase in particle content	2066	C
Ranitidine HCl	GL	1 mg/ml[b]	LI[c]	1 unit/ml[b]	Visually compatible with little or no loss by HPLC of ranitidine in 4 hr at ambient temperature but insulin losses of 9% in 1 hr and 20% in 4 hr, presumably due to sorption	2079	I
Ritodrine HCl	AST	0.3 mg/ml[a]	LI	0.2 unit/ml[b]	Physically compatible for 2 hr at 25 °C	1395	C
Sodium bicarbonate	AB	1 mEq/ml	LI[c]	1 unit/ml	Physically compatible for 3 hr	1316	C
	AB	1 mEq/ml	LI[d]	1 unit/ml[e]	Physically compatible for 3 hr	1316	C
Sodium nitroprusside	RC	0.2 mg/ml[a]	LI	1 unit/ml[a]	Visually compatible for 24 hr at 23 °C	1877	C
Tacrolimus	FUJ	1 mg/ml[b]	LI	0.1 unit/ml[a]	Visually compatible for 24 hr at 25 °C	1630	C
Terbutaline sulfate	CI	0.02 mg/ml[a]	LI	0.2 unit/ml[b]	Physically compatible for 2 hr at 25 °C	1395	C
Ticarcillin disodium	BE	30 mg/ml[b]	LI	0.2 unit/ml[b]	Physically compatible for 2 hr at 25 °C	1395	C
Ticarcillin disodium–clavulanate potassium	BE	31 mg/ml[b]	LI	0.2 unit/ml[b]	Physically compatible for 2 hr at 25 °C	1395	C
Tobramycin sulfate	LI	1.6 and 2 mg/ml[a]	LI	0.2 unit/ml[b]	Physically compatible for 2 hr at 25 °C	1395	C
TNA #218 to #226[j]			NOV	1 unit/ml[a]	Visually compatible with no precipitate or emulsion damage apparent in 4 hr at 23 °C	2215	C
TPN #189[j]			NOV	2 units/ml[k]	Visually compatible for 24 hr at 22 °C	1767	C
TPN #212 to #215[j]			NOV	1 unit/ml[b]	Physically compatible with no change in measured turbidity or increase in particle content in 4 hr at 23 °C	2109	C
Vancomycin HCl	LI	4 mg/ml[a]	LI	0.2 unit/ml[b]	Physically compatible for 2 hr at 25 °C	1395	C
Vitamin B complex with C	RC	2 ml/L[f]	LI	40 units/ml	Physically compatible for at least 4 hr at room temperature by visual and microscopic examination	322	C

[a] *Tested in dextrose 5% in water.*
[b] *Tested in sodium chloride 0.9%.*
[c] *Humulin R.*
[d] *Beef pork.*
[e] *Tested in both dextrose 5% in water and sodium chloride 0.9%.*
[f] *Tested in dextrose 5% in water, sodium chloride 0.9%, and Ringer's injection, lactated.*
[g] *Tested in Ringer's injection, lactated.*
[h] *Tested in sterile water for injection.*
[i] *Tested in dextrose 5% in Ringer's injection, lactated.*
[j] *Refer to Appendix I for the composition of parenteral nutrition solutions. TNA indicates a 3-in-1 admixture, and TPN indicates a 2-in-1 admixture.*
[k] *Tested in Haemaccel (Behring).*
[l] *Regular human insulin.*

Additional Compatibility Information

Parenteral Nutrition Solutions — Regular insulin is not inactivated in amino acid injection (McGaw), but a physical separation may occur if it is not mixed thoroughly; occasional shaking prevents a bolus of insulin from being administered. (189)

Regular insulin (Lilly) 20 to 100 units/L was tested for compatibility in parenteral nutrition solutions composed of protein hydrolysate 7% 590 ml/dextrose 50% 410 ml (Cutter) with calcium, magnesium, phosphate, phytonadione, cyanocobalamin, folic acid, and multivitamin infusion (USV) or Solu B Forte present. The parenteral nutrition solutions were physically compatible with little pH alteration in 24 hours at room temperature. (464)

Mixing Insulin Products — Mixing of the various types of insulin has been utilized. The following compatibility results have been cited (1076):

Insulin Types	Compatibility
Regular with NPH	Mixtures are stable in all ratios
Regular with protamine zinc	Stability is unpredictable
Regular with Lente	Reduces activity of regular due to binding to excess zinc
Lente, Semilente, Ultralente	Mixtures are stable in all ratios
Lente, Semilente, Ultralente with phosphate-buffered insulins[a]	Should not be mixed due to precipitation

[a]*Includes Humulin BR, NPH, protamine zinc, Velosulin insulins.*

It has been stated that neutral regular insulin may be combined with modified insulin in any proportions. (263; 264) However, losses of soluble insulins when mixed with zinc and isophane insulins were reported by Adams et al. These losses generally ranged from about 20 to 50% but were as high as 99%, depending on the ratio and sources of the two insulins in the mixture. The reaction occurred within the first 90 to 120 seconds after mixing, with no further losses occurring after this time. The authors indicated that this phenomenon could explain clinical reports of failure to control postprandial blood sugar levels. (1275)

Nolte et al. reported on the loss of solubility when short-acting insulins were mixed in ratios of 1:1, 1:2, 1:3, and 1:5 with long-acting insulins. Iletin II Regular (Lilly) was mixed with Iletin II Lente, NPH, or Ultralente (Lilly). Actrapid (Novo) was mixed with Monotard (Novo). Velosulin (Nordisk) was mixed with Insulatard (Nordisk). The mixtures were centrifuged after storage times of approximately 20 minutes and 75 seconds. The level of soluble short-acting insulin in the supernatant was determined by radioimmunoassay. In a 1:1 ratio, no significant loss of solubility occurred with the Iletin II Lente combination within 20 minutes and with the Actrapid–Monotard combination in 75 seconds. All other combinations, ratios, and time periods had losses ranging from 10 to 75%. The worst losses were experienced with the highest ratios of long-acting insulins and with the longer time period. The authors noted that the method used to prolong insulin action (precipitation) might affect the solubility of the short-acting insulin when admixed. (1156)

Muhlhauser et al. noted the loss of initial hypoglycemic effect when Actrapid HM (Novo) was mixed with Ultratard HM (Novo), an ultralente insulin, for five minutes before injection. The authors recommended not mixing the two types of insulin to preserve the rapid hypoglycemic effect of regular insulin. (73)

Methylprednisolone — Methylprednisolone sodium succinate (Upjohn) has been stated to be incompatible with insulin. (329)

Octreotide — Radioimmunoassays of insulin levels in a 3-L bag of parenteral nutrition solution showed a marked reduction when octreotide 150 μg was added to the container. Sample parenteral nutrition solutions, with and without octreotide, were prepared with regular insulin 15 units/3-L bag. Subsequent analysis found an insulin level of 3.5 units/L in the plain parenteral nutrition solution, an amount consistent with the losses occurring due to surface adsorption. (See Stability above.) However, in the parenteral nutrition solution containing octreotide, the insulin level was only 0.6 unit/L. The reason for this potential incompatibility is not known. (1377)

Other Information

Mixing Insulin Admixtures — Care is required when adding insulin to infusion solutions, especially in flexible containers. Adding insulin to a polygeline (plasma expander) carrier solution hanging in the use position resulted in stratification, with the insulin floating to the top. Little insulin was delivered initially, and 87% of the insulin appeared in the last 28% of the solution. Repeated inversion and agitation of the container to effect thorough mixture eliminates this stratification, yielding an even distribution and a constant delivery concentration. (85)

Reuse of Disposable Insulin Syringes — Reuse of disposable insulin syringes has been suggested to reduce cost to patients. However, disposable insulin syringes are usually siliconized. Reuse of disposable plastic insulin syringes (Plastipak Microfine II, Becton-Dickinson) has resulted in contamination of vials of insulin with silicone oil, causing a white precipitate and impairment of biological effects. In a test of insulin from several sources, repeated drawing of the insulin into the disposable syringes and then expulsion of it back into the vials introduced substantial amounts of silicone oil; a white precipitate formed within 12 hours at 8 °C. (1110)

INTERFERON ALFA-2B
AHFS 10:00

Products — Interferon alfa-2b is available as a dry powder in vials containing 3, 5, 10, 18, 25, and 50 million International Units (I.U.) packaged with bacteriostatic water for injection containing benzyl alcohol 0.9% diluent. See Table 1. Only the 10-million I.U. vial is recommended for intralesional use. The 50-million I.U. vials are used in malignant melanoma and AIDS-related Kaposi's sarcoma only. (2)

For intramuscular, subcutaneous, or intralesional use, reconstitute the appropriate-size vial contents with the bacteriostatic water for injection diluent using the requisite volume noted in Table 1. Direct the stream at the vial wall and not at the powder in the bottom of the vial. Swirl gently to dissolve the powder; do not shake. (2)

In addition to interferon alfa-2b, the reconstituted solutions also contain in each milliliter glycine 20 mg, sodium phosphate dibasic 2.3 mg, sodium phosphate monobasic 0.55 mg, and albumin human 1 mg. (2)

For intravenous infusion, reconstitute the appropriate-size vial contents with the diluent provided. Swirl gently to dissolve the powder; do not shake. Withdraw the appropriate dose and add it to 100 ml of sodium chloride 0.9%, ensuring that the final concentration is not less than 10 million I.U./100 ml. (2)

Interferon alfa-2b is also available for intramuscular or subcutaneous use as solutions in vials of 3 million I.U./0.5 ml, 5 million I.U./0.5 ml, and 10 million I.U./1 ml. Multidose vials are available labeled as 18 million I.U., which contain 22.8 million I.U./3.8 ml (6 million I.U./ml), and 25 million I.U., which contain 32 million I.U./3.2 ml (10 million I.U./ml). Multidose injection "pens" are also available containing 3, 5, and 10 million I.U. per 0.2 ml injection with a total of 1.5 ml per pen for subcutaneous injection. (2)

In addition to intramuscular and subcutaneous use, the 5-, 10-, and 25-million I.U. vials are also for intralesional use. However, the solution products are not recommended for intravenous administration. Vial size to be used and appropriate concentration are dependent on the intended use of the product. Each milliliter of solution also contains sodium chloride 7.5 mg, sodium phosphate dibasic 1.8 mg, sodium phosphate monobasic 1.3 mg, edetate disodium 0.1 mg, polysorbate 80 0.1 mg, and meta-cresol 1.5 mg. (2)

Specific Activity— Approximately 2×10^8 I.U./mg of protein. (2)

Table 1. Reconstitution of Interferon Alfa-2b Powder for Injection Vials (2)

Vial Size (million I.U.)	Diluent Volume (ml)	Concentration (I.U./ml)
3	1	3
5	1	5
10	2	5
10	1	10 (for intralesional use only)
18	1	18
25	5	5
50	1	50 (for malignant melanoma and AIDS-related Kaposi's sarcoma only)

pH— The reconstituted powder for injection has a pH in the range of 6.9 to 7.5. (4)

Tonicity— Reconstitution of the 10-million I.U. vial with 1 ml of water for injection results in an isotonic solution. (1369)

Trade Name(s)— Intron A.

Administration — The administration of interferon alfa-2b is dependent on the intended use and specific dosage form. The dry powder products, reconstituted as directed, may be administered by intramuscular and subcutaneous injection or intravenous infusion. The contents of the 10-million I.U. vial, reconstituted as directed, may also be given intralesionally. For intravenous infusions, interferon alfa-2b may be diluted further to a concentration of not less than 10 million I.U./100 ml of sodium chloride 0.9% for intravenous infusion over 20 minutes. (2)

The solution products are administered by intramuscular or subcutaneous injection. The 5-million I.U. and 10-million I.U. vials and the 25-million I.U. multidose vials may also be used for intralesional injection. The solution products are not for use in malignant melanoma or AIDS-related Kaposi's sarcoma. (2)

Stability — Interferon alfa-2b dry powder in vials is a white to cream color. (2; 4) It is not photosensitive. (1369) The reconstituted solution is clear and colorless to light yellow. Intact vials should be stored under refrigeration at 2 to 8 °C but are stable up to seven days at 45 °C (4) or 28 days at room temperature. (1369) The reconstituted solution should be stored under refrigeration. In concentrations between 3 and 50 million I.U./ml, reconstituted solutions are stable for up to one month under refrigeration and up to two days at ambient temperatures up to 40 °C. (2)

Interferon alfa-2b solution in vials is colorless. Intact vials of solution should be stored under refrigeration at 2 to 8 °C. The solution products are stable for up to seven days at 35 °C and up to 14 days at 30 °C. Interferon alfa-2b in multidose pens is stable for up to two days at 30 °C. (2)

Interferon alfa-2b (Schering) containing albumin human in the formulation reconstituted with the accompanying diluent and diluted further to 2 million I.U./ml with sterile water for injection was stored at 4 °C for 21 days in polypropylene centrifuge tubes. Biological activity was retained throughout the study period determined by a cell proliferation inhibition bioassay. (2022)

In another study, the retention of bioactivity by albumin-free interferon alfa-2b 6 million units/ml stability was compared to samples of that product to which albumin human 1 mg/ml was added and also to the reconstituted product containing albumin human in the formulation. The solutions were packaged as 0.5 ml in polypropylene syringes and stored at 4 °C for 42 days. In addition, the albumin-free product was diluted to 2 million units/ml with sterile water for injection and stored in a 60-ml polypropylene syringe under the same conditions. No substantial loss of biological activity was found in any of the samples tested by a cell proliferation inhibition bioassay and by a separate interferon-mediated gene induction bioassay. (2188)

pH Effects— Reconstituted interferon alfa-2b is stable over a pH range of 6.5 to 8 (4), with greatest stability between pH 6.9 and 7.5. (1369)

Freezing Solutions— Reconstituted interferon alfa-2b 10 million I.U./ml packaged in plastic syringes is stated to be stable for up to four weeks when frozen at −10 °C or colder. (4) Solutions frozen at

−20 °C are stated to be stable for 56 days including four freeze-thaw cycles. Frozen solutions stored at −80 °C are stable for one year. (1369)

Sorption—Like other interferons, interferon alfa-2b can bind to surfaces, including glass and plastics. Consequently, albumin human is incorporated into the formulation to minimize adsorption and permit the use of glass or plastic syringes for administration without substantial loss. (4)

Compatibility Information

Infusion Solutions— Sodium chloride 0.9% is recommended for preparation of intravenous infusion admixtures. (2)

Interferon alfa-2b is stated to be compatible with sodium chloride 0.9%, Ringer's injection, and Ringer's injection, lactated. It is stated to be incompatible with dextrose solutions. (1369)

IODIPAMIDE MEGLUMINE
AHFS 36:68

Products— Iodipamide meglumine is available in 20-ml vials containing an aqueous solution composed of 52% iodipamide meglumine (5.2 g bound iodine/20 ml) with 0.32% sodium citrate buffer and 0.04% edetate disodium. (4; 29)

pH—From 6.5 to 7.7. (4)

Sodium Content—The 52% solution contains approximately 18.2 mg of sodium per 20 ml. (1-7/00)

Trade Name(s)—Cholografin Meglumine.

Administration— Iodipamide meglumine is administered slowly intravenously only. After warming to body temperature, the 52% injection is injected over 10 minutes. (1-7/00; 4)

Stability— The solutions may vary from colorless to pale yellow or light amber. Darker solutions should not be used. Crystallization may occur in the 52% solution. To redissolve it, place the vial in hot water and shake gently for several minutes. If cloudiness does not disappear, the solution should not be used. (1-7/00; 4)

Plastic syringes have been stated to be unsuitable for accommodating radiopaque solutions for any length of time. The plastic is attacked, and the plunger tends to freeze on prolonged storage. (40) However, when iodipamide meglumine (Squibb) 52% was stored in polystyrene syringes (Pharmaseal) at 25 and 37 °C, no apparent changes were noted visually or spectrophotometrically over five days. (530)

Iodipamide meglumine solutions should be protected from light and excessive heat. (1-7/00)

Compatibility Information

Additive Compatibility

Iodipamide meglumine

Drug	*Mfr*	*Conc/L*	*Mfr*	*Conc/L*	*Test Soln*	*Remarks*	*Ref*	*C/I*
Diphenhydramine HCl	PD	20 to 200 mg	SQ	[a]	NS	Dense putty-like white precipitate forms immediately	309	I

[a]*Amount and percent unspecified.*

Drugs in Syringe Compatibility

Iodipamide meglumine 52%

Drug (in syringe)	*Mfr*	*Amt*	*Mfr*	*Amt*	*Remarks*	*Ref*	*C/I*
Chlorpheniramine maleate	SC	1 ml[a]	SQ	40 to 5 ml	Forms a precipitate initially but clears within 1 hr and remains clear for 48 hr	530	I
	SC	1 ml[a]	SQ	2 and 1 ml	Forms a precipitate initially but clears within 1 hr. Precipitate reforms within 48 hr	530	I
Dimenhydrinate	SE	50 mg/ 1 ml	SQ	40 ml	Forms a precipitate initially but clears within 1 hr and remains clear for 48 hr	530	I
	SE	50 mg/ 1 ml	SQ	20 to 1 ml	Forms a precipitate initially but clears within 1 hr. Precipitate reforms on standing	530	I

Drugs in Syringe Compatibility (Cont.)

Iodipamide meglumine 52%

Drug (in syringe)	*Mfr*	*Amt*	*Mfr*	*Amt*	*Remarks*	*Ref*	*C/I*
Diphenhydramine HCl	PD	5 mg/ 0.1 ml to 50 mg/ 1 ml	SQ	[b]	Dense putty-like white precipitate forms immediately	309	I
	PD	1 ml[a]	SQ	40 to 1 ml	Forms a precipitate initially but clears within 1 hr and remains clear for 48 hr	530	I
Hyaluronidase	WY	150 units/ 1 ml	SQ	40 to 2 ml	Physically compatible for 48 hr	530	C
	WY	150 units/ 1 ml	SQ	1 ml	Physically compatible for at least 1 hr but a precipitate forms within 48 hr	530	I
Promethazine HCl	WY	1 ml[a]	SQ	40 and 20 ml	Forms a precipitate initially but clears within 1 hr and remains clear for 48 hr	530	I
	WY	1 ml[a]	SQ	10 to 1 ml	Immediate precipitation	530	I

[a]*Concentration unspecified.*
[b]*Amount and concentration unspecified.*

Additional Compatibility Information

Antihistamines — Antihistamines have been found to be incompatible with iodipamide meglumine. (4) (See Drugs in Syringe Compatibility table above.) Consequently, the manufacturer recommends that antihistamines be administered separately and not mixed with iodipamide meglumine. (1-7/00)

Iodipamide meglumine (Squibb) was found to be physically incompatible with chlorpheniramine maleate (Schering), diphenhydramine HCl (Parke-Davis), and promethazine HCl (Wyeth). (40)

Gentamicin — Administration of iodipamide meglumine (Squibb) via a Y-injection site of an administration set through which gentamicin sulfate had been previously administered resulted in the immediate formation of a white precipitate downstream to the Y-site. (324)

IOHEXOL
AHFS 36:68

Products — Iohexol is available in concentrations ranging from 30.2% (140 mg/ml organically bound iodine) to 75.5% (350 mg/ml organically bound iodine) in numerous vial and bottle sizes from 10 to 250 ml; not all concentrations are available in all sizes. Also present in each milliliter are tromethamine 1.21 mg, edetate calcium disodium 0.1 mg, and hydrochloric acid or sodium hydroxide to adjust the pH. (1-4/98; 154) Table 1 presents the characteristics of iohexol products.

pH — From 6.8 to 7.7. (1-4/98)

Trade Name(s) — Omnipaque.

Administration — Iohexol at appropriate concentrations may be administered intravenously, intra-arterially, intrathecally (except for Omnipaque 350) slowly over one to two minutes, intra-articularly, or directly into selected areas for visualization. Solutions should be warmed to body temperature prior to administration. (1-4/98)

Table 1. Iohexol Product Characteristics (1-4/98; 154)

Iohexol Concentration (%)	Iodine Concentration (mg/ml)	Osmolality (mOsm/kg)	Specific Gravity (37 °C)
30.2	140	322	1.164
38.8	180	408	1.209
45.3	210	460	1.244
51.8	240	520	1.280
64.7	300	672	1.349
75.5	350	844	1.406

Stability — Iohexol is colorless to pale yellow. Intact vials should be stored at controlled room temperature and protected from direct exposure to sunlight and freezing. The product should not be used if particulate matter is present. If a plastic syringe is to be used, iohexol should be injected immediately after being drawn into it. Do not remove the iohexol containers from the moisture- and light-protective foil overwrap until immediately before use. (1-4/98)

Compatibility Information

Drugs in Syringe Compatibility

Iohexol

Drug (in syringe)	*Mfr*	*Amt*	*Mfr*	*Amt*	*Remarks*	*Ref*	*C/I*
Ampicillin sodium	BR	30 mg/ 1 ml	WI	64.7%, 5 ml	Physically compatible for at least 2 hr	1438	C
Bupivacaine HCl	AST	0.25%, 4 ml		1 ml[a]	Visually compatible with no bupivacaine loss by HPLC in 24 hr at room temperature. Iohexol not tested	1611	C
	AST	0.125%[b], 4 ml		1 ml[a]	Visually compatible with no bupivacaine loss by HPLC in 24 hr at room temperature. Iohexol not tested	1611	C
Chloramphenicol sodium succinate	PD	33 mg/ 1 ml	WI	64.7%, 5 ml	Physically compatible for at least 2 hr	1438	C
Cimetidine HCl	SKF	150 mg/ 1 ml	WI	64.7%, 5 ml	Physically compatible for at least 2 hr	1438	C
Diphenhydramine HCl	PD	12.5 mg/ 0.25 ml	WI	64.7%, 5 ml	Physically compatible for at least 2 hr	1438	C
Epinephrine HCl	PD	1 mg/ 1 ml	WI	64.7%, 5 ml	Physically compatible for at least 2 hr	1438	C
Gentamicin sulfate	SC	0.8 mg/ 1 ml	WI	64.7%, 5 ml	Physically compatible for at least 2 hr	1438	C
Heparin sodium	OR	5000 units/ 0.5 ml	WI	64.7%, 5 ml	Physically compatible for at least 2 hr	1438	C
Hydrocortisone sodium succinate	UP	10 mg/ 1 ml	WI	64.7%, 5 ml	Physically compatible for at least 2 hr	1438	C
Methylprednisolone sodium succinate	UP	10 mg/ 1 ml	WI	64.7%, 5 ml	Physically compatible for at least 2 hr	1438	C
Papaverine HCl	LI	30 mg/ 1 ml	WI	64.7%, 5 ml	Physically compatible for at least 2 hr	1438	C
Protamine sulfate	LI	10 mg/ 1 ml	WI	64.7%, 5 ml	Physically compatible for at least 2 hr	1438	C

[a] *Concentration unspecified.*
[b] *Diluted 1:1 in sodium chloride 0.9%.*

Additional Compatibility Information

Other Drugs — The manufacturer recommends not mixing iohexol products with any other pharmaceutical. (1-4/98)

IOPAMIDOL
AHFS 36:68

Products — Iopamidol products are available in concentrations ranging from 41% (200 mg/ml organically bound iodine) to 76% (370 mg/ml organically bound iodine) in numerous vial and bottle sizes from 20 to 200 ml; not all concentrations are available in all sizes. Also present in each milliliter are tromethamine 1 mg, edetate calcium disodium, with hydrochloric acid and/or sodium hydroxide to adjust the pH. (1-8/99) Table 1 presents the characteristics of iopamidol products.

pH — From 6.5 to 7.5. (1-8/99)

Trade Name(s) — Isovue.

Administration — Iopamidol may be administered intravenously or intra-arterially. Solutions should be warmed to body temperature prior to administration. (1-8/99)

Table 1. Iopamidol Product Characteristics (1-8/99)

Iopamidol Concentration (%)	Iodine Concentration (mg/ml)	Osmolality (mOsm/kg)	Specific Gravity (37 °C)
41	200	413	1.227
51	250	524	1.281
61	300	616	1.339
76	370	796	1.405

Stability — Iopamidol injection is colorless to pale yellow. Intact vials should be stored at controlled room temperature and protected from light. If crystals form, they should be dissolved by warming of the vial in hot (60 to 100 °C) water for about five minutes and gentle shaking. The vials should cool to body temperature before use. If crystals fail to dissolve, the vials should be discarded. (1-8/99)

Compatibility Information

Drugs in Syringe Compatibility

Iopamidol

Drug (in syringe)	*Mfr*	*Amt*	*Mfr*	*Amt*	*Remarks*	*Ref*	*C/I*
Ampicillin sodium	BR	30 mg/ 1 ml	SQ	61%, 5 ml	Physically compatible for at least 2 hr	1438	C
Chloramphenicol sodium succinate	PD	33 mg/ 1 ml	SQ	61%, 5 ml	Physically compatible for at least 2 hr	1438	C
Cimetidine HCl	SKF	150 mg/ 1 ml	SQ	61%, 5 ml	Physically compatible for at least 2 hr	1438	C
Diphenhydramine HCl	PD	12.5 mg/ 0.25 ml	SQ	61%, 5 ml	Physically compatible for at least 2 hr	1438	C
Epinephrine HCl	PD	1 mg/ 1 ml	SQ	61%, 5 ml	Physically compatible for at least 2 hr	1438	C
Gentamicin sulfate	SC	0.8 mg/ 1 ml	SQ	61%, 5 ml	Physically compatible for at least 2 hr	1438	C
Heparin sodium	OR	5000 units/ 0.5 ml	SQ	61%, 5 ml	Physically compatible for at least 2 hr	1438	C
Hydrocortisone sodium succinate	UP	10 mg/ 1 ml	SQ	61%, 5 ml	Physically compatible for at least 2 hr	1438	C
Methylprednisolone sodium succinate	UP	10 mg/ 1 ml	SQ	61%, 5 ml	Physically compatible for at least 2 hr	1438	C
Papaverine HCl	LI	30 mg/ 1 ml	SQ	61%, 5 ml	Physically compatible for at least 2 hr	1438	C
Protamine sulfate	LI	10 mg/ 1 ml	SQ	61%, 5 ml	Physically compatible for at least 2 hr	1438	C

Additional Compatibility Information

Other Drugs — The manufacturer recommends not mixing iopamidol products with any other pharmaceutical. (1-8/99)

IOTHALAMATE MEGLUMINE
AHFS 36:68

Products — Iothalamate meglumine is available in concentrations ranging from 17.2 to 60%. It is also available in combination with other radiopaque contrast agents. The formulations may also contain edetate and phosphate buffers. Some examples of single-agent products are listed in Table 1. (4; 154)

pH — From 6.5 to 7.7. (4)

Osmolarity — The injections have osmolarities from 750 to 1500 mOsm/L. (4)

Table 1. Some Representative Iothalamate Meglumine Products

Iothalamate Meglumine Content (%)	Bound Iodine (mg/ml)	Representative Trade Names
Urogenital solutions (not for intravascular use)		
17.2	81	Cysto-Conray II
43	202	Cysto-Conray
Parenteral solutions		
30	141	Conray 30
43	202	Conray 43
60	282	Conray

Trade Name(s) — See Table 1.

Administration — Iothalamate meglumine solutions may be administered intravenously, intra-arterially, by injection into pancreatic and biliary ducts, and by bladder, ureter, or renal pelvis instillation. Solutions should be warmed to body temperature before administration. (4)

Stability — Iothalamate meglumine solutions are colorless to pale yellow. They should be stored below 30 °C. Crystallization does not occur at room temperature, but exposure to cold temperatures may result in crystallization. Should crystallization occur, the solution should be brought to room temperature, with shaking of the container if necessary to redissolve the crystals. The speed of dissolution may be increased by heating the vials in warm air. (1-1/98; 4)

pH Effects — Iothalamate meglumine is sensitive to low pH values. At pH values reported as about 2.4 to 2.7 (479) and below 3 (4), turbidity or frank precipitation may appear in the 60% product. (479)

Light Effects — Iothalamate meglumine is also sensitive to light and should be protected from strong daylight and direct exposure to sunlight. (4)

Syringes — Iothalamate meglumine 60% (Conray) was stored in polystyrene syringes (Pharmaseal) at 25 and 37 °C. No apparent changes were noted visually or spectrophotometrically over five days. (530)

Compatibility Information

Drugs in Syringe Compatibility

Iothalamate meglumine 60%

Drug (in syringe)	*Mfr*	*Amt*	*Mfr*	*Amt*	*Remarks*	*Ref*	*C/I*
Ampicillin sodium	BR	30 mg/ 1 ml	MA	60%, 5 ml	Physically compatible for at least 2 hr	1438	C
Chloramphenicol sodium succinate	PD	33 mg/ 1 ml	MA	60%, 5 ml	Physically compatible for at least 2 hr	1438	C
Chlorpheniramine maleate	SC	1 ml[a]	MA	40 to 1 ml	Physically compatible for 48 hr	530	C
Cimetidine HCl	SKF	150 mg/ 1 ml	MA	60%, 5 ml	Physically compatible for at least 2 hr	1438	C
Dimenhydrinate	SE	50 mg/ 1 ml	MA	40 to 1 ml	Physically compatible for 48 hr	530	C
Diphenhydramine HCl	PD	1 ml[a]	MA	40 to 1 ml	Physically compatible for 48 hr	530	C
	PD	50 mg/ 1 ml	MA	5 ml[a]	No precipitate observed	309	C
	PD	12.5 mg/ 0.25 ml	MA	60%, 5 ml	Physically compatible for at least 2 hr	1438	C
Epinephrine HCl	PD	1 mg/ 1 ml	MA	60%, 5 ml	Physically compatible for at least 2 hr	1438	C
Gentamicin sulfate	SC	0.8 mg/ 1 ml	MA	60%, 5 ml	Physically compatible for at least 2 hr	1438	C

Drugs in Syringe Compatibility (Cont.)

Iothalamate meglumine 60%

Drug (in syringe)	*Mfr*	*Amt*	*Mfr*	*Amt*	*Remarks*	*Ref*	*C/I*
Heparin sodium	OR	5000 units/ 0.5 ml	MA	60%, 5 ml	Physically compatible for at least 2 hr	1438	C
Hyaluronidase	WY	150 units/ 1 ml	MA	40 to 1 ml	Physically compatible for 48 hr	530	C
Hydrocortisone sodium succinate	UP	10 mg/ 1 ml	MA	60%, 5 ml	Physically compatible for at least 2 hr	1438	C
Methylprednisolone sodium succinate	UP	10 mg/ 1 ml	MA	60%, 5 ml	Physically compatible for at least 2 hr	1438	C
Papaverine HCl	LI	30 mg/ 1 ml	MA	60%, 5 ml	Physically compatible for at least 2 hr	1438	C
Promethazine HCl	WY	1 ml[a]	MA	40 to 1 ml	Immediate precipitation	530	I
Protamine sulfate	LI	10 mg/ 1 ml	MA	60%, 5 ml	Physically compatible for at least 2 hr	1438	C

[a]*Concentration unspecified.*

IOTHALAMATE SODIUM
AHFS 36:68

Products — Iothalamate sodium is available at a concentration of 66.8%, providing 400 mg/ml of organically bound iodine. The formulation also contains edetate calcium disodium and sodium biphosphate buffer. (4; 154)

pH — From 6.5 to 7.7. (4)

Osmolarity — The 66.8% injection has an osmolarity of 1700 mOsm/L. (4)

Sodium Content — Iothalamate sodium contains approximately 1.57 mEq of sodium per gram of drug. (4)

Trade Name(s) — Conray-400.

Administration — Iothalamate sodium solutions may be administered intravenously, intra-arterially, or by injection through a catheter into the chambers of the heart or associated large blood vessels. Solutions should be warmed to body temperature before administration. (4)

Stability — Iothalamate sodium solutions are colorless to pale yellow. Solutions should be protected from strong daylight and direct exposure to the sun and should be stored below 30 °C. Crystallization does not occur at room temperature, but exposure to cold temperatures may result in it. Should crystallization occur, the solution should be warmed to room temperature, with shaking of the container if necessary to redissolve the crystals. (1-1/98; 4) The speed of crystal dissolution may be increased by heating with circulating warm air. Submersion of prefilled syringes in water is not recommended. The prefilled plastic syringes should not be re-autoclaved because of possible damage. (1-1/98)

Syringes — Iothalamate sodium 80% (Angio-Conray) was stored in polystyrene syringes (Pharmaseal) at 25 and 37 °C. No apparent changes were noted visually or spectrophotometrically over five days. (550)

Compatibility Information

Drugs in Syringe Compatibility

Iothalamate sodium

Drug (in syringe)	*Mfr*	*Amt*	*Mfr*	*Amt*	*Remarks*	*Ref*	*C/I*
Chlorpheniramine maleate	SC	1 ml[b]	MA	80%[a], 40 to 1 ml	Physically compatible for 48 hr	530	C

Drugs in Syringe Compatibility (Cont.)

Iothalamate sodium

Drug (in syringe)	*Mfr*	*Amt*	*Mfr*	*Amt*	*Remarks*	*Ref*	*C/I*
Dimenhydrinate	SE	50 mg/ 1 ml	MA	80%[a], 40 to 1 ml	Physically compatible for 48 hr	530	C
Diphenhydramine HCl	PD	1 ml[b]	MA	80%[a], 40 to 1 ml	Physically compatible for 48 hr	530	C
Hyaluronidase	WY	150 units/ 1 ml	MA	80%[a], 40 to 1 ml	Physically compatible for 48 hr	530	C
Papaverine HCl	LI	30 mg/ 1 ml	MA	60%, 3 ml	Physically compatible	1437	C
Promethazine HCl	WY	1 ml[b]	MA	80%[a], 40 to 1 ml	Immediate precipitation	530	I

[a]*This concentration is no longer available.*
[b]*Concentration unspecified.*

IOXAGLATE MEGLUMINE AND IOXAGLATE SODIUM AHFS 36:68

Products — Ioxaglate meglumine 39.3% and ioxaglate sodium 19.6% (Mallinckrodt) is available in containers ranging in size from 20 to 200 ml. Each milliliter contains ioxaglate meglumine 393 mg, ioxaglate sodium 196 mg, and edetate calcium disodium 0.1 mg as a stabilizer. The product provides 32% organically bound iodine. (1-1/98)

pH—From 6 to 7.6. (1-1/98)

Osmolality—The osmolality of the product is approximately 600 mOsm/kg. (1-1/98)

Sodium Content—Each milliliter provides 0.15 mEq (3.48 mg) of sodium. (1-1/98)

Trade Name(s)—Hexabrix.

Administration — The product may be administered intravenously, intra-arterially, or intra-articularly. It also may be injected or instilled directly into selected areas to be visualized. The solutions should be warmed to body temperature before administration. (1-1/98)

Stability — The product should be stored below 30 °C and protected from freezing and direct exposure to sun or strong daylight. The solution is colorless to pale yellow. Crystallization does not occur at normal room temperatures. If the product is frozen or crystallization occurs, bring it to room temperature and shake vigorously to dissolve all crystals. Warming with circulating warm air is recommended to speed dissolution. Submersion of syringes in water is not recommended. (1-1/98)

Compatibility Information

Drugs in Syringe Compatibility

Ioxaglate meglumine 39.3% + Ioxaglate sodium 19.6%

Drug (in syringe)	*Mfr*	*Amt*	*Mfr*	*Amt*	*Remarks*	*Ref*	*C/I*
Ampicillin sodium	BR	30 mg/ 1 ml	MA	5 ml	Physically compatible for at least 2 hr	1438	C
Chloramphenicol sodium succinate	PD	33 mg/ 1 ml	MA	5 ml	Physically compatible for at least 2 hr	1438	C
Cimetidine HCl	SKF	150 mg/ 1 ml	MA	5 ml	Precipitate forms immediately and persists for at least 2 hr	1438	I
Diphenhydramine HCl	PD	12.5 mg/ 0.25 ml	MA	5 ml	Precipitate forms immediately and persists for at least 2 hr	1438	I

Drugs in Syringe Compatibility (Cont.)

			Ioxaglate meglumine 39.3% + Ioxaglate sodium 19.6%				
Drug (in syringe)	*Mfr*	*Amt*	*Mfr*	*Amt*	*Remarks*	*Ref*	*C/I*
Epinephrine HCl	PD	1 mg/ 1 ml	MA	5 ml	Physically compatible for at least 2 hr	1438	C
Gentamicin sulfate	SC	0.8 mg/ 1 ml	MA	5 ml	Transient precipitate clears within 5 min	1438	?
Heparin sodium	OR	5000 units/ 0.5 ml	MA	5 ml	Physically compatible for at least 2 hr	1438	C
Hydrocortisone sodium succinate	UP	10 mg/ 1 ml	MA	5 ml	Physically compatible for at least 2 hr	1438	C
Methylprednisolone sodium succinate	UP	10 mg/ 1 ml	MA	5 ml	Physically compatible for at least 2 hr	1438	C
Papaverine HCl	ME	32 mg/ 1 ml	MA	5 ml	Precipitate forms immediately and persists for at least 2 hr	1438	I
	LI	30 mg/ 1 ml	MA	3 and 5 ml	White amorphous precipitate forms immediately and persists for 24 hr. If shaken, it dissolves in 20 to 30 min	1437	I
	LI	30 mg/2 to 6 ml[a]	MA	5 ml	Precipitate forms	1437	I
	LI	30 mg/11 and 16 ml[a]	MA	5 ml	Precipitate forms	1437	I
	LI	30 mg/ 21 ml[a]	MA	5 ml	Physically compatible	1437	C
	LI	30 mg/ 11 ml[a]	MA	15 and 30 ml	Physically compatible	1437	C
	LI	60 mg/12 and 17 ml[a]	MA	5 ml	Precipitate forms	1437	I
	LI	60 mg/ 22 ml[a]	MA	5 ml	Precipitate forms	1437	I
Protamine sulfate	LI	10 mg/ 1 ml	MA	5 ml	Precipitate forms immediately and persists for at least 2 hr	1438	I

[a]*Diluted in sodium chloride 0.9%.*

IRINOTECAN HCL
AHFS 10:00

Products — Irinotecan HCl is available in 2- and 5-ml single-use vials containing 40 and 100 mg of drug, respectively, on the basis of the trihydrate. Each milliliter of solution contains irinotecan HCl trihydrate 20 mg, sorbitol 45 mg, lactic acid 0.9 mg, and hydrochloric acid or sodium hydroxide to adjust the pH. The product must be diluted prior to use. (2)

pH — From 3 to 3.8. (2)

Trade Name(s) — Camptosar.

Administration — Irinotecan HCl is administered by intravenous infusion over 90 minutes after dilution to a final concentration in the range of 0.12 to 2.8 mg/ml in dextrose 5% in water or sodium chloride 0.9%. In most clinical trials, the doses were given in 500 ml of dextrose 5% in water. (2)

Stability — Irinotecan HCl injection is supplied as a clear pale yellow solution. Intact vials should be stored at controlled room temperature and protected from light. Freezing of irinotecan HCl solutions may result in precipitation and should be avoided. (2)

pH Effects—Irinotecan in solution at acidic pH is stable, but neutral and alkaline solutions are problematic. (1881; 2274) Increasing solution pH to more than pH 6.5 has resulted in 10% loss in as little as three hours. (1881)

Light Effects—Irinotecan HCl is subject to photodegradation, including the formation of a precipitate. (1997; 1998; 2137) Exposure to ultraviolet light for three days produced a darkening in the solution color and the formation of a yellow precipitate composed of several decomposition products. (1997) Photodegradation of irinotecan HCl occurs under any pH condition but is accelerated in neutral and alkaline solutions compared with acidic solutions. At pH 10, photodegradation is very rapid; at pH 3 it is much slower. At pH 7, irinotecan 0.34 mg/ml lost 32% in six hours exposed to a daylight lamp and 19% exposed to a white fluorescent light. In infusion solutions having neutral pH, irinotecan HCl exposed to lighting (such as that of a medical facility) may have rapid decomposition. Protection from light exposure has been recommended to maintain product quality during administration. (1998) The structural changes exhibited by the decomposition products would indicate that they are unlikely to be active antineoplastic compounds. (2137)

Compatibility Information

Y-Site Injection Compatibility (1:1 Mixture)

			Irinotecan				
Drug	*Mfr*	*Conc*	*Mfr*	*Conc*	*Remarks*	*Ref*	*C/I*
Gemcitabine HCl	LI	10 mg/ml[b]	PHU	5 mg/ml[b]	Subvisual haze with green discoloration forms immediately	2226	I

[b]*Tested in sodium chloride 0.9%.*

Additional Compatibility Information

Infusion Solutions — Dextrose 5% in water and sodium chloride 0.9% are recommended for administration of irinotecan HCl. Admixtures of the drug in dextrose 5% in water and sodium chloride 0.9% at concentrations between 0.12 and 2.8 mg/ml are stated to be physically and chemically stable for up to 24 hours at room temperatures around 25 °C exposed to ambient fluorescent light. Under refrigeration and protected from light, admixtures in dextrose 5% in water are stable for 48 hours. However, refrigerated storage of irinotecan HCl in sodium chloride 0.9% is not recommended because of occasional visible precipitation. The manufacturer recommends use of the drug admixtures within six hours at room temperature and 24 hours under refrigeration because of concern for possible microbiological contamination during preparation. (2)

Methylprednisolone — Adding methylprednisolone sodium succinate to irinotecan was found to result in an admixture having a pH greater than 6.5. Approximately 10% irinotecan loss occurs within three hours at this pH. (1881)

IRON DEXTRAN
AHFS 20:04.04

Products — Iron dextran is available in 1- and 2-ml vials for intravenous or intramuscular use. It is composed of a dark brown, slightly viscous liquid complex of ferric hydroxide and dextran in sodium chloride 0.9%, providing 50 mg of elemental iron per milliliter. (2; 29)

pH—From 5.2 to 6.5. (2)

Osmolality—Iron dextran injection has an osmolality exceeding 2000 mOsm/kg. (1689)

Trade Name(s)—INFeD.

Administration — Iron dextran may be administered by slow intravenous injection at a rate of no more than 1 ml/min or by deep intramuscular injection into the upper outer quadrant of the buttock. Subsequent injections should be made into alternate buttocks. Staining of the skin can be minimized by using a separate needle to withdraw the drug from the container and by displacing the skin laterally prior to injection. (2; 4) Iron dextran also has been administered by intravenous infusion over one to six hours after dilution in sodium chloride 0.9%. (4) In adults, a test dose of 25 mg should be given over five minutes (4), with the remainder given after at least one hour has elapsed if no hypersensitivity reaction occurs. (2; 4)

Stability — The commercial injection should be stored at controlled room temperature. (2; 4) High temperatures, such as during autoclaving, precipitate the iron dextran complex. (692)

A stable dilute solution of iron dextran for use in parenteral nutrition has been prepared. A 0.5-mg/ml diluted solution was prepared by diluting 5 ml of iron dextran to 200 ml with sterile water for injection, adding benzyl alcohol 4.5 ml, and adding more sterile water for injection to a final volume of 500 ml. The diluted solution was sterilized by filtration through a 0.22-µm filter. The dilution was stable for at least three months when stored under refrigeration. (692)

Filtration — Iron dextran is reported to be adsorbed to sterilizing membrane filters composed of cellulose nitrate and acetate combined (such as the Millex G.S. and Gelman Acrodisc). The initial concern resulted from a reddish brown stain on the filters. In subsequent studies, an iron dextran solution containing 5 μg/ml in water was estimated to lose 93% of the iron from the first milliliter passed through the filter. As more solution was passed through the filter, a decreasing proportion of the iron was adsorbed, indicating that the filter was approaching saturation. The extent of iron adsorption increased in the presence of electrolytes and trace elements. The authors concluded that adsorption can be significant, especially when small amounts of iron dextran are involved. (918)

Compatibility Information

Solution Compatibility

Iron dextran

Solution	*Mfr*	*Mfr*	*Conc/L*	*Remarks*	*Ref*	*C/I*
TNA #122[a]		FI	50 mg	Lipid oiling out in 18 to 19 hr with formation of yellow-brown layer on admixture surface	1383	I
TNA #159 to #166[a]		FI	2 mg	Physically compatible with no change visually, microscopically, or in particle size distribution in 48 hr at 4 and 25 °C	1648	C
TPN #31 to #33[a]		FI	100 mg	Physically compatible with minimal changes to iron dextran and amino acids for 18 hr at room temperature	692	C
TPN #207 and #208[a]		SCN	10 mg	Rust-colored precipitate forms in 12 hr at 19 °C protected from sunlight	2103	I
TPN #209[a]		SCN	10 mg	Rust-colored precipitate forms in 18 to 24 hr at 19 °C protected from sunlight	2103	I
TPN #210[a]		SCN	10 mg	Visually compatible for 48 hr at 19 °C protected from sunlight. Trace iron precipitation found by filtration and analysis after 48 hr	2103	?
TPN #211[a]		SCN	10 mg	Visually compatible for 48 hr at 19 °C protected from sunlight. No iron precipitation found by filtration and analysis after 48 hr	2103	C

[a]*Refer to Appendix I for the composition of parenteral nutrition solutions. TNA indicates a 3-in-1 admixture, and TPN indicates a 2-in-1 admixture.*

Additive Compatibility

Iron dextran

Drug	*Mfr*	*Conc/L*	*Mfr*	*Conc/L*	*Test Soln*	*Remarks*	*Ref*	*C/I*
Netilmicin sulfate	SC	3 g	MRN	8 ml	D5S	Physically compatible and netilmicin chemically stable for 7 days at 4 and 25 °C. Iron dextran not tested	558	C

Additional Compatibility Information

Infusion Solutions — Sodium chloride 0.9% has been suggested as a diluent for infusion of iron dextran. (75; 76; 429; 919–921) Dilution in dextrose 5% in water results in a greater incidence of pain and phlebitis. (75)

Parenteral Nutrition Solutions — The manufacturer recommends not adding iron dextran injection to parenteral nutrition solutions. (2)

Mayhew and Quick evaluated the effect of amino acid concentration on precipitation of iron from iron dextran (INFeD, Schein) 10 mg/L in neonatal parenteral nutrition mixtures (TPN #207 to #211) formulated with TrophAmine (McGaw). Rust-colored precipitate formed in the neonatal formulations having amino acid concentrations of 1.5% or less. The precipitate formed more rapidly and in greater amounts at lower amino acid concentrations. Parenteral nutrition admixtures with amino acid concentrations of 2 and 2.5% were visually compatible for 48 hr at 19 °C, but trace precipitation was found on filtration and analysis of the 2% admixture. Extrapolation of the information to other iron dextran products may not be appropriate because of possible product differences. (2103)

Iron dextran (Fisons) at a low concentration of 2 mg/L was physically compatible with several fat-containing parenteral nutrition solutions (TNA #159 to #166, Appendix I) for 48 hours at 4 and 25 °C. The order of mixing and deliberate agitation had no effect on physical compatibility and particle size distribution. (1648) At a higher iron dextran concentration of 50 mg/L, the emulsion cracked and lipid oiling out was found. (1383) See Solution Compatibility above.

The influence of six factors on the stability of fat emulsion in 45 different 3-in-1 parenteral nutrition mixtures was evaluated. The factors were amino acid concentration (2.5 to 7%); dextrose (5 to 20%); fat emulsion, intravenous (2 to 5%); monovalent cations (0 to 150 mEq/L); divalent cations (4 to 20 mEq/L); and trivalent cations from iron dextran (0 to 10 mg elemental iron/L). Although many formulations were unstable, visual examination could identify instability in only 65% of the samples. Electronic evaluation of particle size identified the remaining unstable mixtures. Furthermore, only the concentration of trivalent ferric ions significantly and consistently affected the emulsion stability during the 30-hour test period. Of the parenteral nutrition mixtures containing iron dextran, 16% were unstable, exhibiting emulsion cracking. The authors suggested that iron dextran should not be incorporated into 3-in-1 mixtures. (1814)

Other Drugs — Cyanocobalamin is stated to be stable in the presence of iron dextran. (52) The manufacturer recommends not mixing iron dextran injection with other medications. (2)

ISOPROTERENOL HCL (ISOPRENALINE HCL) AHFS 12:12

Products — Isoproterenol HCl is available as a 1:50,000 solution in 10-ml (0.2 mg) unit-of-use syringes. It is also available as a 1:5000 concentrated solution in 5-ml (1 mg) and 10-ml (2 mg) Universal Additive Syringes intended for dilution in an intravenous infusion solution. (1-10/98) The drug is also available in a concentration of 0.2 mg/ml in 1- and 5-ml ampuls. (29; 154)

Each milliliter of isoproterenol HCl solutions contains (1-10/98):

	1:50,000 injection	1:5000 injection
Isoproterenol HCl	0.02 mg (20 μg)	0.2 mg (200 μg)
Sodium chloride	4.7 mg	4.25 mg
Sodium metabisulfite	0.9 mg	0.5 mg
Citric acid, anhydrous	2 mg	2 mg
Sodium citrate dihydrate	0.4 mg	1.6 mg

(Additional citric acid and/or sodium citrate may have been added to adjust pH.)

pH — The 0.02-mg/ml concentration has a pH of 3.2 (range 2.5 to 3.5). The 0.2-mg/ml concentration has a pH of 3.8 (range 3.5 to 4.5). (1-10/98)

Osmolality — The osmolality of isoproterenol HCl (Breon) 0.2 mg/ml was determined to be 277 mOsm/kg by freezing-point depression and 293 mOsm/kg by vapor pressure. (1071)

Trade Name(s) — Isuprel HCl.

Administration — Isoproterenol HCl may be administered by intravenous infusion; by direct intravenous, intramuscular, or subcutaneous injection; and, in extreme emergencies, by intracardiac injection. For direct intravenous injection, 1 ml of the 1:5000 injection should be diluted to 10 ml with sodium chloride 0.9% or dextrose 5% in water to provide a 20-μg/ml solution. Intravenous infusions are prepared by adding 1 to 10 ml of the 1:5000 injection to 500 ml of compatible diluent. (1-10/98; 4)

Stability — Isoproterenol HCl injection in intact containers should be stored in a cool place between 2 and 15 °C and protected from light. Ampuls should be kept in opaque containers until used. The drug should not be used if a color or precipitate is present. Exposure to air, light, or increased temperature may cause a pink to brownish pink color to develop. (1-10/98; 4; 975)

pH Effects — The pH of a solution is the primary determinant of catecholamine stability in intravenous admixtures. (527) Isoproterenol HCl 5 mg/L in dextrose 5% in water was stable for more than 24 hours at 25 °C over a pH range of 3.7 to 5.7. (59) However, isoproterenol HCl displayed significant decomposition at a pH value above approximately 6. (48; 59; 430) Caution should be used when attempting to mix this drug in a solution with a final pH above this value. Drugs that may raise the pH above 6 include sodium bicarbonate, barbiturates, alkaline-buffered antibiotics (59), lidocaine HCl (24), and aminophylline. (6) If these drugs are mixed, they should be administered immediately after preparation (59), or, preferably, separate administration should be considered. (24)

Visual inspection for color changes related to decomposition may be inadequate to assess the compatibility of admixtures. In one evaluation with aminophylline stored at 25 °C, a color change was not noted until 24 hours had elapsed. However, no intact isoproterenol HCl was present in the admixture at 24 hours. (527)

Filtration — Isoproterenol HCl (Winthrop) 2 mg/L in dextrose 5% in water, sodium chloride 0.9%, and Ringer's injection, lactated, filtered over 12 hours through a 5-μm stainless steel depth filter (Argyle Filter Connector), a 0.22-μm cellulose ester membrane filter (Ivex-2 Filter Set), and a 0.22-μm polycarbonate membrane filter (In-Sure Filter Set), showed no significant reduction in potency due to binding to the filters. (320)

In another study, isoproterenol HCl (Winthrop) 4 mg/L in dextrose 5% in water and sodium chloride 0.9% did not display significant sorption to a 0.45-μm cellulose membrane filter (Abbott S-A-I-F) during an eight-hour simulated infusion. (567)

Central Venous Catheter — Isoproterenol HCl (Abbott) 0.02 mg/ml in dextrose 5% in water was found to be compatible with the ARROWg+ard Blue Plus (Arrow International) chlorhexidine-bearing triple-lumen central catheter. HPLC analysis was used to evaluate completeness of drug delivery through the catheter and the amount of chlorhexidine removed from the internal lumens. Essentially complete delivery of the drug was found with little or no drug loss occurring. Furthermore, chlorhexidine delivered from the catheter remained at trace amounts with no substantial increase due to the delivery of the drug through the catheter. (2335)

Compatibility Information

Solution Compatibility

Isoproterenol[a]

Solution	*Mfr*	*Mfr*	*Conc/L*	*Remarks*	*Ref*	*C/I*
Amino acids 4.25%, dextrose 25%	MG	WI	2 mg (H)	No increase in particulate matter in 24 hr at 5 °C	349	C
Dextran 6% in dextrose 5%	AB	AB	0.02 mg (S)	Physically compatible	3	C
Dextran 6% in sodium chloride 0.9%	AB	AB	0.02 mg (S)	Physically compatible	3	C
Dextrose–Ringer's injection combinations	AB	AB	0.02 mg (S)	Physically compatible	3	C
Dextrose–Ringer's injection, lactated, combinations	AB	AB	0.02 mg (S)	Physically compatible	3	C
Dextrose 5% in Ringer's injection, lactated	TR[b]	WI	2 mg (H)	Potency retained for 24 hr at 5 °C	282	C
Dextrose–saline combinations	AB	AB	0.02 mg (S)	Physically compatible	3	C
Dextrose 5% in sodium chloride 0.9%	TR[b]	WI	2 mg (H)	Potency retained for 24 hr at 5 °C	282	C
Dextrose 2½% in water	AB	AB	0.02 mg (S)	Physically compatible	3	C
Dextrose 5% in water	AB	AB	0.02 mg (S)	Physically compatible	3	C
	TR[b]	WI	2 mg (H)	Potency retained for 24 hr at 5 °C	282	C
	AB	BN	2 mg (H)	Physically compatible and chemically stable. 10% decomposition is calculated to occur in 24 hr in the light and 250 hr in the dark at 25 °C	527	C
Dextrose 10% in water	AB	AB	0.02 mg (S)	Physically compatible	3	C
Fructose 10% in sodium chloride 0.9%	AB	AB	0.02 mg (S)	Physically compatible	3	C
Fructose 10% in water	AB	AB	0.02 mg (S)	Physically compatible	3	C
Invert sugar 5 and 10% in sodium chloride 0.9%	AB	AB	0.02 mg (S)	Physically compatible	3	C
Invert sugar 5 and 10% in water	AB	AB	0.02 mg (S)	Physically compatible	3	C
Ionosol products	AB	AB	0.02 mg (S)	Physically compatible	3	C
Ringer's injection	AB	AB	0.02 mg (S)	Physically compatible	3	C
Ringer's injection, lactated	AB	AB	0.02 mg (S)	Physically compatible	3	C
	TR[b]	WI	2 mg (H)	Potency retained for 24 hr at 5 °C	282	C
Sodium bicarbonate 5%		WI	5 mg (H)	Isoproterenol decomposition	48	I

Solution Compatibility (Cont.)

Isoproterenol[a]

Solution	*Mfr*	*Mfr*	*Conc/L*	*Remarks*	*Ref*	*C/I*
Sodium chloride 0.45%	AB	AB	0.02 mg (S)	Physically compatible	3	C
Sodium chloride 0.9%	AB	AB	0.02 mg (S)	Physically compatible	3	C
	TR[b]	WI	2 mg (H)	Potency retained for 24 hr at 5 °C	282	C
Sodium lactate ⅙ M	AB	AB	0.02 mg (S)	Physically compatible	3	C

[a] *Combinations with designation "(H)" in the Conc/L column were tested as the hydrochloride salt; "(S)" indicates the sulfate salt of isoproterenol.*
[b] *Tested in both glass and PVC containers.*

Additive Compatibility

Isoproterenol HCl

Drug	*Mfr*	*Conc/L*	*Mfr*	*Conc/L*	*Test Soln*	*Remarks*	*Ref*	*C/I*
Aminophylline	SE	500 mg	BN	2 mg	D5W	10% isoproterenol decomposition in 2.2 to 2.5 hr in the light and dark at 25 °C	527	I
Atracurium besylate	BW	500 mg		4 mg	D5W	Physically compatible and atracurium chemically stable for 24 hr at 5 and 30 °C	1694	C
Calcium chloride	UP	1 g	WI	4 mg		Physically compatible	59	C
Cibenzoline succinate		2 g	WB	4 mg	D5W, NS	Physically compatible for 24 hr at 25 °C by visual and microscopic examination	1182	C
Cimetidine HCl	SKF	3 g	WI	20 mg	D5W	Physically compatible and cimetidine chemically stable for 24 hr at room temperature. Isoproterenol not tested	551	C
Dobutamine HCl	LI	1 g	ES	2 mg	D5W, NS	Physically compatible for 24 hr at 21 °C	812	C
Floxacillin sodium	BE	20 g	PX	4 mg	D5W	Physically compatible for 24 hr at 15 and 30 °C. Haze forms in 48 hr and precipitate forms in 72 hr	1479	C
Furosemide	HO	1 g	PX	4 mg	D5W	Immediate precipitation	1479	I
Heparin sodium		32,000 units		2 mg	NS	Physically compatible and heparin activity retained for 24 hr	57	C
	AB	20,000 units	WI	4 mg		Physically compatible	59	C
Magnesium sulfate		1 g	WI	4 mg		Physically compatible	59	C
Multivitamins	USV	10 ml	WI	4 mg		Physically compatible	59	C
Netilmicin sulfate	SC	3 g	WI	400 mg	D5S	Physically compatible and netilmicin chemically stable for 7 days at 4 and 25 °C. Isoproterenol not tested	558	C
Potassium chloride	AB	40 mEq	WI	4 mg		Physically compatible	59	C
Ranitidine HCl	GL	50 mg and 2 g		20 mg	D5W	Physically compatible and ranitidine chemically stable by HPLC for 24 hr at 25 °C. Isoproterenol not tested	1515	C
Sodium bicarbonate	AB	2.4 mEq[a]	BN	1 mg	D5W	Isoproterenol inactivated	772	I
Succinylcholine chloride	AB	2 g	WI	4 mg		Physically compatible	59	C

Additive Compatibility (Cont.)

Isoproterenol HCl

Drug	*Mfr*	*Conc/L*	*Mfr*	*Conc/L*	*Test Soln*	*Remarks*	*Ref*	*C/I*
Verapamil HCl	KN	80 mg	BN	10 mg	D5W, NS	Physically compatible for 24 hr	764	C
Vitamin B complex with C	AB	10 ml	WI	4 mg		Physically compatible	59	C
	UP	10 ml	WI	4 mg		Physically compatible	59	C

[a]One vial of Neut added to a liter of admixture.

Drugs in Syringe Compatibility

Isoproterenol[a]

Drug (in syringe)	*Mfr*	*Amt*	*Mfr*	*Amt*	*Remarks*	*Ref*	*C/I*
Ranitidine HCl	GL	50 mg/ 5 ml	BI	0.2 mg	Physically compatible for 4 hr at ambient temperature under fluorescent light	1151	C

[a]Tested as the sulfate salt of isoproterenol.

Y-Site Injection Compatibility (1:1 Mixture)

Isoproterenol HCl

Drug	*Mfr*	*Conc*	*Mfr*	*Conc*	*Remarks*	*Ref*	*C/I*
Amiodarone HCl	LZ	4 mg/ml[c]	ES	0.004 mg/ml[c]	Physically compatible for 24 hr at 21 °C	1032	C
Atracurium besylate	BW	0.5 mg/ml[a]	ES	4 μg/ml[a]	Physically compatible for 24 hr at 28 °C	1337	C
Bretylium tosylate	LY	4 mg/ml[c]	ES	0.032 mg/ml[c]	Physically compatible for 3 hr	1316	C
Cisatracurium besylate	GW	0.1, 2, 5 mg/ ml[a]	AB	0.02 mg/ml[a]	Physically compatible with no change in measured turbidity or increase in particle content in 4 hr at 23 °C	2074	C
Famotidine	MSD	0.2 mg/ml[a]	ES	0.004 mg/ml[a]	Physically compatible for 4 hr at 25 °C	1188	C
Heparin sodium	UP	1000 units/L[d]	WI	0.2 mg/ml	Physically compatible for at least 4 hr at room temperature by visual and microscopic examination	534	C
Hetastarch in lactated electrolyte injection (Hextend)	AB	6%	AB	0.02 mg/ml[a]	Physically compatible with no change in measured turbidity or increase in particle content in 4 hr at 23 °C	2339	C
Hydrocortisone sodium succinate	UP	10 mg/L[d]	WI	0.2 mg/ml	Physically compatible for at least 4 hr at room temperature by visual and microscopic examination	534	C
Inamrinone lactate	WB	3 mg/ml[b]	BR	0.004 mg/ml[a]	Physically compatible for at least 4 hr at 25 °C under fluorescent light	992	C
Levofloxacin	OMN	5 mg/ml[a]	ES	0.2 mg/ml	Visually compatible for 4 hr at 24 °C under fluorescent light	2233	C
Milrinone lactate	SW	0.4 mg/ml[a]	ES	8 μg/ml[a]	Visually compatible with little or no loss of either drug by HPLC in 4 hr at 23 °C	2214	C
Pancuronium bromide	ES	0.05 mg/ml[a]	ES	4 μg/ml[a]	Physically compatible for 24 hr at 28 °C	1337	C
Potassium chloride	AB	40 mEq/L[d]	WI	0.2 mg/ml	Physically compatible for at least 4 hr at room temperature by visual and microscopic examination	534	C
Propofol	ZEN	10 mg/ml	AB	0.004 mg/ml[a]	Physically compatible for 1 hr at 23 °C with no increase in particle content	2066	C

Y-Site Injection Compatibility (1:1 Mixture) (Cont.)

Drug	Mfr	Conc	Isoproterenol HCl Mfr	Isoproterenol HCl Conc	Remarks	Ref	C/I
Remifentanil HCl	GW	0.025 and 0.25 mg/ml[b]	SW	0.02 mg/ml[a]	Physically compatible with no change in measured turbidity or increase in particle content in 4 hr at 23 °C	2075	C
Tacrolimus	FUJ	1 mg/ml[b]	ES	0.04 mg/ml[a]	Visually compatible for 24 hr at 25 °C	1630	C
TNA #73[e]			BR	0.2 mg/50 ml[c]	Physically compatible for 4 hr by visual observation	1009	C
Vecuronium bromide	OR	0.1 mg/ml[a]	ES	4 μg/ml[a]	Physically compatible for 24 hr at 28 °C	1337	C
Vitamin B complex with C	RC	2 ml/L[d]	WI	0.2 mg/ml	Physically compatible for at least 4 hr at room temperature by visual and microscopic examination	534	C

[a]*Tested in dextrose 5% in water.*
[b]*Tested in sodium chloride 0.9%.*
[c]*Tested in both dextrose 5% in water and sodium chloride 0.9%.*
[d]*Tested in dextrose 5% in Ringer's injection, dextrose 5% in Ringer's injection, lactated, dextrose 5% in water, Ringer's injection, lactated, and sodium chloride 0.9%.*
[e]*Refer to Appendix I for the composition of parenteral nutrition solutions. TNA indicates a 3-in-1 admixture.*

Additional Compatibility Information

Infusion Solutions — Dilution of isoproterenol HCl with sodium chloride 0.9% or dextrose 5% in water has been recommended. (1-10/98; 4) Isoproterenol HCl (Winthrop) at 4 mg/L is stated to be physically compatible with all Abbott infusion solutions. (59)

Isoproterenol HCl (Winthrop) 4 mg/L in dextrose 5% in water in PVC bags retained biological activity after 30 months of storage at room temperature. However, spectrophotometric analysis of the PVC-stored solutions was not possible because of interference by substances leached from the plastic. (430)

ITRACONAZOLE
AHFS 8:12.04

Products — Itraconazole is available in a kit containing a 25-ml ampul of itraconazole concentrate 10 mg/ml and a plastic bag containing 50 ml of sodium chloride 0.9% along with a filter-bearing infusion set. Although itraconazole is insoluble in aqueous solutions, the drug is prepared as the concentrate utilizing hydroxypropyl–ß–cyclodextrin 400 mg per 10 mg of drug as a molecular inclusion complex. Each milliliter also contains propylene glycol 25 μL with hydrochloric acid and sodium hydroxide for pH adjustment in water for injection. (2)

To prepare itraconazole for administration, the specially provided bag containing 50 ml of sodium chloride 0.9% must be used. Do *not* substitute any other solution or container for the one provided in the kit. The preparation instructions must be followed completely. Transfer the full contents of the 25-ml ampul of itraconazole concentrate into the 50 ml of 0.9% sodium chloride provided in the infusion bag in the kit. Mix gently after the transfer is complete, yielding 75 ml of a 3.33-mg/ml itraconazole solution for infusion. (2)

pH — 4.5. (2)

Trade Name(s) — Sporanox.

Administration — Itraconazole must be prepared only according the manufacturer's instructions to avoid inadvertent precipitation. See Products above. After dilution of the concentrate using the bag of sodium chloride 0.9% provided in the kit, 60 ml (200 mg) of the itraconazole 3.33-mg/ml solution should be infused intravenously over 60 minutes using a flow control device through a dedicated infusion line; do not give by bolus injection. Administration should be performed using an extension set and the filter-bearing infusion set provided in the kit. No other drugs or solutions should be administered through this dedicated line or added to the bag of itraconazole. After the itraconazole infusion has been completed, the infusion set should be flushed with 15 to 20 ml of sodium chloride 0.9% over 30 seconds to 15 minutes using the two-way stopcock. The entire infusion set should then be discarded. Administration of other drugs through the lumen used to administer itraconazole may only be done after flushing with sodium chloride 0.9% as described above. (2)

Stability — Intact containers of itraconazole in kits should be stored at or below 25 °C protected from light and freezing. The injection is a colorless to slightly yellow solution. It should be inspected for particulates and discoloration prior to use. (2)

After solution preparation, the diluted itraconazole can be stored at controlled room temperature or under refrigeration for as long as 48 hours when protected from exposure to light. Exposure to normal room light during administration is acceptable. (2)

Compatibility Information

Itraconazole was found to be physically incompatible with aqueous solutions at most concentrations. It is essential for the physical stability of itraconazole injection that the preparation instructions be followed accurately to yield the required 3.33-mg/ml concentration in sodium chloride 0.9%. Any variation from this critical concentration, higher or lower, appears to result in rapid gross precipitation, even when no other drug is present and only a simple aqueous diluent is utilized. Consequently, itraconazole should be considered incompatible with all other medications and diluents in admixtures and by Y-site administration. (2314)

The manufacturer specifically notes that itraconazole should not be diluted with dextrose 5% in water or with lactated Ringer's injection alone or in combination with any other diluent. Similarly, the manufacturer recommends that no other drug be added to the itraconazole bag or be administered through the same line. (2)

KANAMYCIN SULFATE
AHFS 8:12.02

Products — Kanamycin sulfate is available in 3-ml vials containing 1 g, 2-ml vials containing 500 mg, and a pediatric injection in 2-ml vials containing 75 mg of kanamycin as the sulfate. The 1-g, 500-mg, and 75-mg products also contain the antioxidant sodium bisulfite 0.45, 0.66, and 0.099%, respectively, and sodium citrate 2.2, 2.2, and 0.33%, respectively. The pH is adjusted during manufacture with sulfuric acid. (1-4/98; 4)

pH — Adjusted by the manufacturer to pH 4.5 with sulfuric acid. (4)

Osmolality — The osmolality of kanamycin sulfate (Beecham) 250 mg/ml was determined to be 858 mOsm/kg by freezing-point depression and 952 mOsm/kg by vapor pressure. (1071)

Trade Name(s) — Kantrex.

Administration — Kanamycin sulfate may be administered by deep intramuscular injection into the upper outer quadrant of the gluteal muscle or by intermittent intravenous infusion over 30 to 60 minutes in dextrose 5% in water or sodium chloride 0.9%. The drug also is administered by intraperitoneal instillation and irrigation. (1-4/98; 4)

Stability — Kanamycin sulfate injection is a clear colorless solution. Although some vials may darken during storage, the manufacturer states that this darkening does not indicate a loss of potency. Kanamycin sulfate injection should be stored at controlled room temperature and protected from temperatures above 40 °C and from freezing. (1-4/98; 4)

Sorption — Kanamycin sulfate (Bristol) 15 mg/L in sodium chloride 0.9% (Travenol) in PVC bags did not exhibit significant sorption to the plastic during one week of storage at room temperature (15 to 20 °C). (536)

In another study, kanamycin sulfate (Bristol) 15 mg/L in sodium chloride 0.9% did not exhibit any loss due to sorption during a seven-hour simulated infusion through an infusion set (Travenol) consisting of a cellulose propionate burette chamber and 170 cm of PVC tubing. (606)

The drug also was tested as a simulated infusion over at least one hour by a syringe pump system. A glass syringe on a syringe pump was fitted with 20 cm of polyethylene tubing or 50 cm of Silastic tubing. No loss of drug due to sorption was observed with either tubing. (606)

A 25-ml aliquot of kanamycin sulfate (Bristol) 15 mg/L in sodium chloride 0.9% was stored in all-plastic syringes composed of polypropylene barrels and polyethylene plungers for 24 hours at room temperature in the dark. No loss due to sorption occurred. (606)

Compatibility Information

Solution Compatibility

Kanamycin sulfate

Solution	*Mfr*	*Mfr*	*Conc/L*	*Remarks*	*Ref*	*C/I*
Amino acids 4.25%, dextrose 25%	MG	BR	500 mg	No increase in particulate matter in 24 hr at 5 °C	349	C
Dextrose 5% in sodium chloride 0.9%	MG	BR	250 mg	Potency retained for 24 hr at 4 and 25 °C	105	C
Dextrose 5% in water	MG	BR	250 mg	Potency retained for 24 hr at 4 and 25 °C	105	C
Dextrose 10% in water	MG	BR	250 mg	Potency retained for 24 hr at 4 and 25 °C	105	C
Isolyte M with dextrose 5%	MG	BR	250 mg	Potency retained for 24 hr at 4 and 25 °C	105	C
Isolyte P with dextrose 5%	MG	BR	250 mg	Potency retained for 24 hr at 4 and 25 °C	105	C
Ringer's injection, lactated	MG	BR	250 mg	Potency retained for 24 hr at 4 and 25 °C	105	C

Solution Compatibility (Cont.)

Kanamycin sulfate

Solution	*Mfr*	*Mfr*	*Conc/L*	*Remarks*	*Ref*	*C/I*
Sodium chloride 0.9%	MG	BR	250 mg	Potency retained for 24 hr at 4 and 25 °C	105	C
TPN #1[a]		BR	400 mg	Antibiotic potency retained for at least 12 hr at 22 °C	313	C
TPN #1, #3, #6, #9[a]		BR	500 mg	Physically incompatible with a precipitate forming in 8 to 12 hr at 22 °C	313	I
TPN #2, #4, #5, #7, #8[a]		BR	500 mg	Physically compatible for 24 hr at 22 °C	313	C
TPN #10[a]		BR	500 mg	Physically compatible for 24 hr and antibiotic potency retained for at least 12 hr at 22 °C	313	C
TPN #21[a]		BR	250 mg	Antibiotic potency retained for 24 hr at 4 °C	87	C
		BR	250 mg	11 to 13% kanamycin decomposition in 24 hr at 25 °C	87	I

[a]Refer to Appendix I for the composition of parenteral nutrition solutions. TPN indicates a 2-in-1 admixture.

Additive Compatibility

Kanamycin sulfate

Drug	*Mfr*	*Conc/L*	*Mfr*	*Conc/L*	*Test Soln*	*Remarks*	*Ref*	*C/I*
Amphotericin B		200 mg	BPC	4 g	D5W	Haze develops over 3 hr	26	I
Ascorbic acid injection	UP	500 mg	BR	4 g	D5W	Physically compatible	15	C
Cefoxitin sodium	MSD	5 g	BR	5 g	D5S	9% cefoxitin decomposition at 25 °C and 1% at 5 °C in 48 hr. 6% kanamycin decomposition at 25 °C and none at 5 °C in 48 hr	308	C
Chloramphenicol sodium succinate	PD	10 g	BR	4 g	D5W	Physically compatible	15	C
	PD	10 g	BR	4 g		Physically compatible	21	C
Chlorpheniramine maleate	SC	100 mg	BR	4 g	D5W	Physically incompatible	15	I
Clindamycin phosphate	UP	2.4 g		1 g	D5W	Physically compatible and clindamycin potency retained for 24 hr at room temperature	104	C
	UP	1.2 g		0.5 g	D5W	Physically compatible and clindamycin potency retained for 24 hr at room temperature	104	C
Colistimethate sodium	WC	500 mg	BR	4 g	D5W	Physically incompatible	15	I
Dopamine HCl	AS	800 mg	BR	2 g	D5W	Kanamycin and dopamine potency retained for 24 hr at 23 to 25 °C	78	C
Furosemide	HO	160 mg	BE	2 g	D5W, NS	Transient cloudiness during admixture. Then physically compatible for 24 hr at 21 °C	876	C
Heparin sodium		12,000 units	BR	250 mg	D5S, D5W, D10W, IM, IP, LR, NS	Immediate precipitation	87	I
	UP	4000 units	BR	4 g	D5W	Physically incompatible	15	I
	BP	20,000 units	BPC	4 g	D5W, NS	Immediate precipitation	26	I

Additive Compatibility (Cont.)

Kanamycin sulfate

Drug	*Mfr*	*Conc/L*	*Mfr*	*Conc/L*	*Test Soln*	*Remarks*	*Ref*	*C/I*
	AB	20,000 units	BR	500 mg		Precipitate forms within 1 hr	21	I
	OR	20,000 units	TE	2 g	NS	Precipitate forms	113	I
Hydrocortisone sodium succinate	UP	500 mg	BR	4 g	D5W	Physically incompatible	15	I
		1.8 g	BR	250 mg	D5S, D5W, D10W, IM, IP, NS	Kanamycin potency retained for 24 hr at 4 and 25 °C	87	C
Methohexital sodium	BR	2 g	BPC	4 g	D5W, NS	Immediate precipitation	26	I
Penicillin G potassium	SQ	20 million units	BR	4 g	D5W	Physically compatible	15	C
	SQ	5 million units	BR	4 g	D	Physically compatible	47	C
Penicillin G sodium	UP	20 million units	BR	4 g	D5W	Physically compatible	15	C
Polymyxin B sulfate	BW	200 mg	BR	4 g	D5W	Physically compatible	15	C
Sodium bicarbonate	AB	80 mEq	BR	4 g	D5W	Physically compatible	15	C
Vitamin B complex with C	AB	5 ml	BR	4 g	D5W	Physically compatible	15	C

Drugs in Syringe Compatibility

Kanamycin sulfate

Drug (in syringe)	*Mfr*	*Amt*	*Mfr*	*Amt*	*Remarks*	*Ref*	*C/I*
Ampicillin sodium	AY	500 mg		1 g/4 ml	Physically incompatible within 1 hr at room temperature	99	I
	AY	500 mg		1 g/2 ml	Precipitate forms in 1 hr at room temperature	300	I
Heparin sodium	AB	20,000 units/ 1 ml	BR	500 mg	Physically incompatible	21	I
Penicillin G sodium		1 million units		1 g/4 ml	No precipitate or color change within 1 hr at room temperature	99	C

Y-Site Injection Compatibility (1:1 Mixture)

Kanamycin sulfate

Drug	*Mfr*	*Conc*	*Mfr*	*Conc*	*Remarks*	*Ref*	*C/I*
Cyclophosphamide	MJ	20 mg/ml[a]	BR	2.5 mg/ml[a]	Physically compatible for 4 hr at 25 °C	1194	C
Furosemide	HO	10 mg/ml	BE	2 mg/ml[a,b]	Physically compatible for 24 hr at 21 °C	876	C
Heparin sodium with hydrocortisone sodium succinate	RI	1000 units + 100 mg/L[c]	BR	250 mg/ml	Physically compatible for at least 4 hr at room temperature by visual and microscopic examination	322	C

Y-Site Injection Compatibility (1:1 Mixture) (Cont.)

			Kanamycin sulfate				
Drug	*Mfr*	*Conc*	*Mfr*	*Conc*	*Remarks*	*Ref*	*C/I*
Hydromorphone HCl	WY	0.2 mg/ml[a]	BR	2.5 mg/ml[a]	Physically compatible for at least 4 hr at 25 °C under fluorescent light	987	C
Magnesium sulfate	IX	16.7, 33.3, 66.7, 100 mg/ml[a]	BR	2.5 mg/ml[a]	Physically compatible for at least 4 hr at 32 °C	813	C
Meperidine HCl	WY	10 mg/ml[a]	BR	2.5 mg/ml[a]	Physically compatible for at least 4 hr at 25 °C under fluorescent light	987	C
Morphine sulfate	WI	1 mg/ml[a]	BR	2.5 mg/ml[a]	Physically compatible for at least 4 hr at 25 °C under fluorescent light	987	C
Perphenazine	SC	0.02 mg/ml[a]	BR	2.5 mg/ml[a]	Physically compatible for 4 hr at 25 °C	1155	C
Potassium chloride		40 mEq/L[c]	BR	250 mg/ml	Physically compatible for at least 4 hr at room temperature by visual and microscopic examination	322	C
TNA #73[d]		32.5 ml[e]	BR	500 mg/50 ml[a]	Physically compatible by visual observation for 4 hr at 25 °C	1008	C
Vitamin B complex with C	RC	2 ml/L[c]	BR	250 mg/ml	Physically compatible for at least 4 hr at room temperature by visual and microscopic examination	322	C

[a]*Tested in dextrose 5% in water.*
[b]*Tested in sodium chloride 0.9%.*
[c]*Tested in dextrose 5% in water, sodium chloride 0.9%, and Ringer's injection, lactated.*
[d]*Refer to Appendix I for the composition of parenteral nutrition solutions. TNA indicates a 3-in-1 admixture.*
[e]*A 32.5-ml sample of parenteral nutrition solution mixed with 50 ml of antibiotic.*

Additional Compatibility Information

Infusion Solutions — Kanamycin sulfate is stated to be stable for 24 hours at room temperature in most intravenous infusion solutions, including dextrose 5% in water and sodium chloride 0.9%. (4)

Concentrated Drug Solutions — The following incompatibility determinations were performed with concentrated solutions. The drugs in dry form were constituted according to the manufacturers' recommendations. One milliliter of kanamycin sulfate (Bristol) was added to 5 ml of sterile distilled water along with 1 ml of each of the following drugs. Particulate matter was noted within two hours (28):

Heparin sodium
Hydrocortisone sodium succinate (Upjohn)
Phenobarbital sodium (Winthrop)
Phenytoin sodium (Parke-Davis)

Other Drugs — It is recommended that other drugs not be physically combined with kanamycin sulfate. (4)

In vitro testing of thiamine HCl, riboflavin-5′-phosphate, pyridoxine HCl, niacinamide, and ascorbic acid individually at concentrations of 0.1% with kanamycin sulfate 0.025% in sterile distilled water showed a significant reduction in antibiotic activity in one hour at 25 °C. (314)

Kanamycin sulfate is stated to be physically incompatible with lincomycin HCl (154) and cefotetan disodium. (4) Kanamycin sulfate also appears to be incompatible with cefazolin sodium. (278)

Cefotaxime sodium (Hoechst-Roussel) should not be mixed with aminoglycosides in the same solution, but they may be administered to the same patient separately. (792)

Although piperacillin sodium and aminoglycosides act synergistically and have been used successfully clinically when recommended doses of each drug were administered, mixing piperacillin sodium directly in a syringe or infusion bottle with an aminoglycoside can result in substantial inactivation of the aminoglycoside. (740)

The comparative inactivation of five aminoglycosides by seven β-lactam antibiotics in human serum at 37 °C was reported by Riff and Thomason. Amikacin, followed by netilmicin, had the lowest degree of inactivation; tobramycin sustained the most pronounced losses. Gentamicin and kanamycin were intermediate in the extent of losses. The six penicillins that were tested all produced aminoglycoside inactivation; the greatest extent of inactivation was caused by carbenicillin followed by ticarcillin, penicillin G, oxacillin, methicillin, and ampicillin, in approximate descending order. Cephalothin produced minimal inactivation (5 to 10% in 24 hours). The rate of inactivation could be reduced by storage at 4 °C and further reduced by storage at −20 °C. The authors suggested processing blood samples rapidly to avoid inaccurate serum determinations. Storage of specimens at low temperature until analysis may be helpful. (1052)

KETAMINE HCL
AHFS 28:04

Products — Ketamine HCl is available in concentrations equivalent to 10, 50, or 100 mg/ml of ketamine base. The injections also contain 0.1 mg/ml of benzethonium chloride. The 10-mg/ml concentration is made isotonic with sodium chloride and is available in 20-ml vials. The 50-mg/ml concentration is available in 10-ml vials, and the 100-mg/ml concentration is available in 5-ml vials. (1-11/99; 29)

The 100-mg/ml concentration must be diluted before intravenous use. Dilution of the dose with an equal volume of sterile water for injection, dextrose 5% in water, or sodium chloride 0.9% is recommended. (1-11/99)

pH — From 3.5 to 5.5. (1-11/99)

Osmolality — The osmolalities of ketamine HCl products were determined to be 300 mOsm/kg for the 10-mg/ml concentration and 387 mOsm/kg for the 50-mg/ml concentration. (1233)

Trade Name(s) — Ketalar.

Administration — Ketamine HCl may be administered intramuscularly or by slow intravenous injection over at least 60 seconds. The 100-mg/ml preparation should not be given undiluted. See Products section above. For intravenous infusion, a 1- or 2-mg/ml solution may be prepared by adding 500 mg of ketamine to 500 ml or to 250 ml, respectively, of dextrose 5% in water or sodium chloride 0.9%. (1-11/99)

Stability — Intact vials of ketamine HCl should be stored at controlled room temperature and protected from light. Ketamine HCl injection is a colorless to slightly yellow solution. Although the drug may darken upon prolonged exposure to light, this darkening does not affect potency. Do not use the product if a precipitate is present. (1-11/99)

Compatibility Information

Additive Compatibility

Ketamine HCl

Drug	*Mfr*	*Conc/L*	*Mfr*	*Conc/L*	*Test Soln*	*Remarks*	*Ref*	*C/I*
Morphine sulfate	SX	1 g	PD	1 g	NS[a]	Variable HPLC assays, but at least 90% of both drugs retained for 6 days at room temperature	2260	C
	SX	25 g	PD	25 g	NS[a]	Variable HPLC assays, but at least 90% of both drugs retained for 6 days at room temperature	2260	C
	SX	25 g	PD	25 g	NS[b]	Variable HPLC assays, but at least 90% of both drugs retained for 6 days at room temperature	2260	C

[a]*Tested in PVC containers.*
[b]*Tested in plastic medication cassette reservoirs (Deltec).*

Drugs in Syringe Compatibility

Ketamine HCl

Drug (in syringe)	*Mfr*	*Amt*	*Mfr*	*Amt*	*Remarks*	*Ref*	*C/I*
Bupivacaine HCl with fentanyl citrate	SW JN	1.5 mg/ml 0.01 mg/ml	PD	2 mg/ml	Diluted to 5 ml with NS. Visually compatible with no new GC/MS peaks appearing in 1 hr at room temperature	1956	C
Clonidine HCl with tetracaine HCl	BI SW	0.03 mg/ml 2 mg/ml	PD	2 mg/ml	Diluted to 5 ml with NS. Visually compatible with no new GC/MS peaks appearing in 1 hr at room temperature	1956	C
Doxapram HCl	RB	400 mg/ 20 ml	PD	200 mg/ 20 ml	Physically compatible with no doxapram loss in 9 hr but 12% loss in 24 hr	1177	I
Lidocaine HCl with morphine sulfate	AST ES	2 mg/ml 0.2 mg/ml	PD	2 mg/ml	Diluted to 5 ml with NS. Visually compatible with no new GC/MS peaks appearing in 1 hr at room temperature	1956	C
Meperidine HCl	DB	12 mg/ml	PD	2 mg/ml	Diluted to 50 ml with NS. Visually compatible for 48 hr at 25 °C	2059	C

Drugs in Syringe Compatibility (Cont.)

Ketamine HCl

Drug (in syringe)	Mfr	Amt	Mfr	Amt	Remarks	Ref	C/I
Morphine sulfate	SX	1 mg/ml[a], 10 mg/ml[a]	PD	1 mg/ml[a]	Variable HPLC assays, but at least 90% of both drugs retained for 6 days at room temperature	2260	C
	SX	25 mg/ml[a]	PD	1 mg/ml[a]	Variable HPLC assays. 5% morphine loss in 6 days at room temperature. Up to 12 to 15% ketamine loss in 2 to 6 days may have occurred	2260	C
	SX	1 mg/ml[a], 10 mg/ml[a], 25 mg/ml[a]	PD	10 mg/ml[a]	Variable HPLC assays, but at least 90% of both drugs retained for 6 days at room temperature	2260	C
	SX	1 mg/ml[a], 10 mg/ml[a], 25 mg/ml[a]	PD	25 mg/ml[a]	Variable HPLC assays, but at least 90% of both drugs retained for 6 days at room temperature	2260	C
Morphine tartrate		240 mg		100 mg	Brought to 9 ml with NS. Visually compatible for 10 days refrigerated and at room temperature protected from light	1899	C

[a]*Diluted in sodium chloride 0.9%.*

Y-Site Injection Compatibility (1:1 Mixture)

Ketamine HCl

Drug	Mfr	Conc	Mfr	Conc	Remarks	Ref	C/I
Propofol	ZEN	10 mg/ml	PD	10 mg/ml	Physically compatible for 1 hr at 23 °C with no increase in particle content	2066	C

Additional Compatibility Information

Infusion Solutions — Dextrose 5% in water and sodium chloride 0.9% have been recommended as diluents for ketamine HCl. (1-11/99)

Barbiturates — Ketamine HCl is incompatible with barbiturates because of precipitate formation. Consequently, they should not be combined in the same syringe. (1-11/99)

Diazepam — Diazepam must be given separately from ketamine HCl and not be mixed in the same syringe or infusion container. (1-11/99)

KETOROLAC TROMETHAMINE
AHFS 28:08.04

Products — Ketorolac tromethamine is available as a 15-mg/ml solution in 1-ml Tubex cartridge-needle units and vials and also as a 30-mg/ml solution in 1- and 2-ml Tubex cartridge-needle units or vials. The 15- and 30-mg/ml concentrations are also available in 1-ml Tubex needle-less cartridges. Each milliliter of the two concentrations contains (2):

Ketorolac tromethamine	15 mg	30 mg
Ethanol	10% (w/v)	10% (w/v)
Sodium chloride	6.68 mg	4.35 mg
Water for injection	qs	qs

The product also contains sodium hydroxide or hydrochloric acid to adjust the pH. The product in vials also contains citric acid 0.1%. (2)

pH — From 6.9 to 7.9. (4)

Tonicity — Both ketorolac tromethamine concentrations are isotonic. (4)

Trade Name(s) — Toradol.

Administration — Ketorolac tromethamine is administered slowly by deep intramuscular injection or by intravenous injection over no less than 15 seconds. (2; 4) The 60 mg/2 ml injection is for intramuscular use only. (2)

Stability — Ketorolac tromethamine injection should be stored at controlled room temperature and protected from light. The injection is clear and has a slight yellow color. (2; 4) Prolonged exposure to light may result in discoloration of the solution and precipitation. Precipitation may also occur in solutions having a relatively low pH. (4)

Sorption — Ketorolac tromethamine (Syntex) 30 mg/50 ml in dextrose 5% in sodium chloride 0.9%, dextrose 5% in water, Plasma-Lyte A (pH 7.4), Ringer's injection, Ringer's injection, lactated, and sodium chloride 0.9% and 30 mg/500 ml in Plasma-Lyte A (pH 7.4) and Ringer's injection did not exhibit sorption to PVC containers over 48 hours or to administration set tubing in static contact or in simulated infusion. (1646)

Compatibility Information

Solution Compatibility

Ketorolac tromethamine

Solution	*Mfr*	*Mfr*	*Conc/L*	*Remarks*	*Ref*	*C/I*
Dextrose 5% in sodium chloride 0.9%	TR[a]	SY	600 mg	Physically compatible by visual examination and particle assessment. No ketorolac loss by HPLC in 48 hr at room temperature	1646	C
Dextrose 5% in water	TR[b]	SY	600 mg	Physically compatible by visual examination and particle assessment. No ketorolac loss by HPLC in 48 hr at room temperature	1646	C
	BA[a]	RC	600 mg	Visually compatible with little or no loss by HPLC in 7 days and 14% loss in 14 days at 25 °C. Less than 2% loss in 50 days at 5 °C	2095	C
Plasma-Lyte A, pH 7.4	TR[a]	SY	600 mg	Physically compatible by visual examination and particle assessment. No ketorolac loss by HPLC in 48 hr at room temperature	1646	C
	TR[b]	SY	60 mg	Physically compatible by visual examination and particle assessment. Little or no ketorolac loss by HPLC in 48 hr at room temperature	1646	C
Ringer's injection	TR[a]	SY	600 mg	Physically compatible by visual examination and particle assessment. No ketorolac loss by HPLC in 48 hr at room temperature	1646	C
	TR[b]	SY	60 mg	Physically compatible by visual examination and particle assessment. Little or no ketorolac loss by HPLC in 48 hr at room temperature	1646	C
Ringer's injection, lactated	TR[a]	SY	600 mg	Physically compatible by visual examination and particle assessment. No ketorolac loss by HPLC in 48 hr at room temperature	1646	C
Sodium chloride 0.9%	TR[b]	SY	600 mg	Physically compatible by visual examination and particle assessment. No ketorolac loss by HPLC in 48 hr at room temperature	1646	C
	BA[a]	RC	600 mg	Visually compatible with no loss by HPLC in 35 days at 25 °C and in 50 days at 25 °C	2095	C

[a]*Tested in PVC containers.*
[b]*Tested in both glass and PVC containers.*

Drugs in Syringe Compatibility

Ketorolac tromethamine

Drug (in syringe)	*Mfr*	*Amt*	*Mfr*	*Amt*	*Remarks*	*Ref*	*C/I*
Diazepam	ES	15 mg/ 3 ml	SY	180 mg/ 6 ml	Visually compatible for 4 hr at 24 °C under ambient light. Spectrophotometric absorbance increases immediately and persists for 30 min but dissipates by 1 hr	1703	?
Haloperidol lactate	SO	5 mg/ 1 ml	SY	30 mg/ 1 ml	White crystalline precipitate forms immediately	1786	I

Drugs in Syringe Compatibility (Cont.)

Ketorolac tromethamine

Drug (in syringe)	*Mfr*	*Amt*	*Mfr*	*Amt*	*Remarks*	*Ref*	*C/I*
Hydromorphone HCl	KN	10 mg/ 1 ml	SY	30 mg/ 1 ml	Cloudiness forms immediately but clears with swirling	1785	?
	KN	1 mg/ 1 ml[a]	SY	30 mg/ 1 ml	Visually compatible for 24 hr at 25 °C	1785	C
	KN	1[a] and 10 mg/ 1 ml	SY	15 mg/ 1 ml[a]	Visually compatible for 24 hr at 25 °C	1785	C
Hydroxyzine HCl	SO	150 mg/ 3 ml	SY	180 mg/ 6 ml	Heavy white precipitate forms immediately, separating into two layers over time	1703	I
Nalbuphine HCl	DU	30 mg/ 3 ml	SY	180 mg/ 6 ml	Solid white precipitate forms immediately and settles to bottom	1703	I
Prochlorperazine edisylate	STS	15 mg/ 3 ml	SY	180 mg/ 6 ml	Heavy white precipitate forms immediately, separating into two layers over time	1703	I
Promethazine HCl	ES	75 mg/ 3 ml	SY	180 mg/ 6 ml	Heavy white precipitate forms immediately, separating into two layers over time	1703	I
Sufentanil citrate	JN	50 μg/ml	SY	30 mg/ml	Physically compatible with no subvisual haze or particle formation in 24 hr at 23 °C	1711	C
Thiethylperazine maleate	ROX	5 mg/ 1 ml	SY	30 mg/ 1 ml	White crystalline precipitate forms immediately	1785	I

[a]*Dilutions prepared with sterile water for injection.*

Y-Site Injection Compatibility (1:1 Mixture)

Ketorolac tromethamine

Drug	*Mfr*	*Conc*	*Mfr*	*Conc*	*Remarks*	*Ref*	*C/I*
Alatrofloxacin mesylate	PF	1.43 mg/ml[a]	AB	15 mg/ml	Visually and microscopically compatible with the ketorolac pushed through a Y-site over 20 sec	2235	C
Cisatracurium besylate	GW	0.1, 2, 5 mg/ml[a]	RC	15 mg/ml[a]	Physically compatible with no change in measured turbidity or increase in particle content in 4 hr at 23 °C	2074	C
Fentanyl citrate	JN	0.025 mg/ml[a]	WY	1 mg/ml[a]	Physically compatible with no change in measured haze or increase in particle content in 48 hr at 22 °C	1706	C
Hetastarch in lactated electrolyte injection (Hextend)	AB	6%	AB	15 mg/ml	Physically compatible with no change in measured turbidity or increase in particle content in 4 hr at 23 °C	2339	C
Hydromorphone HCl	AST	0.5 mg/ml[a]	WY	1 mg/ml[a]	Physically compatible with no change in measured haze or increase in particle content in 48 hr at 22 °C	1706	C
Methadone HCl	LI	1 mg/ml[a]	WY	1 mg/ml[a]	Physically compatible with no change in measured haze or increase in particle content in 48 hr at 22 °C	1706	C
Morphine sulfate	AST	1 mg/ml[a]	WY	1 mg/ml[a]	Physically compatible with no change in measured haze or increase in particle content in 48 hr at 22 °C	1706	C
Remifentanil HCl	GW	0.025 and 0.25 mg/ml[b]	RC	15 mg/ml[a]	Physically compatible with no change in measured turbidity or increase in particle content in 4 hr at 23 °C	2075	C

Y-Site Injection Compatibility (1:1 Mixture) (Cont.)

Ketorolac tromethamine

Drug	*Mfr*	*Conc*	*Mfr*	*Conc*	*Remarks*	*Ref*	*C/I*
Sufentanil citrate	JN	12.5 μg/ml[a]	SY	1 mg/ml[a]	Physically compatible with no subvisual haze or particle formation in 24 hr at 23 °C	1711	C

[a]*Tested in dextrose 5% in water.*
[b]*Tested in sodium chloride 0.9%.*

Additional Compatibility Information

Other Drugs — Ketorolac tromethamine should not be admixed with drugs that result in a relatively low pH such as hydroxyzine HCl, meperidine HCl, morphine sulfate, and promethazine HCl because ketorolac may precipitate. (2; 4)

LABETALOL HCL
AHFS 24:08

Products — Labetalol HCl is available in 20- and 40-ml multiple-dose vials and 4- and 8-ml disposable syringes. Each milliliter of solution contains (2):

Labetalol HCl	5 mg
Dextrose, anhydrous	45 mg
Edetate disodium	0.1 mg
Methylparaben	0.8 mg
Propylparaben	0.1 mg

The product also contains citric acid monohydrate and sodium hydroxide, as necessary, to adjust the pH. (2)

pH — From 3 to 4. (2)

Osmolality — Labetalol HCl 5 mg/ml has an osmolality of 287 mOsm/kg. (1689)

Trade Name(s) — Normodyne, Trandate.

Administration — Labetalol HCl is administered slowly, over two minutes, by direct intravenous injection, or by continuous intravenous infusion at an initial rate of 2 mg/min with subsequent adjustments based on blood pressure response. For continuous infusion, concentrations of 1 mg/ml or 2 mg/3 ml can be made by adding 200 mg (40 ml) to 160 or 250 ml of compatible infusion solution. To facilitate the infusion of labetalol HCl at an accurate rate of administration, a controlled-infusion device, such as a pump, may be used. (2; 4)

Stability — Labetalol HCl may be stored at room temperature or under refrigeration and should be protected from light and freezing. The solution is clear and colorless to slightly yellow. (2)

pH Effects — Labetalol HCl has optimal stability at pH 3 to 4. Addition to an alkaline admixture, such as sodium bicarbonate 5% with a pH of 7.6 to 8, has resulted in a precipitate. (757)

Compatibility Information

Solution Compatibility

Labetalol HCl

Solution	*Mfr*	*Mfr*	*Conc/L*	*Remarks*	*Ref*	*C/I*
Dextrose 5% in Ringer's injection	TR	SC	1.25 and 3.75 g	Physically compatible and chemically stable for 72 hr at 4 and 25 °C	757	C
Dextrose 5% in Ringer's injection, lactated	TR	SC	1.25 and 3.75 g	Physically compatible and chemically stable for 72 hr at 4 and 25 °C	757	C
Dextrose 2½% in sodium chloride 0.45%	TR	SC	1.25 and 3.75 g	Physically compatible and chemically stable for 72 hr at 4 and 25 °C	757	C
Dextrose 5% in sodium chloride 0.2%	TR	SC	1.25 and 3.75 g	Physically compatible and chemically stable for 72 hr at 4 and 25 °C	757	C

Solution Compatibility (Cont.)

Labetalol HCl

Solution	*Mfr*	*Mfr*	*Conc/L*	*Remarks*	*Ref*	*C/I*
Dextrose 5% in sodium chloride 0.33%	TR	SC	1.25 and 3.75 g	Physically compatible and chemically stable for 72 hr at 4 and 25 °C	757	C
Dextrose 5% in sodium chloride 0.9%	TR	SC	1.25 and 3.75 g	Physically compatible and chemically stable for 72 hr at 4 and 25 °C	757	C
Dextrose 5% in water	TR	SC	1.25 and 3.75 g	Physically compatible and chemically stable for 72 hr at 4 and 25 °C	757	C
Polysal in dextrose 5%	CU	SC	1.25 and 3.75 g	Physically compatible and chemically stable for 72 hr at 4 and 25 °C	757	C
Ringer's injection	TR	SC	1.25 and 3.75 g	Physically compatible and chemically stable for 72 hr at 4 and 25 °C	757	C
Ringer's injection, lactated	TR	SC	1.25 and 3.75 g	Physically compatible and chemically stable for 72 hr at 4 and 25 °C	757	C
Sodium bicarbonate 5%	TR	SC	1.25, 2.5, 3.75 g	White precipitate forms within 6 hr after mixing at 4 and 25 °C	757	I

Y-Site Injection Compatibility (1:1 Mixture)

Labetalol HCl

Drug	*Mfr*	*Conc*	*Mfr*	*Conc*	*Remarks*	*Ref*	*C/I*
Amikacin sulfate	BR	5 mg/ml[a]	SC	1 mg/ml[a]	Physically compatible for 24 hr at 18 °C	1171	C
Aminophylline	ES	1 mg/ml[a]	SC	1 mg/ml[a]	Physically compatible for 24 hr at 18 °C	1171	C
Amiodarone HCl	WY	4.8 mg/ml[a]	GL	5 mg/ml	Visually compatible for 24 hr at 23 °C	1877	C
Amphotericin B cholesteryl sulfate complex	SEQ	0.83 mg/ml[a]	AH	5 mg/ml	Gross precipitate forms	2117	I
Ampicillin sodium	WY	10 mg/ml[b]	SC	1 mg/ml[a]	Physically compatible for 24 hr at 18 °C	1171	C
Butorphanol tartrate	BR	0.04 mg/ml[a]	SC	1 mg/ml[a]	Physically compatible for 24 hr at 18 °C	1171	C
Calcium gluconate	AMR	0.23 mEq/ml[a]	SC	1 mg/ml[a]	Physically compatible for 24 hr at 18 °C	1171	C
Cefazolin sodium	LI	10 mg/ml[a]	SC	1 mg/ml[a]	Physically compatible for 24 hr at 18 °C	1171	C
Cefoperazone sodium	RR	10 mg/ml[a]	SC	1 mg/ml[a]	Cloudiness and fine precipitate form immediately	1171	I
Ceftazidime	GL[e]	10 mg/ml[a]	SC	1 mg/ml[a]	Physically compatible for 24 hr at 18 °C	1171	C
Ceftizoxime sodium	SKF	10 mg/ml[a]	SC	1 mg/ml[a]	Physically compatible for 24 hr at 18 °C	1171	C
Ceftriaxone sodium	RC	20[a,b] and 100[c] mg/ml	GL	2.5[c] and 5 mg/ml	Fluffy white precipitate formed immediately	1964	I
Chloramphenicol sodium succinate	PD	10 mg/ml[a]	SC	1 mg/ml[a]	Physically compatible for 24 hr at 18 °C	1171	C
Cimetidine HCl	SKF	3 mg/ml[a]	SC	1 mg/ml[a]	Physically compatible for 24 hr at 18 °C	1171	C
Clindamycin phosphate	UP	9 mg/ml[a]	SC	1 mg/ml[a]	Physically compatible for 24 hr at 18 °C	1171	C
Diltiazem HCl	MMD	1 mg/ml[a]	AH	2 mg/ml[a]	Visually compatible for 4 hr at 27 °C	2062	C
Dobutamine HCl	LI	2.5 mg/ml[a]	GL	1 mg/ml[a]	Visually compatible with little or no loss of either drug by HPLC in 4 hr at room temperature	1762	C
	LI	4 mg/ml[a]	GL	5 mg/ml	Visually compatible for 24 hr at 23 °C	1877	C
	LI	4 mg/ml[a]	AH	2 mg/ml[a]	Visually compatible for 4 hr at 27 °C	2062	C

Y-Site Injection Compatibility (1:1 Mixture) (Cont.)

Labetalol HCl

Drug	*Mfr*	*Conc*	*Mfr*	*Conc*	*Remarks*	*Ref*	*C/I*
Dopamine HCl	IMS	1.6 mg/ml[a]	SC	1 mg/ml[a]	Physically compatible for 24 hr at 18 °C	1171	C
	ES	1.6 mg/ml[a]	GL	1 mg/ml[a]	Visually compatible with little or no loss of either drug by HPLC in 4 hr at room temperature	1762	C
	AB	3.2 mg/ml[a]	AH	2 mg/ml[a]	Visually compatible for 4 hr at 27 °C	2062	C
Enalaprilat	MSD	0.05 mg/ml[b]	GL	1 mg/ml[a]	Physically compatible for 24 hr at room temperature under fluorescent light	1355	C
Epinephrine HCl	AB	0.02 mg/ml[a]	AH	2 mg/ml[a]	Visually compatible for 4 hr at 27 °C	2062	C
Erythromycin lactobionate	AB	5 mg/ml[a]	SC	1 mg/ml[a]	Physically compatible for 24 hr at 18 °C	1171	C
Esmolol HCl	DU	40 mg/ml[a]	GL	5 mg/ml	Visually compatible for 24 hr at 23 °C	1877	C
Famotidine	MSD	0.2 mg/ml[a]	SC	1 mg/ml[a]	Physically compatible for 4 hr at 25 °C	1188	C
Fentanyl citrate	JN	10 µg/ml[a]	SC	1 mg/ml[a]	Physically compatible for 24 hr at 18 °C	1171	C
	ES	0.05 mg/ml	AH	2 mg/ml[a]	Visually compatible for 4 hr at 27 °C	2062	C
Furosemide	AB	10 mg/ml	SC	2.5 mg/ml[a]	White turbidity forms immediately; flocculent precipitate forms in 4 hr	1704	I
	AB	0.5 mg/ml[a]	SC	2.5 mg/ml[a]	Physically compatible with no change in measured turbidity or increase in particle content in 4 hr at 22 °C	1704	C
	AB	0.5[a] and 10 mg/ml	SC	0.25 mg/ml[a]	Physically compatible with no change in measured turbidity or increase in particle content in 4 hr at 22 °C	1704	C
	ES	10 mg/ml[d]	SC	1.6 mg/ml[d]	White precipitate forms immediately	1715	I
	AMR	10 mg/ml	AH	2 mg/ml[a]	Precipitate forms immediately	2062	I
Gatifloxacin	BMS	2 mg/ml[a]	GW	5 mg/ml	Physically compatible with no change in measured haze or increase in particle content in 4 hr at 23 °C	2234	C
Gentamicin sulfate	ES	0.8 mg/ml[a]	SC	1 mg/ml[a]	Physically compatible for 24 hr at 18 °C	1171	C
Heparin sodium	IX	40 units/ml[a]	SC	1 mg/ml[a]	Physically compatible for 24 hr at 18 °C	1171	C
	OR	100 units/ml[a]	GL	5 mg/ml	Cloudiness with particles forms immediately	1877	I
	ES	100 units/ml[a]	AH	2 mg/ml[a]	Visually compatible for 4 hr at 27 °C	2062	C
Hetastarch in lactated electrolyte injection (Hextend)	AB	6%	GW	2 mg/ml[a]	Physically compatible with no change in measured turbidity or increase in particle content in 4 hr at 23 °C	2339	C
Hydromorphone HCl	KN	1 mg/ml	AH	2 mg/ml[a]	Visually compatible for 4 hr at 27 °C	2062	C
Insulin, regular	LI	1 unit/ml[a]	GL	5 mg/ml	Visually compatible for 4 hr. White precipitate forms in 24 hr at 23 °C	1877	?
Lidocaine HCl	AST	20 mg/ml[a]	SC	1 mg/ml[a]	Physically compatible for 24 hr at 18 °C	1171	C
Linezolid	PHU	2 mg/ml	GW	5 mg/ml	Physically compatible with no change in measured turbidity or increase in particle content in 4 hr at 23 °C	2264	C
Lorazepam	WY	0.5 mg/ml[a]	AH	2 mg/ml[a]	Visually compatible for 4 hr at 27 °C	2062	C
Magnesium sulfate	LY	10 mg/ml[a]	SC	1 mg/ml[a]	Physically compatible for 24 hr at 18 °C	1171	C
Meperidine HCl	AB	10 mg/ml	GL	5 mg/ml	Physically compatible for 4 hr at 25 °C	1397	C
Metronidazole	SE	5 mg/ml	SC	1 mg/ml[a]	Physically compatible for 24 hr at 18 °C	1171	C
Midazolam HCl	RC	1 mg/ml[a]	GL	5 mg/ml	Visually compatible for 24 hr at 23 °C	1877	C
	RC	2 mg/ml[a]	AH	2 mg/ml[a]	Visually compatible for 4 hr at 27 °C	2062	C

Y-Site Injection Compatibility (1:1 Mixture) (Cont.)

Labetalol HCl

Drug	*Mfr*	*Conc*	*Mfr*	*Conc*	*Remarks*	*Ref*	*C/I*
Milrinone lactate	SW	0.2 mg/ml[a]	AH	2 mg/ml[a]	Visually compatible for 4 hr at 27 °C	2062	C
Morphine sulfate	WY	1 mg/ml[a]	SC	1 mg/ml[a]	Physically compatible for 24 hr at 18 °C	1171	C
	AB	1 mg/ml	GL	5 mg/ml	Physically compatible for 4 hr at 25 °C	1397	C
	ES	0.5 mg/ml[a]	GL	1 mg/ml[a]	Visually compatible with little or no loss of either drug by HPLC in 4 hr at room temperature	1762	C
	SCN	2 mg/ml[a]	AH	2 mg/ml[a]	Visually compatible for 4 hr at 27 °C	2062	C
Nafcillin sodium	BR	10 mg/ml[a]	SC	1 mg/ml[a]	Cloudiness and fine precipitate form immediately	1171	I
Nicardipine HCl	WY	1 mg/ml[a]	AH	2 mg/ml[a]	Visually compatible for 4 hr at 27 °C	2062	C
Nitroglycerin	DU	0.2 mg/ml[a]	GL	1 mg/ml[a]	Visually compatible with no labetalol loss and 6% nitroglycerin loss by HPLC in 4 hr at room temperature	1762	C
	OM	0.2 mg/ml[a]	GL	5 mg/ml	Visually compatible for 24 hr at 23 °C	1877	C
	AB	0.4 mg/ml[a]	AH	2 mg/ml[a]	Visually compatible for 4 hr at 27 °C	2062	C
Norepinephrine bitartrate	STR	0.064 mg/ml[a]	GL	5 mg/ml	Visually compatible for 24 hr at 23 °C	1877	C
	AB	0.128 mg/ml[a]	AH	2 mg/ml[a]	Visually compatible for 4 hr at 27 °C	2062	C
Oxacillin sodium	BR	10 mg/ml[a]	SC	1 mg/ml[a]	Physically compatible for 24 hr at 18 °C	1171	C
Penicillin G potassium	PF	50,000 units/ml[a]	SC	1 mg/ml[a]	Physically compatible for 24 hr at 18 °C	1171	C
Piperacillin sodium	LE	10 mg/ml[a]	SC	1 mg/ml[a]	Physically compatible for 24 hr at 18 °C	1171	C
Potassium chloride	IX	0.4 mEq/ml[a]	SC	1 mg/ml[a]	Physically compatible for 24 hr at 18 °C	1171	C
Potassium phosphates	LY	0.44 mEq/ml[a]	SC	1 mg/ml[a]	Physically compatible for 24 hr at 18 °C	1171	C
Propofol	ZEN	10 mg/ml	AH	5 mg/ml	Physically compatible for 1 hr at 23 °C with no increase in particle content	2066	C
Ranitidine HCl	GL	0.5 mg/ml[a]	SC	1 mg/ml[a]	Physically compatible for 24 hr at 18 °C	1171	C
	GL	0.6 mg/ml[a]	GL	1 mg/ml[a]	Visually compatible with 5% labetalol loss and little or no ranitidine loss by HPLC in 4 hr at room temperature	1762	C
	GL	1 mg/ml[a]	AH	2 mg/ml[a]	Visually compatible for 4 hr at 27 °C	2062	C
Sodium acetate	LY	0.4 mEq/ml[a]	SC	1 mg/ml[a]	Physically compatible for 24 hr at 18 °C	1171	C
Sodium nitroprusside	RC	0.2 mg/ml[a]	GL	5 mg/ml	Visually compatible for 24 hr at 23 °C	1877	C
Thiopental sodium	AB	25 mg/ml[c]	AH	2 mg/ml[a]	Precipitate forms immediately	2062	I
Tobramycin sulfate	LI	0.8 mg/ml[a]	SC	1 mg/ml[a]	Physically compatible for 24 hr at 18 °C	1171	C
Trimethoprim–sulfamethoxazole	BW	0.8 + 4 mg/ml[a]	SC	1 mg/ml[a]	Physically compatible for 24 hr at 18 °C	1171	C
Vancomycin HCl	LE	5 mg/ml[a]	SC	1 mg/ml[a]	Physically compatible for 24 hr at 18 °C	1171	C
Vecuronium bromide	OR	1 mg/ml	AH	2 mg/ml[a]	Visually compatible for 4 hr at 27 °C	2062	C
Warfarin sodium	DU	2 mg/ml[c]	SC	0.8 mg/ml[a]	Haze forms immediately	2010	I
	DME	2 mg/ml[c]	SC	0.8 mg/ml[a]	Haze forms immediately	2078	I

[a]*Tested in dextrose 5% in water.*
[b]*Tested in sodium chloride 0.9%.*
[c]*Tested in sterile water for injection.*
[d]*Furosemide 0.5 ml injected in the Y-site port of a running infusion of labetalol HCl in dextrose 5% in water.*
[e]*Sodium carbonate–containing formulation tested.*

Additional Compatibility Information

Infusion Solutions — In addition to the solutions noted in the compatibility table, the manufacturer states that labetalol is physically compatible and chemically stable in sodium chloride 0.9% for 24 hours at room temperature or under refrigeration. (2)

Sodium Bicarbonate — The precipitate observed when labetalol HCl is admixed with sodium bicarbonate 5% (757) is believed to be labetalol free base. At the alkaline pH of the sodium bicarbonate solution (pH 7.6 to 8), the amine is no longer protonated but is partially or completely the free base. The free base is unionized and less soluble, precipitating in the aqueous medium. (927)

LEUCOVORIN CALCIUM
AHFS 92:00

Products — Leucovorin calcium is available in lyophilized form in vials containing leucovorin 50, 100, 200, 350, and 500 mg as the calcium salt with sodium chloride and sodium hydroxide or hydrochloric acid to adjust the pH. Reconstitute the vials with bacteriostatic water for injection containing benzyl alcohol or sterile water for injection with the volumes indicated in Table 1. (1-12/97; 1-6/98; 4; 29)

Leucovorin calcium is also available at a concentration of 10 mg/ml containing no preservative in vials of 10, 25, and 30 ml. (4; 29)

pH — The vials have a pH of approximately 8.1. (1-6/98)

Osmolality — Leucovorin calcium 10 mg/ml in sterile water for injection has an osmolality of 274 mOsm/kg. (1689)

Administration — Leucovorin calcium is administered by intramuscular or intravenous injection or infusion at a rate not exceeding 160 mg/min. When doses greater than 10 mg/m^2 are required, diluents containing benzyl alcohol should not be used for reconstitution. (1-6/98; 4)

Stability — Leucovorin calcium injection should be stored at room temperature and protected from light. (1-6/98; 4)

The reconstituted solution of leucovorin calcium is stated to be chemically stable for seven days. However, when reconstituted with diluents that contain no preservatives, immediate use is recommended. (1-6/98) Immunex indicates concentrations of 10 and 50 mg/ml prepared with bacteriostatic water for injection are stable for up to 14 days under refrigeration and at room temperature when protected from light. (31)

Leucovorin calcium (Lederle) 10 mg/ml in sterile water for injection was determined by UV spectroscopy to be stable for seven days at 4 and 25 °C when protected from light. (1669)

Table 1. Recommended Reconstitution of Leucovorin Calcium (1-12/97; 1-6/98; 4)

Vial Size (mg)	Volume of Diluent (ml)	Concentration (mg/ml)
50	5	10
100	10	10
200	20	10
350	17	20
500	50	10

pH Effects — Leucovorin calcium in aqueous solution exhibits good stability at pH 6.5 to 10. The pH of maximum stability was determined to be 7.1 to 7.4. Below pH 6, increased decomposition rates were observed. (1276)

Elastomeric Reservoir Pumps — Leucovorin calcium solutions in elastomeric reservoir pumps have been stated by the pump manufacturers to be stable for the following time periods refrigerated (REF) or at room temperature (RT) (31):

Pump Reservoir(s)	Conc.	REF	RT
Homepump; Homepump Eclipse	4 mg/ml[b]	7 days	7 days
Infusor	2 to 20 mg/ml[a,b]	7 days	2 days
Intermate, Intermate HPC, Intermate LV	2 to 20 mg/ml[a,b]	7 days	2 days

[a] *In dextrose 5% in water.*
[b] *In sodium chloride 0.9%.*

Central Venous Catheter — Leucovorin calcium (Gensia) 2 mg/ml in dextrose 5% in water was found to be compatible with the ARROWg+ard Blue Plus (Arrow International) chlorhexidine-bearing triple-lumen central catheter. HPLC analysis was used to evaluate completeness of drug delivery through the catheter and the amount of chlorhexidine removed from the internal lumens. Essentially complete delivery of the drug was found with little or no drug loss occurring. Furthermore, chlorhexidine delivered from the catheter remained at trace amounts with no substantial increase due to the delivery of the drug through the catheter. (2335)

Compatibility Information

Solution Compatibility

Leucovorin calcium

Solution	*Mfr*	*Mfr*	*Conc/L*	*Remarks*	*Ref*	*C/I*
Dextrose 10% in sodium chloride 0.9%		LE	50 mg	Less than 10% decomposition in 24 hr at room temperature protected from light	488	C

Solution Compatibility (Cont.)

Leucovorin calcium

Solution	*Mfr*	*Mfr*	*Conc/L*	*Remarks*	*Ref*	*C/I*
Dextrose 5% in water	TR[a]	LE	910 mg	Less than 10% decomposition in 24 hr at room temperature	519	**C**
	[a]	LE	0.1, 0.5, 1, 1.5 g	Little or no loss by HPLC in 4 days at 4 and 23 °C protected from light	1596	**C**
	MG[b]		910 mg	Less than 10% loss by HPLC in 24 hr at room temperature exposed to light	1658	**C**
Dextrose 10% in water		LE	50 mg	Less than 10% decomposition in 24 hr at room temperature protected from light	488	**C**
Ringer's injection		LE	50 mg	Less than 10% decomposition in 24 hr at room temperature protected from light	488	**C**
Ringer's injection, lactated		LE	50 mg	Less than 10% decomposition in 24 hr at room temperature protected from light	488	**C**
Sodium chloride 0.9%	[a]	LE	1 and 1.5 g	Little or no loss by HPLC in 4 days at 4 and 23 °C protected from light	1596	**C**
	[c]	LE	0.5 g	Little or no loss by HPLC in 4 days at 4 and 23 °C protected from light	1596	**C**
	[c]	LE	0.1 g	Approximately 9% loss by HPLC in 4 days at 4 and 23 °C protected from light	1596	**C**
	[d]	LE	0.1 and 0.5 g	Variable losses, up to 24%, by HPLC in 4 days at 4 and 23 °C protected from light	1596	**I**
	[b]	LE	1 g	Chemically stable by UV spectroscopy for 7 days at 4 and 25 °C protected from light	1669	**C**

[a]*Tested in both glass and PVC containers.*
[b]*Tested in both glass and polyolefin containers.*
[c]*Tested in glass containers.*
[d]*Tested in PVC containers.*

Additive Compatibility

Leucovorin calcium

Drug	*Mfr*	*Conc/L*	*Mfr*	*Conc/L*	*Test Soln*	*Remarks*	*Ref*	*C/I*
Cisplatin		200 mg		140 mg	NS	Both drugs stable for 15 days at room temperature protected from light	1379	**C**
Cisplatin with floxuridine		200 mg 700 mg		140 mg	NS	All drugs stable for 7 days at room temperature	1379	**C**
Floxuridine	QU	1 g	QU	30 mg	NS	Physically compatible and chemically stable for 48 hr at 4 and 20 °C. No floxuridine loss and 10% leucovorin loss in 48 hr at 40 °C	1317	**C**
	QU	2 g	QU	240 mg	NS	Physically compatible and chemically stable for 48 hr at 4 and 20 °C. No floxuridine loss and 7% leucovorin loss in 48 hr at 40 °C	1317	**C**
	QU	4 g	QU	960 mg	NS	Physically compatible and chemically stable for 48 hr at 4, 20 and 40 °C	1317	**C**
		10 g		200 mg	NS	Both drugs stable for 15 days at room temperature protected from light	1387	**C**
Fluorouracil	AD	16.7 to 46.2 g	LE	1.5 to 13.3 g	[a]	Subvisual particulate matter forms in all combinations in variable periods from 1 to 4 days at 4, 23, and 32 °C	1816	**I**

[a]*Tested with both drugs undiluted and diluted by 25% with dextrose 5% in water.*

Drugs in Syringe Compatibility

Drug (in syringe)	Mfr	Amt	Mfr	Amt	Remarks	Ref	C/I
			Leucovorin calcium				
Bleomycin sulfate		1.5 units/ 0.5 ml		5 mg/ 0.5 ml	Physically compatible for 5 min at room temperature followed by 8 min of centrifugation	980	C
Cisplatin		0.5 mg/ 0.5 ml		5 mg/ 0.5 ml	Physically compatible for 5 min at room temperature followed by 8 min of centrifugation	980	C
Cyclophosphamide		10 mg/ 0.5 ml		5 mg/ 0.5 ml	Physically compatible for 5 min at room temperature followed by 8 min of centrifugation	980	C
Doxorubicin HCl		1 mg/ 0.5 ml		5 mg/ 0.5 ml	Physically compatible for 5 min at room temperature followed by 8 min of centrifugation	980	C
Droperidol		1.25 mg/ 0.5 ml		5 mg/ 0.5 ml	Immediate precipitation	980	I
Fluorouracil		25 mg/ 0.5 ml		5 mg/ 0.5 ml	Physically compatible for 5 min at room temperature followed by 8 min of centrifugation	980	C
Furosemide		5 mg/ 0.5 ml		5 mg/ 0.5 ml	Physically compatible for 5 min at room temperature followed by 8 min of centrifugation	980	C
Heparin sodium		500 units/ 0.5 ml		5 mg/ 0.5 ml	Physically compatible for 5 min at room temperature followed by 8 min of centrifugation	980	C
Methotrexate sodium		12.5 mg/ 0.5 ml		5 mg/ 0.5 ml	Physically compatible for 5 min at room temperature followed by 8 min of centrifugation	980	C
Metoclopramide HCl		2.5 mg/ 0.5 ml		5 mg/ 0.5 ml	Physically compatible for 5 min at room temperature followed by 8 min of centrifugation	980	C
Mitomycin		0.25 mg/ 0.5 ml		5 mg/ 0.5 ml	Physically compatible for 5 min at room temperature followed by 8 min of centrifugation	980	C
Vinblastine sulfate		0.5 mg/ 0.5 ml		5 mg/ 0.5 ml	Physically compatible for 5 min at room temperature followed by 8 min of centrifugation	980	C
Vincristine sulfate		0.5 mg/ 0.5 ml		5 mg/ 0.5 ml	Physically compatible for 5 min at room temperature followed by 8 min of centrifugation	980	C

Y-Site Injection Compatibility (1:1 Mixture)

Drug	Mfr	Conc	Mfr	Conc	Remarks	Ref	C/I
			Leucovorin calcium				
Amifostine	USB	10 mg/ml[a]	LE	2 mg/ml[a]	Physically compatible with no change in measured turbidity or increase in particle content in 4 hr at 23 °C	1845	C
Amphotericin B cholesteryl sulfate complex	SEQ	0.83 mg/ml[a]	IMM	2 mg/ml[a]	Gross precipitate forms	2117	I
Aztreonam	SQ	40 mg/ml[a]	LE	2 mg/ml[a]	Physically compatible with no subvisual haze or particle formation in 4 hr at 23 °C	1758	C
Bleomycin sulfate		3 units/ml		10 mg/ml	Drugs injected sequentially into Y-site with no flush between. No visually apparent precipitate	980	C
Cefepime HCl	BMS	20 mg/ml[a]	LE	2 mg/ml[a]	Physically compatible with no change in measured turbidity or increase in particle content in 4 hr at 22 °C	1689	C
Cisplatin		1 mg/ml		10 mg/ml	Drugs injected sequentially into Y-site with no flush between. No visually apparent precipitate	980	C

Y-Site Injection Compatibility (1:1 Mixture) (Cont.)

Drug	Mfr	Conc	Leucovorin calcium Mfr	Leucovorin calcium Conc	Remarks	Ref	C/I
Cladribine	ORT	0.015[b] and 0.5[c] mg/ml	IMM	2 mg/ml[b]	Physically compatible with no change in measured turbidity or increase in particle content in 4 hr at 23 °C	1969	C
Cyclophosphamide		20 mg/ml		10 mg/ml	Drugs injected sequentially into Y-site with no flush between. No visually apparent precipitate	980	C
Docetaxel	RPR	0.9 mg/ml[a]	ES	2 mg/ml[a]	Physically compatible with no change in measured turbidity or increase in particle content in 4 hr at 23 °C	2224	C
Doxorubicin HCl		2 mg/ml		10 mg/ml	Drugs injected sequentially into Y-site with no flush between. No visually apparent precipitate	980	C
Doxorubicin HCl liposome injection	SEQ	0.4 mg/ml[a]	IMM	2 mg/ml[a]	Physically compatible with little or no change in measured turbidity and no increase in particle content in 4 hr at 23 °C	2087	C
Droperidol		2.5 mg/ml		10 mg/ml	Drugs injected sequentially into Y-site with no flush between. Immediate precipitation	980	I
Etoposide phosphate	BR	5 mg/ml[a]	IMM	2 mg/ml[a]	Physically compatible with no change in measured turbidity or increase in particle content in 4 hr at 23 °C	2218	C
Filgrastim	AMG	30 μg/ml[a]	LE	2 mg/ml[a]	Physically compatible with no change in measured turbidity or increase in particle content in 4 hr at 22 °C	1687	C
Fluconazole	RR	2 mg/ml	LE	10 mg/ml	Physically compatible for 24 hr at 25 °C	1407	C
Fluorouracil		50 mg/ml		10 mg/ml	Drugs injected sequentially into Y-site with no flush between. No visually apparent precipitate	980	C
Foscarnet sodium	AST	24 mg/ml	QU	10 mg/ml	Cloudy yellow solution	1335	I
Furosemide		10 mg/ml		10 mg/ml	Drugs injected sequentially into Y-site with no flush between. No visually apparent precipitate	980	C
Gatifloxacin	BMS	2 mg/ml[a]	GNS	2 mg/ml[a]	Physically compatible with no change in measured haze or increase in particle content in 4 hr at 23 °C	2234	C
Gemcitabine HCl	LI	10 mg/ml[b]	IMM	2 mg/ml[b]	Physically compatible with no change in measured turbidity or increase in particle content in 4 hr at 23 °C	2226	C
Granisetron HCl	SKB	0.05 mg/ml[a]	IMM	2 mg/ml[a]	Physically compatible with no change in measured turbidity or increase in particle content in 4 hr at 23 °C	2000	C
Heparin sodium		1000 units/ml		10 mg/ml	Drugs injected sequentially into Y-site with no flush between. No visually apparent precipitate	980	C
Linezolid	PHU	2 mg/ml	GNS	2 mg/ml[a]	Physically compatible with no change in measured turbidity or increase in particle content in 4 hr at 23 °C	2264	C
Methotrexate sodium		25 mg/ml		10 mg/ml	Drugs injected sequentially into Y-site with no flush between. No visually apparent precipitate	980	C

Y-Site Injection Compatibility (1:1 Mixture) (Cont.)

Leucovorin calcium

Drug	*Mfr*	*Conc*	*Mfr*	*Conc*	*Remarks*	*Ref*	*C/I*
		30 mg/ml	LE	10 mg/ml	Visually compatible for 4 hr at room temperature	1788	C
Metoclopramide HCl		5 mg/ml		10 mg/ml	Drugs injected sequentially into Y-site with no flush between. No visually apparent precipitate	980	C
Mitomycin		0.5 mg/ml		10 mg/ml	Drugs injected sequentially into Y-site with no flush between. No visually apparent precipitate	980	C
Piperacillin sodium–tazobactam sodium	LE	40 + 5 mg/ml[a]	LE	2 mg/ml[a]	Physically compatible with no change in measured turbidity or increase in particle content in 4 hr at 22 °C	1688	C
Sodium bicarbonate		1.4%	LE	10 mg/ml	Yellow precipitate forms in 0.5 hr at room temperature	1788	I
Tacrolimus	FUJ	1 mg/ml[b]	ES	10 mg/ml[a]	Visually compatible for 24 hr at 25 °C	1630	C
Teniposide	BR	0.1 mg/ml[a]	LE	2 mg/ml[a]	Physically compatible with no subvisual haze or particle formation in 4 hr at 23 °C	1725	C
Thiotepa	IMM[d]	1 mg/ml[a]	LE	2 mg/ml[a]	Physically compatible with no change in measured turbidity or increase in particle content in 4 hr at 23 °C	1861	C
TNA #218 to #226[e]			IMM	2 mg/ml[a]	Visually compatible with no precipitate or emulsion damage apparent in 4 hr at 23 °C	2215	C
TPN #212 to #215[e]			IMM	2 mg/ml[a]	Physically compatible with no change in measured turbidity or increase in particle content in 4 hr at 23 °C	2109	C
Vinblastine sulfate		1 mg/ml		10 mg/ml	Drugs injected sequentially into Y-site with no flush between. No visually apparent precipitate	980	C
Vincristine sulfate		1 mg/ml		10 mg/ml	Drugs injected sequentially into Y-site with no flush between. No visually apparent precipitate	980	C

[a]*Tested in dextrose 5% in water.*
[b]*Tested in sodium chloride 0.9%.*
[c]*Tested in bacteriostatic sodium chloride 0.9% preserved with benzyl alcohol 0.9%.*
[d]*Lyophilized formulation tested.*
[e]*Refer to Appendix I for the composition of parenteral nutrition solutions. TNA indicates a 3-in-1 admixture, and TPN indicates a 2-in-1 admixture.*

Additional Compatibility Information

Floxuridine — Leucovorin calcium (Quad) and floxuridine (Quad) in concentrations ranging from 30 mg and 1 g, respectively, to 960 mg and 4 g, respectively, per liter of sodium chloride 0.9% were evaluated for stability under a sequence of temperatures to simulate use conditions as intraperitoneal chemotherapy solutions. The admixtures were stored for 48 hours at 4 °C, followed by 12 hours at 20 °C, and finally followed by 12 hours at 40 °C (near-physiologic temperature). No floxuridine loss and about a 3 to 6% leucovorin calcium loss occurred during the study period. (1317)

Fluorouracil — Several articles reported the chemical stability and physical compatibility of fluorouracil with leucovorin calcium. (980; 1309; 1387; 1817) However, more recent work found substantial amounts of subvisual particles in this drug combination over numerous concentrations when stored at 4, 23, and 32 °C. Particulate formation sometimes clogged filters and disrupted multiple-day treatment. Particulate formation began in about 24 hours in most samples, and particles were found in all samples within seven days. Fluorouracil and leucovorin calcium in the same container can no longer be considered a compatible combination. (1816)

LEVOFLOXACIN
AHFS 8:22

Products — Levofloxacin is available as a 25-mg/ml preservative-free aqueous solution in 20-ml (500-mg) and 30-ml (750-mg) single-use vials. This concentration must be diluted to a 5-mg/ml concentration for administration. Adding 250 mg (10 ml) to 40 ml of diluent, 500 mg (20 ml) to 80 ml of diluent, or 750 mg (30 ml) to 120 ml of diluent will result in a 5-mg/ml concentration. (2)

The drug is also available as premixed infusion solutions of 5 mg/ml in dextrose 5% in water in 50-ml (250-mg), 100-ml (500-mg), and 150-ml (750-mg) flexible plastic bags. The solutions in plastic bags are ready to use and require no dilution. Sodium hydroxide and hydrochloric acid may have been added during manufacture to adjust the pH. (1-1/02; 2)

pH — From 3.8 to 5.8. (2)

The pH of a 5-mg/ml concentration in dextrose or sodium chloride solutions is about 4.6 to 4.7. In solutions with a greater buffering capacity, pH values are higher. A 5-mg/ml concentration had a pH of 4.9 in dextrose 5% in Ringer's injection, lactated, a pH of 5.0 in Plasma-Lyte 56/5% dextrose, and a pH of 5.5 in sodium lactate ⅙ M. (2)

Tonicity — The premixed infusion solutions are nearly isotonic. (2)

Trade Name(s) — Levaquin.

Administration — Levofloxacin is administered only at a concentration of 5-mg/ml by slow intravenous infusion over at least 60 minutes. Doses of 750 mg should be administered over 90 minutes. No other route is recommended. Rapid infusion or bolus administration must not be used because of the potential for hypotension. The 25-mg/ml concentrate must be diluted to 5 mg/ml with a compatible diluent for administration. (2; 4)

Stability — Intact vials should be stored at controlled room temperature and protected from light. The premixed infusion solutions should be stored at or below 25 °C and protected from light, freezing, and excessive heat. A brief exposure to temperatures up to 40 °C does not adversely affect potency. (2) The injection and infusion admixtures are clear and yellow to greenish yellow in appearance. This color does not adversely affect the product. (2; 1986)

Levofloxacin diluted in a compatible diluent to 5 mg/ml is stated to be stable for 72 hours stored at or below 25 °C and for 14 days stored at 5 °C. (2)

pH Effects — Levofloxacin has a solubility of about 100 mg/ml at pH values ranging from 0.6 to 5.8. The solubility increases as pH increases up to 6.7, with a maximum solubility of 272 mg/ml. Above pH 6.7, solubility decreases to a minimum of 50 mg/ml at pH 6.9. (2)

Freezing Solutions — Levofloxacin 5 mg/ml diluted in a compatible diluent in glass bottles or plastic infusion containers is stable for six months frozen at −20 °C. Frozen solutions should be thawed at room temperature or in the refrigerator. Accelerated thawing using microwaves or hot water immersion is not recommended. Thawed solutions should not be refrozen. (2)

Levofloxacin (OMJ Pharmaceuticals) 0.5 and 5 g/L in mannitol 20% and 0.5 g/L in sodium bicarbonate 5% formed a precipitate during frozen storage at −20 °C for 13 weeks. In several other infusion solutions at 0.5 and 5 g/L, no precipitate formed and little or no loss of levofloxacin by HPLC analysis occurred during 26 weeks of storage at −20 °C. (1986) See Solution Compatibility below.

Central Venous Catheter — Levofloxacin (McNeil) 1 mg/ml in dextrose 5% in water was found to be compatible with the ARROWg+ard Blue Plus (Arrow International) chlorhexidine-bearing triple-lumen central catheter. HPLC analysis was used to evaluate completeness of drug delivery through the catheter and the amount of chlorhexidine removed from the internal lumens. Essentially complete delivery of the drug was found with little or no drug loss occurring. Furthermore, chlorhexidine delivered from the catheter remained at trace amounts with no substantial increase due to the delivery of the drug through the catheter. (2335)

Compatibility Information

Solution Compatibility

Levofloxacin

Solution	*Mfr*	*Mfr*	*Conc/L*	*Remarks*	*Ref*	*C/I*
Dextrose 5% in Ringer's injection, lactated	BA[a]	OMJ	0.5 and 5 g	Physically compatible with no loss by HPLC in 3 days at 25 °C, 14 days at 5 °C, and 26 weeks at −20 °C, all protected from light	1986	C
Dextrose 5% in sodium chloride 0.9%	BA[a]	OMJ	0.5 and 5 g	Physically compatible with no loss by HPLC in 3 days at 25 °C, 14 days at 5 °C, and 26 weeks at −20 °C, all protected from light	1986	C
Dextrose 5% in sodium chloride 0.45% with potassium chloride 0.15%	BA[a]	OMJ	0.5 and 5 g	Physically compatible with little or no loss by HPLC in 3 days at 25 °C, 14 days at 5 °C, and 26 weeks at −20 °C, all protected from light	1986	C
Dextrose 5% in water	BA[a]	OMJ	0.5 and 5 g	Physically compatible with no loss by HPLC in 3 days at 25 °C, 14 days at 5 °C, and 26 weeks at −20 °C, all protected from light	1986	C
Mannitol 20%	BA[a]	OMJ	0.5 g	Precipitate forms within a few hours	1986	I

Solution Compatibility (Cont.)

Levofloxacin

Solution	*Mfr*	*Mfr*	*Conc/L*	*Remarks*	*Ref*	*C/I*
	BA[a]	OMJ	5 g	Physically compatible with 4% or less loss by HPLC in 3 days at 25 °C and 14 days at 5 °C protected from light	1986	C
	BA[a]	OMJ	5 g	Precipitate forms within 13 weeks at −20 °C	1986	I
Plasma-Lyte 56 and dextrose 5%	BA[a]	OMJ	0.5 and 5 g	Physically compatible with no loss by HPLC in 3 days at 25 °C, 14 days at 5 °C, and 26 weeks at −20 °C, all protected from light	1986	C
Sodium bicarbonate 5%	BA[a]	OMJ	0.5 g	Physically compatible with no loss by HPLC in 3 days at 25 °C and 14 days at 5 °C, protected from light	1986	C
	BA[a]	OMJ	0.5 g	Precipitate forms within 13 weeks at −20 °C	1986	I
	BA[a]	OMJ	5 g	Physically compatible with no loss by HPLC in 3 days at 25 °C, 14 days at 5 °C, and 26 weeks at −20 °C, all protected from light	1986	C
Sodium chloride 0.9%	BA[a]	OMJ	0.5 and 5 g	Physically compatible with no loss by HPLC in 3 days at 25 °C, 14 days at 5 °C, and 26 weeks at −20 °C, all protected from light	1986	C
Sodium lactate ⅙ M	BA[a]	OMJ	0.5 and 5 g	Physically compatible with 4% or less loss by HPLC in 3 days at 25 °C, 14 days at 5 °C, and 26 weeks at −20 °C, all protected from light	1986	C

[a]*Tested in PVC containers.*

Additive Compatibility

Levofloxacin

Drug	*Mfr*	*Conc/L*	*Mfr*	*Conc/L*	*Test Soln*	*Remarks*	*Ref*	*C/I*
Linezolid	PHU	2 g	OMN	5 g	[a]	Physically compatible with little or no loss of either drug by HPLC in 7 days at 4 and 23°C protected from light	2334	C

[a]*Admixed in the linezolid infusion container.*

Y-Site Injection Compatibility (1:1 Mixture)

Levofloxacin

Drug	*Mfr*	*Conc*	*Mfr*	*Conc*	*Remarks*	*Ref*	*C/I*
Acyclovir sodium	BW	50 mg/ml	OMN	5 mg/ml[a]	Cloudy precipitate forms	2233	I
Alprostadil	UP	0.5 mg/ml	OMN	5 mg/ml[a]	Precipitate forms	2233	I
Amikacin sulfate	BED	50 mg/ml	OMN	5 mg/ml[a]	Visually compatible for 4 hr at 24 °C under fluorescent light	2233	C
Aminophylline	AMR	25 mg/ml	OMN	5 mg/ml[a]	Visually compatible for 4 hr at 24 °C under fluorescent light	2233	C
Ampicillin sodium	MAR	50 mg/ml	OMN	5 mg/ml[a]	Visually compatible for 4 hr at 24 °C under fluorescent light	2233	C
Caffeine citrate		5 mg/ml	OMN	5 mg/ml[a]	Visually compatible for 4 hr at 24 °C under fluorescent light	2233	C
Cefotaxime sodium	HO	200 mg/ml	OMN	5 mg/ml[a]	Visually compatible for 4 hr at 24 °C under fluorescent light	2233	C

Y-Site Injection Compatibility (1:1 Mixture) (Cont.)

Drug	Mfr	Conc	Levofloxacin Mfr	Levofloxacin Conc	Remarks	Ref	C/I
Cimetidine HCl	AMR	150 mg/ml	OMN	5 mg/ml[a]	Visually compatible for 4 hr at 24 °C under fluorescent light	2233	C
Clindamycin phosphate	UP	150 mg/ml	OMN	5 mg/ml[a]	Visually compatible for 4 hr at 24 °C under fluorescent light	2233	C
Dexamethasone sodium phosphate	ES	4 mg/ml	OMN	5 mg/ml[a]	Visually compatible for 4 hr at 24 °C under fluorescent light	2233	C
Dobutamine HCl	AB	12.5 mg/ml	OMN	5 mg/ml[a]	Visually compatible for 4 hr at 24 °C under fluorescent light	2233	C
Dopamine HCl	AMR	80 mg/ml	OMN	5 mg/ml[a]	Visually compatible for 4 hr at 24 °C under fluorescent light	2233	C
Epinephrine HCl	AB	1 mg/ml	OMN	5 mg/ml[a]	Visually compatible for 4 hr at 24 °C under fluorescent light	2233	C
Fentanyl citrate	AB	0.05 mg/ml	OMN	5 mg/ml[a]	Visually compatible for 4 hr at 24 °C under fluorescent light	2233	C
Furosemide	AST	10 mg/ml	OMN	5 mg/ml[a]	Cloudy precipitate forms	2233	I
Gentamicin sulfate	ES	10 mg/ml	OMN	5 mg/ml[a]	Visually compatible for 4 hr at 24 °C under fluorescent light	2233	C
Heparin sodium	ES	10 units/ml	OMN	5 mg/ml[a]	Cloudy precipitate forms	2233	I
Hetastarch in lactated electrolyte injection (Hextend)	AB	6%	OMN	5 mg/ml[a]	Physically compatible with no change in measured turbidity or increase in particle content in 4 hr at 23 °C	2339	C
Indomethacin sodium trihydrate	ME	1 mg/ml	OMN	5 mg/ml[a]	Cloudy precipitate forms	2233	I
Insulin, regular[c]	LI	1 unit/ml	OMN	5 mg/ml[a]	Visually compatible for 4 hours at 24 °C under fluorescent light	2233	C
	LI	100 units/ml	OMN	5 mg/ml[a]	Cloudy precipitate forms	2233	I
Isoproterenol HCl	ES	0.2 mg/ml	OMN	5 mg/ml[a]	Visually compatible for 4 hours at 24 °C under fluorescent light	2233	C
Lidocaine HCl	AB	10 mg/ml[d]	OMN	5 mg/ml[a]	Visually compatible for 4 hours at 24 °C under fluorescent light	2233	C
Linezolid	PHU	2 mg/ml	ORT	5 mg/ml[a]	Physically compatible with no change in measured turbidity or increase in particle content in 4 hr at 23 °C	2264	C
Lorazepam		2 mg/ml	OMN	5 mg/ml[a]	Visually compatible for 4 hours at 24 °C under fluorescent light	2233	C
Metoclopramide HCl	ES	5 mg/ml	OMN	5 mg/ml[a]	Visually compatible for 4 hours at 24 °C under fluorescent light	2233	C
Morphine sulfate	SW	4 mg/ml	OMN	5 mg/ml[a]	Visually compatible for 4 hours at 24 °C under fluorescent light	2233	C
Nitroglycerin	AMR	5 mg/ml	OMN	5 mg/ml[a]	Cloudy precipitate forms	2233	I
Oxacillin sodium	APC	167 mg/ml	OMN	5 mg/ml[a]	Visually compatible for 4 hours at 24 °C under fluorescent light	2233	C
Pancuronium bromide	ES	1 mg/ml	OMN	5 mg/ml[a]	Visually compatible for 4 hours at 24 °C under fluorescent light	2233	C
Penicillin G sodium	MAR	500,000 units/ml	OMN	5 mg/ml[a]	Visually compatible for 4 hours at 24 °C under fluorescent light	2233	C
Phenobarbital sodium	ES	130 mg/ml	OMN	5 mg/ml[a]	Visually compatible for 4 hours at 24 °C under fluorescent light	2233	C

Y-Site Injection Compatibility (1:1 Mixture) (Cont.)

Levofloxacin

Drug	Mfr	Conc	Mfr	Conc	Remarks	Ref	C/I
Phenylephrine HCl	AMR	10 mg/ml	OMN	5 mg/ml[a]	Visually compatible for 4 hours at 24 °C under fluorescent light	2233	C
Propofol	ASZ	10 mg/ml	OMN	5 mg/ml[a]	Emulsion broke and oiled out	1916	I
Sodium bicarbonate	AB	0.5 mEq/ml	OMN	5 mg/ml[a]	Visually compatible for 4 hours at 24 °C under fluorescent light	2233	C
Sodium nitroprusside	ES	10 mg/ml[b]	OMN	5 mg/ml[a]	Fluffy precipitate forms	2233	I
Vancomycin HCl	LI	50 mg/ml	OMN	5 mg/ml[a]	Visually compatible for 4 hours at 24 °C under fluorescent light	2233	C

[a]*Tested in dextrose 5% in water.*
[b]*Tested in sodium chloride 0.9%.*
[c]*Regular human insulin.*
[d]*Preservative free.*

Additional Compatibility Information

Infusion Solutions — The manufacturer recommends the following infusion solutions for dilution of levofloxacin to a 5-mg/ml concentration (2):

Dextrose in Ringer's injection, lactated
Dextrose 5% in sodium chloride 0.9%
Dextrose 5% in sodium chloride 0.45% and potassium chloride 0.15%
Dextrose 5% in water
Plasma-Lyte 56/5% dextrose
Sodium chloride 0.9%
Sodium lactate ⅙ M

Metal Ions — Levofloxacin may form stable coordination compounds with metal ions. The chelation potential is greatest with Al^{3+} and declines from Cu^{2+} to Zn^{2+} to Mg^{2+} to Ca^{2+}. (2)

Other Drugs — The manufacturer recommends that no other drugs be added to levofloxacin or infused simultaneously through the same line. (2)

LEVORPHANOL TARTRATE
AHFS 28:08.08

Products — Levorphanol tartrate is available in 1-ml ampuls and 10-ml multiple-dose vials. Each milliliter of solution contains (2):

Component	Ampul	Vial
Levorphanol tartrate	2 mg	2 mg
Methylparaben	1.8 mg	
Propylparaben	0.2 mg	
Phenol		4.5 mg
Sodium hydroxide	to adjust pH	to adjust pH
Water for injection	qs 1 ml	qs 1 ml

pH — The pH is adjusted to approximately 4.3. (2)

Trade Name(s) — Levo-Dromoran.

Administration — Levorphanol tartrate may be administered by subcutaneous or intramuscular injection or slow intravenous injection or infusion. (2; 4)

Stability — The product should be stored at controlled room temperature. Freezing should be avoided. (4)

Compatibility Information

Additive Compatibility

Levorphanol tartrate

Drug	Mfr	Conc/L	Mfr	Conc/L	Test Soln	Remarks	Ref	C/I
Aminophylline			RC			Physically incompatible	9	I

Additive Compatibility (Cont.)

			Levorphanol tartrate					
Drug	*Mfr*	*Conc/L*	*Mfr*	*Conc/L*	*Test Soln*	*Remarks*	*Ref*	*C/I*
Ammonium chloride			RC			Physically incompatible	9	I
Amobarbital sodium			RC			Physically incompatible	9	I
Chlorothiazide sodium	MSD		RC			Physically incompatible	9	I
Heparin sodium			RC			Physically incompatible	9	I
Pentobarbital sodium			RC			Physically incompatible	9	I
Phenobarbital sodium	WI		RC			Physically incompatible	9	I
Phenytoin sodium	PD		RC			Physically incompatible	9	I
Sodium bicarbonate			RC			Physically incompatible	9	I
Thiopental sodium	AB		RC			Physically incompatible	9	I

Drugs in Syringe Compatibility

			Levorphanol tartrate				
Drug (in syringe)	*Mfr*	*Amt*	*Mfr*	*Amt*	*Remarks*	*Ref*	*C/I*
Glycopyrrolate	RB	0.2 mg/ 1 ml	RC	2 mg/ 1 ml	Physically compatible and pH in stability range for glycopyrrolate for 48 hr at 25 °C	331	C
	RB	0.2 mg/ 1 ml	RC	4 mg/ 2 ml	Physically compatible and pH in stability range for glycopyrrolate for 48 hr at 25 °C	331	C
	RB	0.4 mg/ 2 ml	RC	2 mg/ 1 ml	Physically compatible and pH in stability range for glycopyrrolate for 48 hr at 25 °C	331	C

Y-Site Injection Compatibility (1:1 Mixture)

			Levorphanol tartrate				
Drug	*Mfr*	*Conc*	*Mfr*	*Conc*	*Remarks*	*Ref*	*C/I*
Propofol	ZEN	10 mg/ml	RC	0.5 mg/ml[a]	Physically compatible for 1 hr at 23 °C with no increase in particle content	2066	C
TNA #218 to #226[b]			RC	0.5 mg/ml[a]	Damage to emulsion integrity occurs immediately with free oil formation possible	2215	I
TPN #212 to #215[b]			RC	0.5 mg/ml[a]	Physically compatible with no change in measured turbidity or increase in particle content in 4 hr at 23 °C	2109	C

[a]*Tested in dextrose 5% in water.*
[b]*Refer to Appendix I for the composition of parenteral nutrition solutions. TNA indicates a 3-in-1 admixture, and TPN indicates a 2-in-1 admixture.*

LIDOCAINE HCL (LIGNOCAINE HCL) AHFS 24:04

Products — Lidocaine HCl for direct intravenous use is available in concentrations of 10 and 20 mg/ml in ampuls and vials from 5 to 50 ml and in 5-ml prefilled syringes. The drug is also available as 40-, 100-, and 200-mg/ml concentrates for intravenous admixture preparation. Multiple-dose vials and automatic injection devices may also have methylparaben and EDTA or sulfites. (4; 154)

The pH of these solutions is adjusted with sodium hydroxide and/or hydrochloric acid. (4)

Lidocaine HCl is also available premixed in dextrose 5% in water in concentrations of 0.2, 0.4, and 0.8% (2, 4, and 8 mg/ml, respectively). The solutions come in container sizes ranging from 250 to 1000 ml. (4)

pH—The pH of the injection is about 6.5 but may range from 5 to 7. (2; 4) The premixed infusion solutions in dextrose 5% in water have a pH of 3 to 7. (4; 17)

Osmolality—The osmolalities of lidocaine HCl products were determined to be 296 mOsm/kg for the 10-mg/ml concentration and 352 mOsm/kg for the 20-mg/ml concentration. (1233)

The commercially available lidocaine HCl 0.2, 0.4, and 0.8% premixed solutions have osmolarities of approximately 266, 281, and 308 mOsm/L, respectively. (4)

Trade Name(s)—Xylocaine.

Administration — Lidocaine HCl is administered by direct intravenous injection and continuous intravenous infusion. (4) It may also be administered by intramuscular injection. (4; 118; 119; 120) Products containing 40, 100, or 200 mg/ml should not be administered by direct intravenous injection without prior dilution. Usually 1 or 2 g of lidocaine HCl is added to 1 L of dextrose 5% in water to form a 1- or 2-mg/ml (0.1 or 0.2%) solution, respectively. Concentrations up to 8 mg/ml have been recommended in fluid-restricted patients. Lidocaine HCl products containing preservatives should not be given intravenously. Products containing epinephrine should not be used to treat arrhythmias. (4)

Stability — Lidocaine HCl injection and premixed infusion solutions should be stored at controlled room temperature and protected from excessive heat and freezing. (4) Aqueous solutions are reported to be stable to heat, acids, and alkalies. (24)

pH Effects—Although lidocaine HCl is stable across a broad pH range, its pH of maximum stability was determined to be 3 to 6. (1277)

Bonhomme et al. studied the stability of lidocaine HCl 2%, with and without epinephrine HCl, after alkalinization with sodium bicarbonate. Lidocaine HCl alone was alkalinized to pH 7.2, while the lidocaine–epinephrine combination was adjusted to pH 6.5 and also 7.05. The combinations were compatible, and no loss of lidocaine or epinephrine occurred over six hours. (1401)

Syringes—Lidocaine HCl (Astra) 20 mg/ml retained potency for three months at room temperature when 2 ml of solution was packaged in Tubex syringe cartridges. (13)

Elastomeric Reservoir Pumps—Lidocaine HCl (Lyphomed) 4 mg/ml in both dextrose 5% in water and sodium chloride 0.9% was evaluated for binding potential to natural rubber elastomeric reservoirs (Baxter). Less than 1% binding was found after storage for two weeks at 35 °C with gentle agitation. (2014)

Sorption—Lidocaine HCl (Astra) 200 mg/L did not display significant sorption to a PVC plastic test strip in 24 hours. (12)

Similarly, lidocaine HCl (Sigma) 200 mg/L in sodium chloride 0.9% (Travenol) in PVC bags did not exhibit significant sorption to the plastic during one week of storage at room temperature (15 to 20 °C). (536)

In another study, lidocaine HCl (Sigma) 200 mg/L in sodium chloride 0.9% did not exhibit any loss due to sorption during a seven-hour simulated infusion through an infusion set (Travenol) consisting of a cellulose propionate burette chamber and 170 cm of PVC tubing. (606)

The drug was also tested as a simulated infusion over at least one hour by a syringe pump system. A glass syringe on a syringe pump was fitted with 20 cm of polyethylene tubing or 50 cm of Silastic tubing. No loss of drug due to sorption was observed with either tubing. (606)

In addition, a 25-ml aliquot of lidocaine HCl (Sigma) 200 mg/L in sodium chloride 0.9% was stored in all-plastic syringes composed of polypropylene barrels and polyethylene plungers for 24 hours at room temperature in the dark. No loss due to sorption occurred. (606)

However, in a slightly alkaline (pH 8) cardioplegic solution, the percentage of unionized lidocaine base increased to 58%. This amount compares to less than 3% in dextrose 5% in water and sodium chloride 0.9% at around pH 6. This unionized form is highly lipid soluble and may interact with PVC bags. Storage of the cardioplegic solutions in 500- and 250-ml PVC bags at 22 °C resulted in a 12 to 19% lidocaine loss in two days and a 65 to 75% loss in 21 days. Degradation was not likely because storage of the same solution in glass bottles did not result in any lidocaine loss after 21 days at 22 °C. Refrigeration of the PVC bags at 4 °C slowed the lidocaine loss to 9% or less in 21 days. (776)

Filtration—Lidocaine HCl (Astra) 200 mg/L in dextrose 5% in water and sodium chloride 0.9% did not display significant sorption to a 0.45-µm cellulose membrane filter (Abbott S-A-I-F) during an eight-hour simulated infusion. (567)

Central Venous Catheter—Lidocaine HCl (Astra) 2 mg/ml in dextrose 5% in water was found to be compatible with the ARROWg+ard Blue Plus (Arrow International) chlorhexidine-bearing triple-lumen central catheter. HPLC analysis was used to evaluate completeness of drug delivery through the catheter and the amount of chlorhexidine removed from the internal lumens. Essentially complete delivery of the drug was found with little or no drug loss occurring. Furthermore, chlorhexidine delivered from the catheter remained at trace amounts with no substantial increase due to the delivery of the drug through the catheter. (2335)

Compatibility Information

Solution Compatibility

Lidocaine HCl

Solution	*Mfr*	*Mfr*	*Conc/L*	*Remarks*	*Ref*	*C/I*
Amino acids 4.25%, dextrose 25%	MG	AST	1 g	No increase in particulate matter in 24 hr at 5 °C	349	C
Dextrose 5% in Ringer's injection, lactated	TR[a]	AST	1 g	Potency retained for 24 hr at 5 °C	282	C
	TR[a]	AST	2 g	Physically compatible with little or no lidocaine loss in 14 days at 25 °C	775	C

Solution Compatibility (Cont.)

Lidocaine HCl

Solution	*Mfr*	*Mfr*	*Conc/L*	*Remarks*	*Ref*	*C/I*
Dextrose 5% in sodium chloride 0.45%	CU, AB[a]	AST	2 g	Physically compatible with little or no lidocaine loss in 14 days at 25 °C	775	C
Dextrose 5% in sodium chloride 0.9%	TR[a]	AST	1 g	Potency retained for 24 hr at 5 °C	282	C
Dextrose 5% in water	TR[a]	AST	2 g	Physically compatible with no lidocaine loss in 14 days at 25 °C	775	C
	AB[a]	ES	515 mg	No lidocaine loss over 21 days at 20 to 24 °C	776	C
	TR[a]	AST	1 g	Potency retained for 24 hr at 5 °C	282	C
	TR[b]	ES	4 g	Chemically stable for 120 days at 4 and 30 °C	543	C
	TR[b]	AST	1 and 8 g	Visually compatible with no lidocaine loss by HPLC in 48 hr at room temperature	1802	C
Ringer's injection, lactated	TR[a]	AST	1 g	Potency retained for 24 hr at 5 °C	282	C
	TR[a]	AST	2 g	Physically compatible with no lidocaine loss in 14 days at 25 °C	775	C
Sodium chloride 0.45%	AB[a]	AST	2 g	Physically compatible with no lidocaine loss in 14 days at 25 °C	775	C
Sodium chloride 0.9%	TR[a]	AST	2 g	Physically compatible with no lidocaine loss in 14 days at 25 °C	775	C
	AB[a]	ES	515 mg	No lidocaine loss over 21 days at 20 to 24 °C	776	C
	BA[c]	AST		Potency retained for 24 hr	45	C
	TR[a]	AST	1 g	Potency retained for 24 hr at 5 °C	282	C
	TR[b]	AST	1 g	Potency retained for 24 hr	45	C
	TR[b]	AST	1 and 8 g	Visually compatible with little or no lidocaine loss by HPLC in 48 hr at room temperature	1802	C

[a]*Tested in both glass and PVC containers.*
[b]*Tested in PVC containers.*
[c]*Tested in glass containers.*

Additive Compatibility

Lidocaine HCl

Drug	*Mfr*	*Conc/L*	*Mfr*	*Conc/L*	*Test Soln*	*Remarks*	*Ref*	*C/I*
Alteplase	GEN	0.5 g	AST	4 g	D5W	Visually compatible with no alteplase clotlysis activity loss in 24 hr at 25 °C	1856	C
	GEN	0.5 g	AST	4 g	NS	Visually compatible with 7% alteplase clotlysis activity loss in 24 hr at 25 °C	1856	C
Aminophylline	SE	500 mg	AST	2 g		Physically compatible	24	C
	AQ	1 g	AST	2 g	D5W, LR, NS	Physically compatible for 24 hr at 25 °C	775	C
Amiodarone HCl	LZ	1.8 g	AB	4 g	D5W, NS[a,d]	Physically compatible with 9% or less amiodarone loss in 24 hr at 24 °C under fluorescent light	1031	C
Atracurium besylate	BW	500 mg		2 g	D5W	Physically compatible and atracurium chemically stable for 24 hr at 5 and 30 °C	1694	C
Bretylium tosylate	ACC	10 g	AST	1 g	D5S[b]	Physically compatible and both drugs chemically stable for 48 hr at room temperature and 7 days at 4 °C	522	C
	AS	1 g	AST	2 g	D5W, LR, NS	Physically compatible for 24 hr at 25 °C	775	C
	ACC	1 g	AST	2 g	D5W, NS	Physically compatible for 48 hr at 25 °C	756	C

Additive Compatibility (Cont.)

Lidocaine HCl

Drug	*Mfr*	*Conc/L*	*Mfr*	*Conc/L*	*Test Soln*	*Remarks*	*Ref*	*C/I*
Calcium chloride	UP	1 g	AST	2 g		Physically compatible	24	C
Calcium gluconate	ES	2 g	AST	2 g	D5W, LR, NS	Physically compatible for 24 hr at 25 °C	775	C
Chloramphenicol sodium succinate	PD	1 g	AST	2 g		Physically compatible	24	C
Chlorothiazide sodium	MSD	500 mg	AST	2 g		Physically compatible	24	C
Cibenzoline succinate		2 g	AB	8 g	D5W, NS	Physically compatible for 24 hr at 25 °C by visual and microscopic examination	1182	C
Cimetidine HCl	SKF	3 g	AST	2.5 g	D5W	Physically compatible and cimetidine chemically stable for 24 hr at room temperature. Lidocaine not tested	551	C
Ciprofloxacin	MI	2 g		1 g	NS	Compatible for 24 hr at 25 °C	888	C
	MI	2 g		1.5 g	NS	Compatible for 24 hr at 25 °C	888	C
Dexamethasone sodium phosphate	MSD	4 mg	AST	2 g		Physically compatible	24	C
Digoxin	ES	1 mg	AST	2 g	D5W, LR, NS	Physically compatible for 24 hr at 25 °C	775	C
Diphenhydramine HCl	PD	50 mg	AST	2 g		Physically compatible	24	C
Dobutamine HCl	LI	1 g	ES	4 g	D5W, NS	Physically compatible with no color change in 24 hr at 25 °C	789	C
	LI	1 g	AST	4 and 10 g	D5W, NS	Physically compatible for 24 hr at 21 °C	812	C
Dopamine HCl	ACC	800 mg	AST	2 g	D5W, LR, NS	Physically compatible for 24 hr at 25 °C	775	C
	AS	800 mg	AST	4 g	D5W	No dopamine or lidocaine decomposition in 24 hr at 25 °C	312	C
	AS	800 mg	AST	4 g	D5W[a]	No dopamine or lidocaine decomposition in 24 hr at 25 °C	312	C
Ephedrine sulfate		50 mg	AST	2 g		Physically compatible	24	C
Erythromycin lactobionate	AB	1 g	AST	2 g		Physically compatible	24	C
Fentanyl citrate		2 mg	AST	2.5 g	NS[a]	Physically compatible with no loss of lidocaine or fentanyl at pH 5.8 by HPLC in 30 days at 4 and 23 °C	2305	C
		2 mg	BRN	2.5 g	NS[a]	Physically compatible with little lidocaine loss but 18% fentanyl loss by HPLC at 23 °C and 10% loss at 4 °C in 2 days due to sorption at pH 6.7 from higher pH lidocaine product	2305	I
Floxacillin sodium	BE	20 g	ANT	2 g	NS	Physically compatible for 72 hr at 15 and 30 °C	1479	C
Flumazenil	RC	20 mg	AB	4 g	D5W[a]	Visually compatible with 4% flumazenil loss by HPLC in 24 hr at 23 °C under fluorescent light. Lidocaine not tested	1710	C
Furosemide	HO	1 g	ANT	2 g	NS	Physically compatible for 72 hr at 15 and 30 °C	1479	C
Heparin sodium		32,000 units		4 g	NS	Physically compatible and heparin activity retained for 24 hr	57	C

Additive Compatibility (Cont.)

	Lidocaine HCl							
Drug	*Mfr*	*Conc/L*	*Mfr*	*Conc/L*	*Test Soln*	*Remarks*	*Ref*	*C/I*
	AB	20,000 units	AST	2 g		Physically compatible	24	C
Hydrocortisone sodium succinate	UP	250 mg	AST	2 g		Physically compatible	24	C
Hydroxyzine HCl	PF	100 mg	AST	2 g		Physically compatible	24	C
Insulin, regular	SQ	1000 units	AST	2 g	D5W, LR, NS	Physically compatible for 24 hr at 25 °C	775	C
Mephentermine sulfate	WY	1 g	AST	2 g		Physically compatible	24	C
Metaraminol bitartrate	MSD	100 mg	AST	2 g		Physically compatible	24	C
Methohexital sodium	BP	2 g	BP	2 g	D5W	Immediate precipitation	26	I
Nafcillin sodium	AP	20 g	AST	0.6 g	D5W[a], NS[d]	Visually compatible with little or no nafcillin loss by HPLC in 48 hr at 23 °C. Lidocaine not tested	1806	C
Nitroglycerin	ACC	400 mg	IMS	4 g	D5W, NS[e]	Physically compatible with no nitroglycerin loss in 48 hr at 23 °C. Lidocaine not tested	929	C
Penicillin G potassium	SQ	1 million units	AST	2 g		Physically compatible	24	C
Pentobarbital sodium	AB	500 mg	AST	2 g		Physically compatible	24	C
Phenylephrine HCl	WI	20 mg	AST	2 g		Physically compatible	24	C
Phenytoin sodium	ES	1 g	AST	2 g	D5W, LR, NS	Immediate formation of a white cloudy precipitate	775	I
Potassium chloride	AB	40 mEq	AST	2 g		Physically compatible	24	C
Procainamide HCl	SQ	1 g	AST	2 g	D5W, LR, NS	Physically compatible for 24 hr at 25 °C	775	C
Prochlorperazine edisylate	SKF	10 mg	AST	2 g		Physically compatible	24	C
Promazine HCl	WY	100 mg	AST	2 g		Physically compatible	24	C
Propafenone HCl	KN	0.54 g	AST	4.5 g[c]	D5W	Visually compatible with little or no propafenone loss by HPLC in 24 hr at 22 °C exposed to fluorescent light. Lidocaine not tested	412	C
Ranitidine HCl	GL	50 mg and 2 g	AST	1 and 8 g	D5W, NS[a]	Physically compatible with 3% or less ranitidine loss in 24 hr at room temperature under fluorescent light. Lidocaine not tested	1361	C
	GL	50 mg and 2 g		2.5 g	D5W	Physically compatible and ranitidine chemically stable by HPLC for 24 hr at 25 °C. Lidocaine not tested	1515	C
	GL	50 mg and 2 g	AST	1 and 8 g	D5W, NS[a]	Visually compatible with little or no loss of either drug by HPLC in 48 hr at room temperature	1802	C
Sodium bicarbonate	AB	40 mEq	AST	2 g		Physically compatible	24	C
	AB	2.4 mEq[f]		1 g	D5W	Physically compatible for 24 hr	772	C
Sodium lactate	AB	50 mEq	AST	2 g		Physically compatible	24	C
Theophylline		2 g		380 mg	D5W	Visually compatible with little or no loss of either drug in 48 hr	1909	C

Additive Compatibility (Cont.)

Lidocaine HCl

Drug	*Mfr*	*Conc/L*	*Mfr*	*Conc/L*	*Test Soln*	*Remarks*	*Ref*	*C/I*
Verapamil HCl	KN	80 mg	IMS	2 g	D5W, NS	Physically compatible for 48 hr	739	C
Vitamin B complex with C	AB	10 ml	AST	2 g		Physically compatible	24	C

[a]Tested in PVC containers.
[b]Tested in both glass and PVC containers.
[c]Approximate concentration.
[d]Tested in polyolefin containers.
[e]Tested in glass containers.
[f]One vial of Neut added to a liter of admixture.

Drugs in Syringe Compatibility

Lidocaine HCl

Drug (in syringe)	*Mfr*	*Amt*	*Mfr*	*Amt*	*Remarks*	*Ref*	*C/I*
Ampicillin sodium	BE	500 mg		0.5 and 2.5%/ 1.5 ml	Physically compatible	89	C
	BE	250 mg		0.5 and 2.5%/ 1.5 ml	Occasional turbidity	89	I
Cefazolin sodium	SKF	1 g	AST	0.5%/ 3 ml	Precipitate forms within 3 to 4 hr at 4 °C	532	I
Ceftriaxone sodium	RC	450 mg/ ml	LY	1%	5% or less ceftriaxone loss by HPLC in 8 weeks at −15 °C but solution failed the particulate matter test	1824	I
	RC	250 and 450 mg/ ml	DW	1%	10% ceftriaxone loss in 3 days at 20 °C, 7 to 8% loss in 35 days at 4 °C, and 4 to 6% loss in 168 days at −20 °C. Lidocaine not tested	1991	C
Clonidine HCl with fentanyl citrate	BI JN	0.03 mg/ ml 0.01 mg/ ml	AST	2 mg/ml	Diluted to 5 ml with NS. Visually compatible with no new GC/MS peaks appearing in 1 hr at room temperature	1956	C
Glycopyrrolate	RB	0.2 mg/ 1 ml	ES	10 mg/ 1 ml	Physically compatible and pH in stability range for glycopyrrolate for 48 hr at 25 °C	331	C
	RB	0.2 mg/ 1 ml	ES	20 mg/ 2 ml	Physically compatible and pH in stability range for glycopyrrolate for 48 hr at 25 °C	331	C
	RB	0.4 mg/ 2 ml	ES	10 mg/ 1 ml	Physically compatible and pH in stability range for glycopyrrolate for 48 hr at 25 °C	331	C
	RB	0.2 mg/ 1 ml	ES	20 mg/ 1 ml	Physically compatible and pH in stability range for glycopyrrolate for 48 hr at 25 °C	331	C
	RB	0.2 mg/ 1 ml	ES	40 mg/ 2 ml	Physically compatible and pH in stability range for glycopyrrolate for 48 hr at 25 °C	331	C
	RB	0.4 mg/ 2 ml	ES	20 mg/ 1 ml	Physically compatible and pH in stability range for glycopyrrolate for 48 hr at 25 °C	331	C
Heparin sodium		2500 units/ 1 ml	AST	100 mg/ 5 ml	Physically compatible for at least 5 min	1053	C
Hydroxyzine HCl	PF	50 mg/ 2 ml	AST	2%/2 ml	Physically compatible	771	C
	PF	100 mg/ 2 ml	AST	2%/2 ml	Physically compatible	771	C

Drugs in Syringe Compatibility (Cont.)

			Lidocaine HCl				
Drug (in syringe)	*Mfr*	*Amt*	*Mfr*	*Amt*	*Remarks*	*Ref*	*C/I*
Ketamine HCl with morphine sulfate	PD ES	2 mg/ml 0.2 mg/ml	AST	2 mg/ml	Diluted to 5 ml with NS. Visually compatible with no new GC/MS peaks appearing in 1 hr at room temperature	1956	C
Metoclopramide HCl	RB	10 mg/ 2 ml	ES	50 mg/ 5 ml	Physically compatible for 48 hr at room temperature	924	C
	RB	10 mg/ 2 ml	ES	100 mg/ 10 ml	Physically compatible for 48 hr at room temperature	924	C
	RB	10 mg/ 2 ml	ES	50 mg/ 5 ml	Physically compatible for 48 hr at 25 °C	1167	C
	RB	10 mg/ 2 ml	ES	100 mg/ 10 ml	Physically compatible for 48 hr at 25 °C	1167	C
	RB	160 mg/ 32 ml	ES	50 mg/ 5 ml	Physically compatible for 48 hr at 25 °C	1167	C
	RB	160 mg/ 32 ml	ES	100 mg/ 10 ml	Physically compatible for 48 hr at 25 °C	1167	C
Milrinone lactate	WI	5.25 mg/ 5.25 ml	AB	100 mg/ 10 ml	Physically compatible with no loss of either drug in 20 min at 23 °C under fluorescent light	1410	C
Moxalactam disodium	LI	1 g		0.5 and 1%/3 ml	Physically compatible with 7% moxalactam decomposition in 24 hr at 25 °C and 4% in 96 hr at 5 °C	693	C
Nalbuphine HCl	DU	10 mg/ 1 ml		40 mg	Physically compatible for 48 hr	128	C
	DU	20 mg/ 1 ml		40 mg	Physically compatible for 48 hr	128	C
Sodium bicarbonate	AB	3 mEq/ 3 ml	ES	2%[a], 30 ml	11% lidocaine loss in 1 week and 22% loss in 2 weeks at 25 °C by GC. 28% epinephrine loss by HPLC in 1 week at 25 °C	1712	I
	AB	3 mEq/ 3 ml	ES	2%[a], 30 ml	6% lidocaine loss by GC in 4 weeks at 4 °C. 2% epinephrine loss in 1 week and 12% loss in 3 weeks at 4 °C by HPLC	1712	C
	LY	0.1 mEq/ ml	AST	1%[a], 30 ml	25% epinephrine loss by HPLC in 1 week at room temperature. Lidocaine not tested	1713	I
		0.088 mEq/ml		0.9%	11% lidocaine loss by fluorescence polarization immunoassay in 7 days at room temperature	1723	C
	AST	8.4%, 2 ml	AST	1 and 1.5%[b], 20 ml	Visually compatible for up to 5 hr at room temperature	1724	C
	AST	8.4%, 2 ml	AST	2%[b], 20 ml	Haze forms but clarifies with gentle agitation	1724	?
	AB	4%, 4 ml	AST	1 and 1.5%[b], 20 ml	Visually compatible for up to 5 hr at room temperature	1724	C
	AB	4%, 4 ml	AST	2%[b], 20 ml	Haze forms but clarifies with gentle agitation	1724	?
		1.4 and 8.4%, 1.5 ml	BEL	2%[c], 20 ml	8% epinephrine loss by HPLC in 7 days at room temperature. Lidocaine not tested	1743	C

[a]*Tested with epinephrine HCl 1:100,000 added.*
[b]*Tested with epinephrine HCl 1:200,000 added.*
[c]*Tested with epinephrine HCl 1:80,000 added.*

Y-Site Injection Compatibility (1:1 Mixture)

Lidocaine HCl

Drug	*Mfr*	*Conc*	*Mfr*	*Conc*	*Remarks*	*Ref*	*C/I*
Alteplase	GEN	1 mg/ml	AB	8 mg/ml[a]	Physically compatible for 6 days by spectrophotometric and visual examination	1340	C
Amiodarone HCl	LZ	4 mg/ml[c]	AST	8 mg/ml[c]	Physically compatible for 24 hr at 21 °C	1032	C
Amphotericin B cholesteryl sulfate complex	SEQ	0.83 mg/ml[a]	AST	10 mg/ml	Gross precipitate forms	2117	I
Cefazolin sodium	LI	40 mg/ml[c]	AB	8 mg/ml[c]	Physically compatible for 3 hr	1316	C
Ciprofloxacin	MI	2 mg/ml[c]	AB	4[a] and 20 mg/ml	Visually compatible for 24 hr at 24 °C	1655	C
Cisatracurium besylate	GW	0.1, 2, 5 mg/ml[a]	AST	8 mg/ml[a]	Physically compatible with no change in measured turbidity or increase in particle content in 4 hr at 23 °C	2074	C
Clarithromycin	AB	4 mg/ml[a]	ANT	4 mg/ml[a]	Visually compatible for 72 hr at both 30 and 17 °C	2174	C
Diltiazem HCl	MMD	1 mg/ml[a]	AST	8 mg/ml[a]	Visually compatible for 24 hr at 25 °C	1530	C
	MMD	1[b] and 5 mg/ml	AB	10 mg/ml[b]	Visually compatible	1807	C
	MMD	5 mg/ml	AB, SCN	4 and 8 mg/ml[a]	Visually compatible	1807	C
Dobutamine HCl	LI	4 mg/ml[c]	AB	8 mg/ml[c]	Physically compatible for 3 hr	1316	C
Dobutamine HCl with dopamine HCl	LI DCC	4 mg/ml[c] 3.2 mg/ml[c]	AB	8 mg/ml[c]	Physically compatible for 3 hr	1316	C
Dobutamine HCl with nitroglycerin	LI LY	4 mg/ml[c] 0.4 mg/ml[c]	AB	8 mg/ml[c]	Physically compatible for 3 hr	1316	C
Dobutamine HCl with sodium nitroprusside	LI ES	4 mg/ml[c] 0.4 mg/ml[c]	AB	8 mg/ml[c]	Physically compatible for 3 hr	1316	C
Dopamine HCl	DCC	3.2 mg/ml[c]	AB	8 mg/ml[c]	Physically compatible for 3 hr	1316	C
Dopamine HCl with dobutamine HCl	DCC LI	3.2 mg/ml[c] 4 mg/ml[c]	AB	8 mg/ml[c]	Physically compatible for 3 hr	1316	C
Dopamine HCl with nitroglycerin	DCC LY	3.2 mg/ml[c] 0.4 mg/ml[c]	AB	8 mg/ml[c]	Physically compatible for 3 hr	1316	C
Dopamine HCl with sodium nitroprusside	DCC ES	3.2 mg/ml[c] 0.4 mg/ml[c]	AB	8 mg/ml[c]	Physically compatible for 3 hr	1316	C
Enalaprilat	MSD	0.05 mg/ml[b]	AST	4 mg/ml[a]	Physically compatible for 24 hr at room temperature under fluorescent light	1355	C
Etomidate	AB	2 mg/ml	AST	20 mg/ml	Visually compatible for up to 7 days at 25 °C	1801	C
Famotidine	MSD	0.2 mg/ml[a]	TR	4 mg/ml[a]	Physically compatible for 4 hr at 25 °C	1188	C
	MSD	0.2 mg/ml[a]	LY	1 mg/ml[a]	Physically compatible for 14 hr	1196	C
Gatifloxacin	BMS	2 mg/ml[a]	AST	10 mg/ml[a]	Physically compatible with no change in measured haze or increase in particle content in 4 hr at 23 °C	2234	C
Haloperidol lactate	MN	0.5[a] and 5 mg/ml	AB	4 mg/ml[a]	Visually compatible for 24 hr at 21 °C	1523	C
Heparin sodium	TR	50 units/ml	TR	4 mg/ml	Visually compatible for 4 hr at 25 °C	1793	C
Heparin sodium with hydrocortisone sodium succinate	RI UP	1000 units + 100 mg/L[d]	AST	20 mg/ml	Physically compatible for at least 4 hr at room temperature by visual and microscopic examination	322	C

Y-Site Injection Compatibility (1:1 Mixture) (Cont.)

Drug	Mfr	Conc	Lidocaine HCl Mfr	Lidocaine HCl Conc	Remarks	Ref	C/I
Hetastarch in lactated electrolyte injection (Hextend)	AB	6%	AB	8 mg/ml[a]	Physically compatible with no change in measured turbidity or increase in particle content in 4 hr at 23 °C	2339	C
Inamrinone lactate	WB	3 mg/ml[b]	ES	1 mg/ml[a]	Physically compatible for at least 4 hr at 25 °C under fluorescent light	992	C
Labetalol HCl	SC	1 mg/ml[a]	AST	20 mg/ml[a]	Physically compatible for 24 hr at 18 °C	1171	C
Levofloxacin	OMN	5 mg/ml[a]	AB	10 mg/ml[g]	Visually compatible for 4 hr at 24 °C under fluorescent light	2233	C
Linezolid	PHU	2 mg/ml	AB	10 mg/ml[a]	Physically compatible with no change in measured turbidity or increase in particle content in 4 hr at 23 °C	2264	C
Meperidine HCl	AB	10 mg/ml	AB	1 mg/ml[a]	Physically compatible for 4 hr at 25 °C	1397	C
Morphine sulfate	AB	1 mg/ml	AB	1 mg/ml[a]	Physically compatible for 4 hr at 25 °C	1397	C
Nitroglycerin	LY	0.4 mg/ml[c]	AB	8 mg/ml[c]	Physically compatible for 3 hr	1316	C
Nitroglycerin with dobutamine HCl	LY LI	0.4 mg/ml[c] 4 mg/ml[c]	AB	8 mg/ml[c]	Physically compatible for 3 hr	1316	C
Nitroglycerin with dopamine HCl	LY DCC	0.4 mg/ml[c] 3.2 mg/ml[c]	AB	8 mg/ml[c]	Physically compatible for 3 hr	1316	C
Nitroglycerin with sodium nitroprusside	LY ES	0.4 mg/ml[c] 0.4 mg/ml[c]	AB	8 mg/ml[c]	Physically compatible for 3 hr	1316	C
Potassium chloride		40 mEq/L[d]	AST	20 mg/ml	Physically compatible for at least 4 hr at room temperature by visual and microscopic examination	322	C
Propofol	ZEN	10 mg/ml	AST	10 mg/ml	Physically compatible for 1 hr at 23 °C with no increase in particle content	2066	C
Remifentanil HCl	GW	0.025 and 0.25 mg/ml[b]	AST	8 mg/ml[a]	Physically compatible with no change in measured turbidity or increase in particle content in 4 hr at 23 °C	2075	C
Sodium nitroprusside	ES	0.4 mg/ml[c]	AB	8 mg/ml[c]	Physically compatible for 3 hr	1316	C
Sodium nitroprusside with dobutamine HCl	ES LI	0.4 mg/ml[c] 4 mg/ml[c]	AB	8 mg/ml[c]	Physically compatible for 3 hr	1316	C
Sodium nitroprusside with dopamine HCl	ES DCC	0.4 mg/ml[c] 3.2 mg/ml[c]	AB	8 mg/ml[c]	Physically compatible for 3 hr	1316	C
Sodium nitroprusside with nitroglycerin	ES LY	0.4 mg/ml[c] 0.4 mg/ml[c]	AB	8 mg/ml[c]	Physically compatible for 3 hr	1316	C
Streptokinase	HO	30,000 units/ml[a]	AB	8 mg/ml[a]	Physically compatible for at least 3 days by visual examination	1340	C
Theophylline	TR	4 mg/ml	TR	4 mg/ml	Visually compatible for 6 hr at 25 °C	1793	C
Thiopental sodium	AB	25 mg/ml	AST	20 mg/ml	White cloudiness forms immediately but clears within 24 hr at 25 °C	1801	I
Tirofiban HCl	ME	0.05 mg/ml[a]	AB	1 and 20 mg/ml[a,b]	Physically compatible with little or no loss of either drug by HPLC in 4 hr at room temperature under fluorescent light	2250	C
	ME	0.05 mg/ml[b]	AB	1 and 20 mg/ml[a,b]	Physically compatible with little or no loss of either drug by HPLC in 4 hr at room temperature under fluorescent light	2250	C

Y-Site Injection Compatibility (1:1 Mixture) (Cont.)

Drug	Mfr	Conc	Lidocaine HCl Mfr	Lidocaine HCl Conc	Remarks	Ref	C/I
TNA #73[e]			ES	200 mg/ 50 ml[c]	Physically compatible for 4 hr by visual observation	1009	C
Vitamin B complex with C	RC	2 ml/L[d]	AST	20 mg/ml	Physically compatible for at least 4 hr at room temperature by visual and microscopic examination	322	C
Warfarin sodium	DU	2 mg/ml[f]	AST	2 mg/ml[a]	Visually compatible with no warfarin loss by HPLC in 30 min	2010	C
	DME	2 mg/ml[f]	AST	2 mg/ml[a]	Visually compatible for 24 hr at 24 °C	2078	C

[a] *Tested in dextrose 5% in water.*
[b] *Tested in sodium chloride 0.9%.*
[c] *Tested in both dextrose 5% in water and sodium chloride 0.9%.*
[d] *Tested in dextrose 5% in water, sodium chloride 0.9%, and Ringer's injection, lactated.*
[e] *Refer to Appendix I for the composition of parenteral nutrition solutions. TNA indicates a 3-in-1 admixture.*
[f] *Tested in sterile water for injection.*
[g] *Preservative free.*

Additional Compatibility Information

Infusion Solutions — At a concentration in the range of 1 to 4 mg/ml in dextrose 5% in water, lidocaine HCl appears to be stable for at least 24 hours at room temperature. (4) At a concentration of 2 g/L, lidocaine HCl is physically compatible with most Abbott infusion solutions. (24)

Cardioplegic Solutions — The stability of lidocaine was assessed in a cardioplegic solution of the following composition:

Component	Final Concentration per Liter
Lidocaine (as HCl)	448 mg
Potassium chloride	20 mEq
Sodium bicarbonate	25 mEq
Dextrose	17 g
Sodium chloride	8.3 g

Because insulin is not added to the cardioplegic solution until just before use, it was not included in this study. The cardioplegic solution was stored in glass and PVC containers at 22 and 4 °C for 21 days. No loss of lidocaine occurred in glass containers during this period. However, storage in PVC bags at 22 °C resulted in a 12 to 19% loss in two days and a 65 to 75% loss in 21 days, believed to be due to sorption to the plastic. Refrigeration at 4 °C slowed the loss in PVC bags to 9% or less in 21 days. Concentrations of the other components did not change during the study. (776)

Multiple Drugs — A seven-drug combination consisting of bupivacaine HCl (Sanofi Winthrop) 1.5 mg/1 ml, clonidine HCl (Boehringer Ingelheim) 0.03 mg/1 ml, fentanyl citrate (Janssen) 0.01 mg/1 ml, ketamine (Parke-Davis) 2 mg/ml, lidocaine HCl (Astra) 2 mg/ml, morphine sulfate (Elkins-Sinn) 0.2 mg/ml, and tetracaine HCl (Sanofi Winthrop) 2 mg/ml mixed together in equal quantities was found to be visually compatible with no new GC/MS peaks appearing in one hour at room temperature. (1956)

Sympathomimetic Amines — Lidocaine HCl mixed with certain acid-stable drugs may present a problem. In combination with epinephrine HCl, norepinephrine bitartrate, and isoproterenol HCl, lidocaine HCl is stable, but its buffering action may raise the pH of intravenous admixtures above 5.5, the maximum pH for stability of the other drugs. The final pH is usually about 6. These drugs begin to deteriorate within several hours. Therefore, admixtures should be used promptly after preparation, or the separate administration of the sympathomimetic amines should be considered. Note: This does not apply to commercial lidocaine–epinephrine combinations, which have the pH adjusted to retain the maximum epinephrine potency. (24)

Cefazolin — Cefazolin sodium (SKF) constituted with 0.5% lidocaine HCl (Astra) to a concentration of 1 g/3 ml and frozen at −20 °C in glass syringes (Hy-Pod) did not yield a clear solution on thawing. The solution was unsuitable for injection. (532)

Dobutamine, Dopamine, Nitroglycerin, and Nitroprusside — Dobutamine HCl (Lilly) 4 mg/ml, dopamine HCl (Dupont Critical Care) 3.2 mg/ml, lidocaine HCl (Abbott) 8 mg/ml, nitroglycerin (Lyphomed) 0.4 mg/ml, and sodium nitroprusside (Elkins-Sinn) 0.4 mg/ml, prepared in dextrose 5% in water and sodium chloride 0.9%, were combined in equal quantities in all possible combinations of two, three, four, and five drugs and then evaluated for physical compatibility. No physical incompatibility was observed in any combination within the three-hour study period. (1316)

Phenylephrine — Lidocaine HCl 2% in combination with phenylephrine HCl 0.25% was stable for at least 66 days at 25 °C. No loss of either drug was found by HPLC analysis, and little change in pH occurred during the test period. (1278)

Other Drugs — Dacarbazine is stated to be physically incompatible when mixed with lidocaine HCl 1 or 2%. (524) Also, local anesthetics such as lidocaine HCl cause precipitation of amphotericin B. (107) Lidocaine HCl is stated to be physically compatible with alteplase when administered by Y-site injection into a running alteplase solution. (4)

LINCOMYCIN HCL
AHFS 8:12.28

Products — Lincomycin HCl is available in 2- and 10-ml vials. Each milliliter contains lincomycin HCl equivalent to lincomycin base 300 mg and benzyl alcohol 9.45 mg in water for injection. (1-6/99; 4)

pH — From 3 to 5.5. (4)

Trade Name(s) — Lincocin.

Administration — Lincomycin HCl may be administered by deep intramuscular injection, slow intravenous infusion, or subconjunctival injection. (1-6/99; 4) For intravenous administration, each gram of lincomycin should be diluted in 100 ml or more of compatible infusion solution and infused over at least one hour. (4)

Stability — Lincomycin HCl injection should be stored at controlled room temperature and protected from freezing. (1-6/99; 4)

Compatibility Information

Solution Compatibility

Lincomycin HCl

Solution	*Mfr*	*Mfr*	*Conc/L*	*Remarks*	*Ref*	*C/I*
Dextrose 5% in sodium chloride 0.9%		UP	1.2 g	Potency retained for 24 hr	109	C
Dextrose 5% in water		UP	1.2 g	Potency retained for 24 hr	109	C
Dextrose 10% in water		UP	1.2 g	Potency retained for 24 hr	109	C
Sodium chloride 0.9%		UP	1.2 g	Potency retained for 24 hr	109	C

Additive Compatibility

Lincomycin HCl

Drug	*Mfr*	*Conc/L*	*Mfr*	*Conc/L*	*Test Soln*	*Remarks*	*Ref*	*C/I*
Amikacin sulfate	BR	5 g	UP	10 g	D5LR, D5R, D5S, D5W, D10W, IS10, LR, NS, R, SL	Physically compatible and potency of both retained for 24 hr at 25 °C	294	C
Cimetidine HCl	SKF	3 g	UP	6 g	D5W	Physically compatible and cimetidine chemically stable for 24 hr at room temperature. Lincomycin not tested	551	C
Cytarabine	UP	500 mg		1, 1.5, 2, 2.4, 3 g		Physically compatible for 48 hr	174	C
Heparin sodium	AB	20,000 units	UP	600 mg		Physically compatible	21	C
Penicillin G potassium	SQ	20 million units	UP	6 g	D5W	Physically compatible	15	C
	SQ	5 million units	UP	600 mg	D	Physically compatible	47	C
			UP			Physically incompatible	9	I
Penicillin G sodium	UP	20 million units	UP	6 g	D5W	Physically compatible	15	C
			UP			Physically incompatible	9	I
Phenytoin sodium	PD		UP			Physically incompatible	9	I
Ranitidine HCl	GL	50 mg and 2 g		2.4 g	D5W	Physically compatible and ranitidine chemically stable by HPLC for 24 hr at 25 °C. Lincomycin not tested	1515	C

Drugs in Syringe Compatibility

Lincomycin HCl

Drug (in syringe)	*Mfr*	*Amt*	*Mfr*	*Amt*	*Remarks*	*Ref*	*C/I*
Ampicillin sodium	AY	500 mg	UP	600 mg/ 2 ml	Physically incompatible within 1 hr at room temperature	99	I
	AY	500 mg	UP	600 mg/ 2 ml	Precipitate forms within 1 hr at room temperature	300	I
Doxapram HCl	RB	400 mg/ 20 ml		300 mg/ 1 ml	Physically compatible with no doxapram loss in 24 hr	1177	C
Heparin sodium	AB	20,000 units/ 1 ml	UP	600 mg/ 2 ml	Physically compatible for at least 30 min	21	C
Penicillin G sodium		1 million units	UP	600 mg/ 2 ml	No precipitate or color change within 1 hr at room temperature	99	C

Additional Compatibility Information

Infusion Solutions — Lincomycin HCl is stated to be physically compatible for 24 hours at room temperature with the following infusion solutions and drugs in infusion solutions (1-6/99; 154):

Dextran 6% in sodium chloride 0.9%
Dextrose 5% in sodium chloride 0.9%
Dextrose 10% in sodium chloride 0.9%
Dextrose 5% in water
Dextrose 10% in water
Invert sugar 10% in Electrolyte #1
Ringer's injection
Sodium lactate ⅙ M

Other Drugs — Lincomycin HCl is stated to be physically compatible for 24 hours at room temperature with the following drugs in infusion solutions (1-6/99; 154):

Ampicillin sodium
Chloramphenicol sodium succinate
Polymyxin B sulfate
Vitamin B complex
Vitamin B complex with C

Lincomycin HCl is stated to be physically incompatible with kanamycin sulfate and to be physically compatible for only four hours with colistimethate sodium and penicillin G sodium. (1-6/99; 154)

In vitro testing of riboflavin-5′-phosphate at a concentration of 0.1% with lincomycin HCl 0.025% in sterile distilled water showed significant reduction in antibiotic activity in one hour at 25 °C. (314)

LINEZOLID
AHFS 8:40

Products — Linezolid is available as a single-use, ready-to-use solution for infusion in 100- and 300-ml plastic (Excel) containers. Each milliliter of the ready-to-use infusion provides linezolid 2 mg along with dextrose 50.24 mg, sodium citrate 1.64 mg, and citric acid 0.85 mg in water for injection. (2)

pH — Adjusted to pH 4.8. (2)

Sodium Content — The sodium concentration is 0.38 mg/ml. The sodium content in a 100-ml bag is 1.7 mEq and in a 300-ml bag is 5 mEq. (2)

Trade Name(s) — Zyvox.

Administration — Linezolid ready-to-use solution is administered only by intravenous infusion over a period of 30 to 120 minutes. (2)

Stability — Linezolid ready-to-use solutions may exhibit a yellow color that can intensify over time without affecting the stability of the drug. Intact containers should be kept in their protective overwrap until ready to use, and should be stored at controlled room temperature of 25 °C, with temperature excursions in the range of 15 to 30 °C permitted, and protected from light and freezing. (2)

Sorption — Linezolid was found to be compatible with common types of intravenous administration sets including diethylhexyl phthalate (DEHP) plasticized PVC, trioctyl trimellitate (TOTM) plasticized PVC, and polyolefin sets. The total dose of linezolid was fully delivered with the delivered concentration remaining constant throughout. In addition, no detectable levels of plasticizer were found in the delivered solutions. (2338)

Compatibility Information

Additive Compatibility

Linezolid

Drug	Mfr	Conc/L	Mfr	Conc/L	Test Soln	Remarks	Ref	C/I
Aztreonam	SQ	20 g	PHU	2 g	[a]	Physically compatible with no linezolid loss in 7 days at 4 and 23 °C protected from light. About 9% aztreonam loss at 23 °C and less than 4% loss at 4 °C in 7 days	2263	C
Cefazolin sodium	APC	10 g	PHU	2 g	[a]	Physically compatible with 5% or less loss of both drugs in 3 days at 23 °C and in 7 days at 4 °C protected from light	2262	C
Ceftazidime	GW[b]	20 g	PHU	2 g	[a]	Physically compatible with no linezolid loss in 7 days at 4 °C and 23 °C protected from light. Ceftazidime losses of 5% in 24 hr and 12% loss in 3 days at 23 °C and about 3% in 7 days at 4 °C	2262	C
Ceftriaxone sodium	RC	10 g	PHU	2 g	[a]	Physically compatible, but up to 37% ceftriaxone loss in 24 hr at 23 °C and 10% loss in 3 days at 4 °C	2262	I
Ciprofloxacin	BAY	4 g	PHU	2 g	[a]	Physically compatible with little or no loss of either drug by HPLC in 7 days at 23 °C protected from light. Refrigeration results in precipitation after 1 day	2334	C
Erythromycin lactobionate	AB	5 g	PHU	2 g	[a]	Very rapid erythromycin decomposition; loss of 15% in 1 hr and 30% in 4 hr at 23 °C by HPLC. Losses of about 45% in 1 day at 4 °C	2333	I
Gentamicin sulfate	AB	800 mg	PHU	2 g	[a]	Physically compatible with little or no linezolid loss by HPLC in 7 days at 4 and 23 °C protected from light. Gentamicin losses of about 5 to 7% occurred in 7 days at 4 °C, and losses of about 8% occurred in 5 days at 23 °C	2332	C
Levofloxacin	OMN	5 g	PHU	2 g	[a]	Physically compatible with little or no loss of either drug by HPLC in 7 days at 4 and 23 °C protected from light	2334	C
Ofloxacin	MN	5 g	PHU	2 g	[a]	Physically compatible with little or no loss of either drug by HPLC in 7 days at 4 and 23 °C protected from light	2334	C
Piperacillin sodium	LE	30 g	PHU	2 g	[a]	Physically compatible with little or no loss of either drug in 7 days at 4 °C protected from light. At 23 °C, about 5% piperacillin loss in 3 days and 9 to 12% loss in 5 days	2263	C
Tobramycin sulfate	GNS	800 mg	PHU	2 g	[a]	Physically compatible with little or no linezolid loss by HPLC in 7 days at 4 and 23 °C protected from light. No tobramycin loss occurred in 7 days at 4 °C but losses of about 4% occurred in 1 day and 10 to 12% in 3 days at 23 °C	2332	C
Trimethoprim–sulfamethoxazole	ES	800 mg + 4 g	PHU	2 g	[a]	A large amount of white needle-like crystals forms immediately	2333	I

[a] *Admixed in the linezolid infusion container.*
[b] *Sodium carbonate–containing formulation tested.*

Y-Site Injection Compatibility (1:1 Mixture)

Drug	Mfr	Conc	Linezolid Mfr	Linezolid Conc	Remarks	Ref	C/I
Acyclovir sodium	APP	7 mg/ml[a]	PHU	2 mg/ml	Physically compatible with no change in measured turbidity or increase in particle content in 4 hr at 23 °C	2264	C
Alfentanil HCl	TAY	0.5 mg/ml	PHU	2 mg/ml	Physically compatible with no change in measured turbidity or increase in particle content in 4 hr at 23 °C	2264	C
Amikacin sulfate	AB	5 mg/ml[a]	PHU	2 mg/ml	Physically compatible with no change in measured turbidity or increase in particle content in 4 hr at 23 °C	2264	C
Amino acids 4.9%, dextrose 20%	AB		PHU	2 mg/ml	Physically compatible with no change in measured turbidity or increase in particle content in 4 hr at 23 °C	2264	C
Aminophylline	AB	2.5 mg/ml[a]	PHU	2 mg/ml	Physically compatible with no change in measured turbidity or increase in particle content in 4 hr at 23 °C	2264	C
Amphotericin B	AB	0.6 mg/ml[a]	PHU	2 mg/ml	Yellow flocculent precipitate forms within 5 min	2264	I
Ampicillin sodium	APC	20 mg/ml[b]	PHU	2 mg/ml	Physically compatible with no change in measured turbidity or increase in particle content in 4 hr at 23 °C	2264	C
Ampicillin sodium–sulbactam sodium	PF	20 + 10 mg/ml[b]	PHU	2 mg/ml	Physically compatible with no change in measured turbidity or increase in particle content in 4 hr at 23 °C	2264	C
Aztreonam	SQ	40 mg/ml[a]	PHU	2 mg/ml	Physically compatible with no change in measured turbidity or increase in particle content in 4 hr at 23 °C	2264	C
Bretylium tosylate	AST	50 mg/ml	PHU	2 mg/ml	Physically compatible with no change in measured turbidity or increase in particle content in 4 hr at 23 °C	2264	C
Buprenorphine HCl	RKC	0.04 mg/ml[a]	PHU	2 mg/ml	Physically compatible with no change in measured turbidity or increase in particle content in 4 hr at 23 °C	2264	C
Butorphanol tartrate	APC	0.04 mg/ml[a]	PHU	2 mg/ml	Physically compatible with no change in measured turbidity or increase in particle content in 4 hr at 23 °C	2264	C
Calcium gluconate	AMR	40 mg/ml[a]	PHU	2 mg/ml	Physically compatible with no change in measured turbidity or increase in particle content in 4 hr at 23 °C	2264	C
Carboplatin	BR	5 mg/ml[a]	PHU	2 mg/ml	Physically compatible with no change in measured turbidity or increase in particle content in 4 hr at 23 °C	2264	C
Cefazolin sodium	SKB	20 mg/ml[a]	PHU	2 mg/ml	Physically compatible with no change in measured turbidity or increase in particle content in 4 hr at 23 °C	2264	C
Cefoperazone sodium	RR	40 mg/ml[a]	PHU	2 mg/ml	Physically compatible with no change in measured turbidity or increase in particle content in 4 hr at 23 °C	2264	C
Cefotetan disodium	ZEN	20 mg/ml[a]	PHU	2 mg/ml	Physically compatible with no change in measured turbidity or increase in particle content in 4 hr at 23 °C	2264	C

Y-Site Injection Compatibility (1:1 Mixture) (Cont.)

			Linezolid				
Drug	*Mfr*	*Conc*	*Mfr*	*Conc*	*Remarks*	*Ref*	*C/I*
Cefoxitin sodium	ME	20 mg/ml[a]	PHU	2 mg/ml	Physically compatible with no change in measured turbidity or increase in particle content in 4 hr at 23 °C	2264	C
Ceftazidime	SKB[c]	40 mg/ml[a]	PHU	2 mg/ml	Physically compatible with no change in measured turbidity or increase in particle content in 4 hr at 23 °C	2264	C
	GW[d]	40 mg/ml[a]	PHU	2 mg/ml	Physically compatible with no change in measured turbidity or increase in particle content in 4 hr at 23 °C	2264	C
Ceftizoxime sodium	FUJ	20 mg/ml[a]	PHU	2 mg/ml	Physically compatible with no change in measured turbidity or increase in particle content in 4 hr at 23 °C	2264	C
Ceftriaxone sodium	RC	20 mg/ml[a]	PHU	2 mg/ml	Physically compatible with no change in measured turbidity or increase in particle content in 4 hr at 23 °C	2264	C
Cefuroxime sodium	GL	30 mg/ml[a]	PHU	2 mg/ml	Physically compatible with no change in measured turbidity or increase in particle content in 4 hr at 23 °C	2264	C
Chlorpromazine HCl	ES	2 mg/ml[a]	PHU	2 mg/ml	Measured haze level increases immediately	2264	I
Cimetidine HCl	AMR	12 mg/ml[a]	PHU	2 mg/ml	Physically compatible with no change in measured turbidity or increase in particle content in 4 hr at 23 °C	2264	C
Ciprofloxacin	BAY	1 mg/ml[a]	PHU	2 mg/ml	Physically compatible with no change in measured turbidity or increase in particle content in 4 hr at 23 °C	2264	C
Cisatracurium besylate	GW	2 mg/ml	PHU	2 mg/ml	Physically compatible with no change in measured turbidity or increase in particle content in 4 hr at 23 °C	2264	C
Cisplatin	BR	1 mg/ml	PHU	2 mg/ml	Physically compatible with no change in measured turbidity or increase in particle content in 4 hr at 23 °C	2264	C
Clindamycin phosphate	UP	10 mg/ml[a]	PHU	2 mg/ml	Physically compatible with no change in measured turbidity or increase in particle content in 4 hr at 23 °C	2264	C
Cyclophosphamide	MJ	10 mg/ml[a]	PHU	2 mg/ml	Physically compatible with no change in measured turbidity or increase in particle content in 4 hr at 23 °C	2264	C
Cyclosporine	SZ	5 mg/ml[a]	PHU	2 mg/ml	Physically compatible with no change in measured turbidity or increase in particle content in 4 hr at 23 °C	2264	C
Cytarabine	BED	50 mg/ml	PHU	2 mg/ml	Physically compatible with no change in measured turbidity or increase in particle content in 4 hr at 23 °C	2264	C
Dexamethasone sodium phosphate	FUJ	1 mg/ml[a]	PHU	2 mg/ml	Physically compatible with no change in measured turbidity or increase in particle content in 4 hr at 23 °C	2264	C
Dextrose 5% in sodium chloride 0.45%	BA		PHU	2 mg/ml	Physically compatible with no change in measured turbidity or increase in particle content in 4 hr at 23 °C	2264	C

Y-Site Injection Compatibility (1:1 Mixture) (Cont.)

Linezolid

Drug	*Mfr*	*Conc*	*Mfr*	*Conc*	*Remarks*	*Ref*	*C/I*
Dextrose 5% in sodium chloride 0.9%	BA		PHU	2 mg/ml	Physically compatible with no change in measured turbidity or increase in particle content in 4 hr at 23 °C	2264	C
Dextrose 5% in water	BA		PHU	2 mg/ml	Physically compatible with no change in measured turbidity or increase in particle content in 4 hr at 23 °C	2264	C
Diazepam	AB	5 mg/ml	PHU	2 mg/ml	Turbid precipitate forms immediately	2264	I
Digoxin	ES	0.25 mg/ml	PHU	2 mg/ml	Physically compatible with no change in measured turbidity or increase in particle content in 4 hr at 23 °C	2264	C
Diphenhydramine HCl	ES	2 mg/ml[a]	PHU	2 mg/ml	Physically compatible with no change in measured turbidity or increase in particle content in 4 hr at 23 °C	2264	C
Dobutamine HCl	AST	4 mg/ml[a]	PHU	2 mg/ml	Physically compatible with no change in measured turbidity or increase in particle content in 4 hr at 23 °C	2264	C
Dopamine HCl	AB	3.2 mg/ml[a]	PHU	2 mg/ml	Physically compatible with no change in measured turbidity or increase in particle content in 4 hr at 23 °C	2264	C
Doxorubicin HCl	FUJ	2 mg/ml	PHU	2 mg/ml	Physically compatible with no change in measured turbidity or increase in particle content in 4 hr at 23 °C	2264	C
Doxycycline hyclate	FUJ	1 mg/ml[a]	PHU	2 mg/ml	Physically compatible with no change in measured turbidity or increase in particle content in 4 hr at 23 °C	2264	C
Droperidol	AMR	0.4 mg/ml[a]	PHU	2 mg/ml	Physically compatible with no change in measured turbidity or increase in particle content in 4 hr at 23 °C	2264	C
Enalaprilat	ME	0.1 mg/ml[a]	PHU	2 mg/ml	Physically compatible with no change in measured turbidity or increase in particle content in 4 hr at 23 °C	2264	C
Esmolol HCl	OHM	10 mg/ml	PHU	2 mg/ml	Physically compatible with no change in measured turbidity or increase in particle content in 4 hr at 23 °C	2264	C
Etoposide phosphate	BR	5 mg/ml[a]	PHU	2 mg/ml	Physically compatible with no change in measured turbidity or increase in particle content in 4 hr at 23 °C	2264	C
Famotidine	ME	2 mg/ml[a]	PHU	2 mg/ml	Physically compatible with no change in measured turbidity or increase in particle content in 4 hr at 23 °C	2264	C
Fentanyl citrate	AB	0.05 mg/ml	PHU	2 mg/ml	Physically compatible with no change in measured turbidity or increase in particle content in 4 hr at 23 °C	2264	C
Fluconazole	RR	2 mg/ml	PHU	2 mg/ml	Physically compatible with no change in measured turbidity or increase in particle content in 4 hr at 23 °C	2264	C
Fluorouracil	PH	16 mg/ml[a]	PHU	2 mg/ml	Physically compatible with no change in measured turbidity or increase in particle content in 4 hr at 23 °C	2264	C

Y-Site Injection Compatibility (1:1 Mixture) (Cont.)

			Linezolid				
Drug	*Mfr*	*Conc*	*Mfr*	*Conc*	*Remarks*	*Ref*	*C/I*
Furosemide	AMR	3 mg/ml[a]	PHU	2 mg/ml	Physically compatible with no change in measured turbidity or increase in particle content in 4 hr at 23 °C	2264	C
Ganciclovir sodium	RC	20 mg/ml[a]	PHU	2 mg/ml	Physically compatible with no change in measured turbidity or increase in particle content in 4 hr at 23 °C	2264	C
Gemcitabine HCl	LI	10 mg/ml[a]	PHU	2 mg/ml	Physically compatible with no change in measured turbidity or increase in particle content in 4 hr at 23 °C	2264	C
Gentamicin sulfate	FUJ	5 mg/ml[a]	PHU	2 mg/ml	Physically compatible with no change in measured turbidity or increase in particle content in 4 hr at 23 °C	2264	C
Granisetron HCl	SKB	0.05 mg/ml[a]	PHU	2 mg/ml	Physically compatible with no change in measured turbidity or increase in particle content in 4 hr at 23 °C	2264	C
Haloperidol lactate	MN	0.2 mg/ml[a]	PHU	2 mg/ml	Physically compatible with no change in measured turbidity or increase in particle content in 4 hr at 23 °C	2264	C
Heparin sodium	ES	1000 units/ml[a]	PHU	2 mg/ml	Physically compatible with no change in measured turbidity or increase in particle content in 4 hr at 23 °C	2264	C
Hydrocortisone sodium succinate	UP	1 mg/ml[a]	PHU	2 mg/ml	Physically compatible with no change in measured turbidity or increase in particle content in 4 hr at 23 °C	2264	C
Hydromorphone HCl	AST	0.5 mg/ml[a]	PHU	2 mg/ml	Physically compatible with no change in measured turbidity or increase in particle content in 4 hr at 23 °C	2264	C
Hydroxyzine HCl	ES	2 mg/ml[a]	PHU	2 mg/ml	Physically compatible with no change in measured turbidity or increase in particle content in 4 hr at 23 °C	2264	C
Ifosfamide	MJ	25 mg/ml[a]	PHU	2 mg/ml	Physically compatible with no change in measured turbidity or increase in particle content in 4 hr at 23 °C	2264	C
Imipenem–cilastatin sodium	ME	10 mg/ml[b]	PHU	2 mg/ml	Physically compatible with no change in measured turbidity or increase in particle content in 4 hr at 23 °C	2264	C
Labetalol HCl	GW	5 mg/ml	PHU	2 mg/ml	Physically compatible with no change in measured turbidity or increase in particle content in 4 hr at 23 °C	2264	C
Leucovorin calcium	GNS	2 mg/ml[a]	PHU	2 mg/ml	Physically compatible with no change in measured turbidity or increase in particle content in 4 hr at 23 °C	2264	C
Levofloxacin	ORT	5 mg/ml[a]	PHU	2 mg/ml	Physically compatible with no change in measured turbidity or increase in particle content in 4 hr at 23 °C	2264	C
Lidocaine HCl	AB	10 mg/ml[a]	PHU	2 mg/ml	Physically compatible with no change in measured turbidity or increase in particle content in 4 hr at 23 °C	2264	C

Y-Site Injection Compatibility (1:1 Mixture) (Cont.)

Linezolid

Drug	*Mfr*	*Conc*	*Mfr*	*Conc*	*Remarks*	*Ref*	*C/I*
Lorazepam	WY	0.1 mg/ml[a]	PHU	2 mg/ml	Physically compatible with no change in measured turbidity or increase in particle content in 4 hr at 23 °C	2264	C
Magnesium sulfate	AST	100 mg/ml[a]	PHU	2 mg/ml	Physically compatible with no change in measured turbidity or increase in particle content in 4 hr at 23 °C	2264	C
Mannitol	BA	15%	PHU	2 mg/ml	Physically compatible with no change in measured turbidity or increase in particle content in 4 hr at 23 °C	2264	C
Meperidine HCl	AST	4 mg/ml[a]	PHU	2 mg/ml	Physically compatible with no change in measured turbidity or increase in particle content in 4 hr at 23 °C	2264	C
Meropenem	ZEN	2.5 mg/ml[b]	PHU	2 mg/ml	Physically compatible with no change in measured turbidity or increase in particle content in 4 hr at 23 °C	2264	C
Mesna	MJ	10 mg/ml[a]	PHU	2 mg/ml	Physically compatible with no change in measured turbidity or increase in particle content in 4 hr at 23 °C	2264	C
Methotrexate sodium	IMM	15 mg/ml[a]	PHU	2 mg/ml	Physically compatible with no change in measured turbidity or increase in particle content in 4 hr at 23 °C	2264	C
Methylprednisolone sodium succinate	AB	5 mg/ml[a]	PHU	2 mg/ml	Physically compatible with no change in measured turbidity or increase in particle content in 4 hr at 23 °C	2264	C
Metoclopramide HCl	FAU	5 mg/ml	PHU	2 mg/ml	Physically compatible with no change in measured turbidity or increase in particle content in 4 hr at 23 °C	2264	C
Metronidazole	BA	5 mg/ml	PHU	2 mg/ml	Physically compatible with no change in measured turbidity or increase in particle content in 4 hr at 23 °C	2264	C
Midazolam HCl	RC	2 mg/ml[a]	PHU	2 mg/ml	Physically compatible with no change in measured turbidity or increase in particle content in 4 hr at 23 °C	2264	C
Minocycline HCl	LE	0.2 mg/ml[a]	PHU	2 mg/ml	Physically compatible with no change in measured turbidity or increase in particle content in 4 hr at 23 °C	2264	C
Mitoxantrone HCl	IMM	0.5 mg/ml[a]	PHU	2 mg/ml	Physically compatible with no change in measured turbidity or increase in particle content in 4 hr at 23 °C	2264	C
Morphine sulfate	AST	1 mg/ml[a]	PHU	2 mg/ml	Physically compatible with no change in measured turbidity or increase in particle content in 4 hr at 23 °C	2264	C
Nalbuphine HCl	AST	10 mg/ml	PHU	2 mg/ml	Physically compatible with no change in measured turbidity or increase in particle content in 4 hr at 23 °C	2264	C
Naloxone HCl	DU	0.4 mg/ml	PHU	2 mg/ml	Physically compatible with no change in measured turbidity or increase in particle content in 4 hr at 23 °C	2264	C

Y-Site Injection Compatibility (1:1 Mixture) (Cont.)

Drug	*Mfr*	*Conc*	*Mfr* (Linezolid)	*Conc* (Linezolid)	*Remarks*	*Ref*	*C/I*
Nicardipine HCl	WAY	1 mg/ml[a]	PHU	2 mg/ml	Physically compatible with no change in measured turbidity or increase in particle content in 4 hr at 23 °C	2264	C
Nitroglycerin	FAU	0.4 mg/ml[a]	PHU	2 mg/ml	Physically compatible with no change in measured turbidity or increase in particle content in 4 hr at 23 °C	2264	C
Ofloxacin	MN	4 mg/ml[a]	PHU	2 mg/ml	Physically compatible with no change in measured turbidity or increase in particle content in 4 hr at 23 °C	2264	C
Ondansetron HCl	GW	1 mg/ml[a]	PHU	2 mg/ml	Physically compatible with no change in measured turbidity or increase in particle content in 4 hr at 23 °C	2264	C
Paclitaxel	MJ	0.6 mg/ml[a]	PHU	2 mg/ml	Physically compatible with no change in measured turbidity or increase in particle content in 4 hr at 23 °C	2264	C
Pentamidine isethionate	FUJ	6 mg/ml[a]	PHU	2 mg/ml	Crystalline precipitate forms in 1 to 4 hr	2264	I
Pentobarbital sodium	AB	5 mg/ml[a]	PHU	2 mg/ml	Physically compatible with no change in measured turbidity or increase in particle content in 4 hr at 23 °C	2264	C
Phenobarbital sodium	WY	5 mg/ml[a]	PHU	2 mg/ml	Physically compatible with no change in measured turbidity or increase in particle content in 4 hr at 23 °C	2264	C
Phenytoin sodium	ES	50 mg/ml	PHU	2 mg/ml	Crystalline precipitate forms immediately	2264	I
Piperacillin sodium	LE	40 mg/ml[a]	PHU	2 mg/ml	Physically compatible with no change in measured turbidity or increase in particle content in 4 hr at 23 °C	2264	C
Piperacillin sodium–tazobactam sodium	LE	40 + 5 mg/ml[a]	PHU	2 mg/ml	Physically compatible with no change in measured turbidity or increase in particle content in 4 hr at 23 °C	2264	C
Potassium chloride	FUJ	0.1 mEq/ml[a]	PHU	2 mg/ml	Physically compatible with no change in measured turbidity or increase in particle content in 4 hr at 23 °C	2264	C
Prochlorperazine edisylate	SO	0.5 mg/ml[a]	PHU	2 mg/ml	Physically compatible with no change in measured turbidity or increase in particle content in 4 hr at 23 °C	2264	C
Promethazine HCl	SCN	2 mg/ml[a]	PHU	2 mg/ml	Physically compatible with no change in measured turbidity or increase in particle content in 4 hr at 23 °C	2264	C
Propranolol HCl	WAY	1 mg/ml	PHU	2 mg/ml	Physically compatible with no change in measured turbidity or increase in particle content in 4 hr at 23 °C	2264	C
Ranitidine HCl	GW	2 mg/ml[a]	PHU	2 mg/ml	Physically compatible with no change in measured turbidity or increase in particle content in 4 hr at 23 °C	2264	C
Remifentanil HCl	GW	0.5 mg/ml[a]	PHU	2 mg/ml	Physically compatible with no change in measured turbidity or increase in particle content in 4 hr at 23 °C	2264	C

Y-Site Injection Compatibility (1:1 Mixture) (Cont.)

			Linezolid				
Drug	*Mfr*	*Conc*	*Mfr*	*Conc*	*Remarks*	*Ref*	*C/I*
Ringer's injection	BA		PHU	2 mg/ml	Physically compatible with no change in measured turbidity or increase in particle content in 4 hr at 23 °C	2264	C
Ringer's injection, lactated	BA		PHU	2 mg/ml	Physically compatible with no change in measured turbidity or increase in particle content in 4 hr at 23 °C	2264	C
Sodium bicarbonate	AB	1 mEq/ml	PHU	2 mg/ml	Physically compatible with no change in measured turbidity or increase in particle content in 4 hr at 23 °C	2264	C
Sodium chloride 0.9%	BA		PHU	2 mg/ml	Physically compatible with no change in measured turbidity or increase in particle content in 4 hr at 23 °C	2264	C
Sufentanil citrate	ES	0.05 mg/ml	PHU	2 mg/ml	Physically compatible with no change in measured turbidity or increase in particle content in 4 hr at 23 °C	2264	C
Theophylline	BA	4 mg/ml[a]	PHU	2 mg/ml	Physically compatible with no change in measured turbidity or increase in particle content in 4 hr at 23 °C	2264	C
Ticarcillin disodium	SKB	30 mg/ml[a]	PHU	2 mg/ml	Physically compatible with no change in measured turbidity or increase in particle content in 4 hr at 23 °C	2264	C
Tobramycin sulfate	AB	5 mg/ml[a]	PHU	2 mg/ml	Physically compatible with no change in measured turbidity or increase in particle content in 4 hr at 23 °C	2264	C
Vancomycin HCl	FUJ	10 mg/ml[a]	PHU	2 mg/ml	Physically compatible with no change in measured turbidity or increase in particle content in 4 hr at 23 °C	2264	C
Vecuronium bromide	OR	1 mg/ml	PHU	2 mg/ml	Physically compatible with no change in measured turbidity or increase in particle content in 4 hr at 23 °C	2264	C
Verapamil HCl	AB	2.5 mg/ml	PHU	2 mg/ml	Physically compatible with no change in measured turbidity or increase in particle content in 4 hr at 23 °C	2264	C
Vincristine sulfate	LI	0.05 mg/ml[a]	PHU	2 mg/ml	Physically compatible with no change in measured turbidity or increase in particle content in 4 hr at 23 °C	2264	C
Zidovudine	GW	4 mg/ml[a]	PHU	2 mg/ml	Physically compatible with no change in measured turbidity or increase in particle content in 4 hr at 23 °C	2264	C

[a] *Tested in dextrose 5% in water.*
[b] *Tested in sodium chloride 0.9%.*
[c] *Sodium carbonate–containing formulation tested.*
[d] *Arginine-containing formulation tested.*

Additional Compatibility Information

Infusion Solutions — Linezolid is stated to be compatible with dextrose 5% in water, sodium chloride 0.9%, and Ringer's injection, lactated. (2)

Other Drugs — The manufacturer indicates that linezolid should not be mixed with or administered simultaneously through the same line with other drugs. If linezolid is to be infused sequentially before or after other drugs through a common line, it is recommended that the line be flushed both before and after the linezolid is infused using a solution compatible with linezolid and the other drugs. (2)

LORAZEPAM
AHFS 28:24.08

Products — Lorazepam is available in 2- and 4-mg/ml concentrations in 1- and 10-ml vials. The 2-mg/ml concentration is also available in 0.5- and 1-ml disposable syringe cartridges, and the 4-mg/ml concentration is available in 1-ml syringe cartridges. Each milliliter also contains 0.18 ml of polyethylene glycol 400 and 2% benzyl alcohol in propylene glycol. (2; 29)

For intramuscular use, lorazepam may be injected as is. For intravenous use, however, lorazepam *must* be diluted immediately prior to injection with an equal volume of compatible diluent. To dilute the dose in a syringe cartridge or when aspirated from a vial into a syringe, first eliminate all air and then aspirate the proper volume of diluent. Pull the plunger back slightly to provide some mixing space and gently invert the syringe cartridge or syringe repeatedly to mix the contents thoroughly. To avoid air entrapment, do not shake vigorously. (2)

Trade Name(s) — Ativan.

Administration — Lorazepam may be administered by deep intramuscular injection or by intravenous injection when diluted immediately before use with an equal volume of compatible diluent. Intravenous injection is made directly into a vein or into the tubing of a running intravenous infusion at a rate not exceeding 2 mg/min. Care should be taken to ensure that intra-arterial administration and perivascular infiltration will not occur. (2; 4)

Stability — Intact vials of lorazepam should be refrigerated and protected from light and freezing. (2; 4) The manufacturer has stated that the product may be stored for up to two weeks at room temperature. (1181) However, in response to an inquiry, the manufacturer acknowledged that both physical and chemical stability are acceptable for up to 60 days at room temperature. (1674) As with other parenteral products, lorazepam should be inspected visually for particulate matter and discoloration before use and should not be used if it is discolored or contains a precipitate. (2; 4)

Precipitation — The choice of commercial lorazepam concentration to use in the preparation of dilutions is a critical factor in the physical stability of the dilutions. Both the 2- and 4-mg/ml concentrations utilize the same concentrations of solubilizing solvents. On admixture, the solvents that keep the aqueous insoluble lorazepam in solution are diluted twice as much using the 4-mg/ml concentration than if the 2-mg/ml were used, resulting in different precipitation potentials for the same concentration of lorazepam. Care should be taken to ensure that the compounding procedure that is to be used for lorazepam admixtures has been demonstrated to result in solutions in which the lorazepam remains soluble.

Lorazepam concentrations up to 0.08 mg/ml have been reported to be physically stable, while occasional precipitate formation in admixtures of lorazepam 0.1 to 0.2 mg/ml has been reported. The precipitate has been observed in both containers and in administration set tubing. (1943; 1979; 1980) In one case, a visible precipitate formed in a lorazepam 0.5-mg/ml admixture in sodium chloride 0.9% in a glass bottle. (1945) However, a 0.5-mg/ml concentration may remain in solution longer if prepared from the 2-mg/ml concentration, yielding a higher concentration of organic solvents in the final admixture. (1981; 2207) Concentrations of 1 and 2 mg/ml have been reported to be physically stable for up to 24 hours as well as concentrations below 0.08 mg/ml. (1980; 2208) Concentrations in the middle range of 0.08 to 1 mg/ml may be problematic. (1980) In one report, use of lorazepam 2 mg/ml to prepare lorazepam 1-mg/ml admixtures in dextrose 5% in water or sodium chloride 0.9% was acceptable but use of the lorazepam 4-mg/ml concentration to prepare the same solutions resulted in almost immediate precipitation. (2207) Also see Solubility in Solutions under Additional Compatibility Information below.

Freezing Solutions — Although freezing is not recommended by the manufacturer (2), lorazepam (Wyeth-Ayerst) 0.1 mg/ml in dextrose 5% in water (McGaw) in polyolefin bags exhibited no loss when frozen at −20 °C for seven days. (1684)

Bacteriostatic Water — Dilution of lorazepam (Wyeth) to 1 mg/ml with bacteriostatic water for injection (bacteriostat not noted), packaged in glass vials, resulted in lorazepam losses. HPLC analysis showed losses of about 10% at 4 °C and 12% at 22 °C in seven days. Drug crystals precipitated from solutions in varying periods after the first week of storage. (1840)

Syringes — Lorazepam (Wyeth) 2 mg/ml was packaged as 3 ml in 10-ml polypropylene infusion pump syringes (Pharmacia Deltec). About 12 to 14% loss by HPLC analysis occurred in three days and 25% loss in 10 days at 5 and 30 °C. The authors recommended not storing lorazepam in the syringes for these time periods. (1967)

Lorazepam (Wyeth) 1 mg/ml, prepared from the 2-mg/ml commercial concentration, diluted in dextrose 5% in water or in sodium chloride 0.9% was filled as 40 ml in 60-ml polypropylene syringes (Becton-Dickinson). The filled syringes were stored at 22 °C for 28 hours. Visual inspection found the solutions remained physically stable, and HPLC analysis found less than 3% drug loss in this time period. (2208)

Sorption — Lorazepam (Wyeth-Ayerst) 0.1 mg/ml underwent substantial sorption to PVC containers of infusion solutions. In 50-ml bags of dextrose 5% in water or sodium chloride 0.9%, losses of 11 to 13% in eight hours and of 27 to 29% in 24 hr occurred at 37 °C. At 24 °C, approximately 17% was lost in 24 hr and 30% was lost in 72 hours. At 4 °C, 8 to 9% losses occurred in seven days. In Ringer's injection, lactated, losses due to sorption averaged about 50% more than with the other two infusion solutions. The use of PVC administration sets can be expected to contribute to sorption losses as well, while the use of polyolefin containers reduces losses dramatically. See Compatibility Table. (1684)

Lorazepam (Wyeth) 2- and 4-mg/ml concentrations were diluted 1:1 using dextrose 5% in water, sodium chloride 0.9%, and water for injection. A 2-ml sample of each dilution was injected into the Y-sites of administration sets from five different manufacturers through which dextrose 5% in water, sodium chloride 0.9%, Ringer's injection, or Ringer's injection, lactated, was flowing at rates of 30 and 125 ml/hr. No differences were found among the various infusion sets, infusion solutions, or flow rates. All effluent solutions were visually acceptable and had no loss of lorazepam. (786)

In another study, lorazepam (Wyeth) 2 mg/50 ml in dextrose 5% in water was delivered at rates of 600, 200, and 100 ml/hr using an infusion controller fitted with 180 or 350 cm of PVC tubing. Lorazepam loss due to sorption was greater with the longer tubing and at slower rates. Losses ranged from a high of 5% (350 cm, 100 ml/hr) to a low of 0.7% (180 cm, 600 ml/hr). (787)

In static sorption studies, lorazepam (Wyeth) 2 mg/50 ml in dextrose 5% in water was filled into PVC containers in the following amounts: 50 ml into 50-ml bags, 100 ml into 50-ml bags, and 100 ml into 250-ml bags. The bags were stored at 23 °C. A rapid initial loss of lorazepam occurred (about 3.9 to 5.8% in the first hour) followed by a slower, approximately constant loss after eight hours. Cumulative losses of 6 to 8% occurred in about five hours in the smaller bags with smaller bag surface area to volume ratios. The solution in the larger bags exhibited over a 10% loss in two hours. (787)

Martens et al. found less than a 3% lorazepam loss from a 40-µg/ml solution in 500-ml PVC containers of sodium chloride 0.9% in 24 hours at 21 °C in the dark. In glass and polyethylene-lined laminated containers, virtually no loss was observed. (1392)

Lorazepam (Wyeth) at a high concentration of 1 mg/ml admixed in dextrose 5% in water in PVC containers (Baxter) was stored for 24 hours at 25 °C. HPLC analysis found about 6% loss due to sorption, primarily during the first six hours with little additional loss occurring. This was substantially less loss than if the same solution was evaluated with a spectrophotometric method. The authors attributed the difference to interference of the benzyl alcohol preservative with the spectrophotometric analysis. (2203)

Plasticizer Leaching—Lorazepam (Wyeth-Ayerst) 0.1 mg/ml in dextrose 5% in water did not leach diethylhexyl phthalate (DEHP) plasticizer from 50-ml PVC bags in 24 hours at 24 °C. (1683)

Compatibility Information

Solution Compatibility

Lorazepam

Solution	*Mfr*	*Mfr*	*Conc/L*	*Remarks*	*Ref*	*C/I*
Dextrose 5% in water	BA[a]	WY	0.1 g	Losses due to sorption of 11% in 8 hr and 27% in 24 hr at 37 °C, 8% in 8 hr and 17% in 24 hr at 24 °C, and 3% in 24 hr and 8% in 7 days at 4 °C	1684	I
	MG[b]	WY	0.1 g	3% loss in 24 hr and 9% in 72 hr at 37 °C, little or no loss in 24 hr and 5% in 7 days at 24 °C, and no loss in 7 days at 4 °C	1684	C
	AB[c]	WY	0.16, 0.24, 0.5 g	About 10 to 20% loss due to sorption throughout 24-hr delivery at 24 °C under fluorescent light	1858	I
	BA[a]	WY	0.08 g	10 to 17% loss due to sorption in 4 hr at 4 °C. 17% loss in 1 hr, increasing to over 30% in 24 hr at 21 °C	1873	I
	BA[a]	WY	0.5 g	About 14% loss due to sorption in 4 hr at 21 °C	1873	I
	BA[a]	WY	1 g	Approximately 6% loss by HPLC due to sorption in 6 hr with no further loss in 24 hr at 25 °C	2203	C
	AB[e]	WY	1 g	Prepared with 4-mg/ml lorazepam. White precipitate forms in 8 hours at 22 °C	2208	I
	AB[e]	WY	1 g	Prepared with 2-mg/ml lorazepam. Visually compatible with little or no lorazepam loss by HPLC in 28 hr at 22 °C under fluorescent light	2208	C
	AB[e]	WY	2 g	Prepared with 4-mg/ml lorazepam. Visually compatible with little or no lorazepam loss by HPLC in 28 hr at 22 °C under fluorescent light	2208	C
Ringer's injection, lactated	BA[a]	WY	0.1 g	Losses due to sorption of 25% in 8 hr at 37 °C, 14% in 8 hr at 24 °C, and 5% in 24 hr and 9% in 72 hr at 4 °C	1684	I
	MG[b]	WY	0.1 g	2% loss in 24 hr and 7% in 72 hr at 37 °C, little or no loss in 24 hr and 4% in 7 days at 24 °C, and no loss in 7 days at 4 °C	1684	C
Sodium chloride 0.9%	[d]		40 mg	Physically compatible with less than 3% loss in 24 hr at 21 °C in the dark	1392	C

Solution Compatibility (Cont.)

Lorazepam

Solution	*Mfr*	*Mfr*	*Conc/L*	*Remarks*	*Ref*	*C/I*
	BA[a]	WY	0.1 g	Losses due to sorption of 13% in 8 hr and 29% in 24 hr at 37 °C, 8% in 8 hr and 17% in 24 hr at 24 °C, and 3% in 24 hr and 8% in 7 days at 4 °C	1684	I
	MG[b]	WY	0.1 g	2% loss in 24 hr and 7% in 72 hr at 37 °C, little or no loss in 24 hr and 4% in 7 days at 24 °C, and no loss in 7 days at 4 °C	1684	C
	AB[c]	WY	0.16, 0.24, 0.5 g	About 10 to 20% loss due to sorption throughout 24-hr delivery at 24 °C under fluorescent light	1858	I
	BA[a]	WY	0.08 g	8 to 10% loss due to sorption in 4 hr at 4 °C. 17 to 23% loss in 1 hr, increasing to 25 to 30% loss in 4 hr at 21 °C	1873	I
	BA[a]	WY	0.5 g	17% or more loss due to sorption in 4 hr at 21 °C	1873	I

[a]*Tested in PVC containers.*
[b]*Tested in polyolefin containers.*
[c]*Tested in PVC and glass containers and delivered through PVC administration sets.*
[d]*Tested in PVC, glass, and polyethylene-lined laminated containers.*
[e]*Tested in glass containers.*

Additive Compatibility

Lorazepam

Drug	*Mfr*	*Conc/L*	*Mfr*	*Conc/L*	*Test Soln*	*Remarks*	*Ref*	*C/I*
Dexamethasone sodium phosphate with	AMR	400 mg	WY	40 mg	NS[a]	Rapid lorazepam losses of 8, 10, and 15% at 3, 23, and 30 °C, respectively, in 24 hr by HPLC. Other drugs stable for 14 days by HPLC at all three storage temperatures	1733	I
diphenhydramine HCl and	ES	2 g						
metoclopramide HCl	DU	4 g						

[a]*Tested in Pharmacia-Deltec PVC pump reservoirs.*

Drugs in Syringe Compatibility

Lorazepam

Drug (in syringe)	*Mfr*	*Amt*	*Mfr*	*Amt*	*Remarks*	*Ref*	*C/I*
Cimetidine HCl	SKF	300 mg/2 ml	WY	2 mg/1 ml	Physically compatible for 4 hr at 25 °C	25	C
Haloperidol lactate	MN	5 mg/ml	WY	2 mg/ml	Physically compatible and chemically stable for 16 hr at room temperature	1838	C
Hydromorphone HCl	KN	2, 10, 40 mg/1 ml	WY	4 mg/1 ml	Visually compatible with 10% lorazepam loss by HPLC in 6 days at 4 °C, 4 days at 23 °C, and 24 hr at 37 °C. Little or no hydromorphone loss in 7 days at all three temperatures	1776	C
Ranitidine HCl	GL	50 mg/2 ml	WY	4 mg/1 ml	Lorazepam viscosity caused poor mixing and layering, which disappeared following vortex mixing	978	?
Sufentanil citrate	JN	50 μg/ml	WY	2 mg/ml	Turbidity increases within 0.5 hr and continues to increase over 24 hr at 23 °C	1711	I

Y-Site Injection Compatibility (1:1 Mixture)

			Lorazepam				
Drug	*Mfr*	*Conc*	*Mfr*	*Conc*	*Remarks*	*Ref*	*C/I*
Acyclovir sodium	BW	5 mg/ml[a]	WY	0.04 mg/ml[a]	Physically compatible for 4 hr at 25 °C	1157	C
Alatrofloxacin mesylate	PF	1.43 mg/ml[a]	AB	0.1 mg/ml[a]	Visually and microscopically compatible run through a Y-site over at least 60 min	2235	C
Albumin human		200 mg/ml	WY	0.33 mg/ml[b]	Visually compatible for 24 hr at 22 °C	1855	C
Aldesleukin	CHI	33,800 I.U./ml[a]	WY	2 mg/ml	Globules form immediately	1857	I
Allopurinol sodium	BW	3 mg/ml[b]	WY	0.1 mg/ml[b]	Physically compatible with no change in measured turbidity or increase in particle content in 4 hr at 22 °C	1686	C
Amifostine	USB	10 mg/ml[a]	WY	0.1 mg/ml[a]	Physically compatible with no change in measured turbidity or increase in particle content in 4 hr at 23 °C	1845	C
Amikacin sulfate	BMS	5 mg/ml	WY	0.33 mg/ml[b]	Visually compatible for 24 hr at 22 °C	1855	C
Amoxicillin sodium	SKB	50 mg/ml	WY	0.33 mg/ml[b]	Visually compatible for 24 hr at 22 °C	1855	C
Amoxicillin sodium–clavulanate potassium	SKB	20 + 2 mg/ml	WY	0.33 mg/ml[b]	Visually compatible for 24 hr at 22 °C	1855	C
Amphotericin B cholesteryl sulfate complex	SEQ	0.83 mg/ml[a]	WY	0.1 mg/ml[a]	Physically compatible with little or no change in measured turbidity or increase in particle content in 4 hr at 23 °C under fluorescent light	2117	C
Amsacrine	NCI	1 mg/ml[a]	WY	0.1 mg/ml[a]	Physically compatible for 4 hr at room temperature under fluorescent light	1381	C
Atracurium besylate	BW	0.5 mg/ml[a]	WY	0.5 mg/ml[a]	Physically compatible for 24 hr at 28 °C	1337	C
Aztreonam	SQ	40 mg/ml[a]	WY	0.1 mg/ml[a]	Haze forms within 1 hr	1758	I
Bumetanide	LEO	0.5 mg/ml	WY	0.33 mg/ml[b]	Visually compatible for 24 hr at 22 °C	1855	C
Cefepime HCl	BMS	20 mg/ml[a]	WY	0.1 mg/ml[a]	Physically compatible with no change in measured turbidity or increase in particle content in 4 hr at 22 °C	1689	C
Cefotaxime sodium	RS	10 mg/ml	WY	0.33 mg/ml[b]	Visually compatible for 24 hr at 22 °C	1855	C
Ciprofloxacin	BAY	2 mg/ml	WY	0.33 mg/ml[b]	Visually compatible for 24 hr at 22 °C	1855	C
Cisatracurium besylate	GW	0.1, 2, 5 mg/ml[a]	WY	0.5 mg/ml[a]	Physically compatible with no change in measured turbidity or increase in particle content in 4 hr at 23 °C	2074	C
Cisplatin	BR	1 mg/ml	WY	0.1 mg/ml[a]	Visually compatible for 4 hr at room temperature under fluorescent light	1685	C
Cladribine	WY	0.1 mg/ml[b]	ORT	0.015[b] and 0.5[d] mg/ml	Physically compatible with no change in measured turbidity or increase in particle content in 4 hr at 23 °C	1969	C
Clonidine HCl	BI	0.015 mg/ml	WY	0.33 mg/ml[b]	Visually compatible for 24 hr at 22 °C	1855	C
Cyclophosphamide	MJ	10 mg/ml	WY	0.1 mg/ml[a]	Visually compatible for 4 hr at room temperature under fluorescent light	1685	C
Cytarabine	UP	50 mg/ml	WY	0.1 mg/ml[a]	Visually compatible for 4 hr at room temperature under fluorescent light	1685	C

Y-Site Injection Compatibility (1:1 Mixture) (Cont.)

			Lorazepam				
Drug	*Mfr*	*Conc*	*Mfr*	*Conc*	*Remarks*	*Ref*	*C/I*
Dexamethasone sodium phosphate		4 mg/ml	WY	0.33 mg/ml[b]	Visually compatible for 24 hr at 22 °C	1855	C
Diltiazem HCl	MMD	5 mg/ml	WY	4 mg/ml	Visually compatible	1807	C
	MMD	1 mg/ml[b]	WY	2 mg/ml[b]	Visually compatible	1807	C
	MMD	1 mg/ml[a]	WY	0.5 mg/ml[a]	Visually compatible for 4 hr at 27 °C	2062	C
Dobutamine HCl	LI	4 mg/ml[a]	WY	0.5 mg/ml[a]	Visually compatible for 4 hr at 27 °C	2062	C
Docetaxel	RPR	0.9 mg/ml[a]	WY	0.5 mg/ml[a]	Physically compatible with no change in measured turbidity or increase in particle content in 4 hr at 23 °C	2224	C
Dopamine HCl	AB	3.2 mg/ml[a]	WY	0.5 mg/ml[a]	Visually compatible for 4 hr at 27 °C	2062	C
Doxorubicin HCl	AD	0.2 mg/ml[a]	WY	0.1 mg/ml[a]	Visually compatible for 4 hr at room temperature under fluorescent light	1685	C
Doxorubicin HCl liposome injection	SEQ	0.4 mg/ml[a]	WY	0.1 mg/ml[a]	Physically compatible with little or no change in measured turbidity and no increase in particle content in 4 hr at 23 °C	2087	C
Epinephrine HCl	AB	0.02 mg/ml[a]	WY	0.5 mg/ml[a]	Visually compatible for 4 hr at 27 °C	2062	C
Erythromycin lactobionate	AB	5 mg/ml	WY	0.33 mg/ml[b]	Visually compatible for 24 hr at 22 °C	1855	C
Etomidate	AB	2 mg/ml	WY	2 mg/ml	Visually compatible for up to 7 days at 25 °C	1801	C
Etoposide phosphate	BR	5 mg/ml[a]	WY	0.5 mg/ml[a]	Physically compatible with no change in measured turbidity or increase in particle content in 4 hr at 23 °C	2218	C
Famotidine	ME	2 mg/ml[b]		0.1 mg/ml[a]	Visually compatible for 4 hr at 22 °C	1936	C
Fentanyl citrate		0.05 mg/ml	WY	0.33 mg/ml[b]	Visually compatible for 24 hr at 22 °C	1855	C
	ES	0.05 mg/ml	WY	0.5 mg/ml[a]	Visually compatible for 4 hr at 27 °C	2062	C
	JN	0.025 mg/ml[a]	WY	0.1 mg/ml[a]	Physically compatible with no change in measured haze or increase in particle content in 48 hr at 22 °C	1706	C
Filgrastim	AMG	30 μg/ml[a]	WY	0.1 mg/ml[a]	Physically compatible with no change in measured turbidity or increase in particle content in 4 hr at 22 °C	1687	C
Floxacillin sodium	SKB	50 mg/ml	WY	0.33 mg/ml[b]	White opalescence forms in 4 hr	1855	I
Fluconazole	PF	2 mg/ml	WY	0.33 mg/ml[b]	Visually compatible for 24 hr at 22 °C	1855	C
Fludarabine phosphate	BX	1 mg/ml[a]	WY	0.1 mg/ml[a]	Physically compatible for 4 hr at room temperature under fluorescent light	1439	C
Foscarnet sodium	AST	24 mg/ml	WY	4 mg/ml	Gas production	1335	I
	AST	24 mg/ml	WY	0.08 mg/ml[a]	Physically compatible for 24 hr at 25 °C under fluorescent light by visual and microscopic examination	1393	C
Fosphenytoin sodium	PD	1 mgPE/ml[b,h]	WY	2 mg/ml	Samples remained clear with no loss of either drug by HPLC in 8 hr	2223	C
Furosemide	CNF	10 mg/ml	WY	0.33 mg/ml[b]	Visually compatible for 24 hr at 22 °C	1855	C
	AMR	10 mg/ml	WY	0.5 mg/ml[a]	Visually compatible for 4 hr at 27 °C	2062	C

Y-Site Injection Compatibility (1:1 Mixture) (Cont.)

Lorazepam

Drug	*Mfr*	*Conc*	*Mfr*	*Conc*	*Remarks*	*Ref*	*C/I*
Gatifloxacin	BMS	2 mg/ml[a]	WY	0.1 mg/ml[a]	Physically compatible with no change in measured haze or increase in particle content in 4 hr at 23 °C	2234	C
Gemcitabine HCl	LI	10 mg/ml[b]	WY	0.5 mg/ml[a]	Physically compatible with no change in measured turbidity or increase in particle content in 4 hr at 23 °C	2226	C
Gentamicin sulfate	CNF	3 mg/ml	WY	0.33 mg/ml[b]	Visually compatible for 24 hr at 22 °C	1855	C
Granisetron HCl	SKB	1 mg/ml	WY	0.1 mg/ml[b]	Physically compatible with little or no loss of either drug by HPLC in 4 hr at 22 °C	1883	C
	SKB	0.05 mg/ml[a]	WY	0.1 mg/ml[a]	Physically compatible with no change in measured turbidity or increase in particle content in 4 hr at 23 °C	2000	C
Haloperidol lactate	JN	0.5 and 5 mg/ml	WY	0.33 mg/ml[b]	Visually compatible for 24 hr at 22 °C	1855	C
Heparin sodium		417 units/ml	WY	0.33 mg/ml[b]	Visually compatible for 24 hr at 22 °C	1855	C
	ES	100 units/ml[a]	WY	0.5 mg/ml[a]	Visually compatible for 4 hr at 27 °C	2062	C
Hetastarch in lactated electrolyte injection (Hextend)	AB	6%	OH	0.5 mg/ml[a]	Physically compatible with no change in measured turbidity or increase in particle content in 4 hr at 23 °C	2339	C
Hydrocortisone sodium succinate	UP	50 mg/ml	WY	0.33 mg/ml[b]	Visually compatible for 24 hr at 22 °C	1855	C
Hydromorphone HCl	KN	1 mg/ml	WY	0.5 mg/ml[a]	Visually compatible for 4 hr at 27 °C	2062	C
	AST	0.5 mg/ml[a]	WY	0.1 mg/ml[a]	Physically compatible with no change in measured haze or increase in particle content in 48 hr at 22 °C	1706	C
Idarubicin HCl	AD	1 mg/ml[b]	WY	2 mg/ml	Color changes immediately	1525	I
Imipenem–cilastatin sodium	MSD	5 mg/ml	WY	0.33 mg/ml[b]	Yellow precipitate forms in 24 hr	1855	I
Ketanserin tartrate	JN	1 mg/ml	WY	0.33 mg/ml[b]	Visually compatible for 24 hr at 22 °C	1855	C
Labetalol HCl	AH	2 mg/ml[a]	WY	0.5 mg/ml[a]	Visually compatible for 4 hr at 27 °C	2062	C
Levofloxacin	OMN	5 mg/ml[a]		2 mg/ml	Visually compatible for 4 hr at 24 °C under fluorescent light	2233	C
Linezolid	PHU	2 mg/ml	WY	0.1 mg/ml[a]	Physically compatible with no change in measured turbidity or increase in particle content in 4 hr at 23 °C	2264	C
Melphalan HCl	BW	0.1 mg/ml[b]	WY	0.1 mg/ml[b]	Physically compatible with no change in measured turbidity or increase in particle content in 3 hr at 22 °C	1557	C
Methadone HCl	LI	1 mg/ml[a]	WY	0.1 mg/ml[a]	Physically compatible with no change in measured haze or increase in particle content in 48 hr at 22 °C	1706	C
Methotrexate sodium	AD	15 mg/ml[e]	WY	0.1 mg/ml[a]	Visually compatible for 4 hr at room temperature under fluorescent light	1685	C
Metronidazole	BRN	5 mg/ml	WY	0.33 mg/ml[b]	Visually compatible for 24 hr at 22 °C	1855	C
Midazolam HCl	RC	2 mg/ml[a]	WY	0.5 mg/ml[a]	Visually compatible for 4 hr at 27 °C	2062	C

Y-Site Injection Compatibility (1:1 Mixture) (Cont.)

			Lorazepam				
Drug	*Mfr*	*Conc*	*Mfr*	*Conc*	*Remarks*	*Ref*	*C/I*
Milrinone lactate	SW	0.2 mg/ml[a]	WY	0.5 mg/ml[a]	Visually compatible for 4 hr at 27 °C	2062	C
	SW	0.4 mg/ml[a]	WY	0.2 mg/ml[a]	Visually compatible with little or no loss of either drug by HPLC in 4 hr at 23 °C	2214	C
Morphine HCl	CNF	1 mg/ml	WY	0.33 mg/ml[b]	Visually compatible for 24 hr at 22 °C	1855	C
Morphine sulfate	SCN	2 mg/ml[a]	WY	0.5 mg/ml[a]	Visually compatible for 4 hr at 27 °C	2062	C
	AST	1 mg/ml[a]	WY	0.1 mg/ml[a]	Physically compatible with no change in measured haze or increase in particle content in 48 hr at 22 °C	1706	C
Nicardipine HCl	WY	1 mg/ml[a]	WY	0.5 mg/ml[a]	Visually compatible for 4 hr at 27 °C	2062	C
Nitroglycerin	AB	0.4 mg/ml[a]	WY	0.5 mg/ml[a]	Visually compatible for 4 hr at 27 °C	2062	C
Norepinephrine bitartrate	AB	0.128 mg/ml[a]	WY	0.5 mg/ml[a]	Visually compatible for 4 hr at 27 °C	2062	C
Omeprazole sodium	AST	4 mg/ml	WY	0.33 mg/ml[b]	Yellow discoloration forms	1855	I
Ondansetron HCl	GL	1 mg/ml[b]	WY	0.1 mg/ml[a]	Light haze forms immediately	1365	I
Paclitaxel	NCI	1.2 mg/ml[a]		0.1 mg/ml[a]	Physically compatible with no change in measured turbidity in 4 hr at 22 °C	1528	C
Pancuronium bromide	ES	0.05 mg/ml[a]	WY	0.5 mg/ml[a]	Physically compatible for 24 hr at 28 °C	1337	C
Piperacillin sodium	LE	150 mg/ml	WY	0.33 mg/ml[b]	Visually compatible for 24 hr at 22 °C	1855	C
Piperacillin sodium–tazobactam sodium	LE	40 + 5 mg/ml[a]	WY	0.1 mg/ml[a]	Physically compatible with no change in measured turbidity or increase in particle content in 4 hr at 22 °C	1688	C
Potassium chloride	BRN	1 mEq/ml	WY	0.33 mg/ml[b]	Visually compatible for 24 hr at 22 °C	1855	C
Propofol	ZEN	10 mg/ml	WY	0.1 mg/ml[a]	Physically compatible for 1 hr at 23 °C with no increase in particle content	2066	C
Ranitidine HCl	GL	0.5 mg/ml	WY	0.33 mg/ml[b]	Visually compatible for 24 hr at 22 °C	1855	C
	GL	1 mg/ml[a]	WY	0.5 mg/ml[a]	Visually compatible for 4 hr at 27 °C	2062	C
Remifentanil HCl	GW	0.025 and 0.25 mg/ml[b]	WY	0.5 mg/ml[a]	Physically compatible with no change in measured turbidity or increase in particle content in 4 hr at 23 °C	2075	C
Sargramostim	IMM	10 μg/ml[b]	WY	0.1 mg/ml[b]	Slightly bluish haze, visible with high intensity light, forms in 1 hr	1436	I
Sufentanil citrate	JN	12.5 μg/ml[a]	WY	0.1 mg/ml[a]	Large increase in turbidity occurs immediately and persists for 24 hr at 23 °C	1711	I
Tacrolimus	FUJ	1 mg/ml[b]	WY	1 mg/ml[a]	Visually compatible for 24 hr at 25 °C	1630	C
Teniposide	BR	0.1 mg/ml[a]	WY	0.1 mg/ml[a]	Physically compatible with no subvisual haze or particle formation in 4 hr at 23 °C	1725	C
Thiopental sodium	AB	25 mg/ml	WY	2 mg/ml	Yellow discoloration forms	1801	I
	AB	25 mg/ml[c]	WY	0.5 mg/ml[a]	Visually compatible for 4 hr at 27 °C	2062	C
Thiotepa	IMM[f]	1 mg/ml[a]	WY	0.1 mg/ml[a]	Physically compatible with no change in measured turbidity or increase in particle content in 4 hr at 23 °C	1861	C

Y-Site Injection Compatibility (1:1 Mixture) (Cont.)

Drug	Mfr	Conc	Lorazepam Mfr	Lorazepam Conc	Remarks	Ref	C/I
TNA #218 to #226[g]			WY	0.1 mg/ml[a]	Damage to emulsion integrity occurs in 1 hr	2215	I
TPN #212 to #215[g]			WY	0.1 mg/ml[a]	Physically compatible with no change in measured turbidity or increase in particle content in 4 hr at 23 °C	2109	C
Trimethoprim–sulfamethoxazole	RC	0.8 + 4 mg/ml	WY	0.33 mg/ml[b]	Visually compatible for 24 hr at 22 °C	1855	C
Vancomycin HCl	LI	5 mg/ml	WY	0.33 mg/ml[b]	Visually compatible for 24 hr at 22 °C	1855	C
Vecuronium bromide	OR	0.1 mg/ml[a]	WY	0.5 mg/ml[a]	Physically compatible for 24 hr at 28 °C	1337	C
	OR	4 mg/ml	WY	0.33 mg/ml[b]	Visually compatible for 24 hr at 22 °C	1855	C
	OR	1 mg/ml	WY	0.5 mg/ml[a]	Visually compatible for 4 hr at 27 °C	2062	C
Vinorelbine tartrate	BW	1 mg/ml[b]	WY	0.1 mg/ml[b]	Physically compatible with no change in measured turbidity or increase in particle content in 4 hr at 22 °C	1558	C
Zidovudine	BW	4 mg/ml[a]	WY	80 μg/ml[a]	Physically compatible for 4 hr at 25 °C under fluorescent light by visual and microscopic examination	1193	C

[a]*Tested in dextrose 5% in water.*
[b]*Tested in sodium chloride 0.9%.*
[c]*Tested in sterile water for injection.*
[d]*Tested in bacteriostatic sodium chloride 0.9% preserved with benzyl alcohol 0.9%.*
[e]*Tested in dextrose 5% in water with sodium bicarbonate 0.05 mEq/ml.*
[f]*Lyophilized formulation tested.*
[g]*Refer to Appendix I for the composition of parenteral nutrition solutions. TNA indicates a 3-in-1 admixture, and TPN indicates a 2-in-1 admixture.*
[h]*Concentration expressed in milligrams of phenytoin sodium equivalents (PE) per milliliter.*

Additional Compatibility Information

Infusion Solutions — For dilution of intravenous doses, lorazepam (Wyeth) is stated to be compatible with dextrose 5% in water, sodium chloride 0.9%, and sterile water for injection. (2)

Solubility in Solutions — Lorazepam solubility in common infusion solutions has been reported (Table 1). Its solubility in sodium chloride 0.9% is approximately half that found in the other tested solutions. This result was attributed to the pH of the sodium chloride 0.9% (pH 6.3) being essentially the same as the isoelectric point of lorazepam (pH 6.4), where aqueous solubility would be the lowest. Dextrose 5% in water was the best diluent for lorazepam. (787)

Buprenorphine — Lorazepam is stated to be incompatible with buprenorphine HCl. (4)

Table 1. Lorazepam Equilibrium Solubility (787)

Solution	Lorazepam Solubility (mg/ml)	Solution pH
Deionized water	0.054	7.09
Dextrose 5% in water	0.062	4.41
Ringer's injection, lactated	0.055	7.21
Sodium chloride 0.9%	0.027	6.30

MAGNESIUM SULFATE
AHFS 28:12.92

Products — Magnesium sulfate is available from various manufacturers in concentrations of 50, 20, 12.5, 10, 8, 4, 2, and 1% in a variety of container sizes. (4; 154) The 50% solution provides 500 mg/ml of magnesium sulfate (magnesium 4.06 mEq/ml). The 12.5% solution contains 125 mg/ml of magnesium sulfate (magnesium 1 mEq/ml). Magnesium sulfate 10% contains 100 mg/ml of magnesium sulfate (magnesium 0.8 mEq/ml). The pH of these concentrations may have been adjusted with sodium hydroxide and/or sulfuric acid. (1-8/98; 4; 154)

Magnesium sulfate is also available as 4 and 8% (40 and 80 mg/ml, respectively) solutions in water for injection and 1 and 2% (10 and 20 mg/ml, respectively) solutions in dextrose 5% in water. (4)

pH — Magnesium sulfate injection has a pH adjusted to 5.5 to 7.0 when diluted to a 5% concentration. (1-8/98) The premixed infusion solutions have pH values in the range of 3.5 to 6.5. (17)

Osmotic Values — The osmolality of magnesium sulfate 50% (Invenex) was determined to be 2620 mOsm/kg by freezing-point depression and 2875 mOsm/kg by vapor pressure. (1071)

The 50% solution has a calculated osmolarity of 4060 mOsm/L. (1-8/98)

Administration — Magnesium sulfate may be administered by intramuscular or direct intravenous injection and by continuous or intermittent intravenous infusion. For intravenous injection, a concentration of 20% or less should be used; the rate of injection should not exceed 1.5 ml of a 10% solution (or equivalent) per minute. For intramuscular injection, a 25 or 50% concentration is satisfactory for adults, but dilution to 20% is necessary for infants and children. (1-8/98; 4; 431)

Stability — Magnesium sulfate injection and magnesium sulfate in dextrose 5% in water should be stored at controlled room temperature and protected from temperatures above 40 °C and from freezing. (4) Refrigeration of intact ampuls may result in precipitation or crystallization. (593)

At a concentration of 40 g/L in dextrose 5% in water in polyolefin containers (McGaw), magnesium sulfate (Abbott) was found to be stable for at least 60 days at 0 °C. (922)

Compatibility Information

Solution Compatibility

Magnesium sulfate

Solution	*Mfr*	*Mfr*	*Conc/L*	*Remarks*	*Ref*	*C/I*
Dextrose 5% in water	MG	AB	40 g	Physically compatible and chemically stable for 60 days at 0 °C	922	C
Fat emulsion 10%, intravenous	CU		13.6 mEq[a]	Immediate flocculation with visually apparent layer within 2 hr at room temperature	656	I
Ringer's injection, lactated	BA[b,c]	AMR	37 g	Visually compatible with no consistent change in elemental composition over 3 months stored at room temperature	2184	C
Sodium chloride 0.9%	BA[b,c]	AMR	37 g	Visually compatible with no consistent change in elemental composition over 3 months stored at room temperature	2184	C

[a]*Tested as magnesium chloride.*
[b]*Tested in PVC containers.*
[c]*Tested in glass containers.*

Additive Compatibility

Magnesium sulfate

Drug	*Mfr*	*Conc/L*	*Mfr*	*Conc/L*	*Test Soln*	*Remarks*	*Ref*	*C/I*
Amphotericin B	SQ	40 and 80 mg	IMS	2 and 4 g	D5W	Physically incompatible in 3 hr at 24 °C with decreased clarity and development of supernatant. Total loss of amphotericin B in supernatant by HPLC	1578	I
Calcium gluconate	PR	10, 20, 30, 40 mEq	LI	1, 2, 3, 4 mEq	AA 4%, D 25%	Physically compatible for 24 hr at 22 °C	313	C

Additive Compatibility (Cont.)

Magnesium sulfate

Drug	*Mfr*	*Conc/L*	*Mfr*	*Conc/L*	*Test Soln*	*Remarks*	*Ref*	*C/I*
	PR	4 to 100 mEq	LI	4 to 100 mEq	PH 4%, D 20%	Physically compatible for 24 hr at room temperature	464	C
Chloramphenicol sodium succinate	PD	10 g	LI	16 mEq	D5W	Physically compatible	15	C
Cisplatin	BR	50 and 200 mg		1 and 2 g	D5½S[a]	Compatible for 48 hr at 25 °C and 96 hr at 4 °C followed by 48 hr at 25 °C	1088	C
Cyclosporine	SZ	2 g	LY	30 g	D5W	Transient turbidity appears upon preparation but dissipates in 30 sec and remains clear for 36 hr at 24 °C. 5% cyclosporine loss in 6 hr and 10% loss in 12 hr by HPLC at 24 °C under fluorescent light	1629	I
Dobutamine HCl	LI	167 mg	ES	83 g	NS	Physically compatible for 20 hr. Haze forms at 24 hr	552	I
	LI	1 g	TO	2 g	D5W, NS	Slightly pink in 24 hr at 25 °C	789	I
Heparin sodium		50,000 units		130 mEq	NS[b]	Visually compatible with heparin activity retained for 14 days at 24 °C under fluorescent light	1908	C
Hydrocortisone sodium succinate	UP	100 mg	ES	750 mg	AA 3.5%, D 25%	Physically compatible	302	C
Isoproterenol HCl	WI	4 mg		1 g		Physically compatible	59	C
Linezolid	PHU	2 mg/ml	AST	100 mg/ml[a]		Physically compatible with no change in measured turbidity or increase in particle content in 4 hr at 23 °C	2264	C
Meropenem	ZEN	1 and 20 g	AST	1 g	NS	Visually compatible for 4 hr at room temperature	1994	C
Methyldopate HCl	MSD	1 g		1 g	D, D–S, S	Physically compatible	23	C
Norepinephrine bitartrate	WI	8 mg		1 g	D, D–S, S	Physically compatible	77	C
Penicillin G potassium	PF	500 mg		1 g	W	5% penicillin loss in 1 day and 13% loss in 2 days at 24 °C	999	C
	PF	500 mg		2 to 8 g	W	7 to 8% penicillin loss in 1 day and 20 to 25% loss in 2 days at 24 °C	999	C
Polymyxin B sulfate	BW	200 mg	LI	16 mEq	D5W	Physically incompatible	15	I
Potassium phosphate	MG	10, 20, 30, 40 mEq	LI	1, 2, 3, 4 mEq	AA 4%, D 25%	Physically compatible for 24 hr at 22 °C	313	C
	MG	4 to 100 mEq	LI	4 to 100 mEq	PH 4%, D 20%	Physically compatible for 24 hr at room temperature	464	C
Procaine HCl						Physically incompatible	9	I
	WI	1 g	LI	16 mEq	D5W	Physically incompatible	15	I
Sodium bicarbonate						Physically incompatible	9	I
	AB	80 mEq	LI	16 mEq	D5W	Physically incompatible	15	I
Verapamil HCl	KN	80 mg	IX	10 g	D5W, NS	Physically compatible for 24 hr	764	C

[a]*Tested in PVC containers.*
[b]*Tested in glass bottles.*

Drugs in Syringe Compatibility

Magnesium sulfate

Drug (in syringe)	*Mfr*	*Amt*	*Mfr*	*Amt*	*Remarks*	*Ref*	*C/I*
Metoclopramide HCl	RB	10 mg/ 2 ml	ES	500 mg/ 1 ml	Physically compatible for 48 hr at room temperature	924	**C**
	RB	10 mg/ 2 ml	ES	1 g/2 ml	Physically compatible for 48 hr at room temperature	924	**C**
	RB	10 mg/ 2 ml	ES	500 mg/ 1 ml	Physically compatible for 48 hr at 25 °C	1167	**C**
	RB	10 mg/ 2 ml	ES	1 g/2 ml	Physically compatible for 48 hr at 25 °C	1167	**C**
	RB	160 mg/ 32 ml	ES	1 g/2 ml	Physically compatible for 48 hr at 25 °C	1167	**C**

Y-Site Injection Compatibility (1:1 Mixture)

Magnesium sulfate

Drug	*Mfr*	*Conc*	*Mfr*	*Conc*	*Remarks*	*Ref*	*C/I*
Acyclovir sodium	BW	5 mg/ml[a]	LY	20 mg/ml[a]	Physically compatible for 4 hr at 25 °C	1157	**C**
Alatrofloxacin mesylate	PF	1.43 mg/ml[a]	AMR	20 mg/ml[b]	Microscopic particles form	2235	**I**
Aldesleukin	CHI	33,800 I.U./ ml[a]	LY	20 mg/ml[a]	Visually compatible with little or no loss of aldesleukin activity by bioassay	1857	**C**
Amifostine	USB	10 mg/ml[a]	AST	100 mg/ml[a]	Physically compatible with no change in measured turbidity or increase in particle content in 4 hr at 23 °C	1845	**C**
Amikacin sulfate	BR	5 mg/ml[a]	IX	16.7, 33.3, 66.7, 100 mg/ ml[a]	Physically compatible for at least 4 hr at 32 °C	813	**C**
Amphotericin B cholesteryl sulfate complex	SEQ	0.83 mg/ml[a]	AST	100 mg/ml[a]	Gross precipitate forms	2117	**I**
Ampicillin sodium	WY	20 mg/ml[b]	IX	16.7, 33.3, 66.7, 100 mg/ ml[a]	Physically compatible for at least 4 hr at 32 °C	813	**C**
Aztreonam	SQ	40 mg/ml[a]	AST	100 mg/ml[a]	Physically compatible with no subvisual haze or particle formation in 4 hr at 23 °C	1758	**C**
Cefamandole nafate	LI	20 mg/ml[a]	IX	16.7, 33.3, 66.7, 100 mg/ ml[a]	Physically compatible for at least 4 hr at 32 °C	813	**C**
Cefazolin sodium	LI	20 mg/ml[a]	IX	16.7, 33.3, 66.7, 100 mg/ ml[a]	Physically compatible for at least 4 hr at 32 °C	813	**C**
Cefepime HCl	BMS	20 mg/ml[a]	AST	100 mg/ml[a]	Haze forms immediately	1689	**I**
Cefoperazone sodium	RR	20 mg/ml[a]	IX	16.7, 33.3, 66.7, 100 mg/ ml[a]	Physically compatible for at least 4 hr at 32 °C	813	**C**
Cefotaxime sodium	HO	20 mg/ml[a]	IX	16.7, 33.3, 66.7, 100 mg/ ml[a]	Physically compatible for at least 4 hr at 32 °C	813	**C**
Cefoxitin sodium	MSD	20 mg/ml[a]	IX	16.7, 33.3, 66.7, 100 mg/ ml[a]	Physically compatible for at least 4 hr at 32 °C	813	**C**

Y-Site Injection Compatibility (1:1 Mixture) (Cont.)

Magnesium sulfate

Drug	*Mfr*	*Conc*	*Mfr*	*Conc*	*Remarks*	*Ref*	*C/I*
Chloramphenicol sodium succinate	PD	20 mg/ml[a]	IX	16.7, 33.3, 66.7, 100 mg/ml[a]	Physically compatible for at least 4 hr at 32 °C	813	C
Ciprofloxacin	MI	2 mg/ml[a]	LY	50%	Visually compatible for 2 hr at 25 °C	1628	C
	MI	2 mg/ml[d]	AB	4 mEq/ml	Precipitate forms in 4 hr in D5W and after 4 hr in NS at 24 °C	1655	I
Cisatracurium besylate	GW	0.1, 2, 5 mg/ml[a]	AB	100 mg/ml[a]	Physically compatible with no change in measured turbidity or increase in particle content in 4 hr at 23 °C	2074	C
Clindamycin phosphate	UP	12 mg/ml[a]	IX	16.7, 33.3, 66.7, 100 mg/ml[a]	Physically compatible for at least 4 hr at 32 °C	813	C
Dobutamine HCl	LI	4 mg/ml[d]	LY	40 mg/ml[d]	Physically compatible for 3 hr	1316	C
Docetaxel	RPR	0.9 mg/ml[a]	AST	100 mg/ml[a]	Physically compatible with no change in measured turbidity or increase in particle content in 4 hr at 23 °C	2224	C
Doxorubicin HCl liposome injection	SEQ	0.4 mg/ml[a]	AST	100 mg/ml[a]	Physically compatible with little or no change in measured turbidity and no increase in particle content in 4 hr at 23 °C	2087	C
Doxycycline hyclate	PF	1 mg/ml[a]	IX	16.7, 33.3, 66.7, 100 mg/ml[a]	Physically compatible for at least 4 hr at 32 °C	813	C
Enalaprilat	MSD	0.05 mg/ml[b]	LY	10 mEq/ml[a]	Physically compatible for 24 hr at room temperature under fluorescent light	1355	C
Erythromycin lactobionate	AB	5 mg/ml[a]	IX	16.7, 33.3, 66.7, 100 mg/ml[a]	Physically compatible for at least 4 hr at 32 °C	813	C
Esmolol HCl	DCC	10 mg/ml[a]	LY	10 mg/ml[a]	Physically compatible for 24 hr at 22 °C	1169	C
Etoposide phosphate	BR	5 mg/ml[a]	AST	100 mg/ml[a]	Physically compatible with no change in measured turbidity or increase in particle content in 4 hr at 23 °C	2218	C
Famotidine	MSD	0.2 mg/ml[a]	SO	100 mg/ml[b]	Physically compatible for 14 hr	1196	C
	ME	2 mg/ml[b]		100 mg/ml[a]	Visually compatible for 4 hr at 22 °C	1936	C
Fludarabine phosphate	BX	1 mg/ml[a]	SO	100 mg/ml[a]	Physically compatible for 4 hr at room temperature under fluorescent light	1439	C
Gatifloxacin	BMS	2 mg/ml[a]	AST	100 mg/ml[a]	Physically compatible with no change in measured haze or increase in particle content in 4 hr at 23 °C	2234	C
Gentamicin sulfate	SC	0.8 mg/ml[a]	IX	16.7, 33.3, 66.7, 100 mg/ml[a]	Physically compatible for at least 4 hr at 32 °C	813	C
Granisetron HCl	SKB	1 mg/ml	AB	16 mg/ml[b]	Physically compatible with little or no loss of granisetron by HPLC in 4 hr at 22 °C	1883	C
	SKB	0.05 mg/ml[a]	AB	100 mg/ml[a]	Physically compatible with no change in measured turbidity or increase in particle content in 4 hr at 23 °C	2000	C
Heparin sodium	UP	1000 units/L[e]	AB	500 mg/ml	Physically compatible for at least 4 hr at room temperature by visual and microscopic examination	534	C

Y-Site Injection Compatibility (1:1 Mixture) (Cont.)

			Magnesium sulfate				
Drug	*Mfr*	*Conc*	*Mfr*	*Conc*	*Remarks*	*Ref*	*C/I*
Hetastarch in lactated electrolyte injection (Hextend)	AB	6%	AST	100 mg/ml[a]	Physically compatible with no change in measured turbidity or increase in particle content in 4 hr at 23 °C	2339	C
Hydrocortisone sodium succinate	UP	10 mg/L[e]	AB	500 mg/ml	Physically compatible for at least 4 hr at room temperature by visual and microscopic examination	534	C
Hydromorphone HCl	KN	2 mg/ml[a]	LY	16.7, 33.3, 50, 100 mg/ml[a]	Visually compatible for 4 hr at 25 °C under fluorescent light	1549	C
Idarubicin HCl	AD	1 mg/ml[b]	SO	2 mg/ml[b]	Visually compatible for 24 hr at 25 °C	1525	C
Insulin, regular	LI	0.2 unit/ml[b]	LY	40 mg/ml[f]	Physically compatible for 2 hr at 25 °C	1395	C
Kanamycin sulfate	BR	2.5 mg/ml[a]	IX	16.7, 33.3, 66.7, 100 mg/ml[a]	Physically compatible for at least 4 hr at 32 °C	813	C
Labetalol HCl	SC	1 mg/ml[a]	LY	10 mg/ml[a]	Physically compatible for 24 hr at 18 °C	1171	C
Linezolid	PHU	2 mg/ml	AST	100 mg/ml[a]	Physically compatible with no change in measured turbidity or increase in particle content in 4 hr at 23 °C	2264	C
Meperidine HCl	WI	10 mg/ml[a]	LY	16.7, 33.3, 50, 100 mg/ml[a]	Visually compatible for 4 hr at 25 °C under fluorescent light	1549	C
Metronidazole	SE	5 mg/ml	IX	16.7, 33.3, 66.7, 100 mg/ml[a]	Physically compatible for at least 4 hr at 32 °C	813	C
Milrinone lactate	SW	0.4 mg/ml[a]	SO	40 mg/ml[a]	Visually compatible with no loss of milrinone by HPLC in 4 hr at 23 °C	2214	C
Minocycline HCl	LE	0.2 mg/ml[a]	IX	16.7, 33.3, 66.7, 100 mg/ml[a]	Physically compatible for at least 4 hr at 32 °C	813	C
Morphine sulfate	ES	1 mg/ml[a]	LY	16.7, 33.3, 50, 100 mg/ml[a]	Visually compatible for 4 hr at 25 °C under fluorescent light	1549	C
	[g]	2 mg/ml[b]	AB	2, 4, 8 mg/ml[b]	Visually compatible for 8 hr at room temperature	1719	C
Nafcillin sodium	WY	20 mg/ml[a]	IX	16.7, 33.3, 66.7, 100 mg/ml[a]	Physically compatible for at least 4 hr at 32 °C	813	C
Ondansetron HCl	GL	1 mg/ml[b]	SO	100 mg/ml[a]	Physically compatible for 4 hr at 22 °C	1365	C
Oxacillin sodium	BE	20 mg/ml[a]	IX	16.7, 33.3, 66.7, 100 mg/ml[a]	Physically compatible for at least 4 hr at 32 °C	813	C
Paclitaxel	NCI	1.2 mg/ml[a]	AST	100 mg/ml[a]	Physically compatible with no change in measured turbidity in 4 hr at 22 °C	1556	C
Penicillin G potassium	SQ	100,000 units/ml[a]	IX	16.7, 33.3, 66.7, 100 mg/ml[a]	Physically compatible for at least 4 hr at 32 °C	813	C
Piperacillin sodium	LE	60 mg/ml[a]	IX	16.7, 33.3, 66.7, 100 mg/ml[a]	Physically compatible for at least 4 hr at 32 °C	813	C

Y-Site Injection Compatibility (1:1 Mixture) (Cont.)

Drug	Mfr	Conc	Magnesium sulfate Mfr	Magnesium sulfate Conc	Remarks	Ref	C/I
Piperacillin sodium–tazobactam sodium	LE	40 + 5 mg/ml[a]	AST	100 mg/ml[a]	Physically compatible with no change in measured turbidity or increase in particle content in 4 hr at 22 °C	1688	C
Potassium chloride	AB	40 mEq/L[e]	AB	500 mg/ml	Physically compatible for at least 4 hr at room temperature by visual and microscopic examination	534	C
Propofol	ZEN	10 mg/ml	AST	100 mg/ml[a]	Physically compatible for 1 hr at 23 °C with no increase in particle content	2066	C
Remifentanil HCl	GW	0.025 and 0.25 mg/ml[b]	AB	100 mg/ml[a]	Physically compatible with no change in measured turbidity or increase in particle content in 4 hr at 23 °C	2075	C
Sargramostim	IMM	10 μg/ml[b]	LY	100 mg/ml[b]	Physically compatible for 4 hr at 22 °C	1436	C
Thiotepa	IMM[h]	1 mg/ml[a]	AST	100 mg/ml[a]	Physically compatible with no change in measured turbidity or increase in particle content in 4 hr at 23 °C	1861	C
Ticarcillin disodium	BE	60 mg/ml[a]	IX	16.7, 33.3, 66.7, 100 mg/ml[a]	Physically compatible for at least 4 hr at 32 °C	813	C
TNA #218 to #226[i]			AB	100 mg/ml[a]	Visually compatible with no precipitate or emulsion damage apparent in 4 hr at 23 °C	2215	C
Tobramycin sulfate	DI	0.8 mg/ml[a]	IX	16.7, 33.3, 66.7, 100 mg/ml[a]	Physically compatible for at least 4 hr at 32 °C	813	C
TPN #212 to #215[i]			AB	100 mg/ml[a]	Physically compatible with no change in measured turbidity or increase in particle content in 4 hr at 23 °C	2109	C
Trimethoprim–sulfamethoxazole	RC	0.8 + 4 mg/ml[a]	IX	16.7, 33.3, 66.7, 100 mg/ml[a]	Physically compatible for at least 4 hr at 32 °C	813	C
Vancomycin HCl	LI	5 mg/ml[a]	IX	16.7, 33.3, 66.7, 100 mg/ml[a]	Physically compatible for at least 4 hr at 32 °C	813	C
Vitamin B complex with C	RC	2 ml/L[e]	AB	500 mg/ml	Physically compatible for at least 4 hr at room temperature by visual and microscopic examination	534	C

[a]*Tested in dextrose 5% in water.*
[b]*Tested in sodium chloride 0.9%.*
[c]*Tested in sterile water for injection.*
[d]*Tested in both dextrose 5% in water and sodium chloride 0.9%.*
[e]*Tested in dextrose 5% in Ringer's injection, dextrose 5% in Ringer's injection, lactated, dextrose 5% in water, Ringer's injection, lactated, and sodium chloride 0.9%.*
[f]*Tested in Ringer's injection, lactated.*
[g]*Extemporaneously prepared product.*
[h]*Lyophilized formulation tested.*
[i]*Refer to Appendix I for the composition of parenteral nutrition solutions. TNA indicates a 3-in-1 admixture, and TPN indicates a 2-in-1 admixture.*

Additional Compatibility Information

Hydrocortisone — A white flocculent precipitate was observed when hydrocortisone sodium succinate (Upjohn) 100 mg in 2 ml was drawn into a syringe previously used to add magnesium sulfate 50% (Elkins-Sinn) 1.5 ml to a parenteral nutrition solution. Hydrocortisone sodium succinate (Upjohn) contains phosphate buffers, and it was postulated that insoluble magnesium phosphate was formed. This finding indicates that magnesium sulfate and hydrocortisone sodium succinate should not be admixed as the concentrated solutions but rather should be added separately to large volume parenteral solutions with thorough mixing after each addition. (302)

Potassium Acetate — Potassium acetate 25 mmol/5 ml added to a TPN solution just after the addition of magnesium sulfate 10 mmol/5 ml has resulted in the formation of translucent off-white needle-like crystals of potassium sulfate. The precipitate redissolved readily when adequately mixed. The addition of potassium chloride in similar quantity did not result in crystalline precipitation, but the authors indicated its presence could decrease the solubility of potassium sulfate and promote precipitation, presumably at higher concentrations. (2266)

Other Drugs — Magnesium sulfate is stated to be incompatible with soluble phosphates and with alkali hydroxides and carbonates. (4)

Clindamycin phosphate (Upjohn) has been reported to be physically incompatible with magnesium sulfate. (2)

The activity of tobramycin sulfate apparently is inhibited by magnesium ions. (145)

MANNITOL
AHFS 36:40 and 40:28

Products — Mannitol is available from several manufacturers in concentrations ranging from 5 to 25% (4; 29):

Concentration	Osmolarity	Available Sizes
5%	275 mOsm/L	1000 ml
10%	550 mOsm/L	500 and 1000 ml
15%	825 mOsm/L	500 ml
20%	1100 mOsm/L	250 and 500 ml
25%	1375 mOsm/L	50 ml

pH — From 4.5 to 7. (4)

Trade Name(s) — Osmitrol.

Administration — Mannitol is administered by intravenous infusion. An administration set with a filter should be used for infusion solutions containing mannitol 20% or more. The dosage, concentration, and administration rate are dependent on the patient's condition and response. (4)

Stability — Mannitol solutions should be stored at controlled room temperature and protected from freezing. (4) The solutions are chemically stable. Mannitol 25% (Invenex) was chemically and physically stable after five autoclavings at 250 °F for 15 minutes. In addition, no extracts or visible particles from the rubber closures were found. (83)

Crystallization — In concentrations of 15% or greater, mannitol may crystallize when exposed to low temperatures. (4; 593) Do not use a mannitol solution containing crystals. If such crystallization occurs, the recommended procedure for resolubilization is to heat the mannitol in hot water at 60 to 80 °C with vigorous shaking periodically. The solution should cool to body temperature before use. (1-9/98; 4)

The use of a microwave oven to resolubilize crystallized mannitol in glass ampuls has been suggested. Exposure to microwave radiation followed by shaking satisfactorily resolubilized the crystals in a shorter total time than the water bath and autoclave methods and resulted in no chemical decomposition. (694)

Unfortunately, the use of microwave radiation to solubilize mannitol crystals is a highly risky undertaking. Explosions of mannitol ampuls during microwave exposure have been reported. (695; 697) Such explosions could injure someone as well as ruin the microwave oven. The explosion results from pressure building during the heating of the solution that occurs from the microwave exposure. (696; 697)

One inventive pharmacist redissolved mannitol crystals using a coffeemaker. (1114)

As an alternative to resolubilizing techniques, the use of warming chambers to maintain the solutions in a crystal-free condition has been recommended. (698–700) Various chambers have been described including a wooden cabinet (698), a metal kettle (699), and even a bun warmer. (700) Storage temperatures of 35 and 50 °C have been utilized. (698; 699)

A related but differing effect is seen when supersaturated solutions of mannitol are placed in PVC bags. Within a few minutes, a heavy white flocculent precipitate forms. The needle-like crystals in mannitol solutions result from slow undisturbed growth. The white flocculent mannitol precipitate results from contact with the PVC surfaces, which act as nuclei for rapid rate crystallization of small crystals. Attempts to resolubilize the white flocculent precipitate with the aid of heat are not fruitful because crystallization may recur in a short time. (432)

Compatibility Information

Additive Compatibility

Mannitol

Drug	*Mfr*	*Conc/L*	*Mfr*	*Conc/L*	*Test Soln*	*Remarks*	*Ref*	*C/I*
Amikacin sulfate	BR	250 mg and 5 g		20%		Physically compatible and chemically stable for 24 hr at 25 °C	292	C

Additive Compatibility (Cont.)

Mannitol

Drug	*Mfr*	*Conc/L*	*Mfr*	*Conc/L*	*Test Soln*	*Remarks*	*Ref*	*C/I*
Bretylium tosylate	ACC	10 g	MG	20%		Physically compatible and chemically stable for 48 hr at room temperature. Mannitol crystallized when stored in refrigerator	541	C
Cefamandole nafate	LI	20 g	TR	15%		9% cefamandole decomposition in 72 hr at 25 °C and 2% in 7 days at 5 °C	376	C
		2 g		10 and 20%		Physically compatible and chemically stable for 24 hr at 25 °C	596	C
	LI	20 g	TR	15%		Physically compatible with 9% cefamandole loss in 72 hr at 25 °C and 5% loss in 10 days at 5 °C	788	C
Cefoxitin sodium	MSD	1, 2, 10, 20 g		10%		4 to 5% cefoxitin decomposition in 24 hr and 10 to 11% in 48 hr at 25 °C. 2 to 5% cefoxitin decomposition in 7 days at 5 °C	308	C
Cimetidine HCl	SKF	1.2 and 5 g	TR	10%		Physically compatible and chemically stable for 1 week at room temperature	549	C
Cisplatin	BR	50 and 200 mg		18.75 g		In D5½S.[a] Compatible for 48 hr at 25 °C and 96 hr at 4 °C followed by 48 hr at 25 °C	1088	C
Dopamine HCl	AS	800 mg		20%		5% dopamine decomposition in 48 hr at 25 °C	79	C
Etoposide with cisplatin and potassium chloride	BR BR LY	400 mg 200 mg 20 mEq	LY	1.875%		In NS.[b] Physically compatible and etoposide and cisplatin chemically stable for 8 hr at 22 °C. Precipitate forms within 24 hr	1329	I
Etoposide with cisplatin and potassium chloride	BR BR LY	400 mg 200 mg 20 mEq	LY	1.875%		In D5½S.[b] Physically compatible and etoposide and cisplatin chemically stable for 8 hr at 22 °C. Precipitate forms within 48 hr	1329	C
Fosphenytoin sodium	PD	2, 8, 20 mgPE/ml[g]	BA[a]	20%		Visually compatible with little or no loss of fosphenytoin by HPLC in 7 days at 25 °C under fluorescent light	2083	C
Furosemide	AB	200, 400, 800 mg	BA[a]	20%		Visually compatible for 72 hr at 22 °C	1803	C
Gentamicin sulfate		120 mg		20%		Physically compatible and gentamicin stable by microbiological assay for 24 hr at 25 °C	897	C
Imipenem–cilastatin	MSD	2.5 g	AB[c]	2.5%		9% imipenem loss in 9 hr at 25 °C. 7% imipenem loss in 48 hr and 11% in 72 hr at 4 °C	1141	I[d]
	MSD	5 g	AB[c]	2.5%		6% imipenem loss in 3 hr and 12% in 6 hr at 25 °C. 7% imipenem loss in 24 hr and 10% in 48 hr at 4 °C	1141	I[d]
	MSD	2.5 g	AB[c]	5%		6% imipenem loss in 3 hr and 10% in 6 hr at 25 °C. 9% imipenem loss in 48 hr and 13% in 72 hr at 4 °C	1141	I[d]
	MSD	5 g	AB[c]	5%		7% imipenem loss in 3 hr and 12% in 6 hr at 25 °C. 12% imipenem loss in 48 hr at 4 °C	1141	I[d]

Additive Compatibility (Cont.)

			Mannitol					
Drug	*Mfr*	*Conc/L*	*Mfr*	*Conc/L*	*Test Soln*	*Remarks*	*Ref*	*C/I*
	MSD	2.5 g	AB[c]	10%		6% imipenem loss in 3 hr and 10% in 6 hr at 25 °C. 7% imipenem loss in 24 hr and 12% in 48 hr at 4 °C	1141	I[d]
	MSD	5 g	AB[c]	10%		12% imipenem loss in 3 hr at 25 °C. 13% imipenem loss in 48 hr at 4 °C	1141	I[d]
Meropenem	ZEN	1 g	BA[a]	2.5%		7 to 8% meropenem loss by HPLC in 8 hr at 24 °C and in 24 hr at 4 °C	2089	I[d]
	ZEN	20 g	BA[a]	2.5%		7 to 9% meropenem loss by HPLC in 4 hr at 24 °C and 6% loss in 20 hr at 4 °C	2089	I[d]
	ZEN	1 g	BA[a]	10%		10 to 11% meropenem loss by HPLC in 4 hr at 24 °C and in 20 hr at 4 °C	2089	I[d]
	ZEN	20 g	BA[a]	10%		10% meropenem loss by HPLC in 3 hr at 24 °C and in 20 hr at 4 °C	2089	I[d]
Metoclopramide HCl	RB	40 and 100 mg	AB	20%		Physically compatible for 48 hr at room temperature	924	C
	RB	40 and 100 mg	AB	20%		Physically compatible for 48 hr at 25 °C	1167	C
	RB	640 mg and 1.6 g	AB	20%		Physically compatible for 48 hr at 25 °C	1167	C
Netilmicin sulfate	SC	3 g	TR	10 and 20%		Physically compatible and chemically stable for 7 days at 4 and 25 °C	558	C
Nizatidine	LI	0.75, 1.5, 3 g	MG	20%[c]		Visually compatible and nizatidine potency by HPLC retained for 7 days at 4 and 25 °C	1533	C
Ofloxacin	ORT	0.4 and 4 g	BA[a]	20%		Physically compatible with little or no ofloxacin loss by HPLC in 3 days at 24 °C	1636	C
	ORT	0.4 and 4 g	BA[a]	20%		White mannitol crystals form upon refrigeration at 5 °C and freezing at −20 °C but disappear with warming	1636	C
Ondansetron HCl	GL	16 mg		BP[a]10%		Physically compatible and chemically stable for 7 days at room temperature exposed to light and at 4 °C	1366	C
Sodium bicarbonate	AB	44.6 mEq[e]	AMR	25 g/L[e]		Visually compatible for 24 hr at 24 °C	1853; 1973	C
Tobramycin sulfate	LI	200 mg and 1 g		20%		Physically compatible and chemically stable for 48 hr at 25 °C	147	C
Verapamil HCl	KN	80 mg[f]	IX	25 g[f]		Physically compatible for 24 hr	764	C

[a]*Tested in PVC containers.*
[b]*Tested in both PVC and glass containers.*
[c]*Tested in glass containers.*
[d]*Incompatible by conventional standards but may be used in shorter periods of time.*
[e]*Tested in dextrose 5% in Ringer's injection, lactated, dextrose 5% in sodium chloride 0.225%, dextrose 5% in sodium chloride 0.45%, dextrose 5% in sodium chloride 0.9%, dextrose 5% in water, dextrose 10% in water, sodium chloride 0.45%, and sodium chloride 0.9% in polyolefin containers.*
[f]*Tested in both dextrose 5% in water and sodium chloride 0.9%.*
[g]*Concentration expressed in milligrams of phenytoin sodium equivalents (PE) per milliliter.*

Y-Site Injection Compatibility (1:1 Mixture)

Drug	*Mfr*	*Conc*	Mannitol *Mfr*	Mannitol *Conc*	*Remarks*	*Ref*	*C/I*
Allopurinol sodium	BW	3 mg/ml[b]	BA	15%	Physically compatible with no change in measured turbidity or increase in particle content in 4 hr at 22 °C	1686	C
Amifostine	USB	10 mg/ml[a]	BA	15%	Physically compatible with no change in measured turbidity or increase in particle content in 4 hr at 23 °C	1845	C
Amphotericin B cholesteryl sulfate complex	SEQ	0.83 mg/ml[a]	BA	15%	Physically compatible with little or no change in measured turbidity or increase in particle content in 4 hr at 23 °C under fluorescent light	2117	C
Aztreonam	SQ	40 mg/ml[a]	BA	15%	Physically compatible with no subvisual haze or particle formation in 4 hr at 23 °C	1758	C
Cefepime HCl	BMS	20 mg/ml[a]	BA	15%	Slight haze with particles forms immediately	1689	I
Cisatracurium besylate	GW	0.1, 2, 5 mg/ml[a]	BA	15%	Physically compatible with no change in measured turbidity or increase in particle content in 4 hr at 23 °C	2074	C
Cladribine	ORT	0.015[b] and 0.5[c] mg/ml	BA	15%	Physically compatible with no change in measured turbidity or increase in particle content in 4 hr at 23 °C	1969	C
Docetaxel	RPR	0.9 mg/ml[a]	BA	15%	Physically compatible with no change in measured turbidity or increase in particle content in 4 hr at 23 °C	2224	C
Doxorubicin HCl liposome injection	SEQ	0.4 mg/ml[a]	BA	15%	Partial loss of measured natural turbidity	2087	I
Etoposide phosphate	BR	5 mg/ml[a]	BA	15%	Physically compatible with no change in measured turbidity or increase in particle content in 4 hr at 23 °C	2218	C
Filgrastim	AMG	30 µg/ml[a]	BA	15%	Filaments form immediately	1687	I
Fludarabine phosphate	BX	1 mg/ml[a]	BA	15%	Physically compatible for 4 hr at room temperature under fluorescent light	1439	C
Fluorouracil	SO	1 and 2 mg/ml[d]		20%	Physically compatible both visually and microscopically and fluorouracil chemically stable by HPLC for 24 hr. Mannitol not tested	1526	C
Gatifloxacin	BMS	2 mg/ml[a]	BA	15%	Physically compatible with no change in measured haze or increase in particle content in 4 hr at 23 °C	2234	C
Gemcitabine HCl	LI	10 mg/ml[b]	BA	15%	Physically compatible with no change in measured turbidity or increase in particle content in 4 hr at 23 °C	2226	C
Hetastarch in lactated electrolyte injection (Hextend)	AB	6%	BA	15%	Physically compatible with no change in measured turbidity or increase in particle content in 4 hr at 23 °C	2339	C
Idarubicin HCl	AD	1 mg/ml[b]	AB	12.5 mg/ml[b]	Visually compatible for 24 hr at 25 °C	1525	C
Linezolid	PHU	2 mg/ml	BA	15%	Physically compatible with no change in measured turbidity or increase in particle content in 4 hr at 23 °C	2264	C

Y-Site Injection Compatibility (1:1 Mixture) (Cont.)

			Mannitol				
Drug	*Mfr*	*Conc*	*Mfr*	*Conc*	*Remarks*	*Ref*	*C/I*
Melphalan HCl	BW	0.1 mg/ml[b]	BA	15%	Physically compatible with no change in measured turbidity or increase in particle content in 3 hr at 22 °C	1557	C
Ondansetron HCl	GL	1 mg/ml[b]	BA	15%	Physically compatible for 4 hr at 22 °C	1365	C
Paclitaxel	NCI	1.2 mg/ml[a]	BA	15%	Physically compatible with no change in measured turbidity in 4 hr at 22 °C	1556	C
Piperacillin sodium–tazobactam sodium	LE	40 + 5 mg/ml[a]	BA	15%	Physically compatible with no change in measured turbidity or increase in particle content in 4 hr at 22 °C	1688	C
Propofol	ZEN	10 mg/ml	BA	15%	Physically compatible for 1 hr at 23 °C with no increase in particle content	2066	C
Remifentanil HCl	GW	0.025 and 0.25 mg/ml[b]	BA	15%	Physically compatible with no change in measured turbidity or increase in particle content in 4 hr at 23 °C	2075	C
Sargramostim	IMM	10 μg/ml[b]	BA	15%	Physically compatible for 4 hr at 22 °C	1436	C
Teniposide	BR	0.1 mg/ml[a]	BA	15%	Physically compatible with no subvisual haze or particle formation in 4 hr at 23 °C	1725	C
Thiotepa	IMM[e]	1 mg/ml[b]	BA	15%	Physically compatible with no change in measured turbidity or increase in particle content in 4 hr at 23 °C	1861	C
TNA #218 to #226[f]			BA	15%	Visually compatible with no precipitate or emulsion damage apparent in 4 hr at 23 °C	2215	C
TPN #212 to #215[f]			BA	15%	Physically compatible with no change in measured turbidity or increase in particle content in 4 hr at 23 °C	2109	C
Vinorelbine tartrate	BW	1 mg/ml[b]	BA	15%	Physically compatible with no change in measured turbidity or increase in particle content in 4 hr at 22 °C	1558	C

[a]*Tested in dextrose 5% in water.*
[b]*Tested in sodium chloride 0.9%.*
[c]*Tested in bacteriostatic sodium chloride 0.9% preserved with benzyl alcohol 0.9%.*
[d]*Tested in dextrose 5% in sodium chloride 0.45%, dextrose 5% in water, and sodium chloride 0.9%.*
[e]*Lyophilized formulation tested.*
[f]*Refer to Appendix I for the composition of parenteral nutrition solutions. TNA indicates a 3-in-1 admixture, and TPN indicates a 2-in-1 admixture.*

Additional Compatibility Information

Blood Products — Mannitol should not be mixed with blood. (4)

Other Drugs — The addition of potassium chloride or sodium chloride to mannitol 20 or 25% solutions may cause precipitation of the mannitol. (4)

It has been stated that mannitol is incompatible in strongly acidic and alkaline solutions. (18)

When mannitol 25 g was added to amphotericin B in dextrose 5% in water, serum amphotericin B levels were satisfactory during therapy. (84)

Although short-term combinations of cisplatin and mannitol are feasible and convenient and they reduce renal toxicity of the cisplatin, advanced premixing of the two agents should be avoided because of complex formation. (524)

MECHLORETHAMINE HCL (MUSTINE HCL) AHFS 10:00

Products — Mechlorethamine HCl is available in vials containing 10 mg of drug and sodium chloride qs 100 mg. While taking appropriate protective measures, including wearing protective gloves, reconstitute the vial with 10 ml of water for injection or sodium chloride 0.9%. With the needle in the rubber stopper, shake the vial several times to dissolve the drug. The resultant solution contains mechlorethamine HCl 1 mg/ml. (2)

pH — The reconstituted solution has a pH of 3 to 5. (2; 4)

Osmolality — Mechlorethamine HCl 1 mg/ml in sterile water for injection has an osmolality of 300 mOsm/kg. (1689)

Trade Name(s) — Mustargen.

Administration — Mechlorethamine HCl is administered intravenously or into body cavities. (2; 4) The drug is extremely irritating to tissues and should not be given intramuscularly or subcutaneously. (4) For intravenous use, the drug may be injected over a few minutes directly into the vein or into the tubing of a running infusion solution. (2; 4) After administration, flushing the vein with about 5 to 10 ml of intravenous solution has been recommended. (4) The drug is a powerful vesicant, and extravasation should be avoided. (2; 4; 377) For intracavitary administration, the drug may be diluted up to 100 ml with sodium chloride 0.9%. (2; 4)

Stability — In dry form, the drug is a light yellow-brown and is stable at temperatures up to 40 °C. (4) Solutions of mechlorethamine HCl decompose on standing and should be prepared immediately before use. Mechlorethamine HCl is even less stable in neutral or alkaline solutions than in the acidic reconstituted solution. Do not use if the solution is discolored or if water droplets form within the vial before reconstitution. Discard unused portions after neutralization. (2; 4) (See Other Information section.)

Using HPLC, Kirk determined the stability of mechlorethamine HCl (Boots) 1 mg/ml when reconstituted with water for injection or sodium chloride 0.9% in vials and plastic syringes. About an 8 to 10% loss occurred in samples over six hours at 22 °C; losses of 4 to 6% occurred in six hours in samples stored at 4 °C. (1279)

Freezing Solutions — Using HPLC, Kirk also determined the stability of mechlorethamine HCl (Boots) 1 mg/ml in water for injection and sodium chloride 0.9% frozen at −20 °C. In water for injection, about a 7% loss occurred after 12 weeks; about a 15% loss occurred in eight weeks with sodium chloride 0.9% as the diluent. At a concentration of 10 mg/500 ml in sodium chloride 0.9% in PVC bags, about a 10% loss occurred in eight weeks frozen at −20 °C. (1279)

Sorption — Mechlorethamine HCl apparently does not undergo sorption to PVC infusion containers. During stability studies, mechlorethamine HCl losses were similar for both PVC and glass containers. (1279)

Compatibility Information

Solution Compatibility

Mechlorethamine HCl

Solution	*Mfr*	*Mfr*	*Conc/L*	*Remarks*	*Ref*	*C/I*
Dextrose 5% in water	[a]	BT	20 mg	10% loss in about 5 hr at 22 °C. 4% loss in 6 hr at 4 °C	1279	I
Sodium chloride 0.9%	[a]	BT	20 mg	10% loss in about 3 hr at 22 °C. 10% loss in 4 hr at 4 °C	1279	I

[a]*Tested in PVC containers.*

Additive Compatibility

Mechlorethamine HCl

Drug	*Mfr*	*Conc/L*	*Mfr*	*Conc/L*	*Test Soln*	*Remarks*	*Ref*	*C/I*
Methohexital sodium	BP	2 g	BP	40 mg	D5W, NS	Haze develops within 3 hr	26	I

Y-Site Injection Compatibility (1:1 Mixture)

Mechlorethamine HCl

Drug	*Mfr*	*Conc*	*Mfr*	*Conc*	*Remarks*	*Ref*	*C/I*
Allopurinol sodium	BW	3 mg/ml[b]	MSD	1 mg/ml	Haze and small particles form immediately and become numerous large particles in 4 hr	1686	I

Y-Site Injection Compatibility (1:1 Mixture) (Cont.)

Drug	Mfr	Conc	Mechlorethamine HCl Mfr	Mechlorethamine HCl Conc	Remarks	Ref	C/I
Amifostine	USB	10 mg/ml[a]	MSD	1 mg/ml	Physically compatible with no change in measured turbidity or increase in particle content in 4 hr at 23 °C	1845	C
Aztreonam	SQ	40 mg/ml[a]	MSD	1 mg/ml	Physically compatible with no subvisual haze or particle formation in 4 hr at 23 °C	1758	C
Cefepime HCl	BMS	20 mg/ml[a]	MSD	1 mg/ml	Slight haze with particles forms immediately	1689	I
Filgrastim	AMG	30 μg/ml[a]	MSD	1 mg/ml	Physically compatible with no change in measured turbidity or increase in particle content in 4 hr at 22 °C	1687	C
Fludarabine phosphate	BX	1 mg/ml[a]	MSD	1 mg/ml	Physically compatible for 4 hr at room temperature under fluorescent light	1439	C
Granisetron HCl	SKB	1 mg/ml	MSD	0.5 mg/ml[b]	Physically compatible with little or no loss of either drug by HPLC in 4 hr at 22 °C	1883	C
Melphalan HCl	BW	0.1 mg/ml[b]	MSD	1 mg/ml	Physically compatible with no change in measured turbidity or increase in particle content in 3 hr at 22 °C	1557	C
Ondansetron HCl	GL	1 mg/ml[b]	MSD	1 mg/ml	Physically compatible for 4 hr at 22 °C	1365	C
Sargramostim	IMM	10 μg/ml[b]	MSD	1 mg/ml	Physically compatible for 4 hr at 22 °C	1436	C
Teniposide	BR	0.1 mg/ml[a]	MSD	1 mg/ml	Physically compatible with no subvisual haze or particle formation in 4 hr at 23 °C	1725	C
Vinorelbine tartrate	BW	1 mg/ml[b]	MSD	1 mg/ml	Physically compatible with no change in measured turbidity or increase in particle content in 4 hr at 22 °C	1558	C

[a]*Tested in dextrose 5% in water.*
[b]*Tested in sodium chloride 0.9%.*

Additional Compatibility Information

Infusion Solutions — Because of the rapid decomposition of mechlorethamine HCl in solution, administration in intravenous infusion solutions is not recommended. (4) One report indicated a 7% loss of mechlorethamine in one hour at room temperature when diluted to 0.1 mg/ml in sodium chloride 0.9%. (923) Injecting the drug into the tubing of a running intravenous infusion rather than adding it to the entire volume of the solution minimizes the extent of chemical decomposition. (2)

For intracavitary administration, up to 100 ml of sodium chloride 0.9% has been used for dilution of mechlorethamine. (2; 4)

Aluminum — Ogawa et al. reported that immersion of a needle with an aluminum component in mechlorethamine (MSD) 1 mg/ml resulted in no visually apparent reaction after seven days at 24 °C. (988)

Other Information

Inactivation — Spillage of the drug on gloves, etc., can be neutralized by soaking in an aqueous solution containing equal amounts of sodium thiosulfate 5% and sodium bicarbonate 5% for 45 minutes. Unused injection solution also may be neutralized by mixing with an equal volume of the sodium thiosulfate–sodium bicarbonate solution for 45 minutes. (2; 1200)

MELPHALAN HCL
AHFS 10:00

Products — Melphalan HCl is available as a lyophilized powder in vials containing 50 mg with povidone 20 mg. It is packaged with a vial of special diluent containing sodium citrate 0.2 g, propylene glycol 6 ml, ethanol (96%) 0.52 ml, and sterile water for injection qs to 10 ml. While taking appropriate protective measures, including wearing protective gloves, reconstitute with 10 ml of special diluent and shake vigorously to yield a 5-mg/ml melphalan concentration. (2)

pH—The reconstituted solution has a pH of about 7. (4)

Trade Name(s)—Alkeran.

Administration—Melphalan is administered intravenously. Immediately after reconstitution, the drug should be diluted in sodium chloride 0.9% to a concentration not greater than 0.45 mg/ml. It should be infused over 15 to 20 minutes. (2; 4) Melphalan has also been administered intra-arterially and intraperitoneally. (4)

Stability—Intact vials should be stored at controlled room temperature and protected from light. The reconstituted solution is stable for no more than 90 minutes at room temperature. (4) Refrigeration of the reconstituted solution results in precipitation. (2; 4)

Because of rapid decomposition, the manufacturer recommends that drug administration be completed within 60 minutes of initial reconstitution. Degradation products are detected within 30 minutes. (2); a 10% loss of initial potency occurs within approximately three hours at 30 °C. (234) After dilution in sodium chloride 0.9%, nearly 1% of melphalan HCl is hydrolyzed every 10 minutes. (2)

Melphalan HCl, reconstituted according to the manufacturer's instructions, was cultured with human lymphoblasts to determine whether its cytotoxic activity was retained. The solution retained cytotoxicity for 24 hours at 4 °C and room temperature. (1575)

Melphalan is stated to be compatible with various medical plastic items, including containers, administration sets, and syringes. (1396)

pH Effects—Melphalan is most stable over a pH range of 3 to 7; decomposition increases at pH 9. (971)

Freezing Solutions—Melphalan HCl 20 μg/ml in sodium chloride 0.9% did not undergo significant decomposition after storage at −20 °C for six or seven months. Test samples exhibited about a 2 to 4% loss over this period. Repeated freeze–thaw cycles also had little effect on melphalan concentration. After four such cycles, the loss was less than 2%. (970)

Melphalan HCl (Wellcome) 0.2 mg/ml in sodium chloride 0.9% in PVC containers was frozen at −20 °C for 72 hours. The thawed solutions were visually clear, and no loss was found by HPLC analysis. (1841)

Filtration—Melphalan HCl 20 μg/ml in 1 ml of sodium chloride 0.9% was filtered through the following filters; minimal adsorption occurred in all cases (970):

Filter	Delivered Concentration (% of initial)
Cellulose acetate 0.2 μm (Minisart-N, Sartorius)	99
Polysulfone 0.45 μm (Acrodisc, Gelman)	98
Polytetrafluoroethylene 0.45 μm (Acrodisc-CR, Gelman)	96

Compatibility Information

Solution Compatibility

Melphalan HCl

Solution	*Mfr*	*Mfr*	*Conc/L*	*Remarks*	*Ref*	*C/I*
Dextrose 5% in water		BW	40 and 400 mg	10% loss in 90 min at 20 °C and 36 min at 25 °C	971	I
Ringer's injection, lactated		BW	40 and 400 mg	10% loss in 2.9 hr at 20 °C and 90 min at 25 °C	971	I
Sodium chloride 0.9%		BW	40 and 400 mg	10% loss in 4.5 hr at 20 °C and 2.4 hr at 25 °C	971	I[a]
		BW	100 and 450 mg	10% loss in 45 min at 30 °C	234	I
		BW	100 mg	10% loss in 3 hr at 20 °C	234	I[a]
	[b]	WEL	200 mg	Visually compatible with losses by HPLC of 6% in 3 hr and 17% in 6 hr at room temperature and 6% in 6 hr and 13% in 24 hr at 4 °C	1841	I[a]

[a]*Incompatible by conventional standards. May be used in shorter time periods.*
[b]*Tested in PVC containers.*

Y-Site Injection Compatibility (1:1 Mixture)

Melphalan HCl

Drug	*Mfr*	*Conc*	*Mfr*	*Conc*	*Remarks*	*Ref*	*C/I*
Acyclovir sodium	BW	7 mg/ml[b]	BW	0.1 mg/ml[b]	Physically compatible with no change in measured turbidity or increase in particle content in 3 hr at 22 °C	1557	C
Amikacin sulfate	BR	5 mg/ml[b]	BW	0.1 mg/ml[b]	Physically compatible with no change in measured turbidity or increase in particle content in 3 hr at 22 °C	1557	C

Y-Site Injection Compatibility (1:1 Mixture) (Cont.)

Melphalan HCl

Drug	*Mfr*	*Conc*	*Mfr*	*Conc*	*Remarks*	*Ref*	*C/I*
Aminophylline	AB	2.5 mg/ml[b]	BW	0.1 mg/ml[b]	Physically compatible with no change in measured turbidity or increase in particle content in 3 hr at 22 °C	1557	C
Amphotericin B	SQ	0.6 mg/ml[a]	BW	0.1 mg/ml[b]	Immediate two- to fourfold increase in measured turbidity due to sodium chloride	1557	I
	SQ	0.6 mg/ml[a]	BW	0.1 mg/ml[a]	Physically compatible but rapid melphalan loss in D5W precludes use	1557	I
Ampicillin sodium	WY	20 mg/ml[b]	BW	0.1 mg/ml[b]	Physically compatible with no change in measured turbidity or increase in particle content in 3 hr at 22 °C	1557	C
Aztreonam	SQ	40 mg/ml[b]	BW	0.1 mg/ml[b]	Physically compatible with no change in measured turbidity or increase in particle content in 3 hr at 22 °C	1557	C
Bleomycin sulfate	BR	1 unit/ml[b]	BW	0.1 mg/ml[b]	Physically compatible with no change in measured turbidity or increase in particle content in 3 hr at 22 °C	1557	C
Bumetanide	RC	0.04 mg/ml[b]	BW	0.1 mg/ml[b]	Physically compatible with no change in measured turbidity or increase in particle content in 3 hr at 22 °C	1557	C
Buprenorphine HCl	RKC	0.04 mg/ml[b]	BW	0.1 mg/ml[b]	Physically compatible with no change in measured turbidity or increase in particle content in 3 hr at 22 °C	1557	C
Butorphanol tartrate	BR	0.04 mg/ml[b]	BW	0.1 mg/ml[b]	Physically compatible with no change in measured turbidity or increase in particle content in 3 hr at 22 °C	1557	C
Calcium gluconate	AST	40 mg/ml[b]	BW	0.1 mg/ml[b]	Physically compatible with no change in measured turbidity or increase in particle content in 3 hr at 22 °C	1557	C
Carboplatin	BR	5 mg/ml[b]	BW	0.1 mg/ml[b]	Physically compatible with no change in measured turbidity or increase in particle content in 3 hr at 22 °C	1557	C
Carmustine	BR	1.5 mg/ml[b]	BW	0.1 mg/ml[b]	Physically compatible with no change in measured turbidity or increase in particle content in 3 hr at 22 °C	1557	C
Cefazolin sodium	GEM	20 mg/ml[b]	BW	0.1 mg/ml[b]	Physically compatible with no change in measured turbidity or increase in particle content in 3 hr at 22 °C	1557	C
Cefepime HCl	BMS	20 mg/ml[a]	BW	0.1 mg/ml[a]	Physically compatible with no change in measured turbidity or increase in particle content in 4 hr at 22 °C	1689	C
Cefoperazone sodium	RR	40 mg/ml[b]	BW	0.1 mg/ml[b]	Physically compatible with no change in measured turbidity or increase in particle content in 3 hr at 22 °C	1557	C
Cefotaxime sodium	HO	20 mg/ml[b]	BW	0.1 mg/ml[b]	Physically compatible with no change in measured turbidity or increase in particle content in 3 hr at 22 °C	1557	C
Cefotetan disodium	STU	20 mg/ml[b]	BW	0.1 mg/ml[b]	Physically compatible with no change in measured turbidity or increase in particle content in 3 hr at 22 °C	1557	C

Y-Site Injection Compatibility (1:1 Mixture) (Cont.)

			Melphalan HCl				
Drug	*Mfr*	*Conc*	*Mfr*	*Conc*	*Remarks*	*Ref*	*C/I*
Ceftazidime	LI[c]	40 mg/ml[b]	BW	0.1 mg/ml[b]	Physically compatible with no change in measured turbidity or increase in particle content in 3 hr at 22 °C	1557	C
Ceftizoxime sodium	FUJ	20 mg/ml[b]	BW	0.1 mg/ml[b]	Physically compatible with no change in measured turbidity or increase in particle content in 3 hr at 22 °C	1557	C
Ceftriaxone sodium	RC	20 mg/ml[b]	BW	0.1 mg/ml[b]	Physically compatible with no change in measured turbidity or increase in particle content in 3 hr at 22 °C	1557	C
Cefuroxime sodium	GL	20 mg/ml[b]	BW	0.1 mg/ml[b]	Physically compatible with no change in measured turbidity or increase in particle content in 3 hr at 22 °C	1557	C
Chlorpromazine HCl	ES	2 mg/ml[b]	BW	0.1 mg/ml[b]	Large increase in measured turbidity occurs within 1 hr and grows over 4 hr	1557	I
Cimetidine HCl	SKB	12 mg/ml[b]	BW	0.1 mg/ml[b]	Physically compatible with no change in measured turbidity or increase in particle content in 3 hr at 22 °C	1557	C
Cisplatin	BR	1 mg/ml	BW	0.1 mg/ml[b]	Physically compatible with no change in measured turbidity or increase in particle content in 3 hr at 22 °C	1557	C
Clindamycin phosphate	AB	10 mg/ml[b]	BW	0.1 mg/ml[b]	Physically compatible with no change in measured turbidity or increase in particle content in 3 hr at 22 °C	1557	C
Cyclophosphamide	BR	10 mg/ml[b]	BW	0.1 mg/ml[b]	Physically compatible with no change in measured turbidity or increase in particle content in 3 hr at 22 °C	1557	C
Cytarabine	UP	50 mg/ml	BW	0.1 mg/ml[b]	Physically compatible with no change in measured turbidity or increase in particle content in 3 hr at 22 °C	1557	C
Dacarbazine	MI	4 mg/ml[b]	BW	0.1 mg/ml[b]	Physically compatible with no change in measured turbidity or increase in particle content in 3 hr at 22 °C	1557	C
Dactinomycin	MSD	0.01 mg/ml[b]	BW	0.1 mg/ml[b]	Physically compatible with no change in measured turbidity or increase in particle content in 3 hr at 22 °C	1557	C
Daunorubicin HCl	WY	1 mg/ml[b]	BW	0.1 mg/ml[b]	Physically compatible with little change in measured turbidity or increase in particle content in 3 hr at 22 °C	1557	C
Dexamethasone sodium phosphate	LY	1 mg/ml[b]	BW	0.1 mg/ml[b]	Physically compatible with no change in measured turbidity or increase in particle content in 3 hr at 22 °C	1557	C
Diphenhydramine HCl	WY	2 mg/ml[b]	BW	0.1 mg/ml[b]	Physically compatible with no change in measured turbidity or increase in particle content in 3 hr at 22 °C	1557	C
Doxorubicin HCl	AD	2 mg/ml	BW	0.1 mg/ml[b]	Physically compatible with no change in measured turbidity or increase in particle content in 3 hr at 22 °C	1557	C
Doxycycline hyclate	LY	1 mg/ml[b]	BW	0.1 mg/ml[b]	Physically compatible with no change in measured turbidity or increase in particle content in 3 hr at 22 °C	1557	C

Y-Site Injection Compatibility (1:1 Mixture) (Cont.)

Drug	Mfr	Conc	Mfr	Conc	Remarks	Ref	C/I
			Melphalan HCl				
Droperidol	JN	0.4 mg/ml[b]	BW	0.1 mg/ml[b]	Physically compatible with no change in measured turbidity or increase in particle content in 3 hr at 22 °C	1557	C
Enalaprilat	MSD	0.1 mg/ml[b]	BW	0.1 mg/ml[b]	Physically compatible with no change in measured turbidity or increase in particle content in 3 hr at 22 °C	1557	C
Etoposide	BR	0.4 mg/ml[b]	BW	0.1 mg/ml[b]	Physically compatible with no change in measured turbidity or increase in particle content in 3 hr at 22 °C	1557	C
Famotidine	MSD	2 mg/ml[b]	BW	0.1 mg/ml[b]	Physically compatible with no change in measured turbidity or increase in particle content in 3 hr at 22 °C	1557	C
Floxuridine	RC	3 mg/ml[b]	BW	0.1 mg/ml[b]	Physically compatible with no change in measured turbidity or increase in particle content in 3 hr at 22 °C	1557	C
Fluconazole	RR	2 mg/ml	BW	0.1 mg/ml[b]	Physically compatible with no change in measured turbidity or increase in particle content in 3 hr at 22 °C	1557	C
Fludarabine phosphate	BX	1 mg/ml[b]	BW	0.1 mg/ml[b]	Physically compatible with no change in measured turbidity or increase in particle content in 3 hr at 22 °C	1557	C
Fluorouracil	LY	16 mg/ml[b]	BW	0.1 mg/ml[b]	Physically compatible with no change in measured turbidity or increase in particle content in 3 hr at 22 °C	1557	C
Furosemide	AB	3 mg/ml[b]	BW	0.1 mg/ml[b]	Physically compatible with no change in measured turbidity or increase in particle content in 3 hr at 22 °C	1557	C
Ganciclovir sodium	SY	20 mg/ml[b]	BW	0.1 mg/ml[b]	Physically compatible with no change in measured turbidity or increase in particle content in 3 hr at 22 °C	1557	C
Gentamicin sulfate	LY	5 mg/ml[b]	BW	0.1 mg/ml[b]	Physically compatible with no change in measured turbidity or increase in particle content in 3 hr at 22 °C	1557	C
Granisetron HCl	SKB	0.05 mg/ml[a]	BW	0.1 mg/ml[b]	Physically compatible with no change in measured turbidity or increase in particle content in 4 hr at 23 °C	2000	C
Haloperidol lactate	MN	0.2 mg/ml[b]	BW	0.1 mg/ml[b]	Physically compatible with no change in measured turbidity or increase in particle content in 3 hr at 22 °C	1557	C
Heparin sodium	WY	100 units/ml[b]	BW	0.1 mg/ml[b]	Physically compatible with no change in measured turbidity or increase in particle content in 3 hr at 22 °C	1557	C
Hydrocortisone sodium phosphate	MSD	1 mg/ml[b]	BW	0.1 mg/ml[b]	Physically compatible with no change in measured turbidity or increase in particle content in 3 hr at 22 °C	1557	C
Hydrocortisone sodium succinate	UP	1 mg/ml[b]	BW	0.1 mg/ml[b]	Physically compatible with no change in measured turbidity or increase in particle content in 3 hr at 22 °C	1557	C

Y-Site Injection Compatibility (1:1 Mixture) (Cont.)

Melphalan HCl

Drug	*Mfr*	*Conc*	*Mfr*	*Conc*	*Remarks*	*Ref*	*C/I*
Hydromorphone HCl	KN	0.5 mg/ml[b]	BW	0.1 mg/ml[b]	Physically compatible with no change in measured turbidity or increase in particle content in 3 hr at 22 °C	1557	C
Hydroxyzine HCl	WI	4 mg/ml[b]	BW	0.1 mg/ml[b]	Physically compatible with no change in measured turbidity or increase in particle content in 3 hr at 22 °C	1557	C
Idarubicin HCl	AD	0.5 mg/ml[b]	BW	0.1 mg/ml[b]	Increase in measured turbidity no greater than dilution of idarubicin with sodium chloride 0.9%. No increase in particle content in 3 hr at 22 °C	1557; 1675	C
Ifosfamide	BR	25 mg/ml[b]	BW	0.1 mg/ml[b]	Physically compatible with no change in measured turbidity or increase in particle content in 3 hr at 22 °C	1557	C
Imipenem–cilastatin sodium	MSD	10 mg/ml[b]	BW	0.1 mg/ml[b]	Physically compatible with no change in measured turbidity or increase in particle content in 3 hr at 22 °C	1557	C
Lorazepam	WY	0.1 mg/ml[b]	BW	0.1 mg/ml[b]	Physically compatible with no change in measured turbidity or increase in particle content in 3 hr at 22 °C	1557	C
Mannitol	BA	15%	BW	0.1 mg/ml[b]	Physically compatible with no change in measured turbidity or increase in particle content in 3 hr at 22 °C	1557	C
Mechlorethamine HCl	MSD	1 mg/ml	BW	0.1 mg/ml[b]	Physically compatible with no change in measured turbidity or increase in particle content in 3 hr at 22 °C	1557	C
Meperidine HCl	WY	4 mg/ml[b]	BW	0.1 mg/ml[b]	Physically compatible with no change in measured turbidity or increase in particle content in 3 hr at 22 °C	1557	C
Mesna	BR	10 mg/ml[b]	BW	0.1 mg/ml[b]	Physically compatible with no change in measured turbidity or increase in particle content in 3 hr at 22 °C	1557	C
Methotrexate sodium	LE	15 mg/ml[b]	BW	0.1 mg/ml[b]	Physically compatible with no change in measured turbidity or increase in particle content in 3 hr at 22 °C	1557	C
Methylprednisolone sodium succinate	AB	5 mg/ml[b]	BW	0.1 mg/ml[b]	Physically compatible with no change in measured turbidity or increase in particle content in 3 hr at 22 °C	1557	C
Metoclopramide HCl	RB	5 mg/ml	BW	0.1 mg/ml[b]	Physically compatible with no change in measured turbidity or increase in particle content in 3 hr at 22 °C	1557	C
Metronidazole	AB	5 mg/ml	BW	0.1 mg/ml[b]	Physically compatible with no change in measured turbidity or increase in particle content in 3 hr at 22 °C	1557	C
Minocycline HCl	LE	0.2 mg/ml[b]	BW	0.1 mg/ml[b]	Physically compatible with no change in measured turbidity or increase in particle content in 3 hr at 22 °C	1557	C
Mitomycin	BR	0.5 mg/ml	BW	0.1 mg/ml[b]	Physically compatible with no change in measured turbidity or increase in particle content in 3 hr at 22 °C	1557	C

Y-Site Injection Compatibility (1:1 Mixture) (Cont.)

Melphalan HCl

Drug	*Mfr*	*Conc*	*Mfr*	*Conc*	*Remarks*	*Ref*	*C/I*
Mitoxantrone HCl	LE	0.5 mg/ml[b]	BW	0.1 mg/ml[b]	Physically compatible with no change in measured turbidity or increase in particle content in 3 hr at 22 °C	1557	C
Morphine sulfate	WI	1 mg/ml[b]	BW	0.1 mg/ml[b]	Physically compatible with no change in measured turbidity or increase in particle content in 3 hr at 22 °C	1557	C
Nalbuphine HCl	AST	10 mg/ml	BW	0.1 mg/ml[b]	Physically compatible with no change in measured turbidity or increase in particle content in 3 hr at 22 °C	1557	C
Netilmicin sulfate	SC	5 mg/ml[b]	BW	0.1 mg/ml[b]	Physically compatible with no change in measured turbidity or increase in particle content in 3 hr at 22 °C	1557	C
Ondansetron HCl	GL	1 mg/ml[b]	BW	0.1 mg/ml[b]	Physically compatible with no change in measured turbidity or increase in particle content in 3 hr at 22 °C	1557	C
Pentostatin	PD	0.4 mg/ml[b]	BW	0.1 mg/ml[b]	Physically compatible with no change in measured turbidity or increase in particle content in 3 hr at 22 °C	1557	C
Piperacillin sodium	LE	40 mg/ml[b]	BW	0.1 mg/ml[b]	Physically compatible with no change in measured turbidity or increase in particle content in 3 hr at 22 °C	1557	C
Plicamycin	MI	0.01 mg/ml[b]	BW	0.1 mg/ml[b]	Physically compatible with no change in measured turbidity or increase in particle content in 3 hr at 22 °C	1557	C
Potassium chloride	AB	0.1 mEq/ml[b]	BW	0.1 mg/ml[b]	Physically compatible with no change in measured turbidity or increase in particle content in 3 hr at 22 °C	1557	C
Prochlorperazine edisylate	SKB	0.5 mg/ml[b]	BW	0.1 mg/ml[b]	Physically compatible with no change in measured turbidity or increase in particle content in 3 hr at 22 °C	1557	C
Promethazine HCl	WY	2 mg/ml[b]	BW	0.1 mg/ml[b]	Physically compatible with no change in measured turbidity or increase in particle content in 3 hr at 22 °C	1557	C
Ranitidine HCl	GL	2 mg/ml[b]	BW	0.1 mg/ml[b]	Physically compatible with no change in measured turbidity or increase in particle content in 3 hr at 22 °C	1557	C
Sodium bicarbonate	AB	1 mEq/ml	BW	0.1 mg/ml[b]	Physically compatible with no change in measured turbidity or increase in particle content in 3 hr at 22 °C	1557	C
Streptozocin	UP	40 mg/ml[b]	BW	0.1 mg/ml[b]	Physically compatible with no change in measured turbidity or increase in particle content in 3 hr at 22 °C	1557	C
Teniposide	BR	0.1 mg/ml[a]	BW	0.1 mg/ml[a]	Physically compatible with no subvisual haze or particle formation in 4 hr at 23 °C	1725	C
Thiotepa	LE	10 mg/ml[b]	BW	0.1 mg/ml[b]	Physically compatible with no change in measured turbidity or increase in particle content in 3 hr at 22 °C	1557	C

Y-Site Injection Compatibility (1:1 Mixture) (Cont.)

Melphalan HCl

Drug	*Mfr*	*Conc*	*Mfr*	*Conc*	*Remarks*	*Ref*	*C/I*
Ticarcillin disodium	BE	30 mg/ml[b]	BW	0.1 mg/ml[b]	Physically compatible with no change in measured turbidity or increase in particle content in 3 hr at 22 °C	1557	C
Ticarcillin disodium–clavulanate potassium	SKB	31 mg/ml[b]	BW	0.1 mg/ml[b]	Physically compatible with no change in measured turbidity or increase in particle content in 3 hr at 22 °C	1557	C
Tobramycin sulfate	LI	5 mg/ml[b]	BW	0.1 mg/ml[b]	Physically compatible with no change in measured turbidity or increase in particle content in 3 hr at 22 °C	1557	C
Trimethoprim–sulfamethoxazole	ES	0.8 + 4 mg/ml[b]	BW	0.1 mg/ml[b]	Physically compatible with no change in measured turbidity or increase in particle content in 3 hr at 22 °C	1557	C
Vancomycin HCl	LY	10 mg/ml[b]	BW	0.1 mg/ml[b]	Physically compatible with no change in measured turbidity or increase in particle content in 3 hr at 22 °C	1557	C
Vinblastine sulfate	LI	0.12 mg/ml[b]	BW	0.1 mg/ml[b]	Physically compatible with no change in measured turbidity or increase in particle content in 3 hr at 22 °C	1557	C
Vincristine sulfate	LI	0.05 mg/ml[b]	BW	0.1 mg/ml[b]	Physically compatible with no change in measured turbidity or increase in particle content in 3 hr at 22 °C	1557	C
Vinorelbine tartrate	BW	1 mg/ml[b]	BW	0.1 mg/ml[b]	Physically compatible with no change in measured turbidity or increase in particle content in 4 hr at 22 °C	1558	C
Zidovudine	BW	4 mg/ml[b]	BW	0.1 mg/ml[b]	Physically compatible with no change in measured turbidity or increase in particle content in 3 hr at 22 °C	1557	C

[a]*Tested in dextrose 5% in water.*
[b]*Tested in sodium chloride 0.9%.*
[c]*Sodium carbonate–containing formulation tested.*

MEPERIDINE HCL (PETHIDINE HCL) AHFS 28:08.08

Products — Meperidine HCl is available in concentrations of 10, 25, 50, 75, and 100 mg/ml in a variety of packaging sizes and configurations, including ampuls, vials, and disposable cartridge units. (29) Some products also contain an antioxidant such as sodium metabisulfite and antibacterial preservatives such as phenol and metacresol. (4)

pH — The pH is adjusted to 3.5 to 6. (4)

Osmolality — The osmolality of meperidine HCl 50 mg/ml was determined to be 302 mOsm/kg. (1233)

Trade Name(s) — Demerol Hydrochloride.

Administration — Meperidine HCl is administered by intramuscular injection into a large muscle mass. It may also be given subcutaneously or slowly by intravenous injection or infusion in a diluted solution. A 10-mg/ml concentration has been recommended for slow intravenous injection. The 10-mg/ml commercial injection does not require further dilution and is for use with a compatible infusion device. Intravenous infusion of a 1-mg/ml concentration has been used to supplement anesthesia. (4)

Stability — Meperidine HCl should be stored at controlled room temperature and protected from light and freezing. (4)

Syringes — Meperidine HCl (Wyeth) 5 and 10 mg/ml in dextrose 5% in water and sodium chloride 0.9% was packaged in 30-ml Plastipak (Becton-Dickinson) syringes capped with Monoject (Sherwood) tip caps. Syringes were stored at 23 °C exposed to light and protected from light, 4 °C protected from light, and frozen at −20 °C protected from light for 12 weeks. HPLC analysis found that both concentrations at all storage conditions were stable for at least 12 weeks. (1894)

Preservative-free meperidine HCl (Abbott) was diluted to concentrations of 0.25, 1, 10, 20, and 30 mg/ml with dextrose 5% in water and with sodium chloride 0.9%. The solutions were packaged in 60-ml polypropylene syringes (Becton-Dickinson), sealed with Luer lock caps, and stored at 22 and 4 °C for 28 days protected from light. The solutions were visually colorless and free of precipitation over the course of the study. Stability-indicating HPLC analysis found little or no loss of meperidine HCl in either solution at either temperature in 28 days. (2200)

Ambulatory Pumps— Meperidine HCl 15 mg/ml in sterile water for injection in CADD cassettes (Sims Deltec) has been stated by the pump manufacturer to be stable for 14 days under refrigeration and nine days at room temperature. (31)

Elastomeric Reservoir Pumps— Meperidine HCl 100 mg/ml undiluted and 10 to 50 mg/ml diluted in dextrose 5% in water or sodium chloride 0.9% in Infusor elastomeric reservoir pumps has been stated by the pump manufacturer to be stable for seven days at room temperature and 14 days under refrigeration followed by four days at room temperature. (31)

Implantable Pumps— Meperidine HCl (Sanofi Winthrop) 10 mg/ml in sodium chloride 0.9% was found to undergo no loss over 90 days at 37 °C in an Infusaid implantable pump. (2246)

Sorption— Meperidine HCl (David Bull Laboratories) 71 mg/L in sodium chloride 0.9% (Travenol) in PVC bags did not exhibit significant sorption to the plastic during one week of storage at room temperature (15 to 20 °C). (536)

In another study, meperidine HCl (David Bull Laboratories) 71 mg/L in sodium chloride 0.9% did not exhibit any loss due to sorption during a seven-hour simulated infusion through an infusion set (Travenol) consisting of a cellulose propionate burette chamber and 170 cm of PVC tubing. (606)

The drug was also tested as a simulated infusion over at least one hour by a syringe pump system. A glass syringe on a syringe pump was fitted with 20 cm of polyethylene tubing or 50 cm of Silastic tubing. No loss of drug due to sorption was observed with either tubing. (606)

A 25-ml aliquot of meperidine HCl (David Bull Laboratories) 71 mg/L in sodium chloride 0.9% was stored in all-plastic syringes composed of polypropylene barrels and polyethylene plungers for 24 hours at room temperature in the dark. No loss due to sorption occurred. (606)

Central Venous Catheter— Meperidine HCl (Wyeth) 4 mg/ml in dextrose 5% in water was found to be compatible with the ARROWg+ard Blue Plus (Arrow International) chlorhexidine-bearing triple-lumen central catheter. HPLC analysis was used to evaluate completeness of drug delivery through the catheter and the amount of chlorhexidine removed from the internal lumens. Essentially complete delivery of the drug was found with little or no drug loss occurring. Furthermore, chlorhexidine delivered from the catheter remained at trace amounts with no substantial increase due to the delivery of the drug through the catheter. (2335)

Compatibility Information

Solution Compatibility

Meperidine HCl

Solution	*Mfr*	*Mfr*	*Conc/L*	*Remarks*	*Ref*	*C/I*
Dextran 6% in dextrose 5%	AB	WI	100 mg	Physically compatible	3	C
Dextran 6% in sodium chloride 0.9%	AB	WI	100 mg	Physically compatible	3	C
Dextrose–Ringer's injection combinations	AB	WI	100 mg	Physically compatible	3	C
Dextrose–Ringer's injection, lactated, combinations	AB	WI	100 mg	Physically compatible	3	C
Dextrose–saline combinations	AB	WI	100 mg	Physically compatible	3	C
Dextrose 2½% in water	AB	WI	100 mg	Physically compatible	3	C
Dextrose 4% in water		DB	300 mg	Stable by HPLC for at least 24 hr at 25 °C	53	C
Dextrose 5% in water	AB	WI	100 mg	Physically compatible	3	C
	TR[a]	WI	1.2 g	Physically compatible with no meperidine loss in 36 hr at 22 °C	1000	C
		DB	300 mg	Stable by HPLC for at least 24 hr at 25 °C	53	C
Dextrose 10% in water	AB	WI	100 mg	Physically compatible	3	C
Fructose 10% in sodium chloride 0.9%	AB	WI	100 mg	Physically compatible	3	C
Fructose 10% in water	AB	WI	100 mg	Physically compatible	3	C
Invert sugar 5 and 10% in sodium chloride 0.9%	AB	WI	100 mg	Physically compatible	3	C
Invert sugar 5 and 10% in water	AB	WI	100 mg	Physically compatible	3	C

Solution Compatibility (Cont.)

Meperidine HCl

Solution	*Mfr*	*Mfr*	*Conc/L*	*Remarks*	*Ref*	*C/I*
Ionosol products	AB	WI	100 mg	Physically compatible	3	C
Ringer's injection	AB	WI	100 mg	Physically compatible	3	C
Ringer's injection, lactated	AB	WI	100 mg	Physically compatible	3	C
Sodium chloride 0.18%		DB	300 mg	Stable by HPLC for at least 24 hr at 25 °C	53	C
Sodium chloride 0.45%	AB	WI	100 mg	Physically compatible	3	C
Sodium chloride 0.9%	AB	WI	100 mg	Physically compatible	3	C
	FRE[a]		2.5 g	Visually compatible with little or no loss by GC in 24 days at room temperature	1791	C
		DB	300 mg	Stable by HPLC for at least 24 hr at 25 °C	53	C
	BA	SW	10 g	No loss occurs in 90 days at 37 °C in an implantable pump[c]	2246	C
Sodium lactate ⅙ M	AB	WI	100 mg	Physically compatible	3	C
TPN #71[b]	[a]	WI	100 mg	Physically compatible with no meperidine loss in 36 hr at 22 °C	1000	C

[a]*Tested in PVC bags.*
[b]*Refer to Appendix I for the composition of parenteral nutrition solutions. TPN indicates a 2-in-1 admixture.*
[c]*Tested in an Infusaid implantable pump.*

Additive Compatibility

Meperidine HCl

Drug	*Mfr*	*Conc/L*	*Mfr*	*Conc/L*	*Test Soln*	*Remarks*	*Ref*	*C/I*
Aminophylline			WI			Physically incompatible	9	I
Amobarbital sodium			WI			Physically incompatible	9	I
Cefazolin sodium	FUJ	10 g		0.5 g	D5W	Visually compatible with about 5% loss by HPLC of each drug in 5 days at 25 °C. 5% cefazolin loss and 7% meperidine loss in 20 days at 4 °C.	1966	C
Dobutamine HCl	LI	1 g	ES	50 g	D5W, NS	Physically compatible for 24 hr at 21 °C	812	C
Floxacillin sodium	BE	20 g	RC	5 g	W	Haze forms immediately and precipitate forms in 5 to 24 hr	1479	I
Furosemide	HO	1 g	RC	5 g	W	Fine precipitate forms immediately	1479	I
Heparin sodium			WI			Physically incompatible	9	I
Metoclopramide HCl	DW	150 mg	DW	7.35 g	D5W, NS	Visually compatible with little or no loss of either drug over 48 hr at 32 °C exposed to or protected from fluorescent light	2253	C
Morphine sulfate			WI			Physically incompatible	9	I
Ondansetron HCl	GL	100 mg and 1 g	WY	4 g	NS[a]	Physically compatible with no change in measured turbidity or increase in particle content and no loss of either drug by HPLC in 31 days at 4 and 22 °C and in 7 days at 32 °C	1862	C
Phenobarbital sodium	WI		WI			Physically incompatible	9	I
Phenytoin sodium	PD		WI			Physically incompatible	9	I
Scopolamine HBr		0.43 mg	WI	100 mg		Physically compatible	3	C

Additive Compatibility (Cont.)

Meperidine HCl

Drug	Mfr	Conc/L	Mfr	Conc/L	Test Soln	Remarks	Ref	C/I
Sodium bicarbonate			WI			Physically incompatible	9	I
	AB	2.4 mEq[b]	WI	100 mg	D5W	Physically compatible for 24 hr	772	C
Succinylcholine chloride	AB	2 g	WI	100 mg		Physically compatible	3	C
Thiopental sodium			WI			Physically incompatible	9	I
Triflupromazine HCl	SQ					Physically compatible	40	C
Verapamil HCl	KN	80 mg	WI	150 mg	D5W, NS	Physically compatible for 24 hr	764	C

[a] *Tested in PVC containers.*
[b] *One vial of Neut added to a liter of admixture.*

Drugs in Syringe Compatibility

Meperidine HCl

Drug (in syringe)	Mfr	Amt	Mfr	Amt	Remarks	Ref	C/I
Atropine sulfate		0.6 mg/ 1.5 ml	WY	100 mg/ 1 ml	Physically compatible for at least 15 min	14	C
	ST	0.4 mg/ 1 ml	WI	50 mg/ 1 ml	Physically compatible for at least 15 min	326	C
Atropine sulfate with hydroxyzine HCl[a]	ES PF	0.4 mg 50 mg	WI	50 mg/ 2.5 ml	No alteration of UV spectra in 10 days at 3 and 25 °C	301	C
Atropine sulfate with promethazine HCl	WY	0.6 mg/ 1.5 ml 50 mg/ 2 ml	WY	100 mg/ 1 ml	Physically compatible	14	C
Atropine sulfate with promethazine HCl	LI WY	0.4 mg/ 1 ml 25 mg/ 1 ml	WI	50 mg/ 1 ml	No loss of any drug in 24 hr at 25 °C. Slight haze, not present at 6 hr, developed by 24 hr	991	C
Butorphanol tartrate	BR	4 mg/ 2 ml	WI	50 mg/ 1 ml	Physically compatible both macroscopically and microscopically for 30 min at room temperature	566	C
Chlorpromazine HCl	SKF	50 mg/ 2 ml	WY	100 mg/ 1 ml	Physically compatible for at least 15 min	14	C
	PO	50 mg/ 2 ml	WI	50 mg/ 1 ml	Physically compatible for at least 15 min	326	C
Cimetidine HCl	SKF	300 mg/ 2 ml	WI	100 mg/ 2 ml	Physically compatible for 4 hr at 25 °C	25	C
Dimenhydrinate	HR	50 mg/ 1 ml	WI	50 mg/ 1 ml	Physically compatible for at least 15 min	326	C
	HR	10 mg/ 1 ml	WI	50 mg/ 1 ml	Physically compatible	711	C
Diphenhydramine HCl	PD	50 mg/ 1 ml	WY	100 mg/ 1 ml	Physically compatible for at least 15 min	14	C
	PD	50 mg/ 1 ml	WI	50 mg/ 1 ml	Physically compatible for at least 15 min	326	C
Droperidol	MN	2.5 mg/ 1 ml	WI	50 mg/ 1 ml	Physically compatible for at least 15 min	326	C
Fentanyl citrate	MN	0.05 mg/ 1 ml	WI	50 mg/ 1 ml	Physically compatible for at least 15 min	326	C

Drugs in Syringe Compatibility (Cont.)

			Meperidine HCl				
Drug (in syringe)	*Mfr*	*Amt*	*Mfr*	*Amt*	*Remarks*	*Ref*	*C/I*
Glycopyrrolate	RB	0.2 mg/ 1 ml	WI	50 mg/ 1 ml	Physically compatible and pH in stability range for glycopyrrolate for 48 hr at 25 °C	331	C
	RB	0.2 mg/ 1 ml	WI	100 mg/ 2 ml	Physically compatible and pH in stability range for glycopyrrolate for 48 hr at 25 °C	331	C
	RB	0.4 mg/ 2 ml	WI	50 mg/ 1 ml	Physically compatible and pH in stability range for glycopyrrolate for 48 hr at 25 °C	331	C
Heparin sodium		2500 units/ 1 ml	HO	100 mg/ 2 ml	Turbidity or precipitate forms within 5 min	1053	I
Hydroxyzine HCl	PF	100 mg/ 4 ml	WY	100 mg/ 1 ml	Physically compatible for at least 15 min	14	C
	PF	50 mg/ 1 ml	WI	50 mg/ 1 ml	Physically compatible for at least 15 min	326	C
	PF	50 mg/ 1 ml	WI	100 mg/ 2 ml	Physically compatible	771	C
	PF	100 mg/ 2 ml	WI	50 mg/ 1 ml	Physically compatible	771	C
Hydroxyzine HCl with atropine sulfate[a]	PF ES	50 mg 0.4 mg	WI	50 mg/ 2.5 ml	No alteration of UV spectra in 10 days at 3 and 25 °C	301	C
Ketamine HCl	PD	2 mg/ml	DB	12 mg/ml	Diluted to 50 ml with NS. Visually compatible for 48 hr at 25 °C	2059	C
Metoclopramide HCl	NO	10 mg/ 2 ml	WI	50 mg/ 1 ml	Physically compatible both macroscopically and microscopically for 15 min at room temperature	565	C
	DW	10 mg/ 2 ml	DW	50 mg/ 1 ml	Visually compatible with little or no loss of either drug over 48 hr at 32 °C exposed to or protected from fluorescent light	2253	C
Midazolam HCl	RC	5 mg/ 1 ml	WB	100 mg/ 1 ml	Physically compatible for 4 hr at 25 °C under fluorescent light	1145	C
Morphine sulfate	ST	15 mg/ 1 ml	WI	50 mg/ 1 ml	Physically incompatible within 15 min	326	I
Ondansetron HCl	GW	1.33 mg/ ml[b]	ES	8.33 mg/ ml[b]	Physically compatible with no measured increase in particulates and little or no loss of either drug by HPLC in 24 hr at 4 or 23 °C	2199	C
Papaveretum	RC[c]	20 mg/ 1 ml	WI	50 mg/ 1 ml	Visually compatible for at least 15 min	326	C
Pentazocine lactate	WI	30 mg/ 1 ml	WI	50 mg/ 1 ml	Physically compatible for at least 15 min	326	C
Pentazocine lactate with perphenazine		15 mg 5 mg		150 mg	Physically compatible for at least 15 min	815	C
Pentobarbital sodium	WY	100 mg/ 2 ml	WY	100 mg/ 1 ml	Precipitate forms within 15 min	14	I
	AB	500 mg/ 10 ml	WI	100 mg/ 2 ml	Physically incompatible	55	I
	AB	50 mg/ 1 ml	WI	50 mg/ 1 ml	Physically incompatible within 15 min	326	I
Perphenazine	SC	5 mg/ 1 ml	WI	50 mg/ 1 ml	Physically compatible both macroscopically and microscopically for 30 min at room temperature	566	C

Drugs in Syringe Compatibility (Cont.)

Drug (in syringe)	Mfr	Amt	Meperidine HCl Mfr	Meperidine HCl Amt	Remarks	Ref	C/I
Perphenazine with pentazocine lactate		5 mg 15 mg		150 mg	Physically compatible for at least 15 min	815	C
Prochlorperazine edisylate	SKF		WY	100 mg/ 1 ml	Physically compatible for at least 15 min	14	C
	PO	5 mg/ 1 ml	WI	50 mg/ 1 ml	Physically compatible for at least 15 min	326	C
Promazine HCl	WY	50 mg/ 1 ml	WI	50 mg/ 1 ml	Physically compatible for at least 15 min	326	C
Promethazine HCl	WY	50 mg/ 2 ml	WY	100 mg/ 1 ml	Physically compatible for at least 15 min	14	C
	PO	50 mg/ 2 ml	WI	50 mg/ 1 ml	Physically compatible for at least 15 min	326	C
Promethazine HCl with atropine sulfate	WY	50 mg/ 2 ml 0.6 mg/ 1.5 ml	WY	100 mg/ 1 ml	Physically compatible	14	C
Promethazine HCl with atropine sulfate	WY LI	25 mg/ 1 ml 0.4 mg/ 1 ml	WI	50 mg/ 1 ml	No loss of any drug in 24 hr at 25 °C. Slight haze, not present at 6 hr, developed by 24 hr	991	C
Ranitidine HCl	GL	50 mg/ 2 ml	WI	100 mg/ 1 ml	Physically compatible for 1 hr at 25 °C both macroscopically and microscopically	978	C
Scopolamine HBr		0.6 mg/ 1.5 ml	WY	100 mg/ 1 ml	Physically compatible for at least 15 min	14	C
	ST	0.4 mg/ 1 ml	WI	50 mg/ 1 ml	Physically compatible for at least 15 min	326	C

[a]*Tested in both glass and plastic syringes.*
[b]*Tested in sodium chloride 0.9%.*
[c]*The former formulation was tested.*

Y-Site Injection Compatibility (1:1 Mixture)

Drug	Mfr	Conc	Meperidine HCl Mfr	Meperidine HCl Conc	Remarks	Ref	C/I
Acyclovir sodium	BW	5 mg/ml[a]	WB	1 mg/ml[a]	Physically compatible for 4 hr at 25 °C	1157	C
	BW	5 mg/ml[a]	AB	10 mg/ml	White crystalline precipitate forms within 1 hr at 25 °C under fluorescent light	1397	I
	BW	5 mg/ml[a,b]	WY	100 mg/ml	Visually compatible for 24 hr at room temperature in test tubes. No precipitate found on filter from Y-site delivery	2063	C
Allopurinol sodium	BW	3 mg/ml[b]	WY	4 mg/ml[b]	Tiny particles form immediately and increase in number over 4 hr	1686	I
Amifostine	USB	10 mg/ml[a]	WY	4 mg/ml[a]	Physically compatible with no change in measured turbidity or increase in particle content in 4 hr at 23 °C	1845	C
Amikacin sulfate	BR	5 mg/ml[a]	WY	10 mg/ml[a]	Physically compatible for at least 4 hr at 25 °C under fluorescent light	987	C
Amphotericin B cholesteryl sulfate complex	SEQ	0.83 mg/ml[a]	AST	4 mg/ml[a]	Increased turbidity forms immediately	2117	I
Ampicillin sodium	BR	20 mg/ml[b]	WY	10 mg/ml[a]	Physically compatible for at least 4 hr at 25 °C under fluorescent light	987	C

Y-Site Injection Compatibility (1:1 Mixture) (Cont.)

Drug	Mfr	Conc	Mfr	Conc	Remarks	Ref	C/I
			Meperidine HCl				
Ampicillin sodium–sulbactam sodium	RR	20 + 10 mg/ml[b]	WY	10 mg/ml[b]	Physically compatible for 1 hr at 25 °C	1338	C
Atenolol	ICI	0.5 mg/ml	AB	10 mg/ml	Physically compatible for 4 hr at 25 °C	1397	C
Aztreonam	SQ	20 mg/ml[a]	AB	10 mg/ml	Physically compatible for 4 hr at 25 °C	1397	C
	SQ	40 mg/ml[a]	WY	4 mg/ml[a]	Physically compatible with no subvisual haze or particle formation in 4 hr at 23 °C	1758	C
Bumetanide	RC	0.25 mg/ml	AB	10 mg/ml	Physically compatible for 4 hr at 25 °C	1397	C
Cefamandole nafate	LI	20 mg/ml[a]	WY	10 mg/ml[a]	Physically compatible for at least 4 hr at 25 °C under fluorescent light	987	C
	LI	40 mg/ml[a]	WY	10 mg/ml[b]	Physically compatible for 1 hr at 25 °C	1338	C
Cefazolin sodium	SKF	20 mg/ml[a]	WY	10 mg/ml[a]	Physically compatible for at least 4 hr at 25 °C under fluorescent light	987	C
Cefepime HCl	BMS	20 mg/ml[a]	WY	4 mg/ml[a]	Haze forms immediately with numerous particles in 1 hr	1689	I
Cefoperazone sodium	RR	20 mg/ml[a]	WY	10 mg/ml[a]	Immediate precipitation	987	I
Cefotaxime sodium	HO	20 mg/ml[a]	WY	10 mg/ml[a]	Physically compatible for at least 4 hr at 25 °C under fluorescent light	987	C
Cefotetan disodium	STU	20 and 40 mg/ml[a]	WY	10 mg/ml[b]	Physically compatible for 1 hr at 25 °C	1338	C
Cefoxitin sodium	MSD	20 mg/ml[a]	WY	10 mg/ml[a]	Physically compatible for at least 4 hr at 25 °C under fluorescent light	987	C
Ceftazidime	LI[c]	20 and 40 mg/ml[a]	AB	10 mg/ml	Physically compatible for 4 hr at 25 °C	1397	C
Ceftizoxime sodium	SKF	20 mg/ml[a]	WY	10 mg/ml[a]	Physically compatible for at least 4 hr at 25 °C under fluorescent light	987	C
Ceftriaxone sodium	RC	20 and 40 mg/ml[a]	AB	10 mg/ml	Physically compatible for 4 hr at 25 °C	1397	C
Cefuroxime sodium	GL	30 mg/ml[a]	WY	10 mg/ml[a]	Physically compatible for at least 4 hr at 25 °C under fluorescent light	987	C
Chloramphenicol sodium succinate	LY	20 mg/ml[a]	WY	10 mg/ml[a]	Physically compatible for at least 4 hr at 25 °C under fluorescent light	987	C
Cisatracurium besylate	GW	0.1, 2, 5 mg/ml[a]	AST	4 mg/ml[a]	Physically compatible with no change in measured turbidity or increase in particle content in 4 hr at 23 °C	2074	C
Cladribine	ORT	0.015[b] and 0.5[e] mg/ml	WY	4 mg/ml[b]	Physically compatible with no change in measured turbidity or increase in particle content in 4 hr at 23 °C	1969	C
Clindamycin phosphate	UP	12 mg/ml[a]	WY	10 mg/ml[a]	Physically compatible for at least 4 hr at 25 °C under fluorescent light	987	C
Dexamethasone sodium phosphate	LY	0.2 mg/ml[a]	AB	10 mg/ml	Physically compatible for 4 hr at 25 °C	1397	C
Diltiazem HCl	MMD	1[b] and 5 mg/ml	WY	100 mg/ml	Visually compatible	1807	C
	MMD	5 mg/ml	WY	10 mg/ml[b]	Visually compatible	1807	C
Diphenhydramine HCl	ES	1[a] and 50 mg/ml	AB	10 mg/ml	Physically compatible for 4 hr at 25 °C	1397	C

Y-Site Injection Compatibility (1:1 Mixture) (Cont.)

Drug	Mfr	Conc	Meperidine HCl Mfr	Meperidine HCl Conc	Remarks	Ref	C/I
Dobutamine HCl	LI	1 mg/ml	AB	10 mg/ml	Physically compatible for 4 hr at 25 °C	1397	C
Docetaxel	RPR	0.9 mg/ml[a]	AST	4 mg/ml[a]	Physically compatible with no change in measured turbidity or increase in particle content in 4 hr at 23 °C	2224	C
Dopamine HCl	AB	1.6 mg/ml	AB	10 mg/ml	Physically compatible for 4 hr at 25 °C	1397	C
Doxorubicin HCl liposome injection	SEQ	0.4 mg/ml[a]	AST	4 mg/ml[a]	Increase in measured turbidity	2087	I
Doxycycline hyclate	ES	1 mg/ml[a]	WY	10 mg/ml[a]	Physically compatible for at least 4 hr at 25 °C under fluorescent light	987	C
Droperidol	AMR	2.5 mg/ml[a]	AB	10 mg/ml	Physically compatible for 4 hr at 25 °C	1397	C
Erythromycin lactobionate	AB	5 mg/ml[a]	WY	10 mg/ml[a]	Physically compatible for at least 4 hr at 25 °C under fluorescent light	987	C
Etoposide phosphate	BR	5 mg/ml[a]	AST	4 mg/ml[a]	Physically compatible with no change in measured turbidity or increase in particle content in 4 hr at 23 °C	2218	C
Famotidine	MSD	0.2 mg/ml[a]	AB	10 mg/ml	Physically compatible for 4 hr at 25 °C	1397	C
	ME	2 mg/ml[b]		4 mg/ml[a]	Visually compatible for 4 hr at 22 °C	1936	C
Filgrastim	AMG	3 μg/ml[a]	WY	4 mg/ml[a]	Physically compatible with no change in measured turbidity or increase in particle content in 4 hr at 22 °C	1687	C
Fluconazole	RR	2 mg/ml	AB	10 mg/ml	Physically compatible for 4 hr at 25 °C	1397	C
Fludarabine phosphate	BX	1 mg/ml[a]	WI	4 mg/ml[a]	Physically compatible for 4 hr at room temperature under fluorescent light	1439	C
Furosemide	ES	0.8 mg/ml[a]	AB	10 mg/ml	Physically compatible for 4 hr at 25 °C	1397	C
	ES	2.4 mg/ml[a]	AB	10 mg/ml	White cloudiness forms immediately	1397	I
	ES	10 mg/ml	AB	10 mg/ml	White flocculent precipitate forms immediately	1397	I
Gatifloxacin	BMS	2 mg/ml[a]	AST	4 mg/ml[a]	Physically compatible with no change in measured haze or increase in particle content in 4 hr at 23 °C	2234	C
Gemcitabine HCl	LI	10 mg/ml[b]	AST	4 mg/ml[b]	Physically compatible with no change in measured turbidity or increase in particle content in 4 hr at 23 °C	2226	C
Gentamicin sulfate	TR	0.8 mg/ml[a]	WY	10 mg/ml[a]	Physically compatible for at least 4 hr at 25 °C under fluorescent light	987	C
	ES	1.2 and 2 mg/ml[b]	WY	10 mg/ml[b]	Physically compatible for 1 hr at 25 °C	1338	C
Granisetron HCl	SKB	0.05 mg/ml[a]	WY	4 mg/ml[a]	Physically compatible with no change in measured turbidity or increase in particle content in 4 hr at 23 °C	2000	C
Heparin sodium		50 units/ml/min[b]	HO	100 mg/2 ml[f]	Clear solution	1053	C
	ES	60 units/ml[a]	WY	10 mg/ml[b]	Physically compatible for 1 hr at 25 °C	1338	C
Hetastarch in lactated electrolyte injection (Hextend)	AB	6%	OH	4 mg/ml[a]	Physically compatible with no change in measured turbidity or increase in particle content in 4 hr at 23 °C	2339	C
Hydrocortisone sodium succinate	AB	2 mg/ml[a]	AB	10 mg/ml	Physically compatible for 4 hr at 25 °C	1397	C

Y-Site Injection Compatibility (1:1 Mixture) (Cont.)

Meperidine HCl

Drug	*Mfr*	*Conc*	*Mfr*	*Conc*	*Remarks*	*Ref*	*C/I*
Idarubicin HCl	AD	1 mg/ml[b]	WY	1[a] and 50 mg/ml	Color changes immediately	1525	I
Imipenem–cilastatin sodium	MSD	5 mg/ml[a]	AB	10 mg/ml	Yellow discoloration forms within 2 hr at 25 °C under fluorescent light	1397	I
Insulin, regular	LI	0.2 unit/ml[b]	WY	10 mg/ml[b]	Physically compatible for 1 hr at 25 °C	1338	C
	LI	0.2 unit/ml[b]	AST	50 mg/ml[a]	Physically compatible for 2 hr at 25 °C	1395	C
Kanamycin sulfate	BR	2.5 mg/ml[a]	WY	10 mg/ml[a]	Physically compatible for at least 4 hr at 25 °C under fluorescent light	987	C
Labetalol HCl	GL	5 mg/ml	AB	10 mg/ml	Physically compatible for 4 hr at 25 °C	1397	C
Lidocaine HCl	AB	1 mg/ml[a]	AB	10 mg/ml	Physically compatible for 4 hr at 25 °C	1397	C
Linezolid	PHU	2 mg/ml	AST	4 mg/ml[a]	Physically compatible with no change in measured turbidity or increase in particle content in 4 hr at 23 °C	2264	C
Magnesium sulfate	LY	16.7, 33.3, 50, 100 mg/ml[a]	WI	10 mg/ml[a]	Visually compatible for 4 hr at 25 °C under fluorescent light	1549	C
Melphalan HCl	BW	0.1 mg/ml[b]	WY	4 mg/ml[b]	Physically compatible with no change in measured turbidity or increase in particle content in 3 hr at 22 °C	1557	C
Methyldopate HCl	AMR	2.5 mg/ml[a]	AB	10 mg/ml	Physically compatible for 4 hr at 25 °C	1397	C
Methylprednisolone sodium succinate	UP	2.5 mg/ml[a]	AB	10 mg/ml	Physically compatible for 4 hr at 25 °C	1397	C
Metoclopramide HCl	SN	0.2 mg/ml[a]	AB	10 mg/ml	Physically compatible for 4 hr at 25 °C	1397	C
Metoprolol tartrate	CI	1 mg/ml	AB	10 mg/ml	Physically compatible for 4 hr at 25 °C	1397	C
Metronidazole	SE	5 mg/ml	WY	10 mg/ml[a]	Physically compatible for at least 4 hr at 25 °C under fluorescent light	987	C
Minocycline HCl	LE	0.2 mg/ml[a]	WY	10 mg/ml[a]	Color change from pale yellow to light green within 1 hr at 25 °C	987	I
Nafcillin sodium	WY	20 mg/ml[a]	WY	10 mg/ml[a]	Cloudy haze cleared on mixing and remained clear for 4 hr at 25 °C	987	C
	WY	20 and 30 mg/ml[a]	WY	10 mg/ml[b]	Cloudy solution formed immediately and persisted for at least 1 hr at 25 °C	1338	I
Ondansetron HCl	GL	1 mg/ml[b]	WI	4 mg/ml[a]	Physically compatible for 4 hr at 22 °C	1365	C
Oxacillin sodium	BE	20 mg/ml[a]	WY	10 mg/ml[a]	Physically compatible for at least 4 hr at 25 °C under fluorescent light	987	C
Oxytocin	PD	0.02 mg/ml[h]	WY	10 mg/ml[b]	Physically compatible for 1 hr at 25 °C	1338	C
Paclitaxel	NCI	1.2 mg/ml[a]	WY	4 mg/ml[a]	Physically compatible with no change in measured turbidity in 4 hr at 22 °C	1556	C
Penicillin G potassium	PF	100,000 units/ml[a]	WY	10 mg/ml[a]	Physically compatible for at least 4 hr at 25 °C under fluorescent light	987	C
Piperacillin sodium	LE	60 mg/ml[a]	WY	10 mg/ml[a]	Physically compatible for at least 4 hr at 25 °C under fluorescent light	987	C
Piperacillin sodium–tazobactam sodium	LE	40 + 5 mg/ml[a]	WY	4 mg/ml[a]	Physically compatible with no change in measured turbidity or increase in particle content in 4 hr at 22 °C	1688	C
Potassium chloride	AB	0.4 mEq/ml[a]	AB	10 mg/ml	Physically compatible for 4 hr at 25 °C	1397	C

Y-Site Injection Compatibility (1:1 Mixture) (Cont.)

			Meperidine HCl				
Drug	*Mfr*	*Conc*	*Mfr*	*Conc*	*Remarks*	*Ref*	*C/I*
Propofol	ZEN	10 mg/ml	WY	4 mg/ml[a]	Physically compatible for 1 hr at 23 °C with no increase in particle content	2066	C
Propranolol HCl	WY	1 mg/ml	AB	10 mg/ml	Physically compatible for 4 hr at 25 °C	1397	C
Ranitidine HCl	GL	0.5 mg/ml[i]	WY	10 mg/ml[b]	Physically compatible for 1 hr at 25 °C	1338	C
Remifentanil HCl	GW	0.025 and 0.25 mg/ml[b]	AST	4 mg/ml[a]	Physically compatible with no change in measured turbidity or increase in particle content in 4 hr at 23 °C	2075	C
Sargramostim	IMM	10 μg/ml[b]	WI	4 mg/ml[b]	Physically compatible for 4 hr at 22 °C	1436	C
Teniposide	BR	0.1 mg/ml[a]	WY	4 mg/ml[a]	Physically compatible with no subvisual haze or particle formation in 4 hr at 23 °C	1725	C
Thiotepa	IMM[j]	1 mg/ml[a]	WY	4 mg/ml[a]	Physically compatible with no change in measured turbidity or increase in particle content in 4 hr at 23 °C	1861	C
Ticarcillin disodium	BE	60 mg/ml[a]	WY	10 mg/ml[a]	Physically compatible for at least 4 hr at 25 °C under fluorescent light	987	C
Ticarcillin disodium–clavulanate potassium	BE	31 mg/ml[b]	WY	10 mg/ml[b]	Physically compatible for 1 hr at 25 °C	1338	C
TNA #218 to #226[g]			AST	4 mg/ml[a]	Visually compatible with no precipitate or emulsion damage apparent in 4 hr at 23 °C	2215	C
Tobramycin sulfate	DI	0.8 mg/ml[a]	WY	10 mg/ml[a]	Physically compatible for at least 4 hr at 25 °C under fluorescent light	987	C
	LI	1.6, 2, 2.4 mg/ml[a]	WY	10 mg/ml[b]	Physically compatible for 1 hr at 25 °C	1338	C
TPN #131 and #132[g]			AB	10 mg/ml	Physically compatible for 4 hr at 25 °C	1397	C
TPN #189[g]			DB	50 mg/ml	Visually compatible for 24 hr at 22 °C	1767	C
TPN #212 to #215[g]			AST	4 mg/ml[a]	Physically compatible with no change in measured turbidity or increase in particle content in 4 hr at 23 °C	2109	C
Trimethoprim–sulfamethoxazole	BW	0.8 + 4 mg/ml[a]	WY	10 mg/ml[a]	Physically compatible for at least 4 hr at 25 °C under fluorescent light	987	C
Vancomycin HCl	LI	5 mg/ml[a]	WY	10 mg/ml[a]	Physically compatible for at least 4 hr at 25 °C under fluorescent light	987	C
Verapamil HCl	DU	2.5 mg/ml	AB	10 mg/ml	Physically compatible for 4 hr at 25 °C	1397	C
Vinorelbine tartrate	BW	1 mg/ml[b]	WY	4 mg/ml[b]	Physically compatible with no change in measured turbidity or increase in particle content in 4 hr at 22 °C	1558	C

[a]*Tested in dextrose 5% in water.*
[b]*Tested in sodium chloride 0.9%.*
[c]*Sodium carbonate–containing formulation tested.*
[d]*Tested in sterile water for injection.*
[e]*Tested in bacteriostatic sodium chloride 0.9% preserved with benzyl alcohol 0.9%.*
[f]*Given over three minutes via a Y-site into a running infusion solution.*
[g]*Refer to Appendix I for the composition of parenteral nutrition solutions. TNA indicates a 3-in-1 admixture, and TPN indicates a 2-in-1 admixture.*
[h]*Tested in dextrose 5% in Ringer's injection, lactated.*
[i]*Tested in sodium chloride 0.45%.*
[j]*Lyophilized formulation tested.*

Additional Compatibility Information

Promethazine and Scopolamine — Promethazine HCl (Wyeth) 50 mg/2 ml, meperidine HCl (Wyeth) 100 mg/ml, and scopolamine hydrobromide 0.6 mg/1.5 ml have been reported to be conditionally compatible when packaged in syringes. The mixture is physically compatible when the order of mixing is as stated above. (14)

Chlorpromazine and Hydroxyzine — Chlorpromazine HCl (Elkins-Sinn) 6.25 mg/ml, hydroxyzine HCl (Pfizer) 12.5 mg/ml, and meperidine HCl (Winthrop) 25 mg/ml, in both glass and plastic syringes, have been reported to be physically compatible and chemically stable for at least one year at 4 and 25 °C when protected from light. Significant discoloration, ranging from yellow to brownish yellow, occurred on storage at 44 °C. (989)

Chlorpromazine and Promethazine — Chlorpromazine HCl (Elkins-Sinn), meperidine HCl (Winthrop), and promethazine HCl (Elkins-Sinn), combined as an extemporaneous mixture for preoperative sedation, developed a brownish-yellow color after two weeks of storage with protection from light. The discoloration was attributed to the metacresol preservative content of Winthrop's meperidine HCl. Use of Wyeth's meperidine HCl instead, which contains a different preservative, resulted in a solution that remained clear and colorless for at least three months when protected from light. (1148)

Heparin — If meperidine HCl is injected into a heparinized scalp vein infusion set, a precipitate will form. It has been suggested that these heparinized sets be flushed with sodium chloride 0.9% before and after drug administration. Heparin lock flush solution may then be reinjected into the device. (4; 97)

MEPERIDINE HCL AND PROMETHAZINE HCL
AHFS 4:00, 28:08.08, and 28:24.92

Products — Mepergan is available in 10-ml vials and 2-ml Tubex cartridges. Each milliliter contains meperidine HCl 25 mg and promethazine HCl 25 mg with edetate disodium 0.1 mg, calcium chloride 0.04 mg, sodium metabisulfite 0.25 mg, phenol 5 mg, not more than 0.75 mg sodium formaldehyde sulfoxylate, and sodium acetate buffer. (2)

Trade Name(s) — Mepergan.

Administration — Mepergan may be administered intravenously but is usually given by deep intramuscular injection. When given intravenously, the rate of administration should not exceed 1 ml/min, preferably through the tubing of a running intravenous solution. Subcutaneous administration is contraindicated because of possible tissue necrosis; avoid intra-arterial injection which can result in gangrene. (2)

Stability — Mepergan in intact containers should be stored at controlled room temperature and protected from light. (2)

Compatibility Information

Drugs in Syringe Compatibility

Meperidine HCl and Promethazine HCl

Drug (in syringe)	*Mfr*	*Amt*	*Mfr*	*Amt*	*Remarks*	*Ref*	*C/I*
Glycopyrrolate	RB	0.2 mg/ 1 ml	WY	25 mg + 25 mg/ 1 ml	Physically compatible and pH in stability range for glycopyrrolate for 48 hr at 25 °C	331	C
	RB	0.2 mg/ 1 ml	WY	50 mg + 50 mg/ 2 ml	Physically compatible and pH in stability range for glycopyrrolate for 48 hr at 25 °C	331	C
	RB	0.4 mg/ 2 ml	WY	25 mg + 25 mg/ 1 ml	Physically compatible and pH in stability range for glycopyrrolate for 48 hr at 25 °C	331	C

Additional Compatibility Information

Other Drugs — Mepergan may be combined in the same syringe with 0.3 to 0.4 mg of atropine sulfate or 0.25 to 0.4 mg of scopolamine hydrobromide. (2)

Mepergan is incompatible with barbiturates. Consequently, they should not be mixed in the same syringe. (2)

Also see the monographs on meperidine HCl and promethazine HCl.

MEPHENTERMINE SULFATE
AHFS 12:12

Products — Mephentermine sulfate is available at a concentration of 15 mg/ml in 10-ml vials and 2-ml ampuls. It is also available at a concentration of 30 mg/ml in 10-ml vials. Also present in each milliliter are sodium acetate buffer, methylparaben 1.8 mg, and propylparaben 0.2 mg. (1-5/10/95)

pH — From 4 to 6.5. (1-5/10/95)

Trade Name(s) — Wyamine Sulfate.

Administration — Mephentermine sulfate may be administered by intramuscular or intravenous injection. (1-5/10/95; 4) It may also be administered by intravenous infusion, usually as a solution containing about 1 to 1.2 mg/ml of drug. The flow rate and duration of therapy should be individualized to the response of the patient (1-5/10/95), but mephentermine sulfate is usually infused at 1 to 5 mg/min. (4)

Stability — Intact containers of mephentermine sulfate injection should be stored at controlled room temperature. (4) Mephentermine sulfate is stable at pH 3.5 to 7.5. (48)

Compatibility Information

Solution Compatibility

Mephentermine sulfate

Solution	*Mfr*	*Mfr*	*Conc/L*	*Remarks*	*Ref*	*C/I*
Dextrose 5% in water		WY	1 g	Potency retained for 24 hr at 25 °C	48	C
Sodium bicarbonate 5%		WY	1 g	Potency retained for 48 hr at 25 °C	48	C

Additive Compatibility

Mephentermine sulfate

Drug	*Mfr*	*Conc/L*	*Mfr*	*Conc/L*	*Test Soln*	*Remarks*	*Ref*	*C/I*
Aminophylline		625 mg		750 mg	D5W	Physically compatible and chemically stable for 24 hr at 3 and 30 °C	520	C
Epinephrine HCl	PD		WY			Physically incompatible	10	I
Hydralazine HCl	BP	80 mg	BP	120 mg	D5W	Yellow color produced	26	I
Hydrocortisone sodium succinate		250 mg		750 mg	D5W	Physically compatible and chemically stable for 24 hr at 3 and 30 °C	520	C
Lidocaine HCl	AST	2 g	WY	1 g		Physically compatible	24	C

Additional Compatibility Information

Infusion Solutions — Mephentermine sulfate appears to be compatible with most intravenous infusion solutions. (4) Dextrose 5% in water (1-5/10/95) and sodium chloride 0.9% (4) have been recommended for the preparation of mephentermine sulfate infusions.

Oxidizing Agents — Mephentermine sulfate (Wyeth) has been stated to be incompatible with oxidizing agents because of color formation. (10)

MEPIVACAINE HCL
AHFS 72:00

Products — Mepivacaine HCl is available in concentrations of 1, 1.5, and 2%. Methylparaben is incorporated into multiple-dose containers, but single-dose containers may be preservative free. The pH may have been adjusted with sodium hydroxide and/or hydrochloric acid. (4; 29)

pH — From 4.5 to 6.8. (4)

Trade Name(s) — Carbocaine, Polocaine, Polocaine-MPF.

Administration — Mepivacaine HCl may be administered by infiltration and by peripheral or sympathetic nerve block. Mepivacaine HCl *without* preservatives may be administered by epidural block, including caudal anesthesia; forms containing preservatives should not be administered by this route (4).

Stability — Mepivacaine HCl in intact containers should be stored at controlled room temperature and protected from temperatures above

40 °C and from freezing. Mepivacaine HCl is resistant to hydrolysis and may be autoclaved repeatedly. However, mepivacaine HCl in dental cartridges should not be subjected to autoclaving because of breakdown of the dental cartridge closures. (4)

Syringes—The stability of mepivacaine (salt form unspecified) 10 mg/ml repackaged in polypropylene syringes was evaluated by spectrophotometric and potentiometric methods. Little or no change in concentration was found after four weeks of storage at room temperature not exposed to direct light. (2164)

MEROPENEM
AHFS 8:12.07

Products — Meropenem is available in dosage forms containing 500 mg and 1 g of drug along with sodium carbonate. (2)

Reconstitute the 500-mg vials with 10 ml and the 1-g vials with 20 ml of sterile water for injection, shake the vial, and allow it to stand until the solution is clear. Each milliliter of the resultant solution contains 50 mg of meropenem. (2)

Meropenem is also available in ADD-Vantage vials of 500 mg and 1 g. These vials are to be reconstituted only with sodium chloride 0.45%, sodium chloride 0.9%, and dextrose 5% in water in 50-, 100-, or 250-ml ADD-Vantage flexible diluent containers. (2)

Meropenem is provided in 100-ml infusion vials containing 500 mg and 1 g of drug. The contents may be reconstituted directly with 100 ml of compatible diluent. (2)

pH—The reconstituted solution has a pH from 7.3 to 8.3. (2)

Sodium Content—Each gram of meropenem provides 3.92 mEq (90.2 mg) of sodium from the sodium carbonate present in the formulation. (2)

Trade Name(s)—Merrem.

Administration — Meropenem is administered by direct intravenous injection of 5 to 20 ml over three to five minutes or by intravenous infusion diluted in a compatible infusion solution over 15 to 30 minutes. (2)

Stability — Intact vials should be stored at controlled room temperature between 20 and 25 °C. The drug is a white to pale yellow powder that yields a colorless to yellow solution on reconstitution. (2)

The manufacturer indicates that reconstituted solutions in vials of meropenem up to 50 mg/ml in sterile water for injection are stable for two hours at room temperature and up to 12 hours under refrigeration. The infusion vials diluted in sodium chloride 0.9% to a meropenem concentration of 2.5 to 50 mg/ml are stated to be stable for two hours at room temperature and 18 hours under refrigeration; in dextrose 5% in water at these concentrations, stability is only one hour at room temperature and eight hours under refrigeration. (2)

Solutions of meropenem 2.5 to 20 mg/ml in sodium chloride 0.9% in the Minibag Plus (Baxter) are stable for up to four hours at room temperature and up to 24 hours under refrigeration. In dextrose 5% in water in the same concentration range, the drug is stable for only one hour at room temperature and up to six hours under refrigeration. (2)

Meropenem in ADD-Vantage containers reconstituted to a concentration in the range of 5 to 20 mg/ml in sodium chloride 0.45% or 1 to 20 mg/ml in sodium chloride 0.9% is stable for six or four hours, respectively, at room temperature and up to 24 hours under refrigeration. In dextrose 5% in water at a concentration in the range of 1 to 20 mg/ml, the drug is stable for only one hour at room temperature and up to eight hours under refrigeration. (2)

In addition, the manufacturer notes that meropenem 1 to 20 mg/ml in sterile water for injection or sodium chloride 0.9% is stable for up to four hours and in dextrose 5% in water for up to two hours at room temperature in plastic syringes, plastic administration set tubing, drip chambers, and volume control devices. (2)

The manufacturer recommends that solutions of meropenem not be frozen. (2)

Also see Infusion Solutions under Additional Compatibility Information below.

Ambulatory Pumps—Grant et al. evaluated the stability of meropenem (Zeneca) 2 g/100 ml and 3 g/100 ml in sodium chloride 0.9% in medication cassettes for the CADD-Plus ambulatory pump. Because of the antibiotic's inherent instability at room temperature, the cassettes were kept at a temperature less than 5 °C in cold pouches with two frozen gel packs. The frozen gel packs were changed every eight hours. HPLC analysis found that less than 3% meropenem loss occurred in 24 hours under these conditions. (2261)

Elastomeric Reservoir Pumps—Meropenem (Zeneca) 5 and 10 mg/ml in sodium chloride 0.9% protected from light was evaluated for stability in Intermate SV 200 ml/hr (Baxter) infusion devices having polyisoprene elastomeric reservoirs. By visual inspection, the lower concentration was a faint yellow solution and remained unchanged in color while the higher concentration exhibited an increased yellow coloring on storage. Based on HPLC analysis of the solutions, the calculated time to 10% loss at room temperature (about 24 °C) was 34 hours for the 5-mg/ml concentration and 20 hours for the 10-mg/ml concentration. Under refrigeration, both concentrations had a calculated time to 10% loss of 120 hours. Solutions refrigerated for 96 hours maintained adequate meropenem concentrations for an additional six hours at room temperature but became unacceptable on longer room-temperature storage. The stability characteristics of the meropenem solutions in Intermate SV units was very similar to the solution controls in glass containers. (2152)

Central Venous Catheter—Meropenem (Zeneca) 5 mg/ml in sodium chloride 0.9% was found to be compatible with the ARROWg+ard Blue Plus (Arrow International) chlorhexidine-bearing triple-lumen central catheter. HPLC analysis was used to evaluate completeness of drug delivery through the catheter and the amount of chlorhexidine removed from the internal lumens. Essentially complete delivery of the drug was found with little or no drug loss occurring. Furthermore, chlorhexidine delivered from the catheter remained at trace amounts with no substantial increase due to the delivery of the drug through the catheter. (2335)

Compatibility Information

Solution Compatibility

Meropenem

Solution	*Mfr*	*Mfr*	*Conc/L*	*Remarks*	*Ref*	*C/I*
Dextrose 5% with potassium chloride 0.15%	BA[a]	ZEN	1 g	10 to 11% loss by HPLC in 4 hr at 24 °C and in 18 hr at 4 °C	2089	I[c]
	BA[a]	ZEN	20 g	8 to 10% loss by HPLC in 3 hr at 24 °C and in 18 hr at 4 °C	2089	I[c]
Dextrose 5% in Ringer's injection, lactated	BA[a]	ZEN	1 g	11% loss by HPLC in 8 hr at 24 °C and 4 to 10% loss in 48 hr at 4 °C	2089	I[c]
	BA[a]	ZEN	20 g	15% loss by HPLC in 4 hr at 24 °C and 10% loss in 18 hr at 4 °C	2089	I[c]
Dextrose 5% with sodium bicarbonate 0.02%	BA[a]	ZEN	1 g	11% loss by HPLC in 4 hr at 24 °C and 9% in 18 hr at 4 °C	2089	I[c]
	BA[a]	ZEN	20 g	10 to 12% loss by HPLC in 3 hr at 24 °C and 10% loss in 20 hr at 4 °C	2089	I[c]
Dextrose 2.5% in sodium chloride 0.45%	BA[a]	ZEN	1 g	10% loss by HPLC in 6 hr at 24 °C and 7% loss in 24 hr at 4 °C	2089	I[c]
	BA[a]	ZEN	20 g	8% loss by HPLC in 4 hr at 24 °C and 7% loss in 24 hr at 4 °C	2089	I[c]
Dextrose 5% in sodium chloride 0.2%	BA[a]	ZEN	1 g	10 to 11% loss by HPLC in 4 hr at 24 °C and in 16 hr at 4 °C	2089	I[c]
	BA[a]	ZEN	20 g	Up to 10% loss by HPLC in 3 hr at 24 °C and 9% loss in 18 hr at 4 °C	2089	I[c]
Dextrose 5% in sodium chloride 0.9%	BA[a]	ZEN	1 g	11 to 13% loss by HPLC in 4 hr at 24 °C and in 14 hr at 4 °C	2089	I[c]
	BA[a]	ZEN	20 g	9 to 11% loss by HPLC in 3 hr at 24 °C and in 14 hr at 4 °C	2089	I[c]
Dextrose 5% in water	BA[a]	ZEN	1 g	9% loss by HPLC in 4 hr at 24 °C and in 14 hr at 4 °C	2089	I[c]
	BA[b]	ZEN	2.5 g	6 to 7% loss by HPLC in 4 hr at 24 °C and 8 to 10% in 24 hr at 4 °C	2089	I[c]
	BA[a]	ZEN	20 g	11 to 12% loss by HPLC in 4 hr at 24 °C and in 18 hr at 4 °C	2089	I[c]
	BA[b]	ZEN	50 g	9 to 10% loss by HPLC in 3 hr at 24 °C and in 24 hr at 4 °C	2089	I[c]
Dextrose 10% in water	BA[a]	ZEN	1 g	10 to 12% loss by HPLC in 3 hr at 24 °C and in 8 hr at 4 °C	2089	I[c]
	BA[a]	ZEN	20 g	9 to 10% loss by HPLC in 2 hr at 24 °C and in 8 hr at 4 °C	2089	I[c]
Mannitol 2.5%	BA[a]	ZEN	1 g	7 to 8% loss by HPLC in 8 hr at 24 °C and in 24 hr at 4 °C	2089	I[c]
	BA[a]	ZEN	20 g	7 to 9% loss by HPLC in 4 hr at 24 °C and 6% loss in 20 hr at 4 °C	2089	I[c]
Mannitol 10%	BA[a]	ZEN	1 g	10 to 11% loss by HPLC in 4 hr at 24 °C and in 20 hr at 4 °C	2089	I[c]
	BA[a]	ZEN	20 g	10% loss by HPLC in 3 hr at 24 °C and in 20 hr at 4 °C	2089	I[c]
Normosol M with dextrose 5%	AB[a]	ZEN	1 g	5% loss by HPLC in 8 hr at 24 °C and 4% loss in 48 hr at 4 °C	2089	I[c]
	AB[a]	ZEN	20 g	10% loss by HPLC in 3 hr at 24 °C and 7 to 8% loss in 24 hr at 4°C	2089	I[c]
Ringer's injection	BA[a]	ZEN	1 g	6% loss by HPLC in 10 hr at 24 °C and 4 to 5% loss in 48 hr at 4 °C	2089	I[c]

Solution Compatibility (Cont.)

Meropenem

Solution	*Mfr*	*Mfr*	*Conc/L*	*Remarks*	*Ref*	*C/I*
	BA[a]	ZEN	20 g	7% loss by HPLC in 8 hr at 24 °C and 7% loss in 48 hr at 4 °C	2089	I[c]
Ringer's injection, lactated	BA[a]	ZEN	1 g	10 to 12% loss by HPLC in 10 hr at 24 °C and 9% loss in 48 hr at 4 °C	2089	I[c]
	BA[a]	ZEN	20 g	9% loss by HPLC in 8 hr at 24 °C and 7% loss in 48 hr at 4 °C	2089	I[c]
Sodium bicarbonate 5%	BA[a]	ZEN	1 g	10% loss by HPLC in 4 hr at 24 °C and in 18 hr at 4 °C	2089	I[c]
	BA[a]	ZEN	20 g	9 to 10% loss by HPLC in 3 hr at 24 °C and in 18 hr at 4 °C	2089	I[c]
Sodium chloride 0.45%	AB[d]	ZEN	5 g	9 to 10% loss by HPLC in 22 hr at 24 °C and 3% loss in 48 hr at 4 °C	2089	I[c]
	AB[d]	ZEN	20 g	6 to 8% loss by HPLC in 10 hr at 24 °C and 5 to 6% loss in 48 hr at 4 °C	2089	I[c]
Sodium chloride 0.9%	BA[a]	ZEN	1 g	8 to 10% loss by HPLC in 20 hr at 24 °C and 3 to 4% loss in 48 hr at 4 °C	2089	I[c]
	BA[b]	ZEN	2.5 g	10% loss by HPLC in 24 hr at 24 °C and 2% loss in 48 hr at 4 °C	2089	C
	BA[a]	ZEN	20 g	8% loss by HPLC in 10 hr at 24 °C and 5 to 7% loss in 48 hr at 4 °C	2089	I[c]
	BA[b]	ZEN	50 g	9 to 10% loss by HPLC in 8 hr at 24 °C and in 48 hr at 4 °C	2089	I[c]
	[e]	ZEN	20 and 30 g	Less than 3% meropenem loss in 24 hr when kept at less than 5 °C	2261	C
Sodium lactate ⅙ M	BA[a]	ZEN	1 g	7% loss by HPLC in 8 hr at 24 °C and 6 to 7% loss in 48 hr at 4 °C	2089	I[c]
	BA[a]	ZEN	20 g	9% loss by HPLC in 8 hr at 24 °C and 4 to 5% loss in 24 hr at 4 °C	2089	I[c]

[a]*Tested in PVC containers.*
[b]*Tested in glass containers.*
[c]*Incompatible by conventional standards but recommended for dilution of meropenem with use in shorter periods of time.*
[d]*Tested in Abbott ADD-Vantage system.*
[e]*Tested in CADD-Plus medication cassettes.*

Additive Compatibility

Meropenem

Drug	*Mfr*	*Conc/L*	*Mfr*	*Conc/L*	*Test Soln*	*Remarks*	*Ref*	*C/I*
Acyclovir sodium	BW	5 g	ZEN	1 g	NS	Visually compatible for 4 hr at room temperature	1994	C
	BW	5 g	ZEN	20 g	NS	Immediate precipitation	1994	I
Aminophylline	AMR	1 g	ZEN	1 and 20 g	NS	Visually compatible for 4 hr at room temperature	1994	C
Amphotericin B	SQ	200 mg	ZEN	1 and 20 g	NS	Precipitate forms	2068	I
Atropine sulfate	ES	40 mg	ZEN	1 and 20 g	NS	Visually compatible for 4 hr at room temperature	1994	C
Cimetidine HCl	SKB	3 g	ZEN	1 and 20 g	NS	Visually compatible for 4 hr at room temperature	1994	C

Additive Compatibility (Cont.)

			Meropenem					
Drug	*Mfr*	*Conc/L*	*Mfr*	*Conc/L*	*Test Soln*	*Remarks*	*Ref*	*C/I*
Dexamethasone sodium phosphate	MSD	4 g	ZEN	1 and 20 g	NS	Visually compatible for 4 hr at room temperature	1994	C
Dobutamine HCl	LI	1 g	ZEN	1 and 20 g	NS	Visually compatible for 4 hr at room temperature	1994	C
Dopamine HCl	DU	800 mg	ZEN	1 and 20 g	NS	Visually compatible for 4 hr at room temperature	1994	C
Doxycycline hyclate	RR	200 mg	ZEN	1 g	NS	Visually compatible for 4 hr at room temperature	1994	C
	RR	200 mg	ZEN	20 g	NS	Brown discoloration forms in 1 hr at room temperature	1994	I
Enalaprilat	MSD	50 mg	ZEN	1 and 20 g	NS	Visually compatible for 4 hr at room temperature	1994	C
Fluconazole	RR	2 g	ZEN	1 and 20 g	NS	Visually compatible for 4 hr at room temperature	1994	C
Furosemide	HO	1 g	ZEN	1 and 20 g	NS	Visually compatible for 4 hr at room temperature	1994	C
Gentamicin sulfate	SCH	800 mg	ZEN	1 and 20 g	NS	Visually compatible for 4 hr at room temperature	1994	C
Heparin sodium	ES	20,000 units	ZEN	1 and 20 g	NS	Visually compatible for 4 hr at room temperature	1994	C
Insulin, regular	LI	1000 units	ZEN	1 and 20 g	NS	Visually compatible for 4 hr at room temperature	1994	C
Magnesium sulfate	AST	1 g	ZEN	1 and 20 g	NS	Visually compatible for 4 hr at room temperature	1994	C
Metoclopramide HCl	RB	100 mg	ZEN	1 and 20 g	NS	Visually compatible for 4 hr at room temperature	1994	C
Metronidazole HCl	SE	5 g	ZEN	1 and 20 g	NS	Discoloration forms	2068	I
Morphine sulfate	ES	1 g	ZEN	1 and 20 g	NS	Visually compatible for 4 hr at room temperature	1994	C
Multivitamins	AST	50 ml	ZEN	1 and 20 g	NS	Color darkened in 4 hr at room temperature	1994	I
Norepinephrine bitartrate	WI	8 g	ZEN	1 and 20 g	NS	Visually compatible for 4 hr at room temperature	1994	C
Ondansetron HCl	GL	1 g	ZEN	1 g	NS	Visually compatible for 4 hr at room temperature	1994	C
	GL	1 g	ZEN	20 g	NS	White precipitate forms immediately	1994	I
Phenobarbital sodium	ES	200 mg	ZEN	1 and 20 g	NS	Visually compatible for 4 hr at room temperature	1994	C
Ranitidine HCl	GL	100 mg	ZEN	1 and 20 g	NS	Visually compatible for 4 hr at room temperature	1994	C
Vancomycin HCl	LI	1 g	ZEN	1 and 20 g	NS	Visually compatible for 4 hr at room temperature	1994	C
Zidovudine	BW	4 g	ZEN	1 g	NS	Visually compatible for 4 hr at room temperature	1994	C
	BW	4 g	ZEN	20 g	NS	Dark yellow discoloration forms in 4 hr at room temperature	1994	I

Y-Site Injection Compatibility (1:1 Mixture)

Drug	*Mfr*	*Conc*	Meropenem *Mfr*	Meropenem *Conc*	*Remarks*	*Ref*	*C/I*
Acyclovir sodium	BW	5 mg/ml[c]	ZEN	1 mg/ml[b]	Visually compatible for 4 hr at room temperature	1994	C
	BW	5 mg/ml[c]	ZEN	50 mg/ml[c]	Precipitate forms	2068	I
Aminophylline	AMR	25 mg/ml	ZEN	1 and 50 mg/ml[b]	Visually compatible for 4 hr at room temperature	1994	C
Amphotericin B	SQ	5 mg/ml	ZEN	1 and 50 mg/ml[b]	Precipitate forms	2068	I
Atenolol	ICI	0.5 mg/ml	ZEN	1 and 50 mg/ml[b]	Visually compatible for 4 hr at room temperature	1994	C
Atropine sulfate	ES	0.4 mg/ml	ZEN	1 and 50 mg/ml[b]	Visually compatible for 4 hr at room temperature	1994	C
Calcium gluconate	AMR	4 mg/ml[c]	ZEN	1 mg/ml[b]	Visually compatible for 4 hr at room temperature	1994	C
	AMR	4 mg/ml[c]	ZEN	50 mg/ml[b]	Yellow discoloration forms in 4 hr at room temperature	1994	I
Cimetidine HCl	SKB	150 mg/ml	ZEN	1 and 50 mg/ml[b]	Visually compatible for 4 hr at room temperature	1994	C
Dexamethasone sodium phosphate	MSD	10 mg/ml[c]	ZEN	1 and 50 mg/ml[b]	Visually compatible for 4 hr at room temperature	1994	C
Diazepam	RC	5 mg/ml	ZEN	1 and 50 mg/ml[b]	White precipitate forms immediately	1994	I
Digoxin	BW	0.25 mg/ml	ZEN	1 and 50 mg/ml[b]	Visually compatible for 4 hr at room temperature	1994	C
Diphenhydramine HCl	PD	50 mg/ml	ZEN	1 and 50 mg/ml[b]	Visually compatible for 4 hr at room temperature	1994	C
Docetaxel	RPR	0.9 mg/ml[a]	ZEN	20 mg/ml[b]	Physically compatible with no change in measured turbidity or increase in particle content in 4 hr at 23 °C	2224	C
Doxycycline hyclate	RR	1 mg/ml[c]	ZEN	1 mg/ml[b]	Visually compatible for 4 hr at room temperature	1994	C
	RR	1 mg/ml[c]	ZEN	50 mg/ml[b]	Amber discoloration forms within 30 min	1994	I
Enalaprilat	MSD	0.05 mg/ml[c]	ZEN	1 and 50 mg/ml[b]	Visually compatible for 4 hr at room temperature	1994	C
Fluconazole	RR	2 mg/ml	ZEN	1 and 50 mg/ml[b]	Visually compatible for 4 hr at room temperature	1994	C
Furosemide	HO	10 mg/ml	ZEN	1 and 50 mg/ml[b]	Visually compatible for 4 hr at room temperature	1994	C
Gentamicin sulfate	SCH	4 mg/ml[c]	ZEN	1 and 50 mg/ml[b]	Visually compatible for 4 hr at room temperature	1994	C
Heparin sodium	ES	1 unit/ml[c]	ZEN	1 and 50 mg/ml[b]	Visually compatible for 4 hr at room temperature	1994	C
Insulin, regular	LI	0.2 unit/ml[c]	ZEN	1 and 50 mg/ml[b]	Visually compatible for 4 hr at room temperature	1994	C
Linezolid	PHU	2 mg/ml	ZEN	2.5 mg/ml[b]	Physically compatible with no change in measured turbidity or increase in particle content in 4 hr at 23 °C	2264	C
Metoclopramide HCl	RB	5 mg/ml	ZEN	1 and 50 mg/ml[b]	Visually compatible for 4 hr at room temperature	1994	C

Y-Site Injection Compatibility (1:1 Mixture) (Cont.)

Drug	Mfr	Conc	Meropenem Mfr	Meropenem Conc	Remarks	Ref	C/I
Metronidazole HCl	SE	5 mg/ml[c]	ZEN	1 and 50 mg/ml[b]	Discoloration forms	2068	I
Morphine sulfate	ES	1 mg/ml[c]	ZEN	1 and 50 mg/ml[b]	Visually compatible for 4 hr at room temperature	1994	C
Norepinephrine bitartrate	WI	1 mg/ml	ZEN	1 and 50 mg/ml[b]	Visually compatible for 4 hr at room temperature	1994	C
Ondansetron HCl	GL	1 mg/ml[c]	ZEN	1 mg/ml[b]	Visually compatible for 4 hr at room temperature	1994	C
	GL	1 mg/ml[c]	ZEN	50 mg/ml[b]	White precipitate forms immediately	1994	I
Phenobarbital sodium	ES	0.32 mg/ml[c]	ZEN	1 and 50 mg/ml[b]	Visually compatible for 4 hr at room temperature	1994	C
TNA #218 to #226[d]			ZEN	20 mg/ml[a]	Visually compatible with no precipitate or emulsion damage apparent in 4 hr at 23 °C	2215	C
Vancomycin HCl	LI	5 mg/ml[c]	ZEN	1 and 50 mg/ml[b]	Visually compatible for 4 hr at room temperature	1994	C
Zidovudine	BW	4 mg/ml[c]	ZEN	1 mg/ml[b]	Visually compatible for 4 hr at room temperature	1994	C
	BW	4 mg/ml[c]	ZEN	50 mg/ml[b]	Yellow discoloration forms in 4 hr at room temperature	1994	I

[a] *Tested in dextrose 5% in water.*
[b] *Tested in sodium chloride 0.9%.*
[c] *Tested in sterile water for injection.*
[d] *Refer to Appendix I for the composition of parenteral nutrition solutions. TNA indicates a 3-in-1 admixture.*

Additional Compatibility Information

Infusion Solutions — Meropenem 1 to 20 mg/ml as infusion admixtures is stable for the time periods indicated in the following infusion solutions (2):

Infusion Solution	Time (hr) Stored at 15–25 °C	Time (hr) Stored at 4 °C
Dextrose 2.5% in sodium chloride 0.45%	3	12
Dextrose 5% and potassium chloride 0.15%	1	6
Dextrose 5% in Ringer's injection, lactated	1	4
Dextrose 5% in sodium chloride 0.2%	1	4
Dextrose 5% in sodium chloride 0.9%	1	2
Dextrose 5% in water	1	4
Dextrose 5% in water with sodium bicarbonate 0.02%	1	6
Dextrose 10% in water	1	2
Mannitol 2.5%	2	16
Normosol M with dextrose 5%	1	8
Ringer's injection	4	24
Ringer's injection, lactated	4	12
Sodium bicarbonate 5%	1	4
Sodium chloride 0.9%	4	24
Sodium lactate ⅙ M	2	24

MESNA
AHFS 92:00

Products — Mesna is available as a 100-mg/ml solution in 2-ml ampuls and 10-ml multidose vials. Each milliliter of solution also contains edetate disodium 0.25 mg and sodium hydroxide to adjust the pH. In addition, the multidose vials contain benzyl alcohol 10.4 mg/ml. (2)

pH — From 6.5 to 8.5. (2)

Osmolality — Mesna 100 mg/ml has an osmolality of 1563 mOsm/kg. (1689)

Trade Name(s) — Mesnex.

Administration — Mesna may be administered by intravenous injection or infusion. (2; 4) Infusion is usually performed over 15 to 30 minutes, but continuous infusion has also been utilized. (4) Dilution to a concentration of 20 mg/ml in a compatible solution is recommended for intravenous infusion. (2; 4)

Stability — Intact ampuls of mesna should be stored at controlled room temperature. The solution is clear and colorless (2) and is not light sensitive. (72) When exposed to oxygen, mesna oxidizes to the disulfide form, dimesna. Unused mesna injection in opened ampuls should be discarded after dose preparation. However, the multidose vials may be stored and used for up to eight days after initial entry. (2)

pH Effects — Mesna and ifosfamide have been found to be stable in combined admixtures (72; 1380; 1494–1496). See Additive Compatibility table below. However, mesna has been found to undergo more extensive decomposition when mixed with ifosfamide in an infusion solution made alkaline with sodium bicarbonate. At pH 8, mesna retained adequate potency by HPLC analysis for six hours, but lost about 13% in 24 hours and 23% in 48 hours. Ifosfamide underwent only 6% loss by HPLC in 24 hours, but lost 14% in 24 hours. (2281)

Syringes — The short-term use of plastic syringes for preparing mesna infusions appears to be satisfactory. However, extended storage of mesna in a plastic syringe with a luer tip resulted in the formation of dark or thread-like particles and a change in viscosity after 12 hours at room temperature. Similar behavior also occurred in a glass syringe. (72)

Mesna (Asta Pharma) 100 mg/ml was packaged as 10 ml in 20-ml polypropylene syringes (Becton-Dickinson). Samples having the air expelled from the syringes were stored at 5, 24, and 35 °C, and samples with air drawn into the syringes were stored at 24 °C. After nine days of storage, little or no change in the mesna concentration was determined by colorimetric analysis for thiols and disulfides in all samples with no air present. The maximum loss was less than 4% found in the samples stored at 35 °C. However, the syringes containing air exhibited 10% loss in eight days at 24 °C. Minimizing the exposure of mesna to air during storage was recommended to slow the formation of dimesna. (2181)

Ambulatory Pumps — Ifosfamide (Asta Medica) 20 mg/ml and mesna (Asta Medica) 20 mg/ml in water for injection were evaluated for stability and compatibility in PVC reservoirs for the Graseby 9000 ambulatory pump. The solutions were physically compatible and HPLC analysis found about 3% ifosfamide loss and 9% mesna loss in 7 days at 37 °C. About 2% or less loss of both drugs was found after 14 days at 4 °C. Furthermore, weight losses due to moisture transmission were minimal. (2288)

Compatibility Information

Solution Compatibility

Mesna

Solution	*Mfr*	*Mfr*	*Conc/L*	*Remarks*	*Ref*	*C/I*
Dextrose 5% in sodium chloride 0.45%		AW	1 g	4% loss in 72 hr at room temperature	72	C
		AW	20 g	5% loss in 48 hr at room temperature	72	C
Dextrose 5% in water		AW	1 g	5% loss in 24 hr and 13% in 48 hr at room temperature	72	C
		AW	20 g	5% loss in 48 hr at room temperature	72	C
Ringer's injection, lactated		AW	1 g	4% loss in 24 hr and 11% in 48 hr at room temperature	72	C
Sodium chloride 0.9%		AW	1 g	10% loss in 48 hr at room temperature	72	C

Additive Compatibility

Mesna

Drug	*Mfr*	*Conc/L*	*Mfr*	*Conc/L*	*Test Soln*	*Remarks*	*Ref*	*C/I*
Carboplatin		1 g		1 g	W	More than 10% carboplatin loss within 24 hr at room temperature	1379	I
Cisplatin		67 mg		3.33 g	NS	Cisplatin not detected after 1 hr	1291	I
		67 mg		110 mg	NS	Cisplatin weakly detected after 1 hr	1291	I

Additive Compatibility (Cont.)

Mesna

Drug	Mfr	Conc/L	Mfr	Conc/L	Test Soln	Remarks	Ref	C/I
Hydroxyzine HCl	LY	500 mg	AW	3 g	D5W[a]	Physically compatible for 48 hr	1190	C
Ifosfamide	MJ	3.3 g	AW	3.3 g	D5W, LR	Physically compatible with no ifosfamide loss and about 5% mesna loss in 24 hr at 21 °C exposed to light	72	C
	MJ	5 g	AW	5 g	D5W, LR	Physically compatible with no ifosfamide loss and about 5% mesna loss in 24 hr at 21 °C exposed to light	72	C
		50 g		40 g	NS	Both drugs stable for 14 days at room temperature	1380	C
	BI	83.3 g	BI	79 g	NS	Little or no ifosfamide loss in 9 days at room temperature and 7% loss in 9 days at 37 °C. Mesna not tested	1494	C
		2.6 g		1.6 g	D5S[b]	No increase in decomposition products in 8 hr at room temperature	1495	C
	BR	600 mg	BR	600 mg	D5½S, D5W, LR, NS[c]	Chemically stable for at least 24 hr at room temperature	1496	C
	AM	20 g	AM	20 g	W[d]	Physically compatible with about 3% ifosfamide loss and 9% mesna loss in 7 days at 37 °C. About 2% or less loss of both drugs in 14 days at 4 °C	2288	C
Ifosfamide with epirubicin HCl		50 g 500 mg		80 g	NS	More than 50% epirubicin loss in 7 days at room temperature	1380	I

[a]Tested in glass containers.
[b]Tested in polyethylene containers.
[c]Tested in PVC containers.
[d]Tested in PVC reservoirs for the Graseby 9000 ambulatory pump.

Drugs in Syringe Compatibility

Mesna

Drug (in syringe)	Mfr	Amt	Mfr	Amt	Remarks	Ref	C/I
Ifosfamide		250 mg/ 5 ml		200 mg/ 5 ml	3% ifosfamide loss in 7 days and 12% in 4 weeks at 4 °C and room temperature. No mesna loss	1290	C
		50 mg/ ml[a]		40 mg/ ml[a]	Little or no loss of either drug by HPLC in 28 days at 4 and 20 °C	1564	C
Ifosfamide with epirubicin HCl		50 mg/ ml[a] 1 mg/ml[a]		40 mg/ ml[a]	50% epirubicin loss by HPLC in 7 days at 4 and 20 °C. No loss of other drugs in 7 days	1564	I

[a]Diluted with sodium chloride 0.9%.

Y-Site Injection Compatibility (1:1 Mixture)

Mesna

Drug	Mfr	Conc	Mfr	Conc	Remarks	Ref	C/I
Allopurinol sodium	BW	3 mg/ml[b]	MJ	10 mg/ml[b]	Physically compatible with no change in measured turbidity or increase in particle content in 4 hr at 22 °C	1686	C
Amifostine	USB	10 mg/ml[a]	MJ	10 mg/ml[a]	Physically compatible with no change in measured turbidity or increase in particle content in 4 hr at 23 °C	1845	C

Y-Site Injection Compatibility (1:1 Mixture) (Cont.)

			Mesna				
Drug	*Mfr*	*Conc*	*Mfr*	*Conc*	*Remarks*	*Ref*	*C/I*
Amphotericin B cholesteryl sulfate complex	SEQ	0.83 mg/ml[a]	MJ	10 mg/ml[a]	Microprecipitate forms immediately	2117	I
Aztreonam	SQ	40 mg/ml[a]	MJ	10 mg/ml[a]	Physically compatible with no subvisual haze or particle formation in 4 hr at 23 °C	1758	C
Cefepime HCl	BMS	20 mg/ml[a]	MJ	10 mg/ml[a]	Physically compatible with no change in measured turbidity or increase in particle content in 4 hr at 22 °C	1689	C
Cladribine	ORT	0.015[b] and 0.5[c] mg/ml	MJ	10 mg/ml[b]	Physically compatible with no change in measured turbidity or increase in particle content in 4 hr at 23 °C	1969	C
Docetaxel	RPR	0.9 mg/ml[a]	MJ	10 mg/ml[a]	Physically compatible with no change in measured turbidity or increase in particle content in 4 hr at 23 °C	2224	C
Doxorubicin HCl liposome injection	SEQ	0.4 mg/ml[a]	MJ	10 mg/ml[a]	Physically compatible with little or no change in measured turbidity and no increase in particle content in 4 hr at 23 °C	2087	C
Etoposide phosphate	BR	5 mg/ml[a]	MJ	10 mg/ml[a]	Physically compatible with no change in measured turbidity or increase in particle content in 4 hr at 23 °C	2218	C
Filgrastim	AMG	30 μg/ml[a]	MJ	10 mg/ml[a]	Physically compatible with no change in measured turbidity or increase in particle content in 4 hr at 22 °C	1687	C
Fludarabine phosphate	BR	1 mg/ml[a]	BR	10 mg/ml[a]	Physically compatible for 4 hr at room temperature under fluorescent light	1439	C
Gatifloxacin	BMS	2 mg/ml[a]	MJ	10 mg/ml[a]	Physically compatible with no change in measured haze or increase in particle content in 4 hr at 23 °C	2234	C
Gemcitabine HCl	LI	10 mg/ml[b]	MJ	10 mg/ml[b]	Physically compatible with no change in measured turbidity or increase in particle content in 4 hr at 23 °C	2226	C
Granisetron HCl	SKB	1 mg/ml	MJ	4 mg/ml[b]	Physically compatible with little or no loss of either drug by HPLC in 4 hr at 22 °C	1883	C
Linezolid	PHU	2 mg/ml	MJ	10 mg/ml[a]	Physically compatible with no change in measured turbidity or increase in particle content in 4 hr at 23 °C	2264	C
Melphalan HCl	BW	0.1 mg/ml[b]	BR	10 mg/ml[b]	Physically compatible with no change in measured turbidity or increase in particle content in 3 hr at 22 °C	1557	C
Methotrexate sodium		30 mg/ml		1.8 mg/ml[a]	Visually compatible for 4 hr at room temperature	1788	C
Ondansetron HCl	GL	1 mg/ml[b]	BR	10 mg/ml[a]	Physically compatible for 4 hr at 22 °C	1365	C
Paclitaxel	NCI	1.2 mg/ml[a]	MJ	10 mg/ml[a]	Physically compatible with no change in measured turbidity in 4 hr at 22 °C	1556	C
Piperacillin sodium–tazobactam sodium	LE	40 + 5 mg/ml[a]	MJ	10 mg/ml[a]	Physically compatible with no change in measured turbidity or increase in particle content in 4 hr at 22 °C	1688	C
Sargramostim	IMM	10 μg/ml[b]	MJ	10 mg/ml[b]	Physically compatible for 4 hr at 22 °C	1436	C

Y-Site Injection Compatibility (1:1 Mixture) (Cont.)

Drug	Mfr	Conc	Mesna Mfr	Mesna Conc	Remarks	Ref	C/I
Sodium bicarbonate		1.4%		1.8 mg/ml[a]	Visually compatible for 4 hr at room temperature	1788	C
Teniposide	BR	0.1 mg/ml[a]	MJ	10 mg/ml[a]	Physically compatible with no subvisual haze or particle formation in 4 hr at 23 °C	1725	C
Thiotepa	IMM[d]	1 mg/ml[a]	MJ	10 mg/ml[a]	Physically compatible with no change in measured turbidity or increase in particle content in 4 hr at 23 °C	1861	C
TNA #218 to #226[e]			MJ	10 mg/ml[a]	Visually compatible with no precipitate or emulsion damage apparent in 4 hr at 23 °C	2215	C
TPN #212 to #215[e]			MJ	10 mg/ml[a]	Physically compatible with no change in measured turbidity or increase in particle content in 4 hr at 23 °C	2109	C
Vinorelbine tartrate	BW	1 mg/ml[b]	MJ	10 mg/ml[b]	Physically compatible with no change in measured turbidity or increase in particle content in 4 hr at 22 °C under fluorescent light	1558	C

[a]*Tested in dextrose 5% in water.*
[b]*Tested in sodium chloride 0.9%.*
[c]*Tested in bacteriostatic sodium chloride 0.9% preserved with benzyl alcohol 0.9%.*
[d]*Lyophilized formulation tested.*
[e]*Refer to Appendix I for the composition of parenteral nutrition solutions. TNA indicates a 3-in-1 admixture, and TPN indicates a 2-in-1 admixture.*

Additional Compatibility Information

Infusion Solutions — The manufacturer states that mesna is chemically and physically stable for 24 hours at 25 °C diluted to 20 mg/ml in the following infusion solutions (2):

Dextrose 5% in sodium chloride 0.2%
Dextrose 5% in sodium chloride 0.33%
Dextrose 5% in sodium chloride 0.45%
Dextrose 5% in water
Ringer's injection, lactated
Sodium chloride 0.9%

Other information indicates that admixtures may be stable for a longer time. (72) (See the Solution Compatibility table.)

Cyclophosphamide and Ifosfamide — Mesna is stated to be stable for 24 hours in dextrose 5% in water or Ringer's injection, lactated, when admixed with cyclophosphamide or ifosfamide. (4; 1292)

METARAMINOL BITARTRATE
AHFS 12:12

Products — Metaraminol bitartrate is available in 10-ml vials containing, in each milliliter, metaraminol bitartrate equivalent to metaraminol 10 mg, sodium chloride 4.4 mg, methylparaben 0.15%, propylparaben 0.02%, and sodium bisulfite 0.2% in water for injection. (2)

pH — From 3.2 to 4.5. (4)

Osmolality — Metaraminol bitartrate 10 mg/ml has an osmolality of 290 mOsm/kg. (1689)

Trade Name(s) — Aramine.

Administration — Metaraminol bitartrate may be administered by intramuscular or subcutaneous injection and by direct intravenous injection in severe shock. The drug may also be given by intravenous infusion, usually in 500 ml of dextrose 5% in water or sodium chloride 0.9%, although the volume may be varied depending on the rate of administration and the patient's fluid needs. (2; 4) Some clinicians recommend avoiding subcutaneous injection because of the possibility of local tissue injury. (4)

Stability — Metaraminol bitartrate injection is a clear, colorless solution. Intact containers should be stored at controlled room temperature and protected from light. Temperatures above 40 °C and below

−20 °C should be avoided. (2; 4) Although the drug is sensitive to excessive heat (7), the manufacturer states that the vial can be sterilized by autoclaving as well as by immersion in a sterilizing solution. (2)

pH Effects—Metaraminol bitartrate appears to be stable over a wide pH range. A stability profile of 100 mg/L in dextrose 5% in water at pH 3.6 to 7.6 did not show any significant loss in potency during 24 hours. (7) Another study showed that metaraminol bitartrate 10, 20, and 30 mg/L in various buffer solutions ranging from pH 2.1 to 9.9 was stable for 48 hours. (43)

Sorption—Metaraminol bitartrate 68 mg/L in sodium chloride 0.9% (Travenol) in PVC bags did not exhibit significant sorption to the plastic during one week of storage at room temperature (15 to 20 °C). (536)

In another study, metaraminol bitartrate 68 mg/L in sodium chloride 0.9% did not exhibit any loss due to sorption during a seven-hour simulated infusion through an infusion set (Travenol) consisting of a cellulose propionate burette chamber and 170 cm of PVC tubing. (606)

The drug was also tested as a simulated infusion over at least one hour by a syringe pump system. A glass syringe on a syringe pump was fitted with 20 cm of polyethylene tubing or 50 cm of Silastic tubing. No loss of drug due to sorption was observed with either tubing. (606)

A 25-ml aliquot of metaraminol bitartrate 68 mg/L in sodium chloride 0.9% stored in all-plastic syringes composed of polypropylene barrels and polyethylene plungers for 24 hours at room temperature in the dark did not exhibit any loss due to sorption. (606)

Compatibility Information

Solution Compatibility

Metaraminol bitartrate

Solution	*Mfr*	*Mfr*	*Conc/L*	*Remarks*	*Ref*	*C/I*
Alcohol 5%, dextrose 5%	BA	MSD	1 g	Physically compatible for 24 hr	315	C
Amino acids 4.25%, dextrose 25%	MG	MSD	100 mg	No increase in particulate matter in 24 hr at 5 °C	349	C
Dextran 40,000	PH	MSD		Compatible	44	C
Dextran 6% in sodium chloride 0.9%	AB	MSD	100 mg	Potency retained for 24 hr	7	C
Dextrose 5% in Ringer's injection, lactated	TR[a]	MSD	100 mg	Potency retained for 24 hr at 5 °C	282	C
	BA	MSD	1 g	Physically compatible for 24 hr	315	C
Dextrose 5% in sodium chloride 0.9%	AB	MSD	100 mg	Potency retained for 24 hr	7	C
	AB	MSD	100 mg	Potency retained for 48 hr	46	C
		MSD	100, 200, 300 mg	Potency retained for 48 hr	43	C
	TR[a]	MSD	100 mg	Potency retained for 24 hr at 5 °C	282	C
	BA	MSD	1 g	Physically compatible for 24 hr	315	C
Dextrose 5% in water	AB	MSD	100 mg	Potency retained for 24 hr	7	C
	AB	MSD	100 mg	Potency retained for 48 hr	46	C
	TR[a]	MSD	100 mg	Potency retained for 24 hr	282	C
	BA	MSD	1 g	Physically compatible for 24 hr	315	C
Dextrose 10% in water	BA	MSD	1 g	Physically compatible for 24 hr	315	C
Dextrose 20% in water	BA	MSD	1 g	Physically compatible for 24 hr	315	C
Fructose 10% in water	BA	MSD	1 g	Physically compatible for 24 hr	315	C
Invert sugar 10% in Electrolyte #1	BA	MSD	1 g	Physically compatible for 24 hr	315	C
Invert sugar 10% in Electrolyte #2	BA	MSD	1 g	Physically compatible for 24 hr	315	C
Multielectrolyte solution	AB	MSD	100 mg	Potency retained for 48 hr	46	C
Normosol M in dextrose 5%	AB	MSD	100 mg	Potency retained for 24 hr	7	C
Normosol R	AB	MSD	100 mg	Potency retained for 24 hr	7	C
Normosol R, pH 7.4	AB	MSD	100 mg	Potency retained for 24 hr	7	C
Polysal M with dextrose 5%	CU	MSD	1 g	Physically compatible for 24 hr	315	C
Ringer's injection	AB	MSD	100 mg	Potency retained for 24 hr	7	C
Ringer's injection, lactated	AB	MSD	100 mg	Potency retained for 24 hr	7	C
	TR[a]	MSD	100 mg	Potency retained for 24 hr at 5 °C	282	C

Solution Compatibility (Cont.)

Metaraminol bitartrate

Solution	*Mfr*	*Mfr*	*Conc/L*	*Remarks*	*Ref*	*C/I*
	BA	MSD	1 g	Physically compatible for 24 hr	315	C
	AB	MSD	100 mg	Physically incompatible	15	I
Sodium bicarbonate 5%	AB	MSD	100 mg	Potency retained for 24 hr	7	C
Sodium chloride 0.9%	AB	MSD	100 mg	Potency retained for 24 hr	7	C
	AB	MSD	100 mg	Potency retained for 48 hr	46	C
	BA	MSD		Potency retained for 24 hr	45	C
	TR[a]	MSD	100 mg	Potency retained for 24 hr at 5 °C	282	C
	TR[b]	MSD		Potency retained for 24 hr	45	C
	BA	MSD	1 g	Physically compatible for 24 hr	315	C
Sodium lactate ⅙ M	BA	MSD	1 g	Physically compatible for 24 hr	315	C

[a]*Tested in both glass and PVC containers.*
[b]*Tested in PVC containers.*

Additive Compatibility

Metaraminol bitartrate

Drug	*Mfr*	*Conc/L*	*Mfr*	*Conc/L*	*Test Soln*	*Remarks*	*Ref*	*C/I*
Amikacin sulfate	BR	5 g	BR	200 mg	D5LR, D5R, D5S, D5W, D10W, IS10, LR, NS, R, SL	Physically compatible and potency of both retained for 24 hr at 25 °C	294	C
Amphotericin B		200 mg	BP	200 mg	D5W	Haze develops over 3 hr	26	I
Chloramphenicol sodium succinate	PD	1 g	MSD	100 mg		Physically compatible	7	C
	PD	1 g	MSD	200 mg		Physically compatible	6	C
Cibenzoline succinate		2 g	MSD	1 g	D5W, NS	Physically compatible for 24 hr at 25 °C by visual and microscopic examination	1182	C
Cimetidine HCl	SKF	3 g	MSD	1 g	D5W	Physically compatible and cimetidine chemically stable for 24 hr at room temperature. Metaraminol not tested	551	C
Cyanocobalamin	AB	1000 μg	MSD	100 mg		Physically compatible	7	C
Dexamethasone sodium phosphate	MSD	20 mg	MSD	100 mg	D5W, NS	Altered UV spectrum for dexamethasone within 1 hr at room temperature	42	I
	MSD	100 mg	MSD	500 mg	D5W	Altered UV spectrum for dexamethasone within 1 hr at room temperature	42	I
Dobutamine HCl	LI	1 g	MSD	100 mg	D5W, NS	Physically compatible for 24 hr at 21 °C	812	C
Ephedrine sulfate	AB	50 mg	MSD	100 mg		Physically compatible	7	C
Epinephrine HCl	PD	4 mg	MSD	100 mg		Physically compatible	7	C
Erythromycin lactobionate	AB	750 mg	MSD	100 mg	D5W	92% erythromycin decomposition in 24 hr at 25 °C	20	I
	AB	1 g	MSD	100 mg	D5W	44% erythromycin decomposition in 6 hr at 25 °C	48	I
Fibrinogen	CU	2 g	MSD	200 mg	D5W	Physically incompatible	11	I
Hydrocortisone sodium phosphate	MSD	250 mg	MSD	500 mg	D5W, NS	UV spectra of both not altered in 8 hr at room temperature	42	C

Additive Compatibility (Cont.)

Metaraminol bitartrate

Drug	*Mfr*	*Conc/L*	*Mfr*	*Conc/L*	*Test Soln*	*Remarks*	*Ref*	*C/I*
Hydrocortisone sodium succinate	UP	100 mg	MSD	100 mg	D5S	Potency of both retained for 24 hr	43	**C**
			MSD			Physically incompatible	9	**I**
	UP	250 mg	MSD	100 mg		Precipitate forms within 1 hr	7	**I**
	UP	200 and 300 mg	MSD	100, 200, 300 mg	D5S	Precipitate forms and chemical decomposition of hydrocortisone	43	**I**
		250 mg	MSD	500 mg	D5W, NS	Precipitate forms within 1 hr	42	**I**
Lidocaine HCl	AST	2 g	MSD	100 mg		Physically compatible	24	**C**
Methylprednisolone sodium succinate	UP	125 mg	MSD	400 mg	D5W, NS	Precipitate forms within 4 hr	42	**I**
Oxytocin	PD	5 units	MSD	100 mg		Physically compatible	7	**C**
Penicillin G potassium	SQ	1 million units	MSD	100 mg	D5W	59% penicillin decomposition in 24 hr at 25 °C	47	**I**
	[a]	900,000 units	MSD	100 mg	D5W	17% penicillin decomposition in 6 hr at 25 °C	48	**I**
Phenytoin sodium	PD		MSD			Physically incompatible	9	**I**
Potassium chloride	AB	40 mEq	MSD	100 mg		Physically compatible	7	**C**
Promazine HCl	WY	100 mg	MSD	100 mg		Physically compatible	7	**C**
Sodium bicarbonate	AB	3.75 g	MSD	100 mg		Physically compatible	7	**C**
	AB	4.8 mEq[b]	MSD	100 mg	D5W	Physically compatible for 24 hr	772	**C**
Thiopental sodium	AB	2.5 g	MSD	200 mg	D5W	Precipitate forms within 1 hr	21	**I**
	AB	2.5 g	MSD	100 mg		Precipitate forms within 1 hr	7	**I**
	AB	2.5 g	MSD	200 mg	D5W	Physically incompatible	11	**I**
Verapamil HCl	KN	80 mg	MSD	20 mg	D5W, NS	Physically compatible for 24 hr	764	**C**

[a]*A buffered preparation was specified.*
[b]*Two vials of Neut added to a liter of admixture.*

Y-Site Injection Compatibility (1:1 Mixture)

Metaraminol bitartrate

Drug	*Mfr*	*Conc*	*Mfr*	*Conc*	*Remarks*	*Ref*	*C/I*
Amiodarone HCl	LZ	4 mg/ml[a,b]	MSD	0.2 mg/ml[a,b]	Physically compatible for 24 hr at 21 °C	1032	**C**
Inamrinone lactate	WB	3 mg/ml[b]	MSD	0.2 mg/ml[a]	Physically compatible for at least 4 hr at 25 °C under fluorescent light	992	**C**
Warfarin sodium	DU	0.1[a,b] and 2 mg/ml[c]	MSD	0.2 mg/ml[a,b]	Physically compatible with no change in measured turbidity or increase in particle content in 24 hr at 23 °C	2011	**C**

[a]*Tested in dextrose 5% in water*
[b]*Tested in sodium chloride 0.9%.*
[c]*Tested in sterile water for injection.*

Additional Compatibility Information

Infusion Solutions — At a concentration of 100 mg/L, metaraminol bitartrate is physically compatible with all Abbott infusion solutions. (7) The manufacturer indicates that metaraminol bitartrate (MSD) is physically compatible and chemically stable at a concentration of 100 mg/L in the following infusion solutions (2; 4):

Dextran 6% in sodium chloride 0.9%
Dextrose 5% in sodium chloride 0.9%
Dextrose 5% in water

Normosol M in dextrose 5% in water
Normosol R
Normosol R, pH 7.4
Ringer's injection
Ringer's injection, lactated
Sodium bicarbonate 5%
Sodium chloride 0.9%

Use of the infusions within 24 hours is recommended because no preservatives are present in the solutions. (2)

Acid-Labile Drugs — Physical incompatibilities with metaraminol bitartrate may involve precipitation of drugs with poor solubility in an acidic medium. The incompatibilities occur to varying extents, depending on the concentration of the various additives and metaraminol bitartrate in the infusion solution. Examples include sodium salts of barbituric acid and sulfonamides. In addition, the rate of decomposition of acid-sensitive drugs such as penicillin G, erythromycin lactobionate, and nafcillin sodium may be increased. (6; 7; 20; 27) Metaraminol bitartrate should not be mixed with acid-labile drugs. (7)

Ranitidine — Metaraminol bitartrate is stated to be incompatible with ranitidine HCl. (1515)

Concentrated Drug Solutions — The following incompatibility determinations were performed in concentrated solutions. The drugs in dry form were constituted according to the manufacturers' recommendations. One milliliter of metaraminol bitartrate was added to 5 ml of sterile distilled water along with 1 ml of each of the following drugs. Particulate matter was noted within two hours (28):

Penicillin G potassium
Phenytoin sodium (Parke-Davis)

METHADONE HCL
AHFS 28:08.08

Products — Methadone HCl is available in 20-ml multidose vials. Each milliliter of solution contains methadone HCl 10 mg and sodium chloride 0.9% with sodium hydroxide and/or hydrochloric acid to adjust the pH. In addition, the 20-ml vials contain chlorobutanol 0.5%. (1-5/26/95; 29)

pH — From 3 to 6.5. (4)

Trade Name(s) — Dolophine Hydrochloride.

Administration — Methadone HCl may be administered by subcutaneous or intramuscular injection. (4)

Stability — Methadone HCl in intact vials should be stored at controlled room temperature and protected from light. (1-5/26/95)

Compatibility Information

Solution Compatibility

Methadone HCl

Solution	*Mfr*	*Mfr*	*Conc/L*	*Remarks*	*Ref*	*C/I*
Sodium chloride 0.9%	TR[a]	LI	1, 2, 5 g	Little or no loss by HPLC in 28 days at room temperature exposed to light	1500	C

[a]*Tested in PVC containers.*

Y-Site Injection Compatibility (1:1 Mixture)

Methadone HCl

Drug	*Mfr*	*Conc*	*Mfr*	*Conc*	*Remarks*	*Ref*	*C/I*
Atropine sulfate	LY	0.4 mg/ml	LI	1 mg/ml[a]	Physically compatible with no change in measured haze or increase in particle content in 48 hr at 22 °C	1706	C
Dexamethasone sodium phosphate	AMR	1 mg/ml[a]	LI	1 mg/ml[a]	Physically compatible with no change in measured haze or increase in particle content in 48 hr at 22 °C	1706	C
Diazepam	ES	0.5 mg/ml[a]	LI	1 mg/ml[a]	Physically compatible with no change in measured haze or increase in particle content in 48 hr at 22 °C	1706	C

Y-Site Injection Compatibility (1:1 Mixture) (Cont.)

Methadone HCl

Drug	*Mfr*	*Conc*	*Mfr*	*Conc*	*Remarks*	*Ref*	*C/I*
Diphenhydramine HCl	SCN	2 mg/ml[a]	LI	1 mg/ml[a]	Physically compatible with no change in measured haze or increase in particle content in 48 hr at 22 °C	1706	C
Haloperidol lactate	MN	0.2 mg/ml[a]	LI	1 mg/ml[a]	Physically compatible with no change in measured haze or increase in particle content in 48 hr at 22 °C	1706	C
Hydroxyzine HCl	WI	4 mg/ml[a]	LI	1 mg/ml[a]	Physically compatible with no change in measured haze or increase in particle content in 48 hr at 22 °C	1706	C
Ketorolac tromethamine	WY	1 mg/ml[a]	LI	1 mg/ml[a]	Physically compatible with no change in measured haze or increase in particle content in 48 hr at 22 °C	1706	C
Lorazepam	WY	0.1 mg/ml[a]	LI	1 mg/ml[a]	Physically compatible with no change in measured haze or increase in particle content in 48 hr at 22 °C	1706	C
Methotrimeprazine	LE	0.2 mg/ml[a]	LI	1 mg/ml[a]	Physically compatible with no change in measured haze or increase in particle content in 48 hr at 22 °C	1706	C
Metoclopramide HCl	DU	5 mg/ml	LI	1 mg/ml[a]	Physically compatible with no change in measured haze or increase in particle content in 48 hr at 22 °C	1706	C
Midazolam HCl	RC	0.2 mg/ml[a]	LI	1 mg/ml[a]	Physically compatible with no change in measured haze or increase in particle content in 48 hr at 22 °C	1706	C
Phenobarbital sodium	WY	2 mg/ml[a]	LI	1 mg/ml[a]	Physically compatible with no change in measured haze or increase in particle content in 48 hr at 22 °C	1706	C
Phenytoin sodium	ES	2 mg/ml[a,b]	LI	1 mg/ml[a]	Precipitate forms immediately	1706	I
Scopolamine HBr	LY	0.05 mg/ml[a]	LI	1 mg/ml[a]	Physically compatible with no change in measured haze or increase in particle content in 48 hr at 22 °C	1706	C

[a]*Tested in dextrose 5% in water.*
[b]*Tested in sodium chloride 0.9%.*

METHOHEXITAL SODIUM
AHFS 28:24.04

Products — Methohexital sodium is available in 50-ml vials (with or without accompanying vials of sterile water for injection) containing methohexital sodium 500 mg with anhydrous sodium carbonate 30 mg, in vials containing methohexital sodium 2.5 g with sodium carbonate 150 mg, and in vials containing methohexital sodium 5 g with sodium carbonate 300 mg. (1-3/19/98)

To prepare a 1% (10 mg/ml) solution of methohexital sodium for intravenous use, reconstitute with sterile water for injection, preferably, or dextrose 5% in water or sodium chloride 0.9% in the following amounts. Do not use diluents containing bacteriostats. (1-3/19/98)

Size	Reconstitution Volume	Final Volume of Diluent
500 mg in 50-ml vial		50 ml
2.5 g in vial	15 ml	250 ml
5 g in vial	30 ml	500 ml

The initial dilution of the 2.5- and 5-g vials results in a yellow solution. When further diluted, the solution must be clear and colorless or it should not be used. (1-3/19/98; 4)

To prepare a 0.2% (2 mg/ml) solution of methohexital sodium for intravenous use, add 500 mg to 250 ml of dextrose 5% in water or sodium chloride 0.9%. Sterile water for injection should not be used for this concentration to avoid extreme hypotonicity. (1-3/19/98)

Intramuscular injection of methohexital sodium is described by the manufacturer in the labeling. To prepare a 5% (50-mg/ml) solution for intramuscular use, the 500-mg and 2.5-g vials should be reconstituted with 10 and 50 ml, respectively, of compatible diluent. (1-3/19/98)

pH — A 0.2% solution in dextrose 5% in water has a pH of 9.5 to 10.5; a 1% solution in sterile water for injection has a pH of 10 to 11. (4)

Sodium Content — Methohexital sodium contains 4.652 mEq of sodium per gram of drug; the sodium carbonate provides 1.132 mEq while the balance comes from the drug itself. (869)

Trade Name(s) — Brevital Sodium.

Administration — Methohexital sodium is administered intravenously, by injection or continuous infusion, in concentrations no higher than 1%. Intra-arterial injection and extravasation should be avoided. (1-3/19/98) Intramuscular injection of 5% solutions has also been described. (1-3/19/98)

Stability — Intact vials should be stored at controlled room temperature. (1-3/19/98; 4) Solutions of methohexital sodium in sterile water for injection are stable at 25 °C or below for at least six weeks. In dextrose 5% in water or sodium chloride 0.9%, it is stable for about 24 hours. (4)

pH Effects — Methohexital sodium is alkaline in solution and is incompatible with acidic solutions and phenol-containing solutions. (4)

Sorption — Methohexital sodium (Lilly) 32 mg/L displayed 7.9% sorption to a PVC plastic test strip in 24 hours. (12) However, another test did not confirm this finding. No significant loss in PVC containers and no difference between glass and PVC containers were found. (282)

Compatibility Information

Solution Compatibility

Methohexital sodium

Solution	*Mfr*	*Mfr*	*Conc/L*	*Remarks*	*Ref*	*C/I*
Dextrose 5% in Ringer's injection, lactated	TR[a]	LI	2 g	Potency retained for 24 hr at 5 °C	282	C
Dextrose 5% in sodium chloride 0.9%	TR[a]	LI	2 g	Potency retained for 24 hr at 5 °C	282	C
Dextrose 5% in water	TR[a]	LI	2 g	Potency retained for 24 hr at 5 °C	282	C
Ringer's injection, lactated	TR[a]	LI	2 g	Potency retained for 24 hr at 5 °C	282	C
Sodium chloride 0.9%	TR[a]	LI	2 g	Potency retained for 24 hr at 5 °C	282	C

[a]*Tested in both glass and PVC containers.*

Additive Compatibility

Methohexital sodium

Drug	*Mfr*	*Conc/L*	*Mfr*	*Conc/L*	*Test Soln*	*Remarks*	*Ref*	*C/I*
Chlorpromazine HCl	BP	200 mg	BP	2 g	D5W, NS	Immediate precipitation	26	I
Hydralazine HCl	BP	80 mg	BP	2 g	D5W, NS	Yellow color and precipitate forms within 3 hr	26	I
Kanamycin sulfate	BPC	4 g	BP	2 g	D5W, NS	Immediate precipitation	26	I
Lidocaine HCl	BP	2 g	BP	2 g	D5W	Immediate precipitation	26	I
Mechlorethamine HCl	BP	40 mg	BP	2 g	D5W, NS	Haze develops over 3 hr	26	I
Methyldopate HCl		1 g	BP	2 g	D5W	Haze develops over 3 hr	26	I
		1 g	BP	2 g	NS	Crystals produced	26	I
Prochlorperazine mesylate	BP	100 mg	BP	2 g	D5W	Haze develops over 3 hr	26	I
Promazine HCl	BP	200 mg	BP	2 g	D5W, NS	Immediate precipitation	26	I
Promethazine HCl	BP	100 mg	BP	2 g	D5W, NS	Immediate precipitation	26	I
Streptomycin sulfate	BP	4 g	BP	2 g	NS	Crystals produced	26	I

Drugs in Syringe Compatibility

Methohexital sodium

Drug (in syringe)	*Mfr*	*Amt*	*Mfr*	*Amt*	*Remarks*	*Ref*	*C/I*
Glycopyrrolate	RB	0.2 mg/ 1 ml	LI	10 mg/ 1 ml	Immediate precipitation	331	I
	RB	0.2 mg/ 1 ml	LI	20 mg/ 2 ml	Immediate precipitation	331	I
	RB	0.4 mg/ 2 ml	LI	10 mg/ 1 ml	Immediate precipitation	331	I

Additional Compatibility Information

Infusion Solutions — Although the manufacturer does not recommend the use of Ringer's injection, lactated, as a diluent, methohexital sodium has been determined to be compatible in dextrose 5% in Ringer's injection, lactated, as well as Ringer's injection, lactated. (See the table above.) However, the potential for incompatibility does exist between the sodium carbonate in the drug formulation and the calcium ions of the infusion solutions. (282)

Acidic Drugs — Drugs such as methohexital sodium that exhibit poor solubility in an acidic medium may precipitate in solutions containing acidic drugs. (22) Metaraminol bitartrate is acidic and may cause precipitation, depending on the concentration of the additives. (7) In addition, the acidic methyldopate HCl imparts some buffer capacity to admixtures and may pose solubility problems with barbiturate salts. (23)

Since solubility is maintained only at relatively high pH, mixing methohexital sodium with acidic solutions is not recommended. (4) Mixed with methohexital sodium, a haze or precipitate forms in 15 minutes with atropine sulfate and tubocurarine chloride, in 30 minutes with metocurine iodide and succinylcholine chloride, and in 60 minutes with scopolamine HBr. (1-3/19/98)

When barbiturates are mixed with succinylcholine chloride, either free barbiturate precipitates or the succinylcholine chloride is hydrolyzed, depending on the final pH of the admixture. (4; 21) Similarly, atracurium besylate may be inactivated by alkaline solutions, such as barbiturates, and a free acid of the admixed drug may precipitate, depending on the resultant pH of the admixture. (4)

Alkali-Labile Drugs — Methohexital sodium may raise the pH of admixture solutions to the alkaline range and, therefore, should not be mixed with drugs that are alkali labile such as penicillin G. (47) Significant decomposition of isoproterenol HCl and norepinephrine bitartrate may also occur. If either of these two drugs is mixed with methohexital sodium, the admixture should be used immediately after preparation. (59; 77) Thiamine HCl is also stated to be unstable in the alkaline solutions of barbiturates. (4)

Other Drugs — Other drugs stated to be incompatible with barbiturate salts include clindamycin phosphate (106), pentazocine lactate, fentanyl citrate (4), cimetidine HCl (360), droperidol, and drugs that utilize phenol as a preservative. (4)

A visible precipitate may form if pancuronium bromide is mixed with barbiturates. (4) However, a visible precipitate was not produced when pancuronium bromide was mixed in a syringe with thiopental or methohexital. (134)

Silicone — Methohexital sodium is stated to be incompatible with silicone and, as a consequence, should not contact rubber stoppers or parts of disposable syringes that have been treated with silicone. (4)

METHOTREXATE SODIUM
AHFS 10:00

Products — Methotrexate sodium is available in liquid and lyophilized dosage forms.

The liquid dosage forms contain methotrexate sodium 25 mg/ml and are available in vials of various sizes from 2 to 10 ml. The products also contain sodium chloride, and the preserved products contain benzyl alcohol. The pH has been adjusted during manufacturing with sodium hydroxide and, if necessary, hydrochloric acid. (1-8/99; 4; 29; 154)

The single-use lyophilized dosage forms of methotrexate (as the sodium salt) are available in vials containing 20 mg and 1 g. The pH has been adjusted during manufacturing with sodium hydroxide. Reconstitute the 20-mg vial to a concentration no greater than 25 mg/ml with a sterile, preservative-free medium such as dextrose 5% in water or sodium chloride 0.9%. The 1-g vial requires 19.4 ml of sterile, preservative-free diluent for reconstitution to yield a 50-mg/ml concentration. (154)

pH — The pH of the commercially available dosage forms of methotrexate sodium is adjusted to approximately 8.5 (range 7.5 to 9). (1-8/99; 4)

Tonicity — The liquid dosage forms of methotrexate sodium are isotonic solutions. (4)

Density — Methotrexate sodium (Lederle) 25-mg/ml undiluted injection has a density of 1.00 g/ml. Methotrexate sodium (Lederle) lyophilized powder reconstituted with sterile water for injection to a concentration of 50 mg/ml has a solution density of 1.01 g/ml. (2041; 2248)

Administration — Methotrexate sodium may be administered by intramuscular, intra-arterial, or intrathecal injection, by direct intravenous injection, or by continuous or intermittent intravenous infusion. (1-8/99; 4) For intrathecal injection, a preservative-free form is diluted to a 1-mg/ml concentration in sodium chloride 0.9%, Elliott's B solution, or the patient's own spinal fluid. (1-8/99; 4; 435; 830) For high-dose regimens, it is recommended that preservative-free forms of methotrexate sodium be used (1-8/99; 241; 242); high doses of methotrexate sodium require leucovorin rescue. (1-8/99)

Stability — Storage of the lyophilized powder and injection at controlled room temperature with protection from light is recommended. (1-8/99; 4)

For intrathecal injection, the preservative-free dosage forms should be diluted immediately prior to use. (1-8/99; 4) Although reconstitution of the lyophilized vials immediately prior to use is also recommended because of the absence of antibacterial preservatives, the reconstituted solution is chemically stable for at least one week at room temperature. (234)

Methotrexate sodium, reconstituted according to the manufacturer's instructions, was cultured with human lymphoblasts to determine whether its cytotoxic activity was retained. The solution retained cytotoxicity for 24 hours at 4 °C and room temperature. (1575)

pH Effects — Methotrexate is most stable between pH 6 and 8. Drugs producing extremes of pH should not be added to methotrexate. (1072; 1369; 1379)

Freezing Solutions — Karlsen et al. found that methotrexate sodium (Lederle) 50 mg/100 ml in PVC bags of dextrose 5% in water (Travenol) could be frozen at −20 °C for at least 30 days and thawed by microwave radiation for two minutes with no significant change in concentration. Even after five repetitions of the freeze–thaw treatment, the methotrexate concentration showed no significant change. (818)

Dyvik et al. evaluated the stability of methotrexate 5 mg, 50 mg, and 1 g in 50 ml of sodium chloride 0.9% in PVC bags frozen at −20 °C for up to 12 weeks and thawed in a microwave oven. No loss of methotrexate was found in any of the concentrations. (1281)

Light Effects — Photolability, although unrecognized for many years, is a stability problem that is increased by dilution and mixture with sodium bicarbonate. (1202)

In dilute solutions of 0.1 mg/ml, methotrexate is reported to undergo photodegradation on exposure to light. Decomposition of 5 to 8% in 10 days and 11 to 17% in 20 days has been reported. This effect was not observed in the more concentrated solutions of the commercial preparation (25 mg/ml) (433) or in admixtures of methotrexate during short-term light exposure. Dyvik et al. found no significant loss of methotrexate due to light exposure for four hours in solutions composed of 5 mg, 50 mg, or 1 g of methotrexate in 50 ml of sodium chloride 0.9% in PVC containers. (1281)

McElnay et al. found little methotrexate loss from a 1-mg/ml solution in sodium chloride 0.9% in three burette drip chambers made of cellulose propionate (Avon A200 standard and A2000 Amberset) and methacrylate butadiene styrene (Avon A2001 Sureset) when exposed to normal mixed daylight and fluorescent lighting conditions for 24 hours. However, in 48 hours about 10 and 12% losses were observed in the A200 and A2001, respectively. With exposure to direct sunlight, an 11% loss occurred in the A200 in seven hours. No loss occurred when the Amberset or Sureset was wrapped in foil and exposed to either light condition for 48 hours. (1378)

Exposure of methotrexate 1-mg/ml solution in PVC and polybutadiene tubing to mixed daylight and fluorescent light produced significant losses after eight to 12 hours. Use of the Amberset PVC tubing or of foil wrapping for the polybutadiene tubing to protect static solutions from light reduced losses to 12 to 16% in 48 hours. (1378)

Methotrexate sodium (R. Bellon), reconstituted to a concentration of 1 mg/ml with sodium chloride 0.9%, was evaluated for stability in translucent containers (Perfupack, Baxter) and five opaque containers [green PVC Opafuseur (Bruneau), white EVA Perfu-opaque (Baxter), orange PVC PF170 (Cair), white PVC V86 (Codan), and white EVA Perfecran (Fandre)] when exposed to sunlight for 28 days. Photodegradation was found by HPLC analysis after storage in the translucent Perfupack. Losses ranged from 18.5 to 27% after 24 hours at a methotrexate sodium concentration of 5 mg/ml. At 1 mg/ml, losses of 4% or less occurred in 24 hours in the opaque containers. (1750)

Intrathecal Injections — In a study of solutions for intrathecal injection, the investigational form of preservative-free methotrexate sodium (Ben Venue) was reconstituted to a concentration of 2.5 mg/ml with Elliott's B solution (305 mOsm/kg, pH 7.2), sodium chloride 0.9% injection (303 mOsm/kg, pH 7.6), or Ringer's injection, lactated (270 mOsm/kg, pH 7.6). In all three solutions, methotrexate exhibited no change in concentration by UV spectroscopy over seven days under fluorescent light at 30 °C. (327)

In another study, the stability and compatibility of cytarabine (Upjohn), methotrexate (National Cancer Institute), and hydrocortisone (Upjohn), mixed together in intrathecal injections, were evaluated. Two combinations were tested: (1) cytarabine 50 mg, methotrexate 12 mg (as the sodium salt), and hydrocortisone 25 mg (as the sodium succinate salt); and (2) cytarabine 30 mg, methotrexate 12 mg (as the sodium salt), and hydrocortisone 15 mg (as the sodium succinate salt). Each drug combination was added to 12 ml of Elliott's B solution (National Cancer Institute), sodium chloride 0.9% (Abbott), dextrose 5% in water (Abbott), and Ringer's injection, lactated (Abbott), and stored for 24 hours at 25 °C. Cytarabine and methotrexate were both chemically stable, with no drug loss after the full 24 hours in all solutions. Hydrocortisone was also stable in the sodium chloride 0.9%, dextrose 5% in water, and Ringer's injection, lactated, with about a 2% drug loss. However, in Elliott's B solution, hydrocortisone was significantly less stable, with a 6% loss in the 25-mg concentration over 24 hours. The 15-mg concentration was worse, with a 5% loss in 10 hours and a 13% loss in 24 hours. The higher pH of Elliott's B solution and the lower concentration of hydrocortisone may have been factors in this increased decomposition. All mixtures were physically compatible during this study, but a precipitate formed after several days of storage. (819)

Methotrexate sodium (Lederle) 2 mg/ml diluted in Elliott's B solution (Orphan Medical) was packaged as 20 ml in 30-ml glass vials and 20-ml plastic syringes (Becton-Dickinson) with Red Cap (Burron) Luer-Lok syringe tip caps. The solution was physically compatible with no increase in measured turbidity or particulates and was chemically stable, exhibiting little or no loss by HPLC analysis during storage for 48 hours at 4 and 23 °C. (1976)

Bacterially contaminated intrathecal solutions can pose very grave risks. Consequently, intrathecal solutions should be administered as soon as possible after preparation. (328)

Syringes—Wright and Newton found that methotrexate (Lederle) 50 mg/ml was stable for up to eight months when stored in Monoject (Sherwood) or Plastipak (Becton-Dickinson) plastic syringes at 25 °C. Because of possible alteration in water vapor permeability, use of Sabre (Gillette) and Steriseal (Needle Industries) plastic syringes is limited to 70 days at 25 °C. (1280)

Methotrexate sodium (Lederle) 2.5 mg/ml was repackaged into 10-ml plastic syringes (Becton-Dickinson) and stored at 4 and 25 °C for seven days. No loss of methotrexate was found by HPLC analysis. Furthermore, no contaminants from the syringes were observed. (1913)

Elastomeric Reservoir Pumps—Methotrexate sodium solutions in elastomeric reservoir pumps have been stated by the pump manufacturers to be stable for the following time periods refrigerated (REF) and at room temperature (RT) (31):

Pump Reservoir(s)	Conc.	REF	RT
Homepump; Home pump Eclipse	0.03 mg/ml[a]		7 days
	1.25 to 12.5 mg/ml[b]	105 days	7 days
Infusor	1.25 to 12.5 mg/ml[b]	105 days	10 days

[a]*In dextrose 5% in water.*
[b]*In sodium chloride 0.9%.*

Sorption—Methotrexate sodium 22.5 mg/100 ml and 12 g/500 ml in both dextrose 5% in water and sodium chloride 0.9% in PVC containers (Macroflex, Macopharma) exhibited no loss due to sorption during 30 days of storage at 4 °C protected from light. Simulated infusion of methotrexate sodium 2.25 g/500 ml in dextrose 5% in water and sodium chloride 0.9% over 24 hours through opaque PVC infusion sets (Perfecran, Fandre) also showed no loss of drug due to sorption to the PVC tubing. (1867)

Filtration—Methotrexate sodium (David Bull Laboratories) 50 mg/100 ml in sodium chloride 0.9% in a burette was filtered through a nylon 0.2-μm filter (Pall, ELD96LL). Little or no drug loss due to sorption was found spectrophotometrically. (1568)

Central Venous Catheter—Methotrexate sodium (Immunex) 2.5 mg/ml in dextrose 5% in water was found to be compatible with the ARROWg+ard Blue Plus (Arrow International) chlorhexidine-bearing triple-lumen central catheter. HPLC analysis was used to evaluate completeness of drug delivery through the catheter and the amount of chlorhexidine removed from the internal lumens. Essentially complete delivery of the drug was found with little or no drug loss occurring. Furthermore, chlorhexidine delivered from the catheter remained at trace amounts with no substantial increase due to the delivery of the drug through the catheter. (2335)

Compatibility Information

Solution Compatibility

Methotrexate sodium

Solution	*Mfr*	*Mfr*	*Conc/L*	*Remarks*	*Ref*	*C/I*
Amino acids 4.25%, dextrose 25%	MG	LE	50 mg	No increase in particulate matter in 24 hr at 5 °C	349	C
Dextrose 5% in water	TR[a]	LE	960 mg	Less than 10% decrease in 24 hr at room temperature	519	C
	[b]		225 mg and 24 g	Visually compatible with no loss by HPLC in 30 days at 4 °C protected from light	1867	C
Sodium bicarbonate 0.05 M			2 g	No photodegradation products in 12 hr exposed to room light	433	C
Sodium chloride 0.9%	[a]	FA	1.25 and 12.5 g	Visually compatible with little or no loss by HPLC in 105 days at 4 °C followed by 7 days at 25 °C in the dark	1567	C
	[b]		225 mg and 24 g	Visually compatible with no loss by HPLC in 30 days at 4 °C protected from light	1867	C

[a]*Tested in both glass and PVC containers.*
[b]*Tested in PVC containers.*

Additive Compatibility

Methotrexate sodium

Drug	*Mfr*	*Conc/L*	*Mfr*	*Conc/L*	*Test Soln*	*Remarks*	*Ref*	*C/I*
Bleomycin sulfate	BR	20 and 30 units	LE	250 and 500 mg	NS	About 60% loss of bleomycin activity in 1 week at 4 °C	763	I
Cyclophosphamide		1.67 g		25 mg	NS	6.6% cyclophosphamide loss in 14 days at room temperature	1379; 1389	C

Additive Compatibility (Cont.)

Methotrexate sodium

Drug	*Mfr*	*Conc/L*	*Mfr*	*Conc/L*	*Test Soln*	*Remarks*	*Ref*	*C/I*
Cyclophosphamide with fluorouracil		1.67 g 8.3 g		25 mg	NS	9.3% cyclophosphamide loss in 7 days at room temperature. No loss of other drugs observed	1389	C
Cytarabine	UP	400 mg	LE	200 mg	D5W	Physically compatible. Very little change in UV spectra in 8 hr at room temperature	207	C
Fluorouracil		10 g		30 mg	NS	Both drugs stable for 15 days at room temperature	1379	C
Hydroxyzine HCl	LY	500 mg	BV	1 and 3 g	D5W[a]	Physically compatible for 48 hr	1198	C
Mercaptopurine sodium	BW	1 g	LE	100 mg	D5W	Physically compatible	15	C
Ondansetron HCl	GL	30 and 300 mg	LE	500 mg	D5W[b]	Physically compatible with little or no loss of either drug by HPLC in 48 hr at 23 °C	1876	C
	GL	30 and 300 mg	LE	6 g	D5W[b]	Physically compatible with little or no loss of either drug by HPLC in 48 hr at 23 °C	1876	C
Sodium bicarbonate		50 mEq	LE	750 mg	D5W	1.4% methotrexate decomposition in 72 hr and 6% in 1 week at 5 °C protected from light. At 23 °C exposed to light, 6% methotrexate decomposition in 72 hr and 15% in 1 week	465	C
Vincristine sulfate	LI	10 mg	LE	100 mg	D5W	Physically compatible	15	C
	LI	4 mg	LE	8 mg	D5W	Physically compatible. No change in UV spectra in 8 hr at room temperature	207	C

[a]*Tested in glass containers.*
[b]*Tested in PVC containers.*

Drugs in Syringe Compatibility

Methotrexate sodium

Drug (in syringe)	*Mfr*	*Amt*	*Mfr*	*Amt*	*Remarks*	*Ref*	*C/I*
Bleomycin sulfate		1.5 units/ 0.5 ml		12.5 mg/ 0.5 ml	Physically compatible for 5 min at room temperature followed by 8 min of centrifugation	980	C
Cisplatin		0.5 mg/ 0.5 ml		12.5 mg/ 0.5 ml	Physically compatible for 5 min at room temperature followed by 8 min of centrifugation	980	C
Cyclophosphamide		10 mg/ 0.5 ml		12.5 mg/ 0.5 ml	Physically compatible for 5 min at room temperature followed by 8 min of centrifugation	980	C
Doxapram HCl	RB	400 mg/ 20 ml		50 mg/ 20 ml	Physically compatible with 4% doxapram loss in 24 hr	1177	C
Doxorubicin HCl		1 mg/ 0.5 ml		12.5 mg/ 0.5 ml	Physically compatible for 5 min at room temperature followed by 8 min of centrifugation	980	C
Droperidol		1.25 mg/ 0.5 ml		12.5 mg/ 0.5 ml	Immediate precipitation	980	I
Fluorouracil		25 mg/ 0.5 ml		12.5 mg/ 0.5 ml	Physically compatible for 5 min at room temperature followed by 8 min of centrifugation	980	C
Furosemide		5 mg/ 0.5 ml		12.5 mg/ 0.5 ml	Physically compatible for 5 min at room temperature followed by 8 min of centrifugation	980	C

Drugs in Syringe Compatibility (Cont.)

		Methotrexate sodium					
Drug (in syringe)	*Mfr*	*Amt*	*Mfr*	*Amt*	*Remarks*	*Ref*	*C/I*
Heparin sodium		500 units/ 0.5 ml		12.5 mg/ 0.5 ml	Physically compatible for 5 min at room temperature followed by 8 min of centrifugation	980	C
Leucovorin calcium		5 mg/ 0.5 ml		12.5 mg/ 0.5 ml	Physically compatible for 5 min at room temperature followed by 8 min of centrifugation	980	C
Metoclopramide HCl	RB	10 mg/ 2 ml	LE	50 mg/ 2 ml	Incompatible. If mixed, use immediately	924	I
		2.5 mg/ 0.5 ml		12.5 mg/ 0.5 ml	Physically compatible for 5 min at room temperature followed by 8 min of centrifugation	980	C
	RB	10 mg/ 2 ml	LE	50 mg/ 2 ml	Incompatible. If mixed, use immediately	1167	I
	RB	160 mg/ 32 ml	LE	200 mg/ 8 ml	Incompatible. If mixed, use immediately	1167	I
Mitomycin		0.25 mg/ 0.5 ml		12.5 mg/ 0.5 ml	Physically compatible for 5 min at room temperature followed by 8 min of centrifugation	980	C
Vinblastine sulfate		0.5 mg/ 0.5 ml		12.5 mg/ 0.5 ml	Physically compatible for 5 min at room temperature followed by 8 min of centrifugation	980	C
Vincristine sulfate		0.5 mg/ 0.5 ml		12.5 mg/ 0.5 ml	Physically compatible for 5 min at room temperature followed by 8 min of centrifugation	980	C

Y-Site Injection Compatibility (1:1 Mixture)

			Methotrexate sodium				
Drug	*Mfr*	*Conc*	*Mfr*	*Conc*	*Remarks*	*Ref*	*C/I*
Allopurinol sodium	BW	3 mg/ml[b]	LE	15 mg/ml[b]	Physically compatible with no change in measured turbidity or increase in particle content in 4 hr at 22 °C	1686	C
Amifostine	USB	10 mg/ml[a]	LE	15 mg/ml[a]	Physically compatible with no change in measured turbidity or increase in particle content in 4 hr at 23 °C	1845	C
Amphotericin B cholesteryl sulfate complex	SEQ	0.83 mg/ml[a]	IMM	15 mg/ml[a]	Physically compatible with little or no change in measured turbidity or increase in particle content in 4 hr at 23 °C under fluorescent light	2117	C
Asparaginase	BEL	120 I.U./ml[a]		30 mg/ml	Visually compatible for 4 hr at room temperature	1788	C
Aztreonam	SQ	40 mg/ml[a]	LE	15 mg/ml[a]	Physically compatible with no subvisual haze or particle formation in 4 hr at 23 °C	1758	C
Bleomycin sulfate		3 units/ml		25 mg/ml	Drugs injected sequentially into Y-site with no flush between. No visually apparent precipitate	980	C
Cefepime HCl	BMS	20 mg/ml[a]	LE	15 mg/ml[a]	Physically compatible with no change in measured turbidity or increase in particle content in 4 hr at 22 °C	1689	C
Ceftriaxone sodium	RC	100 mg/ml		30 mg/ml	Visually compatible for 4 hr at room temperature	1788	C

Y-Site Injection Compatibility (1:1 Mixture) (Cont.)

Methotrexate sodium

Drug	*Mfr*	*Conc*	*Mfr*	*Conc*	*Remarks*	*Ref*	*C/I*
Chlorpromazine HCl	SKF	2 mg/ml[a]	AD	15 mg/ml[c]	Turbidity and yellow precipitate form immediately	1685	I
Cimetidine HCl	SKF	12 mg/ml[a]	AD	15 mg/ml[c]	Visually compatible for 4 hr at room temperature under fluorescent light	1685	C
Cisplatin		1 mg/ml		25 mg/ml	Drugs injected sequentially into Y-site with no flush between. No visually apparent precipitate	980	C
Cyclophosphamide		20 mg/ml		25 mg/ml	Drugs injected sequentially into Y-site with no flush between. No visually apparent precipitate	980	C
		20 mg/ml[a]		30 mg/ml	Visually compatible for 4 hr at room temperature	1788	C
Cytarabine	UP	0.6 mg/ml[a]		30 mg/ml	Visually compatible for 4 hr at room temperature	1788	C
Daunorubicin HCl	BEL	0.52 mg/ml[a]		30 mg/ml	Visually compatible for 4 hr at room temperature	1788	C
Dexamethasone sodium phosphate	QU	1 mg/ml[a]	AD	15 mg/ml[c]	Visually compatible for 4 hr at room temperature under fluorescent light	1685	C
	MSD	4 mg/ml		30 mg/ml	Visually compatible for 2 hr at room temperature. Dark yellow precipitate forms in 4 hr	1788	I
Dexchlorpheniramine maleate		5 mg/ml		30 mg/ml	Visually compatible for 4 hr at room temperature	1788	C
Diphenhydramine HCl	PD	2 mg/ml[a]	AD	15 mg/ml[c]	Visually compatible for 4 hr at room temperature under fluorescent light	1685	C
Doxorubicin HCl		2 mg/ml		25 mg/ml	Drugs injected sequentially into Y-site with no flush between. No visually apparent precipitate	980	C
	FA	0.4 mg/ml[a]		30 mg/ml	Visually compatible for 4 hr at room temperature	1788	C
Doxorubicin HCl liposome injection	SEQ	0.4 mg/ml[a]	IMM	15 mg/ml[a]	Physically compatible with little or no change in measured turbidity and no increase in particle content in 4 hr at 23 °C	2087	C
Droperidol		2.5 mg/ml		25 mg/ml	Precipitate forms	977	I
		2.5 mg/ml		25 mg/ml	Drugs injected sequentially into Y-site with no flush between. Immediate precipitation	980	I
	JA	20 μg/ml[a]	AD	15 mg/ml[c]	Visually compatible for 4 hr at room temperature under fluorescent light	1685	C
Etoposide	BR	0.6 mg/ml[b]		30 mg/ml	Visually compatible for 4 hr at room temperature	1788	C
Etoposide phosphate	BR	5 mg/ml[a]	IMM	15 mg/ml[a]	Physically compatible with no change in measured turbidity or increase in particle content in 4 hr at 23 °C	2218	C
Famotidine	MSD	2 mg/ml[a]	AD	15 mg/ml[c]	Visually compatible for 4 hr at room temperature under fluorescent light	1685	C
Filgrastim	AMG	30 μg/ml[a]	LE	15 mg/ml[a]	Physically compatible with no change in measured turbidity or increase in particle content in 4 hr at 22 °C	1687	C

Y-Site Injection Compatibility (1:1 Mixture) (Cont.)

			Methotrexate sodium				
Drug	*Mfr*	*Conc*	*Mfr*	*Conc*	*Remarks*	*Ref*	*C/I*
Fludarabine phosphate	BX	1 mg/ml[a]	CET	15 mg/ml[a]	Physically compatible for 4 hr at room temperature under fluorescent light	1439	C
Fluorouracil		50 mg/ml		25 mg/ml	Drugs injected sequentially into Y-site with no flush between. No visually apparent precipitate	980	C
Furosemide		10 mg/ml		25 mg/ml	Drugs injected sequentially into Y-site with no flush between. No visually apparent precipitate	980	C
	ES	3 mg/ml[a]	AD	15 mg/ml[c]	Visually compatible for 4 hr at room temperature under fluorescent light	1685	C
Ganciclovir sodium	SY	20 mg/ml[a]	AD	15 mg/ml[c]	Visually compatible for 4 hr at room temperature under fluorescent light	1685	C
Gatifloxacin	BMS	2 mg/ml[a]	BV	15 mg/ml[a]	Physically compatible with no change in measured haze or increase in particle content in 4 hr at 23 °C	2234	C
Gemcitabine HCl	LI	10 mg/ml[b]	IMM	15 mg/ml[b]	Gross precipitate forms immediately, redissolves, but reprecipitates within 15 to 20 min	2226	I
Granisetron HCl	SKB	1 mg/ml	CET	12.5 mg/ml[b]	Physically compatible with little or no loss of either drug by HPLC in 4 hr at 22 °C	1883	C
Heparin[d]	CH	500 units/ml[b]		30 mg/ml	Visually compatible for 4 hr at room temperature	1788	C
Heparin sodium		1000 units/ml		25 mg/ml	Drugs injected sequentially into Y-site with no flush between. No visually apparent precipitate	980	C
	SO	40 units/ml[a]	AD	15 mg/ml[c]	Visually compatible for 4 hr at room temperature under fluorescent light	1685	C
Hydromorphone HCl	ES	0.04 mg/ml[a]	AD	15 mg/ml[c]	Visually compatible for 4 hr at room temperature under fluorescent light	1685	C
Idarubicin HCl	AD	1 mg/ml[b]	LE	25 mg/ml	Color changes immediately	1525	I
Ifosfamide		36 mg/ml[a]		30 mg/ml	Visually compatible for 2 hr at room temperature. Dark yellow precipitate forms in 4 hr	1788	I
Imipenem–cilastatin sodium	MSD	5 mg/ml		30 mg/ml	Visually compatible for 4 hr at room temperature	1788	C
Leucovorin calcium		10 mg/ml		25 mg/ml	Drugs injected sequentially into Y-site with no flush between. No visually apparent precipitate	980	C
	LE	10 mg/ml		30 mg/ml	Visually compatible for 4 hr at room temperature	1788	C
Linezolid	PHU	2 mg/ml	IMM	15 mg/ml[a]	Physically compatible with no change in measured turbidity or increase in particle content in 4 hr at 23 °C	2264	C
Lorazepam	WY	0.1 mg/ml[a]	AD	15 mg/ml[c]	Visually compatible for 4 hr at room temperature under fluorescent light	1685	C
Melphalan HCl	BW	0.1 mg/ml[b]	LE	15 mg/ml[b]	Physically compatible with no change in measured turbidity or increase in particle content in 3 hr at 22 °C	1557	C

Y-Site Injection Compatibility (1:1 Mixture) (Cont.)

Drug	Mfr	Conc	Mfr	Conc	Remarks	Ref	C/I
			Methotrexate sodium				
Mesna		1.8 mg/ml[a]		30 mg/ml	Visually compatible for 4 hr at room temperature	1788	C
Methylprednisolone sodium succinate	UP	0.5 mg/ml[a]	AD	15 mg/ml[c]	Visually compatible for 4 hr at room temperature under fluorescent light	1685	C
Metoclopramide HCl		5 mg/ml		25 mg/ml	Drugs injected sequentially into Y-site with no flush between. No visually apparent precipitate	980	C
	RB	2.5 mg/ml[a]	AD	15 mg/ml[c]	Visually compatible for 4 hr at room temperature under fluorescent light	1685	C
Midazolam HCl	RC	5 mg/ml		30 mg/ml	Yellow precipitate forms immediately	1788	I
Mitomycin		0.5 mg/ml		25 mg/ml	Drugs injected sequentially into Y-site with no flush between. No visually apparent precipitate	980	C
Morphine sulfate	ES	0.12 mg/ml[a]	AD	15 mg/ml[c]	Visually compatible for 4 hr at room temperature under fluorescent light	1685	C
Nalbuphine HCl	DU	10 mg/ml		30 mg/ml	Heavy yellow precipitate forms immediately	1788	I
Ondansetron HCl	GL	1 mg/ml[b]	CET	15 mg/ml[a]	Physically compatible for 4 hr at 22 °C	1365	C
	GL	2 mg/ml		30 mg/ml	Visually compatible for 4 hr at room temperature	1788	C
Oxacillin sodium	BR	250 mg/ml		30 mg/ml	Visually compatible for 4 hr at room temperature	1788	C
Paclitaxel	NCI	1.2 mg/ml[a]		15 mg/ml[a]	Physically compatible with no change in measured turbidity in 4 hr at 22 °C	1528	C
Piperacillin sodium–tazobactam sodium	LE	40 + 5 mg/ml[a]	LE	15 mg/ml[a]	Physically compatible with no change in measured turbidity or increase in particle content in 4 hr at 22 °C	1688	C
Prochlorperazine edisylate	SKF	0.5 mg/ml[a]	AD	15 mg/ml[c]	Visually compatible for 4 hr at room temperature under fluorescent light	1685	C
Promethazine HCl	WY	2 mg/ml[a]	AD	15 mg/ml[c]	Turbidity forms in 30 min	1685	I
Propofol	ZEN	10 mg/ml	LE	15 mg/ml[a]	Small amount of white precipitate forms in 1 hr	2066	I
Ranitidine HCl	GL	1 mg/ml[a]	AD	15 mg/ml[c]	Visually compatible for 4 hr at room temperature under fluorescent light	1685	C
Sargramostim	IMM	10 µg/ml[b]	CET	15 mg/ml[b]	Physically compatible for 4 hr at 22 °C	1436	C
Teniposide	BR	0.1 mg/ml[a]	LE	15 mg/ml[a]	Physically compatible with no subvisual haze or particle formation in 4 hr at 23 °C	1725	C
Thiotepa	IMM[e]	1 mg/ml[a]	LE	15 mg/ml[a]	Physically compatible with no change in measured turbidity or increase in particle content in 4 hr at 23 °C	1861	C
TNA #218 to #226[h]			IMM	15 mg/ml[a]	Visually compatible with no precipitate or emulsion damage apparent in 4 hr at 23 °C	2215	C
TPN #212 to #215[h]			LE	15 mg/ml[a]	Substantial loss of natural subvisual turbidity with a hazy subvisual precipitate in 0 to 1 hr	2109	I

Y-Site Injection Compatibility (1:1 Mixture) (Cont.)

			Methotrexate sodium				
Drug	*Mfr*	*Conc*	*Mfr*	*Conc*	*Remarks*	*Ref*	*C/I*
Vancomycin HCl	AB	510 mg[f]	LE	[g]	Physically compatible during 1-hr simultaneous infusion	1405	C
		5 mg/ml[a]		30 mg/ml	Visually compatible for 2 hr at room temperature. Dark yellow precipitate forms in 4 hr	1788	I
Vinblastine sulfate		1 mg/ml		25 mg/ml	Drugs injected sequentially into Y-site with no flush between. No visually apparent precipitate	980	C
Vincristine sulfate		1 mg/ml		25 mg/ml	Drugs injected sequentially into Y-site with no flush between. No visually apparent precipitate	980	C
	LI	0.1 mg/ml		30 mg/ml	Visually compatible for 4 hr at room temperature	1788	C
Vindesine sulfate	LI	0.1 mg/ml		30 mg/ml	Visually compatible for 4 hr at room temperature	1788	C
Vinorelbine tartrate	BW	1 mg/ml[b]	LE	15 mg/ml[b]	Physically compatible with no change in measured turbidity or increase in particle content in 4 hr at 22 °C	1558	C

[a]*Tested in dextrose 5% in water.*
[b]*Tested in sodium chloride 0.9%.*
[c]*Tested in dextrose 5% in water with sodium bicarbonate 0.05 mEq/ml.*
[d]*Salt form unspecified.*
[e]*Lyophilized formulation tested.*
[f]*Infused over one hour simultaneously with methotrexate.*
[g]*Diluted in dextrose 5% in water; concentration not cited.*
[h]*Refer to Appendix I for the composition of parenteral nutrition solutions. TNA indicates a 3-in-1 admixture, and TPN indicates a 2-in-1 admixture.*

Additional Compatibility Information

Infusion Solutions — Methotrexate sodium is stated to be stable in dextrose 5% in water, sodium chloride 0.9%, or dextrose 5% in sodium chloride 0.9% for at least one week at room temperature. (234)

Methotrexate sodium 0.03 mg/ml in dextrose 5% in water exhibited less than a 10% loss in seven days at room temperature when protected from light. (1379)

Dacarbazine — No alteration in the ultraviolet/visible spectra was observed when dacarbazine was combined in solution with methotrexate sodium. (492)

Fluorouracil — The reported incompatibility of fluorouracil (Roche) 250 mg/L with methotrexate sodium (Lederle) 200 mg/L in dextrose 5% in water (207) has been questioned on the grounds that the observed alteration in UV spectra for both drugs might be an artifact of the experiment, merely being a result of methotrexate's altered UV spectra at varying pH values. It was observed that the altered methotrexate spectrum could contribute to an altered spectrum for fluorouracil. (318)

In reply, King noted that the pH of fluorouracil, rather than the drug itself, might be responsible for changes in methotrexate's UV spectrum. However, using a buffered aqueous solution to simulate the admixture with a pH of approximately 8 and decreasing the pH with 0.2 M HCl back to the range of methotrexate sodium in dextrose 5% in water (pH 6.5) failed to return the UV spectrum to that of the pH 6.5 solution; in fact, the UV spectrum was not significantly different than the pH 8 scan. King concluded that irreversible changes were occurring, which make the compatibility of the admixture suspect. (319)

However, it should be noted that the commercial methotrexate sodium (Lederle) used in the studies is formulated in solution at a pH of approximately 8.5, not significantly different than that of the admixture suspected of incompatibility, and yet is stable until expiration, a period of at least two years. (4)

Aluminum — Ogawa et al. reported that immersion of a needle with an aluminum component in methotrexate sodium (Lederle) 25 mg/ml resulted in the formation of orange crystals on the aluminum surface after 36 hours at 24 °C with protection from light. (988)

METHYLDOPATE HCL
AHFS 24:08

Products — Methyldopate HCl is available in 5- and 10-ml vials. Each milliliter of solution contains (2):

Methyldopate HCl	50 mg
Citric acid, anhydrous	5 mg
Sodium bisulfite	3.2 mg
Monothioglycerol	2 mg
Methylparaben	1.5 mg
Disodium edetate	0.5 mg
Propylparaben	0.2 mg
Sodium hydroxide	to adjust pH
Water for injection	qs 1 ml

pH — From 3 to 4.2. (4)

Osmolality — Methyldopate HCl 50 mg/ml has an osmolality of 481 mOsm/kg. (1689)

Trade Name(s) — Aldomet Ester Hydrochloride.

Administration — Methyldopate HCl is administered by intravenous infusion. Intramuscular and subcutaneous injections are not recommended due to erratic absorption. It is recommended that the desired dose be added to 100 ml of dextrose 5% in water. Alternatively, the dose may be administered at a concentration of 100 mg/10 ml in dextrose 5% in water. The dose should be infused slowly over 30 to 60 minutes. (2; 4)

Stability — Intact vials should be stored at controlled room temperature and protected from freezing. (2; 4) In aqueous solutions, the drug is most stable at acid to neutral pH. Oxidation of the catechol ring is the most important degradation process. The rate of such oxidation increases with increasing oxygen supply, increasing pH, and decreasing drug concentration. (1072) Oxidizing agents decompose the drug (4); such oxidation is facilitated in alkaline solutions, yielding inactive dark-colored compounds. (436) In dextrose 5% in water over a pH range of 3.5 to 7.8, no loss of potency occurred over 24 hours. (23) However, at pH 7.8, more than a 5% potency loss occurred after the 24-hour study period. (437)

Compatibility Information

Solution Compatibility

Methyldopate HCl

Solution	*Mfr*	*Mfr*	*Conc/L*	*Remarks*	*Ref*	*C/I*
Amino acids 4.25%, dextrose 25%	MG	MSD	500 mg	No increase in particulate matter in 24 hr at 5 °C	349	C
Dextran 6% in sodium chloride 0.9%	AB	MSD	1 g	Potency retained for 24 hr	23	C
Dextrose 5% in sodium chloride 0.9%	AB	MSD	1 g	Potency retained for 24 hr	23	C
Dextrose 5% in water	AB	MSD	1 g	Potency retained for 24 hr	23	C
	AB	MSD	1 g	Physically compatible and chemically stable. 10% decomposition is calculated to occur in 125 hr at 25 °C	527	C
Normosol M in dextrose 5% in water	AB	MSD	1 g	Potency retained for 24 hr	23	C
Normosol R	AB	MSD	1 g	Potency retained for 24 hr	23	C
Ringer's injection	AB	MSD	1 g	Potency retained for 24 hr	23	C
Sodium bicarbonate 5%	AB	MSD	1 g	Potency retained for 24 hr	23	C
Sodium chloride 0.9%	AB	MSD	1 g	Potency retained for 24 hr	23	C

Additive Compatibility

Methyldopate HCl

Drug	*Mfr*	*Conc/L*	*Mfr*	*Conc/L*	*Test Soln*	*Remarks*	*Ref*	*C/I*
Aminophylline	SE	500 mg	MSD	1 g	D, D–S, S	Physically compatible	23	C
	SE	500 mg	MSD	1 g	D5W	Physically compatible. 10% methyldopate decomposition in 90 hr at 25 °C	527	C
Amphotericin B		200 mg		1 g	D5W	Haze develops over 3 hr	26	I
Ascorbic acid injection	AB	1 g	MSD	1 g	D, D–S, S	Physically compatible	23	C
Chloramphenicol sodium succinate	PD	1 g	MSD	1 g	D, D–S, S	Physically compatible	23	C
Diphenhydramine HCl	PD	50 mg	MSD	1 g	D, D–S, S	Physically compatible	23	C

Additive Compatibility (Cont.)

Methyldopate HCl

Drug	*Mfr*	*Conc/L*	*Mfr*	*Conc/L*	*Test Soln*	*Remarks*	*Ref*	*C/I*
Heparin sodium	AB	20,000 units	MSD	1 g	D, D–S, S	Physically compatible	23	C
Magnesium sulfate		1 g	MSD	1 g	D, D–S, S	Physically compatible	23	C
Methohexital sodium	BP	2 g		1 g	D5W	Haze develops over 3 hr	26	I
	BP	2 g		1 g	NS	Crystals produced	26	I
Multivitamins	USV	10 ml	MSD	1 g	D, D–S, S	Physically compatible	23	C
Netilmicin sulfate	SC	3 g	MSD	1 g	D5S	Physically compatible and netilmicin chemically stable for 7 days at 4 and 25 °C. Methyldopate not tested	558	C
Potassium chloride		40 mEq	MSD	1 g	D, D–S, S	Physically compatible	23	C
Promazine HCl	WY	100 mg	MSD	1 g	D, D–S, S	Physically compatible	23	C
Sodium bicarbonate		50 mEq	MSD	1 g	D, D–S, S	Physically compatible	23	C
Succinylcholine chloride	AB	2 g	MSD	1 g	D, D–S, S	Physically compatible	23	C
Verapamil HCl	KN	80 mg	MSD	500 mg	D5W, NS	Physically compatible for 24 hr	764	C
Vitamin B complex with C	AB	10 ml	MSD	1 g	D, D–S, S	Physically compatible	23	C
	UP	10 ml	MSD	1 g	D, D–S, S	Physically compatible	23	C

Y-Site Injection Compatibility (1:1 Mixture)

Methyldopate HCl

Drug	*Mfr*	*Conc*	*Mfr*	*Conc*	*Remarks*	*Ref*	*C/I*
Esmolol HCl	DCC	10 mg/ml[a]	MSD	5 mg/ml[a]	Physically compatible for 24 hr at 22 °C under fluorescent light	1169	C
Heparin sodium	TR	50 units/ml	ES	5 mg/ml[a]	Visually compatible for 4 hr at 25 °C	1793	C
Meperidine HCl	AB	10 mg/ml	AMR	2.5 mg/ml[a]	Physically compatible for 4 hr at 25 °C under fluorescent light	1397	C
Morphine sulfate	AB	1 mg/ml	AMR	2.5 mg/ml[a]	Physically compatible for 4 hr at 25 °C under fluorescent light	1397	C
Theophylline	TR	4 mg/ml	ES	5 mg/ml[a]	Visually compatible for 6 hr at 25 °C	1793	C
TNA #73[c]			MSD	250 mg/ 50 ml[a]	Cracked the lipid emulsion	1009	I
			MSD	250 mg/ 50 ml[b]	Physically compatible for 4 hr by visual observation	1009	C

[a] *Tested in dextrose 5% in water.*
[b] *Tested in sodium chloride 0.9%.*
[c] *Refer to Appendix I for the composition of parenteral nutrition solutions. TNA indicates a 3-in-1 admixture.*

Additional Compatibility Information

Infusion Solutions — Dextrose 5% in water has been recommended as the diluent for infusion. (2) Methyldopate HCl (MSD) 1 g/L is, however, physically compatible with all Abbott infusion solutions. (23) The drug is stable in most intravenous fluids at pH 3.5 to 6 for 24 hours. (4)

Acid-Labile Drugs — The pH of infusion solutions containing methyldopate HCl tends to be 7 or less, even when alkaline intravenous infusion solutions are used. (4) It has been suggested that drugs poorly soluble in acidic media, such as barbiturate salts and sulfonamides, be mixed cautiously with methyldopate HCl since its acidity imparts some buffer capacity to intravenous admixtures. Furthermore, it should not be used with drugs known to be acid labile. (23)

Metal Ions — Oxidative degradation of methyldopate HCl is catalyzed by manganese, copper, cobalt, nickel, and iron. (436; 437; 1072)

METHYLERGONOVINE MALEATE
AHFS 76:00

Products — Methylergonovine maleate is available in 1-ml ampuls. Each milliliter of solution contains (1-3/99):

Methylergonovine maleate	0.2 mg
Tartaric acid	0.25 mg
Sodium chloride	3 mg
Water for injection	qs 1 ml

pH — From 2.7 to 3.5. (4)

Trade Name(s) — Methergine.

Administration — Methylergonovine maleate may be administered intramuscularly or, in severe or life-threatening situations, intravenously slowly over no less than one minute. (1-3/99; 4) Dilution of the dose to 5 ml with sodium chloride 0.9% has also been recommended for intravenous injection. (4)

Stability — Methylergonovine maleate injection is a clear, colorless solution. If the product becomes discolored, it should not be used. (1-3/99; 4) The drug darkens with age and exposure to light. (4) The manufacturer recommends storage of intact ampuls below 25 °C and protection from light. (1-3/99)

Compatibility Information

Y-Site Injection Compatibility (1:1 Mixture)

Drug	*Mfr*	*Conc*	Methylergonovine maleate *Mfr*	*Conc*	*Remarks*	*Ref*	*C/I*
Heparin sodium	UP	1000 units/L[a]	SZ	0.2 mg/ml	Physically compatible for at least 4 hr at room temperature by visual and microscopic examination	534	C
Hydrocortisone sodium succinate	UP	10 mg/L[a]	SZ	0.2 mg/ml	Physically compatible for at least 4 hr at room temperature by visual and microscopic examination	534	C
Potassium chloride	AB	40 mEq/L[a]	SZ	0.2 mg/ml	Physically compatible for at least 4 hr at room temperature by visual and microscopic examination	534	C
Vitamin B complex with C	RC	2 ml/L[a]	SZ	0.2 mg/ml	Physically compatible for at least 4 hr at room temperature by visual and microscopic examination	534	C

[a]*Tested in dextrose 5% in Ringer's injection, dextrose 5% in Ringer's injection, lactated, dextrose 5% in water, Ringer's injection, lactated, and sodium chloride 0.9%.*

Additional Compatibility Information

Infusion Solutions — Sodium chloride 0.9% has been recommended as a diluent for methylergonovine maleate. (4)

METHYLPREDNISOLONE SODIUM SUCCINATE
AHFS 68:04

Products — Methylprednisolone sodium succinate is available in 40-mg (1 ml), 125-mg (2 ml), 500-mg (4 ml), and 1-g (8 ml) dual-chamber containers and 500-mg (8 ml), 1-g (16 ml), and 2-g (30.6 ml) vials with and without diluent. (2) Use only the special diluent or bacteriostatic water for injection with benzyl alcohol to reconstitute the vials. When reconstituted as directed, each milliliter of solution contains (2):

Component	40 mg	125 mg, 500 mg, 1 g (16 ml)	1 g (8 ml)	2 g
Methylprednisolone equivalent (as sodium succinate)	40 mg	62.5 mg	125 mg	65.3 mg
Monobasic sodium phosphate anhydrous	1.6 mg	0.8 mg	1.6 mg	0.8 mg
Dibasic sodium phosphate dried	17.46 mg	8.7 mg	17.4 mg	9.1 mg
Benzyl alcohol	8.8 mg	8.8 mg	8.4 mg	8.9 mg
Lactose hydrous	25 mg			

pH—The pH is adjusted to 7 to 8 with sodium hydroxide when necessary. (2; 4)

Osmolarity—The osmolarities of the 40-, 62.5-, 125-, and 65.3-mg/ml concentrations are 500, 400, 440, and 420 mOsm/L, respectively. (2)

The osmolality of methylprednisolone sodium succinate was calculated for the following dilutions (1054):

Diluent	Osmolality (mOsm/kg) 50 ml	100 ml
500 mg		
Dextrose 5% in water	291	275
Sodium chloride 0.9%	317	301
1 g		
Dextrose 5% in water	318	292
Sodium chloride 0.9%	345	319

Sodium Content—Each gram of methylprednisolone sodium succinate contains 2.01 mEq of sodium. (846)

Trade Name(s)—A-MethaPred, Solu-Medrol.

Administration — Methylprednisolone sodium succinate may be administered by intramuscular and direct intravenous injection and by intermittent or continuous intravenous infusion. (2; 4) Direct intravenous injection should be performed over at least one minute (4) or over several minutes. (2) High-dose therapy is given intravenously over at least 30 minutes. (2)

Stability — Intact vials should be stored at controlled room temperature between 20 and 25 °C and protected from light. Reconstituted solutions also should be stored between 20 and 25 °C and should used within 48 hours. (2)

The drug is subject to both ester hydrolysis and acyl migration. Degradation products include free methylprednisolone, succinate, and methylprednisolone-17-succinate. (1072) The solution should not be used unless it is clear and free of particulate matter. (4)

Methylprednisolone sodium succinate (Upjohn) diluted to a concentration of 4 mg/ml with sterile water for injection and packaged in glass vials was evaluated for stability by HPLC analysis. The samples stored at 22 °C lost 10% in 24 hours while those stored at 4 °C lost 6% in seven days and 17% in 14 days. (1938)

pH Effects—The minimum rate of hydrolysis occurs at pH 3.5. Between pH 3.4 and 7.4, acyl migration is the dominant effect. (1501)

Freezing Solutions—Reconstituted methylprednisolone sodium succinate (Upjohn) 125 mg/2 ml, when stored frozen, exhibited no loss of potency over four weeks. (69)

When stored frozen at −20 °C, methylprednisolone sodium succinate (Upjohn) 500 mg/108 ml in sodium chloride 0.9% in PVC bags exhibited no loss by HPLC assay after 12 months followed by microwave thawing. Furthermore, the solution was physically compatible, with no increase in subvisual particles. (1612)

Syringes—Methylprednisolone sodium succinate (Pharmacia & Upjohn) 10 mg/ml in sodium chloride 0.9% was packaged in 10-ml polypropylene syringes (Becton-Dickinson) and 12-ml polypropylene syringes (Monoject) and stored at 5 and 25 °C. The drug solutions remained clear, and HPLC analysis found about 10% loss in seven days at 25 °C and about 4% loss in 21 days at 5 °C. The losses were comparable to the drug solution stored in a glass flask, indicating sorption to syringe components did not occur. (2340)

Elastomeric Reservoir Pumps—Methylprednisolone sodium succinate 10 mg/ml in sodium chloride 0.9% in Homepump and Homepump Eclipse elastomeric reservoir pumps has been stated by the pump manufacturer to be stable for 24 hours at room temperature and seven days under refrigeration. (31)

Sorption—Methylprednisolone sodium succinate (Hoechst) 0.125 mg/ml in dextrose 5% in water and sodium chloride 0.9% packaged in PVC, polyethylene, and glass containers exhibited no loss due to sorption to any of the container types when stored at 4 and 22 °C for 24 hours protected from light. (2289)

Central Venous Catheter—Methylprednisolone sodium succinate (Abbott) 5 mg/ml in dextrose 5% in water was found to be compatible with the ARROWg+ard Blue Plus (Arrow International) chlorhexidine-bearing triple-lumen central catheter. HPLC analysis was used to evaluate completeness of drug delivery through the catheter and the amount of chlorhexidine removed from the internal lumens. Essentially complete delivery of the drug was found with little or no drug loss occurring. Furthermore, chlorhexidine delivered from the catheter remained at trace amounts with no substantial increase due to the delivery of the drug through the catheter. (2335)

Compatibility Information

Solution Compatibility

Methylprednisolone sodium succinate

Solution	*Mfr*	*Mfr*	*Conc/L*	*Remarks*	*Ref*	*C/I*
Amino acids 4.25%, dextrose 25%	MG	UP	250 mg	No increase in particulate matter in 24 hr at 5 °C	349	C

Solution Compatibility (Cont.)

Methylprednisolone sodium succinate

Solution	*Mfr*	*Mfr*	*Conc/L*	*Remarks*	*Ref*	*C/I*
Dextrose 5% in sodium chloride 0.45%		UP	5 to 10 g	Physically compatible for at least 4 hr	329	C
Dextrose 5% in sodium chloride 0.9%		UP	80 mg	Physically compatible for 24 hr	329	C
Dextrose 5% in water	AB	AB	500 mg to 1 g	Physically compatible and chemically stable for 24 hr at 25 °C	758	C
	AB	AB	1.25 g	Physically compatible for 12 hr at 25 °C. Turbidity due to free methylprednisolone may develop after 12 hr	758	I
	AB	AB	2 to 20 g	Physically compatible for 8 hr at 25 °C. Turbidity due to free methylprednisolone may develop after 8 hr	758	I
	AB	AB	30 g	Physically compatible and chemically stable for 24 hr at 25 °C	758	C
	TR[a]	UP	400 mg and 1.25 g	Physically compatible with 6 to 8% methylprednisolone 21-succinate ester loss in 24 hr at 24 °C	1418	C
	TR[a]	UP	40 mg and 2 g	Visually compatible with 4% or less loss by HPLC in 48 hr at room temperature	1802	C
	BA[a], BRN[b]	HO	125 mg	Visually compatible with little or no loss by HPLC in 24 hr at 4 and 22 °C	2289	C
Ringer's injection, lactated		UP	80 mg	Physically compatible for 24 hr	329	C
		UP	500 mg to 10 g	Physically incompatible	329	I
Sodium chloride 0.9%	AB	AB	500 mg to 30 g	Physically compatible and chemically stable for 24 hr at 25 °C	758	C
	TR[a]	UP	40 mg	Visually compatible with 6% loss by HPLC in 48 hr at room temperature	1802	C
	TR[a]	UP	2 g	Visually compatible with 9% loss by HPLC in 24 hr and 12% loss in 48 hr at room temperature	1802	C
	BA[a], BRN[b]	HO	125 mg	Visually compatible with little or no loss by HPLC in 24 hr at 4 and 22 °C	2289	C
TNA #237[c]		PHU	25, 63, 125 mg	Physically compatible with no substantial change in lipid particle size. Variable assay results, but less than 10% change in drug concentration by HPLC and less than 8% change in TNA components by colorimetry after 7 days at 4 °C followed by 24 hr at ambient temperature and light	2347	C
TPN #236[c]		PHU	25, 63, 125 mg	Variable assay results, but less than 10% change in drug concentration by HPLC and less than 12% change in TPN components by colorimetry after 7 days at 4 °C followed by 24 hr at ambient temperature and light	2347	C

[a] *Tested in PVC containers.*
[b] *Tested in polyethylene and glass containers.*
[c] *Refer to Appendix I for the composition of parenteral nutrition solutions. TNA indicates a 3-in-1 admixture, and TPN indicates a 2-in-1 admixture.*

Additive Compatibility

Methylprednisolone sodium succinate

Drug	*Mfr*	*Conc/L*	*Mfr*	*Conc/L*	*Test Soln*	*Remarks*	*Ref*	*C/I*
Aminophylline		500 mg	UP	40 to 250 mg	D5W, NS	Clear solution for 24 hr	329	C
		1 g	UP	80 mg	D5W	Clear solution for 24 hr	329	C
	SE	500 mg	UP	125 mg		Precipitate forms after 6 hr but within 24 hr	6	I
		1 g	UP	250 mg to 1 g	D5W	Precipitate forms	329	I
	SE	1 g	UP	500 mg and 2 g	D5W	Physically compatible with no aminophylline or methylprednisolone alcohol loss in 3 hr at room temperature. 7 to 10% ester hydrolysis termed not clinically important	1022	C
	SE	1 g	UP	500 mg and 2 g	NS	Physically compatible with no aminophylline or methylprednisolone alcohol loss in 3 hr at room temperature. 12 to 18% ester hydrolysis termed not clinically important	1022	C
Calcium gluconate		1 g	UP	40 mg	D5S	Physically incompatible	329	I
Chloramphenicol sodium succinate	PD	1 g	UP	40 mg	D5W	Clear solution for 20 hr	329	C
	PD	2 g	UP	80 mg	D5W	Clear solution for 20 hr	329	C
Cimetidine HCl	SKF	3 g	UP	400 mg	D5W	Physically compatible and cimetidine chemically stable for 24 hr at room temperature. Methylprednisolone not tested	551	C
	SKF	3 g	UP	400 mg	D5W[a]	Physically compatible with no cimetidine loss and 3% methylprednisolone 21-succinate ester loss in 24 hr at 24 °C	1418	C
	SKF	3 g	UP	1.25 g	D5W[a]	Physically compatible with no cimetidine loss and 8% methylprednisolone 21-succinate ester loss in 24 hr at 24 °C	1418	C
Clindamycin phosphate	UP	1.2 g	UP	500 mg	D5W, W	Clindamycin stable for 24 hr	101	C
Cytarabine	UP	360 mg	UP	250 mg	D5S, D10S, NS	Clear solution for 24 hr	329	C
	UP	360 mg	UP	250 mg	R, SL	Physically incompatible	329	I
Dopamine HCl	AS	800 mg	UP	500 mg	D5W	Clear solution for 24 hr	329	C
	AS	800 mg	UP	500 mg	D5W	No dopamine decomposition in 18 hr at 25 °C	312	C
Glycopyrrolate	RB	1.33 mg	UP	250 mg	D5½S	Physically incompatible	329	I
Granisetron HCl	BE	56 mg	DAK	2.26 g	D5W, NS[a]	Visually compatible with little or no loss of either drug by HPLC in 72 hr at room temperature	1884	C
Heparin sodium		5000 units	UP	125 mg	D5S, D5W, R, LR	Clear solution for 24 hr	329	C
		10,000 units	UP	40 mg	D5S	Clear solution for 24 hr	329	C
		40,000 units	UP	25 g	NS	Clear solution for 24 hr	329	C
Metaraminol bitartrate	MSD	400 mg	UP	125 mg	D5W, NS	Precipitate forms within 4 hr	42	I
Nafcillin sodium	WY	500 mg	UP	125 mg	D5W	Precipitate forms	329	I
Norepinephrine bitartrate	WI	8 mg	UP	40 mg	D5S	Physically compatible	329	C

Additive Compatibility (Cont.)

Methylprednisolone sodium succinate

Drug	*Mfr*	*Conc/L*	*Mfr*	*Conc/L*	*Test Soln*	*Remarks*	*Ref*	*C/I*
Penicillin G potassium		2 to 10 million units	UP	80 mg	D5S, D5W, LR	Clear solution for 24 hr	329	C
Penicillin G sodium		5 million units	UP	125 mg	D5W, LR	Precipitate forms	329	I
Ranitidine HCl	GL	50 mg	UP	40 mg	D5W[a]	Visually compatible with 7% ranitidine loss and no methylprednisolone loss by HPLC in 48 hr at room temperature	1802	C
	GL	50 mg	UP	2 g	D5W[a]	Visually compatible with 6% ranitidine loss and 10% methylprednisolone loss by HPLC in 48 hr at room temperature	1802	C
	GL	2 g	UP	40 mg and 2 g	D5W[a]	Visually compatible with no loss of either drug by HPLC in 48 hr at room temperature	1802	C
	GL	50 mg and 2 g	UP	40 mg and 2 g	NS[a]	Visually compatible with no ranitidine loss and about 10% methylprednisolone loss by HPLC in 48 hr at room temperature	1802	C
Theophylline	AB	4 g	UP	500 mg and 2 g	D5W[b]	Physically compatible with little or no theophylline or methylprednisolone alcohol loss in 24 hr at room temperature. 8% ester hydrolysis termed not clinically important	1150	C
	AB	400 mg	UP	500 mg and 2 g	D5W[b]	Physically compatible with little or no theophylline or methylprednisolone alcohol loss in 24 hr at room temperature. 11% ester hydrolysis termed not clinically important	1150	C
Verapamil HCl	KN	80 mg	UP	250 mg	D5W, NS	Physically compatible for 24 hr	764	C

[a]*Tested in PVC containers.*
[b]*Premixed theophylline infusion.*

Drugs in Syringe Compatibility

Methylprednisolone sodium succinate

Drug (in syringe)	*Mfr*	*Amt*	*Mfr*	*Amt*	*Remarks*	*Ref*	*C/I*
Diatrizoate meglumine 52%, diatrizoate sodium 8%	MA	5 ml	UP	10 mg/ 1 ml	Physically compatible for at least 2 hr	1438	C
Diatrizoate sodium 60%	WI	5 ml	UP	10 mg/ 1 ml	Physically compatible for at least 2 hr	1438	C
Doxapram HCl	RB	400 mg/ 20 ml	UP	40 mg/ 2 ml	Immediate turbidity and precipitation	1177	I
Granisetron HCl	BE	0.15 mg/ ml[a]	DAK	6 mg/ml[a]	Visually compatible with little or no loss of either drug by HPLC in 72 hr at room temperature	1884	C
Iohexol	WI	64.7%, 5 ml	UP	10 mg/ 1 ml	Physically compatible for at least 2 hr	1438	C
Iopamidol	SQ	61%, 5 ml	UP	10 mg/ 1 ml	Physically compatible for at least 2 hr	1438	C

Drugs in Syringe Compatibility (Cont.)

Methylprednisolone sodium succinate

Drug (in syringe)	*Mfr*	*Amt*	*Mfr*	*Amt*	*Remarks*	*Ref*	*C/I*
Iothalamate meglumine 60%	MA	5 ml	UP	10 mg/ 1 ml	Physically compatible for at least 2 hr	1438	C
Ioxaglate meglumine 39.3%, ioxaglate sodium 19.6%	MA	5 ml	UP	10 mg/ 1 ml	Physically compatible for at least 2 hr	1438	C
Metoclopramide HCl	RB	10 mg/ 2 ml	ES	62.5 mg/ 1 ml	Physically compatible for 24 hr at room temperature	924	C
	RB	10 mg/ 2 ml	ES	250 mg/ 4 ml	Physically compatible for 24 hr at room temperature	924	C
	RB	10 mg/ 2 ml	ES	62.5 mg/ 1 ml	Physically compatible for 24 hr at 25 °C	1167	C
	RB	10 mg/ 2 ml	ES	250 mg/ 4 ml	Physically compatible for 24 hr at 25 °C	1167	C
	RB	160 mg/ 32 ml	ES	250 mg/ 4 ml	Physically compatible for 24 hr at 25 °C	1167	C

[a]*Diluted with water.*

Y-Site Injection Compatibility (1:1 Mixture)

Methylprednisolone sodium succinate

Drug	*Mfr*	*Conc*	*Mfr*	*Conc*	*Remarks*	*Ref*	*C/I*
Acyclovir sodium	BW	5 mg/ml[a]	LY	0.8 mg/ml[a]	Physically compatible for 4 hr at 25 °C	1157	C
Allopurinol sodium	BW	3 mg/ml[b]	AB	5 mg/ml[b]	Haze forms in 1 hr with white precipitate in 24 hr	1686	I
Amifostine	USB	10 mg/ml[a]	AB	5 mg/ml[a]	Physically compatible with no change in measured turbidity or increase in particle content in 4 hr at 23 °C	1845	C
Amphotericin B cholesteryl sulfate complex	SEQ	0.83 mg/ml[a]	PHU	5 mg/ml[a]	Physically compatible with little or no change in measured turbidity or increase in particle content in 4 hr at 23 °C under fluorescent light	2117	C
Amsacrine	NCI	1 mg/ml[a]	UP	5 mg/ml[a]	Immediate orange turbidity and precipitate in 4 hr	1381	I
Aztreonam	SQ	40 mg/ml[a]	AB	5 mg/ml[a]	Physically compatible with no subvisual haze or particle formation in 4 hr at 23 °C	1758	C
Cefepime HCl	BMS	20 mg/ml[a]	AB	5 mg/ml[a]	Physically compatible with no change in measured turbidity or increase in particle content in 4 hr at 22 °C	1689	C
Ciprofloxacin	MI	2 mg/ml[c]	UP	62.5 mg/ml	Transient white cloudiness rapidly dissipates. White crystals form in 2 hr at 24 °C	1655	I
Cisatracurium besylate	GW	0.1 mg/ml[a]	AB	5 mg/ml[a]	Physically compatible with no change in measured turbidity or increase in particle content in 4 hr at 23 °C	2074	C
	GW	2 mg/ml[a]	AB	5 mg/ml[a]	Subvisual haze forms immediately	2074	I
	GW	5 mg/ml[a]	AB	5 mg/ml[a]	Haze forms immediately	2074	I
Cisplatin	BR	1 mg/ml	UP	0.5 mg/ml[a]	Visually compatible for 4 hr at room temperature under fluorescent light	1685	C

Y-Site Injection Compatibility (1:1 Mixture) (Cont.)

Drug	Mfr	Conc	Mfr	Conc	Remarks	Ref	C/I
			Methylprednisolone sodium succinate				
Cladribine	ORT	0.015[b] and 0.5[d] mg/ml	AB	5 mg/ml[b]	Physically compatible with no change in measured turbidity or increase in particle content in 4 hr at 23 °C	1969	C
Cyclophosphamide	MJ	10 mg/ml	UP	0.5 mg/ml[a]	Visually compatible for 4 hr at room temperature under fluorescent light	1685	C
Cytarabine	UP	50 mg/ml	UP	0.5 mg/ml[a]	Visually compatible for 4 hr at room temperature under fluorescent light	1685	C
	UP	16 mg/ml[b]	UP	5 mg/ml[a]	Visually compatible for 24 hr at room temperature in test tubes. No precipitate found on filter from Y-site delivery	2063	C
Diltiazem HCl	MMD	5 mg/ml	UP	2.5 mg/ml[a]	Cloudiness forms	1807	I
	MMD	5 mg/ml	UP	20 mg/ml[b]	Precipitate forms	1807	I
	MMD	5 mg/ml	UP	62.5 mg/ml	Cloudiness forms but clears with swirling	1807	?
	MMD	1 mg/ml[b]	UP	2.5[a], 20[b], 62.5 mg/ml	Visually compatible	1807	C
Docetaxel	RPR	0.9 mg/ml[a]	PHU	5 mg/ml[a]	Partial loss of measured natural turbidity occurs immediately	2224	I
Dopamine HCl	AB	0.8 mg/ml[a]	UP	5 mg/ml[a]	Visually compatible for 24 hr at room temperature in test tubes. No precipitate found on filter from Y-site delivery	2063	C
Doxorubicin HCl	AD	0.2 mg/ml[a]	UP	0.5 mg/ml[a]	Visually compatible for 4 hr at room temperature under fluorescent light	1685	C
Doxorubicin HCl liposome injection	SEQ	0.4 mg/ml[a]	UP	5 mg/ml[a]	Physically compatible with little or no change in measured turbidity and no increase in particle content in 4 hr at 23 °C	2087	C
Enalaprilat	MSD	0.05 mg/ml[b]	UP	0.8 mg/ml[a]	Physically compatible for 24 hr at room temperature under fluorescent light	1355	C
Etoposide phosphate	BR	5 mg/ml[a]	AB	5 mg/ml[a]	Haze with small subvisual particles forms immediately. Particle content increases fivefold over 4 hr at 23 °C	2218	I
Famotidine	MSD	0.2 mg/ml[a]	AB	1 mg/ml[a]	Physically compatible for 4 hr at 25 °C	1188	C
	MSD	0.2 mg/ml[a]	QU	40 mg/ml	Physically compatible for 14 hr	1196	C
	ME	2 mg/ml[b]		5 mg/ml[a]	Visually compatible for 4 hr at 22 °C	1936	C
Filgrastim	AMG	30 μg/ml[a]	AB	5 mg/ml[a]	Haze, particles, and filaments form immediately	1687	I
Fludarabine phosphate	BX	1 mg/ml[a]	UP	5 mg/ml[a]	Physically compatible for 4 hr at room temperature under fluorescent light	1439	C
Gatifloxacin	BMS	2 mg/ml[a]	PHU	5 mg/ml[a]	Physically compatible with no change in measured haze or increase in particle content in 4 hr at 23 °C	2234	C
Gemcitabine HCl	LI	10 mg/ml[b]	AB	5 mg/ml[b]	Gross precipitation occurs immediately	2226	I
Granisetron HCl	SKB	0.05 mg/ml[a]	WY	5 mg/ml[a]	Physically compatible with no change in measured turbidity or increase in particle content in 4 hr at 23 °C	2000	C
Heparin sodium	TR	50 units/ml	UP	2.5 mg/ml[a]	Visually compatible for 4 hr at 25 °C	1793	C
	ES	100 units/ml[c]	UP	5 mg/ml[a]	Visually compatible for 24 hr at room temperature in test tubes. No precipitate found on filter from Y-site delivery	2063	C

Y-Site Injection Compatibility (1:1 Mixture) (Cont.)

Drug	Mfr	Conc	Methylprednisolone sodium succinate Mfr	Conc	Remarks	Ref	C/I
Heparin sodium with hydrocortisone sodium succinate	RI UP	1000 units + 100 mg/L[a]	UP	40 mg/ml	Physically compatible for at least 4 hr at room temperature by visual and microscopic examination	332	C
Heparin sodium with hydrocortisone sodium succinate	RI UP	1000 units + 100 mg/L[e]	UP	40 mg/ml	Physically compatible initially but haziness noted in 4 hr at room temperature	322	I
Hetastarch in lactated electrolyte injection (Hextend)	AB	6%	PHU	5 mg/ml[a]	Physically compatible with no change in measured turbidity or increase in particle content in 4 hr at 23 °C	2339	C
Inamrinone lactate	WB	3 mg/ml[b]	ES	1 mg/ml[a]	Physically compatible for at least 4 hr at 25 °C under fluorescent light	992	C
Linezolid	PHU	2 mg/ml	AB	5 mg/ml[a]	Physically compatible with no change in measured turbidity or increase in particle content in 4 hr at 23 °C	2264	C
Melphalan HCl	BW	0.1 mg/ml[b]	AB	5 mg/ml[b]	Physically compatible with no change in measured turbidity or increase in particle content in 3 hr at 22 °C	1557	C
Meperidine HCl	AB	10 mg/ml	UP	2.5 mg/ml[a]	Physically compatible for 4 hr at 25 °C	1397	C
Methotrexate sodium	AD	15 mg/ml[f]	UP	0.5 mg/ml[a]	Visually compatible for 4 hr at room temperature under fluorescent light	1685	C
		30 mg/ml	UP	20 mg/ml	Visually compatible for 4 hr at room temperature	1788	C
Metronidazole	MG	5 mg/ml	UP	5 mg/ml[a]	Visually compatible for 24 hr at room temperature in test tubes. No precipitate found on filter from Y-site delivery	2063	C
Midazolam HCl	RC	1 mg/ml[a]	UP	40 mg/ml	Visually compatible for 24 hr at 23 °C	1847	C
Morphine sulfate	AB	1 mg/ml	UP	2.5 mg/ml[a]	Physically compatible for 4 hr at 25 °C	1397	C
Ondansetron HCl	GL	1 mg/ml[b]	UP	5 mg/ml[a]	Light haze develops in 30 min	1365	I
Paclitaxel	NCI	1.2 mg/ml[a]	UP	5 mg/ml[a]	Normal inherent haze from paclitaxel decreases immediately	1556	I
Piperacillin sodium–tazobactam sodium	LE	40 + 5 mg/ml[a]	AB	5 mg/ml[a]	Physically compatible with no change in measured turbidity or increase in particle content in 4 hr at 22 °C	1688	C
Potassium chloride		40 mEq/L[a]	UP	40 mg/ml	Physically compatible for at least 4 hr at room temperature by visual and microscopic examination	322	C
		40 mEq/L[b]	UP	40 mg/ml	Physically compatible initially but haziness noted in 4 hr at room temperature	322	I
		40 mEq/L[g]	UP	40 mg/ml	Immediate haze formation	322	I
Propofol	ZEN	10 mg/ml	AB	5 mg/ml[a]	Small amount of white precipitate forms immediately	2066	I
Remifentanil HCl	GW	0.025 and 0.25 mg/ml[b]	AB	5 mg/ml[a]	Physically compatible with no change in measured turbidity or increase in particle content in 4 hr at 23 °C	2075	C
Sargramostim	IMM	10 μg/ml[b]	UP	5 mg/ml[b]	Small amount of particles and filaments form in 4 hr	1436	I
Sodium bicarbonate		1.4%	UP	20 mg/ml	Visually compatible for 4 hr at room temperature	1788	C

Y-Site Injection Compatibility (1:1 Mixture) (Cont.)

			Methylprednisolone sodium succinate				
Drug	*Mfr*	*Conc*	*Mfr*	*Conc*	*Remarks*	*Ref*	*C/I*
Tacrolimus	FUJ	1 mg/ml[b]	UP	0.8 mg/ml[a]	Visually compatible for 24 hr at 25 °C	1630	C
Teniposide	BR	0.1 mg/ml[a]	AB	5 mg/ml[a]	Physically compatible with no subvisual haze or particle formation in 4 hr at 23 °C	1725	C
Theophylline	TR	4 mg/ml	UP	2.5 mg/ml[a]	Visually compatible for 6 hr at 25 °C	1793	C
Thiotepa	IMM[h]	1 mg/ml[a]	AB	5 mg/ml[a]	Physically compatible with no change in measured turbidity or increase in particle content in 4 hr at 23 °C	1861	C
TNA #218 to #226[i]			AB	5 mg/ml[a]	Visually compatible with no precipitate or emulsion damage apparent in 4 hr at 23 °C	2215	C
Topotecan HCl	SKB	56 μg/ml[a,b]	UP	2.4 mg/ml[a,b]	Pale yellow color develops but little or no loss of either drug by HPLC within 4 hr at 22 °C under fluorescent light	2245	C
TPN #212 to #215[i]			AB	5 mg/ml[a]	Physically compatible with no change in measured turbidity or increase in particle content in 4 hr at 23 °C	2109	C
Vinorelbine tartrate	BW	1 mg/ml[b]	AB	5 mg/ml[b]	Heavy white precipitate forms immediately	1558	I
Vitamin B complex with C	RC	2 ml/L[c]	UP	40 mg/ml	Physically compatible for at least 4 hr at room temperature by visual and microscopic examination	322	C
	RC	2 ml/L[g]	UP	40 mg/ml	Physically compatible initially but haziness noted in 4 hr at room temperature	322	I

[a]*Tested in dextrose 5% in water.*
[b]*Tested in sodium chloride 0.9%.*
[c]*Tested in both dextrose 5% in water and sodium chloride 0.9%.*
[d]*Tested in bacteriostatic sodium chloride 0.9% preserved with benzyl alcohol 0.9%.*
[e]*Tested in both Ringer's injection, lactated, and sodium chloride 0.9%.*
[f]*Tested in dextrose 5% in water with sodium bicarbonate 0.05 mEq/ml.*
[g]*Tested in Ringer's injection, lactated.*
[h]*Lyophilized formulation tested.*
[i]*Refer to Appendix I for the composition of parenteral nutrition solutions. TNA indicates a 3-in-1 admixture, and TPN indicates a 2-in-1 admixture.*

Additional Compatibility Information

Infusion Solutions — Dextrose 5% in water, sodium chloride 0.9%, and dextrose 5% in sodium chloride 0.9% have been recommended as diluents for intravenous infusions. (2; 4)

Solution haziness was reported for methylprednisolone sodium succinate admixtures in intravenous fluids.(702; 758) Pharmacia has stated that changes in the manufacturing process for their bulk methylprednisolone sodium succinate powder have resulted in substantial improvements in admixture clarity and absence of the haze formation that developed previously in solutions of Solu-Medrol. (670; 702)

In a study of the turbidity produced by methylprednisolone sodium succinate (Abbott) 500 mg to 30 g/L, turbidity was substantially higher in dextrose 5% in water than in sodium chloride 0.9%. (758) Another important factor was the concentration of methylprednisolone sodium succinate. Turbidity was generally higher at intermediate concentrations (2 to 15 g/L) than at low (300 mg/L) or high (20 g/L) concentrations. (758)

These differences in the development of turbidity cannot be explained by simple increased ester hydrolysis due to differing pH values and drug concentrations. Rather, the solubility of free methylprednisolone in various concentrations of methylprednisolone sodium succinate has been suggested as the primary factor. The solubility of free methylprednisolone is increased as the concentration of the sodium succinate ester increases. The increased solubilization is believed to overshadow increased formation of free methylprednisolone in concentrations over 10 g/L, preventing or minimizing precipitation and turbidity. Differences in turbidity between the drug in dextrose 5% in water and sodium chloride 0.9% are believed to result primarily from the electrolyte content of sodium chloride 0.9% and, to a much lesser extent, the slightly higher pH of the dextrose admixtures. These differences are presumed to affect the solubilizing capacity and reactivity of the ester. (758)

Other Drugs — Amphotericin B in infusions appears to be compatible with limited amounts of methylprednisolone sodium succinate. (4) However, insulin has been stated to be incompatible with methylprednisolone sodium succinate (Upjohn). (329)

Irinotecan admixed with methylprednisolone sodium succinate resulted in an admixture having a pH greater than 6.5. Approximately 10% irinotecan loss occurs within three hours at this pH. (1881)

The compatibility of methylprednisolone sodium succinate (Upjohn) with several drugs added to auxiliary medication infusion units has been studied. Primary admixtures were prepared by adding various drugs to dextrose 5% in water, dextrose 5% in sodium chloride 0.9%, and Ringer's injection, lactated. Up to 100 ml of the primary admixture was added along with methylprednisolone sodium succinate (Upjohn) to the auxiliary medication infusion unit with the following results (329):

Methylprednisolone Sodium Succinate	Primary Solution	Result
	Aminophylline 500 mg/L	
500 mg	D5S, D5W qs 100 ml	Clear solution for 24 hr
500 mg	LR qs 100 ml	Clear solution for 24 hr
500 mg	Added to 100 ml LR	Clear solution for 1 hr
1000 mg	D5W qs 100 ml	Yellow solution, clear for 24 hr
1000 mg	D5S qs 100 ml	Yellow solution, clear for 6 hr
1000 mg	Added to 100 ml D5S	Yellow solution, clear for 24 hr
1000 mg	LR qs 100 ml or added to 100 ml LR	Yellow solution, clear for 4 hr
2000 mg	D5S, D5W, LR qs 100 ml	Yellow solution, clear for 24 hr
	Heparin Sodium 10,000 units/L	
500 mg	D5S, D5W qs 100 ml	Clear solution for 24 hr
500 mg	LR qs 100 ml or added to 100 ml LR	Clear solution for 6 hr
1000 mg	D5S, D5W qs 100 ml	Clear solution for 6 hr
1000 mg	Added to 100 ml D5W	Clear solution for 24 hr
1000 mg	LR qs 100 ml or added to 100 ml LR	Clear solution for 4 to 6 hr
2000 mg	D5W qs 100 ml	Clear solution for 6 hr
2000 mg	D5S, LR qs 100 ml	Clear solution for 24 hr
	Potassium Chloride 40 mEq/L	
500 mg	D5S, D5W, LR qs 100 ml	Clear solution for 24 hr
1000 mg	D5W qs 100 ml	Clear solution for 24 hr
1000 mg	D5S, LR qs 100 ml or added to 100 ml D5S, LR	Clear solution for 6 hr
2000 mg	D5S, D5W, LR qs 100 ml	Clear solution for 24 hr
	Sodium Bicarbonate 44.6 mEq/L	
500 mg	D5S, D5W qs 100 ml	Clear solution for 24 hr
500 mg	LR qs 100 ml or added to 100 ml LR	Clear solution for 1 hr
1000 mg	D5W qs 100 ml	Clear solution for 24 hr
1000 mg	D5S qs 100 ml or added to 100 ml D5S	Clear solution for 24 hr
1000 mg	LR qs 100 ml	Clear solution for 1 hr
1000 mg	Added to 100 ml LR	Clear solution for 4 hr
2000 mg	D5S, D5W qs 100 ml	Clear solution for 24 hr
2000 mg	LR qs 100 ml	Clear solution for 30 min
2000 mg	Added to 100 ml LR	Clear solution for 4 hr
	Ticarcillin Disodium 6 g/L	
500 mg	D5S, D5W qs 100 ml	Clear solution for 24 hr
500 mg	LR qs 100 ml	Clear solution for 6 hr
500 mg	Added to 100 ml LR	Clear solution for 24 hr
1000 mg	D5W qs 100 ml	Clear solution for 24 hr
1000 mg	D5S qs 100 ml or added to 100 ml D5S	Clear solution for 6 hr
1000 mg	LR qs 100 ml	Clear solution for 1 hr
1000 mg	Added to 100 ml LR	Clear solution for 6 hr

METOCLOPRAMIDE HCL
AHFS 56:40

Products — Metoclopramide HCl is available in 2-ml ampuls and syringe cartridges and 2-, 10-, 20-, and 30-ml vials. Each milliliter of solution contains metoclopramide (as the hydrochloride) 5 mg with sodium chloride 8.5 mg in water for injection. The pH may be adjusted with hydrochloric acid and/or sodium hydroxide, if necessary. (2; 29)

pH — From 3 to 6.5. (4) Metoclopramide HCl (Delta West) 1.25, 2.22, and 3.75 mg/ml in sodium chloride 0.9% for continuous subcutaneous infusion had pH values of 4.4, 4.1, and 4.0, respectively. (2161)

Osmolality — The osmolality of metoclopramide HCl 5 mg/ml was determined to be 280 mOsm/kg. (1233) Metoclopramide HCl (Delta West) 1.25, 2.22, and 3.75 mg/ml in sodium chloride 0.9% for continuous subcutaneous infusion had osmolalities of 285, 286, and 294 mOsm/kg, respectively. (2161)

Trade Name(s)— Reglan.

Administration — Metoclopramide HCl is administered by intramuscular injection, by direct intravenous injection undiluted slowly over one or two minutes for 10 mg doses of drug, or by intermittent intravenous infusion over 15 minutes diluted in 50 ml of compatible diluent for larger doses. (2; 4)

Stability — Metoclopramide HCl injection is a clear, colorless solution; it should be stored at controlled room temperature and protected from freezing. The drug is stable over a pH range of 2 to 9. Metoclopramide HCl is photosensitive; protection from light for the product during storage has been recommended. (4) However, the manufacturer no longer recommends light protection for dilutions under normal lighting conditions, stating that they may be stored up to 24 hours. (2)

Freezing Solutions— Metoclopramide HCl diluted in sodium chloride 0.9% in PVC bags is stable for up to four weeks when frozen at −20 °C. However, under the same storage conditions, dilutions in dextrose 5% in water lose up to 40% of their potency. (4)

Metoclopramide HCl (Robins) 10 and 160 mg in 50 ml of sodium chloride 0.9% and dextrose 5% in water in PVC containers was stored frozen at −20 °C. The bags were subsequently thawed for 24 hours at room temperature. In sodium chloride 0.9%, no metoclopramide loss occurred in four weeks. However, in dextrose 5% in water, the lower concentration lost 9% in two weeks and 14% in four weeks. At 160 mg/50 ml in dextrose 5% in water, 11% was lost in one week and 37% in four weeks. The mechanism of this degradation is not fully understood but may be the result of reaction with dextrose breakdown products or impurities. (1167)

Undiluted metoclopramide HCl (Robins) 5 mg/ml packaged as 3 ml in plastic infusion-pump syringes (MiniMed) fitted with Luer-Lok tip caps (Burron) exhibited microprecipitation that did not redissolve upon warming to room temperature when stored frozen at −20 °C for as little as one day. The precipitate was not visible with the unaided eye. Freezing is not an acceptable storage method for undiluted metoclopramide HCl injection. (2001)

Light Effects— Metoclopramide HCl (Robins) 10 and 160 mg/50 ml of dextrose 5% in water, dextrose 5% in sodium chloride 0.45%, and sodium chloride 0.9% was stored exposed to normal room light and to extreme high intensity light. Little or no drug loss occurred in any solution at either concentration exposed to normal room light for 24 hours. The accelerated study under high intensity light showed little or no loss of either concentration in sodium chloride 0.9% or of the high concentration in the dextrose-containing solutions in 24 hours. However, the 10-mg/50 ml concentration in the dextrose-containing solutions exhibited a 1 to 4% loss in four hours and an 11 to 14% loss in 24 hours under the high intensity light. (1167)

Syringes— Undiluted metoclopramide HCl (Robins) 5 mg/ml packaged as 3 ml in plastic infusion-pump syringes (MiniMed) fitted with Luer-Lok tip caps (Burron) was evaluated for physical stability, including subvisual particulates, and chemical stability by HPLC analysis. Stored for seven days at 32 °C to simulate wearing a portable infusion pump close to the body, metoclopramide HCl was physically stable and little or no loss occurred. At 23 °C, metoclopramide HCl was physically and chemically stable for up to 60 days with little or no loss occurring. However, large quantities of subvisual particulates formed after that time, making the drug unsuitable for use. Stored under refrigeration at 4 °C, metoclopramide HCl remained both physically and chemically stable for up to 90 days. (2001)

Metoclopramide HCl (Solopak) 2.5 mg/ml in sodium chloride 0.9% packaged in polypropylene syringes (Sherwood) was physically stable and exhibited not more than 5% loss by stability-indicating HPLC analysis in 24 hours stored at 4 and 23 °C. (2199)

Elastomeric Reservoir Pumps— Metoclopramide HCl 4 mg/ml in dextrose 5% in water in Medflo elastomeric reservoir pumps has been stated by the pump manufacturer to be stable for 24 hours at room temperature and two weeks frozen. When diluted to 4 mg/ml in sodium chloride 0.9% in the Medflo pumps, the drug is stated to be stable for 24 hours at room temperature and four weeks frozen. (31)

Central Venous Catheter— Metoclopramide HCl (Abbott) 0.5 mg/ml in dextrose 5% in water was found to be compatible with the ARROWg+ard Blue Plus (Arrow International) chlorhexidine-bearing triple-lumen central catheter. HPLC analysis was used to evaluate completeness of drug delivery through the catheter and the amount of chlorhexidine removed from the internal lumens. Essentially complete delivery of the drug was found with little or no drug loss occurring. Furthermore, chlorhexidine delivered from the catheter remained at trace amounts with no substantial increase due to the delivery of the drug through the catheter. (2335)

Compatibility Information

Solution Compatibility

Metoclopramide HCl

Solution	*Mfr*	*Mfr*	*Conc/L*	*Remarks*	*Ref*	*C/I*
Amino acids 2.75%, dextrose 25%, electrolytes	TR	RB	5 and 20 mg	Metoclopramide chemically stable for 72 hr at room temperature	854	C
Dextrose 5% in sodium chloride 0.45%	TR[a]	RB	200 mg	Physically compatible with 2% loss in 24 hr at 25 °C exposed to normal room light	1167	C
	TR[a]	RB	3.2 g	Physically compatible with 4 to 5% loss in 24 hr at 25 °C exposed to normal room light	1167	C
Dextrose 5% in water	TR[a]	RB	200 mg	Physically compatible with no loss in 24 hr at 25 °C exposed to normal room light	1167	C
	TR[a]	RB	200 mg	9% loss after 2 weeks and 14% loss after 4 weeks frozen at −20 °C followed by 24 hr at room temperature	1167	C

Solution Compatibility (Cont.)

Metoclopramide HCl

Solution	*Mfr*	*Mfr*	*Conc/L*	*Remarks*	*Ref*	*C/I*
	TR[a]	RB	3.2 g	Physically compatible with 5% loss in 24 hr at 25 °C exposed to normal room light	1167	C
	TR[a]	RB	3.2 g	11% loss after 1 week and 37% loss after 4 weeks frozen at −20 °C followed by 24 hr at room temperature	1167	I
Mannitol 20%	AB	RB	40 and 100 mg	Physically compatible for 48 hr at room temperature	924	C
	AB	RB	40 and 100 mg	Physically compatible for 48 hr at 25 °C	1167	C
	AB	RB	640 mg and 1.6 g	Physically compatible for 48 hr at 25 °C	1167	C
Sodium chloride 0.9%	TR[a]	RB	200 mg and 3.2 g	No loss after 4 weeks frozen at −20 °C followed by 24 hr at room temperature	1167	C
	TR[a]	RB	200 mg and 3.2 g	Physically compatible with no loss in 24 hr at 25 °C exposed to normal room light	1167	C
TPN #89[b]		RB	5 mg	Physically compatible with no metoclopramide loss in 24 hr and 10% loss in 48 hr at 25 °C	1167	C
		RB	20 mg	Physically compatible with no metoclopramide loss in 72 hr at 25 °C	1167	C
TPN #90[b]		RB	5 mg	Physically compatible with no metoclopramide loss in 72 hr at 25 °C	1167	C
		RB	20 mg	Physically compatible with 3% metoclopramide loss in 72 hr at 25 °C	1167	C

[a]*Tested in PVC containers.*
[b]*Refer to Appendix I for the composition of parenteral nutrition solutions. TPN indicates a 2-in-1 admixture.*

Additive Compatibility

Metoclopramide HCl

Drug	*Mfr*	*Conc/L*	*Mfr*	*Conc/L*	*Test Soln*	*Remarks*	*Ref*	*C/I*
Cimetidine HCl	SKF	3 g	RB	100 mg	NS	Physically compatible for 48 hr at room temperature, but bioavailability of cimetidine may be reduced	924	?
	SKF	3 g	RB	100 mg and 1.6 g		Physically compatible for 48 hr at 25 °C	1167	C
Clindamycin phosphate	UP	6 g	RB	100 and 200 mg	NS	Physically compatible for 24 hr at room temperature	924	C
	UP	6 g	RB	100 and 200 mg		Physically compatible for 24 hr at 25 °C	1167	C
	UP	3.5 g	RB	1.9 g		Physically compatible for 24 hr at 25 °C	1167	C
	UP	4.4 g	RB	1.2 g		Physically compatible for 24 hr at 25 °C	1167	C
Dexamethasone sodium phosphate with lorazepam and diphenhydramine HCl	AMR WY ES	400 mg 40 mg 2 g	DU	4 g	NS[a]	Rapid lorazepam losses of 8, 10, and 15% at 3, 23, and 30 °C, respectively, in 24 hr by HPLC. Other drugs stable for 14 days by HPLC at all three storage temperatures	1733	I
Erythromycin lactobionate	AB	4 g	RB	400 mg	NS	Incompatible. If mixed, use immediately	924	I

Additive Compatibility (Cont.)

Metoclopramide HCl

Drug	*Mfr*	*Conc/L*	*Mfr*	*Conc/L*	*Test Soln*	*Remarks*	*Ref*	*C/I*
	AB	4.1 g	RB	416 mg		Incompatible. If mixed, use immediately	1167	I
	AB	5 g	RB	100 mg	NS	Incompatible. If mixed, use immediately	924	I
	AB	5 g	RB	100 mg		Incompatible. If mixed, use immediately	1167	I
	AB	3.5 g	RB	1.1 g		Incompatible. If mixed, use immediately	1167	I
Floxacillin sodium	BE	20 g	ANT	1 g	NS	Immediate white precipitation	1479	I
Fluorouracil	RC	2.5 g	FUJ	100 mg	D5W	10% metoclopramide loss in 6 hr and 27% loss in 24 hr at 25 °C. 5% metoclopramide loss in 120 hr at 4 °C. 5 and 7% fluorouracil losses in 120 hr at 4 and 25 °C, respectively	1780	I
Furosemide	HO	1 g	ANT	1 g	NS	Immediate precipitation	1479	I
Meperidine HCl	DW	7.35 g	DW	150 mg	D5W, NS	Visually compatible with little or no loss of either drug over 48 hr at 32 °C exposed to or protected from fluorescent light	2253	C
Meropenem	ZEN	1 and 20 g	RB	100 mg	NS	Visually compatible for 4 hr at room temperature	1994	C
Morphine sulfate	EV	1 g	SKB	500 mg	NS[b]	Visually compatible with little or no loss of either drug by HPLC in 35 days at 22 °C and 182 days at 4 °C followed by 7 days at 32 °C	1939	C
	EV	1 g	SKB	500 mg	NS[c]	Visually compatible with 8% metoclopramide loss by HPLC in 14 days at 22 °C and 98 days at 4 °C. No morphine loss occurs	1939	C
Multivitamins (M.V.I.)	USV	20 ml	RB	20 and 320 mg	NS	Physically compatible for 48 hr at room temperature	924	C
(M.V.I.)	USV	20 ml	RB	20 and 320 mg		Physically compatible for 48 hr at 25 °C	1167	C
(M.V.I.-12)	USV	20 ml	RB	20 and 320 mg	NS	Physically compatible for 48 hr at room temperature	924	C
(M.V.I.-12)	USV	20 ml	RB	20 and 320 mg		Physically compatible for 48 hr at 25 °C	1167	C
Potassium acetate	IX	20 mEq	RB	10 and 160 mg	NS	Physically compatible for 48 hr at room temperature	924	C
	IX	20 mEq	RB	10 and 160 mg		Physically compatible for 48 hr at 25 °C	1167	C
Potassium chloride	ES	30 mEq	RB	10 and 160 mg	NS	Physically compatible for 48 hr at room temperature	924	C
	ES	30 mEq	RB	10 and 160 mg		Physically compatible for 48 hr at 25 °C	1167	C
Potassium phosphates	IX	15 mM	RB	10 and 160 mg	NS	Physically compatible for 48 hr at room temperature	924	C
	IX	15 mM	RB	10 and 160 mg		Physically compatible for 48 hr at 25 °C	1167	C
Verapamil HCl	KN	80 mg	RB	20 mg	D5W, NS	Physically compatible for 24 hr	764	C

[a]*Tested in Pharmacia-Deltec PVC pump reservoirs.*
[b]*Tested in PVC containers.*
[c]*Tested in PCA Infusors (Baxter).*

Drugs in Syringe Compatibility

Metoclopramide HCl

Drug (in syringe)	*Mfr*	*Amt*	*Mfr*	*Amt*	*Remarks*	*Ref*	*C/I*
Aminophylline	ES	80 mg/ 3.2 ml	RB	10 mg/ 2 ml	Physically compatible for 24 hr at room temperature	924	C
	ES	500 mg/ 20 ml	RB	10 mg/ 2 ml	Physically compatible for 24 hr at room temperature	924	C
	ES	500 mg/ 20 ml	RB	160 mg/ 32 ml	Physically compatible for 24 hr at 25 °C	1167	C
	ES	80 mg/ 3.2 ml	RB	10 mg/ 2 ml	Physically compatible for 24 hr at 25 °C	1167	C
	ES	500 mg/ 20 ml	RB	10 mg/ 2 ml	Physically compatible for 24 hr at 25 °C	1167	C
Ampicillin sodium	BR	250 mg/ 2.5 ml	RB	10 mg/ 2 ml	Incompatible. If mixed, use immediately	1167	I
	BR	1 g/10 ml	RB	10 mg/ 2 ml	Incompatible. If mixed, use immediately	1167	I
	BR	1 g/10 ml	RB	160 mg/ 32 ml	Incompatible. If mixed, use immediately	1167	I
Ascorbic acid injection	AB	250 mg/ 0.5 ml	RB	10 mg/ 2 ml	Physically compatible for 48 hr at room temperature	924	C
	AB	250 mg/ 0.5 ml	RB	160 mg/ 32 ml	Physically compatible for 48 hr at 25 °C	1167	C
	AB	250 mg/ 0.5 ml	RB	10 mg/ 2 ml	Physically compatible for 48 hr at 25 °C	1167	C
Atropine sulfate	GL	0.4 mg/ 1 ml	NO	10 mg/ 2 ml	Physically compatible both macroscopically and microscopically for 15 min at room temperature	565	C
Benztropine mesylate	MSD	2 mg/ 2 ml	RB	10 mg/ 2 ml	Physically compatible for 48 hr at room temperature	924	C
	MSD	2 mg/ 2 ml	RB	160 mg/ 32 ml	Physically compatible for 48 hr at 25 °C	1167	C
	MSD	2 mg/ 2 ml	RB	10 mg/ 2 ml	Physically compatible for 48 hr at 25 °C	1167	C
Bleomycin sulfate		1.5 units/ 0.5 ml		2.5 mg/ 0.5 ml	Physically compatible for 5 min at room temperature followed by 8 min of centrifugation	980	C
Butorphanol tartrate	BR	4 mg/ 2 ml	NO	10 mg/ 2 ml	Physically compatible for 30 min at room temperature both macroscopically and microscopically	566	C
Calcium gluconate	ES	1 g/10 ml	RB	10 mg/ 2 ml	Possible precipitate formation	924	I
	ES	1 g/10 ml	RB	10 mg/ 2 ml	Incompatible. If mixed, use immediately	1167	I
	ES	1 g/10 ml	RB	160 mg/ 32 ml	Incompatible. If mixed, use immediately	1167	I
Chloramphenicol sodium succinate	PD	250 mg/ 2.5 ml	RB	10 mg/ 2 ml	Incompatible. Do not mix	924	I
	PD	2 g/20 ml	RB	10 mg/ 2 ml	Incompatible. Do not mix	924	I
	PD	250 mg/ 2.5 ml	RB	10 mg/ 2 ml	White precipitate forms within 1 hr at 25 °C	1167	I
	PD	2 g/20 ml	RB	10 mg/ 2 ml	White precipitate forms within 1 hr at 25 °C	1167	I
	PD	2 g/20 ml	RB	160 mg/ 32 ml	White precipitate forms within 1 hr at 25 °C	1167	I

Drugs in Syringe Compatibility (Cont.)

Metoclopramide HCl

Drug (in syringe)	*Mfr*	*Amt*	*Mfr*	*Amt*	*Remarks*	*Ref*	*C/I*
Chlorpromazine HCl	MB	25 mg/ 1 ml	NO	10 mg/ 2 ml	Physically compatible both macroscopically and microscopically for 15 min at room temperature	565	C
Cisplatin		0.5 mg/ 0.5 ml		2.5 mg/ 0.5 ml	Physically compatible for 5 min at room temperature followed by 8 min of centrifugation	980	C
Cyclophosphamide	MJ	40 mg/ 2 ml	RB	10 mg/ 2 ml	Physically compatible for 24 hr at room temperature	924	C
		10 mg/ 0.5 ml		2.5 mg/ 0.5 ml	Physically compatible for 5 min at room temperature followed by 8 min of centrifugation	980	C
	MJ	1 g/50 ml	RB	10 mg/ 2 ml	Physically compatible for 24 hr at 25 °C	1167	C
	MJ	1 g/50 ml	RB	160 mg/ 32 ml	Physically compatible for 24 hr at 25 °C	1167	C
	MJ	40 mg/ 2 ml	RB	10 mg/ 2 ml	Physically compatible for 24 hr at 25 °C	1167	C
Cytarabine	UP	50 mg/ 1 ml	RB	10 mg/ 2 ml	Physically compatible for 48 hr at room temperature	924	C
	UP	500 mg/ 10 ml	RB	160 mg/ 32 ml	Physically compatible for 48 hr at 25 °C	1167	C
	UP	50 mg/ 1 ml	RB	10 mg/ 2 ml	Physically compatible for 48 hr at 25 °C	1167	C
Dexamethasone sodium phosphate	ES, MSD	8 mg/ 2 ml	RB	10 mg/ 2 ml	Physically compatible for 48 hr at room temperature	924	C
	ES, MSD	8 mg/ 2 ml	RB	160 mg/ 32 ml	Physically compatible for 48 hr at 25 °C	1167	C
	ES, MSD	8 mg/ 2 ml	RB	10 mg/ 2 ml	Physically compatible for 48 hr at 25 °C	1167	C
Diamorphine HCl	MB	10, 25, 50 mg/ 1 ml	BK	5 mg/ 1 ml	Physically compatible and diamorphine potency retained for 24 hr at room temperature	1454	C
	EV	50 and 150 mg/ 1 ml	LA	5 mg/ 1 ml	Slight discoloration with 8% metoclopramide loss and 9% diamorphine loss in 7 days at room temperature	1455	C
Dimenhydrinate	HR	50 mg/ 1 ml	NO	10 mg/ 2 ml	Physically compatible both macroscopically and microscopically for 15 min at room temperature	565	C
Diphenhydramine HCl	PD	50 mg/ 1 ml	NO	10 mg/ 2 ml	Physically compatible both macroscopically and microscopically for 15 min at room temperature	565	C
	PD	50 mg/ 5 ml	RB	10 mg/ 2 ml	Physically compatible for 48 hr at room temperature	924	C
	PD	250 mg/ 25 ml	RB	10 mg/ 2 ml	Physically compatible for 48 hr at room temperature	924	C
	PD	40 mg/ 4 ml	RB	160 mg/ 32 ml	Physically compatible for 48 hr at 25 °C	1167	C
	PD	200 mg/ 20 ml	RB	160 mg/ 32 ml	Physically compatible for 48 hr at 25 °C	1167	C
	PD	50 mg/ 5 ml	RB	10 mg/ 2 ml	Physically compatible for 48 hr at 25 °C	1167	C
	PD	250 mg/ 25 ml	RB	10 mg/ 2 ml	Physically compatible for 48 hr at 25 °C	1167	C

Drugs in Syringe Compatibility (Cont.)

Metoclopramide HCl

Drug (in syringe)	*Mfr*	*Amt*	*Mfr*	*Amt*	*Remarks*	*Ref*	*C/I*
Doxorubicin HCl	AD	40 mg/ 20 ml	RB	10 mg/ 2 ml	Physically compatible for 48 hr at room temperature	924	**C**
		1 mg/ 0.5 ml		2.5 mg/ 0.5 ml	Physically compatible for 5 min at room temperature followed by 8 min of centrifugation	980	**C**
	AD	90 mg/ 45 ml	RB	160 mg/ 32 ml	Physically compatible for 48 hr at 25 °C	1167	**C**
	AD	40 mg/ 20 ml	RB	10 mg/ 2 ml	Physically compatible for 48 hr at 25 °C	1167	**C**
Droperidol	MN	2.5 mg/ 1 ml	NO	10 mg/ 2 ml	Physically compatible both macroscopically and microscopically for 15 min at room temperature	565	**C**
		1.25 mg/ 0.5 ml		2.5 mg/ 0.5 ml	Physically compatible for 5 min at room temperature followed by 8 min of centrifugation	980	**C**
Fentanyl citrate	MN	0.05 mg/ 1 ml	NO	10 mg/ 2 ml	Physically compatible both macroscopically and microscopically for 15 min at room temperature	565	**C**
Fentanyl citrate with midazolam HCl	DB RC	1 mg/ 20 ml 15 mg/ 3 ml	AST	20 mg/ 4 ml	Visually compatible with 7% or less loss of each drug in 10 days at 32 °C	2268	**C**
Fluorouracil		25 mg/ 0.5 ml		2.5 mg/ 0.5 ml	Physically compatible for 5 min at room temperature followed by 8 min of centrifugation	980	**C**
Furosemide		5 mg/ 0.5 ml		2.5 mg/ 0.5 ml	Immediate precipitation	980	**I**
Heparin sodium	ES	2000 units/ 2 ml	RB	10 mg/ 2 ml	Physically compatible for 48 hr at room temperature	924	**C**
	ES	4000 units/ 4 ml	RB	10 mg/ 2 ml	Physically compatible for 48 hr at room temperature	924	**C**
		500 units/ 0.5 ml		2.5 mg/ 0.5 ml	Physically compatible for 5 min at room temperature followed by 8 min of centrifugation	980	**C**
		2500 units/ 1 ml		10 mg/ 2 ml	Physically compatible for at least 5 min	1053	**C**
	ES	16,000 units/ 16 ml	RB	160 mg/ 32 ml	Physically compatible for 48 hr at 25 °C	1167	**C**
	ES	2000 units/ 2 ml	RB	10 mg/ 2 ml	Physically compatible for 48 hr at 25 °C	1167	**C**
	ES	4000 units/ 4 ml	RB	10 mg/ 2 ml	Physically compatible for 48 hr at 25 °C	1167	**C**
Hydrocortisone sodium phosphate	MSD	10 mg/ 2 ml	RB	10 mg/ 2 ml	Physically compatible for 48 hr at 25 °C	1167	**C**
	MSD	20 mg/ 4 ml	RB	10 mg/ 2 ml	Physically compatible for 48 hr at 25 °C	1167	**C**
	MSD	80 mg/ 16 ml	RB	160 mg/ 32 ml	Physically compatible for 48 hr at 25 °C	1167	**C**

Drugs in Syringe Compatibility (Cont.)

Metoclopramide HCl

Drug (in syringe)	*Mfr*	*Amt*	*Mfr*	*Amt*	*Remarks*	*Ref*	*C/I*
Hydrocortisone sodium succinate	MSD	10 mg/ 2 ml[a]	RB	10 mg/ 2 ml	Physically compatible for 48 hr at room temperature	924	C
	MSD	20 mg/ 4 ml[a]	RB	10 mg/ 2 ml	Physically compatible for 48 hr at room temperature	924	C
Hydroxyzine HCl	PF	50 mg/ 1 ml	NO	10 mg/ 2 ml	Physically compatible both macroscopically and microscopically for 15 min at room temperature	565	C
Insulin, regular	LI	10 units/ 2 ml[a]	RB	10 mg/ 2 ml	Physically compatible for 24 hr at room temperature	924	C
	LI	20 units/ 4 ml[a]	RB	10 mg/ 2 ml	Physically compatible for 24 hr at room temperature	924	C
	LI	80 units/ 16 ml	RB	160 mg/ 32 ml	Physically compatible for 24 hr at 25 °C	1167	C
	LI	10 units/ 2 ml	RB	10 mg/ 2 ml	Physically compatible for 24 hr at 25 °C	1167	C
	LI	20 units/ 4 ml	RB	10 mg/ 2 ml	Physically compatible for 24 hr at 25 °C	1167	C
Leucovorin calcium		5 mg/ 0.5 ml		2.5 mg/ 0.5 ml	Physically compatible for 5 min at room temperature followed by 8 min of centrifugation	980	C
Lidocaine HCl	ES	50 mg/ 5 ml	RB	10 mg/ 2 ml	Physically compatible for 48 hr at room temperature	924	C
	ES	100 mg/ 10 ml	RB	10 mg/ 2 ml	Physically compatible for 48 hr at room temperature	924	C
	ES	50 mg/ 5 ml	RB	160 mg/ 32 ml	Physically compatible for 48 hr at 25 °C	1167	C
	ES	100 mg/ 10 ml	RB	160 mg/ 32 ml	Physically compatible for 48 hr at 25 °C	1167	C
	ES	50 mg/ 5 ml	RB	10 mg/ 2 ml	Physically compatible for 48 hr at 25 °C	1167	C
	ES	100 mg/ 10 ml	RB	10 mg/ 2 ml	Physically compatible for 48 hr at 25 °C	1167	C
Magnesium sulfate	ES	500 mg/ 1 ml	RB	10 mg/ 2 ml	Physically compatible for 48 hr at room temperature	924	C
	ES	1 g/2 ml	RB	10 mg/ 2 ml	Physically compatible for 48 hr at room temperature	924	C
	ES	1 g/2 ml	RB	160 mg/ 32 ml	Physically compatible for 48 hr at 25 °C	1167	C
	ES	500 mg/ 1 ml	RB	10 mg/ 2 ml	Physically compatible for 48 hr at 25 °C	1167	C
	ES	1 g/2 ml	RB	10 mg/ 2 ml	Physically compatible for 48 hr at 25 °C	1167	C
Meperidine HCl	WI	50 mg/ 1 ml	NO	10 mg/ 2 ml	Physically compatible both macroscopically and microscopically for 15 min at room temperature	565	C
	DW	50 mg/ 1 ml	DW	10 mg/ 2 ml	Visually compatible with little or no loss of either drug over 48 hr at 32 °C exposed to or protected from fluorescent light	2253	C
Methotrexate sodium	LE	50 mg/ 2 ml	RB	10 mg/ 2 ml	Incompatible. If mixed, use immediately	924	I
		12.5 mg/ 0.5 ml		2.5 mg/ 0.5 ml	Physically compatible for 5 min at room temperature followed by 8 min of centrifugation	980	C
	LE	200 mg/ 8 ml	RB	160 mg/ 32 ml	Incompatible. If mixed, use immediately	1167	I

Drugs in Syringe Compatibility (Cont.)

Metoclopramide HCl

Drug (in syringe)	*Mfr*	*Amt*	*Mfr*	*Amt*	*Remarks*	*Ref*	*C/I*
	LE	50 mg/ 2 ml	RB	10 mg/ 2 ml	Incompatible. If mixed, use immediately	1167	I
Methotrimeprazine	RP	10 mg/ 2 ml	NO	10 mg/ 2 ml	Physically compatible both microscopically and macroscopically for 15 min at room temperature	565	C
Methylprednisolone sodium succinate	ES	62.5 mg/ 1 ml	RB	10 mg/ 2 ml	Physically compatible for 24 hr at room temperature	924	C
	ES	250 mg/ 4 ml	RB	10 mg/ 2 ml	Physically compatible for 24 hr at room temperature	924	C
	ES	250 mg/ 4 ml	RB	160 mg/ 32 ml	Physically compatible for 24 hr at 25 °C	1167	C
	ES	62.5 mg/ 1 ml	RB	10 mg/ 2 ml	Physically compatible for 24 hr at 25 °C	1167	C
	ES	250 mg/ 4 ml	RB	10 mg/ 2 ml	Physically compatible for 24 hr at 25 °C	1167	C
Midazolam HCl	RC	5 mg/ 1 ml	RB	10 mg/ 2 ml	Physically compatible for 4 hr at 25 °C under fluorescent light	1145	C
Mitomycin		0.25 mg/ 0.5 ml		2.5 mg/ 0.5 ml	Physically compatible for 5 min at room temperature followed by 8 min of centrifugation	980	C
Morphine HCl	STP, FED	5, 10, 20, 30 mg/ 1 ml	SYO	10 mg/ 2 ml	Visually compatible for up to 7 days at 23 °C	2257	C
Morphine sulfate	AH	10 mg/ 1 ml	NO	10 mg/ 2 ml	Physically compatible both macroscopically and microscopically for 15 min at room temperature	565	C
	EV	1 mg/ml	SKB	0.5 mg/ ml	Diluted with NS. 5% or less loss of both drugs by HPLC in 35 days at 22 °C and 182 days at 4 °C followed by 7 days at 32 °C	1938	C
Morphine tartrate	DB	[b]	DB	10 mg/ 2 ml	Visually compatible with about 5% morphine loss by HPLC in 48 hr at room temperature exposed to light. Metoclopramide not tested	1599	C
Ondansetron HCl	GW	1 mg/ml[c]	SO	2.5 mg/ ml[c]	Physically compatible with no measured increase in particulates and less than 6% loss of ondansetron and less than 5% loss of metoclopramide by HPLC in 24 hr at 4 or 23 °C	2199	C
Papaveretum	RC[d]	20 mg/ 1 ml	NO	10 mg/ 2 ml	Physically compatible both macroscopically and microscopically for 30 min at room temperature	565	C
Penicillin G potassium	SQ	250,000 units/ 1 ml	RB	10 mg/ 2 ml	Incompatible. If mixed, use immediately	924; 1167	I
	SQ	1 million units/ 4 ml	RB	10 mg/ 2 ml	Incompatible. If mixed, use immediately	924; 1167	I
	SQ	1 million units/ 4 ml	RB	160 mg/ 32 ml	Incompatible. If mixed, use immediately	1167	I

Drugs in Syringe Compatibility (Cont.)

Metoclopramide HCl

Drug (in syringe)	*Mfr*	*Amt*	*Mfr*	*Amt*	*Remarks*	*Ref*	*C/I*
Pentazocine lactate	WI	30 mg/ 1 ml	NO	10 mg/ 2 ml	Physically compatible both macroscopically and microscopically for 15 min at room temperature	565	C
Perphenazine	SC	5 mg/ 1 ml	NO	10 mg/ 2 ml	Physically compatible both macroscopically and microscopically for 15 min at room temperature	565; 566	C
Prochlorperazine edisylate	MB	10 mg/ 2 ml	NO	10 mg/ 2 ml	Physically compatible both macroscopically and microscopically for 15 min at room temperature	565	C
Promazine HCl	MY	50 mg/ 1 ml	NO	10 mg/ 2 ml	Physically compatible both macroscopically and microscopically for 15 min at room temperature	565	C
Promethazine HCl	WY	25 mg/ 1 ml	NO	10 mg/ 2 ml	Physically compatible both macroscopically and microscopically for 15 min at room temperature	565	C
Ranitidine HCl	GL	50 mg/ 2 ml	RB	10 mg/ 1 ml	Physically compatible for 1 hr at 25 °C both macroscopically and microscopically	978	C
Scopolamine HBr	ST	0.4 mg/ 1 ml	NO	10 mg/ 2 ml	Physically compatible both macroscopically and microscopically for 15 min at room temperature	565	C
Sodium bicarbonate	AB	100 mEq/ 100 ml	RB	10 mg/ 2 ml	Incompatible. Do not mix	924	I
	AB	100 mEq/ 100 ml	RB	10 mg/ 2 ml	Gas evolves	1167	I
	AB	100 mEq/ 100 ml	RB	160 mg/ 32 ml	Gas evolves	1167	I
Sufentanil citrate	JN	50 μg/ml	RB	5 mg/ml	Physically compatible with no subvisual haze or particle formation in 24 hr at 23 °C	1711	C
Vinblastine sulfate		0.5 mg/ 0.5 ml		2.5 mg/ 0.5 ml	Physically compatible for 5 min at room temperature followed by 8 min of centrifugation	980	C
Vincristine sulfate		0.5 mg/ 0.5 ml		2.5 mg/ 0.5 ml	Physically compatible for 5 min at room temperature followed by 8 min of centrifugation	980	C
Vitamin B complex with C	RC	2 ml	RB	10 mg/ 2 ml	Physically compatible for 48 hr at room temperature	924	C
	RC	2 ml	RB	160 mg/ 32 ml	Physically compatible for 48 hr at 25 °C	1167	C
	RC	2 ml	RB	10 mg/ 2 ml	Physically compatible for 48 hr at 25 °C	1167	C

[a] *Brought to volume with distilled water.*
[b] *Amount unspecified.*
[c] *Tested in sodium chloride 0.9%.*
[d] *The former formulation was tested.*

Y-Site Injection Compatibility (1:1 Mixture)

Metoclopramide HCl

Drug	*Mfr*	*Conc*	*Mfr*	*Conc*	*Remarks*	*Ref*	*C/I*
Acyclovir sodium	BW	5 mg/ml[a]	ES	0.2 mg/ml[a]	Physically compatible for 4 hr at 25 °C	1157	C

Y-Site Injection Compatibility (1:1 Mixture) (Cont.)

			Metoclopramide HCl				
Drug	*Mfr*	*Conc*	*Mfr*	*Conc*	*Remarks*	*Ref*	*C/I*
Aldesleukin	CHI	33,800 I.U./ml[a]	DU	5 mg/ml	Visually compatible with little or no loss of aldesleukin activity by bioassay	1857	C
Allopurinol sodium	BW	3 mg/ml[b]	DU	5 mg/ml	Heavy white precipitate forms immediately	1686	I
Amifostine	USB	10 mg/ml[a]	ES	5 mg/ml	Physically compatible with no change in measured turbidity or increase in particle content in 4 hr at 23 °C	1845	C
Amphotericin B cholesteryl sulfate complex	SEQ	0.83 mg/ml[a]	FAU	5 mg/ml	Gross precipitate forms	2117	I
Amsacrine	NCI	1 mg/ml[a]	RB	2.5 mg/ml[a]	Yellow-orange turbidity develops in 15 min, becoming heavy flocculent orange precipitate in 1 hr	1381	I
Aztreonam	SQ	40 mg/ml[a]	ES	5 mg/ml	Physically compatible with no subvisual haze or particle formation in 4 hr at 23 °C	1758	C
Bleomycin sulfate		3 units/ml		5 mg/ml	Drugs injected sequentially into Y-site with no flush between. No visually apparent precipitate	980	C
Cefepime HCl	BMS	20 mg/ml[a]	RB	5 mg/ml	Haze forms immediately	1689	I
Ciprofloxacin	MI	2 mg/ml[c]	DU	5 mg/ml	Visually compatible for 24 hr at 24 °C	1655	C
	BAY	2 mg/ml[b]		5 mg/ml	Visually compatible with no ciprofloxacin loss by HPLC in 15 min. Metoclopramide not tested.	1934	C
Cisatracurium besylate	GW	0.1, 2, 5 mg/ml[a]	AB	5 mg/ml	Physically compatible with no change in measured turbidity or increase in particle content in 4 hr at 23 °C	2074	C
Cisplatin		1 mg/ml		5 mg/ml	Drugs injected sequentially into Y-site with no flush between. No visually apparent precipitate	980	C
	BR	1 mg/ml	RB	2.5 mg/ml[a]	Visually compatible for 4 hr at room temperature under fluorescent light	1685	C
Cladribine	ORT	0.015[b] and 0.5[d] mg/ml	RB	5 mg/ml	Physically compatible with no change in measured turbidity or increase in particle content in 4 hr at 23 °C	1969	C
Clarithromycin	AB	4 mg/ml[a]	ANT	5 mg/ml	Visually compatible for 72 hr at both 30 and 17 °C	2174	C
Cyclophosphamide		20 mg/ml		5 mg/ml	Drugs injected sequentially into Y-site with no flush between. No visually apparent precipitate	980	C
	MJ	10 mg/ml	RB	2.5 mg/ml[a]	Visually compatible for 4 hr at room temperature under fluorescent light	1685	C
Cytarabine	UP	50 mg/ml	RB	2.5 mg/ml[a]	Visually compatible for 4 hr at room temperature under fluorescent light	1685	C
Diltiazem HCl	MMD	1[b] and 5 mg/ml	RB	5 mg/ml	Visually compatible	1807	C
	MMD	5 mg/ml	RB	0.2 mg/ml[b]	Visually compatible	1807	C
Docetaxel	RPR	0.9 mg/ml[a]	AB	5 mg/ml	Physically compatible with no change in measured turbidity or increase in particle content in 4 hr at 23 °C	2224	C

Y-Site Injection Compatibility (1:1 Mixture) (Cont.)

			Metoclopramide HCl				
Drug	*Mfr*	*Conc*	*Mfr*	*Conc*	*Remarks*	*Ref*	*C/I*
Doxorubicin HCl		2 mg/ml		5 mg/ml	Drugs injected sequentially into Y-site with no flush between. No visually apparent precipitate	980	C
	AD	0.2 mg/ml[a]	RB	2.5 mg/ml[a]	Visually compatible for 4 hr at room temperature under fluorescent light	1685	C
Doxorubicin HCl liposome injection	SEQ	0.4 mg/ml[a]	GNS	5 mg/ml	Increase in measured turbidity	2087	I
Droperidol		2.5 mg/ml		5 mg/ml	Drugs injected sequentially into Y-site with no flush between. No visually apparent precipitate	980	C
Etoposide phosphate	BR	5 mg/ml[a]	FAU	5 mg/ml	Physically compatible with no change in measured turbidity or increase in particle content in 4 hr at 23 °C	2218	C
Famotidine	MSD	0.2 mg/ml[a]	RB	5 mg/ml	Physically compatible for 14 hr	1196	C
	ME	2 mg/ml[b]		5 mg/ml	Visually compatible for 4 hr at 22 °C	1936	C
Fentanyl citrate	JN	0.025 mg/ml[a]	DU	5 mg/ml	Physically compatible with no change in measured haze or increase in particle content in 48 hr at 22 °C	1706	C
Filgrastim	AMG	30 μg/ml[a]	ES	5 mg/ml	Physically compatible with no change in measured turbidity or increase in particle content in 4 hr at 22 °C	1687	C
Fluconazole	RR	2 mg/ml	RB	5 mg/ml	Physically compatible for 24 hr at 25 °C	1407	C
Fludarabine phosphate	BX	1 mg/ml[a]	DU	5 mg/ml	Physically compatible for 4 hr at room temperature under fluorescent light	1439	C
Fluorouracil		50 mg/ml		5 mg/ml	Drugs injected sequentially into Y-site with no flush between. No visually apparent precipitate	980	C
Foscarnet sodium	AST	24 mg/ml	RB	4 mg/ml	Physically compatible for 24 hr at room temperature under fluorescent light	1335	C
	AST	24 mg/ml	RB	2 mg/ml[c]	Physically compatible for 24 hr at 25 °C under fluorescent light by visual and microscopic examination	1393	C
Furosemide		10 mg/ml		5 mg/ml	Drugs injected sequentially into Y-site with no flush between. Immediate precipitation	980	I
Gatifloxacin	BMS	2 mg/ml[a]	AB	5 mg/ml	Physically compatible with no change in measured haze or increase in particle content in 4 hr at 23 °C	2234	C
Gemcitabine HCl	LI	10 mg/ml[b]	FAU	5 mg/ml	Physically compatible with no change in measured turbidity or increase in particle content in 4 hr at 23 °C	2226	C
Granisetron HCl	SKB	0.05 mg/ml[a]	AB	5 mg/ml	Physically compatible with no change in measured turbidity or increase in particle content in 4 hr at 23 °C	2000	C
Heparin sodium		1000 units/ml		5 mg/ml	Drugs injected sequentially into Y-site with no flush between. No visually apparent precipitate	980	C

Y-Site Injection Compatibility (1:1 Mixture) (Cont.)

Metoclopramide HCl

Drug	*Mfr*	*Conc*	*Mfr*	*Conc*	*Remarks*	*Ref*	*C/I*
Hetastarch in lactated electrolyte injection (Hextend)	AB	6%	FAU	5 mg/ml	Physically compatible with no change in measured turbidity or increase in particle content in 4 hr at 23 °C	2339	C
Hydromorphone HCl	AST	0.5 mg/ml[a]	DU	5 mg/ml	Physically compatible with no change in measured haze or increase in particle content in 48 hr at 22 °C	1706	C
Idarubicin HCl	AD	1 mg/ml[b]	SO	5 mg/ml	Visually compatible for 24 hr at 25 °C	1525	C
Leucovorin calcium		10 mg/ml		5 mg/ml	Drugs injected sequentially into Y-site with no flush between. No visually apparent precipitate	980	C
Levofloxacin	OMN	5 mg/ml[a]	ES	5 mg/ml	Visually compatible for 4 hr at 24 °C under fluorescent light	2233	C
Linezolid	PHU	2 mg/ml	FAU	5 mg/ml	Physically compatible with no change in measured turbidity or increase in particle content in 4 hr at 23 °C	2264	C
Melphalan HCl	BW	0.1 mg/ml[b]	RB	5 mg/ml	Physically compatible with no change in measured turbidity or increase in particle content in 3 hr at 22 °C	1557	C
Meperidine HCl	AB	10 mg/ml	SN	0.2 mg/ml[a]	Physically compatible for 4 hr at 25 °C	1397	C
Meropenem	ZEN	1 and 50 mg/ml[b]	RB	5 mg/ml	Visually compatible for 4 hr at room temperature	1994	C
Methadone HCl	LI	1 mg/ml[a]	DU	5 mg/ml	Physically compatible with no change in measured haze or increase in particle content in 48 hr at 22 °C	1706	C
Methotrexate sodium		25 mg/ml		5 mg/ml	Drugs injected sequentially into Y-site with no flush between. No visually apparent precipitate	980	C
	AD	15 mg/ml[e]	RB	2.5 mg/ml[a]	Visually compatible for 4 hr at room temperature under fluorescent light	1685	C
Mitomycin		0.5 mg/ml		5 mg/ml	Drugs injected sequentially into Y-site with no flush between. No visually apparent precipitate	980	C
Morphine sulfate	AB	1 mg/ml	SN	0.2 mg/ml[a]	Physically compatible for 4 hr at 25 °C	1397	C
	AST	1 mg/ml[a]	DU	5 mg/ml	Physically compatible with no change in measured haze or increase in particle content in 48 hr at 22 °C	1706	C
Ondansetron HCl	GL	1 mg/ml[b]	DU	5 mg/ml	Physically compatible for 4 hr at 22 °C	1365	C
Paclitaxel	NCI	1.2 mg/ml[a]		5 mg/ml	Physically compatible with no change in measured turbidity in 4 hr at 22 °C	1528	C
Piperacillin sodium–tazobactam sodium	LE	40 + 5 mg/ml[a]	RB	5 mg/ml	Physically compatible with no change in measured turbidity or increase in particle content in 4 hr at 22 °C	1688	C
Propofol	ZEN	10 mg/ml	RB	5 mg/ml	Emulsion broke and oiled out	1916	I
Remifentanil HCl	GW	0.025 and 0.25 mg/ml[b]	AB	5 mg/ml	Physically compatible with no change in measured turbidity or increase in particle content in 4 hr at 23 °C	2075	C
Sargramostim	IMM	10 μg/ml[b]	DU	5 mg/ml	Physically compatible for 4 hr at 22 °C	1436	C

Y-Site Injection Compatibility (1:1 Mixture) (Cont.)

			Metoclopramide HCl				
Drug	*Mfr*	*Conc*	*Mfr*	*Conc*	*Remarks*	*Ref*	*C/I*
Sufentanil citrate	JN	12.5 μg/ml[a]	RB	5 mg/ml	Physically compatible with no subvisual haze or particle formation in 24 hr at 23 °C	1711	C
Tacrolimus	FUJ	1 mg/ml[b]	DU	0.2 mg/ml[a]	Visually compatible for 24 hr at 25 °C	1630	C
Teniposide	BR	0.1 mg/ml[a]	ES	5 mg/ml	Physically compatible with no subvisual haze or particle formation in 4 hr at 23 °C	1725	C
Thiotepa	IMM[f]	1 mg/ml[a]	RB	5 mg/ml	Physically compatible with no change in measured turbidity or increase in particle content in 4 hr at 23 °C	1861	C
TNA #218 to #226[g]			AB	5 mg/ml	Visually compatible with no precipitate or emulsion damage apparent in 4 hr at 23 °C	2215	C
Topotecan HCl	SKB	56 μg/ml[a,b]	RB	1.72 mg/ml[a,b]	Visually compatible with little or no loss of either drug by HPLC in 4 hr at 22 °C under fluorescent light	2245	C
TPN #212 to #215[g]			AB	5 mg/ml	Substantial loss of natural subvisual turbidity occurs immediately	2109	I
Vinblastine sulfate		1 mg/ml		5 mg/ml	Drugs injected sequentially into Y-site with no flush between. No visually apparent precipitate	980	C
Vincristine sulfate		1 mg/ml		5 mg/ml	Drugs injected sequentially into Y-site with no flush between. No visually apparent precipitate	980	C
Vinorelbine tartrate	BW	1 mg/ml[b]	RB	5 mg/ml	Physically compatible with no change in measured turbidity or increase in particle content in 4 hr at 22 °C	1558	C
Zidovudine	BW	4 mg/ml[a]	RB	2 mg/ml[a]	Physically compatible for 4 hr at 25 °C under fluorescent light by visual and microscopic examination	1193	C

[a] *Tested in dextrose 5% in water.*
[b] *Tested in sodium chloride 0.9%.*
[c] *Tested in both dextrose 5% in water and sodium chloride 0.9%.*
[d] *Tested in bacteriostatic sodium chloride 0.9% preserved with benzyl alcohol 0.9%.*
[e] *Tested in dextrose 5% in water with sodium bicarbonate 0.05 mEq/ml.*
[f] *Lyophilized formulation tested.*
[g] *Refer to Appendix I for the composition of parenteral nutrition solutions. TNA indicates a 3-in-1 admixture, and TPN indicates a 2-in-1 admixture.*

Additional Compatibility Information

Infusion Solutions — Metoclopramide HCl has been stated to be compatible for up to 48 hours at room temperature, protected from light, in the following infusion solutions (2; 4):

Dextrose 5% in sodium chloride 0.45%
Dextrose 5% in water
Ringer's injection
Ringer's injection, lactated
Sodium chloride 0.9%

The manufacturer indicates dilutions may be stored under normal light conditions, without light protection, for up to 24 hours. (2)

Cisplatin — The sodium metabisulfite antioxidant present in the former metoclopramide HCl formulation reacted rapidly and extensively with cisplatin, displacing the chloride ligands. At clinically relevant concentrations, a 10% cisplatin loss occurred in less than five minutes. Total cisplatin loss occurred in about 30 minutes. (1175) The current Reglan and Maxolon formulations contain no sulfites. (2; 4; 1247)

Diamorphine HCl — Metoclopramide HCl is stated to be stable and compatible with diamorphine HCl. (1442)

METOPROLOL TARTRATE
AHFS 24:04

Products — Metoprolol tartrate is available in 5-ml ampuls, vials, and syringe cartridges. Each milliliter of solution contains 1 mg of metoprolol tartrate and 9 mg of sodium chloride. (1-6/00)

pH — Approximately 7.5. (175)

Trade Name(s) — Lopressor.

Administration — Metoprolol tartrate is administered intravenously. (2; 4)

Stability — Metoprolol tartrate injection should be stored at controlled room temperature and protected from light and freezing. (2; 4)

Compatibility Information

Solution Compatibility

Metoprolol tartrate

Solution	Mfr	Mfr	Conc/L	Remarks	Ref	C/I
Dextrose 5% in water	BA[a]	CI	300 mg	Visually compatible with little or no metoprolol loss by HPLC in 36 hr at 24 °C under fluorescent light	1679	C
Sodium chloride 0.9%	BA[a]	CI	300 mg	Visually compatible with little or no metoprolol loss by HPLC in 36 hr at 24 °C under fluorescent light	1679	C

[a]*Tested in PVC containers.*

Y-Site Injection Compatibility (1:1 Mixture)

Metoprolol tartrate

Drug	Mfr	Conc	Mfr	Conc	Remarks	Ref	C/I
Alteplase	GEN	1 mg/ml	CI	1 mg/ml	Visually compatible with no alteplase clot-lysis activity loss in 24 hr at 25 °C	1856	C
Amphotericin B cholesteryl sulfate complex	SEQ	0.83 mg/ml[a]	GEM	1 mg/ml	Gross precipitate forms	2117	I
Meperidine HCl	AB	10 mg/ml	CI	1 mg/ml	Physically compatible for 4 hr at 25 °C	1397	C
Morphine sulfate	AB	1 mg/ml	CI	1 mg/ml	Physically compatible for 4 hr at 25 °C	1397	C

[a]*Tested in dextrose 5% in water.*

METRONIDAZOLE
AHFS 8:40

Products — Metronidazole is available as a ready-to-use solution in 100-ml single-dose PVC plastic bags. No dilution or buffering is required. Each bag contains (1-5/96):

Metronidazole	500 mg
Dibasic sodium phosphate	47.6 mg
Citric acid anhydrous	22.9 mg
Sodium chloride	790 mg
Water for injection	qs 100 ml

pH — Metronidazole ready-to-use has a pH of 5.5 (range 4.5 to 7). (1-5/96)

Osmolarity — Metronidazole ready-to-use has an osmolarity of 310 mOsm/L. (1-5/96)

Sodium Content — Metronidazole ready-to-use contains 14 mEq of sodium from the excipients per 500 mg of metronidazole. (1-5/96; 4)

Trade Name(s) — Flagyl I.V. RTU.

Administration — Metronidazole ready-to-use is administered by continuous intravenous infusion or by intermittent intravenous infusion over one hour. Metronidazole ready-to-use may be administered without dilution or buffering. (1-5/96; 4)

Stability — Metronidazole ready-to-use is a clear, colorless solution which should be stored at controlled room temperature and protected from light. (1-5/96; 4) It should not be stored under refrigeration. (1-5/96) Refrigeration may result in crystal formation. However, the crystals redissolve on warming to room temperature. (1115)

Light Effects — Prolonged exposure to light will cause a darkening of the product. (4) However, most manufacturers indicate that short-term exposure to normal room light does not adversely affect metronidazole stability. Direct sunlight should be avoided. (1115)

Elastomeric Reservoir Pumps—Metronidazole 5 mg/ml in Homepump and Homepump Eclipse elastomeric reservoir pumps has been stated by the pump manufacturer to be stable for 24 hours at room temperature and 10 days under refrigeration, although precipitation may occur during refrigerated storage. (31)

Sorption—Metronidazole (May & Baker) 30 mg/L in sodium chloride 0.9% (Travenol) in PVC bags did not exhibit significant sorption to the plastic during one week of storage at room temperature (15 to 20 °C). (536)

In another study, metronidazole (May & Baker) 30 mg/L in sodium chloride 0.9% did not exhibit any loss due to sorption during a seven-hour simulated infusion through an infusion set (Travenol) consisting of a cellulose propionate burette chamber and 170 cm of PVC tubing. (606)

The drug was also tested as a simulated infusion over at least one hour by a syringe pump system. A glass syringe on a syringe pump was fitted with 20 cm of polyethylene tubing or 50 cm of Silastic tubing. No loss of drug due to sorption was observed with either tubing. (606)

A 25-ml aliquot of metronidazole (May & Baker) 30 mg/L in sodium chloride 0.9% was stored in all-plastic syringes composed of polypropylene barrels and polyethylene plungers for 24 hours at room temperature in the dark. No loss due to sorption occurred. (606)

Filtration—Metronidazole (Specia) 5 mg/ml in dextrose 5% in water and sodium chloride 0.9% was filtered through a 0.22-μm cellulose ester membrane filter (Ivex-HP, Millipore) over six hours. No significant drug loss due to binding to the filter was noted. (1034)

Central Venous Catheter—Metronidazole (Baxter) 5 mg/ml in dextrose 5% in water was found to be compatible with the ARROWg+ard Blue Plus (Arrow International) chlorhexidine-bearing triple-lumen central catheter. HPLC analysis was used to evaluate completeness of drug delivery through the catheter and the amount of chlorhexidine removed from the internal lumens. Essentially complete delivery of the drug was found with little or no drug loss occurring. Furthermore, chlorhexidine delivered from the catheter remained at trace amounts with no substantial increase due to the delivery of the drug through the catheter. (2335)

Compatibility Information

Additive Compatibility

Metronidazole

Drug	*Mfr*	*Conc/L*	*Mfr*	*Conc/L*	*Test Soln*	*Remarks*	*Ref*	*C/I*
Amikacin sulfate	BR	5 g	RP	5 g[a]		Physically compatible with little or no pH change for at least 12 hr at 23 °C	807	C
Amoxicillin sodium–clavulanate potassium	BE	20 + 2 g	BAY	5 g		Physically compatible with 8% clavulanate loss in 2 hr and 25% loss in 6 hr at 21 °C by HPLC. 7 to 8% amoxicillin and no metronidazole loss in 6 hr at 21 °C.	1920	I
Ampicillin sodium	AY	20 g	RP	5 g[a]		Physically compatible for at least 24 hr at 23 °C, but pH changed significantly	807	?
	BR	20 g	SE	5 g		9% ampicillin loss in 22 hr at 25 °C and 12 days at 5 °C. No metronidazole loss	993	C
Aztreonam	SQ	10 and 20 g	MG	5 g		Pink color develops in 12 hr, becoming cherry red in 48 hr at 25 °C. Pink color develops in 3 days at 4 °C. No loss of either drug detected	1023	I
Cefamandole nafate	LI	20 g	RP	5 g[a]		Physically compatible with little or no pH change for at least 72 hr at 4 °C	807	C
	LI	20 g	RP	5 g[a]		Physically compatible for at least 24 hr at 23 °C, but pH changed significantly	807	?
	LI	20 g	SE	5 g		10% metronidazole loss in 2 hr at 25 °C and 6 hr at 5 °C with no further loss occurring in up to 3 days. No cefamandole loss	979	I
	LI	800 mg	SE	200 mg	W	No immediate loss of potency of either drug	979	C
	LI	16.7 g	BAY	4.2 g	[b]	Visually compatible with little cefamandole loss and 8% or less metronidazole loss in 4 hr at room temperature by HPLC	1888	C

Additive Compatibility (Cont.)

			Metronidazole					
Drug	*Mfr*	*Conc/L*	*Mfr*	*Conc/L*	*Test Soln*	*Remarks*	*Ref*	*C/I*
Cefazolin sodium	LI	10 g	RP	5 g[a]		Physically compatible with little or no pH change for at least 24 hr at 23 °C and 72 hr at 4 °C	807	C
	LI	10 g	SE	5 g		5% cefazolin loss and no metronidazole loss in 7 days at 25 °C. No loss of either drug in 12 days at 5 °C	993	C
	LI	10 g	AB	5 g		Visually compatible with no loss of either drug by HPLC in 72 hr at 8 °C	1649	C
Cefepime HCl	BR	40 g	AB, ES, SE	5 g		7% cefepime loss by HPLC in 24 hr at room temperature exposed to light and 8% loss in 5 days at 5 °C. Little or no metronidazole loss by HPLC. However, orange color develops in 18 hr at room temperature and 24 hr at 5 °C	1682	?
	BR	4 g	AB, ES, SE	5 g		6% cefepime loss by HPLC in 24 hr at room temperature exposed to light and 3% loss in 5 days at 5 °C. Little or no metronidazole loss by HPLC. However, orange color develops in 18 hr at room temperature and 24 hr at 5 °C	1682	?
	BMS	20 g	SCS	5 g	[e]	Visually compatible. HPLC found 7% cefepime loss in 48 hr and 11% loss in 72 hr at 23 °C; 8% cefepime loss in 7 days at 4 °C. No metronidazole loss in 7 days at 4 and 23 °C	2324	C
	BMS	10 g	SCS	5 g	[e]	Visually compatible. HPLC found 9% cefepime loss in 72 hr at 23 °C and 4% or less loss in 7 days at 4 °C. 7% or less metronidazole loss in 7 days at 4 and 23 °C	2324	C
	BMS	5 g	SCS	5 g	[e]	Visually compatible. HPLC found 9% cefepime loss in 48 hr at 23 °C and 2% or less loss in 7 days at 4 °C. Little or no metronidazole loss in 7 days at 4 and 23 °C	2324	C
	BMS	2.5 g	SCS	5 g	[e]	Visually compatible. HPLC found 8% cefepime loss in 48 hr and 12% loss in 72 hr at 23 °C; 7% cefepime loss in 7 days at 4 °C. 5% or less metronidazole loss in 7 days at 4 and 23 °C	2324	C
Cefotaxime sodium	RS	20 g	RP	5 g[a]		Physically compatible with little or no pH change for at least 24 hr at 4 °C	807	C
	HO	10 g	AB	5 g		Potency of both drugs by HPLC retained for 72 hr at 8 °C	1547	C
	HO	10 g	AB	5 g		Visually compatible with 10% cefotaxime loss by HPLC in 19 hr at 28 °C and 8% loss in 96 hr at 5 °C. No metronidazole loss in 96 hr at 5 or 28 °C	1754	C
Cefotiam HCl	TAK	20 g		5 g		Visually compatible with no little or no loss of either drug by HPLC in 4 hr at room temperature	1737	C
Cefoxitin sodium	FC	30 g	RP	5 g[a]		Physically compatible with little or no pH change for at least 24 hr at 4 °C	807	C

Additive Compatibility (Cont.)

Metronidazole

Drug	Mfr	Conc/L	Mfr	Conc/L	Test Soln	Remarks	Ref	C/I
	FC	30 g	RP	5 g[a]		Physically compatible, but pH changed significantly in 6 to 12 hr at 23 °C	807	?
	MSD	30 g	SE	5 g		9% cefoxitin loss in 48 hr at 25 °C and 3% in 12 days at 5 °C. No metronidazole loss	993	C
Ceftazidime	GL[c]	20 g		5 g		No loss of either drug in 4 hr	1345	C
	LI[c]	10 g	AB	5 g		Visually compatible with little or no loss of either drug by HPLC in 72 hr at 8 °C	1849	C
Ceftizoxime sodium	FUJ	10 g	AB	5 g		Visually compatible with little or no loss of either drug by HPLC in 72 hr at 8 °C	1849	C
	SKB	10 g	AB	5 g		Visually compatible with 8 to 9% loss of both drugs by HPLC in 14 days at 4 °C followed by 48 hr at 25 °C. 3 to 4% loss of both drugs in 3 days and 10 to 13% in 5 days at 25 °C	1879	C
Ceftriaxone sodium	RC	10 g	AB	5 g		Visually compatible with little or no loss of either drug by HPLC in 72 hr at 8 °C	1849	C
	RC	10 g	BA	5 g		Visually compatible with no metronidazole loss by HPLC and with 6% ceftriaxone loss in 3 days and 8% in 4 days at 25 °C	2101	C
Cefuroxime sodium	GL	7.5 g		5 g		Physically compatible with no loss of either drug in 1 hr	1036	C
	GL	15 g		5 g		No loss of either drug in 4 hr at 24 °C	1376	C
	GL	7.5 g		5 g		10% cefuroxime loss by HPLC in 16 days at 4 °C and 35 hr at 25 °C. No metronidazole loss by HPLC in 15 days at 4 and 25 °C	1565	C
	GL	7.5 and 15 g	IVX	5 g		Physically compatible with no visible precipitation or increase in measured particulates. No loss of metronidazole and about 6% cefuroxime loss in 49 days at 5 °C	2192	C
Chloramphenicol sodium succinate	PD	10 g	RP	5 g[a]		Physically compatible with little or no pH change for at least 72 hr at 23 °C	807	C
Ciprofloxacin		2 g		5 g		No loss of either drug in 4 hr at 24 °C	1346	C
	MI	1.6 g	SE	4.2 g		Visually compatible and potency of both drugs by HPLC retained for 48 hr at 25 °C under fluorescent light and 4 °C in the dark	1541	C
Clindamycin phosphate	UP	10 g	RP	5 g[a]		Physically compatible with little or no pH change for at least 24 hr at 23 °C	807	C
Floxacillin sodium	BE	10 g		5 g		Physically compatible for 48 hr. Potency of both drugs retained when assayed after 1 hr at room temperature	1036	C
Fluconazole	PF	1 g	AB	2.5 g		Visually compatible with no fluconazole loss by HPLC in 72 hr at 25 °C under fluorescent light. Metronidazole not tested	1677	C
Gentamicin sulfate	RS	800 mg	RP	5 g[a]		Physically compatible with little or no pH change for at least 72 hr at 23 °C	807	C

Additive Compatibility (Cont.)

Metronidazole

Drug	Mfr	Conc/L	Mfr	Conc/L	Test Soln	Remarks	Ref	C/I
	EX	800 mg[d]		5 g		Physically compatible with no loss of either drug in 1 hr	1036	C
	SC	800 mg and 1.2 g	SE	5 g		Physically compatible with no loss of either drug in 2 days at 18 °C. At 4 °C, no metronidazole loss but up to 10% gentamicin loss in 7 days	1242	C
		800 mg	RP	5 g		Visually compatible with no loss of metronidazole by HPLC in 15 days at 5 and 25 °C. 10% gentamicin loss by immunoassay in 63 hr at 25 °C and 10.6 days at 5 °C	1931	C
Hydrocortisone sodium succinate	UP	10 g	RP	5 g[a]		Physically compatible for at least 72 hr at 23 °C, but pH changed significantly	807	?
	ES	10 g	SE	5 g		No loss of either drug for 7 days at 25 °C and 12 days at 5 °C	993	C
Netilmicin sulfate	SC	1.4 g	RP	5 g[a]		Physically compatible with little or no pH change for at least 24 hr at 23 °C and 72 hr at 4 °C	807	C
	EX	1 g		5 g		Physically compatible with no loss of either drug in 1 hr	1036	C
Penicillin G potassium	AY	12 million units	RP	5 g[a]		Physically compatible for at least 72 hr at 23 °C, but pH changed significantly	807	?
	PF	200 million units	SE	5 g		5% penicillin loss in 22 hr and 8% in 72 hr at 25 °C. 2% penicillin loss in 12 days at 5 °C. No metronidazole loss	993	C
Tobramycin sulfate	LI	800 mg	RP	5 g[a]		Physically compatible with little or no pH change for at least 72 hr at 23 °C	807	C
	LI	1 g	RP	5 g		Visually compatible with no loss of metronidazole by HPLC in 15 days at 5 and 25 °C. 10% tobramycin loss by immunoassay in 73 hr at 25 °C and 12.1 days at 5 °C	1931	C

[a] *Minibags (100 ml) containing metronidazole 500 mg with disodium phosphate 150 mg, citric acid 44 mg, and sodium chloride 740 mg. This product differs from the SCS Pharmaceuticals product.*
[b] *Cefamandole reconstituted with water and added to metronidazole infusion.*
[c] *Sodium carbonate—containing formulation tested.*
[d] *Tested in both dextrose 5% in water and sodium chloride 0.9%.*
[e] *Tested in PVC containers.*

Y-Site Injection Compatibility (1:1 Mixture)

Metronidazole

Drug	Mfr	Conc	Mfr	Conc	Remarks	Ref	C/I
Acyclovir sodium	BW	5 mg/ml[a]	SE	5 mg/ml	Physically compatible for 4 hr at 25 °C	1157	C
Allopurinol sodium	BW	3 mg/ml[b]	BA	5 mg/ml	Physically compatible with no change in measured turbidity or increase in particle content in 4 hr at 22 °C	1686	C
Amifostine	USB	10 mg/ml[a]	BA	5 mg/ml	Physically compatible with no change in measured turbidity or increase in particle content in 4 hr at 23 °C	1845	C

Y-Site Injection Compatibility (1:1 Mixture) (Cont.)

Drug	Mfr	Conc	Metronidazole Mfr	Metronidazole Conc	Remarks	Ref	C/I
Amphotericin B cholesteryl sulfate complex	SEQ	0.83 mg/ml[a]	AB	5 mg/ml	Gross precipitate forms	2117	I
Aztreonam	SQ	40 mg/ml[a]	BA	5 mg/ml	Color changes from colorless to orange in 4 hr	1758	I
Cefepime HCl	BMS	20 mg/ml[a]	BA	5 mg/ml	Physically compatible with no change in measured turbidity or increase in particle content in 4 hr at 22 °C	1689	C
Cisatracurium besylate	GW	0.1, 2, and 5 mg/ml[a]	AB	5 mg/ml	Physically compatible with no change in measured turbidity or increase in particle content in 4 hr at 23 °C	2074	C
Clarithromycin	AB	4 mg/ml[a]	PRK	5 mg/ml	Visually compatible for 72 hr at both 30 and 17 °C	2174	C
Cyclophosphamide	MJ	20 mg/ml[a]	SE	5 mg/ml	Physically compatible for 4 hr at 25 °C	1194	C
Diltiazem HCl	MMD	5 mg/ml	SE	5 mg/ml	Visually compatible	1807	C
Docetaxel	RPR	0.9 mg/ml[a]	BA	5 mg/ml	Physically compatible with no change in measured turbidity or increase in particle content in 4 hr at 23 °C	2224	C
Dopamine HCl	AB	0.8 mg/ml[a]	MG	5 mg/ml	Visually compatible for 24 hr at room temperature in test tubes. No precipitate found on filter from Y-site delivery	2063	C
Doxorubicin HCl liposome injection	SEQ	0.4 mg/ml[a]	AB	5 mg/ml	Physically compatible with little or no change in measured turbidity and no increase in particle content in 4 hr at 23 °C	2087	C
Enalaprilat	MSD	0.05 mg/ml[b]	SE	5 mg/ml	Physically compatible for 24 hr at room temperature under fluorescent light	1355	C
Esmolol HCl	DCC	10 mg/ml[a]	SE	5 mg/ml	Physically compatible for 24 hr at 22 °C	1169	C
Etoposide phosphate	BR	5 mg/ml[a]	AB	5 mg/ml	Physically compatible with no change in measured turbidity or increase in particle content in 4 hr at 23 °C	2218	C
Filgrastim	AMG	30 μg/ml[a]	BA	5 mg/ml	Particles form immediately with filaments in 1 hr	1687	I
Fluconazole	RR	2 mg/ml	AB	5 mg/ml	Physically compatible for 24 hr at 25 °C	1407	C
Foscarnet sodium	AST	24 mg/ml	AB	5 mg/ml	Physically compatible for 24 hr at room temperature under fluorescent light	1335	C
	AST	24 mg/ml	SE	5 mg/ml	Physically compatible for 24 hr at 25 °C under fluorescent light by visual and microscopic examination	1393	C
Gatifloxacin	BMS	2 mg/ml[a]	BA	5 mg/ml	Physically compatible with no change in measured haze or increase in particle content in 4 hr at 23 °C	2234	C
Gemcitabine HCl	LI	10 mg/ml[b]	AB	5 mg/ml	Physically compatible with no change in measured turbidity or increase in particle content in 4 hr at 23 °C	2226	C
Granisetron HCl	SKB	0.05 mg/ml[a]	BA	5 mg/ml	Physically compatible with no change in measured turbidity or increase in particle content in 4 hr at 23 °C	2000	C

Y-Site Injection Compatibility (1:1 Mixture) (Cont.)

Metronidazole

Drug	*Mfr*	*Conc*	*Mfr*	*Conc*	*Remarks*	*Ref*	*C/I*
Heparin sodium	TR	50 units/ml	MG	5 mg/ml	Visually compatible for 4 hr at 25 °C	1793	C
Hetastarch in lactated electrolyte injection (Hextend)	AB	6%	AB	5 mg/ml	Physically compatible with no change in measured turbidity or increase in particle content in 4 hr at 23 °C	2339	C
Hydromorphone HCl	WY	0.2 mg/ml[a]	SE	5 mg/ml	Physically compatible for at least 4 hr at 25 °C under fluorescent light	987	C
Labetalol HCl	SC	1 mg/ml[a]	SE	5 mg/ml	Physically compatible for 24 hr at 18 °C	1171	C
Linezolid	PHU	2 mg/ml	BA	5 mg/ml	Physically compatible with no change in measured turbidity or increase in particle content in 4 hr at 23 °C	2264	C
Lorazepam	WY	0.33 mg/ml[b]	BRN	5 mg/ml	Visually compatible for 24 hr at 22 °C	1855	C
Magnesium sulfate	IX	16.7, 33.3, 66.7, 100 mg/ml[a]	SE	5 mg/ml	Physically compatible for at least 4 hr at 32 °C	813	C
Melphalan HCl	BW	0.1 mg/ml[b]	AB	5 mg/ml	Physically compatible with no change in measured turbidity or increase in particle content in 3 hr at 22 °C	1557	C
Meperidine HCl	WY	10 mg/ml[a]	SE	5 mg/ml	Physically compatible for at least 4 hr at 25 °C under fluorescent light	987	C
Methylprednisolone sodium succinate	UP	5 mg/ml[a]	MG	5 mg/ml	Visually compatible for 24 hr at room temperature in test tubes. No precipitate found on filter from Y-site delivery	2063	C
Midazolam HCl	RC RC	1 mg/ml[a] 5 mg/ml	BA BRN	5 mg/ml 5 mg/ml	Visually compatible for 24 hr at 23 °C Visually compatible for 24 hr at 22 °C	1847 1855	C C
Morphine sulfate	WI	1 mg/ml[a]	SE	5 mg/ml	Physically compatible for at least 4 hr at 25 °C under fluorescent light	987	C
Perphenazine	SC	0.02 mg/ml[a]	SE	5 mg/ml	Physically compatible for 4 hr at 25 °C	1155	C
Piperacillin sodium–tazobactam sodium	LE	40 + 5 mg/ml[a]	BA	5 mg/ml	Physically compatible with no change in measured turbidity or increase in particle content in 4 hr at 22 °C	1688	C
Remifentanil HCl	GW	0.025 and 0.25 mg/ml[b]	AB	5 mg/ml	Physically compatible with no change in measured turbidity or increase in particle content in 4 hr at 23 °C	2075	C
Sargramostim	IMM	10 μg/ml[b]	MG	5 mg/ml	Physically compatible for 4 hr at 22 °C	1436	C
Tacrolimus	FUJ	1 mg/ml[b]	AB	5 mg/ml	Visually compatible for 24 hr at 25 °C	1630	C
Teniposide	BR	0.1 mg/ml[a]	BA	5 mg/ml	Physically compatible with no subvisual haze or particle formation in 4 hr at 23 °C	1725	C
Theophylline	TR	4 mg/ml	MG	5 mg/ml	Visually compatible for 6 hr at 25 °C	1793	C
Thiotepa	IMM[c]	1 mg/ml[a]	BA	5 mg/ml	Physically compatible with no change in measured turbidity or increase in particle content in 4 hr at 23 °C	1861	C
TNA #218 to #226[d]			AB	5 mg/ml	Visually compatible with no precipitate or emulsion damage apparent in 4 hr at 23 °C	2215	C
TPN #189[d]			DB	5 mg/ml	Visually compatible for 24 hr at 22 °C	1767	C

Y-Site Injection Compatibility (1:1 Mixture) (Cont.)

Metronidazole

Drug	*Mfr*	*Conc*	*Mfr*	*Conc*	*Remarks*	*Ref*	*C/I*
TPN #203 and #204[d]			AB	5 mg/ml	Visually compatible for 2 hr at 23 °C	1974	C
TPN #212 to #215[d]			SCS	5 mg/ml	Physically compatible with no change in measured turbidity or increase in particle content in 4 hr at 23 °C	2109	C
Vinorelbine tartrate	BW	1 mg/ml[b]	BA	5 mg/ml	Physically compatible with no change in measured turbidity or increase in particle content in 4 hr at 22 °C	1558	C

[a]*Tested in dextrose 5% in water.*
[b]*Tested in sodium chloride 0.9%.*
[c]*Lyophilized formulation tested.*
[d]*Refer to Appendix I for the composition of parenteral nutrition solutions. TNA indicates a 3-in-1 admixture, and TPN indicates a 2-in-1 admixture.*
[e]*Sodium carbonate–containing formulation tested.*

Additional Compatibility Information

Other Drugs — It is recommended that no other drug be added to infusions of metronidazole ready-to-use. Furthermore, if administration of metronidazole is to be made through the tubing of an ongoing primary infusion, the primary infusion should be stopped, if possible, during metronidazole administration. (1-5/96; 4)

However, ceftazidime (Ceptaz) is stated to be stable for 24 hours at room temperature or for seven days under refrigeration with metronidazole 5 mg/ml. (4)

Aluminum — The discoloration interaction that occurs between reconstituted metronidazole HCl and aluminum in needle hubs does not occur as readily with the ready-to-use metronidazole solution. Discoloration is not apparent when administration is completed within one hour. However, the solution may discolor and a precipitate may form after contact with aluminum for six or more hours. (4; 707; 1116; 1117) Also see Metronidazole HCl monograph.

METRONIDAZOLE HCL
AHFS 8:40

Products — Metronidazole HCl is available in single-dose lyophilized vials containing metronidazole 500 mg as the hydrochloride and mannitol 415 mg. The correct order of mixing must be followed in preparing the dose for administration. (2)

To prepare the solution, add 4.4 ml of one of the following diluents to the vial and mix thoroughly:

Sterile water for injection
Bacteriostatic water for injection
Sodium chloride 0.9%
Bacteriostatic sodium chloride 0.9%

The resulting solution volume of 5 ml will contain 100 mg/ml of metronidazole as the hydrochloride. Further dilute this reconstituted solution to a concentration not more than 8 mg/ml in one of the following infusion solutions:

Dextrose 5% in water
Ringer's injection, lactated
Sodium chloride 0.9%

Addition of 500 mg of metronidazole as the hydrochloride to 100 ml of infusion solution will result in a 5-mg/ml solution. Concentrations exceeding 8 mg/ml may result in precipitation. Use only needles with plastic hubs for this dilution. Do not allow the reconstituted solution to contact aluminum. (2; 4)

The diluted solution has an acidic pH and must be neutralized before administration. Approximately 5 mEq of sodium bicarbonate should be added to the diluted solution for each 500 mg of metronidazole and mixed thoroughly. Carbon dioxide gas will be generated, and it may be necessary to relieve the pressure in the container. (2; 4)

pH — After reconstitution, metronidazole HCl has a pH of 0.5 to 2. On further dilution and subsequent neutralization, the pH is approximately 6 to 7. (2; 4)

Trade Name(s) — Flagyl I.V.

Administration — Metronidazole HCl is administered by continuous intravenous infusion or by intermittent intravenous infusion over one hour. Metronidazole HCl must be diluted to 8 mg/ml or less and neutralized prior to administration. Because of the very low pH of the reconstituted solution, it cannot be given by direct intravenous injection. (2; 4)

Stability — Metronidazole HCl should be stored below 25 °C and protected from light. (2; 4) Prolonged exposure to light will cause darkening of the product. (4) However, most manufacturers indicate that short-term exposure to normal room light does not adversely affect metronidazole stability. Direct sunlight should be avoided. (1115)

Initial reconstitution results in a pale yellow to yellow-green solution, which is chemically stable for 96 hours when stored below 30 °C in normal room light. Once further diluted in infusion solutions and neutralized, the solutions should be stored at room temperature and used within 24 hours. Do not refrigerate the neutralized diluted solution because precipitation may occur. (2; 4)

Do not attempt to neutralize the reconstituted metronidazole HCl solution prior to dilution in intravenous solutions. Direct addition of sodium bicarbonate to the reconstituted solution will result in immediate precipitation along with the formation of carbon dioxide gas. (706)

Elastomeric Reservoir Pumps— Metronidazole HCl 5 mg/ml in dextrose 5% in water and in sodium chloride 0.9% in Medflo and ReadyMed elastomeric reservoir pumps has been stated by the pump manufacturers to be stable for 24 hours at room temperature. (31)

Compatibility Information

Solution Compatibility

Metronidazole HCl

Solution	*Mfr*	*Mfr*	*Conc/L*	*Remarks*	*Ref*	*C/I*
Amino acids 10%	AB	SE	5 g[a]	Initial yellow color becomes dark yellow in 24 hr	765	I

[a]*Reconstituted metronidazole HCl neutralized with sodium bicarbonate 50 mEq/L was tested.*

Additive Compatibility

Metronidazole HCl

Drug	*Mfr*	*Conc/L*	*Mfr*	*Conc/L*	*Test Soln*	*Remarks*	*Ref*	*C/I*
Amikacin sulfate	BR	2.25 g	SE	5 g[a]	D5W, NS	Physically compatible for 48 hr	765	C
Aminophylline	SE	2 g	SE	5 g[a]	D5W, NS	Physically compatible for 48 hr	765	C
Ampicillin sodium	BR	2 g	SE	5 g[a]	D5W, NS	Physically compatible for 48 hr but ampicillin instability may be determining factor	765	?
Cefamandole nafate	LI	2 g	SE	5 g[a]	D5W, NS	Physically compatible for 48 hr. Gradual darkening attributed to normal cephalosporin color change with time	765	C
Cefazolin sodium	SKF	5 g	SE	5 g[a]	D5W, NS	Physically compatible for 48 hr. Gradual darkening attributed to normal cephalosporin color change with time	765	C
Cefepime HCl	BR	40 g	SE	5 g[a]	D5W, NS	7% cefepime loss by HPLC in 24 hr at room temperature exposed to light and 8% loss in 5 days at 5 °C. Little or no metronidazole loss by HPLC. However, orange color develops in 18 hr at room temperature and 24 hr at 5 °C	1682	?
	BR	4 g	SE	8 g[a]	D5W, NS	6% cefepime loss by HPLC in 24 hr at room temperature exposed to light and 3% loss in 5 days at 5 °C. Little or no metronidazole loss by HPLC. However, orange color develops in 18 hr at room temperature and 24 hr at 5 °C. Precipitate forms in 48 hr at 5 °C	1682	?
	BMS	20 g	SCS	5 g	NS[b]	Visually compatible. HPLC found 7% cefepime loss in 24 hr and 17% loss in 48 hr at 23 °C; 4% cefepime loss in 7 days at 4 °C. No metronidazole loss in 7 days at 4 and 23 °C	2324	C

Additive Compatibility (Cont.)

Metronidazole HCl

Drug	*Mfr*	*Conc/L*	*Mfr*	*Conc/L*	*Test Soln*	*Remarks*	*Ref*	*C/I*
	BMS	10 g	SCS	5 g	NS[b]	Visually compatible. HPLC found 9% cefepime loss in 48 hr and 15% loss in 72 hr at 23 °C; 6% cefepime loss in 7 days at 4 °C. 8% or less metronidazole loss in 7 days at 4 and 23 °C	2324	C
	BMS	5 g	SCS	5 g	NS[b]	Visually compatible. HPLC found 8% cefepime loss in 48 hr and 11% loss in 72 hr at 23 °C; 7% cefepime loss in 7 days at 4 °C. 5% or less metronidazole loss in 7 days at 4 and 23 °C	2324	C
	BMS	2.5 g	SCS	5 g	NS[b]	Visually compatible. HPLC found 12% cefepime loss in 48 hr at 23 °C; 7% cefepime loss in 7 days at 4 °C. 6% metronidazole loss in 7 days at 4 and 23 °C	2324	C
	BMS	20 g	SCS	5 g	D5W[b]	Visually compatible. HPLC found 9% cefepime loss in 24 hr and 15% loss in 48 hr at 23 °C; 9% cefepime loss in 7 days at 4 °C. Little or no metronidazole loss in 7 days at 4 and 23 °C	2324	C
	BMS	10 g	SCS	5 g	D5W[b]	Visually compatible. HPLC found 9% cefepime loss in 12 hr and 20% loss in 24 hr at 23 °C; 10% cefepime loss in 72 hr at 4 °C. No metronidazole loss in 7 days at 4 and 23 °C	2324	I
	BMS	5 g	SCS	5 g	D5W[b]	Visually compatible. HPLC found 7% cefepime loss in 12 hr and 13% loss in 24 hr at 23 °C; 9% cefepime loss in 5 days at 4 °C. No metronidazole loss in 7 days at 4 and 23 °C	2324	I
	BMS	2.5 g	SCS	5 g	D5W[b]	Visually compatible. HPLC found 4% cefepime loss in 8 hr and 11% loss in 12 hr at 23 °C; 10% cefepime loss in 6 days at 4 °C. No metronidazole loss in 7 days at 4 and 23 °C	2324	I
Cefotaxime sodium	HO	10 g	SE	5 g[a]	NS	Visually compatible with 10% cefotaxime loss by HPLC in 24 hr at 28 °C and no loss in 96 hr at 5 °C. No metronidazole loss in 96 hr at 5 or 28 °C	1754	C
Cefoxitin sodium	MSD	2 g	SE	5 g[a]	D5W, NS	Physically compatible for 48 hr	765	C
Ceftriaxone sodium	RC	20 g	SCS	15 g	D5W, NS	Metronidazole begins to precipitate immediately and increases with time stored at 4 and 24 °C. 22 to 50% of the metronidazole precipitates in 4 hr	2091	I
	RC	10 g	SCS	7.5 g	D5W, NS	Visually compatible with little or no loss of either drug by HPLC at 24 °C in 72 hr	2091	C
	RC	10 g	SCS	7.5 g	D5W, NS	Visually compatible with little or no loss of either drug by HPLC at 4 °C through 24 hr. Slight precipitation occurred in 48 hr	2091	C
Chloramphenicol sodium succinate	PD	2 g	SE	5 g[a]	D5W, NS	Physically compatible for 48 hr	765	C
Ciprofloxacin	MI	1 g		1 g	D5W	Physically incompatible	888	I
Clindamycin phosphate	UP	2.4 g	SE	5 g[a]	D5W, NS	Physically compatible for 48 hr	765	C

Additive Compatibility (Cont.)

Metronidazole HCl

Drug	Mfr	Conc/L	Mfr	Conc/L	Test Soln	Remarks	Ref	C/I
Disopyramide phosphate	SE	720 mg	SE	5 g[a]	D5W, NS	Physically compatible for 48 hr	765	C
Dopamine HCl	ACC	1 g	SE	5 g[a]	D5W, NS	Becomes markedly discolored, turning yellow then brown	765	I
Gentamicin sulfate	SC	320 mg	SE	5 g[a]	D5W, NS	Physically compatible for 48 hr	765	C
Heparin sodium	UP	30,000 units	SE	5 g[a]	D5W, NS	Physically compatible for 48 hr	765	C
Hydrocortisone sodium succinate	UP	1 g	SE	5 g[a]	D5W, NS	Physically compatible for 48 hr	765	C
Meropenem	ZEN	1 and 20 g	SE	5 g	NS	Discoloration forms	2068	I
Multielectrolyte concentrate	MG	200 ml	SE	5 g[a]	D5W, NS	Physically compatible for 48 hr	765	C
Multivitamins	USV	20 ml	SE	5 g[a]	D5W, NS	Physically compatible for 48 hr	765	C
Penicillin G potassium	SQ	5 million units	SE	5 g[a]	D5W, NS	Physically compatible for 48 hr	765	C
Tobramycin sulfate	LI	700 mg	SE	5 g[a]	D5W, NS	Physically compatible for 48 hr	765	C

[a]*Reconstituted metronidazole HCl neutralized with sodium bicarbonate 50 mEq/L.*
[b]*Tested in PVC containers.*

Y-Site Injection Compatibility (1:1 Mixture)

Metronidazole HCl

Drug	Mfr	Conc	Mfr	Conc	Remarks	Ref	C/I
Amiodarone HCl	LZ	4 mg/ml[a,b]	LY	5 mg/ml[a,b]	Physically compatible for 4 hr at room temperature	1444	C
Diltiazem HCl	MMD	5 mg/ml	SE	8 mg/ml[b]	Visually compatible	1807	C
Meropenem	ZEN	1 and 50 mg/ml[b]	SE	5 mg/ml[c]	Discoloration forms	2068	I
Warfarin sodium	DME	2 mg/ml[c]	SCS	5 mg/ml[b]	Slight haze forms in 24 hr at 24 °C	2078	I

[a]*Tested in dextrose 5% in water.*
[b]*Tested in sodium chloride 0.9%.*
[c]*Tested in sterile water for injection.*

Additional Compatibility Information

Other Drugs — It is recommended that no other drug be added to infusions of metronidazole HCl. Furthermore, if administration of metronidazole HCl is to be made through the tubing of an ongoing primary infusion, the primary infusion should be stopped, if possible, during the metronidazole administration. (2; 4)

Aluminum — Because of the low pH of the initial reconstituted solution of metronidazole HCl, an interaction with aluminum results on contact. Solutions develop a discoloration variously described as bright orange, rust, and reddish brown. Although this interaction is stated not to affect the potency of the solution, aluminum hub needles should not be used in handling this initial solution. Plastic hub needles are recommended. This discoloration interaction does not occur as readily with the diluted and neutralized infusion solution or with metronidazole ready-to-use. It is not apparent when administration is completed within one hour. However, the solution may discolor and a precipitate may form after contact with aluminum for six or more hours. (4; 707; 1116; 1117) Also see the Metronidazole monograph.

MIDAZOLAM HCL
AHFS 28:24.08

Products — Midazolam HCl is available at a concentration equivalent to midazolam 5 mg/ml in vials containing 1, 2, 5, or 10 ml, in 1- and 2-ml syringe cartridges, and in 2-ml disposable syringes. It also is available at a concentration equivalent to midazolam 1 mg/ml in vials containing 2, 5, or 10 ml and 2- and 5-ml syringe cartridges. Each milliliter also contains sodium chloride 0.8%, disodium edetate 0.01%, and benzyl alcohol 1%, with hydrochloric acid and, if necessary, sodium hydroxide to adjust the pH. (2; 4; 29) Preservative-free midazolam HCl 1 and 5 mg/ml is also available. (1-10/01)

pH — The pH of the commercial injection has been adjusted to approximately 3. (2; 4) Midazolam (Roche) 0.625, 1.25, and 1.67 mg/ml in sodium chloride 0.9% had pH values of 3.6, 3.4, and 3.4, respectively. (2161)

Osmolality — The 5-mg/ml concentration has an osmolality of 385 mOsm/kg. (4) Midazolam (Roche) 0.625, 1.25, and 1.67 mg/ml in sodium chloride 0.9% had osmolalities of 274, 262, and 259 mOsm/kg, respectively. (2161)

Sodium Content — Each milliliter of the available products contains about 0.14 mEq of sodium. (4)

Trade Name(s) — Versed.

Administration — Midazolam HCl is administered by intramuscular injection deep into a large muscle mass or by slow intravenous injection in incremental doses (2; 4) or intravenous infusion. (4) Use of the 1-mg/ml concentration is recommended to facilitate slower injection and dosage titration. Both concentrations may be diluted with sodium chloride 0.9% or dextrose 5% in water to facilitate slow administration. (2; 4)

Stability — Midazolam HCl (Roche) is a colorless to light yellow solution. It should be stored at controlled room temperature and protected from light. (2; 4)

pH Effects — Midazolam HCl is stable at pH 3 to 3.6. (4) It is highly water soluble at pH 4 or less; at higher pH values, increased lipid solubility occurs. (1145) The rate of photodecomposition increases with increasing pH from 1.3 to 6.4. (1944)

Light Effects — Midazolam HCl in intact containers should be stored protected from light for long-term stability of the drug. (2; 4) Exposure of the commercial injection (Roche) to sunlight for four months resulted in the yellowing of the solution in one month and a midazolam loss of about 8% by HPLC analysis in four months. (1944) However, admixtures in compatible infusion solutions do not require protection from light for short-term storage and administration. (4)

Midazolam HCl (Roche) 1 mg/ml in PVC bags of sodium chloride 0.9% (Baxter) with benzyl alcohol added to a concentration of 1% was stored for 10 days at 23 °C both protected from and exposed to bright fluorescent light. No difference in midazolam content and no increase in photodecomposition products were found by HPLC analysis. (1859)

Freezing Solutions — The injection was physically stable when frozen for three days followed by room temperature thawing. (4)

Syringes — Midazolam HCl (Roche) 2 mg/ml in sodium chloride 0.9% was packaged as 3 ml in 10-ml polypropylene infusion pump syringes (Pharmacia Deltec). Little or no loss by HPLC analysis occurred during 10 days of storage at 5 and 30 °C. (1967)

Midazolam HCl (Roche) 3 mg/ml in sodium chloride 0.9% exhibited no visual changes and had losses by HPLC analysis of 6.5% at 20 °C and 8.7% at 32 °C in polypropylene syringes (Terumo) and of 8.9% at 32 °C in glass vials after 13 days. (1595)

The stability of midazolam (salt form unspecified) 1 mg/ml repackaged in polypropylene syringes was evaluated by spectrophotometric and potentiometric methods. Little or no change in concentration was found after four weeks of storage at room temperature not exposed to direct light. (2164)

Midazolam HCl (Roche) 5 mg/ml was packaged as 10 ml in 12-ml polypropylene syringes (Sherwood). No loss by HPLC analysis occurred in 36 days when stored at 25 °C protected from light. (2088)

Sorption — Midazolam (Roche) 40 μg/ml in sodium chloride 0.9% exhibited no loss due to sorption in 24 hours at 21 °C when protected from light in PVC, glass, and polyethylene-lined laminated containers. (1392)

Midazolam (Roche) 0.03 mg/ml in sodium chloride 0.9% or dextrose 5% in water was determined by UV spectroscopy to exhibit no loss due to sorption to PVC containers over 72 hours at 20 °C. However, adjustment of the natural pH of 4.3 to 4.8 in the infusion solutions to pH 7 with phosphate buffer resulted in extensive losses. Losses were 8% in one hour, 20% in six hours, and 46% in 24 hours. (1798)

Midazolam (Roche) 1 mg/ml in PVC bags of sodium chloride 0.9% (Baxter) with benzyl alcohol added to a concentration of 1% exhibited little or no loss of drug due to sorption during 10 days of storage at 23 °C. Midazolam losses of about 5% were determined by HPLC analysis. (1859)

Midazolam HCl (Roche) 0.035 mg/ml in dextrose 5% in water and sodium chloride 0.9% packaged in PVC, polyethylene, and glass containers exhibited 4 to 6% loss in all of the container types when stored at 4 and 22 °C for 24 hours. Loss due to sorption to plastic containers did not occur protected from light. (2289)

Compatibility Information

Solution Compatibility

Midazolam HCl

Solution	*Mfr*	*Mfr*	*Conc/L*	*Remarks*	*Ref*	*C/I*
Dextrose 5% in water with potassium chloride 0.15%	BA[a]	RC	0.1 and 0.5 g	13% midazolam loss by HPLC in 24 hr at ambient temperature. 10% loss calculated in 20 hr	1868	I
	BA[a]	RC	1 g	7% midazolam loss by HPLC in 24 hr at ambient temperature. 10% loss calculated in 35 hr	1868	C

Solution Compatibility (Cont.)

Midazolam HCl

Solution	*Mfr*	*Mfr*	*Conc/L*	*Remarks*	*Ref*	*C/I*
Dextrose 5% in sodium chloride 0.9%	GRI	RC	0.1 and 0.5 g	8 to 10% midazolam loss by HPLC in 24 hr at ambient temperature	1868	C
	GRI	RC	1 g	4% midazolam loss by HPLC in 24 hr at ambient temperature. 10% loss calculated in 54 hr	1868	C
Dextrose 5% in water	MG[b]	RC	0.5 g	Visually compatible with no midazolam loss by HPLC in 30 days at 23 °C in the dark or at 4 °C	1717	C
	[c]	RC	30 mg	No loss by UV spectroscopy in 72 hr at 20 °C	1798	C
	AB	RC	0.1 and 0.5 g	Visually compatible with no midazolam loss by HPLC in 3 hr at 24 °C	1852	C
	GRI	RC	0.1, 0.5, 1 g	3 to 5% midazolam loss by HPLC in 24 hr at ambient temperature. 10% loss calculated in 63 to 112 hr (0.1 to 1 g/L)	1868	C
	BA[g]	RC	500 mg	Visually compatible with no loss by HPLC in 36 days at 4, 25, and 40 °C protected from light	2088	C
	BA[a], BRN[g,h]	RC	35 mg	Visually compatible with 4 to 6% loss by HPLC in 24 hr at 4 and 22 °C	2289	C
Ringer's injection, lactated	GRI	RC	0.1 g	10% midazolam loss calculated in 2 hr at ambient temperature	1868	I
	GRI	RC	0.5 g	10% midazolam loss calculated in 6 hr at ambient temperature	1868	I
	GRI	RC	1 g	10% midazolam loss calculated in 10 hr at ambient temperature	1868	I
Sodium chloride 0.9%	[d]	RC	40 mg	Physically compatible with no midazolam loss in 24 hr at 21 °C in the dark	1392	C
	MG[b]	RC	0.5 g	Visually compatible with no midazolam loss by HPLC in 30 days at 23 °C in the dark or at 4 °C	1717	C
	[c]	RC	30 mg	No loss by UV spectroscopy in 72 hr at 20 °C	1798	C
	BA[a]	RC	1 g[e]	Visually compatible with 5% or less midazolam loss by HPLC in 10 days at 23 °C both protected from and exposed to fluorescent light	1859	C
	BA[a]	RC	1 g	Visually compatible with 4 to 6% midazolam loss by HPLC in 49 days at 4 and 20 °C exposed to fluorescent light and at 20 °C protected from light	1863	C
	GRI	RC	0.1, 0.5, 1 g	8 to 10% midazolam loss by HPLC in 24 hr at ambient temperature	1868	C
	BA[g]	RC	500 mg	Visually compatible with no loss by HPLC in 36 days at 4, 25, and 40 °C protected from light	2088	C
	BA[a], BRN[g,h]	RC	35 mg	Visually compatible with 4 to 6% loss by HPLC in 24 hr at 4 and 22 °C	2289	C
TPN #174 to #176[f]		RC	600 mg to 1 g	Immediate precipitation	1624	I
		RC	100 and 500 mg	Visually compatible with little or no midazolam loss by HPLC and less than 10% loss of any amino acid by HPLC in 5 hr at 22 °C under fluorescent light	1624	C

[a]*Tested in PVC containers.*
[b]*Tested in polyolefin containers.*
[c]*Tested in both glass and PVC containers.*
[d]*Tested in PVC, glass, and polyethylene-lined laminated containers.*
[e]*Also contained benzyl alcohol 1%.*
[f]*Refer to Appendix I for the composition of parenteral nutrition solutions. TPN indicates a 2-in-1 admixture.*
[g]*Tested in glass bottles.*
[h]*Tested in polyethylene containers.*

Additive Compatibility

Midazolam HCl

Drug	Mfr	Conc/L	Mfr	Conc/L	Test Soln	Remarks	Ref	C/I
Hydromorphone HCl	KN	0.5 to 45 g	RC	0.1 to 4.5 g	D5W, NS	Visually compatible for 24 hr at room temperature	2086	C
	KN	2 and 20 g	RC	100 mg	D5W, NS	Visually compatible with less than 7% hydromorphone loss and less than 3% midazolam loss by HPLC in 23 days at 4 and 23 °C	2086	C
	KN	2 and 20 g	RC	500 mg	D5W, NS	Visually compatible with less than 6% hydromorphone loss and less than 7% midazolam loss by HPLC in 23 days at 4 and 23 °C	2086	C

Drugs in Syringe Compatibility

Midazolam HCl

Drug (in syringe)	Mfr	Amt	Mfr	Amt	Remarks	Ref	C/I
Alfentanil HCl	JN	0.5 mg/ml	RC	0.2 mg/ml[a]	Visually compatible with 8% midazolam and 2% alfentanil loss in 3 weeks at 20 °C exposed to light. No alfentanil loss and 7% midazolam loss in 4 weeks at 6 °C in the dark	2133	C
Atracurium besylate	BW	10 mg/1 ml		5 mg/1 ml	Physically compatible and atracurium chemically stable for 24 hr at 5 and 25 °C	1694	C
Atropine sulfate	IX	0.4 mg/1 ml	RC	5 mg/1 ml	Physically compatible for 4 hr at 25 °C under fluorescent light	1145	C
Buprenorphine HCl	NE	0.3 mg/1 ml	RC	5 mg/1 ml	Physically compatible for 4 hr at 25 °C under fluorescent light	1145	C
Butorphanol tartrate	BR	2 mg/1 ml	RC	5 mg/1 ml	Physically compatible for 4 hr at 25 °C under fluorescent light	1145	C
Chlorpromazine HCl	SKF	50 mg/2 ml	RC	5 mg/1 ml	Physically compatible for 4 hr at 25 °C under fluorescent light	1145	C
Cimetidine HCl	SKF	300 mg/2 ml	RC	5 mg/1 ml	Physically compatible for 4 hr at 25 °C under fluorescent light	1145	C
Diamorphine HCl	EV	10 mg	RC	10[b] and 75[c] mg	Visually compatible with 10% diamorphine loss and no midazolam loss by HPLC in 15.9 days at 22 °C	1792	C
	EV	500 mg	RC	10[b] and 75[c] mg	Visually compatible with 10% diamorphine loss and no midazolam loss in 22.2 days at 22 °C	1792	C
Dimenhydrinate	SE	50 mg/1 ml	RC	5 mg/1 ml	White precipitate forms immediately	1145	I
Diphenhydramine HCl	ES	50 mg/1 ml	RC	5 mg/1 ml	Physically compatible for 4 hr at 25 °C under fluorescent light	1145	C
Droperidol	JN	2.5 mg/1 ml	RC	5 mg/1 ml	Physically compatible for 4 hr at 25 °C under fluorescent light	1145	C
Fentanyl citrate	ES	0.1 mg/2 ml	RC	5 mg/1 ml	Physically compatible for 4 hr at 25 °C under fluorescent light	1145	C
	DB	12.5 μg/ml[a]	RC	0.625 and 0.938 mg/ml[a]	Visually compatible with little fentanyl loss and 7 to 9% midazolam loss by HPLC in 7 days at 5 and 22 °C, respectively	2202	C

Drugs in Syringe Compatibility (Cont.)

Midazolam HCl

Drug (in syringe)	*Mfr*	*Amt*	*Mfr*	*Amt*	*Remarks*	*Ref*	*C/I*
	DB	37.5 μg/ml[a]	RC	0.625 mg/ml[a]	Visually compatible with no fentanyl loss and 5 to 8% midazolam loss by HPLC in 7 days at 5 and 22 °C, respectively	2202	C
	DB	37.5 μg/ml[a]	RC	0.938 mg/ml[a]	Visually compatible with little fentanyl loss and 7 to 9% midazolam loss by HPLC in 7 days at 5 and 22 °C, respectively	2202	C
	DB	33.3 μg/ml[a]	RC	0.278 and 0.833 mg/ml[a]	Visually compatible with no fentanyl loss and not more than 5 to 7% midazolam loss by HPLC in 7 days at 5 and 22 °C, respectively	2202	C
Fentanyl citrate with	DB	1 mg/20 ml	RC	15 mg/3 ml	Visually compatible with 9% or less loss of each drug in 7 days at 32 °C	2268	C
hyoscine butylbromide	BI	30 mg/1.5 ml					
Fentanyl citrate with	DB	1 mg/20 ml	RC	15 mg/3 ml	Visually compatible with 7% or less loss of each drug in 10 days at 32 °C	2268	C
metoclopramide HCl	AST	20 mg/4 ml					
Glycopyrrolate	RB	0.2 mg/1 ml	RC	5 mg/1 ml	Physically compatible for 4 hr at 25 °C under fluorescent light	1145	C
Heparin sodium		2500 units/1 ml	RC	15 mg/3 ml	Turbidity or precipitate forms within 5 min	1053	I
Hydromorphone HCl	WB	2 mg/0.5 ml	RC	5 mg/1 ml	Physically compatible for 4 hr at 25 °C under fluorescent light	1145	C
Hydroxyzine HCl	ES	100 mg/2 ml	RC	5 mg/1 ml	Physically compatible for 4 hr at 25 °C under fluorescent light	1145	C
Meperidine HCl	WB	100 mg/1 ml	RC	5 mg/1 ml	Physically compatible for 4 hr at 25 °C under fluorescent light	1145	C
Metoclopramide HCl	RB	10 mg/2 ml	RC	5 mg/1 ml	Physically compatible for 4 hr at 25 °C under fluorescent light	1145	C
Morphine sulfate	WB	10 mg/1 ml	RC	5 mg/1 ml	Physically compatible for 4 hr at 25 °C under fluorescent light	1145	C
		5 and 10 mg/1 ml[d]	RC	5 mg/1 ml	Visually compatible with 9% or less morphine loss and 8% or less midazolam loss by HPLC in 14 days at 22 °C protected from light. Subvisual microprecipitate may form, requiring filtration	1901	C
		5 and 10 mg/1 ml[e]	RC	5 mg/1 ml	Visually compatible with 8% or less morphine loss and 3% or less midazolam loss by HPLC in 14 days at 22 °C protected from light. Subvisual microprecipitate may form, requiring filtration	1901	C
Morphine tartrate	DB	24 mg/ml	RC	3 mg/ml[a]	Visually compatible with 4.4% midazolam loss by HPLC in 13 days at 32 °C. Morphine not tested	1595	C
Nalbuphine HCl	DU	10 mg/1 ml	RC	5 mg/1 ml	Physically compatible for 4 hr at 25 °C under fluorescent light	1145	C
Ondansetron HCl	GW	1.33 mg/ml[a]	RC	1.66 mg/ml[a]	Physically compatible with no measured increase in particulates and less than 4% loss of ondansetron and less than 7% loss of midazolam by HPLC in 24 hr at 4 or 23 °C	2199	C

Drugs in Syringe Compatibility (Cont.)

Midazolam HCl

Drug (in syringe)	*Mfr*	*Amt*	*Mfr*	*Amt*	*Remarks*	*Ref*	*C/I*
Pentobarbital sodium	WY	100 mg/ 2 ml	RC	5 mg/ 1 ml	White precipitate forms immediately	1145	**I**
Perphenazine	SC	5 mg/ 1 ml	RC	5 mg/ 1 ml	White precipitate forms immediately	1145	**I**
Prochlorperazine edisylate	SKF	10 mg/ 2 ml	RC	5 mg/ 1 ml	White precipitate forms immediately	1145	**I**
Promazine HCl	WY	50 mg/ 1 ml	RC	5 mg/ 1 ml	Physically compatible for 4 hr at 25 °C under fluorescent light	1145	**C**
Promethazine HCl	WY	25 mg/ 1 ml	RC	5 mg/ 1 ml	Physically compatible for 4 hr at 25 °C under fluorescent light	1145	**C**
Ranitidine HCl	GL	50 mg/ 2 ml	RC	5 mg/ 1 ml	White precipitate forms immediately	1145	**I**
Scopolamine HBr	BW	0.43 mg/ 0.5 ml	RC	5 mg/ 1 ml	Physically compatible for 4 hr at 25 °C under fluorescent light	1145	**C**
Sufentanil citrate	JN	50 μg/ml	RC	5 mg/ml	Physically compatible with no subvisual haze or particle formation in 24 hr at 23 °C	1711	**C**
Thiethylperazine malate	BI	10 mg/ 2 ml	RC	5 mg/ 1 ml	Physically compatible for 4 hr at 25 °C under fluorescent light	1145	**C**
Trimethobenzamide HCl	BE	200 mg/ 2 ml	RC	5 mg/ 1 ml	Physically compatible for 4 hr at 25 °C under fluorescent light	1145	**C**

[a]*Diluted with sodium chloride 0.9%.*
[b]*Diluted with sterile water to 15 ml.*
[c]*Diamorphine HCl constituted with midazolam injection.*
[d]*Morphine sulfate powder dissolved in dextrose 5% in water.*
[e]*Morphine sulfate powder dissolved in water and sodium chloride 0.9%.*

Y-Site Injection Compatibility (1:1 Mixture)

Midazolam HCl

Drug	*Mfr*	*Conc*	*Mfr*	*Conc*	*Remarks*	*Ref*	*C/I*
Alatrofloxacin mesylate	PF	1.43 mg/ml[a]	RC	0.5 mg/ml[b]	Visually and microscopically compatible run through a Y-site over at least 60 min	2235	**C**
Albumin human		200 mg/ml	RC	5 mg/ml	White precipitate forms immediately	1855	**I**
Amikacin sulfate	BMS	5 mg/ml	RC	5 mg/ml	Visually compatible for 24 hr at 22 °C	1855	**C**
Amiodarone HCl	WY	4.8 mg/ml[a]	RC	1 mg/ml[a]	Visually compatible for 24 hr at 23 °C	1877	**C**
Amoxicillin sodium	SKB	50 mg/ml	RC	5 mg/ml	White precipitate forms immediately	1855	**I**
Amoxicillin sodium–clavulanate potassium	SKB	20 + 2 mg/ ml	RC	5 mg/ml	White precipitate forms immediately	1855	**I**
Amphotericin B cholesteryl sulfate complex	SEQ	0.83 mg/ml[a]	RC	2 mg/ml[a]	Gross precipitate forms	2117	**I**
Ampicillin sodium	WY	20 mg/ml[b]	RC	1 mg/ml[a]	Haze forms immediately	1847	**I**
Atracurium besylate	BW	0.5 mg/ml[a]	RC	0.05 mg/ml[a]	Physically compatible for 24 hr at 28 °C	1337	**C**
	GW	1 and 5 mg/ ml[a]	RC	0.1 mg/ml[a]	Visually compatible with no loss of either drug by HPLC in 3 hr at 25 °C under fluorescent light	2112	**C**

Y-Site Injection Compatibility (1:1 Mixture) (Cont.)

Midazolam HCl

Drug	*Mfr*	*Conc*	*Mfr*	*Conc*	*Remarks*	*Ref*	*C/I*
	GW	5 mg/ml[a]	RC	0.5 mg/ml[a]	Visually compatible with no loss of either drug by HPLC in 3 hr at 25 °C under fluorescent light	2112	C
	GW	1 mg/ml[a]	RC	0.5 mg/ml[a]	Visually compatible with no loss of midazolam and 4% loss of atracurium by HPLC in 3 hr at 25 °C under fluorescent light	2112	C
Bumetanide	LEO	0.5 mg/ml	RC	5 mg/ml	White precipitate forms immediately	1855	I
Butorphanol tartrate	BR	[f]	RC	[f]	Crystalline precipitate identified by HPLC as midazolam formed in infusion line several hours after administration was completed	2144	I
Calcium gluconate	FUJ	100 mg/ml	RC	1 mg/ml[a]	Visually compatible for 24 hr at 23 °C	1847	C
Cefazolin sodium	MAR	20 mg/ml[a]	RC	1 mg/ml[a]	Visually compatible for 24 hr at 23 °C	1847	C
Cefotaxime sodium	HO	20 mg/ml[a]	RC	1 mg/ml[a]	Visually compatible for 24 hr at 23 °C	1847	C
	RS	10 mg/ml	RC	5 mg/ml	Visually compatible for 24 hr at 22 °C	1855	C
Ceftazidime	LI[d]	20 mg/ml[a]	RC	1 mg/ml[a]	Haze forms in 1 hr	1847	I
Cefuroxime sodium	LI	15 mg/ml[a]	RC	1 mg/ml[a]	Particles form in 8 hr	1847	I
Cimetidine HCl	SKB	15 mg/ml[a]	RC	1 mg/ml[a]	Visually compatible for 24 hr at 23 °C	1847	C
Ciprofloxacin	BAY	2 mg/ml	RC	5 mg/ml	Visually compatible for 24 hr at 22 °C	1855	C
Cisatracurium besylate	GW	0.1, 2, 5 mg/ml[a]	RC	1 mg/ml[a]	Physically compatible with no change in measured turbidity or increase in particle content in 4 hr at 23 °C	2074	C
Clindamycin phosphate	UP	9 mg/ml[a]	RC	1 mg/ml[a]	Visually compatible for 24 hr at 23 °C	1847	C
Clonidine HCl	BI	0.015 mg/ml	RC	5 mg/ml	Orange discoloration forms in 24 hr at 22 °C	1855	I
Dexamethasone sodium phosphate	ES	4 mg/ml	RC	1 mg/ml[a]	Haze forms immediately. Precipitate forms in 8 hr	1847	I
		4 mg/ml	RC	5 mg/ml	White precipitate forms immediately	1855	I
Digoxin	BW	0.1 mg/ml	RC	1 mg/ml[a]	Visually compatible for 24 hr at 23 °C	1847	C
Diltiazem HCl	MMD	1 mg/ml[a]	RC	2 mg/ml[a]	Visually compatible for 4 hr at 27 °C	2062	C
Dobutamine HCl	GNS	2 mg/ml[a]	RC	1 mg/ml[a]	Particles form in 8 hr	1847	I
	LI	4 mg/ml[a]	RC	1 mg/ml[a]	Visually compatible for 24 hr at 23 °C	1877	C
	LI	4 mg/ml[a]	RC	2 mg/ml[a]	Visually compatible for 4 hr at 27 °C	2062	C
Dopamine HCl	AB	1.6 mg/ml[a]	RC	1 mg/ml[a]	Visually compatible for 24 hr at 23 °C	1847	C
	DU	3.2 mg/ml[a]	RC	1 mg/ml[a]	Visually compatible for 24 hr at 23 °C	1877	C
	AB	3.2 mg/ml[a]	RC	2 mg/ml[a]	Visually compatible for 4 hr at 27 °C	2062	C
Epinephrine HCl	AB	0.02 mg/ml[a]	RC	2 mg/ml[a]	Visually compatible for 4 hr at 27 °C	2062	C
Erythromycin lactobionate	AB	5 mg/ml	RC	5 mg/ml	Visually compatible for 24 hr at 22 °C	1855	C
Esmolol HCl	DU	40 mg/ml[a]	RC	1 mg/ml[a]	Visually compatible for 24 hr at 23 °C	1877	C
Etomidate	AB	2 mg/ml	RC	5 mg/ml	Visually compatible for up to 7 days at 25 °C	1801	C
Famotidine	MSD	0.2 mg/ml[a]	RC	0.15 mg/ml[a]	Physically compatible for 4 hr at 25 °C	1188	C
	ME	2 mg/ml[b]		1.5 mg/ml[a]	Visually compatible for 4 hr at 22 °C	1936	C

Y-Site Injection Compatibility (1:1 Mixture) (Cont.)

			Midazolam HCl				
Drug	*Mfr*	*Conc*	*Mfr*	*Conc*	*Remarks*	*Ref*	*C/I*
Fentanyl citrate	ES	0.05 mg/ml	RC	1 mg/ml[a]	Visually compatible for 24 hr at 23 °C	1847	C
	JN	0.02 mg/ml[a]	RC	0.1 and 0.5 mg/ml[a]	Visually compatible with no midazolam loss and 3 to 4% fentanyl loss by HPLC in 3 hr at 24 °C	1852	C
	JN	0.04 mg/ml[a]	RC	0.1 and 0.5 mg/ml[a]	Visually compatible with no loss of either drug by HPLC in 3 hr at 24 °C	1852	C
		0.05 mg/ml	RC	5 mg/ml	Visually compatible for 24 hr at 22 °C	1855	C
	ES	0.05 mg/ml	RC	2 mg/ml[a]	Visually compatible for 4 hr at 27 °C	2062	C
	JN	0.025 mg/ml[a]	RC	0.2 mg/ml[a]	Physically compatible with no change in measured haze or increase in particle content in 48 hr at 22 °C	1706	C
Floxacillin sodium	SKB	50 mg/ml	RC	5 mg/ml	White precipitate forms immediately	1855	I
Fluconazole	RR	2 mg/ml	RC	5 mg/ml	Physically compatible for 24 hr at 25 °C	1407	C
	PF	2 mg/ml	RC	5 mg/ml	Visually compatible for 24 hr at 22 °C	1855	C
Foscarnet sodium	AST	24 mg/ml	RC	5 mg/ml	Gas production	1335	I
Fosphenytoin sodium	PD	1 mgPE/ml[b,g]	RC	2 mg/ml[b]	Midazolam base precipitates immediately	2223	I
Furosemide	AST	10 mg/ml	RC	1 mg/ml[a]	Haze forms immediately. Precipitate forms in 2 hr	1847	I
	CNF	10 mg/ml	RC	5 mg/ml	White precipitate forms immediately	1855	I
	AMR	10 mg/ml	RC	2 mg/ml[a]	Precipitate forms immediately	2062	I
Gatifloxacin	BMS	2 mg/ml[a]	RC	2 mg/ml[a]	Physically compatible with no change in measured haze or increase in particle content in 4 hr at 23 °C	2234	C
Gentamicin sulfate	ES	10 mg/ml	RC	1 mg/ml[a]	Visually compatible for 24 hr at 23 °C	1847	C
	CNF	3 mg/ml	RC	5 mg/ml	Visually compatible for 24 hr at 22 °C	1855	C
Haloperidol lactate	JN	0.5 and 5 mg/ml	RC	5 mg/ml	Visually compatible for 24 hr at 22 °C	1855	C
Heparin sodium		417 units/ml	RC	5 mg/ml	Visually compatible for 24 hr at 22 °C	1855	C
	ES	100 units/ml[a]	RC	2 mg/ml[a]	Visually compatible for 4 hr at 27 °C	2062	C
		50 units/ml/min[b]	RC	15 mg/3 ml[h]	Clear solution	1053	C
Hetastarch in lactated electrolyte injection (Hextend)	AB	6%	RC	1 mg/ml[a]	Physically compatible with no change in measured turbidity or increase in particle content in 4 hr at 23 °C	2339	C
Hydrocortisone sodium succinate	UP	50 mg/ml	RC	5 mg/ml	White precipitate forms immediately	1855	I
Hydromorphone HCl	KN	1 mg/ml	RC	2 mg/ml[a]	Visually compatible for 4 hr at 27 °C	2062	C
	AST	0.5 mg/ml[a]	RC	0.2 mg/ml[a]	Physically compatible with no change in measured haze or increase in particle content in 48 hr at 22 °C	1706	C
Imipenem–cilastatin sodium	MSD	5 mg/ml	RC	5 mg/ml	Haze forms in 24 hr	1855	I
Insulin, regular	LI	1 unit/ml[a]	RC	1 mg/ml[a]	Visually compatible for 24 hr at 23 °C	1877	C
Ketanserin tartrate	JN	1 mg/ml	RC	5 mg/ml	Visually compatible for 24 hr at 22 °C	1855	C
Labetalol HCl	GL	5 mg/ml	RC	1 mg/ml[a]	Visually compatible for 24 hr at 23 °C	1877	C
	AH	2 mg/ml[a]	RC	2 mg/ml[a]	Visually compatible for 4 hr at 27 °C	2062	C
Linezolid	PHU	2 mg/ml	RC	2 mg/ml[a]	Physically compatible with no change in measured turbidity or increase in particle content in 4 hr at 23 °C	2264	C
Lorazepam	WY	0.5 mg/ml[a]	RC	2 mg/ml[a]	Visually compatible for 4 hr at 27 °C	2062	C

Y-Site Injection Compatibility (1:1 Mixture) (Cont.)

			Midazolam HCl				
Drug	*Mfr*	*Conc*	*Mfr*	*Conc*	*Remarks*	*Ref*	*C/I*
Methadone HCl	LI	1 mg/ml[a]	RC	0.2 mg/ml[a]	Physically compatible with no change in measured haze or increase in particle content in 48 hr at 22 °C	1706	C
Methotrexate sodium		30 mg/ml	RC	5 mg/ml	Yellow precipitate forms immediately	1788	I
Methylprednisolone sodium succinate	UP	40 mg/ml	RC	1 mg/ml[a]	Visually compatible for 24 hr at 23 °C	1847	C
Metronidazole	BA	5 mg/ml	RC	1 mg/ml[a]	Visually compatible for 24 hr at 23 °C	1847	C
	BRN	5 mg/ml	RC	5 mg/ml	Visually compatible for 24 hr at 22 °C	1855	C
Milrinone lactate	SW	0.2 mg/ml[a]	RC	2 mg/ml[a]	Visually compatible for 4 hr at 27 °C	2062	C
	SW	0.4 mg/ml[a]	RC	1 mg/ml	Visually compatible with little or no loss of either drug by HPLC in 4 hr at 23 °C	2214	C
Morphine HCl	CNF	1 mg/ml	RC	5 mg/ml	Visually compatible for 24 hr at 22 °C	1855	C
Morphine sulfate	AST	1 mg/ml[a]	RC	0.2 mg/ml[a]	Physically compatible with no change in measured haze or increase in particle content in 48 hr at 22 °C	1706	C
	ES	0.25 mg/ml[a]	RC	0.1 and 0.5 mg/ml[a]	Visually compatible with no loss of either drug by HPLC in 3 hr at 24 °C	1789	C
	ES	1 mg/ml[a]	RC	0.1 and 0.5 mg/ml[a]	Visually compatible with no loss of either drug by HPLC in 3 hr at 24 °C	1789	C
	SX	1 mg/ml[a]	RC	1 mg/ml[a]	Visually compatible for 24 hr at 23 °C	1877	C
	SCN	2 mg/ml[a]	RC	2 mg/ml[a]	Visually compatible for 4 hr at 27 °C	2062	C
Nafcillin sodium	WY	20 mg/ml[a]	RC	1 mg/ml[a]	Haze forms immediately. Particles form in 4 hr	1847	I
Nicardipine HCl	WY	1 mg/ml[a]	RC	2 mg/ml[a]	Visually compatible for 4 hr at 27 °C	2062	C
Nitroglycerin	SO	0.2 mg/ml[a]	RC	1 mg/ml[a]	Visually compatible for 24 hr at 23 °C	1847	C
	OM	0.2 mg/ml[a]	RC	1 mg/ml[a]	Visually compatible for 24 hr at 23 °C	1877	C
	AB	0.4 mg/ml[a]	RC	2 mg/ml[a]	Visually compatible for 4 hr at 27 °C	2062	C
Norepinephrine bitartrate	STR	0.064 mg/ml[a]	RC	1 mg/ml[a]	Visually compatible for 24 hr at 23 °C	1877	C
	AB	0.128 mg/ml[a]	RC	2 mg/ml[a]	Visually compatible for 4 hr at 27 °C	2062	C
Omeprazole sodium	AST	4 mg/ml	RC	5 mg/ml	Brown discoloration forms, followed by a brown precipitate	1855	I
Pancuronium bromide	ES	0.05 mg/ml[a]	RC	0.05 mg/ml[a]	Physically compatible for 24 hr at 28 °C	1337	C
Piperacillin sodium	LE	150 mg/ml	RC	5 mg/ml	Visually compatible for 24 hr 22 °C	1855	C
Potassium chloride	BRN	1 mEq/ml	RC	5 mg/ml	Visually compatible for 24 hr at 22 °C	1855	C
Propofol	STU	2 mg/ml	RC	5 mg/ml	Oil droplets form within 7 days at 25 °C. No visible change in 24 hr	1801	?
	ZEN	10 mg/ml	RC	2 mg/ml[a]	Physically compatible for 1 hr at 23 °C with no increase in particle content	2066	C
Ranitidine HCl	GL	0.5 mg/ml	RC	5 mg/ml	Visually compatible for 24 hr at 22 °C	1855	C
	GL	1 mg/ml[a]	RC	2 mg/ml[a]	Visually compatible for 4 hr at 27 °C	2062	C
Remifentanil HCl	GW	0.025 and 0.25 mg/ml[b]	RC	1 mg/ml[a]	Physically compatible with no change in measured turbidity or increase in particle content in 4 hr at 23 °C	2075	C
Sodium bicarbonate		1.4%	RC	5 mg/ml	White precipitate forms immediately	1788	I
	IMS	1 mEq/ml	RC	1 mg/ml[a]	Haze forms immediately. Precipitate forms in 2 hr	1847	I

Y-Site Injection Compatibility (1:1 Mixture) (Cont.)

Midazolam HCl

Drug	*Mfr*	*Conc*	*Mfr*	*Conc*	*Remarks*	*Ref*	*C/I*
Sodium nitroprusside	ES	0.2 mg/ml[a]	RC	1 mg/ml[a]	Visually compatible for 24 hr at 23 °C	1847	C
	RC	0.2 mg/ml[a]	RC	1 mg/ml[a]	Visually compatible for 24 hr at 23 °C	1877	C
Sufentanil citrate	JN	12.5 µg/ml[a]	RC	0.2 mg/ml[a]	Physically compatible with no subvisual haze or particle formation in 24 hr at 23 °C	1711	C
Theophylline	BA	1.6 mg/ml[a]	RC	1 mg/ml[a]	Visually compatible for 24 hr at 23 °C	1847	C
Thiopental sodium	AB	25 mg/ml	RC	5 mg/ml	White precipitate forms immediately	1801	I
	AB	25 mg/ml[b]	RC	2 mg/ml[a]	Precipitate forms immediately	2062	I
TNA #218 to #226[e]			RC	2 mg/ml[a]	Damage to emulsion integrity occurs immediately with free oil formation possible	2215	I
Tobramycin sulfate	LI	10 mg/ml	RC	1 mg/ml[a]	Visually compatible for 24 hr at 23 °C	1847	C
TPN #189[e]			RC	5 mg/ml	White haze and light, white precipitate form immediately. Crystals form in 24 hr	1767	I
TPN #212 to #215[e]			RC	2 mg/ml[a]	White cloudiness forms rapidly	2109	I
Trimethoprim–sulfamethoxazole	RC	0.8 + 4 mg/ml	RC	5 mg/ml	White precipitate forms immediately	1855	I
Vancomycin HCl	LI	5 mg/ml[a]	RC	1 mg/ml[a]	Visually compatible for 24 hr at 23 °C	1847	C
	LI	5 mg/ml	RC	5 mg/ml	Visually compatible for 24 hr at 22 °C	1855	C
Vecuronium bromide	OR	0.1 mg/ml[a]	RC	0.05 mg/ml[a]	Physically compatible for 24 hr at 28 °C	1337	C
	OR	4 mg/ml	RC	5 mg/ml	Visually compatible for 24 hr at 22 °C	1855	C
	OR	1 mg/ml	RC	2 mg/ml[a]	Visually compatible for 4 hr at 27 °C	2062	C

[a]*Tested in dextrose 5% in water.*
[b]*Tested in sodium chloride 0.9%.*
[c]*Tested in sterile water for injection.*
[d]*Sodium carbonate-containing formulation tested.*
[e]*Refer to Appendix I for the composition of parenteral nutrition solutions. TNA indicates a 3-in-1 admixture, and TPN indicates a 2-in-1 admixture.*
[f]*Concentration unspecified.*
[g]*Concentration expressed in milligrams of phenytoin sodium equivalents (PE) per milliliter.*
[h]*Given over three minutes into a heparin infusion run at 1 ml/min.*

Additional Compatibility Information

Infusion Solutions — Midazolam HCl 0.5 mg/ml or less is physically compatible and chemically stable at 25 °C for 24 hours in dextrose 5% in water and sodium chloride 0.9% and for four hours in Ringer's injection, lactated, in both glass and PVC containers. (4)

Other Drugs — Midazolam HCl has been stated to be compatible mixed in the same syringe for 30 minutes with atropine sulfate, meperidine HCl, morphine sulfate, and scopolamine HBr and for eight hours with fentanyl citrate, glycopyrrolate, hydroxyzine HCl, ketamine HCl, nalbuphine HCl, promethazine HCl, and sufentanil citrate. (4) Published research studies tend to support this statement, although longer and shorter tested time frames have been reported. See Drugs in Syringe Compatibility table above.

MILRINONE LACTATE
AHFS 24:04

Products — Milrinone lactate is available as a solution containing the equivalent of milrinone 1 mg/ml in 10-, 20-, and 50-ml single-dose vials and 5-ml syringe cartridge units with and without needles. Each milliliter also contains dextrose, anhydrous, 47 mg in water for injection. Lactic acid or sodium hydroxide may have been used to adjust the pH. The total lactic acid concentration may vary between 0.95 and 1.29 mg/ml. The 1-mg/ml concentration must be diluted for use. (2)

Milrinone lactate is also available as a ready-to-use solution in 100-

and 200-ml flexible PVC plastic containers at a concentration equivalent to milrinone 0.2 mg/ml (200 μg/ml). The solution has a nominal lactic acid concentration of 0.282 mg/ml and also contains dextrose, anhydrous 49.4 mg/ml. (2)

pH — From 3.2 to 4. (2)

Trade Name(s) — Primacor.

Administration — Milrinone lactate is administered intravenously. For maintenance administration by continuous intravenous infusion, milrinone lactate in vials is diluted in a compatible diluent, usually to 200 μg/ml. The premixed 200-μg/ml infusion in flexible plastic containers need not be diluted for use. When milrinone lactate is administered by continuous infusion, the use of a calibrated electronic infusion device is recommended. (2)

Stability — Milrinone lactate solutions are colorless to pale yellow. The 1-mg/ml concentration should be stored at controlled room temperature and protected from freezing. The 0.2-mg/ml concentration in PVC containers should be stored at room temperature of 25 °C and should be protected from freezing and exposure to excessive heat. Brief exposure to temperatures up to 40 °C does not adversely affect the product. (2)

Milrinone lactate (Sterling Winthrop) 0.2 mg/ml in sodium chloride 0.45 or 0.9% or dextrose 5% in water was stored in glass (Abbott), Accumed (McGaw), or PVC (Travenol) containers for 72 hours at room temperature in normal light. The milrinone concentration remained constant at about 100% of the initial amount over the study period by HPLC analysis. In addition, the solutions remained physically compatible and the pH remained constant. (1468)

Sorption — Milrinone lactate (Sterling Winthrop) 0.2 mg/ml in sodium chloride 0.45 or 0.9% or dextrose 5% in water did not exhibit any loss due to sorption to glass, PVC, or Accumed containers during storage for 72 hours at room temperature. (1468)

Compatibility Information

Solution Compatibility

Milrinone lactate

Solution	*Mfr*	*Mfr*	*Conc/L*	*Remarks*	*Ref*	*C/I*
Dextrose 5% in water	[c]	WI	200 mg	Physically compatible and potency retained for 72 hr at room temperature under normal light or in the dark	1468	C
	[a]	SW	0.2 g	Visually compatible with little or no loss by HPLC after 14 days at 23 °C in normal room light and at 4 °C	2106	C
	BA[a]	SW	0.4, 0.6, 0.8 g	Visually compatible with little or no loss by HPLC after 14 days at 23 °C and at 4 °C	2107	C
	BA[a]	SW	0.4 g	Visually compatible with no loss by HPLC after 7 days at 23 °C under fluorescent light	2214	C
Ringer's injection, lactated	BA[a]	SW	0.4 g	Visually compatible with 3% loss by HPLC after 7 days at 23 °C under fluorescent light	2214	C
Sodium chloride 0.45%	[c]	WI	200 mg	Physically compatible and potency retained for 72 hr at room temperature under normal light or in the dark	1468	C
	BA[a]	SW	0.4 g	Visually compatible with no loss by HPLC after 7 days at 23 °C under fluorescent light	2214	C
Sodium chloride 0.9%	[c]	WI	200 mg	Physically compatible and potency retained for 72 hr at room temperature under normal light or in the dark	1468	C
	[a]	SW	0.2 g	Visually compatible with little or no loss by HPLC after 14 days at 23 °C in normal room light and at 4 °C	2106	C
	MG[b]	SW	0.4, 0.6, 0.8 g	Visually compatible with little or no loss by HPLC after 14 days at 23 and 4 °C	2107	C
	BA[a]	SW	0.4 g	Visually compatible with no loss by HPLC after 7 days at 23 °C under fluorescent light	2214	C

[a]*Tested in PVC containers.*
[b]*Tested in polyolefin containers.*
[c]*Tested in glass (Abbott), Accumed (McGaw), and PVC (Travenol) containers.*

Additive Compatibility

			Milrinone lactate					
Drug	*Mfr*	*Conc/L*	*Mfr*	*Conc/L*	*Test Soln*	*Remarks*	*Ref*	*C/I*
Procainamide HCl	SQ	2 and 4 g	WI	200 mg	D5W	2 to 3% procainamide loss in 1 hr and 10 to 11% loss in 4 hr at 23 °C. No milrinone loss	1191	I
Quinidine gluconate	LI	16 g	WI	200 mg	D5W	Physically compatible with no loss of either drug in 4 hr at 23 °C	1191	C

Drugs in Syringe Compatibility

			Milrinone lactate				
Drug (in syringe)	*Mfr*	*Amt*	*Mfr*	*Amt*	*Remarks*	*Ref*	*C/I*
Atropine sulfate	IX	2 mg/ 2 ml	WI	5.25 mg/ 5.25 ml	Physically compatible with no loss of either drug in 20 min at 23 °C under fluorescent light	1410	C
Calcium chloride	AB	3 g/30 ml	WI	5.25 mg/ 5.25 ml	Physically compatible with no milrinone loss in 20 min at 23 °C under fluorescent light	1410	C
Digoxin	BW	0.5 mg/ 2 ml	WI	3.5 mg/ 3.5 ml	Brought to 10-ml total volume with D5W. Physically compatible with no loss of either drug in 4 hr at 23 °C	1191	C
Epinephrine HCl	AB	0.5 mg/ 0.5 ml	WI	5.25 mg/ 5.25 ml	Physically compatible with no loss of either drug in 20 min at 23 °C under fluorescent light	1410	C
Furosemide	LY	40 mg/ 4 ml	WI	3.5 mg/ 3.5 ml	Brought to 10-ml total volume with D5W. Immediate precipitation	1191	I
Lidocaine HCl	AB	100 mg/ 10 ml	WI	5.25 mg/ 5.25 ml	Physically compatible with no loss of either drug in 20 min at 23 °C under fluorescent light	1410	C
Morphine sulfate	WI	40 mg/ 5 ml	WI	5.25 mg/ 5.25 ml	Physically compatible with no loss of either drug in 20 min at 23 °C under fluorescent light	1410	C
Propranolol HCl	AY	3 mg/ 3 ml	WI	3.5 mg/ 3.5 ml	Brought to 10-ml total volume with D5W. Physically compatible with no loss of either drug in 4 hr at 23 °C	1191	C
Sodium bicarbonate	AB	3.75 g/ 50 ml	WI	5.25 mg/ 5.25 ml	Physically compatible with no milrinone loss in 20 min at 23 °C under fluorescent light	1410	C
Verapamil HCl	KN	10 mg/ 4 ml	WI	3.5 mg/ 3.5 ml	Brought to 10-ml total volume with D5W. Physically compatible with no loss of either drug in 4 hr at 23 °C	1191	C

Y-Site Injection Compatibility (1:1 Mixture)

			Milrinone lactate				
Drug	*Mfr*	*Conc*	*Mfr*	*Conc*	*Remarks*	*Ref*	*C/I*
Atracurium besylate	BW	1 mg/ml[a]	SW	0.4 mg/ml[a]	Visually compatible with little or no loss of either drug by HPLC in 4 hr at 23 °C	2214	C
Bumetanide	RC	0.25 mg/ml	SW	0.4 mg/ml[a]	Visually compatible with little or no loss of either drug by HPLC in 4 hr at 23 °C	2214	C
Calcium gluconate	LY	0.465 mEq/ ml	SW	0.4 mg/ml[a]	Visually compatible with no loss of milrinone by HPLC in 4 hr at 23 °C	2214	C

Y-Site Injection Compatibility (1:1 Mixture) (Cont.)

Milrinone lactate

Drug	*Mfr*	*Conc*	*Mfr*	*Conc*	*Remarks*	*Ref*	*C/I*
Cimetidine HCl	SKB	6 mg/ml[a]	SW	0.4 mg/ml[a]	Visually compatible with little or no loss of either drug by HPLC in 4 hr at 23 °C	2214	C
Digoxin	BW	0.25 mg/ml	WI	200 μg/ml[a]	Physically compatible with no loss of either drug in 4 hr at 23 °C	1191	C
Diltiazem HCl	MMD	1 mg/ml[a]	SW	0.2 mg/ml[a]	Visually compatible for 4 hr at 27 °C	2062	C
	MMD	1 mg/ml[a]	SW	0.4 mg/ml[a]	Visually compatible with little or no loss of either drug by HPLC in 4 hr at 23 °C	2214	C
Dobutamine HCl	LI	4 mg/ml[a]	SW	0.2 mg/ml[a]	Visually compatible for 4 hr at 27 °C	2062	C
	GEN	8 mg/ml[a]	SW	0.4 mg/ml[a]	Visually compatible with little or no loss of either drug by HPLC in 4 hr at 23 °C	2214	C
Dopamine HCl	AB	3.2 mg/ml[a]	SW	0.2 mg/ml[a]	Visually compatible for 4 hr at 27 °C	2062	C
	SO	6.4 mg/ml[a]	SW	0.4 mg/ml[a]	Visually compatible with little or no loss of either drug by HPLC in 4 hr at 23 °C	2214	C
Epinephrine HCl	AB	0.02 mg/ml[a]	SW	0.2 mg/ml[a]	Visually compatible for 4 hr at 27 °C	2062	C
	AB	0.064 mg/ml[a]	SW	0.4 mg/ml[a]	Visually compatible with little or no loss of either drug by HPLC in 4 hr at 23 °C	2214	C
Fentanyl citrate	ES	0.05 mg/ml	SW	0.2 mg/ml[a]	Visually compatible for 4 hr at 27 °C	2062	C
	ES	50 μg/ml	SW	0.4 mg/ml[a]	Visually compatible with little or no loss of either drug by HPLC in 4 hr at 23 °C	2214	C
Furosemide	LY	10 mg/ml	WI	200 μg/ml[a]	Immediate precipitation	1191	I
	AMR	10 mg/ml	SW	0.2 mg/ml[a]	Precipitate forms in 4 hr at 27 °C	2062	I
Heparin sodium	ES	100 units/ml[a]	SW	0.2 mg/ml[a]	Visually compatible for 4 hr at 27 °C	2062	C
	ES	100 units/ml[a]	SW	0.4 mg/ml[a]	Visually compatible with little or no loss of milrinone by HPLC and heparin by immunoassay in 4 hr at 23 °C	2214	C
Hetastarch in lactated electrolyte injection (Hextend)	AB	6%	SAN	0.2 mg/ml[a]	Physically compatible with no change in measured turbidity or increase in particle content in 4 hr at 23 °C	2339	C
Hydromorphone HCl	KN	1 mg/ml	SW	0.2 mg/ml[a]	Visually compatible for 4 hr at 27 °C	2062	C
Insulin, regular human	NOV	1 unit/ml[b]	SW	0.4 mg/ml[a]	Visually compatible with little or no loss of either drug by HPLC in 4 hr at 23 °C	2214	C
Isoproterenol HCl	ES	8 μg/ml[a]	SW	0.4 mg/ml[a]	Visually compatible with little or no loss of either drug by HPLC in 4 hr at 23 °C	2214	C
Labetalol HCl	AH	2 mg/ml[a]	SW	0.2 mg/ml[a]	Visually compatible for 4 hr at 27 °C	2062	C
Lorazepam	WY	0.5 mg/ml[a]	SW	0.2 mg/ml[a]	Visually compatible for 4 hr at 27 °C	2062	C
	WY	0.2 mg/ml[a]	SW	0.4 mg/ml[a]	Visually compatible with little or no loss of either drug by HPLC in 4 hr at 23 °C	2214	C
Magnesium sulfate	SO	40 mg/ml[a]	SW	0.4 mg/ml[a]	Visually compatible with no loss of milrinone by HPLC in 4 hr at 23 °C	2214	C
Midazolam HCl	RC	2 mg/ml[a]	SW	0.2 mg/ml[a]	Visually compatible for 4 hr at 27 °C	2062	C
	RC	1 mg/ml	SW	0.4 mg/ml[a]	Visually compatible with little or no loss of either drug by HPLC in 4 hr at 23 °C	2214	C
Morphine sulfate	SCN	2 mg/ml[a]	SW	0.2 mg/ml[a]	Visually compatible for 4 hr at 27 °C	2062	C
	AST	1 mg/ml[a]	SW	0.4 mg/ml[a]	Visually compatible with little or no loss of either drug by HPLC in 4 hr at 23 °C	2214	C
Nicardipine HCl	WY	1 mg/ml[a]	SW	0.2 mg/ml[a]	Visually compatible for 4 hr at 27 °C	2062	C
Nitroglycerin	AB	0.4 mg/ml[a]	SW	0.2 mg/ml[a]	Visually compatible for 4 hr at 27 °C	2062	C
	SO	0.8 mg/ml[a]	SW	0.4 mg/ml[a]	Visually compatible with little or no loss of either drug by HPLC in 4 hr at 23 °C	2214	C

Y-Site Injection Compatibility (1:1 Mixture) (Cont.)

			Milrinone lactate				
Drug	*Mfr*	*Conc*	*Mfr*	*Conc*	*Remarks*	*Ref*	*C/I*
Norepinephrine bitartrate	AB	0.128 mg/ml[a]	SW	0.2 mg/ml[a]	Visually compatible for 4 hr at 27 °C	2062	C
	SW	0.064 mg/ml[a]	SW	0.4 mg/ml[a]	Visually compatible with little or no loss of either drug by HPLC in 4 hr at 23 °C	2214	C
Pancuronium bromide	GNS	1 mg/ml	SW	0.4 mg/ml[a]	Visually compatible with little or no loss of either drug by HPLC in 4 hr at 23 °C	2214	C
Potassium chloride	AB	1 mEq/ml[a]	SW	0.4 mg/ml[a]	Visually compatible with no loss of milrinone by HPLC in 4 hr at 23 °C	2214	C
Procainamide HCl	SQ	2 and 4 mg/ml[a]	WI	350 μg/ml[a]	3 to 6% procainamide loss in 1 hr and 10 to 13% loss in 4 hr at 23 °C. No milrinone loss	1191	I
Propofol	ZEN	10 mg/ml	SW	0.4 mg/ml[a]	Little or no loss of either drug by HPLC in 4 hr at 23 °C	2214	C
Propranolol HCl	AY	1 mg/ml[a]	WI	200 μg/ml[a]	Physically compatible with no loss of either drug in 4 hr at 23 °C	1191	C
Quinidine gluconate	LI	16 mg/ml[a]	WI	350 μg/ml[a]	Physically compatible with no loss of either drug in 4 hr at 23 °C	1191	C
Ranitidine HCl	GL	1 mg/ml[a]	SW	0.2 mg/ml[a]	Visually compatible for 4 hr at 27 °C	2062	C
	GL	2 mg/ml[a]	SW	0.4 mg/ml[a]	Visually compatible with little or no loss of either drug by HPLC in 4 hr at 23 °C	2214	C
Rocuronium bromide	OR	2 mg/ml[a]	SW	0.4 mg/ml[a]	Visually compatible with little or no loss of either drug by HPLC in 4 hr at 23 °C	2214	C
Sodium bicarbonate	AB	1 mEq/ml	SW	0.4 mg/ml[a]	Visually compatible with 4% loss of milrinone by HPLC in 4 hr at 23 °C	2214	C
Sodium nitroprusside	AB	0.8 mg/ml[a]	SW	0.4 mg/ml[a]	Visually compatible with little or no loss of either drug by HPLC in 4 hr at 23 °C protected from light	2214	C
Theophylline	AB	1.6 mg/ml[a]	SW	0.4 mg/ml[a]	Visually compatible with little or no loss of milrinone by HPLC and theophylline by immunoassay in 4 hr at 23 °C	2214	C
Thiopental sodium	AB	25 mg/ml[c]	SW	0.2 mg/ml[a]	Visually compatible for 4 hr at 27 °C	2062	C
Torsemide	BM	10 mg/ml	SW	0.4 mg/ml[a]	Visually compatible with little or no loss of either drug by HPLC in 4 hr at 23 °C	2214	C
TPN #217[d]			SW	0.4 mg/ml[a]	Visually compatible with no loss of milrinone by HPLC in 4 hr at 23 °C	2214	C
Vecuronium bromide	OR	1 mg/ml	SW	0.2 mg/ml[a]	Visually compatible for 4 hr at 27 °C	2062	C
	OR	1 mg/ml	SW	0.4 mg/ml[a]	Visually compatible with little or no loss of either drug by HPLC in 4 hr at 23 °C	2214	C

[a]Tested in dextrose 5% in water.
[b]Tested in sodium chloride 0.9%.
[c]Tested in sterile water for injection.
[d]Refer to Appendix I for the composition of parenteral nutrition solutions. TPN indicates a 2-in-1 admixture.

Additional Compatibility Information

Infusion Solutions — Dextrose 5% in water and sodium chloride 0.45 and 0.9% are recommended for milrinone lactate dilution for intravenous infusion. (2)

Other Drugs — Furosemide and bumetanide may precipitate if mixed with milrinone lactate infusions. (1442)

MINOCYCLINE HCL
AHFS 8:12.24

Products — Minocycline HCl is available in vials containing 100 mg of drug in lyophilized form. The vials should be reconstituted with 5 ml of sterile water for injection to yield a 20-mg/ml solution. (2; 4)

pH — From 2 to 2.8. (2; 4)

Osmolality — Minocycline HCl 20 mg/ml in sterile water for injection has an osmolality of 107 mOsm/kg. (1689)

Trade Name(s) — Minocin.

Administration — Minocycline HCl is administered by intravenous infusion. The reconstituted drug is further diluted to a concentration of 100 to 200 μg/ml in 500 to 1000 ml of a compatible infusion solution. Minocycline HCl is infused slowly, usually over a six-hour period. (2; 4)

Stability — Minocycline HCl in intact vials should be stored at controlled room temperature and protected from temperatures above 40 °C and from light. (4) The reconstituted solution is stable for 24 hours at room temperature. (2; 4)

Central Venous Catheter — Minocycline HCl (Lederle) 0.2 mg/ml in dextrose 5% in water was found to be compatible with the ARROWg+ard Blue Plus (Arrow International) chlorhexidine-bearing triple-lumen central catheter. HPLC analysis was used to evaluate completeness of drug delivery through the catheter and the amount of chlorhexidine removed from the internal lumens. Essentially complete delivery of the drug was found with little or no drug loss occurring. Furthermore, chlorhexidine delivered from the catheter remained at trace amounts with no substantial increase due to the delivery of the drug through the catheter. (2335)

Compatibility Information

Solution Compatibility

Minocycline HCl

Solution	*Mfr*	*Mfr*	*Conc/L*	*Remarks*	*Ref*	*C/I*
Dextrose 5% in water	BA[a]	LE	0.1 g	Physically compatible with approximately 8% minocycline loss at 24 °C and 2% loss at 4 °C in 7 days	1559	C
Sodium chloride 0.9%	BA[a]	LE	0.1 g	Physically compatible with approximately 8% minocycline loss at 24 °C and 2% loss at 4 °C in 7 days	1559	C

[a]*Tested in PVC containers.*

Additive Compatibility

Minocycline HCl

Drug	*Mfr*	*Conc/L*	*Mfr*	*Conc/L*	*Test Soln*	*Remarks*	*Ref*	*C/I*
Rifampin	MMD	0.1 g	LE	0.1 g	NS	Brownish color appears in 4 hr at 37 and 24 °C and 8 hr at 4 °C. 10% rifampin loss by HPLC in 3 days at 4 °C and 8 hr at 24 °C; 14% loss in 4 hr at 37 °C. Less than 2% minocycline loss by HPLC under these conditions	1559	I

Drugs in Syringe Compatibility

Minocycline HCl

Drug (in syringe)	*Mfr*	*Amt*	*Mfr*	*Amt*	*Remarks*	*Ref*	*C/I*
Doxapram HCl	RB	400 mg/ 20 ml		100 mg/ 5 ml	8% doxapram loss in 3 hr and 13% loss in 6 hr	1177	I

Y-Site Injection Compatibility (1:1 Mixture)

			Minocycline HCl				
Drug	*Mfr*	*Conc*	*Mfr*	*Conc*	*Remarks*	*Ref*	*C/I*
Allopurinol sodium	BW	3 mg/ml[b]	LE	0.2 mg/ml[b]	Greenish-yellow color forms in 4 hr	1686	I
Amifostine	USB	10 mg/ml[b]	LE	0.2 mg/ml[b]	Bright yellow discoloration forms immediately	1845	I
Aztreonam	SQ	40 mg/ml[a]	LE	0.2 mg/ml[a]	Physically compatible with no subvisual haze or particle formation in 4 hr at 23 °C	1758	C
Cisatracurium besylate	GW	0.1, 2, 5 mg/ml[a]	LE	0.2 mg/ml[a]	Physically compatible with no change in measured turbidity or increase in particle content in 4 hr at 23 °C	2074	C
Cyclophosphamide	MJ	20 mg/ml[a]	LE	0.2 mg/ml[a]	Physically compatible for 4 hr at 25 °C	1194	C
Docetaxel	RPR	0.9 mg/ml[a]	LE	0.2 mg/ml[a]	Physically compatible with no change in measured turbidity or increase in particle content in 4 hr at 23 °C	2224	C
Etoposide phosphate	BR	5 mg/ml[a]	LE	0.2 mg/ml[a]	Physically compatible with no change in measured turbidity or increase in particle content in 4 hr at 23 °C	2218	C
Filgrastim	AMG	30 μg/ml[a]	LE	0.2 mg/ml[a]	Physically compatible with no change in measured turbidity or increase in particle content in 4 hr at 22 °C	1687	C
Fludarabine phosphate	BX	1 mg/ml[a]	LE	0.2 mg/ml[a]	Physically compatible for 4 hr at room temperature under fluorescent light	1439	C
Gemcitabine HCl	LI	10 mg/ml[b]	LE	0.2 mg/ml[b]	Physically compatible with no change in measured turbidity or increase in particle content in 4 hr at 23 °C	2226	C
Granisetron HCl	SKB	0.05 mg/ml[a]	LE	0.2 mg/ml[a]	Physically compatible with no change in measured turbidity or increase in particle content in 4 hr at 23 °C	2000	C
Heparin sodium	UP	1000 units/L[c]	LE	50 mg/ml	Physically compatible for at least 4 hr at room temperature by visual and microscopic examination	534	C
Hydrocortisone sodium succinate	UP	10 mg/L[c]	LE	50 mg/ml	Physically compatible for at least 4 hr at room temperature by visual and microscopic examination	534	C
Hydromorphone HCl	WY	0.2 mg/ml[a]	LE	0.2 mg/ml[a]	Color changed from pale yellow to light green within 1 hr at 25 °C	987	I
Linezolid	PHU	2 mg/ml	LE	0.2 mg/ml[a]	Physically compatible with no change in measured turbidity or increase in particle content in 4 hr at 23 °C	2264	C
Magnesium sulfate	IX	16.7, 33.3, 66.7, 100 mg/ml[a]	LE	0.2 mg/ml[a]	Physically compatible for at least 4 hr at 32 °C	813	C
Melphalan HCl	BW	0.1 mg/ml[b]	LE	0.2 mg/ml[b]	Physically compatible with no change in measured turbidity or increase in particle content in 3 hr at 22 °C	1557	C
Meperidine HCl	WY	10 mg/ml[a]	LE	0.2 mg/ml[a]	Color changed from pale yellow to light green within 1 hr at 25 °C	987	I
Morphine sulfate	WI	1 mg/ml[a]	LE	0.2 mg/ml[a]	Color changed from pale yellow to light green within 1 hr at 25 °C	987	I

Y-Site Injection Compatibility (1:1 Mixture) (Cont.)

Minocycline HCl

Drug	*Mfr*	*Conc*	*Mfr*	*Conc*	*Remarks*	*Ref*	*C/I*
Perphenazine	SC	0.02 mg/ml[a]	LE	0.2 mg/ml[a]	Physically compatible for 4 hr at 25 °C	1155	C
Piperacillin sodium–tazobactam sodium	LE	40 + 5 mg/ml[a]	LE	1 mg/ml[a]	Particles form immediately, becoming numerous in 4 hr	1688	I
Potassium chloride	AB	40 mEq/L[c]	LE	50 mg/ml	Physically compatible for at least 4 hr at room temperature by visual and microscopic examination	534	C
Propofol	ZEN	10 mg/ml	LE	0.2 mg/ml[a]	Small amount of white particles forms immediately	2066	I
Remifentanil HCl	GW	0.025 and 0.25 mg/ml[b]	LE	0.2 mg/ml[a]	Physically compatible with no change in measured turbidity or increase in particle content in 4 hr at 23 °C	2075	C
Sargramostim	IMM	10 μg/ml[b]	LE	0.2 mg/ml[b]	Physically compatible for 4 hr at 22 °C	1436	C
Teniposide	BR	0.1 mg/ml[a]	LE	0.2 mg/ml[a]	Physically compatible with no subvisual haze or particle formation in 4 hr at 23 °C	1725	C
Thiotepa	IMM[d]	1 mg/ml[a]	LE	0.2 mg/ml[a]	Yellow-green discoloration forms in 1 hr at 23 °C	1861	I
TNA #218 to #226[e]			LE	0.2 mg/ml[a]	Damage to emulsion integrity occurs immediately with free oil formation possible	2215	I
TPN #212 to #215[e]			LE	0.2 mg/ml[a]	Bright yellow discoloration forms immediately	2109	I
Vinorelbine tartrate	BW	1 mg/ml[b]	LE	0.2 mg/ml[b]	Physically compatible with no change in measured turbidity or increase in particle content in 4 hr at 22 °C	1558	C
Vitamin B complex with C	RC	2 ml/L[c]	LE	50 mg/ml	Physically compatible for at least 4 hr at room temperature by visual and microscopic examination	534	C

[a]*Tested in dextrose 5% in water.*
[b]*Tested in sodium chloride 0.9%.*
[c]*Tested in dextrose 5% in Ringer's injection, dextrose 5% in Ringer's injection, lactated, dextrose 5% in water, Ringer's injection, lactated, and sodium chloride 0.9%.*
[d]*Lyophilized formulation tested.*
[e]*Refer to Appendix I for the composition of parenteral nutrition solutions. TNA indicates a 3-in-1 admixture, and TPN indicates a 2-in-1 admixture.*

Additional Compatibility Information

Infusion Solutions — The manufacturer recommends further dilution of the reconstituted minocycline HCl solution in the following infusion solutions (2):

Dextrose 5% in sodium chloride 0.9%
Dextrose 5% in water
Ringer's injection
Ringer's injection, lactated
Sodium chloride 0.9%

Other calcium-containing solutions are not recommended because of possible precipitate formation. (2; 4)

MITOMYCIN
AHFS 10:00

Products — Mitomycin is available in 5-mg vials with mannitol 10 mg, 20-mg vials with mannitol 40 mg, and 40-mg vials with mannitol 80 mg. Reconstitute the 5-mg vials with 10 ml, the 20-mg vials with 40 ml, and the 40-mg vials with 80 ml of sterile water for injection and shake to aid dissolution. The product should be allowed to stand at room temperature if dissolution does not take place immediately. The reconstituted solution contains 500 μg/ml of mitomycin. (2; 4)

pH — From 6 to 8. (4)

Osmolality — Mitomycin (Bristol) 0.5 mg/ml in sterile water for injection has an osmolality of 9 mOsm/kg. (2043)

Density — Mitomycin (Bristol) reconstituted with sterile water for injection to a concentration of 0.5 mg/ml has a solution density of 1.00 g/ml. (2041; 2248)

Trade Name(s) — Mutamycin.

Administration — Mitomycin is administered intravenously through a functioning intravenous catheter. Extravasation should be avoided because cellulitis, ulceration, and sloughing may occur. It has been recommended that mitomycin be administered through the tubing of a running infusion solution to avoid this problem. (2; 4)

Stability — Intact vials of mitomycin should be stored at controlled room temperature and protected from light. Temperatures exceeding 40 °C should be avoided. Reconstituted solutions are stable for two weeks when stored under refrigeration at 2 to 8 °C or for one week at room temperature. (2; 4)

Mitomycin (Kyowa) 0.6 and 0.8 mg/ml in water for injection exhibited 10% loss in seven days at 21 °C in the dark. When stored at 4 °C in the dark, the 0.6-mg/ml concentration lost 7% in seven days. Although exhibiting no loss in 24 hours when stored at 4 °C in the dark, the 0.8-mg/ml concentration developed a fine, pink, needle-like precipitate in three days. At a higher concentration of 1 mg/ml in water for injection similar results were obtained. Refrigeration resulted in fine, pink, needle-like precipitate formation in 24 hours. The 1-mg/ml concentration stored at 21 °C exposed to fluorescent light exhibited 6% loss in 24 hours and developed the fine, pink, needle-like precipitate in four days. Stored at a higher temperature of 25 °C in the dark, losses of 6% in 24 hours and 10% in seven days were found with no precipitate forming. (1503)

Mitomycin, reconstituted according to the manufacturer's instructions, was cultured with human lymphoblasts to determine whether its cytotoxic activity was retained. The solution retained cytotoxicity for 24 hours at 4 °C and room temperature. (1575)

pH Effects — Mitomycin is very stable in solution at a neutral pH but undergoes more rapid decomposition at acidic and basic pH. (1119; 1203; 1204; 1866) The decomposition is complex and pH dependent, producing different decomposition products in acidic and basic solutions. (1119; 1283; 1284) The pH of maximum stability is approximately pH 7. (1072; 1203; 1204; 1379) At pH 7, a 10% mitomycin loss occurs in seven days at room temperature. (1072) At a concentration of 0.05 mg/ml in dextrose 5% in water buffered to pH 7.8 with a mixture of phosphates, mitomycin was stable for 15 days at room temperature and over 120 days when refrigerated. (1118)

Temperature Effects — Heating mitomycin 0.6 mg/ml in sodium chloride 0.9% to 100 °C resulted in a 24% drug loss in 30 minutes and a 58% loss in one hour. (1285)

Freezing Solutions — Mitomycin 0.6 mg/ml in sodium chloride 0.9% crystallized out of solution when frozen at −20 °C. The particles did not redissolve after thawing in a microwave oven. Freezing to −30 °C, below the eutectic temperature, resulted in no loss of mitomycin during four weeks of storage, microwave thawing, and refreezing at −30 °C for another four weeks. (1285)

Light Effects — The stability of mitomycin is not adversely affected by the presence or absence of normal fluorescent light. (1503)

Syringes — Mitomycin (Bristol-Myers Squibb) reconstituted to a concentration of 0.5 mg/ml with sterile water was repackaged in 1-ml polypropylene tuberculin syringes (Sherwood). Syringes were stored at both 5 and 25 °C protected from light. Stability-indicating HPLC analysis found about 7% mitomycin loss in 11 days at 25 °C and about 8% loss in 42 days at 5 °C. (2179)

Sorption — Mitomycin (Kyowa) 20 to 50 mg in 50 ml of sterile water for injection or sodium chloride 0.9% in PVC containers exhibited no loss due to sorption. (1503)

Filtration — Mitomycin 10 to 75 μg/ml exhibited little or no loss due to sorption to either cellulose nitrate/cellulose acetate ester (Millex OR) or Teflon (Millex FG) filters. (1415; 1416)

Compatibility Information

Solution Compatibility

Mitomycin

Solution	Mfr	Mfr	Conc/L	Remarks	Ref	C/I
Dextrose 3.3% in sodium chloride 0.3%		BR	50 mg	10% mitomycin loss in 1.6 hr at 25 °C	1205	I
Dextrose 5% in water	TR[a]	BR	400 mg	10% mitomycin loss in 1 or 2 hr at room temperature	519	I
	TR[b]	CH	50 mg	Violet color appeared in 4 hr and intensified over 12 hr. 74% mitomycin loss in 12 hr at 28 °C under fluorescent light and 33% in 12 hr at 5 °C in the dark	1118	I

Solution Compatibility (Cont.)

Mitomycin

Solution	*Mfr*	*Mfr*	*Conc/L*	*Remarks*	*Ref*	*C/I*
		BR	50 mg	10% mitomycin loss in 2.6 hr at 25 °C	1205	I
	MG[c]	BR	20 mg	10% mitomycin loss by HPLC in 3 hr at 25 °C	1866	I
	MG[c]	BR	40 mg	10% mitomycin loss by HPLC in 24 hr at 4 °C	1866	C
	TR[b]	BR	20 mg	10% mitomycin loss by HPLC in 7 hr at 25 °C	1866	I
	TR[b]	BR	40 mg	10% mitomycin loss by HPLC in 23 hr at 4 °C	1866	C
Ringer's injection, lactated		BR	50 mg	10% mitomycin loss in 43 hr at 25 °C	1205	C
	MG[c]	BR	20 mg	10% mitomycin loss by HPLC in 143 hr at 25 °C	1866	C
	MG[c]	BR	40 mg	10% mitomycin loss by HPLC in 480 hr at 4 °C	1866	C
	TR[b]	BR	20 mg	10% mitomycin loss by HPLC in 142 hr at 25 °C	1866	C
	TR[b]	BR	40 mg	10% mitomycin loss by HPLC in 370 hr at 4 °C	1866	C
Sodium chloride 0.4%	[a,d]	KY	600 mg	6 to 8% loss in 7 days at 4 °C in the dark	1503	C
Sodium chloride 0.6%	[b,d]	KY	400 mg	9% loss in 7 days at 4 °C in the dark	1503	C
Sodium chloride 0.9%	TR[a]	BR	400 mg	Less than 10% mitomycin loss in 24 hr at room temperature	519	C
	TR[b]	CH	50 mg	Violet color appeared in 4 hr and intensified over 12 hr. 10% mitomycin loss in 12 hr at 5 °C in the dark	1118	I
		BR	50 mg	10% mitomycin loss in 5 days at 25 °C	1205	C
	[a]	KY	600 mg	5% loss in 24 hr and 9% loss in 4 days at 4 °C in the dark	1503	C
	MG[c]	BR	40 mg	10% mitomycin loss by HPLC in 128 hr at 4 °C	1866	C
	TR[b]	BR	40 mg	10% mitomycin loss by HPLC in 126 hr at 4 °C	1866	C

[a]*Tested in both glass and PVC containers.*
[b]*Tested in PVC containers.*
[c]*Tested in glass containers.*
[d]*Prepared from sodium chloride 0.9% and water for injection.*

Additive Compatibility

Mitomycin

Drug	*Mfr*	*Conc/L*	*Mfr*	*Conc/L*	*Test Soln*	*Remarks*	*Ref*	*C/I*
Bleomycin sulfate	BR	20 and 30 units	BR	10 mg	NS	20% loss of bleomycin activity in 1 week at 4 °C	763	I
	BR	20 and 30 units	BR	50 mg	NS	52% loss of bleomycin activity in 1 week at 4 °C	763	I
Dexamethasone sodium phosphate	LY	5 g	BR	100 mg	NS[a]	Visually compatible with 10% mitomycin loss calculated in 68 hr and 10% dexamethasone loss calculated in 250 hr at 25 °C	1866	C
	LY	5 g	BR	100 mg	NS[b]	Visually compatible with 10% mitomycin loss calculated in 91 hr and 10% dexamethasone loss calculated in 154 hr at 25 °C	1866	C
	LY	5 g	BR	100 mg	NS[a]	Visually compatible with 10% mitomycin loss calculated in 211 hr and 10% dexamethasone loss calculated in 98 hr at 4 °C	1866	C
	LY	5 g	BR	100 mg	NS[b]	Visually compatible with 10% mitomycin loss calculated in 238 hr and 10% dexamethasone loss calculated in 355 hr at 25 °C	1866	C

Additive Compatibility (Cont.)

Mitomycin

Drug	Mfr	Conc/L	Mfr	Conc/L	Test Soln	Remarks	Ref	C/I
Heparin sodium	ES	33,300 units	BR	167 mg	NS[a]	Visually compatible with 10% mitomycin loss calculated in 21 hr and no decrease in heparin bioactivity at 25 °C	1866	I
	ES	33,300 units	BR	167 mg	NS[b]	Visually compatible with 10% mitomycin loss calculated in 25 hr and no decrease in heparin bioactivity at 25 °C	1866	C
	ES	33,300 units	BR	500 mg	NS[a]	Visually compatible with 10% mitomycin loss calculated in 42 hr and no decrease in heparin bioactivity at 25 °C	1866	C
	ES	33,300 units	BR	500 mg	NS[b]	Visually compatible with 10% mitomycin loss calculated in 61 hr and no decrease in heparin bioactivity at 25 °C	1866	C
Hydrocortisone sodium succinate	AB	33.3 g	BR	1 g	W[a]	Visually compatible with 10% mitomycin loss calculated in 172 hr and 10% hydrocortisone loss calculated in 212 hr at 25 °C	1866	C
	AB	33.3 g	BR	1 g	W[b]	Visually compatible with 10% mitomycin loss calculated in 206 hr and 10% hydrocortisone loss calculated in 218 hr at 25 °C	1866	C
	AB	33.3 g	BR	1 g	W[a]	Visually compatible with 10% mitomycin loss calculated in 1423 hr and 10% hydrocortisone loss calculated in 176 hr at 4 °C	1866	C
	AB	33.3 g	BR	1 g	W[b]	Visually compatible with 10% mitomycin loss calculated in 820 hr and 10% hydrocortisone loss calculated in 807 hr at 4 °C	1866	C

[a]*Tested in glass containers.*
[b]*Tested in PVC containers.*

Drugs in Syringe Compatibility

Mitomycin

Drug (in syringe)	Mfr	Amt	Mfr	Amt	Remarks	Ref	C/I
Bleomycin sulfate		1.5 units/ 0.5 ml		0.25 mg/ 0.5 ml	Physically compatible for 5 min at room temperature followed by 8 min of centrifugation	980	C
Cisplatin		0.5 mg/ 0.5 ml		0.25 mg/ 0.5 ml	Physically compatible for 5 min at room temperature followed by 8 min of centrifugation	980	C
Cyclophosphamide		10 mg/ 0.5 ml		0.25 mg/ 0.5 ml	Physically compatible for 5 min at room temperature followed by 8 min of centrifugation	980	C
Doxorubicin HCl		1 mg/ 0.5 ml		0.25 mg/ 0.5 ml	Physically compatible for 5 min at room temperature followed by 8 min of centrifugation	980	C
Droperidol		1.25 mg/ 0.5 ml		0.25 mg/ 0.5 ml	Physically compatible for 5 min at room temperature followed by 8 min of centrifugation	980	C
Fluorouracil		25 mg/ 0.5 ml		0.25 mg/ 0.5 ml	Physically compatible for 5 min at room temperature followed by 8 min of centrifugation	980	C
Furosemide		5 mg/ 0.5 ml		0.25 mg/ 0.5 ml	Physically compatible for 5 min at room temperature followed by 8 min of centrifugation	980	C

Drugs in Syringe Compatibility (Cont.)

Mitomycin

Drug (in syringe)	*Mfr*	*Amt*	*Mfr*	*Amt*	*Remarks*	*Ref*	*C/I*
Heparin sodium		500 units/ 0.5 ml		0.25 mg/ 0.5 ml	Physically compatible for 5 min at room temperature followed by 8 min of centrifugation	980	C
Leucovorin calcium		5 mg/ 0.5 ml		0.25 mg/ 0.5 ml	Physically compatible for 5 min at room temperature followed by 8 min of centrifugation	980	C
Methotrexate sodium		12.5 mg/ 0.5 ml		0.25 mg/ 0.5 ml	Physically compatible for 5 min at room temperature followed by 8 min of centrifugation	980	C
Metoclopramide HCl		2.5 mg/ 0.5 ml		0.25 mg/ 0.5 ml	Physically compatible for 5 min at room temperature followed by 8 min of centrifugation	980	C
Vinblastine sulfate		0.5 mg/ 0.5 ml		0.25 mg/ 0.5 ml	Physically compatible for 5 min at room temperature followed by 8 min of centrifugation	980	C
Vincristine sulfate		0.5 mg/ 0.5 ml		0.25 mg/ 0.5 ml	Physically compatible for 5 min at room temperature followed by 8 min of centrifugation	980	C

Y-Site Injection Compatibility (1:1 Mixture)

Mitomycin

Drug	*Mfr*	*Conc*	*Mfr*	*Conc*	*Remarks*	*Ref*	*C/I*
Amifostine	USB	10 mg/ml[a]	BR	0.5 mg/ml	Physically compatible with no change in measured turbidity or increase in particle content in 4 hr at 23 °C	1845	C
Aztreonam	SQ	40 mg/ml[a]	BMS	0.5 mg/ml	Color changes from pale blue to reddish purple in 4 hr	1758	I
Bleomycin sulfate		3 units/ml		0.5 mg/ml	Drugs injected sequentially into Y-site with no flush between. No visually apparent precipitate	980	C
Cefepime HCl	BMS	20 mg/ml[a]	BR	0.5 mg/ml	Color changes to pinkish purple in 1 hr	1684	I
Cisplatin		1 mg/ml		0.5 mg/ml	Drugs injected sequentially into Y-site with no flush between. No visually apparent precipitate	980	C
Cyclophosphamide		20 mg/ml		0.5 mg/ml	Drugs injected sequentially into Y-site with no flush between. No visually apparent precipitate	980	C
Doxorubicin HCl		2 mg/ml		0.5 mg/ml	Drugs injected sequentially into Y-site with no flush between. No visually apparent precipitate	980	C
Droperidol		2.5 mg/ml		0.5 mg/ml	Drugs injected sequentially into Y-site with no flush between. No visually apparent precipitate	980	C
Etoposide phosphate	BR	5 mg/ml[a]	BR	0.5 mg/ml	Color changed from light blue to reddish purple in 4 hr at 23 °C	2218	I
Filgrastim	AMG	30 µg/ml[a]	BR	0.5 mg/ml	Color changes to reddish purple in 1 hr	1687	I
Fluorouracil		50 mg/ml		0.5 mg/ml	Drugs injected sequentially into Y-site with no flush between. No visually apparent precipitate	980	C

Y-Site Injection Compatibility (1:1 Mixture) (Cont.)

			Mitomycin				
Drug	*Mfr*	*Conc*	*Mfr*	*Conc*	*Remarks*	*Ref*	*C/I*
Furosemide		10 mg/ml		0.5 mg/ml	Drugs injected sequentially into Y-site with no flush between. No visually apparent precipitate	980	C
Gemcitabine HCl	LI	10 mg/ml[b]	BR	0.5 mg/ml	Reddish-purple discoloration forms in 1 hr	2226	I
Granisetron HCl	SKB	0.05 mg/ml[a]	BMS	0.5 mg/ml	Physically compatible with no change in measured turbidity or increase in particle content in 4 hr at 23 °C	2000	C
Heparin sodium		1000 units/ml		0.5 mg/ml	Drugs injected sequentially into Y-site with no flush between. No visually apparent precipitate	980	C
Leucovorin calcium		10 mg/ml		0.5 mg/ml	Drugs injected sequentially into Y-site with no flush between. No visually apparent precipitate	980	C
Melphalan HCl	BW	0.1 mg/ml[b]	BR	0.5 mg/ml	Physically compatible with no change in measured turbidity or increase in particle content in 3 hr at 22 °C	1557	C
Methotrexate sodium		25 mg/ml		0.5 mg/ml	Drugs injected sequentially into Y-site with no flush between. No visually apparent precipitate	980	C
Metoclopramide HCl		5 mg/ml		0.5 mg/ml	Drugs injected sequentially into Y-site with no flush between. No visually apparent precipitate	980	C
Ondansetron HCl	GL	1 mg/ml[b]	BR	0.5 mg/ml	Physically compatible for 4 hr at 22 °C	1365	C
Piperacillin sodium–tazobactam sodium	LE	40 + 5 mg/ml[a]	BR	0.5 mg/ml	Blue color darkens in 4 hr, becoming reddish purple in 24 hr	1688	I
Sargramostim	IMM	10 μg/ml[b]	BR	0.5 mg/ml	Slight haze, visible with high intensity light, forms in 30 min	1436	I
Teniposide	BR	0.1 mg/ml[a]	BR	0.5 mg/ml	Physically compatible with no subvisual haze or particle formation in 4 hr at 23 °C	1725	C
Thiotepa	IMM[c]	1 mg/ml[a]	BMS	0.5 mg/ml	Physically compatible with no change in measured turbidity or increase in particle content in 4 hr at 23 °C	1861	C
Topotecan HCl	SKB	56 μg/ml[a,b]	BR	84 μg/ml[a,b]	Pale purple discoloration forms immediately becoming a dark pinkish-lavender in 4 hr. About 15 to 20% loss of mitomycin occurs in 4 hr at 22 °C under fluorescent light	2245	I
Vinblastine sulfate		1 mg/ml		0.5 mg/ml	Drugs injected sequentially into Y-site with no flush between. No visually apparent precipitate	980	C
Vincristine sulfate		1 mg/ml		0.5 mg/ml	Drugs injected sequentially into Y-site with no flush between. No visually apparent precipitate	980	C
Vinorelbine tartrate	BW	1 mg/ml[b]	BR	0.5 mg/ml	Color changes from pale blue to reddish purple in 1 hr	1558	I

[a] *Tested in dextrose 5% in water.*
[b] *Tested in sodium chloride 0.9%.*
[c] *Lyophilized formulation tested.*

Additional Compatibility Information

Infusion Solutions — The manufacturer indicates that mitomycin 20 to 40 μg/ml is stable at room temperature for three hours in dextrose 5% in water, 12 hours in sodium chloride 0.9%, and 24 hours in sodium lactate ⅙ M. (2) Other reports indicated differing stability information. (519; 1118; 1205; 1503) See both Stability and Solution Compatibility tables.

Heparin — Combining mitomycin 5 to 15 mg and heparin sodium 1000 to 10,000 units in 30 ml of sodium chloride 0.9% results in a solution that is stable for 48 hours at room temperature. (2)

Other Information

Inactivation — In the event of spills or leaks, Bristol-Myers Squibb recommends the use of sodium hypochlorite 5% (household bleach) or potassium permanganate 1% to inactivate mitomycin. (1200)

MITOXANTRONE HCL
AHFS 10:00

Products — Mitoxantrone HCl is supplied as a concentrate for further dilution in 10-, 12.5-, and 15-ml multidose vials. Each milliliter of the dark blue aqueous solution contains mitoxantrone 2 mg (as the hydrochloride salt), sodium chloride 0.8%, sodium acetate 0.005%, and acetic acid 0.046%. (2)

pH — From 3 to 4.5. (2)

Osmolality — Mitoxantrone HCl 2 mg/ml has an osmolality of 270 mOsm/kg. (1689)

Sodium Content — Each milliliter of solution contains 0.14 mEq of sodium. (2)

Density — Mitoxantrone HCl (Immunex) 2 mg/ml undiluted injection has a solution density of 0.99 g/ml. (2041; 2248)

Trade Name(s) — Novantrone.

Administration — Mitoxantrone HCl must be diluted for use. The drug is administered by slow intravenous infusion after dilution to at least 50 ml in dextrose 5% in water or sodium chloride 0.9%. Mitoxantrone HCl is usually administered over 15 to 30 minutes through the tubing of a freely running intravenous solution (2; 4) or by continuous intravenous infusion over 24 hours. (4) It should not be given over less than three minutes. (2; 4)

Stability — Intact vials of the dark blue concentrate should be stored at controlled room temperature and protected from freezing. (2) Refrigeration of the concentrate may cause a precipitate, which redissolves upon warming to room temperature. (72; 1369)

The manufacturer indicates that mitoxantrone HCl concentrate remaining in partially used vials may be stored for up to seven days at 15 to 25 °C and up to 14 days under refrigeration but should not be stored frozen. (4)

Mitoxantrone HCl was cultured with human lymphoblasts to determine whether its cytotoxic activity was retained. The solution retained cytotoxicity for 24 hours at 4 °C and room temperature. (1575)

pH Effects — The pH range of maximum stability is 2 to 4.5. Mitoxantrone HCl was unstable when the pH was increased to 7.4. (1379)

Light Effects — Mitoxantrone HCl is not photolabile. Exposure of the product to direct sunlight for one month caused no change in its appearance or potency. (72; 1293)

Syringes — Mitoxantrone HCl 0.2 mg/ml in sodium chloride 0.9% in polypropylene syringes (Braun Omnifix) is reported to be stable for 28 days at 4 and 20 °C (1564) and for 24 hours at 37 °C. (1369)

Mitoxantrone HCl (Lederle) 2 mg/ml in glass vials and drawn into 12-ml plastic syringes (Monoject) exhibited no visual changes and little or no loss by HPLC when stored for 42 days at 4 and 23 °C. Potential extractable materials from the syringes were not detectable during the study period. (1593)

Ambulatory Pumps — Mitoxantrone HCl (Lederle) 0.2 mg/ml in sterile water for injection was stable in Parker Micropump PVC reservoirs for 14 days at 4 and 37 °C, exhibiting no loss by HPLC. (1696)

Elastomeric Reservoir Pumps — Mitoxantrone HCl 0.1 to 0.5 mg/ml in sodium chloride 0.9% in Infusor elastomeric reservoir pumps has been stated by the pump manufacturer to be stable for two days at room temperature followed by five days at 33 °C. At a concentration of 0.2 mg/ml in sodium chloride 0.9% in Infusors, the pump manufacturer has stated that the drug is stable for eight days at room temperature. (31)

Sorption — Mitoxantrone HCl (Lederle) 1 mg/ml in sodium chloride 0.9% exhibited no loss by UV spectroscopy due to sorption to PVC and polyethylene administration lines during simulated infusion at 0.875 ml/hr for 2.5 hours via a syringe pump. (1795)

Filtration — Although binding of mitoxantrone HCl to filters has been reported (1249; 1415; 1416), the manufacturer states that filtration of mitoxantrone HCl through a 0.22-μm filter (Millipore) results in no loss of potency. (1293)

Mitoxantrone HCl (Lederle) 5 mg/100 ml in sodium chloride 0.9% in a burette was filtered through a nylon 0.2-μm filter (Pall, ELD96LL). No drug loss due to sorption was found spectrophotometrically. (1568)

Mitoxantrone HCl (Lederle) 1 mg/ml in sodium chloride 0.9%, during simulated infusion at 0.875 ml/hr for 2.5 hours via a syringe pump, exhibited no loss by UV spectroscopy due to sorption to cellulose acetate (Minisart 45, Sartorius), polysulfone (Acrodisc 45, Gelman), and nylon (Posidyne ELD96, Pall) filters. (1795)

Compatibility Information

Solution Compatibility

Mitoxantrone HCl

Solution	*Mfr*	*Mfr*	*Conc/L*	*Remarks*	*Ref*	*C/I*
Dextrose 5% in sodium chloride 0.9%	[a]	LE	20 to 500 mg	Physically compatible and at least 90% potency retained for 48 hr at room temperature	1293	C
Dextrose 5% in water	[a]	LE	20 to 500 mg	Physically compatible and at least 90% potency retained for 7 days at room temperature and under refrigeration	72; 1293	C
		LE	5 mg	Physically compatible and no decomposition in 48 hr	72	C
Sodium chloride 0.9%	[a]	LE	20 to 500 mg	Physically compatible and at least 90% potency retained for 7 days at room temperature and under refrigeration	72; 1293	C
	[b]	LE	20 to 500 mg	Physically compatible and at least 90% potency retained for 48 hr at room temperature	1293	C
		LE	5 mg	Physically compatible and no decomposition in 48 hr	72	C

[a]*Tested in PVC containers.*
[b]*Tested in glass containers.*

Additive Compatibility

Mitoxantrone HCl

Drug	*Mfr*	*Conc/L*	*Mfr*	*Conc/L*	*Test Soln*	*Remarks*	*Ref*	*C/I*
Cyclophosphamide	AD	10 g	LE	500 mg	D5W	Visually compatible and mitoxantrone potency by HPLC retained for 24 hr at room temperature. Cyclophosphamide not tested	1531	C
Cytarabine	UP	500 mg	LE	500 mg	D5W	Visually compatible and mitoxantrone potency by HPLC retained for 24 hr at room temperature. Cytarabine not tested	1531	C
Etoposide	BR	500 mg	LE	50 mg	NS	Visually compatible with no loss of either drug by HPLC in 22 hr at room temperature	2271	C
Fluorouracil		25 g	LE	500 mg	D5W	Visually compatible and mitoxantrone potency by HPLC retained for 24 hr at room temperature. Fluorouracil not tested	1531	C
Hydrocortisone sodium phosphate		100 mg to 2 g	LE	50 to 200 mg	NS[a]	Physically compatible and potency of both drugs retained for 24 hr at room temperature	1293	C
		100 mg to 2 g	LE	50 to 200 mg	D5W[a]	Small blue particles form on inner surface of bag	1293	I
		100 mg to 2 g	LE	50 to 200 mg	D5W[b]	Physically compatible	1293	C
Hydrocortisone sodium succinate		100 mg to 2 g	LE	50 to 200 mg	D5W, NS[a]	Physically compatible and potency of both drugs retained for 24 hr at room temperature	1293	C

Additive Compatibility (Cont.)

Mitoxantrone HCl

Drug	*Mfr*	*Conc/L*	*Mfr*	*Conc/L*	*Test Soln*	*Remarks*	*Ref*	*C/I*
Potassium chloride		50 mEq	LE	500 mg	D5W	Visually compatible and mitoxantrone potency by HPLC retained for 24 hr at room temperature. Potassium chloride not tested	1531	C

[a]*Tested in PVC containers.*
[b]*Tested in glass containers.*

Y-Site Injection Compatibility (1:1 Mixture)

Mitoxantrone HCl

Drug	*Mfr*	*Conc*	*Mfr*	*Conc*	*Remarks*	*Ref*	*C/I*
Allopurinol sodium	BW	3 mg/ml[b]	LE	0.5 mg/ml[b]	Physically compatible with no change in measured turbidity or increase in particle content in 4 hr at 22 °C	1686	C
Amifostine	USB	10 mg/ml[a]	LE	0.5 mg/ml[a]	Physically compatible with no change in measured turbidity or increase in particle content in 4 hr at 23 °C	1845	C
Amphotericin B cholesteryl sulfate complex	SEQ	0.83 mg/ml[a]	IMM	0.5 mg/ml[a]	Gross precipitate forms	2117	I
Aztreonam	SQ	40 mg/ml[a]	LE	0.5 mg/ml[a]	Heavy precipitate forms in 1 hr	1758	I
Cefepime HCl	BMS	20 mg/ml[a]	LE	0.5 mg/ml[a]	Haze forms immediately and becomes flocculent precipitate in 4 hr	1689	I
Cladribine	ORT	0.015[b] and 0.5[c] mg/ml	LE	0.5 mg/ml[b]	Physically compatible with no change in measured turbidity or increase in particle content in 4 hr at 23 °C	1969	C
Doxorubicin HCl liposome injection	SEQ	0.4 mg/ml[a]	IMM	0.5 mg/ml[a]	Partial loss of measured natural turbidity	2087	I
Etoposide	BR	20 mg/ml	LE	2 mg/ml	Visually compatible with no loss of either drug by HPLC in 22 hr at room temperature	2271	C
Etoposide phosphate	BR	5 mg/ml[a]	IMM	0.5 mg/ml[a]	Physically compatible with no change in measured turbidity or increase in particle content in 4 hr at 23 °C	2218	C
Filgrastim	AMG	30 μg/ml[a]	LE	0.5 mg/ml[a]	Physically compatible with no change in measured turbidity or increase in particle content in 4 hr at 22 °C	1687	C
Fludarabine phosphate	BX	1 mg/ml[a]	LE	0.5 mg/ml[a]	Physically compatible for 4 hr at room temperature under fluorescent light	1439	C
Gatifloxacin	BMS	2 mg/ml[a]	IMM	0.5 mg/ml[a]	Physically compatible with no change in measured haze or increase in particle content in 4 hr at 23 °C	2234	C
Gemcitabine HCl	LI	10 mg/ml[b]	IMM	0.5 mg/ml[b]	Physically compatible with no change in measured turbidity or increase in particle content in 4 hr at 23 °C	2226	C
Granisetron HCl	SKB	0.05 mg/ml[a]	IMM	0.5 mg/ml[a]	Physically compatible with no change in measured turbidity or increase in particle content in 4 hr at 23 °C	2000	C

Y-Site Injection Compatibility (1:1 Mixture) (Cont.)

Drug	Mfr	Conc	Mfr (Mitoxantrone HCl)	Conc (Mitoxantrone HCl)	Remarks	Ref	C/I
Linezolid	PHU	2 mg/ml	IMM	0.5 mg/ml[a]	Physically compatible with no change in measured turbidity or increase in particle content in 4 hr at 23 °C	2264	C
Melphalan HCl	BW	0.1 mg/ml[b]	LE	0.5 mg/ml[b]	Physically compatible with no change in measured turbidity or increase in particle content in 3 hr at 22 °C	1557	C
Ondansetron HCl	GL	1 mg/ml[b]	LE	0.5 mg/ml[a]	Physically compatible for 4 hr at 22 °C	1365	C
Paclitaxel	NCI	1.2 mg/ml[a]	LE	0.5 mg/ml[a]	Normal inherent haze from paclitaxel decreases immediately	1556	I
Piperacillin sodium–tazobactam sodium	LE	40 + 5 mg/ml[a]	LE	0.5 mg/ml[a]	Haze and particles form immediately. Large particles form in 4 hr	1688	I
Propofol	ZEN	10 mg/ml	IMM	0.5 mg/ml[a]	Small amount of particles forms immediately	2066	I
Sargramostim	IMM	10 μg/ml[b]	LE	0.5 mg/ml[b]	Physically compatible for 4 hr at 22 °C	1436	C
Teniposide	BR	0.1 mg/ml[a]	LE	0.5 mg/ml[a]	Physically compatible with no subvisual haze or particle formation in 4 hr at 23 °C	1725	C
Thiotepa	IMM[d]	1 mg/ml[a]	IMM	0.5 mg/ml[a]	Physically compatible with no change in measured turbidity or increase in particle content in 4 hr at 23 °C	1861	C
TNA #218 to #226[e]			IMM	0.5 mg/ml[a]	Visually compatible with no precipitate or emulsion damage apparent in 4 hr at 23 °C	2215	C
TPN #212 to #215[e]			IMM	0.5 mg/ml[a]	Substantial loss of natural subvisual turbidity occurs immediately	2109	I
Vinorelbine tartrate	BW	1 mg/ml[b]	LE	0.5 mg/ml[b]	Physically compatible with little change in measured turbidity or increase in particle content in 4 hr at 22 °C	1558	C

[a] *Tested in dextrose 5% in water.*
[b] *Tested in sodium chloride 0.9%.*
[c] *Tested in bacteriostatic sodium chloride 0.9% preserved with benzyl alcohol 0.9%.*
[d] *Lyophilized formulation tested.*
[e] *Refer to Appendix I for the composition of parenteral nutrition solutions. TNA indicates a 3-in-1 admixture, and TPN indicates a 2-in-1 admixture.*

Additional Compatibility Information

Infusion Solutions — The manufacturer recommends the use of dextrose 5% in sodium chloride 0.9%, dextrose 5% in water, or sodium chloride 0.9% for dilution of mitoxantrone HCl concentrate. (2)

Heparin — The manufacturer does not recommend combining heparin with mitoxantrone HCl in the same admixture because of possible precipitate formation. (2; 1293)

Other Information

Inactivation — The manufacturer recommends that mitoxantrone HCl spilled on equipment or surfaces be inactivated with an aqueous solution of calcium hypochlorite, 5.5 parts in 13 parts (by weight) of water for each one part of mitoxantrone HCl. (2; 1293)

MIVACURIUM CHLORIDE
AHFS 12:20

Products — Mivacurium chloride is available in 5- and 10-ml single-use vials and 20- and 50-ml multiple-use vials. Each milliliter contains mivacurium 2 mg (as the chloride) with hydrochloric acid, if necessary, to adjust the pH. The multiple-use vials also contain benzyl alcohol 0.9%. (1-00)

pH — From 3.5 to 5. (1-00)

Trade Name(s) — Mivacron.

Administration — Mivacurium chloride is administered by rapid intravenous injection or by intravenous infusion. (1-00; 4)

Stability — Mivacurium chloride solutions are clear and colorless. Intact vials of mivacurium chloride should be stored at controlled room temperature and protected from exposure to direct sunlight and freezing. (1-00)

pH Effects — Mivacurium chloride is incompatible with alkaline solutions having a pH greater than 8.5. (1-00)

Compatibility Information

Y-Site Injection Compatibility (1:1 Mixture)

Drug	Mfr	Conc	Mivacurium chloride Mfr	Mivacurium chloride Conc	Remarks	Ref	C/I
Etomidate	AB	2 mg/ml	BW	2 mg/ml	Visually compatible for up to 7 days at 25 °C	1801	C
Hetastarch in lactated electrolyte injection (Hextend)	AB	6%	GW	0.5 mg/ml[a]	Physically compatible with no change in measured turbidity or increase in particle content in 4 hr at 23 °C	2339	C
Thiopental sodium	AB	25 mg/ml	BW	2 mg/ml	Visually compatible for up to 7 days at 25 °C	1801	C

[a] *Tested in dextrose 5% in water.*

Additional Compatibility Information

Infusion Solutions — The manufacturer states that mivacurium chloride 0.5 mg/ml is physically and chemically stable for 24 hours at 5 to 25 °C in the following infusion solutions (1-00):

Dextrose 5% in Ringer's injection, lactated
Dextrose 5% in sodium chloride 0.9%
Dextrose 5% in water
Ringer's injection, lactated
Sodium chloride 0.9%

Other Drugs — The manufacturer recommends that, in general, no drugs should be admixed with mivacurium chloride. However, alfentanil HCl, droperidol, fentanyl citrate, midazolam HCl, and sufentanil citrate are compatible by Y-site administration with mivacurium chloride. (1-00)

MORPHINE SULFATE
AHFS 28:08.08

Products — Morphine sulfate is available in a variety of concentrations and sizes ranging from 0.5 to 50 mg/ml. The Astramorph PF and Duramorph 0.5- and 1-mg/ml concentrations and the Infumorph 200 (10 mg/ml) and Infumorph 500 (25 mg/ml) formulations are preservative free. Other morphine sulfate products may contain various preservatives, antioxidants, and buffers, including chlorobutanol, phenol, sodium bisulfite, sodium phosphates, and sodium formaldehyde sulfoxylate. (4; 154)

pH — From 2.5 to 6 for most products. Duramorph has a pH of 3.5 to 7, and Infumorph has a pH of about 4.5. (4) Morphine sulfate (David Bull) 7.5 mg/ml in sodium chloride 0.9% had a pH of 3.5. (2161)

Osmolality — The osmolality of morphine (as the hydrochloride) 10 mg/ml was determined to be 54 mOsm/kg. (1233) Morphine sulfate (David Bull) 7.5 mg/ml in sodium chloride 0.9% had an osmolality of 236 mOsm/kg. (2161)

Morphine sulfate solutions prepared from powder for intrathecal use had the following measured osmolalities (2290):

Solution	Osmolality (mOsm/kg)
Morphine sulfate 50 mg/ml in 0.9% sodium chloride	401
Morphine sulfate 5 mg/ml in 0.9% sodium chloride	310
Morphine sulfate 50 mg/ml in sterile water for injection	104
Morphine sulfate 5 mg/ml in sterile water for injection	7

Solubility—The maximum aqueous solubility of morphine sulfate at room temperature has been reported to be about 62.5 mg/ml. (4) However, a lower practical morphine sulfate solubility was found during an evaluation of concentrations ranging from 10 to 50 mg/ml in water, dextrose 5% in water, and sodium chloride 0.9%. The maximum practical solubility in dextrose 5% in water was essentially the same as in water over the temperature range of 4 to 40 °C and was about 50 mg/ml at 22 °C. However, the solubility in sodium chloride 0.9% was markedly reduced about 40% to about 30 mg/ml at 22 °C. Under refrigeration, the maximum solubilities were reduced to 30 mg/ml in water and dextrose 5% in water and to 20 mg/ml in sodium chloride 0.9%. (2162)

Trade Name(s)—Astramorph PF, Duramorph, Infumorph.

Administration — Morphine sulfate is usually administered subcutaneously but may be administered by intramuscular or slow intravenous injection and by slow continuous subcutaneous or intravenous infusion. For continuous intravenous infusion, a concentration of 0.1 to 1 mg/ml in dextrose 5% in water may be infused using an infusion control device, although more concentrated solutions also have been used. Duramorph, Infumorph, and Astramorph PF contain no preservatives and may be administered intrathecally or epidurally. (2; 4)

High-concentration morphine sulfate is not recommended for subcutaneous, intramuscular, or intravenous injection of individual doses or for intrathecal or epidural administration. The products are intended for continuous intravenous infusion using a suitable microinfusion control device. (4)

Stability — Morphine sulfate injections are clear, colorless solutions. Intact containers should be stored at controlled room temperature and protected from freezing and light. Morphine sulfate darkens upon prolonged exposure to light. (4)

Undiluted morphine sulfate (Allen & Hanburys) 10 mg/ml, stored in 100-ml glass vials and PVC bags, exhibited no loss in 30 days at 23 °C. (1394)

Morphine sulfate (Wyeth) 1 mg/ml in bacteriostatic sodium chloride 0.9% containing benzyl alcohol 0.9%, when stored in glass vials with protection from light, exhibited no loss by HPLC at 4 °C and a 4% loss at 22 °C after 91 days. (1583)

Duafala et al. studied the stability of morphine sulfate 15 and 2 mg/ml diluted with sterile water for injection at 4 and 24 °C in 200-ml PVC bags (Baxter). Both concentrations were stable at both temperatures with little or no loss in 15 days. (1504)

Morphine sulfate physical and chemical stability were evaluated at concentrations ranging from 10 to 50 mg/ml in water, dextrose 5% in water, and sodium chloride 0.9% for use in subcutaneous infusion. The solutions were stored in glass containers, polypropylene syringes, and PVC containers at 4, 22, and 40 °C for up to three months in the absence of light. At concentrations above 20 mg/ml, refrigerated storage resulted in the formation of visually apparent precipitation that was difficult to redissolve. Precipitation also occurred at concentrations above 30 mg/ml using sodium chloride 0.9% as the diluent. The solution color increased progressively from colorless to pale yellow initially to darker yellow and to brown in the 40 °C samples. HPLC analysis of morphine sulfate 30-mg/ml aqueous solutions found no substantial decomposition of morphine sulfate within three months at 22 °C, but the authors recommended that refrigerated storage be avoided because of the potential for precipitation. In addition, the solutions in PVC containers exhibited a gradual increase in drug concentration and osmolality possibly indicating a loss of water through the PVC. The morphine concentration increased to over 105% after storage of one month and one week at 22 and 40 °C, respectively. In addition, a white precipitate formed, possibly because of water evaporation. Storage in PVC containers for longer time periods was not recommended. (2162)

pH Effects—Morphine sulfate is relatively stable at acidic pH, especially below pH 4, but degradation increases greatly at neutral or basic pH. Degradation is often accompanied by a yellow to brown discoloration in the normally colorless solution. (1072; 2170)

Freezing Solutions—Morphine sulfate (Lilly) 1 and 2 mg/ml in dextrose 5% in water and sodium chloride 0.9% in PVC bags exhibited no loss during 14 weeks of frozen storage at −20 °C. (1286)

Syringes—Prefilled into plastic syringes with syringe caps (Braun), morphine sulfate is stated to remain within acceptable limits of degradation for at least 69 days at room temperature. (982)

In another study, less than a 3% loss of morphine sulfate occurred in 12 weeks when stored in plastic syringes at 22 °C and exposed to light. A smaller loss occurred when the morphine sulfate was stored at 3 °C with light protection. (1287)

Duafala et al. studied the stability of morphine sulfate 15 and 2 mg/ml diluted with sterile water for injection at 4 and 24 °C in 3-ml disposable glass syringes (Hypod). Both concentrations were stable at both temperatures with little or no loss in 12 days. (1504)

Morphine sulfate (Lilly) 1 and 5 mg/ml in dextrose 5% in water and sodium chloride 0.9% was packaged in 30-ml Plastipak (Becton-Dickinson) syringes capped with Monoject (Sherwood) tip caps. Syringes were stored at 23 °C exposed to light and protected from light, 4 °C protected from light, and frozen at −20 °C protected from light for 12 weeks. HPLC analysis found that both concentrations at all three temperatures were stable for at least six weeks when protected from light. However, the samples at 23 °C exposed to light were stable for a week, but some developed unacceptable losses after that. (1894)

Grassby and Hutchings reported the stability of morphine sulfate 2 mg/ml in sodium chloride 0.9% packaged in 50-ml (Becton-Dickinson) and 30-ml (Becton-Dickinson and Sherwood) polypropylene syringes for use in patient-controlled analgesia and in stoppered glass vials. The morphine sulfate solution packaged in the syringes and glass vials was stored at room temperature in the dark for six weeks. Using HPLC analysis, the authors found little or no loss of morphine sulfate content in the 50-ml syringes and the glass vials in six weeks. About 5% loss occurred when packaged in both brands of 30-ml syringes. Addition of sodium metabisulfite 0.1% as an antioxidant substantially increased the rate of drug loss; up to 10% loss occurred in two weeks. (2040)

The stability of morphine hydrochloride 1, 5, and 10 mg/ml in dextrose 5% in water and 0.9% sodium chloride packaged in 50-ml polypropylene syringes (B. Braun and Becton-Dickinson) was evaluated. HPLC analysis found little or no loss, with degradation products being less than 2% of the concentration when stored at 37 °C for two days. (2169)

Morphine tartrate (David Bull) 80 mg/ml (undiluted) and 4 mg/ml diluted in sodium chloride 0.9% was packaged as 10 ml of solution in polypropylene syringes (Terumo) sealed with tip caps (Terumo). Samples were stored in the dark at 4 and 22 °C for 21 days. The refrigerated samples at both concentrations and the 4-mg/ml concentration at 22 °C underwent no visible changes and HPLC analysis found little or no loss. The 80-mg/ml samples stored at 22 °C developed a slight yellow discoloration within 21 days that was considered to be within the normal color range for this product. HPLC analysis found about 7% loss after 21 days. (1461)

Preservative-free morphine (salt form unspecified) 0.1 to 1 mg/ml in sodium chloride 0.9% was packaged in 60-ml polypropylene syringes (Monoject) and stored at room temperature. HPLC analysis found no loss of morphine after 36 hours. (631)

Ambulatory Pumps—Walker et al. reported the stability of morphine sulfate (Sabex) 50 and 25 mg/ml and 10 mg/ml diluted in dextrose 5% in water and sodium chloride 0.9%, with and without sodium metabisulfite preservative, in portable infusion pump cassettes (Pharmacia) stored at 4 and 23 °C. At all concentrations with or without preservatives at both temperatures, samples remained clear and colorless. Morphine sulfate losses of approximately 5 to 8% were found during 31 days of storage. (1505)

Altman et al. evaluated the stability of morphine sulfate 0.5, 15, 30, and 60 mg/ml in sodium chloride 0.9% stored in Kalex (Cormed III) bags at 5 and 37 °C. The 60-mg/ml concentration exhibited precipitation in four to eight days when refrigerated. The maximum solubility of morphine sulfate at room temperature is 62.5 mg/ml; refrigeration reduced the solubility, causing precipitation. All other solutions were clear, with no evidence of precipitation. HPLC analysis showed no loss during 14 days of storage at either temperature. A small concentration increase in samples stored at 37 °C was attributed to water evaporation. (1506)

Stiles et al. studied the stability of morphine sulfate 25, 15, 5 and 1 mg/ml (with the latter two concentrations prepared in sodium chloride 0.9%) in pump reservoirs (Pharmacia Deltec) stored at 5 and 25 °C for 30 days. After the initial storage period, the solutions were subsequently stored at 37 °C and pumped at a flow rate of 0.4 ml/hr to simulate patient use. No color change or precipitation occurred in any sample. No losses were detected by HPLC; in fact, increased concentrations were observed, especially at room temperature. The concentration increases were attributed to water evaporation during storage. The authors recommended a maximum storage of 30 days under refrigeration and 14 days at room temperature because of the evaporation. (1507)

Morphine HCl (Merck) 20 mg/ml was filled into 50-ml ambulatory infusion pump cassette reservoirs (Pharmacia Deltec) and stored at room temperature and protected from light for 90 days. HPLC analysis found no loss of the drug. Instead, the drug concentration increased 13% during the observation period, possibly due to loss of water from the solutions. (1850)

The stability of morphine HCl 20 mg/ml (undiluted) and 1 mg/ml diluted with dextrose 5% in water or sodium chloride 0.9% packaged in ambulatory infusion pump cassettes (B. Braun and Deltec) was evaluated. HPLC analysis found no evidence of drug loss, with degradation products being less than 2% of the concentration when stored at 37 °C for 14 days. However, morphine concentration increases of up to 12% over the study period were observed in some samples presumably because of loss of water. (2169)

Hor et al. reported the stability of morphine sulfate 1 and 10 mg/ml in sodium chloride 0.9% filled in 100-ml Deltec medication cassette reservoirs. The reservoirs were stored at 32 °C at 37% relative humidity and protected from light for 16 days to simulate use conditions. HPLC analysis found no morphine loss and no formation of decomposition products. However, a 4% increase in morphine sulfate concentration occurred during the study period that is consistent with a small amount of evaporation occurring. (2254)

Morphine HCl (Centrafarm) 0.5, 1.5, and 2.5 mg/ml in sodium chloride 0.9% was packaged in PVC/Kalex phthalate ester medication cassette reservoirs (Pharmacia Deltec) and stored at 32 °C to simulate in use conditions close to the body. No visually apparent change occurred, and HPLC analysis found no morphine decomposition after 60 days of storage. However, evaporation of about 0.8 ml/week was found, resulting in a concentration effect on the morphine HCl of about 1% per week. After 60 days, morphine HCl concentrations were generally near 107 to 109% of the initial concentration. (1312)

Elastomeric Reservoir Pumps—Duafala et al. studied the stability of morphine sulfate 15 and 2 mg/ml diluted with sterile water for injection at 4 and 24 °C in Intermate 200 (Infusion Systems) and Infusor (Baxter) disposable elastomeric infusion devices. In the Intermate 200 with 100 ml of morphine sulfate solution, little or no loss occurred in 15 days at either 4 or 24 °C and even at 31 °C (simulating use next to a patient's skin or clothing). In the Infusor, with 50 ml, losses of 5% or more were observed in 12 days in some containers. (1504)

Morphine sulfate 0.5 mg/ml in both dextrose 5% in water and sodium chloride 0.9% was evaluated for binding potential to natural rubber elastomeric reservoirs (Baxter). No binding was found after storage for two weeks at 35 °C with gentle agitation. (2014)

Morphine HCl 2.5 and 5 mg/ml in 0.9% sodium chloride with and without the antioxidant sodium metabisulfite was filled into 60-ml Infusors (Baxter) and stored at room temperature exposed to or protected from light. HPLC analysis found 6% or less variation in the morphine concentration over a month. The formation of the decomposition product pseudomorphine was greatest without the metabisulfite in the samples exposed to light. Up to 1.5% formed in 30 days. No decomposition products formed if the metabisulfite was present. (2176)

Morphine sulfate solutions in elastomeric reservoir pumps have been stated by the pump manufacturers to be stable for the following time periods frozen, refrigerated (REF), or at room temperature (RT) (31):

Pump Reservoir(s)	Conc.	Frozen	REF	RT
Homepump; Homepump Eclipse	20 mg/ml[b]			7 days
Infusor	1 to 20 mg/ml[a]		57 days[c]	7 days
	1 to 20 mg/ml[b]		87 days[c]	7 days
	5 to 20 mg/ml[b]	177 days[c]		7 days

[a]*In dextrose 5% in water.*
[b]*In sodium chloride 0.9%.*
[c]*Stable for an additional three days at room temperature after low temperature storage.*

Implantable Pumps—Morphine sulfate 10 mg/ml was filled into a VIP 30 implantable infusion pump (Fresenius) and associated capillary tubing and stored at 37 °C. Samples were analyzed using an HPLC assay. No morphine loss and no contamination from components of pump materials occurred during eight weeks of storage. (1903)

Undiluted morphine sulfate (unspecified concentration) was stated to be stable for 90 days at room temperature or at body temperature in the Synchromed pump (Medtronic). (31)

Baclofen (Ciba) 0.2 mg/ml with morphine sulfate (David Bull) 1 mg/ml in an implantable pump (Infusaid) was physically compatible and exhibited little or no loss of either drug within 30 days at 37 °C. (1911)

In a follow-up study at higher concentrations, baclofen (Ciba) 1 mg/ml with morphine sulfate (David Bull) 15 mg/ml in an implantable pump (Infusaid) was physically compatible, with only a slight yellowing of the solution observed. HPLC analysis found no change in the baclofen concentration and 5% or less morphine loss after 30 days at 37 °C. (2170)

Other Devices—Caute et al. evaluated the stability of two intrathecal solutions of morphine sulfate 10 mg/ml in sodium chloride 0.9% (isobaric) and 5 mg/ml in dextrose 7% in water (hyperbaric). The solutions were stored at 4 and 37 °C in glass ampuls and pump reservoirs composed of silicone rubber reinforced with polyester (Cordis Europa). No precipitation or discoloration and no loss of morphine sulfate or increase in degradation products occurred in the solutions in glass ampuls after two months at either temperature. However, in the pump reservoirs, the isobaric solution in sodium chloride 0.9% developed a yellow color. Furthermore, a decomposition product, pseudomorphine, was detectable in three days and increased to 1% in one month at 37 °C. This level was 20 times that of the pseudomorphine found in the hyperbaric dextrose 7% in water solution under the same conditions. The decomposition was attributed to dissolved oxygen, ethylene oxide sterilant, and silicone rubber. (1508)

Sorption—Morphine HCl (British Drug Houses) 75 mg/L in sodium chloride 0.9% (Travenol) in PVC bags did not exhibit significant sorption to the plastic during one week of storage at room temperature (15 to 20 °C). (536)

In another study, morphine HCl (British Drug Houses) 75 mg/L in sodium chloride 0.9% did not exhibit any loss due to sorption during a seven-hour simulated infusion through an infusion set (Travenol) consisting of a cellulose propionate burette chamber and 170 cm of PVC tubing. (606)

The drug was also tested as a simulated infusion over at least one hour by a syringe pump system. A glass syringe on a syringe pump was fitted with 20 cm of polyethylene tubing or 50 cm of Silastic tubing. No loss of drug due to sorption was observed with either tubing. (606)

A 25-ml aliquot of morphine HCl (British Drug Houses) 75 mg/L in sodium chloride 0.9% was stored in all-plastic syringes composed of polypropylene barrels and polyethylene plungers for 24 hours at room temperature in the dark. No loss due to sorption occurred. (606)

Filtration—Adsorption to cellulose acetate membrane filters was less than 3% for morphine sulfate 10 to 50 mg/ml in water, dextrose 5% in water, and sodium chloride 0.9%. (2162)

Central Venous Catheter—Morphine sulfate (Astra) 1 mg/ml in dextrose 5% in water was found to be compatible with the ARROWg+ard Blue Plus (Arrow International) chlorhexidine-bearing triple-lumen central catheter. HPLC analysis was used to evaluate completeness of drug delivery through the catheter and the amount of chlorhexidine removed from the internal lumens. Essentially complete delivery of the drug was found with little or no drug loss occurring. Furthermore, chlorhexidine delivered from the catheter remained at trace amounts with no substantial increase due to the delivery of the drug through the catheter. (2335)

Compatibility Information

Solution Compatibility

Morphine sulfate

Solution	*Mfr*	*Mfr*	*Conc/L*	*Remarks*	*Ref*	*C/I*
Dextran 6% in dextrose 5%	AB		16.2 mg	Physically compatible	3	C
Dextran 6% in sodium chloride 0.9%	AB		16.2 mg	Physically compatible	3	C
Dextrose–Ringer's injection combinations	AB		16.2 mg	Physically compatible	3	C
Dextrose–Ringer's injection, lactated, combinations	AB		16.2 mg	Physically compatible	3	C
Dextrose–saline combinations	AB		16.2 mg	Physically compatible	3	C
Dextrose 2½% in water	AB		16.2 mg	Physically compatible	3	C
Dextrose 5% in water	AB		16.2 mg	Physically compatible	3	C
	TR[a]	LI	1.2 g	Physically compatible and no morphine loss in 36 hr at 22 °C	1000	C
	TR[b]	AB, AH	40 and 400 mg	Physically compatible with little or no loss in 7 days at 23 and 4 °C	1349	C
	[a]	AH	5 g	No morphine loss in 30 days at 23 °C	1394	C
	[g]	SX	10 g	Visually compatible with morphine losses of 5 to 8% by HPLC in 31 days at 4 and 23 °C	1505	C
	[e,j]	[c]	1 g	Little or no decomposition by HPLC in 14 days at 37 °C, but concentration increased by up to 12% due to evaporation	2169	C
Dextrose 10% in water	AB		16.2 mg	Physically compatible	3	C
Fructose 10% in sodium chloride 0.9%	AB		16.2 mg	Physically compatible	3	C
Fructose 10% in water	AB		16.2 mg	Physically compatible	3	C
Invert sugar 5 and 10% in sodium chloride 0.9%	AB		16.2 mg	Physically compatible	3	C

Solution Compatibility (Cont.)

Morphine sulfate

Solution	*Mfr*	*Mfr*	*Conc/L*	*Remarks*	*Ref*	*C/I*
Invert sugar 5 and 10% in water	AB		16.2 mg	Physically compatible	3	**C**
Ionosol products	AB		16.2 mg	Physically compatible	3	**C**
Ringer's injection	AB		16.2 mg	Physically compatible	3	**C**
Ringer's injection, lactated	AB		16.2 mg	Physically compatible	3	**C**
Sodium chloride 0.45%	AB		16.2 mg	Physically compatible	3	**C**
Sodium chloride 0.9%	AB		16.2 mg	Physically compatible	3	**C**
	TR[b]	AB, AH	40 and 400 mg	Physically compatible with little or no loss in 7 days at 23 and 4 °C	1349	**C**
	[a]	AH	5 g	No morphine loss in 30 days at 23 °C	1394	**C**
	GRI[a]		140 and 190 mg[c]	No change in concentration by UV in 28 days at 4 °C and room temperature	1910	**C**
	AB[a]	SCN	100 and 500 mg	Visually compatible with no loss by HPLC in 72 hr at 24 °C under fluorescent light	2058	**C**
	[e]	PHS	1 and 10 g	Visually compatible with no loss by HPLC within 16 days at 32 °C protected from light. A 4% increase in concentration was consistent with a small amount of evaporation	2254	**C**
	[f]	CNF	0.5, 1.5, 2.5 g	Visually compatible with no loss by HPLC within 60 days at 32° C. About 8% increase in concentration was found due to evaporation	1312	**C**
	[g]	SX	10 g	Visually compatible with morphine losses of 5 to 8% by HPLC at 4 and 23 °C	1505	**C**
	[h]		0.5, 1, 30 g[i]	No morphine loss by HPLC in 14 days at 5 °C and a small increase in concentration at 37 °C due to evaporation. Light brown discoloration observed after 5 days at 37 °C	1506	**C**
	[h]		60 g[i]	At 37 °C, a small increase in morphine concentration in 14 days due to evaporation. Light brown discoloration observed after 5 days	1506	**C**
	[h]		60 g[i]	At 5 °C, morphine precipitates in as little as 4 days with morphine losses by HPLC of over 40%	1506	**I**
	[e]	ES	1 and 5 g	Visually compatible for 30 days at 5 and 25 °C. HPLC found increased morphine concentration due to evaporation. Maximum storage of 30 days at 5 °C and 14 days at 25 °C	1507	**C**
	[e,j]	[c]	1 g	Little or no decomposition by HPLC in 14 days at 37 °C, but concentration increased by up to 12% due to evaporation	2169	**C**
Sodium lactate ⅙ M	AB		16.2 mg	Physically compatible	3	**C**
TPN #71[d]	[a]	LI	100 mg	Physically compatible and no morphine loss in 36 hr at 22 °C	1000	**C**

[a]*Tested in PVC containers.*
[b]*Tested in both glass and PVC containers.*
[c]*Tested as the HCl salt.*
[d]*Refer to Appendix I for the composition of parenteral nutrition solutions. TPN indicates a 2-in-1 admixture.*
[e]*Tested in Pharmacia or SIMS Deltec medication cassette reservoirs.*
[f]*Tested in Pharmacia Deltec PVC/Kalex phthalate ester medication cassette reservoirs.*
[g]*Tested in Pharmacia cassette reservoirs.*
[h]*Tested in Cormed III Kalex reservoirs.*
[i]*Prepared from morphine sulfate powder.*
[j]*Tested in B. Braun pump cassettes.*

Additive Compatibility

Morphine sulfate

Drug	Mfr	Conc/L	Mfr	Conc/L	Test Soln	Remarks	Ref	C/I
Alteplase	GEN	0.5 g	WY	1 g	NS	Visually compatible with 5 to 8% alteplase clot-lysis activity loss in 24 hr at 25 °C	1856	C
Aminophylline						Physically incompatible	9	I
Amobarbital sodium						Physically incompatible	9	I
Atracurium besylate	BW	500 mg		1 g	D5W	Physically compatible and atracurium chemically stable for 24 hr at 5 and 30 °C	1694	C
Baclofen	CI	200 mg	DB	1 and 1.5 g	NS[d]	Physically compatible with little or no loss of either drug by HPLC in 30 days at 37 °C	1911	C
	CI	800 mg	DB	1 g	NS[d]	Physically compatible with little or no baclofen loss and less than 7% morphine loss by HPLC in 29 days at 37 °C	1911	C
	CI	800 mg	DB	1.5 g	NS[d]	Physically compatible with little or no loss of either drug by HPLC in 30 days at 37 °C	1911	C
	CI	1.5 g	DB	7.5 g	NS[d]	Physically compatible with little or no loss of either drug by HPLC in 30 days at 37 °C	2170	C
	CI	1 g	DB	15 g	NS[d]	Physically compatible with little or no loss of either drug by HPLC in 30 days at 37 °C	2170	C
	CI	200 mg	DB	21 g	NS[d]	Physically compatible with about 7% baclofen loss and little or no morphine loss by HPLC in 30 days at 37 °C	2170	C
Bupivacaine HCl		850 mg		140 and 190 mg[a]	NS[b]	No change in concentration by UV in 28 days at 4 °C and room temperature	1910	C
	AST	3 g		1 g	[a]	Little or no loss of either drug by HPLC in 30 days at 18 °C	1932	C
	AB	625 mg and 1.25 g	SCN	100 mg	NS[b]	Visually compatible with no loss of either drug by HPLC in 72 hr at 24 °C under fluorescent light	2058	C
	AB	625 mg and 1.25 g	SCN	500 mg	NS[b]	Visually compatible with no loss of either drug by HPLC in 72 hr at 24 °C under fluorescent light	2058	C
Chlorothiazide sodium	MSD					Physically incompatible	9	I
Dobutamine HCl	LI	1 g	ES	5 g	D5W, NS	Physically compatible for 24 hr at 21 °C	812	C
Floxacillin sodium	BE	20 g	EV	1 g	W	Haze forms in 24 hr and precipitate forms in 48 hr at 30 °C. No change at 15 °C	1479	I
Fluconazole	PF	1 g	ES	0.25 g	D5W[b]	Fluconazole chemically stable by gas chromatography for at least 24 hr at 25 °C under fluorescent light. Morphine not tested	1676	C
Fluorouracil	AB	1 and 16 g	AST	1 g	D5W, NS[b]	Subvisual morphine precipitate forms immediately, becoming grossly visible within 24 hr. Morphine losses by HPLC of 60 to 80% occur within 1 day	1977	I
Furosemide	HO	1 g	EV	1 g	W	Physically compatible for 72 hr at 15 and 30 °C	1479	C
Heparin sodium						Physically incompatible	9	I

Additive Compatibility (Cont.)

Morphine sulfate

Drug	*Mfr*	*Conc/L*	*Mfr*	*Conc/L*	*Test Soln*	*Remarks*	*Ref*	*C/I*
Ketamine HCl	PD	1 g	SX	1 g	NS[b]	Variable HPLC assays, but at least 90% of both drugs retained for 6 days at room temperature	2260	C
	PD	25 g	SX	25 g	NS[b]	Variable HPLC assays, but at least 90% of both drugs retained for 6 days at room temperature	2260	C
	PD	25 g	SX	25 g	NS[e]	Variable HPLC assays, but at least 90% of both drugs retained for 6 days at room temperature	2260	C
Meperidine HCl	WI					Physically incompatible	9	I
Meropenem	ZEN	1 and 20 g	ES	1 g	NS	Visually compatible for 4 hr at room temperature	1994	C
Metoclopramide HCl	SKB	500 mg	EV	1 g	NS[b]	Visually compatible with little or no loss of either drug by HPLC in 35 days at 22 °C and 182 days at 4 °C followed by 7 days at 32 °C	1939	C
	SKB	500 mg	EV	1 g	NS[c]	Visually compatible with 8% metoclopramide loss by HPLC in 14 days at 22 °C and 98 days at 4 °C. No morphine loss occurs	1939	C
Ondansetron HCl	GL	100 mg and 1 g	AST	1 g	NS[b]	Physically compatible with no ondansetron loss and 5% or less morphine loss by HPLC in 7 days at 32 °C or 31 days at 4 and 22 °C protected from light	1690	C
Phenobarbital sodium	WI					Physically incompatible	9	I
Phenytoin sodium	PD					Physically incompatible	9	I
Sodium bicarbonate						Physically incompatible	9	I
Succinylcholine chloride	AB	2 g		16.2 mg		Physically compatible	3	C
Thiopental sodium	AB					Physically incompatible	9	I
Verapamil HCl	KN	80 mg	KN	30 mg	D5W, NS	Physically compatible for 24 hr	764	C

[a]*Tested as the HCl salt.*
[b]*Tested in PVC containers.*
[c]*Tested in PCA Infusors (Baxter).*
[d]*Tested in glass containers.*
[e]*Tested in Deltec plastic medication cassette reservoirs.*

Drugs in Syringe Compatibility

Morphine sulfate

Drug (in syringe)	*Mfr*	*Amt*	*Mfr*	*Amt*	*Remarks*	*Ref*	*C/I*
Atropine sulfate		0.6 mg/ 1.5 ml	WY	15 mg/ 1 ml	Physically compatible for at least 15 min	14	C
	ST	0.4 mg/ 1 ml	ST	15 mg/ 1 ml	Physically compatible for at least 15 min	326	C
	FED	1 mg/ 1 ml	STP, FED[h]	5, 10, 20, 30 mg/ 1 ml	Visually compatible for up to 7 days at 23 °C. (Morphine HCl tested)	2257	C
Bupivacaine HCl	AST	3 mg/ml		1 mg/ml	Little or no loss of either drug by HPLC in 30 days at 18 °C	1932	C

Drugs in Syringe Compatibility (Cont.)

Drug (in syringe)	*Mfr*	*Amt*	Morphine sulfate *Mfr*	Morphine sulfate *Amt*	*Remarks*	*Ref*	*C/I*
Bupivacaine HCl with	SW	1.5 mg/ ml	ES	0.2 mg/ ml	Diluted to 5 ml with NS. Visually compatible with no new GC/MS peaks appearing in 1 hr at room temperature	1956	C
clonidine HCl	BI	0.03 mg/ ml					
Butorphanol tartrate	BR	4 mg/ 2 ml	AH	15 mg/ 1 ml	Physically compatible both macroscopically and microscopically for 30 min at room temperature	566	C
Chlorpromazine HCl	SKF	50 mg/ 2 ml	WY	15 mg/ 1 ml	Physically compatible for at least 15 min	14	C
	PO	50 mg/ 2 ml	STS	15 mg/ 1 ml	Physically compatible for at least 15 min	326	C
	DB	10 mg/ 2 ml	DB	[a,b]	Discoloration develops, although no morphine loss by HPLC in 48 hr at room temperature exposed to light. Chlorpromazine not tested	1599	?
Cimetidine HCl	SKF	300 mg/ 2 ml	WI	10 mg/ 1 ml	Physically compatible for 4 hr at 25 °C	25	C
Dimenhydrinate	HR	50 mg/ 1 ml	ST	15 mg/ 1 ml	Physically compatible for at least 15 min	326	C
Diphenhydramine HCl	PD	50 mg/ 1 ml	WY	15 mg/ 1 ml	Physically compatible for at least 15 min	14	C
	PD	50 mg/ 1 ml	ST	15 mg/ 1 ml	Physically compatible for at least 15 min	326	C
Droperidol	MN	2.5 mg/ 1 ml	ST	15 mg/ 1 ml	Physically compatible for at least 15 min	326	C
Fentanyl citrate	MN	0.05 mg/ 1 ml	ST	15 mg/ 1 ml	Physically compatible for at least 15 min	326	C
Glycopyrrolate	RB	0.2 mg/ 1 ml	LI	15 mg/ 1 ml	Physically compatible and pH in stability range for glycopyrrolate for 48 hr at 25 °C	326	C
	RB	0.2 mg/ 1 ml	LI	30 mg/ 2 ml	Physically compatible and pH in stability range for glycopyrrolate for 48 hr at 25 °C	326	C
	RB	0.4 mg/ 2 ml	LI	15 mg/ 1 ml	Physically compatible and pH in stability range for glycopyrrolate for 48 hr at 25 °C	326	C
Haloperidol lactate	MN	5 mg/ 1 ml		5 and 10 mg/ 1 ml[c,d]	Cloudiness forms immediately, becoming a crystalline precipitate of haloperidol and parabens	1901	I
	JC	5 mg/ 1 ml	STP, FED[h]	5, 10, 20, 30 mg/ 1 ml	Visually compatible for up to 7 days at 23 °C. (Morphine HCl tested)	2257	C
Heparin sodium	WY	100 and 200 units		1, 2, 5, 10 mg	Brought to 5 ml with sodium chloride 0.9%. Physically compatible with no morphine loss in 24 hr at 23 °C	985	C
	WY	100 and 200 units		1, 2, 5 mg	Brought to 5 ml with sterile water for injection. Physically compatible with no morphine loss in 24 hr at 23 °C	985	C
	WY	100 and 200 units		10 mg	Brought to 5 ml with sterile water for injection. Immediate haze with white precipitate and 5 to 7% loss of morphine potency	985	I
Hydroxyzine HCl	PF	100 mg/ 4 ml	WY	15 mg/ 1 ml	Physically compatible for at least 15 min	14	C
	PF	50 mg/ 1 ml	ST	15 mg/ 1 ml	Physically compatible for at least 15 min	326	C

Drugs in Syringe Compatibility (Cont.)

Morphine sulfate

Drug (in syringe)	*Mfr*	*Amt*	*Mfr*	*Amt*	*Remarks*	*Ref*	*C/I*
	PF	50 mg/ 1 ml		10 mg/ 0.7 ml	Physically compatible	771	C
	PF	100 mg/ 2 ml		5 mg/ 0.3 ml	Physically compatible	771	C
Hyoscine butylbromide	BI	20 mg/ 1 ml	STP, FED[h]	5 and 10 mg/ 1 ml	Visually compatible for up to 24 hr at 23 °C. (Morphine HCl tested)	2257	C
	BI	20 mg/ 1 ml	STP, FED[h]	20 and 30 mg/ 1 ml	Visually compatible for up to 7 days at 23 °C. (Morphine HCl tested)	2257	C
Ketamine HCl		100 mg		240 mg[a]	Brought to 9 ml with NS. Visually compatible for 10 days refrigerated and at room temperature protected from light	1899	C
	PD	1 mg/ml[e]	SX	1 mg/ml[e], 10 mg/ ml[e]	Variable HPLC assays, but at least 90% of both drugs retained for 6 days at room temperature	2260	C
	PD	1 mg/ml[e]	SX	25 mg/ ml[e]	Variable HPLC assays. 5% morphine loss in 6 days at room temperature. Up to 12 to 15% ketamine loss in 2 to 6 days may have occurred	2260	C
	PD	10 mg/ ml[e]	SX	1, 10, 25 mg/ ml[e]	Variable HPLC assays, but at least 90% of both drugs retained for 6 days at room temperature	2260	C
	PD	25 mg/ ml[e]	SX	1, 10, 25 mg/ ml[e]	Variable HPLC assays, but at least 90% of both drugs retained for 6 days at room temperature	2260	C
Ketamine HCl with lidocaine HCl	PD AST	2 mg/ml 2 mg/ml	ES	0.2 mg/ ml	Diluted to 5 ml with NS. Visually compatible with no new GC/MS peaks appearing in 1 hr at room temperature	1956	C
Meperidine HCl	WI	50 mg/ 1 ml	ST	15 mg/ 1 ml	Physically incompatible within 15 min	326	I
Metoclopramide HCl	NO	10 mg/ 2 ml	AH	10 mg/ 1 ml	Physically compatible both macroscopically and microscopically for 15 min at room temperature	565	C
	DB	10 mg/ 2 ml	DB	[a,b]	Visually compatible with about 5% morphine loss by HPLC in 48 hr at room temperature exposed to light. Metoclopramide not tested	1599	C
	SKB	0.5 mg/ ml	EV	1 mg/ml	Diluted with NS. 5% or less loss of both drugs by HPLC in 35 days at 22 °C and 182 days at 4 °C followed by 7 days at 32 °C	1939	C
	SYO	10 mg/ 2 ml	STP, FED[h]	5, 10, 20, 30 mg/ 1 ml	Visually compatible for up to 7 days at 23 °C. (Morphine HCl tested)	2257	C
Midazolam HCl	RC	5 mg/ 1 ml	WB	10 mg/ 1 ml	Physically compatible for 4 hr at 25 °C under fluorescent light	1145	C
	RC	3 mg/ml[e]	DB	24 mg/ ml[a]	Visually compatible with 4.4% midazolam loss by HPLC in 13 days at 32 °C. Morphine not tested	1595	C
	RC	5 mg/ 1 ml		5 and 10 mg/ 1 ml[c]	Visually compatible with 9% or less morphine loss and 8% or less midazolam loss by HPLC in 14 days at 22 °C protected from light. Subvisual microprecipitate may form, requiring filtration	1901	C

Drugs in Syringe Compatibility (Cont.)

Drug (in syringe)	Mfr	Amt	Mfr	Amt	Remarks	Ref	C/I
				Morphine sulfate			
	RC	5 mg/ 1 ml		5 and 10 mg/ 1 ml[d]	Visually compatible with 8% or less morphine loss and 3% or less midazolam loss by HPLC in 14 days at 22 °C protected from light. Subvisual microprecipitate may form, requiring filtration	1901	C
Milrinone lactate	WI	5.25 mg/ 5.25 ml	WI	40 mg/ 5 ml	Physically compatible with no loss of either drug in 20 min at 23 °C under fluorescent light	1410	C
Ondansetron HCl	GW	1.33 mg/ ml[e]	ES	2.67 mg/ ml[e]	Physically compatible with no measured increase in particulates and less than 5% loss of ondansetron and less than 4% loss of morphine by HPLC in 24 hr at 4 or 23 °C	2199	C
Papaveretum	RC[i]	20 mg/ 1 ml	ST	15 mg/ 1ml	Visually compatible for at least 15 min	326	C
Pentazocine lactate	WI	30 mg/ 1 ml	ST	15 mg/ 1 ml	Physically compatible for at least 15 min	326	C
Pentobarbital sodium	AB	500 mg/ 10 ml		16.2 mg/ 1 ml	Physically compatible	55	C
	WY	100 mg/ 2 ml	WY	15 mg/ 1 ml	Precipitate forms within 15 min	14	I
	AB	50 mg/ 1 ml	ST	15 mg/ 1 ml	Physically incompatible within 15 min	326	I
Perphenazine	SC	5 mg/ 1 ml	AH	15 mg/ 1 ml	Physically compatible both macroscopically and microscopically for 30 min at room temperature	566	C
Prochlorperazine edisylate	SKF		WY	15 mg/ 1 ml	Physically compatible for at least 15 min	14	C
	PO	5 mg/ 1 ml	ST	15 mg/ 1 ml	Physically compatible for at least 15 min	326	C
	ES, SKF	10 mg/ 2 ml	WB	10 mg/ 1 ml	Immediate precipitation probably due to phenol in morphine formulation	1006	I
	SKF	5 mg/ 1 ml	WY	8, 10, 15 mg/ 1 ml	Physically compatible for 24 hr at 25 °C	1086	C
	DB	10 mg/ 2 ml	DB	[a,b]	Discoloration develops with 22% morphine loss by HPLC in 48 hr at room temperature exposed to light. Prochlorperazine not tested	1599	I
Promazine HCl	WY	50 mg/ 1 ml	ST	15 mg/ 1 ml	Physically compatible for at least 15 min	326	C
Promethazine HCl	WY	50 mg/ 2 ml	WY	15 mg/ 1 ml	Physically compatible for at least 15 min	14	C
	PO	50 mg/ 2 ml	ST	15 mg/ 1 ml	Physically compatible for at least 15 min	326	C
	WY	12.5 mg	WY	8 mg	Cloudiness develops	98	I
Ranitidine HCl	GL	50 mg/ 2 ml	AH	10 mg/ 1 ml	Physically compatible for 1 hr at 25 °C both macroscopically and microscopically	978	C
	GW	50 mg/ 2 ml	STP, FED[h]	5, 10, 20, 30 mg/ 1 ml	Visually compatible for 24 hr at 23 °C. Yellow discoloration forms in 7 days. (Morphine HCl tested)	2257	C
Salbutamol	GL	2.5 mg/ 2.5 ml[f]	AB	5 mg/ 0.5 ml	Visually compatible for 1 hr both macroscopically and microscopically	1904	C

Drugs in Syringe Compatibility (Cont.)

Morphine sulfate

Drug (in syringe)	*Mfr*	*Amt*	*Mfr*	*Amt*	*Remarks*	*Ref*	*C/I*
Scopolamine HBr		0.6 mg/ 1.5 ml	WY	15 mg/ 1 ml	Physically compatible for at least 15 min	14	C
	ST	0.4 mg/ 1 ml	ST	15 mg/ 1 ml	Physically compatible for at least 15 min	326	C
	BP	5 mg/ 5 ml	BP[g]	500 mg/ 5 ml	Little or no scopolamine loss by HPLC in 14 days at room temperature and 37 °C. Morphine not tested	1609	C
Thiopental sodium	AB	75 mg/ 3 ml	LI	16.2 mg/ 1 ml	Physically incompatible	21	I

[a]Present as the tartrate salt.
[b]Amount unspecified.
[c]Morphine sulfate powder dissolved in dextrose 5% in water.
[d]Morphine sulfate powder dissolved in water and sodium chloride 0.9%.
[e]Diluted in sodium chloride 0.9%.
[f]Both preserved (benzyl alcohol 0.9%; benzalkonium chloride 0.01%) and unpreserved sodium chloride 0.9% were used as a diluent.
[g]Tested as both sulfate and hydrochloride salts.
[h]Tested as the hydrochloride salt.
[i]The former formulation was tested.

Y-Site Injection Compatibility (1:1 Mixture)

Morphine sulfate

Drug	*Mfr*	*Conc*	*Mfr*	*Conc*	*Remarks*	*Ref*	*C/I*
Acyclovir sodium	BW	5 mg/ml[a]	WB	0.08 mg/ml[a]	Physically compatible for 4 hr at 25 °C	1157	C
	BW	5 mg/ml[a]	AB	1 mg/ml	White crystalline precipitate forms within 2 hr at 25 °C under fluorescent light	1397	I
Alatrofloxacin mesylate	PF	1.43 mg/ml[a]	WY	1 mg/ml	Microscopic particles form	2235	I
Allopurinol sodium	BW	3 mg/ml[b]	WI	1 mg/ml[b]	Physically compatible with no change in measured turbidity or increase in particle content in 4 hr at 22 °C	1686	C
Amifostine	USB	10 mg/ml[a]	AST	1 mg/ml[a]	Physically compatible with no change in measured turbidity or increase in particle content in 4 hr at 23 °C	1845	C
Amikacin sulfate	BR	5 mg/ml[a]	WI	1 mg/ml[a]	Physically compatible for at least 4 hr at 25 °C under fluorescent light	987	C
Aminophylline	ES	4 mg/ml[c]	WY	0.2 mg/ml[c]	Physically compatible for 3 hr	1316	C
Amiodarone HCl	WY	4.8 mg/ml[a]	SX	1 mg/ml[a]	Visually compatible for 24 hr at 23 °C	1877	C
Amphotericin B cholesteryl sulfate complex	SEQ	0.83 mg/ml[a]	ES	1 mg/ml[a]	Increased turbidity forms immediately	2117	I
Ampicillin sodium	BR	20 mg/ml[b]	WI	1 mg/ml[a]	Physically compatible for at least 4 hr at 25 °C under fluorescent light	987	C
Ampicillin sodium–sulbactam sodium	RR	20 + 10 mg/ ml[b]	ES	1 mg/ml[b]	Physically compatible for 1 hr at 25 °C	1338	C
Amsacrine	NCI	1 mg/ml[a]	ES	1 mg/ml[a]	Physically compatible for 4 hr at room temperature under fluorescent light	1381	C
Atenolol	ICI	0.5 mg/ml	AB	1 mg/ml	Physically compatible for 4 hr at 25 °C	1397	C
Atracurium besylate	BW	0.5 mg/ml[a]	WY	1 mg/ml[a]	Physically compatible for 24 hr at 28 °C	1337	C
Atropine sulfate	LY	0.4 mg/ml	AST	1 mg/ml[a]	Physically compatible with no change in measured haze or increase in particle content in 48 hr at 22 °C	1706	C

Y-Site Injection Compatibility (1:1 Mixture) (Cont.)

			Morphine sulfate				
Drug	*Mfr*	*Conc*	*Mfr*	*Conc*	*Remarks*	*Ref*	*C/I*
Aztreonam	SQ	20 mg/ml[a]	AB	1 mg/ml	Physically compatible for 4 hr at 25 °C	1397	C
	SQ	40 mg/ml[a]	AST	1 mg/ml[a]	Physically compatible with no subvisual haze or particle formation in 4 hr at 23 °C	1758	C
Bumetanide	RC	0.25 mg/ml	AB	1 mg/ml	Physically compatible for 4 hr at 25 °C	1397	C
Calcium chloride	AB	4 mg/ml[c]	WY	0.2 mg/ml[c]	Physically compatible for 3 hr	1316	C
Cefamandole nafate	LI	20 mg/ml[a]	WI	1 mg/ml[a]	Physically compatible for at least 4 hr at 25 °C under fluorescent light	987	C
	LI	40 mg/ml[a]	ES	1 mg/ml[b]	Physically compatible for 1 hr at 25 °C	1338	C
Cefazolin sodium	SKF	20 mg/ml[a]	WI	1 mg/ml[a]	Physically compatible for at least 4 hr at 25 °C under fluorescent light	987	C
Cefepime HCl	BMS	20 mg/ml[a]	AST	1 mg/ml[a]	Haze forms immediately with numerous particles in 1 hr	1689	I
Cefoperazone sodium	RR	20 mg/ml[a]	WI	1 mg/ml[a]	Physically compatible for at least 4 hr at 25 °C under fluorescent light	987	C
Cefotaxime sodium	HO	20 mg/ml[a]	WI	1 mg/ml[a]	Physically compatible for at least 4 hr at 25 °C under fluorescent light	987	C
Cefotetan disodium	STU	20 and 40 mg/ml[a]	ES	1 mg/ml[b]	Physically compatible for 1 hr at 25 °C	1338	C
Cefoxitin sodium	MSD	20 mg/ml[a]	WI	1 mg/ml[a]	Physically compatible for at least 4 hr at 25 °C under fluorescent light	987	C
	MSD	40 mg/ml[a]	ES	1 mg/ml[b]	Physically compatible for 1 hr at 25 °C	1338	C
Ceftazidime	LI[l]	20 and 40 mg/ml[a]	AB	1 mg/ml	Physically compatible for 4 hr at 25 °C	1397	C
Ceftizoxime sodium	SKF	20 mg/ml[a]	WI	1 mg/ml[a]	Physically compatible for at least 4 hr at 25 °C under fluorescent light	987	C
Ceftriaxone sodium	RC	20 and 40 mg/ml[a]	AB	1 mg/ml	Physically compatible for 4 hr at 25 °C	1397	C
Cefuroxime sodium	GL	30 mg/ml[a]	WI	1 mg/ml[a]	Physically compatible for at least 4 hr at 25 °C under fluorescent light	987	C
Chloramphenicol sodium succinate	LY	20 mg/ml[a]	WI	1 mg/ml[a]	Physically compatible for at least 4 hr at 25 °C under fluorescent light	987	C
Cisatracurium besylate	GW	0.1, 2, 5 mg/ml[a]	AST	1 mg/ml[a]	Physically compatible with no change in measured turbidity or increase in particle content in 4 hr at 23 °C	2074	C
Cisplatin	BR	1 mg/ml	ES	0.12 mg/ml[a]	Visually compatible for 4 hr at room temperature under fluorescent light	1685	C
Cladribine	ORT	0.015[b] and 0.5[e] mg/ml	AST	1 mg/ml[b]	Physically compatible with no change in measured turbidity or increase in particle content in 4 hr at 23 °C	1969	C
Clindamycin phosphate	UP	12 mg/ml[a]	WI	1 mg/ml[a]	Physically compatible for at least 4 hr at 25 °C under fluorescent light	987	C
Cyclophosphamide	MJ	10 mg/ml	ES	0.12 mg/ml[a]	Visually compatible for 4 hr at room temperature under fluorescent light	1685	C
Cytarabine	UP	50 mg/ml	ES	0.12 mg/ml[a]	Visually compatible for 4 hr at room temperature under fluorescent light	1685	C

Y-Site Injection Compatibility (1:1 Mixture) (Cont.)

Drug	*Mfr*	*Conc*	Morphine sulfate *Mfr*	*Conc*	*Remarks*	*Ref*	*C/I*
Dexamethasone sodium phosphate	LY	0.2 mg/ml[a]	AB	1 mg/ml	Physically compatible for 4 hr at 25 °C	1397	C
	AMR	1 mg/ml[a]	AST	1 mg/ml[a]	Physically compatible with no change in measured haze or increase in particle content in 48 hr at 22 °C	1706	C
Diazepam	ES	0.5 mg/ml[a]	AST	1 mg/ml[a]	Physically compatible with no change in measured haze or increase in particle content in 48 hr at 22 °C	1706	C
Digoxin	BW	0.25 mg/ml	AB	1 mg/ml	Physically compatible for 4 hr at 25 °C	1397	C
Diltiazem HCl	MMD	1[b] and 5 mg/ml	SCN	15 mg/ml	Visually compatible	1807	C
	MMD	5 mg/ml	SCN	0.4 mg/ml[b]	Visually compatible	1807	C
	MMD	1 mg/ml[a]	SCN	2 mg/ml[a]	Visually compatible for 4 hr at 27 °C	2062	C
Diphenhydramine HCl	SCN	2 mg/ml[a]	AST	1 mg/ml[a]	Physically compatible with no change in measured haze or increase in particle content in 48 hr at 22 °C	1706	C
Dobutamine HCl	LI	4 mg/ml[a]	SCN	2 mg/ml[a]	Visually compatible for 4 hr at 27 °C	2062	C
Docetaxel	RPR	0.9 mg/ml[a]	ES	1 mg/ml[a]	Physically compatible with no change in measured turbidity or increase in particle content	2224	C
Dopamine HCl	AB	1.6 mg/ml[a]	AB	1 mg/ml	Physically compatible for 4 hr at 25 °C	1397	C
	AB	3.2 mg/ml[a]	SCN	2 mg/ml[a]	Visually compatible for 4 hr at 27 °C	2062	C
Doxorubicin HCl	AD	0.2 mg/ml[a]	ES	0.12 mg/ml[a]	Visually compatible for 4 hr at room temperature under fluorescent light	1685	C
Doxorubicin HCl liposome injection	SEQ	0.4 mg/ml[a]	ES	1 mg/ml[a]	Partial loss of measured natural turbidity	2087	I
Doxycycline hyclate	ES	1 mg/ml[a]	WI	1 mg/ml[a]	Physically compatible for at least 4 hr at 25 °C under fluorescent light	987	C
Enalaprilat	MSD	0.05 mg/ml[b]	WY	0.2 mg/ml[a]	Physically compatible for 24 hr at room temperature under fluorescent light	1355	C
Epinephrine HCl	AB	0.02 mg/ml[a]	SCN	2 mg/ml[a]	Visually compatible for 4 hr at 27 °C	2062	C
Erythromycin lactobionate	AB	5 mg/ml[a]	WI	1 mg/ml[a]	Physically compatible for at least 4 hr at 25 °C under fluorescent light	987	C
Esmolol HCl	DCC	1 g/100 ml[f]	ES	15 mg/1 ml	Physically compatible when morphine is injected into Y-site of flowing admixture[g]	1168	C
	DCC	10 mg/ml[f]	ES	15 mg/ml	Physically compatible with no loss of either drug in 8 hr at ambient temperature exposed to light	1168	C
Etomidate	AB	2 mg/ml	ES	10 mg/ml	Visually compatible for up to 7 days at 25 °C	1801	C
Etoposide phosphate	BR	5 mg/ml[a]	ES	1 mg/ml[a]	Physically compatible with no change in measured turbidity or increase in particle content in 4 hr at 23 °C	2218	C
Famotidine	MSD	0.2 mg/ml[a]	ES	0.2 mg/ml[a]	Physically compatible for 4 hr at 25 °C	1188	C
	MSD	0.2 mg/ml[a]	AB	1 mg/ml	Physically compatible for 4 hr at 25 °C	1397	C
	ME	2 mg/ml[b]		1 mg/ml[a]	Visually compatible for 4 hr at 22 °C	1936	C
Fentanyl citrate	ES	0.05 mg/ml	SCN	2 mg/ml[a]	Visually compatible for 4 hr at 27 °C	2062	C

Y-Site Injection Compatibility (1:1 Mixture) (Cont.)

			Morphine sulfate				
Drug	*Mfr*	*Conc*	*Mfr*	*Conc*	*Remarks*	*Ref*	*C/I*
Filgrastim	AMG	30 μg/ml[a]	WY	1 mg/ml[a]	Physically compatible with no change in measured turbidity or increase in particle content in 4 hr at 22 °C	1687	C
Fluconazole	RR	2 mg/ml	IMS	25 mg/ml	Physically compatible for 24 hr at 25 °C	1407	C
	RR	2 mg/ml	AB	1 mg/ml	Physically compatible for 4 hr at 25 °C	1397	C
Fludarabine phosphate	BX	1 mg/ml[a]	WI	1 mg/ml[a]	Physically compatible for 4 hr at room temperature under fluorescent light	1439	C
Foscarnet sodium	AST	24 mg/ml	IMS	1 mg/ml	Physically compatible for 24 hr at room temperature under fluorescent light	1335	C
	AST	24 mg/ml	ES	1 mg/ml[c]	Physically compatible for 24 hr at 25 °C under fluorescent light by visual and microscopic examination	1393	C
	AST	24 mg/ml	ES	5[b] and 15 mg/ml	Visually compatible for 24 hr at 23 °C under fluorescent light	1529	C
Furosemide	ES	0.8[a], 2.4[a], 10 mg/ml	AB	1 mg/ml	White precipitate forms within 1 hr at 25 °C under fluorescent light	1397	I
	AMR	10 mg/ml	SCN	2 mg/ml[a]	Visually compatible for 4 hr at 27 °C	2062	C
Gatifloxacin	BMS	2 mg/ml[a]	WY	1 mg/ml[a]	Physically compatible with no change in measured haze or increase in particle content in 4 hr at 23 °C	2234	C
Gemcitabine HCl	LI	10 mg/ml[b]	ES	1 mg/ml[b]	Physically compatible with no change in measured turbidity or increase in particle content in 4 hr at 23 °C	2226	C
Gentamicin sulfate	TR	0.8 mg/ml[a]	WI	1 mg/ml[a]	Physically compatible for at least 4 hr at 25 °C under fluorescent light	987	C
	ES	1.2 and 2 mg/ml[b]	ES	1 mg/ml[b]	Physically compatible for 1 hr at 25 °C	1338	C
Granisetron HCl	SKB	1 mg/ml	AST	1 mg/ml[b]	Physically compatible with little or no loss of either drug by HPLC in 4 hr at 22 °C	1883	C
	SKB	0.05 mg/ml[a]	AST	1 mg/ml[a]	Physically compatible with no change in measured turbidity or increase in particle content in 4 hr at 23 °C	2000	C
Haloperidol lactate	MN	0.2 mg/ml[a]	AST	1 mg/ml[a]	Physically compatible with no change in measured haze or increase in particle content in 48 hr at 22 °C	1706	C
Heparin sodium	UP	1000 units/L[h]	WY	15 mg/ml	Physically compatible for at least 4 hr at room temperature by visual and microscopic examination	534	C
	ES	50 units/ml[c]	WY	0.2 mg/ml[c]	Physically compatible for 3 hr	1316	C
	ES	60 units/ml[a]	ES	1 mg/ml[b]	Physically compatible for 1 hr at 25 °C	1338	C
	ES	100 units/ml[a]	SCN	2 mg/ml[a]	Visually compatible for 4 hr at 27 °C	2062	C
Hetastarch in lactated electrolyte injection (Hextend)	AB	6%	AST	1 mg/ml[a]	Physically compatible with no change in measured turbidity or increase in particle content in 4 hr at 23 °C	2339	C
Hydrocortisone sodium succinate	UP	10 mg/L[f]	WY	15 mg/ml	Physically compatible for at least 4 hr at room temperature by visual and microscopic examination	534	C
Hydromorphone HCl	KN	1 mg/ml	SCN	2 mg/ml[a]	Visually compatible for 4 hr at 27 °C	2062	C

Y-Site Injection Compatibility (1:1 Mixture) (Cont.)

Morphine sulfate

Drug	*Mfr*	*Conc*	*Mfr*	*Conc*	*Remarks*	*Ref*	*C/I*
Hydroxyzine HCl	WI	4 mg/ml[a]	AST	1 mg/ml[a]	Physically compatible with no change in measured haze or increase in particle content in 48 hr at 22 °C	1706	C
IL-2	RC	4800 I.U./ml[b]	SCN	1 mg/ml	Visually compatible and IL-2 activity by bioassay retained. Morphine not tested	1552	C
Insulin, regular	LI	0.2 unit/ml[b]	ES	1 mg/ml[b]	Physically compatible for 1 hr at 25 °C	1338	C
	LI	0.2 unit/ml[b]	ES	5 mg/ml[b]	Physically compatible for 2 hr at 25 °C	1395	C
	LI	1 unit/ml[a]	SX	1 mg/ml[a]	Visually compatible for 24 hr at 23 °C	1877	C
Kanamycin sulfate	BR	2.5 mg/ml[a]	WI	1 mg/ml[a]	Physically compatible for at least 4 hr at 25 °C under fluorescent light	987	C
Ketorolac tromethamine	WY	1 mg/ml[a]	AST	1 mg/ml[a]	Physically compatible with no change in measured haze or increase in particle content in 48 hr at 22 °C	1706	C
Labetalol HCl	SC	1 mg/ml[a]	WY	1 mg/ml[a]	Physically compatible for 24 hr at 18 °C	1171	C
	GL	5 mg/ml	AB	1 mg/ml	Physically compatible for 4 hr at 25 °C	1397	C
	GL	1 mg/ml[a]	ES	0.5 mg/ml[a]	Visually compatible with little or no loss of either drug by HPLC in 4 hr at room temperature	1762	C
	AH	2 mg/ml[a]	SCN	2 mg/ml[a]	Visually compatible for 4 hr at 27 °C	2062	C
Levofloxacin	OMN	5 mg/ml[a]	SW	4 mg/ml	Visually compatible for 4 hr at 24 °C under fluorescent light	2233	C
Lidocaine HCl	AB	1 mg/ml[a]	AB	1 mg/ml	Physically compatible for 4 hr at 25 °C	1397	C
Linezolid	PHU	2 mg/ml	AST	1 mg/ml[a]	Physically compatible with no change in measured turbidity or increase in particle content in 4 hr at 23 °C	2264	C
Lorazepam	WY	0.33 mg/ml[b]	CNF	1 mg/ml[i]	Visually compatible for 24 hr at 22 °C	1855	C
	WY	0.5 mg/ml[a]	SCN	2 mg/ml[a]	Visually compatible for 4 hr at 27 °C	2062	C
	WY	0.1 mg/ml[a]	AST	1 mg/ml[a]	Physically compatible with no change in measured haze or increase in particle content in 48 hr at 22 °C	1706	C
Magnesium sulfate	LY	16.7, 33.3, 50, 100 mg/ml[a]	ES	1 mg/ml[a]	Visually compatible for 4 hr at 25 °C under fluorescent light	1549	C
	AB	2, 4, 8 mg/ml[b]	[j]	2 mg/ml[b]	Visually compatible for 8 hr at room temperature	1719	C
Melphalan HCl	BW	0.1 mg/ml[b]	WI	1 mg/ml[b]	Physically compatible with no change in measured turbidity or increase in particle content in 3 hr at 22 °C	1557	C
Meropenem	ZEN	1 and 50 mg/ml[b]	ES	1 mg/ml[d]	Visually compatible for 4 hr at room temperature	1994	C
Methotrexate sodium	AD	15 mg/ml[k]	ES	0.12 mg/ml[a]	Visually compatible for 4 hr at room temperature under fluorescent light	1685	C
Methotrimeprazine	LE	0.2 mg/ml[a]	AST	1 mg/ml[a]	Physically compatible with no change in measured haze or increase in particle content in 48 hr at 22 °C	1706	C
Methyldopate HCl	AMR	2.5 mg/ml[a]	AB	1 mg/ml	Physically compatible for 4 hr at 25 °C	1397	C
Methylprednisolone sodium succinate	UP	2.5 mg/ml[a]	AB	1 mg/ml	Physically compatible for 4 hr at 25 °C	1397	C

Y-Site Injection Compatibility (1:1 Mixture) (Cont.)

Morphine sulfate

Drug	*Mfr*	*Conc*	*Mfr*	*Conc*	*Remarks*	*Ref*	*C/I*
Metoclopramide HCl	SN	0.2 mg/ml[a]	AB	1 mg/ml	Physically compatible for 4 hr at 25 °C	1397	C
	DU	5 mg/ml	AST	1 mg/ml[a]	Physically compatible with no change in measured haze or increase in particle content in 48 hr at 22 °C	1706	C
Metoprolol tartrate	CI	1 mg/ml	AB	1 mg/ml	Physically compatible for 4 hr at 25 °C	1397	C
Metronidazole	SE	5 mg/ml	WI	1 mg/ml[a]	Physically compatible for at least 4 hr at 25 °C under fluorescent light	987	C
Midazolam HCl	RC	0.2 mg/ml[a]	AST	1 mg/ml[a]	Physically compatible with no change in measured haze or increase in particle content in 48 hr at 22 °C	1706	C
	RC	0.1 and 0.5 mg/ml[a]	ES	0.25 mg/ml[a]	Visually compatible with no loss of either drug by HPLC in 3 hr at 24 °C	1789	C
	RC	0.1 and 0.5 mg/ml[a]	ES	1 mg/ml[a]	Visually compatible with no loss of either drug by HPLC in 3 hr at 24 °C	1789	C
	RC	5 mg/ml	CNF	1 mg/ml[i]	Visually compatible for 24 hr at 22 °C	1855	C
	RC	1 mg/ml[a]	SX	1 mg/ml[a]	Visually compatible for 24 hr at 23 °C	1877	C
	RC	2 mg/ml[a]	SCN	2 mg/ml[a]	Visually compatible for 4 hr at 27 °C	2062	C
Milrinone lactate	SW	0.2 mg/ml[a]	SCN	2 mg/ml[a]	Visually compatible for 4 hr at 27 °C	2062	C
	SW	0.4 mg/ml[a]	AST	1 mg/ml[a]	Visually compatible with little or no loss of either drug by HPLC in 4 hr at 23 °C	2214	C
Minocycline HCl	LE	0.2 mg/ml[a]	WI	1 mg/ml[a]	Color changed from pale yellow to light green in 1 hr	987	I
Nafcillin sodium	WY	20 mg/ml[a]	WI	1 mg/ml[a]	Physically compatible for at least 4 hr at 25 °C under fluorescent light	987	C
	WY	30 mg/ml[a]	ES	1 mg/ml[b]	Physically compatible for 1 hr at 25 °C	1338	C
Nicardipine HCl	WY	1 mg/ml[a]	SCN	2 mg/ml[a]	Visually compatible for 4 hr at 27 °C	2062	C
Nitroglycerin	AB	0.4 mg/ml[a]	SCN	2 mg/ml[a]	Visually compatible for 4 hr at 27 °C	2062	C
Norepinephrine bitartrate	STR	0.064 mg/ml[a]	SX	1 mg/ml[a]	Visually compatible for 24 hr at 23 °C	1877	C
	AB	0.128 mg/ml[a]	SCN	2 mg/ml[a]	Visually compatible for 4 hr at 27 °C	2062	C
Ondansetron HCl	GL	1 mg/ml[b]	WI	1 mg/ml[a]	Physically compatible for 4 hr at 22 °C	1365	C
Oxacillin sodium	BE	20 mg/ml[a]	WI	1 mg/ml[a]	Physically compatible for at least 4 hr at 25 °C under fluorescent light	987	C
Oxytocin	PD	0.02 mg/ml[m]	ES	1 mg/ml[b]	Physically compatible for 1 hr at 25 °C	1338	C
Paclitaxel	NCI	1.2 mg/ml[a]	WY	1 mg/ml[a]	Physically compatible with no change in measured turbidity in 4 hr at 22 °C	1556	C
Pancuronium bromide	ES	0.05 mg/ml[a]	WY	1 mg/ml[a]	Physically compatible for 24 hr at 28 °C	1337	C
Penicillin G potassium	PF	100,000 units/ml[a]	WI	1 mg/ml[a]	Physically compatible for at least 4 hr at 25 °C under fluorescent light	987	C
Phenobarbital sodium	WY	2 mg/ml[a]	AST	1 mg/ml[a]	Physically compatible with no change in measured haze or increase in particle content in 48 hr at 22 °C	1706	C
Phenytoin sodium	ES	2 mg/ml[a,b]	AST	1 mg/ml[a]	Precipitate forms after 1 hr	1706	I
Piperacillin sodium	LE	60 mg/ml[a]	WI	1 mg/ml[a]	Physically compatible for at least 4 hr at 25 °C under fluorescent light	987	C
Piperacillin sodium–tazobactam sodium	LE	40 + 5 mg/ml[a]	WY	1 mg/ml[a]	Physically compatible with no change in measured turbidity or increase in particle content in 4 hr at 22 °C	1688	C

Y-Site Injection Compatibility (1:1 Mixture) (Cont.)

Morphine sulfate

Drug	*Mfr*	*Conc*	*Mfr*	*Conc*	*Remarks*	*Ref*	*C/I*
Potassium chloride	AB	40 mEq/L[f]	WY	15 mg/ml	Physically compatible for at least 4 hr at room temperature by visual and microscopic examination	534	C
Propofol	ASZ	10 mg/ml		15 mg/ml	Precipitate formed and emulsion broke and oiled out	1916	I
	ZEN	10 mg/ml	AST	1 mg/ml[a]	Physically compatible for 1 hr at 23 °C with no increase in particle content	2066	C
Propranolol HCl	WY	1 mg/ml	AB	1 mg/ml	Physically compatible for 4 hr at 25 °C	1397	C
Ranitidine HCl	GL	0.5 mg/ml[n]	ES	1 mg/ml[b]	Physically compatible for 1 hr at 25 °C	1338	C
	GL	1 mg/ml[a]	SCN	2 mg/ml[a]	Visually compatible for 4 hr at 27 °C	2062	C
Remifentanil HCl	GW	0.025 and 0.25 mg/ml[b]	AST	1 mg/ml[a]	Physically compatible with no change in measured turbidity or increase in particle content in 4 hr at 23 °C	2075	C
Sargramostim	IMM	10 μg/ml[b]	WI	1 mg/ml[b]	Slight haze, visible with high intensity light, and small amount of particles formed in 1 hr in one of two samples	1436	I
Scopolamine HBr	LY	0.05 mg/ml[a]	AST	1 mg/ml[a]	Physically compatible with no change in measured haze or increase in particle content in 48 hr at 22 °C	1706	C
Sodium bicarbonate	AB	1 mEq/ml	WY	0.2 mg/ml[c]	Physically compatible for 3 hr	1316	C
Sodium nitroprusside	RC	0.2 mg/ml[a]	SX	1 mg/ml[a]	Visually compatible for 24 hr at 23 °C	1877	C
Tacrolimus	FUJ	10 and 40 μg/ml[b]	SCN	1 mg/ml[b]	Visually compatible with no loss of either drug by HPLC in 4 hr at 24 °C under fluorescent light	2216	C
	FUJ	10 and 40 μg/ml[b]	SCN	3 mg/ml[b]	Visually compatible with no loss of either drug by HPLC in 4 hr at 24 °C under fluorescent light	2216	C
Teniposide	BR	0.1 mg/ml[a]	AST	1 mg/ml[a]	Physically compatible with no subvisual haze or particle formation in 4 hr at 23 °C	1725	C
Thiopental sodium	AB	25 mg/ml	ES	10 mg/ml	White precipitate forms immediately	1801	I
	AB	25 mg/ml[d]	SCN	2 mg/ml[a]	Visually compatible for 4 hr at 27 °C	2062	C
Thiotepa	IMM[o]	1 mg/ml[a]	AST	1 mg/ml[a]	Physically compatible with no change in measured turbidity or increase in particle content in 4 hr at 23 °C	1861	C
Ticarcillin disodium	BE	60 mg/ml[a]	WI	1 mg/ml[a]	Physically compatible for at least 4 hr at 25 °C under fluorescent light	987	C
Ticarcillin disodium–clavulanate potassium	BE	31 mg/ml[b]	ES	1 mg/ml[b]	Physically compatible for 1 hr at 25 °C	1338	C
TNA #218 to #226[p]			ES	1 mg/ml[a]	Visually compatible with no precipitate or emulsion damage apparent in 4 hr at 23 °C	2215	C
			ES	15 mg/ml	Damage to emulsion integrity occurs immediately with free oil formation possible	2215	I
Tobramycin sulfate	DI	0.8 mg/ml[a]	WI	1 mg/ml[a]	Physically compatible for at least 4 hr at 25 °C under fluorescent light	987	C
	LI	1.6, 2, 2.4 mg/ml[a]	ES	1 mg/ml[b]	Physically compatible for 1 hr at 25 °C	1338	C

Y-Site Injection Compatibility (1:1 Mixture) (Cont.)

Drug	Mfr	Conc	Morphine sulfate Mfr	Morphine sulfate Conc	Remarks	Ref	C/I
TPN #131 and #132[p]			AB	1 mg/ml	Physically compatible for 4 hr at 25 °C	1397	C
TPN #189[p]			DB	30 mg/ml	Visually compatible for 24 hr at 22 °C	1767	C
TPN #203 and #204[p]			ES	1 mg/ml	Visually compatible for 2 hr at 23 °C	1974	C
TPN #212 to #215[p]			AST	1 mg/ml[a]	Physically compatible with no change in measured turbidity or increase in particle content in 4 hr at 23 °C	2109	C
Trimethoprim–sulfamethoxazole	BW	0.8 + 4 mg/ml[a]	WI	1 mg/ml[a]	Physically compatible for at least 4 hr at 25 °C under fluorescent light	987	C
Vancomycin HCl	LI	5 mg/ml[a]	WI	1 mg/ml[a]	Physically compatible for at least 4 hr at 25 °C under fluorescent light	987	C
Vecuronium bromide	OR	0.1 mg/ml[a]	WY	1 mg/ml[a]	Physically compatible for 24 hr at 28 °C	1337	C
	OR	1 mg/ml	SCN	2 mg/ml[a]	Visually compatible for 4 hr at 27 °C	2062	C
Vinorelbine tartrate	BW	1 mg/ml[b]	WI	1 mg/ml[b]	Physically compatible with no change in measured turbidity or increase in particle content in 4 hr at 22 °C	1558	C
Vitamin B complex with C	RC	2 ml/L[f]	WY	15 mg/ml	Physically compatible for at least 4 hr at room temperature by visual and microscopic examination	534	C
Warfarin sodium	DU	2 mg/ml[d]	ES	2 mg/ml[a]	Visually compatible with no warfarin loss by HPLC in 30 min	2010	C
	DME	2 mg/ml[d]	ES	2 mg/ml[a]	Visually compatible for 24 hr at 24 °C	2078	C
Zidovudine	BW	4 mg/ml[a]	ES	1 mg/ml[a]	Physically compatible for 4 hr at 25 °C under fluorescent light by visual and microscopic examination	1193	C

[a] *Tested in dextrose 5% in water.*
[b] *Tested in sodium chloride 0.9%.*
[c] *Tested in both dextrose 5% in water and sodium chloride 0.9%.*
[d] *Tested in sterile water for injection.*
[e] *Tested in bacteriostatic sodium chloride 0.9% preserved with benzyl alcohol 0.9%.*
[f] *Tested in dextrose 5% in sodium chloride 0.9%.*
[g] *Flowing at 1.6 ml/min.*
[h] *Tested in dextrose 5% in Ringer's injection, dextrose 5% in Ringer's injection, lactated, dextrose 5% in water, Ringer's injection, lactated, and sodium chloride 0.9%.*
[i] *Tested as the hydrochloride salt.*
[j] *Extemporaneously prepared product.*
[k] *Tested in dextrose 5% in water with sodium bicarbonate 0.05 mEq/ml.*
[l] *Sodium carbonate–containing formulation tested.*
[m] *Tested in dextrose 5% in Ringer's injection, lactated.*
[n] *Tested in sodium chloride 0.45%.*
[o] *Lyophilized formulation tested.*
[p] *Refer to Appendix I for the composition of parenteral nutrition solutions. TNA indicates a 3-in-1 admixture, and TPN indicates a 2-in-1 admixture.*

Additional Compatibility Information

Multiple Drugs — A seven-drug combination consisting of bupivacaine HCl (Sanofi Winthrop) 1.5 mg/1 ml, clonidine HCl (Boehringer Ingelheim) 0.03 mg/1 ml, fentanyl citrate (Janssen) 0.01 mg/1 ml, ketamine (Parke-Davis) 2 mg/1 ml, lidocaine HCl (Astra) 2 mg/1 ml, morphine sulfate (Elkins-Sinn) 0.2 mg/1 ml, and tetracaine HCl (Sanofi Winthrop) 2 mg/1 ml mixed together was found to be visually compatible with no new GC/MS peaks appearing in one hour at room temperature. (1956)

Clonidine HCl (Boehringer) 30 μg/ml, bupivacaine HCl (Astra) 3 mg/ml, and morphine HCl (Merck) 6.66 mg/ml were combined in 50-ml ambulatory infusion pump cassette reservoirs (Pharmacia Deltec). The reservoirs were stored at room temperature and protected from light for 90 days. HPLC analysis found no loss of any of the drugs. Instead, drug concentrations increased 12 to 16% during the observation period, possibly due to loss of water from the solutions. (1850)

Morphine tartrate (David Bull) 4 and 40 mg/ml was admixed with four other drugs and packaged in 10-ml polypropylene syringes with tip caps (Terumo). The formulas of the two admixtures to make 10 ml total volume are shown in Table 1. Samples were stored at 21 to 23 °C and 4 to 8 °C for two weeks. Most samples remained unchanged on visual inspection except Formulation 1 stored at room temperature that developed a slight straw color within 10 days. HPLC analysis found that the morphine tartrate and the other drug components except midazolam remained stable (less than 10% loss) throughout the 14-day study. Midazolam HCl was also stable for 14 days under refrigeration but was only stable through 12 days in Formulation 1 and five days in Formulation 2 stored at room temperature. (2180)

Clonidine HCl — Clonidine HCl (Fujisawa) 100 μg/ml and morphine sulfate (Elkins-Sinn) 10 mg/ml were mixed in equal quantities, transferred to flint glass vials with rubber stoppers, and stored for 14 days at controlled room temperature protected from light. The solutions remained clear and colorless with no increase in particulate content. HPLC analysis found little or no change in concentration for either drug during the study period. (2067)

Table 1. Formulas of Morphine Tartrate with Multiple Drug Admixtures Tested for Stability (2180)

Component	Formulation 1	Formulation 2
Morphine tartrate	400 mg	40 mg
Dexamethasone sodium phosphate	8 mg	8 mg
Droperidol HCl	2 mg	2 mg
Scopolamine butylbromide	20 mg	20 mg
Midazolam HCl	8 mg	5 mg
Sodium chloride 0.9%		qs to 10 ml

MULTIVITAMINS
AHFS 88:28

Products — Multivitamin products for parenteral administration are available in a variety of compositions and sizes from several manufacturers. (154) The following products are representative formulations.

M.V.I.-12 is available as a package of two vials (labeled Vial 1 and Vial 2) that are prepared for use by transferring the contents of Vial 1 into Vial 2 and mixing gently. M.V.I.-12 is also available as a two-chambered, single-dose 10-ml vial that must be mixed prior to use. To mix, remove the plastic cap, turn the plunger stopper 90 degrees, and press down to force the fluid in the upper chamber along with the center seal into the lower chamber. Gently mix the solution. The manufacturer states that the stopper must be "sterilized in the usual manner" before inserting a needle to withdraw the contents. After mixing, the products contain (1-4/98):

Ascorbic acid	100 mg
Vitamin A (retinol)	1 mg
Vitamin D (ergocalciferol)	5 μg
Thiamine (as HCl)	3 mg
Riboflavin (as 5-phosphate sodium)	3.6 mg
Pyridoxine HCl	4 mg
Niacinamide	40 mg
Dexpanthenol	15 mg
Vitamin E (*dl*-alpha tocopheryl acetate)	10 mg
Biotin	60 μg
Folic acid	400 μg
Cyanocobalamin (vitamin B_{12})	5 μg

M.V.I.-12 also contains propylene glycol 30%, gentisic acid ethanolamide 1%, polysorbate 80 0.8%, polysorbate 20 0.014%, butylated hydroxytoluene 0.001%, butylated hydroxyanisole 0.0003%, and citric acid, sodium citrate, and sodium hydroxide to adjust pH. (1-4/98) The M.V.I.-12 mixed solution must be diluted for use; do not give it undiluted. (1-4/98)

M.V.I. Pediatric is available as a lyophilized powder in vials containing a single dose. Each single dose contains (1-11/00):

Ascorbic acid	80 mg
Vitamin A (retinol)	0.7 mg
Vitamin D (ergocalciferol)	10 μg
Thiamine (as HCl)	1.2 mg
Riboflavin (as 5-phosphate sodium)	1.4 mg
Pyridoxine (as HCl)	1 mg
Niacinamide	17 mg
Dexpanthenol	5 mg
Vitamin E (*dl*-alpha tocopheryl acetate)	7 mg
Biotin	20 μg
Folic acid	140 μg
Cyanocobalamin	1 μg
Phytonadione	200 μg

M.V.I. Pediatric also contains, in each vial, mannitol 375 mg, polysorbate 80 50 mg, polysorbate 20 0.8 mg, butylated hydroxytoluene 58 μg, butylated hydroxyanisole 14 μg, and sodium hydroxide for pH adjustment. (1-11/00)

Reconstitute the single-dose vial with 5 ml of sterile water for injection, dextrose 5% in water, or sodium chloride 0.9% and swirl gently. The solution is ready within three minutes. This solution must be further diluted for use; do not give it undiluted. (1-11/00)

Osmolality — The osmolality of M.V.I.-12 was determined to be 4820 mOsm/kg by freezing-point depression and 4210 mOsm/kg by vapor pressure. (1071)

Trade Name(s) — Berocca Parenteral Nutrition, M.V.I.-12, M.V.I. Pediatric, Cernevit-12.

Administration — Multivitamin infusion preparations are administered by intravenous infusion only. They should not be given by direct intravenous injection. M.V.I.-12 is diluted in not less than 500 ml but preferably 1000 ml of intravenous infusion solution for administration. M.V.I. Pediatric should be added to at least 100 ml of a compatible intravenous infusion solution for administration. (1-4/98; 1-11/00)

Stability — Multivitamin products for infusion should be stored under refrigeration and protected from light. Since some of the vitamins, especially A, D, and riboflavin, are light sensitive, light protection is necessary. (1-4/98; 1-11/00) After reconstitution of M.V.I. Pediatric, use of the product without delay is recommended. However, if this is not possible, the manufacturer permits use within a maximum of four hours from the initial penetration of the closure. (1-11/00)

Light Effects — The effects of photoirradiation on a FreAmine II–dextrose 10% parenteral nutrition solution containing 1 ml/500 ml of multivitamins (USV) were evaluated. During simulated continuous administration to an infant at 0.156 ml/min, the amino acids were stable when the bottle, infusion tubing, and collection bottle were shielded with foil. Only 20 cm of tubing in the incubator was exposed to light. However, if the flow was stopped, marked reductions in methionine (40%), tryptophan (44%), and histidine (22%) occurred in the solution exposed to light for 24 hours. In a similar solution without vitamins, only the tryptophan concentration decreased. The difference was attributed to the presence of riboflavin, a photosensitizer. The authors recommended administering the multivitamins separately and shielding from light. (833)

The stability of five B vitamins was studied over eight hours in representative parenteral nutrition solutions exposed to fluorescent light, indirect sunlight, or direct sunlight. One 5-ml vial of multivitamin concentrate (Lyphomed) and 1 mg of folic acid (Lederle) were added to a liter of parenteral nutrition solution composed of amino acids 4.25% and dextrose 25% (Travenol) with standard electrolytes and trace elements. The five B vitamins were stable for eight hours at room temperature when exposed to fluorescent light. In addition, folic acid and niacinamide were stable over eight hours in direct or indirect sunlight. Exposure to indirect sunlight appeared to have little or no effect on thiamine HCl and pyridoxine HCl in eight hours, but riboflavin-5-phosphate lost 47%. Direct sunlight caused a 26% loss of thiamine HCl and an 86% loss of pyridoxine HCl in eight hours. A four-hour exposure of riboflavin-5-phosphate to direct sunlight resulted in a 98% loss. (842)

Samples from 24 1-L and four 2-L parenteral nutrition solutions, containing one vial each of multivitamin concentrate (USV), were evaluated for thiamine HCl content 48 to 72 hours after mixing. The parenteral nutrition solutions contained amino acids 2.75 to 5%, dextrose 15 to 25%, and electrolytes. Thiamine HCl was stable in all of the solutions tested in spite of approximately 0.05% sulfite content. (843)

Kishi et al. reported on a parenteral nutrition solution in glass bottles exposed to sunlight. Vitamin A decomposed rapidly, losing more than 50% in three hours. The decomposition could be slowed by covering the bottle with a light-resistant vinyl bag, resulting in about a 25% loss in three hours. (1040)

Kishi et al. also reported that vitamin E was stable in the parenteral nutrition solution in glass bottles exposed to sunlight, with no loss occurring during six hours of exposure. (1040)

Allwood found that vitamin A was rapidly and significantly decomposed when exposed to daylight. The extent and rate of loss were dependent on the degree of exposure to daylight which, in turn, depended on various factors such as the direction of the radiation, time of day, and climatic conditions. Delivery of less than 10% of the expected amount was reported. (1047) In controlled light experiments, the decomposition initially progressed exponentially. Subsequently, the rate of decomposition slowed. This result was attributed to a protective effect of the degradation products on the remaining vitamin A. The presence of amino acids provided greater protection. Compared to degradation rates in dextrose 5% in water, decomposition was reduced by up to 50% in some amino acid mixtures. (1048)

The stability of several water-soluble vitamins in dextrose 5% in water and sodium chloride 0.9% in PVC and ClearFlex containers was evaluated. HPLC analysis showed that thiamine, riboflavin, ascorbic acid, and folic acid were stable at 23 °C when protected from light, exhibiting 10% or less loss in 24 hours. When exposed to light, thiamine and folic acid were stable but ascorbic acid was reduced by approximately 50 to 65% and riboflavin was completely lost. (1509)

The stability of phytonadione in a TPN solution containing amino acids 2%, dextrose 12.5%, "standard" electrolytes, and M.V.I. Pediatric over 24 hours while exposed to light was evaluated by HPLC analysis. Vitamin loss was about 7% in four hours and 27% in 24 hours. Some loss was attributed to the light sensitivity of the phytonadione. (1815)

Billion-Rey et al. reported substantial loss by HPLC analysis of retinol all-*trans* palmitate and phytonadione from both TPN and TNA admixtures due to exposure to sunlight. In three hours of exposure to sunlight, essentially total loss of retinol and 50% loss of phytonadione had occurred. The presence or absence of lipids did not affect stability. In contrast, tocopherol concentrations remained essentially unchanged by exposure to sunlight through 12 hours. The container material used to store the nutrition admixtures affected the concentration of the vitamins as well. Losses were greatest (10 to 25%) in PVC containers and were slightly better in EVA and glass containers. (2049)

Sorption — Vitamin A (as the acetate) (Sigma) 7.5 mg/L displayed 66.7% sorption to a PVC plastic test strip in 24 hours. The presence of dextrose 5% and sodium chloride 0.9% increased the extent of the sorption. (12)

In another report, vitamin A acetate displayed 78% sorption to 200-ml PVC containers after 24 hours at 25 °C with gentle shaking. The initial concentration was 3 mg/L. The sorption was increased by approximately 10% in sodium chloride 0.9% and by 20% in dextrose 5% in water. (133)

However, Nedich noted that vitamin A delivery is also reduced in glass intravenous containers. At a concentration of 10,000 units/L in glass and PVC plastic containers protected from light with aluminum foil, 77 and 71%, respectively, of the vitamin A were delivered over a 10-hour period. Without light protection, 61% was delivered from glass and 49% from PVC plastic containers over a 10-hour period. (290)

In another test using multivitamin infusion (USV), one ampul per liter of sodium chloride 0.9% in glass and PVC plastic containers not protected from light, 69.4 and 67.9% of the vitamin A were delivered from glass and PVC containers, respectively, over a 10-hour period. The amount of vitamin A was constant over the test period; it did not decrease with time. (282)

Similar results were observed in a parenteral nutrition solution composed of protein hydrolysate 2%, dextrose 20%, electrolytes, and multivitamin infusion (USV) 10 ml in 1-L glass containers. Approximately 50 to 65% of the vitamin A content in the solution was lost in 24 hours and then it remained stable for three to seven days. When added to the cellulose propionate burette chambers of infusion sets, about 60% of the vitamin A was lost in six hours. Further, the effluent from the PVC tubing of the set was even worse. The concentration dropped from an initial 3 μg/ml to 1 μg/ml in two hours. Wrapping foil around the chambers to exclude light did not alter the vitamin A disappearance. About 50% of the lost vitamin A was recovered by hexane extraction of the administration sets. (438)

The following vitamins did not reveal significant sorption to a PVC plastic test strip in 24 hours (12):

Ascorbic acid
Niacinamide
Pyridoxine HCl
Riboflavin
Thiamine HCl
Vitamin D
Vitamin E acetate

However, Gillis et al. evaluated the delivery of vitamins A, D, and E from a parenteral nutrition solution composed of 3% amino acid solution (Pharmacia) in dextrose 10% with electrolytes, trace elements, vitamin K, folate, and vitamin B_{12}. To this solution was added 6 ml of multivitamin infusion (USV). The solution was prepared in PVC bags (Travenol), and administration was simulated through a fluid chamber (Buretrol) and infusion tubing with a 0.5-μm filter at 10 ml/hr. During the first 60 to 90 minutes, minimal delivery of the vitamins occurred. This was followed by a rise and plateau in the delivered vitamins, which were attributed to an increasing saturation of adsorptive binding sites in the tubing. The total amounts delivered over 24 hours were 31% for vitamin A, 68% for vitamin D, and 64% for vitamin E. Sorption of the vitamins was found in the PVC bag, fluid chamber, and tubing. Decomposition was not a factor. (836)

Riboflavin (Sigma) 5 mg/L in sodium chloride 0.9% (Travenol) in PVC bags wrapped in aluminum foil for light protection did not exhibit significant sorption to the plastic during one week of storage at room temperature (15 to 20 °C). (536)

In another study, riboflavin (Sigma) 5 mg/L in sodium chloride 0.9% did not exhibit any loss due to sorption during a seven-hour simulated infusion through an infusion set (Travenol) consisting of a cellulose propionate burette chamber and 170 cm of PVC tubing. (606)

The riboflavin solution was also tested as a simulated infusion over at least one hour by a syringe pump system. A glass syringe on a syringe pump was fitted with 20 cm of polyethylene tubing or 50 cm of Silastic tubing. No loss of riboflavin due to sorption was observed with either tubing. (606)

A 25-ml aliquot of riboflavin (Sigma) 5 mg/L in sodium chloride 0.9% was stored in all-plastic syringes composed of polypropylene barrels and polyethylene plungers for 24 hours at room temperature in the dark. No loss due to sorption occurred. (606)

Howard et al. reported on a patient receiving 3000 I.U. of retinol daily in a parenteral nutrition solution; nevertheless, this patient experienced two episodes of night blindness. The pharmacy prepared the parenteral nutrition solution in 1-L PVC bags in weekly batches and stored them at 4 °C in the dark until use. A subsequent in vitro study showed losses of vitamin A of 23 and 77% in three- and 14-day periods, respectively, under these conditions. About 30% of the lost vitamin A could be extracted from the PVC bag. (1038)

Shenai et al. reported on losses of vitamin A from multivitamin infusion (USV) in a neonatal parenteral nutrition solution. The solution was prepared in colorless glass bottles and run through an administration set with a burette (Travenol). The total loss of vitamin A was 75% in 24 hours, with about 16% as decomposition in the glass bottle. The decomposition was not noticeable during the first 12 hours, but then vitamin A levels fell rather precipitously to about one-third of the initial amount. The balance of the loss, averaging about 59%, occurred during transit through the administration set. Removal of the inline filter and treatment of the set with albumin human had no effect on vitamin A delivery. The authors recommended a three- to fourfold increase in the amount of vitamin A to compensate for the losses. (1039)

Riggle et al. noted a 50% loss of vitamin A from a bottle of parenteral nutrition solution prepared with multivitamin infusion (USV) after 5.5 hours of infusion. The amount delivered through an Ivex-2 filter set was only 6.3% of the added amount. Similar quantities were found after 20 hours of infusion. A reduced light exposure and use of ^{3}H-labeled vitamin A confirmed binding to the infusion bottles and tubing. (704)

Subsequently, Riggle and Brandt incubated solutions containing multivitamin infusion (USV) spiked with ^{3}H-labeled retinol in intravenous tubing protected from light and agitated to simulate flow for five hours. About half of the vitamin A was lost in 30 minutes, and 88 to 96% was lost in five hours. Spectrophotometric assays correlated closely with the radioisotope assays. Hexane rinses and radioactivity determinations on the tubing accounted for the decrease in radioactivity. (1049)

McGee et al. evaluated the stability of vitamin E (alpha-tocopherol acetate from M.V.I.-1000 or Soluzyme) and selenium (from Selepen) in amino acids (Abbott) and dextrose in PVC bags. Exposure to fluorescent light and room temperature (23 °C) for 24 hours and simulated infusion at 50 ml/hr for eight hours through a Medlon TPN administration set with a 0.22-μm filter did not affect the concentrations of vitamin E and selenium. (1224)

Dahl et al. reported the stability of numerous vitamins in parenteral nutrition solutions composed of amino acids (Kabi-Vitrum), dextrose 30%, and fat emulsion 20% (Kabi-Vitrum) in a 2:1:1 ratio with electrolytes, trace elements, and both fat- and water-soluble vitamins. The admixtures were stored in darkness at 2 to 8 °C for 96 hours with no significant loss of retinyl palmitate, alpha-tocopherol, thiamine mononitrate, sodium riboflavin-5′-phosphate, pyridoxine HCl, nicotinamide, folic acid, biotin, sodium pantothenate, and cyanocobalamin. Sodium ascorbate and its biologically active degradation product, dehydroascorbic acid, totaled 59 and 42% of the nominal starting concentration at 24 and 96 hours, respectively. However, the actual initial concentration was only 66% of the nominal concentration. (1225)

When the admixture was subjected to simulated infusion over 24 hours at 20 °C, either exposed to room light or light protected, or stored for six days in the dark under refrigeration and then subjected to the same simulated infusion, once again the retinyl palmitate, alpha-tocopherol, and sodium riboflavin-5′-phosphate did not undergo significant loss. However, sodium ascorbate and its degradation product, dehydroascorbic acid, had initial combined concentrations of 51 to 65% of the nominal initial concentration, with further declines during infusion. Light protection did not significantly alter the loss of total ascorbic acid. (1225)

In another experiment, neonatal parenteral nutrition solutions containing multivitamin infusion prepared in bags were delivered at 10 ml/hr through Buretrol sets (Travenol). The bags and sets were protected from light. Spectrophotometric and radioisotope assays showed that about 26% of the vitamin A was lost before the flow was started. At 10 ml/hr, about 67% was lost from the effluent. More rapid flow reduced the extent of loss. Analysis of clinical samples of parenteral nutrition solutions showed losses of 21 to 57% after 20 hours. Because losses after five hours were of the same magnitude, the authors concluded that the loss occurs fairly rapidly and is not due to gradual decomposition. (1049)

McKenna and Bieri reported that 40% retinol losses occurred in two hours and 60% in five hours from parenteral nutrition solutions pumped at 10 ml/hr through standard infusion sets at room temperature. The retinol concentration in the bottle remained constant while the retinol in the effluent decreased. Antioxidants had no effect. Much of the vitamin A was recoverable from hexane washings of the tubing. (1050)

Interestingly, no loss of vitamin A to PVC delivery systems of *enteral* feeding solutions, after six hours of storage without protection from light and with exposure to ambient temperature, was reported by Bryant and Neufeld. The authors attributed this result to the presence of other (undefined) substances in the enteral feeding mixtures. (1051)

To minimize the importance of this sorption, Allwood suggested using vitamin A palmitate instead of acetate; he stated that vitamin A palmitate does not sorb to PVC. However, this does not alter the problem of degradation from exposure to light. Alternatively, an excess of vitamin A could be used. (1033)

Plasticizer Leaching—Multivitamins (Lyphomed) 1 ml in 50 ml of dextrose 5% in water leached insignificant amounts of diethylhexyl phthalate (DEHP) plasticizer. This leaching was due to the surfactant polysorbate 80 in the formulation. This finding is consistent with the low surfactant concentration (0.032%) in the final admixture solution. (1683)

Compatibility Information

Solution Compatibility

Multivitamins

Solution	*Mfr*	*Mfr*	*Conc/L*	*Remarks*	*Ref*	*C/I*
Alcohol 5%, dextrose 5% in water	BA	USV	20 ml	Physically compatible for 24 hr	315	C
Amino acids 10%	TR	USV	1 vial	40% thiamine loss in 22 hr at 30 °C due to sulfite content	843	I
Amino acids 8.5% (FreAmine III)	MG	RC	4 ml[a]	97% thiamine loss in 24 hr at 23 °C due to bisulfite content of solution. 63% loss in 24 hr at 7 °C	774	I
	MG	AB	[b]	96% thiamine loss in 24 hr at 23 °C due to bisulfite content of solution	774	I
	MG	USV	[c]	92% thiamine loss in 24 hr at 23 °C due to bisulfite content of solution	774	I
Amino acids 5.5% (Travasol)	TR	RC	4 ml[a]	About 70% thiamine loss in 24 hr at 23 °C due to bisulfite content of solution. 33% loss in 24 hr at 7 °C	774	I
Amino acids 4.25%, dextrose 25%	TR	USV	1 vial	No thiamine loss in 22 hr at 30 °C	843	C
Amino acids 2%, dextrose 12.5%		ROR	5 ml[d]	7% phytonadione loss in 4 hr and 27% loss in 24 hr by HPLC under ambient temperature and light	1815	I
Dextrose 5% in Ringer's injection, lactated	BA	USV	20 ml	Physically compatible for 24 hr	315	C
Dextrose 5% in sodium chloride 0.9%	BA	USV	20 ml	Physically compatible for 24 hr	315	C
Dextrose 5% in water	BA	USV	20 ml	Physically compatible for 24 hr	315	C
	TR[e]	RC	4 ml[a]	8% or less thiamine loss in 24 hr at 23 °C	774	C
Dextrose 10% in water	BA	USV	20 ml	Physically compatible for 24 hr	315	C
	TR[e]	RC	4 ml[a]	5% or less thiamine loss in 24 hr at 23 °C	774	C
	MG[f]	RC	4 ml[a]	11% or less thiamine loss in 24 hr at 23 °C	774	C
Dextrose 20% in water	BA	USV	20 ml	Physically compatible for 24 hr	315	C
Fat emulsion 10%, intravenous	VT	USV	4 ml	Physically compatible for 48 hr at 4 °C and room temperature	32	C
	KA	KA		Physically compatible for 24 hr at 26 °C with little loss of most vitamins by HPLC; up to 52% ascorbate loss	2050	C
Fructose 10% in water	BA	USV	20 ml	Physically compatible for 24 hr	315	C
Invert sugar 10% in Electrolyte #1	BA	USV	20 ml	Physically compatible for 24 hr	315	C
Invert sugar 10% in Electrolyte #2	BA	USV	20 ml	Physically compatible for 24 hr	315	C
Polysal M with dextrose 5%	CU	USV	20 ml	Physically compatible for 24 hr	315	C

Solution Compatibility (Cont.)

Multivitamins

Solution	*Mfr*	*Mfr*	*Conc/L*	*Remarks*	*Ref*	*C/I*
Ringer's injection, lactated	BA	USV	20 ml	Physically compatible for 24 hr	315	C
	TR[e]	RC	4 ml[a]	5% or less thiamine loss in 24 hr at 23 °C	774	C
Sodium chloride 0.9%	BA	USV	20 ml	Physically compatible for 24 hr	315	C
	TR[e]	RC	4 ml[a]	Thiamine losses of 6 to 11% in 24 hr at 23 °C	774	C
Sodium lactate ⅙ M	BA	USV	20 ml	Physically compatible for 24 hr	315	C

[a] *Berocca Parenteral Nutrition.*
[b] *Multivitamin Additive.*
[c] *M.V.I.-12.*
[d] *M.V.I. Pediatric.*
[e] *Tested in both glass and PVC containers.*
[f] *Tested in polyolefin containers.*

Additive Compatibility

Multivitamins

Drug	*Mfr*	*Conc/L*	*Mfr*	*Conc/L*	*Test Soln*	*Remarks*	*Ref*	*C/I*
Cefoxitin sodium	MSD	10 g	USV	50 ml[a]	W	5% cefoxitin decomposition in 24 hr and 10% in 48 hr at 25 °C; 3% in 48 hr at 5 °C. TLC showed no other transformation products	308	C
Isoproterenol HCl	WI	4 mg	USV	10 ml		Physically compatible	59	C
Meropenem	ZEN	1 and 20 g	AST	50 ml	NS	Color darkened in 4 hr at room temperature	1994	I
Methyldopate HCl	MSD	1 g	USV	10 ml	D, D–S, S	Physically compatible	23	C
Metoclopramide HCl	RB	20 and 320 mg	USV	20 ml[b]	NS	Physically compatible for 48 hr at room temperature	924; 1167	C
	RB	20 and 320 mg	USV	20 ml[c]	NS	Physically compatible for 48 hr at room temperature	924; 1167	C
Metronidazole HCl with sodium bicarbonate	SE AB	5 g 50 mEq	USV	20 ml	D5W, NS	Physically compatible for 48 hr	765	C
Netilmicin sulfate	SC	3 g	USV	40 ml	D5S	Physically compatible and netilmicin chemically stable for 24 hr at 25 and 4 °C. 20% loss noted after 3 days. Multivitamins not tested	558	C
Norepinephrine bitartrate	WI	8 mg	USV	10 ml	D, D–S, S	Physically compatible	77	C
Sodium bicarbonate	AB	4.8 mEq[d]	USV	10 ml	D5W	Physically compatible for 24 hr	772	C
Verapamil HCl	KN	80 mg	USV	10 ml	D5W, NS	Physically compatible for 24 hr	764	C

[a] *Concentrate.*
[b] *M.V.I.*
[c] *M.V.I.-12.*
[d] *Two vials of Neut added to a liter of admixture.*

Y-Site Injection Compatibility (1:1 Mixture)

Multivitamins

Drug	*Mfr*	*Conc*	*Mfr*	*Conc*	*Remarks*	*Ref*	*C/I*
Acyclovir sodium	BW	5 mg/ml[a]	LY	0.01 ml/ml[a]	Physically compatible for 4 hr at 25 °C	1157	C

Y-Site Injection Compatibility (1:1 Mixture) (Cont.)

			Multivitamins				
Drug	*Mfr*	*Conc*	*Mfr*	*Conc*	*Remarks*	*Ref*	*C/I*
Ampicillin sodium	AY	1 g/50 ml[a,b]	USV	5 ml/L[a]	Physically compatible for 24 hr at room temperature	323	C
Cefazolin sodium	SKF	1 g/50 ml[a]	USV	5 ml/L[a]	Physically compatible for 24 hr at room temperature	323	C
Diltiazem HCl	MMD	5 mg/ml		[c]	Visually compatible	1807	C
Erythromycin lactobionate	AB	500 mg/ 250 ml[b]	USV	5 ml/L[a]	Physically compatible for 24 hr at room temperature	323	C
Fludarabine phosphate	BX	1 mg/ml[a]	RR	0.01 ml/ml[a]	Physically compatible for 4 hr at room temperature under fluorescent light	1439	C
Gentamicin sulfate	SC	80 mg/ 100 ml[a]	USV	5 ml/L[a]	Physically compatible for 24 hr at room temperature	323	C
Tacrolimus	FUJ	1 mg/ml[b]	LY	0.001 ml/ml[a]	Visually compatible for 24 hr at 25 °C	1630	C
TPN #189[d]			RR	[e]	Visually compatible for 24 hr at 22 °C	1767	C

[a]*Tested in dextrose 5% in water.*
[b]*Tested in sodium chloride 0.9%.*
[c]*Concentration unspecified.*
[d]*Refer to Appendix I for the composition of parenteral nutrition solutions. TPN indicates a 2-in-1 admixture.*
[e]*M.V.I.-12.*

Additional Compatibility Information

Infusion Solutions — Dextrose and saline infusion solutions have been recommended as diluents for infusion of multivitamins. (1-4/98)

Feroz et al. evaluated the stability of the vitamins in M.V.C. 9 + 3 (Lyphomed) in several infusion solutions. The contents of one package of two vials of M.V.C. 9 + 3 were added to 1000 ml of the following infusion solutions:

Amino acid injection (Abbott) 2.5%, dextrose 25% (in glass, PVC, and polyolefin containers)
Amino acid injection (McGaw) 4.25%, dextrose 25% (in glass, PVC, and polyolefin containers)
Dextrose 5% in sodium chloride 0.9% (in glass and PVC containers)
Dextrose 5% in water (in polyolefin containers)

The admixtures were stored for 24 hours at room temperature in the light and in the dark and at 4 °C. Under all three storage conditions, cyanocobalamin, biotin, folic acid, riboflavin, vitamin E, niacinamide, and dexpanthenol were stable in all solutions. Pyridoxine and vitamin D were moderately stable; vitamin A, ascorbic acid, and thiamine were unstable, with the higher temperature and light exposure adversely affecting their activity. However, all vitamins retained at least 90% of the labeled amounts for 24 hours when the admixtures were stored at 4 °C. (926)

Parenteral Nutrition Solutions — Multivitamin infusion concentrate (USV) 5 and 10 ml/L was tested in parenteral nutrition solutions #38 through #42. (Refer to Appendix I for the composition of parenteral nutrition solutions.) The admixtures were physically compatible for 24 hours at 22 °C. However, the UV spectra for both the amino acids–dextrose and the vitamins altered markedly. Whether this result indicates an incompatibility is uncertain. (313)

Additional tests were conducted with multivitamin infusion concentrate (USV) 10 ml/L in parenteral nutrition solutions #43 through #47. Once again, no physical incompatibility was observed in 24 hours at 22 °C. However, TLC changes were observed in similar solutions in 12 hours. (313)

In a parenteral nutrition solution composed of amino acids, dextrose, electrolytes, trace elements, and multivitamins in PVC bags stored at 4 and 25 °C, vitamin A rapidly deteriorated to 10% of the initial concentration in eight hours at 25 °C when exposed to light. The decomposition was slowed by light protection and refrigeration, with a loss of about 25% in four days. Folic acid concentration dropped 40% initially on admixture and then remained relatively constant for 28 days of storage. About 35% of the ascorbic acid was lost in 39 hours at 25 °C when exposed to light. The loss was reduced substantially, to a negligible amount in four days, by refrigeration and light protection. Thiamine content dropped by about 50% initially but then remained unchanged over 120 hours of storage. (1063)

The stability of ascorbic acid in parenteral nutrition solutions, with and without fat emulsion, was studied using HPLC analysis. Both with and without fat emulsion, the total vitamin C content (ascorbic acid plus dehydroascorbic acid) remained above 90% for 12 hours when the solutions were exposed to fluorescent light and for 24 hours when they were protected from light. When stored in a cool dark place, the solutions were stable for seven days. (1227)

Erythromycin — Erythromycin 5 mg/ml as the lactobionate in pH 8 buffer was combined with riboflavin in concentrations varying from 1 mg/ml to 20 μg/ml. On exposure to light for four hours, almost total decomposition of the erythromycin occurred, with only 4 to 12% remaining. Protection from light resulted in 12 to 25% decomposition. When no riboflavin was present, 10% or less decomposition of the erythromycin occurred. It was concluded that a photodynamic decomposition reaction was taking place. (564)

Penicillin G — The times to 10% decomposition of combinations of penicillin G potassium buffered (Lilly, Pfizer, Squibb) with multivitamin infusion concentrate (USV) in dextrose 5% in water and sodium chloride 0.9% have been mathematically predicted on the basis of the final pH of the admixture (304):

Penicillin G Potassium	Multivitamin Infusion Concentrate	pH	Time to 10% Decomposition
1 million units/L	1 ml/L	5.1	6.51 hr
	5 ml/L	4.9	4.56 hr
3 million units/L	1 ml/L	5.4	13.54 hr
	5 ml/L	5.0	6.38 hr
5 million units/L	1 ml/L	5.7	22.01 hr
	5 ml/L	5.1	6.51 hr
10 million units/L	1 ml/L	5.9	over 24 hr
	5 ml/L	5.4	13.54 hr

Other Antibiotics — In vitro testing of thiamine HCl, riboflavin-5′-phosphate, pyridoxine HCl, niacinamide, and ascorbic acid individually at concentrations of 0.1% and the following antibiotics at 0.025% in sterile distilled water showed significant reduction in antibiotic activity in one hour at 25 °C (314):

Erythromycin (as estolate)
Kanamycin sulfate
Streptomycin sulfate

Riboflavin-5′-phosphate, but not the other vitamins, caused significant reduction in antibiotic activity of the following (314):

Doxycycline HCl
Lincomycin HCl

Bisulfite Effects — A study of the stability of thiamine HCl in the multivitamin products Berocca Parenteral Nutrition (Roche), Multivitamin Additive (Abbott), and M.V.I-12 (USV) showed extensive decomposition when these products were admixed in infusion solutions containing sodium bisulfite. After 24 hours at 23 °C, thiamine losses ranged from 70% in Travasol 5.5% (pH 5.5) to 97% in FreAmine III 8.5% (pH 6.5). The extent of decomposition increased as the pH neared neutrality. The rate of decomposition could be slowed, but not eliminated, by refrigeration. When admixed in solutions not containing bisulfite, the thiamine was much more stable, showing losses of 0 to 11% in 24 hours at 23 °C. The authors noted that if bisulfite-containing solutions are necessary to administer the multivitamin preparations, the admixtures should be used immediately after preparation and patients on long-term therapy should be monitored for thiamine deficiency. (774)

In another experiment, multivitamin concentrate (USV) was added to 500-ml glass bottles of amino acids 10% (Travenol) containing 0.1% sulfite and also to 1000-ml PVC bags containing amino acids 4.25%–dextrose 25% (Travenol) with about 0.05% sulfite. After 22 hours at 30 °C, a 40% loss of thiamine HCl occurred in the amino acids 10% solution, but no loss occurred in the PVC bags of parenteral nutrition solution. The authors concluded that the thiamine HCl content is retained in usual clinical parenteral nutrition solutions, probably because of the dilution of the sulfite and buffering of pH. However, direct addition to solutions with a high sulfite content (0.1%) may result in significant decomposition. (843)

Other Drugs — Bleomycin sulfate is inactivated in vitro by ascorbic acid and riboflavin. (4) In addition, some of the vitamins may react with vitamin K bisulfite. Folic acid has been reported to be unstable in the presence of calcium salts. A physical incompatibility may result from addition to moderately alkaline solutions such as a sodium bicarbonate solution and other alkaline drugs such as acetazolamide sodium, aminophylline, ampicillin sodium, and chlorothiazide sodium. (1-4/98; 1-11/00)

NAFCILLIN SODIUM
AHFS 8:12.16

Products — Nafcillin sodium is available in vials containing the equivalent of 1 and 2 g of nafcillin. (4; 29) Reconstitute the 1-g vial with 3.4 ml and the 2-g vial with 6.8 ml of sterile water for injection, sodium chloride 0.9%, or bacteriostatic water for injection containing parabens or benzyl alcohol. The solution then contains nafcillin sodium equivalent to nafcillin 250 mg/ml with sodium citrate buffer. The final volumes of the 1- and 2-g vials are 4 and 8 ml, respectively. (4)

A 10-g pharmacy bulk vial is also available and is reconstituted with 93 ml of sterile water for injection or sodium chloride 0.9% to yield a 100-mg/ml solution with sodium citrate buffer 4 mg/ml. (4; 29)

Nafcillin sodium is also available as frozen premixed solutions containing 1 and 2 g of nafcillin per minibag in dextrose 3.6% or 2%, respectively. (4; 29)

pH — The pH of the reconstituted solution and frozen premixed solution is 6 to 8.5. (4)

Osmolality — The osmolality of nafcillin sodium (Wyeth) 250 mg/ml in sterile water for injection was determined to be 709 mOsm/kg by freezing-point depression and 665 mOsm/kg by vapor pressure. (1071)

The frozen premixed solutions have an osmolality of 300 mOsm/kg. (4)

The osmolality of nafcillin sodium (Wyeth) 40 mg/ml was determined to be 403 mOsm/kg in dextrose 5% in water and 402 mOsm/kg in sodium chloride 0.9%. (1375)

The osmolality of nafcillin sodium was calculated for the following dilutions (1054):

Diluent	Osmolality (mOsm/kg) 50 ml	100 ml
2 g		
Dextrose 5% in water	399	334
Sodium chloride 0.9%	425	361
3 g		
Dextrose 5% in water	458	371
Sodium chloride 0.9%	485	398

Robinson et al. recommended the following maximum nafcillin sodium concentrations to achieve osmolalities suitable for peripheral infusion in fluid-restricted patients (1180):

Diluent	Maximum Concentration (mg/ml)	Osmolality (mOsm/kg)
Dextrose 5% in water	71	491
Sodium chloride 0.9%	64	470
Sterile water for injection	128	319

Sodium Content — Each gram of nafcillin sodium with sodium citrate buffer contains 2.9 mEq (66 mg) of sodium. (4; 27)

Trade Name(s) — Nallpen.

Administration — Nafcillin sodium may be administered intramuscularly by deep intragluteal injection, by direct intravenous injection, or by intermittent intravenous infusion. For direct intravenous injection, the dose should be diluted with 15 to 30 ml of sterile water for injection or sodium chloride 0.45 or 0.9% and given over five to 10 minutes into the tubing of a running intravenous infusion. Intermittent intravenous infusion in a concentration between 2 and 40 mg/ml should be administered slowly, over 30 to 60 minutes. (4)

Stability — Intact containers should be stored at controlled room temperature or lower. (4) When reconstituted to a concentration of 250 mg/ml, nafcillin sodium is stable for three days at room temperature or seven days when refrigerated at 2 to 8 °C. (4; 27) For the piggyback concentrations of 2 to 40 mg/ml, nafcillin sodium is stable for 24 hours at room temperature or 96 hours under refrigeration, although longer periods have also been cited. (4)

Commercially available frozen premixed nafcillin sodium solutions, thawed at room temperature or under refrigeration, are stable for 72 hours at 25 °C and 21 days at 5 °C. (4)

pH Effects — The stability of nafcillin sodium is pH dependent, with a maximum stability at pH 6 and a preferred range of pH 5 to 8. Drug decomposition is rapidly increased as pH values vary from this range. (27)

Freezing Solutions — At a concentration of 250 mg/ml in sterile water for injection and frozen at −20 °C, the drug is stable for up to three months. (27; 123)

In one study, however, when nafcillin sodium (Wyeth) 1 g/4 ml was frozen at −20 °C in glass syringes (Hy-Pod), the potency was retained for nine months. (532)

In another study, nafcillin sodium (Wyeth) 1 g/50 ml of dextrose 5% in water in PVC bags frozen at −20 °C for 30 days and then thawed by exposure to ambient temperature or microwave radiation showed no evidence of precipitation or color change but had a 2 to 3% loss of potency as determined microbiologically. Subsequent storage of the admixture at room temperature for 24 hours also yielded physically compatible solutions with no additional loss of activity. (555)

Nafcillin sodium (Wyeth) 20 mg/ml in dextrose 5% in water and sodium chloride 0.9% frozen at −20 °C for 12 weeks exhibited little or no loss of potency by HPLC analysis in latex elastomeric reservoirs (Secure Medical) and in glass containers. (1970)

Syringes — Nafcillin sodium (Apothecon) 10 mg/ml in sodium chloride 0.9% was packaged in 10-ml polypropylene syringes (Becton-Dickinson) and stored at 5 and 25 °C. The solutions remained clear under refrigeration for 44 days and at room temperature for seven days. But they developed a yellow discoloration after 14 days at room temperature. HPLC analysis found about 2% loss of nafcillin sodium after seven days and 18% loss in 14 days at 25 °C. Under refrigeration at 5 °C, about 1% loss occurred after 44 days. Stability in glass containers was found to be comparable. (2325)

Ambulatory Pumps — Stiles et al. evaluated the stability of nafcillin sodium (Wyeth) 80 mg/ml in sterile water for injection and sodium chloride 0.9% in 100-ml portable pump reservoirs (Pharmacia Deltec) during simulated administration for 48 hours. The drug solutions were tested by HPLC analysis immediately after preparation and after storage for 24 hours at 5 °C before 48-hour simulated administration. During simulated administration, some reservoirs were kept at 30 °C; others were placed in insulated pouches with frozen (−20 °C) gel packs to keep them chilled below the ambient temperature. The nafcillin sodium solutions exhibited a 5% or less loss by HPLC under all study conditions during 24 hours of simulated administration and an 8% or less loss during 48 hours of such administration. Chilling of the drug reservoirs was not necessary to complete the infusions, nor did it enhance stability substantially during the study period. (1779)

Nafcillin sodium (Marsam) 20 mg/ml in sterile water for injection in PVC portable pump reservoirs (Pharmacia Deltec) exhibited no loss by HPLC analysis in three days stored at 25 °C and in 14 days at 5 °C. However, at a concentration of 120 mg/ml, 6% loss was found in three days at 25 °C, and 2% loss occurred in 14 days at 5 °C. (2080)

Elastomeric Reservoir Pumps — Nafcillin sodium (Wyeth) 20 mg/ml in 100 ml of dextrose 5% in water and sodium chloride 0.9% was packaged in latex elastomeric reservoirs (Secure Medical). Little or no loss by HPLC analysis occurred in 24 hours at 25 °C and in four days at 5 °C. (1970)

Nafcillin sodium solutions in elastomeric reservoir pumps have been stated by the pump manufacturers to be stable for the following time periods frozen, refrigerated (REF), or at room temperature (RT) (31):

Pump Reservoir(s)	Conc.	Frozen	REF	RT
Homepump; Homepump Eclipse	10 mg/ml[b]		3 days	24 hr
Intermate	5 to 40 mg/ml[a,b]	30 days	10 days	
Intermate HPC	10 to 40 mg/ml[a]	30 days	14 days	2 days[c]
Medflo	10 to 20 mg/ml[a,b]	12 weeks	4 days	24 hr
ReadyMed	250 mg/ml[a,b,d]	30 days	7 days	3 days

[a] *In dextrose 5% in water.*
[b] *In sodium chloride 0.9%.*
[c] *After 14 days refrigerated storage.*
[d] *In sterile water for injection.*

Compatibility Information

Solution Compatibility

Nafcillin sodium

Solution	*Mfr*	*Mfr*	*Conc/L*	*Remarks*	*Ref*	*C/I*
Alcohol 5% in dextrose 5%	AB	WY	2 and 30 g	Physically compatible and potency retained for 24 hr at 25 °C	27	C
Dextran 40 10% in dextrose 5%	PH	WY	2 and 30 g	Physically compatible and potency retained for 24 hr at 25 °C	27	C
Dextrose 5% in Ringer's injection	AB	WY	2 and 30 g	Physically compatible and potency retained for 24 hr at 25 °C	27	C
Dextrose 5% in half-strength Ringer's injection, lactated	AB	WY	2 and 30 g	Physically compatible	27	C
Dextrose 5% in Ringer's injection, lactated	AB	WY	2 and 30 g	Physically compatible	27	C
Dextrose 5% in sodium chloride 0.225%	AB	WY	2 and 30 g	Physically compatible	27	C
Dextrose 5% in sodium chloride 0.45%	AB	WY	2 and 30 g	Physically compatible and potency retained for 24 hr at 25 °C	27	C
Dextrose 5% in sodium chloride 0.9%	AB	WY	2 and 30 g	Physically compatible and potency retained for 24 hr at 25 °C	27	C
Dextrose 5% in water		WY	1 g	Potency retained for 24 hr	109	C
	AB	WY	2 and 30 g	Physically compatible and potency retained for 24 hr at 25 °C	27	C
	TR[a]	WY	20 g	Physically compatible and no loss of potency in 24 hr at room temperature	555	C
	AB[b]	WY	20 g	4% or less nafcillin loss by HPLC in 24 hr at 25 °C and in 4 days at 5 °C	1970	C
Dextrose 10% in sodium chloride 0.9%	AB	WY	2 and 30 g	Physically compatible	27	C
Dextrose 10% in water	AB	WY	2 and 30 g	Physically compatible	27	C
Ionosol T with dextrose 5%	AB	WY	2 and 30 g	Physically compatible	27	C
Normosol M in dextrose 5% in water	AB	WY	2 and 30 g	Physically compatible and potency retained for 24 hr at 25 °C	27	C
Normosol M, 900 cal	AB	WY	2 and 30 g	Physically compatible	27	C
Normosol R	AB	WY	2 and 30 g	Physically compatible	27	C
Normosol R in dextrose 5% in water	AB	WY	2 and 30 g	Physically compatible	27	C
Normosol R, pH 7.4	AB	WY	2 and 30 g	Physically compatible	27	C
Polysal M in dextrose 5% in water	CU	WY	30 g	Physically compatible and potency retained for 24 hr at 25 °C	27	C
Ringer's injection	AB	WY	2 and 30 g	Physically compatible and potency retained for 24 hr at 25 °C	27	C
Ringer's injection, lactated	AB	WY	2 and 30 g	Physically compatible and potency retained for 24 hr at 25 °C	27	C

Solution Compatibility (Cont.)

Nafcillin sodium

Solution	*Mfr*	*Mfr*	*Conc/L*	*Remarks*	*Ref*	*C/I*
Sodium chloride 0.9%		WY	1 g	Potency retained for 24 hr	109	C
	AB	WY	2 and 30 g	Physically compatible and potency retained for 24 hr at 25 °C	27	C
	AB[c]	WY	80 g	5% or less loss by HPLC with 24-hr storage at 5 °C followed by 48-hr simulated administration at 30 °C via portable pump	1779	C
	AB[b]	WY	20 g	4% or less nafcillin loss by HPLC in 24 hr at 25 °C and in 4 days at 5 °C	1970	C
Sodium lactate ⅙ M	AB	WY	2 and 30 g	Physically compatible and potency retained for 24 hr at 25 °C	27	C
TPN #107[d]			1 and 2 g	Physically compatible and nafcillin activity retained for 24 hr at 21 °C by microbiological assay	1326	C

[a]*Tested in PVC containers.*
[b]*Tested in glass containers and latex elastomeric reservoirs (Secure Medical).*
[c]*Tested in portable pump reservoirs (Pharmacia Deltec).*
[d]*Refer to Appendix I for the composition of parenteral nutrition solutions. TPN indicates a 2-in-1 admixture.*

Additive Compatibility

Nafcillin sodium

Drug	*Mfr*	*Conc/L*	*Mfr*	*Conc/L*	*Test Soln*	*Remarks*	*Ref*	*C/I*
Aminophylline	SE	500 mg	WY	30 g	D5W	Nafcillin potency retained for 24 hr at 25 °C	27	C
	SE	500 mg	WY	2 g	D5W	14% nafcillin decomposition in 24 hr at 25 °C	27	I
Ascorbic acid injection	UP	500 mg	WY	5 g	D5W	Physically incompatible	15	I
Aztreonam	SQ	20 g	BR	20 g	D5W, NS[a]	Cloudiness with a fine precipitate forms gradually. 6 to 7% aztreonam loss and 10 to 11% nafcillin loss in 24 hr at room temperature	1028	I
Bleomycin sulfate	BR	20 and 30 units	BR	2.5 g	NS	Substantial loss of bleomycin activity in 1 week at 4 °C	763	I
Chloramphenicol sodium succinate	PD	1 g	WY	500 mg		Physically compatible	27	C
Chlorothiazide sodium	MSD	500 mg	WY	500 mg		Physically compatible	27	C
Cytarabine	UP	100 mg		4 g	D5W	Heavy crystalline precipitation	174	I
Dexamethasone sodium phosphate	MSD	4 mg	WY	500 mg		Physically compatible	27	C
Diphenhydramine HCl	PD	50 mg	WY	500 mg		Physically compatible	27	C
Ephedrine sulfate		50 mg	WY	500 mg		Physically compatible	27	C
Gentamicin sulfate		75 mg		1 g	TPN #107[b]	10% gentamicin loss in 24 hr at 21 °C by microbiological assay	1326	I
Heparin sodium	AB, WY	20,000 units	WY	500 mg		Physically compatible	27	C
	AB	20,000 units	WY	500 mg		Physically compatible	21	C
Hydrocortisone sodium succinate	UP	250 mg	WY	500 mg		Precipitate forms within 1 hr	27	I

Additive Compatibility (Cont.)

Nafcillin sodium

Drug	*Mfr*	*Conc/L*	*Mfr*	*Conc/L*	*Test Soln*	*Remarks*	*Ref*	*C/I*
Hydroxyzine HCl	PF	100 mg	WY	500 mg		Physically compatible	27	C
Lidocaine HCl	AST	0.6 g	AP	20 g	D5W[a], NS[c]	Visually compatible with little or no nafcillin loss by HPLC in 48 hr at 23 °C. Lidocaine not tested	1806	C
Methylprednisolone sodium succinate	UP	125 mg	WY	500 mg	D5W	Precipitate forms	329	I
Potassium chloride	TR	40 mEq	WY	30 g	NS	Nafcillin potency retained for 24 hr at 25 °C	27	C
	AB	40 mEq	WY	500 mg		Physically compatible	27	C
Prochlorperazine edisylate	SKF	10 mg	WY	500 mg		Physically compatible	27	C
Promazine HCl	WY	100 mg	WY	500 mg		Physically compatible for only 6 hr	27	I
Sodium bicarbonate	AB	40 mEq	WY	500 mg		Physically compatible	27	C
Sodium lactate	AB	50 mEq	WY	500 mg		Physically compatible	27	C
Verapamil HCl	KN	80 mg	WY	4 g	D5W, NS	Physically compatible for 24 hr	764	C
	SE	[d]	WY	40 g	D5W, NS	Cloudy solution clears with agitation	1166	?
Vitamin B complex with C	WY	2 ml	WY	2 and 30 g	D5W	Nafcillin potency retained for 24 hr at 25 °C	27	C
	WY	2 ml	WY	2 g	NS	Nafcillin potency retained for 24 hr at 25 °C	27	C
	AB	5 ml	WY	5 g	D5W	Physically incompatible	15	I

[a]*Tested in PVC containers.*
[b]*Refer to Appendix I for the composition of parenteral nutrition solutions. TPN indicates a 2-in-1 admixture.*
[c]*Tested in polyolefin containers.*
[d]*Final concentration unspecified.*

Drugs in Syringe Compatibility

Nafcillin sodium

Drug (in syringe)	*Mfr*	*Amt*	*Mfr*	*Amt*	*Remarks*	*Ref*	*C/I*
Cimetidine HCl	SKF	300 mg/ 2 ml		1 g/5 ml	Physically compatible for 48 hr at room temperature	516	C
Heparin sodium	AB	20,000 units/ 1 ml	WY	500 mg	Physically compatible for at least 30 min	21	C

Y-Site Injection Compatibility (1:1 Mixture)

Nafcillin sodium

Drug	*Mfr*	*Conc*	*Mfr*	*Conc*	*Remarks*	*Ref*	*C/I*
Acyclovir sodium	BW	5 mg/ml[a]	WY	20 mg/ml[a]	Physically compatible for 4 hr at 25 °C	1157	C
Atropine sulfate		0.4 mg/ml	WY	33 mg/ml[b]	No precipitation	547	C
Cyclophosphamide	MJ	20 mg/ml[a]	WY	20 mg/ml[a]	Physically compatible for 4 hr at 25 °C	1194	C
Diazepam		5 mg/ml	WY	33 mg/ml[b]	No precipitation	547	C
Diltiazem HCl	MMD	5 mg/ml	WY	10 mg/ml[b]	Cloudiness forms and persists	1807	I
	MMD	5 mg/ml	WY	200 mg/ml[b]	Cloudiness forms but clears with swirling	1807	?
	MMD	1 mg/ml[b]	WY	10 and 200 mg/ml[b]	Visually compatible	1807	C

Y-Site Injection Compatibility (1:1 Mixture) (Cont.)

			Nafcillin sodium				
Drug	*Mfr*	*Conc*	*Mfr*	*Conc*	*Remarks*	*Ref*	*C/I*
Droperidol		2.5 mg/ml	WY	33 mg/ml[b]	Precipitate forms, probably free nafcillin	547	I
Enalaprilat	MSD	0.05 mg/ml[b]	BR	10 mg/ml[a]	Physically compatible for 24 hr at room temperature under fluorescent light	1355	C
Esmolol HCl	DCC	10 mg/ml[a]	BR	10 mg/ml[a]	Physically compatible for 24 hr at 22 °C	1169	C
Famotidine	MSD	0.2 mg/ml[a]	WY	15 mg/ml[b]	Physically compatible for 14 hr	1196	C
Fentanyl citrate		0.05 mg/ml	WY	33 mg/ml[b]	No precipitation	547	C
Fluconazole	RR	2 mg/ml	BR	20 mg/ml	Physically compatible for 24 hr at 25 °C	1407	C
Foscarnet sodium	AST	24 mg/ml	BR	20 mg/ml[c]	Physically compatible for 24 hr at 25 °C under fluorescent light by visual and microscopic examination	1393	C
Heparin sodium	TR	50 units/ml	WY	20 mg/ml[a]	Visually compatible for 4 hr at 25 °C	1793	C
Hydromorphone HCl	WY	0.2 mg/ml[a]	WY	20 mg/ml[a]	Physically compatible for at least 4 hr at 25 °C under fluorescent light	987	C
Insulin, regular	LI	0.2 unit/ml[b]	BA	20 and 40 mg/ml[a]	Immediate precipitation	1395	I
Labetalol HCl	SC	1 mg/ml[a]	BR	10 mg/ml[a]	Cloudiness and fine precipitate form immediately	1171	I
Magnesium sulfate	IX	16.7, 33.3, 66.7, 100 mg/ml[a]	WY	20 mg/ml[a]	Physically compatible for at least 4 hr at 32 °C	813	C
Meperidine HCl	WY	10 mg/ml[a]	WY	20 mg/ml[a]	Cloudy haze cleared on mixing and remained clear for 4 hr at 25 °C	987	C
	WY	10 mg/ml[b]	WY	20 and 30 mg/ml[a]	Cloudy solution formed immediately and persisted for at least 1 hr at 25 °C	1338	I
Midazolam HCl	RC	1 mg/ml[a]	WY	20 mg/ml[a]	Haze forms immediately. Particles form in 4 hr	1847	I
Morphine sulfate	WI	1 mg/ml[a]	WY	20 mg/ml[a]	Physically compatible for at least 4 hr at 25 °C under fluorescent light	987	C
	ES	1 mg/ml[b]	WY	30 mg/ml[a]	Physically compatible for 1 hr at 25 °C	1338	C
Nalbuphine HCl		10 mg/ml	WY	33 mg/ml[b]	Precipitate forms, probably free nafcillin	547	I
Pentazocine lactate		30 mg/ml	WY	33 mg/ml[b]	Precipitate forms, probably free nafcillin	547	I
Perphenazine	SC	0.02 mg/ml[a]	WY	20 mg/ml[a]	Physically compatible for 4 hr at 25 °C	1155	C
Propofol	ZEN	10 mg/ml	MAR	20 mg/ml[a]	Physically compatible for 1 hr at 23 °C with no increase in particle content	2066	C
Theophylline	TR	4 mg/ml	WY	20 mg/ml[a]	Visually compatible for 6 hr at 25 °C	1793	C
TNA #218 to #226[d]			BE, APC	20 mg/ml[a]	Visually compatible with no precipitate or emulsion damage apparent in 4 hr at 23 °C	2215	C
TPN #54[d]				250 mg/ml	Physically compatible and nafcillin activity retained over 6 hr at 22 °C by microbiological assay	1045	C
TPN #61[d]		[e]	WY	250 mg/1 ml[f]	Physically compatible	1012	C
		[g]	WY	1.5 g/6 ml[f]	Physically compatible	1012	C
TPN #212 to #215[d]			BE	20 mg/ml[a]	Physically compatible with no change in measured turbidity or increase in particle content in 4 hr at 23 °C	2109	C

Y-Site Injection Compatibility (1:1 Mixture) (Cont.)

Drug	Mfr	Conc	Mfr	Conc	Remarks	Ref	C/I
			Nafcillin sodium				
Vancomycin HCl	AB	20 mg/ml[a]	BE	250 mg/ml[i]	Transient precipitate forms followed by a visibly hazy solution	2189	I
	AB	20 mg/ml[a]	BE	10 and 50 mg/ml[b]	Gross white precipitate forms immediately	2189	I
	AB	20 mg/ml[a]	BE	1 mg/ml[b]	Physically compatible with no change in measured turbidity or increase in particle content in 4 hr at 23 °C	2189	C
	AB	2 mg/ml[a]	BE	10[b], 50[b], 250[i] mg/ml	Subvisual measured haze forms immediately	2189	I
	AB	2 mg/ml[a]	BE	1 mg/ml[b]	Physically compatible with no change in measured turbidity or increase in particle content in 4 hr at 23 °C	2189	C
Verapamil HCl				[h]	White milky precipitate forms immediately	840	I
	SE	2.5 mg/ml	WY	40 mg/ml[c]	White milky precipitate forms immediately and persists. 20% of verapamil precipitated	1166	I
Zidovudine	BW	4 mg/ml[a]	BR	20 mg/ml[a]	Physically compatible for 4 hr at 25 °C under fluorescent light by visual and microscopic examination	1193	C

[a]*Tested in dextrose 5% in water.*
[b]*Tested in sodium chloride 0.9%.*
[c]*Tested in both dextrose 5% in water and sodium chloride 0.9%.*
[d]*Refer to Appendix I for the composition of parenteral nutrition solutions. TNA indicates a 3-in-1 admixture, and TPN indicates a 2-in-1 admixture.*
[e]*Run at 21 ml/hr.*
[f]*Given over five minutes by syringe pump.*
[g]*Run at 94 ml/hr.*
[h]*Injected into a line being used to infuse nafcillin sodium.*
[i]*Tested in sterile water for injection.*

Additional Compatibility Information

Infusion Solutions — Nafcillin sodium (Wyeth) 500 mg/L is physically compatible with most Abbott infusion solutions. A precipitate forms within several hours when nafcillin sodium is mixed with infusion solutions containing vitamin B complex or vitamin C. (27)

It is stated that nafcillin sodium, at concentrations of 2 to 40 mg/ml, will lose less than 10% potency in 24 hours at room temperature or 96 hours under refrigeration in the following infusion solutions (4):

Dextrose 5% in sodium chloride 0.45%
Dextrose 5% in water
Ringer's injection
Sodium chloride 0.9%
Sodium lactate ⅙ M

However, individual package labeling should be consulted because manufacturers' recommended stability periods for nafcillin sodium vary. (4)

Care should be exercised when mixing nafcillin sodium (Wyeth) at concentrations of 500 mg/L or less in dextrose–polyelectrolyte solutions. These solutions have their pH adjusted to maintain dextrose stability and have a relatively high buffer capacity. Small amounts of nafcillin sodium may not have enough buffer capability to adjust the pH adequately. (27)

Peritoneal Dialysis Solutions — The activity of nafcillin 100 mg/L was evaluated in peritoneal dialysis fluids containing dextrose 1.5 or 4.25% (Dianeal 137, Travenol). Storage at 25 °C resulted in no loss of antimicrobial activity in 24 hours. (515)

The stability of nafcillin sodium (Wyeth) 100 mg/L in peritoneal dialysis solutions (Dianeal 137 and PD2) with heparin sodium 500 units/L was evaluated by microbiological assay. Approximately 98 ± 7% activity remained after 24 hours at 25 °C. (1228)

Acidic and Alkaline Drugs — Additives that may result in a final pH of above 8 or below 5 should not be mixed with nafcillin sodium. These additives include metaraminol bitartrate, succinylcholine chloride, and ascorbic acid. (22; 27)

Nafcillin sodium (Wyeth) 500 mg/L has been reported to be conditionally compatible with norepinephrine bitartrate (Winthrop) 8 mg/L. The admixture is physically compatible for 24 hours, but the pH is 5.3 and the solution should therefore be used within six hours. (27)

Aminoglycosides — Lundergan et al. studied the interaction of tobramycin sulfate with several penicillins in vitro in human serum under clinical laboratory conditions. Tobramycin sulfate 10 μg/ml was combined with carbenicillin disodium 200 μg/ml, oxacillin sodium (Bristol) 50 μg/ml, and nafcillin sodium (Wyeth) 50 μg/ml. Samples were evaluated over 72 hours at −23, 6, and 23 °C. Although results were somewhat variable, only the carbenicillin sample at 23 °C exhibited substantial decomposition after 72 hours. None of the other carbenicillin, oxacillin, and nafcillin samples showed significant differences over the study period. (814)

To determine if spurious aminoglycoside levels could result from a delay in assaying blood samples, Tindula et al. evaluated the inactivation of amikacin 35 μg/ml and gentamicin and tobramycin 10 μg/ml in human serum by 400-μg/ml concentrations of several penicillins and cephalosporins. Samples were stored for 24 hours at room temperature or frozen at −20 °C. For the room temperature samples, cefazolin and cefamandole caused relatively little inactivation. Nafcillin, cephapirin, and cefoxitin caused moderate inactivation, 20% or less. Penicillin, ampicillin, carbenicillin, and ticarcillin generally caused 25% or more inactivation of gentamicin and tobramycin. Amikacin was somewhat less affected. Freezing samples at −20 °C prevented significant inactivation of amikacin and gentamicin by any of the drugs. Freezing the tobramycin samples was satisfactory for most of the drugs except penicillin, ampicillin, and carbenicillin, which still exhibited a 15 to 20% loss in 24 hours. (824)

The clinical significance of these interactions in patients appears to be confined primarily to those with renal failure. (218; 334; 361; 364; 616; 847) Literature reports of greatly reduced aminoglycoside levels in such patients have appeared frequently. (363; 365–367; 614; 615; 962) In addition, the interaction may be clinically important if assays for aminoglycoside levels in serum are sufficiently delayed. (517; 618; 824; 832; 847; 1052)

Vancomycin — The compatibility or incompatibility of vancomycin HCl mixed with or administered simultaneously with nafcillin sodium is concentration dependent. (2189) See Y-Site Compatibility above. Vancomycin HCl has a low pH and is variably compatible with drugs having neutral to mildly alkaline pH, including cephalosporins and penicillins. The compatibility may depend on a number of factors, including concentration of each drug, dilution vehicle, actual pH of solutions, and completeness of mixing during administration. Combinations that are compatible when well mixed may result in precipitation if only partially mixed, presumably due to regionally different concentrations and pH values. If attempting to administer vancomycin HCl with nafcillin sodium, take care to ensure that the specific combination and the concentrations are compatible under the exact administration conditions to be used. An inline filter should be used as a final safety measure. (2189)

Verapamil — A milky white precipitate formed immediately when verapamil HCl was given by intravenous push into an infusion line being used for nafcillin sodium. (840)

NALBUPHINE HCL
AHFS 28:08.12

Products — Nalbuphine HCl is available as a 10-mg/ml concentration in 1-ml ampuls and 10-ml vials and as a 20-mg/ml concentration in 1-ml ampuls and 10-ml vials. Each milliliter of solution in vials contains (2):

Nalbuphine HCl	10 mg	20 mg
Sodium chloride	0.2%	
Sodium citrate hydrous	0.94%	0.94%
Citric acid anhydrous	1.26%	1.26%
Methyl- and propylparabens (9:1)	0.2%	0.2%
Hydrochloric acid	to adjust pH	to adjust pH

Nalbuphine HCl in ampuls is provided without the parabens. (2)

pH — The pH is adjusted to 3.5 to 3.7. (2; 4)

Osmolality — Nalbuphine HCl (Abbott) 10 mg/ml has an osmolality of 290 mOsm/kg. (2043)

Trade Name(s) — Nubain.

Administration — Nalbuphine HCl is administered by subcutaneous, intramuscular, or intravenous injection. (2; 4)

Stability — Intact vials and ampuls should be protected from excessive light and stored at 15 to 30 °C. (2; 4)

Central Venous Catheter — Nalbuphine HCl (Astra) 1 mg/ml in dextrose 5% in water was found to be compatible with the ARROWg+ard Blue Plus (Arrow International) chlorhexidine-bearing triple-lumen central catheter. HPLC analysis was used to evaluate completeness of drug delivery through the catheter and the amount of chlorhexidine removed from the internal lumens. Essentially complete delivery of the drug was found with little or no drug loss occurring. Furthermore, chlorhexidine delivered from the catheter remained at trace amounts with no substantial increase due to the delivery of the drug through the catheter. (2335)

Compatibility Information

Drugs in Syringe Compatibility

Nalbuphine HCl

Drug (in syringe)	*Mfr*	*Amt*	*Mfr*	*Amt*	*Remarks*	*Ref*	*C/I*
Atropine sulfate	WY	0.2 mg	EN	10 mg/ 1 ml	Physically compatible for 36 hr at 27 °C	762	C
	WY	0.2 mg	EN	5 mg/ 0.5 ml	Physically compatible for 36 hr at 27 °C	762	C

Drugs in Syringe Compatibility (Cont.)

Nalbuphine HCl

Drug (in syringe)	*Mfr*	*Amt*	*Mfr*	*Amt*	*Remarks*	*Ref*	*C/I*
	WY	0.5 mg	EN	10 mg/ 1 ml	Physically compatible for 36 hr at 27 °C	762	C
	WY	0.5 mg	EN	5 mg/ 0.5 ml	Physically compatible for 36 hr at 27 °C	762	C
		0.4 and 1 mg	DU	10 mg/ 1 ml	Physically compatible for 48 hr	128	C
		0.4 and 1 mg	DU	20 mg/ 1 ml	Physically compatible for 48 hr	128	C
Cimetidine HCl	SKF	300 mg/ 2 ml	EN	10 mg/ 1 ml	Physically compatible for 4 hr at 25 °C	25	C
		300 mg/ 2 ml	DU	10 mg/ 1 ml	Physically compatible for 48 hr	128	C
		300 mg/ 2 ml	DU	20 mg/ 1 ml	Physically compatible for 48 hr	128	C
Diazepam	RC	5 mg/ 1 ml	EN	10 mg/ 1 ml	Immediate white milky precipitate that persists for 36 hr at 27 °C	762	I
	RC	5 mg/ 1 ml	EN	5 mg/ 0.5 ml	Immediate white milky precipitate that clears upon vigorous shaking. Remains clear for 36 hr at 27 °C	762	I
	RC	5 mg/ 1 ml	EN	2.5 mg/ 0.25 ml	Immediate white milky precipitate that clears upon vigorous shaking. Remains clear for 36 hr at 27 °C	762	I
	RC	10 mg/ 2 ml	DU	10 mg/ 1 ml	Physically incompatible	128	I
	RC	10 mg/ 2 ml	DU	20 mg/ 1 ml	Physically incompatible	128	I
Dimenhydrinate	HR	50 mg/ 1 ml	EN	10 mg/ 1 ml	Physically incompatible	711	I
	HR	50 mg/ 1 ml	EN	20 mg/ 1 ml	Physically incompatible	711	I
Diphenhydramine HCl	PD	50 mg/ 1 ml	DU	10 mg/ 1 ml	Physically compatible for 48 hr	128	C
	PD	50 mg/ 1 ml	DU	20 mg/ 1 ml	Physically compatible for 48 hr	128	C
Droperidol	JN	5 mg/ 2 ml	EN	5 mg/ 0.5 ml	Physically compatible for 36 hr at 27 °C	762	C
	JN	2.5 mg/ 1 ml	EN	10 mg/ 1 ml	Physically compatible for 36 hr at 27 °C	762	C
	JN	2.5 mg/ 1 ml	EN	5 mg/ 0.5 ml	Physically compatible for 36 hr at 27 °C	762	C
	JN	5 mg/ 2 ml	DU	10 mg/ 1 ml	Physically compatible for 48 hr	128	C
	JN	5 mg/ 2 ml	DU	20 mg/ 1 ml	Physically compatible for 48 hr	128	C
Glycopyrrolate	RB	0.2 mg/ 1 ml	DU	10 mg/ 1 ml	Physically compatible for 48 hr	128	C
	RB	0.2 mg/ 1 ml	DU	20 mg/ 1 ml	Physically compatible for 48 hr	128	C
Hydroxyzine HCl	PF	50 mg	EN	10 mg/ 1 ml	Physically compatible for 36 hr at 27 °C	762	C
	PF	50 mg	EN	5 mg/ 0.5 ml	Physically compatible for 36 hr at 27 °C	762	C

Drugs in Syringe Compatibility (Cont.)

Nalbuphine HCl

Drug (in syringe)	*Mfr*	*Amt*	*Mfr*	*Amt*	*Remarks*	*Ref*	*C/I*
	PF	50 mg	EN	2.5 mg/ 0.25 ml	Physically compatible for 36 hr at 27 °C	762	C
	PF	25 mg/ 1 ml	DU	10 mg/ 1 ml	Physically compatible for 48 hr	128	C
	PF	25 mg/ 1 ml	DU	20 mg/ 1 ml	Physically compatible for 48 hr	128	C
Ketorolac tromethamine	SY	180 mg/ 6 ml	DU	30 mg/ 3 ml	White solid precipitate forms immediately and settles to bottom	1703	I
Lidocaine HCl		40 mg	DU	10 mg/ 1 ml	Physically compatible for 48 hr	128	C
		40 mg	DU	20 mg/ 1 ml	Physically compatible for 48 hr	128	C
Midazolam HCl	RC	5 mg/ 1 ml	DU	10 mg/ 1 ml	Physically compatible for 4 hr at 25 °C under fluorescent light	1145	C
Pentobarbital sodium	WY	50 mg/ 1 ml	EN	10 mg/ 1 ml	Immediate white milky precipitate that persists for 36 hr at 27 °C	762	I
	WY	50 mg/ 1 ml	EN	2.5 mg/ 0.25 ml	Immediate white milky precipitate that clears upon vigorous shaking	762	I
	WY	50 mg/ 1 ml	EN	5 mg/ 0.5 ml	Immediate white milky precipitate that persists for 36 hr at 27 °C	762	I
Prochlorperazine edisylate	WY	5 mg/ 1 ml	EN	10 mg/ 1 ml	Physically compatible for 36 hr at 27 °C	762	C
	WY	5 mg/ 1 ml	EN	5 mg/ 0.5 ml	Physically compatible for 36 hr at 27 °C	762	C
	WY	5 mg/ 1 ml	EN	2.5 mg/ 0.25 ml	Physically compatible for 36 hr at 27 °C	762	C
	SKF	10 mg/ 2 ml	DU	10 mg/ 1 ml	Physically compatible for 48 hr	128	C
	SKF	10 mg/ 2 ml	DU	20 mg/ 1 ml	Physically compatible for 48 hr	128	C
Promethazine HCl	ES	25 mg	EN	10 mg/ 1 ml	Physically compatible for 36 hr at 27 °C	762	C
	ES	25 mg	EN	5 mg/ 0.5 ml	Physically compatible for 36 hr at 27 °C	762	C
	ES	12.5 mg	EN	10 mg/ 1 ml	Physically compatible for 36 hr at 27 °C	762	C
	WY	25 and 50 mg	DU	10 mg/ 1 ml	Physically incompatible	128	I
	WY	25 and 50 mg	DU	20 mg/ 1 ml	Physically incompatible	128	I
	WY	25 mg/ 1 ml	DU	10 mg/ 1 ml	White flocculent precipitate forms immediately	1184	I
	ES	25 mg/ 1 ml	DU	10 mg/ 1 ml	Physically compatible for 24 hr at room temperature	1184	C
Ranitidine HCl	GL	50 mg/ 2 ml	EN	10 mg/ 1 ml	Physically compatible for 1 hr at 25 °C both macroscopically and microscopically	978	C
Scopolamine HBr	BW	0.86 mg/ 1 ml	EN	10 mg/ 1 ml	Physically compatible for 36 hr at 27 °C	762	C
	BW	0.86 mg/ 1 ml	EN	5 mg/ 0.5 ml	Physically compatible for 36 hr at 27 °C	762	C
	BW	0.43 mg/ 0.5 ml	EN	10 mg/ 1 ml	Physically compatible for 36 hr at 27 °C	762	C

Drugs in Syringe Compatibility (Cont.)

Nalbuphine HCl

Drug (in syringe)	*Mfr*	*Amt*	*Mfr*	*Amt*	*Remarks*	*Ref*	*C/I*
		0.4 mg	DU	10 mg/ 1 ml	Physically compatible for 48 hr	128	C
		0.4 mg	DU	20 mg/ 1 ml	Physically compatible for 48 hr	128	C
Thiethylperazine malate	BI	5 mg/ 1 ml	EN	10 mg/ 1 ml	Physically compatible for 36 hr at 27 °C	762	C
	BI	5 mg/ 1 ml	EN	5 mg/ 0.5 ml	Crystals form in 24 hr at 27 °C. Physically compatible for at least 12 hr	762	I
	BI	5 mg/ 1 ml	EN	2.5 mg/ 0.25 ml	Crystals form in 24 hr at 27 °C. Physically compatible for at least 12 hr	762	I
		10 mg/ 2 ml	DU	10 mg/ 1 ml	Physically compatible for 48 hr	128	C
		10 mg/ 2 ml	DU	20 mg/ 1 ml	Physically compatible for 48 hr	128	C
Trimethobenzamide HCl	BE	100 mg/ 1 ml	EN	10 mg/ 1 ml	Physically compatible for 36 hr at 27 °C	762	C
	BE	100 mg/ 1 ml	EN	5 mg/ 0.5 ml	Physically compatible for 36 hr at 27 °C	762	C
	BE	100 mg/ 1 ml	EN	2.5 mg/ 0.25 ml	Physically compatible for 36 hr at 27 °C	762	C
		200 mg/ 2 ml	DU	10 mg/ 1 ml	Physically compatible for 48 hr	128	C
		200 mg/ 2 ml	DU	20 mg/ 1 ml	Physically compatible for 48 hr	128	C

Y-Site Injection Compatibility (1:1 Mixture)

Nalbuphine HCl

Drug	*Mfr*	*Conc*	*Mfr*	*Conc*	*Remarks*	*Ref*	*C/I*
Allopurinol sodium	BW	3 mg/ml[b]	DU	10 mg/ml	Tiny particles form in 1 hr, becoming numerous crystals in 4 hr	1686	I
Amifostine	USB	10 mg/ml[a]	AST	10 mg/ml	Physically compatible with no change in measured turbidity or increase in particle content in 4 hr at 23 °C	1845	C
Amphotericin B cholesteryl sulfate complex	SEQ	0.83 mg/ml[a]	AST	10 mg/ml	Gross precipitate forms	2117	I
Aztreonam	SQ	40 mg/ml[a]	AST	10 mg/ml	Physically compatible with no subvisual haze or particle formation in 4 hr at 23 °C	1758	C
Cefepime HCl	BMS	20 mg/ml[a]	DU	10 mg/ml	Haze forms immediately and becomes flocculent precipitate in 4 hr	1689	I
Cisatracurium besylate	GW	0.1, 2, 5 mg/ ml[a]	AST	10 mg/ml	Physically compatible with no change in measured turbidity or increase in particle content in 4 hr at 23 °C	2074	C
Cladribine	ORT	0.015[b] and 0.5[c] mg/ml	AST	10 mg/ml	Physically compatible with no change in measured turbidity or increase in particle content in 4 hr at 23 °C	1969	C
Docetaxel	RPR	0.9 mg/ml[a]	AST	10 mg/ml	Increase in measured subvisual turbidity occurs immediately	2224	I

Y-Site Injection Compatibility (1:1 Mixture) (Cont.)

			Nalbuphine HCl				
Drug	*Mfr*	*Conc*	*Mfr*	*Conc*	*Remarks*	*Ref*	*C/I*
Etoposide phosphate	BR	5 mg/ml[a]	AST	10 mg/ml	Physically compatible with no change in measured turbidity or increase in particle content in 4 hr at 23 °C	2218	C
Filgrastim	AMG	30 μg/ml[a]	DU	10 mg/ml	Physically compatible with no change in measured turbidity or increase in particle content in 4 hr at 22 °C	1687	C
Fludarabine phosphate	BX	1 mg/ml[a]	DU	10 mg/ml	Physically compatible for 4 hr at room temperature under fluorescent light	1439	C
Gatifloxacin	BMS	2 mg/ml[a]	AST	10 mg/ml	Physically compatible with no change in measured haze or increase in particle content in 4 hr at 23 °C	2234	C
Gemcitabine HCl	LI	10 mg/ml[b]	AST	10 mg/ml	Physically compatible with no change in measured turbidity or increase in particle content in 4 hr at 23 °C	2226	C
Granisetron HCl	SKB	0.05 mg/ml[a]	AB	10 mg/ml	Physically compatible with no change in measured turbidity or increase in particle content in 4 hr at 23 °C	2000	C
Hetastarch in lactated electrolyte injection (Hextend)	AB	6%	AST	10 mg/ml	Physically compatible with no change in measured turbidity or increase in particle content in 4 hr at 23 °C	2339	C
Linezolid	PHU	2 mg/ml	AST	10 mg/ml	Physically compatible with no change in measured turbidity or increase in particle content in 4 hr at 23 °C	2264	C
Melphalan HCl	BW	0.1 mg/ml[b]	AST	10 mg/ml	Physically compatible with no change in measured turbidity or increase in particle content in 3 hr at 22 °C	1557	C
Methotrexate sodium		30 mg/ml	DU	10 mg/ml	Heavy yellow precipitate forms immediately	1788	I
Nafcillin sodium	WY	33 mg/ml[b]		10 mg/ml	Precipitate forms, probably free nafcillin	547	I
Paclitaxel	NCI	1.2 mg/ml[a]	AST	10 mg/ml	Physically compatible with no change in measured turbidity in 4 hr at 22 °C	1556	C
Piperacillin sodium–tazobactam sodium	LE	40 + 5 mg/ml[a]	DU	10 mg/ml	Heavy white turbidity forms immediately and particles form in 4 hr	1688	I
Propofol	ZEN	10 mg/ml	AB	10 mg/ml	Physically compatible for 1 hr at 23 °C with no increase in particle content	2066	C
Remifentanil HCl	GW	0.025 and 0.25 mg/ml[b]	AST	10 mg/ml	Physically compatible with no change in measured turbidity or increase in particle content in 4 hr at 23 °C	2075	C
Sargramostim	IMM	10 μg/ml[b]	DU	10 mg/ml	Slight haze, visible with high intensity light, formed in 30 min. Filament formed in 4 hr in one of two samples	1436	I
Sodium bicarbonate		1.4%	DU	10 mg/ml	Gas evolves	1788	I
Teniposide	BR	0.1 mg/ml[a]	DU	10 mg/ml	Physically compatible with no subvisual haze or particle formation in 4 hr at 23 °C	1725	C
Thiotepa	IMM[d]	1 mg/ml[a]	AST	10 mg/ml	Physically compatible with no change in measured turbidity or increase in particle content in 4 hr at 23 °C	1861	C

Y-Site Injection Compatibility (1:1 Mixture) (Cont.)

Nalbuphine HCl

Drug	*Mfr*	*Conc*	*Mfr*	*Conc*	*Remarks*	*Ref*	*C/I*
TNA #218 to #226[e]			AB, AST	10 mg/ml	Damage to emulsion integrity occurs immediately with free oil formation possible	2215	I
TPN #212 to #215[e]			AB	10 mg/ml	Physically compatible with no change in measured turbidity or increase in particle content in 4 hr at 23 °C	2109	C
Vinorelbine tartrate	BW	1 mg/ml[b]	AST	10 mg/ml	Physically compatible with no change in measured turbidity or increase in particle content in 4 hr at 22 °C	1558	C

[a] *Tested in dextrose 5% in water.*
[b] *Tested in sodium chloride 0.9%.*
[c] *Tested in bacteriostatic sodium chloride 0.9% preserved with benzyl alcohol 0.9%.*
[d] *Lyophilized formulation tested.*
[e] *Refer to Appendix I for the composition of parenteral nutrition solutions. TNA indicates a 3-in-1 admixture, and TPN indicates a 2-in-1 admixture.*

Additional Compatibility Information

Infusion Solutions — Nalbuphine HCl (DuPont) 10 and 20 mg/ml was physically compatible for 48 hours when diluted in 1:1 and 1:2 ratios with the following diluents (128):

Dextrose 5% in sodium chloride 0.9%
Dextrose 10% in water
Ringer's injection, lactated
Sodium chloride 0.9%

Promethazine — The compatibility of nalbuphine HCl with promethazine HCl appears to be conditional on the specific formulation of promethazine HCl being used. When Elkins-Sinn promethazine HCl is combined with nalbuphine HCl, the admixture is compatible. However, if the Wyeth promethazine HCl is combined, a precipitate forms immediately. (128; 762; 1183)

NALMEFENE HCL
AHFS 28:10

Products — Nalmefene HCl is available as 100 μg/ml (of nalmefene) in 1-ml ampuls and as 1 mg/ml (of nalmefene) in 2-ml ampuls. Both concentrations also contain sodium chloride 9 mg/ml and hydrochloric acid to adjust the pH. (1-4/95)

pH — Adjusted to pH 3.9. (1-4/95)

Osmolality — Nalmefene HCl injections are made nearly isotonic by the presence of sodium chloride 9 mg/ml. (2134)

Trade Name(s) — Revex.

Administration — Nalmefene HCl injection may be administered by subcutaneous, intramuscular, or intravenous injection. (4)

Stability — Intact containers of nalmefene HCl should be stored at controlled room temperature. (1-4/95)

Nalmefene HCl has been determined to be stable in solution, with significant decomposition occurring only at elevated temperatures. For solutions containing 0.1 or 1 mg/ml, essentially no decomposition occurred when stored at 4 °C, and very little loss occurred after 35 months stored at 30 °C. Significant losses were found if either concentration was stored exposed to temperatures of 40 °C and above. In addition, the decomposition product of nalmefene HCl is less toxic than nalmefene itself. (2134)

Compatibility Information

Solution Compatibility

Nalmefene HCl

Solution	*Mfr*	*Mfr*	*Conc/L*	*Remarks*	*Ref*	*C/I*
Dextrose 5% in Ringer's injection, lactated	AB[a]	OHM	10 mg	Little or no loss by HPLC in 72 hr at 4, 21, and 40 °C	1962	C
Dextrose 5% in sodium chloride 0.45%	AB[a]	OHM	10 mg	Little or no loss by HPLC in 72 hr at 4, 21, and 40 °C	1962	C
Dextrose 5% in water	AB[a]	OHM	10 mg	Little or no loss by HPLC in 72 hr at 4, 21, and 40 °C	1962	C
Ringer's injection, lactated	AB[a]	OHM	10 mg	Little or no loss by HPLC in 72 hr at 4, 21, and 40 °C	1962	C
Sodium bicarbonate 5%	AB[a]	OHM	10 mg	Little or no loss by HPLC in 72 hr at 4, 21, and 40 °C	1962	C
Sodium chloride 0.45%	AB[a]	OHM	10 mg	Little or no loss by HPLC in 72 hr at 4, 21, and 40 °C	1962	C
Sodium chloride 0.9%	AB[a]	OHM	10 mg	Little or no loss by HPLC in 72 hr at 4, 21, and 40 °C	1962	C

[a]*Tested in glass containers.*

NALOXONE HCL
AHFS 28:10

Products — Naloxone HCl is available in the following formulations (2):

Component	Preserved (mg/ml)		Paraben-Free (mg/ml)		
Naloxone HCl	1	0.4	1	0.4	0.02
Sodium chloride	8.35	8.6	9	9	9
Methyl- and propylparabens (9:1)	2	2			
Sizes (ml)	10	10	2	1	2

pH — The pH is adjusted to 3 to 4 with hydrochloric acid. (2)

Osmolality — The osmolality of the 0.02-mg/ml concentration was determined to be 293 mOsm/kg by freezing-point depression and 289 mOsm/kg by vapor pressure. (1071)

The osmolality of naloxone HCl 0.4 mg/ml was determined to be 301 mOsm/kg. (1233)

Trade Name(s) — Narcan.

Administration — Naloxone HCl may be administered by subcutaneous, intramuscular, or intravenous injection or by continuous intravenous infusion. Solutions for continuous intravenous infusion may be prepared as 2 mg/500 ml (4 µg/ml) of sodium chloride 0.9% or dextrose 5% in water. (2; 4)

Stability — Naloxone HCl should be stored at room temperature and protected from excessive light. It is stable at pH 2.5 to 5. It should not be mixed with any alkaline solutions. Naloxone HCl solutions diluted in infusion solutions for administration should be discarded after 24 hours. (2; 4)

Syringes — Naloxone HCl (Astra) 0.133 mg/ml in sodium chloride 0.9% packaged in polypropylene syringes (Sherwood) was physically stable and exhibited little or no loss by stability-indicating HPLC analysis in 24 hours stored at 4 and 23 °C. (2199)

Compatibility Information

Additive Compatibility

Naloxone HCl

Drug	Mfr	Conc/L	Mfr	Conc/L	Test Soln	Remarks	Ref	C/I
Verapamil HCl	KN	80 mg	EN	0.8 mg	D5W, NS	Physically compatible for 24 hr	764	C

Drugs in Syringe Compatibility

Naloxone HCl

Drug (in syringe)	Mfr	Amt	Mfr	Amt	Remarks	Ref	C/I
Heparin sodium		2500 units/ 1 ml	DU	0.4 mg/ 1 ml	Physically compatible for at least 5 min	1053	C
Ondansetron HCl	GW	1.33 mg/ ml[a]	AST	0.133 mg/ml[a]	Physically compatible with no measured increase in particulates and 6% or less loss of ondansetron and 5% or less loss of naloxone by HPLC in 24 hr at 4 or 23 °C	2199	C

[a]*Tested in sodium chloride 0.9%.*

Y-Site Injection Compatibility (1:1 Mixture)

Naloxone HCl

Drug	Mfr	Conc	Mfr	Conc	Remarks	Ref	C/I
Amphotericin B cholesteryl sulfate complex	SEQ	0.83 mg/ml[a]	AST	0.4 mg/ml	Gross precipitate forms	2117	I
Gatifloxacin	BMS	2 mg/ml[a]	AST	0.4 mg/ml	Physically compatible with no change in measured haze or increase in particle content in 4 hr at 23 °C	2234	C
Linezolid	PHU	2 mg/ml	DU	0.4 mg/ml	Physically compatible with no change in measured turbidity or increase in particle content in 4 hr at 23 °C	2264	C
Propofol	ZEN	10 mg/ml	AST	0.4 mg/ml	Physically compatible for 1 hr at 23 °C with no increase in particle content	2066	C

[a]*Tested in dextrose 5% in water.*

Additional Compatibility Information

Infusion Solutions — Sterile water for injection is recommended as a diluent for naloxone HCl. For intravenous infusion, dextrose 5% in water and sodium chloride 0.9% are recommended as vehicles. (2; 4)

Other Drugs — It has been stated that naloxone HCl should not be mixed with bisulfite, sulfite, or long-chain or high molecular weight anions or any solution with an alkaline pH. (2; 4)

NEOSTIGMINE METHYLSULFATE
AHFS 12:04

Products — Neostigmine methylsulfate is available in a concentration of 1:2000 and 1:4000 in 1-ml ampuls and in concentrations of 1:1000 and 1:2000 in 10-ml multiple-dose vials. Each milliliter of these products contains (2):

Ampuls	1:2000	1:4000
Neostigmine methylsulfate	0.5 mg	0.25 mg
Methyl- and propylparabens	0.2%	0.2%

Vials	1:1000	1:2000
Neostigmine methylsulfate	1 mg	0.5 mg
Phenol	0.45%	0.45%
Sodium acetate	0.2 mg	0.2 mg

In addition, these products contain sodium hydroxide (ampuls) or acetic acid and sodium hydroxide (vials) to adjust the pH. (2)

pH — The pH is adjusted to approximately 5.9. (2)

Osmolality — The osmolality of neostigmine (salt form unspecified) 0.5 mg/ml was determined to be 251 mOsm/kg. (1233)

Trade Name(s) — Prostigmin.

Administration — Neostigmine methylsulfate may be administered intramuscularly, subcutaneously, or slowly intravenously. (2; 4)

Stability — Neostigmine methylsulfate in intact containers should be stored at controlled room temperature and protected from light, freezing, and temperatures of 40 °C or more. (4)

Syringes — The stability of neostigmine (salt form unspecified) 0.5 mg/ml repackaged in polypropylene syringes was evaluated by spectrophotometric and potentiometric methods. Little or no change in concentration was found after four weeks of storage at room temperature not exposed to direct light. (2164)

Neostigmine methylsulfate (Elkins-Sinn) 0.167 mg/ml in sodium chloride 0.9% packaged in polypropylene syringes (Sherwood) was physically stable and exhibited no loss by stability-indicating HPLC analysis in 24 hours stored at 4 and 23 °C. (2199)

Compatibility Information

Additive Compatibility

Neostigmine methylsulfate

Drug	*Mfr*	*Conc/L*	*Mfr*	*Conc/L*	*Test Soln*	*Remarks*	*Ref*	*C/I*
Netilmicin sulfate	SC	3 g	RC	40 mg	D5S	Physically compatible and netilmicin chemically stable for 3 days at 4 and 25 °C. Neostigmine not tested	558	C

Drugs in Syringe Compatibility

Neostigmine methylsulfate

Drug (in syringe)	*Mfr*	*Amt*	*Mfr*	*Amt*	*Remarks*	*Ref*	*C/I*
Glycopyrrolate	RB	0.2 mg/ 1 ml	RC	0.5 mg/ 1 ml	Physically compatible and pH in stability range for glycopyrrolate for 48 hr at 25 °C	331	C
	RB	0.2 mg/ 1 ml	RC	1 mg/ 2 ml	Physically compatible and pH in stability range for glycopyrrolate for 48 hr at 25 °C	331	C
	RB	0.4 mg/ 2 ml	RC	0.5 mg/ 1 ml	Physically compatible and pH in stability range for glycopyrrolate for 48 hr at 25 °C	331	C
Heparin sodium		2500 units/ 1 ml	RC	0.5 mg/ 1 ml	Physically compatible for at least 5 min	1053	C
Ondansetron HCl	GW	1.33 mg/ ml[a]	ES	0.167 mg/ml[a]	Physically compatible with no measured increase in particulates and less than 3% loss of ondansetron and less than 5% loss of neostigmine by HPLC in 24 hr at 4 or 23 °C	2199	C
Pentobarbital sodium	AB	500 mg/ 10 ml	RC	0.5 mg/ 1 ml	Physically compatible	55	C
Thiopental sodium	AB	75 mg/ 3 ml	RC	0.5 mg/ 1 ml	Physically compatible	55	C

[a]*Tested in sodium chloride 0.9%.*

Y-Site Injection Compatibility (1:1 Mixture)

Neostigmine methylsulfate

Drug	*Mfr*	*Conc*	*Mfr*	*Conc*	*Remarks*	*Ref*	*C/I*
Heparin sodium	UP	1000 units/L[a]	RC	0.5 mg/ml	Physically compatible for at least 4 hr at room temperature by visual and microscopic examination	534	C
Hydrocortisone sodium succinate	UP	10 mg/L[a]	RC	0.5 mg/ml	Physically compatible for at least 4 hr at room temperature by visual and microscopic examination	534	C
Potassium chloride	AB	40 mEq/L[a]	RC	0.5 mg/ml	Physically compatible for at least 4 hr at room temperature by visual and microscopic examination	534	C
Vitamin B complex with C	RC	2 ml/L[a]	RC	0.5 mg/ml	Physically compatible for at least 4 hr at room temperature by visual and microscopic examination	534	C

[a]*Tested in dextrose 5% in Ringer's injection, dextrose 5% in Ringer's injection, lactated, dextrose 5% in water, Ringer's injection, lactated, and sodium chloride 0.9%.*

NICARDIPINE HCL
AHFS 24:04

Products — Nicardipine HCl is available as a 2.5-mg/ml concentrate in 10-ml ampuls. Each milliliter also contains sorbitol 48 mg, citric acid monohydrate 0.525 mg, and sodium hydroxide 0.09 mg in water for injection. Additional citric acid and/or sodium hydroxide may have been added to adjust solution pH. (2)

pH — Buffered to pH 3.5. (2)

Trade Name(s) — Cardene I.V.

Administration — Nicardipine HCl must be diluted for use. It is administered as a slow continuous intravenous infusion at a concentration of 0.1 mg/ml. The infusion is prepared by adding 10 ml of nicardipine HCl (25 mg) to 240 ml of compatible infusion solution, making 250 ml of a 0.1-mg/ml solution. If nicardipine HCl is administered via a peripheral vein, the infusion site should be changed every 12 hours to avoid venous irritation. (2; 4)

Stability — Intact ampuls of the clear, yellow solution should be stored at controlled room temperature and protected from light. Freezing does not adversely affect the product, but exposure to elevated temperatures should be avoided. (2)

Light Effects — Deliberate exposure of a 0.1-mg/ml nicardipine HCl solution to daylight resulted in about 8% loss in seven hours and 21% loss in 14 hours by HPLC analysis. The authors recommended that protection from light be considered for pharmaceutical dosage forms. (2193)

Compatibility Information

Y-Site Injection Compatibility (1:1 Mixture)

Nicardipine HCl

Drug	*Mfr*	*Conc*	*Mfr*	*Conc*	*Remarks*	*Ref*	*C/I*
Diltiazem HCl	MMD	1 mg/ml[a]	WY	1 mg/ml[a]	Visually compatible for 4 hr at 27 °C	2062	C
Dobutamine HCl	LI	4 mg/ml[a]	WY	1 mg/ml[a]	Visually compatible for 4 hr at 27 °C	2062	C
Dopamine HCl	AB	3.2 mg/ml[a]	WY	1 mg/ml[a]	Visually compatible for 4 hr at 27 °C	2062	C
Epinephrine HCl	AB	0.02 mg/ml[a]	WY	1 mg/ml[a]	Visually compatible for 4 hr at 27 °C	2062	C
Fentanyl citrate	ES	0.05 mg/ml	WY	1 mg/ml[a]	Visually compatible for 4 hr at 27 °C	2062	C
Furosemide	AMR	10 mg/ml	WY	1 mg/ml[a]	Precipitate forms immediately	2062	I
Gatifloxacin	BMS	2 mg/ml[a]	WY	1 mg/ml[a]	Physically compatible with no change in measured haze or increase in particle content in 4 hr at 23 °C	2234	C

Y-Site Injection Compatibility (1:1 Mixture) (Cont.)

			Nicardipine HCl				
Drug	*Mfr*	*Conc*	*Mfr*	*Conc*	*Remarks*	*Ref*	*C/I*
Heparin sodium	ES	100 units/ml[a]	WY	1 mg/ml[a]	Precipitate forms immediately	2062	I
Hydromorphone HCl	KN	1 mg/ml	WY	1 mg/ml[a]	Visually compatible for 4 hr at 27 °C	2062	C
Labetalol HCl	AH	2 mg/ml[a]	WY	1 mg/ml[a]	Visually compatible for 4 hr at 27 °C	2062	C
Linezolid	PHU	2 mg/ml	WAY	1 mg/ml[a]	Physically compatible with no change in measured turbidity or increase in particle content in 4 hr at 23 °C	2264	C
Lorazepam	WY	0.5 mg/ml[a]	WY	1 mg/ml[a]	Visually compatible for 4 hr at 27 °C	2062	C
Midazolam HCl	RC	2 mg/ml[a]	WY	1 mg/ml[a]	Visually compatible for 4 hr at 27 °C	2062	C
Milrinone lactate	SW	0.2 mg/ml[a]	WY	1 mg/ml[a]	Visually compatible for 4 hr at 27 °C	2062	C
Morphine sulfate	SCN	2 mg/ml[a]	WY	1 mg/ml[a]	Visually compatible for 4 hr at 27 °C	2062	C
Nitroglycerin	AB	0.4 mg/ml[a]	WY	1 mg/ml[a]	Visually compatible for 4 hr at 27 °C	2062	C
Norepinephrine bitartrate	AB	0.128 mg/ml[a]	WY	1 mg/ml[a]	Visually compatible for 4 hr at 27 °C	2062	C
Ranitidine HCl	GL	1 mg/ml[a]	WY	1 mg/ml[a]	Visually compatible for 4 hr at 27 °C	2062	C
Thiopental sodium	AB	25 mg/ml[b]	WY	1 mg/ml[a]	Precipitate forms immediately	2062	I
Vecuronium bromide	OR	1 mg/ml	WY	1 mg/ml[a]	Visually compatible for 4 hr at 27 °C	2062	C

[a]*Tested in dextrose 5% in water.*
[b]*Tested in sterile water for injection.*

Additional Compatibility Information

Infusion Solutions — The manufacturer states that nicardipine HCl is stable for 24 hours at room temperature diluted to a 0.1-mg/ml concentration in glass and PVC containers in the following infusion solutions (2):

Dextrose 5% with potassium chloride 40 mEq
Dextrose 5% in sodium chloride 0.45%
Dextrose 5% in sodium chloride 0.9%
Dextrose 5% in water
Sodium chloride 0.45%
Sodium chloride 0.9%

Nicardipine HCl is incompatible with Ringer's injection, lactated, and sodium bicarbonate 5%. (2)

NITROGLYCERIN
AHFS 24:12

Products — Nitroglycerin injection is available in a 5-mg/ml concentration in 5- and 10-ml vials. The product also contains ethanol 30% and propylene glycol 30% in water for injection. The pH may have been adjusted during manufacture with sodium hydroxide and/or hydrochloric acid. Nitroglycerin injection must be diluted before use. (1-6/99; 4)

Nitroglycerin is available premixed in dextrose 5% in water at concentrations of 100, 200, and 400 μg/ml in 250- and 500-ml containers. The premixed infusions also contain propylene glycol and ethanol. The Baxter premixed infusion also contains citric acid as a buffer and sodium hydroxide and hydrochloric acid, if necessary, to adjust the pH during manufacturing. (1-1/00; 4)

pH — The concentrate for injection has a pH of 3 to 6.5. (1-6/99; 4) The Baxter premixed infusion solution has a pH of 4 (range 3 to 5). (1-1/00)

Osmolarity — The osmolarities of the nitroglycerin premixed infusions solutions in dextrose 5% in water vary by manufacturer but are all within the normal range for infusions (1-3/95; 1-1/00):

Nitroglycerin Concentration	Osmolarity (mOsm/L) Abbott	Baxter
100 μg/ml	264	428
200 μg/ml	277	440
400 μg/ml	301	465

Administration — Nitroglycerin injection is administered by intravenous infusion after dilution in dextrose 5% in water or sodium chloride 0.9% contained in glass bottles, using an infusion control device.

The use of filters should be avoided. Various concentrations and administration rates are utilized, depending on the fluid requirements of the patient and the duration of therapy. An initial concentration of 50 to 100 μg/ml, with adjustment to the concentration if necessary, has been recommended. The concentration should not exceed 400 μg/ml. (1-6/99; 4)

Because of nitroglycerin sorption into PVC plastic, dosing is higher with standard PVC administration sets and should be reduced when nonabsorbing administration sets are used. (2; 4)

Inaccurate nitroglycerin dosing may occur with nonabsorbing high-density polyethylene plastic administration sets. Such tubing is less pliable than PVC and may not work well with some infusion control devices designed for PVC tubing, resulting in overinfusion. (729–731; 1120)

Stability — Nitroglycerin injections are practically colorless and stable in the intact containers. The solutions are not explosive. Storage should be at controlled room temperature; the containers should be protected from freezing. (1-6/99; 1-1/00; 4) Exposure to light, even high intensity light, does not adversely affect nitroglycerin stability. (506; 510; 928; 930; 1941) Dilution of the nitroglycerin injections with dextrose 5% in water or sodium chloride 0.9% in glass containers results in physically and chemically stable solutions for 48 hours at room temperature and seven days under refrigeration. (4)

pH Effects — The rate of nitroglycerin hydrolysis becomes significant at low pH values and is also quite rapid in alkaline solutions. (933) In neutral to weakly acidic solutions, the drug is stable. No loss was observed over 136 days at room temperature at pH 3 to 5. (1072)

Syringes — Nitroglycerin concentrate 5 mg/ml from four manufacturers (Abbott, DuPont, Goldline, Marion) was filled as 10 ml in 10-ml glass syringes (Becton-Dickinson) and in 10-ml (Becton-Dickinson) and 12-ml (Monoject) polypropylene plastic syringes. No loss of nitroglycerin content by HPLC analysis occurred in 23 hours when stored at 25 °C protected from light. Mean nitroglycerin concentrations were greater than 99% and were the same for both the glass and plastic syringes. (2055)

Sorption — Nitroglycerin readily undergoes sorption to many soft plastics (943), especially PVC which is commonly used to make infusion solution bags and intravenous tubing.

Hard solid plastics such as polyethylene and polypropylene generally do not absorb nitroglycerin. Consequently, it is recommended that only infusion solution containers made from glass or a plastic known to be compatible with nitroglycerin (i.e., polyolefin) be used for mixing infusions.

To circumvent the significant loss to PVC tubing, use of the special high-density polyethylene administration sets provided by the various nitroglycerin injection manufacturers is recommended. Nitroglycerin is not significantly sorbed to these special sets, but the rate of loss to conventional PVC sets is significant (40 to 80%), although not constant nor self-limiting. Many factors including flow rate, concentration, and length of the set affect the extent of sorption. The greatest amount of sorption occurs early in the infusion. A slow rate of flow and long tubing length increase the loss. Simple calculations or corrections cannot be applied to this complex phenomenon to determine or control the actual amount of nitroglycerin delivered through PVC tubing. (2; 4)

Numerous articles have described or evaluated nitroglycerin sorption characteristics.

Sturek et al. reported the stability of a 0.4-mg/ml solution in sterile water for injection prepared from solubilized sublingual tablets. The solution was sterilized by filtration through a 0.22-μm filter and stored in 10-ml glass ampuls or rubber-stoppered vials at room temperature. While the authors did not feel an adequate prediction of the stability of aqueous nitroglycerin solutions could be made from their data, they did note a significantly increased rate of loss of nitroglycerin in the rubber-stoppered vials. About 10% of the nitroglycerin was lost over eight days in glass ampuls, while about 25% was lost in the vials stored in the inverted position. The solution also appeared to reach an equilibrium after four weeks of storage in ampuls or vials at about 75 or 55%, respectively. The presence or absence of light had no apparent effect on the loss of the drug. (506)

These authors also found no difference in the stability of nitroglycerin 46.5 mg/100 ml in dextrose 5% in water or sodium chloride 0.9% in 500-ml glass bottles. A loss of about 13% was noted in 50 hours at room temperature. (506)

A profound impact of the container size and type on the loss of nitroglycerin was reported in this article, however. Compared with the 13% loss mentioned above, the same solutions in 150-ml PVC bags exhibited an 83.5% loss. At the other end of the spectrum, a 5.35-mg/10 ml solution in 10-ml glass ampuls showed about a 3% loss. The differences were attributed to variations in the amount of sorption occurring among the different containers. The authors recommended the use of only glass containers for injections of nitroglycerin. (506)

This work supports other reports that indicated substantial sorption of nitroglycerin by plastics.

Crouthamel et al. prepared nitroglycerin 50 μg/ml in dextrose 5% in water in PVC bags and glass bottles. Using HPLC analysis, they determined that nearly half of the drug had disappeared from solution within two hours when stored in PVC bags. In glass bottles, little change was noted. Because degradation products were not observed, it was concluded that sorption of nitroglycerin to the plastic was occurring. Upon testing nitroglycerin solutions infused through PVC infusion sets (Travenol, 2.4 m), a similar effect was noted. At a rate of 2 ml/min from a glass bottle, a 20% loss of nitroglycerin was noted. (508)

Cossum et al. noted this effect of infusion sets on nitroglycerin 0.01% in dextrose 5% in water in glass bottles. The nitroglycerin content decreased rapidly during the first hour and then reached a plateau. The level of the plateau varied from 20 to 70% of the initial amount for flow rates from 0.07 to 0.91 ml/min, respectively. However, little nitroglycerin was lost from the solution when a glass syringe pump system fitted with a high-density polyethylene cannula was used to deliver a constant flow rate of 0.05 ml/min. (509)

Boylan et al. reported a 50% loss of nitroglycerin in 24 hours at room temperature from a solution stored in PVC bags that originally contained 32 μg/ml in dextrose 5% in water. Potency loss was negligible upon storing the solution in glass bottles. (510)

McNiff et al. found little or no loss in nitroglycerin solutions prepared from sublingual tablets and stored in glass bottles. The solutions varied in initial concentration from about 35 to 87 μg/ml in dextrose 5% in water and sodium chloride 0.9% and were stored in closed-system or open-airway type bottles for about 70 days at room temperature or under refrigeration. However, solutions of about 35 μg/ml in dextrose 5% in water in PVC bags exhibited approximately 10% loss during the first hour. Further, solutions stored at room temperature exhibited a greater loss of drug after seven days (55%) than those stored under refrigeration (30%). The drug lost in the PVC containers could be recovered by methanol extraction over 13 days, indicating that a reversible adsorption phenomenon was occurring. (503)

The work of Ludwig and Ueda, however, did not support a difference between glass and plastic containers. Using solutions of approximately 10 μg/ml in dextrose 5% in water, they found essentially similar rates of drug loss for both glass bottles and PVC bags. About 10% was lost in one hour and about 25% in five hours at room temperature. Refrigeration of the solutions resulted in about a 20% loss in five hours in both. (511) However, in light of both previous and subsequent work, this anomalous result is questionable.

Yuen et al. evaluated the type of sorption that occurs. Aqueous solutions of nitroglycerin in concentrations of 61 to 473 μg/ml were tested with PVC test strips from Viaflex bags. The authors believed that their results showed that the nitroglycerin loss was primarily an absorption or partitioning process into the matrix of the plastic. However, the results did not rule out some adsorption. (723)

Baaske et al. evaluated the extent of nitroglycerin sorption to various filters, sets, and containers. Filtration of 250 ml of a 485-μg/ml aqueous solution through three different 142-mm, 0.2-μm filters was performed. A loss of 55% resulted with the Gelman GA filter composed of cellulose triacetate. Losses of only 5% occurred with a Millipore GS filter (a mixture of cellulose acetate and cellulose nitrate), and 2% losses occurred with a Gelman Tuffryn filter (a high-temperature aromatic polymer). (724)

Baaske et al. also found extensive sorption to PVC bags (Travenol) from nitroglycerin 50 μg/ml in dextrose 5% in water and sodium chloride 0.9%. The sorption process was quite rapid and interfered with obtaining accurate time-zero assays. After 24 hours, the solutions had lost 43 to 45% at 4 °C and 54 to 64% at 25 °C, indicating that increases in temperature also increased the loss of nitroglycerin. Varying the PVC bag size and, therefore, surface area impacted on the loss of nitroglycerin from solutions. The larger the volume of the bags, the slower was the rate of sorption. However, over a seven-day period, the total amount of drug lost increased with the increasing size of the PVC bag. The authors stated that neither small nor large PVC bags of infusion solutions are suitable for the infusion of nitroglycerin. (724)

Eight different intravenous infusion sets were tested with a nitroglycerin 100-μg/ml aqueous solution at a flow rate of 1 ml/min. Four of the sets were obtained from the United States and four came from Europe, but all were believed to be manufactured from PVC. All of the sets caused a substantial fall in the amount of nitroglycerin delivered, to about 50 to 70% of the nominal concentration during the first 25 minutes. After that time, the rate of loss gradually became less and delivery of approximately 60 to 90% of the nominal concentration occurred after about 120 minutes of infusion. The authors indicated that this result was consistent with an initial rapid adsorption which soon saturated available sites. This was then followed by an absorption into the plastic matrix at a slower rate. Differences in sorption characteristics between sets were attributed to differences in plastic formulations, tubing length and size, and composition of the drip chamber. (724) A theoretical treatment of these data and a model consisting of surface adsorption followed by partitioning into the plastic have been developed. (944; 945)

The rate of infusion (and, therefore, the contact time with the PVC tubing) also is an important factor. Delivered amounts of nitroglycerin were much lower at a flow rate of 0.5 ml/min (20 to 30%) than at 2 ml/min (60 to 70%). The authors noted that small adjustments in flow rates could greatly increase or decrease the concentration of the solution delivered to the patient. Moreover, control of the flow rate did not actually provide accurate control of the amount of nitroglycerin delivered through PVC tubing. It was speculated that this result could be a factor in the variability of responses. (724)

Roberts et al. noted significant sorption to PVC bags and tubing and, in addition, to cellulose propionate burette chambers from Buretrol sets. In static experiments with each, nitroglycerin from a 200-μg/ml solution in water, sodium chloride 0.9%, or dextrose 5% in water was initially lost rapidly but then leveled and became constant, indicating sorption to the plastic. The most rapid and extensive sorption occurred with the tubing, which yielded only 8% of the initial amount of nitroglycerin after five hours. Roberts et al. also confirmed that the loss of nitroglycerin from solution is related to the surface area of plastic in contact with the solution. For the PVC bags, nitroglycerin was lost at a more rapid rate from smaller volumes. However, the rate of loss appeared to be independent of the nitroglycerin concentration. (725)

In addition, Roberts et al. simulated infusions of nitroglycerin 200 μg/ml in sodium chloride 0.9% from glass containers through Buretrol sets. The delivered concentration of nitroglycerin dropped to about 50 to 60% of the initial concentration during the first hour of infusion. Thereafter, the delivered concentration gradually increased until nitroglycerin accumulated in the plastic to such an extent that sorption from the solution diminished. Flow rate was an important factor in determining the amount of delivered nitroglycerin. The slower flow rates provided the greatest contact time with the plastic and delivered the lowest concentrations of nitroglycerin during the first 24 hours. Given sufficient time, the delivered concentration eventually returned to the initial concentration with any flow rate. Also, the total cumulative amount of drug that was sorbed was independent of flow rate. (725)

One comparison of nitroglycerin sorption characteristics by Amann et al. involved glass, PVC, and polyolefin containers. Nitroglycerin (American Critical Care) 50 μg/ml in both dextrose 5% in water and sodium chloride 0.9% was tested for 48 hours at 25 and 4 °C in containers made of the three different materials. Nitroglycerin in both glass and polyolefin containers remained stable for the study period, exhibiting less than a 6% loss. However, in the PVC bags, losses of 38 to 44% at 4 °C and of up to 68 to 70% at 25 °C occurred. Polyolefin containers appeared to work equally as well as glass containers for nitroglycerin administration. (721)

Christiansen et al. tested the delivered concentration of nitroglycerin from a 100-μg/ml solution in dextrose 5% in water in glass, polyethylene, and PVC containers. They found a rapid fall during the first hour, followed by a continual decline in nitroglycerin content to about 65% of the initial amount after eight hours of storage in the PVC bag. In the glass container, no loss was apparent; in the polyethylene containers, about a 5% loss occurred during the first two hours with no further decline thereafter. These authors also confirmed that the concentration of nitroglycerin delivered through an infusion set declines rapidly during the first hour to about 50% of the initial amount and then begins to increase gradually until equilibrium is reached after about four hours. Attempts to presaturate the tubing by rinsing it with a nitroglycerin solution yielded a more quickly achieved equilibrium (within one hour) but still only delivered about half of the intended amount. The authors also confirmed the greater extent of sorption at slower flow rates. (726)

Sokoloski et al. attempted to define the mechanism and quantitate the rate of sorption to PVC intravenous infusion tubing. The mechanism was described as a highly complex adsorption process. Complicating factors include the existence of different solid forms of nitroglycerin, temperature, and the complex composition of the plastic, including not only PVC but also plasticizers, fillers, and other ingredients, as well as its complex surface characteristics. Therefore, precise quantitative kinetic and equilibrium characterization was not possible. However, the rate of nitroglycerin sorption by PVC tubing was quite rapid. At 21 °C, the observed half-life to the attainment of equilibrium with nitroglycerin solutions was 2.8 minutes. (727)

The lack of significant sorption of nitroglycerin by high-density polyethylene has been observed. (509; 726) An administration set made of polyethylene (Tridilset) was tested by Baaske et al. Evaluation of the delivered concentration of nitroglycerin 100 μg/ml in sodium chloride 0.9% showed little or no sorption at flow rates of 0.2, 0.6, and 1 ml/min over three hours. When conventional PVC sets were used, variable and unpredictable amounts of nitroglycerin were delivered, although the greatest losses occurred at the slower rates. When a 24-hour infusion of the 100-μg/ml solution (flow rate of 0.17 ml/min) through polyethylene tubing was evaluated, delivered concentrations were 94% or greater at all time intervals. (728)

Although the presaturation of PVC intravenous infusion sets has been suggested (935), other work shows that such attempts complicate the titration of nitroglycerin infusions, leading to greater variation in the delivered amount of nitroglycerin. (936)

Kowaluk et al. also found negligible nitroglycerin sorption using a polyethylene administration set (Tridilset). Nitroglycerin 50 mg/L in sodium chloride 0.9% in a glass bottle was delivered at 1 ml/min through the set over eight hours at 15 to 20 °C. (769)

The sorption of nitroglycerin 200 mg/L in sodium chloride 0.9% was evaluated in 100-ml PVC infusion bags (Travenol). After eight hours at 20 to 24 °C, 54% of the nitroglycerin was lost. Nitroglycerin showed a negligible (less than 3%) loss if the aqueous solution was stored in polypropylene infusion bags. (770)

Plastic syringes having polypropylene barrels and polyethylene plungers (Pharma-Plast, AHS Australia) and all-glass containers were compared in an investigation of the possible sorption of nitroglycerin. After 24 hours of storage of aqueous nitroglycerin solutions (concentrations unspecified), no drug loss was found in either the plastic syringes or glass containers. The authors indicated that these plastic syringes could be substituted for glass syringes for use with syringe pumps. (782)

Yliruusi et al. found a negligible loss of nitroglycerin to glass or polyethylene containers from 90-mg/L concentrations in dextrose 5% in water or sodium chloride 0.9%. However, in PVC containers, drug losses of around 28% occurred in 24 hours at 25 °C. (797)

Scheife et al. found nitroglycerin losses of 38 to 44% from solutions of 200 mg/L in sodium chloride 0.9% in PVC bags after 52 hours at 29 °C. Losses were reduced to 14% when the solutions were stored at 6 °C. Similar solutions stored in glass bottles exhibited no loss of nitroglycerin. Losses to PVC tubing during simulated infusion ranged up to 50%. However, two one-minute exposures of a 1-mg/ml nitroglycerin solution to a 50-ml plastic syringe resulted in no loss. (930)

Ingram and Miller reported no loss of nitroglycerin from 50- and 200-μg/ml solutions after storage for five hours in both glass and polypropylene (Monoject) syringes. However, PVC bags and tubing and cellulose propionate drip chambers caused nitroglycerin losses of 40 to 80%. Slower infusion rates caused greater decrements in the nitroglycerin concentration. (931)

Using a solution of nitroglycerin 0.625 mg/ml in dextrose 5% in water, Mathot et al. also noted no nitroglycerin loss from a delivery system consisting of a syringe pump, polypropylene syringe, and polyethylene tubing. This result was contrasted with a PVC bag and tubing system in which losses of up to 75% were found. When silicone rubber tubing was tested, only 14% of the nitroglycerin was delivered. (932)

Cavello and Bonn demonstrated the difference in sorption of nitroglycerin by PVC and polyethylene tubing. At slow rates of infusion through PVC, losses of up to 60% were observed. Polyethylene tubing did not show this reduction in concentration. (934)

The comparative sorption of nitroglycerin 50 mg/500 ml in sodium chloride 0.9% from PVC and polybutadiene (PBD) administration sets (Avon Medicals, U.K.) has been reported. The nitroglycerin admixture in glass bottles was run through PVC administration sets, with and without a cellulose propionate burette chamber, and through PBD sets, with and without a methacrylate butadiene styrene (MBS) burette chamber. At a flow rate of 1 ml/min, the delivered concentration was about 50% of the expected amount initially, climbing to about 70 to 75% after four hours. Slowing the flow rate to 0.5 ml/min decreased the delivered concentration at four hours to about 60 to 65%. If a cellulose propionate burette chamber was used to prepare the admixture, 10 to 15% sorption occurred in the burette. Conversely, use of the PBD set, with or without the MBS burette chamber, resulted in no detectable loss of nitroglycerin potency. (1027)

Nix et al. reported on a solution of nitroglycerin 50 mg/500 ml in dextrose 5% in water in glass bottles. When the solution was infused at rates of 6, 12, and 24 ml/hr through PVC sets over 24 hours, delivered nitroglycerin was about 42, 63, and 76%, respectively. Polyethylene administration sets delivered about 97% in 24 hours at all of the infusion rates. (1121)

Schaber et al. compared the sorption of nitroglycerin, from a solution of 100 mg/L in dextrose 5% in water, to sets of plain PVC tubing and a set lined with 87% of polyethylene/ethylene vinyl acetate (AVI 290). Nitroglycerin was absorbed by all sets, but the extent of sorption was considerably less with the set lined with polyethylene/ethylene vinyl acetate. At a rate of 12 ml/hr, the delivered concentration dropped to about 50% at about 90 minutes and then increased to about 70 to 80% over 24 hr through the lined set. The delivered concentration through the plain PVC sets initially fell to about 20% at 90 minutes and then increased to about 25 to 50% over 24 hours. Increasing the flow rate to 60 ml/hr and flushing the sets with nitroglycerin solution immediately prior to use increased the amount of drug delivered. (1122)

Martens et al. reported that nitroglycerin 100 μg/ml in sodium chloride 0.9% in PVC containers exhibited a 10% loss in one hour and a 51% loss in 24 hr at 21 °C due to sorption. Only a 2% loss occurred in glass bottles and a 5% loss occurred in polyethylene-lined laminated bags in 24 hours under the study conditions. (1392)

DeRudder et al. evaluated several infusion sets and burettes, composed of various plastic materials, for the sorption of nitroglycerin from a solution of 250 μg/ml in dextrose 5% in water. In cellulose propionate (Travenol) and polystyrolbutadiene (Braun) burettes, losses of about 70 and 50%, respectively, occurred in five hours; in a high density polyethylene burette (Miramed), no loss was observed. Similarly, PVC infusion sets from various manufacturers showed losses of about 50 to 70% when run at 15 and 3 ml/min. (1512)

Tracy et al. compared the nitroglycerin (Parke-Davis) losses from solutions of 50, 125, and 200 μg/ml in sodium chloride 0.9% in glass bottles run through PVC sets and polyethylene-lined administration sets (IMED) over 24 hours at 24 °C at 12 and 60 ml/hr. Nitroglycerin sorption losses to the PVC sets were approximately 40%; losses to the polyethylene-lined sets were about 2%. (1510)

Nitroglycerin (DuPont) (concentration unspecified) was filled into 3-ml plastic syringes (Becton-Dickinson, Sherwood Monoject, and Terumo) and stored at −20, 4, and 25 °C in the dark. Nitroglycerin losses by spectroscopy in one day ranged from 10 to 15% at 25 °C, to 2 to 3% at 4 °C, to 2% or less at −20 °C. Long-term storage for seven days at 4 °C and 30 days at −20 °C resulted in losses of 5 to 7% and 2% or less, respectively. The losses were presumably due to sorption to surfaces and/or the elastomeric plunger. (1562)

Nitroglycerin (DuPont) 50 mg/50 ml in dextrose 5% in water exhibited no change in appearance and about a 3.6% loss in potency by HPLC when stored in 60-ml plastic syringes (Becton-Dickinson) for 24 hours at 25 °C. (1579)

Loucas et al. determined the effect of the diluent and ionic strength on nitroglycerin sorption from a 0.4-mg/ml solution delivered at 100 ml/hr through a PVC set. During the initial 10 minutes, the greatest losses (about 40%) were observed when dextrose 5% in water was the diluent; slightly lower losses (about 35%) occurred from a sodium chloride 0.9% solution. After 18 minutes, the pattern reversed, with higher losses for sodium chloride 0.9% and lower losses for dextrose 5% in water. When sodium chloride solutions of 0.25, 0.9, and 5% were the diluents, the losses appeared as an inverse function of ionic strength. The highest losses occurred with the 0.25% solution and the lowest with the 5% solution. (1511)

Nitroglycerin 0.5 mg/ml was delivered at 5 ml per hour by syringe pump through Terumo administration sets 100 cm in length with an internal diameter of 2.1 mm. HPLC analysis of the effluent found about 90% loss during the first hour, gradually changing to about 70% loss over eight hours. (2143)

In addition to PVC bags and infusion tubing, nitroglycerin has been demonstrated to undergo similar sorption to PVC pulmonary artery catheters (937) and central venous pressure catheters (Intracath, Deseret) (938), a polyurethane sponge used to defoam blood in a bubble oxygenator (939), a silicone rubber membrane in a membrane oxygenator (940), an infusion pump cassette (Accuset C-924, IMED) (941), and silicone rubber microbore intravenous infusion tubing. (942)

Nitroglycerin (Orion) 100 µg/ml in sodium chloride 0.9% exhibited no loss due to sorption by HPLC analysis in 120 hours at 21 °C in glass bottles and polypropylene trilayer bags (Softbag, Orion). However, about a 75% loss due to sorption occurred under these conditions in PVC bags. (1796)

However, the clinical importance of the sorption to PVC has been questioned because nitroglycerin administration is titrated to clinical response, not in a fixed dosage. (1120; 1123; 2015; 2016; 2054) Young et al. reported 25 to 35% loss to PVC tubing at rates of nitroglycerin administration of 80 and 60 µg/min, respectively. Polyethylene tubing delivered essentially 100% of the nitroglycerin. Nevertheless, there was no statistically significant difference in physiologic response in patients when a variety of parameters were evaluated. The authors concluded that the type of tubing used does not influence the ultimate hemodynamic responses significantly, because even the PVC delivered a significant amount of the drug. The authors advised that physiologic endpoints be monitored in patients on intravenous nitroglycerin. (1120)

Similar results were reported by McCollom et al. (2015), Altavela et al. (2016), and Haas et al. (2054) Adequate clinical response was achieved using PVC containers and tubing. However, changes in patient hemodynamic status could occur if containers for nitroglycerin infusions were changed during the treatment course; switching from PVC to glass or vice versa could require substantial adjustment in the rate of administration to achieve a similar clinical response. (2016)

Nitroglycerin 0.01 mg/ml in dextrose 5% in water and sodium chloride 0.9% packaged in PVC, polyethylene, and glass containers exhibited no loss in glass and polyethylene containers but 76% loss due to sorption in PVC containers when stored at 4 and 22 °C for 24 hours protected from light. (2289)

Filtration— Some filters absorb nitroglycerin and should be avoided. (4) In one study, a filter material specially treated with a proprietary agent was evaluated for a possible reduction in nitroglycerin binding. Nitroglycerin (Abbott) 62.5 mg/250 ml in dextrose 5% in water and in sodium chloride 0.9% was run through an administration set with a treated 0.22-µm cellulose ester inline filter at a rate of 3 ml/min. Cumulative nitroglycerin losses of less than 6% occurred from 200 ml of either solution. However, equilibrium binding studies showed no significant differences in drug affinity between treated and untreated filter material in either solution. (904) Ivex integral filter and extension sets use the treated filter material. (1074)

Compatibility Information

Solution Compatibility

Nitroglycerin

Solution	*Mfr*	*Mfr*	*Conc/L*	*Remarks*	*Ref*	*C/I*
Dextrose 5% in Ringer's injection, lactated	MG	ACC	200 and 400 mg	Physically compatible with little or no loss after 28 days at 4 °C and room temperature in glass and polyolefin containers	928	C
Dextrose 5% in sodium chloride 0.45%	MG	ACC	200 and 400 mg	Physically compatible with little or no loss after 28 days at 4 °C and room temperature in glass and polyolefin containers	928	C
Dextrose 5% in sodium chloride 0.9%	MG	ACC	200 and 400 mg	Physically compatible with little or no loss after 28 days at 4 °C and room temperature in glass and polyolefin containers	928	C
Dextrose 5% in water		LI	32 mg	Negligible loss over 24 hr at room temperature in glass bottles	510	C
		[a]	100 mg	Less than 1% loss of nitroglycerin in 24 hr at room temperature in glass bottles	509	C

Solution Compatibility (Cont.)

Nitroglycerin

Solution	*Mfr*	*Mfr*	*Conc/L*	*Remarks*	*Ref*	*C/I*
	TR		50 mg	Little change in 2 hr in glass containers	508	**C**
	TR	[a]	465 mg	About 8% loss in 24 hr and 13% in 50 hr at room temperature in glass containers	506	**C**
		[a]	35 to 87 mg	Little or no loss after 70 days at room temperature or under refrigeration in glass bottles	503	**C**
	MG	ACC	50 mg	0 to 3% loss in 48 hr at 4 and 25 °C in glass bottles	721	**C**
	MG	ACC	50 mg	1 to 6% loss in 48 hr at 4 and 25 °C in polyolefin containers	721	**C**
	MG	[a]	50 mg	Nitroglycerin stable for 48 hr at 4 and 25 °C in glass containers	724	**C**
			100 mg	Little or no loss in 8 hr in glass containers	726	**C**
	ON	[a]	90 mg	No precipitate and negligible drug loss in 24 hr at 25 °C in glass and polyethylene containers	797	**C**
	MG	ACC	200 and 400 mg	Physically compatible with little or no loss after 28 days at 4 °C and room temperature in glass and polyolefin containers	928	**C**
	TR	[a]	200 mg	No loss of nitroglycerin after 52 hr at 29 °C in glass bottles	930	**C**
			200 to 800 mg	Physically compatible with 4% or less loss in 24 hr in glass bottles exposed to light	1412	**C**
			250 mg	3% or less loss in 24 hr at 6, 20, and 40 °C in glass containers exposed to light or in the dark	1512	**C**
	TR	LI	32 mg	Approximately 50% loss in 24 hr at room temperature in PVC containers	510	**I**
	TR		50 mg	Almost 50% loss in 2 hr in PVC containers	508	**I**
	TR	[a]	465 mg	Over 50% loss in 8 hr and over 83% in 50 hr at room temperature in PVC containers	506	**I**
		[a]	35 mg	Approximately 10% loss in 1 hr in PVC bags. In 7 days, 55% loss at room temperature and 30% under refrigeration	503	**I**
	TR	ACC	50 mg	Rapid loss in PVC bags with approximately 44% loss in 48 hr at 4 °C and about 70% loss at 25 °C	721	**I**
	TR	[a]	50 mg	Approximately 43% loss at 4 °C and 64% at 25 °C in 24 hr in PVC bags	724	**I**
	TR	[a]	100 and 500 mg	Approximately 50% loss in 24 hr at 20 to 24 °C in PVC bags	725	**I**
	TR		100 mg	Approximately 20% loss in 1 hr and 35% in 8 hr in PVC bags	726	**I**
		[a]	90 mg	No precipitate but 10% potency loss in 3 hr and 27% loss in 24 hr at 25 °C in PVC containers	797	**I**
	BA[b]	AMR	800 mg	No nitroglycerin loss by HPLC in 24 hr at 23 °C in glass bottles	2085	**C**
	BA[b]	PB	10 mg	Visually compatible but 66% loss of drug due to sorption to the PVC container at 22 °C and 33% at 4 °C in 24 hr	2289	**I**
	BRN[c,d]	PB	10 mg	Visually compatible with no loss by HPLC in 24 hr at 4 and 22 °C in glass and polyethylene containers	2289	**C**
Ringer's injection, lactated	MG	ACC	200 and 400 mg	Physically compatible with little or no loss after 28 days at 4 °C and room temperature in glass and polyolefin containers	928	**C**

Solution Compatibility (Cont.)

Nitroglycerin

Solution	*Mfr*	*Mfr*	*Conc/L*	*Remarks*	*Ref*	*C/I*
Sodium chloride 0.45%	MG	ACC	200 and 400 mg	Physically compatible with little or no loss after 28 days at 4 °C and room temperature in glass and polyolefin containers	928	C
Sodium chloride 0.9%	TR	[a]	465 mg	About 8% loss in 24 hr and 13% in 50 hr at room temperature in glass containers	506	C
		[a]	35 to 87 mg	Little or no loss after 70 days of storage at room temperature or under refrigeration in glass bottles	503	C
	MG	ACC	50 mg	Approximately 5% loss in 48 hr at 4 and 25 °C in glass bottles	721	C
	MG	ACC	50 mg	No loss in 48 hr at 4 and 25 °C in polyolefin containers	721	C
		[a]	200 mg	No loss in 24 hr and about 5% loss in 3 months in glass bottles stored at room temperature or under refrigeration	722	C
		[a]	3.6 to 95 mg	Little or no loss in 48 hr at 35 °C in glass flasks	723	C
		[a]	0.2 mg	About 10% loss in 24 hr and 13% in 48 hr at 35 °C in glass flasks	723	C
	MG	[a]	50 mg	Nitroglycerin stable for 48 hr at 4 and 25 °C in glass containers	724	C
	ON	[a]	90 mg	No precipitate and 2 to 3% drug loss in 24 hr at 25 °C in glass and polyethylene containers	797	C
	MG	ACC	200 and 400 mg	Physically compatible with little or no loss after 28 days at 4 °C and room temperature in glass and polyolefin containers	928	C
	TR	[a]	200 mg	No loss of nitroglycerin after 52 hr at 29 °C in glass bottles	930	C
			200 to 800 mg	Physically compatible with 8% or less loss in 24 hr in glass bottles exposed to light	1412	C
			100 mg	Physically compatible with 2% loss in glass bottles and 5% loss in polyethylene-lined bags in 24 hr at 21 °C in the dark	1392	C
			250 mg	4% loss at 6 °C and 7% loss at 40 °C in 6 hr in glass bottles; no further loss in 24 hr	1512	C
	TR	[a]	465 mg	Over 50% loss in 8 hr and over 83% in 50 hr at room temperature in PVC containers	506	I
	TR	ACC	50 mg	Rapid loss in PVC bags with approximately 38% loss in 48 hr at 4 °C and about 68% at 25 °C	721	I
	TR	[a]	50 mg	Approximately 45% loss at 4 °C and 54% at 25 °C in 24 hr in PVC bags	724	I
	TR	[a]	100 and 500 mg	Approximately 50% loss in 24 hr at 20 to 24 °C in PVC bags	725	I
		[a]	90 mg	No precipitate but 10% potency loss in 3 hr and 28% loss in 24 hr at 25 °C in PVC containers	797	I
	TR	[a]	200 mg	38 to 44% nitroglycerin loss in 8 hr at 29 °C in PVC bags. At 6 °C, 14% loss in 8 hr	930	I
			100 mg	10% loss in 1 hr and 51% loss in 24 hr at 21 °C in PVC containers in the dark	1392	I
		PD	50, 125, 200 mg	About 14% loss in 8 hr at 24 °C in glass bottles	1510	I
	ON	ON	100 mg	Visually compatible with no loss by UV and HPLC in 24 hr at 21 °C in glass and polypropylene trilayer containers	1796	C

Solution Compatibility (Cont.)

Nitroglycerin

Solution	Mfr	Mfr	Conc/L	Remarks	Ref	C/I
	ON[b]	ON	100 mg	Visually compatible but 50% loss in 24 hr and 75% loss in 120 hr by HPLC at 21 °C in PVC bags due to sorption	1796	I
	BA[b]	PB	10 mg	Visually compatible but 66% loss of drug due to sorption to the PVC container in 24 hr at 4 and 22 °C	2289	I
	BRN[c,d]	PB	10 mg	Visually compatible with 4 to 5% loss by HPLC in 24 hr at 4 and 22 °C in glass and polyethylene containers	2289	C
Sodium lactate ⅙ M	MG	ACC	200 and 400 mg	Physically compatible with little or no loss after 28 days at 4 °C and room temperature in glass and polyolefin containers	928	C

[a]*An extemporaneous preparation was tested.*
[b]*Tested in PVC containers.*
[c]*Tested in glass containers.*
[d]*Tested in polyethylene containers.*

Additive Compatibility

Nitroglycerin

Drug	Mfr	Conc/L	Mfr	Conc/L	Test Soln	Remarks	Ref	C/I
Alteplase	GEN	0.5 g	ACC	400 mg	D5W, NS	Visually compatible with 2% or less alteplase clot-lysis activity loss in 24 hr at 25 °C	1856	C
Aminophylline	IX	1 g	ACC	400 mg	D5W[a]	Physically compatible with 4% nitroglycerin loss in 24 hr and 6% loss in 48 hr at 23 °C. Aminophylline not tested	929	C
	IX	1 g	ACC	400 mg	NS[a]	Physically compatible with no nitroglycerin loss in 24 hr and 5% loss in 48 hr at 23 °C. Aminophylline not tested	929	C
Bretylium tosylate	ACC	10 g	ACC	400 mg	D5W, NS[a]	Physically compatible with little or no nitroglycerin loss in 48 hr at 23 °C. Bretylium not tested	929	C
	ACC	10 g	ACC	100 mg	D5S[a]	Physically compatible and both drugs chemically stable for 48 hr at room temperature and 7 days at 4 °C	522	C
	ACC	10 g	ACC	100 mg	D5S[b]	Physically compatible and bretylium chemically stable for 48 hr at room temperature and 7 days at 4 °C. 40% loss of nitroglycerin at room temperature and 10% loss at 4 °C in 24 hr due to sorption to PVC	522	I
Cibenzoline succinate		2 g	ACC	500 mg	D5W, NS	Physically compatible for 24 hr at 25 °C by visual and microscopic examination	1182	C
Dobutamine HCl	LI	1 g	AB	120 mg	D5W, NS	Physically compatible for 24 hr at 21 °C	812	C
	LI	500 mg	ACC	100 mg	D5S	Chemically stable with no loss of either drug after 24 hr at 25 °C. Pale pink color developed after 4 hr	990	C
Dobutamine HCl with sodium nitroprusside		2 to 8 g 200 to 800 mg		200 to 800 mg	D5W[a]	Pale pink discoloration with small amount of dark brown precipitate and 11 to 19% sodium nitroprusside loss in 24 hr exposed to light	1412	I

Additive Compatibility (Cont.)

Nitroglycerin

Drug	*Mfr*	*Conc/L*	*Mfr*	*Conc/L*	*Test Soln*	*Remarks*	*Ref*	*C/I*
Dobutamine HCl with sodium nitroprusside		2 to 8 g 200 to 800 mg		200 to 800 mg	NS[a]	Pale pink discoloration with all drugs remaining stable for 24 hr exposed to light. Not more than 8% loss for either drug	1412	C
Dopamine HCl	ACC	800 mg	ACC	400 mg	D5W, NS[a]	Physically compatible with little or no nitroglycerin loss in 48 hr at 23 °C. Dopamine not tested	929	C
Enalaprilat	MSD	12 mg	DU	200 mg	D5W[a]	Visually compatible with about 4% enalaprilat loss by HPLC in 24 hr at room temperature under fluorescent light. Nitroglycerin not tested	1572	C
Furosemide	HO	1 g	ACC	400 mg	D5W[a]	Physically compatible with no nitroglycerin loss in 48 hr at 23 °C. Furosemide not tested	929	C
	HO	1 g	ACC	400 mg	NS[a]	Physically compatible with 3% nitroglycerin loss in 48 hr at 23 °C. Furosemide not tested	929	C
Hydralazine HCl	CI	1 g	ACC	400 mg	D5W[a]	Deep yellow color produced. 4% nitroglycerin loss in 48 hr at 23 °C. Hydralazine not tested	929	I
	CI	1 g	ACC	400 mg	NS[a]	Pale yellow color produced. No nitroglycerin loss in 48 hr at 23 °C. Hydralazine not tested.	929	I
Lidocaine HCl	IMS	4 g	ACC	400 mg	D5W, NS[a]	Physically compatible with no nitroglycerin loss in 48 hr at 23 °C. Lidocaine not tested	929	C
Phenytoin sodium	PD	1 g	ACC	400 mg	D5W, NS[a]	Phenytoin crystals produced in 24 hr. 3 to 4% nitroglycerin loss in 24 hr and 9% loss in 48 hr at 23 °C. Phenytoin not tested	929	I
Verapamil HCl	KN	80 mg	ACC	100 mg	D5W, NS	Physically compatible for 24 hr	764	C

[a]*Tested in glass containers.*
[b]*Tested in PVC containers.*

Drugs in Syringe Compatibility

Nitroglycerin

Drug (in syringe)	*Mfr*	*Amt*	*Mfr*	*Amt*	*Remarks*	*Ref*	*C/I*
Heparin sodium		2500 units/ 1 ml		25 mg/ 25 ml	Physically compatible for at least 5 min	1053	C

Y-Site Injection Compatibility (1:1 Mixture)

Nitroglycerin

Drug	*Mfr*	*Conc*	*Mfr*	*Conc*	*Remarks*	*Ref*	*C/I*
Alatrofloxacin mesylate	PF	1.43 mg/ml[a]	BA	0.2 mg/ml	Visually and microscopically compatible run through a Y-site over at least 60 min	2235	C

Y-Site Injection Compatibility (1:1 Mixture) (Cont.)

			Nitroglycerin				
Drug	*Mfr*	*Conc*	*Mfr*	*Conc*	*Remarks*	*Ref*	*C/I*
Alteplase	GEN	1 mg/ml	DU	0.2 mg/ml[a]	Haze noted in 24 hr by visual examination. Erratic spectrophotometer readings	1340	I
Amiodarone HCl	LZ	4 mg/ml[c]	AB	0.24 mg/ml[c]	Physically compatible for 24 hr at 21 °C	1032	C
Amphotericin B cholesteryl sulfate complex	SEQ	0.83 mg/ml[a]	AMR	0.4 mg/ml[a]	Physically compatible with little or no change in measured turbidity or increase in particle content in 4 hr at 23 °C under fluorescent light	2117	C
Atracurium besylate	BW	0.5 mg/ml[a]	SO	0.4 mg/ml[a]	Physically compatible for 24 hr at 28 °C	1337	C
Cisatracurium besylate	GW	0.1, 2, 5 mg/ml[a]	DU	0.4 mg/ml[a]	Physically compatible with no change in measured turbidity or increase in particle content in 4 hr at 23 °C	2074	C
Diltiazem HCl	MMD	1 mg/ml[a]	DU	0.032 mg/ml[a]	Visually compatible for 24 hr at 25 °C	1530	C
	MMD	1[b] and 5 mg/ml	DU	400 μg/ml[b]	Visually compatible	1807	C
	MMD	5 mg/ml	DU	400 μg/ml[a]	Visually compatible	1807	C
	MMD	1 mg/ml[a]	AB	0.4 mg/ml[a]	Visually compatible for 4 hr at 27 °C	2062	C
Dobutamine HCl	LI	4 mg/ml[c]	LY	0.4 mg/ml[c]	Physically compatible for 3 hr	1316	C
	LI	4 mg/ml[a]	AB	0.4 mg/ml[a]	Visually compatible for 4 hr at 27 °C	2062	C
Dobutamine HCl with dopamine HCl	LI DCC	4 mg/ml[c] 3.2 mg/ml[c]	LY	0.4 mg/ml[c]	Physically compatible for 3 hr	1316	C
Dobutamine HCl with lidocaine HCl	LI AB	4 mg/ml[c] 8 mg/ml[c]	LY	0.4 mg/ml[c]	Physically compatible for 3 hr	1316	C
Dobutamine HCl with sodium nitroprusside	LI ES	4 mg/ml[c] 0.4 mg/ml[c]	LY	0.4 mg/ml[c]	Physically compatible for 3 hr	1316	C
Dopamine HCl	DCC	3.2 mg/ml[c]	LY	0.4 mg/ml[c]	Physically compatible for 3 hr	1316	C
	AB	3.2 mg/ml[a]	AB	0.4 mg/ml[a]	Visually compatible for 4 hr at 27 °C	2062	C
Dopamine HCl with dobutamine HCl	DCC LI	3.2 mg/ml[c] 4 mg/ml[c]	LY	0.4 mg/ml[c]	Physically compatible for 3 hr	1316	C
Dopamine HCl with lidocaine HCl	DCC AB	3.2 mg/ml[c] 8 mg/ml[c]	LY	0.4 mg/ml[c]	Physically compatible for 3 hr	1316	C
Dopamine HCl with sodium nitroprusside	DCC ES	3.2 mg/ml[c] 0.4 mg/ml[c]	LY	0.4 mg/ml[c]	Physically compatible for 3 hr	1316	C
Epinephrine HCl	AB	0.02 mg/ml[a]	AB	0.4 mg/ml[a]	Visually compatible for 4 hr at 27 °C	2062	C
Esmolol HCl	DU	40 mg/ml[a]	OM	0.2 mg/ml[a]	Visually compatible for 24 hr at 23 °C	1877	C
Famotidine	MSD	0.2 mg/ml[a]	IMS	0.8 mg/ml[a]	Physically compatible for 4 hr at 25 °C	1188	C
	MSD	0.2 mg/ml[a]	PD	85 μg/ml[b]	Physically compatible for 14 hr	1196	C
Fentanyl citrate	ES	0.05 mg/ml	AB	0.4 mg/ml[a]	Visually compatible for 4 hr at 27 °C	2062	C
Fluconazole	RR	2 mg/ml	AMR	0.2 mg/ml[a]	Visually compatible for 24 hr at 28 °C under fluorescent light	1760	C
Furosemide	AMR	10 mg/ml	AB	0.4 mg/ml[a]	Visually compatible for 4 hr at 27 °C	2062	C
Gatifloxacin	BMS	2 mg/ml[a]	FAU	0.4 mg/ml[a]	Physically compatible with no change in measured haze or increase in particle content in 4 hr at 23 °C	2234	C
Haloperidol lactate	MN	0.5[a] and 5 mg/ml	DU	0.4 mg/ml[a]	Visually compatible for 24 hr at 21 °C	1523	C
Heparin sodium	OR	100 units/ml[a]	OM	0.2 mg/ml[a]	Visually compatible for 24 hr at 23 °C	1877	C
	ES	100 units/ml[a]	AB	0.4 mg/ml[a]	Visually compatible for 4 hr at 27 °C	2062	C

Y-Site Injection Compatibility (1:1 Mixture) (Cont.)

			Nitroglycerin				
Drug	*Mfr*	*Conc*	*Mfr*	*Conc*	*Remarks*	*Ref*	*C/I*
Hetastarch in lactated electrolyte injection (Hextend)	AB	6%	AMR	0.4 mg/ml[a]	Physically compatible with no change in measured turbidity or increase in particle content in 4 hr at 23 °C	2339	C
Hydralazine HCl	SO	1 mg/ml[a]	LY	0.4 mg/ml[a]	Physically compatible for 3 hr	1316	C
	SO	1 mg/ml[b]	LY	0.4 mg/ml[b]	Slight precipitate in 3 hr	1316	I
Hydromorphone HCl	KN	1 mg/ml	AB	0.4 mg/ml[a]	Visually compatible for 4 hr at 27 °C	2062	C
Inamrinone lactate	WB	3 mg/ml[b]		0.8 mg/ml[a]	Physically compatible for at least 4 hr at 25 °C under fluorescent light	992	C
Insulin, regular	LI	1 unit/ml[a]	OM	0.2 mg/ml[a]	Visually compatible for 24 hr at 23 °C	1877	C
Labetalol HCl	GL	1 mg/ml[a]	DU	0.2 mg/ml[a]	Visually compatible with no labetalol loss and 6% nitroglycerin loss by HPLC in 4 hr at room temperature	1762	C
	GL	5 mg/ml	OM	0.2 mg/ml[a]	Visually compatible for 24 hr at 23 °C	1877	C
	AH	2 mg/ml[a]	AB	0.4 mg/ml[a]	Visually compatible for 4 hr at 27 °C	2062	C
Levofloxacin	OMN	5 mg/ml[a]	AMR	5 mg/ml	Cloudy precipitate forms	2233	I
Lidocaine HCl	AB	8 mg/ml[c]	LY	0.4 mg/ml[c]	Physically compatible for 3 hr	1316	C
Lidocaine HCl with dobutamine HCl	AB LI	8 mg/ml[c] 4 mg/ml[c]	LY	0.4 mg/ml[c]	Physically compatible for 3 hr	1316	C
Lidocaine HCl with dopamine HCl	AB DCC	8 mg/ml[c] 3.2 mg/ml[c]	LY	0.4 mg/ml[c]	Physically compatible for 3 hr	1316	C
Lidocaine HCl with sodium nitroprusside	AB ES	8 mg/ml[c] 0.4 mg/ml[c]	LY	0.4 mg/ml[c]	Physically compatible for 3 hr	1316	C
Linezolid	PHU	2 mg/ml	FAU	0.4 mg/ml[a]	Physically compatible with no change in measured turbidity or increase in particle content in 4 hr at 23 °C	2264	C
Lorazepam	WY	0.5 mg/ml[a]	AB	0.4 mg/ml[a]	Visually compatible for 4 hr at 27 °C	2062	C
Midazolam HCl	RC	1 mg/ml[a]	SO	0.2 mg/ml[a]	Visually compatible for 24 hr at 23 °C	1847	C
	RC	1 mg/ml[a]	OM	0.2 mg/ml[a]	Visually compatible for 24 hr at 23 °C	1877	C
	RC	2 mg/ml[a]	AB	0.4 mg/ml[a]	Visually compatible for 4 hr at 27 °C	2062	C
Milrinone lactate	SW	0.2 mg/ml[a]	AB	0.4 mg/ml[a]	Visually compatible for 4 hr at 27 °C	2062	C
	SW	0.4 mg/ml[a]	SO	0.8 mg/ml[a]	Visually compatible with little or no loss of either drug by HPLC in 4 hr at 23 °C	2214	C
Morphine sulfate	SCN	2 mg/ml[a]	AB	0.4 mg/ml[a]	Visually compatible for 4 hr at 27 °C	2062	C
Nicardipine HCl	WY	1 mg/ml[a]	AB	0.4 mg/ml[a]	Visually compatible for 4 hr at 27 °C	2062	C
Norepinephrine bitartrate	AB	0.128 mg/ml[a]	AB	0.4 mg/ml[a]	Visually compatible for 4 hr at 27 °C	2062	C
Pancuronium bromide	ES	0.05 mg/ml[a]	SO	0.4 mg/ml[a]	Physically compatible for 24 hr at 28 °C	1337	C
Propofol	ZEN	10 mg/ml	DU	0.4 mg/ml[a]	Physically compatible for 1 hr at 23 °C with no increase in particle content	2066	C
Ranitidine HCl	GL	0.5 mg/ml[e]	SO	0.2 mg/ml[a]	Physically compatible for 24 hr	1323	C
	GL	1 mg/ml[a]	AB	0.4 mg/ml[a]	Visually compatible for 4 hr at 27 °C	2062	C
Remifentanil HCl	GW	0.025 and 0.25 mg/ml[b]	DU	0.4 mg/ml[a]	Physically compatible with no change in measured turbidity or increase in particle content in 4 hr at 23 °C	2075	C

Y-Site Injection Compatibility (1:1 Mixture) (Cont.)

Drug	*Mfr*	*Conc*	Nitroglycerin *Mfr*	*Conc*	*Remarks*	*Ref*	*C/I*
Sodium nitroprusside	ES	0.4 mg/ml[c]	LY	0.4 mg/ml[c]	Physically compatible for 3 hr	1316	C
Sodium nitroprusside with dobutamine HCl	ES LI	0.4 mg/ml[c] 4 mg/ml[c]	LY	0.4 mg/ml[c]	Physically compatible for 3 hr	1316	C
Sodium nitroprusside with dopamine HCl	ES DCC	0.4 mg/ml[c] 3.2 mg/ml[c]	LY	0.4 mg/ml[c]	Physically compatible for 3 hr	1316	C
Sodium nitroprusside with lidocaine HCl	ES AB	0.4 mg/ml[c] 8 mg/ml[c]	LY	0.4 mg/ml[c]	Physically compatible for 3 hr	1316	C
Streptokinase	HO	30,000 units/ml[a]	DU	0.2 mg/ml[a]	Physically compatible for at least 5 days by visual examination	1340	C
Tacrolimus	FUJ	1 mg/ml[b]	DU	0.1 mg/ml[a]	Visually compatible for 24 hr at 25 °C	1630	C
Theophylline	TR	4 mg/ml	LY	0.2 mg/ml[a]	Visually compatible for 6 hr at 25 °C	1793	C
Thiopental sodium	AB	25 mg/ml[d]	AB	0.4 mg/ml[a]	Visually compatible for 4 hr at 27 °C	2062	C
TNA #218 to #226[f]			DU	0.4 mg/ml[a]	Visually compatible with no precipitate or emulsion damage apparent in 4 hr at 23 °C	2215	C
TPN #212 to #215[f]			DU	0.4 mg/ml[a]	Physically compatible with no change in measured turbidity or increase in particle content in 4 hr at 23 °C	2109	C
Vecuronium bromide	OR OR	0.1 mg/ml[a] 1 mg/ml	SO AB	0.4 mg/ml[a] 0.4 mg/ml[a]	Physically compatible for 24 hr at 28 °C Visually compatible for 4 hr at 27 °C	1337 2062	C C
Warfarin sodium	DU DME	2 mg/ml[d] 2 mg/ml[d]	FAU DU	0.4 mg/ml[a] 0.4 mg/ml[a]	Visually compatible with no warfarin loss by HPLC in 30 min Visually compatible for 24 hr at 24 °C	2010 2078	C C

[a] *Tested in dextrose 5% in water.*
[b] *Tested in sodium chloride 0.9%.*
[c] *Tested in both dextrose 5% in water and sodium chloride 0.9%.*
[d] *Tested in sterile water for injection.*
[e] *Premixed infusion solution.*
[f] *Refer to Appendix I for the composition of parenteral nutrition solutions. TNA indicates a 3-in-1 admixture, and TPN indicates a 2-in-1 admixture.*

Additional Compatibility Information

Infusion Solutions — Dextrose 5% in water or sodium chloride 0.9% is recommended for dilution. (4) It is also recommended that no other drug be admixed with nitroglycerin. (1-1/00)

Dobutamine, Dopamine, Lidocaine, and Nitroprusside — Dobutamine HCl (Lilly) 4 mg/ml, dopamine HCl (Dupont Critical Care) 3.2 mg/ml, lidocaine HCl (Abbott) 8 mg/ml, nitroglycerin (Lyphomed) 0.4 mg/ml, and sodium nitroprusside (Elkins-Sinn) 0.4 mg/ml, prepared in dextrose 5% in water and sodium chloride 0.9%, were combined in equal quantities in all possible combinations of two, three, four, and five drugs and then evaluated for physical compatibility. No physical incompatibility was observed in any combination within the three-hour study period. (1316)

NOREPINEPHRINE BITARTRATE (NORADRENALINE ACID TARTRATE) AHFS 12:12

Products — Norepinephrine bitartrate (Levophed) is available in 4-ml ampuls. Each milliliter of solution contains (1-7/99; 29):

Norepinephrine base	1 mg
(as norepinephrine bitartrate, 2 mg)	
Sodium chloride	≈7.4 mg
Sodium metabisulfite	2 mg
Water for injection	qs 1 ml

Generic norepinephrine bitartrate injection is available in 4-ml ampuls that has a different formulation. Each milliliter of the generic norepinephrine bitartrate injection contains (1-10/92; 29):

Norepinephrine base (as bitartrate)	1 mg
Sodium chloride	8.2 mg
Sodium metabisulfite	0.46 mg
Citric acid, anhydrous	1.3 mg
Sodium citrate, dihydrate	0.9 mg
Water for injection	qs 1 ml

pH — From 3 to 4.5. (4; 77)

Osmolality — The osmolality of norepinephrine (salt form unspecified) 1 mg/ml was determined to be 319 mOsm/kg. (1233)

Trade Name(s) — Levophed.

Administration — Norepinephrine bitartrate is administered by intravenous infusion into a large vein, using a pump or other flow rate control device. Extravasation may cause tissue damage and should be avoided. A 4-μg/ml dilution of norepinephrine base for infusion is usually prepared by adding 4 mg of base (4 ml) to 1000 ml of dextrose 5% in water with or without sodium chloride. The concentration and infusion rate depend on the patient's requirements. (4)

Stability — Norepinephrine bitartrate in intact containers should be stored at controlled room temperature and protected from light. (1-7/99; 4) The drug gradually darkens upon exposure to light or air and must not be used if it is discolored or has a precipitate. (4)

pH Effects — Norepinephrine bitartrate is stable at pH 3.6 to 6 in dextrose 5% in water. (48; 77) The pH of a solution is the primary determinant of catecholamine stability in intravenous admixtures. (527) At a concentration of 5 mg/L in dextrose 5% in water at pH 6.5, norepinephrine bitartrate loses 5% potency in six hours; at pH 7.5, it loses 5% potency in four hours. (77) The rate of decomposition also increases with exposure to increasing temperatures. (1929)

Filtration — Norepinephrine bitartrate (Winthrop) 4 mg/L in dextrose 5% in water and sodium chloride 0.9% was filtered at a rate of 120 ml/hr for six hours through a 0.22-μm cellulose ester membrane filter (Ivex-2). No significant reduction in potency due to binding to the filter was noted. (533)

Central Venous Catheter — Norepinephrine bitartrate 0.1 mg/ml in dextrose 5% in water was found to be compatible with the ARROWg+ard Blue Plus (Arrow International) chlorhexidine-bearing triple-lumen central catheter. HPLC analysis was used to evaluate completeness of drug delivery through the catheter and the amount of chlorhexidine removed from the internal lumens. Essentially complete delivery of the drug was found with little or no drug loss occurring. Furthermore, chlorhexidine delivered from the catheter remained at trace amounts with no substantial increase due to the delivery of the drug through the catheter. (2335)

Compatibility Information

Solution Compatibility

Norepinephrine bitartrate

Solution	*Mfr*	*Mfr*	*Conc/L*	*Remarks*	*Ref*	*C/I*
Amino acids 4.25%, dextrose 25%	MG	WI	4 mg	No increase in particulate matter in 24 hr at 5 °C	349	C
Dextrose 5% in sodium chloride 0.9%		WI	8 mg	Physically compatible	74	C
Dextrose 5% in water		WI	8 mg	Physically compatible	74	C
	AB	WI	8 mg	Physically compatible and chemically stable. 10% decomposition is calculated to occur in 2500 hr at 25 °C	527	C
	TR[a]	WI	4 and 8 mg	2 to 4% loss in 24 hr at room temperature exposed to light	1163	C
	BA[a]	WI	16 mg	5% loss by HPLC in 47.2 days at 5 °C protected from light	1610	C
	BA[a]	WI	40 mg	5% loss by HPLC in 87.7 days at 5 °C protected from light	1610	C
	TR[a]	RC	4 and 8 mg	Visually compatible with no norepinephrine loss by HPLC in 48 hr at room temperature	1802	C
	BA[a]	SW	42 mg	No norepinephrine loss by HPLC in 24 hr at 23 °C protected from light	2085	C
Ringer's injection, lactated		WI	8 mg	Physically compatible	74	C

Solution Compatibility (Cont.)

Norepinephrine bitartrate

Solution	*Mfr*	*Mfr*	*Conc/L*	*Remarks*	*Ref*	*C/I*
Sodium chloride 0.9%		WI	8 mg	Physically compatible	74	C
	TR[a]	WI	4 and 8 mg	2% loss in 24 hr at room temperature exposed to light	1163	C

[a]*Tested in PVC containers.*

Additive Compatibility

Norepinephrine bitartrate

Drug	*Mfr*	*Conc/L*	*Mfr*	*Conc/L*	*Test Soln*	*Remarks*	*Ref*	*C/I*
Amikacin sulfate	BR	5 g	WI	8 mg	D5LR, D5R, D5S, D5W, D10W, IS10, LR, NS, R, SL	Physically compatible and potency of both retained for 24 hr at 25 °C	294	C
Aminophylline	SE	500 mg	WI	8 mg	D5W	10% norepinephrine decomposition in 3.6 hr at 25 °C	527	I
Amobarbital sodium			WI			Physically incompatible	9	I
	LI	1 g	WI	2 mg	D5W	Physically incompatible	15	I
Blood, whole			WI			Physically incompatible	9	I
Calcium chloride	UP	1 g	WI	8 mg	D, D–S, S	Physically compatible	77	C
Calcium gluconate		1 g	WI	8 mg	D5W	Physically compatible	74	C
Chlorothiazide sodium	MSD		WI			Physically incompatible	9	I
Chlorpheniramine maleate			WI			Physically incompatible	9	I
	SC	100 mg	WI	2 mg	D5W	Physically incompatible	15	I
Cibenzoline succinate		2 g	WB	80 mg	D5W, NS	Physically compatible for 24 hr at 25 °C by visual and microscopic examination	1182	C
Cimetidine HCl	SKF	3 g	WI	40 mg	D5W	Physically compatible and cimetidine chemically stable for 24 hr at room temperature. Norepinephrine not tested	551	C
Corticotropin		500 units	WI	8 mg	D5W	Physically compatible	74	C
Dimenhydrinate	SE	50 mg	WI	8 mg	D5W	Physically compatible	74	C
Dobutamine HCl	LI	1 g	BN	32 mg	D5W, NS	Physically compatible for 24 hr at 21 °C	812	C
Heparin sodium		12,000 units	WI	8 mg	D5W	Physically compatible	74	C
	AB	20,000 units	WI	8 mg	D, D–S, S	Physically compatible	77	C
Hydrocortisone sodium succinate	UP	100 mg	WI	8 mg	D5W	Physically compatible	74	C
Magnesium sulfate		1 g	WI	8 mg	D, D–S, S	Physically compatible	77	C
Meropenem	ZEN	1 and 20 g	WI	8 g	NS	Visually compatible for 4 hr at room temperature	1994	C
Methylprednisolone sodium succinate	UP	40 mg	WI	8 mg	D5S	Physically compatible	329	C
Multivitamins	USV	10 ml	WI	8 mg	D, D–S, S	Physically compatible	77	C

Additive Compatibility (Cont.)

			Norepinephrine bitartrate					
Drug	*Mfr*	*Conc/L*	*Mfr*	*Conc/L*	*Test Soln*	*Remarks*	*Ref*	*C/I*
Netilmicin sulfate	SC	3 g	WI	64 mg	D5S	Physically compatible and netilmicin chemically stable for 7 days at 4 and 25 °C. Norepinephrine not tested	558	C
Pentobarbital sodium			WI			Physically incompatible	9	I
Phenobarbital sodium	WI		WI			Physically incompatible	9	I
Phenytoin sodium	PD		WI			Physically incompatible	9	I
Potassium chloride		3 g	WI	8 mg	D5W	Physically compatible	74	C
	AB	40 mEq	WI	8 mg	D, D–S, S	Physically compatible	77	C
Ranitidine HCl	GL	2 g	WI	4 and 8 mg	D5W, NS[a]	Physically compatible with no ranitidine loss in 48 hr at room temperature under fluorescent light. Norepinephrine not tested	1361	C
	GL	50 mg	WI	4 and 8 mg	D5W, NS[a]	Physically compatible with 2 to 6% ranitidine loss in 48 hr at room temperature under fluorescent light. Norepinephrine not tested	1361	C
	GL	50 mg and 2 g		4 mg	D5W	Physically compatible and ranitidine chemically stable by HPLC for 24 hr at 25 °C. Norepinephrine not tested	1515	C
	GL	50 mg	RC	4 and 8 mg	D5W[a]	Visually compatible with 5 to 7% ranitidine loss and little or no norepinephrine loss by HPLC in 48 hr at room temperature	1802	C
	GL	2 g	RC	4 mg	D5W[a]	Visually compatible but 7% norepinephrine loss in 4 hr and 13% loss in 12 hr by HPLC at room temperature. No ranitidine loss in 48 hr	1802	I
	GL	2 g	RC	8 mg	D5W[a]	Visually compatible but 6% norepinephrine loss in 12 hr and 11% loss in 24 hr by HPLC at room temperature. No ranitidine loss in 48 hr	1802	I
Sodium bicarbonate			WI			Physically incompatible	9	I
	AB	80 mEq	WI	2 mg	D5W	Physically incompatible	15	I
	AB	2.4 mEq[b]	BN	8 mg	D5W	Norepinephrine inactivated	772	I
Streptomycin sulfate			WI			Physically incompatible	9	I
Succinylcholine chloride	AB	2 g	WI	8 mg	D, D–S, S	Physically compatible	77	C
Thiopental sodium	AB		WI			Physically incompatible	9	I
Verapamil HCl	KN	80 mg	BN	8 mg	D5W, NS	Physically compatible for 24 hr	764	C
Vitamin B complex with C		1 vial	WI	8 mg	D5W	Physically compatible	74	C
	AB	10 ml	WI	8 mg	D, D–S, S	Physically compatible	77	C
	UP	10 ml	WI	8 mg	D, D–S, S	Physically compatible	77	C

[a] *Tested in PVC containers.*
[b] *One vial of Neut added to a liter of admixture.*

Drugs in Syringe Compatibility

Norepinephrine bitartrate

Drug (in syringe)	*Mfr*	*Amt*	*Mfr*	*Amt*	*Remarks*	*Ref*	*C/I*
Heparin sodium		2500 units/ 1 ml	HO[a]	1 mg/ 1 ml	Physically compatible for at least 5 min	1053	C

[a]*Tested as the hydrochloride salt.*

Y-Site Injection Compatibility (1:1 Mixture)

Norepinephrine bitartrate

Drug	*Mfr*	*Conc*	*Mfr*	*Conc*	*Remarks*	*Ref*	*C/I*
Amiodarone HCl	LZ	4 mg/ml[c]	BN	0.064 mg/ml[c]	Physically compatible for 24 hr at 21 °C	1032	C
Cisatracurium besylate	GW	0.1, 2, 5 mg/ ml[a]	SW	0.12 mg/ml[a]	Physically compatible with no change in measured turbidity or increase in particle content in 4 hr at 23 °C	2074	C
Diltiazem HCl	MMD	1 mg/ml[a]	WI	0.12 mg/ml[a]	Visually compatible for 24 hr at 25 °C	1530	C
	MMD	1 mg/ml[a]	AB	0.128 mg/ml[a]	Visually compatible for 4 hr at 27 °C	2062	C
Dobutamine HCl	LI	4 mg/ml[a]	AB	0.128 mg/ml[a]	Visually compatible for 4 hr at 27 °C	2062	C
Dopamine HCl	DU	3.2 mg/ml[a]	STR	0.064 mg/ml[a]	Visually compatible for 24 hr at 23 °C	1877	C
	AB	3.2 mg/ml[a]	AB	0.128 mg/ml[a]	Visually compatible for 4 hr at 27 °C	2062	C
Epinephrine HCl	AB	0.02 mg/ml[a]	AB	0.128 mg/ml[a]	Visually compatible for 4 hr at 27 °C	2062	C
Esmolol HCl	DU	40 mg/ml[a]	STR	0.064 mg/ml[a]	Visually compatible for 24 hr at 23 °C	1877	C
Famotidine	MSD	0.2 mg/ml[a]	WI	0.004 mg/ml[a]	Physically compatible for 4 hr at 25 °C	1188	C
Fentanyl citrate	ES	0.05 mg/ml	AB	0.128 mg/ml[a]	Visually compatible for 4 hr at 27 °C	2062	C
Furosemide	AMR	10 mg/ml	AB	0.128 mg/ml[a]	Visually compatible for 4 hr at 27 °C	2062	C
Haloperidol lactate	MN	0.5[a] and 5 mg/ml	WI	0.032 mg/ml[a]	Visually compatible for 24 hr at 21 °C	1523	C
Heparin sodium	UP	1000 units/L[d]	WI	1 mg/ml	Physically compatible for at least 4 hr at room temperature by visual and microscopic examination	534	C
	ES	100 units/ml[a]	AB	0.128 mg/ml[a]	Visually compatible for 4 hr at 27 °C	2062	C
Hetastarch in lactated electrolyte injection (Hextend)	AB	6%	AB	0.12 mg/ml[a]	Physically compatible with no change in measured turbidity or increase in particle content in 4 hr at 23 °C	2339	C
Hydrocortisone sodium succinate	UP	10 mg/L[d]	WI	1 mg/ml	Physically compatible for at least 4 hr at room temperature by visual and microscopic examination	534	C
Hydromorphone HCl	KN	1 mg/ml	AB	0.128 mg/ml[a]	Visually compatible for 4 hr at 27 °C	2062	C
Inamrinone lactate	WB	3 mg/ml[b]	BN	0.004 mg/ml[a]	Physically compatible for at least 4 hr at 25 °C under fluorescent light	992	C
Insulin, regular	LI	1 unit/ml[a]	STR	0.064 mg/ml[a]	White precipitate forms immediately	1877	I
Labetalol HCl	GL	5 mg/ml	STR	0.064 mg/ml[a]	Visually compatible for 24 hr at 23 °C	1877	C
	AH	2 mg/ml[a]	AB	0.128 mg/ml[a]	Visually compatible for 4 hr at 27 °C	2062	C
Lorazepam	WY	0.5 mg/ml[a]	AB	0.128 mg/ml[a]	Visually compatible for 4 hr at 27 °C	2062	C
Meropenem	ZEN	1 and 50 mg/ ml[b]	WI	1 mg/ml	Visually compatible for 4 hr at room temperature	1994	C
Midazolam HCl	RC	1 mg/ml[a]	STR	0.064 mg/ml[a]	Visually compatible for 24 hr at 23 °C	1877	C
	RC	2 mg/ml[a]	AB	0.128 mg/ml[a]	Visually compatible for 4 hr at 27 °C	2062	C

Y-Site Injection Compatibility (1:1 Mixture) (Cont.)

Drug	Mfr	Conc	Norepinephrine bitartrate Mfr	Norepinephrine bitartrate Conc	Remarks	Ref	C/I
Milrinone lactate	SW	0.2 mg/ml[a]	AB	0.128 mg/ml[a]	Visually compatible for 4 hr at 27 °C	2062	C
	SW	0.4 mg/ml[a]	SW	0.064 mg/ml[a]	Visually compatible with little or no loss of either drug by HPLC in 4 hr at 23 °C	2214	C
Morphine sulfate	SX	1 mg/ml[a]	STR	0.064 mg/ml[a]	Visually compatible for 24 hr at 23 °C	1877	C
	SCN	2 mg/ml[a]	AB	0.128 mg/ml[a]	Visually compatible for 4 hr at 27 °C	2062	C
Nicardipine HCl	WY	1 mg/ml[a]	AB	0.128 mg/ml[a]	Visually compatible for 4 hr at 27 °C	2062	C
Nitroglycerin	AB	0.4 mg/ml[a]	AB	0.128 mg/ml[a]	Visually compatible for 4 hr at 27 °C	2062	C
Potassium chloride	AB	40 mEq/L[d]	WI	1 mg/ml	Physically compatible for at least 4 hr at room temperature by visual and microscopic examination	534	C
Propofol	ZEN	10 mg/ml	AB	0.016 mg/ml[a]	Physically compatible for 1 hr at 23 °C with no increase in particle content	2066	C
Ranitidine HCl	GL	1 mg/ml[a]	AB	0.128 mg/ml[a]	Visually compatible for 4 hr at 27 °C	2062	C
Remifentanil HCl	GW	0.025 and 0.25 mg/ml[b]	SW	0.12 mg/ml[a]	Physically compatible with no change in measured turbidity or increase in particle content in 4 hr at 23 °C	2075	C
Thiopental sodium	AB	25 mg/ml[e]	AB	0.128 mg/ml[a]	Precipitate forms in 4 hr at 27 °C	2062	I
TNA #73[e]			BN	0.4 mg/50 ml[c]	Physically compatible for 4 hr by visual observation	1009	C
TPN #212 to #215[e]			AB	0.016 mg/ml[a]	Physically compatible with no change in measured turbidity or increase in particle content in 4 hr at 23 °C	2109	C
Vecuronium bromide	OR	1 mg/ml	AB	0.128 mg/ml[a]	Visually compatible for 4 hr at 27 °C	2062	C
Vitamin B complex with C	RC	2 ml/L[d]	WI	1 mg/ml	Physically compatible for at least 4 hr at room temperature by visual and microscopic examination	534	C

[a] *Tested in dextrose 5% in water.*
[b] *Tested in sodium chloride 0.9%.*
[c] *Tested in both dextrose 5% in water and sodium chloride 0.9%.*
[d] *Tested in dextrose 5% in Ringer's injection, dextrose 5% in Ringer's injection, lactated, dextrose 5% in water, Ringer's injection, lactated, and sodium chloride 0.9%.*
[e] *Refer to Appendix I for the composition of parenteral nutrition solutions. TNA indicates a 3-in-1 admixture, and TPN indicates a 2-in-1 admixture.*

Additional Compatibility Information

Infusion Solutions — At a concentration of 8 mg/L, norepinephrine bitartrate is stated to be compatible with all Abbott infusion solutions. (77) However, dextrose 5% in water and dextrose 5% in sodium chloride 0.9% are the recommended diluents for infusion because their dextrose content provides protection against significant loss of potency due to oxidation. Administration of norepinephrine bitartrate in sodium chloride 0.9% is not recommended because of the lack of oxidation protection. (2) However, other information indicates that norepinephrine bitartrate may be stable in sodium chloride 0.9%. (1163) (See the Solution Compatibility table.)

Blood Products — If whole blood or plasma is indicated, it should be administered from a separate flask through a Y-tube. (2; 4)

Alkaline Drugs — Caution should be employed in mixing additives that may result in a final pH above 6 since norepinephrine bitartrate is alkali labile. These additives include sodium bicarbonate, barbiturates, alkaline-buffered antibiotics (77), lidocaine HCl (24), and aminophylline. (6) Such admixtures should be administered immediately after preparation to assure full potency of norepinephrine bitartrate (77), or separate administration should be considered. (24)

Visual inspection for color change may be inadequate to assess compatibility of admixtures. In one evaluation with aminophylline stored at 25 °C, a color change was not noted until 48 hours had elapsed. However, no intact norepinephrine bitartrate was present in the admixture at 48 hours. (527)

Nafcillin Sodium — Norepinephrine bitartrate (Winthrop) 8 mg/L has been reported to be conditionally compatible with nafcillin sodium (Wyeth) 500 mg/L. The admixture is physically compatible for 24 hours, but the pH is 5.3 and the solution should therefore be used within six hours. (27)

OCTREOTIDE ACETATE
AHFS 92:00

Products — Octreotide acetate injection is available in 1-ml ampuls containing 0.05 mg (50 μg), 0.1 mg (100 μg), and 0.5 (500 μg) mg of octreotide and in 5-ml multiple-dose vials containing 0.2 mg (200 μg) and 1 (1000 μg) mg/ml of octreotide. Each milliliter also contains (2):

	Ampul	Vial
Lactic acid	3.4 mg	3.4 mg
Mannitol	45 mg	45 mg
Phenol		5 mg
Sodium bicarbonate	to adjust pH	to adjust pH
Water for injection	qs 1 ml	qs 1 ml

pH — From 3.9 to 4.5. (2)

Osmolality — Octreotide acetate injection 0.5 mg/ml has an osmolality of 279 mOsm/kg. (1689)

Trade Name(s) — Sandostatin.

Administration — Octreotide acetate injection is usually administered by subcutaneous injection in the smallest volume that will deliver the dose. Subcutaneous injection sites should be rotated. Multiple subcutaneous injections at the same site within a short time should be avoided. Administration by intravenous injection over three minutes or by infusion over 15 to 30 minutes after further dilution with 50 to 200 ml of dextrose 5% in water or sodium chloride 0.9% also has been recommended. (2; 4) NOTE: Do not confuse octreotide acetate injection with the injectable depot suspension product, which cannot be given by these routes of administration. (2)

Stability — Octreotide acetate injection is a clear solution. Ampuls and vials should be stored under refrigeration and protected from light. However, octreotide acetate injection can be stored at room temperature for up to 14 days when protected from light. (2; 4)

Syringes — When stored in Travenol, Minimed, and Becton-Dickinson (Plastipak) plastic syringes of polypropylene and natural rubber, octreotide 100 and 500 μg/ml as the acetate injection retained its potency for 30 days. (1370)

The stability of octreotide acetate injection (Sandoz) 0.2 mg/ml packaged 1 ml in 3-ml polypropylene syringes (Becton-Dickinson) sealed with tip caps (Becton-Dickinson) was evaluated at 3 and 23 °C both exposed to and protected from normal room light. Using HPLC analysis, the authors found no octreotide acetate loss in 29 days stored at 3 °C protected from light but about 7 to 9% loss in 15 to 22 days exposed to light. At 23 °C, the drug was less stable. Although results were somewhat variable, more than 10% loss occurred in about two weeks. The authors recommended a maximum storage time of one week at 23 °C, whether protected from light or not. (2020)

In a similar study, the stability of octreotide acetate injection (Sandoz) 0.2 mg/ml was evaluated for 60 days stored at 5 and −20 °C (light conditions were not stated). The undiluted octreotide acetate injection was packaged 1 ml in 3-ml polypropylene syringes (Terumo) and sealed with a cap. HPLC analysis found losses of about 6% at both storage conditions after 60 days. (2021)

Sorption — The manufacturer indicates that octreotide, a peptide, has the potential for adsorption to plastic and, possibly, glass. (1540) However, in both static and dynamic tests, octreotide did not adsorb to Travenol, Minimed, and Becton-Dickinson (Plastipak) syringes of polypropylene and natural rubber, Travenol 3-ml insulin pump containers of polypropylene and polycarbonate, and Microflex PVC and Minimed polyolefin-lined PVC administration tubing. (1370) Neither was it adsorbed to glass infusion bottles or a PVC administration set at a concentration of 5 μg/ml in sodium chloride 0.9%. (1371)

Compatibility Information

Solution Compatibility

Octreotide acetate injection

Solution	*Mfr*	*Mfr*	*Conc/L*	*Remarks*	*Ref*	*C/I*
Fat emulsion 10%, intravenous	KV	SZ	1.5 mg	Octreotide content unstable with time	1373	I
Sodium chloride 0.9%	TR[a]	SZ	1.5 mg	Little octreotide loss over 48 hr at room temperature in ambient room light	1373	C
		SZ	5, 50, 100 μg	Physically compatible with no octreotide loss in 96 hr at room temperature exposed to light	1372	C
TNA #139[b]	[c]	SZ	450 μg	Physically compatible with no change in lipid particle size in 48 hr at 22 °C under fluorescent light and 7 days at 4 °C. Octreotide activity highly variable by radioimmunoassay	1540	?
TPN #119 and #120[b]	[a]	SZ	1.5 mg	Little octreotide loss over 48 hr at room temperature in ambient room light	1373	C

[a]*Tested in PVC containers.*
[b]*Refer to Appendix I for the composition of parenteral nutrition solutions. TNA indicates a 3-in-1 admixture, and TPN indicates a 2-in-1 admixture.*
[c]*Tested in both glass and ethylene vinyl acetate (EVA) containers.*

Additive Compatibility

Octreotide acetate injection

Drug	*Mfr*	*Conc/L*	*Mfr*	*Conc/L*	*Test Soln*	*Remarks*	*Ref*	*C/I*
Heparin sodium	ES	1000 units	SZ	1.5 mg	TPN #120[a]	Little octreotide loss over 48 hr at room temperature in ambient light	1373	C

[a]*Refer to Appendix I for the composition of parenteral nutrition solutions. TPN indicates a 2-in-1 admixture.*

Y-Site Injection Compatibility (1:1 Mixture)

Octreotide acetate injection

Drug	*Mfr*	*Conc*	*Mfr*	*Conc*	*Remarks*	*Ref*	*C/I*
TNA #218 to #226[b]			SZ	0.01 mg/ml[a]	Visually compatible with no precipitate or emulsion damage apparent in 4 hr at 23 °C	2215	C
TPN #212 to #215[b]			SZ	0.01 mg/ml[a]	Physically compatible with no change in measured turbidity or increase in particle content in 4 hr at 23 °C	2109	C

[a]*Tested in dextrose 5% in water.*
[b]*Refer to Appendix I for the composition of parenteral nutrition solutions. TNA indicates a 3-in-1 admixture, and TPN indicates a 2-in-1 admixture.*

Additional Compatibility Information

Infusion Solutions — Octreotide acetate injection (Sandoz) is physically compatible and chemically stable in concentrations of 5, 50, and 100 µg/ml in sodium chloride 0.9%, exhibiting no decomposition in 96 hours at room temperature when exposed to light. (1372)

Parenteral Nutrition Solutions — The manufacturer states that octreotide acetate injection should not be added to total parenteral nutrition solutions because of the formation of a glycosyl octreotide conjugate that may decrease the product's efficacy (2), although the clinical value of this administration approach continues to be debated. (2136)

Insulin — Radioimmunoassays of insulin levels in 3-L bags of parenteral nutrition solutions showed a marked reduction when octreotide 150 µg was added. Sample parenteral nutrition solutions, with and without octreotide, were prepared with regular insulin 15 units/3-L bag. Subsequent analysis found an insulin level of 3.5 units/L in the plain parenteral nutrition solution, an amount consistent with losses occurring due to surface adsorption. However, in the parenteral nutrition solution containing octreotide, the insulin level was only 0.6 unit/L. The reason for this incompatibility is not known. (1377)

ONDANSETRON HCL
AHFS 56:22

Products — Ondansetron HCl is available in 20-ml multiple-dose vials and 2-ml single-dose vials. Each milliliter of solution in multiple-dose vials contains ondansetron (as the hydrochloride dihydrate) 2 mg with sodium chloride 8.3 mg, citric acid monohydrate 0.5 mg, sodium citrate dihydrate 0.25 mg, methylparaben 1.2 mg, and propylparaben 0.15 mg. Each milliliter of solution in single-dose vials contains ondansetron (as the hydrochloride dihydrate) 2 mg with sodium chloride 9 mg, citric acid monohydrate 0.5 mg, and sodium citrate dihydrate 0.25 mg. (2)

Ondansetron HCl (Glaxo Wellcome) is also available as a premixed infusion solution in dextrose 5% containing in each 50 ml of solution ondansetron 32 mg (as the hydrochloride dihydrate), dextrose 2.5 g, citric acid 26 mg, and sodium citrate 11.5 mg in water for injection. (2)

pH — From 3.3 to 4. (2)

Osmolality — Ondansetron HCl 2 mg/ml has an osmolality of 281 mOsm/kg. (1689) The osmolarity of the premixed ondansetron HCl 32 mg/50 ml solution is 270 mOsm/L. (2)

Trade Name(s) — Zofran.

Administration — Ondansetron hydrochloride is administered intravenously over 15 minutes after further dilution with 50 ml of sodium chloride 0.9% or dextrose 5% in water. By intravenous injection, it is administered undiluted over at least 30 seconds and preferably over two to five minutes. (2; 4)

Stability — Ondansetron HCl is a clear, colorless solution. It should be stored at room temperature or under refrigeration and protected from light, excessive heat, and from freezing. (2) Although ondansetron HCl is unstable under intense light, it is stable for about a month in daylight with added fluorescent light. (1366)

Ondansetron HCl (Glaxo) 0.03 and 0.3 mg/ml in dextrose 5% in water or sodium chloride 0.9% was stable when frozen at −20 °C, exhibiting a 10% or less loss in three months. (1642)

pH Effects — The natural pH of ondansetron HCl solutions is about 4.5 to 4.6. (1366; 1367) If the pH is increased, a precipitate of ondansetron free base has been reported to develop at pH 5.7 (1366) and pH 7. (1513) Redissolution of the ondansetron precipitate occurs at pH 6.2 when titrated with hydrochloric acid. (1513) Precipitation by combination with alkaline drugs has been observed. (1365; 1513)

Syringes — Casto reported the stability of ondansetron HCl undiluted at 2 mg/ml and diluted in dextrose 5% in water and sodium chloride 0.9% at 1, 0.5, and 0.25 mg/ml packaged in polypropylene syringes. Representative syringes were stored at 24 °C for 48 hours, 4 °C for 14 days, and frozen at −20 °C for 90 days. Visually, the solutions exhibited no precipitate or color or clarity changes. HPLC analysis found ondansetron HCl concentrations in all samples remained above 90% throughout the study periods; most samples were above 95%. Sequentially storing sample syringes for 90 days at −20 °C followed by 14 days at 4 °C followed by 48 hours at 24 °C did not alter the stability. (2056)

When diluted with compatible infusion solutions, ondansetron HCl is stable for up to seven days at room temperature or under refrigeration in polypropylene–neoprene syringes (Plastipak) with syringe caps. (1366)

Ambulatory Pumps — Ondansetron HCl (Glaxo) 2 mg/ml in medication cassette reservoirs (Pharmacia Deltec CADD-1) was pumped by portable infusion pumps (CADD-Plus) and maintained at 30 °C to simulate use conditions. Approximately 95% of the initial concentration was retained by HPLC after seven days. (1553)

Ondansetron HCl (Glaxo) 0.24 mg/ml diluted in sodium chloride 0.9% and packaged in medication cassette reservoirs (CADD-1) exhibited no loss by HPLC stored for 24 hours at 30 °C or for 30 days at 3 °C followed by 24 hours at 30 °C. (1553)

Elastomeric Reservoir Pumps — Ondansetron HCl (Glaxo) 0.03 and 0.3 mg/ml in dextrose 5% in water and in sodium chloride 0.9% was packaged in Kraton polymer elastomeric reservoirs for the Homepump. The solutions were visually compatible, and no ondansetron loss by HPLC occurred in 14 days at 4 °C under fluorescent light. In addition, no microbial growth was found. (1722)

Ondansetron HCl solutions in elastomeric reservoir pumps have been stated by the pump manufacturers to be stable for the following time periods frozen, refrigerated (REF), or at room temperature (RT) (31):

Pump Reservoir(s)	Conc.	Frozen	REF	RT
Infusor	0.1 to 0.7 mg/ml[a,b]		10 days	24 hr[c]
Intermate	0.1 to 0.7 mg/ml[a,b]		10 days	24 hr[c]
Medflo	0.3 mg/ml[a,b]	90 days	14 days	7 days
ReadyMed	0.08 mg/ml[a]		7 days	7 days
	0.25 mg/ml[b]		14 days	2 days

[a]*In dextrose 5% in water.*
[b]*In sodium chloride 0.9%.*
[c]*After refrigerated storage for 10 days.*

Filtration — Ondansetron HCl (Glaxo) 0.03 and 0.2 mg/ml (30 and 200 µg/ml) in sodium chloride 0.9% was delivered over 15 minutes through five 0.2-µm inline filters: Continu-Flo Solution Set (Baxter, 2C5561S), Filtered Extension Sets (Burron, PFE-2007 and FE-2024), Universal Primary infusion set (IVAC, 52023), and Ivex-HP Filterset-SL (Abbott, 4524). Little or no ondansetron loss was found by HPLC. (1678)

Central Venous Catheter — Ondansetron HCl (Glaxo Wellcome) 0.2 mg/ml in dextrose 5% in water was found to be compatible with the ARROWg+ard Blue Plus (Arrow International) chlorhexidine-bearing triple-lumen central catheter. HPLC analysis was used to evaluate completeness of drug delivery through the catheter and the amount of chlorhexidine removed from the internal lumens. Essentially complete delivery of the drug was found with little or no drug loss occurring. Furthermore, chlorhexidine delivered from the catheter remained at trace amounts with no substantial increase due to the delivery of the drug through the catheter. (2335)

Compatibility Information

Solution Compatibility

Ondansetron HCl

Solution	*Mfr*	*Mfr*	*Conc/L*	*Remarks*	*Ref*	*C/I*
Dextrose 5% in water	BP[a]	GL	16 and 80 mg	Physically compatible and chemically stable for 7 days at room temperature exposed to light and at 4 °C	1366	C
		GL	24 and 96 mg	Visually compatible with no loss by HPLC in 14 days at 24 °C or 14 days at 5 °C followed by 2 days at 24 °C	1560	C
	BA[a]	GL	30 and 300 mg	Visually compatible with 5% or less loss by HPLC in 48 hr at 25 °C or 14 days at 5 °C	1642	C
	MG[b]	GL	0.03 and 0.3 g	Visually compatible with no ondansetron loss by HPLC in 14 days at 4 °C under fluorescent light and no microbial growth	1722	C
Dextrose 5% in water with potassium chloride 0.3%	BP[a]	GL	16 mg	Physically compatible and chemically stable for 7 days at room temperature exposed to light and at 4 °C	1366	C

Solution Compatibility (Cont.)

Ondansetron HCl

Solution	*Mfr*	*Mfr*	*Conc/L*	*Remarks*	*Ref*	*C/I*
Mannitol 10%	BP[a]	GL	16 mg	Physically compatible and chemically stable for 7 days at room temperature exposed to light and at 4 °C	1366	C
Ringer's injection	BP[a]	GL	16 mg	Physically compatible and chemically stable for 7 days at room temperature exposed to light and at 4 °C	1366	C
Ringer's injection, lactated		GL	24 and 96 mg	Visually compatible with no loss by HPLC in 14 days at 24 °C or 14 days at 5 °C followed by 2 days at 24 °C	1560	C
Sodium chloride 0.9%	BP[a]	GL	16 and 80 mg	Physically compatible and chemically stable for 7 days at room temperature exposed to light and at 4 °C	1366	C
		GL	24 and 96 mg	Visually compatible with no loss by HPLC in 14 days at 24 °C or 14 days at 5 °C followed by 2 days at 24 °C	1560	C
	BA[c]	GL	240 mg	No loss by HPLC in 24 hr at 30 °C or 30 days at 3 °C followed by 24 hr at 30 °C	1553	C
	BA[a]	GL	30 and 300 mg	Visually compatible with 4% or less loss by HPLC in 48 hr at 25 °C or 14 days at 5 °C	1642	C
	MG[b]	GL	0.03 and 0.3 g	Visually compatible with no ondansetron loss by HPLC in 14 days at 4 °C under fluorescent light and no microbial growth	1722	C
	BA[a]	CER	100 mg	Visually compatible with about 6 to 7% loss by HPLC after 30 days at 4 °C followed by 2 days at 23 °C	1882	C
	BA[a]	CER	200, 400, 640 mg	Visually compatible with not more than 4% loss by HPLC after 30 days at 4 °C followed by 2 days at 23 °C	1882	C
Sodium chloride 0.9% with potassium chloride 0.3%	BP[a]	GL	16 mg	Physically compatible and chemically stable for 7 days at room temperature exposed to light and at 4 °C	1366	C
TNA #190[d]		GL	0.03 and 0.3 g	Physically compatible with little or no ondansetron loss by HPLC in 48 hr at 24 °C under fluorescent light	1766	C

[a]Tested in PVC containers.
[b]Tested in a Kraton polymer elastomeric infusion device (Homepump, Block).
[c]Tested in a medication cassette reservoir (Pharmacia Deltec CADD-1).
[d]Refer to Appendix I for the composition of parenteral nutrition solutions. TNA indicates a 3-in-1 admixture.

Additive Compatibility

Ondansetron HCl

Drug	*Mfr*	*Conc/L*	*Mfr*	*Conc/L*	*Test Soln*	*Remarks*	*Ref*	*C/I*
Cisplatin	BR	485 mg	GL	1.031 g	NS[a]	Physically compatible with little or no loss of either drug by HPLC in 24 hr at 4 °C followed by 7 days at 30 °C	1846	C
	BR	219 mg	GL	479 mg	NS[b]	Physically compatible with little or no loss of either drug by HPLC in 24 hr at 4 °C followed by 7 days at 30 °C	1846	C

Additive Compatibility (Cont.)

Ondansetron HCl

Drug	*Mfr*	*Conc/L*	*Mfr*	*Conc/L*	*Test Soln*	*Remarks*	*Ref*	*C/I*
Cyclophosphamide	MJ	300 mg	GL	50 mg	D5W[a], NS[a]	Visually compatible with 9 to 10% cyclophosphamide loss and no ondansetron loss by HPLC in 5 days at 24 °C. No loss of either drug in 8 days at 4 °C	1812	C
	MJ	2 g	GL	400 mg	D5W[a], NS[a]	Visually compatible with 10% cyclophosphamide loss and no ondansetron loss by HPLC in 5 days at 24 °C. No loss of either drug in 8 days at 4 °C	1812	C
Cytarabine	UP	200 mg	GL	30 and 300 mg	D5W[a]	Physically compatible with little or no loss of either drug by HPLC in 48 hr at 23 °C	1876	C
	UP	40 g	GL	30 and 300 mg	D5W[a]	Physically compatible with little or no loss of either drug by HPLC in 48 hr at 23 °C	1876	C
Dacarbazine	MI	1 g	GL	30 and 300 mg	D5W[a]	Physically compatible with little or no loss of ondansetron by HPLC in 48 hr at 23 °C. 8 to 12% dacarbazine loss in 24 hr and 20% loss in 48 hr at 23 °C	1876	C
	MI	3 g	GL	30 and 300 mg	D5W[a]	Physically compatible with little or no loss of ondansetron by HPLC in 48 hr at 23 °C. 8% dacarbazine loss in 24 hr and 15% loss in 48 hr at 23 °C	1876	C
Dacarbazine with doxorubicin HCl	LY AD	8 g 800 mg	GL	640 mg	D5W[a]	Visually compatible with greater than 90% ondansetron and doxorubicin potency by HPLC over 24 hr at 30 °C and after 7 days at 4 °C followed by 24 hr at 30 °C. Dacarbazine stable for 8 hr but up to 13% loss in 24 hr	2092	I
Dacarbazine with doxorubicin HCl	LY AD	20 g 1.5 g	GL	640 mg	D5W[a]	Visually compatible with greater than 90% potency of all drugs by HPLC over 24 hr at 30 °C and after 7 days at 4 °C followed by 24 hr at 30 °C.	2092	C
Dacarbazine with doxorubicin HCl	LY AD	8 g 800 mg	GL	640 mg	D5W[b]	Visually compatible with greater than 90% potency of all drugs by HPLC over 24 hr at 30 °C and after 7 days at 4 °C followed by 24 hr at 30 °C.	2092	C
Dacarbazine with doxorubicin HCl	LY AD	20 g 1.5 g	GL	640 mg	D5W[b]	Visually compatible with greater than 90% potency of all drugs by HPLC over 24 hr at 30 °C and after 7 days at 4 °C followed by 24 hr at 30 °C.	2092	C
Dexamethasone sodium phosphate		20 and 40 mg	GL	48 mg	D5W, NS	Visually compatible for 24 hr at 22 °C	1608	C
		200 and 400 mg	GL	160 mg	NS	Visually compatible for 24 hr at 22 °C	1608	C
	ES	200 mg	CER	100 mg	NS[a]	Visually compatible with no dexamethasone loss and 8% ondansetron loss by HPLC after 30 days at 4 °C followed by 2 days at 23 °C	1882	C
	ES	400 mg	CER	100 and 200 mg	NS[a]	Visually compatible with no dexamethasone loss and 7 to 10% ondansetron loss by HPLC after 30 days at 4 °C followed by 2 days at 23 °C	1882	C

Additive Compatibility (Cont.)

Drug	*Mfr*	*Conc/L*	*Mfr*	*Conc/L*	*Test Soln*	*Remarks*	*Ref*	*C/I*
				Ondansetron HCl				
	ES	200 mg	CER	200, 400, and 640 mg	NS[a]	Visually compatible with no dexamethasone loss and not more than 5% ondansetron loss by HPLC after 30 days at 4 °C followed by 2 days at 23 °C	1882	C
	ES	400 mg	CER	400 and 640 mg	NS[a]	Visually compatible with no dexamethasone loss and not more than 3% ondansetron loss by HPLC after 30 days at 4 °C followed by 2 days at 23 °C	1882	C
	ES	200 and 400 mg	CER	640 mg	D5W[c]	Visually compatible with 7% dexamethasone loss and no ondansetron loss by HPLC after 30 days at 4 °C followed by 2 days at 23 °C	1882	C
	MSD	400 mg	GL	150 mg	NS[a]	Visually compatible with 4% or less loss of either drug by HPLC in 28 days at 4 and 22 °C	2084	C
	MSD	400 mg	GL	150 mg	D5W[a]	Visually compatible with 4% or less loss of either drug by HPLC in 28 days at 4 °C. Up to 10% ondansetron loss in 3 days at 22 °C	2084	C
	MSD	230 mg	GL	750 mg	NS[a]	Visually compatible with 4% or less loss of either drug by HPLC in 28 days at 4 °C. Up to 10% ondansetron loss in 7 days at 22 °C	2084	C
	MSD	230 mg	GL	750 mg	D5W[a]	Visually compatible with up to 13% ondansetron loss by HPLC in 3 days at 4 and 22 °C	2084	?
Doxorubicin HCl	MJ	100 mg	GL	30 and 300 mg	D5W[a]	Physically compatible with little or no loss of either drug by HPLC in 48 hr at 23 °C	1876	C
	MJ	2 g	GL	30 and 300 mg	D5W[a]	Physically compatible with little or no loss of either drug by HPLC in 48 hr at 23 °C	1876	C
Doxorubicin HCl with vincristine sulfate	AD LI	400 mg 14 mg	GL	480 mg	D5W[b]	Visually compatible with greater than 90% potency of all drugs by HPLC after 5 days at 4 °C followed by 24 hr at 30 °C	2092	C
Doxorubicin HCl with vincristine sulfate	AD LI	800 mg 28 mg	GL	960 mg	D5W[a]	Visually compatible with greater than 90% potency of all drugs by HPLC after 120 hr at 30 °C	2092	C
Etoposide	BR	100 mg	GL	30 and 300 mg	D5W[a]	Physically compatible with little or no loss of ondansetron by HPLC in 48 hr at 23 °C. 4% etoposide loss in 24 hr and 6% loss in 48 hr at 23 °C	1876	C
	BR	400 mg	GL	30 and 300 mg	D5W[a]	Physically compatible with little or no loss of either drug by HPLC in 48 hr at 23 °C	1876	C
Fluconazole with ranitidine HCl	RR GL	2 g 500 mg	GL	100 mg	[a]	Visually compatible with no loss of any drug by HPLC in 4 hr	1730	C
Hydromorphone HCl	ES	500 mg	GL	100 mg and 1 g	NS	Physically compatible with no loss of either drug by HPLC in 7 days at 32 °C or 31 days at 4 and 22 °C protected from light	1690	C

Additive Compatibility (Cont.)

Ondansetron HCl

Drug	Mfr	Conc/L	Mfr	Conc/L	Test Soln	Remarks	Ref	C/I
Meperidine HCl	WY	4 g	GL	100 mg and 1 g	NS[a]	Physically compatible with no change in measured turbidity or increase in particle content and no loss of either drug by HPLC in 31 days at 4 and 22 °C and in 7 days at 32 °C	1862	C
Meropenem	ZEN	1 g	GL	1 g	NS	Visually compatible for 4 hr at room temperature	1994	C
	ZEN	20 g	GL	1 g	NS	White precipitate forms immediately	1994	I
Methotrexate sodium	LE	500 mg	GL	30 and 300 mg	D5W[a]	Physically compatible with little or no loss of either drug by HPLC in 48 hr at 23 °C	1876	C
	LE	6 g	GL	30 and 300 mg	D5W[a]	Physically compatible with little or no loss of either drug by HPLC in 48 hr at 23 °C	1876	C
Morphine sulfate	AST	1 g	GL	100 mg and 1 g	NS	Physically compatible with no ondansetron loss and 5% or less morphine loss by HPLC in 7 days at 32 °C or 31 days at 4 and 22 °C protected from light	1690	C

[a]Tested in PVC containers.
[b]Tested in polyisoprene reservoirs (Travenol Infusors).
[c]Tested in ondansetron HCl ready-to-use CR3 polyester bags.

Drugs in Syringe Compatibility

Ondansetron HCl

Drug (in syringe)	Mfr	Amt	Mfr	Amt	Remarks	Ref	C/I
Alfentanil HCl	JN	0.167 mg/ml[b]	GW	1.33 mg/ml[b]	Physically compatible with no measured increase in particulates and little or no loss of either drug by HPLC in 24 hr at 4 or 23 °C	2199	C
Atropine sulfate	GNS	0.133 mg/ml[b]	GW	1.33 mg/ml[b]	Physically compatible with no measured increase in particulates and less than 6% loss of ondansetron and less than 7% loss of atropine by HPLC in 24 hr at 4 or 23 °C	2199	C
Dexamethasone sodium phosphate	ES	0.33 and 0.67 mg/ml[a]	CER	0.17 mg/ml[a]	Visually compatible with no loss of either drug by HPLC after 30 days at 4 °C followed by 2 days at 23 °C	1882	C
	ES	0.5 mg/ml[a]	CER	0.25 mg/ml[a]	Visually compatible with no loss of either drug by HPLC after 30 days at 4 °C followed by 2 days at 23 °C	1882	C
	ES	1 mg/ml[a]	CER	0.25 mg/ml[a]	Visually compatible for 3 days at 4 °C. Precipitation of ondansetron observed at 7 days as opaque white ring	1882	C
	ES	0.33 and 0.67 mg/ml[a]	CER	0.33 mg/ml[a]	Visually compatible with no loss of either drug by HPLC after 30 days at 4 °C followed by 2 days at 23 °C	1882	C
	ES	0.5 mg/ml[a]	CER	0.5 mg/ml[a]	Visually compatible with no loss of either drug by HPLC after 30 days at 4 °C followed by 2 days at 23 °C	1882	C
	ES	1 mg/ml[a]	CER	0.5 mg/ml[a]	Visually compatible for 3 days at 4 °C. Precipitation of ondansetron observed at 5 days as opaque white ring	1882	C

Drugs in Syringe Compatibility (Cont.)

Ondansetron HCl

Drug (in syringe)	*Mfr*	*Amt*	*Mfr*	*Amt*	*Remarks*	*Ref*	*C/I*
	ES	0.33 and 0.67 mg/ ml[a]	CER	0.67 mg/ ml[a]	Visually compatible with no loss of either drug by HPLC after 30 days at 4 °C followed by 2 days at 23 °C	1882	C
	ES	0.33 mg/ ml[a]	CER	1.07 mg/ ml[a]	Visually compatible with no loss of either drug by HPLC after 30 days at 4 °C followed by 2 days at 23 °C	1882	C
	ES	0.67 mg/ ml[a]	CER	1.07 mg/ ml[a]	Heavy white flocculent precipitate within 72 hr at 4 °C. 25 to 30% loss of both drugs by HPLC	1882	I
Droperidol	AMR	1.25 mg/ ml[b]	GW	1 mg/ml[b]	Droperidol precipitates in less than 4 hr at 4 °C. At 23 °C, little or no loss of either drug by HPLC in 8 hr, but droperidol precipitates after that time	2199	I
Fentanyl citrate	ES	0.0167 mg/ml[b]	GW	1.33 mg/ ml[b]	Physically compatible with no measured increase in particulates and little or no loss of either drug by HPLC in 24 hr at 4 or 23 °C	2199	C
Glycopyrrolate	AMR	0.1 mg/ ml[b]	GW	1 mg/ml[b]	Physically compatible with no measured increase in particulates and little or no loss of either drug by HPLC in 24 hr at 4 or 23 °C	2199	C
Meperidine HCl	ES	8.33 mg/ ml[b]	GW	1.33 mg/ ml[b]	Physically compatible with no measured increase in particulates and little or no loss of either drug by HPLC in 24 hr at 4 or 23 °C	2199	C
Metoclopramide HCl	SO	2.5 mg/ ml[b]	GW	1 mg/ml[b]	Physically compatible with no measured increase in particulates and less than 6% loss of ondansetron and less than 5% loss of metoclopramide by HPLC in 24 hr at 4 or 23 °C	2199	C
Midazolam HCl	RC	1.66 mg/ ml[b]	GW	1.33 mg/ ml[b]	Physically compatible with no measured increase in particulates and less than 4% loss of ondansetron and less than 7% loss of midazolam by HPLC in 24 hr at 4 or 23 °C	2199	C
Morphine sulfate	ES	2.67 mg/ ml[b]	GW	1.33 mg/ ml[b]	Physically compatible with no measured increase in particulates and less than 5% loss of ondansetron and less than 4% loss of morphine by HPLC in 24 hr at 4 or 23 °C	2199	C
Naloxone HCl	AST	0.133 mg/ml[b]	GW	1.33 mg/ ml[b]	Physically compatible with no measured increase in particulates and 6% or less loss of ondansetron and 5% or less loss of naloxone by HPLC in 24 hr at 4 or 23 °C	2199	C
Neostigmine methylsulfate	ES	0.167 mg/ml[b]	GW	1.33 mg/ ml[b]	Physically compatible with no measured increase in particulates and less than 3% loss of ondansetron and less than 5% loss of neostigmine by HPLC in 24 hr at 4 or 23 °C	2199	C
Propofol	STU	1 and 5 mg/ml[b]	GW	1 mg/ml[b]	Physically compatible with no measured increase in particulates and little or no loss of either drug by HPLC in 4 hr at 23 °C	2199	C

[a]*Diluted with sodium chloride 0.9% drawn into a syringe prior to drugs to yield the concentrations cited.*
[b]*Tested in sodium chloride 0.9%.*

Y-Site Injection Compatibility (1:1 Mixture)

Drug	Mfr	Conc	Mfr (Ondansetron HCl)	Conc (Ondansetron HCl)	Remarks	Ref	C/I
Acyclovir sodium	BW	7 mg/ml[a]	GL	1 mg/ml[b]	Immediate precipitation	1365	I
Alatrofloxacin mesylate	PF	1.43 mg/ml[a]	GL	2 mg/ml	Visually and microscopically compatible with the ondansetron HCl pushed through a Y-site over 5 min	2235	C
Aldesleukin	CHI	33,800 I.U./ml[a]	GL	0.7 mg/ml[a]	Visually compatible with little or no loss of aldesleukin activity by bioassay	1857	C
Allopurinol sodium	BW	3 mg/ml[b]	GL	1 mg/ml[b]	Heavy turbidity forms immediately, becoming white flocculent precipitate	1686	I
Amifostine	USB	10 mg/ml[a]	GL	1 mg/ml[a]	Physically compatible with no change in measured turbidity or increase in particle content in 4 hr at 23 °C	1845	C
Amikacin sulfate	BR	5 mg/ml[a]	GL	1 mg/ml[b]	Physically compatible for 4 hr at 22 °C	1365	C
Aminophylline	AMR	2.5 mg/ml[a]	GL	1 mg/ml[b]	Immediate turbidity and precipitation	1365	I
Amphotericin B	SQ	0.6 mg/ml[a]	GL	1 mg/ml[a]	Immediate pale yellow turbidity and precipitation	1365	I
Amphotericin B cholesteryl sulfate complex	SEQ	0.83 mg/ml[a]	CER	1 mg/ml[a]	Gross precipitate forms	2117	I
Ampicillin sodium	BR	20 mg/ml[b]	GL	1 mg/ml[b]	Immediate turbidity and precipitation	1365	I
Ampicillin sodium–sulbactam sodium	RR	20 + 10 mg/ml[b]	GL	1 mg/ml[b]	Immediate turbidity and precipitation	1365	I
Amsacrine	NCI	1 mg/ml[a]	GL	1 mg/ml[a]	Orange precipitate forms within 30 min	1365	I
Aztreonam	SQ	40 mg/ml[a]	GL	1 mg/ml[b]	Physically compatible for 4 hr at 22 °C	1365	C
	SQ	40 mg/ml[a]	GL	0.03 and 0.3 mg/ml[a]	Visually compatible with little or no loss of either drug by HPLC in 4 hr at 25 °C	1732	C
	SQ	40 mg/ml[a]	GL	1 mg/ml[a]	Physically compatible with no subvisual haze or particle formation in 4 hr at 23 °C	1758	C
Bleomycin sulfate	BR	1 unit/ml[b]	GL	1 mg/ml[b]	Physically compatible for 4 hr at 22 °C	1365	C
Carboplatin	BR	5 mg/ml[a]	GL	1 mg/ml[b]	Physically compatible for 4 hr at 22 °C	1365	C
		0.18 to 9.9 mg/ml	GL	16 to 160 μg/ml	Physically compatible when carboplatin given over 10 to 60 min via Y-site	1366	C
Carmustine	BR	1.5 mg/ml[a]	GL	1 mg/ml[b]	Physically compatible for 4 hr at 22 °C	1365	C
Cefazolin sodium	LEM	20 mg/ml[a]	GL	1 mg/ml[b]	Physically compatible for 4 hr at 22 °C	1365	C
	LI	20 mg/ml[a]	GL	0.03 and 0.3 mg/ml[a]	Visually compatible with little or no loss of either drug by HPLC in 4 hr at 25 °C	1732	C
Cefepime HCl	BMS	20 mg/ml[a]	GL	1 mg/ml[a]	Haze forms immediately	1689	I
Cefoperazone sodium	RR	40 mg/ml[a]	GL	1 mg/ml[b]	Immediate turbidity and precipitation	1365	I
Cefotaxime sodium	HO	20 mg/ml[a]	GL	1 mg/ml[b]	Physically compatible for 4 hr at 22 °C	1365	C
Cefoxitin sodium	MSD	20 mg/ml[a]	GL	1 mg/ml[b]	Physically compatible for 4 hr at 22 °C	1365	C
Ceftazidime	GL[i]	40 mg/ml[a]	GL	1 mg/ml[b]	Physically compatible for 4 hr at 22 °C	1365	C
	[i]	100 to 200 mg/ml	GL	16 to 160 μg/ml	Physically compatible when ceftazidime given as 5-min bolus via Y-site	1366	C
	LI[i]	40 mg/ml[a]	GL	0.03 and 0.3 mg/ml[a]	Visually compatible with less than 10% loss of either drug by HPLC in 4 hr at 25 °C	1732	C
	GL[h]	40 mg/ml[a]	GL	1 mg/ml[b]	Physically compatible for 4 hr at 22 °C	1365	C

Y-Site Injection Compatibility (1:1 Mixture) (Cont.)

			Ondansetron HCl				
Drug	*Mfr*	*Conc*	*Mfr*	*Conc*	*Remarks*	*Ref*	*C/I*
Ceftizoxime sodium	FUJ	20 mg/ml[a]	GL	1 mg/ml[b]	Physically compatible for 4 hr at 22 °C	1365	C
Cefuroxime sodium	LI	30 mg/ml[a]	GL	1 mg/ml[b]	Physically compatible for 4 hr at 22 °C	1365	C
Chlorpromazine HCl	ES	2 mg/ml[a]	GL	1 mg/ml[b]	Physically compatible for 4 hr at 22 °C	1365	C
Cimetidine HCl	SKF	12 mg/ml[a]	GL	1 mg/ml[b]	Physically compatible for 4 hr at 22 °C	1365	C
Cisatracurium besylate	GW	0.1, 2, 5 mg/ml[a]	CER	1 mg/ml[a]	Physically compatible with no change in measured turbidity or increase in particle content in 4 hr at 23 °C	2074	C
Cisplatin	BR	1 mg/ml 0.48 mg/ml	GL GL	1 mg/ml[b] 16 to 160 μg/ml	Physically compatible for 4 hr at 22 °C Physically compatible when cisplatin given over 1 to 8 hr via Y-site	1365 1366	C C
Cladribine	ORT	0.015[b] and 0.5[d] mg/ml	CER	1 mg/ml[b]	Physically compatible with no change in measured turbidity or increase in particle content in 4 hr at 23 °C	1969	C
Clindamycin phosphate	LY	10 mg/ml[a]	GL	1 mg/ml[b]	Physically compatible for 4 hr at 22 °C	1365	C
Cyclophosphamide	MJ	10 mg/ml[a] 20 mg/ml	GL GL	1 mg/ml[b] 16 to 160 μg/ml	Physically compatible for 4 hr at 22 °C Physically compatible when cyclophosphamide given as 5-min bolus via Y-site	1365 1366	C C
Cytarabine	UP	50 mg/ml	GL	1 mg/ml[b]	Physically compatible for 4 hr at 22 °C	1365	C
Dacarbazine	MI	4 mg/ml[a]	GL	1 mg/ml[b]	Physically compatible for 4 hr at 22 °C	1365	C
Dactinomycin	MSD	0.01 mg/ml[a]	GL	1 mg/ml[b]	Physically compatible for 4 hr at 22 °C	1365	C
Daunorubicin HCl	WY	2 mg/ml[a]	GL	1 mg/ml[b]	Physically compatible for 4 hr at 22 °C	1365	C
Dexamethasone sodium phosphate	MSD	1 mg/ml[a]	GL	1 mg/ml[b]	Physically compatible for 4 hr at 22 °C	1365	C
Diphenhydramine HCl	PD	2 mg/ml[a]	GL	1 mg/ml[b]	Physically compatible for 4 hr at 22 °C	1365	C
Docetaxel	RPR	0.9 mg/ml[a]	GW	1 mg/ml[a]	Physically compatible with no change in measured turbidity or increase in particle content in 4 hr at 23 °C	2224	C
Dopamine HCl	AB	0.8 mg/ml[a]	GL	0.32 mg/ml[c]	Visually compatible for 24 hr at room temperature in test tubes. No precipitate found on filter from Y-site delivery	2063	C
Doxorubicin HCl	CET	2 mg/ml 2 mg/ml	GL GL	1 mg/ml[b] 16 to 160 μg/ml	Physically compatible for 4 hr at 22 °C Physically compatible when doxorubicin given as 5-min bolus via Y-site	1365 1366	C C
Doxorubicin HCl liposome injection	SEQ	0.4 mg/ml[a]	CER	1 mg/ml[a]	Physically compatible with little or no change in measured turbidity and no increase in particle content in 4 hr at 23 °C	2087	C
Doxycycline hyclate	ES	1 mg/ml[a]	GL	1 mg/ml[b]	Physically compatible for 4 hr at 22 °C	1365	C
Droperidol	JN	0.4 mg/ml[a]	GL	1 mg/ml[b]	Physically compatible for 4 hr at 22 °C	1365	C
Etoposide	BR	0.4 mg/ml[a] 0.144 to 0.25 mg/ml	GL GL	1 mg/ml[b] 16 to 160 μg/ml	Physically compatible for 4 hr at 22 °C Physically compatible when etoposide given over 30 to 60 min via Y-site	1365 1366	C C
Etoposide phosphate	BR	5 mg/ml[a]	GW	1 mg/ml[a]	Physically compatible with no change in measured turbidity or increase in particle content in 4 hr at 23 °C	2218	C

Y-Site Injection Compatibility (1:1 Mixture) (Cont.)

Ondansetron HCl

Drug	*Mfr*	*Conc*	*Mfr*	*Conc*	*Remarks*	*Ref*	*C/I*
Famotidine	MSD	2 mg/ml[a]	GL	1 mg/ml[b]	Physically compatible for 4 hr at 22 °C	1365	C
Filgrastim	AMG	30 μg/ml[a]	GL	1 mg/ml[a]	Physically compatible with no change in measured turbidity or increase in particle content in 4 hr at 22 °C	1687	C
Floxuridine	RC	3 mg/ml[a]	GL	1 mg/ml[b]	Physically compatible for 4 hr at 22 °C	1365	C
Fluconazole	PF	2 mg/ml	GL	1 mg/ml[b]	Physically compatible for 4 hr at 22 °C	1365	C
	RR	2 mg/ml[b]	GL	0.03 and 0.3 mg/ml[a]	Visually compatible with little or no loss of either drug by HPLC in 4 hr at 25 °C	1732	C
	RR	2 mg/ml	GL	0.03, 0.1, 0.3 mg/ml[a,b]	Visually compatible with little or no ondansetron or fluconazole loss by HPLC in 4 hr and 5% or less loss of both drugs in 12 hr at room temperature	2168	C
Fludarabine phosphate	BX	1 mg/ml[a]	GL	0.5 mg/ml[a]	Physically compatible for 4 hr at room temperature under fluorescent light	1439	C
Fluorouracil	SO	16 mg/ml[a]	GL	1 mg/ml[b]	Immediate precipitation	1365	I
		≤0.8 mg/ml	GL	16 to 160 μg/ml	Physically compatible when fluorouracil given at 20 ml/hr via Y-site	1366	C
Furosemide	AB	3 mg/ml[a]	GL	1 mg/ml[b]	Immediate turbidity and precipitation	1365	I
Ganciclovir sodium	SY	20 mg/ml[a]	GL	1 mg/ml[b]	Immediate turbidity and precipitation	1365	I
Gatifloxacin	BMS	2 mg/ml[a]	GW	1 mg/ml[a]	Physically compatible with no change in measured haze or increase in particle content in 4 hr at 23 °C	2234	C
Gemcitabine HCl	LI	10 mg/ml[b]	GW	1 mg/ml[b]	Physically compatible with no change in measured turbidity or increase in particle content in 4 hr at 23 °C	2226	C
Gentamicin sulfate	ES	5 mg/ml[a]	GL	1 mg/ml[b]	Physically compatible for 4 hr at 22 °C	1365	C
Haloperidol lactate	LY	0.2 mg/ml[a]	GL	1 mg/ml[b]	Physically compatible for 4 hr at 22 °C	1365	C
Heparin sodium	SO	40 units/ml[a]	GL	1 mg/ml[b]	Physically compatible for 4 hr at 22 °C	1365	C
Hetastarch in lactated electrolyte injection (Hextend)	AB	6%	GW	1 mg/ml[a]	Physically compatible with no change in measured turbidity or increase in particle content in 4 hr at 23 °C	2339	C
Hydrocortisone sodium phosphate	MSD	1 mg/ml[a]	GL	1 mg/ml[b]	Physically compatible for 4 hr at 22 °C	1365	C
Hydrocortisone sodium succinate	UP	1 mg/ml[a]	GL	1 mg/ml[b]	Physically compatible for 4 hr at 22 °C	1365	C
Hydromorphone HCl	KN	0.5 mg/ml[a]	GL	1 mg/ml[b]	Physically compatible for 4 hr at 22 °C	1365	C
Hydroxyzine HCl	WI	4 mg/ml[a]	GL	1 mg/ml[b]	Physically compatible for 4 hr at 22 °C	1365	C
Ifosfamide	MJ	25 mg/ml[a]	GL	1 mg/ml[b]	Physically compatible for 4 hr at 22 °C	1365	C
Imipenem–cilastatin sodium	MSD	5 mg/ml[b]	GL	1 mg/ml[b]	Physically compatible for 4 hr at 22 °C	1365	C
Linezolid	PHU	2 mg/ml	GW	1 mg/ml[a]	Physically compatible with no change in measured turbidity or increase in particle content in 4 hr at 23 °C	2264	C
Lorazepam	WY	0.1 mg/ml[a]	GL	1 mg/ml[b]	Light haze develops immediately	1365	I
Magnesium sulfate	SO	100 mg/ml[a]	GL	1 mg/ml[b]	Physically compatible for 4 hr at 22 °C	1365	C
Mannitol	BA	15%	GL	1 mg/ml[b]	Physically compatible for 4 hr at 22 °C	1365	C
Mechlorethamine HCl	MSD	1 mg/ml	GL	1 mg/ml[b]	Physically compatible for 4 hr at 22 °C	1365	C

Y-Site Injection Compatibility (1:1 Mixture) (Cont.)

Drug	Mfr	Conc	Ondansetron HCl Mfr	Ondansetron HCl Conc	Remarks	Ref	C/I
Melphalan HCl	BW	0.1 mg/ml[b]	GL	1 mg/ml[b]	Physically compatible with no change in measured turbidity or increase in particle content in 3 hr at 22 °C	1557	C
Meperidine HCl	WI	4 mg/ml[a]	GL	1 mg/ml[b]	Physically compatible for 4 hr at 22 °C	1365	C
Meropenem	ZEN	1 mg/ml[b]	GL	1 mg/ml[c]	Visually compatible for 4 hr at room temperature	1994	C
	ZEN	50 mg/ml[b]	GL	1 mg/ml[c]	White precipitate forms immediately	1994	I
Mesna	BR	10 mg/ml[a]	GL	1 mg/ml[b]	Physically compatible for 4 hr at 22 °C	1365	C
Methotrexate sodium	CET	15 mg/ml[a]	GL	1 mg/ml[b]	Physically compatible for 4 hr at 22 °C	1365	C
		30 mg/ml	GL	2 mg/ml	Visually compatible for 4 hr at room temperature	1788	C
Methylprednisolone sodium succinate	UP	5 mg/ml[a]	GL	1 mg/ml[b]	Light haze develops in 30 min	1365	I
Metoclopramide HCl	DU	5 mg/ml	GL	1 mg/ml[b]	Physically compatible for 4 hr at 22 °C	1365	C
Mitomycin	BR	0.5 mg/ml	GL	1 mg/ml[b]	Physically compatible for 4 hr at 22 °C	1365	C
Mitoxantrone HCl	LE	0.5 mg/ml[a]	GL	1 mg/ml[b]	Physically compatible for 4 hr at 22 °C	1365	C
Morphine sulfate	WI	1 mg/ml[a]	GL	1 mg/ml[b]	Physically compatible for 4 hr at 22 °C	1365	C
Paclitaxel	NCI	1.2 mg/ml[a]	GL	0.5 mg/ml[a]	Physically compatible with no change in measured turbidity in 4 hr at 22 °C	1556	C
	BR	0.3 mg/ml[a]	GL	0.03 and 0.3 mg/ml[a]	Visually compatible with no loss of either drug in 4 hr at 23 °C	1741	C
	BR	1.2 mg/ml[a]	GL	0.03 and 0.3 mg/ml[a]	Visually compatible with no loss of either drug in 4 hr at 23 °C	1741	C
Paclitaxel with ranitidine HCl	BR GL	1.2 mg/ml[a] 2 mg/ml[a]	GL	0.3 mg/ml[a]	Visually compatible with no loss of any drug by HPLC in 4 hr at 23 °C	1741	C
Pentostatin	NCI	0.4 mg/ml[b]	GL	1 mg/ml[b]	Physically compatible for 4 hr at 22 °C	1365	C
Piperacillin sodium	LE	40 mg/ml[a]	GL	1 mg/ml[b]	Slight turbidity appears in 30 min	1365	I
Piperacillin sodium–tazobactam sodium	LE	40 + 5 mg/ml[a]	GL	1 mg/ml[a]	Physically compatible with no change in measured turbidity or increase in particle content in 4 hr at 22 °C	1688	C
	LE	40 + 5 mg/ml[b]	GL	0.03, 0.1, 0.3 mg/ml[b]	Visually compatible with no loss of any component by HPLC in 4 hr	1752	C
	LE	80 + 10 mg/ml[b]	GL	0.03, 0.1, 0.3 mg/ml[b]	Visually compatible with no loss of any component by HPLC in 4 hr	1752	C
Potassium chloride	AB	0.1 mEq/ml[a]	GL	1 mg/ml[b]	Physically compatible for 4 hr at 22 °C	1365	C
Prochlorperazine edisylate	SKF	0.5 mg/ml[a]	GL	1 mg/ml[b]	Physically compatible for 4 hr at 22 °C	1365	C
Promethazine HCl	ES	2 mg/ml[a]	GL	1 mg/ml[b]	Physically compatible for 4 hr at 22 °C	1365	C
Ranitidine HCl	GL	2 mg/ml[a]	GL	1 mg/ml[b]	Physically compatible for 4 hr at 22 °C	1365	C
	GL	0.5 mg/ml[a]	GL	0.03, 0.1, 0.3 mg/ml[a]	Visually compatible with no loss of either drug by HPLC in 4 hr	1730	C
	GL	2 mg/ml[a]	GL	0.03, 0.1, 0.3 mg/ml[a]	Visually compatible with no loss of either drug by HPLC in 4 hr	1730	C
Remifentanil HCl	GW	0.025 and 0.25 mg/ml[b]	CER	1 mg/ml[a]	Physically compatible with no change in measured turbidity or increase in particle content in 4 hr at 23 °C	2075	C
Sargramostim	IMM	10 µg/ml[b]	GL	0.5 mg/ml[b]	Filaments form in 30 to 60 min	1436	I

Y-Site Injection Compatibility (1:1 Mixture) (Cont.)

			Ondansetron HCl				
Drug	*Mfr*	*Conc*	*Mfr*	*Conc*	*Remarks*	*Ref*	*C/I*
Sodium acetate		0.1 and 1 mEq/ml[a]	GL	0.1 mg/ml[a]	Visually compatible with no increase in 10-, 25-, and 50-μm particles in 4 hr at room temperature	1661	C
Sodium bicarbonate		0.05 mmol/ml[e]	GL	0.32 mg/ml[a]	White precipitate forms immediately	1513	I
		0.1 mEq/ml[a]	GL	0.1 mg/ml[a]	Large increase in 10-, 25-, and 50-μm particles. Visible particles in 30 to 60 min at room temperature	1661	I
		1.4%	GL	2 mg/ml	Heavy white precipitate forms immediately	1788	I
Streptozocin	UP	30 mg/ml[a]	GL	1 mg/ml[b]	Physically compatible for 4 hr at 22 °C	1365	C
Teniposide	BR	0.1 mg/ml[a]	GL	1 mg/ml[b]	Physically compatible for 4 hr at 22 °C	1365	C
	BR	0.1 mg/ml[a]	GL	1 mg/ml[a]	Physically compatible with no subvisual haze or particle formation in 4 hr at 23 °C	1725	C
Thiotepa	IMM[f]	1 mg/ml[a]	GL	1 mg/ml[a]	Physically compatible with no change in measured turbidity or increase in particle content in 4 hr at 23 °C	1861	C
Ticarcillin disodium	BE	30 mg/ml[a]	GL	1 mg/ml[b]	Physically compatible for 4 hr at 22 °C	1365	C
Ticarcillin disodium–clavulanate potassium	BE	31 mg/ml[a]	GL	1 mg/ml[b]	Physically compatible for 4 hr at 22 °C	1365	C
TNA #218 to #226[g]			CER	1 mg/ml[a]	Damage to emulsion integrity occurs immediately with free oil formation possible	2215	I
Topotecan HCl	SKB	56 μg/ml[a,b]	CER	0.48 mg/ml[a,b]	Visually compatible with little or no loss of either drug by HPLC within 4 hr at 22 °C under fluorescent light	2245	C
TPN #212 to #215[g]			GL	1 mg/ml[a]	Physically compatible with no change in measured turbidity or increase in particle content in 4 hr at 23 °C	2109	C
Vancomycin HCl	LI	10 mg/ml[a]	GL	1 mg/ml[b]	Physically compatible for 4 hr at 22 °C	1365	C
Vinblastine sulfate	LY	0.12 mg/ml[a]	GL	1 mg/ml[b]	Physically compatible for 4 hr at 22 °C	1365	C
Vincristine sulfate	LY	0.05 mg/ml[a]	GL	1 mg/ml[b]	Physically compatible for 4 hr at 22 °C	1365	C
Vinorelbine tartrate	BW	1 mg/ml[b]	GL	1 mg/ml[b]	Physically compatible with no change in measured turbidity or increase in particle content in 4 hr at 22 °C	1558	C
Zidovudine	BW	4 mg/ml[a]	GL	1 mg/ml[b]	Physically compatible for 4 hr at 22 °C	1365	C

[a] *Tested in dextrose 5% in water.*
[b] *Tested in sodium chloride 0.9%.*
[c] *Tested in sterile water for injection.*
[d] *Tested in bacteriostatic sodium chloride 0.9% preserved with benzyl alcohol 0.9%.*
[e] *Tested in dextrose 5% in water with potassium chloride 0.02 mM/ml.*
[f] *Lyophilized formulation tested.*
[g] *Refer to Appendix I for the composition of parenteral nutrition solutions. TNA indicates a 3-in-1 admixture, and TPN indicates a 2-in-1 admixture.*
[h] *Arginine-containing formulation tested.*
[i] *Sodium carbonate–containing formulation tested.*

Additional Compatibility Information

Infusion Solutions — The manufacturer states that ondansetron HCl is stable at room temperature and exposed to normal light for 48 hours when diluted in the following infusion solutions (2):

Dextrose 5% in sodium chloride 0.45%
Dextrose 5% in sodium chloride 0.9%
Dextrose 5% in water
Sodium chloride 0.9%
Sodium chloride 3%

OXACILLIN SODIUM
AHFS 8:12.16

Products — Oxacillin sodium is available in vials containing the equivalent of oxacillin 500 mg, 1 g, and 2 g. A 10-g hospital bulk package also is available. The products also contain dibasic sodium phosphate 40 mg/g of drug. (4)

For intramuscular use, reconstitute the vials with the appropriate amount of sterile water for injection or sodium chloride 0.45 or 0.9% as listed below and shake until a clear solution is obtained. A 250-mg/1.5 ml (167 mg/ml) solution results. (4)

Vial Size	Volume of Diluent
500 mg	2.8 ml
1 g	5.7 ml
2 g	11.4 ml

For direct intravenous injection, reconstitute the 500-mg and 1- and 2-g vials with 5, 10, or 20 ml, respectively, of sterile water for injection, sodium chloride 0.45%, or sodium chloride 0.9% and shake until a clear solution is obtained to yield a 100-mg/ml concentration. (4)

The 10-g hospital bulk package is reconstituted with 93 ml of sterile water for injection to yield a 100-mg/ml solution. (4)

Frozen premixed solutions of oxacillin 1 g/50 ml in dextrose 3% and 2 g/50 ml in dextrose 0.6% are also available. The solutions also contain sodium citrate buffer and hydrochloric acid and/or sodium hydroxide to adjust the pH. (4)

pH—From 6 to 8.5. (4) At a concentration of 10 g/L in dextrose 5% in water, the pH has been variously reported as 7.4 (149) and 7.94. (153) At this concentration in sodium chloride 0.9%, the pH has been reported as 7.73. (153)

Osmolality—The osmolality of oxacillin sodium (Bristol) 250 mg/1.5 ml in sterile water for injection was determined to be 596 mOsm/kg by freezing-point depression and 657 mOsm/kg by vapor pressure. (1071)

The osmolality of oxacillin sodium (Beecham) 50 mg/ml was determined to be 381 mOsm/kg in dextrose 5% in water and 396 mOsm/kg in sodium chloride 0.9%. (1375)

The osmolality of oxacillin sodium was calculated for the following dilutions (1054):

Diluent	Osmolality (mOsm/kg) 50 ml	100 ml
1 g		
Dextrose 5% in water	326	295
Sodium chloride 0.9%	353	321
2 g		
Dextrose 5% in water	379	329
Sodium chloride 0.9%	406	356

Robinson et al. recommended the following maximum oxacillin sodium concentrations to achieve osmolalities suitable for peripheral infusion in fluid-restricted patients (1180):

Diluent	Maximum Concentration (mg/ml)	Osmolality (mOsm/kg)
Dextrose 5% in water	59	530
Sodium chloride 0.9%	53	519
Sterile water for injection	106	422

The frozen premixed solutions are iso-osmotic, having an osmolality of about 300 mOsm/kg. (4)

Sodium Content—Each gram of oxacillin sodium powder contains approximately 2.5 to 3.1 mEq of sodium. (4; 154)

Administration — Oxacillin sodium may be administered by deep intramuscular injection, direct intravenous injection, or by continuous or intermittent intravenous infusion. By direct intravenous injection, the dose should be given over a 10-minute period. To minimize vein irritation, intravenous injections should be made as slowly as possible. For intermittent infusion, the drug should be further diluted with a compatible solution to a concentration of 0.5 to 40 mg/ml. (4)

Stability — Oxacillin sodium in intact vials should be stored at controlled room temperature. After reconstitution, oxacillin sodium is stable for three days at room temperature and for one week under refrigeration at concentrations used for intramuscular or direct intravenous injection. In ADD-Vantage vials, oxacillin sodium reconstituted with sodium chloride 0.9% or dextrose 5% in water is stated to be stable for three days or 24 hours, respectively, at room temperature. The reconstituted hospital bulk package is stable for 24 hours at room temperature. (4)

The frozen premixed injection is stable at −20 °C for at least 90 days after shipping. The frozen premixed infusions should be thawed at room temperature or under refrigeration and should not be refrozen after being thawed initially. The thawed solutions are stated to be stable for 48 hours at room temperature and 21 days under refrigeration. (4)

Freezing Solutions—Oxacillin sodium (Bristol), 500 mg/2.5 ml and 1 g/5 ml in sterile water for injection packaged in glass and plastic syringes and 200 mg/ml in the original vial, was frozen at −20 °C. Chemical analysis indicated that adequate stability was maintained over three months of storage. (303)

In another study, oxacillin sodium (Bristol) 1 g/100 ml of dextrose 5% in water in PVC bags was frozen at −20 °C for 30 days. The bags were then thawed by exposure to ambient temperature or microwave radiation. The solutions showed no evidence of precipitation or color change and no loss of potency as determined microbiologically. Subsequent storage of the admixture at room temperature for 24 hours yielded a physically compatible solution, which exhibited a 3 to 4% loss of potency. (554)

Ambulatory Pumps—The stability of oxacillin sodium (Marsam) 120 mg/ml in sterile water for injection was evaluated in PVC portable infusion pump reservoirs (Pharmacia Deltec). HPLC analysis found no oxacillin loss in three days at 25 °C and 5% loss in 14 days at 5 °C. (2080)

Elastomeric Reservoir Pumps—Oxacillin sodium solutions in elastomeric reservoir pumps have been stated by the pump manufacturers to be stable for the following time periods frozen, refrigerated (REF), or at room temperature (RT) (31):

Pump Reservoir(s)	Conc.	Frozen	REF	RT
Intermate	10 to 80 mg/ml[a,b]	30 days	10 days	24 hr
Medflo	20 mg/ml[a]	4 weeks	3 days	24 hr
	20 mg/ml[b]	4 weeks	8 days	3 days
ReadyMed	10 to 50 mg/ml[a,c]	30 days	8 days	2 days
	10 to 50 mg/ml[b,d]	30 days	8 days	7 days

[a]*In dextrose 5% in water.*
[b]*In sodium chloride 0.9%.*
[c]*In lactated Ringer's injection.*
[d]*In sterile water for injection.*

Sorption—Picard et al. reported little or no loss due to sorption of oxacillin sodium (Bristol) 1 g/100 ml in dextrose 5% in water and sodium chloride 0.9% in trilayer solution bags (Bieffe Medital) composed of polyethylene, polyamide, and polypropylene. The admixtures were evaluated by HPLC analysis up to two hours after preparation. Similarly, no loss was found during a one-hour simulated infusion. (1918)

Compatibility Information

Solution Compatibility

Oxacillin sodium

Solution	Mfr	Mfr	Conc/L	Remarks	Ref	C/I
Amino acids 4.25%, dextrose 25%	MG	BR	500 mg	No increase in particulate matter in 24 hr at 5 °C	349	C
Dextran 70 6% in dextrose 5%			4 g	Approximately 1 to 3% decomposition in 24 hr at 20 °C	834	C
Dextran 40 10% in dextrose 5%			4 g	3% decomposition in 24 hr at 20 °C	834	C
Dextrose 5% in Ringer's injection, lactated	TR[a]	BR	1 g	Potency retained for 24 hr at 5 °C	282	C
Dextrose 5% in sodium chloride 0.9%	TR[a]	BR	1 g	Potency retained for 24 hr at 5 °C	282	C
		BR	2 g	12% decomposition in 12 hr and 14% in 24 hr	109	I
Dextrose 5% in water		BR	2 g	Potency retained for 24 hr	109	C
		BR	1, 10, 50 g	4 to 9% oxacillin decomposition in 24 hr at 23 °C	153	C
	TR[a]	BR	1 g	Potency retained for 24 hr at 5 °C	282	C
	TR[b]	BR	10 g	Physically compatible with approximately 8% potency loss in 24 hr at room temperature	554	C
			4 g	8% loss in 6 hr and 14% loss in 24 hr at room temperature	768	I
	[b]	BR	20 g	No drug loss by HPLC during 2-hr storage and 1-hr simulated infusion	1774	C
Dextrose 10% in water		BR	2 g	Potency retained for 24 hr	109	C
Hetastarch 6% in sodium chloride 0.9%			4 g	1% decomposition in 24 hr at 20 °C	834	C
Ringer's injection, lactated	TR[a]	BR	1 g	Potency retained for 24 hr at 5 °C	282	C
Sodium chloride 0.9%		BR	2 g	Potency retained for 24 hr	109	C
		BR	1, 10, 50 g	2 to 4% oxacillin decomposition in 24 hr at 23 °C	153	C
	TR[a]	BR	1 g	Potency retained for 24 hr at 5 °C	282	C
			4 g	10% loss in 8 hr and 12% loss in 24 hr at room temperature	768	I
	[b]	BR	20 g	No drug loss by HPLC during 2-hr storage and 1-hr simulated infusion	1774	C

[a]*Tests performed in both glass and PVC containers.*
[b]*Tested in PVC containers.*

Additive Compatibility

			Oxacillin sodium					
Drug	*Mfr*	*Conc/L*	*Mfr*	*Conc/L*	*Test Soln*	*Remarks*	*Ref*	*C/I*
Amikacin sulfate	BR	5 g	BR	2 g	D5LR, D5R, D5S, D5W, D10W, IS10, LR, NS, R	Physically compatible and potency of both retained for 24 hr at 25 °C	293	C
	BR	5 g	BR	2 g	NR, SL	Oxacillin potency retained through 8 hr at 25 °C. Greater than 10% decomposition in 24 hr	293	I
Chloramphenicol sodium succinate	PD	500 mg	BR	500 mg	D5S, D5W	Therapeutic availability maintained	110	C
	PD	1 g	BR	2 g	D5S, D5W	Therapeutic availability maintained	110	C
	PD	1 g	BR	2 g		Physically compatible	6	C
Cytarabine	UP	100 mg		2 g	D5W	pH outside stability range for oxacillin	174	I
Dopamine HCl	AS	800 mg	BR	2 g	D5W	No dopamine decomposition and 2% oxacillin decomposition in 24 hr at 25 °C	312	C
Potassium chloride		20, 40, 80 mEq	BR	1, 2.5, 4 g	D5S, D5W	Therapeutic availability maintained	110	C
Sodium bicarbonate	AB	2.4 mEq[a]	BR	500 mg	D5W	Physically compatible for 24 hr	772	C
Verapamil HCl	KN	80 mg	BR	4 g	D5W, NS	Physically compatible for 24 hr	764	C
	SE	[b]	BR	40 g	D5W, NS	Cloudy solution clears with agitation	1166	?

[a]*One vial of Neut added to a liter of admixture.*
[b]*Final concentration unspecified.*

Y-Site Injection Compatibility (1:1 Mixture)

			Oxacillin sodium				
Drug	*Mfr*	*Conc*	*Mfr*	*Conc*	*Remarks*	*Ref*	*C/I*
Acyclovir sodium	BW	5 mg/ml[a]	BE	20 mg/ml[a]	Physically compatible for 4 hr at 25 °C	1157	C
Cyclophosphamide	MJ	20 mg/ml[a]	BE	20 mg/ml[a]	Physically compatible for 4 hr at 25 °C	1194	C
Diltiazem HCl	MMD	1[b] and 5 mg/ml		100 mg/ml[b]	Visually compatible	1807	C
	MMD	5 mg/ml		10 mg/L[b]	Visually compatible	1807	C
Famotidine	MSD	0.2 mg/ml[a]	BE	20 mg/ml[b]	Physically compatible for 14 hr	1196	C
Fluconazole	RR	2 mg/ml	BE	40 mg/ml	Physically compatible for 24 hr at 25 °C	1407	C
Foscarnet sodium	AST	24 mg/ml	BR	40 mg/ml	Physically compatible for 24 hr at room temperature under fluorescent light	1335	C
	AST	24 mg/ml	BE	20 mg/ml[c]	Physically compatible for 24 hr at 25 °C under fluorescent light by visual and microscopic examination	1393	C
Heparin sodium	UP	1000 units/L[d]	BR	100 mg/ml	Physically compatible for at least 4 hr at room temperature by visual and microscopic examination	534	C
Hydrocortisone sodium succinate	UP	10 mg/L[d]	BR	100 mg/ml	Physically compatible for at least 4 hr at room temperature by visual and microscopic examination	534	C

Y-Site Injection Compatibility (1:1 Mixture) (Cont.)

			Oxacillin sodium				
Drug	*Mfr*	*Conc*	*Mfr*	*Conc*	*Remarks*	*Ref*	*C/I*
Hydromorphone HCl	WY	0.2 mg/ml[a]	BE	20 mg/ml[a]	Physically compatible for at least 4 hr at 25 °C under fluorescent light	987	C
Labetalol HCl	SC	1 mg/ml[a]	BR	10 mg/ml[a]	Physically compatible for 24 hr at 18 °C	1171	C
Levofloxacin	OMN	5 mg/ml[a]	APC	167 mg/ml	Visually compatible for 4 hr at 24 °C under fluorescent light	2233	C
Magnesium sulfate	IX	16.7, 33.3, 66.7, 100 mg/ml[a]	BE	20 mg/ml[a]	Physically compatible for at least 4 hr at 32 °C	813	C
Meperidine HCl	WY	10 mg/ml[a]	BE	20 mg/ml[a]	Physically compatible for at least 4 hr at 25 °C under fluorescent light	987	C
Methotrexate sodium		30 mg/ml	BR	250 mg/ml	Visually compatible for 4 hr at room temperature	1788	C
Morphine sulfate	WI	1 mg/ml[a]	BE	20 mg/ml[a]	Physically compatible for at least 4 hr at 25 °C under fluorescent light	987	C
Perphenazine	SC	0.02 mg/ml[a]	BE	20 mg/ml[a]	Physically compatible for 4 hr at 25 °C	1155	C
Potassium chloride	AB	40 mEq/L[d]	BR	100 mg/ml	Physically compatible for at least 4 hr at room temperature by visual and microscopic examination	534	C
Sodium bicarbonate		1.4%	BR	250 mg/ml	Gas evolves	1788	I
Tacrolimus	FUJ	1 mg/ml[b]	BR	40 mg/ml[a]	Visually compatible for 24 hr at 25 °C	1630	C
TNA #73[e]		32.5 ml[f]	BE	1 g/50 ml[a]	Physically compatible by visual observation for 4 hr at 25 °C	1008	C
TPN #54[e]				100 and 150 mg/ml	Physically compatible with 88 to 94% oxacillin activity retained over 6 hr at 22 °C by microbiological assay	1045	C
TPN #61[e]		[g]	BE	250 mg/1.5 ml[h]	Physically compatible	1012	C
		[i]	BE	1.5 g/9 ml[h]	Physically compatible	1012	C
Verapamil HCl	SE	2.5 mg/ml	BR	40 mg/ml[c]	White milky precipitate forms immediately and persists. 39% of verapamil precipitated	1166	I
Vitamin B complex with C	RC	2 ml/L[d]	BR	100 mg/ml	Physically compatible for at least 4 hr at room temperature by visual and microscopic examination	534	C
Zidovudine	BW	4 mg/ml[a]	BR	20 mg/ml[a]	Physically compatible for 4 hr at 25 °C under fluorescent light by visual and microscopic examination	1193	C

[a] *Tested in dextrose 5% in water.*
[b] *Tested in sodium chloride 0.9%.*
[c] *Tested in both dextrose 5% in water and sodium chloride 0.9%.*
[d] *Tested in dextrose 5% in Ringer's injection, dextrose 5% in Ringer's injection, lactated, dextrose 5% in water, Ringer's injection, lactated, and sodium chloride 0.9%.*
[e] *Refer to Appendix I for the composition of parenteral nutrition solutions. TNA indicates a 3-in-1 admixture, and TPN indicates a 2-in-1 admixture.*
[f] *A 32.5-ml sample of parenteral nutrition solution mixed with 50 ml of antibiotic solution.*
[g] *Run at 21 ml/hr.*
[h] *Given over five minutes by syringe pump.*
[i] *Run at 94 ml/hr.*

Additional Compatibility Information

Infusion Solutions — Oxacillin sodium in concentrations of 0.5 to 40 mg/ml loses less than 10% activity at room temperature in six hours in the following infusion solutions (4):

Dextrose 5% in sodium chloride 0.9%
Dextrose 5% in water
Fructose 10% in sodium chloride 0.9%
Fructose 10% in water
Invert sugar 10% in Electrolyte #1
Invert sugar 10% in Electrolyte #2
Invert sugar 10% in Electrolyte #3
Invert sugar 10% and potassium chloride 0.3%
Invert sugar 10% in sodium chloride 0.9%
Invert sugar 10% in water
Ringer's injection, lactated
Sodium chloride 0.9%

It has been stated that the decomposition of oxacillin sodium in solutions is independent of concentration. However, dextrose has a catalytic effect on the hydrolysis of the drug. It was predicted that oxacillin sodium in solutions with dextrose 5% or less would be stable for at least 24 hours at room temperature. In higher dextrose concentrations, the drug would not be stable for 24 hours at room temperature. (153)

Acidic Drugs — Acid-labile drugs such as oxacillin sodium may degrade in infusion solutions containing acidic additives. (22)

Aminoglycosides — Lundergan et al. studied, in vitro, the interaction of tobramycin sulfate with several penicillins in human serum under clinical laboratory conditions. Tobramycin sulfate 10 μg/ml was combined with carbenicillin disodium 200 μg/ml, oxacillin sodium (Bristol) 50 μg/ml, and nafcillin sodium (Wyeth) 50 μg/ml. Samples were evaluated over 72 hours at −23, 6, and 23 °C. Although the results were somewhat variable, only the carbenicillin sample at 23 °C exhibited substantial decomposition after 72 hours. None of the other carbenicillin, oxacillin, or nafcillin samples showed significant differences over the study period. (814)

The comparative inactivation of five aminoglycosides by seven β-lactam antibiotics in human serum at 37 °C was reported by Riff and Thomason. Amikacin, followed by netilmicin, had the lowest degree of inactivation; tobramycin sustained the most pronounced losses. Gentamicin and kanamycin were intermediate in the extent of losses. The six penicillins that were tested all produced aminoglycoside inactivation; the greatest extent of inactivation was caused by carbenicillin followed by ticarcillin, penicillin G, oxacillin, methicillin, and ampicillin, in approximate descending order. Cephalothin produced minimal inactivation (5 to 10% in 24 hours). The rate of inactivation could be reduced by storage at 4 °C and further reduced by storage at −20 °C. The authors suggested processing blood samples rapidly to avoid inaccurate serum determinations. Storage of specimens at low temperature until analysis may be helpful. (1052)

OXYMORPHONE HCL
AHFS 28:08.08

Products — Oxymorphone HCl is available in a concentration of 1 mg/ml in 1-ml ampuls. It is also available in a concentration of 1.5 mg/ml in 10-ml vials. Each milliliter of solution contains (2):

	1-ml Ampul	10-ml Vial
Oxymorphone HCl	1 mg	1.5 mg
Sodium chloride	8 mg	8 mg
Methylparaben		1.8 mg
Propylparaben		0.2 mg
Hydrochloric acid	to adjust pH	to adjust pH

pH — From 2.7 to 4.5. (4)

Trade Name(s) — Numorphan.

Administration — Oxymorphone HCl may be administered by subcutaneous, intramuscular, or intravenous injection. (2; 4)

Stability — Intact containers of oxymorphone HCl should be stored at controlled room temperature and protected from light and freezing. (2; 4)

Compatibility Information

Drugs in Syringe Compatibility

Oxymorphone HCl

Drug (in syringe)	*Mfr*	*Amt*	*Mfr*	*Amt*	*Remarks*	*Ref*	*C/I*
Glycopyrrolate	RB	0.2 mg/ 1 ml	EN	1 mg/ 1 ml	Physically compatible and pH in stability range for glycopyrrolate for 48 hr at 25 °C	331	C
	RB	0.2 mg/ 1 ml	EN	2 mg/ 2 ml	Physically compatible and pH in stability range for glycopyrrolate for 48 hr at 25 °C	331	C
	RB	0.4 mg/ 2 ml	EN	1 mg/ 1 ml	Physically compatible and pH in stability range for glycopyrrolate for 48 hr at 25 °C	331	C

Drugs in Syringe Compatibility (Cont.)

Oxymorphone HCl

Drug (in syringe)	*Mfr*	*Amt*	*Mfr*	*Amt*	*Remarks*	*Ref*	*C/I*
	RB	0.2 mg/ 1 ml	EN	1.5 mg/ 1 ml	Physically compatible and pH in stability range for glycopyrrolate for 48 hr at 25 °C	331	C
	RB	0.2 mg/ 1 ml	EN	3 mg/ 2 ml	Physically compatible and pH in stability range for glycopyrrolate for 48 hr at 25 °C	331	C
	RB	0.4 mg/ 2 ml	EN	1.5 mg/ 1 ml	Physically compatible and pH in stability range for glycopyrrolate for 48 hr at 25 °C	331	C
Hydroxyzine HCl	PF	100 mg/ 2 ml	EN	0.75 mg/ 0.5 ml	Physically compatible	771	C
Ranitidine HCl	GL	50 mg/ 2 ml	EN	1.5 mg/ 1 ml	Physically compatible for 1 hr at 25 °C both macroscopically and microscopically	978	C

OXYTOCIN
AHFS 76:00

Products — Oxytocin is available in 1-ml ampuls and 1- and 10-ml vials. Each milliliter contains oxytocin 10 units with chlorobutanol 0.5%. Acetic acid may have been added to adjust the pH during manufacture. (1-1/00; 4; 29)

Units — One unit of oxytocin is equivalent to 2 to 2.2 μg of pure oxytocin. (4)

pH — The USP cites the official pH range as 3 to 5 (17), and the commercial products are also listed as pH 3 to 5. (1-1/00) The AHFS cites the pH range as being 2.5 to 4.5. (4)

Osmolality — Oxytocin 10 units/ml has an osmolality of 24 mOsm/kg. (1689)

Trade Name(s) — Pitocin.

Administration — Oxytocin is administered by intravenous infusion using an infusion control device (1-1/00; 4) or intramuscular injection (1-1/00), although intramuscular injection is usually not recommended for induction or augmentation of labor because the drug's effects are unpredictable and difficult to control. (4) For intravenous administration the injection should be diluted to a usual concentration of 10 milliunits/ml by adding 10 units (1 ml) to 1000 ml of dextrose 5% in water, Ringer's injection, lactated, or sodium chloride 0.9%. (1-1/00; 4) A higher concentration range of 10 to 40 milliunits/ml has been cited to control postpartum uterine bleeding. (1-1/00)

Stability — Oxytocin injection should be stored at controlled room temperature and protected from freezing. Do not use the solution if it is discolored or contains a precipitate. (1-1/00; 4)

Filtration — Oxytocin (Parke-Davis) 25 units/100 ml in dextrose 5% in water and sodium chloride 0.9% was filtered at about 3 ml/min through a 0.22-μm cellulose ester membrane filter (Ivex-2). At this concentration, 25 times higher than normally used, oxytocin appeared to bind initially to the filter from the sodium chloride 0.9% solution. Results in dextrose 5% in water were equivocal. From these data, it is not possible to draw a definite conclusion regarding substantial binding of oxytocin during normal usage. (533)

Compatibility Information

Solution Compatibility

Oxytocin

Solution	*Mfr*	*Mfr*	*Conc/L*	*Remarks*	*Ref*	*C/I*
Dextran 6% in dextrose 5%	AB	PD	5 units	Physically compatible	3	C
Dextran 6% in sodium chloride 0.9%	AB	PD	5 units	Physically compatible	3	C
Dextrose–Ringer's injection combinations	AB	PD	5 units	Physically compatible	3	C
Dextrose–Ringer's injection, lactated, combinations	AB	PD	5 units	Physically compatible	3	C
Dextrose–saline combinations	AB	PD	5 units	Physically compatible	3	C
Dextrose 2½% in water	AB	PD	5 units	Physically compatible	3	C

Solution Compatibility (Cont.)

Oxytocin

Solution	*Mfr*	*Mfr*	*Conc/L*	*Remarks*	*Ref*	*C/I*
Dextrose 5% in water	AB	PD	5 units	Physically compatible	3	C
		CN	10.4 units	Stable for at least 6 hr at room temperature	333	C
Dextrose 10% in water	AB	PD	5 units	Physically compatible	3	C
Fructose 10% in sodium chloride 0.9%	AB	PD	5 units	Physically compatible	3	C
Fructose 10% in water	AB	PD	5 units	Physically compatible	3	C
Invert sugar 5 and 10% in sodium chloride 0.9%	AB	PD	5 units	Physically compatible	3	C
Invert sugar 5 and 10% in water	AB	PD	5 units	Physically compatible	3	C
Ionosol products	AB	PD	5 units	Physically compatible	3	C
Ringer's injection	AB	PD	5 units	Physically compatible	3	C
Ringer's injection, lactated	AB	PD	5 units	Physically compatible	3	C
Sodium chloride 0.45%	AB	PD	5 units	Physically compatible	3	C
Sodium chloride 0.9%	AB	PD	5 units	Physically compatible	3	C
Sodium lactate ⅙ M	AB	PD	5 units	Physically compatible	3	C

Additive Compatibility

Oxytocin

Drug	*Mfr*	*Conc/L*	*Mfr*	*Conc/L*	*Test Soln*	*Remarks*	*Ref*	*C/I*
Chloramphenicol sodium succinate	PD	1 g	PD	5 units		Physically compatible	6	C
Fibrinolysin, human	MSD	2 g	PD	5 units	D5W	Physically incompatible	11	I
Metaraminol bitartrate	MSD	100 mg	PD	5 units		Physically compatible	7	C
Netilmicin sulfate	SC	3 g	PD	4 ml	D5S	Physically compatible and netilmicin chemically stable for 7 days at 4 and 25 °C. Oxytocin not tested	558	C
Sodium bicarbonate	AB	2.4 mEq[a]	PD	5 units	D5W	Physically compatible for 24 hr	772	C
Thiopental sodium	AB	2.5 g	PD	5 units	D5W	Physically compatible	21	C
Verapamil HCl	KN	80 mg	SZ	40 units	D5W, NS	Physically compatible for 24 hr	764	C

[a]*One vial of Neut added to a liter of admixture.*

Y-Site Injection Compatibility (1:1 Mixture)

Oxytocin

Drug	*Mfr*	*Conc*	*Mfr*	*Conc*	*Remarks*	*Ref*	*C/I*
Heparin sodium	UP	1000 units/L[d]	SZ	1 mg/ml	Physically compatible for at least 4 hr at room temperature by visual and microscopic examination	534	C
Hydrocortisone sodium succinate	UP	10 mg/L[d]	SZ	1 mg/ml	Physically compatible for at least 4 hr at room temperature by visual and microscopic examination	534	C
Insulin, regular	LI	0.2 unit/ml[b]	PD	0.02 unit/ml[c]	Physically compatible for 2 hr at 25 °C	1395	C

Y-Site Injection Compatibility (1:1 Mixture) (Cont.)

Oxytocin

Drug	*Mfr*	*Conc*	*Mfr*	*Conc*	*Remarks*	*Ref*	*C/I*
Meperidine HCl	WY	10 mg/ml[b]	PD	0.02 mg/ml[c]	Physically compatible for 1 hr at 25 °C	1338	C
Morphine sulfate	ES	1 mg/ml[b]	PD	0.02 mg/ml[c]	Physically compatible for 1 hr at 25 °C	1338	C
Potassium chloride	AB	40 mEq/L[d]	SZ	1 mg/ml	Physically compatible for at least 4 hr at room temperature by visual and microscopic examination	534	C
Vitamin B complex with C	RC	2 ml/L[d]	SZ	1 mg/ml	Physically compatible for at least 4 hr at room temperature by visual and microscopic examination	534	C
Warfarin sodium	DU	0.1[a,b] and 2[e] mg/ml	FUJ	1 unit/ml[a,b]	Physically compatible with no change in measured turbidity or increase in particle content in 24 hr at 23 °C	2011	C

[a]*Tested in dextrose 5% in water.*
[b]*Tested in sodium chloride 0.9%.*
[c]*Tested in dextrose 5% in Ringer's injection, lactated.*
[d]*Tested in dextrose 5% in Ringer's injection, dextrose 5% in Ringer's injection, lactated, dextrose 5% in water, Ringer's injection, lactated, and sodium chloride 0.9%.*
[e]*Tested in sterile water for injection.*

Additional Compatibility Information

Infusion Solutions — Sodium chloride 0.9% and dextrose 5% in water have been recommended as diluents for oxytocin infusion. (4)

Phytonadione — Oxytocin (Parke-Davis) 5 units/L has been reported to be conditionally compatible with phytonadione (Abbott) 50 mg/L. The mixture is physically compatible in most Abbott infusion solutions except dextran 12%, in which a haze or precipitate forms within one hour. (3)

Sodium Bisulfite — Oxytocin appears to be rapidly decomposed in the presence of sodium bisulfite. (333)

Other Drugs — Oxytocin is stated to be incompatible with fibrinolysin, norepinephrine bitartrate, prochlorperazine edisylate, and warfarin sodium. (4)

PACLITAXEL
AHFS 10:00

Products — Paclitaxel is available as 6-mg/ml non-aqueous concentrated solutions that must be diluted for use. Taxol is available in 5-, 16.7-, and 50-ml multiple-dose vials while Onxol is available in 5-, 25-, and 50-ml multiple-dose vials. One milliliter of either formulation provides paclitaxel 6 mg with polyoxyl 35 castor oil (Cremophor EL; polyoxyethylated castor oil) surfactant 527 mg and dehydrated alcohol 49.7% (v/v). The Onxol formulation also incorporates citric acid anhydrous 2 mg/ml. (1-4/01; 2; 4)

pH — Paclitaxel admixtures at concentrations of 0.6 and 1.2 mg/ml in dextrose 5% in water, sodium chloride 0.9%, and dextrose 5% in lactated Ringer's injection have a pH of 4.4 to 5.6. (4)

Density — Paclitaxel 6 mg/ml (undiluted) injection has a solution density of 0.92 g/ml. (2041; 2248)

Trade Name(s) — Onxol, Taxol.

Administration — Paclitaxel is administered by intravenous infusion. The concentrate must be diluted to a final paclitaxel concentration of 0.3 to 1.2 mg/ml in dextrose 5% in water, sodium chloride 0.9%, dextrose 5% in sodium chloride 0.9%, or dextrose 5% in lactated Ringer's injection. Administration over three hours is often recommended (1-4/01; 2; 4), although other duration periods have been used. (4) An inline 0.22-µm filter should be used for administration. The intravenous solution containers and administration sets should be free of the plasticizer diethylhexyl phthalate (DEHP). (1-4/01; 2) See Plasticizer Leaching under Stability below.

Use of self-venting sets spiked into glass bottles of paclitaxel admixtures has occasionally resulted in solution dripping from the air vent. Presumably, the surfactant content wetted the hydrophobic filter, allowing the solution to drip. (1843) In another observation, the spikes of administration sets were made sufficiently slippery by surfactant in the paclitaxel formulation that the spike slipped out after it had been seated through the rubber bung of the glass bottle. The admixture also leaked due to a poor seal. The authors recommend use of non-PVC plastic solution containers (Excel, McGaw) to avoid the problem. (2052)

Stability — Intact vials should be stored between 20 and 25 °C and protected from light. Stability is not adversely affected by refrigeration or freezing. Refrigeration may result in the precipitation of formulation components. However, warming to room temperature redissolves the material and does not adversely affect the product. If a precipitate is insoluble, the product should be discarded. (1-4/01; 2)

Turbidity — Paclitaxel concentrate is a clear, colorless to slightly yellow viscous liquid. After dilution in an infusion solution, the drug may exhibit haziness because of the surfactant content of the formulation. (2; 1528) This haziness increases until the maximum turbidity of around 6 to 8 nephelometric turbidity units occurs between 0.3 and 0.9 mg/ml. This level of haze may be visible in normal room light. Continued dilution below 0.3 mg/ml results in a continual decline of measured turbidity through 0.01 mg/ml, the lowest concentration evaluated. (1528)

Precipitation — Although paclitaxel in aqueous solutions is chemically stable for 27 hours (1-4/01; 2) or longer (1746; 1842), precipitation has occurred irregularly and unpredictably. Such precipitation occurs within the recommended range of 0.3 to 1.2 mg/ml and at even lower paclitaxel concentrations. These precipitates often have been observed in the infusion tubing distal to the pump chamber. (1716) Although the precipitation of insoluble drugs in an aqueous medium is a foregone conclusion, the time to precipitation is irregular. It may be accelerated by various factors including the presence or formation of crystallization nuclei, agitation, and contact with incompatible drugs or materials. (1374; 1521) Since the mechanism of this irregular paclitaxel precipitation has not been identified (1739), care and vigilance throughout its infusion are required.

Sorption — No paclitaxel loss due to sorption to containers or sets has been observed. (1520; 2230–2232)

Plasticizer Leaching — Contact of undiluted paclitaxel concentrate with plasticized PVC equipment and devices is not recommended. (1-4/01; 2; 4)

Paclitaxel itself does not contribute to the extraction of the plasticizer DEHP. (1520) However, the surfactant, Cremophor EL, in the paclitaxel formulation extracts DEHP from PVC containers and sets. The amount of DEHP extracted increases with time and drug concentration. (2; 1520; 1683; 2146) Consequently, the use of DEHP-plasticized PVC containers and sets is not recommended for infusion of paclitaxel solutions. Instead, the manufacturer recommends the use of glass, polypropylene, or polyolefin containers and non-PVC administration sets such as those that are polyethylene lined. (2)

The use of inline filters, such as the Ivex-2 filter set that incorporates about 10 inches of PVC inlet and outlet tubing, has resulted in a small amount of DEHP extraction. Since the extracted DEHP is at a sufficiently low level, however, the manufacturer considers the Ivex-2 filter set to be acceptable. (1-4/01; 2)

A study was performed on the compatibility of paclitaxel 0.3- and 1.2-mg/ml infusions with various non-PVC infusion sets. The paclitaxel infusions were run through the study sets, and the effluent was then analyzed by HPLC for leached DEHP plasticizer. The following sets had significant and unacceptable amounts of leached DEHP: Baxter vented nitroglycerin (2C7552S), Baxter vented basic solution (1C8355S), McGaw Horizon pump vented nitroglycerin (V7450), and McGaw Intelligent pump vented nitroglycerin (V7150). Although these sets were largely non-PVC, their highly plasticized pumping segments contributed the DEHP. The administration and extension sets cited in Tables 1 and 2 exhibited no more leached DEHP than the Ivex-2 filter set specified in the product labeling. (1843)

Mazzo et al. evaluated the leaching of DEHP plasticizer by paclitaxel 0.3 and 1.2 mg/ml in dextrose 5% in water and in sodium chloride 0.9%. PVC bags of the solutions were used to prepare the admixtures. The leaching of the plasticizer was found to be time and concentration dependent; however, there was little difference between the two infusion solutions. After storage for eight hours at 21 °C, HPLC analysis found leached DEHP in the range from 73 to 108 µg/ml for the 1.2 mg/ml concentration and from 21 to 30 µg/ml for the 0.3 mg/ml concentration. During a simulated one-hour infusion using DEHP plasticized administration sets, the amount of leached DEHP did not exceed 18 µg/ml at the 0.3 mg/ml paclitaxel concentration but resulted in a maximum of 114 µg/ml with the 1.2 mg/ml concentration. (1825)

Allwood and Martin confirmed the leaching of DEHP plasticizer from PVC containers and administration sets, and the amount of DEHP leached was again found to depend on surfactant concentration and length of contact period. They also reported leaching of up to

Table 1. Administration Sets Compatible with Paclitaxel Infusions by Manufacturer (1843)

Abbott
LifeCare 5000 Plum PVC specialty set (11594)
Life Shield anesthesia pump set OL with cartridge (13503)
LifeCare model 4P specialty set, non-PVC (11434)
Omni-Flow universal primary intravenous pump short minibore patient line (40527)
Baxter
Vented volumetric pump nitroglycerin set (2C1042)
Block Medical
Verifuse nonvented administration set with 0.22-µm filter, check valve, injection site, and non-DEHP PVC tubing (V021015)
I-Flow
Vivus-4000 polyethylene-lined infusion set (5000-784)
IMED
Standard PVC set (9215)
Closed-system non-PVC fluid path nonvented quick-spike administration set (9635)
Non-PVC set with inline filter (9986)
Gemini 20 nonvented primary administration set for nitroglycerin and emulsions (2262)
IVAC
Universal set with low-sorbing tubing (52053, 59953, and S75053)
Ivion/Medex
WalkMed spike set (SP-06) with pump set (PS-401, PS-360, FPS-560, or FPX-560)
Siemens
Reduced-PVC full set MiniMed Uni-Set macrobore (28-60-190)

Table 2. Extension Sets Compatible with Paclitaxel Infusions by Manufacturer (1843)

Abbott
- Ivex-HP filter set (4524)
- Ivex-2 filter set (2679)

Becton-Dickinson
- Intima intravenous catheter placement set (38-6918-1)
- J-loop connector (38-1252-2)
- E-Z infusion set shorty (38-53741)
- E-Z infusion set (38-53121)

Baxter
- Polyethylene-lined extension set with 0.22-μm air-eliminating filter (1C8363)

Braun
- 0.2-μm filter extension set (FE-2012L)
- Small-bore 0.2-μm filter extension set (PFE-2007)
- Whin-winged extension set with 90° Huber needle (HW-2267)
- Whin extension set with Y-site and Huber needle (HW-2276 YHR)
- Y-extension set with valve (ET-08-YL)
- Small-bore extension set with T-fitting (ET-04T)
- Small-bore extension set with reflux valve (ET-116L)

Gish Biomedical
- VasTack noncoring portal-access needle system (VT-2022)

IMED
- 0.2-μm add-on filter set (9400 XL)

IVAC
- Spec-Sets extension set with 0.22-μm inline filter (C20028 and C20350)

Ivion/Medex
- Extension set with 0.22-μm filter (IV4A07-IV3)

PALL
- SetSaver extended-life disposable set with 0.2-μm filter (ELD-96P and ELD-96LL)
- SetSaver extended-life disposable microbore extension tubing with 0.2-μm Posidyne filter (ELD-96LYL and ELD-96LYLN)

Pfizer/Strato Medical
- Lifeport vascular-access system infusion set with Y-site (LPS 3009)

30 mg of DEHP per dose from Flo-Gard Low Adsorption Sets (Baxter), a set with a reduced amount of PVC present in its construction. (2146)

An acceptability limit of no more than 5 parts per million (5 μg/ml) for DEHP plasticizer released from PVC containers, administration sets, and other equipment has been proposed. The limit was proposed based on a review of metabolic and toxicologic considerations. (2185)

The acceptability of two reduced-phthalate administration sets for the Acclaim (Abbott) pump was evaluated. Administration set model 11993-48 (Abbott) is composed of polyethylene tubing but has a DEHP-plasticized pumping segment. Administration set model L-12060 (Abbott) is composed of tris(2-ethylhexyl)trimellitate (TOTM)–plasticized PVC tubing and a DEHP-plasticized pumping segment. Paclitaxel diluent at concentrations equivalent to 0.3 and 1.2 mg/ml in dextrose 5% in water delivered rapidly over three hours at 23 °C did not leach detectable levels of TOTM from model L-12060 or DEHP from either set using HPLC analysis. Similarly, slow delivery over four days of the 0.3-mg/ml concentration yielded detectable but not quantifiable amounts of plasticizer. However, slow delivery of the equivalent of 1.2 mg/ml over four days yielded large but variable amounts of DEHP from both sets; DEHP concentrations ranged from 30 to 150 μg/ml. Consequently, these two reduced-phthalate sets are suitable for short-term delivery up to three hours of paclitaxel at concentrations up to 1.2 mg/ml. However, these sets should not be used for slow delivery of higher concentrations. (2198)

The admonition of the paclitaxel labeling (2) to avoid PVC administration sets was found not to extend to a TOTM-plasticized PVC set (SoloPak). Paclitaxel vehicle equivalent to paclitaxel 0.3 and 1.2 mg/ml in dextrose 5% in water did not leach TOTM plasticizer from the set during simulated three-hour administration. During extremely slow delivery at 5.2 ml/hr for four days, no detectable TOTM was found in the 0.3-mg/ml equivalent concentration, and only a barely detectable, unquantifiable, trace amount of TOTM was found with the 1.2-mg/ml equivalent solution. (2232)

Paclitaxel (Faulding) 0.3 and 1.2 mg/ml in dextrose 5% in water or in sodium chloride 0.9% in ethylene vinyl acetate (EVA) plastic containers was found to leach an unknown material after storage at 25 and 32 °C for 24 hours. (2182)

Filtration — The manufacturer recommends the use of a 0.22-μm inline filter for paclitaxel administration. (2) No loss of paclitaxel due to filtration through 0.22-μm filters has been observed. (2; 1520)

The acceptability of the 0.22-μm IV Express Filter Unit (Millipore) for the administration of paclitaxel was evaluated. Paclitaxel vehicle equivalent to paclitaxel 1.2 mg/ml (for plasticizer leaching) and paclitaxel 0.3 mg/ml (for sorption potential) in 500 ml of dextrose 5% in water in polyolefin containers (McGaw) was delivered through the filter units over a three-hour period at a rate of 167 ml/hr at about 23 °C to simulate paclitaxel administration. HPLC analysis found no leached plasticizer and no loss of paclitaxel due to sorption. The filter unit was determined to be acceptable for the administration of paclitaxel infusions. (2231)

Central Venous Catheter — The acceptability of the Arrow-Howes triple-lumen, 7 French, 30-cm polyurethane central catheter (Arrow International) for the administration of paclitaxel was evaluated. Paclitaxel vehicle equivalent to paclitaxel 0.3 and 1.2 mg/ml (for catheter component leaching) and paclitaxel 0.3 mg/ml (for sorption potential) were prepared in polyolefin bags of dextrose 5% in water (McGaw). The solutions were delivered through the polyurethane central venous catheters for periods of three hours and of 24 hours at 23 °C to simulate rapid and slow administration. HPLC analysis found no leached catheter components in the effluent solution and no loss of paclitaxel due to sorption. The Arrow-Howes polyurethane central venous catheter was determined to be acceptable for the administration of paclitaxel infusions in the concentration range of 0.3 to 1.2 mg/ml over short or long delivery periods. (2230)

Compatibility Information

Solution Compatibility

Paclitaxel

Solution	*Mfr*	*Mfr*	*Conc/L*	*Remarks*	*Ref*	*C/I*
Dextrose 5% in water	MG, TR[a]	NCI	0.3, 0.6, 0.9 g	Visually compatible with no paclitaxel loss by HPLC over 12 hr at 22 °C	1520	C
	MG[b]	NCI	0.6 g	Visually compatible with no paclitaxel loss by HPLC over 25 hr at 22 °C	1520	C
	MG, TR[c]	NCI	1.2 g	Visually compatible with no paclitaxel loss by HPLC over 12 hr at 22 °C	1520	C
		BR	0.2 to 0.58 g	Fluffy, white precipitate forms occasionally in administration set just distal to pump chamber	1716	I
	MG[b]	BR	0.1 and 1 g	Physically compatible with no change in subvisual haze or particle content and stable by HPLC for 3 days at 4, 22, and 32 °C. Small, needlelike crystals form after 3 days	1746	C
	MG[b]	BR	0.3 and 1.2 g	Physically compatible and chemically stable for 48 hr at 22 °C	1842	C
	BA[d]	FAU	0.3 and 1.2 g	Physically compatible with no change in subvisual haze or particle content and stable by HPLC for 3 days at 25 and 32 °C. Unknown material leached from EVA container by 24 hr	2182	?
Sodium chloride 0.9%	MG, TR[a]	NCI	0.3, 0.6, 0.9, 1.2 g	Visually compatible with no paclitaxel loss by HPLC over 12 hr at 22 °C	1520	C
	MG[b]	NCI	0.6 and 1.2 g	Visually compatible with no paclitaxel loss by HPLC over 26 hr at 22 °C	1520	C
	MG[b]	BR	0.1 and 1 g	Physically compatible with no change in subvisual haze or particle content and stable by HPLC for 3 days at 4, 22, and 32 °C. Small, needlelike crystals form after 3 days	1746	C
	MG[b]	BR	0.3 and 1.2 g	Physically compatible and chemically stable for 48 hr at 22 °C	1842	C
	BA[d]	FAU	0.3 and 1.2 g	Physically compatible with no change in subvisual haze or particle content and stable by HPLC for 3 days at 25 and 32 °C. Unknown material leached from EVA container by 24 hr	2182	?

[a]*Tested in both glass and PVC containers.*
[b]*Tested in polyolefin containers.*
[c]*Tested in glass, PVC, and polyolefin containers.*
[d]*Tested in Baxter ethylene vinyl acetate (EVA) containers.*

Additive Compatibility

Paclitaxel

Drug	*Mfr*	*Conc/L*	*Mfr*	*Conc/L*	*Test Soln*	*Remarks*	*Ref*	*C/I*
Carboplatin	BMS	2 g	BMS	300 mg and 1.2 g	NS	No paclitaxel loss but carboplatin losses of 2, 5, and 7% at 4, 24, and 32 °C, respectively, in 24 hr by HPLC. Physically compatible for 24 hr but subvisual particulates of paclitaxel form after 3 to 5 days	2094	C

Additive Compatibility (Cont.)

Paclitaxel

Drug	*Mfr*	*Conc/L*	*Mfr*	*Conc/L*	*Test Soln*	*Remarks*	*Ref*	*C/I*
	BMS	2 g	BMS	300 mg and 1.2 g	D5W	No paclitaxel and carboplatin loss by HPLC at 4, 24, and 32 °C in 24 hr. Physically compatible for 24 hr but subvisual particulates of paclitaxel form after 3 to 5 days	2094	C
Cisplatin	BMS	200 mg	BMS	300 mg	NS	No paclitaxel loss and cisplatin losses of 1, 4, and 5% at 4, 24 and 32 °C, respectively, in 24 hr by HPLC. Physically compatible for 24 hr but subvisual particulates of paclitaxel form after 3 to 5 days	2094	C
	BMS	200 mg	BMS	1.2 g	NS	No paclitaxel loss but cisplatin losses of 10, 19, and 22% at 4, 24, and 32 °C, respectively, in 24 hr by HPLC. Physically compatible for 24 hr but subvisual particulates of paclitaxel form after 3 to 5 days	2094	I
Doxorubicin HCl	PH	200 mg	BMS	300 mg	D5W, NS	Visually compatible for at least 1 day with microprecipitation appearing in 3 to 5 days and gross precipitation in 7 days at 4, 23, and 32 °C protected from light. No paclitaxel loss and less than 8% doxorubicin loss in 7 days	2247	C
	PH	200 mg	BMS	1.2 g	D5W, NS	Visually compatible for at least 1 day with microprecipitation appearing in 3 to 5 days and gross precipitation in 7 days at 4, 23, and 32 °C protected from light. No paclitaxel loss and less than 7% doxorubicin loss in 7 days	2247	C

Y-Site Injection Compatibility (1:1 Mixture)

Paclitaxel

Drug	*Mfr*	*Conc*	*Mfr*	*Conc*	*Remarks*	*Ref*	*C/I*
Acyclovir sodium	BW	7 mg/ml[a]	NCI	1.2 mg/ml[a]	Physically compatible with no change in measured turbidity in 4 hr at 22 °C	1556	C
Amikacin sulfate	BR	5 mg/ml[a]	NCI	1.2 mg/ml[a]	Physically compatible with no change in measured turbidity in 4 hr at 22 °C	1556	C
Aminophylline	AB	2.5 mg/ml[a]	NCI	1.2 mg/ml[a]	Physically compatible with no change in measured turbidity in 4 hr at 22 °C	1556	C
Amphotericin B	SQ	0.6 mg/ml[a]	NCI	1.2 mg/ml[a]	Immediate increase in measured turbidity followed by separation into two layers in 24 hr at 22 °C	1556	I
Amphotericin B cholesteryl sulfate complex	SEQ	0.83 mg/ml[a]	MJ	0.6 mg/ml[a]	Decreased natural turbidity occurs immediately	2117	I
Ampicillin sodium–sulbactam sodium	RR	20 + 10 mg/ml[b]	NCI	1.2 mg/ml[a]	Physically compatible with no change in measured turbidity in 4 hr at 22 °C	1556	C
Bleomycin sulfate	MJ	1 unit/ml[a]	NCI	1.2 mg/ml[a]	Physically compatible with no change in measured turbidity in 4 hr at 22 °C	1556	C

Y-Site Injection Compatibility (1:1 Mixture) (Cont.)

			Paclitaxel				
Drug	*Mfr*	*Conc*	*Mfr*	*Conc*	*Remarks*	*Ref*	*C/I*
Butorphanol tartrate	BR	0.04 mg/ml[a]	NCI	1.2 mg/ml[a]	Physically compatible with no change in measured turbidity in 4 hr at 22 °C	1556	C
Calcium chloride	AST	20 mg/ml[a]	NCI	1.2 mg/ml[a]	Physically compatible with no change in measured turbidity in 4 hr at 22 °C	1556	C
Carboplatin		5 mg/ml[a]	NCI	1.2 mg/ml[a]	Physically compatible with no change in measured turbidity in 4 hr at 22 °C	1528	C
Cefepime HCl	BMS	20 mg/ml[a]	BR	0.6 mg/ml[a]	Physically compatible with no change in measured turbidity or increase in particle content in 4 hr at 22 °C	1689	C
Cefotetan disodium	STU	20 mg/ml[a]	NCI	1.2 mg/ml[a]	Physically compatible with no change in measured turbidity in 4 hr at 22 °C	1556	C
Ceftazidime	LI[f]	40 mg/ml[a]	NCI	1.2 mg/ml[a]	Physically compatible with no change in measured turbidity in 4 hr at 22 °C	1556	C
Ceftriaxone sodium	RC	20 mg/ml[a]	NCI	1.2 mg/ml[a]	Physically compatible with no change in measured turbidity in 4 hr at 22 °C	1556	C
Chlorpromazine HCl	ES	2 mg/ml[a]	NCI	1.2 mg/ml[a]	Normal inherent haze from paclitaxel decreases immediately	1556	I
Cimetidine HCl		12 mg/ml[a]	NCI	1.2 mg/ml[a]	Physically compatible with no change in measured turbidity in 4 hr at 22 °C	1528	C
Cisplatin		1 mg/ml	NCI	1.2 mg/ml[a]	Physically compatible with no change in measured turbidity in 4 hr at 22 °C	1528	C
Cladribine	ORT	0.015[b] and 0.5[c] mg/ml	BR	0.6 mg/ml[b]	Physically compatible with no change in measured turbidity or increase in particle content in 4 hr at 23 °C	1969	C
Cyclophosphamide		10 mg/ml[a]	NCI	1.2 mg/ml[a]	Physically compatible with no change in measured turbidity in 4 hr at 22 °C	1528	C
Cytarabine		50 mg/ml	NCI	1.2 mg/ml[a]	Physically compatible with no change in measured turbidity in 4 hr at 22 °C	1528	C
Dacarbazine	MI	4 mg/ml[a]	NCI	1.2 mg/ml[a]	Physically compatible with no change in measured turbidity in 4 hr at 22 °C	1556	C
Dexamethasone sodium phosphate		1 mg/ml[a]	NCI	1.2 mg/ml[a]	Physically compatible with no change in measured turbidity in 4 hr at 22 °C	1528	C
Diphenhydramine HCl		2 mg/ml[a]	NCI	1.2 mg/ml[a]	Physically compatible with no change in measured turbidity in 4 hr at 22 °C	1528	C
Doxorubicin HCl		2 mg/ml	NCI	1.2 mg/ml[a]	Physically compatible with no change in measured turbidity in 4 hr at 22 °C	1528	C
Doxorubicin HCl liposome injection	SEQ	0.4 mg/ml[a]	MJ	0.6 mg/ml[a]	Partial loss of measured natural turbidity	2087	I
Droperidol	JN	0.4 mg/ml[a]	NCI	1.2 mg/ml[a]	Physically compatible with no change in measured turbidity in 4 hr at 22 °C	1556	C
Etoposide		0.4 mg/ml[a]	NCI	1.2 mg/ml[a]	Physically compatible with no change in measured turbidity in 4 hr at 22 °C	1528	C
Etoposide phosphate	BR	5 mg/ml[a]	MJ	1.2 mg/ml[a]	Physically compatible with no change in measured turbidity or increase in particle content in 4 hr at 23 °C	2218	C
Famotidine	MSD	2 mg/ml[a]	NCI	1.2 mg/ml[a]	Physically compatible with no change in measured turbidity in 4 hr at 22 °C	1556	C

Y-Site Injection Compatibility (1:1 Mixture) (Cont.)

Paclitaxel

Drug	*Mfr*	*Conc*	*Mfr*	*Conc*	*Remarks*	*Ref*	*C/I*
Floxuridine	RC	3 mg/ml[a]	NCI	1.2 mg/ml[a]	Physically compatible with no change in measured turbidity in 4 hr at 22 °C	1556	C
Fluconazole	RR	2 mg/ml	NCI	1.2 mg/ml[a]	Physically compatible with no change in measured turbidity in 4 hr at 22 °C	1556	C
	PF	2 mg/ml	BR	0.3 and 1.2 mg/ml[a]	Visually compatible with no loss of either drug by HPLC in 4 hr at 23 °C	1790	C
Fluorouracil		16 mg/ml[a]	NCI	1.2 mg/ml[a]	Physically compatible with no change in measured turbidity in 4 hr at 22 °C	1528	C
Furosemide	AST	3 mg/ml[a]	NCI	1.2 mg/ml[a]	Physically compatible with no change in measured turbidity in 4 hr at 22 °C	1556	C
Ganciclovir sodium	SY	20 mg/ml[a]	NCI	1.2 mg/ml[a]	Physically compatible with no change in measured turbidity in 4 hr at 22 °C	1556	C
Gatifloxacin	BMS	2 mg/ml[a]	MJ	0.6 mg/ml[a]	Physically compatible with no change in measured haze or increase in particle content in 4 hr at 23 °C	2234	C
Gemcitabine HCl	LI	10 mg/ml[b]	MJ	1.2 mg/ml[a]	Physically compatible with no change in measured turbidity or increase in particle content in 4 hr at 23 °C	2226	C
Gentamicin sulfate	ES	5 mg/ml[a]	NCI	1.2 mg/ml[a]	Physically compatible with no change in measured turbidity in 4 hr at 22 °C	1556	C
Granisetron HCl	SKB	1 mg/ml	MJ	0.3 mg/ml[b]	Physically compatible with little or no loss of either drug by HPLC in 4 hr at 22 °C	1883	C
	SKB	0.05 mg/ml[a]	MJ	1.2 mg/ml[a]	Physically compatible with no change in measured turbidity or increase in particle content in 4 hr at 23 °C	2000	C
Haloperidol lactate		0.2 mg/ml[a]	NCI	1.2 mg/ml[a]	Physically compatible with no change in measured turbidity in 4 hr at 22 °C	1528	C
Heparin sodium	WY	100 units/ml[a]	NCI	1.2 mg/ml[a]	Physically compatible with no change in measured turbidity in 4 hr at 22 °C	1556	C
Hydrocortisone sodium phosphate	MSD	1 mg/ml[a]	NCI	1.2 mg/ml[a]	Physically compatible with no change in measured turbidity in 4 hr at 22 °C	1556	C
Hydrocortisone sodium succinate	AB	1 mg/ml[a]	NCI	1.2 mg/ml[a]	Physically compatible with no change in measured turbidity in 4 hr at 22 °C	1556	C
Hydromorphone HCl	KN	0.5 mg/ml[a]	NCI	1.2 mg/ml[a]	Physically compatible with no change in measured turbidity in 4 hr at 22 °C	1556	C
Hydroxyzine HCl	ES	4 mg/ml[a]	NCI	1.2 mg/ml[a]	Normal inherent haze from paclitaxel decreases immediately	1556	I
Ifosfamide	BR	25 mg/ml[a]	NCI	1.2 mg/ml[a]	Physically compatible with no change in measured turbidity in 4 hr at 22 °C	1556	C
Linezolid	PHU	2 mg/ml	MJ	0.6 mg/ml[a]	Physically compatible with no change in measured turbidity or increase in particle content in 4 hr at 23 °C	2264	C
Lorazepam		0.1 mg/ml[a]	NCI	1.2 mg/ml[a]	Physically compatible with no change in measured turbidity in 4 hr at 22 °C	1528	C
Magnesium sulfate	AST	100 mg/ml[a]	NCI	1.2 mg/ml[a]	Physically compatible with no change in measured turbidity in 4 hr at 22 °C	1556	C
Mannitol	BA	15%	NCI	1.2 mg/ml[a]	Physically compatible with no change in measured turbidity in 4 hr at 22 °C	1556	C

Y-Site Injection Compatibility (1:1 Mixture) (Cont.)

			Paclitaxel				
Drug	*Mfr*	*Conc*	*Mfr*	*Conc*	*Remarks*	*Ref*	*C/I*
Meperidine HCl	WY	4 mg/ml[a]	NCI	1.2 mg/ml[a]	Physically compatible with no change in measured turbidity in 4 hr at 22 °C	1556	C
Mesna	MJ	10 mg/ml[a]	NCI	1.2 mg/ml[a]	Physically compatible with no change in measured turbidity in 4 hr at 22 °C	1556	C
Methotrexate sodium		15 mg/ml[a]	NCI	1.2 mg/ml[a]	Physically compatible with no change in measured turbidity in 4 hr at 22 °C	1528	C
Methylprednisolone sodium succinate	UP	5 mg/ml[a]	NCI	1.2 mg/ml[a]	Normal inherent haze from paclitaxel decreases immediately	1556	I
Metoclopramide HCl		5 mg/ml	NCI	1.2 mg/ml[a]	Physically compatible with no change in measured turbidity in 4 hr at 22 °C	1528	C
Mitoxantrone HCl	LE	0.5 mg/ml[a]	NCI	1.2 mg/ml[a]	Normal inherent haze from paclitaxel decreases immediately	1556	I
Morphine sulfate	WY	1 mg/ml[a]	NCI	1.2 mg/ml[a]	Physically compatible with no change in measured turbidity in 4 hr at 22 °C	1556	C
Nalbuphine HCl	AST	10 mg/ml	NCI	1.2 mg/ml[a]	Physically compatible with no change in measured turbidity in 4 hr at 22 °C	1556	C
Ondansetron HCl	GL	0.5 mg/ml[a]	NCI	1.2 mg/ml[a]	Physically compatible with no change in measured turbidity in 4 hr at 22 °C	1556	C
	GL	0.03 and 0.3 mg/ml[a]	BR	0.3 mg/ml[a]	Visually compatible with no loss of either drug in 4 hr at 23 °C	1741	C
	GL	0.03 and 0.3 mg/ml[a]	BR	1.2 mg/ml[a]	Visually compatible with no loss of either drug in 4 hr at 23 °C	1741	C
Ondansetron HCl with ranitidine HCl	GL GL	0.3 mg/ml[a] 2 mg/ml[a]	BR	1.2 mg/ml[a]	Visually compatible with no loss of any drug by HPLC in 4 hr at 23 °C	1741	C
Pentostatin	NCI	0.4 mg/ml[b]	NCI	1.2 mg/ml[a]	Physically compatible with no change in measured turbidity in 4 hr at 22 °C	1556	C
Potassium chloride	AB	0.1 mEq/ml[a]	NCI	1.2 mg/ml[a]	Physically compatible with no change in measured turbidity in 4 hr at 22 °C	1556	C
Prochlorperazine edisylate		0.5 mg/ml[a]	NCI	1.2 mg/ml[a]	Physically compatible with no change in measured turbidity in 4 hr at 22 °C	1528	C
Propofol	ZEN	10 mg/ml	MJ	1.2 mg/ml[a]	Physically compatible for 1 hr at 23 °C with no increase in particle content	2066	C
Ranitidine HCl		2 mg/ml[a]	NCI	1.2 mg/ml[a]	Physically compatible with no change in measured turbidity in 4 hr at 22 °C	1528	C
	GL	0.5 and 2 mg/ml[a]	BR	0.3 mg/ml[a]	Visually compatible with no loss of either drug in 4 hr at 23 °C	1741	C
	GL	0.5 and 2 mg/ml[a]	BR	1.2 mg/ml[a]	Visually compatible with no loss of either drug in 4 hr at 23 °C	1741	C
Sodium bicarbonate	LY	1 mEq/ml	NCI	1.2 mg/ml[a]	Physically compatible with no change in measured turbidity in 4 hr at 22 °C	1556	C
Thiotepa	IMM[d]	1 mg/ml[a]	MJ	0.6 mg/ml[a]	Physically compatible with no change in measured turbidity or increase in particle content in 4 hr at 23 °C	1861	C
TNA #218 to #226[e]			MJ	1.2 mg/ml[a]	Visually compatible with no precipitate or emulsion damage apparent in 4 hr at 23 °C	2215	C

Y-Site Injection Compatibility (1:1 Mixture) (Cont.)

Drug	Mfr	Conc	Paclitaxel Mfr	Paclitaxel Conc	Remarks	Ref	C/I
Topotecan HCl	SKB	56 μg/ml[a,b]	MJ	0.54 mg/ml[a,b]	Visually compatible with little or no loss of either drug by HPLC in 4 hr at 22 °C under fluorescent light	2245	C
TPN #212 to #215[e]			MJ	1.2 mg/ml[a]	Physically compatible with no change in measured turbidity or increase in particle content in 4 hr at 23 °C	2109	C
Vancomycin HCl		10 mg/ml[a]	NCI	1.2 mg/ml[a]	Physically compatible with no change in measured turbidity in 4 hr at 22 °C	1528	C
Vinblastine sulfate	LI	0.12 mg/ml[b]	NCI	1.2 mg/ml[a]	Physically compatible with no change in measured turbidity in 4 hr at 22 °C	1556	C
Vincristine sulfate	LI	0.05 mg/ml[a]	NCI	1.2 mg/ml[a]	Physically compatible with no change in measured turbidity in 4 hr at 22 °C	1556	C
Zidovudine	BW	4 mg/ml[a]	NCI	1.2 mg/ml[a]	Physically compatible with no change in measured turbidity in 4 hr at 22 °C	1556	C

[a]*Tested in dextrose 5% in water.*
[b]*Tested in sodium chloride 0.9%.*
[c]*Tested in bacteriostatic sodium chloride 0.9% preserved with benzyl alcohol 0.9%.*
[d]*Lyophilized formulation tested.*
[e]*Refer to Appendix I for the composition of parenteral nutrition solutions. TNA indicates a 3-in-1 admixture, and TPN indicates a 2-in-1 admixture.*
[f]*Sodium carbonate–containing formulation tested.*

Additional Compatibility Information

Infusion Solutions — The manufacturer recommends dilution of paclitaxel to a concentration between 0.3 and 1.2 mg/ml in dextrose 5% in water, dextrose 5% in sodium chloride 0.9%, dextrose 5% in Ringer's injection, or sodium chloride 0.9%. These solutions are stated to be physically and chemically stable for up to 27 hours at room temperature (about 25 °C) under normal room light. (1-4/01; 2)

Other Information

Microbial Growth — Paclitaxel (Bristol) 0.7 mg/ml diluted in sodium chloride 0.9% did not exhibit an antimicrobial effect on the growth of three of four organisms (*Enterococcus faecium, Staphylococcus aureus, Pseudomonas aeruginosa,* and *Candida albicans*) inoculated into the solution. *S. aureus* remained viable for 4 hours. *E. faecium* and *P. aeruginosa* remained viable for 48 hours, and *C. albicans* remained viable to the end of the study at 120 hours. The author recommended that diluted solutions of paclitaxel be stored under refrigeration whenever possible and that the potential for microbiological growth be considered when assigning expiration periods. (2160)

PANCURONIUM BROMIDE
AHFS 12:20

Products — Pancuronium bromide is available in 2- and 5-ml ampuls and vials containing 2 mg/ml of drug. It is also available in 10-ml vials at a concentration of 1 mg/ml. Each milliliter also contains sodium acetate anhydrous 2 mg, benzyl alcohol 1%, and sodium chloride 4 mg for isotonicity. Acetic acid and/or sodium hydroxide is added to adjust the pH. (1-9/98; 4; 29)

pH — The solution has been adjusted to pH 3.8 to 4.2 by the manufacturer. (1-9/98; 4)

Osmolality — The osmolality of pancuronium bromide (Organon) 1 mg/ml was determined to be 277 mOsm/kg by freezing-point depression and 273 mOsm/kg by vapor pressure. (1071)

The osmolality of pancuronium bromide 2 mg/ml was determined to be 338 mOsm/kg. (1233)

Administration — Pancuronium bromide is administered intravenously. (1-9/98; 4)

Stability — Pancuronium bromide should be stored under refrigeration at 2 to 8 °C. (4) However, the manufacturer indicates that the drug is stable for six months at room temperature. (1-9/98; 853; 1181; 1433)

Sorption—The manufacturer indicates that pancuronium bromide in compatible infusion solutions does not undergo sorption to glass or plastic containers during short-term storage over 48 hours at room temperature. (1-9/98; 4) However, the drug may exhibit sorption to plastic containers with prolonged contact. (4)

Compatibility Information

Additive Compatibility

			Pancuronium bromide					
Drug	*Mfr*	*Conc/L*	*Mfr*	*Conc/L*	*Test Soln*	*Remarks*	*Ref*	*C/I*
Verapamil HCl	KN	80 mg	OR	8 mg	D5W, NS	Physically compatible for 24 hr	764	C

Drugs in Syringe Compatibility

			Pancuronium bromide				
Drug (in syringe)	*Mfr*	*Amt*	*Mfr*	*Amt*	*Remarks*	*Ref*	*C/I*
Heparin sodium		2500 units/ 1 ml		4 mg/ 2 ml	Physically compatible for at least 5 min	1053	C

Y-Site Injection Compatibility (1:1 Mixture)

			Pancuronium bromide				
Drug	*Mfr*	*Conc*	*Mfr*	*Conc*	*Remarks*	*Ref*	*C/I*
Aminophylline	AB	1 mg/ml[a]	ES	0.05 mg/ml[a]	Physically compatible for 24 hr at 28 °C	1337	C
Cefazolin sodium	LY	10 mg/ml[a]	ES	0.05 mg/ml[a]	Physically compatible for 24 hr at 28 °C	1337	C
Cefuroxime sodium	GL	7.5 mg/ml[a]	ES	0.05 mg/ml[a]	Physically compatible for 24 hr at 28 °C	1337	C
Cimetidine HCl	SKF	6 mg/ml[a]	ES	0.05 mg/ml[a]	Physically compatible for 24 hr at 28 °C	1337	C
Diazepam	ES	5 mg/ml	ES	0.05 mg/ml[a]	Cloudy solution forms immediately	1337	I
Dobutamine HCl	LI	1 mg/ml[a]	ES	0.05 mg/ml[a]	Physically compatible for 24 hr at 28 °C	1337	C
Dopamine HCl	SO	1.6 mg/ml[a]	ES	0.05 mg/ml[a]	Physically compatible for 24 hr at 28 °C	1337	C
Epinephrine HCl	AB	4 μg/ml[a]	ES	0.05 mg/ml[a]	Physically compatible for 24 hr at 28 °C	1337	C
Esmolol HCl	DCC	10 mg/ml[a]	ES	0.05 mg/ml[a]	Physically compatible for 24 hr at 28 °C	1337	C
Etomidate	AB	2 mg/ml	GNS	2 mg/ml	Visually compatible for up to 7 days at 25 °C	1801	C
Fentanyl citrate	ES	10 μg/ml[a]	ES	0.05 mg/ml[a]	Physically compatible for 24 hr at 28 °C	1337	C
Fluconazole	RR	2 mg/ml	GNS	0.5 mg/ml[b]	Visually compatible for 24 hr at 28 °C	1760	C
Gentamicin sulfate	ES	2 mg/ml[a]	ES	0.05 mg/ml[a]	Physically compatible for 24 hr at 28 °C	1337	C
Heparin sodium	SO	40 units/ml[a]	ES	0.05 mg/ml[a]	Physically compatible for 24 hr at 28 °C	1337	C
Hetastarch in lactated electrolyte injection (Hextend)	AB	6%	ES	0.1 mg/ml[a]	Physically compatible with no change in measured turbidity or increase in particle content in 4 hr at 23 °C	2339	C
Hydrocortisone sodium succinate	AB	1 mg/ml[a]	ES	0.05 mg/ml[a]	Physically compatible for 24 hr at 28 °C	1337	C
Isoproterenol HCl	ES	4 μg/ml	ES	0.05 mg/ml[a]	Physically compatible for 24 hr at 28 °C	1337	C
Levofloxacin	OMN	5 mg/ml[a]	ES	1 mg/ml	Visually compatible for 4 hr at 24 °C under fluorescent light	2233	C
Lorazepam	WY	0.5 mg/ml[a]	ES	0.05 mg/ml[a]	Physically compatible for 24 hr at 28 °C	1337	C

Y-Site Injection Compatibility (1:1 Mixture) (Cont.)

Pancuronium bromide

Drug	*Mfr*	*Conc*	*Mfr*	*Conc*	*Remarks*	*Ref*	*C/I*
Midazolam HCl	RC	0.05 mg/ml[a]	ES	0.05 mg/ml[a]	Physically compatible for 24 hr at 28 °C	1337	C
Milrinone lactate	SW	0.4 mg/ml[a]	GNS	1 mg/ml	Visually compatible with little or no loss of either drug by HPLC in 4 hr at 23 °C	2214	C
Morphine sulfate	WY	1 mg/ml[a]	ES	0.05 mg/ml[a]	Physically compatible for 24 hr at 28 °C	1337	C
Nitroglycerin	SO	0.4 mg/ml[a]	ES	0.05 mg/ml[a]	Physically compatible for 24 hr at 28 °C	1337	C
Propofol	STU	2 mg/ml	GNS	2 mg/ml	Oil droplets form within 7 days at 25 °C. No visible change in 24 hr	1801	?
	ZEN	10 mg/ml	AST	1 mg/ml	Physically compatible for 1 hr at 23 °C with no increase in particle content	2066	C
Ranitidine HCl	GL	0.5 mg/ml[a]	ES	0.05 mg/ml[a]	Physically compatible for 24 hr at 28 °C	1337	C
Sodium nitroprusside	ES	0.2 mg/ml[a]	ES	0.05 mg/ml[a]	Physically compatible for 24 hr at 28 °C	1337	C
Thiopental sodium	AB	25 mg/ml	GNS	2 mg/ml	White precipitate forms immediately	1801	I
Trimethoprim–sulfamethoxazole	ES	0.64 + 3.2 mg/ml[a]	ES	0.05 mg/ml[a]	Physically compatible for 24 hr at 28 °C	1337	C
Vancomycin HCl	ES	5 mg/ml[a]	ES	0.05 mg/ml[a]	Physically compatible for 24 hr at 28 °C	1337	C

[a]*Tested in dextrose 5% in water.*
[b]*Tested in sodium chloride 0.9%.*

Additional Compatibility Information

Infusion Solutions — The manufacturer states that pancuronium bromide exhibits no decomposition for 48 hours mixed in the following infusion solutions (1-9/98; 4):

Dextrose 5% in sodium chloride 0.45%
Dextrose 5% in sodium chloride 0.9%
Dextrose 5% in water
Ringer's injection, lactated
Sodium chloride 0.9%

Other Drugs — It is stated that a precipitate may be formed if pancuronium bromide is mixed with barbiturates. (4) However, a precipitate was not visible when pancuronium bromide was mixed in a syringe with thiopental or methohexital as well as succinylcholine, meperidine, opium alkaloids HCl, neostigmine, gallamine, tubocurarine, alcuronium, hydrocortisone, or promethazine. (134)

PAPAVERINE HCL
AHFS 24:12

Products — Papaverine HCl is available in 2-ml single-dose ampuls and vials and 10-ml multiple-dose vials. Each milliliter of solution contains 30 mg of papaverine as the hydrochloride. (1-3/99; 4; 29) The multiple-dose vials also contain edetate disodium 0.005%, chlorobutanol 0.5%, and sodium hydroxide to adjust the pH. (1-3/99) The single-dose containers are preservative free. (4)

pH — Not below 3. (17)

Osmolality — Papaverine HCl 30 mg/ml has an osmolality of 99 mOsm/kg. (1689)

Administration — Papaverine HCl may be administered by intramuscular or slow intravenous injection over one to two minutes. (1-3/99; 4)

Stability — Papaverine HCl injection should be stored at controlled room temperature and protected from temperatures of 40 °C or higher and from freezing. (4) It should not be refrigerated because of a reduction in solubility with possible precipitation. (593) The solutions should be clear and colorless to pale yellow. (1-7/99) The yellow discoloration of papaverine HCl injection does not appear to be related to drug decomposition. HPLC analysis of a yellow injection found nearly 100% of the labeled potency. Furthermore, yellow discoloration is not produced by intentional degradation from boiling with acid or base. (1996)

Compatibility Information

Solution Compatibility

Papaverine HCl

Solution	*Mfr*	*Mfr*	*Conc/L*	*Remarks*	*Ref*	*C/I*
Dextran 6% in dextrose 5%	AB		96 mg	Physically compatible	3	C
Dextran 6% in sodium chloride 0.9%	AB		96 mg	Physically compatible	3	C
Dextrose–Ringer's injection combinations	AB		96 mg	Physically compatible	3	C
Dextrose–saline combinations	AB		96 mg	Physically compatible	3	C
Dextrose 2½% in water	AB		96 mg	Physically compatible	3	C
Dextrose 5% in water	AB		96 mg	Physically compatible	3	C
Dextrose 10% in water	AB		96 mg	Physically compatible	3	C
Fructose 10% in sodium chloride 0.9%	AB		96 mg	Physically compatible	3	C
Fructose 10% in water	AB		96 mg	Physically compatible	3	C
Invert sugar 5 and 10% in sodium chloride 0.9%	AB		96 mg	Physically compatible	3	C
Invert sugar 5 and 10% in water	AB		96 mg	Physically compatible	3	C
Ionosol products	AB		96 mg	Physically compatible	3	C
Ringer's injection	AB		96 mg	Physically compatible	3	C
Sodium chloride 0.45%	AB		96 mg	Physically compatible	3	C
Sodium chloride 0.9%	AB		96 mg	Physically compatible	3	C
Sodium lactate ⅙ M	AB		96 mg	Physically compatible	3	C

Additive Compatibility

Papaverine HCl

Drug	*Mfr*	*Conc/L*	*Mfr*	*Conc/L*	*Test Soln*	*Remarks*	*Ref*	*C/I*
Aminophylline with trimecaine HCl		480 mg 600 mg		120 mg	D5W	Papaverine precipitates within 3 hr due to alkaline pH	835	I
Theophylline		2 g		160 mg	D5W	Visually compatible with little or no loss of either drug in 48 hr	1909	C

Drugs in Syringe Compatibility

Papaverine HCl

Drug (in syringe)	*Mfr*	*Amt*	*Mfr*	*Amt*	*Remarks*	*Ref*	*C/I*
Diatrizoate meglumine 66%, diatrizoate sodium 10%	SQ	3 ml	LI	30 mg/ 1 ml	White precipitate disappears after 1 to 2 min	1437	?
Diatrizoate meglumine 52%, diatrizoate sodium 8%	MA	5 ml	ME	32 mg/ 1 ml	Transient precipitate clears and then reforms after 2 hr	1438	I
Diatrizoate sodium 60%	WI	5 ml	ME	32 mg/ 1 ml	Transient precipitate clears within 5 min	1438	?
Iohexol 64.7%	WI	5 ml	LI	30 mg/ 1 ml	Physically compatible for at least 2 hr	1438	C
Iopamidol 61%	SQ	5 ml	LI	30 mg/ 1 ml	Physically compatible for at least 2 hr	1438	C

Drugs in Syringe Compatibility (Cont.)

Papaverine HCl

Drug (in syringe)	*Mfr*	*Amt*	*Mfr*	*Amt*	*Remarks*	*Ref*	*C/I*
Iothalamate sodium 60%	MA	3 ml	LI	30 mg/ 1 ml	Physically compatible	1437	C
Ioxaglate meglumine 39.3%, ioxaglate sodium 19.6%	MA	5 ml	LI	32 mg/ 1 ml	Precipitate forms immediately and persists for at least 2 hr	1438	I
	MA	3 and 5 ml	LI	30 mg/ 1 ml	White amorphous precipitate forms immediately and persists for 24 hr. If shaken, it redissolves in 20 to 30 min	1437	I
	MA	5 ml	LI	30 mg/2 to 6 ml[a]	Precipitate forms	1437	I
	MA	5 ml	LI	30 mg/11 and 16 ml[a]	Precipitate forms and then redissolves	1437	?
	MA	5 ml	LI	30 mg/ 21 ml[a]	Physically compatible	1437	C
	MA	15 and 30 ml	LI	30 mg/ 11 ml[a]	Physically compatible	1437	C
	MA	5 ml	LI	60 mg/12 and 17 ml[a]	Precipitate forms	1437	I
	MA	5 ml	LI	60 mg/ 22 ml[a]	Precipitate forms and then redissolves	1437	?
Metrizamide 48.25%	WI	3 ml	LI	30 mg/ 1 ml	Physically compatible	1437	C
Phentolamine mesylate	BV, CI	0.5 mg/ ml[b]	LI	30 mg/ml	Physically compatible with virtually no papaverine loss at 5 and 25 °C and 1 to 3% phentolamine loss at 5 °C and 4 to 5% loss at 25 °C in 30 days	1161	C

[a]*Diluted in sodium chloride 0.9%.*
[b]*Reconstituted with the papaverine HCl injection.*

Additional Compatibility Information

Infusion Solutions — Papaverine HCl should not be added to Ringer's injection, lactated, because precipitation results. (4)

PENICILLIN G POTASSIUM (BENZYLPENICILLIN POTASSIUM) AHFS 8:12.16

Products — Penicillin G potassium is available from several manufacturers in vial sizes ranging from 1 to 20 million units. (4; 29) The commercial products contain sodium citrate and citric acid as buffers. Depending on the route of administration, reconstitute the vials with sterile water for injection, dextrose 5% in water, or sodium chloride 0.9%. The recommended reconstitution volumes vary slightly among manufacturers; the amount of diluent recommended by the manufacturer should be used for reconstitution. To reconstitute the product, loosen the powder in the vials. While holding the vial horizontally, rotate it and add the diluent slowly, directing the stream against the wall of the vial. Shake the vial vigorously. When the required volume of solvent is greater than the capacity of the vial, a portion of the total volume of diluent may be added to the vial first to dissolve the drug. The resulting solution should then be withdrawn and mixed with the remainder of the needed diluent in a larger container. (2; 4)

Penicillin G potassium is also available as frozen premixed infusion solutions of 1, 2, and 3 million units in 50 ml of dextrose 4, 2.3, and 0.7%, respectively. The products also contain sodium citrate buffer;

hydrochloric acid and/or sodium hydroxide may have been used to adjust the pH during manufacture. (4; 29)

Units—Each milligram of penicillin G potassium has a potency of 1440 to 1680 USP units. Each milligram of the powder for injection (which contains sodium citrate buffer) has a potency of 1355 to 1595 USP units. (4)

pH—The reconstituted powder for injection has a pH of 6 to 8.5. The frozen premixed infusion solutions have a pH of 5.5 to 8. (4)

Osmolality—The frozen premixed penicillin G potassium infusion solutions are iso-osmotic having an osmolality of 300 mOsm/kg. (4)

The osmolality of penicillin G potassium (Pfizer) 250,000 units/ml in sterile water for injection was determined to be 776 mOsm/kg by freezing-point depression and 767 mOsm/kg by vapor pressure. (1071) Another report cited the osmolality of this concentration as 749 mOsm/kg. (50)

The osmolality of penicillin G potassium (Roerig) 50,000 units/ml was determined to be 402 mOsm/kg in dextrose 5% in water and 414 mOsm/kg in sodium chloride 0.9%. At 100,000 units/ml, the osmolality was determined to be 535 mOsm/kg in dextrose 5% in water and 554 mOsm/kg in sodium chloride 0.9%. (1375)

The osmolality of penicillin G potassium was calculated for the following dilutions (1054):

	Osmolality (mOsm/kg)	
Diluent	50 ml	100 ml
3 million units		
Dextrose 5% in water	411	340
Sodium chloride 0.9%	437	367
5 million units		
Dextrose 5% in water	501	394
Sodium chloride 0.9%	527	420

Robinson et al. recommended the following maximum penicillin G potassium concentrations to achieve osmolalities suitable for peripheral infusion in fluid-restricted patients (1180):

Diluent	Maximum Concentration (units/ml)	Osmolality (mOsm/kg)
Dextrose 5% in water	81,568	566
Sodium chloride 0.9%	73,455	545
Sterile water for injection	147,205	513

Sodium and Potassium Content—Penicillin G potassium contains, in each million units, 1.7 mEq of potassium and 0.3 mEq of sodium. (4)

Trade Name(s)—Pfizerpen.

Administration — NOTE: Do not confuse other forms of penicillin G with penicillin G potassium.

Penicillin G potassium is administered by intramuscular injection or continuous or intermittent intravenous infusion. (2) It may also be administered by intrathecal, intra-articular, and intrapleural injections and other local instillations. Vials containing 10 or 20 million units are intended for intravenous administration. For intramuscular injections, concentrations of up to 100,000 units/ml will cause a minimum of discomfort. Higher concentrations may be used when needed. (2; 4)

In high doses, intravenous administration should be performed slowly to avoid electrolyte imbalance from the potassium content. For daily doses of 10 million units or more, the drug may be diluted in 1 or 2 L of infusion solution and administered in a 24-hour period. (2; 4) By intermittent intravenous infusion, one-fourth or one-sixth of the daily dose may be given over one to two hours and repeated every six to four hours, respectively. Divided doses are generally infused over 15 to 30 minutes in children and neonates. (4)

Stability — The dry powder is stable when stored at room temperature. (4) After reconstitution, penicillin G potassium is stable for seven days under refrigeration at 2 to 8 °C. (4; 47)

However, penicillin G potassium approximately 500,000 units/ml was stored at room temperature and 4 °C. After 24 hours at room temperature, HPLC analysis revealed a new peak, which increased in size by 72 hours. Storage at 4 °C significantly reduced the rate of formation of this new compound. Although the therapeutic potency of penicillin G potassium was retained over the time period studied, the authors indicated that its potential as an antigen may change due to possible formation of polymers or conjugation products that may cause allergic sensitization reactions. It was recommended that the drug be freshly prepared before use or refrigerated during interim storage. (785)

Another study found increased formation of specific antipenicillin antibodies in patients administered aged penicillin solutions, not only at room temperature but also 4 °C. The authors indicated that the causative antigens were degradation or transformation products of penicillin G. Freshly prepared solutions did not seem to be immunogenic. (946)

pH Effects—The stability of penicillin G potassium 500,000 units/ml is greatest at pH 7. (160) Penicillin G activity rapidly declines at pH 5.5 and below. Penicillin inactivation also occurs at pH values above 8. (47)

Freezing Solutions—Frozen premixed infusion solutions of penicillin G potassium are stable for at least 90 days from shipping stored at −20 °C. The frozen solutions should be thawed at room temperature or under refrigeration and, once thawed, should not be refrozen. Thawing should not be performed using a warm water bath or microwave radiation. Thawed solutions are stated to be stable for 24 hours at room temperature and for 14 days under refrigeration. (4)

Shoup and Thur reported that penicillin G potassium 1 million units/ml is stable for 12 weeks when frozen at −18 °C. (161) Aisenstein and Kahn reported penicillin G potassium (Lilly), reconstituted to a concentration of 500,000 units/ml with sterile water for injection, to be stable for at least 35 days. (325) However, the validity of these results has been questioned because the highly inaccurate serial dilution method was employed. (162; 299) Boylan et al. cited a report by Grant et al. that showed a loss of penicillin G in 17 hours when frozen at −18 °C with imidazole or histidine. (163) However, other reports indicate that the freezing of penicillin G potassium may be satisfactory. One report showed that penicillin G potassium in concentrations of 1 to 10%, buffered to pH 6.85, lost no more than 1% potency in one month when frozen at −20 °C. (99) Another study of penicillin G potassium at a concentration of 5 million units in 50 ml of dextrose 5% in water, in PVC containers frozen at −20 °C, showed no loss of potency after 14 days of storage. It was noted, however, that this study was not conclusive evidence of the safety of using such a technique. (155) Additional information has come from a report of penicillin G potassium 2 million units/50 ml of dextrose 5% in water and sodium chloride 0.9% in PVC containers frozen at −20 °C for 30 days. The results indicate that potency was retained for the duration of the study. (299)

Penicillin G potassium (Squibb) 1 million units/100 ml of dextrose 5% in water in PVC bags was also frozen at −20 °C for 30 days and then thawed by exposure to ambient temperature or microwave radiation. No evidence of precipitation or color change was observed, and a 3 to 4% loss of potency, as determined microbiologically, was reported. Subsequent storage of the thawed admixture at room temperature for 24 hours yielded a physically compatible solution, which exhibited no further loss of potency. (554)

Miller and Pesko reported an approximate fivefold increase in particles of 2 to 60 μm produced by freezing and thawing penicillin G potassium (Squibb) 2 million units/100 ml of dextrose 5% in water (Travenol). The constituted drug was filtered through a 0.45-μm filter into PVC bags of solution and frozen for seven days at −20 °C. Thawing was performed at 29 °C for 12 hours. Although the total number of particles increased significantly, no particles greater than 60 μm were observed; the solutions complied with USP standards for particle sizes and numbers in large volume parenteral solutions. (822)

Penicillin G potassium (Parke-Davis) 1 million units/50 ml of sodium chloride 0.9% lost 5% in 16 days and 7% in 25 days (by HPLC) when frozen at −7 °C. However, samples of the same solution stored at 4 °C showed similar results, indicating a lack of advantage for frozen storage. (1035)

Ambulatory Pumps — The stability of penicillin G potassium (Marsam) 100,000 and 200,000 units/ml in sterile water for injection was evaluated in PVC portable pump reservoirs (Pharmacia Deltec). HPLC analysis found 6% loss in three days at 25 °C. The 200,000-unit/ml concentration was also tested stored at 5 °C. About 3% loss occurred in 14 days. (2080)

Elastomeric Reservoir Pumps — Penicillin G potassium (Pfizer) 40,000 units/ml in both dextrose 5% in water and sodium chloride 0.9% was evaluated for binding potential to natural rubber elastomeric reservoirs (Baxter). No binding was found after storage for two weeks at 35 °C with gentle agitation. (2014)

Penicillin G potassium solutions in elastomeric reservoir pumps have been stated by the pump manufacturers to be stable for the following time periods frozen, refrigerated (REF), and at room temperature (RT) (31):

Pump Reservoir(s)	Conc.	Frozen	REF	RT
Homepump; Homepump Eclipse	10,000 units/ml[a]	30 days	24 hr	24 hr
Intermate	100,000 units/ml[a,b]	30 days	10 days	24 hr
Medflo	10,000 units/ml[a]	4 weeks	7 days	24 hr
ReadyMed	50,000 units/ml[b]	4 weeks	14 days	48 hr

[a]*In dextrose 5% in water.*
[b]*In sodium chloride 0.9%.*

Filtration — Filtering penicillin G potassium (Pfizer) through 5-μm stainless steel and 0.22-μm cellulose ester inline filters resulted in no significant reduction in activity under conditions of varying doses, temperatures, flow rates, and administration methods. (167)

Compatibility Information

Solution Compatibility

Penicillin G potassium

Solution	*Mfr*	*Mfr*	*Conc/L*	*Remarks*	*Ref*	*C/I*
Alcohol 5%, dextrose 5%	AB		1 MU[b]	34% decomposition in 24 hr. Potency retained for 6 hr	46	I
Amino acids 4.25%, dextrose 25%	MG	LI	1 MU[b]	No increase in particulate matter in 24 hr at 5 °C	349	C
Dextran 6% in dextrose 5%	AB		1 MU[b]	Physically compatible	3	C
Dextran 6% in sodium chloride 0.9%	AB		1 MU[b]	Physically compatible	3	C
Dextran 70 6% in dextrose 5%			~6 MU[b]	7% decomposition in 6 hr and 18% in 24 hr at 20 °C	834	I
Dextran 40 10% in dextrose 5%			~6 MU[b]	34% decomposition in 24 hr at 20 °C	834	I
Dextrose–Ringer's injection combinations	AB		1 MU[b]	Physically compatible	3	C
Dextrose–Ringer's injection, lactated, combinations	AB		1 MU[b]	Physically compatible	3	C
Dextrose 5% in Ringer's injection, lactated	TR[c]	SQ	10 MU[b]	Potency retained for 24 hr at 5 °C	282	C
Dextrose–saline combinations	AB		1 MU[b]	Physically compatible	3	C
Dextrose 5% in sodium chloride 0.9%	MG	SQ	5 MU[b]	Potency retained for 24 hr at 4 and 25 °C	105	C
		SQ	2 MU[b]	Potency retained for 24 hr	109	C
	AB, BA, CU	(B)	5 MU[b]	Potency retained for 48 hr at 25 °C	164	C
			1 MU[b]	Physically compatible	74	C
	TR[c]	SQ	10 MU[b]	Potency retained for 24 hr at 5 °C	282	C

Solution Compatibility (Cont.)

Penicillin G potassium

Solution	*Mfr*	*Mfr*	*Conc/L*	*Remarks*	*Ref*	*C/I*
Dextrose 2½% in water	AB		1 MU[b]	Physically compatible	3	C
Dextrose 5% in water	AB		1 MU[b]	Physically compatible	3	C
			10 MU[b]	No decomposition in 12 hr	165	C
			100 MU[b]	7.5% decomposition in 48 hr at 25 °C and none at 5 °C	141	C
	MG	SQ	5 MU[b]	Potency retained for 24 hr at 4 and 25 °C	105	C
		SQ	2 MU[b]	Potency retained for 24 hr	109	C
		(B)	900,000 units	Potency retained for 24 hr at 25 °C	48	C
			1 MU[b]	Physically compatible	74	C
	TR[c]	SQ	10 MU[b]	Potency retained for 24 hr at 5 °C	282	C
	BA[c], TR	AY	40 MU[b]	Potency retained for 24 hr at 5 and 22 °C	298	C
	TR[d]	SQ	10 MU[b]	Physically compatible with approximately 5% potency loss in 24 hr at room temperature	554	C
Dextrose 10% in water	AB		1 MU[b]	Physically compatible	3	C
	MG	SQ	5 MU[b]	Potency retained for 24 hr at 4 and 25 °C	105	C
		SQ	2 MU[b]	Potency retained for 24 hr	109	C
Fat emulsion 10%, intravenous	VT	SQ	10 MU[b]	Physically compatible for 48 hr at 4 °C and room temperature	32	C
	VT		2 MU[b]	Microscopic globule coalescence in 24 hr at 8 and 25 °C	825	I
Fructose 10% in sodium chloride 0.9%	AB		1 MU[b]	Physically compatible	3	C
Fructose 10% in water	AB		1 MU[b]	Physically compatible	3	C
Hetastarch 6%			~6 MU[b]	7% decomposition in 24 hr at 20 °C	834	C
Invert sugar 5 and 10% in sodium chloride 0.9%	AB		1 MU[b]	Physically compatible	3	C
Invert sugar 5 and 10% in water	AB		1 MU[b]	Physically compatible	3	C
Isolyte M with dextrose 5%	MG	SQ	5 MU[b]	Potency retained for 24 hr at 4 and 25 °C	105	C
Isolyte P with dextrose 5%	MG	SQ	5 MU[b]	Potency retained for 24 hr at 4 and 25 °C	105	C
Ionosol products	AB		1 MU[b]	Physically compatible	3	C
Ringer's injection	AB		1 MU[b]	Physically compatible	3	C
Ringer's injection, lactated	AB		1 MU[b]	Physically compatible	3	C
	MG	SQ	5 MU[b]	Potency retained for 24 hr at 4 and 25 °C	105	C
			1 MU[b]	Physically compatible	74	C
	TR[c]	SQ	10 MU[b]	Potency retained for 24 hr at 5 °C	282	C
Sodium chloride 0.45%	AB		1 MU[b]	Physically compatible	3	C
Sodium chloride 0.9%	AB		1 MU[b]	Physically compatible	3	C
			100 MU[b]	Potency retained for 48 hr at 5 °C	141	C
	MG	SQ	5 MU[b]	Potency retained for 24 hr at 4 and 25 °C	105	C
		SQ	2 MU[b]	Potency retained for 24 hr	109	C
	AB, BA, CU	(B)	5 MU[b]	Potency retained for 48 hr at 25 °C	164	C
			1 MU[b]	Physically compatible	74	C
	TR[c]	SQ	10 MU[b]	Potency retained for 24 hr at 5 °C	282	C
	BA[c], TR	AY	40 MU[b]	Potency retained for 24 hr at 5 and 22 °C	298	C
	TR[d]	PD	20 MU[b]	5% penicillin loss at 24 °C and no loss at 4 °C in 4 days	1035	C

Solution Compatibility (Cont.)

Penicillin G potassium

Solution	*Mfr*	*Mfr*	*Conc/L*	*Remarks*	*Ref*	*C/I*
TPN #21[e]		SQ	5 MU[b]	Antibiotic potency retained for 24 hr at 4 and 25 °C	87	**C**
TPN #22[e]		AY	25 MU[b]	Physically compatible with no activity loss by microbiological assay in 24 hr at 22 °C in the dark	837	**C**
TPN #107[e]			2 g	Physically compatible and penicillin G activity retained for 24 hr at 21 °C by microbiological assay	1326	**C**

[a]Citations with the notation "(B)" in the penicillin G potassium manufacturer's column specified a buffered preparation.
[b]Million units.
[c]Tested in both glass and PVC containers.
[d]Tested in PVC containers.
[e]Refer to Appendix I for the composition of parenteral nutrition solutions. TPN indicates a 2-in-1 admixture.

Additive Compatibility

Penicillin G potassium

Drug	*Mfr*	*Conc/L*	*Mfr*	*Conc/L*	*Test Soln*	*Remarks*	*Ref*	*C/I*
Amikacin sulfate	BR	5 g	LI	20 MU[b]	D5LR, D5R, D5S, D5W, D10W, LR, NS, R, SL	Physically compatible and potency of both retained for 24 hr at 25 °C	293	**C**
	BR	5 g	LI	20 MU[b]	IG–D5W, IS10	Potency of penicillin retained through 8 hr at 25 °C. Greater than 10% decomposition in 24 hr	293	**I**
Aminophylline	SE	500 mg	(B)	900,000 units	D5W	22% penicillin decomposition in 6 hr at 25 °C	48	**I**
	SE	500 mg	SQ	1 MU[b]	D5W	44% penicillin decomposition in 24 hr at 25 °C	47	**I**
Amphotericin B		200 mg	BP	10 MU[b]	D5W	Haze develops over 3 hr	26	**I**
	SQ	50 mg	SQ	5 MU[b]		Precipitate forms within 1 hr	47	**I**
	SQ	100 mg	SQ	20 MU[b]	D5W	Physically incompatible	15	**I**
Ascorbic acid injection	AB	1 g		1 MU[b]		Physically compatible	3	**C**
	PD	500 mg	SQ	10 MU[b]	D5W	99% penicillin potency retained for at least 8 hr	166	**C**
Calcium chloride	UP	1 g	SQ	20 MU[b]	D5W	Physically compatible	15	**C**
	UP	1 g	SQ	5 MU[b]	D	Physically compatible	47	**C**
Calcium gluconate	UP	1 g	SQ	20 MU[b]	D5W	Physically compatible	15	**C**
		1 g		1 MU[b]	D5W	Physically compatible	74	**C**
Chloramphenicol sodium succinate	PD	10 g	SQ	20 MU[b]	D5W	Physically compatible	15	**C**
	PD	1 g	SQ	5 MU[b]		Physically compatible	47	**C**
	PD	500 mg	SQ	1 MU[b]	D5S, D5W	Therapeutic availability maintained	110	**C**
	PD	1 g	SQ	5 and 10 MU[b]	D5S, D5W	Therapeutic availability maintained	110	**C**
	PD	1 g		1 MU[b]		Physically compatible	3	**C**
	PD	1 g	SQ	10 MU[b]		Physically compatible	6	**C**

Additive Compatibility (Cont.)

Penicillin G potassium

Drug	*Mfr*	*Conc/L*	*Mfr*	*Conc/L*	*Test Soln*	*Remarks*	*Ref*	*C/I*
Chlorpromazine HCl	BP	200 mg	BP	10 MU[b]	NS	Haze develops over 3 hr	26	**I**
Cimetidine HCl	SKF	1.2 and 5 g	LI	2.4 MU[b]	D5W, NS	Physically compatible and cimetidine chemically stable for 24 hr at room temperature. Penicillin not tested	551	**C**
Clindamycin phosphate	UP	1.2 g		10 MU[b]	D5W	Physically compatible and clindamycin potency retained for 24 hr at room temperature	104	**C**
	UP	2.4 g		20 MU[b]	D5W	Physically compatible and clindamycin potency retained for 24 hr at room temperature	104	**C**
Colistimethate sodium	WC	500 mg	SQ	20 MU[b]	D5W	Physically compatible	15	**C**
	WC	500 mg	SQ	5 MU[b]	D	Physically compatible	47	**C**
Corticotropin		500 units		1 MU[b]	D5W	Physically compatible	74	**C**
Dimenhydrinate	SE	50 mg		1 MU[b]	D5W	Physically compatible	74	**C**
Diphenhydramine HCl	PD	80 mg	SQ	20 MU[b]	D5W	Physically compatible	15	**C**
	PD	50 mg	SQ	1 MU[b]	D5W	Physically compatible. Penicillin potency retained for 24 hr at 25 °C	47	**C**
Dopamine HCl	AS	800 mg	LI	20 MU[b]	D5W	14% penicillin decomposition in 24 hr at 23 to 25 °C. Dopamine potency retained for 24 hr	78	**I**
Ephedrine sulfate		50 mg		1 MU[b]		Physically compatible	3	**C**
	AB	50 mg	SQ	5 MU[b]		Physically compatible	47	**C**
Erythromycin lactobionate	AB	5 g	SQ	20 MU[b]	D5W	Physically compatible	15	**C**
	AB	1 g	SQ	5 MU[b]		Physically compatible	20; 47	**C**
	AB	1 g		1 MU[b]		Physically compatible	3	**C**
Floxacillin sodium	BE	20 g	GL	12 g[c]	NS	Haze forms in 24 hr and precipitate forms in 48 hr at 30 °C. No change at 15 °C	1479	**I**
Furosemide	HO	1 g	GL	12 g[c]	NS	Physically compatible for 24 hr at 15 and 30 °C. Precipitate forms in 48 to 72 hr at 30 °C. No change at 15 °C	1479	**C**
Heparin sodium		12,000 units		1 MU[b]	D5W	Physically compatible	74	**C**
	AB	20,000 units	SQ	1 MU[b]	D5W	Penicillin potency retained for 24 hr at 25 °C	47	**C**
		32,000 units		20 MU[b]	NS	Physically compatible and heparin activity retained for 24 hr	57	**C**
	UP	4000 units	SQ	20 MU[b]	D5W	Physically incompatible	15	**I**
Hydrocortisone sodium succinate	UP	500 mg	SQ	20 MU[b]	D5W	Physically compatible	15	**C**
	UP	250 mg	SQ	5 MU[b]	D	Physically compatible	47	**C**
	UP	100 mg		1 MU[b]	D5W	Physically compatible	74	**C**
Hydroxyzine HCl	RR	250 mg	SQ	20 MU[b]	D5W	Physically incompatible	15	**I**
Kanamycin sulfate	BR	4 g	SQ	20 MU[b]	D5W	Physically compatible	15	**C**
	BR	4 g	SQ	5 MU[b]	D	Physically compatible	47	**C**
Lidocaine HCl	AST	2 g	SQ	1 MU[b]		Physically compatible	24	**C**

Additive Compatibility (Cont.)

Penicillin G potassium

Drug	*Mfr*	*Conc/L*	*Mfr*	*Conc/L*	*Test Soln*	*Remarks*	*Ref*	*C/I*
Lincomycin HCl	UP	6 g	SQ	20 MU[b]	D5W	Physically compatible	15	C
	UP	600 mg	SQ	5 MU[b]	D	Physically compatible	47	C
	UP					Physically incompatible	9	I
Magnesium sulfate		1 g	PF	500 mg	W	5% penicillin loss in 1 day and 13% in 2 days at 24 °C	999	C
		2 to 8 g	PF	500 mg	W	7 to 8% penicillin loss in 1 day and 20 to 25% in 2 days at 24 °C	999	C
Metaraminol bitartrate	MSD	100 mg	SQ	1 MU[b]	D5W	59% penicillin decomposition in 24 hr at 25 °C	47	I
	MSD	100 mg	(B)	900,000 units	D5W	17% penicillin decomposition in 6 hr at 25 °C	48	I
Methylprednisolone sodium succinate	UP	80 mg		2 to 10 MU[b]	D5S, D5W, LR	Clear solution for 24 hr	329	C
Metronidazole	RP	5 g[d]	AY	12 MU[b]		Physically compatible for at least 72 hr at 23 °C, but pH changed significantly	807	?
	SE	5 g[e]	PF	200 MU[b]		5% penicillin loss in 22 hr and 8% in 72 hr at 25 °C. 2% penicillin loss in 12 days at 5 °C. No metronidazole loss	993	C
Metronidazole HCl with sodium bicarbonate	SE AB	5 g 50 mEq	SQ	5 MU[b]	D5W, NS	Physically compatible for 48 hr	765	C
Pentobarbital sodium	AB	500 mg	(B)	900,000 units	D5W	17% penicillin decomposition in 6 hr at 25 °C	48	I
	AB	500 mg	SQ	1 MU[b]	D5W	42% penicillin decomposition in 24 hr at 25 °C	47	I
Polymyxin B sulfate	BW	200 mg	SQ	20 MU[b]	D5W	Physically compatible	15	C
	BW	200 mg	SQ	5 MU[b]	D	Physically compatible	47	C
Potassium chloride		20 mEq	SQ	1 MU[b]	D5S, D5W	Therapeutic availability maintained	110	C
		40 mEq	SQ	5 MU[b]	D5S, D5W	Therapeutic availability maintained	110	C
	AB	40 mEq	SQ	5 MU[b]		Physically compatible	47	C
Potassium chloride with vitamin B complex with C	 TR	20 mEq 1 ampul	SQ	2 MU[b]	D5S, D5W	Therapeutic availability maintained	110	C
Potassium chloride with vitamin B complex with C	 TR	40 mEq 1 ampul	SQ	8 MU[b]	D5S, D5W	Therapeutic availability maintained	110	C
Procaine HCl	WI	1 g	SQ	20 MU[b]	D5W	Physically compatible	15	C
		1 g		1 MU[b]		Physically compatible	3	C
Prochlorperazine edisylate	SKF	10 mg	SQ	5 MU[b]	D5W	Physically compatible. Penicillin potency retained for 24 hr at 25 °C	47	C
	SKF	10 mg	(B)	900,000 units	D5W	Penicillin potency retained for 24 hr at 25 °C	48	C
Prochlorperazine mesylate	BP	100 mg	BP	10 MU[b]	NS	Haze develops over 3 hr	26	I
Promethazine HCl	WY	100 mg	SQ	5 MU[b]		Physically compatible	47	C
	WY	100 mg		1 MU[b]		Physically compatible	3	C
	WY	250 mg		20 MU[b]	D5W	Physically incompatible	15	I
Ranitidine HCl	GL	50 mg and 2 g		24 MU[b]	D5W, NS	Physically compatible and ranitidine chemically stable by HPLC for 24 hr at 25 °C. Penicillin not tested	1515	C

Additive Compatibility (Cont.)

Penicillin G potassium

Drug	Mfr	Conc/L	Mfr	Conc/L	Test Soln	Remarks	Ref	C/I
Sodium bicarbonate		0.5 and 0.75 g	SQ	1 MU[b]	D5W	Penicillin decomposition at 20 °C due to pH	135	I
		3.75 g	(B)	900,000 units	D5W	26% penicillin decomposition in 24 hr at 25 °C	48	I
	AB	3.75 g	SQ	1 MU[b]	D5W	26% penicillin decomposition in 24 hr at 25 °C	47	I
	AB	2.4 mEq[f]		100 MU[b]	D5W	Physically compatible for 24 hr	772	C
Thiopental sodium	AB	2.5 g	SQ	20 MU[b]	D5W	Precipitate forms within 1 hr	21	I
	AB	2.5 g	PF	20 MU[b]	D5W	Physically incompatible	11	I
Verapamil HCl	KN	80 mg	SQ	10 MU[b]	D5W, NS	Physically compatible for 24 hr	764	C
	SE	[g]	PD	62.5 g	D5W, NS	Physically compatible for 24 hr at 21 °C under fluorescent light	1166	C
Vitamin B complex with C	AB	5 ml	SQ	20 MU[b]	D5W	Physically compatible	15	C
	TR	1 ampul	SQ	2 and 8 MU[b]	D5S, D5W	Therapeutic availability maintained	110	C
	AB	2 ml		1 MU[b]		Physically compatible	3	C
		1 vial		1 MU[b]	D5W	Physically compatible	74	C
		10 ml	(B)	900,000 units	D5W	37% penicillin decomposition in 6 hr at 25 °C	48	I
	AB	10 ml	SQ	1 MU[b]	D5W	86% penicillin decomposition in 24 hr at 25 °C	47	I
Vitamin B complex with C with oxytetracycline HCl	TR PF	1 ampul 500 mg and 1 g	SQ	5 MU[b]	D5W, NS	Therapeutic availability lost	110	I
Vitamin B complex with C with potassium chloride	TR	1 ampul 20 mEq	SQ	2 MU[b]	D5S, D5W	Therapeutic availability maintained	110	C
Vitamin B complex with C with potassium chloride	TR	1 ampul 40 mEq	SQ	8 MU[b]	D5S, D5W	Therapeutic availability maintained	110	C

[a] Citations with the notation "(B)" in the penicillin G potassium manufacturer's column specified a buffered preparation.
[b] Million units.
[c] Salt form unspecified.
[d] Minibags (100 ml) containing metronidazole 500 mg with disodium phosphate 150 mg, citric acid 44 mg, and sodium chloride 740 mg. This product differs from the Searle product.
[e] Searle's ready-to-use formulation tested.
[f] One vial of Neut added to a liter of admixture.
[g] Final concentration unspecified.

Drugs in Syringe Compatibility

Penicillin G potassium

Drug (in syringe)	Mfr	Amt	Mfr	Amt	Remarks	Ref	C/I
Heparin sodium		2500 units/ 1 ml		10 million units	Physically compatible for at least 5 min	1053	C
Metoclopramide HCl	RB	10 mg/ 2 ml	SQ	250,000 units/ 1 ml	Incompatible. If mixed, use immediately	924	I
	RB	10 mg/ 2 ml	SQ	1 million units/ 4 ml	Incompatible. If mixed, use immediately	924	I

Drugs in Syringe Compatibility (Cont.)

Drug (in syringe)	Mfr	Amt	Penicillin G potassium Mfr	Penicillin G potassium Amt	Remarks	Ref	C/I
	RB	10 mg/ 2 ml	SQ	250,000 units/ 1 ml	Incompatible. If mixed, use immediately	1167	I
	RB	10 mg/ 2 ml	SQ	1 million units/ 4 ml	Incompatible. If mixed, use immediately	1167	I
	RB	160 mg/ 32 ml	SQ	1 million units/ 4 ml	Incompatible. If mixed, use immediately	1167	I

Y-Site Injection Compatibility (1:1 Mixture)

Drug	Mfr	Conc	Penicillin G potassium Mfr	Penicillin G potassium Conc	Remarks	Ref	C/I
Acyclovir sodium	BW	5 mg/ml[a]	PF	40,000 units/ ml[a]	Physically compatible for 4 hr at 25 °C	1157	C
Amiodarone HCl	LZ	4 mg/ml[c]	PF	100,000 units/ml[c]	Physically compatible for 4 hr at room temperature	1444	C
Cyclophosphamide	MJ	20 mg/ml[a]	PF	100,000 units/ml[a]	Physically compatible for 4 hr at 25 °C	1194	C
Diltiazem HCl	MMD	1[b] and 5 mg/ ml	RR	1 million units/ml	Visually compatible	1807	C
	MMD	5 mg/ml	RR	100,000 units/ml[b]	Visually compatible	1807	C
Enalaprilat	MSD	0.05 mg/ml[b]	PF	50,000 units/ ml[a]	Physically compatible for 24 hr at room temperature under fluorescent light	1355	C
Esmolol HCl	DCC	10 mg/ml[a]	PF	50,000 units/ ml[a]	Physically compatible for 24 hr at 22 °C	1169	C
Fluconazole	RR	2 mg/ml	RR	100,000 units/ml	Physically compatible for 24 hr at 25 °C	1407	C
Foscarnet sodium	AST	24 mg/ml	SQ	100,000 units/ml	Physically compatible for 24 hr at room temperature under fluorescent light	1335	C
Heparin sodium	TR	50 units/ml	RR	40,000 units/ ml[b]	Visually compatible for 4 hr at 25 °C	1793	C
Heparin sodium with hydrocortisone sodium succinate	RI UP	1000 units + 100 mg/L[d]	LI	200,000 units/ml	Physically compatible for at least 4 hr at room temperature by visual and microscopic examination	322	C
Hydromorphone HCl	WY	0.2 mg/ml[a]	PF	100,000 units/ml[a]	Physically compatible for at least 4 hr at 25 °C under fluorescent light	987	C
Labetalol HCl	SC	1 mg/ml[a]	PF	50,000 units/ ml[a]	Physically compatible for 24 hr at 18 °C	1171	C
Magnesium sulfate	IX	16.7, 33.3, 66.7, 100 mg/ ml[a]	SQ	100,000 units/ml[a]	Physically compatible for at least 4 hr at 32 °C	813	C
Meperidine HCl	WY	10 mg/ml[a]	PF	100,000 units/ml[a]	Physically compatible for at least 4 hr at 25 °C under fluorescent light	987	C
Morphine sulfate	WI	1 mg/ml[a]	PF	100,000 units/ml[a]	Physically compatible for at least 4 hr at 25 °C under fluorescent light	987	C

Y-Site Injection Compatibility (1:1 Mixture) (Cont.)

Penicillin G potassium

Drug	*Mfr*	*Conc*	*Mfr*	*Conc*	*Remarks*	*Ref*	*C/I*
Perphenazine	SC	0.02 mg/ml[a]	PF	100,000 units/ml[a]	Physically compatible for 4 hr at 25 °C	1155	C
Potassium chloride		40 mEq/L[d]	LI	200,000 units/ml	Physically compatible for at least 4 hr at room temperature by visual and microscopic examination	322	C
Tacrolimus	FUJ	1 mg/ml[b]	BR	100,000 units/ml[a]	Visually compatible for 24 hr at 25 °C	1630	C
Theophylline	TR	4 mg/ml	RR	40,000 units/ml[b]	Visually compatible for 6 hr at 25 °C	1793	C
TNA #73[e]		32.5 ml[f]	SQ	2 million units/50 ml[a]	Physically compatible for 4 hr at 25 °C by visual observation	1008	C
TPN #54[e]				320,000 and 500,000 units/ml	Physically compatible and 88% penicillin activity retained over 6 hr at 22 °C by microbiological assay	1045	C
TPN #61[e]		[g]	PF	200,000 units/2 ml[h]	Physically compatible	1012	C
		[i]	PF	1.2 million units/1.2 ml[h]	Physically compatible	1012	C
TPN #189[e]				300 mg/ml[b]	Visually compatible for 24 hr at 22 °C	1767	C
Verapamil HCl	SE	2.5 mg/ml	PD	62.5 mg/ml[c]	Physically compatible for 15 min at 21 °C under fluorescent light	1166	C
Vitamin B complex with C	RC	2 ml/L[d]	LI	200,000 units/ml	Physically compatible for at least 4 hr at room temperature by visual and microscopic examination	322	C

[a]*Tested in dextrose 5% in water.*
[b]*Tested in sodium chloride 0.9%.*
[c]*Tested in both dextrose 5% in water and sodium chloride 0.9%.*
[d]*Tested in dextrose 5% in water, Ringer's injection, lactated, and sodium chloride 0.9%.*
[e]*Refer to Appendix I for the composition of parenteral nutrition solutions. TNA indicates a 3-in-1 admixture, and TPN indicates a 2-in-1 admixture.*
[f]*A 32.5-ml sample of parenteral nutrition solution mixed with 50 ml of antibiotic solution.*
[g]*Run at 21 ml/hr.*
[h]*Given over five minutes by syringe pump.*
[i]*Run at 94 ml/hr.*

Additional Compatibility Information

Infusion Solutions — Penicillin G potassium (Squibb) in concentrations up to 5 million units/L is stated to be physically compatible in all Abbott infusion solutions. Although physical compatibility does not indicate nonvisual deterioration, the citrate buffer is sufficient to adjust the pH of most intravenous solutions to the optimum pH range. (47)

Although the stability of penicillin G potassium (buffered) in dextrose 5% in water and sodium chloride 0.9% has been reported to be 60 days at 5 °C (144), studies using more accurate assay methods indicate substantial (as much as 30% in 28 days) potency losses during this period. (141)

Peritoneal Dialysis Solutions — The activity of penicillin G 6 mg/L was evaluated in peritoneal dialysis fluids containing dextrose 1.5 and 4.25% (Dianeal 137, Travenol). Storage at 25 °C resulted in about a 25% loss of antimicrobial activity in 24 hours. The loss of activity was attributed to the pH (5.2) of the dialysis fluids. (515)

Acidic and Alkaline Drugs — Penicillin G potassium is both an acid- and alkali-labile drug. It should not be mixed with drugs that may result in a final pH outside of its stability range of pH 5.5 to 8. (47) Unfortunately, the citrate buffer is of little value in the presence of strongly acidic or alkaline drugs. (48) These drugs include the acidic drugs metaraminol bitartrate and ascorbic acid (not ascorbate sodium) and the alkaline drugs aminophylline, sodium bicarbonate, sodium salts of barbituric acid derivatives, and THAM. (6; 7; 22; 47)

Vitamins — Penicillin G potassium is inactivated by the low pH of ascorbic acid in solution. However, it is compatible with ascorbic acid injection, which has a pH of 5.5 to 7. (166)

The times to 10% decomposition of combinations of penicillin G potassium buffered (Lilly, Pfizer, and Squibb) with multivitamin infusion concentrate (USV) or vitamin B complex with C (Betalin Com-

Table 1. Time to 10% Decomposition of Penicillin G Potassium with Vitamin Products (304)

Penicillin G Potassium	Multi-vitamin Infusion Concentrate	or	Vitamin B Complex with C	pH	Time to 10% Decompo-sition
1 million units/L	1 ml/L	or	2 ml/L	5.1	6.51 hr
	5 ml/L	or	10 ml/L	4.9	4.56 hr
3 million units/L	1 ml/L	or	2 ml/L	5.4	13.56 hr
	5 ml/L	or	10 ml/L	5.0	6.38 hr
5 million units/L	1 ml/L	or	2 ml/L	5.7	22.01 hr
	5 ml/L	or	10 ml/L	5.1	6.51 hr
10 million units/L	1 ml/L	or	2 ml/L	5.9	>24 hr
	5 ml/L	or	10 ml/L	5.4	13.54 hr

plex F.C., Lilly) in dextrose 5% in water and sodium chloride 0.9% have been mathematically predicted on the basis of the final pH of the admixture (Table 1). (304)

Aminoglycosides — Penicillin G 100 μg/ml mixed with gentamicin 5 μg/ml in distilled water had no appreciable effect on gentamicin potency over 72 hours at 20 °C. (362)

To determine if spurious aminoglycoside levels could result from a delay in assaying blood samples, Tindula et al. evaluated the inactivation of amikacin 35 μg/ml and gentamicin and tobramycin 10 μg/ml in human serum by 400-μg/ml concentrations of several penicillins and cephalosporins. Samples were stored for 24 hours at room temperature and frozen at −20 °C. For the room temperature samples, cefazolin and cefamandole caused relatively little inactivation. Nafcillin, cephapirin, and cefoxitin caused moderate inactivation, 20% or less. Penicillin, ampicillin, carbenicillin, and ticarcillin generally caused 25% or more inactivation of gentamicin and tobramycin. Amikacin was somewhat less affected. Freezing samples at −20 °C prevented significant inactivation of amikacin and gentamicin by any of the drugs. Freezing the tobramycin samples was satisfactory for most of the drugs except penicillin, ampicillin, and carbenicillin, which still exhibited a 15 to 20% loss in 24 hours. (824)

The inactivation of tobramycin sulfate 8 μg/ml in human serum by ampicillin, carbenicillin disodium, and penicillin G potassium, each at 200 μg/ml, was studied at 0, 23, and 37 °C by O'Bey et al. For the tobramycin–ampicillin mixture, essentially no differences were observed at the various temperatures. The t_{90} values were 19, 16.5, and 20 hours at 0, 23, and 37 °C, respectively. Carbenicillin displayed a temperature-dependent inactivation of tobramycin. At 0 °C, the t_{90} was 36 hours; but at 23 and 37 °C, the t_{90} values were 10 and 12 hours, respectively. With penicillin G potassium, the t_{90} values for tobramycin inactivation at 0, 23, and 37 °C were 48, 44, and 16 hours, respectively. Inaccurate pharmacokinetic dosing of tobramycin may occur if serum samples are not properly handled. (832)

The inactivation of tobramycin, gentamicin, and amikacin 10 μg/ml in sterile distilled water by penicillin G 500 and 100 μg/ml stored at 37 °C was investigated by Jorgensen and Crawford. Penicillin G 500 μg/ml caused a 23% tobramycin loss in six hours, but no significant loss occurred at the 100-μg/ml concentration. Gentamicin and amikacin were not inactivated in either concentration of penicillin G. No loss of penicillin G activity was detected in any combination. (973)

The comparative inactivation of five aminoglycosides by seven β-lactam antibiotics in human serum at 37 °C was reported by Riff and Thomason. Amikacin, followed by netilmicin, had the lowest degree of inactivation; tobramycin sustained the most pronounced losses. Gentamicin and kanamycin were intermediate in the extent of losses. The six penicillins that were tested all produced aminoglycoside inactivation; the greatest extent of inactivation was caused by carbenicillin followed by ticarcillin, penicillin G, oxacillin, methicillin, and ampicillin, in approximate descending order. Cephalothin produced minimal inactivation (5 to 10% in 24 hours). The rate of inactivation could be reduced by storage at 4 °C and further reduced by storage at −20 °C. The authors suggested processing blood samples rapidly to avoid inaccurate serum determinations. Storage of specimens at low temperature until analysis may be helpful. (1052)

Hydrocortisone — Penicillin G potassium 1 million units/L has also been reported to be conditionally compatible with hydrocortisone sodium succinate (Upjohn) 250 mg/L. The mixture is physically compatible in most Abbott infusion solutions except as noted here (3):

Ionosol B with invert sugar 10%	Haze or precipitate forms within 24 hr
Ionosol D-CM with dextrose 5%	Haze or precipitate forms within 24 hr
Ionosol D with invert sugar 10%	Haze or precipitate forms within 24 hr
Ionosol G with invert sugar 10%	Haze or precipitate forms within 24 hr

Concentrated Drug Solutions — The following incompatibility determinations were performed with concentrated solutions. The drugs in dry form were constituted according to manufacturers' recommendations. One milliliter of penicillin G potassium was added to 5 ml of sterile distilled water along with 1 ml of each of the following drugs. Particulate matter was noted within two hours (28):

Hydroxyzine HCl (Pfizer)
Metaraminol bitartrate (MSD)
Phenytoin sodium (Parke-Davis)
Prochlorperazine edisylate (SKF)
Promazine HCl (Wyeth)
Promethazine HCl (Wyeth)
Vancomycin HCl (Lilly)

Other Drugs — Penicillin G potassium is rapidly inactivated by oxidizing and reducing agents, alcohols, and glycols. (281) High concentrations of penicillin G in combination with vancomycin HCl may result in a precipitate. Five to 10 million units of penicillin G added to vancomycin HCl, especially in dextrose solutions, will cause precipitation. (143) The degradation of penicillin G may be accelerated by the presence of zinc, copper, chromium, manganese, and, especially, iron ions in solutions. (81)

PENICILLIN G SODIUM (BENZYLPENICILLIN SODIUM) AHFS 8:12.16

Products — Penicillin G sodium is available in vials containing 5 million units of drug with sodium citrate and citric acid as buffers. Depending on the route of administration, reconstitute the vials with sterile water for injection, dextrose 5% in water, or sodium chloride 0.9%; reconstitution of the 5 million-unit vial with 3 or 8 ml of diluent results in a final concentration of 1 million or 500,000 units/ml, respectively. Loosen the powder in the vial while holding the vial horizontally, rotate it and add the diluent slowly, directing the stream against the wall of the vial. Shake the vial vigorously. (1-4/01; 4)

Units— Each milligram of penicillin G sodium has a potency of 1500 to 1750 USP units. Each milligram of the powder for injection (which contains sodium citrate buffer) has a potency of 1420 to 1667 USP units. (4)

pH— From 5 to 7.5. (1-4/01)

Osmolality— Penicillin G sodium (Squibb) 250,000 units/ml in sterile water for injection has an osmolality of 795 mOsm/kg. (50)

The osmolality of penicillin G sodium was calculated for the following dilutions (1054):

	Osmolality (mOsm/kg)	
Diluent	50 ml	100 ml
3 million units		
Dextrose 5% in water	413	341
Sodium chloride 0.9%	439	368
5 million units		
Dextrose 5% in water	502	394
Sodium chloride 0.9%	529	421

Robinson et al. recommended the following maximum penicillin G sodium concentrations to achieve osmolalities suitable for peripheral infusion in fluid-restricted patients (1180):

Diluent	Maximum Concentration (units/ml)	Osmolality (mOsm/kg)
Dextrose 5% in water	85,383	573
Sodium chloride 0.9%	76,891	563
Sterile water for injection	154,091	545

Sodium Content— Penicillin G sodium contains 1.68 mEq of sodium per million units. (1-4/01)

Administration — NOTE: Do not confuse other forms of penicillin G with penicillin G sodium.

Penicillin G sodium is administered by intramuscular injection or by continuous or intermittent intravenous infusion. For intramuscular injections, concentrations of up to 100,000 units/ml will cause a minimum of discomfort. Higher concentrations may be used when needed. In high doses, intravenous administration should be performed slowly to avoid electrolyte imbalance from the sodium content. For daily doses of 10 million units or more, the drug may be diluted in 1 or 2 L of infusion solution and administered in a 24-hour period. By intermittent intravenous infusion, one-fourth or one-sixth of the daily dose may be given over one to two hours and repeated every six to four hours, respectively. Divided doses are generally infused over 15 to 30 minutes in children and neonates. (4)

Stability — The dry powder may be stored at controlled room temperature without significant potency loss. After reconstitution, solutions may be stored for three days (1-4/01) to seven days (4) under refrigeration. Intravenous infusions containing this drug are stable at room temperature for at least 24 hours. (4)

pH Effects— At 25 °C, the maximum stability of penicillin G sodium is attained at pH 6.8 (131), but little difference in the rate of decomposition occurs in the pH range of 6.5 to 7.5. (1947) Not more than 10% loss of activity occurs in 24 hours in a pH range of approximately 5.4 to 8.5. (131) Unbuffered penicillin G sodium injection 12 and 48 mg/ml in sodium chloride 0.9% had an initial pH between 5.4 and 5.8. Approximately 7% loss determined by HPLC analysis occurred in two days in samples stored at 5 °C. However, reconstituting with citrate buffers having pH values of 6.5, 7.0, and 7.5 resulted in great stability improvement. At these same concentrations in sodium chloride 0.9% in minibags stored at 5 °C, losses of 5 to 7% occurred in 28 days and 10% in 56 days. (1671)

Freezing Solutions— It has been shown that penicillin G sodium in concentrations of 1 to 10%, buffered to pH 6.85, loses not more than 1% potency in one month when frozen at −20 °C. (99) Another report stated that solutions of penicillin G sodium at a concentration of 50,000 units/ml in water, sodium chloride 0.9%, and 0.05 M citrate buffer and also at a concentration of 500,000 units/ml with sodium citrate 15 mg are stable for at least 12 weeks when frozen at −25 °C. At −5 °C in the citrate buffer, the rate of decomposition is considerably higher than at either −25 or 5 °C. (156)

Rayani et al. reported that penicillin G sodium 2.5 million units/50 ml of dextrose 5% in water in PVC containers was physically compatible and chemically stable for 39 days when frozen at −20 °C. Subsequent thawing and storage at 4 °C resulted in a 3 to 4% loss in 10 to 15 days and up to a 10% loss in 31 days. (1125)

Stiles et al. reported little or no penicillin G sodium loss from a solution containing 180,000 units/ml in sterile water for injection in PVC and glass containers after 30 days at −20 °C. Subsequent thawing and storage for four days at 5 °C, followed by 24 hours at 37 °C to simulate the use of a portable infusion pump, resulted in about a 12 to 16% penicillin loss. (1391)

Ambulatory Pumps— The stability of penicillin G sodium (Marsam) 100,000 and 200,000 units/ml in sterile water for injection was evaluated in PVC portable pump reservoirs (Pharmacia Deltec). HPLC analysis found about 4 to 6% loss in three days at 25 °C. (2080)

Exposure of penicillin G sodium (Squibb-Marsam) 180,000 units/ml in sterile water for injection to 37 °C for 24 hours, to simulate the use of an ambulatory pump, resulted in a 10 to 13% penicillin loss. (1391)

Elastomeric Reservoir Pumps— Penicillin G sodium 10,000 units/ml in dextrose 5% in water in Medflo elastomeric reservoir pumps has been stated by the pump manufacturer to be stable for four weeks frozen at −20 °C, seven days under refrigeration, and 24 hours at room temperature. (31)

Compatibility Information

Solution Compatibility

Penicillin G sodium

Solution	*Mfr*	*Mfr*	*Conc/L*	*Remarks*	*Ref*	*C/I*
Dextran 40 10%	PH	KA	6 MU[a]	Potency retained for 24 hr at 25 °C	131	C
Dextrose 5% in water		KA	6 MU[a]	Potency retained for 24 hr at 25 °C	131	C
		BE	20 MU[a]	25% decomposition in 24 hr at 25 °C	113	I
			4 MU[a,b]	7% loss in 6 hr and 29% loss in 24 hr at room temperature	768	I
	TR[c]	AY	50 MU[a]	No penicillin loss in 39 days at −20 °C. Up to 10% loss on subsequent storage for 31 days at 5 °C	1125	C
Fat emulsion 10%, intravenous	VT		2 MU[a]	Microscopic globule coalescence in 24 hr at 8 and 25 °C	825	I
Invert sugar 10%		KA	6 MU[a]	10% decomposition in 6 to 12 hr at 25 °C	131	I
Sodium chloride 0.9%		BE	20 MU[a]	Potency retained for 24 hr at 25 °C	131	C
			4 MU[a,b]	10% loss in 8 hr and 16% loss in 24 hr at room temperature	768	I
	TR[c]	GL	20 and 80 MU[a]	In unbuffered solution. 7 to 8% loss by HPLC in 48 hr and 18% loss in 96 hr at 5 °C	1671	C
	TR[c]	GL	20 MU[a]	Reconstituted with citrate buffer (pH 6.5 to 7.5). 5% loss by HPLC in 28 days and 10% loss in 56 days at 5 °C	1671	C
TPN #107[e]			2 g	Physically compatible and penicillin G activity retained for 24 hr at 21 °C by microbiological assay	1326	C
TPN #189[e]			300 mg/ml[f]	Visually compatible for 24 hr at 22 °C	1767	C

[a] *Million units.*
[b] *An unbuffered preparation was specified.*
[c] *Tested in PVC containers.*
[d] *Tested in both PVC and glass containers.*
[e] *Refer to Appendix I for the composition of parenteral nutrition solutions. TPN indicates a 2-in-1 admixture.*
[f] *Tested in sodium chloride 0.9%.*

Additive Compatibility

Penicillin G sodium

Drug	*Mfr*	*Conc/L*	*Mfr*	*Conc/L*	*Test Soln*	*Remarks*	*Ref*	*C/I*
Amphotericin B	SQ	100 mg	UP	20 MU[a]	D5W	Physically incompatible	15	I
		200 mg	BP	10 MU[a]	D5W	Haze develops over 3 hr	26	I
Bleomycin sulfate	BR	20 and 30 units	SQ	2 MU[a]	NS	77% loss of bleomycin activity in 1 week at 4 °C	763	I
	BR	20 and 30 units	SQ	5 MU[a]	NS	41% loss of bleomycin activity in 1 week at 4 °C	763	I
Calcium chloride	UP	1 g	UP	20 MU[a]	D5W	Physically compatible	15	C
Calcium gluconate	UP	1 g	UP	20 MU[a]	D5W	Physically compatible	15	C
Chloramphenicol sodium succinate	PD	10 g	UP	20 MU[a]	D5W	Physically compatible	15	C
Chlorpromazine HCl	BP	200 mg	BP	10 MU[a]	NS	Haze develops over 3 hr	26	I

Additive Compatibility (Cont.)

Penicillin G sodium

Drug	*Mfr*	*Conc/L*	*Mfr*	*Conc/L*	*Test Soln*	*Remarks*	*Ref*	*C/I*
Clindamycin phosphate	UP	1.2 g		10 MU[a]	D5W	Physically compatible and clindamycin potency retained for 24 hr at room temperature	104	C
	UP	2.4 g		20 MU[a]	D5W	Physically compatible and clindamycin potency retained for 24 hr at room temperature	104	C
Colistimethate sodium	WC	500 mg	UP	20 MU[a]	D5W	Physically compatible	15	C
Cytarabine	UP	200 mg		2 MU[a]	D5W	pH outside stability range for penicillin G	174	I
Diphenhydramine HCl	PD	80 mg	UP	20 MU[a]	D5W	Physically compatible	15	C
Erythromycin lactobionate	AB	5 g	UP	20 MU[a]	D5W	Physically compatible	15	C
Floxacillin sodium	BE	20 g	GL	12 g[b]	NS	Haze forms in 24 hr and precipitate forms in 48 hr at 30 °C. No change at 15 °C	1479	I
Furosemide	HO	1 g	GL	12 g[b]	NS	Physically compatible for 24 hr at 15 and 30 °C. Precipitate forms in 48 to 72 hr at 30 °C. No change at 15 °C	1479	C
Gentamicin sulfate	RS	160 mg	GL	13 and 40 MU[a]	D5¼S, D5W, NS	Gentamicin potency retained for 24 hr at room temperature	157	C
Heparin sodium	OR	20,000 units	BE	20 MU[a]	NS	Potency of both retained for 24 hr at 25 °C	113	C
		32,000 units		20 MU[a]	NS	Physically compatible and heparin activity retained for 24 hr	57	C
	UP	4000 units	UP	20 MU[a]	D5W	Physically incompatible	15	I
Hydrocortisone sodium succinate	UP	500 mg	UP	20 MU[a]	D5W	Physically compatible	15	C
Hydroxyzine HCl	RR	250 mg	UP	20 MU[a]	D5W	Physically incompatible	15	I
Kanamycin sulfate	BR	4 g	UP	20 MU[a]	D5W	Physically compatible	15	C
Lincomycin HCl	UP	6 g	UP	20 MU[a]	D5W	Physically compatible	15	C
	UP					Physically incompatible	9	I
Methylprednisolone sodium succinate	UP	125 mg		5 MU[a]	D5W, LR	Precipitate forms	329	I
Polymyxin B sulfate	BW	200 mg	UP	20 MU[a]	D5W	Physically compatible	15	C
Potassium chloride		40 mEq	KA	6 MU[a]	D5W	Penicillin potency retained for at least 24 hr at 25 °C	131	C
		40 mEq	KA	5 MU[a]	IS10	pH outside stability range for penicillin	131	I
Procaine HCl	WI	1 g	UP	20 MU[a]	D5W	Physically compatible	15	C
Prochlorperazine mesylate	BP	100 mg	BP	10 MU[a]	NS	Haze develops over 3 hr	26	I
Promethazine HCl	WY	25 mg	UP	20 MU[a]	D5W	Physically incompatible	15	I
Ranitidine HCl	GL	100 mg		2.4 MU[a]	D5W	Physically compatible for 24 hr at ambient temperature under fluorescent light	1151	C
Verapamil HCl	KN	80 mg	SQ	10 MU[a]	D5W, NS	Physically compatible for 24 hr	764	C
Vitamin B complex with C	AB	5 ml	UP	20 MU[a]	D5W	Physically compatible	15	C

[a] *Million units.*
[b] *Salt form unspecified.*

Drugs in Syringe Compatibility

Penicillin G sodium

Drug (in syringe)	Mfr	Amt	Mfr	Amt	Remarks	Ref	C/I
Chloramphenicol sodium succinate	PD	250 and 400 mg/ 1.5 to 2 ml		1 million units	No precipitate or color change within 1 hr at room temperature	99	C
Cimetidine HCl	SKF	300 mg/ 2 ml		1 million units/ 5 ml	Precipitate forms between 36 and 48 hr at room temperature	516	C
Colistimethate sodium	PX	40 mg/ 2 ml		1 million units	No precipitate or color change within 1 hr at room temperature	99	C
Gentamicin sulfate		80 mg/ 2 ml		1 million units	No precipitate or color change within 1 hr at room temperature	99	C
Heparin sodium		2500 units/ 1 ml		10 million units	Physically compatible for at least 15 min	1053	C
Kanamycin sulfate		1 g/4 ml		1 million units	No precipitate or color change within 1 hr at room temperature	99	C
Lincomycin HCl	UP	600 mg/ 2 ml		1 million units	No precipitate or color change within 1 hr at room temperature	99	C
Polymyxin B sulfate	BW	25 mg/ 1.5 to 2 ml		1 million units	No precipitate or color change within 1 hr at room temperature	99	C
Streptomycin sulfate		1 g/2 ml		1 million units	No precipitate or color change within 1 hr at room temperature	99	C

Y-Site Injection Compatibility (1:1 Mixture)

Penicillin G sodium

Drug	Mfr	Conc	Mfr	Conc	Remarks	Ref	C/I
Clarithromycin	AB	4 mg/ml[a]	BRT	24 mg/ml[a]	Visually compatible for 72 hr at both 30 and 17 °C	2174	C
Levofloxacin	OMN	5 mg/ml[a]	MAR	500,000 units/ml	Visually compatible for 4 hr at 24 °C under fluorescent light	2233	C
TPN #54[e]				320,000 and 500,000 units/ml	Physically compatible and 88% penicillin activity retained over 6 hr at 22 °C by microbiological assay	1045	C
TPN #61[e]	[b]		PF	200,000 units/2 ml[c]	Physically compatible	1012	C
	[d]		PF	1.2 million units/12 ml[c]	Physically compatible	1012	C

[a]*Tested in dextrose 5% in water.*
[b]*Run at 21 ml/hr.*
[c]*Given over five minutes by syringe pump.*
[d]*Run at 94 ml/hr.*
[e]*Refer to Appendix I for the composition of parenteral nutrition solutions. TPN indicates a 2-in-1 admixture.*

Additional Compatibility Information

Infusion Solutions — Penicillin G sodium degradation was unaffected by the presence of dextrose 5 and 10%, fructose 5 and 15%, invert sugar 4 and 8%, or ethanol 2.5, 5, 10, and 20% in solutions at 25 °C at a constant pH of 5.4. (131)

Peritoneal Dialysis Solutions — The activity of penicillin G 6 mg/L was evaluated in peritoneal dialysis fluids containing dextrose 1.5 and

4.25% (Dianeal 137, Travenol). Storage at 25 °C resulted in about a 25% loss of antimicrobial activity in 24 hours. The loss of activity was attributed to the pH (5.2) of the dialysis fluids. (515)

Acidic Drugs — The rate of decomposition of acid-sensitive drugs such as penicillin G sodium may be increased by mixing with acidic additives such as metaraminol bitartrate, oxytetracycline HCl, and tetracycline HCl. (7; 22)

Aminoglycosides — Penicillin G 100 μg/ml mixed with gentamicin 5 μg/ml in distilled water had no appreciable effect on gentamicin potency over 72 hours at 20 °C. (362)

Rank et al. evaluated the inactivation of tobramycin 6 μg/ml in human serum with the sodium salts of cloxacillin and piperacillin 150 and 300 μg/ml, ampicillin 100 and 200 μg/ml, and penicillin G 75 and 150 I.U./ml at 25 and 37 °C for up to 12 hours. Piperacillin induced the greatest inactivation among the penicillins, with up to a 15% loss in 12 hours at 37 °C in the 300-μg/ml concentration. Cloxacillin and ampicillin had an intermediate effect, causing about a 5% loss in 12 hours at 37 °C in the highest concentrations. Penicillin G did not yield significant tobramycin inactivation. (817)

To determine if spurious aminoglycoside levels could result from a delay in assaying blood samples, Tindula et al. evaluated the inactivation of amikacin 35 μg/ml and gentamicin and tobramycin 10 μg/ml in human serum by 400-μg/ml concentrations of several penicillins and cephalosporins. Samples were stored for 24 hours at room temperature and frozen at −20 °C. For the room temperature samples, cefazolin and cefamandole caused relatively little inactivation. Nafcillin, cephapirin, and cefoxitin caused moderate inactivation, 20% or less. Penicillin, ampicillin, carbenicillin, and ticarcillin generally caused 25% or more inactivation of gentamicin and tobramycin. Amikacin was somewhat less affected. Freezing samples at −20 °C prevented significant inactivation of amikacin and gentamicin by any of the drugs. Freezing the tobramycin sample was satisfactory for most of the drugs except penicillin, ampicillin, and carbenicillin, which still exhibited a 15 to 20% loss in 24 hours. (824)

The inactivation of tobramycin, gentamicin, and amikacin 10 μg/ml in sterile distilled water by penicillin G 500 and 100 μg/ml stored at 37 °C was investigated by Jorgensen and Crawford. Penicillin G 500 μg/ml caused a 23% tobramycin loss in six hours, but no significant loss occurred at the 100-μg/ml concentration. Gentamicin and amikacin were not inactivated in either concentration of penicillin G. No loss of penicillin G activity was detected in any combination. (973)

The comparative inactivation of five aminoglycosides by seven β-lactam antibiotics in human serum at 37 °C was reported by Riff and Thomason. Amikacin, followed by netilmicin, had the lowest degree of inactivation; tobramycin sustained the most pronounced losses. Gentamicin and kanamycin were intermediate in the extent of losses. The six penicillins that were tested all produced aminoglycoside inactivation; the greatest extent of inactivation was caused by carbenicillin followed by ticarcillin, penicillin G, oxacillin, methicillin, and ampicillin, in approximate descending order. Cephalothin produced minimal inactivation (5 to 10% in 24 hours). The rate of inactivation could be reduced by storage at 4 °C and further reduced by storage at −20 °C. The authors suggested processing blood samples rapidly to avoid inaccurate serum determinations. Storage of specimens at low temperature until analysis may be helpful. (1052)

Other Drugs — High concentrations of penicillin G in combination with vancomycin HCl may result in a precipitate. Five to 10 million units of penicillin G added to vancomycin HCl, especially in dextrose solutions, will cause precipitation. (143) Also, lincomycin HCl is reported to be physically compatible for only four hours in infusion solutions. (154)

In addition, penicillin G is inactivated by oxidizing and reducing agents, alcohols, and glycols. (281) Also, the degradation of penicillin G may be accelerated by the presence of zinc, copper, chromium, manganese, and, especially, iron ions in solutions. (81)

PENTAMIDINE ISETHIONATE
AHFS 8:40

Products — Pentamidine isethionate is available in vials containing 300 mg in lyophilized form; sodium hydroxide and/or hydrochloric acid may have been added during manufacture to adjust the pH. (1-8/99) For intramuscular injection, the contents of a vial should be reconstituted with 3 ml of sterile water for injection to yield a 100-mg/ml concentration. For intravenous injection, the contents of a vial should be reconstituted with 3, 4, or 5 ml of sterile water for injection or dextrose 5% in water to yield solutions containing 100, 75, or 60 mg/ml, respectively. The dose should be withdrawn and further diluted in 50 to 250 ml of dextrose 5% in water for administration. (1-8/99; 4)

pH — Reconstituted solutions of 60 to 100 mg/ml have a pH of approximately 5.4 in sterile water for injection and of 4.09 to 4.38 in dextrose 5% in water. (4)

Osmolality — At a concentration of 100 mg/ml in sterile water for injection and dextrose 5% in water, the osmolalities are 160 and 455 mOsm/kg, respectively. (4)

Equivalency — Pentamidine isethionate 1.74 mg is equivalent to pentamidine 1 mg. (4)

Trade Name(s) — Pentam 300.

Administration — Pentamidine isethionate injection may be administered by slow intravenous infusion or deep intramuscular injection using the Z-track technique. Intravenously, the calculated dose should be diluted in 50 to 250 ml of dextrose 5% in water and infused over 60 to 120 minutes. The drug should not be administered by rapid intravenous injection or infusion. (4)

Stability — The sterile dry powder should be stored at controlled room temperature and protected from light. (1-8/99; 4)

Reconstituted solutions containing 60 to 100 mg/ml are stable for 48 hours at room temperature protected from light. The reconstituted solution should be kept between 22 and 30°C to avoid crystallization. (1-8/99; 4) Because the product does not contain a preservative, the manufacturer recommends discarding any unused portion of the solution. (4)

Pentamidine isethionate at concentrations of 1 and 2.5 mg/ml in dextrose 5% in water is stated to be stable at room temperature for up to 24 hours (4), but other information indicates that the drug may be stable for a longer period at room temperature exposed to fluorescent light. See Compatibility Information.

Elastomeric Reservoir Pumps—Pentamidine isethionate (Fujisawa) 3 mg/ml in dextrose 5% in water and 2 mg/ml in sodium chloride 0.9% was evaluated for binding potential to natural rubber elastomeric reservoirs (Baxter). No binding was found after storage for two weeks at 35 °C with gentle agitation. (2014)

Pentamidine isethionate solutions in elastomeric reservoir pumps have been stated by the pump manufacturers to be stable for the following time periods frozen, refrigerated (REF), or at room temperature (RT) (31):

Pump Reservoir(s)	Conc.	Frozen	REF	RT
Homepump; Homepump Eclipse	2.5 mg/ml[a]	90 days	30 days	24 hr
	2 mg/ml[a,b]			48 hr
Intermate	2 to 6 mg/ml[a]	30 days	10 days	24 hr

[a]In dextrose 5% in water.
[b]In sodium chloride 0.9%.

Sorption—The possible sorption of small amounts of pentamidine isethionate to PVC tubing has been reported. (1142) However, other work indicated that no significant loss occurs due to sorption to PVC containers and tubing. (1311)

Compatibility Information

Solution Compatibility

Pentamidine isethionate

Solution	*Mfr*	*Mfr*	*Conc/L*	*Remarks*	*Ref*	*C/I*
Dextrose 5% in water	TR[a]	LY	1 g	Physically compatible with 3% loss in 48 hr at 24 °C under fluorescent light	1142	C
	TR[a]	LY	2 g	Physically compatible with 1% loss in 48 hr at 24 °C under fluorescent light	1142	C
	TR[a]	MB	2 g	Physically compatible with little or no loss in 24 hr at 20 °C	1311	C
Sodium chloride 0.9%	TR[a]	LY	1 g	Physically compatible with 2% loss in 48 hr at 24 °C under fluorescent light	1142	C
	TR[a]	LY	2 g	Physically compatible with no loss in 48 hr at 24 °C under fluorescent light	1142	C
	TR[a]	MB	2 g	Physically compatible with little or no loss in 24 hr at 20 °C	1311	C

[a]Tested in PVC containers.

Y-Site Injection Compatibility (1:1 Mixture)

Pentamidine isethionate

Drug	*Mfr*	*Conc*	*Mfr*	*Conc*	*Remarks*	*Ref*	*C/I*
Aldesleukin	CHI	33,800 I.U./ml[a]	FUJ	6 mg/ml[a]	Aldesleukin bioactivity inhibited	1857	I
Cefazolin sodium	SKB	20 mg/ml[a]	FUJ	3 mg/ml[a]	Cloudiness and gelatin-like precipitate form immediately	1880	I
Cefoperazone sodium	RR	20 mg/ml[e]	FUJ	3 mg/ml[a]	Heavy white precipitate forms immediately	1880	I
Cefotaxime sodium	HO	20 mg/ml[a]	FUJ	3 mg/ml[a]	Fine precipitate, difficult to see, forms immediately	1880	I
Cefoxitin sodium	ME	20 mg/ml[c]	FUJ	3 mg/ml[a]	Cloudiness and powder-like precipitate form immediately	1880	I
Ceftazidime	LI[d]	20 mg/ml[a]	FUJ	3 mg/ml[a]	Fine precipitate, difficult to see, forms immediately	1880	I
Ceftriaxone sodium	RC	20 mg/ml[a]	FUJ	3 mg/ml[a]	Heavy white precipitate forms immediately	1880	I

Y-Site Injection Compatibility (1:1 Mixture) (Cont.)

Drug	Mfr	Conc	Mfr	Conc	Remarks	Ref	C/I
			Pentamidine isethionate				
Diltiazem HCl	MMD	5 mg/ml	LY	6 and 30 mg/ml[a]	Visually compatible	1807	C
Fluconazole	RR	2 mg/ml	LY	6 mg/ml	Cloudiness develops	1407	I
Foscarnet sodium	AST	24 mg/ml	LY	6 mg/ml	Immediate precipitation	1335	I
	AST	24 mg/ml	LY	6 mg/ml[a,b]	Pentamidine crystals form immediately	1393	I
Gatifloxacin	BMS	2 mg/ml[a]	FUJ	6 mg/ml[a]	Physically compatible with no change in measured haze or increase in particle content in 4 hr at 23 °C	2234	C
Linezolid	PHU	2 mg/ml	FUJ	6 mg/ml[a]	Crystalline precipitate forms in 1 to 4 hr	2264	I
Zidovudine	BW	4 mg/ml[a]	LY	6 mg/ml[a]	Physically compatible for 4 hr at 25 °C under fluorescent light by visual and microscopic examination	1193	C

[a] *Tested in dextrose 5% in water.*
[b] *Tested in sodium chloride 0.9%.*
[c] *Tested in dextrose 4% in water.*
[d] *Sodium carbonate-containing formulation tested.*
[e] *Tested in dextrose 4.6% in water.*

PENTAZOCINE LACTATE
AHFS 28:08.12

Products — Pentazocine lactate is supplied in 1-ml ampuls, 1- and 2-ml syringe cartridges, and 10-ml multiple-dose vials. Each milliliter of solution contains (1-6/98):

Component	Ampul	Cartridge Unit	Vial
Pentazocine (as lactate)	30 mg	30 mg	30 mg
Sodium chloride	2.8 mg	2.2 mg	1.5 mg
Acetone sodium bisulfite	1 mg	2 mg	
Methylparaben			1 mg
Water for injection	qs 1 ml	qs 1 ml	qs 1 ml

pH — The pH is adjusted to between 4 and 5 with lactic acid or sodium hydroxide. (1-6/98)

Osmolality — The osmolality of pentazocine lactate 30 mg/ml was determined to be 307 mOsm/kg. (1233)

Trade Name(s) — Talwin.

Administration — Pentazocine lactate may be administered by intramuscular, subcutaneous, or intravenous injection. For repeated administration, the drug should be given by intramuscular injection with constant rotation of the injection sites. Subcutaneous injection should be used only when necessary because of possible tissue damage. (1-6/98; 4)

Stability — Pentazocine lactate injection should be stored at controlled room temperature (1-6/98) and protected from temperatures of 40 °C or above and from freezing. (4)

Syringes — Pentazocine lactate (Winthrop) 30 mg/ml was found to retain potency for three months at room temperature when 1 ml of solution was packaged in Tubex cartridges. (13)

Pentazocine lactate (Winthrop) 30 mg/1 ml, repackaged in 3-ml clear glass syringes (Hy-Pod) and stored at 25 °C, exhibited no significant changes in pH, physical appearance, or drug concentration during 360 days of storage. (535)

Compatibility Information

Additive Compatibility

Drug	Mfr	Conc/L	Mfr	Conc/L	Test Soln	Remarks	Ref	C/I
			Pentazocine lactate					
Aminophylline	SE	1 g	WI	300 mg	D5W	Physically incompatible	15	I
Amobarbital sodium	LI	1 g	WI	300 mg	D5W	Physically incompatible	15	I
Pentobarbital sodium	AB	1 g	WI	300 mg	D5W	Physically incompatible	15	I

Additive Compatibility (Cont.)

Pentazocine lactate

Drug	Mfr	Conc/L	Mfr	Conc/L	Test Soln	Remarks	Ref	C/I
Phenobarbital sodium	WI	200 mg	WI	300 mg	D5W	Physically incompatible	15	I
Sodium bicarbonate	AB	80 mEq	WI	300 mg	D5W	Physically incompatible	15	I

Drugs in Syringe Compatibility

Pentazocine lactate

Drug (in syringe)	Mfr	Amt	Mfr	Amt	Remarks	Ref	C/I
Atropine sulfate		0.6 mg/ 1.5 ml	WI	30 mg/ 1 ml	Physically compatible for at least 15 min	14	C
	ST	0.4 mg/ 1 ml	WI	30 mg/ 1 ml	Physically compatible for at least 15 min	326	C
Butorphanol tartrate	BR	4 mg/ 2 ml	WI	30 mg/ 1 ml	Physically compatible both macroscopically and microscopically for 30 min at room temperature	566	C
Chlorpromazine HCl	SKF	50 mg/ 2 ml	WI	30 mg/ 1 ml	Physically compatible for at least 15 min	14	C
	PO	50 mg/ 2 ml	WI	30 mg/ 1 ml	Physically compatible for at least 15 min	326	C
Cimetidine HCl	SKF	300 mg/ 2 ml	WI	60 mg/ 2 ml	Physically compatible for 4 hr at 25 °C	25	C
Dimenhydrinate	HR	50 mg/ 1 ml	WI	30 mg/ 1 ml	Physically compatible for at least 15 min	326	C
Diphenhydramine HCl	PD	50 mg/ 1 ml	WI	30 mg/ 1 ml	Physically compatible for at least 15 min	326	C
Droperidol	MN	2.5 mg/ 1 ml	WI	30 mg/ 1 ml	Physically compatible for at least 15 min	326	C
Fentanyl citrate	MN	0.05 mg/ 1 ml	WI	30 mg/ 1 ml	Physically compatible for at least 15 min	326	C
Glycopyrrolate	RB	0.2 mg/ 1 ml	WI	30 mg/ 1 ml	Immediate precipitation	331	I
	RB	0.2 mg/ 1 ml	WI	60 mg/ 2 ml	Immediate precipitation	331	I
	RB	0.4 mg/ 2 ml	WI	30 mg/ 1 ml	Immediate precipitation	331	I
Heparin sodium		2500 units/ 1 ml	WI	30 mg/ 1 ml	Turbidity or precipitate forms within 5 min	1053	I
Hydromorphone HCl	KN	4 mg/ 2 ml	WI	30 mg/ 1 ml	Physically compatible for 30 min	517	C
Hydroxyzine HCl	PF	100 mg/ 4 ml	WI	30 mg/ 1 ml	Physically compatible for at least 15 min	14	C
	PF	50 mg/ 1 ml	WI	30 mg/ 1 ml	Physically compatible for at least 15 min	326	C
	PF	50 mg/ 1 ml	WI	60 mg/ 2 ml	Physically compatible	771	C
	PF	100 mg/ 2 ml	WI	30 mg/ 1 ml	Physically compatible	771	C
Meperidine HCl	WI	50 mg/ 1 ml	WI	30 mg/ 1 ml	Physically compatible for at least 15 min	326	C

Drugs in Syringe Compatibility (Cont.)

Pentazocine lactate

Drug (in syringe)	*Mfr*	*Amt*	*Mfr*	*Amt*	*Remarks*	*Ref*	*C/I*
Meperidine HCl with perphenazine		150 mg 5 mg		15 mg	Physically compatible for at least 15 min	815	C
Metoclopramide HCl	NO	10 mg/ 2 ml	WI	30 mg/ 1 ml	Physically compatible both macroscopically and microscopically for 15 min at room temperature	565	C
Morphine sulfate	ST	15 mg/ 1 ml	WI	30 mg/ 1 ml	Physically compatible for at least 15 min	326	C
Papaveretum	RC[a]	20 mg/ 1 ml	WI	30 mg/ 1 ml	Visually compatible for at least 15 min	326	C
Pentobarbital sodium	WY	100 mg/ 2 ml	WI	30 mg/ 1 ml	Precipitate forms within 15 min	14	I
	AB	50 mg/ 1 ml	WI	30 mg/ 1 ml	Physically incompatible within 15 min	326	I
Perphenazine	SC	5 mg/ 1 ml	WI	30 mg/ 1 ml	Physically compatible both macroscopically and microscopically for 30 min at room temperature	566	C
Perphenazine with meperidine HCl		5 mg 150 mg		15 mg	Physically compatible for at least 15 min	815	C
Prochlorperazine edisylate	PO	5 mg/ 1 ml	WI	30 mg/ 1 ml	Physically compatible for at least 15 min	326	C
Promazine HCl	WY	25 mg/ 1 ml	WI	30 mg/ 1 ml	Potency retained for 3 months at room temperature in Tubex	13	C
	WY	50 mg/ 1 ml	WI	30 mg/ 1 ml	Potency retained for 3 months at room temperature in Tubex	13	C
	WY	50 mg/ 1 ml	WI	30 mg/ 1 ml	Physically compatible for at least 15 min	326	C
Promethazine HCl	WY	50 mg/ 2 ml	WI	30 mg/ 1 ml	Physically compatible for at least 15 min	14	C
	WY	25 mg/ 0.5 ml	WI	30 mg/ 1 ml	Potency retained for 3 months at room temperature in Tubex	13	C
	WY	25 mg/ 1 ml	WI	30 mg/ 1 ml	Potency retained for 3 months at room temperature in Tubex	13	C
	WY	50 mg/ 1 ml	WI	30 mg/ 1 ml	Potency retained for 3 months at room temperature in Tubex	13	C
	WY	25 mg/ 0.5 ml	WI	45 mg/ 1.5 ml	Potency retained for 3 months at room temperature in Tubex	13	C
	PO	50 mg/ 2 ml	WI	30 mg/ 1 ml	Physically compatible for at least 15 min	326	C
Propiomazine HCl	WY	20 mg/ 1 ml	WI	30 mg/ 1 ml	Potency retained for 3 months at room temperature in Tubex	13	C
	WY	10 mg/ 0.5 ml	WI	30 mg/ 1 ml	Potency retained for 3 months at room temperature in Tubex	13	C
Ranitidine HCl	GL	50 mg/ 2 ml	WI	60 mg/ 2 ml	Physically compatible for 1 hr at 25 °C both macroscopically and microscopically	978	C
Scopolamine HBr		0.6 mg/ 1.5 ml	WI	30 mg/ 1 ml	Physically compatible for at least 15 min	14	C
	ST	0.4 mg/ 1 ml	WI	30 mg/ 1 ml	Physically compatible for at least 15 min	326	C

[a]*The former formulation was tested.*

Y-Site Injection Compatibility (1:1 Mixture)

Drug	Mfr	Conc	Pentazocine lactate Mfr	Pentazocine lactate Conc	Remarks	Ref	C/I
Heparin sodium	UP	1000 units/L[a]	WI	30 mg/ml	Physically compatible for at least 4 hr at room temperature by visual and microscopic examination	534	C
Hydrocortisone sodium succinate	UP	10 mg/L[a]	WI	30 mg/ml	Physically compatible for at least 4 hr at room temperature by visual and microscopic examination	534	C
Nafcillin sodium	WY	33 mg/ml[b]		30 mg/ml	Precipitate forms, probably free nafcillin	547	I
Potassium chloride	AB	40 mEq/L[a]	WI	30 mg/ml	Physically compatible for at least 4 hr at room temperature by visual and microscopic examination	534	C
Vitamin B complex with C	RC	2 ml/L[a]	WI	30 mg/ml	Physically compatible for at least 4 hr at room temperature by visual and microscopic examination	534	C

[a]*Tested in dextrose 5% in Ringer's injection, dextrose 5% in Ringer's injection, lactated, dextrose 5% in water, Ringer's injection, lactated, and sodium chloride 0.9%.*
[b]*Tested in sodium chloride 0.9%.*

Additional Compatibility Information

Other Drugs — Pentazocine lactate is incompatible with alkaline substances such as aminophylline and barbiturates. (4) Mixing pentazocine lactate and barbiturates in the same syringe may result in precipitation. (1-6/98)

PENTOBARBITAL SODIUM
AHFS 28:24.04

Products — Pentobarbital sodium is available in 20-ml (1 g) and 50-ml (2.5 g) multiple-dose vials. Each milliliter of solution contains (2):

Pentobarbital sodium	50 mg
Propylene glycol	40% (v/v)
Alcohol	10%
Hydrochloric acid and/or sodium hydroxide	to adjust pH
Water for injection	qs

pH — Adjusted to approximately 9.5. (2); range 9 to 10.5. (4)

Trade Name(s) — Nembutal.

Administration — Pentobarbital sodium may be administered by deep intramuscular injection into a large muscle or by slow intravenous injection. It is usually administered in a concentration of 50 mg/ml. The rate of intravenous administration should not exceed 50 mg/min. No more than 5 ml of solution (250 mg) should be injected intramuscularly at any one site. (2; 4)

Stability — Intact vials of pentobarbital sodium should be stored at controlled room temperature and protected from excessive heat and freezing. Brief exposures to temperatures up to 40 °C does not adversely affect the product. (2)

Aqueous solutions of pentobarbital sodium are not stable. The commercially available pentobarbital sodium in a propylene glycol vehicle is more stable. In an acidic medium, pentobarbital sodium may precipitate. (4) No solution containing a precipitate or that is cloudy should be used. (2; 4)

Sorption — Pentobarbital sodium (Abbott) 25 mg/L did not display significant sorption to a PVC plastic test strip in 24 hours. (12)

The sorption of pentobarbital sodium 30 mg/L in sodium chloride 0.9% was evaluated in 100-ml PVC infusion bags (Travenol). After eight hours at 20 to 24 °C, no loss of pentobarbital had occurred. (770)

Plasticizer Leaching — Pentobarbital sodium (Abbott) 2 mg/ml in dextrose 5% in water did not leach diethylhexyl phthalate (DEHP) plasticizer from 50-ml PVC bags in 24 hours at 24 °C. (1683)

Filtration — Pentobarbital sodium (Abbott) 600 mg/L and 1.25 g/L in dextrose 5% in water and also sodium chloride 0.9% was filtered through a 0.45-μm filter. The delivered concentration did not decrease. (754)

Compatibility Information

Solution Compatibility

Pentobarbital sodium

Solution	*Mfr*	*Mfr*	*Conc/L*	*Remarks*	*Ref*	*C/I*
Dextran 6% in dextrose 5%	AB	AB	500 mg	Physically compatible	3	C
Dextran 6% in sodium chloride 0.9%	AB	AB	500 mg	Physically compatible	3	C
Dextrose–Ringer's injection combinations	AB	AB	500 mg	Physically compatible	3	C
Dextrose–Ringer's injection, lactated, combinations	AB	AB	500 mg	Physically compatible	3	C
Dextrose–saline combinations	AB	AB	500 mg	Physically compatible	3	C
Dextrose 2½% in water	AB	AB	500 mg	Physically compatible	3	C
Dextrose 5% in water	AB	AB	500 mg	Physically compatible	3	C
	MG[a]	AB	600 mg and 1.25 g	Physically compatible and chemically stable for 12-hr study period	754	C
	BA[b]	AB	4 and 8 g	Visually compatible with no loss by HPLC in 24 hr	1590	C
	BA[b]	AB	>8 g	Occasional visible precipitation	1590	I
Dextrose 10% in water	AB	AB	500 mg	Physically compatible	3	C
Fructose 10% in sodium chloride 0.9%	AB	AB	500 mg	Physically compatible	3	C
Fructose 10% in water	AB	AB	500 mg	Physically compatible	3	C
Invert sugar 5 and 10% in sodium chloride 0.9%	AB	AB	500 mg	Physically compatible	3	C
Invert sugar 5 and 10% in water	AB	AB	500 mg	Physically compatible	3	C
Ionosol products	AB	AB	500 mg	Physically compatible	3	C
Ringer's injection	AB	AB	500 mg	Physically compatible	3	C
Ringer's injection, lactated	AB	AB	500 mg	Physically compatible	3	C
Sodium chloride 0.45%	AB	AB	500 mg	Physically compatible	3	C
Sodium chloride 0.9%	AB	AB	500 mg	Physically compatible	3	C
	MG[a]	AB	600 mg and 1.25 g	Physically compatible and chemically stable for 12-hr study period	754	C
	BA[b]	AB	4 and 8 g	Visually compatible with no loss by HPLC in 24 hr	1590	C
	BA[b]	AB	>8 g	Occasional visible precipitation	1590	I
Sodium lactate ⅙ M	AB	AB	500 mg	Physically compatible	3	C

[a]*Tested in polyolefin containers.*
[b]*Tested in PVC containers.*

Additive Compatibility

Pentobarbital sodium

Drug	*Mfr*	*Conc/L*	*Mfr*	*Conc/L*	*Test Soln*	*Remarks*	*Ref*	*C/I*
Amikacin sulfate	BR	5 g	AB	100 mg	D5LR, D5R, D5S, D5W, D10W, IS10, LR, NS, R, SL	Physically compatible and potency of both drugs retained for 24 hr at 25 °C	294	C

Additive Compatibility (Cont.)

Pentobarbital sodium

Drug	*Mfr*	*Conc/L*	*Mfr*	*Conc/L*	*Test Soln*	*Remarks*	*Ref*	*C/I*
Aminophylline		500 mg	AB	500 mg		Physically compatible	3	**C**
	SE	500 mg	AB	500 mg		Physically compatible	6	**C**
	SE	1 g	AB	1 g	D5W	Physically compatible	15	**C**
Calcium chloride	UP	1 g	AB	1 g	D5W	Physically compatible	15	**C**
Chloramphenicol sodium succinate	PD	1 g	AB	200 mg		Physically compatible	6	**C**
Chlorpheniramine maleate						Physically incompatible	9	**I**
	SC	100 mg	AB	1 g	D5W	Physically incompatible	15	**I**
Dimenhydrinate	SE	500 mg	AB	1 g	D5W	Physically compatible	15	**C**
Ephedrine sulfate						Physically incompatible	9	**I**
	LI	250 mg	AB	1 g	D5W	Physically incompatible	15	**I**
Erythromycin lactobionate	AB	1 g	AB	500 mg		Physically compatible. Erythromycin stable for 24 hr at 25 °C	20	**C**
Hydrocortisone sodium succinate						Physically incompatible	9	**I**
	UP	500 mg	AB	1 g	D5W	Physically incompatible	15	**I**
Hydroxyzine HCl	PF					Physically incompatible	9	**I**
	RR	250 mg	AB	1 g	D5W	Physically incompatible	15	**I**
Insulin, regular[a]						Physically incompatible	9	**I**
Levorphanol bitartrate	RC					Physically incompatible	9	**I**
Lidocaine HCl	AST	2 g	AB	500 mg		Physically compatible	24	**C**
Norepinephrine bitartrate	WI					Physically incompatible	9	**I**
Penicillin G potassium	(B)[b]	900,000 units	AB	500 mg	D5W	17% penicillin decomposition in 6 hr at 25 °C	48	**I**
	SQ	1 million units	AB	500 mg	D5W	42% penicillin decomposition in 24 hr at 25 °C	47	**I**
Pentazocine lactate	WI	300 mg	AB	1 g	D5W	Physically incompatible	15	**I**
Phenytoin sodium	PD					Physically incompatible	9	**I**
Promazine HCl	WY	1 g	AB	200 mg	D5W	Physically incompatible	11	**I**
Promethazine HCl	WY	250 mg	AB	1 g	D5W	Physically incompatible	15	**I**
Sodium bicarbonate						Physically incompatible	9	**I**
	AB	80 mEq	AB	1 g	D5W	Physically incompatible	15	**I**
	AB	2.4 mEq[c]	AB	500 mg	D5W	Physically compatible for 24 hr	772	**C**
Streptomycin sulfate						Physically incompatible	9	**I**
Succinylcholine chloride	AB	2 g	AB	500 mg		Physically compatible	3	**C**
						Physically incompatible	9	**I**
Thiopental sodium	AB	2.5 g	AB	200 mg	D5W	Physically compatible	21	**C**
Triflupromazine HCl	SQ					Precipitate forms	40	**I**
Vancomycin HCl	LI					Physically incompatible	9	**I**
Verapamil HCl	KN	80 mg	AB	200 mg	D5W, NS	Physically compatible for 24 hr	764	**C**

[a] *Test performed prior to availability of neutral regular insulin.*
[b] *A buffered preparation was specified.*
[c] *One vial of Neut added to a liter of admixture.*

Drugs in Syringe Compatibility

Pentobarbital sodium

Drug (in syringe)	Mfr	Amt	Mfr	Amt	Remarks	Ref	C/I
Aminophylline		500 mg/ 2 ml	AB	500 mg/ 10 ml	Physically compatible	55	C
Atropine sulfate		0.6 mg/ 1.5 ml	WY	100 mg/ 2 ml	Physically compatible for at least 15 min	14	C
	ST	0.4 mg/ 1 ml	AB	50 mg/ 1 ml	Physically compatible for at least 15 min	326	C
	LI	0.6 mg/ 1.5 ml	AB	100 mg/ 2 ml	Precipitate forms within 24 hr at room temperature	542	I
Atropine sulfate with cimetidine HCl	LI SKF	0.6 mg/ 1.5 ml 300 mg/ 2 ml	AB	100 mg/ 2 ml	Immediate precipitation	542	I
Butorphanol tartrate	BR	4 mg/ 2 ml	AB	50 mg/ 1 ml	Immediate precipitation	761	I
Chlorpromazine HCl	SKF	50 mg/ 2 ml	AB	500 mg/ 10 ml	Physically incompatible	55	I
	SKF	50 mg/ 2 ml	WY	100 mg/ 2 ml	Precipitate forms within 15 min	14	I
	PO	50 mg/ 2 ml	AB	50 mg/ 1 ml	Physically incompatible within 15 min	326	I
Cimetidine HCl	SKF	300 mg/ 2 ml	AB	100 mg/ 2 ml	Immediate precipitation	542	I
Cimetidine HCl with atropine sulfate	SKF LI	300 mg/ 2 ml 0.6 mg/ 1.5 ml	AB	100 mg/ 2 ml	Immediate precipitation	542	I
Dimenhydrinate	SE	50 mg/ 1 ml	AB	500 mg/ 10 ml	Physically incompatible	55	I
	HR	50 mg/ 1 ml	AB	50 mg/ 1 ml	Physically incompatible within 15 min	326	I
Diphenhydramine HCl	PD	50 mg/ 1 ml	AB	500 mg/ 10 ml	Physically incompatible	55	I
	PD	50 mg/ 1 ml	AB	50 mg/ 1 ml	Physically incompatible within 15 min	326	I
Droperidol	MN	2.5 mg/ 1 ml	AB	50 mg/ 1 ml	Physically incompatible within 15 min	326	I
Ephedrine sulfate		50 mg/ 1 ml	AB	500 mg/ 10 ml	Physically compatible	55	C
Fentanyl citrate	MN	0.05 mg/ 1 ml	AB	50 mg/ 1 ml	Physically incompatible within 15 min	326	I
Glycopyrrolate	RB	0.2 mg/ 1 ml	AB	50 mg/ 1 ml	Immediate precipitation	331	I
	RB	0.4 mg/ 2 ml	AB	50 mg/ 1 ml	Immediate precipitation	331	I
	RB	0.2 mg/ 1 ml	AB	100 mg/ 2 ml	Immediate precipitation	331	I
Hyaluronidase		150 units	AB	500 mg/ 10 ml	Physically compatible	55	C
Hydromorphone HCl	KN	4 mg/ 2 ml[a]	AB	50 mg/ 1 ml	Physically compatible for 30 min	517	C

Drugs in Syringe Compatibility (Cont.)

Pentobarbital sodium

Drug (in syringe)	*Mfr*	*Amt*	*Mfr*	*Amt*	*Remarks*	*Ref*	*C/I*
	KN	4 mg/ 2 ml[b]	AB	50 mg/ 1 ml	Transient precipitate dissipates after mixing. Physically compatible for 30 min	517	C
Hydroxyzine HCl	PF	100 mg/ 4 ml	WY	100 mg/ 2 ml	Precipitate forms within 15 min	14	I
	PF	50 mg/ 1 ml	AB	50 mg/ 1 ml	Physically incompatible within 15 min	326	I
Meperidine HCl	WI	100 mg/ 2 ml	AB	500 mg/ 10 ml	Physically incompatible	55	I
	WY	100 mg/ 1 ml	WY	100 mg/ 2 ml	Precipitate forms within 15 min	14	I
	WI	50 mg/ 1 ml	AB	50 mg/ 1 ml	Physically incompatible within 15 min	326	I
Midazolam HCl	RC	5 mg/ 1 ml	WY	100 mg/ 2 ml	White precipitate forms immediately	1145	I
Morphine sulfate		16.2 mg/ 1 ml	AB	500 mg/ 10 ml	Physically compatible	55	C
	WY	15 mg/ 1 ml	WY	100 mg/ 2 ml	Precipitate forms within 15 min	14	I
	ST	15 mg/ 1 ml	AB	50 mg/ 1 ml	Physically incompatible within 15 min	326	I
Nalbuphine HCl	EN	10 mg/ 1 ml	WY	50 mg/ 1 ml	Immediate white milky precipitate that persists for 36 hr at 27 °C	762	I
	EN	2.5 mg/ 0.25 ml	WY	50 mg/ 1 ml	Immediate white milky precipitate that clears upon vigorous shaking	762	I
	EN	5 mg/ 0.5 ml	WY	50 mg/ 1 ml	Immediate white milky precipitate that persists for 36 hr at 27 °C	762	I
Neostigmine methylsulfate	RC	0.5 mg/ 1 ml	AB	500 mg/ 10 ml	Physically compatible	55	C
Papaveretum	RC[c]	20 mg/ 1 ml	AB	50 mg/ 1 ml	Incompatible within 15 min	326	I
Pentazocine lactate	WI	30 mg/ 1 ml	WY	100 mg/ 2 ml	Precipitate forms within 15 min	14	I
	WI	30 mg/ 1 ml	AB	50 mg/ 1 ml	Physically incompatible within 15 min	326	I
Perphenazine	SC	5 mg/ 1 ml	AB	50 mg/ 1 ml	Immediate precipitation	761	I
Prochlorperazine edisylate	SKF	10 mg/ 2 ml	AB	500 mg/ 10 ml	Physically incompatible	55	I
	SKF		WY	100 mg/ 2 ml	Precipitate forms within 15 min	14	I
	PO	5 mg/ 1 ml	AB	50 mg/ 1 ml	Physically incompatible within 15 min	326	I
Promazine HCl	WY	50 mg/ 1 ml	AB	50 mg/ 1 ml	Physically incompatible within 15 min	326	I
Promethazine HCl	WY	100 mg/ 4 ml	AB	500 mg/ 10 ml	Physically incompatible	55	I
	WY	50 mg/ 2 ml	WY	100 mg/ 2 ml	Precipitate forms within 15 min	14	I
	PO	50 mg/ 2 ml	AB	50 mg/ 1 ml	Physically incompatible within 15 min	326	I

Drugs in Syringe Compatibility (Cont.)

Drug (in syringe)	Mfr	Amt	Pentobarbital sodium Mfr	Pentobarbital sodium Amt	Remarks	Ref	C/I
Ranitidine HCl	GL	50 mg/ 5 ml	AB	100 mg	Immediate precipitation	1151	I
Scopolamine HBr		0.6 mg/ 1.5 ml	WY	100 mg/ 2 ml	Physically compatible for at least 15 min	14	C
		0.13 mg/ 0.26 ml	AB	500 mg/ 10 ml	Physically compatible	55	C
	STE	0.4 mg/ 1 ml	AB	50 mg/ 1 ml	Physically compatible for at least 15 min	326	C
Sodium bicarbonate		3.75 g/ 50 ml	AB	500 mg/ 10 ml	Physically compatible	55	C
Thiopental sodium	AB	75 mg/ 3 ml	AB	50 mg/ 1 ml	Physically compatible for at least 30 min	21	C
	AB	75 mg/ 3 ml	AB	37.5 mg/ 0.75 ml	Physically compatible	55	C

[a]*Vial formulation was tested.*
[b]*Ampul formulation was tested.*
[c]*The former formulation was tested.*

Y-Site Injection Compatibility (1:1 Mixture)

Drug	Mfr	Conc	Pentobarbital sodium Mfr	Pentobarbital sodium Conc	Remarks	Ref	C/I
Acyclovir sodium	BW	5 mg/ml[a]	WY	2 mg/ml[a]	Physically compatible for 4 hr at 25 °C	1157	C
Amphotericin B cholesteryl sulfate complex	SEQ	0.83 mg/ml[a]	AB	5 mg/ml[a]	Decreased natural turbidity occurs immediately	2117	I
Gatifloxacin	BMS	2 mg/ml[a]	WY	5 mg/ml[a]	Physically compatible with no change in measured haze or increase in particle content in 4 hr at 23 °C	2234	C
Insulin, regular (Humulin R)	LI	1 unit/ml[b]	WY	2 mg/ml[b]	Physically compatible for 3 hr	1316	C
(beef, pork)	LI	1 unit/ml[b]	WY	2 mg/ml[b]	Physically compatible for 3 hr	1316	C
Linezolid	PHU	2 mg/ml	AB	5 mg/ml[a]	Physically compatible with no change in measured turbidity or increase in particle content in 4 hr at 23 °C	2264	C
Propofol	ZEN	10 mg/ml	WY	5 mg/ml[a]	Physically compatible for 1 hr at 23 °C with no increase in particle content	2066	C
TNA #218 to #226[c]			AB	5 mg/ml[a]	Damage to emulsion integrity occurs immediately with free oil formation possible	2215	I
TPN #212 to #215[c]			AB	5 mg/ml[a]	Physically compatible with no change in measured turbidity or increase in particle content in 4 hr at 23 °C	2109	C

[a]*Tested in dextrose 5% in water.*
[b]*Tested in sodium chloride 0.9%.*
[c]*Refer to Appendix I for the composition of parenteral nutrition solutions. TNA indicates a 3-in-1 admixture, and TPN indicates a 2-in-1 admixture.*

Additional Compatibility Information

Acidic Drugs — Drugs such as pentobarbital sodium that exhibit poor solubility in an acidic medium may precipitate in solutions containing acidic additives. (4; 22) Metaraminol bitartrate is acidic and may cause precipitation, depending on the concentrations of the additives. (7) Also, the acidic methyldopate HCl imparts some buffer capacity to admixtures and may pose solubility problems with barbiturate salts. (23)

Alkali-Labile Drugs — Pentobarbital sodium may raise the pH of admixture solutions to the alkaline range and, therefore, should not be mixed with alkali-labile drugs such as penicillin G. (47) Significant decomposition of isoproterenol HCl and norepinephrine bitartrate may also occur. If either of these two drugs is mixed with pentobarbital sodium, the admixture should be used immediately after preparation. (59; 77)

Atracurium besylate also may be inactivated by alkaline solutions such as barbiturates; precipitation of a free acid of the admixed drug may occur, depending on the resultant pH of the admixture. (4)

Hydrocortisone — Pentobarbital sodium (Abbott) has also been reported to be conditionally compatible with hydrocortisone sodium succinate (Upjohn) 250 mg/L. The mixture is physically compatible in most Abbott infusion solutions except Ionosol G with invert sugar 10%, in which a haze or precipitate forms within six hours. (3)

Promethazine and Chlorpromazine — Pentobarbital sodium (Abbott) 500 mg/L has been reported to be conditionally compatible with promethazine HCl (Wyeth) 100 mg/L and chlorpromazine HCl 50 mg/L. The mixtures are physically incompatible in most Abbott infusion solutions except as noted below (3):

Ionosol MB with dextrose 5%	Physically compatible
Ionosol T with dextrose 5%	Physically compatible

Succinylcholine Chloride — When barbiturates are mixed with succinylcholine chloride, either the free barbiturate will precipitate or the succinylcholine chloride will be hydrolyzed, depending on the final pH of the admixture. (4; 21)

Other Drugs — The manufacturer recommends that pentobarbital sodium be mixed with no other medication or solution. (2) Drugs stated to be incompatible with pentobarbital sodium or barbiturate salts include clindamycin phosphate (106), cefazolin sodium (278), fentanyl citrate (4), pancuronium bromide (4), droperidol (4), and cimetidine HCl. (360)

Pentobarbital sodium should not be mixed in the same syringe with pentazocine lactate because precipitation occurs. (4)

PENTOSTATIN
AHFS 10:00

Products — Pentostatin is available as a lyophilized powder in vials containing 10 mg of drug. Also present are 50 mg of mannitol and sodium hydroxide or hydrochloric acid to adjust the pH. Reconstitute the vial contents with 5 ml of sterile water for injection and shake well to yield a 2-mg/ml solution. (2)

pH — From 7 to 8.5. (2)

Trade Name(s) — Nipent.

Administration — Pentostatin is administered intravenously by injection over five minutes or by infusion over 20 to 30 minutes when diluted in 25 to 50 ml of dextrose 5% in water or sodium chloride 0.9%. Adequate hydration is necessary prior to administering pentostatin. Administration of 500 to 1000 ml of dextrose 5% in sodium chloride 0.45% or similar solution prior to drug administration with an additional 500 ml of dextrose 5% in water or similar solution after drug administration is recommended. (2; 4)

Stability — The manufacturer recommends that pentostatin be stored under refrigeration (2), but other information indicates that the drug in intact vials is stable for at least three years at room temperature. (234)

The white to off-white powder yields a colorless solution when reconstituted. The manufacturer states that reconstituted pentostatin solutions are stable at room temperature for up to eight hours only because of the absence of antibacterial preservatives. (2) Other information indicates that the reconstituted solution is stable for 72 hours at room temperature, exhibiting a 2 to 4% loss. (234; 1453)

pH Effects — Pentostatin displays greater decomposition under acidic conditions compared to alkaline conditions. The pH range of maximum stability is about 6.5 to 11.5. At pH 6 to 8, hydrolysis is not sensitive to the ionic strength of the solution. (1453)

Sorption — Pentostatin does not undergo sorption to PVC containers or administration sets at concentrations between 0.18 and 0.33 mg/ml in dextrose 5% water or sodium chloride 0.9%. (2)

Compatibility Information

Solution Compatibility

Pentostatin

Solution	*Mfr*	*Mfr*	*Conc/L*	*Remarks*	*Ref*	*C/I*
Dextrose 5% in water		NCI	20 mg	Approximately 2% loss in 24 hr and 8 to 10% loss in 48 hr at room temperature. No loss in 96 hr under refrigeration	234	**C**
	TR[a], BA[b]	NCI	20 mg	10% loss in 54 hr at 23 °C	1453	**C**
	TR[a], BA[b]	NCI	2 mg	10% loss in 11 hr at 23 °C	1453	**I**

Solution Compatibility (Cont.)

Solution	Mfr	Pentostatin Mfr	Conc/L	Remarks	Ref	C/I
Ringer's injection, lactated		NCI	20 mg	Approximately 0 to 4% loss in 48 hr at room temperature	234	C
Sodium chloride 0.9%		NCI	20 mg	Approximately 0 to 4% loss in 48 hr at room temperature. No loss in 96 hr under refrigeration	234	C
	AB[a], BA[b]	NCI	20 mg	1 to 4% loss in about 49 hr at 23 °C	1453	C
	AB[a], BA[b]	NCI	2 mg	3 to 6% loss in 48 hr at 23 °C	1453	C

[a]*Tested in glass containers.*
[b]*Tested in PVC containers.*

Y-Site Injection Compatibility (1:1 Mixture)

Drug	Mfr	Conc	Pentostatin Mfr	Pentostatin Conc	Remarks	Ref	C/I
Fludarabine phosphate	BX	1 mg/ml[a]	NCI	0.4 mg/ml[b]	Physically compatible for 4 hr at room temperature under fluorescent light	1439	C
Melphalan HCl	BW	0.1 mg/ml[b]	PD	0.4 mg/ml[b]	Physically compatible with no change in measured turbidity or increase in particle content in 3 hr at 22 °C under fluorescent light	1557	C
Ondansetron HCl	GL	1 mg/ml[b]	NCI	0.4 mg/ml[b]	Physically compatible for 4 hr at 22 °C	1365	C
Paclitaxel	NCI	1.2 mg/ml[a]	NCI	0.4 mg/ml[b]	Physically compatible with no change in measured turbidity in 4 hr at 22 °C	1556	C
Sargramostim	IMM	10 μg/ml[b]	NCI	0.4 mg/ml[b]	Physically compatible for 4 hr at 22 °C	1436	C

[a]*Tested in dextrose 5% in water.*
[b]*Tested in sodium chloride 0.9%.*

Additional Compatibility Information

Infusion Solutions — Dextrose 5% in water and sodium chloride 0.9% are recommended as diluents for the infusion of pentostatin. The manufacturer recommends use within eight hours. (2)

Other information indicates that the drug is stable for much longer periods (234; 1453) except in very low concentrations (approximately 0.002 mg/ml) in dextrose 5% in water when buffering to neutral pH may be desirable. (1453) (See Solution Compatibility.)

Other Information

Microbial Growth — Pentostatin (Parke-Davis) 0.03 mg/ml diluted in sodium chloride 0.9% and stored at 22 °C did not exhibit a substantial antimicrobial effect on the growth of four organisms (*Enterococcus faecium, Staphylococcus aureus, Pseudomonas aeruginosa,* and *Candida albicans*) inoculated into the solution. *C. albicans* maintained viability for 24 hours, and the others were viable for 48 to 120 hours. The author recommended that diluted solutions of pentostatin be stored under refrigeration whenever possible and that the potential for microbiological growth be considered when assigning expiration periods. (2160)

PERPHENAZINE
AHFS 28:16.08

Products — Perphenazine is available as a 5-mg/ml solution in 1-ml ampuls. Each milliliter also contains citric acid, sodium bisulfite, and water for injection. (2)

pH — From 4.2 to 5.6. (4)

Osmolality — Perphenazine 5 mg/ml has an osmolality of 263 mOsm/kg. (1689)

Trade Name(s) — Trilafon.

Administration — Perphenazine is given by deep intramuscular injection or, rarely, by fractional intravenous injection or slow intravenous infusion. The intravenous route is used only when necessary in severe cases and limited to recumbent hospitalized adult patients. By fractional intravenous injection, a 0.5-mg/ml dilution in sodium chloride 0.9% is administered; a maximum of 1 mg per injection should be given slowly at intervals of at least one to two minutes. (2; 4)

Stability — Perphenazine should be stored at controlled room temperature or under refrigeration and protected from temperatures above 40 °C and from freezing. (2; 4) Perphenazine is light sensitive and should be protected from light. Exposure to light may cause a discoloration. Potency or therapeutic efficacy is not altered by a slight yellowish discoloration, but the drug should be discarded if a marked discoloration appears. (2)

Compatibility Information

Drugs in Syringe Compatibility

			Perphenazine				
Drug (in syringe)	*Mfr*	*Amt*	*Mfr*	*Amt*	*Remarks*	*Ref*	*C/I*
Atropine sulfate	ST	0.4 mg/ 1 ml	SC	5 mg/ 1 ml	Physically compatible both macroscopically and microscopically for 30 min at room temperature	566	C
Benztropine mesylate	MSD	2 mg/ 2 ml	SC	10 mg/ 2 ml	Visually compatible for 60 min	1784	C
Butorphanol tartrate	BR	4 mg/ 2 ml	SC	5 mg/ 1 ml	Physically compatible both macroscopically and microscopically for 30 min at room temperature	761	C
Chlorpromazine HCl	MB	25 mg/ 1 ml	SC	5 mg/ 1 ml	Physically compatible both macroscopically and microscopically for 30 min at room temperature	566	C
Cimetidine HCl	SKF	300 mg/ 2 ml	SC	5 mg/ 1 ml	Physically compatible for 4 hr at 25 °C	25	C
Dimenhydrinate	HR	50 mg/ 1 ml	SC	5 mg/ 1 ml	Physically compatible both macroscopically and microscopically for 30 min at room temperature	761	C
Diphenhydramine HCl	PD	50 mg/ 1 ml	SC	5 mg/ 1 ml	Physically compatible both macroscopically and microscopically for 30 min at room temperature	566	C
	ES	100 mg/ 2 ml	SC	10 mg/ 2 ml	Visually compatible for 60 min	1784	C
Droperidol	MN	5 mg/ 2 ml	SC	5 mg/ 1 ml	Physically compatible both macroscopically and microscopically for 30 min at room temperature	566	C
Fentanyl citrate	MN	0.1 mg/ 2 ml	SC	5 mg/ 1 ml	Physically compatible both macroscopically and microscopically for 30 min at room temperature	566	C
Hydroxyzine HCl	ES	100 mg/ 2 ml	SC	10 mg/ 2 ml	Visually compatible for 60 min	1784	C
Meperidine HCl	WI	50 mg/ 1 ml	SC	5 mg/ 1 ml	Physically compatible both macroscopically and microscopically for 30 min at room temperature	566	C
Meperidine HCl with pentazocine lactate		150 mg 15 mg		5 mg	Physically compatible for at least 15 min	815	C
Methotrimeprazine		25 mg/ 1 ml	SC	5 mg/ 1 ml	Physically compatible for 30 min at room temperature both macroscopically and microscopically	566	C
Metoclopramide HCl	NO	10 mg/ 2 ml	SC	5 mg/ 1 ml	Physically compatible both macroscopically and microscopically for 30 min at room temperature	565; 566	C

Drugs in Syringe Compatibility (Cont.)

			Perphenazine				
Drug (in syringe)	*Mfr*	*Amt*	*Mfr*	*Amt*	*Remarks*	*Ref*	*C/I*
Midazolam HCl	RC	5 mg/ 1 ml	SC	5 mg/ 1 ml	White precipitate forms immediately	1145	I
Morphine sulfate	AH	15 mg/ 1 ml	SC	5 mg/ 1 ml	Physically compatible both macroscopically and microscopically for 30 min at room temperature	566	C
Papaveretum	RC[a]	20 mg/ 1 ml	SC	5 mg/ 1 ml	Yellow discoloration within 15 min	761	I
Pentazocine lactate	WI	30 mg/ 1 ml	SC	5 mg/ 1 ml	Physically compatible both macroscopically and microscopically for 30 min at room temperature	566	C
Pentazocine lactate with meperidine HCl		15 mg 150 mg		5 mg	Physically compatible for at least 15 min	815	C
Pentobarbital sodium	AB	50 mg/ 1 ml	SC	5 mg/ 1 ml	Immediate precipitation	761	I
Prochlorperazine edisylate	MB	5 mg/ 1 ml	SC	5 mg/ 1 ml	Physically compatible both macroscopically and microscopically for 30 min at room temperature	566	C
Promethazine HCl	WY	25 mg/ 1 ml	SC	5 mg/ 1 ml	Physically compatible both macroscopically and microscopically for 30 min at room temperature	566	C
Ranitidine HCl	GL	50 mg/ 2 ml	SC	5 mg/ 1 ml	Physically compatible for 1 hr at 25 °C both macroscopically and microscopically	978	C
Scopolamine HBr	STE	0.4 mg/ 1 ml	SC	5 mg/ 1 ml	Physically compatible both macroscopically and microscopically for 30 min at room temperature	566	C
Thiethylperazine malate	BI	10 mg/ 1 ml	SC	5 mg/ 1 ml	Yellow discoloration within 15 min	761	I

[a]*The former formulation was tested.*

Y-Site Injection Compatibility (1:1 Mixture)

			Perphenazine				
Drug	*Mfr*	*Conc*	*Mfr*	*Conc*	*Remarks*	*Ref*	*C/I*
Acyclovir sodium	BW	5 mg/ml[a]	SC	0.1 mg/ml[a]	Physically compatible for 4 hr at 25 °C	1157	C
Amikacin sulfate	BR	5 mg/ml[a]	SC	0.02 mg/ml[a]	Physically compatible for 4 hr at 25 °C	1155	C
Ampicillin sodium	BR	20 mg/ml[b]	SC	0.02 mg/ml[a]	Physically compatible for 4 hr at 25 °C	1155	C
Azlocillin sodium	MI	20 mg/ml[a]	SC	0.02 mg/ml[a]	Physically compatible for 4 hr at 25 °C	1155	C
Cefamandole nafate	LI	20 mg/ml[a]	SC	0.02 mg/ml[a]	Physically compatible for 4 hr at 25 °C	1155	C
Cefazolin sodium	SKF	20 mg/ml[c]	SC	0.02 mg/ml[a]	Physically compatible for 4 hr at 25 °C	1155	C
Cefoperazone sodium	RR	20 mg/ml[a]	SC	0.02 mg/ml[a]	Cloudy solution forms immediately with fine precipitate persisting for 4 hr at 25 °C	1155	I
Cefotaxime sodium	HO	20 mg/ml[a]	SC	0.02 mg/ml[a]	Physically compatible for 4 hr at 25 °C	1155	C
Cefoxitin sodium	MSD	20 mg/ml[c]	SC	0.02 mg/ml[a]	Physically compatible for 4 hr at 25 °C	1155	C
Cefuroxime sodium	GL	30 mg/ml[a]	SC	0.02 mg/ml[a]	Physically compatible for 4 hr at 25 °C	1155	C

Y-Site Injection Compatibility (1:1 Mixture) (Cont.)

Perphenazine

Drug	*Mfr*	*Conc*	*Mfr*	*Conc*	*Remarks*	*Ref*	*C/I*
Chloramphenicol sodium succinate	ES	20 mg/ml[a]	SC	0.02 mg/ml[a]	Physically compatible for 4 hr at 25 °C	1155	C
Clindamycin phosphate	UP	12 mg/ml[a]	SC	0.02 mg/ml[a]	Physically compatible for 4 hr at 25 °C	1155	C
Doxycycline hyclate	ES	1 mg/ml[a]	SC	0.02 mg/ml[a]	Physically compatible for 4 hr at 25 °C	1155	C
Erythromycin lactobionate	AB	5 mg/ml[a]	SC	0.02 mg/ml[a]	Physically compatible for 4 hr at 25 °C	1155	C
Famotidine	MSD	0.2 mg/ml[a]	SC	0.04 mg/ml[a]	Physically compatible for 4 hr at 25 °C	1188	C
Gentamicin sulfate	TR	1.6 mg/ml[a]	SC	0.02 mg/ml[a]	Physically compatible for 4 hr at 25 °C	1155	C
Kanamycin sulfate	BR	2.5 mg/ml[a]	SC	0.02 mg/ml[a]	Physically compatible for 4 hr at 25 °C	1155	C
Metronidazole	SE	5 mg/ml	SC	0.02 mg/ml[a]	Physically compatible for 4 hr at 25 °C	1155	C
Minocycline HCl	LE	0.2 mg/ml[a]	SC	0.02 mg/ml[a]	Physically compatible for 4 hr at 25 °C	1155	C
Nafcillin sodium	WY	20 mg/ml[a]	SC	0.02 mg/ml[a]	Physically compatible for 4 hr at 25 °C	1155	C
Oxacillin sodium	BE	20 mg/ml[a]	SC	0.02 mg/ml[a]	Physically compatible for 4 hr at 25 °C	1155	C
Penicillin G potassium	PF	100,000 units/ml[a]	SC	0.02 mg/ml[a]	Physically compatible for 4 hr at 25 °C	1155	C
Piperacillin sodium	LE	60 mg/ml[a]	SC	0.02 mg/ml[a]	Physically compatible for 4 hr at 25 °C	1155	C
Tacrolimus	FUJ	1 mg/ml[b]	SC	2.5 mg/ml[a]	Visually compatible for 24 hr at 25 °C	1630	C
Ticarcillin disodium	BE	30 mg/ml[a]	SC	0.02 mg/ml[a]	Physically compatible for 4 hr at 25 °C	1155	C
Ticarcillin disodium–clavulanate potassium	BE	31 mg/ml[a]	SC	0.02 mg/ml[a]	Physically compatible for 4 hr at 25 °C	1155	C
Tobramycin sulfate	DI	0.8 mg/ml[a]	SC	0.02 mg/ml[a]	Physically compatible for 4 hr at 25 °C	1155	C
Trimethoprim–sulfamethoxazole	BW	0.8 + 4 mg/ml[a]	SC	0.02 mg/ml[a]	Physically compatible for 4 hr at 25 °C	1155	C
Vancomycin HCl	LI	5 mg/ml[a]	SC	0.02 mg/ml[a]	Physically compatible for 4 hr at 25 °C	1155	C

[a]*Tested in dextrose 5% in water.*
[b]*Tested in sodium chloride 0.9%.*
[c]*Manufacturer's premixed solution.*

PHENOBARBITAL SODIUM
AHFS 28:12.04 and 28:24.04

Products — Phenobarbital sodium injection is available in various dosage forms and sizes, including 30, 60, 65, and 130 mg/ml, from several manufacturers. (4; 29) The product formulations also contain ethanol 10%, propylene glycol 67.8 to 75%, and water for injection. Some products also contain benzyl alcohol 1.5% as a preservative. (1-5/99; 4; 29)

pH — The USP cites the official pH range as 9.2 to 10.2. (17) The AHFS cites the pH range as being 8.5 to 10.5. (4)

Osmolality — The osmolality of phenobarbital sodium (Elkins-Sinn) 65 mg/ml was determined to be 15,570 mOsm/kg by freezing-point depression and 9285 mOsm/kg by vapor pressure. (1071)

The osmolality of phenobarbital sodium 200 mg/ml was determined to be 10,800 mOsm/kg. (1233)

The osmolality of phenobarbital sodium 100 mg was calculated for the following dilutions (1054):

	Osmolality (mOsm/kg)	
Diluent	50 ml	100 ml
Dextrose 5% in water	296	289
Sodium chloride 0.9%	325	317

Trade Name(s) — Luminal Sodium.

Administration — Phenobarbital sodium is administered by intramuscular injection into a large muscle and slow intravenous injection. The commercial injection is highly alkaline and may cause local tissue damage. Do not administer subcutaneously. When given intravenously, the rate of injection should not exceed 60 mg/min. (1-5/99; 4)

Stability — Phenobarbital sodium injection in intact containers should be stored at controlled room temperature and protected from light. (1-5/99)

Phenobarbital sodium is not generally considered stable in aqueous solutions. (4) However, a test of phenobarbital sodium 10% (w/v) in aqueous solution showed 7% decomposition in four weeks when stored at 20 °C. There was no measurable decomposition in eight weeks with storage at −25 °C. (233)

In addition, Nahata et al. studied the stability of phenobarbital sodium (Elkins-Sinn) diluted to a 10-mg/ml concentration in sodium chloride 0.9% for use in infants. When stored at 4 °C, the dilution was physically compatible with no loss of phenobarbital during the 28-day test period. (1294)

Phenobarbital sodium in the special propylene glycol base is more stable. (4)

Phenobarbital may be precipitated from solutions of phenobarbital sodium, depending on the concentration and pH (29):

Concentration	pH at which Precipitate Forms
3 mg/ml	7.5 or below
6 mg/ml	7.9 or below
10 mg/ml	8.3 or below
20 mg/ml	8.6 or below

No solution containing a precipitate or that is more than slightly discolored should be used. (1-5/99; 4)

Plasticizer Leaching — Phenobarbital sodium (Wyeth-Ayerst) 6 mg/ml in dextrose 5% in water did not leach diethylhexyl phthalate (DEHP) plasticizer from 50-ml PVC bags in 24 hours at 24 °C. (1683)

Filtration — Phenobarbital sodium (Mallinckrodt) 130 mg/L in dextrose 5% in water, sodium chloride 0.9%, and Ringer's injection, lactated, filtered over 12 hours through a 5-µm stainless steel depth filter (Argyle Filter Connector), a 0.22-µm cellulose ester membrane filter (Ivex-2 Filter Set), and a 0.22-µm polycarbonate membrane filter (In-Sure Filter Set), showed no significant potency loss due to binding to the filters. (320)

Compatibility Information

Solution Compatibility

Phenobarbital sodium

Solution	*Mfr*	*Mfr*	*Conc/L*	*Remarks*	*Ref*	*C/I*
Alcohol 5%, dextrose 5%	AB		320 mg	Color changes	3	I
Dextran 6% in dextrose 5%	AB		320 mg	Physically compatible	3	C
Dextran 6% in sodium chloride 0.9%	AB		320 mg	Physically compatible	3	C
Dextrose–Ringer's injection combinations	AB		320 mg	Physically compatible	3	C
Dextrose–Ringer's injection, lactated, combinations	AB		320 mg	Physically compatible	3	C
Dextrose–saline combinations	AB		320 mg	Physically compatible	3	C
Dextrose 2½% in water	AB		320 mg	Physically compatible	3	C
Dextrose 5% in water	AB		320 mg	Physically compatible	3	C
Dextrose 10% in water	AB		320 mg	Physically compatible	3	C
Fructose 10% in sodium chloride 0.9%	AB		320 mg	Physically compatible	3	C
Fructose 10% in water	AB		320 mg	Physically compatible	3	C
Invert sugar 5 and 10% in sodium chloride 0.9%	AB		320 mg	Physically compatible	3	C
Invert sugar 5 and 10% in water	AB		320 mg	Physically compatible	3	C
Ionosol products	AB		320 mg	Physically compatible	3	C
Ringer's injection	AB		320 mg	Physically compatible	3	C
Ringer's injection, lactated	AB		320 mg	Physically compatible	3	C
Sodium chloride 0.45%	AB		320 mg	Physically compatible	3	C
Sodium chloride 0.9%	AB		320 mg	Physically compatible	3	C
Sodium lactate ⅙ M	AB		320 mg	Physically compatible	3	C

Additive Compatibility

Phenobarbital sodium

Drug	*Mfr*	*Conc/L*	*Mfr*	*Conc/L*	*Test Soln*	*Remarks*	*Ref*	*C/I*
Amikacin sulfate	BR	5 g	LI	300 mg	D5LR, D5R, D5S, D5W, D10W, IS10, LR, NS, R, SL	Physically compatible and potency of both retained for 24 hr at 25 °C	294	C
Aminophylline	SE	500 mg	AB	100 mg		Physically compatible	6	C
	SE	1 g	WI	200 mg	D5W	Physically compatible	15	C
Calcium chloride	UP	1 g	WI	200 mg	D5W	Physically compatible	15	C
Calcium gluconate	UP	1 g	WI	200 mg	D5W	Physically compatible	15	C
Chlorpromazine HCl	BP	200 mg	BP	800 mg	D5W, NS	Immediate precipitation	26	I
Colistimethate sodium	WC	500 mg	WI	200 mg	D5W	Physically compatible	15	C
Dimenhydrinate	SE	500 mg	WI	200 mg	D5W	Physically compatible	15	C
Ephedrine HCl			WI			Physically incompatible	9	I
	LI	250 mg	WI	200 mg	D5W	Physically incompatible	15	I
Hydralazine HCl	BP	80 mg	BP	800 mg	D5W	Yellow color and precipitate forms within 3 hr	26	I
Hydrocortisone sodium succinate			WI			Physically incompatible	9	I
	UP	500 mg	WI	200 mg	D5W	Physically incompatible	15	I
Hydroxyzine HCl	RR	250 mg	WI	200 mg	D5W	Physically incompatible	15	I
Insulin, regular[a]			WI			Physically incompatible	9	I
Levorphanol bitartrate	RC		WI			Physically incompatible	9	I
Meperidine HCl	WI		WI			Physically incompatible	9	I
Meropenem	ZEN	1 and 20 g	ES	200 mg	NS	Visually compatible for 4 hr at room temperature	1994	C
Morphine sulfate			WI			Physically incompatible	9	I
Norepinephrine bitartrate	WI		WI			Physically incompatible	9	I
Pentazocine lactate	WI	300 mg	WI	200 mg	D5W	Physically incompatible	15	I
Polymyxin B sulfate	BW	200 mg	WI	200 mg	D5W	Physically compatible	15	C
Procaine HCl			WI			Physically incompatible	9	I
Prochlorperazine mesylate	BP	100 mg	BP	800 mg	D5W	Haze develops over 3 hr	26	I
	BP	100 mg	BP	800 mg	NS	Immediate precipitation	26	I
Promazine HCl	BP	200 mg	BP	800 mg	NS	Immediate precipitation	26	I
Promethazine HCl	WY	250 mg	WI	200 mg	D5W	Physically incompatible	15	I
	BP	100 mg	BP	800 mg	D5W	Haze develops over 3 hr	26	I
	BP	100 mg	BP	800 mg	NS	Immediate precipitation	26	I
Sodium bicarbonate	AB	2.4 mEq[b]		320 mg	D5W	Physically compatible for 24 hr	772	C
Streptomycin sulfate			WI			Physically incompatible	9	I
Thiopental sodium	AB	2.5 g	AB	100 mg	D5W	Physically compatible	21	C
Vancomycin HCl	LI		WI			Physically incompatible	9	I
Verapamil HCl	KN	80 mg	ES	260 mg	D5W, NS	Physically compatible for 24 hr	764	C

[a]*Test performed prior to availability of neutral regular insulin.*
[b]*One vial of Neut added to a liter of admixture.*

Drugs in Syringe Compatibility

Phenobarbital sodium

Drug (in syringe)	*Mfr*	*Amt*	*Mfr*	*Amt*	*Remarks*	*Ref*	*C/I*
Heparin sodium		2500 units/ 1 ml		200 mg/ 1 ml	Physically compatible for at least 5 min	1053	C
Hydromorphone HCl	KN	2, 10, 40 mg/ 1 ml	AB	120 mg/ 1 ml	Precipitate forms immediately but dissipates with shaking. A white precipitate of phenobarbital re-forms after 6 hr at room temperature	2082	I
Ranitidine HCl	GL	50 mg/ 2 ml	AB	120 mg/ 1 ml	Immediate white haze	978	I
Sufentanil citrate	JN	50 μg/ml	WY	60 mg/ml	Haze forms immediately and particles form in 24 hr at 23 °C	1711	I

Y-Site Injection Compatibility (1:1 Mixture)

Phenobarbital sodium

Drug	*Mfr*	*Conc*	*Mfr*	*Conc*	*Remarks*	*Ref*	*C/I*
Amphotericin B cholesteryl sulfate complex	SEQ	0.83 mg/ml[a]	WY	5 mg/ml[a]	Increased turbidity forms immediately	2117	I
Enalaprilat	MSD	1.25 mg/ml	WY	0.32 mg/ml[a,b]	Physically compatible for 4 hr at 21 °C under fluorescent light by microscopic and macroscopic examination	1409	C
Fentanyl citrate	JN	0.025 mg/ml[a]	WY	2 mg/ml[a]	Physically compatible with no change in measured haze or increase in particle content in 48 hr at 22 °C	1706	C
Fosphenytoin sodium	PD	10 mg PE/ ml[b,e]		130 mg/ml	Visually compatible wtih no loss of either drug by HPLC in 8 hr at room temperature	2212	C
Gatifloxacin	BMS	2 mg/ml[a]	WY	5 mg/ml[a]	Physically compatible with no change in measured haze or increase in particle content in 4 hr at 23 °C	2234	C
Hydromorphone HCl	KN	2, 10, 40 mg/ ml	AB	120 mg/ml	Turbidity forms immediately but dissipates; phenobarbital precipitate develops in 6 hr	1532	I
	AST	0.5 mg/ml[a]	WY	2 mg/ml[a]	Physically compatible with no change in measured haze or increase in particle content in 48 hr at 22 °C	1706	C
Levofloxacin	OMN	5 mg/ml[a]	ES	130 mg/ml	Visually compatible for 4 hr at 24 °C under fluorescent light	2233	C
Linezolid	PHU	2 mg/ml	WY	5 mg/ml[a]	Physically compatible with no change in measured turbidity or increase in particle content in 4 hr at 23 °C	2264	C
Meropenem	ZEN	1 and 50 mg/ ml[b]	ES	0.32 mg/ml[c]	Visually compatible for 4 hr at room temperature	1994	C
Methadone HCl	LI	1 mg/ml[a]	WY	2 mg/ml[a]	Physically compatible with no change in measured haze or increase in particle content in 48 hr at 22 °C	1706	C
Morphine sulfate	AST	1 mg/ml[a]	WY	2 mg/ml[a]	Physically compatible with no change in measured haze or increase in particle content in 48 hr at 22 °C	1706	C

Y-Site Injection Compatibility (1:1 Mixture) (Cont.)

Phenobarbital sodium

Drug	*Mfr*	*Conc*	*Mfr*	*Conc*	*Remarks*	*Ref*	*C/I*
Propofol	ZEN	10 mg/ml	WY	5 mg/ml[a]	Physically compatible for 1 hr at 23 °C with no increase in particle content	2066	C
Sufentanil citrate	JN	12.5 μg/ml[a]	WY	2 mg/ml[a]	Physically compatible with no subvisual haze or particle formation in 24 hr at 23 °C	1711	C
TNA #218 to #226[d]			WY	5 mg/ml[a]	Damage to emulsion integrity occurs immediately with free oil formation possible	2215	I
TPN #212 to #215[d]			WY	5 mg/ml[a]	Physically compatible with no change in measured turbidity or increase in particle content in 4 hr at 23 °C	2109	C

[a]*Tested in dextrose 5% in water.*
[b]*Tested in sodium chloride 0.9%.*
[c]*Tested in sterile water for injection.*
[d]*Refer to Appendix I for the composition of parenteral nutrition solutions. TNA indicates a 3-in-1 admixture, and TPN indicates a 2-in-1 admixture.*
[e]*Concentration expressed in milligrams of phenytoin sodium equivalents (PE) per milliliter.*

Additional Compatibility Information

Acidic Drugs — Drugs such as phenobarbital sodium that exhibit poor solubility in an acidic medium may precipitate in solutions containing acidic additives. (4; 22) Metaraminol bitartrate is acidic and may cause precipitation, depending on the concentration of the additives. (7) Also, the acidic methyldopate HCl imparts some buffer capacity to admixtures and may pose solubility problems with barbiturate salts. (23)

Alkali-Labile Drugs — Phenobarbital sodium may raise the pH of admixture solutions to the alkaline range and, therefore, should not be mixed with alkali-labile drugs such as penicillin G. (47) Significant decomposition of isoproterenol HCl and norepinephrine bitartrate may also occur. If either of these two drugs is mixed with phenobarbital sodium, the admixture should be used immediately after preparation. (59; 77)

Atracurium besylate also may be inactivated by alkaline solutions such as barbiturates; precipitation of a free acid of the admixed drug may occur, depending on the resultant pH of the admixture. (4)

Ephedrine — Titration of 50 ml of a 0.5 M aqueous solution of ephedrine HCl (BP) with 30.8 ml or more of a 0.5 M aqueous solution of phenobarbital sodium (BP) resulted in precipitation of an ephedrine–phenobarbital complex. The point at which precipitation began corresponded to the point at which the pH of the ephedrine HCl solution had been increased from its initial pH 7 to 8.5. Further addition of phenobarbital sodium resulted in additional precipitation but did not alter the pH. (332)

Succinylcholine Chloride — When barbiturates are mixed with succinylcholine chloride, either the free barbiturate will precipitate or the succinylcholine chloride will be hydrolyzed, depending on the final pH of the admixture. (4; 21)

Concentrated Drug Solutions — The following incompatibility determinations were performed with concentrated solutions. The drugs in dry form were constituted according to manufacturer's recommendations. One milliliter of phenobarbital sodium (Winthrop) was added to 5 ml of sterile distilled water along with 1 ml of each of the following drugs. Particulate matter was noted within two hours (28):

Dimenhydrinate (Searle)
Diphenhydramine HCl (Parke-Davis)
Hydroxyzine HCl (Pfizer)
Kanamycin sulfate (Bristol)
Phenytoin sodium (Parke-Davis)
Prochlorperazine edisylate (SKF)
Promazine HCl (Wyeth)
Promethazine HCl (Wyeth)

Other Drugs — Drugs stated to be incompatible with barbiturate salts include clindamycin phosphate (106), droperidol (4), pancuronium bromide (4), and cimetidine HCl. (360)

Phenobarbital sodium should not be mixed in the same syringe with pentazocine lactate because precipitation occurs. (4)

Other Information

Heating Plasma — Heating plasma samples to 56 °C for one hour to inactivate potential HIV content resulted in no phenobarbital loss as determined by fluorescence polarization immunoassay. (1615)

PHENTOLAMINE MESYLATE
AHFS 12:16

Products — Phentolamine mesylate is available in vials containing 5 mg of drug with 25 mg of mannitol as a lyophilized powder. Reconstitution with 1 ml of sterile water for injection results in a 5-mg/ml solution. (1-5/99; 4)

pH — From 4.5 to 6.5. (4)

Osmolality — Phentolamine mesylate 5 mg/ml has an osmolality of 169 mOsm/kg. (1689)

Administration — Phentolamine mesylate may be administered by intramuscular or intravenous injection. (1-5/99; 4)

Stability — The intact vials should be stored at controlled room temperature. (1-5/99; 4) Although the manufacturer recommends that reconstituted solutions be used immediately and not stored (1-5/99), other information indicates that such solutions are stable for 48 hours at room temperature and one week at 2 to 8 °C. (4)

Sorption — Phentolamine mesylate (Novartis) 18 mg/L in sodium chloride 0.9% (Travenol) in PVC bags did not exhibit significant sorption to the plastic during one week of storage at room temperature (15 to 20 °C). (536)

In another study, phentolamine mesylate (Novartis) 18 mg/L in sodium chloride 0.9% did not exhibit any loss due to sorption during a seven-hour simulated infusion through an infusion set (Travenol) consisting of a cellulose propionate burette chamber and 170 cm of PVC tubing. (606)

The drug was also tested as a simulated infusion over at least one hour by a syringe pump system. A glass syringe on a syringe pump was fitted with 20 cm of polyethylene tubing or 50 cm of Silastic tubing. No loss of drug due to sorption was observed with either tubing. (606)

A 25-ml aliquot of phentolamine mesylate (Novartis) 18 mg/L in sodium chloride 0.9% was stored in all-plastic syringes composed of polypropylene barrels and polyethylene plungers for 24 hours at room temperature in the dark. No loss due to sorption occurred. (606)

Compatibility Information

Additive Compatibility

Phentolamine mesylate

Drug	Mfr	Conc/L	Mfr	Conc/L	Test Soln	Remarks	Ref	C/I
Cibenzoline succinate		2 g	CI	40 mg	D5W, NS	Physically compatible for 24 hr at 25 °C by visual and microscopic examination	1182	C
Dobutamine HCl	LI	1 g	CI	20 mg	D5W, NS	Physically compatible for 24 hr at 21 °C	812	C
Verapamil HCl	KN	80 mg	CI	10 mg	D5W, NS	Physically compatible for 24 hr	764	C

Drugs in Syringe Compatibility

Phentolamine mesylate

Drug (in syringe)	Mfr	Amt	Mfr	Amt	Remarks	Ref	C/I
Papaverine HCl	LI	30 mg/ml	BV, CI	0.5 mg/ml[a]	Physically compatible with virtually no papaverine loss at 5 and 25 °C and 1 to 3% phentolamine loss at 5 °C and 4 to 5% loss at 25 °C in 30 days	1161	C

[a]*Constituted with the papaverine HCl injection.*

Y-Site Injection Compatibility (1:1 Mixture)

Phentolamine mesylate

Drug	Mfr	Conc	Mfr	Conc	Remarks	Ref	C/I
Amiodarone HCl	LZ	4 mg/ml[a,b]	CI	0.04 mg/ml[a,b]	Physically compatible for 24 hr at 21 °C under fluorescent light	1032	C

[a]*Tested in dextrose 5% in water.*
[b]*Tested in sodium chloride 0.9%.*

Additional Compatibility Information

Infusion Solutions — Sodium chloride 0.9% has been recommended for the dilution of phentolamine mesylate. (1-5/99; 4)

Norepinephrine — The admixture of 10 mg/L of phentolamine mesylate with norepinephrine has been stated to not affect the pressor ability of norepinephrine. (1-5/99; 4)

PHENYLEPHRINE HCL
AHFS 12:12

Products — Phenylephrine HCl is available as a 1% solution in 1-ml ampuls and 1- and 5-ml vials. (29) Each milliliter of solution contains phenylephrine HCl 10 mg with sodium citrate and citric acid buffer, sodium chloride, and sodium metabisulfite antioxidant. The pH may have been adjusted during manufacture. (1-7/98; 4)

pH — From 3 to 6.5. (1-7/98; 4)

Osmolality — Phenylephrine HCl 10 mg/ml has an osmolality of 284 mOsm/kg. (1689)

Trade Name(s) — Neo-Synephrine.

Administration — Phenylephrine HCl is administered by subcutaneous, intramuscular, or direct slow intravenous injection or by intravenous infusion. For direct intravenous injection, a 0.1% solution (1 mg/ml) may be prepared by diluting 1 ml of phenylephrine HCl with 9 ml of sterile water for injection. Solutions for intravenous infusion are usually prepared by adding 10 mg of drug to 500 ml of dextrose 5% in water or sodium chloride 0.9%. (1-7/98; 4)

Stability — Intact containers of phenylephrine HCl should be stored at controlled room temperature and protected from light. (1-7/98; 4) Solutions of the drug must not be used if they are brown or contain a precipitate. However, oxidation may occur, resulting in loss of activity even though no color change is evident. (4)

Phenylephrine HCl (Winthrop) was stable for up to 84 days at 60 °C in a 250-mg/100 ml concentration in sterile water for injection. (132) At pH 2, no loss of potency occurred in 10 days at 97 °C. A rise in pH, especially above 9, increased decomposition. (29)

Phenylephrine HCl in dextrose 5% in water is stated to be stable for at least 48 hours at pH 3.5 to 7.5. (4)

Central Venous Catheter — Phenylephrine HCl (Ohmeda) 1 mg/ml in dextrose 5% in water was found to be compatible with the ARROWg+ard Blue Plus (Arrow International) chlorhexidine-bearing triple-lumen central catheter. HPLC analysis was used to evaluate completeness of drug delivery through the catheter and the amount of chlorhexidine removed from the internal lumens. Essentially complete delivery of the drug was found with little or no drug loss occurring. Furthermore, chlorhexidine delivered from the catheter remained at trace amounts with no substantial increase due to the delivery of the drug through the catheter. (2335)

Compatibility Information

Solution Compatibility

Phenylephrine HCl

Solution	*Mfr*	*Mfr*	*Conc/L*	*Remarks*	*Ref*	*C/I*
Dextran 6% in dextrose 5%	AB	WI	1 mg	Physically compatible	3	C
Dextran 6% in sodium chloride 0.9%	AB	WI	1 mg	Physically compatible	3	C
Dextrose–Ringer's injection combinations	AB	WI	1 mg	Physically compatible	3	C
Dextrose–Ringer's injection, lactated, combinations	AB	WI	1 mg	Physically compatible	3	C
Dextrose–saline combinations	AB	WI	1 mg	Physically compatible	3	C
Dextrose 2½% in water	AB	WI	1 mg	Physically compatible	3	C
Dextrose 5% in water	AB	WI	1 mg	Physically compatible	3	C
Dextrose 10% in water	AB	WI	1 mg	Physically compatible	3	C
Fructose 10% in sodium chloride 0.9%	AB	WI	1 mg	Physically compatible	3	C
Fructose 10% in water	AB	WI	1 mg	Physically compatible	3	C
Invert sugar 5 and 10% in sodium chloride 0.9%	AB	WI	1 mg	Physically compatible	3	C

Solution Compatibility (Cont.)

Phenylephrine HCl

Solution	*Mfr*	*Mfr*	*Conc/L*	*Remarks*	*Ref*	*C/I*
Invert sugar 5 and 10% in water	AB	WI	1 mg	Physically compatible	3	C
Ionosol products	AB	WI	1 mg	Physically compatible	3	C
Ringer's injection	AB	WI	1 mg	Physically compatible	3	C
Ringer's injection, lactated	AB	WI	1 mg	Physically compatible	3	C
Sodium bicarbonate 5%		WI	20 mg	Potency retained for 24 hr at 25 °C	48	C
Sodium chloride 0.45%	AB	WI	1 mg	Physically compatible	3	C
Sodium chloride 0.9%		WI	2.5 g	Potency retained for 24 hr at 22 °C	132	C
	AB	WI	1 mg	Physically compatible	3	C
Sodium lactate ⅙ M	AB	WI	1 mg	Physically compatible	3	C

Additive Compatibility

Phenylephrine HCl

Drug	*Mfr*	*Conc/L*	*Mfr*	*Conc/L*	*Test Soln*	*Remarks*	*Ref*	*C/I*
Chloramphenicol sodium succinate	PD	500 mg	WI	2.5 g	D5W, NS	Phenylephrine potency retained for over 24 hr at 22 °C	132	C
Chloramphenicol sodium succinate with sodium bicarbonate	PD AB	500 mg 7.5 g	WI	2.5 g	D5W	Phenylephrine potency retained for over 24 hr at 22 °C	132	C
Cibenzoline succinate		2 g	WB	40 mg	D5W, NS	Physically compatible for 24 hr at 25 °C by visual and microscopic examination	1182	C
Dobutamine HCl	LI	1 g	WI	20 mg	D5W, NS	Physically compatible for 24 hr at 21 °C	812	C
Lidocaine HCl	AST	2 g	WI	20 mg		Physically compatible	24	C
Potassium chloride	AB	40 mEq	WI	2.5 g	D5W	Phenylephrine potency retained for over 24 hr at 22 °C	132	C
Sodium bicarbonate	AB	2.4 mEq[a]	WI	10 mg	D5W	Physically compatible for 24 hr	772	C
Sodium bicarbonate with chloramphenicol sodium succinate	AB PD	7.5 g 500 mg	WI	2.5 g	D5W	Phenylephrine potency retained for over 24 hr at 22 °C	132	C

[a]*One vial of Neut added to a liter of admixture.*

Y-Site Injection Compatibility (1:1 Mixture)

Phenylephrine HCl

Drug	*Mfr*	*Conc*	*Mfr*	*Conc*	*Remarks*	*Ref*	*C/I*
Amiodarone HCl	LZ	4 mg/ml[a,b]	WI	0.04 mg/ml[a,b]	Physically compatible for 24 hr at 21 °C	1032	C
Cisatracurium besylate	GW	0.1, 2, 5 mg/ml[a]	GNS	1 mg/ml[a]	Physically compatible with no change in measured turbidity or increase in particle content in 4 hr at 23 °C	2074	C
Etomidate	AB	2 mg/ml	ES	10 mg/ml	Visually compatible for up to 7 days at 25 °C	1801	C
Famotidine	MSD	0.2 mg/ml[a]	WI	0.02 mg/ml[a]	Physically compatible for 4 hr at 25 °C	1188	C
Haloperidol lactate	MN	0.5[a] and 5 mg/ml	WB	0.02 mg/ml[a]	Visually compatible for 24 hr at 21 °C	1523	C

Y-Site Injection Compatibility (1:1 Mixture) (Cont.)

Phenylephrine HCl

Drug	*Mfr*	*Conc*	*Mfr*	*Conc*	*Remarks*	*Ref*	*C/I*
Hetastarch in lactated electrolyte injection (Hextend)	AB	6%	OH	1 mg/ml[a]	Physically compatible with no change in measured turbidity or increase in particle content in 4 hr at 23 °C	2339	C
Inamrinone lactate	WB	3 mg/ml[b]	WI	0.02 mg/ml[a]	Physically compatible for at least 4 hr at 25 °C under fluorescent light	992	C
Levofloxacin	OMN	5 mg/ml[a]	AMR	10 mg/ml	Visually compatible for 4 hr at 24 °C under fluorescent light	2233	C
Propofol	STU	2 mg/ml	ES	10 mg/ml	Bright yellow discoloration forms within 7 days at 25 °C. No visible change in 24 hr	1801	?
	ZEN	10 mg/ml	ES	0.1 mg/ml[a]	Physically compatible for 1 hr at 23 °C with no increase in particle content	2066	C
Remifentanil HCl	GW	0.025 and 0.25 mg/ml[b]	AMR	1 mg/ml[a]	Physically compatible with no change in measured turbidity or increase in particle content in 4 hr at 23 °C	2075	C
Thiopental sodium	AB	25 mg/ml	ES	10 mg/ml	White precipitate forms immediately	1801	I
Zidovudine	BW	4 mg/ml[a]	WI	1 mg/ml[a]	Physically compatible for 4 hr at 25 °C under fluorescent light by visual and microscopic examination	1193	C

[a]*Tested in dextrose 5% in water.*
[b]*Tested in sodium chloride 0.9%.*

Additional Compatibility Information

Infusion Solutions — Dextrose 5% in water and sodium chloride 0.9% have been recommended as diluents for infusion solutions. Phenylephrine HCl may be added to anesthetics for local or spinal anesthesia. (1-7/98; 4)

Lidocaine — Lidocaine HCl 2% in combination with phenylephrine HCl 0.25% was stable for at least 66 days at 25 °C. No loss of either drug was found by HPLC analysis, and little change in pH occurred during the test period. (1278)

Concentrated Drug Solutions — The following incompatibility determination was performed with concentrated solutions. One milliliter of phenylephrine HCl (Winthrop) was added to 5 ml of sterile distilled water along with 1 ml of phenytoin sodium (Parke-Davis). Particulate matter was noted within two hours. (28)

Other Drugs — Phenylephrine HCl has been stated to be incompatible with alkalies, ferric salts, and other metals. (4)

PHENYTOIN SODIUM
AHFS 28:12.12

Products — Phenytoin sodium is available as a ready-mixed solution in 100-mg (2 ml) vials, ampuls, and syringe cartridges and 250-mg (5 ml) vials. Each milliliter of solution contains (1-9/98; 29):

Phenytoin sodium	50 mg
Propylene glycol	40%
Alcohol	10%
Sodium hydroxide	to adjust pH
Water for injection	qs

CAUTION: Care should be taken to avoid confusion between phenytoin sodium and fosphenytoin sodium to prevent dosing errors.

pH — From 10 to 12.3. (1-9/98; 17) The pH is adjusted to about 12 during manufacture. (4)

The apparent pH of multiple lots of phenytoin sodium from several manufacturers was evaluated. The lower apparent pH of some products may play a role in microcrystal formation on dilution (1514):

Manufacturer	Apparent pH
Elkins-Sinn	11.39 ± 0.21
Lyphomed	11.68 ± 0.36
Parke-Davis	12.00 ± 0.06
SoloPak	11.38 ± 0.33

Osmolality — The osmolality of phenytoin sodium (Parke-Davis)

50 mg/ml was determined to be 9740 mOsm/kg by freezing-point depression and 6175 mOsm/kg by vapor pressure. (1071)

Another report indicated that the osmolality of phenytoin sodium 50 mg/ml was 3035 mOsm/kg by freezing-point depression. (1233)

The osmolality of phenytoin sodium 500 mg was calculated for the following dilutions (1054):

	Osmolality (mOsm/kg)	
Diluent	50 ml	100 ml
Sodium chloride 0.9%	336	312

Sodium Content—Each milliliter of phenytoin sodium injection contains 0.2 mEq of sodium. (4)

Administration — Phenytoin sodium is preferably administered by direct intravenous injection into a large vein through a large-gauge needle or intravenous catheter. Although intramuscular injection can be used, erratic or delayed absorption may occur. Subcutaneous injection should be avoided because of the possibility of local tissue damage. (1-9/98; 4) The rate of intravenous injection should not exceed 50 mg/min in adults or 1 to 3 mg/kg/min in neonates. Following intravenous injection, sodium chloride 0.9% should be injected through the same needle or catheter to reduce irritation. (1-9/98; 4)

Because of the drug's low solubility and possible precipitation (1-9/98; 4), intravenous infusion is usually not recommended. However, some clinicians have suggested that intravenous infusion is reasonable in an appropriately diluted, compatible infusion solution for short periods using inline filtration; they have advocated infusion to circumvent the adverse effects associated with direct intravenous injection. (See Additional Compatibility Information.)

Stability — Intact containers should be stored at controlled room temperature and protected from freezing. Phenytoin sodium is stable as long as it remains free of haziness and precipitation. If refrigerated or frozen, a precipitate may form, but it dissolves on standing at room temperature. On dissolution of the precipitate, the product is still suitable for use. Also, a faint yellow color, which has no effect on potency, may sometimes develop in the injection. (1-9/98; 4)

Precipitation of free phenytoin occurs at pH 11.5 or less. (4)

Phenytoin precipitate may form if the injection contacts more acidic drugs or infusion solutions such as dextrose 5% in water during administration. (See Additional Compatibility Information.) Such precipitation has been found to occlude catheters. Instilling 5 ml of 8.4% sodium bicarbonate injection at 15- to 30-minute intervals has cleared catheters occluded with phenytoin precipitate. The sodium bicarbonate apparently raised the pH enough to result in dissolution of a sufficient amount of the phenytoin precipitate to reopen the catheter. (2299; 2300) However, the safety of using this method of catheter clearance is uncertain because it is not known if some of the precipitated phenytoin is delivered into the bloodstream upon opening the occlusion.

Sorption—Phenytoin sodium (Sigma) 114 mg/L in sodium chloride 0.9% (Travenol) in PVC bags did not exhibit significant sorption to the plastic during one week of storage at room temperature (15 to 20 °C). (536)

In another study, phenytoin sodium (Sigma) 114 mg/L in sodium chloride 0.9% did not exhibit any loss due to sorption during a seven-hour simulated infusion through an infusion set (Travenol) consisting of a cellulose propionate burette chamber and 170 cm of PVC tubing. (606)

The drug was also tested as a simulated infusion over at least one hour by a syringe pump system. A glass syringe on a syringe pump was fitted with 20 cm of polyethylene tubing or 50 cm of Silastic tubing. No loss of drug due to sorption was observed with either tubing. (606)

A 25-ml aliquot of phenytoin sodium (Sigma) 114 mg/L in sodium chloride 0.9% was stored in all-plastic syringes composed of polypropylene barrels and polyethylene plungers for 24 hours at room temperature in the dark. No loss due to sorption occurred. (606)

Plasticizer Leaching—Phenytoin sodium (Elkins-Sinn) 10 mg/ml in sodium chloride 0.9% did not leach diethylhexyl phthalate (DEHP) plasticizer from 50-ml PVC bags in 24 hours at 24 °C. (1683)

Filtration—Phenytoin sodium (Parke-Davis) 250 mg/5 ml in a 5-ml syringe was filtered at a rate of 1 ml/min through a 5-µm stainless steel depth filter (Argyle Filter Connector). No significant reduction in potency due to binding to the filter was observed. (320)

Compatibility Information

Solution Compatibility

Phenytoin sodium

Solution	*Mfr*	*Mfr*	*Conc/L*	*Remarks*	*Ref*	*C/I*
Dextrose 5% in sodium chloride 0.9%	TR	PD	1 g	Visible crystals in minutes. 21% crystallized in 8 hr and 38% in 24 hr	306	I
Dextrose 5% in water	TR	PD	1 g	Visible crystals in minutes. 15% crystallized in 8 hr and 36% in 24 hr	306	I
	TR	PD	4.6, 9.2, 18.4 g	Phenytoin crystal formation. Erratic concentrations delivered through 0.2-µm filter over 24 hr at 29 °C	305	I
	MG	PD	1 g	No visible precipitate or reduction in phenytoin in 8 hr at room temperature. Precipitate forms within 24 hr with 15% loss of phenytoin	446	I
	TR	PD	1 g	Substantial crystal formation in 1 hr found upon filtration	450; 451	I

Solution Compatibility (Cont.)

Solution	Mfr	Phenytoin sodium Mfr	Conc/L	Remarks	Ref	C/I
	AB	PD	1 g	Visible crystals in less than 12 min. 18% loss of phenytoin in 14 hr and 22% in 24 hr	452	I
			1 g	10% of phenytoin removed by filtration in 2 hr and 15 to 18% in 4 hr	453	I
		PD	670 mg to 4 g	Phenytoin crystals within 5 to 25 min. Reduced phenytoin concentration	708	I
	AB, CU, MG, TR	ES, PD	0.4 to 4.55 g	Visible precipitate forms within 10 to 60 min with significant reduction in phenytoin concentration in 20 to 45 min	710	I
	TR	PD	1, 1.5, 2, 4, 10 g	Visible crystals in 30 min. 12 to 20% crystallized in 4 hr	951	I
Fat emulsion 10%, intravenous	VT	PD	1 g	Phenytoin crystal formation	32	I
Ringer's injection, lactated	TR	PD	4.6, 9.2, 18.4 g	Phenytoin crystal formation. Erratic concentration delivered through 0.2-μm filter over 24 hr at 29 °C	305	I
	TR	PD	1 g	Visible crystals in 6 to 9 hr. Approximately 0.8% crystallized in 8 hr and 7% in 24 hr	306	I
	TR	ES, PD	0.4 to 4.55 g	No significant reduction in phenytoin concentration for 12 to 24 hr at 23 °C. Visible precipitate inconsistently formed	710	I
Sodium chloride 0.45%	TR	PD	4.6, 9.2, 18.4 g	Phenytoin crystal formation. Less than 10% phenytoin reduction delivered through 0.2-μm filter over 24 hr at 29 °C	305	I
Sodium chloride 0.9%		PD	1 to 10 g	Phenytoin crystal formation in 20 to 30 min	63	I
		PD	200 mg to 10 g	Phenytoin crystal formation in 30 min	65; 447	I
		PD	2 and 4 g	Phenytoin crystal formation in 10 to 15 min	66	I
	TR	PD	1 g	Visible crystals in 6 to 9 hr. Approximately 0.8% crystallized in 8 hr and 7% in 24 hr	306	I
	TR	PD	4.6, 9.2, 18.4 g	Phenytoin crystal formation. Less than 10% phenytoin reduction delivered through 0.2-μm filter over 24 hr at 29 °C	305	I
			1 g	10% of phenytoin removed by filtration in 4 hr	453	I
		PD	670 mg to 4 g	No crystals observed during 1-hr study period	708	C
	TR	PD	1 to 10 g	Crystals formed in unfiltered solutions in 18 hr. Filtered solutions stored at 6 °C had no crystals and no reduction in phenytoin in 24 hr	709	I
	TR	ES, PD	0.4 to 4.55 g	No significant reduction in phenytoin for 8 to 24 hr at 23 °C. Visible precipitate inconsistently formed	710	I
	TR	PD	1, 1.5, 2, 4, 10 g	Visible precipitation appeared in some samples in 3 hr	951	I
	TR	PD	9.2 and 18.4 g	Physically compatible for 2 hr by microscopic and macroscopic examination. Filtration did not significantly reduce phenytoin concentration	1514	C
	TR	ES, LY, SO	9.2 and 18.4 g	Microcrystals formed repeatedly, but inconsistently, over 2 hr. Filtration did not significantly reduce phenytoin concentration	1514	?

Additive Compatibility

Phenytoin sodium

Drug	*Mfr*	*Conc/L*	*Mfr*	*Conc/L*	*Test Soln*	*Remarks*	*Ref*	*C/I*
Amikacin sulfate	BR	5 g	PD	250 mg	D5LR, D5R, D5S, D5W, D10W, IS10, LR, NS, R, SL	Immediate precipitation	294	I
Bleomycin sulfate	BR	20 and 30 units	PD	500 mg	NS	Physically compatible and bleomycin activity retained for 1 week at 4 °C. Phenytoin not tested	763	C
Bretylium tosylate	ACC	1 g	PD	2 g	D5W, NS	Immediate precipitation	756	I
Dobutamine HCl	LI	1 g	ES	1 g	D5W, NS	White precipitate forms within 5 to 10 min	789	I
	LI	1 g	AHP	25 g	D5W, NS	White precipitate forms rapidly, with brown solution in 6 hr at 21 °C	812	I
Insulin, regular[a]			PD			Physically incompatible	9	I
Levorphanol bitartrate	RC		PD			Physically incompatible	9	I
Lidocaine HCl	AST	2 g	ES	1 g	D5W, LR, NS	Immediate formation of white cloudy precipitate	775	I
Lincomycin HCl	UP		PD			Physically incompatible	9	I
Meperidine HCl	WI		PD			Physically incompatible	9	I
Metaraminol bitartrate	MSD		PD			Physically incompatible	9	I
Morphine sulfate			PD			Physically incompatible	9	I
Nitroglycerin	ACC	400 mg	PD	1 g	D5W, NS[b]	Phenytoin crystal formation in 24 hr. 3 to 4% nitroglycerin loss in 24 hr and 9% loss in 48 hr at 23 °C. Phenytoin not tested	929	I
Norepinephrine bitartrate	WI		PD			Physically incompatible	9	I
Pentobarbital sodium			PD			Physically incompatible	9	I
Procaine HCl			PD			Physically incompatible	9	I
Sodium bicarbonate	AB	2.4 mEq[c]	PD	250 mg	D5W	Physically compatible for 24 hr	772	C
Streptomycin sulfate			PD			Physically incompatible	9	I
Verapamil HCl	KN	80 mg	PD	500 mg	D5W, NS	Physically compatible for 48 hr	739	C

[a]*Test performed prior to availability of neutral regular insulin.*
[b]*Tested in glass containers.*
[c]*One vial of Neut added to a liter of admixture.*

Drugs in Syringe Compatibility

Phenytoin sodium

Drug (in syringe)	*Mfr*	*Amt*	*Mfr*	*Amt*	*Remarks*	*Ref*	*C/I*
Hydromorphone HCl	KN	2, 10, 40 mg/ 1 ml	AB	50 mg/ 1 ml	White precipitate of phenytoin forms immediately	2082	I
Sufentanil citrate	JN	50 μg/ml	SO	50 mg/ml	Small crystals form immediately. Large crystals settle to bottom in 24 hr at 23 °C	1711	I

Y-Site Injection Compatibility (1:1 Mixture)

			Phenytoin sodium				
Drug	*Mfr*	*Conc*	*Mfr*	*Conc*	*Remarks*	*Ref*	*C/I*
Amphotericin B cholesteryl sulfate complex	SEQ	0.83 mg/ml[a]	ES	50 mg/ml[a]	Gross precipitate forms	2117	I
Ciprofloxacin	MI	2 mg/ml[c]	PD	50 mg/ml	Immediate crystal formation	1655	I
Clarithromycin	AB	4 mg/ml[a]	ANT	20 mg/ml[a]	White cloudiness forms immediately, becoming a white precipitate in 1 hr at both 30 and 17 °C	2174	I
Diltiazem HCl	MMD	1 mg/ml[b]	PD	50 mg/ml	Precipitate forms	1807	I
Enalaprilat	MSD	1.25 mg/ml	PD	1 mg/ml[b]	Crystalline precipitate forms immediately	1409	I
Esmolol HCl	DCC	10 mg/ml[a]	IX	1 mg/ml[a]	Physically compatible for 24 hr at 22 °C	1169	C
Famotidine	MSD	0.2 mg/ml[a]	PD	50 mg/ml	Physically compatible for 14 hr	1196	C
Fentanyl citrate	JN	0.0.25 mg/ml[a]	ES	2 mg/ml[a,b]	Precipitate forms within 1 hr	1706	I
Fluconazole	RR	2 mg/ml	PD	50 mg/ml	Physically compatible for 24 hr at 25 °C	1407	C
Foscarnet sodium	AST	24 mg/ml	PD	50 mg/ml	Physically compatible for 24 hr at room temperature under fluorescent light	1335	C
Gatifloxacin	BMS	2 mg/ml[a]	ESI	50 mg/ml	Large amount of crystalline precipitate forms immediately	2234	I
Heparin sodium	TR	50 units/ml	ES	2 mg/ml[b]	Cloudiness forms immediately and becomes dense, white, flocculent precipitate in 4 hr at 25 °C	1793	I
Heparin sodium with hydrocortisone sodium succinate	RI UP	1000 units + 100 mg/L[d]	PD	50 mg/ml	Immediate formation of phenytoin crystals	322	I
Hydromorphone HCl	KN	2, 10, 40 mg/ml	AB	50 mg/ml	Turbidity forms immediately and phenytoin precipitate develops	1532	I
	AST	0.5 mg/ml[a]	ES	2 mg/ml[a,b]	Precipitate forms within 1 hr	1706	I
Linezolid	PHU	2 mg/ml	ES	50 mg/ml	Crystalline precipitate forms immediately	2264	I
Methadone HCl	LI	1 mg/ml[a]	ES	2 mg/ml[a,b]	Precipitate forms immediately	1706	I
Morphine sulfate	AST	1 mg/ml[a]	ES	2 mg/ml[a,b]	Precipitate forms after 1 hr	1706	I
Potassium chloride		40 mEq/L[a]	PD	50 mg/ml	Immediate formation of phenytoin crystals	322	I
		40 mEq/L[e]	PD	50 mg/ml	Phenytoin crystals form within 4 hr at room temperature	322	I
Propofol	ZEN	10 mg/ml	ES	50 mg/ml	Needle-like crystals form immediately	2066	I
Sufentanil citrate	JN	12.5 μg/ml[a]	ES	2 mg/ml[a]	Numerous tiny crystals form immediately and become larger over 24 hr at 23 °C under fluorescent light	1711	I
Tacrolimus	FUJ	1 mg/ml[b]	ES	5 mg/ml[a]	Visually compatible for 4 hr at 25 °C. White haze forms by 24 hr	1630	C
Theophylline	TR	4 mg/ml	ES	2 mg/ml[b]	Cloudiness forms immediately and becomes dense, flocculent precipitate in 6 hr at 25 °C	1793	I
TPN #189[f]			PD	50 mg/ml	Heavy white precipitate forms immediately	1767	I

Y-Site Injection Compatibility (1:1 Mixture) (Cont.)

			Phenytoin sodium				
Drug	*Mfr*	*Conc*	*Mfr*	*Conc*	*Remarks*	*Ref*	*C/I*
Vitamin B complex with C	RC	2 ml/L[g]	PD	50 mg/ml	Phenytoin crystals form within 4 hr at room temperature	322	I
	RC	2 ml/L[c]	PD	50 mg/ml	Immediate formation of phenytoin crystals	322	I

[a]*Tested in dextrose 5% in water.*
[b]*Tested in sodium chloride 0.9%.*
[c]*Tested in both dextrose 5% in water and sodium chloride 0.9%.*
[d]*Tested in dextrose 5% in water, Ringer's injection, lactated, and sodium chloride 0.9%.*
[e]*Tested in both Ringer's injection, lactated, and sodium chloride 0.9%.*
[f]*Refer to Appendix I for the composition of parenteral nutrition solutions. TPN indicates a 2-in-1 admixture.*
[g]*Tested in Ringer's injection, lactated.*

Additional Compatibility Information

Infusion Solutions — The mixing of phenytoin sodium with other drugs or with intravenous infusion solutions is not recommended (1-9/98; 4) because the solubility of phenytoin sodium is such that crystallization or precipitation may result if the special vehicle is altered or the pH is lowered. (62; 63; 613) Unfortunately, direct intravenous injection of phenytoin sodium is inconvenient and is occasionally associated with significant cardiovascular side effects. (1-9/98; 4) In spite of the caveat against dilution, some clinicians have advocated the infusion of phenytoin sodium (443; 444; 448; 611; 947–950; 1295) or administration into the tubing of a running infusion solution. (63; 65; 338; 445)

Reports of phenytoin crystallization in infusion solutions are numerous. Tobias and Kellick microscopically examined solutions composed of 10 mg of phenytoin sodium in 1 to 50 ml of sodium chloride 0.9% 30 minutes after mixing. They found rod-shaped crystals in all concentrations. They did not find crystals when phenytoin was injected into a running sodium chloride 0.9% infusion. (65) Frank repeated the experiment and confirmed the results. (447) However, a more recent study pointed out that this crystallization may have occurred from evaporation and the consequent increase in concentration of free phenytoin. (306)

Chan noted that the addition of 100 mg of phenytoin sodium to 25 to 50 ml of sodium chloride 0.9% resulted in immediate microcrystal formation with subsequent visually apparent macrocrystal formation in 10 to 15 minutes. (66)

In contrast, Bighley et al. added phenytoin sodium 100 mg/L to sodium chloride 0.9% in PVC bags and, by visual observation, did not detect any precipitate formation. (449)

Furthermore, Greenblatt and Shader added 500 mg of phenytoin sodium (Parke-Davis) to 490 ml of dextrose 5% in water and, by visual inspection, found no precipitation for at least eight hours at room temperature. Analysis of the solution showed the phenytoin concentration to be 105% of the predicted concentration. They did note a fine crystalline precipitate after 24 hours. Also, the concentration had declined to 85% at that time. (446)

Using this same 500-mg/500 ml in dextrose 5% in water admixture, both Schondelmeyer et al. (450) and Baumann et al. (451) found substantial crystal formation in one hour by filtering the solution through 0.45- and 0.22-μm filters, respectively. Crystals could be detected in as little as five minutes, and the quantity increased with time.

More recent studies examined the problem in depth. Baumann et al. (306) evaluated phenytoin sodium at a concentration of 1 g/L in dextrose 5% in water, sodium chloride 0.9%, dextrose 5% in sodium chloride 0.9%, and Ringer's injection, lactated. At various time intervals, samples were withdrawn and filtered through a 0.22-μm filter. The filtrate was then analyzed for phenytoin content. In both sodium chloride 0.9% and Ringer's injection, lactated, there was no detected crystallization in four hours and only 0.8% crystallization in eight hours. Visible crystal formation did not occur until six to nine hours after admixture. In contrast, the dextrose solutions had 5 to 9% and 15 to 21% crystallization in one and eight hours, respectively. Visible crystals were observed within minutes. The authors suggested that, at a concentration of 1 mg/ml, the critical pH for aqueous solubility of phenytoin is 10. It would, therefore, be expected that phenytoin solubility would increase as this pH is approached. Their results were consistent with the pH values of the four admixtures:

Solution	pH of Phenytoin Sodium 1 mg/ml
Ringer's injection, lactated	10.4
Sodium chloride 0.9%	10.0
Dextrose 5% in water	9.3
Dextrose 5% in sodium chloride 0.9%	9.3

It was noted that the pH of infusion solutions may vary (as may the pH of the drug) (452), and it is not possible to predict the final pH of the admixture accurately. The authors concluded that intravenous infusion of phenytoin sodium was feasible at a concentration of 1 mg/ml in sodium chloride 0.9% or Ringer's injection, lactated, provided the administration of the solutions was started immediately after preparation and watched carefully. (306)

Subsequent studies, performed by Sistare and Greene (452) and Biberdorf and Spurbeck (453), tended to corroborate this result.

Cloyd et al. also studied phenytoin sodium in infusion solutions but in higher concentrations. The concentrations tested were 4.6, 9.2, and 18.4 mg/ml in sodium chloride 0.45 and 0.9%, dextrose 5% in water, and Ringer's injection, lactated. The test was conducted over 24 hours at 29 °C, and the pH values of all solutions were between 10.15 and 11.50. Crystallization was observed in all admixtures but was not sufficient to permit precise quantitation. Analysis of the admixtures yielded rather erratic results, but it was felt that phenytoin sodium retained sufficient potency for 24 hours in both sodium chloride solutions. The extent of crystallization was not believed to be large enough to reduce significantly the phenytoin concentration when an inline filter was used. (305)

Carmichael et al. diluted phenytoin sodium 100 mg in 25, 50, 100, and 150 ml of dextrose 5% in water and sodium chloride 0.9%. The dextrose admixtures were noted to have consistently lower pH values than those in sodium chloride. Further, as the volume of diluent increased, the pH decreased. In the dextrose 5% in water admixtures, visible crystals were observed within five to 25 minutes. In sodium chloride 0.9%, no crystals were visually apparent within the one-hour study period. During simulated infusion of a 100-mg/50 ml solution in dextrose 5% in water or sodium chloride 0.9% through a burette administration set, a reduced concentration of phenytoin sodium was delivered in the dextrose solution, but no significant reduction occurred in the sodium chloride solution. The use of a 1-μm inline filter had no significant effect on the delivered concentrations. The authors concluded that dextrose 5% in water was an unacceptable diluent for phenytoin sodium infusion. However, they indicated that sodium chloride 0.9% could be acceptable as a diluent if the phenytoin sodium concentration was no less than 100 mg/100 ml and, preferably, at 100 mg/25 or 50 ml. Moreover, such solutions should be prepared immediately before use and infused within one hour, and an inline filter should be used because of the possibility of microcrystal formation. (708)

Salem et al. evaluated the compatibility of phenytoin sodium at concentrations of 1, 2.5, 5, 7.5, and 10 mg/ml in sodium chloride 0.9% over 24 hours at 6 °C. At the one-hour interval in all concentrations, a small increase in concentration was observed and attributed to supersaturation. But at eight through 24 hours, the phenytoin concentrations had returned to expected values and remained consistent. Observation of additional 1- and 10-mg/ml concentrations for the Tyndall effect demonstrated light scattering, which the authors indicated would suggest a colloidal dispersion rather than a true solution. Also crystals formed in those solutions within 18 hours. However, unlike the initial test solutions, these latter two solutions were unfiltered. In filtered solutions, crystal formation took up to three days to occur, which the authors indicated explained why no crystals appeared in the original dilutions in 24 hours. It was noted that while the time to crystal formation may be variable and difficult to predict, it was nonetheless inevitable. The authors recommended using phenytoin sodium infusions as soon as possible after preparation, observing closely for particulate matter, and avoiding conditions that would enhance precipitation such as refrigeration. (709)

Phenytoin sodium concentrations of 0.40, 0.98, 2.38, and 4.55 mg/ml in dextrose 5% in water, sodium chloride 0.9%, and Ringer's injection, lactated, were evaluated by Pfeifle et al. Concentrations of the drug in sodium chloride 0.9% or Ringer's injection, lactated, did not significantly vary from the initial amount for at least eight hours and usually for 12 to 24 hours at 23 °C. In dextrose 5% in water, however, significant reductions in concentration appeared in as little as 20 minutes. Further, visible precipitation occurred within 10 minutes at all concentrations in dextrose 5% in water, except 0.4 mg/ml in which 15 to 60 minutes elapsed before crystallization occurred. With phenytoin sodium from Elkins-Sinn, the precipitate flocculated and sank or floated; the Parke-Davis product produced a precipitate that remained suspended. In sodium chloride 0.9% and Ringer's injection, lactated, visible precipitation was not consistently observed. However, nephelometer determinations indicated that some particulate matter was present in all admixtures. Although not precisely predictable, the authors concluded that formation of a visible precipitate did coincide with a phenytoin concentration decline but did not correlate with the differences in pH observed in this study. While dextrose 5% in water was determined to be unacceptable for phenytoin sodium dilution, the authors indicated that sodium chloride 0.9% and Ringer's injection, lactated, were suitable. (710)

In a paper by Newton and Kluza, the relationship of phenytoin sodium solubility to various solution characteristics was explored. It was noted that the effect of the special solvent system could be disregarded in dilutions of 1:5 or more. The pH of the admixture was stated to be the primary determinant of the occurrence or absence of crystallization. With a given solution, the pH is dependent on the volume of dilution, with a lower pH resulting from greater dilution. Phenytoin becomes less soluble in aqueous solution as the pH drops. Equations for predicting the compatibility of phenytoin sodium in admixture solutions were presented, but the authors noted that it is not possible to predict the time required to develop precipitation. (713)

Giacona et al. evaluated phenytoin sodium (Parke-Davis) and two European preparations of phenytoin utilizing tromethamine in dextrose 5% in water and sodium chloride 0.9% (Travenol) in PVC bags. Phenytoin concentrations ranged from 1 to 10 mg/ml. The two European preparations did not develop visually apparent crystals for four or five days in either solution. Microscopic examination revealed no crystals in 24 hours in either solution. Phenytoin sodium (Parke-Davis) in dextrose 5% in water developed visible particles in 30 minutes, with 12 to 20% of the phenytoin crystallizing in four hours. In sodium chloride 0.9%, macroscopic and microscopic examination showed that phenytoin crystals did not develop within 24 hours when the solution was sealed from the atmosphere. However, in an open container, crystals formed in three hours. This result was attributed to the absorption of atmospheric carbon dioxide decreasing the solution pH. (951)

Markowsky et al. evaluated the pH variability among six lots each of phenytoin sodium from four suppliers (Elkins-Sinn, Lyphomed, Parke-Davis, and SoloPak) and the impact of microcrystal formation on dilution. The Parke-Davis product had the highest apparent pH and the least variability. At concentrations of 9.2 and 18.4 mg/ml in sodium chloride 0.9% over two hours, the Parke-Davis lots had no microcrystal formation while the other products had inconsistent but repeated episodes. Microcrystallization was observed most frequently when the apparent pH of the initial product was less than 11.35 and the admixture apparent pH was less than 10.8. Filtration did not remove significant amounts of phenytoin even from the solutions containing microcrystals. (1514)

Collins and Lutz demonstrated that phenytoin sodium 50 mg/ml precipitated when injected simultaneously with a total parenteral nutrition solution through a double-lumen catheter using separate ports in a simulated venous flow model. White clouds of precipitated phenytoin and clumps of phenytoin crystals were observed. With a triple-lumen catheter, no clumps were noted, but a white coating formed on the catheter. (1421)

Although some feel that infusion of phenytoin sodium is, perhaps, too dangerous to perform clinically (452), others indicate that such administration may be feasible provided proper precautions are taken such as using a suitable vehicle (i.e., sodium chloride 0.9% or Ringer's injection, lactated), using a sufficiently concentrated solution, starting the infusion immediately after preparation and completing administration within a relatively short time, using a 0.22-μm inline filter, and watching the admixture very carefully. (305; 306; 453; 611–613; 708–710; 947–950; 1295)

Clindamycin — Clindamycin phosphate (Cleocin) has been stated to be incompatible with phenytoin sodium. (2)

Gentamicin — A 2-ml fluid barrier of dextrose 5% in water in a microbore retrograde infusion set failed to prevent precipitation between gentamicin sulfate 5 mg/0.5 ml and phenytoin sodium 5 mg/0.1 ml. (1385)

Concentrated Drug Solutions — The following incompatibility determinations were performed with concentrated solutions. The drugs in dry form were constituted according to manufacturers' recommendations. One milliliter of phenytoin sodium was added to 5 ml of sterile distilled water along with 1 ml of each of the following drugs. Particulate matter was noted within two hours (28):

- Aminophylline
- Chloramphenicol sodium succinate (Parke-Davis)
- Dimenhydrinate (Searle)
- Diphenhydramine HCl (Parke-Davis)
- Hydroxyzine HCl (Pfizer)
- Kanamycin sulfate (Bristol)
- Metaraminol bitartrate (MSD)
- Penicillin G potassium
- Phenobarbital sodium (Winthrop)
- Phenylephrine HCl (Winthrop)
- Phytonadione (MSD)
- Procainamide HCl (Squibb)
- Prochlorperazine edisylate (SKF)
- Promazine HCl (Wyeth)
- Promethazine HCl (Wyeth)
- Vancomycin HCl (Lilly)
- Vitamin B complex with C (Lederle)

Other Information

Heating Plasma — Heating plasma samples to 56 °C for one hour to inactivate potential HIV content resulted in no phenytoin loss as determined by fluorescence polarization immunoassay. (1615)

PHYTONADIONE (PHYTOMENADIONE) AHFS 88:24

Products — Phytonadione is available as a 2-mg/ml aqueous dispersion in 0.5-ml ampuls and as a 10-mg/ml aqueous dispersion in 1-ml ampuls and 2.5- and 5-ml vials. Each milliliter contains (2):

Phytonadione	2 or 10 mg
Polyoxyethylated fatty acid	70 mg
Dextrose	37.5 mg
Benzyl alcohol	0.9%
Water for injection	qs 1 ml

pH — The USP cites the official pH range as 3.5 to 7. (17) Phytonadione (Merck) has a pH of 5 to 7. (2)

Osmolality — The osmolality of phytonadione (MSD) 10 mg/ml was determined to be 325 mOsm/kg by freezing-point depression and 303 mOsm/kg by vapor pressure. (1071)

Trade Name(s) — AquaMEPHYTON.

Administration — The intramuscular or subcutaneous routes are preferred for phytonadione. If intravenous injection is unavoidable, phytonadione may be given by direct intravenous injection at a rate not exceeding 1 mg/min or by intravenous infusion. (2; 4)

Stability — Phytonadione injection is available as an essentially clear yellow liquid. Phytonadione is stable in the presence of heat and moisture and may be autoclaved (4), but it is photosensitive and should be protected from light at all times. (2; 4) When dilutions are indicated, administration should start immediately after mixing with the diluent; unused portions of the dilution, as well as unused contents of the ampul, should be discarded. (4)

Light Effects — A study of phytonadione in intravenous solutions showed 50% decomposition in 15 days under fluorescent light and 43 to 63% in three hours on exposure to sunlight. (463) The manufacturer indicates that about a 10 to 15% loss occurs over 24 hours on exposure to fluorescent light or sunlight. (854) It has been recommended that infusion solutions containing phytonadione require wrapping the container with aluminum foil or other opaque material for light protection. (4)

Martinelli et al. evaluated the loss of phytonadione (Roche) 0.05 to 0.1 mg/ml from solutions in glass and polypropylene containers unprotected or packaged in light-protective overwraps when exposed to neon light and daylight. HPLC evaluation found losses approached 80% in one day unprotected from light exposure. A brown polyethylene light protection bag (specific mass 6.6 g/cm^2) provided the best protection, yielding no phytonadione loss during a seven-day exposure period. A white "light-tight" light-protective overwrap (6 g/cm^2) and a black plastic waste disposal bag (2.7 g/cm^2) failed to protect the phytonadione completely. In the black bag, phytonadione losses of over 30% occurred in seven days; the white light-protective overwrap was worse, allowing loss of nearly half of the phytonadione in one day. The authors concluded that substantial differences in light protection are afforded by the different materials and that the efficacy of purported light-protection barriers for light-sensitive drugs should be validated prior to use. (1923)

Syringes — Phytonadione (MSD) 10 mg/ml was found to retain potency for three weeks at room temperature when 1 and 2 ml were packaged in Tubex cartridges. After one month, however, an insoluble precipitate was noted. (13)

Filtration — The manufacturer states that phytonadione passes through an inline filter (porosity and filter media unspecified) with negligible loss occurring. (854)

Compatibility Information

Solution Compatibility

Phytonadione

Solution	*Mfr*	*Mfr*	*Conc/L*	*Remarks*	*Ref*	*C/I*
Amino acids 2%, dextrose 12.5%		ROR	5 ml[a]	7% phytonadione loss in 4 hr and 27% loss in 24 hr by HPLC under ambient temperature and light	1815	I
Amino acids 4.25%, dextrose 25%	MG	MSD	10 mg	No increase in particulate matter in 24 hr at 4 °C	349	C
Dextran 12%	AB	AB	50 mg	Haze or precipitate forms within 1 hr	3	I
Dextran 6% in dextrose 5%	AB	AB	50 mg	Physically compatible	3	C
Dextran 6% in sodium chloride 0.9%	AB	AB	50 mg	Physically compatible	3	C
Dextrose 2½% in water	AB	AB	50 mg	Physically compatible	3	C
Dextrose 5% in water	AB	AB	50 mg	Physically compatible	3	C
Dextrose 10% in water	AB	AB	50 mg	Physically compatible	3	C
Dextrose–Ringer's injection combinations	AB	AB	50 mg	Physically compatible	3	C
Dextrose–Ringer's injection, lactated, combinations	AB	AB	50 mg	Physically compatible	3	C
Dextrose–saline combinations	AB	AB	50 mg	Physically compatible	3	C
Fat emulsion 10%, intravenous	KA	KA[a]	16 mg	Physically compatible for 24 hr at 26 °C with little loss of phytonadione and of most other vitamins by HPLC; up to 52% ascorbate loss	2050	C
Fructose 10% in sodium chloride 0.9%	AB	AB	50 mg	Physically compatible	3	C
Fructose 10% in water	AB	AB	50 mg	Physically compatible	3	C
Invert sugar 5 and 10% in sodium chloride 0.9%	AB	AB	50 mg	Physically compatible	3	C
Invert sugar 5 and 10% in water	AB	AB	50 mg	Physically compatible	3	C
Ionosol products	AB	AB	50 mg	Physically compatible	3	C
Ringer's injection	AB	AB	50 mg	Physically compatible	3	C
Ringer's injection, lactated	AB	AB	50 mg	Physically compatible	3	C
Sodium chloride 0.45%	AB	AB	50 mg	Physically compatible	3	C
Sodium chloride 0.9%	AB	AB	50 mg	Physically compatible	3	C
Sodium lactate ⅙ M	AB	AB	50 mg	Physically compatible	3	C
TPN #11 to #15[b]		MSD	5 and 10 mg	Physically compatible for 24 hr at 22 °C. TLC changes of amino acids in similar solutions attributed to M.V.I. or vitamin B complex with C	313	C
TPN #16 to #20[b]		MSD	5 and 10 mg	Physically compatible for 24 hr at 22 °C. UV spectra for amino acids solution unaltered	313	C

[a]*From multivitamins.*
[b]*Refer to Appendix I for the composition of parenteral nutrition solutions. TPN indicates a 2-in-1 admixture.*

Additive Compatibility

			Phytonadione					
Drug	*Mfr*	*Conc/L*	*Mfr*	*Conc/L*	*Test Soln*	*Remarks*	*Ref*	*C/I*
Amikacin sulfate	BR	5 g	MSD	200 mg	D5LR, D5R, D5S, D5W, D10W, IS10, LR, NS, R, SL	Physically compatible and amikacin potency retained for 24 hr at 25 °C. Phytonadione not analyzed	294	C
Chloramphenicol sodium succinate	PD	1 g	MSD	50 mg		Physically compatible	6	C
Cimetidine HCl	SKF	3 g	MSD	100 mg	D5W	Physically compatible and cimetidine chemically stable for 24 hr at room temperature. Phytonadione not tested	551	C
Netilmicin sulfate	SC	3 g	MSD	100 mg	D5S	Physically compatible and netilmicin chemically stable for 7 days at 4 and 25 °C. Phytonadione not tested	558	C
Ranitidine HCl	GL	50 mg and 2 g		100 mg	D5W	Ranitidine chemically stable by HPLC for only 6 hr at 25 °C. Phytonadione not tested	1515	I
Sodium bicarbonate	AB	2.4 mEq[a]	MSD	10 mg	D5W	Physically compatible for 24 hr	772	C

[a] *One vial of Neut added to a liter of admixture.*

Drugs in Syringe Compatibility

			Phytonadione				
Drug (in syringe)	*Mfr*	*Amt*	*Mfr*	*Amt*	*Remarks*	*Ref*	*C/I*
Doxapram HCl	RB	400 mg/20 ml		10 mg/1 ml	Physically compatible with no doxapram loss in 24 hr	1177	C

Y-Site Injection Compatibility (1:1 Mixture)

			Phytonadione				
Drug	*Mfr*	*Conc*	*Mfr*	*Conc*	*Remarks*	*Ref*	*C/I*
Ampicillin sodium	WY	40 mg/ml[b]	MSD	0.4 mg/ml[c]	Physically compatible for 3 hr	1316	C
Dobutamine HCl	LI	4 mg/ml[c]	MSD	0.4 mg/ml[c]	Slight haze in 3 hr	1316	I
Epinephrine HCl	ES	0.032 mg/ml[c]	MSD	0.4 mg/ml[c]	Physically compatible for 3 hr	1316	C
Famotidine	MSD	0.2 mg/ml[a]	MSD	2 mg/ml	Physically compatible for 14 hr	1196	C
Heparin sodium	UP	1000 units/L[d]	RC	10 mg/ml	Physically compatible for at least 4 hr at room temperature by visual and microscopic examination	534	C
Hydrocortisone sodium succinate	UP	10 mg/L[d]	RC	10 mg/ml	Physically compatible for at least 4 hr at room temperature by visual and microscopic examination	534	C
Potassium chloride	AB	40 mEq/L[d]	RC	10 mg/ml	Physically compatible for at least 4 hr at room temperature by visual and microscopic examination	534	C
Tolazoline HCl		0.1 mg/ml[a]	MSD	2 mg/ml	Physically compatible for 24 hr at 22 °C	1363	C

Y-Site Injection Compatibility (1:1 Mixture) (Cont.)

			Phytonadione				
Drug	*Mfr*	*Conc*	*Mfr*	*Conc*	*Remarks*	*Ref*	*C/I*
Vitamin B complex with C	RC	2 ml/L[d]	RC	10 mg/ml	Physically compatible for at least 4 hr at room temperature by visual and microscopic examination	534	C

[a]*Tested in dextrose 5% in water.*
[b]*Tested in sodium chloride 0.9%*
[c]*Tested in both dextrose 5% in water and sodium chloride 0.9%.*
[d]*Tested in dextrose 5% in Ringer's injection, dextrose 5% in Ringer's injection, lactated, dextrose 5% in water, Ringer's injection, lactated, and sodium chloride 0.9%.*

Additional Compatibility Information

Infusion Solutions — If intravenous infusion is necessary, preservative-free solutions only should be used; dextrose 5% in water, sodium chloride 0.9%, and dextrose 5% in sodium chloride 0.9% have been recommended as diluents. Other diluents are not recommended by the manufacturer. (2)

The stability of phytonadione was evaluated in a TPN solution containing amino acids 2%, dextrose 12.5%, "standard" electrolytes, and multivitamins (M.V.I. Pediatric) by HPLC analysis over 24 hours while exposed to light. Vitamin losses were about 7 and 27% in four and 24 hours, respectively. Some loss was attributed to the light sensitivity of phytonadione. (1815)

Billion-Rey et al. reported substantial loss by HPLC analysis of retinol all-*trans* palmitate and phytonadione from both TPN and TNA admixtures due to exposure to sunlight. In three hours of exposure to sunlight, essentially total loss of retinol and 50% loss of phytonadione had occurred. The presence or absence of lipids did not affect stability. In contrast, tocopherol concentrations remained essentially unchanged by exposure to sunlight through 12 hours. The container material used to store the nutrition admixtures affected the concentration of the vitamins as well. Losses were greatest (10 to 25%) in PVC containers and were slightly better in EVA and glass containers. (2049)

See Light Effects above.

Oxytocin — Phytonadione (Abbott) 50 mg/L has been reported to be conditionally compatible with oxytocin (Parke-Davis) 5 USP units/L. The mixture is physically compatible in most Abbott infusion solutions except dextran 12%, in which a haze or precipitate forms within one hour. (3)

Phenytoin Sodium — Phytonadione (MSD) has been reported to be incompatible with phenytoin sodium (Parke-Davis) in concentrated solutions. Phenytoin sodium was constituted according to the manufacturer's directions, and 1 ml was added to a solution of 5 ml of sterile distilled water along with 1 ml of phytonadione. Particulate matter was noted within two hours. (28)

PIPERACILLIN SODIUM
AHFS 8:12.16

Products — Piperacillin sodium is available in 2-, 3-, and 4-g vials and infusion bottles and 40-g bulk packages. (2)

For intramuscular use, reconstitute the appropriate vial with sterile water for injection, sodium chloride 0.9%, bacteriostatic sterile water for injection or bacteriostatic sodium chloride 0.9% (preserved with parabens or benzyl alcohol), dextrose 5% in sodium chloride 0.9%, dextrose 5% in water, or lidocaine HCl 0.5 to 1% (without epinephrine) and shake well until dissolved. Reconstitute the 2-, 3-, and 4-g vials with 4, 6, and 8 ml of diluent, respectively, to yield solutions containing 1 g/2.5 ml. (2; 4)

For intravenous use, each gram of piperacillin sodium should be reconstituted with at least 5 ml of sterile water for injection, sodium chloride 0.9%, bacteriostatic sterile water for injection, bacteriostatic sodium chloride 0.9% (preserved with parabens or benzyl alcohol), dextrose 5% in water, or dextrose 5% in sodium chloride 0.9%. Shake well until dissolved. This solution may be administered by direct intravenous injection, or it may be further diluted with at least 50 ml of compatible infusion solution for intermittent intravenous infusion. (2; 4)

The 40-g bulk pharmacy package is reconstituted with 172 ml of a compatible diluent (except lidocaine HCl) to provide a 200-mg/ml concentration. (2; 4)

pH — The pH of the reconstituted solution is 5.5 to 7.5. (2)

Osmolality — The osmolality of piperacillin sodium (Lederle) 45 mg/ml was determined to be 346 mOsm/kg in dextrose 5% in water and 361 mOsm/kg in sodium chloride 0.9%. At 70 mg/ml, the osmolality was determined to be 389 mOsm/kg in dextrose 5% in water and 399 mOsm/kg in sodium chloride 0.9%. (1375)

The osmolality of piperacillin sodium was calculated for the following dilutions (1054):

Diluent	Osmolality (mOsm/kg) 50 ml	100 ml
3 g		
Dextrose 5% in water	425	348
Sodium chloride 0.9%	452	375
4 g		
Dextrose 5% in water	475	377
Sodium chloride 0.9%	502	404

Robinson et al. recommended the following maximum piperacillin sodium concentrations to achieve osmolalities suitable for peripheral infusion in fluid-restricted patients (1180):

Diluent	Maximum Concentration (mg/ml)	Osmolality (mOsm/kg)
Dextrose 5% in water	91	536
Sodium chloride 0.9%	81	515
Sterile water for injection	163	439

Sodium Content—Each gram of piperacillin sodium contains 1.85 mEq (42.5 mg) of sodium. (2)

Trade Name(s)—Pipracil.

Administration—Piperacillin sodium may be administered by direct intravenous injection slowly over three to five minutes, by intermittent intravenous infusion diluted in at least 50 ml of compatible diluent and given over about 20 to 30 minutes, or by intramuscular injection, preferably into the upper outer quadrant of the buttock. No more than 2 g should be administered intramuscularly at any one site. (2; 4)

Stability—Piperacillin sodium is a white to off-white powder which may be stored at controlled room temperature. (2) Storage of the powder for two months at 56 °C and for four months at 2 °C resulted in retention of at least 95% potency. Exposure of the powder to sunlight for one month resulted in a slight darkening of the powder but no loss of potency. (740)

Reconstitution yields a colorless to pale yellow solution which is chemically stable and remains clear for at least 24 hours at room temperature, one week under refrigeration, and one month if frozen. (Pharmacy bulk packages should not be frozen, and ADD-Vantage vials should not be refrigerated or frozen.) Slight darkening of the solution does not indicate a potency loss. Shorter storage periods of 24 hours at room temperature and 48 hours under refrigeration may be appropriate when aseptic technique and sterility considerations indicate. (2; 4) In solution the drug is stable over a pH range of 4.5 to 8.5. (740)

Dilution of the piggyback infusion bottles to a 12% (6 g/50 ml) concentration with the following infusion diluents also results in solutions that are chemically stable for at least 24 hours at room temperature, one week under refrigeration, and one month if frozen (740):

Dextran 6% in sodium chloride 0.9%
Dextrose 5% in sodium chloride 0.9%
Dextrose 5% in water
Ringer's injection, lactated
Sodium chloride 0.9%

Piperacillin sodium in a concentration of 0.2% in various admixture solutions has been shown to be stable in both glass and PVC containers for 24 hours at room temperature, 48 hours under refrigeration, and one month if frozen. (740)

Das Gupta et al. evaluated the stability of piperacillin sodium (Lederle) 10 g/L in dextrose 5% in water and sodium chloride 0.9% when frozen at −10 °C. After 71 days of storage, the solutions were thawed by warming under tap water and by microwave exposure for four minutes. No loss of potency was noted with either thawing technique. (1126)

Piperacillin sodium (Lederle) 41.5 mg/ml in dextrose 5% in water was visually compatible and showed no potency loss by HPLC after frozen storage (−20 °C) for 30 days followed by seven days of refrigeration at 4 °C. (1539)

Syringes—Piperacillin sodium reconstituted to a 40% (2 g/50 ml) concentration with sterile water for injection retains chemical stability for at least 32 days when frozen in both glass (Glaspak) and plastic (Plastipak) syringes. (740)

Borst et al. reported that piperacillin sodium (Lederle) 2 and 3 g/10 ml in sterile water for injection, packaged in plastic syringes (Monoject), exhibited a 10% piperacillin loss in two days at 24 °C and 10 days at 4 °C as determined by HPLC. Frozen at −15 °C, the drug exhibited less than a 10% loss during the three-month study period. (1178)

Piperacillin sodium (Lederle) 40 mg/ml in sodium chloride 0.9% was packaged in 10-ml polypropylene syringes (Becton-Dickinson) and stored at 5 and 25 °C. The drug solutions remained clear, and HPLC analysis found about 9% loss in five days and 13% loss in nine days at 25 °C. Less than 2% loss was found after 28 days at 5 °C. The losses were comparable to the drug solution stored in a glass flask, indicating sorption to syringe components did not occur. (2345)

Elastomeric Reservoir Pumps—Piperacillin sodium (Lederle) 30 mg/ml in dextrose 5% in water and sodium chloride 0.9% 100 ml was packaged in latex elastomeric reservoirs (Secure Medical). Little or no loss by HPLC analysis occurred in 24 hours at 25 °C, 4% or less loss occurred in seven days at 5 °C, and 7% or less loss occurred in 12 weeks frozen at −20 °C. (1970)

Piperacillin sodium (Lederle) 16 mg/ml in both dextrose 5% in water and sodium chloride 0.9% was evaluated for binding potential to natural rubber elastomeric reservoirs (Baxter). No binding was found after storage for two weeks at 35 °C with gentle agitation. (2014)

Piperacillin sodium solutions in elastomeric reservoir pumps have been stated by the pump manufacturers to be stable for the following time periods frozen, refrigerated (REF), or at room temperature (RT) (31):

Pump Reservoir(s)	Conc.	Frozen	REF	RT
Homepump; Homepump Eclipse	10 to 80 mg/ml[b]	30 days	14 days	24 hr
Intermate	10 to 80 mg/ml[a,b]	30 days	14 days	24 hr
Intermate HPC	10 to 80 mg/ml[a]		14 days	24 hr
Medflo	>30 to 40 mg/ml[a,b]	4 weeks	14 days	48 hr
ReadyMed	2 mg/ml[a,b]	4 weeks	48 hr	24 hr
	120 mg/ml[a,b]	4 weeks	7 days	24 hr

[a] *In dextrose 5% in water.*
[b] *In sodium chloride 0.9%.*

Sorption — Picard et al. reported little or no loss due to sorption of piperacillin sodium (Lederle) 4 g/100 ml in dextrose 5% in water and sodium chloride 0.9% in trilayer solution bags (Bieffe Medital) composed of polyethylene, polyamide, and polypropylene. The admixtures were evaluated by HPLC analysis up to two hours after preparation. Similarly, no loss was found during one-hour simulated infusion. (1918)

Filtration — Piggyback infusions at a 4% (2 g/50 ml) concentration in dextrose 5% in sodium chloride 0.9%, Ringer's injection, lactated, and sodium chloride 0.9% exhibited no changes in potency or pH when passed through an intravenous administration set with a 0.45-μm inline final filter (Abbott). (740)

Central Venous Catheter — Piperacillin sodium (Lederle) 10 mg/ml in dextrose 5% in water was found to be compatible with the ARROWg+ard Blue Plus (Arrow International) chlorhexidine-bearing triple-lumen central catheter. HPLC analysis was used to evaluate completeness of drug delivery through the catheter and the amount of chlorhexidine removed from the internal lumens. Essentially complete delivery of the drug was found with little or no drug loss occurring. Furthermore, chlorhexidine delivered from the catheter remained at trace amounts with no substantial increase due to the delivery of the drug through the catheter. (2335)

Compatibility Information

Solution Compatibility

Piperacillin sodium

Solution	*Mfr*	*Mfr*	*Conc/L*	*Remarks*	*Ref*	*C/I*
Dextran 6% in sodium chloride 0.9%		LE	120 g[a]	Physically compatible and chemically stable for 24 hr at room temperature and 1 week under refrigeration	740	C
Dextrose 5% in sodium chloride 0.9%		LE	120 g[a]	Physically compatible and chemically stable for 24 hr at room temperature and 1 week under refrigeration	740	C
Dextrose 5% in water		LE	120 g[a]	Physically compatible and chemically stable for 24 hr at room temperature and 1 week under refrigeration	740	C
	TR[b]	LE	2 g	Physically compatible and chemically stable for 24 hr at room temperature and 48 hr under refrigeration	740	C
	MG[c]	LE	40 g	Physically compatible and less than 2% drug loss in 48 hr at 25 °C under fluorescent light	1026	C
	TR[b]	LE	10 g	Physically compatible with 4% loss in 48 hr and 9% in 5 days at 25 °C. 3% loss in 28 days and 8% in 49 days at 5 °C. No loss in 71 days at −10 °C	1126	C
	MG[d]	LE	41.5 g	Visually compatible with no piperacillin loss by HPLC after 30 days at −20 °C followed by 7 days at 4 °C	1539	C
	[b]	LE	80 g	No drug loss by HPLC during 2-hr storage and 1-hr simulated infusion	1774	C
	AB[e]	LE	30 g	7% or less drug loss by HPLC in 24 hr at 25 °C and in 7 days at 5 °C	1970	C
Ringer's injection, lactated		LE	120 g[a]	Physically compatible and chemically stable for 24 hr at room temperature and 1 week under refrigeration	740	C
	TR[b]	LE	2 g	Physically compatible and chemically stable for 24 hr at room temperature and 48 hr under refrigeration	740	C
Sodium chloride 0.9%		LE	120 g[a]	Physically compatible and chemically stable for 24 hr at room temperature and 1 week under refrigeration	740	C
	TR[b]	LE	2 g	Physically compatible and chemically stable for 24 hr at room temperature and 48 hr under refrigeration	740	C
	MG[c]	LE	40 g	Physically compatible and less than 2% drug loss in 48 hr at 25 °C under fluorescent light	1026	C

Solution Compatibility (Cont.)

Piperacillin sodium

Solution	Mfr	Mfr	Conc/L	Remarks	Ref	C/I
	TR[b]	LE	10 g	Physically compatible with 3.5% loss in 48 hr and 8% in 5 days at 25 °C. 2% loss in 28 days and 6% in 49 days at 5 °C. No loss in 71 days at −10 °C	1126	C
	[b]	LE	80 g	No drug loss by HPLC during 2-hr storage and 1-hr simulated infusion	1774	C
	AB[e]	LE	30 g	Little or no drug loss by HPLC in 24 hr at 25 °C and in 7 days at 5 °C	1970	C
TPN #107[f]			2 g	43% piperacillin loss in 24 hr at 21 °C by microbiological assay	1326	I

[a]*The piggyback concentration of 12% (6 g/50 ml).*
[b]*Tested in PVC containers.*
[c]*Tested in glass containers.*
[d]*Tested in polyolefin containers.*
[e]*Tested in glass containers and latex elastomeric reservoirs (Secure Medical).*
[f]*Refer to Appendix I for the composition of parenteral nutrition solutions. TPN indicates a 2-in-1 admixture.*

Additive Compatibility

Piperacillin sodium

Drug	Mfr	Conc/L	Mfr	Conc/L	Test Soln	Remarks	Ref	C/I
Ciprofloxacin	MI	2 g		40 g	D5W	Physically incompatible	888	I
	MI	1 g	LE	40 g	D5W, NS	Physically compatible for 24 hr at 22 °C	1189	C
Clindamycin phosphate	UP	9 g	LE	40 g	D5W, NS	Physically compatible with 2% clindamycin loss and 3 to 5% piperacillin loss in 48 hr at 25 °C under fluorescent light	1026	C
Flucloxacillin sodium	BE	50 g	LE	120 g	W	10% piperacillin loss and 6% flucloxacillin loss by HPLC in 12 days at 5 °C. 3% piperacillin loss and 6% flucloxacillin loss by HPLC in 1 day at 30 °C	1748	C
Fluconazole	PF	1 g	LE	40 g	D5W	Visually compatible with no fluconazole loss by HPLC in 72 hr at 25 °C under fluorescent light. Piperacillin not tested	1677	C
Hydrocortisone sodium succinate	UP	40 mg	LE	40 g	D5S[a]	Physically compatible and piperacillin chemically stable for 24 hr at room temperature and 1 week under refrigeration. Hydrocortisone not tested	740	C
Linezolid	PHU	2 g	LE	30 g	[c]	Physically compatible with little or no loss of either drug by HPLC in 7 days at 4 °C protected from light. At 23 °C, about 5% piperacillin loss in 3 days and 9 to 12% loss in 5 days.	2263	C
Ofloxacin	HO	1.67 g	LE	16.7 g	W	Visually compatible with little or no loss of either drug by HPLC in 48 hr	1613	C
Potassium chloride		40 mEq	LE	2 g	D5S, D5W, LR, R, NS	Physically compatible and piperacillin chemically stable for 24 hr at room temperature and 48 hr under refrigeration	740	C
Verapamil HCl	SE	[b]	LE	40 g	D5W, NS	Physically compatible for 24 hr at 21 °C	1166	C

[a]*Tested in PVC containers.*
[b]*Final concentration unspecified.*
[c]*Admixed in the linezolid infusion container.*

Drugs in Syringe Compatibility

Drug (in syringe)	Mfr	Amt	Piperacillin sodium Mfr	Piperacillin sodium Amt	Remarks	Ref	C/I
Heparin sodium		2500 units/ 1 ml	LE	2 g	Physically compatible for at least 5 min	1053	C

Y-Site Injection Compatibility (1:1 Mixture)

Drug	Mfr	Conc	Piperacillin sodium Mfr	Piperacillin sodium Conc	Remarks	Ref	C/I
Acyclovir sodium	BW	5 mg/ml[a]	LE	60 mg/ml[a]	Physically compatible for 4 hr at 25 °C	1157	C
Allopurinol sodium	BW	3 mg/ml[b]	LE	40 mg/ml[b]	Physically compatible with no change in measured turbidity or increase in particle content in 4 hr at 22 °C	1686	C
Amifostine	USB	10 mg/ml[a]	LE	40 mg/ml[a]	Physically compatible with no change in measured turbidity or increase in particle content in 4 hr at 23 °C	1845	C
Amphotericin B cholesteryl sulfate complex	SEQ	0.83 mg/ml[a]	LE	40 mg/ml[a]	Microprecipitate forms in 4 hr at 23 °C under fluorescent light	2117	I
Aztreonam	SQ	40 mg/ml[a]	LE	40 mg/ml[a]	Physically compatible with no subvisual haze or particle formation in 4 hr at 23 °C	1758	C
Ciprofloxacin	MI	1 mg/ml[a]	LE	40 mg/ml[c]	Physically compatible for 24 hr at 22 °C	1189	C
Cisatracurium besylate	GW	0.1 mg/ml[a]	LE	40 mg/ml[a]	Physically compatible with no change in measured turbidity or increase in particle content in 4 hr at 23 °C	2074	C
	GW	2 mg/ml[a]	LE	40 mg/ml[a]	Subvisual haze forms immediately	2074	I
	GW	5 mg/ml[a]	LE	40 mg/ml[a]	Haze forms immediately	2074	I
Cyclophosphamide	MJ	20 mg/ml[a]	LE	60 mg/ml[a]	Physically compatible for 4 hr at 25 °C	1194	C
Diltiazem HCl	MMD	1[b] and 5 mg/ml	LE	200 mg/ml[b]	Visually compatible	1807	C
	MMD	5 mg/ml	LE	20 mg/ml[b]	Visually compatible	1807	C
Docetaxel	RPR	0.9 mg/ml[a]	LE	40 mg/ml[a]	Physically compatible with no change in measured turbidity or increase in particle content in 4 hr at 23 °C	2224	C
Doxorubicin HCl liposome injection	SEQ	0.4 mg/ml[a]	LE	40 mg/ml[a]	Physically compatible with little or no change in measured turbidity and no increase in particle content in 4 hr at 23 °C	2087	C
Enalaprilat	MSD	0.05 mg/ml[b]	LE	12 mg/ml[a]	Physically compatible for 24 hr at room temperature under fluorescent light	1355	C
Esmolol HCl	DCC	10 mg/ml[a]	LE	30 mg/ml[a]	Physically compatible for 24 hr at 22 °C	1169	C
Etoposide phosphate	BR	5 mg/ml[a]	LE	40 mg/ml[a]	Physically compatible with no change in measured turbidity or increase in particle content in 4 hr at 23 °C	2218	C
Famotidine	MSD	0.2 mg/ml[a]	LE	40 mg/ml[b]	Physically compatible for 14 hr	1196	C
	ME	2 mg/ml[b]		40 mg/ml[a]	Visually compatible for 4 hr at 22 °C	1936	C
Filgrastim	AMG	30 μg/ml[a]	LE	40 mg/ml[a]	Particles and filaments form immediately	1687	I
Fluconazole	RR	2 mg/ml	LE	80 mg/ml	Viscous gel-like substance forms	1407	I

Y-Site Injection Compatibility (1:1 Mixture) (Cont.)

			Piperacillin sodium				
Drug	*Mfr*	*Conc*	*Mfr*	*Conc*	*Remarks*	*Ref*	*C/I*
Fludarabine phosphate	BX	1 mg/ml[a]	LE	40 mg/ml[a]	Physically compatible for 4 hr at room temperature under fluorescent light	1439	C
Foscarnet sodium	AST	24 mg/ml	LE	80 mg/ml	Physically compatible for 24 hr at room temperature under fluorescent light	1335	C
Gatifloxacin	BMS	2 mg/ml[a]	LE	40 mg/ml[a]	Haze increases immediately becoming a microprecipitate in 4 hours	2234	I
Gemcitabine HCl	LI	10 mg/ml[b]	LE	40 mg/ml[b]	Cloudiness forms immediately, becoming precipitated clumps in 4 hr	2226	I
Granisetron HCl	SKB	0.05 mg/ml[a]	LE	40 mg/ml[a]	Physically compatible with no change in measured turbidity or increase in particle content in 4 hr at 23 °C	2000	C
Heparin sodium	TR	50 units/ml	LE	60 mg/ml[a]	Visually compatible for 4 hr at 25 °C	1793	C
Hetastarch in lactated electrolyte injection (Hextend)	AB	6%	LE	40 mg/ml[a]	Physically compatible with no change in measured turbidity or increase in particle content in 4 hr at 23 °C	2339	C
Hydromorphone HCl	WY	0.2 mg/ml[a]	LE	60 mg/ml[a]	Physically compatible for at least 4 hr at 25 °C under fluorescent light	987	C
IL-2	RC	4800 I.U./ml[b]	LE	200 mg/ml	Visually compatible and IL-2 activity by bioassay retained. Piperacillin not tested	1552	C
Labetalol HCl	SC	1 mg/ml[a]	LE	10 mg/ml[a]	Physically compatible for 24 hr at 18 °C	1171	C
Linezolid	PHU	2 mg/ml	LE	40 mg/ml[a]	Physically compatible with no change in measured turbidity or increase in particle content in 4 hr at 23 °C	2264	C
Lorazepam	WY	0.33 mg/ml[b]	LE	150 mg/ml	Visually compatible for 24 hr at 22 °C	1855	C
Magnesium sulfate	IX	16.7, 33.3, 66.7, 100 mg/ml[a]	LE	60 mg/ml[a]	Physically compatible for at least 4 hr at 32 °C	813	C
Melphalan HCl	BW	0.1 mg/ml[b]	LE	40 mg/ml[b]	Physically compatible with no change in measured turbidity or increase in particle content in 3 hr at 22 °C	1557	C
Meperidine HCl	WY	10 mg/ml[a]	LE	60 mg/ml[a]	Physically compatible for at least 4 hr at 25 °C under fluorescent light	987	C
Midazolam HCl	RC	5 mg/ml	LE	150 mg/ml	Visually compatible for 24 hr at 22 °C	1855	C
Morphine sulfate	WI	1 mg/ml[a]	LE	60 mg/ml[a]	Physically compatible for at least 4 hr at 25 °C under fluorescent light	987	C
Ondansetron HCl	GL	1 mg/ml[b]	LE	40 mg/ml[a]	Slight turbidity appears in 30 min	1365	I
Perphenazine	SC	0.02 mg/ml[a]	LE	60 mg/ml[a]	Physically compatible for 4 hr at 25 °C	1155	C
Propofol	ZEN	10 mg/ml	LE	40 mg/ml[a]	Physically compatible for 1 hr at 23 °C with no increase in particle content	2066	C
Ranitidine HCl	GL	1 mg/ml[b]	LE	30 mg/ml[a]	Little or no loss of either drug by HPLC in 4 hr at 22 °C under fluorescent light	1632	C
Remifentanil HCl	GW	0.025 and 0.25 mg/ml[b]	LE	40 mg/ml[a]	Physically compatible with no change in measured turbidity or increase in particle content in 4 hr at 23 °C	2075	C
Sargramostim	IMM	10 μg/ml[b]	LE	40 mg/ml[b]	Small amount of particles form in 4 hr	1436	I

Y-Site Injection Compatibility (1:1 Mixture) (Cont.)

			Piperacillin sodium				
Drug	*Mfr*	*Conc*	*Mfr*	*Conc*	*Remarks*	*Ref*	*C/I*
Tacrolimus	FUJ	1 mg/ml[b]	LE	80 mg/ml[a]	Visually compatible for 24 hr at 25 °C	1630	C
Teniposide	BR	0.1 mg/ml[a]	LE	40 mg/ml[a]	Physically compatible with no subvisual haze or particle formation in 4 hr at 23 °C	1725	C
Theophylline	TR	4 mg/ml	LE	60 mg/ml[a]	Visually compatible for 6 hr at 25 °C	1793	C
Thiotepa	IMM[d]	1 mg/ml[a]	LE	40 mg/ml[a]	Physically compatible with no change in measured turbidity or increase in particle content in 4 hr at 23 °C	1861	C
TNA #218 to #226[e]			LE	40 mg/ml[a]	Visually compatible with no precipitate or emulsion damage apparent in 4 hr at 23 °C	2215	C
TPN #54[e]				133 and 200 mg/ml	Physically compatible and 90 to 100% piperacillin activity retained over 6 hr at 22 °C by microbiological assay	1045	C
TPN #61[e]		[f]	LE	250 mg/ 1.25 ml[g]	Physically compatible	1012	C
		[h]	LE	1.5 g/7.5 ml[g]	Physically compatible	1012	C
TPN #212 to #215[e]			LE	40 mg/ml[a]	Physically compatible with no change in measured turbidity or increase in particle content in 4 hr at 23 °C	2109	C
Vancomycin HCl	AB	20 mg/ml[a]	LE	200 mg/ml[i]	Transient precipitate forms, followed by clear solution	2189	?
	AB	20 mg/ml[a]	LE	10 and 50 mg/ml[a]	Gross white precipitate forms immediately	2189	I
	AB	20 mg/ml[a]	LE	1 mg/ml[a]	Physically compatible with no change in measured turbidity or increase in particle content in 4 hr at 23 °C	2189	C
	AB	2 mg/ml[a]	LE	1[a], 10[a], 50[a], 200[i] mg/ml	Physically compatible with no change in measured turbidity or increase in particle content in 4 hr at 23 °C	2189	C
Verapamil HCl	SE	2.5 mg/ml	LE	40 mg/ml[c]	Physically compatible for 15 min at 21 °C under fluorescent light	1166	C
Vinorelbine tartrate	BW	1 mg/ml[b]	LE	40 mg/ml[b]	Heavy white turbidity forms immediately, becoming white flocculent precipitate in 4 hr at 22 °C	1558	I
Zidovudine	BW	4 mg/ml[a]	LE	4 mg/ml[a]	Physically compatible for 4 hr at 25 °C under fluorescent light by visual and microscopic examination	1193	C

[a] *Tested in dextrose 5% in water.*
[b] *Tested in sodium chloride 0.9%.*
[c] *Tested in both dextrose 5% in water and sodium chloride 0.9%.*
[d] *Lyophilized formulation tested.*
[e] *Refer to Appendix I for the composition of parenteral nutrition solutions. TNA indicates a 3-in-1 admixture, and TPN indicates a 2-in-1 admixture.*
[f] *Run at 21 ml/hr.*
[g] *Given over five minutes by syringe pump.*
[h] *Run at 94 ml/hr.*
[i] *Tested in sterile water for injection.*

Additional Compatibility Information

Peritoneal Dialysis Solutions — The stability of piperacillin sodium (Lederle) 200 mg/L in peritoneal dialysis solutions (Dianeal 137 and PD2) with heparin sodium 500 units/L was evaluated at 25 °C by microbiological assay. Approximately 94 ± 11% activity remained after 24 hours. (1228)

Aminoglycosides — Although piperacillin sodium and aminoglycosides act synergistically and have been used successfully clinically when recommended doses of each drug were administered, mixing piperacillin sodium directly in a syringe or infusion bottle with an aminoglycoside can result in substantial inactivation of the aminoglycoside. (740)

Using bioassay and radioimmunoassay, Hale et al. evaluated piperacillin and carbenicillin at concentrations of 62.5 to 1000 μg/ml in human serum in combination with amikacin, gentamicin, or tobramycin 10 μg/ml at 37 °C for up to 24 hours. Penicillin concentrations of 62.5 and 125 μg/ml had relatively little effect on the aminoglycoside concentration, even after 24 hours. However, increasing the penicillin concentration to 250 or 500 μg/ml greatly increased decomposition. After 24 hours with carbenicillin 500 μg/ml, the amounts of aminoglycosides remaining were: amikacin, 82%; gentamicin, 43%; and tobramycin, 27%. After 24 hours with piperacillin 500 μg/ml, the remaining concentrations were 95, 45, and 52%, respectively. Even greater inactivation occurred at 1000 μg/ml of the penicillins, including the essentially complete loss of tobramycin in 24 hours. The authors concluded that amikacin is much more resistant to inactivation than the other aminoglycosides tested and that carbenicillin is more aggressive in its inactivation than piperacillin. (816)

Pickering and Rutherford evaluated several aminoglycosides combined with a number of penicillins. Gentamicin sulfate, netilmicin sulfate, and tobramycin sulfate 5 and 10 μg/ml and amikacin 10 and 20 μg/ml were combined in human serum with 125, 250, and 500 μg/ml of azlocillin, carbenicillin disodium, amdinocillin, mezlocillin, and piperacillin individually. Tobramycin and gentamicin sustained greater losses than netilmicin and amikacin at each of the penicillin concentrations. Significant decomposition of all aminoglycosides occurred in 24 hours at 37 °C at a penicillin concentration of 500 μg/ml. Tobramycin and gentamicin had losses of 40 to 60%, while 15 to 30% losses occurred for netilmicin. Amikacin sustained the least inactivation with losses of about 10 to 20%. At penicillin concentrations of 125 to 250 μg/ml, smaller losses of aminoglycosides were observed. (68)

Rank et al. evaluated the inactivation of tobramycin 6 μg/ml in human serum with the sodium salts of cloxacillin and piperacillin 150 and 300 μg/ml, ampicillin 100 and 200 μg/ml, and penicillin G 75 and 150 I.U./ml at 25 and 37 °C for up to 12 hours. Piperacillin induced the greatest inactivation among the penicillins, with up to a 15% loss in 12 hours at 37 °C in the 300-μg/ml concentration. Cloxacillin and ampicillin had an intermediate effect, causing about a 5% loss in 12 hours at 37 °C in the highest concentrations. Penicillin G did not yield significant tobramycin inactivation. (817)

The inactivation of gentamicin, tobramycin, and amikacin, each 5 μg/ml, by seven β-lactam antibiotics, 250 and 500 μg/ml, in serum at 25 °C over 24 hours was studied using bioassay, enzyme-mediated immunoassay technique (EMIT), fluorescence polarization immunoassay (TDx), and radioimmunoassay. Results with the penicillins varied, depending on the assay technique used. The bioassay was the most sensitive to loss, TDx and radioimmunoassay were intermediate, and EMIT was the least sensitive. Azlocillin, carbenicillin, mezlocillin, and piperacillin all caused variable but extensive inactivation (up to 70%) of gentamicin and tobramycin in 24 hours. Amikacin, however, had only minor losses compared to the other aminoglycosides. (654)

The clinical significance of these interactions in patients appears to be confined primarily to those with renal failure. (218; 334; 361; 364; 616; 816; 847; 952) Literature reports of greatly reduced aminoglycoside levels in such patients have appeared frequently. (363; 365–367; 614; 615; 962) In addition, the interaction may be clinically important if assays for aminoglycoside levels in serum are sufficiently delayed. (576; 618; 735; 814; 824; 832; 847; 1052)

Most authors believe that in vitro mixing of penicillins, such as piperacillin sodium, with aminoglycoside antibiotics should be avoided but that clinical use of the drugs in combination can be of great value. It is generally recommended that the drugs be given separately in such combined therapy. (157; 218; 222; 224; 361; 364; 368–370)

Vancomycin — The compatibility or incompatibility of vancomycin HCl mixed with or administered simultaneously with piperacillin sodium is concentration dependent. (2189) See Y-Site Compatibility above. Vancomycin HCl has a low pH and is variably compatible with drugs having neutral to mildly alkaline pH, including cephalosporins and penicillins. The compatibility may depend on a number of factors, including concentration of each drug, dilution vehicle, actual pH of solutions, and completeness of mixing during administration. Combinations that are compatible when well mixed may result in precipitation if only partially mixed, presumably because of regionally different concentrations and pH values. If attempting to administer vancomycin HCl with piperacillin sodium, take care to ensure that the specific combination and the concentrations are compatible under the exact administration conditions to be used. An inline filter should be used as a final safety measure. (2189)

PIPERACILLIN SODIUM–TAZOBACTAM SODIUM AHFS 8:12.16

Products — Piperacillin sodium–tazobactam sodium is available in vials containing 2.25 g (piperacillin 2 g plus tazobactam 250 mg), 3.375 g (piperacillin 3 g plus tazobactam 375 mg), and 4.5 g (piperacillin 4 g plus tazobactam 500 mg) as sodium salts. The drug is also available in a pharmacy bulk package containing 40.5 g (piperacillin 36 plus tazobactam 4.5) as sodium salts. The products contain no preservatives. The pH may have been adjusted during manufacture with sodium bicarbonate and hydrochloric acid. (2; 4)

Each gram of piperacillin should be reconstituted with at least 5 ml of sterile water for injection, sodium chloride 0.9%, bacteriostatic water for injection (preserved with benzyl alcohol or parabens), bacteriostatic sodium chloride 0.9% (preserved with benzyl alcohol or parabens), or dextrose 5% in water and shaken well until dissolved. The solution should be diluted in at least 50 ml of compatible infusion solution for intermittent infusion. (2)

The pharmacy bulk package is reconstituted with 152 ml of compatible diluent to yield a solution containing 200 mg/ml of piperacillin and 25 mg/ml of tazobactam. The reconstituted pharmacy bulk package solution must be diluted further for use. (4)

Piperacillin sodium–tazobactam sodium (Lederle) is also available as frozen iso-osmotic injections containing piperacillin sodium 40 mg/ml with tazobactam 5 mg/ml and piperacillin sodium 60 mg/ml with tazobactam sodium 7.5 mg/ml. (2; 4)

pH — From 4.5 to 6.8. (4)

Sodium Content — The combination product contains 2.35 mEq (54 mg) of sodium per gram of piperacillin. (2)

Trade Name(s) — Zosyn.

Administration — Piperacillin sodium–tazobactam sodium should be administered by intravenous infusion over at least 30 minutes after dilution to at least 50 ml in a compatible diluent. It can also be infused using ambulatory infusion pumps. (2; 4)

Stability — The white to off-white lyophilized powder in intact vials should be stored at controlled room temperature. (2)

Single-dose vials of the solution should be used immediately after reconstitution. Any remaining portion should be discarded after 24 hours at room temperature or 48 hours under refrigeration at 2 to 8 °C. In ADD-Vantage vials, the product has been found to be stable for 24 hours at room temperature but should not be refrigerated or frozen. (2; 4)

In compatible infusion solutions, the drug is stable for up to 24 hours at room temperature or one week under refrigeration. Glass and plastic (including syringes, intravenous solution bags, and tubing) do not affect stability. (2)

Freezing Solutions — The commercially available frozen injections should be stored at or below −20 °C. The frozen solutions should be thawed at room temperature or under refrigeration but should not be thawed in a warm water bath or by exposure to microwave radiation. Thawed solutions should not be refrozen. After thawing, the solutions are stable for 24 hours at room temperature or 14 days under refrigeration. (4)

Piperacillin sodium–tazobactam sodium (American Cyanamid) 80 + 10 mg/ml in PVC bags of dextrose 5% in water and sodium chloride 0.9% was frozen at −15 °C for 30 days and thawed by microwave radiation for 45 seconds. HPLC analysis showed no loss of either component. (1768)

Piperacillin sodium–tazobactam sodium (American Cyanamid) 150 + 18.75 mg/ml and 200 + 25 mg/ml in dextrose 5% in water and sodium chloride 0.9% was drawn as 20-ml aliquots into polypropylene syringes (Becton-Dickinson). The syringes were frozen at −15 °C for 30 days and then stored at 4 °C for seven days. HPLC analysis showed no loss of either component. (1768)

Syringes — Piperacillin sodium–tazobactam sodium (American Cyanamid) 150 + 18.75 mg/ml and 200 + 25 mg/ml in dextrose 5% in water and sodium chloride 0.9% was drawn as 20-ml aliquots into polypropylene syringes (Becton-Dickinson). The syringes were stored at 25 °C for one day and at 4 °C for seven days. HPLC analysis showed no loss of either drug in the dextrose 5% in water samples. Similarly, no tazobactam loss occurred in the sodium chloride 0.9% solutions. However, piperacillin losses of 7% in one day at 25 °C and 4% in seven days at 4 °C were found in the sodium chloride 0.9% solutions. (1768)

Ambulatory Pumps — The product was shown to be stable for up to 12 hours in an ambulatory infusion pump. Each dose was diluted to 25 or 37.5 ml, and stability was not affected. (2)

Elastomeric Reservoir Pumps — Piperacillin sodium–tazobactam sodium solutions in elastomeric reservoir pumps have been stated by the pump manufacturers to be stable for the following time periods refrigerated (REF) or at room temperature (RT) (31):

Pump Reservoir(s)	Conc.	REF	RT
Homepump; Homepump Eclipse	18 mg/ml[a]		7 days
Intermate	10 to 80 mg/ml[a,b]	7 days	24 hr

[a] *In dextrose 5% in water.*
[b] *In sodium chloride 0.9%.*

Central Venous Catheter — Piperacillin sodium–tazobactam sodium (Lederle) 10 + 1.25 mg/ml in dextrose 5% in water was found to be compatible with the ARROWg+ard Blue Plus (Arrow International) chlorhexidine-bearing triple-lumen central catheter. HPLC analysis was used to evaluate completeness of drug delivery through the catheter and the amount of chlorhexidine removed from the internal lumens. Essentially complete delivery of the drug was found with little or no drug loss occurring. Furthermore, chlorhexidine delivered from the catheter remained at trace amounts with no substantial increase due to the delivery of the drug through the catheter. (2335)

Compatibility Information

Y-Site Injection Compatibility (1:1 Mixture)

Drug	Mfr	Conc	Mfr	Conc	Remarks	Ref	C/I
			Piperacillin sodium–tazobactam sodium				
Acyclovir sodium	BW	7 mg/ml[a]	LE	40 + 5 mg/ml[a]	Particles form in 1 hr	1688	I
Alatrofloxacin mesylate	PF	1.43 mg/ml[a]	LE	40 + 5 mg/ml[e]	White precipitate forms	2235	I
Aminophylline	AB	2.5 mg/ml[a]	LE	40 + 5 mg/ml[a]	Physically compatible with no change in measured turbidity or increase in particle content in 4 hr at 22 °C	1688	C
Amphotericin B	SQ	0.6 mg/ml[a]	LE	40 + 5 mg/ml[a]	Heavy yellow flocculent precipitate forms immediately	1688	I
Amphotericin B cholesteryl sulfate complex	SEQ	0.83 mg/ml[a]	CY	40 + 5 mg/ml[a]	Microprecipitate forms immediately	2117	I
Aztreonam	SQ	40 mg/ml[a]	LE	40 + 5 mg/ml[a]	Physically compatible with no change in measured turbidity or increase in particle content in 4 hr at 22 °C	1688	C
Bleomycin sulfate	BR	1 unit/ml[b]	LE	40 + 5 mg/ml[a]	Physically compatible with no change in measured turbidity or increase in particle content in 4 hr at 22 °C	1688	C
Bumetanide	RC	0.04 mg/ml[a]	LE	40 + 5 mg/ml[a]	Physically compatible with no change in measured turbidity or increase in particle content in 4 hr at 22 °C	1688	C
Buprenorphine HCl	RKC	0.04 mg/ml[a]	LE	40 + 5 mg/ml[a]	Physically compatible with no change in measured turbidity or increase in particle content in 4 hr at 22 °C	1688	C
Butorphanol tartrate	BR	0.04 mg/ml[a]	LE	40 + 5 mg/ml[a]	Physically compatible with no change in measured turbidity or increase in particle content in 4 hr at 22 °C	1688	C
Calcium gluconate	AMR	40 mg/ml[a]	LE	40 + 5 mg/ml[a]	Physically compatible with no change in measured turbidity or increase in particle content in 4 hr at 22 °C	1688	C
Carboplatin	BR	5 mg/ml[a]	LE	40 + 5 mg/ml[a]	Physically compatible with no change in measured turbidity or increase in particle content in 4 hr at 22 °C	1688	C
Carmustine	BR	1.5 mg/ml[a]	LE	40 + 5 mg/ml[a]	Physically compatible with no change in measured turbidity or increase in particle content in 4 hr at 22 °C	1688	C
Cefepime HCl	BMS	20 mg/ml[a]	LE	40 + 5 mg/ml[a]	Physically compatible with no change in measured turbidity or increase in particle content in 4 hr at 22 °C	1689	C
Chlorpromazine HCl	RU	2 mg/ml[a]	LE	40 + 5 mg/ml[a]	Heavy white turbidity forms immediately. White precipitate forms in 4 hr	1688	I
Cimetidine HCl	SKB	12 mg/ml[a]	LE	40 + 5 mg/ml[a]	Physically compatible with no change in measured turbidity or increase in particle content in 4 hr at 22 °C	1688	C
Cisatracurium besylate	GW	0.1 and 2 mg/ml[a]	CY	40 + 5 mg/ml[a]	Physically compatible with no change in measured turbidity or increase in particle content in 4 hr at 23 °C	2074	C
	GW	5 mg/ml[a]	CY	40 + 5 mg/ml[a]	Tiny particles and subvisual haze within 4 hr	2074	I

Y-Site Injection Compatibility (1:1 Mixture) (Cont.)

			Piperacillin sodium–tazobactam sodium				
Drug	*Mfr*	*Conc*	*Mfr*	*Conc*	*Remarks*	*Ref*	*C/I*
Cisplatin	BR	1 mg/ml	LE	40 + 5 mg/ml[a]	Haze and particles form in 1 hr	1688	**I**
Clindamycin phosphate	AB	10 mg/ml[a]	LE	40 + 5 mg/ml[a]	Physically compatible with no change in measured turbidity or increase in particle content in 4 hr at 22 °C	1688	**C**
Cyclophosphamide	MJ	10 mg/ml[a]	LE	40 + 5 mg/ml[a]	Physically compatible with no change in measured turbidity or increase in particle content in 4 hr at 22 °C	1688	**C**
Cytarabine	SCN	50 mg/ml	LE	40 + 5 mg/ml[a]	Physically compatible with no change in measured turbidity or increase in particle content in 4 hr at 22 °C	1688	**C**
Dacarbazine	MI	4 mg/ml[a]	LE	40 + 5 mg/ml[a]	Turbidity and particles form immediately and increase over 4 hr	1688	**I**
Daunorubicin HCl	WY	1 mg/ml[a]	LE	40 + 5 mg/ml[a]	Turbidity increases immediately	1688	**I**
Dexamethasone sodium phosphate	LY	1 mg/ml[a]	LE	40 + 5 mg/ml[a]	Physically compatible with no change in measured turbidity or increase in particle content in 4 hr at 22 °C	1688	**C**
Diphenhydramine HCl	WY	2 mg/ml[a]	LE	40 + 5 mg/ml[a]	Physically compatible with no change in measured turbidity or increase in particle content in 4 hr at 22 °C	1688	**C**
Dobutamine HCl	LI	4 mg/ml[a]	LE	40 + 5 mg/ml[a]	Heavy white turbidity forms immediately	1688	**I**
Docetaxel	RPR	0.9 mg/ml[a]	CY	40 + 5 mg/ml[a]	Physically compatible with no change in measured turbidity or increase in particle content in 4 hr at 23 °C	2224	**C**
Dopamine HCl	AST	3.2 mg/ml[a]	LE	40 + 5 mg/ml[a]	Physically compatible with no change in measured turbidity or increase in particle content in 4 hr at 22 °C	1688	**C**
Doxorubicin HCl	CET	2 mg/ml	LE	40 + 5 mg/ml[a]	Turbidity forms immediately	1688	**I**
Doxorubicin HCl liposome injection	SEQ	0.4 mg/ml[a]	CY	40 + 5 mg/ml[a]	Partial loss of measured natural turbidity	2087	**I**
Doxycycline hyclate	ES	1 mg/ml[a]	LE	40 + 5 mg/ml[a]	Heavy white turbidity forms immediately	1688	**I**
Droperidol	JN	0.4 mg/ml[a]	LE	40 + 5 mg/ml[a]	Heavy white turbidity with white precipitate forms immediately	1688	**I**
Enalaprilat	MSD	0.1 mg/ml[a]	LE	40 + 5 mg/ml[a]	Physically compatible with no change in measured turbidity or increase in particle content in 4 hr at 22 °C	1688	**C**
Etoposide	BR	0.4 mg/ml[a]	LE	40 + 5 mg/ml[a]	Physically compatible with no change in measured turbidity or increase in particle content in 4 hr at 22 °C	1688	**C**
Etoposide phosphate	BR	5 mg/ml[a]	LE	40 + 5 mg/ml[b]	Physically compatible with no change in measured turbidity or increase in particle content in 4 hr at 23 °C	2218	**C**
Famotidine	MSD	2 mg/ml[a]	LE	40 + 5 mg/ml[a]	Particles form immediately	1688	**I**

Y-Site Injection Compatibility (1:1 Mixture) (Cont.)

			Piperacillin sodium–tazobactam sodium				
Drug	*Mfr*	*Conc*	*Mfr*	*Conc*	*Remarks*	*Ref*	*C/I*
Floxuridine	RC	3 mg/ml[a]	LE	40 + 5 mg/ml[a]	Physically compatible with no change in measured turbidity or increase in particle content in 4 hr at 22 °C	1688	C
Fluconazole	RR	2 mg/ml	LE	40 + 5 mg/ml[a]	Physically compatible with no change in measured turbidity or increase in particle content in 4 hr at 22 °C	1688	C
Fludarabine phosphate	BX	1 mg/ml[a]	LE	40 + 5 mg/ml[a]	Physically compatible with no change in measured turbidity or increase in particle content in 4 hr at 22 °C	1688	C
Fluorouracil	LY	16 mg/ml[a]	LE	40 + 5 mg/ml[a]	Physically compatible with no change in measured turbidity or increase in particle content in 4 hr at 22 °C	1688	C
Furosemide	AB	3 mg/ml[a]	LE	40 + 5 mg/ml[a]	Physically compatible with no change in measured turbidity or increase in particle content in 4 hr at 22 °C	1688	C
Ganciclovir sodium	SY	20 mg/ml[a]	LE	40 + 5 mg/ml[a]	Large crystals form in 1 hr and become heavy white precipitate in 4 hr	1688	I
Gatifloxacin	BMS	2 mg/ml[a]	LE	40+5 mg/ml[a]	Haze increases and microprecipitate forms immediately	2234	I
Gemcitabine HCl	LI	10 mg/ml[b]	LE	40 + 5 mg/ml[b]	Cloudiness forms immediately, becoming flocculent precipitate in 1 hr	2226	I
Granisetron HCl	SKB	0.05 mg/ml[a]	CY	40 + 5 mg/ml[a]	Physically compatible with no change in measured turbidity or increase in particle content in 4 hr at 23 °C	2000	C
Haloperidol lactate	MN	0.2 mg/ml[a]	LE	40 + 5 mg/ml[a]	White turbidity and particles form immediately	1688	I
Heparin sodium	ES	100 units/ml[a]	LE	40 + 5 mg/ml[a]	Physically compatible with no change in measured turbidity or increase in particle content in 4 hr at 22 °C	1688	C
Hetastarch in lactated electrolyte injection (Hextend)	AB	6%	LE	40+5 mg/ml[a]	Physically compatible with no change in measured turbidity or increase in particle content in 4 hr at 23 °C	2339	C
Hydrocortisone sodium phosphate	MSD	1 mg/ml[a]	LE	40 + 5 mg/ml[a]	Physically compatible with no change in measured turbidity or increase in particle content in 4 hr at 22 °C	1688	C
Hydrocortisone sodium succinate	UP	1 mg/ml[a]	LE	40 + 5 mg/ml[a]	Physically compatible with no change in measured turbidity or increase in particle content in 4 hr at 22 °C	1688	C
Hydromorphone HCl	ES	0.5 mg/ml[a]	LE	40 + 5 mg/ml[a]	Physically compatible with no change in measured turbidity or increase in particle content in 4 hr at 22 °C	1688	C
Hydroxyzine HCl	WI	4 mg/ml[a]	LE	40 + 5 mg/ml[a]	Haze and particles form immediately	1688	I
Idarubicin HCl	AD	0.5 mg/ml[a]	LE	40 + 5 mg/ml[a]	Immediate increase in haze much larger than from simple dilution alone	1688	I
Ifosfamide	MJ	25 mg/ml[a]	LE	40 + 5 mg/ml[a]	Physically compatible with no change in measured turbidity or increase in particle content in 4 hr at 22 °C	1688	C

Y-Site Injection Compatibility (1:1 Mixture) (Cont.)

			Piperacillin sodium–tazobactam sodium				
Drug	*Mfr*	*Conc*	*Mfr*	*Conc*	*Remarks*	*Ref*	*C/I*
Leucovorin calcium	LE	2 mg/ml[a]	LE	40 + 5 mg/ml[a]	Physically compatible with no change in measured turbidity or increase in particle content in 4 hr at 22 °C	1688	C
Linezolid	PHU	2 mg/ml	LE	40+5 mg/ml[a]	Physically compatible with no change in measured turbidity or increase in particle content in 4 hr at 23 °C	2264	C
Lorazepam	WY	0.1 mg/ml[a]	LE	40 + 5 mg/ml[a]	Physically compatible with no change in measured turbidity or increase in particle content in 4 hr at 22 °C	1688	C
Magnesium sulfate	AST	100 mg/ml	LE	40 + 5 mg/ml[a]	Physically compatible with no change in measured turbidity or increase in particle content in 4 hr at 22 °C	1688	C
Mannitol	BA	15%	LE	40 + 5 mg/ml[a]	Physically compatible with no change in measured turbidity or increase in particle content in 4 hr at 22 °C	1688	C
Meperidine HCl	WY	4 mg/ml[a]	LE	40 + 5 mg/ml[a]	Physically compatible with no change in measured turbidity or increase in particle content in 4 hr at 22 °C	1688	C
Mesna	MJ	10 mg/ml[a]	LE	40 + 5 mg/ml[a]	Physically compatible with no change in measured turbidity or increase in particle content in 4 hr at 22 °C	1688	C
Methotrexate sodium	LE	15 mg/ml[a]	LE	40 + 5 mg/ml[a]	Physically compatible with no change in measured turbidity or increase in particle content in 4 hr at 22 °C	1688	C
Methylprednisolone sodium succinate	AB	5 mg/ml[a]	LE	40 + 5 mg/ml[a]	Physically compatible with no change in measured turbidity or increase in particle content in 4 hr at 22 °C	1688	C
Metoclopramide HCl	RB	5 mg/ml	LE	40 + 5 mg/ml[a]	Physically compatible with no change in measured turbidity or increase in particle content in 4 hr at 22 °C	1688	C
Metronidazole	BA	5 mg/ml	LE	40 + 5 mg/ml[a]	Physically compatible with no change in measured turbidity or increase in particle content in 4 hr at 22 °C	1688	C
Minocycline HCl	LE	1 mg/ml[a]	LE	40 + 5 mg/ml[a]	Particles form immediately, becoming numerous in 4 hr	1688	I
Mitomycin	BR	0.5 mg/ml	LE	40 + 5 mg/ml[a]	Blue color darkens in 4 hr, becoming reddish purple in 24 hr	1688	I
Mitoxantrone HCl	LE	0.5 mg/ml[a]	LE	40 + 5 mg/ml[a]	Haze and particles form immediately. Large particles form in 4 hr	1688	I
Morphine sulfate	WY	1 mg/ml[a]	LE	40 + 5 mg/ml[a]	Physically compatible with no change in measured turbidity or increase in particle content in 4 hr at 22 °C	1688	C
Nalbuphine HCl	DU	10 mg/ml	LE	40 + 5 mg/ml[a]	Heavy white turbidity forms immediately. Particles form in 4 hr	1688	I
Ondansetron HCl	GL	1 mg/ml[a]	LE	40 + 5 mg/ml[a]	Physically compatible with no change in measured turbidity or increase in particle content in 4 hr at 22 °C	1688	C
	GL	0.03, 0.1, 0.3 mg/ml[b]	LE	40 + 5 mg/ml[b]	Visually compatible with no loss of any component by HPLC in 4 hr	1751	C

Y-Site Injection Compatibility (1:1 Mixture) (Cont.)

			Piperacillin sodium–tazobactam sodium				
Drug	*Mfr*	*Conc*	*Mfr*	*Conc*	*Remarks*	*Ref*	*C/I*
	GL	0.03, 0.1, 0.3 mg/ml[b]	LE	80 + 10 mg/ml[b]	Visually compatible with no loss of any component by HPLC in 4 hr	1751	C
Plicamycin	MI	0.01 mg/ml[a]	LE	40 + 5 mg/ml[a]	Physically compatible with no change in measured turbidity or increase in particle content in 4 hr at 22 °C	1688	C
Potassium chloride	AB	0.1 mEq/ml[a]	LE	40 + 5 mg/ml[a]	Physically compatible with no change in measured turbidity or increase in particle content in 4 hr at 22 °C	1688	C
Prochlorperazine edisylate	SCN	0.5 mg/ml[a]	LE	40 + 5 mg/ml[a]	White turbidity forms immediately	1688	I
Promethazine HCl	SCN	2 mg/ml[a]	LE	40 + 5 mg/ml[a]	Heavy white turbidity forms immediately. Particles form in 4 hr	1688	I
Ranitidine HCl	GL	2 mg/ml[a]	LE	40 + 5 mg/ml[a]	Physically compatible with no change in measured turbidity or increase in particle content in 4 hr at 22 °C	1688	C
	GL	0.5 and 2 mg/ml[b]	LE	80 + 10 mg/ml[b]	Visually compatible with little or no loss of any component by HPLC in 4 hr at 23 °C	1759	C
	GL	0.5 and 2 mg/ml[b]	LE	40 + 5 mg/ml[b]	Visually compatible with little or no loss of ranitidine and tazobactam by HPLC in 4 hr at 23 °C. Piperacillin not tested	1759	C
Remifentanil HCl	GW	0.025 and 0.25 mg/ml[b]	CY	40 + 5 mg/ml[a]	Physically compatible with no change in measured turbidity or increase in particle content in 4 hr at 23 °C	2075	C
Sargramostim	HO	10 μg/ml[a]	LE	40 + 5 mg/ml[a]	Physically compatible with no change in measured turbidity or increase in particle content in 4 hr at 22 °C	1688	C
Sodium bicarbonate	AB	1 mEq/ml	LE	40 + 5 mg/ml[a]	Physically compatible with no change in measured turbidity or increase in particle content in 4 hr at 22 °C	1688	C
Streptozocin	UP	40 mg/ml[a]	LE	40 + 5 mg/ml[a]	Particles form in 1 hr	1688	I
Thiotepa	LE	1 mg/ml[a]	LE	40 + 5 mg/ml[a]	Physically compatible with no change in measured turbidity or increase in particle content in 4 hr at 22 °C	1688	C
TNA #218 to #226[c]			LE	40 + 5 mg/ml[a]	Visually compatible with no precipitate or emulsion damage apparent in 4 hr at 23 °C	2215	C
TPN #212 to #215[c]			CY	40 + 5 mg/ml[a]	Physically compatible with no change in measured turbidity or increase in particle content in 4 hr at 23 °C	2109	C
Trimethoprim–sulfamethoxazole	ES	0.8 + 4 mg/ml[a]	LE	40 + 5 mg/ml[a]	Physically compatible with no change in measured turbidity or increase in particle content in 4 hr at 22 °C	1688	C
Vancomycin HCl	AB	10 mg/ml[a]	LE	40 + 5 mg/ml[a]	White turbidity forms immediately. White precipitate forms in 4 hr	1688	I
	AB	20 mg/ml[a]	LE	200 + 25 mg/ml[d]	Transient precipitate forms, followed by clear solution	2189	?

Y-Site Injection Compatibility (1:1 Mixture) (Cont.)

			Piperacillin sodium–tazobactam sodium				
Drug	*Mfr*	*Conc*	*Mfr*	*Conc*	*Remarks*	*Ref*	*C/I*
	AB	20 mg/ml[a]	LE	50 + 6.25 and 10 + 1.25 mg/ml[a]	Gross white precipitate forms immediately	2189	I
	AB	20 mg/ml[a]	LE	1 + 0.125 mg/ml[a]	Physically compatible with no change in measured turbidity or increase in particle content in 4 hr at 23 °C	2189	C
	AB	2 mg/ml[a]	LE	1 + 0.125[a], 10 + 1.25[a], 50 + 6.25[a], and 200 + 25[d] mg/ml	Physically compatible with no change in measured turbidity or increase in particle content in 4 hr at 23 °C	2189	C
Vinblastine sulfate	LI	0.12 mg/ml[a]	LE	40 + 5 mg/ml[a]	Physically compatible with no change in measured turbidity or increase in particle content in 4 hr at 22 °C	1688	C
Vincristine sulfate	LI	0.05 mg/ml[a]	LE	40 + 5 mg/ml[a]	Physically compatible with no change in measured turbidity or increase in particle content in 4 hr at 22 °C	1688	C
Zidovudine	BW	4 mg/ml[a]	LE	40 + 5 mg/ml[a]	Physically compatible with no change in measured turbidity or increase in particle content in 4 hr at 22 °C	1688	C

[a]*Tested in dextrose 5% in water.*
[b]*Tested in sodium chloride 0.9%.*
[c]*Refer to Appendix I for the composition of parenteral nutrition solutions. TNA indicates a 3-in-1 admixture, and TPN indicates a 2-in-1 admixture.*
[d]*Tested in sterile water for injection.*
[e]*Tested in sodium chloride 0.45%.*

Additional Compatibility Information

Also see Piperacillin Sodium monograph.

Infusion Solutions — The manufacturer states that the following intravenous solutions are compatible with piperacillin sodium–tazobactam sodium (2):

Bacteriostatic sodium chloride 0.9% (benzyl alcohol or parabens)
Bacteriostatic water for injection (benzyl alcohol or parabens)
Dextran 6% in sodium chloride 0.9%
Dextrose 5% in water
Sodium chloride 0.9%
Sterile water for injection

The manufacturer also states that piperacillin sodium–tazobactam sodium is incompatible with Ringer's injection, lactated. (2)

Peritoneal Dialysis Solutions — The physical and chemical stability of piperacillin sodium–tazobactam sodium (Lederle) at concentrations of 200 and 25 μg/ml, respectively, were evaluated in Dianeal PD-2 with dextrose 1.5% and Dianeal PD-2 with dextrose 4.25% (Baxter). Samples were stored at 4 °C for 14 days, 23 °C for seven days, and 37 °C for one day. The samples were physically and chemically stable. Little or no loss of either component occurred in the 4 °C samples throughout the 14-day period. At 23 °C, losses of each component were in the range of 3 to 6% in seven days. The one-day losses at 37 °C were similarly small. (2018)

Aminoglycosides — Aminoglycosides should not be combined with piperacillin sodium–tazobactam sodium because substantial aminoglycoside inactivation may occur. Concomitant therapy should be performed with separate administration. (2)

Potassium Chloride — Potassium chloride injection is stated to be compatible with piperacillin sodium–tazobactam sodium. (2)

Vancomycin — The compatibility or incompatibility of vancomycin HCl mixed with or administered simultaneously with piperacillin sodium–tazobactam sodium is concentration dependent. (2189) See Y-Site Compatibility above. Vancomycin HCl has a low pH and is variably compatible with drugs having neutral to mildly alkaline pH, including cephalosporins and penicillins. The compatibility may depend on a number of factors, including concentration of each drug, dilution vehicle, actual pH of solutions, and completeness of mixing during administration. Combinations that are compatible when well mixed may result in precipitation if only partially mixed, presumably because of regionally different concentrations and pH values. If attempting to administer vancomycin HCl with piperacillin sodium–tazobactam sodium, take care to ensure that the specific combination and the concentrations are compatible under the exact administration conditions to be used. An inline filter should be used as a final safety measure. (2189)

PLICAMYCIN (MITHRAMYCIN) AHFS 10:00

Products — Plicamycin is available in vials containing 2500 μg (2.5 mg) of the drug in a freeze-dried preparation. Also present are mannitol 100 mg and disodium phosphate to adjust the pH. (2)

Reconstitute with 4.9 ml of water for injection and shake to dissolve the drug. The vials contain an excess of drug so that the concentration of reconstituted vials is 500 μg/ml. (2; 4)

pH — 7. (2)

Osmolality — Plicamycin (Bayer) 0.5 mg/ml in sterile water for injection has an osmolality of 104 mOsm/kg. (2043)

Trade Name(s) — Mithracin.

Administration — Plicamycin is administered by intravenous infusion. The appropriate dose is added to 1000 ml of dextrose 5% in water or sodium chloride 0.9% and administered over four to six hours. Extravasation should be avoided because of local tissue irritation and cellulitis. Rapid direct intravenous push administration is associated with a higher incidence and greater severity of side effects and is not recommended. (2; 4)

Stability — The intact vials should be stored at 2 to 8 °C. (2) Although refrigeration is recommended, intact vials of plicamycin have been variously reported by the manufacturer to be stable at room temperatures less than 25 °C for five days (1433) or longer. (60; 1369)

Plicamycin contains no antibacterial preservative. The manufacturer recommends that the plicamycin solution be prepared freshly each day of therapy and that any remaining unused solution be discarded. (2) Reconstituting the solution immediately before injection has also been recommended. (4) However, reconstituted solutions have been found to be chemically stable for two days under refrigeration. (1369)

pH Effects — Plicamycin is rapidly hydrolyzed in acidic solutions below pH 4. (4) At pH 4 to 5, 13% losses in 24 hours have been reported. At pH 5 to 7.5, the drug is stable in solution for at least two days at 2 to 6 °C. (1369)

Sorption — Storage of plicamycin (Dome) 23.4 μg/ml in dextrose 5% in water and sodium chloride 0.9% in both glass and PVC containers did not result in substantial differences in drug loss by HPLC analysis in 24 hours. (519)

Filtration — Plicamycin (Pfizer) 2.5 mg/L in dextrose 5% in water and sodium chloride 0.9% was filtered at 120 ml/hr for six hours through a 0.22-μm cellulose ester membrane filter (Ivex-2). Significant losses of plicamycin due to binding to the filters were noted with both solutions. In dextrose 5% in water, a total of 14.3% of the dose was bound over the six-hour period; a 9.9% loss occurred over this time from the sodium chloride 0.9% solution. (533)

In static equilibrium experiments, 100 mg of 0.22-μm cellulose ester membrane filter (Ivex-2) was soaked in 25 ml of plicamycin (Pfizer) 25 and 50 μg/ml in both dextrose 5% in water and sodium chloride 0.9%. In dextrose 5% in water, about 60 and 40% were bound to the filter for each strength, respectively, in 24 hours. In sodium chloride 0.9%, about 33 to 39% was bound for both strengths in the same time. (533)

In a followup study, a filter material specially treated with a proprietary agent was evaluated for a reduction in plicamycin binding. Plicamycin (Miles) 2.5 mg/L in dextrose 5% in water and sodium chloride 0.9% was run through an administration set with a treated 0.22-μm cellulose ester inline filter at a rate of 2 ml/min. Cumulative plicamycin losses of about 4% occurred from both solutions compared to the much higher losses previously reported for untreated cellulose ester filter material. Furthermore, equilibrium binding studies showed five- and sevenfold reductions in binding from sodium chloride 0.9% and dextrose 5% in water, respectively. (904) All Abbott Ivex integral filter and extension sets currently use this treated filter material. (1074)

Compatibility Information

Solution Compatibility

Plicamycin

Solution	*Mfr*	*Mfr*	*Conc/L*	*Remarks*	*Ref*	*C/I*
Dextrose 5% in water	TR[a]	DM	23.4 mg	Less than 10% loss by HPLC in 24 hr at room temperature exposed to light	519	C
Sodium chloride 0.9%	TR[a]	DM	23.4 mg	Less than 10% loss by HPLC in 24 hr at room temperature exposed to light	519	C

[a]*Tested in both glass and PVC containers.*

Y-Site Injection Compatibility (1:1 Mixture)

Plicamycin

Drug	*Mfr*	*Conc*	*Mfr*	*Conc*	*Remarks*	*Ref*	*C/I*
Allopurinol sodium	BW	3 mg/ml[b]	MI	0.01 mg/ml[b]	Physically compatible with no change in measured turbidity or increase in particle content in 4 hr at 22 °C	1686	C

Y-Site Injection Compatibility (1:1 Mixture) (Cont.)

Drug	Mfr	Conc	Plicamycin Mfr	Plicamycin Conc	Remarks	Ref	C/I
Amifostine	USB	10 mg/ml[a]	MI	0.01 mg/ml[a]	Physically compatible with no change in measured turbidity or increase in particle content in 4 hr at 23 °C	1845	C
Aztreonam	SQ	40 mg/ml[a]	MI	0.01 mg/ml[a]	Physically compatible with no subvisual haze or particle formation in 4 hr at 23 °C	1758	C
Cefepime HCl	BMS	20 mg/ml[a]	MI	0.01 mg/ml[a]	Haze forms immediately. Particles form in 1 hr	1689	I
Etoposide phosphate	BR	5 mg/ml[a]	MI	0.01 mg/ml[a]	Physically compatible with no change in measured turbidity or increase in particle content in 4 hr at 23 °C	2218	C
Filgrastim	AMG	30 μg/ml[a]	MI	0.01 mg/ml[a]	Physically compatible with no change in measured turbidity or increase in particle content in 4 hr at 22 °C	1687	C
Gemcitabine HCl	LI	10 mg/ml[b]	BAY	0.01 mg/ml[b]	Physically compatible with no change in measured turbidity or increase in particle content in hr at 23 °C	2226	C
Granisetron HCl	SKB	0.05 mg/ml[a]	BAY	0.01 mg/ml[a]	Physically compatible with no change in measured turbidity or increase in particle content in 4 hr at 23 °C	2000	C
Melphalan HCl	BW	0.1 mg/ml[b]	MI	0.01 mg/ml[b]	Physically compatible with no change in measured turbidity or increase in particle content in 3 hr at 22 °C	1557	C
Piperacillin sodium–tazobactam sodium	LE	40 + 5 mg/ml[a]	MI	0.01 mg/ml[a]	Physically compatible with no change in measured turbidity or increase in particle content in 4 hr at 22 °C	1688	C
Teniposide	BR	0.1 mg/ml[a]	MI	0.01 mg/ml[a]	Physically compatible with no subvisual haze or particle formation in 4 hr at 23 °C	1725	C
Thiotepa	IMM[c]	1 mg/ml[a]	MI	0.01 mg/ml[a]	Physically compatible with no change in measured turbidity or increase in particle content in 4 hr at 23 °C	1861	C
Vinorelbine tartrate	BW	1 mg/ml[b]	MI	0.01 mg/ml[b]	Physically compatible with no change in measured turbidity or increase in particle content in 4 hr at 22 °C	1558	C

[a]*Tested in dextrose 5% in water.*
[b]*Tested in sodium chloride 0.9%.*
[c]*Lyophilized formulation tested.*

Additional Compatibility Information

Plicamycin has a strong ability to chelate metal ions, especially iron. (4; 1369)

Other Information

Inactivation — In the event of spills or leaks, Miles recommends the use of trisodium phosphate 10%, in contact for 24 hours, to inactivate plicamycin. (1200)

POLYMYXIN B SULFATE
AHFS 8:12.28

Products — Polymyxin B sulfate is available in 10-ml vials containing 500,000 units of polymyxin B. For intramuscular injection, reconstitute the vial with 2 ml of sterile water for injection, sodium chloride 0.9%, or procaine HCl 1% solution. For intravenous infusion, dilute 500,000 units in 300 to 500 ml of dextrose 5% in water. For intrathecal administration, reconstitute the vial with 10 ml of sodium chloride 0.9%. Procaine HCl should not be used for intrathecal injection. (1-8/99; 4; 29)

Units— Each milligram of polymyxin base is equivalent to 10,000 units. Each microgram is equivalent to 10 units. (4)

pH— From 5 to 7.5. (4; 54)

Osmolality— Polymyxin B sulfate 50,000 units/ml in sterile water for injection has an osmolality of 10 mOsm/kg. (1689)

Administration — Polymyxin B sulfate is usually administered by intravenous infusion; 500,000 units is added to 300 to 500 ml of dextrose 5% in water (providing 1667 to 1000 units/ml) and is administered over 60 to 90 minutes. The drug may also be administered intrathecally as a 50,000-units/ml solution in sodium chloride 0.9%. Although it may be administered by deep intramuscular injection in the upper outer quadrant of the gluteal muscles, this route is generally not recommended, because severe pain at the injection site results. (4)

Stability — Intact vials should be stored at controlled room temperature and protected from light. Aqueous solutions of polymyxin B sulfate in the pH range of 5 to 7.5 are stable for six to 12 months under refrigeration. However, it is recommended that unused portions of the reconstituted solution be discarded after 72 hours. Polymyxin B sulfate is inactivated in strongly acidic or alkaline solutions. (4) In the pH range of 2 to 7, pH has little effect on the rate of decomposition. However, as pH values become more alkaline, the rate of decomposition increases markedly. (1946)

Compatibility Information

Solution Compatibility

Polymyxin B sulfate

Solution	*Mfr*	*Mfr*	*Conc/L*	*Remarks*	*Ref*	*C/I*
Invert sugar 7.5% with electrolytes		NOV	40 mg	Physically compatible with no polymyxin B loss in 24 hr at 29 °C by microbiological assay	440	C
TPN #52 and #53[a]		NOV	40 mg	Physically compatible with no polymyxin B loss in 24 hr at 29 °C by microbiological assay	440	C

[a]*Refer to Appendix I for the composition of parenteral nutrition solutions. TPN indicates a 2-in-1 admixture.*

Additive Compatibility

Polymyxin B sulfate

Drug	*Mfr*	*Conc/L*	*Mfr*	*Conc/L*	*Test Soln*	*Remarks*	*Ref*	*C/I*
Amikacin sulfate	BR	5 g	BW	200 mg	D5LR, D5R, D5S, D5W, D10W, IS10, LR, NS, R, SL	Physically compatible and amikacin potency retained for 24 hr at 25 °C. Polymyxin not analyzed	293	C
Amphotericin B		200 mg	BP	20 mg	D5W	Haze develops over 3 hr	26	I
Ascorbic acid injection	UP	500 mg	BW	200 mg	D5W	Physically compatible	15	C
Chloramphenicol sodium succinate	PD	10 g	BW	200 mg	D5W	Physically incompatible	15	I
	PD	10 g	BW	200 mg		Precipitate forms within 1 hr	6	I
Chlorothiazide sodium	BP	2 g	BP	20 mg	D5W	Yellow color produced	26	I
Colistimethate sodium	WC	500 mg	BW	200 mg	D5W	Physically compatible	15	C
Diphenhydramine HCl	PD	80 mg	BW	200 mg	D5W	Physically compatible	15	C
Erythromycin lactobionate	AB	5 g	BW	200 mg	D5W	Physically compatible	15	C
Heparin sodium	BP	20,000 units	BP	20 mg	D5W	Immediate precipitation	26	I
	BP	20,000 units	BP	20 mg	NS	Haze develops over 3 hr	26	I

Additive Compatibility (Cont.)

Polymyxin B sulfate

Drug	*Mfr*	*Conc/L*	*Mfr*	*Conc/L*	*Test Soln*	*Remarks*	*Ref*	*C/I*
Hydrocortisone sodium succinate	UP	500 mg	BW	200 mg	D5W	Physically compatible	15	C
Kanamycin sulfate	BR	4 g	BW	200 mg	D5W	Physically compatible	15	C
Magnesium sulfate	LI	16 mEq	BW	200 mg	D5W	Physically incompatible	15	I
Penicillin G potassium	SQ	20 million units	BW	200 mg	D5W	Physically compatible	15	C
	SQ	5 million units	BW	200 mg	D	Physically compatible	47	C
Penicillin G sodium	UP	20 million units	BW	200 mg	D5W	Physically compatible	15	C
Phenobarbital sodium	WI	200 mg	BW	200 mg	D5W	Physically compatible	15	C
Ranitidine HCl	GL	50 mg and 2 g		1 million units	D5W	Physically compatible and ranitidine chemically stable by HPLC for 24 hr at 25 °C. Polymyxin B not tested	1515	C
Vitamin B complex with C	AB	5 ml	BW	200 mg	D5W	Physically compatible	15	C

Drugs in Syringe Compatibility

Polymyxin B sulfate

Drug (in syringe)	*Mfr*	*Amt*	*Mfr*	*Amt*	*Remarks*	*Ref*	*C/I*
Ampicillin sodium	AY	500 mg	BW	25 mg/ 1.5 ml	Physically compatible for 1 hr at room temperature	300	C
	AY	250 mg	BW	25 mg/ 1.5 ml	Precipitate forms within 1 hr at room temperature	300	I
Penicillin G sodium		1 million units	BW	25 mg/ 1.5 to 2 ml	No precipitate or color change within 1 hr at room temperature	99	C

Y-Site Injection Compatibility (1:1 Mixture)

Polymyxin B sulfate

Drug	*Mfr*	*Conc*	*Mfr*	*Conc*	*Remarks*	*Ref*	*C/I*
Esmolol HCl	DCC	10 mg/ml[a]	PF	0.005 unit/ ml[a]	Physically compatible for 24 hr at 22 °C	1169	C

[a]*Tested in dextrose 5% in water.*

Additional Compatibility Information

Parenteral Nutrition Solutions — Polymyxin B sulfate has been reported to be visually compatible and stable for 24 hours at 29 °C in a parenteral nutrition solution. (854)

Lincomycin HCl — Polymyxin B sulfate is stated to be physically compatible for 24 hours at room temperature with lincomycin HCl in infusion solutions. (154)

Other Drugs — Solutions of polymyxin B sulfate are stated to be inactivated by alkalies and strong acids. (4) Cefazolin sodium also appears to be incompatible with polymyxin B sulfate (278) as are calcium and magnesium salts. (4)

POTASSIUM ACETATE
AHFS 40:12

Products — Potassium acetate additive solution is available in 20-, 50-, and 100-ml single-dose vials at a concentration of 2 mEq/ml in water for injection. Each milliliter provides potassium acetate 196 mg. It is also available in 50-ml vials at a concentration of 4 mEq/ml in water for injection. Each milliliter provides 392 mg of potassium acetate. The pH of the solutions may have been adjusted with acetic acid when necessary. These concentrated solutions must be diluted for administration. (1-3/99; 29)

pH — The pH of potassium acetate additive solution has been stated to be approximately 7.1 to 7.7 (4) with a range of 5.5 to 8. (1-3/99)

Osmolarity — The calculated osmolarity of the 2-mEq/ml solution is 4000 mOsm/L and for the 4-mEq/ml solution is 8000 mOsm/L. (1-3/99)

Administration — Potassium acetate is administered as a dilute solution by slow intravenous infusion. It must not be administered undiluted. (1-3/99; 4) In most cases, the maximum recommended concentration is 40 mEq/L. Solutions generally may be infused at a rate up to 20 mEq/hr. (4)

Stability — Potassium acetate additive solution should be stored at room temperature and protected from freezing. It should not be administered unless the solution is clear. (1-3/99)

Compatibility Information

Additive Compatibility

Potassium acetate

Drug	*Mfr*	*Conc/L*	*Mfr*	*Conc/L*	*Test Soln*	*Remarks*	*Ref*	*C/I*
Metoclopramide HCl	RB	10 and 160 mg	IX	20 mEq	NS	Physically compatible for 48 hr at room temperature	924	C
	RB	10 and 160 mg	IX	20 mEq		Physically compatible for 48 hr at 25 °C	1167	C

Y-Site Injection Compatibility (1:1 Mixture)

Potassium acetate

Drug	*Mfr*	*Conc*	*Mfr*	*Conc*	*Remarks*	*Ref*	*C/I*
Ciprofloxacin	MI	2 mg/ml[a]	LY	2 mEq/ml	Visually compatible for 2 hr at 25 °C	1628	C

[a]*Tested in dextrose 5% in water.*

Additional Compatibility Information

Magnesium Sulfate — Potassium acetate 25 mmol/5 ml added to a TPN solution just after the addition of magnesium sulfate 10 mmol/5 ml has resulted in the formation of translucent off-white needle-like crystals of potassium sulfate. The precipitate redissolved readily when adequately mixed. The addition of a similar quantity of potassium chloride did not result in crystalline precipitation, but the authors indicated the presence of potassium chloride could decrease the solubility of potassium sulfate and promote precipitation, presumably at higher concentrations. (2266)

POTASSIUM CHLORIDE
AHFS 40:12

Products — Potassium chloride is available as concentrated solutions of 1.5 and 2 mEq/ml in 10-, 20-, 30-, and 40-mEq sizes in water for injection in ampuls, vials, and syringes. It is also available in a 30-ml (60-mEq) multiple-dose vial containing methylparaben 0.05% and propylparaben 0.005% as preservatives and 250-ml pharmacy bulk packages. (29) The pH may have been adjusted with hydrochloric acid and if necessary potassium hydroxide during manufacture. The concentrated solutions must be diluted for use. (1-10/98)

Potassium chloride is also available premixed in infusion solutions in concentrations of 10, 20, 30, and 40 mEq/L. (4)

pH — From 4 to 8. (4)

Osmolarity — The injections are very hypertonic; the 2-mEq/ml concentration has an osmolarity of 4000 mOsm/L. The injection must be diluted for use. (1-10/98)

The osmolality of potassium chloride (Abbott) 2 mEq/ml was determined to be 4355 mOsm/kg by freezing-point depression and 3440 mOsm/kg by vapor pressure. (1071)

The osmolality of a potassium chloride 7.5% solution was determined to be 1895 mOsm/kg. (1233)

Administration — Potassium chloride in the concentrated injections must be diluted before slow intravenous administration. Mix potassium chloride injection thoroughly with the infusion solution before administration. See Other Information below. The usual maximum concentration is 40 mEq/L. Extravasation should be avoided. (1-10/98; 4)

Stability — The solution should be stored at controlled room temperature and used only if it is clear. (1-10/98)

Potassium chloride injection 80 mEq/L added to dextrose 5% in water contained in glass bottles results in a leaching of precipitates consisting of silica and alumina. (129)

Compatibility Information

Solution Compatibility

Potassium chloride

Solution	*Mfr*	*Mfr*	*Conc/L*	*Remarks*	*Ref*	*C/I*
Alcohol 5% and dextrose 5%	BA	LI	80 mEq	Physically compatible for 24 hr	315	C
Dextran 6% in dextrose 5%	AB	AB	160 mEq	Physically compatible	3	C
Dextran 6% in sodium chloride 0.9%	AB	AB	160 mEq	Physically compatible	3	C
Dextrose–Ringer's injection combinations	AB	AB	160 mEq	Physically compatible	3	C
Dextrose–Ringer's injection, lactated, combinations	AB	AB	160 mEq	Physically compatible	3	C
Dextrose 5% in Ringer's injection, lactated	BA	LI	80 mEq	Physically compatible for 24 hr	315	C
Dextrose–saline combinations	AB	AB	160 mEq	Physically compatible	3	C
Dextrose 5% in sodium chloride 0.9%			3 g	Physically compatible	74	C
	BA	LI	80 mEq	Physically compatible for 24 hr	315	C
Dextrose 2½% in water	AB	AB	160 mEq	Physically compatible	3	C
Dextrose 5% in water			3 g	Physically compatible	74	C
	AB	AB	160 mEq	Physically compatible	3	C
	BA	LI	80 mEq	Physically compatible for 24 hr	315	C
Dextrose 10% in water	AB	AB	160 mEq	Physically compatible	3	C
	BA	LI	80 mEq	Physically compatible for 24 hr	315	C
Dextrose 20% in water	BA	LI	80 mEq	Physically compatible for 24 hr	315	C
Fat emulsion 10%, intravenous	VT		7.5 g	Physically compatible for 48 hr at 4 °C and room temperature	32	C
	CU		200 mEq	Globule coalescence with noticeable surface creaming in 4 hr at room temperature. Oil globules noted on surface at 48 hr	656	I
	CU		100 mEq	No significant change in emulsion for 24 hr at room temperature. Significant globule coalescence noted at 48 hr	656	C
	VT	DB	4 g	Microscopic globule coalescence in 24 hr at 8 and 25 °C	825	I
Fructose 10% in sodium chloride 0.9%	AB	AB	160 mEq	Physically compatible	3	C
Fructose 10% in water	AB	AB	160 mEq	Physically compatible	3	C
	BA	LI	80 mEq	Physically compatible for 24 hr	315	C
Invert sugar 10% in Electrolyte #1	BA	LI	80 mEq	Physically compatible for 24 hr	315	C
Invert sugar 10% in Electrolyte #2	BA	LI	80 mEq	Physically compatible for 24 hr	315	C
Invert sugar 5 and 10% in sodium chloride 0.9%	AB	AB	160 mEq	Physically compatible	3	C
Invert sugar 5 and 10% in water	AB	AB	160 mEq	Physically compatible	3	C
Ionosol products	AB	AB	160 mEq	Physically compatible	3	C
Polysal M with dextrose 5%	CU	LI	80 mEq	Physically compatible for 24 hr	315	C

Solution Compatibility (Cont.)

Potassium chloride

Solution	*Mfr*	*Mfr*	*Conc/L*	*Remarks*	*Ref*	*C/I*
Ringer's injection	AB	AB	160 mEq	Physically compatible	3	C
			3 g	Physically compatible	74	C
Ringer's injection, lactated	AB	AB	160 mEq	Physically compatible	3	C
	BA	LI	80 mEq	Physically compatible for 24 hr	315	C
Sodium chloride 0.45%	AB	AB	160 mEq	Physically compatible	3	C
Sodium chloride 0.9%			3 g	Physically compatible	74	C
	AB	AB	160 mEq	Physically compatible	3	C
	BA	LI	80 mEq	Physically compatible for 24 hr	315	C
Sodium chloride 3%	BA	LI	80 mEq	Physically compatible for 24 hr	315	C
Sodium lactate ⅙ M	AB	AB	160 mEq	Physically compatible	3	C
	BA	LI	80 mEq	Physically compatible for 24 hr	315	C

Additive Compatibility

Potassium chloride

Drug	*Mfr*	*Conc/L*	*Mfr*	*Conc/L*	*Test Soln*	*Remarks*	*Ref*	*C/I*
Amikacin sulfate	BR	5 g	LI	3 g	D5LR, D5R, D5S, D5W, D10W, IS10, LR, NS, R, SL	Physically compatible and potency of both retained for 24 hr at 25 °C	294	C
	BR	5 g	LI	3 g	DXN–S	14% amikacin decomposition in 4 hr at 25 °C	294	I
Aminophylline		250 mg		3 g	D5W	Physically compatible	74	C
	SE	500 mg	AB	40 mEq		Physically compatible	6	C
Amiodarone HCl	LZ	1.8 g	AB	40 mEq	D5W, NS[a]	Physically compatible with no amiodarone loss in 24 hr at 24 °C under fluorescent light	1031	C
Amoxicillin sodium		10, 20, 50 g		0.3%	NS	4 and 9% amoxicillin losses in 8 hr at 10 and 20 g/L, respectively, and 9% loss in 3 hr at 50 g/L at 25 °C	1469	I
Amphotericin B		200 mg	BP	4 g	D5W	Haze develops over 3 hr	26	I
	SQ	100 mg	AB	100 mEq	D5W	Physically incompatible	15	I
Atracurium besylate	BW	500 mg		80 mEq	D5W	Physically compatible and atracurium chemically stable for 24 hr at 5 and 30 °C	1694	C
Bretylium tosylate	ACC	10 g	AB	40 mEq	D5W[b]	Physically compatible and chemically stable for 48 hr at room temperature and 7 days at 4 °C	541	C
Calcium gluconate		1 g		3 g	D5W	Physically compatible	74	C
Cefepime HCl	BR	4 g	AB	40 mEq	D5W, NS	Visually compatible with 2% cefepime loss by HPLC in 24 hr at room temperature or 7 days at 5 °C	1681	C
	BR	4 g	AB	10 mEq	D5W	Visually compatible with 2% cefepime loss by HPLC in 24 hr at room temperature or 7 days at 5 °C	1681	C

Additive Compatibility (Cont.)

Potassium chloride

Drug	*Mfr*	*Conc/L*	*Mfr*	*Conc/L*	*Test Soln*	*Remarks*	*Ref*	*C/I*
Chloramphenicol sodium succinate	PD	500 mg		3 g	D5W	Physically compatible	74	C
	PD	1 g	AB	40 mEq		Physically compatible	6	C
	PD	500 mg and 1 g		20 and 40 mEq	D2.5½S, D5W	Therapeutic availability maintained	110	C
Cibenzoline succinate		2 g	IX	160 mEq	D5W, NS	Physically compatible for 24 hr at 25 °C by visual and microscopic examination	1182	C
Cimetidine HCl	SKF	1.2 and 5 g	SKF	20 mEq	D5S, D5W, NS	Physically compatible and cimetidine chemically stable for 24 hr at room temperature. Potassium chloride not tested	551	C
	SKF	1.2 and 5 g	SKF	80 mEq	D5S, D5W, NS	Physically compatible and cimetidine chemically stable for 24 hr at room temperature. Potassium chloride not tested	551	C
Ciprofloxacin	MI	2 g		40 mEq	NS	Compatible for 24 hr at 25 °C	888	C
	BAY	2 g	AB	40 mEq	NS	Visually compatible with little or no ciprofloxacin loss by HPLC in 24 hr at 25 °C	1934	C
Clindamycin phosphate	UP	600 mg		40 mEq	D5½S	Physically compatible and clindamycin potency retained for 24 hr at room temperature	104	C
	UP	600 mg		100 mEq	D5W, NS	Physically compatible	101	C
	UP	6 g		400 mEq	D5½S	Clindamycin stability maintained for 24 hr	101	C
Corticotropin		500 units		3 g	D5W	Physically compatible	74	C
Cytarabine	UP	2 g		100 mEq	D5S	Physically compatible and chemically stable for 8 days	174	C
	UP	170 mg		80 mEq	D5S	Physically compatible for 24 hr	174	C
Dimenhydrinate	SE	50 mg		3 g	D5W	Physically compatible	74	C
Dobutamine HCl	LI	1 g	ES	160 mEq	D5W, NS	Slightly pink in 24 hr at 25 °C	789	I
	LI	1 g	AB	20 mEq	D5W, NS	Physically compatible for 24 hr at 21 °C	812	C
Dopamine HCl	AS	800 mg	MG		D5W	No dopamine decomposition in 24 hr at 25 °C	312	C
Enalaprilat	MSD	12 mg	AB	3 g	D5W[a]	Visually compatible with little or no enalaprilat loss by HPLC in 24 hr at room temperature under fluorescent light. Potassium chloride not tested	1572	C
Erythromycin lactobionate	AB	1 g	AB	40 mEq		Physically compatible	20	C
Etoposide with cisplatin and mannitol	BR BR LY	400 mg 200 mg 1.875%	LY	20 mEq	NS[b]	Physically compatible and etoposide and cisplatin chemically stable for 8 hr at 22 °C. Precipitate forms within 24 hr	1329	I
Etoposide with cisplatin and mannitol	BR BR LY	400 mg 200 mg 1.875%	BR	20 mEq	D5½S[b]	Physically compatible and etoposide and cisplatin chemically stable for 24 hr at 22 °C. Precipitate forms within 48 hr	1329	C
Floxacillin sodium	BE	20 g	ANT	40 mM	W	Physically compatible for 72 hr at 15 and 30 °C	1479	C
Fluconazole	PF	1 g	AB	10 mEq	D5W[a]	Fluconazole chemically stable by gas chromatography for at least 24 hr at 25 °C under fluorescent light	1676	C

Additive Compatibility (Cont.)

Potassium chloride

Drug	*Mfr*	*Conc/L*	*Mfr*	*Conc/L*	*Test Soln*	*Remarks*	*Ref*	*C/I*
Foscarnet sodium	AST	12 g		20, 40, 60, 80, 120 mmol	NS	Foscarnet stability was maintained for at least 65 hr. UV analysis found concentrations of 93 to 99% throughout	2156	C
Fosphenytoin sodium	PD	1, 8, 20 mg PE/ml[e]	BA	20 and 40 mEq	D5½S[a]	Visually compatible with little or no loss of fosphenytoin by HPLC in 7 days at 25 °C under fluorescent light	2083	C
Furosemide	HO	1 g	ANT	40 mmol	W	Physically compatible for 72 hr at 15 and 30 °C	1479	C
Heparin sodium		12,000 units		3 g	D5W	Physically compatible	74	C
	AB	20,000 units	AB	40 mEq		Physically compatible	21	C
		32,000 units		80 mEq	NS	Physically compatible and heparin activity retained for 24 hr	57	C
Hydrocortisone sodium succinate	UP	100 mg		3 g	D5W	Physically compatible	74	C
Hydrocortisone sodium succinate with netilmicin sulfate	UP SC	400 mg 3 g	AB	160 mEq	D5S	Physically compatible and netilmicin chemically stable for 7 days at 4 and 25 °C. Other drugs not tested	558	C
Isoproterenol HCl	WI	4 mg	AB	40 mEq		Physically compatible	59	C
Lidocaine HCl	AST	2 g	AB	40 mEq		Physically compatible	24	C
Metaraminol bitartrate	MSD	100 mg	AB	40 mEq		Physically compatible	7	C
Methyldopate HCl	MSD	1 g		40 mEq	D, D–S, S	Physically compatible	23	C
Metoclopramide HCl	RB	10 and 160 mg	ES	30 mEq	NS	Physically compatible for 48 hr at room temperature	924	C
	RB	10 and 160 mg	ES	30 mEq		Physically compatible for 48 hr at 25 °C	1167	C
Mitoxantrone HCl	LE	500 mg		50 mEq	D5W	Visually compatible and mitoxantrone potency by HPLC retained for 24 hr at room temperature. Potassium chloride not tested	1531	C
Nafcillin sodium	WY	500 mg	AB	40 mEq		Physically compatible	27	C
	WY	30 g	TR	40 mEq	NS	Nafcillin potency retained for 24 hr at 25 °C	27	C
Netilmicin sulfate	SC	3 g	AB	160 mEq	D5S	Physically compatible and netilmicin chemically stable for 7 days at 4 and 25 °C. Potassium chloride not tested	558	C
Netilmicin sulfate with hydrocortisone sodium succinate	SC UP	3 g 400 mg	AB	160 mEq	D5S	Physically compatible and netilmicin chemically stable for 7 days at 4 and 25 °C. Other drugs not tested	558	C
Norepinephrine bitartrate	WI	8 mg		3 g	D5W	Physically compatible	74	C
	WI	8 mg	AB	40 mEq	D, D–S, S	Physically compatible	77	C
Oxacillin sodium	BR	1, 2.5, 4 g		20, 40, 80 mEq	D5S, D5W	Therapeutic availability maintained	110	C
Penicillin G potassium	SQ	5 million units	AB	40 mEq		Physically compatible	47	C

Additive Compatibility (Cont.)

Potassium chloride

Drug	*Mfr*	*Conc/L*	*Mfr*	*Conc/L*	*Test Soln*	*Remarks*	*Ref*	*C/I*
	SQ	5 million units		40 mEq	D5S, D5W	Therapeutic availability maintained	110	C
	SQ	1 million units		20 mEq	D5S, D5W	Therapeutic availability maintained	110	C
Penicillin G potassium with vitamin B complex with C	SQ TR	2 million units 1 ampul		20 mEq	D5S, D5W	Therapeutic availability maintained	110	C
Penicillin G potassium with vitamin B complex with C	SQ TR	8 million units 1 ampul		40 mEq	D5S, D5W	Therapeutic availability maintained	110	C
Penicillin G sodium	KA	6 million units		40 mEq	D5W	Penicillin potency retained for at least 24 hr at 25 °C	131	C
	KA	5 million units		40 mEq	IS10	pH outside stability range for penicillin	131	I
Phenylephrine HCl	WI	2.5 g	AB	40 mEq	D5W	Phenylephrine potency retained for over 24 hr at 22 °C	132	C
Piperacillin sodium	LE	2 g		40 mEq	D5S, D5W, LR, R, NS	Physically compatible and piperacillin chemically stable for 24 hr at room temperature and 48 hr under refrigeration	740	C
Propafenone HCl	KN	0.54 g	AST	18 mmol[f]	D5W	Visually compatible for 24 hr at 22 °C exposed to fluorescent light	412	C
Ranitidine HCl	GL	2 g	LY	10 and 60 mEq	D5W, NS[a]	Physically compatible with 2% or less ranitidine loss in 48 hr at room temperature under fluorescent light	1361	C
	GL	50 mg	LY	10 and 60 mEq	NS[a]	Physically compatible with no ranitidine loss in 48 hr at room temperature under fluorescent light	1361	C
	GL	50 mg	LY	10 and 60 mEq	D5W[a]	Physically compatible with 7% ranitidine loss in 48 hr at room temperature under fluorescent light	1361	C
	GL	50 mg and 2 g		80 mEq	D5S, D5W, NS	Physically compatible and ranitidine chemically stable by HPLC for 24 hr at 25 °C. Potassium chloride not tested	1515	C
Sodium bicarbonate	AB	2.4 mEq[d]		120 mEq	D5W	Physically compatible for 24 hr	772	C
Thiopental sodium	AB	2.5 g	AB	40 mEq	D5W	Physically compatible	21	C
Vancomycin HCl	LI	1 g		3 g	D5W	Physically compatible	74	C
Verapamil HCl	KN	80 mg	TR	80 mEq	D5W, NS	Physically compatible for 24 hr	764	C
Vitamin B complex with C		1 vial		3 g	D5W	Physically compatible	74	C
Vitamin B complex with C with penicillin G potassium	TR SQ	1 ampul 2 million units		20 mEq	D5S, D5W	Therapeutic availability maintained	110	C

Additive Compatibility (Cont.)

			Potassium chloride					
Drug	*Mfr*	*Conc/L*	*Mfr*	*Conc/L*	*Test Soln*	*Remarks*	*Ref*	*C/I*
Vitamin B complex with C with penicillin G potassium	TR SQ	1 ampul 8 million units		40 mEq	D5S, D5W	Therapeutic availability maintained	110	C

[a]*Tested in PVC containers.*
[b]*Tested in both glass and PVC containers.*
[c]*Tested in both polyolefin and PVC containers.*
[d]*One vial of Neut added to a liter of admixture.*
[e]*Concentration expressed in milligrams of phenytoin sodium equivalents (PE) per milliliter.*
[f]*Approximate concentration.*

Y-Site Injection Compatibility (1:1 Mixture)

			Potassium chloride				
Drug	*Mfr*	*Conc*	*Mfr*	*Conc*	*Remarks*	*Ref*	*C/I*
Acyclovir sodium	BW	5 mg/ml[a]	IX	0.04 mEq/ml[a]	Physically compatible for 4 hr at 25 °C	1157	C
Alatrofloxacin mesylate	PF	1.43 mg/ml[a]		0.02 mEq/ml[n]	Visually and microscopically compatible run through a Y-site over at least 60 min	2235	C
	PF	1.43 mg/ml[a]	BA	0.4 mEq/ml	Visually and microscopically compatible run through a Y-site over at least 60 min	2235	C
Aldesleukin	CHI	33,800 I.U./ml[a]	AB	0.2 mEq/ml	Visually compatible with little or no loss of aldesleukin activity by bioassay	1857	C
Allopurinol sodium	BW	3 mg/ml[b]	AB	0.1 mEq/ml[b]	Physically compatible with no change in measured turbidity or increase in particle content in 4 hr at 22 °C	1686	C
Amifostine	USB	10 mg/ml[a]	AB	0.1 mEq/ml[a]	Physically compatible with no change in measured turbidity or increase in particle content in 4 hr at 23 °C	1845	C
Aminophylline	SE	25 mg/ml		40 mEq/L[c]	Physically compatible for at least 4 hr at room temperature by visual and microscopic examination	322	C
Amiodarone HCl	LZ	4 mg/ml[d]	AB	0.04 mEq/ml[d]	Physically compatible for 24 hr at 21 °C	1032	C
Amphotericin B cholesteryl sulfate complex	SEQ	0.83 mg/ml[a]	AB	0.1 mEq/ml[a]	Gross precipitate forms	2117	I
Ampicillin sodium	BR	25, 50, 100, 125 mg/ml		40 mEq/L[c]	Physically compatible for at least 4 hr at room temperature by visual and microscopic examination	322	C
Atropine sulfate	BW	0.5 mg/ml	AB	40 mEq/L[f]	Physically compatible for at least 4 hr at room temperature by visual and microscopic examination	534	C
Aztreonam	SQ	40 mg/ml[a]	AB	0.1 mEq/ml[a]	Physically compatible with no subvisual haze or particle formation in 4 hr at 23 °C	1758	C
Betamethasone sodium phosphate	SC	3 mg/ml	AB	40 mEq/L[f]	Physically compatible for at least 4 hr at room temperature by visual and microscopic examination	534	C

Y-Site Injection Compatibility (1:1 Mixture) (Cont.)

Potassium chloride

Drug	*Mfr*	*Conc*	*Mfr*	*Conc*	*Remarks*	*Ref*	*C/I*
Calcium gluconate	UP	100 mg/ml		40 mEq/L[c]	Physically compatible for at least 4 hr at room temperature by visual and microscopic examination	322	C
Chlordiazepoxide HCl	RC	10 mg/ml	AB	40 mEq/L[f]	Physically compatible for at least 4 hr at room temperature by visual and microscopic examination	534	C
Chlorpromazine HCl	SKF	25 mg/ml	AB	40 mEq/L[f]	Physically compatible for at least 4 hr at room temperature by visual and microscopic examination	534	C
	RPR	0.13 mg/ml[a]	BRN	0.625 mEq/ml[a]	Visually compatible for 150 min	2244	C
Ciprofloxacin	MI	2 mg/ml[d]	LY	0.04 mEq/ml	Visually compatible for 24 hr at 24 °C	1655	C
	MI	2 mg/ml[a]	AMR	2 mEq/ml	Visually compatible for 2 hr at 25 °C	1628	C
Cisatracurium besylate	GW	0.1, 2, 5 mg/ml[a]	AB	0.1 mEq/ml[a]	Physically compatible with no change in measured turbidity or increase in particle content in 4 hr at 23 °C	2074	C
Cladribine	ORT	0.015[b] and 0.5[h] mg/ml	AB	0.1 mEq/ml[b]	Physically compatible with no change in measured turbidity or increase in particle content in 4 hr at 23 °C	1969	C
Clarithromycin	AB	4 mg/ml[a]	ANT	0.08 mmol/ml[a]	Visually compatible for 72 hr at both 30 and 17 °C	2174	C
Cyanocobalamin	PD	0.1 mg/ml	AB	40 mEq/L[f]	Physically compatible for at least 4 hr at room temperature by visual and microscopic examination	534	C
Dexamethasone sodium phosphate	MSD	4 mg/ml		40 mEq/L[c]	Physically compatible for at least 4 hr at room temperature by visual and microscopic examination	322	C
Diazepam	RC	5 mg/ml		40 mEq/L[c]	Immediate haziness and globule formation	322	I
Digoxin	BW	0.25 mg/ml		40 mEq/L[c]	Physically compatible for at least 4 hr at room temperature by visual and microscopic examination	322	C
Diltiazem HCl	MMD	5 mg/ml	LY	0.08[a] and 2 mEq/ml	Visually compatible	1807	C
Diphenhydramine HCl	PD	50 mg/ml	AB	40 mEq/L[f]	Physically compatible for at least 4 hr at room temperature by visual and microscopic examination	534	C
Dobutamine HCl	LI	4 mg/ml[d]	AB	0.06 mEq/ml[d]	Physically compatible for 3 hr	1316	C
Docetaxel	RPR	0.9 mg/ml[a]	AB	0.1 mEq/ml[a]	Physically compatible with no change in measured turbidity or increase in particle content in 4 hr at 23 °C	2224	C
Dopamine HCl	ACC	40 mg/ml	AB	40 mEq/L[f]	Physically compatible for at least 4 hr at room temperature by visual and microscopic examination	534	C
Doxorubicin HCl liposome injection	SEQ	0.4 mg/ml[a]	AB	0.1 mEq/ml[a]	Physically compatible with little or no change in measured turbidity and no increase in particle content in 4 hr at 23 °C	2087	C

Y-Site Injection Compatibility (1:1 Mixture) (Cont.)

			Potassium chloride				
Drug	*Mfr*	*Conc*	*Mfr*	*Conc*	*Remarks*	*Ref*	*C/I*
Droperidol	CR	1.25 mg/ml	AB	40 mEq/L[f]	Physically compatible for at least 4 hr at room temperature by visual and microscopic examination	534	C
Edrophonium chloride	RC	10 mg/ml	AB	40 mEq/L[f]	Physically compatible for at least 4 hr at room temperature by visual and microscopic examination	534	C
Enalaprilat	MSD	0.05 mg/ml[b]	LY	0.4 mEq/ml[a]	Physically compatible for 24 hr at room temperature under fluorescent light	1355	C
Epinephrine HCl	AB	0.1 mg/ml	AB	40 mEq/L[f]	Physically compatible for at least 4 hr at room temperature by visual and microscopic examination	534	C
Ergotamine tartrate	SZ	0.5 mg/ml	AB	40 mEq/L[f]	Crystal formation and brown discoloration in 4 hr at room temperature	534	I
Esmolol HCl	DCC	10 mg/ml[a]	IX	0.4 mEq/ml[a]	Physically compatible for 24 hr at 22 °C	1169	C
Estrogens, conjugated	AY	5 mg/ml		40 mEq/L[c]	Physically compatible for at least 4 hr at room temperature by visual and microscopic examination	322	C
Ethacrynate sodium	MSD	1 mg/ml		40 mEq/L[c]	Physically compatible for at least 4 hr at room temperature by visual and microscopic examination	322	C
Etoposide phosphate	BR	5 mg/ml[a]	AB	0.1 mEq/ml[a]	Physically compatible with no change in measured turbidity or increase in particle content in 4 hr at 23 °C	2218	C
Famotidine	MSD	0.2 mg/ml[a]	AB	0.04 mEq/ml[a]	Physically compatible for 4 hr at 25 °C	1188	C
	ME	2 mg/ml[b]		0.1 mEq/ml[a]	Visually compatible for 4 hr at 22 °C	1936	C
Fentanyl citrate	MN	0.05 mg/ml	AB	40 mEq/L[f]	Physically compatible for at least 4 hr at room temperature by visual and microscopic examination	534	C
Filgrastim	AMG	30 μg/ml[a]	AB	0.1 mEq/ml[a]	Physically compatible with no change in measured turbidity or increase in particle content in 4 hr at 22 °C	1687	C
Fludarabine phosphate	BX	1 mg/ml[a]	AB	0.1 mEq/ml[a]	Physically compatible for 4 hr at room temperature under fluorescent light	1439	C
Fluorouracil	RC	50 mg/ml	AB	40 mEq/L[f]	Physically compatible for at least 4 hr at room temperature by visual and microscopic examination	534	C
Furosemide	HO	10 mg/ml	AB	40 mEq/L[f]	Physically compatible for at least 4 hr at room temperature by visual and microscopic examination	534	C
	HMR	2.6 mg/ml[a]	BRN	0.625 mEq/ml[a]	Visually compatible for 150 min	2244	C
Gatifloxacin	BMS	2 mg/ml[a]	AB	0.1 mEq/ml[a]	Physically compatible with no change in measured haze or increase in particle content in 4 hr at 23 °C	2234	C
Gemcitabine HCl	LI	10 mg/ml[b]	AB	0.1 mEq/ml[b]	Physically compatible with no change in measured turbidity or increase in particle content in 4 hr at 23 °C	2226	C
Granisetron HCl	SKB	1 mg/ml	LY	0.04 mEq/ml[b]	Physically compatible with little or no loss of granisetron by HPLC in 4 hr at 22 °C	1883	C

Y-Site Injection Compatibility (1:1 Mixture) (Cont.)

Potassium chloride

Drug	*Mfr*	*Conc*	*Mfr*	*Conc*	*Remarks*	*Ref*	*C/I*
Heparin sodium	TR	50 units/ml	AB	0.2 mEq/ml[a]	Visually compatible for 4 hr at 25 °C	1793	C
	NOV	29.2 units/ml[a]	BRN	0.625 mEq/ml[a]	Visually compatible for 150 min	2244	C
Hetastarch in lactated electrolyte injection (Hextend)	AB	6%	AB	0.1 mEq/ml[a]	Physically compatible with no change in measured turbidity or increase in particle content in 4 hr at 23 °C	2339	C
Hydralazine HCl	CI	20 mg/ml	AB	40 mEq/L[f]	Physically compatible for at least 4 hr at room temperature by visual and microscopic examination	534	C
Idarubicin HCl	AD	1 mg/ml[b]	AB	0.03 mEq/ml[b]	Visually compatible for 24 hr at 25 °C	1525	C
Inamrinone lactate	WB	3 mg/ml[b]	IX	0.04 mEq/ml	Physically compatible for at least 4 hr at 25 °C under fluorescent light	992	C
	WI	5 mg/ml	LY	0.08 mEq/ml[e]	Physically compatible with little or no loss of either drug in 4 hr at 22 °C	1419	C
	WI	2.5 mg/ml[e]	LY	0.08 mEq/ml[e]	Physically compatible with little or no loss of either drug in 4 hr at 22 °C	1419	C
Indomethacin sodium trihydrate	MSD	1 mg/ml[b]	AB	0.2 mEq/ml[a]	Visually compatible for 24 hr at 28 °C	1527	C
Insulin, regular	LI	40 units/ml		40 mEq/L[c]	Physically compatible for at least 4 hr at room temperature by visual and microscopic examination	322	C
Isoproterenol HCl	WI	0.2 mg/ml	AB	40 mEq/L[f]	Physically compatible for at least 4 hr at room temperature by visual and microscopic examination	534	C
Kanamycin sulfate	BR	250 mg/ml		40 mEq/L[c]	Physically compatible for at least 4 hr at room temperature by visual and microscopic examination	322	C
Labetalol HCl	SC	1 mg/ml[a]	IX	0.4 mEq/ml[a]	Physically compatible for 24 hr at 18 °C	1171	C
Lidocaine HCl	AST	20 mg/ml		40 mEq/L[c]	Physically compatible for at least 4 hr at room temperature by visual and microscopic examination	322	C
Linezolid	PHU	2 mg/ml	FUJ	0.1 mEq/ml[a]	Physically compatible with no change in measured turbidity or increase in particle content in 4 hr at 23 °C	2264	C
Lorazepam	WY	0.33 mg/ml[b]	BRN	1 mEq/ml	Visually compatible for 24 hr at 22 °C	1855	C
Magnesium sulfate	AB	500 mg/ml	AB	40 mEq/L[f]	Physically compatible for at least 4 hr at room temperature by visual and microscopic examination	534	C
Melphalan HCl	BW	0.1 mg/ml[b]	AB	0.1 mEq/ml[b]	Physically compatible with no change in measured turbidity or increase in particle content in 3 hr at 22 °C	1557	C
Menadiol sodium diphosphate	RC	5 mg/ml	AB	40 mEq/L[f]	Physically compatible for at least 4 hr at room temperature by visual and microscopic examination	534	C
Meperidine HCl	AB	10 mg/ml	AB	0.4 mEq/ml[a]	Physically compatible for 4 hr at 25 °C	1397	C
Methoxamine HCl	BW	10 mg/ml	AB	40 mEq/L[f]	Physically compatible for at least 4 hr at room temperature by visual and microscopic examination	534	C

Y-Site Injection Compatibility (1:1 Mixture) (Cont.)

			Potassium chloride				
Drug	*Mfr*	*Conc*	*Mfr*	*Conc*	*Remarks*	*Ref*	*C/I*
Methylergonovine maleate	SZ	0.2 mg/ml	AB	40 mEq/L[f]	Physically compatible for at least 4 hr at room temperature by visual and microscopic examination	534	C
Methylprednisolone sodium succinate	UP	40 mg/ml		40 mEq/L[a]	Physically compatible for at least 4 hr at room temperature by visual and microscopic examination	322	C
	UP	40 mg/ml		40 mEq/L[b]	Physically compatible initially but haze forms within 4 hr at room temperature	322	I
	UP	40 mg/ml		40 mEq/L[i]	Immediate haze formation	322	I
Midazolam HCl	RC	5 mg/ml	BRN	1 mEq/ml	Visually compatible for 24 hr at 22 °C	1855	C
Milrinone lactate	SW	0.4 mg/ml[a]	AB	1 mEq/ml[a]	Visually compatible with no loss of milrinone by HPLC in 4 hr at 23 °C	2214	C
Minocycline HCl	LE	50 mg/ml	AB	40 mEq/L[f]	Physically compatible for at least 4 hr at room temperature by visual and microscopic examination	534	C
Morphine sulfate	WY	15 mg/ml	AB	40 mEq/L[f]	Physically compatible for at least 4 hr at room temperature by visual and microscopic examination	534	C
Neostigmine methylsulfate	RC	0.5 mg/ml	AB	40 mEq/L[f]	Physically compatible for at least 4 hr at room temperature by visual and microscopic examination	534	C
Norepinephrine bitartrate	WI	1 mg/ml	AB	40 mEq/L[f]	Physically compatible for at least 4 hr at room temperature by visual and microscopic examination	534	C
Ondansetron HCl	GL	1 mg/ml[b]	AB	0.1 mEq/ml[a]	Physically compatible for 4 hr at 22 °C	1365	C
Oxacillin sodium	BR	100 mg/ml	AB	40 mEq/L[f]	Physically compatible for at least 4 hr at room temperature by visual and microscopic examination	534	C
Oxytocin	SZ	1 mg/ml	AB	40 mEq/L[f]	Physically compatible for at least 4 hr at room temperature by visual and microscopic examination	534	C
Paclitaxel	NCI	1.2 mg/ml[a]	AB	0.1 mEq/ml[a]	Physically compatible with no change in measured turbidity in 4 hr at 22 °C	1556	C
Penicillin G potassium	LI	200,000 units		40 mEq/L[c]	Physically compatible for at least 4 hr at room temperature by visual and microscopic examination	322	C
Pentazocine lactate	WI	30 mg/ml	AB	40 mEq/L[f]	Physically compatible for at least 4 hr at room temperature by visual and microscopic examination	534	C
Phenytoin sodium	PD	50 mg/ml		40 mEq/L[a]	Immediate formation of phenytoin crystals	322	I
	PD	50 mg/ml		40 mEq/L[b,i]	Phenytoin crystals form in 4 hr at room temperature	322	I
Phytonadione	RC	10 mg/ml	AB	40 mEq/L[f]	Physically compatible for at least 4 hr at room temperature by visual and microscopic examination	534	C
Piperacillin sodium–tazobactam sodium	LE	40 + 5 mg/ml[a]	AB	0.1 mEq/ml[a]	Physically compatible with no change in measured turbidity or increase in particle content in 4 hr at 22 °C	1688	C

Y-Site Injection Compatibility (1:1 Mixture) (Cont.)

Potassium chloride

Drug	*Mfr*	*Conc*	*Mfr*	*Conc*	*Remarks*	*Ref*	*C/I*
Procainamide HCl	SQ	100 mg/ml	AB	40 mEq/L[f]	Physically compatible for at least 4 hr at room temperature by visual and microscopic examination	534	C
Prochlorperazine edisylate	SKF	5 mg/ml	AB	40 mEq/L[f]	Physically compatible for at least 4 hr at room temperature by visual and microscopic examination	534	C
Promethazine HCl	SV	50 mg/ml	AB	40 mEq/L[j]	Physically compatible initially, but cloudiness developed in 4 hr at room temperature	534	I
	SV	50 mg/ml	AB	40 mEq/L[k]	Physically compatible for at least 4 hr at room temperature by visual and microscopic examination	534	C
Propofol	ZEN	10 mg/ml	AB	0.1 mEq/ml[a]	Physically compatible for 1 hr at 23 °C with no increase in particle content	2066	C
Propranolol HCl	AY	1 mg/ml	AB	40 mEq/L[f]	Physically compatible for at least 4 hr at room temperature by visual and microscopic examination	534	C
Pyridostigmine bromide	RC	5 mg/ml	AB	40 mEq/L[f]	Physically compatible for at least 4 hr at room temperature by visual and microscopic examination	534	C
Remifentanil HCl	GW	0.025 and 0.25 mg/ml[b]	AB	0.1 mEq/ml[a]	Physically compatible with no change in measured turbidity or increase in particle content in 4 hr at 23 °C	2075	C
Sargramostim	IMM	10 μg/ml[b]	AB	0.1 mEq/ml[b]	Physically compatible for 4 hr at 22 °C under fluorescent light	1436	C
Scopolamine HBr	BW	0.86 mg/ml	AB	40 mEq/L[f]	Physically compatible for at least 4 hr at room temperature by visual and microscopic examination	534	C
Sodium bicarbonate	BR	75 mg/ml		40 mEq/L[c]	Physically compatible for at least 4 hr at room temperature by visual and microscopic examination	322	C
Succinylcholine chloride	BW	20 mg/ml		40 mEq/L[c]	Physically compatible for at least 4 hr at room temperature by visual and microscopic examination	322	C
Tacrolimus	FUJ	1 mg/ml[b]	AB	2 mEq/ml	Visually compatible for 24 hr at 25 °C	1630	C
Teniposide	BR	0.1 mg/ml[a]	AB	0.1 mEq/ml[a]	Physically compatible with no subvisual haze or particle formation in 4 hr at 23 °C	1725	C
Theophylline	TR	4 mg/ml	AB	0.2 mEq/ml[a]	Visually compatible for 6 hr at 25 °C	1793	C
Thiotepa	IMM[l]	1 mg/ml[a]	AMR	0.1 mEq/ml[a]	Physically compatible with no change in measured turbidity or increase in particle content in 4 hr at 23 °C	1861	C
Tirofiban HCl	ME	0.05 mg/ml[a]	AB	0.01 and 0.04 mEq/ml[a,b]	Physically compatible with no tirofiban loss by HPLC in 4 hr at room temperature under fluorescent light	2250	C
	ME	0.05 mg/ml[b]	AB	0.01 and 0.04 mEq/ml[a,b]	Physically compatible with no tirofiban loss by HPLC in 4 hr at room temperature under fluorescent light	2250	C

Y-Site Injection Compatibility (1:1 Mixture) (Cont.)

Drug	Mfr	Conc	Potassium chloride Mfr	Potassium chloride Conc	Remarks	Ref	C/I
TNA #218 to #226[m]			AB	0.1 mEq/ml[a]	Visually compatible with no precipitate or emulsion damage apparent in 4 hr at 23 °C	2215	C
TPN #189[m]			AST	30 mg/ml[b]	Visually compatible for 24 hr at 22 °C	1767	C
TPN #212 to #215[m]			AB	0.1 mEq/ml[a]	Physically compatible with no change in measured turbidity or increase in particle content in 4 hr at 23 °C	2109	C
Trimethobenzamide HCl	RC	100 mg/ml	AB	40 mEq/L[f]	Physically compatible for at least 4 hr at room temperature by visual and microscopic examination	534	C
Vinorelbine tartrate	BW	1 mg/ml[b]	AB	0.1 mEq/ml[b]	Physically compatible with no change in measured turbidity or increase in particle content in 4 hr at 22 °C	1558	C
Warfarin sodium	DME	2 mg/ml[g]	BA	0.04 mEq/ml[n]	Visually compatible for 24 hr at 24 °C	2078	C
Zidovudine	BW	4 mg/ml[a]	IMS	0.67 mEq/ml[a]	Physically compatible for 4 hr at 25 °C under fluorescent light by visual and microscopic examination	1193	C

[a]*Tested in dextrose 5% in water.*
[b]*Tested in sodium chloride 0.9%.*
[c]*Tested in dextrose 5% in water, sodium chloride 0.9%, and Ringer's injection, lactated.*
[d]*Tested in both dextrose 5% in water and sodium chloride 0.9%.*
[e]*Tested in sodium chloride 0.45%.*
[f]*Tested in dextrose 5% in Ringer's injection, dextrose 5% in Ringer's injection, lactated, dextrose 5% in water, Ringer's injection, lactated, and sodium chloride 0.9%.*
[g]*Tested in sterile water for injection.*
[h]*Tested in bacteriostatic sodium chloride 0.9% preserved with benzyl alcohol 0.9%.*
[i]*Tested in Ringer's injection, lactated.*
[j]*Tested in dextrose 5% in Ringer's injection.*
[k]*Tested in dextrose 5% in Ringer's injection, lactated, dextrose 5% in water, Ringer's injection, lactated, and sodium chloride 0.9%.*
[l]*Lyophilized formulation tested.*
[m]*Refer to Appendix I for the composition of parenteral nutrition solutions. TNA indicates a 3-in-1 admixture, and TPN indicates a 2-in-1 admixture.*
[n]*Tested in dextrose 5% in sodium chloride 0.45%.*

Additional Compatibility Information

Infusion Solutions — Great care is required when adding potassium chloride to infusion solutions, whether in flexible plastic containers or in rigid bottles. Adding potassium chloride to running infusion solutions hanging in the use position, especially in flexible containers, has resulted in the pooling of potassium chloride and a resultant high-concentration bolus of the drug being administered to patients, with serious and even fatal consequences. Attempts to mix adequately the potassium chloride in flexible containers by squeezing the container in the hanging position were unsuccessful. It is recommended that drugs be admixed with solutions in flexible containers when positioned with the injection arm of the container uppermost. With both rigid bottles and flexible containers, subsequent repeated inversion and agitation to effect thorough mixture are necessary. (85; 130; 454–456; 714; 715; 1127; 1778; 2151)

Methylprednisolone — The compatibility of methylprednisolone sodium succinate (Upjohn) with potassium chloride added to an auxiliary medication infusion unit has been studied. Primary admixtures were prepared by adding potassium chloride 40 mEq/L to dextrose 5% in water, dextrose 5% in sodium chloride 0.9%, and Ringer's injection, lactated. The primary admixture was added along with methylprednisolone sodium succinate (Upjohn) to the auxiliary medication infusion unit with the following results (329):

Methylprednisolone Sodium Succinate	Potassium Chloride 40 mEq/L Primary Solution	Results
500 mg	D5S, D5W, LR qs 100 ml	Clear solution for 24 hr
1000 mg	D5W qs 100 ml	Clear solution for 24 hr
1000 mg	D5S, LR qs 100 ml	Clear solution for 6 hr
2000 mg	D5S, D5W, LR qs 100 ml	Clear solution for 24 hr

Other Drugs — Potassium chloride appears to be physically compatible with ceftazidime. (4)

The addition of potassium chloride to mannitol 20 or 25% solutions may cause precipitation of the mannitol. (38)

POTASSIUM PHOSPHATES
AHFS 40:12

Products — Potassium phosphates injection is available from several manufacturers in single-dose flip-top vials containing 5 or 15 ml of solution and 50-ml bulk additive solution containers. (29) Each milliliter of solution contains monobasic potassium phosphate 224 mg and dibasic potassium phosphate 236 mg in water for injection. The phosphate concentration of the solution is 3 mmol/ml, and the potassium content is 4.4 mEq/ml. This concentrated solution must be diluted for use. (1-11/98; 4)

pH — Potassium phosphates injection is stated to have a pH of approximately 7 to 7.8. (4) However, some products cite a pH range of 6.2 to 6.8. (1-11/98)

Osmolarity — The osmolarity of potassium phosphates injection has been variously cited as 12 mOsm/ml (1-2/94) and 7.4 mOsm/ml. (1-11/98)

Administration — Potassium phosphates injection is administered slowly intravenously diluted in infusion solutions. (4)

The relationship between milliequivalents and millimoles of phosphate is expressed in the following equation:

$$\text{mEq phosphate} = \text{mmol phosphate} \times \text{valence}$$

However, the average valence of phosphate changes with changes in pH. Consequently, it is necessary to specify a pH before the valence, and therefore the milliequivalents, can be determined. To avoid this problem, it has been suggested that doses of phosphate be expressed in terms of millimoles, which is independent of valence. (178; 716–718) Alternatively, the dose may be expressed in terms of milligrams of phosphorus. One millimole of phosphorus equals 31 mg. (205; 717)

Stability — Potassium phosphates injection should be stored at controlled room temperature. The solutions should be clear and free of particulate matter. (1-11/98)

Compatibility Information

Solution Compatibility

Potassium phosphates

Solution	*Mfr*	*Mfr*	*Conc/L*	*Remarks*	*Ref*	*C/I*
Amino acids 4%, dextrose 25%	CU	MG	100 mEq	Physically compatible for 24 hr at 22 °C	313	C
Dextran 6% in dextrose 5%	AB	AB	160 mEq	Physically compatible	3	C
Dextran 6% in sodium chloride 0.9%	AB	AB	160 mEq	Physically compatible	3	C
Dextrose 2½% in half-strength Ringer's injection	AB	AB	160 mEq	Haze or precipitate forms within 1 hr	3	I
Dextrose 5% in Ringer's injection	AB	AB	160 mEq	Haze or precipitate forms within 1 hr	3	I
Dextrose 2½% in half-strength Ringer's injection, lactated	AB	AB	160 mEq	Haze or precipitate forms within 24 hr	3	I
Dextrose 5% in Ringer's injection, lactated	AB	AB	160 mEq	Haze or precipitate forms within 24 hr	3	I
Dextrose 10% in Ringer's injection	AB	AB	160 mEq	Physically compatible	3	C
Dextrose 10% in Ringer's injection, lactated	AB	AB	160 mEq	Physically compatible	3	C
Dextrose–saline combinations (except as noted below)	AB	AB	160 mEq	Physically compatible	3	C
Dextrose 10% in sodium chloride 0.9%	AB	AB	160 mEq	Haze or precipitate forms within 24 hr	3	I
Dextrose 2½% in water	AB	AB	160 mEq	Physically compatible	3	C
Dextrose 5% in water	AB	AB	160 mEq	Physically compatible	3	C
Dextrose 10% in water	AB	AB	160 mEq	Physically compatible	3	C
Fructose 10% in sodium chloride 0.9%	AB	AB	160 mEq	Physically compatible	3	C
Fructose 10% in water	AB	AB	160 mEq	Physically compatible	3	C
Invert sugar 5 and 10% in sodium chloride 0.9%	AB	AB	160 mEq	Physically compatible	3	C
Invert sugar 5 and 10% in water	AB	AB	160 mEq	Physically compatible	3	C
Ionosol products (except as noted below)	AB	AB	160 mEq	Physically compatible	3	C
Ionosol D-CM	AB	AB	160 mEq	Haze or precipitate forms within 1 hr	3	I
Ionosol D-CM with dextrose 5%	AB	AB	160 mEq	Haze or precipitate forms within 6 hr	3	I

Solution Compatibility (Cont.)

Potassium phosphates

Solution	*Mfr*	*Mfr*	*Conc/L*	*Remarks*	*Ref*	*C/I*
Ionosol D with invert sugar 10%	AB	AB	160 mEq	Color change	3	I
Ionosol D modified with invert sugar 10%	AB	AB	160 mEq	Haze or precipitate forms within 24 hr	3	I
Ringer's injection	AB	AB	160 mEq	Haze or precipitate forms within 1 hr	3	I
Ringer's injection, lactated	AB	AB	160 mEq	Haze or precipitate forms within 24 hr	3	I
Sodium chloride 0.45%	AB	AB	160 mEq	Physically compatible	3	C
Sodium chloride 0.9%	AB	AB	160 mEq	Physically compatible	3	C
Sodium lactate ⅙ M	AB	AB	160 mEq	Physically compatible	3	C
TPN #11 to #15[a]		MG	10 to 40 mEq	Physically compatible for 24 hr at 22 °C. TLC changes of amino acids in similar solutions attributed to M.V.I. or vitamin B complex with C	313	C
TPN #81 to #85[a]		MG	10 to 40 mEq	Physically compatible for 24 hr at 22 °C. Changes in UV spectra of amino acids and vitamins in solutions with M.V.I. and vitamin B complex with C. TLC changes in similar solutions attributed to vitamins	313	C

[a]*Refer to Appendix I for the composition of parenteral nutrition solutions. TPN indicates a 2-in-1 admixture.*

Additive Compatibility

Potassium phosphates

Drug	*Mfr*	*Conc/L*	*Mfr*	*Conc/L*	*Test Soln*	*Remarks*	*Ref*	*C/I*
Dobutamine HCl	LI	200 mg	AB	100 mmol	NS	Small particles form after 1 hr. White precipitate noted after 15 hr	552	I
Magnesium sulfate	LI	1, 2, 3, 4 mEq	MG	10, 20, 30, 40 mEq	AA 4%, D 25%	Physically compatible for 24 hr at 22 °C	313	C
Metoclopramide HCl	RB	10 and 160 mg	IX	15 mmol	NS	Physically compatible for 48 hr at room temperature	924	C
	RB	10 and 160 mg	IX	15 mmol		Physically compatible for 48 hr at 25 °C	1167	C
Verapamil HCl	KN	80 mg	AB	88 mEq	D5W, NS	Physically compatible for 24 hr	764	C

Y-Site Injection Compatibility (1:1 Mixture)

Potassium phosphates

Drug	*Mfr*	*Conc*	*Mfr*	*Conc*	*Remarks*	*Ref*	*C/I*
Ciprofloxacin	BAY	2 mg/ml[a,b]	APP	3 mmol/ml	Transient precipitate forms on first contact, becoming crystalline precipitate within 1 hr	2290	I
	BAY	2 mg/ml[a,d]	APP	0.06 mmol/ml[a,b]	Transient precipitate forms on first contact, becoming crystalline precipitate within 1 hr	2290	I
Diltiazem HCl	MMD	5 mg/ml	AMR	0.015 mmol/ml	Visually compatible	1807	C
Enalaprilat	MSD	0.05 mg/ml[b]	LY	0.44 mEq/ml[a]	Physically compatible for 24 hr at room temperature under fluorescent light	1355	C

Y-Site Injection Compatibility (1:1 Mixture) (Cont.)

Potassium phosphates

Drug	*Mfr*	*Conc*	*Mfr*	*Conc*	*Remarks*	*Ref*	*C/I*
Esmolol HCl	DCC	10 mg/ml[a]	LY	0.44 mEq/ml[a]	Physically compatible for 24 hr at 22 °C	1169	C
Famotidine	MSD	0.2 mg/ml[a]	LY	3 mmol/ml	Physically compatible for 14 hr	1196	C
Gatifloxacin	BMS	2 mg/ml[a]	AB	3 mmol/ml	Microprecipitate formed in 1 of 6 replicates	2234	I
Labetalol HCl	SC	1 mg/ml[a]	LY	0.44 mEq/ml[a]	Physically compatible for 24 hr at 18 °C	1171	C
TNA #218 to #226[c]			AB	3 mmol/ml	Damage to emulsion integrity occurs immediately with free oil formation possible	2215	I
TPN #212 to #215[c]			AB	3 mmol/ml	Increased turbidity forms immediately	2109	I

[a]*Tested in dextrose 5% in water.*
[b]*Tested in sodium chloride 0.9%.*
[c]*Refer to Appendix I for the composition of parenteral nutrition solutions. TNA indicates a 3-in-1 admixture, and TPN indicates a 2-in-1 admixture.*
[d]*Manufacturer's premixed solution.*

Additional Compatibility Information

Calcium and Phosphate — UNRECOGNIZED CALCIUM PHOSPHATE PRECIPITATION IN A 3-IN-1 PARENTERAL NUTRITION MIXTURE RESULTED IN PATIENT DEATH. The potential for the formation of a calcium phosphate precipitate in parenteral nutrition solutions is well studied and documented (1771; 1777), but the information is complex and difficult to apply to the clinical situation. (1770; 1772; 1777) The incorporation of fat emulsion in 3-in-1 parenteral nutrition solutions obscures any precipitate that is present which has led to substantial debate on the dangers associated with 3-in-1 parenteral nutrition mixtures and when or if the danger to the patient is warranted therapeutically. (1770–1772; 2031–2036) Because such precipitation may be life-threatening to patients (2037; 2291), the Food and Drug Administration issued a Safety Alert containing the following recommendations (1769):

"1. The amounts of phosphorus and of calcium added to the admixture are critical. The solubility of the added calcium should be calculated from the volume at the time the calcium is added. It should not be based upon the final volume.

Some amino acid injections for TPN admixtures contain phosphate ions (as a phosphoric acid buffer). These phosphate ions and the volume at the time the phosphate is added should be considered when calculating the concentration of phosphate additives. Also, when adding calcium and phosphate to an admixture, the phosphate should be added first.

The line should be flushed between the addition of any potentially incompatible components.

2. A lipid emulsion in a three-in-one admixture obscures the presence of a precipitate. Therefore, if a lipid emulsion is needed, either (1) use a two-in-one admixture with the lipid infused separately, or (2) if a three-in-one admixture is medically necessary, then add the calcium before the lipid emulsion and according to the recommendations in number 1 above.

If the amount of calcium or phosphate which must be added is likely to cause a precipitate, some or all of the calcium should be administered separately. Such separate infusions must be properly diluted and slowly infused to avoid serious adverse events related to the calcium.

3. When using an automated compounding device, the above steps should be considered when programming the device. In addition, automated compounders should be maintained and operated according to the manufacturer's recommendations.

Any printout should be checked against the programmed admixture and weight of components.

4. During the mixing process, pharmacists who mix parenteral nutrition admixtures should periodically agitate the admixture and check for precipitates. Medical or home care personnel who start and monitor these infusions should carefully inspect for the presence of precipitates both before and during infusion. Patients and care givers should be trained to visually inspect for signs of precipitation. They also should be advised to stop the infusion and seek medical assistance if precipitates are noted.

5. A filter should be used when infusing either central or peripheral parenteral nutrition admixtures. At this time, data have not been submitted to document which size filter is most effective in trapping precipitates.

Standards of practice vary, but the following is suggested: a 1.2-µm air-eliminating filter for lipid-containing admixtures and a 0.22-µm air-eliminating filter for non-lipid-containing admixtures.

6. Parenteral nutrition admixtures should be administered within the following time frames: if stored at room temperature, the infusion should be started within 24 hours after mixing; if stored at refrigerated temperatures, the infusion should be started within 24 hours of rewarming. Because warming parenteral nutrition admixtures may contribute to the formation of precipitates, once administration begins, care should be taken to avoid excessive warming of the admixture.

Persons administering home care parenteral nutrition admixtures may need to deviate from these time frames. Pharmacists who initially prepare these admixtures should check a reserve sample for precipitates over the duration and under the conditions of storage.

7. If symptoms of acute respiratory distress, pulmonary emboli, or interstitial pneumonitis develop, the infusion should be stopped

immediately and thoroughly checked for precipitates. Appropriate medical interventions should be instituted. Home care personnel and patients should immediately seek medical assistance."

Calcium Phosphate Precipitation Fatalities—Hill et al. reported fatal cases of paroxysmal respiratory failure in two previously healthy women receiving peripheral vein parenteral nutrition. The patients experienced sudden cardiopulmonary arrest consistent with pulmonary emboli. The authors used in vitro simulations and an animal model to conclude that unrecognized calcium phosphate precipitation in a 3-in-1 total nutrition admixture caused the fatalities. The precipitation resulted during compounding by introducing calcium and phosphate near to one another in the compounding sequence and prior to complete fluid addition. This resulted in a temporarily high concentration of the drugs and precipitation of calcium phosphate. Observation of the precipitate was obscured by the incorporation of 20% fat emulsion, intravenous into the nutrition mixture. No filter was used during infusion of the fatal nutrition admixtures. (2037)

In a follow-up retrospective review, Shay et al. reported that five patients were identified that had respiratory distress associated with the infusion of the 3-in-1 admixtures at around the same time. Four of these five patients died, although the cause of death could be definitively determined for only two of them. (2291)

Calcium and Phosphate Conditional Compatibility—Calcium salts are conditionally compatible with phosphate in parenteral nutrition solutions. The incompatibility is dependent on a solubility and concentration phenomenon and is not entirely predictable. Precipitation may occur during compounding or at some time after compounding is completed.

NOTE: Some amino acids solutions inherently contain calcium and phosphate, which must be considered in any projection of compatibility. See the Amino Acid Injection monograph, Table 1.

It has been noted that the order of mixing of calcium gluconate and potassium phosphate may affect compatibility at elevated concentrations. Addition of potassium phosphate should precede calcium gluconate. (313)

Eggert et al. (609) evaluated the compatibility of calcium and phosphate in several parenteral nutrition formulas for newborn infants. Calcium gluconate 10% (Cutter) and potassium phosphate (Abbott) were used to achieve concentrations of 2.5 to 100 mEq/L of calcium and 2.5 to 100 mmol/L of phosphorus added. The parenteral nutrition solutions evaluated were as shown in Table 1.

Eggert et al. noted the pH dependence of the phosphate–calcium precipitation. Dibasic calcium phosphate is very insoluble while monobasic calcium phosphate is relatively soluble. At low pH, the soluble monobasic form predominates; but as the pH increases, more dibasic phosphate becomes available to bind with calcium and precipitate. Therefore, the lower the pH of the parenteral nutrition solution, the more calcium and phosphate can be solubilized. Once again, the effects of temperature were also observed. As the temperature is increased, more calcium ion becomes available and more dibasic calcium phosphate is formed. Therefore, temperature increases increase the amount of precipitate. (609)

Table 1. Parenteral Nutrition Solutions Evaluated by Eggert et al. (609)

	Solution Number			
Component	#1	#2	#3	#4
FreAmine III	4%	2%	1%	1%
Dextrose	25%	20%	10%	10%
pH	6.3	6.4	6.6	7.0[a]

[a]*Adjusted with sodium hydroxide.*

Fitzgerald and MacKay reported calcium and phosphate solubility curves for neonatal parenteral nutrition solutions using TrophAmine (McGaw) 2, 1.5, and 0.8% as the sources of amino acids. The solutions also contained dextrose 10%, with cysteine and pH adjustment in some admixtures. Calcium and phosphate solubility followed the patterns reported by Eggert et al. (609) A slightly greater concentration of phosphate could be used in some mixtures, but this finding was not consistent. (1024)

Using a similar study design, Fitzgerald and MacKay also studied six neonatal parenteral nutrition solutions based on Aminosyn-PF (Abbott) 2, 1.5, and 0.8%, with and without added cysteine HCl and dextrose 10%. Calcium concentrations ranged from 2.5 to 50 mEq/L, and phosphate concentrations ranged from 2.5 to 50 mmol/L. Solutions sat for 18 hours at 25 °C and then were warmed to 37 °C in a water bath to simulate the clinical situation of warming prior to infusion into a child. Solubility curves were markedly different than those for TrophAmine in the previous study. (1024) Solubilities were reported to decrease by 15 mEq/L for calcium and 15 mmol/L for phosphate. The solutions remained clear during room temperature storage, but crystals often formed on warming to 37 °C. (1211)

However, these data were questioned by Mikrut, who noted the similarities between the Aminosyn-PF and TrophAmine products and found little difference in calcium and phosphate solubilities in a preliminary report. (1212) In the full report (1213), parenteral nutrition solutions containing Aminosyn-PF or TrophAmine 1 or 2.5% with dextrose 10 or 25%, respectively, plus electrolytes and trace metals, with or without cysteine HCl, were evaluated under the same conditions used by Fitzgerald and MacKay. Calcium concentrations ranged from 2.5 to 50 mEq/L, and phosphate concentrations ranged from 5 to 50 mmol/L. In contrast to the results of Fitzgerald and MacKay, the solubility curves were very similar for the Aminosyn-PF and TrophAmine parenteral nutrition solutions but very different from those of the previous Aminosyn-PF study. (1211) The authors again showed that the solubility of calcium and phosphate is greater in solutions containing higher concentrations of amino acids and dextrose. (1213)

Dunham et al. also reported calcium and phosphate solubility curves for TrophAmine 1 and 2% with dextrose 10% and electrolytes, vitamins, heparin, and trace elements. Calcium concentrations ranged from 10 to 60 mEq/L, and phosphorus concentrations ranged from 10 to 40 mmol/L. Calcium and phosphate solubilities were assessed by analysis of the calcium concentrations and followed patterns similar to those reported by Henry et al. (608) and Eggert et al. (609) The higher percentage of amino acids (TrophAmine 2%) permitted a slightly greater solubility of calcium and phosphate, especially in the 10 to 50 mEq/L and 10 to 35 mmol/L ranges, respectively. (1614)

Knight et al. reported the maximal product of the amount of calcium (as gluconate) times phosphate (as potassium) that can be added to a parenteral nutrition solution, composed of amino acids 1% (Travenol) and dextrose 10%, for preterm infants. Turbidity was observed on initial mixing when the solubility product was around 115 to 130 $mmol^2$ or greater. After storage at 7 °C for 20 hours, visible precipitates formed at solubility products of 130 $mmol^2$ or greater. If the solution was administered through a barium-impregnated silicone rubber catheter, crystalline precipitates obstructed the catheters in 12 hours at a solubility product of 100 mmol^2 and in 10 days at 79 mmol^2, much lower than the in vitro results. (1041)

Alexander and Arena evaluated the compatibility of calcium gluconate (American Quinine) and potassium phosphate (Lyphomed) in a parenteral nutrition solution, composed of dextrose 12.5% and amino acid injection (FreAmine III, McGaw) 1.33% and having a pH of 6.6, for premature infants. Potassium phosphate was added in varying amounts to samples of this solution. The samples were then titrated with calcium gluconate 10%. From the resulting data, an equation was derived to predict when precipitation would occur:

$$Y = -0.455X + 2.951$$

where Y is the Log_{10} of the calcium gluconate concentration (as mg/100 ml) and X is the phosphate concentration (as mmol/100 ml). The equation can be solved to determine the maximum concentration of calcium gluconate for a given phosphate concentration or vice versa. If either additive is sufficiently dilute, then the other can be added in high concentrations without precipitation occurring, obviating the need for the equation. These lower limits were set at 60 mg/100 ml for calcium gluconate and 0.6 mmol/100 ml for phosphate. (1004)

While the authors noted that this equation technically applies to the specific solution being tested and that other variables such as temperature can affect precipitation, in practice they found it applicable to a variety of parenteral nutrition solutions, having similar components and pH values, for premature infants. The equation is *not* applicable to parenteral nutrition solutions with amino acid and dextrose concentrations, other components, or pH values that are much different. (1004)

Venkataraman et al. evaluated the solubility of calcium and phosphorus in neonatal parenteral nutrition solutions composed of amino acids (Abbott) 1.25 and 2.5% with dextrose 5 and 10%, respectively. Also present were multivitamins and trace elements. The solutions contained calcium (as gluconate) in amounts ranging from 25 to 200 mg/100 ml. The phosphorus (as potassium phosphate) concentrations evaluated ranged from 25 to 150 mg/100 ml. If calcium gluconate was added first, cloudiness occurred immediately. If potassium phosphate was added first, substantial quantities could be added with no precipitate formation in 48 hours at 4 °C (Table 2). However, if stored at 22 °C, the solutions were stable for only 24 hours, and all contained precipitates after 48 hours. (1210)

Kirkpatrick et al. reported the physical compatibility of calcium gluconate 10 to 40 mEq/L and potassium phosphates 10 to 40 mmol/L in three neonatal parenteral nutrition solutions (TPN #123 to #125 in Appendix I), alone and with retrograde administration of aminophylline 7.5 mg diluted with 1.5 ml of sterile water for injection. Contact of the alkaline aminophylline solution with the parenteral nutrition solutions resulted in the precipitation of calcium phosphate at much lower concentrations than were compatible in the parenteral nutrition solutions alone. (1404)

Koorenhof and Timmer reported the maximum allowable concentrations of calcium and phosphate in a 3-in-1 parenteral nutrition mixture for children (TNA #192 in Appendix I). Added calcium was varied from 1.5 to 150 mmol/L, while added phosphate was varied from 21 to 300 mmol/L. The mixtures were stable for 48 hours at 22 and 37 °C as long as the pH was not greater than 5.7, the calcium concentration was below 16 mmol/L, the phosphate concentration was below 52 mmol/L, and the product of the calcium and phosphate concentrations was below 250 mmol^2/L^2. (1773)

MacKay et al. reported additional calcium and phosphate solubility curves for specialty parenteral nutrition solutions based on NephrAmine and also HepatAmine at concentrations of 0.8, 1.5, and 2% as the sources of amino acids. The solutions also contained dextrose 10%, with cysteine and pH adjustment to simulate addition of fat emulsion used in some admixtures. Calcium and phosphate solubility followed the hyperbolic patterns reported by Eggert et al. (609) Temperature, time, and pH affected calcium and phosphate solubility, with pH having the greatest effect. (2038)

Shatsky et al. reported the maximum sodium phosphate concentrations for given amounts of calcium gluconate that could be admixed in parenteral nutrition solutions containing TrophAmine in varying quantities (with cysteine HCl 40 mg/g of amino acid) and dextrose 10%. The solutions also contained magnesium sulfate 4 mEq/L, potassium acetate 24 mEq/L, sodium chloride 32 mEq/L, pediatric multivitamins, and trace elements. The presence of cysteine HCl reduces the solution pH and increases the amount of calcium and phosphate that can be incorporated before precipitation occurs. The results of this study cannot be safely extrapolated to TPN solutions with compositions other than the ones tested. The admixtures were compounded with the sodium phosphate added last, after thorough mixing of all other components. The authors noted this is not the preferred order of mixing (usually phosphate is added first and thoroughly mixed before adding calcium last); however, they believed this reversed order of mixing would provide a margin of error in cases in which the proper order is not followed. After compounding, the solutions were stored for 24 hours at 40 °C. The maximum calcium and phosphate amounts that could be mixed in the various solutions were reported tabularly and are shown in Table 3. (2039) However, these results are not entirely consistent with the study of Hoie and Narducci. (2196) See below.

The temperature dependence of the calcium–phosphate precipitation has resulted in the occlusion of a subclavian catheter by a solution apparently free of precipitation. The parenteral nutrition solution con-

Table 2. Maximum Calcium and Phosphorus Concentrations Physically Compatible for 48 Hours at 4 °C (1210)

Calcium (mg/100 ml)	Phosphorus (mg/100 ml): Amino Acids 1.25% + Dextrose 5%[a]	Amino Acids 2.5% + Dextrose 10%[a]
200[b]	50	75
150	50	100
100	75	100
50	100	125
25	150[b]	150[b]

[a]*Plus multivitamins and trace elements.*
[b]*Maximum concentration tested.*

Table 3. Maximum Amount of Phosphate (as Sodium) (mmol/L) Not Resulting in Precipitation According to the Study of Shatsky et al. (2039) See CAUTION below.[a]

Calcium (as gluconate)	Amino Acid (as TrophAmine) with Cysteine HCl 40 mg/g of Amino Acid: 0%	0.4%	1%	2%	3%
9.8 mEq/L	0	27	42	60	66
14.7 mEq/L	0	15	18	30	36
19.6 mEq/L	0	6	15	27	30
29.4 mEq/L	0	3	6	21	24

[a]*CAUTION: The results cannot be safely extrapolated to other solutions. See text.*

sisted of FreAmine III 500 ml, dextrose 70% 500 ml, sodium chloride 50 mEq, sodium phosphate 40 mmol, potassium acetate 10 mEq, potassium phosphate 40 mmol, calcium gluconate 10 mEq, magnesium sulfate 10 mEq, and Shil's trace metals solution 1 ml. Although there was no evidence of precipitation in the bottle, tubing and pump cassette, and filter (all at approximately 26 °C) during administration, the occluded catheter and Vicra Loop Lock (next to the patient's body at 37 °C) had numerous crystals identified as calcium phosphate. In vitro, it was found that this parenteral nutrition solution had a precipitate in 12 hours at 37 °C but was clear for 24 hours at 26 °C. (610)

Similarly, a parenteral nutrition solution that was clear and free of particulates after two weeks under refrigeration developed a precipitate in four to six hours when stored at room temperature. When the solution was warmed in a 37 °C water bath, precipitation occurred in one hour. Administration of the solution before the precipitate was noticed led to interstitial pneumonitis due to deposition of calcium phosphate crystals. (1427)

Fausel et al. evaluated calcium phosphate precipitation phenomena in a series of parenteral nutrition admixtures composed of dextrose 22%, amino acids (FreAmine III) 2.7%, and fat emulsion (Abbott) 0, 1, and 3.2%. Incorporation of calcium gluconate 19 to 24 mEq/L and phosphate (as sodium) 22 to 28 mmol/L resulted in visible precipitation in the fat-free admixtures. New precipitate continued to form over 14 days, even after repeated filtrations of the solutions through 0.2-μm filters. The presence of the amino acids increased calcium and phosphate solubility compared to simple aqueous solutions. However, the incorporation of the fat emulsion did not result in a statistically significant increase in calcium and phosphate solubility. The authors noted that the pharmacokinetics of calcium phosphate precipitate formation do not appear to be entirely predictable; both transient and permanent precipitation can occur either during the compounding process or at some time afterward. Because calcium phosphate precipitation can be clinically very dangerous, the use of inline filters was recommended. The filters should have a porosity appropriate to the parenteral nutrition admixture: 1.2 μm for fat-containing and 0.2 or 0.45 μm for fat-free nutrition mixtures. (2061)

Hoie and Narducci used laser particle analysis to evaluate the formation of calcium phosphate precipitation in pediatric TPN solutions containing TrophAmine in concentrations ranging from 0.5 to 3% with dextrose 10% and also containing L-cysteine HCl 1 g/L. The solutions also contained in each liter sodium chloride 20 mEq, sodium acetate 20 mEq, magnesium sulfate 3 mEq, trace elements 3 ml, and heparin sodium 500 units. The presence of L-cysteine HCl reduces the solution pH and increases the amount of calcium and phosphate that can be incorporated before precipitation occurs. The results of this study cannot be safely extrapolated to TPN solutions with compositions other than the ones tested. The maximum amounts of phosphate that were incorporated without the appearance of a measurable increase in particulates in 24 hours at 37 °C for each of the amino acids concentrations is shown in Table 4. (2196) These results are not entirely consistent with those of Shatsky et al. See above. The use of more sensitive electronic particle measurement for the formation of subvisual particulates in this study may contribute to the differences in the results.

Zhang et al. evaluated calcium and phosphate compatibility in a series of parenteral nutrition admixtures composed of Aminosyn II in concentrations ranging from 2% up to 5% (TPN #227 to #231 in Appendix I). The solutions also contained dextrose ranging from 10% up to 25%. Also present were sodium chloride, potassium chloride, and magnesium sulfate in common amounts. Phosphates as the potassium salt and calcium as the acetate salt were added in variable quantities to determine the maximum amounts of calcium and phosphates that could be added to the representative TPN admixtures. The samples were evaluated at 23 and 37 °C over 48 hours by visual inspection in ambient light and using a Tyndall beam and electronically measured for turbidity and microparticulates. The boundaries between the compatible and incompatible concentrations were presented graphically as hyperbolic curves. (2265)

Table 4. Maximum Amount of Phosphate (as Potassium) (mmol/L) Not Resulting in Precipitation According to the Study of Hoie and Narducci. (2196) See CAUTION below.[a]

Calcium (as Gluconate) (mEq/L)	Amino Acid (as TrophAmine) plus Cysteine HCl 1 g/L					
	0.5%	1%	1.5%	2%	2.5%	3%
10	22	28	38	38	38	43
14	18	18	18	38	38	43
19	18	18	18	33	33	38
24	12	18	18	22	28	28
28	12	18	18	18	18	18
33	12	12	12	12	12	12
37	12	12	12	12	12	12
41	9	9	9	12	12	12
45	0	9	9	12	12	12
49	0	9	9	9	12	12
53	0	9	9	9	9	9

[a]*CAUTION: The results cannot be safely extrapolated to solutions with formulas other than the ones tested. See text.*

The presence of magnesium in solutions may also influence the reaction between calcium and phosphate, including the nature and extent of precipitation. (158; 159)

The interaction of calcium and phosphate in parenteral nutrition solutions is a complex phenomenon. Various factors have been identified as playing a role in the solubility or precipitation of a given combination, including (608; 609; 1042; 1063; 1404; 1427):

1. Concentration of calcium
2. Salt form of calcium
3. Concentration of phosphate
4. Concentration of amino acids
5. Amino acids composition
6. Concentration of dextrose
7. Temperature of solution
8. pH of solution
9. Presence of other additives
10. Order of mixing

Enhanced precipitate formation would be expected from such factors as high concentrations of calcium and phosphate, increases in solution pH, decreased amino acid concentrations, increases in temperature, addition of calcium prior to the phosphate, lengthy standing times or slow infusion rates, and use of calcium as the chloride salt. (854)

Even if precipitation does not occur in the container, it has been reported that crystallization of calcium phosphate may occur in a Silastic infusion pump chamber or tubing if the rate of administration is slow, as for premature infants. Water vapor may be transmitted outward and be replaced by air rapidly enough to produce supersaturation. (202) Several other cases of catheter occlusion have been reported. (610; 1427–1429)

The UV spectrum of an equal parts mixture of amino acids 8%–

dextrose 50% solution was not altered in 24 hours at 22 °C by the addition of calcium gluconate 20 mEq and potassium phosphate 25 mEq. (313)

Also see the monograph on sodium phosphates.

Ciprofloxacin — Although ciprofloxacin was reported to be compatible with potassium phosphates (1628), subsequent testing has found that crystalline precipitation forms during simultaneous administration with either potassium or sodium phosphates. (671; 1971; 1972; 2290) See Y-Site Injection Compatibility Table above.

Ciprofloxacin (Bayer) 2 mg/ml in sodium chloride 0.9% or dextrose 5% in water was evaluated for compatibility with potassium phosphates 3 mmol/ml (undiluted) and diluted to 0.06 mg/ml in sodium chloride 0.9% or dextrose 5% in water in simulated simultaneous administration. All samples exhibited transient white precipitate upon first contact that became a crystalline precipitate within an hour. (2290) Precipitation was also reported during clinical administration of a premixed solution of ciprofloxacin 2 mg/ml in dextrose 5% in water (Bayer) with potassium phosphates 0.06 mg/ml in dextrose 5% in water. (671) In addition, the manufacturer has had reports of precipitation of these drugs. (2009) Sodium phosphates 3 mmol/ml was similarly incompatible with ciprofloxacin (Bayer) 2 mg/ml in dextrose 5% in water or sodium chloride 0.9%, resulting in crystalline precipitation. (1971; 1972)

Consequently, ciprofloxacin and phosphates should be considered incompatible across a broad range of phosphate concentrations.

PROCAINAMIDE HCL
AHFS 24:04

Products — Procainamide HCl is available in 10-ml vials providing 100 mg/ml or 2-ml vials and 2-ml syringe cartridges providing 500 mg/ml. The 100-mg/ml form also contains benzyl alcohol 0.9% and sodium metabisulfite 0.09%. The 500-mg/ml form contains benzyl alcohol 0.9% and sodium metabisulfite 0.2%. In both forms, the pH is adjusted with hydrochloric acid and/or sodium hydroxide. (1-2/98; 4; 29)

pH — From 4 to 6. (4)

Osmolality — Procainamide HCl 500 mg/ml has an osmolality exceeding 2000 mOsm/kg. (1689)

Trade Name(s) — Pronestyl.

Administration — Procainamide HCl may be administered by intramuscular or direct intravenous injection or intravenous infusion. Both the 100- and 500-mg/ml forms may be diluted prior to intravenous use to facilitate control of the administration rate. The intravenous rate of administration should not exceed 50 mg/min. (1-2/98; 4)

Stability — Procainamide HCl may be stored at controlled room temperature. (1-2/98; 4) However, refrigeration retards oxidation, which causes color formation. The solution is initially colorless but may turn slightly yellow on standing. Injection of air into the vial causes the solution to darken. Solutions darker than a light amber should be discarded. (4)

Sorption — Procainamide HCl (Sigma) 8 mg/L in sodium chloride 0.9% (Travenol) in PVC bags did not exhibit significant sorption to the plastic during one week of storage at room temperature (15 to 20 °C). (536)

In another study, procainamide HCl (Sigma) 8 mg/L in sodium chloride 0.9% did not exhibit any loss due to sorption during a seven-hour simulated infusion through an infusion set (Travenol) consisting of a cellulose propionate burette chamber and 170 cm of PVC tubing. (606)

The drug was also tested as a simulated infusion over at least one hour by a syringe pump system. A glass syringe on a syringe pump was fitted with 20 cm of polyethylene tubing or 50 cm of Silastic tubing. No loss of drug due to sorption was observed with either tubing. (606)

A 25-ml aliquot of procainamide HCl (Sigma) 8 mg/L in sodium chloride 0.9% was stored in all-plastic syringes composed of polypropylene barrels and polyethylene plungers for 24 hours at room temperature in the dark. No loss due to sorption occurred. (606)

Compatibility Information

Solution Compatibility

Procainamide HCl

Solution	*Mfr*	*Mfr*	*Conc/L*	*Remarks*	*Ref*	*C/I*
Dextrose 5% in sodium chloride 0.9%	MG[a]	SQ	4 g	Approximately 17% decomposition in 24 hr at room temperature	522	I
	MG[a]	SQ	4 g	Approximately 5% decomposition in 24 hr at 4 °C	522	C
	TR[b]	SQ	4 g	Approximately 17% decomposition in 24 hr at room temperature	522	I
	TR[b]	SQ	4 g	Approximately 5% decomposition in 24 hr at 4 °C	522	C
	MG[a]	SQ	4 g	Approximately 20% decomposition in 24 hr at room temperature	546	I

Solution Compatibility (Cont.)

Procainamide HCl

Solution	Mfr	Mfr	Conc/L	Remarks	Ref	C/I
	MG[a]	SQ	4 g	Approximately 5% decomposition in 24 hr at 4 °C	546	**C**
Dextrose 5% in water	TR[a]	SQ	1 g	No decomposition in 8 hr but 12% loss in 24 hr at room temperature	545	**I**
	BA[b]	ASC	4 and 8 g	12 to 14% loss in 12 hr at room temperature. 6 to 10% loss in 24 hr under refrigeration	1327	**I**
(neutralized)[c]	BA[b]	ASC	4 g	10% or less loss in 24 hr at room temperature and under refrigeration	1327	**C**
(neutralized)[c]	BA[b]	ASC	8 g	Little or no loss in 24 hr at room temperature and under refrigeration	1327	**C**
	TR	ES	4 g	24% loss in 24 hr at room temperature under fluorescent light	1358	**I**
		LY	4 and 10 g	Physically compatible with 14 to 15% loss in 4 hr at 22 °C	1419	**I**
	AB	SQ	2 g	10% procainamide loss in 5 hr and 30% loss in 24 hr at 25 °C by HPLC due to reaction with dextrose	1896	**I**
Sodium chloride 0.45%		LY	4 and 10 g	Physically compatible with no loss in 4 hr at 22 °C	1419	**C**
Sodium chloride 0.9%	TR[a]	SQ	1 g	No decomposition in 24 hr at room temperature	545	**C**

[a]*Tested in glass containers.*
[b]*Tested in PVC containers.*
[c]*With pH adjusted to approximately 7.5 with sodium bicarbonate 8.4%.*

Additive Compatibility

Procainamide HCl

Drug	Mfr	Conc/L	Mfr	Conc/L	Test Soln	Remarks	Ref	C/I
Amiodarone HCl	LZ	1.8 g	SQ	4 g	D5W, NS[a]	Physically compatible with amiodarone losses of 5% or less in 24 hr at 24 °C under fluorescent light	1031	**C**
Atracurium besylate	BW	500 mg		4 g	D5W	Physically compatible	1694	**C**
Bretylium tosylate	ACC	10 g	SQ	4 g	D5S[b]	Physically compatible and bretylium chemically stable for 48 hr at room temperature. Approximately 14% procainamide loss in 24 hr	522	**I**
	ACC	10 g	SQ	4 g	D5S[b]	Physically compatible and bretylium chemically stable for 7 days at 4 °C. Approximately 7% procainamide loss in 24 hr	522	**C**
	ACC	1 g	SQ	1 g	D5W, NS	Physically compatible for 48 hr at 25 °C	756	**C**
Cibenzoline succinate		2 g	SQ	8 g	D5W, NS	Physically compatible for 24 hr at 25 °C by visual and microscopic examination	1182	**C**
Dobutamine HCl	LI	1 g	SQ	1 g	D5W, NS	Physically compatible with no color change in 24 hr at 25 °C	789	**C**
	LI	1 g	AHP	4 and 50 g	D5W, NS	Physically compatible for 24 hr at 21 °C	812	**C**
Esmolol HCl	DU	6 g	ES	4 g	D5W	43% procainamide loss in 24 hr at room temperature under fluorescent light	1358	**I**
Ethacrynate sodium	MSD	50 mg	SQ	1 g	NS	Altered UV spectra for both drugs at room temperature	16	**I**

Additive Compatibility (Cont.)

Procainamide HCl

Drug	*Mfr*	*Conc/L*	*Mfr*	*Conc/L*	*Test Soln*	*Remarks*	*Ref*	*C/I*
Flumazenil	RC	20 mg	ES	4 g	D5W[c]	Visually compatible with no flumazenil loss by HPLC in 24 hr at 23 °C under fluorescent light. Procainamide not tested	1710	C
Lidocaine HCl	AST	2 g	SQ	1 g	D5W, LR, NS	Physically compatible for 24 hr at 25 °C	775	C
Milrinone lactate	WI	200 mg	SQ	2 and 4 g	D5W	2 to 3% procainamide loss in 1 hr and 10 to 11% in 4 hr at 23 °C. No milrinone loss	1191	I
Netilmicin sulfate	SC	3 g	SQ	4 g	D5S	Physically compatible and netilmicin chemically stable for 7 days at 4 and 25 °C. Procainamide not tested	558	C
Verapamil HCl	KN	80 mg	SQ	2 g	D5W, NS	Physically compatible for 48 hr	739	C

[a] *Tested in both polyolefin and PVC containers.*
[b] *Tested in both glass and PVC containers.*
[c] *Tested in PVC containers.*

Y-Site Injection Compatibility (1:1 Mixture)

Procainamide HCl

Drug	*Mfr*	*Conc*	*Mfr*	*Conc*	*Remarks*	*Ref*	*C/I*
Amiodarone HCl	LZ	4 mg/ml[c]	AHP	8 mg/ml[c]	Physically compatible for 24 hr at 21 °C	1032	C
Cisatracurium besylate	GW	0.1, 2, 5 mg/ml[a]	ES	10 mg/ml[a]	Physically compatible with no change in measured turbidity or increase in particle content in 4 hr at 23 °C	2074	C
Diltiazem HCl	MMD	5 mg/ml	ES	500 mg/ml	Cloudiness forms but clears within 2 min	1807	?
	MMD	1 mg/ml[b]	ES	50 mg/ml[a]	Visually compatible	1807	C
	MMD	5 mg/ml	ES	2 mg/ml[a]	Visually compatible	1807	C
Famotidine	MSD	0.2 mg/ml[a]	ASC	5 mg/ml[a]	Physically compatible for 4 hr at 25 °C	1188	C
Heparin sodium	UP	1000 units/L[e]	SQ	100 mg/ml	Physically compatible for at least 4 hr at room temperature by visual and microscopic examination	534	C
Hetastarch in lactated electrolyte injection (Hextend)	AB	6%	ES	10 mg/ml[a]	Physically compatible with no change in measured turbidity or increase in particle content in 4 hr at 23 °C	2339	C
Hydrocortisone sodium succinate	UP	10 mg/L[e]	SQ	100 mg/ml	Physically compatible for at least 4 hr at room temperature by visual and microscopic examination	534	C
Inamrinone lactate	WB	3 mg/ml[b]	SQ	4 mg/ml[a]	Physically compatible for at least 4 hr at 25 °C under fluorescent light	992	C
	WI	2.5 mg/ml[d]	LY	20 mg/ml[d]	Physically compatible with little or no loss of either drug in 4 hr at 22 °C	1419	C
	WI	2.5 mg/ml[a]	LY	20 mg/ml[a]	18% procainamide loss and 10% inamrinone loss in 4 hr at 22 °C due to dextrose diluent	1419	I
	WI	5 mg/ml	LY	4 mg/ml[d]	Physically compatible with little or no loss of either drug in 4 hr at 22 °C	1419	C

Y-Site Injection Compatibility (1:1 Mixture) (Cont.)

			Procainamide HCl				
Drug	*Mfr*	*Conc*	*Mfr*	*Conc*	*Remarks*	*Ref*	*C/I*
	WI	5 mg/ml	LY	4 mg/ml[a]	20% procainamide loss and 8% inamrinone loss in 4 hr at 22 °C due to dextrose diluent	1419	I
	WI	2.5 mg/ml[d]	LY	4 mg/ml[d]	Physically compatible with little or no loss of either drug in 4 hr at 22 °C	1419	C
	WI	2.5 mg/ml[a]	LY	4 mg/ml[a]	17% procainamide loss in 4 hr at 22 °C due to dextrose diluent	1419	I
Milrinone	WI	350 μg/ml[a]	SQ	2 and 4 mg/ml[a]	3 to 6% procainamide loss in 1 hr and 10 to 13% in 4 hr at 23 °C. No milrinone loss	1191	I
Potassium chloride	AB	40 mEq/L[e]	SQ	100 mg/ml	Physically compatible for at least 4 hr at room temperature by visual and microscopic examination	534	C
Ranitidine HCl	GL	0.5 mg/ml[f]	BA	4 mg/ml[a]	Physically compatible for 24 hr	1323	C
Remifentanil HCl	GW	0.025 and 0.25 mg/ml[b]	ES	10 mg/ml[a]	Physically compatible with no change in measured turbidity or increase in particle content in 4 hr at 23 °C	2075	C
Vitamin B complex with C	RC	2 ml/L[e]	SQ	100 mg/ml	Physically compatible for at least 4 hr at room temperature by visual and microscopic examination	534	C

[a] *Tested in dextrose 5% in water.*
[b] *Tested in sodium chloride 0.9%.*
[c] *Tested in dextrose 5% in water and sodium chloride 0.9%.*
[d] *Tested in sodium chloride 0.45%.*
[e] *Tested in dextrose 5% in Ringer's injection, dextrose 5% in Ringer's injection, lactated, dextrose 5% in water, Ringer's injection, lactated, and sodium chloride 0.9%.*
[f] *Premixed infusion solution.*

Additional Compatibility Information

Infusion Solutions — Procainamide HCl 2 to 4 mg/ml in sodium chloride 0.9% or sterile water for injection is stated to be stable for 24 hours at room temperature or seven days under refrigeration. (4)

Similarly, procainamide HCl in dextrose 5% in water has been stated to be stable for 24 hours at room temperature or seven days under refrigeration. However, other information indicates that procainamide HCl may be subject to greater decomposition in dextrose 5% in water unless the admixture is refrigerated (1327) or the pH is adjusted. (1327; 1358; 1422; 1423)

Raymond et al. found that neutralization of the acidic pH of procainamide HCl 0.4 and 0.8% in dextrose 5% in water to approximately pH 7.5 with sodium bicarbonate 8.4% increased stability. The neutralized admixtures maintained their stability for at least 24 hours at 24 °C; the acidic admixtures lost greater than 10% procainamide HCl in six to 12 hours at 24 °C. Similar increased stability could be obtained by refrigeration. (1327)

Procainamide HCl forms α- and β-glucosylamine compounds with dextrose. The reaction proceeds rapidly, with about 10% procainamide loss in dextrose 5% in water occurring in about five hours and 30% loss in 24 hours at 25 °C. Equilibrium is achieved with about 62% of the procainamide present as glucosylamines. (1896) The bioavailability, activity, and metabolic fate of these compounds is not known. (546; 1896) The α- and β-glucosylamine compounds that form are reversible (1422; 1896), although the extent of reversibility in plasma has been questioned. (2051) The rate and extent of complex formation are dependent on the dextrose concentration and the solution pH but are independent of the procainamide HCl concentration. (1422) In dextrose concentrations ranging from 1 to 5%, the extent of procainamide complex formation ranged from 6% in two days in dextrose 1% up to 35% (1422) to 60% (1896) in dextrose 5%. Lowering the pH from the normal 4.5 to 1.4 with 0.01 *N* hydrochloric acid completely prevented complex formation. (1422) Similarly, increasing the solution pH to 8 is reported to block complexation. (1423) Maximum complex formation occurred at pH 3 to 5 (1423) or 4 to 5.2 (1358), the natural pH of procainamide HCl admixtures in dextrose 5% in water.

The clinical importance of this complexation, if any, is uncertain. Consequently, the manufacturer continues to state that procainamide HCl 2 to 4 mg/ml in dextrose 5% in water can be considered stable for 24 hours at room temperature or seven days under refrigeration. (4)

Oxidizing Agents — Oxidizing agents may cause discoloration, though usually without a significant loss of potency. (40)

Phenytoin — The following incompatibility determination was performed with concentrated solutions. One milliliter of procainamide HCl (Squibb) was added to 5 ml of sterile distilled water along with 1 ml of phenytoin sodium (Parke-Davis). Particulate matter was observed within two hours. (28)

PROCAINE HCL
AHFS 72:00

Products — Procaine HCl is available as a 2% solution in 30-ml multiple-dose vials. This solution is made isotonic with sodium chloride and contains not more than 2 mg/ml of acetone sodium bisulfite and chlorobutanol 0.25%. It is also available as a 1% solution in 2- and 6-ml single-dose ampuls and in 30-ml multiple-dose vials. The solutions are made isotonic with sodium chloride. The ampuls contain not more than 1 mg/ml of acetone sodium bisulfite. The vials contain not more than 2 mg/ml of acetone sodium bisulfite and chlorobutanol 0.25%. (1-11/98; 4)

Procaine HCl (Abbott) is also provided as a 10% solution in 2-ml single-dose ampuls for spinal anesthesia. Each milliliter contains 100 mg of drug and not more than 1 mg of acetone sodium bisulfite. (4; 29; 154)

pH — From 3 to 5.5. (4)

Osmolality — Procaine HCl 10 mg/ml has an osmolality of 279 mOsm/kg. (1689)

Trade Name(s) — Novocain.

Administration — Procaine HCl may be administered by infiltration, peripheral or sympathetic nerve block, or subarachnoid block. Less concentrated solutions may be prepared by diluting the 1% solution. (1-11/98; 4)

For intraspinal use, doses of the 10% solution are diluted with 0.5 to 1 ml of appropriate diluent, depending on site of injection, and are delivered at a rate of injection of 1 ml/5 sec. For spinal anesthesia, sodium chloride 0.9%, sterile water for injection, spinal fluid, and (for hyperbaric technique) dextrose injection may be used as diluents. (4)

Stability — Intact containers should be stored at controlled room temperature and protected from exposure to temperatures of 40 °C or more, from freezing, and from exposure to light. The solutions may be autoclaved at 121 °C and 15 psi for 15 minutes, but reautoclaving increases the possibility of crystal formation. Solutions of procaine HCl should not be used if crystal formation, cloudiness, or discoloration is observed. (1-11/98; 4)

pH Effects — The pH of maximum stability is 3.5, with the best range being approximately 3 to 5. Procaine HCl solutions are subject to acid and base catalysis at pH values outside of this range. (1072)

Compatibility Information

Solution Compatibility

Procaine HCl

Solution	*Mfr*	*Mfr*	*Conc/L*	*Remarks*	*Ref*	*C/I*
Dextran 6% in dextrose 5%	AB		1 g	Physically compatible	3	C
Dextran 6% in sodium chloride 0.9%	AB		1 g	Physically compatible	3	C
Dextrose–Ringer's injection combinations	AB		1 g	Physically compatible	3	C
Dextrose–Ringer's injection, lactated, combinations	AB		1 g	Physically compatible	3	C
Dextrose–saline combinations	AB		1 g	Physically compatible	3	C
Dextrose 2½% in water	AB		1 g	Physically compatible	3	C
Dextrose 5% in water	AB		1 g	Physically compatible	3	C
Dextrose 10% in water	AB		1 g	Physically compatible	3	C
Fructose 10% in sodium chloride 0.9%	AB		1 g	Physically compatible	3	C
Fructose 10% in water	AB		1 g	Physically compatible	3	C
Invert sugar 5 and 10% in sodium chloride 0.9%	AB		1 g	Physically compatible	3	C
Invert sugar 5 and 10% in water	AB		1 g	Physically compatible	3	C
Ionosol products	AB		1 g	Physically compatible	3	C
Ringer's injection	AB		1 g	Physically compatible	3	C
Ringer's injection, lactated	AB		1 g	Physically compatible	3	C
Sodium chloride 0.45%	AB		1 g	Physically compatible	3	C
Sodium chloride 0.9%	AB		1 g	Physically compatible	3	C
Sodium lactate ⅙ M	AB		1 g	Physically compatible	3	C

Additive Compatibility

Procaine HCl

Drug	*Mfr*	*Conc/L*	*Mfr*	*Conc/L*	*Test Soln*	*Remarks*	*Ref*	*C/I*
Aminophylline	SE	500 mg	AB	1 g		Physically compatible	6	C
						Physically incompatible	9	I
	SE	1 g	WI	1 g	D5W	Physically incompatible	15	I
Amobarbital sodium						Physically incompatible	9	I
	LI	1 g	WI	1 g	D5W	Physically incompatible	15	I
Ascorbic acid injection	UP	500 mg	WI	1 g	D5W	Physically compatible	15	C
Chlorothiazide sodium	MSD					Physically incompatible	9	I
Hydrocortisone sodium succinate	UP	500 mg	WI	1 g	D5W	Physically compatible	15	C
Magnesium sulfate						Physically incompatible	9	I
	LI	16 mEq	WI	1 g	D5W	Physically incompatible	15	I
Penicillin G potassium		1 million units		1 g		Physically compatible	3	C
	SQ	20 million units	WI	1 g	D5W	Physically compatible	15	C
Penicillin G sodium	UP	20 million units	WI	1 g	D5W	Physically compatible	15	C
Phenobarbital sodium	WI					Physically incompatible	9	I
Phenytoin sodium	PD					Physically incompatible	9	I
Sodium bicarbonate						Physically incompatible	9	I
	AB	80 mEq	WI	1 g	D5W	Physically incompatible	15	I
Vitamin B complex with C	AB	2 ml		1 g		Physically compatible	3	C
	AB	5 ml	WI	1 g	D5W	Physically compatible	15	C

Drugs in Syringe Compatibility

Procaine HCl

Drug (in syringe)	*Mfr*	*Amt*	*Mfr*	*Amt*	*Remarks*	*Ref*	*C/I*
Ampicillin sodium	BE				Physically compatible	89	C
Glycopyrrolate	RB	0.2 mg/ 1 ml	ES	10 mg/ 1 ml	Physically compatible and pH in stability range for glycopyrrolate for 48 hr at 25 °C	331	C
	RB	0.2 mg/ 1 ml	ES	20 mg/ 2 ml	Physically compatible and pH in stability range for glycopyrrolate for 48 hr at 25 °C	331	C
	RB	0.4 mg/ 2 ml	ES	10 mg/ 1 ml	Physically compatible and pH in stability range for glycopyrrolate for 48 hr at 25 °C	331	C
	RB	0.2 mg/ 1 ml	ES	20 mg/ 1 ml	Physically compatible and pH in stability range for glycopyrrolate for 48 hr at 25 °C	331	C
	RB	0.2 mg/ 1 ml	ES	40 mg/ 2 ml	Physically compatible and pH in stability range for glycopyrrolate for 48 hr at 25 °C	331	C
	RB	0.4 mg/ 2 ml	ES	20 mg/ 1 ml	Physically compatible and pH in stability range for glycopyrrolate for 48 hr at 25 °C	331	C
Hydroxyzine HCl	PF	50 mg/ 2 ml	WI	2%/2 ml	Physically compatible	771	C
	PF	100 mg/ 2 ml	WI	2%/2 ml	Physically compatible	771	C

Additional Compatibility Information

Cardioplegic Solutions — The stability of procaine HCl in cardioplegic solutions composed of Ringer's injection with added increments of potassium and magnesium was assessed. The procaine HCl underwent little or no decomposition after 101 days of storage. (719)

In another study, the cardioplegic solutions were similarly formulated except that the pH was buffered with tromethamine from the inherent pH of 5 to a physiological pH of 7.3 to 7.6. The procaine HCl underwent 10% decomposition in 10 days when stored under refrigeration. It was calculated that a 10% loss would occur in about two days at room temperature. The authors recommended that if the cardioplegic solution is to be buffered to the physiological range, then the procaine HCl should be added to the formulation at the time of dispensing to permit a minimal loss of the drug. (720)

Synave et al. evaluated the stability of procaine HCl 270 mg/L in cardioplegic solutions containing sodium bicarbonate (pH 7.6) and stored at 37, 21, 6, and −10 °C. At 37 °C, 70% of the procaine HCl was lost in one week. At 21 and 6 °C, 10% was lost in one and five weeks, respectively. When frozen at −10 °C, the solutions lost less than 10% in nine weeks. However, thawing in a microwave oven resulted in the formation of a white crystalline precipitate. Exposure to light did not affect the rate of procaine hydrolysis. (1128)

Hydrocortisone — Procaine HCl 1 g/L has been reported to be conditionally compatible with hydrocortisone sodium succinate (Upjohn) 250 mg/L. The mixture is physically compatible in most Abbott infusion solutions except as noted below (3):

Beclysyl 5 and 10%	Haze or precipitate forms within 24 hr
Ionosol B with invert sugar 10%	Haze or precipitate forms within 24 hr
Ionosol G with invert sugar 10%	Haze or precipitate forms within 24 hr

Other Drugs — Local anesthetics such as procaine HCl cause precipitation of amphotericin B. (107) Procaine HCl is incompatible with alkali hydroxides and their carbonates. (4)

PROCHLORPERAZINE EDISYLATE
AHFS 28:16.08 and 56:22

Products — Prochlorperazine edisylate is available in 2-ml vials and syringe cartridges and 10-ml multiple-dose vials (1-10/99; 29). Each milliliter of solution contains (1-10/99):

Prochlorperazine (as edisylate)	5 mg
Sodium biphosphate	5 mg
Sodium tartrate	12 mg
Sodium saccharin	0.9 mg
Benzyl alcohol	0.75%

pH — From 4.2 to 6.2. (4)

Osmolality — Prochlorperazine edisylate 5 mg/ml has an osmolality of 282 mOsm/kg. (1689)

Trade Name(s) — Compazine.

Administration — Prochlorperazine edisylate may be given intramuscularly deep into the upper outer quadrant of the buttock. It may also be given by direct intravenous injection at a rate not exceeding 5 mg/min. It can be given undiluted or diluted in a compatible diluent. It should not be given as a bolus intravenous injection. (1-10/99; 4) For intravenous infusion, dilution of 20 mg in a liter of compatible infusion solution is recommended. (4) Because the drug causes local irritation, subcutaneous injection is not recommended. (1-10/99; 4)

Stability — Intact containers should be stored at controlled room temperature and protected from temperatures of 40 °C or more and from freezing. Solutions of prochlorperazine edisylate are light sensitive and, therefore, should be protected from light. A slightly yellow solution has not had its potency altered. However, a markedly discolored solution should be discarded. (1-10/99; 4)

Syringes — Prochlorperazine edisylate (SKF) 5 mg/ml retained potency for three months at room temperature when 1 and 2 ml of solution were packaged in Tubex cartridges. (13)

Filtration — Prochlorperazine edisylate (SKF) 5 mg/L in dextrose 5% in water and sodium chloride 0.9% did not display significant sorption to a 0.45-μm cellulose membrane filter during an eight-hour simulated infusion. (567)

Central Venous Catheter — Prochlorperazine edisylate (SoloPak) 0.5 mg/ml in dextrose 5% in water was found to be compatible with the ARROWg+ard Blue Plus (Arrow International) chlorhexidine-bearing triple-lumen central catheter. HPLC analysis was used to evaluate completeness of drug delivery through the catheter and the amount of chlorhexidine removed from the internal lumens. Essentially complete delivery of the drug was found with little or no drug loss occurring. Furthermore, chlorhexidine delivered from the catheter remained at trace amounts with no substantial increase due to the delivery of the drug through the catheter. (2335)

Compatibility Information

Solution Compatibility

Prochlorperazine edisylate

Solution	*Mfr*	*Mfr*	*Conc/L*	*Remarks*	*Ref*	*C/I*
Dextran 6% in dextrose 5%	AB	SKF	10 mg	Physically compatible	3	C
Dextran 6% in sodium chloride 0.9%	AB	SKF	10 mg	Physically compatible	3	C
Dextrose–Ringer's injection combinations	AB	SKF	10 mg	Physically compatible	3	C
Dextrose–Ringer's injection, lactated, combinations	AB	SKF	10 mg	Physically compatible	3	C
Dextrose–saline combinations	AB	SKF	10 mg	Physically compatible	3	C
Dextrose 2½% in water	AB	SKF	10 mg	Physically compatible	3	C
Dextrose 5% in water	AB	SKF	10 mg	Physically compatible	3	C
Dextrose 10% in water	AB	SKF	10 mg	Physically compatible	3	C
Fructose 10% in sodium chloride 0.9%	AB	SKF	10 mg	Physically compatible	3	C
Fructose 10% in water	AB	SKF	10 mg	Physically compatible	3	C
Invert sugar 5 and 10% in sodium chloride 0.9%	AB	SKF	10 mg	Physically compatible	3	C
Invert sugar 5 and 10% in water	AB	SKF	10 mg	Physically compatible	3	C
Ionosol products	AB	SKF	10 mg	Physically compatible	3	C
Ringer's injection	AB	SKF	10 mg	Physically compatible	3	C
Ringer's injection, lactated	AB	SKF	10 mg	Physically compatible	3	C
Sodium chloride 0.45%	AB	SKF	10 mg	Physically compatible	3	C
Sodium chloride 0.9%	AB	SKF	10 mg	Physically compatible	3	C
Sodium lactate ⅙ M	AB	SKF	10 mg	Physically compatible	3	C

Additive Compatibility

Prochlorperazine edisylate[a]

Drug	*Mfr*	*Conc/L*	*Mfr*	*Conc/L*	*Test Soln*	*Remarks*	*Ref*	*C/I*
Amikacin sulfate	BR	5 g	SKF	20 mg	D5LR, D5R, D5S, D5W, D10W, IS10, LR, NS, R, SL	Physically compatible and potency of both drugs retained for 24 hr at 25 °C	294	C
Aminophylline	SE	1 g	SKF	100 mg	D5W	Physically incompatible	15	I
	BP	1 g	BP	100 mg (M)	D5W, NS	Immediate precipitation	26	I
Amphotericin B		200 mg	BP	100 mg (M)	D5W	Haze develops over 3 hr	26	I
Ampicillin sodium	BP	2 g	BP	100 mg (M)	D5W, NS	Immediate precipitation	26	I
Ascorbic acid injection	UP	500 mg	SKF	100 mg	D5W	Physically compatible	15	C
Calcium gluconate			SKF			Physically incompatible	9	I
	UP	1 g	SKF	100 mg	D5W	Physically compatible	15	C

Additive Compatibility (Cont.)

Prochlorperazine edisylate[a]

Drug	*Mfr*	*Conc/L*	*Mfr*	*Conc/L*	*Test Soln*	*Remarks*	*Ref*	*C/I*
Chloramphenicol sodium succinate	PD	10 g	SKF	100 mg	D5W	Physically incompatible	15	I
	BP	4 g	BP	100 mg (M)	NS	Haze develops over 3 hr	26	I
Chlorothiazide sodium	MSD		SKF			Physically incompatible	9	I
	BP	2 g	BP	100 mg (M)	D5W	Immediate precipitation	26	I
	BP	2 g	BP	100 mg (M)	NS	Haze develops over 3 hr	26	I
Dexamethasone sodium phosphate	MSD	20 mg	SKF	100 mg	D5W	Physically compatible	15	C
Dimenhydrinate	SE	500 mg	SKF	100 mg	D5W	Physically compatible	15	C
Erythromycin lactobionate	AB	1 g	SKF	10 mg		Physically compatible. Erythromycin potency retained for 24 hr at 25 °C	20	C
Ethacrynate sodium	MSD	80 mg	SKF	20 mg	NS	Little alteration of UV spectra within 8 hr at room temperature	16	C
Floxacillin sodium	BE	20 g	MB	1.25 g	W	Precipitate forms immediately	1479	I
Furosemide	HO	1 g	MB	1.25 g	W	Yellow globular precipitate forms immediately	1479	I
Hydrocortisone sodium succinate			SKF			Physically incompatible	9	I
Lidocaine HCl	AST	2 g	SKF	10 mg		Physically compatible	24	C
Methohexital sodium	BP	2 g	BP	100 mg (M)	D5W	Haze develops over 3 hr	26	I
Nafcillin sodium	WY	500 mg	SKF	10 mg		Physically compatible	27	C
Penicillin G potassium	SQ	1 million units	SKF	10 mg	D5W	Physically compatible. Penicillin potency retained for 24 hr at 25 °C	47	C
	(B)[b]	900,000 units	SKF	10 mg	D5W	Penicillin potency retained for 24 hr at 25 °C	48	C
	BP	10 million units	BP	100 mg (M)	NS	Haze develops over 3 hr	26	I
Penicillin G sodium	BP	10 million units	BP	100 mg (M)	NS	Haze develops over 3 hr	26	I
Phenobarbital sodium	BP	800 mg	BP	100 mg (M)	D5W	Haze develops over 3 hr	26	I
	BP	800 mg	BP	100 mg (M)	NS	Immediate precipitation	26	I
Sodium bicarbonate	AB	2.4 mEq[c]	SKF	10 mg	D5W	Physically compatible for 24 hr	772	C
Thiopental sodium	AB		SKF			Physically incompatible	9	I
Vitamin B complex with C	AB	5 ml	SKF	100 mg	D5W	Physically compatible	15	C

[a] *Entries with the notation "(M)" in the prochlorperazine Conc/L column were tested as the mesylate salt.*
[b] *A buffered preparation was specified.*
[c] *One vial of Neut added to a liter of admixture.*

Drugs in Syringe Compatibility

Prochlorperazine edisylate

Drug (in syringe)	*Mfr*	*Amt*	*Mfr*	*Amt*	*Remarks*	*Ref*	*C/I*
Atropine sulfate		0.6 mg/ 1.5 ml	SKF		Physically compatible for at least 15 min	14	C
	ST	0.4 mg/ 1 ml	PO	5 mg/ 1 ml	Physically compatible for at least 15 min	326	C
Butorphanol tartrate	BR	4 mg/ 2 ml	MB	5 mg/ 1 ml	Physically compatible both macroscopically and microscopically for 30 min at room temperature	566	C
Chlorpromazine HCl	SKF	50 mg/ 2 ml	SKF		Physically compatible for at least 15 min	14	C
	PO	50 mg/ 2 ml	PO	5 mg/ 1 ml	Physically compatible for at least 15 min	326	C
Cimetidine HCl	SKF	300 mg/ 2 ml	SKF	10 mg/ 2 ml	Physically compatible for 4 hr at 25 °C	25	C
Diamorphine HCl	MB	10, 25, 50 mg/ 1 ml	MB	1.25 mg/ 1 ml[a]	Physically compatible and diamorphine content retained for 24 hr at room temperature	1454	C
Dimenhydrinate	HR	50 mg/ 1 ml	PO	5 mg/ 1 ml	Physically incompatible within 15 min	326	I
Diphenhydramine HCl	PD	50 mg/ 1 ml	PO	5 mg/ 1 ml	Physically compatible for at least 15 min	326	C
Droperidol	MN	2.5 mg/ 1 ml	PO	5 mg/ 1 ml	Physically compatible for at least 15 min	326	C
Fentanyl citrate	MN	0.05 mg/ 1 ml	PO	5 mg/ 1 ml	Physically compatible for at least 15 min	326	C
Glycopyrrolate	RB	0.2 mg/ 1 ml	SKF	5 mg/ 1 ml	Physically compatible and pH in stability range for glycopyrrolate for 48 hr at 25 °C	331	C
	RB	0.2 mg/ 1 ml	SKF	10 mg/ 2 ml	Physically compatible and pH in stability range for glycopyrrolate for 48 hr at 25 °C	331	C
	RB	0.4 mg/ 2 ml	SKF	5 mg/ 1 ml	Physically compatible and pH in stability range for glycopyrrolate for 48 hr at 25 °C	331	C
Hydromorphone HCl	KN	4 mg/ 2 ml[b]	SKF	5 mg/ 1 ml	Immediate precipitation	517	I
	KN	4 mg/ 2 ml[c]	SKF	5 mg/ 1 ml	Physically compatible for 30 min	517	C
	KN	2, 10, 40 mg/ 1 ml	RP	5 mg/ 1 ml[d]	Visually compatible with little or no loss of either drug by HPLC in 7 days at 4, 23, and 37 °C	1776	C
	SX	0.5 mg/ ml[f]	RP	1.5 mg/ ml[d,f]	Visually and microscopically compatible for 96 hr at room temperature exposed to light	2171	C
Hydroxyzine HCl	PF	50 mg/ 1 ml	PO	5 mg/ 1 ml	Physically compatible for at least 15 min	326	C
Ketorolac tromethamine	SY	180 mg/ 6 ml	STS	15 mg/ 3 ml	Heavy white precipitate forms immediately, separating into two layers over time	1703	I
Meperidine HCl	WY	100 mg/ 1 ml	SKF		Physically compatible for at least 15 min	14	C
	WI	50 mg/ 1 ml	PO	5 mg/ 1 ml	Physically compatible for at least 15 min	326	C
Metoclopramide HCl	NO	10 mg/ 2 ml	MB	10 mg/ 2 ml	Physically compatible both macroscopically and microscopically for 15 min at room temperature	565	C

Drugs in Syringe Compatibility (Cont.)

Prochlorperazine edisylate

Drug (in syringe)	*Mfr*	*Amt*	*Mfr*	*Amt*	*Remarks*	*Ref*	*C/I*
Midazolam HCl	RC	5 mg/ 1 ml	SKF	10 mg/ 2 ml	White precipitate forms immediately	1145	I
Morphine sulfate	WY	15 mg/ 1 ml	SKF		Physically compatible for at least 15 min	14	C
	ST	15 mg/ 1 ml	PO	5 mg/ 1 ml	Physically compatible for at least 15 min	326	C
	WB	10 mg/ 1 ml	ES, SKF	10 mg/ 2 ml	Immediate precipitation, probably due to phenol in morphine formulation	1006	I
	WY	8, 10, 15 mg/ 1 ml	SKF	5 mg/ 1 ml	Physically compatible for 24 hr at 25 °C	1086	C
Morphine tartrate	DB	[e]	DB	10 mg/ 2 ml	Visually discolored with 22% morphine loss by HPLC in 48 hr at room temperature protected from light. Prochlorperazine not tested	1599	I
Nalbuphine HCl	EN	10 mg/ 1 ml	WY	5 mg/ 1 ml	Physically compatible for 36 hr at 27 °C	762	C
	EN	5 mg/ 0.5 ml	WY	5 mg/ 1 ml	Physically compatible for 36 hr at 27 °C	762	C
	EN	2.5 mg/ 0.25 ml	WY	5 mg/ 1 ml	Physically compatible for 36 hr at 27 °C	762	C
	DU	10 mg/ 1 ml	SKF	10 mg/ 2 ml	Physically compatible for 48 hr	128	C
	DU	20 mg/ 1 ml	SKF	10 mg/ 2 ml	Physically compatible for 48 hr	128	C
Papaveretum	RC[g]	20 mg/ 1 ml	PO	5 mg/ 1 ml	Visually compatible for at least 15 min	326	C
Pentazocine lactate	WI	30 mg/ 1 ml	PO	5 mg/ 1 ml	Physically compatible for at least 15 min	326	C
Pentobarbital sodium	WY	100 mg/ 2 ml	SKF		Precipitate forms within 15 min	14	I
	AB	500 mg/ 10 ml	SKF	10 mg/ 2 ml	Physically incompatible	55	I
	AB	50 mg/ 1 ml	PO	5 mg/ 1 ml	Physically incompatible within 15 min	326	I
Perphenazine	SC	5 mg/ 1 ml	MB	5 mg/ 1 ml	Physically compatible both macroscopically and microscopically for 30 min at room temperature	566	C
Promazine HCl	WY	50 mg/ 1 ml	PO	5 mg/ 1 ml	Physically compatible for at least 15 min	326	C
Promethazine HCl	PO	50 mg/ 2 ml	PO	5 mg/ 1 ml	Physically compatible for at least 15 min	326	C
Ranitidine HCl	GL	50 mg/ 2 ml	RP	10 mg/ 2 ml	Physically compatible for 1 hr at 25 °C both macroscopically and microscopically	978	C
Scopolamine HBr		0.6 mg/ 1.5 ml	SKF		Physically compatible for at least 15 min	14	C
	ST	0.4 mg/ 1 ml	PO	5 mg/ 1 ml	Physically compatible for at least 15 min	326	C
Sufentanil citrate	JN	50 µg/ml	SCN	5 mg/ml	Physically compatible with no subvisual haze or particle formation in 24 hr at 23 °C	1711	C

Drugs in Syringe Compatibility (Cont.)

Prochlorperazine edisylate

Drug (in syringe)	*Mfr*	*Amt*	*Mfr*	*Amt*	*Remarks*	*Ref*	*C/I*
Thiopental sodium	AB	75 mg/ 3 ml	SKF	10 mg/ 2 ml	Physically incompatible	21	I

[a]*Diluted with sterile water for injection.*
[b]*The vial formulation was tested.*
[c]*The ampul formulation was tested.*
[d]*Tested as the mesylate salt.*
[e]*Amount unspecified.*
[f]*Diluted in sodium chloride 0.9%.*
[g]*The former formulation was tested.*

Y-Site Injection Compatibility (1:1 Mixture)

Prochlorperazine edisylate

Drug	*Mfr*	*Conc*	*Mfr*	*Conc*	*Remarks*	*Ref*	*C/I*
Aldesleukin	CHI	33,800 I.U./ ml[a]	SKB	5 mg/ml	Aldesleukin bioactivity inhibited	1857	I
Allopurinol sodium	BW	3 mg/ml[b]	SKB	0.5 mg/ml[b]	Heavy turbidity forms immediately	1686	I
Amifostine	USB	10 mg/ml[a]	SN	0.5 mg/ml[a]	Immediate increase in subvisual haze	1845	I
Amphotericin B cholesteryl sulfate complex	SEQ	0.83 mg/ml[a]	SKB	0.5 mg/ml[a]	Gross precipitate forms	2117	I
Amsacrine	NCI	1 mg/ml[a]	SKF	0.5 mg/ml[a]	Physically compatible for 4 hr at room temperature under fluorescent light	1381	C
Aztreonam	SQ	40 mg/ml[a]	ES	0.5 mg/ml[a]	Haze and tiny particles form within 4 hr	1758	I
Calcium gluconate	AMR	10 mg/ml[b]	SCN	5 mg/ml	Visually compatible for 24 hr at room temperature in test tubes. No precipitate found on filter from Y-site delivery	2063	C
Cefepime HCl	BMS	20 mg/ml[a]	SN	0.5 mg/ml[a]	Haze forms immediately. Flocculent precipitate forms in 4 hr	1689	I
Cisatracurium besylate	GW	0.1, 2, 5 mg/ ml[a]	SO	0.5 mg/ml[a]	Physically compatible with no change in measured turbidity or increase in particle content in 4 hr at 23 °C	2074	C
Cisplatin	BR	1 mg/ml	SKF	0.5 mg/ml[a]	Visually compatible for 4 hr at room temperature under fluorescent light	1685	C
Cladribine	ORT	0.015[b] and 0.5[d] mg/ml	SCN	0.5 mg/ml[b]	Physically compatible with no change in measured turbidity or increase in particle content in 4 hr at 23 °C	1969	C
Clarithromycin	AB	4 mg/ml[a]	ANT[i]	12.5 mg/ml	Visually compatible for 72 hr at both 30 and 17 °C	2174	C
Cyclophosphamide	MJ	10 mg/ml	SKF	0.5 mg/ml[a]	Visually compatible for 4 hr at room temperature under fluorescent light	1685	C
Cytarabine	UP	50 mg/ml	SKF	0.5 mg/ml[a]	Visually compatible for 4 hr at room temperature under fluorescent light	1685	C
Docetaxel	RPR	0.9 mg/ml[a]	SO	0.5 mg/ml[a]	Physically compatible with no change in measured turbidity or increase in particle content in 4 hr at 23 °C	2224	C
Doxorubicin HCl	AD	0.2 mg/ml[a]	SKF	0.5 mg/ml[a]	Visually compatible for 4 hr at room temperature under fluorescent light	1685	C

Y-Site Injection Compatibility (1:1 Mixture) (Cont.)

Drug	Mfr	Conc	Prochlorperazine edisylate Mfr	Prochlorperazine edisylate Conc	Remarks	Ref	C/I
Doxorubicin HCl liposome injection	SEQ	0.4 mg/ml[a]	SO	0.5 mg/ml[a]	Physically compatible with little or no change in measured turbidity and no increase in particle content in 4 hr at 23 °C	2087	C
Etoposide phosphate	BR	5 mg/ml[a]	ES	0.5 mg/ml[a]	White cloudy solution forms immediately with precipitate in 4 hr	2218	I
Fluconazole	RR	2 mg/ml	SKF	5 mg/ml	Physically compatible for 24 hr at 25 °C	1407	C
Fludarabine phosphate	BX	1 mg/ml[a]	WY	0.5 mg/ml[a]	Slight haze forms within 30 min	1439	I
Foscarnet sodium	AST	24 mg/ml	SKF	5 mg/ml	Cloudy brown solution	1335	I
Filgrastim	AMG	30 μg/ml[a]	SCN	0.5 mg/ml[a]	Particles form immediately. Filaments form in 1 hr	1687	I
Gatifloxacin	BMS	2 mg/ml[a]	SO	0.5 mg/ml[a]	Physically compatible with no change in measured haze or increase in particle content in 4 hr at 23 °C	2234	C
Gemcitabine HCl	LI	10 mg/ml[b]	SCN	0.5 mg/ml[b]	Subvisual haze forms immediately and increases over 4 hr	2226	I
Granisetron HCl	SKB	0.05 mg/ml[a]	SCN	0.5 mg/ml[a]	Physically compatible with no change in measured turbidity or increase in particle content in 4 hr at 23 °C	2000	C
Heparin sodium	UP	1000 units/L[e]	SKF	5 mg/ml	Physically compatible for at least 4 hr at room temperature by visual and microscopic examination	534	C
Hetastarch in lactated electrolyte injection (Hextend)	AB	6%	SO	0.5 mg/ml[a]	Physically compatible with no change in measured turbidity or increase in particle content in 4 hr at 23 °C	2339	C
Hydrocortisone sodium succinate	UP	10 mg/L[e]	SKF	5 mg/ml	Physically compatible for at least 4 hr at room temperature by visual and microscopic examination	534	C
Linezolid	PHU	2 mg/ml	SO	0.5 mg/ml[a]	Physically compatible with no change in measured turbidity or increase in particle content in 4 hr at 23 °C	2264	C
Melphalan HCl	BW	0.1 mg/ml[b]	SKB	0.5 mg/ml[b]	Physically compatible with no change in measured turbidity or increase in particle content in 3 hr at 22 °C	1557	C
Methotrexate sodium	AD	15 mg/ml[f]	SKF	0.5 mg/ml[a]	Visually compatible for 4 hr at room temperature under fluorescent light	1685	C
Ondansetron HCl	GL	1 mg/ml[b]	SKF	0.5 mg/ml[a]	Physically compatible for 4 hr at 22 °C	1365	C
Paclitaxel	NCI	1.2 mg/ml[a]		0.5 mg/ml[a]	Physically compatible with no change in measured turbidity in 4 hr at 22 °C	1528	C
Piperacillin sodium–tazobactam sodium	LE	40 + 5 mg/ml[a]	SCN	0.5 mg/ml[a]	White turbidity forms immediately	1688	I
Potassium chloride	AB	40 mEq/L[e]	SKF	5 mg/ml	Physically compatible for at least 4 hr at room temperature by visual and microscopic examination	534	C
Propofol	ZEN	10 mg/ml	SCN	0.5 mg/ml[a]	Physically compatible for 1 hr at 23 °C with no increase in particle content	2066	C

Y-Site Injection Compatibility (1:1 Mixture) (Cont.)

Drug	Mfr	Conc	Prochlorperazine edisylate Mfr	Prochlorperazine edisylate Conc	Remarks	Ref	C/I
Remifentanil HCl	GW	0.025 and 0.25 mg/ml[b]	SO	0.5 mg/ml[a]	Physically compatible with no change in measured turbidity or increase in particle content in 4 hr at 23 °C	2075	C
Sargramostim	IMM	10 μg/ml[b]	ES	0.5 mg/ml[b]	Physically compatible for 4 hr at 22 °C	1436	C
Sufentanil citrate	JN	12.5 μg/ml[a]	SCN	0.5 mg/ml[a]	Physically compatible with little subvisual haze or particle formation in 24 hr at 23 °C	1711	C
Teniposide	BR	0.1 mg/ml[a]	SCN	0.5 mg/ml[a]	Physically compatible with no subvisual haze or particle formation in 4 hr at 23 °C	1725	C
Thiotepa	IMM[g]	1 mg/ml[a]	SCN	0.5 mg/ml[a]	Physically compatible with no change in measured turbidity or increase in particle content in 4 hr at 23 °C	1861	C
TNA #218 to #226[h]			SCN, SO	0.5 mg/ml[a]	Visually compatible with no precipitate or emulsion damage apparent in 4 hr at 23 °C	2215	C
Topotecan HCl	SKB	56 μg/ml[a,b]	SKB	0.192 mg/ml[a,b]	Visually compatible with little or no loss of either drug by HPLC in 4 hr at 22 °C under fluorescent light	2245	C
TPN #212 to #215[h]			SCN	0.5 mg/ml[a]	Physically compatible with no change in measured turbidity or increase in particle content in 4 hr at 23 °C	2109	C
Vinorelbine tartrate	BW	1 mg/ml[b]	SKB	0.5 mg/ml[b]	Physically compatible with no change in measured turbidity or increase in particle content in 4 hr at 22 °C	1558	C
Vitamin B complex with C	RC	2 ml/L[e]	SKF	5 mg/ml	Physically compatible for at least 4 hr at room temperature by visual and microscopic examination	534	C

[a] *Tested in dextrose 5% in water.*
[b] *Tested in sodium chloride 0.9%.*
[c] *Tested in sterile water for injection.*
[d] *Tested in bacteriostatic sodium chloride 0.9% preserved with benzyl alcohol 0.9%.*
[e] *Tested in dextrose 5% in Ringer's injection, dextrose 5% in Ringer's injection, lactated, dextrose 5% in water, Ringer's injection, lactated, and sodium chloride 0.9%.*
[f] *Tested in dextrose 5% in water with sodium bicarbonate 0.05 mEq/ml.*
[g] *Lyophilized formulation tested.*
[h] *Refer to Appendix I for the composition of parenteral nutrition solutions. TNA indicates a 3-in-1 admixture, and TPN indicates a 2-in-1 admixture.*
[i] *Salt form unspecified.*

Additional Compatibility Information

Diamorphine HCl — Prochlorperazine edisylate is stated to be compatible with diamorphine HCl. (1442)

Parabens — Dilution of prochlorperazine edisylate (SKF) to a 1-mg/ml concentration with bacteriostatic sodium chloride 0.9% containing methyl- and propylparabens resulted in a distinctly cloudy solution. This cloudiness did not occur when sodium chloride 0.9% preserved with benzyl alcohol was used for the dilution. (752)

Concentrated Drug Solutions — The following incompatibility determinations were performed with concentrated solutions. The drugs in dry form were reconstituted according to manufacturers' recommendations. One milliliter of prochlorperazine edisylate (SKF) was added to 5 ml of sterile distilled water along with 1 ml of each of the following drugs. Particulate matter was noted within two hours (28):

Aminophylline
Chloramphenicol sodium succinate (Parke-Davis)
Dexamethasone sodium phosphate (MSD)
Dimenhydrinate (Searle)
Heparin sodium
Penicillin G potassium
Phenobarbital sodium (Winthrop)
Phenytoin sodium (Parke-Davis)
Vitamin B complex with C (Lederle)

Other Drugs — The manufacturer recommends that other agents not be mixed in a syringe with prochlorperazine edisylate. (1-10/99)

PROMETHAZINE HCL
AHFS 4:00 and 28:24.92

Products — Promethazine HCl is available from several manufacturers in vials, ampuls, and syringe cartridges in concentrations of 25 and 50 mg/ml. Each milliliter also contains disodium edetate 0.1 mg, calcium chloride 0.04 mg, sodium metabisulfite 0.25 mg, phenol 5 mg, and acetic acid–sodium acetate buffer in water for injection. (1-3/00; 2; 29)

pH — From 4 to 5.5. (4)

Osmolality — The osmolality of promethazine HCl 25 mg/ml was determined to be 291 mOsm/kg. (1233)

Trade Name(s) — Pentazine, Phenazine, Phenergan, Prorex, others.

Administration — Promethazine HCl is administered by deep intramuscular or intravenous injection. It should not be given subcutaneously or intra-arterially. When given by intravenous injection, a concentration not exceeding 25 mg/ml should be given into the tubing of a running infusion solution at a rate not exceeding 25 mg/min. (2; 4) Extravasation should be avoided. (4; 2312)

Stability — The product should be stored at controlled room temperature and protected from freezing and light. The injection should be inspected prior to administration for particulate matter formation and discoloration; the injection should be discarded if particulate matter or discoloration is observed. (2; 4) In general, promethazine HCl exhibits increasing stability with decreasing pH. (1072)

Syringes — Promethazine HCl (Fellows) 25 mg/1 ml repackaged in 3-ml amber glass syringes (Hy-Pod) and stored at 25 °C exhibited no significant changes in pH or physical appearance during 360 days of storage. A possible reduction in drug concentration to about 95% of initial was noted during this period. (535)

Sorption — Promethazine HCl (May & Baker) 8 mg/L in sodium chloride 0.9% (Travenol) in PVC bags exhibited only about 5% sorption to the plastic during one week of storage at room temperature (15 to 20 °C). However, when the solution was buffered from its initial pH of 5 to 7.4, approximately 59% of the drug was lost in one week due to sorption. (536)

In another study, promethazine HCl (May & Baker) 8 mg/L in sodium chloride 0.9% exhibited a cumulative 22% loss during a seven-hour simulated infusion through an infusion set (Travenol) consisting of a cellulose propionate burette chamber and 170 cm of PVC tubing due to sorption. Both the burette and the tubing contributed to the loss. The extent of sorption was found to be independent of concentration. (606)

The drug was also tested as a simulated infusion over at least one hour by a syringe pump system. A glass syringe on a syringe pump was fitted with 20 cm of polyethylene tubing or 50 cm of Silastic tubing. Only 5% of the drug was lost with the polyethylene tubing, but a cumulative loss of 72% occurred during the one-hour infusion through the Silastic tubing. (606)

A 25-ml aliquot of promethazine HCl (May & Baker) 8 mg/L in sodium chloride 0.9% was stored in all-plastic syringes composed of polypropylene barrels and polyethylene plungers for 24 hours at room temperature in the dark. No loss due to sorption occurred. (606)

Martens et al. reported that promethazine HCl 100 µg/ml in sodium chloride 0.9% in PVC, glass, and polyethylene-lined laminated containers exhibited little or no loss due to sorption in 24 hours at 21 °C when protected from light. (1392)

Central Venous Catheter — Promethazine HCl (Schein) 2 mg/ml in dextrose 5% in water was found to be compatible with the ARROWg+ard Blue Plus (Arrow International) chlorhexidine-bearing triple-lumen central catheter. HPLC analysis was used to evaluate completeness of drug delivery through the catheter and the amount of chlorhexidine removed from the internal lumens. Essentially complete delivery of the drug was found with little or no drug loss occurring. Furthermore, chlorhexidine delivered from the catheter remained at trace amounts with no substantial increase due to the delivery of the drug through the catheter. (2335)

Compatibility Information

Solution Compatibility

Promethazine HCl

Solution	*Mfr*	*Mfr*	*Conc/L*	*Remarks*	*Ref*	*C/I*
Dextran 6% in dextrose 5%	AB	WY	100 mg	Physically compatible	3	C
Dextran 6% in sodium chloride 0.9%	AB	WY	100 mg	Physically compatible	3	C
Dextrose–Ringer's injection combinations	AB	WY	100 mg	Physically compatible	3	C
Dextrose–Ringer's injection, lactated, combinations	AB	WY	100 mg	Physically compatible	3	C
Dextrose–saline combinations	AB	WY	100 mg	Physically compatible	3	C
Dextrose 2½% in water	AB	WY	100 mg	Physically compatible	3	C
Dextrose 5% in water	AB	WY	100 mg	Physically compatible	3	C
Dextrose 10% in water	AB	WY	100 mg	Physically compatible	3	C
Fructose 10% in sodium chloride 0.9%	AB	WY	100 mg	Physically compatible	3	C
Fructose 10% in water	AB	WY	100 mg	Physically compatible	3	C

Solution Compatibility (Cont.)

Promethazine HCl

Solution	*Mfr*	*Mfr*	*Conc/L*	*Remarks*	*Ref*	*C/I*
Invert sugar 5 and 10% in sodium chloride 0.9%	AB	WY	100 mg	Physically compatible	3	C
Invert sugar 5 and 10% in water	AB	WY	100 mg	Physically compatible	3	C
Ionosol products	AB	WY	100 mg	Physically compatible	3	C
Ringer's injection	AB	WY	100 mg	Physically compatible	3	C
Ringer's injection, lactated	AB	WY	100 mg	Physically compatible	3	C
Sodium chloride 0.45%	AB	WY	100 mg	Physically compatible	3	C
Sodium chloride 0.9%	AB	WY	100 mg	Physically compatible	3	C
	a		100 mg	Physically compatible with little or no drug loss in 24 hr at 21 °C in the dark	1392	C
Sodium lactate ⅙ M	AB	WY	100 mg	Physically compatible	3	C

[a]*Tested in PVC, glass, and polyethylene-lined laminated containers.*

Additive Compatibility

Promethazine HCl

Drug	*Mfr*	*Conc/L*	*Mfr*	*Conc/L*	*Test Soln*	*Remarks*	*Ref*	*C/I*
Amikacin sulfate	BR	5 g	WY	100 mg	D5LR, D5R, D5S, D5W, D10W, IS10, LR, NS, R, SL	Physically compatible and potency of both drugs retained for 24 hr at 25 °C	294	C
Aminophylline	SE	1 g	WY	250 mg	D5W	Physically incompatible	15	I
	BP	1 g	BP	100 mg	D5W, NS	Immediate precipitation	26	I
Ascorbic acid injection	UP	500 mg	WY	250 mg	D5W	Physically compatible	15	C
Chloramphenicol sodium succinate	PD	10 g	WY	250 mg	D5W	Physically incompatible	15	I
Chloroquine phosphate		5 mg		5 mg	W	Visually compatible with no change in UV spectra	1745	C
		25 mg		5 mg	W	Visually compatible with no change in UV spectra	1745	C
		5 mg		25 mg	W	Visually compatible with no change in UV spectra	1745	C
Chlorothiazide sodium	MSD		WY			Physically incompatible	9	I
	BP	2 g	BP	100 mg	D5W, NS	Immediate precipitation	26	I
Floxacillin sodium	BE	20 g	MB	5 g	W	White precipitate forms immediately	1479	I
Furosemide	HO	1 g	MB	5 g	W	White precipitate forms immediately	1479	I
Heparin sodium	UP	4000 units	WY	250 mg	D5W	Physically incompatible	15	I
Hydrocortisone sodium succinate	UP	500 mg	WY	250 mg	D5W	Physically incompatible	15	I
Hydromorphone HCl	KN	1 g	ES	300 mg	NS[a]	Visually compatible for 21 days at 4 and 25 °C	1992	C
Methohexital sodium	BP	2 g	BP	100 mg	D5W	Immediate precipitation	26	I

Additive Compatibility (Cont.)

Promethazine HCl

Drug	*Mfr*	*Conc/L*	*Mfr*	*Conc/L*	*Test Soln*	*Remarks*	*Ref*	*C/I*
Netilmicin sulfate	SC	3 g	WY	100 mg	D5S	Physically compatible and netilmicin chemically stable for 7 days at 4 and 25 °C. Promethazine not tested	558	C
Penicillin G potassium	SQ	20 million units	WY	250 mg	D5W	Physically incompatible	15	I
		1 million units	WY	100 mg		Physically compatible	3	C
	SQ	5 million units	WY	100 mg		Physically compatible	47	C
Penicillin G sodium	UP	20 million units	WY	250 mg	D5W	Physically incompatible	15	I
Pentobarbital sodium	AB	1 g	WY	250 mg	D5W	Physically incompatible	15	I
Phenobarbital sodium	WI	200 mg	WY	250 mg	D5W	Physically incompatible	15	I
	BP	800 mg	BP	100 mg	D5W	Haze develops over 3 hr	26	I
	BP	800 mg	BP	100 mg	NS	Immediate precipitation	26	I
Thiopental sodium	AB		WY			Physically incompatible	9	I
Vitamin B complex with C	AB	2 ml	WY	100 mg		Physically compatible	3	C
	AB	5 ml	WY	250 mg	D5W	Physically compatible	15	C

[a]*Tested in PVC containers.*

Drugs in Syringe Compatibility

Promethazine HCl

Drug (in syringe)	*Mfr*	*Amt*	*Mfr*	*Amt*	*Remarks*	*Ref*	*C/I*
Atropine sulfate		0.6 mg/ 1.5 ml	WY	50 mg/ 2 ml	Physically compatible for at least 15 min	14	C
	ST	0.4 mg/ 1 ml	PO	50 mg/ 2 ml	Physically compatible for at least 15 min	326	C
Atropine sulfate with meperidine HCl	WY	0.6 mg/ 1.5 ml 100 mg/ 1 ml	WY	50 mg/ 2 ml	Physically compatible	14	C
Atropine sulfate with meperidine HCl	LI WI	0.4 mg/ 1 ml 50 mg/ 1 ml	WY	25 mg/ 1 ml	No loss of any drug in 24 hr at 25 °C. Slight haze not present at 6 hr but developed by 24 hr	991	C
Butorphanol tartrate	BR	4 mg/ 2 ml	WY	25 mg/ 1 ml	Physically compatible both macroscopically and microscopically for 30 min at room temperature	566	C
Cefotetan disodium	ZE	10 mg/ ml[a]	ES	25 mg/ 1 ml	White precipitate, resembling cottage cheese, forms immediately	1753	I
Chloroquine phosphate		250 mg/ 5 ml		50 mg/ 2 ml	Greenish-yellow discoloration becomes precipitate in 22 hr	1745	I
		50 mg/ 1 ml		50 mg/ 2 ml	Greenish-yellow discoloration becomes precipitate in 17 hr	1745	I

Drugs in Syringe Compatibility (Cont.)

Promethazine HCl

Drug (in syringe)	*Mfr*	*Amt*	*Mfr*	*Amt*	*Remarks*	*Ref*	*C/I*
Chlorpromazine HCl	PO	50 mg/ 2 ml	PO	50 mg/ 2 ml	Physically compatible for at least 15 min	326	C
Cimetidine HCl	SKF	300 mg/ 2 ml	WY	25 mg/ 1 ml	Physically compatible for 4 hr at 25 °C	25	C
Diatrizoate sodium 75% (Hypaque)	WI	40 to 1 ml	WY	1 ml[b]	Immediate precipitation	530	I
Diatrizoate meglumine 52%, diatrizoate sodium 8% (Renografin-60)	SQ	40 to 1 ml	WY	1 ml[b]	Immediate precipitation	530	I
Diatrizoate meglumine 34.3%, diatrizoate sodium 35% (Renovist)	SQ	40 to 1 ml	WY	1 ml[b]	Immediate precipitation	530	I
Dihydroergotamine mesylate	SZ	1 mg/ 1 ml	ES	25 mg/ 1 ml	Visually compatible with no loss of either drug by HPLC in 24 hr at 4 and 23 °C protected from light	2240	C
	SZ	1 mg/ 1 ml	ES	50 mg/ 1 ml	Visually compatible with no loss of either drug by HPLC in 24 hr at 4 and 23 °C protected from light	2240	C
Dimenhydrinate	HR	50 mg/ 1 ml	PO	50 mg/ 2 ml	Physically incompatible within 15 min	326	I
	HR	50 mg/ 1 ml	WY	25 mg/ 1 ml	Physically incompatible	711	I
Diphenhydramine HCl	PD	50 mg/ 1 ml	WY	50 mg/ 2 ml	Physically compatible for at least 15 min	14	C
	PD	50 mg/ 1 ml	PO	50 mg/ 2 ml	Physically compatible for at least 15 min	326	C
Droperidol	MN	2.5 mg/ 1 ml	PO	50 mg/ 2 ml	Physically compatible for at least 15 min	326	C
Fentanyl citrate	MN	0.05 mg/ 1 ml	PO	50 mg/ 2 ml	Physically compatible for at least 15 min	326	C
Glycopyrrolate	RB	0.2 mg/ 1 ml	WY	25 mg/ 1 ml	Physically compatible and pH in stability range for glycopyrrolate for 48 hr at 25 °C	331	C
	RB	0.2 mg/ 1 ml	WY	50 mg/ 2 ml	Physically compatible and pH in stability range for glycopyrrolate for 48 hr at 25 °C	331	C
	RB	0.4 mg/ 2 ml	WY	25 mg/ 1 ml	Physically compatible and pH in stability range for glycopyrrolate for 48 hr at 25 °C	331	C
Heparin sodium		2500 units/ 1 ml		50 mg/ 2 ml	Turbidity or precipitate forms within 5 min	1053	I
Hydromorphone HCl	KN	4 mg/ 2 ml	WY	50 mg/ 1 ml	Physically compatible for 30 min	517	C
	KN	4 mg/ 2 ml	WY	25 mg/ 1 ml	Physically compatible for 30 min	517	C
Hydroxyzine HCl	PF	100 mg/ 4 ml	WY	50 mg/ 2 ml	Physically compatible for at least 15 min	14	C
	PF	50 mg/ 1 ml	PO	50 mg/ 2 ml	Physically compatible for at least 15 min	326	C
Iodipamide meglumine 52% (Cholografin)	SQ	40 and 20 ml	WY	1 ml[b]	Forms a precipitate initially but clears within 1 hr and remains clear for 48 hr	530	I
	SQ	10 to 1 ml	WY	1 ml[b]	Immediate precipitation	530	I

Drugs in Syringe Compatibility (Cont.)

Promethazine HCl

Drug (in syringe)	*Mfr*	*Amt*	*Mfr*	*Amt*	*Remarks*	*Ref*	*C/I*
Iothalamate meglumine 60% (Conray)	MA	40 to 1 ml	WY	1 ml[b]	Immediate precipitation	530	I
Iothalamate sodium 80% (Angio-Conray)	MA	40 to 1 ml	WY	1 ml[b]	Immediate precipitation	530	I
Ketorolac tromethamine	SY	180 mg/ 6 ml	ES	75 mg/ 3 ml	Heavy white precipitate forms immediately, separating into two layers over time	1703	I
Meperidine HCl	WY	100 mg/ 1 ml	WY	50 mg/ 2 ml	Physically compatible for at least 15 min	14	C
	WI	50 mg/ 1 ml	PO	50 mg/ 2 ml	Physically compatible for at least 15 min	326	C
Meperidine HCl with atropine sulfate	WY	100 mg/ 1 ml 0.6 mg/ 1.5 ml	WY	50 mg/ 2 ml	Physically compatible	14	C
Meperidine HCl with atropine sulfate	WI LI	50 mg/ 1 ml 0.4 mg/ 1 ml	WY	25 mg/ 1 ml	No loss of any drug in 24 hr at 25 °C. Slight haze not present at 6 hr but developed by 24 hr	991	C
Metoclopramide HCl	NO	10 mg/ 2 ml	WY	25 mg/ 1 ml	Physically compatible both macroscopically and microscopically for 30 min at room temperature	565	C
Midazolam HCl	RC	5 mg/ 1 ml	WY	25 mg/ 1 ml	Physically compatible for 4 hr at 25 °C under fluorescent light	1145	C
Morphine sulfate	WY	15 mg/ 1 ml	WY	50 mg/ 2 ml	Physically compatible for at least 15 min	14	C
	ST	15 mg/ 1 ml	PO	50 mg/ 2 ml	Physically compatible for at least 15 min	326	C
	WY	8 mg	WY	12.5 mg	Cloudiness develops	98	I
Nalbuphine HCl	EN	10 mg/ 1 ml	ES	25 mg	Physically compatible for 36 hr at 27 °C	762	C
	EN	5 mg/ 0.5 ml	ES	25 mg	Physically compatible for 36 hr at 27 °C	762	C
	EN	10 mg/ 1 ml	ES	12.5 mg	Physically compatible for 36 hr at 27 °C	762	C
	DU	10 mg/ 1 ml	WY	25 and 50 mg	Physically incompatible	128	I
	DU	20 mg/ 1 ml	WY	25 and 50 mg	Physically incompatible	128	I
	DU	10 mg/ 1 ml	WY	25 mg/ 1 ml	White flocculent precipitate forms immediately	1184	I
	DU	10 mg/ 1 ml	ES	25 mg/ 1 ml	Physically compatible for 24 hr at room temperature	1184	C
Papaveretum	RC[c]	20 mg/ 1 ml	PO	50 mg/ 2 ml	Visually compatible for at least 15 min	326	C
Pentazocine lactate	WI	30 mg/ 1 ml	WY	50 mg/ 2 ml	Physically compatible for at least 15 min	14	C
	WI	30 mg/ 1 ml	WY	25 mg/ 0.5 or 1 ml	Potency retained for 3 months at room temperature in Tubex	13	C
	WI	30 mg/ 1 ml	WY	50 mg/ 1 ml	Potency retained for 3 months at room temperature in Tubex	13	C

Drugs in Syringe Compatibility (Cont.)

Promethazine HCl

Drug (in syringe)	*Mfr*	*Amt*	*Mfr*	*Amt*	*Remarks*	*Ref*	*C/I*
	WI	45 mg/ 1.5 ml	WY	25 mg/ 0.5 ml	Potency retained for 3 months at room temperature in Tubex	13	C
	WI	30 mg/ 1 ml	PO	50 mg/ 2 ml	Physically compatible for at least 15 min	326	C
Pentobarbital sodium	AB	500 mg/ 10 ml	WY	100 mg/ 4 ml	Physically incompatible	55	I
	WY	100 mg/ 2 ml	WY	50 mg/ 2 ml	Precipitate forms within 15 min	14	I
	AB	50 mg/ 1 ml	PO	50 mg/ 2 ml	Physically incompatible within 15 min	326	I
Perphenazine	SC	5 mg/ 1 ml	WY	25 mg/ 1 ml	Physically compatible both macroscopically and microscopically for 30 min at room temperature	566	C
Prochlorperazine edisylate	PO	5 mg/ 1 ml	PO	50 mg/ 2 ml	Physically compatible for at least 15 min	326	C
Promazine HCl	WY	50 mg/ 1 ml	PO	50 mg/ 2 ml	Physically compatible for at least 15 min	326	C
Ranitidine HCl	GL	50 mg/ 2 ml	RP	25 mg/ 1 ml	Physically compatible for 1 hr at 25 °C both macroscopically and microscopically	978	C
	GL	50 mg/ 5 ml	RP	25 mg	Physically compatible for 4 hr at ambient temperature under fluorescent light	1151	C
Scopolamine HBr		0.6 mg/ 1.5 ml	WY	50 mg/ 2 ml	Physically compatible for at least 15 min	14	C
	ST	0.4 mg/ 1 ml	PO	50 mg/ 2 ml	Physically compatible for at least 15 min	326	C
Thiopental sodium	AB	75 mg/ 3 ml	WY	100 mg/ 4 ml	Physically incompatible	21	I

[a] *Tested in dextrose 5% in water.*
[b] *Promethazine HCl concentration unspecified.*
[c] *The former formulation was tested.*

Y-Site Injection Compatibility (1:1 Mixture)

Promethazine HCl

Drug	*Mfr*	*Conc*	*Mfr*	*Conc*	*Remarks*	*Ref*	*C/I*
Aldesleukin	CHI	33,800 I.U./ml[a]	ES	25 mg/ml	Aldesleukin bioactivity inhibited	1857	I
Allopurinol sodium	BW	3 mg/ml[b]	WY	2 mg/ml[b]	Heavy turbidity forms immediately, developing white particles in 4 hr	1686	I
Amifostine	USB	10 mg/ml[a]	ES	2 mg/ml[a]	Physically compatible with no change in measured turbidity or increase in particle content in 4 hr at 23 °C	1845	C
Amphotericin B cholesteryl sulfate complex	SEQ	0.83 mg/ml[a]	ES	2 mg/ml[a]	Gross precipitate forms	2117	I
Amsacrine	NCI	1 mg/ml[a]	ES	2 mg/ml[a]	Physically compatible for 4 hr at room temperature under fluorescent light	1381	C
Aztreonam	SQ	40 mg/ml[a]	SCN	2 mg/ml[a]	Physically compatible with no subvisual haze or particle formation in 4 hr at 23 °C	1758	C

Y-Site Injection Compatibility (1:1 Mixture) (Cont.)

Promethazine HCl

Drug	*Mfr*	*Conc*	*Mfr*	*Conc*	*Remarks*	*Ref*	*C/I*
Cefazolin sodium	LI	10 mg/ml[a]	ES	25 mg	Fine cloudy precipitate forms immediately and dissolves in seconds	1753	?
Cefepime HCl	BMS	20 mg/ml[a]	WY	2 mg/ml[a]	Haze forms immediately and becomes flocculent precipitate in 4 hr	1689	I
Cefoperazone sodium	RR	[a,c]		6.25 mg	White precipitate forms due to ionic complex formation	1336	I
Cefotetan disodium	ZE	10 mg/ml[a]	ES	25 mg	White precipitate forms immediately	1753	I
Ceftizoxime sodium	FUJ	10 mg/ml[a]	ES	25 mg	Fine cloudy precipitate forms immediately and dissolves in seconds	1753	?
Ciprofloxacin	MI	2 mg/ml[a,b]	ES	25 mg/ml	Visually compatible for 24 hr at 24 °C	1655	C
Cisatracurium besylate	GW	0.1, 2, 5 mg/ml[a]	ES	2 mg/ml[a]	Physically compatible with no change in measured turbidity or increase in particle content in 4 hr at 23 °C	2074	C
Cisplatin	BR	1 mg/ml	WY	2 mg/ml[a]	Visually compatible for 4 hr at room temperature under fluorescent light	1685	C
Cladribine	ORT	0.015[b] and 0.5[d] mg/ml	SCN	2 mg/ml[b]	Physically compatible with no change in measured turbidity or increase in particle content in 4 hr at 23 °C	1969	C
Cyclophosphamide	MJ	10 mg/ml	WY	2 mg/ml[a]	Visually compatible for 4 hr at room temperature under fluorescent light	1685	C
Cytarabine	UP	50 mg/ml	WY	2 mg/ml[a]	Visually compatible for 4 hr at room temperature under fluorescent light	1685	C
Docetaxel	RPR	0.9 mg/ml[a]	SCN	2 mg/ml[a]	Physically compatible with no change in measured turbidity or increase in particle content in 4 hr at 23 °C	2224	C
Doxorubicin HCl	AD	0.2 mg/ml[a]	WY	2 mg/ml[a]	Visually compatible for 4 hr at room temperature under fluorescent light	1685	C
Doxorubicin HCl liposome injection	SEQ	0.4 mg/ml[a]	ES	2 mg/ml[a]	Increase in measured turbidity	2087	I
Etoposide phosphate	BR	5 mg/ml[a]	SCN	2 mg/ml[a]	Physically compatible with no change in measured turbidity or increase in particle content in 4 hr at 23 °C	2218	C
Filgrastim	AMG	30 μg/ml[a]	SCN	2 mg/ml[a]	Physically compatible with no change in measured turbidity or increase in particle content in 4 hr at 22 °C	1687	C
Fluconazole	RR	2 mg/ml	ES	50 mg/ml	Physically compatible for 24 hr at 25 °C	1407	C
Fludarabine phosphate	BX	1 mg/ml[a]	WY	2 mg/ml[a]	Physically compatible for 4 hr at room temperature under fluorescent light	1439	C
Foscarnet sodium	AST	24 mg/ml	ES	50 mg/ml	Gas production	1335	I
Gatifloxacin	BMS	2 mg/ml[a]	SCN	2 mg/ml[a]	Physically compatible with no change in measured haze or increase in particle content in 4 hr at 23 °C	2234	C
Gemcitabine HCl	LI	10 mg/ml[b]	SCN	2 mg/ml[b]	Physically compatible with no change in measured turbidity or increase in particle content in 4 hr at 23 °C	2226	C

Y-Site Injection Compatibility (1:1 Mixture) (Cont.)

			Promethazine HCl				
Drug	*Mfr*	*Conc*	*Mfr*	*Conc*	*Remarks*	*Ref*	*C/I*
Granisetron HCl	SKB	0.05 mg/ml[a]	WY	2 mg/ml[a]	Physically compatible with no change in measured turbidity or increase in particle content in 4 hr at 23 °C	2000	C
Heparin sodium		50 units/ml/min[b]		50 mg/2 ml[e]	Distinct turbidity	1053	I
	UP	1000 units/L[f]	SV	50 mg/ml	Physically compatible for at least 4 hr at room temperature by visual and microscopic examination	534	C
	UP	1000 units/L[g]	SV	50 mg/ml	Physically compatible initially, but cloudiness developed within 4 hr at room temperature	534	I
Hetastarch in lactated electrolyte injection (Hextend)	AB	6%	SCN	2 mg/ml[a]	Physically compatible with no change in measured turbidity or increase in particle content in 4 hr at 23 °C	2339	C
Hydrocortisone sodium succinate	UP	10 mg/L[f]	SV	50 mg/ml	Physically compatible for at least 4 hr at room temperature by visual and microscopic examination	534	C
	UP	10 mg/L[g]	SV	50 mg/ml	Physically compatible initially, but cloudiness developed within 4 hr at room temperature	534	I
Linezolid	PHU	2 mg/ml	SCN	2 mg/ml[a]	Physically compatible with no change in measured turbidity or increase in particle content in 4 hr at 23 °C	2264	C
Melphalan HCl	BW	0.1 mg/ml[b]	WY	2 mg/ml[b]	Physically compatible with no change in measured turbidity or increase in particle content in 3 hr at 22 °C	1557	C
Methotrexate sodium	AD	15 mg/ml[h]	WY	2 mg/ml[a]	Turbidity forms within 30 min	1685	I
Ondansetron HCl	GL	1 mg/ml[b]	ES	2 mg/ml[a]	Physically compatible for 4 hr at 22 °C	1365	C
Piperacillin sodium–tazobactam sodium	LE	40 + 5 mg/ml[a]	SCN	2 mg/ml[a]	Heavy white turbidity forms immediately. Particles form in 4 hr	1688	I
Potassium chloride	AB	40 mEq/L[f]	SV	50 mg/ml	Physically compatible for at least 4 hr at room temperature by visual and microscopic examination	534	C
	AB	40 mEq/L[g]	SV	50 mg/ml	Physically compatible initially, but cloudiness developed within 4 hr at room temperature	534	I
Remifentanil HCl	GW	0.025 and 0.25 mg/ml[b]	SCN	2 mg/ml[a]	Physically compatible with no change in measured turbidity or increase in particle content in 4 hr at 23 °C	2075	C
Sargramostim	IMM	10 μg/ml[b]	ES	2 mg/ml[b]	Physically compatible for 4 hr at 22 °C	1436	C
Teniposide	BR	0.1 mg/ml[a]	WY	2 mg/ml[a]	Physically compatible with no subvisual haze or particle formation in 4 hr at 23 °C	1725	C
Thiotepa	IMM[i]	1 mg/ml[a]	WY	2 mg/ml[a]	Physically compatible with no change in measured turbidity or increase in particle content in 4 hr at 23 °C	1861	C
TNA #218 to #226[j]			SCN	2 mg/ml[a]	Visually compatible with no precipitate or emulsion damage apparent in 4 hr at 23 °C	2215	C

Y-Site Injection Compatibility (1:1 Mixture) (Cont.)

Promethazine HCl

Drug	*Mfr*	*Conc*	*Mfr*	*Conc*	*Remarks*	*Ref*	*C/I*
TPN #212 and #214[j]			SCN	2 mg/ml[a]	Physically compatible with no change in measured turbidity or increase in particle content in 4 hr at 23 °C	2109	C
TPN #213 and #215[j]			SCN	2 mg/ml[a]	Amber discoloration forms in 4 hr	2109	I
Vinorelbine tartrate	BW	1 mg/ml[b]	ES	2 mg/ml[b]	Physically compatible with no change in measured turbidity or increase in particle content in 4 hr at 22 °C	1558	C
Vitamin B complex with C	RC	2 ml/L[f]	SV	50 mg/ml	Physically compatible for at least 4 hr at room temperature by visual and microscopic examination	534	C
	RC	2 ml/L[g]	SV	50 mg/ml	Physically compatible initially, but cloudiness developed within 4 hr at room temperature	534	I

[a] *Tested in dextrose 5% in water.*
[b] *Tested in sodium chloride 0.9%.*
[c] *Concentration unspecified.*
[d] *Tested in bacteriostatic sodium chloride 0.9% preserved with benzyl alcohol 0.9%.*
[e] *Given over three minutes into running infusion solution.*
[f] *Tested in dextrose 5% in Ringer's injection, lactated, dextrose 5% in water, Ringer's injection, lactated, and sodium chloride 0.9%.*
[g] *Tested in dextrose 5% in Ringer's injection.*
[h] *Tested in dextrose 5% in water with sodium bicarbonate 0.05 mEq/ml.*
[i] *Lyophilized formulation tested.*
[j] *Refer to Appendix I for the composition of parenteral nutrition solutions. TNA indicates a 3-in-1 admixture, and TPN indicates a 2-in-1 admixture.*

Additional Compatibility Information

Nalbuphine — The compatibility of nalbuphine HCl with promethazine HCl appears to be conditional on the specific formulation of promethazine HCl being used. When Elkins-Sinn's promethazine HCl is combined with nalbuphine HCl, the admixture is compatible. However, if Wyeth's promethazine HCl is combined, a precipitate forms immediately. (128; 762; 1183)

Chlorpromazine and Meperidine — Chlorpromazine HCl (Elkins-Sinn), meperidine HCl (Winthrop), and promethazine HCl (Elkins-Sinn), combined as an extemporaneous mixture for preoperative sedation, developed a brownish-yellow color after two weeks of storage with protection from light. The discoloration was attributed to the metacresol preservative content of Winthrop's meperidine HCl. Use of Wyeth's meperidine HCl instead, which contains a different preservative, resulted in a solution that remained clear and colorless for at least three months when protected from light. (1148)

Heparin Lock — It has been reported that if promethazine HCl is injected into a heparinized scalp vein infusion set, a precipitate will form. It has been suggested that these heparinized sets be flushed with sterile water for injection or sodium chloride 0.9% both before and after drug administration. A heparin lock flush solution may then be reinjected into the device. (4; 97)

Pentobarbital — Promethazine HCl (Wyeth) 100 mg/L has been reported to be conditionally compatible with pentobarbital sodium (Abbott) 500 mg/L. The mixture is physically incompatible in most Abbott infusion solutions except as noted below (3):

Ionosol MB with dextrose 5%	Physically compatible
Ionosol T with dextrose 5%	Physically compatible

Concentrated Drug Solutions — The following incompatibility determinations were performed with concentrated solutions. The drugs in dry form were reconstituted according to manufacturers' recommendations. One milliliter of promethazine HCl (Wyeth) was added to 5 ml of sterile distilled water along with 1 ml of each of the following drugs. Particulate matter was noted within two hours (28):

Aminophylline
Chloramphenicol sodium succinate (Parke-Davis)
Dimenhydrinate (Searle)
Heparin sodium
Hydrocortisone sodium succinate (Upjohn)
Penicillin G potassium
Phenobarbital sodium (Winthrop)
Phenytoin sodium (Parke-Davis)
Vitamin B complex with C (Lederle)

Other Drugs — Promethazine HCl has been stated to be physically and chemically compatible with butorphanol tartrate (Bristol) (481) and buprenorphine HCl. (4) However, promethazine HCl is stated to be incompatible with diatrizoate meglumine products (Squibb) and iodipamide meglumine (Squibb). (40) Metal ions such as iron and especially copper, even in trace quantities, accelerate the degradation rate of promethazine HCl. (1072)

Promethazine HCl (Wyeth) 50 mg/2 ml, meperidine HCl (Wyeth) 100 mg/1 ml, and scopolamine HBr 0.6 mg/1.5 ml have been reported to be conditionally compatible when packaged in syringes. The mixture is physically compatible when the order of mixing is as listed above. (14)

PROPOFOL
AHFS 28:04

Products — Propofol (Diprivan) 1% is available as a ready-to-use oil-in-water emulsion in 20-ml ampuls, 50-ml prefilled syringes, and 50- and 100-ml infusion vials. Each milliliter contains propofol 10 mg along with soybean oil 100 mg, glycerol 22.5 mg, egg lecithin 12 mg, and disodium edetate 0.005% with sodium hydroxide to adjust the pH. (2)

Generic propofol 1% is also available as a ready-to-use oil-in-water emulsion in 20-ml vials and 50- and 100-ml infusion vials. However, the product differs from the Diprivan formulation. Each milliliter contains propofol 10 mg along with soybean oil 100 mg, glycerol 22.5 mg, and egg yolk phospholipid 12 mg, but incorporates sodium metabisulfite 0.25 mg. Sodium hydroxide is used to adjust the pH during manufacture. (2)

The two propofol products are not identical. Diprivan utilizes disodium edetate as an antimicrobial agent; the generic product utilizes sodium metabisulfite for this purpose. Diprivan has a pH in the range of 7 to 8.5. For the sodium metabisulfite to be comparable to disodium edetate as an antimicrobial agent, the pH of the generic product has been adjusted to 4.5 to 6.4 during manufacture. (2348; 2349)

NOTE: Most of the compatibility information for propofol with other drug products has been developed using Diprivan and cannot be automatically extrapolated to the other product because of the formulation differences. The formulation differences have been demonstrated to result in some differing compatibilities with other drugs. (2336)

pH — The Diprivan formulation has a pH of 7 to 8.5. The generic formulation has a pH of 4.5 to 6.4. (2)

Tonicity — Propofol 1% injectable emulsion from both suppliers is isotonic. (2)

Trade Name(s) — Diprivan.

Administration — Before use, propofol should be shaken well. It may be administered undiluted by intravenous injection or infusion or diluted with dextrose 5% in water to no less than 2 mg/ml. (2)

Numerous outbreaks of serious postoperative infections have resulted from inadvertent contamination of propofol during preparation. The contamination resulted from risky preparation practices and lapses in aseptic technique. The product's lipid base supports microbiological growth. (2; 1930) The disodium edetate and sodium metabisulfite in the Diprivan and generic formulations, respectively, retard the growth of microorganisms, but the products can still support growth and are not antimicrobially preserved. Strict aseptic procedures are required during preparation. (2)

Stability — Propofol 1% injection is a white, oil-in-water emulsion. Intact containers should be stored between 4 and 22 °C and protected from freezing. The emulsion should not be used if phase separation is evident. (2)

Propofol is subject to oxidative degradation when exposed to oxygen. Intact containers are packaged using nitrogen to avoid oxygen exposure. If propofol is administered directly from the vial, administration should be completed within 12 hours after the vial is spiked. The tubing and any unused propofol should be discarded after 12 hours. (2)

Generic propofol formulated with sodium metabisulfite antioxidant is subject to a differing decomposition reaction compared to the edetate-containing formulation (Diprivan). Exposure to air results in the formation of a yellow discoloration in less than 24 hours. The yellow discoloration is possibly due to the formation of the oxidized dimer of propofol, which does not occur in the Diprivan formulation. Stability information developed for the Diprivan formulation should not be extrapolated to the sodium metabisulfite-containing generic formulation. (2344)

If propofol emulsion is transferred to a syringe or other container prior to use, administration should be begun promptly and completed within six hours after the container is opened. After six hours, the product should be discarded and the lines should be flushed or discarded. (2)

Propofol emulsion is a single-use product and can support the growth of microorganisms. (2; 1930) Strict aseptic procedures, including wiping of the ampul neck or vial stopper with isopropanol 70%, are essential. (2)

Plastic and Glass Containers — Diluted in dextrose 5% in water, propofol has been shown to be more stable in glass than in plastic containers. The manufacturers indicate that the potency is only 95% after only two hours in plastic. However, the type of plastic container subject to this increased rate of decomposition is not specified. (2) See Syringes and Sorption below.

Syringes — Propofol (Zeneca) 10 mg/ml was repackaged into 60-ml polypropylene syringes (Monoject, Sherwood Medical) and stored at 23 °C under fluorescent light and at 4 °C protected from light. No visually apparent changes occurred to the emulsion under either storage condition. Propofol losses by HPLC analysis were 7% in five days and 12% in seven days in the room-temperature samples. No propofol losses occurred in 13 days in the refrigerated samples. (1984) Propofol supports microbial growth; see Administration.

Propofol (Zeneca) 1% was repackaged into 2- and 10-ml Plastipak (Becton-Dickinson) and 2-ml Inject (B. Braun) plastic syringes and was stored at 5 °C. Propofol losses by HPLC analysis were about 7 to 8% in the Plastipak syringes and about 2% in the Inject syringes after 28 days of refrigerated storage. (2118)

Sorption — In a study by Bailey et al., Diprivan injection was diluted to 2 mg/ml with dextrose 5% in water and stored in PVC tubing (Kendall-McGaw). HPLC analysis showed a propofol loss exceeding 31% after static storage for two hours. In simulated infusions using the same initial concentration, administration through 72-inch PVC administration sets at a rate of 1.75 ml/min resulted in an average propofol loss of 7.7% over the two-hour period. (2057)

When tested undiluted at 10 mg/ml, Parsons et al. found that propofol (Diprivan) sorption to administration tubing composed principally of PVC did not represent a substantial portion of the total amount of drug delivered. Any losses that did occur were within the error of the method and were not clinically relevant. (2297) This result is consistent with the small propofol loss to PVC tubing during dynamic flow through the tubing that was found by Bailey et al.

Filtration — The manufacturer recommends that filters with a pore size less than 5 μm should not be used with propofol emulsion. These filters may restrict its administration and/or cause the breakdown of the emulsion. (2) However, Bailey et al. reported that 10 ml of propofol injection (Stuart) 10 mg/ml filtered through a 5-μm filter needle

(Burron Medical) underwent no potency loss by HPLC analysis. (2057) Whether this also applies to other filters is not known.

Opening propofol packaged in glass ampuls has been shown to yield a substantially higher amount of larger particulates compared to the product packaged in vials. The larger particulates are probably glass associated with opening the ampuls. Drawing the propofol into a syringe using a 5-μm filter significantly reduced the amount of these particles in the product. The authors recommend that the use of a 5-μm filter needle be a standard part of propofol preparation. (2311)

Compatibility Information

Drugs in Syringe Compatibility

			Propofol				
Drug (in syringe)	*Mfr*	*Amt*	*Mfr*	*Amt*	*Remarks*	*Ref*	*C/I*
Ondansetron HCl	GW	1 mg/ml[b]	STU	1 and 5 mg/ml[b]	Physically compatible with no measured increase in particulates and little or no loss of either drug by HPLC in 4 hr at 23 °C	2199	C
Thiopental sodium	AB	12.5 mg/ml[a]	ZEN	5 mg/ml[a]	Visually compatible. 10% loss by HPLC of thiopental in 10 days and of propofol in 7 days at 23 °C under fluorescent light. No thiopental loss and 4% propofol loss in 13 days at 4 °C protected from light	1984	C
	AB	37.5 mg/ 1.5 ml	ICI	5 mg/ 0.5 ml	Little or no increase in measured emulsion droplet size in 24 hr at 4 °C.	1985	C
	AB	31.25 mg/ 1.25 ml	ICI	7.5 mg/ 0.75 ml	Little or no increase in measured emulsion droplet size in 24 hr at 4 °C.	1985	C
	AB	25 mg/ 1 ml	ICI	10 mg/ 1 ml	Little or no increase in measured emulsion droplet size in 24 hr at 4 °C. Little or no loss of either drug by HPLC in 24 hr at 4 °C	1985	C
	AB	18.75 mg/ 0.75 ml	ICI	12.5 mg/ 1.25 ml	Little or no increase in measured emulsion droplet size in 24 hr at 4 °C.	1985	C
	AB	12.5 mg/ 0.5 ml	ICI	15 mg/ 1.5 ml	Little or no increase in measured emulsion droplet size in 24 hr at 4 °C.	1985	C

[a]*Final concentrations after mixing.*
[b]*Tested in sodium chloride 0.9%.*

Y-Site Injection Compatibility (1:1 Mixture)

			Propofol				
Drug	*Mfr*	*Conc*	*Mfr*	*Conc*	*Remarks*	*Ref*	*C/I*
Acyclovir sodium	BW	7 mg/ml[a]	ZEN	10 mg/ml	Physically compatible for 1 hr at 23 °C with no increase in particle content	2066	C
Alatrofloxacin mesylate	PF	2 mg/ml[a]	ASZ	10 mg/ml	Physically compatible for 1 hr at 23 °C with no increase in particle content	1916	C
Alfentanil HCl	JN	0.5 mg/ml	ZEN	10 mg/ml	Physically compatible for 1 hr at 23 °C with no increase in particle content	2066	C
Amikacin sulfate	DU	5 mg/ml[a]	ZEN	10 mg/ml	White precipitate and yellow color form immediately	2066	I
Aminophylline	AMR	2.5 mg/ml[a]	ZEN	10 mg/ml	Physically compatible for 1 hr at 23 °C with no increase in particle content	2066	C
Amphotericin B	APC	0.6 mg/ml[a]	ZEN	10 mg/ml	Gel-like precipitate forms immediately	2066	I
Ampicillin sodium	WY	20 mg/ml[b]	ZEN	10 mg/ml	Physically compatible for 1 hr at 23 °C with no increase in particle content	2066	C
Ascorbic acid	AB	500 mg/ml	STU	2 mg/ml	Yellow discoloration forms within 7 days at 25 °C	1801	?
Atracurium besylate	BW	10 mg/ml	STU	2 mg/ml	Oil droplets form within 24 hr, followed by phase separation at 25 °C	1801	I

Y-Site Injection Compatibility (1:1 Mixture) (Cont.)

Drug	*Mfr*	*Conc*	Propofol *Mfr*	Propofol *Conc*	*Remarks*	*Ref*	*C/I*
	BW	10 mg/ml	ZEN	10 mg/ml	Emulsion broke and oiled out	2066	I
		10 mg/ml	ASZ, BA	10 mg/ml	Emulsion disruption upon mixing	2336	I
		5 mg/ml[a]	ASZ, BA	10 mg/ml	Emulsion disruption upon mixing	2336	I
		0.5 mg/ml[a]	BA	10 mg/ml	Emulsion disruption upon mixing	2336	I
		0.5 mg/ml[a]	ASZ	10 mg/ml	Physically compatible for at least 1 hr at room temperature	2336	C
Atropine sulfate	GNS	0.4 mg/ml	STU	2 mg/ml	Oil droplets form within 7 days at 25 °C	1801	?
	AST	0.1 mg/ml[a]	ZEN	10 mg/ml	Physically compatible for 1 hr at 23 °C with no increase in particle content	2066	C
Aztreonam	SQ	40 mg/ml[a]	ZEN	10 mg/ml	Physically compatible for 1 hr at 23 °C with no increase in particle content	2066	C
Bretylium tosylate	AST	50 mg/ml	ZEN	10 mg/ml	Emulsion broke and oiled out	2066	I
Bumetanide	RC	0.04 mg/ml[a]	ZEN	10 mg/ml	Physically compatible for 1 hr at 23 °C with no increase in particle content	2066	C
Buprenorphine HCl	RKC	0.04 mg/ml[a]	ZEN	10 mg/ml	Physically compatible for 1 hr at 23 °C with no increase in particle content	2066	C
Butorphanol tartrate	APC	0.04 mg/ml[a]	ZEN	10 mg/ml	Physically compatible for 1 hr at 23 °C with no increase in particle content	2066	C
Calcium chloride	AST	40 mg/ml[a]	ZEN	10 mg/ml	White precipitate formed in 1 hr	2066	I
Calcium gluconate	AMR	40 mg/ml[a]	ZEN	10 mg/ml	Physically compatible for 1 hr at 23 °C with no increase in particle content	2066	C
Carboplatin	BR	5 mg/ml[a]	ZEN	10 mg/ml	Physically compatible for 1 hr at 23 °C with no increase in particle content	2066	C
Cefazolin sodium	MAR	20 mg/ml[a]	ZEN	10 mg/ml	Physically compatible for 1 hr at 23 °C with no increase in particle content	2066	C
Cefepime HCl	BMS	20 mg/ml[a]	ASZ	10 mg/ml	Physically compatible for 1 hr at 23 °C with no increase in particle content	1916	C
Cefoperazone sodium	RR	40 mg/ml[a]	ZEN	10 mg/ml	Physically compatible for 1 hr at 23 °C with no increase in particle content	2066	C
Cefotaxime sodium	HO	20 mg/ml[a]	ZEN	10 mg/ml	Physically compatible for 1 hr at 23 °C with no increase in particle content	2066	C
Cefotetan disodium	STU	20 mg/ml[a]	ZEN	10 mg/ml	Physically compatible for 1 hr at 23 °C with no increase in particle content	2066	C
Cefoxitin sodium	ME	20 mg/ml[a]	ZEN	10 mg/ml	Physically compatible for 1 hr at 23 °C with no increase in particle content	2066	C
Ceftazidime[c]	SKB	40 mg/ml[a]	ZEN	10 mg/ml	Physically compatible for 1 hr at 23 °C with no increase in particle content	2066	C
Ceftizoxime sodium	FUJ	20 mg/ml[a]	ZEN	10 mg/ml	Physically compatible for 1 hr at 23 °C with no increase in particle content	2066	C
Ceftriaxone sodium	RC	20 mg/ml[a]	ZEN	10 mg/ml	Physically compatible for 1 hr at 23 °C with no increase in particle content	2066	C
Cefuroxime sodium	LI	30 mg/ml[a]	ZEN	10 mg/ml	Physically compatible for 1 hr at 23 °C with no increase in particle content	2066	C
Chlorpromazine HCl	SCN	2 mg/ml[a]	ZEN	10 mg/ml	Physically compatible for 1 hr at 23 °C with no increase in particle content	2066	C

Y-Site Injection Compatibility (1:1 Mixture) (Cont.)

			Propofol				
Drug	*Mfr*	*Conc*	*Mfr*	*Conc*	*Remarks*	*Ref*	*C/I*
Cimetidine HCl	SKB	12 mg/ml[a]	ZEN	10 mg/ml	Physically compatible for 1 hr at 23 °C with no increase in particle content	2066	C
Ciprofloxacin	MI	1 mg/ml[a]	ZEN	10 mg/ml	Emulsion broke and oiled out	1916	I
Cisatracurium besylate	GW	5 mg/ml[a]	ASZ, BA	10 mg/ml	Emulsion disruption upon mixing	2336	I
	GW	0.5 mg/ml[a]	BA	10 mg/ml	Emulsion disruption upon mixing	2336	I
	GW	0.5 mg/ml[a]	ASZ	10 mg/ml	Physically compatible for at least 1 hr at room temperature	2336	C
Cisplatin	BR	1 mg/ml	ZEN	10 mg/ml	Physically compatible for 1 hr at 23 °C with no increase in particle content	2066	C
Clindamycin phosphate	AST	10 mg/ml[a]	ZEN	10 mg/ml	Physically compatible for 1 hr at 23 °C with no increase in particle content	2066	C
Cyclophosphamide	MJ	10 mg/ml[a]	ZEN	10 mg/ml	Physically compatible for 1 hr at 23 °C with no increase in particle content	2066	C
Cyclosporine	SZ	5 mg/ml[a]	ZEN	10 mg/ml	Physically compatible for 1 hr at 23 °C with no increase in particle content	2066	C
Cytarabine	CHI	50 mg/ml	ZEN	10 mg/ml	Physically compatible for 1 hr at 23 °C with no increase in particle content	2066	C
Dexamethasone sodium phosphate	AMR	1 mg/ml[a]	ZEN	10 mg/ml	Physically compatible for 1 hr at 23 °C with no increase in particle content	2066	C
Diazepam	ES	5 mg/ml	ZEN	10 mg/ml	Emulsion broke and oiled out	2066	I
Digoxin	ES	0.25 mg/ml	ZEN	10 mg/ml	Emulsion broke and oiled out	1916	I
Diphenhydramine HCl	SCN	2 mg/ml[a]	ZEN	10 mg/ml	Physically compatible for 1 hr at 23 °C with no increase in particle content	2066	C
Dobutamine HCl	LI	4 mg/ml[a]	ZEN	10 mg/ml	Physically compatible for 1 hr at 23 °C with no increase in particle content	2066	C
Dopamine HCl	AST	3.2 mg/ml[a]	ZEN	10 mg/ml	Physically compatible for 1 hr at 23 °C with no increase in particle content	2066	C
Doxacurium chloride	BW	1 mg/ml	STU	2 mg/ml	Separation into layers occurs within 7 days at 25 °C	1801	?
Doxorubicin HCl	CHI	2 mg/ml	ZEN	10 mg/ml	Emulsion broke and oiled out	1916	I
Doxycycline hyclate	LY	1 mg/ml[a]	ZEN	10 mg/ml	Physically compatible for 1 hr at 23 °C with no increase in particle content	2066	C
Droperidol	JN	0.4 mg/ml[a]	ZEN	10 mg/ml	Physically compatible for 1 hr at 23 °C with no increase in particle content	2066	C
Enalaprilat	MSD	0.1 mg/ml[a]	ZEN	10 mg/ml	Physically compatible for 1 hr at 23 °C with no increase in particle content	2066	C
Ephedrine HCl	AB	5 mg/ml[a]	ZEN	10 mg/ml	Physically compatible for 1 hr at 23 °C with no increase in particle content	2066	C
Epinephrine HCl	AMR	0.1 mg/ml	ZEN	10 mg/ml	Physically compatible for 1 hr at 23 °C with no increase in particle content	2066	C
Esmolol HCl	OHM	10 mg/ml	ZEN	10 mg/ml	Physically compatible for 1 hr at 23 °C with no increase in particle content	2066	C
Famotidine	AB	2 mg/ml[a]	ZEN	10 mg/ml	Physically compatible for 1 hr at 23 °C with no increase in particle content	2066	C

Y-Site Injection Compatibility (1:1 Mixture) (Cont.)

			Propofol				
Drug	*Mfr*	*Conc*	*Mfr*	*Conc*	*Remarks*	*Ref*	*C/I*
Fentanyl citrate	AB	0.05 mg/ml	ZEN	10 mg/ml	Physically compatible for 1 hr at 23 °C with no increase in particle content	2066	C
Fluconazole	PF	2 mg/ml[a]	ZEN	10 mg/ml	Physically compatible for 1 hr at 23 °C with no increase in particle content	2066	C
Fluorouracil	AD	16 mg/ml[a]	ZEN	10 mg/ml	Physically compatible for 1 hr at 23 °C with no increase in particle content	2066	C
Furosemide	AB	3 mg/ml[a]	ZEN	10 mg/ml	Physically compatible for 1 hr at 23 °C with no increase in particle content	2066	C
Ganciclovir sodium	SY	20 mg/ml[a]	ZEN	10 mg/ml	Physically compatible for 1 hr at 23 °C with no increase in particle content	2066	C
Gentamicin sulfate	ES	5 mg/ml[a]	ZEN	10 mg/ml	White precipitate forms immediately	2066	I
Glycopyrrolate	RB	0.2 mg/ml	ZEN	10 mg/ml	Physically compatible for 1 hr at 23 °C with no increase in particle content	2066	C
Granisetron HCl	SKB	0.05 mg/ml[a]	ZEN	10 mg/ml	Physically compatible for 1 hr at 23 °C with no increase in particle content	2066	C
Haloperidol lactate	MN	0.2 mg/ml[a]	ZEN	10 mg/ml	Physically compatible for 1 hr at 23 °C with no increase in particle content	2066	C
Heparin sodium	ES	100 units/ml[a]	ZEN	10 mg/ml	Physically compatible for 1 hr at 23 °C with no increase in particle content	2066	C
Hydrocortisone sodium succinate	UP	1 mg/ml[a]	ZEN	10 mg/ml	Physically compatible for 1 hr at 23 °C with no increase in particle content	2066	C
Hydromorphone HCl	AST	0.5 mg/ml[a]	ZEN	10 mg/ml	Physically compatible for 1 hr at 23 °C with no increase in particle content	2066	C
Hydroxyzine HCl	ES	2 mg/ml[a]	ZEN	10 mg/ml	Physically compatible for 1 hr at 23 °C with no increase in particle content	2066	C
Ifosfamide	MJ	25 mg/ml[a]	ZEN	10 mg/ml	Physically compatible for 1 hr at 23 °C with no increase in particle content	2066	C
Imipenem–cilastatin sodium	ME	10 mg/ml[b]	ZEN	10 mg/ml	Physically compatible for 1 hr at 23 °C with no increase in particle content	2066	C
Inamrinone lactate	WI	1 mg/ml[a]	ZEN	10 mg/ml	Physically compatible for 1 hr at 23 °C with no increase in particle content	2066	C
Insulin	NOV	1 unit/ml[a]	ZEN	10 mg/ml	Physically compatible for 1 hr at 23 °C with no increase in particle content	2066	C
Isoproterenol HCl	AB	0.004 mg/ml[a]	ZEN	10 mg/ml	Physically compatible for 1 hr at 23 °C with no increase in particle content	2066	C
Ketamine HCl	PD	10 mg/ml	ZEN	10 mg/ml	Physically compatible for 1 hr at 23 °C with no increase in particle content	2066	C
Labetalol HCl	AH	5 mg/ml	ZEN	10 mg/ml	Physically compatible for 1 hr at 23 °C with no increase in particle content	2066	C
Levofloxacin	OMN	5 mg/ml[a]	ASZ	10 mg/ml	Emulsion broke and oiled out	1916	I
Levorphanol tartrate	RC	0.5 mg/ml[a]	ZEN	10 mg/ml	Physically compatible for 1 hr at 23 °C with no increase in particle content	2066	C
Lidocaine HCl	AST	10 mg/ml	ZEN	10 mg/ml	Physically compatible for 1 hr at 23 °C with no increase in particle content	2066	C
Lorazepam	WY	0.1 mg/ml[a]	ZEN	10 mg/ml	Physically compatible for 1 hr at 23 °C with no increase in particle content	2066	C

Y-Site Injection Compatibility (1:1 Mixture) (Cont.)

Propofol

Drug	*Mfr*	*Conc*	*Mfr*	*Conc*	*Remarks*	*Ref*	*C/I*
Magnesium sulfate	AST	100 mg/ml[a]	ZEN	10 mg/ml	Physically compatible for 1 hr at 23 °C with no increase in particle content	2066	C
Mannitol	BA	15%	ZEN	10 mg/ml	Physically compatible for 1 hr at 23 °C with no increase in particle content	2066	C
Meperidine HCl	WY	4 mg/ml[a]	ZEN	10 mg/ml	Physically compatible for 1 hr at 23 °C with no increase in particle content	2066	C
Methotrexate sodium	LE	15 mg/ml[a]	ZEN	10 mg/ml	Small amount of white precipitate forms in 1 hr	2066	I
Methylprednisolone sodium succinate	AB	5 mg/ml[a]	ZEN	10 mg/ml	Small amount of white precipitate forms immediately	2066	I
Metoclopramide HCl	RB	5 mg/ml	ZEN	10 mg/ml	Emulsion broke and oiled out	1916	I
Midazolam HCl	RC	5 mg/ml	STU	2 mg/ml	Oil droplets form within 7 days at 25 °C	1801	?
	RC	2 mg/ml[a]	ZEN	10 mg/ml	Physically compatible for 1 hr at 23 °C with no increase in particle content	2066	C
Milrinone lactate	SW	0.4 mg/ml[a]	ZEN	10 mg/ml	Little or no loss of either drug by HPLC in 4 hr at 23 °C	2214	C
Minocycline HCl	LE	0.2 mg/ml[a]	ZEN	10 mg/ml	Small amount of white particles forms immediately	2066	I
Mitoxantrone HCl	IMM	0.5 mg/ml[a]	ZEN	10 mg/ml	Small amount of particles forms immediately	2066	I
Morphine sulfate		15 mg/ml	ASZ	10 mg/ml	Precipitate formed and emulsion broke and oiled out	1916	I
	AST	1 mg/ml[a]	ZEN	10 mg/ml	Physically compatible for 1 hr at 23 °C with no increase in particle content	2066	C
Nafcillin sodium	MAR	20 mg/ml[a]	ZEN	10 mg/ml	Physically compatible for 1 hr at 23 °C with no increase in particle content	2066	C
Nalbuphine HCl	AB	10 mg/ml	ZEN	10 mg/ml	Physically compatible for 1 hr at 23 °C with no increase in particle content	2066	C
Naloxone HCl	AST	0.4 mg/ml	ZEN	10 mg/ml	Physically compatible for 1 hr at 23 °C with no increase in particle content	2066	C
Netilmicin sulfate	SC	5 mg/ml[a]	ZEN	10 mg/ml	Precipitate forms immediately	2066	I
Nitroglycerin	DU	0.4 mg/ml[a]	ZEN	10 mg/ml	Physically compatible for 1 hr at 23 °C with no increase in particle content	2066	C
Norepinephrine bitartrate	AB	0.016 mg/ml[a]	ZEN	10 mg/ml	Physically compatible for 1 hr at 23 °C with no increase in particle content	2066	C
Ofloxacin	ORT	4 mg/ml[a]	ZEN	10 mg/ml	Physically compatible for 1 hr at 23 °C with no increase in particle content	2066	C
Paclitaxel	MJ	1.2 mg/ml[a]	ZEN	10 mg/ml	Physically compatible for 1 hr at 23 °C with no increase in particle content	2066	C
Pancuronium bromide	GNS	2 mg/ml	STU	2 mg/ml	Oil droplets form within 7 days at 25 °C	1801	?
	AST	1 mg/ml	ZEN	10 mg/ml	Physically compatible for 1 hr at 23 °C with no increase in particle content	2066	C
Pentobarbital sodium	WY	5 mg/ml[a]	ZEN	10 mg/ml	Physically compatible for 1 hr at 23 °C with no increase in particle content	2066	C
Phenobarbital sodium	WY	5 mg/ml[a]	ZEN	10 mg/ml	Physically compatible for 1 hr at 23 °C with no increase in particle content	2066	C

Y-Site Injection Compatibility (1:1 Mixture) (Cont.)

Drug	*Mfr*	*Conc*	*Mfr*	*Conc*	*Remarks*	*Ref*	*C/I*
			Propofol				
Phenylephrine HCl	ES	10 mg/ml	STU	2 mg/ml	Bright yellow discoloration forms within 7 days at 25 °C	1801	?
	ES	0.1 mg/ml[a]	ZEN	10 mg/ml	Physically compatible for 1 hr at 23 °C with no increase in particle content	2066	C
Phenytoin sodium	ES	50 mg/ml	ZEN	10 mg/ml	Needle-like crystals form immediately	2066	I
Piperacillin sodium	LE	40 mg/ml[a]	ZEN	10 mg/ml	Physically compatible for 1 hr at 23 °C with no increase in particle content	2066	C
Potassium chloride	AB	0.1 mEq/ml[a]	ZEN	10 mg/ml	Physically compatible for 1 hr at 23 °C with no increase in particle content	2066	C
Prochlorperazine edisylate	SCN	0.5 mg/ml[a]	ZEN	10 mg/ml	Physically compatible for 1 hr at 23 °C with no increase in particle content	2066	C
Propranolol HCl	SO	1 mg/ml	ZEN	10 mg/ml	Physically compatible for 1 hr at 23 °C with no increase in particle content	2066	C
Ranitidine HCl	GL	2 mg/ml[a]	ZEN	10 mg/ml	Physically compatible for 1 hr at 23 °C with no increase in particle content	2066	C
Scopolamine HBr	LY	0.4 mg/ml	ZEN	10 mg/ml	Physically compatible for 1 hr at 23 °C with no increase in particle content	2066	C
Sodium bicarbonate	AB	1 mEq/ml	ZEN	10 mg/ml	Physically compatible for 1 hr at 23 °C with no increase in particle content	2066	C
Sodium nitroprusside	ES	0.4 mg/ml[a]	ZEN	10 mg/ml	Physically compatible for 1 hr at 23 °C with no increase in particle content	2066	C
Succinylcholine chloride	AB	20 mg/ml[a]	ZEN	10 mg/ml	Physically compatible for 1 hr at 23 °C with no increase in particle content	2066	C
Sufentanil citrate	JN	0.05 mg/ml	ZEN	10 mg/ml	Physically compatible for 1 hr at 23 °C with no increase in particle content	2066	C
Thiopental sodium	AB	25 mg/ml	ASZ	10 mg/ml	Physically compatible for 1 hr at 23 °C with no increase in particle content	1916	C
Ticarcillin disodium	SKB	30 mg/ml[a]	ZEN	10 mg/ml	Physically compatible for 1 hr at 23 °C with no increase in particle content	2066	C
Ticarcillin disodium–clavulanate potassium	SKB	31 mg/ml[a]	ZEN	10 mg/ml	Physically compatible for 1 hr at 23 °C with no increase in particle content	2066	C
Tobramycin sulfate	AB	5 mg/ml[a]	ZEN	10 mg/ml	Precipitate forms immediately	2066	I
TPN #186[d]			STU	500 mg	Physically compatible with no change in particle size distribution but 28% propofol loss by HPLC in 5 hr at 22 °C	1805	I
TPN #187 and #188[d]			STU	500 mg	Physically compatible with no change in particle size distribution and 6% or less propofol loss by HPLC in 5 hr at 22 °C	1805	C
TPN #186 to #188[d]			STU	2 and 3 g	Physically compatible with no change in particle size distribution and 6% or less propofol loss by HPLC in 5 hr at 22 °C	1805	C
Vancomycin HCl		10 mg/ml[a]	BA	10 mg/ml	Emulsion disruption within 1 to 4 hr at room temperature	2336	I
	AB	10 mg/ml[a]	ZEN	10 mg/ml	Physically compatible for 1 hr at 23 °C with no increase in particle content	2066	C
		10 mg/ml[a]	ASZ	10 mg/ml	Physically compatible for up to 30 days at room temperature	2336	C

Y-Site Injection Compatibility (1:1 Mixture) (Cont.)

Drug	Mfr	Conc	Propofol Mfr	Propofol Conc	Remarks	Ref	C/I
Vecuronium bromide	OR	1 mg/ml	ZEN	10 mg/ml	Physically compatible for 1 hr at 23 °C with no increase in particle content	2066	C
Verapamil HCl	AMR	2.5 mg/ml	ZEN	10 mg/ml	Emulsion broke and oiled out	1916	I

[a]Tested in dextrose 5% in water.
[b]Tested in sodium chloride 0.9%.
[c]Sodium carbonate–containing formulation.
[d]Refer to Appendix I for the composition of parenteral nutrition solutions. TPN indicates a 2-in-1 admixture.

Additional Compatibility Information

Infusion Solutions — The propofol emulsions are compatible with the following infusion solutions (2):

Dextrose 5% in Ringer's injection, lactated
Dextrose 5% in sodium chloride 0.2%
Dextrose 5% in sodium chloride 0.45%
Dextrose 5% in water
Ringer's injection, lactated

The manufacturers recommend that only dextrose 5% in water be used to dilute propofol and that the concentration not be less than 2 mg/ml. (2)

Blood Products — The manufacturers recommend that propofol not be mixed with blood, plasma, or serum. Aggregates of the emulsion have been found when propofol has been in contact with blood, plasma, and serum. (2)

Atracurium Besylate and Cisatracurium Besylate — The incompatibility of atracurium besylate and cisatracurium besylate with propofol is both concentration dependent and specific to the formulation of propofol. A low atracurium besylate or cisatracurium besylate concentration of 0.5 mg/ml with the sulfite-containing formulation of generic propofol results in emulsion disruption whereas the edetate-containing formulation of propofol (Diprivan) remains compatible. However, a high atracurium besylate or cisatracurium besylate concentration of 5 or 10 mg/ml disrupts the emulsions of both formulations of propofol. (2336) See Y-site Table above.

Other Drugs — Most compatibility information for propofol with other drug products has been developed using Diprivan from AstraZeneca and cannot be automatically extrapolated to the other product because of the formulation differences. The formulation differences have been demonstrated to result in some differing compatibilities. (2336) The manufacturers recommend that propofol not be mixed with other therapeutic agents. (2)

PROPRANOLOL HCL
AHFS 24:04

Products — Propranolol HCl is available in 1-ml ampuls containing 1 mg of the drug with citric acid to adjust the pH in water for injection. (2)

pH — From 2.8 to 3.5. (4)

Osmolality — The osmolality of propranolol HCl 1 mg/ml was determined to be 12 mOsm/kg. (1233)

Trade Name(s) — Inderal.

Administration — Propranolol HCl is administered by intravenous injection at a rate not exceeding 1 mg/min for life-threatening arrhythmias or those occurring during anesthesia. (2; 4)

Stability — Propranolol HCl should be stored at controlled room temperature around 25 °C and protected from light, freezing, or excessive heat. (2; 4) Solutions of the drug have maximum stability at pH 3 and decompose rapidly at alkaline pH. Decomposition in aqueous solutions is accompanied by a lowered pH and discoloration. Solutions fluoresce at pH 4 to 5. (4)

Sorption — Propranolol HCl (Sigma) 20 mg/L in sodium chloride 0.9% (Travenol) in PVC bags did not exhibit significant sorption to the plastic during one week of storage at room temperature (15 to 20 °C). (536)

In another study, propranolol HCl (Sigma) 20 mg/L in sodium chloride 0.9% did not exhibit any loss due to sorption during a seven-hour simulated infusion through an infusion set (Travenol) consisting of a cellulose propionate burette chamber and 170 cm of PVC tubing. (606)

The drug was also tested as a simulated infusion over at least one hour by a syringe pump system. A glass syringe on a syringe pump was fitted with 20 cm of polyethylene tubing or 50 cm of Silastic tubing. No loss of drug due to sorption was observed with either tubing. (606)

A 25-ml aliquot of propranolol HCl (Sigma) 20 mg/L in sodium chloride 0.9% was stored in all-plastic syringes composed of polypropylene barrels and polyethylene plungers for 24 hours at room temperature in the dark. No loss due to sorption occurred. (606)

Propranolol HCl (Ayerst) 0.5 and 20 mg/L was evaluated for 24 hours at room temperature in PVC (Abbott and Travenol) and polyolefin (McGaw) containers of the following solutions:

Dextrose 5% in sodium chloride 0.45 and 0.9%
Dextrose 5% in water
Ringer's injection, lactated
Sodium chloride 0.9%

Samples for HPLC analysis were taken through administration sets and 0.2-μm filters attached to the admixture containers. The results indicated no sorption of propranolol HCl to the plastic solution containers, sets, or filters. (746)

Compatibility Information

Solution Compatibility

Propranolol HCl

Solution	*Mfr*	*Mfr*	*Conc/L*	*Remarks*	*Ref*	*C/I*
Dextrose 5% in sodium chloride 0.45%	AB[a], TR[a]	AY	0.5 and 20 mg	Physically compatible and chemically stable for 24 hr at room temperature	746	C
	MG[b]	AY	0.5 and 20 mg	Physically compatible and chemically stable for 24 hr at room temperature	746	C
Dextrose 5% in sodium chloride 0.9%	AB[a], TR[a]	AY	0.5 and 20 mg	Physically compatible and chemically stable for 24 hr at room temperature	746	C
	MG[b]	AY	0.5 and 20 mg	Physically compatible and chemically stable for 24 hr at room temperature	746	C
Dextrose 5% in water	AB[a], TR[a]	AY	0.5 and 20 mg	Physically compatible and chemically stable for 24 hr at room temperature	746	C
	MG[b]	AY	0.5 and 20 mg	Physically compatible and chemically stable for 24 hr at room temperature	746	C
Ringer's injection, lactated	AB[a], TR[a]	AY	0.5 and 20 mg	Physically compatible and chemically stable for 24 hr at room temperature	746	C
	MG[b]	AY	0.5 and 20 mg	Physically compatible and chemically stable for 24 hr at room temperature	746	C
Sodium chloride 0.45%		LY	500 mg	Physically compatible with no loss in 4 hr at 22 °C	1419	C
Sodium chloride 0.9%	AB[a], TR[a]	AY	0.5 and 20 mg	Physically compatible and chemically stable for 24 hr at room temperature	746	C
	MG[b]	AY	0.5 and 20 mg	Physically compatible and chemically stable for 24 hr at room temperature	746	C

[a] *Tested in PVC containers.*
[b] *Tested in polyolefin containers.*

Additive Compatibility

Propranolol HCl

Drug	*Mfr*	*Conc/L*	*Mfr*	*Conc/L*	*Test Soln*	*Remarks*	*Ref*	*C/I*
Dobutamine HCl	LI	1 g	AY	50 mg	D5W, NS	Physically compatible for 24 hr at 21 °C	812	C
Verapamil HCl	KN	80 mg	AY	4 mg	D5W, NS	Physically compatible for 24 hr	764	C

Drugs in Syringe Compatibility

Propranolol HCl

Drug (in syringe)	*Mfr*	*Amt*	*Mfr*	*Amt*	*Remarks*	*Ref*	*C/I*
Inamrinone lactate	WI	5 mg/ 1 ml	LY	1 mg/ 1 ml	Physically compatible with little or no loss of either drug in 4 hr at 22 °C	1419	C
Milrinone lactate	WI	3.5 mg/ 3.5 ml	AY	3 mg/ 3 ml	Brought to 10-ml total volume with D5W. Physically compatible with no loss of either drug in 4 hr at 23 °C	1191	C

Y-Site Injection Compatibility (1:1 Mixture)

Drug	*Mfr*	*Conc*	Propranolol HCl *Mfr*	*Conc*	*Remarks*	*Ref*	*C/I*
Alteplase	GEN	1 mg/ml	AY	1 mg/ml	Visually compatible with 2% or less alteplase clot-lysis activity loss in 24 hr at 25 °C	1856	C
Amphotericin B cholesteryl sulfate complex	SEQ	0.83 mg/ml[a]	WY	1 mg/ml	Gross precipitate forms	2117	I
Diazoxide	SC	15 mg/ml[a]	AY	0.08 mg/ml[a]	Moderate precipitate and slight color change in 1 hr	1316	I
	SC	15 mg/ml[b]	AY	0.08 mg/ml[b]	Moderate precipitate in 1 hr	1316	I
Gatifloxacin	BMS	2 mg/ml[a]	WAY	1 mg/ml	Physically compatible with no change in measured haze or increase in particle content in 4 hr at 23 °C	2234	C
Heparin sodium	UP	1000 units/L[d]	AY	1 mg/ml	Physically compatible for at least 4 hr at room temperature by visual and microscopic examination	534	C
Hydrocortisone sodium succinate	UP	10 mg/L[d]	AY	1 mg/ml	Physically compatible for at least 4 hr at room temperature by visual and microscopic examination	534	C
Inamrinone lactate	WI	2.5 mg/ml[c]	LY	1 mg/ml	Physically compatible with little or no loss of either drug in 4 hr at 22 °C	1419	C
Linezolid	PHU	2 mg/ml	WAY	1 mg/ml	Physically compatible with no change in measured turbidity or increase in particle content in 4 hr at 23 °C	2264	C
Meperidine HCl	AB	10 mg/ml	WY	1 mg/ml	Physically compatible for 4 hr at 25 °C	1397	C
Milrinone lactate	WI	200 μg/ml[a]	AY	1 mg/ml	Physically compatible with no loss of either drug in 4 hr at 23 °C	1191	C
Morphine sulfate	AB	1 mg/ml	WY	1 mg/ml	Physically compatible for 4 hr at 25 °C	1397	C
Potassium chloride	AB	40 mEq/L[d]	AY	1 mg/ml	Physically compatible for at least 4 hr at room temperature by visual and microscopic examination	534	C
Propofol	ZEN	10 mg/ml	SO	1 mg/ml	Physically compatible for 1 hr at 23 °C with no increase in particle content	2066	C
Tacrolimus	FUJ	1 mg/ml[b]	AY	1 mg/ml	Visually compatible for 24 hr at 25 °C	1630	C
Vitamin B complex with C	RC	2 ml/L[d]	AY	1 mg/ml	Physically compatible for at least 4 hr at room temperature by visual and microscopic examination	534	C

[a] *Tested in dextrose 5% in water.*
[b] *Tested in sodium chloride 0.9%.*
[c] *Tested in sodium chloride 0.45%*
[d] *Tested in dextrose 5% in Ringer's injection, dextrose 5% in Ringer's injection, lactated, dextrose 5% in water, Ringer's injection, lactated, and sodium chloride 0.9%.*

Additional Compatibility Information

Alteplase — Propranolol HCl is stated to be physically compatible with alteplase when administered by Y-site injection into a running alteplase solution. (4)

PROTAMINE SULFATE
AHFS 20:12.08

Products — Protamine sulfate is available in 5- and 25-ml vials and 25-ml ampuls. Each milliliter contains 10 mg of protamine sulfate with sodium chloride 0.9% and sodium phosphate and/or sulfuric acid to adjust the pH. (2; 29)

pH — From 6 to 7. (2)

Osmolality — The osmolality of protamine sulfate (Lilly) 10 mg/ml was determined to be 290 mOsm/kg by freezing-point depression and 292 mOsm/kg by vapor pressure. (1071)

Administration — Protamine sulfate is administered by slow intravenous injection undiluted as the 10-mg/ml concentration given over one to three minutes. No more than 50 mg should be administered in any 10-minute period. It has also been given by intravenous infusion after dilution in sodium chloride 0.9% or dextrose 5% in water. (2; 4)

Stability — Protamine sulfate should be stored under refrigeration; freezing should be avoided. (2) However, protamine sulfate has been stated to be stable for 10 days (1433) to two weeks (853) at room temperature.

Filtration — Protamine sulfate (Fournier Freres) 0.2 mg/ml in dextrose 5% in water and sodium chloride 0.9% was filtered through a 0.22-μm cellulose ester membrane filter (Ivex-HP, Millipore) over six hours. No significant drug loss due to binding to the filter was noted. (1034)

Compatibility Information

Additive Compatibility

Protamine sulfate

Drug	*Mfr*	*Conc/L*	*Mfr*	*Conc/L*	*Test Soln*	*Remarks*	*Ref*	*C/I*
Cimetidine HCl	SKF	3 g	LI	500 mg	D5W	Physically compatible and cimetidine chemically stable for 24 hr at room temperature. Protamine not tested	551	C
Ranitidine HCl	GL	50 mg and 2 g		500 mg	D5W	Physically compatible and ranitidine chemically stable by HPLC for 24 hr at 25 °C. Protamine not tested	1515	C
Verapamil HCl	KN	80 mg	LI	100 mg	D5W, NS	Physically compatible for 24 hr	764	C

Drugs in Syringe Compatibility

Protamine sulfate

Drug (in syringe)	*Mfr*	*Amt*	*Mfr*	*Amt*	*Remarks*	*Ref*	*C/I*
Diatrizoate meglumine 52%, diatrizoate sodium 8%	MA	5 ml	LI	10 mg/ 1 ml	Precipitate forms immediately and persists for at least 2 hr	1438	I
Diatrizoate sodium 60%	WI	5 ml	LI	10 mg/ 1 ml	Precipitate forms immediately and persists for at least 2 hr	1438	I
Iohexol 64.7%	WI	5 ml	LI	10 mg/ 1 ml	Physically compatible for at least 2 hr	1438	C
Iopamidol 61%	SQ	5 ml	LI	10 mg/ 1 ml	Physically compatible for at least 2 hr	1438	C
Iothalamate meglumine 60%	MA	5 ml	LI	10 mg/ 1 ml	Physically compatible for at least 2 hr	1438	C
Ioxaglate meglumine 39.3%, ioxaglate sodium 19.6%	MA	5 ml	LI	10 mg/ 1 ml	Precipitate forms immediately and persists for at least 2 hr	1438	I

Additional Compatibility Information

Infusion Solutions — Dextrose 5% in water and sodium chloride 0.9% have been recommended for the infusion of protamine sulfate. (2; 4)

Other Drugs — The manufacturer recommends that protamine sulfate not be mixed with other drugs unless their compatibility is known. Protamine sulfate is incompatible with some antibiotics including several cephalosporins and penicillins. (2)

PYRIDOSTIGMINE BROMIDE
AHFS 12:04

Products — Pyridostigmine bromide is available in 2-ml ampuls and 5-ml vials. Each milliliter of solution contains pyridostigmine bromide 5 mg, citric acid and sodium hydroxide, if necessary, to adjust pH, and methyl- and propylparabens 0.2% or benzyl alcohol 1% as a preservative. (4; 29; 154)

pH — Approximately 5. (4)

Osmolality — Pyridostigmine bromide 5 mg/ml has an osmolality of 132 mOsm/kg. (1689)

Trade Name(s) — Mestinon, Regonol.

Administration — Pyridostigmine bromide is administered intramuscularly or by very slow intravenous injection. (4)

Stability — Pyridostigmine bromide is unstable in alkaline solutions. (4)

Compatibility Information

Drugs in Syringe Compatibility

Drug (in syringe)	Mfr	Amt	Pyridostigmine bromide Mfr	Amt	Remarks	Ref	C/I
Glycopyrrolate	RB	0.2 mg/ 1 ml	RC	5 mg/ 1 ml	Physically compatible and pH in stability range for glycopyrrolate for 48 hr at 25 °C	331	C
	RB	0.2 mg/ 1 ml	RC	10 mg/ 2 ml	Physically compatible and pH in stability range for glycopyrrolate for 48 hr at 25 °C	331	C
	RB	0.4 mg/ 2 ml	RC	5 mg/ 1 ml	Physically compatible and pH in stability range for glycopyrrolate for 48 hr at 25 °C	331	C

Y-Site Injection Compatibility (1:1 Mixture)

Drug	Mfr	Conc	Pyridostigmine bromide Mfr	Conc	Remarks	Ref	C/I
Heparin sodium	UP	1000 units/L[a]	RC	5 mg/ml	Physically compatible for at least 4 hr at room temperature by visual and microscopic examination	534	C
Hydrocortisone sodium succinate	UP	10 mg/L[a]	RC	5 mg/ml	Physically compatible for at least 4 hr at room temperature by visual and microscopic examination	534	C
Potassium chloride	AB	40 mEq/L[a]	RC	5 mg/ml	Physically compatible for at least 4 hr at room temperature by visual and microscopic examination	534	C
Vitamin B complex with C	RC	2 ml/L[a]	RC	5 mg/ml	Physically compatible for at least 4 hr at room temperature by visual and microscopic examination	534	C

[a]*Tested in dextrose 5% in Ringer's injection, dextrose 5% in Ringer's injection, lactated, dextrose 5% in water, Ringer's injection, lactated, and sodium chloride 0.9%.*

PYRIDOXINE HCL
AHFS 88:08

Products — Pyridoxine HCl injection is available from several manufacturers in 1-, 10-, and 30-ml multiple-dose vials as an aqueous solution providing 100 mg/ml. Also present are antimicrobial preservatives, such as benzyl alcohol 1.5% or chlorobutanol 0.5%. Sodium hydroxide and/or hydrochloric acid may have been used to adjust pH. (1-1/99; 4; 29; 154)

pH — From 2 to 3.8. (1-1/99; 4)

Osmolality — The osmolality of pyridoxine HCl (Lilly) 100 mg/ml was determined to be 870 mOsm/kg by freezing-point depression and 852 mOsm/kg by vapor pressure. (1071)

Administration — Pyridoxine HCl may be administered by intramuscular, subcutaneous, or intravenous injection. (4)

Stability — The product should be stored at controlled room temperature and protected from freezing and from light. (1-1/99; 4)

Because pyridoxine HCl is photosensitive and degrades slowly when exposed to light, protection from light has been recommended. (4)

Sorption — Pyridoxine HCl (Sigma) 40 mg/L did not display significant sorption to a PVC plastic test strip in 24 hours. (12)

Compatibility Information

Solution Compatibility

Pyridoxine HCl

Solution	*Mfr*	*Mfr*	*Conc/L*	*Remarks*	*Ref*	*C/I*
Fat emulsion 10%, intravenous	KA	KA[a]	98 mg	Physically compatible for 24 hr at 26 °C with little loss of pyridoxine HCl and of most other vitamins by HPLC; up to 52% ascorbate loss	2050	C

[a] *From multivitamins.*

Drugs in Syringe Compatibility

Pyridoxine HCl

Drug (in syringe)	*Mfr*	*Amt*	*Mfr*	*Amt*	*Remarks*	*Ref*	*C/I*
Doxapram HCl	RB	400 mg/ 20 ml		10 mg/ 1 ml	Physically compatible with 6% doxapram loss in 24 hr	1177	C

Additional Compatibility Information

Infusion Solutions — Pyridoxine HCl in infusion solutions under hospital conditions is reported to be stable. However, addition of riboflavin phosphate sodium promoted decomposition of the pyridoxine so that approximately 8% remained after three hours in the light. Addition of an antioxidant such as ascorbic acid or protection from light reduced the rate of degradation of pyridoxine. (563)

Parenteral Nutrition Solutions — The stability of pyridoxine HCl 15 mg/L was studied in representative parenteral nutrition solutions exposed to fluorescent light, indirect sunlight, and direct sunlight for eight hours. One 5-ml vial of multivitamin concentrate (Lyphomed) containing 15 mg of pyridoxine HCl and also 1 mg of folic acid (Lederle) was added to a liter of parenteral nutrition solution composed of amino acids 4.25%–dextrose 25% (Travenol) with standard electrolytes and trace elements. Pyridoxine HCl was stable over the eight-hour study at room temperature under fluorescent light and indirect sunlight. However, eight hours of exposure to direct sunlight caused an 86% loss of pyridoxine HCl. (842)

Dahl et al. reported the stability of numerous vitamins in parenteral nutrition solutions composed of amino acids (Kabi-Vitrum), dextrose 30%, and fat emulsion 20% (Kabi-Vitrum) in a 2:1:1 ratio with electrolytes, trace elements, and both fat- and water-soluble vitamins. The admixtures were stored in darkness at 2 to 8 °C for 96 hours with no significant loss of retinyl palmitate, alpha-tocopherol, thiamine mononitrate, sodium riboflavin-5′-phosphate, pyridoxine HCl, nicotinamide, folic acid, biotin, sodium pantothenate, and cyanocobalamin. Sodium ascorbate and its biologically active degradation product, dehydroascorbic acid, totaled 59 and 42% of the nominal starting concentration at 24 and 96 hours, respectively. However, the actual initial concentration was only 66% of the nominal concentration. (1225)

Antibiotics — In vitro testing of pyridoxine HCl at a concentration of 0.1% with the following antibiotics at a concentration of 0.025% in sterile distilled water showed significant reduction in antibiotic activity in one hour at 25 °C (314):

Erythromycin (as estolate)
Kanamycin sulfate
Streptomycin sulfate

Other Drugs — Pyridoxine HCl is stated to be incompatible with alkaline solutions, iron salts, and oxidizing agents. (4; 18)

QUINIDINE GLUCONATE
AHFS 24:04

Products — Quinidine gluconate is available in 10-ml vials. Each milliliter contains 80 mg of drug with edetate disodium 0.005% and phenol 0.25% in sterile water for injection. D-gluconic acid delta-lactone may have been added to adjust the pH. (2)

Equivalency — Quinidine gluconate 800 mg is equivalent to 500 mg of anhydrous quinidine. (2)

pH — Quinidine gluconate injection has a pH of 5.5 to 7. (4)

Osmolality — Quinidine gluconate 80 mg/ml has an osmolality of 220 mOsm/kg. (1689)

Administration — Quinidine gluconate injection may be administered by intermittent or continuous intravenous infusion. (4) For intravenous administration in treating arrhythmias, 800 mg (10 ml) is diluted with 40 ml of dextrose 5% in water for a total of 50 ml to yield a 16-mg/ml solution. The drug has also been given by intramuscular injection, but this route is not recommended because of variable absorption. (2; 4)

For the treatment of malaria, continuous and intermittent infusion regimens have been used. A loading dose is prepared as a dilution in about 250 ml of sodium chloride 0.9% and given as a one- or two-hour (continuous regimen) or four-hour (intermittent regimen) infusion. This is followed by continuous or intermittent intravenous infusions. (4)

Infusions of quinidine gluconate must be delivered slowly at a rate no faster than 0.25 mg/kg/min, preferably using a volumetric pump to control the rate of administration. (2)

Stability — Quinidine gluconate should be stored at controlled room temperature. Quinidine salts slowly discolor on exposure to light, acquiring a brownish tint. Only clear, colorless solutions are suitable for injection. (4)

Sorption — Quinidine (as the sulfate) 4.5 mg/L in sodium chloride 0.9% (Travenol) in PVC bags did not exhibit significant sorption to the plastic during one week of storage at room temperature (15 to 20 °C). (536)

In another study, quinidine (as the sulfate) 4.5 mg/L in sodium chloride 0.9% did not exhibit any loss due to sorption during a seven-hour simulated infusion through an infusion set (Travenol) consisting of a cellulose propionate burette chamber and 170 cm of PVC tubing. (606)

The drug was also tested as a simulated infusion over at least one hour by a syringe pump system. A glass syringe on a syringe pump was fitted with 20 cm of polyethylene tubing or 50 cm of Silastic tubing. No loss of drug due to sorption was observed with either tubing. (606)

In addition, a 25-ml aliquot of quinidine (as the sulfate) 4.5 mg/L in sodium chloride 0.9% was stored in all-plastic syringes composed of polypropylene barrels and polyethylene plungers for 24 hours at room temperature in the dark. No loss due to sorption occurred. (606)

Darbar et al. noted a substantial loss of quinidine gluconate due to sorption to PVC containers and administration sets. Quinidine gluconate (Lilly) 6 mg/ml in dextrose 5% in water in 100-ml PVC bags (Baxter) exhibited about 5 to 7% loss determined by UV spectroscopy. Administration of the solution over 30 minutes through 112-inch PVC administration sets (Gemini, IMED) resulted in an additional loss of over 30% of the quinidine gluconate from the delivered solution. Losses totaled over 40% for both bag and catheter. Use of a glass syringe on a syringe pump and a winged administration catheter having only 12 inches of PVC tubing reduced the loss to about 3%. (2005)

Compatibility Information

Additive Compatibility

Quinidine gluconate

Drug	Mfr	Conc/L	Mfr	Conc/L	Test Soln	Remarks	Ref	C/I
Amiodarone HCl	LZ	1.8 g	LI	1 g	D5W[a]	Precipitation caused a milky appearance. 13% amiodarone loss in 6 hr and 23% in 24 hr at 24 °C under fluorescent light	1031	I
	LZ	1.8 g	LI	1 g	D5W[b]	Precipitation caused a milky appearance. No amiodarone loss in 24 hr at 24 °C under fluorescent light	1031	I
	LZ	1.8 g	LI	1 g	NS[a]	Physically compatible but 4% amiodarone loss in 6 hr and 13% in 24 hr at 24 °C under fluorescent light	1031	I
	LZ	1.8 g	LI	1 g	NS[b]	Physically compatible with no amiodarone loss in 24 hr at 24 °C under fluorescent light	1031	C
Atracurium besylate	BW	500 mg		8.3 g	D5W	Particles form and atracurium chemically unstable at 5 and 30 °C	1694	I
Bretylium tosylate	ACC	1 g	LI	800 mg	D5W, NS	Physically compatible for 48 hr at 25 °C	756	C
Cimetidine HCl	SKF	3 g	LI	3.2 g	D5W	Physically compatible and cimetidine chemically stable for 24 hr at room temperature. Quinidine not tested	551	C

Additive Compatibility (Cont.)

			Quinidine gluconate					
Drug	*Mfr*	*Conc/L*	*Mfr*	*Conc/L*	*Test Soln*	*Remarks*	*Ref*	*C/I*
Milrinone lactate	WI	200 mg	LI	16 g	D5W	Physically compatible with no loss of either drug in 4 hr at 23 °C	1191	C
Ranitidine HCl	GL	50 mg and 2 g		3.2 mg	D5W	Physically compatible and ranitidine chemically stable by HPLC for 24 hr at 25 °C. Quinidine not tested	1515	C
Verapamil HCl	KN	80 mg	LI	800 mg	D5W, NS	Physically compatible for 48 hr	739	C

[a]Tested in PVC containers.
[b]Tested in polyolefin containers.

Y-Site Injection Compatibility (1:1 Mixture)

			Quinidine gluconate				
Drug	*Mfr*	*Conc*	*Mfr*	*Conc*	*Remarks*	*Ref*	*C/I*
Diazepam	ES	0.2 mg/ml[a,b]	LI	6 mg/ml[a,b]	Physically compatible for 3 hr	1316	C
Furosemide	ES	4 mg/ml[a,b]	LI	6 mg/ml[a,b]	Immediate gross precipitation	1316	I
Heparin sodium	ES	50 units/ml[b]	LI	6 mg/ml[b]	Physically compatible for 3 hr	1316	C
	ES	50 units/ml[a]	LI	6 mg/ml[a]	Immediate gross haze	1316	I
Milrinone lactate	WI	350 μg/ml[a]	LI	16 mg/ml[a]	Physically compatible with no loss of either drug in 4 hr at 23 °C	1191	C

[a]Tested in dextrose 5% in water.
[b]Tested in sodium chloride 0.9%.

Additional Compatibility Information

Infusion Solutions — At a concentration of 16 mg/ml in dextrose 5% in water, quinidine gluconate is reported to be stable for 24 hours at room temperature and for 48 hours under refrigeration. (4)

RANITIDINE HCL
AHFS 56:40

Products — Ranitidine HCl is available in 2-ml single-dose vials, 6-ml multiple-dose vials, and 40-ml pharmacy bulk packages. Each milliliter of solution contains (2):

Ranitidine (as the hydrochloride)	25 mg
Phenol	5 mg
Dibasic sodium phosphate	2.4 mg
Monobasic potassium phosphate	0.96 mg

Ranitidine HCl is also available at a 1-mg/ml concentration in 50-ml (50 mg) plastic containers premixed in sodium chloride 0.45%. The solution also contains citric acid 15 mg and dibasic sodium phosphate 90 mg as buffers. (2)

Equivalency — Ranitidine HCl 168 mg is approximately equivalent to 150 mg of ranitidine. (4)

pH — From 6.7 to 7.3. (2; 4)

Osmolality — The osmolality of ranitidine HCl 10 mg/ml was determined to be 59 mOsm/kg. (1233)

The osmolality of ranitidine HCl (Glaxo) 1 mg/ml was determined to be 260 mOsm/kg in dextrose 5% in water and 302 mOsm/kg in sodium chloride 0.9%. At 2 mg/ml, the osmolality was determined to be 257 mOsm/kg in dextrose 5% in water and 294 mOsm/kg in sodium chloride 0.9%. (1375)

The premixed ranitidine 1-mg/ml solution (Glaxo Wellcome) in sodium chloride 0.45% has an osmolarity of 180 mOsm/L. (2)

Trade Name(s)—Zantac.

Administration — Ranitidine HCl is administered intramuscularly undiluted or slowly intravenously after dilution. For direct intravenous injection, 50 mg is usually diluted to a total of at least 20 ml with a compatible intravenous infusion fluid and given over at least five minutes (4 ml/min). For intermittent intravenous infusion, 50 mg may be added to at least 100 ml of appropriate intravenous solution and infused over 15 to 20 minutes. For continuous intravenous infusion, 150 mg of ranitidine HCl may be diluted in 250 ml of intravenous fluid and infused at 6.25 mg/hr for 24 hours. (2; 4)

Stability — Ranitidine HCl injection should be stored between 4 and 30 °C and protected from light and excessive heat. Brief exposure to temperatures up to 40 °C will not adversely affect the stability of the injection. The product is a clear, colorless to yellow solution. Slight darkening does not affect potency. The pharmacy bulk package should be used as soon as possible after initial entry; unused portions should be discarded within 24 hours. The premixed infusion solution should be stored between 2 and 25 °C. (2; 4)

Ranitidine HCl (Glaxo) was diluted to a concentration of 2.5 mg/ml with bacteriostatic water for injection and repackaged in 30-ml glass vials and 10-ml polypropylene syringes (Becton-Dickinson) (closure not specified). The vials and syringes were stored at 4 °C for 91 days. Approximately 5 to 6% ranitidine loss determined by HPLC analysis occurred after 91 days of storage under refrigeration. Freshly prepared syringes and syringes stored at 4 °C for 91 days were also stored at 22 °C for 72 hours. No ranitidine loss was found in the freshly prepared syringes, and about 2% additional loss was found in syringes stored under refrigeration for 91 days. (1965)

Freezing Solutions—Ranitidine HCl (Glaxo) 0.5, 1, and 2 mg/ml in dextrose 5% in water and sodium chloride 0.9% in PVC bags showed no significant change in appearance or potency when frozen for 30 days at −30 °C. An additional 14 days of refrigerated storage at 4 °C for these previously frozen solutions also resulted in no potency loss. (1143)

At a concentration of 2 mg/ml in dextrose 5% in water and sodium chloride 0.9% in PVC containers, no significant change in appearance or potency occurred even after 100 days of frozen storage at −30 °C. (1143)

Ranitidine HCl (Glaxo) 441 μg/ml in dextrose 5% in water was visually compatible and showed no potency loss by HPLC after frozen storage (−20 °C) for 30 days followed by 10 days of refrigeration at 4 °C. (1539)

Stewart et al. studied the stability of ranitidine HCl (Glaxo) 0.5, 1, and 2 mg/ml in several infusion fluids when frozen at −20 °C for 60 days followed by seven days at 23 °C or 14 days at 4 °C. In dextrose 5% in sodium chloride 0.45%, dextrose 5% in water, dextrose 10% in water, and sodium chloride 0.9%, ranitidine was physically compatible and chemically stable, retaining more than 90% of the initial concentration under these storage conditions. However, in dextrose 5% in Ringer's injection, lactated, the thawed solutions were slightly yellow with ranitidine HCl losses of up to 25% at 0.5 mg/ml and 16% at 1 mg/ml. At 2 mg/ml, losses were 9% or less. (1516)

Ranitidine HCl (Glaxo) 1.5 mg/ml in dextrose 5% in water or in sodium chloride 0.9% was packaged in PVC infusion pump reservoirs. The reservoirs were frozen at −20 °C and stored for 30 days. The frozen solutions were then thawed by storing at 3 °C for 24 hours followed by 24 hours at 30 °C to simulate use conditions. No loss of ranitidine HCl was found by HPLC analysis of the solutions. (1865)

Sorption—Ranitidine HCl (Glaxo Wellcome) 0.25 mg/ml in dextrose 5% in water and sodium chloride 0.9% packaged in PVC, polyethylene, and glass containers exhibited little or no loss due to sorption to polyethylene or glass containers when stored at 4 and 22 °C for 24 hours. About 4 to 5% loss occurred in the PVC bags under these conditions protected from light. (2289)

Elastomeric Reservoir Pumps—Ranitidine HCl solutions in elastomeric reservoir pumps have been stated by the pump manufacturers to be stable for the following time periods frozen, refrigerated (REF), and at room temperature (RT) (31):

Pump Reservoir(s)	Conc.	Frozen	REF	RT
Homepump; Homepump Eclipse	0.5 to 2 mg/ml[a,b]	30 days	30 days	7 days
Medflo	0.5 mg/ml[a,b]	12 weeks	30 days	7 days
ReadyMed	0.5 mg/ml[a,b]	4 weeks	14 days	2 days

[a] *In dextrose 5% in water.*
[b] *In sodium chloride 0.9%.*

Filtration—Filtration of ranitidine HCl (Glaxo) 0.25, 0.5, and 2.5 mg/ml in sodium chloride 0.9% through 0.2-μm polysulfone filters (IVS Set-P Supor Filter, Codan) at a rate of 4 ml/hr for five hours did not result in any loss of drug due to sorption to the filter. (2229)

Central Venous Catheter—Ranitidine HCl (Glaxo Wellcome) 0.2 mg/ml in dextrose 5% in water was found to be compatible with the ARROWg+ard Blue Plus (Arrow International) chlorhexidine-bearing triple-lumen central catheter. HPLC analysis was used to evaluate completeness of drug delivery through the catheter and the amount of chlorhexidine removed from the internal lumens. Essentially complete delivery of the drug was found with little or no drug loss occurring. Furthermore, chlorhexidine delivered from the catheter remained at trace amounts with no substantial increase due to the delivery of the drug through the catheter. (2335)

Compatibility Information

Solution Compatibility

Ranitidine HCl

Solution	*Mfr*	*Mfr*	*Conc/L*	*Remarks*	*Ref*	*C/I*
Amino acids 8.5%	TR	GL	50 mg and 2 g	Physically compatible and ranitidine chemically stable by HPLC for 24 hr at 25 °C	1515	C

Solution Compatibility (Cont.)

Ranitidine HCl

Solution	*Mfr*	*Mfr*	*Conc/L*	*Remarks*	*Ref*	*C/I*
Dextrose 5% in Ringer's injection, lactated	TR[a]	GL	50 mg	15% ranitidine loss in 2 days at room temperature under fluorescent light	1362	I
	TR[a]	GL	500 mg, 1 g, 2 g	Physically compatible with 5% or less ranitidine loss in 7 days at 23 °C and 8% or less loss in 30 days at 4 °C	1516	C
Dextrose 5% in sodium chloride 0.45%	TR[a]	GL	50 mg	8 to 10% ranitidine loss in 7 days at room temperature under fluorescent light	1362	C
	TR[a]	GL	500 mg, 1 g, 2 g	Physically compatible with 5% or less ranitidine loss in 7 days at 23 °C and 8% or less loss in 30 days at 4 °C	1516	C
Dextrose 5% in water	TR[a]	GL	1 g	Little or no ranitidine loss in 10 days at 4 °C	1143	C
	TR[a]		1 g	Physically compatible with 8% loss in 18 days at 25 °C and 3% loss in 66 days at 5 °C	1342	C
	TR[a]	GL	1 g	Physically compatible with no loss in 92 days at 4 °C	1350	C
	TR[a]	GL	50 mg	Physically compatible with 6% loss in 48 hr at room temperature under fluorescent light	1361	C
	TR[a]	GL	2 g	Physically compatible with 2% loss in 48 hr at room temperature under fluorescent light	1361	C
	TR[a]	GL	500 mg, 1 g, 2 g	5% or less ranitidine loss in 28 days at room temperature under fluorescent light	1362	C
	TR[a]	GL	50 mg	8 to 10% ranitidine loss in 7 days at room temperature under fluorescent light	1362	C
	TR[a]	GL	500 mg, 1 g, 2 g	Physically compatible with 5% or less ranitidine loss in 7 days at 23 °C and 6% or less loss in 30 days at 4 °C	1516	C
	MG	GL	441 mg	Visually compatible with no ranitidine loss by HPLC after 30 days at −20 °C followed by 10 days at 4 °C	1539	C
	TR[a]	GL	2 g	Visually compatible with little or no ranitidine loss by HPLC in 48 hr at room temperature	1802	C
	TR[a]	GL	50 mg	Visually compatible with 6% ranitidine loss by HPLC in 48 hr at room temperature	1802	C
	AB[a]	GL	1.5 g	Little or no ranitidine loss by HPLC in 24 hr at 30 °C and for 7 days at 3 °C followed by 24 hr at 30 °C	1865	C
	BA[a]	GW	250 mg	Visually compatible with about 4 to 5% loss by HPLC in 24 hr at 4 and 22 °C	2289	C
	BRN[b]	GW	250 mg	Visually compatible with little or no loss by HPLC in 24 hr at 4 and 22 °C	2289	C
Dextrose 10% in water	TR[a]	GL	50 mg	7% ranitidine loss in 2 days at room temperature under fluorescent light	1362	C
	TR[a]	GL	500 mg, 1 g, 2 g	Physically compatible with 4% or less ranitidine loss in 7 days at 23 °C and 8% or less loss in 30 days at 4 °C	1516	C
Fat emulsion 10%, intravenous	KV	GL	50 mg	Physically compatible with no effect on emulsion stability and 2 to 4% ranitidine loss in 48 hr at 25 °C with or without light protection	1360	C
	KV	GL	100 mg	Physically compatible with no effect on emulsion stability and no ranitidine loss in 48 hr under refrigeration and at 25 °C with or without light protection	1360	C

Solution Compatibility (Cont.)

Ranitidine HCl

Solution	*Mfr*	*Mfr*	*Conc/L*	*Remarks*	*Ref*	*C/I*
Sodium chloride 0.9%	TR	GL	50 and 100 mg	No ranitidine loss in 48 hr at 24 °C under fluorescent light	1010	**C**
	TR[a]	GL	1 g	Little or no ranitidine loss in 10 days at 4 °C	1143	**C**
	TR[a]		1 g	Physically compatible with no loss in 18 days at 25 °C and in 66 days at 5 °C	1342	**C**
	TR[a]	GL	1 g	Physically compatible with no loss in 92 days at 4 °C	1350	**C**
	TR	GL	50 mg	Physically compatible with no loss in 48 hr at 25 °C protected from light	1360	**C**
	TR	GL	100 mg	Physically compatible with no loss in 48 hr at 25 °C with or without light protection and under refrigeration for 24 hr followed by 24 hr at 25 °C with or without light protection	1360	**C**
	TR[a]	GL	50 mg and 2 g	Physically compatible with no loss in 48 hr at room temperature under fluorescent light	1361	**C**
	TR[a]	GL	500 mg, 1 g, 2 g	No ranitidine loss in 28 days at room temperature under fluorescent light	1362	**C**
	TR[a]	GL	50 mg	3% or less ranitidine loss in 28 days at room temperature under fluorescent light	1362	**C**
	TR[a]	GL	500 mg, 1 g, 2 g	Physically compatible with no ranitidine loss in 7 days at 23 °C and 3% or less loss in 30 days at 4 °C	1516	**C**
	TR[a]	GL	50 mg and 2 g	Visually compatible with little or no ranitidine loss in 48 hr at room temperature	1802	**C**
	AB[a]	GL	1.5 g	Little or no ranitidine loss by HPLC in 24 hr at 30 °C and for 7 days at 3 °C followed by 24 hr at 30 °C	1865	**C**
	BA[a]	GL	600 mg	Visually compatible with little or no loss of ranitidine by HPLC in 24 hr at ambient temperature	2079	**C**
	BA[a]	GL	1 g	Visually compatible with little or no loss of ranitidine by HPLC in 4 hr at ambient temperature	2079	**C**
	BA[a]	GW	250 mg	Visually compatible with about 4 to 5% loss by HPLC in 24 hr at 4 and 22 °C	2289	**C**
	BRN[b]	GW	250 mg	Visually compatible with little or no loss by HPLC in 24 hr at 4 and 22 °C	2289	**C**
TNA #92[d]	[c]	GL	50 and 100 mg	7 to 10% ranitidine loss in 12 hr and 20 to 28% in 24 hr at 23 °C under fluorescent light	1183	**I**
TNA #118[d]		GL	50 and 100 mg	Physically compatible with no effect on emulsion stability and about 6 to 10% ranitidine loss in 36 hr under refrigeration and at 25 °C with or without light protection	1360	**C**
TNA #197 to #200[d]		GL	75 mg	Physically compatible with 7% or less ranitidine loss by HPLC in 24 hr at 22 °C exposed to light. About 15% loss in 48 hr	1921	**C**
TPN #58[d]		GL	83, 167, 250 mg	10% ranitidine loss in 48 hr at 23 °C	997	**C**
TPN #59 and #60[d]	[a]	GL	50 and 100 mg	No color change and 7 to 9% ranitidine loss in 24 hr at 24 °C under fluorescent light. Amino acids not substantially affected. Darkened color and 10 to 12% ranitidine loss in 48 hr	1010	**C**
TPN #117[d]		GL	50 and 100 mg	Physically compatible and 5% or less ranitidine loss in 48 hr at 25 °C and under refrigeration	1360	**C**

Solution Compatibility (Cont.)

Ranitidine HCl

Solution	Mfr	Mfr	Conc/L	Remarks	Ref	C/I
TPN #196[d]		GL	75 mg	Physically compatible with 7% or less ranitidine loss by HPLC in 24 hr at 22 °C exposed to light. About 12% loss in 48 hr	1921	C

[a]*Tested in PVC containers.*
[b]*Tested in polyethylene and glass containers.*
[c]*Tested in ethylene vinyl acetate containers.*
[d]*Refer to Appendix I for the composition of parenteral nutrition solutions. TNA indicates a 3-in-1 admixture, and TPN indicates a 2-in-1 admixture.*

Additive Compatibility

Ranitidine HCl

Drug	Mfr	Conc/L	Mfr	Conc/L	Test Soln	Remarks	Ref	C/I
Acetazolamide sodium		5 g	GL	50 mg and 2 g	D5W	Physically compatible and ranitidine chemically stable by HPLC for 24 hr at 25 °C. Acetazolamide not tested	1515	C
Amikacin sulfate	BR	1 g	GL	100 mg	D5W	Physically compatible for 24 hr at ambient temperature under fluorescent light	1151	C
		2.5 g	GL	50 mg and 2 g	D5W	Physically compatible and ranitidine chemically stable by HPLC for 24 hr at 25 °C. Amikacin not tested	1515	C
Aminophylline	ES	500 mg and 2 g	GL	50 mg and 2 g	D5W, NS[a]	Physically compatible with 4% or less ranitidine loss in 24 hr at room temperature under fluorescent light. Aminophylline not tested	1361	C
	ES	0.5 and 2 g	GL	50 mg and 2 g	D5W, NS[a]	Visually compatible with little or no loss of either drug by HPLC in 48 hr at room temperature	1802	C
Amphotericin B	SQ	200 mg	GL	100 mg	D5W	Color change and particle formation	1151	I
Ampicillin sodium		2 g	GL	100 mg	D5W	Physically compatible for 24 hr at ambient temperature under fluorescent light. Ampicillin instability is determining factor	1151	?
		1 g	GL	50 mg and 2 g	NS	Physically compatible and ranitidine chemically stable by HPLC for 24 hr at 25 °C. Ampicillin not tested	1515	C
Atracurium besylate	BW	500 mg		500 mg	D5W	Atracurium chemically unstable due to high pH	1694	I
Cefamandole nafate		1 g	GL	50 mg and 2 g	D5W	Ranitidine chemically stable by HPLC for only 6 hr at 25 °C. Cefamandole not tested	1515	I
Cefazolin sodium		2 g	GL	100 mg	D5W	Color change within 24 hr at ambient temperature under fluorescent light	1151	?
		1 g	GL	50 mg and 2 g	D5W	Ranitidine chemically stable by HPLC for only 6 hr at 25 °C. Cefazolin not tested	1515	I
Cefoxitin sodium		10 g	GL	50 mg and 2 g	D5W	Ranitidine chemically stable by HPLC for only 4 hr at 25 °C. Cefoxitin not tested	1515	I
Ceftazidime	GL[c]	10 g	GL	500 mg	D2.5½S	8% ranitidine loss in 4 hr and 39% loss in 24 hr by HPLC at 22 °C	1632	I
Cefuroxime sodium	GL	1.5 g	GL	100 mg	D5W	Color change within 24 hr at ambient temperature under fluorescent light	1151	?

Additive Compatibility (Cont.)

Ranitidine HCl

Drug	*Mfr*	*Conc/L*	*Mfr*	*Conc/L*	*Test Soln*	*Remarks*	*Ref*	*C/I*
		6 g	GL	50 mg and 2 g	D5W	Ranitidine chemically stable by HPLC for only 6 hr at 25 °C. Cefuroxime not tested	1515	I
Chloramphenicol sodium succinate		2 g	GL	100 mg	D5W	Physically compatible for 24 hr at ambient temperature	1151	C
Chlorothiazide sodium		5 g	GL	50 mg and 2 g	D5W	Physically compatible and ranitidine chemically stable by HPLC for 24 hr at 25 °C. Chlorothiazide not tested	1515	C
Ciprofloxacin	BAY	2 g	GL	500 mg and 1 g	NS	Visually compatible with little or no ciprofloxacin loss by HPLC in 24 hr at 25 °C. Ranitidine not tested	1934	C
Clindamycin phosphate	UP	1.2 g	GL	100 mg	D5W	Color change and gas formation	1151	I
		1.2 g	GL	50 mg and 2 g	D5W, NS	Physically compatible and ranitidine chemically stable by HPLC for 24 hr at 25 °C. Clindamycin not tested	1515	C
Colistimethate sodium		1.5 g	GL	50 mg and 2 g	D5W	Physically compatible and ranitidine chemically stable by HPLC for 24 hr at 25 °C. Colistimethate not tested	1515	C
Dexamethasone sodium phosphate		40 mg	GL	50 mg and 2 g	D5W	Physically compatible and ranitidine chemically stable by HPLC for 24 hr at 25 °C. Dexamethasone not tested	1515	C
Digoxin		2.5 mg	GL	50 mg and 2 g	D5W	Physically compatible and ranitidine chemically stable by HPLC for 24 hr at 25 °C. Digoxin not tested	1515	C
Dobutamine HCl	LI	250 mg and 1 g	GL	2 g	D5W, NS[a]	Physically compatible with no ranitidine loss in 48 hr at room temperature under fluorescent light. Dobutamine not tested	1361	C
	LI	250 mg and 1 g	GL	50 mg	D5W[a]	Physically compatible with 5 to 7% ranitidine loss in 48 hr at room temperature under fluorescent light. Dobutamine not tested	1361	C
	LI	250 mg and 1 g	GL	50 mg	NS[a]	Physically compatible with no ranitidine loss in 48 hr at room temperature under fluorescent light. Dobutamine not tested	1361	C
	LI	0.25 to 1 g	GL	50 mg and 2 g	D5W, NS[a]	Visually compatible with little or no loss of either drug by HPLC in 48 hr at room temperature	1802	C
Dopamine HCl	ES	400 mg and 3.2 g	GL	50 mg and 2 g	D5W, NS[a]	Physically compatible with 6% or less ranitidine loss in 48 hr at room temperature under fluorescent light. Dopamine not tested	1361	C
	ES	0.4 and 3.2 g	GL	50 mg and 2 g	D5W, NS[a]	Visually compatible with 5 to 7% ranitidine loss and little or no dopamine loss by HPLC in 48 hr at room temperature	1802	C
Doxycycline hyclate	PF	200 mg	GL	100 mg	D5W	Physically compatible for 24 hr at ambient temperature under fluorescent light	1151	C
Epinephrine HCl		50 mg	GL	50 mg and 2 g	D5W	Physically compatible and ranitidine chemically stable by HPLC for 24 hr at 25 °C. Epinephrine not tested	1515	C

Additive Compatibility (Cont.)

			Ranitidine HCl					
Drug	*Mfr*	*Conc/L*	*Mfr*	*Conc/L*	*Test Soln*	*Remarks*	*Ref*	*C/I*
Erythromycin lactobionate		5 g	GL	50 mg and 2 g	NS	Physically compatible and ranitidine chemically stable by HPLC for 24 hr at 25 °C. Erythromycin not tested	1515	C
Ethacrynate sodium		500 mg	GL	50 mg and 2 g	D5W	Ranitidine chemically stable by HPLC for only 6 hr at 25 °C. Ethacrynate not tested	1515	I
Floxacillin sodium	BE	20 g	GL	500 mg	NS	Physically compatible for 72 hr at 15 and 30 °C	1479	C
Fluconazole with ondansetron HCl	RR GL	2 g 100 mg	GL	500 mg	[a]	Visually compatible with no loss of any drug by HPLC in 4 hr	1730	C
Flumazenil	RC	20 mg	GL	300 mg	D5W[a]	Visually compatible with 3% flumazenil loss by HPLC in 24 hr at 23 °C under fluorescent light. Ranitidine not tested	1710	C
Furosemide	HO	1 g	GL	500 mg	NS	Physically compatible for 72 hr at 15 and 30 °C	1479	C
		400 mg	GL	50 mg and 2 g	D5W	Physically compatible and ranitidine chemically stable by HPLC for 24 hr at 25 °C. Furosemide not tested	1515	C
Gentamicin sulfate		160 mg	GL	100 mg	D5W	Physically compatible for 24 hr at ambient temperature under fluorescent light	1151	C
		80 mg	GL	50 mg and 2 g	D5W, NS	Physically compatible and ranitidine chemically stable by HPLC for 24 hr at 25 °C. Gentamicin not tested	1515	C
Heparin sodium	ES	10,000 and 40,000 units	GL	2 g	D5W, NS[a]	Physically compatible with 2% or less ranitidine loss in 48 hr at room temperature under fluorescent light. Heparin not tested	1361	C
	ES	10,000 and 40,000 units	GL	50 mg	NS[a]	Physically compatible with no ranitidine loss in 48 hr at room temperature under fluorescent light. Heparin not tested	1361	C
	ES	10,000 and 40,000 units	GL	50 mg	D5W[a]	Physically compatible with 7% ranitidine loss in 24 hr and about 12% loss in 48 hr at room temperature under fluorescent light. Heparin not tested	1361	C
Insulin, regular		100 units	GL	50 mg and 2 g	NS	Physically compatible and ranitidine chemically stable by HPLC for 24 hr at 25 °C. Insulin not tested	1515	C
	LI[b]	1000 units	GL	600 mg	NS[a]	Visually compatible with little or no loss by HPLC of ranitidine in 24 hr at ambient temperature but insulin losses of 9% in 4 hr and 14% in 24 hr presumably due to sorption	2079	I
Isoproterenol HCl		20 mg	GL	50 mg and 2 g	D5W	Physically compatible and ranitidine chemically stable by HPLC for 24 hr at 25 °C. Isoproterenol not tested	1515	C
Lidocaine HCl	AST	1 and 8 g	GL	50 mg and 2 g	D5W, NS[a]	Physically compatible with 3% or less ranitidine loss in 24 hr at room temperature under fluorescent light. Lidocaine not tested	1361	C

Additive Compatibility (Cont.)

			Ranitidine HCl					
Drug	*Mfr*	*Conc/L*	*Mfr*	*Conc/L*	*Test Soln*	*Remarks*	*Ref*	*C/I*
		2.5 g	GL	50 mg and 2 g	D5W	Physically compatible and ranitidine chemically stable by HPLC for 24 hr at 25 °C. Lidocaine not tested	1515	C
	AST	1 and 8 g	GL	50 mg and 2 g	D5W, NS[a]	Visually compatible with little or no loss of either drug by HPLC in 48 hr at room temperature	1802	C
Lincomycin HCl		2.4 g	GL	50 mg and 2 g	D5W	Physically compatible and ranitidine chemically stable by HPLC for 24 hr at 25 °C. Lincomycin not tested	1515	C
Meropenem	ZEN	1 and 20 g	GL	100 mg	NS	Visually compatible for 4 hr at room temperature	1994	C
Methylprednisolone sodium succinate	UP	40 mg	GL	50 mg	D5W[a]	Visually compatible with 7% ranitidine loss and no methylprednisolone loss by HPLC in 48 hr at room temperature	1802	C
	UP	2 g	GL	50 mg	D5W[a]	Visually compatible with 6% ranitidine loss and 10% methylprednisolone loss by HPLC in 48 hr at room temperature	1802	C
	UP	40 mg and 2 g	GL	2 g	D5W[a]	Visually compatible with no loss of either drug by HPLC in 48 hr at room temperature	1802	C
	UP	40 mg and 2 g	GL	50 mg and 2 g	NS[a]	Visually compatible with no ranitidine loss and about 10% methylprednisolone loss by HPLC in 48 hr at room temperature	1802	C
Norepinephrine bitartrate	WI	4 and 8 mg	GL	2 g	D5W, NS[a]	Physically compatible with no ranitidine loss in 48 hr at room temperature under fluorescent light. Norepinephrine not tested	1361	C
	WI	4 and 8 mg	GL	50 mg	D5W, NS[a]	Physically compatible with 2 to 6% ranitidine loss in 48 hr at room temperature under fluorescent light. Norepinephrine not tested	1361	C
		4 mg	GL	50 mg and 2 g	D5W	Physically compatible and ranitidine chemically stable by HPLC for 24 hr at 25 °C. Norepinephrine not tested	1515	C
	RC	4 and 8 mg	GL	50 mg	D5W[a]	Visually compatible with 5 to 7% ranitidine loss and little or no norepinephrine loss by HPLC in 48 hr at room temperature	1802	C
	RC	4 mg	GL	2 g	D5W[a]	Visually compatible but 7% norepinephrine loss in 4 hr and 13% loss in 12 hr by HPLC at room temperature. No ranitidine loss in 48 hr	1802	I
	RC	8 mg	GL	2 g	D5W[a]	Visually compatible but 6% norepinephrine loss in 12 hr and 11% loss in 24 hr by HPLC at room temperature. No ranitidine loss in 48 hr	1802	I
Penicillin G potassium		24 million units	GL	50 mg and 2 g	D5W, NS	Physically compatible and ranitidine chemically stable by HPLC for 24 hr at 25 °C. Penicillin not tested	1515	C
Penicillin G sodium		2.4 million units	GL	100 mg	D5W	Physically compatible for 24 hr at ambient temperature under fluorescent light	1151	C

Additive Compatibility (Cont.)

Ranitidine HCl

Drug	Mfr	Conc/L	Mfr	Conc/L	Test Soln	Remarks	Ref	C/I
Phytonadione		100 mg	GL	50 mg and 2 g	D5W	Ranitidine chemically stable by HPLC for only 6 hr at 25 °C. Phytonadione not tested	1515	I
Polymyxin B sulfate		1 million units	GL	50 mg and 2 g	D5W	Physically compatible and ranitidine chemically stable by HPLC for 24 hr at 25 °C. Polymyxin B not tested	1515	C
Potassium chloride	LY	10 and 60 mEq	GL	2 g	D5W, NS[a]	Physically compatible with 2% or less ranitidine loss in 48 hr at room temperature under fluorescent light	1361	C
	LY	10 and 60 mEq	GL	50 mg	NS[a]	Physically compatible with no ranitidine loss in 48 hr at room temperature under fluorescent light	1361	C
	LY	10 and 60 mEq	GL	50 mg	D5W[a]	Physically compatible with 7% ranitidine loss in 48 hr at room temperature under fluorescent light	1361	C
		80 mEq	GL	50 mg and 2 g	D5S, D5W, NS	Physically compatible and ranitidine chemically stable by HPLC for 24 hr at 25 °C. Potassium chloride not tested	1515	C
Protamine sulfate		500 mg	GL	50 mg and 2 g	D5W	Physically compatible and ranitidine chemically stable by HPLC for 24 hr at 25 °C. Protamine not tested	1515	C
Quinidine gluconate		3.2 g	GL	50 mg and 2 g	D5W	Physically compatible and ranitidine chemically stable by HPLC for 24 hr at 25 °C. Quinidine not tested	1515	C
Sodium nitroprusside	RC	50 and 400 mg	GL	2 g	D5W, NS[a]	Physically compatible with no ranitidine loss in 48 hr at room temperature protected from light. Nitroprusside not tested	1361	C
	RC	50 and 400 mg	GL	50 mg	NS[a]	Physically compatible with no ranitidine loss in 48 hr at room temperature protected from light. Nitroprusside not tested	1361	C
	RC	50 and 400 mg	GL	50 mg	D5W[a]	Physically compatible with 7% or less ranitidine loss in 48 hr protected from light. Nitroprusside not tested	1361	C
		50 mg and 1 g	GL	50 mg and 2 g	D5W, NS	Physically compatible and both drugs chemically stable for 48 hr at room temperature protected from light	1515	C
		100 mg	GL	50 mg and 2 g	D5W	Physically compatible and ranitidine chemically stable by HPLC for 24 hr at 25 °C. Sodium nitroprusside not tested	1515	C
	RC	50 and 400 mg	GL	50 mg and 2 g	D5W[a]	Visually compatible with 5 to 7% ranitidine loss and 8% or less nitroprusside loss in 48 hr at room temperature protected from light	1802	C
	RC	50 and 400 mg	GL	50 mg and 2 g	NS[a]	Visually compatible with no loss of either drug by HPLC in 48 hr at room temperature protected from light	1802	C
Ticarcillin disodium	BE	10 g	GL	100 mg	D5W	Physically compatible for 24 hr at ambient temperature under fluorescent light	1151	C

Additive Compatibility (Cont.)

Ranitidine HCl

Drug	Mfr	Conc/L	Mfr	Conc/L	Test Soln	Remarks	Ref	C/I
Tobramycin sulfate	DI	200 mg	GL	100 mg	D5W	Physically compatible for 24 hr at ambient temperature under fluorescent light	1151	C
Vancomycin HCl	DI	1 g	GL	100 mg	D5W	Physically compatible for 24 hr at ambient temperature under fluorescent light	1151	C
		5 g	GL	50 mg and 2 g	D5W	Physically compatible and ranitidine chemically stable by HPLC for 24 hr at 25 °C. Vancomycin not tested	1515	C

[a]*Tested in PVC containers.*
[b]*Regular human insulin.*
[c]*Sodium carbonate–containing formulation tested.*

Drugs in Syringe Compatibility

Ranitidine HCl

Drug (in syringe)	Mfr	Amt	Mfr	Amt	Remarks	Ref	C/I
Atropine sulfate	GL	0.4 mg/ 1 ml	GL	50 mg/ 2 ml	Physically compatible for 1 hr at 25 °C both macroscopically and microscopically	978	C
Chlorpromazine HCl	RP	25 mg/ 1 ml	GL	50 mg/ 2 ml	Physically compatible for 1 hr at 25 °C both macroscopically and microscopically	978	C
	RP	25 mg	GL	50 mg/ 5 ml	Gas formation	1151	I
Cyclizine lactate	CA	50 mg/ 1 ml	GL	50 mg/ 2 ml	Physically compatible for 1 hr at 25 °C both macroscopically and microscopically	978	C
Dexamethasone sodium phosphate	ME	4 mg	GL	50 mg/ 5 ml	Physically compatible for 4 hr at ambient temperature under fluorescent light	1151	C
Diazepam	RC	10 mg/ 2 ml	GL	50 mg/ 2 ml	Immediate white haze which disappeared following vortex mixing	978	I
		10 mg	GL	50 mg/ 5 ml	Physically compatible for 4 hr at ambient temperature under fluorescent light	1151	C
Dimenhydrinate	HR	50 mg/ 1 ml	GL	50 mg/ 2 ml	Physically compatible for 1 hr at 25 °C both macroscopically and microscopically	978	C
Diphenhydramine HCl	PD	50 mg/ 1 ml	GL	50 mg/ 2 ml	Physically compatible for 1 hr at 25 °C both macroscopically and microscopically	978	C
Dobutamine HCl	LI	25 mg	GL	50 mg/ 5 ml	Physically compatible for 4 hr at ambient temperature under fluorescent light	1151	C
Dopamine HCl		40 mg	GL	50 mg/ 5 ml	Physically compatible for 4 hr at ambient temperature under fluorescent light	1151	C
Fentanyl citrate	JN	0.1 mg/ 2 ml	GL	50 mg/ 2 ml	Physically compatible for 1 hr at 25 °C both macroscopically and microscopically	978	C
Glycopyrrolate	RB	0.2 mg/ 1 ml	GL	50 mg/ 2 ml	Physically compatible for 1 hr at 25 °C both macroscopically and microscopically	978	C
Heparin sodium		2500 units/ 1 ml	GL	50 mg/ 5 ml	Visually compatible for at least 5 min	1053	C
Hydromorphone HCl		2 mg/ 1 ml	GL	50 mg/ 2 ml	Physically compatible for 1 hr at 25 °C both macroscopically and microscopically	978	C

Drugs in Syringe Compatibility (Cont.)

Ranitidine HCl

Drug (in syringe)	*Mfr*	*Amt*	*Mfr*	*Amt*	*Remarks*	*Ref*	*C/I*
Hydroxyzine HCl	PF	50 mg/ 1 ml	GL	50 mg/ 2 ml	Immediate white haze which disappeared following vortex mixing	978	I
Isoproterenol sulfate	BI	0.2 mg	GL	50 mg/ 5 ml	Physically compatible for 4 hr at ambient temperature under fluorescent light	1151	C
Lorazepam	WY	4 mg/ 1 ml	GL	50 mg/ 2 ml	Lorazepam viscosity caused poor mixing and layering which disappeared following vortex mixing	978	?
Meperidine HCl	WI	100 mg/ 1 ml	GL	50 mg/ 2 ml	Physically compatible for 1 hr at 25 °C both macroscopically and microscopically	978	C
Methotrimeprazine	RP	25 mg/ 1 ml	GL	50 mg/ 2 ml	Immediate white turbidity	978	I
Metoclopramide HCl	RB	10 mg/ 1 ml	GL	50 mg/ 2 ml	Physically compatible for 1 hr at 25 °C both macroscopically and microscopically	978	C
Midazolam HCl	RC	5 mg/ 1 ml	GL	50 mg/ 2 ml	White precipitate forms immediately	1145	I
Morphine HCl	STP, FED	5, 10, 20, 30 mg/ 1 ml	GW	50 mg/ 2 ml	Visually compatible for 24 hr at 23 °C. Yellow discoloration forms in 7 days	2257	C
Morphine sulfate	AH	10 mg/ 1 ml	GL	50 mg/ 2 ml	Physically compatible for 1 hr at 25 °C both macroscopically and microscopically	978	C
Nalbuphine HCl	EN	10 mg/ 1 ml	GL	50 mg/ 2 ml	Physically compatible for 1 hr at 25 °C both macroscopically and microscopically	978	C
Oxymorphone HCl	EN	1.5 mg/ 1 ml	GL	50 mg/ 2 ml	Physically compatible for 1 hr at 25 °C both macroscopically and microscopically	978	C
Papaveretum	RC[a]	20 mg/ 1 ml	GL	50 mg/ 2 ml	White haze and precipitate form immediately	978	I
Pentazocine lactate	WI	60 mg/ 2 ml	GL	50 mg/ 2 ml	Physically compatible for 1 hr at 25 °C both macroscopically and microscopically	978	C
Pentobarbital sodium	AB	100 mg	GL	50 mg/ 5 ml	Immediate precipitation	1151	I
Perphenazine	SC	5 mg/ 1 ml	GL	50 mg/ 2 ml	Physically compatible for 1 hr at 25 °C both macroscopically and microscopically	978	C
Phenobarbital sodium	AB	120 mg/ 1 ml	GL	50 mg/ 2 ml	Immediate white haze	978	I
Prochlorperazine edisylate	RP	10 mg/ 2 ml	GL	50 mg/ 2 ml	Physically compatible for 1 hr at 25 °C both macroscopically and microscopically	978	C
Promethazine HCl	RP	25 mg/ 1 ml	GL	50 mg/ 2 ml	Physically compatible for 1 hr at 25 °C both macroscopically and microscopically	978	C
	RP	25 mg	GL	50 mg/ 5 ml	Physically compatible for 4 hr at ambient temperature under fluorescent light	1151	C
Scopolamine HBr	AB	0.4 mg/ 1 ml	GL	50 mg/ 2 ml	Physically compatible for 1 hr at 25 °C both macroscopically and microscopically	978	C
		0.5 mg	GL	50 mg/ 5 ml	Physically compatible for 4 hr at ambient temperature under fluorescent light	1151	C
Thiethylperazine malate	SZ	10 mg/ 1 ml	GL	50 mg/ 2 ml	Physically compatible for 1 hr at 25 °C both macroscopically and microscopically	978	C

[a] *The former formulation was tested.*

Y-Site Injection Compatibility (1:1 Mixture)

Drug	Mfr	Conc	Ranitidine HCl Mfr	Ranitidine HCl Conc	Remarks	Ref	C/I
Acyclovir sodium	BW	5 mg/ml[a]	GL	1 mg/ml[a]	Physically compatible for 4 hr at 25 °C	1157	C
Aldesleukin	CHI	33,800 I.U./ml[a]	AB	1 mg/ml[c]	Visually compatible with little or no loss of aldesleukin activity by bioassay	1857	C
Allopurinol sodium	BW	3 mg/ml[b]	GL	2 mg/ml[b]	Physically compatible with no change in measured turbidity or increase in particle content in 4 hr at 22 °C	1686	C
Amifostine	USB	10 mg/ml[a]	GL	2 mg/ml[a]	Physically compatible with no change in measured turbidity or increase in particle content in 4 hr at 23 °C	1845	C
Aminophylline	LY	4 mg/ml[a]	GL	0.5 mg/ml[d]	Physically compatible for 24 hr	1323	C
Amphotericin B cholesteryl sulfate complex	SEQ	0.83 mg/ml[a]	GL	2 mg/ml[a]	Microprecipitate and increased turbidity form immediately	2117	I
Amsacrine	NCI	1 mg/ml[a]	GL	2 mg/ml[a]	Physically compatible for 4 hr at room temperature under fluorescent light	1381	C
Atracurium besylate	BW	0.5 mg/ml[a]	GL	0.5 mg/ml[a]	Physically compatible for 24 hr at 28 °C	1337	C
Aztreonam	SQ	16.7 mg/ml[b]	GL	1 mg/ml[b]	No loss of either drug by HPLC in 4 hr at 22 °C under fluorescent light	1632	C
	SQ	40 mg/ml[a]	GL	2 mg/ml[a]	Physically compatible with no subvisual haze or particle formation in 4 hr at 23 °C	1758	C
Bretylium tosylate	LY	4 mg/ml[a]	GL	0.5 mg/ml[d]	Physically compatible for 24 hr	1323	C
Cefazolin sodium	FUJ	20 mg/ml[b]	GL	1 mg/ml[b]	Visually compatible with little or no loss of either drug by HPLC in 4 hr at 25 °C exposed to fluorescent light	2259	C
Cefepime HCl	BMS	20 mg/ml[a]	GL	2 mg/ml[a]	Physically compatible with no change in measured turbidity or increase in particle content in 4 hr at 22 °C	1689	C
Cefoperazone sodium	TAK	20 mg/ml[b]	GL	1 mg/ml[b]	Visually compatible with no loss of either drug by HPLC in 4 hr at 25 °C	2209	C
Cefoxitin sodium	BAN	20 mg/ml[b]	GL	1 mg/ml[b]	Visually compatible with no cefoxitin loss and less than 8% ranitidine loss by HPLC in 4 hr at 25 °C exposed to fluorescent light	2259	C
Ceftazidime	GL[k]	20 mg/ml[a]	GL	1 mg/ml[b]	No ceftazidime loss and 8% ranitidine loss by HPLC in 4 hr at 22 °C	1632	C
Ceftizoxime sodium	FUJ	20 mg/ml[b]	GL	1 mg/ml[b]	Visually compatible with no loss of either drug by HPLC in 4 hr at 25 °C	2209	C
Ciprofloxacin	MI	2 mg/ml[e]	GL	0.5 mg/ml[e]	Visually compatible for 24 hr at 24 °C	1655	C
Cisatracurium besylate	GW	0.1, 2, 5 mg/ml[a]	GL	2 mg/ml[a]	Physically compatible with no change in measured turbidity or increase in particle content in 4 hr at 23 °C	2074	C
Cisplatin	BR	1 mg/ml	GL	1 mg/ml[a]	Visually compatible for 4 hr at room temperature under fluorescent light	1685	C
Cladribine	ORT	0.015[b] and 0.5[f] mg/ml	GL	2 mg/ml[b]	Physically compatible with no change in measured turbidity or increase in particle content in 4 hr at 23 °C	1969	C

Y-Site Injection Compatibility (1:1 Mixture) (Cont.)

Ranitidine HCl

Drug	*Mfr*	*Conc*	*Mfr*	*Conc*	*Remarks*	*Ref*	*C/I*
Clarithromycin	AB	4 mg/ml[a]	GW	5 mg/ml[a]	Visually compatible for 72 hr at both 30 and 17 °C	2174	C
Cyclophosphamide	MJ	10 mg/ml	GL	1 mg/ml[a]	Visually compatible for 4 hr at room temperature under fluorescent light	1685	C
Cytarabine	UP	50 mg/ml	GL	1 mg/ml[a]	Visually compatible for 4 hr at room temperature under fluorescent light	1685	C
Diltiazem HCl	MMD	1[b] and 5 mg/ml	GL	25 mg/ml	Visually compatible	1807	C
	MMD	5 mg/ml	GL	0.5[c] and 1[b] mg/ml	Visually compatible	1807	C
	MMD	1 mg/ml[a]	GL	1 mg/ml[a]	Visually compatible for 4 hr at 27 °C	2062	C
Dobutamine HCl	LI	1 mg/ml[a]	GL	0.5 mg/ml[d]	Physically compatible for 24 hr	1323	C
	LI	4 mg/ml[a]	GL	1 mg/ml[a]	Visually compatible for 4 hr at 27 °C	2062	C
Docetaxel	RPR	0.9 mg/ml[a]	GL	2 mg/ml[a]	Physically compatible with no change in measured turbidity or increase in particle content in 4 hr at 23 °C	2224	C
Dopamine HCl	ES	1.6 mg/ml[a]	GL	0.5 mg/ml[d]	Physically compatible for 24 hr	1323	C
	AB	3.2 mg/ml[a]	GL	1 mg/ml[a]	Visually compatible for 4 hr at 27 °C	2062	C
Doxorubicin HCl	AD	0.2 mg/ml[a]	GL	1 mg/ml[a]	Visually compatible for 4 hr at room temperature under fluorescent light	1685	C
Doxorubicin HCl liposome injection	SEQ	0.4 mg/ml[a]	GL	2 mg/ml[a]	Physically compatible with little or no change in measured turbidity and no increase in particle content in 4 hr at 23 °C	2087	C
Enalaprilat	MSD	0.05 mg/ml[b]	GL	0.5 mg/ml[a]	Physically compatible for 24 hr at room temperature under fluorescent light	1355	C
Epinephrine HCl	AB	0.02 mg/ml[a]	GL	1 mg/ml[a]	Visually compatible for 4 hr at 27 °C	2062	C
Esmolol HCl	DCC	10 mg/ml[a]	GL	0.5 mg/ml[a]	Physically compatible for 24 hr at 22 °C	1169	C
Etoposide phosphate	BR	5 mg/ml[a]	GL	2 mg/ml[a]	Physically compatible with no change in measured turbidity or increase in particle content in 4 hr at 23 °C	2218	C
Fentanyl citrate	ES	0.05 mg/ml	GL	1 mg/ml[a]	Visually compatible for 4 hr at 27 °C	2062	C
Filgrastim	AMG	30 µg/ml[a]	GL	2 mg/ml[a]	Physically compatible with no change in measured turbidity or increase in particle content in 4 hr at 22 °C	1687	C
Fluconazole	BR	2 mg/ml[b]	GL	0.5 and 2 mg/ml[a]	Visually compatible with no loss of either drug by HPLC in 4 hr	1730	C
Fludarabine phosphate	BX	1 mg/ml[a]	GL	2 mg/ml[a]	Physically compatible for 4 hr at room temperature under fluorescent light	1439	C
Foscarnet sodium	AST	24 mg/ml	GL	2 mg/ml[e]	Physically compatible for 24 hr at 25 °C under fluorescent light by visual and microscopic examination	1393	C
Furosemide	AMR	10 mg/ml	GL	1 mg/ml[a]	Visually compatible for 4 hr at 27 °C	2062	C
Gatifloxacin	BMS	2 mg/ml[a]	GW	2 mg/ml[a]	Physically compatible with no change in measured haze or increase in particle content in 4 hr at 23 °C	2234	C

Y-Site Injection Compatibility (1:1 Mixture) (Cont.)

Ranitidine HCl

Drug	*Mfr*	*Conc*	*Mfr*	*Conc*	*Remarks*	*Ref*	*C/I*
Gemcitabine HCl	LI	10 mg/ml[b]	GL	2 mg/ml[b]	Physically compatible with no change in measured turbidity or increase in particle content in 4 hr at 23 °C	2226	C
Granisetron HCl	SKB	0.05 mg/ml[a]	GL	2 mg/ml[a]	Physically compatible with no change in measured turbidity or increase in particle content in 4 hr at 23 °C	2000	C
Heparin sodium	LY	50 units/ml[a]	GL	0.5 mg/ml[d]	Physically compatible for 24 hr	1323	C
	TR	50 units/ml	GL	1 mg/ml	Visually compatible for 4 hr at 25 °C	1793	C
	ES	100 units/ml[a]	GL	1 mg/ml[a]	Visually compatible for 4 hr at 27 °C	2062	C
Hetastarch in lactated electrolyte injection (Hextend)	AB	6%	GW	2 mg/ml[a]	Physically compatible with no change in measured turbidity or increase in particle content in 4 hr at 23 °C	2339	C
Hetastarch in sodium chloride 0.9%	DCC	6%	GL	0.5 mg/ml[d]	Barely visible single particle appeared after 1 hr but disappeared when vial was rotated	1313	?
	DCC	6%	GL	0.5 mg/ml[d]	Barely visible particles appeared and disappeared in three of five vials	1314	I
	DCC	6%	GL	0.5 mg/ml[d]	Small white particle in two of five test vials. Small white fiber formed on needle during Y-site infusion	1315	I
Hydromorphone HCl	KN	1 mg/ml	GL	1 mg/ml[a]	Visually compatible for 4 hr at 27 °C	2062	C
Idarubicin HCl	AD	1 mg/ml[b]	GL	1 mg/ml[a]	Visually compatible for 24 hr at 25 °C	1525	C
Insulin, regular	LI[l]	1 unit/ml[b]	GL	1 mg/ml[b]	Visually compatible with little or no loss by HPLC of ranitidine in 4 hr at ambient temperature but insulin losses of 9% in 1 hr and 20% in 4 hr presumably due to sorption	2079	I
Labetalol HCl	SC	1 mg/ml[a]	GL	0.5 mg/ml[a]	Physically compatible for 24 hr at 18 °C	1171	C
	GL	1 mg/ml[a]	GL	0.6 mg/ml[a]	Visually compatible with 5% labetalol loss and little or no ranitidine loss by HPLC in 4 hr at room temperature	1762	C
	AH	2 mg/ml[a]	GL	1 mg/ml[a]	Visually compatible for 4 hr at 27 °C	2062	C
Linezolid	PHU	2 mg/ml	GW	2 mg/ml[a]	Physically compatible with no change in measured turbidity or increase in particle content in 4 hr at 23 °C	2264	C
Lorazepam	WY	0.33 mg/ml[b]	GL	0.5 mg/ml	Visually compatible for 24 hr at 22 °C	1855	C
	WY	0.5 mg/ml[a]	GL	1 mg/ml[a]	Visually compatible for 4 hr at 27 °C	2062	C
Melphalan HCl	BW	0.1 mg/ml[b]	GL	2 mg/ml[b]	Physically compatible with no change in measured turbidity or increase in particle content in 3 hr at 22 °C	1557	C
Meperidine HCl	WY	10 mg/ml[b]	GL	0.5 mg/ml[c]	Physically compatible for 1 hr at 25 °C	1338	C
Methotrexate sodium	AD	15 mg/ml[g]	GL	1 mg/ml[a]	Visually compatible for 4 hr at room temperature under fluorescent light	1685	C
Midazolam HCl	RC	5 mg/ml	GL	0.5 mg/ml	Visually compatible for 24 hr at 22 °C	1855	C
	RC	2 mg/ml[a]	GL	1 mg/ml[a]	Visually compatible for 4 hr at 27 °C	2062	C
Milrinone lactate	SW	0.2 mg/ml[a]	GL	1 mg/ml[a]	Visually compatible for 4 hr at 27 °C	2062	C
	SW	0.4 mg/ml[a]	GL	2 mg/ml[a]	Visually compatible with little or no loss of either drug by HPLC in 4 hr at 23 °C	2214	C

Y-Site Injection Compatibility (1:1 Mixture) (Cont.)

			Ranitidine HCl				
Drug	*Mfr*	*Conc*	*Mfr*	*Conc*	*Remarks*	*Ref*	*C/I*
Morphine sulfate	ES	1 mg/ml[b]	GL	0.5 mg/ml[c]	Physically compatible for 1 hr at 25 °C	1338	C
	SCN	2 mg/ml[a]	GL	1 mg/ml[a]	Visually compatible for 4 hr at 27 °C	2062	C
Nicardipine HCl	WY	1 mg/ml[a]	GL	1 mg/ml[a]	Visually compatible for 4 hr at 27 °C	2062	C
Nitroglycerin	SO	0.2 mg/ml[a]	GL	0.5 mg/ml[d]	Physically compatible for 24 hr	1323	C
	AB	0.4 mg/ml[a]	GL	1 mg/ml[a]	Visually compatible for 4 hr at 27 °C	2062	C
Norepinephrine bitartrate	AB	0.128 mg/ml[a]	GL	1 mg/ml[a]	Visually compatible for 4 hr at 27 °C	2062	C
Ondansetron HCl	GL	1 mg/ml[b]	GL	2 mg/ml[a]	Physically compatible for 4 hr at 22 °C	1365	C
	GL	0.03, 0.1, 0.3 mg/ml[a]	GL	0.5 mg/ml[a]	Visually compatible with no loss of either drug by HPLC in 4 hr	1730	C
	GL	0.03, 0.1, 0.3 mg/ml[a]	GL	2 mg/ml[a]	Visually compatible with no loss of either drug by HPLC in 4 hr	1730	C
Ondansetron HCl with paclitaxel	GL BR	0.3 mg/ml[a] 1.2 mg/ml[a]	GL	2 mg/ml[a]	Visually compatible with no loss of any drug by HPLC in 4 hr at 23 °C under fluorescent light	1741	C
Paclitaxel	NCI	1.2 mg/ml[a]		2 mg/ml[a]	Physically compatible with no change in measured turbidity in 4 hr at 22 °C	1528	C
	BR	0.3 mg/ml[a]	GL	0.5 and 2 mg/ml[a]	Visually compatible with no loss of either drug in 4 hr at 23 °C under fluorescent light	1741	C
	BR	1.2 mg/ml[a]	GL	0.5 and 2 mg/ml[a]	Visually compatible with no loss of either drug in 4 hr at 23 °C under fluorescent light	1741	C
Pancuronium bromide	ES	0.05 mg/ml[a]	GL	0.5 mg/ml[a]	Physically compatible for 24 hr at 28 °C	1337	C
Piperacillin sodium	LE	30 mg/ml[a]	GL	1 mg/ml[b]	Little or no loss of either drug by HPLC in 4 hr at 22 °C under fluorescent light	1632	C
Piperacillin sodium–tazobactam sodium	LE	40 + 5 mg/ml[a]	GL	2 mg/ml[a]	Physically compatible with no change in measured turbidity or increase in particle content in 4 hr at 22 °C	1688	C
	LE	80 + 10 mg/ml[b]	GL	0.5 and 2 mg/ml[b]	Visually compatible with little or no loss of any component by HPLC in 4 hr at 23 °C under fluorescent light	1759	C
	LE	40 + 5 mg/ml[b]	GL	0.5 and 2 mg/ml[b]	Visually compatible with little or no loss of ranitidine and tazobactam by HPLC in 4 hr at 23 °C under fluorescent light. Piperacillin not tested	1759	C
Procainamide HCl	BA	4 mg/ml[a]	GL	0.5 mg/ml[d]	Physically compatible for 24 hr	1323	C
Propofol	ZEN	10 mg/ml	GL	2 mg/ml[a]	Physically compatible for 1 hr at 23 °C with no increase in particle content	2066	C
Remifentanil HCl	GW	0.025 and 0.25 mg/ml[b]	GL	2 mg/ml[a]	Physically compatible with no change in measured turbidity or increase in particle content in 4 hr at 23 °C	2075	C
Sargramostim	IMM	10 μg/ml[b]	GL	2 mg/ml[b]	Physically compatible for 4 hr at 22 °C	1436	C
Tacrolimus	FUJ	1 mg/ml[b]	GL	25 mg/ml	Visually compatible for 24 hr at 25 °C	1630	C
Teniposide	BR	0.1 mg/ml[a]	GL	2 mg/ml[a]	Physically compatible with no subvisual haze or particle formation in 4 hr at 23 °C	1725	C
Theophylline	TR	4 mg/ml	GL	1 mg/ml	Visually compatible for 6 hr at 25 °C	1793	C
Thiopental sodium	AB	25 mg/ml[h]	GL	1 mg/ml[a]	Visually compatible for 4 hr at 27 °C	2062	C

Y-Site Injection Compatibility (1:1 Mixture) (Cont.)

Drug	Mfr	Conc	Ranitidine HCl Mfr	Ranitidine HCl Conc	Remarks	Ref	C/I
Thiotepa	IMM[i]	1 mg/ml[a]	GL	2 mg/ml[a]	Physically compatible with no change in measured turbidity or increase in particle content in 4 hr at 23 °C	1861	C
TNA #218 to #226[j]			GL	2 mg/ml[a]	Visually compatible with no precipitate or emulsion damage apparent in 4 hr at 23 °C	2215	C
TPN #189[j]			GL	2.5 mg/ml[b]	Visually compatible for 24 hr at 22 °C	1767	C
TPN #203 and #204[j]			GL	25 mg/ml	Visually compatible for 2 hr at 23 °C	1974	C
TPN #212 to #215[j]			GL	2 mg/ml[a]	Physically compatible with no change in measured turbidity or increase in particle content in 4 hr at 23 °C	2109	C
Vecuronium bromide	OR	0.1 mg/ml[a]	GL	0.5 mg/ml[a]	Physically compatible for 24 hr at 28 °C	1337	C
	OR	1 mg/ml	GL	1 mg/ml[a]	Visually compatible for 4 hr at 27 °C	2062	C
Vinorelbine tartrate	BW	1 mg/ml[b]	GL	2 mg/ml[b]	Physically compatible with no change in measured turbidity or increase in particle content in 4 hr at 22 °C	1558	C
Warfarin sodium	DU	2 mg/ml[h]	GL	1 mg/ml[a]	Visually compatible with no warfarin loss by HPLC in 30 min	2010	C
	DME	2 mg/ml[h]	GL	1 mg/ml[a]	Visually compatible for 24 hr at 24 °C	2078	C
Zidovudine	BW	4 mg/ml[a]	GL	1 mg/ml[a]	Physically compatible for 4 hr at 25 °C under fluorescent light by visual and microscopic examination	1193	C

[a]*Tested in dextrose 5% in water.*
[b]*Tested in sodium chloride 0.9%.*
[c]*Tested in sodium chloride 0.45%.*
[d]*Premixed infusion solution.*
[e]*Tested in both dextrose 5% in water and sodium chloride 0.9%.*
[f]*Tested in bacteriostatic sodium chloride 0.9% preserved with benzyl alcohol 0.9%.*
[g]*Tested in dextrose 5% in water with sodium bicarbonate 0.05 mEq/ml.*
[h]*Tested in sterile water for injection.*
[i]*Lyophilized formulation tested.*
[j]*Refer to Appendix I for the composition of parenteral nutrition solutions. TNA indicates a 3-in-1 admixture, and TPN indicates a 2-in-1 admixture.*
[k]*Sodium carbonate–containing formulation tested.*
[l]*Regular human insulin.*

Additional Compatibility Information

Infusion Solutions — The manufacturer states that ranitidine HCl is stable for 48 hours at room temperature in most infusion solutions such as dextrose 5 and 10% in water, Ringer's injection, lactated, sodium bicarbonate 5%, and sodium chloride 0.9%. (2; 4)

Parenteral Nutrition Solutions — The stability of ranitidine HCl has been evaluated in a number of TPN solutions with variable results. See Solution Compatibility table above. The major mechanism of ranitidine HCl decomposition is oxidation. A number of factors have been found to contribute to ranitidine HCl instability in TPN solutions including the presence or absence of antioxidants (such as sodium metabisulfite) in the amino acids, the addition of trace elements (which can catalyze ranitidine oxidation), solution pH, and the type of plastic container used. In a study of rantidine HCl stability in several TPN solutions stored at 5 °C, the drug was most stable in FreAmine III–based (contains sodium metabisulfite) admixtures with additives when packaged in multilayer, gas-impermeable plastic containers (Ultrastab), with about 8% ranitidine HCl loss by HPLC in 28 days. In contrast, in ethylene vinyl acetate (EVA) bags, which are permeable to oxygen, ranitidine HCl losses of approximately 50% occurred in this time period. If Vamin 14 with no antioxidant present was used as the amino acid source and the solution was packaged in EVA bags, ranitidine HCl losses of approximately 65% occurred in 28 days. Similarly, the addition of air to the bags during compounding increased rantidine HCl oxidation substantially. (2195)

Other Drugs — Ranitidine HCl is stated to be incompatible with amphotericin B and metaraminol bitartrate. (1515)

REMIFENTANIL HCL
AHFS 28:08.08

Products — Remifentanil HCl is available in vials containing 1, 2, or 5 mg of remifentanil base present as the hydrochloride. Each vial also contains glycine 15 mg and hydrochloric acid for pH adjustment. The contents of the vials should be reconstituted with 1 ml of compatible diluent per milligram of remifentanil to yield a 1-mg/ml solution. (1-1/00)

pH — From 2.5 to 3.5. (1-1/00)

Trade Name(s) — Ultiva.

Administration — Remifentanil HCl is administered intravenously only. Single doses may be given over 30 to 60 seconds. Remifentanil HCl may also be given by continuous intravenous infusion using an infusion device. The manufacturer recommends that the injection site be near the venous cannula and that all tubing be cleared at the time the infusion is discontinued. Bolus doses and continuous infusion should not be administered simultaneously to spontaneously breathing patients. (1-1/00)

For intravenous administration, remifentanil HCl should be diluted to a final concentration of 20, 25, 50, or 250 μg/ml. It should not be administered without dilution. (1-1/00)

Stability — Remifentanil HCl is a white to off-white lyophilized powder that forms a clear, colorless solution upon reconstitution. Intact vials should be stored between 2 and 25 °C. (1-1/00)

Compatibility Information

Y-Site Injection Compatibility (1:1 Mixture)

			Remifentanil HCl				
Drug	*Mfr*	*Conc*	*Mfr*	*Conc*	*Remarks*	*Ref*	*C/I*
Acyclovir sodium	BW	7 mg/ml[a]	GW	0.025 and 0.25 mg/ml[b]	Physically compatible with no change in measured turbidity or increase in particle content in 4 hr at 23 °C	2075	C
Alfentanil HCl	JN	0.125 mg/ml[a]	GW	0.025 and 0.25 mg/ml[b]	Physically compatible with no change in measured turbidity or increase in particle content in 4 hr at 23 °C	2075	C
Amikacin sulfate	AB	5 mg/ml[a]	GW	0.025 and 0.25 mg/ml[b]	Physically compatible with no change in measured turbidity or increase in particle content in 4 hr at 23 °C	2075	C
Aminophylline	AB	2.5 mg/ml[a]	GW	0.025 and 0.25 mg/ml[b]	Physically compatible with no change in measured turbidity or increase in particle content in 4 hr at 23 °C	2075	C
Amphotericin B	PHT	0.6 mg/ml[a]	GW	0.025 mg/ml[a]	Physically compatible with no change in measured turbidity or increase in particle content in 4 hr at 23 °C	2075	C
	PHT	0.6 mg/ml[a]	GW	0.25 mg/ml[a]	Yellow precipitate forms immediately	2075	I
Amphotericin B cholesteryl sulfate complex	SEQ	0.83 mg/ml[a]	GW	0.5 mg/ml[a]	Gross precipitate forms	2117	I
Ampicillin sodium	SKB	20 mg/ml[b]	GW	0.025 and 0.25 mg/ml[b]	Physically compatible with no change in measured turbidity or increase in particle content in 4 hr at 23 °C	2075	C
Ampicillin sodium–sulbactam sodium	RR	20 + 10 mg/ml[b]	GW	0.025 and 0.25 mg/ml[b]	Physically compatible with no change in measured turbidity or increase in particle content in 4 hr at 23 °C	2075	C
Aztreonam	SQ	40 mg/ml[a]	GW	0.025 and 0.25 mg/ml[b]	Physically compatible with no change in measured turbidity or increase in particle content in 4 hr at 23 °C	2075	C
Bretylium tosylate	AST	4 mg/ml[a]	GW	0.025 and 0.25 mg/ml[b]	Physically compatible with no change in measured turbidity or increase in particle content in 4 hr at 23 °C	2075	C
Bumetanide	RC	0.04 mg/ml[a]	GW	0.025 and 0.25 mg/ml[b]	Physically compatible with no change in measured turbidity or increase in particle content in 4 hr at 23 °C	2075	C

Y-Site Injection Compatibility (1:1 Mixture) (Cont.)

Remifentanil HCl

Drug	*Mfr*	*Conc*	*Mfr*	*Conc*	*Remarks*	*Ref*	*C/I*
Buprenorphine HCl	RKC	0.04 mg/ml[a]	GW	0.025 and 0.25 mg/ml[b]	Physically compatible with no change in measured turbidity or increase in particle content in 4 hr at 23 °C	2075	C
Butorphanol tartrate	APC	0.04 mg/ml[a]	GW	0.025 and 0.25 mg/ml[b]	Physically compatible with no change in measured turbidity or increase in particle content in 4 hr at 23 °C	2075	C
Calcium gluconate	AB	40 mg/ml[a]	GW	0.025 and 0.25 mg/ml[b]	Physically compatible with no change in measured turbidity or increase in particle content in 4 hr at 23 °C	2075	C
Cefazolin sodium	SKB	20 mg/ml[a]	GW	0.025 and 0.25 mg/ml[b]	Physically compatible with no change in measured turbidity or increase in particle content in 4 hr at 23 °C	2075	C
Cefoperazone sodium	RR	40 mg/ml[a]	GW	0.025 mg/ml[b]	Physically compatible with no change in measured turbidity or increase in particle content in 4 hr at 23 °C	2075	C
	RR	40 mg/ml[a]	GW	0.25 mg/ml[b]	Subvisual haze forms in 1 hr	2075	I
Cefotaxime sodium	HO	20 mg/ml[a]	GW	0.025 and 0.25 mg/ml[b]	Physically compatible with no change in measured turbidity or increase in particle content in 4 hr at 23 °C	2075	C
Cefotetan sodium	ZEN	20 mg/ml[a]	GW	0.025 and 0.25 mg/ml[b]	Physically compatible with no change in measured turbidity or increase in particle content in 4 hr at 23 °C	2075	C
Cefoxitin sodium	ME	20 mg/ml[a]	GW	0.025 and 0.25 mg/ml[b]	Physically compatible with no change in measured turbidity or increase in particle content in 4 hr at 23 °C	2075	C
Ceftazidime	GW[c]	40 mg/ml[a]	GW	0.025 and 0.25 mg/ml[b]	Physically compatible with no change in measured turbidity or increase in particle content in 4 hr at 23 °C	2075	C
Ceftizoxime sodium	FUJ	20 mg/ml[a]	GW	0.025 and 0.25 mg/ml[b]	Physically compatible with no change in measured turbidity or increase in particle content in 4 hr at 23 °C	2075	C
Ceftriaxone sodium	RC	20 mg/ml[a]	GW	0.025 and 0.25 mg/ml[b]	Physically compatible with no change in measured turbidity or increase in particle content in 4 hr at 23 °C	2075	C
Cefuroxime sodium	LI	30 mg/ml[a]	GW	0.025 and 0.25 mg/ml[b]	Physically compatible with no change in measured turbidity or increase in particle content in 4 hr at 23 °C	2075	C
Chlorpromazine HCl	SCN	2 mg/ml[a]	GW	0.025 mg/ml[b]	Slight subvisual haze forms in 1 hr	2075	I
	SCN	2 mg/ml[a]	GW	0.25 mg/ml[b]	Physically compatible with no change in measured turbidity or increase in particle content in 4 hr at 23 °C	2075	C
Cimetidine HCl	SKB	12 mg/ml[a]	GW	0.025 and 0.25 mg/ml[b]	Physically compatible with no change in measured turbidity or increase in particle content in 4 hr at 23 °C	2075	C
Ciprofloxacin	BAY	1 mg/ml[a]	GW	0.025 and 0.25 mg/ml[b]	Physically compatible with no change in measured turbidity or increase in particle content in 4 hr at 23 °C	2075	C

Y-Site Injection Compatibility (1:1 Mixture) (Cont.)

Remifentanil HCl

Drug	*Mfr*	*Conc*	*Mfr*	*Conc*	*Remarks*	*Ref*	*C/I*
Cisatracurium besylate	GW	2 mg/ml[a]	GW	0.025 and 0.25 mg/ml[b]	Physically compatible with no change in measured turbidity or increase in particle content in 4 hr at 23 °C	2075	C
Clindamycin phosphate	AST	10 mg/ml[a]	GW	0.025 and 0.25 mg/ml[b]	Physically compatible with no change in measured turbidity or increase in particle content in 4 hr at 23 °C	2075	C
Dexamethasone sodium phosphate	FUJ	2 mg/ml[a]	GW	0.025 and 0.25 mg/ml[b]	Physically compatible with no change in measured turbidity or increase in particle content in 4 hr at 23 °C	2075	C
Diazepam	ES	5 mg/ml	GW	0.025 and 0.25 mg/ml[b]	White turbidity forms immediately	2075	I
	ES	0.25 mg/ml[a]	GW	0.025 and 0.25 mg/ml[b]	Physically compatible with no change in measured turbidity or increase in particle content in 4 hr at 23 °C	2075	C
Digoxin	ES	0.25 mg/ml	GW	0.025 and 0.25 mg/ml[b]	Physically compatible with no change in measured turbidity or increase in particle content in 4 hr at 23 °C	2075	C
Diphenhydramine HCl	SCN	2 mg/ml[a]	GW	0.025 and 0.25 mg/ml[b]	Physically compatible with no change in measured turbidity or increase in particle content in 4 hr at 23 °C	2075	C
Dobutamine HCl	LI	4 mg/ml[a]	GW	0.025 and 0.25 mg/ml[b]	Physically compatible with no change in measured turbidity or increase in particle content in 4 hr at 23 °C	2075	C
Dopamine HCl	AB	3.2 mg/ml[a]	GW	0.025 and 0.25 mg/ml[b]	Physically compatible with no change in measured turbidity or increase in particle content in 4 hr at 23 °C	2075	C
Doxycycline hyclate	FUJ	1 mg/ml[a]	GW	0.025 and 0.25 mg/ml[b]	Physically compatible with no change in measured turbidity or increase in particle content in 4 hr at 23 °C	2075	C
Droperidol	AST	2.5 mg/ml	GW	0.025 and 0.25 mg/ml[b]	Physically compatible with no change in measured turbidity or increase in particle content in 4 hr at 23 °C	2075	C
Enalaprilat	ME	0.1 mg/ml[a]	GW	0.025 and 0.25 mg/ml[b]	Physically compatible with no change in measured turbidity or increase in particle content in 4 hr at 23 °C	2075	C
Epinephrine HCl	AMR	0.05 mg/ml[a]	GW	0.025 and 0.25 mg/ml[b]	Physically compatible with no change in measured turbidity or increase in particle content in 4 hr at 23 °C	2075	C
Esmolol HCl	OHM	10 mg/ml[a]	GW	0.025 and 0.25 mg/ml[b]	Physically compatible with no change in measured turbidity or increase in particle content in 4 hr at 23 °C	2075	C
Famotidine	MSD	2 mg/ml[a]	GW	0.025 and 0.25 mg/ml[b]	Physically compatible with no change in measured turbidity or increase in particle content in 4 hr at 23 °C	2075	C
Fentanyl citrate	ES	0.0125 mg/ml[a]	GW	0.025 and 0.25 mg/ml[b]	Physically compatible with no change in measured turbidity or increase in particle content in 4 hr at 23 °C	2075	C

Y-Site Injection Compatibility (1:1 Mixture) (Cont.)

Remifentanil HCl

Drug	*Mfr*	*Conc*	*Mfr*	*Conc*	*Remarks*	*Ref*	*C/I*
Fluconazole	RR	2 mg/ml	GW	0.025 and 0.25 mg/ml[b]	Physically compatible with no change in measured turbidity or increase in particle content in 4 hr at 23 °C	2075	C
Furosemide	AMR	3 mg/ml[a]	GW	0.025 and 0.25 mg/ml[b]	Physically compatible with no change in measured turbidity or increase in particle content in 4 hr at 23 °C	2075	C
Ganciclovir sodium	SY	20 mg/ml[a]	GW	0.025 and 0.25 mg/ml[b]	Physically compatible with no change in measured turbidity or increase in particle content in 4 hr at 23 °C	2075	C
Gatifloxacin	BMS	2 mg/ml[a]	GW	0.5 mg/ml[a]	Physically compatible with no change in measured haze or increase in particle content in 4 hr at 23 °C	2234	C
Gentamicin sulfate	ES	5 mg/ml[a]	GW	0.025 and 0.25 mg/ml[b]	Physically compatible with no change in measured turbidity or increase in particle content in 4 hr at 23 °C	2075	C
Haloperidol lactate	MN	0.2 mg/ml[a]	GW	0.025 and 0.25 mg/ml[b]	Physically compatible with no change in measured turbidity or increase in particle content in 4 hr at 23 °C	2075	C
Heparin sodium	AB	100 units/ml	GW	0.025 and 0.25 mg/ml[b]	Physically compatible with no change in measured turbidity or increase in particle content in 4 hr at 23 °C	2075	C
Hydrocortisone sodium succinate	AB	1 mg/ml[a]	GW	0.025 and 0.25 mg/ml[b]	Physically compatible with no change in measured turbidity or increase in particle content in 4 hr at 23 °C	2075	C
Hydromorphone HCl	ES	0.5 mg/ml[a]	GW	0.025 and 0.25 mg/ml[b]	Physically compatible with no change in measured turbidity or increase in particle content in 4 hr at 23 °C	2075	C
Hydroxyzine HCl	ES	2 mg/ml[a]	GW	0.025 and 0.25 mg/ml[b]	Physically compatible with no change in measured turbidity or increase in particle content in 4 hr at 23 °C	2075	C
Imipenem–cilastatin sodium	ME	10 mg/ml[a]	GW	0.025 and 0.25 mg/ml[b]	Physically compatible with no change in measured turbidity or increase in particle content in 4 hr at 23 °C	2075	C
Inamrinone lactate	SW	2.5 mg/ml[a]	GW	0.025 and 0.25 mg/ml[b]	Physically compatible with no change in measured turbidity or increase in particle content in 4 hr at 23 °C	2075	C
Isoproterenol HCl	SW	0.02 mg/ml[a]	GW	0.025 and 0.25 mg/ml[b]	Physically compatible with no change in measured turbidity or increase in particle content in 4 hr at 23 °C	2075	C
Ketorolac tromethamine	RC	15 mg/ml[a]	GW	0.025 and 0.25 mg/ml[b]	Physically compatible with no change in measured turbidity or increase in particle content in 4 hr at 23 °C	2075	C
Lidocaine HCl	AST	8 mg/ml[a]	GW	0.025 and 0.25 mg/ml[b]	Physically compatible with no change in measured turbidity or increase in particle content in 4 hr at 23 °C	2075	C
Linezolid	PHU	2 mg/ml	GW	0.5 mg/ml[a]	Physically compatible with no change in measured turbidity or increase in particle content in 4 hr at 23 °C	2264	C

Y-Site Injection Compatibility (1:1 Mixture) (Cont.)

Remifentanil HCl

Drug	*Mfr*	*Conc*	*Mfr*	*Conc*	*Remarks*	*Ref*	*C/I*
Lorazepam	WY	0.5 mg/ml[a]	GW	0.025 and 0.25 mg/ml[b]	Physically compatible with no change in measured turbidity or increase in particle content in 4 hr at 23 °C	2075	C
Magnesium sulfate	AB	100 mg/ml[a]	GW	0.025 and 0.25 mg/ml[b]	Physically compatible with no change in measured turbidity or increase in particle content in 4 hr at 23 °C	2075	C
Mannitol	BA	15%	GW	0.025 and 0.25 mg/ml[b]	Physically compatible with no change in measured turbidity or increase in particle content in 4 hr at 23 °C	2075	C
Meperidine HCl	AST	4 mg/ml[a]	GW	0.025 and 0.25 mg/ml[b]	Physically compatible with no change in measured turbidity or increase in particle content in 4 hr at 23 °C	2075	C
Methylprednisolone sodium succinate	AB	5 mg/ml[a]	GW	0.025 and 0.25 mg/ml[b]	Physically compatible with no change in measured turbidity or increase in particle content in 4 hr at 23 °C	2075	C
Metoclopramide HCl	AB	5 mg/ml	GW	0.025 and 0.25 mg/ml[b]	Physically compatible with no change in measured turbidity or increase in particle content in 4 hr at 23 °C	2075	C
Metronidazole	AB	5 mg/ml	GW	0.025 and 0.25 mg/ml[b]	Physically compatible with no change in measured turbidity or increase in particle content in 4 hr at 23 °C	2075	C
Mezlocillin disodium	MI	40 mg/ml[a]	GW	0.025 and 0.25 mg/ml[b]	Physically compatible with no change in measured turbidity or increase in particle content in 4 hr at 23 °C	2075	C
Midazolam HCl	RC	1 mg/ml[a]	GW	0.025 and 0.25 mg/ml[b]	Physically compatible with no change in measured turbidity or increase in particle content in 4 hr at 23 °C	2075	C
Minocycline HCl	LE	0.2 mg/ml[a]	GW	0.025 and 0.25 mg/ml[b]	Physically compatible with no change in measured turbidity or increase in particle content in 4 hr at 23 °C	2075	C
Morphine sulfate	AST	1 mg/ml[a]	GW	0.025 and 0.25 mg/ml[b]	Physically compatible with no change in measured turbidity or increase in particle content in 4 hr at 23 °C	2075	C
Nalbuphine HCl	AST	10 mg/ml	GW	0.025 and 0.25 mg/ml[b]	Physically compatible with no change in measured turbidity or increase in particle content in 4 hr at 23 °C	2075	C
Netilmicin sulfate	SC	5 mg/ml[a]	GW	0.025 and 0.25 mg/ml[b]	Physically compatible with no change in measured turbidity or increase in particle content in 4 hr at 23 °C	2075	C
Nitroglycerin	DU	0.4 mg/ml[a]	GW	0.025 and 0.25 mg/ml[b]	Physically compatible with no change in measured turbidity or increase in particle content in 4 hr at 23 °C	2075	C
Norepinephrine bitartrate	SW	0.12 mg/ml[a]	GW	0.025 and 0.25 mg/ml[b]	Physically compatible with no change in measured turbidity or increase in particle content in 4 hr at 23 °C	2075	C
Ofloxacin	ORT	4 mg/ml[a]	GW	0.025 and 0.25 mg/ml[b]	Physically compatible with no change in measured turbidity or increase in particle content in 4 hr at 23 °C	2075	C

Y-Site Injection Compatibility (1:1 Mixture) (Cont.)

Remifentanil HCl

Drug	*Mfr*	*Conc*	*Mfr*	*Conc*	*Remarks*	*Ref*	*C/I*
Ondansetron HCl	CER	1 mg/ml[a]	GW	0.025 and 0.25 mg/ml[b]	Physically compatible with no change in measured turbidity or increase in particle content in 4 hr at 23 °C	2075	C
Phenylephrine HCl	AMR	1 mg/ml[a]	GW	0.025 and 0.25 mg/ml[b]	Physically compatible with no change in measured turbidity or increase in particle content in 4 hr at 23 °C	2075	C
Piperacillin sodium	LE	40 mg/ml[a]	GW	0.025 and 0.25 mg/ml[b]	Physically compatible with no change in measured turbidity or increase in particle content in 4 hr at 23 °C	2075	C
Piperacillin sodium–tazobactam sodium	CY	40 + 5 mg/ml[a]	GW	0.025 and 0.25 mg/ml[b]	Physically compatible with no change in measured turbidity or increase in particle content in 4 hr at 23 °C	2075	C
Potassium chloride	AB	0.1 mg/ml[a]	GW	0.025 and 0.25 mg/ml[b]	Physically compatible with no change in measured turbidity or increase in particle content in 4 hr at 23 °C	2075	C
Procainamide HCl	ES	10 mg/ml[a]	GW	0.025 and 0.25 mg/ml[b]	Physically compatible with no change in measured turbidity or increase in particle content in 4 hr at 23 °C	2075	C
Prochlorperazine edisylate	SO	0.5 mg/ml[a]	GW	0.025 and 0.25 mg/ml[b]	Physically compatible with no change in measured turbidity or increase in particle content in 4 hr at 23 °C	2075	C
Promethazine HCl	SCN	2 mg/ml[a]	GW	0.025 and 0.25 mg/ml[b]	Physically compatible with no change in measured turbidity or increase in particle content in 4 hr at 23 °C	2075	C
Ranitidine HCl	GL	2 mg/ml[a]	GW	0.025 and 0.25 mg/ml[b]	Physically compatible with no change in measured turbidity or increase in particle content in 4 hr at 23 °C	2075	C
Sodium bicarbonate	AB	1 mEq/ml	GW	0.025 and 0.25 mg/ml[b]	Physically compatible with no change in measured turbidity or increase in particle content in 4 hr at 23 °C	2075	C
Sufentanil citrate	ES	0.0125 mg/ml[a]	GW	0.025 and 0.25 mg/ml[b]	Physically compatible with no change in measured turbidity or increase in particle content in 4 hr at 23 °C	2075	C
Theophylline	AB	3.2 mg/ml[a]	GW	0.025 and 0.25 mg/ml[b]	Physically compatible with no change in measured turbidity or increase in particle content in 4 hr at 23 °C	2075	C
Thiopental sodium	AB	50 mg/ml[a]	GW	0.025 and 0.25 mg/ml[b]	Physically compatible with no change in measured turbidity or increase in particle content in 4 hr at 23 °C	2075	C
Ticarcillin disodium	SKB	30 mg/ml[a]	GW	0.025 and 0.25 mg/ml[b]	Physically compatible with no change in measured turbidity or increase in particle content in 4 hr at 23 °C	2075	C
Ticarcillin disodium–clavulanate potassium	SKB	31 mg/ml[a]	GW	0.025 and 0.25 mg/ml[b]	Physically compatible with no change in measured turbidity or increase in particle content in 4 hr at 23 °C	2075	C
Tobramycin sulfate	AB	5 mg/ml[a]	GW	0.025 and 0.25 mg/ml[b]	Physically compatible with no change in measured turbidity or increase in particle content in 4 hr at 23 °C	2075	C

Y-Site Injection Compatibility (1:1 Mixture) (Cont.)

Remifentanil HCl

Drug	Mfr	Conc	Mfr	Conc	Remarks	Ref	C/I
Trimethoprim–sulfamethoxazole	ES	0.8 + 4 mg/ml[a]	GW	0.025 and 0.25 mg/ml[b]	Physically compatible with no change in measured turbidity or increase in particle content in 4 hr at 23 °C	2075	C
Vancomycin HCl	AB	10 mg/ml[a]	GW	0.025 and 0.25 mg/ml[b]	Physically compatible with no change in measured turbidity or increase in particle content in 4 hr at 23 °C	2075	C
Zidovudine	BW	4 mg/ml[a]	GW	0.025 and 0.25 mg/ml[b]	Physically compatible with no change in measured turbidity or increase in particle content in 4 hr at 23 °C	2075	C

[a]*Tested in dextrose 5% in water.*
[b]*Tested in sodium chloride 0.9%.*
[c]*L-Arginine–containing formulation tested.*

Additional Compatibility Information

Infusion Solutions — Remifentanil HCl is compatible and stable for 24 hours after reconstitution and dilution to concentrations from 20 to 250 μg/ml in the following diluents:

Dextrose 5% in Ringer's injection, lactated
Dextrose 5% in sodium chloride 0.9%
Dextrose 5% in water
Sodium chloride 0.45%
Sodium chloride 0.9%
Sterile water for injection

In Ringer's injection, lactated, remifentanil HCl is stable for four hours at room temperature. (2)

Other Drugs — Propofol (Zeneca) has been stated to be compatible with remifentanil HCl. However, administration of remifentanil HCl into the same tubing with blood is not recommended, because of the possibility of hydrolysis. (2)

RIFAMPIN
AHFS 8:16

Products — Rifampin is available as a lyophilized powder in vials containing rifampin 600 mg, sodium formaldehyde sulfoxylate 10 mg, and sodium hydroxide to adjust the pH. Reconstitute with 10 ml of sterile water for injection; swirl gently to dissolve the vial contents for a 60-mg/ml solution. (2)

Trade Name(s) — Rifadin I.V.

Administration — Rifampin is administered by intravenous infusion. It must not be given intramuscularly or subcutaneously, and extravasation should be avoided. The reconstituted solution may be diluted in 500 ml of dextrose 5% in water or sodium chloride 0.9% and infused over three hours. Alternatively, the desired dose may be diluted in 100 ml and administered over 30 minutes. (2; 4)

Stability — Rifampin powder is reddish brown. Intact vials should be stored at room temperature and protected from excessive heat and light. (2)

The reconstituted solution is stable for 24 hours at room temperature. (2)

Compatibility Information

Solution Compatibility

Rifampin

Solution	Mfr	Mfr	Conc/L	Remarks	Ref	C/I
Dextrose 5% in water	AB	MMD	6 g	Gelatinous precipitate adhered to PVC container wall after overnight room temperature storage protected from light	1543	I
	AB	MMD	1.2 g	Clear with no visible precipitation during 3-hr administration period	1543	C

Solution Compatibility (Cont.)

Rifampin

Solution	*Mfr*	*Mfr*	*Conc/L*	*Remarks*	*Ref*	*C/I*
	BA[a]	MMD	0.1 g	Brownish color appears in 4 hr and darkens over 3 days. 5% rifampin loss in 8 hr and 15 to 17% loss in 24 hr at 24 °C by HPLC. 8% loss in 3 days at 4 °C	1559	I[b]
Sodium chloride 0.9%	BA[a]	MMD	0.1 g	Brownish color appears in 4 hr and darkens over 3 days. 5 to 7% rifampin loss in 8 hr and 11 to 13% loss in 24 hr at 24 °C by HPLC. 7% loss in 3 days at 4 °C	1559	I[b]

[a]Tested in PVC containers.
[b]Incompatible by conventional standards. May be used in shorter time periods.

Additive Compatibility

Drug	*Mfr*	*Conc/L*	*Mfr*	*Conc/L*	*Test Soln*	*Remarks*	*Ref*	*C/I*
			Rifampin					
Minocycline HCl	LE	0.1 g	MMD	0.1 g	NS	Brownish color appears in 4 hr at 37 and 24 °C and 8 hr at 4 °C. 10% rifampin loss by HPLC in 3 days at 4 °C and 8 hr at 24 °C; 14% loss in 4 hr at 37 °C. Less than 2% minocycline loss by HPLC under these conditions	1559	I

Y-Site Injection Compatibility (1:1 Mixture)

Drug	*Mfr*	*Conc*	*Mfr*	*Conc*	*Remarks*	*Ref*	*C/I*
			Rifampin				
Diltiazem HCl	MMD	1[a] and 5 mg/ml	MMD	6 mg/ml[a]	Precipitate forms	1807	I

[a]Tested in sodium chloride 0.9%.

Additional Compatibility Information

Infusion Solutions — The manufacturer recommends use of rifampin dilutions in dextrose 5% in water within four hours due to the potential for precipitation beyond this time period. (2) However, the manufacturer recommends use of rifampin diluted in sodium chloride 0.9% within 24 hours (2) although other information indicates substantial (11 to 13%) rifampin decomposition occurs in 24 hours at room temperature in this infusion solution. (1559) The administration of rifampin admixtures in either infusion solution within three hours of preparation seems to be a reasonable time frame based on both precipitation potential and drug decomposition.

ROCURONIUM BROMIDE
AHFS 12:20

Products — Rocuronium bromide is available in 5- and 10-ml vials. Each milliliter contains rocuronium bromide 10 mg with sodium acetate 2 mg, sodium chloride for isotonicity, and acetic acid and/or sodium hydroxide to adjust the pH. (2)

pH — Adjusted during manufacture to pH 4. (2)

Osmolality — The injection is isotonic. (2)

Trade Name(s) — Zemuron.

Administration — Rocuronium bromide is administered intravenously only by rapid intravenous injection or by intravenous infusion when admixed in an appropriate intravenous infusion solution. Infusion rates should be individualized for each patient according to the requirements and response. (2; 4)

Stability — Intact vials of rocuronium bromide should be stored under refrigeration at 2 to 8 °C and protected from freezing. Intact vials stored at room temperature should be used within 60 days. (2)

Compatibility Information

Y-Site Injection Compatibility (1:1 Mixture)

Rocuronium bromide

Drug	*Mfr*	*Conc*	*Mfr*	*Conc*	*Remarks*	*Ref*	*C/I*
Hetastarch in lactated electrolyte injection (Hextend)	AB	6%	OR	1 mg/ml[a]	Physically compatible with no change in measured turbidity or increase in particle content in 4 hr at 23 °C	2339	C
Milrinone lactate	SW	0.4 mg/ml[a]	OR	2 mg/ml[a]	Visually compatible with little or no loss of either drug by HPLC in 4 hr at 23 °C	2214	C

[a]*Tested in dextrose 5% in water.*

Additional Compatibility Information

Infusion Solutions — Rocuronium bromide is stated to be compatible and stable for 24 hours in the following infusion solutions (2):

Dextrose 5% in water
Dextrose 5% in sodium chloride 0.9%
Ringer's injection, lactated
Sodium chloride 0.9%

SARGRAMOSTIM
(GM-CSF)
AHFS 20:16

Products — Sargramostim is available in single-dose vials labeled as 250 µg. Reconstitute the vial with 1 ml of sterile water for injection or bacteriostatic water for injection containing benzyl alcohol 0.9% directed at the sides of the vial. Gently swirl to avoid foaming during dissolution, and do not shake. Each milliliter of the reconstituted solution contains sargramostim 250 µg, mannitol 40 mg, sucrose 10 mg, and tromethamine 1.2 mg. (2; 4) The contents of vials reconstituted with different diluents should not be mixed. (2)

Sargramostim is also available as a preserved liquid formulation in 1-ml vials containing in each milliliter sargramostim 500 µg along with mannitol 40 mg, sucrose 10 mg, tromethamine 1.2 mg, and benzyl alcohol 1.1% as an antimicrobial preservative. (2; 4)

Specific Activity — The specific activity is approximately 5.6×10^6 units per milligram. (2)

pH — From 7.1 to 7.7. (17)

Trade Name(s) — Leukine.

Administration — Sargramostim may be administered by subcutaneous injection undiluted or by intravenous infusion usually over two to four hours after dilution in sodium chloride 0.9%. (2; 4) Intravenous infusion also has been performed over 30 to 60 minutes, over five to 12 hours, and as a continuous infusion over 24 hours. (4) For infusion concentrations below 10 µg/ml, albumin human at a final concentration of 0.1% should be added to the intravenous solution prior to the addition of sargramostim to prevent adsorption. (2; 4)

The preparations containing benzyl alcohol (Leukine liquid, and lyophilized Leukine reconstituted with bacteriostatic water for injection containing benzyl alcohol) should not be used in neonates. (2)

Stability — Intact vials, reconstituted solutions, and sargramostim diluted in sodium chloride 0.9% should be stored under refrigeration. Solutions should be protected from freezing and not shaken. The liquid formulation is a clear, colorless solution. The white lyophilized powder forms a clear, colorless solution on reconstitution. The manufacturer recommends administration within six hours following reconstitution with sterile water for injection and/or dilution in an infusion solution and discarding any unused solution. When reconstituted with bacteriostatic water for injection preserved with benzyl alcohol 0.9%, the manufacturer states that the solution may be stored for up to 20 days under refrigeration. (2)

Other information indicates that sargramostim reconstituted with sterile water for injection or bacteriostatic water for injection retains potency for 30 days at room temperature (25 °C) or under refrigeration. (226)

Syringes — Sargramostim reconstituted with bacteriostatic water for injection preserved with benzyl alcohol 0.9% and repackaged into 1-ml tuberculin syringes remained sterile for 14 days under refrigeration. (1764) However, because of the limited nature of the tests performed, the results may apply to a single institution only. Other institutions that repackage sargramostim injection need to establish specific testing results for their own sterile facilities, equipment, procedures, and personnel. (1765)

Sargramostim 250 μg and 500 μg reconstituted with 1 ml of bacteriostatic water for injection with benzyl alcohol 0.9% and repackaged in 1-ml tuberculin syringes (Becton-Dickinson) is stated to retain potency for 14 days when stored under refrigeration. (226)

Sorption—Sargramostim will adsorb to containers and tubing if the concentration is below 10 μg/ml. Albumin human 0.1% should be added to the intravenous solution to prevent this adsorption. (2)

Filtration—Sargramostim should not be infused through an inline filter because of possible absorption. (2; 4)

Compatibility Information

Y-Site Injection Compatibility (1:1 Mixture)

			Sargramostim				
Drug	*Mfr*	*Conc*	*Mfr*	*Conc*	*Remarks*	*Ref*	*C/I*
Acyclovir sodium	BW	7 mg/ml[b]	IMM	10 μg/ml[b]	Few small white particles in 4 hr	1436	I
Amikacin sulfate	BR	5 mg/ml[b]	IMM	10 μg/ml[b]	Physically compatible for 4 hr at 22 °C	1436	C
Aminophylline	ES	2.5 mg/ml[b]	IMM	10 μg/ml[b]	Physically compatible for 4 hr at 22 °C	1436	C
Amphotericin B	SQ	0.6 mg/ml[a]	IMM	10 μg/ml[b]	Moderately heavy yellow precipitate forms immediately	1436	I
	SQ	0.6 mg/ml[a]	IMM	10 μg/ml[a]	Physically compatible for 4 hr at 22 °C	1436	C
Ampicillin sodium	BR	20 mg/ml[b]	IMM	10 μg/ml[b]	Few small particles in 4 hr	1436	I
Ampicillin sodium–sulbactam sodium	RR	20 + 10 mg/ml[b]	IMM	10 μg/ml[b]	Few small particles in 4 hr in one of two samples	1436	I
Amsacrine	NCI	1 mg/ml[a]	IMM	10 μg/ml[b]	Immediate haze with heavy yellow flocculent precipitate in 30 min	1436	I
	NCI	1 mg/ml[a]	IMM	10 μg/ml[a]	Physically compatible for 4 hr at 22 °C	1436	C
Aztreonam	SQ	40 mg/ml[b]	IMM	10 μg/ml[b]	Physically compatible for 4 hr at 22 °C	1436	C
	SQ	40 mg/ml[a]	IMM	10 μg/ml[b]	Physically compatible with no subvisual haze or particle formation in 4 hr at 23 °C	1758	C
Bleomycin sulfate	MJ	1 unit/ml[b]	IMM	10 μg/ml[b]	Physically compatible for 4 hr at 22 °C	1436	C
Butorphanol tartrate	BR	0.04 mg/ml[b]	IMM	10 μg/ml[b]	Physically compatible for 4 hr at 22 °C	1436	C
Calcium gluconate	AMR	40 mg/ml[b]	IMM	10 μg/ml[b]	Physically compatible for 4 hr at 22 °C	1436	C
Carboplatin	BR	5 mg/ml[b]	IMM	10 μg/ml[b]	Physically compatible for 4 hr at 22 °C	1436	C
Carmustine	BR	1.5 mg/ml[b]	IMM	10 μg/ml[b]	Physically compatible for 4 hr at 22 °C	1436	C
Cefazolin sodium	LEM	20 mg/ml[b]	IMM	10 μg/ml[b]	Physically compatible for 4 hr at 22 °C	1436	C
Cefepime HCl	BMS	20 mg/ml[a]	IMM	10 μg/ml[b]	Physically compatible with no change in measured turbidity or increase in particle content in 4 hr at 22 °C	1689	C
Cefoperazone sodium	RR	40 mg/ml[b]	IMM	10 μg/ml[b]	Slight haze, visible with high intensity light, forms immediately	1436	I
Cefotaxime sodium	HO	20 mg/ml[b]	IMM	10 μg/ml[b]	Physically compatible for 4 hr at 22 °C	1436	C
Cefotetan disodium	STU	20 mg/ml[b]	IMM	10 μg/ml[b]	Physically compatible for 4 hr at 22 °C	1436	C
Ceftazidime	GL[c]	40 mg/ml[b]	IMM	10 μg/ml[b]	Particles and filaments form in 4 hr	1436	I
	LI[c]	40 mg/ml[d]	IMM	6[b,e] and 15[b] μg/ml	Visually compatible for 2 hr	1618	C
Ceftizoxime sodium	FUJ	20 mg/ml[b]	IMM	10 μg/ml[b]	Physically compatible for 4 hr at 22 °C	1436	C
Ceftriaxone sodium	RC	20 mg/ml[b]	IMM	10 μg/ml[b]	Physically compatible for 4 hr at 22 °C	1436	C
Cefuroxime sodium	GL	30 mg/ml[b]	IMM	10 μg/ml[b]	Physically compatible for 4 hr at 22 °C	1436	C
Chlorpromazine HCl	ES	2 mg/ml[b]	IMM	10 μg/ml[b]	Slight haze, visible with high intensity light, forms immediately	1436	I

Y-Site Injection Compatibility (1:1 Mixture) (Cont.)

Drug	Mfr	Conc	Sargramostim Mfr	Sargramostim Conc	Remarks	Ref	C/I
Cimetidine HCl	SKF	12 mg/ml[b]	IMM	10 μg/ml[b]	Physically compatible for 4 hr at 22 °C	1436	C
Cisplatin	BR	1 mg/ml	IMM	10 μg/ml[b]	Physically compatible for 4 hr at 22 °C	1436	C
Clindamycin phosphate	LY	10 mg/ml[b]	IMM	10 μg/ml[b]	Physically compatible for 4 hr at 22 °C	1436	C
Cyclophosphamide	MJ	10 mg/ml[b]	IMM	10 μg/ml[b]	Physically compatible for 4 hr at 22 °C	1436	C
Cyclosporine	SZ	5 mg/ml[b]	IMM	6[b,e] and 15[b] μg/ml	Visually compatible for 2 hr	1618	C
Cytarabine	SCN	50 mg/ml	IMM	10 μg/ml[b]	Physically compatible for 4 hr at 22 °C	1436	C
Dacarbazine	MI	4 mg/ml[b]	IMM	10 μg/ml[b]	Physically compatible for 4 hr at 22 °C	1436	C
Dactinomycin	MSD	0.01 mg/ml[b]	IMM	10 μg/ml[b]	Physically compatible for 4 hr at 22 °C	1436	C
Dexamethasone sodium phosphate	ES	1 mg/ml[b]	IMM	10 μg/ml[b]	Physically compatible for 4 hr at 22 °C	1436	C
Diphenhydramine HCl	RU	1 mg/ml[b]	IMM	10 μg/ml[b]	Physically compatible for 4 hr at 22 °C	1436	C
Dopamine HCl	DU	1.6 mg/ml[d]	IMM	6[b,e] and 15[b] μg/ml	Visually compatible for 2 hr	1618	C
Doxorubicin HCl	CET	2 mg/ml	IMM	10 μg/ml[b]	Physically compatible for 4 hr at 22 °C	1436	C
Doxycycline hyclate	LY	1 mg/ml[b]	IMM	10 μg/ml[b]	Physically compatible for 4 hr at 22 °C	1436	C
Droperidol	DU	0.4 mg/ml[b]	IMM	10 μg/ml[b]	Physically compatible for 4 hr at 22 °C	1436	C
Etoposide	BR	0.4 mg/ml[b]	IMM	10 μg/ml[b]	Physically compatible for 4 hr at 22 °C	1436	C
Famotidine	MSD	2 mg/ml	IMM	10 μg/ml[b]	Physically compatible for 4 hr at 22 °C	1436	C
Fentanyl citrate	ES	50 μg/ml	IMM	6[b,e] and 15[b] μg/ml	Visually compatible for 2 hr	1618	C
Floxuridine	RC	3 mg/ml[b]	IMM	10 μg/ml[b]	Physically compatible for 4 hr at 22 °C	1436	C
Fluconazole	PF	2 mg/ml	IMM	10 μg/ml[b]	Physically compatible for 4 hr at 22 °C	1436	C
Fluorouracil	SO	16 mg/ml	IMM	10 μg/ml[b]	Physically compatible for 4 hr at 22 °C	1436	C
Furosemide	AB	3 mg/ml[b]	IMM	10 μg/ml[b]	Physically compatible for 4 hr at 22 °C	1436	C
Ganciclovir sodium	SY	20 mg/ml[b]	IMM	10 μg/ml[b]	Very small amount of particles formed in 4 hr in one of two samples	1436	I
Gentamicin sulfate	SO	5 mg/ml[a]	IMM	10 μg/ml[b]	Physically compatible for 4 hr at 22 °C	1436	C
Granisetron HCl	SKB	0.05 mg/ml[a]	IMM	10 μg/ml[b]	Physically compatible with no change in measured turbidity or increase in particle content in 4 hr at 23 °C	2000	C
Haloperidol lactate	LY	0.2 mg/ml[b]	IMM	10 μg/ml[b]	Small particles formed in 4 hr in one of two samples	1436	I
Heparin sodium	WY	100 units/ml[b]	IMM	10 μg/ml[b]	Physically compatible for 4 hr at 22 °C	1436	C
	ES	100 units/ml[d]	IMM	6[b,e] and 15[b] μg/ml	Visually compatible for 2 hr	1618	C
Hydrocortisone sodium phosphate	MSD	1 mg/ml[b]	IMM	10 μg/ml[b]	Filament formed in 4 hr in one of two samples	1436	I
Hydrocortisone sodium succinate	UP	1 mg/ml[b]	IMM	10 μg/ml[b]	Few small particles in 1 hr	1436	I
Hydromorphone HCl	WI	0.5 mg/ml[b]	IMM	10 μg/ml[b]	Few small particles in 30 min	1436	I
Hydroxyzine HCl	ES	4 mg/ml[b]	IMM	10 μg/ml[b]	Slight haze, visible with high intensity light, and small flake-like particles formed in 4 hr in one of two samples	1436	I

Y-Site Injection Compatibility (1:1 Mixture) (Cont.)

Drug	*Mfr*	*Conc*	*Mfr*	*Conc*	*Remarks*	*Ref*	*C/I*
			Sargramostim				
Idarubicin HCl	AD	0.5 mg/ml[b]	IMM	10 µg/ml[b]	Increase in measured turbidity no greater than dilution of idarubicin with sodium chloride 0.9%	1675	C
Ifosfamide	MJ	25 mg/ml[b]	IMM	10 µg/ml[b]	Physically compatible for 4 hr at 22 °C	1436	C
Imipenem–cilastatin sodium	MSD	5 mg/ml[b]	IMM	10 µg/ml[b]	Large particle and fibrous clump form in 4 hr	1436	I
Immune globulin intravenous	CU	50 mg/ml	IMM	6[b,e] and 15[b] µg/ml	Visually compatible for 2 hr	1618	C
Lorazepam	WY	0.1 mg/ml[b]	IMM	10 µg/ml[b]	Slightly bluish haze, visible with high intensity light, forms in 1 hr	1436	I
Magnesium sulfate	LY	100 mg/ml[b]	IMM	10 µg/ml[b]	Physically compatible for 4 hr at 22 °C	1436	C
Mannitol	BA	15%	IMM	10 µg/ml[b]	Physically compatible for 4 hr at 22 °C	1436	C
Mechlorethamine HCl	MSD	1 mg/ml	IMM	10 µg/ml[b]	Physically compatible for 4 hr at 22 °C	1436	C
Meperidine HCl	WI	4 mg/ml[b]	IMM	10 µg/ml[b]	Physically compatible for 4 hr at 22 °C	1436	C
Mesna	MJ	10 mg/ml[b]	IMM	10 µg/ml[b]	Physically compatible for 4 hr at 22 °C	1436	C
Methotrexate sodium	CET	15 mg/ml[b]	IMM	10 µg/ml[b]	Physically compatible for 4 hr at 22 °C	1436	C
Methylprednisolone sodium succinate	UP	5 mg/ml[b]	IMM	10 µg/ml[b]	Small amounts of particles and filaments form in 4 hr	1436	I
Metoclopramide HCl	DU	5 mg/ml[b]	IMM	10 µg/ml[b]	Physically compatible for 4 hr at 22 °C	1436	C
Metronidazole	MG	5 mg/ml	IMM	10 µg/ml[b]	Physically compatible for 4 hr at 22 °C	1436	C
Minocycline HCl	LE	0.2 mg/ml[b]	IMM	10 µg/ml[b]	Physically compatible for 4 hr at 22 °C	1436	C
Mitomycin	BR	0.5 mg/ml	IMM	10 µg/ml[b]	Slight haze, visible with high intensity light, forms in 30 min	1436	I
Mitoxantrone HCl	LE	0.5 mg/ml[b]	IMM	10 µg/ml[b]	Physically compatible for 4 hr at 22 °C	1436	C
Morphine sulfate	WI	1 mg/ml[b]	IMM	10 µg/ml[b]	Slight haze, visible with high intensity light, and small amount of particles formed in 1 hr in one of two samples	1436	I
Nalbuphine HCl	DU	10 mg/ml	IMM	10 µg/ml[b]	Slight haze, visible with high intensity light, forms in 30 min. Filament formed in 4 hr in one of two samples	1436	I
Netilmicin sulfate	SC	5 mg/ml[b]	IMM	10 µg/ml[b]	Physically compatible for 4 hr at 22 °C	1436	C
Ondansetron HCl	GL	0.5 mg/ml[b]	IMM	10 µg/ml[b]	Filaments form in 30 to 60 min	1436	I
Pentostatin	NCI	0.4 mg/ml[b]	IMM	10 µg/ml[b]	Physically compatible for 4 hr at 22 °C	1436	C
Piperacillin sodium	LE	40 mg/ml[b]	IMM	10 µg/ml[b]	Small amount of particles forms in 4 hr	1436	I
Piperacillin sodium–tazobactam sodium	LE	40 + 5 mg/ml[a]	HO	10 µg/ml[a]	Physically compatible with no change in measured turbidity or increase in particle content in 4 hr at 22 °C	1688	C
Potassium chloride	AB	0.1 mEq/ml[b]	IMM	10 µg/ml[b]	Physically compatible for 4 hr at 22 °C	1436	C
Prochlorperazine edisylate	ES	0.5 mg/ml[b]	IMM	10 µg/ml[b]	Physically compatible for 4 hr at 22 °C	1436	C
Promethazine HCl	ES	2 mg/ml[b]	IMM	10 µg/ml[b]	Physically compatible for 4 hr at 22 °C	1436	C
Ranitidine HCl	GL	2 mg/ml[b]	IMM	10 µg/ml[b]	Physically compatible for 4 hr at 22 °C	1436	C
Sodium bicarbonate	LY	1 mEq/ml	IMM	10 µg/ml[b]	Small amount of particles forms in 4 hr	1436	I
Teniposide	BR	0.1 mg/ml[b]	IMM	10 µg/ml[b]	Physically compatible for 4 hr at 22 °C	1436	C

Y-Site Injection Compatibility (1:1 Mixture) (Cont.)

			Sargramostim				
Drug	*Mfr*	*Conc*	*Mfr*	*Conc*	*Remarks*	*Ref*	*C/I*
Ticarcillin disodium	BE	30 mg/ml[b]	IMM	10 μg/ml[b]	Physically compatible for 4 hr at 22 °C	1436	C
Ticarcillin disodium–clavulanate potassium	BE	31 mg/ml[b]	IMM	10 μg/ml[b]	Physically compatible for 4 hr at 22 °C	1436	C
Tobramycin sulfate	LI	5 mg/ml[b]	IMM	10 μg/ml[b]	Particles and filaments form in 4 hr	1436	I
TPN #133[f]			IMM	10 μg/ml[b]	Physically compatible for 4 hr at 22 °C	1436	C
TPN #181[f]			IMM	6[b,e] and 15[b] μg/ml	Visually compatible for 2 hr	1618	C
Trimethoprim–sulfamethoxazole	ES	0.8 + 4 mg/ml[b]	IMM	10 μg/ml[b]	Physically compatible for 4 hr at 22 °C	1436	C
Vancomycin HCl	LI	10 mg/ml[b]	IMM	10 μg/ml[b]	Physically compatible for 4 hr at 22 °C	1436	C
	LI	20 mg/ml[d]	IMM	15 μg/ml[b]	Visually compatible for 2 hr	1618	C
	LI	20 mg/ml[d]	IMM	6 μg/ml[b,e]	Haze forms within 15 min and increases due to vancomycin incompatibility with albumin human	1618; 1701	I
Vinblastine sulfate	LY	0.12 mg/ml[b]	IMM	10 μg/ml[b]	Physically compatible for 4 hr at 22 °C	1436	C
Vincristine sulfate	LY	0.05 mg/ml[b]	IMM	10 μg/ml[b]	Physically compatible for 4 hr at 22 °C	1436	C
Zidovudine	BW	4 mg/ml[b]	IMM	10 μg/ml[b]	Physically compatible for 4 hr at 22 °C	1436	C

[a]*Tested in dextrose 5% in water.*
[b]*Tested in sodium chloride 0.9%.*
[c]*Sodium carbonate–containing formulation tested.*
[d]*Tested in both dextrose 5% in water and sodium chloride 0.9%.*
[e]*Tested with 0.1% albumin human added.*
[f]*Refer to Appendix I for the composition of parenteral nutrition solutions. TPN indicates a 2-in-1 admixture.*

Additional Compatibility Information

Infusion Solutions — The manufacturer recommends that only sodium chloride 0.9% be used for dilution of sargramostim for infusion. (2) When diluted for infusion, sargramostim is stable for 48 hours at room temperature or under refrigeration. (4) The manufacturer recommends use within six hours due to microbiological concerns. (2; 4)

Sargramostim concentrations below 10 μg/ml require albumin human 0.1% to prevent adsorption. This albumin concentration may be obtained by adding 1 mg of albumin human per 1 ml of solution. For example, 1 ml of albumin human 5% is added to 50 ml of sodium chloride 0.9%. (2)

Other Drugs — The manufacturer recommends that no other medication be added to sargramostim infusions in the absence of compatibility and stability information. (2)

SCOPOLAMINE HYDROBROMIDE (HYOSCINE HYDROBROMIDE) AHFS 12:08.08

Products — Scopolamine hydrobromide is available in 1-ml multiple-dose vials containing 0.4- and 1-mg/ml concentrations. Also present in the products are methylparaben 0.18% and propylparaben 0.02%. Hydrobromic acid may have been used to adjust the pH. (1-1/99; 4)

pH — From 3.5 to 6.5. (1-1/99; 4)

Osmolality — The osmolality of scopolamine hydrobromide 0.5 mg/ml was determined to be 303 mOsm/kg. (1233)

Administration — Scopolamine hydrobromide may be administered subcutaneously, intramuscularly, or intravenously by direct intravenous injection after dilution with sterile water for injection. (4)

Stability — The product should be stored at controlled room temperature and protected from light. (1-1/99) Scopolamine hydrobromide decomposition is primarily due to hydrolysis below pH 3 and to both hydrolysis and inversion about the chiral carbon above pH 3. The minimum rate of decomposition occurs at pH 3.5. (1071)

Compatibility Information

Additive Compatibility

Drug	Mfr	Conc/L	Scopolamine HBr Mfr	Scopolamine HBr Conc/L	Test Soln	Remarks	Ref	C/I
Floxacillin sodium	BE	20 g	BI	2 g[a]	W	Physically compatible for 24 hr at 15 and 30 °C. Precipitate forms in 48 hr at 30 °C. No change at 15 °C in 48 hr	1479	C
Furosemide	HO	1 g	BI	2 g[a]	W	Physically compatible for 72 hr at 15 and 30 °C	1479	C
Meperidine HCl	WI	100 mg		0.43 mg		Physically compatible	3	C
Succinylcholine chloride	AB	2 g		0.43 mg		Physically compatible	3	C

[a]*Present as the butylbromide salt.*

Drugs in Syringe Compatibility

Drug (in syringe)	Mfr	Amt	Scopolamine HBr Mfr	Scopolamine HBr Amt	Remarks	Ref	C/I
Atropine sulfate	ST	0.4 mg/ 1 ml	ST	0.4 mg/ 1 ml	Physically compatible for at least 15 min	326	C
Butorphanol tartrate	BR	4 mg/ 2 ml	ST	0.4 mg/ 1 ml	Physically compatible both macroscopically and microscopically for 30 min at room temperature	566	C
Chlorpromazine HCl	SKF	50 mg/ 2 ml		0.6 mg/ 1.5 ml	Physically compatible for at least 15 min	14	C
	PO	50 mg/ 2 ml	ST	0.4 mg/ 1 ml	Physically compatible for at least 15 min	326	C
Cimetidine HCl	SKF	300 mg/ 2 ml	BW	0.43 mg/ 0.5 ml	Physically compatible for 4 hr at 25 °C	25	C
Diamorphine HCl	MB	10, 25, 50 mg/ 1 ml	EV	60 μg/ 1 ml[a]	Physically compatible and diamorphine potency retained for 24 hr at room temperature	1454	C
	EV	50 and 150 mg/ 1 ml	EV	0.4 mg/ 1 ml	Physically compatible with 7% diamorphine loss in 7 days at room temperature	1455	C
	EV	50 and 150 mg/ 1 ml	BI	20 mg/ 1 ml[b]	Physically compatible with no scopolamine loss and 4% diamorphine loss in 7 days at room temperature	1455	C
Dimenhydrinate	HR	50 mg/ 1 ml	ST	0.4 mg/ 1 ml	Physically compatible for at least 15 min	326	C
	HR	50 mg/ 1 ml		0.6 mg/ 1 ml	Physically compatible	711	C
Diphenhydramine HCl	PD	50 mg/ 1 ml	ST	0.4 mg/ 1 ml	Physically compatible for at least 15 min	326	C
Droperidol	MN	2.5 mg/ 1 ml	ST	0.4 mg/ 1 ml	Physically compatible for at least 15 min	326	C
Fentanyl citrate	MN	100 μg/ 1 ml		0.6 mg/ 1.5 ml	Physically compatible for at least 15 min	14	C
	MN	0.05 mg/ 1 ml	ST	0.4 mg/ 1 ml	Physically compatible for at least 15 min	326	C
Glycopyrrolate	RB	0.2 mg/ 1 ml	ES	0.4 mg/ 1 ml	Physically compatible and pH in stability range for glycopyrrolate for 48 hr at 25 °C	331	C

Drugs in Syringe Compatibility (Cont.)

Scopolamine HBr

Drug (in syringe)	*Mfr*	*Amt*	*Mfr*	*Amt*	*Remarks*	*Ref*	*C/I*
	RB	0.2 mg/ 1 ml	ES	0.8 mg/ 2 ml	Physically compatible and pH in stability range for glycopyrrolate for 48 hr at 25 °C	331	C
	RB	0.4 mg/ 2 ml	ES	0.4 mg/ 1 ml	Physically compatible and pH in stability range for glycopyrrolate for 48 hr at 25 °C	331	C
Hydromorphone HCl	KN	4 mg/ 2 ml	BW	0.43 mg/ 0.5 ml	Physically compatible for 30 min	517	C
Hydroxyzine HCl	PF	100 mg/ 4 ml		0.6 mg/ 1.5 ml	Physically compatible for at least 15 min	14	C
	PF	50 mg/ 1 ml	ST	0.4 mg/ 1 ml	Physically compatible for at least 15 min	326	C
	PF	100 mg/ 2 ml		0.65 mg/ 1 ml	Physically compatible	771	C
	PF	50 mg/ 1 ml		0.65 mg/ 1 ml	Physically compatible	771	C
Meperidine HCl	WY	100 mg/ 1 ml		0.6 mg/ 1.5 ml	Physically compatible for at least 15 min	14	C
	WI	50 mg/ 1 ml	ST	0.4 mg/ 1 ml	Physically compatible for at least 15 min	326	C
Metoclopramide HCl	NO	10 mg/ 2 ml	ST	0.4 mg/ 1 ml	Physically compatible both macroscopically and microscopically for 15 min at room temperature	565	C
Midazolam HCl	RC	5 mg/ 1 ml	BW	0.43 mg/ 0.5 ml	Physically compatible for 4 hr at 25 °C under fluorescent light	1145	C
Morphine HCl	BP	500 mg/ 5 ml	BP	5 mg/ 5 ml	Little or no scopolamine loss by HPLC in 14 days at room temperature or 37 °C. Morphine not tested	1609	C
Morphine sulfate	WY	15 mg/ 1 ml		0.6 mg/ 1.5 ml	Physically compatible for at least 15 min	14	C
	ST	15 mg/ 1 ml	ST	0.4 mg/ 1 ml	Physically compatible for at least 15 min	326	C
	BP	500 mg/ 5 ml	BP	5 mg/ 5 ml	Little or no scopolamine loss by HPLC in 14 days at room temperature or 37 °C. Morphine not tested	1609	C
Nalbuphine HCl	EN	10 mg/ 1 ml	BW	0.86 mg/ 1 ml	Physically compatible for 36 hr at 27 °C	762	C
	EN	5 mg/ 0.5 ml	BW	0.86 mg/ 1 ml	Physically compatible for 36 hr at 27 °C	762	C
	EN	10 mg/ 1 ml	BW	0.43 mg/ 0.5 ml	Physically compatible for 36 hr at 27 °C	762	C
	DU	10 mg/ 1 ml		0.4 mg	Physically compatible for 48 hr	128	C
	DU	20 mg/ 1 ml		0.4 mg	Physically compatible for 48 hr	128	C
Papaveretum	RC[c]	20 mg/ 1 ml	ST	0.4 mg/ 1 ml	Visually compatible for at least 15 min	326	C
Pentazocine lactate	WI	30 mg/ 1 ml		0.6 mg/ 1.5 ml	Physically compatible for at least 15 min	14	C
	WI	30 mg/ 1 ml	ST	0.4 mg/ 1 ml	Physically compatible for at least 15 min	326	C
Pentobarbital sodium	AB	500 mg/ 10 ml		0.13 mg/ 0.26 ml	Physically compatible	55	C

Drugs in Syringe Compatibility (Cont.)

Drug (in syringe)	Mfr	Amt	Scopolamine HBr Mfr	Scopolamine HBr Amt	Remarks	Ref	C/I
	WY	100 mg/2 ml		0.6 mg/1.5 ml	Physically compatible for at least 15 min	14	C
	AB	50 mg/1 ml	ST	0.4 mg/1 ml	Physically compatible for at least 15 min	326	C
Perphenazine	SC	5 mg/1 ml	ST	0.4 mg/1 ml	Physically compatible both macroscopically and microscopically for 30 min at room temperature	566	C
Prochlorperazine edisylate	SKF			0.6 mg/1.5 ml	Physically compatible for at least 15 min	14	C
	PO	5 mg/1 ml	ST	0.4 mg/1 ml	Physically compatible for at least 15 min	326	C
Promazine HCl	WY	50 mg/1 ml	ST	0.4 mg/1 ml	Physically compatible for at least 15 min	326	C
Promethazine HCl	WY	50 mg/2 ml		0.6 mg/1.5 ml	Physically compatible for at least 15 min	14	C
	PO	50 mg/2 ml	ST	0.4 mg/1 ml	Physically compatible for at least 15 min	326	C
Ranitidine HCl	GL	50 mg/2 ml	AB	0.4 mg/1 ml	Physically compatible for 1 hr at 25 °C both macroscopically and microscopically	978	C
	GL	50 mg/5 ml		0.5 mg	Physically compatible for 4 hr at ambient temperature under fluorescent light	1151	C
Sufentanil citrate	JN	50 μg/ml	LY	0.43 mg/ml	Physically compatible with no subvisual haze or particle formation in 24 hr at 23 °C	1711	C
Thiopental sodium	AB	75 mg/3 ml		0.13 mg/0.26 ml	Physically compatible for at least 30 min	21	C
	AB	75 mg/3 ml		0.13 mg/0.26 ml	Physically compatible	55	C

[a]*Diluted with sterile water for injection.*
[b]*Present as the butylbromide salt.*
[c]*The former formulation was tested.*

Y-Site Injection Compatibility (1:1 Mixture)

Drug	Mfr	Conc	Scopolamine HBr Mfr	Scopolamine HBr Conc	Remarks	Ref	C/I
Fentanyl citrate	JN	0.025 mg/ml[a]	LY	0.05 mg/ml[a]	Physically compatible with no change in measured haze or increase in particle content in 48 hr at 22 °C	1706	C
Heparin sodium	UP	1000 units/L[a]	BW	0.86 mg/ml	Physically compatible for at least 4 hr at room temperature by visual and microscopic examination	534	C
Hydrocortisone sodium succinate	UP	10 mg/L[a]	BW	0.86 mg/ml	Physically compatible for at least 4 hr at room temperature by visual and microscopic examination	534	C
Hydromorphone HCl	AST	0.5 mg/ml[a]	LY	0.05 mg/ml[a]	Physically compatible with no change in measured haze or increase in particle content in 48 hr at 22 °C	1706	C
Methadone HCl	LI	1 mg/ml[a]	LY	0.05 mg/ml[a]	Physically compatible with no change in measured haze or increase in particle content in 48 hr at 22 °C	1706	C

Y-Site Injection Compatibility (1:1 Mixture) (Cont.)

			Scopolamine HBr				
Drug	*Mfr*	*Conc*	*Mfr*	*Conc*	*Remarks*	*Ref*	*C/I*
Morphine sulfate	AST	1 mg/ml[a]	LY	0.05 mg/ml[a]	Physically compatible with no change in measured haze or increase in particle content in 48 hr at 22 °C	1706	C
Potassium chloride	AB	40 mEq/L[a]	BW	0.86 mg/ml	Physically compatible for at least 4 hr at room temperature by visual and microscopic examination	534	C
Propofol	ZEN	10 mg/ml	LY	0.4 mg/ml	Physically compatible for 1 hr at 23 °C with no increase in particle content	2066	C
Sufentanil citrate	JN	12.5 μg/ml[b]	LY	0.05 mg/ml[b]	Physically compatible with no subvisual haze or particle formation in 24 hr at 23 °C	1711	C
Vitamin B complex with C	RC	2 ml/L[a]	BW	0.86 mg/ml	Physically compatible for at least 4 hr at room temperature by visual and microscopic examination	534	C

[a]*Tested in dextrose 5% in water.*
[b]*Tested in dextrose 5% in Ringer's injection, lactated, dextrose 5% in Ringer's injection, dextrose 5% in water, Ringer's injection, lactated, and sodium chloride 0.9%.*

Additional Compatibility Information

Other Drugs — Scopolamine hydrobromide is stated to be physically and chemically compatible with buprenorphine HCl (4) and diamorphine HCl. (1442)

Scopolamine hydrobromide is stated to be incompatible with alkalies. (4) A haze forms in one hour when scopolamine hydrobromide is mixed with methohexital sodium. (4)

A mixture of promethazine HCl (Wyeth) 50 mg/2 ml, meperidine HCl (Wyeth) 100 mg/1 ml, and scopolamine hydrobromide 0.6 mg/1.5 ml has been reported to be conditionally compatible when packaged in syringes. The mixture is physically compatible when the order of mixing is as stated above. (14)

SODIUM ACETATE
AHFS 40:08

Products — Sodium acetate is available as a 16.4% solution in 20-, 50-, 100-, and 250-ml vials. Each milliliter of solution contains 2 mEq of sodium acetate in water for injection. Sodium acetate is also available as a 32.8% solution in 50- and 100-ml vials. Each milliliter of solution contains 4 mEq of sodium acetate in water for injection. The pH may have been adjusted with acetic acid. (1-12/98; 29)

pH — From 6 to 7. (1-12/98)

Osmolarity — Sodium acetate injection is very hypertonic and must be diluted for use. The 2-mEq/ml concentration has a calculated osmolarity of 4 mOsm/ml, and the 4-mEq/ml concentration has a calculated osmolarity of 8 mOsm/ml. (1-12/98)

Administration — Sodium acetate is administered by slow intravenous infusion after addition to a larger volume of fluid. It must not be given undiluted. (1-12/98)

Stability — The product should be stored at controlled room temperature and protected from freezing and excessive heat. Discarding the vials four hours after initial entry has been recommended. (1-12/98)

Compatibility Information

Drugs in Syringe Compatibility

			Sodium acetate				
Drug (in syringe)	*Mfr*	*Amt*	*Mfr*	*Amt*	*Remarks*	*Ref*	*C/I*
Cimetidine HCl	SKF	300 mg/ 2 ml		10 mEq/ 5 ml	Physically compatible for 48 hr at room temperature	516	C

Y-Site Injection Compatibility (1:1 Mixture)

			Sodium acetate				
Drug	*Mfr*	*Conc*	*Mfr*	*Conc*	*Remarks*	*Ref*	*C/I*
Enalaprilat	MSD	0.05 mg/ml[b]	LY	0.4 mEq/ml[a]	Physically compatible for 24 hr at room temperature under fluorescent light	1355	C
Esmolol HCl	DCC	10 mg/ml[a]	LY	0.4 mEq/ml[a]	Physically compatible for 24 hr at 22 °C	1169	C
Labetalol HCl	SC	1 mg/ml[a]	LY	0.4 mEq/ml[a]	Physically compatible for 24 hr at 18 °C	1171	C
Ondansetron HCl	GL	0.1 mg/ml[a]		0.1 and 1 mEq/ml[a]	Visually compatible with no increase in 10-, 25-, and 50-μm particles in 4 hr at room temperature	1661	C

[a]*Tested in dextrose 5% in water.*
[b]*Tested in sodium chloride 0.9%.*

SODIUM BICARBONATE
AHFS 40:08

Products — Sodium bicarbonate injections are available from various manufacturers in vials, ampuls, bottles, and disposable syringes as aqueous solutions in concentrations ranging from 4.2% to 8.4%. (1-7/98; 4; 29)

Concentration	Bicarbonate (and Sodium) Concentration	Total Container Content	Osmolarity
8.4%	1 mEq/ml	10 mEq/10 ml 50 mEq/50 ml	2000 mOsm/L
7.5%	0.892 mEq/ml	44.6 mEq/50 ml	1790 mOsm/L
5.0%	0.595 mEq/ml	297.5 mEq/500 ml	1200 mOsm/L
4.2%	0.5 mEq/ml	5 mEq/10 ml	1000 mOsm/L

The osmolality of sodium bicarbonate (Invenex) 1 mEq/ml was determined to be 1555 mOsm/kg by freezing-point depression and 1538 mOsm/kg by vapor pressure. (1071)

The osmolalities of sodium bicarbonate solutions were determined to be 815, 1095, and 1815 mOsm/kg for concentrations of 4.2, 6, and 8.4%, respectively. (1233)

Sodium bicarbonate injection is available in a 5% concentration as a large volume parenteral in 500-ml bottles. The solution provides 0.6 mEq/ml or 297.5 mEq/500 ml of bicarbonate and sodium and also contains 0.9 mg/ml of edetate disodium. It has an osmolarity of about 1190 to 1203 mOsm/L. (4; 29)

Sodium bicarbonate 4% neutralizing additive solution is available in 5-ml vials. Each milliliter of solution provides 0.48 mEq of bicarbonate and sodium. Sodium bicarbonate 4.2% neutralizing additive solution is available in 5-ml vials. Each milliliter of solution provides 0.5 mEq of bicarbonate and sodium. (1-9/98; 4; 29) The sodium bicarbonate-neutralizing additive solutions are used to raise the pH of acidic solutions.

Equivalency—Each 84 mg of sodium bicarbonate provides 1 mEq of sodium and bicarbonate ions. Each gram of sodium bicarbonate provides about 12 mEq of sodium and bicarbonate ions. (4)

pH—From 7 to 8.5. (4)

Administration — Sodium bicarbonate is administered intravenously, either undiluted or diluted in other fluids. It may also be given subcutaneously if diluted to isotonicity (1.5%). (4)

Stability — Sodium bicarbonate injection should be stored at controlled room temperature and protected from freezing and excessive temperatures of 40 °C or above. Do not use a solution that is unclear or that contains a precipitate. (4)

Combining sodium bicarbonate with acids in aqueous solutions results in the liberation of carbon dioxide gas. The bubbles can be evolved in sufficient quantity to cause effervescence. (4)

The stability of sodium bicarbonate 7.5% in polypropylene syringes is inversely related to the storage temperature. (136) Estimates of room temperature stability range from one week (137) to one month. (136) Refrigeration may increase the stability to 60 (137) to 90 days. (136) Stability may also be increased by refrigerating the sodium bicarbonate injection and the syringes before preparation, rinsing the syringes twice with refrigerated sterile water for injection, minimizing the contact of the solution with the air by expelling the air from the syringes, and taping the plunger in place to minimize its movement from escaping carbon dioxide. (137)

Compatibility Information

Solution Compatibility

Sodium bicarbonate

Solution	*Mfr*	*Mfr*	*Conc/L*	*Remarks*	*Ref*	*C/I*
Alcohol 5%, dextrose 5%	AB		3.75 g	Color change	3	I
Dextran 6% in dextrose 5%	AB		3.75 g	Physically compatible	3	C
Dextran 6% in sodium chloride 0.9%	AB		3.75 g	Physically compatible	3	C
Dextrose–Ringer's injection combinations	AB		3.75 g	Physically compatible	3	C
Dextrose–Ringer's injection, lactated, combinations	AB		3.75 g	Physically compatible	3	C
Dextrose 5% in Ringer's injection, lactated	AB	AB	80 mEq	Physically incompatible	15	I
Dextrose–saline combinations	AB		3.75 g	Physically compatible	3	C
Dextrose 5% in sodium chloride 0.9%	TR[a]	AB	4 g	Potency retained for 24 hr at 5 °C	282	C
Dextrose 2½% in water	AB		3.75 g	Physically compatible	3	C
Dextrose 5% in water	AB		3.75 g	Physically compatible	3	C
	TR[a]	AB	4 g	Potency retained for 24 hr at 5 °C	282	C
Dextrose 10% in water	AB		3.75 g	Physically compatible	3	C
Fat emulsion 10%, intravenous	VT	BR	7.5 g	Physically compatible for 48 hr at 4 °C and room temperature	32	C
	VT		3.4 g	Microscopic globule coalescence in 24 hr at 8 and 25 °C	825	I
Fructose 10% in sodium chloride 0.9%	AB		3.75 g	Physically compatible	3	C
Fructose 10% in water	AB		3.75 g	Physically compatible	3	C
Invert sugar 5 and 10% in sodium chloride 0.9%	AB		3.75 g	Physically compatible	3	C
Invert sugar 5 and 10% in water	AB		3.75 g	Physically compatible	3	C
Ionosol products	AB		3.75 g	Physically compatible	3	C
Ringer's injection	AB		3.75 g	Physically compatible	3	C
				Physically incompatible	9	I
Ringer's injection, lactated	AB		3.75 g	Physically compatible	3	C
				Physically incompatible	9	I
	AB	AB	80 mEq	Physically incompatible	15	I
Sodium chloride 0.45%	AB		3.75 g	Physically compatible	3	C
Sodium chloride 0.9%	AB		3.75 g	Physically compatible	3	C
	TR[a]	AB	4 g	Potency retained for 24 hr at 5 °C	282	C
Sodium lactate ⅙ M	AB		3.75 g	Physically compatible	3	C
				Physically incompatible	9	I
TNA #66 to #68[b]			50 and 150 mEq	Physically compatible with 10% or less carbon dioxide loss and unchanged pH in 7 days at 25 °C protected from light	1011	C
TPN #62 to #65[b]			50 and 150 mEq	Physically compatible with 10% or less carbon dioxide loss and unchanged pH in 7 days at 25 °C protected from light	1011	C

[a] *Tested in both glass and PVC containers.*
[b] *Refer to Appendix I for the composition of parenteral nutrition solutions. TNA indicates a 3-in-1 admixture, and TPN indicates a 2-in-1 admixture.*

Additive Compatibility

Sodium bicarbonate

Drug	Mfr	Conc/L	Mfr	Conc/L	Test Soln	Remarks	Ref	C/I
Amikacin sulfate	BR	5 g	BR	15 g	D5LR, D5R, D5S, D5W, D10W, IS10, LR, NS, R, SL	Physically compatible and potency of both drugs retained for 24 hr at 25 °C	294	C
Aminophylline	SE	1 g	AB	80 mEq	D5W	Physically compatible	15	C
	SE	500 mg	AB	40 mEq		Physically compatible	6	C
		500 mg	AB	2.4 mEq[a]	D5W	Physically compatible for 24 hr	772	C
Amobarbital sodium	LI	500 mg	AB	2.4 mEq[a]	D5W	Physically compatible for 24 hr	772	C
Amoxicillin sodium		10, 20, 50 g		2.74%		9% amoxicillin loss in 6 and 4 hr at 10 and 20 g/L, respectively, and 15% loss in 4 hr at 50 g/L at 25 °C	1469	I
		10, 20, 50 g		8.4%		10 and 13% amoxicillin loss in 4 hr at 10 and 20 g/L, respectively, and 17% loss in 3 hr at 50 g/L at 25 °C	1469	I
Amphotericin B	SQ	50 mg	AB	2.4 mEq[a]	D5W	Physically compatible for 24 hr	772	C
Ampicillin sodium	BR	500 mg	AB	2.4 mEq[a]	D5W	Physically compatible for 24 hr. Ampicillin instability is determining factor	772	?
Ascorbic acid injection	UP	500 mg	AB	80 mEq	D5W	Physically incompatible	15	I
Atropine sulfate		0.4 mg	AB	2.4 mEq[a]	D5W	Physically compatible for 24 hr	772	C
Bretylium tosylate	ACC	10 g	MG	5%		Physically compatible and chemically stable for 48 hr at room temperature and 7 days at 4 °C	541	C
Calcium chloride		1 g	AB	2.4 mEq[a]	D5W	Physically compatible for 24 hr	772	C
Carboplatin		1 g		200 mM		13% carboplatin loss in 24 hr at 27 °C	1379	I
Carmustine	BR	100 mg	AB	100 mEq	D5W, NS	10% carmustine decomposition in 15 min and 27% in 90 min	523	I
Cefoxitin sodium	MSD	1, 2, 10, 20 g	AB	200 mg/g cefoxitin	W	5 to 6% cefoxitin decomposition in 24 hr and 11 to 12% in 48 hr at 25 °C. 2 to 3% decomposition in 7 days at 5 °C	308	C
Ceftazidime	GL[i]	20 g		4.2%		3% ceftazidime loss in 6 hr and 11% in 24 hr at 25 °C. 1% loss in 24 hr and 3% in 48 hr at 4 °C	1136	C
Chloramphenicol sodium succinate	PD	10 g	AB	80 mEq	D5W	Physically compatible	15	C
	PD	1 g	AB	80 mEq		Physically compatible	6	C
Chlorothiazide sodium	MSD	500 mg	AB	2.4 mEq[a]	D5W	Physically compatible for 24 hr	772	C
Cimetidine HCl	SKF	1.2 and 5 g	TR	5%		Physically compatible and chemically stable for 1 week at room temperature	549	C
Ciprofloxacin	MI	2 g		[j]	D5W	Physically incompatible	888	I
Cisplatin		50 and 500 mg		5%		Bright gold precipitate forms in 8 to 24 hr at 25 °C	635	I
Clindamycin phosphate	UP	1.2 g		44 mEq	D5S, D5W	Clindamycin stability maintained for 24 hr	101	C

Additive Compatibility (Cont.)

Sodium bicarbonate

Drug	*Mfr*	*Conc/L*	*Mfr*	*Conc/L*	*Test Soln*	*Remarks*	*Ref*	*C/I*
Corticotropin	AR	250 units	AB	80 mEq	D5W	Physically incompatible	15	I
	AR	40 units	AB	2.4 mEq[a]	D5W	Physically compatible for 24 hr	772	C
Cytarabine	UP	200 mg and 1 g	AB	50 mEq	D5W[b]	Physically compatible with no cytarabine loss in 7 days at 8 and 22 °C	748	C
	UP	200 mg	AB	50 mEq	D5¼S[b]	Physically compatible with no cytarabine loss in 7 days at 8 and 22 °C	748	C
Dobutamine HCl	LI	1 g	MG	5%		Cloudy brownish solution with precipitate forms within 3 hr at 25 °C. 18% dobutamine loss with dense precipitate in 24 hr	789	I
	LI	1 g	IX	500 mEq	D5W, NS	White precipitate forms within 6 hr at 21 °C	812	I
Dopamine HCl	AS	800 mg	MG	5%		Color change 5 min after mixing. Also second spot appeared on TLC	79	I
Epinephrine HCl		4 mg	AB	2.4 mEq[a]	D5W	Epinephrine inactivated	772	I
Ergonovine maleate		0.2 mg	AB	2.4 mEq[a]	D5W	Physically compatible for 24 hr	772	C
Erythromycin lactobionate	AB	1 g	AB	3.75 g		Physically compatible. Erythromycin potency retained for 24 hr at 25 °C	20	C
	AB	1 g	AB	2.4 mEq[a]	D5W	Physically compatible for 24 hr	772	C
Esmolol HCl	ACC	10 g	MG[c]	5%		Visually compatible with 5 and 8% esmolol losses by HPLC in 7 days at 4 and 27 °C, respectively. 9 and 4% losses in 24 hr at 40 °C and under intense light, respectively	1831	C
Floxacillin sodium	BE	20 g	IMS	8.4%		Physically compatible for 72 hr at 15 and 30 °C	1479	C
Furosemide	HO	1 g	IMS	8.4%		Physically compatible for 72 hr at 15 and 30 °C	1479	C
Heparin sodium	AB	20,000 units	AB	2.4 mEq[a]	D5W	Physically compatible for 24 hr	772	C
Hyaluronidase	WY	150 units	AB	2.4 mEq[a]	D5W	Physically compatible for 24 hr	772	C
Hydrocortisone sodium phosphate	MSD	100 mg	AB	2.4 mEq[a]	D5W	Physically compatible for 24 hr	772	C
Hydrocortisone sodium succinate	UP	250 mg	AB	2.4 mEq[a]	D5W	Physically compatible for 24 hr	772	C
Hydromorphone HCl						Physically incompatible	9	I
Imipenem–cilastatin sodium	MSD	2.5 g	AB	5%		43% imipenem loss in 3 hr at 25 °C and 52% in 24 hr at 4 °C	1141	I
	MSD	5 g	AB	5%		45% imipenem loss in 3 hr at 25 °C and 50% in 24 hr at 4 °C	1141	I
Isoproterenol HCl	BN	1 mg	AB	2.4 mEq[a]	D5W	Isoproterenol inactivated	772	I
Kanamycin sulfate	BR	4 g	AB	80 mEq	D5W	Physically compatible	15	C
Labetalol HCl	SC	1.25, 2.5, 3.75 g	TR	5%		White precipitate forms within 6 hr after mixing at 4 and 25 °C	757	I
Levorphanol bitartrate	RC					Physically incompatible	9	I
Lidocaine HCl	AST	2 g	AB	40 mEq		Physically compatible	24	C
		1 g	AB	2.4 mEq[a]	D5W	Physically compatible for 24 hr	772	C

Additive Compatibility (Cont.)

Sodium bicarbonate

Drug	*Mfr*	*Conc/L*	*Mfr*	*Conc/L*	*Test Soln*	*Remarks*	*Ref*	*C/I*
Magnesium sulfate						Physically incompatible	9	I
	LI	16 mEq	AB	80 mEq	D5W	Physically incompatible	15	I
Mannitol	AMR	25 g	AB	44.6 mEq	D5LR, D5¼S, D5½S, D5S, D5W, D10W, NS, ½S[d]	Visually compatible for 24 hr at 24 °C	1853; 1973	C
Meperidine HCl	WI					Physically incompatible	9	I
	WI	100 mg	AB	2.4 mEq[a]	D5W	Physically compatible for 24 hr	772	C
Meropenem	ZEN	1 g	BA[f]	5%		10% meropenem loss by HPLC in 4 hr at 24 °C and 18 hr at 4 °C	2089	I[h]
	ZEN	20 g	BA[f]	5%		9 to 10% meropenem loss by HPLC in 3 hr at 24 °C and 18 hr at 4 °C	2089	I[h]
Metaraminol bitartrate	MSD	100 mg	AB	3.75 g		Physically compatible	7	C
	MSD	100 mg	AB	4.8 mEq[e]	D5W	Physically compatible for 24 hr	772	C
Methotrexate sodium	LE	750 mg		50 mEq	D5W	1.4% methotrexate decomposition in 72 hr and 6% in 1 week at 5 °C protected from light. At 23 °C exposed to light, 6% methotrexate decomposition in 72 hr and 15% in 1 week	465	C
Methyldopate HCl	MSD	1 g		50 mEq	D, D–S, S	Physically compatible	23	C
Morphine sulfate						Physically incompatible	9	I
Multivitamins	USV	10 ml	AB	4.8 mEq[e]	D5W	Physically compatible for 24 hr	772	C
Nafcillin sodium	WY	500 mg	AB	40 mEq		Physically compatible	27	C
Nalmefene HCl	OHM	10 mg	AB	5%	[c]	Little or no nalmefene loss by HPLC in 72 hr at 4, 21, and 40 °C	1962	C
Netilmicin sulfate	SC	3 g	TR	5%		Physically compatible and chemically stable for 7 days at 4 and 25 °C	558	C
Nizatidine	LI	0.75, 1.5, 3 g	MG[c]	5%		Visually compatible and nizatidine potency by HPLC retained for 7 days at 4 and 25 °C	1533	C
Norepinephrine bitartrate	WI					Physically incompatible	9	I
	WI	2 mg	AB	80 mEq	D5W	Physically incompatible	15	I
	BN	8 mg	AB	2.4 mEq[a]	D5W	Norepinephrine inactivated	772	I
Ofloxacin	ORT	0.4 and 4 g	BA[f]	5%		Physically compatible with little or no ofloxacin loss by HPLC in 3 days at 24 °C and 14 days at 5 °C	1636	C
Oxacillin sodium	BR	500 mg	AB	2.4 mEq[a]	D5W	Physically compatible for 24 hr	772	C
Oxytocin	PD	5 units	AB	2.4 mEq[a]	D5W	Physically compatible for 24 hr	772	C
Penicillin G potassium		100 million units	AB	2.4 mEq[a]	D5W	Physically compatible for 24 hr	772	C
	SQ	1 million units	AB	3.75 g	D5W	26% penicillin decomposition in 24 hr at 25 °C	47	I

Additive Compatibility (Cont.)

Sodium bicarbonate

Drug	*Mfr*	*Conc/L*	*Mfr*	*Conc/L*	*Test Soln*	*Remarks*	*Ref*	*C/I*
	SQ	1 million units		0.5 and 0.75 g	D5W	Penicillin decomposition at 20 °C due to pH	135	I
	[g]	900,000 units		3.75 g	D5W	26% penicillin decomposition in 24 hr at 25 °C	48	I
Pentazocine lactate	WI	300 mg	AB	80 mEq	D5W	Physically incompatible	15	I
Pentobarbital sodium						Physically incompatible	9	I
	AB	1 g	AB	80 mEq	D5W	Physically incompatible	15	I
	AB	500 mg	AB	2.4 mEq[a]	D5W	Physically compatible for 24 hr	772	C
Phenobarbital sodium		320 mg	AB	2.4 mEq[a]	D5W	Physically compatible for 24 hr	772	C
Phenylephrine HCl	WI	10 mg	AB	2.4 mEq[a]	D5W	Physically compatible for 24 hr	772	C
	WI	20 mg		5%		Potency retained for 24 hr at 25 °C	48	C
Phenytoin sodium	PD	250 mg	AB	2.4 mEq[a]	D5W	Physically compatible for 24 hr	772	C
Phytonadione	MSD	10 mg	AB	2.4 mEq[a]	D5W	Physically compatible for 24 hr	772	C
Potassium chloride		120 mEq	AB	2.4 mEq[a]	D5W	Physically compatible for 24 hr	772	C
Procaine HCl						Physically incompatible	9	I
	WI	1 g	AB	80 mEq	D5W	Physically incompatible	15	I
Prochlorperazine edisylate	SKF	10 mg	AB	2.4 mEq[a]	D5W	Physically compatible for 24 hr	772	C
Promazine HCl	WY	100 mg	AB	2.4 mEq[a]	D5W	Physically compatible for 24 hr	772	C
	WY	1 g	AB	3.75 g	D5W	Physically incompatible	11	I
Streptomycin sulfate						Physically incompatible	9	I
Succinylcholine chloride	AB	1 g	AB	2.4 mEq[a]	D5W	Succinylcholine inactivated	772	I
Thiopental sodium	AB	2.5 g	AB	40 mEq	D5W	Physically compatible	21	C
	AB	1 g	AB	2.4 mEq[a]	D5W	Physically compatible for 24 hr	772	C
Vancomycin HCl	LI					Physically incompatible	9	I
	LI	500 mg	AB	2.4 mEq[a]	D5W	Physically compatible for 24 hr	772	C
Verapamil HCl	KN	80 mg	BR	89.2 mEq	D5W, NS	Physically compatible for 24 hr	764	C
Vitamin B complex with C	LE					Physically incompatible	9	I
	AB	5 ml	AB	80 mEq	D5W	Physically incompatible	15	I

[a]*One vial of Neut added to a liter of admixture.*
[b]*Tested in both glass and PVC containers.*
[c]*Tested in glass containers.*
[d]*Tested in polyolefin containers.*
[e]*Two vials of Neut added to a liter of admixture.*
[f]*Tested in PVC bags.*
[g]*A buffered preparation was specified.*
[h]*Incompatible by conventional standards but may be used in shorter periods of time.*
[i]*Sodium carbonate–containing formulation tested.*
[j]*Final sodium bicarbonate concentration not specified.*

Drugs in Syringe Compatibility

Sodium bicarbonate

Drug (in syringe)	*Mfr*	*Amt*	*Mfr*	*Amt*	*Remarks*	*Ref*	*C/I*
Bupivacaine HCl	AST, WI	0.25, 0.5[a], 0.75%[a]; 20 ml	AB	4%, 0.05 to 0.6 ml	Precipitate forms in 1 to 2 min up to 2 hr at lowest amount of bicarbonate	1724	I

Drugs in Syringe Compatibility (Cont.)

Sodium bicarbonate

Drug (in syringe)	*Mfr*	*Amt*	*Mfr*	*Amt*	*Remarks*	*Ref*	*C/I*
	BEL	0.5%[b], 20 ml		1.4%, 1.5 ml	Little or no epinephrine loss by HPLC in 7 days at room temperature. Bupivacaine not tested	1743	C
	BEL	0.5%[b], 20 ml		4.2 and 8.4%, 1.5 ml	5 to 7% epinephrine loss by HPLC in 7 days at room temperature. Bupivacaine not tested	1743	C
Chlorprocaine HCl	AST	2 and 3%, 20 ml	AST	8.4%, 0.5 and 1 ml	Visually compatible for up to 5 hr at room temperature	1724	C
	AST	2 and 3%, 20 ml	AST	8.4%, 2 ml	Haze forms but clarifies with gentle agitation	1724	?
	AST	2 and 3%, 20 ml	AB	4%, 1 and 2 ml	Visually compatible for up to 5 hr at room temperature	1724	C
	AST	2 and 3%, 20 ml	AB	4%, 4 ml	Haze forms but clarifies with gentle agitation	1724	?
Etidocaine HCl	AST	1 and 1.5%[a], 20 ml	AB	4%, 0.015 to 0.2 ml	Precipitate forms in 1 to 2 min to over 4 hr at lowest amount of bicarbonate	1724	I
Glycopyrrolate	RB	0.2 mg/ 1 ml	AB	75 mg/ 1 ml	Gas evolves	331	I
	RB	0.2 mg/ 1 ml	AB	150 mg/ 2 ml	Gas evolves	331	I
	RB	0.4 mg/ 2 ml	AB	75 mg/ 1 ml	Gas evolves	331	I
Lidocaine HCl	ES	2%[c], 30 ml	ES	3 mEq/ 3 ml	11% lidocaine loss in 1 week and 22% loss in 2 weeks at 25 °C by GC. 28% epinephrine loss by HPLC in 1 week at 25 °C	1712	I
	ES	2%[c], 30 ml	AB	3 mEq/ 3 ml	6% lidocaine loss by GC in 4 weeks at 4 °C. 2% epinephrine loss in 1 week and 12% loss in 3 weeks at 4 °C by HPLC	1712	C
	AST	1%[c], 30 ml	LY	0.1 mEq/ ml	25% epinephrine loss by HPLC in 1 week at room temperature. Lidocaine not tested	1713	I
		0.9%		0.088 mEq/ml	11% lidocaine loss by fluorescence polarization immunoassay in 7 days at room temperature	1723	C
	AST	1 and 1.5%[a], 20 ml	AST	8.4%, 2 ml	Visually compatible for up to 5 hr at room temperature	1724	C
	AST	2%[a], 20 ml	AST	8.4%, 2 ml	Haze forms but clarifies with gentle agitation	1724	?
	AST	1 and 1.5%[a], 20 ml	AB	4%, 4 ml	Visually compatible for up to 5 hr at room temperature	1724	C
	AST	2%[a], 20 ml	AB	4%, 4 ml	Haze forms but clarifies with gentle agitation	1724	?
	BEL	2%[d], 20 ml		1.4 and 8.4%, 1.5 ml	8% epinephrine loss by HPLC in 7 days at room temperature. Lidocaine not tested	1743	C
Mepivacaine HCl	AST, WI	1 and 1.5%, 20 ml	AST	8.4%; 0.5, 1, 2 ml	Precipitate forms within approximately 1 hr	1724	I

Drugs in Syringe Compatibility (Cont.)

Sodium bicarbonate

Drug (in syringe)	*Mfr*	*Amt*	*Mfr*	*Amt*	*Remarks*	*Ref*	*C/I*
	AST, WI	1 and 1.5%, 20 ml	AB	4%; 1, 2, 4 ml	Precipitate forms within approximately 1 hr	1724	I
Metoclopramide HCl	RB	10 mg/ 2 ml	AB	100 mEq/ 100 ml	Incompatible. Do not mix	924	I
	RB	10 mg/ 2 ml	AB	100 mEq/ 100 ml	Gas evolves	1167	I
	RB	160 mg/ 32 ml	AB	100 mEq/ 100 ml	Gas evolves	1167	I
Milrinone lactate	WI	5.25 mg/ 5.25 ml	AB	3.75 g/ 50 ml	Physically compatible with no milrinone loss in 20 min at 23 °C under fluorescent light	1410	C
Pentobarbital sodium	AB	500 mg/ 10 ml		3.75 g/ 50 ml	Physically compatible	55	C
Thiopental sodium	AB	75 mg/ 3 ml		3.75 g/ 50 ml	Physically incompatible	55	I

[a]Tested with and without epinephrine HCl 1:200,000 added.
[b]Tested with epinephrine HCl 1:200,000 added.
[c]Tested with epinephrine HCl 1:100,000 added.
[d]Tested with epinephrine HCl 1:80,000 added.

Y-Site Injection Compatibility (1:1 Mixture)

Sodium bicarbonate

Drug	*Mfr*	*Conc*	*Mfr*	*Conc*	*Remarks*	*Ref*	*C/I*
Acyclovir sodium	BW	5 mg/ml[a]	IX	0.5 mEq/ml[a]	Physically compatible for 4 hr at 25 °C	1157	C
Alatrofloxacin mesylate	PF	1.43 mg/ml[a]	AB	0.13 mEq/ml[a]	Visually and microscopically compatible run through a Y-site over at least 60 min	2235	C
Allopurinol sodium	BW	3 mg/ml[b]	AB	1 mEq/ml	Small and large crystals form in 1 hr	1686	I
Amifostine	USB	10 mg/ml[a]	AST	1 mEq/ml	Physically compatible with no change in measured turbidity or increase in particle content in 4 hr at 23 °C	1845	C
Amiodarone HCl	WY	3 mg/ml[a]	AB	1 mEq/ml	Precipitate forms immediately	1851	I
Amphotericin B cholesteryl sulfate complex	SEQ	0.83 mg/ml[a]	AB	1 mEq/ml	Gross precipitate forms	2117	I
Asparaginase	BEL	120 I.U./ml[a]		1.4%	Visually compatible for 4 hr at room temperature	1788	C
Aztreonam	SQ	40 mg/ml[a]	AB	1 mEq/ml	Physically compatible with no subvisual haze or particle formation in 4 hr at 23 °C	1758	C
Calcium chloride	AB	4 mg/ml[d]	AB	1 mEq/ml	Slight haze or precipitate in 1 hr	1316	I
Cefepime HCl	BMS	20 mg/ml[a]	AB	1 mEq/ml	Physically compatible with no change in measured turbidity or increase in particle content in 4 hr at 22 °C	1689	C
Ceftriaxone sodium	RC	100 mg/ml		1.4%	Visually compatible for 4 hr at room temperature	1788	C
Ciprofloxacin	MI	2 mg/ml[a]	AB	1 mEq/ml	Visually compatible for 24 hr at 24 °C	1655	C
	MI	2 mg/ml[b]	AB	1 mEq/ml	Very fine crystals form in 20 min in NS	1655	I

Y-Site Injection Compatibility (1:1 Mixture) (Cont.)

			Sodium bicarbonate				
Drug	*Mfr*	*Conc*	*Mfr*	*Conc*	*Remarks*	*Ref*	*C/I*
	MI	2 mg/ml[a]	AB	1 mEq/ml	Physically compatible with no change in measured turbidity or increase in particle content in 4 hr at 23 °C	1869	C
	MI	2 mg/ml[a]	AB	0.1 mEq/ml[a]	Subvisual haze forms immediately, becoming a white crystalline precipitate in 4 hr at 23 °C	1869	I
	BAY	1 and 2 mg/ml[a]	AB	1 and 0.75[a] mEq/ml	Physically compatible with no change in measured turbidity or increase in particle content in 4 hr at 23 °C	2065	C
	BAY	1 mg/ml[b]	AB	1 and 0.75[b] mEq/ml	Physically compatible with no change in measured turbidity or increase in particle content in 4 hr at 23 °C	2065	C
	BAY	2 mg/ml[b]	AB	1 and 0.75[b] mEq/ml	Small amount of particles forms immediately, becoming more numerous over 4 hr at 23 °C	2065	I
	BAY	1 and 2 mg/ml[a]	AB	0.5, 0.25, 0.1 mEq/ml[a]	Small amount of particles forms immediately, becoming more numerous over 4 hr at 23 °C	2065	I
	BAY	1 mg/ml[b]	AB	0.5, 0.25, 0.1 mEq/ml[b]	Small amount of particles forms in 1 hr, becoming more numerous over 4 hr at 23 °C	2065	I
	BAY	2 mg/ml[b]	AB	0.5, 0.25, 0.1 mEq/ml[b]	Precipitate forms immediately	2065	I
Cisatracurium besylate	GW	0.1 mg/ml[a]	AB	1 mEq/ml	Physically compatible with no change in measured turbidity or increase in particle content in 4 hr at 23 °C	2074	C
	GW	2 mg/ml[a]	AB	1 mEq/ml	Subvisual light brown discoloration with subvisual haze in 1 hr	2074	I
	GW	5 mg/ml[a]	AB	1 mEq/ml	Subvisual haze forms immediately; subvisual light brown discoloration with turbidity forms in 4 hr	2074	I
Cladribine	ORT	0.015[b] and 0.5[f] mg/ml	AB	1 mEq/ml	Physically compatible with no change in measured turbidity or increase in particle content in 4 hr at 23 °C	1969	C
Cyclophosphamide		20 mg/ml[a]		1.4%	Visually compatible for 4 hr at room temperature	1788	C
Cytarabine	UP	0.6 mg/ml[a]		1.4%	Visually compatible for 4 hr at room temperature	1788	C
Daunorubicin HCl	BEL	0.52 mg/ml[a]		1.4%	Visually compatible for 4 hr at room temperature	1788	C
Dexamethasone sodium phosphate	MSD	4 mg/ml		1.4%	Visually compatible for 4 hr at room temperature	1788	C
Dexchlorpheniramine maleate		5 mg/ml		1.4%	Visually compatible for 4 hr at room temperature	1788	C
Diltiazem HCl	MMD	5 mg/ml	LY	1 mEq/ml	Precipitate forms	1807	I
	MMD	1 mg/ml[b]	LY	1 mEq/ml	Visually compatible	1807	C
	MMD	5 mg/ml	LY	0.05 mEq/ml[a]	Visually compatible	1807	C
Docetaxel	RPR	0.9 mg/ml[a]	AB	1 mEq/ml	Physically compatible with no change in measured turbidity or increase in particle content in 4 hr at 23 °C	2224	C
Doxorubicin HCl	FA	0.4 mg/ml[a]		1.4%	Visually compatible for 2 hr at room temperature	1788	C

Y-Site Injection Compatibility (1:1 Mixture) (Cont.)

Drug	Mfr	Conc	Mfr	Conc	Remarks	Ref	C/I
			Sodium bicarbonate				
Doxorubicin HCl liposome injection	SEQ	0.4 mg/ml[a]	AB	1 mEq/ml	Partial loss of measured natural turbidity	2087	I
Etoposide	BR	0.6 mg/ml[b]		1.4%	Visually compatible for 4 hr at room temperature	1788	C
Etoposide phosphate	BR	5 mg/ml[a]	AB	1 mEq/ml	Physically compatible with no change in measured turbidity or increase in particle content in 4 hr at 23 °C	2218	C
Famotidine	MSD	0.2 mg/ml[a]	AB	1 mEq/ml	Physically compatible for 4 hr at 25 °C	1188	C
Filgrastim	AMG	30 μg/ml[a]	AB	1 mEq/ml	Physically compatible with no change in measured turbidity or increase in particle content in 4 hr at 22 °C	1687	C
Fludarabine phosphate	BX	1 mg/ml[a]	AB	1 mEq/ml	Physically compatible for 4 hr at room temperature under fluorescent light	1439	C
Gatifloxacin	BMS	2 mg/ml[a]	AB	1 mEq/ml	Physically compatible with no change in measured haze or increase in particle content in 4 hr at 23 °C	2234	C
	BMS	2 mg/ml[a]	AB	0.25 mEq/ml[a]	Physically compatible with no change in measured haze or increase in particle content in 4 hr at 23 °C	2234	C
Gemcitabine HCl	LI	10 mg/ml[b]	AB	1 mEq/ml	Physically compatible with no change in measured turbidity or increase in particle content in 4 hr at 23 °C	2226	C
Granisetron HCl	SKB	0.05 mg/ml[a]	AB	1 mEq/ml	Physically compatible with no subvisual haze or particle formation in 4 hr at 23 °C	1804	C
	SKB	1 mg/ml	AB	0.33 mEq/ml[b]	Physically compatible with 8% loss of granisetron by HPLC in 4 hr at 22 °C	1883	C
	SKB	0.05 mg/ml[a]	AB	1 mEq/ml	Physically compatible with no change in measured turbidity or increase in particle content in 4 hr at 23 °C	2000	C
Heparin[g]	CH	500 units/ml[b]		1.4%	Visually compatible for 4 hr at room temperature	1788	C
Heparin sodium with hydrocortisone sodium succinate	RI UP	1000 units + 100 mg/L[h]	BR	75 mg/ml	Physically compatible for at least 4 hr at room temperature by visual and microscopic examination	322	C
Hetastarch in lactated electrolyte injection (Hextend)	AB	6%	AB	1 mEq/ml	Microprecipitation develops rapidly	2339	I
Idarubicin HCl	AD	1 mg/ml[b]	AB	0.09 mEq/ml[a]	Haze forms and color changes immediately. Precipitate forms in 20 min	1525	I
Ifosfamide		36 mg/ml[a]		1.4%	Visually compatible for 4 hr at room temperature	1788	C
Imipenem–cilastatin sodium	MSD	5 mg/ml[a]		1.4%	Pale yellow precipitate forms in 1 hr at room temperature	1788	I
Inamrinone lactate	WB	3 mg/ml[b]	AB	1 mEq/ml	Immediate change from yellow to colorless	992	I
	WI	5 mg/ml	AST	75 mg/ml	Immediate precipitation	1419	I
	WI	2.5 mg/ml[c]	AST	75 mg/ml	Precipitate forms in 10 min	1419	I
Indomethacin sodium trihydrate	MSD	1 mg/ml[b]	AB	0.5 mEq/ml[a]	Visually compatible for 24 hr at 28 °C	1527	C
Insulin, regular (Humulin R)	LI	1 unit/ml[d]	AB	1 mEq/ml	Physically compatible for 3 hr	1316	C

Y-Site Injection Compatibility (1:1 Mixture) (Cont.)

			Sodium bicarbonate				
Drug	*Mfr*	*Conc*	*Mfr*	*Conc*	*Remarks*	*Ref*	*C/I*
Insulin, regular (beef, pork)	LI	1 unit/ml[d]	AB	1 mEq/ml	Physically compatible for 3 hr	1316	C
Leucovorin calcium	LE	10 mg/ml		1.4%	Yellow precipitate forms in 0.5 hr at room temperature	1788	I
Levofloxacin	OMN	5 mg/ml[a]	AB	0.5 mEq/ml	Visually compatible for 4 hr at 24 °C under fluorescent light	2233	C
Linezolid	PHU	2 mg/ml	AB	1 mEq/ml	Physically compatible with no change in measured turbidity or increase in particle content in 4 hr at 23 °C	2264	C
Melphalan HCl	BW	0.1 mg/ml[b]	AB	1 mEq/ml	Physically compatible with no change in measured turbidity or increase in particle content in 3 hr at 22 °C	1557	C
Mesna		1.8 mg/ml[a]		1.4%	Visually compatible for 4 hr at room temperature	1788	C
Methylprednisolone sodium succinate	UP	20 mg/ml		1.4%	Visually compatible for 4 hr at room temperature	1788	C
Midazolam HCl	RC	5 mg/ml		1.4%	White precipitate forms immediately	1788	I
	RC	1 mg/ml[a]	IMS	1 mEq/ml	Haze forms immediately. Precipitate forms in 2 hr	1847	I
Milrinone lactate	SW	0.4 mg/ml[a]	AB	1 mEq/ml	Visually compatible with 4% loss of milrinone by HPLC in 4 hr at 23 °C	2214	C
Morphine sulfate	WY	0.2 mg/ml[d]	AB	1 mEq/ml	Physically compatible for 3 hr	1316	C
Nalbuphine HCl	DU	10 mg/ml		1.4%	Gas evolves	1788	I
Ondansetron HCl	GL	0.32 mg/ml[a]		0.05 mmol/ml[i]	White precipitate forms immediately	1513	I
	GL	0.1 mg/ml[a]		0.1 mEq/ml[a]	Large increase in 10-, 25-, and 50-μm particles. Visible particles in 30 to 60 min at room temperature	1661	I
	GL	2 mg/ml		1.4%	Heavy white precipitate forms immediately	1788	I
Oxacillin sodium	BR	250 mg/ml		1.4%	Gas evolves	1788	I
Paclitaxel	NCI	1.2 mg/ml[a]	LY	1 mEq/ml	Physically compatible with no change in measured turbidity in 4 hr at 22 °C	1556	C
Piperacillin sodium–tazobactam sodium	LE	40 + 5 mg/ml[a]	AB	1 mEq/ml	Physically compatible with no change in measured turbidity or increase in particle content in 4 hr at 22 °C	1688	C
Potassium chloride		40 mEq/L[h]	BR	75 mg/ml	Physically compatible for at least 4 hr at room temperature by visual and microscopic examination	322	C
Propofol	ZEN	10 mg/ml	AB	1 mEq/ml	Physically compatible for 1 hr at 23 °C with no increase in particle content	2066	C
Remifentanil HCl	GW	0.025 and 0.25 mg/ml[b]	AB	1 mEq/ml	Physically compatible with no change in measured turbidity or increase in particle content in 4 hr at 23 °C	2075	C
Sargramostim	IMM	10 μg/ml[b]	LY	1 mEq/ml	Small amount of particles forms in 4 hr	1436	I
Tacrolimus	FUJ	1 mg/ml[b]	AB	1 mEq/ml	Visually compatible for 24 hr at 25 °C	1630	C
Teniposide	BR	0.1 mg/ml[a]	AB	1 mEq/ml	Physically compatible with no subvisual haze or particle formation in 4 hr at 23 °C	1725	C

Y-Site Injection Compatibility (1:1 Mixture) (Cont.)

Drug	Mfr	Conc	Sodium bicarbonate Mfr	Sodium bicarbonate Conc	Remarks	Ref	C/I
Thiotepa	IMM[j]	1 mg/ml[a]	AB	1 mEq/ml	Physically compatible with no change in measured turbidity or increase in particle content in 4 hr at 23 °C	1861	C
TNA #218 to #226[k]			AB	1 mEq/ml	Visually compatible with no precipitate or emulsion damage apparent in 4 hr at 23 °C	2215	C
Tolazoline HCl		0.1 mg/ml[a]	AB	0.5 mEq/ml	Physically compatible for 24 hr at 22 °C	1363	C
TPN #212 and #214[k]			AB	1 mEq/ml	Small amount of hazy subvisual precipitate forms in 1 hr and settles	2109	I
TPN #213 and #215[k]			AB	1 mEq/ml	Physically compatible with no change in measured turbidity or increase in particle content in 4 hr at 23 °C	2109	C
Vancomycin HCl		5 mg/ml[a]		1.4%	Visually compatible for 4 hr at room temperature	1788	C
Verapamil HCl	SE	5 mg/2 ml		88 mEq/L[c]	Crystalline precipitate forms when verapamil injected into infusion line	839	I
Vincristine sulfate	LI	0.1 mg/ml		1.4%	White precipitate forms in 0.5 hr at room temperature	1788	I
Vindesine sulfate	LI	0.1 mg/ml		1.4%	White precipitate forms in 0.5 hr at room temperature	1788	I
Vinorelbine tartrate	BW	1 mg/ml[b]	AB	1 mEq/ml	Tiny particles and light blue haze form immediately, developing into large particles in 4 hr at 22 °C	1558	I
Vitamin B complex with C	RC	2 ml/L[h]	BR	75 mg/ml	Physically compatible for at least 4 hr at room temperature by visual and microscopic examination	322	C

[a]*Tested in dextrose 5% in water.*
[b]*Tested in sodium chloride 0.9%.*
[c]*Tested in sodium chloride 0.45%.*
[d]*Tested in both dextrose 5% in water and sodium chloride 0.9%.*
[e]*Tested in sterile water for injection.*
[f]*Tested in bacteriostatic sodium chloride 0.9% preserved with benzyl alcohol 0.9%.*
[g]*Salt form not specified.*
[h]*Tested in dextrose 5% in water, sodium chloride 0.9%, and Ringer's injection, lactated.*
[i]*Tested in dextrose 5% in water with potassium chloride 0.02 mM/ml.*
[j]*Lyophilized formulation tested.*
[k]*Refer to Appendix I for the composition of parenteral nutrition solutions. TNA indicates a 3-in-1 admixture, and TPN indicates a 2-in-1 admixture.*

Additional Compatibility Information

Infusion Solutions — Raymond and DeGennaro reported the change in pH that occurred when 5 ml of Neut was added to a liter of 10 common infusion solutions. The results were as follows:

Solution	Initial pH	pH after Neut Added	pH Increase
Dextrose 5% in Electrolyte #48	5.0	6.1	1.1
Dextrose 5% in Electrolyte #75	4.7	5.5	0.8
Dextrose 5% in Ringer's injection	4.3	7.3	3.0
Dextrose 5% in Ringer's injection, lactated	5.0	6.2	1.2
Dextrose 5% in water	4.4	7.5	3.1
Dextrose 10% in water	3.9	7.1	3.2
Ringer's injection	5.6	7.5	1.9
Ringer's injection, lactated	6.3	7.4	1.1
Sodium chloride 0.45%	5.6	7.8	2.2
Sodium chloride 0.9%	5.4	7.6	2.2

The observed pH increase persisted over the 24-hour study period. Solutions with a low buffer capacity exhibited pH increases of about two to three pH units. Solutions with a higher buffer capacity showed pH changes of approximately one pH unit. (1129)

Parenteral Nutrition Solutions — Because of the acidity of amino acid injection, the addition of bicarbonate ion may result in the loss of some of this ion as carbon dioxide. Moreover, adding bicarbonate ion to solutions containing calcium or magnesium may result in the precipitation of insoluble carbonates. (189)

Alkali-Labile Drugs — Drugs such as sodium bicarbonate that may raise the pH of an admixture above 6 may cause significant decomposition of isoproterenol HCl and norepinephrine bitartrate. If they are combined, the mixture should be administered immediately after preparation. (59; 77) Also, dopamine HCl is inactivated in alkaline solutions such as sodium bicarbonate 5%. (79)

Amiodarone HCl — The manufacturer states that amiodarone HCl may precipitate if mixed with sodium bicarbonate. (2)

Calcium Salts — The manufacturer recommends avoiding the addition of sodium bicarbonate to infusion solutions that contain calcium unless compatibility has been established. Haze formation or precipitation may result from such combinations. (4)

Sodium bicarbonate (Abbott) in dextrose 5% in water has been reported to be conditionally compatible with calcium chloride (Upjohn) and calcium gluconate (Upjohn). The incompatibility is dependent on the concentration of the additives. Therefore, if attempting to combine sodium bicarbonate with either of these drugs, mix the solution thoroughly and observe it closely for any sign of incompatibility. (15) A white precipitate and turbidity were found in concentrated solutions. (845)

Cefotaxime — Cefotaxime sodium should not be mixed in alkaline solutions such as sodium bicarbonate injection. (4)

Ciprofloxacin — Ciprofloxacin mixed with sodium bicarbonate in lower concentrations has resulted in the formation of a haze and precipitate, while 10-fold higher concentrations of sodium bicarbonate appear to be physically compatible with the same amount of ciprofloxacin. (1869) Although not unprecedented, it is less common for high concentrations of drugs to be compatible while lower concentrations are incompatible. The differing compatibility results have been ascribed to pH dependency of ciprofloxacin solubility. (2012) However, a thorough evaluation of the compatibility of ciprofloxacin with a wide range of sodium bicarbonate concentrations found that incompatibility cannot be predicted by pH of the solutions alone; the solutions were generally in a very narrow pH range (8.0 to 8.3). Because the interaction between ciprofloxacin and sodium bicarbonate appears to be complex and variable, simultaneous administration of these drugs should be avoided. (2065)

Dobutamine HCl — Dobutamine HCl has been stated to be incompatible with alkaline solutions and should not be mixed with sodium bicarbonate 5% or other alkaline solutions. (4)

Methylprednisolone — The compatibility of methylprednisolone sodium succinate (Upjohn) with sodium bicarbonate added to an auxiliary medication infusion unit has been studied. Primary admixtures were prepared by adding sodium bicarbonate 44.6 mEq/L to dextrose 5% in water, dextrose 5% in sodium chloride 0.9%, and Ringer's injection, lactated. Up to 100 ml of the primary admixture was added along with methylprednisolone sodium succinate (Upjohn) to the auxiliary medication infusion unit with the following results (329):

Methylprednisolone Sodium Succinate	Sodium Bicarbonate 44.6 mEq/L Primary Solution	Results
500 mg	D5S, D5W qs 100 ml	Clear solution for 24 hr
500 mg	LR qs 100 ml or added to 100 ml LR	Clear solution for 1 hr
1000 mg	D5W qs 100 ml	Clear solution for 24 hr
1000 mg	D5S qs 100 ml or added to 100 ml D5S	Clear solution for 24 hr
1000 mg	LR qs 100 ml	Clear solution for 1 hr
1000 mg	Added to 100 ml LR	Clear solution for 4 hr
2000 mg	D5S, D5W qs 100 ml	Clear solution for 24 hr
2000 mg	LR qs 100 ml	Clear solution for 30 min
2000 mg	Added to 100 ml LR	Clear solution for 4 hr

Timentin — Ticarcillin disodium–clavulanate potassium (SmithKline Beecham) is stated to be incompatible with sodium bicarbonate. (4)

Other Drugs — Sodium bicarbonate is stated to be incompatible with acids, acidic salts, and many alkaloidal salts. (4)

Other Information

Preparing Isotonic Solutions — An isotonic 1.5% sodium bicarbonate solution may be prepared by diluting the concentrated injections with sterile water for injection in the following amounts:

Sodium Bicarbonate Concentration (%)	Amount of Sodium Bicarbonate Concentrate (ml)	Amount of Sterile Water for Injection (ml)
8.4	1	4.61
7.5	1	4
4.2	1	1.8

SODIUM CHLORIDE
AHFS 40:12

Products — Sodium chloride additive solution is available in various size containers in concentrations of 14.6 and 23.4%. The 14.6% concentration contains sodium chloride 146 mg/ml and provides 2.5 mEq/ml of sodium and chloride ions. The 23.4% concentration contains sodium chloride 234 mg/ml and provides 4 mEq/ml of sodium and chloride ions. (1-6/99; 4; 29)

NOTE: Do not confuse these high concentration additive solutions with other sodium chloride products with lower concentrations.

Sodium chloride 0.45 and 0.9% infusion solutions are available in a variety of sizes from 25 to 1000 ml. The 0.45 and 0.9% concentrations provide 77 and 154 mEq of sodium and chloride per liter, respectively. (4; 29)

pH — From 4.5 to 7. (1-6/99; 4)

Osmolarity — Sodium chloride additive solutions are very hypertonic and must be diluted for use. The osmolarities of the 14.6 and 23.4% concentrations have been calculated to be about 5000 and 8000 mOsm/L, respectively. (4) The osmolality of the 14.6% concentration was determined to be 5370 mOsm/kg by freezing-point depression and 4783 mOsm/kg by vapor pressure. (1071) A 0.9% sodium chloride solution is isotonic, having an osmolarity of 308 mOsm/L. A 0.45% sodium chloride solution is hypotonic, having a calculated osmolarity of 154 mOsm/L. (4)

Administration — Sodium chloride additive solutions of 14.6 and 23.4% are administered by intravenous infusion only after dilution in a larger volume of fluid. When concentrations of 3 or 5% are indicated, these hypertonic solutions should be administered into a large vein, at a rate not exceeding 100 ml/hr. Infiltration should be avoided. (4)

Stability — Sodium chloride additive solution should be stored at controlled room temperature and protected from excessive heat and freezing. (1-6/99; 17)

Elastomeric Reservoir Pumps — Sodium chloride 0.9% (Baxter) 250 ml was filled into Intermate LV 250 (Baxter) elastomeric infusion devices and stored at 5 and 23 °C for 90 days. The solution remained visually compatible with no change in pH and sodium or chloride concentration and less than 0.1% water loss. (1993)

Compatibility Information

Solution Compatibility

Sodium chloride

Solution	*Mfr*	*Mfr*	*Conc/L*	*Remarks*	*Ref*	*C/I*
Dextran 6% in dextrose 5%	AB	AB	200 mEq	Physically compatible	3	C
Dextran 6% in sodium chloride 0.9%	AB	AB	200 mEq	Physically compatible	3	C
Dextrose–Ringer's injection combinations	AB	AB	200 mEq	Physically compatible	3	C
Dextrose–Ringer's injection, lactated, combinations	AB	AB	200 mEq	Physically compatible	3	C
Dextrose–saline combinations	AB	AB	200 mEq	Physically compatible	3	C
Dextrose 2½% in water	AB	AB	200 mEq	Physically compatible	3	C
Dextrose 5% in water	AB	AB	200 mEq	Physically compatible	3	C
Dextrose 10% in water	AB	AB	200 mEq	Physically compatible	3	C
Fat emulsion 10%, intravenous	CU		200 mEq	Globule coalescence with noticeable surface creaming in 4 hr at room temperature. Oil globules noted on surface at 48 hr	656	I
	CU		100 mEq	No significant change in emulsion for 24 hr at room temperature. Significant emulsion globule coalescence noted at 48 hr	656	C
Fructose 10% in sodium chloride 0.9%	AB	AB	200 mEq	Physically compatible	3	C
Fructose 10% in water	AB	AB	200 mEq	Physically compatible	3	C
Invert sugar 5 and 10% in sodium chloride 0.9%	AB	AB	200 mEq	Physically compatible	3	C
Invert sugar 5 and 10% in water	AB	AB	200 mEq	Physically compatible	3	C
Ionosol products	AB	AB	200 mEq	Physically compatible	3	C
Ringer's injection	AB	AB	200 mEq	Physically compatible	3	C
Ringer's injection, lactated	AB	AB	200 mEq	Physically compatible	3	C
Sodium chloride 0.45%	AB	AB	200 mEq	Physically compatible	3	C

Solution Compatibility (Cont.)

Sodium chloride

Solution	*Mfr*	*Mfr*	*Conc/L*	*Remarks*	*Ref*	*C/I*
Sodium chloride 0.9%	AB	AB	200 mEq	Physically compatible	3	C
Sodium lactate ⅙ M	AB	AB	200 mEq	Physically compatible	3	C

Drugs in Syringe Compatibility

Sodium chloride

Drug (in syringe)	*Mfr*	*Amt*	*Mfr*	*Amt*	*Remarks*	*Ref*	*C/I*
Cimetidine HCl	SKF	300 mg/ 2 ml		12.5 mEq/5 ml	Precipitate forms between 36 and 48 hr at room temperature	516	C

Y-Site Injection Compatibility (1:1 Mixture)

Sodium chloride

Drug	*Mfr*	*Conc*	*Mfr*	*Conc*	*Remarks*	*Ref*	*C/I*
Ciprofloxacin	MI	2 mg/ml[a]	AMR	4 mEq/ml	Visually compatible for 2 hr at 25 °C	1628	C

[a]*Tested in dextrose 5% in water.*

Additional Compatibility Information

Mannitol — The addition of sodium chloride to mannitol 20 or 25% may cause precipitation of the mannitol. (4)

SODIUM LACTATE
AHFS 40:08

Products — Sodium lactate additive solution is available in 10-ml vials. (29) Each milliliter of solution contains 5 mEq of sodium lactate. The 10-ml vial contains a total of 50 mEq each of Na^+ and lactate ion (5.6 g of sodium lactate). The pH is adjusted with hydrochloric acid, lactic acid, or sodium hydroxide if necessary. (4)

Sodium lactate ⅙ M (1.9%) infusion solution is available in 500- and 1000-ml containers. It provides 167 mEq of sodium and lactate per liter. (4)

pH — From 6 to 7.3. (4)

Osmolality — Sodium lactate additive solution is very hypertonic and must be diluted for use. The osmolality was determined to be 11,490 mOsm/kg by freezing-point depression and 10,665 mOsm/kg by vapor pressure. (1071)

Sodium lactate ⅙ M (1.9%) is approximately isotonic with a calculated osmolarity of 330 mOsm/L. (4)

Administration — Sodium lactate additive solution is administered by intravenous infusion only after dilution in a larger volume of fluid. A ⅙ M (1.9%) solution may be prepared by diluting 50 mEq of the additive solution to 300 ml with a nonelectrolyte solution or sterile water for injection. Sodium lactate ⅙ M infusion solution does not require dilution prior to use. The rate of infusion should not exceed 300 ml/hr in adults. (4)

Stability — Sodium lactate additive solution should be stored at controlled room temperature and protected from freezing and excessive temperatures of 40 °C or more. (4)

Compatibility Information

Solution Compatibility

Sodium lactate

Solution	*Mfr*	*Mfr*	*Conc/L*	*Remarks*	*Ref*	*C/I*
Dextran 6% in dextrose 5%	AB	AB	200 mEq	Physically compatible	3	C
Dextran 6% in sodium chloride 0.9%	AB	AB	200 mEq	Physically compatible	3	C
Dextrose–Ringer's injection combinations	AB	AB	200 mEq	Physically compatible	3	C
Dextrose–Ringer's injection, lactated, combinations	AB	AB	200 mEq	Physically compatible	3	C
Dextrose–saline combinations	AB	AB	200 mEq	Physically compatible	3	C
Dextrose 2½% in water	AB	AB	200 mEq	Physically compatible	3	C
Dextrose 5% in water	AB	AB	200 mEq	Physically compatible	3	C
Dextrose 10% in water	AB	AB	200 mEq	Physically compatible	3	C
Fructose 10% in sodium chloride 0.9%	AB	AB	200 mEq	Physically compatible	3	C
Fructose 10% in water	AB	AB	200 mEq	Physically compatible	3	C
Invert sugar 5 and 10% in sodium chloride 0.9%	AB	AB	200 mEq	Physically compatible	3	C
Invert sugar 5 and 10% in water	AB	AB	200 mEq	Physically compatible	3	C
Ionosol products	AB	AB	200 mEq	Physically compatible	3	C
Ringer's injection	AB	AB	200 mEq	Physically compatible	3	C
Ringer's injection, lactated	AB	AB	200 mEq	Physically compatible	3	C
Sodium chloride 0.45%	AB	AB	200 mEq	Physically compatible	3	C
Sodium chloride 0.9%	AB	AB	200 mEq	Physically compatible	3	C

Additive Compatibility

Sodium lactate

Drug	*Mfr*	*Conc/L*	*Mfr*	*Conc/L*	*Test Soln*	*Remarks*	*Ref*	*C/I*
Lidocaine HCl	AST	2 g	AB	50 mEq		Physically compatible	24	C
Nafcillin sodium	WY	500 mg	AB	50 mEq		Physically compatible	27	C
Sodium bicarbonate						Physically incompatible	9	I

Drugs in Syringe Compatibility

Sodium lactate

Drug (in syringe)	*Mfr*	*Amt*	*Mfr*	*Amt*	*Remarks*	*Ref*	*C/I*
Cimetidine HCl	SKF	300 mg/ 2 ml		25 mEq/ 5 ml	Physically compatible for 48 hr at room temperature	516	C

SODIUM NITROPRUSSIDE
AHFS 24:08

Products — Sodium nitroprusside (Nitropress) is available in vials containing 50 mg of sodium nitroprusside dihydrate. Reconstitute with 2 to 3 ml of dextrose 5% in water (4) or sterile water for injection (without preservative). (4; 457) Bacteriostatic water for injection should not be used, because preservatives increase the rate of decomposition. (4)

Sodium nitroprusside is also available in 2-ml vials as a 25-mg/ml solution of sodium nitroprusside dihydrate in sterile water for injection. (1-9/98)

For administration, dilute the reconstituted solution or the liquid form in dextrose 5% in water. Sodium nitroprusside 50 mg added to 250, 500, and 1000 ml of dextrose 5% in water results in concentrations of 200, 100, and 50 μg/ml, respectively. The infusion containers should be wrapped in aluminum foil or other opaque material for light protection. It is not necessary to cover the infusion drip chamber or tubing. (1-9/98; 4)

pH — The pH of sodium nitroprusside diluted with dextrose 5% in water is 3.5 to 6. (4)

Osmolality — Sodium nitroprusside 25 mg/ml in sterile water for injection has an osmolality of 214 mOsm/kg. (1689)

Sodium Content — Sodium nitroprusside contains 0.335 mEq of sodium per 50 mg of drug. (846)

Trade Name(s) — Nitropress.

Administration — Sodium nitroprusside is administered only as an intravenous infusion by freshly reconstituting the drug and diluting 50 mg in 250 to 1000 ml of dextrose 5% in water. An infusion pump, microdrip regulator, or similar device should be used to control the flow rate precisely. Extravasation should be avoided. (1-9/98; 4)

Stability — Sodium nitroprusside is a reddish-brown color. Sodium nitroprusside in intact containers should be stored at controlled room temperature and protected from light and heat (1-9/98; 4) and from freezing for the liquid product. (1-9/98)

It was previously stated that solutions of sodium nitroprusside should be discarded four hours after reconstitution. (4; 90) However, numerous studies reported the stability, protected from light, to be from 12 to 24 hours (93; 460; 1296; 1579), to 48 hours (958), to 13 days (95), or even longer. (94; 458; 459; 732) It is now recommended that reconstituted sodium nitroprusside solutions be used within 24 hours when stored adequately protected from light. (4) Similarly, the freshly diluted liquid injection is stated to be stable for 24 hours when protected from light. (1-9/98)

Temperature Effects — Sodium nitroprusside solutions are heat sensitive. Autoclaving a solution of 100 mg/250 ml in dextrose 5% in water at 115 °C for 30 minutes results in decomposition to a pale blue-green precipitate. (458) It has been stated that autoclaving is less deleterious than even moderate exposure to light. (94)

Light Effects — Solutions of sodium nitroprusside exhibit a color variously described as brownish (4), brown (90), brownish-pink (91), light orange (95), and straw. (92) These solutions are highly sensitive to light. Exposure to light causes decomposition, resulting in a highly colored solution of orange (92), dark brown (91), or blue. (4; 90–92) A blue color indicates almost complete degradation. (92)

The rate of decomposition of sodium nitroprusside when exposed to light is dependent on such factors as the wavelength and intensity of light, temperature, infusion fluid, pH, and container material. The amount of loss occurring in the administration tubing can be affected additionally by the nature and thickness of the tubing wall, duration of light exposure, volume of fluid, and flow rate. (1297)

In one study, sodium nitroprusside 0.01% in both water and dextrose 5% in water in glass bottles exhibited 9 to 10% decomposition in two hours and 18 to 20% decomposition in four hours on exposure to fluorescent light. No decomposition was detected in either solution in 24 hours when protected from light. In PVC bags, even greater decomposition occurred on exposure to light. (460)

In another study, 10-mg/ml aqueous solutions of sodium nitroprusside lost 3% in 24 hours on exposure to fluorescent light and 10% in 24 hours when exposed to both fluorescent light and indirect daylight. At a concentration of 200 mg/L in infusion solutions, exposure to bright daylight increased the loss to approximately 15 to 30% in five hours. The rate of breakdown was related to the amount of illumination. When the containers were protected from light by wrapping with foil, no decomposition was observed in infusion solutions for seven days at room temperature and for two years at 10 mg/ml in glass tubes at room temperature or 4 °C. (732)

Davidson and Lyall studied the rate of decomposition of sodium nitroprusside (David Bull Laboratories) 1 mg/ml in dextrose 5% in water when exposed to fluorescent light and natural daylight. The solutions were stored at 23 °C in the burette chambers of an amber light-protective set, a clear colorless set, and a clear set covered with a foil overwrap. With exposure to fluorescent light, losses in the clear burette chamber totaled 11% in 150 minutes and 100% in 24 hours. Both the amber and foil-wrapped clear sets sustained virtually no loss in four hours and about a 3 to 4% loss in 24 hours. Natural daylight caused a more rapid drug loss in the unprotected burette; essentially all drug was lost in 30 to 150 minutes, depending on the daylight intensity. The amber set slowed the degradation rate, but 32% was still lost in two hours with exposure to intense direct sunlight. (1296)

Solutions of sodium nitroprusside should be protected from light by wrapping the container with aluminum foil or some other opaque material. (1-9/98; 4; 90; 91; 1297) The container should be wrapped as soon as practical without delaying therapy. (959) Amber plastic bags, which are often used for light protection, have been stated not to provide sufficient protection for sodium nitroprusside against photodegradation. Only opaque materials should be used. (733)

The effect of the light exposure that sodium nitroprusside infusions receive while flowing through a 3-m long PVC infusion set tubing was evaluated. Sodium nitroprusside infusions in dextrose 5% in water, sodium chloride 0.9%, and Ringer's injection, lactated, were studied for 24 and eight hours at flow rates of 10 and 50 ml/hr, respectively. The delivered amount of sodium nitroprusside was not reduced. (958)

Baaske et al. evaluated the stability of sodium nitroprusside (Roche) 100 μg/ml in dextrose 5% in water when delivered through tubing exposed to normal room light. No degradation occurred in the infusion container wrapped in foil, but concentration differences in the delivered solution of about 2% were noted at each time point sampled over the five-hour study. When the effects of different light sources on a 50-μg/ml solution in dextrose 5% in water were compared, about a 7% loss occurred on exposure to fluorescent light for six hours but a 32% loss occurred in one hour on exposure to direct sunlight. (1131)

Sewell et al. evaluated the stability of sodium nitroprusside (Roche) 0.5 and 1.67 mg/ml in dextrose 5% in water administered by a syringe pump system. In polypropylene syringes (Sherwood Medical) exposed to both artificial light and daylight, sodium nitroprusside losses after 24 hours were 26.0 and 18.7% at 0.5 and 1.67 mg/ml, respectively. The level of free cyanide exceeded 2 μg/ml. The time to 10% decomposition was about four hours. Syringes wrapped in foil exhibited less than a 5% loss in 24 hours. A comparison of the decomposition occurring in the delivery tubing showed that about 10.3 and 3.7% were lost from the 0.5- and 1.67-mg/ml concentrations, respectively, when delivered by pumps at 3 ml/hr through tubing exposed to the light. Wrapping the line with foil prevented any decomposition over the 24-hour study. (1130)

Sodium nitroprusside (Roche) 50 mg/50 ml in dextrose 5% in water exhibited no change in appearance and no loss in potency by HPLC when stored for 24 hours at 25 °C in 60-ml plastic syringes (Becton-Dickinson) wrapped in foil. However, if the syringes were not wrapped in foil for light protection, the solution turned yellow in 12 hours and had 11 and 17% losses in six and 12 hours, respectively. (1579)

Sorption— Sodium nitroprusside (May & Baker) 5 g/L in dextrose 5% in water (Travenol) in PVC bags wrapped in aluminum foil for light protection did not exhibit significant sorption to the plastic during one week of storage at room temperature (15 to 20 °C). (536)

In another study, sodium nitroprusside (May & Baker) 5 g/L in dextrose 5% in water did not exhibit any loss due to sorption during a seven-hour simulated infusion through an infusion set (Travenol) consisting of a cellulose propionate burette chamber and 170 cm of PVC tubing. (606)

The drug was also tested as a simulated infusion over at least one hour by a syringe pump system. A glass syringe on a syringe pump was fitted with 20 cm of polyethylene tubing or 50 cm of Silastic tubing. No loss of drug due to sorption was observed with either tubing. (606)

In addition, a 25-ml aliquot of sodium nitroprusside (May & Baker) 5 g/L in dextrose 5% in water was stored in all-plastic syringes composed of polypropylene barrels and polyethylene plungers for 24 hours at room temperature in the dark. No loss due to sorption was observed. (606)

Baaske et al. noted a 2% loss of sodium nitroprusside (Roche) 50 μg/ml when delivered through administration sets exposed to normal room light. Examination of the HPLC chromatogram showed the loss to be due to photodecomposition. No evidence of any sorption to the plastic was noted. (1131)

Compatibility Information

Solution Compatibility

Sodium nitroprusside

Solution	*Mfr*	*Mfr*	*Conc/L*	*Remarks*	*Ref*	*C/I*
Dextrose 4% in sodium chloride 0.18%	TR		200 mg	No decomposition in 7 days at room temperature in foil-wrapped bottles	732	C
	TR		200 mg	20 to 25% decomposition in 5 hr exposed to bright daylight	732	I
Dextrose 5% in water			100 mg	No decomposition in 24 hr protected from light	460	C
			100 mg	9 to 10% decomposition in 2 hr exposed to light	460	I
	TR		200 mg	No decomposition in 7 days at room temperature in foil-wrapped bottles	732	C
	TR		200 mg	14 to 16% decomposition in 5 hr exposed to bright daylight	732	I
	TR[a]		88 mg	18% loss in 24 hr when bag was hung adjacent to a window exposed to both daylight and fluorescent light	732	I
	TR	RC	165 mg	4% loss in 65 min in bright daylight	732	I
	AB[b]	RC	50 and 100 mg	No decomposition in 48 hr in foil-wrapped bottles and bags at room temperature	958	C
	MG	RC	50 mg	Little or no loss over 6 days at room temperature protected from light	1131	C
	MG	RC	50 mg	10% loss in 7 hr at room temperature exposed to fluorescent light. 32% loss in 1 hr exposed to direct sunlight	1131	I
	BT[c]	DB	100 mg	11% loss in 2.5 hr and 100% in 24 hr at 23 °C under fluorescent light. 100% loss in 0.5 to 2.5 hr in daylight	1296	I
	BT[c]	DB	100 mg	3 to 4% loss in 24 hr at 23 °C protected from light with foil wrapping or amber light-protective set	1296	C
	BT[c]	DB	100 mg	32% loss in 2 hr at 23 °C in intense daylight in amber light-protective set	1296	I
	[d]		200 to 800 mg	Physically compatible with 7% or less loss in 24 hr exposed to light	1412	C

Solution Compatibility (Cont.)

Sodium nitroprusside

Solution	*Mfr*	*Mfr*	*Conc/L*	*Remarks*	*Ref*	*C/I*
	TR[a]	RC	50 and 400 mg	Visually compatible with little or no drug loss in 48 hr at room temperature	1802	C
Ringer's injection, lactated	AB[b]	RC	50 and 100 mg	No decomposition in 48 hr in foil-wrapped bottles and bags at room temperature	958	C
Sodium chloride 0.9%	TR		200 mg	No decomposition in 7 days at room temperature in foil-wrapped bottles	732	C
	TR		200 mg	24 to 28% decomposition in 5 hr exposed to bright daylight	732	I
	TR		289 mg	4% loss in 3 hr exposed to both daylight and fluorescent light	732	I
	TR		206 mg	2% loss in 60 min exposed to both daylight and fluorescent light	732	I
	TR		183 mg	1% loss in 2 hr in fluorescent light only	732	I
	AB[b]	RC	50 and 100 mg	No decomposition in 48 hr in foil-wrapped bottles and bags at room temperature	958	C
	[d]		200 to 800 mg	Physically compatible with 8% or less loss in 24 hr exposed to light	1412	C
	TR[a]	RC	50 and 400 mg	Visually compatible with little or no drug loss in 48 hr at room temperature	1802	C

[a]Tested in PVC containers.
[b]Tested in both glass and PVC containers.
[c]Tested in burette chambers of administration sets.
[d]Tested in glass containers.

Additive Compatibility

Sodium nitroprusside

Drug	*Mfr*	*Conc/L*	*Mfr*	*Conc/L*	*Test Soln*	*Remarks*	*Ref*	*C/I*
Atracurium besylate	BW	500 mg		2 g	D5W	Physically incompatible. Haze, particles, and yellow color form	1694	I
Cimetidine HCl	SKF	3 g	RC	500 mg	D5W	Physically compatible and cimetidine chemically stable for 24 hr at room temperature. Sodium nitroprusside not tested	551	C
Dobutamine HCl with nitroglycerin		2 to 8 g 200 to 800 mg		200 to 800 mg	D5W[a]	Pale pink discoloration with small amount of dark brown precipitate and 11 to 19% nitroprusside loss in 24 hr exposed to light	1412	I
Dobutamine HCl with nitroglycerin		2 to 8 g 200 to 800 mg		200 to 800 mg	NS[a]	Pale pink discoloration with all drugs stable for 24 hr exposed to light. 8% or less loss for any drug in any combination	1412	C
Enalaprilat	MSD	12 mg	ES	1 g	D5W[b]	Visually compatible with little or no enalaprilat loss by HPLC in 24 hr at room temperature protected from light. Sodium nitroprusside not tested	1572	C
Ranitidine HCl	GL	2 g	RC	50 and 400 mg	D5W, NS[b]	Physically compatible with no ranitidine loss in 48 hr at room temperature protected from light. Nitroprusside not tested	1361	C
	GL	50 mg	RC	50 and 400 mg	NS[b]	Physically compatible with no ranitidine loss in 48 hr at room temperature protected from light. Nitroprusside not tested	1361	C

Additive Compatibility (Cont.)

Sodium nitroprusside

Drug	*Mfr*	*Conc/L*	*Mfr*	*Conc/L*	*Test Soln*	*Remarks*	*Ref*	*C/I*
	GL	50 mg	RC	50 and 400 mg	D5W[b]	Physically compatible with 7% or less ranitidine loss in 48 hr protected from light. Nitroprusside not tested	1361	C
	GL	50 mg and 2 g		50 mg and 1 g	D5W, NS	Physically compatible and both drugs chemically stable for 48 hr at room temperature protected from light	1515	C
	GL	50 mg and 2 g		100 mg	D5W	Physically compatible and ranitidine chemically stable by HPLC for 24 hr at 25 °C. Sodium nitroprusside not tested	1515	C
	GL	50 mg and 2 g	RC	50 and 400 mg	D5W[a]	Visually compatible with 5 to 7% ranitidine losses and 8% or less nitroprusside loss by HPLC in 48 hr at room temperature protected from light	1802	C
	GL	50 mg and 2 g	RC	50 and 400 mg	NS[a]	Visually compatible with no loss of either drug by HPLC in 48 hr at room temperature protected from light	1802	C
Verapamil HCl	KN	80 mg	RC	100 mg	D5W, NS	Physically compatible for 24 hr	764	C

[a]*Tested in glass containers.*
[b]*Tested in PVC containers.*

Drugs in Syringe Compatibility

Sodium nitroprusside

Drug (in syringe)	*Mfr*	*Amt*	*Mfr*	*Amt*	*Remarks*	*Ref*	*C/I*
Heparin sodium		2500 units/ 1 ml		60 mg/ 5 ml	Physically compatible for at least 5 min	1053	C

Y-Site Injection Compatibility (1:1 Mixture)

Sodium nitroprusside

Drug	*Mfr*	*Conc*	*Mfr*	*Conc*	*Remarks*	*Ref*	*C/I*
Atracurium besylate	BW	0.5 mg/ml[a]	ES	0.2 mg/ml[a]	Physically compatible for 24 hr at 28 °C	1337	C
Cisatracurium besylate	GW	0.1 mg/ml[a]	AB	2 mg/ml[a]	Physically compatible with no change in measured turbidity or increase in particle content in 4 hr at 23 °C protected from light	2074	C
	GW	2 and 5 mg/ ml[a]	AB	2 mg/ml[a]	White cloudiness forms immediately	2074	I
Diltiazem HCl	MMD	5 mg/ml	AB	0.2 mg/ml[a]	Visually compatible	1807	C
Dobutamine HCl	LI	4 mg/ml[c]	ES	0.4 mg/ml[c]	Physically compatible for 3 hr	1316	C
Dobutamine HCl with dopamine HCl	LI DCC	4 mg/ml[c] 3.2 mg/ml[c]	ES	0.4 mg/ml[c]	Physically compatible for 3 hr	1316	C
Dobutamine HCl with lidocaine HCl	LI AB	4 mg/ml[c] 8 mg/ml[c]	ES	0.4 mg/ml[c]	Physically compatible for 3 hr	1316	C
Dobutamine HCl with nitroglycerin	LI LY	4 mg/ml[c] 0.4 mg/ml[c]	ES	0.4 mg/ml[c]	Physically compatible for 3 hr	1316	C
Dopamine HCl	DCC	3.2 mg/ml[c]	ES	0.4 mg/ml[c]	Physically compatible for 3 hr	1316	C

Y-Site Injection Compatibility (1:1 Mixture) (Cont.)

			Sodium nitroprusside				
Drug	*Mfr*	*Conc*	*Mfr*	*Conc*	*Remarks*	*Ref*	*C/I*
Dopamine HCl with dobutamine HCl	DCC LI	3.2 mg/ml[c] 4 mg/ml[c]	ES	0.4 mg/ml[c]	Physically compatible for 3 hr	1316	C
Dopamine HCl with lidocaine HCl	DCC AB	3.2 mg/ml[c] 8 mg/ml[c]	ES	0.4 mg/ml[c]	Physically compatible for 3 hr	1316	C
Dopamine HCl with nitroglycerin	DCC LY	3.2 mg/ml[c] 0.4 mg/ml[c]	ES	0.4 mg/ml[c]	Physically compatible for 3 hr	1316	C
Enalaprilat	MSD	0.05 mg/ml[b]	LY	0.2 mg/ml[a]	Physically compatible for 24 hr at room temperature under fluorescent light	1355	C
Esmolol HCl	DU	40 mg/ml[a]	RC	0.2 mg/ml[a]	Visually compatible for 24 hr at 23 °C	1877	C
Famotidine	MSD	0.2 mg/ml[a]	ES	0.2 mg/ml[a]	Physically compatible for 4 hr at 25 °C protected from light	1188	C
Haloperidol lactate	MN	5 mg/ml	AB	0.2 mg/ml[d]	Turbidity forms immediately and persists, developing fine precipitate in 24 hr at 21 °C under fluorescent light	1523	I
	MN	0.5 mg/ml[a]	AB	0.2 mg/ml[d]	Visually compatible for 24 hr at 21 °C	1523	C
Heparin sodium	TR	50 units/ml	ES	0.2 mg/ml[a]	Visually compatible for 4 hr at 25 °C protected from light	1793	C
	OR	100 units/ml[a]	RC	0.2 mg/ml[a]	Visually compatible for 24 hr at 23 °C	1877	C
Hetastarch in lactated electrolyte injection (Hextend)	AB	6%	OH	2 mg/ml[a]	Physically compatible with no change in measured turbidity or increase in particle content in 4 hr at 23 °C protected from light	2339	C
Inamrinone lactate	WB	3 mg/ml[b]	AB	0.2 mg/ml[a]	Physically compatible for at least 4 hr at 25 °C under fluorescent light	992	C
Indomethacin sodium trihydrate	MSD	1 mg/ml[b]	AB	0.2 mg/ml[a]	Visually compatible for 24 hr at 28 °C	1527	C
Insulin, regular	LI	1 unit/ml[a]	RC	0.2 mg/ml[a]	Visually compatible for 24 hr at 23 °C	1877	C
Labetalol HCl	GL	5 mg/ml	RC	0.2 mg/ml[a]	Visually compatible for 24 hr at 23 °C	1877	C
Levofloxacin	OMN	5 mg/ml[a]	ES	10 mg/ml[b]	Fluffy precipitate forms	2233	I
Lidocaine HCl	AB	8 mg/ml[c]	ES	0.4 mg/ml[c]	Physically compatible for 3 hr	1316	C
Lidocaine HCl with dobutamine HCl	AB LI	8 mg/ml[c] 4 mg/ml[c]	ES	0.4 mg/ml[c]	Physically compatible for 3 hr	1316	C
Lidocaine HCl with dopamine HCl	AB DCC	8 mg/ml[c] 3.2 mg/ml[c]	ES	0.4 mg/ml[c]	Physically compatible for 3 hr	1316	C
Lidocaine HCl with nitroglycerin	AB LY	8 mg/ml[c] 0.4 mg/ml[a]	ES	0.4 mg/ml[c]	Physically compatible for 3 hr	1316	C
Midazolam HCl	RC	1 mg/ml[a]	ES	0.2 mg/ml[a]	Visually compatible for 24 hr at 23 °C	1847	C
	RC	1 mg/ml[a]	RC	0.2 mg/ml[a]	Visually compatible for 24 hr at 23 °C	1877	C
Milrinone lactate	SW	0.4 mg/ml[a]	AB	0.8 mg/ml[a]	Visually compatible with little or no loss of either drug by HPLC in 4 hr at 23 °C protected from light	2214	C
Morphine sulfate	SX	1 mg/ml[a]	RC	0.2 mg/ml[a]	Visually compatible for 24 hr at 23 °C	1877	C
Nitroglycerin	LY	0.4 mg/ml[c]	ES	0.4 mg/ml[c]	Physically compatible for 3 hr	1316	C
Nitroglycerin with dobutamine HCl	LY LI	0.4 mg/ml[c] 4 mg/ml[c]	ES	0.4 mg/ml[c]	Physically compatible for 3 hr	1316	C
Nitroglycerin with dopamine HCl	LY DCC	0.4 mg/ml[c] 3.2 mg/ml[c]	ES	0.4 mg/ml[c]	Physically compatible for 3 hr	1316	C

Y-Site Injection Compatibility (1:1 Mixture) (Cont.)

Sodium nitroprusside

Drug	*Mfr*	*Conc*	*Mfr*	*Conc*	*Remarks*	*Ref*	*C/I*
Nitroglycerin with lidocaine HCl	LY AB	0.4 mg/ml[c] 8 mg/ml[c]	ES	0.4 mg/ml[c]	Physically compatible for 3 hr	1316	C
Pancuronium bromide	ES	0.05 mg/ml[a]	ES	0.2 mg/ml[a]	Physically compatible for 24 hr at 28 °C	1337	C
Propofol	ZEN	10 mg/ml	ES	0.4 mg/ml[a]	Physically compatible for 1 hr at 23 °C with no increase in particle content	2066	C
Tacrolimus	FUJ	1 mg/ml[b]	ES	0.004 mg/ml[a]	Visually compatible for 24 hr at 25 °C	1630	C
Theophylline	TR	4 mg/ml	ES	0.2 mg/ml[a]	Visually compatible for 6 hr at 25 °C protected from light	1793	C
TNA #218 to #226[e]			AB	0.4 mg/ml[a]	Visually compatible with no precipitate or emulsion damage apparent in 4 hr at 23 °C protected from light	2215	C
TPN #212 to #215[e]			AB	0.4 mg/ml[a]	Physically compatible with no change in measured turbidity or increase in particle content in 4 hr at 23 °C protected from light	2109	C
Vecuronium bromide	OR	0.1 mg/ml[a]	ES	0.2 mg/ml[a]	Physically compatible for 24 hr at 28 °C	1337	C

[a] *Tested in dextrose 5% in water.*
[b] *Tested in sodium chloride 0.9%.*
[c] *Tested in both dextrose 5% in water and sodium chloride 0.9%.*
[d] *Tested in sterile water for injection.*
[e] *Refer to Appendix I for the composition of parenteral nutrition solutions. TNA indicates a 3-in-1 admixture, and TPN indicates a 2-in-1 admixture.*

Additional Compatibility Information

Infusion Solutions — Dextrose 5% in water is the recommended infusion solution for admixture. (1-9/98; 4; 90; 91) However, it has been reported that solutions of sodium nitroprusside in either dextrose or saline exposed to light exhibit decomposition similar in rate and degree. The dextrose admixture turns blue more rapidly than the drug in saline solution. (732)

Another study found no decomposition of sodium nitroprusside 50 and 100 mg/L in dextrose 5% in water, sodium chloride 0.9%, and Ringer's injection, lactated, after 48 hours of storage when protected from light. The authors concluded that there was no factual basis for the restriction of sodium nitroprusside infusions to dextrose 5% in water. (958)

Sodium nitroprusside 1 mg/ml in six solutions in PVC bags was evaluated for production of cyanide, produced by sodium nitroprusside degradation from exposure to 300 foot-candles of light for 72 hours. The solutions tested included three nonelectrolyte solutions (dextrose 5% in water, dextrose 10% in water, distilled water) and three electrolyte solutions (sodium chloride 0.9%, Ringer's injection, lactated, Ringer's injection, lactated, with dextrose 5%). Analysis was performed with a cyanide ion-specific electrode. There was no difference in the amount of cyanide produced among the solutions throughout the first 24 hours. However, the electrolyte solutions exhibited statistically significant lower mean cyanide ion concentrations, about 2 to 5 ppm, than the nonelectrolyte solutions (about 7 to 9 ppm). These levels of cyanide are an order of magnitude greater than in light-protected solutions. The authors concluded that electrolyte solutions may be preferable to dextrose 5% in water for sodium nitroprusside administration and that all doses should be prepared as fresh as possible and protected from light. (2023)

Additives and Trace Contaminants — Sodium nitroprusside reacts with even minute quantities of a wide variety of inorganic and organic substances, forming highly colored reaction products (usually blue, green, or dark red). Such solutions should not be used. It is, therefore, recommended that no drug or preservative be added to sodium nitroprusside solutions. (1-9/98; 4)

Dobutamine, Dopamine, Lidocaine, and Nitroglycerin — Dobutamine HCl (Lilly) 4 mg/ml, dopamine HCl (Dupont Critical Care) 3.2 mg/ml, lidocaine HCl (Abbott) 8 mg/ml, nitroglycerin (Lyphomed) 0.4 mg/ml, and sodium nitroprusside (Elkins-Sinn) 0.4 mg/ml, prepared in dextrose 5% in water and sodium chloride 0.9%, were combined in equal quantities in all possible combinations of two, three, four, and five drugs and then evaluated for physical compatibility. No physical incompatibility was observed in any combination within the three-hour study period. (1316)

SODIUM PHOSPHATES
AHFS 40:12

Products — Sodium phosphates additive solution is available in 5-, 15-, and 50-ml vials. Each milliliter contains monobasic sodium phosphate monohydrate 276 mg and dibasic sodium phosphate anhydrous 142 mg. The phosphorus concentration is 3 mmol/ml (93 mg/ml), and the sodium content is 4 mEq/ml (92 mg/ml). (1-9/98)

The additive solution is a concentrate and must be diluted for use. (1-9/98)

pH — Approximately 5.7. (1-9/98)

Osmolarity — Sodium phosphates additive solution is very hypertonic. The osmolarity of sodium phosphates additive solution is calculated to be 12 mOsm/ml. (1-9/98)

Administration — Sodium phosphates additive solution must be diluted and thoroughly mixed in a larger volume of fluid before use (1-9/98).

Stability — Sodium phosphates additive solution should be stored at controlled room temperature. The solution should be inspected for discoloration or particulate matter prior to use and should be used only if it is clear. The injection contains no antibacterial preservative. After the vials have been entered, discard any unused portions. (1-9/98)

Compatibility Information

Y-Site Injection Compatibility (1:1 Mixture)

Sodium phosphates

Drug	*Mfr*	*Conc*	*Mfr*	*Conc*	*Remarks*	*Ref*	*C/I*
Ciprofloxacin	BAY	2 mg/ml[a]	AB	3 mmol/ml	Subvisual microcrystals form in 1 hr at 23 °C	1972	I
	BAY	2 mg/ml[b]	AB	3 mmol/ml	White crystalline precipitate forms immediately	1971; 1972	I
Gatifloxacin	BMS	2 mg/ml[a]	AB	3 mmol/ml	Physically compatible with no change in measured haze or increase in particle content in 4 hr at 23 °C	2234	C
TNA #218 to #226[c]			AB	3 mmol/ml	Damage to emulsion integrity occurs immediately with free oil formation possible	2215	I
TPN #212 to #215[c]			AB	3 mmol/ml	Increased turbidity forms immediately	2109	I

[a]*Tested in dextrose 5% in water.*
[b]*Tested in both sodium chloride 0.9% and 0.45%.*
[c]*Refer to Appendix I for the composition of parenteral nutrition solutions. TNA indicates a 3-in-1 admixture, and TPN indicates a 2-in-1 admixture.*

Additional Compatibility Information

Calcium and Phosphate — Phosphates may be incompatible with metal ions such as magnesium and calcium. A number of studies using potassium phosphate have been performed. For additional information, refer to the potassium phosphate monograph.

UNRECOGNIZED CALCIUM PHOSPHATE PRECIPITATION IN A 3-IN-1 PARENTERAL NUTRITION MIXTURE RESULTED IN PATIENT DEATH.

The potential for the formation of a calcium phosphate precipitate in parenteral nutrition solutions is well studied and documented (1771; 1777), but the information is complex and difficult to apply to the clinical situation. (1770; 1772; 1777) The incorporation of fat emulsion in 3-in-1 parenteral nutrition solutions obscures any precipitate that is present, which has led to substantial debate on the dangers associated with 3-in-1 parenteral nutrition mixtures and when or if the danger to the patient is warranted therapeutically. (1770–1772; 2031–2036) Because such precipitation may be life-threatening to patients (2037; 2291), the Food and Drug Administration issued a Safety Alert containing the following recommendations (1769):

"1. The amounts of phosphorus and of calcium added to the admixture are critical. The solubility of the added calcium should be calculated from the volume at the time the calcium is added. It should not be based upon the final volume.

Some amino acid injections for TPN admixtures contain phosphate ions (as a phosphoric acid buffer). These phosphate ions and the volume at the time the phosphate is added should be considered when calculating the concentration of phosphate additives. Also, when adding calcium and phosphate to an admixture, the phosphate should be added first.

The line should be flushed between the addition of any potentially incompatible components.

2. A lipid emulsion in a three-in-one admixture obscures the presence of a precipitate. Therefore, if a lipid emulsion is needed, either (1) use a two-in-one admixture with the lipid infused separately, or (2) if a three-in-one admixture is medically necessary, then add the calcium before the lipid emulsion and according to the recommendations in number 1 above.

If the amount of calcium or phosphate which must be added is likely to cause a precipitate, some or all of the calcium should be administered separately. Such separate infusions must be properly diluted and slowly infused to avoid serious adverse events related to the calcium.

3. When using an automated compounding device, the above steps should be considered when programming the device. In addition, automated compounders should be maintained and operated according to the manufacturer's recommendations.

   Any printout should be checked against the programmed admixture and weight of components.
4. During the mixing process, pharmacists who mix parenteral nutrition admixtures should periodically agitate the admixture and check for precipitates. Medical or home care personnel who start and monitor these infusions should carefully inspect for the presence of precipitates both before and during infusion. Patients and care givers should be trained to visually inspect for signs of precipitation. They also should be advised to stop the infusion and seek medical assistance if precipitates are noted.
5. A filter should be used when infusing either central or peripheral parenteral nutrition admixtures. At this time, data have not been submitted to document which size filter is most effective in trapping precipitates.

   Standards of practice vary, but the following is suggested: a 1.2-μm air-eliminating filter for lipid-containing admixtures and a 0.22-μm air-eliminating filter for non-lipid-containing admixtures.
6. Parenteral nutrition admixtures should be administered within the following time frames: if stored at room temperature, the infusion should be started within 24 hours after mixing; if stored at refrigerated temperatures, the infusion should be started within 24 hours of rewarming. Because warming parenteral nutrition admixtures may contribute to the formation of precipitates, once administration begins, care should be taken to avoid excessive warming of the admixture.

   Persons administering home care parenteral nutrition admixtures may need to deviate from these time frames. Pharmacists who initially prepare these admixtures should check a reserve sample for precipitates over the duration and under the conditions of storage.
7. If symptoms of acute respiratory distress, pulmonary emboli, or interstitial pneumonitis develop, the infusion should be stopped immediately and thoroughly checked for precipitates. Appropriate medical interventions should be instituted. Home care personnel and patients should immediately seek medical assistance."

Calcium Phosphate Precipitation Fatalities—Hill et al. reported fatal cases of paroxysmal respiratory failure in two previously healthy women receiving peripheral vein parenteral nutrition. The patients experienced sudden cardiopulmonary arrest consistent with pulmonary emboli. The authors used in vitro simulations and an animal model to conclude that unrecognized calcium phosphate precipitation in a 3-in-1 total nutrition admixture caused the fatalities. The precipitation resulted during compounding by introducing calcium and phosphate near to one another in the compounding sequence and prior to complete fluid addition. This resulted in a temporarily high concentration of the drugs and precipitation of calcium phosphate. Observation of the precipitate was obscured by the incorporation of 20% fat emulsion, intravenous into the nutrition mixture. No filter was used during infusion of the fatal nutrition admixtures. (2037)

In a follow-up retrospective review, Shay et al. reported that five patients were identified that had respiratory distress associated with the infusion of the 3-in-1 admixtures at around the same time. Four of these five patients died, although the cause of death could be definitively determined for only two of them. (2291)

Calcium and Phosphate Conditional Compatibility—Calcium salts are conditionally compatible with phosphates in parenteral nutrition solutions. The incompatibility is dependent on a solubility and concentration phenomenon and is not entirely predictable. Precipitation may occur during compounding or at some time after compounding is completed.

NOTE: Some amino acid solutions inherently contain calcium and phosphate, which must be considered in any projection of compatibility. See the Amino Acid Injection monograph, Table 1.

It has been noted that the order of mixing of calcium and phosphate may affect compatibility at elevated concentrations. Addition of phosphate should precede calcium. (313)

Sodium phosphate was used in a study by Henry et al. (608) The maximum concentrations of calcium (as chloride and gluconate) and phosphate that can be maintained without precipitation in a parenteral nutrition solution consisting of FreAmine II 4.25% and dextrose 25% for 24 hours at 30 °C were determined. The results are depicted in Figure 1.

Henry et al. noted that the amino acids in parenteral nutrition solutions form soluble complexes with calcium and phosphate, reducing the available free calcium and phosphate that can form insoluble precipitates. The concentration of calcium available for precipitation is greater with the chloride salt compared to the gluconate salt, at least in part because of differences in dissociation characteristics. This can be seen in Figure 1 by the greater concentration of calcium gluconate that can be mixed with sodium phosphate. (608)

In addition to the concentrations of phosphate and calcium and the salt form of the calcium, Henry et al. noted that the concentration of amino acids and the time and temperature of storage altered the formation of calcium phosphate in parenteral nutrition solutions. As the temperature was increased, the incidence of precipitate formation also increased. This result was attributed, at least in part, to a greater degree of dissociation of the calcium and phosphate complexes and the decreased solubility of calcium phosphate. Therefore, it is possible for a solution to be stored at 4 °C with no precipitation but, on warming to room temperature, a precipitate will form over time. (608)

Poole et al. determined the solubility characteristics of calcium and

Figure 1. ***Maximum solubilities of calcium chloride (○) and calcium gluconate (△) with sodium phosphate in an amino acid 4.25% – dextrose 25% solution at 30 °C***

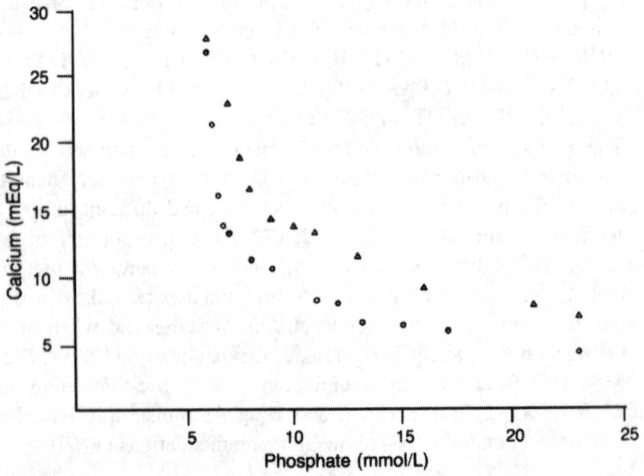

phosphate in pediatric parenteral nutrition solutions composed of Aminosyn 0.5, 2, and 4% with dextrose 10 to 25%. Also present were electrolytes and vitamins. Sodium phosphate was added sequentially in phosphorus concentrations from 10 to 30 mmol/L. Calcium gluconate was added last in amounts ranging from 1 to 10 g/L. The solutions were stored at 25 °C for 30 hours and examined visually and microscopically for precipitation. The authors found that higher concentrations of Aminosyn increased the solubility of calcium and phosphate. Precipitation occurred at lower calcium and phosphate concentrations in the 0.5% solution compared to the 2 and 4% solutions. For example, at a phosphorus concentration of 30 mmol/L, precipitation occurred at calcium gluconate concentrations of about 1, 2, and 4 g/L in the 0.5, 2, and 4% Aminosyn mixtures, respectively. Similarly, at a calcium gluconate concentration of 8 g/L and above, precipitation occurred at phosphorus concentrations of about 13, 17, and 22 mmol/L in the 0.5, 2, and 4% solutions, respectively. The dextrose concentration did not appear to affect the calcium and phosphate solubility significantly. (1042)

Koorenhof and Timmer reported the maximum allowable concentrations of calcium and phosphate in a 3-in-1 parenteral nutrition mixture for children (TNA #192 in Appendix I). Added calcium was varied from 1.5 to 150 mmol/L, while added phosphate was varied from 21 to 300 mmol/L. The mixtures were stable for 48 hours at 22 and 37 °C as long as the pH was not greater than 5.7, the calcium concentration was below 16 mmol/L, the phosphate concentration was below 52 mmol/L, and the product of the calcium and phosphate concentrations was below 250 $mmol^2/L^2$. (1773)

MacKay et al. reported additional calcium and phosphate solubility curves for specialty parenteral nutrition solutions based on NephrAmine and also HepatAmine at concentrations of 0.8, 1.5, and 2% as the sources of amino acids. The solutions also contained dextrose 10%, with cysteine and pH adjustment to simulate addition of fat emulsion used in some admixtures. Calcium and phosphate solubility followed the hyperbolic patterns reported by Eggert et al. (609) Temperature, time, and pH affected calcium and phosphate solubility, with pH having the greatest effect. (2038)

Shatsky et al. reported the maximum sodium phosphate concentrations for given amounts of calcium gluconate that could be admixed in parenteral nutrition solutions containing TrophAmine in varying quantities (with cysteine HCl 40 mg/g of amino acid) and dextrose 10%. The solutions also contained magnesium sulfate 4 mEq/L, potassium acetate 24 mEq/L, sodium chloride 32 mEq/L, pediatric multivitamins, and trace elements. The presence of cysteine HCl reduces the solution pH and increases the amount of calcium and phosphate that can be incorporated before precipitation occurs. The results of this study cannot be safely extrapolated to TPN solutions with compositions other than the ones tested. The admixtures were compounded with the sodium phosphate added last after thorough mixing of all other components. The authors noted this is not the preferred order of mixing (usually phosphate is added first and thoroughly mixed before adding calcium last); however, they believed this reversed order of mixing would provide a margin of error in cases where the proper order is not followed. After compounding, the solutions were stored for 24 hours at 40 °C. The maximum calcium and phosphate amounts that could be mixed in the various solutions were reported tabularly and are shown in Table 1. (2039) However, these results are not entirely consistent with the study of Hoie and Narducci using potassium phosphates. (2196) See Potassium Phosphates monograph.

Fausel et al. evaluated calcium phosphate precipitation phenomena in a series of parenteral nutrition admixtures composed of dextrose 22%, amino acids (FreAmine III) 2.7%, and fat emulsion (Abbott) 0, 1, and 3.2%. Incorporation of calcium gluconate 19 to 24 mEq/L and phosphate (as sodium) 22 to 28 mmol/L resulted in visible precipitation in the fat-free admixtures. New precipitate continued to form over 14 days, even after repeated filtrations of the solutions through 0.2-µm filters. The presence of the amino acids increased calcium and phosphate solubility compared with simple aqueous solutions. However, the incorporation of the fat emulsion did not result in a statistically significant increase in calcium and phosphate solubility. The authors noted that the kinetics of calcium phosphate precipitate formation do not appear to be entirely predictable; both transient and permanent precipitation can occur either during the compounding process or at some time afterward. Because calcium phosphate precipitation can be clinically very dangerous, the use of inline filters was recommended. The filters should have a porosity appropriate to the parenteral nutrition admixture—1.2 µm for fat-containing and 0.2 or 0.45 µm for fat-free nutrition mixtures. (2061)

Table 1. Maximum Amount of Phosphate (as Sodium) (mmol/L) Not Resulting in Precipitation According to the Study of Shatsky et al. (2039) See CAUTION below.[a]

Calcium (as gluconate)	Amino Acid (as TrophAmine) plus Cysteine HCl 40 mg/g of Amino Acid				
	0%	0.4%	1%	2%	3%
9.8 mEq/L	0	27	42	60	66
14.7 mEq/L	0	15	18	30	36
19.6 mEq/L	0	6	15	27	30
29.4 mEq/L	0	3	6	21	24

[a]*CAUTION: The results cannot be safely extrapolated to solutions with formulas other than the ones tested. See text.*

A 2-ml fluid barrier of dextrose 5% in water in a microbore retrograde infusion set failed to prevent precipitation when used between calcium gluconate 200 mg/2 ml and sodium phosphate 0.3 mmol/0.1 ml. (1385)

The presence of magnesium in solutions may also influence the reaction between calcium and phosphate, including the nature and extent of precipitation. (158; 159)

The interaction of calcium and phosphate in parenteral nutrition solutions is a complex phenomenon. Various factors have been identified as playing a role in the solubility or precipitation of a given combination, including (608; 609; 1042; 1063; 1427):

1. Concentration of calcium
2. Salt form of calcium
3. Concentration of phosphate
4. Concentration of amino acids
5. Amino acids composition
6. Concentration of dextrose
7. Temperature of solution
8. pH of solution
9. Presence of other additives
10. Order of mixing

Enhanced precipitate formation would be expected from such factors as high concentrations of calcium and phosphate, increases in solution pH, decreased amino acid concentrations, increases in temperature, addition of calcium prior to phosphate, lengthy standing times or slow infusion rates, and use of calcium as the chloride salt. (854)

Ciprofloxacin — Although ciprofloxacin was reported to be compatible with potassium phosphates (1628), subsequent testing has found that crystalline precipitation forms during simultaneous administration with either potassium or sodium phosphates. (671; 1971; 1972; 2290) See Y-Site Injection Compatibility Table above.

Ciprofloxacin (Bayer) 2 mg/ml in sodium chloride 0.9% or dextrose 5% in water was evaluated for compatibility with potassium phosphates 3 mmol/ml (undiluted) and diluted to 0.06 mg/ml in sodium chloride 0.9% or dextrose 5% in water in simulated simultaneous administration. All samples exhibited transient white precipitate upon first contact that became a crystalline precipitate within an hour. (2290) Precipitation was also reported during clinical administration of a premixed solution of ciprofloxacin 2 mg/ml in dextrose 5% in water (Bayer) with potassium phosphates 0.06 mg/ml in dextrose 5% in water. (671) In addition, the manufacturer has had reports of precipitation of these drugs. (2009) Sodium phosphates 3 mmol/ml was similarly incompatible with ciprofloxacin (Bayer) 2 mg/ml in dextrose 5% in water or sodium chloride 0.9%, resulting in crystalline precipitation. (1971; 1972)

Consequently, ciprofloxacin and phosphates should be considered incompatible across a broad range of phosphate concentrations.

SOMATROPIN
AHFS 68:28

Products — Somatropin derived from *Escherichia coli* is available in vials and cartridges in sizes ranging from 1.5 to 24 mg, depending on the specific product. Each milligram represents about three units of activity. The commercially available dosage forms are variable in components and concentrations; care should be taken to follow the directions for the specific product being used. Most products are supplied in dry form requiring reconstitution using a diluent that is supplied with the product. Manufacturers' specific reconstitution instructions for each product should be followed. For products in vials, the specified amount of the diluent is injected into the somatropin container, aiming the stream at the container wall. The drug is reconstituted by gentle swirling using a rotary motion for most products but vigorous swirling for two minutes for Nutropin Depot. Vial inversion is recommended for reconstitution of Norditropin. Shaking is not recommended for any product and may damage the product. (2)

Norditropin Cartridges and Nutropin AQ are available as liquid injections not requiring dilution for use. (2; 29)

Somatropin derived from mammalian cells (Saizen; Serostim) is available in vials in varying sizes from 4 to 8.8 mg, depending on the specific product. The manufacturer's specific reconstitution instructions for each product using the diluents provided should be followed. The specified amount of the diluent is injected into the somatropin container, aiming the stream at the container wall. The drug is dissolved by gentle swirling using a rotary motion, *not* shaking. Shaking is not recommended for any product and may damage the protein. (2; 29)

pH — The pH values cited by the manufacturers are as follows (2):

Products	pH
Genotropin	about 6.7
Humatrope	about 7.5
Norditropin	about 7.3
Nutropin	about 7.4
Nutropin AQ	about 6.0
Nutropin Depot	5.8 to 7.2
Saizen	6.5 to 8.5
Serostim	7.4 to 8.5

Trade Name(s) — Genotropin, Humatrope, Norditropin, Nutropin, Saizen, Serostim.

Administration — Somatropin products are usually administered by subcutaneous injection. Humatrope and Saizen may also be administered intramuscularly. (2)

Stability — Intact containers of somatropin products derived from *E. coli* should be stored under refrigeration and protected from freezing. Genotropin and Norditropin should also be protected from light during storage. Most somatropin products result in clear solutions when reconstituted correctly. Shaking may result in cloudiness, rendering the products unacceptable for use. Reconstituted Nutropin Depot is a thick, milky suspension. (2)

Stability after reconstitution is variable among the products and depends on whether a preservative-containing diluent is used. See Table 1. Unpreserved reconstituted products of Genotropin and Humatrope should be stored under refrigeration and used within 24 hours. Nutropin Depot suspension should be used immediately upon reconstitution, discarding any unused remainder. Products reconstituted with the specified preserved diluents are stable for longer periods. After reconstitution with the appropriate preserved diluent, Norditropin and Nutropin are stable for 14 days, Genotropin for 21 days, and Humatrope for 28 days stored under refrigeration. Nutropin AQ is stable for 28 days after initial stopper penetration when stored under refrigeration. (2)

Table 1. Recommended Stability Periods for Somatropin Products Using Diluents with and without Preservatives and Stored under Refrigeration (2)

Product	Stability Period
Diluent with Preservative	
Genotropin 5.8 and 13.8 mg	21 days
Humatrope	28 days
Norditropin	14 days
Nutropin	14 days
Nutropin AQ	28 days[a]
Saizen	14 days
Diluent without Preservative	
Genotropin 1.5 mg	24 hr
Humatrope	24 hr
Nutropin Depot	Immediate use only
Serostim	24 hr

[a] *Period after initial penetration of the vial stopper of this liquid product.*

Intact containers of somatropin products derived from mammalian cells should be stored at controlled room temperature. Saizen reconstituted with the preserved diluent provided is stable for 14 days after reconstitution when stored under refrigeration. Serostim reconstituted with the unpreserved diluent provided is stable for 24 hours stored under refrigeration. Freezing of reconstituted solutions should be avoided. (2)

Syringes — Somatropin (Humatrope) was reconstituted to concentrations of 1 and 3.33 mg/ml with the accompanying diluent; the diluent contains glycerin 1.7% and *m*-cresol 0.3% as a preservative. The reconstituted product at each concentration was packaged in 1-ml plastic syringes with barrels composed of polypropylene (Becton-Dickinson) or propylene–ethylene copolymer (Terumo) and capped and stored under refrigeration at about 5 °C for 28 days. HPLC analysis found little or no loss of somatropin stored in either syringe. The solutions remained visually acceptable for 28 days in the polypropylene syringes, but an unacceptable turbidity formed within 21 days in the propylene–ethylene copolymer syringes, which became a precipitate by 28 days. The preservative, *m*-cresol, concentrations fell up to 4% but remained above the minimum acceptable concentration. The authors stated that somatropin should be stored no more than 14 days at 5 °C in propylene–ethylene copolymer syringes. Storage up to 28 days was acceptable in the polypropylene syringes. (2210)

STREPTOKINASE
AHFS 20:40

Products — Streptokinase is available as a lyophilized powder in 6.5-ml vials containing 250,000, 750,000, or 1,500,000 I.U. and in 50-ml infusion bottles containing 1,500,000 I.U. Each vial or infusion bottle of the products also contains cross-linked gelatin polypeptides 25 mg, sodium L-glutamate 25 mg, and albumin human 100 mg as stabilizers with sodium hydroxide to adjust pH. (2)

Reconstitute streptokinase in vials or in the infusion bottles with 5 ml of sodium chloride 0.9% or dextrose 5% in water, directing the diluent against the sides of the vials rather than the drug powder. Roll and tilt the vials gently to effect dissolution; do not shake, to avoid foam formation. The reconstituted solution may be diluted further for administration; the contents of the vials may be diluted up to 500 ml in glass bottles or 50 ml in plastic bags, while the streptokinase infusion bottle may have an additional 40 ml added after reconstitution yielding a total volume of 45 ml. (2)

Units — One International Unit (I.U.) is equivalent to one Christensen Unit, which is the amount of streptokinase that activates sufficient human plasminogen to lyse a standard fibrin clot within 10 minutes in vitro. (4)

pH — The pH of the reconstituted solution is dependent on the diluent used. (4)

Trade Name(s) — Streptase.

Administration — Streptokinase is administered by intravenous, intra-arterial, or intracoronary infusion after dilution with sodium chloride 0.9% or dextrose 5% in water, using a volumetric infusion control device. (2; 4) Reconstituted streptokinase solutions may adversely affect the accuracy of drop-counting infusion devices (both manual and instrument controlled) by altering drop size. Consequently, use of volumetric infusion control devices or syringe pumps is recommended for administration of streptokinase. (4)

To clear an occluded intravenous cannula, streptokinase 250,000 I.U. is administered over 25 to 35 minutes in 2 ml of solution. The drug is infused directly into the cannula, which is then clamped for 2 hours, aspirated, and flushed with sodium chloride solution. (2; 4)

Stability — Streptokinase, a white lyophilized powder, may have a slight yellow color in solution due to the presence of albumin human. (4) Intact vials should be stored at room temperature. Reconstituted solutions should be refrigerated and are stable for 24 hours. (4) However, the manufacturers recommend use within eight hours. (2)

Streptokinase is most stable in solution at pH 6 to 8. Small amounts of flocculation may occur; solutions with large amounts of flocculation should be discarded. Streptokinase may be filtered through a 0.8-μm or larger filter. (2; 4)

Streptokinase flocculation was observed after transfer to 250-ml evacuated glass bottles. The flocculation was delayed in some cases but was always visible within 10 to 15 minutes. Although filtration removed the filaments, more flocculation occurred afterward. The flocculation was attributed to the acetic acid–sodium acetate buffer present in the evacuated glass bottles for glass preservation during sterilization. (1517)

Compatibility Information

Y-Site Injection Compatibility (1:1 Mixture)

Drug	Mfr	Conc	Streptokinase Mfr	Streptokinase Conc	Remarks	Ref	C/I
Dobutamine HCl	LI	2 mg/ml[a]	HO	30,000 units/ml[a]	Physically compatible for at least 48 hr by spectrophotometric and visual examination	1340	C
Dopamine HCl	DU	8 mg/ml[a]	HO	30,000 units/ml[a]	Physically compatible for at least 4 days by visual examination	1340	C

Y-Site Injection Compatibility (1:1 Mixture) (Cont.)

		Streptokinase					
Drug	*Mfr*	*Conc*	*Mfr*	*Conc*	*Remarks*	*Ref*	*C/I*
Heparin sodium	ES	100 units/ml[a]	HO	30,000 units/ml[a]	Physically compatible for at least 5 days by visual examination	1340	C
Lidocaine HCl	AB	8 mg/ml[a]	HO	30,000 units/ml[a]	Physically compatible for at least 3 days by visual examination	1340	C
Nitroglycerin	DU	0.2 mg/ml[a]	HO	30,000 units/ml[a]	Physically compatible for at least 5 days by visual examination	1340	C

[a]*Tested in dextrose 5% in water.*

Additional Compatibility Information

Infusion Solutions — Sodium chloride 0.9% is the preferred diluent for streptokinase, although dextrose 5% in water may be used. Solutions are stable for 24 hours under refrigeration. (4)

Dextrans — Streptokinase is reported to be incompatible with dextrans. (4)

STREPTOMYCIN SULFATE
AHFS 8:12.02

Products — Streptomycin sulfate (Pfizer) is available as a solution in ampuls containing 1 g/2.5 ml (400 mg/ml). Each milliliter also contains sodium citrate dihydrate 12 mg, phenol 0.25% (w/v), and sodium metabisulfite 2 mg in water for injection. (2)

Streptomycin sulfate (Pharma-Tek) is available as a lyophilized powder for injection in vials containing 1 g of drug with no preservatives. Reconstitute with 4.2, 3.2, or 1.8 ml of sterile water for injection to yield solutions containing 200, 250, or 400 mg/ml, respectively. (1-5/99; 4)

pH — The injection from Pfizer has a pH of 5 to 8. (2) The reconstituted Pharma-Tek injection at a concentration of 200 mg/ml has a pH of 4.5 to 7. (1-5/99; 4)

Administration — Streptomycin sulfate is administered by deep intramuscular injection well within the body of a relatively large muscle, such as the upper outer quadrant of the buttock in adults or the midlateral thigh in adults or children. Injection sites should be alternated. (1-5/99; 2; 4) Intravenous injection is not recommended (4), although it has been performed. (1603)

Stability — Intact containers of streptomycin sulfate injection (Pfizer) should be stored under refrigeration at 2 to 8 °C. Intact vials of streptomycin sulfate lyophilized powder (Pharma-Tek) should be stored at controlled room temperature and protected from light. (4)

Reconstituted solutions of streptomycin sulfate are stated to be stable for one week at room temperature and protected from light. However, no preservatives are present and the possibility of microbiological contamination must be considered. (4)

Compatibility Information

Additive Compatibility

			Streptomycin sulfate					
Drug	*Mfr*	*Conc/L*	*Mfr*	*Conc/L*	*Test Soln*	*Remarks*	*Ref*	*C/I*
Amobarbital sodium						Physically incompatible	9	I
Amphotericin B		200 mg	BP	4 g	D5W	Haze develops over 3 hr	26	I
Bleomycin sulfate	BR	20 and 30 units	PF	4 g	NS	Physically compatible and bleomycin activity retained for 1 week at 4 °C. Streptomycin not tested	763	C

Additive Compatibility (Cont.)

Drug	*Mfr*	*Conc/L*	*Mfr*	*Conc/L*	*Test Soln*	*Remarks*	*Ref*	*C/I*
			Streptomycin sulfate					
Chlorothiazide sodium	MSD					Physically incompatible	9	I
Heparin sodium						Physically incompatible	9	I
	AB	20,000 units		1 g		Precipitate forms within 1 hr	21	I
	BP	20,000 units	BP	4 g	D5W, NS	Immediate precipitation	26	I
Methohexital sodium	BP	2 g	BP	4 g	NS	Crystals produced	26	I
Norepinephrine bitartrate	WI					Physically incompatible	9	I
Pentobarbital sodium						Physically incompatible	9	I
Phenobarbital sodium	WI					Physically incompatible	9	I
Phenytoin sodium	PD					Physically incompatible	9	I
Sodium bicarbonate						Physically incompatible	9	I

Drugs in Syringe Compatibility

Drug (in syringe)	*Mfr*	*Amt*	*Mfr*	*Amt*	*Remarks*	*Ref*	*C/I*
			Streptomycin sulfate				
Ampicillin sodium	AY	500 mg		1 g/2 ml	No precipitate or color change within 1 hr at room temperature	99	C
	AY	500 mg	BP	1 g/2 ml	Physically compatible for 1 hr at room temperature	300	C
	AY	500 mg	BP[a]	0.75 g/ 1.5 ml	Precipitate forms within 1 hr at room temperature	300	I
	AY	500 mg	BP	1 g/ 1.5 ml	Syrupy solution forms	300	I
Heparin sodium	AB	20,000 units/ 1 ml		1 g	Physically incompatible	21	I
Penicillin G sodium		1 million units		1 g/2 ml	No precipitate or color change within 1 hr at room temperature	99	C

[a]*Stabilized injection.*

Y-Site Injection Compatibility (1:1 Mixture)

Drug	*Mfr*	*Conc*	*Mfr*	*Conc*	*Remarks*	*Ref*	*C/I*
			Streptomycin sulfate				
Esmolol HCl	DCC	10 mg/ml[a]	PF	10 mg/ml[a]	Physically compatible for 24 hr at 22 °C	1169	C

[a]*Tested in dextrose 5% in water.*

Additional Compatibility Information

Other Drugs — In vitro testing of thiamine HCl, riboflavin-5′-phosphate, pyridoxine HCl, niacinamide, and ascorbic acid individually at concentrations of 0.1% with streptomycin sulfate 0.025% in sterile distilled water showed significant reduction in antibiotic activity in one hour at 25 °C. (314)

Although piperacillin sodium and aminoglycosides act synergistically and have been used successfully clinically when recommended doses of each drug were administered, mixing piperacillin sodium directly in a syringe or infusion bottle with an aminoglycoside can result in substantial inactivation of the aminoglycoside. (740)

STREPTOZOCIN
AHFS 10:00

Products — Streptozocin is available in single-dose vials containing 1 g of drug and 220 mg of citric acid anhydrous. Sodium hydroxide may have been used to adjust the pH. (1-2/99)

Reconstitute with 9.5 ml of sodium chloride 0.9% or dextrose 5% in water to provide a 100-mg/ml solution. (1-2/99; 4)

pH— From 3.5 to 4.5. (2)

Density— Streptozocin (Upjohn) reconstituted with 0.9% sodium chloride injection to a concentration of 100 mg/ml has a solution density of 1.04 g/ml. (2041; 2248)

Trade Name(s)— Zanosar.

Administration — Streptozocin may be administered by rapid intravenous injection or intravenous infusion over 15 minutes to six hours. (1-2/99; 4) Streptozocin has also been administered intra-arterially. (4)

Stability — Intact vials containing a pale yellow powder should be refrigerated and protected from light. (1-2/99; 4)

The pale gold reconstituted solution is stable for 48 hours at room temperature or 96 hours under refrigeration. (4) However, the manufacturer recommends use within 12 hours because the product does not contain an antibacterial preservative. (1-2/99; 4)

Filtration— Streptozocin 10 to 200 µg/ml exhibited no loss due to sorption to either cellulose nitrate/cellulose acetate ester (Millex OR) or Teflon (Millex FG) filters. (1415; 1416)

Compatibility Information

Y-Site Injection Compatibility (1:1 Mixture)

Drug	*Mfr*	*Conc*	Streptozocin *Mfr*	Streptozocin *Conc*	*Remarks*	*Ref*	*C/I*
Allopurinol sodium	BW	3 mg/ml[b]	UP	40 mg/ml[b]	Haze and small particles form in 1 hr and increase in 4 hr	1686	I
Amifostine	USB	10 mg/ml[a]	UP	40 mg/ml[a]	Physically compatible with no change in measured turbidity or increase in particle content in 4 hr at 23 °C	1845	C
Aztreonam	SQ	40 mg/ml[a]	UP	40 mg/ml[a]	Color changes from pale gold to red in 1 hr	1758	I
Cefepime HCl	BMS	20 mg/ml[a]	UP	40 mg/ml[a]	Haze forms immediately and particles form in 1 hr. Deep red color forms in 4 hr	1689	I
Etoposide phosphate	BR	5 mg/ml[a]	UP	40 mg/ml[a]	Physically compatible with no change in measured turbidity or increase in particle content in 4 hr at 23 °C	2218	C
Filgrastim	AMG	30 µg/ml[a]	UP	40 mg/ml[a]	Physically compatible with no change in measured turbidity or increase in particle content in 4 hr at 22 °C	1687	C
Gemcitabine HCl	LI	10 mg/ml[b]	UP	40 mg/ml[b]	Physically compatible with no change in measured turbidity or increase in particle content in 4 hr at 23 °C	2226	C
Granisetron HCl	SKB	1 mg/ml	UP	9.1 mg/ml[b]	Physically compatible with little or no loss of either drug by HPLC in 4 hr at 22 °C	1883	C
Melphalan HCl	BW	0.1 mg/ml[b]	UP	40 mg/ml[b]	Physically compatible with no change in measured turbidity or increase in particle content in 3 hr at 22 °C	1557	C
Ondansetron HCl	GL	1 mg/ml[b]	UP	30 mg/ml[a]	Physically compatible for 4 hr at 22 °C	1365	C
Piperacillin sodium–tazobactam sodium	LE	40 + 5 mg/ml[a]	UP	40 mg/ml[a]	Particles form in 1 hr	1688	I
Teniposide	BR	0.1 mg/ml[a]	UP	40 mg/ml[a]	Physically compatible with no subvisual haze or particle formation in 4 hr at 23 °C	1725	C

Y-Site Injection Compatibility (1:1 Mixture) (Cont.)

Streptozocin

Drug	*Mfr*	*Conc*	*Mfr*	*Conc*	*Remarks*	*Ref*	*C/I*
Thiotepa	IMM[c]	1 mg/ml[a]	UP	40 mg/ml[a]	Physically compatible with no change in measured turbidity or increase in particle content in 4 hr at 23 °C	1861	C
Vinorelbine tartrate	BW	1 mg/ml[b]	UP	40 mg/ml[b]	Physically compatible with no change in measured turbidity or increase in particle content in 4 hr at 22 °C	1558	C

[a] *Tested in dextrose 5% in water.*
[b] *Tested in sodium chloride 0.9%.*
[c] *Lyophilized formulation tested.*

Additional Compatibility Information

Infusion Solutions — Dextrose 5% in water and sodium chloride 0.9% are recommended for dilution of streptozocin for infusion. (1-2/99) In these solutions, streptozocin 2 mg/ml is stable for at least 48 hours at room temperature or 96 hours under refrigeration. (4) The manufacturer recommends use within 12 hours, however, because the product does not contain an antibacterial preservative. (1-2/99; 4)

SUCCINYLCHOLINE CHLORIDE
AHFS 12:20

Products — Succinylcholine chloride is available in a concentration of 20 mg/ml in 5- and 10-ml multiple-dose vials and 5-ml syringes. The vials are preserved with parabens or benzyl alcohol and may contain sodium chloride for isotonicity and hydrochloric acid for pH adjustment. Succinylcholine chloride is also available in higher concentrations of 50 mg/ml in 10-ml ampuls and 100 mg/ml in 10-ml single-dose vials. (2; 4; 29; 154)

pH — From 3 to 4.5. (4) The pH of Anectine is adjusted to 3.5. (2)

Osmolality — The osmolality of succinylcholine chloride 50 mg/ml was determined to be 409 mOsm/kg. (1233)

Trade Name(s) — Anectine, Quelicin.

Administration — Succinylcholine chloride is usually administered by direct intermittent intravenous injection or intravenous infusion. For continuous intravenous infusion, a 1- to 2-mg/ml (0.1 to 0.2%) solution is prepared, usually in 250 to 1000 ml of compatible fluid. If necessary, when a suitable vein is inaccessible, a maximum of 150 mg of the drug may be administered by deep intramuscular injection, preferably high into the deltoid muscle. (2; 4)

Stability — Commercially available injections of succinylcholine chloride should be stored at 2 to 8 °C to retard potency loss. (2; 4) Anectine is stable for up to 14 days at room temperature. (2; 1433) Quelicin is stable for three months at temperatures up to 25 °C. (1239) In one study, storage for seven days at 40 °C followed by storage at 25 °C for four weeks was used to simulate the worst case of shipping followed by storage on an emergency cart. Calculated loss of potency at room temperature was 1%/week; at 40 °C, it was 3.2%/week. Therefore, the loss was estimated to be about 7% under such conditions. (960)

After dilution of succinylcholine chloride to a concentration of 1 or 2 mg/ml in sodium chloride 0.9%, the drug is stated to be chemically stable for four weeks at 5 °C and one week at 25 °C. However, use within 24 hours of preparation is recommended along with discarding any unused solution. (2; 4)

pH Effects — Succinylcholine chloride is unstable in alkaline solutions (2; 4) and decomposes in solutions with a pH greater than 4.5. (4) The pH of maximum stability was found to be 3.75 to 4.50. (960)

Syringes — Succinylcholine chloride (Abbott) 20 mg/ml was packaged in both glass and polypropylene syringes (Becton-Dickinson) sealed with rubber luer-tip caps (Becton-Dickinson). The syringes were stored for 45 days at 4 °C, 22 °C and 50% relative humidity, and 37 °C and 85% relative humidity. At 4 °C, there was little or no succinylcholine chloride loss after 45 days in either glass or plastic syringes. At 22 °C and 50% relative humidity, about a 5% loss occurred in 45 days. However, at 37 °C and 85% relative humidity, the drug concentration fell below the acceptable USP limit after about 30 days. (1209)

Succinylcholine chloride (Burroughs Wellcome) 20 mg/ml in dextrose 5% in water and in sodium chloride 0.9% (Baxter) was packaged as 10 ml in 12-ml plastic syringes (Monoject) and wrapped in aluminum foil. Samples were evaluated by HPLC analysis. Little or no loss of succinylcholine chloride occurred during 107 days of storage at 5 °C. At 25 °C, about 5 to 6% loss occurred in 100 days. Samples at an elevated temperature of 40 °C were stable through 22 days with only 3 to 4% loss but exhibited 12 to 14% loss at the next assay point of 63 days. (1892)

Compatibility Information

Solution Compatibility

Succinylcholine chloride

Solution	Mfr	Mfr	Conc/L	Remarks	Ref	C/I
Dextran 6% in dextrose 5%	AB	AB	2 g	Physically compatible	3	C
Dextran 6% in sodium chloride 0.9%	AB	AB	2 g	Physically compatible	3	C
Dextrose–Ringer's injection combinations	AB	AB	2 g	Physically compatible	3	C
Dextrose–Ringer's injection, lactated, combinations	AB	AB	2 g	Physically compatible	3	C
Dextrose 5% in Ringer's injection, lactated	TR[a]	TR	1 g	Potency retained for 24 hr at 5 °C	282	C
Dextrose–saline combinations	AB	AB	2 g	Physically compatible	3	C
Dextrose 5% in sodium chloride 0.9%	TR[a]	TR	1 g	Potency retained for 24 hr at 5 °C	282	C
Dextrose 2½% in water	AB	AB	2 g	Physically compatible	3	C
Dextrose 5% in water	AB	AB	2 g	Physically compatible	3	C
	TR[a]	TR	1 g	Potency retained for 24 hr at 5 °C	282	C
Dextrose 10% in water	AB	AB	2 g	Physically compatible	3	C
Fructose 10% in sodium chloride 0.9%	AB	AB	2 g	Physically compatible	3	C
Fructose 10% in water	AB	AB	2 g	Physically compatible	3	C
Invert sugar 5 and 10% in sodium chloride 0.9%	AB	AB	2 g	Physically compatible	3	C
Invert sugar 5 and 10% in water	AB	AB	2 g	Physically compatible	3	C
Ionosol products	AB	AB	2 g	Physically compatible	3	C
Ringer's injection	AB	AB	2 g	Physically compatible	3	C
Ringer's injection, lactated	AB	AB	2 g	Physically compatible	3	C
	TR[a]	TR	1 g	Potency retained for 24 hr at 5 °C	282	C
Sodium chloride 0.45%	AB	AB	2 g	Physically compatible	3	C
Sodium chloride 0.9%	AB	AB	2 g	Physically compatible	3	C
	TR[a]	TR	1 g	Potency retained for 24 hr at 5 °C	282	C
Sodium lactate ⅙ M	AB	AB	2 g	Physically compatible	3	C

[a]*Tested in both glass and PVC containers.*

Additive Compatibility

Succinylcholine chloride

Drug	Mfr	Conc/L	Mfr	Conc/L	Test Soln	Remarks	Ref	C/I
Amikacin sulfate	BR	5 g	SQ	2 g	D5LR, D5R, D5S, D5W, D10W, IS10, LR, NS, R, SL	Physically compatible and potency of both retained for 24 hr at 25 °C	294	C
Isoproterenol HCl	WI	4 mg	AB	2 g		Physically compatible	59	C
Meperidine HCl	WI	100 mg	AB	2 g		Physically compatible	3	C
Methyldopate HCl	MSD	1 g	AB	2 g	D, D–S, S	Physically compatible	23	C
Morphine sulfate		16.2 mg	AB	2 g		Physically compatible	3	C

Additive Compatibility (Cont.)

Drug	Mfr	Conc/L	Mfr (Succinylcholine chloride)	Conc/L (Succinylcholine chloride)	Test Soln	Remarks	Ref	C/I
Norepinephrine bitartrate	WI	8 mg	AB	2 g	D, D–S, S	Physically compatible	77	C
Pentobarbital sodium						Physically incompatible	9	I
	AB	500 mg	AB	2 g		Physically compatible	3	C
Scopolamine HBr		0.43 mg	AB	2 g		Physically compatible	3	C
Sodium bicarbonate	AB	2.4 mEq[a]	AB	1 g	D5W	Succinylcholine inactivated	772	I
Thiopental sodium	AB	25 g	AB	2 g		Haze or precipitate forms within 1 to 6 hr	3	I

[a]*One vial of Neut added to a liter of admixture.*

Drugs in Syringe Compatibility

Drug (in syringe)	Mfr	Amt	Mfr (Succinylcholine chloride)	Amt (Succinylcholine chloride)	Remarks	Ref	C/I
Heparin sodium		2500 units/ 1 ml		100 mg/ 5 ml	Physically compatible for at least 5 min	1053	C

Y-Site Injection Compatibility (1:1 Mixture)

Drug	Mfr	Conc	Mfr (Succinylcholine chloride)	Conc (Succinylcholine chloride)	Remarks	Ref	C/I
Etomidate	AB	2 mg/ml	AB	20 mg/ml	Visually compatible for up to 7 days at 25 °C	1801	C
Heparin sodium with hydrocortisone sodium succinate	RI UP	1000 units + 100 mg/L[a,b,c]	BW	20 mg/ml	Physically compatible for at least 4 hr at room temperature by visual and microscopic examination	322	C
Hetastarch in lactated electrolyte injection (Hextend)	AB	6%	AB	2 mg/ml[a]	Physically compatible with no change in measured turbidity or increase in particle content in 4 hr at 23 °C	2339	C
Potassium chloride		40 mEq/L[a,b,c]	BW	20 mg/ml	Physically compatible for at least 4 hr at room temperature by visual and microscopic examination	322	C
Propofol	ZEN	10 mg/ml	AB	20 mg/ml[a]	Physically compatible for 1 hr at 23 °C with no increase in particle content	2066	C
Thiopental sodium	AB	25 mg/ml	AB	20 mg/ml	White cloudiness forms immediately followed by fine crystalline particles	1801	I
Vitamin B complex with C	RC	2 ml/L[a,b,c]	BW	20 mg/ml	Physically compatible for at least 4 hr at room temperature by visual and microscopic examination	322	C

[a]*Tested in dextrose 5% in water.*
[b]*Tested in sodium chloride 0.9%.*
[c]*Tested in Ringer's injection, lactated.*

Additional Compatibility Information

Infusion Solutions — Dextrose 5% in water, sodium chloride 0.9% (2; 4), dextrose 5% in sodium chloride 0.9%, and sodium lactate ⅙ M have been recommended as diluents for infusing succinylcholine chloride. (4)

Barbiturates — Succinylcholine chloride is unstable in alkaline solutions (2; 4) and decomposes in solutions with a pH greater than 4.5. (4) In combination with barbiturates, either free barbituric acid will precipitate or the succinylcholine chloride will be hydrolyzed, depending on the final pH of the admixture. (2; 4; 21) Succinylcholine chloride should not be mixed with barbiturates in the same syringe or given simultaneously through the same needle. (2)

A haze forms in 30 minutes when succinylcholine chloride is mixed with methohexital sodium. (4)

Nafcillin — Additives, such as succinylcholine chloride, that may result in a final admixture pH below 5 should not be mixed with nafcillin sodium because of an increased rate of nafcillin decomposition. (27)

SUFENTANIL CITRATE
AHFS 28:08.08

Products — Sufentanil citrate is available as a preservative-free aqueous injection in 1-, 2-, and 5-ml ampuls and vials from several manufacturers. Each milliliter of solution contains sufentanil citrate equivalent to 50 μg of sufentanil base. (4; 29)

pH — From 3.5 to 6. (17)

Trade Name(s) — Sufenta.

Administration — Sufentanil citrate is administered intravenously by slow injection or infusion. For labor and delivery, it may be administered epidurally. The drug has also been given intramuscularly. (4)

Stability — Sufentanil citrate is a stable, clear, aqueous, preservative-free injection. The product should be stored at controlled room temperature and protected from light. It is hydrolyzed in acidic solutions. (4)

pH Effects — Sufentanil citrate 5 μg/ml in a solution with a pH greater than 3 lost less than 1% potency in 48 weeks at 90 °C. However, at a pH of less than 2, the drug loss was 14% at 60 °C and 32% at 90 °C in 48 weeks. (1755)

Freezing Solutions — Sufentanil citrate (Janssen) 5 μg/ml in sodium chloride 0.9% became nonhomogeneous and difficult to restore to homogeneity when frozen at −20 °C. The authors cautioned against freezing these solutions. (1755)

Syringes — Sufentanil citrate (Janssen) 2 μg/ml in sodium chloride 0.9% was packaged in 50-ml polypropylene syringes (Omnifix, B. Braun) and stored at 21 °C. HPLC analysis, although variable, reported less than 10% sufentanil loss in 24 hours. (2201)

Sorption — Sufentanil citrate (Janssen) 5 μg/ml in sodium chloride 0.9% in PVC/Kalex 3000 (phthalate ester) CADD pump reservoirs (Pharmacia) exhibited a 13% drug loss in two days at 32 °C due to sorption to the container. A slight white precipitate also formed in several containers. However, little or no loss occurred in reservoirs stored at 4 °C. In glass and polyethylene containers, the drug was stable by HPLC for at least 21 days at 4 and 32 °C. (1755)

Sufentanil citrate (Janssen) at concentrations near 5 μg/ml in dextrose 5% in water in PVC/Kalex 3000 CADD pump reservoirs (Pharmacia) also sorbed to the container, although to a lesser extent than the sodium chloride 0.9% solution. HPLC analysis found losses of 5 to 6% in 7 days and 10% in 30 days at 32 °C. At 4 °C, little or no loss occurred in 30 days. In simulated epidural administration, losses in the first 5 ml of priming solution were 25 to 30%, but the concentration returned to about 94% after two hours and 99% after 48 hours. (1756)

Sufentanil citrate (Janssen) 20 μg/ml in sodium chloride 0.9% in PVC/Kalex 3000 CADD pump reservoirs (Pharmacia) lost approximately 10 and 18% potency after 24 hours at 26 and 37 °C, respectively. Losses increased to about 22 and 30% after 10 days at 26 and 37 °C, respectively. In contrast, only about a 5% loss occurred after 10 days at 5 °C. The sufentanil losses, determined by HPLC analysis, were attributed to sorption to the container. The addition of bupivacaine HCl 3 mg/ml reduced sufentanil losses to no more than 5% at any of the three temperatures during 10 days of storage. (1751)

In another study, sufentanil citrate (Janssen) again demonstrated loss from solutions in concentrations from 1 to 20 μg/ml due to sorption to PVC/Kalex 3000 reservoirs for use with CADD pumps (Pharmacia Deltec) and administration tubing. (790)

The extent of sufentanil citrate sorption into PVC containers from aqueous solutions is influenced by the pH of the solution. Sufentanil citrate 5 μg/ml in sodium chloride 0.9% exhibited about 30% loss due to sorption to a PVC/phthalate ester container (CADD pump reservoir, Pharmacia Deltec) in one day at its natural pH of about 6. The extent of loss increased to 80% after 21 days of storage. However, combined with pH 4.6 citrate buffer, about 5% loss due to sorption occurred initially with little change thereafter. (2042)

Sufentanil citrate (Janssen) 2 μg/ml in sodium chloride 0.9% was delivered from 50-ml polypropylene syringes (Omnifix, B. Braun) by a syringe pump (JMS-Syringe-Pump Model SP-100, Japan Medical Supply Company) through polyethylene extension sets (Original-Perfusor-Leitung, Type PE, B. Braun) or polyvinyl chloride extension sets (Original-Perfusor-Leitung, Type N, B. Braun), 0.2-μm epidural filters (Sterifix, B. Braun), and epidural catheters (Perifix, B. Braun) over 24 hours. The pump, syringes, and extension sets were kept at 21 °C while the filters and epidural catheters were kept at 36 °C. Running at 1 ml/hr, the delivered sufentanil concentration using PVC tubing was about 7 to 10% below the theoretical concentration throughout 24 hours. Using polyethylene tubing, losses were about 16% initially but the concentration returned to expected levels within one to two hours and remained stable throughout the 24-hour delivery. (2201)

Filtration— Sufentanil citrate (Janssen) 50 μg/10 ml in sodium chloride 0.9% was evaluated for drug loss when administered through filters or epidural catheters; 2.5-g cellulose acetate/cellulose nitrate 0.2-μm filters (Millex, Millipore) were utilized. Approximately 20% of the sufentanil was lost to the void volume and/or adsorption. This loss should be considered when a new filter is used. (1667)

Sufentanil citrate (Janssen) 2 μg/ml in sodium chloride 0.9% delivered at 1 ml/hr through 0.2-μm epidural filters (Sterifix, B. Braun) during the first hour was 83% of the theoretical concentration and remained at reduced concentrations of 85 to 89% of theoretical through at least six hours. By 24 hours the concentration was near 96% of theoretical. The authors attributed the lower concentrations to sorption of sufentanil onto the filter. (2201)

In addition, sufentanil citrate (Janssen) demonstrated varying amounts of loss from solutions in concentrations from 1 to 20 μg/ml due to sorption to several filters including Millex-OR, Minisart NML, Schleicher & Schuell FP 30/3, and Sterifix EF. (790)

Compatibility Information

Solution Compatibility

Sufentanil citrate

Solution	*Mfr*	*Mfr*	*Conc/L*	*Remarks*	*Ref*	*C/I*
Dextrose 5% in water	[a]	JN	5 mg	10% sufentanil loss by HPLC in 30 days at 32 °C and little or no loss in 30 days at 4 °C	1756	C
Sodium chloride 0.9%	[a]	JN	20 mg	10 and 18% sufentanil losses by HPLC in 24 hr at 26 and 37 °C, respectively, due to sorption. 5% loss in 10 days at 5 °C	1751	I
	[a]	JN	5 mg	13% sufentanil loss by HPLC in 2 days at 32 °C due to sorption. Little or no loss in 25 days at 4 °C. Slight white precipitate forms within 6 days in some containers	1755	I
	FRE[b]	JN	5 mg	No sufentanil loss by HPLC in 21 days at 4 and 32 °C	1755	C
	[c]	JN	5 mg	No sufentanil loss by HPLC in 21 days at 4 and 32 °C	1755	C
	[a]	JN	5 mg	Visually compatible with 11% sufentanil loss over 48 hr at 32 °C. No loss over 48 hr when buffered to pH 4.6	2042	C

[a]*Tested in PVC/Kalex 3000 (phthalate ester) CADD pump reservoirs.*
[b]*Tested in glass bottles.*
[c]*Tested in high-density polyethylene containers.*

Additive Compatibility

Sufentanil citrate

Drug	*Mfr*	*Conc/L*	*Mfr*	*Conc/L*	*Test Soln*	*Remarks*	*Ref*	*C/I*
Bupivacaine HCl		3 g	JN	20 mg	NS[a]	5% sufentanil loss and no bupivacaine loss by HPLC in 10 days at 5, 26, and 37 °C	1751	C
	AST	2 g	JN	5 mg	D5W[a]	9% sufentanil loss and 5% bupivacaine loss by HPLC in 30 days at 32 °C. Little or no loss of either drug in 30 days at 4 °C	1756	C
	AST	2 g	JN	5 mg	NS[a]	Buffered with pH 4.6 citrate buffer. Visually compatible with little or no loss of either drug by HPLC in 48 hr at 32 °C	2042	C

[a]*Tested in PVC/Kalex 3000 (phthalate ester) CADD pump reservoirs.*

Drugs in Syringe Compatibility

Sufentanil citrate

Drug (in syringe)	*Mfr*	*Amt*	*Mfr*	*Amt*	*Remarks*	*Ref*	*C/I*
Atracurium besylate	BW	10 mg/ml		50 μg/ml	Physically compatible and atracurium chemically stable for 24 hr at 5 and 25 °C	1694	C

Drugs in Syringe Compatibility (Cont.)

Sufentanil citrate

Drug (in syringe)	*Mfr*	*Amt*	*Mfr*	*Amt*	*Remarks*	*Ref*	*C/I*
Atropine sulfate	LY	0.4 mg/ml	JN	50 μg/ml	Physically compatible with no subvisual haze or particle formation in 24 hr at 23 °C	1711	**C**
Dexamethasone sodium phosphate	AMR	4 mg/ml	JN	50 μg/ml	Physically compatible with no subvisual haze or particle formation in 24 hr at 23 °C	1711	**C**
Diazepam	ES	5 mg/ml	JN	50 μg/ml	White turbidity forms immediately. Precipitate forms in 24 hr at 23 °C	1711	**I**
Diphenhydramine HCl	SCN	50 mg/ml	JN	50 μg/ml	Physically compatible with no subvisual haze or particle formation in 24 hr at 23 °C	1711	**C**
Haloperidol lactate	MN	5 mg/ml	JN	50 μg/ml	Physically compatible with no subvisual haze or particle formation in 24 hr at 23 °C	1711	**C**
Hydroxyzine HCl	ES	50 mg/ml	JN	50 μg/ml	Physically compatible with no subvisual haze or particle formation in 24 hr at 23 °C	1711	**C**
Ketorolac tromethamine	SY	30 mg/ml	JN	50 μg/ml	Physically compatible with no subvisual haze or particle formation in 24 hr at 23 °C	1711	**C**
Lorazepam	WY	2 mg/ml	JN	50 μg/ml	Turbidity increases within 0.5 hr and continues to increase over 24 hr at 23 °C	1711	**I**
Methotrimeprazine	LE	20 mg/ml	JN	50 μg/ml	Physically compatible with no subvisual haze or particle formation in 24 hr at 23 °C	1711	**C**
Metoclopramide HCl	RB	5 mg/ml	JN	50 μg/ml	Physically compatible with no subvisual haze or particle formation in 24 hr at 23 °C	1711	**C**
Midazolam HCl	RC	5 mg/ml	JN	50 μg/ml	Physically compatible with no subvisual haze or particle formation in 24 hr at 23 °C	1711	**C**
Phenobarbital sodium	WY	60 mg/ml	JN	50 μg/ml	Haze forms immediately and particles form in 24 hr at 23 °C	1711	**I**
Phenytoin sodium	SO	50 mg/ml	JN	50 μg/ml	Small crystals form immediately. Large crystals settle to bottom in 24 hr at 23 °C	1711	**I**
Prochlorperazine edisylate	SCN	5 mg/ml	JN	50 μg/ml	Physically compatible with no subvisual haze or particle formation in 24 hr at 23 °C	1711	**C**
Scopolamine HBr	LY	0.43 mg/ml	JN	50 μg/ml	Physically compatible with no subvisual haze or particle formation in 24 hr at 23 °C	1711	**C**

Y-Site Injection Compatibility (1:1 Mixture)

Sufentanil citrate

Drug	*Mfr*	*Conc*	*Mfr*	*Conc*	*Remarks*	*Ref*	*C/I*
Amphotericin B cholesteryl sulfate complex	SEQ	0.83 mg/ml[a]	JN	0.05 mg/ml	Physically compatible with little or no change in measured turbidity or increase in particle content in 4 hr at 23 °C under fluorescent light	2117	**C**
Atropine sulfate	LY	0.4 mg/ml[a]	JN	12.5 μg/ml[a]	Physically compatible with no subvisual haze or particle formation in 24 hr at 23 °C	1711	**C**
Cisatracurium besylate	GW	0.1, 2, 5 mg/ml[a]	ES	0.0125 mg/ml[a]	Physically compatible with no change in measured turbidity or increase in particle content in 4 hr at 23 °C	2074	**C**

Y-Site Injection Compatibility (1:1 Mixture) (Cont.)

Sufentanil citrate

Drug	*Mfr*	*Conc*	*Mfr*	*Conc*	*Remarks*	*Ref*	*C/I*
Dexamethasone sodium phosphate	AMR	1 mg/ml[a]	JN	12.5 µg/ml[a]	Physically compatible with no subvisual haze or particle formation in 24 hr at 23 °C	1711	C
Diazepam	ES	0.5 mg/ml[a]	JN	12.5 µg/ml[a]	Physically compatible with no subvisual haze or particle formation in 24 hr at 23 °C	1711	C
Diphenhydramine HCl	SCN	2 mg/ml[a]	JN	12.5 µg/ml[a]	Physically compatible with no subvisual haze or particle formation in 24 hr at 23 °C	1711	C
Etomidate	AB	2 mg/ml	JN	0.05 mg/ml	Visually compatible for up to 7 days at 25 °C	1801	C
Gatifloxacin	BMS	2 mg/ml[a]	ES	0.05 mg/ml	Physically compatible with no change in measured haze or increase in particle content in 4 hr at 23 °C	2234	C
Haloperidol lactate	MN	0.2 mg/ml[a]	JN	12.5 µg/ml[a]	Physically compatible with no subvisual haze or particle formation in 24 hr at 23 °C	1711	C
Hetastarch in lactated electrolyte injection (Hextend)	AB	6%	BA	12.5 µg/ml[a]	Physically compatible with no change in measured turbidity or increase in particle content in 4 hr at 23 °C	2339	C
Hydroxyzine HCl	ES	4 mg/ml[a]	JN	12.5 µg/ml[a]	Physically compatible with little subvisual haze or particle formation in 24 hr at 23 °C	1711	C
Ketorolac tromethamine	SY	1 mg/ml[a]	JN	12.5 µg/ml[a]	Physically compatible with no subvisual haze or particle formation in 24 hr at 23 °C	1711	C
Linezolid	PHU	2 mg/ml	ES	0.05 mg/ml	Physically compatible with no change in measured turbidity or increase in particle content in 4 hr at 23 °C	2264	C
Lorazepam	WY	0.1 mg/ml[a]	JN	12.5 µg/ml[a]	Large increase in measured turbidity occurs immediately and persists for 24 hr at 23 °C under fluorescent light	1711	I
Methotrimeprazine	LE	0.2 mg/ml[a]	JN	12.5 µg/ml[a]	Physically compatible with no subvisual haze or particle formation in 24 hr at 23 °C	1711	C
Metoclopramide HCl	RB	5 mg/ml	JN	12.5 µg/ml[a]	Physically compatible with no subvisual haze or particle formation in 24 hr at 23 °C	1711	C
Midazolam HCl	RC	0.2 mg/ml[a]	JN	12.5 µg/ml[a]	Physically compatible with no subvisual haze or particle formation in 24 hr at 23 °C	1711	C
Phenobarbital sodium	WY	2 mg/ml[a]	JN	12.5 µg/ml[a]	Physically compatible with no subvisual haze or particle formation in 24 hr at 23 °C	1711	C
Phenytoin sodium	ES	2 mg/ml[a]	JN	12.5 µg/ml[a]	Numerous tiny crystals form immediately and become larger over 24 hr at 23 °C under fluorescent light	1711	I

Y-Site Injection Compatibility (1:1 Mixture) (Cont.)

			Sufentanil citrate				
Drug	*Mfr*	*Conc*	*Mfr*	*Conc*	*Remarks*	*Ref*	*C/I*
Prochlorperazine edisylate	SCN	0.5 mg/ml[a]	JN	12.5 μg/ml[a]	Physically compatible with little subvisual haze or particle formation in 24 hr at 23 °C	1711	C
Propofol	ZEN	10 mg/ml	JN	0.05 mg/ml	Physically compatible for 1 hr at 23 °C with no increase in particle content	2066	C
Remifentanil HCl	GW	0.025 and 0.25 mg/ml[b]	ES	0.0125 mg/ml[a]	Physically compatible with no change in measured turbidity or increase in particle content in 4 hr at 23 °C	2075	C
Scopolamine HBr	LY	0.05 mg/ml[a]	JN	12.5 μg/ml[a]	Physically compatible with no subvisual haze or particle formation in 24 hr at 23 °C	1711	C
Thiopental sodium	AB	25 mg/ml	JN	0.05 mg/ml	White pellets form within 24 hr at 25 °C	1801	I

[a]*Tested in dextrose 5% in water.*
[b]*Tested in sodium chloride 0.9%.*

SUMATRIPTAN SUCCINATE
AHFS 28:92

Products — Sumatriptan succinate is available at a concentration of 6 mg/0.5 ml in single-dose vials and prefilled syringes. Each 0.5 ml of solution also contains sodium chloride 3.5 mg in water for injection. (2)

pH — Approximately 4.2 to 5.3. (2)

Osmolality — The solution is nearly isotonic with an osmolality of 291 mOsm/kg.

Trade Name(s) — Imitrex.

Administration — Sumatriptan succinate is administered subcutaneously. It should not be given by other routes of administration. (2)

Stability — Intact containers of sumatriptan succinate should be stored between 2 and 30 °C and protected from light. The injection is a clear, colorless to light yellow solution. (2)

Syringes — The stability of sumatriptan succinate (Glaxo Wellcome) 12 mg/ml packaged as 1 ml of solution drawn into 1-ml polypropylene tuberculin syringes was evaluated stored under refrigeration and at room temperature of 25 °C both exposed to and protected from fluorescent light. The room temperature samples were evaluated over 24 hours while the refrigerated samples were evaluated over 72 hours. No visible indications of physical instability were observed, and HPLC analysis found no loss of sumatriptan. (2276)

TACROLIMUS
AHFS 92:00

Products — Tacrolimus injection is available in 1-ml ampuls containing the equivalent of 5 mg of anhydrous tacrolimus per milliliter. In addition to tacrolimus, each milliliter contains polyoxyl 60 hydrogenated castor oil (surfactant) 200 mg and dehydrated alcohol, USP, 80% (v/v). The product is a concentrate that must be diluted for use in dextrose 5% in water or sodium chloride 0.9%. (2)

Trade Name(s) — Prograf.

Administration — Tacrolimus is administered by intravenous infusion diluted to a final concentration of 0.004 to 0.02 mg/ml (4 to 20 μg/ml) in dextrose 5% in water or sodium chloride 0.9%. Intravenous solution containers should be made of glass or polyethylene; PVC containers plasticized with diethylhexyl phthalate (DEHP) should be avoided due to leaching of plasticizer and decreased stability. For dilute solutions of tacrolimus, non-PVC tubing should also be used to minimize the potential for significant drug sorption. (2)

Stability — Intact ampuls should be stored at temperatures between 5 and 25 °C. (2) Tacrolimus exhibits a minimum rate of decomposition at pH values between 2 and 6; the rate of decomposition increases substantially at higher pH values (1926) and is unstable above pH 9. (2216) The manufacturer recommends that tacrolimus not be mixed with or even co-infused with solutions having a pH of 9 or greater. (2)

Syringes—Tacrolimus (Fujisawa) 100 μg/ml in sodium chloride 0.9% was packaged 20 ml in 30-ml plastic syringes (Becton-Dickinson) and stored at 24 °C exposed to normal room light and protected from light. No decrease in tacrolimus concentration was found by HPLC analysis after storage for 24 hours. (1864)

Sorption—Tacrolimus (Fujisawa) 100 μg/ml in dextrose 5% in water was delivered through PVC anesthesia extension tubing (Abbott), PVC intravenous administration set tubing (Venoset, Abbott), and fat emulsion tubing (Abbott). HPLC analysis of the delivered solutions found no loss of tacrolimus using the PVC administration set tubing and the fat emulsion tubing and only 2.5% drug loss from the PVC anesthesia extension tubing. (1864)

However, tacrolimus has demonstrated drug loss in PVC containers that did not occur with other container materials. (1864) See Solution Compatibility below. The manufacturer recommends that non-PVC tubing be used for low concentrations of tacrolimus to minimize the potential for significant drug sorption. (2)

Plasticizer Leaching—Parenteral products containing a large amount of surfactant in the formulation such as tacrolimus injection will extract the plasticizer DEHP from PVC containers and administration sets. Consequently, their use should be avoided for tacrolimus. Instead, glass or polyethylene containers and non-DEHP plasticized administration sets are recommended. (2; 4; 1683)

Compatibility Information

Solution Compatibility

Tacrolimus

Solution	*Mfr*	*Mfr*	*Conc/L*	*Remarks*	*Ref*	*C/I*
Dextrose 5% in water	AB[a]	FUJ	100 mg	5 to 8% loss by HPLC in 48 hr at 24 °C	1864	C
	AB[b]	FUJ	100 mg	15% loss in 6 hr and 19% loss in 24 hr by HPLC at 24 °C	1864	I
Sodium chloride 0.9%	BA[c]	FUJ	10 mg	Visually compatible with 4% loss by HPLC in 48 hr	1854	C
	AB[c]	FUJ	100 mg	10 to 12% loss by HPLC in 24 hr at 24 °C	1864	C
	AB[b]	FUJ	100 mg	12% loss in 6 hr and 16% loss in 24 hr by HPLC at 24 °C	1864	I
TPN #201[d]	[c]	FUJ	100 mg	Visually compatible with no loss by HPLC in 24 hr at 24 °C	1922	C

[a]*Tested in glass and polyolefin containers.*
[b]*Tested in PVC containers.*
[c]*Tested in glass containers.*
[d]*Refer to Appendix I for the composition of parenteral nutrition solutions. TPN indicates a 2-in-1 admixture.*

Additive Compatibility

Tacrolimus

Drug	*Mfr*	*Conc/L*	*Mfr*	*Conc/L*	*Test Soln*	*Remarks*	*Ref*	*C/I*
Cimetidine HCl	SKB	600 mg	FUJ	10 mg	NS[a]	Visually compatible with no cimetidine loss and 3% tacrolimus loss by HPLC in 48 hr at 24 °C	1854	C

[a]*Tested in glass containers.*

Y-Site Injection Compatibility (1:1 Mixture)

Tacrolimus

Drug	*Mfr*	*Conc*	*Mfr*	*Conc*	*Remarks*	*Ref*	*C/I*
Acyclovir sodium	BW	10 mg/ml[a]	FUJ	1 mg/ml[b]	Visually compatible for 24 hr at 25 °C	1630	C
Aminophylline	ES	2 mg/ml[a]	FUJ	1 mg/ml[b]	Visually compatible for 24 hr at 25 °C	1630	C
Amphotericin B	LY	5 mg/ml[a]	FUJ	1 mg/ml[c]	Visually compatible for 24 hr at 25 °C	1630	C
Ampicillin sodium	WY	20 mg/ml[a]	FUJ	1 mg/ml[b]	Visually compatible for 24 hr at 25 °C	1630	C

Y-Site Injection Compatibility (1:1 Mixture) (Cont.)

Drug	Mfr	Conc	Tacrolimus Mfr	Tacrolimus Conc	Remarks	Ref	C/I
Ampicillin sodium–sulbactam sodium	RR	33.3 + 16.7 mg/ml[a]	FUJ	1 mg/ml[b]	Visually compatible for 24 hr at 25 °C	1630	C
Benztropine mesylate	MSD	1 mg/ml[a]	FUJ	1 mg/ml[b]	Visually compatible for 24 hr at 25 °C	1630	C
Calcium gluconate	ES	100 mg/ml	FUJ	1 mg/ml[b]	Visually compatible for 24 hr at 25 °C	1630	C
Cefazolin sodium	BR	40 mg/ml[a]	FUJ	1 mg/ml[b]	Visually compatible for 24 hr at 25 °C	1630	C
Cefotetan disodium	STU	40 mg/ml[a]	FUJ	1 mg/ml[b]	Visually compatible for 24 hr at 25 °C	1630	C
Ceftazidime	GL[e]	20 mg/ml[a]	FUJ	1 mg/ml[b]	Visually compatible for 24 hr at 25 °C	1630	C
	GW[e]	40 mg/ml[a]	FUJ	10 and 40 μg/ml[a]	Visually compatible with no loss of either drug by HPLC in 4 hr at 24 °C under fluorescent light	2216	C
	GW[e]	200 mg/ml[a]	FUJ	10 and 40 μg/ml[a]	Visually compatible with no loss of either drug by HPLC in 4 hr at 24 °C under fluorescent light	2216	C
Ceftriaxone sodium	RC	40 mg/ml[a]	FUJ	1 mg/ml[b]	Visually compatible for 24 hr at 25 °C	1630	C
Cefuroxime sodium	LI	30 mg/ml[a]	FUJ	1 mg/ml[b]	Visually compatible for 24 hr at 25 °C	1630	C
Chloramphenicol sodium succinate	PD	20 mg/ml[a]	FUJ	1 mg/ml[b]	Visually compatible for 24 hr at 25 °C	1630	C
Cimetidine HCl	SKB	150 mg/ml[a]	FUJ	1 mg/ml[b]	Visually compatible for 24 hr at 25 °C	1630	C
Ciprofloxacin	MI	1 mg/ml[a]	FUJ	1 mg/ml[b]	Visually compatible for 24 hr at 25 °C	1630	C
Clindamycin phosphate	ES	12 mg/ml[a]	FUJ	1 mg/ml[b]	Visually compatible for 24 hr at 25 °C	1630	C
Dexamethasone sodium phosphate	ES	4 mg/ml[a]	FUJ	1 mg/ml[b]	Visually compatible for 24 hr at 25 °C	1630	C
Digoxin	WY	0.25 mg/ml	FUJ	1 mg/ml[b]	Visually compatible for 24 hr at 25 °C	1630	C
Diphenhydramine HCl	ES	1 mg/ml[a]	FUJ	1 mg/ml[b]	Visually compatible for 24 hr at 25 °C	1630	C
Dobutamine HCl	LI	1 mg/ml[a]	FUJ	1 mg/ml[b]	Visually compatible for 24 hr at 25 °C	1630	C
Dopamine HCl	ES	1.6 mg/ml[a]	FUJ	1 mg/ml[b]	Visually compatible for 24 hr at 25 °C	1630	C
Doxycycline hyclate	RR	5 mg/ml[a]	FUJ	1 mg/ml[b]	Visually compatible for 24 hr at 25 °C	1630	C
Erythromycin lactobionate	AB	20 mg/ml[a]	FUJ	1 mg/ml[b]	Visually compatible for 24 hr at 25 °C	1630	C
Esmolol HCl	DU	10 mg/ml[a]	FUJ	1 mg/ml[b]	Visually compatible for 24 hr at 25 °C	1630	C
Fluconazole	RR	2 mg/ml[a]	FUJ	1 mg/ml[b]	Visually compatible for 24 hr at 25 °C	1630	C
	PF	1 mg/ml[b]	FUJ	10 and 40 μg/ml[b]	Visually compatible with no loss of either drug by HPLC in 3 hr at 24 °C under fluorescent light	2225	C
	PF	15 mg/ 7.5 ml[b]	FUJ	50 and 200 μg/2.5 ml[b]	Mixed in the amounts indicated.[f] Visually compatible with no loss of either drug by HPLC in 3 hr at 24 °C under fluorescent light	2225	C
	PF	0.5 mg/ml[b]	FUJ	5 μg/ml[b]	Visually compatible with no loss of either drug in 3 hr at 24 °C under fluorescent light	2236	C
	PF	1.5 mg/ml[b]	FUJ	5 μg/ml[b]	Visually compatible with no loss of either drug in 3 hr at 24 °C under fluorescent light	2236	C
	PF	0.5 mg/ml[b]	FUJ	20 μg/ml[b]	Visually compatible with no loss of either drug in 3 hr at 24 °C under fluorescent light	2236	C

Y-Site Injection Compatibility (1:1 Mixture) (Cont.)

Tacrolimus

Drug	*Mfr*	*Conc*	*Mfr*	*Conc*	*Remarks*	*Ref*	*C/I*
	PF	1.5 mg/ml[b]	FUJ	20 μg/ml[b]	Visually compatible with no loss of either drug in 3 hr at 24 °C under fluorescent light	2236	C
Furosemide	ES	10 mg/ml	FUJ	1 mg/ml[b]	Visually compatible for 24 hr at 25 °C	1630	C
Ganciclovir sodium	SY	50 mg/ml[a]	FUJ	1 mg/ml[b]	Visually compatible for 24 hr at 25 °C	1630	C
Gentamicin sulfate	SCN	4 mg/ml[a]	FUJ	1 mg/ml[b]	Visually compatible for 24 hr at 25 °C	1630	C
Haloperidol lactate	SO	2.5 mg/ml[a]	FUJ	1 mg/ml[b]	Visually compatible for 24 hr at 25 °C	1630	C
Heparin sodium	ES	10 units/ml[a]	FUJ	1 mg/ml[b]	Visually compatible for 24 hr at 25 °C	1630	C
Hydrocortisone sodium succinate	AB	50 mg/ml[a]	FUJ	1 mg/ml[b]	Visually compatible for 24 hr at 25 °C	1630	C
Hydromorphone HCl	KN	200 μg/ml[a]	FUJ	10 and 40 μg/ml[a]	Visually compatible with no loss of either drug by HPLC in 4 hr at 24 °C under fluorescent light	2216	C
	KN	2 mg/ml[a]	FUJ	10 and 40 μg/ml[a]	Visually compatible with no loss of either drug by HPLC in 4 hr at 24 °C under fluorescent light	2216	C
Imipenem–cilastatin sodium	MSD	10 mg/ml[b]	FUJ	1 mg/ml[b]	Visually compatible for 24 hr at 25 °C	1630	C
Insulin, regular	LI	0.1 unit/ml[a]	FUJ	1 mg/ml[b]	Visually compatible for 24 hr at 25 °C	1630	C
Isoproterenol HCl	ES	0.04 mg/ml[a]	FUJ	1 mg/ml[b]	Visually compatible for 24 hr at 25 °C	1630	C
Leucovorin calcium	ES	10 mg/ml[a]	FUJ	1 mg/ml[b]	Visually compatible for 24 hr at 25 °C	1630	C
Lorazepam	WY	1 mg/ml[a]	FUJ	1 mg/ml[b]	Visually compatible for 24 hr at 25 °C	1630	C
Methylprednisolone sodium succinate	UP	0.8 mg/ml[a]	FUJ	1 mg/ml[b]	Visually compatible for 24 hr at 25 °C	1630	C
Metoclopramide HCl	DU	0.2 mg/ml[a]	FUJ	1 mg/ml[b]	Visually compatible for 24 hr at 25 °C	1630	C
Metronidazole	AB	5 mg/ml	FUJ	1 mg/ml[b]	Visually compatible for 24 hr at 25 °C	1630	C
Morphine sulfate	SCN	1 mg/ml[b]	FUJ	10 and 40 μg/ml[b]	Visually compatible with no loss of either drug by HPLC in 4 hr at 24 °C under fluorescent light	2216	C
	SCN	3 mg/ml[b]	FUJ	10 and 40 μg/ml[b]	Visually compatible with no loss of either drug by HPLC in 4 hr at 24 °C under fluorescent light	2216	C
Multivitamins	LY	0.001 ml/ml[a]	FUJ	1 mg/ml[b]	Visually compatible for 24 hr at 25 °C	1630	C
Nitroglycerin	DU	0.1 mg/ml[a]	FUJ	1 mg/ml[b]	Visually compatible for 24 hr at 25 °C	1630	C
Oxacillin sodium	BR	40 mg/ml[a]	FUJ	1 mg/ml[b]	Visually compatible for 24 hr at 25 °C	1630	C
Penicillin G potassium	BR	100,000 units/ml[a]	FUJ	1 mg/ml[b]	Visually compatible for 24 hr at 25 °C	1630	C
Perphenazine	SC	2.5 mg/ml[a]	FUJ	1 mg/ml[b]	Visually compatible for 24 hr at 25 °C	1630	C
Phenytoin sodium	ES	5 mg/ml[a]	FUJ	1 mg/ml[b]	Visually compatible for 4 hr at 25 °C. White haze forms by 24 hr	1630	C
Piperacillin sodium	LE	80 mg/ml[a]	FUJ	1 mg/ml[b]	Visually compatible for 24 hr at 25 °C	1630	C
Potassium chloride	AB	2 mEq/ml	FUJ	1 mg/ml[b]	Visually compatible for 24 hr at 25 °C	1630	C
Propranolol HCl	AY	1 mg/ml	FUJ	1 mg/ml[b]	Visually compatible for 24 hr at 25 °C	1630	C
Ranitidine HCl	GL	25 mg/ml	FUJ	1 mg/ml[b]	Visually compatible for 24 hr at 25 °C	1630	C
Sodium bicarbonate	AB	1 mEq/ml	FUJ	1 mg/ml[b]	Visually compatible for 24 hr at 25 °C	1630	C
Sodium nitroprusside	ES	0.004 mg/ml[a]	FUJ	1 mg/ml[b]	Visually compatible for 24 hr at 25 °C	1630	C

Y-Site Injection Compatibility (1:1 Mixture) (Cont.)

Tacrolimus

Drug	*Mfr*	*Conc*	*Mfr*	*Conc*	*Remarks*	*Ref*	*C/I*
Sodium tetradecyl sulfate	ES	10 mg/ml	FUJ	1 mg/ml[b]	Visually compatible for 24 hr at 25 °C	1630	C
TNA #218 to #226[d]			FUJ	1 mg/ml[a]	Visually compatible with no precipitate or emulsion damage apparent in 4 hr at 23 °C	2215	C
Tobramycin sulfate	BR	40 mg/ml	FUJ	1 mg/ml[b]	Visually compatible for 24 hr at 25 °C	1630	C
TPN #212 to #215[d]			FUJ	1 mg/ml[a]	Physically compatible with no change in measured turbidity or increase in particle content in 4 hr at 23 °C	2109	C
Trimethoprim–sulfamethoxazole	RC	1.6 + 8 mg/ml[a]	FUJ	1 mg/ml[b]	Visually compatible for 24 hr at 25 °C	1630	C
Vancomycin HCl	LI	5 mg/ml[a]	FUJ	1 mg/ml[b]	Visually compatible for 24 hr at 25 °C	1630	C

[a]*Tested in dextrose 5% in water.*
[b]*Tested in sodium chloride 0.9%.*
[c]*Diluted with sterile water for injection.*
[d]*Refer to Appendix I for the composition of parenteral nutrition solutions. TNA indicates a 3-in-1 admixture, and TPN indicates a 2-in-1 admixture.*
[e]*Sodium carbonate–containing formulation tested.*
[f]*Final concentrations were 1.5 mg/ml of fluconazole and 5 and 20 μg/ml of tacrolimus.*

Additional Compatibility Information

Infusion Solutions — The manufacturer recommends dilution of tacrolimus to 0.004 to 0.02 mg/ml in dextrose 5% in water or sodium chloride 0.9%. Tacrolimus in these solutions is reported to be stable for 24 hours. (2)

TENIPOSIDE (VM-26) AHFS 10:00

Products — Teniposide is available in a nonaqueous solution in 5-ml ampuls containing 50 mg of drug. Each milliliter of solution contains teniposide 10 mg, benzyl alcohol 30 mg, *N,N*-dimethylacetamide 60 mg, polyoxyethylated castor oil (Cremophor EL) 500 mg, and dehydrated alcohol 42.7%. The pH is adjusted with maleic acid. (2)

The product is a concentrate that must be diluted for use. (2)

pH — Approximately 5. (2)

Density — Teniposide (Bristol) 10-mg/ml undiluted injection has a solution density of 0.94 g/ml. (2041; 2248)

Trade Name(s) — Vumon.

Administration — Teniposide is administered by slow intravenous infusion over at least 30 to 60 minutes after dilution in dextrose 5% in water or sodium chloride 0.9% to a final concentration of 0.1, 0.2, 0.4, or 1 mg/ml. (2) Extended infusions of 0.1- and 0.2-mg/ml solutions over 24 hours have resulted in precipitation. (2; 1502; 1521) The intravenous solution containers and sets used to administer teniposide should not contain the plasticizer diethylhexyl phthalate (DEHP). (2; 4) Extravasation should be avoided because of local tissue irritation and phlebitis. Tissue necrosis is unlikely. (2; 4; 1561; 1562)

Stability — The teniposide concentrate is clear (2) but may exhibit a slight opalescence when diluted in infusion solutions due to the surfactant content. (234)

Intact ampuls should be stored under refrigeration in the original package to protect from light. Teniposide stability is not adversely affected by freezing (2) or exposure to normal room fluorescent light during administration. (1374)

The manufacturer does not recommend refrigeration of teniposide diluted in infusion solutions. (2)

Precipitation — Although teniposide is chemically stable for at least 24 hours, precipitation from aqueous solutions has occurred irregularly and unpredictably even at 0.1 and 0.2 mg/ml, the lowest recommended concentrations. (2; 1502; 1521) The precipitation rate depends on the formation of crystallization nuclei. Precipitation then proceeds rapidly. The formation of crystallization nuclei may be accelerated by agitation, contact with incompatible drugs or material surfaces, and, possibly, other factors. (1374; 1502; 1521) The manufacturer recommends avoiding an inordinate amount of agitation during preparation, minimizing storage time prior to administration, and avoiding contact with other drugs and solutions. Even the compatibility of teniposide infusions with some infusion set materials and pumps cannot be assured. (2; 1502; 1521)

Sorption—No teniposide loss due to sorption to PVC containers has been observed. (1374; 2053)

Plasticizer Leaching—The surfactant, Cremophor EL, in the teniposide formulation leaches the plasticizer DEHP from PVC containers and sets. The amount leached increases with time and drug concentration and is similar for sodium chloride 0.9% and dextrose 5% in water. Consequently, the manufacturer recommends the use of non-PVC containers, such as glass bottles and polyolefin bags, and non-PVC administration sets, such as lipid administration sets and nitroglycerin sets. (2)

Teniposide (Bristol) 0.1 mg/ml in dextrose 5% in water leached relatively large amounts of DEHP from PVC bags due to the Cremophor EL surfactant in the formulation. After eight hours at 24 °C, the DEHP concentration in 50-ml bags of infusion solution was as much as 7.5 μg/ml; it continued to increase through 24 hours to 22.2 μg/ml. This finding is consistent with the surfactant concentration (1%) of the final admixture solution. The actual amount of DEHP leached from PVC containers and administration sets may vary in clinical situations, depending on surfactant concentration, bag size, and contact time. (1683)

Faouzi et al. reported substantial leaching of DEHP plasticizer from PVC bags of dextrose 5% in water and sodium chloride 0.9% and PVC administration sets by teniposide admixtures containing 0.4 mg/ml of the drug due to the Cremophor EL surfactant used in the formulation. DEHP levels increased throughout the one-hour infusion time to over 20 μg/ml from both the bags and sets. There was no difference in plasticizer leaching between the two infusion solutions. Storage of the teniposide 0.4-mg/ml admixtures for 48 hours at both 4 and 24 °C resulted in substantially greater DEHP leaching. DEHP concentrations ranged from about 60 μg/ml in the refrigerated samples to over 200 μg/ml (a total of 52 mg) in the room temperature samples. The authors noted that the actual amount of DEHP a patient will receive is dependent on a number of factors, including Cremophor EL concentration, storage temperature, and contact time. No plasticizer was leached from glass bottles or polyolefin infusion containers. To minimize plasticizer leaching if PVC containers and sets must be used, it is recommended that teniposide admixtures be used immediately after preparation and administered over no more than one hour. (2053)

An acceptability limit of no more than 5 parts per million (5 μg/ml) for DEHP plasticizer released from PVC containers, administration sets, and other equipment has been proposed. The limit was proposed based on a review of metabolic and toxicologic considerations. (2185)

Compatibility Information

Solution Compatibility

Teniposide

Solution	*Mfr*	*Mfr*	*Conc/L*	*Remarks*	*Ref*	*C/I*
Dextrose 5% in water	a	BR	400 mg	Physically compatible with up to 6% teniposide loss in 4 days at 21 °C under fluorescent light or in the dark	1374	C
Ringer's injection, lactated	a	BR	400 mg	Physically compatible with 1 to 3% teniposide loss in 4 days at 21 °C under fluorescent light or in the dark	1374	C
Sodium chloride 0.9%	b	BR	400 mg	Physically compatible with 2 to 4% teniposide loss in 4 days at 21 °C under fluorescent light or in the dark	1374	C
	a	BR	500, 600, 700 mg	Physically compatible for 4 days at 21 °C	1374	C

[a]*Tested in glass containers.*
[b]*Tested in both glass and PVC containers.*

Y-Site Injection Compatibility (1:1 Mixture)

Teniposide

Drug	*Mfr*	*Conc*	*Mfr*	*Conc*	*Remarks*	*Ref*	*C/I*
Acyclovir sodium	BW	7 mg/ml[a]	BR	0.1 mg/ml[a]	Physically compatible with no subvisual haze or particle formation in 4 hr at 23 °C	1725	C

Y-Site Injection Compatibility (1:1 Mixture) (Cont.)

			Teniposide				
Drug	*Mfr*	*Conc*	*Mfr*	*Conc*	*Remarks*	*Ref*	*C/I*
Allopurinol	BW	3 mg/ml[a]	BR	0.1 mg/ml[a]	Physically compatible with no subvisual haze or particle formation in 4 hr at 23 °C	1725	C
Amifostine	USB	10 mg/ml[a]	BR	0.1 mg/ml[a]	Physically compatible with no change in measured turbidity or increase in particle content in 4 hr at 23 °C	1845	C
Amikacin sulfate	BR	5 mg/ml[a]	BR	0.1 mg/ml[a]	Physically compatible with no subvisual haze or particle formation in 4 hr at 23 °C	1725	C
Aminophylline	AB	2.5 mg/ml[a]	BR	0.1 mg/ml[a]	Physically compatible with no subvisual haze or particle formation in 4 hr at 23 °C	1725	C
Amphotericin B	SQ	0.6 mg/ml[a]	BR	0.1 mg/ml[a]	Physically compatible with no subvisual haze or particle formation in 4 hr at 23 °C	1725	C
Ampicillin sodium	WY	20 mg/ml[b]	BR	0.1 mg/ml[a]	Physically compatible with no subvisual haze or particle formation in 4 hr at 23 °C	1725	C
Ampicillin sodium–sulbactam sodium	RR	20 + 10 mg/ml[b]	BR	0.1 mg/ml[a]	Physically compatible with no subvisual haze or particle formation in 4 hr at 23 °C	1725	C
Aztreonam	SQ	40 mg/ml[a]	BR	0.1 mg/ml[a]	Physically compatible with no subvisual haze or particle formation in 4 hr at 23 °C	1725; 1758	C
Bleomycin sulfate	BR	1 unit/ml[b]	BR	0.1 mg/ml[a]	Physically compatible with no subvisual haze or particle formation in 4 hr at 23 °C	1725	C
Bumetanide	RC	0.04 mg/ml[a]	BR	0.1 mg/ml[a]	Physically compatible with no subvisual haze or particle formation in 4 hr at 23 °C	1725	C
Buprenorphine HCl	RKC	0.04 mg/ml[a]	BR	0.1 mg/ml[a]	Physically compatible with no subvisual haze or particle formation in 4 hr at 23 °C	1725	C
Butorphanol tartrate	BR	0.04 mg/ml[a]	BR	0.1 mg/ml[a]	Physically compatible with no subvisual haze or particle formation in 4 hr at 23 °C	1725	C
Calcium gluconate	AMR	40 mg/ml[a]	BR	0.1 mg/ml[a]	Physically compatible with no subvisual haze or particle formation in 4 hr at 23 °C	1725	C
Carboplatin	BR	5 mg/ml[a]	BR	0.1 mg/ml[a]	Physically compatible with no subvisual haze or particle formation in 4 hr at 23 °C	1725	C
Carmustine	BR	1.5 mg/ml[a]	BR	0.1 mg/ml[a]	Physically compatible with no subvisual haze or particle formation in 4 hr at 23 °C	1725	C
Cefazolin sodium	MAR	20 mg/ml[a]	BR	0.1 mg/ml[a]	Physically compatible with no subvisual haze or particle formation in 4 hr at 23 °C	1725	C

Y-Site Injection Compatibility (1:1 Mixture) (Cont.)

			Teniposide				
Drug	*Mfr*	*Conc*	*Mfr*	*Conc*	*Remarks*	*Ref*	*C/I*
Cefoperazone sodium	RR	40 mg/ml[a]	BR	0.1 mg/ml[a]	Physically compatible with no subvisual haze or particle formation in 4 hr at 23 °C	1725	C
Cefotaxime sodium	HO	20 mg/ml[a]	BR	0.1 mg/ml[a]	Physically compatible with no subvisual haze or particle formation in 4 hr at 23 °C	1725	C
Cefotetan disodium	STU	20 mg/ml[a]	BR	0.1 mg/ml[a]	Physically compatible with no subvisual haze or particle formation in 4 hr at 23 °C	1725	C
Cefoxitin sodium	MSD	20 mg/ml[a]	BR	0.1 mg/ml[a]	Physically compatible with no subvisual haze or particle formation in 4 hr at 23 °C	1725	C
Ceftazidime	LI[d]	40 mg/ml[a]	BR	0.1 mg/ml[a]	Physically compatible with no subvisual haze or particle formation in 4 hr at 23 °C	1725	C
Ceftizoxime sodium	FUJ	20 mg/ml[a]	BR	0.1 mg/ml[a]	Physically compatible with no subvisual haze or particle formation in 4 hr at 23 °C	1725	C
Ceftriaxone sodium	RC	20 mg/ml[a]	BR	0.1 mg/ml[a]	Physically compatible with no subvisual haze or particle formation in 4 hr at 23 °C	1725	C
Cefuroxime sodium	GL	20 mg/ml[a]	BR	0.1 mg/ml[a]	Physically compatible with no subvisual haze or particle formation in 4 hr at 23 °C	1725	C
Chlorpromazine HCl	SCN	2 mg/ml[a]	BR	0.1 mg/ml[a]	Physically compatible with no subvisual haze or particle formation in 4 hr at 23 °C	1725	C
Cimetidine HCl	SKB	12 mg/ml[a]	BR	0.1 mg/ml[a]	Physically compatible with no subvisual haze or particle formation in 4 hr at 23 °C	1725	C
Ciprofloxacin	MI	2 mg/ml[a]	BR	0.1 mg/ml[a]	Physically compatible with no subvisual haze or particle formation in 4 hr at 23 °C	1725	C
Cisplatin	BR	1 mg/ml	BR	0.1 mg/ml[a]	Physically compatible with no subvisual haze or particle formation in 4 hr at 23 °C	1725	C
Cladribine	ORT	0.015[b] and 0.5[c] mg/ml	BR	0.1 mg/ml[b]	Physically compatible with no change in measured turbidity or increase in particle content in 4 hr at 23 °C	1969	C
Clindamycin phosphate	AST	10 mg/ml[a]	BR	0.1 mg/ml[a]	Physically compatible with no subvisual haze or particle formation in 4 hr at 23 °C	1725	C
Cyclophosphamide	MJ	10 mg/ml[a]	BR	0.1 mg/ml[a]	Physically compatible with no subvisual haze or particle formation in 4 hr at 23 °C	1725	C
Cytarabine	CET	50 mg/ml	BR	0.1 mg/ml[a]	Physically compatible with no subvisual haze or particle formation in 4 hr at 23 °C	1725	C

Y-Site Injection Compatibility (1:1 Mixture) (Cont.)

			Teniposide				
Drug	*Mfr*	*Conc*	*Mfr*	*Conc*	*Remarks*	*Ref*	*C/I*
Dacarbazine	MI	4 mg/ml[a]	BR	0.1 mg/ml[a]	Physically compatible with no subvisual haze or particle formation in 4 hr at 23 °C	1725	C
Dactinomycin	MSD	0.01 mg/ml[a]	BR	0.1 mg/ml[a]	Physically compatible with no subvisual haze or particle formation in 4 hr at 23 °C	1725	C
Daunorubicin HCl	WY	1 mg/ml[a]	BR	0.1 mg/ml[a]	Physically compatible with no subvisual haze or particle formation in 4 hr at 23 °C	1725	C
Dexamethasone sodium phosphate	LY	1 mg/ml[a]	BR	0.1 mg/ml[a]	Physically compatible with no subvisual haze or particle formation in 4 hr at 23 °C	1725	C
Diphenhydramine HCl	ES	2 mg/ml[a]	BR	0.1 mg/ml[a]	Physically compatible with no subvisual haze or particle formation in 4 hr at 23 °C	1725	C
Doxorubicin HCl	CET	2 mg/ml	BR	0.1 mg/ml[a]	Physically compatible with no subvisual haze or particle formation in 4 hr at 23 °C	1725	C
Doxycycline hyclate	LY	1 mg/ml[a]	BR	0.1 mg/ml[a]	Physically compatible with no subvisual haze or particle formation in 4 hr at 23 °C	1725	C
Droperidol	JN	0.4 mg/ml[a]	BR	0.1 mg/ml[a]	Physically compatible with no subvisual haze or particle formation in 4 hr at 23 °C	1725	C
Enalaprilat	MSD	0.1 mg/ml[a]	BR	0.1 mg/ml[a]	Physically compatible with no subvisual haze or particle formation in 4 hr at 23 °C	1725	C
Etoposide	BR	0.4 mg/ml[a]	BR	0.1 mg/ml[a]	Physically compatible with no subvisual haze or particle formation in 4 hr at 23 °C	1725	C
Etoposide phosphate	BR	5 mg/ml[a]	BR	0.1 mg/ml[a]	Physically compatible with no change in measured turbidity or increase in particle content in 4 hr at 23 °C	2218	C
Famotidine	MSD	2 mg/ml[a]	BR	0.1 mg/ml[a]	Physically compatible with no subvisual haze or particle formation in 4 hr at 23 °C	1725	C
Floxuridine	RC	3 mg/ml[a]	BR	0.1 mg/ml[a]	Physically compatible with no subvisual haze or particle formation in 4 hr at 23 °C	1725	C
Fluconazole	RR	2 mg/ml	BR	0.1 mg/ml[a]	Physically compatible with no subvisual haze or particle formation in 4 hr at 23 °C	1725	C
Fludarabine phosphate	BX	1 mg/ml[a]	BR	0.1 mg/ml[a]	Physically compatible with no subvisual haze or particle formation in 4 hr at 23 °C	1725	C
Fluorouracil	AD	16 mg/ml[a]	BR	0.1 mg/ml[a]	Physically compatible with no subvisual haze or particle formation in 4 hr at 23 °C	1725	C

Y-Site Injection Compatibility (1:1 Mixture) (Cont.)

Drug	Mfr	Conc	Teniposide Mfr	Teniposide Conc	Remarks	Ref	C/I
Furosemide	AB	3 mg/ml[a]	BR	0.1 mg/ml[a]	Physically compatible with no subvisual haze or particle formation in 4 hr at 23 °C	1725	C
Ganciclovir sodium	SY	20 mg/ml[a]	BR	0.1 mg/ml[a]	Physically compatible with no subvisual haze or particle formation in 4 hr at 23 °C	1725	C
Gemcitabine HCl	LI	10 mg/ml[b]	BR	0.1 mg/ml[a]	Physically compatible with no change in measured turbidity or increase in particle content in 4 hr at 23 °C	2226	C
Gentamicin sulfate	LY	5 mg/ml[a]	BR	0.1 mg/ml[a]	Physically compatible with no subvisual haze or particle formation in 4 hr at 23 °C	1725	C
Granisetron HCl	SKB	0.05 mg/ml[a]	BMS	0.1 mg/ml[a]	Physically compatible with no change in measured turbidity or increase in particle content in 4 hr at 23 °C	2000	C
Haloperidol lactate	MN	0.2 mg/ml[a]	BR	0.1 mg/ml[a]	Physically compatible with no subvisual haze or particle formation in 4 hr at 23 °C	1725	C
Hydrocortisone sodium phosphate	MSD	1 mg/ml[a]	BR	0.1 mg/ml[a]	Physically compatible with no subvisual haze or particle formation in 4 hr at 23 °C	1725	C
Hydrocortisone sodium succinate	UP	1 mg/ml[a]	BR	0.1 mg/ml[a]	Physically compatible with no subvisual haze or particle formation in 4 hr at 23 °C	1725	C
Hydromorphone HCl	KN	0.5 mg/ml[a]	BR	0.1 mg/ml[a]	Physically compatible with no subvisual haze or particle formation in 4 hr at 23 °C	1725	C
Hydroxyzine HCl	WI	4 mg/ml[a]	BR	0.1 mg/ml[a]	Physically compatible with no subvisual haze or particle formation in 4 hr at 23 °C	1725	C
Idarubicin HCl	AD	0.5 mg/ml[a]	BR	0.1 mg/ml[a]	Unacceptable increase in turbidity occurs immediately	1725	I
Ifosfamide	MJ	25 mg/ml[a]	BR	0.1 mg/ml[a]	Physically compatible with no subvisual haze or particle formation in 4 hr at 23 °C	1725	C
Imipenem–cilastatin sodium	MSD	10 mg/ml[b]	BR	0.1 mg/ml[a]	Physically compatible with no subvisual haze or particle formation in 4 hr at 23 °C	1725	C
Leucovorin calcium	LE	2 mg/ml[a]	BR	0.1 mg/ml[a]	Physically compatible with no subvisual haze or particle formation in 4 hr at 23 °C	1725	C
Lorazepam	WY	0.1 mg/ml[a]	BR	0.1 mg/ml[a]	Physically compatible with no subvisual haze or particle formation in 4 hr at 23 °C	1725	C
Mannitol	WY	15%	BR	0.1 mg/ml[a]	Physically compatible with no subvisual haze or particle formation in 4 hr at 23 °C	1725	C

Y-Site Injection Compatibility (1:1 Mixture) (Cont.)

			Teniposide				
Drug	*Mfr*	*Conc*	*Mfr*	*Conc*	*Remarks*	*Ref*	*C/I*
Mechlorethamine HCl	MSD	1 mg/ml	BR	0.1 mg/ml[a]	Physically compatible with no subvisual haze or particle formation in 4 hr at 23 °C	1725	C
Melphalan HCl	BW	0.1 mg/ml[a]	BR	0.1 mg/ml[a]	Physically compatible with no subvisual haze or particle formation in 4 hr at 23 °C	1725	C
Meperidine HCl	WY	4 mg/ml[a]	BR	0.1 mg/ml[a]	Physically compatible with no subvisual haze or particle formation in 4 hr at 23 °C	1725	C
Mesna	MJ	10 mg/ml[a]	BR	0.1 mg/ml[a]	Physically compatible with no subvisual haze or particle formation in 4 hr at 23 °C	1725	C
Methotrexate sodium	LE	15 mg/ml[a]	BR	0.1 mg/ml[a]	Physically compatible with no subvisual haze or particle formation in 4 hr at 23 °C	1725	C
Methylprednisolone sodium succinate	AB	5 mg/ml[a]	BR	0.1 mg/ml[a]	Physically compatible with no subvisual haze or particle formation in 4 hr at 23 °C	1725	C
Metoclopramide HCl	ES	5 mg/ml	BR	0.1 mg/ml[a]	Physically compatible with no subvisual haze or particle formation in 4 hr at 23 °C	1725	C
Metronidazole	BA	5 mg/ml	BR	0.1 mg/ml[a]	Physically compatible with no subvisual haze or particle formation in 4 hr at 23 °C	1725	C
Minocycline HCl	LE	0.2 mg/ml[a]	BR	0.1 mg/ml[a]	Physically compatible with no subvisual haze or particle formation in 4 hr at 23 °C	1725	C
Mitomycin	BR	0.5 mg/ml	BR	0.1 mg/ml[a]	Physically compatible with no subvisual haze or particle formation in 4 hr at 23 °C	1725	C
Mitoxantrone HCl	LE	0.5 mg/ml[a]	BR	0.1 mg/ml[a]	Physically compatible with no subvisual haze or particle formation in 4 hr at 23 °C	1725	C
Morphine sulfate	AST	1 mg/ml[a]	BR	0.1 mg/ml[a]	Physically compatible with no subvisual haze or particle formation in 4 hr at 23 °C	1725	C
Nalbuphine HCl	DU	10 mg/ml	BR	0.1 mg/ml[a]	Physically compatible with no subvisual haze or particle formation in 4 hr at 23 °C	1725	C
Netilmicin sulfate	SC	5 mg/ml[a]	BR	0.1 mg/ml[a]	Physically compatible with no subvisual haze or particle formation in 4 hr at 23 °C	1725	C
Ondansetron HCl	GL	1 mg/ml[b]	BR	0.1 mg/ml[a]	Physically compatible for 4 hr at 22 °C	1365	C
	GL	1 mg/ml[a]	BR	0.1 mg/ml[a]	Physically compatible with no subvisual haze or particle formation in 4 hr at 23 °C	1725	C
Piperacillin sodium	LE	40 mg/ml[a]	BR	0.1 mg/ml[a]	Physically compatible with no subvisual haze or particle formation in 4 hr at 23 °C	1725	C

Y-Site Injection Compatibility (1:1 Mixture) (Cont.)

Drug	Mfr	Conc	Teniposide Mfr	Teniposide Conc	Remarks	Ref	C/I
Plicamycin	MI	0.01 mg/ml[a]	BR	0.1 mg/ml[a]	Physically compatible with no subvisual haze or particle formation in 4 hr at 23 °C	1725	C
Potassium chloride	AB	0.1 mEq/ml[a]	BR	0.1 mg/ml[a]	Physically compatible with no subvisual haze or particle formation in 4 hr at 23 °C	1725	C
Prochlorperazine edisylate	SCN	0.5 mg/ml[a]	BR	0.1 mg/ml[a]	Physically compatible with no subvisual haze or particle formation in 4 hr at 23 °C	1725	C
Promethazine HCl	WY	2 mg/ml[a]	BR	0.1 mg/ml[a]	Physically compatible with no subvisual haze or particle formation in 4 hr at 23 °C	1725	C
Ranitidine HCl	GL	2 mg/ml[a]	BR	0.1 mg/ml[a]	Physically compatible with no subvisual haze or particle formation in 4 hr at 23 °C	1725	C
Sargramostim	IMM	10 μg/ml[b]	BR	0.1 mg/ml[b]	Physically compatible for 4 hr at 22 °C	1436	C
Sodium bicarbonate	AB	1 mEq/ml	BR	0.1 mg/ml[a]	Physically compatible with no subvisual haze or particle formation in 4 hr at 23 °C	1725	C
Streptozocin	UP	40 mg/ml[a]	BR	0.1 mg/ml[a]	Physically compatible with no subvisual haze or particle formation in 4 hr at 23 °C	1725	C
Thiotepa	LE	1 mg/ml[a]	BR	0.1 mg/ml[a]	Physically compatible with no subvisual haze or particle formation in 4 hr at 23 °C	1725	C
Ticarcillin disodium	BE	30 mg/ml[a]	BR	0.1 mg/ml[a]	Physically compatible with no subvisual haze or particle formation in 4 hr at 23 °C	1725	C
Ticarcillin disodium–clavulanate potassium	SKB	31 mg/ml[a]	BR	0.1 mg/ml[a]	Physically compatible with no subvisual haze or particle formation in 4 hr at 23 °C	1725	C
Tobramycin sulfate	LI	5 mg/ml[a]	BR	0.1 mg/ml[a]	Physically compatible with no subvisual haze or particle formation in 4 hr at 23 °C	1725	C
Trimethoprim–sulfamethoxazole	ES	0.8 + 4 mg/ml[a]	BR	0.1 mg/ml[a]	Physically compatible with no subvisual haze or particle formation in 4 hr at 23 °C	1725	C
Vancomycin HCl	AB	10 mg/ml[a]	BR	0.1 mg/ml[a]	Physically compatible with no subvisual haze or particle formation in 4 hr at 23 °C	1725	C
Vinblastine sulfate	LI	0.12 mg/ml[a]	BR	0.1 mg/ml[a]	Physically compatible with no subvisual haze or particle formation in 4 hr at 23 °C	1725	C
Vincristine sulfate	LI	0.05 mg/ml[a]	BR	0.1 mg/ml[a]	Physically compatible with no subvisual haze or particle formation in 4 hr at 23 °C	1725	C
Vinorelbine tartrate	BW	1 mg/ml[a]	BR	0.1 mg/ml[a]	Physically compatible with no subvisual haze or particle formation in 4 hr at 23 °C	1725	C

Y-Site Injection Compatibility (1:1 Mixture) (Cont.)

Teniposide

Drug	*Mfr*	*Conc*	*Mfr*	*Conc*	*Remarks*	*Ref*	*C/I*
Zidovudine	BW	4 mg/ml[a]	BR	0.1 mg/ml[a]	Physically compatible with no subvisual haze or particle formation in 4 hr at 23 °C	1725	C

[a]*Tested in dextrose 5% in water.*
[b]*Tested in sodium chloride 0.9%.*
[c]*Tested in bacteriostatic sodium chloride 0.9% preserved with benzyl alcohol 0.9%.*
[d]*Sodium carbonate–containing formulation tested.*

Additional Compatibility Information

Infusion Solutions — Dextrose 5% in water and sodium chloride 0.9% are recommended for dilution of teniposide. Concentrations of 0.1, 0.2, and 0.4 mg/ml in these solutions are stable for 24 hours at room temperature. At 1 mg/ml, teniposide administration should be completed within four hours because of the potential for precipitation. Solutions should not be refrigerated. (2)

Heparin — Heparin sodium can cause precipitation of teniposide. Administration apparatus should be thoroughly flushed before and after teniposide administration with dextrose 5% in water or sodium chloride 0.9%. (2; 1502)

Plastics — Contact of the undiluted teniposide concentrate with plastic equipment and devices during preparation has resulted in softening of the plastic, cracking, and leakage. Damage to plastic equipment has not been reported with diluted solutions. (2)

TERBUTALINE SULFATE
AHFS 12:12

Products — Terbutaline sulfate is available in 1-ml ampuls. Each milliliter contains terbutaline sulfate 1 mg, sodium chloride for isotonicity, and hydrochloric acid to adjust the pH. (2)

pH — The pH is adjusted to 3 to 5. (2; 4)

Osmolality — The injection is isotonic. (2) Terbutaline sulfate 1 mg/ml has an osmolality of 283 mOsm/kg. (1689)

Trade Name(s) — Brethine.

Administration — Terbutaline sulfate injection is administered subcutaneously only, usually into the lateral deltoid area. (2; 4) Intravenous administration is not recommended by the manufacturer (2) but has been used in selected patients with careful monitoring. (4)

Stability — Although relatively stable compared to corresponding catecholamines (738), terbutaline sulfate is nonetheless sensitive to light and excessive heat. The injection should be stored at controlled room temperature and protected from light. Discolored solutions should not be used. (2; 4) Terbutaline sulfate is stated to be stable over the pH range of 1 to 7. (4)

Syringes — Glascock et al. studied the stability of terbutaline sulfate (Geigy) 1 mg/ml packaged in polypropylene syringes (Becton-Dickinson) fitted with luer-tip caps (Becton-Dickinson). The samples were stored at 4 °C in the dark, 25 °C in the dark, and 25 °C with exposure to fluorescent light. Samples stored in the dark at both temperatures were stable, exhibiting a 5 to 6% drug loss in 60 days. The 25 °C samples exposed to light showed a 5% loss in 28 days and an 11% loss in 60 days, with a yellow discoloration at the latter time point. (1298)

Raymond (1299) also evaluated the stability of terbutaline sulfate (Geigy) 1 mg/ml repackaged in syringes. A 0.25-ml sample was drawn into each plastic tuberculin syringe (Becton-Dickinson) and sealed with a luer-tip cap (Becton-Dickinson). Samples were stored at 4 and 24 °C with exposure to light and light protection. Little difference was reported in the terbutaline sulfate content among the four storage conditions. Drug losses of 5% or less were observed after seven weeks of storage. Although no discoloration was reported, as found by Glascock et al. (1298), it may not have been observed in the small sample present in the tuberculin syringe.

Compatibility Information

Solution Compatibility

Terbutaline sulfate

Solution	*Mfr*	*Mfr*	*Conc/L*	*Remarks*	*Ref*	*C/I*
Dextrose 5% in water	AB	CI	4 mg	Physically compatible and chemically stable exposed to light. 10% decomposition calculated to occur in 328 hr at 25 °C	527	C
	TR[a]	MRD	30 mg	Less than 10% terbutaline loss in 7 days at 25 °C under fluorescent light	1133	C
Sodium chloride 0.45%	TR[a]	MRD	30 mg	Less than 5% terbutaline loss in 7 days at 25 °C under fluorescent light or at 4 °C	1133	C
Sodium chloride 0.9%	TR[a]	MRD	30 mg	Less than 6% terbutaline loss in 7 days at 25 °C under fluorescent light	1133	C

[a]*Tested in PVC containers.*

Additive Compatibility

Terbutaline sulfate

Drug	*Mfr*	*Conc/L*	*Mfr*	*Conc/L*	*Test Soln*	*Remarks*	*Ref*	*C/I*
Aminophylline	SE	500 mg	CI	4 mg	D5W	Physically compatible. 10% terbutaline decomposition in 44 hr at 25 °C exposed to light	527	C
Bleomycin sulfate	BR	20 and 30 units	GG	7.5 mg	NS	36% loss of bleomycin activity in 1 week at 4 °C	763	I

Drugs in Syringe Compatibility

Terbutaline sulfate

Drug (in syringe)	*Mfr*	*Amt*	*Mfr*	*Amt*	*Remarks*	*Ref*	*C/I*
Doxapram HCl	RB	400 mg/ 20 ml		0.2 mg/ 1 ml	Physically compatible with 6% doxapram loss in 24 hr	1177	C

Y-Site Injection Compatibility (1:1 Mixture)

Terbutaline sulfate

Drug	*Mfr*	*Conc*	*Mfr*	*Conc*	*Remarks*	*Ref*	*C/I*
Insulin, regular	LI	0.2 unit/ml[b]	CI	0.02 mg/ml[a]	Physically compatible for 2 hr at 25 °C under fluorescent light	1395	C

[a]*Tested in dextrose 5% in water.*
[b]*Tested in sodium chloride 0.9%.*

THEOPHYLLINE
AHFS 86:16

Products — Theophylline is available, premixed in dextrose 5% in water, in various concentrations (expressed as anhydrous theophylline) and container sizes (4; 154):

Concentration	Container Size	Total Theophylline
4 mg/ml	50 ml	200 mg
	100 ml	400 mg
3.2 mg/ml	250 ml	800 mg
2 mg/ml	100 ml	200 mg
1.6 mg/ml	250 ml	400 mg
	500 ml	800 mg
0.8 mg/ml	500 ml	400 mg
	1000 ml	800 mg
0.4 mg/ml	1000 ml	400 mg

pH — From 3.5 to 6.5. (17)

Administration — Theophylline may be administered by continuous or intermittent intravenous infusion. Slow administration, not exceeding 20 mg/min, has been recommended. Loading doses are usually given over 20 to 30 minutes. (4)

Stability — Theophylline injection should be stored at controlled room temperature and protected from freezing. Avoid excessive heat. (17)

At a concentration of 1 g/L in dextrose 5% in water, theophylline was stable during autoclaving for 20 minutes at 120 °C. No decrease in the theophylline content was detected. (1173)

Compatibility Information

Additive Compatibility

Theophylline

Drug	*Mfr*	*Conc/L*	*Mfr*	*Conc/L*	*Test Soln*	*Remarks*	*Ref*	*C/I*
Ascorbic acid injection		1.9 g		2 g	D5W	Yellow discoloration with 8% ascorbic acid loss in 6 hr and 15% in 24 hr. No loss of theophylline	1909	I
Cefepime HCl	BR	4 g	BA	800 mg	D5W	Visually compatible with 3% cefepime loss by HPLC in 24 hr at room temperature and 7 days at 5 °C. No theophylline loss	1681	C
Ceftriaxone sodium	RC	40 g	BA[a]	4 g		Yellow color forms immediately. 14% ceftriaxone loss and no theophylline loss by HPLC in 24 hr	1727	I
Chlorpromazine HCl		200 mg		2 g	D5W	Visually compatible with little or no theophylline loss and 7% chlorpromazine loss in 48 hr	1909	C
Deslanoside		1.6 mg		2 g	D5W	Visually compatible with little or no theophylline loss and 4% deslanoside loss in 48 hr	1909	C
Fluconazole	PF	1 g	BA	0.4 g	D5W[a,b]	Fluconazole chemically stable by gas chromatography for at least 72 hr at 25 °C under fluorescent light. Theophylline not tested	1676	C
Furosemide		330 mg		2 g	D5W	Visually compatible with little or no theophylline loss and 10% furosemide loss in 48 hr	1909	C
Hydrocortisone hemisuccinate		390 mg		2 g	D5W	Visually compatible with little or no loss of either drug in 48 hr	1909	C
Lidocaine HCl		380 mg		2 g	D5W	Visually compatible with little or no loss of either drug in 48 hr	1909	C
Methylprednisolone sodium succinate	UP	500 mg and 2 g	AB	4 g	D5W[b]	Physically compatible with little or no theophylline or methylprednisolone alcohol loss in 24 hr at room temperature. 8% ester hydrolysis termed not clinically important	1150	C

Additive Compatibility (Cont.)

Theophylline

Drug	*Mfr*	*Conc/L*	*Mfr*	*Conc/L*	*Test Soln*	*Remarks*	*Ref*	*C/I*
	UP	500 mg and 2 g	AB	400 mg	D5W[b]	Physically compatible with little or no theophylline or methylprednisolone alcohol loss in 24 hr at room temperature. 11% ester hydrolysis termed not clinically important	1150	C
Papaverine HCl		160 mg		2 g	D5W	Visually compatible with little or no loss of either drug in 48 hr	1909	C
Verapamil HCl	KN	100 and 400 mg	AB	400 mg and 4 g	D5W[b]	Physically compatible both visually and microscopically with little or no loss of either drug in 24 hr at 24 °C under fluorescent light	1172	C

[a]*Tested in PVC containers.*
[b]*Premixed theophylline infusion.*

Y-Site Injection Compatibility (1:1 Mixture)

Theophylline

Drug	*Mfr*	*Conc*	*Mfr*	*Conc*	*Remarks*	*Ref*	*C/I*
Acyclovir sodium	BW	5 mg/ml[a]	TR	1.6 mg/ml[a]	Physically compatible for 4 hr at 25 °C	1157	C
Ampicillin sodium	WY	20 mg/ml[b]	TR	4 mg/ml	Visually compatible for 6 hr at 25 °C	1793	C
Ampicillin sodium–sulbactam sodium	PF	20 + 10 mg/ml[b]	TR	4 mg/ml	Visually compatible for 6 hr at 25 °C	1793	C
Aztreonam	BV	20 mg/ml[a]	TR	4 mg/ml	Visually compatible for 6 hr at 25 °C	1793	C
Cefazolin sodium	SKB	20 mg/ml	TR	4 mg/ml	Visually compatible for 6 hr at 25 °C	1793	C
Cefotetan disodium	STU	40 mg/ml[a]	TR	4 mg/ml	Visually compatible for 6 hr at 25 °C	1793	C
Ceftazidime	LI[d]	20 mg/ml	TR	4 mg/ml	Visually compatible for 6 hr at 25 °C	1793	C
Ceftriaxone sodium	RC	20 mg/ml	TR	4 mg/ml	Visually compatible for 6 hr at 25 °C	1793	C
Cimetidine HCl	SKB	6 mg/ml[a]	TR	4 mg/ml	Visually compatible for 6 hr at 25 °C	1793	C
Cisatracurium besylate	GW	0.1, 2, 5 mg/ml[a]	AB	3.2 mg/ml	Physically compatible with no change in measured turbidity or increase in particle content in 4 hr at 23 °C	2074	C
Clindamycin phosphate	UP	12 mg/ml[a]	TR	4 mg/ml	Visually compatible for 6 hr at 25 °C	1793	C
Dexamethasone sodium phosphate	ES	0.08 mg/ml[a]	TR	4 mg/ml	Visually compatible for 6 hr at 25 °C	1793	C
Diltiazem HCl	MMD	5 mg/ml	AB	0.8 mg/ml[a]	Visually compatible	1807	C
Dobutamine HCl	LI	1 mg/ml[a]	TR	4 mg/ml	Visually compatible for 6 hr at 25 °C	1793	C
Dopamine HCl	BA	1.6 mg/ml	TR	4 mg/ml	Visually compatible for 6 hr at 25 °C	1793	C
Doxycycline hyclate	ES	1 mg/ml[a]	TR	4 mg/ml	Visually compatible for 6 hr at 25 °C	1793	C
Erythromycin lactobionate	AB	3.3 mg/ml[b]	TR	4 mg/ml	Visually compatible for 6 hr at 25 °C	1793	C
Famotidine	MSD	0.2 mg/ml[a]	TR	1.6 mg/ml[a]	Physically compatible for 4 hr at 25 °C	1188	C
Fluconazole	RR	2 mg/ml	AMR	1.6 mg/ml[a]	Visually compatible for 24 hr at 28 °C under fluorescent light	1760	C
	PF	2 mg/ml	TR	4 mg/ml	Visually compatible for 6 hr at 25 °C	1793	C

Y-Site Injection Compatibility (1:1 Mixture) (Cont.)

Drug	*Mfr*	*Conc*	Theophylline *Mfr*	Theophylline *Conc*	*Remarks*	*Ref*	*C/I*
Gatifloxacin	BMS	2 mg/ml[a]	BA	4 mg/ml[a]	Physically compatible with no change in measured haze or increase in particle content in 4 hr at 23 °C	2334	C
Gentamicin sulfate	TR	2 mg/ml	TR	4 mg/ml	Visually compatible for 6 hr at 25 °C	1793	C
Haloperidol lactate	MN	0.5[a] and 5 mg/ml	TR	1.6 mg/ml[a]	Visually compatible for 24 hr at 21 °C	1523	C
Heparin sodium	TR	50 units/ml	TR	4 mg/ml	Visually compatible for 4 hr at 25 °C	1793	C
Hetastarch in lactated electrolyte injection (Hextend)	AB	6%	BA	4 mg/ml[a]	Physically compatible with no change in measured turbidity or increase in particle content in 4 hr at 23 °C	2339	C
Hetastarch in sodium chloride 0.9%	DCC	6%	TR	4 mg/ml[c]	Precipitation after 2 hr at room temperature	1313	I
Hydrocortisone sodium succinate	UP	2 mg/ml[a]	TR	4 mg/ml	Visually compatible for 6 hr at 25 °C	1793	C
Lidocaine HCl	TR	4 mg/ml	TR	4 mg/ml	Visually compatible for 6 hr at 25 °C	1793	C
Linezolid	PHU	2 mg/ml	BA	4 mg/ml[a]	Physically compatible with no change in measured turbidity or increase in particle content in 4 hr at 23 °C	2264	C
Methyldopate HCl	ES	5 mg/ml[a]	TR	4 mg/ml	Visually compatible for 6 hr at 25 °C	1793	C
Methylprednisolone sodium succinate	UP	2.5 mg/ml[a]	TR	4 mg/ml	Visually compatible for 6 hr at 25 °C	1793	C
Metronidazole	MG	5 mg/ml	TR	4 mg/ml	Visually compatible for 6 hr at 25 °C	1793	C
Midazolam HCl	RC	1 mg/ml[a]	BA	1.6 mg/ml[a]	Visually compatible for 24 hr at 23 °C	1847	C
Milrinone lactate	SW	0.4 mg/ml[a]	AB	1.6 mg/ml[a]	Visually compatible with little or no loss of milrinone by HPLC and theophylline by immunoassay in 4 hr at 23 °C	2214	C
Nafcillin sodium	WY	20 mg/ml[a]	TR	4 mg/ml	Visually compatible for 6 hr at 25 °C	1793	C
Nitroglycerin	LY	0.2 mg/ml[a]	TR	4 mg/ml	Visually compatible for 6 hr at 25 °C	1793	C
Penicillin G potassium	RR	40,000 units/ml[a]	TR	4 mg/ml	Visually compatible for 6 hr at 25 °C	1793	C
Phenytoin sodium	ES	2 mg/ml[b]	TR	4 mg/ml	Cloudiness forms immediately and becomes dense, flocculent precipitate in 6 hr at 25 °C	1793	I
Piperacillin sodium	LE	60 mg/ml[a]	TR	4 mg/ml	Visually compatible for 6 hr at 25 °C	1793	C
Potassium chloride	AB	0.2 mEq/ml[a]	TR	4 mg/ml	Visually compatible for 6 hr at 25 °C	1793	C
Ranitidine HCl	GL	1 mg/ml	TR	4 mg/ml	Visually compatible for 6 hr at 25 °C	1793	C
Remifentanil HCl	GW	0.025 and 0.25 mg/ml[b]	AB	3.2 mg/ml[a]	Physically compatible with no change in measured turbidity or increase in particle content in 4 hr at 23 °C	2075	C
Sodium nitroprusside	ES	0.2 mg/ml[a]	TR	4 mg/ml	Visually compatible for 6 hr at 25 °C protected from light	1793	C
Ticarcillin disodium	BE	20 mg/ml[a]	TR	4 mg/ml	Visually compatible for 6 hr at 25 °C	1793	C
Ticarcillin disodium–clavulanate potassium	BE	31 mg/ml[a]	TR	4 mg/ml	Visually compatible for 6 hr at 25 °C	1793	C
Tobramycin sulfate	LI	0.8 mg/ml[a]	TR	4 mg/ml	Visually compatible for 6 hr at 25 °C	1793	C

Y-Site Injection Compatibility (1:1 Mixture) (Cont.)

Theophylline

Drug	*Mfr*	*Conc*	*Mfr*	*Conc*	*Remarks*	*Ref*	*C/I*
Vancomycin HCl	LI	6.6 mg/ml[a]	TR	4 mg/ml	Visually compatible for 6 hr at 25 °C	1793	C

[a]*Tested in dextrose 5% in water.*
[b]*Tested in sodium chloride 0.9%.*
[c]*Premixed infusion solution.*
[d]*Sodium carbonate–containing formulation tested.*

Additional Compatibility Information

Cimetidine — Complex formation between cimetidine and theophylline was noted in pH 7.4 phosphate buffer solution and human plasma. (1043)

Other Information

Heating Plasma — Heating plasma samples to 56 °C for one hour to inactivate potential HIV content resulted in no theophylline loss as determined by fluorescence polarization immunoassay. (1615)

THIAMINE HCL
AHFS 88:08

Products — Thiamine HCl is available in a concentration of 100 mg/ml in 1-ml syringe cartridge units and 1- and 2-ml vials. Each milliliter of solution may also contain chlorobutanol 0.5% as an antibacterial preservative and monothioglycerol 0.5%. Sodium hydroxide and/or hydrochloric acid may be added to adjust the pH. (1-1/99; 4; 29)

pH — From 2.5 to 4.5. (1-1/99; 17)

Osmolality — Thiamine HCl 100 mg/ml has an osmolality of 777 mOsm/kg. (1689)

Administration — Thiamine HCl injection may be administered by intramuscular or slow intravenous injection. An intradermal test dose has been recommended for patients with suspected thiamine sensitivity. (1-1/99; 4)

Stability — Thiamine HCl in intact containers should be stored at controlled room temperature and protected from light and freezing. (4)

pH Effects — Thiamine HCl is stable in acid solutions (1-3/91), losing activity very slowly at pH 4 or less. It is maximally stable at pH 2. (1072) Thiamine HCl is unstable in neutral or alkaline solutions. (1-1/99; 4; 1072)

Syringes — Thiamine HCl (Lilly) 100 mg/ml was repackaged in glass syringes (Glaspak), back-fill glass syringes (Hy-Pod), and plastic syringes (Stylex). Half of the syringes were filled with thiamine HCl injection filtered through 5-μm stainless steel depth filters (Extemp filter pin), and the rest were filled with unfiltered drug. The syringes containing 1 ml of thiamine HCl injection were stored protected from light (amber UV-light-inhibiting plastic bags) at 22 to 24 °C for 84 days. No color changes were observed, and changes in pH were minimal. Furthermore, no differences between filtered or unfiltered samples occurred, with all solutions retaining approximately 100% of the initial potency over the 84 days. (734)

Sorption — Thiamine HCl (Merck) 30 mg/L did not display significant sorption to a PVC plastic test strip in 24 hours. (12)

Compatibility Information

Solution Compatibility

Thiamine HCl

Solution	*Mfr*	*Mfr*	*Conc/L*	*Remarks*	*Ref*	*C/I*
Dextran 6% in dextrose 5%	AB		100 mg	Physically compatible	3	C
Dextran 6% in sodium chloride 0.9%	AB		100 mg	Physically compatible	3	C
Dextrose–Ringer's injection combinations	AB		100 mg	Physically compatible	3	C
Dextrose–Ringer's injection, lactated, combinations	AB		100 mg	Physically compatible	3	C
Dextrose–saline combinations	AB		100 mg	Physically compatible	3	C

Solution Compatibility (Cont.)

Thiamine HCl

Solution	*Mfr*	*Mfr*	*Conc/L*	*Remarks*	*Ref*	*C/I*
Dextrose 2½% in water	AB		100 mg	Physically compatible	3	C
Dextrose 5% in water	AB		100 mg	Physically compatible	3	C
Dextrose 10% in water	AB		100 mg	Physically compatible	3	C
Fat emulsion 10%, intravenous	KA	KA[a]	118 mg	Physically compatible for 24 hr at 26 °C with little loss of thiamine HCl and of most other vitamins by HPLC; up to 52% ascorbate loss	2050	C
Fructose 10% in sodium chloride 0.9%	AB		100 mg	Physically compatible	3	C
Fructose 10% in water	AB		100 mg	Physically compatible	3	C
Invert sugar 5 and 10% in sodium chloride 0.9%	AB		100 mg	Physically compatible	3	C
Invert sugar 5 and 10% in water	AB		100 mg	Physically compatible	3	C
Ionosol products	AB		100 mg	Physically compatible	3	C
Ringer's injection	AB		100 mg	Physically compatible	3	C
Ringer's injection, lactated	AB		100 mg	Physically compatible	3	C
Sodium chloride 0.45%	AB		100 mg	Physically compatible	3	C
Sodium chloride 0.9%	AB		100 mg	Physically compatible	3	C
Sodium lactate ⅙ M	AB		100 mg	Physically compatible	3	C

[a]From multivitamins.

Drugs in Syringe Compatibility

Thiamine HCl

Drug (in syringe)	*Mfr*	*Amt*	*Mfr*	*Amt*	*Remarks*	*Ref*	*C/I*
Doxapram HCl	RB	400 mg/ 20 ml		10 mg/ 2 ml	Physically compatible with 6% doxapram loss in 24 hr	1177	C

Y-Site Injection Compatibility (1:1 Mixture)

Thiamine HCl

Drug	*Mfr*	*Conc*	*Mfr*	*Conc*	*Remarks*	*Ref*	*C/I*
Famotidine	MSD	0.2 mg/ml[a]	ES	100 mg/ml	Physically compatible for 14 hr	1196	C

[a]Tested in dextrose 5% in water.

Additional Compatibility Information

Infusion Solutions — A study of the stability of thiamine HCl in the multivitamin products Berocca-PN (Roche), Multivitamin Additive (Abbott), and M.V.I.-12 (USV) showed extensive decomposition when these products were admixed in infusion solutions containing sodium bisulfite. After 24 hours at 23 °C, thiamine losses ranged from 70% in Travasol 5.5% (pH 5.5) to 97% in FreAmine III 8.5% (pH 6.5). The extent of decomposition increased as the pH neared neutrality. The rate of decomposition could be slowed, but not eliminated, by refrigeration. When admixed in solutions without bisulfite, the thiamine was much more stable, showing losses of 0 to 11% in 24 hours at 23 °C. The authors noted that if bisulfite-containing solutions are necessary to administer multivitamin preparations, the admixtures should be used immediately after preparation and patients on long-term therapy should be monitored for thiamine deficiency. (774)

The stability of thiamine HCl 50 mg/L was studied in representative parenteral nutrition solutions exposed to fluorescent light, indirect sunlight, and direct sunlight for eight hours. One 5-ml vial of multivitamin concentrate (Lyphomed) containing 50 mg of thiamine HCl and also 1 mg of folic acid (Lederle) were added to a liter of parenteral nutrition solution composed of amino acids 4.25%–dextrose 25% (Travenol) with standard electrolytes and trace elements. Thiamine HCl was stable over the eight-hour study period at room temperature under fluorescent light and indirect sunlight, but direct sunlight caused a 26% loss. (842)

Samples from 24 1-L and four 2-L parenteral nutrition solutions containing one vial each of multivitamin concentrate (USV) were evaluated for thiamine HCl content 48 to 72 hours after mixing. The parenteral nutrition solutions contained amino acids 2.75 to 5%, dextrose 15 to 25%, and electrolytes. Thiamine HCl was stable in all of the solutions tested in spite of an approximately 0.05% sulfite content. (843)

In another experiment, multivitamin concentrate (USV) was added to 500-ml glass bottles of amino acids 10% (Travenol) containing 0.1% sulfite and also 1000-ml PVC bags containing amino acids 4.25%–dextrose 25% (Travenol) with about 0.05% sulfite. After 22 hours at 30 °C, a 40% loss of thiamine HCl occurred in the amino acid 10% solution, but no loss occurred in the PVC bags of parenteral nutrition solution. The authors concluded that the thiamine HCl content is retained in usual clinical parenteral nutrition solutions, probably because of the dilution of the sulfite and buffering of pH. However, direct addition to solutions with a high sulfite content (0.1%) may result in significant decomposition. (843)

Shine and Farwell reported a 50% initial drop in thiamine concentration immediately after admixture of multivitamins in a parenteral nutrition solution composed of amino acids, dextrose, electrolytes, and trace elements in PVC bags. The thiamine concentration then remained relatively constant for 120 hours when stored at both 4 and 25 °C. (1063)

Dahl et al. reported the stability of numerous vitamins in parenteral nutrition solutions composed of amino acids (Kabi-Vitrum), dextrose 30%, and fat emulsion 20% (Kabi-Vitrum) in a 2:1:1 ratio with electrolytes, trace elements, and both fat- and water-soluble vitamins. The admixtures were stored in darkness at 2 to 8 °C for 96 hours with no significant loss of retinyl palmitate, alpha-tocopherol, thiamine mononitrate, sodium riboflavin-5′-phosphate, pyridoxine HCl, nicotinamide, folic acid, biotin, sodium pantothenate, and cyanocobalamin. Sodium ascorbate and its biologically active degradation product, dehydroascorbic acid, totaled 59 and 42% of the nominal starting concentration at 24 and 96 hours, respectively. However, the actual initial concentration was only 66% of the nominal concentration. (1225)

Smith et al. reported the stability of several vitamins from M.V.I.-12 (Armour) admixed in parenteral nutrition solutions composed of different amino acid products, with or without Intralipid 10%, when stored in glass bottles and PVC bags at 25 and 5 °C for 48 hours. Thiamine HCl was stable in the parenteral nutrition solutions prepared with amino acid products without bisulfite. However, amino acid products containing bisulfite (Travasol and FreAmine III) had a 25% thiamine loss in 12 hours and a 50% loss in 24 hours when the solutions were stored at 25 °C; no loss occurred when the solutions were stored at 5 °C. (1431)

The stability of thiamine HCl from a multiple vitamin product in dextrose 5% in water and sodium chloride 0.9% in PVC and ClearFlex containers was evaluated. HPLC analysis showed that thiamine HCl was stable at 23 °C when exposed to or protected from light, exhibiting losses of 11% or less in 24 hours. (1509)

Other Drugs — Thiamine HCl is stated to be incompatible with alkaline or neutral solutions (4) (i.e., barbiturates, carbonates and bicarbonates, etc.) and with copper ions. (461)

Thiamine HCl is also stated to be incompatible with oxidizing and reducing agents. (4) In solutions with sulfites or bisulfites, it is rapidly inactivated. (52; 1072; 1925) Oxidation of thiamine HCl results in the formation of the highly blue-colored and biologically inactive compound thiochrome. (734; 1072)

In vitro testing of thiamine HCl at a concentration of 0.1% with the following antibiotics at a concentration of 0.025% in sterile distilled water showed significant reduction in antibiotic activity in one hour at 25 °C (314):

Erythromycin (as estolate)
Kanamycin sulfate
Streptomycin sulfate

THIETHYLPERAZINE MALATE
AHFS 56:22

Products — Thiethylperazine malate is available in 2-ml ampuls. Each milliliter of solution contains (1-6/00):

Thiethylperazine malate	5 mg
Sodium metabisulfite	0.25 mg
Ascorbic acid	1 mg
Sorbitol	20 mg
Carbon dioxide	qs
Water for injection	qs 1 ml

pH — From 3 to 4. (4)

Trade Name(s) — Torecan.

Administration — Thiethylperazine malate is administered by deep intramuscular injection. Subcutaneous or intravenous injection is not recommended. (1-6/00; 4)

Stability — The solution should be stored below 30 °C protected from light and used only if clear and colorless. (1-6/00)

Thiethylperazine malate (Sandoz) 5 mg/ml was found to retain potency for two weeks under refrigeration when 2 ml of solution was packaged in Tubex cartridges. Room temperature storage for one week and refrigerated storage for three weeks resulted in a darkening in color. (13)

Compatibility Information

Drugs in Syringe Compatibility

Thiethylperazine malate

Drug (in syringe)	*Mfr*	*Amt*	*Mfr*	*Amt*	*Remarks*	*Ref*	*C/I*
Butorphanol tartrate	BR	4 mg/ 2 ml	BI	10 mg/ 1 ml	Physically compatible both macroscopically and microscopically for 30 min at room temperature	761	C
Hydromorphone HCl	KN	4 mg/ 2 ml	SZ	5 mg/ 1 ml	Physically compatible for 30 min	517	C
Ketorolac tromethamine	SY	30 mg/ 1 ml	ROX	5 mg/ 1 ml	White crystalline precipitate forms immediately	1785	I
Midazolam HCl	RC	5 mg/ 1 ml	BI	10 mg/ 2 ml	Physically compatible for 4 hr at 25 °C under fluorescent light	1145	C
Nalbuphine HCl	EN	10 mg/ 1 ml	BI	5 mg/ 1 ml	Physically compatible for 36 hr at 27 °C	762	C
	EN	5 mg/ 0.5 ml	BI	5 mg/ 1 ml	Crystals form within 24 hr at 27 °C. Physically compatible for at least 12 hr	762	I
	EN	2.5 mg/ 0.25 ml	BI	5 mg/ 1 ml	Crystals form within 24 hr at 27 °C. Physically compatible for at least 12 hr	762	I
	DU	10 mg/ 1 ml		10 mg/ 2 ml	Physically compatible for 48 hr	128	C
	DU	20 mg/ 1 ml		10 mg/ 2 ml	Physically compatible for 48 hr	128	C
Perphenazine	SC	5 mg/ 1 ml	BI	10 mg/ 1 ml	Yellow discoloration within 15 min	761	I
Ranitidine HCl	GL	50 mg/ 2 ml	SZ	10 mg/ 1 ml	Physically compatible for 1 hr at 25 °C both macroscopically and microscopically	978	C

Y-Site Injection Compatibility (1:1 Mixture)

Thiethylperazine malate

Drug	*Mfr*	*Conc*	*Mfr*	*Conc*	*Remarks*	*Ref*	*C/I*
Aldesleukin	CHI	33,800 I.U./ml[a]	SZ	0.4 mg/ml[a]	Visually compatible with little or no loss of aldesleukin activity by bioassay	1857	C

[a]*Tested in dextrose 5% in water.*

THIOPENTAL SODIUM
AHFS 28:24.04

Products — Thiopental sodium is available in 250-, 400-, and 500-mg syringes, 500-mg and 1-g vials, and 1-, 2.5-, and 5-g containers in kits. (29; 154) The products also contain anhydrous sodium carbonate as a buffer. (1-8/96; 17) Reconstitute only with sterile water for injection, sodium chloride 0.9%, or dextrose 5% in water for solutions in the 2 to 5% range or with dextrose 5% in water, sodium chloride 0.9%, or Normosol R, pH 7.4, for solutions of 0.2 or 0.4%. Do not use sterile water for injection to prepare thiopental sodium solutions less than 2% because such solutions would be very hypotonic and would cause hemolysis. (1-8/96; 21; 154)

Thiopental Sodium	Volume of Diluent	Concentration
1 g	500 ml	2 mg/ml (0.2%)
1 g	250 ml	4 mg/ml (0.4%)
2 g	500 ml	4 mg/ml (0.4%)
5 g	250 ml	20 mg/ml (2.0%)
10 g	500 ml	20 mg/ml (2.0%)
1 g	40 ml	25 mg/ml (2.5%)
5 g	200 ml	25 mg/ml (2.5%)
1 g	20 ml	50 mg/ml (5.0%)
5 g	100 ml	50 mg/ml (5.0%)

pH—A thiopental sodium 80 mg/ml solution in water has an official pH range of 10.2 to 11.2. (17) The pH of a 2.5% solution in sterile water for injection is 10 to 11. (21)

Osmolality—The osmolality of thiopental sodium 25 and 100 mg/ml was determined to be 215 and 942 mOsm/kg, respectively. (1233) A 3.4% solution in sterile water for injection is isotonic. A thiopental sodium concentration less than 2% in sterile water for injection is very hypotonic and will cause hemolysis. (1-8/96; 154) Sterile water for injection should not be used to prepare thiopental sodium solutions less than 2%.

Sodium Content—Each gram of thiopental sodium contains 4.9 mEq of sodium. (846)

Trade Name(s)—Pentothal Sodium.

Administration — Thiopental sodium is given by slow intravenous infusion only. For intermittent intravenous administration, the concentrations used range between 2 and 5% in sterile water for injection, dextrose 5% in water, or sodium chloride 0.9%, with 2 or 2.5% being the most common. By continuous intravenous drip, concentrations of 0.2 or 0.4% in dextrose 5% in water, sodium chloride 0.9%, or a pH 7.4 combined electrolyte solution such as Normosol R are used. Sterile water for injection should not be used for these concentrations, because of resulting hemolysis from the hypotonic solution. Extravasation and intra-arterial administration should be avoided because of the high alkalinity of the solutions. (1-8/96)

Stability — Thiopental sodium is a yellowish-colored powder. Intact containers should be stored at controlled room temperature. Factors that affect the stability of solutions of thiopental sodium include the diluent, storage temperature, and the amount of carbon dioxide from room air that gains access to the solution and combines with water to form carbonic acid, lowering the pH of the solution. The drug is most stable when reconstituted with sterile water for injection or sodium chloride 0.9%, stored under refrigeration, and tightly sealed. (1-8/96) Reconstituted solutions are stated to be stable for three days at room temperature (18 to 22 °C) and for seven days under refrigeration (5 to 6 °C). (108) Since no preservative is present, however, use within 24 hours is recommended. (1-8/96; 21) Also, glass attack has been noted in 48 hours. (46) Sterilization by heating should not be attempted. (1-8/96)

The pH of thiopental sodium must be very alkaline or the insoluble acid form will precipitate. (21)

Syringes—Thiopental sodium (Abbott) 25 mg/ml (2.5%) in water for injection, repackaged in 20-ml syringes (Monoject and Becton-Dickinson), was stable for up to five days at 25 °C and 45 days at 5 °C, sustaining potency losses of 6 to 7%. No physical changes occurred during the study period. (1300)

Thiopental sodium (Abbott) 25 mg/ml was repackaged into 60-ml polypropylene syringes (Monoject, Sherwood Medical) and stored at 23 °C under fluorescent light and at 4 °C protected from light. No visually apparent changes occurred under either storage condition. Thiopental sodium losses by HPLC analysis were 9% in 10 days in the room temperature samples. No thiopental sodium losses occurred in 13 days in the refrigerated samples. (1984)

The stability of thiopental sodium 25 mg/ml repackaged in polypropylene syringes was evaluated by spectrophotometric and potentiometric methods. About 7% loss of drug concentration was found after four weeks of storage at room temperature not exposed to direct light. (2164)

Sorption—Thiopental sodium (May & Baker) 7 mg/L in sodium chloride 0.9% (Travenol) in PVC bags exhibited approximately 23% loss in 24 hours and 37% loss in one week at room temperature (15 to 20 °C) due to sorption. (536)

In another study, thiopental sodium (May & Baker) 7 mg/L in sodium chloride 0.9%, buffered to pH 6.1, exhibited a cumulative 16% loss during a seven-hour simulated infusion through an infusion set (Travenol) consisting of a cellulose propionate burette chamber and 170 cm of PVC tubing due to sorption. Thiopental sorption was attributed mainly to the burette. The extent of sorption was dependent on the pH of the solution. As the pH decreased, the percentage of unionized drug increased. In turn, the extent of sorption also increased. (606)

The drug was also tested as a simulated infusion over at least one hour by a syringe pump system. A glass syringe on a syringe pump was fitted with 20 cm of polyethylene tubing or 50 cm of Silastic tubing. Only 5% of the drug was lost with the polyethylene tubing, but a cumulative loss of 50% occurred during the one-hour infusion through the Silastic tubing. (606)

In contrast, a 25-ml aliquot of thiopental sodium (May & Baker) 7 mg/L in sodium chloride 0.9% was stored in all-plastic syringes composed of polypropylene barrels and polyethylene plungers for 24 hours at room temperature in the dark. No loss due to sorption occurred. (606)

In a continuation of this work, thiopental sodium (May & Baker) 9 mg/L in sodium chloride 0.9% in a glass bottle was delivered through a polyethylene administration set (Tridilset) over eight hours at 15 to 20 °C. The flow rate was set at 1 ml/min. No appreciable loss because of sorption occurred. (769) This finding is in contrast to the 16% loss with a conventional administration set. (606)

The sorption of thiopental sodium 30 mg/L in sodium chloride 0.9% (pH 4 and 7.2) was evaluated in 100-ml PVC infusion bags (Travenol). After eight hours at 20 to 24 °C, 25% of the thiopental was lost. Thiopental sodium showed a negligible (less than 3%) loss if the aqueous solution was stored in polypropylene infusion bags. (770)

Martens et al. (1392) reported that thiopental sodium 2 mg/ml in sodium chloride 0.9% in PVC, glass, and polyethylene-lined laminated containers exhibited no loss due to sorption in 24 hours at 21 °C when protected from light. This finding differs from that of Kowaluk et al. who reported a significant loss in PVC containers. (536) Martens et al. attribute the difference to their use of a much higher concentration, representing a therapeutic dosage, which resulted in a sharply different solution pH (pH 9.1); the more dilute solution in the Kowaluk et al. study had a pH of 6. At lower pH, more drug remains unionized, increasing the rate of sorption. (1392)

Compatibility Information

Solution Compatibility

Thiopental sodium

Solution	*Mfr*	*Mfr*	*Conc/L*	*Remarks*	*Ref*	*C/I*
Alcohol 5%, dextrose 5%	AB	AB	25 g	Physically compatible	21	C
Dextran 6% in dextrose 5%	AB	AB	25 g	Physically compatible	3; 21	C
Dextran 6% in sodium chloride 0.9%	AB	AB	25 g	Physically compatible	3; 21	C
Dextrose–Ringer's injection combinations	AB	AB	25 g	Haze or precipitate forms within 1 hr	3; 21	I
Dextrose–Ringer's injection, lactated, combinations	AB	AB	25 g	Haze or precipitate forms within 1 hr	3; 21	I
Dextrose 5% in Ringer's injection, lactated	TR	AB		Precipitate forms within variable time periods	544	I
Dextrose 2½% in sodium chloride 0.45%	AB	AB	25 g	Physically compatible	3	C
Dextrose 2½% in sodium chloride 0.9%	AB	AB	25 g	Physically compatible	3	C
Dextrose 5% in sodium chloride 0.225%	AB	AB	25 g	Physically compatible	3; 21	C
Dextrose 5% in sodium chloride 0.45%	AB	AB	25 g	Physically compatible	3; 21	C
Dextrose 5% in sodium chloride 0.9%	AB	AB	2 g	Potency retained for 48 hr	46	C
	TR[a]	AB	2 g	Potency retained for 24 hr at 5 °C	282	C
	AB	AB	25 g	Haze or precipitate forms within 24 hr. Physically compatible for 6 hr	3; 21	I
Dextrose 10% in sodium chloride 0.9%		AB		Physically incompatible	9	I
	AB	AB	25 g	Haze or precipitate forms within 1 hr	3; 21	I
Dextrose 2½% in water	AB	AB	25 g	Physically compatible	3	C
Dextrose 5% in water	AB	AB	25 g	Physically compatible	3; 21	C
	AB	AB	2 g	Potency retained for 48 hr	46	C
	TR[a]	AB	2 g	Potency retained for 24 hr at 5 °C	282	C
Dextrose 10% in water	AB	AB	25 g	Haze or precipitate forms within 1 hr	3; 21	I
Fructose 10% in sodium chloride 0.9%	AB	AB	25 g	Haze or precipitate forms within 1 hr	3	I
Fructose 10% solutions	AB	AB	25 g	Precipitate forms within 1 hr	21	I
Fructose 10% in water	BA	AB	1 g	Physically incompatible	10	I
Invert sugar 5 and 10% in sodium chloride 0.9%	AB	AB	25 g	Haze or precipitate forms within 1 to 6 hr	3	I
	AB	AB	25 g	Precipitate forms within 1 hr	21	I
Invert sugar 5 and 10% in water	AB	AB	25 g	Haze or precipitate forms within 1 to 6 hr	3	I
	AB	AB	25 g	Precipitate forms within 1 hr	21	I
Ionosol products	AB	AB	25 g	Haze or precipitate forms within 1 hr	3; 21	I
Multielectrolyte solution	AB	AB	2 g	Potency retained for 48 hr	46	C
Normosol solutions (except R)	AB	AB	25 g	Precipitate forms within 1 hr	21	I
Normosol R	AB	AB	25 g	Physically compatible	21	C
Ringer's injection	AB	AB	25 g	Haze or precipitate forms within 1 hr	3	I

Solution Compatibility (Cont.)

Thiopental sodium

Solution	*Mfr*	*Mfr*	*Conc/L*	*Remarks*	*Ref*	*C/I*
Ringer's injection, lactated		AB		Physically incompatible	9	I
	AB	AB	25 g	Haze or precipitate forms within 1 hr	3	I
Sodium chloride 0.45%	AB	AB	25 g	Physically compatible	3	C
Sodium chloride 0.9%	AB	AB	25 g	Physically compatible	3; 21	C
	AB	AB	2 g	Potency retained for 48 hr	46	C
	TR[a]	AB	2 g	Potency retained for 24 hr at 5 °C	282	C
	[b]		2 g	Physically compatible with little or no drug loss in 24 hr at 21 °C in the dark	1392	C
Sodium lactate ⅙ M	AB	AB	25 g	Physically compatible	3; 21	C

[a]*Tested in both glass and PVC containers.*
[b]*Tested in PVC, glass, and polyethylene-lined laminated containers.*

Additive Compatibility

Thiopental sodium

Drug	*Mfr*	*Conc/L*	*Mfr*	*Conc/L*	*Test Soln*	*Remarks*	*Ref*	*C/I*
Amikacin sulfate	BR	5 g	AB	4 g	D5LR, D5R, D5S, D5W, D10W, IS10, LR, NS, R, SL	Immediate precipitation	294	I
Chloramphenicol sodium succinate	PD	1 g	AB	2.5 g	D5W	Physically compatible	21	C
Dimenhydrinate	SE		AB			Physically incompatible	9	I
Diphenhydramine HCl	PD		AB			Physically incompatible	9	I
Ephedrine sulfate			AB			Physically incompatible	9	I
	AB	50 mg	AB	2.5 g	D5W	Physically compatible	21	C
Fibrinolysin, human	MSD	2 g	AB	2.5 g	D5W	Physically incompatible	11	I
Hydrocortisone sodium succinate	UP	100 mg	AB	2.5 g	D5W	Physically compatible	21	C
Hydromorphone HCl			AB			Physically incompatible	9	I
Insulin, regular[a]			AB			Physically incompatible	9	I
Levorphanol bitartrate	RC		AB			Physically incompatible	9	I
Meperidine HCl	WI		AB			Physically incompatible	9	I
Metaraminol bitartrate	MSD	100 mg	AB	2.5 g		Precipitate forms within 1 hr	7	I
	MSD	200 mg	AB	2.5 g	D5W	Physically incompatible	11	I
	MSD	200 mg	AB	2.5 g	D5W	Precipitate forms within 1 hr	21	I
Morphine sulfate			AB			Physically incompatible	9	I
Norepinephrine bitartrate	WI		AB			Physically incompatible	9	I
Oxytocin	PD	5 units	AB	2.5 g	D5W	Physically compatible	21	C
Penicillin G potassium	SQ	20 million units	AB	2.5 g	D5W	Precipitate forms within 1 hr	21	I

Additive Compatibility (Cont.)

Thiopental sodium

Drug	*Mfr*	*Conc/L*	*Mfr*	*Conc/L*	*Test Soln*	*Remarks*	*Ref*	*C/I*
	PF	20 million units	AB	2.5 g	D5W	Physically incompatible	11	I
Pentobarbital sodium	AB	200 mg	AB	2.5 g	D5W	Physically compatible	21	C
Phenobarbital sodium	AB	100 mg	AB	2.5 g	D5W	Physically compatible	21	C
Potassium chloride	AB	40 mEq	AB	2.5 g	D5W	Physically compatible	21	C
Prochlorperazine edisylate	SKF		AB			Physically incompatible	9	I
Promazine HCl	WY	100 mg	AB	2.5 g	D5W	Precipitate forms within 1 hr	21	I
	WI	1 g	AB	2.5 g	D5W	Physically incompatible	11	I
Promethazine HCl	WY		AB			Physically incompatible	9	I
Sodium bicarbonate	AB	40 mEq	AB	2.5 g	D5W	Physically compatible	21	C
	AB	2.4 mEq[b]	AB	1 g	D5W	Physically compatible for 24 hr	772	C
Succinylcholine chloride	AB	2 g	AB	25 g		Haze or precipitate forms within 1 to 6 hr	3	I

[a]*Test performed prior to availability of neutral regular insulin.*
[b]*One vial of Neut added to a liter of admixture.*

Drugs in Syringe Compatibility

Thiopental sodium

Drug (in syringe)	*Mfr*	*Amt*	*Mfr*	*Amt*	*Remarks*	*Ref*	*C/I*
Aminophylline	SE	500 mg/ 2 ml	AB	75 mg/ 3 ml	Physically compatible for at least 30 min	21	C
		500 mg/ 2 ml	AB	75 mg/ 3 ml	Physically compatible	55	C
Chlorpromazine HCl	SKF	50 mg/ 2 ml	AB	75 mg/ 3 ml	Physically incompatible	21	I
Dimenhydrinate	SE	50 mg/ 1 ml	AB	75 mg/ 3 ml	Physically incompatible	21	I
Diphenhydramine HCl	PD	50 mg/ 1 ml	AB	75 mg/ 3 ml	Physically incompatible	21	I
Doxapram HCl	RB	400 mg/ 20 ml		300 mg/ 12 ml	Immediate precipitation	1177	I
Ephedrine sulfate	AB	50 mg/ 1 ml	AB	75 mg/ 3 ml	Physically incompatible	21	I
Glycopyrrolate	RB	0.2 mg/ 1 ml	AB	25 mg/ 1 ml	Immediate precipitation	331	I
	RB	0.2 mg/ 1 ml	AB	50 mg/ 2 ml	Immediate precipitation	331	I
	RB	0.4 mg/ 2 ml	AB	25 mg/ 1 ml	Immediate precipitation	331	I
Hyaluronidase	AB	150 units	AB	75 mg/ 3 ml	Physically compatible	55	C
Hydrocortisone sodium succinate	UP	250 mg/ 2 ml	AB	75 mg/ 3 ml	Physically compatible for at least 30 min	21	C
Meperidine HCl	WI	100 mg/ 2 ml	AB	75 mg/ 3 ml	Physically incompatible	21	I

Drugs in Syringe Compatibility (Cont.)

Thiopental sodium

Drug (in syringe)	*Mfr*	*Amt*	*Mfr*	*Amt*	*Remarks*	*Ref*	*C/I*
Morphine sulfate	LI	16.2 mg/ 1 ml	AB	75 mg/ 3 ml	Physically incompatible	21	I
Neostigmine methylsulfate	RC	0.5 mg/ 1 ml	AB	75 mg/ 3 ml	Physically compatible	55	C
Pentobarbital sodium	AB	50 mg/ 1 ml	AB	75 mg/ 3 ml	Physically compatible for at least 30 min	21	C
	AB	37.5 mg/ 0.75 ml	AB	75 mg/ 3 ml	Physically compatible	55	C
Prochlorperazine edisylate	SKF	10 mg/ 2 ml	AB	75 mg/ 3 ml	Physically incompatible	21	I
Promethazine HCl	WY	100 mg/ 4 ml	AB	75 mg/ 3 ml	Physically incompatible	21	I
Propofol	ZEN	5 mg/ml[a]	AB	12.5 mg/ ml[a]	Visually compatible with 10% loss by HPLC of thiopental in 10 days and of propofol in 7 days at 23 °C under fluorescent light. No thiopental loss and 4% propofol loss in 13 days at 4 °C protected from light	1984	C
	ICI	5 mg/ 0.5 ml	AB	37.5 mg/ 1.5 ml	Little or no increase in measured emulsion droplet size in 24 hr at 4 °C.	1985	C
	ICI	7.5 mg/ 0.75 ml	AB	31.25 mg/ 1.25 ml	Little or no increase in measured emulsion droplet size in 24 hr at 4 °C.	1985	C
	ICI	10 mg/ 1 ml	AB	25 mg/ 1 ml	Little or no increase in measured emulsion droplet size in 24 hr at 4 °C. Little or no loss of either drug by HPLC in 24 hr at 4 °C	1985	C
	ICI	12.5 mg/ 1.25 ml	AB	18.75 mg/ 0.75 ml	Little or no increase in measured emulsion droplet size in 24 hr at 4 °C.	1985	C
	ICI	15 mg/ 1.5 ml	AB	12.5 mg/ 0.5 ml	Little or no increase in measured emulsion droplet size in 24 hr at 4 °C.	1985	C
Scopolamine HBr		0.13 mg/ 0.26 ml	AB	75 mg/ 3 ml	Physically compatible for at least 30 min	21	C
		0.13 mg/ 0.26 ml	AB	75 mg/ 3 ml	Physically compatible	55	C
Sodium bicarbonate		3.75 g/ 50 ml	AB	75 mg/ 3 ml	Physically incompatible	55	I
Tubocurarine chloride		2.25 mg/ 0.15 ml	AB	75 mg/ 3 ml	Physically compatible for at least 30 min	21	C
		2.25 mg/ 0.15 ml	AB	75 mg/ 3 ml	Physically compatible	55	C

[a]*Final concentrations after mixing.*

Y-Site Injection Compatibility (1:1 Mixture)

Thiopental sodium

Drug	*Mfr*	*Conc*	*Mfr*	*Conc*	*Remarks*	*Ref*	*C/I*
Alfentanil HCl	JN	0.5 mg/ml	AB	25 mg/ml	White pellets form within 24 hr at 25 °C	1801	I
Ascorbic acid	AB	500 mg/ml	AB	25 mg/ml	Yellow discoloration and fine precipitate form in 24 hr	1801	I

Y-Site Injection Compatibility (1:1 Mixture) (Cont.)

			Thiopental sodium				
Drug	*Mfr*	*Conc*	*Mfr*	*Conc*	*Remarks*	*Ref*	*C/I*
Atracurium besylate	BW	10 mg/ml	AB	25 mg/ml	White cloudiness forms immediately but clears within 24 hr at 25 °C	1801	I
Atropine sulfate	GNS	0.4 mg/ml	AB	25 mg/ml	White particles form immediately and yellow discoloration forms within 24 hr at 25 °C	1801	I
Cisatracurium besylate	GW	0.1 mg/ml[a]	AB	25 mg/ml[a]	Physically compatible with no change in measured turbidity or increase in particle content in 4 hr at 23 °C	2074	C
	GW	2 mg/ml[a]	AB	25 mg/ml[a]	White turbidity forms immediately but dissipates within 1 min; subvisual haze remains	2074	I
	GW	5 mg/ml[a]	AB	25 mg/ml[a]	White cloudiness forms immediately	2074	I
Diltiazem HCl	MMD	1 mg/ml[a]	AB	25 mg/ml[c]	Precipitate forms immediately	2062	I
Dobutamine HCl	LI	4 mg/ml[a]	AB	25 mg/ml[c]	Precipitate forms immediately	2062	I
Dopamine HCl	AB	3.2 mg/ml[a]	AB	25 mg/ml[c]	Precipitate forms immediately	2062	I
Doxacurium chloride	BW	1 mg/ml	AB	25 mg/ml	Visually compatible for up to 7 days at 25 °C	1801	C
Ephedrine sulfate	AB	50 mg/ml	AB	25 mg/ml	White cloudiness forms immediately, followed by fine crystalline particles	1801	I
Epinephrine HCl	AB	0.02 mg/ml[a]	AB	25 mg/ml[c]	Yellow color forms in 4 hr at 27 °C	2062	I
Fentanyl citrate	ES	0.05 mg/ml	AB	25 mg/ml	Visually compatible for up to 7 days at 25 °C	1801	C
	ES	0.05 mg/ml	AB	25 mg/ml[c]	Visually compatible for 4 hr at 27 °C	2062	C
Furosemide	AMR	10 mg/ml	AB	25 mg/ml[c]	Precipitate forms immediately	2062	I
Heparin sodium	ES	100 units/ml[a]	AB	25 mg/ml[c]	Visually compatible for 4 hr at 27 °C	2062	C
Hetastarch in lactated electrolyte injection (Hextend)	AB	6%	OH	25 mg/ml	Physically compatible with no change in measured turbidity or increase in particle content in 4 hr at 23 °C	2339	C
Hydromorphone HCl	KN	1 mg/ml	AB	25 mg/ml[c]	Precipitate forms in 4 hr at 27 °C	2062	I
Labetalol HCl	AH	2 mg/ml[a]	AB	25 mg/ml[c]	Precipitate forms immediately	2062	I
Lidocaine HCl	AST	20 mg/ml	AB	25 mg/ml	White cloudiness forms immediately but clears within 24 hr at 25 °C	1801	I
Lorazepam	WY	2 mg/ml	AB	25 mg/ml	Yellow discoloration forms	1801	I
	WY	0.5 mg/ml[a]	AB	25 mg/ml[c]	Visually compatible for 4 hr at 27 °C	2062	C
Midazolam HCl	RC	5 mg/ml	AB	25 mg/ml	White precipitate forms immediately	1801	I
	RC	2 mg/ml[a]	AB	25 mg/ml[c]	Precipitate forms immediately	2062	I
Milrinone lactate	SW	0.2 mg/ml[a]	AB	25 mg/ml[c]	Visually compatible for 4 hr at 27 °C	2062	C
Mivacurium chloride	BW	2 mg/ml	AB	25 mg/ml	Visually compatible for up to 7 days at 25 °C	1801	C
Morphine sulfate	ES	10 mg/ml	AB	25 mg/ml	White precipitate forms immediately	1801	I
	SCN	2 mg/ml[a]	AB	25 mg/ml[c]	Visually compatible for 4 hr at 27 °C	2062	C
Nicardipine HCl	WY	1 mg/ml[a]	AB	25 mg/ml[c]	Precipitate forms immediately	2062	I
Nitroglycerin	AB	0.4 mg/ml[a]	AB	25 mg/ml[c]	Visually compatible for 4 hr at 27 °C	2062	C
Norepinephrine bitartrate	AB	0.128 mg/ml[a]	AB	25 mg/ml[c]	Precipitate forms in 4 hr at 27 °C	2062	I
Pancuronium bromide	GNS	2 mg/ml	AB	25 mg/ml	White precipitate forms immediately	1801	I

Y-Site Injection Compatibility (1:1 Mixture) (Cont.)

			Thiopental sodium				
Drug	*Mfr*	*Conc*	*Mfr*	*Conc*	*Remarks*	*Ref*	*C/I*
Phenylephrine HCl	ES	10 mg/ml	AB	25 mg/ml	White precipitate forms immediately	1801	I
Propofol	ASZ	10 mg/ml	AB	25 mg/ml	Physically compatible for 1 hr at 23 °C with no increase in particle content	1916	C
Ranitidine HCl	GL	1 mg/ml[a]	AB	25 mg/ml[c]	Visually compatible for 4 hr at 27 °C	2062	C
Remifentanil HCl	GW	0.025 and 0.25 mg/ml[b]	AB	50 mg/ml[a]	Physically compatible with no change in measured turbidity or increase in particle content in 4 hr at 23 °C	2075	C
Succinylcholine chloride	AB	20 mg/ml	AB	25 mg/ml	White cloudiness forms immediately, followed by fine crystalline particles	1801	I
Sufentanil citrate	JN	0.05 mg/ml	AB	25 mg/ml	White pellets form within 24 hr at 25 °C	1801	I
Vecuronium bromide	OR	1 mg/ml	AB	25 mg/ml	White particles form immediately	1801	I
	OR	1 mg/ml	AB	25 mg/ml[c]	Precipitate forms immediately	2062	I

[a]Tested in dextrose 5% in water.
[b]Tested in sodium chloride 0.9%.
[c]Tested in sterile water for injection.

Additional Compatibility Information

Any thiopental sodium solution containing a visible precipitate should not be administered. (1-8/96; 21)

The physical incompatibilities of thiopental sodium are of three types (21):

1. Acid solutions that precipitate thiopental acid
2. Calcium and magnesium solutions that form insoluble carbonates
3. Amine salts that liberate the insoluble free base in alkaline solution

Infusion Solutions — Dextrose 5% in water, sodium chloride 0.9%, and Normosol R, pH 7.4, have been recommended as diluents for the continuous infusion of thiopental sodium. (1-8/96)

Thiopental sodium is incompatible or possesses limited compatibility with solutions containing sugars in concentrations above 5%. This is due to the relatively high titratable acidity of the solutions, which converts part of the thiopental sodium to the insoluble acid form. The acidity of dextrose–multielectrolyte solutions and vitamin infusion solutions (pH adjusted with hydrochloric acid) also causes such precipitation. (21) The absorption of carbon dioxide, which can combine with water to form carbonic acid, may also lower the pH of the solution and cause precipitation. (1-8/96)

In addition, calcium ions in solutions such as Ringer's injection and Ringer's injection, lactated, may form insoluble carbonates. Thiopental sodium may sometimes be administered into the tubing of the administration set of these solutions, although the titratable acidity of each lot of solution, the rate of injection, and the amount of thiopental sodium will affect the outcome. (21)

Acidic Drugs — The acidity of various additives may also result in an incompatibility. Drugs such as thiopental sodium that exhibit poor solubility in an acidic medium may precipitate in solutions containing acidic additives. (4; 22) Metaraminol bitartrate is acidic and may cause precipitation, depending on the concentration of the additives. (7) In addition, the acidic methyldopate HCl imparts some buffer capacity to admixtures and may pose solubility problems for barbiturate salts. (23)

Alkali-Labile Drugs — Thiopental sodium may raise the pH of admixture solutions to the alkaline range and, therefore, should not be mixed with alkali-labile drugs such as penicillin G. (47) Significant decomposition of isoproterenol HCl and norepinephrine bitartrate may also occur. If either of these two drugs is mixed with thiopental sodium, the admixture should be administered immediately after preparation. (59; 77)

Atracurium Besylate — Atracurium besylate also may be inactivated by alkaline solutions, such as barbiturates, and precipitation of a free acid of the admixed drug may occur, depending on the resultant pH of the admixture. (4)

Pancuronium Bromide — It is stated that a visible precipitate may form if pancuronium bromide is mixed with barbiturates. (4) However, a precipitate was not visible when pancuronium bromide was mixed in a syringe with thiopental or methohexital. (134)

Succinylcholine Chloride — When barbiturates are mixed in combination with succinylcholine chloride, either the free barbiturate precipitates (4) or the succinylcholine chloride is hydrolyzed, depending on the final pH of the admixture. (4; 21)

Tubocurarine Chloride — Tubocurarine chloride 15 mg/ml has been reported to be conditionally compatible with thiopental sodium 2.5% in a 1:19 ratio. This mixture is usually satisfactory, but occasional precipitation does occur if the pH of the tubocurarine chloride is at its lower limit. The overall pH of the mixture is then reduced below 9.7, resulting in thiopental precipitation. As long as the final pH is above 9.7, there is no precipitate over 48 hours. (40)

In infusion solutions, tubocurarine chloride 9 mg/L has also been reported to be conditionally compatible with thiopental sodium (Abbott) 25 g/L. The mixture is physically incompatible in most Abbott infusion solutions except as noted below (3):

Dextran 6% in dextrose 5%	Physically compatible
Dextran 6% in sodium chloride 0.9%	Physically compatible
Dextrose 2½% in sodium chloride 0.45%	Physically compatible
Dextrose 2½% in sodium chloride 0.9%	Physically compatible
Dextrose 5% in sodium chloride 0.225%	Physically compatible
Dextrose 5% in sodium chloride 0.45%	Physically compatible
Dextrose 2½% in water	Physically compatible
Dextrose 5% in water	Physically compatible
Ionosol PSL	Physically compatible
Sodium chloride 0.45%	Physically compatible
Sodium chloride 0.9%	Physically compatible
Sodium lactate ⅙ M	Physically compatible

Other Drugs — Other drugs stated to be incompatible with thiopental sodium or barbiturate salts include clindamycin phosphate (106), fentanyl citrate (4), droperidol (4), and cimetidine HCl. (360) In addition, thiopental sodium should not be mixed in the same syringe with pentazocine lactate because precipitation will occur. (4)

THIOTEPA
AHFS 10:00

Products — Thiotepa is available in vials containing 15 mg of drug and sodium carbonate 0.03 mg as a lyophilized powder. Reconstitute the vials with 1.5 ml of sterile water for injection. The approximate withdrawable volume is 1.4 ml. Because of a small excess of drug, the reconstituted solution contains thiotepa 10.4 mg/ml, yielding a withdrawable amount of approximately 14.7 mg from each vial. (1-10/00)

pH — Approximately 5.5 to 7.5. (1-10/00)

Tonicity — Reconstitution with sterile water for injection results in a hypotonic solution; it should be diluted in sodium chloride 0.9% prior to use. (1-10/00) Reconstitution with other diluents may result in a hypertonic solution which can cause mild to moderate discomfort upon administration. (4)

Thiotepa concentrations, 0.5 and 1 mg/ml diluted in sodium chloride 0.9%, are nearly isotonic, having osmolalities of 277 and 269 mOsm/kg, respectively. However, thiotepa concentrations of 3 and 5 mg/ml in sodium chloride 0.9% are hypotonic. (2006)

Trade Name(s) — Thioplex.

Administration — Thiotepa is usually given by rapid intravenous administration but may also be given by the intracavitary or intravesical route. (1-10/00; 4) The drug has also been given by intramuscular, intrathecal, and intratumoral administration. (4)

Stability — Intact vials should be stored under refrigeration and protected from light at all times. Reconstituted solutions should be stored under refrigeration and protected from light until used. (1-10/00; 4) The reconstituted solution in sterile water for injection is stated to be stable for up to 28 days stored under refrigeration or frozen and seven days at room temperature. (1369) However, the manufacturer recommends storage under refrigeration and use within eight hours because of the absence of an antimicrobial preservative. (1-10/00; 4) Thiotepa may undergo polymerization forming inactive and insoluble polymeric derivatives (1369), especially at high temperatures. (4) Solutions that are grossly opaque or contain a precipitate should not be used. (1-10/00; 4)

Thiotepa is stable in alkaline media but unstable in acidic media (1-10/00; 4), undergoing increased rates of hydrolysis. (1389)

In sodium chloride–containing solutions, thiotepa reacts to form a chloro-adduct product. The amount and rate of chloro-adduct formation are inversely related to the thiotepa concentration. Refrigerated storage slows but does not eliminate chloro-adduct formation. Substantial chloro-adduct formation occurred in as little as eight hours in a 0.5 mg/ml solution at room temperature but did not occur until 24 hours or more than 48 hours in 1 and 3 mg/ml solutions, respectively. (2077)

Syringes — Thiotepa reconstituted to a concentration of 10 mg/ml with sterile water for injection was found to be stable for 24 hours under refrigeration at 8 °C and at room temperature of 23 °C in both the original vials and transferred to plastic syringes. (2006)

Sorption — An evaluation of the stability of thiotepa (Immunex) 0.5 and 5 mg/ml in dextrose 5% in water in both PVC and polyolefin containers found no difference in concentration between the two containers, indicating no loss due to sorption to PVC. (2007)

Filtration — Thiotepa 10 to 300 µg/ml exhibited no loss due to sorption to either cellulose nitrate/cellulose acetate ester (Millex OR) or Teflon (Millex FG) filters. (1415; 1416)

Compatibility Information

Solution Compatibility

Thiotepa

Solution	*Mfr*	*Mfr*	*Conc/L*	*Remarks*	*Ref*	*C/I*
Dextrose 5% in water	BA[a], MG[b]	IMM	0.5 g	Physically stable with losses of 10% or less by HPLC in 8 hr at 4 and 23 °C. Losses ranged up to 17% in 24 hr	2007	I
	BA[a], MG[b]	IMM	5 g	Physically stable with losses of less than 10% by HPLC in 14 days at 4 °C and in 3 days at 23 °C	2007	C
Sodium chloride 0.9%	BA[a]	IMM	1 and 3 g	Physically stable with 7 to 10% loss by HPLC in 24 hrs at 25 °C and 4% or less in 48 hr at 4 °C	2077	C
	BA[a]	IMM	0.5 g	Physically stable but up to 7% loss by HPLC in 8 hr with substantial chloro-adduct formation. Up to 13% loss in 24 hr at 25 °C	2077	I
	BA[a]	IMM	0.5 g	Physically stable with 4% or less loss by HPLC in 48 hr at 8 °C	2077	C

[a]*Tested in PVC containers.*
[b]*Tested in polyolefin containers.*

Additive Compatibility

Thiotepa

Drug	*Mfr*	*Conc/L*	*Mfr*	*Conc/L*	*Test Soln*	*Remarks*	*Ref*	*C/I*
Cisplatin		200 mg		1 g	NS	Yellow precipitation	1379	I

Y-Site Injection Compatibility (1:1 Mixture)

Thiotepa

Drug	*Mfr*	*Conc*	*Mfr*	*Conc*	*Remarks*	*Ref*	*C/I*
Acyclovir sodium	BW	7 mg/ml[a]	IMM[c]	1 mg/ml[a]	Physically compatible with no change in measured turbidity or increase in particle content in 4 hr at 23 °C	1861	C
Allopurinol sodium	BW	3 mg/ml[b]	LE[d]	1 mg/ml[c]	Physically compatible with no change in measured turbidity or increase in particle content in 4 hr at 22 °C	1686	C
Amifostine	USB	10 mg/ml[a]	LE[d]	1 mg/ml[a]	Physically compatible with no change in measured turbidity or increase in particle content in 4 hr at 23 °C	1845	C
Amikacin sulfate	DU	5 mg/ml[a]	IMM[c]	1 mg/ml[a]	Physically compatible with no change in measured turbidity or increase in particle content in 4 hr at 23 °C	1861	C
Aminophylline	AMR	2.5 mg/ml[a]	IMM[c]	1 mg/ml[a]	Physically compatible with no change in measured turbidity or increase in particle content in 4 hr at 23 °C	1861	C
Amphotericin B	APC	0.6 mg/ml[a]	IMM[c]	1 mg/ml[a]	Physically compatible with no change in measured turbidity or increase in particle content in 4 hr at 23 °C	1861	C
Ampicillin sodium	WY	20 mg/ml[b]	IMM[c]	1 mg/ml[a]	Physically compatible with no change in measured turbidity or increase in particle content in 4 hr at 23 °C	1861	C

Y-Site Injection Compatibility (1:1 Mixture) (Cont.)

			Thiotepa				
Drug	*Mfr*	*Conc*	*Mfr*	*Conc*	*Remarks*	*Ref*	*C/I*
Ampicillin sodium–sulbactam sodium	RR	20 + 10 mg/ml[b]	IMM[c]	1 mg/ml[a]	Physically compatible with no change in measured turbidity or increase in particle content in 4 hr at 23 °C	1861	C
Aztreonam	SQ	40 mg/ml[a]	LE[d]	1 mg/ml[a]	Physically compatible with no subvisual haze or particle formation in 4 hr at 23 °C	1758	C
	SQ	40 mg/ml[a]	IMM[c]	1 mg/ml[a]	Physically compatible with no change in measured turbidity or increase in particle content in 4 hr at 23 °C	1861	C
Bleomycin sulfate	MJ	1 unit/ml[b]	IMM[c]	1 mg/ml[a]	Physically compatible with no change in measured turbidity or increase in particle content in 4 hr at 23 °C	1861	C
Bumetanide	RC	0.04 mg/ml[a]	IMM[c]	1 mg/ml[a]	Physically compatible with no change in measured turbidity or increase in particle content in 4 hr at 23 °C	1861	C
Buprenorphine HCl	RKC	0.04 mg/ml[a]	IMM[c]	1 mg/ml[a]	Physically compatible with no change in measured turbidity or increase in particle content in 4 hr at 23 °C	1861	C
Butorphanol tartrate	APC	0.04 mg/ml[a]	IMM[c]	1 mg/ml[a]	Physically compatible with no change in measured turbidity or increase in particle content in 4 hr at 23 °C	1861	C
Calcium gluconate	AMR	40 mg/ml[a]	IMM[c]	1 mg/ml[a]	Physically compatible with no change in measured turbidity or increase in particle content in 4 hr at 23 °C	1861	C
Carboplatin	BMS	5 mg/ml[a]	IMM[c]	1 mg/ml[a]	Physically compatible with no change in measured turbidity or increase in particle content in 4 hr at 23 °C	1861	C
Carmustine	BMS	1.5 mg/ml[a]	IMM[c]	1 mg/ml[a]	Physically compatible with no change in measured turbidity or increase in particle content in 4 hr at 23 °C	1861	C
Cefazolin sodium	MAR	20 mg/ml[a]	IMM[c]	1 mg/ml[a]	Physically compatible with no change in measured turbidity or increase in particle content in 4 hr at 23 °C	1861	C
Cefepime HCl	BMS	20 mg/ml[a]	LE[d]	1 mg/ml[a]	Physically compatible with no change in measured turbidity or increase in particle content in 4 hr at 22 °C	1689	C
Cefoperazone sodium	RR	40 mg/ml[a]	IMM[c]	1 mg/ml[a]	Physically compatible with no change in measured turbidity or increase in particle content in 4 hr at 23 °C	1861	C
Cefotaxime sodium	HO	20 mg/ml[a]	IMM[c]	1 mg/ml[a]	Physically compatible with no change in measured turbidity or increase in particle content in 4 hr at 23 °C	1861	C
Cefotetan sodium	STU	20 mg/ml[a]	IMM[c]	1 mg/ml[a]	Physically compatible with no change in measured turbidity or increase in particle content in 4 hr at 23 °C	1861	C
Cefoxitin sodium	ME	20 mg/ml[a]	IMM[c]	1 mg/ml[a]	Physically compatible with no change in measured turbidity or increase in particle content in 4 hr at 23 °C	1861	C

Y-Site Injection Compatibility (1:1 Mixture) (Cont.)

Thiotepa

Drug	*Mfr*	*Conc*	*Mfr*	*Conc*	*Remarks*	*Ref*	*C/I*
Ceftazidime	LI[e]	40 mg/ml[a]	IMM[c]	1 mg/ml[a]	Physically compatible with no change in measured turbidity or increase in particle content in 4 hr at 23 °C	1861	C
Ceftizoxime sodium	FUJ	20 mg/ml[a]	IMM[c]	1 mg/ml[a]	Physically compatible with no change in measured turbidity or increase in particle content in 4 hr at 23 °C	1861	C
Ceftriaxone sodium	RC	20 mg/ml[a]	IMM[c]	1 mg/ml[a]	Physically compatible with no change in measured turbidity or increase in particle content in 4 hr at 23 °C	1861	C
Cefuroxime sodium	MI	30 mg/ml[a]	IMM[c]	1 mg/ml[a]	Physically compatible with no change in measured turbidity or increase in particle content in 4 hr at 23 °C	1861	C
Chlorpromazine HCl	SCN	2 mg/ml[a]	IMM[c]	1 mg/ml[a]	Physically compatible with no change in measured turbidity or increase in particle content in 4 hr at 23 °C	1861	C
Cimetidine HCl	SKB	12 mg/ml[a]	IMM[c]	1 mg/ml[a]	Physically compatible with no change in measured turbidity or increase in particle content in 4 hr at 23 °C	1861	C
Ciprofloxacin	MI	1 mg/ml[a]	IMM[c]	1 mg/ml[a]	Physically compatible with no change in measured turbidity or increase in particle content in 4 hr at 23 °C	1861	C
Cisplatin	BMS	1 mg/ml	IMM[c]	1 mg/ml[a]	White cloudiness appears in 4 hr at 23 °C	1861	I
Clindamycin phosphate	AST	10 mg/ml[a]	IMM[c]	1 mg/ml[a]	Physically compatible with no change in measured turbidity or increase in particle content in 4 hr at 23 °C	1861	C
Cyclophosphamide	MJ	10 mg/ml[a]	IMM[c]	1 mg/ml[a]	Physically compatible with no change in measured turbidity or increase in particle content in 4 hr at 23 °C	1861	C
Cytarabine	CET	50 mg/ml	IMM[c]	1 mg/ml[a]	Physically compatible with no change in measured turbidity or increase in particle content in 4 hr at 23 °C	1861	C
Dacarbazine	MI	4 mg/ml[a]	IMM[c]	1 mg/ml[a]	Physically compatible with no change in measured turbidity or increase in particle content in 4 hr at 23 °C	1861	C
Dactinomycin	ME	0.01 mg/ml[a]	IMM[c]	1 mg/ml[a]	Physically compatible with no change in measured turbidity or increase in particle content in 4 hr at 23 °C	1861	C
Daunorubicin HCl	WY	1 mg/ml[a]	IMM[c]	1 mg/ml[a]	Physically compatible with no change in measured turbidity or increase in particle content in 4 hr at 23 °C	1861	C
Dexamethasone sodium phosphate	AMR	1 mg/ml[a]	IMM[c]	1 mg/ml[a]	Physically compatible with no change in measured turbidity or increase in particle content in 4 hr at 23 °C	1861	C
Diphenhydramine HCl	WY	2 mg/ml[a]	IMM[c]	1 mg/ml[a]	Physically compatible with no change in measured turbidity or increase in particle content in 4 hr at 23 °C	1861	C
Dobutamine HCl	LI	4 mg/ml[a]	IMM[c]	1 mg/ml[a]	Physically compatible with no change in measured turbidity or increase in particle content in 4 hr at 23 °C	1861	C

Y-Site Injection Compatibility (1:1 Mixture) (Cont.)

Drug	Mfr	Conc	Thiotepa Mfr	Thiotepa Conc	Remarks	Ref	C/I
Dopamine HCl	AST	3.2 mg/ml[a]	IMM[c]	1 mg/ml[a]	Physically compatible with no change in measured turbidity or increase in particle content in 4 hr at 23 °C	1861	C
Doxorubicin HCl	CHI	2 mg/ml	IMM[c]	1 mg/ml[a]	Physically compatible with no change in measured turbidity or increase in particle content in 4 hr at 23 °C	1861	C
Doxycycline hyclate	LY	1 mg/ml[a]	IMM[c]	1 mg/ml[a]	Physically compatible with no change in measured turbidity or increase in particle content in 4 hr at 23 °C	1861	C
Droperidol	JN	0.4 mg/ml[a]	IMM[c]	1 mg/ml[a]	Physically compatible with no change in measured turbidity or increase in particle content in 4 hr at 23 °C	1861	C
Enalaprilat	ME	0.1 mg/ml[a]	IMM[c]	1 mg/ml[a]	Physically compatible with no change in measured turbidity or increase in particle content in 4 hr at 23 °C	1861	C
Etoposide	BMS	0.4 mg/ml[a]	IMM[c]	1 mg/ml[a]	Physically compatible with no change in measured turbidity or increase in particle content in 4 hr at 23 °C	1861	C
Etoposide phosphate	BR	5 mg/ml[a]	IMM[c]	1 mg/ml[a]	Physically compatible with no change in measured turbidity or increase in particle content in 4 hr at 23 °C	2218	C
Famotidine	ME	2 mg/ml[a]	IMM[c]	1 mg/ml[a]	Physically compatible with no change in measured turbidity or increase in particle content in 4 hr at 23 °C	1861	C
Filgrastim	AMG	30 μg/ml[a]	LE[d]	1 mg/ml[a]	Particles and filaments form immediately	1687	I
Floxuridine	RC	3 mg/ml[a]	IMM[c]	1 mg/ml[a]	Physically compatible with no change in measured turbidity or increase in particle content in 4 hr at 23 °C	1861	C
Fluconazole	RR	2 mg/ml	IMM[c]	1 mg/ml[a]	Physically compatible with no change in measured turbidity or increase in particle content in 4 hr at 23 °C	1861	C
Fludarabine phosphate	BX	1 mg/ml[a]	IMM[c]	1 mg/ml[a]	Physically compatible with no change in measured turbidity or increase in particle content in 4 hr at 23 °C	1861	C
Fluorouracil	AD	16 mg/ml[a]	IMM[c]	1 mg/ml[a]	Physically compatible with no change in measured turbidity or increase in particle content in 4 hr at 23 °C	1861	C
Furosemide	AMR	3 mg/ml[a]	IMM[c]	1 mg/ml[a]	Physically compatible with no change in measured turbidity or increase in particle content in 4 hr at 23 °C	1861	C
Ganciclovir sodium	SY	20 mg/ml[a]	IMM[c]	1 mg/ml[a]	Physically compatible with no change in measured turbidity or increase in particle content in 4 hr at 23 °C	1861	C
Gemcitabine HCl	LI	10 mg/ml[b]	IMM[c]	1 mg/ml[b]	Physically compatible with no change in measured turbidity or increase in particle content in 4 hr at 23 °C	2226	C
Gentamicin sulfate	ES	5 mg/ml[a]	IMM[c]	1 mg/ml[a]	Physically compatible with no change in measured turbidity or increase in particle content in 4 hr at 23 °C	1861	C

Y-Site Injection Compatibility (1:1 Mixture) (Cont.)

Drug	*Mfr*	*Conc*	*Mfr*	*Conc*	*Remarks*	*Ref*	*C/I*
			Thiotepa				
Granisetron HCl	SKB	0.05 mg/ml[a]	IMM[c]	1 mg/ml[a]	Physically compatible with no change in measured turbidity or increase in particle content in 4 hr at 23 °C	1861; 2000	C
Haloperidol lactate	MN	0.2 mg/ml[a]	IMM[c]	1 mg/ml[a]	Physically compatible with no change in measured turbidity or increase in particle content in 4 hr at 23 °C	1861	C
Heparin sodium	ES	100 units/ml[a]	IMM[c]	1 mg/ml[a]	Physically compatible with no change in measured turbidity or increase in particle content in 4 hr at 23 °C	1861	C
Hydrocortisone sodium phosphate	MSD	1 mg/ml[a]	IMM[c]	1 mg/ml[a]	Physically compatible with no change in measured turbidity or increase in particle content in 4 hr at 23 °C	1861	C
Hydrocortisone sodium succinate	UP	1 mg/ml[a]	IMM[c]	1 mg/ml[a]	Physically compatible with no change in measured turbidity or increase in particle content in 4 hr at 23 °C	1861	C
Hydromorphone HCl	AST	0.5 mg/ml[a]	IMM[c]	1 mg/ml[a]	Physically compatible with no change in measured turbidity or increase in particle content in 4 hr at 23 °C	1861	C
Hydroxyzine HCl	ES	4 mg/ml[a]	IMM[c]	1 mg/ml[a]	Physically compatible with no change in measured turbidity or increase in particle content in 4 hr at 23 °C	1861	C
Idarubicin HCl	AD	0.5 mg/ml[a]	IMM[c]	1 mg/ml[a]	Increase in turbidity no greater than dilution with D5W alone. No increase in particle content in 4 hr at 23 °C	1861	C
Ifosfamide	MJ	25 mg/ml[a]	IMM[c]	1 mg/ml[a]	Physically compatible with no change in measured turbidity or increase in particle content in 4 hr at 23 °C	1861	C
Imipenem–cilastatin sodium	ME	10 mg/ml[a]	IMM[c]	1 mg/ml[a]	Physically compatible with no change in measured turbidity or increase in particle content in 4 hr at 23 °C	1861	C
Leucovorin calcium	LE	2 mg/ml[a]	IMM[c]	1 mg/ml[a]	Physically compatible with no change in measured turbidity or increase in particle content in 4 hr at 23 °C	1861	C
Lorazepam	WY	0.1 mg/ml[a]	IMM[c]	1 mg/ml[a]	Physically compatible with no change in measured turbidity or increase in particle content in 4 hr at 23 °C	1861	C
Magnesium sulfate	AST	100 mg/ml[a]	IMM[c]	1 mg/ml[a]	Physically compatible with no change in measured turbidity or increase in particle content in 4 hr at 23 °C	1861	C
Mannitol	BA	15%	IMM[c]	1 mg/ml[a]	Physically compatible with no change in measured turbidity or increase in particle content in 4 hr at 23 °C	1861	C
Melphalan HCl	BW	0.1 mg/ml[b]	LE[d]	10 mg/ml[b]	Physically compatible with no change in measured turbidity or increase in particle content in 3 hr at 22 °C	1557	C
Meperidine HCl	WY	4 mg/ml[a]	IMM[c]	1 mg/ml[a]	Physically compatible with no change in measured turbidity or increase in particle content in 4 hr at 23 °C	1861	C

Y-Site Injection Compatibility (1:1 Mixture) (Cont.)

			Thiotepa				
Drug	*Mfr*	*Conc*	*Mfr*	*Conc*	*Remarks*	*Ref*	*C/I*
Mesna	MJ	10 mg/ml[a]	IMM[c]	1 mg/ml[a]	Physically compatible with no change in measured turbidity or increase in particle content in 4 hr at 23 °C	1861	C
Methotrexate sodium	LE	15 mg/ml[a]	IMM[c]	1 mg/ml[a]	Physically compatible with no change in measured turbidity or increase in particle content in 4 hr at 23 °C	1861	C
Methylprednisolone sodium succinate	AB	5 mg/ml[a]	IMM[c]	1 mg/ml[a]	Physically compatible with no change in measured turbidity or increase in particle content in 4 hr at 23 °C	1861	C
Metoclopramide HCl	RB	5 mg/ml	IMM[c]	1 mg/ml[a]	Physically compatible with no change in measured turbidity or increase in particle content in 4 hr at 23 °C	1861	C
Metronidazole	BA	5 mg/ml	IMM[c]	1 mg/ml[a]	Physically compatible with no change in measured turbidity or increase in particle content in 4 hr at 23 °C	1861	C
Minocycline HCl	LE	0.2 mg/ml[a]	IMM[c]	1 mg/ml[a]	Yellow-green discoloration forms in 1 hr at 23 °C	1861	I
Mitomycin	BMS	0.5 mg/ml	IMM[c]	1 mg/ml[a]	Physically compatible with no change in measured turbidity or increase in particle content in 4 hr at 23 °C	1861	C
Mitoxantrone HCl	IMM	0.5 mg/ml[a]	IMM[c]	1 mg/ml[a]	Physically compatible with no change in measured turbidity or increase in particle content in 4 hr at 23 °C	1861	C
Morphine sulfate	AST	1 mg/ml[a]	IMM[c]	1 mg/ml[a]	Physically compatible with no change in measured turbidity or increase in particle content in 4 hr at 23 °C	1861	C
Nalbuphine HCl	AST	10 mg/ml	IMM[c]	1 mg/ml[a]	Physically compatible with no change in measured turbidity or increase in particle content in 4 hr at 23 °C	1861	C
Netilmicin sulfate	SC	5 mg/ml[a]	IMM[c]	1 mg/ml[a]	Physically compatible with no change in measured turbidity or increase in particle content in 4 hr at 23 °C	1861	C
Ofloxacin	ORT	4 mg/ml	IMM[c]	1 mg/ml[a]	Physically compatible with no change in measured turbidity or increase in particle content in 4 hr at 23 °C	1861	C
Ondansetron HCl	GL	1 mg/ml[a]	IMM[c]	1 mg/ml[a]	Physically compatible with no change in measured turbidity or increase in particle content in 4 hr at 23 °C	1861	C
Paclitaxel	MJ	0.6 mg/ml[a]	IMM[c]	1 mg/ml[a]	Physically compatible with no change in measured turbidity or increase in particle content in 4 hr at 23 °C	1861	C
Piperacillin sodium	LE	40 mg/ml[a]	IMM[c]	1 mg/ml[a]	Physically compatible with no change in measured turbidity or increase in particle content in 4 hr at 23 °C	1861	C
Piperacillin sodium–tazobactam sodium	LE	40 + 5 mg/ml[a]	LE[d]	1 mg/ml[a]	Physically compatible with no change in measured turbidity or increase in particle content in 4 hr at 22 °C	1688	C

Y-Site Injection Compatibility (1:1 Mixture) (Cont.)

Thiotepa

Drug	*Mfr*	*Conc*	*Mfr*	*Conc*	*Remarks*	*Ref*	*C/I*
Plicamycin	MI	0.01 mg/ml[a]	IMM[c]	1 mg/ml[a]	Physically compatible with no change in measured turbidity or increase in particle content in 4 hr at 23 °C	1861	C
Potassium chloride	AMR	0.1 mEq/ml[a]	IMM[c]	1 mg/ml[a]	Physically compatible with no change in measured turbidity or increase in particle content in 4 hr at 23 °C	1861	C
Prochlorperazine edisylate	SCN	0.5 mg/ml[a]	IMM[c]	1 mg/ml[a]	Physically compatible with no change in measured turbidity or increase in particle content in 4 hr at 23 °C	1861	C
Promethazine HCl	WY	2 mg/ml[a]	IMM[c]	1 mg/ml[a]	Physically compatible with no change in measured turbidity or increase in particle content in 4 hr at 23 °C	1861	C
Ranitidine HCl	GL	2 mg/ml[a]	IMM[c]	1 mg/ml[a]	Physically compatible with no change in measured turbidity or increase in particle content in 4 hr at 23 °C	1861	C
Sodium bicarbonate	AB	1 mEq/ml	IMM[c]	1 mg/ml[a]	Physically compatible with no change in measured turbidity or increase in particle content in 4 hr at 23 °C	1861	C
Streptozocin	UP	40 mg/ml[a]	IMM[c]	1 mg/ml[a]	Physically compatible with no change in measured turbidity or increase in particle content in 4 hr at 23 °C	1861	C
Teniposide	BR	0.1 mg/ml[a]	LE[d]	1 mg/ml[a]	Physically compatible with no subvisual haze or particle formation in 4 hr at 23 °C	1725	C
Ticarcillin disodium	SKB	30 mg/ml[a]	IMM[c]	1 mg/ml[a]	Physically compatible with no change in measured turbidity or increase in particle content in 4 hr at 23 °C	1861	C
Ticarcillin disodium–clavulanate potassium	SKB	31 mg/ml[a]	IMM[c]	1 mg/ml[a]	Physically compatible with no change in measured turbidity or increase in particle content in 4 hr at 23 °C	1861	C
Tobramycin sulfate	LI	5 mg/ml[a]	IMM[c]	1 mg/ml[a]	Physically compatible with no change in measured turbidity or increase in particle content in 4 hr at 23 °C	1861	C
TPN #193[f]			IMM[c]	1 mg/ml[a]	Physically compatible with no change in measured turbidity or increase in particle content in 4 hr at 23 °C	1861	C
Trimethoprim–sulfamethoxazole	ES	0.8 + 4 mg/ml[a]	IMM[c]	1 mg/ml[a]	Physically compatible with no change in measured turbidity or increase in particle content in 4 hr at 23 °C	1861	C
Vancomycin HCl	AB	10 mg/ml[a]	IMM[c]	1 mg/ml[a]	Physically compatible with no change in measured turbidity or increase in particle content in 4 hr at 23 °C	1861	C
Vinblastine sulfate	LI	0.12 mg/ml[a]	IMM[c]	1 mg/ml[a]	Physically compatible with no change in measured turbidity or increase in particle content in 4 hr at 23 °C	1861	C
Vincristine sulfate	LI	0.05 mg/ml[a]	IMM[c]	1 mg/ml[a]	Physically compatible with no change in measured turbidity or increase in particle content in 4 hr at 23 °C	1861	C

Y-Site Injection Compatibility (1:1 Mixture) (Cont.)

			Thiotepa				
Drug	*Mfr*	*Conc*	*Mfr*	*Conc*	*Remarks*	*Ref*	*C/I*
Vinorelbine tartrate	BW	1 mg/ml[b]	LE[d]	10 mg/ml[b]	Cloudy solution with particles forms immediately	1558	I
Zidovudine	BW	4 mg/ml[a]	IMM[c]	1 mg/ml[a]	Physically compatible with no change in measured turbidity or increase in particle content in 4 hr at 23 °C	1861	C

[a]*Tested in dextrose 5% in water.*
[b]*Tested in sodium chloride 0.9%.*
[c]*Lyophilized formulation tested.*
[d]*Powder fill formulation tested.*
[e]*Sodium carbonate–containing formulation tested.*
[f]*Refer to Appendix I for the composition of parenteral nutrition solutions. TPN indicates a 2-in-1 admixture.*

Additional Compatibility Information

Infusion Solutions — The reconstituted thiotepa solution may be diluted for administration with dextrose or dextrose and sodium chloride injections, sodium chloride injection, Ringer's injection, or lactated Ringer's injection if larger volumes of fluid are desired. (4)

The manufacturer has stated that thiotepa 1 and 3 mg/ml in sodium chloride 0.9% in PVC containers is stable for up to 24 hours at 25 °C and up to 48 hours at 8 °C, while at a concentration of 5 mg/ml in sodium chloride 0.9% thiotepa is stable for 24 hours at either 8 or 23 °C. However, thiotepa 0.5 mg/ml in sodium chloride 0.9% is unstable and should be used immediately if mixed at this concentration. (2006) Similar results have been reported for admixtures in dextrose 5% in water. (2007) See Compatibility Information above.

Other Drugs — Reconstituted thiotepa may be mixed with 2% procaine HCl and/or 0.1% epinephrine HCl for local administration. (4)

TICARCILLIN DISODIUM
AHFS 8:12.16

Products — Ticarcillin disodium is available in 1-, 3-, and 6-g standard vials, 3-g piggyback bottles, and 20- and 30-g bulk pharmacy packages. (1-8/98; 4)

For intramuscular injections, each gram of ticarcillin disodium in standard vials should be reconstituted with 2 ml of sterile water for injection, sodium chloride 0.9%, lidocaine HCl 1% (without epinephrine), or another compatible intravenous infusion solution to yield a solution containing ticarcillin 1 g/2.6 ml (385 mg/ml). (1-8/98; 4)

For intravenous use, each gram of drug in standard vials should be reconstituted with at least 4 ml of sodium chloride 0.9%, dextrose 5% in water, or lactated Ringer's injection to yield a solution containing ticarcillin approximately 200 mg/ml. (1-8/98; 4)

The 3-g piggyback bottles should be reconstituted with a compatible intravenous infusion solution in the following amounts (2; 4):

Amount of Diluent	Solution Concentration
100 ml	1 g/34 ml
60 ml	1 g/20 ml
30 ml	1 g/10 ml

The 20- or 30-g bulk pharmacy packages should be reconstituted with 85 or 75 ml, respectively, of sodium chloride 0.9%, dextrose 5% in water, or lactated Ringer's injection (added in two portions, with shaking after each addition) to yield a 200- or 300-mg/ml ticarcillin concentration, respectively. This concentrated solution must be diluted further in a compatible infusion solution for administration. (4)

pH — From 6 to 8. (1-8/98; 4)

Osmolality — The osmolality of ticarcillin disodium 3 g was calculated for the following dilutions (1054):

	Osmolality (mOsm/kg)	
Diluent	50 ml	100 ml
Dextrose 5% in water	558	420
Sodium chloride 0.9%	579	442

Robinson et al. recommended the following maximum ticarcillin disodium concentrations to achieve osmolalities suitable for peripheral infusion in fluid-restricted patients (1180):

Diluent	Maximum Concentration (mg/ml)	Osmolality (mOsm/kg)
Dextrose 5% in water	50	558
Sodium chloride 0.9%	45	538
Sterile water for injection	90	541

Sodium Content — Each gram of ticarcillin disodium contains 5.2 (120 mg) to 6.5 mEq of sodium. (4; 371; 462; 846)

Trade Name(s)—Ticar.

Administration—Ticarcillin disodium is administered by deep intramuscular injection or direct intravenous injection as slowly as possible or by continuous or intermittent intravenous infusion. (1-8/98; 4) Intramuscular injection should be made well within the body of a relatively large muscle. Doses should not exceed 2 g per injection by this route. By direct intravenous injection, concentrations of 50 mg/ml or less should be administered to minimize vein irritation. For intravenous infusion, the reconstituted solution is diluted with an appropriate volume of a suitable diluent to a concentration of 10 to 100 mg/ml and administered continuously or intermittently over 30 to 120 minutes in adults or over 10 to 20 minutes in neonates. (1-8/98; 4)

Stability—Intact vials of ticarcillin disodium may be stored at controlled room temperature or below. The manufacturer recommends that intramuscular solutions be used promptly. (1-8/98) Storage of ticarcillin disodium solutions, especially high concentrations at room temperature, may form polymer conjugation products that play a role in hypersensitivity reactions even though the potency remains acceptable. Consequently, refrigeration or use within 30 minutes of reconstituting solutions has been recommended by some clinicians. (4)

Nicholas et al. reported on ticarcillin disodium 250 mg/ml stored at room temperature and 4 °C. After 24 hours at room temperature, HPLC analysis revealed a new peak, which increased in size by 72 hours. Storage at 4 °C significantly reduced the formation rate of this new compound. Although the therapeutic potency of ticarcillin disodium is retained over the time period studied, the potential as an antigen may change because of the possible formation of polymers or conjugation products that may cause allergic sensitization reactions. The authors recommended that the drug be freshly prepared before use or refrigerated during interim storage. (785)

Lynn reported on the chemical stability of a ticarcillin disodium concentration of 500 mg/ml in sterile water for injection. Approximately 3% decomposition occurred at 5 °C and 7% at 25 °C in 24 hours. When stored at 5 °C for seven days, 9% decomposition occurred. However, at 25 °C for only three days, 27% decomposition was noted. (334)

Reconstitution of the bulk pharmacy package to a 200- or 300-mg/ml concentration results in a solution that should be used or discarded within 24 hours at room temperature or 72 hours under refrigeration. (4)

Freezing Solutions—Ticarcillin disodium (Beecham) 3 g/50 ml of dextrose 5% in water, in PVC bags frozen at −20 °C for 30 days and then thawed by exposure to ambient temperature or microwave radiation, showed no evidence of precipitation or color change and showed no loss of potency as determined microbiologically. Subsequent storage of the admixture at room temperature for 24 hours also yielded a physically compatible solution which exhibited little or no additional loss of activity. (555)

Solutions of ticarcillin disodium 1.5 g/50 ml in dextrose 5% in water and sodium chloride 0.9% in PVC containers were stored at −27 °C for 270 days and then thawed in a microwave oven for 2.5 minutes. Both solutions retained their ticarcillin potency for the 270 days. Some loss of ticarcillin was observed during further storage of the thawed solutions for 24 hours at 4 °C, usually between 2 and 7%, but no sample fell below 90% of the labeled concentration. (1176)

Borst et al. reported that ticarcillin disodium (Beecham) 2 and 3 g/10 ml in sterile water for injection, packaged in plastic syringes (Monoject) and frozen at −15 °C, was stable for the three-month study period, exhibiting less than a 10% loss as determined by HPLC. (1178)

Ticarcillin disodium (Beecham) 100 mg/ml in sterile water for injection and 25 mg/ml in sodium chloride 0.45% in polypropylene syringes was physically and chemically stable for 30 days when frozen at −20 °C. (2019)

At concentrations of 10 to 100 mg/ml in the following infusion solutions, ticarcillin disodium will not lose potency for up to 30 days when frozen immediately after preparation (2; 4):

Dextrose 5% in water
Ringer's injection
Ringer's injection, lactated
Sodium chloride 0.9%
Sterile water for injection

The stabilities of thawed solutions are identical with those of solutions that have not been frozen, although use within 24 hours of thawing is recommended. (2; 4) (See Additional Compatibility Information.)

Syringes—Borst et al. reported that ticarcillin disodium (Beecham) 2 and 3 g/10 ml in sterile water for injection, packaged in plastic syringes (Monoject), exhibited 10% ticarcillin loss in four days at 24 °C and six days at 4 °C as determined by HPLC. (1178)

Ticarcillin disodium (Beecham) 100 mg/ml in sterile water for injection and 25 mg/ml in sodium chloride 0.45% was packaged as 10 ml in 12-ml polypropylene syringes and sealed with syringe tip caps (Sherwood). Samples were stored at 24 °C for one day, 4 °C for seven days, and −20 °C for 30 days. All samples at all three temperatures remained physically and chemically stable throughout the study. HPLC analysis found no loss of ticarcillin disodium. (2019)

Elastomeric Reservoir Pumps—Ticarcillin disodium solutions in elastomeric reservoir pumps have been stated by the pump manufacturers to be stable for the following time periods frozen, refrigerated (REF), or at room temperature (RT) (31):

Pump Reservoir(s)	Conc.	Frozen	REF	RT
Intermate	5 to 50 mg/ml[a,b]	30 days	15 days	
	5 to 70 mg/ml[b]	7 weeks	14 days	
Medflo	30 mg/ml[a,b]	4 weeks	7 days	24 hr
ReadyMed	30 mg/ml[a,b]	4 weeks	3 days	24 hr

[a]*In dextrose 5% in water.*
[b]*In sodium chloride 0.9%.*

Central Venous Catheter—Ticarcillin disodium (SmithKline Beecham) 10 mg/ml in dextrose 5% in water was found to be compatible with the ARROWg+ard Blue Plus (Arrow International) chlorhexidine-bearing triple-lumen central catheter. HPLC analysis was used to evaluate completeness of drug delivery through the catheter and the amount of chlorhexidine removed from the internal lumens. Essentially complete delivery of the drug was found with little or no drug loss occurring. Furthermore, chlorhexidine delivered from the catheter remained at trace amounts with no substantial increase due to the delivery of the drug through the catheter. (2335)

Compatibility Information

Solution Compatibility

Ticarcillin disodium

Solution	Mfr	Mfr	Conc/L	Remarks	Ref	C/I
Dextrose 4.3% in sodium chloride 0.18%		BE	20 g	No decomposition in 24 hr at 25 °C	334	C
Dextrose 5% in water		BE	20 g	3% decomposition in 24 hr at 25 °C	334	C
	TR[a]	BE	30 g	Physically compatible and potency retained for 24 hr at room temperature	518	C
	TR[a]	BE	60 g	Physically compatible and no potency loss in 24 hr at room temperature	555	C
Sodium chloride 0.9%		BE	20 g	6% decomposition in 24 hr at 25 °C	334	C
	TR[a]	BE	30 g	Physically compatible and potency retained for 24 hr at room temperature	518	C
Sodium lactate ⅙ M		BE	20 g	11% decomposition in 24 hr at 25 °C	334	C
TPN #86 to #88[b]		BE	10 mg	10% ticarcillin loss in 24 hr at room temperature exposed to light	1160	C
		BE	20 mg	12 to 15% ticarcillin loss in 4 hr at room temperature exposed to light	1160	I
TPN #107[b]			2 g	50% ticarcillin loss in 24 hr at 21 °C by microbiological assay	1326	I

[a]Tested in PVC containers.
[b]Refer to Appendix I for the composition of parenteral nutrition solutions. TPN indicates a 2-in-1 admixture.

Additive Compatibility

Ticarcillin disodium

Drug	Mfr	Conc/L	Mfr	Conc/L	Test Soln	Remarks	Ref	C/I
Ciprofloxacin	MI	2 g		30 g	D5W	Physically incompatible	888	I
Gentamicin sulfate		100 mg		2 g	TPN #107[a]	Over 98% gentamicin loss in 24 hr at 21 °C by microbiological assay	1326	I
Ranitidine HCl	GL	100 mg	BE	10 g	D5W	Physically compatible for 24 hr at ambient temperature under fluorescent light	1151	C
Verapamil HCl	KN	80 mg	BE	6 g	D5W, NS	Physically compatible for 24 hr	764	C
	SE	[b]	BE	40 g	D5W, NS	Physically compatible for 24 hr at 21 °C	1166	C

[a]Refer to Appendix I for the composition of parenteral nutrition solutions. TPN indicates a 2-in-1 admixture.
[b]Final concentration unspecified.

Drugs in Syringe Compatibility

Ticarcillin disodium

Drug (in syringe)	Mfr	Amt	Mfr	Amt	Remarks	Ref	C/I
Doxapram HCl	RB	400 mg/ 20 ml		1 g/20 ml	18% doxapram loss in 3 hr	1177	I

Y-Site Injection Compatibility (1:1 Mixture)

Ticarcillin disodium

Drug	Mfr	Conc	Mfr	Conc	Remarks	Ref	C/I
Acyclovir sodium	BW	5 mg/ml[a]	TR	30 mg/ml[a]	Physically compatible for 4 hr at 25 °C	1157	C

Y-Site Injection Compatibility (1:1 Mixture) (Cont.)

			Ticarcillin disodium				
Drug	*Mfr*	*Conc*	*Mfr*	*Conc*	*Remarks*	*Ref*	*C/I*
Allopurinol sodium	BW	3 mg/ml[b]	BE	30 mg/ml[b]	Physically compatible with no change in measured turbidity or increase in particle content in 4 hr at 22 °C	1686	C
Amifostine	USB	10 mg/ml[a]	BE	30 mg/ml[a]	Physically compatible with no change in measured turbidity or increase in particle content in 4 hr at 23 °C	1845	C
Amphotericin B cholesteryl sulfate complex	SEQ	0.83 mg/ml[a]	SKB	30 mg/ml[a]	Microprecipitate forms immediately	2117	I
Aztreonam	SQ	40 mg/ml[a]	BE	30 mg/ml[a]	Physically compatible with no subvisual haze or particle formation in 4 hr at 23 °C	1758	C
Cisatracurium besylate	GW	0.1, 2, 5 mg/ml[a]	SKB	30 mg/ml[a]	Physically compatible with no change in measured turbidity or increase in particle content in 4 hr at 23 °C	2074	C
Cyclophosphamide	MJ	20 mg/ml[a]	BE	30 mg/ml[a]	Physically compatible for 4 hr at 25 °C	1194	C
Diltiazem HCl	MMD	1[b] and 5 mg/ml	BE	200 mg/ml[b]	Visually compatible	1807	C
	MMD	5 mg/ml	BE	10 mg/ml[b]	Visually compatible	1807	C
Docetaxel	RPR	0.9 mg/ml[a]	SKB	30 mg/ml[a]	Physically compatible with no change in measured turbidity or increase in particle content in 4 hr at 23 °C	2224	C
Doxorubicin HCl liposome injection	SEQ	0.4 mg/ml[a]	SKB	30 mg/ml[a]	Physically compatible with little or no change in measured turbidity and no increase in particle content in 4 hr at 23 °C	2087	C
Etoposide phosphate	BR	5 mg/ml[a]	SKB	30 mg/ml[a]	Physically compatible with no change in measured turbidity or increase in particle content in 4 hr at 23 °C	2218	C
Famotidine	MSD	0.2 mg/ml[a]	BE	30 mg/ml[b]	Physically compatible for 14 hr	1196	C
Filgrastim	AMG	30 μg/ml[a]	BE	30 mg/ml[a]	Physically compatible with no change in measured turbidity or increase in particle content in 4 hr at 22 °C	1687	C
Fluconazole	RR	2 mg/ml	BE	15 mg/ml	Viscous gel-like substance forms	1407	I
Fludarabine phosphate	BX	1 mg/ml[a]	BE	30 mg/ml[a]	Physically compatible for 4 hr at room temperature under fluorescent light	1439	C
Gatifloxacin	BMS	2 mg/ml[a]	SKB	30 mg/ml[a]	Physically compatible with no change in measured haze or increase in particle content in 4 hr at 23 °C	2234	C
Gemcitabine HCl	LI	10 mg/ml[b]	SKB	30 mg/ml[b]	Physically compatible with no change in measured turbidity or increase in particle content in 4 hr at 23 °C	2226	C
Granisetron HCl	SKB	0.05 mg/ml[a]	SKB	30 mg/ml[a]	Physically compatible with no change in measured turbidity or increase in particle content in 4 hr at 23 °C	2000	C
Heparin sodium	TR	50 units/ml	BE	20 mg/ml[a]	Visually compatible for 4 hr at 25 °C	1793	C
Hetastarch in lactated electrolyte injection (Hextend)	AB	6%	SKB	30 mg/ml[a]	Physically compatible with no change in measured turbidity or increase in particle content in 4 hr at 23 °C	2339	C

Y-Site Injection Compatibility (1:1 Mixture) (Cont.)

Drug	*Mfr*	*Conc*	*Mfr*	*Conc*	*Remarks*	*Ref*	*C/I*
			Ticarcillin disodium				
Hydromorphone HCl	WY	0.2 mg/ml[a]	BE	60 mg/ml[a]	Physically compatible for at least 4 hr at 25 °C under fluorescent light	987	C
IL-2	RC	4800 I.U./ml[b]	BE	200 mg/ml	Visually compatible and IL-2 activity by bioassay retained. Ticarcillin not tested	1552	C
Insulin, regular	LI	0.2 unit/ml[b]	BE	30 mg/ml[b]	Physically compatible for 2 hr at 25 °C	1395	C
Linezolid	PHU	2 mg/ml	SKB	30 mg/ml[a]	Physically compatible with no change in measured turbidity or increase in particle content in 4 hr at 23 °C	2264	C
Magnesium sulfate	IX	16.7, 33.3, 66.7, 100 mg/ml[a]	BE	60 mg/ml[a]	Physically compatible for at least 4 hr at 32 °C	813	C
Melphalan HCl	BW	0.1 mg/ml[b]	BE	30 mg/ml[b]	Physically compatible with no change in measured turbidity or increase in particle content in 3 hr at 22 °C	1557	C
Meperidine HCl	WY	10 mg/ml[a]	BE	60 mg/ml[a]	Physically compatible for at least 4 hr at 25 °C under fluorescent light	987	C
Morphine sulfate	WI	1 mg/ml[a]	BE	60 mg/ml[a]	Physically compatible for at least 4 hr at 25 °C under fluorescent light	987	C
Ondansetron HCl	GL	1 mg/ml[b]	BE	30 mg/ml[a]	Physically compatible for 4 hr at 22 °C	1365	C
Perphenazine	SC	0.02 mg/ml[a]	BE	30 mg/ml[a]	Physically compatible for 4 hr at 25 °C	1155	C
Propofol	ZEN	10 mg/ml	SKB	30 mg/ml[a]	Physically compatible for 1 hr at 23 °C with no increase in particle content	2066	C
Remifentanil HCl	GW	0.025 and 0.25 mg/ml[b]	SKB	30 mg/ml[a]	Physically compatible with no change in measured turbidity or increase in particle content in 4 hr at 23 °C	2075	C
Sargramostim	IMM	10 μg/ml[b]	BE	30 mg/ml[b]	Physically compatible for 4 hr at 22 °C	1436	C
Teniposide	BR	0.1 mg/ml[a]	BE	30 mg/ml[a]	Physically compatible with no subvisual haze or particle formation in 4 hr at 23 °C	1725	C
Theophylline	TR	4 mg/ml	BE	20 mg/ml[a]	Visually compatible for 6 hr at 25 °C	1793	C
Thiotepa	IMM[c]	1 mg/ml[a]	SKB	30 mg/ml[a]	Physically compatible with no change in measured turbidity or increase in particle content in 4 hr at 23 °C	1861	C
TNA #73[d]		32.5 ml[e]	BE	3 g/50 ml[a]	Physically compatible for 4 hr at 25 °C by visual observation	1008	C
TNA #218 to #226[d]			SKB	30 mg/ml[a]	Visually compatible with no precipitate or emulsion damage apparent in 4 hr at 23 °C	2215	C
TPN #54[d]				267 and 400 mg/ml	Physically compatible and 89 to 94% ticarcillin activity retained over 6 hr at 22 °C by microbiological assay	1045	C
TPN #61[d]		[f]	BE	250 mg/1 ml[g]	Physically compatible	1012	C
		[h]	BE	1.5 g/6 ml[g]	Physically compatible	1012	C
TPN #212 to #215[d]			SKB	30 mg/ml[a]	Physically compatible with no change in measured turbidity or increase in particle content in 4 hr at 23 °C	2109	C

Y-Site Injection Compatibility (1:1 Mixture) (Cont.)

Drug	Mfr	Conc	Ticarcillin disodium Mfr	Ticarcillin disodium Conc	Remarks	Ref	C/I
Vancomycin HCl	AB	20 mg/ml[a]	SKB	50[a] and 200[j] mg/ml	Transient precipitate forms followed by clear solution	2189	?
	AB	20 mg/ml[a]	SKB	1 and 10 mg/ml[a]	Gross white precipitate forms immediately	2189	I
	AB	2 mg/ml[a]	SKB	1[a], 10[a], 50[a], and 200[j] mg/ml	Physically compatible with no change in measured turbidity or increase in particle content in 4 hr at 23 °C	2189	C
Verapamil HCl	SE	2.5 mg/ml	BE	40 mg/ml[i]	Physically compatible for 15 min at 21 °C under fluorescent light	1166	C
Vinorelbine tartrate	BW	1 mg/ml[b]	BE	30 mg/ml[b]	Physically compatible with no change in measured turbidity or increase in particle content in 4 hr at 22 °C	1558	C

[a]*Tested in dextrose 5% in water.*
[b]*Tested in sodium chloride 0.9%.*
[c]*Lyophilized formulation tested.*
[d]*Refer to Appendix I for the composition of parenteral nutrition solutions. TNA indicates a 3-in-1 admixture, and TPN indicates a 2-in-1 admixture.*
[e]*A 32.5-ml sample of parenteral nutrition solution mixed with 50 ml of antibiotic solution.*
[f]*Run at 21 ml/hr.*
[g]*Given over five minutes by syringe pump.*
[h]*Run at 94 ml/hr.*
[i]*Tested in both dextrose 5% in water and sodium chloride 0.9%.*
[j]*Tested in sterile water for injection.*

Additional Compatibility Information

Infusion Solutions — The manufacturer indicates that ticarcillin disodium in the following infusion solutions will provide sufficient activity at room temperature in the indicated concentrations and time periods (4):

Solution	Time Period
Between 10 and 100 mg/ml	
Dextrose 5% in water	72 hr
Ringer's injection	48 hr
Ringer's injection, lactated	48 hr
Sodium chloride 0.9%	72 hr
Sterile water for injection	72 hr
Between 10 and 50 mg/ml	
Alcohol 5%, dextrose 5% in sodium chloride 0.9%	72 hr
Dextrose 5% in Electrolyte #48	48 hr
Dextrose 5% in Electrolyte #75	48 hr
Dextrose 5% in sodium chloride 0.225%	72 hr
Dextrose 5% in sodium chloride 0.45%	72 hr
Fructose 5% in Electrolyte #75	48 hr
Invert sugar 10% in water	48 hr

These solutions are stable for 14 days when stored at 4 °C but should not be used for multidose purposes. (2; 4)

Peritoneal Dialysis Solutions — The activity of ticarcillin 200 mg/L was evaluated in peritoneal dialysis fluids containing 1.5 or 4.25% dextrose (Dianeal 137, Travenol). Storage at 25 °C resulted in virtually no loss of antimicrobial activity in 24 hours. (515)

Aminoglycosides — Like carbenicillin, ticarcillin disodium is incompatible with gentamicin sulfate, tobramycin sulfate, and other aminoglycoside antibiotics. Inactivation of aminoglycosides is dependent on the concentration of ticarcillin, temperature, and time of exposure. (2; 4)

In vitro, a 50% reduction in gentamicin activity results in 15 to 20 hours when ticarcillin 200 μg/ml is incubated with gentamicin 10 μg/ml at 37 °C in phosphate-buffered saline (pH 7.3). (365)

In a study by Holt et al., ticarcillin 500 mg/L in sodium chloride 0.9% was incubated at 37 °C for 24 hours with amikacin, sisomicin, gentamicin sulfate, and tobramycin sulfate individually at concentrations of 10 mg/L. Aminoglycoside activity was reduced by about 50 to 70% for all except amikacin, which showed a 25% reduction. Substituting serum for the sodium chloride solution slowed the loss of activity, but the loss of activity was accentuated when buffered to pH 7.4 in aqueous solution. (574)

In another study, ticarcillin 100 to 600 μg/ml was combined with amikacin 10 and 20 μg/ml, netilmicin sulfate 5 and 10 μg/ml, gentamicin sulfate 5 and 10 μg/ml, and tobramycin sulfate 5 and 10 μg/ml, individually in human serum. Incubation at 37 °C demonstrated greater rates of aminoglycoside decomposition with higher concentrations of ticarcillin. In 72 hours, little or no loss of amikacin, netilmicin, or gentamicin occurred when combined with ticarcillin 100 μg/ml. Tobramycin lost about 11% of its initial activity with this concentration of ticarcillin. At 600 μg/ml of ticarcillin, however, losses were increased to 10% for amikacin, 17% for netilmicin, and about 70% for gentamicin and tobramycin. In general, ticarcillin exerted a less severe adverse effect on aminoglycoside activity than did carbenicillin under these conditions. (575)

Murillo et al. determined that lower serum levels of gentamicin occurred in patients with normal renal function when concomitant ticarcillin disodium was administered compared to cephalothin sodium. The dose of ticarcillin disodium was 12 g/m²/day while cephalothin sodium was given at 7 g/m²/day. The gentamicin sulfate dose was 180 mg/m²/day. In one hour, gentamicin serum levels of 3.1 μg/ml resulted in patients receiving cephalothin while only 2 μg/ml was achieved in patients on ticarcillin. Ticarcillin levels were also substantially reduced. (667)

To determine if spurious aminoglycoside levels could result from a delay in assaying blood samples, Tindula et al. evaluated the inactivation of amikacin 35 μg/ml and gentamicin and tobramycin 10 μg/ml in human serum by 400-μg/ml concentrations of several penicillins and cephalosporins. Samples were stored for 24 hours at room temperature or frozen at −20 °C. For the room temperature samples, cefazolin and cefamandole caused relatively little inactivation. Nafcillin, cephapirin, and cefoxitin caused moderate inactivation, 20% or less. Penicillin, ampicillin, carbenicillin, and ticarcillin generally caused 25% or more inactivation of gentamicin and tobramycin. Amikacin was somewhat less affected. Freezing samples at −20 °C prevented significant inactivation of amikacin and gentamicin by any of the drugs. Freezing the tobramycin samples was satisfactory for most of the drugs except penicillin, ampicillin, and carbenicillin, which still exhibited a 15 to 20% loss in 24 hours. (824)

The inactivation of tobramycin, gentamicin, and amikacin 10 μg/ml in sterile distilled water by ticarcillin 500 and 100 μg/ml stored at 37 °C was reported by Jorgensen and Crawford. Ticarcillin 500 μg/ml caused about a 45% tobramycin loss in two hours and a 75% loss in six hours. At 100 μg/ml, 47% tobramycin inactivation occurred in six hours. The gentamicin loss was 34 and 15% in six hours for ticarcillin 500- and 100-μg/ml concentrations, respectively. The amikacin loss was 16% in six hours with ticarcillin 500 μg/ml but was insignificant with the 100-μg/ml concentration. No loss of ticarcillin activity was detected in any combination. (973)

The comparative inactivation of five aminoglycosides by seven β-lactam antibiotics in human serum at 37 °C was reported by Riff and Thomason. Amikacin, followed by netilmicin, had the lowest degree of inactivation; tobramycin sustained the most pronounced losses. Gentamicin and kanamycin were intermediate in the extent of losses. The six penicillins that were tested all produced aminoglycoside inactivation; the greatest extent of inactivation was caused by carbenicillin followed by ticarcillin, penicillin G, oxacillin, methicillin, and ampicillin, in approximate descending order. Cephalothin produced minimal inactivation (5 to 10% in 24 hours). The rate of inactivation could be reduced by storage at 4 °C and further reduced by storage at −20 °C. The authors suggested processing blood samples rapidly to avoid inaccurate serum determinations. Storage of specimens at low temperature until analysis may be helpful. (1052)

The clinical significance of these interactions in patients appears to be primarily confined to those with renal failure. (218; 334; 361; 364; 616; 847) Literature reports of greatly reduced aminoglycoside levels in such patients have appeared frequently. (363; 365; 366; 367; 614; 615; 962) In addition, the interaction may be clinically important if assays for aminoglycoside levels in serum are sufficiently delayed. (576; 618; 824; 847; 1052)

Most authors believe that in vitro mixing of penicillins such as ticarcillin disodium with aminoglycoside antibiotics should be avoided but that clinical use of the drugs in combination can be of great value. In such combined therapy, it is generally recommended that the drugs be given separately. (2; 157; 218; 222; 224; 361; 364; 368; 369; 370)

Methylprednisolone — The compatibility of methylprednisolone sodium succinate (Upjohn) with ticarcillin disodium added to an auxiliary medication infusion unit has been studied. Primary admixtures were prepared by adding ticarcillin disodium 6 g/L to dextrose 5% in water, dextrose 5% in sodium chloride 0.9%, and Ringer's injection, lactated. Up to 100 ml of the primary admixture was added, along with the methylprednisolone sodium succinate (Upjohn), to the auxiliary medication infusion unit with the following results (329):

Methylprednisolone Sodium Succinate	Ticarcillin Disodium 6 g/L Primary Solution	Results
500 mg	D5S, D5W qs 100 ml	Clear solution for 24 hr
500 mg	LR qs 100 ml	Clear solution for 6 hr
500 mg	Added to 100 ml LR	Clear solution for 24 hr
1000 mg	D5W qs 100 ml	Clear solution for 24 hr
1000 mg	D5S qs 100 ml or added to 100 ml D5S	Clear solution for 6 hr
1000 mg	LR qs 100 ml	Clear solution for 1 hr
1000 mg	Added to 100 ml LR	Clear solution for 6 hr

Vancomycin — Direct mixture of vancomycin HCl and ticarcillin disodium reportedly does not result in precipitate formation. However, sequential administration of ticarcillin disodium 4.25 g/50 ml and then vancomycin HCl 500 mg/50 ml in dextrose 5% in sodium chloride 0.3% through a calibrated chamber set (Buretrol) can result in a white precipitate. In that study, the precipitate did not appear during the initial infusion but formed after repeated administration through the same set. The sequence of administration (ticarcillin first, followed by vancomycin), drug concentrations, and repetitive administration all appear to affect the appearance of the precipitate. (972)

The compatibility or incompatibility of vancomycin HCl mixed with or administered simultaneously with ticarcillin disodium is concentration dependent. (2189) See Y-Site Injection Compatibility above. Vancomycin HCl has a low pH and is variably compatible with drugs having neutral to mildly alkaline pH, including cephalosporins and penicillins. The compatibility may depend on a number of factors, including concentration of each drug, dilution vehicle, actual pH of solutions, and completeness of mixing during administration. Combinations that are compatible when well mixed may result in precipitation if only partially mixed, presumably because of regionally different concentrations and pH values. If attempting to administer vancomycin HCl with ticarcillin disodium, care should be taken to ensure that the specific combination and the concentrations are compatible under the exact administration conditions to be used. An inline filter should be used as a final safety measure. (2189)

TICARCILLIN DISODIUM–CLAVULANATE POTASSIUM AHFS 8:12.16

Products — Ticarcillin disodium–clavulanate potassium is available in vials and piggyback bottles containing 3.1 g (ticarcillin 3 g as the disodium salt plus clavulanic acid 100 mg as the potassium salt). Reconstitute the vials with 13 ml of sterile water for injection or sodium chloride 0.9% and shake well. When dissolution is completed, the solution will contain ticarcillin 200 mg/ml with clavulanic acid 6.7 mg/ml. (2)

The 3.1-g piggyback bottles may be reconstituted with 50 to 100 ml of sodium chloride 0.9%, dextrose 5% in water, or lactated Ringer's injection. (4)

The product is also available in a pharmacy bulk package containing 31 g (ticarcillin 30 g as the disodium salt plus clavulanic acid 1 g as the potassium salt). It should be reconstituted with 76 ml of sterile water for injection or sodium chloride 0.9%, added in two portions, and shaken well. Each milliliter of this concentrate contains ticarcillin 300 mg plus clavulanic acid 10 mg. (4)

Ticarcillin disodium–clavulanate potassium is available as a frozen premixed infusion containing 3.1 g in 100 ml of water (30 mg/ml of ticarcillin plus 1 mg/ml of clavulanic acid) with sodium citrate buffer and hydrochloric acid or sodium hydroxide to adjust pH. Thawing for use should be performed at room temperature or under refrigeration and not by warming in a water bath or by exposure to microwave radiation. Any precipitate that has formed during freezing should redissolve upon reaching room temperature. The container and ports should be checked for leaking by squeezing the bag. (4)

pH — From 5.5 to 7.5. (2)

Osmolality — Robinson et al. recommended the following maximum ticarcillin disodium–clavulanate potassium concentrations to achieve osmolalities suitable for peripheral infusion in fluid-restricted patients (1180):

Diluent	Maximum Concentration[a] (mg/ml)	Osmolality (mOsm/kg)
Dextrose 5% in water	48	562
Sodium chloride 0.9%	43	546
Sterile water for injection	86	573

[a]*Ticarcillin concentration.*

Sodium and Potassium Content — Each gram of this combination product contains 4.75 mEq of sodium. The 3.1-g vial contains 0.15 mEq of potassium. (2)

The 3.1 g/100 ml frozen injection contains 0.187 mEq of sodium and 0.005 mEq of potassium. (4)

Trade Name(s) — Timentin.

Administration — Reconstituted ticarcillin disodium–clavulanate potassium solutions should be further diluted to concentrations of 10 to 100 mg/ml of ticarcillin and given over 30 minutes by intermittent intravenous infusion directly into a vein or through a Y-type administration set. Other solutions should be temporarily discontinued during the infusion of ticarcillin disodium–clavulanate potassium. (2; 4)

Stability — The commercially available combination product as a powder is white to pale yellow. It should be stored at 24 °C or less. Higher temperatures may cause darkening, an indication of clavulanate potassium degradation. (4)

The concentrated reconstituted solutions, which are colorless to pale yellow, are stable for up to six hours after reconstitution when stored at room temperatures of 21 to 24 °C or for up to 72 hours when refrigerated at 4 °C. (2; 4)

pH Effects — Clavulanic acid exhibits maximum stability at pH 6.4. (1797)

Freezing Solutions — Ticarcillin disodium–clavulanate potassium solutions of 10 to 100 mg/ml (based on ticarcillin content) in sodium chloride 0.9% or Ringer's injection, lactated, are stable for up to 30 days when frozen at −18 °C. Diluted to this concentration range in dextrose 5% in water, the drug is stable for up to seven days when frozen. Frozen solutions should be thawed at room temperature, and thawed solutions should be used within eight hours and not be refrozen. (2; 4)

The frozen premixed infusion solutions should be stored at −20 °C. After thawing at room temperature or under refrigeration, the solutions are stable for 24 hours at room temperature or seven days under refrigeration. Thawed solutions should not be refrozen. (4)

Elastomeric Reservoir Pumps — Ticarcillin disodium–clavulanate potassium (Beecham) 15 mg/ml in both dextrose 5% in water and sodium chloride 0.9% was evaluated for binding potential to natural rubber elastomeric reservoirs (Baxter). No binding was found after storage for two weeks at 35 °C with gentle agitation. (2014)

Ticarcillin disodium – clavulanate potassium solutions in elastomeric reservoir pumps have been stated by the pump manufacturers to be stable for the following time periods frozen, refrigerated (REF), or at room temperature (RT) (31):

Pump Reservoir(s)	Conc.	Frozen	REF	RT
Homepump; Homepump Eclipse	30 mg/ml[b]		7 days	24 hr
Medflo	30 mg/ml[a,b]	4 weeks	7 days	24 hr
ReadyMed	30 mg/ml[b]	4 weeks	3 days	24 hr
	30 mg/ml[a]	4 weeks	3 days	12 hr

[a]*In dextrose 5% in water.*
[b]*In sodium chloride 0.9%.*

Central Venous Catheter — Ticarcillin disodium–clavulanate potassium (SmithKline Beecham) 10.33 mg/ml in dextrose 5% in water was found to be compatible with the ARROWg+ard Blue Plus (Arrow International) chlorhexidine-bearing triple-lumen central catheter. HPLC analysis was used to evaluate completeness of drug delivery through the catheter and the amount of chlorhexidine removed from the internal lumens. Essentially complete delivery of the drug was found with little or no drug loss occurring. Furthermore, chlorhexidine delivered from the catheter remained at trace amounts with no substantial increase due to the delivery of the drug through the catheter. (2335)

Compatibility Information

Y-Site Injection Compatibility (1:1 Mixture)

Drug	Mfr	Conc	Mfr	Conc	Remarks	Ref	C/I
			Ticarcillin disodium–clavulanate potassium				
Alatrofloxacin mesylate	PF	1.43 mg/ml[a]	SKB	103.3 mg/ml[g]	Yellow precipitate forms	2235	I
Allopurinol sodium	BW	3 mg/ml[b]	SKB	31 mg/ml[b]	Physically compatible with no change in measured turbidity or increase in particle content in 4 hr at 22 °C	1686	C
Amifostine	USB	10 mg/ml[a]	SKB	31 mg/ml[a]	Physically compatible with no change in measured turbidity or increase in particle content in 4 hr at 23 °C	1845	C
Amphotericin B cholesteryl sulfate complex	SEQ	0.83 mg/ml[a]	SKB	31 mg/ml[a]	Gross precipitate forms	2117	I
Aztreonam	SQ	40 mg/ml[a]	SKB	31 mg/ml[a]	Physically compatible with no subvisual haze or particle formation in 4 hr at 23 °C	1758	C
Cefepime HCl	BMS	20 mg/ml[a]	SKB	31 mg/ml[a]	Physically compatible with no change in measured turbidity or increase in particle content in 4 hr at 22 °C	1689	C
Cisatracurium besylate	GW	0.1 and 2 mg/ml[a]	SKB	31 mg/ml[a]	Physically compatible with no change in measured turbidity or increase in particle content in 4 hr at 23 °C	2074	C
	GW	5 mg/ml[a]	SKB	31 mg/ml[a]	Subvisual haze forms immediately	2074	I
Clarithromycin	AB	4 mg/ml[a]	BE	32 mg/ml[a]	Visually compatible for 72 hr at both 30 and 17 °C	2174	C
Cyclophosphamide	MJ	20 mg/ml[a]	BE	31 mg/ml[a]	Physically compatible for 4 hr at 25 °C	1194	C
Diltiazem HCl	MMD	1[b] and 5 mg/ml	BE	200 mg/ml[b]	Visually compatible	1807	C
	MMD	5 mg/ml	BE	10 mg/ml[b]	Visually compatible	1807	C
Docetaxel	RPR	0.9 mg/ml[a]	SKB	31 mg/ml[a]	Physically compatible with no change in measured turbidity or increase in particle content in 4 hr at 23 °C	2224	C
Doxorubicin HCl liposome injection	SEQ	0.4 mg/ml[a]	SKB	31 mg/ml[a]	Physically compatible with little or no change in measured turbidity and no increase in particle content in 4 hr at 23 °C	2087	C
Etoposide phosphate	BR	5 mg/ml[a]	SKB	31 mg/ml[a]	Physically compatible with no change in measured turbidity or increase in particle content in 4 hr at 23 °C	2218	C
Famotidine	MSD	0.2 mg/ml[a]	BE	31 mg/ml[b]	Physically compatible for 14 hr	1196	C
Filgrastim	AMG	30 µg/ml[a]	SKB	31 mg/ml[a]	Physically compatible with no change in measured turbidity or increase in particle content in 4 hr at 22 °C	1687	C
Fluconazole	RR	2 mg/ml	BE	60 mg/ml	Physically compatible for 24 hr at 25 °C	1407	C
Fludarabine phosphate	BX	1 mg/ml[a]	BE	31 mg/ml[a]	Physically compatible for 4 hr at room temperature under fluorescent light	1439	C
Foscarnet sodium	AST	24 mg/ml	BE	100 mg/ml[c]	Physically compatible for 24 hr at 25 °C under fluorescent light by visual and microscopic examination	1393	C

Y-Site Injection Compatibility (1:1 Mixture) (Cont.)

Drug	Mfr	Conc	Ticarcillin disodium–clavulanate potassium Mfr	Conc	Remarks	Ref	C/I
Gatifloxacin	BMS	2 mg/ml[a]	SKB	31 mg/ml[a]	Physically compatible with no change in measured haze or increase in particle content in 4 hr at 23 °C	2234	C
Gemcitabine HCl	LI	10 mg/ml[b]	SKB	31 mg/ml[b]	Physically compatible with no change in measured turbidity or increase in particle content in 4 hr at 23 °C	2226	C
Granisetron HCl	SKB	1 mg/ml	SKB	27 mg/ml[b]	Physically compatible with little or no loss of either drug by HPLC in 4 hr at 22 °C	1883	C
	SKB	0.05 mg/ml[a]	SKB	31 mg/ml[a]	Physically compatible with no change in measured turbidity or increase in particle content in 4 hr at 23 °C	2000	C
Heparin sodium	TR	50 units/ml	BE	31 mg/ml[b]	Visually compatible for 4 hr at 25 °C	1793	C
Hetastarch in lactated electrolyte injection (Hextend)	AB	6%	SKB	31 mg/ml[a]	Physically compatible with no change in measured turbidity or increase in particle content in 4 hr at 23 °C	2339	C
Insulin, regular	LI	0.2 unit/ml[b]	BE	31 mg/ml[b]	Physically compatible for 2 hr at 25 °C	1395	C
Melphalan HCl	BW	0.1 mg/ml[b]	SKB	31 mg/ml[b]	Physically compatible with no change in measured turbidity or increase in particle content in 3 hr at 22 °C	1557	C
Meperidine HCl	WY	10 mg/ml[b]	BE	31 mg/ml[b]	Physically compatible for 1 hr at 25 °C	1338	C
Morphine sulfate	ES	1 mg/ml[b]	BE	31 mg/ml[b]	Physically compatible for 1 hr at 25 °C	1338	C
Ondansetron HCl	GL	1 mg/ml[b]	BE	31 mg/ml[a]	Physically compatible for 4 hr at 22 °C	1365	C
Perphenazine	SC	0.02 mg/ml[a]	BE	31 mg/ml[a]	Physically compatible for 4 hr at 25 °C	1155	C
Propofol	ZEN	10 mg/ml	SKB	31 mg/ml[a]	Physically compatible for 1 hr at 23 °C with no increase in particle content	2066	C
Remifentanil HCl	GW	0.025 and 0.25 mg/ml[b]	SKB	31 mg/ml[a]	Physically compatible with no change in measured turbidity or increase in particle content in 4 hr at 23 °C	2075	C
Sargramostim	IMM	10 µg/ml[b]	BE	31 mg/ml[b]	Physically compatible for 4 hr at 22 °C	1436	C
Teniposide	BR	0.1 mg/ml[a]	SKB	31 mg/ml[a]	Physically compatible with no subvisual haze or particle formation in 4 hr at 23 °C	1725	C
Theophylline	TR	4 mg/ml	BE	31 mg/ml[b]	Visually compatible for 6 hr at 25 °C	1793	C
Thiotepa	IMM[d]	1 mg/ml[a]	SKB	31 mg/ml[a]	Physically compatible with no change in measured turbidity or increase in particle content in 4 hr at 23 °C	1861	C
TNA #218 to #226[e]			SKB	31 mg/ml[a]	Visually compatible with no precipitate or emulsion damage apparent in 4 hr at 23 °C	2215	C
Topotecan HCl	SKB	56 µg/ml[a]	SKB	24.6 mg/ml[a]	Pale yellow color occurs immediately. 11% loss of topotecan occurs in 4 hr at 22 °C under fluorescent light	2245	I
	SKB	56 µg/ml[b]	SKB	24.6 mg/ml[b]	Pale yellow color occurs immediately. 5% or less loss of all drug components in 4 hr at 22 °C under fluorescent light	2245	C
TPN #189[e]			BE	30 mg/ml[b]	Visually compatible for 24 hr at 22 °C	1767	C

Y-Site Injection Compatibility (1:1 Mixture) (Cont.)

			Ticarcillin disodium–clavulanate potassium				
Drug	*Mfr*	*Conc*	*Mfr*	*Conc*	*Remarks*	*Ref*	*C/I*
TPN #212 to #215[e]			SKB	31 mg/ml[a]	Physically compatible with no change in measured turbidity or increase in particle content in 4 hr at 23 °C	2109	C
Vancomycin HCl	AB	20 mg/ml[a]	SKB	206.7 mg/ml[f]	Transient precipitate forms followed by clear solution	2189	?
	AB	20 mg/ml[a]	SKB	1.034, 10.335, and 51.675 mg/ml[a]	Gross white precipitate forms	2189	I
		5 mg/ml[b]	SKB	31 mg/ml[b]	White precipitate formed sporadically	2167	I
	AB	2 mg/ml[a]	SKB	1.034[a], 10.335[a], 51.675[a], and 206.7[f] mg/ml	Physically compatible with no change in measured turbidity or increase in particle content in 4 hr at 23 °C	2189	C
Vinorelbine tartrate	BW	1 mg/ml[b]	SKB	31 mg/ml[b]	Physically compatible with no change in measured turbidity or increase in particle content in 4 hr at 22 °C	1558	C

[a]*Tested in dextrose 5% in water.*
[b]*Tested in sodium chloride 0.9%.*
[c]*Tested in both dextrose 5% in water and sodium chloride 0.9%.*
[d]*Lyophilized formulation tested.*
[e]*Refer to Appendix I for the composition of parenteral nutrition solutions. TNA indicates a 3-in-1 admixture, and TPN indicates a 2-in-1 admixture.*
[f]*Tested in sterile water for injection.*
[g]*Tested in sodium chloride 0.45%.*

Additional Compatibility Information

The compatibility information on ticarcillin disodium should be considered. See previous monograph.

Infusion Solutions — Dextrose 5% in water, Ringer's injection, lactated, sodium chloride 0.9%, and sterile water for injection are recommended for dilution of ticarcillin disodium–clavulanate potassium. (2; 4)

The manufacturer indicates that storage of the 200-mg/ml (based on ticarcillin content) reconstituted solution for up to six hours at room temperature, followed by dilution to 10 to 100 mg/ml in the following infusion solutions, results in the stability periods noted (2):

Solution	Room Temperature	Refrigeration
Dextrose 5% in water	24 hr	3 days
Ringer's injection, lactated	24 hr	7 days
Sodium chloride 0.9%	24 hr	7 days

If the 300-mg/ml (based on ticarcillin content) reconstituted solution in the pharmacy bulk package is stored for six hours at room temperature, followed by dilution to 10 to 100 mg/ml, the following stability periods result (2):

Solution	Room Temperature	Refrigeration
Dextrose 5% in water	24 hr	3 days
Ringer's injection, lactated	24 hr	4 days
Sodium chloride 0.9%	24 hr	4 days
Sterile water for injection	24 hr	4 days

Vancomycin HCl — Ticarcillin disodium–clavulanate potassium when admixed with vancomycin HCl has been reported to exhibit occasional precipitate formation. This observation from practice was made with a combination of vancomycin HCl 5 mg/ml and ticarcillin disodium–clavulanate potassium 30 + 1 mg/ml and also with combinations at variable but unrecorded concentrations. The occurrence of precipitate formation was characterized as sporadic and unpredictable. (2167)

The compatibility or incompatibility of vancomycin HCl mixed with or administered simultaneously with ticarcillin disodium–clavulanate potassium is concentration dependent. (2189) See Y-Site Injection Compatibility above. Vancomycin HCl has a low pH and is variably compatible with drugs having neutral to mildly alkaline pH, including cephalosporins and penicillins. The compatibility may depend on a number of factors, including concentration of each drug, dilution vehicle, actual pH of solutions, and completeness of mixing during administration. Combinations that are compatible when well mixed may result in precipitation if only partially mixed, presumably because of regionally different concentrations and pH values. If attempting to administer vancomycin HCl with ticarcillin disodium–clavulanate potassium, take care to ensure that the specific combination and the concentrations are compatible under the exact administration conditions to be used. An inline filter should be used as a final safety measure. (2189)

Other Drugs — Ticarcillin disodium–clavulanate potassium is incompatible with sodium bicarbonate. (2; 4) Because of the potential for incompatibility, the manufacturer recommends that other anti-infectives, such as aminoglycosides, not be admixed with ticarcillin disodium–clavulanate potassium. (2)

TIROFIBAN HCL
AHFS 92:00

Products — Tirofiban HCl is available in 50-ml single-use vials as a concentrated solution that must be diluted for administration. Each milliliter of injection provides tirofiban 0.25 mg (as the hydrochloride monohydrate) along with citric acid anhydrous 0.16 mg, sodium citrate dihydrate 2.7 mg, sodium chloride 8 mg and sodium hydroxide and/or hydrochloric acid to adjust pH in water for injection. (2)

Tirofiban HCl is also available premixed as a ready-to-use solution for infusion in 250- and 500-ml (IntraVia) plastic containers. Each milliliter of the ready-to-use infusion provides tirofiban 0.05 mg (50 µg) as the hydrochloride monohydrate along with sodium chloride 9 mg, sodium citrate dihydrate 0.54 mg, citric acid anhydrous 0.032 mg, and sodium hydroxide and/or hydrochloric acid to adjust pH in water for injection. (2)

pH — From 5.5 to 6.5. (2)

Osmolality — The osmolality of tirofiban HCl concentrated solution after dilution for administration and of the premixed infusion solution is approximately 280 and 300 mOsm/kg, respectively. (4)

Trade Name(s) — Aggrastat.

Administration — Tirofiban HCl is administered only by intravenous infusion. The concentrated injection in vials should be diluted to a final concentration of 0.05 mg/ml (50 µg/ml) using a compatible infusion solution. Before adding the tirofiban HCl to the infusion solution, remove an amount of infusion solution equivalent to the volume of tirofiban HCl concentrated solution that is to be added. This volume would be 50 ml for a 250-ml container and 100 ml for a 500-ml container. The premixed infusion solution is ready to use and does not require dilution. (2)

Stability — Tirofiban HCl concentrated solution and the ready-to-use infusion are clear and colorless solutions. Both intact vials and plastic containers should be stored at controlled room temperature of 25 °C, with temperature excursions in the range of 15 to 30 °C permitted, and protected from light and freezing. (2)

Sorption — Tirofiban HCl (Merck) 0.05 mg/ml in dextrose 5% in water, dextrose 5% in sodium chloride 0.45%, and sodium chloride 0.9% was found to be compatible with PVC administration sets from Baxter, IVAC, and Abbott. The drug concentration was delivered completely with no loss due to sorption; extractables from the plastic sets were comparable to control solutions without the drug. (2249)

Compatibility Information

Solution Compatibility

Tirofiban HCl

Solution	*Mfr*	*Mfr*	*Conc/L*	*Remarks*	*Ref*	*C/I*
Dextrose 5% in 0.45% sodium chloride	AB[a]	ME	50 mg	Visually compatible with no loss by HPLC within 24 hr at 23 °C exposed to fluorescent light	2249	C
Dextrose 5% in water	BA[a]	ME	50 mg	Visually compatible with no loss by HPLC within 24 hr at 23 °C exposed to fluorescent light	2249	C
Sodium chloride	AB[a]	ME	50 mg	Visually compatible with no loss by HPLC within 24 hr at 23 °C exposed to fluorescent light	2249	C

[a]*Tested in PVC containers.*

Y-Site Injection Compatibility (1:1 Mixture)

Tirofiban HCl

Drug	*Mfr*	*Conc*	*Mfr*	*Conc*	*Remarks*	*Ref*	*C/I*
Dopamine HCl	AMR	0.2 and 3.2 mg/ml[a]	ME	0.05 mg/ml[b]	Physically compatible with little or no loss of either drug by HPLC in 4 hr at room temperature under fluorescent light	2250	C
	AMR	0.2 and 3.2 mg/ml[b]	ME	0.05 mg/ml[a]	Physically compatible with little or no loss of either drug by HPLC in 4 hr at room temperature under fluorescent light	2250	C
Famotidine HCl	ME	2 and 4 mg/ml[a]	ME	0.05 mg/ml[b]	Physically compatible with little or no loss of either drug by HPLC in 4 hr at room temperature under fluorescent light	2250	C
	ME	2 and 4 mg/ml[b]	ME	0.05 mg/ml[a]	Physically compatible with little or no loss of either drug by HPLC in 4 hr at room temperature under fluorescent light	2250	C

Y-Site Injection Compatibility (1:1 Mixture) (Cont.)

			Tirofiban HCl				
Drug	*Mfr*	*Conc*	*Mfr*	*Conc*	*Remarks*	*Ref*	*C/I*
Heparin sodium	AB	40 units/ml[a]	ME	0.05 mg/ml[a,b]	Physically compatible with no tirofiban loss by HPLC or loss of heparin activity in 4 hr at room temperature under fluorescent light	2250	C
	AB	50 units/ml[b]	ME	0.05 mg/ml[b]	Physically compatible with no tirofiban loss by HPLC or loss of heparin activity in 4 hr at room temperature under fluorescent light	2250	C
	AB	100 units/ml[a,b]	ME	0.05 mg/ml[a,b]	Physically compatible with no tirofiban loss by HPLC or loss of heparin activity in 4 hr at room temperature under fluorescent light	2250	C
Lidocaine HCl	AB	1 and 20 mg/ml[a,b]	ME	0.05 mg/ml[a]	Physically compatible with little or no loss of either drug by HPLC in 4 hr at room temperature under fluorescent light	2250	C
	AB	1 and 20 mg/ml[a,b]	ME	0.05 mg/ml[b]	Physically compatible with little or no loss of either drug by HPLC in 4 hr at room temperature under fluorescent light	2250	C
Potassium chloride	AB	0.01 and 0.04 mEq/ml[a,b]	ME	0.05 mg/ml[a]	Physically compatible with no tirofiban loss by HPLC in 4 hr at room temperature under fluorescent light. Potassium chloride not tested	2250	C
	AB	0.01 and 0.04 mEq/ml[a,b]	ME	0.05 mg/ml[b]	Physically compatible with no tirofiban loss by HPLC in 4 hr at room temperature under fluorescent light. Potassium chloride not tested	2250	C

[a]*Tested in dextrose 5% in water.*
[b]*Tested in sodium chloride 0.9%.*

Additional Compatibility Information

Infusion Solutions — Dextrose 5% in water and sodium chloride 0.9% are recommended for dilution of tirofiban HCl concentrated solution to a concentration of 0.05 mg/ml for infusion. (2) Discard any unadministered solution remaining 24 hours after initiation of the infusion. (4)

Other Drugs — The manufacturer indicates that tirofiban HCl may be infused through the same line with dopamine HCl, famotidine HCl, lidocaine HCl, and potassium chloride. (2) Other information indicates that heparin sodium may also be infused through the same line. (4) Tirofiban HCl should not be adminstered simultaneously with diazepam. (2) It has been recommended that additives should not be added directly to the container of tirofiban HCl. (4)

TOBRAMYCIN SULFATE
AHFS 8:12.02

Products — Tobramycin sulfate is available in a concentration equivalent to tobramycin base 40 mg/ml in 2- and 30-ml vials as well as 50-ml bulk vials and 1- and 2-ml disposable syringes. It is also available as a pediatric injection containing tobramycin sulfate equivalent to tobramycin base 10 mg/ml in 2-, 6-, and 8-ml vials. Each milliliter of Nebcin contains phenol 5 mg, sodium bisulfite 3.2 mg, and disodium edetate 0.1 mg in water for injection. Sodium hydroxide and/or sulfuric acid may have been added during manufacture for pH adjustment. (2)

The drug is also supplied in 60- and 80-mg ADD-Vantage vials with phenol 1.25 mg, sodium bisulfite 1.6 mg, and edetate disodium 0.1 mg in water for injection. Sodium hydroxide and/or sulfuric acid may have been added during manufacture for pH adjustment. (2)

Tobramycin sulfate is also available premixed in sodium chloride 0.9% in 0.8-mg/ml (80 mg), 1.2-mg/ml (60 mg), and 1.6-mg/ml (80 mg) concentrations. (4)

Tobramycin sulfate is also available in a pharmacy bulk package as a dry powder in vials containing the equivalent of tobramycin 1.2 g. (2) The vial contents should be diluted with 30 ml of sterile water for injection to yield a 40-mg/ml solution. The reconstituted solution is intended to be diluted in a suitable intravenous infusion solution for administration. (4)

pH—The pH of the injection is adjusted to 3 to 6.5. The reconstituted solution from powder has a pH of 6 to 8. (4)

Osmolality—The osmolality of tobramycin sulfate (Dista) 10 mg/ml was determined to be 133 mOsm/kg by freezing-point depression and 213 mOsm/kg by vapor pressure. (1071)

The osmolality of tobramycin sulfate (Lilly) 1 mg/ml was determined to be 254 mOsm/kg in dextrose 5% in water and 288 mOsm/kg in sodium chloride 0.9%. At 2.5 mg/ml, the osmolality was determined to be 261 mOsm/kg in dextrose 5% in water and 283 mOsm/kg in sodium chloride 0.9%. (1375)

The osmolality of tobramycin sulfate 80 mg was calculated for the following dilutions (1054):

	Osmolality (mOsm/kg)	
Diluent	50 ml	100 ml
Dextrose 5% in water	289	285
Sodium chloride 0.9%	319	315

The premixed products in sodium chloride 0.9% have an osmolarity of approximately 316 mOsm/kg. (4)

Sodium Content—The premixed products contain about 15.4 mEq of sodium per 100 ml of solution. (4)

Trade Name(s)—Nebcin.

Administration — Tobramycin sulfate may be administered by intramuscular injection or intermittent intravenous infusion. Intramuscular doses should be withdrawn only from multiple-dose vials; alternatively, the commercial prefilled syringes may be used. When given by intravenous infusion, the dose should be added to 50 to 100 ml of infusion solution and administered over 20 to 60 minutes. In children, the volume should be proportionately less but should allow an infusion period of 20 to 60 minutes. Infusion periods should not be less than 20 minutes; such shorter periods could result in excessive peak serum concentrations. (2; 4)

Stability — Tobramycin sulfate is stable at room temperature both as the clear, colorless solution and as the dry powder. Intact containers should be stored at controlled room temperature between 15 and 30 °C; premixed infusion solutions may be stored at temperatures up to 25 °C. Freezing and excessive temperatures above 40 °C should be avoided. The injections should not be used if they are discolored. The manufacturer recommends use of the 40-mg/ml reconstituted solution within 24 hours when stored at room temperature or 96 hours if refrigerated. (2; 4) Tobramycin sulfate is stable for several weeks at pH 1 to 11 at temperatures from 5 to 27 °C. It can be autoclaved without loss of potency. (145)

Freezing Solutions—Tobramycin sulfate reconstituted to a concentration of 40 mg/ml and immediately frozen in the original container is stable for up to 12 weeks when stored at −10 to −20 °C. (4)

Holmes et al. evaluated tobramycin sulfate (Lilly) 160 mg/50 ml of dextrose 5% in water in PVC bags frozen at −20 °C for 30 days and then thawed by exposure to ambient temperature or microwave radiation. The solutions showed no evidence of precipitation or color change and showed 6% or less loss of potency determined microbiologically. Subsequent storage of the admixture at room temperature for 24 hours also yielded a physically compatible solution which exhibited little or no additional loss of activity. (555)

Marble et al. reported that tobramycin sulfate (Dista) 120 mg/50 ml in dextrose 5% in water and sodium chloride 0.9% in PVC bags lost 9% activity in 28 days when frozen at −20 °C. (981)

Minibags of tobramycin sulfate in dextrose 5% in water or sodium chloride 0.9%, frozen at −20 °C for up to 35 days, were thawed at room temperature and in a microwave oven, with care taken that the thawed solution temperature never exceeded 25 °C. No significant differences in tobramycin sulfate concentrations occurred between the two thawing methods. (1192)

Syringes—Samples of a 40-mg/ml solution of tobramycin sulfate (Lilly) from a reconstituted 1.2-g vial were stored in Monoject plastic syringes at both 25 and 4 °C. After two months, no significant change in potency was detected in samples at either storage temperature. The authors did note that the manufacturer does not recommend storage in plastic syringes because of possible incompatibility with the plunger heads. (736)

Tobramycin sulfate (Dista) 120 mg diluted with 1 ml of sodium chloride 0.9% to a final volume of 4 ml was stable (less than a 10% loss) when stored in polypropylene syringes (Becton-Dickinson) for 48 hours at 25 °C under fluorescent light. (1159)

Elastomeric Reservoir Pumps—Tobramycin sulfate (Lilly) 0.8 mg/ml in sodium chloride 0.9% 100 ml was packaged in latex elastomeric reservoirs (Secure Medical). Little or no loss by HPLC analysis occurred in 24 hours at 25 °C. (1970)

Tobramycin sulfate (Lilly) 0.8 mg/ml in both dextrose 5% in water and sodium chloride 0.9% was evaluated for binding potential to natural rubber elastomeric reservoirs (Baxter). No binding was found after storage for two weeks at 35 °C with gentle agitation. (2014)

Tobramycin sulfate solutions in elastomeric reservoir pumps have been stated by the pump manufacturers to be stable for the following time periods frozen, refrigerated (REF), or at room temperature (RT) (31):

Pump Reservoir(s)	Conc.	Frozen	REF	RT
Homepump;	0.8 mg/ml[b]		14 days	24 hr
Homepump	0.2 mg/ml[b]		7 days	24 hr
Eclipse	4.8 mg/ml[b]		7 days	
Intermate	0.5 to 4.8 mg/ml[a,b]		10 days	24 hr
Intermate HPC	0.8 to 2.4 mg/ml[b]		14 days	7 days
Medflo	0.8 mg/ml[a,b]	12 weeks	4 days	48 hr
ReadyMed	1 mg/ml[b]	4 weeks	14 days	48 hr

[a]*In dextrose 5% in water.*
[b]*In sodium chloride 0.9%.*

Sorption—Tobramycin sulfate (Lilly) 20 mg/L in sodium chloride 0.9% (Travenol) in PVC bags did not exhibit significant sorption to the plastic during one week of storage at room temperature (15 to 20 °C). (536)

In another study, tobramycin sulfate (Lilly) 20 mg/L in sodium chloride 0.9% did not exhibit any loss due to sorption during a seven-hour simulated infusion through an infusion set (Travenol) consisting of a cellulose propionate burette chamber and 170 cm of PVC tubing. (606)

The drug was also tested as a simulated infusion over at least one hour by a syringe pump system. A glass syringe on a syringe pump was fitted with 20 cm of polyethylene tubing or 50 cm of Silastic tubing. No loss of drug due to sorption was observed with either tubing. (606)

Furthermore, a 25-ml aliquot of tobramycin sulfate (Lilly) 20 mg/L in sodium chloride 0.9% was stored in all-plastic syringes composed of polypropylene barrels and polyethylene plungers for 24 hours at room temperature in the dark. No loss due to sorption occurred. (606)

Tobramycin sulfate (Qualimed) 1.5 mg/ml in dextrose 5% in water and in sodium chloride 0.9% was packaged in PVC bags (Macropharma) and in multilayer bags composed of polyethylene, polyamide, and polypropylene (Bieffe Medital). The solutions were delivered through PVC administration sets (Abbott) over one hour and evaluated for drug loss by HPLC. No loss due to sorption to any of the plastic materials was found. (2269)

Filtration—Tobramycin sulfate (Lilly) 0.3 mg/ml in dextrose 5% in water and sodium chloride 0.9% was filtered through a 0.22-µm cellulose ester membrane filter (Ivex-HP, Millipore) over six hours. No significant drug loss due to binding to the filter was noted. (1034)

Thompson et al. evaluated tobramycin sulfate 5 and 10 mg/55 ml in dextrose 5% in water and sodium chloride 0.9% filtered over 20 minutes through a 0.22-µm cellulose ester filter set (Ivex-2, Millipore). Enzyme-mediated immunoassays showed that little or no binding of the drug to the filter occurred. (1003)

Elenbaas et al. found no significant loss due to sorption to a 0.22-µm cellulose ester filter (Continu-Flo 2C0252s, Travenol) from a solution containing tobramycin sulfate (Dista) 80 mg/100 ml of dextrose 5% in water administered over 30 minutes. An enzyme immunoassay found no difference in drug recovery between filtered and unfiltered solutions. However, the authors did note that 10% or more of the solution may remain in the tubing unless the sets are flushed. (1132)

Central Venous Catheter—Tobramycin sulfate (Lilly) 1 mg/ml in dextrose 5% in water was found to be compatible with the ARROWg+ard Blue Plus (Arrow International) chlorhexidine-bearing triple-lumen central catheter. HPLC analysis was used to evaluate completeness of drug delivery through the catheter and the amount of chlorhexidine removed from the internal lumens. Essentially complete delivery of the drug was found with little or no drug loss occurring. Furthermore, chlorhexidine delivered from the catheter remained at trace amounts with no substantial increase due to the delivery of the drug through the catheter. (2335)

Compatibility Information

Solution Compatibility

Tobramycin sulfate

Solution	*Mfr*	*Mfr*	*Conc/L*	*Remarks*	*Ref*	*C/I*
Alcohol 5% in dextrose 5%		LI	200 mg and 1 g	Opalescent haze develops immediately	147	I
Amino acids 4.25%, dextrose 25%	MG	LI	80 mg	No increase in particulate matter in 24 hr at 25 °C	349	C
Dextran 40 10% in dextrose 5% in water	TR	LI	200 mg and 1 g	Physically compatible and chemically stable for 24 hr at 25 °C. Not more than 9% loss occurs	147	C
Dextrose 5% in Polysal	CU	LI	200 mg and 1 g	12 to 15% decomposition in 24 hr at 25 °C. Potency retained through 4 hr	147	I
Dextrose 5% in Polysal M	CU	LI	200 mg and 1 g	11% decomposition in 24 hr at 25 °C. Potency retained through 4 hr	147	I
Dextrose 5% in sodium chloride 0.9%	TR[a]	LI	200 mg and 1 g	Physically compatible and chemically stable for 48 hr at 25 °C. Not more than 7% loss occurs	147	C
Dextrose 5% in water	TR[a]	LI	200 mg and 1 g	Physically compatible and chemically stable for 48 hr at 25 °C. Not more than 4% loss occurs	147	C
	TR[a]	LI	3.2 g	Physically compatible and no potency loss in 24 hr at room temperature	555	C
		LI	1 and 5 g	Physically compatible with no loss of tobramycin activity in 60 min at room temperature	984	C
	AB[a]	DI	1.2 g	Visually compatible and potency by immunoassay retained for 48 hr at 25 °C under fluorescent light and 4 °C in the dark	1541	C
Dextrose 10% in water	TR[a]	LI	200 mg and 1 g	Physically compatible and chemically stable for 48 hr at 25 °C. Not more than 4% loss occurs	147	C
	SO	LI	60 mg/21.5 ml[b]	Visually compatible with little or no tobramycin loss by TDx in 30 days at 5 °C in the dark	1731	C
	SO	LI	60 mg/18.5 ml[b]	Visually compatible with little or no tobramycin loss by TDx in 30 days at 5 °C in the dark	1731	C

Solution Compatibility (Cont.)

Tobramycin sulfate

Solution	*Mfr*	*Mfr*	*Conc/L*	*Remarks*	*Ref*	*C/I*
	SO	LI	120 mg/ 23 ml[b]	Visually compatible with little or no tobramycin loss by TDx in 30 days at 5 °C in the dark	1731	C
	SO	LI	120 mg/ 20 ml[b]	Visually compatible with little or no tobramycin loss by TDx in 30 days at 5 °C in the dark	1731	C
Invert sugar 5% in Electrolyte #2	TR	LI	200 mg and 1 g	Physically compatible and chemically stable for 24 hr at 25 °C. Not more than 2% loss occurs	147	C
Invert sugar 10% in Electrolyte #3	TR	LI	200 mg and 1 g	Physically compatible and chemically stable for 24 hr at 25 °C	147	C
Isolyte E in dextrose 5% in water	MG	LI	1 g	12% decomposition in 24 hr at 25 °C. Potency retained through 4 hr	147	I
Isolyte M in dextrose 5% in water	MG	LI	200 mg and 1 g	12% decomposition in 24 hr at 25 °C. Potency retained through 4 hr	147	I
Isolyte P in dextrose 5% in water	MG	LI	200 mg and 1 g	11 to 12% decomposition in 24 hr at 25 °C. Potency retained through 4 hr	147	I
Mannitol 15%, dextrose 5% in sodium chloride 0.45%		LI	200 mg and 1 g	Physically compatible and chemically stable for 48 hr at 25 °C. Not more than 6% loss occurs	147	C
Mannitol 20%		LI	200 mg and 1 g	Physically compatible and chemically stable for 48 hr at 25 °C	147	C
Normosol M in dextrose 5% in water	AB	LI	200 mg and 1 g	Physically compatible and chemically stable for 24 hr at 25 °C. Not more than 10% loss occurs	147	C
Normosol R	AB	LI	200 mg and 1 g	Physically compatible and chemically stable for 24 hr at 25 °C	147	C
Normosol R in dextrose 5% in water	AB	LI	200 mg and 1 g	Physically compatible and chemically stable for 24 hr at 25 °C. Not more than 8% loss occurs	147	C
Normosol R, pH 7.4	AB	LI	200 mg and 1 g	Physically compatible and chemically stable for 24 hr at 25 °C	147	C
Ringer's injection	TR[a]	LI	200 mg and 1 g	Physically compatible and chemically stable for 24 hr at 25 °C	147	C
Ringer's injection, lactated		LI	200 mg and 1 g	Physically compatible and chemically stable for 24 hr at 25 °C	147	C
Sodium chloride 0.9%	TR[a]	LI	200 mg and 1 g	Physically compatible and chemically stable for 48 hr at 25 °C	147	C
	AB[a]	DI	1.2 g	Visually compatible and potency by immunoassay retained for 48 hr at 25 °C under fluorescent light and 4 °C in the dark	1541	C
	AB[c]	LI	800 mg	Little or no loss of drug by HPLC in 24 hr at 25 °C	1970	C
	AB[d]	MAR	1 and 10 g	Little or no loss by HPLC in 3 days at 25 °C and 14 days at 5 °C in PVC portable infusion pump reservoirs	2080	C
Sodium lactate ⅙ M		LI	200 mg and 1 g	Physically compatible and chemically stable for 48 hr at 25 °C	147	C

[a]*Tested in PVC containers.*
[b]*Tested in glass vials as a concentrate.*
[c]*Tested in glass containers and latex elastomeric reservoirs (Secure Medical).*
[d]*Tested in PVC portable pump reservoirs (Pharmacia Deltec).*

Additive Compatibility

Tobramycin sulfate

Drug	*Mfr*	*Conc/L*	*Mfr*	*Conc/L*	*Test Soln*	*Remarks*	*Ref*	*C/I*
Aztreonam	SQ	10 and 20 g	LI	200 and 800 mg	D5W, NS	Little or no loss of either drug in 48 hr at 25 °C and 7 days at 4 °C	1023	C
Bleomycin sulfate	BR	20 and 30 units	LI	500 mg	NS	Physically compatible and bleomycin activity retained for 1 week at 4 °C. Tobramycin not tested	763	C
Calcium gluconate		16 g	LI	5 g	D5W	Physically compatible with no loss of tobramycin activity in 60 min at room temperature	984	C
		33 g	LI	1 g	D5W	Physically compatible with no loss of tobramycin activity in 60 min at room temperature	984	C
Cefamandole nafate	LI	2 and 20 g	LI	80 mg	D5W, NS, W	Haze or precipitate forms within 4 hr	376; 788	I
Cefepime HCl	BR	40 g	AB	0.4 g	D5W, NS	Cloudiness forms immediately	1682	I
	BR	2.5 g	AB	2 g	D5W, NS, W	Cloudiness forms immediately	1682	I
Cefoxitin sodium	MSD	5 g	LI	400 mg	D5S	5% cefoxitin decomposition in 24 hr and 13% in 48 hr at 25 °C. 3% in 48 hr at 5 °C. 8% tobramycin decomposition in 24 hr and 37% in 48 hr at 25 °C. 3% in 48 hr at 5 °C	308	C
Ciprofloxacin	MI	1 g	LI	1.6 g	D5W, NS	Physically compatible for 24 hr at 22 °C under fluorescent light	1189	C
	MI	1.6 g	LI	1 g	D5W, NS	Visually compatible and ciprofloxacin potency by HPLC and tobramycin potency by immunoassay retained for 48 hr at 25 °C under fluorescent light and 4 °C in the dark	1541	C
Clindamycin phosphate	UP	18 g	DI	2.4 g	D5W[a]	8% tobramycin activity lost in 14 days and 17% in 28 days frozen at −20 °C. Clindamycin potency retained	981	C
	UP	18 g	DI	2.4 g	NS[a]	Potency of both drugs retained for 28 days frozen at −20 °C	981	C
	UP	9 g	DI	1 g	D5W, NS[b]	Physically compatible and potency of both drugs retained for 48 hr at room temperature exposed to light and for 1 week frozen	174	C
	UP	9 g	DI	1.2 g	D5W[c]	Physically compatible and potency of clindamycin retained for 28 days frozen. About 8% tobramycin loss in 14 days and 17% in 28 days	174	C
	UP	9 g	DI	1.2 g	NS[c]	Physically compatible and potency of both drugs retained for 28 days frozen	174	C
Floxacillin sodium	BE	20 g	LI	8 g	NS	White precipitate forms in 7 hr	1479	I
Furosemide	HO	1 g	LI	8 g	NS	Physically compatible for 72 hr at 15 and 30 °C	1479	C
	HO	800 mg	DI	1.6 g	D5W, NS	Transient cloudiness during admixture; then physically compatible for 24 hr at 21 °C	876	C

Additive Compatibility (Cont.)

Tobramycin sulfate

Drug	Mfr	Conc/L	Mfr	Conc/L	Test Soln	Remarks	Ref	C/I
Linezolid	PHU	2 g	GNS	800 mg	[f]	Physically compatible with little or no linezolid loss by HPLC in 7 days at 4 and 23 °C protected from light. No tobramycin loss occurred in 7 days at 4 °C but losses of about 4% occurred in 1 day and 10 to 12% in 3 days at 23 °C	2332	C
Metronidazole	RP	5 g[d]	LI	800 mg		Physically compatible with little or no pH change for at least 72 hr at 23 °C	807	C
	RP	5 g[e]	LI	1 g		Visually compatible with no loss of metronidazole by HPLC in 15 days at 5 and 25 °C. 10% tobramycin loss by immunoassay in 73 hr at 25 °C and 12.1 days at 5 °C	1931	C
Metronidazole HCl with sodium bicarbonate	SE AB	5 g 50 mEq	LI	700 mg	D5W, NS	Physically compatible for 48 hr	765	C
Ofloxacin	HO	2 g	LI	800 mg	W	Visually compatible with little or no loss of either drug by HPLC in 48 hr	1613	C
Ranitidine HCl	GL	100 mg	DI	200 mg	D5W	Physically compatible for 24 hr at ambient temperature under fluorescent light	1151	C
Verapamil HCl	KN	80 mg	LI	160 mg	D5W, NS	Physically compatible for 24 hr	764	C

[a]Tested in PVC containers.
[b]Tested in both glass and PVC containers.
[c]Tested in glass containers.
[d]Minibags (100 ml) containing metronidazole 500 mg with disodium phosphate 150 mg, citric acid 44 mg, and sodium chloride 740 mg. This product differs from the Searle product.
[e]Tested in ready-to-use metronidazole injection.
[f]Admixed in the linezolid infusion container.

Drugs in Syringe Compatibility

Tobramycin sulfate

Drug (in syringe)	Mfr	Amt	Mfr	Amt	Remarks	Ref	C/I
Cefamandole nafate	LI	1 g/10 ml	LI	80 mg/ 2 ml	Haze or precipitate forms within 4 hr	376; 788	I
	LI	1 g/3 ml	LI	80 mg/ 2 ml	Haze or precipitate forms within 4 hr	376; 788	I
Clindamycin phosphate	UP	900 mg/ 6 ml	DI	120 mg/ 4 ml[a]	Cloudy white precipitate forms immediately and changes to gel-like precipitate	1159	I
Doxapram HCl	RB	400 mg/ 20 ml		60 mg/ 1.5 ml	Physically compatible with no doxapram loss in 24 hr	1177	C
Heparin sodium		10 units/ 1 ml		80 mg/ 2 ml	Turbidity or fine white precipitate due to formation of an insoluble salt	845	I
		2500 units/ 1 ml	LI	40 mg	Turbidity or precipitate forms within 5 min	1053	I

[a]Diluted to 4 ml with 1 ml of sodium chloride 0.9%.

Y-Site Injection Compatibility (1:1 Mixture)

			Tobramycin sulfate				
Drug	*Mfr*	*Conc*	*Mfr*	*Conc*	*Remarks*	*Ref*	*C/I*
Acyclovir sodium	BW	5 mg/ml[a]	DI	1.6 mg/ml[a]	Physically compatible for 4 hr at 25 °C	1157	C
Alatrofloxacin mesylate	PF	1.43 mg/ml[a]	LI	21 mg/ml[n]	Visually and microscopically compatible run through a Y-site over 33 min	2235	C
Allopurinol sodium	BW	3 mg/ml[b]	LI	5 mg/ml[b]	Haze and crystals form in 1 hr	1686	I
Amifostine	USB	10 mg/ml[a]	LI	5 mg/ml[a]	Physically compatible with no change in measured turbidity or increase in particle content in 4 hr at 23 °C	1845	C
Amiodarone HCl	LZ	4 mg/ml[c]	LI	0.8 mg/ml[c]	Physically compatible for 4 hr at room temperature	1441	C
Amphotericin B cholesteryl sulfate complex	SEQ	0.83 mg/ml[a]	AB	5 mg/ml[a]	Gross precipitate forms	2117	I
Amsacrine	NCI	1 mg/ml[a]	LI	5 mg/ml[a]	Physically compatible for 4 hr at room temperature under fluorescent light	1381	C
Aztreonam	SQ	40 mg/ml[a]	LI	5 mg/ml[a]	Physically compatible with no subvisual haze or particle formation in 4 hr at 23 °C	1758	C
Ciprofloxacin	MI	1 mg/ml[a]	LI	1.6 mg/ml[c]	Physically compatible for 24 hr at 22 °C	1189	C
Cisatracurium besylate	GW	0.1, 2, 5 mg/ml[a]	AB	5 mg/ml[a]	Physically compatible with no change in measured turbidity or increase in particle content in 4 hr at 23 °C	2074	C
Cyclophosphamide	MJ	20 mg/ml[a]	DI	0.8 mg/ml[a]	Physically compatible for 4 hr at 25 °C	1194	C
Diltiazem HCl	MMD	5 mg/ml	LI	2.4[b] and 40 mg/ml	Visually compatible	1807	C
Docetaxel	RPR	0.9 mg/ml[a]	LI	5 mg/ml[a]	Physically compatible with no change in measured turbidity or increase in particle content in 4 hr at 23 °C	2224	C
Doxorubicin HCl liposome injection	SEQ	0.4 mg/ml[a]	AB	5 mg/ml[a]	Physically compatible with little or no change in measured turbidity and no increase in particle content in 4 hr at 23 °C	2087	C
Enalaprilat	MSD	0.05 mg/ml[b]	LI	0.8 mg/ml[a]	Physically compatible for 24 hr at room temperature under fluorescent light	1355	C
Esmolol HCl	DCC	10 mg/ml[a]	LI	0.8 mg/ml[a]	Physically compatible for 24 hr at 22 °C	1169	C
Etoposide phosphate	BR	5 mg/ml[a]	LI	5 mg/ml[a]	Physically compatible with no change in measured turbidity or increase in particle content in 4 hr at 23 °C	2218	C
Filgrastim	AMG	30 μg/ml[a]	LI	5 mg/ml[a]	Physically compatible with no change in measured turbidity or increase in particle content in 4 hr at 22 °C	1687	C
	AMG	10[d] and 40[a] μg/ml	LI	1.6 mg/ml[a]	Visually compatible with little or no loss of filgrastim activity by bioassay and tobramycin by immunoassay in 4 hr at 25 °C	2060	C
Fluconazole	RR	2 mg/ml	LI	40 mg/ml	Physically compatible for 24 hr at 25 °C	1407	C
Fludarabine phosphate	BX	1 mg/ml[a]	LI	5 mg/ml[a]	Physically compatible for 4 hr at room temperature under fluorescent light	1439	C

Y-Site Injection Compatibility (1:1 Mixture) (Cont.)

Tobramycin sulfate

Drug	*Mfr*	*Conc*	*Mfr*	*Conc*	*Remarks*	*Ref*	*C/I*
Foscarnet sodium	AST	24 mg/ml	LI	40 mg/ml	Physically compatible for 24 hr at room temperature under fluorescent light	1335	C
Furosemide	HO	10 mg/ml	DI	1.6 mg/ml[a]	Physically compatible for 24 hr at 21 °C	876	C
Gatifloxacin	BMS	2 mg/ml[a]	GNS	5 mg/ml[a]	Physically compatible with no change in measured haze or increase in particle content in 4 hr at 23 °C	2234	C
Gemcitabine HCl	LI	10 mg/ml[b]	LI	5 mg/ml[b]	Physically compatible with no change in measured turbidity or increase in particle content in 4 hr at 23 °C	2226	C
Granisetron HCl	SKB	0.05 mg/ml[a]	AB	5 mg/ml[a]	Physically compatible with no change in measured turbidity or increase in particle content in 4 hr at 23 °C	2000	C
Heparin sodium	ES	50 units/ml[c]	LI	3.2 mg/ml[c]	Immediate gross haze	1316	I
	TR	50 units/ml	LI	0.8 mg/ml[a]	Visually incompatible within 4 hr at 25 °C	1793	I
Hetastarch in lactated electrolyte injection (Hextend)	AB	6%	GNS	5 mg/ml[a]	Physically compatible with no change in measured turbidity or increase in particle content in 4 hr at 23 °C	2339	C
Hetastarch in sodium chloride 0.9%	DCC	6%	LI	0.8 mg/ml[e]	Small crystals formed immediately after mixing and persisted for 4 hr	1313	I
Hydromorphone HCl	WY	0.2 mg/ml[a]	DI	0.8 mg/ml[a]	Physically compatible for at least 4 hr at 25 °C under fluorescent light	987	C
IL-2	RC	4800 I.U./ml[b]	LI	40 mg/ml	Visually compatible and IL-2 activity by bioassay retained. Tobramycin not tested	1552	C
Indomethacin sodium trihydrate	MSD	0.5 and 1 mg/ml[a]		1 mg/ml[a]	White turbidity forms immediately and becomes white flakes in 1 hr	1550	I
Insulin, regular	LI	0.2 unit/ml[b]	LI	1.6 and 2 mg/ml[a]	Physically compatible for 2 hr at 25 °C	1395	C
Labetalol HCl	SC	1 mg/ml[a]	LI	0.8 mg/ml[a]	Physically compatible for 24 hr at 18 °C	1171	C
Linezolid	PHU	2 mg/ml	AB	5 mg/ml[a]	Physically compatible with no change in measured turbidity or increase in particle content in 4 hr at 23 °C	2264	C
Magnesium sulfate	IX	16.7, 33.3, 66.7, 100 mg/ml[a]	DI	0.8 mg/ml[a]	Physically compatible for at least 4 hr at 32 °C	813	C
Melphalan HCl	BW	0.1 mg/ml[b]	LI	5 mg/ml[b]	Physically compatible with no change in measured turbidity or increase in particle content in 3 hr at 22 °C	1557	C
Meperidine HCl	WY	10 mg/ml[a]	DI	0.8 mg/ml[a]	Physically compatible for at least 4 hr at 25 °C under fluorescent light	987	C
	WY	10 mg/ml[b]	LI	1.6, 2, 2.4 mg/ml[a]	Physically compatible for 1 hr at 25 °C	1338	C
Midazolam HCl	RC	1 mg/ml[a]	LI	10 mg/ml	Visually compatible for 24 hr at 23 °C	1847	C
Morphine sulfate	WI	1 mg/ml[a]	DI	0.8 mg/ml[a]	Physically compatible for at least 4 hr at 25 °C under fluorescent light	987	C
	ES	1 mg/ml[b]	LI	1.6, 2, 2.4 mg/ml[a]	Physically compatible for 1 hr at 25 °C	1338	C
Perphenazine	SC	0.02 mg/ml[a]	DI	0.8 mg/ml[a]	Physically compatible for 4 hr at 25 °C	1155	C

Y-Site Injection Compatibility (1:1 Mixture) (Cont.)

			Tobramycin sulfate				
Drug	*Mfr*	*Conc*	*Mfr*	*Conc*	*Remarks*	*Ref*	*C/I*
Propofol	ZEN	10 mg/ml	AB	5 mg/ml[a]	Precipitate forms immediately	2066	I
Remifentanil HCl	GW	0.025 and 0.25 mg/ml[b]	AB	5 mg/ml[a]	Physically compatible with no change in measured turbidity or increase in particle content in 4 hr at 23 °C	2075	C
Sargramostim	IMM	10 μg/ml[b]	LI	5 mg/ml[b]	Particles and filaments form in 4 hr	1436	I
Tacrolimus	FUJ	1 mg/ml[b]	BR	40 mg/ml	Visually compatible for 24 hr at 25 °C	1630	C
Teniposide	BR	0.1 mg/ml[a]	LI	5 mg/ml[a]	Physically compatible with no subvisual haze or particle formation in 4 hr at 23 °C	1725	C
Theophylline	TR	4 mg/ml	LI	0.8 mg/ml[a]	Visually compatible for 6 hr at 25 °C	1793	C
Thiotepa	IMM[c]	1 mg/ml[a]	LI	5 mg/ml[a]	Physically compatible with no change in measured turbidity or increase in particle content in 4 hr at 23 °C	1861	C
TNA #73[g]		32.5 ml[h]	LI	80 mg/50 ml[a]	Physically compatible by visual observation for 4 hr at 25 °C	1008	C
TNA #97 to #104[g]			LI	40 mg/ml	Physically compatible and tobramycin content retained for 6 hr at 21 °C by TDx	1324	C
TNA #218 to #226[g]			AB	5 mg/ml[a]	Visually compatible with no precipitate or emulsion damage apparent in 4 hr at 23 °C	2215	C
Tolazoline HCl		0.1 mg/ml[a]	LI	10 mg/ml[a]	Physically compatible for 24 hr at 22 °C	1363	C
TPN #54[g]				20 mg/ml	Physically compatible and tobramycin activity retained over 6 hr at 22 °C by microbiological assay	1045	C
TPN #61[g]		[i]	DI	12.5 mg/1.25 ml[j]	Physically compatible	1012	C
		[k]	DI	75 mg/1.9 ml[j]	Physically compatible	1012	C
TPN #91[g]		[l]	LI	5 mg[m]	Physically compatible	1170	C
TPN #212 to #215[g]			AB	5 mg/ml[a]	Physically compatible with no change in measured turbidity or increase in particle content in 4 hr at 23 °C	2109	C
Vinorelbine tartrate	BW	1 mg/ml[b]	LI	5 mg/ml[b]	Physically compatible with no change in measured turbidity or increase in particle content in 4 hr at 22 °C	1558	C
Zidovudine	BW	4 mg/ml[a]	LI	2 mg/ml[a]	Physically compatible for 4 hr at 25 °C under fluorescent light by visual and microscopic examination	1193	C

[a] *Tested in dextrose 5% in water.*
[b] *Tested in sodium chloride 0.9%.*
[c] *Tested in both dextrose 5% in water and sodium chloride 0.9%.*
[d] *Tested in dextrose 5% in water with albumin human 2 mg/ml.*
[e] *Premixed infusion solution.*
[f] *Lyophilized formulation tested.*
[g] *Refer to Appendix I for the composition of parenteral nutrition solutions. TNA indicates a 3-in-1 admixture, and TPN indicates a 2-in-1 admixture.*
[h] *A 32.5-ml sample of parenteral nutrition solution mixed with 50 ml of antibiotic solution.*
[i] *Run at 21 ml/hr.*
[j] *Given over 30 minutes by syringe pump.*
[k] *Run at 94 ml/hr.*
[l] *Run at 10 ml/hr.*
[m] *Given over one hour by syringe pump.*
[n] *Tested in sodium chloride 0.45%.*

Additional Compatibility Information

Peritoneal Dialysis Solutions — Tobramycin base (Lilly) 3 and 10 mg/L in peritoneal dialysis concentrate with dextrose 50% (McGaw) retained about 50 to 60% of initial activity in seven hours and about 15 to 30% in 24 hours at room temperature as determined by microbiological assay. (1044)

The stability of tobramycin sulfate (Lilly) 10 mg/L in peritoneal dialysis solutions (Dianeal 137 and PD2) with heparin sodium 500 units/L was evaluated by microbiological assay. Approximately 102 ± 20% activity remained after 24 hours at 25 °C. (1228)

In another study, the stability of tobramycin sulfate (Lilly) was evaluated in peritoneal dialysis concentrates containing dextrose 30 and 50% (Dianeal) as well as in a diluted solution containing dextrose 2.5%. The tobramycin sulfate concentrations were 100 and 160 mg/L in the peritoneal dialysate concentrates and 5 and 8 mg/L in the diluted solution. With immunoassay techniques, tobramycin sulfate was found to be stable in the diluted peritoneal dialysis solution for at least 24 hours at 23 °C. However, greater decomposition occurred in the concentrates, with a 10% loss in as little as 9 to 15 hours. (1229)

Drake et al., using a disc diffusion bioassay, evaluated the retention of antimicrobial activity of tobramycin sulfate (Lilly) 120 mg/L alone and with vancomycin HCl (Lilly) 1 g/L in Dianeal PD-2 (Travenol) with dextrose 1.5%. Little or no loss of either antibiotic occurred in eight hours at 37 °C. Tobramycin sulfate alone retained activity for at least 48 hours at 4 and 25 °C. With vancomycin HCl, the antimicrobial activity of both antibiotics was retained for up to 48 hours; however, the authors recommended refrigeration at 4 °C for storage longer than 24 hours. (1414)

Ceftazidime (Fortaz) 125 mg/L and tobramycin sulfate (Lilly) 8 mg/L in Dianeal PD-2 with dextrose 2.5% (Baxter) were visually compatible and chemically stable by HPLC (ceftazidime) and fluorescence polarization immunoassay (tobramycin). After 16 hours of storage at 25 °C under fluorescent light, the loss of both drugs was less than 3%. Additional storage for eight hours at 37 °C, to simulate the maximum peritoneal dwell time, showed tobramycin sulfate concentrations of 96% and ceftazidime concentrations of 92 to 96%. (1652)

Tobramycin sulfate (Lilly) 25 μg/ml combined separately with the cephalosporins cefazolin sodium (Lilly), cefamandole nafate (Lilly), and cefoxitin sodium (MSD) at a concentration of 125 μg/ml in peritoneal dialysis solution (Dianeal 1.5%) exhibited enhanced rates of lethality to *Staphylococcus aureus, Escherichia coli,* and *Pseudomonas aeruginosa* compared to any of the drugs alone. (1623)

β-Lactam Antibiotics — In common with other aminoglycoside antibiotics, tobramycin sulfate activity may be impaired by the β-lactam antibiotics. The inactivation is dependent on concentration, temperature, and time of exposure.

Levison et al. evaluated tobramycin 10 μg/ml in combination with carbenicillin in concentrations ranging from 200 to 800 μg/ml in a bacterial growth medium incubated at 37 °C for 24 hours. At carbenicillin concentrations of 200 to 400 μg/ml, no loss of tobramycin activity (determined microbiologically) occurred over the 24-hour period. However, at a carbenicillin concentration of 600 μg/ml, tobramycin activity was retained for only six hours. The solution had lost 90% of the activity by 24 hours. At 800 μg/ml, 50% of the tobramycin concentration was lost in two hours. (737)

Holt et al. found that tobramycin sulfate 10 mg/L in sodium chloride 0.9%, incubated with 500 mg/L of carbenicillin or ticarcillin at 37 °C for 24 hours, resulted in about a 60 to 70% reduction in tobramycin activity. When serum was substituted for the sodium chloride solution, a 40 to 50% reduction in activity was reported. However, about 80% of the activity was lost when buffered to pH 7.4 in aqueous solution. (574)

In another study, tobramycin sulfate 5 and 10 μg/ml, dissolved in human serum and incubated with carbenicillin and ticarcillin 100 to 600 μg/ml at 37 °C, demonstrated greater decomposition rates at the higher penicillin concentrations. In 24 hours, about a 3 to 7% loss of tobramycin activity occurred at 100 μg/ml and about a 70% loss occurred at 600 μg/ml of carbenicillin. Approximately a 12% loss at 100 μg/ml to a 90% loss at 600 μg/ml occurred in 72 hours with carbenicillin. When tobramycin sulfate was combined with ticarcillin under these conditions, about an 11% loss of tobramycin activity occurred at 100 μg/ml of ticarcillin in 72 hours. The tobramycin loss increased to 25% at 300 μg/ml and to 75% at 600 μg/ml of ticarcillin in 72 hours. (575)

Several aminoglycosides in combination with several penicillins were evaluated by Henderson et al. Gentamicin sulfate, netilmicin sulfate, and tobramycin sulfate 5 μg/ml were combined with carbenicillin disodium, azlocillin sodium, and mezlocillin sodium 50, 250, and 500 μg/ml in human plasma. Samples were evaluated over nine days at 27 and 37 °C. All of the aminoglycosides underwent significant inactivation during the evaluation. Aminoglycoside decomposition of 17 to 61% in 24 hours occurred at the higher two concentrations of penicillins—the highest inactivation was sustained by tobramycin and the lowest by netilmicin. Little if any aminoglycoside inactivation occurred at 50 μg/ml of penicillin. Carbenicillin caused a greater degree of aminoglycoside decomposition than did azlocillin or mezlocillin. (616)

Flournoy noted the relative degree of inactivation of tobramycin, gentamicin, netilmicin, and amikacin 10 mg/L in serum when combined with carbenicillin 125 to 1000 mg/L over temperatures ranging from −20 to 42 °C. Tobramycin was more susceptible to inactivation than the others. Amikacin was the least susceptible, and gentamicin and netilmicin were similar in intermediate susceptibility to inactivation. (617)

Although piperacillin sodium and aminoglycosides act synergistically and have been used successfully clinically when recommended doses of each drug were administered, mixing piperacillin sodium directly in a syringe or infusion bottle with an aminoglycoside can result in substantial inactivation of the aminoglycoside. (740)

While most evaluations of aminoglycoside and penicillin combinations have centered on aminoglycoside decomposition, Das Gupta and Stewart evaluated the stability of carbenicillin in the presence of tobramycin. Carbenicillin disodium (Roerig) 100 to 1000 μg/ml was combined with tobramycin sulfate (Lilly) 40 to 160 μg/ml in dextrose 5% in water, sodium chloride 0.9%, and pH 6.6 phosphate buffer. At 24 °C, the rate of decomposition of carbenicillin increased by 0.5% for each microgram per milliliter of tobramycin. The decomposition of tobramycin apparently is dependent on the carbenicillin concentration, and the decomposition of carbenicillin apparently is dependent on the tobramycin concentration. (783)

The inactivation of tobramycin 10 μg/ml in sterile distilled water by several β-lactam antibiotics stored at 37 °C was reported by Jorgensen and Crawford. Ticarcillin and carbenicillin 500 μg/ml caused about a 45% tobramycin loss in two hours and a 75% loss in six hours, while 100 μg/ml caused a 47 and 39% loss, respectively, after six hours. Penicillin G 500 μg/ml caused a 23% tobramycin loss in six hours, but no significant loss occurred at 100 μg/ml. Tobramycin was not inactivated by 500- or 100-μg/ml concentrations of cephalothin, cefotaxime, and moxalactam. No loss of β-lactam antibiotic activity was detected in any combination. (973)

Pickering and Rutherford evaluated several aminoglycosides combined with a number of penicillins. Gentamicin sulfate, netilmicin sulfate, and tobramycin sulfate 5 and 10 μg/ml and amikacin 10 and 20 μg/ml were combined in human serum with 125, 250, and 500 μg/ml of azlocillin, carbenicillin disodium, amdinocillin, mezlocillin, and piperacillin individually. Tobramycin and gentamicin sustained greater losses than netilmicin and amikacin at each of the penicillin concentrations. Significant decomposition of all aminoglycosides occurred in 24 hours at 37 °C at a penicillin concentration of 500 μg/ml. Tobramycin and gentamicin had losses of 40 to 60%, while 15 to 30% losses occurred for netilmicin. Amikacin sustained the least inactivation with losses of about 10 to 20%. At penicillin concentrations of 125 to 250 μg/ml, smaller losses of aminoglycosides were observed. (68)

Lundergan et al. studied, in vitro, the interaction of tobramycin sulfate with several penicillins in human serum under clinical laboratory conditions. Tobramycin sulfate 10 μg/ml was combined with carbenicillin disodium 200 μg/ml, oxacillin sodium (Bristol) 50 μg/ml, and nafcillin sodium (Wyeth) 50 μg/ml. Samples were evaluated over 72 hours at −23, 6, and 23 °C. Although results were variable, only the carbenicillin sample at 23 °C exhibited substantial decomposition after 72 hours. None of the other samples of carbenicillin, oxacillin, or nafcillin showed significant differences over the study period. (814)

Using bioassay and radioimmunoassay, Hale et al. evaluated piperacillin and carbenicillin at concentrations of 62.5 to 1000 μg/ml in human serum in combination with amikacin, gentamicin, or tobramycin 10 μg/ml at 37 °C for up to 24 hours. Penicillin concentrations of 62.5 and 125 μg/ml had relatively little effect on the aminoglycoside concentration, even after 24 hours. However, increasing the penicillin concentration to 250 or 500 μg/ml greatly increased decomposition. After 24 hours with carbenicillin 500 μg/ml, the amounts of aminoglycosides remaining were amikacin 82%, gentamicin 43%, and tobramycin 27%. After 24 hours with piperacillin 500 μg/ml, the remaining concentrations were 95, 45, and 52%, respectively. Even greater inactivation occurred at 1000 μg/ml of the penicillins, including the essentially complete loss of tobramycin in 24 hours. The authors concluded that amikacin is much more resistant to inactivation than the other aminoglycosides tested and that carbenicillin is somewhat more aggressive in its inactivation than piperacillin. (816)

Rank et al. evaluated the inactivation of tobramycin 6 μg/ml in human serum with the sodium salts of cloxacillin and piperacillin 150 and 300 μg/ml, ampicillin 100 and 200 μg/ml, and penicillin G 75 and 150 I.U./ml at 25 and 37 °C for up to 12 hours. Piperacillin induced the greatest inactivation among the penicillins, with up to a 15% loss in 12 hours at 37 °C in the 300-μg/ml concentration. Cloxacillin and ampicillin had an intermediate effect, causing about a 5% loss in 12 hours at 37 °C in the highest concentrations. Penicillin G did not yield significant tobramycin inactivation. (817)

The inactivation of tobramycin sulfate 8 μg/ml in human serum by ampicillin, carbenicillin disodium, and penicillin G potassium, each at 200 μg/ml, was studied at 0, 23, and 37 °C by O'Bey et al. For the tobramycin–ampicillin mixture, essentially no differences were observed at the various temperatures. The t_{90} values were 19, 16.5, and 20 hours at 0, 23, and 37 °C, respectively. Carbenicillin displayed a temperature-dependent inactivation of tobramycin. At 0 °C, the t_{90} was 36 hours; but at 23 and 37 °C, the t_{90} values were 10 and 12 hours, respectively. With penicillin G potassium, the t_{90} values for tobramycin inactivation at 0, 23, and 37 °C were 48, 44, and 16 hours, respectively. Inaccurate pharmacokinetic dosing of tobramycin may occur if serum samples are not handled properly. (832)

The comparative inactivation of five aminoglycosides by seven β-lactam antibiotics in human serum at 37 °C was reported by Riff and Thomason. Amikacin, followed by netilmicin, had the lowest degree of inactivation; tobramycin sustained the most pronounced losses. Gentamicin and kanamycin were intermediate in the extent of losses. The six penicillins that were tested all produced aminoglycoside inactivation; the greatest extent of inactivation was caused by carbenicillin followed by ticarcillin, penicillin G, oxacillin, methicillin, and ampicillin, in approximate descending order. Cephalothin produced minimal inactivation (5 to 10% in 24 hours). The rate of inactivation could be reduced by storage at 4 °C and further reduced by storage at −20 °C. The authors suggested processing blood samples rapidly to avoid inaccurate serum determinations. Storage of specimens at low temperature until analysis may be helpful. (1052)

Spruill et al. evaluated the effect of various cephalosporins on tobramycin sulfate 7.7 μg/ml in human serum. At concentrations of 250 and 1000 μg/ml, cefazolin, cefoxitin, cefamandole, cefoperazone, and cefotaxime caused about a 10 to 15% loss of tobramycin over 48 hours at 0 and 21 °C. Moxalactam caused about a 15% loss at 0 °C and a 20 to 30% loss at 21 °C over 48 hours. (1005)

Pennell et al. evaluated the potential for inactivation of tobramycin sulfate (Lilly) 9 μg/ml with 100- and 200-μg/ml concentrations of ceftazidime (Lilly), cefoperazone sodium (Roerig), and cefotaxime sodium (Hoechst-Roussel) in human serum. No loss of tobramycin sulfate was determined by TDx fluorescence polarization immunoassay over 48 hours when stored at 4, 24, and 37 °C. (1420)

To determine if spurious aminoglycoside levels could result from a delay in assaying blood samples, Tindula et al. evaluated the inactivation of amikacin 35 μg/ml and gentamicin and tobramycin 10 μg/ml in human serum by 400-μg/ml concentrations of several penicillins and cephalosporins. Samples were stored for 24 hours at room temperature or frozen at −20 °C. For the room temperature samples, cefazolin and cefamandole caused relatively little inactivation. Nafcillin, cephapirin, and cefoxitin caused moderate inactivation, 20% or less. Penicillin, ampicillin, carbenicillin, and ticarcillin generally caused 25% or more inactivation of gentamicin and tobramycin. Amikacin was somewhat less affected. Freezing samples at −20 °C prevented significant inactivation of amikacin and gentamicin by any of the drugs. Freezing the tobramycin samples was satisfactory for most of the drugs except penicillin, ampicillin, and carbenicillin, which still exhibited a 15 to 20% tobramycin loss in 24 hours. (824)

The inactivation of gentamicin, tobramycin, and amikacin, each 5 μg/ml, by seven β-lactam antibiotics, 250 and 500 μg/ml, in serum at 25 °C over 24 hours was studied using bioassay, enzyme-mediated immunoassay technique (EMIT), TDx, and radioimmunoassay. No inactivation of any aminoglycoside by the cephalosporins moxalactam, cefotaxime, and cefazolin occurred within the study period. Results with the penicillins varied, depending on the assay technique used. The bioassay was the most sensitive to loss, TDx and radioimmunoassay were intermediate, and EMIT was the least sensitive. Azlocillin, carbenicillin, mezlocillin, and piperacillin all caused variable but extensive inactivation (up to 70%) of gentamicin and tobramycin in 24 hours. Amikacin, however, had only minor losses compared to the other aminoglycosides. (654)

The clinical significance of these interactions appears to be primarily confined to patients with renal failure. (218; 334; 361; 364; 616; 737; 816; 847; 952) Literature reports of greatly reduced aminoglycoside levels in such patients have appeared frequently. (363; 365–367; 614; 615; 962) In addition, the interaction may be clinically important if assays for aminoglycoside levels in serum are sufficiently delayed. (576; 618; 735; 824; 832; 847; 1052)

Most authors believe that in vitro mixing of penicillins such as ticarcillin disodium with aminoglycoside antibiotics should be avoided but that clinical use of the drugs in combination can be of great value. It is generally recommended that the drugs be given separately in such combined therapy. (157; 218; 222; 224; 361; 364; 368–370)

Cephalosporins — Cefotaxime sodium should not be mixed with aminoglycosides in the same solution, but they may be administered to the same patient separately. (2; 792)

When tobramycin sulfate (Lilly) 80 mg/100 ml in dextrose 5% in water was run through an administration set previously used to administer cefoperazone (Roerig) 4 g/100 ml in dextrose 5% in water, an immediate precipitate formed in the infusion tubing where the two solutions mixed. A retest using cefoperazone 1 g/100 ml produced the same result. (831)

Cefotetan is stated to be physically incompatible with tobramycin sulfate. (4)

Clindamycin — Clindamycin phosphate (Upjohn) 600 mg/L has been reported to be conditionally compatible with tobramycin sulfate 80 mg/L. Clindamycin stability is maintained for 24 hours in sodium chloride 0.9%, but an unstable mixture results in dextrose 5% in water. (101)

Heparin — Tobramycin sulfate is stated to be physically incompatible with heparin sodium. (147) A white precipitate may result from the administration of tobramycin sulfate through a heparinized intravenous cannula. (976) Flushing heparin locks with sterile water for injection or sodium chloride 0.9% before and after administering drugs incompatible with heparin has been recommended. (4)

Imipenem — The potential for inactivation of tobramycin sulfate by the carbapenem antibiotic imipenem–cilastatin sodium was investigated by Ariano et al. Tobramycin sulfate 10 μg/ml was incubated at 37 °C for five days with imipenem–cilastatin sodium concentrations ranging from 10 to 40 μg/ml in human serum. Degradation rates of tobramycin sulfate determined by fluorescence polarization immunoassay were not enhanced by the presence of imipenem–cilastatin sodium. (2013)

Other Drugs — The manufacturer recommends that other drugs not be mixed with tobramycin sulfate. (2) In addition, its activity appears to be inhibited by calcium and magnesium ions. (145)

Other Information

Heating Plasma — Heating plasma samples to 56 °C for one hour to inactivate potential HIV content resulted in no tobramycin loss as determined by TDx. (1615)

TOLAZOLINE HCL
AHFS 24:12

Products — Tolazoline HCl is supplied in 4-ml ampuls containing tolazoline HCl 25 mg/ml. Also present in each milliliter of solution are tartaric acid 6.5 mg and hydrous sodium citrate 6.5 mg. (1-9/98; 4)

pH — From 3 to 4. (4)

Osmolality — The osmolality of tolazoline HCl (Ciba) 25 mg/ml was determined to be 402 mOsm/kg by freezing-point depression and 353 mOsm/kg by vapor pressure. (1071)

Trade Name(s) — Priscoline Hydrochloride.

Administration — Tolazoline HCl may be administered intravenously. It has also been given by subcutaneous, intramuscular, or intra-arterial injection. (4)

Stability — Intact ampuls of tolazoline HCl should be stored at controlled room temperature and protected from light. (1-9/98; 4)

Compatibility Information

Solution Compatibility

Tolazoline HCl

Solution	*Mfr*	*Mfr*	*Conc/L*	*Remarks*	*Ref*	*C/I*
Dextran 6% in dextrose 5%	AB	CI	50 mg	Physically compatible	3	C
Dextran 6% in sodium chloride 0.9%	AB	CI	50 mg	Physically compatible	3	C
Dextrose–Ringer's injection combinations	AB	CI	50 mg	Physically compatible	3	C
Dextrose–Ringer's injection, lactated, combinations	AB	CI	50 mg	Physically compatible	3	C
Dextrose–saline combinations	AB	CI	50 mg	Physically compatible	3	C
Dextrose 2½% in water	AB	CI	50 mg	Physically compatible	3	C

Solution Compatibility (Cont.)

Tolazoline HCl

Solution	*Mfr*	*Mfr*	*Conc/L*	*Remarks*	*Ref*	*C/I*
Dextrose 5% in water	AB	CI	50 mg	Physically compatible	3	C
Dextrose 10% in water	AB	CI	50 mg	Physically compatible	3	C
Fructose 10% in sodium chloride 0.9%	AB	CI	50 mg	Physically compatible	3	C
Fructose 10% in water	AB	CI	50 mg	Physically compatible	3	C
Invert sugar 5 and 10% in sodium chloride 0.9%	AB	CI	50 mg	Physically compatible	3	C
Invert sugar 5 and 10% in water	AB	CI	50 mg	Physically compatible	3	C
Ionosol products	AB	CI	50 mg	Physically compatible	3	C
Ringer's injection	AB	CI	50 mg	Physically compatible	3	C
Ringer's injection, lactated	AB	CI	50 mg	Physically compatible	3	C
Sodium chloride 0.45%	AB	CI	50 mg	Physically compatible	3	C
Sodium chloride 0.9%	AB	CI	50 mg	Physically compatible	3	C
Sodium lactate ⅙ M	AB	CI	50 mg	Physically compatible	3	C

Additive Compatibility

Tolazoline HCl

Drug	*Mfr*	*Conc/L*	*Mfr*	*Conc/L*	*Test Soln*	*Remarks*	*Ref*	*C/I*
Ethacrynate sodium	MSD	50 mg	CI	400 mg	NS	Altered UV spectra for both at room temperature	16	I
Verapamil HCl	KN	80 mg	CI	160 mg	D5W, NS	Physically compatible for 24 hr	764	C

Y-Site Injection Compatibility (1:1 Mixture)

Tolazoline HCl

Drug	*Mfr*	*Conc*	*Mfr*	*Conc*	*Remarks*	*Ref*	*C/I*
Aminophylline	AB	5[a] and 25 mg/ml		0.1 mg/ml[a]	Physically compatible for 24 hr at 22 °C	1363	C
Ampicillin sodium	WY	30 mg/ml[b]		0.1 mg/ml[a]	Physically compatible for 24 hr at 22 °C	1363	C
Calcium gluconate	AMR	100 mg/ml		0.1 mg/ml[a]	Physically compatible for 24 hr at 22 °C	1363	C
Cefotaxime sodium	HO	60 mg/ml[a]		0.1 mg/ml[a]	Physically compatible for 24 hr at 22 °C	1363	C
Cimetidine HCl	SKF	15 mg/ml[a]		0.1 mg/ml[a]	Physically compatible for 24 hr at 22 °C	1363	C
Dobutamine HCl	LI	1.2 mg/ml[a]		0.1 mg/ml[a]	Physically compatible for 24 hr at 22 °C	1363	C
Dopamine HCl	AB	1.2 mg/ml[a]		0.1 mg/ml[a]	Physically compatible for 24 hr at 22 °C	1363	C
Furosemide	AB	10 mg/ml		0.1 mg/ml[a]	Physically compatible for 24 hr at 22 °C	1363	C
Gentamicin sulfate	ES	10 mg/ml[a]		0.1 mg/ml[a]	Physically compatible for 24 hr at 22 °C	1363	C
Indomethacin sodium trihydrate	MSD	1 mg/ml		0.1 mg/ml[a]	White precipitate forms within 30 min	1363	I
Phytonadione	MSD	2 mg/ml		0.1 mg/ml[a]	Physically compatible for 24 hr at 22 °C	1363	C
Sodium bicarbonate	AB	0.5 mEq/ml		0.1 mg/ml[a]	Physically compatible for 24 hr at 22 °C	1363	C
Tobramycin sulfate	LI	10 mg/ml[a]		0.1 mg/ml[a]	Physically compatible for 24 hr at 22 °C	1363	C
Vancomycin HCl	LE	5 mg/ml[a]		0.1 mg/ml[a]	Physically compatible for 24 hr at 22 °C	1363	C

[a]*Tested in dextrose 5% in water.*
[b]*Tested in sodium chloride 0.9%.*

TOPOTECAN HCL
AHFS 10:00

Products — Topotecan HCl is available in vials containing 4 mg of topotecan base (present as the hydrochloride) as a lyophilized powder. Reconstitute with 4 ml of sterile water for injection to yield a 1-mg/ml topotecan (as the hydrochloride) solution. In addition to topotecan HCl, each milliliter of the reconstituted solution contains mannitol 12 mg and tartaric acid 5 mg. Hydrochloric acid and sodium hydroxide may have been used during manufacture to adjust the pH. The reconstituted solution must be diluted for use. (2)

pH — From 2.5 to 3.5. (2)

Trade Name(s) — Hycamtin.

Administration — Topotecan HCl is administered by intravenous infusion over 30 minutes after dilution in 50 to 250 ml of either sodium chloride 0.9% or dextrose 5% in water. Extravasation should be avoided; local reactions including erythema and bruising may result. (2; 4)

Stability — Topotecan HCl in intact vials should be stored in the original cartons at controlled room temperature and protected from light. The lyophilized drug is a light yellow to greenish powder. The reconstituted solution is yellow to yellow-green in color. (2) The reconstituted solution should be inspected for particulate matter in the vial and again in the transferring syringe prior to preparing admixtures. As for all parenteral products, the admixtures should also be inspected for particulate matter and discoloration prior to administration. (4)

Reconstituted topotecan HCl is stated to be stable for 24 hours at 20 to 25 °C exposed to ambient light. (4) However, the manufacturer recommends use immediately after reconstitution because the product contains no antibacterial preservative. (2)

Other information indicates the reconstituted drug may be stable for longer periods. Vials of reconstituted topotecan HCl (SmithKline Beecham) at a concentration of 1 mg/ml were stored at 5, 25, and 30 °C both upright and inverted for 28 days. The solutions remained visually clear with no change in color, and HPLC analysis found little or no loss of topotecan HCl at any condition. (2211)

Topotecan HCl (SmithKline Beecham) 1 mg/ml reconstituted with sterile water for injection was physically and chemically stable for 28 days at 4 and 25 °C protected from light. No loss of topotecan by HPLC was found, and no visible precipitation or color change occurred. (2243)

pH Effects — Topotecan HCl has a pH near 3 maintained with tartaric acid to ensure adequate solubility of greater than 2.5 mg/ml. The solubility decreases as the pH increases, becoming virtually insoluble at pH 4.5. (1747) Hydrolysis of the topotecan HCl lactone ring is known to occur at pH values above 4. (2140)

Light Effects — Topotecan HCl is subject to photodegradation. Topotecan HCl (SmithKline Beecham) 10 µg/ml in sodium chloride 0.9% in a PVC bag stored at room temperature was exposed to mixed daylight and fluorescent light for 28 days. Unlike light-protected solutions that retain drug concentration for 28 days, 10% loss of topotecan occurred after 17 days of mixed light exposure. It was recommended that topotecan HCl solutions be protected from light during storage, but light protection during administration was deemed to be unnecessary. (2243)

Elastomeric Reservoir Pumps — Topotecan (SmithKline Beecham) HCl 10, 20, and 50 µg/ml in dextrose 5% in water and in sodium chloride 0.9% in elastomeric pump reservoirs (Infusors LV 2) was evaluated for stability at 4 and 25 °C for 28 days followed by five days at 37 °C protected from light. The solutions contained no visually apparent precipitation or color changes, and HPLC analysis found little or no topotecan loss. (2243)

Plasticizer Leaching — Topotecan HCl (SmithKline Beecham) 0.025 and 0.05 mg/ml in dextrose 5% in water or in sodium chloride 0.9% did not result in measurable amounts of diethylhexyl phthalate plasticizer leached from PVC containers. (2140)

Compatibility Information

Solution Compatibility

Topotecan HCl

Solution	*Mfr*	*Mfr*	*Conc/L*	*Remarks*	*Ref*	*C/I*
Dextrose 5% in water	BA[a], MG[b], MG[c]	SKB	50 mg	Visually compatible with no loss by HPLC in 24 hr at 24 °C exposed to light and 7 days at 5 °C protected from light	2140	C
	BA[a]	SKB	25 mg	Visually compatible with no loss by HPLC in 24 hr at 24 °C exposed to light and 7 days at 5 °C protected from light	2140	C
	BA[a]	SKB	10, 25, 50 mg	Visually compatible with little or no loss by HPLC in 28 days at 4 and 25 °C protected from light	2243	C
	BA[d]	SKB	10, 25, 50 mg	Visually compatible with little or no loss by HPLC in 28 days at 4 and 25 °C protected from light followed by 5 days at 37 °C	2243	C
Sodium chloride 0.9%	BA[a], MG[b], MG[c]	SKB	50 mg	Visually compatible with no loss by HPLC in 24 hr at 24 °C exposed to light and 7 days at 5 °C protected from light	2140	C

Solution Compatibility (Cont.)

Topotecan HCl

Solution	Mfr	Mfr	Conc/L	Remarks	Ref	C/I
	BA[a]	SKB	25 mg	Visually compatible with no loss by HPLC in 24 hr at 24 °C exposed to light and 7 days at 5 °C protected from light	2140	C
	BA[a]	SKB	10, 25, 50 mg	Visually compatible with little or no loss by HPLC in 28 days at 4 and 25 °C protected from light	2243	C
	BA[d]	SKB	10, 25, 50 mg	Visually compatible with little or no loss by HPLC in 28 days at 4 and 25 °C protected from light followed by 5 days at 37°C	2243	C
	BA[a]	SKB	10 mg	Visually compatible. A 10% topotecan loss due to photodegradation occurred in 17 days at room temperature exposed to mixed daylight and fluorescent light	2243	C

[a] *Tested in PVC containers.*
[b] *Tested in polyolefin containers.*
[c] *Tested in glass containers.*
[d] *Tested in elastomeric infusion devices (Infusors LV 2, Baxter)*

Y-Site Injection Compatibility (1:1 Mixture)

Topotecan HCl

Drug	Mfr	Conc	Mfr	Conc	Remarks	Ref	C/I
Carboplatin	BR	0.9 mg/ml[a,b]	SKB	56 μg/ml[a,b]	Visually compatible with little or no loss of either drug by HPLC in 4 hr at 22 °C under fluorescent light	2245	C
Cimetidine HCl	SKB	5.76 mg/ml[a,b]	SKB	56 μg/ml[a,b]	Visually compatible with little or no loss of either drug by HPLC in 4 hr at 22 °C under fluorescent light	2245	C
Cisplatin	BR	0.168 mg/ml[b]	SKB	56 μg/ml[b]	Visually compatible with little or no loss of either drug by HPLC in 4 hr at 22 °C under fluorescent light	2245	C
Cyclophosphamide	MJ	20 mg/ml	SKB	56 μg/ml[a,b]	Visually compatible with little or no loss of either drug by HPLC in 4 hr at 22 °C under fluorescent light	2245	C
Dexamethasone sodium phosphate	RU	4 mg/ml	SKB	56 μg/ml[b]	Haze and color change to intense yellow occur immediately	2245	I
Doxorubicin HCl	PH	2 mg/ml	SKB	56 μg/ml[a,b]	Visually compatible with little or no loss of either drug by HPLC in 4 hr at 22 °C under fluorescent light	2245	C
Etoposide	BR	0.4 mg/ml[a,b]	SKB	56 μg/ml[a,b]	Visually compatible with little or no loss of either drug by HPLC in 4 hr at 22 °C under fluorescent light	2245	C
Fluorouracil	RC	50 mg/ml	SKB	56 μg/ml[b]	Haze and color change to intense yellow occur immediately	2245	I
Gemcitabine HCl	LI	10 mg/ml[b]	SKB	0.1 mg/ml[b]	Physically compatible with no change in measured turbidity or increase in particle content in 4 hr at 23 °C	2226	C
Granisetron HCl	SKB	20 μg/ml[a,b]	SKB	56 μg/ml[a,b]	Visually compatible with little or no loss of either drug by HPLC in 4 hr at 22 °C under fluorescent light	2245	C

Y-Site Injection Compatibility (1:1 Mixture) (Cont.)

Drug	Mfr	Conc	Topotecan HCl Mfr	Topotecan HCl Conc	Remarks	Ref	C/I
Ifosfamide	MJ	14.28 mg/ml[a,b]	SKB	56 µg/ml[a,b]	Visually compatible with little or no loss of either drug by HPLC in 4 hr at 22 °C under fluorescent light	2245	C
Methylprednisolone sodium succinate	UP	2.4 mg/ml[a,b]	SKB	56 µg/ml[a,b]	Pale yellow color develops but little or no loss of either drug by HPLC in 4 hr at 22 °C under fluorescent light	2245	C
Metoclopramide HCl	RB	1.72 mg/ml[a,b]	SKB	56 µg/ml[a,b]	Visually compatible with little or no loss of either drug by HPLC in 4 hr at 22 °C under fluorescent light	2245	C
Mitomycin	BR	84 µg/ml[a,b]	SKB	56 µg/ml[a,b]	Pale purple discoloration forms immediately becoming a dark pinkish-lavender in 4 hours. About 15 to 20% loss of mitomycin occurs in 4 hr at 22 °C under fluorescent light	2245	I
Ondansetron HCl	CER	0.48 mg/ml[a,b]	SKB	56 µg/ml[a,b]	Visually compatible with little or no loss of either drug by HPLC in 4 hr at 22 °C under fluorescent light	2245	C
Paclitaxel	MJ	0.54 mg/ml[a,b]	SKB	56 µg/ml[a,b]	Visually compatible with little or no loss of either drug by HPLC in 4 hr at 22 °C under fluorescent light	2245	C
Prochlorperazine edisylate	SKB	0.192 mg/ml[a,b]	SKB	56 µg/ml[a,b]	Visually compatible with little or no loss of either drug by HPLC in 4 hr at 22 °C under fluorescent light	2245	C
Ticarcillin disodium–clavulanate potassium	SKB	24.6 mg/ml[a]	SKB	56 µg/ml[a]	Pale yellow color occurs immediately. 11% loss of topotecan occurs in 4 hr at 22 °C under fluorescent light	2245	I
	SKB	24.6 mg/ml[b]	SKB	56 µg/ml[b]	Pale yellow color occurs immediately. 5% or less loss of all drug components in 4 hr at 22 °C under fluorescent light	2245	C
Vincristine sulfate	LI	1 mg/ml	SKB	56 µg/ml[a,b]	Visually compatible with little or no loss of either drug by HPLC in 4 hr at 22 °C under fluorescent light	2245	C

[a]*Tested in dextrose 5% in water.*
[b]*Tested in sodium chloride 0.9%.*

Additional Compatibility Information

Infusion Solutions — The manufacturer states that topotecan HCl reconstituted and further diluted for infusion is stable for 24 hours stored at 20 to 25 °C under ambient lighting conditions. (2) However, other information indicates that topotecan HCl diluted for infusion in dextrose 5% in water or sodium chloride 0.9% in PVC bags at concentrations of 10 to 500 µg/ml is stable for up to four days at room temperature. (4)

Other Information

Microbial Growth — Whether any antimicrobial effect of topotecan HCl exists is uncertain but could be concentration dependent. Two studies that have been performed seem to have different results, perhaps due to the very different topotecan HCl concentrations being tested.

Topotecan HCl (SmithKline Beecham) 0.01 mg/ml diluted in sodium chloride 0.9% and stored at 22 °C did not exhibit an antimicrobial effect on the growth of four organisms (*Enterococcus faecium, Staphylococcus aureus, Pseudomonas aeruginosa,* and *Candida albicans*) inoculated into the solution. The author recommended that diluted solutions of topotecan HCl be stored under refrigeration whenever possible and that the potential for microbiological growth be considered when assigning expiration periods. (2160)

Topotecan HCl (SmithKline Beecham) 1 mg/ml reconstituted with sterile water did not support the growth of five organisms inoculated into the solution. The USP Preservative Effectiveness Test found that *Pseudomonas aeruginosa, Staphylococcus aureus,* and *Escherichia coli* were not viable after 16 hours, 24 hours, and 28 days, respectively. *Candida albicans* and *Aspergillus niger* did not lose viability but did not exhibit growth during the test. (2211)

Handling Precautions — As for other toxic drugs, topotecan HCl should be prepared using protective measures to avoid inadvertent contact with the drug. The use of gloves, protective clothing, and vertical laminar flow hoods or biological safety cabinets is recommended. If skin contact with the drug does occur, wash the area thoroughly with soap and water. For mucous membrane contact, flush thoroughly with water. Disposal should also be performed safely to avoid inadvertent exposure. (2; 4)

TORSEMIDE
AHFS 40:28

Products — Torsemide is available in 2- and 5-ml ampuls. Each milliliter of solution contains torsemide 10 mg along with polyethylene glycol 400, tromethamine, water for injection, and sodium hydroxide if needed to adjust pH during manufacture. (2)

pH — Approximately 8.3. (2)

Trade Name(s) — Demadex.

Administration — Torsemide is administered intravenously either slowly as a bolus over two minutes or as a continuous infusion. If given through an intravenous line, flushing with sodium chloride 0.9% before and after torsemide administration is recommended. (2)

Stability — Intact containers of torsemide should be stored at controlled room temperature and protected from freezing. At concentrations of 0.1 and 0.8 mg/ml in dextrose 5% in water and sodium chloride 0.9% and at concentrations of 0.1 and 0.4 mg/ml in sodium chloride 0.45%, torsemide is stated to be stable for 24 hours at room temperature in plastic containers. (2)

Compatibility Information

Solution Compatibility

Torsemide

Solution	*Mfr*	*Mfr*	*Conc/L*	*Remarks*	*Ref*	*C/I*
Dextrose 5% in water	AB[a]	BM	200 mg	6% loss by HPLC occurs in 72 hr at 24 °C	2108	C
	AB[a]	BM	5 g	3% loss by HPLC occurs in 72 hr at 24 °C	2108	C

[a]*Tested in PVC containers.*

Y-Site Injection Compatibility (1:1 Mixture)

Torsemide

Drug	*Mfr*	*Conc*	*Mfr*	*Conc*	*Remarks*	*Ref*	*C/I*
Milrinone lactate	BM	10 mg/ml	SW	0.4 mg/ml[a]	Visually compatible with little or no loss of either drug by HPLC in 4 hr at 23 °C	2214	C

[a]*Tested in dextrose 5% in water.*

TRIFLUOPERAZINE HCL
AHFS 28:16.08

Products — Trifluoperazine HCl is available in 10-ml multiple-dose vials. Each milliliter of the aqueous solution contains trifluoperazine 2 mg as the hydrochloride, sodium tartrate 4.75 mg, sodium biphosphate 11.6 mg, sodium saccharin 0.3 mg, and benzyl alcohol 0.75% as a preservative. (2)

pH — From 4 to 5. (4)

Osmolality — Trifluoperazine HCl 2 mg/ml has an osmolality of 288 mOsm/kg. (1689)

Trade Name(s) — Stelazine.

Administration — Trifluoperazine HCl is administered by deep intramuscular injection. (2; 4)

Stability — Trifluoperazine HCl should be stored at controlled room temperature and protected from light and freezing. (2; 4) Exposure to ultraviolet light results in discoloration; trifluoperazine HCl solutions gradually become yellowish-red and then reddish-brown, depending on the length of exposure time. (1957) A slight yellowish color does not indicate significant alteration in potency, but a markedly discolored solution should not be used. (2; 4)

Sorption—Trifluoperazine HCl (SKF) 10 mg/L in sodium chloride 0.9% (Travenol) in PVC bags did not exhibit significant sorption to the plastic during one week of storage at room temperature (15 to 20 °C). However, when the solution was buffered from its initial pH of 5 to 7.4, approximately 91% of the drug was lost in one week due to sorption. (536)

In another study, trifluoperazine HCl (SKF) 10 mg/L in sodium chloride 0.9% exhibited a cumulative 45% loss during a seven-hour simulated infusion through an infusion set (Travenol) consisting of a cellulose propionate burette chamber and 170 cm of PVC tubing due to sorption. Both the burette and the tubing contributed to the loss. The extent of sorption was found to be independent of concentration. (606)

The drug was also tested as a simulated infusion over at least one hour by a syringe pump system. A glass syringe on a syringe pump was fitted with 20 cm of polyethylene tubing or 50 cm of Silastic tubing. Only 5% of the drug was lost with the polyethylene tubing, but a cumulative loss of 78% occurred during the one-hour infusion through the Silastic tubing. (606)

In addition, a 25-ml aliquot of trifluoperazine HCl (SKF) 10 mg/L in sodium chloride 0.9% was stored in all-plastic syringes composed of polypropylene barrels and polyethylene plungers for 24 hours at room temperature in the dark. No loss due to sorption occurred. (606)

TRIMETHOBENZAMIDE HCL
AHFS 56:22

Products — Trimethobenzamide HCl is available in 2-ml (200 mg) ampuls and 20-ml (100 mg/ml) multiple-dose vials. Each milliliter of solution contains (2):

Component	Ampul	Vial
Trimethobenzamide HCl	100 mg	100 mg
Methyl- and propylparabens	0.2%	
Phenol		0.45%
Sodium citrate	0.5 mg	0.5 mg
Citric acid	0.2 mg	0.2 mg
Edetate disodium		
Sodium hydroxide	to adjust pH	to adjust pH

pH—The official pH range is 4.5 to 5.5. (17) The manufacturer indicates the actual pH is approximately 5. (2)

Osmolality—Trimethobenzamide HCl 100 mg/ml has an osmolality of 244 mOsm/kg. (1689)

Trade Name(s)—Tigan.

Administration — Trimethobenzamide HCl is administered by intramuscular injection deep into the upper outer quadrant of the gluteal region. Intravenous injection is not recommended. (2; 4)

Stability — Trimethobenzamide HCl should be stored at controlled room temperature and protected from freezing. (4)

Trimethobenzamide HCl (Roche) 100 mg/ml was found to retain potency for three months at room temperature when 1 or 2 ml of solution was packaged in Tubex cartridges. (13)

Compatibility Information

Drugs in Syringe Compatibility

Trimethobenzamide HCl

Drug (in syringe)	*Mfr*	*Amt*	*Mfr*	*Amt*	*Remarks*	*Ref*	*C/I*
Glycopyrrolate	RB	0.2 mg/ 1 ml	BE	100 mg/ 1 ml	Physically compatible and pH in stability range for glycopyrrolate for 48 hr at 25 °C	331	C
	RB	0.2 mg/ 1 ml	BE	200 mg/ 2 ml	Physically compatible and pH in stability range for glycopyrrolate for 48 hr at 25 °C	331	C
	RB	0.4 mg/ 2 ml	BE	100 mg/ 1 ml	Physically compatible and pH in stability range for glycopyrrolate for 48 hr at 25 °C	331	C
Hydromorphone HCl	KN	4 mg/ 2 ml	BE	100 mg/ 1 ml	Physically compatible for 30 min	517	C
Midazolam HCl	RC	5 mg/ 1 ml	BE	200 mg/ 2 ml	Physically compatible for 4 hr at 25 °C under fluorescent light	1145	C
Nalbuphine HCl	EN	10 mg/ 1 ml	BE	100 mg/ 1 ml	Physically compatible for 36 hr at 27 °C	762	C
	EN	5 mg/ 0.5 ml	BE	100 mg/ 1 ml	Physically compatible for 36 hr at 27 °C	762	C
	EN	2.5 mg/ 0.25 ml	BE	100 mg/ 1 ml	Physically compatible for 36 hr at 27 °C	762	C

Drugs in Syringe Compatibility (Cont.)

Drug (in syringe)	Mfr	Amt	Mfr	Amt	Remarks	Ref	C/I
			Trimethobenzamide HCl				
	DU	10 mg/ 1 ml		200 mg/ 2 ml	Physically compatible for 48 hr	128	C
	DU	20 mg/ 1 ml		200 mg/ 2 ml	Physically compatible for 48 hr	128	C

Y-Site Injection Compatibility (1:1 Mixture)

Drug	Mfr	Conc	Mfr	Conc	Remarks	Ref	C/I
			Trimethobenzamide HCl				
Heparin sodium	UP	1000 units/L[a]	RC	100 mg/ml	Physically compatible for at least 4 hr at room temperature by visual and microscopic examination	534	C
Hydrocortisone sodium succinate	UP	10 mg/L[a]	RC	100 mg/ml	Physically compatible for at least 4 hr at room temperature by visual and microscopic examination	534	C
Potassium chloride	AB	40 mEq/L[a]	RC	100 mg/ml	Physically compatible for at least 4 hr at room temperature by visual and microscopic examination	534	C
Vitamin B complex with C	RC	2 ml/L[a]	RC	100 mg/ml	Physically compatible for at least 4 hr at room temperature by visual and microscopic examination	534	C

[a] *Tested in dextrose 5% in Ringer's injection, dextrose 5% in Ringer's injection, lactated, dextrose 5% in water, Ringer's injection, lactated, and sodium chloride 0.9%.*

TRIMETHOPRIM–SULFAMETHOXAZOLE (CO-TRIMOXAZOLE) AHFS 8:40

Products — Trimethoprim–sulfamethoxazole is available as a concentrate in 10-, 20-, and 30-ml vials. Each milliliter contains (2):

Trimethoprim	16 mg
Sulfamethoxazole	80 mg
Propylene glycol	40%
Ethyl alcohol	10%
Diethanolamine	0.3%
Benzyl alcohol	1%
Sodium metabisulfite	0.1%
Sodium hydroxide	to adjust pH
Water for injection	qs

pH — Approximately 10. (2)

Osmolality — The osmolalities of trimethoprim–sulfamethoxazole (Burroughs Wellcome) in concentrations of 0.8 + 4, 1.1 + 5.5, and 1.6 + 8 mg/ml in dextrose 5% in water were determined to be 541, 669, and 798 mOsm/kg, respectively. At 1.6 + 8 mg/ml in sodium chloride 0.9%, the osmolality was determined to be 833 mOsm/kg. (1375)

Trade Name(s) — Bactrim I.V. Infusion, Septra I.V. Infusion.

Administration — Trimethoprim–sulfamethoxazole is administered by intravenous infusion only after dilution in dextrose 5% in water. The drug should not be injected intramuscularly. Infusion over 60 to 90 minutes is recommended; rapid or direct intravenous injection must not be used. It is recommended that each 5-ml vial be diluted in 125 ml or, if fluid restriction is required, in 75 ml of dextrose 5% in water. Infusion admixtures should be inspected for cloudiness or crystallization before and during administration. (2; 4)

Stability — Trimethoprim–sulfamethoxazole in intact vials should be stored at controlled room temperature and not refrigerated. The multiple-dose vials should be used within 48 hours of initial entry. (2)

The solubility of trimethoprim in aqueous solutions is partially dependent on the pH of the solution. Trimethoprim is a weak base, and its solubility is lower in solutions with a more alkaline pH. (553)

Syringes — Undiluted trimethoprim–sulfamethoxazole (Elkins-Sinn) (16 + 80 mg/ml) was stored in polypropylene syringes (Becton-Dickinson) for 2.5 days at room temperature. The syringes were exposed to fluorescent light during the day but kept in the dark at night. No loss by HPLC was observed. (1582)

Sorption — Trimethoprim (Sigma) 25 mg/L in sodium chloride 0.9%

(Travenol) in PVC bags did not exhibit significant sorption to the plastic during one week of storage at room temperature (15 to 20 °C). (536)

In another study, trimethoprim (Sigma) 25 mg/L in sodium chloride 0.9% did not exhibit any loss due to sorption during a seven-hour simulated infusion through an infusion set (Travenol) consisting of a cellulose propionate burette chamber and 170 cm of PVC tubing. (606)

The drug was also tested as a simulated infusion over at least one hour by a syringe pump system. A glass syringe on a syringe pump was fitted with 20 cm of polyethylene tubing or 50 cm of Silastic tubing. No loss of drug due to sorption was observed with either tubing. (606)

In addition, a 25-ml aliquot of trimethoprim (Sigma) 25 mg/L in sodium chloride 0.9% was stored in all-plastic syringes composed of polypropylene barrels and polyethylene plungers for 24 hours at room temperature in the dark. No loss due to sorption occurred. (606)

A 1:10 (v/v) dilution of trimethoprim–sulfamethoxazole (Roche) in dextrose 5% in water prepared in a glass container and also in a burette chamber administration set (Travenol) showed no loss of either drug because of sorption during 24 hours at 23 to 25 °C. (747)

Plasticizer Leaching— Trimethoprim–sulfamethoxazole (Elkins-Sinn) 0.8 + 4 mg/ml in dextrose 5% in water did not leach diethylhexyl phthalate (DEHP) plasticizer from 50-ml PVC bags in 24 hours at 24 °C. (1683)

Filtration— Filtration of dilutions of trimethoprim–sulfamethoxazole (Roche), ranging from 1:25 (v/v) to 1:10 (v/v) in several common intravenous infusion solutions, did not appear to result in loss of either drug because of sorption to the filter. Filtration of a visibly precipitated solution resulted in a substantial loss of trimethoprim. (747)

Trimethoprim–sulfamethoxazole (Roche) 1.88 mg/ml in dextrose 5% in water and sodium chloride 0.9% was filtered through a 0.22-μm cellulose ester membrane filter (Ivex-HP, Millipore) over six hours. No significant drug loss due to binding to the filter was noted. (1034)

Compatibility Information

Solution Compatibility

Trimethoprim + Sulfamethoxazole

Solution	*Mfr*	*Mfr*	*Conc/L*	*Remarks*	*Ref*	*C/I*
Dextrose 5% in sodium chloride 0.45%	AB	RC	640 mg + 3.2 g	Physically compatible with 6% trimethoprim loss and little or no sulfamethoxazole loss in 24 hr at 23 to 25 °C	747	C
	AB	RC	800 mg + 4 g	Physically compatible with 4% trimethoprim loss and little or no sulfamethoxazole loss in 24 hr at 23 to 25 °C	747	C
Dextrose 5% in water	AB	RC	640 mg + 3.2 g	Physically compatible with little or no trimethoprim and sulfamethoxazole loss in 24 hr at 23 to 25 °C	747	C
	AB	RC	800 mg + 4 g	Physically compatible with little or no trimethoprim and sulfamethoxazole loss in 24 hr at 23 to 25 °C	747	C
	TR	RC	640 mg + 3.2 g	Admixture clear and colorless for 4 hr at 22 °C. Turbidity and precipitation appear after this time. 5% trimethoprim loss in 4 hr and 28% in 24 hr. About 1% sulfamethoxazole loss in 24 hr	553	I[a]
	TR	RC	1.6 + 8 g	Admixture clear and colorless for 2 hr at 22 °C. Turbidity and precipitation appear after this time. 5% trimethoprim loss in 2 hr and 64% in 24 hr. About 3% sulfamethoxazole loss in 24 hr	553	I[a]
	TR	RC	3.2 + 16 g	Rapid precipitation and 32% trimethoprim loss in 1 hr. 9% sulfamethoxazole loss in 24 hr	553	I
	AB[b]	BW, RC	640 mg + 3.2 g	Physically compatible with little or no trimethoprim and sulfamethoxazole loss in 48 hr at 24 °C	1201	C
	AB[b]	BW, RC	800 mg + 4 g	Physically compatible with little or no trimethoprim and sulfamethoxazole loss in 24 hr at 24 °C. Precipitate forms within 48 hr	1201	C
	AB[b]	BW, RC	1.07 + 5.33 g	Physically compatible with little or no trimethoprim and sulfamethoxazole loss in 4 hr at 24 °C. Precipitate forms within 8 hr	1201	I[a]
	AB[b]	BW, RC	1.6 + 8 g	Precipitate forms as early as 2 hr at 24 °C. Up to 75% trimethoprim loss in 4 hr	1201	I

Solution Compatibility (Cont.)

Trimethoprim + Sulfamethoxazole

Solution	*Mfr*	*Mfr*	*Conc/L*	*Remarks*	*Ref*	*C/I*
Ringer's injection, lactated	AB	RC	640 mg + 3.2 g	Physically compatible with 4% trimethoprim loss and little or no sulfamethoxazole loss in 24 hr at 23 to 25 °C	747	C
	AB	RC	800 mg + 4 g	Physically compatible with little or no trimethoprim loss and about 4% sulfamethoxazole loss in 24 hr at 23 to 25 °C	747	C
Sodium chloride 0.45%	AB	RC	640 mg + 3.2 g	Physically compatible with little or no trimethoprim and sulfamethoxazole loss in 24 hr at 23 to 25 °C	747	C
	AB	RC	800 mg + 4 g	Physically compatible with 4% trimethoprim loss and little or no sulfamethoxazole loss in 24 hr at 23 to 25 °C	747	C
Sodium chloride 0.9%	AB	RC	640 mg + 3.2 g	Physically compatible with 5% trimethoprim loss and 4% sulfamethoxazole loss in 24 hr at 23 to 25 °C	747	C
	AB	RC	800 mg + 4 g	Physically compatible with little or no trimethoprim and sulfamethoxazole loss in 24 hr at 23 to 25 °C	747	C
	TR	RC	640 mg + 3.2 g	Admixture clear and colorless for 4 hr at 22 °C. Turbidity and precipitation appear after this time. 1% trimethoprim loss in 4 hr and 36% in 24 hr. No sulfamethoxazole loss in 24 hr	553	I[a]
	TR	RC	1.6 + 8 g	Admixture clear and colorless for 1 to 2 hr at 22 °C. Turbidity appears after this time. 15% trimethoprim loss in 2 hr and 76% in 24 hr. 5% sulfamethoxazole loss in 24 hr	553	I
	TR	RC	3.2 + 16 g	Rapid precipitation and 74% trimethoprim loss in 1 hr. 6% sulfamethoxazole loss in 24 hr	553	I
	AB[b]	BW, RC	640 mg + 3.2 g	Physically compatible with little or no trimethoprim and sulfamethoxazole loss in 48 hr at 24 °C	1201	C
	AB[b]	BW, RC	800 mg + 4 g	Physically compatible with little or no trimethoprim and sulfamethoxazole loss in 14 hr at 24 °C. Precipitate forms within 24 hr	1201	I[a]
	AB[b]	BW, RC	1.07 + 5.33 g	Physically compatible with little or no trimethoprim and sulfamethoxazole loss in 2 hr at 24 °C. Precipitate forms within 4 hr	1201	I[a]
	AB[b]	BW, RC	1.6 + 8 g	Precipitate forms as early as 2 hr at 24 °C. Up to 18% trimethoprim loss in 4 hr	1201	I
	[b]	BW	1.6 + 8 g	Precipitate forms in 1.5 hr at 20 °C. 10% trimethoprim loss by HPLC in 1.5 hr, 21% loss in 3 hr, and 60% loss in 24 hr	1555	I

[a]*Incompatible by conventional standards. May be used in shorter time periods.*
[b]*Tested in glass containers.*

Additive Compatibility

Trimethoprim + Sulfamethoxazole

Drug	*Mfr*	*Conc/L*	*Mfr*	*Conc/L*	*Test Soln*	*Remarks*	*Ref*	*C/I*
Fluconazole	PF	1 g	ES	0.4 + 2 g	D5W	Delayed cloudiness and precipitation. No fluconazole loss by HPLC in 72 hr at 25 °C under fluorescent light	1677	I

Additive Compatibility (Cont.)

Trimethoprim + Sulfamethoxazole

Drug	*Mfr*	*Conc/L*	*Mfr*	*Conc/L*	*Test Soln*	*Remarks*	*Ref*	*C/I*
Linezolid	PHU	2 g	ES	800 mg + 4 g	[a]	A large amount of white needle-like crystals forms immediately	2333	I
Verapamil HCl	KN	80 mg	BW	160 + 800 mg	D5W, NS	Transient precipitate	764	I

[a]*Admixed in the linezolid infusion container.*

Drugs in Syringe Compatibility

Trimethoprim + Sulfamethoxazole

Drug (in syringe)	*Mfr*	*Amt*	*Mfr*	*Amt*	*Remarks*	*Ref*	*C/I*
Heparin sodium		2500 units/ 1 ml		80 + 400 mg/ 5 ml	Physically compatible for at least 5 min	1053	C

Y-Site Injection Compatibility (1:1 Mixture)

Trimethoprim + Sulfamethoxazole

Drug	*Mfr*	*Conc*	*Mfr*	*Conc*	*Remarks*	*Ref*	*C/I*
Acyclovir sodium	BW	5 mg/ml[a]	RC	0.8 + 4 mg/ ml[a]	Physically compatible for 4 hr at 25 °C	1157	C
Aldesleukin	CHI	33,800 I.U./ ml[a]	BW	1.6 + 8 mg/ ml[a]	Visually compatible with little or no loss of aldesleukin activity by bioassay	1857	C
Allopurinol sodium	BW	3 mg/ml[b]	ES	0.8 + 4 mg/ ml[b]	Physically compatible with no change in measured turbidity or increase in particle content in 4 hr at 22 °C	1686	C
Amifostine	USB	10 mg/ml[a]	ES	0.8 + 4 mg/ ml[a]	Physically compatible with no change in measured turbidity or increase in particle content in 4 hr at 23 °C	1845	C
Amphotericin B cholesteryl sulfate complex	SEQ	0.83 mg/ml[a]	ES	0.8 + 4 mg/ ml[a]	Physically compatible with little or no change in measured turbidity or increase in particle content in 4 hr at 23 °C under fluorescent light	2117	C
Atracurium besylate	BW	0.5 mg/ml[a]	ES	0.64 + 3.2 mg/ml[a]	Physically compatible for 24 hr at 28 °C	1337	C
Aztreonam	SQ	40 mg/ml[a]	ES	0.8 + 4 mg/ ml[a]	Physically compatible with no subvisual haze or particle formation in 4 hr at 23 °C	1758	C
Cefepime HCl	BMS	20 mg/ml[a]	ES	0.8 + 4 mg/ ml[a]	Physically compatible with no change in measured turbidity or increase in particle content in 4 hr at 22 °C	1689	C
Cisatracurium besylate	GW	0.1 mg/ml[a]	ES	0.8 + 4 mg/ ml[a]	Physically compatible with no change in measured turbidity or increase in particle content in 4 hr at 23 °C	2074	C
	GW	2 mg/ml[a]	ES	0.8 + 4 mg/ ml[a]	Subvisual haze forms in 1 hr	2074	I
	GW	5 mg/ml[a]	ES	0.8 + 4 mg/ ml[a]	Subvisual haze forms immediately	2074	I

Y-Site Injection Compatibility (1:1 Mixture) (Cont.)

Trimethoprim + Sulfamethoxazole

Drug	*Mfr*	*Conc*	*Mfr*	*Conc*	*Remarks*	*Ref*	*C/I*
Cyclophosphamide	MJ	20 mg/ml[a]	BW	0.8 + 4 mg/ml[a]	Physically compatible for 4 hr at 25 °C	1194	C
Diltiazem HCl	MMD	5 mg/ml	BW, RC	0.21 + 1 mg/ml[a] and 0.63 + 3.2 mg/ml[a]	Visually compatible	1807	C
Docetaxel	RPR	0.9 mg/ml[a]	ES	0.8 + 4 mg/ml[a]	Physically compatible with no change in measured turbidity or increase in particle content in 4 hr at 23 °C	2224	C
Doxorubicin HCl liposome injection	SEQ	0.4 mg/ml[a]	ES	0.8 + 4 mg/ml[a]	Physically compatible with little or no change in measured turbidity and no increase in particle content in 4 hr at 23 °C	2087	C
Enalaprilat	MSD	0.05 mg/ml[b]	QU	0.16 + 0.8 mg/ml[a]	Physically compatible for 24 hr at room temperature under fluorescent light	1355	C
Esmolol HCl	DCC	10 mg/ml[a]	BW	0.64 + 3.2 mg/ml[a]	Physically compatible for 24 hr at 22 °C	1169	C
Etoposide phosphate	BR	5 mg/ml[a]	ES	0.8 + 4 mg/ml[a]	Physically compatible with no change in measured turbidity or increase in particle content in 4 hr at 23 °C	2218	C
Filgrastim	AMG	30 μg/ml[a]	ES	0.8 + 4 mg/ml[a]	Physically compatible with no change in measured turbidity or increase in particle content in 4 hr at 22 °C	1687	C
Fluconazole	RR	2 mg/ml	BW	16 + 80 mg/ml	Viscous gel-like substance forms	1407	I
Fludarabine phosphate	BX	1 mg/ml[a]	ES	0.8 + 4 mg/ml[a]	Physically compatible for 4 hr at room temperature under fluorescent light	1439	C
Foscarnet sodium	AST	24 mg/ml	RC	16 + 80 mg/ml	Immediate precipitation and gas production	1335	I
	AST	24 mg/ml	BW	0.53 + 2.6 mg/ml[a]	Physically compatible for 24 hr at 25 °C under fluorescent light by visual and microscopic examination	1393	C
Gatifloxacin	BMS	2 mg/ml[a]	ES	0.8 + 4 mg/ml[a]	Physically compatible with no change in measured haze or increase in particle content in 4 hr at 23 °C	2234	C
Gemcitabine HCl	LI	10 mg/ml[b]	ES	0.8 + 4 mg/ml[b]	Physically compatible with no change in measured turbidity or increase in particle content in 4 hr at 23 °C	2226	C
Granisetron HCl	SKB	0.05 mg/ml[a]	ES	0.8 + 4 mg/ml[a]	Physically compatible with no change in measured turbidity or increase in particle content in 4 hr at 23 °C	2000	C
Hetastarch in lactated electrolyte injection (Hextend)	AB	6%	ES	0.8 + 4 mg/ml[a]	Physically compatible with no change in measured turbidity or increase in particle content in 4 hr at 23 °C	2339	C
Hydromorphone HCl	WY	0.2 mg/ml[a]	BW	0.8 + 4 mg/ml[a]	Physically compatible for at least 4 hr at 25 °C under fluorescent light	987	C
Labetalol HCl	SC	1 mg/ml[a]	BW	0.8 + 4 mg/ml[a]	Physically compatible for 24 hr at 18 °C	1171	C
Lorazepam	WY	0.33 mg/ml[b]	RC	0.8 + 4 mg/ml	Visually compatible for 24 hr at 22 °C	1855	C

Y-Site Injection Compatibility (1:1 Mixture) (Cont.)

Trimethoprim + Sulfamethoxazole

Drug	*Mfr*	*Conc*	*Mfr*	*Conc*	*Remarks*	*Ref*	*C/I*
Magnesium sulfate	IX	16.7, 33.3, 66.7, 100 mg/ml[a]	RC	0.8 + 4 mg/ml[a]	Physically compatible for at least 4 hr at 32 °C	813	C
Melphalan HCl	BW	0.1 mg/ml[b]	ES	0.8 + 4 mg/ml[b]	Physically compatible with no change in measured turbidity or increase in particle content in 3 hr at 22 °C	1557	C
Meperidine HCl	WY	10 mg/ml[a]	BW	0.8 + 4 mg/ml[a]	Physically compatible for at least 4 hr at 25 °C under fluorescent light	987	C
Midazolam HCl	RC	5 mg/ml	RC	0.8 + 4 mg/ml	White precipitate forms immediately	1855	I
Morphine sulfate	WI	1 mg/ml[a]	BW	0.8 + 4 mg/ml[a]	Physically compatible for at least 4 hr at 25 °C under fluorescent light	987	C
Pancuronium bromide	ES	0.05 mg/ml[a]	ES	0.64 + 3.2 mg/ml[a]	Physically compatible for 24 hr at 28 °C	1337	C
Perphenazine	SC	0.02 mg/ml[a]	BW	0.8 + 4 mg/ml[a]	Physically compatible for 4 hr at 25 °C	1155	C
Piperacillin sodium–tazobactam sodium	LE	40 + 5 mg/ml[a]	ES	0.8 + 4 mg/ml[a]	Physically compatible with no change in measured turbidity or increase in particle content in 4 hr at 22 °C	1688	C
Remifentanil HCl	GW	0.025 and 0.25 mg/ml[b]	ES	0.8 + 4 mg/ml[a]	Physically compatible with no change in measured turbidity or increase in particle content in 4 hr at 23 °C	2075	C
Sargramostim	IMM	10 μg/ml[b]	ES	0.8 + 4 mg/ml[b]	Physically compatible for 4 hr at 22 °C	1436	C
Tacrolimus	FUJ	1 mg/ml[b]	RC	1.6 + 8 mg/ml[a]	Visually compatible for 24 hr at 25 °C	1630	C
Teniposide	BR	0.1 mg/ml[a]	ES	0.8 + 4 mg/ml[a]	Physically compatible with no subvisual haze or particle formation in 4 hr at 23 °C	1725	C
Thiotepa	IMM[c]	1 mg/ml[a]	ES	0.8 + 4 mg/ml[a]	Physically compatible with no change in measured turbidity or increase in particle content in 4 hr at 23 °C	1861	C
TNA #218 to #226[d]			ES	0.8 + 4 mg/ml[a]	Visually compatible with no precipitate or emulsion damage apparent in 4 hr at 23 °C	2215	C
TPN #212 to #215[d]			ES	0.8 + 4 mg/ml[a]	Physically compatible with no change in measured turbidity or increase in particle content in 4 hr at 23 °C	2109	C
Vecuronium bromide	OR	0.1 mg/ml[a]	ES	0.64 + 3.2 mg/ml[a]	Physically compatible for 24 hr at 28 °C	1337	C
Vinorelbine tartrate	BW	1 mg/ml[b]	ES	0.8 + 4 mg/ml[b]	Heavy white turbidity forms immediately, developing particles in 1 hr	1558	I
Zidovudine	BW	4 mg/ml[a]	BW	0.53 + 2.6 mg/ml[a]	Physically compatible for 4 hr at 25 °C under fluorescent light by visual and microscopic examination	1193	C

[a]*Tested in dextrose 5% in water.*
[b]*Tested in sodium chloride 0.9%.*
[c]*Lyophilized formulation tested.*
[d]*Refer to Appendix I for the composition of parenteral nutrition solutions. TNA indicates a 3-in-1 admixture, and TPN indicates a 2-in-1 admixture.*

Additional Compatibility Information

Infusion Solutions — The manufacturers recommend only dextrose 5% in water for dilution and infusion of trimethoprim–sulfamethoxazole. No other drugs or solutions should be mixed with the product. (2)

Precipitation occurs in the diluted infusion solution in varying time periods, depending on the final concentration. For dilutions of 5 ml per 125 ml of dextrose 5% in water (trimethoprim 640 mg/L, sulfamethoxazole 3.2 g/L), use within six hours is recommended. (2) However, precipitation within four hours has been observed at this concentration. (553) For dilutions of 5 ml per 100 ml of dextrose 5% in water (trimethoprim 800 mg/L, sulfamethoxazole 4 g/L), use within four hours is recommended. For dilutions of 5 ml per 75 ml of dextrose 5% in water (trimethoprim 1.067 g/L, sulfamethoxazole 5.33 g/L), use within two hours is recommended. All infusions should be inspected carefully and watched closely for turbidity and precipitation. Infusion admixtures in dextrose 5% in water should not be refrigerated. (2; 4)

Lesko et al. (553) and Deans et al. (747) reported dramatically different results for the compatibility of trimethoprim–sulfamethoxazole in aqueous solution, and Jarosinski et al. (1201) showed results between these two reports. Highly concentrated admixtures, at 1:15 or greater, apparently precipitate in only two to four hours. (553; 1201) For more dilute trimethoprim–sulfamethoxazole admixtures, caution and close inspection are still warranted.

The use of trimethoprim–sulfamethoxazole in glass, PVC, and polyolefin containers was found to be satisfactory. (2)

Precipitation has also been found in intravenous infusion set tubing that was not flushed or changed after administration of a trimethoprim–sulfamethoxazole infusion. The authors recommended thorough flushing of the total infusion tubing or replacement after drug administration. (963)

Giordano et al. evaluated the nature of the precipitate that forms from seven infusion solutions containing trimethoprim–sulfamethoxazole (Roche). In all cases, the sulfamethoxazole concentrations were within 5% of expected values, but the trimethoprim concentrations dropped to about 30% of the initial values. Further evaluation of the solid phases showed them to be trimethoprim alone or with trimethoprim monohydrate. (1895)

TRIMETREXATE GLUCURONATE
AHFS 8:40

Products — Trimetrexate glucuronate is available in 5-ml vials containing the equivalent of trimetrexate 25 mg and 30-ml vials containing the equivalent of trimetrexate 200 mg. Reconstitute the 25-mg vials with 2 ml of sterile water for injection or dextrose 5% in water. Reconstitute the 200-mg vials in accordance with the label instructions with dextrose 5% in water or sterile water for injection. The reconstituted vials yield a solution containing trimetrexate 12.5 mg/ml as the glucuronate. Complete dissolution should occur within 30 seconds. Do not reconstitute or dilute with chloride-containing solutions or with leucovorin because precipitate forms immediately. The reconstituted solution should be passed through a 0.22-μm filter prior to further dilution. It should not be used if cloudiness or precipitate is observed before or after filtration. (2; 4)

pH — From 3.5 to 5.5. (234)

Trade Name(s) — Neutrexin.

Administration — Trimetrexate glucuronate is administered by intravenous infusion at a concentration of 0.25 to 2 mg/ml in dextrose 5% in water. Do not dilute in chloride-containing infusion solutions. Flush the intravenous line with at least 10 ml of dextrose 5% in water both before and after administering trimetrexate glucuronate. The diluted trimetrexate glucuronate solution is infused intravenously over 60 to 90 minutes. Leucovorin calcium must also be administered to avoid serious, even life-threatening, toxicities. (2; 4)

Stability — Intact vials of trimetrexate glucuronate should be stored at controlled room temperature and protected from exposure to light. Trimetrexate glucuronate is a pale greenish-yellow cake or powder; the reconstituted solution is a pale greenish-yellow clear solution. Do not use if cloudiness or precipitate is present. The drug is stable after reconstitution for 48 hours at room temperature, five days under refrigeration at 2 to 8 °C, and eight days frozen at −10 to −20 °C. (2)

Chloride-Containing Solutions — Precipitation will occur immediately if trimetrexate glucuronate is reconstituted or diluted with chloride-containing solutions. (2; 4)

Compatibility Information

Y-Site Injection Compatibility (1:1 Mixture)

Trimetrexate glucuronate

Drug	*Mfr*	*Conc*	*Mfr*	*Conc*	*Remarks*	*Ref*	*C/I*
Amifostine	USB	10 mg/ml[a]	USB	2 mg/ml[a]	Physically compatible with no change in measured turbidity or increase in particle content in 4 hr at 23 °C	1845	C
Foscarnet	AST	24 mg/ml	WL	1 mg/ml[a]	Trimetrexate crystals form immediately	1393	I

Y-Site Injection Compatibility (1:1 Mixture) (Cont.)

Trimetrexate glucuronate

Drug	Mfr	Conc	Mfr	Conc	Remarks	Ref	C/I
Zidovudine	BW	4 mg/ml[a]	WL	1 mg/ml[a]	Physically compatible for 4 hr at 25 °C under fluorescent light by visual and microscopic examination	1193	C

[a]*Tested in dextrose 5% in water.*

Additional Compatibility Information

Infusion Solutions — Trimetrexate glucuronate reconstituted as directed and further diluted in dextrose 5% in water to a concentration of 0.25 to 2 mg/ml is stable for 24 hours at room temperature or under refrigeration. Discard any unused solution after 24 hours. Diluted solutions for infusion should not be frozen. Precipitation will occur immediately if admixed in any chloride-containing infusion solution. (2; 4)

Leucovorin — Trimetrexate glucuronate will precipitate immediately if reconstituted or mixed with leucovorin calcium. The manufacturer recommends flushing the intravenous line with at least 10 ml of dextrose 5% in water both before and after trimetrexate glucuronate, particularly if leucovorin is to be administered through the same line. (2; 4)

Other Information

Handling Precautions — If contact with the drug occurs, wash the area thoroughly with soap and water. Disposal should also be performed safely to avoid inadvertent exposure. (2)

TUBOCURARINE CHLORIDE
AHFS 12:20

Products — Tubocurarine chloride is available as a 3-mg/ml solution in 10- and 20-ml multiple-dose vials and 5-ml syringes. (4; 29) Each milliliter of solution contains (1-6/99):

Component	Amount
Tubocurarine chloride	3 mg
Benzyl alcohol	9 mg
Sodium metabisulfite	1 mg
Sodium chloride	qs[a]
Sodium citrate, dihydrate	0.3 mg
Citric acid, anhydrous	1 mg
Water for injection	qs

[a]*Sufficient to adjust tonicity.*

Units — Each 3 mg of tubocurarine chloride is equivalent to approximately 20 units of crude curare extract. (4)

pH — From 2.5 to 5. (4)

Osmolality — The osmolality of tubocurarine chloride 3 mg/ml was determined to be 296 mOsm/kg. (1233)

Administration — Tubocurarine chloride is usually administered intravenously, although intramuscular injection may be performed for infants or other patients if a suitable vein is not available. Undiluted at a concentration of 3 mg/ml, tubocurarine chloride should be given over approximately 60 to 90 seconds when administered by direct intravenous injection. (4)

Stability — Store this product at controlled room temperature. Freezing and excessive heat of 40 °C or more should be avoided. The drug should not be used if it is more than faintly discolored. (4)

Sorption — Tubocurarine chloride (Abbott) 80 mg/L did not display significant sorption to a PVC plastic test strip in 24 hours. (12)

Compatibility Information

Solution Compatibility

Tubocurarine chloride

Solution	Mfr	Mfr	Conc/L	Remarks	Ref	C/I
Dextran 6% in dextrose 5%	AB		9 mg	Physically compatible	3	C
Dextran 6% in sodium chloride 0.9%	AB		9 mg	Physically compatible	3	C
Dextrose–Ringer's injection combinations	AB		9 mg	Physically compatible	3	C

Solution Compatibility (Cont.)

Tubocurarine chloride

Solution	*Mfr*	*Mfr*	*Conc/L*	*Remarks*	*Ref*	*C/I*
Dextrose–Ringer's injection, lactated, combinations	AB		9 mg	Physically compatible	3	C
Dextrose–saline combinations	AB		9 mg	Physically compatible	3	C
Dextrose 2½% in water	AB		9 mg	Physically compatible	3	C
Dextrose 5% in water	AB		9 mg	Physically compatible	3	C
Dextrose 10% in water	AB		9 mg	Physically compatible	3	C
Fructose 10% in sodium chloride 0.9%	AB		9 mg	Physically compatible	3	C
Fructose 10% in water	AB		9 mg	Physically compatible	3	C
Invert sugar 5 and 10% in sodium chloride 0.9%	AB		9 mg	Physically compatible	3	C
Invert sugar 5 and 10% in water	AB		9 mg	Physically compatible	3	C
Ionosol products	AB		9 mg	Physically compatible	3	C
Ringer's injection	AB		9 mg	Physically compatible	3	C
Ringer's injection, lactated	AB		9 mg	Physically compatible	3	C
Sodium chloride 0.45%	AB		9 mg	Physically compatible	3	C
Sodium chloride 0.9%	AB		9 mg	Physically compatible	3	C
Sodium lactate ⅙ M	AB		9 mg	Physically compatible	3	C

Additive Compatibility

Tubocurarine chloride

Drug	*Mfr*	*Conc/L*	*Mfr*	*Conc/L*	*Test Soln*	*Remarks*	*Ref*	*C/I*
Trimethaphan camsylate	BP	1 g	BP	60 mg	D5W	Haze develops within 3 hr	26	I

Drugs in Syringe Compatibility

Tubocurarine chloride

Drug (in syringe)	*Mfr*	*Amt*	*Mfr*	*Amt*	*Remarks*	*Ref*	*C/I*
Pentobarbital sodium	AB	500 mg/ 10 ml		2.25 mg/ 0.15 ml	Physically compatible	55	C
Thiopental sodium	AB	75 mg/ 3 ml		2.25 mg/ 0.15 ml	Physically compatible for at least 30 min	21	C
	AB	75 mg/ 3 ml		2.25 mg/ 0.15 ml	Physically compatible	55	C

Additional Compatibility Information

Alkaline Solutions — Because of the high pH of barbiturates, a precipitate may form if a barbiturate is combined with tubocurarine chloride. (1-6/99; 4)

A haze forms in 15 minutes when tubocurarine chloride is mixed with methohexital sodium. (4)

Tubocurarine chloride 9 mg/L has been reported to be conditionally compatible with thiopental sodium (Abbott) 25 g/L. The mixture is physically incompatible in most Abbott infusion solutions except as noted below (3):

Dextran 6% in dextrose 5%	Physically compatible
Dextran 6% in sodium chloride 0.9%	Physically compatible
Dextrose 2½% in sodium chloride 0.45%	Physically compatible
Dextrose 2½% in sodium chloride 0.9%	Physically compatible
Dextrose 5% in sodium chloride 0.225%	Physically compatible

Dextrose 5% in sodium chloride 0.45%	Physically compatible
Dextrose 2½% in water	Physically compatible
Dextrose 5% in water	Physically compatible
Ionosol PSL (Darrow's)	Physically compatible
Sodium chloride 0.45%	Physically compatible
Sodium chloride 0.9%	Physically compatible
Sodium lactate ⅙ M	Physically compatible

Tubocurarine chloride 15 mg/ml has been reported to be conditionally compatible with thiopental sodium 2.5% in a 1:19 ratio. This mixture is usually satisfactory, but occasional precipitation occurs if the pH of the tubocurarine chloride is at its lower pH limit. The overall pH of the mixture is then reduced below 9.7, resulting in thiopental precipitation. As long as the final pH is above 9.7, no precipitate forms over 48 hours. (40)

VALPROATE SODIUM
AHFS 28:12.92

Products — Valproate sodium is available in 5-ml single-dose vials. Each milliliter of solution contains valproate sodium equivalent to valproic acid 100 mg and edetate disodium 0.4 mg in water for injection. Sodium hydroxide and/or hydrochloric acid may have been used to adjust pH during manufacture. The product should be diluted for use. (2)

pH — 7.6. (2; 4)

Trade Name(s) — Depacon.

Administration — Valproate sodium is usually administered as an intravenous infusion over 60 minutes at a rate that does not exceed 20 mg/min diluted in at least 50 ml of a compatible infusion solution. (2) More rapid infusion at a rate of 1.5 to 3 mg/kg/min over 5 to 10 minutes has been used in one study. (1-2/02)

Stability — Intact vials should be stored at controlled room temperature. The injection is a clear, colorless solution. Because no antibacterial preservatives are present in the formulation, any unused solution remaining in a vial after entry should be discarded. (2)

Compatibility Information

Solution Compatibility

Valproate sodium

Solution	*Mfr*	*Mfr*	*Conc/L*	*Remarks*	*Ref*	*C/I*
Dextrose 3.3% in sodium chloride 0.3%	GRI[a]	SW	1.6 g	10% or less loss by immunoassay in 6 days at room temperature	2287	C
Dextrose 5% in water	GRI[a]	SW	1.6 g	10% or less loss by immunoassay in 6 days at room temperature	2287	C
Ringer's injection, lactated	GRI[a]	SW	1.6 g	10% or less loss by immunoassay in 6 days at room temperature	2287	C
Sodium chloride 0.9%	GRI[a]	SW	1.6 g	10% or less loss by immunoassay in 6 days at room temperature	2287	C

[a]*Tested in glass, polyethylene (polyolefin), and PVC containers.*

Additional Compatibility Information

Infusion Solutions — Valproate sodium is stated by the manufacturer to be stable for at least 24 hours in dextrose 5% in water, Ringer's injection, lactated, and sodium chloride 0.9% in PVC bags and glass bottles. (2) However, other information indicates the drug may be stable for longer periods. See Compatibility Information above.

VANCOMYCIN HCL
AHFS 8:12.28

Products — Vancomycin HCl is available in vials containing drug equivalent to 500 mg or 1 g of vancomycin base. Reconstitute the vials with 10 or 20 ml, respectively, of sterile water for injection to yield a solution containing 50 mg of base (as the hydrochloride) per milliliter. Vancomycin HCl is also available in 5- and 10-g pharmacy bulk packages. (2; 4; 29)

Vancomycin HCl is also available as a frozen premixed infusion solution containing 500 mg in 100 ml and 1 g in 200 ml of dextrose 5% in water; the pH is adjusted with hydrochloric acid and/or sodium hydroxide. The frozen solution should not be thawed by warming in a water bath or exposure to microwave radiation. A precipitate may form during freezing, but it should redissolve upon warming to room temperature. After thawing, the bag should be checked for leaks by squeezing. The bag should be discarded if any leaks are found or if a precipitate or discoloration occurs. (4; 29)

pH — Vancomycin HCl (Lilly) in distilled water or sodium chloride 0.9% has a pH of about 3.9. (143) A 5% solution in water has a pH of 2.5 to 4.5. The commercial frozen vancomycin HCl premixed solution has a pH of 3 to 5. (4)

Vancomycin HCl (Lilly) reconstituted with sterile water for injection to a concentration of 50 mg/ml exhibited a measured pH of 3.3. Vancomycin HCl (Lilly) reconstituted with sterile water for injection and admixed at concentrations of 10 and 20 mg/ml in dextrose 5% in water and sodium chloride 0.9% injection exhibited pH values of 3.3 to 3.5. (1689)

Osmolality — Vancomycin HCl (Lilly) 50 mg/ml in sterile water for injection has an osmolality of 57 mOsm/kg. (50)

The osmolality of vancomycin HCl (Lederle) 5 mg/ml was determined to be 249 mOsm/kg in dextrose 5% in water and 291 mOsm/kg in sodium chloride 0.9%. (1375)

The osmolalities of vancomycin HCl (Lilly) reconstituted with sterile water for injection and admixed in dextrose 5% in water and sodium chloride 0.9% were determined (1689):

	Osmolality (mOsm/kg)	
Vancomycin HCl Concentration	Dextrose 5% in water	Sodium chloride 0.9%
10 mg/ml	230	254
20 mg/ml	187	227

Trade Name(s) — Lyphocin, Vancocin HCl.

Administration — Vancomycin HCl is administered by intermittent (2; 4) or continuous (4) intravenous infusion. The drug is extremely irritating to tissue and may cause necrosis. Therefore, it should not be given by intramuscular injection, and extravasation should be avoided during intravenous administration. For intermittent intravenous infusion, 500 mg to 1 g should be added to 100 to 200 ml, respectively, of dextrose 5% in water or sodium chloride 0.9% and administered over at least one hour. (2; 4) For continuous infusion, 1 to 2 g may be added to a fluid volume sufficient to permit administration of the daily dose over 24 hours. (4) Thrombophlebitis can be minimized by using dilute solutions of 2.5 to 5 mg/ml and rotating injection sites. (2; 4)

Stability — Intact vials should be stored at controlled room temperature. The manufacturer indicates that reconstituted solutions of vancomycin HCl are stable for 14 days under refrigeration (2); other information indicates that the drug is also stable in solution for 14 days at room temperature. (4; 141)

The frozen premixed infusion solution should be stored at −20 °C and is stable for 90 days from the date of shipping. The frozen solutions should be thawed at room temperature or under refrigeration. After thawing, they should not be refrozen. The thawed solutions are stable for 72 hours at room temperature and 30 days under refrigeration. (4)

pH Effects — In the pH range of 2 to 10, vancomycin HCl degradation is principally deamidation. (1927) Vancomycin HCl has been reported to be most stable at pH 3 to 5 (141) and at pH 5.5 (1927), with relatively pH-independent decomposition in the range of 3 to 8. (1927) The stability of a 1-mg/ml concentration was evaluated in buffer solutions having pH values of 1.4, 5.6, and 7.1 at 24 °C. Little or no loss occurred in 24 hours in any solution. However, the pH 1.4 buffer had a 19% loss in five days, the pH 5.6 buffer had a 10% loss in 17 days, and the pH 7.1 buffer had an 11% loss in five days. (1134)

Vancomycin HCl has a low pH and may cause a physical incompatibility with other drugs, especially drugs with an alkaline pH. (2; 4; 873)

In an accelerated study at 66 °C, the half-life of vancomycin B (the largest component of the commercial product) was 400 minutes in a phosphate buffer with a pH of 2.2 and 650 minutes in a phosphate buffer with a pH of 7. (1354)

Freezing Solutions — Vancomycin HCl (Lilly) at a concentration of 5 mg/ml in dextrose 5% in water or sodium chloride 0.9% exhibited no loss after 63 days of storage when frozen at −10 °C. However, neither did a loss occur in the same time period when the solution was stored at 5 °C. (1134)

Vancomycin HCl (Elkins-Sinn) 5 mg/ml in dextrose 5% in water and sodium chloride 0.9% frozen at −20 °C for 12 weeks exhibited 4% or less loss of potency by HPLC analysis in latex elastomeric reservoirs (Secure Medical) and in glass containers. (1970)

Syringes — Nahata et al. studied the stability of vancomycin HCl (Lilly) 5 mg/ml in dextrose concentrations ranging from 5 to 30% and packaged in plastic syringes. The syringes were stored at 4 °C for 24 hours followed by two hours at room temperature. Little or no change in the vancomycin concentration occurred during the study period. (1301)

Wood et al. reported the stability of vancomycin HCl (Lilly) reconstituted to a concentration of 10 mg/ml with sterile water for injection, dextrose 5% in water, and 0.9% sodium chloride repackaged into plastic syringes. Five milliliters of the solutions were filled into three-piece Plastipak (Becton-Dickinson) and two-piece Injekt (Braun) syringes that were then sealed with Luer-Lok hubs (Vigon) and stored at 4 and 25 °C for 84 days. Under refrigeration, vancomycin HCl prepared with all three solutions and packaged in both kinds of syringes was physically and chemically stable for the 84-day period; losses determined by HPLC analysis were 4% or less for all samples.

However, stored at 25 °C in the Plastipak syringes, 10% loss occurred in about 47 days in water, 55 days in dextrose 5% in water, and 62 days in sodium chloride 0.9%. In the Injekt syringes, stability was less; 10% loss occurred in 29 days in water, 33 days in dextrose

5% in water, and 34 days in sodium chloride 0.9%. In addition, a degradation product appeared as a white flocculent precipitate in all room temperature samples after about eight weeks of storage. (1893)

Ambulatory Pumps— Stiles et al. evaluated the stability of vancomycin HCl (Elkins-Sinn) 10 mg/ml in sterile water for injection and sodium chloride 0.9% in 100-ml portable pump reservoirs (Pharmacia Deltec) during simulated administration for 24 hours. The drug solutions were tested by HPLC analysis when administered immediately after preparation and after storage for 24 hours at 5 °C before 24-hour administration. During simulated administration, some reservoirs were kept at 30 °C; others were placed in insulated pouches with frozen (−20 °C) gel packs to keep them chilled below the ambient temperature. The vancomycin HCl solutions exhibited little or no loss by HPLC under all study conditions throughout the observation periods. To complete the infusions, chilling of the drug reservoirs was not necessary nor did it enhance stability during the study period. (1779)

Vancomycin HCl (Abbott) 20 and 40 mg/ml in dextrose 5% in water stored in SIMS Deltec Medication Cassette reservoirs exhibited little or no loss by HPLC analysis after 96 hours of storage at 25 °C and 30 days stored at 5 °C. (2097)

Elastomeric Reservoir Pumps— Vancomycin HCl (Elkins-Sinn) 5 mg/ml in dextrose 5% in water and sodium chloride 0.9% 100 ml was packaged in latex elastomeric reservoirs (Secure Medical). Little or no loss by HPLC analysis occurred in 24 hours at 25 °C and in 14 days at 5 °C. (1970)

Vancomycin HCl (Lilly) 10 mg/ml in both dextrose 5% in water and sodium chloride 0.9% was evaluated for binding potential to natural rubber elastomeric reservoirs (Baxter). No binding was found after storage for two weeks at 35 °C with gentle agitation. (2014)

Vancomycin HCl solutions in elastomeric reservoir pumps have been stated by the pump manufacturers to be stable for the following time periods frozen, refrigerated (REF), or at room temperature (RT) (31):

Pump Reservoir(s)	Conc.	Frozen	REF	RT
Homepump; Homepump Eclipse	5 mg/ml[b]		14 days	24 hr
Intermate	10 to 20 mg/ml[a,b]	30 days	10 days	24 hr
Intermate HPC; Intermate LV	10 to 20 mg/ml[a]		14 days	3 days
Medflo	5 mg/ml[a,b]	9 weeks	14 days	7 days
ReadyMed	5 mg/ml[a]		63 days	17 days

[a] *In dextrose 5% in water.*
[b] *In sodium chloride 0.9%.*

Implantable Pumps— Vancomycin HCl (Lilly) 1 mg/ml in water in an implantable pump (Infusaid model 100) was incubated in a water bath at 37 °C for 28 days. Vancomycin losses were substantial—about 25% in seven days and 40% in 28 days. At the end of the test period, a colloidal precipitate also was found in the pumps. (1302)

Sorption— Vancomycin HCl (Lilly) 15 mg/ml in dextrose 5% in water is reported to undergo substantial sorption to Teflon tubing used in an automatic dilutor (Syva). The vancomycin HCl was apparently released from the tubing into subsequent solutions resulting in vancomycin toxicity. (2153)

Plasticizer Leaching— Vancomycin HCl (Qualimed Laboratories) 8 mg/ml in dextrose 5% in water and sodium chloride 0.9% in PVC containers (Macropharma) did not leach detectable amounts of DEHP plasticizer during simulated administration over 24 hours. If any DEHP was present, the concentration was less than 1 μg/ml, the limit of detection in this study. (2148)

Filtration— Vancomycin HCl (Lilly) 2 mg/ml in dextrose 5% in water or sodium chloride 0.9% was filtered through a 0.22-μm cellulose ester filter (Ivex-HP, Millipore) over six hours. No significant drug loss due to binding to the filter was noted. (1034)

Central Venous Catheter— Vancomycin HCl (Fujisawa) 2 mg/ml in dextrose 5% in water was found to be compatible with the ARROWg+ard Blue Plus (Arrow International) chlorhexidine-bearing triple-lumen central catheter. HPLC analysis was used to evaluate completeness of drug delivery through the catheter and the amount of chlorhexidine removed from the internal lumens. Essentially complete delivery of the drug was found with little or no drug loss occurring. Furthermore, chlorhexidine delivered from the catheter remained at trace amounts with no substantial increase due to the delivery of the drug through the catheter. (2335)

Compatibility Information

Solution Compatibility

Vancomycin HCl

Solution	*Mfr*	*Mfr*	*Conc/L*	*Remarks*	*Ref*	*C/I*
Dextran 6% in sodium chloride 0.9%		LI	5 g	Physically compatible	143	C
Dextrose 5% in sodium chloride 0.9%		LI	1 g	Physically compatible	74	C
Dextrose 5% in water		LI	1 g	Physically compatible	74	C
		LI	5 g	Potency retained for at least 7 days at 5 and 25 °C	141	C
	TR[a]	LI	5 g	Physically compatible and potency retained for 24 hr at room temperature	518	C
	TR[b]	LI	5 g	Physically compatible with no vancomycin loss in 7 days and 5% loss in 17 days at 24 °C. In glass containers, no loss in 63 days at 5 °C	1134	C

Solution Compatibility (Cont.)

Solution	Mfr	Vancomycin HCl Mfr	Conc/L	Remarks	Ref	C/I
	TR	LI	4 and 5 g	Physically compatible with 8% loss in 17 days at 23 °C and 11% loss in 30 days at 4 °C	1354	C
	AB[c]	ES	5 g	Little or no loss of drug by HPLC in 24 hr at 25 °C and in 14 days at 5 °C	1970	C
	AB[f]	AB	20 and 40 g	Little or no loss by HPLC in 96 hr at 25 °C and in 30 days at 5 °C	2097	C
	[a]	QLM	8 g	Visually compatible and no loss by HPLC during a 24 hr simulated infusion at 22 °C	2148	C
	[a]	QLM	5 g	Visually compatible and no loss by HPLC during a 1 hr simulated infusion at 22 °C	2148	C
	[a]	QLM	5 g	Visually compatible and no loss by HPLC during storage for 48 hr at 22 °C exposed to light and 7 days at 4 °C protected from light	2148	C
	BA[a]	LI	5 and 10 g	Visually compatible with less than 3% vancomycin loss in 58 days at 4 °C	2252	C
	BA[g]	QLM	2 g	Visually compatible with no loss by HPLC at 4 °C and 4 to 6% loss at room temperature in 48 hr. No stability difference found among the various containers	2278	C
Dextrose 10% in water		LI	5 g	Physically compatible	143	C
Ringer's injection, lactated		LI	5 g	Physically compatible	143	C
		LI	1 g	Physically compatible	74	C
Sodium bicarbonate 3.75%		LI	5 g	Physically compatible	143	C
Sodium chloride 0.9%		LI	5 g	Potency retained for at least 7 days at 5 and 25 °C	141	C
		LI	1 g	Physically compatible	74	C
	TR[a]	LI	5 g	Physically compatible and potency retained for 24 hr at room temperature	518	C
	TR[b]	LI	5 g	Physically compatible with no vancomycin loss in 7 days and 5% loss in 17 days at 24 °C. In glass containers, no loss in 63 days at 5 °C	1134	C
	TR	LI	4 and 5 g	Physically compatible with 9% loss in 24 days at 23 °C and 5 to 6% loss in 30 days at 4 °C	1354	C
	AB[d]	ES	10 g	Little or no drug loss by HPLC with 24-hr storage at 5 °C followed by 24-hr simulated administration at 30 °C via portable pump	1779	C
	AB[c]	ES	5 g	Little or no loss of drug by HPLC in 24 hr at 25 °C and in 14 days at 5 °C	1970	C
	[a]	QLM	8 g	Visually compatible and no loss by HPLC during a 24 hr simulated infusion at 22 °C	2148	C
	[a]	QLM	5 g	Visually compatible and no loss by HPLC during a 1 hr simulated infusion at 22 °C	2148	C
	[a]	QLM	5 g	Visually compatible and no loss by HPLC during storage for 48 hr at 22 °C exposed to light and 7 days at 4 °C protected from light	2148	C
	BA[g]	QLM	2 g	Visually compatible with no loss by HPLC at 4 °C and at room temperature in 48 hr. No stability difference found among the various containers	2278	C
Sodium lactate ⅙ M		LI	5 g	Physically compatible	143	C
TPN #95 and #96[e]		LE	400 mg	Physically compatible and vancomycin content retained for 8 days at room temperature and under refrigeration, with and without heparin, by TDx	1321	C

Solution Compatibility (Cont.)

Vancomycin HCl

Solution	Mfr	Mfr	Conc/L	Remarks	Ref	C/I
TPN #105 and #106[e]		LI	1 and 6 g	Physically compatible with little or no vancomycin loss in 4 hr at 22 °C by HPLC	1325	C
TPN #107[e]			200 mg	Physically compatible and vancomycin content retained for 24 hr at 21 °C by microbiological assay	1326	C
TPN #202[a,e]		LI	500 mg and 1 g	Visually compatible and vancomycin activity by bioassay and immunoassay retained for 35 days at 4 °C and an additional 24 hr at 22 °C	1933	C

[a] *Tested in PVC containers.*
[b] *Tested in both glass and PVC containers.*
[c] *Tested in glass containers and latex elastomeric reservoirs (Secure Medical).*
[d] *Tested in portable pump reservoirs (Pharmacia Deltec).*
[e] *Refer to Appendix I for the composition of parenteral nutrition solutions. TPN indicates a 2-in-1 admixture.*
[f] *Tested in SIMS Deltec Medication Cassette reservoirs.*
[g] *Tested in PVC, polyolefin, and glass containers.*

Additive Compatibility

Vancomycin HCl

Drug	Mfr	Conc/L	Mfr	Conc/L	Test Soln	Remarks	Ref	C/I
Amikacin sulfate	BR	5 g	LI	2 g	D5LR, D5R, D5S, D5W, D10W, IS10, LR, NS, R, SL	Physically compatible and amikacin potency retained for 24 hr at 25 °C. Vancomycin not tested	293	C
Aminophylline		250 mg	LI	1 g	D5W	Physically compatible	74	C
	SE	1 g	LI	5 g	D5W	Physically incompatible	15	I
Amobarbital sodium			LI			Physically incompatible	9	I
	LI	1 g	LI	5 g	D5W	Physically incompatible	15	I
Atracurium besylate	BW	500 mg		5 g	D5W	Physically compatible and atracurium chemically stable for 24 hr at 5 and 30 °C	1694	C
Aztreonam	SQ	40 g	AB	10 g	D5W, NS	Microcrystalline precipitate forms immediately. Gross turbidity and precipitate form over 24 hr	1848	I
	SQ	4 g	AB	1 g	D5W	Physically compatible with little or no loss of either drug in 31 days at 4 °C. 8 to 10% aztreonam loss in 14 days at 23 °C and 7 days at 32 °C	1848	C
	SQ	4 g	AB	1 g	NS	Physically compatible with little or no loss of either drug in 31 days at 4 °C. About 5 to 8% aztreonam loss in 31 days at 23 °C and 7 days at 32 °C	1848	C
Calcium gluconate		1 g	LI	1 g	D5W	Physically compatible	74	C
Cefepime HCl	BR	4 g	LI	5 g	D5W, NS	4% cefepime loss by HPLC in 24 hr at room temperature exposed to light and 2% loss in 7 days at 5 °C. No vancomycin loss by HPLC, but cloudiness develops in 5 days at 5 °C	1682	C

Additive Compatibility (Cont.)

			Vancomycin HCl					
Drug	*Mfr*	*Conc/L*	*Mfr*	*Conc/L*	*Test Soln*	*Remarks*	*Ref*	*C/I*
	BR	40 g	LI	1 g	D5W, NS	4% cefepime loss by HPLC in 24 hr at room temperature exposed to light and 2% loss in 7 days at 5 °C. No vancomycin loss by HPLC and no cloudiness	1682	C
Chloramphenicol sodium succinate	PD	10 g	LI	5 g	D5W	Physically incompatible	15	I
Chlorothiazide sodium	MSD		LI			Physically incompatible	9	I
Cimetidine HCl	SKF	3 g	LI	5 g	D5W	Physically compatible and cimetidine chemically stable for 24 hr at room temperature. Vancomycin not tested	551	C
Corticotropin		500 units	LI	1 g	D5W	Physically compatible	74	C
Dexamethasone sodium phosphate			LI			Physically incompatible	9	I
Dimenhydrinate	SE	50 mg	LI	1 g	D5W	Physically compatible	74	C
Famotidine	YAM	200 mg	AB	5 g	D5W[d]	Visually compatible with 9% vancomycin loss and 6% famotidine loss by HPLC in 14 days at 25 °C. At 4 °C, 3 to 4% loss of both drugs occurred in 14 days	2111	C
Heparin sodium		12,000 units	LI	1 g	D5W	Immediate precipitate	74	I
	IX	1000 units	LE	400 mg	TPN #95[a]	Physically compatible and vancomycin content retained for 8 days at room temperature and under refrigeration by TDx	1321	C
	OR	500 to 14,300 units	LI	15 mg to 5.3 g	[b]	Physically compatible for 24 hr at 25 °C	1322	C
	OR	500 to 14,300 units	LI	6.9 to 14.3 g	[b]	Immediate white precipitation	1322	I
Hydrocortisone sodium succinate	UP	100 mg	LI	1 g	D5W	Physically compatible	74	C
Meropenem	ZEN	1 and 20 g	LI	1 g	NS	Visually compatible for 4 hr at room temperature	1994	C
Ofloxacin	HO	1.67 g	LI	4.2 g	W	Visually compatible with little or no loss of either drug by HPLC in 48 hr	1613	C
Pentobarbital sodium			LI			Physically incompatible	9	I
Phenobarbital sodium	WI		LI			Physically incompatible	9	I
Potassium chloride		3 g	LI	1 g	D5W	Physically compatible	74	C
Ranitidine HCl	GL	100 mg	DI	1 g	D5W	Physically compatible for 24 hr at ambient temperature under fluorescent light	1151	C
	GL	50 mg and 2 g		5 g	D5W	Physically compatible and ranitidine chemically stable by HPLC for 24 hr at 25 °C. Vancomycin not tested	1515	C
Sodium bicarbonate			LI			Physically incompatible	9	I
	AB	2.4 mEq[c]	LI	500 mg	D5W	Physically compatible for 24 hr	772	C
Verapamil HCl	KN	80 mg	LI	1 g	D5W, NS	Physically compatible for 24 hr	764	C

Additive Compatibility (Cont.)

Vancomycin HCl

Drug	*Mfr*	*Conc/L*	*Mfr*	*Conc/L*	*Test Soln*	*Remarks*	*Ref*	*C/I*
Vitamin B complex with C		1 vial	LI	1 g	D5W	Physically compatible	74	C

[a]*Refer to Appendix I for the composition of parenteral nutrition solutions. TPN indicates a 2-in-1 admixture.*
[b]*Tested in Dianeal with dextrose 2.5 and 4.25%.*
[c]*One vial of Neut added to a liter of admixture.*
[d]*Tested in methyl-methacrylate-butadiene-styrene plastic containers.*

Drugs in Syringe Compatibility

Vancomycin HCl

Drug (in syringe)	*Mfr*	*Amt*	*Mfr*	*Amt*	*Remarks*	*Ref*	*C/I*
Heparin sodium		2500 units/ 1 ml	LI	500 mg	Turbidity or precipitate forms within 5 min	1053	I

Y-Site Injection Compatibility (1:1 Mixture)

Vancomycin HCl

Drug	*Mfr*	*Conc*	*Mfr*	*Conc*	*Remarks*	*Ref*	*C/I*
Acyclovir sodium	BW	5 mg/ml[a]	LI	5 mg/ml[a]	Physically compatible for 4 hr at 25 °C	1157	C
Alatrofloxacin mesylate	PF	1.43 mg/ml[a]	AB	4 mg/ml[b]	Visually and microscopically compatible run through a Y-site over at least 60 min	2235	C
Albumin human		0.1 and 1%[b]		20 mg/ml[a]	Heavy turbidity forms immediately and precipitate develops subsequently	1701	I
Allopurinol sodium	BW	3 mg/ml[b]	LY	10 mg/ml[b]	Physically compatible with no change in measured turbidity or increase in particle content in 4 hr at 22 °C	1686	C
Amifostine	USB	10 mg/ml[a]	AB	10 mg/ml[a]	Physically compatible with no change in measured turbidity or increase in particle content in 4 hr at 23 °C	1845	C
Amiodarone HCl	LZ	4 mg/ml[c]	LI	5 mg/ml[c]	Physically compatible for 4 hr at room temperature	1444	C
Ampicillin sodium	SKB	250 mg/ml[d]	AB	20 mg/ml[a]	Transient precipitate forms followed by clear solution	2189	?
	SKB	1, 10, 50 mg/ml[b]	AB	20 mg/ml[a]	Physically compatible with no change in measured turbidity or increase in particle content in 4 hr at 23 °C	2189	C
	SKB	1[b], 10[b], 50[b], 250[d] mg/ml	AB	2 mg/ml[a]	Physically compatible with no change in measured turbidity or increase in particle content in 4 hr at 23 °C	2189	C
Ampicillin sodium–sulbactam sodium	PF	250 + 125 mg/ml[d]	AB	20 mg/ml[a]	Transient precipitate forms followed by clear solution	2189	?
	PF	1 + 0.5, 10 + 5, and 50 + 25 mg/ml[b]	AB	20 mg/ml[a]	Physically compatible with no change in measured turbidity or increase in particle content in 4 hr at 23 °C	2189	C
	PF	1 + 0.5[b], 10 + 5[b], and 50 + 25[b], and 250 + 125[d] mg/ml	AB	2 mg/ml[a]	Physically compatible with no change in measured turbidity or increase in particle content in 4 hr at 23 °C	2189	C

Y-Site Injection Compatibility (1:1 Mixture) (Cont.)

Drug	Mfr	Conc	Vancomycin HCl Mfr	Vancomycin HCl Conc	Remarks	Ref	C/I
Amphotericin B cholesteryl sulfate complex	SEQ	0.83 mg/ml[a]	AB	10 mg/ml[a]	Gross precipitate forms	2117	I
Amsacrine	NCI	1 mg/ml[a]	LI	10 mg/ml[a]	Physically compatible for 4 hr at room temperature under fluorescent light	1381	C
Atracurium besylate	BW	0.5 mg/ml[a]	ES	5 mg/ml[a]	Physically compatible for 24 hr at 28 °C	1337	C
Aztreonam	SQ	200 mg/ml[b]	LI	67 mg/ml[b]	White granular precipitate forms immediately in tubing when given sequentially	1364	I
	SQ	40 mg/ml[a]	AB	10 mg/ml[a]	Physically compatible with no subvisual haze or particle formation in 4 hr at 23 °C	1758	C
Cefazolin sodium	SKB	200 mg/ml[d]	AB	20 mg/ml[a]	Transient precipitate forms followed by clear solution	2189	?
	SKB	10 and 50 mg/ml[a]	AB	20 mg/ml[a]	Gross white precipitate forms immediately	2189	I
	SKB	1 mg/ml[a]	AB	20 mg/ml[a]	Physically compatible with no change in measured turbidity or increase in particle content in 4 hr at 23 °C	2189	C
	SKB	200 mg/ml[d]	AB	2 mg/ml[a]	Physically compatible with no change in measured turbidity or increase in particle content in 4 hr at 23 °C	2189	C
	SKB	50 mg/ml[a]	AB	2 mg/ml[a]	Subvisual measured haze forms immediately	2189	I
	SKB	1 and 10 mg/ml[a]	AB	2 mg/ml[a]	Physically compatible with no change in measured turbidity or increase in particle content in 4 hr at 23 °C	2189	C
Cefepime HCl	BMS	20 mg/ml[a]	AB	10 mg/ml[a]	Haze forms immediately and flocculent precipitate forms in 4 hr	1689	I
Cefotaxime sodium		100 mg/ml[d]		12.5, 25, 30, 50 mg/ml[d]	White precipitate forms immediately	1721	I
		100 mg/ml[d]		5 mg/ml[d]	No precipitate visually observed over 7 days at room temperature, but nonvisual incompatibility cannot be ruled out	1721	?
	HO	200 mg/ml[d]	AB	20 mg/ml[a]	Transient precipitate forms followed by clear solution	2189	?
	HO	50 mg/ml[a]	AB	20 mg/ml[a]	White cloudiness forms immediately	2189	I
	HO	1 and 10 mg/ml[a]	AB	20 mg/ml[a]	Physically compatible with no change in measured turbidity or increase in particle content in 4 hr at 23 °C	2189	C
	HO	1[a], 10[a], 50[a], 200[d] mg/ml	AB	2 mg/ml[a]	Physically compatible with no change in measured turbidity or increase in particle content in 4 hr at 23 °C	2189	C
Cefotetan sodium	ZEN	200 mg/ml[d]	AB	20 mg/ml[a]	Transient precipitate forms followed by clear solution. White precipitate forms in 4 hr	2189	I
	ZEN	10 and 50 mg/ml[a]	AB	20 mg/ml[a]	Gross white precipitate forms immediately	2189	I
	ZEN	1 mg/ml[a]	AB	20 mg/ml[a]	Subvisual measured haze forms immediately followed by white precipitate in 4 hr	2189	I
	ZEN	1[a], 10[a], 50[a], 200[d] mg/ml	AB	2 mg/ml[a]	Physically compatible with no change in measured turbidity or increase in particle content in 4 hr at 23 °C	2189	C

Y-Site Injection Compatibility (1:1 Mixture) (Cont.)

Vancomycin HCl

Drug	*Mfr*	*Conc*	*Mfr*	*Conc*	*Remarks*	*Ref*	*C/I*
Cefoxitin sodium	ME	180 mg/ml[d]	AB	20 mg/ml[a]	Transient precipitate forms followed by clear solution	2189	?
	ME	50 mg/ml[a]	AB	20 mg/ml[a]	Gross white precipitate forms immediately	2189	I
	ME	10 mg/ml[a]	AB	20 mg/ml[a]	Visible haze forms in 4 hr at 23 °C	2189	I
	ME	1 mg/ml[a]	AB	20 mg/ml[a]	Physically compatible with no change in measured turbidity or increase in particle content in 4 hr at 23 °C	2189	C
	ME	1[a], 10[a]. 50[a], 180[d] mg/ml	AB	2 mg/ml[a]	Physically compatible with no change in measured turbidity or increase in particle content in 4 hr at 23 °C	2189	C
Cefpirome sulfate	HO	50 mg/ml[e]	AB	5 mg/ml[e]	Visually and microscopically compatible with little or no cefpirome and vancomycin loss by HPLC in 8 hr at 23 °C	2044	C
Ceftazidime	GL[p]	25 and 60 mg/ml[a]	AB	3 mg/ml[a]	Physically compatible with no subvisual haze or particle formation in 4 hr at 23 °C	1563	C
	GL[p]	25 mg/ml[a]	AB	10 mg/ml[a]	Subvisual haze forms immediately	1563	I
	GL[p]	60 mg/ml[a]	AB	10 mg/ml[a]	Dense turbidity and white particles form immediately and become gross precipitate in 1 hr	1563	I
	SKB[p]	10[a], 50[a], 200[d] mg/ml	AB	20 mg/ml[a]	Gross white precipitate forms immediately	2189	I
	SKB[p]	1 mg/ml[a]	AB	20 mg/ml[a]	Physically compatible with no change in measured turbidity or increase in particle content in 4 hr at 23 °C	2189	C
	SKB[p]	1[a], 10[a], 50[a], 200[d] mg/ml	AB	2 mg/ml[a]	Physically compatible with no change in measured turbidity or increase in particle content in 4 hr at 23 °C	2189	C
Ceftizoxime sodium	FUJ	280 mg/ml[d]	AB	20 mg/ml[a]	Transient precipitate forms followed by clear solution	2189	?
	FUJ	1, 10, 50 mg/ml[a]	AB	20 mg/ml[a]	Physically compatible with no change in measured turbidity or increase in particle content in 4 hr at 23 °C	2189	C
	FUJ	1[a], 10[a], 50[a], 280[d] mg/ml	AB	2 mg/ml[a]	Physically compatible with no change in measured turbidity or increase in particle content in 4 hr at 23 °C	2189	C
Ceftriaxone sodium	RC	250 mg/ml[d]	AB	20 mg/ml[a]	Transient precipitate forms followed by clear solution	2189	?
	RC	10 and 50 mg/ml[a]	AB	20 mg/ml[a]	Gross white precipitate forms immediately	2189	I
	RC	1 mg/ml[a]	AB	20 mg/ml[a]	Subvisual measured haze forms immediately	2189	I
	RC	1[a], 10[a], 50[a], 250[d] mg/ml	AB	2 mg/ml[a]	Physically compatible with no change in measured turbidity or increase in particle content in 4 hr at 23 °C	2189	C
Cefuroxime sodium	GW	150 mg/ml[d]	AB	20 mg/ml[a]	Transient precipitate forms followed by a subvisual measured haze	2189	I
	GW	50 mg/ml[a]	AB	20 mg/ml[a]	Gross white precipitate forms immediately	2189	I
	GW	10 mg/ml[a]	AB	20 mg/ml[a]	Subvisual measured haze forms immediately	2189	I
	GW	1 mg/ml[a]	AB	20 mg/ml[a]	Physically compatible with no change in measured turbidity or increase in particle content in 4 hr at 23 °C	2189	C

Y-Site Injection Compatibility (1:1 Mixture) (Cont.)

Drug	Mfr	Conc	Mfr	Conc	Remarks	Ref	C/I
				Vancomycin HCl			
	GW	1[a], 10[a], 50[a], 150[d] mg/ml	AB	2 mg/ml[a]	Physically compatible with no change in measured turbidity or increase in particle content in 4 hr at 23 °C	2189	C
Cisatracurium besylate	GW	0.1, 2, 5 mg/ml[a]	AB	10 mg/ml[a]	Physically compatible with no change in measured turbidity or increase in particle content in 4 hr at 23 °C	2074	C
Clarithromycin	AB	4 mg/ml[a]	DB	10 mg/ml[a]	Visually compatible for 72 hr at both 30 and 17 °C	2174	C
Cyclophosphamide	MJ	20 mg/ml[a]	LI	5 mg/ml[a]	Physically compatible for 4 hr at 25 °C	1194	C
Diltiazem HCl	MMD	5 mg/ml	LI	5 and 50 mg/ml[b]	Visually compatible	1807	C
Docetaxel	RPR	0.9 mg/ml[a]	LI	10 mg/ml[a]	Physically compatible with no change in measured turbidity or increase in particle content in 4 hr at 23 °C	2224	C
Doxorubicin HCl liposome injection	SEQ	0.4 mg/ml[a]	AB	10 mg/ml[a]	Physically compatible with little or no change in measured turbidity and no increase in particle content in 4 hr at 23 °C	2087	C
Enalaprilat	MSD	0.05 mg/ml[b]	LE	5 mg/ml[a]	Physically compatible for 24 hr at room temperature under fluorescent light	1355	C
Esmolol HCl	DCC	10 mg/ml[a]	LE	5 mg/ml[a]	Physically compatible for 24 hr at 22 °C	1169	C
Etoposide phosphate	BR	5 mg/ml[a]	LI	10 mg/ml[a]	Physically compatible with no change in measured turbidity or increase in particle content in 4 hr at 23 °C	2218	C
Filgrastim	AMG	30 μg/ml[a]	AB	10 mg/ml[a]	Physically compatible with no change in measured turbidity or increase in particle content in 4 hr at 22 °C	1687	C
Fluconazole	RR	2 mg/ml	LY	20 mg/ml	Physically compatible for 24 hr at 25 °C	1407	C
Fludarabine phosphate	BX	1 mg/ml[a]	LI	10 mg/ml[a]	Physically compatible for 4 hr at room temperature under fluorescent light	1439	C
Foscarnet sodium	AST	24 mg/ml	LE	20 mg/ml	Immediate precipitation	1335	I
	AST	24 mg/ml	LE	15 mg/ml[c]	Physically compatible for 24 hr at 25 °C under fluorescent light by visual and microscopic examination	1393	C
	AST	24 mg/ml	LE	10 mg/ml[b]	Visually compatible for 24 hr at room temperature in test tubes. No precipitate found on filter	2063	C
Gatifloxacin	BMS	2 mg/ml[a]	LI	10 mg/ml[a]	Measured haze increases and microprecipitate forms immediately	2234	I
Gemcitabine HCl	LI	10 mg/ml[b]	LI	10 mg/ml[b]	Physically compatible with no change in measured turbidity or increase in particle content in 4 hr at 23 °C	2226	C
Granisetron HCl	SKB	0.05 mg/ml[a]	AB	10 mg/ml[a]	Physically compatible with no change in measured turbidity or increase in particle content in 4 hr at 23 °C	2000	C
Heparin sodium	TR	50 units/ml	LI	6.6 mg/ml[a]	Visually incompatible within 4 hr at 25 °C	1793	I
	ES	100 units/ml[c]	LE	10 mg/ml[b]	Precipitate forms	2063	I

Y-Site Injection Compatibility (1:1 Mixture) (Cont.)

			Vancomycin HCl				
Drug	*Mfr*	*Conc*	*Mfr*	*Conc*	*Remarks*	*Ref*	*C/I*
Hetastarch in lactated electrolyte injection (Hextend)	AB	6%	LI	10 mg/ml[a]	Physically compatible with no change in measured turbidity or increase in particle content in 4 hr at 23 °C	2339	C
Hydromorphone HCl	WY	0.2 mg/ml[a]	LI	5 mg/ml[a]	Physically compatible for at least 4 hr at 25 °C under fluorescent light	987	C
Idarubicin HCl	AD	1 mg/ml[b]	AD	4 mg/ml[a]	Color changes immediately	1525	I
Insulin, regular	LI	0.2 unit/ml[b]	LI	4 mg/ml[a]	Physically compatible for 2 hr at 25 °C	1395	C
Labetalol HCl	SC	1 mg/ml[a]	LE	5 mg/ml[a]	Physically compatible for 24 hr at 18 °C	1171	C
Levofloxacin	OMN	5 mg/ml[a]	LI	50 mg/ml	Visually compatible for 4 hr at 24 °C under fluorescent light	2233	C
Linezolid	PHU	2 mg/ml	FUJ	10 mg/ml[a]	Physically compatible with no change in measured turbidity or increase in particle content in 4 hr at 23 °C	2264	C
Lorazepam	WY	0.33 mg/ml[b]	LI	5 mg/ml	Visually compatible for 24 hr at 22 °C	1855	C
Magnesium sulfate	IX	16.7, 33.3, 66.7, 100 mg/ml[a]	LI	5 mg/ml[a]	Physically compatible for at least 4 hr at 32 °C	813	C
Melphalan HCl	BW	0.1 mg/ml[b]	LY	10 mg/ml[b]	Physically compatible with no change in measured turbidity or increase in particle content in 3 hr at 22 °C	1557	C
Meperidine HCl	WY	10 mg/ml[a]	LI	5 mg/ml[a]	Physically compatible for at least 4 hr at 25 °C under fluorescent light	987	C
Meropenem	ZEN	1 and 50 mg/ml[b]	LI	5 mg/ml[d]	Visually compatible for 4 hr at room temperature	1994	C
Methotrexate sodium	LE	[a,f]	AB	510 mg[g]	Physically compatible during 1-hr simultaneous infusion	1405	C
		30 mg/ml		5 mg/ml[a]	Visually compatible for 2 hr at room temperature. Dark yellow precipitate forms in 4 hr	1788	I
Midazolam HCl	RC	1 mg/ml[a]	LI	5 mg/ml[a]	Visually compatible for 24 hr at 23 °C	1847	C
	RC	5 mg/ml	LI	5 mg/ml	Visually compatible for 24 hr at 22 °C	1855	C
Morphine sulfate	WI	1 mg/ml[a]	LI	5 mg/ml[a]	Physically compatible for at least 4 hr at 25 °C under fluorescent light	987	C
Nafcillin sodium	BE	250 mg/ml[d]	AB	20 mg/ml[a]	Transient precipitate forms followed by a visibly hazy solution	2189	I
	BE	10 and 50 mg/ml[b]	AB	20 mg/ml[a]	Gross white precipitate forms immediately	2189	I
	BE	1 mg/ml[b]	AB	20 mg/ml[a]	Physically compatible with no change in measured turbidity or increase in particle content in 4 hr at 23 °C	2189	C
	BE	10[b], 50[b], 250[d] mg/ml	AB	2 mg/ml[a]	Subvisual measured haze forms immediately	2189	I
	BE	1 mg/ml[b]	AB	2 mg/ml[a]	Physically compatible with no change in measured turbidity or increase in particle content in 4 hr at 23 °C	2189	C
Omeprazole		4 mg/ml		10 mg/ml[a]	White precipitate forms within 5 min	2173	I
Ondansetron HCl	GL	1 mg/ml[b]	LI	10 mg/ml[a]	Physically compatible for 4 hr at 22 °C	1365	C

Y-Site Injection Compatibility (1:1 Mixture) (Cont.)

Vancomycin HCl

Drug	*Mfr*	*Conc*	*Mfr*	*Conc*	*Remarks*	*Ref*	*C/I*
Paclitaxel	NCI	1.2 mg/ml[a]		10 mg/ml[a]	Physically compatible with no change in measured turbidity in 4 hr at 22 °C	1528	C
Pancuronium bromide	ES	0.05 mg/ml[a]	ES	5 mg/ml[a]	Physically compatible for 24 hr at 28 °C	1337	C
Perphenazine	SC	0.02 mg/ml[a]	LI	5 mg/ml[a]	Physically compatible for 4 hr at 25 °C	1155	C
Piperacillin sodium	LE	200 mg/ml[d]	AB	20 mg/ml[a]	Transient precipitate forms followed by clear solution	2189	?
	LE	10 and 50 mg/ml[a]	AB	20 mg/ml[a]	Gross white precipitate forms immediately	2189	I
	LE	1 mg/ml[a]	AB	20 mg/ml[a]	Physically compatible with no change in measured turbidity or increase in particle content in 4 hr at 23 °C	2189	C
	LE	1[a], 10[a], 50[a], 200[d] mg/ml	AB	2 mg/ml[a]	Physically compatible with no change in measured turbidity or increase in particle content in 4 hr at 23 °C	2189	C
Piperacillin sodium–tazobactam sodium	LE	40 + 5 mg/ml[a]	AB	10 mg/ml[a]	White turbidity forms immediately and white precipitate forms in 4 hr	1688	I
	LE	200 + 25 mg/ml[d]	AB	20 mg/ml[a]	Transient precipitate forms followed by clear solution	2189	?
	LE	10 + 1.25 and 50 + 6.25 mg/ml[a]	AB	20 mg/ml[a]	Gross white precipitate forms immediately	2189	I
	LE	1 + 0.125 mg/ml[a]	AB	20 mg/ml[a]	Physically compatible with no change in measured turbidity or increase in particle content in 4 hr at 23 °C	2189	C
	LE	1 + 0.125[a], 10 + 1.25[a], 50 + 6.25[a], and 200 + 25[d] mg/ml	AB	2 mg/ml[a]	Physically compatible with no change in measured turbidity or increase in particle content in 4 hr at 23 °C	2189	C
Propofol	ZEN	10 mg/ml	AB	10 mg/ml[a]	Physically compatible for 1 hr at 23 °C with no increase in particle content	2066	C
	GNS	10 mg/ml		10 mg/ml[a]	Emulsion disruption within 1 to 4 hr at room temperature	2336	I
	ASZ	10 mg/ml		10 mg/ml[a]	Physically compatible for up to 30 days at room temperature	2336	C
Remifentanil HCl	GW	0.025 and 0.25 mg/ml[b]	AB	10 mg/ml[a]	Physically compatible with no change in measured turbidity or increase in particle content in 4 hr at 23 °C	2075	C
Sargramostim	IMM	10 μg/ml[b]	LI	10 mg/ml[b]	Physically compatible for 4 hr at 22 °C	1436	C
	IMM	15 μg/ml[b]	LI	20 mg/ml[c]	Visually compatible for 2 hr	1618	C
	IMM	6 μg/ml[b,h]	LI	20 mg/ml[c]	Haze forms within 15 min and increases due to vancomycin incompatibility with albumin human	1618; 1701	I
Sodium bicarbonate		1.4%		5 mg/ml[a]	Visually compatible for 4 hr at room temperature	1788	C
Tacrolimus	FUJ	1 mg/ml[b]	LI	5 mg/ml[a]	Visually compatible for 24 hr at 25 °C	1630	C

Y-Site Injection Compatibility (1:1 Mixture) (Cont.)

Vancomycin HCl

Drug	*Mfr*	*Conc*	*Mfr*	*Conc*	*Remarks*	*Ref*	*C/I*
Teniposide	BR	0.1 mg/ml[a]	AB	10 mg/ml[a]	Physically compatible with no subvisual haze or particle formation in 4 hr at 23 °C	1725	C
Theophylline	TR	4 mg/ml	LI	6.6 mg/ml[a]	Visually compatible for 6 hr at 25 °C	1793	C
Thiotepa	IMM[i]	1 mg/ml[a]	AB	10 mg/ml[a]	Physically compatible with no change in measured turbidity or increase in particle content in 4 hr at 23 °C	1861	C
Ticarcillin disodium	SKB	50[a] and 200[d] mg/ml	AB	20 mg/ml[a]	Transient precipitate forms followed by clear solution	2189	?
	SKB	1 and 10 mg/ml[a]	AB	20 mg/ml[a]	Gross white precipitate forms immediately	2189	I
	SKB	1[a], 10[a], 50[a], 200[d] mg/ml	AB	2 mg/ml[a]	Physically compatible with no change in measured turbidity or increase in particle content in 4 hr at 23 °C	2189	C
Ticarcillin disodium–clavulanate potassium	SKB	206.7 mg/ml[d]	AB	20 mg/ml[a]	Transient precipitate forms followed by clear solution	2189	?
	SKB	1.034, 10.335, and 51.675 mg/ml[a]	AB	20 mg/ml[a]	Gross white precipitate forms	2189	I
	SKB	31 mg/ml[b]		5 mg/ml[b]	White precipitate formed sporadically	2167	I
	SKB	1.034[a], 10.335[a], 51.675[a], and 206.7[d] mg/ml	AB	2 mg/ml[a]	Physically compatible with no change in measured turbidity or increase in particle content in 4 hr at 23 °C	2189	C
Tolazoline HCl		0.1 mg/ml[a]	LE	5 mg/ml[a]	Physically compatible for 24 hr at 22 °C	1363	C
TNA #218 to #226[j]			AB	10 mg/ml[a]	Visually compatible with no precipitate or emulsion damage apparent in 4 hr at 23 °C	2215	C
TPN #61[j]		[k]	LI	50 mg/1 ml[l]	Physically compatible	1012	C
		[m]	LI	300 mg/6 ml[l]	Physically compatible	1012	C
TPN #91[j]		[n]	LI	30 mg[o]	Physically compatible	1170	C
TPN #189[j]			DB	10 mg/ml[b]	Visually compatible for 24 hr at 22 °C	1767	C
TPN #212 to #215[j]			AB	10 mg/ml[a]	Physically compatible with no change in measured turbidity or increase in particle content in 4 hr at 23 °C	2109	C
Vecuronium bromide	OR	0.1 mg/ml[a]	ES	5 mg/ml[a]	Physically compatible for 24 hr at 28 °C	1337	C
Vinorelbine tartrate	BW	1 mg/ml[b]	LY	10 mg/ml[b]	Physically compatible with no change in measured turbidity or increase in particle content in 4 hr at 22 °C	1558	C
Warfarin sodium	DU	2 mg/ml[d]	LI	4 mg/ml[a]	Haze forms immediately	2010	I
	DU	0.1 mg/ml[c]	AB	10 mg/ml[c]	Physically compatible with no change in measured turbidity or increase in particle content in 24 hr at 23 °C	2011	C
	DU	2 mg/ml[d]	AB	10 mg/ml[c]	Heavy white turbidity forms immediately	2011	I
	DME	2 mg/ml[d]	LI	4 mg/ml[a]	Haze forms immediately	2078	I

Y-Site Injection Compatibility (1:1 Mixture) (Cont.)

Vancomycin HCl

Drug	Mfr	Conc	Mfr	Conc	Remarks	Ref	C/I
Zidovudine	BW	4 mg/ml[a]	LI	15 mg/ml[a]	Physically compatible for 4 hr at 25 °C under fluorescent light by visual and microscopic examination	1193	C

[a]*Tested in dextrose 5% in water.*
[b]*Tested in sodium chloride 0.9%.*
[c]*Tested in both dextrose 5% in water and sodium chloride 0.9%.*
[d]*Tested in sterile water for injection.*
[e]*Tested in dextrose 5% in water, Ringer's injection, lactated, sodium chloride 0.45%, and sodium chloride 0.9%.*
[f]*Concentration unspecified.*
[g]*Infused over one hour simultaneously with methotrexate.*
[h]*Tested with 0.1% albumin human added.*
[i]*Lyophilized formulation tested.*
[j]*Refer to Appendix I for the composition of parenteral nutrition solutions. TNA indicates a 3-in-1 admixture, and TPN indicates a 2-in-1 admixture.*
[k]*Run at 21 ml/hr.*
[l]*Given over 30 minutes by syringe pump.*
[m]*Run at 94 ml/hr.*
[n]*Run at 10 ml/hr.*
[o]*Given over one hour by syringe pump.*
[p]*Sodium carbonate–containing formulation tested.*

Additional Compatibility Information

Infusion Solutions — Dextrose 5% in water and sodium chloride 0.9% are recommended as diluents for the intravenous infusion of vancomycin HCl. The manufacturer indicates that vancomycin HCl, at a concentration of no more than 5 mg/ml, is stable for 14 days under refrigeration in either of these solutions. (2)

Vancomycin HCl 5 mg/ml is stated to be stable for 96 hours under refrigeration in the following solutions (2):

Acetated Ringer's injection
Dextrose 5% in Ringer's injection, lactated
Dextrose 5% in sodium chloride 0.9%
Isolyte E
Normosol M in dextrose 5%
Ringer's injection, lactated

Peritoneal Dialysis Solutions — The activity of vancomycin 15 mg/L was evaluated in peritoneal dialysis fluids containing dextrose 1.5 or 4.25% (Dianeal 137, Travenol). Storage at 25 °C resulted in virtually no loss of antimicrobial activity in 24 hours. (738)

Vancomycin HCl with aztreonam admixed in Dianeal 137 with dextrose 4.25% is stated to be stable for 24 hours at room temperature. (2)

Vancomycin HCl (Lilly) 10 and 50 mg/L in peritoneal dialysis concentrate with dextrose 50% (McGaw) retained 93 to 100% of its initial activity (by microbiological assay) after 24 hours of storage at room temperature. (1044)

The stability of vancomycin HCl (Lilly) 20 mg/L in peritoneal dialysis solutions (Dianeal 137 and PD2) with heparin sodium 500 units/L was evaluated by microbiological assay. Approximately 95 ± 12% activity remained after 24 hours at 25 °C. (1228)

Drake et al. evaluated the retention of antimicrobial activity, using a disc diffusion bioassay, of vancomycin HCl (Lilly) 1 g/L alone and with each of the aminoglycosides gentamicin sulfate (SoloPak) 120 mg/L and tobramycin sulfate (Lilly) 120 mg/L in Dianeal PD-2 (Travenol) with dextrose 1.5%. Little or no loss of any antibiotic occurred in eight hours at 37 °C. Vancomycin HCl alone retained activity for at least 48 hours at 4 and 25 °C. In combination with gentamicin sulfate and tobramycin sulfate, antimicrobial activity of both vancomycin and the aminoglycosides was retained for up to 48 hours. However, the authors recommended refrigeration at 4 °C for storage periods greater than 24 hours. (1414)

The stability of vancomycin HCl (Lilly) 25 mg/L in Dianeal 137 (Baxter) with dextrose 1.36 and 3.86%, while protected from direct sunlight, was evaluated by HPLC and enzyme immunoassay. At both dextrose concentrations, less than 4% vancomycin HCl was lost in 42 days at 4 °C. At 20 °C, a 5% or less loss occurred in 28 days. At 37 °C, a 10% loss occurred in six to seven days. (1654)

Vancomycin HCl (Lilly) 1 mg/ml admixed with ceftazidime (sodium carbonate–containing formulation) (Lilly) 0.5 mg/ml in Dianeal PD-2 (Baxter) with 1.5% and also 4.25% dextrose were evaluated for compatibility and stability. Samples were stored under fluorescent light at 4 and 24 °C for 24 hours and at 37 °C for 12 hours. No precipitation or other change was observed by visual inspection in any sample. HPLC analysis found no loss of either drug in the samples stored at 4 °C and no loss of vancomycin HCl and about 4 to 5% ceftazidime loss in the samples stored at 24 °C in 24 hours. Vancomycin HCl losses of 3% or less and ceftazidime loss of about 6% were found in the samples stored at 37 °C for 12 hours. No difference in stability was found between samples at either dextrose concentration. (2217)

Vancomycin HCl (Lederle) 0.05 mg/ml in Dianeal PD-2 with dextrose 1.5% with or without heparin sodium 1 unit/ml in PVC bags was chemically stable by HPLC analysis for up to six days at 4 °C (about 3 to 5% loss) and 25 °C (up to 7% loss) and five days at body temperature of 37 °C. (866)

The addition of ceftazidime (sodium carbonate formulation) (Glaxo) 0.1 mg/ml to this peritoneal dialysis solution demonstrated a somewhat reduced stability with the ceftazidime being the defining component. The ceftazidime was chemically stable by HPLC analysis for up to six days at 4 °C (about 3% loss), three days at 25 °C (about 9 to 10% loss), and 12 hours at body temperature of 37 °C with the vancomycin exhibiting less loss throughout. (866)

pH and Concentration Dependency — The concentration dependency of compatibility or incompatibility of vancomycin HCl mixed with or administered simultaneously with a number of penicillins and cephalosporins has been demonstrated. (2189) See Y-Site Injection Compatibility table above. Vancomycin HCl has a low pH and is variably compatible with drugs having neutral to mildly alkaline pH, including cephalosporins and penicillins. The compatibility may depend on a number of factors including concentration of each drug, dilution vehicle, actual pH of solutions, and completeness of mixing during administration. Combinations that are compatible when well mixed may result in precipitation if only partially mixed, presumably due to regionally different concentrations and pH values. If attempting to administer vancomycin HCl with another drug product, care should be taken to ensure that the specific combination and concentrations are compatible under the exact administration conditions to be used. An inline filter should be used as a final safety measure. (2189)

Ceftazidime — A precipitate formed instantaneously when ceftazidime 2 g/50 ml in sterile water for injection was added to a burette previously used to administer vancomycin HCl 1 g/100 ml in dextrose 5% in water. The authors suggested that vancomycin may have precipitated because of the alkaline pH due to the sodium carbonate in the ceftazidime formulation. (873) However, the manufacturer of Ceptaz also notes precipitation with vancomycin HCl, even though no sodium carbonate is present in the Ceptaz formulation. (2)

The concentration dependency of precipitation for these drugs has been demonstrated. (2189) For more information, see pH and Concentration Dependency and also the Y-Site Injection Compatibility table above.

Chloramphenicol and Penicillin G — Chloramphenicol sodium succinate and high concentrations of penicillin G in combination with vancomycin HCl may result in the formation of a precipitate. Five to 10 million units of penicillin G added to vancomycin HCl, especially in dextrose solutions, cause precipitation. (143)

Heparin — Heparin sodium approximately 5000 units/L has been reported to be conditionally compatible with vancomycin HCl 2 g/L. A satisfactory solution is obtained if the infusion solution used is sodium chloride 0.9%. However, if dextrose 5% in water is used, a precipitate may form. (143)

Vancomycin HCl (Lilly) 15 mg/L to 5.3 g/L in Dianeal with dextrose 2.5 or 4.25% was physically compatible with heparin sodium (Organon) 500 to 14,300 units/L for 24 hours at 25 °C under fluorescent light. However, a white precipitate formed immediately in combinations of heparin sodium with vancomycin HCl 6.9 to 14.3 g/L. (1322)

Vancomycin HCl (Lilly) 25 μg/ml and heparin sodium (Elkins-Sinn) 100 units/ml in 0.9% sodium chloride injection as a catheter flush solution was evaluated for stability when stored at 4 °C for 14 days. The flush solution was visually clear, and the vancomycin activity (by bioassay and immunoassay) and heparin activity (by colorimetric assay) were retained throughout the storage period. However, an additional 24 hours at 37 °C to simulate use conditions resulted in losses of both agents ranging from 20 to 37%. (1933)

Vancomycin HCl (Lilly) 25 μg/ml and preservative-free heparin sodium (Elkins-Sinn) 100 units/ml in 0.9% sodium chloride in 2-ml glass vials for use as a central catheter flush solution were evaluated for compatibility and stability at 4 and 28 °C. Visual inspection found no evidence of color change or particulate formation throughout the study. Heparin activity assessed by serial activated, partial thromboplastin times remained unchanged for 100 days. EMIT immunoassay of vancomycin activity found that acceptable antibiotic levels were maintained for 30 days at 28 °C and for 63 days at 4 °C. However, unacceptable losses occurred after those times. The activity of both drugs was unaffected by the presence of the other when compared to the activity of single drug controls. (2279)

Ticarcillin — Sequential administration of ticarcillin disodium 4.25 g/50 ml and then vancomycin HCl 500 mg/50 ml in dextrose 5% in sodium chloride 0.3% through a calibrated chamber set (Buretrol) has resulted in a white precipitate. The precipitate did not appear during the initial infusion but formed after repeated administration through the same set. The sequence of administration (ticarcillin first, followed by vancomycin), drug concentrations, and repetitive administration all appear to affect the appearance of the precipitate. (972)

The concentration dependency of precipitation for these drugs has been demonstrated. (2189) For more information, see pH and Concentration Dependency and also the Y-Site Injection Compatibility table above.

Ticarcillin Disodium–Clavulanate Potassium — Vancomycin HCl when admixed with ticarcillin disodium–clavulanate potassium has been reported to exhibit occasional precipitate formation. This observation from practice was made with a combination of vancomycin HCl 5 mg/ml and ticarcillin disodium–clavulanate potassium 30 + 1 mg/ml and also with combinations at variable but unrecorded concentrations. The occurrence of precipitate formation was characterized as sporadic and unpredictable. (2167)

The concentration dependency of precipitation for these drugs has been demonstrated. (2189) For more information, see pH and Concentration Dependency and also the Y-Site Injection Compatibility table above.

Concentrated Drug Solutions — The following incompatibility determinations were performed with concentrated solutions. The drugs in dry form were reconstituted according to manufacturers' recommendations. One milliliter of vancomycin HCl (Lilly) was added to 5 ml of sterile distilled water along with 1 ml of each of the following drugs. Particulate matter was noted within two hours (28):

Aminophylline
Chloramphenicol sodium succinate (Parke-Davis)
Dexamethasone sodium phosphate (MSD)
Heparin sodium
Hydrocortisone sodium succinate (Upjohn)
Penicillin G potassium
Phenytoin sodium (Parke-Davis)
Vitamin B complex with C (Lederle)

VASOPRESSIN
AHFS 68:28

Products — Vasopressin is available in 0.5-, 1-, and 10-ml vials. Each milliliter of solution contains vasopressin 20 pressor units, sodium chloride 0.9%, chlorobutanol 0.5%, in water for injection. Acetic acid may have been used to adjust pH during manufacture. (1-8/98)

pH — From 2.5 to 4.5. (1-8/98; 4)

Osmolality — Vasopressin 20 units/ml has an osmolality of 30 mOsm/kg. (1689)

Administration — Vasopressin may be given subcutaneously or intramuscularly. (1-8/98; 4) or by continuous intravenous or intra-arterial infusion using a controlled infusion device. For infusion, the drug is usually diluted to a concentration of 0.1 to 1 unit/ml with sodium chloride 0.9% or dextrose 5% in water. (4)

Stability — Vasopressin injection is a clear, colorless or practically colorless solution. Intact containers should be stored at controlled room temperature and protected from freezing. (1-8/98; 4)

Compatibility Information

Additive Compatibility

Drug	Mfr	Conc/L	Vasopressin Mfr	Vasopressin Conc/L	Test Soln	Remarks	Ref	C/I
Verapamil HCl	KN	80 mg	PD	40 units	D5W, NS	Physically compatible for 24 hr	764	C

VECURONIUM BROMIDE
AHFS 12:20

Products — Vecuronium bromide is available in 10-mg vials as a lyophilized cake, both with and without accompanying bacteriostatic water for injection with benzyl alcohol 0.9% for use as a diluent. It also is available in 20-mg vials without a diluent. The vials contain (2):

Component	10 mg	20 mg
Vecuronium bromide	10 mg	20 mg
Citric acid anhydrous	20.75 mg	41.5 mg
Mannitol	97 mg	194 mg
Sodium phosphate dibasic anhydrous	16.25 mg	32.5 mg

Sodium hydroxide and/or phosphoric acid also may be present to adjust the pH. (2)

The 10- and 20-mg vials should be reconstituted with 10 and 20 ml, respectively, of the accompanying bacteriostatic water for injection or sterile water for injection to yield a 1-mg/ml solution. (2; 4) The bacteriostatic water for injection, which contains benzyl alcohol 0.9%, is not for use in newborns. (2)

pH — Approximately 4. (2; 4)

Osmolality — The osmolality of vecuronium bromide 4 mg/ml was determined to be 292 mOsm/kg. (1233)

Trade Name(s) — Norcuron.

Administration — Vecuronium bromide may be administered by rapid intravenous injection or by intravenous infusion using an infusion control device after dilution to a concentration of 0.1 to 0.2 mg/ml in a compatible infusion solution. It should not be administered intramuscularly. (4)

Stability — Vecuronium bromide should be stored at room temperature and protected from light. The reconstituted solution is clear and colorless. When reconstituted with bacteriostatic water for injection, the solution may be used for up to five days when stored at room temperature or under refrigeration. When reconstituted with sterile water for injection, the vial is a single-use container and should be stored under refrigeration and used within 24 hours. (2)

pH Effects — Vecuronium bromide is unstable in the presence of bases and should not be combined with alkaline drugs or simultaneously administered through the same line as an alkaline solution. (4)

Syringes — Vecuronium solutions reconstituted with sterile water for injection are stable for 48 hours at room temperature or under refrigeration, but the manufacturer recommends that they be used within 24 hours. (4)

Compatibility Information

Y-Site Injection Compatibility (1:1 Mixture)

Vecuronium bromide

Drug	Mfr	Conc	Mfr	Conc	Remarks	Ref	C/I
Aminophylline	AB	1 mg/ml[a]	OR	0.1 mg/ml[a]	Physically compatible for 24 hr at 28 °C	1337	C
Amphotericin B cholesteryl sulfate complex	SEQ	0.83 mg/ml[a]	MAR	1 mg/ml[a]	Gross precipitate forms	2117	I
Cefazolin sodium	LY	10 mg/ml[a]	OR	0.1 mg/ml[a]	Physically compatible for 24 hr at 28 °C	1337	C
Cefuroxime sodium	GL	7.5 mg/ml[a]	OR	0.1 mg/ml[a]	Physically compatible for 24 hr at 28 °C	1337	C
Cimetidine HCl	SKF	6 mg/ml[a]	OR	0.1 mg/ml[a]	Physically compatible for 24 hr at 28 °C	1337	C
Clarithromycin	AB	4 mg/ml[a]	ORG	2 mg/ml[a]	Visually compatible for 72 hr at both 30 and 17 °C	2174	C
Diazepam	ES	5 mg/ml[a]	OR	0.1 mg/ml[a]	Cloudy solution forms immediately	1337	I
Diltiazem HCl	MMD	1 mg/ml[a]	OR	1 mg/ml	Visually compatible for 4 hr at 27 °C	2062	C
Dobutamine HCl	LI	1 mg/ml[a]	OR	0.1 mg/ml[a]	Physically compatible for 24 hr at 28 °C	1337	C
	LI	4 mg/ml[a]	OR	1 mg/ml	Visually compatible for 4 hr at 27 °C	2062	C
Dopamine HCl	SO	1.6 mg/ml[a]	OR	0.1 mg/ml[a]	Physically compatible for 24 hr at 28 °C	1337	C
	AB	3.2 mg/ml[a]	OR	1 mg/ml	Visually compatible for 4 hr at 27 °C	2062	C
Epinephrine HCl	AB	4 μg/ml[a]	OR	0.1 mg/ml[a]	Physically compatible for 24 hr at 28 °C	1337	C
	AB	0.02 mg/ml[a]	OR	1 mg/ml	Visually compatible for 4 hr at 27 °C	2062	C
Esmolol HCl	DCC	10 mg/ml[a]	OR	0.1 mg/ml[a]	Physically compatible for 24 hr at 28 °C	1337	C
Etomidate	AB	2 mg/ml	OR	1 mg/ml	Slight turbidity and white particles form	1801	I
Fentanyl citrate	ES	10 μg/ml[a]	OR	0.1 mg/ml[a]	Physically compatible for 24 hr at 28 °C	1337	C
	ES	0.05 mg/ml	OR	1 mg/ml	Visually compatible for 4 hr at 27 °C	2062	C
Fluconazole	RR	2 mg/ml	OR	1 mg/ml[a]	Visually compatible for 24 hr at 28 °C under fluorescent light	1760	C
Furosemide	AMR	10 mg/ml	OR	1 mg/ml	Precipitate forms immediately	2062	I
Gatifloxacin	BMS	2 mg/ml[a]	MAR	1 mg/ml	Physically compatible with no change in measured haze or increase in particle content in 4 hr at 23 °C	2234	C
Gentamicin sulfate	ES	2 mg/ml[a]	OR	0.1 mg/ml[a]	Physically compatible for 24 hr at 28 °C	1337	C
Heparin sodium	SO	40 units/ml[a]	OR	0.1 mg/ml[a]	Physically compatible for 24 hr at 28 °C	1337	C
	ES	100 units/ml[a]	OR	1 mg/ml	Visually compatible for 4 hr at 27 °C	2062	C
Hetastarch in lactated electrolyte injection (Hextend)	AB	6%	OR	0.2 mg/ml[a]	Physically compatible with no change in measured turbidity or increase in particle content in 4 hr at 23 °C	2339	C
Hydrocortisone sodium succinate	AB	1 mg/ml[a]	OR	0.1 mg/ml[a]	Physically compatible for 24 hr at 28 °C	1337	C
Hydromorphone HCl	KN	1 mg/ml	OR	1 mg/ml	Visually compatible for 4 hr at 27 °C	2062	C
Isoproterenol HCl	ES	4 μg/ml[a]	OR	0.1 mg/ml[a]	Physically compatible for 24 hr at 28 °C	1337	C
Labetalol HCl	AH	2 mg/ml[a]	OR	1 mg/ml	Visually compatible for 4 hr at 27 °C	2062	C
Linezolid	PHU	2 mg/ml	OR	1 mg/ml	Physically compatible with no change in measured turbidity or increase in particle content in 4 hr at 23 °C	2264	C
Lorazepam	WY	0.5 mg/ml[a]	OR	0.1 mg/ml[a]	Physically compatible for 24 hr at 28 °C	1337	C
	WY	0.33 mg/ml[a]	OR	4 mg/ml	Visually compatible for 24 hr at 22 °C	1855	C
	WY	0.5 mg/ml[a]	OR	1 mg/ml	Visually compatible for 4 hr at 27 °C	2062	C

Y-Site Injection Compatibility (1:1 Mixture) (Cont.)

			Vecuronium bromide				
Drug	*Mfr*	*Conc*	*Mfr*	*Conc*	*Remarks*	*Ref*	*C/I*
Midazolam HCl	RC	0.05 mg/ml[a]	OR	0.1 mg/ml[a]	Physically compatible for 24 hr at 28 °C	1337	C
	RC	5 mg/ml	OR	4 mg/ml	Visually compatible for 24 hr at 22 °C	1855	C
	RC	2 mg/ml[a]	OR	1 mg/ml	Visually compatible for 4 hr at 27 °C	2062	C
Milrinone lactate	SW	0.2 mg/ml[a]	OR	1 mg/ml	Visually compatible for 4 hr at 27 °C	2062	C
	SW	0.4 mg/ml[a]	OR	1 mg/ml	Visually compatible with little or no loss of either drug by HPLC in 4 hr at 23 °C	2214	C
Morphine sulfate	WY	1 mg/ml[a]	OR	0.1 mg/ml[a]	Physically compatible for 24 hr at 28 °C	1337	C
	SCN	2 mg/ml[a]	OR	1 mg/ml	Visually compatible for 4 hr at 27 °C	2062	C
Nicardipine HCl	WY	1 mg/ml[a]	OR	1 mg/ml	Visually compatible for 4 hr at 27 °C	2062	C
Nitroglycerin	SO	0.4 mg/ml[a]	OR	0.1 mg/ml[a]	Physically compatible for 24 hr at 28 °C	1337	C
	AB	0.4 mg/ml[a]	OR	1 mg/ml	Visually compatible for 4 hr at 27 °C	2062	C
Norepinephrine bitartrate	AB	0.128 mg/ml[a]	OR	1 mg/ml	Visually compatible for 4 hr at 27 °C	2062	C
Propofol	ZEN	10 mg/ml	OR	1 mg/ml	Physically compatible for 1 hr at 23 °C with no increase in particle content	2066	C
Ranitidine HCl	GL	0.5 mg/ml[a]	OR	0.1 mg/ml[a]	Physically compatible for 24 hr at 28 °C	1337	C
	GL	1 mg/ml[a]	OR	1 mg/ml	Visually compatible for 4 hr at 27 °C	2062	C
Sodium nitroprusside	ES	0.2 mg/ml[a]	OR	0.1 mg/ml[a]	Physically compatible for 24 hr at 28 °C	1337	C
Thiopental sodium	AB	25 mg/ml	OR	1 mg/ml	White particles form immediately	1801	I
	AB	25 mg/ml[d]	OR	1 mg/ml	Precipitate forms immediately	2062	I
TPN #189[c]			OR	2 mg/ml[b]	Visually compatible for 24 hr at 22 °C	1767	C
Trimethoprim–sulfamethoxazole	ES	0.64 + 3.2 mg/ml[a]	OR	0.1 mg/ml[a]	Physically compatible for 24 hr at 28 °C	1337	C
Vancomycin HCl	ES	5 mg/ml[a]	OR	0.1 mg/ml[a]	Physically compatible for 24 hr at 28 °C	1337	C

[a]*Tested in dextrose 5% in water.*
[b]*Tested in sodium chloride 0.9%.*
[c]*Refer to Appendix I for the composition of parenteral nutrition solutions. TPN indicates a 2-in-1 admixture.*
[d]*Tested in sterile water for injection.*

Additional Compatibility Information

Infusion Solutions — Vecuronium bromide is physically compatible and chemically stable for at least 24 hours in the following solutions (2; 4):

Dextrose 5% in sodium chloride 0.9%
Dextrose 5% in water
Ringer's injection, lactated
Sodium chloride 0.9%

VERAPAMIL HCL
AHFS 24:04

Products — Verapamil HCl is available in single-dose containers including 2-ml ampuls, vials, and syringes and in 4-ml vials and syringes. Each milliliter contains verapamil HCl 2.5 mg with sodium chloride 8.5 mg in water for injection. Hydrochloric acid may have been used to adjust pH during manufacture. (1-11/98)

pH — From 4 to 6.5. Target pH is 4.9. (1-11/98)

Osmolality — The osmolality of verapamil HCl 2.5 mg/ml was determined to be 290 mOsm/kg. (1233)

Trade Name(s) — Isoptin I.V.

Administration — Verapamil HCl is administered slowly intravenously. Direct intravenous injection should be performed over at least two minutes and at least three minutes in older patients. (1-11/98; 4) Intravenous infusion has also been performed. (4)

Stability — Verapamil HCl should be stored at controlled room temperature and protected from light. (1-11/98) Freezing should be avoided. (4) Infusion solution stability studies indicate that verapamil HCl does not adsorb to glass, PVC, or polyolefin containers. (548) It is physically compatible in solution over a pH range of 3 to 6 but may precipitate in solutions having a pH greater than 6 (1-11/98; 4) or 7. (1384)

Compatibility Information

Solution Compatibility

Verapamil HCl

Solution	*Mfr*	*Mfr*	*Conc/L*	*Remarks*	*Ref*	*C/I*
Dextran 40 10% in sodium chloride 0.9%	TR	KN	80 mg	Physically compatible for 24 hr	764	C
Dextran 75 6% in sodium chloride 0.9%	TR	KN	80 mg	Physically compatible for 24 hr	764	C
Dextrose 5% in Ringer's injection	MG	KN	40 mg	Physically compatible and chemically stable for 48 hr at 25 °C protected from light	548	C
Dextrose 5% in Ringer's injection, lactated	MG	KN	40 mg	Physically compatible and chemically stable for 24 hr at 25 °C protected from light	548	C
Dextrose 5% in sodium chloride 0.45%	MG	KN	40 mg	Physically compatible and chemically stable for 24 hr at 25 °C protected from light	548	C
Dextrose 5% in sodium chloride 0.9%	MG	KN	40 mg	Physically compatible and chemically stable for 24 hr at 25 °C protected from light	548	C
Dextrose 5% in water	CU	KN	40 mg	Physically compatible and chemically stable for 48 hr at 25 °C protected from light	548	C
	MG[a]	KN	40 mg	Physically compatible and chemically stable for 24 hr at 25 °C protected from light	548	C
	TR[b]	KN	40 mg	Physically compatible and chemically stable for 24 hr at 25 °C protected from light	548	C
	TR[b]	KN	160 mg	Physically compatible with no drug loss in 7 days at 24 °C	811	C
	AB	KN	100 and 400 mg	Physically compatible with no drug loss in 24 hr at 24 °C under fluorescent light	1198	C
Ringer's injection	MG	KN	40 mg	Physically compatible and chemically stable for 24 hr at 25 °C protected from light	548	C
Ringer's injection, lactated	MG	KN	40 mg	Physically compatible and chemically stable for 24 hr at 25 °C protected from light	548	C
Sodium chloride 0.45%	MG	KN	40 mg	Physically compatible and chemically stable for 24 hr at 25 °C protected from light	548	C
		LY	1.25 and 2 g	Physically compatible with no drug loss in 4 hr at 22 °C	1419	C
Sodium chloride 0.9%	CU	KN	40 mg	Physically compatible and chemically stable for 48 hr at 25 °C protected from light	548	C
	MG[a]	KN	40 mg	Physically compatible and chemically stable for 24 hr at 25 °C protected from light	548	C
	TR[b]	KN	40 mg	Physically compatible and chemically stable for 24 hr at 25 °C protected from light	548	C

Solution Compatibility (Cont.)

Verapamil HCl

Solution	Mfr	Mfr	Conc/L	Remarks	Ref	C/I
	TR[b]	KN	160 mg	Physically compatible with little or no drug loss in 7 days at 24 °C	811	C
Sodium lactate ⅙ M	MG	KN	40 mg	Physically compatible and chemically stable for 48 hr at 25 °C protected from light	548	C

[a]*Tested in polyolefin containers.*
[b]*Tested in PVC containers.*

Additive Compatibility

Verapamil HCl

Drug	Mfr	Conc/L	Mfr	Conc/L	Test Soln	Remarks	Ref	C/I
Albumin human	ARC	25 g	KN	80 mg	D5W, NS	Cloudiness develops within 8 hr	764	I
Amikacin sulfate	BR	2 g	KN	80 mg	D5W, NS	Physically compatible for 24 hr	764	C
Aminophylline	SE	1 g	KN	80 mg	D5W, NS	Transient precipitate clears rapidly. Solution physically compatible for 48 hr	739	C
	SE	1 g	KN	400 mg	D5W	Visible turbidity forms immediately. Filtration removes all verapamil	1198	I
	SE	1 g	KN	100 mg	D5W	Visually clear, but precipitate found by microscopic examination. Filtration removes all verapamil	1198	I
Amiodarone HCl	LZ	1.8 g	KN	50 mg	D5W, NS[a]	Physically compatible with 8% or less amiodarone loss in 24 hr at 24 °C under fluorescent light	1031	C
Amphotericin B	SQ	100 mg	KN	80 mg	D5W	Physically incompatible after 8 hr	764	I
	SQ	100 mg	KN	80 mg	NS	Physically incompatible immediately	764	I
Ampicillin sodium	BR	4 g	KN	80 mg	D5W, NS	Physically compatible for 24 hr	764	C
	WY	40 g	SE	[b]	D5W, NS	Cloudy solution clears with agitation	1166	?
Ascorbic acid	LI	1 g	KN	80 mg	D5W, NS	Physically compatible for 24 hr	764	C
Atropine sulfate	IX	0.8 mg	KN	80 mg	D5W, NS	Physically compatible for 24 hr	764	C
Bretylium tosylate	ACC	2 g	KN	80 mg	D5W, NS	Physically compatible for 48 hr	739	C
Calcium chloride	ES	2 g	KN	80 mg	D5W, NS	Physically compatible for 24 hr	764	C
Calcium gluconate	IX	2 g	KN	80 mg	D5W, NS	Physically compatible for 48 hr	739	C
Cefamandole nafate	LI	4 g	KN	80 mg	D5W, NS	Physically compatible for 24 hr	764	C
Cefazolin sodium	SKF	2 g	KN	80 mg	D5W, NS	Physically compatible for 24 hr	764	C
Cefotaxime sodium	HO	4 g	KN	80 mg	D5W, NS	Physically compatible for 24 hr	764	C
Cefoxitin sodium	MSD	4 g	KN	80 mg	D5W, NS	Physically compatible for 24 hr	764	C
Chloramphenicol sodium succinate	PD	2 g	KN	80 mg	D5W, NS	Physically compatible for 24 hr	764	C
Cimetidine HCl	SKF	2.4 g	KN	80 mg	D5W, NS	Physically compatible for 24 hr	764	C
Clindamycin phosphate	UP	1.2 g	KN	80 mg	D5W, NS	Physically compatible for 24 hr	764	C
Dexamethasone sodium phosphate	MSD	40 mg	KN	80 mg	D5W, NS	Physically compatible for 24 hr	764	C
Diazepam	RC	20 mg	KN	80 mg	D5W, NS	Physically compatible for 24 hr	764	C
Digoxin	BW	2 mg	KN	80 mg	D5W, NS	Physically compatible for 48 hr	739	C

Additive Compatibility (Cont.)

Verapamil HCl

Drug	*Mfr*	*Conc/L*	*Mfr*	*Conc/L*	*Test Soln*	*Remarks*	*Ref*	*C/I*
Dobutamine HCl	LI	500 mg	KN	80 mg	D5W, NS	Slight pink color develops after 24 hr because of dobutamine oxidation	764	I
	LI	250 mg	KN	160 mg	D5W	No decomposition of either drug in 48 hr at 24 °C or 7 days at 5 °C. Transient light pink color noted	811	C
	LI	250 mg	KN	160 mg	NS	No verapamil decomposition and 3% dobutamine loss in 48 hr at 24 °C. Initially colorless solution becomes pink with time. At 5 °C, no loss of either drug in 7 days	811	C
	LI	1 g	KN	1.25 g	D5W, NS	Physically compatible for 24 hr at 21 °C	812	C
Dopamine HCl	ES	400 mg	KN	80 mg	D5W, NS	Physically compatible for 24 hr	764	C
Epinephrine HCl	PD	2 mg	KN	80 mg	D5W, NS	Physically compatible for 24 hr	764	C
Erythromycin lactobionate	AB	2 g	KN	80 mg	D5W, NS	Physically compatible for 24 hr	764	C
Floxacillin sodium	BE	20 g	AB	500 mg	NS	Haze and precipitate form in 24 hr at 30 °C. No change at 15 °C	1479	I
Furosemide	HO	200 mg	KN	80 mg	D5W, NS	Physically compatible for 24 hr	764	C
	HO	1 g	AB	500 mg	NS	Slight precipitate forms but dissipates	1479	?
Gentamicin sulfate	SC	160 mg	KN	80 mg	D5W, NS	Physically compatible for 24 hr	764	C
Heparin sodium	ES	20,000 units	KN	80 mg	D5W, NS	Physically compatible for 24 hr	764	C
Hydralazine HCl	CI	40 mg	KN	80 mg	D5W, NS	Yellow discoloration	764	I
Hydrocortisone sodium phosphate	MSD	200 mg	KN	80 mg	D5W, NS	Physically compatible for 24 hr	764	C
Hydrocortisone sodium succinate	UP	200 mg	KN	80 mg	D5W, NS	Physically compatible for 24 hr	764	C
Hydromorphone HCl	KN	16 mg	KN	80 mg	D5W, NS	Physically compatible for 24 hr	764	C
Insulin, regular	SQ	200 units	KN	80 mg	D5W, NS	Physically compatible for 48 hr	739	C
Isoproterenol HCl	BN	10 mg	KN	80 mg	D5W, NS	Physically compatible for 24 hr	764	C
Lidocaine HCl	IMS	2 g	KN	80 mg	D5W, NS	Physically compatible for 48 hr	739	C
Magnesium sulfate	IX	10 g	KN	80 mg	D5W, NS	Physically compatible for 24 hr	764	C
Mannitol	IX	25 g	KN	80 mg	D5W, NS	Physically compatible for 24 hr	764	C
Meperidine HCl	WI	150 mg	KN	80 mg	D5W, NS	Physically compatible for 24 hr	764	C
Metaraminol bitartrate	MSD	20 mg	KN	80 mg	D5W, NS	Physically compatible for 24 hr	764	C
Methyldopate HCl	MSD	500 mg	KN	80 mg	D5W, NS	Physically compatible for 24 hr	764	C
Methylprednisolone sodium succinate	UP	250 mg	KN	80 mg	D5W, NS	Physically compatible for 24 hr	764	C
Metoclopramide HCl	RB	20 mg	KN	80 mg	D5W, NS	Physically compatible for 24 hr	764	C
Morphine sulfate	KN	30 mg	KN	80 mg	D5W, NS	Physically compatible for 24 hr	764	C
Multivitamins	USV	10 ml	KN	80 mg	D5W, NS	Physically compatible for 24 hr	764	C
Nafcillin sodium	WY	4 g	KN	80 mg	D5W, NS	Physically compatible for 24 hr	764	C
	WY	40 g	SE	[b]	D5W, NS	Cloudy solution clears with agitation	1166	?
Naloxone HCl	EN	0.8 mg	KN	80 mg	D5W, NS	Physically compatible for 24 hr	764	C
Nitroglycerin	ACC	100 mg	KN	80 mg	D5W, NS	Physically compatible for 24 hr	764	C

Additive Compatibility (Cont.)

Verapamil HCl

Drug	*Mfr*	*Conc/L*	*Mfr*	*Conc/L*	*Test Soln*	*Remarks*	*Ref*	*C/I*
Norepinephrine bitartrate	BN	8 mg	KN	80 mg	D5W, NS	Physically compatible for 24 hr	764	C
Oxacillin sodium	BR	4 g	KN	80 mg	D5W, NS	Physically compatible for 24 hr	764	C
	BR	40 g	SE	[b]	D5W, NS	Cloudy solution clears with agitation	1166	?
Oxytocin	SZ	40 units	KN	80 mg	D5W, NS	Physically compatible for 24 hr	764	C
Pancuronium bromide	OR	8 mg	KN	80 mg	D5W, NS	Physically compatible for 24 hr	764	C
Penicillin G potassium	SQ	10 million units	KN	80 mg	D5W, NS	Physically compatible for 24 hr	764	C
	PD	62.5 g	SE	[b]	D5W, NS	Physically compatible for 24 hr at 21 °C under fluorescent light	1166	C
Penicillin G sodium	SQ	10 million units	KN	80 mg	D5W, NS	Physically compatible for 24 hr	764	C
Pentobarbital sodium	AB	200 mg	KN	80 mg	D5W, NS	Physically compatible for 24 hr	764	C
Phenobarbital sodium	ES	260 mg	KN	80 mg	D5W, NS	Physically compatible for 24 hr	764	C
Phentolamine mesylate	RC	10 mg	KN	80 mg	D5W, NS	Physically compatible for 24 hr	764	C
Phenytoin sodium	PD	500 mg	KN	80 mg	D5W, NS	Physically compatible for 48 hr	739	C
Piperacillin sodium	LE	40 g	SE	[b]	D5W, NS	Physically compatible for 24 hr at 21 °C	1166	C
Potassium chloride	TR	80 mEq	KN	80 mg	D5W, NS	Physically compatible for 24 hr	764	C
Potassium phosphates	AB	88 mEq	KN	80 mg	D5W, NS	Physically compatible for 24 hr	764	C
Procainamide HCl	SQ	2 g	KN	80 mg	D5W, NS	Physically compatible for 48 hr	739	C
Propranolol HCl	AY	4 mg	KN	80 mg	D5W, NS	Physically compatible for 24 hr	764	C
Protamine sulfate	LI	100 mg	KN	80 mg	D5W, NS	Physically compatible for 24 hr	764	C
Quinidine gluconate	LI	800 mg	KN	80 mg	D5W, NS	Physically compatible for 48 hr	739	C
Sodium bicarbonate	BR	89.2 mEq	KN	80 mg	D5W, NS	Physically compatible for 24 hr	764	C
Sodium nitroprusside	RC	100 mg	KN	80 mg	D5W, NS	Physically compatible for 24 hr	764	C
Theophylline	AB	400 mg and 4 g[c]	KN	100 and 400 mg	D5W	Physically compatible both visually and microscopically with little or no loss of either drug in 24 hr at 24 °C under fluorescent light	1172	C
Ticarcillin disodium	BE	6 g	KN	80 mg	D5W, NS	Physically compatible for 24 hr	764	C
	BE	40 g	SE	[b]	D5W, NS	Physically compatible for 24 hr at 21 °C	1166	C
Tobramycin sulfate	LI	160 mg	KN	80 mg	D5W, NS	Physically compatible for 24 hr	764	C
Tolazoline HCl	CI	160 mg	KN	80 mg	D5W, NS	Physically compatible for 24 hr	764	C
Trimethoprim–sulfamethoxazole	BW	160 + 800 mg	KN	80 mg	D5W, NS	Transient precipitate	764	I
Vancomycin HCl	LI	1 g	KN	80 mg	D5W, NS	Physically compatible for 24 hr	764	C
Vasopressin	PD	40 units	KN	80 mg	D5W, NS	Physically compatible for 24 hr	764	C
Vitamin B complex with C	RC	4 ml	KN	80 mg	D5W, NS	Physically compatible for 24 hr	764	C

[a] *Tested in both polyolefin and PVC containers.*
[b] *Final concentration unspecified.*
[c] *Premixed theophylline infusion.*

Drugs in Syringe Compatibility

Verapamil HCl

Drug (in syringe)	*Mfr*	*Amt*	*Mfr*	*Amt*	*Remarks*	*Ref*	*C/I*
Heparin sodium		2500 units/ 1 ml	KN	5 mg/ 2 ml	Physically compatible for at least 5 min	1053	C
Inamrinone lactate	WI	5 mg/ 1 ml	LY	10 mg/ 4 ml	Physically compatible with little or no loss of either drug in 4 hr at 22 °C	1419	C
Milrinone lactate	WI	3.5 mg/ 3.5 ml	KN	10 mg/ 4 ml	Brought to 10 ml total volume with D5W. Physically compatible with no loss of either drug in 4 hr at 23 °C	1191	C

Y-Site Injection Compatibility (1:1 Mixture)

Verapamil HCl

Drug	*Mfr*	*Conc*	*Mfr*	*Conc*	*Remarks*	*Ref*	*C/I*
Albumin human	HY	250 mg/ml[a]	LY	0.2 mg/ml[a]	Slight haze in 1 hr	1316	I
	HY	250 mg/ml[b]	LY	0.2 mg/ml[b]	Slight haze in 3 hr	1316	I
Amphotericin B cholesteryl sulfate complex	SEQ	0.83 mg/ml[a]	AMR	2.5 mg/ml	Gross precipitate forms	2117	I
Ampicillin sodium	WY	40 mg/ml[c]	SE	2.5 mg/ml	White milky precipitate forms immediately and persists. 91% of verapamil precipitated	1166	I
Ciprofloxacin	MI	2 mg/ml[c]	KN	2.5 mg/ml	Visually compatible for 24 hr at 24 °C	1655	C
Clarithromycin	AB	4 mg/ml[a]	BKN	2.5 mg/ml	Visually compatible for 72 hr at both 30 and 17 °C	2174	C
Dobutamine HCl	LI	4 mg/ml[c]	LY	0.2 mg/ml[c]	Physically compatible for 3 hr	1316	C
Dopamine HCl		[e]			Physically compatible	840	C
Famotidine	MSD	0.2 mg/ml[a]	KN	0.1 mg/ml[a]	Physically compatible for 4 hr at 25 °C	1188	C
Gatifloxacin	BMS	2 mg/ml[a]	AB	2.5 mg/ml	Physically compatible with no change in measured haze or increase in particle content in 4 hr at 23 °C	2234	C
Hetastarch in lactated electrolyte injection (Hextend)	AB	6%	AMR	1.25 mg/ml[a]	Physically compatible with no change in measured turbidity or increase in particle content in 4 hr at 23 °C	2239	C
Hydralazine HCl	SO	1 mg/ml[c]	LY	0.2 mg/ml[c]	Physically compatible for 3 hr	1316	C
Inamrinone lactate	WB	3 mg/ml[b]	SE	0.1 mg/ml[a]	Physically compatible for at least 4 hr at 25 °C under fluorescent light	992	C
	WI	2.5 mg/ml[d]	LY	2.5 mg/ml	Physically compatible with little or no loss of either drug in 4 hr at 22 °C	1419	C
Linezolid	PHU	2 mg/ml	AB	2.5 mg/ml	Physically compatible with no change in measured turbidity or increase in particle content in 4 hr at 23 °C	2264	C
Meperidine HCl	AB	10 mg/ml	DU	2.5 mg/ml	Physically compatible for 4 hr at 25 °C	1397	C
Milrinone	WI	200 µg/ml[a]	KN	2.5 mg/ml[a]	Physically compatible with no loss of either drug in 4 hr at 23 °C	1191	C
Nafcillin sodium		[f]			White milky precipitate forms immediately	840; 1303	I

Y-Site Injection Compatibility (1:1 Mixture) (Cont.)

Drug	Mfr	Conc	Verapamil HCl Mfr	Verapamil HCl Conc	Remarks	Ref	C/I
	WY	40 mg/ml[c]	SE	2.5 mg/ml	White milky precipitate forms immediately and persists. 20% of verapamil precipitated	1166	I
Oxacillin sodium	BR	40 mg/ml[c]	SE	2.5 mg/ml	White milky precipitate forms immediately and persists. 39% of verapamil precipitated	1166	I
Penicillin G potassium	PD	62.5 mg/ml[c]	SE	2.5 mg/ml	Physically compatible for 15 min at 21 °C under fluorescent light	1166	C
Piperacillin sodium	LE	40 mg/ml[c]	SE	2.5 mg/ml	Physically compatible for 15 min at 21 °C under fluorescent light	1166	C
Propofol	AMR	2.5 mg/ml	ZEN	10 mg/ml	Emulsion broke and oiled out	1916	I
Sodium bicarbonate		88 mEq/L[d]	SE	5 mg/2 ml	Crystalline precipitate forms when verapamil injected into infusion line	839	I
Ticarcillin disodium	BE	40 mg/ml[c]	SE	2.5 mg/ml	Physically compatible for 15 min at 21 °C under fluorescent light	1166	C

[a] *Tested in dextrose 5% in water.*
[b] *Tested in sodium chloride 0.9%.*
[c] *Tested in both dextrose 5% in water and sodium chloride 0.9%.*
[d] *Tested in sodium chloride 0.45%.*
[e] *Injected into a line being used to infuse dopamine HCl in dextrose 5% in sodium chloride 0.3% with potassium chloride 20 mEq.*
[f] *Injected into a line being used to infuse nafcillin sodium.*

VINBLASTINE SULFATE
AHFS 10:00

Products — Vinblastine sulfate is available in 10-ml vials containing 10 mg of lyophilized drug without excipients. It should be reconstituted with 10 ml of sodium chloride 0.9% or bacteriostatic sodium chloride 0.9% (preserved with benzyl alcohol) to yield a 1-mg/ml solution. (2)

Vinblastine sulfate is also available as a 1-mg/ml solution with benzyl alcohol 0.9% in 10-ml vials. (4; 29)

pH — The pH of the reconstituted lyophilized product is 3.5 to 5. The pH of the vinblastine sulfate injection is 3 to 5.5. (4)

Osmolality — Vinblastine sulfate 1 mg/ml in sodium chloride 0.9% has an osmolality of 278 mOsm/kg. (1689)

Density — Vinblastine sulfate (Lilly) reconstituted with 0.9% sodium chloride injection to a concentration of 1 mg/ml has a solution density of 1.00 g/ml. (2041; 2248)

Administration — Vinblastine sulfate is administered intravenously only. It should not be given by any other route. A sticker is provided in the vinblastine sulfate package that must be affixed directly to the container of the individual dose that states (2):

Fatal if given intrathecally. For intravenous use only.

In addition, the container holding an individual dose must be enclosed in an overwrap which is labeled (2):

Do not remove covering until moment of injection.
Fatal if given intrathecally. For intravenous use only.

The drug may be administered over one minute directly into a vein or into the tubing of a running infusion solution. Generally, dilution of vinblastine sulfate in larger amounts of intravenous fluid and administration over longer time periods are not recommended. Extravasation should be avoided. (2; 4)

Stability — The vials should be refrigerated to ensure extended stability. (2) Room temperature stability of intact vials has been variously reported for the Lilly product to be at least one month (853) and only 14 days. (1433) The Lyphomed product has been reported to be stable for up to three months (1181) and for less than two months. (1433) The solution reconstituted with bacteriostatic sodium chloride injection is stable under refrigeration for 28 days. If reconstituted with unpreserved sodium chloride injection, any remaining unused drug should be discarded immediately. (2)

Vinblastine sulfate, reconstituted according to the manufacturer's instructions, was cultured with human lymphoblasts to determine whether its cytotoxic activity was retained. The solution retained cytotoxicity for 24 hours at 4 °C and room temperature. (1575)

pH Effects — The range of maximum stability for vinblastine sulfate in aqueous solutions was determined to be pH 2 to 4. Vinblastine sulfate in solution at pH 3 retained 90% potency after 39 days at 20 °C. (1307)

Vinblastine sulfate in solutions having a pH above 6 may form a precipitate of vinblastine base. (1369)

Freezing Solutions— Vinblastine sulfate (Lilly) 20 μg/ml in dextrose 5% in water, Ringer's injection, lactated, and sodium chloride 0.9% underwent no degradation after four weeks when frozen at −20 °C. (1195)

Light Effects— It is recommended that vinblastine sulfate, both in the dry state and in solution, be protected from light. (4)

Black et al. studied the effects of light exposure on a 1.197-mg/ml vinblastine sulfate solution in sterile water for injection. Samples at 25 °C were exposed to indirect incandescent (not fluorescent) light intermittently for at least 12 hours each day; another group was exposed to direct incandescent light intermittently for 12 hours daily with at least two additional hours of exposure to sunlight. A third group of samples at 30 °C were exposed to continuous direct incandescent light. Both groups of samples exposed directly to light showed substantial losses of vinblastine sulfate. Samples exposed to continuous direct light sustained a 10% loss in about one day and a 71% loss in 14 days. Samples intermittently exposed to direct light and sunlight sustained a 10% loss in eight days and a 23% loss in 15 days. However, samples exposed to intermittent indirect light showed no drug loss in 70 days. (1306)

McElnay et al. found less than a 6% vinblastine loss in 48 hours from a 3-μg/ml solution in sodium chloride 0.9% contained as a static solution in polybutadiene tubing when exposed to normal mixed daylight and fluorescent light. The authors concluded that photodegradation is not a problem with vinblastine sulfate. (1378)

Syringes— Vinblastine sulfate (David Bull Laboratories) 1 mg/ml in polypropylene syringes was stable by HPLC for 31 days at 8 °C and for at least 23 days at 21 °C in the dark; little or no loss occurred. (1566)

Vinblastine sulfate (Lilly) 1 mg/ml in sodium chloride 0.9% was packaged in polypropylene syringes (Plastipak, Becton-Dickinson) and stored at 25 °C protected from light. HPLC analysis found no vinblastine sulfate loss after storage for 30 days. (2155)

Elastomeric Reservoir Pumps— Vinblastine sulfate 0.2 mg/ml in both dextrose 5% in water and sodium chloride 0.9% was evaluated for binding potential to natural rubber elastomeric reservoirs (Baxter). Less than 1% binding was found after storage for two weeks at 35 °C with gentle agitation. (2014)

Vinblastine sulfate 0.15 to 0.5 mg/ml in sodium chloride 0.9% water in Infusor elastomeric reservoir pumps has been stated by the pump manufacturer to be stable for 21 days at room temperature and five days at body temperature when protected from light. (31)

Implantable Pumps— Vinblastine sulfate (Lilly) 1 mg/ml in bacteriostatic sodium chloride 0.9% was evaluated for stability in an implantable pump (Infusaid model 400). In this in vitro assessment, a 24% vinblastine loss occurred in 24 hours at 37 °C with mild agitation. In 12 days, the loss totaled 48%. In comparison, control solutions in glass vials had no drug loss in 24 hours and a 20% loss in 12 days at 37 °C. The authors believed that this result indicated an acute interaction of vinblastine with some component of the Infusaid model 400, rendering it unsuitable for administration with this infusion device. (767)

Sorption— McElnay et al. evaluated the stability of vinblastine sulfate (Lilly) 3 μg/ml in methacrylate butadiene styrene (Avon A2001 Sureset) and cellulose propionate (Avon A200 standard and A2000 Amberset) when exposed to normal mixed daylight and fluorescent light for up to 48 hours. A maximum vinblastine loss of about 5% resulted in the Sureset, with as little as a 2.25% loss occurring with foil wrapping. However, significant losses occurred in both cellulose propionate burettes in 24 hours, and losses of 15 to 20% occurred in 48 hours. The vinblastine sulfate solution in the polybutadiene tubing of the Sureset showed no more than a 6% drug loss with or without light protection. However, in the PVC tubing of the standard or Amberset, losses were significant within four hours; at 48 hours, losses were 42 to 44%. (1378)

Vinblastine sulfate (Lilly) 10 mg/250 ml in dextrose 5% in water or sodium chloride 0.9%, in PVC bags at 22 °C with protection from light, was infused over two hours at 2.08 ml/min through PVC sets. HPLC analysis of the effluent solution found no loss due to sorption. (1631)

Vinblastine sulfate (Lederle) 250 μg/ml in sodium chloride 0.9% exhibited no loss by UV spectroscopy due to sorption to PVC and polyethylene administration lines during simulated infusions at 0.875 ml/hr for 2.5 hours via a syringe pump. (1795)

Filtration— Vinblastine sulfate (Lilly) 10 mg/50 ml in dextrose 5% in water and sodium chloride 0.9%, filtered at a rate of about 3 ml/min through a 0.22-μm cellulose ester membrane filter (Ivex-2), showed no significant reduction in potency due to binding to the filter. (533)

Vinblastine sulfate 10 to 300 μg/ml exhibited no loss due to sorption to either cellulose nitrate/cellulose acetate ester (Millex OR) or Teflon (Millex FG) filters. (1415; 1416)

Vinblastine sulfate (Lederle) 250 μg/ml in sodium chloride 0.9% exhibited no loss by UV spectroscopy due to sorption to cellulose acetate (Minisart 45, Sartorius) and polysulfone (Acrodisc 45, Gelman) filters. However, a 10 to 20% loss due to sorption occurred during the first 30 to 60 minutes of infusion through nylon filters (Nylaflo, Gelman, and Utipore, Pall). About a 30% loss was found during the first hour using a positively-charged nylon filter (Posidyne ELD96, Pall). The delivered concentrations gradually returned to the full concentrations within 2 to 2.5 hours. (1795)

Central Venous Catheter— Vinblastine sulfate (Lilly) 0.12 mg/ml in dextrose 5% in water was found to be compatible with the ARROWg+ard Blue Plus (Arrow International) chlorhexidine-bearing triple-lumen central catheter. HPLC analysis was used to evaluate completeness of drug delivery through the catheter and the amount of chlorhexidine removed from the internal lumens. Essentially complete delivery of the drug was found with little or no drug loss occurring. Furthermore, chlorhexidine delivered from the catheter remained at trace amounts with no substantial increase due to the delivery of the drug through the catheter. (2335)

Compatibility Information

Solution Compatibility

Vinblastine sulfate

Solution	*Mfr*	*Mfr*	*Conc/L*	*Remarks*	*Ref*	*C/I*
Dextrose 5% in water	TR[a]	LI	170 mg	Less than 10% decrease in 24 hr at room temperature	519	C
		LI	20 mg	Physically compatible with little or no drug loss in 21 days at 4 and 25 °C in the dark	1195	C
	[b]	LI	100 mg	6 to 8% loss by HPLC in 7 days at 4 °C protected from light	1631	C
	MG[c]		170 mg	Less than 10% loss by HPLC in 24 hr at room temperature exposed to light	1658	C
Ringer's injection, lactated		LI	20 mg	Physically compatible with 2 to 3% drug loss in 21 days at 4 and 25 °C in the dark	1195	C
Sodium chloride 0.9%		LI	20 mg	Physically compatible with little or no drug loss in 21 days at 4 and 25 °C in the dark	1195	C
	[b]	LI	100 mg	No loss by HPLC in 7 days at 4 °C protected from light	1631	C
	[d]		50 mg	5% loss of vinblastine at 23 °C and 3% loss at 4 °C in 21 days protected from light	2256	C

[a]*Tested in both glass and PVC containers.*
[b]*Tested in PVC containers.*
[c]*Tested in both glass and polyolefin containers.*
[d]*Tested in glass containers.*

Additive Compatibility

Vinblastine sulfate

Drug	*Mfr*	*Conc/L*	*Mfr*	*Conc/L*	*Test Soln*	*Remarks*	*Ref*	*C/I*
Bleomycin sulfate	BR	20 and 30 mg	LI	10 and 100 mg	NS	Physically compatible and bleomycin activity retained for 1 week at 4 °C. Vinblastine not tested	763	C
Doxorubicin HCl	AD	500 mg	LI	75 mg	NS[a]	Physically compatible for at least 10 days at 8, 25, and 32 °C. HPLC assays highly erratic	838	?
	AD	1.5 g	LI	150 mg	NS[a]	Physically compatible for at least 10 days at 8, 25, and 32 °C. HPLC assays highly erratic	838	?

[a]*Tested in PVC containers.*

Drugs in Syringe Compatibility

Vinblastine sulfate

Drug (in syringe)	*Mfr*	*Amt*	*Mfr*	*Amt*	*Remarks*	*Ref*	*C/I*
Bleomycin sulfate		1.5 units/ 0.5 ml		0.5 mg/ 0.5 ml	Physically compatible for 5 min at room temperature followed by 8 min of centrifugation	980	C
Cisplatin		0.5 mg/ 0.5 ml		0.5 mg/ 0.5 ml	Physically compatible for 5 min at room temperature followed by 8 min of centrifugation	980	C
Cyclophosphamide		10 mg/ 0.5 ml		0.5 mg/ 0.5 ml	Physically compatible for 5 min at room temperature followed by 8 min of centrifugation	980	C

Drugs in Syringe Compatibility (Cont.)

Vinblastine sulfate

Drug (in syringe)	*Mfr*	*Amt*	*Mfr*	*Amt*	*Remarks*	*Ref*	*C/I*
Doxorubicin HCl	AD	45 mg/ 22.5 ml	LI	4.5 mg/ 4.5 ml	(Brought to 30-ml total volume with NS) Physically compatible for at least 10 days at 8, 25, and 32 °C. HPLC assays highly erratic	838	?
	AD	15 mg/ 7.5 ml	LI	2.25 mg/ 2.25 ml	(Brought to 30-ml total volume with NS) Physically compatible for at least 10 days at 8, 25, and 32 °C. HPLC assays highly erratic	838	?
		1 mg/ 0.5 ml		0.5 mg/ 0.5 ml	Physically compatible for 5 min at room temperature followed by 8 min of centrifugation	980	C
Droperidol		1.25 mg/ 0.5 ml		0.5 mg/ 0.5 ml	Physically compatible for 5 min at room temperature followed by 8 min of centrifugation	980	C
Fluorouracil		25 mg/ 0.5 ml		0.5 mg/ 0.5 ml	Physically compatible for 5 min at room temperature followed by 8 min of centrifugation	980	C
Furosemide		5 mg/ 0.5 ml		0.5 mg/ 0.5 ml	Immediate precipitation	980	I
Heparin sodium		200 units/ 1 ml[a]		1 mg/ 1 ml	Turbidity appears in 2 to 3 min	767	I
		500 units/ 0.5 ml		0.5 mg/ 0.5 ml	Physically compatible for 5 min at room temperature followed by 8 min of centrifugation	980	C
Leucovorin calcium		5 mg/ 0.5 ml		0.5 mg/ 0.5 ml	Physically compatible for 5 min at room temperature followed by 8 min of centrifugation	980	C
Methotrexate sodium		12.5 mg/ 0.5 ml		0.5 mg/ 0.5 ml	Physically compatible for 5 min at room temperature followed by 8 min of centrifugation	980	C
Metoclopramide HCl		2.5 mg/ 0.5 ml		0.5 mg/ 0.5 ml	Physically compatible for 5 min at room temperature followed by 8 min of centrifugation	980	C
Mitomycin		0.25 mg/ 0.5 ml		0.5 mg/ 0.5 ml	Physically compatible for 5 min at room temperature followed by 8 min of centrifugation	980	C
Vincristine sulfate		0.5 mg/ 0.5 ml		0.5 mg/ 0.5 ml	Physically compatible for 5 min at room temperature followed by 8 min of centrifugation	980	C

[a]Tested in bacteriostatic sodium chloride 0.9%.

Y-Site Injection Compatibility (1:1 Mixture)

Vinblastine sulfate

Drug	*Mfr*	*Conc*	*Mfr*	*Conc*	*Remarks*	*Ref*	*C/I*
Allopurinol sodium	BW	3 mg/ml[b]	LI	0.12 mg/ml[b]	Physically compatible with no change in measured turbidity or increase in particle content in 4 hr at 22 °C	1686	C
Amifostine	USB	10 mg/ml[a]	LI	0.12 mg/ml[a]	Physically compatible with no change in measured turbidity or increase in particle content in 4 hr at 23 °C	1845	C
Amphotericin B cholesteryl sulfate complex	SEQ	0.83 mg/ml[a]	FAU	0.12 mg/ml[a]	Physically compatible with little or no change in measured turbidity or increase in particle content in 4 hr at 23 °C under fluorescent light	2117	C
Aztreonam	SQ	40 mg/ml[a]	LI	0.12 mg/ml[a]	Physically compatible with no subvisual haze or particle formation in 4 hr at 23 °C	1758	C

Y-Site Injection Compatibility (1:1 Mixture) (Cont.)

			Vinblastine sulfate				
Drug	*Mfr*	*Conc*	*Mfr*	*Conc*	*Remarks*	*Ref*	*C/I*
Bleomycin sulfate		3 units/ml		1 mg/ml	Drugs injected sequentially into Y-site with no flush between. No visually apparent precipitate	980	C
Cefepime HCl	BMS	20 mg/ml[a]	LI	0.12 mg/ml[a]	Haze with numerous particles forms immediately	1689	I
Cisplatin		1 mg/ml		1 mg/ml	Drugs injected sequentially into Y-site with no flush between. No visually apparent precipitate	980	C
Cyclophosphamide		20 mg/ml		1 mg/ml	Drugs injected sequentially into Y-site with no flush between. No visually apparent precipitate	980	C
Doxorubicin HCl		2 mg/ml		1 mg/ml	Drugs injected sequentially into Y-site with no flush between. No visually apparent precipitate	980	C
Doxorubicin HCl liposome injection	SEQ	0.4 mg/ml[a]	FAU	0.12 mg/ml[a]	Physically compatible with little or no change in measured turbidity and no increase in particle content in 4 hr at 23 °C	2087	C
Droperidol		2.5 mg/ml		1 mg/ml	Drugs injected sequentially into Y-site with no flush between. No visually apparent precipitate	980	C
Etoposide phosphate	BR	5 mg/ml[a]	FAU	0.12 mg/ml[a]	Physically compatible with no change in measured turbidity or increase in particle content in 4 hr at 23 °C	2218	C
Filgrastim	AMG	30 μg/ml[a]	LI	0.12 mg/ml[a]	Physically compatible with no change in measured turbidity or increase in particle content in 4 hr at 22 °C	1687	C
Fludarabine phosphate	BX	1 mg/ml[a]	LY	0.12 mg/ml[a]	Physically compatible for 4 hr at room temperature under fluorescent light	1439	C
Fluorouracil		50 mg/ml		1 mg/ml	Drugs injected sequentially into Y-site with no flush between. No visually apparent precipitate	980	C
Furosemide		10 mg/ml		1 mg/ml	Drugs injected sequentially into Y-site with no flush between. Immediate precipitation	980	I
Gatifloxacin	BMS	2 mg/ml[a]	LI	0.12 mg/ml[b]	Physically compatible with no change in measured haze or increase in particle content in 4 hr at 23 °C	2234	C
Gemcitabine HCl	LI	10 mg/ml[b]	FAU	0.12 mg/ml[b]	Physically compatible with no change in measured turbidity or increase in particle content in 4 hr at 23 °C	2226	C
Granisetron HCl	SKB	0.05 mg/ml[a]	LI	0.12 mg/ml[a]	Physically compatible with no change in measured turbidity or increase in particle content in 4 hr at 23 °C	2000	C
Heparin sodium		1000 units/ml		1 mg/ml	Drugs injected sequentially into Y-site with no flush between. No visually apparent precipitate	980	C

Y-Site Injection Compatibility (1:1 Mixture) (Cont.)

Drug	Mfr	Conc	Vinblastine sulfate Mfr	Vinblastine sulfate Conc	Remarks	Ref	C/I
Leucovorin calcium		10 mg/ml		1 mg/ml	Drugs injected sequentially into Y-site with no flush between. No visually apparent precipitate	980	C
Melphalan HCl	BW	0.1 mg/ml[b]	LI	0.12 mg/ml[b]	Physically compatible with no change in measured turbidity or increase in particle content in 3 hr at 22 °C	1557	C
Methotrexate sodium		25 mg/ml		1 mg/ml	Drugs injected sequentially into Y-site with no flush between. No visually apparent precipitate	980	C
Metoclopramide HCl		5 mg/ml		1 mg/ml	Drugs injected sequentially into Y-site with no flush between. No visually apparent precipitate	980	C
Mitomycin HCl		0.5 mg/ml		1 mg/ml	Drugs injected sequentially into Y-site with no flush between. No visually apparent precipitate	980	C
Ondansetron HCl	GL	1 mg/ml[b]	LY	0.12 mg/ml[a]	Physically compatible for 4 hr at 22 °C	1365	C
Paclitaxel	NCI	1.2 mg/ml[a]	LI	0.12 mg/ml[b]	Physically compatible with no change in measured turbidity in 4 hr at 22 °C	1556	C
Piperacillin sodium–tazobactam sodium	LE	40 + 5 mg/ml[a]	LI	0.12 mg/ml[a]	Physically compatible with no change in measured turbidity or increase in particle content in 4 hr at 22 °C	1688	C
Sargramostim	IMM	10 µg/ml[b]	LY	0.12 mg/ml[b]	Physically compatible for 4 hr at 22 °C	1436	C
Teniposide	BR	0.1 mg/ml[a]	LI	0.12 mg/ml[a]	Physically compatible with no subvisual haze or particle formation in 4 hr at 23 °C	1725	C
Thiotepa	IMM[c]	1 mg/ml[a]	LI	0.12 mg/ml[a]	Physically compatible with no change in measured turbidity or increase in particle content in 4 hr at 23 °C	1861	C
Vincristine sulfate		1 mg/ml		1 mg/ml	Drugs injected sequentially into Y-site with no flush between. No visually apparent precipitate	980	C
Vinorelbine tartrate	BW	1 mg/ml[b]	LI	0.12 mg/ml[b]	Physically compatible with no change in measured turbidity or increase in particle content in 4 hr at 22 °C	1558	C

[a]Tested in dextrose 5% in water.
[b]Tested in sodium chloride 0.9%.
[c]Lyophilized formulation tested.

Additional Compatibility Information

Dacarbazine — No alteration in the ultraviolet/visible spectra was observed when dacarbazine was combined in solution with vinblastine sulfate. (492)

Aluminum — Ogawa et al. reported that immersion of a needle with an aluminum component in vinblastine sulfate (Lilly) 1 mg/ml resulted in no visually apparent reaction after seven days at 24 °C. (988)

Other Information

Microbial Growth — Vinblastine sulfate (Lilly) 0.015 and 0.5 mg/ml in sodium chloride 0.9% did not inhibit the growth of deliberately inoculated *Staphylococcus epidermidis* (10^6 to 10^7 CFU/ml) during 21 days at 35 °C (representing near body temperature). (1659)

Inactivation — In the event of spills or leaks, Lilly recommends the use of sodium hypochlorite 5% (household bleach) to inactivate vinblastine sulfate. (1200)

VINCRISTINE SULFATE
AHFS 10:00

Products — Vincristine sulfate is available as a preservative-free solution in a 1-mg/ml concentration. The ready-to-use solution is available in 1- and 2-ml single-dose vials. (4; 29)

pH — From 3.5 to 5.5. (4)

Osmolality — Vincristine sulfate 1 mg/ml has an osmolality of 610 mOsm/kg. (1689)

Density — Undiluted vincristine sulfate (Lilly) 1-mg/ml injection has a solution density of 1.02 g/ml. (2041; 2248)

Administration — Vincristine sulfate is administered intravenously only. It should not be given by any other route. A sticker is provided in the vincristine sulfate package that must be affixed directly to the container of the individual dose that states (2):

Fatal if given intrathecally. For intravenous use only.

In addition, the container holding an individual dose must be enclosed in an overwrap which is labeled (2):

Do not remove covering until moment of injection.
Fatal if given intrathecally. For intravenous use only.

The drug may be administered over one minute directly into a vein or into the tubing of a running infusion solution. (2; 4) It can also be diluted in dextrose 5% in water or sodium chloride 0.9% and given by intermittent or continuous intravenous infusion. (4) Extravasation should be avoided. (2; 4)

Stability — The ready-to-use solution should be stored under refrigeration and protected from light. Vincristine sulfate and its solutions are light sensitive; light protection has been recommended. (4) The pH range of maximum stability is 4 to 6. (1195) Precipitation may occur at alkaline pH values. (1369)

Room temperature stability has been variously reported for the Lilly product to be at least one month (853) and only three days. (1433) The Adria product has been stated to be stable at room temperature for seven days, while the Lyphomed product is stable for 30 days. (1433) These differences are likely due more to varying study periods and regulatory changes than real stability variations of such magnitudes.

Vincristine sulfate was cultured with human lymphoblasts to determine whether its cytotoxic activity was retained. The solution retained cytotoxicity for 24 hours at 4 °C and room temperature. (1575)

Freezing Solutions — Vincristine sulfate (Lilly) 20 µg/ml in dextrose 5% in water, Ringer's injection, lactated, and sodium chloride 0.9% underwent no degradation after four weeks when frozen at −20 °C. (1195)

Light Effects — An evaluation of etoposide phosphate (Bristol-Myers Squibb) 2 mg/ml, doxorubicin HCl 0.4 mg/ml, and vincristine sulfate 0.016 mg/ml (16 µg/ml) in sodium chloride 0.9% in polyolefin plastic bags (McGaw) found little or no effect of constant exposure to normal fluorescent room light for 124 hours. The admixtures were physically compatible, and all three drugs in the admixture remained stable throughout the time period stored at an elevated temperature of 35 to 40 °C. (2343)

Syringes — Vincristine sulfate (Lilly) 0.5, 1, 2, and 3 mg diluted to 20 ml with sodium chloride 0.9% and packaged in 30-ml polypropylene syringes (Becton-Dickinson) was stored for seven days at 4 °C followed by two days at 23 °C. All samples remained physically compatible with no increase in measured turbidity or particle content. HPLC analysis found no loss after seven days at 4 °C and not more than 5% loss after two additional days at room temperature. (2350)

Ambulatory Pumps — Doxorubicin HCl (Pharmacia & Upjohn) 2 mg/ml and vincristine sulfate (Faulding) 0.2 mg/ml in water for injection were evaluated for stability and compatibility in PVC reservoirs for the Graseby 9000 ambulatory pumps. The solutions were physically compatible, and no loss of either drug was found by HPLC analysis in 7 days at 37 °C. About 4% loss of both drugs was found after 14 days at 4 °C. Furthermore, weight losses due to moisture transmission were minimal. (2288)

Elastomeric Reservoir Pumps — Vincristine sulfate 0.04 to 0.2 mg/ml in sodium chloride 0.9% in Infusor elastomeric reservoir pumps has been stated by the pump manufacturer to be stable for 29 days under refrigeration and 10 days at room temperature. (31)

Sorption — Vincristine sulfate (Lilly) 2 mg/250 ml in dextrose 5% in water or sodium chloride 0.9%, in PVC bags at 22 °C with protection from light, was infused over two hours at 2.08 ml/min through PVC sets. HPLC analysis of the effluent solution found no loss due to sorption. (1631)

Vincristine sulfate (David Bull Laboratories) 25 µg/ml in sodium chloride 0.9% exhibited no loss by UV spectroscopy due to sorption to a polyethylene administration line (Vygon) during simulated infusions at 0.875 ml/hr for 2.5 hours via a syringe pump. However, about a 9% loss of delivered concentration due to sorption occurred during the first hour using a PVC administration line (Baxter). The delivered concentration returned to the full concentration within 1.5 hours. (1795)

Filtration — Vincristine sulfate (Lilly) 1 mg/50 ml in dextrose 5% in water and sodium chloride 0.9% was filtered at about 3 ml/min through a 0.22-µm cellulose ester membrane filter (Ivex-2). Losses of vincristine sulfate due to binding to the filters were noted in both solutions. In dextrose 5% in water, about 6.5% of the vincristine sulfate was bound; about 12% of the drug was lost from the sodium chloride 0.9% solution. (533)

In static equilibrium experiments, 100 mg of 0.22-µm cellulose ester membrane filter (Ivex-2) was soaked in 25 ml of vincristine sulfate (Lilly) 10 and 20 µg/ml in both dextrose 5% in water and sodium chloride 0.9%. The higher concentration exhibited about 20 to 30% binding to the filter in 24 to 48 hours. The lower concentration had about 30 to 45% binding in the same period. (533)

In a followup study, a filter material specially treated with a proprietary agent was evaluated for a reduction in vincristine sulfate binding. Vincristine sulfate (Lilly) 1 mg/50 ml in dextrose 5% in water and sodium chloride 0.9% was run through an administration set with a treated 0.22-µm cellulose ester inline filter at a rate of 3 ml/min. Cumulative vincristine sulfate losses of about 1% occurred from both solutions compared to the much higher losses previously reported for untreated cellulose ester filter material. Furthermore, equilibrium binding studies showed five- and sevenfold reductions in binding from dextrose 5% in water and sodium chloride 0.9%, respectively. (904) All Abbott Ivex integral filter and extension sets currently use this treated filter material. (1074)

Vincristine sulfate 1.5 mg/3 ml was injected as a bolus through a 0.2-µm nylon, air-eliminating, filter (Ultipor, Pall) to evaluate the effect of filtration on simulated intravenous push delivery. Spectrophotometric evaluation showed that about 90% of the drug was delivered through the filter after flushing with 10 ml of sodium chloride 0.9%. (809)

Vincristine sulfate 10 to 200 μg/ml exhibited a 10 to 15% loss due to sorption to both cellulose nitrate/cellulose acetate ester (Millex OR) and Teflon (Millex FG) filters. (1415; 1416)

Vincristine sulfate (David Bull Laboratories) 250 μg/ml in sodium chloride 0.9% exhibited little or no loss by UV spectroscopy due to sorption to cellulose acetate (Minisart 45, Sartorius) and polysulfone (Acrodisc 45, Gelman) filters. However, a 5 to 20% loss due to sorption occurred during the first 30 to 60 minutes of infusion through nylon filters (Nylaflo, Gelman, and Utipore, Pall). About a 20 to 25% loss was found during the first hour using a nylon filter (Posidyne ELD96, Pall). The delivered concentrations gradually returned to the full concentrations within 2 to 2.5 hours. (1795)

Central Venous Catheter—Vincristine sulfate (Lilly) 0.05 mg/ml in dextrose 5% in water was found to be compatible with the ARROWg+ard Blue Plus (Arrow International) chlorhexidine-bearing triple-lumen central catheter. HPLC analysis was used to evaluate completeness of drug delivery through the catheter and the amount of chlorhexidine removed from the internal lumens. Essentially complete delivery of the drug was found with little or no drug loss occurring. Furthermore, chlorhexidine delivered from the catheter remained at trace amounts with no substantial increase due to the delivery of the drug through the catheter. (2335)

Compatibility Information

Solution Compatibility

		Vincristine sulfate				
Solution	*Mfr*	*Mfr*	*Conc/L*	*Remarks*	*Ref*	*C/I*
Dextrose 5% in water	TR[a]	LI	16.7 mg	No loss of vincristine in 24 hr at room temperature	806	C
		LI	20 mg	Physically compatible with 3 to 5% drug loss in 21 days at 4 and 25 °C in the dark	1195	C
	[b]	LI	20 mg	Little or no loss by HPLC in 7 days at 4 °C protected from light	1631	C
	MG, TR[c]		20 mg	Less than 10% loss by HPLC in 24 hr at room temperature exposed to light	1658	C
Ringer's injection, lactated		LI	20 mg	Physically compatible with little or no drug loss in 21 days at 4 and 25 °C in the dark	1195	C
Sodium chloride 0.9%		LI	20 mg	Physically compatible with little or no drug loss in 21 days at 4 and 25 °C in the dark	1195	C
	[b]	LI	20 mg	8% or less loss by HPLC in 7 days at 4 °C protected from light	1631	C
	BA[b]	LI	10, 20, 40, 60, 80, 120 mg	Physically compatible with no loss of vincristine by HPLC after 7 days at 4 °C followed by 2 days at 23 °C	2350	C

[a]*Tested in both glass and PVC containers.*
[b]*Tested in PVC containers.*
[c]*Tested in glass, polyolefin, and PVC containers.*

Additive Compatibility

			Vincristine sulfate					
Drug	*Mfr*	*Conc/L*	*Mfr*	*Conc/L*	*Test Soln*	*Remarks*	*Ref*	*C/I*
Bleomycin sulfate	BR	20 and 30 units	LI	50 and 100 mg	NS	Physically compatible and bleomycin activity retained for 1 week at 4 °C	763	C
Cytarabine	UP	16 mg	LI	4 mg	D5W	Physically compatible. No alteration in UV spectra in 8 hr at room temperature	207	C
Doxorubicin HCl	PHU	2 g	FAU	200 mg	W[c]	Physically compatible with no loss of either drug by HPLC in 7 days at 37 °C. About 4% loss of both drugs in 14 days at 4 °C	2288	C
Doxorubicin HCl with etoposide	PHU BMS	40 mg 200 mg	LI	1.6 mg	NS[d]	Visually compatible and all drugs chemically stable by HPLC for up to 72 hr at 30 °C protected from light	2239	C

Additive Compatibility (Cont.)

Vincristine sulfate

Drug	*Mfr*	*Conc/L*	*Mfr*	*Conc/L*	*Test Soln*	*Remarks*	*Ref*	*C/I*
Doxorubicin HCl with etoposide	PHU BMS	25 mg 125 mg	LI	1 mg	NS[d]	Visually compatible and all drugs chemically stable by HPLC for up to 96 hr at 24 °C protected from or exposed to light	2239	C
Doxorubicin HCl with etoposide	PHU BMS	35 mg 175 mg	LI	1.4 mg	NS[d]	Visually compatible and all drugs chemically stable by HPLC for up to 96 hr at 24 °C protected from or exposed to light	2239	C
Doxorubicin HCl with etoposide	PHU BMS	50 mg 250 mg	LI	2 mg	NS[d]	Visually compatible and all drugs chemically stable by HPLC for up to 48 hr at 24 °C protected from or exposed to light. Etoposide precipitate formed in 72 hr	2239	C
Doxorubicin HCl with etoposide	PHU BMS	70 mg 350 mg	LI	2.8 mg	NS[d]	Visually compatible and all drugs chemically stable by HPLC for up to 24 hr at 24 °C protected from or exposed to light. Etoposide precipitate formed in 36 hr	2239	C
Doxorubicin HCl with etoposide	PHU BMS	100 mg 500 mg	LI	4 mg	NS[d]	Etoposide precipitate formed in 12 hr at 24 °C protected from or exposed to light	2239	I
Doxorubicin HCl with etoposide phosphate	PHU BMS	120 mg 600 mg	LI	5 mg	NS[d]	Physically compatible with little or no loss of any drug by HPLC under refrigeration or at 35 to 40 °C in 124 hr	2343	C
Doxorubicin HCl with etoposide phosphate	PHU BMS	240 mg 1.2 g	LI	10 mg	NS[d]	Physically compatible with little or no loss of any drug by HPLC under refrigeration or at 35 to 40 °C in 124 hr	2343	C
Doxorubicin HCl with etoposide phosphate	PHU BMS	400 mg 2 g	LI	16 mg	NS[d]	Physically compatible with not more than 4% loss of any drug by HPLC under refrigeration or at 35 to 40 °C in 124 hr	2343	C
Doxorubicin HCl with ondansetron HCl	AD GL	400 mg 480 mg	LI	14 mg	D5W[b]	Visually compatible with >90% potency of all drugs by HPLC after 5 days at 4 °C followed by 24 hr at 30 °C	2092	C
Doxorubicin HCl with ondansetron HCl	AD GL	800 mg 960 mg	LI	28 mg	D5W[a]	Visually compatible with >90% potency of all drugs by HPLC after 120 hr at 30 °C	2092	C
Fluorouracil	RC	10 mg	LI	4 mg	D5W	Physically compatible. No alteration in UV spectra in 8 hr at room temperature	207	C
Methotrexate sodium	LE	100 mg	LI	10 mg	D5W	Physically compatible	15	C
	LE	8 mg	LI	4 mg	D5W	Physically compatible. No alteration in UV spectra in 8 hr at room temperature	207	C

[a]Tested in PVC containers.
[b]Tested in polyisoprene infusion pump reservoirs.
[c]Tested in PVC reservoirs for the Graseby 9000 ambulatory pumps.
[d]Tested in polyolefin-lined plastic bags.

Drugs in Syringe Compatibility

Vincristine sulfate

Drug (in syringe)	*Mfr*	*Amt*	*Mfr*	*Amt*	*Remarks*	*Ref*	*C/I*
Bleomycin sulfate		1.5 units/ 0.5 ml		0.5 mg/ 0.5 ml	Physically compatible for 5 min at room temperature followed by 8 min of centrifugation	980	C
Cisplatin		0.5 mg/ 0.5 ml		0.5 mg/ 0.5 ml	Physically compatible for 5 min at room temperature followed by 8 min of centrifugation	980	C
Cyclophosphamide		10 mg/ 0.5 ml		0.5 mg/ 0.5 ml	Physically compatible for 5 min at room temperature followed by 8 min of centrifugation	980	C

Drugs in Syringe Compatibility (Cont.)

Drug (in syringe)	Mfr	Amt	Vincristine sulfate Mfr	Vincristine sulfate Amt	Remarks	Ref	C/I
Doxapram HCl	RB	400 mg/ 20 ml		1 mg/ 10 ml	Physically compatible with 7% doxapram loss in 24 hr	1177	C
Doxorubicin HCl		1 mg/ 0.5 ml		0.5 mg/ 0.5 ml	Physically compatible for 5 min at room temperature followed by 8 min of centrifugation	980	C
Droperidol		1.25 mg/ 0.5 ml		0.5 mg/ 0.5 ml	Physically compatible for 5 min at room temperature followed by 8 min of centrifugation	980	C
Fluorouracil		25 mg/ 0.5 ml		0.5 mg/ 0.5 ml	Physically compatible for 5 min at room temperature followed by 8 min of centrifugation	980	C
Furosemide		5 mg/ 0.5 ml		0.5 mg/ 0.5 ml	Immediate precipitation	980	I
Heparin sodium		500 units/ 0.5 ml		0.5 mg/ 0.5 ml	Physically compatible for 5 min at room temperature followed by 8 min of centrifugation	980	C
Leucovorin calcium		5 mg/ 0.5 ml		0.5 mg/ 0.5 ml	Physically compatible for 5 min at room temperature followed by 8 min of centrifugation	980	C
Methotrexate sodium		12.5 mg/ 0.5 ml		0.5 mg/ 0.5 ml	Physically compatible for 5 min at room temperature followed by 8 min of centrifugation	980	C
Metoclopramide HCl		2.5 mg/ 0.5 ml		0.5 mg/ 0.5 ml	Physically compatible for 5 min at room temperature followed by 8 min of centrifugation	980	C
Mitomycin		0.25 mg/ 0.5 ml		0.5 mg/ 0.5 ml	Physically compatible for 5 min at room temperature followed by 8 min of centrifugation	980	C
Vinblastine sulfate		0.5 mg/ 0.5 ml		0.5 mg/ 0.5 ml	Physically compatible for 5 min at room temperature followed by 8 min of centrifugation	980	C

Y-Site Injection Compatibility (1:1 Mixture)

Drug	Mfr	Conc	Vincristine sulfate Mfr	Vincristine sulfate Conc	Remarks	Ref	C/I
Allopurinol sodium	BW	3 mg/ml[b]	LI	0.05 mg/ml[b]	Physically compatible with no change in measured turbidity or increase in particle content in 4 hr at 22 °C	1686	C
Amifostine	USB	10 mg/ml[a]	LI	0.05 mg/ml[a]	Physically compatible with no change in measured turbidity or increase in particle content in 4 hr at 23 °C	1845	C
Amphotericin B cholesteryl sulfate complex	SEQ	0.83 mg/ml[a]	FAU	0.05 mg/ml[a]	Physically compatible with little or no change in measured turbidity or increase in particle content in 4 hr at 23 °C under fluorescent light	2117	C
Aztreonam	SQ	40 mg/ml[a]	LI	0.05 mg/ml[a]	Physically compatible with no subvisual haze or particle formation in 4 hr at 23 °C	1758	C
Bleomycin sulfate		3 units/ml		1 mg/ml	Drugs injected sequentially into Y-site with no flush between. No visually apparent precipitate	980	C
Cefepime HCl	BMS	20 mg/ml[b]	LI	0.05 mg/ml[b]	Small particles form immediately	1689	I

Y-Site Injection Compatibility (1:1 Mixture) (Cont.)

Vincristine sulfate

Drug	*Mfr*	*Conc*	*Mfr*	*Conc*	*Remarks*	*Ref*	*C/I*
Cisplatin		1 mg/ml		1 mg/ml	Drugs injected sequentially into Y-site with no flush between. No visually apparent precipitate	980	C
Cladribine	ORT	0.015[b] and 0.5[c] mg/ml	LI	0.05 mg/ml[b]	Physically compatible with no change in measured turbidity or increase in particle content in 4 hr at 23 °C	1969	C
Cyclophosphamide		20 mg/ml		1 mg/ml	Drugs injected sequentially into Y-site with no flush between. No visually apparent precipitate	980	C
Doxorubicin HCl		2 mg/ml		1 mg/ml	Drugs injected sequentially into Y-site with no flush between. No visually apparent precipitate	980	C
Doxorubicin HCl liposome injection	SEQ	0.4 mg/ml[a]	FAU	0.05 mg/ml[a]	Physically compatible with little or no change in measured turbidity and no increase in particle content in 4 hr at 23 °C	2087	C
Droperidol		2.5 mg/ml		1 mg/ml	Drugs injected sequentially into Y-site with no flush between. No visually apparent precipitate	980	C
Etoposide phosphate	BR	5 mg/ml[a]	FAU	0.05 mg/ml[a]	Physically compatible with no change in measured turbidity or increase in particle content in 4 hr at 23 °C	2218	C
Filgrastim	AMG	30 μg/ml[a]	LI	0.05 mg/ml[a]	Physically compatible with no change in measured turbidity or increase in particle content in 4 hr at 22 °C	1687	C
Fludarabine phosphate	BX	1 mg/ml[a]	LY	1 mg/ml[a]	Physically compatible for 4 hr at room temperature under fluorescent light	1439	C
Fluorouracil		50 mg/ml		1 mg/ml	Drugs injected sequentially into Y-site with no flush between. No visually apparent precipitate	980	C
Furosemide		10 mg/ml		1 mg/ml	Drugs injected sequentially into Y-site with no flush between. Immediate precipitation	980	I
Gatifloxacin	BMS	2 mg/ml[a]	LI	0.05 mg/ml[a]	Physically compatible with no change in measured haze or increase in particle content in 4 hr at 23 °C	2234	C
Gemcitabine HCl	LI	10 mg/ml[b]	FAU	0.05 mg/ml[b]	Physically compatible with no change in measured turbidity or increase in particle content in 4 hr at 23 °C	2226	C
Granisetron HCl	SKB	1 mg/ml	LI	0.34 mg/ml[b]	Physically compatible with little or no loss of either drug by HPLC in 4 hr at 22 °C	1883	C
	SKB	1 mg/ml	LI	0.01 mg/ml[b]	Physically compatible with little or no loss of granisetron by HPLC in 4 hr at 22 °C	1883	C
Heparin sodium		1000 units/ml		1 mg/ml	Drugs injected sequentially into Y-site with no flush between. No visually apparent precipitate	980	C
Idarubicin HCl	AD	1 mg/ml[b]	AD	1 mg/ml	Color changes immediately	1525	I

Y-Site Injection Compatibility (1:1 Mixture) (Cont.)

Drug	Mfr	Conc	Vincristine sulfate Mfr	Vincristine sulfate Conc	Remarks	Ref	C/I
Leucovorin calcium		10 mg/ml		1 mg/ml	Drugs injected sequentially into Y-site with no flush between. No visually apparent precipitate	980	C
Linezolid	PHU	2 mg/ml	LI	0.05 mg/ml[a]	Physically compatible with no change in measured turbidity or increase in particle content in 4 hr at 23 °C	2264	C
Melphalan HCl	BW	0.1 mg/ml[b]	LI	0.05 mg/ml[b]	Physically compatible with no change in measured turbidity or increase in particle content in 3 hr at 22 °C	1557	C
Methotrexate sodium		25 mg/ml		1 mg/ml	Drugs injected sequentially into Y-site with no flush between. No visually apparent precipitate	980	C
		30 mg/ml	LI	0.1 mg/ml	Visually compatible for 4 hr at room temperature	1788	C
Metoclopramide HCl		5 mg/ml		1 mg/ml	Drugs injected sequentially into Y-site with no flush between. No visually apparent precipitate	980	C
Mitomycin		0.5 mg/ml		1 mg/ml	Drugs injected sequentially into Y-site with no flush between. No visually apparent precipitate	980	C
Ondansetron HCl	GL	1 mg/ml[b]	LY	0.05 mg/ml[a]	Physically compatible for 4 hr at 22 °C	1365	C
Paclitaxel	NCI	1.2 mg/ml[a]	LI	0.05 mg/ml[a]	Physically compatible with no change in measured turbidity in 4 hr at 22 °C	1556	C
Piperacillin sodium–tazobactam sodium	LE	40 + 5 mg/ml[a]	LI	0.05 mg/ml[a]	Physically compatible with no change in measured turbidity or increase in particle content in 4 hr at 22 °C	1688	C
Sargramostim	IMM	10 μg/ml[b]	LY	0.05 mg/ml[b]	Physically compatible for 4 hr at 22 °C	1439	C
Sodium bicarbonate		1.4%	LI	0.1 mg/ml	White precipitate forms in 30 min at room temperature	1788	I
Teniposide	BR	0.1 mg/ml[a]	LI	0.05 mg/ml[a]	Physically compatible with no subvisual haze or particle formation in 4 hr at 23 °C	1725	C
Thiotepa	IMM[d]	1 mg/ml[a]	LI	0.05 mg/ml[a]	Physically compatible with no change in measured turbidity or increase in particle content in 4 hr at 23 °C	1861	C
Topotecan HCl	SKB	56 μg/ml[a,b]	LI	1 mg/ml	Visually compatible with little or no loss of either drug by HPLC in 4 hr at 22 °C under fluorescent light	2245	C
Vinblastine sulfate		1 mg/ml		1 mg/ml	Drugs injected sequentially into Y-site with no flush between. No visually apparent precipitate	980	C
Vinorelbine tartrate	BW	1 mg/ml[b]	LI	0.05 mg/ml[b]	Physically compatible with no change in measured turbidity or increase in particle content in 4 hr at 22 °C	1558	C

[a]*Tested in dextrose 5% in water.*
[b]*Tested in sodium chloride 0.9%.*
[c]*Tested in bacteriostatic sodium chloride 0.9% preserved with benzyl alcohol 0.9%.*
[d]*Lyophilized formulation tested.*

Additional Compatibility Information

Infusion Solutions — Vincristine sulfate should not be added to solutions that would raise or lower the pH outside the 3.5 to 5.5 range. Only dextrose 5% in water and sodium chloride 0.9% are recommended. (2)

Doxorubicin — The compatibility of doxorubicin HCl (Farmitalia) 1.4 mg/ml with vincristine sulfate (Lilly) 0.033 mg/ml in three infusion solutions, under conditions simulating prolonged infusion via an implanted device (37 °C) or via a pump kept under clothing (30 °C) as well as at 25 °C, has been reported. In sodium chloride 0.9% and dextrose 2.5% in sodium chloride 0.45%, there was no precipitate or color change; the concentration of both drugs showed 10% or less loss after 14 days of storage at any of the temperatures. The greatest losses of doxorubicin HCl and vincristine sulfate were about 10 and 6 to 8%, respectively, in the 37 °C samples. (1030)

However, when sodium chloride 0.45% and Ringer's acetate was used as the infusion solution, the stability of both drugs was much worse, probably because of the substantially higher solution pH. At 37 °C, a red-pink precipitate formed after two to three days, with about 40% doxorubicin HCl and 14% vincristine sulfate losses occurring in four days. The lower temperatures showed 17 to 27% doxorubicin HCl losses in four days, followed eventually by opalescence in the solutions. Also, the degradation products of doxorubicin adsorbed extensively to the walls of the low density polyethylene–polysiloxane bags. (1030)

Increasing the concentration of doxorubicin HCl from 1.4 to 1.88 and 2.37 mg/ml increased the extent of decomposition at 37 °C from 10% at the lowest concentration to 12 and 16%, respectively, after 14 days. Increasing the vincristine sulfate concentration to 0.05 mg/ml did not alter the stability of either drug. (1030)

Doxorubicin HCl (Nycomed) was combined with vincristine sulfate (Lilly) in both PVC (Pharmacia Deltec) and polyisoprene (Infusor, Baxter) infusion reservoirs. The drug solution concentrates were diluted slightly with sodium chloride 0.9% to yield a doxorubicin HCl concentration of 1.67 mg/ml and a vincristine sulfate concentration of 0.036 mg/ml. The reservoirs were stored at 4 °C for seven days. This was followed by incubation for four days at 35 °C to simulate near-body temperature during use. No visible changes occurred and neither drug sustained any loss by HPLC analysis throughout the course of the study in either reservoir. (1874)

Aluminum — Ogawa et al. reported that immersion of a needle with an aluminum component in vincristine sulfate (Lilly) 1 mg/ml resulted in no visually apparent reaction after seven days at 24 °C. (988)

Other Information

Microbial Growth — Admixtures containing doxorubicin HCl, etoposide phosphate, and vincristine sulfate in a variety of concentration combinations in sodium chloride 0.9% were unable to pass the USP test for antimicrobial growth effectiveness. Mixtures of these drugs are not "self-preserving" and will permit microbial growth. (2343)

Inactivation — In the event of spills or leaks, Lilly recommends the use of sodium hypochlorite 5% (household bleach) to inactivate vincristine sulfate. (1200)

VINORELBINE TARTRATE
AHFS 10:00

Products — Vinorelbine tartrate is available in a 10-mg/ml concentration in water for injection in 1- and 5-ml single-use vials. No preservatives or other additives are present. (2)

Vinorelbine tartrate should be diluted with a compatible diluent for administration. Because skin reactions may occur, gloves should be worn during preparation. (2)

pH — The injection has a pH of approximately 3.5. (2)

Density — Vinorelbine tartrate 10-mg/ml undiluted injection has a solution density of 0.99 g/ml. (2041; 2248)

Trade Name(s) — Navelbine.

Administration — Vinorelbine tartrate is administered intravenously, after dilution, from a syringe (at a concentration of 1.5 to 3 mg/ml) or infusion solution minibag (at a concentration of 0.5 to 2 mg/ml) over six to 10 minutes into the side port of a free-flowing infusion solution closest to the infusion container. After administration, 75 to 125 ml of solution should be used as a flush. Extravasation should be avoided due to tissue irritation, necrosis, and thrombophlebitis. (2)

Intrathecal injection of other vinca alkaloids has resulted in death. When vinorelbine tartrate is dispensed in a syringe containing an individual dose, the syringe must be labeled with this statement (2; 4):

Warning: Navelbine for intravenous use only.
Fatal if given intrathecally

Stability — Vinorelbine tartrate injection is a colorless to pale yellow clear solution. Intact vials should be refrigerated at 2 to 8 °C and protected from light (by storage in the carton) and freezing. Intact vials are stable at room temperature (up to 25 °C) for up to 72 hours. (2)

When diluted to 1.5 to 3 mg/ml in polypropylene syringes or to 0.5 to 2 mg/ml in PVC infusion containers, vinorelbine tartrate is stable for 24 hours at 5 to 30 °C with exposure to normal room light. (2)

Sorption — Vinorelbine tartrate (Pierre Fabre) 50 mg/250 ml in dextrose 5% in water or sodium chloride 0.9% in PVC bags was infused through PVC sets over two hours at 2.08 ml/min at 22 °C with protection from light. HPLC analysis of the effluent solution found no loss due to sorption to plastic. (1631)

Compatibility Information

Solution Compatibility

Vinorelbine tartrate

Solution	Mfr	Mfr	Conc/L	Remarks	Ref	C/I
Dextrose 5% in water	[a]		500 mg	Little or no loss by HPLC in 7 days at 4 °C protected from light	1631	C
	[a]	GW	0.5 and 2 g	Visually compatible with 6% or less loss by HPLC in 120 hr at 24 °C under fluorescent light	2213	C
Sodium chloride 0.9%	[a]		500 mg	4% loss in 3 days and 14% loss in 7 days by HPLC at 4 °C protected from light	1631	C
	[a]	GW	0.5 and 2 g	Visually compatible with 3% or less loss by HPLC in 120 hr at 24 °C under fluorescent light	2213	C

[a]Tested in PVC containers.

Y-Site Injection Compatibility (1:1 Mixture)

Vinorelbine tartrate

Drug	Mfr	Conc	Mfr	Conc	Remarks	Ref	C/I
Acyclovir sodium	BW	7 mg/ml[b]	BW	1 mg/ml[b]	Heavy white precipitate forms immediately	1558	I
Allopurinol sodium	BW	3 mg/ml[b]	BW	1 mg/ml[b]	Heavy gelatinous white precipitate forms immediately	1686	I
Amikacin sulfate	BR	5 mg/ml[b]	BW	1 mg/ml[b]	Physically compatible with no change in measured turbidity or increase in particle content in 4 hr at 22 °C	1558	C
Aminophylline	AB	2.5 mg/ml[b]	BW	1 mg/ml[b]	Initial light haze becomes visible in room light along with large particles in 1 hr	1558	I
Amphotericin B	SQ	0.6 mg/ml[a,b]	BW	1 mg/ml[b]	Heavy yellow precipitate forms immediately	1558	I
Amphotericin B cholesteryl sulfate complex	SEQ	0.83 mg/ml[a]	BW	1 mg/ml[a]	Gross precipitate forms	2117	I
Ampicillin sodium	WY	20 mg/ml[b]	BW	1 mg/ml[b]	Tiny particles form immediately, becoming large white particles in cloudy solution in 1 hr	1558	I
Aztreonam	SQ	40 mg/ml[b]	BW	1 mg/ml[b]	Physically compatible with no change in measured turbidity or increase in particle content in 4 hr at 22 °C	1558	C
Bleomycin sulfate	BR	1 unit/ml[b]	BW	1 mg/ml[b]	Physically compatible with no change in measured turbidity or increase in particle content in 4 hr at 22 °C	1558	C
Bumetanide	RC	0.04 mg/ml[b]	BW	1 mg/ml[b]	Physically compatible with no change in measured turbidity or increase in particle content in 4 hr at 22 °C	1558	C
Buprenorphine HCl	RKC	0.04 mg/ml[b]	BW	1 mg/ml[b]	Physically compatible with no change in measured turbidity or increase in particle content in 4 hr at 22 °C	1558	C
Butorphanol tartrate	BR	0.04 mg/ml[b]	BW	1 mg/ml[b]	Physically compatible with no change in measured turbidity or increase in particle content in 4 hr at 22 °C	1558	C
Calcium gluconate	AMR	40 mg/ml[b]	BW	1 mg/ml[b]	Physically compatible with no change in measured turbidity or increase in particle content in 4 hr at 22 °C	1558	C

Y-Site Injection Compatibility (1:1 Mixture) (Cont.)

			Vinorelbine tartrate				
Drug	*Mfr*	*Conc*	*Mfr*	*Conc*	*Remarks*	*Ref*	*C/I*
Carboplatin	BR	5 mg/ml[b]	BW	1 mg/ml[b]	Physically compatible with no change in measured turbidity or increase in particle content in 4 hr at 22 °C	1558	C
Carmustine	BR	1.5 mg/ml[b]	BW	1 mg/ml[b]	Physically compatible with no change in measured turbidity or increase in particle content in 4 hr at 22 °C	1558	C
Cefazolin sodium	GEM	20 mg/ml[b]	BW	1 mg/ml[b]	Large increase in measured turbidity occurs immediately and grows over 4 hr at 22 °C	1558	I
Cefoperazone sodium	RR	40 mg/ml[b]	BW	1 mg/ml[b]	Heavy white flocculent precipitate forms immediately	1558	I
Cefotaxime sodium	HO	20 mg/ml[b]	BW	1 mg/ml[b]	Physically compatible with no change in measured turbidity or increase in particle content in 4 hr at 22 °C	1558	C
Cefotetan disodium	STU	20 mg/ml[b]	BW	1 mg/ml[b]	Tiny particles form immediately, becoming numerous in cloudy solution in 4 hr at 22 °C	1558	I
Ceftazidime	LI[c]	40 mg/ml[b]	BW	1 mg/ml[b]	Physically compatible with no change in measured turbidity or increase in particle content in 4 hr at 22 °C	1558	C
Ceftizoxime sodium	FUJ	20 mg/ml[b]	BW	1 mg/ml[b]	Physically compatible with no change in measured turbidity or increase in particle content in 4 hr at 22 °C	1558	C
Ceftriaxone sodium	RC	20 mg/ml[b]	BW	1 mg/ml[b]	Tiny particles form immediately, becoming more numerous in 4 hr at 22 °C	1558	I
Cefuroxime sodium	GL	20 mg/ml[b]	BW	1 mg/ml[b]	Large increase in measured turbidity occurs immediately and grows over 4 hr at 22 °C	1558	I
Chlorpromazine HCl	RU	2 mg/ml[b]	BW	1 mg/ml[b]	Physically compatible with no change in measured turbidity or increase in particle content in 4 hr at 22 °C	1558	C
Cimetidine HCl	SKB	12 mg/ml[b]	BW	1 mg/ml[b]	Physically compatible with no change in measured turbidity or increase in particle content in 4 hr at 22 °C	1558	C
Cisplatin	BR	1 mg/ml	BW	1 mg/ml[b]	Physically compatible with no change in measured turbidity or increase in particle content in 4 hr at 22 °C	1558	C
Clindamycin phosphate	AB	10 mg/ml[b]	BW	1 mg/ml[b]	Physically compatible with no change in measured turbidity or increase in particle content in 4 hr at 22 °C	1558	C
Cyclophosphamide	MJ	10 mg/ml[b]	BW	1 mg/ml[b]	Physically compatible with no change in measured turbidity or increase in particle content in 4 hr at 22 °C	1558	C
Cytarabine	CET	50 mg/ml	BW	1 mg/ml[b]	Physically compatible with no change in measured turbidity or increase in particle content in 4 hr at 22 °C	1558	C
Dacarbazine	MI	4 mg/ml[b]	BW	1 mg/ml[b]	Physically compatible with no change in measured turbidity or increase in particle content in 4 hr at 22 °C	1558	C

Y-Site Injection Compatibility (1:1 Mixture) (Cont.)

Drug	*Mfr*	*Conc*	*Mfr*	*Conc*	*Remarks*	*Ref*	*C/I*
			Vinorelbine tartrate				
Dactinomycin	MSD	0.01 mg/ml[b]	BW	1 mg/ml[b]	Physically compatible with no change in measured turbidity or increase in particle content in 4 hr at 22 °C	1558	C
Daunorubicin HCl	WY	1 mg/ml[b]	BW	1 mg/ml[b]	Physically compatible with little change in measured turbidity or increase in particle content in 4 hr at 22 °C	1558	C
Dexamethasone sodium phosphate	LY	1 mg/ml[b]	BW	1 mg/ml[b]	Physically compatible with no change in measured turbidity or increase in particle content in 4 hr at 22 °C	1558	C
Diphenhydramine HCl	ES	2 mg/ml[b]	BW	1 mg/ml[b]	Physically compatible with no change in measured turbidity or increase in particle content in 4 hr at 22 °C	1558	C
Doxorubicin HCl	CET	2 mg/ml	BW	1 mg/ml[b]	Physically compatible with no change in measured turbidity or increase in particle content in 4 hr at 22 °C	1558	C
Doxorubicin HCl liposome injection	SEQ	0.4 mg/ml[a]	BW	1 mg/ml[a]	Physically compatible with little or no change in measured turbidity and no increase in particle content in 4 hr at 23 °C	2087	C
Doxycycline hyclate	ES	1 mg/ml[b]	BW	1 mg/ml[b]	Physically compatible with no change in measured turbidity or increase in particle content in 4 hr at 22 °C	1558	C
Droperidol	JN	0.4 mg/ml[b]	BW	1 mg/ml[b]	Physically compatible with no change in measured turbidity or increase in particle content in 4 hr at 22 °C	1558	C
Enalaprilat	MSD	0.1 mg/ml[b]	BW	1 mg/ml[b]	Physically compatible with no change in measured turbidity or increase in particle content in 4 hr at 22 °C	1558	C
Etoposide	BR	0.4 mg/ml[b]	BW	1 mg/ml[b]	Physically compatible with no change in measured turbidity or increase in particle content in 4 hr at 22 °C	1558	C
Famotidine	MSD	2 mg/ml[b]	BW	1 mg/ml[b]	Physically compatible with no change in measured turbidity or increase in particle content in 4 hr at 22 °C	1558	C
Filgrastim	AMG	30 μg/ml[a]	BW	1 mg/ml[b]	Physically compatible with no change in measured turbidity or increase in particle content in 4 hr at 22 °C	1687	C
Floxuridine	RC	3 mg/ml[b]	BW	1 mg/ml[b]	Physically compatible with no change in measured turbidity or increase in particle content in 4 hr at 22 °C	1558	C
Fluconazole	RR	2 mg/ml	BW	1 mg/ml[b]	Physically compatible with no change in measured turbidity or increase in particle content in 4 hr at 22 °C	1558	C
Fludarabine phosphate	BX	1 mg/ml[b]	BW	1 mg/ml[b]	Physically compatible with no change in measured turbidity or increase in particle content in 4 hr at 22 °C	1558	C
Fluorouracil	RC	16 mg/ml[b]	BW	1 mg/ml[b]	Heavy white precipitate forms immediately	1558	I
Furosemide	ES	3 mg/ml[b]	BW	1 mg/ml[b]	Heavy white precipitate forms immediately	1558	I

Y-Site Injection Compatibility (1:1 Mixture) (Cont.)

			Vinorelbine tartrate				
Drug	*Mfr*	*Conc*	*Mfr*	*Conc*	*Remarks*	*Ref*	*C/I*
Ganciclovir sodium	SY	20 mg/ml[b]	BW	1 mg/ml[b]	White turbid solution with precipitate forms immediately	1558	I
Gatifloxacin	BMS	2 mg/ml[a]	GW	1 mg/ml[a]	Physically compatible with no change in measured haze or increase in particle content in 4 hr at 23 °C	2234	C
Gemcitabine HCl	LI	10 mg/ml[b]	GW	1 mg/ml[b]	Physically compatible with no change in measured turbidity or increase in particle content in 4 hr at 23 °C	2226	C
Gentamicin sulfate	ES	5 mg/ml[b]	BW	1 mg/ml[b]	Physically compatible with no change in measured turbidity or increase in particle content in 4 hr at 22 °C	1558	C
Granisetron HCl	SKB	0.05 mg/ml[a]	BW	1 mg/ml[a]	Physically compatible with no change in measured turbidity or increase in particle content in 4 hr at 23 °C	2000	C
Haloperidol lactate	MN	0.2 mg/ml[b]	BW	1 mg/ml[b]	Physically compatible with no change in measured turbidity or increase in particle content in 4 hr at 22 °C	1558	C
Heparin sodium	ES	100 units/ml[b]	BW	1 mg/ml[b]	Physically compatible with no change in measured turbidity or increase in particle content in 4 hr at 22 °C	1558	C
		100 units/ml[b]	GW	3 mg/ml[b]	A fine haze forms immediately, becoming cloudy in 15 min	2238	I
		100 units/ml[b]	GW	2 mg/ml[b]	Visually compatible for at least 15 min	2238	C
		100 units/ml[b]	GW	1 mg/ml[b]	Visually compatible for at least 15 min	2238	C
		100 units/ 1 ml[b]	GW	4 mg/4 ml[b]	Volumes mixed as cited. Visually compatible for at least 15 min	2238	C
		100 units/ 1 ml[b]	GW	8 mg/4 ml[b]	Volumes mixed as cited. Precipitate forms	2238	I
		100 units/ 1 ml[b]	GW	12 mg/4 ml[b]	Volumes mixed as cited. Precipitate forms	2238	I
Hydrocortisone sodium phosphate	MSD	1 mg/ml[b]	BW	1 mg/ml[b]	Physically compatible with no change in measured turbidity or increase in particle content in 4 hr at 22 °C	1558	C
Hydrocortisone sodium succinate	UP	1 mg/ml[b]	BW	1 mg/ml[b]	Physically compatible with no change in measured turbidity or increase in particle content in 4 hr at 22 °C	1558	C
Hydromorphone HCl	KN	0.5 mg/ml[b]	BW	1 mg/ml[b]	Physically compatible with no change in measured turbidity or increase in particle content in 4 hr at 22 °C	1558	C
Hydroxyzine HCl	ES	4 mg/ml[b]	BW	1 mg/ml[b]	Physically compatible with no change in measured turbidity or increase in particle content in 4 hr at 22 °C	1558	C
Idarubicin HCl	AD	0.5 mg/ml[b]	BW	1 mg/ml[b]	Increase in measured turbidity no greater than dilution of idarubicin with sodium chloride 0.9%. No increase in particle content in 4 hr at 22 °C	1558; 1675	C
Ifosfamide	MJ	25 mg/ml[b]	BW	1 mg/ml[b]	Physically compatible with no change in measured turbidity or increase in particle content in 4 hr at 22 °C	1558	C

Y-Site Injection Compatibility (1:1 Mixture) (Cont.)

			Vinorelbine tartrate				
Drug	*Mfr*	*Conc*	*Mfr*	*Conc*	*Remarks*	*Ref*	*C/I*
Imipenem–cilastatin sodium	MSD	10 mg/ml[b]	BW	1 mg/ml[b]	Physically compatible with no change in measured turbidity or increase in particle content in 4 hr at 22 °C	1558	C
Lorazepam	WY	0.1 mg/ml[b]	BW	1 mg/ml[b]	Physically compatible with no change in measured turbidity or increase in particle content in 4 hr at 22 °C	1558	C
Mannitol	BA	15%	BW	1 mg/ml[b]	Physically compatible with no change in measured turbidity or increase in particle content in 4 hr at 22 °C	1558	C
Mechlorethamine HCl	MSD	1 mg/ml	BW	1 mg/ml[b]	Physically compatible with no change in measured turbidity or increase in particle content in 4 hr at 22 °C	1558	C
Melphalan HCl	BW	0.1 mg/ml[b]	BW	1 mg/ml[b]	Physically compatible with no change in measured turbidity or increase in particle content in 4 hr at 22 °C	1558	C
Meperidine HCl	WY	4 mg/ml[b]	BW	1 mg/ml[b]	Physically compatible with no change in measured turbidity or increase in particle content in 4 hr at 22 °C	1558	C
Mesna	MJ	10 mg/ml[b]	BW	1 mg/ml[b]	Physically compatible with no change in measured turbidity or increase in particle content in 4 hr at 22 °C	1558	C
Methotrexate sodium	LE	15 mg/ml[b]	BW	1 mg/ml[b]	Physically compatible with no change in measured turbidity or increase in particle content in 4 hr at 22 °C	1558	C
Methylprednisolone sodium succinate	AB	5 mg/ml[b]	BW	1 mg/ml[b]	Heavy white precipitate forms immediately	1558	I
Metoclopramide HCl	RB	5 mg/ml	BW	1 mg/ml[b]	Physically compatible with no change in measured turbidity or increase in particle content in 4 hr at 22 °C	1558	C
Metronidazole	BA	5 mg/ml	BW	1 mg/ml[b]	Physically compatible with no change in measured turbidity or increase in particle content in 4 hr at 22 °C	1558	C
Minocycline HCl	LE	0.2 mg/ml[b]	BW	1 mg/ml[b]	Physically compatible with no change in measured turbidity or increase in particle content in 4 hr at 22 °C	1558	C
Mitomycin	BR	0.5 mg/ml	BW	1 mg/ml[b]	Color changes from pale blue to reddish purple in 1 hr	1558	I
Mitoxantrone HCl	LE	0.5 mg/ml[b]	BW	1 mg/ml[b]	Physically compatible with little change in measured turbidity or increase in particle content in 4 hr at 22 °C	1558	C
Morphine sulfate	WI	1 mg/ml[b]	BW	1 mg/ml[b]	Physically compatible with no change in measured turbidity or increase in particle content in 4 hr at 22 °C	1558	C
Nalbuphine HCl	AST	10 mg/ml	BW	1 mg/ml[b]	Physically compatible with no change in measured turbidity or increase in particle content in 4 hr at 22 °C	1558	C

Y-Site Injection Compatibility (1:1 Mixture) (Cont.)

			Vinorelbine tartrate				
Drug	*Mfr*	*Conc*	*Mfr*	*Conc*	*Remarks*	*Ref*	*C/I*
Netilmicin sulfate	SC	5 mg/ml[b]	BW	1 mg/ml[b]	Physically compatible with no change in measured turbidity or increase in particle content in 4 hr at 22 °C	1558	C
Ondansetron HCl	GL	1 mg/ml[b]	BW	1 mg/ml[b]	Physically compatible with no change in measured turbidity or increase in particle content in 4 hr at 22 °C	1558	C
Piperacillin sodium	LE	40 mg/ml[b]	BW	1 mg/ml[b]	Heavy white turbidity forms immediately, becoming white flocculent precipitate in 4 hr at 22 °C	1558	I
Plicamycin	MI	0.01 mg/ml[b]	BW	1 mg/ml[b]	Physically compatible with no change in measured turbidity or increase in particle content in 4 hr at 22 °C	1558	C
Sodium bicarbonate	AB	1 mEq/ml	BW	1 mg/ml[b]	Tiny particles and light blue haze form immediately, developing into large particles in 4 hr at 22 °C	1558	I
Streptozocin	UP	40 mg/ml[b]	BW	1 mg/ml[b]	Physically compatible with no change in measured turbidity or increase in particle content in 4 hr at 22 °C	1558	C
Teniposide	BR	0.1 mg/ml[a]	BW	1 mg/ml[a]	Physically compatible with no change in measured turbidity or increase in particle content in 4 hr at 23 °C	1725	C
Thiotepa	LE	10 mg/ml[b]	BW	1 mg/ml[b]	Cloudy solution with particles forms immediately	1558	I
Ticarcillin disodium	BE	30 mg/ml[b]	BW	1 mg/ml[b]	Physically compatible with no change in measured turbidity or increase in particle content in 4 hr at 22 °C	1558	C
Ticarcillin disodium–clavulanate potassium	SKB	31 mg/ml[b]	BW	1 mg/ml[b]	Physically compatible with no change in measured turbidity or increase in particle content in 4 hr at 22 °C	1558	C
Tobramycin sulfate	LI	5 mg/ml[b]	BW	1 mg/ml[b]	Physically compatible with no change in measured turbidity or increase in particle content in 4 hr at 22 °C	1558	C
Trimethoprim–sulfamethoxazole	ES	0.8 + 4 mg/ml[b]	BW	1 mg/ml[b]	Heavy white turbidity forms immediately, developing particles in 1 hr	1558	I
Vancomycin HCl	LY	10 mg/ml[b]	BW	1 mg/ml[b]	Physically compatible with no change in measured turbidity or increase in particle content in 4 hr at 22 °C	1558	C
Vinblastine sulfate	LI	0.12 mg/ml[b]	BW	1 mg/ml[b]	Physically compatible with no change in measured turbidity or increase in particle content in 4 hr at 22 °C	1558	C
Vincristine sulfate	LI	0.05 mg/ml[b]	BW	1 mg/ml[b]	Physically compatible with no change in measured turbidity or increase in particle content in 4 hr at 22 °C	1558	C
Zidovudine	BW	4 mg/ml[b]	BW	1 mg/ml[b]	Physically compatible with no change in measured turbidity or increase in particle content in 4 hr at 22 °C	1558	C

[a] *Tested in dextrose 5% in water.*
[b] *Tested in sodium chloride 0.9%.*
[c] *Sodium carbonate–containing formulation tested.*

Additional Compatibility Information

Infusion Solutions — Vinorelbine tartrate, diluted to between 1.5 and 3 mg/ml in dextrose 5% in water or sodium chloride 0.9% for intravenous injection from a syringe, is reported to be stable for 24 hours at 5 to 30 °C when exposed to normal room light. (2)

Vinorelbine tartrate injection, diluted to between 0.5 and 2 mg/ml for intravenous infusion, is reported to be stable for up to 24 hours at 5 to 30 °C when exposed to normal room light in the following infusion solutions: (2):

Dextrose 5% in sodium chloride 0.45%
Dextrose 5% in water
Ringer's injection
Ringer's injection, lactated
Sodium chloride 0.45%
Sodium chloride 0.9%

Other Information

Microbial Growth — Vinorelbine tartrate (Pierre Fabre) 0.1 mg/ml diluted in sodium chloride 0.9% and stored at 22 °C did not exhibit an antimicrobial effect on the growth of four organisms (*Enterococcus faecium, Staphylococcus aureus, Pseudomonas aeruginosa,* and *Candida albicans*) inoculated into the solution. The author recommended that diluted solutions of vinorelbine tartrate be stored under refrigeration whenever possible and that the potential for microbiological growth be considered when assigning expiration periods. (2160)

VITAMIN A
AHFS 88:04

Products — Vitamin A is available in 2-ml single-dose vials. Each milliliter contains (2):

Vitamin A (retinol present as the palmitate)	50,000 I.U.
Polysorbate 80	12%
Chlorobutanol	0.5%
Citric acid	0.1%
Butylated hydroxyanisole	0.03%
Butylated hydroxytoluene	0.03%
Sodium hydroxide	to adjust pH

Units — Vitamin A activity is usually expressed in USP or International Units or retinol equivalents. The USP and International Units are equivalent and are equal to the biological activity of 300 ng of all-*trans*-retinol, 334 ng of all-*trans*-retinol acetate, or 600 ng of β-carotene. One retinol equivalent equals 1 μg of all-*trans*-retinol, 6 μg of β-carotene, or 12 μg of other provitamin A carotenoids. (4)

pH — From 6.5 to 7.1. (4)

Trade Name(s) — Aquasol A Parenteral.

Administration — Vitamin A is administered intramuscularly. (2; 4) Intravenous administration is not recommended. (2)

Stability — Vitamin A is a light yellow to amber or red oil. It is sensitive to, and should be protected from, light and air. (4) Intact vials should be stored under refrigeration and protected from light and freezing. (2; 4)

Light Effects — Kishi et al. reported on a parenteral nutrition solution in glass bottles exposed to sunlight. Vitamin A decomposed rapidly, losing more than 50% in three hours. The decomposition could be slowed to approximately a 25% loss in three hours by covering the bottle with a light-resistant vinyl bag. (1040)

Allwood found that vitamin A was rapidly and significantly decomposed when exposed to daylight. The extent and rate of loss were dependent on the degree of exposure to daylight which, in turn, depended on various factors such as the direction of the radiation, time of day, and climatic conditions. Delivery of less than 10% of the expected amount was reported. (1047) In controlled light experiments, the decomposition initially progressed exponentially. Subsequently, the rate of decomposition slowed. This result was attributed to a protective effect of the degradation products on the remaining vitamin A. The presence of amino acids provided greater protection. Compared to degradation rates in dextrose 5% in water, decomposition was reduced by up to 50% in some amino acid mixtures. (1048)

In a parenteral nutrition solution composed of amino acids, dextrose, electrolytes, trace elements, and multivitamins in PVC bags stored at 4 and 25 °C, vitamin A rapidly deteriorated to 10% of the initial concentration in eight hours at 25 °C while exposed to light. The decomposition was slowed by light protection and refrigeration, with a loss of about 25% in four days. (1063)

Billion-Rey et al. reported substantial loss by HPLC analysis of retinol all-*trans* palmitate and phytonadione from both TPN and TNA admixtures due to exposure to sunlight. In three hours' exposure to sunlight, essentially total loss of retinol and 50% loss of phytonadione had occurred. The presence or absence of lipids did not affect stability. In contrast, tocopherol concentrations remained essentially unchanged by exposure to sunlight through 12 hours. The container material used to store the nutrition admixtures affected the concentration of the vitamins as well. Losses were greatest (10 to 25%) in PVC containers and were slightly better in EVA and glass containers. (2049)

Sorption — Vitamin A (as the acetate) (Sigma) 7.5 mg/L displayed 66.7% sorption to a PVC plastic test strip in 24 hours. The presence of dextrose 5% and sodium chloride 0.9% increased the extent of sorption. (12)

In another study, vitamin A acetate displayed 78% sorption to 200-ml PVC containers after 24 hours at 25 °C with gentle shaking. The initial concentration was 3 mg/L. The sorption was increased by approximately 10% in sodium chloride 0.9% and by 20% in dextrose 5% in water. (133)

However, Nedich noted that vitamin A delivery is also reduced in glass intravenous containers. At a concentration of 10,000 units/L in glass and PVC plastic containers protected from light with aluminum foil, 77 and 71%, respectively, of the vitamin A were delivered in 10 hours. Without light protection, 61% was delivered from glass and 49% from PVC plastic containers over a 10-hour period. (290)

In another test using multivitamin infusion (USV), one ampul/L of sodium chloride 0.9% in glass and PVC containers not protected from light, 69.4 and 67.9% of the vitamin A were delivered from the glass and PVC containers, respectively, in 10 hours. The amount of vitamin A was constant over this test period, not decreasing with time. (282)

Similar results were observed in a parenteral nutrition solution composed of protein hydrolysate 2%, dextrose 20%, electrolytes, and multivitamin infusion (USV) 10 ml in 1-L glass containers. Approximately 50 to 65% of the vitamin A content in the solution was lost in 24 hours, and then it remained stable for three to seven days. When added to the cellulose propionate burette chambers of infusion sets, about 60% of the vitamin A was lost in six hours. Further, the effluent from the PVC tubing of the set was even worse. The concentration dropped from an initial 3 μg/ml to 1 μg/ml in two hours. Wrapping foil around the chambers to exclude light did not alter the vitamin A disappearance. About 50% of the lost vitamin A was recovered by hexane extraction of the administration sets. (438)

Gillis et al. evaluated the delivery of vitamins A, D, and E from a parenteral nutrition solution composed of 3% amino acid solution (Pharmacia) in dextrose 10% with electrolytes, trace elements, vitamin K, folate, and vitamin B_{12}. To this solution was added 6 ml of multivitamin infusion (USV). The solution was prepared in PVC bags (Travenol), and administration was simulated through a fluid chamber (Buretrol) and infusion tubing with a 0.5-μm filter at 10 ml/hr. During the first 60 to 90 minutes, minimal delivery of the vitamins occurred. Then a rise and a plateau in the delivered vitamins followed and were attributed to an increasing saturation of adsorptive binding sites in the tubing. Total amounts delivered over 24 hours were: vitamin A, 31%; vitamin D, 68%; and vitamin E, 64%. Sorption of the vitamins was found in the PVC bag, fluid chamber, and tubing. Decomposition was not a factor. (836)

Howard et al. reported on a patient receiving 3000 I.U. of retinol daily in a parenteral nutrition solution; nevertheless, this patient experienced two episodes of night blindness. The pharmacy prepared the parenteral nutrition solution in 1-L PVC bags in weekly batches and stored them at 4 °C in the dark until use. A subsequent in vitro study showed losses of vitamin A of 23 and 77% in three- and 14-day periods, respectively, under these conditions. About 30% of the lost vitamin A could be extracted from the PVC bag. (1038)

Shenai et al. reported on losses of vitamin A from neonatal parenteral nutrition solutions containing multivitamins (USV). The solution was prepared in colorless glass bottles and run through an administration set with a burette (Travenol). The total loss of vitamin A was 75% in 24 hours, with about 16% as decomposition in the glass bottle. The decomposition was not noticeable during the first 12 hours, but then vitamin A levels fell rather precipitously to about one-third of the initial amount. The balance of the loss, averaging about 59%, occurred during transit through the administration set. Removal of the inline filter and treatment of the set with albumin had no effect on vitamin A delivery. The authors recommended a three- to fourfold increase in the amount of vitamin A to compensate for the losses. (1039)

Riggle et al. noted a 50% loss of vitamin A from a bottle of parenteral nutrition solution prepared with multivitamin infusion (USV) after 5.5 hours of infusion. The amount delivered through an Ivex-2 filter set was only 6.3% of the added amount. Similar quantities were found after 20 hours of infusion. A reduced light exposure and use of ^{3}H-labeled vitamin A confirmed binding to the infusion bottles and tubing. (704)

Subsequently, Riggle and Brandt incubated solutions containing multivitamins (USV) spiked with ^{3}H-labeled retinol in intravenous tubing protected from light and agitated to simulate flow for five hours. About half of the vitamin A was lost in 30 minutes, and 88 to 96% was lost in five hours. Spectrophotometric assays correlated closely with the radioisotope assays. Hexane rinses and radioactivity determinations on the tubing accounted for the decrease in radioactivity. (1049)

In another experiment, neonatal parenteral nutrition solutions containing multivitamins prepared in bags were delivered at 10 ml/hr through Buretrol sets (Travenol). The bags and sets were protected from light. Spectrophotometric and radioisotope assays showed that about 26% of the vitamin A was lost before the flow was started. At 10 ml/hr, about 67% was lost from the effluent. More rapid flow reduced the extent of loss. Analysis of clinical samples of parenteral nutrition solutions showed losses of 21 to 57% after 20 hours. Because losses after five hours were of the same magnitude, the authors concluded that the loss occurs fairly rapidly and is not due to gradual decomposition. (1049)

Dahl et al. reported the stability of numerous vitamins in parenteral nutrition solutions composed of amino acids (Kabi-Vitrum), dextrose 30%, and fat emulsion 20% (Kabi-Vitrum) in a 2:1:1 ratio with electrolytes, trace elements, and both fat- and water-soluble vitamins. The admixtures were stored in darkness at 2 to 8 °C for 96 hours with no significant loss of retinyl palmitate, alpha-tocopherol, thiamine mononitrate, sodium riboflavin-5′-phosphate, pyridoxine HCl, nicotinamide, folic acid, biotin, sodium pantothenate, and cyanocobalamin. Sodium ascorbate and its biologically active degradation product, dehydroascorbic acid, totaled 59 and 42% of the nominal starting concentration at 24 and 96 hours, respectively. However, the actual initial concentration was only 66% of the nominal concentration. (1225)

When the admixture was subjected to simulated infusion over 24 hours at 20 °C, either exposed to room light or light protected, or stored for six days in the dark under refrigeration and then subjected to the same simulated infusion, once again the retinyl palmitate, alpha-tocopherol, and sodium riboflavin-5′-phosphate did not undergo significant loss. However, sodium ascorbate and its degradation product, dehydroascorbic acid, had initial combined concentrations of 51 to 65% of the nominal initial concentration, with further declines during infusion. Light protection did not significantly alter the loss of total ascorbic acid. (1225)

McKenna and Bieri reported that 40% retinol losses occurred in two hours and 60% in five hours from parenteral nutrition solutions pumped at 10 ml/hr through standard infusion sets at room temperature. The retinol concentration in the bottle remained constant while the retinol in the effluent decreased. Antioxidants had no effect. Much of the vitamin A was recoverable from hexane washings of the tubing. (1050)

Smith et al. reported the stability of several vitamins from M.V.I.-12 (Armour) admixed in parenteral nutrition solutions composed of different amino acid products, with or without Intralipid 10%, when stored in glass bottles and PVC bags at 25 and 5 °C for 48 hours. No vitamin A was lost from any formula in glass bottles, but samples in PVC containers lost as much as 35 and 60% at 5 and 25 °C, respectively, in 48 hours. (1431)

Bluhm et al. studied the stability of vitamin A in two parenteral nutrition solutions. In TPN #172 (see Appendix I), a 10% loss of vitamin A palmitate by HPLC occurred in about 20 days in PVC bags while no loss occurred in Buretrol chambers in 21 days at 30 °C with exposure to normal ward light. In TPN #173 (see Appendix I), a 10% loss of vitamin A palmitate occurred in about 12 days in both glass and PVC containers at 2 to 8 °C with protection from light. (1606)

Bluhm et al. also evaluated the effects of the fat emulsion concentration on vitamin A stability in several parenteral nutrition solutions. Vitamin A palmitate was not absorbed into PVC containers from Intralipid 10%. Among TPN solutions with lower Intralipid contents, no correlation existed between the fat emulsion content and the extent of vitamin A loss during refrigerated storage. The fat emulsion content afforded vitamin A some protection from decomposition due to light exposure at 30 °C. (1607)

The quantity of retinol delivered from an M.V.I.-containing 2-in-1 parenteral nutrition solution and when M.V.I. was added to Intralipid 10% was evaluated during simulated administration through a PVC administration set. The parenteral nutrition solution was composed of amino acids 2.8%, dextrose 10%, and standard electrolytes; M.V.I. was added to yield a nominal retinol concentration of 455 μg/150 ml. Retinol losses were about 80% of the admixed amount after being delivered through the PVC set. When M.V.I. was added to Intralipid 10% in a retinol concentration of 455 μg/20 ml, retinol losses were reduced to about 10% of the admixed amount. As in the study by Bluhm et al. (1607), the fat emulsion provided retinol protection from sorption to the PVC administration set. (2027)

Substantially higher amounts of retinol were found to be delivered using polyolefin administration set tubing than with PVC tubing during simulated neonatal intensive care administration. Retinol was added to a 2-in-1 parenteral nutrition solution (TPN #206) in concentrations of 25 and 50 I.U./ml and run at 4 and 10 ml/hr through three meter lengths of polyolefin (MiniMed) and PVC (Baxter) intravenous extension set tubing protected from light and passed through a 37 °C water bath. Using HPLC analysis, delivered quantities of retinol varied from 19 to 74% through the PVC tubing and 47 to 87% through the polyolefin tubing. The authors noted that the loss of retinol to the PVC tubing appeared to be saturable. Even so, the use of polyolefin tubing increases the amount of retinol delivered during simulated neonatal administration. (2028)

Interestingly, no loss of vitamin A to PVC delivery systems of *enteral* feeding solutions, after six hours of storage without protection from light and with exposure to ambient temperature, was reported by Bryant and Neufeld. The authors attributed this result to the presence of other (undefined) substances in the enteral feeding mixtures. (1051)

To minimize the importance of this sorption, Allwood suggested using vitamin A palmitate, which he and others have noted does not sorb as extensively to PVC (1033; 1606; 2026), instead of the acetate. However, this change does not alter the problem of degradation from exposure to light. Alternatively, an excess of vitamin A could be used. (1033)

Plasticizer Leaching — Vitamin A leached significant amounts of diethylhexyl phthalate (DEHP) plasticizer from PVC bags and administration set tubing. (1621)

Compatibility Information

Solution Compatibility

Vitamin A

Solution	*Mfr*	*Mfr*	*Conc/L*	*Remarks*	*Ref*	*C/I*
Fat emulsion 10%, intravenous	KA	KA[a]	101 mg	Physically compatible for 24 hr at 26 °C with little loss of retinol and of most other vitamins by HPLC; up to 52% ascorbate loss	2050	C

[a] *From multivitamins.*

WARFARIN SODIUM
AHFS 20:12.04

Products — Warfarin sodium is available as a lyophilized powder in vials containing a total of 5.4 mg of drug. When reconstituted with 2.7 ml of sterile water for injection, each milliliter of solution contains (2):

Warfarin sodium	2 mg
Sodium phosphate, dibasic, heptahydrate	4.98 mg
Sodium phosphate, monobasic, monohydrate	0.194 mg
Sodium chloride	0.1 mg
Mannitol	38 mg
Sodium hydroxide	to adjust pH

The maximum amount of withdrawable solution is about 2.5 ml. (2)

pH — From 8.1 to 8.3. (2)

Trade Name(s) — Coumadin.

Administration — Warfarin sodium is administered by slow intravenous injection over one to two minutes into a peripheral vein. It should not be given intramuscularly. (2)

Stability — Intact vials should be stored at controlled room temperature and protected from exposure to light. After reconstitution, warfarin sodium is physically and chemically stable for only four hours at room temperature. The reconstituted solution should not be refrigerated. If either particulates or discoloration is noted, the drug should be discarded. Unused solution also should be discarded. (2)

pH Effects — A precipitate may form in solution due to formation of the poorly soluble enol form of warfarin at pH values below 8. At pH 8 or higher, clear stable solutions result because the warfarin is in the soluble enolate form. (964)

Table 1. Extent of Equilibrium Sorption of Warfarin Sodium in Sodium Chloride 0.9% in PVC Bags (770)

Initial Concentration (mg/ml)	pH	Extent of Sorption (%)
1.31	6.95	4
0.433	6.55	6
0.190	6.27	18
0.093	6.04	24
0.048	5.90	30
0.024	5.78	45
0.009	5.65	66

Sorption—Warfarin sodium (Abbott) 25 mg/L displayed 11.7% sorption to a PVC plastic test strip in 24 hours. The presence of dextrose 5% increased the extent of the sorption. (12)

Warfarin sodium 22 mg/L in sodium chloride 0.9% (Travenol) in PVC bags exhibited approximately a 15% loss in one week at room temperature (15 to 20 °C) due to sorption. However, when the solution was buffered from its initial pH of 6.7 to 7.4, no significant loss of drug due to sorption was observed over the one-week study period. (536)

In another study, warfarin sodium 22 mg/L in sodium chloride 0.9% did not exhibit any loss due to sorption during a seven-hour simulated infusion through an infusion set (Travenol) consisting of a cellulose propionate burette chamber and 170 cm of PVC tubing. (606)

The drug was also tested as a simulated infusion over at least one hour by a syringe pump system. A glass syringe on a syringe pump was fitted with 20 cm of polyethylene tubing or 50 cm of Silastic tubing. No loss of drug due to sorption was observed with either tubing. (606)

In addition, a 25-ml aliquot of warfarin sodium 22 mg/L in sodium chloride 0.9% was stored in all-plastic syringes composed of polypropylene barrels and polyethylene plungers for 24 hours at room temperature in the dark. No loss due to sorption occurred. (606)

The sorption of warfarin sodium 20 mg/L in sodium chloride 0.9% was evaluated in 100-ml PVC infusion bags (Travenol). After eight hours at 20 to 24 °C, 29% of the warfarin was lost. Adjusting the pH of the solution to 2 or 4 increased the sorption in eight hours to 49% because of the increased amount of un-ionized warfarin present in the solution at these low pH values. The un-ionized form is most favorably sorbed by the plastic. The concentration of warfarin sodium in solution also affects the pH and, thereby, the extent of sorption. Table 1 shows that as the warfarin sodium concentration is reduced, small changes in the pH of the solution occur. Even these small pH changes result in a greatly increased extent of sorption at equilibrium (about 100 hours of exposure). (770)

Like the old formulation, the new phosphate-buffered formulation of warfarin sodium (DuPont) undergoes sorption to PVC containers and administration sets. At a concentration of 0.02 mg/ml in dextrose 5% in water in PVC containers, about 2.4% loss occurred in six hours. In sodium chloride 0.9% in PVC containers, the loss was only 1% in six hours. At 0.6 mg/ml, no potency loss was found in either solution. Similarly, a 0.02-mg/ml concentration exhibited a 6% loss in dextrose 5% in water and a 2% loss in sodium chloride 0.9% to PVC administration sets in two hours of contact; potency continued to decrease at four and six hours of contact. Once again, the 0.6-mg/ml concentration did not exhibit potency loss due to sorption in six hours in either solution. It would appear that low concentrations and dextrose 5% in water used as the infusion vehicle may increase loss due to sorption to PVC. (2010)

Warfarin sodium showed a negligible (less than 3%) loss if the aqueous solutions at pH 2 to 7 were stored in polypropylene infusion bags. (770)

Warfarin sodium (Orion) 25 µg/ml in sodium chloride 0.9% exhibited no loss by UV spectroscopy and HPLC analysis due to sorption in 120 hours at 21 °C in glass bottles and polypropylene trilayer bags (Softbag, Orion). However, about a 70% loss due to sorption occurred under these conditions in PVC bags. (1796)

Compatibility Information

Solution Compatibility

Warfarin sodium

Solution	*Mfr*	*Mfr*	*Conc/L*	*Remarks*	*Ref*	*C/I*
Dextrose 5% in Ringer's injection, lactated	BA	DU	100 mg	Physically compatible with no change in measured turbidity or increase in particle content in 24 hr at 23 °C	2011	C
Dextrose 5% in sodium chloride 0.45%	BA	DU	100 mg	Physically compatible with no change in measured turbidity or increase in particle content in 24 hr at 23 °C	2011	C
Dextrose 5% in sodium chloride 0.9%	BA	DU	100 mg	Physically compatible with no change in measured turbidity or increase in particle content in 24 hr at 23 °C	2011	C
Dextrose 5% in water	[a]	DU	20 mg	Visually compatible with about 2.4% loss due to sorption in 6 hr	2010	C
	[b]	DU	20 mg	Visually compatible with no loss in 6 hr	2010	C
	[a]	DU	600 mg	Visually compatible with no loss in 6 hr	2010	C
	MG	DU	100 mg	Physically compatible with no change in measured turbidity or increase in particle content in 24 hr at 23 °C	2011	C

Solution Compatibility (Cont.)

Warfarin sodium

Solution	*Mfr*	*Mfr*	*Conc/L*	*Remarks*	*Ref*	*C/I*
Dextrose 10% in water	BA	DU	100 mg	Physically compatible with no change in measured turbidity or increase in particle content in 24 hr at 23 °C	2011	C
Ringer's injection		DU	1 g	Haze forms immediately	2010	I
	BA	DME	1 g	Haze forms immediately	2078	I
Ringer's injection, lactated	BA	DU	100 mg	Physically compatible with no change in measured turbidity or increase in particle content in 24 hr at 23 °C	2011	C
	BA	DME	1 g	Slight haze may form in 1 hr	2078	I
Sodium chloride 0.9%	[c]	ON	100 mg	Visually compatible with no drug loss by UV and HPLC in 24 hr at 21 °C	1796	C
	[a]	ON	100 mg	Visually compatible but 50% drug loss in 24 hr and 70% loss in 120 hr by UV and HPLC at 21 °C due to sorption	1796	I
	[a]	DU	20 mg	Visually compatible with about 1% loss due to sorption in 6 hr	2010	C
	[b]	DU	20 mg	Visually compatible with no loss in 6 hr	2010	C
	[a]	DU	600 mg	Visually compatible with no loss in 6 hr	2010	C
	MG	DU	100 mg	Physically compatible with no change in measured turbidity or increase in particle content in 24 hr at 23 °C	2011	C
	AB	DME	1 g	Haze may form in 24 hr	2078	I

[a]*Tested in PVC containers.*
[b]*Tested in glass containers.*
[c]*Tested in glass containers and polypropylene trilayer containers.*

Drugs in Syringe Compatibility

Warfarin sodium

Drug (in syringe)	*Mfr*	*Amt*	*Mfr*	*Amt*	*Remarks*	*Ref*	*C/I*
Heparin sodium	ES	5000 units/ 1 ml	DU	2 mg/ 1 ml[a]	Low-level haze forms immediately and becomes visible in ambient light in 1 hr	2010	I

[a]*Tested in sterile water for injection.*

Y-Site Injection Compatibility (1:1 Mixture)

Warfarin sodium

Drug	*Mfr*	*Conc*	*Mfr*	*Conc*	*Remarks*	*Ref*	*C/I*
Amikacin sulfate	AB	5 mg/ml[a,b]	DU	0.1[a,b] and 2[d] mg/ml	Physically compatible with no change in measured turbidity or increase in particle content in 24 hr at 23 °C	2011	C
Aminophylline	ES	4 mg/ml[a]	DME	2 mg/ml[d]	Haze forms in 4 hr	2078	I
Ammonium chloride	AB	5 mEq/ml	DU	0.1 mg/ml[a]	Subvisual haze forms immediately	2011	I
	AB	5 mEq/ml	DU	0.1 mg/ml[b]	Physically compatible with no change in measured turbidity in 24 hr at 23 °C	2011	C
	AB	5 mEq/ml	DU	2 mg/ml[d]	Heavy white turbidity forms immediately and becomes flocculent precipitate in 24 hr at 23 °C	2011	I

Y-Site Injection Compatibility (1:1 Mixture) (Cont.)

			Warfarin sodium				
Drug	*Mfr*	*Conc*	*Mfr*	*Conc*	*Remarks*	*Ref*	*C/I*
Ascorbic acid injection	SCN	0.5 mg/ml[a,b]	DU	0.1[a,b] and 2[d] mg/ml	Physically compatible with no change in measured turbidity or increase in particle content in 24 hr at 23 °C	2011	C
Bretylium tosylate	FAU	10 mg/ml[a]	DU	2 mg/ml[d]	Haze forms immediately	2010	I
	DU	10 mg/ml[a]	DME	2 mg/ml[d]	Haze forms immediately	2078	I
Cefazolin sodium	SKB	20 mg/ml[a]	DU	2 mg/ml[d]	Visually compatible with no warfarin loss by HPLC in 30 min	2010	C
	SKB	20 mg/ml[a]	DME	2 mg/ml[d]	Visually compatible for 24 hr at 24 °C	2078	C
Ceftazidime	SKB[c]	20 mg/ml[a]	DME	2 mg/ml[d]	Haze forms in 24 hr at 24 °C	2078	I
Ceftriaxone sodium	RC	20 mg/ml[a]	DME	2 mg/ml[d]	Visually compatible for 24 hr at 24 °C	2078	C
Cimetidine HCl	SKB	3.6 mg/ml[a]	DU	2 mg/ml[d]	Haze forms in 1 hr	2010	I
	EN	3.6 mg/ml[a]	DU	2 mg/ml[d]	Haze forms immediately	2010	I
	SKB	3.6 mg/ml[a]	DME	2 mg/ml[d]	Haze forms in 1 hr	2078	I
Ciprofloxacin	MI	2 mg/ml[a]	DU	2 mg/ml[d]	Haze forms immediately; crystals form in 1 hr	2010	I
	MI	2 mg/ml[a]	DME	2 mg/ml[d]	Haze forms immediately; crystals form in 1 hr	2078	I
Dobutamine HCl	LI	1 mg/ml[a]	DU	2 mg/ml[d]	Haze and precipitate form immediately	2010	I
	LI	1 mg/ml[a]	DME	2 mg/ml[d]	Haze and precipitate form immediately	2078	I
Dopamine HCl	FAU	1.6 mg/ml[a]	DU	2 mg/ml[d]	Visually compatible with no warfarin loss by HPLC in 30 min	2010	C
	DU	1.6 mg/ml[a]	DME	2 mg/ml[d]	Visually compatible for 24 hr at 24 °C	2078	C
Epinephrine HCl	AMR	0.1 mg/ml[a,b]	DU	0.1[a,b] and 2[d] mg/ml	Physically compatible with no change in measured turbidity or increase in particle content in 24 hr at 23 °C	2011	C
Esmolol HCl	OHM	10 mg/ml[a]	DU	2 mg/ml[d]	Haze forms immediately	2010	I
	OHM	10 mg/ml[a]	DME	2 mg/ml[d]	Haze forms immediately	2078	I
Gentamicin sulfate	SC	1.6 mg/ml[a]	DU	2 mg/ml[d]	Haze forms immediately	2010	I
	SC	1.6 mg/ml[a]	DME	2 mg/ml[d]	Haze forms immediately	2078	I
Heparin sodium	AB	100 units/ml[a]	DU	2 mg/ml[d]	Visually compatible with no warfarin loss by HPLC in 30 min	2010	C
	AB	100 units/ml[a]	DME	2 mg/ml[d]	Visually compatible for 24 hr at 24 °C	2078	C
Labetalol HCl	SC	0.8 mg/ml[a]	DU	2 mg/ml[d]	Haze forms immediately	2010	I
	SC	0.8 mg/ml[a]	DME	2 mg/ml[d]	Haze forms immediately	2078	I
Lidocaine HCl	AST	2 mg/ml[a]	DU	2 mg/ml[d]	Visually compatible with no warfarin loss by HPLC in 30 min	2010	C
	AST	2 mg/ml[a]	DME	2 mg/ml[d]	Visually compatible for 24 hr at 24 °C	2078	C
Metaraminol tartrate	MSD	0.2 mg/ml[a,b]	DU	0.1[a,b] and 2[d] mg/ml	Physically compatible with no change in measured turbidity or increase in particle content in 24 hr at 23 °C	2011	C
Metronidazole HCl	SCS	5 mg/ml[b]	DME	2 mg/ml[d]	Slight haze forms in 24 hr at 24 °C	2078	I
Morphine sulfate	ES	2 mg/ml[a]	DU	2 mg/ml[d]	Visually compatible with no warfarin loss by HPLC in 30 min	2010	C
	ES	2 mg/ml[a]	DME	2 mg/ml[d]	Visually compatible for 24 hr at 24 °C	2078	C
Nitroglycerin	FAU	0.4 mg/ml[a]	DU	2 mg/ml[d]	Visually compatible with no warfarin loss by HPLC in 30 min	2010	C
	DU	0.4 mg/ml[a]	DME	2 mg/ml[d]	Visually compatible for 24 hr at 24 °C	2078	C

Y-Site Injection Compatibility (1:1 Mixture) (Cont.)

Warfarin sodium

Drug	*Mfr*	*Conc*	*Mfr*	*Conc*	*Remarks*	*Ref*	*C/I*
Oxytocin	FUJ	1 unit/ml[a,b]	DU	0.1[a,b] and 2[d] mg/ml	Physically compatible with no change in measured turbidity or increase in particle content in 24 hr at 23 °C	2011	C
Potassium chloride	BA	0.04 mEq/ml[e]	DME	2 mg/ml[d]	Visually compatible for 24 hr at 24 °C	2078	C
Promazine HCl	WY	5 mg/ml[a,b]	DU	0.1[a,b] and 2[d] mg/ml	Heavy white turbidity forms immediately	2011	I
Ranitidine HCl	GL	1 mg/ml[a]	DU	2 mg/ml[d]	Visually compatible with no warfarin loss by HPLC in 30 min	2010	C
	GL	1 mg/ml[a]	DME	2 mg/ml[d]	Visually compatible for 24 hr at 24 °C	2078	C
Ringer's injection	BA		DU	2 mg/ml[d]	Haze forms immediately	2010	I
Vancomycin HCl	LI	4 mg/ml[a]	DU	2 mg/ml[d]	Haze forms immediately	2010	I
	AB	10 mg/ml[a,b]	DU	0.1 mg/ml[a,b]	Physically compatible with no change in measured turbidity or increase in particle content in 24 hr at 23 °C	2011	C
	AB	10 mg/ml[a,b]	DU	2 mg/ml[d]	Heavy white turbidity forms immediately	2011	I
	LI	4 mg/ml[a]	DME	2 mg/ml[d]	Haze forms immediately	2078	I

[a]*Tested in dextrose 5% in water.*
[b]*Tested in sodium chloride 0.9%.*
[c]*Sodium carbonate–containing formulation tested.*
[d]*Tested in sterile water for injection.*
[e]*Tested in dextrose 5% in sodium chloride 0.45%.*

ZIDOVUDINE
AHFS 8:18.08

Products — Zidovudine is available in 20-ml single-use vials. Each milliliter of solution contains zidovudine 10 mg in water for injection. Hydrochloric acid and/or sodium hydroxide may be present to adjust the pH. (2)

pH — Approximately 5.5. (2)

Osmolality — Zidovudine 10 mg/ml has an osmolality of 34 mOsm/kg. (1689)

Trade Name(s) — Retrovir.

Administration — Zidovudine must be diluted in dextrose 5% in water to a concentration no greater than 4 mg/ml prior to administration. The drug is administered by intravenous infusion at a constant rate over one hour. (2; 4) Zidovudine has also been administered by continuous intravenous infusion. (4) Intramuscular injection, intravenous bolus, and rapid intravenous infusion should be avoided. (2; 4)

Stability — Intact vials of zidovudine should be stored at 15 to 25 °C and protected from light. (2)

Elastomeric Reservoir Pumps — Zidovudine HCl 1 to 4 mg/ml in dextrose 5% in water in Intermate HPC elastomeric reservoir pumps has been stated by the pump manufacturer to be stable for 10 days under refrigeration and 24 hours at room temperature. (31)

Central Venous Catheter — Zidovudine (Glaxo Wellcome) 1 mg/ml in dextrose 5% in water was found to be compatible with the ARROWg+ard Blue Plus (Arrow International) chlorhexidine-bearing triple-lumen central catheter. HPLC analysis was used to evaluate completeness of drug delivery through the catheter and the amount of chlorhexidine removed from the internal lumens. Essentially complete delivery of the drug was found with little or no drug loss occurring. Furthermore, chlorhexidine delivered from the catheter remained at trace amounts with no substantial increase due to the delivery of the drug through the catheter. (2335)

Compatibility Information

Solution Compatibility

Zidovudine

Solution	*Mfr*	*Mfr*	*Conc/L*	*Remarks*	*Ref*	*C/I*
Dextrose 5% in water	[a]	BW	4 g	Physically compatible with no drug loss in 8 days at 4 and 25 °C	1411	C
Sodium chloride 0.9%	[a]	BW	4 g	Physically compatible with no drug loss in 8 days at 4 and 25 °C	1411	C

[a]*Tested in PVC containers.*

Additive Compatibility

Zidovudine

Drug	*Mfr*	*Conc/L*	*Mfr*	*Conc/L*	*Test Soln*	*Remarks*	*Ref*	*C/I*
Meropenem	ZEN	1 g	BW	4 g	NS	Visually compatible for 4 hr at room temperature	1994	C
	ZEN	20 g	BW	4 g	NS	Dark yellow discoloration forms in 4 hr at room temperature	1994	I

Y-Site Injection Compatibility (1:1 Mixture)

Zidovudine

Drug	*Mfr*	*Conc*	*Mfr*	*Conc*	*Remarks*	*Ref*	*C/I*
Acyclovir sodium	BW	7 mg/ml[a]	BW	4 mg/ml[a]	Physically compatible for 4 hr at 25 °C under fluorescent light by visual and microscopic examination	1193	C
Allopurinol sodium	BW	3 mg/ml[b]	BW	4 mg/ml[b]	Physically compatible with no change in measured turbidity or increase in particle content in 4 hr at 22 °C	1686	C
Amifostine	USB	10 mg/ml[a]	BW	4 mg/ml[a]	Physically compatible with no change in measured turbidity or increase in particle content in 4 hr at 23 °C	1845	C
Amikacin sulfate	BR	4 mg/ml[a]	BW	4 mg/ml[a]	Physically compatible for 4 hr at 25 °C under fluorescent light by visual and microscopic examination	1193	C
Amphotericin B	SQ	600 µg/ml[a]	BW	4 mg/ml[a]	Physically compatible for 4 hr at 25 °C under fluorescent light by visual and microscopic examination	1193	C
Amphotericin B cholesteryl sulfate complex	SEQ	0.83 mg/ml[a]	BW	4 mg/ml[a]	Physically compatible with little or no change in measured turbidity or increase in particle content in 4 hr at 23 °C under fluorescent light	2117	C
Aztreonam	SQ	40 mg/ml[a]	BW	4 mg/ml[a]	Physically compatible for 4 hr at 25 °C under fluorescent light by visual and microscopic examination	1193	C
	SQ	40 mg/ml[a]	BW	4 mg/ml[a]	Physically compatible with no subvisual haze or particle formation in 4 hr at 23 °C	1758	C
Cefepime HCl	BMS	20 mg/ml[a]	BW	4 mg/ml[a]	Physically compatible with no change in measured turbidity or increase in particle content in 4 hr at 22 °C	1689	C

Y-Site Injection Compatibility (1:1 Mixture) (Cont.)

Drug	Mfr	Conc	Zidovudine Mfr	Zidovudine Conc	Remarks	Ref	C/I
Ceftazidime	GL[g]	20 mg/ml[a]	BW	4 mg/ml[a]	Physically compatible for 4 hr at 25 °C under fluorescent light by visual and microscopic examination	1193	C
Ceftriaxone sodium	RC	20 mg/ml[a]	BW	4 mg/ml[a]	Physically compatible for 4 hr at 25 °C under fluorescent light by visual and microscopic examination	1193	C
Cimetidine HCl	SKF	6 mg/ml[a]	BW	4 mg/ml[a]	Physically compatible for 4 hr at 25 °C under fluorescent light by visual and microscopic examination	1193	C
Cisatracurium besylate	GW	0.1, 2, 5 mg/ml[a]	BW	4 mg/ml[a]	Physically compatible with no change in measured turbidity or increase in particle content in 4 hr at 23 °C	2074	C
Clindamycin phosphate	UP	12 mg/ml[a]	BW	4 mg/ml[a]	Physically compatible for 4 hr at 25 °C under fluorescent light by visual and microscopic examination	1193	C
Dexamethasone sodium phosphate	ES	0.16 mg/ml[a]	BW	4 mg/ml[a]	Physically compatible for 4 hr at 25 °C under fluorescent light by visual and microscopic examination	1193	C
Dobutamine HCl	LI	5 mg/ml[a]	BW	4 mg/ml[a]	Physically compatible for 4 hr at 25 °C under fluorescent light by visual and microscopic examination	1193	C
Docetaxel	RPR	0.9 mg/ml[a]	GW	4 mg/ml[a]	Physically compatible with no change in measured turbidity or increase in particle content in 4 hr at 23 °C	2224	C
Dopamine HCl	AB	1.6 mg/ml[a]	BW	4 mg/ml[a]	Physically compatible for 4 hr at 25 °C under fluorescent light by visual and microscopic examination	1193	C
Doxorubicin HCl liposome injection	SEQ	0.4 mg/ml[a]	BW	4 mg/ml[a]	Physically compatible with little or no change in measured turbidity and no increase in particle content in 4 hr at 23 °C	2087	C
Erythromycin lactobionate	AB	20 mg/ml[a,c]	BW	4 mg/ml[a]	Physically compatible for 4 hr at 25 °C under fluorescent light by visual and microscopic examination	1193	C
Etoposide phosphate	BR	5 mg/ml[a]	BW	4 mg/ml[a]	Physically compatible with no change in measured turbidity or increase in particle content in 4 hr at 23 °C	2218	C
Filgrastim	AMG	30 μg/ml[a]	BW	4 mg/ml[a]	Physically compatible with no change in measured turbidity or increase in particle content in 4 hr at 22 °C	1687	C
Fluconazole	RR	2 mg/ml	BW	10 mg/ml	Physically compatible for 24 hr at 25 °C	1407	C
Fludarabine phosphate	BX	1 mg/ml[a]	BW	4 mg/ml[a]	Physically compatible for 4 hr at room temperature under fluorescent light	1439	C
Gatifloxacin	BMS	2 mg/ml[a]	GW	4 mg/ml[a]	Physically compatible with no change in measured haze or increase in particle content in 4 hr at 23 °C	2234	C
Gemcitabine HCl	LI	10 mg/ml[b]	GW	4 mg/ml[b]	Physically compatible with no change in measured turbidity or increase in particle content in 4 hr at 23 °C	2226	C

Y-Site Injection Compatibility (1:1 Mixture) (Cont.)

			Zidovudine				
Drug	*Mfr*	*Conc*	*Mfr*	*Conc*	*Remarks*	*Ref*	*C/I*
Gentamicin sulfate	IMS	2 mg/ml[a]	BW	4 mg/ml[a]	Physically compatible for 4 hr at 25 °C under fluorescent light by visual and microscopic examination	1193	C
Granisetron HCl	SKB	0.05 mg/ml[a]	BW	4 mg/ml[a]	Physically compatible with no change in measured turbidity or increase in particle content in 4 hr at 23 °C	2000	C
Heparin sodium	LY	100 units/ml[a]	BW	4 mg/ml[a]	Physically compatible for 4 hr at 25 °C under fluorescent light by visual and microscopic examination	1193	C
Imipenem–cilastatin sodium	MSD	5 mg/ml[a]	BW	4 mg/ml[a]	Physically compatible for 4 hr at 25 °C under fluorescent light by visual and microscopic examination	1193	C
Linezolid	PHU	2 mg/ml	GW	4 mg/ml[a]	Physically compatible with no change in measured turbidity or increase in particle content in 4 hr at 23 °C	2264	C
Lorazepam	WY	80 μg/ml[a]	BW	4 mg/ml[a]	Physically compatible for 4 hr at 25 °C under fluorescent light by visual and microscopic examination	1193	C
Melphalan HCl	BW	0.1 mg/ml[b]	BW	4 mg/ml[b]	Physically compatible with no change in measured turbidity or increase in particle content in 3 hr at 22 °C	1557	C
Meropenem	ZEN	1 mg/ml[b]	BW	4 mg/ml[d]	Visually compatible for 4 hr at room temperature	1994	C
	ZEN	50 mg/ml[b]	BW	4 mg/ml[d]	Yellow discoloration forms in 4 hr at room temperature	1994	I
Metoclopramide HCl	RB	2 mg/ml[a]	BW	4 mg/ml[a]	Physically compatible for 4 hr at 25 °C under fluorescent light by visual and microscopic examination	1193	C
Morphine sulfate	ES	1 mg/ml[a]	BW	4 mg/ml[a]	Physically compatible for 4 hr at 25 °C under fluorescent light by visual and microscopic examination	1193	C
Nafcillin sodium	BR	20 mg/ml[a]	BW	4 mg/ml[a]	Physically compatible for 4 hr at 25 °C under fluorescent light by visual and microscopic examination	1193	C
Ondansetron HCl	GL	1 mg/ml[b]	BW	4 mg/ml[a]	Physically compatible for 4 hr at 22 °C	1365	C
Oxacillin sodium	BR	20 mg/ml[a]	BW	4 mg/ml[a]	Physically compatible for 4 hr at 25 °C under fluorescent light by visual and microscopic examination	1193	C
Paclitaxel	NCI	1.2 mg/ml[a]	BW	4 mg/ml[a]	Physically compatible with no change in measured turbidity in 4 hr at 22 °C under fluorescent light	1556	C
Pentamidine isethionate	LY	6 mg/ml[a]	BW	4 mg/ml[a]	Physically compatible for 4 hr at 25 °C under fluorescent light by visual and microscopic examination	1193	C
Phenylephrine HCl	WI	1 mg/ml[a]	BW	4 mg/ml[a]	Physically compatible for 4 hr at 25 °C under fluorescent light by visual and microscopic examination	1193	C

Y-Site Injection Compatibility (1:1 Mixture) (Cont.)

			Zidovudine				
Drug	*Mfr*	*Conc*	*Mfr*	*Conc*	*Remarks*	*Ref*	*C/I*
Piperacillin sodium	LE	4 mg/ml[a]	BW	4 mg/ml[a]	Physically compatible for 4 hr at 25 °C under fluorescent light by visual and microscopic examination	1193	C
Piperacillin sodium–tazobactam sodium	LE	40 + 5 mg/ml[a]	BW	4 mg/ml[a]	Physically compatible with no change in measured turbidity or increase in particle content in 4 hr at 22 °C	1688	C
Potassium chloride	IMS	0.67 mEq/ml[a]	BW	4 mg/ml[a]	Physically compatible for 4 hr at 25 °C under fluorescent light by visual and microscopic examination	1193	C
Ranitidine HCl	GL	1 mg/ml[a]	BW	4 mg/ml[a]	Physically compatible for 4 hr at 25 °C under fluorescent light by visual and microscopic examination	1193	C
Remifentanil HCl	GW	0.025 and 0.25 mg/ml[b]	BW	4 mg/ml[a]	Physically compatible with no change in measured turbidity or increase in particle content in 4 hr at 23 °C	2075	C
Sargramostim	IMM	10 μg/ml[b]	BW	4 mg/ml[b]	Physically compatible for 4 hr at 22 °C	1436	C
Teniposide	BR	0.1 mg/ml[a]	BW	4 mg/ml[a]	Physically compatible with no subvisual haze or particle formation in 4 hr at 23 °C	1725	C
Thiotepa	IMM[e]	1 mg/ml[a]	BW	4 mg/ml[a]	Physically compatible with no change in measured turbidity or increase in particle content in 4 hr at 23 °C	1861	C
TNA #218 to #226[f]			GW	4 mg/ml[a]	Visually compatible with no precipitate or emulsion damage apparent in 4 hr at 23 °C	2215	C
Tobramycin sulfate	LI	2 mg/ml[a]	BW	4 mg/ml[a]	Physically compatible for 4 hr at 25 °C under fluorescent light by visual and microscopic examination	1193	C
TPN #212 to #215[f]			BW	4 mg/ml[a]	Physically compatible with no change in measured turbidity or increase in particle content in 4 hr at 23 °C	2109	C
Trimethoprim–sulfamethoxazole	BW	0.53 + 2.6 mg/ml[a]	BW	4 mg/ml[a]	Physically compatible for 4 hr at 25 °C under fluorescent light by visual and microscopic examination	1193	C
Trimetrexate	WL	1 mg/ml[a]	BW	4 mg/ml[a]	Physically compatible for 4 hr at 25 °C under fluorescent light by visual and microscopic examination	1193	C
Vancomycin HCl	LI	15 mg/ml[a]	BW	4 mg/ml[a]	Physically compatible for 4 hr at 25 °C under fluorescent light by visual and microscopic examination	1193	C
Vinorelbine tartrate	BW	1 mg/ml[b]	BW	4 mg/ml[b]	Physically compatible with no change in measured turbidity or increase in particle content in 4 hr at 22 °C	1558	C

[a] *Tested in dextrose 5% in water.*
[b] *Tested in sodium chloride 0.9%.*
[c] *Sodium bicarbonate 2.5 mEq added to adjust pH.*
[d] *Tested in sterile water for injection.*
[e] *Lyophilized formulation tested.*
[f] *Refer to Appendix I for the composition of parenteral nutrition solutions. TNA indicates a 3-in-1 admixture, and TPN indicates a 2-in-1 admixture.*
[g] *Sodium carbonate–containing formulation tested.*

Additional Compatibility Information

Infusion Solutions — The manufacturer indicates that zidovudine is physically and chemically stable in dextrose 5% in water for 24 hours at room temperature and 48 hours under refrigeration at 2 to 8 °C. However, the manufacturer also recommends that zidovudine diluted for infusion be administered within eight hours if stored at 25 °C or 24 hours if refrigerated because no antibacterial preservative is present in the formulation. (2; 4) Other information indicates that the drug is chemically stable diluted for infusion for longer time periods. (1411) See Solution Compatibility table above.

Zidovudine injection and diluted solutions should not be mixed with biological or colloidal fluids such as blood products and protein solutions. (4)

Drugs Available Outside the United States

The monographs in this section describe drugs available in much of the world, but not the United States, for which substantial stability and/or compatibility information has been published. The drug names cited in this section are primarily those in use in the United Kingdom. The drug names in use in the United States have been cross-referenced elsewhere in the book.

L-ALANYL-L-GLUTAMINE

Products — Dipeptiven contains the dipeptide *N*(2)-L-alanyl-L-glutamine. The product is available in 50- and 100-ml glass bottles. Each milliliter of solution contains 200 mg of the dipeptide and provides the equivalent of 82 mg of L-alanine and 134.6 mg of L-glutamine. L-Alanyl-L-glutamine solution is a concentrate that must be diluted for administration. For infusion, the product is diluted with at least five times its volume of a suitable amino acid solution or parenteral nutrition solution. The concentration of L-alanyl-L-glutamine should not exceed 3.5%. (182)

pH — From 5.4 to 6.0. (182)

Osmolarity — The osmolarity of L-alanyl-L-glutamine solution is 921 mOsm/L. (182)

Trade Name(s) — Dipeptiven.

Administration — L-Alanyl-L-glutamine may be administered intravenously after dilution to a concentration not exceeding 3.5%. Each 100 ml of L-alanyl-L-glutamine should be mixed with at least 500 ml of amino acid solution or parenteral nutrition admixture. (182)

Stability — Intact containers of L-alanyl-L-glutamine solution should be stored at room temperature (20 °C). (182)

Compatibility Information

Solution Compatibility

L-Alanyl-L-glutamine solution

Solution	*Mfr*	*Mfr*	*Conc/L*	*Remarks*	*Ref*	*C/I*
AKE 4 GX		FRE	50 ml	Compatible for 24 hr at room temperature	2047	C
AKE 1100 with glucose		FRE	50 ml	Compatible for 24 hr at room temperature	2047	C
Aminomel 10%		FRE	100 ml	Compatible for 24 hr at room temperature	2047	C
Aminosteril KE 10%		FRE	100 ml	Compatible for 24 hr at room temperature	2047	C
Aminosteril 10%		FRE	100 ml	Compatible for 24 hr at room temperature	2047	C
Combiplasmal 4,5 GXE		FRE	50 ml	Compatible for 24 hr at room temperature	2047	C
Intrafusin 10%		FRE	100 ml	Compatible for 24 hr at room temperature	2047	C
Nutriflex 32/125 G-E		FRE	100 ml	Compatible for 24 hr at room temperature	2047	C
Nutriflex 48/150 G-E		FRE	100 ml	Compatible for 24 hr at room temperature	2047	C
Nutri Twin Forte		FRE	100 ml	Compatible for 24 hr at room temperature	2047	C
Nutri Twin G		FRE	100 ml	Compatible for 24 hr at room temperature	2047	C
Nutri Twin GX		FRE	100 ml	Compatible for 24 hr at room temperature	2047	C
Salviamin 3,5 G-E		FRE	50 ml	Compatible for 24 hr at room temperature	2047	C
Salviamin 3,5 GX-E		FRE	50 ml	Compatible for 24 hr at room temperature	2047	C
Salviamin 3,5 X-E		FRE	50 ml	Compatible for 24 hr at room temperature	2047	C

Additional Compatibility Information

Parenteral Nutrition Solutions — L-Alanyl-L-glutamine solution in amounts up to 200 ml/L per liter has been reported to be compatible with a wide and varied array of parenteral nutrition admixtures for nine days under refrigeration followed by one day at room temperature. The parenteral nutrition admixtures contained 500 to 1000 ml of the amino acid sources Aminosteril KE 10%, Vamin 14, Vamin 14 EF, Vamin 18 EF, Vamin glucose, and Vamin N. Dextrose sources ranged from 10 to 70%. Lipovenoes 10% PLR or Lipovenoes 20% was incorporated in some combinations. The following electrolytes were also included (2047):

Sodium chloride	20 to 120 mmol/L
Potassium chloride	20 to 90 mmol/L
Sodium glycerophosphate	6.3 to 25 mmol/L
Calcium chloride	1.5 to 7.5 mmol/L
Magnesium sulphate	1.23 to 6.0 mmol/L

ALIZAPRIDE HCL

Products — Alizapride HCl is available as a 25-mg/ml solution of alizapride as the hydrochloride in 2-ml ampuls. Also present in the formulation are sodium chloride and water for injection. (116)

Trade Name(s) — Limican, Litican, Plitican, Vergentan.

Administration — Alizapride HCl is administered by intramuscular injection and intravenously. (5; 116)

Stability — Alizapride HCl 0.5 and 2 mg/ml in sodium chloride 0.9% stored at room temperature was found to undergo about 7% loss in four days when exposed to light. (2304)

Compatibility Information

Solution Compatibility

Alizapride HCl

Solution	*Mfr*	*Mfr*	*Conc/L*	*Remarks*	*Ref*	*C/I*
Sodium chloride 0.9%	FRE[a]	SS	500 mg	Physically compatible with no loss of drug by HPLC in 28 days at 4 °C, 7 days at room temperature, and 4 days at 40 °C protected from light	2304	C
	FRE[a]	SS	2 g	Physically compatible with no loss of drug by HPLC in 28 days at 4 °C, 7 days at room temperature, and 4 days at 40 °C protected from light	2304	C

[a] *Tested in PVC containers.*

AMOXYCILLIN SODIUM

Products — Amoxycillin sodium is available in vials containing the equivalent of amoxycillin 250 mg, 500 mg, and 1 g. (38; 115)

For intramuscular injection, reconstitute the vials with the following volumes of sterile water for injection (38):

Vial Size	Volume of Diluent	Final Volume
250 mg	1.5 ml	1.7 ml
500 mg	2.5 ml	2.9 ml
1 g	2.5 ml	3.3 ml

Alternatively, the 1-g vial may be reconstituted with lignocaine HCl 1% or procaine HCl 0.5%. However, a greater volume of local anesthetic is required to dissolve amoxycillin 1 g than sterile water for injection. Dividing a 1-g dose into two 500-mg portions given at different sites has been suggested. (38)

For intravenous injection, reconstitute the vials with the following volumes of sterile water for injection (38):

Vial Size	Volume of Diluent	Final Volume
250 mg	5 ml	5.2 ml
500 mg	10 ml	10.4 ml
1 g	20 ml	20.8 ml

For intravenous infusion, the reconstituted drug may be added to an intravenous solution in a minibag or burette chamber of an administration set. (38)

Sodium Content — Amoxycillin sodium contains 3.3 mmol of sodium per gram of drug. (38)

Trade Name(s) — Amoxil, Clamoxyl, Ibiamox, many others.

Administration — Amoxycillin sodium may be administered by intramuscular injection, direct intravenous injection over three to four minutes, or intermittent intravenous infusion over 30 to 60 minutes. (38)

Stability — After reconstitution with sterile water for injection, a transient pink color or slight opalescence may appear. Reconstituted solutions are normally a pale straw color. The reconstituted solution should be administered or diluted immediately in a suitable infusion solution. (38)

Concentration Effects — Amoxycillin sodium 50 mg/ml is substantially less stable in all infusion solutions than at lower concentrations of 10 or 20 mg/ml. (1469)

Freezing Solutions — Amoxycillin sodium 10 mg/ml in sterile water for injection was unstable when stored frozen at between 0 and −20 °C but was stable for 13 days when stored below −30 °C. Amoxycillin sodium 10 mg/ml in sterile water for injection was stable for only two days at 0 °C in the unfrozen state. (1470)

McDonald et al. showed that amoxycillin sodium 10 mg/ml in sodium chloride 0.9% was stable for 10.5 days at 0 °C (unfrozen) and for 14 hours when frozen at −19 °C; in dextrose 5% in water, the comparative times were 12.5 and 8.4 hours, respectively. (1471)

The processes of freezing and thawing increase the degradation rate of amoxycillin sodium 10 mg/ml in sodium chloride 0.9% in PVC bags (Travenol). Freezing and thawing (natural or microwave) could account for a 5 to 10% loss of amoxycillin; the losses will be affected by the time to reach the equilibrium frozen temperature. (1472)

Sorption—Amoxycillin trihydrate (Beecham) 400 mg/L in sodium chloride 0.9% (Travenol) in PVC bags did not exhibit significant sorption to the plastic during one week at room temperature (15 to 20 °C). (536)

Amoxycillin sodium (Beecham) 400 mg/L in sodium chloride 0.9% did not exhibit any loss due to sorption during a seven-hour simulated infusion through an infusion set (Travenol) consisting of a cellulose propionate burette chamber and 170 cm of PVC tubing. (606)

The drug also was tested as a simulated infusion over at least one hour by a syringe pump system. A glass syringe on a syringe pump was fitted with 20 cm of polyethylene tubing or 50 cm of Silastic tubing. No drug loss due to sorption was observed with either tubing. (606)

A 25-ml aliquot of amoxycillin sodium (Beecham) 400 mg/L in sodium chloride 0.9% was stored in all-plastic syringes composed of polypropylene barrels and polyethylene plungers for 24 hours at room temperature in the dark. The solution did not exhibit any loss due to sorption. (606)

Picard et al. reported little or no loss due to sorption of amoxycillin sodium (Beecham) 1 g/100 ml in sodium chloride 0.9% in trilayer solution bags (Bieffe Medital) composed of polyethylene, polyamide, and polypropylene. The admixtures were evaluated by HPLC analysis up to two hours after preparation. Similarly, no loss was found after one hour of simulated infusion. (1918)

Filtration—Amoxycillin sodium 1.98 mg/ml in sodium chloride 0.9% was filtered through a 0.22-µm cellulose ester membrane filter (Ivex-HP, Millipore) over five hours. No significant drug loss due to sorption to the filter was noted. (1034)

Compatibility Information

Solution Compatibility

Amoxycillin sodium

Solution	*Mfr*	*Mfr*	*Conc/L*	*Remarks*	*Ref*	*C/I*
Compound sodium lactate			10, 20, 50 g	5, 9, and 22% losses at 10, 20, and 50 g/L, respectively, in 6 hr at 25 °C	1469	I
Dextran 40 10% in dextrose 5% in water			10, 20, 50 g	9 to 12% loss in 1 hr at 25 °C	1469	I
Dextran 40 10% in sodium chloride 0.9%			10, 20, 50 g	12, 14, and 20% losses at 10, 20, and 50 g/L, respectively, in 3 hr at 25 °C	1469	I
Dextrose 5% in water			1 g	9% loss in 4 hr and 34% loss in 24 hr at room temperature	768	I
			10, 20, 50 g	14 and 18% losses in 3 hr at 10 and 20 g/L, respectively, and 14% loss in 1.5 hr at 50 g/L at 25 °C	1469	I
	[a]	BE	20 g	No drug loss by HPLC during 2-hr storage and 1-hr simulated infusion	1774	C
Sodium bicarbonate 2.74%			10, 20, 50 g	9% loss in 6 and 4 hr at 10 and 20 g/L, respectively, and 15% loss in 4 hr at 50 g/L at 25 °C	1469	I
Sodium bicarbonate 8.4%			10, 20, 50 g	10 and 13% losses in 4 hr at 10 and 20 g/L, respectively, and 17% loss in 3 hr at 50 g/L at 25 °C	1469	I
Sodium chloride 0.9%			1 g	10% loss in 24 hr at room temperature	768	C
			10, 20, 50 g	3 and 7% losses in 6 hr at 10 and 20 g/L, respectively, and 12% loss in 4 hr at 50 g/L at 25 °C	1469	I
	TR	PR	10 g	Less than 3% loss in 24 hr at 0 °C	1472	C
Sodium chloride 0.9% with potassium chloride 0.3%			10, 20, 50 g	4 and 9% losses in 8 hr at 10 and 20 g/L, respectively, and 9% loss in 3 hr at 50 g/L at 25 °C	1469	I
Sodium lactate ⅙ M			10, 20, 50 g	10% loss in 6 hr at 10 and 20 g/L and 14% loss in 4 hr at 50 g/L at 25 °C	1469	I
Sorbitol 30%			10 and 20 g	11 and 16% losses in 1 hr at 10 and 20 g/L, respectively, at 25 °C	1469	I

[a] *Tested in PVC containers.*

Additive Compatibility

			Amoxycillin sodium					
Drug	*Mfr*	*Conc/L*	*Mfr*	*Conc/L*	*Test Soln*	*Remarks*	*Ref*	*C/I*
Ciprofloxacin		2 g		10 g	[a]	Immediate precipitation	1473	I
Ofloxacin	HO	1.67 g	BE	8.3 g	W	Visually compatible with little or no loss of either drug by HPLC in 48 hr	1613	C
Pefloxacin		4 g		10 g	D5W, NS	Precipitate forms within 1 hr	1473	I

[a]*Amoxycillin sodium added to ciprofloxacin solution.*

Y-Site Injection Compatibility (1:1 Mixture)

			Amoxycillin sodium				
Drug	*Mfr*	*Conc*	*Mfr*	*Conc*	*Remarks*	*Ref*	*C/I*
Lorazepam	WY	0.33 mg/ml[a]	SKB	50 mg/ml	Visually compatible for 24 hr at 22 °C	1855	C
Midazolam HCl	RC	5 mg/ml	SKB	50 mg/ml	White precipitate forms immediately	1855	I
TPN #189[b]				50 mg/ml[a]	Visually compatible for 24 hr at 22 °C	1767	C

[a]*Tested in sodium chloride 0.9%.*
[b]*Refer to Appendix I for the composition of parenteral nutrition solutions. TPN indicates a 2-in-1 admixture.*

Additional Compatibility Information

Aminoglycosides — It is recommended that amoxycillin sodium not be mixed with aminoglycoside antibiotics in the same syringe, intravenous infusion container, or set because aminoglycoside activity may be lost. (38)

AMOXYCILLIN SODIUM–CLAVULANIC ACID (CO-AMOXICLAV)

Products — Amoxycillin sodium–clavulanic acid is available in 600-mg vials containing amoxycillin sodium 500 mg and clavulanic acid 100 mg as the potassium salt and in 1.2-g vials containing amoxycillin sodium 1 g and clavulanic acid 200 mg as the potassium salt. Reconstitute the 600-mg vials with 10 ml and the 1.2-g vials with 20 ml of sterile water for injection. (38)

Sodium and Potassium Content — Amoxycillin sodium–clavulanic acid contains 3.1 mmol of sodium and 1 mmol of potassium in 1.2 g of drug product. (38)

Trade Name(s) — Augmentin, Clavulin, Flanamox, many others.

Administration — Amoxycillin sodium–clavulanic acid may be administered by intravenous injection or intermittent infusion. It is not suitable for intramuscular administration. When given by intravenous injection directly into a vein or via a drip tube, it should be injected slowly over three to four minutes. For intravenous infusion, add the contents of the 600-mg or 1.2-g vial to 50 or 100 ml, respectively, of sterile water for injection or sodium chloride 0.9% and then infuse over 30 to 40 minutes, completing the administration within four hours of reconstitution. (38)

Stability — Amoxycillin sodium–clavulanic acid in intact vials should be stored at 25 °C or below.The injection should be used within 20 minutes after reconstitution with sterile water for injection. (38)

Ashwin et al. reported that the stability of amoxycillin sodium–clavulanic acid is governed by the more rapid degradation of clavulanic acid compared with amoxycillin. Amoxycillin sodium–clavulanic acid 1.2 g reconstituted with 20 ml of sterile water for injection and added to 100 ml of sodium chloride 0.9% in PVC bags showed 10% degradation of amoxycillin in 390 minutes and of clavulanic acid in 261 minutes at 25 °C. However, the drug was more stable when stored at 5 °C. Amoxycillin sodium–clavulanic acid 1.2 g reconstituted with 20 ml of sterile water for injection and added to 100 ml of sterile water for injection, sodium chloride 0.9%, or dextrose 5% in water lost 10% activity in 15, 12.5, and 1.2 hours, respectively, when stored at 5 °C. (1474)

Stability is also concentration dependent; amoxycillin sodium–clavulanic acid is less stable in high concentrations. Therefore, it is suggested that reconstituted solutions be used immediately or diluted without delay. (1474)

Freezing Solutions — Amoxycillin sodium–clavulanic acid 1.2 g reconstituted with 20 ml and diluted in 100 ml of sterile water for injection was frozen at −20 °C for four hours, followed by microwave thawing. Solutions retained only 65% of the initial clavulanic acid content. (1474)

Sorption — Amoxycillin sodium–clavulanic acid 1.2 g in 100 ml of sodium chloride 0.9% stored at 25 °C in PVC bags (Baxter) did not show evidence of sorption compared to solutions stored in glass containers. Furthermore, identical solutions infused at 1 ml/min through a standard administration set (Continuflo, Baxter) did not show drug loss due to sorption. (1474)

Compatibility Information

Solution Compatibility

Amoxycillin sodium–clavulanic acid

Solution	*Mfr*	*Mfr*	*Conc/L*	*Remarks*	*Ref*	*C/I*
Dextrose 5% in water	BT[a]	BE	8.33 + 1.67 g	Physically compatible with 10% loss within 30 min at 25 °C and 1.2 hr at 5 °C	1474	I
Ringer's injection	BT[a]	BE	8.33 + 1.67 g	Physically compatible with 10% loss in 4.1 hr at 25 °C	1474	I[b]
Ringer's injection, lactated	BT[a]	BE	8.33 + 1.67 g	Physically compatible with 10% loss in 4.1 hr	1474	I[b]
Sodium chloride 0.9%	BT[a]	BE	8.33 + 1.67 g	Physically compatible with 10% loss in 4.4 hr at 25 °C and 12.5 hr at 5 °C	1474	I[b]
Sodium chloride 0.9% with potassium chloride 0.3%	BT[a]	BE	8.33 + 1.67 g	Physically compatible with 10% loss in 3.9 hr at 25 °C	1474	I[b]
Sodium lactate ⅙ M	BT[a]	BE	8.33 + 1.67 g	Physically compatible with 10% loss in 4.3 hr at 25 °C	1474	I[b]

[a] *Tested in polyethylene containers.*
[b] *Incompatible by conventional standards; may be used in shorter time periods.*

Additive Compatibility

Amoxycillin sodium–clavulanic acid

Drug	*Mfr*	*Conc/L*	*Mfr*	*Conc/L*	*Test Soln*	*Remarks*	*Ref*	*C/I*
Ciprofloxacin		2 g		10 + 2 g	[a]	Immediate precipitation	1473	I
Metronidazole	BAY	5 g	BE	20 + 2 g		Physically compatible with 8% clavulanate loss in 2 hr and 25% loss in 6 hr at 21 °C by HPLC. 7 to 8% amoxycillin and no metronidazole loss in 6 hr at 21 °C.	1920	I
Ofloxacin	HO	1.67 g	BE	8.33 + 1.67 g	W	Visually compatible with little or no loss of either drug by HPLC in 48 hr	1613	C
Pefloxacin		4 g		10 + 2 g	D5W, NS	Precipitate forms within 1 hr	1473	I

[a] *Amoxycillin sodium–clavulanic acid added to ciprofloxacin solution.*

Y-Site Injection Compatibility (1:1 Mixture)

Amoxycillin sodium–clavulanic acid

Drug	*Mfr*	*Conc*	*Mfr*	*Conc*	*Remarks*	*Ref*	*C/I*
Clarithromycin	AB	4 mg/ml[a]	BE	20 + 4 mg/ml[a]	Visually compatible for 72 hr at both 30 and 17 °C	2174	C
Lorazepam	WY	0.33 mg/ml[b]	SKB	20 + 2 mg/ml	Visually compatible for 24 hr at 22 °C	1855	C
Midazolam HCl	RC	5 mg/ml	SKB	20 + 2 mg/ml	White precipitate formed immediately	1855	I

[a] *Tested in dextrose 5% in water.*
[b] *Tested in sodium chloride 0.9%.*

Additional Compatibility Information

Infusion Solutions — Amoxycillin sodium–clavulanic acid should not be added to infusion solutions containing dextrose, dextran, sodium bicarbonate, blood products, proteinaceous fluids, or intravenous fat emulsions. (38)

Ashwin et al. reported that administration should be completed within the following periods after further dilution in infusion solutions and storage at room temperature (25 °C). (1474):

Ringer's injection	3 hr
Ringer's injection, lactated	3 hr
Sodium chloride 0.9%	4 hr
Sodium chloride 0.9% with potassium chloride 0.3%	3 hr
Sodium lactate ⅙ M	4 hr

The manufacturer indicates that infusions of amoxycillin sodium–clavulanic acid in sterile water for injection or sodium chloride 0.9% are stable at 5 °C for up to eight hours. Amoxycillin sodium–clavulanic acid is less stable in dextrose, dextran, or bicarbonate-containing infusion solutions and should not be added to them. However, it may be injected into the tubing of running infusions of these solutions. (38; 115)

Aminoglycosides — The manufacturer states that amoxycillin sodium–clavulanic acid should not be mixed in a syringe, intravenous fluid container, or administration set with aminoglycosides because of possible aminoglycoside activity loss. (38)

AMSACRINE
(ACRIDINYL ANISIDIDE; m-AMSA)

Products — Amsacrine is available in ampuls containing 1.5 ml of a 50-mg/ml solution (75 mg total) in anhydrous *N,N*-dimethylacetamide (DMA). It is packaged with a vial containing 13.5 ml of 0.0353 M L-lactic acid diluent. (115; 116)

To prepare the drug for use, aseptically add 1.5 ml of the amsacrine solution to the vial of L-lactic acid diluent. The resulting orange-red solution contains amsacrine 5 mg/ml in 10% (v/v) *N,N*-dimethylacetamide and 0.0318 M L-lactic acid. This concentrated solution must be diluted in dextrose 5% in water for infusion; do not use chloride-containing solutions. (115; 234)

Direct contact of amsacrine solutions with skin or mucous membranes may result in skin sensitization and should be avoided. (234)

Trade Name(s) — Amsidine, Amsidyl.

Administration — Amsacrine is administered by central vein infusion over 60 to 90 minutes after the dose is diluted in 500 ml of dextrose 5% in water. (115; 116)

Stability — Amsacrine in intact ampuls should be stored at room temperature. When mixed with the L-lactic acid diluent, the amsacrine solution is physically and chemically stable for at least 48 hours at room temperature under ambient light. (234)

Light Effects — The effect of diffuse daylight and fluorescent light on amsacrine 150 μg/ml in dextrose 5% in water was studied for 48 hours at 19 to 21 °C; no loss due to light exposure occurred. The authors concluded that light protection has no relevance to the normal clinical use of amsacrine. (1308)

Syringes — Glass syringes are recommended for the transfer of amsacrine concentrate to the L-lactic acid diluent. (115) The DMA solvent may extract UV-absorbing species from plastics and rubber used in plastic syringes. (967)

The compatibility of amsacrine (Gödecke) concentrated solution in DMA with rubber-free plastic syringes (Injekt, B. Braun) was evaluated at 37 °C and ambient temperature. Storage of the DMA diluent in the plastic syringes resulted in no visible changes to the drug or syringes and did not adversely affect the performance of the syringes. HPLC, GC–MS, and GC–MS–SIMS analysis found a trace amount of oleic acid amide lubricant, about 50 μg in the 2-ml syringe content, after storage for 24 hours at 37 °C. Storage at ambient temperature resulted in substantially lower amounts of oleic acid amide. The authors concluded the rubber-free Injekt plastic syringes were acceptable alternatives to glass syringes to transfer the amsacrine concentrate. Other plastic syringes incorporating rubber components are not recommended because of the extraction of materials into the drug solution. (2284)

Sorption — Amsacrine 150 μg/ml in dextrose 5% in water was evaluated for sorption to cellulose propionate and methacrylate butadiene styrene burette chambers and PVC and polybutadiene tubing. No amsacrine loss due to sorption was found during 48 hours at 19 to 21 °C. (1308)

Compatibility Information

Solution Compatibility

Amsacrine

Solution	*Mfr*	*Mfr*	*Conc/L*	*Remarks*	*Ref*	*C/I*
Dextrose 5% in water		PD	150 mg[a]	Physically compatible with little or no loss in 48 hr at 20 °C exposed to light	1308	C

Solution Compatibility (Cont.)

Amsacrine

Solution	*Mfr*	*Mfr*	*Conc/L*	*Remarks*	*Ref*	*C/I*
		NCI	150 mg	Physically compatible and chemically stable for at least 48 hours at room temperature under ambient light	234	C

[a]*Tested in burette chambers composed of cellulose propionate, PVC, or methacrylate butadiene styrene.*

Additive Compatibility

Amsacrine

Drug	*Mfr*	*Conc/L*	*Mfr*	*Conc/L*	*Test Soln*	*Remarks*	*Ref*	*C/I*
Sodium bicarbonate		2 mEq	NCI	[a]	D5W	Amsacrine chemically stable for 96 hr at room temperature	234	C

[a]*Concentration unspecified.*

Y-Site Injection Compatibility (1:1 Mixture)

Amsacrine

Drug	*Mfr*	*Conc*	*Mfr*	*Conc*	*Remarks*	*Ref*	*C/I*
Acyclovir sodium	BW	7 mg/ml[a]	NCI	1 mg/ml[a]	Immediate dark orange turbidity, becoming brownish orange in 1 hr	1381	I
Amikacin sulphate	BR	5 mg/ml[a]	NCI	1 mg/ml[a]	Physically compatible for 4 hr at room temperature under fluorescent light	1381	C
Amphotericin B	SQ	0.6 mg/ml[a]	NCI	1 mg/ml[a]	Immediate light yellow turbidity, becoming yellow flocculent precipitate in 15 min	1381	I
Aztreonam	SQ	40 mg/ml[a]	NCI	1 mg/ml[a]	Immediate light yellow-orange turbidity, developing into flocculent precipitate in 4 hr	1381	I
Ceftazidime	GL[c]	40 mg/ml[a]	NCI	1 mg/ml[a]	Light flocculent orange precipitate forms immediately, becoming heavier with time	1381	I
Ceftriaxone sodium	RC	40 mg/ml[a]	NCI	1 mg/ml[a]	Immediate orange turbidity, developing into flocculent precipitate in 4 hr	1381	I
Chlorpromazine HCl	ES	2 mg/ml[a]	NCI	1 mg/ml[a]	Physically compatible for 4 hr at room temperature under fluorescent light	1381	C
Cimetidine HCl	SKF	12 mg/ml[a]	NCI	1 mg/ml[a]	Initially clear, but yellow-orange turbidity develops in 1 hr, becoming flocculent precipitate in 4 hr	1381	I
Clindamycin phosphate	UP	10 mg/ml[a]	NCI	1 mg/ml[a]	Physically compatible for 4 hr at room temperature under fluorescent light	1381	C
Cytarabine	QU	50 mg/ml	NCI	1 mg/ml[a]	Physically compatible for 4 hr at room temperature under fluorescent light	1381	C
Dexamethasone sodium phosphate	QU	1 mg/ml[a]	NCI	1 mg/ml[a]	Physically compatible for 4 hr at room temperature under fluorescent light	1381	C
Diphenhydramine HCl	PD	2 mg/ml[a]	NCI	1 mg/ml[a]	Physically compatible for 4 hr at room temperature under fluorescent light	1381	C
Famotidine	MSD	2 mg/ml[a]	NCI	1 mg/ml[a]	Physically compatible for 4 hr at room temperature under fluorescent light	1381	C

Y-Site Injection Compatibility (1:1 Mixture) (Cont.)

			Amsacrine				
Drug	*Mfr*	*Conc*	*Mfr*	*Conc*	*Remarks*	*Ref*	*C/I*
Fludarabine phosphate	BX	1 mg/ml[a]	NCI	1 mg/ml[a]	Physically compatible for 4 hr at room temperature under fluorescent light	1439	C
Frusemide	ES	3 mg/ml[a]	NCI	1 mg/ml[a]	Heavy yellow-orange turbidity forms initially, becoming colorless liquid with yellow precipitate	1381	I
Ganciclovir sodium	SY	20 mg/ml[a]	NCI	1 mg/ml[a]	Immediate dark orange turbidity	1381	I
Gentamicin sulphate	SO	5 mg/ml[a]	NCI	1 mg/ml[a]	Physically compatible for 4 hr at room temperature under fluorescent light	1381	C
Granisetron HCl	SKB	0.05 mg/ml[a]	NCI	1 mg/ml[a]	Physically compatible with no change in measured turbidity or increase in particle content in 4 hr at 23 °C. Precipitate forms in 24 hr	2000	C
Haloperidol lactate	MN	0.2 mg/ml[a]	NCI	1 mg/ml[a]	Physically compatible for 4 hr at room temperature under fluorescent light	1381	C
Heparin sodium	SO	40 units/ml[a]	NCI	1 mg/ml[a]	Light flocculent orange precipitate forms immediately	1381	I
Hydrocortisone sodium succinate	UP	1 mg/ml[a]	NCI	1 mg/ml[a]	Physically compatible for 4 hr at room temperature under fluorescent light	1381	C
Hydromorphone HCl	AST	0.5 mg/ml[a]	NCI	1 mg/ml[a]	Physically compatible for 4 hr at room temperature under fluorescent light	1381	C
Lorazepam	WY	0.1 mg/ml[a]	NCI	1 mg/ml[a]	Physically compatible for 4 hr at room temperature under fluorescent light	1381	C
Methylprednisolone sodium succinate	UP	5 mg/ml[a]	NCI	1 mg/ml[a]	Immediate orange turbidity and precipitate in 4 hr	1381	I
Metoclopramide HCl	RB	2.5 mg/ml[a]	NCI	1 mg/ml[a]	Yellow-orange turbidity develops in 15 min, becoming heavy flocculent orange precipitate in 1 hr	1381	I
Morphine sulphate	ES	1 mg/ml[a]	NCI	1 mg/ml[a]	Physically compatible for 4 hr at room temperature under fluorescent light	1381	C
Ondansetron HCl	GL	1 mg/ml[a]	NCI	1 mg/ml[a]	Orange precipitate forms within 30 min	1365	I
Prochlorperazine edisylate	SKF	0.5 mg/ml[a]	NCI	1 mg/ml[a]	Physically compatible for 4 hr at room temperature under fluorescent light	1381	C
Promethazine HCl	ES	2 mg/ml[a]	NCI	1 mg/ml[a]	Physically compatible for 4 hr at room temperature under fluorescent light	1381	C
Ranitidine HCl	GL	2 mg/ml[a]	NCI	1 mg/ml[a]	Physically compatible for 4 hr at room temperature under fluorescent light	1381	C
Sargramostim	IMM	10 µg/ml[a]	NCI	1 mg/ml[a]	Physically compatible for 4 hr at 22 °C under fluorescent light	1436	C
	IMM	10 µg/ml[b]	NCI	1 mg/ml[a]	Immediate haze with heavy yellow flocculent precipitate in 30 min	1436	I
Tobramycin sulphate	LI	5 mg/ml[a]	NCI	1 mg/ml[a]	Physically compatible for 4 hr at room temperature under fluorescent light	1381	C
Vancomycin HCl	LI	10 mg/ml[a]	NCI	1 mg/ml[a]	Physically compatible for 4 hr at room temperature under fluorescent light	1381	C

[a] *Tested in dextrose 5% in water.*
[b] *Tested in sodium chloride 0.9%.*
[c] *Sodium carbonate–containing formulation tested.*

Additional Compatibility Information

Infusion Solutions — Amsacrine is physically incompatible with sodium chloride 0.9% and other chloride-containing solutions. The hydrochloride salt is poorly soluble, and precipitation may result. (115; 234)

Evacuated flasks may contain a small amount of chloride-containing solution from the manufacturing process. This residual chloride ion caused precipitation when amsacrine solutions were prepared in evacuated flasks. (234)

CEFPIROME SULPHATE

Products — Cefpirome as the sulphate is available in 1- and 2-g vials for intravenous injection. Each vial also contains anhydrous sodium carbonate. (38)

For intravenous use, reconstitute the 1- and 2-g vials with 10 and 20 ml, respectively, of sterile water for injection. The reconstituted drug may be diluted further in a compatible infusion solution. (38)

Although the vials have a slight negative pressure, reconstitution releases carbon dioxide, increasing the pressure in the vial. Effervescence occurs during dissolution, and the container should be tipped gently from side to side for approximately one minute to assure complete dissolution of the drug. The reconstituted solution may still retain some bubbles of carbon dioxide, but these have no adverse effects on efficacy. (38)

Sodium Content — Cefpirome sulphate contains 4.7 mEq (107 mg) of sodium per gram of drug. (1442)

Trade Name(s) — Cefrom.

Administration — Cefpirome sulphate may be administered by intravenous injection over three to five minutes or by intermittent intravenous infusion over 20 to 30 minutes. (38)

Stability — Intact containers of cefpirome sulphate should be stored at 25 °C or below and protected from light. The drug is a white to pale yellow powder that becomes a faint yellow to yellow solution upon reconstitution. Some color intensification of both the powder and its solutions may occur during storage. However, this does not indicate a change in potency or safety. (38)

The manufacturer recommends storage of the reconstituted solution under refrigeration at 2 to 8 °C and use within 24 hours. (38)

Sorption — Cefpirome sulphate (Roussel) 2 mg/ml in dextrose 5% in water and sodium chloride 0.9% stored in PVC bags for 48 hours under refrigeration and at room temperature for eight hours and during simulated 30-minute and 1-hour infusion through a PVC administration set exhibited no loss due to sorption. (2315)

Plasticizer Leaching — Cefpirome sulphate (Roussel) 2 mg/ml in dextrose 5% in water and sodium chloride 0.9% stored in PVC bags for 48 hours under refrigeration and at room temperature for eight hours and during simulated 30-minute and 1-hour infusion through a PVC administration set did not leach measurable diethylhexyl phthlate (DEHP) plasticizer from the bags or tubing. (2315)

Compatibility Information

Solution Compatibility

Cefpirome sulphate

Solution	*Mfr*	*Mfr*	*Conc/L*	*Remarks*	*Ref*	*C/I*
Dextrose 5% in water	MAC[a]	RS	20 g	Visually compatible with 5% or less loss by HPLC in 8 hr at 21 °C protected from light and 4% or less loss in 48 hr at 4 °C protected from light	2315	C
Sodium chloride 0.9%	MAC[a]	RS	20 g	Visually compatible with 4% or less loss by HPLC in 8 hr at 21 °C protected from light and 9% or less loss in 48 hr at 4 °C protected from light	2315	C

[a]Tested in PVC containers.

Y-Site Injection Compatibility (1:1 Mixture)

Cefpirome sulphate

Drug	*Mfr*	*Conc*	*Mfr*	*Conc*	*Remarks*	*Ref*	*C/I*
Amikacin sulphate	APC	0.5 mg/ml[a]	HO	50 mg/ml[a]	Visually and microscopically compatible with less than 6% cefpirome loss and less than 10% amikacin loss by HPLC in 8 hr at 23 °C	2044	C

Y-Site Injection Compatibility (1:1 Mixture) (Cont.)

Cefpirome sulphate

Drug	*Mfr*	*Conc*	*Mfr*	*Conc*	*Remarks*	*Ref*	*C/I*
Amphotericin B	SQ	0.1 mg/ml[a]	HO	50 mg/ml[a]	Little or no cefpirome loss but up to 45% amphotericin B loss by HPLC in 4 hr at 23 °C possibly due to precipitation	2044	I
Cefazolin sodium	LI	10 mg/ml[a]	HO	50 mg/ml[a]	Visually and microscopically compatible with 7% or less cefpirome loss and little or no cefazolin loss by HPLC in 8 hr at 23 °C	2044	C
Clindamycin phosphate	AB	12 mg/ml[a]	HO	50 mg/ml[a]	Visually and microscopically compatible with 5% or less cefpirome loss and 4% or less clindamycin loss by HPLC in 8 hr at 23 °C	2044	C
Dexamethasone sodium phosphate	LY	4 mg/ml[a]	HO	50 mg/ml[a]	Visually and microscopically compatible with 5% or less cefpirome loss and little or no dexamethasone loss by HPLC in 8 hr at 23 °C	2044	C
Dopamine HCl	AB	0.8 mg/ml[a]	HO	50 mg/ml[a]	Visually and microscopically compatible with 7% or less cefpirome loss and 6% or less dopamine loss by HPLC in 8 hr at 23 °C	2044	C
Epinephrine HCl	AB	0.1 mg/ml[a]	HO	50 mg/ml[a]	Visually and microscopically compatible with 6% or less cefpirome loss and 5% or less epinephrine loss by HPLC in 8 hr at 23 °C	2044	C
Fluconazole	RR	2 mg/ml	HO	50 mg/ml[a]	Visually and microscopically compatible with little or no cefpirome loss and 8% or less fluconazole loss by HPLC in 8 hr at 23 °C	2044	C
Gentamicin sulphate	LY	1 mg/ml[a]	HO	50 mg/ml[a]	Visually and microscopically compatible with little or no cefpirome and cefazolin loss by HPLC in 8 hr at 23 °C	2044	C
Vancomycin HCl	AB	5 mg/ml[a]	HO	50 mg/ml[a]	Visually and microscopically compatible with little or no cefpirome and vancomycin loss by HPLC in 8 hr at 23 °C	2044	C

[a]*Tested in dextrose 5% in water, Ringer's injection, lactated, sodium chloride 0.45%, and sodium chloride 0.9%.*

Additional Compatibility Information

Infusion Solutions — The manufacturer states that cefpirome sulphate is chemically stable and physically compatible for 24 hours stored under refrigeration at 2 to 8 °C in the following solutions (38):

Dextrose 6% with sodium chloride 0.9%
Dextrose 5% in water
Dextrose 10% in water
Fructose 5% in water
Ringer's injection
Sodium chloride 0.9%
Sterile water for injection

Cefpirome sulphate should not be administered in sodium bicarbonate injection. (38)

CHLORMETHIAZOLE EDISYLATE (CLOMETHIAZOLE)

Products — Chlormethiazole edisylate is available in 500-ml glass infusion bottles. Each milliliter contains chlormethiazole edisylate 8 mg with dextrose and sodium hydroxide to adjust pH in water for injection. (115)

Chlormethiazole edisylate is also available as a lyophilized powder in vials containing 3.75 g. The vials are accompanied by 250 ml of a special vehicle composed of arginine and ethanol in water for injection. (116)

Sodium Content — Chlormethiazole edisylate contains 0.032 mmol of sodium per milliliter. (115)

Trade Name(s) — Distraneurin, Hemineurin, Heminevrin.

Administration — Chlormethiazole edisylate is administered by intravenous infusion. In general, the infusion is given as a loading dose followed by a maintenance dose. Patients receiving the drug by continuous infusion should be kept under close and constant observation and monitoring. (115)

Stability — Chlormethiazole edisylate is stored under refrigeration and protected from freezing. (115)

Electrolytes such as sodium, potassium, and chloride can be added to chlormethiazole edisylate infusions without affecting the drug's stability adversely over a 24-hour period. (115)

Syringes — A 25-ml aliquot of chlormethiazole edisylate (Astra) 8 g/L in the supplied infusion solution, stored in all-plastic syringes composed of polypropylene barrels and polyethylene plungers (Pharma-Plast, AHS Australia) for 24 hours at room temperature in the dark, did not exhibit any loss due to sorption or decomposition. (606) These same syringes were compared with glass containers in an investigation of the possible sorption of the drug. After 24 hours of storage of aqueous solutions of chlormethiazole edisylate (concentration unspecified), no drug loss due to sorption or decomposition was found in either the plastic syringes or glass containers. The authors indicated that these plastic syringes could be substituted for glass syringes for use with syringe pumps. (782)

Sorption — Chlormethiazole edisylate is sorbed to PVC administration sets, resulting in some concentration loss before the drug reaches the patient. (115)

Chlormethiazole edisylate (Astra) 8 g/L in the infusion solution supplied by the manufacturer and placed into PVC bags (Travenol) exhibited approximately a 33% loss in 24 hours and a 43% loss in one week at room temperature (15 to 20 °C) due to sorption. (536)

Chlormethiazole edisylate (Astra) 8 g/L in the infusion solution supplied by the manufacturer was delivered through a polyethylene administration set (Tridilset) over eight hours at 15 to 20 °C. The flow rate was 1 ml/min. No appreciable loss due to sorption occurred. (769)

This result is in contrast to that of a study using conventional PVC sets. Chlormethiazole edisylate (Astra) 8 g/L in the infusion solution supplied by the manufacturer exhibited a cumulative 34% loss due to sorption during a seven-hour simulated infusion through an infusion set (Travenol) consisting of a cellulose propionate burette chamber and 170 cm of PVC tubing. Both the burette chamber and the tubing contributed to the loss. The extent of sorption increased with increasing concentration. (606)

Chlormethiazole edisylate (Astra) 8 g/L in the infusion solution supplied by the manufacturer was delivered at a flow rate of 0.8 ml/min through a polybutadiene set, with and without a methacrylate butadiene styrene burette chamber (Avon Medical). For tests in the burette sets, 150 ml was run into the burette before simulated administration was begun. Losses of chlormethiazole to polybutadiene sets were 7 to 13%. Drug delivery was not affected by the burette. In contrast, losses up to 50% to PVC sets were observed. (1027)

In a similar study, losses due to sorption of chlormethiazole edisylate infusion to a volume infusion set (Ivac), blood administration set (Travenol), and Metriset (McGaw) were investigated. Flow rates were 1.25 to 2.5 ml/min. Following 500 ml of infusion, the average recoveries of chlormethiazole were 78.5, 82.2, and 71.2%, respectively. (1446)

The drug was also tested as a simulated infusion over at least one hour by a syringe pump system. A glass syringe on a syringe pump was fitted with 20 cm of polyethylene tubing or 50 cm of Silastic tubing. A negligible amount of drug was lost with the polyethylene tubing, but a cumulative 32% loss occurred during the one-hour infusion through the Silastic tubing. (606)

Other Information

It was reported that PVC bags containing chlormethiazole edisylate solutions become softer and more pliable during storage. The distinctive odor of the solution was also detectable in the immediate vicinity of the bags. (536) Penetration of chlormethiazole edisylate through the walls of silicone catheters might be responsible for the high incidence of thrombophlebitis. (1447) The manufacturer recommends that a glass syringe connected to a Teflon intravenous cannula using a polyethylene extension set be used for administration to small children. (115)

CHLORPHENIRAMINE MALEATE (CHLORPHENAMINE MALEATE)

Products — Chlorpheniramine maleate is available in 1-ml ampuls containing 10 mg/ml of drug along with sodium chloride in water for injection. (38)

pH — From 4 to 5.2. (19)

Osmolality — Chlorpheniramine maleate 10 mg/ml has an osmolality of 44 mOsm/kg. (1689)

Trade Name(s) — Piriton.

Administration — Chlorpheniramine maleate 10 mg/ml may be administered by subcutaneous, intramuscular, or intravenous injection slowly over a period of one minute. (38)

Stability — Intact containers of chlorpheniramine maleate should be stored below 25 °C and protected from light. (38)

Compatibility Information

Additive Compatibility

Chlorpheniramine maleate

Drug	Mfr	Conc/L	Mfr	Conc/L	Test Soln	Remarks	Ref	C/I
Amikacin sulphate	BR	5 g	SC	40 mg	D5LR, D5R, D5S, D5W, D10W, IS10, LR, NS, R, SL	Physically compatible and potency of both retained for 24 hr at 25 °C	294	C
Calcium chloride						Physically incompatible	9	I
	UP	1 g	SC	100 mg	D5W	Physically incompatible	15	I
Kanamycin sulphate	BR	4 g	SC	100 mg	D5W	Physically incompatible	15	I
Norepinephrine bitartrate	WI					Physically incompatible	9	I
	WI	2 mg	SC	100 mg	D5W	Physically incompatible	15	I
Pentobarbital sodium						Physically incompatible	9	I
	AB	1 g	SC	100 mg	D5W	Physically incompatible	15	I

Drugs in Syringe Compatibility

Chlorpheniramine maleate

Drug (in syringe)	Mfr	Amt	Mfr	Amt	Remarks	Ref	C/I
Diatrizoate meglumine 52%, diatrizoate sodium 8% (Renografin-60)	SQ	40 to 1 ml	SC	1 ml[a]	Physically compatible for 48 hr	530	C
Diatrizoate meglumine 34.3%, diatrizoate sodium 35% (Renovist)	SQ	40 to 1 ml	SC	1 ml[a]	Physically compatible for 48 hr	530	C
Diatrizoate sodium 75% (Hypaque)	WI	40 to 1 ml	SC	1 ml[a]	Physically compatible for 48 hr	530	C
Iodipamide meglumine 52% (Cholografin)	SQ	40 to 5 ml	SC	1 ml[a]	Forms a precipitate initially but clears within 1 hr and remains clear for 48 hr	530	I
	SQ	2 and 1 ml	SC	1 ml[a]	Forms a precipitate initially but clears within 1 hr. Precipitate reforms within 48 hr	530	I
Iothalamate meglumine 60% (Conray)	MA	40 to 1 ml	SC	1 ml[a]	Physically compatible for 48 hr	530	C
Iothalamate sodium 80% (Angio-Conray)	MA	40 to 1 ml	SC	1 ml[a]	Physically compatible for 48 hr	530	C

[a] *Chlorpheniramine maleate concentration unspecified.*

Additional Compatibility Information

Infusion Solutions — Chlorpheniramine maleate is reportedly compatible with most intravenous infusion solutions. (19)

Other Drugs — Chlorpheniramine maleate (Schering) was found to be compatible with diatrizoate meglumine products (Squibb) but incompatible with iodipamide meglumine (Squibb). (40)

CLARITHROMYCIN

Products — Clarithromycin is available in 500-mg vials with lactobionic acid as a solubilizing agent and sodium hydroxide to adjust pH. Reconstitute with 10 ml of sterile water for injection, and shake to dissolve the powder. Do not use diluents containing preservatives or inorganic salts. Each milliliter of the resultant solution contains 50 mg of clarithromycin. This solution must be diluted before use. See Administration below. (38; 115)

Trade Name(s) — Klacid, Klaricid, Zeclar.

Administration — Clarithromycin is administered by intravenous infusion after dilution in an appropriate infusion solution. See Additional Compatibility Information below. It should not be given by intravenous bolus or intramuscular injection. The reconstituted drug solution (500 mg) is added to 250 ml of compatible infusion solution yielding a 2-mg/ml final solution. The final diluted solution is administered by intravenous infusion over 60 minutes into one of the larger proximal veins. (38; 115)

Stability — Intact containers of the white to off-white lyophilized powder should be stored at 30 °C or below and protected from light. When reconstituted as directed, the 50-mg/ml solution should be used within 24 hours stored at room temperature of 25 °C (38; 115) and 48 hours stored under refrigeration at 5 °C. (115) After final dilution to a 2-mg/ml concentration for administration, the solution should be used within six hours stored at room temperature (25 °C) or 24 (38) to 48 (115) hours if stored under refrigeration at 5 °C.

Compatibility Information

Y-Site Injection Compatibility (1:1 Mixture)

Drug	Mfr	Conc	Clarithromycin Mfr	Clarithromycin Conc	Remarks	Ref	C/I
Aminophylline	EV	2 mg/ml[a]	AB	4 mg/ml[a]	Needle-like crystals form in 2 hr at 30 °C and 4 hr at 17 °C	2174	I
Amiodarone HCl	SW	3 mg/ml[a]	AB	4 mg/ml[a]	Visually compatible for 72 hr at both 30 and 17 °C	2174	C
Amoxycillin sodium–clavulanate potassium	BE	20 + 4 mg/ml[a]	AB	4 mg/ml[a]	Visually compatible for 72 hr at both 30 and 17 °C	2174	C
Ampicillin sodium	BE	40 mg/ml[a]	AB	4 mg/ml[a]	Visually compatible for 72 hr at both 30 and 17 °C	2174	C
Atracurium besylate	GW	1 mg/ml[a]	AB	4 mg/ml[a]	Visually compatible for 72 hr at both 30 and 17 °C	2174	C
Bumetanide	LEO	0.5 mg/ml	AB	4 mg/ml[a]	Visually compatible for 72 hr at both 30 and 17 °C	2174	C
Cefuroxime sodium	GW	60 mg/ml[a]	AB	4 mg/ml[a]	White precipitate forms in 3 hr at 30 °C and 24 hr at 17 °C	2174	I
Cimetidine HCl	SKB	8 mg/ml[a]	AB	4 mg/ml[a]	Visually compatible for 72 hr at both 30 and 17 °C	2174	C
Ciprofloxacin	BAY	2 mg/ml[a]	AB	4 mg/ml[a]	Visually compatible for 72 hr at both 30 and 17 °C	2174	C
Dobutamine HCl	BI	2 mg/ml[a]	AB	4 mg/ml[a]	Visually compatible for 72 hr at both 30 and 17 °C	2174	C
Dopamine HCl	DB	3.2 mg/ml[a]	AB	4 mg/ml[a]	Visually compatible for 72 hr at both 30 and 17 °C	2174	C
Flucloxacillin sodium	BE	40 mg/ml[a]	AB	4 mg/ml[a]	Translucent precipitate forms in 1 to 2 hr becoming a gel in 3 hr at both 30 and 17 °C	2174	I
Frusemide	ANT	10 mg/ml	AB	4 mg/ml[a]	White cloudiness forms immediately becoming an obvious precipitate in 15 min	2174	I
Gentamicin sulphate	RS	40 mg/ml	AB	4 mg/ml[a]	Visually compatible for 72 hr at both 30 and 17 °C	2174	C
Heparin sodium	CPP	1000 units/ml[a]	AB	4 mg/ml[a]	White cloudiness forms immediately	2174	I

Y-Site Injection Compatibility (1:1 Mixture) (Cont.)

Drug	Mfr	Conc	Clarithromycin Mfr	Clarithromycin Conc	Remarks	Ref	C/I
Hydrocortisone sodium phosphate	GL	100 mg/ml	AB	4 mg/ml[a]	Visually compatible for 72 hr at both 30 and 17 °C	2174	C
Insulin, human	NOV	4 units/ml[a]	AB	4 mg/ml[a]	Visually compatible for 72 hr at both 30 and 17 °C	2174	C
Lignocaine HCl	ANT	4 mg/ml[a]	AB	4 mg/ml[a]	Visually compatible for 72 hr at both 30 and 17 °C	2174	C
Metoclopramide HCl	ANT	5 mg/ml	AB	4 mg/ml[a]	Visually compatible for 72 hr at both 30 and 17 °C	2174	C
Metronidazole	PRK	5 mg/ml	AB	4 mg/ml[a]	Visually compatible for 72 hr at both 30 and 17 °C	2174	C
Penicillin G sodium	BRT	24 mg/ml[a]	AB	4 mg/ml[a]	Visually compatible for 72 hr at both 30 and 17 °C	2174	C
Phenytoin sodium	ANT	20 mg/ml[a]	AB	4 mg/ml[a]	White cloudiness forms immediately becoming a white precipitate in 1 hr at both 30 and 17 °C	2174	I
Prochlorperazine (salt unspecified)	ANT	12.5 mg/ml	AB	4 mg/ml[a]	Visually compatible for 72 hr at both 30 and 17 °C	2174	C
Potassium chloride	ANT	0.08 mmol/ml[a]	AB	4 mg/ml[a]	Visually compatible for 72 hr at both 30 and 17 °C	2174	C
Ranitidine HCl	GW	5 mg/ml[a]	AB	4 mg/ml[a]	Visually compatible for 72 hr at both 30 and 17 °C	2174	C
Ticarcillin disodium–clavulanate potassium	BE	32 mg/ml[a]	AB	4 mg/ml[a]	Visually compatible for 72 hr at both 30 and 17 °C	2174	C
Vancomycin HCl	DB	10 mg/ml[a]	AB	4 mg/ml[a]	Visually compatible for 72 hr at both 30 and 17 °C	2174	C
Vecuronium bromide	ORG	2 mg/ml[a]	AB	4 mg/ml[a]	Visually compatible for 72 hr at both 30 and 17 °C	2174	C
Verapamil HCl	BKN	2.5 mg/ml	AB	4 mg/ml[a]	Visually compatible for 72 hr at both 30 and 17 °C	2174	C

[a]*Tested in dextrose 5% in water.*

Additional Compatibility Information

Infusion Solutions — The following diluents are recommended by the manufacturer for the preparation of the final dilution of clarithromycin to 2 mg/ml (115):

Dextrose 5% in Ringer's injection, lactated
Dextrose 5% in sodium chloride 0.3%
Dextrose 5% in sodium chloride 0.45%
Dextrose 5% in water
Normosol M in dextrose 5%
Normosol R in dextrose 5%
Ringer's injection, lactated
Sodium chloride 0.9%

CLOMIPRAMINE HCL

Products — Clomipramine HCl is available as a 12.5-mg/ml solution in 2-ml ampuls containing 25 mg of drug with glycerine in water. (38; 116)

For intravenous administration, the drug should be diluted in dextrose 5% in water or sodium chloride 0.9%. After addition of the drug, the admixture should be agitated to ensure even distribution. (38)

Trade Name(s) — Anafranil.

Administration — Clomipramine HCl is administered by intramuscular injection or intravenous infusion. By intravenous infusion, the dose should initially be diluted in 250 to 500 ml of infusion solution and infused over 1.5 to 3 hours. If tolerated satisfactorily, the volume of fluid for subsequent doses may be reduced to a minimum of 125 ml and the infusion time decreased to a minimum of 45 minutes. (38)

Stability — Intact ampuls of clomipramine HCl should be stored protected from light. (38)

Sorption — Clomipramine HCl (Ciba-Geigy) (concentration unspecified) in dextrose 5% in water in PVC containers was delivered over four hours through PVC administration sets. Loss due to sorption ranged from about 1 to 8% determined by UV spectroscopy. (2045)

The manufacturer states that any standard administration set can be used to deliver clomipramine HCl. (38)

Compatibility Information

Infusion Solutions — The manufacturer recommends dextrose 5% in water or sodium chloride 0.9% for preparing intravenous infusion admixtures. 38

CLONAZEPAM

Products — Clonazepam is available in 1-ml ampuls containing 1 mg of drug in a solvent composed of absolute alcohol, glacial acetic acid, benzyl alcohol, and propylene glycol. An ampul containing 1 ml of sterile water for injection is included as a diluent. (38; 115)

pH — Clonazepam (Roche) 0.125, 0.222, and 0.5 mg/ml in sodium chloride 0.9% for continuous subcutaneous infusion had pH values of 3.6, 3.5, and 3.6, respectively. (2161)

Trade Name(s) — Rivotril.

Administration — Clonazepam is administered by slow intravenous injection. For bolus administration, the content of the diluent ampul is added to the drug immediately before administration. The injection is administered at a rate not exceeding 0.25 to 0.5 ml/min into a large vein of the antecubital fossa. Clonazepam is also administered as a slow intravenous infusion; up to 3 mg of clonazepam is added to 250 ml of dextrose 5 or 10% in water, sodium chloride 0.9%, or dextrose 2.5% in sodium chloride 0.45%. (38; 115) In exceptional cases and if intravenous administration is not possible, intramuscular injection has been cited. (115)

Stability — The colorless to slightly greenish-yellow solution in intact ampuls should be stored below 30 °C and protected from light. The manufacturer recommends that the drug be used immediately after mixing with the supplied diluent. (38; 115) After dilution in a recommended infusion solution in a glass container, the infusion should be completed within 12 (38) to 24 (115) hours. If prepared in an infusion solution in a PVC container, the infusion should be completed without delay after preparation, usually within two (38) to four (115) hours of addition to the container due to sorption loss.

Syringes — Clonazepam (Roche) 5 and 10 mg, diluted to 48 ml with sodium chloride 0.9% and stored in polyethylene syringes, was physically compatible and exhibited no clonazepam loss in 10 hours at room temperature. (1708)

In another study, the stability of reconstituted clonazepam (Roche) 0.5 mg/ml packaged in polypropylene syringes was evaluated. HPLC analysis found less than 2% clonazepam loss in 48 hours stored at room temperature exposed to normal room light. (2172)

Sorption — Clonazepam shows evidence of sorption losses when in contact with PVC. It is recommended that glass containers be used for infusions. If PVC bags are used, the admixture should be infused without delay after preparation and usually over a period no longer than two (38) to four (115) hours.

Nation et al. reported that clonazepam (Roche) 3 mg in 500 ml of dextrose 5% in water or sodium chloride 0.9%, stored at room temperature and protected from light in PVC bags, showed losses of 17 to 20% after 24 hours and 31 to 33% after six days. (1707)

It was further reported that clonazepam 3 mg in 500 ml of dextrose 5% in water or sodium chloride 0.9% in glass bottles, delivered through PVC infusion sets at 40 ml/hr, had losses of approximately 20 to 25% in delivered potency over 20 to 30 minutes. Thereafter, the effluent concentrations increased over time to stabilize at 92 to 94% of the original concentration. An even greater loss of delivered potency, but in a similar pattern, was reported when admixtures were prepared in PVC bags. Losses of 25 to 30% occurred over the first 20 to 30 minutes but decreased to about a 16 to 20% loss of delivered potency over 6.5 hours. (1707)

Hooymans et al. compared losses of clonazepam to PVC and polyethylene-lined infusion tubing. Clonazepam (Roche) 5 and 10 mg, diluted in sodium chloride 0.9% to a final volume of 48 ml in polyethylene syringes, was delivered at room temperature through tubing at flow rates of 2 or 4 ml/hr (5 mg in 48 ml) and 2 ml/hr (10 mg in 48 ml). No losses were observed in the plastic syringes or to the polyethylene-lined tubing over 10 hours. Losses to the PVC tubing depended on the flow rate and concentration, being greater at 2 ml/hr and at 5 mg/48 ml, respectively. Potency decreased to approximately 40 and 55% of the original strength after 0.6 hour for the 5-mg/48 ml concentration at 2 and 4 ml/hr, respectively. After 0.6 hour, the 10-mg/48 ml concentration was at 55% of original potency when delivered at 2 ml/hr. Effluent concentrations gradually increased after the first hour, reaching approximately 80 to 90% of original concentrations after 10 hours. (1708)

Clonazepam (Roche) (concentration unspecified) in dextrose 5% in water in PVC containers was delivered over four hours through PVC administration sets. Losses due to sorption ranged from about 13 to 18% determined by UV spectroscopy. (2045)

Compatibility Information

Solution Compatibility

Clonazepam

Solution	Mfr	Mfr	Conc/L	Remarks	Ref	C/I
Dextrose 5% in water	AB[a]	RC	6 mg	Physically compatible with no loss in 10 hr	1707	C
	TR[b]	RC	6 mg	7% loss in 7 hr, 17 to 20% loss in 24 hr, and 31 to 33% loss in 6 days at room temperature protected from light	1707	I
Sodium chloride 0.9%	AB[a]	RC	6 mg	Physically compatible with no loss in 10 hr	1707	C
	TR[b]	RC	6 mg	14% loss in 7 hr, 17 to 20% loss in 24 hr, and 31 to 33% loss in 6 days at room temperature protected from light	1707	I

[a]*Tested in glass containers.*
[b]*Tested in PVC containers.*

Drugs in Syringe Compatibility

Clonazepam

Drug (in syringe)	Mfr	Amt	Mfr	Amt	Remarks	Ref	C/I
Heparin sodium		2500 units/ 1 ml	RC	1 mg/ 2 ml	Visually compatible for at least 5 min	1053	C

Y-Site Injection Compatibility (1:1 Mixture)

Clonazepam

Drug	Mfr	Conc	Mfr	Conc	Remarks	Ref	C/I
TPN #189[a]			RC	10 mg/ml[b]	Visually compatible for 24 hr at 22 °C	1767	C

[a]*Refer to Appendix I for the composition of parenteral nutrition solutions. TPN indicates a 2-in-1 admixture.*
[b]*Tested in sterile water for injection.*

Additional Compatibility Information

Infusion Solutions — Dextrose 2.5% in sodium chloride 0.45%, dextrose 5 or 10% in water, and sodium chloride 0.9% have been recommended as diluents for the intravenous infusion of clonazepam. Infusions should be completed usually within 12 (38) to 24 (115) hours of preparation.

Clonazepam should not be admixed with sodium bicarbonate because of the potential for precipitation. (115)

CYCLIZINE LACTATE

Products — Cyclizine lactate is available in 1-ml ampuls containing 50 mg of drug in water for injection. (38; 115)

pH — From 3.3 to 3.7. (176)

Trade Name(s) — Marzine, Valoid.

Administration — Cyclizine lactate is administered by intramuscular or intravenous injection. When administered intravenously, it should be injected slowly, with minimal withdrawal of blood in the syringe. (38; 115)

Stability — Cyclizine lactate injection, a colorless solution, should be stored below 25 °C and protected from light. (38; 115) Although a slight yellow tint may develop during storage, this color change is stated not to indicate a potency loss. (19)

Crystallization — Cyclizine lactate has an aqueous solubility of 8 mg/ml. When the drug was diluted to concentrations of 7.5 and 3.75 mg/ml in water or dextrose 5% in water, it remained in solution for at least 24 hours at 23 °C. However, when these dilutions were made with sodium chloride 0.9%, crystals formed within 24 hours at 23 °C. (1761)

pH Effects — Cyclizine lactate is incompatible with any solution having a pH of 6.8 or greater. (19)

Compatibility Information

Drugs in Syringe Compatibility

Cyclizine lactate

Drug (in syringe)	*Mfr*	*Amt*	*Mfr*	*Amt*	*Remarks*	*Ref*	*C/I*
Diamorphine HCl	MB	10, 25, 50 mg/ 1 ml	CA	5 mg/ 1 ml[a]	Physically compatible and diamorphine potency retained for 24 hr at room temperature	1454	C
	EV	15 mg/ 1 ml	CA	15 mg/ 1 ml	Physically compatible for 24 hr at room temperature	1455	C
	EV	37.5 to 150 mg/ 1 ml	CA	12.5 to 50 mg/ 1 ml	Precipitate forms within 24 hr	1455	I
	HC	25 to 100 mg/ ml	CA	10 mg/ml	Visually incompatible	1672	I
	HC	20 mg/ml	CA	10 mg/ml	Visually compatible for 48 hr at 5 and 20 °C	1672	C
	HC	≤100 mg/ ml	CA	6.7 mg/ ml	Visually compatible for 48 hr at 5 and 20 °C	1672	C
	HC	2 mg/ml	CA	6.7 mg/ ml	5% diamorphine loss by HPLC in 9.9 days at 20 °C. Cyclizine potency by HPLC retained for at least 45 days	1672	C
	HC	20 mg/ml	CA	6.7 mg/ ml	5% diamorphine loss by HPLC in 13.6 days at 20 °C. Cyclizine potency by HPLC retained for at least 45 days	1672	C
	BP	6 mg/ml	WEL	51 mg/ml	Physically compatible with 10% diamorphine loss in 1.7 days and little or no cyclizine loss by HPLC at 23 °C	2071	C
	BP	9 mg/ml	WEL	32 mg/ml	Physically compatible with less than 10% diamorphine loss and little or no cyclizine loss by HPLC in 4 days at 23 °C	2071	C
	BP	10 mg/ml	WEL	39 mg/ml	Physically compatible with less than 10% diamorphine loss and little or no cyclizine loss by HPLC in 4 days at 23 °C	2071	C
	BP	10 mg/ml	WEL	28 mg/ml	Physically compatible with 10% diamorphine loss in 3.1 days and little or no cyclizine loss by HPLC at 23 °C	2071	C
	BP	12 mg/ml	WEL	51 mg/ml	Physically compatible with 10% diamorphine loss in 2.2 days and little or no cyclizine loss by HPLC at 23 °C	2071	C
	BP	14 mg/ml	WEL	40 mg/ml	Crystals form	2071	I
	BP	17 mg/ml	WEL	26 mg/ml	Physically compatible with 10% diamorphine loss in 1.1 days and 10% cyclizine loss in 2.5 days by HPLC at 23 °C	2071	C
	BP	18 mg/ml	WEL	52 mg/ml	Crystals form	2071	I
	BP	20 mg/ml	WEL	10 mg/ml	Physically compatible with less than 10% diamorphine loss and little or no cyclizine loss by HPLC in 7 days at 23 °C	2071	C
	BP	20 mg/ml	WEL	15 mg/ml	Physically compatible with little or no diamorphine loss and 10% cyclizine loss in 0.5 days by HPLC at 23 °C	2071	I
	BP	21 mg/ml	WEL	26 mg/ml	Physically compatible with 10% diamorphine loss in 4.9 days and 10% cyclizine loss in 3.2 days by HPLC at 23 °C	2071	C
	BP	18 mg/ml	WEL	23 mg/ml	Physically compatible with little or no diamorphine loss and 10% cyclizine loss by HPLC in 3.2 days at 23 °C	2071	C
	BP	26 mg/ml	WEL	23 mg/ml	Physically compatible with 10% diamorphine loss in 1.9 days and 10% cyclizine loss in 0.4 days by HPLC at 23 °C	2071	I

Drugs in Syringe Compatibility (Cont.)

			Cyclizine lactate				
Drug (in syringe)	*Mfr*	*Amt*	*Mfr*	*Amt*	*Remarks*	*Ref*	*C/I*
	BP	30 mg/ml	WEL	30 mg/ml	Physically compatible with 10% diamorphine loss in 0.9 days and 10% cyclizine loss in 0.4 days by HPLC at 23 °C	2071	I
	BP	49 mg/ml	WEL	10 mg/ml	Physically compatible with little or no diamorphine loss and 10% cyclizine loss in 5.5 days by HPLC at 23 °C	2071	C
	BP	51 mg/ml	WEL	4 mg/ml	Physically compatible with little or no diamorphine or cyclizine loss in 7 days by HPLC at 23 °C	2071	C
	BP	61 mg/ml	WEL	8 mg/ml	Physically compatible with 10% diamorphine loss in 1.4 days and 10% cyclizine loss in 1.1 days by HPLC at 23 °C	2071	C
	BP	65 mg/ml	WEL	13 mg/ml	Physically compatible with 10% diamorphine loss in 1.6 days and 10% cyclizine loss in 0.5 days by HPLC at 23 °C	2071	I
	BP	92 mg/ml	WEL	10 mg/ml	Physically compatible with little or no diamorphine loss and 10% cyclizine loss in 2.4 days by HPLC at 23 °C	2071	C
	BP	99 mg/ml	WEL	4 mg/ml	Physically compatible with little or no diamorphine or cyclizine loss in 7 days by HPLC at 23 °C	2071	C
Diamorphine HCl with haloperidol lactate	BP JC	11 mg/ml 2.2 mg/ml	WEL	16 mg/ml	Physically compatible with less than 10% loss of any drug by HPLC in 7 days at 23 °C	2071	C
Diamorphine HCl with haloperidol lactate	BP JC	25 mg/ml 2.2 mg/ml	WEL	16 mg/ml	Physically compatible with less than 10% loss of any drug by HPLC in 7 days at 23 °C	2071	C
Diamorphine HCl with haloperidol lactate	BP JC	40 mg/ml 2.2 mg/ml	WEL	11 mg/ml	Physically compatible with less than 10% loss of any drug by HPLC in 7 days at 23 °C	2071	C
Diamorphine HCl with haloperidol lactate	BP JC	42 mg/ml 2.1 mg/ml	WEL	13 mg/ml	Physically compatible with less than 10% loss of any drug by HPLC in 6 days at 23 °C	2071	C
Diamorphine HCl with haloperidol lactate	BP JC	55 mg/ml 2.1 mg/ml	WEL	9 mg/ml	Physically compatible with less than 10% loss of any drug by HPLC in 7 days at 23 °C	2071	C
Diamorphine HCl with haloperidol lactate	BP JC	56 mg/ml 2.1 mg/ml	WEL	13 mg/ml	Physically compatible with less than 10% loss of any drug by HPLC in 7 days at 23 °C	2071	C
Haloperidol lactate	SE	1.5 mg/ 0.3 ml	WEL	150 mg/ 3 ml	Diluted with 17 ml of NS. Crystals of cyclizine form within 24 hr at 25 °C	1761	I
	SE	1.5 mg/ 0.3 ml	WEL	150 mg/ 3 ml	Diluted with 17 ml of D5W or W. Visually compatible for 24 hr at 25 °C	1761	C
Ranitidine HCl	GL	50 mg/ 2 ml	CA	50 mg/ 1 ml	Physically compatible for 1 hr at 25 °C both macroscopically and microscopically	978	C

[a]*Diluted with sterile water for injection.*

Additional Compatibility Information

Diamorphine — Grassby and Hutchings reported that cyclizine lactate is conditionally compatible with diamorphine HCl, depending on the concentrations of the two drugs. Diamorphine HCl to cyclizine lactate concentration ratios of 1:1 are stable in concentrations up to 20 mg/ml. However, an increase in the diamorphine HCl concentration necessitates a reduction in the cyclizine lactate concentration to 10 mg/ml. Similarly, an increase in the cyclizine lactate concentration necessitates a reduction in the diamorphine HCl concentration to 15 mg/ml for the combinations to remain stable for at least 24 hours at room temperature. (2071) See Compatibility Information above.

DIAMORPHINE HCL (DIACETYLMORPHINE HCL)

Products — Diamorphine HCl is available as a lyophilized product in 5-, 10-, 30-, 100-, 250-, and 500-mg ampuls. (38)

Diamorphine HCl is very soluble in water. Up to 100 mg can be reconstituted in 1 ml of diluent; a minimum of 2 ml of diluent is recommended for the 500-mg size. The preferred diluent is dextrose 5% in water, but sodium chloride 0.9% also may be used. (1442)

Administration — Diamorphine HCl is given by intramuscular, intravenous, or subcutaneous injection. Administration can also be by slow continuous subcutaneous or intravenous injection with an infusion control device. (38)

Stability — Ampuls of lyophilized diamorphine HCl should be stored at or below 25 °C. (38)

Diamorphine HCl 1 mg/ml as a simple aqueous solution in flint glass ampuls stored at 25 °C exhibited a 10% loss in about 50 days. (1958)

In another study, diamorphine HCl up to 50 mg/ml in sterile water for injection was stable for longer than two days at ambient temperature when protected from light. (1454)

pH Effects — The stability of the reconstituted injection depends on its pH; it is most stable at acidic pH, around 3.8 to 4.4 (1442) to pH 4.5 (1958). Degradation increases greatly at neutral or basic pH (1448).

Diamorphine HCl exhibits a pH-dependent incompatibility in sodium chloride injection. To remain in solution, the pH must be below 6. (1458) Solutions containing up to 250 mg/ml of diamorphine HCl have been shown to be compatible in sodium chloride 0.9%. (1457–1459)

Temperature Effects — Solutions of diamorphine HCl in sterile water for injection at concentrations greater than 15 mg/ml exhibited precipitation when stored at 21 and 37 °C for longer than two weeks. At concentrations of 1 to 250 mg/ml in sterile water for injection in glass containers, diamorphine HCl was stable for eight weeks at −20 °C, exhibiting less than 10% degradation. At 4 °C, degradation was inversely related to concentration. Diamorphine HCl 31 and 250 mg/ml was stable, but solutions containing 1 and 7.81 mg/ml showed 15 and 12% losses, respectively, after eight weeks of storage. (1452)

Syringes — The stability of diamorphine HCl solutions containing 1 and 20 mg/ml in sodium chloride 0.9% in glass syringes was determined. At ambient temperature, diamorphine HCl in glass syringes was stable for seven days at 1 mg/ml and for 12 days at 20 mg/ml. This was somewhat less than the drug's stability at these concentrations in PVC containers; adequate stability was maintained for at least 15 days in PVC containers. (1449) See Compatibility Information below.

Diamorphine HCl stability also was investigated in plastic syringes. Gove et al. reported the stability of diamorphine HCl solutions to be 14 days at room temperature and greater than 40 days at 4 °C, although no details of concentrations were cited. (982)

Diamorphine HCl (Hillcross) 2 and 20 mg/ml in water for injection also was stored in plastic syringes (Becton-Dickinson) sealed with blind hubs. HPLC showed a 5% potency loss in about 18 days at 20 °C. (1672)

Infusion Pumps — Solutions containing diamorphine HCl 250 mg/ml in an Act-a-Pump (Pharmacia) reservoir were stable for at least 14 days during simulated patient use. (1450) Jones et al. also reported that degradation was both temperature and concentration dependent. Solutions of diamorphine HCl 1 mg/ml in water stored at 21 °C for 42 days in the Act-a-Pump reservoir showed 10.6% degradation. At 37 °C, 32.6% degradation occurred. (1451)

Diamorphine HCl (Evans Medical) 5 mg/ml in sterile water for injection was stable in Parker Micropump PVC reservoirs for 14 days at 4 °C, exhibiting no loss by HPLC analysis. At 37 °C, about a 2% loss occurred in seven days and a 7% loss occurred in 14 days. (1696)

However, at a concentration of 250 mg/ml, diamorphine HCl losses of 11 and 85.8% at 21 and 37 °C, respectively (1451), were partially attributed to precipitation. (1452)

Elastomeric Reservoir Pumps — Diamorphine HCl 1 and 20 mg/ml in sodium chloride 0.9% was evaluated for stability in two elastomeric disposable infusion devices, Infusor (Travenol) and Intermate 200 (I.S.C.). The drug was stable for 15 days in most cases. However, solutions containing diamorphine HCl 1 mg/ml in the Intermate reservoir stored at 31 °C were only stable for two days. (1449)

Compatibility Information

Solution Compatibility

Diamorphine HCl

Solution	*Mfr*	*Mfr*	*Conc/L*	*Remarks*	*Ref*	*C/I*
Sodium chloride 0.9%	TR[a]	EV	1 and 20 g	Little or no loss in 15 days at 4 and 24 °C	1449	C

[a]*Tested in PVC bags.*

Additive Compatibility

Diamorphine HCl

Drug	*Mfr*	*Conc/L*	*Mfr*	*Conc/L*	*Test Soln*	*Remarks*	*Ref*	*C/I*
Bupivacaine HCl	GL	1.25 g		0.125 g	NS	Visually compatible with 8% diamorphine loss and no bupivacaine loss by HPLC in 28 days at room temperature	1791	C

Additive Compatibility (Cont.)

Drug	Mfr	Conc/L	Diamorphine HCl Mfr	Diamorphine HCl Conc/L	Test Soln	Remarks	Ref	C/I
	AST	150 mg	NAP	20 mg	NS[a]	5% diamorphine and no bupivacaine loss by HPLC in 14 days at 7 °C. Both drugs were stable for 6 months at −20 °C	2070	C
Flucloxacillin sodium	BE	20 g	EV	500 mg	W	Physically compatible for 24 hr at 15 and 30 °C. Haze forms in 48 hr at 30 °C. No change at 15 °C	1479	C
Frusemide	HO	1 g	EV	500 mg	W	Physically compatible for 72 hr at 15 and 30 °C	1479	C

[a]*Tested in PVC containers.*

Drugs in Syringe Compatibility

Drug (in syringe)	Mfr	Amt	Diamorphine HCl Mfr	Diamorphine HCl Amt	Remarks	Ref	C/I
Bupivacaine HCl	AST	0.5%	EV	1 and 10 mg/ml	10 to 11% diamorphine loss by HPLC in 5 weeks at 20 °C and 3 to 7% loss in 8 weeks at 6 °C. Little or no bupivacaine loss at 6 or 20 °C in 8 weeks	1952	C
Cyclizine lactate	CA	5 mg/1 ml[a]	MB	10, 25, 50 mg/1 ml	Physically compatible and diamorphine potency retained for 24 hr at room temperature	1454	C
	CA	15 mg/1 ml	EV	15 mg/1 ml	Physically compatible for 24 hr at room temperature	1455	C
	CA	12.5 to 50 mg/1 ml	EV	37.5 to 150 mg/1 ml	Precipitate forms within 24 hr	1455	I
	CA	10 mg/ml	HC	25 to 100 mg/ml	Visually incompatible	1672	I
	CA	10 mg/ml	HC	20 mg/ml	Visually compatible for 48 hr at 5 and 20 °C	1672	C
	CA	6.7 mg/ml	HC	≤100 mg/ml	Visually compatible for 48 hr at 5 and 20 °C	1672	C
	CA	6.7 mg/ml	HC	2 mg/ml	5% diamorphine loss by HPLC in 9.9 days at 20 °C. Cyclizine potency by HPLC retained for at least 45 days	1672	C
	CA	6.7 mg/ml	HC	20 mg/ml	5% diamorphine loss by HPLC in 13.6 days at 20 °C. Cyclizine potency by HPLC retained for at least 45 days	1672	C
	WEL	51 mg/ml	BP	6 mg/ml	Physically compatible with 10% diamorphine loss in 1.7 days and little or no cyclizine loss by HPLC at 23 °C	2071	C
	WEL	32 mg/ml	BP	9 mg/ml	Physically compatible with less than 10% diamorphine loss and little or no cyclizine loss by HPLC in 4 days at 23 °C	2071	C
	WEL	39 mg/ml	BP	10 mg/ml	Physically compatible with less than 10% diamorphine loss and little or no cyclizine loss by HPLC in 4 days at 23 °C	2071	C
	WEL	28 mg/ml	BP	10 mg/ml	Physically compatible with 10% diamorphine loss in 3.1 days and little or no cyclizine loss by HPLC at 23 °C	2071	C
	WEL	51 mg/ml	BP	12 mg/ml	Physically compatible with 10% diamorphine loss in 2.2 days and little or no cyclizine loss by HPLC at 23 °C	2071	C

Drugs in Syringe Compatibility (Cont.)

Diamorphine HCl

Drug (in syringe)	*Mfr*	*Amt*	*Mfr*	*Amt*	*Remarks*	*Ref*	*C/I*
	WEL	40 mg/ml	BP	14 mg/ml	Crystals form	2071	I
	WEL	26 mg/ml	BP	17 mg/ml	Physically compatible with 10% diamorphine loss in 1.1 days and 10% cyclizine loss in 2.5 days by HPLC at 23 °C	2071	C
	WEL	52 mg/ml	BP	18 mg/ml	Crystals form	2071	I
	WEL	10 mg/ml	BP	20 mg/ml	Physically compatible with less than 10% diamorphine loss and little or no cyclizine loss by HPLC in 7 days at 23 °C	2071	C
	WEL	15 mg/ml	BP	20 mg/ml	Physically compatible with little or no diamorphine loss and 10% cyclizine loss in 0.5 days by HPLC at 23 °C	2071	I
	WEL	26 mg/ml	BP	21 mg/ml	Physically compatible with 10% diamorphine loss in 4.9 days and 10% cyclizine loss in 3.2 days by HPLC at 23 °C	2071	C
	WEL	23 mg/ml	BP	18 mg/ml	Physically compatible with little or no diamorphine loss and 10% cyclizine loss by HPLC in 3.2 days at 23 °C	2071	C
	WEL	23 mg/ml	BP	26 mg/ml	Physically compatible with 10% diamorphine loss in 1.9 days and 10% cyclizine loss in 0.4 days by HPLC at 23 °C	2071	I
	WEL	30 mg/ml	BP	30 mg/ml	Physically compatible with 10% diamorphine loss in 0.9 days and 10% cyclizine loss in 0.4 days by HPLC at 23 °C	2071	I
	WEL	10 mg/ml	BP	49 mg/ml	Physically compatible with little or no diamorphine loss and 10% cyclizine loss in 5.5 days by HPLC at 23 °C	2071	C
	WEL	4 mg/ml	BP	51 mg/ml	Physically compatible with little or no loss of either drug by HPLC in 7 days at 23 °C	2071	C
	WEL	8 mg/ml	BP	61 mg/ml	Physically compatible with 10% diamorphine loss in 1.4 days and 10% cyclizine loss in 1.1 days by HPLC at 23 °C	2071	C
	WEL	13 mg/ml	BP	65 mg/ml	Physically compatible with 10% diamorphine loss in 1.6 days and 10% cyclizine loss in 0.5 days by HPLC at 23 °C	2071	I
	WEL	10 mg/ml	BP	92 mg/ml	Physically compatible with little or no diamorphine loss and 10% cyclizine loss in 2.4 days by HPLC at 23 °C	2071	C
	WEL	4 mg/ml	BP	99 mg/ml	Physically compatible with little or no loss of either drug by HPLC in 7 days at 23 °C	2071	C
Cyclizine lactate with haloperidol lactate	WEL JC	16 mg/ml 2.2 mg/ml	BP	11 mg/ml	Physically compatible with less than 10% loss of any drug by HPLC in 7 days at 23 °C	2071	C
Cyclizine lactate with haloperidol lactate	WEL JC	16 mg/ml 2.2 mg/ml	BP	25 mg/ml	Physically compatible with less than 10% loss of any drug by HPLC in 7 days at 23 °C	2071	C
Cyclizine lactate with haloperidol lactate	WEL JC	11 mg/ml 2.2 mg/ml	BP	40 mg/ml	Physically compatible with less than 10% loss of any drug by HPLC in 7 days at 23 °C	2071	C
Cyclizine lactate with haloperidol lactate	WEL JC	13 mg/ml 2.1 mg/ml	BP	42 mg/ml	Physically compatible with less than 10% loss of any drug by HPLC in 6 days at 23 °C	2071	C
Cyclizine lactate with haloperidol lactate	WEL JC	9 mg/ml 2.1 mg/ml	BP	55 mg/ml	Physically compatible with less than 10% loss of any drug by HPLC in 7 days at 23 °C	2071	C
Cyclizine lactate with haloperidol lactate	WEL JC	13 mg/ml 2.1 mg/ml	BP	56 mg/ml	Physically compatible with less than 10% loss of any drug by HPLC in 7 days at 23 °C	2071	C
Haloperidol lactate	SE	1.5 mg/ 1 ml[a]	MB	10, 25, 50 mg/ 1 ml	Physically compatible and diamorphine content retained for 24 hr at room temperature	1454	C

Drugs in Syringe Compatibility (Cont.)

			Diamorphine HCl				
Drug (in syringe)	*Mfr*	*Amt*	*Mfr*	*Amt*	*Remarks*	*Ref*	*C/I*
	SE	2 mg/ 1 ml	EV	20 mg/ 1 ml	Crystallization with 58% haloperidol loss in 7 days at room temperature	1455	I
	SE	5 mg/ 1 ml	EV	50 and 150 mg/ 1 ml	Immediate precipitation	1455	I
	SE	2.5 mg/ 8 ml	EV	100 mg/ 8 ml	Physically compatible for 24 hr at room temperature and 7 days at 6 °C	1456	C
	SE	0.75 mg/ ml	HC	20 to 100 mg/ ml	Visually compatible for 48 hr at 5 and 20 °C	1672	C
	SE	0.75 mg/ ml	HC	2 mg/ml	5% diamorphine loss by HPLC in 14.8 days at 20 °C. Haloperidol potency by HPLC retained for at least 45 days	1672	C
	SE	0.75 mg/ ml	HC	20 mg/ml	5% diamorphine loss by HPLC in 20.7 days at 20 °C. Haloperidol potency by HPLC retained for at least 45 days	1672	C
	JC	2 mg/ml	BP	20, 50, and 100 mg/ ml	Physically compatible with no loss of either drug by HPLC in 7 days at 23 °C	2071	C
	JC	3 mg/ml	BP	20, 50, and 100 mg/ ml	Physically compatible with no loss of either drug by HPLC in 7 days at 23 °C	2071	C
	JC	4 mg/ml	BP	20 and 50 mg/ml	Physically compatible with no loss of either drug by HPLC in 7 days at 23 °C	2071	C
Hyoscine butylbromide	BI	20 mg/ 1 ml	EV	50 and 150 mg/ 1 ml	Physically compatible with no hyoscine loss and 4% diamorphine loss in 7 days at room temperature	1455	C
Hyoscine HBr	EV	60 μg/ 1 ml[a]	MB	10, 25, 50 mg/ 1 ml	Physically compatible and diamorphine content retained for 24 hr at room temperature	1454	C
	EV	0.4 mg/ 1 ml	EV	50 and 150 mg/ 1 ml	Physically compatible with 7% diamorphine loss in 7 days at room temperature	1455	C
Methotrimeprazine	MB	2.5 and 1.25 mg/ 1 ml[a]	MB	50 mg/ 1 ml	Physically compatible and diamorphine content retained for 24 hr at room temperature	1454	C
Metoclopramide HCl	BK	5 mg/ 1 ml	MB	10, 25, 50 mg/ 1 ml	Physically compatible and diamorphine content retained for 24 hr at room temperature	1454	C
	LA	5 mg/ 1 ml	EV	50 and 150 mg/ 1 ml	Slight discoloration with 8% metoclopramide loss and 9% diamorphine loss in 7 days at room temperature	1455	C
Midazolam HCl	RC	10[b] and 75[c] mg	EV	10 mg	Visually compatible with 10% diamorphine loss and no midazolam loss by HPLC in 15.9 days at 22 °C	1792	C
	RC	10[b] and 75[c] mg	EV	500 mg	Visually compatible with 10% diamorphine loss and no midazolam loss by HPLC in 22.2 days at 22 °C	1792	C

Drugs in Syringe Compatibility (Cont.)

Diamorphine HCl

Drug (in syringe)	*Mfr*	*Amt*	*Mfr*	*Amt*	*Remarks*	*Ref*	*C/I*
Prochlorperazine edisylate	MB	1.25 mg/ 1 ml[a]	MB	10, 25, 50 mg/ 1 ml	Physically compatible and diamorphine content retained for 24 hr at room temperature	1454	C

[a]Diluted with sterile water for injection.
[b]Diluted with sterile water to 15 ml.
[c]Diamorphine HCl constituted with midazolam injection.

Additional Compatibility Information

Other Drugs — The manufacturer indicates that hyoscine HBr, methotrimeprazine, and metoclopramide HCl are stable and compatible with diamorphine HCl. Chlorpromazine HCl and prochlorperazine edisylate also are stated to be compatible. (1442)

FLECAINIDE ACETATE

Products — Flecainide acetate is available as a 10-mg/ml solution in 4- and 15-ml ampuls. The product also contains sodium acetate and acetic acid in water for injection. (38; 115; 116)

Trade Name(s) — Flecaine, Tambocor.

Administration — Flecainide acetate may be administered intravenously as a bolus injection and by intravenous infusion. For rapid effect, the drug is administered as a slow intravenous injection over not less than 10 minutes or in divided doses. It may also be diluted in 20 to 100 ml of dextrose 5% in water and given as a mini-infusion. Flecainide acetate administration by intravenous infusion usually should not exceed 24 hours. (38; 115; 116)

Stability — Flecainide acetate injection is clear and colorless. Intact containers of the drug should be stored between 5 and 30 °C and protected from freezing and exposure to light. (38; 115)

Dextrose 5% in water is the preferred diluent for flecainide acetate. If a chloride-containing solution such as 0.9% sodium chloride or lactated Ringer's injection is used, the dose must be diluted in at least 500 ml to prevent the formation of a precipitate. (38; 115)

Compatibility Information

Drugs in Syringe Compatibility

Flecainide acetate

Drug (in syringe)	*Mfr*	*Amt*	*Mfr*	*Amt*	*Remarks*	*Ref*	*C/I*
Heparin sodium		2500 units/ 1 ml		10 mg/ 5 ml	Turbidity or precipitate forms within 5 min	1053	I

Y-Site Injection Compatibility (1:1 Mixture)

Flecainide acetate

Drug	*Mfr*	*Conc*	*Mfr*	*Conc*	*Remarks*	*Ref*	*C/I*
Heparin sodium		50 units/1 ml/ min[b]		10 mg/5 ml[a]	Clear solution	1053	C

[a]Given over three minutes into a heparin infusion run at 1 ml/min.
[b]Tested in sodium chloride 0.9%.

FLUCLOXACILLIN SODIUM (FLOXACILLIN SODIUM)

Products — Flucloxacillin sodium is available in vials containing 250 mg, 500 mg, and 1 g of flucloxacillin as the sodium salt. To reconstitute for intramuscular use, add 1.5 ml of sterile water for injection to the 250-mg vial or 2 ml to the 500-mg vial. (38; 115)

For intravenous use, reconstitute the 250- or 500-mg vial with 5 to 10 ml of sterile water for injection; reconstitute the 1-g vial with 15 to 20 ml of sterile water for injection. For intravenous infusion, the solution may be diluted further in a compatible infusion fluid. (38; 115) (See Compatibility Information.)

For intrapleural use, reconstitute the 250-mg vial with 5 to 10 ml of sterile water for injection. For intra-articular use, reconstitute the 250- or 500-mg vial with up to 5 ml of sterile water for injection or lignocaine HCl 0.5% injection. Do not use lignocaine HCl to reconstitute the drug for other routes of administration. (38; 115)

For smaller doses, the reconstitution volumes cited in Table 1 will yield the indicated amount of flucloxacillin sodium in a volume of 1 ml. (115)

Sodium and Magnesium Content — Each gram of flucloxacillin sodium contains 2.2 mmol (51 mg) of sodium and 1 mmol of magnesium. (38; 89; 115)

Trade Name(s) — Floxapen, Ladropen.

Administration — Flucloxacillin sodium may be administered by intramuscular injection, direct intravenous injection slowly over three to four minutes, continuous intravenous infusion, and intrapleural and intra-articular injection. (38)

Stability — Flucloxacillin sodium in intact vials should be stored below 25 °C. (115) The injection reconstituted for intramuscular or direct intravenous injection should be freshly prepared (115) and administered within 30 minutes. (38) However, reconstituted flucloxacillin sodium injection is stated to be stable for 24 hours when stored under refrigeration. (38)

Lynn reported losses of 8% in three days for reconstituted solutions containing flucloxacillin sodium (Beecham) 100 mg/ml stored at 20 to 25 °C. (89)

Table 1. Flucloxacillin Reconstitution Volumes for Smaller Doses (115)

	Concentration (mg/1 ml)					
Vial Size	50	100	125	200	250	500
250 mg	4.8 ml	2.3 ml	1.8 ml	1.05 ml		
500 mg		4.7 ml	3.7 ml	2.2 ml	1.7 ml	
1 g		9.3 ml			3.3 ml	1.3 ml

Freezing Solutions — Flucloxacillin sodium (Beecham) 10 mg/ml in sodium chloride 0.9% or dextrose 5% in water in PVC bags (Travenol) retained greater than 90% potency after being frozen and stored at −27 °C for up to 270 days. Thawing by microwave radiation and subsequent storage for 24 hours at 4 °C did not cause drug potency to fall below 90% of the stated concentration. However, a distinct yellow discoloration was produced after 90 days of storage, rendering the solutions unacceptable. (1176)

Flucloxacillin sodium (Beecham) 1 g in 50 ml of sodium chloride 0.9% or dextrose 5% in water in PVC bags (Travenol) was stored at −20 °C for 30 days, followed by natural thawing and storage at 5 °C for 21 hours. The drug was stable under these conditions for the duration of the study. (299)

Syringes — Flucloxacillin sodium (Berck) 125 mg/ml in sterile water for injection, packaged as 0.16 ml in 1-ml Injekt syringes (Braun) sealed with blind hubs and stored at about 6 °C, retained antibiotic activity against *Staphylococcus aureus* for nine days but lost 13% by day 14. (1697)

Ambulatory Pumps — Flucloxacillin sodium at a concentration of 120 mg/ml in sodium chloride 0.9% and packaged in polyvinyl chloride bags (Baxter) for use in ambulatory and in-home treatment was evaluated for stability. After preparation, the containers were stored under refrigeration at about 4 °C for six days followed by 24 hours at 37 °C to simulate use conditions. HPLC analysis found that the flucloxacillin sodium solutions remained stable during refrigerated storage, but about 28% loss occurred during the 24-hour simulated in-use condition. The authors recommended not administering flucloxacillin sodium infusions as single 24-hour infusions. The use of divided dose reservoirs, which expose the drug solution to elevated temperatures for shorter time periods, was recommended. (2206)

Sorption — Flucloxacillin sodium (Beecham) 200 mg/L in sodium chloride 0.9% (Travenol) in PVC bags did not exhibit significant sorption to the plastic during one week at room temperature (15 to 20 °C). (536)

Flucloxacillin sodium (Beecham) 200 mg/L in sodium chloride 0.9% did not exhibit any loss due to sorption during a seven-hour simulated infusion through an infusion set (Travenol) consisting of a cellulose propionate burette chamber and 170 cm of PVC tubing. (606)

The drug also was tested as a simulated infusion over at least one hour by a syringe pump system. A glass syringe on a syringe pump was fitted with 20 cm of polyethylene tubing or 50 cm of Silastic tubing. No drug loss due to sorption was observed with either tubing. (606)

Furthermore, a 25-ml aliquot of flucloxacillin sodium (Beecham) 200 mg/L in sodium chloride 0.9% was stored in all-plastic syringes composed of polypropylene barrels and polyethylene plungers for 24 hours at room temperature in the dark. The solution did not exhibit any loss due to sorption. (606)

Compatibility Information

Solution Compatibility

Flucloxacillin sodium

Solution	*Mfr*	*Mfr*	*Conc/L*	*Remarks*	*Ref*	*C/I*
Dextrose 2.5% in sodium chloride 0.45%		BE	1 g	6% loss in 24 hr at 20 to 25 °C	89	C
Dextrose 5% in water		BE	1 g	1% loss in 24 hr at 20 to 25 °C	89	C

Solution Compatibility (Cont.)

Flucloxacillin sodium

Solution	Mfr	Mfr	Conc/L	Remarks	Ref	C/I
Sodium chloride 0.9%		BE	1 g	3% loss in 24 hr at 20 to 25 °C	89	C
	BA	BE	20 g	Visually compatible with 3% drug loss in 14 days and 9% loss in 28 days by HPLC at 5 °C	1844	C
	BA	BE	10 g	Visually compatible with 3% drug loss in 14 days and 8% loss in 28 days by HPLC at 5 °C	1844	C
	BA	BE	5 g	Visually compatible with 2% drug loss in 14 days and 7% loss in 28 days by HPLC at 5 °C	1844	C
	BA[a]		120 g	Stable for at least 6 days at 4 °C by HPLC analysis. 28% loss in 24 hours at 37 °C	2206	C
Sodium lactate ⅙ M		BE	1 g	4% loss in 24 hr at 20 to 25 °C	89	C

[a]*Tested in PVC containers.*

Additive Compatibility

Flucloxacillin sodium

Drug	Mfr	Conc/L	Mfr	Conc/L	Test Soln	Remarks	Ref	C/I
Aminophylline	ANT	1 g	BE	20 g	NS	Physically compatible for 72 hr at 15 and 30 °C	1479	C
Amiodarone HCl	LZ	4 g	BE	20 g	D5W	Immediate precipitation	1479	I
Ampicillin sodium	BE	20 g	BE	20 g	NS	Physically compatible for 72 hr at 15 and 30 °C	1479	C
Atropine sulphate	ANT	60 mg	BE	20 g	W	Haze forms in 24 hr and precipitate forms in 48 hr at 30 °C. No change at 15 °C	1479	I
Bumetanide	LEO	6 mg	BE	20 g	NS	Physically compatible for 72 hr at 15 and 30 °C	1479	C
Buprenorphine HCl		75 mg	BE	20 g	W	Thick haze forms in 24 hr and precipitate forms in 47 hr at 30 °C. No change at 15 °C	1479	I
Calcium gluconate	ANT	2 g	BE	20 g	NS	Thick white precipitate forms immediately	1479	I
Cefamandole nafate	DI	20 g	BE	20 g	W	Physically compatible for 24 hr at 15 and 30 °C. Haze forms in 48 hr and precipitate forms in 72 hr at 30 °C. No change at 15 °C	1479	C
Cefuroxime sodium	GL	37.5 g	BE	20 g	W	Physically compatible for 72 hr at 15 and 30 °C	1479	C
	GL	7.5 g	BE	10 g	D5W, NS	Physically compatible for 48 hr. Potency of both drugs retained when assayed after 1 hr at room temperature	1036	C
Chlorpromazine HCl	ANT	5 g	BE	20 g	W	Sticky yellow precipitate forms immediately	1479	I
Cimetidine HCl	SKF	4 g	BE	20 g	NS	Physically compatible for 72 hr at 15 and 30 °C	1479	C
Ciprofloxacin		2 g	BE	10 g	[a]	Immediate precipitation	1473	I
Dexamethasone sodium phosphate	MSD	4 g	BE	20 g	NS	Physically compatible for 72 hr at 15 and 30 °C	1479	C
Diamorphine HCl	EV	500 mg	BE	20 g	W	Physically compatible for 24 hr at 15 and 30 °C. Haze forms in 48 hr at 30 °C. No change at 15 °C	1479	C

Additive Compatibility (Cont.)

			Flucloxacillin sodium					
Drug	*Mfr*	*Conc/L*	*Mfr*	*Conc/L*	*Test Soln*	*Remarks*	*Ref*	*C/I*
Diazepam	PHX	1 g	BE	20 g	D5W	Haze forms in 7 hr at 30 °C and 48 hr at 15 °C	1479	I
Digoxin	BW	25 mg	BE	20 g	NS	Physically compatible for 72 hr at 15 and 30 °C	1479	C
Dobutamine HCl	LI	500 mg	BE	20 g	NS	Haze forms immediately and precipitate forms in 24 to 48 hr at 15 and 30 °C	1479	I
Epinephrine HCl	ANT	8 mg	BE	20 g	W	Physically compatible for 72 hr at 15 and 30 °C	1479	C
Erythromycin lactobionate	AB	5 g	BE	20 g	NS	Immediate precipitation. Crystals form in 5 hr at 15 °C	1479	I
Gentamicin sulphate	RS	8 g	BE	20 g	NS	Haze forms immediately and precipitate forms in 2 hr	1479	I
	EX	8 g	BE	10 g	NS	Physically compatible for 48 hr. Potency of both drugs retained when assayed after 1 hr at room temperature	1036	C
	EX	8 g	BE	10 g	D5W	Immediate precipitation	1036	I
Heparin sodium	WED	20,000 units	BE	20 g	NS	Physically compatible for 24 hr at 15 and 30 °C. Haze forms in 48 hr at 30 °C. No change at 15 °C	1479	C
Hydrocortisone sodium succinate	UP	50 g	BE	20 g	NS	Physically compatible for 72 hr at 15 and 30 °C	1479	C
Hyoscine butylbromide	BI	2 g	BE	20 g	W	Physically compatible for 24 hr at 15 and 30 °C. Precipitate forms in 48 hr. No change at 15 °C	1479	C
Isoprenaline HCl	PX	4 mg	BE	20 g	D5W	Physically compatible for 24 hr at 15 and 30 °C. Haze forms in 48 hr and precipitate forms in 72 hr	1479	C
Isosorbide dinitrate		1 g	BE	20 g		Physically compatible for 24 hr at 15 and 30 °C. Haze forms in 48 hr and precipitate forms in 72 hr at 30 °C. No change at 15 °C	1479	C
Lignocaine HCl	ANT	2 g	BE	20 g	NS	Physically compatible for 72 hr at 15 and 30 °C	1479	C
Metoclopramide HCl	ANT	1 g	BE	20 g	NS	White precipitate forms immediately	1479	I
Metronidazole		5 g	BE	10 g		Physically compatible for 48 hr. Potency of both drugs retained when assayed after 1 hr at room temperature	1036	C
Morphine sulphate	EV	1 g	BE	20 g	W	Haze forms in 24 hr and precipitate forms in 48 hr at 30 °C. No change at 15 °C	1479	I
Netilmicin sulphate	EX	1 g	BE	10 g	NS	Physically compatible for 48 hr. Potency of both drugs retained when assayed after 1 hr at room temperature	1036	C
	EX	1 g	BE	10 g	D5W	Immediate precipitation	1036	I
Ofloxacin	HO	1.67 g	BE	8.3 g	W	Visually compatible for 7 hr. Precipitate forms by 24 hr with about 75% ofloxacin loss and 20% flucloxacillin loss by HPLC	1613	I
Papaveretum	RC[b]	2 g	BE	20 g	W	White precipitate forms immediately	1479	I

Additive Compatibility (Cont.)

Flucloxacillin sodium

Drug	*Mfr*	*Conc/L*	*Mfr*	*Conc/L*	*Test Soln*	*Remarks*	*Ref*	*C/I*
Pefloxacin		4 g	BE	10 g	D5W, NS	Immediate precipitation	1473	I
Penicillin G	GL	12 g	BE	20 g	NS	Haze forms in 24 hr and precipitate forms in 48 hr at 30 °C. No change at 15 °C	1479	I
Pethidine HCl	RC	5 g	BE	20 g	W	Haze forms immediately and precipitate forms in 5 to 24 hr	1479	I
Piperacillin sodium	LE	120 g	BE	50 g	W	10% piperacillin loss and 6% flucloxacillin loss by HPLC in 12 days at 5 °C. 3% piperacillin loss and 6% flucloxacillin loss by HPLC in 1 day at 30 °C	1748	C
Potassium chloride	ANT	40 mM	BE	20 g	W	Physically compatible for 72 hr at 15 and 30 °C	1479	C
Prochlorperazine edisylate	MB	1.25 g	BE	20 g	W	Immediate precipitation	1479	I
Promethazine HCl	MB	5 g	BE	20 g	W	White precipitate forms immediately	1479	I
Ranitidine HCl	GL	500 mg	BE	20 g	NS	Physically compatible for 72 hr at 15 and 30 °C	1479	C
Sodium bicarbonate	IMS	84 g	BE	20 g		Physically compatible for 72 hr at 15 and 30 °C	1479	C
Sulphadimidine	ICI	100 g	BE	20 g	W	Crystals form in 48 hr and globular precipitate forms in 72 hr at 30 °C. No change at 15 °C	1479	I
Tobramycin sulphate	LI	8 g	BE	20 g	NS	White precipitate forms in 7 hr	1479	I
Verapamil HCl	AB	500 mg	BE	20 g	NS	Haze and precipitate form in 24 hr at 30 °C. No change at 15 °C	1479	I

[a]*Flucloxacillin sodium added to ciprofloxacin solvent.*
[b]*The former formulation was tested.*

Drugs in Syringe Compatibility

Flucloxacillin sodium

Drug (in syringe)	*Mfr*	*Amt*	*Mfr*	*Amt*	*Remarks*	*Ref*	*C/I*
Heparin sodium		2500 units/ 1 ml	BE	1 g	Visually compatible for at least 5 min	1053	C

Y-Site Injection Compatibility (1:1 Mixture)

Flucloxacillin sodium

Drug	*Mfr*	*Conc*	*Mfr*	*Conc*	*Remarks*	*Ref*	*C/I*
Clarithromycin	AB	4 mg/ml[a]	BE	40 mg/ml[a]	Translucent precipitate forms in 1 to 2 hr becoming a gel in 3 hr at both 30 and 17 °C	2174	I
Lorazepam	WY	0.33 mg/ml[b]	SKB	50 mg/ml	White opalescence forms in 4 hr	1855	I
Midazolam HCl	RC	5 mg/ml	SKB	50 mg/ml	White precipitate forms immediately	1855	I
TPN #189[c]			BE	50 mg/ml[b]	Visually compatible for 24 hr at 22 °C	1767	C

[a]*Tested in dextrose 5% in water.*
[b]*Tested in sodium chloride 0.9%.*
[c]*Refer to Appendix I for the composition of parenteral nutrition solutions. TPN indicates a 2-in-1 admixture.*

Additional Compatibility Information

Infusion Solutions — Flucloxacillin sodium is stated to be stable over 24 hours at room temperature, exhibiting less than a 10% potency loss when administered with the following intravenous infusion fluids (1475):

Dextran 40 10% in dextrose 5%
Dextran 40 10% in sodium chloride 0.9%
Dextrose 5% in water
Ringer's injection, lactated
Sodium chloride 0.18% in dextrose 4%
Sodium chloride 0.9%
Sodium lactate ⅙ M

Flucloxacillin sodium should not be mixed with proteinaceous solutions or with intravenous lipid emulsions. (38)

Aminoglycosides — Flucloxacillin sodium and aminoglycosides should not be mixed in the same syringe, intravenous fluid container, or administration set because precipitation may occur. (38; 115)

Other Drugs — The manufacturer recommends that flucloxacillin sodium not be mixed with other drugs for parenteral administration. (38; 115)

FOSFOMYCIN DISODIUM

Products — Fosfomycin disodium is available in vials containing the equivalent of 1 g of fosfomycin as the disodium salt with an accompanying 10-ml ampul of diluent for reconstitution and in vials containing the equivalent of 4 g of fosfomycin as the disodium salt with an accompanying 20-ml ampul of diluent for reconstitution. Also present in the formulation is succinic acid. (116)

Sodium Content — Fosfomycin disodium contains 14.4 mEq or mmol (330 mg) of sodium per gram of drug product. (116)

Trade Name(s) — Fosfocine, Monuril.

Administration — Fosfomycin disodium is administered intramuscularly (5) and by intravenous infusion after dilution of the reconstituted product in a compatible infusion solution. A recommended minimum volume for dilution for infusion is 250 ml. (5; 116)

Stability — The reconstituted drug in vials and the solution diluted for infusion in dextrose 5% in water or sodium chloride 0.9% are stable for 24 hours at room temperature. (116)

Table 1. Stability of Fosfomycin Disodium 50 mg/1 ml and 50 mg/3 ml in Water for Injection in Infusion Pump Syringes (2303)

Storage Conditions and Durations	Fosfomycin Remaining
Room temperature, light protected for 6 hr	97 to 98%
Room temperature, light exposed for 8 hr	88 to 91%
Refrigerated at 4 to 8 °C for 96 hr plus room temperature, light protected for 6 hr	95 to 96%
Frozen at −20 °C for 31 days plus 4 to 8 °C for 96 hr plus room temperature, light protected for 6 hr	94 to 95%

Syringes — Fosfomycin disodium diluted to concentrations of 50 mg/1 ml and 50 mg/3 ml in water for injection were packaged in infusion pump syringes (Braun Melsungen) and were evaluated for stability under a variety of storage conditions. The stability results are presented in Table 1. No concentration dependency was found, but exposure to light appeared to increase the rate of decomposition. (2303)

Compatibility Information

Drugs in Syringe Compatibility

Fosfomycin disodium

Drug (in syringe)	*Mfr*	*Amt*	*Mfr*	*Amt*	*Remarks*	*Ref*	*C/I*
Heparin sodium		2500 units/1 ml	BM	3 g	Visually compatible for at least 5 min	1053	C

FOTEMUSTINE

Products — Fotemustine is available in vials containing 208 mg of drug. The vials are accompanied by an ampul of diluent for reconstitution composed of 95% ethanol 3.35 ml and water for injection 0.65 ml. Reconstitution with the special ethanol-containing diluent yields a solution with a total volume of 4.16 ml and containing fotemustine 50 mg/ml. This concentrated solution must be diluted for use. (115; 116)

pH — A 0.3% aqueous solution of fotemustine has a pH of 6.3. (115)

Trade Name(s) — Muphoran.

Administration — Fotemustine is administered by intravenous infusion over one hour and intra-arterial infusion over four hours after dilution of the dose in 250 to 400 ml of dextrose 5% in water. Solutions must be protected from light during storage and infusion. (115; 116)

Stability — Fotemustine is supplied as a pale yellow powder in amber vials. Intact vials of fotemustine should be stored under refrigeration. Solutions of fotemustine are not stable. Use of the drug immediately upon reconstitution is recommended. Fotemustine diluted in dextrose 5% in water for administration is light sensitive and must be protected from light during administration. Completion of administration within a few hours of preparation is recommended. (115; 116)

Light Effects — Fotemustine is light sensitive. (115; 116) At concentrations of 0.8 and 2 mg/ml in dextrose 5% in water stored at 22 °C exposed to ambient room light and also exposed to direct sunlight, fotemustine underwent substantial decomposition. Exposed to ambient light, about 10% decomposition occurred in one hour and about 30% loss in eight hours. Losses were much greater and occurred rapidly when solutions were exposed to direct sunlight. About 35% loss of fotemustine occurred in one hour and near total loss occurred within four hours. The loss of drug was accompanied by discoloration of the solution. (2320)

Sorption — No loss due to sorption to PVC containers was found in solutions of 0.8 and 2 mg/ml prepared in dextrose 5% in water in PVC bags and delivered through PVC administration sets over one hour, stored for eight hours at 22 °C, and stored at 4 °C for 48 hours. (2320)

Plasticizer Leaching — No leaching of diethylhexyl phthlate (DEHP) plasticizer from PVC containers was found in solutions of 0.8 and 2 mg/ml prepared in dextrose 5% in water in PVC bags and delivered through PVC administration sets over one hour, stored for eight hours at 22 °C, and stored at 4 °C for 48 hours. (2320)

Compatibility Information

Solution Compatibility

Fotemustine

Solution	*Mfr*	*Mfr*	*Conc/L*	*Remarks*	*Ref*	*C/I*
Dextrose 5% in water	[a]	SER	800 mg and 2 g	Visually compatible with no substantial loss in 8 hr at 22 °C protected from light and 48 hr at 4 °C protected from light	2320	C

[a] *Tested in PVC containers.*

HYALURONIDASE

Products — Hyaluronidase is supplied in ampuls containing 1500 I.U. as a white lyophilized plug of powder. For subcutaneous infusion (hypodermoclysis), the content of the ampul is reconstituted with 1 ml of water for injection or sodium chloride 0.9%. For use with subcutaneous or intramuscular injections and local anesthetics, the hyaluronidase is dissolved in the solution to be injected. (38; 115)

pH — From 6.4 to 7.4. (4)

Osmolality — Hyaluronidase 150 units/ml has an osmolality of 300 mOsm/kg. (1689)

Trade Name(s) — Hyalase.

Administration — Hyaluronidase is administered subcutaneously, intradermally, or intramuscularly along with other drugs or solutions. The solutions should be isotonic for subcutaneous administration. It should not be administered intravenously. (4; 38; 115)

Stability — Hyaluronidase injection in intact ampuls should be stored at 25 °C or below. Use immediately after reconstitution is recommended. (38; 115) It should not be used if it is discolored or contains a precipitate. When reconstituted with sodium chloride 0.9%, the solution is stated to be stable for up to two weeks at temperatures below 25 °C. (4)

Hyaluronidase (Wyeth) 75 units/ml in citric acid/sodium citrate buffer (pH ≈ 4.5) was found to lose about 7 to 8% activity in 24 hours at 4 and 23 °C. Hyaluronidase activity decreased by 25 to 33% in 48 hours. (1907)

Compatibility Information

Solution Compatibility

Hyaluronidase

Solution	*Mfr*	*Mfr*	*Conc/L*	*Remarks*	*Ref*	*C/I*
Dextran 6% in dextrose 5%	AB	AB	150 units	Physically compatible	3	C
Dextran 6% in sodium chloride 0.9%	AB	AB	150 units	Physically compatible	3	C

Solution Compatibility (Cont.)

Solution	Mfr	Hyaluronidase Mfr	Conc/L	Remarks	Ref	C/I
Dextrose–Ringer's injection combinations	AB	AB	150 units	Physically compatible	3	C
Dextrose–Ringer's injection, lactated, combinations	AB	AB	150 units	Physically compatible	3	C
Dextrose–saline combinations	AB	AB	150 units	Physically compatible	3	C
Dextrose 2½% in water	AB	AB	150 units	Physically compatible	3	C
Dextrose 5% in water	AB	AB	150 units	Physically compatible	3	C
Dextrose 10% in water	AB	AB	150 units	Physically compatible	3	C
Fructose 10% in sodium chloride 0.9%	AB	AB	150 units	Physically compatible	3	C
Fructose 10% in water	AB	AB	150 units	Physically compatible	3	C
Invert sugar 5 and 10% in sodium chloride 0.9%	AB	AB	150 units	Physically compatible	3	C
Invert sugar 5 and 10% in water	AB	AB	150 units	Physically compatible	3	C
Ionosol products	AB	AB	150 units	Physically compatible	3	C
Ringer's injection	AB	AB	150 units	Physically compatible	3	C
Ringer's injection, lactated	AB	AB	150 units	Physically compatible	3	C
Sodium chloride 0.45%	AB	AB	150 units	Physically compatible	3	C
Sodium chloride 0.9%	AB	AB	150 units	Physically compatible	3	C
Sodium lactate ⅙ M	AB	AB	150 units	Physically compatible	3	C

Additive Compatibility

Drug	Mfr	Conc/L	Hyaluronidase Mfr	Conc/L	Test Soln	Remarks	Ref	C/I
Amikacin sulphate	BR	5 g	SE	150 units	D5LR, D5R, D5S, D5W, D10W, IS10, LR, NS, R, SL	Physically compatible and amikacin potency retained for 24 hr at 25 °C. Hyaluronidase not analyzed	294	C
Epinephrine HCl	PD					Physically incompatible	10	I
	PD		WY			Physically incompatible	9	I

Additive Compatibility (Cont.)

Hyaluronidase

Drug	*Mfr*	*Conc/L*	*Mfr*	*Conc/L*	*Test Soln*	*Remarks*	*Ref*	*C/I*
Heparin sodium						Physically incompatible	10	I
			WY			Physically incompatible	9	I
Sodium bicarbonate	AB	2.4 mEq[a]	WY	150 units	D5W	Physically compatible for 24 hr	772	C

[a]One vial of Neut added to a liter of admixture.

Drugs in Syringe Compatibility

Hyaluronidase

Drug (in syringe)	*Mfr*	*Amt*	*Mfr*	*Amt*	*Remarks*	*Ref*	*C/I*
Diatrizoate meglumine 52%, diatrizoate sodium 8% (Renografin-60)	SQ	40 to 5 ml	WY	150 units/ 1 ml	Physically compatible for 48 hr	530	C
	SQ	2 and 1 ml	WY	150 units/ 1 ml	Physically compatible for at least 1 hr but a precipitate forms within 48 hr	530	I
Diatrizoate meglumine 34.3%, diatrizoate sodium 35% (Renovist)	SQ	40 to 1 ml	WY	150 units/ 1 ml	Physically compatible for 48 hr	530	C
Diatrizoate sodium 75% (Hypaque)	WI	40 to 5 ml	WY	150 units/ 1 ml	Physically compatible for 48 hr	530	C
	WI	2 and 1 ml	WY	150 units/ 1 ml	Physically compatible for at least 1 hr but a precipitate forms within 48 hr	530	I
Hydromorphone HCl	KN	2 mg/ml[a]	WY	150 units/ml[a]	43 and 56% hyaluronidase loss in 24 hr at 4 and 23 °C, respectively	1907	I
	KN	10 and 40 mg/ml[a]	WY	150 units/ml[a]	70 to 82% hyaluronidase loss in 24 hr at 4 and 23 °C	1907	I
Iodipamide meglumine 52% (Cholografin)	SQ	40 to 2 ml	WY	150 units/ 1 ml	Physically compatible for 48 hr	530	C
	SQ	1 ml	WY	150 units/ 1 ml	Physically compatible for at least 1 hr but a precipitate forms within 48 hr	530	I
Iothalamate meglumine 60% (Conray)	MA	40 to 1 ml	WY	150 units/ 1 ml	Physically compatible for 48 hr	530	C
Iothalamate sodium 80% (Angio-Conray)	MA	40 to 1 ml	WY	150 units/ 1 ml	Physically compatible for 48 hr	530	C
Pentobarbital sodium	AB	500 mg/ 10 ml	AB	150 units	Physically compatible	55	C
Thiopental sodium	AB	75 mg/ 3 ml	AB	150 units	Physically compatible	55	C

[a]Mixed in equal quantities.

Additional Compatibility Information

Other Drugs — Hyaluronidase has been mixed with morphine (form unspecified), diamorphine HCl, hydromorphone HCl, chlorpromazine HCl, metoclopramide HCl, promazine HCl, dexamethasone sodium phosphate, and local anesthetics (38; 115) and with diatrizoate meglumine products (40). It has also been mixed in epinephrine HCl in low concentrations (38; 115), although reports of incompatibility of this combination also exist. (9; 10; 115)

Hyaluronidase is stated to be physically incompatible with benzodiazepines, frusemide, heparin sodium, and phenytoin sodium. (115)

HYOSCINE BUTYLBROMIDE (SCOPOLAMINE BUTYLBROMIDE)

Products — Hyoscine butylbromide is available in 1-ml ampuls as a 20-mg/ml solution with sodium chloride in water for injection. (38; 115; 116)

Trade Name(s) — Buscopan, Scoburen.

Administration — Hyoscine butylbromide is administered by intramuscular or subcutaneous injection or slowly intravenously. Dextrose 5% in water and sodium chloride 0.9% are recommended for dilution if needed. (38; 115; 116)

Stability — Hyoscine butylbromide injection is a clear, colorless or nearly colorless solution. (38; 115) Intact containers should be stored below 25 °C (116) or 30 °C and protected from light. (38; 115)

Compatibility Information

Drugs in Syringe Compatibility

Hyoscine butylbromide

Drug (in syringe)	*Mfr*	*Amt*	*Mfr*	*Amt*	*Remarks*	*Ref*	*C/I*
Dimenhydrinate	HR	50 mg/ 1 ml	BI	20 mg/ 1 ml	Physically compatible	711	C
	HR	10 mg/ 1 ml	BI	20 mg/ 1 ml	Physically compatible	711	C
Fentanyl citrate with midazolam HCl	DB RC	1 mg/ 20 ml 15 mg/ 3 ml	BI	30 mg/ 1.5 ml	Visually compatible with 9% or less loss of each drug in 7 days at 32 °C	2268	C
Morphine HCl	FED, STP	5 and 10 mg/ 1 ml	BI	20 mg/ 1 ml	Visually compatible for up to 24 hr at 23 °C	2257	C
	FED, STP	20 and 30 mg/ 1 ml	BI	20 mg/ 1 ml	Visually compatible for up to 7 days at 23 °C	2257	C

ISOSORBIDE DINITRATE

Products — Isosorbide dinitrate is available as a 0.1% solution in 10-ml ampuls and 50- and 100-ml vials. Each milliliter contains isosorbide dinitrate 1 mg. It also is available as a 0.05% solution in 50-ml vials and 10-ml prefilled syringes. Each milliliter contains isosorbide dinitrate 0.5 mg in sodium chloride 0.9%. (38)

Trade Name(s) — Isoket, Risordan.

Administration — Isosorbide dinitrate is administered by intravenous infusion when diluted to a maximum concentration of 0.05% in sodium chloride 0.9% or dextrose 5% in water. The delivery rate should be controlled using an infusion or syringe pump. (38)

Isosorbide dinitrate is also administered as an intracoronary bolus injection during percutaneous transluminal coronary angioplasty. (38)

Stability — Isosorbide dinitrate injections are colorless and stable in the intact ampuls or vials when stored at room temperature. Once opened, ampuls and vials should be used immediately, and any remainder should be discarded. (38)

Syringes — Isosorbide dinitrate (Rhone-Poulenc) 10 mg/ml was repackaged in polypropylene syringes (Plastipak, Becton-Dickinson) and stored for eight hours at room temperature and 4 °C. HPLC analysis found no loss of drug. (1799)

Sorption — Isosorbide dinitrate is readily sorbed to PVC; sorption to polyethylene, polypropylene, and glass appears to be negligible. Consequently, it is recommended that nonabsorbing polyethylene or polybutadiene administration sets and polyethylene bags or glass containers be used for infusion. Alternatively, glass or polypropylene syringes can be used with a syringe pump to control the delivery rate. Sorption losses are affected by many factors, especially concentration, flow rate, time of infusion, and length of the administration set. The greatest amount of sorption occurs early in the infusion. Losses are greater if the flow rate is slow and the tubing is long. Simple calculations or corrections cannot be applied to this complex phenomenon to determine or control the actual delivery rate of isosorbide dinitrate if PVC bags or sets are used. However, losses of 15 to 30% can occur. (1442)

Several articles have described or evaluated isosorbide dinitrate sorption characteristics. Lee and Fenton-May reported on losses of isosorbide dinitrate from an 80-mg/L solution in sodium chloride 0.9% to PVC (Viaflex, Steriflex), glass containers, and polyethylene (Polyfusor) bags. Losses of 20 to 30% in PVC bags were recorded after six hours at room temperature. Losses to glass or polyethylene bags were negligible. Isosorbide dinitrate injection was not sorbed to polypropylene syringes over six hours at room temperature. In addition, sorption to conventional PVC administration sets during simulated infusion at 1.5 ml/min accounted for 70 to 80% losses during the first 15 to 30 minutes of the infusion. Delivery then increased slowly as the set became partially saturated. (1464)

Kowaluk et al. reported on isosorbide dinitrate 50 mg/ml in sodium chloride 0.9% in glass bottles delivered through a polyethylene administration set (Tridilset) over eight hours at 15 to 20 °C. The flow rate was 1 ml/min. No appreciable loss due to sorption occurred. (769) This result is in contrast to the 30% loss that occurred using a conventional PVC administration set. The same authors reported losses up to 50% in a PVC bag with conventional PVC administration set combination, depending on the flow rate. The delivered dose of isosorbide dinitrate fell rapidly over the first hour and then became almost constant as the infusion continued. (795)

Lee reported on isosorbide dinitrate 100 mg/L in sodium chloride 0.9% in glass bottles delivered at 0.8 ml/min through conventional PVC and polybutadiene administration sets (Avon Medical). While losses of isosorbide dinitrate of 15 to 25% to PVC sets over a four-hour period were observed, there was no appreciable loss to polybutadiene sets. Tests were also conducted in burette administration sets with polybutadiene tubing and acrylate butadiene styrene burette chambers (Avon Medical). Each chamber was primed with 100 ml of isosorbide dinitrate 100-mg/L solution, and the flow rate was 0.7 ml/min. Losses of isosorbide dinitrate were negligible over 90 minutes. (1027)

Martens et al. stored isosorbide dinitrate 100 mg/L in PVC bags, Clear-Flex bags (laminated polyethylene, nylon, and polypropylene), and glass bottles at 21 °C in the dark for 24 hours. Losses due to sorption amounted to 9% in two hours and 23% in 24 hours in the PVC containers but were negligible in the Clear-Flex and glass containers. (1392)

De Muynck et al. also studied the sorption of isosorbide dinitrate 100 mg/L in sodium chloride 0.9% and dextrose 10% in water at room temperature to various containers and administration sets. Losses due to sorption of less than 1 and 10% were observed for glass and high density polyethylene, respectively, while losses to PVC and polyamide bags amounted to 20 to 26%. Isosorbide dinitrate solutions containing 250 mg/L exhibited variable losses to burette chambers after seven hours of storage, depending on the burette composition. The loss to methacrylate butadiene styrene burettes was less than 2%, while burettes composed of cellulose propionate yielded 13 to 16% losses. Butadiene styrene burettes yielded 22 to 26% losses. During simulated infusion of isosorbide dinitrate solutions containing 250 mg/L in sodium chloride 0.9% at a flow rate of 20 ml/hr, sorption to administration set tubing composed of polybutadiene was 2 to 4%. However, sorption to the Venisystem (Abbott) and Dosifix (B. Braun) was 50 to 60%. (1465)

Struhar et al. reported that the infusion of isosorbide dinitrate 50 mg/L from glass containers through PVC administration sets resulted in an accumulated drug loss of about 16% over three hours. The maximum loss occurred in the first hour. (1466)

Lee and Fenton-May investigated the sorption of isosorbide dinitrate to syringes and extension sets used when administering the drug via syringe pump. Sabre (Gillette), Plastipak (Becton-Dickinson), and Brunswick (Sherwood) plastic syringes containing isosorbide dinitrate 1 mg/ml were stored for six hours. No drug loss due to sorption was observed. (1464)

Pharma-Plast (AHS Australia) plastic syringes having polypropylene barrels and polyethylene plungers were compared to glass containers for the possible sorption of isosorbide dinitrate. After 24 hours of storage of aqueous solutions of the drug (concentration unspecified), no drug loss was found in either plastic syringes or glass containers. The authors indicated that these plastic syringes could be substituted for glass syringes for use with syringe pumps. (782)

Allwood also investigated the sorption of isosorbide dinitrate during simulated syringe pump injection. Solutions containing drug concentrations of 100 mg/L to 1 g/L in Plastipak (Becton-Dickinson) plastic syringes were administered at 0.75 ml/hr through PVC (Kimel), nylon (Portex), and polyethylene (Lectrocath) extension sets. Losses of up to 90% were observed when the solution was delivered through the PVC sets, but sorption to nylon and polyethylene sets was negligible over 24 hours. There was no detectable sorption to plastic syringes during the study. (1467)

DeMuynck et al. studied isosorbide dinitrate 250 μg/ml in sodium chloride 0.9% and dextrose 10% in water delivered at 20 ml/hr through PVC tubing. The tubing was plasticized with diethylhexyl phthalate (DEHP). Losses due to sorption varied from 5.5 to 35% and were directly related to the hardness (and DEHP content) of the PVC. The harder the PVC, the lower was the loss. Similar results were noted with triethyl trimellitate plasticized PVC. The sorption to polybutadiene tubing was small (1 to 2%) but increased to 9% in some polybutadiene–PVC laminates. Polyethylene tubing also sorbed little isosorbide dinitrate, with losses of 1.6 to 1.9%. (1619)

Isosorbide dinitrate 1 mg/ml was delivered by syringe pump at 5 ml/hr through Terumo administration sets 100 cm in length with an internal diameter of 2.1 mm. HPLC analysis of the effluent found about 70% loss during the first hour, gradually changing to about 40% loss over eight hours. Administration tubing of greater length resulted in more isosorbide dinitrate loss, whereas shorter tubing caused less loss. (2143)

Isosorbide dinitrate (Schwarz Pharma) 0.02 mg/ml in dextrose 5% in water and sodium chloride 0.9% packaged in PVC, polyethylene, and glass containers exhibited little or no loss in glass and polyethylene containers but about 43% loss due to sorption in PVC containers when stored at 4 and 22 °C for 24 hours protected from light. (2289)

Filtration—Losses due to sorption of isosorbide dinitrate 250 mg/L in sodium chloride 0.9% delivered at 20 ml/hr through cellulose acetate filters (Sterifix, Ivex HP) were 15 to 26%. Losses to polyamide filters (Pall) were 9 to 13% under the same conditions. (1465)

The loss of isosorbide dinitrate due to sorption to filters extends to filters used in hemodialysis. HPLC analysis of isosorbide dinitrate 0.1 mg/ml in sodium chloride 0.9% during simulated hemodialysis using five different filter media found substantial drug losses from the solution and binding to some of the filters. Losses of approximately 86% with polysulfone (Fresenius), 72% with cellulose acetate (Baxter), 43% with polyacrylonitrile (Hospal), and 12% cuprophan (Gambro) were found. However, with hemophan filters (Gambro), no loss of drug due to sorption occurred. (2138)

Compatibility Information

Solution Compatibility

Isosorbide dinitrate

Solution	Mfr	Mfr	Conc/L	Remarks	Ref	C/I
Dextrose 5% in water	BA[a]	BRN	20 mg	Visually compatible but 43% loss of drug due to sorption to the PVC container at 22 °C and 17% loss at 4 °C in 24 hr	2289	I
	BRN[b,c]	BRN	20 mg	Visually compatible with 2 to 3% loss by HPLC in 24 hr at 4 and 22 °C	2289	C
Sodium chloride 0.9%	TR[a], BT[a]	TL	80 mg	44% loss in 24 hr at room temperature	1464	I
	TR[b], BT[c]	TL	80 mg	Physically compatible with little or no loss in 6 hr at room temperature	1464	C
	TR[a]	TL	100 mg	9% loss in 2 hr and 23% loss in 24 hr at 21 °C in the dark	1392	I
	[b,d]	TL	100 mg	Physically compatible with little or no loss in 24 hr at 21 °C in the dark	1392	C
	BA[a]	BRN	20 mg	Visually compatible but 43% loss of drug due to sorption to the PVC container at 22 °C and 17% loss at 4 °C in 24 hr	2289	I
	BRN[b,c]	BRN	20 mg	Visually compatible with 2 to 3% loss by HPLC in 24 hr at 4 and 22 °C	2289	C

[a]*Tested in PVC containers.*
[b]*Tested in glass containers.*
[c]*Tested in polyethylene containers.*
[d]*Tested in Clear-Flex polyethylene-lined laminated containers.*

Additive Compatibility

Isosorbide dinitrate

Drug	Mfr	Conc/L	Mfr	Conc/L	Test Soln	Remarks	Ref	C/I
Flucloxacillin sodium	BE	20 g		1 g		Physically compatible for 24 hr at 15 and 30 °C. Haze forms in 48 hr and precipitate forms in 72 hr at 30 °C. No change at 15 °C	1479	C
Frusemide	HO	1 g		1 g		Physically compatible for 72 hr at 15 and 30 °C	1479	C

Y-Site Injection Compatibility (1:1 Mixture)

Isosorbide dinitrate

Drug	Mfr	Conc	Mfr	Conc	Remarks	Ref	C/I
Heparin sodium	LEO	300 units/ml[a]	RP	10 mg/ml	Erratic availability of both drugs delivered through PVC tubing	1799	I

[a]*Tested in dextrose 5% in water.*

LENOGRASTIM

Products — Lenograstim (rHuG-CSF) is available as a lyophilized powder in single-use vials containing 13.4 million I.U. (Granocyte-13) or 33.6 million I.U. (Granocyte-34). In addition to lenograstim, each vial of the product contains mannitol 2.5%, arginine 1%, phenylalanine 1%, methionine 0.1%, polysorbate 20 0.01%, and hydrochloric acid to adjust pH. (38)

Lenograstim vials of either strength should be reconstituted with 1.05 ml of the accompanying water for injection diluent. Gently mix to effect dissolution, usually about 5 seconds. Do not shake the vials vigorously. Both the lenograstim vials and the diluent are overfilled by 5% to permit withdrawal of a full 1 ml of the reconstituted product containing 13.4 or 33.6 million I.U. (38)

Units—Each 13.4-million I.U. vial contains 105 μg of lenograstim. Each 33.6-million I.U. vial contains 263 μg of lenograstim. (38)

pH—The reconstituted solution has a pH buffered to 6.5. (38)

Trade Name(s)—Granocyte-13, Granocyte-34.

Administration — Lenograstim is administered by subcutaneous injection and intravenous infusion after dilution in sodium chloride 0.9% in glass or PVC containers or dextrose 5% in water in glass containers. Granocyte 13 should not be diluted to a concentration lower than 0.26 million I.U. per milliliter (2 μg/ml); Granocyte-34 should not be diluted to a concentration lower than 0.32 million I.U. per milliliter (2.5 μg/ml). The dilution volume should not exceed 50 ml for each vial of Granocyte-13 and 100 ml for each vial of Granocyte-34. (38)

Stability — Intact vials of lenograstim should be stored at 30 °C or below and protected from freezing. When reconstituted as directed and diluted for administration to concentrations not less than 0.26 million I.U. (Granocyte-13) or 0.32 million I.U. (Granocyte-34) per milliliter, lenograstim is stable for up to 24 hours at 5 or 25 °C. (38)

Ambulatory Pumps—The stability of lenograstim (Rhône-Poulenc Rorer) 33.6 million I.U. (263 μg) and 67.2 million I.U. (526 μg) each in 100 ml of sodium chloride 0.9% filled into Intermate elastomeric infusion devices (Baxter) was evaluated stored at 4 °C for 14 days. Bioassay of the solutions found no loss of lenograstim. (2048)

Sorption—The manufacturer states that lenograstim prepared in sodium chloride 0.9% as directed for administration is compatible with PVC containers and common administration sets. (38)

Compatibility Information

Infusion Solutions — At concentrations not less than 0.26 million I.U. (Granocyte-13) or 0.32 million I.U. (Granocyte-34) per milliliter, lenograstim is stable for up to 24 hours at 5 or 25 °C in sodium chloride 0.9% in both PVC and glass containers and in dextrose 5% in water in glass containers. (38)

METHOTRIMEPRAZINE (LEVOMEPROMAZINE HCL)

Products — Methotrimeprazine is available in 1-ml ampuls as a 25-mg/ml (2.5% w/v) solution. The injection also contains ascorbic acid, sodium sulphite, and sodium chloride in water for injection. (38; 115)

pH—From 3 to 5. (17)

Osmolality—Methotrimeprazine is an isotonic solution. (38; 115)

Trade Name(s)—Nozinan.

Administration — Methotrimeprazine is administered by intramuscular injection or intravenously after dilution with an equal volume of sodium chloride 0.9% immediately before use. It may also be given by continuous subcutaneous infusion diluted with the appropriate volume of sodium chloride 0.9%. (38; 115)

Stability — Methotrimeprazine injection is a clear, colorless solution. It should be stored at controlled room temperature and protected from light. On exposure to light, methotrimeprazine HCl rapidly develops a pink or yellow discoloration; discolored solutions should be discarded. The drug is incompatible with alkaline solutions. (38; 115)

Compatibility Information

Drugs in Syringe Compatibility

			Methotrimeprazine				
Drug (in syringe)	*Mfr*	*Amt*	*Mfr*	*Amt*	*Remarks*	*Ref*	*C/I*
Butorphanol tartrate	BR	4 mg/ 2 ml		25 mg/ 1 ml	Physically compatible for 30 min at room temperature both microscopically and macroscopically	566	C
Diamorphine HCl	MB	50 mg/ 1 ml	MB	1.25 and 2.5 mg/ 1 ml[a]	Physically compatible and diamorphine potency retained for 24 hr at room temperature	1454	C
Heparin sodium		2500 units/ 1 ml		25 mg/ 1 ml	Turbidity or precipitate forms within 5 min	1053	I
Hydroxyzine HCl	PF	50 mg/ 1 ml	LE	20 mg/ 1 ml	Physically compatible	771	C

Drugs in Syringe Compatibility (Cont.)

Methotrimeprazine

Drug (in syringe)	*Mfr*	*Amt*	*Mfr*	*Amt*	*Remarks*	*Ref*	*C/I*
	PF	100 mg/ 2 ml	LE	10 mg/ 0.5 ml	Physically compatible	771	C
Metoclopramide HCl	NO	10 mg/ 2 ml	RP	10 mg/ 2 ml	Physically compatible for 15 min at room temperature both microscopically and macroscopically	565	C
Perphenazine	SC	5 mg/ 1 ml		25 mg/ 1 ml	Physically compatible for 30 min at room temperature both microscopically and macroscopically	566	C
Ranitidine HCl	GL	50 mg/ 2 ml	RP	25 mg/ 1 ml	Immediate white turbidity	978	I
Sufentanil citrate	JN	50 μg/ml	LE	20 mg/ml	Physically compatible with no subvisual haze or particle formation in 24 hr at 23 °C	1711	C

[a]*Diluted with sterile water for injection.*

Y-Site Injection Compatibility (1:1 Mixture)

Methotrimeprazine

Drug	*Mfr*	*Conc*	*Mfr*	*Conc*	*Remarks*	*Ref*	*C/I*
Fentanyl citrate	JN	0.025 mg/ml[a]	LE	0.2 mg/ml[a]	Physically compatible with no change in measured haze or increase in particle content in 48 hr at 22 °C	1706	C
Heparin sodium		50 units/ml/ min		25 mg/1 ml[b]	White precipitate forms	1053	I
Hydromorphone HCl	AST	0.5 mg/ml[a]	LE	0.2 mg/ml[a]	Physically compatible with no change in measured haze or increase in particle content in 48 hr at 22 °C	1706	C
Methadone HCl	LI	1 mg/ml[a]	LE	0.2 mg/ml[a]	Physically compatible with no change in measured haze or increase in particle content in 48 hr at 22 °C	1706	C
Morphine sulphate	AST	1 mg/ml[a]	LE	0.2 mg/ml[a]	Physically compatible with no change in measured haze or increase in particle content in 48 hr at 22 °C	1706	C
Sufentanil citrate	JN	12.5 μg/ml[a]	LE	0.2 mg/ml[a]	Physically compatible with no subvisual haze or particle formation in 24 hr at 23 °C	1711	C

[a]*Tested in dextrose 5% in water.*
[b]*Given over three minutes via Y-site into a running infusion solution of heparin sodium in sodium chloride 0.9%.*

Additional Compatibility Information

Other Drugs — Atropine sulphate or scopolamine HBr may be mixed in the same syringe with methotrimeprazine for intramuscular administration. (19)

Methotrimeprazine is stated to be stable and compatible with diamorphine HCl for 24 hours. (38; 115)

METHOXAMINE HCL

Products — Methoxamine HCl is available in 1-ml ampuls. Each milliliter of aqueous solution contains methoxamine HCl 20 mg with sodium chloride in water for injection. (38)

pH — A 2% (20-mg/ml) solution in water has a pH of 4 to 6. (5)

Trade Name(s) — Vasoxine.

Administration — Methoxamine HCl is administered intramuscularly or, in emergencies, intravenously by direct injection slowly at a rate of 1 mg/min. (38) In addition, the slow intravenous infusion of methoxamine HCl diluted in dextrose 5% in water has been described. (4)

Stability — Methoxamine HCl in intact containers should be stored at controlled room temperature of 25 °C and protected from freezing. (38) The drug is stated to be sensitive to light and should be stored protected from light. (4)

Compatibility Information

Y-Site Injection Compatibility (1:1 Mixture)

Methoxamine HCl

Drug	*Mfr*	*Conc*	*Mfr*	*Conc*	*Remarks*	*Ref*	*C/I*
Heparin sodium	UP	1000 units/L[a]	BW	10 mg/ml	Physically compatible for at least 4 hr at room temperature by visual and microscopic examination	534	C
Hydrocortisone sodium succinate	UP	10 mg/L[a]	BW	10 mg/ml	Physically compatible for at least 4 hr at room temperature by visual and microscopic examination	534	C
Potassium chloride	AB	40 mEq/L[a]	BW	10 mg/ml	Physically compatible for at least 4 hr at room temperature by visual and microscopic examination	534	C
Vitamin B complex with C	RC	2 ml/L[a]	BW	10 mg/ml	Physically compatible for at least 4 hr at room temperature by visual and microscopic examination	534	C

[a]Tested in dextrose 5% in Ringer's injection, dextrose 5% in Ringer's injection, lactated, dextrose 5% in water, Ringer's injection, lactated, and sodium chloride 0.9%.

MEXILETINE HCL

Products — Mexiletine HCl is available as a 25-mg/ml solution in 10-ml (250-mg) ampuls. The product also contains sodium chloride and water for injection. (38; 115; 116)

Trade Name(s) — Mexitil.

Administration — Mexiletine HCl is administered intravenously. It should never be given as a bolus. A loading dose is given by intravenous injection at a rate of 1 ml (25 mg) per minute. This is followed by intravenous infusion of a 500-mg/500 ml (1-mg/ml) dilution in a suitable infusion solution. The initial infusion rate of the first 250 ml of the admixture is 4 ml/min over the first hour followed by infusion of the next 250 ml at 2 ml/min over the next two hours. (38; 115) Maintenance is performed using a 250-mg/500 ml (0.5-mg/ml) dilution administered at a rate of 1 ml/min (38) or, alternatively, 50 mg/hr has been recommended. (115)

Stability — Mexiletine HCl injection is a clear, colorless solution in intact containers that should be stored below 25 °C and protected from light. Dilutions for infusion are stable for up to eight hours. (38; 115)

Compatibility Information

Drugs in Syringe Compatibility

Mexiletine HCl

Drug (in syringe)	*Mfr*	*Amt*	*Mfr*	*Amt*	*Remarks*	*Ref*	*C/I*
Heparin sodium		2500 units/ 1 ml	BI	250 mg/ 10 ml	Turbidity or precipitate forms within 5 min	1053	I

Y-Site Injection Compatibility (1:1 Mixture)

Mexiletine HCl

Drug	Mfr	Conc	Mfr	Conc	Remarks	Ref	C/I
Heparin sodium		50 units/ml/min[b]	BI	250 mg/10 ml[a]	Opalescent solution	1053	I

[a]*Given over three minutes into a heparin infusion run at 1 ml/min.*
[b]*Tested in sodium chloride 0.9%.*

Additional Compatibility Information

Infusion Solutions — Mexiletine HCl is stated to be compatible for up to eight hours in the following intravenous infusion solutions (38; 115; 116):

Dextrose 5% in water
Sodium bicarbonate (concentration unspecified)
Sodium chloride 0.9%
Sodium chloride 0.9% with potassium chloride 0.3 or 0.6%
Sodium lactate ⅙ M

NETILMICIN SULPHATE

Products — Netilmicin (as the sulphate) is available in concentrations of 100, 50, 25, and 10 mg/ml in ampuls of various sizes. (38; 116) The solution also contains sodium chloride to adjust tonicity when needed, sodium hydroxide, sodium sulphite, and benzyl alcohol in water for injection. (116)

pH—From 3.5 to 6. (4)

Osmolality—Netilmicin sulphate (Schering) 100 mg/ml has an osmolality of 430 mOsm/kg. (2043)

Trade Name(s)—Netillin, Netromycine.

Administration — Netilmicin sulphate may be administered by intramuscular injection or intravenous infusion. (38; 116) For intravenous administration to adults, the dose is added to a compatible infusion solution and infused over 30 minutes. (116)

Stability — Netilmicin sulphate injection is a clear, colorless to pale yellow solution. It should be stored between 2 and 30 °C, i.e., at room temperature or under refrigeration, and should be protected from freezing. (4; 38)

Compatibility Information

Solution Compatibility

Netilmicin sulphate

Solution	Mfr	Mfr	Conc/L	Remarks	Ref	C/I
Amino acids 8.5%	MG	SC	3 g	Physically compatible and chemically stable for 7 days at 4 and 25 °C	558	C
Dextran 6% in dextrose 5%	AB	SC	3 g	Physically compatible and chemically stable for 7 days at 4 and 25 °C	558	C
Dextran 40 10% in dextrose 5%	PH, TR	SC	3 g	Physically compatible and chemically stable for 7 days at 4 and 25 °C	558	C
Dextrose 50%	TR	SC	3 g	Physically compatible and chemically stable for 7 days at 4 and 25 °C	558	C
Dextrose 5% in Electrolyte #48	TR	SC	3 g	Physically compatible and chemically stable for 7 days at 4 and 25 °C	558	C
Dextrose 5% in Ringer's injection, lactated	TR	SC	3 g	Physically compatible and chemically stable for 7 days at 4 and 25 °C	558	C
Dextrose 5% in sodium chloride 0.9%	TR	SC	3 g	Physically compatible and chemically stable for 7 days at 4 and 25 °C	558	C
Dextrose 5% in water	TR	SC	3 g	Physically compatible and chemically stable for 7 days at 4 and 25 °C	558	C
	AB[a]	SC	3 g	Physically compatible with no netilmicin loss in 24 hr at 25 °C	994	C

Solution Compatibility (Cont.)

Netilmicin sulphate

Solution	*Mfr*	*Mfr*	*Conc/L*	*Remarks*	*Ref*	*C/I*
Dextrose 10% in water	TR	SC	3 g	Physically compatible and chemically stable for 7 days at 4 and 25 °C	558	C
Fructose 10% in water	TR	SC	3 g	Physically compatible and chemically stable for 7 days at 4 and 25 °C	558	C
Invert sugar 10% in Electrolyte #2	TR	SC	3 g	Physically compatible and chemically stable for 7 days at 4 and 25 °C	558	C
Invert sugar 10% in Electrolyte #3	TR	SC	3 g	Physically compatible and chemically stable for 7 days at 4 and 25 °C	558	C
Ionosol B in dextrose 5%	AB	SC	3 g	Physically compatible and chemically stable for 7 days at 4 and 25 °C	558	C
Ionosol T in dextrose 5%	AB	SC	3 g	Physically compatible and chemically stable for 7 days at 4 and 25 °C	558	C
Isolyte E with dextrose 5%	MG	SC	3 g	Physically compatible and chemically stable for 7 days at 4 and 25 °C	558	C
Isolyte M with dextrose 5%	MG	SC	3 g	Physically compatible and chemically stable for 7 days at 4 and 25 °C	558	C
Isolyte P with dextrose 5%	MG	SC	3 g	Physically compatible and chemically stable for 7 days at 4 and 25 °C	558	C
Mannitol 10%	TR	SC	3 g	Physically compatible and chemically stable for 7 days at 4 and 25 °C	558	C
Mannitol 20%	TR	SC	3 g	Physically compatible and chemically stable for 7 days at 4 and 25 °C	558	C
Normosol R	AB	SC	3 g	Physically compatible and chemically stable for 7 days at 4 and 25 °C	558	C
Normosol R, pH 7.4	AB	SC	3 g	Physically compatible and chemically stable for 7 days at 4 and 25 °C	558	C
Plasma-Lyte 56 in dextrose 5%	TR	SC	3 g	Physically compatible and chemically stable for 7 days at 4 and 25 °C	558	C
Plasma-Lyte 148 in dextrose 5%	TR	SC	3 g	Physically compatible and chemically stable for 7 days at 4 and 25 °C	558	C
Plasma-Lyte M in dextrose 5%	TR	SC	3 g	Physically compatible and chemically stable for 7 days at 4 and 25 °C	558	C
Polysal	CU	SC	3 g	Physically compatible and chemically stable for 7 days at 4 and 25 °C	558	C
Polysal in dextrose 5%	CU	SC	3 g	Physically compatible and chemically stable for 7 days at 4 and 25 °C	558	C
Ringer's injection	TR	SC	3 g	Physically compatible and chemically stable for 7 days at 4 and 25 °C	558	C
Ringer's injection, lactated	CU	SC	3 g	Physically compatible and chemically stable for 7 days at 4 and 25 °C	558	C
Sodium bicarbonate 5%	TR	SC	3 g	Physically compatible and chemically stable for 7 days at 4 and 25 °C	558	C
Sodium chloride 0.9%	TR	SC	3 g	Physically compatible and chemically stable for 7 days at 4 and 25 °C	558	C
	AB[a]	SC	3 g	Physically compatible with no netilmicin loss in 24 hr at 25 °C	994	C

Solution Compatibility (Cont.)

Netilmicin sulphate

Solution	*Mfr*	*Mfr*	*Conc/L*	*Remarks*	*Ref*	*C/I*
TPN #107[b]			75 mg	Physically compatible and netilmicin activity retained for 24 hr at 21 °C by microbiological assay	1326	C

[a]*Tested in both glass and PVC containers.*
[b]*Refer to Appendix I for the composition of parenteral nutrition solutions. TPN indicates a 2-in-1 admixture.*

Additive Compatibility

Netilmicin sulphate

Drug	*Mfr*	*Conc/L*	*Mfr*	*Conc/L*	*Test Soln*	*Remarks*	*Ref*	*C/I*
Aminocaproic acid	LE	10 g	SC	3 g	D5S	Physically compatible and netilmicin chemically stable for 7 days at 25 and 4 °C. Aminocaproic acid not tested	558	C
Atropine sulphate	BW	40 mg	SC	3 g	D5S	Physically compatible and netilmicin chemically stable for 7 days at 4 and 25 °C. Atropine sulphate not tested	558	C
Cefepime HCl	BR	40 g	SC	1 g	D5W, NS	Cloudiness forms immediately	1682	I
	BR	2.5 g	SC	5 g	D5W, NS	Cloudiness forms immediately	1682	I
Cefuroxime sodium	GL	7.5 g	EX	1 g	D5W, NS[a]	Physically compatible with no loss of either drug in 1 hr	1036	C
Chlorpromazine HCl	SKF	100 mg	SC	3 g	D5S	Physically compatible and netilmicin chemically stable for 7 days at 4 and 25 °C. Chlorpromazine not tested	558	C
Ciprofloxacin	BAY	2 g	SC	2.5 g	NS	Visually compatible with little or no ciprofloxacin loss by HPLC in 24 hr at 25 °C. Netilmicin not tested	1934	C
Clindamycin phosphate	UP	9 g	SC	3 g	D5W, NS[b]	Physically compatible with no clindamycin loss and 2 to 5% netilmicin loss in 24 hr at 25 °C	994	C
Dexamethasone sodium phosphate	MSD	80 mg	SC	3 g	D5S	Physically compatible and netilmicin chemically stable for 7 days at 4 and 25 °C. Dexamethasone not tested	558	C
Diazepam	RC	40 mg	SC	3 g	D5S	Physically compatible and netilmicin chemically stable for 7 days at 4 and 25 °C. Diazepam not tested	558	C
Diphenhydramine HCl	PD	400 mg	SC	3 g	D5S	Physically compatible and netilmicin chemically stable for 3 days at 4 and 25 °C. 17% loss after 7 days at 25 °C. Diphenhydramine not tested	558	C
Edetate calcium disodium	RI	4 g	SC	3 g	D5S	Physically compatible and netilmicin chemically stable for 7 days at 4 and 25 °C. Edetate not tested	558	C
Fibrinolysin and deoxyribonuclease combined	PD	40 ml	SC	3 g	D5S	Physically compatible and netilmicin chemically stable for 7 days at 4 and 25 °C. Enzymes not tested	558	C
Flucloxacillin sodium	BE	10 g	EX	1 g	NS	Physically compatible for 48 hr. Potency of both drugs retained when assayed after 1 hr at room temperature	1036	C
	BE	10 g	EX	1 g	D5W	Immediate precipitation	1036	I

Additive Compatibility (Cont.)

Netilmicin sulphate

Drug	*Mfr*	*Conc/L*	*Mfr*	*Conc/L*	*Test Soln*	*Remarks*	*Ref*	*C/I*
Frusemide	HO	400 mg	SC	1.5 g	D5W, NS	Immediate precipitation of frusemide	876	I
Hydrocortisone sodium succinate	UP	400 mg	SC	3 g	D5S	Physically compatible and netilmicin chemically stable for 7 days at 4 and 25 °C. Hydrocortisone not tested	558	C
Hydrocortisone sodium succinate with potassium chloride	UP AB	400 mg 160 mEq	SC	3 g	D5S	Physically compatible and netilmicin chemically stable for 7 days at 4 and 25 °C. Other drugs not tested	558	C
Iron dextran	MRN	8 ml	SC	3 g	D5S	Physically compatible and netilmicin chemically stable for 7 days at 4 and 25 °C. Iron dextran not tested	558	C
Isoproterenol HCl	WI	400 mg[c]	SC	3 g	D5S	Physically compatible and netilmicin chemically stable for 7 days at 4 and 25 °C. Isoproterenol not tested	558	C
Methyldopate HCl	MSD	1 g	SC	3 g	D5S	Physically compatible and netilmicin chemically stable for 7 days at 4 and 25 °C. Methyldopate not tested	558	C
Metronidazole	RP	5 g[d]	SC	1.4 g		Physically compatible with little or no pH change for at least 24 hr at 23 °C and 72 hr at 4 °C	807	C
		5 g	EX	1 g	[a]	Physically compatible with no loss of either drug in 1 hr	1036	C
Multivitamins	USV	40 ml	SC	3 g	D5S	Physically compatible and netilmicin chemically stable for 24 hr at 4 and 25 °C. 20% loss after 3 days. Multivitamins not tested	558	C
Neostigmine methylsulphate	RC	40 mg	SC	3 g	D5S	Physically compatible and netilmicin chemically stable for 3 days at 4 and 25 °C. Neostigmine not tested	558	C
Norepinephrine bitartrate	WI	64 mg	SC	3 g	D5S	Physically compatible and netilmicin chemically stable for 7 days at 4 and 25 °C. Norepinephrine not tested	558	C
Oxytocin	PD	4 ml	SC	3 g	D5S	Physically compatible and netilmicin chemically stable for 7 days at 4 and 25 °C. Oxytocin not tested	558	C
Phytonadione	MSD	100 mg	SC	3 g	D5S	Physically compatible and netilmicin chemically stable for 7 days at 4 and 25 °C. Phytonadione not tested	558	C
Potassium chloride	AB	160 mEq	SC	3 g	D5S	Physically compatible and netilmicin chemically stable for 7 days at 4 and 25 °C. Potassium chloride not tested	558	C
Potassium chloride with hydrocortisone sodium succinate	AB UP	160 mEq 400 mg	SC	3 g	D5S	Physically compatible and netilmicin chemically stable for 7 days at 4 and 25 °C. Other drugs not tested	558	C
Procainamide HCl	SQ	4 g	SC	3 g	D5S	Physically compatible and netilmicin chemically stable for 7 days at 4 and 25 °C. Procainamide not tested	558	C
Promethazine HCl	WY	100 mg	SC	3 g	D5S	Physically compatible and netilmicin chemically stable for 7 days at 4 and 25 °C. Promethazine not tested	558	C

Additive Compatibility (Cont.)

Netilmicin sulphate

Drug	Mfr	Conc/L	Mfr	Conc/L	Test Soln	Remarks	Ref	C/I
Triflupromazine HCl	SQ	400 mg	SC	3 g	D5S	Physically compatible and netilmicin chemically stable for 7 days at 4 and 25 °C. Triflupromazine not tested	558	C
Vitamin B complex	PD	40 ml	SC	3 g	D5S	Physically compatible and netilmicin chemically stable for 7 days at 4 and 25 °C. Vitamins not tested	558	C
	UP	8 ml	SC	3 g	D5S	Physically compatible with 10 to 12% netilmicin loss in 24 hr at 4 and 25 °C. Vitamins not tested	558	I
Vitamin B complex with C	LI	40 ml	SC	3 g	D5S	Physically compatible and netilmicin chemically stable for 7 days at 4 and 25 °C. Vitamins not tested	558	C
	RC	8 ml	SC	3 g	D5S	Physically compatible and netilmicin chemically stable for 7 days at 4 and 25 °C. Vitamins not tested	558	C

[a]*Tested in PVC containers.*
[b]*Tested in both glass and PVC containers.*
[c]*Isoproterenol HCl 1% inhalation solution tested. Injection is also expected to be compatible.*
[d]*Minibags (100 ml) containing metronidazole 500 mg with disodium phosphate 150 mg, citric acid 44 mg, and sodium chloride 740 mg. This product differs from the Searle product.*

Drugs in Syringe Compatibility

Netilmicin sulphate

Drug (in syringe)	Mfr	Amt	Mfr	Amt	Remarks	Ref	C/I
Doxapram HCl	RB	400 mg/ 20 ml		100 mg/ 2 ml	Physically compatible with 2% decomposition in 24 hr	1177	C
Heparin sodium		2500 units/ 1 ml		150 mg	Turbidity or precipitate forms within 5 min	1053	I

Y-Site Injection Compatibility (1:1 Mixture)

Netilmicin sulphate

Drug	Mfr	Conc	Mfr	Conc	Remarks	Ref	C/I
Allopurinol sodium	BW	3 mg/ml[b]	SC	5 mg/ml[b]	Haze increases and flakes form in 1 hr	1686	I
Amifostine	USB	10 mg/ml[a]	SC	5 mg/ml[a]	Physically compatible with no change in measured turbidity or increase in particle content in 4 hr at 23 °C	1845	C
Aminophylline	ES	800 μg/ml[c]	SC	5 mg/ml[c]	Physically compatible and no netilmicin loss in 2 hr at 24 °C	1021	C
Amphotericin B cholesteryl sulphate complex	SEQ	0.83 mg/ml[a]	SC	5 mg/ml[a]	Gross precipitate forms	2117	I
Aztreonam	SQ	40 mg/ml[c]	SC	5 mg/ml[c]	Physically compatible with no subvisual haze or particle formation in 4 hr at 23 °C	1758	C
Calcium gluconate	WY	40 mg/ml[c]	SC	5 mg/ml[c]	Physically compatible and no netilmicin loss in 2 hr at 24 °C	1021	C

Y-Site Injection Compatibility (1:1 Mixture) (Cont.)

			Netilmicin sulphate				
Drug	*Mfr*	*Conc*	*Mfr*	*Conc*	*Remarks*	*Ref*	*C/I*
Cisatracurium besylate	GW	0.1, 2, 5 mg/ml[a]	SC	5 mg/ml[a]	Physically compatible with no change in measured turbidity or increase in particle content in 4 hr at 23 °C	2074	C
Docetaxel	RPR	0.9 mg/ml[a]	SC	5 mg/ml[a]	Physically compatible with no change in measured turbidity or increase in particle content in 4 hr at 23 °C	2224	C
Doxorubicin HCl liposome injection	SEQ	0.4 mg/ml[a]	SC	5 mg/ml[a]	Physically compatible with little or no change in measured turbidity and no increase in particle content in 4 hr at 23 °C	2087	C
Etoposide phosphate	BR	5 mg/ml[a]	SC	5 mg/ml[a]	Physically compatible with no change in measured turbidity or increase in particle content in 4 hr at 23 °C	2218	C
Filgrastim	AMG	30 µg/ml[a]	SC	5 mg/ml[a]	Physically compatible with no change in measured turbidity or increase in particle content in 4 hr at 22 °C	1687	C
Fludarabine phosphate	BX	1 mg/ml[a]	SC	5 mg/ml[a]	Physically compatible for 4 hr at room temperature under fluorescent light	1439	C
Frusemide	HO	10 mg/ml	SC	1.5 mg/ml[d]	White precipitate of frusemide forms immediately	876	I
Gemcitabine HCl	LI	10 mg/ml[b]	SC	5 mg/ml[b]	Physically compatible with no change in measured turbidity or increase in particle content in 4 hr at 23 °C	2226	C
Granisetron HCl	SKB	0.05 mg/ml[a]	SC	5 mg/ml[a]	Physically compatible with no change in measured turbidity or increase in particle content in 4 hr at 23 °C	2000	C
Melphalan HCl	BW	0.1 mg/ml[b]	SC	5 mg/ml[b]	Physically compatible with no change in measured turbidity or increase in particle content in 3 hr at 22 °C	1557	C
Propofol	ZEN	10 mg/ml	SC	5 mg/ml[a]	Precipitate forms immediately	2066	I
Remifentanil HCl	GW	0.025 and 0.25 mg/ml[b]	SC	5 mg/ml[a]	Physically compatible with no change in measured turbidity or increase in particle content in 4 hr at 23 °C	2075	C
Sargramostim	IMM	10 µg/ml[b]	SC	5 mg/ml[b]	Physically compatible for 4 hr at 22 °C	1436	C
Teniposide	BR	0.1 mg/ml[a]	SC	5 mg/ml[a]	Physically compatible with no subvisual haze or particle formation in 4 hr at 23 °C	1725	C
Thiotepa	IMM[e]	1 mg/ml[b]	SC	5 mg/ml[b]	Physically compatible with no change in measured turbidity or increase in particle content in 4 hr at 23 °C	1861	C
TNA #218 to #226[f]			SC	5 mg/ml[a]	Visually compatible with no precipitate or emulsion damage apparent in 4 hr at 23 °C	2215	C
TPN #61[f]	[g]		SC	12.5 mg/0.13 ml[h]	Physically compatible	1012	C
	[i]		SC	75 mg/0.75 ml[h]	Physically compatible	1012	C
TPN #212 to #215[f]			SC	5 mg/ml[a]	Physically compatible with no change in measured turbidity or increase in particle content in 4 hr at 23 °C	2109	C

Y-Site Injection Compatibility (1:1 Mixture) (Cont.)

Netilmicin sulphate

Drug	*Mfr*	*Conc*	*Mfr*	*Conc*	*Remarks*	*Ref*	*C/I*
Vinorelbine tartrate	BW	1 mg/ml[b]	SC	5 mg/ml[b]	Physically compatible with no change in measured turbidity or increase in particle content in 4 hr at 22 °C	1558	C

[a]*Tested in dextrose 5% in water.*
[b]*Tested in sodium chloride 0.9%.*
[c]*Tested in dextrose 5% in sodium chloride 0.2%.*
[d]*Tested in both dextrose 5% in water and sodium chloride 0.9%.*
[e]*Lyophilized formulation tested.*
[f]*Refer to Appendix I for the composition of parenteral nutrition solutions. TNA indicates a 3-in-1 admixture, and TPN indicates a 2-in-1 admixture.*
[g]*Run at 21 ml/hr.*
[h]*Given over 30 minutes by syringe pump.*
[i]*Run at 94 ml/hr.*

Additional Compatibility Information

Peritoneal Dialysis Solutions — Netilmicin sulphate (Schering) 3 and 10 mg/L in peritoneal dialysis concentrate with dextrose 50% (McGaw) retained about 90% of its initial activity for seven hours and about 80% for 24 hours at room temperature as determined by microbiological assay. (1044)

β-Lactam Antibiotics — In common with other aminoglycoside antibiotics, netilmicin activity may be impaired by the β-lactam antibiotics (penicillins or cephalosporins). (4) This inactivation is dependent on concentration, temperature, and time of exposure.

Netilmicin sulphate 5 and 10 μg/ml dissolved in human serum and incubated with carbenicillin and ticarcillin 100 to 600 μg/ml at 37 °C demonstrated greater rates of netilmicin decomposition at the higher concentrations of the penicillins. In 24 hours, little or no loss of netilmicin activity occurred at 100 μg/ml but about a 25% loss occurred at 600 μg/ml of carbenicillin. Approximately 5% loss at 100 μg/ml to 60% loss at 600 μg/ml occurred in 72 hours with carbenicillin. Ticarcillin affected netilmicin less under these conditions. Little or no loss of netilmicin activity occurred at 100 μg/ml, but about a 17% loss occurred at 600 μg/ml in 72 hours. (575)

Pickering and Rutherford evaluated several aminoglycosides combined with a number of penicillins. Gentamicin sulphate, netilmicin sulphate, and tobramycin sulphate 5 and 10 μg/ml and amikacin 10 and 20 μg/ml were combined in human serum with 125, 250, and 500 μg/ml of azlocillin, carbenicillin disodium, amdinocillin, mezlocillin, and piperacillin individually. Tobramycin and gentamicin sustained greater losses than netilmicin and amikacin at each of the penicillin concentrations. Significant decomposition of all aminoglycosides occurred in 24 hours at 37 °C at a penicillin concentration of 500 μg/ml. Tobramycin and gentamicin had losses of 40 to 60%, while 15 to 30% losses occurred for netilmicin. Amikacin sustained the least inactivation with losses of about 10 to 20%. At penicillin concentrations of 125 to 250 μg/ml, smaller losses of aminoglycosides were observed. (68)

Several aminoglycosides were evaluated in combination with several penicillins. Gentamicin sulphate, netilmicin sulphate, and tobramycin sulphate 5 μg/ml were combined with carbenicillin disodium, azlocillin sodium, and mezlocillin sodium 50, 250, and 500 μg/ml in human plasma. Samples were evaluated over nine days at 27 and 37 °C. All of the aminoglycosides underwent significant inactivation during the evaluation. Aminoglycoside decomposition of 17 to 61% in 24 hours occurred at the higher two concentrations of penicillins—the highest inactivation was sustained by tobramycin and the lowest by netilmicin. Little if any aminoglycoside inactivation occurred at 50 μg/ml of penicillin. Carbenicillin caused a greater degree of aminoglycoside decomposition than did azlocillin or mezlocillin. (616)

Flournoy noted the relative degree of inactivation of tobramycin, gentamicin, netilmicin, and amikacin 10 mg/L in serum when combined with carbenicillin 125 to 1000 mg/L over temperatures ranging from −20 to 42 °C. Tobramycin was more susceptible to inactivation than the others. Amikacin was the least susceptible, and gentamicin and netilmicin were similar in intermediate susceptibility to inactivation. (617)

Although piperacillin sodium and aminoglycosides act synergistically and have been used successfully when recommended doses of each drug were administered, mixing piperacillin sodium directly in a syringe or infusion bottle with an aminoglycoside can result in substantial inactivation of the aminoglycoside. (740)

The comparative inactivation of five aminoglycosides by seven β-lactam antibiotics in human serum at 37 °C was reported by Riff and Thomason. Amikacin, followed by netilmicin, had the lowest degree of inactivation; tobramycin sustained the most pronounced losses. Gentamicin and kanamycin were intermediate in the extent of losses. The six penicillins that were tested all produced aminoglycoside inactivation; the greatest extent of inactivation was caused by carbenicillin followed by ticarcillin, penicillin G, oxacillin, methicillin, and ampicillin, in approximate descending order. Cephalothin produced minimal inactivation (5 to 10% in 24 hours). The rate of inactivation could be reduced by storage at 4 °C and further reduced by storage at −20 °C. The authors suggested processing blood samples rapidly to avoid inaccurate serum determinations. Storage of specimens at low temperature until analysis may be helpful. (1052)

Roberts et al. studied the stability of azlocillin sodium 500 mg/L combined with the aminoglycosides amikacin sulphate 20 mg/L, gentamicin sulphate 8 mg/L, and netilmicin sulphate 7.5 mg/L in peritoneal dialysis solution (Dianeal 1.36%) stored at 37 °C. No azlocillin sodium loss occurred by HPLC during the eight-hour study period. However, the aminoglycosides tested by the enzyme-multiplied immunoassay technique (EMIT) showed 10% losses in about six hours for gentamicin sulphate and netilmicin sulphate and in about 30 minutes for amikacin sulphate. (1179)

Cefotetan disodium is stated to be physically incompatible with aminoglycosides (4), including netilmicin sulphate. (283)

Cefotaxime sodium (Hoechst-Roussel) should not be mixed with aminoglycosides in the same solution, but they may be administered to the same patient separately. (792)

The clinical significance of these interactions in patients appears to be confined primarily to those with renal failure. (218; 334; 361; 364; 616; 847) Literature reports of greatly reduced aminoglycoside levels in such patients have appeared frequently. (303; 365–367; 614; 615; 962) In addition, the interaction may be clinically important if assays for aminoglycoside levels in serum are sufficiently delayed. (576; 618; 847; 1052)

Most authors believe that in vitro mixing of penicillins such as ticarcillin disodium with aminoglycoside antibiotics should be avoided but that clinical use of the drugs in combination can be of great value. It is generally recommended that the drugs be given separately in such combined therapy. (157; 218; 222; 224; 361; 364; 368–370)

Heparin — A white precipitate may result from the administration of netilmicin sulphate through a heparinized intravenous cannula. (976) Flushing heparin locks with sterile water for injection or sodium chloride 0.9% before and after administering drugs incompatible with heparin has been recommended. (4)

NIMODIPINE

Products — Nimodipine is available at a concentration of 0.02% (0.2 mg/ml) in 50-ml brown glass vials and 250-ml brown glass bottles. The product also contains ethanol 20% (w/v), polyethylene glycol 400, sodium citrate, citric acid, and water for injection. (38; 115; 116)

Trade Name(s) — Nimotop.

Administration — Nimodipine is given by intravenous infusion via a central catheter (38; 115); use of an infusion pump has been recommended. (115) Intracisternal instillation has also been described. (115; 116) The drug must not be added to an infusion bag or bottle. For administration, nimodipine injection is drawn into a 50-ml syringe and connected to a three-way stopcock and polyethylene tube that permits simultaneous administration of the nimodipine and a co-infusion running at a rate of 40 ml/hr. Dextrose 5% in water, sodium chloride 0.9%, lactated Ringer's injection, lactated Ringer's injection with magnesium, dextran 40, mannitol 10%, albumin human 5%, and hetastarch 6% in sodium chloride 0.9% have been recommended for use as the co-infusion solution. (38; 115; 116)

Stability — Nimodipine injection is a clear yellow solution. Intact containers of the drug should be stored at or below 25 °C. The drug is light sensitive and should be stored in the light-protective container within the carton that is supplied with the product. Nimodipine should not be added to infusion solution bags or bottles or mixed with other drugs. The 250-ml bottles are intended for single use only and should be pierced only once. Once pierced, the bottle should be used for no longer than 25 hours regardless of whether all of the solution has been administered. (38; 115)

Light Effects — Nimodipine is light sensitive. The drug drawn into a syringe for administration must be protected from direct sunlight during administration but is stable for up to 10 hours exposed to diffuse daylight and artificial light. The 250-ml infusion bottle should also be protected from direct sunlight at all times. Opaque coverings for infusion pumps and tubing or black, brown, yellow, or red infusion lines can be used when needed. (38; 115)

Sorption — Nimodipine reacts with PVC equipment but is compatible with polyethylene and polypropylene containers, syringes, and administration sets as well as glass containers. (38; 115)

Nimodipine (Bayer) 0.01 mg/ml in dextrose 5% in water and sodium chloride 0.9% packaged in PVC, polyethylene, and glass containers exhibited only 3 to 5% loss in glass and polyethylene containers but 94% loss due to sorption in PVC containers when stored at 4 and 22 °C for 24 hours protected from light. (2289)

Compatibility Information

Solution Compatibility

Nimodipine

Solution	*Mfr*	*Mfr*	*Conc/L*	*Remarks*	*Ref*	*C/I*
Dextrose 5% in water	BA[a]	BAY	10 mg	Visually compatible but 94% loss of drug due to sorption to the PVC container at 22 °C and 81% loss at 4 °C in 24 hr	2289	I
	BRN[b,c]	BAY	10 mg	Visually compatible with 3 to 5% loss by HPLC in 24 hr at 4 and 22 °C	2289	C
Sodium chloride 0.9%	BA[a]	BAY	10 mg	Visually compatible but 94% loss of drug due to sorption to the PVC container at 22 °C and 81% loss at 4 °C in 24 hr	2289	I
	BRN[b,c]	BAY	10 mg	Visually compatible with 3 to 5% loss by HPLC in 24 hr at 4 and 22 °C	2289	C

[a]*Tested in PVC containers.*
[b]*Tested in glass containers.*
[c]*Tested in polyethylene containers.*

NIZATIDINE

Products — Nizatidine is available as a 25-mg/ml solution with hydrochloric acid and/or sodium hydroxide in water for injection packaged in 4-, 6-, and 12-ml ampuls. (38)

pH — From 6.5 to 7.5. (38)

Trade Name(s) — Axid, Nizax, Nizaxid, others.

Administration — Nizatidine is administered by continuous or intermittent intravenous infusion. For continuous infusion, the manufacturer recommends diluting 300 mg of drug in 150 ml of compatible diluent and infusing at a rate of 10 mg/hr. For intermittent intravenous infusion, the manufacturer recommends diluting 100 mg of drug in 50 ml of compatible diluent and infusing over 15 minutes. (38)

Stability — Intact containers of nizatidine should be stored below 25 °C and protected from light. Nizatidine injection is a clear and colorless to yellow solution. It may tend to darken slightly, but this does not adversely affect potency. (38)

Freezing Solutions — Nizatidine (Lilly) 0.75 and 3 mg/ml in dextrose 5% in water, sodium chloride 0.9%, and sterile water for injection in PVC containers was stored frozen at −20 °C for 30 days. Little or no nizatidine loss was found using HPLC analysis after frozen storage. An additional seven days of storage under refrigeration at 4 °C resulted in no additional loss of drug. (1533)

Sorption — Nizatidine (Lilly) 0.75, 1.5, and 3 mg/ml in dextrose 5% in water, sodium chloride 0.9%, and sterile water for injection exhibited no loss due to sorption during seven days of storage at 4 and 25 °C in both glass and PVC containers. (1533)

Compatibility Information

Solution Compatibility

Nizatidine

Solution	*Mfr*	*Mfr*	*Conc/L*	*Remarks*	*Ref*	*C/I*
Amino acids 8.5%	TR[a]	LI	0.75 and 1.5 g	Visually compatible and nizatidine potency by HPLC retained for 7 days at 4 and 25 °C. Amino acids not tested	1533	C
	TR[a]	LI	3 g	Visually compatible with 8% nizatidine loss in 3 days and 13% loss in 7 days at 25 °C by HPLC. 5% nizatidine loss in 7 days at 4 °C. Amino acids not tested	1533	C
Dextrose 5% in Ringer's injection, lactated	TR[a]	LI	0.75, 1.5, 3 g	Visually compatible with 5% or less loss by HPLC in 7 days at 4 and 25 °C	1533	C
Dextrose 5% in sodium chloride 0.2%	TR[a]	LI	0.75, 1.5, 3 g	Visually compatible with little or no loss by HPLC in 7 days at 4 and 25 °C	1533	C
Dextrose 5% in sodium chloride 0.45%	TR[a]	LI	0.75, 1.5, 3 g	Visually compatible with 6% or less loss by HPLC in 7 days at 25 °C and little or no loss in 7 days at 4 °C	1533	C
Dextrose 5% in sodium chloride 0.45% with potassium chloride 0.15%	TR[a]	LI	0.75, 1.5, 3 g	Visually compatible with 7% or less loss by HPLC in 7 days at 4 and 25 °C	1533	C
Dextrose 5% in sodium chloride 0.9%	TR[a]	LI	0.75, 1.5, 3 g	Visually compatible with little or no loss by HPLC in 7 days at 4 and 25 °C	1533	C
Dextrose 5% in water	TR[a,b]	LI	0.75, 1.5, 3 g	Visually compatible with little or no loss by HPLC in 7 days at 4 and 25 °C	1533	C
Dextrose 10% in water	TR[a]	LI	0.75, 1.5, 3 g	Visually compatible with little or no loss by HPLC in 7 days at 4 and 25 °C	1533	C
Mannitol 20%	MG[a]	LI	0.75, 1.5, 3 g	Visually compatible with little or no loss by HPLC in 7 days at 4 and 25 °C	1533	C
Plasma-Lyte 56 with dextrose 5%	TR[a]	LI	0.75, 1.5, 3 g	Visually compatible with 7% or less loss by HPLC at 25 °C in 7 days and little or no loss at 4 °C in 7 days	1533	C
Ringer's injection, lactated	TR[a]	LI	0.75, 1.5, 3 g	Visually compatible with little or no loss by HPLC in 7 days at 4 and 25 °C	1533	C
Sodium bicarbonate 5%	TR[a]	LI	0.75, 1.5, 3 g	Visually compatible with little or no loss by HPLC in 7 days at 4 and 25 °C	1533	C
Sodium chloride 0.9%	TR[a,b]	LI	0.75, 1.5, 3 g	Visually compatible with little or no loss by HPLC in 7 days at 4 and 25 °C	1533	C

Solution Compatibility (Cont.)

Nizatidine

Solution	Mfr	Mfr	Conc/L	Remarks	Ref	C/I
Sodium lactate ⅙ M	TR[a]	LI	0.75, 1.5, 3 g	Visually compatible with little or no loss by HPLC in 7 days at 4 and 25 °C	1533	C
TNA #135 to #138 and TPN #134[c]		LI	150 mg	Physically compatible with no increase in fat particle size and 2 to 7% nizatidine loss by HPLC in 48 hr at 22 °C under fluorescent light	1534; 1921	C

[a]*Tested in glass containers.*
[b]*Tested in PVC containers.*
[c]*Refer to Appendix I for the composition of parenteral nutrition solutions. TNA indicates a 3-in-1 admixture, and TPN indicates a 2-in-1 admixture.*

Additional Compatibility Information

Infusion Solutions — The manufacturer states that nizatidine admixtures in the following solutions are stable for 24 hours stored under refrigeration at 2 to 8 °C. However, other information indicates the drug may be stable for longer periods. See the following solutions in the Solution Compatibility table above (38):

Dextrose 5% in water
Ringer's injection, lactated (Compound sodium lactate injection)
Sodium bicarbonate 5%
Sodium chloride 0.9%

OFLOXACIN

Products — Ofloxacin is available as a 2-mg/ml solution in 50- and 100-ml containers (30; 38) and as a 5-mg/ml solution in 40-ml containers. (116) Also present in the solutions are sodium chloride, hydrochloric acid, and water for injection. (38; 116)

Osmolality — The osmolality of ofloxacin (Ortho-McNeil) 0.4 and 4 mg/ml in several infusion solutions has been reported (1636):

	Osmolality (mOsm/kg)	
Diluent	0.4 mg/ml	4 mg/ml
Dextrose 5% in Ringer's injection, lactated	523	489
Dextrose 5% in sodium chloride 0.9%	547	512
Dextrose 5% in sodium chloride 0.45% with potassium chloride 0.15%	439	412
Dextrose 5% in water	259	252
Mannitol 20%	1303	1196
Plasma-Lyte 56 with dextrose 5%	372	353
Sodium chloride 0.9%	281	270
Sodium lactate ⅙ M	311	294

Trade Name(s) — Oflocet, Tarivid.

Administration — Ofloxacin is administered by intravenous infusion over 30 minutes for a 200-mg dose (38; 116) to 60 minutes for a 400-mg dose. (5)

Stability — Ofloxacin solutions are light yellow to amber. (2) Intact containers should be stored at controlled room temperature and protected from light. (38)

Ofloxacin has aqueous solubilities of 60 mg/ml at pH 2 to 5, 4 mg/ml at pH 7, and 303 mg/ml at pH 9.8. (4)

Sorption — Ofloxacin (Diamant) 200 mg/250 ml in dextrose 5% in water and sodium chloride 0.9% in PVC bags was infused through infusion sets at about 4 ml/min. No drug loss due to sorption was detected by HPLC. (1698)

Central Venous Catheter — Ofloxacin (McNeil) 1 mg/ml in dextrose 5% in water was found to be compatible with the ARROWg+ard Blue Plus (Arrow International) chlorhexidine-bearing triple-lumen central catheter. HPLC analysis was used to evaluate completeness of drug delivery through the catheter and the amount of chlorhexidine removed from the internal lumens. Essentially complete delivery of the drug was found with little or no drug loss occurring. Furthermore, chlorhexidine delivered from the catheter remained at trace amounts with no substantial increase due to the delivery of the drug through the catheter. (2335)

Compatibility Information

Solution Compatibility

Ofloxacin

Solution	Mfr	Mfr	Conc/L	Remarks	Ref	C/I
Dextrose 5% in Ringer's injection, lactated	BA[a]	ORT	0.4 and 4 g	Physically compatible with little or no ofloxacin loss by HPLC in 3 days at 24 °C or 14 days at 5 °C	1636	C

Solution Compatibility (Cont.)

Ofloxacin

Solution	*Mfr*	*Mfr*	*Conc/L*	*Remarks*	*Ref*	*C/I*
Dextrose 5% in sodium chloride 0.9%	BA[a]	ORT	0.4 and 4 g	Physically compatible with little or no ofloxacin loss by HPLC in 3 days at 24 °C or 14 days at 5 °C	1636	C
Dextrose 5% in sodium chloride 0.45% with potassium chloride 0.15%	BA[a]	ORT	0.4 and 4 g	Physically compatible with little or no ofloxacin loss by HPLC in 3 days at 24 °C or 14 days at 5 °C	1636	C
Dextrose 5% in water	BA[a]	ORT	0.4 and 4 g	Physically compatible with little or no ofloxacin loss by HPLC in 3 days at 24 °C or 14 days at 5 °C	1636	C
	[a]	DIA	800 mg	Visually compatible with no significant ofloxacin loss by HPLC in 6 hr at 22 °C exposed to light	1698	C
Mannitol 20%	BA[a]	ORT	0.4 and 4 g	Physically compatible with little or no ofloxacin loss by HPLC in 3 days at 24 °C. White mannitol crystals form upon refrigeration at 5 °C or freezing at −20 °C but disappear upon warming	1636	C
Plasma-Lyte 56 with dextrose 5%	BA[a]	ORT	0.4 and 4 g	Physically compatible with little or no ofloxacin loss by HPLC in 3 days at 24 °C or 14 days at 5 °C	1636	C
Sodium bicarbonate 5%	BA[a]	ORT	0.4 and 4 g	Physically compatible with little or no ofloxacin loss by HPLC in 3 days at 24 °C or 14 days at 5 °C	1636	C
Sodium chloride 0.9%	BA[a]	ORT	0.4 and 4 g	Physically compatible with little or no ofloxacin loss by HPLC in 3 days at 24 °C or 14 days at 5 °C	1636	C
	[a]	DIA	800 mg	Visually compatible with no significant ofloxacin loss by HPLC in 6 hr at 22 °C exposed to light	1698	C
Sodium lactate ⅙ M	BA[a]	ORT	0.4 and 4 g	Physically compatible with little or no ofloxacin loss by HPLC in 3 days at 24 °C or 14 days at 5 °C	1636	C

[a]*Tested in PVC containers.*

Additive Compatibility

Ofloxacin

Drug	*Mfr*	*Conc/L*	*Mfr*	*Conc/L*	*Test Soln*	*Remarks*	*Ref*	*C/I*
Amoxycillin sodium	BE	8.3 g	HO	1.67 g	W	Visually compatible with little or no loss of either drug by HPLC in 48 hr	1613	C
Amoxycillin sodium–clavulanic acid	BE	8.33 + 1.67 g	HO	1.67 g	W	Visually compatible with little or no loss of either drug by HPLC in 48 hr	1613	C
Ceftazidime	GL[a]	8.3 g	HO	1.67 g	W	Visually compatible with little or no loss of either drug by HPLC in 48 hr	1613	C
Clindamycin phosphate	UP	6 g	HO	2 g	W	Visually compatible with little or no loss of either drug by HPLC in 48 hr	1613	C
Flucloxacillin sodium	BE	8.3 g	HO	1.67 g	W	Visually compatible for 7 hr. Precipitate forms by 24 hr with about 75% ofloxacin loss and 20% flucloxacillin loss by HPLC	1613	I
Gentamicin sulphate	ESX	800 mg	HO	2 g	W	Visually compatible with little or no loss of either drug by HPLC in 48 hr	1613	C

Additive Compatibility (Cont.)

Ofloxacin

Drug	*Mfr*	*Conc/L*	*Mfr*	*Conc/L*	*Test Soln*	*Remarks*	*Ref*	*C/I*
Linezolid	PHU	2 g	MN	4 g	[b]	Physically compatible with little or no loss of either drug by HPLC in 7 days at 4 and 23 °C protected from light	2334	C
Piperacillin sodium	LE	16.7 g	HO	1.67 g	W	Visually compatible with little or no loss of either drug by HPLC in 48 hr	1613	C
Tobramycin sulphate	LI	800 mg	HO	2 g	W	Visually compatible with little or no loss of either drug by HPLC in 48 hr	1613	C
Vancomycin HCl	LI	4.2 g	HO	1.67 g	W	Visually compatible with little or no loss of either drug by HPLC in 48 hr	1613	C

[a]Sodium carbonate–containing formulation tested.
[b]Admixed in the linezolid infusion container.

Drugs in Syringe Compatibility

Ofloxacin

Drug (in syringe)	*Mfr*	*Amt*	*Mfr*	*Amt*	*Remarks*	*Ref*	*C/I*
Cefotaxime sodium	HO	2 g	HO	200 mg	Visually compatible with no loss of either drug by HPLC in 4 hr at room temperature	1735	C

Y-Site Injection Compatibility (1:1 Mixture)

Ofloxacin

Drug	*Mfr*	*Conc*	*Mfr*	*Conc*	*Remarks*	*Ref*	*C/I*
Amphotericin B cholesteryl sulphate complex	SEQ	0.83 mg/ml[a]	ORT	4 mg/ml[a]	Gross precipitate forms	2117	I
Ampicillin sodium	HO	21.3 mg/ml	HO	2.2 mg/ml	Visually compatible with no loss of either drug by HPLC in 2 hr at room temperature	1734	C
Cefepime HCl	BMS	20 mg/ml[a]	ORT	4 mg/ml[a]	Haze forms immediately and becomes flocculent precipitate in 4 hr	1689	I
Cisatracurium besylate	GW	0.1, 2, 5 mg/ml[a]	ORT	4 mg/ml[a]	Physically compatible with no change in measured turbidity or increase in particle content in 4 hr at 23 °C	2074	C
Docetaxel	RPR	0.9 mg/ml[a]	MN	4 mg/ml[a]	Physically compatible with no change in measured turbidity or increase in particle content in 4 hr at 23 °C	2224	C
Doxorubicin HCl liposome injection	SEQ	0.4 mg/ml[a]	ORT	4 mg/ml[a]	Increase in measured turbidity	2087	I
Etoposide phosphate	BR	5 mg/ml[a]	MN	4 mg/ml[a]	Physically compatible with no change in measured turbidity or increase in particle content in 4 hr at 23 °C	2218	C
Gemcitabine HCl	LI	10 mg/ml[b]	MN	4 mg/ml[b]	Physically compatible with no change in measured turbidity or increase in particle content in 4 hr at 23 °C	2226	C
Granisetron HCl	SKB	0.05 mg/ml[a]	ORT	4 mg/ml[a]	Physically compatible with no change in measured turbidity or increase in particle content in 4 hr at 23 °C	2000	C

Y-Site Injection Compatibility (1:1 Mixture) (Cont.)

Drug	Mfr	Conc	Ofloxacin Mfr	Ofloxacin Conc	Remarks	Ref	C/I
Hetastarch in lactated electrolyte injection (Hextend)	AB	6%	OMN	4 mg/ml[a]	Physically compatible with no change in measured turbidity or increase in particle content in 4 hr at 23 °C	2339	C
Linezolid	PHU	2 mg/ml	MN	4 mg/ml[a]	Physically compatible with no change in measured turbidity or increase in particle content in 4 hr at 23 °C	2264	C
Propofol	ZEN	10 mg/ml	ORT	4 mg/ml[a]	Physically compatible for 1 hr at 23 °C with no increase in particle content	2066	C
Remifentanil HCl	GW	0.025 and 0.25 mg/ml[b]	ORT	4 mg/ml[a]	Physically compatible with no change in measured turbidity or increase in particle content in 4 hr at 23 °C	2075	C
Thiotepa	IMM[c]	1 mg/ml[a]	ORT	4 mg/ml	Physically compatible with no change in measured turbidity or increase in particle content in 4 hr at 23 °C	1861	C
TNA #218 to #226[d]			ORT	4 mg/ml[a]	Visually compatible with no precipitate or emulsion damage apparent in 4 hr at 23 °C	2215	C
TPN #212 to #215[d]			ORT	4 mg/ml[a]	Physically compatible with no change in measured turbidity or increase in particle content in 4 hr at 23 °C	2109	C

[a] *Tested in dextrose 5% in water.*
[b] *Tested in sodium chloride 0.9%.*
[c] *Lyophilized formulation tested.*
[d] *Refer to Appendix I for the composition of parenteral nutrition solutions. TNA indicates a 3-in-1 admixture, and TPN indicates a 2-in-1 admixture.*

Additional Compatibility Information

Infusion Solutions — The manufacturer states that ofloxacin 4 mg/ml is compatible with sodium chloride 0.9%, dextrose 5% in water, and Ringer's injection. (38)

Heparin — Ofloxacin is stated to be incompatible with heparin sodium. (38)

OMEPRAZOLE

Products — Omeprazole infusion is available in vials containing 40 mg of drug as the sodium salt. Also present in the formulation are sodium hydroxide and disodium edetate. Reconstitute the vials with 5 ml from a 100-ml bag or bottle of sodium chloride 0.9% or dextrose 5% in water. Mix thoroughly, ensuring that all of the omeprazole has dissolved; do not use if any particles remain in the reconstituted solution. The reconstituted solution should be transferred into the infusion bag or bottle making 100 ml of the admixture solution. (38; 115)

Omeprazole injection is also available in vials containing 40 mg of drug as the sodium salt with an accompanying 10-ml ampul of special solvent. Each milliliter of the solvent contains citric acid monohydrate 0.5 mg and polyethylene glycol 400 0.4 g in water for injection. The vial of omeprazole should be reconstituted with 10 ml of the solvent provided in the accompanying ampul in two 5-ml increments withdrawing air pressure back into the syringe between the increments. No other diluent should be used for reconstitution. Rotate and shake the vial to ensure all of the omeprazole has dissolved; do not use if any particles remain in the reconstituted solution. (38; 115)

Sodium Content — Each 40 mg of omeprazole provides sodium 2.6 mg. (115)

Trade Name(s) — Losec, Mopral, Omeprazen, many others.

Administration — Omeprazole is administered by intravenous infusion and intravenous injection. The drug must not be given by any other route. (38; 115)

After dilution of the omeprazole infusion to 100 ml with sodium chloride 0.9% or dextrose 5% in water, omeprazole is administered only as a 20- to 30-minute intravenous infusion. (38; 115).

After dilution with the accompanying special diluent, omeprazole injection is administered intravenously over 2.5 to 5 minutes at a maximum rate of 4 ml/min. (38; 115)

Stability — Intact vials of omeprazole infusion and injection should be stored at room temperature not exceeding 25 °C and protected from light. Discoloration of the reconstituted solution may occur if reconstituted incorrectly. Dilution of omeprazole infusion with sodium chloride 0.9% results in a solution that is stable for 12 hours (38; 115); diluted in dextrose 5% in water omeprazole is stable for three (38) to six (115) hours. Other solutions must not be used for dilution of omeprazole infusion. Omeprazole injection reconstituted with the accompanying special diluent is stable for four hours. Do not use the reconstituted solution if particles are present. (38; 115)

Compatibility Information

Y-Site Injection Compatibility (1:1 Mixture)

Drug	*Mfr*	*Conc*	**Omeprazole** *Mfr*	*Conc*	*Remarks*	*Ref*	*C/I*
Lorazepam	WY	0.33 mg/ml[b]	AST	4 mg/ml	Yellow discoloration forms	1855	I
Midazolam HCl	RC	5 mg/ml	AST	4 mg/ml	Brown discoloration forms, followed by brown precipitate	1855	I
Vancomycin HCl		10 mg/ml[a]		4 mg/ml	White precipitate forms within 5 min	2173	I

[a]*Tested in dextrose 5% in water.*
[b]*Tested in sodium chloride 0.9%.*

Additional Compatibility Information

Other Drugs — It is recommended that no other drugs be mixed with omeprazole infusion or injection. (38; 115)

PAPAVERETUM

Products — Papaveretum injection is available in 1-ml ampuls containing a mixture of hydrochlorides of opium alkaloids. The reformulated mixture is composed of 253 parts of morphine hydrochloride, 23 parts of papaverine hydrochloride, and 20 parts of codeine hydrochloride. The product contains 15.4 mg of alkaloids per milliliter providing the equivalent of 10 mg of anhydrous morphine. (5; 30)

pH — A 1.5% solution in water has a pH of 3.7 to 4.7. (5)

Administration — Papaveretum injection may be administered by subcutaneous and intramuscular injection. It may also be administered by intravenous injection in doses reduced by 25 to 50%. (5; 30)

Stability — Papaveretum injection in intact ampuls should be stored at room temperature and protected from light. Freezing should be avoided. (4; 5)

Syringes — The former formulation of papaveretum injection (Roche) 20 mg/ml was found to retain potency for three months at room temperature when 1 and 2 ml of the injection were packaged in Tubex cartridges. (13)

Compatibility Information

Additive Compatibility

Drug	*Mfr*	*Conc/L*	**Papaveretum** *Mfr*	*Conc/L*	*Test Soln*	*Remarks*	*Ref*	*C/I*
Flucloxacillin sodium	BE	20 g	RC[a]	2 g	W	White precipitate forms immediately	1479	I
Frusemide	HO	1 g	RC[a]	2 g	W	Thick white precipitate forms immediately	1479	I

[a]*The former formulation was tested.*

Drugs in Syringe Compatibility

			Papaveretum				
Drug (in syringe)	*Mfr*	*Amt*	*Mfr*	*Amt*	*Remarks*	*Ref*	*C/I*
Atropine sulphate	ST	0.4 mg/ 1 ml	RC[a]	20 mg/ 1 ml	Visually compatible for at least 15 min	326	C
Butorphanol tartrate	BR	4 mg/ 2 ml	RC[a]	20 mg/ 1 ml	Physically compatible both macroscopically and microscopically for 30 min at room temperature	761	C
Chlorpromazine HCl	PO	50 mg/ 2 ml	RC[a]	20 mg/ 1 ml	Visually compatible for at least 15 min	326	C
Cimetidine HCl	SKF	300 mg/ 2 ml	RC[a]	20 mg/ 1 ml	Visually compatible for 4 hr at 25 °C	25	C
Dimenhydrinate	HR	50 mg/ 1 ml	RC[a]	20 mg/ 1 ml	Incompatible within 15 min	326	I
Diphenhydramine HCl	PD	50 mg/ 1 ml	RC[a]	20 mg/ 1 ml	Visually compatible for at least 15 min	326	C
Droperidol	MN	2.5 mg/ 1 ml	RC[a]	20 mg/ 1 ml	Visually compatible for at least 15 min	326	C
Fentanyl citrate	MN	0.05 mg/ 1 ml	RC[a]	20 mg/ 1 ml	Visually compatible for at least 15 min	326	C
Glycopyrrolate	RB	0.2 mg/ 1 ml	RC[a]	20 mg/ 1 ml	Visually compatible and pH in stability range for glycopyrrolate for 48 hr at 25 °C	331	C
	RB	0.2 mg/ 1 ml	RC[a]	40 mg/ 2 ml	Visually compatible and pH in stability range for glycopyrrolate for 48 hr at 25 °C	331	C
	RB	0.4 mg/ 2 ml	RC[a]	20 mg/ 1 ml	Visually compatible and pH in stability range for glycopyrrolate for 48 hr at 25 °C	331	C
Hydroxyzine HCl	PF	50 mg/ 1 ml	RC[a]	20 mg/ 1 ml	Visually compatible for at least 15 min	326	C
Meperidine HCl	WI	50 mg/ 1 ml	RC[a]	20 mg/ 1 ml	Visually compatible for at least 15 min	326	C
Metoclopramide HCl	NO	10 mg/ 2 ml	RC[a]	20 mg/ 1 ml	Physically compatible both macroscopically and microscopically for 30 min at room temperature	565	C
Morphine sulphate	ST	15 mg/ 1 ml	RC[a]	20 mg/ 1 ml	Visually compatible for at least 15 min	326	C
Pentazocine lactate	WI	30 mg/ 1 ml	RC[a]	20 mg/ 1 ml	Visually compatible for at least 15 min	326	C
Pentobarbital sodium	AB	50 mg/ 1 ml	RC[a]	20 mg/ 1 ml	Incompatible within 15 min	326	I
Perphenazine	SC	5 mg/ 1 ml	RC[a]	20 mg/ 1 ml	Yellow discoloration within 15 min	761	I
Prochlorperazine edisylate	PO	5 mg/ 1 ml	RC[a]	20 mg/ 1 ml	Visually compatible for at least 15 min	326	C
Promazine HCl	WY	50 mg/ 1 ml	RC[a]	20 mg/ 1 ml	Visually compatible for at least 15 min	326	C
Promethazine HCl	PO	50 mg/ 2 ml	RC[a]	20 mg/ 1 ml	Visually compatible for at least 15 min	326	C
Ranitidine HCl	GL	50 mg/ 2 ml	RC[a]	20 mg/ 1 ml	White haze and precipitate form immediately	978	I
Scopolamine HBr	ST	0.4 mg/ 1 ml	RC[a]	20 mg/ 1 ml	Visually compatible for at least 15 min	326	C

[a]*The former formulation was tested.*

PENTOXIFYLLINE (OXPENTIFYLLINE)

Products — Pentoxifylline is available as a 20-mg/ml solution in 5-ml (100-mg) and 15-ml (300-mg) ampuls. The products also contain sodium chloride, sodium hydroxide, or hydrochloric acid in water for injection. (115; 116)

Trade Name(s) — Rentylin, Torental, Trental.

Administration — Pentoxifylline injection may be given intravenously slowly over not less than five minutes with the patient in a prone position. Initially, a test dose of 50 mg may be diluted to 10 ml with 0.9% sodium chloride to test for individual susceptibility. If there are no ill effects, the dose may be gradually increased. (115) Administration of pentoxifylline by intravenous infusion after dilution in 250 to 500 ml of a compatible infusion solution such as dextrose 5% in water is also recommended. (5; 116)

Stability — Pentoxifylline in intact containers should be stored below 30 °C and protected from light. (115) Pentoxifylline 1 mg/ml and 3 mg/ml in sodium chloride 0.9% for intravenous infusion was found to undergo no loss by HPLC analysis after exposure to fluorescent light for 24 hours. (2302)

Sorption — Although loss of pentoxifylline due to sorption to containers and delivery devices was previously reported (146), no loss determined by HPLC analysis occurred in PVC containers stored for extended periods. (2302)

Compatibility Information

Solution Compatibility

Pentoxifylline

Solution	*Mfr*	*Mfr*	*Conc/L*	*Remarks*	*Ref*	*C/I*
Sodium chloride 0.9%	FRE[a]	DRA	1 g	Physically compatible with no loss by HPLC in 9 days at 4 °C, 4 days at room temperature, and 1 day at 40 °C protected from light	2302	C
	FRE[a]	DRA	3 g	Physically compatible with no loss by HPLC in 9 days at 4 °C, 4 days at room temperature, and 1 day at 40 °C protected from light	2302	C

[a]*Tested in PVC containers.*

Drugs in Syringe Compatibility

Pentoxifylline

Drug (in syringe)	*Mfr*	*Amt*	*Mfr*	*Amt*	*Remarks*	*Ref*	*C/I*
Heparin sodium		2500 units/ 1 ml	RS	300 mg/ 15 ml	Visually compatible for at least 5 min	1053	C

PROMAZINE HCL

Products — Promazine HCl is available in a concentration of 50 mg/ml in 1-ml ampuls. (30)

pH — From 4 to 5.5. (17)

Administration — Promazine HCl is administered by deep intramuscular injection (19; 30) or slowly by direct intravenous injection at a concentration not exceeding 25 mg/ml. Extravasation should be avoided. It should not be given intra-arterially. (19)

Stability — The product should be stored at controlled room temperature and protected from freezing and light. (19) Promazine HCl is maximally stable at pH 6.5. (67) It oxidizes after prolonged exposure to air. (4) A slight yellowish discoloration does not affect potency or efficacy, but markedly discolored solutions or solutions containing a precipitate should not be used. (19)

Sorption — Promazine HCl (Wyeth) 6.4 mg/L in sodium chloride 0.9% (Travenol) in PVC bags did not exhibit significant sorption to the plastic during one week of storage at room temperature (15 to 20 °C). However, when the solution was buffered from its initial pH of 5 to 7.4, approximately 48% of the drug was lost in one week due to sorption. (536)

Promazine HCl (Wyeth) 6.4 mg/L in sodium chloride 0.9% exhibited a cumulative 11% loss during a seven-hour simulated infusion through an infusion set (Travenol) consisting of a cellulose propionate burette chamber and 170 cm of PVC tubing due to sorption. Both the burette and the tubing contributed to the loss. The extent of sorption was found to be independent of concentration. (606)

The drug was also tested as a simulated infusion over at least one hour by a syringe pump system. A glass syringe on a syringe pump was fitted with 20 cm of polyethylene tubing or 50 cm of Silastic tubing. A negligible amount of drug was lost with the polyethylene tubing, but a cumulative loss of 59% occurred during the one-hour infusion through the Silastic tubing. (606)

A 25-ml aliquot of promazine HCl (Wyeth) 6.4 mg/L in sodium chloride 0.9%, stored in all-plastic syringes composed of polypropylene barrels and polyethylene plungers for 24 hours at room temperature in the dark, did not exhibit any loss due to sorption. (606)

Compatibility Information

Solution Compatibility

Promazine HCl

Solution	*Mfr*	*Mfr*	*Conc/L*	*Remarks*	*Ref*	*C/I*
Dextran 6% in dextrose 5%	AB	WY	300 mg	Physically compatible	3	C
Dextran 6% in sodium chloride 0.9%	AB	WY	300 mg	Physically compatible	3	C
Dextrose–Ringer's injection combinations	AB	WY	300 mg	Physically compatible	3	C
Dextrose–Ringer's injection, lactated, combinations	AB	WY	300 mg	Physically compatible	3	C
Dextrose–saline combinations	AB	WY	300 mg	Physically compatible	3	C
Dextrose 2½% in water	AB	WY	300 mg	Physically compatible	3	C
Dextrose 5% in water	AB	WY	300 mg	Physically compatible	3	C
	TR	WY	1 g	10% loss in 3 days at room temperature exposed to daylight. No loss in 6 days at room temperature or 4 °C in the dark	1149	C
Dextrose 10% in water	AB	WY	300 mg	Physically compatible	3	C
Fructose 10% in sodium chloride 0.9%	AB	WY	300 mg	Physically compatible	3	C
Fructose 10% in water	AB	WY	300 mg	Physically compatible	3	C
Invert sugar 5 and 10% in sodium chloride 0.9%	AB	WY	300 mg	Physically compatible	3	C
Invert sugar 5 and 10% in water	AB	WY	300 mg	Physically compatible	3	C
Ionosol products (except as noted below)	AB	WY	300 mg	Physically compatible	3	C
Ionosol B with dextrose 5%	AB	WY	300 mg	Haze or precipitate forms within 6 hr	3	I
Ringer's injection	AB	WY	300 mg	Physically compatible	3	C
Ringer's injection, lactated	AB	WY	300 mg	Physically compatible	3	C
Sodium chloride 0.45%	AB	WY	300 mg	Physically compatible	3	C
Sodium chloride 0.9%	AB	WY	300 mg	Physically compatible	3	C
	TR	WY	1 g	8% loss in 8 hr and 15% in 24 hr at room temperature exposed to daylight	1149	I
	TR	WY	1 g	10% loss in 6 days at room temperature or 4 °C in the dark	1149	C
Sodium lactate ⅙ M	AB	WY	300 mg	Physically compatible	3	C

Additive Compatibility

Promazine HCl

Drug	*Mfr*	*Conc/L*	*Mfr*	*Conc/L*	*Test Soln*	*Remarks*	*Ref*	*C/I*
Aminophylline	SE	1 g	WY	1 g	D5W	Physically incompatible	15	I
	BP	1 g	BP	200 mg	D5W, NS	Immediate precipitation	26	I
Chloramphenicol sodium succinate	PD	1 g	WY	100 mg		Physically compatible	6	C
Chlorothiazide sodium	BP	2 g	BP	200 mg	D5W, NS	Immediate precipitation	26	I
Erythromycin lactobionate	AB	1 g	WY	100 mg		Physically compatible	20	C

Additive Compatibility (Cont.)

Promazine HCl

Drug	*Mfr*	*Conc/L*	*Mfr*	*Conc/L*	*Test Soln*	*Remarks*	*Ref*	*C/I*
Ethacrynate sodium	MSD	50 mg	WY	50 mg	NS	Little alteration of UV spectra in 8 hr at room temperature	16	C
Fibrinogen	CU	2 g	WY	1 g	D5W	Physically incompatible	11	I
Fibrinolysin, human	MSD	2 g	WY	1 g	D5W	Physically incompatible	11	I
Heparin sodium	AB	20,000 units	WY	100 mg		Physically compatible	21	C
Lignocaine HCl	AST	2 g	WY	100 mg		Physically compatible	24	C
Metaraminol bitartrate	MSD	100 mg	WY	100 mg		Physically compatible	7	C
Methohexital sodium	BP	2 g	BP	200 mg	D5W, NS	Immediate precipitation	26	I
Methyldopate HCl	MSD	1 g	WY	100 mg	D, D–S, S	Physically compatible	23	C
Nafcillin sodium	WY	500 mg	WY	100 mg		Physically compatible for only 6 hr	27	I
Penicillin G potassium	PF	20 million units	WY	1 g	D5W	Physically incompatible	11	I
Pentobarbital sodium	AB	200 mg	WY	1 g	D5W	Physically incompatible	11	I
Phenobarbital sodium	BP	800 mg	BP	200 mg	NS	Immediate precipitation	26	I
Sodium bicarbonate	AB	3.75 g	WY	1 g	D5W	Physically incompatible	11	I
	AB	2.4 mEq[a]	WY	100 mg	D5W	Physically compatible for 24 hr	772	C
Thiopental sodium	AB	2.5 g	WY	1 g	D5W	Physically incompatible	11	I
	AB	2.5 g	WY	100 mg	D5W	Precipitate forms within 1 hr	21	I

[a]*One vial of Neut added to a liter of admixture.*

Drugs in Syringe Compatibility

Promazine HCl

Drug (in syringe)	*Mfr*	*Amt*	*Mfr*	*Amt*	*Remarks*	*Ref*	*C/I*
Atropine sulphate	ST	0.4 mg/ 1 ml	WY	50 mg/ 1 ml	Physically compatible for at least 15 min	326	C
Chlorpromazine HCl	PO	50 mg/ 2 ml	WY	50 mg/ 1 ml	Physically compatible for at least 15 min	326	C
Cimetidine HCl	SKF	300 mg/ 2 ml	WY	25 mg/ 1 ml	Physically compatible for 4 hr at 25 °C	25	C
Dimenhydrinate	HR	50 mg/ 1 ml	WY	50 mg/ 1 ml	Physically incompatible within 15 min	326	I
Diphenhydramine HCl	PD	50 mg/ 1 ml	WY	50 mg/ 1 ml	Physically compatible for at least 15 min	326	C
Droperidol	MN	2.5 mg/ 1 ml	WY	50 mg/ 1 ml	Physically compatible for at least 15 min	326	C
Fentanyl citrate	MN	0.05 mg/ 1 ml	WY	50 mg/ 1 ml	Physically compatible for at least 15 min	326	C
Glycopyrrolate	RB	0.2 mg/ 1 ml	WY	50 mg/ 1 ml	Physically compatible and pH in stability range for glycopyrrolate for 48 hr at 25 °C	331	C
	RB	0.2 mg/ 1 ml	WY	100 mg/ 2 ml	Physically compatible and pH in stability range for glycopyrrolate for 48 hr at 25 °C	331	C
	RB	0.4 mg/ 2 ml	WY	50 mg/ 1 ml	Physically compatible and pH in stability range for glycopyrrolate for 48 hr at 25 °C	331	C

Drugs in Syringe Compatibility (Cont.)

			Promazine HCl				
Drug (in syringe)	*Mfr*	*Amt*	*Mfr*	*Amt*	*Remarks*	*Ref*	*C/I*
Hydroxyzine HCl	PF	50 mg/ 1 ml	WY	50 mg/ 1 ml	Physically compatible for at least 15 min	326	C
Meperidine HCl	WI	50 mg/ 1 ml	WY	50 mg/ 1 ml	Physically compatible for at least 15 min	326	C
Metoclopramide HCl	NO	10 mg/ 2 ml	MY	50 mg/ 1 ml	Physically compatible both macroscopically and microscopically for 15 min at room temperature	565	C
Midazolam HCl	RC	5 mg/ 1 ml	WY	50 mg/ 1 ml	Physically compatible for 4 hr at 25 °C under fluorescent light	1145	C
Morphine sulphate	ST	15 mg/ 1 ml	WY	50 mg/ 1 ml	Physically compatible for at least 15 min	326	C
Papaveretum	RC[a]	20 mg/ 1 ml	WY	50 mg/ 1 ml	Visually compatible for at least 15 min	326	C
Pentazocine lactate	WI	30 mg/ 1 ml	WY	25 mg/ 1 ml	Potency retained for 3 months at room temperature in Tubex	13	C
	WI	30 mg/ 1 ml	WY	50 mg/ 1 ml	Potency retained for 3 months at room temperature in Tubex	13	C
	WI	30 mg/ 1 ml	WY	50 mg/ 1 ml	Physically compatible for at least 15 min	326	C
Pentobarbital sodium	AB	50 mg/ 1 ml	WY	50 mg/ 1 ml	Physically incompatible within 15 min	326	I
Prochlorperazine edisylate	PO	5 mg/ 1 ml	WY	50 mg/ 1 ml	Physically compatible for at least 15 min	326	C
Promethazine HCl	PO	50 mg/ 2 ml	WY	50 mg/ 1 ml	Physically compatible for at least 15 min	326	C
Scopolamine HBr	ST	0.4 mg/ 1 ml	WY	50 mg/ 1 ml	Physically compatible for at least 15 min	326	C

[a]The former formulation was tested

Y-Site Injection Compatibility (1:1 Mixture)

			Promazine HCl				
Drug	*Mfr*	*Conc*	*Mfr*	*Conc*	*Remarks*	*Ref*	*C/I*
Warfarin sodium	DU	0.1[a,b] and 2[c] mg/ml	WY	5 mg/ml[a,b]	Heavy white turbidity forms immediately	2011	I

[a]Tested in dextrose 5% in water.
[b]Tested in sodium chloride 0.9%.
[c]Tested in sterile water for injection.

Additional Compatibility Information

Concentrated Drug Solutions — The following incompatibility determinations were performed with concentrated solutions. The drugs in dry form were reconstituted according to manufacturers' recommendations. One milliliter of promazine HCl was added to 5 ml of sterile distilled water along with 1 ml of each of the following drugs. Particulate matter was noted within two hours (28):

Aminophylline
Chloramphenicol sodium succinate (Parke-Davis)
Dimenhydrinate (Searle)
Heparin sodium
Hydrocortisone sodium succinate (Upjohn)
Penicillin G potassium
Phenobarbital sodium (Winthrop)
Phenytoin sodium (Parke-Davis)
Vitamin B complex with C (Lederle)

PROPAFENONE HCL

Products — Propafenone HCl is available as a 3.5-mg/ml solution in 20-ml (70-mg) ampuls. Each milliliter of solution also contains dextrose monohydrate 53.8 mg in water for injection. (411; 412; 441)

pH — Propafenone HCl 70-mg/20 ml injection has a pH of 4.7 to 6. (411; 412)

Trade Name(s) — Rhythmol, Rytmonorm, others.

Administration — Propafenone HCl is administered by intravenous injection as a bolus given slowly over three to five minutes. Intervals between doses should be about 90 to 120 minutes. Blood pressure and electrocardiogram parameters should be monitored. (441)

Propafenone HCl may also be given as a short-term infusion over one to three hours or as a long-term infusion continuously over periods up to several days. The drug is diluted in dextrose 5% in water or fructose 5% in water for intravenous infusion. (441)

Stability — The manufacturer indicates that propafenone HCl is incompatible with chloride-containing infusion solutions because of the potential for precipitation. (441)

Freezing Solutions — Propafenone HCl (Knoll) 2 mg/ml in dextrose 5% in 0.2% sodium chloride in PVC bags was found to have precipitated on thawing of frozen solutions. Precipitation was not observed when lower drug concentrations (0.5 and 1 mg/ml) in polypropylene syringes (Becton-Dickinson) were frozen and when dextrose 5% in water was used as the diluent for concentrations of 0.5, 1, and 2 mg/ml. Nevertheless, avoiding the freezing of propafenone HCl solutions should be considered. (411)

Syringes — Propafenone HCl (Knoll) at concentrations of 0.5, 1, and 2 mg/ml in dextrose 5% in water and in dextrose 5% in 0.2% sodium chloride was packaged as 7 ml of solution in 10-ml polypropylene syringes (Becton-Dickinson). The solutions were visually compatible and HPLC analysis found 4% or less loss in 48 hours stored at 21 °C exposed to fluorescent light. (411)

Compatibility Information

Solution Compatibility

Propafenone HCl

Solution	*Mfr*	*Mfr*	*Conc/L*	*Remarks*	*Ref*	*C/I*
Dextrose 5% in water	BA[a]	KN	0.5, 1, and 2 g	Visually compatible with 4% or less loss by HPLC in 48 hr at 21 °C under fluorescent light	411	C
Dextrose 5% in 0.2% sodium chloride	BA[a]	KN	0.5 and 1 g	Visually compatible with no loss by HPLC in 48 hr at 21 °C under fluorescent light	411	C

[a]*Tested in PVC containers.*

Additive Compatibility

Propafenone HCl

Drug	*Mfr*	*Conc/L*	*Mfr*	*Conc/L*	*Test Soln*	*Remarks*	*Ref*	*C/I*
Amiodarone HCl	LZ	1.25 g[a]	KN	0.625 g	D5W	Visually compatible with no propafenone loss by HPLC in 24 hr at 22 °C exposed to fluorescent light. Amiodarone not tested	412	C
Dopamine HCl	DU	0.9 and 2.3 g[a]	KN	0.54 g	D5W	Visually compatible with little or no propafenone loss by HPLC in 24 hr at 22 °C exposed to fluorescent light. Dopamine not tested	412	C
Inamrinone lactate	SW	1 and 2.5 g[a]	KN	0.5 g	NS	Visually compatible with little or no propafenone loss by HPLC in 24 hr at 22 °C exposed to fluorescent light. Inamrinone not tested	412	C
Lignocaine HCl	AST	4.5 g[a]	KN	0.54 g	D5W	Visually compatible with little or no propafenone loss by HPLC in 24 hr at 22 °C exposed to fluorescent light. Lignocaine not tested	412	C
Potassium chloride	AST	18 mmol[a]	KN	0.54 g	D5W	Visually compatible for 24 hr at 22 °C exposed to fluorescent light	412	C

[a]*Approximate concentration.*

Drugs in Syringe Compatibility

Propafenone HCl

Drug (in syringe)	*Mfr*	*Amt*	*Mfr*	*Amt*	*Remarks*	*Ref*	*C/I*
Heparin sodium		2500 units/ 1 ml	KN	70 mg/ 20 ml	Turbidity or precipitate forms within 5 min	1053	I

Y-Site Injection Compatibility (1:1 Mixture)

Propafenone HCl

Drug	*Mfr*	*Conc*	*Mfr*	*Conc*	*Remarks*	*Ref*	*C/I*
Heparin sodium		50 units/ml/ min[b]	KN	70 mg/20 ml[a]	White opalescence forms	1053	I

[a]*Given over three minutes into a heparin infusion run at 1 ml/min.*
[b]*Tested in sodium chloride 0.9%.*

SALBUTAMOL

Products — Salbutamol injection is available as a 50-μg/ml solution in 5-ml ampuls and as a 500-μg/ml solution in 1-ml ampuls as the sulphate. In addition, the products contain sodium chloride, sodium hydroxide, and sulphuric acid in water for injection. (38; 115)

Salbutamol infusion is available as a 1-mg/ml solution as the sulphate in 5-ml vials for use in infusions. In addition, the product for infusion also contains sodium chloride, sodium hydroxide, and sulphuric acid in water for injection. This concentrate must be diluted in a suitable intravenous infusion solution for use. (38; 115)

pH — About 3.5. (115)

Tonicity — Both salbutamol injection and infusion are isotonic. (38; 115)

Trade Name(s) — Salbumol, Ventolin, others.

Administration — Salbutamol injection is administered by subcutaneous, intramuscular, or slow intravenous injection. The 50-μg/ml concentration is suitable for slow intravenous injection; dilution of the 500-μg/ml concentration with water for injection has been recommended for intravenous injection. (38; 115)

Salbutamol 1-mg/ml for intravenous infusion is used to prepare intravenous infusion solutions of the drug. It should not be given undiluted. It should be diluted to a concentration of 10 or 20 μg/ml with a compatible infusion solution. Dextrose 5% in water is recommended but sodium chloride 0.9% or dextrose 5% in sodium chloride 0.9% may also be used. (38; 115) Dilution to a 200-μg/ml concentration is recommended for use in a syringe pump. (38)

Stability — Salbutamol injection and infusion are clear, colorless, or pale straw-colored solutions. The intact containers should be stored below 30 °C and protected from light. (38; 115)

Compatibility Information

Drugs in Syringe Compatibility

Salbutamol

Drug (in syringe)	*Mfr*	*Amt*	*Mfr*	*Amt*	*Remarks*	*Ref*	*C/I*
Hydromorphone HCl	KN	1 mg/ 0.5 ml	GL	2.5 mg/ 2.5 ml[a]	Visually compatible for 1 hr both macroscopically and microscopically	1904	C
Morphine sulphate	AB	5 mg/ 0.5 ml	GL	2.5 mg/ 2.5 ml[a]	Visually compatible for 1 hr both macroscopically and microscopically	1904	C

[a]*Both preserved (benzyl alcohol 0.9%; benzalkonium chloride 0.01%) and unpreserved sodium chloride 0.9% were used as a diluent.*

Additional Compatibility Information

Infusion Solutions — The manufacturer states that salbutamol is stable for use within 24 hours diluted in the following infusion solutions (38; 115):

Dextrose 5% in water
Sodium chloride 0.18% and dextrose 4%
Sodium chloride 0.9%

SODIUM FUSIDATE

Products — Sodium fusidate is available as a dry powder in vials containing 500 mg (equivalent to 480 mg of fusidic acid). It is packaged with a diluent vial containing 10 ml of phosphate–citrate buffer (pH 7.4 to 7.6). The drug should be reconstituted with the diluent and diluted further with sodium chloride 0.9% or other compatible diluent for administration. (38; 115)

Sodium and Phosphate Content— Each vial of reconstituted sodium fusidate contains 3.1 mmol of sodium and 1.1 mmol of phosphate. (38)

Administration — Sodium fusidate is administered by slow intravenous infusion over not less than six hours if a superficial vein is employed. If a central venous line is used, the infusion should be given over two to four hours. The reconstituted sodium fusidate in 10 ml of buffer solution is diluted in 250 ml (115) to 500 ml of sodium chloride 0.9% or other compatible infusion solution for administration. The drug must not be given by other routes. (38; 115)

Stability — Sodium fusidate should be stored below 25 °C and protected from light. (38) Reconstituted solutions that are added to 500 ml of compatible infusion solutions are stable for 24 hours at room temperature. (38; 115) Unused portions of the reconstituted solution should be discarded. (38)

pH Effects— Precipitation may occur upon dilution if the resulting pH is less than 7.4. (38)

Freezing Solutions— Sodium fusidate (Leo) 1 mg/ml in sodium chloride 0.9%, dextrose 5% in water, and sodium chloride 0.18% and dextrose 4% is stated to be stable frozen at −20 °C for 24 hours followed by thawing in a microwave oven. (1800)

Fusidic acid (Leo) 500 mg, reconstituted in buffer and diluted to 550 ml in sodium chloride 0.9% in PVC bags, was stored frozen at −20 °C. No loss was found by HPLC after 12 months of storage followed by microwave thawing. Furthermore, the solution was physically compatible, with no increase in subvisual particles. In addition, there was no loss of sodium fusidate after six months of storage at −20 °C followed by three freeze–thaw cycles. (1612)

Compatibility Information

Solution Compatibility

Sodium fusidate

Solution	*Mfr*	*Mfr*	*Conc/L*	*Remarks*	*Ref*	*C/I*
Compound sodium lactate intravenous infusion (Ringer's lactate)	BP	LEO	1 g	Physically compatible and chemically stable for 48 hr at room temperature	1800	C
Darrow-glucose intravenous infusion		LEO	2 g	Physically compatible and chemically stable for 48 hr at room temperature	1800	C
Dextrose 5% in water	BA[a]	LEO	1.16 and 2.32 g	Physically compatible with less than 10% loss in 162 days at 4 °C and 10% loss in 10.4 days at 25 °C or 2.1 days at 37 °C	1709	C
	BP	LEO	1 or 2 g	Physically compatible and chemically stable for 48 hr at room temperature	1800	C
Electrolyte Solution B with dextrose 20%	TR	LEO	1 g	Physically incompatible	1800	I
Fat emulsion, intravenous 10% (Intralipid)		LEO	1 g	Physically incompatible	1800	I
Potassium chloride 0.3% and dextrose 5%	BP	LEO	1 g	Physically compatible and chemically stable for 48 hr at room temperature	1800	C
Potassium chloride 0.3% and sodium chloride 0.9%	BP	LEO	1 and 2 g	Physically compatible and chemically stable for 48 hr at room temperature	1800	C
Sodium chloride 0.9%	BP	LEO	1 and 2 g	Physically compatible and chemically stable for 48 hr at room temperature	1800	C
Sodium chloride 0.18% and dextrose 4%	BP	LEO	1 g	Physically compatible and chemically stable for 48 hr at room temperature	1800	C
Sodium lactate intravenous infusion	BP	LEO	1 g	Physically compatible and chemically stable for 48 hr at room temperature	1800	C

[a]*Tested in PVC containers.*

Additive Compatibility

			Sodium fusidate					
Drug	*Mfr*	*Conc/L*	*Mfr*	*Conc/L*	*Test Soln*	*Remarks*	*Ref*	*C/I*
Amdinocillin		50 g	LEO	500 mg	D–S	Physically incompatible	1800	I
Cefotaxime sodium		2.5 g	LEO	500 mg	D–S	Physically compatible and chemically stable for 48 hr at room temperature	1800	C
Erythromycin lactobionate		5 g	LEO	1 g	D–S	Physically compatible and chemically stable for 48 hr at room temperature	1800	C
Flucloxacillin sodium		2.5 g	LEO	500 mg	D–S	Physically compatible and chemically stable for 48 hr at room temperature	1800	C
Gentamicin sulphate		160 mg	LEO	1 g	D–S	Physically compatible and chemically stable for 48 hr at room temperature	1800	C
		1.5 g	LEO	1 g	D–S	Physically incompatible	1800	I
Vancomycin HCl		25 g	LEO	500 mg	D–S	Physically incompatible	1800	I

Additional Compatibility Information

Infusion Solutions — The manufacturer indicates that sodium fusidate is stable for at least 24 hours at room temperature in the following infusion solutions at the concentrations cited. (38) It should be noted that other research indicates that the drug is stable for longer periods when diluted for infusion. See Solution Compatibility table above.

Infusion Solution	Soduim Fusidate Concentration
Compound sodium lactate intravenous infusion (Ringer's injection, lactated)	1 to 2 mg/ml
Dextrose 5% in water	1 to 2 mg/ml
Potassium chloride 0.3% and dextrose 5%	1 mg/ml
Sodium chloride 0.18% and dextrose 4%	1 mg/ml
Sodium chloride 0.9%	1 to 2 mg/ml
Sodium lactate intravenous infusion	1 mg/ml

Sodium fusidate reconstituted with the buffer solution to 50 mg/ml is physically incompatible with infusion solutions containing amino acids solutions, dextrose 20% or greater, and lipid infusions. (38; 115)

Peritoneal Dialysis Solutions — Sodium fusidate (Leo) at a concentration of 0.125 mg/ml is stated to be physically incompatible with the following peritoneal dialysis solutions (1800):

Dianeal PD2 with dextrose 1.36%
Dianeal PD3 with dextrose 1.36%
Dianeal with dextrose 3.86%
Peritoneal Dialysis Solution 6.36%
Peritoneal Dialysis Solution 6.36% + acetate
Peritoneal Dialysis Solution with dextrose 2.27%

Blood Products — Sodium fusidate should not be infused with whole blood. (38)

Other Drugs — Sodium fusidate is physically incompatible with acidic drug solutions and should not be mixed with kanamycin sulphate or gentamicin sulphate. (115)

TEICOPLANIN

Products — Teicoplanin is available as a lyophilized powder in vials containing teicoplanin 200 and 400 mg. The vials are accompanied by an ampul of water for injection for use as a diluent. Reconstitute by adding the diluent slowly down the side of the vial of teicoplanin and then rolling the vial gently until the powder is completely dissolved. Do not shake the vial. Care should be taken to avoid the formation of foam; if foam does form, the solution should stand for about 15 minutes for the foam to subside. The teicoplanin vials contain a calculated excess so that when reconstituted as directed the full amount of drug can be withdrawn from the vial using a syringe and needle. The concentration of teicoplanin is 100 mg in 1.5 ml (from the 200-mg vials) and 400 mg in 3 ml (from the 400-mg vial). (38; 115)

Trade Name(s) — Targocid.

Administration — Teicoplanin may be administered after reconstitution either intramuscularly with a maximum of 3 ml in a single site or by direct intravenous injection as a bolus over 3 to 5 minutes. It may also be administered as an intravenous infusion over 30 minutes after dilution of the reconstituted solution in a compatible infusion solution. (38; 115)

Stability — Intact vials of teicoplanin should be stored below 25 °C. The manufacturer recommends that reconstituted teicoplanin be used immediately after preparation and any unused portion be discarded. However, the manufacturer also states that the reconstituted solution may be stored under refrigeration at 4 °C for up to 24 hours if the situation makes discarding the reconstituted drug impractical. (38; 115)

Compatibility Information

Solution Compatibility

Teicoplanin

Solution	*Mfr*	*Mfr*	*Conc/L*	*Remarks*	*Ref*	*C/I*
Dextrose 5% in water	BA[a]	HO	2 g	Visually compatible with no loss of teicoplanin by HPLC and microbiological assays in 24 hr at 25 °C	2165	C
Sodium chloride 0.9%	BA[a]	HO	2 g	Visually compatible with no loss of teicoplanin by HPLC and microbiological assays in 24 hr at 25 °C	2165	C

[a]*Tested in glass containers.*

Additive Compatibility

Teicoplanin

Drug	*Mfr*	*Conc/L*	*Mfr*	*Conc/L*	*Test Soln*	*Remarks*	*Ref*	*C/I*
Heparin sodium	CPP	20,000 and 40,000 units	HO	2 g	D5W, NS	Visually compatible with no loss of teicoplanin by HPLC and microbiological assay and no loss of heparin activity in 24 hr at 25 °C	2165	C

Y-Site Injection Compatibility (1:1 Mixture)

Teicoplanin

Drug	*Mfr*	*Conc*	*Mfr*	*Conc*	*Remarks*	*Ref*	*C/I*
Ciprofloxacin	BAY	2 mg/ml[a]	GRP	60 mg/ml	White precipitate forms immediately but disappears with shaking	1934	?

[a]*Tested in sodium chloride 0.9%.*

Additional Compatibility Information

Infusion Solutions — The manufacturer recommends the following infusion solutions for diluting teicoplanin for intravenous infusion (38; 115):

Dextrose 5% in water
Ringer's injection, lactated (Compound sodium lactate injection)
Sodium chloride 0.18% and dextrose 4%
Sodium chloride 0.9%

Teicoplanin forms dextrose aldehyde adducts when diluted in dextrose-containing solutions. Equilibrium is reached faster at room temperature (seven days) than with refrigerated storage (30 days). The equilibrium concentration of the adduct is directly related to the dextrose concentration. The reaction is reversible with dilution. (2046)

Peritoneal Dialysis Solutions — The manufacturer recommends use of peritoneal dialysis solutions containing 1.36 or 3.86% dextrose. (38)

Teicoplanin (Marion Merrell Dow) 0.025 mg/ml in Dianeal PD-2 with dextrose 1.5% in PVC containers was physically and chemically stable by HPLC analysis for 24 hours at 25 °C exposed to light, exhibiting no loss; additional storage for eight hours at 37 °C resulted in losses of 6% or less. Under refrigeration at 4 °C protected from light, no loss occurred in seven days. Additional storage for 16 hours at 25 °C followed by eight hours at 37 °C resulted in about 7% loss. (1989)

Ceftazidime (sodium carbonate formulation) (Glaxo) 0.1 mg/ml admixed with teicoplanin (Marion Merrell Dow) 0.025 mg/ml in Dianeal PD-2 with dextrose 1.5% in PVC containers did not result in a stable mixture. Using HPLC analysis, large (but variable) teicoplanin losses generally in the 20% range were noted in as little as two hours at 25 °C exposed to light. Ceftazidime losses of about 9% occurred in 16 hours. Refrigeration and protection from light of the peritoneal dialysis admixture reduced losses of both drugs to negligible levels. Even so, the authors did not recommend admixing these two drugs because of the high levels of teicoplanin loss at room temperature. (1989)

Teicoplanin (Merrell Dow) 25 mg/L in Dianeal 137 with dextrose 1.36% (Baxter) was evaluated for stability over 42 days using a stability-indicating bioassay. Stored at 4 °C, teicoplanin retained stability with a loss of less than 5% in 42 days. At 20 °C, 10% loss occurred in about 25 days with 17% loss in 42 days. At an elevated temperature of 37 °C, a much greater rate of decomposition occurs with over 40% loss occurring in 42 days. (2145)

Aminoglycosides — Solutions of teicoplanin and aminoglycosides are incompatible and should not be directly mixed prior to injection. (38)

Heparin Sodium — The stability of catheter flush solutions composed of teicoplanin 133 mg/ml in water for injection, or heparin sodium 10 units/ml or 100 units/ml, was evaluated in Hickman catheters at 25 °C over 24 hours. No decomposition products formed by HPLC analysis, and no loss was found by HPLC or microbiological assays. Indeed, a small (11%) increase in teicoplanin concentration was observed which the authors attributed to loss of water. (2165)

TRAMADOL HCL

Products — Tramadol HCl is available as a 50-mg/ml aqueous solution in 2-ml (100 mg) ampuls. Sodium acetate and water for injection are also present in the formulation. (38)

Osmolarity — Tramadol HCl has an osmolarity of 320 to 380 mOsm/L. (38)

Trade Name(s) — Contramal, Topalgic, Tramal, Zamadol, Zydol, others.

Administration — Tramadol HCl is administered intramuscularly, by direct intravenous injection slowly over two to three minutes, or by intravenous infusion after dilution. (38)

Stability — Tramadol HCl is a clear, colorless solution. The intact ampuls should be stored below 30 °C. (38)

Exposure to or protection from light did not affect the stability of tramadol HCl 0.5- and 4-mg/ml infusion solutions in dextrose 5% in water or sodium chloride 0.9%. (434)

Ambulatory Pumps — Tramadol HCl (Mundipharma) 0.5 and 4 mg/ml in dextrose 5% in water or sodium chloride 0.9% was evaluated by HPLC analysis for stability in PVC portable infusion pump reservoirs (Ultraflow, Fresenius). No visible changes were observed, and HPLC analysis found little or no loss of tramadol HCl in 14 days at 4 °C followed by six hours at room temperature and in seven days stored at room temperature. At 40 °C, 3 to 5% loss was found in sodium chloride 0.9% but little or no loss occurred in dextrose 5% in water. (434)

Compatibility Information

Solution Compatibility

Tramadol HCl

Solution	*Mfr*	*Mfr*	*Conc/L*	*Remarks*	*Ref*	*C/I*
Dextrose 5% in water	[a]	MUN	0.5 and 4 g	Visually compatible with no loss by HPLC in 14 days at 4 °C and 7 days at room temperature or 40 °C	434	C
Sodium chloride 0.9%	[a]	MUN	0.5 and 4 g	Visually compatible with little or no loss by HPLC in 14 days at 4 °C and 7 days at room temperature. 3 to 5% loss in 7 days at 40 °C	434	C

[a]*Tested in PVC containers.*

Drugs in Syringe Compatibility

Tramadol HCl

Drug (in syringe)	*Mfr*	*Amt*	*Mfr*	*Amt*	*Remarks*	*Ref*	*C/I*
Heparin sodium		2500 units/ 1 ml	GRU	100 mg/ 2 ml	Visually compatible for at least 5 min	1053	C

Y-Site Injection Compatibility (1:1 Mixture)

Tramadol HCl

Drug	*Mfr*	*Conc*	*Mfr*	*Conc*	*Remarks*	*Ref*	*C/I*
Heparin sodium		50 units/ml/ min[b]	GRU	100 mg/2 ml[a]	Turbidity forms	1053	I

[a]*Given over three minutes into a heparin infusion run at 1 ml/min.*
[b]*Tested in sodium chloride 0.9%.*

Additional Compatibility Information

Infusion Solutions — Tramadol HCl (Zydol) is stated to be physically compatible and chemically stable for up to five days in the following infusion solutions (38):

Compound sodium lactate (Ringer's lactate)
Dextrose 5% in water
Haemaccel
Sodium chloride 0.9%
Sodium chloride 0.18% and dextrose 4%

Tramadol HCl is stated to be physically compatible and chemically stable for up to 24 hours in Ringer's solution and sodium bicarbonate 4.2%. (38)

Other Drugs — Tramadol HCl should not be mixed in the same syringe with diazepam, diclofenac sodium, indomethacin sodium, midazolam, and piroxicam. (38)

TROPISETRON HCL

Products — Tropisetron HCl is available as an aqueous solution in 2- and 5-ml ampuls. Each milliliter of solution provides 1 mg of tropisetron (present as 1.13 mg of the hydrochloride). Also present in the formulation are acetic acid, sodium acetate, sodium chloride, and water for injection. (38; 115)

Trade Name(s) — Navoban.

Administration — Tropisetron HCl is administered either as a slow intravenous injection over not less than 30 seconds for a 2-mg dose (38; 115) or one minute for a 5-mg dose (115) or as an intravenous infusion over 15 minutes. (38)

Stability — Tropisetron HCl injection is a colorless or faintly brown-yellow solution. Intact ampules should be stored at room temperature. (38)

Tropisetron HCl is stated to be physically compatible and chemically stable for 24 hours under refrigeration diluted in several common infusion solutions. (See Additional Compatibility Information below.) However, the manufacturer recommends use within eight hours of preparing the infusion because of microbiological contamination concerns. (38)

Syringes — Tropisetron HCl (Sandoz) 1 mg/ml was packaged in polypropylene syringes (Becton-Dickinson) and stored under refrigeration at 4 °C and at room temperature about 23 °C exposed to daylight and protected from light for 15 days. HPLC analysis found 4% or less loss of tropisetron HCl in 15 days under any of the storage conditions. (2298)

Sorption — The manufacturer indicates that tropisetron HCl solutions are compatible with both glass and PVC containers and infusion sets. (38)

Compatibility Information

Solution Compatibility

Tropisetron HCl

Solution	*Mfr*	*Mfr*	*Conc/L*	*Remarks*	*Ref*	*C/I*
Dextrose 5% in water	AGT[a], BFM[b]	SZ	50 mg	Visually compatible with no loss by HPLC in 90 days at 4 and −20 °C	470	C
	BA[a], BRN[c]	SZ	50 mg	10% or less change in drug concentration in 15 days at 4 and 23 °C exposed to or protected from light	2298	C
Sodium chloride 0.9%	AGT[a], BFM[b]	SZ	50 mg	Visually compatible with no loss by HPLC in 90 days at 4 and −20 °C	470	C
	BA[a], BRN[c]	SZ	50 mg	10% or less change in drug concentration in 15 days at 4 and 23 °C exposed to or protected from light	2298	C

[a]*Tested in PVC containers.*
[b]*Tested in three-layer (Clear-Flex) laminate containers having a polyethylene inner surface.*
[c]*Tested in glass and polyethylene containers.*

Additional Compatibility Information

Infusion Solutions — Tropisetron HCl 0.05 mg/ml is physically compatible and chemically stable for 24 hours under refrigeration with the following infusion solutions (38):

Dextrose 5% in water
Fructose 5% in water
Ringer's injection
Sodium chloride 0.9%

Tropisetron HCl 0.05 mg/ml was also stated to be compatible with mannitol 10% and sodium chloride 0.9% and potassium chloride 0.3% and with levulose 5%, although no stability period was cited. (115)

VINDESINE SULPHATE

Products — Vindesine sulphate is available in lyophilized form in vials containing 5 mg with mannitol 25 mg and sodium hydroxide and/or sulphuric acid to adjust the pH. The drug should be reconstituted with 5 ml of sterile diluent to yield a 1-mg/ml solution. (38; 1442)

pH — From 4.2 to 4.5. (234)

Trade Name(s) — Eldisine.

Administration — Vindesine sulphate is administered intravenously. It must not be given intramuscularly, subcutaneously, or intrathecally. Administration of the reconstituted injection directly into a vein or into the tubing of a running intravenous solution is recommended. Extravasation must be avoided because of possible severe tissue irritation. (38)

A sticker is provided in the vindesine sulphate package that must be affixed directly to the container of the individual dose that states (38):

Fatal if given intrathecally. For intravenous use only.

In addition, the container holding an individual dose must be packaged in an overwrap which is labeled (38):

Do not remove covering until moment of injection.
Fatal if given intrathecally. For intravenous use only.

Stability — Intact vials should be refrigerated at 2 to 8 °C. The reconstituted solution is stable under refrigeration for 28 days when reconstituted with bacteriostatic sodium chloride 0.9% containing benzyl alcohol 2%. If reconstituted with a non-bacteriostatic diluent, the reconstituted solution is stable for 24 hours under refrigeration. (38)

Vindesine sulphate, reconstituted according to the manufacturer's instructions, was cultured with human lymphoblasts to determine whether its cytotoxic activity was retained. The solution retained cytotoxicity for 24 hours at 4 °C and room temperature. (1575)

pH Effects — Vindesine sulphate is most stable at pH 1.9. (1369) It may precipitate in a solution with a pH greater than 6. Therefore, multi-electrolyte solutions such as Ringer's injection, lactated, are not recommended. (234)

Freezing Solutions — Vindesine sulphate (Lilly) 20 μg/ml in dextrose 5% in water, Ringer's injection, lactated, or sodium chloride 0.9% underwent no degradation after four weeks when frozen at −20 °C. (1195)

Sorption — Vindesine sulphate (Lilly) 4 mg/250 ml in dextrose 5% in water or sodium chloride 0.9% in PVC bags was infused over two hours at 2.08 ml/min through PVC sets at 22 °C while protected from light. HPLC of the effluent solution found no loss due to sorption to the plastic. (1631)

Compatibility Information

Solution Compatibility

Vindesine sulphate

Solution	*Mfr*	*Mfr*	*Conc/L*	*Remarks*	*Ref*	*C/I*
Dextrose 5% in water		LI	20 mg	Physically compatible with little or no loss in 21 days at 4 and 25 °C in the dark	1195	C
	[a]	LI	20 mg	Little or no loss by HPLC in 7 days at 4 °C protected from light	1631	C
	MG, TR[b]	LI	47.6 mg	Less than 10% loss by HPLC in 24 hr at room temperature exposed to light	1658	C
Ringer's injection, lactated		LI	20 mg	Physically compatible with little or no loss in 21 days at 4 and 25 °C in the dark	1195	C
Sodium chloride 0.9%		LI	20 mg	Physically compatible with little or no loss in 21 days at 4 and 25 °C in the dark	1195	C
	[a]	LI	20 mg	No loss by HPLC in 7 days at 4 °C protected from light	1631	C

[a]*Tested in PVC containers.*
[b]*Tested in both glass and PVC containers.*

APPENDIX I: Parenteral Nutrition Formulas

The following tables summarize the composition of the total parenteral nutrition mixtures that are referenced throughout the *Handbook on Injectable Drugs*. Each unique formula that has been tested for stability and/or compatibility characteristics, alone or in combination with other drugs, is described and assigned a code number. These code numbers are used in the drug monographs to denote the TNA (3-in-1) or TPN (2-in-1) formulation being discussed (i.e., TPN #183, TPN #184, etc.). The TNA and TPN formulations are described as completely as possible from the original published sources.

The consolidation of the formulations into a single appendix is designed to avoid unnecessary repetition and to facilitate comparisons among different mixtures.

		Concentration per Liter									
Component	Mfr	#1	#2	#3	#4	#5	#6	#7	#8	#9	#10
Amino acids	CU	4%	4%	4%	4%	4%	4%	4%	4%	4%	4%
Dextrose	CU	25%	25%	25%	25%	25%	25%	25%	25%	25%	25%
Calcium gluconate	PR	10 mEq	20 mEq	15 mEq	10 mEq	20 mEq	15 mEq	10 mEq	20 mEq	15 mEq	
Potassium phosphate	MG	20 mEq	25 mEq	40 mEq	20 mEq	25 mEq	40 mEq	20 mEq	25 mEq	40 mEq	
Folic acid	LE				5 mg	5 mg	5 mg	5 mg	5 mg	5 mg	
Cyanocobalamin	SQ				1 mg	1 mg	1 mg	1 mg	1 mg	1 mg	
Multivitamin concentrate	USV							5 ml	5 ml	5 ml	
Vitamin B complex with C	UP				10 ml	10 ml	10 ml				

		Concentration per Liter									
Component	Mfr	#11	#12	#13	#14	#15	#16	#17	#18	#19	#20
Amino acids	CU	4%	4%	4%	4%	4%	4%	4%	4%	4%	4%
Dextrose	CU	25%	25%	25%	25%	25%	25%	25%	25%	25%	25%
Calcium gluconate	PR	10 mEq	20 mEq	25 mEq	15 mEq	40 mEq	10 mEq	20 mEq	25 mEq	15 mEq	40 mEq
Potassium phosphate	MG	10 mEq	25 mEq	20 mEq	40 mEq	15 mEq	10 mEq	25 mEq	20 mEq	40 mEq	15 mEq
Folic acid	LE	5 mg	5 mg	5 mg	5 mg	5 mg					
Cyanocobalamin	SQ	1 mg	1 mg	1 mg	1 mg	1 mg					
Phytonadione	MSD	10 mg	10 mg	10 mg	10 mg	10 mg					
Multivitamin concentrate	USV										
or		10 ml	10 ml	10 ml	10 ml	10 ml					
Vitamin B complex with C	UP										

		Concentration per Liter			
Component	Mfr	#21	#22	#23	#24
Amino acids	MG	200 ml			
Amino acids 8.5%	TR		500 ml		
Amino acids 8.5% with electrolytes	TR			500 ml	500 ml
Dextrose 50% in water		400 ml		500 ml	500 ml
Dextrose 33.3% in water			500 ml		
Phosphate		15 mEq[a]	30 mEq		30 mEq[a]
Acetate		15 mEq[a]	67.5 mEq		
Calcium gluconate		2 g	9 mEq	1 g	
Calcium chloride			7.2 mEq		
Potassium chloride			70 mEq		20 mEq
Sodium chloride		40 mEq	55 mEq		60 mEq
Magnesium sulfate		8.1 mEq			
Multivitamins		10 ml			
Multivitamin concentrate				5 ml	
Water for injection		qs 1000 ml			
Trace elements			present		

[a]*Potassium salt.*

Component	Mfr	Concentration per Liter #25	#26	#27	#28	#29	#30
Amino acids (Aminosyn)	AB	3.5%			1%		
Amino acids (FreAmine III)	MG		4.25%			1%	
Amino acids (Travasol)	TR			4.25%			1%
Dextrose		25%	25%	25%	25%	25%	25%
Sodium phosphate	AB	10 mmol	10 mmol	10 mmol	10 mmol	10 mmol	10 mmol
Multivitamins (M.V.I.-12)	USV	10 ml	10 ml	10 ml	10 ml	10 ml	10 ml
Multielectrolyte concentrate[a]	SE	25 ml	25 ml	25 ml	25 ml	25 ml	25 ml
Trace mineral injection[b]		3.5 ml	3.5 ml	3.5 ml	3.5 ml	3.5 ml	3.5 ml

[a]*Each 25 ml provides: sodium, 25 mEq; potassium, 40.5 mEq; calcium, 5 mEq; magnesium, 8 mEq; chloride, 33.5 mEq; acetate, 40.6 mEq; and gluconate, 5 mEq.*
[b]*Each 3.5 ml provides: zinc, 2 mg; copper, 1 mg; manganese, 0.5 mg; and chromium, 10 μg.*

Component	Mfr	Concentration per Liter #31	#32	#33	#34	#35	#36	#37
Amino acids	TR	4.2%	4.2%	4.2%	4.2%	4.2%	4.2%	4.2%
Dextrose		25%	25%	25%	25%	25%	25%	25%
Sodium		29 mEq	29 mEq	29 mEq	29 mEq	69 mEq	69 mEq	69 mEq
Potassium		25 mEq	25 mEq	25 mEq	25 mEq	46 mEq	46 mEq	46 mEq
Calcium		9 mEq	9 mEq	9 mEq	4.5 mEq	9.5 mEq	9.5 mEq	9.5 mEq
Magnesium		4 mEq	4 mEq	4 mEq	4 mEq	12 mEq	12 mEq	12 mEq
Phosphorus		388 mg	388 mg	388 mg	388 mg	388 mg	388 mg	388 mg
Chloride		29 mEq	29 mEq	29 mEq	29 mEq	103 mEq	103 mEq	103 mEq
Acetate		63 mEq	63 mEq	63 mEq	63 mEq	63 mEq	63 mEq	63 mEq
Trace elements			a,b	a		a,b	a,b	a,b
Multivitamins	USV			10 ml			5 ml	5 ml
Vitamin B complex with C plus folic acid (Soluzyme)	UP			5 ml				5 ml

[a]*Trace elements: selenium, 120 μg; chromium, 2 μg; zinc, 3 mg; and manganese, 0.7 mg.*
[b]*Trace elements: iodine, 120 μg; and copper, 1 mg.*

Component	Mfr	Concentration per Liter #38	#39	#40	#41	#42	#43	#44	#45	#46	#47
Amino acids	CU	4%	4%	4%	4%	4%	4%	4%	4%	4%	4%
Dextrose	CU	25%	25%	25%	25%	25%	25%	25%	25%	25%	25%
Calcium gluconate	PR	10 mEq	20 mEq	25 mEq	15 mEq	40 mEq	10 mEq	20 mEq	25 mEq	15 mEq	40 mEq
Potassium phosphate	MG	10 mEq	25 mEq	20 mEq	40 mEq	15 mEq	10 mEq	25 mEq	20 mEq	40 mEq	15 mEq
Folic acid	LE						5 mg	5 mg	5 mg	5 mg	5 mg
Cyanocobalamin	SQ						1 mg	1 mg	1 mg	1 mg	1 mg
Phytonadione	MSD						10 mg	10 mg	10 mg	10 mg	10 mg
Multivitamin concentrate	USV										
or		5 and	5 and	5 and	5 and	5 and	10 ml	10 ml	10 ml	10 ml	10 ml
Vitamin B complex with C	UP	10 ml	10 ml	10 ml	10 ml	10 ml					

Component	Concentration per Liter #48	#49	#50	#51
Amino acids	5%	5%	5%	5%
Dextrose	5%	5%	25%	25%
Vitamins	present		present	
Trace elements		present		present

Component	Mfr	Concentration per Liter #52	#53	#54	#55	#56
Amino acids	VT	7%	2.3%			
Amino acids	AB			1.5%		
Amino acids (FreAmine III)	MG				3%	3%
Dextrose			6.5%	15%	25%	25%
Fructose		10%	3.2%			
Sodium		50 mmol	16.2 mmol	[a]	35 mEq	35 mEq
Potassium		20 mmol	18.4 mmol	[a]		
Calcium		2.5 mmol	4.9 mmol	300 mg	5 mEq[b]	5 mEq[b]
Magnesium		1.5 mmol	2.1 mmol		8 mEq	8 mEq
Phosphorus				155 mg		
Phosphate			12.1 mmol[c]		40 mEq[d]	40 mEq[d]
Chloride		55 mmol	17.8 mmol	[e]	35 mEq	35 mEq
Laevulate calcium			9.8 mmol			
Folic acid				0.5 mg		
Cyanocobalamin				[f]		
Phytonadione				0.2 mg		
Multivitamins			present	4 ml		10 ml
Vitamin B complex with C (Berocca-C)				0.2 ml		

[a]*Adjusted to provide 2.5 mEq/kg/day.*
[b]*Present as the gluconate.*
[c]*Anion not specified.*
[d]*Present as the potassium salt.*
[e]*Adjusted to provide 5 mEq/kg/day.*
[f]*Present but concentration not specified.*

Component	Mfr	Concentration per Liter #57	#58[a]	#59	#60	#61
Amino acids	MG	2.125%	4.25%			
Amino acids	TR				2.125%	
Amino acids	AB					3%
Amino acids with electrolytes	TR			4.25%		
Dextrose		10%	25%	25%	25%	20%
Sodium		40 mEq	100 mmol	50 mEq	50 mEq	30 mEq
Potassium		30 mEq	60 to 80 mmol			25 mEq
Calcium		15 mEq	5 mmol	5 mEq	5 mEq	15 mEq
Magnesium		12.5 mEq	5 mmol	5 mEq	5 mEq	10 mEq
Phosphorus		6 mmol	10 mmol	465 mg	465 mg	15 mmol
Chloride		40 mEq	100 mmol	50 mEq	50 mEq	
Heparin sodium			1000 units	500 units	500 units	
Phytonadione				1 mg	1 mg	
Multivitamins			10 ml	10 ml	10 ml	2 ml
Multivitamin concentrate		2 ml				
Iron			1 mg			
Trace elements		present	present	present	present	present

[a]*Concentration per 1200 ml.*

Component	Mfr	Component Amounts #62	#63	#64	#65	#66	#67	#68
Amino acids 8.5% (FreAmine III)	MG	500 ml	500 ml			500 ml		
Amino acids 5.4% (Nephramine)	MG			500 ml			500 ml	
Amino acids 5.2% (Aminosyn RF)	AB				500 ml			500 ml
Dextrose 50%	MG	500 ml	500 ml	500 ml	500 ml	500 ml	500 ml	500 ml
Hyperlyte (electrolyte) concentrate	MG		25 ml					
Fat emulsion 10%, intravenous	CU					500 ml	500 ml	500 ml
Multivitamins (M.V.I.-12)	USV	[a]	[a]	[a]	[a]	[a]	[a]	[a]

[a]*Tested both with and without multivitamins.*

Component	Mfr	Component Amounts		
		#69	#70	#71
Amino acids 8.5% (FreAmine II)	MG	1000 ml		
Amino acids 8.5% with electrolytes	TR			1500 ml[a]
Amino acids 7%	AB		500 ml	
Dextrose 50% in water		500 ml	500 ml	1500 ml
Dextrose 20% with electrolyte pattern A	TR	500 ml[b]		
Dextrose 20% in water		500 ml		
Sodium chloride 0.9%		500 ml		
Potassium chloride		20 mmol		
Calcium gluconate 10%				30 ml
Multivitamins		1 ampul		10 ml
Multivitamin concentrate			5 ml	
Folic acid		1 mg	0.25, 0.5, 0.75, 1 mg	
Trace elements				present

[a]*Each 1500 ml provides: sodium, 105 mEq; potassium, 90 mEq; magnesium, 15 mEq; chloride, 105 mEq; acetate, 203 mEq; and phosphate, 45 mmol.*
[b]*Each 500 ml provides: magnesium, 14 mmol; calcium, 13 mmol; chloride, 54 mmol; acetate, 0.08 mmol; zinc, 0.04 mmol; and manganese, 0.02 mmol.*

Component	Mfr	Component Amounts			
		#72	#73	#74	#75
Amino acids 10%	TR	750 ml	750 ml		
Amino acids 8.5%	TR			500 ml	
Amino acids 8.5%	MG				500 ml
Dextrose 70%		429 ml	429 ml		300 ml
Dextrose 50%				500 ml	
Fat emulsion 20%, intravenous	TR	225 ml	225 ml		
Sterile water for injection		24.2 ml	15 ml		300 ml
Calcium gluconate 10%		20 ml	20 ml		
Calcium gluceptate					8 mEq
Sodium phosphate			15 mmol		
Potassium phosphate		20 mmol		30 mEq	18 mEq
Potassium chloride		30 mEq	40 mEq	20 mEq	20 mEq
Magnesium sulfate 50%		2 ml	2 ml		8 mEq
Sodium chloride		60 mEq	60 mEq	40 mEq	60 mEq
Sodium acetate					5 mEq
Heparin sodium			6000 units		
Multivitamins		10 ml	10 ml		
Trace elements		present	present		

Component	Mfr	Concentration per Liter				
		#76	#77	#78	#79	#80
Amino acids	CU	4%	4%	4%	4%	4%
Dextrose	CU	25%	25%	25%	25%	25%
Calcium gluconate	PR	10 mEq	20 mEq	25 mEq	15 mEq	40 mEq
Potassium phosphate	MG	10 mEq	25 mEq	20 mEq	40 mEq	15 mEq
Cyanocobalamin	SQ	0.5 and 1 mg	0.5 and 1 mg	0.5 and 1 mg	0.5 and 1 mg	0.5 and 1 mg

Component	Mfr	Concentration per Liter				
		#81	#82	#83	#84	#85
Amino acids	CU	4%	4%	4%	4%	4%
Dextrose	CU	25%	25%	25%	25%	25%
Calcium gluconate	PR	10 mEq	20 mEq	25 mEq	40 mEq	15 mEq
Potassium phosphate	MG	10 mEq	25 mEq	20 mEq	15 mEq	40 mEq
Other components		a	a	a	a	a

[a]*Tested with each of the following individually: folic acid (Lederle), 2.5 and 5 mg; cyanocobalamin (Squibb), 0.5 and 1 mg; phytonadione (MSD), 5 and 10 mg; multivitamin concentrate (USV), 5 and 10 ml; and vitamin B complex with C (Upjohn), 5 and 10 ml.*

Component	Mfr	Concentration per Liter		
		#86	#87	#88
Amino acids (Aminosyn)	AB	2.5%	4.25%	5%
Dextrose		10%	25%	35%
Calcium		4.5 mEq	4.5 mEq	4.5 mEq
Magnesium		5 mEq	5 mEq	5 mEq
Potassium		23 mEq	40 mEq	40 mEq
Sodium		47 mEq	35 mEq	35 mEq
Acetate		82 mEq	74.5 mEq	74.5 mEq
Chloride		35 mEq	52.5 mEq	52.5 mEq
Phosphorus		9 mmol	12 mmol	12 mmol
Heparin sodium		1000 units	1000 units	1000 units
Insulin		[a]	[a]	[a]

[a]*Insulin 10 to 40 units/L.*

Component	Concentration per Liter	
	#89	#90
Amino acids (Travasol)	4.25%	
Amino acids with electrolytes (Travasol with electrolytes)		4.25%
Dextrose	25%	25%

Component	Mfr	Concentration per 100 ml	Concentration per 2L
		#91	#92
Amino acids 10%		1.6 ml	
Nitrogen (from amino acids)	PFM		14 g
Dextrose 5% in water		15 ml	
Dextrose 50% in water			500 ml
Fat emulsion 20%, intravenous	KA		500 ml
Sodium		3 mEq	150 mEq
Potassium		2.2 mEq	120 mEq
Calcium		1 mEq	15 mEq
Magnesium		0.3 mEq	30 mEq
Phosphate		0.5 mmol	30 mmol
Chloride		2.5 mEq	150 mEq
Sulfate			30 mEq
Acetate			90 mEq
Pediatric multivitamins		5 ml	
Multivitamins			present
Trace elements		[a]	present
Heparin sodium		100 units	
Water for injection			qs 2000 ml

[a]*Trace elements: zinc, 600 μg; copper, 40 μg; manganese, 10 μg; and chromium, 0.4 μg.*

Component	Mfr	Concentration per Liter #93	#94	#95	#96
Amino acids	TR	4.25%	4.25%		
Amino acids	AB			3%	3%
Dextrose		25%	25%	20%	20%
Potassium chloride		15 mEq	15 mEq	25 mEq	25 mEq
Sodium chloride		15 mEq	15 mEq	30 mEq	30 mEq
Calcium gluconate		4.7 mEq	4.7 mEq	15 mEq	15 mEq
Magnesium sulfate		4.05 mEq	4.05 mEq	10 mEq	10 mEq
Potassium phosphate		5 mEq	5 mEq	15 mmol	15 mmol
Sodium phosphate		10 mEq	10 mEq		
Zinc		1.5 mg	1.5 mg	3 mg	3 mg
Manganese		150 μg	150 μg	50 μg	50 μg
Chromium		6 μg	6 μg	2 μg	2 μg
Selenium		30 μg	30 μg		
Copper			600 μg	200 μg	200 μg
Multivitamins	LY			2 ml	2 ml
Heparin sodium	IX			1000 units	

Component	Mfr	Milliliters per Container #97	#98	#99	#100	#101	#102	#103	#104
Amino acids 8.5% (FreAmine III)	MG	10	10	10	10	75	75	75	75
Dextrose 70%		89	36	89	36	89	36	89	36
Fat emulsion 20%, intravenous (Intralipid)	KV	5	5	75	75	5	5	50	50
Sterile water qs ad		250	250	250	250	250	250	250	250
Other components		[a]	[a]	[a]	[a]	[a]	[a]	[a]	[a]

[a]*Each TNA admixture also contained: sodium, 25 mEq; potassium, 25 mEq; calcium, 5 mEq; magnesium, 25 mEq; chloride, 30 mEq; acetate, 7.5 mEq; lactate, 10.5 mEq; phosphate 1.5 mmol; multivitamins (M.V.I. Pediatric), 2.5 ml; trace elements; and heparin sodium, 250 units.*

Component	Mfr	Concentration per Liter #105	#106	#107	#108
Amino acids	TR	1.65%	4.25%	1.5%	1.5%
Dextrose		10%	10%	15%	15%
Sodium		21 mEq	35 mEq		
Potassium		18 mEq	30 mEq		
Magnesium		3 mEq	5 mEq		
Calcium		15 mEq	10 mEq		
Phosphate		10 mmol	15 mmol		
Chloride		21 mEq	35 mEq		
Acetate		30 mEq	68 mEq		
Pediatric multivitamins		1 ml	1 ml		
Trace elements		0.1 ml	0.1 ml		
Unspecified electrolytes and vitamins				present	present

Component	Mfr	Concentration per Liter				
		#109	#110	#111	#112	#113
Amino acids (FreAmine III)	MG	4.25%	2%	4.25%	2.125%	
Amino acids (Travasol)	TR					4.25%
Fat emulsion 20%, intravenous (Intralipid)	KV			200 ml	125 ml	
Dextrose		25%	25%	20%	25%	25%
Sodium		50 mEq	50 mEq	50 mEq	50 mEq	35 mEq
Potassium		40 mEq	40 mEq	40 mEq	40 mEq	30 mEq
Chloride		40 mEq	40 mEq	[a]	[a]	35 mEq
Phosphorus		13 mmol	13 mmol	6 mmol	6 mmol	15 mmol
Acetate		31 mEq	31 mEq	[a]	[a]	70.5 mEq
Calcium		16.7 mEq	16.7 mEq	10 mEq	10 mEq	4.7 mEq
Magnesium		10 mEq	10 mEq	5 mEq	5 mEq	5 mEq
Multivitamins		4 ml	4 ml	3.33 ml	3.33 ml	
Trace elements		present	present	present	present	present
Heparin sodium		1000 units	1000 units	1000 units	1000 units	
Sterile water		qs	qs	qs	qs	

[a] *Not cited.*

Component	Concentration per Liter				
	#114	#115	#116	#117	#118
Nitrogen (from amino acids)	7 g				
Amino acids (Travasol)		3.5%	3.5%	4.5%	3.7%
Dextrose	12.5%	17.5%	35%	22.7%	18.5%
Fat emulsion, intravenous	50 g[a]				3.7%
Sodium	75 mEq	66.7 mmol	66.7 mmol	45 mEq	45 mEq
Potassium	60 mEq	50 mmol	50 mmol	40 mEq	40 mEq
Magnesium	15 mEq	4.16 mmol	4.16 mmol	8 mEq	8 mEq
Calcium	7.5 mEq	4.16 mmol	4.16 mmol	5 mEq	5 mEq
Chloride	75 mEq	66.7 mmol	66.7 mmol	53 mEq	53 mEq
Phosphorus	15 mmol	8.3 mmol	8.3 mmol	15 mmol	15 mmol
Sulfate	15 mEq				
Acetate	45 mEq	90.8 mmol	90.8 mmol	84 mEq	84 mEq
Trace elements	present	present	present		
Multivitamins	present	8.3 ml	8.3 ml		
Sterile water for injection	qs				
Iron		833 µg	833 µg		
Heparin sodium		1000 units	1000 units		

[a]*Both Intralipid (long-chain triglycerides) and MCT/LCT (medium- and long-chain triglycerides) tested.*

Component	Mfr	Concentration per Liter						
		#119	#120	#121	#122	#123	#124	#125
Amino acids	TR	4.25%	4.25%	5%	5%	1%	2%	
Amino acids (TrophAmine)	MG							2%
Dextrose		35%	35%	20%	14.3%	10%	10%	10%
Fat emulsion					5.7%			
Sodium chloride		50 mEq	50 mEq	20 mEq	4 mEq	16 mEq	16 mEq	16 mEq
Potassium chloride				20 mEq	30 mEq	5 mEq	5 mEq	5 mEq
Potassium phosphate		30 mEq	30 mEq		3 mmol	10 to 40 mmol	10 to 40 mmol	10 to 40 mmol
Magnesium sulfate		10 mEq	10 mEq	8 mEq	12 mEq	4 mEq	4 mEq	4 mEq
Calcium gluconate		4.7 mEq	4.7 mEq	4.8 mEq	4 mEq	10 to 40 mEq	10 to 40 mEq	10 to 40 mEq
Sodium phosphates				20 mEq				
Sodium acetate					20 mEq	10 mEq	10 mEq	10 mEq
Cysteine HCl								1 g
Mixed electrolytes	LY				27 ml			
Trace Elements		1 ml	1 ml	present	3 ml			
Heparin sodium			1000 units					
Multivitamins				10 ml	10 ml			
Phytonadione					1 mg			
Cimetidine HCl					1 g			

Component	Mfr	Concentration per Liter							
		#126	#127	#128	#129	#130	#131	#132	#133
Amino acids (Aminosyn II)	AB	2%	3.3%	3.6%	3.6%	5%	3.5%	3.5%	
Amino acids (Travasol)	TR								4.25%
Dextrose		14.8%	3.3%	23.3%	20.8%	10%	25%	25%	25%
Fat emulsion, intravenous (Liposyn II)	AB	1.2%	3.3%	3.3%	2%	7.1%			
Sodium		39.5 mEq	51.7 mEq	48.4 mEq	96.3 mEq	49.4 mEq	33.6 mEq	33.6 mEq	75 mEq
Potassium		27 mEq	13.3 mEq	21.4 mEq	60 mEq	78.6 mEq	35.6 mEq	35.6 mEq	20 mEq
Calcium		6.6 mEq	3 mEq	6.7 mEq	10 mEq	13.4 mEq	4.5 mEq	4.5 mEq	9.6 mEq
Magnesium		3.2 mEq	3.3 mEq	10 mEq	12 mEq	14.5 mEq	5 mEq	5 mEq	10 mEq
Phosphate		5.5 mmol	10 mmol	10 mmol	15 mmol	21.4 mmol	12 mmol	12 mmol	10 mEq
Chloride		57.9 mEq	23.3 mEq	40 mEq	80 mEq	73.9 mEq	35 mEq	35 mEq	85 mEq
Acetate		21.9 mEq	43.6 mEq	23.9 mEq	65.8 mEq	35.9 mEq	35.7 mEq	35.7 mEq	
Trace elements		present	present	present	present	present		present	3 ml
Multivitamins (M.V.I.-12)								present	10 ml

Component	Mfr	Concentration per Liter						
		#134	#135	#136	#137	#138	#139	#140
Amino acids (Travasol)	BA	5.8%	5.8%	5.8%	5.8%	5.8%	5.7%	6%
Dextrose	BA	23.7%	23.7%	23.7%	23.7%	23.7%	23.4%	25%
Fat emulsion, intravenous (Intralipid)	KV		3%	5%			3%	
Fat emulsion, intravenous (Liposyn II)	AB				3%	5%		
Potassium chloride		54.2 mEq	54.2 mEq	54.2 mEq	54.2 mEq	54.2 mEq	32.2 mEq	30 mEq
Sodium chloride		108 mEq	108 mEq	108 mEq	108 mEq	108 mEq	64.4 mEq	110 mEq
Calcium gluconate 10%		13.6 ml	13.6 ml	13.6 ml	13.6 ml	13.6 ml	8 ml	10 ml
Magnesium sulfate 50%		1.4 ml	1.4 ml	1.4 ml	1.4 ml	1.4 ml	0.8 ml	4 ml
Potassium phosphate		20.3 mmol	20.3 mmol	20.3 mmol	20.3 mmol	20.3 mmol	36 mmol	
Multivitamins		6.8 ml	6.8 ml	6.8 ml	6.8 ml	6.8 ml	4 ml	1 vial
Trace elements		present	present	present	present	present	present	present
Phytonadione								1 mg

Component	Mfr	Concentration per Liter			
		#141	#142	#143	#144
Amino acids	AB		2.5%	5%	
Amino acids (Travasol)	TR				4.25%
Dextrose		25%	25%	25%	25%
Sodium		50 mEq	50 mEq	50 mEq	22.5 mEq
Potassium		40 mEq	40 mEq	40 mEq	20 mEq
Magnesium		5 mEq	5 mEq	5 mEq	2.85 mEq
Calcium		5 mEq	5 mEq	5 mEq	4.25 mEq
Phosphorus		15 mmol	15 mmol	15 mmol	15.75 mmol
Chloride		58 mEq	58 mEq	58 mEq	17 mEq
Acetate					58 mEq
Multivitamins		10 ml	10 ml	10 ml	
Trace elements		1 ml	1 ml	1 ml	present
Heparin sodium	UP	500 units	500 units	500 units	
Sterile water for injection					qs

Component	Mfr	Concentration per Liter			
		#145	#146	#147	#148
Amino acids (Travasol)	BA	5%			
Amino acids	AB		5%	2.5%	1%
Dextrose		15%	25%	25%	25%
Sodium		45 mEq	35 mEq	35 mEq	35 mEq
Potassium		15 mEq	40 mEq	40 mEq	40 mEq
Chloride		20 mEq	35 mEq	35 mEq	35 mEq
Phosphorus		16 mmol	12 mmol	12 mmol	12 mmol
Acetate		81 mEq	82 mEq	82 mEq	82 mEq
Calcium		20 mEq	9 mEq	9 mEq	9 mEq
Magnesium			5 mEq	5 mEq	5 mEq

Component	Component Amounts									
	#149	#150	#151	#152	#153	#154	#155	#156	#157	#158
Amino acids 10% (TrophAmine)	50 ml	50 ml	50 ml	50 ml	350 ml	350 ml	350 ml	350 ml	50 ml	350 ml
Dextrose	10%	10%	10%	10%	25%	25%	25%	25%	25%	25%
Fat emulsion 20%, intravenous[a]	25 ml	25 ml	70 ml	70 ml	25 ml	25 ml	70 ml	70 ml	100 ml	100 ml
Sodium	25 mEq	100 mEq	25 mEq	100 mEq	25 mEq	100 mEq	25 mEq	100 mEq	100 mEq	100 mEq
Potassium	15 mEq	80 mEq	15 mEq	80 mEq	15 mEq	80 mEq	15 mEq	80 mEq	80 mEq	80 mEq
Chloride	25 mEq	100 mEq	25 mEq	100 mEq	25 mEq	100 mEq	25 mEq	100 mEq	100 mEq	100 mEq
Calcium	7 mEq	18 mEq	7 mEq	18 mEq	7 mEq	18 mEq	7 mEq	18 mEq	18 mEq	18 mEq
Magnesium	2.5 mEq	13 mEq	2.5 mEq	13 mEq	2.5 mEq	13 mEq	2.5 mEq	13 mEq	13 mEq	13 mEq
Phosphate	3.4 mmol	9 mmol	3.4 mmol	9 mmol	3.4 mmol	9 mmol	3.4 mmol	9 mmol	9 mmol	9 mmol
Trace elements	present	present	present	present	present	present	present	present	present	present
Multivitamins (M.V.I. Pediatric)	5 ml	5 ml	5 ml	5 ml	5 ml	5 ml	5 ml	5 ml	5 ml	5 ml
Heparin	1000 units	1000 units	1000 units	1000 units	1000 units	1000 units	1000 units	1000 units	1000 units	1000 units

[a]*Intralipid 20%, Liposyn II 20%, and Nutrilipid 20% were each tested.*

Component	Mfr	Component Amounts							
		#159	#160	#161	#162	#163	#164	#165	#166
Amino acids 5.5% with electrolytes (Travasol)	BA	100 ml	100 ml	400 ml	400 ml	400 ml	400 ml	100 ml	100 ml
Fat emulsion 20%, intravenous (Intralipid)	KV	100 ml		200 ml		100 ml		200 ml	
Fat emulsion 20%, intravenous (Liposyn II)	AB		100 ml		200 ml		100 ml		200 ml
Heparin sodium 1000 units/ml	ES	5 ml	5 ml	5 ml	5 ml	5 ml	5 ml	5 ml	5 ml
Dextrose 10%		795 ml	795 ml					695 ml	695 ml
Dextrose 20%				395 ml	395 ml	495 ml	495 ml		

Component	Component Amounts						
	#167	#168	#169	#170	#171	#172	#173
Aminoplex 12			500 ml		1000 ml		
Aminoplex 24	500 ml	500 ml	500 ml	500 ml			
Vamin glucose							1000 ml
Lipofundin S 20%	500 ml	500 ml	500 ml	500 ml	500 ml		
Fat emulsion 10%, intravenous (Intralipid)						300 ml	
Glucoplex 1000	1000 ml						
Glucoplex 1600		1000 ml	1000 ml		500 ml		
Dextrose 5%					1000 ml		
Dextrose 50%				500 ml			1000 ml
Potassium chloride 15%		37.5 ml		10 ml			
Potassium phosphate 17%	20 ml	20 ml	20 ml	20 ml	10 ml		
Sodium chloride 30%		27 ml		15 ml			
Addamel	10 ml	10 ml	10 ml	10 ml	10 ml		10 ml
Soluvit						7.5 ml	
Vitalipid infant						15 ml	
Pancebrin							10 ml

Component	Mfr	Concentration per Liter					
		#174	#175	#176	#177	#178	#179
Amino acids	AB	25 g	50 g	15 g			
Amino acids	TR				3%		
Nitrogen						7.9 g	7 g
Dextrose		125 g	250 g	100 g	5%	100 g	125 g
Fat emulsion, intravenous (Intralipid)	KV					50 g	5 g
TPN II electrolytes	AB	20 ml	20 ml				
Sodium		26.3 mEq	37.5 mEq	40 mEq	46 mEq	24 mmol	75 mEq
Potassium		35.5 mEq	40 mEq	50 mEq	40 mEq	12.5 mmol	60 mEq
Magnesium		5 mEq	5 mEq	10 mEq	8 mEq	2.5 mmol	15 mEq
Calcium		9 mEq	4.5 mEq	10 mEq	5 mEq		7.5 mEq
Phosphorus		12 mmol	45 mmol	5 mmol	12 mmol	4.5 mmol	15 mmol
Chloride		35 mEq	35 mEq	47.6 mEq	57 mEq	7 mmol	75 mEq
Acetate		25 mEq	43 mEq	31.8 mEq	61 mEq	40.5 mmol	45 mEq
Gluconate				10 mEq			
Sulfate				10 mEq			15 mEq
Trace elements			present	present	present	present	present
Multivitamins (M.V.I. Pediatric)		3 ml		3 ml			
Multivitamins (M.V.I. 9+3)			10 ml				
Multivitamins					10 ml	present	present
Vitamin K			5 mg				
Heparin sodium		1000 units	1000 units	1000 units	1000 units		
Sterile water qs ad		1000 ml	1000 ml	1000 ml		1000 ml	1000 ml

Component	Component Amounts	
	#180	#181
Amino acids 10%	1000 ml	400 ml
Dextrose 50% in water	500 ml	500 ml
Fat emulsion 20%, intravenous (Intralipid)	500 ml	
Sodium	40 mmol	41 mEq
Potassium	70 mmol	22.7 mEq
Calcium	4.6 mmol	5 mEq
Magnesium	5 mmol	5 mEq
Phosphorus	17.5 mmol	12 mmol
Chloride	120 mmol	30 mEq
Acetate	45 mmol	89 mEq
Trace elements		present
Multivitamins		10 ml

Component	Mfr	Concentration per Liter
		#182
Amino acids	KV	5%
Dextrose		25%
Fat emulsion, intravenous (Intralipid)	KV	2.25%
Potassium phosphate		10 mmol
Potassium chloride		45 mEq
Sodium chloride		75 mEq
Magnesium sulfate		8 mEq
Calcium gluconate		47 mg
Trace elements		present
Multivitamins		5 ml
Sterile water qs ad		1000 ml

Component	Mfr	Component Amounts #183	#184	#185	#186[a]	#187[b]	#188[c]	#189
Amino acids (Aminosyn II)	AB	1%	2.5%	5%				
Amino acids (Aminosyn)	AB				15 g	25 g	50 g	
Amino acids 10% with electrolytes (Synthamin 17 with electrolytes)								500 ml
Dextrose	AB	10%	10%	25%	125 g	125 g	250 g	
Dextrose 50%								500 ml
TPN II electrolytes						1 ml	1 ml	
Calcium		9 mEq	4.4 mEq	5 mEq	1 mEq	9 mEq	4.5 mEq	2.2 mmol
Magnesium		5 mEq	5 mEq	5 mEq	1 mEq	5 mEq	5 mEq	2.5 mmol
Potassium		27 mEq	18 mEq	40 mEq	5 mEq	30 mEq	40 mEq	42.5 mmol
Sodium		24 mEq	38 mEq	42 mEq	4 mEq	35 mEq	37.65 mEq	45 mmol
Phosphorus		6 mmol	9 mmol	15 mmol	2 mmol	6 mmol	12 mmol	15 mmol
Chloride		35 mEq	35 mEq	43 mEq	5.7 mEq	46.9 mEq	39.4 mEq	55.65 mmol
Acetate		22 mEq	25 mEq	38 mEq	11.1 mEq	25.6 mEq	43.5 mEq	81.25 mmol
Gluconate					1.1 mEq	2.5 mEq	0.05 mEq	
Sulfate					1.1 mEq			
Trace elements		1 ml	1 ml	1 ml	0.6 ml	1 ml	1 ml	present
Multivitamins (M.V.I. Pediatric)	AST				3 ml	3 ml		
Multivitamins (M.V.I. 9+3)	AST						10 ml	
Heparin sodium	ES				1000 units	1000 units	1000 units	
Sterile water					qs	qs	qs	

[a]*Neonatal formula.*
[b]*Pediatric formula.*
[c]*Adult formula.*

Component	Mfr	Component Amounts #190	#191	#192
Amino acids (Aminosyn II 15%)	AB	333 ml		
Amino acids (Azonutril 25)			500 ml	
Amino acids				17 g
Dextrose 70%		500 ml		
Dextrose 50%			250 ml	
Dextrose 30%			750 ml	
Dextrose				42.4 g
Fat emulsion 20%, intravenous (Intralipid)			500 ml	24.2 g
Fat emulsion 20%, intravenous (Liposyn II)	AB	400 ml		
Sterile water		133 ml		
Sodium				55.7 mmol
Potassium				19.4 mmol
Magnesium				2.3 mmol
Calcium				1.5 to 150 mmol
Phosphate				21 to 300 mmol
Unspecified electrolytes		present		
Vitamins		present		present
Trace elements			present	present

Component	Mfr	Component Amounts #193
Amino acids 10%	CL	1000 ml
Dextrose 50%	CL	750 ml
Sodium chloride	AB	140 mEq
Potassium phosphates	AB	20 mmol
Calcium gluconate		4.8 mEq
Magnesium sulfate		40 mEq
Multivitamins	AST	10 ml
Trace elements	LY	3 ml
Famotidine		40 mg

Component	Concentration per Liter #194	#195
Amino acids	2.2%	2.2%
Dextrose	12.5%	20%
Sodium chloride	26 mEq	26 mEq
Potassium phosphates	15 mmol	15 mmol
Calcium gluconate	25 mEq	25 mEq
Magnesium sulfate	8 mEq	8 mEq
Potassium chloride	2 mEq	2 mEq
Heparin sodium	1000 units	1000 units
Cysteine	660 mg	660 mg
Trace elements	present	present
Multivitamins	20 ml	20 ml

Component	Mfr	Concentration per Liter				
		#196	#197	#198	#199	#200
Amino acids	BA	6%	6%	6%	6%	6%
Dextrose	BA	24%	24%	24%	24%	24%
Intralipid	KV		3%	5%		
Liposyn II	AB				3%	5%
Sodium chloride	LY	108 mEq	108 mEq	108 mEq	108 mEq	108 mEq
Potassium phosphates	AB	20 mmol	20 mmol	20 mmol	20 mmol	20 mmol
Calcium gluconate	LY	6.3 mEq	6.3 mEq	6.3 mEq	6.3 mEq	6.3 mEq
Magnesium sulfate	AST	5.6 mEq	5.6 mEq	5.6 mEq	5.6 mEq	5.6 mEq
Potassium chloride	AB	54 mEq	54 mEq	54 mEq	54 mEq	54 mEq
Trace elements	SO	present	present	present	present	present
Multivitamins	AR	6.8 ml	6.8 ml	6.8 ml	6.8 ml	6.8 ml

Component	Mfr	Concentration per Liter			
		#201	#202	#203[a]	#204[b]
Amino acids	BA	4.25%			
Amino acids	AB		4.25%		
Amino acids (TrophAmine)	MG			2%	3%
Dextrose		25%	25%	10%	20%
Sodium		35 mEq	35 mEq	38 mEq	77 mEq
Potassium		30 mEq	30 mEq	20 mEq	40 mEq
Calcium		5 mEq	9.4 mEq	600 mg	600 mg
Magnesium		3 mEq	10 mEq	2.5 mEq	2.5 mEq
Chloride		47 mEq	[c]	38 mEq	77 mEq
Phosphate		14.3 mEq	15 mmol	400 mg	400 mg
Acetate		67 mEq	50 mEq	29 mEq	58 mEq
L-cysteine				200 mg	300 mg
Trace elements			present	present	present
Multivitamins			present	present	present
Heparin					500 units

[a]*Calculated quantities from a pediatric peripheral line formula.*
[b]*Calculated quantities from a pediatric central line formula.*
[c]*Unspecified.*

Component	Mfr	Concentration per Liter	
		#205	#206
Amino acids	BA	5%	
Aminosyn	AB		2.125%
Dextrose		25%	20%
Intralipid	KA		
Liposyn II	AB		
Sodium chloride		75 mEq	30 mEq
Potassium chloride		60 mEq	30 mEq
Potassium phosphates		20 mmol	
Sodium phosphates			15 mmol
Calcium gluconate		10 mEq	14 mEq
Magnesium sulfate		10 mEq	50 mg
Trace elements		present	present
Multivitamins			
Heparin sodium		3000 to 20,000 units	

Component	Mfr	Concentration per Liter				
		#207	#208	#209	#210	#211
Amino acids (TrophAmine)	MG	0.5%	1%	1.5%	2%	2.5%
Dextrose		10%	10%	10%	10%	10%
Sodium chloride		20 mEq	20 mEq	20 mEq	20 mEq	20 mEq
Sodium acetate		10 mEq	10 mEq	10 mEq	10 mEq	10 mEq
Potassium acetate		5 mEq	5 mEq	5 mEq	5 mEq	5 mEq
Potassium phosphates		10 mmol	10 mmol	10 mmol	10 mmol	10 mmol
Calcium gluconate		20 mEq	20 mEq	20 mEq	20 mEq	20 mEq
Magnesium sulfate		4 mEq	4 mEq	4 mEq	4 mEq	4 mEq
Trace elements	FUJ	[a]	[a]	[a]	[a]	[a]
Multivitamins	AST	[b]	[b]	[b]	[b]	[b]
Heparin sodium		1000 units	1000 units	1000 units	1000 units	1000 units
L-Cysteine[c]		200 mg	400 mg	600 mg	800 mg	1 g

[a]*Tested with and without trace elements (Neotrace, Fujisawa).*
[b]*Tested with and without multivitamins (M.V.I. Pediatric, Astra) 3.5 ml/L.*
[c]*40 mg/g of protein.*

Component	Mfr	Concentration per Liter				
		#212	#213	#214	#215	#216[a]
Amino acids (Aminosyn II)	AB	3.5%		4.25%		
Amino acids (FreAmine III)	MG		3.5%		4.25%	
Amino acids (Travasol)	BA					0.5 to 5%
Dextrose		5%	5%	25%	25%	10 to 20%
Sterile water for injection		516.8 ml	516.75 ml	161 ml	158.6 ml	q.s.
Potassium phosphates		3.5 mmol	[b]	15 mmol	5.75 mmol[c]	0 to 20 mEq K[d]
Sodium chloride		25 mEq	37.5 mEq	25 mEq	40 mEq	0 to 44 mEq
Sodium acetate						0 to 40 mEq
Potassium chloride		35 mEq	40 mEq	18 mEq	25 mEq	0 to 20 mEq
Magnesium sulfate		8 mEq	8 mEq	8 mEq	8 mEq	4 mEq
Calcium gluconate		9.3 mEq	5 mEq	9.15 mEq	7.5 mEq	19.2 to 28.8 mEq
Multivitamins	AST	10 ml	10 ml	10 ml	10 ml	14 ml
Trace elements		present	present	present	present	present
Heparin sodium	ES					500 units
Ranitidine (as HCl)	GL					0 to 84 mg

[a]*Forty parenteral nutrition formulations within the ranges cited were tested. Specific formulations were not reported.*
[b]*No phosphates added. Phosphates from FreAmine III formulation yielded 3.5 mmol/L.*
[c]*Added phosphates indicated. All phosphates from addition plus FreAmine III formulation totaled 10 mmol/L.*
[d]*Reported as potassium concentration.*

Component	Mfr	Concentration per Liter			
		#217	#218	#219	#220
Amino acids		5%			
Amino acids	MG		3%	3%	
Amino acids	AB				3%
Dextrose		25%	5%	5%	5%
Intralipid	KA		2%		
Liposyn II	AB			2%	
Liposyn III	AB				2%
Sodium		50 mEq	43 mEq	43 mEq	41.6 mEq
Potassium		40 mEq	40 mEq	40 mEq	40 mEq
Chloride		58 mEq	45 mEq	45 mEq	35 mEq
Phosphorus		15 mmol	7.5 mmol	7.5 mmol	15 mmol
Calcium		5 mEq	5 mEq	5 mEq	9.15 mEq
Magnesium		8 mEq	8 mEq	8 mEq	8 mEq
Acetate			51.7 mEq	51.7 mEq	42 mEq
Heparin sodium		1000 units			
Multivitamins		10 ml	10 ml	10 ml	10 ml
Phytonadione		1 mg			
Trace elements		2 ml	1 ml	1 ml	1 ml
Sterile water for injection			qs	qs	qs

Component	Mfr	Concentration per Liter #221	#222	#223	#224	#225	#226
Amino acids	MG	4.9%	4.9%			6%	6%
Amino acids	AB			4.9%	6%		
Dextrose		20%	20%	20%	11%	10.7%	10.7%
Intralipid	KA		3.5%				4%
Liposyn II	AB	3.5%				4%	
Liposyn III	AB			3.5%	4%		
Sodium		39.8 mEq	39.8 mEq	39.7 mEq	45 mEq	45 mEq	45 mEq
Potassium		40 mEq	40 mEq	40 mEq	40 mEq	40.2 mEq	40.2 mEq
Calcium		7.5 mEq	7.5 mEq	9.15 mEq	9.15 mEq	7.5 mEq	7.5 mEq
Magnesium		8 mEq	8 mEq	8 mEq	8 mEq	8 mEq	8 mEq
Chloride		45 mEq	45 mEq	35 mEq	35 mEq	51 mEq	51 mEq
Acetate		67.7 mEq	67.7 mEq	45 mEq	53.2 mEq	78.4 mEq	78.4 mEq
Phosphate		10 mmol	10 mmol	15 mmol	15 mmol	10 mmol	10 mmol
Multivitamins		10 ml	10 ml	10 ml	10 ml	10 ml	10 ml
Trace elements		1 ml	1 ml	1 ml	1 ml	1 ml	1 ml

Component	Mfr	Concentration per Liter #227	#228	#229	#230	#231
Aminosyn II	AB	2%	3.5%	4.25%	4.25%	5%
Dextrose	AB	10%	10%	15%	25%	25%
Sodium (as chloride)	AB	40 mEq	40 mEq	70 mEq	70 mEq	70 mEq
Potassium (as chloride)	AB	20 mEq	20 mEq	50 mEq	50 mEq	50 mEq
Magnesium (as sulfate)	AB	8 mEq	8 mEq	12 mEq	12 mEq	12 mEq
Phosphates (as potassium)	AB	up to 40 mmol	up to 40 mmol	up to 40 mmol	up to 40 mmol	up to 40 mmol
Calcium (as acetate)	AB	up to 40 mEq	up to 40 mEq	up to 40 mEq	up to 40 mEq	up to 40 mEq

Component	Mfr	Component Amounts #232	#233	#234	#235	#236	#237
Synthamin 17		500 ml	500 ml	500 ml	500 ml		
Vaminolact	FRE					150 ml	150 ml
Dextrose 50%		500 ml	500 ml	500 ml	500 ml	180 ml	154 ml
Sterile water for injection		500 ml	500 ml	500 ml	500 ml		
Intralipid 20%		500 ml	500 ml	500 ml	500 ml		
Medialipide	BRN						50 ml
Albumin, human		100 ml	100 ml	200 ml	200 ml		
Sodium chloride 10%						6.08 ml	6.08 ml
Potassium chloride 10%						18.66 ml	18.66 ml
Calcium chloride			7 mmol		7 mmol		
Calcium gluconate/glucoheptonate						16.1 ml	16.1 ml
Magnesium sulfate			10 mmol		10 mmol		
Magnesium sulfate 15%						1.64 ml	1.64 ml
Phosphorus (Phocytan)						14.56 ml	14.56 ml
Vitamins (Soluvit)						5 ml	5 ml
Trace elements, pediatric (OEP)						10 ml	10 ml

Component	Mfr	Component Amounts		
		#238	#239	#240
Aminoplex 12	GEI	200 ml		
FreAmine III	FRE		200 ml	
Vamin 14	PH			200 ml
Dextrose 20%	BA	300 ml	300 ml	300 ml
Addiphos	PH	4 ml	4 ml	4 ml
Additrace	PH	2 ml	2 ml	2 ml

Component	Mfr	Concentration per Liter	
		#241	#242
Aminosyn	AB	4.25%	5%
Dextrose		25%	25%
Calcium		4.5 mEq	4.5 mEq
Magnesium		5 mEq	5 mEq
Potassium		40 mEq	40 mEq
Sodium		35 mEq	35 mEq
Acetate		74.5 mEq	74.5 mEq
Chloride		52.5 mEq	52.5 mEq
Phosphorus		12 mmol	12 mmol
Heparin sodium		1000 units	1000 units

REFERENCES

1. Package insert (for brands listed after the nonproprietary name heading a monograph; date of package insert given as part of citation).
2. Physicians' Desk Reference, 55th edition, Medical Economics Company, Montvale, New Jersey, 2001.
3. Kirkland WD, Jones RW, Ellis JR, et al.: Compatibility studies of parenteral admixtures, *Am J Hosp Pharm 18*:694–699 (Dec) 1961.
4. McEvoy GK (ed): AHFS drug information 2001, American Society of Health-System Pharmacists, Bethesda, Maryland, 2001.
5. Parfait K (ed): Martindale: the complete drug reference, 32nd ed, The Pharmaceutical Press, London, England, 1999.
6. Parker EA: Compatibility digest, *Am J Hosp Pharm 27*:67–69 (Jan) 1970.
7. Parker EA: Compatibility digest, *Am J Hosp Pharm 27*:672–673 (Aug) 1970.
8. Trissel's stability of compounded formulations, 2nd ed, American Pharmaceutical Association, Washington, DC, 2000.
9. Patel JA and Phillips GL: Guide to physical compatibility of intravenous drug admixtures, *Am J Hosp Pharm 23*:409–411 (Aug) 1966.
10. Bogash RC: Compatibilities and incompatibilities of some parenteral medication, *Bull Am Soc Hosp Pharm 12*:445–448 (July–Aug) 1955.
11. Dunworth RD and Kenna FR: Preliminary report: incompatibility of combinations of medications in intravenous solutions, *Am J Hosp Pharm 22*:190–191 (Apr) 1965.
12. Moorhatch P and Chiou WL: Interactions between drugs and plastic intravenous fluid bags, part i: sorption studies on 17 drugs, *Am J Hosp Pharm 31*:72–78 (Jan) 1974.
13. Levin HJ, Fieber RA, and Levi RS: Stability data for Tubex filled by hospital pharmacists, *Hosp Pharm 8*:310–311, 314 (Oct) 1973.
14. Powers S: Incompatibilities of pre-op medications, *Hosp Formul Manage 5*:22 (May) 1970.
15. Anon: Intravenous additive incompatibilities, Pharmacy Department, National Institutes of Health (Jan) 1970.
16. Cantina PN and King JC: Physico-chemical incompatibilities of selected cardiovascular and psychotherapeutic agents with sodium ethacrynate, *Am J Hosp Pharm 29*:141–146 (Feb) 1972.
17. The United States Pharmacopeia, 24th rev, United States Pharmacopeial Convention, Rockville, Maryland, 2000.
18. Kramer W, Inglott A, and Cluxton R: Some physical and chemical incompatibilities of drugs for i.v. administration, *Drug Intell Clin Pharm 5*:211–228 (July) 1971 and 1999.
19. McEvoy GK (ed): American hospital formulary service drug information 97, American Society of Health-System Pharmacists, Bethesda, Maryland, 1997.
20. Parker EA: Compatibility digest, *Am J Hosp Pharm 26*:412–413 (July) 1969.
21. Parker EA: Compatibility digest, *Am J Hosp Pharm 26*:653–655 (Nov) 1969.
22. Parker EA: Compatibility digest, *Am J Hosp Pharm 27*:327–329 (Apr) 1970.
23. Parker EA: Compatibility digest, *Am J Hosp Pharm 31*:1076 (Nov) 1974.
24. Parker EA: Compatibility digest, *Am J Hosp Pharm 28*:805 (Oct) 1971.
25. Souney PF, Solomon MA, and Stancher D: Visual compatibility of cimetidine hydrochloride with common preoperative injectable medications, *Am J Hosp Pharm 41*:1840–1841 (Sep) 1984.
26. Riley BB: Incompatibilities in intravenous solutions, *J Hosp Pharm 28*:228–240 (Aug) 1970.
27. Parker EA and Levin HJ: Compatibility digest, *Am J Hosp Pharm 32*:943–944 (Sep) 1975.
28. Misgen R: Compatibilities and incompatibilities of some intravenous solution admixtures, *Am J Hosp Pharm 22*:92–94 (Feb) 1965.
29. Drug Topics Red Book, Medical Economics Company, Montvale, New Jersey, 2001.
30. Mehta DK (ed.): British National Formulary 41, British Medical Association and Royal Pharmaceutical Society of Great Britain, London, England, March, 2001.
31. Bing CM: Extended stability for parenteral drugs, American Society of Health-System Pharmacists, Bethesda, Maryland, 2001.
32. Frank JT: Intralipid compatibility study, *Drug Intell Clin Pharm 7*:351–352 (Aug) 1973.
33. Yeo MT, Gazzaniga AB, Bartlett RH, et al.: Total intravenous nutrition experience with fat emulsions and hypertonic glucose, *Arch Surg 106*:792–796 (June) 1973.
34. Melly MA, Meng HC, and Schaffner W: Microbial growth in lipid emulsions used in parenteral nutrition, *Arch Surg 110*:1479–1481 (Dec) 1975.
35. Deitel M and Kaminsky V: Total nutrition by peripheral vein—the lipid system, *Can Med Assoc J 111*:152–154 (July 20) 1974.
36. Cashore WJ, Sedaghatian MR, and Usher RA: Nutritional supplements with intravenously administered lipid, protein hydrolysate, and glucose in small premature infants, *Pediatrics 56*:8–16 (July) 1975.
37. Lynn B: Intralipid compatibility study, *Drug Intell Clin Pharm 8*:75, 78 (Feb) 1974.
38. Electronic Medicines Compendium, Datapharm Communications Ltd., London, England. Available at http://www.emc.vhn.net.
39. Fortner CL, Grove WR, Bowie D, et al.: Fat emulsion vehicle for intravenous administration of an aqueous insoluble drug, *Am J Hosp Pharm 32*:582–584 (June) 1975.
40. Riffkin C: Incompatibilities of manufactured parenteral products, *Am J Hosp Pharm 20*:19–22 (Jan) 1963.
41. Edward M: pH—an important factor in the compatibility of additives in intravenous therapy, *Am J Hosp Pharm 24*:440–449 (Aug) 1967.
42. Turner FE and King JC: Spectrophotometric analysis of intravenous admixtures containing metaraminol and corticosteroids, *Am J Hosp Pharm 27*:540–547 (July) 1970.
43. Anderson RW and Latiolais CJ: Physico-chemical incompatibilities of parenteral admixtures—Aramine and Solu-Cortef, *Am J Hosp Pharm 30*:128–133 (Feb) 1973.
44. Smith MC: The dextrans, *Am J Hosp Pharm 22*:273–275 (May) 1965.
45. Stokes TF, Sumner ED, and Needham TE: Particulate contamination and stability of three additives in 0.9% sodium chloride injection in plastic and glass large-volume containers, *Am J Hosp Pharm 32*:821–826 (Aug) 1975.
46. Parker EA: Solution additive chemical incompatibility study, *Am J Hosp Pharm 24*:434–439 (Aug) 1967.
47. Parker EA: Compatibility digest, *Am J Hosp Pharm 26*:543–544 (Sep) 1969.
48. Parker EA: Parenteral incompatibilities, *Hosp Pharm 4*:14–22 (Aug) 1969.
49. Beatrice MG, Stanaszek WF, Allen LV, et al.: Physicochemical stability of a preanesthetic mixture of hydroxyzine hydrochloride and atropine sulfate, *Am J Hosp Pharm 32*:1133–1137 (Nov) 1975.
50. Leff RD and Roberts RJ: Effect of intravenous fluid and drug solution coadministration on final-infusate osmolality, specific gravity, and pH, *Am J Hosp Pharm 39*:468–471 (Mar) 1982.
51. Crevar GE and Slotnick IJ: A note on the stability of actinomycin D, *J Pharm Pharmacol 16*:429, 1964.
52. Coles CLJ and Lees KA: Additives to intravenous fluids, *Pharm J 206*:153–154 (Mar 27) 1971.
53. Rudd L, Simpson P: Pethidine stability in intravenous solutions, *Med J Aust 2*:34 (July 1) 1978.
54. Webb JW: A pH pattern for i.v. additives, *Am J Hosp Pharm 26*:31–35 (Jan) 1969.
55. Jones RW, Stanko GL, and Gross HM: Pharmaceutical compatibilities of Pentothal and Nembutal, *Am J Hosp Pharm 18*:700–704 (Dec) 1961.
56. Turco SJ, Sherman NE, Zagar L, et al.: Stability of aminophylline in 5% dextrose in water, *Hosp Pharm 10*:374–375 (Sep) 1975.
57. Hodby ED, Hirsch J, and Adeniyi-Jones C: Influence of drugs upon the anticoagulant activity of heparin, *Can Med Assoc J 106*:562–564 (Mar 4) 1972.
58. Piafsky KM and Ogilvie RI: Dosage of theophylline in bronchial asthma, *N Engl J Med 292*:1218–1222 (June 5) 1975.
59. Parker EA: Compatibility digest, *Am J Hosp Pharm 31*:775 (Aug) 1974.
60. Wolfert RR and Cox RM: Room temperature stability of drug products labeled for refrigerated storage, *Am J Hosp Pharm 32*:585–587 (June) 1975.
61. Anon: Intravenous fat, *Lancet 1*:1059–1060 (May 15) 1976.
62. Sachtler G: Dilantin for i.v. use, *Drug Intell Clin Pharm 7*:418 (Sep) 1973.
63. Burke WA: I.V. drug incompatibilities—Dilantin, *Am J IV Ther 2*:16–18 (Oct/Nov) 1975.
64. Baldwin J and Amerson AB: Intramuscular use of diphenylhydantoin, *Am J Hosp Pharm 30*:837–838 (Sep) 1973.
65. Tobias DC and Kellick KA: Dilantin for i.v. use, *Drug Intell Clin Pharm 7*:418 (Sep) 1973.
66. Chan NL: Dilantin for i.v. use, *Drug Intell Clin Pharm 7*:419 (Sep) 1973.
67. Ammar HO, Salama HA, and El-Nimr AE: Studies on the stability of injectable solutions of some phenothiazines, part i: effect of pH and buffer systems, *Pharmazie 30*:368–369 (June) 1975.
68. Pickering LK and Rutherford I: Effect of concentration and time upon inactivation of tobramycin, gentamicin, netilmicin, and amikacin by azlocillin, carbenicillin, mecillinam, mezlocillin, and piperacillin, *J Pharmacol Exp Ther 217*:345–349 (May) 1981.
69. Ho NFH and Goeman JA: Prediction of pharmaceutical stability of parenteral solutions, *Drug Intell Clin Pharm 4*:69–71 (Mar) 1970.
70. Wilson CO and Jones TE: American drug index, J.B. Lippincott Company, Philadelphia, Pennsylvania, 1975.

71. Product Information Office (Astra Pharmaceutical Products, Westborough, Massachusetts): Personal communication, October 16, 1991.
72. Trissel LA, Davignon JP, Kleinman LM, et al.: NCI investigational drugs pharmaceutical data, National Cancer Institute, Bethesda, Maryland, 1988.
73. Muhlhauser I, Broermann C, Tsotsalas M, et al.: Miscibility of human and bovine ultralente insulin with soluble insulin, *Br Med J 289*:1656–1657 (Dec 15) 1984.
74. Grant HR: Compatibilities of intravenous admixtures, *Hosp Pharmacist 15*: 67–70, 94 (Mar–Apr) 1962.
75. Hanson DB and Hendeles L: Guide to total dose intravenous iron dextran therapy, *Am J Hosp Pharm 31*:592–595 (June) 1974.
76. Duke AB, Kelleher J, Bauminger BB, et al.: Serum iron and iron binding capacity after total dose infusion of iron–dextran for iron deficiency anaemia in pregnancy, *J Obstet Gynaecol Br Commonwealth 81*:895–900 (Nov) 1974.
77. Parker EA: Compatibility digest, *Am J Hosp Pharm 32*:214 (Feb) 1975.
78. Gardella LA, Kesler H, Carter JE, et al.: Intropin (dopamine hydrochloride) intravenous admixture compatibility, part ii: stability with some commonly used antibiotics in 5% dextrose injection, *Am J Hosp Pharm 33*:537–540 (June) 1976.
79. Gardella LA, Zaroslinski JF, and Possley LH: Intropin (dopamine hydrochloride) intravenous admixture compatibility, part i: stability with common intravenous fluids, *Am J Hosp Pharm 32*:575–578 (June) 1975.
80. Garnett W: Diluents for antineoplastic drugs, *Drug Intell Clin Pharm 5*:261 (Aug) 1971.
81. Landersjo L, Stjernstrom G, and Lundgren P: Studies on the stability and compatibility of drugs in infusion fluids V. Effect of lactate and metal ions on the stability of benzylpenicillin, *Acta Pharm Suec 15*:161–168 (3) 1978.
82. Notari RE, Chin ML, and Wittebort R: Arabinosylcytosine stability in aqueous solutions: pH profile and shelf life predictions, *J Pharm Sci 61*:1189–1196 (Aug) 1972.
83. Murty BSR and Kapoor JN: Properties of mannitol injection (25%) after repeated autoclavings, *Am J Hosp Pharm 32*:826–827 (Aug) 1975.
84. Rosch JM, Pazin GJ, and Fireman P: Reduction of amphotericin B nephrotoxicity with mannitol, *J Am Med Assoc 235*:1995–1996 (May 3) 1976.
85. Bergman N and Vellar ID: Potential life-threatening variations of drug concentrations in intravenous infusion systems—potassium chloride, insulin, and heparin, *Med J Aust 2*:270–272 (Sep 18) 1982.
86. Parker EA: Compatibility digest, *Am J Hosp Pharm 27*:492–493 (June) 1970.
87. Feigen RD, Moss KS, and Shackelford PG: Antibiotic stability in solutions used for intravenous nutrition and fluid therapy, *Pediatrics 51*:1016–1026 (June) 1973.
88. Zost ED and Yanchick VA: Compatibility and stability of disodium carbenicillin in combination with other drugs and large volume parenteral solutions, *Am J Hosp Pharm 29*:135–140 (Feb) 1972.
89. Lynn B: Recent work on parenteral penicillins, *J Hosp Pharm 29*:183–194 (July) 1971.
90. Tourville J: Sodium nitroprusside, *Drug Intell Clin Pharm 9*:361–364 (July) 1975.
91. Anon: Sodium nitroprusside in anaesthesia, *Br Med J 2*:524–525 (June 7) 1975.
92. Hargrave RE: Degradation of solutions of sodium nitroprusside, *J Hosp Pharm 32*:188–189, 191 (Oct) 1974.
93. Anon: Sodium nitroprusside for hypertensive crisis, *Med Letter Drug Ther 17*: 82–83 (Sep 26) 1975.
94. Anderson RA and Rae W: Stability of sodium nitroprusside solutions, *Aust J Pharm Sci NS1*:45–46 (July) 1972.
95. Schumacher GE: Sodium nitroprusside injection, *Am J Hosp Pharm 23*:532 (Sep) 1966.
96. Johnson DE: Nitroprusside in hypertensive emergencies, *Hosp Formul 10*: 272–273 (June) 1975.
97. Thomas R: Meperidine HCl and heparin sodium precipitation, *Hosp Pharm 9*: 356 (Sep) 1974.
98. Fleischer NM: Promethazine hydrochloride–morphine sulfate incompatibility, *Am J Hosp Pharm 30*:665 (Aug) 1973.
99. Lynn B: Pharmaceutical aspects of semi-synthetic penicillins, *J Hosp Pharm 28*:71–86 (Mar) 1970.
100. Meisler JM and Skolaut MW: Extemporaneous sterile compounding in intravenous additives, *Am J Hosp Pharm 23*:557–563 (Oct) 1966.
101. Guthaus MR (Medical Services, The Upjohn Company, Kalamazoo, Michigan): Personal communication, August 9, 1973.
102. Hamlin WE, Riebe KW, Scothorn WW, et al.: Pharmacy profile of Cleocin Phosphate, Presented at 10th Annual ASHP Midyear Clinical Meeting, December 11, 1975, Washington, D.C.
103. Riebe KW and Oesterling TO: Parenteral development of clindamycin-2-phosphate, *Bull Parenter Drug Assoc 26*:139–145 (May–June) 1972.
104. Anon: Therapeutic profile: Cleocin Phosphate, The Upjohn Company, Kalamazoo, Michigan, 1973.
105. Wyatt RG, Okamato GA, and Feigen RD: Stability of antibiotics in parenteral solutions, *Pediatrics 49*:22–29 (Jan) 1972.
106. Murty BSR, Kapoor JN, and DeLuca PP: Compliance with USP osmolarity labeling requirements, *Am J Hosp Pharm 33*:546–551 (June) 1976.
107. Whiting DA: Treatment of chromoblastomycosis with local concentrations of amphotericin B, *Br J Dermatol 79*:345–351, 1967.
108. Kirschenbaum BE and Latiolais CJ: Injectable medications—a guide to stability and reconstitution, McMahon Group, New York, New York, 1993.
109. Bair JN and Carew DP: Therapeutic availability of antibiotics in parenteral solutions, *Bull Parenter Drug Assoc 19*:153–163 (Nov–Dec) 1965.
110. Dancey JW and Carew DP: Availability of antibiotics in combination with other additives in intravenous solutions, *Am J Hosp Pharm 23*:543–551 (Oct) 1966.
111. Prasad VK, Granatek AP, and Mihotic MM: Physical compatibility and chemical stability of cephapirin sodium in combination with antibiotics and large-volume parenteral solutions, part i, *Curr Ther Res Clin Exp 16*:505–539 (May) 1974.
112. Lynn B: Carbenicillin plus gentamicin, *Lancet 1*:654 (Mar 27) 1971.
113. Jacobs J, Kletter D, Superstine E, et al.: Intravenous infusions of heparin and penicillins, *J Clin Pathol 26*:742–746, 1973.
114. Lynn B: Penicillin instability in infusions, *Br Med J 1*:174 (Jan 16) 1971.
115. Information for health professionals, New Zealand Medicines and Medical Devices Safety Authority, Wellington, New Zealand. Available at http://www.medsafe.govt.nz.
116. l'Universite et l'Industrie Pharmaceutique, Banque de donnes automatisee sur-les medicaments (BIAM), Paris, France. Available at http://www2.biam2.org.
117. McEvoy GK (ed): American hospital formulary service drug information 95, American Society of Health-System Pharmacists, Bethesda, Maryland, 1995.
118. Harrison DC: Practical guidelines for the use of lidocaine, *J Am Med Assoc 233*:1202–1204 (Sep 15) 1975.
119. Collinsworth K: Clinical pharmacology of lidocaine as an antiarrhythmic drug, *West J Med 124*:36–43 (Jan) 1976.
120. Anon: Prophylactic use of lidocaine in myocardial infarction, *Med Letter Drug Ther 18*:1–2 (Jan 2) 1976.
121. Dundee JW, Gamble JAS, and Assaf RAE: Plasma diazepam levels following intramuscular injection by nurses and doctors, *Lancet 2*:1461 (Dec 14) 1974.
122. Product information, Trophamine, McGaw, Irvine, California, March 1992.
123. Tortorici MP: Stability data on frozen i.m. and i.v. solutions, *Pharm Times 41*: 68–72 (Aug) 1975.
124. Barbara AC, Clemente C, and Wagman E: Physical incompatibility of sulfonamide compounds and polyionic solutions, *N Engl J Med 274*:1316–1317 (June 9) 1966.
125. Brooke D, Bequette RJ, and Davis RE: Chemical stability of cyclophosphamide in parenteral solutions, *Am J Hosp Pharm 30*:134–137 (Feb) 1973.
126. Brooke D, Scott JA, and Bequette RJ: Effect of briefly heating cyclophosphamide solutions, *Am J Hosp Pharm 32*:44–45 (Jan) 1975.
127. Gallelli JF: Stability studies of drugs used in intravenous solutions, part i, *Am J Hosp Pharm 24*:425–433 (Aug) 1967.
128. Anon: Nubain, physical compatibility, Dupont Pharmaceuticals, Wilmington, Delaware.
129. Kramer W, Tanja JJ, and Harrison WL: Precipitates found in admixtures of potassium chloride and dextrose 5% in water, *Am J Hosp Pharm 27*:548–553 (July) 1970.
130. Lawson DH: Clinical use of potassium supplements, *Am J Hosp Pharm 32*: 708–711 (July) 1975.
131. Lundgren P and Landersjo L: Studies on the stability and compatibility of drugs in infusion fluids, ii: factors affecting the stability of benzylpenicillin, *Acta Pharm Suec 7*:509–526 (Nov) 1970.
132. Weber CR and Gupta VD: Stability of phenylephrine hydrochloride in intravenous solutions, *J Hosp Pharm 28*:200–208 (July) 1970.
133. Chiou WL and Moorhatch P: Interaction between vitamin A and plastic intravenous fluid bags, *J Am Med Assoc 223*:328 (Jan 15) 1973.
134. Komesaroff D and Field JE: Pancuronium bromide: a new non-depolarizing muscle relaxant, *Med J Aust 1*:908–911 (May 3) 1969.
135. Simberkoff MS, Thomas L, McGregor D, et al.: Inactivation of penicillins by carbohydrate solutions at alkaline pH, *N Engl J Med 283*:116–119 (July 16) 1970.
136. Hicks CI, Gallardo JPB, and Guillory JK: Stability of sodium bicarbonate injection stored in polypropylene syringes, *Am J Hosp Pharm 29*:210–216 (Mar) 1972.

137. DeLuca PP and Kowalski RJ: Problems arising from the transfer of sodium bicarbonate injection from ampuls to plastic disposable syringes, *Am J Hosp Pharm 29*:217–222 (Mar) 1972.
138. D'Arcy PF and Thompson KM: Stability of chlorpromazine hydrochloride added to intravenous infusion fluids, *Pharm J 210*:28 (Jan 13) 1973.
139. Bergstrom RF and Fites AL: Stability of erythromycin gluceptate in sodium chloride injection and dextrose injection, *Am J Hosp Pharm 32*:241 (Mar) 1975.
140. Murabito AS (Medical Correspondence, Smith Kline & French Laboratories, Philadelphia, Pennsylvania): Personal communication, December 15, 1986.
141. Mann JM, Coleman DL, and Boylan JC: Stability of parenteral solutions of sodium cephalothin, cephaloridine, potassium penicillin G (buffered), and vancomycin HCl, *Am J Hosp Pharm 28*:760–763 (Oct) 1971.
142. Appleby DH and John JF: Effect of peritoneal dialysis solution on the antimicrobial activity of cephalosporins, *Nephron 30*:341–344, 1982.
143. Upshaw MD (Medical Information Services, Eli Lilly and Company, Indianapolis, Indiana): Personal communication, January 10, 1972.
144. Gallelli JF, MacLowry JD, and Skolaut MW: Stability of antibiotics in parenteral solutions, *Am J Hosp Pharm 26*:630–635 (Nov) 1969.
145. Dienstag JL and Neu HC: Tobramycin: new aminoglycoside antibiotic, *Clin Med 82*:13–19 (Dec) 1975.
146. Struhar M, Heinrich J, and Krenek P: K sorpcii pentoxifyllinu na infuznu supravu Luer, *Farm Obz 57*:405–410 (9) 1988.
147. Bergstrom RF, Fites AL, and Lamb JW: Stability of parenteral solutions of tobramycin sulfate, *Am J Hosp Pharm 32*:887–888 (Sep) 1975.
148. Huber RC and Riffkin C: Inline final filters for removing particles from amphotericin B infusions, *Am J Hosp Pharm 32*:173–176 (Feb) 1975.
149. Rebagay T, Rapp R, Bivins B, et al.: Residues in antibiotic preparations, i: scanning electron microscopic studies of surface topography, *Am J Hosp Pharm 33*:433–443 (May) 1976.
150. Gallelli JF: Assay and stability of amphotericin B in aqueous solutions, *Drug Intell 1*:102–105 (Mar) 1967.
151. Piecoro JJ, Goodman NL, Wheeler WE, et al.: Particulate matter in reconstituted amphotericin B and assay of filtered solutions of amphotericin B, *Am J Hosp Pharm 32*:381–384 (Apr) 1975.
152. Gotz V and Simon W: Inline filtration of amphotericin B infusions, *Am J Hosp Pharm 32*:458 (May) 1975.
153. Chatterji D, Hiranaka PK, and Gallelli JF: Stability of sodium oxacillin in intravenous solutions, *Am J Hosp Pharm 32*:1130–1132 (Nov) 1975.
154. Drug Facts and Comparisons, St. Louis, MO, Facts and Comparisons, 1999.
155. Parodi JF: Stability of frozen antibiotic solutions in Viaflex infusion containers, *Hosp Pharm 11*:178–179 (May) 1976.
156. Larsen SS: Studies on stability of drugs in frozen systems, iv: the stability of benzylpenicillin sodium in frozen aqueous solutions, *Dansk Tidsskr Farm 45*: 307–316 (9) 1971.
157. Noone P and Pattison JR: Therapeutic implications of interaction of gentamicin and penicillins, *Lancet 2*:575–578 (Sep 11) 1971.
158. Boulet M, Marier JR, and Rose D: Effect of magnesium on formation of calcium phosphate precipitates, *Arch Biochem Biophys 96*:629–636, 1962.
159. van den Berg L and Soliman FS: Composition and pH changes during freezing of solutions containing calcium and magnesium phosphate, *Cryobiology 6*:10–14 (1) 1969.
160. Ong JTH and Kostenbauder HB: Effect of self-association on rate of penicillin G degradation in concentrated aqueous solutions, *J Pharm Sci 64*:1378–1380 (Aug) 1975.
161. Shoup LK and Thur MP: Stability of frozen buffered penicillin G potassium injection, *Hosp Formul Manage 3*:38–39 (May) 1968.
162. Boylan JC, Simmons JL, and Winely CL: Stability of frozen solutions of sodium cephalothin and cephaloridine, *Am J Hosp Pharm 29*:687–689 (Aug) 1972.
163. Grant NH, Clark DE, and Alburn HE: Imidazole- and base-catalyzed hydrolysis of penicillin in frozen systems, *J Am Chem Soc 83*:4476–4477 (Nov) 1961.
164. Lindsay RE and Hem SL: Dosage form for potassium penicillin G intravenous infusion solutions, *Drug Devel Commun 1*:211–222 (3) 1974–1975.
165. Im S and Latiolais CJ: Physico-chemical incompatibilities of parenteral admixtures—penicillin and tetracyclines, *Am J Hosp Pharm 23*:333–343 (July) 1966.
166. Pfeifer HJ and Webb JW: Compatibility of penicillin and ascorbic acid injection, *Am J Hosp Pharm 33*:448–450 (May) 1976.
167. Rusmin S and DeLuca PP: Effect of inline filtration on the potency of potassium penicillin G, *Bull Parenter Drug Assoc 30*:64–71 (Mar–Apr) 1976.
168. Stolar MH, Carlin HS, and Blake MI: Effect of freezing on the stability of sodium methicillin injection, *Am J Hosp Pharm 25*:32–35 (Jan) 1968.
169. Lynn B: Stability of methicillin in dextrose solutions at alkaline pH, *J Hosp Pharm 30*:81–83 (Mar) 1972.
170. Lynn B: Pharmaceutics of the semi-synthetic penicillins, *Chem Drug 187*:134–136 (Feb 11) 1967.
171. Lynn B: Inactivation of methicillin in dextrose solutions at alkaline pH, *N Engl J Med 285*:690 (Sep 16) 1971.
172. Mattson CJ, Clark ST, and Colangelo A: Stability of clindamycin phosphate in plastic syringes, Presented at 20th Annual ASHP Midyear Clinical Meeting, December 1985, New Orleans, Louisiana.
173. Clark ST and Colangelo A: Stability of clindamycin phosphate in plastic syringes, Presented at 20th Annual ASHP Midyear Clinical Meeting, December 1985, New Orleans, Louisiana.
174. Cohon MS (Drug Information Services, Upjohn Company, Kalamazoo, Michigan): Personal communications, December 12, 1986, January 27, 1988, February 3, 1988.
175. Trissel LA: Unpublished data.
176. Owen RT (UK Medical Information Section, The Wellcome Foundation Ltd., Cheshire, England): Personal communication, August 19, 1993.
177. Lesson LJ and Weidenheimer JF: Stability of tetracycline and riboflavin, *J Pharm Sci 58*:355–357 (Mar) 1969.
178. Turco SJ and Burke WA: Methods of ordering and use of intravenous phosphate (mEq vs mM), *Hosp Pharm 10*:320, 322, 326 (Aug) 1975.
179. Pinkus TF and Jeffrey LP: Incompatibility of calcium and phosphate in parenteral alimentation solutions, *Am J IV Ther 3*:22–24 (Feb–Mar) 1976.
180. Kaminski MV, Harris DF, Collin CF, et al.: Electrolyte compatibility in synthetic amino acid hyperalimentation solution, *Am J Hosp Pharm 31*:244–246 (Mar) 1974.
181. Schlicht JR: Adjustments in etoposide infusion flow rates when using controllers, *Am J Hosp Pharm 47*:2656 (Dec) 1990.
182. FASS, Karolinska Institutet, Huddinge, Sweden. Available at http://edu.ofa.ki.effica/.
183. Lee FA and Gwinn JL: Roentgen patterns of extravasation of calcium gluconate in the tissues of the neonate, *J Pediatr 86*:598–601 (Apr) 1975.
184. Weiss Y, Ackerman C, and Shmilovitz L: Localized necrosis of scalp in neonates due to calcium gluconate infusions: a cautionary note, *Pediatrics 56*: 1084–1086 (Dec) 1975.
185. Ramamurthy RS, Harris V, and Pildes RS: Subcutaneous calcium deposition in the neonate associated with intravenous administration of calcium gluconate, *Pediatrics 55*:802–806 (June) 1975.
186. Laegeler WL, Tio JM, and Blake MI: Stability of certain amino acids in a parenteral nutrition solution, *Am J Hosp Pharm 31*:776–779 (Aug) 1974.
187. Kleinman LM, Tangrea JA, Gallelli JF, et al.: Stability of solutions of essential amino acids, *Am J Hosp Pharm 30*:1054–1057 (Nov) 1973.
188. Rowlands DA: Compatibility of calcium and phosphate in amino acids solution, *Am J Hosp Pharm 32*:360 (Apr) 1975.
189. FreAmine brochure, McGaw Laboratories, Santa Ana, California, April 1971.
190. Rowlands DA, Wilkinson WR, and Yoshimura N: Storage stability of mixed hyperalimentation solutions, *Am J Hosp Pharm 30*:436–438 (May) 1973.
191. Ravin RL: Parenteral hyperalimentation, *Drug Intell Clin Pharm 6*:186–189 (May) 1972.
192. Hull RL: Physicochemical considerations in intravenous hyperalimentation, *Am J Hosp Pharm 31*:236–243 (Mar) 1974.
193. Dryps JS and Hoffman RP: Hyperalimentation review, *Drug Intell Clin Pharm 7*:413–417 (Sep) 1973.
194. Hull RL: Use of trace elements in intravenous hyperalimentation solutions, *Am J Hosp Pharm 31*:759–761 (Aug) 1974.
195. Johnson C, Cloyd J, and Rapp RP: Parenteral hyperalimentation, *Drug Intell Clin Pharm 9*:493–499 (Sep) 1975.
196. Hankins DA, Riella MC, Scribner BH, et al.: Whole blood trace element concentrations during total parenteral nutrition, *Surgery 79*:674–677 (June) 1976.
197. Hamann MA: Trace element requirements in hyperalimentation, *Am J Hosp Pharm 31*:1035, 1038 (Nov) 1974.
198. Hull RL: Trace element requirements in hyperalimentation, *Am J Hosp Pharm 31*:1038 (Nov) 1974.
199. Heird WC and Winters RW: Total intravenous alimentation in pediatric patients, *South Med J 68*:1173–1176 (Sep) 1975.
200. Baker JA, Kirkman H, Woodley C, et al.: Computer-assisted pediatric hyperalimentation, *Am J Hosp Pharm 31*:752–758 (Aug) 1974.
201. Parish R: Hyperalimentation procedures, *Am J Hosp Pharm 31*:1160, 1166 (Dec) 1974.
202. Pomerance HH and Rader RE: Crystal formation: a new complication of total parenteral nutrition, *Pediatrics 52*:864–866 (Dec) 1973.
203. Bohart RD and Ogawa G: An observation on the stability of cis-dichlorodiam-

mineplatinum (II): a caution regarding its administration, *Cancer Treat Rep 63*:2117–2118 (Nov–Dec) 1979.

204. Prestayko AW, Cadiz M, and Crooke ST: Incompatibility of aluminum-containing iv administration equipment with cis-dichlorodiammineplatinum (II) administration, *Cancer Treat Rep 63*:2118–2119 (Nov–Dec) 1979.
205. Shils ME: Minerals in total parenteral nutrition, *Drug Intell Clin Pharm 6*: 385–393 (Nov) 1972.
206. Flack HL, Gans VA, Serlick SE, et al.: Current status of parenteral hyperalimentation, *Am Hosp Pharm 28*:326–335 (May) 1971.
207. McRae MP and King JC: Compatibility of antineoplastic, antibiotic, and corticosteroid drugs in intravenous admixtures, *Am J Hosp Pharm 33*:1010–1013 (Oct) 1976.
208. Warren E, Synder RJ, Thompson CO, et al.: Stability of ampicillin in intravenous solutions, *Mayo Clin Proc 47*:34–35 (Jan) 1972.
209. Raffanti EF and King JC: Effect of pH on the stability of sodium ampicillin solutions, *Am J Hosp Pharm 31*:745–751 (Aug) 1974.
210. Savello DR and Shangraw RF: Stability of sodium ampicillin solutions in the frozen and liquid states, *Am J Hosp Pharm 28*:754–759 (Oct) 1971.
211. Jacobs J, Nathan I, Superstine E, et al.: Ampicillin and carbenicillin stability in commonly used infusion solutions, *Drug Intell Clin Pharm 4*:204–208 (Aug) 1970.
212. Hiranaka P, Frazier AG, and Gallelli JF: Stability of ampicillin in aqueous solutions, *Am J Hosp Pharm 29*:321–322 (Apr) 1972.
213. Stratton M and Sandmann BJ: Stability studies of ampicillin sodium in intravenous fluids using optical activity, *Bull Parenter Drug Assoc 29*:286–295 (Nov–Dec) 1975.
214. Pincock RE and Kiovsky TE: Kinetics of reactions in frozen solutions, *J Chem Educ 43*:358–360 (July) 1966.
215. Hou JP and Poole JW: Kinetics and mechanism of degradation of ampicillin in solution, *J Pharm Sci 58*:447–454 (Apr) 1969.
216. Shils ME, Wright WL, Turnbull A, et al.: Long-term parenteral nutrition through an external arteriovenous shunt, *N Engl J Med 283*:341–344 (Aug 13) 1970.
217. Zia H, Tehrani M, and Zargarbashi R: Kinetics of carbenicillin degradation in aqueous solutions, *Can J Pharm Sci 9*:112–117 (4) 1974.
218. Riff LJ and Jackson GG: Laboratory and clinical conditions for gentamicin inactivation by carbenicillin, *Arch Intern Med 130*:887–891 (Dec) 1972.
219. McLaughlin JE and Reeves DS: Clinical and laboratory evidence for inactivation of gentamicin by carbenicillin, *Lancet 1*:261–264 (Feb 6) 1971.
220. Klastersky J: Carbenicillin plus gentamicin, *Lancet 1*:653–654 (Mar 27) 1971.
221. Levison ME and Kaye D: Carbenicillin plus gentamicin, *Lancet 2*:45–46 (July 3) 1971.
222. Eykyn S, Phillips I, and Ridley M: Gentamicin plus carbenicillin, *Lancet 1*: 545–546 (Mar 13) 1971.
223. Riff L and Jackson GG: Gentamicin plus carbenicillin, *Lancet 1*:592 (Mar 20) 1971.
224. Zost ED and Yanchick VA: Stability of gentamicin in combination with carbenicillin, *Am J Hosp Pharm 29*:388–390 (May) 1972.
225. Jacoby GA: Carbenicillin and gentamicin, *N Engl J Med 284*:1096–1098 (May 13) 1971.
226. Kleinberg ML (Director, Professional Services, Immunex, Seattle, Washington): Personal communication, June 14, 1993.
227. Baldini JT (Professional Services, Schering Laboratories, Kenilworth, New Jersey): Personal communication, February 11, 1972.
228. Koup JR and Gerbracht L: Combined use of heparin and gentamicin in peritoneal dialysis solutions, *Drug Intell Clin Pharm 9*:388 (July) 1975.
229. Reeves DS, Bywater MJ, Wise R, et al.: Availability of three antibiotics after intramuscular injection into thigh and buttock, *Lancet 2*:1421–1422 (Dec 14) 1974.
230. Jackson GG: Gentamicin, *Practitioner 198*:855–866 (June) 1967.
231. Preskey D and Kayes JB: Stability of sulfadiazine sodium as used in admixture with intravenous infusion fluids, *J Clin Pharm 1*:39–48 (Mar) 1976.
232. Physicians' desk reference, 49th ed, Medical Economics Company, Oradell, New Jersey, 1995.
233. Larsen SS and Jensen VG: Studies on the stability of drugs in frozen systems, ii: the stabilities of hexobarbital sodium and phenobarbital sodium in frozen aqueous solutions, *Dansk Tidsskr Farm 44*:21–31 (2) 1970.
234. NCI investigational drugs pharmaceutical data, National Cancer Institute, Bethesda, Maryland, 1988, 1990, 1994.
235. Shapiro WR, Young DF, and Mehta BM: Methotrexate: distribution in cerebrospinal fluid after intravenous, ventricular and lumbar injections, *N Engl J Med 293*:161–165 (July 24) 1975.
236. Anon: Kidney toxicity—main source of methotrexate complications, *J Am Med Assoc 223*:1036–1037, 1040 (Sep 8) 1975.
237. Frei E, Jaffe N, Tattersall MHN, et al.: New approaches to cancer chemotherapy with methotrexate, *N Engl J Med 292*:846–851 (Apr 17) 1975.
238. Rosen G, Ghavimi F, Vanucci R, et al.: Pontine glioma—high-dose methotrexate and leucovorin rescue, *J Am Med Assoc 230*:1149–1152 (Nov 25) 1974.
239. Jaffe N, Frei E, Traggis D, et al.: Adjuvant methotrexate and citrovorum-factor treatment of osteogenic sarcoma, *N Engl J Med 291*:994–997 (Nov 7) 1974.
240. Rosen G, Suwansirikul S, Kwon C, et al.: High-dose methotrexate with citrovorum factor rescue and adriamycin in childhood osteogenic sarcoma, *Cancer (Philadelphia) 33*:1151–1163 (Apr) 1974.
241. Lapidas B: Cautions regarding the preparation of high-dose methotrexate infusions, *Am J Hosp Pharm 33*:760 (Aug) 1976.
242. Pelsor FR: Cautions regarding the preparation of high-dose methotrexate infusions, *Am J Hosp Pharm 33*:760 (Aug) 1976.
243. Pritchard J: Stability of heparin solutions, *J Pharm Pharmacol 16*:487–489 (July) 1964.
244. Turco SJ: I.V. drug incompatibilities—heparin sodium USP, *Am J IV Ther 3*: 16–19 (Dec–Jan) 1976.
245. Kakkar VV, Corrigan TP, and Fossard DP: Prevention of fatal postoperative pulmonary embolism by low doses of heparin: an international multicentre trial, *Lancet 2*:45–51 (July 12) 1975.
246. Sherry S: Low-dose heparin prophylaxis for postoperative venous thromboembolism, *N Engl J Med 293*:300–302 (Aug 7) 1975.
247. Gallus AS, Hirsch J, O'Brien SE, et al.: Prevention of venous thrombosis with small, subcutaneous doses of heparin, *J Am Med Assoc 235*:1980–1982 (May 3) 1976.
248. Hopefl AW: Low-dose heparin for the prevention of venous thromboembolism, *Hosp Pharm 11*:223, 226 (June) 1976.
249. Wessler S: Heparin as an antithrombotic agent, *J Am Med Assoc 236*:389–391 (July 26) 1976.
250. Erdi A, Kakkar VV, Thomas DP, et al.: Effect of low-dose subcutaneous heparin on whole-blood viscosity, *Lancet 2*:342–344 (Aug 14) 1976.
251. Hadgraft JW: Adding drugs to intravenous infusions, *Lancet 2*:1254 (Dec 12) 1970.
252. Stock SL and Warner N: Heparin in acid solutions, *Br Med J 3*:307 (July 31) 1971.
253. Chessells JM, Braithwaite TA, and Chamberlain DA: Dextrose and sorbitol as diluents for continuous intravenous heparin infusion, *Br Med J 2*:81–82 (Apr 8) 1972.
254. Mitchell JF, Barger RC, and Cantwell L: Heparin stability in 5% dextrose and 0.9% sodium chloride, *Am J Hosp Pharm 33*:540–542 (June) 1976.
255. Thomas RB and Salter FJ: Heparin locks: their advantages and disadvantages, *Hosp Formul 10*:536–538 (Nov) 1975.
256. Deeb EN and DiMattia PE: The key question: how much heparin in the lock?, *Am J IV Ther 3*:22–26 (Dec–Jan) 1976.
257. DeFina E: How we use heparin locks, *Am J IV Ther 3*:27, 33 (Dec–Jan) 1976.
258. Hanson RL, Grant AM, and Majors KR: Heparin-lock maintenance with ten units of sodium heparin in one milliliter of normal saline solution, *Surg Gynecol Obstet 142*:373–376 (Mar) 1976.
259. Rebagay T and DeLuca PP: Residues in antibiotic preparations, ii: effect of pH on the nature and level of particulate matter in sodium cephalothin intravenous solutions, *Am J Hosp Pharm 33*:443–448 (May) 1976.
260. Gaines K (Parenteral Products Development, Eli Lilly and Company, Indianapolis, Indiana): Personal communication, August 13, 1976.
261. Hopefl AW: Room temperature stability of drug products, *Am J Hosp Pharm 32*:1084, 1089 (Nov) 1975.
262. Barger RC: Room temperature stability of drug products, *Am J Hosp Pharm 32*:1089 (Nov) 1975.
263. Rosenbloom AL: Advances in commercial insulin preparations, *Am J Dis Child 128*:631–633 (Nov) 1974.
264. Rosenberg JM, Simon WA, Sangkachand P, et al.: Mixing insulin preparations, *Hosp Pharm 11*:186, 191 (May) 1976.
265. Shainfeld FJ: Errors in insulin doses due to the design of insulin syringes, *Pediatrics 56*:302–303 (Aug) 1975.
266. Weisenfeld S, Podolsky S, Goldsmith L, et al.: Adsorption of insulin to infusion bottles and tubing, *Diabetes 17*:766–771 (Dec) 1968.
267. Petty C and Cunningham NL: Insulin adsorption by glass infusion bottles, polyvinylchloride infusion containers, and intravenous tubing, *Anesthesiology 40*:400–404 (Apr) 1974.
268. Kraegen EW, Lazarus L, Meler H, et al.: Carrier solutions for low-level intravenous insulin infusion, *Br Med J 3*:464–466 (Aug 23) 1975.
269. Semple P, Ratcliffe JG, and Manderson WG: Carrier solutions for low-level intravenous insulin infusion, *Br Med J 4*:228–229 (Oct 25) 1975.
270. Hays DP and Mehl B: I.V. drug incompatibilities—insulin, *Am J IV Ther 3*: 30–32 (Apr–May) 1976.

271. Owen JA: The insulin revolution, *Hosp Formul 11*:343 (July) 1976.
272. Galloway JA (Medical Research Division, Eli Lilly and Company, Indianapolis, Indiana): Personal communication, August 29, 1967.
273. Kaplan MA and Granatek AP: Stability of frozen solutions of cephapirin sodium, *Curr Ther Res Clin Exp 16*:573–579 (May) 1974.
274. Prasad VK, Johns WH, Wingate MW, et al.: Pharmaceutics of cephapirin sodium (Cefadyl) a new semisynthetic cephalosporin part iii, *Curr Ther Res Clin Exp 16*:1214–1237 (Nov) 1974.
275. Kochevar M and Fry LK: Insulin and dead space volume, *Drug Intell Clin Pharm 8*:33–34 (Jan) 1974.
276. Bornstein M, Thomas PN, Coleman DL, et al.: Stability of parenteral solutions of cefazolin sodium, *Am J Hosp Pharm 31*:296–298 (Mar) 1974.
277. Carone SM, Bornstein M, Coleman DL, et al.: Stability of frozen solutions of cefazolin sodium, *Am J Hosp Pharm 33*:639–641 (July) 1976.
278. Royston DA (Consumer Technical Services, Eli Lilly and Company, Indianapolis, Indiana): Personal communication, February 19, 1976.
279. Brudney N, Eustace BT, and Gilmour WN: Some formulations and compatibility problems with dimenhydrinate (Gravol), *Can Pharm J 96*:470–471, 1963.
280. Acred P, Brown DM, Knudsen ET, et al.: New semi-synthetic penicillin active against pseudomonas pyocyanea, *Nature (London) 215*:25–30 (July) 1967.
281. Schwartz MA and Buckwalter FH: Pharmaceutics of penicillin, *J Pharm Sci 51*:1119–1128 (Dec) 1962.
282. Thur MP (Parenteral Products, Travenol Laboratories, Deerfield, Illinois): Personal communication, September 20, 1976.
283. Ziemba LJ (Medical Information, ICI Pharmaceuticals Group, Wilmington, Delaware): Personal communication, March 15, 1990.
284. Yamana T and Tsuji A: Comparative stability of cephalosporins in aqueous solution: kinetics and mechanisms of degradation, *J Pharm Sci 65*:1563–1574 (Nov) 1976.
285. Kleinman LM, Davignon JP, Cradock JC, et al.: Investigational drug information, *Drug Intell Clin Pharm 10*:48–49 (Jan) 1976.
286. Chang SY, Evans TL, and Alberts DS: The stability of melphalan in the presence of chloride ion, *J Pharm Pharmacol 31*:853–854, 1979.
287. Mitenko PA and Ogilvie RI: Rational intravenous doses of theophylline, *N Engl J Med 289*:600–603 (Sep 20) 1973.
288. Simons FER, Pierson WE, and Bierman CW: Current status of the use of intravenously administered aminophylline, *South Med J 68*:802–804 (July) 1975.
289. Weinberger MW, Matthay RA, Ginchansky EJ, et al.: Intravenous aminophylline dosage use of serum theophylline measurement for guidance, *J Am Med Assoc 235*:2110–2113 (May 10) 1976.
290. Nedich RL: Vitamin A absorption from plastic i.v. bags, *J Am Med Assoc 224*: 1531–1532 (June 11) 1973.
291. Kaplan MA, Coppola WP, Nunning BC, et al.: Pharmaceutical properties and stability of amikacin, part i, *Curr Ther Res Clin Exp 20*:352–358 (Oct) 1976.
292. Nunning BC and Granatek AP: Physical compatibility and chemical stability of amikacin sulfate in large-volume parenteral solutions, part ii, *Curr Ther Res Clin Exp 20*:359–368 (Oct) 1976.
293. Nunning BC, Granatek AP, and Ricci RA: Physical compatibility and chemical stability of amikacin sulfate in combination with antibiotics in large-volume parenteral solutions, part iii, *Curr Ther Res Clin Exp 20*:369–416 (Oct) 1976.
294. Nunning BC and Granatek AP: Physical compatibility and chemical stability of amikacin sulfate in combination with non-antibiotic drugs in large-volume parenteral solutions, part iv, *Curr Ther Res Clin Exp 20*:417–491 (Oct) 1976.
295. Koup JR and Gerbracht L: Reduction in heparin activity by gentamicin, *Drug Intell Clin Pharm 9*:568 (Oct) 1975.
296. McKinley JD (M.D. Anderson Hospital and Tumor Institute, Houston, Texas): Personal communication, August 23, 1976.
297. Weiner B, McNeely DJ, Kluge RM, et al.: Stability of gentamicin sulfate following unit dose repackaging, *Am J Hosp Pharm 33*:1254–1259 (Dec) 1976.
298. Dinel BA, Ayotte DL, Behme RJ, et al.: Comparative stability of antibiotic admixtures in minibags and minibottles, *Drug Intell Clin Pharm 11*:226–239 (Apr) 1977.
299. Dinel BA, Ayotte DL, Behme RJ, et al.: Stability of antibiotic admixtures frozen in minibags, *Drug Intell Clin Pharm 11*:542–548 (Sep) 1977.
300. Lynn B: Pharmaceutics of the semi-synthetic penicillins, *Chem Drug 187*:157–160 (Feb 18) 1967.
301. Stanaszek WF and Pan IH: Analysis of hydroxyzine hydrochloride, meperidine hydrochloride and atropine sulfate in glass and plastic syringes, *Am J Hosp Pharm 35*:1084–1087 (Sep) 1978.
302. Fraser GL: Incompatibility of magnesium sulfate and hydrocortisone sodium succinate, *Am J Hosp Pharm 35*:783 (July) 1978.
303. Kresel JJ, McDermott JS, Huffer LM, et al.: Stability of carbenicillin and oxacillin frozen in syringes, *Am J Hosp Pharm 35*:310–312 (Mar) 1978.
304. Manning RE: Predicted expiration times for penicillin G in combination with multivitamin injections, *Am J Hosp Pharm 33*:870, 874 (Sep) 1976.
305. Cloyd JC, Bosch DE, and Sawchuk RJ: Concentration–time profile of phenytoin after admixture with small volumes of intravenous fluids, *Am J Hosp Pharm 35*:45–48 (Jan) 1978.
306. Bauman JL, Siepler JK, and Fitzloff J: Phenytoin crystallization in intravenous fluids, *Drug Intell Clin Pharm 11*:646–649 (Nov) 1977.
307. Ashwin J and Lynn B: Ampicillin stability in saline or dextrose infusions, *Pharm J 214*:487–489 (May 31) 1975.
308. O'Brien MJ, Portnoff JB, and Cohen EM: Cefoxitin sodium compatibility with intravenous infusions and additives, *Am J Hosp Pharm 36*:33–38 (Jan) 1979.
309. Stevens JS: Incompatibility of diphenhydramine hydrochloride (Benadryl) with meglumine iodipamide (Cholografin), *Radiology 117*:224–225 (Oct) 1975.
310. Petrick RJ, Wolleben JE, and Vargas TA: Stability of frozen solutions of doxycycline hyclate for injection, *Am J Hosp Pharm 35*:1386–1387 (Nov) 1978.
311. Chrai SS, Phelan KR, Speicher ER, et al.: Stability of gentamicin sulfate admixture, *Am J Hosp Pharm 34*:348 (Apr) 1977.
312. Gardella LA, Kesler H, Amann A, et al.: Intropin (dopamine hydrochloride) intravenous admixture compatibility, part 3: stability with miscellaneous additives, *Am J Hosp Pharm 35*:581–584 (May) 1978.
313. Schuetz DH and King JC: Compatibility and stability of electrolytes, vitamins and antibiotics in combination with 8% amino acids solution, *Am J Hosp Pharm 35*:33–44 (Jan) 1978.
314. El-Nakeeb MA, Souccar N, and Yousef RT: Inactivation of various antibiotics by some vitamins, *Can J Pharm Sci 11*:85–89 (July) 1976.
315. Dixon FW and Weshalek J: Physical compatibility of nine drugs in various intavenous solutions, *Am J Hosp Pharm 29*:822–823 (Oct) 1972.
316. Earhart RH: Instability of cis-dichlorodiammineplatinum in dextrose solution, *Cancer Treat Rep 62*:1105–1106 (July) 1978.
317. Greene RF, Chatterji DC, Hiranaka PK, et al.: Stability of cisplatin in aqueous solution, *Am J Hosp Pharm 36*:38–43 (Jan) 1979.
318. Morrison RA, Oseekey KB, and Fung HL: 5-Fluorouracil and methotrexate sodium: an admixture incompatibility?, *Am J Hosp Pharm 35*:15, 18 (Jan) 1978.
319. King JC: 5-Fluorouracil and methotrexate sodium: an admixture incompatibility?, *Am J Hosp Pharm 35*:18 (Jan) 1978.
320. Rusmin S, Welton S, DeLuca P, et al.: Effect of inline filtration on the potency of drugs administered intravenously, *Am J Hosp Pharm 34*:1071–1074 (Oct) 1977.
321. Morris ME: Compatibility and stability of diazepam injection following dilution with intravenous fluids, *Am J Hosp Pharm 35*:669–672 (June) 1978.
322. Allen LV, Levinson RS, and Phisutsinthop D: Compatibility of various admixtures with secondary additives at Y-injection sites of intravenous administration sets, *Am J Hosp Pharm 34*:939–943 (Sep) 1977.
323. Arnold TR, Eder J, and Lower B: Compatibility of primary-piggyback solution combinations, *Am J Hosp Pharm 35*:249–250 (Mar) 1978.
324. Jansen JR: Volume control sets and incompatibilities, *Am J Hosp Pharm 32*: 1225 (Dec) 1975.
325. Aisenstein A and Kahn S: Study of the stability of some frozen antibiotics, *Hosp Pharm 4*:17–21 (Feb) 1969.
326. Parker WA: Physical compatibilities of preanesthetic medications, *Can J Hosp Pharm 29*:91–92 (May–June) 1976.
327. Cradock JC, Kleinman LM, and Rahman A: Evaluation of some pharmaceutical aspects of intrathecal methotrexate sodium, cytarabine and hydrocortisone sodium succinate, *Am J Hosp Pharm 35*:402–406 (Apr) 1978.
328. Sarubbi FA, Wilson MB, Lee M, et al.: Noscomial meningitis and bacteremia due to contaminated amphotericin B, *J Am Med Assoc 239*:416–418 (Jan 30) 1978.
329. The Upjohn Company, Solu-Medrol IV admixture, dilution, and compatibility information, August 1978.
330. Parker WA, Morris ME, and Shearer CA: Incompatibility of diazepam injection in plastic intravenous bags, *Am J Hosp Pharm 36*:505–507 (Apr) 1979.
331. Ingallinera T, Kapadia AJ, Hagman D, et al.: Compatibility of glycopyrrolate injection with commonly used infusion solutions and additives, *Am J Hosp Pharm 36*:508–510 (Apr) 1979.
332. Bateman NE and Graham MD: Solubility of an ephedrine–phenobarbitone complex in water, *Australas J Pharm 48*:S68–S69 (June 30) 1967.
333. Chang CH, Ashford WR, Ives DAJ, et al.: Stability of oxytocin in various infusion solutions, *Can J Hosp Pharm 25*:152 (July–Aug) 1972.
334. Lynn B: Administration of carbenicillin and ticarcillin—pharmaceutical aspects, *Europ J Cancer 9*:425–433 (June) 1973.

335. Block ER and Bennett JE: Stability of amphotericin B in infusion bottles, *Antimicrob Agents Chemother 4*:648–649 (Dec) 1973.
336. Prue B and Elliott RK: Bethesda Hospital IV reference, *Am J IV Ther 4*:22–34 (Dec–Jan) 1977.
337. Anon: Label changes on albumin—a reminder, *FDA Drug Bull 8*:32 (Oct–Nov) 1978.
338. Van Der Linde LP, Campbell RK, and Jackson E: Guidelines for the intravenous administration of drugs, *Drug Intell Clin Pharm 11*:30–55 (Jan) 1977.
339. Koup JR, Schentag JJ, Vance JW, et al.: System for clinical pharmacokinetic monitoring of theophylline therapy, *Am J Hosp Pharm 33*:949–956 (Sep) 1976.
340. Jusko WJ, Koup JR, Vance JW, et al.: Intravenous theophylline therapy: nomogram guidelines, *Ann Intern Med 86*:400–404 (Apr) 1977.
341. Product information, Travasol, Travenol Laboratories, Deerfield, Illinois, January 1994.
342. Product information, FreAmine III, McGaw Laboratories, Irvine, California, September 1991.
343. Odne MAL, Lee SC, and Jeffrey LP: Rationale for adding trace elements to total parenteral nutrient solutions—a brief review, *Am J Hosp Pharm 35*:1057–1059 (Sep) 1978.
344. Jeejeebhoy KN, Langer B, Tsallas G, et al.: Total parenteral nutrition at home: studies in patients surviving 4 months to 5 years; *Gastroenterology 71*:943–953 (Dec) 1976.
345. Hull RL and Cassidy D: Trace element deficiencies during total parenteral nutrition, *Drug Intell Clin Pharm 11*:536–541 (Sep) 1977.
346. Shils ME: More on trace elements in total parenteral nutrition solutions, *Am J Hosp Pharm 32*:141–142 (Feb) 1975.
347. Okada A, Takagi Y, Itakura T, et al.: Skin lesions during intravenous hyperalimentation: zinc deficiency, *Surgery 80*:629–635 (Nov) 1976.
348. Matoi JR and Jeffreys LP: Formulation of a trace element solution for long-term parenteral nutrition, *Am J Hosp Pharm 35*:165–168 (Feb) 1978.
349. Athanikar N, Boyer B, Deamer R, et al: Visual compatibility of 30 additives with a parenteral nutrient solution, *Am J Hosp Pharm 36*:511–513 (Apr) 1979.
350. Finlayson JS: The birth and demise of "salt-poor" albumin, *Am J Hosp Pharm 35*:898–900 (Aug) 1978.
351. Winsnes M, Jeppsson R, and Sjoberg B: Diazepam adsorption to infusion sets and plastic syringes, *Acta Anaesthesiol Scand 25*:93–96 (Apr) 1981.
352. Bonner DP, Mechlinski W, and Schaffner CP: Stability studies with amphotericin B and amphotericin B methyl ester, *J Antibiotics 28*:132–135 (Feb) 1975.
353. Shadomy S, Brummer DL, and Ingroff AV: Light sensitivity of prepared solutions of amphotericin B, *Am Rev Resp Dis 107*:303–304, 1973.
354. Fields BT, Bates JH, and Abernathy RS: Effect of rapid intravenous infusion on serum concentrations of amphotericin B, *App Microbiol 22*:615–617 (Oct) 1971.
355. Barreuther AD, Dodge RR, and Blondeaux AM: Administration of amphotericin B, *Drug Intell Clin Pharm 11*:368–369 (June) 1977.
356. Arbuthnot R, Dullea A, and Rippel S: Controlling thrombophlebitis from amphotericin B, *Am J Hosp Pharm 35*:129 (Feb) 1978.
357. Rosch JM, Pazin G, and Fireman P: Mannitol and amphotericin B, *J Am Med Assoc 237*:27 (Jan 3) 1977.
358. Package insert, Cenolate, Abbott Laboratories, North Chicago, Illinois, December 1991.
359. Roberts JR: Cutaneous and subcutaneous complications of calcium infusions, *J Am Col Emerg Phys 6*:16–20 (Jan) 1977.
360. Product information, Tagamet, Smith Kline & French Laboratories, Philadelphia, Pennsylvania, October 1978.
361. Winters RE, Chow AW, Hecht RH, et al.: Combined use of gentamicin and carbenicillin, *Ann Intern Med 75*:925–927 (Dec) 1971.
362. Waitz JA, Drube CG, Moss EL, et al.: Biological aspects of the interaction between gentamicin and carbenicillin, *J Antibiot 25*:219–225 (Apr) 1972.
363. Ervin FR, Bullock WE, and Nuttall CE: Inactivation of gentamicin by penicillins in patients with renal failure, *Antimicrob Agents Chemother 9*:1004–1011 (June) 1976.
364. Peterson CD, Kaatz BL, and Angaran DM: Ticarcillin and carbenicillin, *Drug Intell Clin Pharm 11*:482–486 (Aug) 1977.
365. Davies M, Morgan JR, and Anand C: Interactions of carbenicillin and ticarcillin with gentamicin, *Antimicrob Agents Chemother 7*:431–434 (Apr) 1975.
366. Weibert R, Keane W, and Shapiro F: Carbenicillin inactivation of aminoglycosides in patients with severe renal failure, *Trans Am Soc Artif Int Organs 22*:439–443 1976.
367. Weibert RT and Keane WF: Carbenicillin–gentamicin interaction in acute renal failure, *Am J Hosp Pharm 34*:1137–1139 (Oct) 1977.
368. Bodey GP, Feld R, and Burgess MA: β-Lactam antibiotics alone or in combination with gentamicin for therapy of gram-negative bacillary infections in neutropenic patients, *Am J Med Sci 271*:179–186 (Mar–Apr) 1976.
369. Schimpff S, Satterlee W, Young UM, et al.: Empiric therapy with carbenicillin and gentamicin for febrile patients with cancer and granulocytopenia, *N Eng J Med 284*:1061–1065 (May 13) 1971.
370. Hendeles L: Are carbenicillin and gentamicin synergists or antagonists? *Hosp Pharm 7*:297–298 (Sep) 1972.
371. Kole-James A: Electrolyte content of common intravenous solutions and antibiotics, *Hosp Pharm 12*:394 (Aug) 1977.
372. Anon: Correction: Sodium in ticarcillin and carbenicillin, *Med Letter Drug Ther 19*:28 (Mar 25) 1977.
373. Turco SJ and Hasan I: Comparison of features of Kefzol and Ancef, *Hosp Pharm 11*:482, 484 (Nov) 1976.
374. Vukovich RA, Sugerman AA, and Fields LA: Effect of 2% procaine hydrochloride solution on the bioavailability of cephradine after intramuscular injection, *Curr Ther Res Clin Exp 18*:711–719 (Nov) 1975.
375. Stennett DJ, Simonson W, and Ayres JW: Effect of membrane filtration on 10-mg/ml cefazolin admixtures, *Am J Hosp Pharm 36*:657–660 (May) 1979.
376. Klink PR, Frable RA, and Bornstein M: Stability of Mandol in parenteral fluids, frozen solutions and admixtures containing other drugs, Presented at 13th Annual ASHP Midyear Clinical Meeting, December 1978, San Antonio, Texas.
377. Henney JE, Von Hoff DD, Rozencweig M, et al.: Thrombophlebitic potential of intravenous cytotoxic agents, *Drug Intell Clin Pharm 11*:266–267 (May) 1977.
378. Sillers BR: Irritant properties of diazepam, *Br Dent J 124*:295 (Apr 2) 1968.
379. Roche Products Ltd: Irritant properties of diazepam—reply, *Br Dent J 124*: 295 (Apr 2) 1968.
380. Friedenberg W and Barker JD: Intravenous diazepam administration, *J Am Med Assoc 224*:901 (May 7) 1973.
381. Jusko WJ, Gretch M, and Gassett R: Precipitation of diazepam from intravenous preparations, *J Am Med Assoc 225*:176 (July 9) 1973.
382. Kortilla K, Sothman A, and Andersson P: Polyethylene glycol as a solvent for diazepam: bioavailability and clinical effects after intramuscular administration, comparison of oral, intramuscular and rectal administration, and precipitation from intravenous solutions, *Acta Pharmacol Toxicol 39*:104–117 (Aug) 1976.
383. Hillestad L, Hansen T, Melsome H, et al.: Diazepam metabolism in normal man I. Serum concentrations and clinical effects after intravenous, intramuscular and oral administration, *Clin Pharmacol Ther 16*:479–484 (Sep) 1974.
384. Assaf RAE, Dundee JW, and Gamble JAS: Influence of route of administration on the clinical action of diazepam, *Anesthesia 30*:152–158 (Mar) 1975.
385. Baxter MT, McKenzie DD, and Mikish RA: Dilution of diazepam in intravenous fluids, *Am J Hosp Pharm 34*:124 (Feb) 1977.
386. Thong YH and Abramson DC: Continuous infusion of diazepam in infants with severe recurrent convulsions, *Med Ann DC 43*:63–65 (Feb) 1974.
387. Khalid MS and Schultz H: Treatment and management of emergency status epilepticus, *Epilepsia 17*:73–76 (Mar) 1976.
388. Gibberd FB: Diseases of the central nervous system—epilepsy, *Br Med J 4*: 270–272 (Nov 1) 1975.
389. Kawathekar P, Anusuya SR, Sriniwas P, et al.: Diazepam (Calmpose) in eclampsia: a preliminary report of 16 cases, *Curr Ther Res Clin Exp 15*:845–855 (Nov) 1973.
390. Baskett TF and Bradford CR: Active management of severe pre-eclampsia, *Can Med Assoc J 109*:1209–1211 (Dec 15) 1973.
391. Prensky AL, Raff MC, Moore MJ, et al.: Intravenous diazepam in the treatment of prolonged seizure activity, *N Eng J Med 276*:779–784 (Apr 6) 1967.
392. Tehrani JB and Cavanaugh A: Diazepam infusion in the treatment of tetanus, *Drug Intell Clin Pharm 11*:491 (Aug) 1977.
393. McLean WN: Safety of diazepam infusion questioned, *Drug Intell Clin Pharm 11*:690 (Nov) 1977.
394. Trissel LA, Kleinman LM, Davignon JP, et al.: Investigational drug information—daunorubicin hydrochloride and streptozotocin, *Drug Intell Clin Pharm 12*:404–406 (July) 1978.
395. Elsberry VA, Grangeia JM, Giorgianni SJ, et al.: The lipid phase in TPN, *Am J IV Ther 4*:22–28 (Apr–May) 1977.
396. Belin RP, Bivins BA, Jona JZ, et al.: Fat overload with a 10% soybean oil emulsion, *Arch Surg 111*:1391–1393 (Dec) 1976.
397. McNiff BL: Clinical use of 10% soybean oil emulsion, *Am J Hosp Pharm 34*: 1080–1086 (Oct) 1977.
398. Roche Laboratories, Personal communication.
399. Anon: McGaw compatibility studies. A preliminary report, McGaw Laboratories, Irvine, California, 1978.

400. Cooperman LB and Rubin I: Toxicity of ethacrynic acid and furosemide, *Am Heart J 85*:831–834 (June) 1973.
401. Kresel JJ, Smith AL, and Siber GR: Stability of gentamicin in plastic syringes, *Am J Hosp Pharm 34*:570 (June) 1977.
402. McNeely DJ, Weiner B, Stewart RB, et al.: Stability of gentamicin in plastic syringes, *Am J Hosp Pharm 34*:570, 575 (June) 1977.
403. Chrai SS and Ambrosio TJ: Gentamicin sulfate injection repackaging in syringes, *Am J Hosp Pharm 34*:920 (Sep) 1977.
404. Product information, Heparin Lock Flush Solution, Wyeth Laboratories, Philadelphia, Pennsylvania, 1978.
405. Sohn C and Cupit GC: Concentration of heparin in heparin-locks, *Drug Intell Clin Pharm 12*:112 (Feb) 1978.
406. Okuno T and Nelson CA: Anticoagulant activity of heparin in intravenous fluids, *J Clin Pathol 28*:494–497 (June) 1975.
407. Joy RT, Hyneck ML, Berardi RR, et al.: Effect of pH on the stability of heparin in 5% dextrose solutions, *Am J Hosp Pharm 36*:618–621 (May) 1979.
408. Brown J and Stead K: Anti-human lymphocyte globulin-heparin precipitate, *Drug Intell Clin Pharm 10*:654 (Nov) 1976.
409. Raab WP and Windisch J: Antagonism of neomycin by heparin, *Drug Res 23*: 1326–1328 (9) 1973.
410. Stella VJ: A case for prodrugs: Fosphenytoin, *Adv Drug Del Rev 19*:311–330, 1996.
411. Dupuis LL, Wong B, and Trope A: Stability of propafenone hydrochloride in i.v. solutions, *Am J Health-Syst Pharm 54*:1293–1295 (June 1) 1997.
412. Dupuis LL, Trope A, Giesbrecht E, and Wong B: Compatibility and stability of propafenone hydrochloride with five critical-care medications, *Can J Hosp Pharm 51*:55–57 (Apr) 1998.
413. Storvick WO and Henry HJ: Effect of storage temperature on stability of commercial insulin preparations, *Diabetes 17*:499–502 (Aug) 1968.
414. Jackson RL, Storvick WO, Hollinden CS, et al.: Neutral regular insulin, *Diabetes 21*:235–245 (Apr) 1972.
415. Page MM, Alberti KGMM, Greenwood R, et al.: Treatment of diabetic coma with continuous low-dose infusion of insulin, *Br Med J 2*:687–690 (June 29) 1974.
416. Kidson W, Casey J, Kraegen E, et al.: Treatment of severe diabetes mellitus by insulin infusion, *Br Med J 2*:691–694 (June 29) 1974.
417. Semple PF, White C, and Manderson WG: Continuous intravenous infusion of small doses of insulin in treatment of diabetic ketoacidosis, *Br Med J 2*: 694–698 (June 29) 1974.
418. Campbell LV, Lazarus L, Casey JH, et al.: Routine use of low-dose intravenous insulin infusion in severe hyperglycaemia, *Med J Aust 2*:519–522 (Oct 2) 1976.
419. Martin MM and Martin ALA: Continuous low-dose infusion of insulin in the treatment of diabetic ketoacidosis in children, *J Pediatr 89*:560–564 (Oct) 1976.
420. Drop SLS, Duval-Arnould BJM, Gober AE, et al.: Low-dose intravenous insulin infusion versus subcutaneous insulin injection: A controlled comparative study of diabetic ketoacidosis, *Pediatrics 59*:733–738 (May) 1977.
421. Fisher JN, Shahshahani MN, and Kitabchi AE: Diabetic ketoacidosis: low-dose insulin therapy by various routes, *N Engl J Med 297*:238–241 (Aug 4) 1977.
422. Goldberg NJ and Levin SR: Insulin adsorption to an inline membrane filter, *N Engl J Med 298*:1480 (June 29) 1978.
423. Kristofferson J, Skobba TJ, and Johansen T: Adsorption of insulin to infusion equipment, *Nor Farm Tidsskr 85*:220–224 (7) 1977.
424. Hirsch JI, Fratkin MJ, Wood JH, et al.: Clinical significance of insulin adsorption by polyvinyl chloride infusion systems, *Am J Hosp Pharm 34*:583–588 (June) 1977.
425. Weber SS, Wood WA, and Jackson EA: Availability of insulin from parenteral nutrient solutions, *Am J Hosp Pharm 34*:353–357 (Apr) 1977.
426. Whalen FJ, LeCain WK, and Latiolais CJ: Availability of insulin from continuous low-dose insulin infusions, *Am J Hosp Pharm 36*:330–337 (Mar) 1979.
427. Clarke BF, Campbell IW, Fraser DM, et al.: Direct addition of small doses of insulin to intravenous infusion in severe uncontrolled diabetes, *Br Med J 2*: 1395–1396 (Nov 26) 1977.
428. Peterson L, Caldwell J, and Hoffman J: Insulin adsorbance to polyvinyl chloride surfaces with implications for constant-infusion therapy, *Diabetes 25*:72–74 (Jan) 1976.
429. Sadeghi A, Mehrbanpour J, Behmard S, et al.: A trial of total dose infusion iron therapy as an outpatient procedure in rural Iranian villages (a three month follow-up), *Curr Ther Res Clin Exp 19*:595–602 (June) 1976.
430. Leach JK, Strickland RD, Millis DL, et al.: Biological activity of dilute isoproterenol solution stored for long periods in plastic bags, *Am J Hosp Pharm 34*:709–712 (July) 1977.
431. Browning ML: IM $MgSO_4$ ampuls for IV use, *Hosp Pharm 11*:325 (Aug) 1976.
432. Epperson E and Nedich RL: Mannitol crystallization in plastic containers, *Am J Hosp Pharm 35*:1337 (Nov) 1978.
433. Chatterji DC and Gallelli JF: Thermal and photolytic decomposition of methotrexate in aqueous solutions, *J Pharm Sci 67*:526–531 (Apr) 1978.
434. Muller HJ and Berg J: Stabilitatsstudie zu tramadolhydrochlorid im PVC-infusionbeutel, *Krankenhauspharmazie 18*:75–79, 1997.
435. Duttera MJ, Gallelli JF, Kleinman LM, et al.: Intrathecal methotrexate, *Lancet 2*:540 (Mar 4) 1972.
436. Hartshorn EA: Oxidation of methyldopate hydrochloride in alkaline media, *Am J Hosp Pharm 32*:244 (Mar) 1975.
437. Parker EA: Oxidation of methyldopate hydrochloride in alkaline media, *Am J Hosp Pharm 32*:244 (Mar) 1975.
438. Hartline JV and Zachman RD: Vitamin A delivery in total parenteral nutrition solution, *Pediatrics 58*:448–451 (Sep) 1976.
439. Sina A, Youssef MK, Kassem AA, et al.: Stability of oxytetracycline in solutions and injections, *Can J Pharm Sci 9*:44–49 (2) 1974.
440. Colding H and Anderson GE: Stability of antibiotics and amino acids in two synthetic L-amino acid solutions commonly used for total parenteral nutrition in children, *Antimicrob Agents Chemother 13*:555–558 (Apr) 1978.
441. Schneider E (Knoll AG, Milan, Italy): Personal communication, February 25, 2000.
442. Perrier D, Rapp R, Young B, et al.: Maintenance of therapeutic phenytoin plasma levels via intramuscular administration, *Ann Intern Med 85*:318–321 (Sep) 1976.
443. Sellers EM and Kalant H: Alcohol intoxication and withdrawal, *N Eng J Med 294*:757–762, 1976.
444. Greenblatt DJ and Shader RI: Treatment of the alcohol withdrawal syndrome, *in* Manual of psychiatric therapeutics, Little, Brown and Company, Boston, Massachusetts, 1975, pp 211–235.
445. Cooper PE: Intravenous phenytoin, *N Eng J Med 295*:1078 (Nov 4) 1976.
446. Greenblatt DJ and Shader RI: Intravenous phenytoin, *N Eng J Med 295*:1078 (Nov 4) 1976.
447. Frank JT: Author's response, *Drug Intell Clin Pharm 7*:419 (Sep) 1973.
448. Woo E and Greenblatt DJ: Choosing the right phenytoin dosage, *Drug Ther 7*:131–139 (Oct) 1977.
449. Bighley LD, Wille J, and Lach JL: Mixing of additives in glass and plastic intravenous fluid containers, *Am J Hosp Pharm 31*:736–739 (Aug) 1974.
450. Schondelmeyer S, Gatlin L, and Gwilt P: Intravenous phenytoin (concluded), *N Eng J Med 296*:111 (Jan 13) 1977.
451. Bauman JL and Siepler JK: Intravenous phenytoin (concluded), *N Eng J Med 296*:111 (Jan 13) 1977.
452. Sistare F and Greene R: Phenytoin crystallization in intravenous fluids, *Drug Intell Clin Pharm 12*:120 (Feb) 1978.
453. Biberdorf RI and Spurbeck GH: Phenytoin in IV fluids: results endorsed, *Drug Intell Clin Pharm 12*:300–301 (May) 1978.
454. Williams RHP: Potassium overdosage: a potential hazard of non-rigid parenteral fluid containers, *Br Med J 1*:714–715 (Mar 24) 1973.
455. Woodside W, King JA, and Barr A: Addition of potassium to non-rigid plastic intravenous infusion containers: a potential hazard, *J Hosp Pharm 31*:192–194 (Sep) 1973.
456. Lankton JW, Siler JN, and Neigh JL: Hyperkalemia after administration of potassium from nonrigid parenteral-fluid containers, *Anesthesiology 39*:660–661, 1973.
457. Vrabel RB and Amerson AB: Reconstitution of sodium nitroprusside, *Am J Hosp Pharm 32*:140–141 (Feb) 1975.
458. Challen RG: Stability of sodium nitroprusside solutions, *Australas J Pharm 48*:S110 (Oct 30) 1967.
459. Martin T and Patel JA: Determination of sodium nitroprusside in aqueous solution, *Am J Hosp Pharm 26*:51–53 (Jan) 1969.
460. Frank MJ, Johnson JB, and Rubin SH: Spectrophotometric determination of sodium nitroprusside and its photodegradation products, *J Pharm Sci 65*:44–48 (Jan) 1976.
461. Ammar HO: Stability of injection solutions of vitamin B_1, *Pharmazie 31*:373–374 (June) 1976.
462. Anon: Correction: sodium in ticarcillin and carbenicillin, *Med Letter Drug Ther 19*:28 (Mar 25) 1977.
463. Yamaji A, Yasuko F, Okuda H, et al.: Photodegradation of vitamin K^1 and vitamin K^2 injections in preservation and in intravenous admixtures, *J Nippon Hosp Pharm Assoc Sci Ed 4*:7–11 (5) 1978.
464. Kobayashi NH and King JC: Compatibility of common additives in protein hydrolysate/dextrose solutions, *Am J Hosp Pharm 34*:589–594 (June) 1977.

465. Humphreys A, Marty JJ, Gooey SL, et al.: Stability of methotrexate in an intravenous fluid, *Aust J Hosp Pharm 8*:66–67 (2) 1978.
466. Clayton SK: Stability of intravenous additive preparations; studies on hydralazine as an additive, *J Clin Pharm 2*:247–256 (4) 1978.
467. Anon: Mixing chlorpromazine and morphine, *Br Med J 3*:681 (Sep 14) 1974.
468. Crapper JB: Mixing chlorpromazine and morphine, *Br Med J 1*:33 (Jan 4) 1975.
469. Baird GM and Willoughby MLN: Photodegradation of dacarbazine, *Lancet 2*: 681 (Sep 23) 1978.
470. Georget S, Vigneron J, Blaise N, et al.: Stability of refrigerated and frozen solutions of tropisetron in either polyvinylchloride or polyolefin infusion bags, *J Clin Pharm Ther 22*:257–260, 1997.
471. Bergman HD: Cefamandole, *Drug Intell Clin Pharm 13*:144–149 (Mar) 1979.
472. Indelicato JM, Wilham WL, and Cerimele BJ: Conversion of cefamandole nafate to cefamandole sodium, *J Pharm Sci 65*:1175–1178 (Aug) 1976.
473. Palmer MA and Fraterrigo CC: Production of carbon dioxide gas after reconstitution of cefamandole nafate, *Am J Hosp Pharm 36*:596–597 (May) 1979.
474. Klink PR and McKeechan CW: Production of carbon dioxide gas after reconstitution of cefamandole nafate, *Am J Pharm 36*:597 (May) 1979.
475. Bornstein M, Klink PR, Farrell BT, et al.: Stability of frozen solutions of cefamandole nafate, *Am J Hosp Pharm, 37*:98–101 (Jan) 1980.
476. Buckles J and Walters V: Stability of amitriptyline hydrochloride in aqueous solution, *J Clin Pharm 1*:107–112 (June) 1976.
477. Enever RP, Po ALW, Millard BJ, et al.: Decomposition of amitriptyline hydrochloride in aqueous solution: identification of decomposition products, *J Pharm Sci 64*:1497–1499 (Sep) 1975.
478. Enever RP, Po ALW, and Shotton E: Factors influencing decomposition rate of amitriptyline hydrochloride in aqueous solution, *J Pharm Sci 66*:1087–1089 (Aug) 1977.
479. Holman BL and Dewanjee MK: Potential pH incompatibility of pharmacological and isotopic adjuncts to arteriography, *Radiology 110*:722–723 (Mar) 1974.
480. Kawilarang CRT, Georghiou K, and Groves MJ: The effect of additives on the physical properties of a phospholipid-stabilized soybean oil emulsion, *J Clin Hosp Pharm 5*:151–160, 1980.
481. Anon: Stadol Q&A, Bristol Laboratories, Syracuse, New York, November 1978, p 7.
482. Jacobs RS: Calcitonin-Salmon, *Drug Intell Clin Pharm 9*:557–559 (Oct) 1975.
483. Honda DH, Jansen JR, Minor DR, et al.: Preprinted physician's order form for intravenous cisplatin therapy, *Am J Hosp Pharm 36*:742–743 (June) 1979.
484. Davignon JP, Yang KW, Wood HB, et al.: Formulation of three nitrosoureas for intravenous use, *Cancer Chemother Rep*, Part 3, *4*:7–11 (May) 1973.
485. Buckles J and Walters V: Stability of imipramine hydrochloride solutions, *J Clin Pharm 1*:113–118 (June) 1976.
486. Shand DG: Propranolol, *N Eng J Med 293*:280–285 (Aug 7) 1975.
487. Vidarabine monohydrate for infusion, *Fed Register 44*:1374 (Jan 5) 1979.
488. Lauper RD: Leucovorin calcium administration and preparation, *Am J Hosp Pharm 35*:377 (Apr) 1978.
489. Tavoloni N, Guarino AM, and Berk PD: Photolytic degradation of adriamycin, *J Pharm Pharmacol 32*:860–862, 1980.
490. Black CD and Popovich NG: Stability of intravenous fat emulsions, *Arch Surg 115*:891 (July) 1980.
491. Bacon L: A review of two safety factors in the use of paraldehyde, *J Royal Col Gen Pract 30*:622–624 (Oct) 1980.
492. Horton JK and Stevens MFG: Search for drug interactions between the antitumor agent DTIC and other cytotoxic agents, *J Pharm Pharmacol 31(Suppl)*: 64P, 1979.
493. Zaccardelli DS, Krcmarik CS, Wolk R, et al.: Stability of imipenem and cilastatin sodium in total parenteral nutrient solution, *J Parenter Enter Nutr 14*: 306–309 (May/June) 1990.
494. Kuehnle C and Moore TD: Sodium chloride residue provides potential for drug incompatibilities, *Am J Hosp Pharm 36*:881 (July) 1979.
495. Trissel LA, Kleinman LM, Cradock JC, et al.: Investigational drug information—ifosfamide and semustine, *Drug Intell Clin Pharm 13*:340–343 (June) 1979.
496. Kohno M, Haneda I, Koyama Y, et al.: Basic studies on the stability of the high molecular weight antineoplastic agent neocarzinostatin. I. The stability of aqueous solutions of neocarzinostatin, *Japan J Antibiotics 27*:707–714 (6) 1974.
497. Dean TW and Baun DC: Preparation and standardization of nitroglycerin injection, *Am J Hosp Pharm 32*:1036–1038 (Oct) 1975.
498. Fung HL and Rhodes CT: Preparation of intravenous nitroglycerin solutions, *Am J Hosp Pharm 32*:139–140 (Feb) 1975.
499. Christensson B, Nordenfelt I, Westling H, et al.: Intravenous infusion of nitroglycerin in normal subjects, *Scand J Clin Lab Invest 23*:49–53, 1969.
500. Flaherty JT, Reid PR, Kelly DT, et al.: Intravenous nitroglycerin in acute myocardial infarction, *Circulation 51*:132–139 (Jan) 1975.
501. Kaplan JA and Treasure RL: Intravenous nitroglycerin during coronary artery surgery, *Mil Med 142*:152–153 (Feb) 1977.
502. Kaplan JA, Dunbar RW, and Jones EL: Nitroglycerin infusion during coronary-artery surgery, *Anesthesiology 45*:14–21 (July) 1976.
503. McNiff BL, McNiff EF, and Fung HL: Potency and stability of extemporaneous nitroglycerin infusions, *Am J Hosp Pharm 36*:173–177 (Feb) 1979.
504. Stach PE: Stability of nitroglycerin in aqueous solution, *Am J Hosp Pharm 30*:579 (July) 1973.
505. Cottrell JE and Turndorff H: Intravenous nitroglycerin, *Am Heart J 96*:550–553 (Oct) 1978.
506. Sturek JK, Sokolski TD, Winsley WT, et al.: Stability of nitroglycerin injection determined by gas chromatography, *Am J Hosp Pharm 35*:537–541 (May) 1978.
507. Fung HL: Potency and stability of extemporaneously prepared nitroglycerin intravenous solutions (editorial), *Am J Hosp Pharm 35*:528–529 (May) 1978.
508. Crouthamel WG, Dorsch B, and Shangraw R: Loss of nitroglycerin from plastic intravenous bags, *N Eng J Med 299*:262 (Aug 3) 1978.
509. Cossum PA, Galbraith AJ, Roberts MS, et al.: Loss of nitroglycerin from intravenous infusion sets, *Lancet 2*:349–350 (Aug 12) 1978.
510. Boylan JC, Robison RL, and Terrill PM: Stability of nitroglycerin solutions in Viaflex plastic containers, *Am J Hosp Pharm 35*:1031 (Sep) 1978.
511. Ludwig DJ and Ueda CT: Apparent stability of nitroglycerin in dextrose 5% in water, *Am J Hosp Pharm 35*:541–544 (May) 1978.
512. Brillaud AR: Interaction of Platinol (cisplatin) and the metal aluminum, Bristol Laboratories, Syracuse, New York, July 1979.
513. Product information, Intralipid 10% and 20%, Clintec Nutrition Company, Deerfield, Illinois, December 1998.
514. Product information, Liposyn II 10% and 20%, Abbott Laboratories, North Chicago, Illinois, August 1989.
515. Sewell DL and Golper TA: Stability of antimicrobial agents in peritoneal dialysate, *Antimicrob Agents Chemother 21*:528–529 (Mar) 1982.
516. El-Mallakh R: Incompatibilities with cimetidine hydrochloride injection, *Am J Hosp Pharm 36*:1024 (Aug) 1979.
517. Cutie MR: Letters, *Hosp Formul 15*:502–503 (June) 1980.
518. Tung EC, Gurwich EL, Sula JA, et al.: Stability of five antibiotics in plastic intravenous solution containers of dextrose and sodium chloride, *Drug Intell Clin Pharm 14*:848–850 (Dec) 1980.
519. Benvenuto JA, Anderson RW, Kerkof K, et al.: Stability and compatibility of antitumor agents in glass and plastic containers, *Am J Hosp Pharm 38*:1914–1918 (Dec) 1981.
520. Jhunjhunwala VP and Bhalla HL: Compatibility of mephentermine sulfate with hydrocortisone sodium succinate or aminophylline in 5% dextrose injection, *Am J Hosp Pharm 38*:1922–1924 (Dec) 1981.
521. Jhunjhunwala VP and Bhalla HL: Compatibility of aminophylline with hydrocortisone sodium succinate or dexamethasone sodium phosphate in 5% dextrose injection, *Am J Hosp Pharm 38*:900–901 (June) 1981.
522. Lee YC, Malick AW, Amann AH, et al.: Bretylium tosylate intravenous admixture compatibility. II. Dopamine, lidocaine, procainamide and nitroglycerin, *Am J Hosp Pharm 38*:183–187 (Feb) 1981.
523. Colvin M, Hartner J, and Summerfield M: Stability of carmustine in the presence of sodium bicarbonate, *Am J Hosp Pharm 37*:677–678 (May) 1980.
524. Dorr RT: Incompatibilities with parenteral anticancer drugs, *Am J IV Ther 6*: 42, 45, 46, 52 (Feb–Mar) 1979.
525. Das Gupta V and Stewart KR: Stability of cefamandole nafate and cefoxitin sodium solutions, *Am J Hosp Pharm 38*:875–879 (June) 1981.
526. Poochikian GK, Cradock JC, and Flora KP: Stability of anthracycline antitumor agents in four infusion fluids, *Am J Hosp Pharm 38*:483–486 (Apr) 1981.
527. Newton DW, Fung EYY, and Williams DA: Stability of five catecholamines and terbutaline sulfate in 5% dextrose injection in the absence and presence of aminophylline, *Am J Hosp Pharm 38*:1314–1319 (Sep) 1981.
528. Neil JM: A rational approach to intravenous additives, *Proc Guild 7*:3–33 (Winter) 1979.
529. Otterman GE and Samuelson DW: Incompatibility between carbenicillin injection and promethazine injection, *Am J Hosp Pharm 36*:1156 (Sep) 1979.
530. Marshall TR, Ling IT, Follis G, et al.: Pharmacological incompatibility of contrast media with various drugs and agents, *Radiology 84*:536–539 (Mar) 1965.
531. Monder C: Stability of corticosteroids in aqueous solutions, *Endocrinology 82*:318–326 (Feb) 1968.
532. Kleinberg ML, Stauffer GL, Prior RB, et al.: Stability of antibiotics frozen and

stored in disposable hypodermic syringes, *Am J Hosp Pharm 37*:1087–1088 (Aug) 1980.
533. Butler LD, Munson JM, and DeLuca PP: Effect of inline filtration on the potency of low-dose drugs, *Am J Hosp Pharm 37*:935–941 (July) 1980.
534. Allen LV and Stiles ML: Compatibility of various admixtures with secondary additives at Y-injection sites of intravenous administration sets. Part 2, *Am J Hosp Pharm 38*:380–381 (Mar) 1981.
535. Kleinberg, ML, Stauffer GL, and Latiolais CJ: Stability of five liquid drug products after unit dose repackaging, *Am J Hosp Pharm 37*:680–682 (May) 1980.
536. Kowaluk EA, Roberts MS, Blackburn HD, et al.: Interactions between drugs and polyvinyl chloride infusion bags, *Am J Hosp Pharm 38*:1308–1314 (Sep) 1981.
537. Zatz L, Sethia P, and Sherman NE: Stability of refrigerated aminophylline in 5% dextrose in water: a 96-hour study, *Hosp Pharm 16*:548 (Oct) 1981.
538. Scott KR, Bell AF, and Telang VG: Drug interactions I: Folic acid and calcium gluconate, *J Pharm Sci 69*:234 (Feb) 1980.
539. Jurgens RW, DeLuca PP, and Papadimitriou D: Compatibility of amphotericin B with certain large-volume parenterals, *Am J Hosp Pharm 38*:377–378 (Mar) 1981.
540. Gotz VP, Mar DD, and Roche JJ: Compatibility of amphotericin B with drugs used to reduce adverse reactions, *Am J Hosp Pharm 38*:378–379 (Mar) 1981.
541. Lee YC, Baaske DM, Amann AH, et al.: Bretylium tosylate intravenous admixture compatibility. I. Stability in common large-volume parenteral solutions, *Am J Hosp Pharm 37*:803–808 (June) 1980.
542. Yuhas EM, Lofton FT, Baldinus JG, et al.: Cimetidine hydrochloride compatibility with preoperative medications, *Am J Hosp Pharm 38*:1173–1174 (Aug) 1981.
543. Smith FM and Nuessle NO: Stability of lidocaine hydrochloride in 5% dextrose injection in plastic bags, *Am J Hosp Pharm 38*:1745–1747 (Nov) 1981.
544. Finch ME: Sodium thiopental in 5% dextrose in lactated Ringer's precipitate, *Hosp Pharm 14*:559–560 (Sep) 1979.
545. Kirschenbaum HL, Lesko LJ, Mendes RW, et al.: Stability of procainamide in 0.9% sodium chloride or dextrose 5% in water, *Am J Hosp Pharm 36*:1464–1465 (Nov) 1979.
546. Baaske DM, Malick AW, and Carter JE: Stability of procainamide hydrochloride in dextrose solutions, *Am J Hosp Pharm 37*:1050–1052 (Aug) 1980.
547. Jeglum EL, Winter E, and Kotos M: Nafcillin sodium incompatibility with acidic solutions, *Am J Hosp Pharm 38*:462, 464 (Apr) 1981.
548. Cutie MR and Lordi NG: Compatibility of verapamil hydrochloride injection in commonly used large-volume parenterals, *Am J Hosp Pharm 37*:675–676 (May) 1980.
549. Rosenberg HA, Dougherty JT, Mayron D, et al.: Cimetidine hydrochloride compatibility I: Chemical aspects and room temperature stability in intravenous infusion fluids, *Am J Hosp Pharm 37*:390–393 (Mar) 1980.
550. Yuhas EM, Lofton FT, Mayron D, et al.: Cimetidine hydrochloride compatibility II: Room temperature stability in intravenous infusion fluids, *Am J Hosp Pharm 38*:879–881 (June) 1981.
551. Yuhas EM, Lofton FT, Rosenberg HA, et al.: Cimetidine hydrochloride compatibility III: Room temperature stability in drug admixtures, *Am J Hosp Pharm 38*:1919–1922 (Dec) 1981.
552. Dahlin PA and Paredes SM: Visual compatibility of dobutamine with seven parenteral drug products, *Am J Hosp Pharm 37*:460, 464 (Apr) 1980.
553. Lesko LJ, Marion A, Ericson J, et al.: Stability of trimethoprim–sulfamethoxazole injection in two infusion fluids, *Am J Hosp Pharm 38*:1004–1006 (July) 1981.
554. Holmes CJ, Ausman RK, Walter CW, et al.: Activity of antibiotic admixtures subjected to different freeze-thaw treatments, *Drug Intell Clin Pharm 14*:353–357 (May) 1980.
555. Holmes CJ, Ausman RK, Kundsin RB, et al.: Effect of freezing and microwave thawing on the stability of six antibiotic admixtures in plastic bags, *Am J Hosp Pharm 39*:104–108 (Jan) 1982.
556. Boddapati S, Yang K, and Murty R: Physiochemical properties of aminophylline–dextrose injection admixtures, *Am J Hosp Pharm 39*:108–112 (Jan) 1982.
557. Canton EM and Baluch WM: Effect of freezing on particle formation in three antibiotic injections, *Am J Hosp Pharm 39*:124–125 (Jan) 1982.
558. Chaudry IA, Bruey KP, Hurlburt LE, et al.: Compatibility of netilmicin sulfate injection with commonly used intravenous injections and additives, *Am J Hosp Pharm 38*:1737–1742 (Nov) 1981.
559. Cutie MR: Effects of cold and freezing temperatures on pharmaceutical dosage forms, *US Pharmacist 4*:38–40, 48 (Oct) 1979.
560. Gove L, Walls ADF, and Scott W: Mixing parenteral nutrition products, *Pharm J 223*:587 (Dec 8) 1979.
561. Lauder AD: Mixing parenteral nutrition products, *Pharm J 223*:587 (Dec 8) 1979.
562. Hardin TC and Clibon U: Stability of 5-fluorouracil in a crystalline amino acid solution, *Am J IV Ther Clin Nutr 9*:39–40, 43 (Jan) 1982.
563. Yamaji A, Fujii Y, Kurata Y, et al.: Stability of pyridoxine hydrochloride in infusion solution under practical circumstances in wards, *Yakuzaigaku 40*:143–150 (Oct 20) 1980.
564. Dony J and Devleeschouwer MJ: Etude de la degradation photochimique de macrolides en presence de riboflavine, *J Pharm Belg 31*:479–484 (Sep–Oct) 1976.
565. Parker WA and Shearer CA: Metoclopramide compatibility, *Can J Hosp Pharm 32*:38 (Mar–Apr) 1979.
566. Parker WA: Compatibility of perphenazine and butorphanol admixtures, *Can J Hosp Pharm 33*:152 (Sep–Oct) 1980.
567. Stiles ML and Allen LV: Retention of drugs during inline filtration of parenteral solutions, *Infusion 3*:67–69 (May–June) 1979.
568. Somani P, Leathem WD, and Barlow AL: Safflower oil emulsion: single and multiple infusions with or without added heparin in normal human volunteers, *J Parenter Enter Nutr 4*:307–311 (May–June) 1980.
569. Rubin M, Bilik R, Gruenewald Z, et al.: Use of 5-micron filter in administering 'all-in-one' mixtures for total parenteral nutrition, *Clin Nutr 4*:163–168, 1985.
570. Moore RA, Feldman S, Treuting J, et al.: Cimetidine and parenteral nutrition, *J Parenter Enter Nutr 5*:61–63 (Jan–Feb) 1981.
571. Das Gupta V and Stewart KR: Stability of haloperidol in 5% dextrose injection, *Am J Hosp Pharm 39*:292–294 (Feb) 1982.
572. Cutie MR and Waranis R: Compatibility of hydromorphone hydrochloride in large-volume parenterals, *Am J Hosp Pharm 39*:307–308 (Feb) 1982.
573. Mirtallo JM, Caryer K, Schneider PJ, et al.: Growth of bacteria and fungi in parenteral nutrition solutions containing albumin, *Am J Hosp Pharm 38*:1907–1910 (Dec) 1981.
574. Holt HA, Broughall JM, McCarthy MM, et al.: Interactions between aminoglycoside antibiotics and carbenicillin or ticarcillin, *Infection 4*:107–109 (2) 1976.
575. Pickering LK and Gearhart P: Effect of time and concentration upon interaction between gentamicin, tobramycin, netilmicin, or amikacin and carbenicillin or ticarcillin, *Antimicrob Agents Chemother 15*:592–596 (Apr) 1979.
576. Pieper JA, Vidal RA, and Schentag JJ: Animal model distinguishing in vitro from in vivo carbenicillin–aminoglycoside interactions, *Antimicrob Agents Chemother 18*:604–609 (Oct) 1980.
577. Sturgeon RJ, Athanikar NK, Henry RS, et al.: Titratable acidities of crystalline amino acid admixtures, *Am J Hosp Pharm 37*:388–390 (Mar) 1980.
578. Ausman RK, Kerkhof K, Holmes CJ, et al.: Frozen storage and microwave thawing of parenteral nutrition solutions in plastic containers, *Drug Intell Clin Pharm 15*:440–443 (June) 1981.
579. Tortorici MP, Fearing D, Inman M, et al.: Photoreaction involving essential amino acid injection, *Am J Hosp Pharm 35*:1030 (Sep) 1978.
580. West KR, Sansom LN, Cosh DG, et al.: Some aspects of the stability of parenteral nutrition solutions, *Pharm Acta Helv 5*:19–22 (1–2) 1976.
581. Jurgens RW, Henry RS, and Welco A: Amino acid stability in a mixed parenteral nutrition solution, *Am J Hosp Pharm 38*:1358–1359 (Sep) 1981.
582. Mirtallo JM, Rogers KR, Johnson JA, et al.: Stability of amino acids and the availability of acid in total parenteral nutrition solutions containing hydrochloric acid, *Am J Hosp Pharm 38*:1729–1731 (Nov) 1981.
583. Rusho WJ, Standish R, and Bair JN: A comparison of crystalline amino acid solutions for total parenteral nutrition, *Hosp Formul 16*:29–33 (Jan) 1981.
584. Shils ME, Burke AW, Greene HL, et al.: Guidelines for essential trace element preparations for parenteral use: A statement by an expert panel, *J Am Med Assoc 241*:2051–2054 (May 11) 1979.
585. Freund H, Atamian S, and Fischer JE: Chromium deficiency during total parenteral nutrition, *J Am Med Assoc 241*:496–498 (Feb 2) 1979.
586. Heller RM, Kirchner SG, O'Neill JA, et al.: Skeletal changes of copper deficiency in infants receiving prolonged total parenteral nutrition, *J Pediatr 92*: 947–949 (June) 1978.
587. Moran DM, Russo J, and Bell LV: Zinc deficiency dermatitis accompanying parenteral nutrition supplemented with trace elements, *Clin Pharm 1*:169–176 (Mar–Apr) 1982.
588. Askari A, Long CL, and Blakemore WS: Zinc, copper and parenteral nutrition in cancer: a review, *J Parenter Enter Nutr 4*:561–571 (Nov–Dec) 1980.
589. Wolman SL, Anderson GH, Marliss EB, et al.: Zinc in total parenteral nutrition: requirements and metabolic effects, *Gastroenterology 76*:458–467 (Mar) 1979.
590. Fliss DM and Lamy PP: Trace elements and total parenteral nutrition, *Hosp Formul 14*:698–717 (July) 1979.

591. Schneider PJ: Total parenteral nutrition: Part II: What goes into parenteral nutrition solutions?, *J Postgrad Pharm (Hosp Ed) 1*:18–27 (Mar) 1979.

592. Isaacs JW, Millikan WJ, Stackhouse J, et al.: Parenteral nutrition of adults with a 900 milliosmolar solution via peripheral veins, *Am J Clin Nutr 30*:552–559 1977.

593. Romankiewicz JA, McManus J, Gotz VP, et al.: Medications not to be refrigerated, *Am J Hosp Pharm 36*:1541–1545 (Nov) 1979.

594. Swerling R: Dilution of oral and intravenous aminophylline preparations, *Am J Hosp Pharm 38*:1359–1360 (Sep) 1981.

595. Alcorn BT, Barnes SG, and du Plessis DJ: Pharmacy-initiated intravenous infusion guidelines, *Hosp Pharm 17*:60–76 (Feb) 1982.

596. Bowtle WJ, Heasman MJ, Prince AP, et al.: Compatibility of the cephalosporin, cefamandole nafate, with injections, *Int J Pharm 4*:263–265 (Jan) 1980.

597. Anon: I.V. dosage guidelines for theophylline products, *FDA Drug Bulletin 10*:4–5 (Feb) 1980.

598. Tipple M, Shadomy S, and Espinel-Ingroff A: Availability of active amphotericin B after filtration through membrane filters, *Am Rev Resp Dis 115*:879–881, 1977.

599. Maddux MS and Barriere SL: A review of complications of amphotericin B therapy: recommendations for prevention and management, *Drug Intell Clin Pharm 14*:177–181 (Mar) 1980.

600. Lufter CH and Ball WD: Activity of amphotericin B after filtration, *Drug Intell Clin Pharm 14*:719 (Oct) 1980.

601. Kuchinskas EJ and Levy GN: Comparative stabilities of ampicillin and hetacillin in aqueous solutions, *J Pharm Sci 61*:727–729 (May) 1972.

602. Schwartz MA and Hayton WL: Relative stability of hetacillin and ampicillin in solution, *J Pharm Sci 61*:906–909 (June) 1972.

603. Bundgaard H: Polymerization of penicillins: kinetics and mechanism of di- and polymerization of ampicillin in aqueous solution, *Acta Pharm Suec 13*:9–26, 1976.

604. Stjernstrom G, Olson OT, Nyqvist H, et al.: Studies on the stability and compatibility of drugs in infusion fluids 6. Factors affecting the stability of ampicillin, *Acta Pharm Suec 15*:33–50, 1978.

605. Johnson CA and Porter WA: Compatibility of azathioprine sodium with intravenous fluids, *Am J Hosp Pharm 38*:871–875 (June) 1981.

606. Kowaluk EA, Roberts MS, and Polack AE: Interactions between drugs and intravenous delivery systems, *Am J Hosp Pharm 39*:460–467 (Mar) 1982.

607. Bryan CK and Darby MH: Bretylium tosylate: a review, *Am J Hosp Pharm 36*:1189–1192 (Sep) 1979.

608. Henry RS, Jurgens RW, Sturgeon R, et al.: Compatibility of calcium chloride and calcium gluconate with sodium phosphate in a mixed TPN solution, *Am J Hosp Pharm 37*:673–674 (May) 1980.

609. Eggert LD, Rusho WJ, MacKay MW, et al.: Calcium and phosphorus compatibility in parenteral nutrition solutions for neonates, *Am J Hosp Pharm 39*:49–53 (Jan) 1982.

610. Robinson LA and Wright BT: Central venous catheter occlusion caused by body-heat-mediated calcium phosphate precipitation, *Am J Hosp Pharm 39*:120–121 (Jan) 1982.

611. Tuttle CB: Guidelines for phenytoin infusions, *Can J Hosp Pharm 37*:137–139 (4) 1984.

612. Stewart P, Lourwood D, and Skolly S: Guidelines for the administration of a phenytoin loading dose via IVPB, *Hosp Pharm 21*:1003–1004 (Oct) 1986.

613. Goldschmied S: An evaluation of the stability and safety of phenytoin infusion, *NY State J Pharm 7*:45–47 (2) 1987.

614. Kradjan WA and Burger R: In vivo inactivation of gentamicin by carbenicillin and ticarcillin, *Arch Intern Med 140*:1668–1670 (Dec) 1980.

615. Young LS, Decker G, and Hewitt WL: Inactivation of gentamicin by carbenicillin in the urinary tract, *Chemotherapy 20*:212–220, 1974.

616. Henderson JL, Polk RE, and Kline BJ: In vitro inactivation of gentamicin, tobramycin, and netilmicin by carbenicillin, azlocillin, or mezlocillin, *Am J Hosp Pharm 38*:1167–1170 (Aug) 1981.

617. Flournoy DJ: Inactivation of netilmicin by carbenicillin, *Infection 6*:241 (5) 1978.

618. Russo ME: Penicillin–aminoglycoside inactivation: another possible mechanism of interaction, *Am J Hosp Pharm 37*:702–704 (May) 1980.

619. Laskar PA and Ayres JW: Degradation of carmustine in aqueous media, *J Pharm Sci 66*:1073–1076 (Aug) 1977.

620. Cardi V and Willcox GS: Reconstituting cefamandole and protecting from light, *Am J Hosp Pharm 37*:334 (Mar) 1980.

621. Kaiser GV, Gorman M, and Webber JA: Cefamandole—a review of chemistry and microbiology, *J Infect Dis 137*:S10–S16 (May) 1978.

622. Wold JS, Joost RR, Black HR, et al.: Hydrolysis of cefamandole nafate to cefamandole in vivo, *J Infect Dis 137*:S17–S24 (May) 1978.

623. Palmer MA and Fraterrigo CC: Clarification of "explosive-like" reaction occurring when reconstituted cefamandole nafate was stored in syringes, *Am J Hosp Pharm 36*:1025 (Aug) 1979.

624. Fites AL: Reconstituting cefamandole and protecting from light, *Am J Hosp Pharm 37*:334 (Mar) 1980.

625. Foster TS, Shrewsbury RP, and Coonrod JD: Bioavailability and pain study of cefamandole nafate, *J Clin Pharm 20*:526–533 (Aug–Sep) 1980.

626. Indelicato JM, Stewart BA, and Engel GL: Formylation of glucose by cefamandole nafate at alkaline pH, *J Pharm Sci 69*:1183–1188 (Oct) 1980.

627. Tomecko GW, Kleinberg ML, Latiolais CL, et al.: Stability of cefazolin sodium admixtures in plastic bags after thawing by microwave radiation, *Am J Hosp Pharm 37*:211–215 (Feb) 1980.

628. Janousek JP and Minisci MP: An evaluation of cefazolin sodium injection in an IV piggyback bottle, *Infusion 2*:67–73 (Mar–Apr) 1978.

629. Stiles ML: Effect of microwave radiation on the stability of frozen cefoxitin sodium solution in plastic bags, *Am J Hosp Pharm 38*:1743–1745 (Nov) 1981.

630. Oberholtzer ER and Brenner GS: Cefoxitin sodium: solution and solid state chemical stability studies, *J Pharm Sci 68*:863–866 (July) 1979.

631. Bray RJ, Davies PA, and Seviour JA: The stability of preservative-free morphine in plastic syringes, *Anaesthesia 41*:294–295, 1986.

632. Walker SE, Paton TW, Fabian TM, et al.: Stability and sterility of cimetidine admixtures frozen in minibags, *Am J Hosp Pharm 38*:881–883 (June) 1981.

633. Cohen MR: Error 148—More on cisplatin storage, *Hosp Pharm 15*:158–159 (Mar) 1980.

634. LeRoy AF: Some quantitative data on cis-dichlorodiammineplatinum (II) species in solution, *Cancer Treat Rep 63*:231–233 (Feb) 1979.

635. Hincal AA, Long DF, and Repta AJ: Cis-platin stability in aqueous parenteral vehicles, *J Parenter Drug Assoc 33*:107–116 (May–June) 1979.

636. Mariani EP, Southard BJ, Woolever JT, et al.: Physical compatibility and chemical stability of cisplatin in various diluents and in large-volume parenteral solutions, *in* Cisplatin current status and new developments, Prestayko AW, Crooke ST, and Carter SK (eds), Academic Press, New York, New York, 1980, pp 305–316.

637. Repta AJ, Long DF, and Hincal AA: cis-Dichlorodiammineplatinum (II) stability in aqueous vehicles, *Cancer Treat Rep 63*:229–230 (Feb) 1979.

638. Gamble JAS, Dundee JW, and Assaf RAE: Plasma diazepam levels after single dose oral and intramuscular administration, *Anesthesia 30*:164–169, 1975.

639. Langdon DE, Harlan JR, and Bailey RL: Thrombophlebitis with diazepam used intravenously, *J Am Med Assoc 223*:184–185 (Jan 8) 1973.

640. Dam M and Christiansen J: Diazepam: intravenous infusion in the treatment of status epilepticus, *Acta Neurol Scandinav 54*:278–280, 1976.

641. Huber JW and Raymond GG: Additional conclusions on diazepam injectable precipitate: GC–MS confirmation, *Clin Toxicol 14*:439–444 (4) 1979.

642. Raymond G and Huber JW: Identification of injectable Valium precipitate, *Drug Intell Clin Pharm 13*:612 (Oct) 1979.

643. Newton DW, Driscoll DF, Goudreau JL, et al.: Solubility characteristics of diazepam in aqueous admixture solutions: theory and practice, *Am J Hosp Pharm 38*:179–182 (Feb) 1981.

644. Mason NA, Cline S, Hyneck ML, et al.: Factors affecting diazepam infusion: solubility, administration-set composition, and flow rate, *Am J Hosp Pharm 38*:1449–1454 (Oct) 1981.

645. MacKichan J, Duffner PK, and Cohen ME: Adsorption of diazepam to plastic tubing, *N Eng J Med 301*:332–333 (Aug 9) 1979.

646. Parker WA and MacCara ME: Compatibility of diazepam with intravenous fluid containers and administration sets, *Am J Hosp Pharm 37*:496–500 (Apr) 1980.

647. Cloyd JC, Vezeau C, and Miller KW: Availability of diazepam from plastic containers, *Am J Hosp Pharm 37*:492–496 (Apr) 1980.

648. Cloyd JC: Diluting diazepam injection, *Am J Hosp Pharm 38*:32 (Jan) 1981.

649. Dasta JF, Brier K, and Schonfield S: Loss of diazepam to drug delivery systems, *Am J Hosp Pharm 37*:1176, 1178 (Sep) 1980.

650. Boatman JA and Johnson JB: A four-stage approach to new-drug development, *Pharm Tech 5*:46–56 (Jan) 1981.

651. Martin CM: Chemical incompatibility of Renografin 76 and protamine sulfate, *Am Heart J 91*:675–677 (May) 1976.

652. Hoffman DM, Grossano DD, Damin L, et al.: Stability of refrigerated and frozen solutions of doxorubicin hydrochloride, *Am J Hosp Pharm 36*:1536–1538 (Nov) 1979.

653. Gardiner WA: Possible incompatibility of doxorubicin hydrochloride with aluminum, *Am J Hosp Pharm 38*:1276 (Sep) 1981.

654. Pfaller MA, Granich GG, Valdes R, et al.: Comparative study of the ability of four aminoglycoside assay techniques to detect the inactivation of aminoglycosides by β-lactam antibiotics, *Diag Microbiol Infect Dis 2*:93–100, 1984.

655. Product information, Liposyn III 10% and 20%, Abbott Laboratories, North Chicago, Illinois, June 1989.

656. Black CD and Popovich NG: Study of intravenous emulsion compatibility: effects of dextrose, amino acids and selected electrolytes, *Drug Intell Clin Pharm 15*:184–193 (Mar) 1981.
657. Black CD and Popovich NG: Comment on intravenous emulsion compatibility, *Drug Intell Clin Pharm 15*:908–909 (Nov) 1981.
658. Pelham LD: Rational use of intravenous fat emulsions, *Am J Hosp Pharm 38*: 198–208 (Feb) 1981.
659. Solussol C, et al: Long-term parenteral nutrition: an artificial gut, *Int Surg 61*: 266–270, 1976.
660. Wretlind A: Current status of Intralipid and other fat emulsions, *in* Fat emulsion in parenteral nutrition, Meng HC and Wilmore DW (eds), American Medical Association, Chicago, Illinois, 1975, pp 109–119.
661. Higbee KC and Lamy PP: Use of Intralipid in neonates and infants, *Hosp Formul 15*:117–119, 122, 127 (Feb) 1980.
662. Kleinberg ML, Stauffer GL, and Latiolais CJ: Effect of microwave radiation on redissolving precipitated matter in fluorouracil injection, *Am J Hosp Pharm 37*:678–679 (May) 1980.
663. Driessen O, deVos D, and Timmermans PJA: Adsorption of fluorouracil on glass surfaces, *J Pharm Sci 67*:1494–1495 (Oct) 1978.
664. Ghanekar AG, Das Gupta V, and Gibbs CW: Stability of furosemide in aqueous systems, *J Pharm Sci 67*:808–811 (June) 1978.
665. McLaughlin JE and Reeves DS: Gentamicin plus carbenicillin, *Lancet 1*:864–865 (Apr 24) 1971.
666. Young LS, Decker G, and Hewitt WL: Inactivation of gentamicin by carbenicillin in the urinary tract, *Chemotherapy 20*:212–220, 1974.
667. Murillo J, Standiford HC, Schimpff SC, et al.: Gentamicin and ticarcillin serum levels, *J Amer Med Assoc 241*:2401–2403 (June 1) 1979.
668. Gomez-Perez F: Anticoagulant activity of two commercially available heparin preparations: a controlled study, *J Clin Pharm 12*:413–416 (Oct) 1972.
669. Bangham DR and Woodward PM: Collaborative study of heparins from different sources, *Bull WHO 42*:129–149, 1972.
670. Dormarunno CG (Associate Medical Information Scientist, Medical and Drug Information, Pharmacia Corp., Kalamazoo, MI): Personal communication, March 21, 2002.
671. Liles S (Clinical Coordinator, Department of Pharmacy, Christ Hospital, Cincinnati, OH): Personal communication, February 20, 2002.
672. Hayes DM, Reilly RM, and Lee MMC: The pharmaceutical stability of deferoxamine mesylate, *Can J Hosp Pharm 47*:9–14 (Feb) 1994.
673. Downie G, McRae N, and Will I: Leaching of plasticizers by fat emulsion from polyvinyl chloride, *Br J Parenter Ther 6*:142–144 (Nov) 1985.
674. Anderson W, Harthill JE, Couper IA, et al.: Heparin stability in dextrose solutions, *J Pharm Pharmacol 29*:31P (Dec) 1977.
675. Bowie HM and Haylor V: Stability of heparin in sodium chloride solution, *J Clin Pharm 3*:211–214 (3) 1978.
676. Tunbridge LJ, Lloyd JV, Penhall RK, et al.: Stability of diluted heparin sodium stored in plastic syringes, *Am J Hosp Pharm 38*:1001–1004 (July) 1981.
677. Deeb EN and DiMattia PE: Standardization of heparin-lock maintenance solution, *N Eng J Med 294*:448 (Feb 19) 1976.
678. Holford NHG, Vozeh S, Coates P, et al.: More on heparin lock, *N Eng J Med 296*:1300–1301 (June 2) 1977.
679. Lynch CL, Linder GE, and Scheller JC: Frequently asked questions about insulin, *Hosp Pharm 15*:213–214 (Apr) 1980.
680. Graham DT and Pomeroy AR: Effects of freezing on commercial insulin suspensions, *Int J Pharm 1*:315–322, 1978.
681. Hill JB: Adsorption of insulin to glass, *Proc Soc Exp Biol Med 102*:75–77 (Oct) 1959.
682. Hill JB: The adsorption of I^{131}-insulin to glass, *Endocrinology 65*:515–517 (Sep) 1959.
683. Wiseman R and Baltz BE: Prevention of insulin-I^{131} adsorption to glass, *Endocrinology 68*:354–356 (Feb) 1961.
684. Sonksen PH, Ellis JP, Lowy C, et al.: Quantitative evaluation of the relative efficiency of gelatine and albumin in preventing insulin adsorption to glass, *Diabetologia 1*:208–210, 1965.
685. Suess V and Froesch ER: Zur therapie des coma diabeticum: quantitative bedeutung des insulinuerlusts am infusionsbesteck, *Schweizer Med Wochanschr 105*:1315–1318, 1975.
686. Okamoto H, Kikuchi T, and Tanizawa H: Adsorption of insulin to infusion bottles and plastic intravenous tubing, *Yakuzaigaku 39*:107–111 (July 30) 1979.
687. Wingert TD and Levin SR: Insulin adsorption to an air-eliminating inline filter, *Am J Hosp Pharm 38*:382–383 (Mar) 1981.
688. Hirsch JI, Wood JH, and Thomas RB: Insulin adsorption to polyolefin infusion bottles and polyvinyl chloride administration sets, *Am J Hosp Pharm 38*:995–997 (July) 1981.
689. Kerchner J, Cocaluca DM, and Juhl RP: Effect of whole blood on insulin adsorption onto intravenous infusion systems, *Am J Hosp Pharm 37*:1323–1325 (Oct) 1980.
690. Galloway JA and Bressler R: Insulin treatment in diabetes, *Med Clinics N Amer 62*:663–680 (July) 1978.
691. Sonksen P: Carrier solutions for low-level intravenous insulin infusion, *Br Med J 1*:151–152 (Jan 17) 1976.
692. Wan KK and Tsallas G: Dilute iron dextran formulation for addition to parenteral nutrient solutions, *Am J Hosp Pharm 37*:206–210 (Feb) 1980.
693. Bornstein M, Lo AY, Thomas PN, et al.: Moxalactam disodium compatibility with intramuscular and intravenous diluents, *Am J Hosp Pharm 39*:1495–1498 (Sep) 1982.
694. Kleinberg ML, Latiolais CJ, and Stauffer GL: Use of a microwave oven to redissolve crystallized mannitol injection (25%) in ampuls, *Hosp Pharm 14*: 391–392 (July) 1979.
695. Hanson GG: Microwave oven explosion, *Hosp Pharm 14*:612 (Oct) 1979.
696. Kleinberg ML, Latiolais CJ, and Stauffer GL: Microwave oven explosion, *Hosp Pharm 14*:612 (Oct) 1979.
697. Kana MJ: Microwave oven explosion, *Hosp Pharm 15*:104 (Feb) 1980.
698. Post RE, Stephen SP, and McKinley JD: A warming cabinet for storing mannitol ampuls, *Hosp Pharm 10*:102–103 (Mar) 1975.
699. Scott KR, Bell AF, and Thomas AJ: Warming kettle for storing mannitol injection, *Am J Hosp Pharm 37*:16, 19, 22 (Jan) 1980.
700. Herring P: Keeping mannitol in solution, *Hosp Pharm 15*:530–531 (Oct) 1980.
701. Church JJ: Continuous narcotic infusions for relief of postoperative pain, *Br Med J 1*:977–979 (Apr 14) 1979.
702. Townsend RJ, Puchala AH, and Nail SL: Stability of methylprednisolone sodium succinate in small volumes of 5% dextrose and 0.9% sodium chloride injections, *Am J Hosp Pharm 38*:1319–1322 (Sep) 1981.
703. Knutsen CV, Epps DR, McCormick DC, et al.: Total nutrient admixture guidelines, *Drug Intell Clin Pharm 18*:253–254 (Mar) 1984.
704. Riggle MA, Brandt RB, and Mueller DG: Decomposition of TPN solutions, *J Pediatr 100*:670 (Apr) 1982.
705. Gralla RJ, Itri LM, Pisko SH, et al.: Antiemetic efficacy of high-dose metoclopramide: randomized trials with placebo and prochlorperazine in patients with chemotherapy-induced nausea and vomiting, *N Eng J Med 305*:905–909 (Oct 15) 1981.
706. Cohen MR: Hazard warning—Flagyl IV (metronidazole hydrochloride) product reconstitution, *Hosp Pharm 16*:398, 400 (July) 1981.
707. Little GB and Boylan JC: I.V. Flagyl reacts with aluminum, *Hosp Pharm 16*: 627 (Nov) 1981.
708. Carmichael RR, Mahoney CD, and Jeffrey LP: Solubility and stability of phenytoin sodium when mixed with intravenous solutions, *Am J Hosp Pharm 37*: 95–98 (Jan) 1980.
709. Salem RB, Yost RL, Torosian G, et al.: Investigation of the crystallization of phenytoin in normal saline, *Drug Intell Clin Pharm 14*:605–608 (Sep) 1980.
710. Pfeifle CE, Adler DS, and Gannaway WL: Phenytoin sodium solubility in three intravenous solutions, *Am J Hosp Pharm 38*:358–362 (Mar) 1981.
711. Anon. Gravol, Carter-Horner, Inc., Montreal, Quebec. http://www.mdmultimedia.com/a/momo/mg5.htm (accessed 2000 Aug 20).
712. Gupta VD and Stewart KR: Stability of cefuroxime sodium in some aqueous buffered solutions and intravenous admixtures, *J Clin Hosp Pharm 11*:47–54, 1986.
713. Newton DW and Kluza RB: Prediction of phenytoin solubility in intravenous admixtures: physicochemical theory, *Am J Hosp Pharm 37*:1647–1651 (Dec) 1980.
714. Cohen MR: Make sure your nurses mix drug additions to infusing I.V. solutions, *Hosp Pharm 16*:164 (Mar) 1981.
715. Schuna A, Nappi J, and Kolstad J: Potassium pooling in non-rigid parenteral fluid containers, *J Parenter Drug Assn 33*:184–186 (July–Aug) 1979.
716. McCloskey WW and Jeffrey LP: Rational ordering of phosphate supplements, *Hosp Pharm 14*:486–487 (Aug) 1979.
717. Herman JJ: Phosphate: its valence and methods of quantification in parenteral solutions, *Drug Intell Clin Pharm 13*:579–585 (Oct) 1979.
718. Benderev K: Hypophosphatemia and phosphorus supplementation, *Hosp Pharm 15*:611–613 (Dec) 1980.
719. Swerling R: Use and preparation of cardioplegic solutions in cardiac surgery, *Hosp Pharm 15*:497–503 (Oct) 1980.
720. Loucas SP, Mehl B, Maager P, et al.: Stability of procaine HCl in a buffered cardioplegia formulation, *Am J Hosp Pharm 38*:1924–1928 (Dec) 1981.
721. Amann AH, Baaske DM, and Wagenknecht DM: Plastic i.v. container for nitroglycerin, *Am J Hosp Pharm 37*:618 (May) 1980.
722. Cacace LG, Harralson A, and Clougherty T: Stability of NTG, *Am Heart J 97*:816–818 (June) 1979.

723. Yuen PH, Denman SL, Sokoloski TD, et al.: Loss of nitroglycerin from aqueous solution into plastic intravenous delivery systems, *J Pharm Sci 68*:1163–1166 (Sep) 1979.
724. Baaske DM, Amann AH, Wagenknecht DM, et al.: Nitroglycerin compatibility with intravenous fluid filters, containers, and administration sets, *Am J Hosp Pharm 37*:201–205 (Feb) 1980.
725. Roberts MS, Cossum PA, Galbraith AJ, et al.: Availability of nitroglycerin from parenteral solutions, *J Pharm Pharmacol 32*:237–244, 1980.
726. Christiansen H, Skobba TJ, Andersen R, et al.: Nitroglycerin infusion—factors influencing the concentration of nitroglycerin available to the patient, *J Clin Hosp Pharm 5*:209–215 (Sep) 1980.
727. Sokoloski TD, Wu CC, and Burkman AM: Rapid adsorptive loss of nitroglycerin from aqueous solution to plastic, *Int J Pharm 6*:63–76 (July) 1980.
728. Baaske DM, Amann AH, Karnatz NN, et al.: Administration set for use with intravenous nitroglycerin, *Am J Hosp Pharm 39*:121–122 (Jan) 1982.
729. Little LA and Hatheway GJ: Problems with administration devices for commercially available nitroglycerin injection, *Am J Hosp Pharm 39*:400 (Mar) 1982.
730. Schad RF and Jennings R: Problems with administration devices for commercially available nitroglycerin injection, *Am J Hosp Pharm 39*:400 (Mar) 1982.
731. Turco SJ: Problems with administration devices for commercially available nitroglycerin injection, *Am J Hosp Pharm 39*:977 (June) 1982.
732. Vesey CJ and Batistoni GA: Determination and stability of sodium nitroprusside in aqueous solutions (determination and stability of SNP), *J Clin Pharm 2*:105–117 (2) 1977.
733. Milewski B and Jones D: Photodecomposition, *Hosp Pharm 16*:178 (Mar) 1981.
734. Nolly RJ, Stach PE, Latiolais CJ, et al.: Stability of thiamine hydrochloride repackaged in disposable syringes, *Am J Hosp Pharm 39*:471–474 (Mar) 1982.
735. Polk RE and Kline BJ: Mail order tobramycin serum levels: low values caused by ticarcillin, *Am J Hosp Pharm 37*:920, 922 (July) 1980.
736. Seitz DJ, Archambault JR, Kresel JJ, et al.: Stability of tobramycin sulfate in plastic syringes, *Am J Hosp Pharm 37*:1614–1615 (Dec) 1980.
737. Levison ME, Knight R, and Kaye D: In vitro evaluation of tobramycin, a new aminoglycoside antibiotic, *Antimicrob Agents Chemother 1*:381–384 (May) 1972.
738. Svensson LA: Stressed oxidative degradation of terbutaline in aqueous solution, *Acta Pharm Suec 9*:141–146 (Apr) 1972.
739. Cutie MR: Compatibility of verapamil with other additives, *Am J Hosp Pharm 38*:231 (Feb) 1981.
740. Anon: Hospital formulary monograph—Pipracil, Lederle Laboratories, Wayne, New Jersey, November 1981.
741. Chan KK, Giannini DD, Staroscik JA, et al.: 5-Azacytidine hydrolysis kinetics measured by high-pressure liquid chromatography and ^{13}C-NMR spectroscopy, *J Pharm Sci 68*:807–812 (July) 1979.
742. Poochikian GK and Cradock JC: -Diaziridinyl-3,6-bis(carboethoxy amino)-1,4-benzoquinone I: Kinetics in aqueous solutions by high-performance liquid chromatography, *J Pharm Sci 70*:159–162 (Feb) 1981.
743. Flora KP, Smith SL, and Cradock JC: Application of a simple high-performance liquid chromatographic method for the determination of melphalan in the presence of its hydrolysis products, *J Chromatogr 177*:91–97, 1979.
744. Kohno M, Ishii F, Haneda I, et al.: Studies on the stability of the high molecular weight antineoplastic antibiotic neocarzinostatin. II. The stability of neocarzinostatin injection, *Jap J Antibiot 27*:715–724 (6) 1974.
745. Morris ME and Parker WA: Compatibility of chlordiazepoxide HCl injection following dilution, *Can J Pharm Sci 16*:43–45 (1) 1981.
746. Cummings DS, Park MK, and Howard AB: Compatibility of propranolol hydrochloride injection with intravenous infusion fluids in plastic containers, *Am J Hosp Pharm 39*:1685–1687 (Oct) 1982.
747. Deans KW, Lang JR, and Smith DE: Stability of trimethoprim–sulfamethoxazole injection in five infusion fluids, *Am J Hosp Pharm 39*:1681–1684 (Oct) 1982.
748. Munson JW, Kubiak EJ, and Cohon MS: Cytosine arabinoside stability in intravenous admixtures with sodium bicarbonate and in plastic syringes, *Drug Intell Clin Pharm 16*:765–767 (Oct) 1982.
749. Kirschenbaum HL, Aronoff W, Perentesis GP, et al.: Stability of dobutamine hydrochloride in selected large-volume parenterals, *Am J Hosp Pharm 39*:1923–1925 (Nov) 1982.
750. Ray JB, Newton DW, Nye MT, et al.: Droperidol stability in intravenous admixtures, *Am J Hosp Pharm 40*:94–97 (Jan) 1983.
751. Das Gupta V, Stewart KR, and Gunter JM: Stability of cefotaxime sodium and moxalactam disodium in 5% dextrose and 0.9% sodium chloride injections, *Am J IV Ther Clin Nutr 10*:20, 27–29 (Jan) 1983.
752. Jett S, Eng SS, and Milewski B: Prochlorperazine edisylate incompatibility, *Am J Hosp Pharm 40*:210 (Feb) 1983.
753. Porter WR, Johnson CA, Cohon MS, et al.: Compatibility and stability of clindamycin phosphate with intravenous fluids, *Am J Hosp Pharm 40*:91–94 (Jan) 1983.
754. Hittel WP, Iafrate RP, Karnes HT, et al.: Stability of pentobarbital sodium in 5% dextrose injection and 0.9% sodium chloride injection, *Am J Hosp Pharm 40*:294–296 (Feb) 1983.
755. Niemiec PW, Vanderveen TW, Hohenwarter MW, et al.: Stability of aminophylline injection in three parenteral nutrition solutions, *Am J Hosp Pharm 40*:428–432 (Mar) 1983.
756. Perentesis GP, Piltz GW, Kirschenbaum HL, et al.: Stability and visual compatibility of bretylium tosylate with selected large-volume parenterals and additives, *Am J Hosp Pharm 40*:1010–1012 (June) 1983.
757. Yuen PC, Taddei CR, Wyka BE, et al.: Compatibility and stability of labetalol hydrochloride in commonly used intravenous solutions, *Am J Hosp Pharm 40*:1007–1009 (June) 1983.
758. Pyter RA, Hsu LCC, and Buddenhagen JD: Stability of methylprednisolone sodium succinate in 5% dextrose and 0.9% sodium chloride injection, *Am J Hosp Pharm 40*:1329–1333 (Aug) 1983.
759. Gannon PM and Sesin GP: Stability of cytarabine following repackaging in plastic syringes and glass containers, *Am J IV Ther Clin Nutr 10*:11–16 (June) 1983.
760. Sesin GP, Millette LA, and Weiner B: Stability study of 5-fluorouracil following repackaging in plastic disposable syringes and multidose vials, *Am J IV Ther Clin Nutr 9*:23–25, 29–30 (Sep) 1982.
761. Parker WA: Compatibility of perphenazine and butorphanol admixtures, *Can J Hosp Pharm 34*:38 (Mar–Apr) 1981.
762. Jump WG, Plaza VM, and Poremba A: Compatibility of nalbuphine hydrochloride with other preoperative medications, *Am J Hosp Pharm 39*:841–843 (May) 1982.
763. Dorr RT, Peng YM, and Alberts DS: Bleomycin compatibility with selected intravenous medications, *J Med 13*:121–130 (1–2) 1982.
764. Cutie MR: Compatibility of verapamil hydrochloride injection with commonly used additives, *Am J Hosp Pharm 40*:1205–1207 (July) 1983.
765. Shively CD, Redford A, and Mancini A: Flagyl I.V., drug–drug physical compatibility, *Am J IV Ther Clin Nutr 8*:9–16 (Aug) 1981.
766. Souney PF, Steele L, and Polk BF: Effect of vitamin B complex and ascorbic acid on the antimicrobial activity of cefazolin sodium, *Am J Hosp Pharm 39*:840–841 (May) 1982.
767. Keller JH and Ensminger WD: Stability of cancer chemotherapeutic agents in a totally implanted drug delivery system, *Am J Hosp Pharm 39*:1321–1323 (Aug) 1982.
768. Rodanelli R, Comelli M, Pascale W, et al.: Clinical pharmacology of some antibiotics: problems relating to their intravenous use in hospitals, *Farmaco Ed Prat 37*:185–188 (June) 1982.
769. Kowaluk EA, Roberts MS, and Polack AE: Drug loss in polyolefin infusion systems, *Am J Hosp Pharm 40*:118–119 (Jan) 1983.
770. Illum L and Bundgaard H: Sorption of drugs by plastic infusion bags, *Int J Pharm 10*:339–351, 1982.
771. Anon: Vistaril IM, table of physical compatibilities, Pfizer Laboratories, New York, New York, July 1979.
772. Package insert, Neut, Abbott Laboratories, North Chicago, Illinois, October 1988.
773. Jhunjhuowala VP and Bhalla HL: Sodium ampicillin: its stability in some large volume parenteral solutions, *Indian J Hosp Pharm 8*:55–57 (Mar–Apr) 1981.
774. Scheiner JM, Araujo MM, and DeRitter E: Thiamine destruction by sodium bisulfite in infusion solutions, *Am J Hosp Pharm 38*:1911–1913 (Dec) 1981.
775. Kirschenbaum HL, Aronoff W, Perentesis GP, et al.: Stability and compatibility of lidocaine hydrochloride with selected large-volume parenterals and drug additives, *Am J Hosp Pharm 39*:1013–1015 (June) 1982.
776. Lackner TE, Baldus D, Butler CD, et al.: Lidocaine stability in cardioplegic solution stored in glass bottles and polyvinyl chloride bags, *Am J Hosp Pharm 40*:97–101 (Jan) 1983.
777. Russell WJ and Meyer-Witting M: The stability of atracurium in clinical practice, *Anaesth Intens Care 18*:550–552 (Nov) 1990.
778. Shank WA and Coupal JJ: Stability of digoxin in common large-volume injections, *Am J Hosp Pharm 39*:844–846 (May) 1982.
779. Solomon DA and Nasinnyk KK: Compatibility of haloperidol lactate and heparin sodium, *Am J Hosp Pharm 39*:843–844 (May) 1982.
780. Elliott GT, McKenzie MW, Curry SH, et al.: Stability of cimetidine hydrochloride in admixtures after microwave thawing, *Am J Hosp Pharm 40*:1002–1006 (June) 1983.

781. Tsallas G and Allen LC: Stability of cimetidine hydrochloride in parenteral nutrition solutions, *Am J Hosp Pharm 39*:484–485 (Mar) 1982.
782. Roberts MS, Cossum PA, Kowaluk EA, et al.: Plastic syringes and intravenous infusions, *Med J Aust 2*:580–581 (Nov 28) 1981.
783. Das Gupta V and Stewart KR: Effect of tobramycin on the stability of carbenicillin disodium, *Am J Hosp Pharm 40*:1013–1016 (June) 1983.
784. Simmons A and Allwood MC: Sorption to plastic syringes of drugs administered by syringe pump, *J Clin Hosp Pharm 6*:71–73 (Mar) 1981.
785. Nicholas E, Hess G, and Colten HR: Degradation of penicillin, ticarcillin and carbenicillin resulting from storage of unit doses, *N Eng J Med 306*:547–548 (Mar 4) 1982.
786. Carpenter JP, Gomez EA, and Levin HJ: Administration of lorazepam injection through intravenous tubing, *Am J Hosp Pharm 38*:1514–1516 (Oct) 1981.
787. Newton DW, Narducci WA, Leet WA, et al.: Lorazepam solubility in and sorption from intravenous admixture solutions, *Am J Hosp Pharm 40*:424–427 (Mar) 1983.
788. Frable RA, Klink PR, Engel GL, et al.: Stability of cefamandole nafate injection with parenteral solutions and additives, *Am J Hosp Pharm 39*:622–627 (Apr) 1982.
789. Kirschenbaum HL, Aronoff W, Piltz GW, et al.: Compatibility and stability of dobutamine hydrochloride with large-volume parenterals and selected additives, *Am J Hosp Pharm 40*:1690–1691 (Oct) 1983.
790. Bosch EH, van Doorne H, Brouwers JRBJ, et al.: Vermindering van het sufentanilgehalte bij de bereiding en tijdens het gebruik van een epidurale toedieningsvorm. Een orienterend onderzoek, *Ziekenhuisfarmacie 9*:97–101 (3) 1993.
791. Cairns CJ: Incompatibility of amiodarone, *Pharm J 236*:68 (Jan 18) 1986.
792. Roney JV (Scientific Services, Hoechst-Roussel Pharmaceuticals, Somerville, New Jersey): Personal communication, December 4, 1983.
793. Berge SM, Henderson NL, and Frank MJ: Kinetics and mechanism of degradation of cefotaxime sodium in aqueous solution, *J Pharm Sci 72*:59–63 (Jan) 1983.
794. Smith FM and Nuessle NO: Stability of diazepam injection repackaged in glass unit-dose syringes, *Am J Hosp Pharm 39*:1687–1690 (Oct) 1982.
795. Cossum PA and Roberts MS: Availability of isosorbide dinitrate, diazepam and chlormethiazole from I.V. delivery systems, *Eur J Clin Pharmacol 19*: 181–185 (3) 1981.
796. Smith A and Bird G: Compatibility of diazepam with infusion fluids and their containers, *J Clin Hosp Pharm 7*:181–186 (Sep) 1982.
797. Yliruusi JK, Sothmann AG, Laine RH, et al.: Sorptive loss of diazepam and nitroglycerin from solutions to three types of containers, *Am J Hosp Pharm 39*:1018–1021 (June) 1982.
798. Kuhlman J, Abshagen U, and Rietbrock N: Cleavage of glycosidic bonds of digoxin and derivatives as function of pH and time, *Naunyn Schmiedebergs Arch Pharmacol 276*:149–156, 1973.
799. Gault MH, Charles JD, Sugden DL, et al.: Hydrolysis of digoxin by acid, *J Pharm Pharmacol 29*:27–32 (Jan) 1977.
800. Sternson LA and Shaffer RD: Kinetics of digoxin stability in aqueous solution, *J Pharm Sci 67*:327–330 (Mar) 1978.
801. Khalil SA and El-Masry S: Instability of digoxin in acid medium using a nonisotopic method, *J Pharm Sci 67*:1358–1360 (Oct) 1978.
802. Fagerman KE and Dean RE: Daily digoxin administration in parenteral nutrition solution, *Am J Hosp Pharm 38*:1955 (Dec) 1981.
803. Patterson MJ, Tjokrosetio R, and Hett KF: Stability of adrenaline injection BP following resterilization, *Aust J Hosp Pharm 11*:21–22 (Mar) 1981.
804. Nazeravich DR and Otlen NHH: Effect of inline filtration on delivery of gentamicin at a slow infusion rate, *Am J Hosp Pharm 40*:1961–1964 (Nov) 1983.
805. Zell M and Paone RP: Stability of insulin in plastic syringes, *Am J Hosp Pharm 40*:637–638 (Apr) 1983.
806. Benvenuto JA: Errors in oncolytic agent stability study, *Am J Hosp Pharm 40*:1628 (Oct) 1983.
807. Bisaillon S and Sarrazin R: Compatibility of several antibiotics or hydrocortisone when added to metronidazole solution for intravenous infusion, *J Parenter Sci Technol 37*:129–132 (July–Aug) 1983.
808. Gove L: Antibiotic interactions, *Pharm J 231*:233 (Sep 3) 1983.
809. Ennis CE, Merritt RJ, and Neff ON: In vitro study of inline filtration of medications commonly administered to pediatric cancer patients, *J Parenter Enter Nutr 7*:156–158 (Mar–Apr) 1983.
810. Buxton PC, Conduit SM, and Hathaway J: Stability of parentrovite in infusion fluids, *Br J IV Ther 4*:5, 12 (Jan) 1983.
811. Das Gupta V and Stewart KR: Stability of dobutamine hydrochloride and verapamil hydrochloride in 0.9% sodium chloride and 5% dextrose injections, *Am J Hosp Pharm 41*:686–689 (Apr) 1984.
812. Hasegawa GR and Eder JF: Visual compatibility of dobutamine hydrochloride with other injectable drugs, *Am J Hosp Pharm 41*:949–951 (May) 1984.
813. Souney PF, Colucci RD, Mariani G, et al.: Compatibility of magnesium sulfate solutions with various antibiotics during simulated Y-site injection, *Am J Hosp Pharm 41*:323–324 (Feb) 1984.
814. Lundergan FS, Lombardi TP, Neilan GE, et al.: Stability of tobramycin sulfate mixed with oxacillin sodium and nafcillin sodium in human serum, *Am J Hosp Pharm 41*:144–145 (Jan) 1981.
815. Parker WA: Physical compatibility update of preoperative medications, *Hosp Pharm 19*:475–478 (July) 1984.
816. Hale DC, Jenkins R, and Matsen JM: In-vitro inactivation of aminoglycoside antibiotics by piperacillin and carbenicillin, *Am J Clin Pathol 74*:316–319 (Sep) 1980.
817. Rank DM, Packer AM, and Tierney MG: In vitro inactivation of tobramycin by penicillins, *Am J Hosp Pharm 41*:1187–1188 (June) 1984.
818. Karlsen J, Thonnesen HH, Olsen IR, et al.: Stability of cytotoxic intravenous solutions subjected to freeze–thaw treatment, *Nor Pharm Acta 45*:61–67 (2) 1983.
819. Cheung YW, Vishnuvajjala BR, and Flora KP: Stability of cytarabine, methotrexate sodium, and hydrocortisone sodium succinate admixtures, *Am J Hosp Pharm 41*:1802–1806 (Sep) 1984.
820. Bundgaard H and Larsen C: Influence of carbohydrates and polyhydric alcohols on the stability of cephalosporins in aqueous solution, *Int J Pharm 16*: 319–325 (Oct) 1983.
821. Hamilton G: Adverse reactions to intravenous pyelography contrast agents, *Can Med Assoc J 129*:405–406 (Sep 1) 1983.
822. Miller B and Pesko L: Effect of freezing on particulate matter concentrations in five antibiotic solutions, *Am J IV Ther Clin Nutr 11*:19–22 (Mar) 1984.
823. Wagman GH, Bailey JV, and Weinstein MJ: Binding of aminoglycoside antibiotics to filtration materials, *Antimicrob Agents Chemother 7*:316–319 (Mar) 1975.
824. Tindula RJ, Ambrose PJ, and Harralson AF: Aminoglycoside inactivation by penicillins and cephalosporins and its impact on drug-level monitoring, *Drug Intell Clin Pharm 17*:906–908 (Dec) 1983.
825. Gillies IR: Physical stability of Intralipid following drug addition, *Aust J Hosp Pharm 10*:118–120 (Sep) 1980.
826. Hardin TC, Clibon U, Page CP, et al.: Compatibility of 5-fluorouracil and total parenteral nutrition solutions, *J Parenter Enter Nutr 6*:163–165 (Mar–Apr) 1982.
827. Gaj E, Sesin GP, and Griffin RE: Evaluation of growth of five microorganisms in doxorubicin and floxuridine media, *Pharm Manufacturing 1*:50, 52–53 (Mar) 1984.
828. Gaj E and Griffin RE: Evaluation of growth of six microorganisms in fluorouracil, bacteriostatic sodium chloride 0.9% and sodium chloride 0.9% media, *Hosp Pharm 18*:348–349 (July) 1983.
829. Turco SJ: Drug adsorption to membrane filters, *Am J IV Ther Clin Nutr 9*:6, 9 (May) 1982.
830. Robinson WA and Krebs LU: The "real stuff" for intrathecal injection during leukaemia therapy, *Lancet 1*:283 (Jan 30) 1982.
831. Frear RS: Cefoperazone–aminoglycoside incompatibility, *Am J Hosp Pharm 40*:564 (Apr) 1983.
832. O'Bey KA, Jim LK, Gee JP, et al.: Temperature dependence of the stability of tobramycin mixed with penicillins in human serum, *Am J Hosp Pharm 39*: 1005–1008 (June) 1982.
833. Bhatia J, Mims LC, and Roesel RA: Effect of phototherapy on amino acid solutions containing multivitamins, *J Pediatr 96*:284–286 (Feb) 1980.
834. Koshiro A and Fujita T: Interaction of penicillins with the components of plasma expanders, *Drug Intell Clin Pharm 17*:351–356 (May) 1983.
835. Szucsova S, Slana M, and Lehky M: Stability of infusion mixtures of 5% glucose solution with injection solutions, *Farm Obzor 52*:209–213 (May) 1983.
836. Gillis J, Jones G, and Pencharz P: Delivery of vitamin A, D, and E in total parenteral nutrition solutions, *J Parenter Enter Nutr 7*:11–14 (Jan–Feb) 1983.
837. Farago S: Compatibility of antibiotics and other drugs in total parenteral nutrition solutions, *Can J Hosp Pharm 36*:43–51 (2) 1983.
838. Gaj E and Sesin GP: Compatibility of doxorubicin hydrochloride and vinblastine sulfate—stability of a solution stored in Cormed reservoir bags or Monoject plastic syringes, *Am J IV Ther Clin Nutr 11*:8–9, 13–14, 19–20 (May) 1984.
839. Bar-Or D, Kulig K, Marx JA, et al.: Precipitation of verapamil, *Ann Intern Med 97*:619 (Oct) 1982.
840. Tucker R and Gentile JF: Precipitation of verapamil with nafcillin, *Am J Hosp Pharm 41*:2588 (Dec) 1984.

841. Hasegawa GR and Eder JF: Dobutamine–heparin mixture inadvisable, *Am J Hosp Pharm 41*:2588, 2590 (Dec) 1984.
842. Chen MF, Boyce HW, and Triplett L: Stability of B vitamins in mixed parenteral nutrition solution, *J Parenter Enter Nutr 7*:462–464 (Sep–Oct) 1983.
843. Bowman BB and Nguyen P: Stability of thiamine in parenteral nutrition solutions, *J Parenter Enter Nutr 7*:567–568 (Nov–Dec) 1983.
844. Newton DW: Physicochemical determinants of incompatibility and instability in injectable drug solutions and admixtures, *Am J Hosp Pharm 35*:1213–1222 (Oct) 1978.
845. Newton DW: Physicochemical determinants of incompatibility and instability of drugs for injection and infusion, *in* Trissel LA: Handbook on injectable drugs, 3rd ed, American Society of Hospital Pharmacists, Bethesda, Maryland, 1983, pp XI–XXI.
846. Raymond G, Day P, and Rabb M: Sodium content of commonly administered intravenous drugs, *Hosp Pharm 17*:560–561 (Oct) 1982.
847. Rich DS: Recent information about inactivation of aminoglycosides by carbenicillin and ticarcillin: clinical implications, *Hosp Pharm 18*:41–43 (Jan) 1983.
848. Lawrence RI, Flukes WK, Rust VJ, et al.: Total parenteral nutrition using a combined nutrient solution, *Aust J Hosp Pharm 11*:540–542 (4) 1981.
849. Davis SS and Galloway M: Total parenteral nutrition, *Pharm J 230*:6 (Jan 1 & 8) 1983.
850. Anon: 3-in-1 admixture guide from Travenol, Travenol Laboratories, November 1983.
851. Chan JCM, Malekzadeh M, and Hurley J: pH and titratable acidity of amino acid mixtures used in hyperalimentation, *J Am Med Assoc 220*:1119–1120 (May 22) 1972.
852. Kirk B and Sprake JM: Stability of aminophylline, *Br J IV Ther 3*:4, 6, 8 (Nov) 1982.
853. Vogenberg FR and Souney PF: Stability guidelines for routinely refrigerated drug products, *Am J Hosp Pharm 40*:101–102 (Jan) 1983.
854. Niemiec PW and Vanderveen TW: Compatibility considerations in parenteral nutrient solutions, *Am J Hosp Pharm 41*:893–911 (May) 1984.
855. Irving JD and Reynolds PV: Disposable syringe danger, *Lancet 1*:362 (Feb 12) 1966.
856. Salter F (Bristol Myers Squibb, Princeton, New Jersey): Personal communication, February 27, 1991.
857. Hopefl AW: Clinical use of intravenous acyclovir, *Drug Intell Clin Pharm 17*: 623–628 (Sep) 1983.
858. Larsen C and Bundgaard H: Polymerization of penicillins VI. Time-course of formation of antigenic di- and polymerization products in aqueous ampicillin sodium solutions, *Arch Pharm Chemi Sci Ed 5*:201–209, 1977.
859. Carthy BJ and Hill GT: Some aspects of the analysis and stability of atracurium besylate, *Anal Proc 20*:177–179 (Apr) 1983.
860. D'Arcy PF: Comment on handling of anticancer drugs, *Drug Intell Clin Pharm 18*:417 (May) 1984.
861. Adams J, Wilson JP, and Solimando DA: Instability of bleomycin in plastic containers, *Am J Hosp Pharm 39*:1636 (Oct) 1982.
862. Levin VA, Zackheim HS, and Liu J: Stability of carmustine for topical application, *Arch Dermatol 118*:450–451 (July) 1982.
863. Chan KK and Zackheim HS: Stability of nitrosourea solutions, *Arch Dermatol 107*:298, 1973.
864. Teil SM, Arwood LL, and Visconti JA: Stability of gentamicin and cefamandole in serum, *Am J Hosp Pharm 39*:485–486 (Mar) 1982.
865. Portnoff JB, Henley MW, and Restaino FA: Development of sodium cefoxitin as a dosage form, *J Parenter Sci Technol 37*:180–185 (Sep–Oct) 1983.
866. Vaughan LM and Poon CY: Stability of ceftazidime and vancomycin alone and in combination in heparinized and nonheparinized peritoneal dialysis solution, *Ann Pharmacother 28*:572–576 (May) 1994.
867. Wang YJ and Monkhouse DC: Solution stability of cephradine neutralized with arginine or sodium bicarbonate, *Am J Hosp Pharm 40*:432–434 (Mar) 1983.
868. Sorkin EM and Darvey DC: Review of cimetidine drug interactions, *Drug Intell Clin Pharm 17*:110–120 (Feb) 1983.
869. Raymond G and Day P: Multiple sources of sodium in injectable drugs, *Drug Intell Clin Pharm 16*:703 (Sep) 1982.
870. Eshaque M, McKay MJ, and Theophanides T: D-Mannitol platinum complexes, *Wadley Med Bull 7*:338–348 (1) 1977.
871. Ferguson DE: Degradation of clindamycin in frozen admixtures, *Am J Hosp Pharm 38*:1156 (July) 1982.
872. Ausman RK, Holmes CJ, Kundsin RB, et al.: Degradation of clindamycin in frozen admixtures, *Am J Hosp Pharm 39*:1156 (July) 1982.
873. Cairns CJ and Robertson J: Incompatibility of ceftazidime and vancomycin, *Pharm J 238*:577 (May 9) 1987.
874. Anon: Sandimmune—pharmacy fact sheet, Sandoz, East Hanover, New Jersey, November 1983.
875. Senholzi CS and Kerus MP: Crystal formation after reconstituting cefazolin sodium with 0.9% sodium chloride injection, *Am J Hosp Pharm 42*:129–130 (Jan) 1985.
876. Thompson DF, Allen LV, Desai SR, et al.: Compatibility of furosemide with aminoglycoside admixtures, *Am J Hosp Pharm 42*:116–119 (Jan) 1985.
877. Geary TG, Akood MA, and Jensen JB: Characteristics of chloroquine binding to glass and plastic, *Am J Trop Med Hyg 32*:19–23 (Jan) 1984.
878. Yayon A and Ginsburg A: A method for the measurement of chloroquin uptake in erythrocytes, *Anal Biochem 107*:332–336, 1980.
879. D'Arcy PF: Drug interactions with medical plastics, *Drug Intell Clin Pharm 17*:726–731 (Oct) 1983.
880. Kowaluk EA, Roberts MS, and Polack AE: Factors affecting the availability of diazepam stored in plastic bags and administered through intravenous sets, *Am J Hosp Pharm 40*:417–423 (Mar) 1983.
881. Kasahara K and Ruiz-Torres A: Einwirkung der verdauungssafe auf die bestandigkeit des digoxin-und digitoxin-molekuls, *Klin Wochenschr 47*:1109–1111, 1969.
882. Berman W, Whitman V, Marks KH, et al.: Inadvertent overadministration of digoxin to low-birth-weight infants, *J Pediatr 92*:1024–1025 (June) 1978.
883. Berman W, Dubynsky O, Whitman V, et al.: Digoxin therapy in low-birth-weight infants with patent ductus arteriosus, *J Pediatr 93*:652–655 (Oct) 1978.
884. Hajratwala BR: Stability of prostaglandins, *Aust J Pharm Sci NS5*:39–41 (June) 1975.
885. Roseman TJ, Sims B, and Stehle RG: Stability of prostaglandins, *Am J Hosp Pharm 30*:236–239 (Mar) 1973.
886. Gupta VD and Stewart KR: Stability of cefsulodin in aqueous buffered solutions and some intravenous admixtures, *J Clin Hosp Pharm 9*:21–27 (Jan) 1984.
887. Williamson MJ, Luce JK, and Hausmann WK: Doxorubicin hydrochloride–aluminum interaction, *Am J Hosp Pharm 40*:214 (Feb) 1983.
888. Chin TH (Professional Services, Miles Inc., West Haven, Connecticut): Personal communication, December 3, 1993.
889. Hausrani PK, Davis SS, and Groves J: Preparation and properties of sterile intravenous emulsions, *J Parenter Sci Technol 37*:145–150 (July–Aug) 1983.
890. Gray MS and Singleton WS: Creaming of phosphatide stabilized fat emulsions by electrolyte solutions, *J Pharm Sci 56*:1428–1431 (Nov) 1967.
891. Knutsen C, Miller P, and Kaminski MV: Compatibility, stability, and effect of mixing 10% fat emulsion in TPN solutions, *J Parenter Enter Nutr 5*:579 (Nov–Dec) 1981.
892. Burnham WR, Hansrani PK, Knott CE, et al.: Stability of a fat emulsion based intravenous feeding mixture, *Int J Pharm 13*:9–22 (Dec) 1983.
893. Hardin TC: Complex parenteral nutrition solutions: II. Addition of fat emulsions, *Nutr Supp Serv 3*:50–51 (May) 1983.
894. Quebbeman EJ, Hamid AAR, Hoffman NE, et al.: Stability of fluorouracil in plastic containers used for continuous infusion at home, *Am J Hosp Pharm 41*:1153–1156 (June) 1984.
895. Barker A, Hebron BS, Beck PR, et al.: Folic acid and total parenteral nutrition, *J Parenter Enter Nutr 8*:3–7 (Jan–Feb) 1984.
896. Louie N and Stennett DJ: Stability of folic acid in 25% dextrose, 3.5% amino acids, and multivitamin solutions, *J Parenter Enter Nutr 8*:421–426 (July–Aug) 1984.
897. Koshiro A, Oie S, Harima Y, et al.: Compatibility of gentamicin sulfate injection in parenteral solutions, *Jap J Hosp Pharm 7*:377–380 (6) 1982.
898. Godefroid RJ: Intravenous gentamicin dilution requirements, *Am J Hosp Pharm 39*:1457, 1459 (Sep) 1982.
899. Godefroid RJ: Comment on IV guidelines, *Drug Intell Clin Pharm 18*:925 (Nov) 1984.
900. Matthews H: Heparin anticoagulant activity in intravenous fluids utilising a chromagenic substrate assay method, *Aust J Hosp Pharm 12*:S17–S22 (June) 1982.
901. Turco SJ: Heparin locks, *Am J IV Ther Clin Nutr 10*:9, 12 (Jan) 1983.
902. Swerling R: Normal saline or dilute heparin for heparin lock flush? *Infusion 6*:123–124 (July–Aug) 1982.
903. Epperson EL: Efficacy of 0.9% sodium chloride injection with and without heparin for maintaining indwelling intermittent injection sites, *Clin Pharm 3*: 626–629 (Nov–Dec) 1984.
904. Kanke M, Eubanks JL, and DeLuca PP: Binding of selected drugs to a "treated" inline filter, *Am J Hosp Pharm 40*:1323–1328 (Aug) 1983.
905. Anderson W and Harthill JE: Anticoagulant activity of heparins in dextrose solutions, *J Pharm Pharmacol 34*:90–96 (Feb) 1982.

906. Enderlin G: Discoloration of hydralazine injection, *Am J Hosp Pharm 41*:634 (Apr) 1984.

907. Pingel M and Volund A: Stability of insulin preparations, *Diabetes 21*:805–813 (July) 1972.

908. Weber SS and Wood WA: Insulin adsorption controversy, *Drug Intell Clin Pharm 10*:232–233 (Apr) 1976.

909. Schildt B, Ahlgren T, Berghem L, et al.: Adsorption of insulin by infusion materials, *Acta Anaesthesiol Scand 22*:556–562, 1978.

910. Mitrano FP and Newton DW: Factors affecting insulin adherence to type I glass bottles, *Am J Hosp Pharm 39*:1491–1495 (Sep) 1982.

911. Twardowski ZJ, Nolph KD, McGary TJ, et al.: Insulin binding to plastic bags: a methodologic study, *Am J Hosp Pharm 40*:575–579 (Apr) 1983.

912. Twardowski ZJ, Nolph KD, McGary TJ, et al.: Nature of insulin binding to plastic bags, *Am J Hosp Pharm 40*:579–582 (Apr) 1983.

913. Twardowski ZJ, Nolph KD, McGary TJ, et al.: Influence of temperature and time on insulin adsorption to plastic bags, *Am J Hosp Pharm 40*:583–586 (Apr) 1983.

914. Sato S, Ebert CD, and Kim SW: Prevention of insulin self-association and surface adsorption, *J Pharm Sci 72*:228–232 (Mar) 1983.

915. Phillips NC and Lauper RD: Review of etoposide, *Clin Pharm 2*:112–119 (Mar–Apr) 1983.

916. McCollam PL and Garrison TJ: Etoposide: A new chemotherapeutic agent, *Am J IV Ther Clin Nutr 11*:24, 27–28 (Mar) 1984.

917. Stroup JW and Mighton-Eryou LM: Expiry date guidelines for a centralized IV admixture service, *Can J Hosp Pharm 39*:57–59 (June) 1986.

918. Bishop BG: Adsorption of iron-dextran on membrane filters, *NZ Pharm 1*:49 (Mar) 1981.

919. Reed MD, Bertino JS, and Halpin TC: Use of intravenous iron dextran injection in children receiving total parenteral nutrition, *Am J Dis Child 135*:829–831 (Sep) 1981.

920. Halpin TC: Use of intravenous iron dextran in sick patients receiving TPN, *Nutr Supp Serv 2*:19–20 (Jan) 1982.

921. Shimada A: Adverse reactions to total-dose infusion of iron dextran, *Clin Pharm 1*:248–249 (May–June) 1982.

922. Thompson DF and Shimanek M: Stability of sterility study with magnesium sulfate admixtures, *Infusion 7*:83, 86 (May–June) 1983.

923. Ausman RK, Crevar GE, Hagedorn H, et al.: Studies in the pharmacodynamics of mechlorethamine and AB100, *J Am Med Assoc 178*:143–146 (Nov 18) 1961.

924. Anon: Compatibility chart for Reglan injectable 5 mg/ml, A.H. Robins Pharmaceutical Division, Richmond, Virginia, October 1983.

925. Bonati M, Gaspari F, D'Aranno V, et al.: Physicochemical and analytical characteristics of amiodarone, *J Pharm Sci 73*:829–831 (June) 1984.

926. Feroz RM, Puppala S, Chaudhry MA, et al.: Compatibility of M.V.C. 9+3 (multivitamin concentrate for infusion) in different large volume parenteral solutions, LyphoMed, Inc., 1984.

927. Alam AS: Identification of labetalol precipitate, *Am J Hosp Pharm 41*:74 (Jan) 1984.

928. Wagenknecht DM, Baaske DM, Alam AS, et al.: Stability of nitroglycerin solutions in polyolefin and glass containers, *Am J Hosp Pharm 41*:1807–1811 (Sep) 1984.

929. Klamerus KJ, Ueda CT, and Newton DW: Stability of nitroglycerin in intravenous admixtures, *Am J Hosp Pharm 41*:303–305 (Feb) 1984.

930. Scheife AH, Grisafe JA, and Shargel L: Stability of intravenous nitroglycerin solutions, *J Pharm Sci 71*:55–59 (Jan) 1982.

931. Ingram JK and Miller JD: Plastic absorption adsorption of nitroglycerin solution, *Anesthesiology 51*:S132 (Sep) 1979.

932. Mathot F, Bonnard J, Hans P, et al.: Les perfusions de nitroglycerine: Etude de l'absorption par differents materiaux plastiques, *J Pharm Belg 35*:389–393 (Sep–Oct) 1980.

933. Sokoloski TD and Wu CC: Nitroglycerin stability: effects on bioavailability, assay and biological dissolution, *J Clin Hosp Pharm 6*:227–232 (Dec) 1981.

934. Cawello VW and Bonn R: Bioverfugbarkeitseinflusse durch die wahl des infusionsmaterials bei der therapie mit nitroglycerin, *Arzneim-Forsch 33*:595–597 (4) 1983.

935. Rock CM and Gull J: Reducing IV-nitroglycerin loss to an intravenous administration set by preliminary preparation, *Am J IV Ther Clin Nutr 9*:36, 40–42 (Oct) 1982.

936. Nix DE, Tharpe WN, and Francisco GE: Effects of presaturation on nitroglycerin delivery by polyvinyl chloride infusion sets, *Am J Hosp Pharm 41*: 1835–1837 (Sep) 1984.

937. Jacobi J, Dasta JF, Reilley TE, et al.: Loss of nitroglycerin to pulmonary artery delivery systems, *Am J Hosp Pharm 40*:1980–1982 (Nov) 1983.

938. Jacobi J, Dasta JF, Wu LS, et al.: Loss of nitroglycerin to central venous pressure catheter, *Drug Intell Clin Pharm 16*:331–332 (Apr) 1982.

939. Dasta JF, Jacobi J, Sokolowski TD, et al.: Loss of nitroglycerin to cardiopulmonary bypass apparatus, *Crit Care Med 11*:50–52, 1983.

940. Dasta JF, Jacobi J, Sokoloski TD, et al.: Extraction of nitroglycerin by a membrane oxygenator, *J Extra-Corp Tech 15*:101–103 (4) 1983.

941. St. Peter JV and Cochran TG: Nitroglycerin loss from intravenous solutions administered with a volumetric infusion pump, *Am J Hosp Pharm 39*:1328–1330 (Aug) 1982.

942. Hola ET: Loss of nitroglycerin during microinfusion, *Am J Hosp Pharm 41*: 142–144 (Jan) 1984.

943. Yacobi A, Amann AH, and Baaske DM: Pharmaceutical considerations of nitroglycerin, *Drug Intell Clin Pharm 17*:255–263 (Apr) 1983.

944. Malick AW, Amann AH, Baaske DM, et al.: Loss of nitroglycerin from solutions to intravenous plastic containers: a theoretical treatment, *J Pharm Sci 70*:798–800 (July) 1981.

945. Amann AH and Baaske DM: Loss of nitroglycerin from intravenous administration sets during infusion: a theoretical treatment, *J Pharm Sci 71*:473–474 (Apr) 1982.

946. Neftel KA, Walti M, Spengler H, et al.: Effect of storage of penicillin G solutions on sensitization to penicillin G after intravenous administration, *Lancet 1*:986–988 (May 1) 1982.

947. Salem RB, Wilder BJ, Yost RL, et al.: Rapid infusion of phenytoin sodium loading doses, *Am J Hosp Pharm 38*:354–357 (Mar) 1981.

948. Gannaway WL, Wilding DC, Siepler JK, et al.: Clinical use of intravenous phenytoin sodium infusions, *Clin Pharm 2*:135–138 (Mar–Apr) 1983.

949. Boike SC, Rybak MJ, Tintinalli JE, et al.: Evaluation of a method for intravenous phenytoin infusion, *Clin Pharm 2*:444–446 (Sep–Oct) 1983.

950. Earnest MP, Marx JA, and Drury LR: Complications of intravenous phenytoin for acute treatment of seizures, *J Am Med Assoc 249*:762–765 (Feb 11) 1983.

951. Giacona N, Bauman JL, and Siepler JK: Crystallization of three phenytoin preparations in intravenous solutions, *Am J Hosp Pharm 39*:630–634 (Apr) 1982.

952. Lau A, Lee M, Flascha S, et al.: Effect of piperacillin on tobramycin pharmacokinetics in patients with normal renal function, *Antimicrob Agents Chemother 24*:533–537 (Oct) 1983.

953. Autian J and Dhorda CN: Evaluation of disposable plastic syringes as to physical incompatibilities with parenteral products, *Am J Hosp Pharm 16*:176–179, 1959.

954. Addy DP, Alesbury P, and Winter L: Paraldehyde and plastic syringes, *Br Med J 2*:1434 (Nov 18) 1978.

955. Fenton-May VT and Lee F: Paraldehyde and plastic syringes, *Br Med J 2*: 1166 (Oct 21) 1978.

956. Evans RJ: Effect of paraldehyde on disposable syringes and needles, *Lancet 2*:1451 (Dec 30) 1961.

957. Johnson CE and Vigoreaux JA: Compatibility of paraldehyde with plastic syringes and needle hubs, *Am J Hosp Pharm 41*:306–308 (Feb) 1984.

958. Mahony C, Brown JE, Starget WW, et al.: In vitro stability of sodium nitroprusside solutions for intravenous administration, *J Pharm Sci 73*:838–839 (June) 1984.

959. Fricker MP and Swerling R: Sodium nitroprusside reconstitution and administration, *Infusion 5*:56 (2–3) 1981.

960. Boehm JJ, Dutton DM, and Poust RI: Shelf life of unrefrigerated succinylcholine chloride injection, *Am J Hosp Pharm 41*:300–302 (Feb) 1984.

961. Roach M: IV tetracycline, *Pharm J 220*:143 (Feb 18) 1978.

962. Chow MSS, Qwintiliani R, and Nightingale CH: In vivo inactivation of tobramycin by ticarcillin, *J Am Med Assoc 247*:658–659 (Feb 5) 1982.

963. Baumgartner TG and Russell WL: Intravenous trimethoprim–sulfamethoxazole administration alert, *Am J IV Ther Clin Nutr 10*:14–15 (Feb) 1983.

964. Hiskey CF, Bullock E, and Whitman G: Spectrophotometric study of aqueous solutions of warfarin sodium, *J Pharm Sci 51*:43–46 (Jan) 1962.

965. Nahata MC: Stability of ceftriaxone sodium in intravenous solutions, *Am J Hosp Pharm 40*:2193–2194 (Dec) 1983.

966. Smith BR: Effect of storage temperature and time on stability of cefmenoxime, ceftriaxone, and cefotetan in 5% dextrose injection, *Am J Hosp Pharm 40*: 1024–1025 (June) 1983.

967. Vishnuvajjala BR and Cradock JC: Compatibility of plastic infusion devices with diluted *N*-methylformamide and *N,N*-dimethylacetamide, *Am J Hosp Pharm 41*:1160–1163 (June) 1984.

968. Godefroid RJ: Vindesine: A new antineoplastic drug, *Cancer Chemother Update 2*:4–7 (Jan–Feb) 1984.

969. Cheung YW, Vishnuvajjala BR, Morris NL, et al.: Stability of azacitidine in infusion fluids, *Am J Hosp Pharm 41*:1156–1159 (June) 1984.

970. Bosanquet AG: Stability of melphalan solutions during preparation and storage, *J Pharm Sci 74*:348–351 (Mar) 1985.
971. Tabibi SE and Cradock JC: Stability of melphalan in infusion fluids, *Am J Hosp Pharm 41*:1380–1382 (July) 1984.
972. Teresi M and Allison J: Interaction between vancomycin and ticarcillin, *Am J Hosp Pharm 42*:2420, 2422 (Nov) 1985.
973. Jorgensen JH and Crawford SA: Selective inactivation of aminoglycosides by newer beta-lactam antibiotics, *Curr Ther Res Clin Exp 32*:25–35 (July) 1982.
974. Bhatia J, Stegink LD, and Zeigler EE: Riboflavin enhances photo-oxidation of amino acids under simulated clinical conditions, *J Parenter Enter Nutr 7*: 277–279 (May–June) 1983.
975. Smith G, Hasson K, and Clements JA: Effects of ascorbic acid and disodium edetate on the stability of isoprenaline hydrochloride injection, *J Clin Hosp Pharm 9*:209–215 (Sep) 1984.
976. Hutchinson SMW: Heparin and aminoglycosides instability, *Drug Intell Clin Pharm 20*:886 (Nov) 1986.
977. Johnston-Early A, McKenzie MA, Krasnow SH, et al.: Drug trapping in intravenous infusion side arms, *J Am Med Assoc 252*:2392 (Nov 2) 1984.
978. Parker WA: Physical compatibility of ranitidine HCl with preoperative injectable medications, *Can J Hosp Pharm 38*:160–161 (Dec) 1985.
979. Das Gupta V, Stewart KR, and Torre MD: Chemical stabilities of cefamandole nafate and metronidazole when mixed together for intravenous infusion, *J Clin Hosp Pharm 10*:379–383 (Dec) 1985.
980. Cohen MH, Johnston-Early A, Hood MA, et al.: Drug precipitation within iv tubing: a potential hazard of chemotherapy administration, *Cancer Treat Rep 69*:1325–1326 (Nov) 1985.
981. Marble DA, Bosso JA, and Townsend RJ: Compatibility of clindamycin phosphate with amikacin sulfate at room temperature and with gentamicin sulfate and tobramycin sulfate under frozen conditions, *Drug Intell Clin Pharm 20*: 960–963 (Dec) 1986.
982. Gove LF, Gordon NH, Miller J, et al.: Pre-filled syringes for self-administration of epidural opiates, *Pharm J 234*:378–379 (Mar 23) 1985.
983. Bosso JA and Townsend RJ: Stability of clindamycin phosphate and ceftizoxime sodium, cefoxitin sodium, cefamandole nafate, or cefazolin sodium in two intravenous solutions, *Am J Hosp Pharm 42*:2211–2214 (Oct) 1985.
984. Nahata MC and Durrell DE: Stability of tobramycin sulfate in admixtures with calcium gluconate, *Am J Hosp Pharm 42*:1987–1988 (Sep) 1985.
985. Baker DE, Yost GS, Craig VL, et al.: Compatibility of heparin sodium and morphine sulfate, *Am J Hosp Pharm 42*:1352–1355 (June) 1985.
986. Carlson GH and Matzke GR: Particle formation of third-generation cephalosporin injections, *Am J Hosp Pharm 42*:1578–1579 (July) 1985.
987. Nieves-Cordero AL, Luciw HM, and Souney PF: Compatibility of narcotic analgesic solutions with various antibiotics during simulated Y-site injection, *Am J Hosp Pharm 42*:1108–1109 (May) 1985.
988. Ogawa GS, Young R, and Munar M: Dispensing-pin problems, *Am J Hosp Pharm 42*:1042, 1045 (May) 1985.
989. Conklin CA, Kerege JF, and Christensen JM: Stability of an analgesic–sedative combination in glass and plastic single-dose syringes, *Am J Hosp Pharm 42*: 339–342 (Feb) 1985.
990. Thompson M, Smith M, Gragg R, et al.: Stability of nitroglycerin and dobutamine in 5% dextrose and 0.9% sodium chloride injection, *Am J Hosp Pharm 42*:361–362 (Feb) 1985.
991. Rhodes RS, Rhodes PJ, and McCurdy HH: Stability of meperidine hydrochloride, promethazine hydrochloride, and atropine sulfate in plastic syringes, *Am J Hosp Pharm 42*:112–115 (Jan) 1985.
992. Kiel D, Connolly BJ, and Souney PF: Visual compatibility of amrinone lactate with various i.v. secondary additives, *Parenterals 3*:1, 5–6 (May–June) 1985.
993. Das Gupta V and Stewart KR: Chemical stabilities of hydrocortisone sodium succinate and several antibiotics when mixed with metronidazole injection for intravenous infusion, *J Parenter Sci Technol 39*:145–148 (May–June) 1985.
994. Foley PT, Bosso JA, Bair JN, et al.: Compatibility of clindamycin phosphate with cefotaxime sodium or netilmicin sulfate in small-volume admixtures, *Am J Hosp Pharm 42*:839–843 (Apr) 1985.
995. Mansur JM, Abramowitz PW, Lerner SA, et al.: Stability and cost analysis of clindamycin–gentamicin admixtures given every eight hours, *Am J Hosp Pharm 42*:332–335 (Feb) 1985.
996. Quock JR and Sakai RI: Stability of cytarabine in a parenteral nutrient solution, *Am J Hosp Pharm 42*:592–594 (Mar) 1985.
997. Walker SE and Bayliff CD: Stability of ranitidine hydrochloride in total parenteral nutrient solution, *Am J Hosp Pharm 42*:590–592 (Mar) 1985.
998. Baptista RJ, Palumbo JD, Tahan SR, et al.: Stability of cimetidine hydrochloride in a total nutrient admixture, *Am J Hosp Pharm 42*:2208–2210 (Oct) 1985.
999. Das Gupta V and Stewart KR: pH-Dependent effect of magnesium sulfate on the stability of penicillin G potassium solution, *Am J Hosp Pharm 42*:598–602 (Mar) 1985.
1000. Macias JM, Martin WJ, and Lloyd CW: Stability of morphine sulfate and meperidine hydrochloride in a parenteral nutrient formulation, *Am J Hosp Pharm 42*:1087–1094 (May) 1985.
1001. James MJ and Riley CM: Stability of intravenous admixtures of aztreonam and ampicillin, *Am J Hosp Pharm 42*:1095–1110 (May) 1985.
1002. James MJ and Riley CM: Stability of intravenous admixtures of aztreonam and clindamycin phosphate, *Am J Hosp Pharm 42*:1984–1986 (Sep) 1985.
1003. Thompson DF, Thompson GD, and Hedrick PJ: Effect of inline filtration on pediatric doses of gentamicin and tobramycin, *Infusion 8*:31–32 (Jan–Feb) 1984.
1004. Alexander SR and Arena R: Predicting calcium phosphate precipitation in premature infant parenteral nutrition solutions, *Hosp Pharm 20*:656–658 (Sep) 1985.
1005. Spruill WJ, McCall CY, and Francisco GE: In vitro inactivation of tobramycin by cephalosporins, *Am J Hosp Pharm 42*:2506–2509 (Nov) 1985.
1006. Stevenson JG and Patriarca C: Incompatibility of morphine sulfate and prochlorperazine edisylate in syringes, *Am J Hosp Pharm 42*:2651 (Dec) 1985.
1007. Beijnen JH, Rosing H, deVries PA, et al.: Stability of anthracycline antitumor agents in infusion fluids, *J Parenter Sci Technol 39*:220–222 (Nov–Dec) 1985.
1008. Baptista RJ and Lawrence RW: Compatibility of total nutrient admixtures and secondary antibiotic infusions, *Am J Hosp Pharm 42*:362–363 (Feb) 1985.
1009. Baptista RJ, Dumas GJ, Bistrian BR, et al.: Compatibility of total nutrient admixtures and secondary cardiovascular medications, *Am J Hosp Pharm 42*: 777–778 (Apr) 1985.
1010. Bullock L, Parks RB, Lampasona V, et al.: Stability of ranitidine hydrochloride and amino acids in parenteral nutrient solutions, *Am J Hosp Pharm 42*:2683–2687 (Dec) 1985.
1011. Henann NE and Jacks TT: Compatibility and availability of sodium bicarbonate in total parenteral nutrient solutions, *Am J Hosp Pharm 42*:2718–2720 (Dec) 1985.
1012. Watson D: Piggyback compatibility of antibiotics with pediatric parenteral nutrition solutions, *J Parenter Enter Nutr 9*:220–224 (Mar–Apr) 1985.
1013. Turner SA: Stability and clinical use of intravenous admixtures containing lipid emulsion, *Pharm J 234*:799–800 (June 22) 1985.
1014. El Eini D and Knott CE: Stability of iv lipid emulsions, *Pharm J 235*:170 (Aug 10) 1985.
1015. Hobbiss JH: Stability of iv lipid emulsions, *Pharm J 235*:170 (Aug 10) 1985.
1016. Allwood MC: Drop size of infusions containing fat emulsion, *Br J Parenter Ther 5*:113–114, 116 (May) 1984.
1017. Iliano L, Delanghe M, van Den Baviere H, et al.: Effect of electrolytes in the presence of some trace elements on the stability of all-in-one emulsion mixtures for total parenteral nutrition, *J Clin Hosp Pharm 9*:87–93 (June) 1984.
1018. Whateley TL, Steele G, Urwin J, et al.: Particle size stability of Intralipid and mixed total parenteral nutrition mixtures, *J Clin Hosp Pharm 9*:113–126 (June) 1984.
1019. Harrie KR, Jacob M, McCormick D, et al.: Comparison of total nutrient admixture stability using two intravenous fat emulsions, Soyacal and Intralipid 20%, *J Parenter Enter Nutr 10*:381–387 (July–Aug) 1986.
1020. Riley CM and James MJ: Stability of intravenous admixtures containing aztreonam and cefazolin, *Am J Hosp Pharm 43*:925–927 (Apr) 1986.
1021. Kuhn RJ and Nahata MC: Stability of netilmicin sulfate in admixtures with calcium gluconate and aminophylline, *Am J Hosp Pharm 43*:1241–1242 (May) 1986.
1022. Johnson CE, Cohen IA, Craft DA, et al.: Compatibility of aminophylline and methylprednisolone sodium succinate intravenous admixtures, *Am J Hosp Pharm 43*:1482–1485 (June) 1986.
1023. Bell RG, Lipford LC, Massanari MJ, et al.: Stability of intravenous admixtures of aztreonam and cefoxitin, gentamicin, metronidazole, or tobramycin, *Am J Hosp Pharm 43*:1444–1453 (June) 1986.
1024. Fitzgerald KA and MacKay MW: Calcium and phosphate solubility in neonatal parenteral nutrient solutions containing TrophAmine, *Am J Hosp Pharm 43*:88–93 (Jan) 1986.
1025. Sayeed FA, Johnson HW, Sukumaran KB, et al.: Stability of Liposyn II fat emulsion in total nutrient admixtures, *Am J Hosp Pharm 43*:1230–1235 (May) 1986.
1026. Marble DA, Bosso JA, and Townsend RJ: Stability of clindamycin phosphate with aztreonam, ceftazidime sodium, ceftriaxone sodium, or piperacillin sodium in two intravenous solutions, *Am J Hosp Pharm 43*:1732–1736 (July) 1986.
1027. Lee MG: Sorption of four drugs to polyvinyl chloride and polybutadiene intravenous administration sets, *Am J Hosp Pharm 43*:1945–1950 (Aug) 1986.

1028. Riley CM and Lipford LC: Interaction of aztreonam with nafcillin in intravenous admixtures, *Am J Hosp Pharm 43*:2221–2224 (Sep) 1986.

1029. Walker PC, Kaufmann RE, and Massoud N: Compatibility of cefazolin and gentamicin in peritoneal dialysis solutions, *Drug Intell Clin Pharm 20*:697–700 (Sep) 1986.

1030. Beijnen JH, Neef C, Menwissen OJAT, et al.: Stability of intravenous admixtures of doxorubicin and vincristine, *Am J Hosp Pharm 43*:3022–3027 (Dec) 1986.

1031. Campbell S, Nolan PE, Bliss M, et al.: Stability of amiodarone hydrochloride in admixtures with other injectable drugs, *Am J Hosp Pharm 43*:917–921 (Apr) 1986.

1032. Hasegawa GR and Eder JF: Visual compatibility of amiodarone hydrochloride injection with other injectable drugs, *Am J Hosp Pharm 41*:1379–1380 (July) 1984.

1033. Allwood MC: Sorption of drugs to intravenous delivery systems, *Pharm Int 4*:83–85 (Apr) 1983.

1034. Khue NV and Jung L: Study of the retention of child-dose drugs on cellulose ester membranes during inline intravenous filtration, *S-T-P-Pharma 1*:201–207 (Mar) 1985.

1035. Das Gupta V, Shah KA, and de la Torre M: Stability of ampicillin sodium and penicillin G potassium solutions using high-pressure liquid chromatography, *Can J Pharm Sci 16*:61–65 (1) 1981.

1036. Janknegt R and Neil MJLE: De verenigbaarheid van antimicrobiele middelen in infusievloeistoffen, *Pharm Weekbl 120*:638–640 (Aug) 1985.

1037. Bouma J, Beijnen JH, Bult A, et al.: Anthracycline antitumor agents, a review of physicochemical, analytical and stability properties, *Pharm Weekbl Sci Ed 8*:109–133, 1986.

1038. Howard L, Chu R, Feman S, et al.: Vitamin A deficiency from long-term parenteral nutrition, *Ann Intern Med 93*:576–577 (Oct) 1980.

1039. Shenai JP, Stahlman MT, and Chytil F: Vitamin A delivery from parenteral alimentation solution, *J Pediatr 99*:661–663 (Oct) 1981.

1040. Kishi H, Yamaji A, Kataoka K, et al.: Vitamin A and E requirements during total parenteral nutrition, *J Parenter Enter Nutr 5*:420–423 (Sep–Oct) 1981.

1041. Knight P, Heer D, and Abdenour G: CaXP and Ca/P in the parenteral feeding of preterm infants, *J Parenter Enter Nutr 7*:110–114 (Mar–Apr) 1983.

1042. Poole RK, Rupp CA, and Kerner JA: Calcium and phosphorus in neonatal parenteral nutrition solutions, *J Parenter Enter Nutr 7*:358–360 (July–Aug) 1983.

1043. Ritschel WA, Alcorn GJ, Streng WH, et al.: Cimetidine–theophylline complex formation, *Methods Find Exp Clin Pharmacol 5*:55–58 (1) 1983.

1044. Glew RH and Pavuk RA: Stability of vancomycin and aminoglycoside antibiotics in peritoneal dialysis concentrate, *Nephron 28*:241–243, 1981.

1045. Kamen BA, Gunther N, Sowinsky N, et al.: Analysis of antibiotic stability in a parenteral nutrition solution, *Pediatr Infect Dis 4*:387–389 (July) 1985.

1046. Baumgartner TG, Sitren HS, Hall J, et al.: Stability of urokinase in parenteral nutrition solutions, *Nutr Supp Serv 5*:41–43 (Jan) 1985.

1047. Allwood MC: Influence of light on vitamin A degradation during administration, *Clin Nutr 1*:63–70, 1982.

1048. Allwood MC and Plane JH: Degradation of vitamin A exposed to ultraviolet radiation, *Int J Pharm 19*:207–213 (Apr) 1984.

1049. Riggle MA and Brandt RB: Decrease of available vitamin A in parenteral nutrition solutions, *J Parenter Enter Nutr 10*:388–392 (July–Aug) 1986.

1050. McKenna MC and Bieri JC: Loss of vitamin A from total parenteral nutrition (TPN) solutions, *Fed Proc 39*:561, 1980.

1051. Bryant CA and Neufeld NJ: Differences in vitamin A content of enteral feeding solutions following exposure to a polyvinyl chloride enteral feeding system, *J Parenter Enter Nutr 6*:403–405 (Sep–Oct) 1982.

1052. Riff LJ and Thomason JL: Comparative aminoglycoside inactivation by beta-lactam antibiotics—effect of cephalosporin and six penicillins on five aminoglycosides, *J Antibiot (Tokyo) 35*:850–857 (July) 1982.

1053. Schutz VH and Schroder F: Heparin–natrium kompatibilitat bei gleichzeitiger applikation anderer pharmaka, *Krankenhauspharmazie 6*:7–11 (Jan) 1985.

1054. Wermeling DP, Rapp RP, DeLuca PP, et al.: Osmolality of small-volume intravenous admixtures, *Am J Hosp Pharm 42*:1739–1744 (Aug) 1985.

1055. Johnston SJ: Stability of tryptophan in total parenteral nutrient solutions, *Am J Hosp Pharm 43*:1424 (June) 1986.

1056. Allwood MC: Factors influencing the stability of ascorbic acid in total parenteral nutrition solutions, *J Clin Hosp Pharm 9*:75–85 (June) 1984.

1057. Parr MD, Bertch KE, and Rapp RP: Amino acid stability and microbial growth in total parenteral nutrient solutions, *Am J Hosp Pharm 42*:2688–2691 (Dec) 1985.

1058. Nordfjeld K, Rasmussen M, and Jensen VG: Storage of mixtures for total parenteral nutrition: long-term stability of a total parenteral nutrition mixture, *J Clin Hosp Pharm 8*:265–274 (Sep) 1983.

1059. Nordfjeld K, Pedersen JL, Rasmussen M, et al.: Storage of mixtures for total parenteral nutrition III. Stability of vitamins in TPN mixtures, *J Clin Hosp Pharm 9*:293–301 (Dec) 1984.

1060. Das Gupta V: Stability of vitamins in total parenteral nutrient solutions, *Am J Hosp Pharm 43*:2132 (Sep) 1986.

1061. Allwood MC: Stability of vitamins in total parenteral nutrient solutions, *Am J Hosp Pharm 43*:2138 (Sep) 1986.

1062. Louie N: Stability of vitamins in total parenteral nutrient solutions, *Am J Hosp Pharm 43*:2138, 2143 (Sep) 1986.

1063. Shine B and Farwell JA: Stability and compatibility in parenteral nutrition solutions, *Br J Parenter Ther 5*:4, 44–46, 50 (Mar) 1984.

1064. Pamperl H and Kleinberger G: Stability of intravenous fat emulsions, *Arch Surg 117*:859–860 (June) 1982.

1065. Hardy G, Cotter R, and Dawe R: The stability and comparative clearance of TPN mixtures with lipid, in: *Advances in Clinical Nutrition—Selected Proceedings of the 2nd International Symposium*, Johnson ID (ed), MTP Press, Lancaster, England, 1983, pp 241–260.

1066. Hardy G and Klim RA: Stability studies of parenteral nutrition mixtures with lipids, *J Parenter Enter Nutr 5*:569 (Nov–Dec) 1981.

1067. Jeppsson RI and Sjoberg B: Compatibility of parenteral nutrition solutions when mixed in a plastic bag, *Clin Nutr 2*:149–158, 1984.

1068. Parry VA, Harrie KR, and McIntosh-Lowe NL: Effect of various nutrient ratios on the emulsion stability of total nutrient admixtures, *Am J Hosp Pharm 43*:3017–3022 (Dec) 1986.

1069. Bettner FS and Stennett DJ: Effects of pH, temperature, concentration, and time on particle counts in lipid-containing total parenteral nutrition admixtures, *J Parenter Enter Nutr 10*:375–380 (July–Aug) 1986.

1070. Schneider PJ: Three-in-one TPN formulations, *Infusion 8*:94–95, 101 (May–June) 1984.

1071. Ernst JA, Williams JM, Glick MR, et al.: Osmolality of substances used in the intensive care nursery, *Pediatrics 72*:347–352 (Sep) 1983.

1072. Connors KA, Amidon GL, and Stella VJ: *Chemical Stability of Pharmaceuticals, A Handbook for Pharmacists*, John Wiley & Sons, New York, 1986.

1073. Bosanquet AG: Stability of solutions of antineoplastic agents during preparation and storage for in vitro assays II. Assay methods, adriamycin and the other antitumor antibiotics, *Cancer Chemother Pharmacol 17*:1–10, 1986.

1074. Grant AM (Manager, Medical Affairs, Abbott Laboratories, Abbott Park, Illinois): Personal communication, March 23, 1987.

1075. Bornstein M and Templeton RJ: Crystal formation after reconstituting cefazolin sodium with 0.9% sodium chloride injection, *Am J Hosp Pharm 42*:2436 (Nov) 1985.

1076. White JR and Campbell RK: Guide to mixing insulins, *Hosp Pharm 26*:1046–1048 (Dec) 1991.

1077. Das Gupta V: Stability of cefotaxime sodium as determined by high-performance liquid chromatography, *J Pharm Sci 73*:565–567 (Apr) 1984.

1078. Carlson GH and Matzke GR: Particle formation of ceftizoxime sodium injections, *Am J Hosp Pharm 42*:2651–2652 (Dec) 1985.

1079. Swenson E, Gooch WM, and Higbee MD: Visual compatibility of ceftizoxime sodium in four electrolyte injections, *Am J Hosp Pharm 43*:2242–2244 (Sep) 1986.

1080. Barbero JR, Marino EL, and Dominguez-Gil A: Accelerated stability studies on Rocephin by high-efficiency liquid chromatography, *Int J Pharm 19*:199–206 (Apr) 1984.

1081. Smith RC: Overfill in cefuroxime sodium vials, *Am J Hosp Pharm 42*:1045–1046 (May) 1985.

1082. Smith RC: No more overfill in cefuroxime sodium vials, *Am J Hosp Pharm 43*:2154 (Sep) 1986.

1083. DeVane CL and Wailand LA: Stability of chlorpromazine in five milliliter vials, *Can J Hosp Pharm 37*:9 (1) 1984.

1084. Mu-Chow KJ and Baptista RJ: Cost-effectiveness of parenteral nutrient solutions containing cimetidine hydrochloride, *Am J Hosp Pharm 41*:1321, 1324 (July) 1984.

1085. Parasrampuria J, Das Gupta V, and Stewart KR: Stability of acetazolamide sodium in 5% dextrose or 0.9% sodium chloride injection, *Am J Hosp Pharm 44*:358–360 (Feb) 1987.

1086. Zuber DEL: Compatibility of morphine sulfate injection and prochlorperazine edisylate injection, *Am J Hosp Pharm 44*:67 (Jan) 1987.

1087. Cheung YW, Cradock JC, Vishnuvajjala BR, et al.: Stability of cisplatin, iproplatin, carboplatin, and tetraplatin in commonly used intravenous infusion solutions, *Am J Hosp Pharm 44*:124–130 (Jan) 1987.

1088. LaFollette JM, Arbus MH, and Lauper RD: Stability of cisplatin admixtures in polyvinyl chloride bags, *Am J Hosp Pharm 42*:2652 (Dec) 1985.

1089. Hussain AA, Haddadin M, and Iga K: Reaction of cis-platinum with sodium bisulfite, *J Pharm Sci 69*:364 (Mar) 1980.

1090. Kirk B, Melia CD, Wilson JV, et al.: Chemical stability of cyclophosphamide injection, *Br J Parenter Ther 5*:90–97 (May) 1984.

1091. Ptachcinski RJ, Logue LW, Burckart GJ, et al.: Stability and availability of cyclosporine in 5% dextrose injection or 0.9% sodium chloride injection, *Am J Hosp Pharm 43*:94–97 (Jan) 1986.

1092. Venkataramanan R, Burckart GJ, Ptachcinski RJ, et al.: Leaching of diethylhexyl phthalate from polyvinyl chloride bags into intravenous cyclosporine solution, *Am J Hosp Pharm 43*:2800–2802 (Nov) 1986.

1093. Stevens MFG and Peatey L: Photodegradation of solutions of the antitumor drug DTIC, *J Pharm Pharmacol 30(Suppl)*:47P, 1978.

1094. Williams BA and Tritton TR: Photoinactivation of anthracyclines, *Photochem Photobiol 34*:131–134, 1981.

1095. Maloney TJ: Dilution of diazepam injection prior to intravenous administration, *Aust J Hosp Pharm 13*:79 (June) 1983.

1096. Hancock BG and Black CD: Effect of polyethylene-lined administration set on the availability of diazepam injection, *Am J Hosp Pharm 42*:335–339 (Feb) 1985.

1097. Yliruusi JK, Uotila JA, and Kristoffersson ER: Effect of tubing length on adsorption of diazepam to polyvinyl chloride administration sets, *Am J Hosp Pharm 43*:2789–2794 (Nov) 1986.

1098. Yliruusi JK, Uotila JA, and Kristoffersson ER: Effect of flow rate and type of i.v. container on adsorption of diazepam to i.v. administration systems, *Am J Hosp Pharm 43*:2795–2799 (Nov) 1986.

1099. Bell HE and Bertino JS: Constant diazepam infusion in the treatment of continuous seizure activity, *Drug Intell Clin Pharm 18*:965–970 (Dec) 1984.

1100. Dandurand KR and Stennett DJ: Stability of dopamine hydrochloride exposed to blue-light phototherapy, *Am J Hosp Pharm 42*:595–597 (Mar) 1985.

1101. Pluta PL and Morgan PK: Stability of erythromycin in intravenous admixtures, *Am J Hosp Pharm 43*:2732, 2738 (Nov) 1986.

1102. Deitel M, Faksa M, Kaminsky VM, et al.: Growth of microorganisms in soybean oil emulsion and clinical implications, *Int Surg 64*:27–32, 1979.

1103. Keammerer D, Mayhall CG, Hall GO, et al.: Microbial growth patterns in intravenous fat emulsions, *Am J Hosp Pharm 40*:1650–1653 (Oct) 1983.

1104. Kim CH, Lewis DE, and Kumar A: Bacterial and fungal growth in intravenous fat emulsions, *Am J Hosp Pharm 40*:2159–2161 (Dec) 1983.

1105. Allwood MC: Release of DEHP plasticizer into fat emulsion from iv administration sets, *Pharm J 235*:600 (Nov 2) 1985.

1106. Driscoll DF, Baptista RJ, Bistrian BR, et al.: Practical considerations regarding the use of total nutrient admixtures, *Am J Hosp Pharm 43*:416–419 (Feb) 1986.

1107. Morgan DE, Bergdale S, and Zeigler EE: Effect of syringe-pump position on infusion of fat emulsion with a primary solution, *Am J Hosp Pharm 42*:1110–1111 (May) 1985.

1108. Neil JM, Fell AF, and Smith G: Evaluation of the stability of frusemide in intravenous infusions by reversed-phase high-performance liquid chromatography, *Int J Pharm 22*:105–126 (Nov) 1984.

1109. Dean T and Ridley P: Use of 0.9% sodium chloride injection without heparin for maintaining indwelling intermittent injection sites, *Clin Pharm 4*:488 (Sep–Oct) 1985.

1110. Chantelau EA and Berger M: Pollution of insulin with silicone oil, a hazard of disposable plastic syringes, *Lancet 1*:1459 (June 22) 1985.

1111. Furberg H, Jensen AK, and Salbu B: Effect of pretreatment with 0.9% sodium chloride or insulin solutions on the delivery of insulin from an infusion system, *Am J Hosp Pharm 43*:2209–2213 (Sep) 1986.

1112. Kane M, Jay M, and DeLuca PP: Binding of insulin to a continuous ambulatory peritoneal dialysis system, *Am J Hosp Pharm 43*:81–88 (Jan) 1986.

1113. Hutchinson KG: Assessment of gelling in insulin solutions for infusion pumps, *J Pharm Pharmacol 37*:528–531, 1985.

1114. Kamerman B: Dissolving mannitol crystals, *Hosp Pharm 20*:360 (May) 1985.

1115. Cano SB and Glogiewicz FL: Storage requirements for metronidazole injection, *Am J Hosp Pharm 43*:2983, 2985 (Dec) 1986.

1116. Schell KH and Copland JR: Metronidazole hydrochloride–aluminum interaction, *Am J Hosp Pharm 42*:1040, 1042 (May) 1985.

1117. Struthers BJ and Parr RJ: Clarifying the metronidazole hydrochloride–aluminum interaction, *Am J Hosp Pharm 42*:2660 (Dec) 1985.

1118. Quebbeman EJ, Hoffman NE, Ausman RK, et al.: Stability of mitomycin admixtures, *Am J Hosp Pharm 42*:1750–1754 (Aug) 1985.

1119. Edwards D, Selkirk AB, and Taylor RB: Determination of the stability of mitomycin C by high-performance liquid chromatography, *Int J Pharm 4*:21–26, 1979.

1120. Young JB, Pratt CM, Farmer JA, et al.: Specialized delivery systems for intravenous nitroglycerin—are they necessary?, *Am J Med 75*:27–37 (June 22) 1984.

1121. Nix DE, Tharpe WN, and Francisco GE: Intravenous nitroglycerin delivery: dynamics and cost considerations, *Hosp Pharm 20*:230–232 (Apr) 1985.

1122. Schaber DE, Uden DL, and McCoy HG: Nitroglycerin adsorption to a combination polyvinyl chloride, polyethylene intravenous administration set, *Drug Intell Clin Pharm 19*:572–575 (July–Aug) 1985.

1123. Mendel S and Green JA: Comment: Nitroglycerin iv tubing adsorption, *Drug Intell Clin Pharm 19*:946–947 (Dec) 1985.

1124. Tarr BD, Campbell RK, and Workman TM: Stability and sterility of biosynthetic human insulin stored in plastic insulin syringes for 28 days, *Am J Hosp Pharm 48*:2631–2634 (Dec) 1991.

1125. Rayani S and Fakhreddin J: Stability of penicillin G sodium in 5% dextrose in water minibags after freezing, *Can J Hosp Pharm 38*:162–163 (Dec) 1985.

1126. Das Gupta V, Davis DD, and Stewart KR: Stability of piperacillin sodium in dextrose 5% and sodium chloride 0.9% injections, *Am J IV Ther Clin Nutr 11*: 14–15, 18–19 (Feb) 1984.

1127. Deardorff DL and Schmidt CN: Mixing additives by squeezing plastic bags, *Am J Hosp Pharm 42*:533–534 (Mar) 1985.

1128. Synave R, Vergote A, and Remon JP: Stability of procaine hydrochloride in a cardioplegic solution containing bicarbonate, *J Clin Hosp Pharm 10*:385–388 (Dec) 1985.

1129. Raymond G and DeGennaro M: Effect of Neut on the pH of some commercially available intravenous solutions, *Infusion 9*:144–146 (Sep–Oct) 1985.

1130. Sewell GJ, Forbes DR, and Munton TJ: Stability of sodium nitroprusside infusion during the administration by motorized syringe-pump, *J Clin Hosp Pharm 10*:351–360 (Dec) 1985.

1131. Baaske DM, Smith MD, Karnatz N, et al.: High-performance liquid chromatographic determination of sodium nitroprusside, *J Chromatogr 212*:339–346, 1981.

1132. Elenbaas JK, Lander RD, and Elenbaas RM: Effect of inline filtration on tobramycin delivery, *Drug Intell Clin Pharm 19*:122–125 (Feb) 1985.

1133. Mehta J, Searcy CJ, and Jung DT: Stability of terbutaline sulfate admixtures stored in polyvinyl chloride bags, *Am J Hosp Pharm 43*:1760–1762 (July) 1986.

1134. Das Gupta V, Stewart KR, and Nohria S: Stability of vancomycin hydrochloride in 5% dextrose and 0.9% sodium chloride injections, *Am J Hosp Pharm 43*:1729–1731 (July) 1986.

1135. Hazlet TK and Tankersley DL: Possible incompatibilities with immune globulin for i.v. use. *Am J Hosp Pharm 50*:654, 659, 660 (Apr) 1993.

1136. Richardson BL, Woodford JD, and Andrews GD: Pharmacy of ceftazidime, *J Antimicrob Chemother 8*:233–236 (Suppl B) 1981.

1137. Cox ME, Roesner M, and McAllister JC: Production of carbon dioxide gas after reconstitution of ceftazidime, *Am J Hosp Pharm 43*:1422 (June) 1986.

1138. Fites AL: Production of carbon dioxide gas after reconstitution of ceftazidime, *Am J Hosp Pharm 43*:1422–1423 (June) 1986.

1139. Marwaha RK, Johnson BF, and Wright GE: Simple stability-indicating assay for histamine solutions, *Am J Hosp Pharm 42*:1568–1571 (July) 1985.

1140. Marwaha RK and Johnson BF: Long-term stability study of histamine in sterile bronchoprovocation solutions, *Am J Hosp Pharm 43*:380–383 (Feb) 1986.

1141. Bigley FP, Forsyth RJ, and Henley MW: Compatibility of imipenem–cilastatin sodium with commonly used intravenous solutions, *Am J Hosp Pharm 43*: 2803–2809 (Nov) 1986.

1142. De NC, Alam AS, and Kapoor JN: Stability of pentamidine isethionate in 5% dextrose and 0.9% sodium chloride injections, *Am J Hosp Pharm 43*:1486–1488 (June) 1986.

1143. Lampasona V, Mullins RE, and Parks RB: Stability of ranitidine admixtures frozen and refrigerated in minibags, *Am J Hosp Pharm 43*:921–925 (Apr) 1986.

1144. Gralla RJ, Tyson LB, Kris MG, et al.: Management of chemotherapy-induced nausea and vomiting, *Med Clinics N Am 71*:289–301 (Mar) 1987.

1145. Forman JK and Souney PF: Visual compatibility of midazolam hydrochloride with common preoperative injectable medications, *Am J Hosp Pharm 44*: 2298–2299 (Oct) 1987.

1146. Thompson DF and Thompson GD: Visual compatibility of esmolol hydrochloride and furosemide in 5% dextrose or 0.9% sodium chloride injections, *Am J Hosp Pharm 44*:2740 (Dec) 1987.

1147. Ahmed I and Day P: Stability of cefazolin sodium in various artificial tear solutions and aqueous vehicles, *Am J Hosp Pharm 44*:2287–2290 (Oct) 1987.

1148. McSherry TJ: Incompatibility between chlorpromazine and metacresol, *Am J Hosp Pharm 44*:1574 (July) 1987.

1149. Tebbett IR, Melrose E, and Reeves DE: Stability of promazine as an intravenous infusion, *Pharm J 237*:172, 174 (Aug 9) 1986.

1150. Johnson CE, Cohen IA, Michelini TJ, et al.: Compatibility of premixed theophylline and methylprednisolone sodium succinate intravenous admixtures, *Am J Hosp Pharm 44*:1620–1624 (July) 1987.

1151. Marti E and Cervera P: Compatibility of ranitidine hydrochloride with other

injectable pharmaceuticals in common use, *Rev Assoc Esp Farm Hosp 9*:169–172 (Oct–Dec) 1985.
1152. Navarro JN, Aznar MT, Ruiz MD, et al.: Stability of 5-fluorouracil in large volume intravenous solutions, *Rev Assoc Esp Farm Hosp 9*:69–72 (Apr–June) 1985.
1153. Biondi L and Nairn JG: Stability of 5-fluorouracil and flucytosine in parenteral solutions, *Can J Hosp Pharm 39*:60–63, 66 (June) 1986.
1154. Parr MD, Barton SD, Haver VM, et al.: Cyclosporine binding to components in medication administration sets, *Drug Intell Clin Pharm 22*:173–174 (Feb) 1988.
1155. Gasca M, Fanikos J, and Souney PF: Visual compatibility of perphenazine with various antimicrobials during simulated Y-site injection, *Am J Hosp Pharm 44*:574–575 (Mar) 1987.
1156. Nolte MS, Poon V, Grodsky GM, et al.: Reduced solubility of short-acting soluble insulins when mixed with longer-acting insulins, *Diabetes 32*:1177–1181 (Dec) 1983.
1157. Forman JK, Lachs JR, and Souney PF: Visual compatibility of acyclovir sodium with commonly used intravenous drugs during simulated Y-site injection, *Am J Hosp Pharm 44*:1408–1409 (June) 1987.
1158. Nelson RW, Young R, and Lamnin M: Visual incompatibility of dacarbazine and heparin, *Am J Hosp Pharm 44*:2028 (Sep) 1987.
1159. Zbrozek AS, Marble DA, Bosso JA, et al.: Compatibility and stability of clindamycin phosphate–aminoglycoside combinations within polypropylene syringes, *Drug Intell Clin Pharm 21*:806–810 (Oct) 1987.
1160. Perry M, Khalidi N, and Sanders CA: Stability of penicillins in total parenteral nutrient solution, *Am J Hosp Pharm 44*:1625–1628 (July) 1987.
1161. Tu YH, Allen LV, and Wang DP: Stability of papaverine hydrochloride and phentolamine mesylate in injectable mixtures, *Am J Hosp Pharm 44*:2524–2527 (Nov) 1987.
1162. Seargeant LE, Kobrinsky NL, Sus CJ, et al.: In vitro stability and compatibility of daunorubicin, cytarabine, and etoposide, *Cancer Treat Rep 71*:1189–1192 (Dec) 1987.
1163. Baumgartner TG, Knudsen AK, Dunn AJ, et al.: Norepinephrine stability in saline solutions, *Hosp Pharm 23*:44, 49, 59 (Jan) 1988.
1164. Marble DA, Bosso JA, and Townsend RJ: Compatibility of clindamycin phosphate with aztreonam in polypropylene syringes and with cefoperazone sodium, cefonicid sodium, and cefuroxime sodium in partial-fill glass bottles, *Drug Intell Clin Pharm 22*:54–57 (Jan) 1988.
1165. Welty TE, Cloyd JC, and Abdel-Monem MM: Delivery of paraldehyde in 5% dextrose and 0.9% sodium chloride injections through polyvinyl chloride i.v. sets and burettes, *Am J Hosp Pharm 45*:131–135 (Jan) 1988.
1166. Thompson DF, Stiles ML, Allen LV, et al.: Compatibility of verapamil hydrochloride with penicillin admixtures during simulated Y-site injection, *Am J Hosp Pharm 45*:142–145 (Jan) 1988.
1167. Pesko LJ, Arend KA, Hagman DE, et al.: Physical compatibility and stability of metoclopramide injection, *Parenterals 5*:1–3, 6–8 (Dec–Jan) 1988.
1168. Karnatz NN, Wong J, Kesler H, et al.: Compatibility of esmolol hydrochloride with morphine sulfate and fentanyl citrate during simulated Y-site administration, *Am J Hosp Pharm 45*:368–371 (Feb) 1988.
1169. Colucci RD, Cobuzzi LE, and Halpern NA: Visual compatibility of esmolol hydrochloride and various injectable drugs during simulated Y-site injection, *Am J Hosp Pharm 45*:630–632 (Mar) 1988.
1170. Schilling CG: Compatibility of drugs with a heparin-containing neonatal total parenteral nutrient solution, *Am J Hosp Pharm 45*:313–314 (Feb) 1988.
1171. Colucci RD, Cobuzzi LE, and Halpern NA: Visual compatibility of labetalol hydrochloride injection with various injectable drugs during simulated Y-site injection, *Am J Hosp Pharm 45*:1357–1358 (June) 1988.
1172. Johnson CE, Lloyd CW, Aviles AI, et al.: Compatibility of premixed theophylline and verapamil intravenous admixtures, *Am J Hosp Pharm 45*:609–612 (Mar) 1988.
1173. Askerud L, Finholt P, and Karlsen J: Intravenous infusion of theophylline in 5% dextrose solution—formulation and stability, *Medd Nor Farm Selsk 43*: 17–24, 1981.
1174. Morgan GJ, McClellan JD, and Hutton RD: Stability of a heparin urokinase mixture, *Br J Parenter Ther 8*:89 (May–June) 1987.
1175. Garren KW and Repta AJ: Incompatibility of cisplatin and Reglan injectable, *Int J Pharm 24*:91–99, 1985.
1176. Sanburg AL, Lyndon RC, and Sunderland B: Effects of freezing, long-term storage and microwave thawing on the stability of three antibiotics reconstituted in minibags, *Aust J Hosp Pharm 17*:31–34 (Mar) 1987.
1177. Murase S, Ochiai K, Aoki M, et al.: Study on compatibility of dopram with other drugs, *Jap J Hosp Pharm 13*:244–260 (Aug) 1987.
1178. Borst DL, Sesin GP, and Cersosimo RJ: Stability of selected beta-lactam antibiotics stored in plastic syringes, *NITA 10*:368–372 (Sep–Oct) 1987.
1179. Roberts DE, Cross MD, Thomas PH, et al.: Azlocillin–aminoglycoside combinations in CAPD fluid, *Br J Pharm Pract 9*:98–99 (Apr) 1987.
1180. Robinson DC, Cookson TL, and Grisafe JA: Concentration guidelines for parenteral antibiotics in fluid-restricted patients, *Drug Intell Clin Pharm 21*:985–989 (Dec) 1987.
1181. Sterchele JA: Update on stability guidelines for routinely refrigerated drug products, *Am J Hosp Pharm 44*:2698, 2701 (Dec) 1987.
1182. Dahl JM, Roche VF, and Hilleman DE: Visual compatibility of cibenzoline succinate with commonly used acute care medications, *Am J Hosp Pharm 44*: 1123–1125 (May) 1987.
1183. Cano SM, Montoro JB, Pastor C, et al.: Stability of ranitidine hydrochloride in total nutrient admixtures, *Am J Hosp Pharm 45*:1100–1102 (May) 1988.
1184. Jimenez MD: Visual compatibility of nalbuphine hydrochloride and promethazine hydrochloride, *Am J Hosp Pharm 45*:1278 (June) 1988.
1185. Pereira-Rosario R, Utamura T, and Perrin JH: Interaction of heparin sodium and dopamine hydrochloride in admixtures studied by microcalorimetry, *Am J Hosp Pharm 45*:1350–1352 (June) 1988.
1186. Baptista RJ and Mitrano FP: Stability and compatibility of cimetidine hydrochloride and aminophylline in dextrose 5% in water injection, *Drug Intell Clin Pharm 22*:592–593 (July–Aug) 1988.
1187. Holmes CJ, Kubey WY, and Love DI: Viability of microorganisms in fluorouracil and cisplatin small-volume injections, *Am J Hosp Pharm 45*:1089–1091 (May) 1988.
1188. Jay GT, Fanikos J, and Souney PF: Visual compatibility of famotidine with commonly used critical-care medications during simulated Y-site injection, *Am J Hosp Pharm 45*:1556–1557 (July) 1988.
1189. Tucker DR and Sieradzan R: Visual compatibility of ciprofloxacin lactate with five broad-spectrum antimicrobial agents during simulated Y-site injection, *Am J Hosp Pharm 45*:1910–1911 (Sep) 1988.
1190. Marquardt ED: Visual compatibility of hydroxyzine hydrochloride with various antineoplastic agents, *Am J Hosp Pharm 45*:2127 (Oct) 1988.
1191. Riley CM: Stability of milrinone and digoxin, furosemide, procainamide hydrochloride, propranolol hydrochloride, quinidine gluconate, or verapamil hydrochloride in 5% dextrose injection, *Am J Hosp Pharm 45*:2079–2091 (Oct) 1988.
1192. Awang DVC and Graham KC: Microwave thawing of frozen drug solutions, *Am J Hosp Pharm 44*:2256 (Oct) 1987.
1193. Bashaw ED, Amantea MA, Minor JR, et al.: Visual compatibility of zidovudine with other injectable drugs during simulated Y-site administration, *Am J Hosp Pharm 45*:2532–2533 (Dec) 1988.
1194. Souney PF, Fanikos J, and Gasca M: Compatibility of cyclophosphamide solution with antibiotics during simulated Y-site injection, *Parenterals 6*:1, 2, 8 (Aug–Sep) 1988.
1195. Beijnen JH, Vendrig DEMM, and Underberg WJM: Stability of Vinca alkaloid anticancer drugs in three commonly used infusion fluids, *J Parenter Sci Technol 43*:84–87 (Mar–Apr) 1989.
1196. Fong PA and Ward J: Visual compatibility of intravenous famotidine with selected drugs, *Am J Hosp Pharm 46*:125–126 (Jan) 1989.
1197. Karnatz NN, Wong J, Baaske DM, et al.: Stability of esmolol hydrochloride and sodium nitroprusside in intravenous admixtures, *Am J Hosp Pharm 46*: 101–104 (Jan) 1989.
1198. Johnson CE, Lloyd CW, Mesaros JL, et al.: Compatibility of aminophylline and verapamil in intravenous admixtures, *Am J Hosp Pharm 46*:97–100 (Jan) 1989.
1199. Parti R and Wolf W: Caveats with respect to storage of cisplatin and fluorouracil admixtures, *Am J Hosp Pharm 46*:259 (Feb) 1989.
1200. Johnson EG and Janosik JE: Manufacturer's recommendations for handling spilled antineoplastic agents, *Am J Hosp Pharm 46*:318–319 (Feb) 1989.
1201. Jarosinski PF, Kennedy PF, and Gallelli JF: Stability of concentrated trimethoprim–sulfamethoxazole admixtures, *Am J Hosp Pharm 46*:732–737 (Apr) 1989.
1202. Bosanquet AG: Stability of solutions of antineoplastic agents during preparation and storage for in vitro assays III. Antimetabolites, tubulin-binding agents, platinum drugs, amsacrine, L-asparaginase, interferons, steroids and other miscellaneous antitumor agents, *Cancer Chemother Pharmacol 23*:197–207, 1989.
1203. Beijnen JH and Underberg WJM: Degradation of mitomycin C in acidic solution, *Int J Pharm 24*:219–229, 1985.
1204. Beijnen JH, den Hartigh J, and Underberg WJM: Quantitative aspects of the degradation of mitomycin C in alkaline solution, *J Pharm Biomed Anal 3*:59–69, 1985.
1205. Beijnen JH, Rosing H, and Underberg WJM: Stability of mitomycins in infusion fluids, *Arch Pharm Chemi Sci Ed 13*:58–66, 1985.
1206. Janssen MJH, Crommelin DJA, Storm G, et al.: Doxorubicin decomposition

on storage. Effect of pH, type of buffer and liposome encapsulation, *Int J Pharm 23*:1–11, 1985.

1207. Beijnen JH, van der Houwen OAGJ, Voskuilen MCH, et al.: Aspects of the degradation kinetics of daunorubicin in aqueous solution, in: Chemical stability of mitomycin and anthracycline antineoplastic drugs, Beijnen JH (ed), Drukkerij Elkinkwijk BV, Utrecht, The Netherlands, 1986, pp 245–260.

1208. Beijnen JH, van der Houwen OAGJ, and Underberg WJM: Aspects of the degradation kinetics of doxorubicin in aqueous solution, *Int J Pharm 32*:123–131, 1986.

1209. Fritz BL, Lockhart HE, and Giacin JR: Chemical stability of selected pharmaceuticals repackaged in glass and plastic, *Pharm Tech 12*:44, 46, 48, 50–52 (Nov) 1988.

1210. Venkataraman PS, Brissie EO, and Tsang RC: Stability of calcium and phosphorus in neonatal parenteral nutrition solutions, *J Pediatr Gastroenterol Nutr* 2:640–643 (4) 1983.

1211. Fitzgerald KA and MacKay MW: Calcium and phosphate solubility in neonatal parenteral nutrient solutions containing Aminosyn PF, *Am J Hosp Pharm 44*:1396–1400 (June) 1987.

1212. Mikrut BA: Calcium and phosphate solubility in neonatal parenteral nutrient solutions containing Aminosyn PF or TrophAmine, *Am J Hosp Pharm 44*: 2702–2704 (Dec) 1987.

1213. Lenz GT and Mikrut BA: Calcium and phosphate solubility in neonatal parenteral nutrient solutions containing Aminosyn-PF or TrophAmine, *Am J Hosp Pharm 45*:2367–2371 (Nov) 1988.

1214. Raupp P, von Kries R, Schmidt E, et al.: Incompatibility between fat emulsion and calcium plus heparin in parenteral nutrition of premature babies, *Lancet 1*:700 (Mar 26) 1988.

1215. Waller DJ and Smith SR: Use of infusion devices with total nutrient admixtures, *Am J Hosp Pharm 44*:1570, 1574 (July) 1987.

1216. Gilbert M, Gallagher SC, Eads M, et al.: Microbial growth patterns in a total parenteral nutrition formulation containing lipid emulsion, *J Parenter Enter Nutr 10*:494–497 (Sep–Oct) 1986.

1217. Barat AC, Harrie K, Jacob M, et al.: Effect of amino acid solutions on total nutrient admixture stability, *J Parenter Enter Nutr 11*:384–388 (July–Aug) 1987.

1218. Cripps AL: Stability studies on total parenteral nutrition mixtures containing fat emulsions, *Br J Pharm Pract 6*:187–195 (June) 1984.

1219. Davis SS and Galloway M: Studies on fat emulsions in combined nutrition solutions, *J Clin Hosp Pharm 11*:33–45 (Feb) 1986.

1220. Ang SD, Canham JE, and Daly JM: Parenteral infusion with an admixture of amino acids, dextrose, fat emulsion solution: compatibility and clinical safety, *J Parenter Enter Nutr 11*:23–27 (Jan–Feb) 1987.

1221. du Plessis J, Van Wyk CJ, and Ackermann C: The stability of parenteral fat emulsions in nutrition admixtures, *J Clin Pharm Ther 12*:307–318 (Oct) 1987.

1222. Sayeed FA, Tripp MG, Sukumaran KB, et al.: Stability of total nutrient admixtures using various intravenous fat emulsions, *Am J Hosp Pharm 44*:2271–2280 (Oct) 1987.

1223. Sayeed FA, Tripp MG, Sukumaran KB, et al.: Stability of various total nutrient admixture formulations using Liposyn II and Aminosyn II, *Am J Hosp Pharm 44*:2280–2286 (Oct) 1987.

1224. McGee CD, Mascarenhas MG, Ostro MJ, et al.: Selenium and vitamin E stability in parenteral solutions, *J Parenter Enter Nutr 9*:568–570 (Sep–Oct) 1985.

1225. Dahl GB, Jeppsson RI, and Tengborn HJ: Vitamin stability in a TPN mixture stored in an EVA plastic bag, *J Clin Hosp Pharm 11*:271–279 (Aug) 1986.

1226. Shenkin A, Fraser WD, McLelland AJD, et al.: Maintenance of vitamin and trace element status in intravenous nutrition using a complete nutritive mixture, *J Parenter Enter Nutr 11*:238–242 (May–June) 1987.

1227. Yamaoka K, Nakajima Y, Okinaga S, et al.: Variation by combination of hyperalimentation with fat emulsion, *Jap J Hosp Pharm 13*:211–215 (Aug) 1987.

1228. Sewell DL, Golper TA, Brown SD, et al.: Stability of single and combination antimicrobial agents in various peritoneal dialysates in the presence of insulin and heparin, *Am J Kidney Dis 111*:209–212 (Nov) 1983.

1229. Nance KS and Matzke GR: Stability of gentamicin and tobramycin in concentrate solutions for automated peritoneal dialysis, *Am J Nephrol 4*:240–243, 1984.

1230. Das Gupta V and Parasrampuria J: Quantitation of acetazolamide in pharmaceutical dosage forms using high-performance liquid chromatography, *Drug Dev Ind Pharm 13*:147–157 (1) 1987.

1231. Boak LR: Aminophylline stability, *Can J Hosp Pharm 40*:155 (5) 1987.

1232. Moore BR and Tindula R: Incompatibility between amphotericin B and evacuated i.v. containers, *Am J Hosp Pharm 44*:1312 (June) 1987.

1233. Bretschneider H: Osmolalities of commercially supplied drugs often used in anesthesia, *Anaesth Analg 66*:361–362, 1987.

1234. Odgers C: Drug/nutrient interactions and incompatibilities complicating TPN, *N.Z. Pharm 6*:64–68 (Jan) 1986.

1235. Kedzierewicz F, Finance C, Nicolas A, et al.: Etude comparative de la stabilite de solutions de carbenicilline en fonction de la temperature. Interet du cycle congelation-decongelation au four a micro-ondes, *Pharm Acta Helv 62*:109–115 (4) 1987.

1236. Arbus MH: Room temperature stability guidelines for carmustine, *Am J Hosp Pharm 45*:531 (Mar) 1988.

1237. Frederiksson K, Lundgren P, and Landersjo L: Stability of carmustine—kinetics and compatibility during administration, *Acta Pharm Suec 23*:115–124 (2) 1986.

1238. Sewell GJ, Riley CM, and Rowland CG: The stability of carboplatin in ambulatory continuous infusion regimes, *J Clin Pharm Ther 12*:427–432, 1987.

1239. Ross MB: Additional stability guidelines for routinely refrigerated drug products, *Am J Hosp Pharm 45*:1498–1499 (July) 1988.

1240. Goodell JA, Harry DJ, and Low JR: More on production of a carbon dioxide gas after reconstitution of ceftazidime, *Am J Hosp Pharm 44*:510, 512 (Mar) 1987.

1241. Savello DR: More on production of carbon dioxide gas after reconstitution of ceftazidime, *Am J Hosp Pharm 44*:512 (Mar) 1987.

1242. Rovers JP, Menielly G, Souney PF, et al.: The use of stability-indicating assays to determine the in vitro compatibility and stability of metronidazole/gentamicin admixtures, *Can J Hosp Pharm 42*:143–146 (Aug) 1989.

1243. Walker SE and Dranitsaris G: Stability of reconstituted ceftriaxone in dextrose and saline solutions, *Can J Hosp Pharm 40*:161–166 (Oct) 1987.

1244. Martinez-Pancheco R, Vila-Jato JL, and Gomez-Amoza JL: Effect of different factors on stability of ceftriaxone in solution, *Farmaco Ed Prat 42*:131–137 (May) 1987.

1245. Kedzierewicz F, Finance C, Nicolas A, et al.: Stability of parenteral ceftriaxone disodium solutions in frozen and liquid states: effect of freezing and microwave thawing, *J Pharm Sci 78*:73–77 (Jan) 1989.

1246. Kristjansson F, Sternson LA, and Lindenbaum S: An investigation on possible oligomer formation in pharmaceutical formulations of cisplatin, *Int J Pharm 41*:67–74 (Jan) 1988.

1247. Anon: High-dose Maxolon mixes with cisplatin, *Pharm J 234*:593 (May 11) 1985.

1248. Kirk B: The evaluation of a light-protective giving set. The photosensitivity of intravenous dacarbazine solutions, *Br J Parenter Ther 8*:78, 81–82, 85–86 (May–June) 1987.

1249. Bosanquet AG: Stability of solutions of antineoplastic agents during preparation and storage for in vitro assays. General considerations, the nitrosoureas and alkylating agents, *Cancer Chemother Pharmacol 14*:83–95, 1985.

1250. Beijnen JH, Potman RP, van Ooijen RD, et al.: Structure elucidation and characterization of daunorubicin degradation products, *Int J Pharm 34*:247–257, 1987.

1251. Haronikova K, Pikulikova Z, Kral L, et al.: Sorption of diazepam on the surface of the plastic infusion unit, part 2, *Farm Obz 55*:485–494 (11) 1986.

1252. Mathot F, Bonnard J, Paris P, et al.: Influence des materiaux de perfusion sur les solutions de diazepam, *J Pharm Belg 37*:153–156 (Mar–Apr) 1982.

1253. Murphy A, Maltby S, and Launchbury AP: Dissolution time, on reconstitution, of a new parenteral formulation of doxorubicin (Doxorubicin Rapid Dissolution), *Int J Pharm 38*:257–259, 1987.

1254. Baumann TJ, Smythe MA, Kaufmann K, et al.: Dissolution times of Adriamycin and Adriamycin RDF, *Am J Hosp Pharm 45*:1667 (Aug) 1988.

1255. Vogelzang NJ, Ruane M, and DeMeester TR: Phase I trial of an implanted battery-powered, programmable drug delivery system for continuous doxorubicin administration, *J Clin Oncol 3*:407–414 (Mar) 1985.

1256. Keusters L, Stolk LML, Umans R, et al.: Stability of solutions of doxorubicin and epirubicin in plastic minibags for intravesical use after storage at −20 °C and thawing by microwave radiation, *Pharm Weekbl Sci Ed 8*:194–197 (June 20) 1986.

1257. Williamson M and Luce JK: Microwave thawing of doxorubicin hydrochloride admixtures not recommended, *Am J Hosp Pharm 44*:505, 510 (Mar) 1987.

1258. Adams S and Fernandez F: Intravenous use of haloperidol, *Hosp Pharm 22*: 306–307 (Mar) 1987.

1259. Thoma K and Struve M: Untersuchungen zur photo- und thermostabilitat von adrenalin-losungen, *Pharm Acta Helv 61*:2–9 (1) 1986.

1260. David LM: Phlebitis with intravenous erythromycin, *Am J Hosp Pharm 44*: 732, 738 (Apr) 1987.

1261. Schwinghammer TL, Reilly M, and Rosenfeld CS: Cracking of ABS plastic devices used to infuse undiluted etoposide injection, *Am J Hosp Pharm 45*: 1277 (June) 1988.

1262. Beijnen JH, Holthuis JJM, Kerkdijk HG, et al.: Degradation kinetics of etoposide in aqueous solution, *Int J Pharm 41*:169–178, 1988.
1263. Brown DH and Simkover RA: Maximum hang times for i.v. fat emulsions, *Am J Hosp Pharm 44*:282, 284 (Feb) 1987.
1264. Allwood MC: The release of phthalate ester plasticizer from intravenous administration sets into fat emulsion, *Int J Pharm 29*:233–236, 1986.
1265. Nahata MC, Hipple TF, and Strausbaugh SD: Stability of gentamicin diluted in 0.9% sodium chloride injection in glass syringes, *Hosp Pharm 22*:1131–1132 (Nov) 1987.
1266. Dunn DL and Lenihan SF: The case for the saline flush, *Am J Nurs 87*:798–799 (June) 1987.
1267. Shearer J: Normal saline flush versus dilute heparin flush. A study of peripheral intermittent I.V. devices, *NITA 10*:425–427 (Nov–Dec) 1987.
1268. Hamilton RA, Plis JM, Clay C, et al.: Heparin sodium versus 0.9% sodium chloride injection for maintaining patency of indwelling intermittent infusion devices, *Clin Pharm 7*:439–443, 1988.
1269. Lombardi TP, Gundersen B, Zammett LO, et al.: Efficacy of 0.9% sodium chloride injection with or without heparin sodium for maintaining patency of intravenous catheters in children, *Clin Pharm 7*:832–836, 1988.
1270. Cyganski JM, Donahue JM, and Heaton JS: The case for the heparin flush, *Am J Nurs 87*:796–797 (June) 1987.
1271. Bullock LS, Fitzgerald JF, and Glick MR: Stability of famotidine in minibags refrigerated and/or frozen, *DICP, Ann Pharmacother 23*:132–135 (Feb) 1989.
1272. Swanson DJ, DeAngelis C, Smith IL, et al.: Degradation kinetics of imipenem in normal saline and human serum, *Antimicrob Agents Chemother 29*:936–937 (May) 1986.
1273. Smith GB and Schoenewaldt EF: Stability of N-formimidoylthienamycin in aqueous solution, *J Pharm Sci 70*:272–276 (Mar) 1981.
1274. McElnay JC, Elliott DS, and D'Arcy PF: Binding of human insulin to burette administration sets, *Int J Pharm 36*:199–203 (May) 1987.
1275. Adams PS, Haines-Nutt RF, and Town R: Stability of insulin mixtures in disposable plastic insulin syringes, *J Pharm Pharmacol 39*:158–163 (Mar) 1987.
1276. Mozzi G, Conegliani B, Lomi R, et al.: Stabilita del calcio folinato in soluzioni acquose in funzione del pH e delta temperatura, *Boll Chim Farm 125*:424–428 (Dec) 1986.
1277. Powell MF: Stability of lidocaine in aqueous solution: effect of temperature, pH, buffer, and metal ions on amide hydrolysis, *Pharm Res 4*:42–45 (Feb) 1987.
1278. Das Gupta V and Stewart KR: Chemical stabilities of lignocaine hydrochloride and phenylephrine hydrochloride in aqueous solution, *J Clin Hosp Pharm 11*:449–452 (Dec) 1986.
1279. Kirk B: Stability of reconstituted mustine injection BP during storage, *Br J Parenter Ther 7*:86–87, 90–92 (July–Aug) 1986.
1280. Wright MP and Newton JM: Stability of methotrexate injection in prefilled, plastic disposable syringes, *Int J Pharm 45*:237–244 (3) 1988.
1281. Dyvik O, Grislingaas AL, Tonnesen HH, et al.: Methotrexate in infusion solutions—a stability test for the hospital pharmacy, *J Clin Hosp Pharm 11*:343–348 (5) 1986.
1282. Cabeza Barrera J, Bautista Paloma J, Garcia de Pesquera F, et al.: Disminucion de la adsorcion de insulina a los envases de nutricion parenteral, *Rev Assoc Esp Farm Hosp 12*:251–254 (Oct-Dec) 1988.
1283. Beijnen JH, Fokkens RH, Rosing H, et al.: Degradation of mitomycin C in acid phosphate and acetate buffer solutions, *Int J Pharm 32*:111–121, 1986.
1284. Beijnen JH, Lingeman H, Van Munster HA, et al.: Mitomycin antitumor agents: a review of their physico-chemical and analytical properties and stability, *J Pharm Biomed Anal 4*:275–295, 1986.
1285. Stolk LML, Fruijtier A, and Umans R: Stability after freezing and thawing of solutions of mitomycin C in plastic minibags for intravesical use, *Pharm Weekbl Sci Ed 8*:286–288, 1986.
1286. Depiero D, Rekhi GS, Souney PF, et al.: Stability of morphine sulfate solutions frozen in polyvinyl chloride intravenous bags, *Pharm Pract News 14*:1, 39–40 (Oct) 1987.
1287. Hung CT, Young M, and Gupta PK: Stability of morphine solutions in plastic syringes determined by reversed-phase ion-pair liquid chromatography, *J Pharm Sci 77*:719–723 (Aug) 1988.
1288. Visor GC, Lin LH, Jackson SE, et al.: Stability of ganciclovir sodium (DHPG sodium) in 5% dextrose or 0.9% sodium chloride injections, *Am J Hosp Pharm 43*:2810–2812 (Nov) 1986.
1289. Behme RJ, Brooke D, Kensler TT, et al.: Incompatibility of ifosfamide with benzyl-alcohol-preserved bacteriostatic water for injection, *Am J Hosp Pharm 45*:627–628 (Mar) 1988.
1290. Rowland CG, Bradford E, Adams P, et al.: Infusion of ifosfamide plus mesna, *Lancet 2*:468 (Aug 25) 1984.
1291. Anon: Mesnex (Mesna), Bristol-Myers Oncology Division, Evansville, Indiana, June 1989.
1292. Dorr RT: Mesnex dosing and administration guide, Bristol Myers Company, Evansville, Indiana, 1989.
1293. Anon: Novantrone, Lederle Laboratories, American Cyanamid Company, Pearl River, New York, 1988.
1294. Nahata MC, Hipple TF, and Strausbaugh SD: Stability of phenobarbital sodium diluted in 0.9% sodium chloride injection, *Am J Hosp Pharm 43*:384–385 (Feb) 1986.
1295. Dela Cruz FG, Kanter MZ, Fischer JH, et al.: Efficacy of individualized phenytoin sodium loading doses administered by intravenous infusion, *Clin Pharm 7*:219–224 (Mar) 1988.
1296. Davidson SW and Lyall D: Sodium nitroprusside stability in light-protective administration sets, *Pharm J 239*:599–601 (Nov 14) 1987.
1297. Saunders A: Stability and light sensitivity of sodium nitroprusside infusions, *Aust J Hosp Pharm 16*:55–56 (Mar) 1986.
1298. Glascock JC, DiPiro JT, Cadwallader DE, et al.: Stability of terbutaline sulfate repackaged in disposable plastic syringes, *Am J Hosp Pharm 44*:2291–2293 (Oct) 1987.
1299. Raymond GG: Stability of terbutaline sulfate injection stored in plastic tuberculin syringes, *Drug Intell Clin Pharm 22*:303–305 (Apr) 1988.
1300. Das Gupta V, Gardner SN, Jalowsky CM, et al.: Chemical stability of thiopental sodium injection in disposable plastic syringes, *J Clin Pharm Ther 12*:339–342 (Oct) 1987.
1301. Nahata MC, Miller MA, and Durrell DE: Stability of vancomycin hydrochloride in various concentrations of dextrose injection, *Am J Hosp Pharm 44*:802–804 (Apr) 1987.
1302. Greenberg RN, Saeed AMK, Kennedy DJ, et al.: Instability of vancomycin in Infusaid drug pump model 100, *Antimicrob Agents Chemother 31*:610–611 (Apr) 1987.
1303. Tucker R and Gentile JF: Precipitation of verapamil in an intravenous line, *Ann Intern Med 101*:880 (Dec) 1984.
1304. Patel SD and Yalkowsky SH: Development of an intravenous formulation for the antiviral drug 9-(beta-D-arabinofuranosyl)-adenine, *J Parenter Sci Technol 41*:15–20 (Jan–Feb) 1987.
1305. Stolk LML, Huisman W, Nordemann HD, et al.: Formulation of a stable vidarabine infusion fluid, *Pharm Weekbl Sci Ed 5*:57–60 (Apr 29) 1983.
1306. Black J, Buechter DD, and Thurston DE: Stability of vinblastine sulfate when exposed to light, *Drug Intell Clin Pharm 22*:634–636 (July–Aug) 1988.
1307. Vindrig DEMM, Smeets BPGH, Beijnen JH, et al.: Degradation kinetics of vinblastine sulphate in aqueous solutions, *Int J Pharm 43*:131–138, 1988.
1308. Cartwight-Shamoon JM, McElnay JC, and D'Arcy PF: Examination of sorption and photodegradation of amsacrine during storage in intravenous burette administration sets, *Int J Pharm 42*:41–46, 1988.
1309. Milano G, Etienne MC, Cassuto-Viguier E, et al.: Long-term stability of 5-fluorouracil and folinic acid admixtures, *Eur J Cancer 29A*:129–132 (1) 1993.
1310. Kraynak MA: Pharmaceutical aspects of docetaxel, *Am J Health-Syst Pharm 54*:S7–S10 (Dec 15 Suppl 2) 1997.
1311. Leigh PH and Buddle GC: Pentamidine infusion stability, *Br J Pharm Pract 10*:22–23 (Jan) 1988.
1312. Roos PJ, Glerum JH, and Meilink JW: Stability of morphine hydrochloride in a portable pump reservoir, *Pharmaceut Weekbl Sci Ed 14*:23–26 (1) 1992.
1313. Wohlford JG and Fowler MD: Visual compatibility of hetastarch with injectable critical-care drugs, *Am J Hosp Pharm 46*:995–996 (May) 1989.
1314. Wohlford JG: Clarification of visual compatibility of hetastarch and ranitidine hydrochloride, *Am J Hosp Pharm 46*:1772 (Sep) 1989.
1315. Wohlford JG, Wright JC, and Wilson MR: More information on the visual compatibility of hetastarch with injectable critical-care drugs, *Am J Hosp Pharm 47*:297–298 (Feb) 1990.
1316. Dasta JF, Hale KN, Stauffer GL, et al.: Comparison of visual and turbidimetric methods for determining short-term compatibility of intravenous critical-care drugs, *Am J Hosp Pharm 45*:2361–2366 (Nov) 1988.
1317. Smith JA, Morris A, Duafala ME, et al.: Stability of floxuridine and leucovorin calcium admixtures for intraperitoneal administration, *Am J Hosp Pharm 46*:985–989 (May) 1989.
1318. Perrin JH, Pereira-Rosario R, and Utamura T: The interaction of dobutamine hydrochloride and heparin sodium in parenteral fluids, *Drug Dev Indust Pharm 14*:1617–1622 (11) 1988.
1319. Lesko AB, Sesin GP, and Cersosimo RJ: Ceftizoxime stability in iv solutions, *DICP, Ann Pharmacother 23*:615, 617–618 (July–Aug) 1989.
1320. Mitrano FP and Baptista RJ: Stability of cimetidine HCl and copper sulfate in a TPN solution, *DICP, Ann Pharmacother 23*:429–430 (May) 1989.
1321. Schilling CG, Watson DM, McCoy HG, et al.: Stability and delivery of van-

comycin hydrochloride when admixed in a total parenteral nutrition solution, *J Parenter Enter Nutr 13*:63–64 (1) 1989.

1322. Strong DK, Ho W, and Nairn JG: Visual compatibility of vancomycin and heparin in peritoneal dialysis solutions, *Am J Hosp Pharm 46*:1832–1833 (Sep) 1989.

1323. Chilvers MR and Lysne JM: Visual compatibility of ranitidine hydrochloride with commonly used critical-care medications, *Am J Hosp Pharm 46*:2057–2058 (Oct) 1989.

1324. Bullock L, Clark JH, Fitzgerald JF, et al.: The stability of amikacin, gentamicin, and tobramycin in total nutrient admixture, *J Parenter Enter Nutr 13*: 505–509 (Sep–Oct) 1989.

1325. Nahata MC: Stability of vancomycin hydrochloride in total parenteral nutrient solutions, *Am J Hosp Pharm 46*:2055–2057 (Oct) 1989.

1326. Fox AS, Boyer KM, and Sweeney HM: Antibiotic stability in a pediatric parenteral alimentation solution, *J Pediatr 112*:813–817 (May) 1988.

1327. Raymond GG, Reed MT, Teagarden JR, et al.: Stability of procainamide hydrochloride in neutralized 5% dextrose injection, *Am J Hosp Pharm 45*:2513–2517 (Dec) 1988.

1328. Zbrozek AS, Marble DA, and Bosso JA: Compatibility and stability of cefazolin sodium, clindamycin phosphate, and gentamicin sulfate in two intravenous solutions, *Drug Intell Clin Pharm 22*:873–875 (Nov) 1988.

1329. Stewart CF and Hampton EM: Stability of cisplatin and etoposide in intravenous admixtures, *Am J Hosp Pharm 46*:1400–1404 (July) 1989.

1330. Shea BF, Ptachcinski RJ, O'Neill S, et al.: Stability of cyclosporine in 5% dextrose injection, *Am J Hosp Pharm 46*:2053–2055 (Oct) 1989.

1331. Bullock L, Fitzgerald JF, Glick MR, et al.: Stability of famotidine 20 and 40 mg/L and amino acids in total parenteral nutrient solutions, *Am J Hosp Pharm 46*:2321–2325 (Nov) 1989.

1332. Bullock L, Fitzgerald JF, and Glick MR: Stability of famotidine 20 and 50 mg/L in total nutrient admixtures, *Am J Hosp Pharm 46*:2326–2329 (Nov) 1989.

1333. Montoro JB, Pou L, Salvador P, et al.: Stability of famotidine 20 and 40 mg/L in total nutrient admixtures, *Am J Hosp Pharm 46*:2329–2332 (Nov) 1989.

1334. DiStefano JE, Mitrano FP, Baptista RJ, et al.: Long-term stability of famotidine 20 mg/L in a total parenteral nutrient solution, *Am J Hosp Pharm 46*:2333–2335 (Nov) 1989.

1335. Lor E and Takagi J: Visual compatibility of foscarnet with other injectable drugs, *Am J Hosp Pharm 47*:157–159 (Jan) 1990.

1336. Scott SM: Incompatibility of cefoperazone and promethazine, *Am J Hosp Pharm 47*:519 (Mar) 1990.

1337. Savitsky ME: Visual compatibility of neuromuscular blocking agents with various injectable drugs during simulated Y-site injection, *Am J Hosp Pharm 47*:820–821 (Apr) 1990.

1338. Smythe MA, Patel MA, and Gasloli RA: Visual compatibility of narcotic analgesics with selected intravenous admixtures, *Am J Hosp Pharm 47*:819–820 (Apr) 1990.

1339. Stewart CF and Fleming RA: Compatibility of cisplatin and fluorouracil in 0.9% sodium chloride injection, *Am J Hosp Pharm 47*:1373–1377 (June) 1990.

1340. Lee CY, Mauro VF, and Alexander KS: Visual and spectrophotometric determination of compatibility of alteplase and streptokinase with other injectable drugs, *Am J Hosp Pharm 47*:606–608 (Mar) 1990.

1341. Gupta VD, Bethea C, and dela Torre M: Chemical stabilities of cefoperazone sodium and ceftazidime in 5% dextrose and 0.9% sodium chloride injections, *J Clin Pharm Ther 13*:199–205 (June) 1988.

1342. Gupta VD, Parasrampuria J, and Bethea C: Chemical stabilities of famotidine and ranitidine hydrochloride in intravenous admixtures, *J Clin Pharm Ther 13*:329–334 (Oct) 1988.

1343. Gupta VD, Pramar Y, and Bethea C: Stability of acyclovir sodium in dextrose and sodium chloride injections, *J Clin Pharm Ther 14*:451–456 (6) 1989.

1344. Underberg WJM, Koomen JM, and Beijnen JH: Stability of famotidine in commonly used nutritional infusion fluids, *J Parenter Sci Technol 42*:94–97 (May–June) 1988.

1345. Messerschmidt W: Pharmazeutische kompatibilitat von ceftazidim und metronidazol, *Pharm Ztg 135*:36–38 (Mar 8) 1990.

1346. Messerschmidt W: Kompatibilitat von ciprofloxacin und metronidazol in mischinfusionen, *Pharm Ztg 133*:26, 28 (May 26) 1988.

1347. Murdoch JM and Garner ST: Calcium gluconate compatibility, *Pharm J 242*: 634 (June 3) 1989.

1348. Stoberski P, Zakrzewski Z, and Szulc A: Bandanie stabilnosci furosemidu i soli sodowej hemibursztynianu hydrokortyzonu metoda RP-HPLC w wybranych plynach infuzyjnych, *Farm Pol 44*:398–401 (7) 1988.

1349. Veechio M, Walker SE, Iazzetta J, et al.: The stability of morphine intravenous infusion solutions, *Can J Hosp Pharm 41*:5–9, 43 (Feb) 1988.

1350. Walker SE and Kirby K: Stability of ranitidine hydrochloride admixtures refrigerated in polyvinyl chloride minibags, *Can J Hosp Pharm 41*:105–108 (June) 1988.

1351. Gupta VD, Parasrampuria J, Bethea C, et al.: Stability of clindamycin phosphate in dextrose and saline solutions, *Can J Hosp Pharm 42*:109–112 (June) 1989.

1352. Walker SE, Iazzetta J, Lau DWC, et al.: Famotidine stability in total parenteral nutrient solutions, *Can J Hosp Pharm 42*:97–103 (June) 1989.

1353. Walker SE and Dranitsaris G: Ceftazidime stability in normal saline and dextrose 5% in water, *Can J Hosp Pharm 41*:65–71 (Apr) 1988.

1354. Walker SE and Birkhans B: Stability of intravenous vancomycin, *Can J Hosp Pharm 41*:233–238, 242 (Oct) 1988.

1355. Halpern NA, Colucci RD, Alicea M, et al.: Visual compatibility of enalaprilat with commonly used critical care medications during simulated Y-site injection, *Int J Clin Pharmacol Ther Toxicol 27*:294–297 (June) 1989.

1356. Allen LV Jr, Stiles ML, and Tu YH: Stability of fentanyl citrate in 0.9% sodium chloride solution in portable infusion pumps, *Am J Hosp Pharm 47*: 1572–1574 (July) 1990.

1357. Kowalski SR and Gourlay GK: Stability of fentanyl citrate in glass and plastic containers and in a patient-controlled delivery system, *Am J Hosp Pharm 47*: 1584–1587 (July) 1990.

1358. Schaaf LJ, Robinson DH, Vogel GJ, et al.: Stability of esmolol hydrochloride in the presence of aminophylline, bretylium tosylate, heparin sodium, and procainamide hydrochloride, *Am J Hosp Pharm 47*:1567–1571 (July) 1990.

1359. Rosenberg LS, Hostetler CK, Wagenknecht DM, et al.: An accurate prediction of the pH change due to degradation: correction for a "produced" secondary buffering system, *Pharm Res 5*:514–517 (Aug) 1988.

1360. Williams MF, Hak LJ, and Dukes G: In vitro evaluation of the stability of ranitidine hydrochloride in total parenteral nutrient mixtures, *Am J Hosp Pharm 47*:1574–1579 (July) 1990.

1361. Galante LJ, Stewart JT, Warren FW, et al.: Stability of ranitidine hydrochloride with eight medications in intravenous admixtures, *Am J Hosp Pharm 47*:1606–1610 (July) 1990.

1362. Galante LJ, Stewart JT, Warren FW, et al.: Stability of ranitidine hydrochloride at dilute concentration in intravenous infusion fluids at room temperature, *Am J Hosp Pharm 47*:1580–1584 (July) 1990.

1363. Marquardt ED: Visual compatibility of tolazoline hydrochloride with various medications during simulated Y-site injection, *Am J Hosp Pharm 47*:1802–1803 (Aug) 1990.

1364. Chandler SW, Folstad J, and Trissel LA: Aztreonam–vancomycin incompatibility, *Am J Hosp Pharm 47*:1970 (Sep) 1990.

1365. Trissel LA, Tramonte SM, and Grilley BJ: Visual compatibility of ondansetron hydrochloride with other selected drugs during simulated Y-site injection, *Am J Hosp Pharm 48*:988–992 (May) 1991.

1366. Leak RE and Woodford JD: Pharmaceutical development of ondansetron injection, *Eur J Cancer Clin Oncol 25 (Suppl 1)*:S67–S69, 1989.

1367. MacKinnon JWM and Collin DT: The chemistry of ondansetron, *Eur J Cancer Clin Oncol 25 (Suppl 1)*:S61, 1989.

1368. Anon: Idamycin—hospital formulary product information form, Adria Laboratories, Columbus, Ohio, October 19, 1990.

1369. Allwood M, Stanley A, and Wright P: The cytotoxics handbook, 3rd ed, Radcliffe Medical Press, Oxford, England, 1997.

1370. Garinot O, Vitzling C, Mottu R, et al.: Sandostatine: compatibility of Sandostatine 100 μg/ml and 500 μg/ml infusions with various plastic syringes and infusion apparatus, Sandoz Pharmaceutical Research Center, Basle, Switzerland, September 1988.

1371. Anon: Sandostatin—compatibility between octreotide in the infusion and the giving set/container, Sandoz Laboratories, Basle, Switzerland, April 3, 1986.

1372. Anon: Sandostatin—stability in physiological salt solutions, Sandoz Laboratories, Basle, Switzerland, March 26, 1986.

1373. Marchiarullo M: Stability of octreotide in various infusion supplies, Sandoz Pharmaceuticals Corporation, East Hanover, New Jersey, March 20, 1990.

1374. Beijnen JH, Beijnen-Bandhoe AU, Dubbelman AC, et al.: Chemical and physical stability of etoposide and teniposide in commonly used infusion fluids, *J Parenter Sci Technol 45*:108–112 (Mar–Apr) 1991.

1375. Santiero ML, Sagraves R, and Allen LV Jr: Osmolality of small-volume i.v. admixtures for pediatric patients, *Am J Hosp Pharm 47*:1359–1364 (June) 1990.

1376. Messerschmidt W: Kompatibilitat von cefuroxim mit metronidazole, *Krankenhauspharmazie 8*:45–47 (2) 1987.

1377. Rosen GH: Potential incompatibility of insulin and octreotide in total parenteral nutrient solutions, *Am J Hosp Pharm 46*:1128 (June) 1989.

1378. McElnay JC, Elliott DS, Cartwright-Shamoon J, et al.: Stability of methotrexate and vinblastine in burette administration sets, *Int J Pharm 47*:239–247 (Nov) 1988.

1379. Williams DA: Stability and compatibility of admixtures of antineoplastic drugs, *in* Lokich JJ (ed), Cancer chemotherapy by infusion, 2nd ed, Precept Press, Chicago, Illinois, 1990, pp 52–73.
1380. Adams PS, Haines-Nutt RF, Bradford E., et al.: Pharmaceutical aspects of home infusion therapy for cancer patients, *Pharm J 11*:476–478, 1987.
1381. Trissel LA, Chandler SW, and Folstad JT: Visual compatibility of amsacrine with selected drugs during simulated Y-site injection, *Am J Hosp Pharm 47*: 2525–2528 (Nov) 1990.
1382. Townsend RS: In vitro inactivation of gentamicin by ampicillin, *Am J Hosp Pharm 46*:2250–2251 (Nov) 1989.
1383. Vaughn LM, Small C, and Plunkett V: Incompatibility of iron dextran and a total nutrient admixture, *Am J Hosp Pharm 47*:1745–1746 (Aug) 1990.
1384. Cutie MR: Verapamil precipitation, *Ann Intern Med 98*:672 (May) 1983.
1385. Garner SS and Wiest DB: Compatibility of drugs separated by a fluid barrier in a retrograde intravenous infusion system, *Am J Hosp Pharm 47*:604–606 (Mar) 1990.
1386. Lokich J, Anderson N, Bern M, et al.: Combined floxuridine and cisplatin in a 14-day infusion, *Cancer 62*:2309–2312 (Dec 1) 1988.
1387. Anderson N, Lokich J, Bern M, et al.: A phase I clinical trial of combined fluoropyrimidines with leucovorin in a 14-day infusion, *Cancer 63*:233–237 (Jan 15) 1989.
1388. Lokich J, Anderson N, Bern M, et al.: Etoposide admixed with cisplatin, *Cancer 63*:818–821 (Mar 1) 1989.
1389. Lokich J, Bern M, Anderson N, et al.: Cyclophosphamide, methotrexate, and 5-fluorouracil in a three-drug admixture, *Cancer 63*:822–824 (Mar 1) 1989.
1390. Anderson N, Lokich J, Bern M, et al.: Combined 5-fluorouracil and floxuridine administered as a 14-day infusion, *Cancer 63*:825–827 (Mar 1) 1989.
1391. Stiles ML, Tu YH, and Allen LV Jr: Stability of cefazolin sodium, cefoxitin sodium, ceftazidime, and penicillin G sodium in portable pump reservoirs, *Am J Hosp Pharm 46*:1408–1412 (July) 1989.
1392. Martens HJ, De Goede PN, and van Loenen AC: Sorption of various drugs in polyvinyl chloride, glass, and polyethylene-lined infusion containers, *Am J Hosp Pharm 47*:369–373 (Feb) 1990.
1393. Baltz JK, Kennedy P, Minor JR, et al.: Visual compatibility of foscarnet with other injectable drugs during simulated Y-site administration, *Am J Hosp Pharm 47*:2075–2077 (Sep) 1990.
1394. Walker SE, Coons C, Matte D, et al.: Hydromorphone and morphine stability in portable infusion pump casettes and minibags, *Can J Hosp Pharm 41*:177–182 (Aug) 1988.
1395. Smythe M and Malouf E: Visual compatibility of insulin with secondary intravenous drugs in admixtures, *Am J Hosp Pharm 48*:125–126 (Jan) 1991.
1396. Tu YH, Stiles ML, and Allen LV Jr: Stability of fentanyl citrate and bupivacaine hydrochloride in portable pump reservoirs, *Am J Hosp Pharm 47*:2037–2040 (Sep) 1990.
1397. Pugh CB, Pabis DJ, and Rodriguez C: Visual compatibility of morphine sulfate and meperidine hydrochloride with other injectable drugs during simulated Y-site injection, *Am J Hosp Pharm 48*:123–125 (Jan) 1991.
1398. Pritts D and Hancock D: Incompatibility of ceftriaxone with vancomycin, *Am J Hosp Pharm 48*:77 (Jan) 1991.
1399. DeMuynck C, De Vroe C, Remon JP, et al.: Binding of drugs to end-line filters: a study of four commonly administered drugs in intensive care units, *J Clin Pharm Ther 13*:335–340 (Oct) 1988.
1400. Aki H, Sawai N, Yamamoto K, et al.: Structural confirmation of ampicillin polymers formed in aqueous solution, *Pharm Res 8*:119–122 (Jan) 1991.
1401. Bonhomme L, Postaire E, Touratier S, et al.: Chemical stability of lignocaine (lidocaine) and adrenaline (epinephrine) in pH-adjusted parenteral solutions, *J Clin Pharm Ther 13*:257–261, 1988.
1402. Lee DKT, Lee A, and Wang DP: Compatibility of cefoperazone sodium and furosemide in 5% dextrose injection, *Am J Hosp Pharm 48*:108–110 (Jan) 1991.
1403. Lee DKT, Wang DP, and Lee A: Compatibility of cefoperazone sodium and cimetidine hydrochloride in 5% dextrose injection, *Am J Hosp Pharm 48*:111–113 (Jan) 1991.
1404. Kirkpatrick AE, Holcome BJ, and Sawyer WT: Effect of retrograde aminophylline administration on calcium and phosphate solubility in neonatal total parenteral nutrient solutions, *Am J Hosp Pharm 46*:2496–2500 (Dec) 1989.
1405. Seay R and Bostrom B: Apparent compatibility of methotrexate and vancomycin, *Am J Hosp Pharm 47*:2656, 2658 (Dec) 1990.
1406. Johnson OL, Washington C, Davis SS, et al.: The destabilization of parenteral feeding emulsions by heparin, *Int J Pharm 53*:237–240 (Aug 1) 1989.
1407. Lor E, Sheybani T, and Takagi J: Visual compatibility of fluconazole with commonly used injectable drugs during simulated Y-site administration, *Am J Hosp Pharm 48*:744–746 (Apr) 1991.
1408. Tol A, Quik RFP, and Thyssen JHH: Adsorption of human and porcine insulins to intravenous administration sets, *Pharm Weekbl Sci Ed 10*:213–216 (Oct 14) 1988.
1409. Thompson DF, Allen LV Jr, and Stiles ML: Visual compatibility of enalaprilat with selected intravenous medications during simulated Y-site injection, *Am J Hosp Pharm 47*:2530–2531 (Nov) 1990.
1410. Wilson TD and Forde MD: Stability of milrinone and epinephrine, atropine sulfate, lidocaine hydrochloride, or morphine sulfate injection, *Am J Hosp Pharm 47*:2504–2507 (Nov) 1990.
1411. Lam NP, Kennedy PE, Jarosinski PF, et al.: Stability of zidovudine in 5% dextrose injection and 0.9% sodium chloride injection, *Am J Hosp Pharm 48*: 280–282 (Feb) 1991.
1412. Horrow JC, Digregorio GJ, Barbieri EJ, et al.: Intravenous infusions of nitroprusside, dobutamine, and nitroglycerin are compatible, *Crit Care Med 18*: 858–861 (Aug) 1990.
1413. Halstead DC, Guzzo J, Giardina JA, et al.: In vitro bactericidal activities of gentamicin, cefazolin, and imipenem in peritoneal dialysis fluids, *Antimicrob Agents Chemother 33*:1553–1556 (Sep) 1989.
1414. Drake JM, Myre SA, Staneck JL, et al.: Antimicrobial activity of vancomycin, gentamicin, and tobramycin in peritoneal dialysis solution, *Am J Hosp Pharm 47*:1604–1606 (July) 1990.
1415. Pavlik EJ, van Nagell JR, Hanson MB, et al.: Sensitivity to anticancer agents in vitro: standardizing the cytotoxic response and characterizing the sensitivities of a reference cell line, *Gynecol Oncol 14*:243–261 (Oct) 1982.
1416. Pavlik EJ, Kenady DE, van Nagell JR, et al.: Properties of anticancer agents relevant to in vitro determinations of human tumor cell sensitivity, *Cancer Chemother Pharmacol 11*:8–15 (1) 1983.
1417. Gora ML, Seth S, Visconti JA, et al.: Stability of dobutamine hydrochloride in peritoneal dialysis solutions, *Am J Hosp Pharm 48*:1234–1237 (June) 1991.
1418. Strom JG Jr and Miller SW: Stability and compatibility of methylprednisolone sodium succinate and cimetidine hydrochloride in 5% dextrose injection, *Am J Hosp Pharm 48*:1237–1241 (June) 1991.
1419. Riley CM and Junkin P: Stability of amrinone and digoxin, procainamide hydrochloride, propranolol hydrochloride, sodium bicarbonate, potassium chloride, or verapamil hydrochloride in intravenous admixtures, *Am J Hosp Pharm 48*:1245–1252 (June) 1991.
1420. Pennell AT, Allington DR, and Chandler MHH: Effect of ceftazidime, cefotaxime, and cefoperazone on serum tobramycin concentrations, *Am J Hosp Pharm 48*:520–522 (Mar) 1991.
1421. Collins JL and Lutz RJ: In vitro study of simultaneous infusion of incompatible drugs in multilumen catheters, *Heart Lung 20*:271–277 (May) 1991.
1422. Gupta VD: Complexation of procainamide with dextrose, *J Pharm Sci 71*: 994–996 (Sep) 1982.
1423. Gupta VD: Complexation of procainamide with hydroxide-containing compounds, *J Pharm Sci 72*:205–207 (Feb) 1983.
1424. Parasrampuria J and Gupta VD: Preformulation studies of acetazolamide: effect of pH, two buffer species, ionic strength, and temperature on its stability, *J Pharm Sci 78*:855–857 (Oct) 1989.
1425. Franzin BS: Maximal dilution of Activase, *Am J Hosp Pharm 47*:1016 (May) 1990.
1426. Tripp MG: Automated 3-in-1 admixture compounding: a comparative study of simultaneous versus sequential pumping of core substrates on admixture stability, *Hosp Pharm 25*:1090–1093, 1096 (Dec) 1990.
1427. Knowles JB, Cusson G, Smith M, et al.: Pulmonary deposition of calcium phosphate crystals as a complication of home total parenteral nutrition, *J Parenter Enter Nutr 13*:209–213 (Mar–Apr) 1989.
1428. Knight PJ, Buchanan S, and Clatworthy HW: Calcium and phosphate requirements of preterm infants who require prolonged hyperalimentation, *J Am Med Assoc 243*:1244–1246, 1980.
1429. Stennett DJ, Gerwick WH, Egging PK, et al.: Precipitate analysis from an indwelling total parenteral nutrition catheter, *J Parenter Enter Nutr 12*:88–92, 1988.
1430. Mazur HI, Stennett DJ, and Egging PK: Extraction of diethylhexylphthalate from total nutrient solution-containing polyvinyl chloride bags, *J Parenter Enter Nutr 13*:59–62 (Jan–Feb) 1989.
1431. Smith JL, Canham JE, Kirkland WD, et al.: Effect of Intralipid, amino acids, container, temperature, and duration of storage on vitamin stability in total parenteral nutrition admixtures, *J Parenter Enter Nutr 12*:478–483 (Sep–Oct) 1988.
1432. Tripp MG, Menon SK, and Mikrut BA: Stability of total nutrient admixtures in a dual-chamber flexible container, *Am J Hosp Pharm 47*:2496–2503 (Nov) 1990.
1433. Dalton-Bunnow MF and Halvacks FJ: Update on room-temperature stability of drug products labeled for refrigerated storage, *Am J Hosp Pharm 47*:2522–2524 (Nov) 1990.

1434. Kintzel PE and Kennedy PE: Stability of amphotericin B in 5% dextrose injection at concentrations used for administration through a central venous line, *Am J Hosp Pharm 48*:283–285 (Feb) 1991.
1435. Rice JK: Visual compatibility of amphotericin B and flush solutions, *Am J Hosp Pharm 46*:2461 (Dec) 1989.
1436. Trissel LA, Bready BB, Kwan JW, et al.: The visual compatibility of sargramostim with selected chemotherapeutic drugs, anti-infectives, and other drugs during simulated Y-site injection, *Am J Hosp Pharm 49*:402–406 (Feb) 1992.
1437. Pilla TJ, Beshany SE, and Shields JB: Incompatibility of Hexabrix and papaverine, *Am J Roentgenol 146*:1300–1301 (June) 1986.
1438. Irving HD and Burbridge BE: Incompatibility of contrast agents with intravascular medications, *Radiology 173*:91–92, 1989.
1439. Trissel LA, Parks NPT, and Santiago NM: Visual compatibility of fludarabine phosphate with antineoplastic drugs, anti-infectives, and other selected drugs during simulated Y-site injection, *Am J Hosp Pharm 48*:2186–2189 (Oct) 1991.
1440. Tidy PJ, Sewell GJ, and Jeffries TM: Microwave freeze–thaw studies on azlocillin infusion, *Pharm J 241*:R22–R23 (Nov 12 Suppl) 1988.
1441. Koberda M, Zieske PA, Raghavan NV, et al.: Stability of bleomycin sulfate reconstituted in 5% dextrose injection or 0.9% sodium chloride injection stored in glass vials or polyvinyl chloride containers, *Am J Hosp Pharm 47*:2528–2529 (Nov) 1990.
1442. Anon: ABPI compendium of data sheets and summaries of product characteristics 1999/2000, Datapharm Publications Ltd., London, England, 1999.
1443. Weir SJ, Szucs Myers VA, Bengston KD, et al.: Sorption of amiodarone to polyvinyl chloride infusion bags and administration sets, *Am J Hosp Pharm 42*:2679–2683 (Dec) 1985.
1444. Benedict MK, Roche VF, Banakar UV, et al.: Visual compatibility of amiodarone hydrochloride with various antimicrobial agents during simulated Y-site injection, *Am J Hosp Pharm 45*:1117–1118 (May) 1988.
1445. Capps PA and Robertson AL: Influence of amiodarone injection on delivery rate of intravenous fluids, *Pharm J 234*:14–15 (Jan 5) 1985.
1446. Tsuei SE, Nation RL, and Thomas J: Sorption of chlormethiazole by intravenous infusion giving sets, *Eur J Clin Pharmacol 18*:333–338 (Aug) 1980.
1447. Lingam S, Bertwistle H, Elliston HM, et al.: Problems with intravenous chlormethiazole (Heminevrin) in status epilepticus, *Br Med J 1*:155–156 (Jan) 1980.
1448. Beaumont IM: Stability study of aqueous solutions of diamorphine and morphine using HPLC, *Pharm J 229*:39–41 (July 10) 1982.
1449. Kleinberg ML, Duafala ME, Nacov C, et al.: Stability of heroin hydrochloride in infusion devices and containers for intravenous administration, *Am J Hosp Pharm 47*:377–381 (Feb) 1990.
1450. Jones VA and Hanks GW: New portable infusion pump for prolonged subcutaneous administration of opiod analgesics in patients with advanced cancer, *Br Med J 292*:1496 (June 7) 1986.
1451. Jones VA, Hoskin PJ, Omar OA, et al.: Diamorphine stability in aqueous solution for subcutaneous infusion, *Abs Br Soc Pharmacol Meet* 66 (Dec) 1986.
1452. Omar OA, Hoskin PJ, Johnston A, et al.: Diamorphine stability in aqueous solution for subcutaneous infusion, *J Pharm Pharmacol 41*:275–277 (Apr) 1989.
1453. Al-Razzak LA, Benedetti AE, Waugh WN, et al.: Chemical stability of pentostatin (NSC-218321), a cytotoxic and immunosuppressive agent, *Pharm Res 7*:452–460 (May) 1990.
1454. Allwood MC: Diamorphine mixed with antiemetic drugs in plastic syringes, *Br J Pharm Prac 6*:88–90 (Mar) 1984.
1455. Regnard C, Pashley S, and Westrope F: Anti-emetic/diamorphine mixture compatibility in infusion pumps, *Br J Pharm Pract 8*:218–220 (Aug) 1986.
1456. Collins AJ, Abathell JA, Holmes SG, et al.: Stability of diamorphine hydrochloride with haloperidol in prefilled syringes for continuous subcutaneous administration, *J Pharm Pharmacol 38(S)*:51P (Nov) 1986.
1457. Page J and Hudson SA: Diamorphine hydrochloride compatibility with saline, *Pharm J 228*:238–239 (Feb 27) 1982.
1458. Kirk B and Hain WR: Diamorphine injection BP incompatibility, *Pharm J 235*:171 (Aug 10) 1985.
1459. Jones V, Murphy A, and Hanks GW: Solubility of diamorphine, *Pharm J 235*: 426 (Oct 5) 1985.
1460. Wood MJ, Irwin WJ, and Scott DK: Stability of doxorubicin, daunorubicin and epirubicin in plastic syringes and minibags, *J Clin Pharm Ther 15*:279–289, 1990.
1461. Targett PL, Keefe PA, and Merridew CG: Stability of two concentrations of morphine tartrate in 10 ml polypropylene syringes, *Aust J Hosp Pharm 27*: 452–454 (6) 1997.
1462. Keusters L, Stolk LML, Umans R, et al.: Stability of solutions of doxorubicin and epirubicin in plastic minibags for intravesical use after storage at −20 °C and thawing by microwave radiation, *Pharm Weekbl Sci Ed 8*:194–197 (June) 1986.
1463. Wood MJ, Irwin WJ, and Scott DK: Photodegradation of doxorubicin, daunorubicin, and epirubicin measured by high-performance liquid chromatography, *J Clin Pharm Ther 35*:291–300, 1990.
1464. Lee MG and Fenton-May V: Absorption of isosorbide dinitrate by PVC infusion bags and administration sets, *J Clin Hosp Pharm 6*:209–211 (Sep) 1981.
1465. DeMuynck C, Remon JP, and Colardyn F: The sorption of isosorbide dinitrate to intravenous delivery systems, *J Pharm Pharmacol 40*:601–604 (Sep) 1988.
1466. Struhar M, Mandak M, Heinrich J, et al.: Sorption of isosorbide dinitrate on infusion sets, *Farm Obz 58*:443–446 (Oct) 1989.
1467. Allwood MC: Sorption of parenteral nitrates during administration with a syringe pump and extension set, *Int J Pharm 39*:183–186 (Feb) 1987.
1468. Wilson TD, Forde MD, Crain AVR, et al.: Stability of milrinone in 0.45% sodium chloride, 0.9% sodium chloride, or 5% dextrose injections, *Am J Hosp Pharm 43*:2218–2220 (Sep) 1986.
1469. Cook B, Hill SA, and Lynn B: The stability of amoxycillin sodium in intravenous infusion fluids, *J Clin Hosp Pharm 7*:245–250 (Dec) 1982.
1470. Concannon J, Lovitt H, Ramage M, et al.: Stability of aqueous solutions of amoxicillin sodium in the frozen and liquid states, *Am J Hosp Pharm 43*:3027–3030 (Dec) 1986.
1471. McDonald C, Sunderland VB, Lau H, et al.: The stability of amoxicillin sodium in normal saline and glucose (5%) solutions in the liquid and frozen states, *J Clin Pharm Ther 14*:45–52 (Feb) 1989.
1472. McDonald C, Sunderland VB, Marshall CA, et al.: Freezing rates of 50-ml infusion bags and some implications for drug stability as shown with amoxycillin, *Aust J Hosp Pharm 19*:194–197 (Apr) 1989.
1473. Janknegt R, Schrouff GGM, Hooymans PM, et al.: Quinolones and penicillins incompatibility, *DICP, Ann Pharmacother 23*:91–92 (Jan) 1989.
1474. Ashwin J, Lynn B, and Taskis CB: Stability and administration of intravenous Augmentin, *Pharm J 238*:116–118 (Jan 24) 1987.
1475. Lynn B: The stability and administration of intravenous penicillins, *Br J IV Ther 2*:22–39 (Mar) 1981.
1476. Landersjo L, Kallstrand G, and Lundgren P: Studies on the stability and compatibility of drugs in infusion fluids III. Factors affecting the stability of cloxacillin, *Acta Pharm Suec 11*:563–580 (Dec) 1974.
1477. Bundgaard H and Ilver K: Kinetics of degradation of cloxacillin sodium in aqueous solution, *Dansk Tidsskr Farm 44*:365–380, 1970.
1478. Brown AF, Harvey DA, Hoddinott DJ, et al.: Freeze–thaw stability of antibiotics used in an IV additive service, *Br J Parenter Ther 7*:42–44 (Mar–Apr) 1986.
1479. Beatson C and Taylor A: A physical compatibility study of frusemide and flucloxacillin injections, *Br J Pharm Pract 9*:223–226, 236 (July) 1987.
1480. Nahata MC and Ahalt PA: Stability of cefazolin sodium in peritoneal dialysis solutions, *Am J Hosp Pharm 48*:291–292 (Feb) 1991.
1481. Paap CM and Nahata MC: Stability of cefotaxime in two peritoneal dialysis solutions, *Am J Hosp Pharm 47*:147–150 (Jan) 1990.
1482. Mehta AC, McCarty M, and Calvert RT: The chemical stability of cephradine injection solutions, *Intensive Ther Clin Monit 9*:195–196 (Oct) 1988.
1483. Lyall D and Blythe J: Ciprofloxacin lactate infusion, *Pharm J 238*:290 (Mar 7) 1987.
1484. Veljkovic VB, Lazic ML, and Cakic MD: Stability of bottled dextran solutions with respect to insoluble particle formations: a review, *Pharmazie 44*:305–310 (May) 1989.
1485. Veljkovic VB, Lazic ML, and Cakic MD: Mechanism of insoluble particle formation in bottled dextran solutions, *Pharmazie 43*:840–842 (Dec) 1988.
1486. Shea BF and Souney PF: Stability of famotidine frozen in polypropylene syringes, *Am J Hosp Pharm 47*:2073–2074 (Sep) 1990.
1487. Bullock LS, Fitzgerald JF, and Mazur HI: Stability of intravenous famotidine stored in polyvinyl-chloride syringes, *DICP, Ann Pharmacother 23*:588–590 (July–Aug) 1989.
1488. Thomas SMB: Stability of Intralipid in a parenteral nutrition solution, *Aust J Hosp Pharm 17*:115–117 (July) 1987.
1489. Stiles ML, Allen LV Jr, and Tu YH: Stability of fluorouracil administered through four portable infusion pumps, *Am J Hosp Pharm 46*:2036–2040 (Oct) 1989.
1490. Tu YH, Stiles ML, Allen LV Jr, et al.: Stability study of gentamicin sulfate administered via Pharmacia Deltec CADD-VT pump, *Hosp Pharm 25*:843–845 (Sep) 1990.
1491. Parkinson R, Wilson JV, Ross M, et al.: Stability of low-dosage heparin in pre-filled syringes, *Br J Pharm Pract 11*:34, 36 (Jan) 1989.
1492. Menzies AR, Benoliel DM, and Edwards HE: The effects of autoclaving on the physical properties and biological activity of parenteral heparin preparations, *J Pharm Pharmacol 41*:512–516, 1989.

1493. Anon: Stability of 4-demethoxydaunorubicin hydrochloride reconstituted solutions with water for injections, sodium chloride, dextrose, and sodium chloride with dextrose injections, Farmitalia Carlo Erba, June 1985.

1494. Radford JA, Margison JM, Swindell R, et al.: The stability of ifosfamide in aqueous solution and its suitability for continuous 7-day infusion by ambulatory pump, *Cancer Chemother Pharmacol 26*:144–146 (May) 1990.

1495. Shaw IC and Rose JWP: Infusion of ifosfamide plus mesna, *Lancet 1*:1353–1354 (June 16) 1984.

1496. Anon: IFEX (Ifosfamide), Bristol Myers Oncology, Evansville, Indiana, February 1990.

1497. Doglietto GB, Bellantone R, Bossola M, et al.: Insulin adsorption to three-liter ethylene vinyl acetate bags during 24-hour infusion, *J Parenter Enter Nutr 13*: 539–543 (Sep–Oct) 1989.

1498. Donnelly RF: Immune globulin solubility in 5% dextrose injection, *Am J Hosp Pharm 47*:1976 (Sep) 1990.

1499. Prouix SM: Reconstitution of intravenous immunoglobulins, *Hosp Pharm 22*: 1133–1134 (Nov) 1987.

1500. Denson DD, Crews JC, Grummich KW, et al.: Stability of methadone hydrochloride in 0.9% sodium chloride injection in single-dose plastic containers, *Am J Hosp Pharm 48*:515–517 (Mar) 1991.

1501. Anderson BD and Taphouse V: Initial rate studies of hydrolysis and acyl migration in methylprednisolone 21-hemisuccinate and 17-hemisuccinate, *J Pharm Sci 70*:181–186 (Feb) 1981.

1502. Bogardus JB, Kaplan MA, and Carpenter JP: Precipitation of teniposide during infusion, *Am J Hosp Pharm 48*:518 (Mar) 1990.

1503. Beijnen JH, van Gijn R, and Underberg WJM: Chemical stability of the antitumor drug mitomycin C in solutions for intravesical installation, *J Parenter Sci Technol 44*:332–335 (Nov–Dec) 1990.

1504. Duafala ME, Kleinberg ML, Nacov C, et al.: Stability of morphine sulfate in infusion devices and containers for intravenous administration, *Am J Hosp Pharm 47*:143–146 (Jan) 1990.

1505. Walker SE, Iazetta J, and Lau DWC: Stability of sulfite free high potency morphine sulfate solutions in portable infusion pump casettes, *Can J Hosp Pharm 42*:195–200, 218–219 (Oct) 1989.

1506. Altman L, Hopkins RJ, Ahmed S, et al.: Stability of morphine sulfate in Cormed III (Kalex) intravenous bags, *Am J Hosp Pharm 47*:2040–2042 (Sep) 1990.

1507. Stiles ML, Tu YH, and Allen LV Jr: Stability of morphine sulfate in portable pump reservoirs during storage and simulated administration, *Am J Hosp Pharm 46*:1404–1407 (July) 1989.

1508. Cante B, Monsarrat B, Lazorthes Y, et al.: The stability of morphine in isobaric and hyperbaric solutions in a drug delivery system, *J Pharm Pharmacol 40*: 644–645, 1988.

1509. Martens HJ: Stabilitat wasserloslicher vitamine in verschiedenen infusionsbenteln, *Krankenhauspharmazie 10*:359–361 (Sep) 1989.

1510. Tracy TS, Bowman L, and Black CD: Nitroglycerin delivery through a polyethylene-lined intravenous administration set, *Am J Hosp Pharm 46*:2031–2035 (Oct) 1989.

1511. Loucas SP, Maager P, Mehl B, et al.: Effect of vehicle ionic strength on sorption on nitroglycerin to a polyvinyl chloride administration set, *Am J Hosp Pharm 47*:1559–1562 (July) 1990.

1512. DeRudder D, Remon JP, and Neyt EN: The sorption of nitroglycerin by infusion sets, *J Pharm Pharmacol 39*:556–558 (July) 1987.

1513. Jarosinski PF and Hirschfield S: Precipitation of ondansetron in alkaline solutions, *N Engl J Med 325*:1315–1316 (Oct 31) 1991.

1514. Markowsky SJ, Kohls PR, Ehresman D, et al.: Compatibility and pH variability of four injectable phenytoin sodium products, *Am J Hosp Pharm 48*:510–514 (Mar) 1991.

1515. Stolshek BS (Professional Services, Glaxo Inc.): Personal communication, August 27, 1990.

1516. Stewart JT, Warren FW, Johnson SM, et al.: Stability of ranitidine in intravenous admixtures stored frozen, refrigerated, and at room temperature, *Am J Hosp Pharm 47*:2043–2046 (Sep) 1990.

1517. Thibault L: Streptokinase flocculation in evacuated glass bottles, *Am J Hosp Pharm 42*:278, 280 (Feb) 1985.

1518. Camacho-Sanchez MA, Torres-Suarez AI, and Sanz MP: Stability of amonafide solutions in front of light and temperature, *Cienc Ind Farm 8*:104–109 (Mar–Apr) 1989.

1519. Den Hartigh J, Brandenburg HCR, and Vermeij P: Stability of azacitidine in lactated Ringer's injection frozen in polypropylene syringes, *Am J Hosp Pharm 46*:2500–2505 (Dec) 1989.

1520. Waugh WN, Trissel LA, and Stella VJ: Stability, compatibility, and plasticizer extraction of taxol (NSC-125973) injection diluted in infusion solutions and stored in various containers, *Am J Hosp Pharm 48*:1520–1524 (July) 1991.

1521. Strong DK and Morris LA: Precipitation of teniposide during infusion, *Am J Hosp Pharm 47*:512 (Mar) 1990.

1522. Outman WR, Mitrano FP, and Baptista RJ: Visual compatibility of ganciclovir sodium and total parenteral nutrient solution during simulated Y-site injection, *Am J Hosp Pharm 48*:1538–1539 (July) 1991.

1523. Outman WR and Monolakis J: Visual compatibility of haloperidol lactate with 0.9% sodium chloride injection or injectable critical-care drugs during simulated Y-site injection, *Am J Hosp Pharm 48*:1539–1541 (July) 1991.

1524. Neels JT: Compatibility of hydromorphone hydrochloride and tetracaine hydrochloride, *Am J Hosp Pharm 48*:1682–1683 (Aug) 1991.

1525. Turowski RC and Durthaler JM: Visual compatibility of idarubicin hydrochloride with selected drugs during simulated Y-site injection, *Am J Hosp Pharm 48*:2181–2184 (Oct) 1991.

1526. Woloschuk DMM, Wermeling JR, and Pruemer JM: Stability and compatibility of fluorouracil and mannitol during simulated Y-site administration, *Am J Hosp Pharm 48*:2158–2160 (Oct) 1991.

1527. Ishisaka DY, van Fleet J, and Marquardt E: Visual compatibility of indomethacin sodium trihydrate with drugs given to neonates by continuous infusion, *Am J Hosp Pharm 48*:2442–2443 (Nov) 1991.

1528. Trissel LA and Bready BB: Turbidimetric assessment of the compatibility of taxol with selected other drugs during simulated Y-site injection, *Am J Hosp Pharm 49*:1716–1719 (July) 1992.

1529. DiStefano JE and Outman WR: Additional data on visual compatibility of foscarnet sodium with morphine sulfate, *Am J Hosp Pharm 49*:1672 (July) 1992.

1530. Farquhar Zanetti LA: Visual compatibility of diltiazem with commonly used injectable drugs during simulated Y-site administration, *Am J Hosp Pharm 49*: 1911 (Aug) 1992.

1531. Martin KM (Product Information Services, Lederle Laboratories, Pearl River, New York): Personal communication, January 14, 1992.

1532. Walker SE, DeAngelis C, and Iazzetta J: Stability and compatibility of combinations of hydromorphone and a second drug, *Can J Hosp Pharm 44*:289–295 (Dec) 1991.

1533. Raineri DL, Cwik MJ, Rodvold KA, et al.: Stability of nizatidine in commonly used intravenous fluids and containers, *Am J Hosp Pharm 45*:1523–1529 (July) 1988.

1534. Hatton J, Holstad SG, Rosenbloom AD, et al.: Stability of nizatidine in total nutrient admixtures, *Am J Hosp Pharm 48*:1507–1510 (July) 1991.

1535. Wade CS, Lampasona V, Mullins RE, et al.: Stability of ceftazidime and amino acids in parenteral nutrient solutions, *Am J Hosp Pharm 48*:1515–1519 (July) 1991.

1536. Patel JP, Tran LT, Sinai WJ, et al.: Activity of urokinase diluted in 0.9% sodium chloride injection or 5% dextrose injection and stored in glass or plastic syringes, *Am J Hosp Pharm 48*:1511–1514 (July) 1991.

1537. Kintzel PE and Kennedy PE: Stability of amphotericin B in 5% dextrose injection at 25 °C, *Am J Hosp Pharm 48*:1681 (Aug) 1991.

1538. Stiles ML and Allen LV: Stability of doxorubicin hydrochloride in portable pump reservoirs, *Am J Hosp Pharm 48*:1976–1977 (Sep) 1991.

1539. Sarkar MA, Rogers E, Reinhard M, et al.: Stability of clindamycin phosphate, ranitidine hydrochloride, and piperacillin sodium in polyolefin containers, *Am J Hosp Pharm 48*:2184–2186 (Oct) 1991.

1540. Ritchie DJ, Holstad SG, Westrich TJ, et al.: Activity of octreotide acetate in a total nutrient admixture, *Am J Hosp Pharm 48*:2172–2175 (Oct) 1991.

1541. Goodwin SD, Nix DE, Heyd A, et al.: Compatibility of ciprofloxacin injection with selected drugs and solutions, *Am J Hosp Pharm 48*:2166–2171 (Oct) 1991.

1542. Walker SE, DeAngelis C, Iazzetta J, et al.: Compatibility of dexamethasone sodium phosphate with hydromorphone hydrochloride or diphenhydramine hydrochloride, *Am J Hosp Pharm 48*:2161–2166 (Oct) 1991.

1543. Harkness BJ, Williams D, Stewart MC, et al.: Change needed for i.v. rifampin preparation instructions, *Am J Hosp Pharm 48*:2127–2128 (Oct) 1991.

1544. Wiest DB, Maish WA, Garner SS, et al.: Stability of amphotericin B in four concentrations of dextrose injection, *Am J Hosp Pharm 48*:2430–2433 (Nov) 1991.

1545. Silvestri AP, Mitrano FP, Baptista RJ, et al.: Stability and compatibility of ganciclovir sodium in 5% dextrose injection over 35 days, *Am J Hosp Pharm 48*:2641–2643 (Dec) 1991.

1546. Mitrano FP, Outman WR, Baptista RJ, et al.: Chemical and visual stability of amphotericin B in 5% dextrose injection stored at 4 °C for 35 days, *Am J Hosp Pharm 48*:2635–2637 (Dec) 1991.

1547. Rivers TE, McBride HA, and Trang JM: Stability of cefotaxime sodium and metronidazole in an i.v. admixture at 8 °C, *Am J Hosp Pharm 48*:2638–2640 (Dec) 1991.

1548. Rochard EB, Barthes DMC, and Courtois PY: Stability of fluorouracil, cytarabine, or doxorubicin hydrochloride in ethylene vinyl acetate portable infusion-pump reservoirs, *Am J Hosp Pharm 49*:619–623 (Mar) 1992.

1549. Letourneau M, Milot L, and Souney PF: Visual compatibility of magnesium sulfate with narcotic analgesics, *Am J Hosp Pharm 49*:838–839 (Apr) 1992.

1550. Thompson DF and Heflin NR: Incompatibility of injectable indomethacin with gentamicin sulfate or tobramycin sulfate, *Am J Hosp Pharm 49*:836, 838 (Apr) 1992.

1551. Munoz M, Girona V, Pujol M, et al.: Stability of ifosfamide in 0.9% sodium chloride solution or water for injection in a portable i.v. pump cassette, *Am J Hosp Pharm 49*:1137–1139 (May) 1992.

1552. Anderson PM, Rogosheske JR, Ramsay NKC, et al.: Biological activity of recombinant interleukin-2 in intravenous admixtures containing antibiotic, morphine sulfate, or total parenteral nutrient solution, *Am J Hosp Pharm 49*: 608–612 (Mar) 1992.

1553. Stiles ML, Allen LV, and Fox JL: Stability of ondansetron hydrochloride in portable infusion-pump reservoirs, *Am J Hosp Pharm 49*:1471–1473 (June) 1992.

1554. Couch P, Jacobson P, and Johnson CE: Stability of fluconazole and amino acids in parenteral nutrient solutions, *Am J Hosp Pharm 49*:1459–1462 (June) 1992.

1555. McDonald C and Faridah: Solubilities of trimethoprim and sulfamethoxazole at various pH values and crystallization of trimethoprim from infusion fluids, *J Parenter Sci Tech 45*:147–151 (May–June) 1991.

1556. Trissel LA and Martinez JF: Turbidimetric assessment of the compatibility of taxol with 42 drugs during simulated Y-site injection, *Am J Hosp Pharm 50*: 300–304 (Feb) 1993.

1557. Trissel LA and Martinez JF: Melphalan physical compatibility with selected drugs during simulated Y-site administration, *Am J Hosp Pharm 50*:2359–2363 (Nov) 1993.

1558. Trissel LA and Martinez JF: Visual, turbidimetric, and particle-content assessment of compatibility of vinorelbine tartrate with selected drugs during simulated Y-site injection, *Am J Hosp Pharm 51*:495–499 (Feb 15) 1994.

1559. Pearson SD and Trissel LA: Stability and compatibility of minocycline hydrochloride and rifampin in intravenous solutions at various temperatures, *Am J Hosp Pharm 50*:698–702 (Apr) 1993.

1560. Graham CL, Dukes GE, Kao CF, et al.: Stability of ondansetron in large-volume parenteral solutions, *Ann Pharmacother 26*:768–771 (June) 1992.

1561. Halasi S and Nairn JG: Stability of hydralazine hydrochloride in parenteral solutions, *Can J Hosp Pharm 43*:237–241 (Oct) 1990.

1562. Speaker TJ, Turco SJ, Nardone DA, et al.: A study of the interaction of selected drugs and plastic syringes, *J Parenter Sci Tech 45*:212–217 (Sep–Oct) 1991.

1563. Trissel LA, Martinez JF, and Gilbert D: Data on file, Pharmaceutical Analysis Laboratory, University of Texas, M. D. Anderson Cancer Center, Houston, Texas, August 1995.

1564. Adams PS, Haines-Nutt RF, Bradford E, et al.: Pharmaceutical aspects of home infusion therapy for cancer patients, *Pharm J 238*:476–478, 1987.

1565. Barnes AR: Chemical stabilities of cefuroxime sodium and metronidazole in an admixture for intravenous infusion, *J Clin Pharm Ther 15*:187–196, 1990.

1566. Weir PJ and Ireland DS: Chemical stability of cytarabine and vinblastine injections, *Br J Pharm Pract 12*:53, 54, 60 (Feb) 1990.

1567. Vincke BJ, Verstraeten AE, El Eini DID, et al.: Extended stability of 5-fluorouracil and methotrexate solutions in PVC containers, *Int J Pharm 54*:181–189, 1989.

1568. Stevens RF and Wilkins KM: Use of cytotoxic drugs with an end-line filter—a study of four drugs commonly administered to paediatric patients, *J Clin Pharm Ther 14*:475–479, 1989.

1569. Garner ST and Murdoch JM: Dopamine dilutions, *Pharm J 244*:218 (Feb 24) 1990.

1570. Schroder F and Schutz H: Kompatibilitat von heparin und gentamicin sulfat, *Pharm Ztg 134*:24–26 (July 27) 1989.

1571. Adams PS, Haines-Nutt RF, and Ross ID: The stability of aminophylline intravenous infusion solutions, *Proc Guild 25*:41–44 (Autumn) 1988.

1572. Schaaf LJ, Tremel LC, Wulf BG, et al.: Compatibility of enalaprilat with dobutamine, dopamine, heparin, nitroglycerin, potassium chloride, and nitroprusside, *J Clin Pharm Ther 15*:371–376 (5) 1990.

1573. Kern JW, Lee KJ, Martinoff JT, et al.: The in vivo availability of gentamicin when admixed with total nutrient solutions: a comparative study, *J Parenter Enter Nutr 14*:523–526 (Sep–Oct) 1990.

1574. Montoro JB, Galard R, Catalan R, et al.: Stability of somatostatin in total parenteral nutrition, *Pharm Weekbl Sci Ed 12*:240–242 (Dec 14) 1990.

1575. Sauer H: Aufbewahrung von zytostatika-losungen, *Krankenhauspharmazie 11*:373–375 (Sep) 1990.

1576. Shea BF and Souney PF: Stability of famotidine in a 3-in-1 total nutrient admixture, *DICP Ann Pharmacother 24*:232–235 (Mar) 1990.

1577. De Vroe C, De Muynck C, Remon JP, et al.: A study on the stability of three antineoplastic drugs and on their sorption by i.v. delivery systems and end-line filters, *Int J Pharm 65*:49–56 (Nov 28) 1990.

1578. Raymond GG and Davis RL: Physical compatibility and chemical stability of amphotericin B in combination with magnesium sulfate in 5% dextrose injection, *DICP Ann Pharmacother 25*:123–126 (Feb) 1991.

1579. Prammar Y, Gupta VD, Gardner SN, et al.: Stabilities of dobutamine, dopamine, nitroglycerin, and sodium nitroprusside in disposable plastic syringes, *J Clin Pharm Ther 16*:203–207 (3) 1991.

1580. Stewart JT, Warren FW, Johnson SM, et al.: Stability of ceftazidime in plastic syringes and glass vials under various storage conditions, *Am J Hosp Pharm 49*:2765–2768 (Nov) 1992.

1581. Stiles ML, Allen LV Jr, and Fox JL: Stability of ceftazidime (with arginine) and cefuroxime sodium in infusion-pump reservoirs, *Am J Hosp Pharm 49*: 2761–2764 (Nov) 1992.

1582. Kaufman MB, Scavone JM, and Foley JJ: Stability of undiluted trimethoprim–sulfamethoxazole for injection in plastic syringes, *Am J Hosp Pharm 49*:2782–2783 (Nov) 1992.

1583. Nahata MC, Morosco RS, and Hipple TF: Stability of morphine sulfate in bacteriostatic 0.9% sodium chloride injection stored in glass vials at two temperatures, *Am J Hosp Pharm 49*:2785–2786 (Nov) 1992.

1584. Nahata MC, Morosco RS, and Fox JF: Stability of ceftazidime (with arginine) stored in plastic syringes at three temperatures, *Am J Hosp Pharm 49*:2954–2956 (Dec) 1992.

1585. Mawhinney WM, Adair CG, Gorman SP, et al.: Stability of ciprofloxacin in peritoneal dialysis solutions, *Am J Hosp Pharm 49*:2956–2959 (Dec) 1992.

1586. Nahata MC, Morosco RS, and Hipple TF: Stability of aminophylline in bacteriostatic water for injection stored in plastic syringes at two temperatures, *Am J Hosp Pharm 49*:2962–2963 (Dec) 1992.

1587. Allwood MC: The influence of buffering on the stability of erythromycin injection in small-volume infusions, *Int J Pharm 80*:R7–R9 (Feb 10) 1992.

1588. Toki N: Glass adsorption of highly purified urokinase, *Thromb Haemost 43*: 67, 1980.

1589. Zimmerman R, Schoffel G, and Harenberg J: Urokinase therapy: dose reduction by administration in plastic material, *Thromb Haemost 45*:296 (3) 1981.

1590. Walker SE and Iazzetta J: Compatibility and stability of pentobarbital infusions, *Anesthesiology 55*:487–489 (Oct) 1981.

1591. Walker SE and Iazzetta J: Cefotetan stability in normal saline and five percent dextrose in water, *Can J Hosp Pharm 45*:9–13, 37 (1) 1992.

1592. Nahata MC: Stability of ceftriaxone sodium in peritoneal dialysis solutions, *DICP Ann Pharmacother 25*:741–742 (July–Aug) 1991.

1593. Walker SE, Lau DWC, DeAngelis C, et al.: Mitoxantrone stability in syringes and glass vials and evaluation of chemical contamination, *Can J Hosp Pharm 44*:143–151 (June) 1991.

1594. Walker S, Lau D, DeAngelis C, et al.: Doxorubicin stability in syringes and glass vials and evaluation of chemical contamination, *Can J Hosp Pharm 44*: 71–78, 88 (Apr) 1991.

1595. Peterson GM, Khoo BHC, Galloway JG, et al.: A preliminary study of the stability of midazolam in polypropylene syringes, *Aust J Hosp Pharm 21*:115–118 (Apr) 1991.

1596. Lecompte D, Bousselet M, Gayrard D, et al.: Stability study of reconstituted and diluted solutions of calcium folinate, *Pharm Ind 53*:90–94 (1) 1991.

1597. Allwood MC: The stability of erythromycin injection in small-volume infusions, *Int J Pharm 62*:R1–R3 (July 15) 1990.

1598. Gupta VD, Pramar Y, Odom C, et al.: Chemical stability of cefotetan disodium in 5% dextrose and 0.9% sodium chloride injections, *J Clin Pharm Ther 15*: 109–114, 1990.

1599. Poggi GL: Compatibility of morphine tartrate admixtures in polypropylene syringes, *Aust J Hosp Pharm 21*:316 (Oct) 1991.

1600. McLaughlin JP and Simpson C: The stability of reconstituted aztreonam, *Br J Pharm Pract 12*:328, 330, 334 (Oct) 1990.

1601. Biejnen JH, van Gijn R, Horenblas S, et al.: Chemical stability of suramin in commonly used infusion fluids, *DICP Ann Pharmacother 24*:1056–1058 (Nov) 1990.

1602. Patel JP: Urokinase: stability studies in solution and lyophilized formulations, *Drug Dev Ind Pharm 16*:2613–2626, 1990.

1603. Driver AG and Worden JP Jr: Intravenous streptomycin, *DICP Ann Pharmacother 24*:826–828 (Sep) 1990.

1604. Bosso JA: Clindamycin stability, *DICP Ann Pharmacother 24*:1008–1009 (Oct) 1990.

1605. Theuer H, Scherbel G, Distler F, et al.: Cisplatin-injektionslosung, *Krankenhauspharmazie 11*:288–291 (July) 1990.

1606. Bluhm DP, Summers RS, Lowes MMJ, et al.: Influence of container on vitamin A stability in TPN admixtures, *Int J Pharm 68*:281–283 (Feb 1) 1991.

1607. Bluhm DP, Summers RS, Lowes MMJ, et al.: Lipid emulsion content and vitamin A stability in TPN admixtures, *Int J Pharm 68*:277–280 (Feb 1) 1991.

1608. Beijnen J and Koks CHW: Visual compatibility of ondansetron and dexamethasone, *DICP Ann Pharmacother 25*:869 (July–Aug) 1991.

1609. Lawson WA, Longmore RB, McDonald C, et al.: Stability of hyoscine in mixtures with morphine for continuous subcutaneous administration, *Aust J Hosp Pharm 21*:395–396 (Dec) 1991.

1610. Allwood MC: The stability of four catecholamines in 5% glucose infusions, *J Clin Pharm Ther 16*:337–340 (5) 1991.

1611. Van Asten P, Glerum JH, Spaanderman ER, et al.: Compatibility of bupivacaine and iohexol in two mixtures for paediatric regional anaesthesia, *Pharm Weekbl Sci Ed 13*:254–256 (6) 1991.

1612. Sewell GJ and Palmer AJ: The chemical and physical stability of three intravenous infusions subjected to frozen storage and microwave thawing, *Int J Pharm 72*:57–63 (May 13) 1991.

1613. Janknegt R, Stratermans T, Cilissen J, et al.: Ofloxacin intravenous—compatibility with other antibacterial agents, *Pharm Weekbl Sci Ed 13*:207–209 (Oct 18) 1991.

1614. Dunham B, Marcuard S, Khazanie PG, et al.: The solubility of calcium and phosphorus in neonatal total parenteral nutrition solutions, *J Parenter Enter Nutr 15*:608–611 (Nov–Dec) 1991.

1615. Delaney RA, Mikkelsen SL, and Jackson MB: Effects of heat treatment on selected plasma therapeutic drug concentrations, *Ann Pharmacother 26*:338–340 (Mar) 1992.

1616. McLeod HL, McGuire TR, and Yee GC: Stability of cyclosporine in dextrose 5%, NaCl 0.9%, dextrose/amino acid solution, and lipid emulsion, *Ann Pharmacother 26*:172–175 (Feb) 1992.

1617. Andreu A, Cardona D, Pastor C, et al.: Intravenous aminophylline: in vitro stability in fat-containing TPN, *Ann Pharmacother 26*:127–128 (Jan) 1992.

1618. Matsuura G: Visual compatibility of sargramostim (GM-CSF) during simulated Y-site administration with selected agents, *Hosp Pharm 27*:200, 202, 209 (Mar) 1992.

1619. De Muynck C, Colardyn F, and Remon JP: Influence of intravenous administration set composition on the sorption of isosorbide dinitrate, *J Pharm Pharmacol 43*:601–604 (Sep) 1991.

1620. Bullock L, Fitzgerald JF, and Walter WV: Emulsion stability in total nutrient admixtures containing a pediatric amino acid formulation, *J Parenter Enter Nutr 16*:64–68 (Jan–Feb) 1992.

1621. Olbrich A: Weichmacher als problematische bestandteile von mischinfusionen, *Krankenhauspharmazie 12*:192–194 (May) 1991.

1622. Cano SM, Montoro JB, Pastor C, et al.: Stability of cimetidine in total parenteral nutrition, *J Clin Nutr Gastroenter 2*:40–43 (1) 1987.

1623. Loeppky C, Tarka E, and Everett ED: Compatibility of cephalosporins and aminoglycosides in peritoneal dialysis fluid, *Perit Dial Bull 3*:128–129, 1983.

1624. Bhatt-Mehta V, Rosen DA, King RS, et al.: Stability of midazolam hydrochloride in parenteral nutrient solutions, *Am J Hosp Pharm 50*:285–288 (Feb) 1993.

1625. Jacobson PA, Maksym CJ, Landvay A, et al.: Compatibility of cyclosporine with fat emulsion, *Am J Hosp Pharm 50*:687–690 (Apr) 1993.

1626. Johnson CE, Jacobson PA, Pillen HA, et al.: Stability and compatibility of fluconazole and aminophylline in intravenous admixtures, *Am J Hosp Pharm 50*:703–706 (Apr) 1993.

1627. Allen LV Jr, Stiles ML, Wang DP, et al.: Stability of bupivacaine hydrochloride, epinephrine hydrochloride, and fentanyl citrate in portable infusion-pump reservoirs, *Am J Hosp Pharm 50*:714–715 (Apr) 1993.

1628. Percy LA and Rho JP: Visual compatibility of ciprofloxacin with selected components of total parenteral nutrient solutions during simulated Y-site injection, *Am J Hosp Pharm 50*:715–716 (Apr) 1993.

1629. Nieforth KA, Shea BF, Souney PF, et al.: Stability of cyclosporine with magnesium sulfate in 5% dextrose injection, *Am J Hosp Pharm 50*:470–472 (Mar) 1993.

1630. Min DI, Brown T, and Hwang GC: Visual compatibility of tacrolimus with commonly used drugs during simulated Y-site injection, *Am J Hosp Pharm 49*:2964–2966 (Dec) 1992.

1631. Dine T, Luyckx M, Cazin JC, et al.: Stability and compatibility studies of vinblastine, vincristine, vindesine and vinorelbine with PVC infusion bags, *Int J Pharm 77*:279–285 (Nov 15) 1991.

1632. Inagaki K, Gill MA, Okamoto MP, et al.: Stability of ranitidine hydrochloride with aztreonam, ceftazidime, or piperacillin sodium during simulated Y-site administration, *Am J Hosp Pharm 49*:2769–2772 (Nov) 1992.

1633. Mitra AK and Narurkar MM: Kinetics of azathioprine degradation in aqueous solution, *Int J Pharm 35*:165–171, 1986.

1634. Snyder RL: Filter clogging caused by albumin in i.v. nutrient solution, *Am J Hosp Pharm 50*:63–64 (Jan) 1993.

1635. Feldman F and Bergman G: Filter clogging caused by albumin in i.v. nutrient solution, *Am J Hosp Pharm 50*:64 (Jan) 1993.

1636. Bornstein M, Kao SH, Mercorelli M, et al.: Stability of an ofloxacin injection in various infusion fluids, *Am J Hosp Pharm 49*:2756–2760 (Nov) 1992.

1637. Heni J: Rekonstituierte ganciclovirlosung, *Krankenhauspharmazie 12*:342–344 (Aug) 1991.

1638. Theuer H, Scherbel G, and Windsheimer U: Stabilitatsuntersuchungen von fentanylcitrat i.v., *Krankenhauspharmazie 12*:233–245 (June) 1991.

1639. Burger DM, Brandjes DPM, Koks CHW, et al.: Heparine in het heparineslot? *Pharm Weekbl 126*:624–627 (July 5) 1991.

1640. Witmer DR: Heparin lock flush solution versus 0.9% sodium chloride injection for maintaining patency, *Am J Hosp Pharm 50*:241 (Feb) 1993.

1641. Weber DR: Is heparin really necessary in the lock and, if so, how much? *DICP Ann Pharmacother 25*:399–407 (Apr) 1991.

1642. Bosso JA, Prince RA, and Fox JL: Stability of ondansetron hydrochloride in injectable solutions at −20, 5, and 25 °C, *Am J Hosp Pharm 49*:2223–2225 (Sep) 1992.

1643. Parasrampuria J, Li LC, Stelmach AH, et al.: Stability of ganciclovir sodium in 5% dextrose injection and in 0.9% sodium chloride injection over 35 days, *Am J Hosp Pharm 49*:116–118 (Jan) 1992.

1644. Guo-jie JL: Compatibility of bumetanide injection and dextrose injection, *Yaoxue Tongbao 24*:86–87 (Feb) 1989.

1645. Buck GW and Wolfe KR: Interaction of sodium ascorbate with stainless steel particulate-filter needles, *Am J Hosp Pharm 48*:1191 (June) 1991.

1646. Floy BJ, Royko CG, and Fleitman JS: Compatibility of ketorolac tromethamine injection with common infusion fluids and administration sets, *Am J Hosp Pharm 47*:1097–1100 (May) 1990.

1647. Zieske PA, Koberda M, Hines JL, et al.: Characterization of cisplatin degradation as affected by pH and light, *Am J Hosp Pharm 48*:1500–1506 (July) 1991.

1648. Tu YH, Knox NL, Biringer JM, et al.: Compatibility of iron dextran with total nutrient admixtures, *Am J Hosp Pharm 49*:2233–2235 (Sep) 1992.

1649. Rivers TE, McBride HA, and Trang JM: Stability of cefazolin sodium and metronidazole at 8 °C for use as an IV admixture, *J Parenter Sci Tech 47*:135–137 (May–June) 1993.

1650. Helbock HJ, Motchnik PA, and Ames BN: Toxic hydroperoxides in intravenous lipid emulsions used in preterm infants, *Pediatrics 91*:83–87 (Jan) 1993.

1651. Washington C and Sizer T: Stability of TPN mixtures compounded from Lipofundin S and Aminoplex amino-acid solutions: comparison of laser diffraction and Coulter counter droplet size analysis, *Int J Pharm 83*:227–231 (June 30) 1992.

1652. Mason NA, Johnson CE, and O'Brien MA: Stability of ceftazidime and tobramycin sulfate in peritoneal dialysis solution, *Am J Hosp Pharm 49*:1139–1142 (May) 1992.

1653. Brawley V, Bhatia J, and Karp WB: Hydrogen peroxide generation in a model paediatric parenteral amino acid solution, *Clin Sci 85*:709–712, 1993.

1654. Mawhinney WM, Adair CG, Gorman SP, et al.: Stability of vancomycin hydrochloride in peritoneal dialysis solution, *Am J Hosp Pharm 49*:137–139 (Jan) 1992.

1655. Cervenka P, DeJong DJ, Butler BL, et al.: Visual compatibility of injectable ciprofloxacin lactate with selected injectable drugs during simulated Y-site administration, *Hosp Pharm 27*:957–958, 961–962 (Nov) 1992.

1656. Garrelts JC, LaRocca J, Ast D, et al.: Comparison of heparin and 0.9% sodium chloride injection in the maintenance of indwelling intermittent i.v. devices, *Clin Pharm 8*:34–39 (Jan) 1989.

1657. Lewis JS: Justification for use of 1.2 micron end-line filters on total nutrient admixtures, *Hosp Pharm 28*:656–658, 697 (July) 1993.

1658. Benvenuto JA, Adams SC, Vyas HM, et al.: Pharmaceutical issues in infusion chemotherapy stability and compatibility, *in* Lokich JJ (ed), Cancer chemotherapy by infusion, Precept Press, Chicago, Illinois, 1987, pp 100–113.

1659. Briceland LL, Fudin J, and Johnson KR: Evaluation of microbial growth in select inoculated antineoplastic solutions, *Hosp Pharm 25*:338–340, 359 (Apr) 1990.

1660. Neels JT: Compatibility of bupivacaine hydrochloride with hydromorphone hydrochloride or morphine sulfate, *Am J Hosp Pharm 49*:2149 (Sep) 1992.

1661. Hauser AR, Trissel LA, and Martinez JF: Ondansetron compatible with sodium acetate, *J Clin Oncol 11*:197 (Jan) 1993.

1662. Pecosky DA, Parasrampuria J, Li LC, et al.: Stability and sorption of calcitriol in plastic tuberculin syringes, *Am J Hosp Pharm 49*:1463–1466 (June) 1992.

1663. Gregory R, Edwards S, and Yateman NA: Demonstration of insulin transformation products in insulin vials by high-performance liquid chromatography, *Diabetes Care 14*:42–48 (Jan) 1991.

1664. Seres DS: Insulin adsorption to parenteral infusion systems: case report and review of the literature, *Nutr Clin Pract 5*:111–117 (June) 1990.

1665. Lazorova L, Haronikova K, and Mandak M: Studium sorpcie inzulinu v priebehu infuznej terapie, *Farm Obz 59*:157–164 (Apr) 1990.

1666. Stolk LML and Chandi LS: Stabiliteit van fluorouracil (0,55 mg) in polypropyleen spuiten bij −20 °C, *Ziekenhuisfarmacie 7*:12–13 (1) 1991.

1667. de Vogel EM, Hendrikx MMP, van Dellen RT, et al.: Adsorptie van sufentanil aan bacteriefilters, *Ziekenhuisfarmacie 7*:65–70 (3) 1991.

1668. Hehenberger H: Fettemulsionen kompatibilitat wahrend der bypass-infusion, *Krankenhauspharmazie 10*:513–518 (Dec) 1989.

1669. Carstens G: Calcium-folinat uberlegungen zur stabilitat und zum einsatz verschiedener zubereitungen, *Krankenhauspharmazie 10*:478–482 (Nov) 1989.

1670. Washington C: The stability of intravenous fat emulsions in total parenteral nutrition mixtures, *Int J Pharm 66*:1–21 (Dec 1) 1990.

1671. Allwood MC and Brown PW: The effect of buffering on the stability of reconstituted benzylpenicillin injection, *Int J Pharm Pract 1*:242–244 (Aug) 1992.

1672. Allwood MC: The stability of diamorphine alone and in combination with anti-emetics in plastic syringes, *Palliative Med 5*:330–333, 1991.

1673. Lober CA and Dollard PA: Visual compatibility of gallium nitrate with selected drugs during simulated Y-site injection, *Am J Hosp Pharm 50*:1208–1210 (June) 1993.

1674. Jahns BE and Bakst CM: Extension of expiration time for lorazepam injection at room temperature, *Am J Hosp Pharm 50*:1134 (June) 1993.

1675. Trissel LA and Martinez JF: Idarubicin hydrochloride turbidity versus incompatibility, *Am J Hosp Pharm 50*:1134, 1137 (June) 1993.

1676. Hunt-Fugate AK, Hennessey CK, and Kazarian CM: Stability of fluconazole injectable solutions, *Am J Hosp Pharm 50*:1186–1187 (June) 1993.

1677. Inagaki K, Takagi J, Lor E, et al.: Stability of fluconazole in commonly used intravenous antibiotic solutions, *Am J Hosp Pharm 50*:1206–1208 (June) 1993.

1678. Liao E, Fox JL, and Dukes GE: Inline filtration of ondansetron hydrochloride during simulated i.v. administration, *Am J Hosp Pharm 50*:906, 909 (May) 1993.

1679. Belliveau PP, Shea BF, and Scavone JM: Stability of metoprolol tartrate in 5% dextrose injection or 0.9% sodium chloride injection, *Am J Hosp Pharm 50*:950–952 (May) 1993.

1680. Ringwood MA: Stability of cefepime for injection for IM or IV use following constitution/dilution, Bristol-Myers Company, Syracuse, New York, August 16, 1990.

1681. Ringwood MA and Vance VH: Cefepime IM, IV, and compatibility studies for U.S. registrational filing, Bristol-Myers Squibb Company, Syracuse, New York, May 13, 1992.

1682. Vance VH: Stability of cefepime admixed with vancomycin, metronidazole, ampicillin, clindamycin, tobramycin, netilmicin, TPN solution, and PD solution, Bristol-Myers Squibb Company, Syracuse, New York, October 14, 1992.

1683. Pearson SD and Trissel LA: Leaching of diethylhexyl phthalate from polyvinyl chloride containers by selected drugs and formulation components, *Am J Hosp Pharm 50*:1405–1409 (July) 1993.

1684. Trissel LA and Pearson SD: Storage of lorazepam in three injectable solutions in polyvinyl chloride and polyolefin bags, *Am J Hosp Pharm 51*:368–372 (Feb 1) 1994.

1685. Reilly MD and Trissel LA: Visual compatibility of cisplatin, cyclophosphamide, doxorubicin HCl, and methotrexate sodium with selected drugs during simulated Y-site injection, Data on file, Pharmaceutical Analysis Laboratory, University of Texas, M. D. Anderson Cancer Center, Houston, Texas, January 15, 1990.

1686. Trissel LA and Martinez JF: Compatibility of allopurinol sodium with selected drugs during simulated Y-site administration, *Am J Hosp Pharm 51*:792–799 (July 15) 1994.

1687. Trissel LA and Martinez JF: Compatibility of filgrastim with selected drugs during simulated Y-site administration, *Am J Hosp Pharm 51*:1907–1913 (Aug 1) 1994.

1688. Trissel LA and Martinez JF: Compatibility of piperacillin sodium plus tazobactam sodium with selected drugs during simulated Y-site injection, *Am J Hosp Pharm 51*:672–678 (Mar 1) 1994.

1689. Trissel LA: Data on file, Pharmaceutical Analysis Laboratory, University of Texas, M. D. Anderson Cancer Center, Houston, Texas.

1690. Trissel LA, Xu Q, Martinez JF, et al.: Compatibility and stability of ondansetron hydrochloride with morphine sulfate and hydromorphone hydrochloride in 0.9% sodium chloride injection at various temperatures, *Am J Hosp Pharm 51*:2138–2142 (Sep 1) 1994.

1691. Belliveau PP, Nightingale CH, and Quintiliani R: Stability of aztreonam and ampicillin/sulbactam in 0.9% saline for injection, *Am J Hosp Pharm 51*:901–904 (Apr 1) 1994.

1692. Fisher DM, Canfell C, and Miller RD: Stability of atracurium administered by infusion, *Anesthesiology 61*:347–348 (Sep) 1984.

1693. Harper NJN, Pollard BJ, Edwards D, et al.: Stability of atracurium in dilute solutions, *Br J Anaesth 60*:344P–345P (Feb) 1988.

1694. Talton MA (Drug Information, Burroughs Wellcome Company, Research Triangle Park, North Carolina): Personal communication, June 11, 1993.

1695. Perrone RK, Kaplan MA, and Bogardus JB: Extent of cisplatin formation in carboplatin admixtures, *Am J Hosp Pharm 46*:258–259 (Feb) 1989.

1696. Northcott M, Allsopp MA, Powell H, et al.: The stability of carboplatin, diamorphine, 5-fluorouracil and mitozantrone infusions in an ambulatory pump under storage and prolonged "in-use" conditions, *J Clin Pharm Ther 16*:123–129, 1991.

1697. Ahmed ST and Parkinson R: The stability of drugs in pre-filled syringes: flucloxacillin, ampicillin, cefuroxime, cefotaxime, and ceftazidime, *Hosp Pharm Pract 2*:285–289 (Apr) 1992.

1698. Faouzi MA, Dine T, Luyckx M, et al.: Stability and compatibility studies of pefloxacin, ofloxacin and ciprofloxacin with PVC infusion bags, *Int J Pharm 89*:125–131, 1993.

1699. Stiles ML, Allen LV Jr, and Fox JL: Gas production of three brands of ceftazidime, *Am J Hosp Pharm 48*:1727–1729 (Aug) 1991.

1700. Dine T, Cazin JC, Gressier B, et al.: Stability and compatibility of four anthracyclines: doxorubicin, epirubicin, daunorubicin, and pirarubicin with PVC infusion bags, *Pharm Weekbl Sci Ed 14*:365–369 (6) 1992.

1701. Trissel LA and Martinez JF: Sargramostim incompatibility, *Hosp Pharm 27*: 929 (Oct) 1992.

1702. Trissel LA: Alternative interpretation for data, *Am J Hosp Pharm 49*:570 (Mar) 1992.

1703. Knapp AJ, Mauro VF, and Alexander KS: Incompatibility of ketorolac tromethamine with selected postoperative drugs, *Am J Hosp Pharm 49*:2960–2962 (Dec) 1992.

1704. Trissel LA: Data on file, Pharmaceutical Analysis Laboratory, University of Texas, M. D. Anderson Cancer Center, Houston, Texas, October 29, 1993.

1705. Cohon MS (Clinical Development and Medical Affairs, The Upjohn Company, Kalamazoo, Michigan): Personal communication, December 6, 1993.

1706. Chandler SW, Trissel LA, and Weinstein SM: Combined administration of opioids with selected drugs to manage pain and other cancer symptoms: initial safety screening for compatibility, *J Pain Symptom Manag 12*:168–171 (Sep) 1996.

1707. Nation RL, Hackett LP, and Dusci LJ: Uptake of clonazepam by plastic intravenous infusion bags and administration sets, *Am J Hosp Pharm 40*:1692–1693 (Oct) 1983.

1708. Hooymans PM, Janknegt R, and Lohman JJHM: Comparison of clonazepam sorption to polyvinyl chloride-coated and polyethylene-coated tubings, *Pharm Weekbl Sci Ed 12*:188–189 (July) 1990.

1709. McLaughlin JP and Simpson C: The stability of reconstituted diethanolamine fusidate in a 5% dextrose infusion, *Hosp Pharm Pract 2*:59–62 (Jan) 1992.

1710. Olsen KM, Gurley BJ, Davis GA, et al.: Stability of flumazenil with selected drugs in 5% dextrose injection, *Am J Hosp Pharm 50*:1907–1912 (Sep) 1993.

1711. Trissel LA and Martinez JF: Sufentanil data on file, Pharmaceutical Analysis Laboratory, University of Texas, M. D. Anderson Cancer Center, Houston, Texas, February 1995.

1712. Larson PO, Ragi G, Swandby M, et al.: Stability of buffered lidocaine and epinephrine used for local anesthesia, *J Dermatol Surg Oncol 17*:411–414, 1991.

1713. Stewart JH, Cole GW, and Klein JA: Neutralized lidocaine with epinephrine for local anesthesia, *J Dermatol Surg Oncol 15*:1081–1083 (Oct) 1989.

1714. Nahata MC, Morosco RS, and Hipple TF: Stability of cimetidine hydrochloride and of clindamycin phosphate in water for injection stored in glass vials at two temperatures, *Am J Hosp Pharm 50*:2559–2561 (Dec) 1993.

1715. Zeisler J and Alagna C: Incompatibility of labetalol hydrochloride and furosemide, *Am J Hosp Pharm 50*:2521–2522 (Dec) 1993.

1716. Pfeifer RW and Hale KN: Precipitation of paclitaxel during infusion by pump, *Am J Hosp Pharm 50*:2518, 2521 (Dec) 1993.

1717. Hagan RL, Jacobs LF, Pimsler M, et al.: Stability of midazolam hydrochloride in 5% dextrose injection or 0.9% sodium chloride injection over 30 days, *Am J Hosp Pharm 50*:2379–2381 (Nov) 1993.

1718. Jones JW and Davis AT: Stability of bupivacaine hydrochloride in polypropylene syringes, *Am J Hosp Pharm 50*:2364–2365 (Nov) 1993.

1719. Vogt C, Skipper PM, and Ruggaber S: Compatibility of magnesium sulfate and morphine sulfate in 0.9% sodium chloride injection, *Am J Hosp Pharm 50*:2311 (Nov) 1993.

1720. Bailey LC, Tang KT, and Medwick T: Stability of ceftriaxone sodium in infusion-pump syringes, *Am J Hosp Pharm 50*:2092–2094 (Oct) 1993.

1721. Szof C and Walker PC: Incompatibility of cefotaxime sodium and vancomycin sulfate during Y-site administration, *Am J Hosp Pharm 50*:2054, 2057 (Oct) 1993.

1722. Jhee SS, Jeong EW, Chin A, et al.: Stability of ondansetron hydrochloride stored in a disposable, elastomeric infusion device at 4 °C, *Am J Hosp Pharm 50*:1918–1920 (Sep) 1993.
1723. Bartfield JM, Homer PJ, Ford DT, et al.: Buffered lidocaine as a local anesthetic: an investigation of shelf life, *Ann Emerg Med 21*:16–19 (Jan) 1992.
1724. Peterfreund RA, Datta S, and Ostheimer GW: pH adjustment of local anesthetic solutions with sodium bicarbonate: laboratory evaluation of alkalinization and precipitation, *Reg Anesth 14*:265–270 (Nov–Dec) 1989.
1725. Trissel LA and Martinez JF: Screening teniposide for Y-site physical incompatibilities, *Hosp Pharm 29*:1012–1014, 1017 (Nov) 1994.
1726. Woods K, Steinman W, Bruns L, et al.: Stability of foscarnet sodium in 0.9% sodium chloride injection, *Am J Hosp Pharm 51*:88–90 (Jan 1) 1994.
1727. Parrish MA, Bailey LC, and Medwick T: Stability of ceftriaxone sodium and aminophylline or theophylline in intravenous admixtures, *Am J Hosp Pharm 51*:92–94 (Jan 1) 1994.
1728. Lee MD, Hess MM, Boucher BA, et al.: Stability of amphotericin B in 5% dextrose injection stored at 4 or 25 °C for 120 hours, *Am J Hosp Pharm 51*: 394–396 (Feb 1) 1994.
1729. Trissel LA and Martinez JF: Data on file, Pharmaceutical Analysis Laboratory, University of Texas, M. D. Anderson Cancer Center, Houston, Texas, November 1994.
1730. Pompilio FM, Fox JL, Inagaki K, et al.: Stability of ranitidine hydrochloride with ondansetron hydrochloride or fluconazole during simulated Y-site administration, *Am J Hosp Pharm 51*:391–394 (Feb 1) 1994.
1731. Wolff DJ, Kline SS, and Mauro LS: Stability of amikacin, gentamicin, or tobramycin in 10% dextrose injection, *Am J Hosp Pharm 51*:518–519 (Feb 15) 1994.
1732. Bosso JA, Prince RA, and Fox JL: Compatibility of ondansetron hydrochloride with fluconazole, ceftazidime, aztreonam, and cefazolin sodium under simulated Y-site conditions, *Am J Hosp Pharm 51*:389–391 (Feb 1) 1994.
1733. Stiles ML, Allen LV Jr, Prince SJ, et al.: Stability of dexamethasone sodium phosphate, diphenhydramine hydrochloride, lorazepam, and metoclopramide hydrochloride in portable infusion-pump reservoirs, *Am J Hosp Pharm 51*: 514–517 (Feb 15) 1994.
1734. Messerschmidt W: Kompatibilitat von ofloxacin mit ampicillin, *Krankenhauspharmazie 15*:337–340 (6) 1994.
1735. Messerschmidt W: Kompatibilitat von cefotaxim mit ofloxacin, *Pharmazie 136*:42–44 (Sep) 1991.
1736. Trissel LA, Gilbert D, and Martinez JF: Data on file, Pharmaceutical Analysis Laboratory, University of Texas, M. D. Anderson Cancer Center, Houston, Texas, August 1995.
1737. Messerschmidt W: Kompatibilitat von cefotiam mit metronidazol, *Krankenhauspharmazie 7*:263–265 (6) 1986.
1738. Messerschmidt W: Pharmazeutische kompatibilitat der kombination cefotiam und ampicillin, *Krankenhauspharmazie 13*:98–100 (3) 1992.
1739. Cronquist SE and Daniels M: Precipitation of paclitaxel during infusion by pump, *Am J Hosp Pharm 50*:2521 (Dec) 1993.
1740. Fraser GL and Riker RR: Visual compatibility of haloperidol lactate with injectable solutions, *Am J Hosp Pharm 51*:905–906 (Apr 1) 1994.
1741. Burm JP, Jhee SS, Chin A, et al.: Stability of paclitaxel with ondansetron hydrochloride or ranitidine hydrochloride during simulated Y-site administration, *Am J Hosp Pharm 51*:1201–1204 (May 1) 1994.
1742. Mulye NV, Turco SJ, and Speaker TJ: Stability of ganciclovir sodium in an infusion-pump syringe, *Am J Hosp Pharm 51*:1348–1349 (May 15) 1994.
1743. Bonhomme L, Benhamou D, Comoy E, et al.: Stability of adrenaline pH-adjusted solutions of local anaesthetics, *J Pharm Biomed Anal 9*:497–499 (6) 1991.
1744. Johnson CE, Jacobson PA, and Chan E: Stability of ganciclovir sodium and amino acids in parenteral nutrient solutions, *Am J Hosp Pharm 51*:503–508 (Feb 15) 1994.
1745. Abubakar AA, Mustapha A, and Wambebe OC: An in vitro chemical interaction between promethazine hydrochloride and chloroquine phosphate, *Int J Pharm 7*:14–19 (1) 1993.
1746. Xu Q, Trissel LA, and Martinez JF: Stability of paclitaxel in 5% dextrose injection or 0.9% sodium chloride injection at 4, 22, or 32 °C, *Am J Hosp Pharm 51*:3058–3060 (Dec 15) 1994.
1747. Kearney AS, Patel K, and Palepu NR: Preformulation studies to aid in the development of a ready-to-use injectable solution of the antitumor agent, topotecan, *Int J Pharm 127*:229–237 (Feb 17) 1996.
1748. Cilissen J, Hooymans PM, and Lohman JJHM: Indicatie van de stabiliteit van een mengsel van piperacilline en flucloxacilline in een reservoir voor een draagbare infusiepomp, *Ziekenhuisfarmacie 10*:10–11, 1994.
1749. Banerjee PS, Ghosh LK, and Gupta BK: Studies on the effects of some additives on the stability of injectable formulations of diazepam, *Indian Drugs 29*:361–364 (8) 1992.
1750. Lorillon P, Corbel JC, Mordelet MF, et al.: Photosensibilite du 5-fluoro-uracile et du methotrexate dans des perfuseurs translucides ou opaques, *J Pharm Clin 11*:285–295, 1992.
1751. Brouwers JRBJ, van Doorne H, Meevis RF, et al.: Stability of sufentanil citrate and sufentanil citrate/bupivacaine mixture in portable infusion pump reservoirs, *Eur Hosp Pharm 1*:12–14 (Jan) 1995.
1752. Chung KC, Moon YSK, Chin A, et al.: Compatibility of ondansetron hydrochloride and piperacillin sodium–tazobactam sodium during simulated Y-site administration, *Am J Health-Syst Pharm 52*:1554–1556 (July 15) 1995.
1753. Erickson SH and Ulici D: Incompatibility of cefotetan disodium and promethazine hydrochloride, *Am J Health-Syst Pharm 52*:1347 (June 15) 1995.
1754. Belliveau PP, Nightingale CH, and Quintiliani R: Stability of cefotaxime sodium and metronidazole in 0.9% sodium chloride injection or in ready-to-use metronidazole bags, *Am J Health-Syst Pharm 52*:1561–1563 (July 15) 1995.
1755. Roos PJ, Glerum JH, and Meilink JW: Stability of sufentanil citrate in a portable pump reservoir, a glass container and a polyethylene container, *Pharm Weekbl Sci Ed 14*:196–200 (4) 1992.
1756. Roos PJ, Glerum JH, and Schroeders MJH: Effect of glucose 5% solution and bupivacaine hydrochloride on adsorption of sufentanil citrate in a portable pump reservoir during storage and simulated infusion by an epidural catheter, *Pharm World Sci Ed 15*:269–275 (6) 1993.
1757. Benaji B, Dine T, Luyckx M, et al.: Stability and compatibility of cisplatin and carboplatin with PVC infusion bags, *J Clin Pharm Ther 19*:95–100, 1994.
1758. Trissel LA and Martinez JF: Compatibility of aztreonam with selected drugs during simulated Y-site administration, *Am J Health-Syst Pharm 52*:1086–1090 (May 15) 1995.
1759. Choi JS, Burm JP, Jhee SS, et al.: Stability of piperacillin sodium–tazobactam sodium and ranitidine hydrochloride in 0.9% sodium chloride injection during simulated Y-site administration, *Am J Hosp Pharm 51*:2273–2276 (Sep 15) 1994.
1760. Ishisaka DY: Visual compatibility of fluconazole with drugs given by continuous infusion, *Am J Hosp Pharm 51*:2290, 2292 (Sep 15) 1994.
1761. Fawcett JP, Woods DJ, Munasiri B, et al.: Compatibility of cyclizine lactate and haloperidol lactate, *Am J Hosp Pharm 51*:2292 (Sep 15) 1994.
1762. Hassan E, Leslie J, and Martir-Herrero ML: Stability of labetalol hydrochloride with selected critical care drugs during simulated Y-site injection, *Am J Hosp Pharm 51*:2143–2145 (Sep 1) 1994.
1763. Wang DP, Chang LC, Wong CY, et al.: Stability of cefazolin sodium–famotidine admixture, *Am J Hosp Pharm 51*:2205, 2209 (Sep 1) 1994.
1764. Singh RF, Corelli RL, and Guglielmo BJ: Sterility of unit dose syringes of filgrastim and sargramostim, *Am J Hosp Pharm 51*:2811–2812 (Nov 15) 1994.
1765. Kleinberg ML: Sterility of repackaged filgrastim and sargramostim, *Am J Health-Syst Pharm 52*:1101 (May 15) 1995.
1766. Kirkham JC, Rutherford ET, Cunningham GN, et al.: Stability of ondansetron hydrochloride in a total parenteral nutrient admixture, *Am J Health-Syst Pharm 52*:1557–1558 (July 15) 1995.
1767. Gilbar PJ and Groves CF: Visual compatibility of total parenteral nutrition solution (Synthamin 17 premix) with selected drugs during simulated Y-site injection, *Aust J Hosp Pharm 24*:167–170 (2) 1994.
1768. Moon YSK, Chung KC, Chin A, et al.: Stability of piperacillin sodium–tazobactam sodium in polypropylene syringes and polyvinyl chloride minibags, *Am J Health-Syst Pharm 52*:999–1001 (May 1) 1995.
1769. Lumpkin MM and Burlington DB: Safety alert: hazards of precipitation associated with parenteral nutrition, *Am J Hosp Pharm 51*:1427–1428 (June 1) 1994.
1770. Hasegawa GR: Caring about stability and compatibility, *Am J Hosp Pharm 51*:1533–1534 (June 15) 1994.
1771. Trissel LA: Compounding our problems, *Am J Hosp Pharm 51*:1534 (June 15) 1994.
1772. Mirtallo JM: The complexity of mixing calcium and phosphate, *Am J Hosp Pharm 51*:1535–1536 (June 15) 1994.
1773. Koorenhof MJC and Timmer JG: Stability of total parenteral nutrition supplied as "all-in-one" for children with chemotherapy-linked hyperhydration, *Pharm Weekbl Sci Ed 14*:50–54 (2) 1992.
1774. Picard C, Brazier M, Hary L, et al.: Stabilite de quatre solutions de penicillines dans des poches et tubulures de perfusion en PVC plastifie, *J Pharm Clin 11*: 302–305, 1992.
1775. Szucsova S and Sykora J: Stablita injekcneho pripravku celaskon v infuznych zmesiach, *Farm Obzor 61*:109–112, 1992.
1776. Walker SE, Iazzetta J, De Angelis C, et al.: Stability and compatibility of combinations of hydromorphone and dimenhydrinate, lorazepam or prochlorperazine, *Can J Hosp Pharm. 46*:61–65 (Apr) 1993.

1777. Maswoswe JJ, Okpara AU, and Hilliard MA: An old nemesis: calcium and phosphate interaction in TPN admixtures, *Hosp Pharm 30*:579–580, 582–586 (July) 1995.

1778. Deardorff DL, Schmidt CN, and Wiley RA: Effect of preparation techniques on mixing of additives in intravenous fluids in nonrigid containers, *Hosp Pharm 28*:306, 309–310, 312–313 (Apr) 1993.

1779. Stiles ML, Allen LV Jr, and Prince SJ: Stability of various antibiotics kept in an insulated pouch during administration via portable infusion pump, *Am J Health-Syst Pharm 52*:70–74 (Jan 1) 1995.

1780. Wang DP, Chang LC, Lee DKT, et al.: Stability of fluorouracil–metoclopramide hydrochloride admixture, *Am J Health-Syst Pharm 52*:98–99 (Jan 1) 1995.

1781. Jackson CW and Cunningham K: Compatibility of haloperidol lactate with benztropine mesylate, *Am J Hosp Pharm 51*:2962–2963 (Dec 1) 1994.

1782. Mirtallo JM: Should the use of total nutrient admixtures be limited? *Am J Hosp Pharm 51*:2831–2834 (Nov 15) 1994.

1783. Driscoll DF, Newton DW, and Bistrian BR: Precipitation of calcium phosphate from parenteral nutrient fluids, *Am J Hosp Pharm 51*:2834–2836 (Nov 15) 1994.

1784. Gibler B, Kim MS, and Raleigh F: Visual compatibility of neuroleptics with anticholinergics or antihistamines in polyethylene syringes, *Am J Hosp Pharm 51*:2709–2710 (Nov 1) 1994.

1785. Huang E and Anderson RP: Compatibility of hydromorphone hydrochloride with haloperidol lactate and ketorolac tromethamine, *Am J Hosp Pharm 51*: 2963 (Dec 1) 1994.

1786. Mendenhall A and Hoyt DB: Incompatibility of ketorolac tromethamine with haloperidol lactate and thiethylperazine maleate, *Am J Hosp Pharm 51*:2964 (Dec 1) 1994.

1787. Harraki B, Guiraud P, Rochat MH, et al.: Influence of copper, iron, and zinc on the physicochemical properties of parenteral admixture, *J Parenter Sci Technol 47*:199–204 (Sep–Oct) 1993.

1788. Aujoulat P, Coze C, Braguer D, et al.: Compatibilite physico-chimique du methotrexate avec les medicaments co-administres dans les protocols de chimiotherapie, *J Pharm Clin 12*:31–35, 1993.

1789. Johnson CE, Bhatt-Mehta V, Mancari SC, et al.: Stability of midazolam hydrochloride and morphine sulfate during simulated intravenous coadministration, *Am J Hosp Pharm 51*:2812–2813 (Nov 15) 1994.

1790. Burm JP, Choi JS, Jhee SS, et al.: Stability of paclitaxel and fluconazole during simulated Y-site administration, *Am J Hosp Pharm 51*:2704–2706 (Nov 1) 1994.

1791. Grassby PF and Roberts DE: Stability of epidural opiate solutions in 0.9 per cent sodium chloride infusion bags, *Int J Pharm Pract 3*:174–177 (July) 1995.

1792. Allwood MC, Brown PW, and Lee M: Stability of injections containing diamorphine and midazolam in plastic syringes, *Int J Pharm Pract 3*:57–59 (Oct) 1994.

1793. Kershaw BP, Monnier HL, and Mason JH: Visual compatibility of premixed theophylline or heparin with selected drugs for i.v. administration, *Am J Hosp Pharm 50*:1360, 1362–1363 (July) 1993.

1794. Trissel LA: Were the bubbles evolved or entrained? *Am J Health-Syst Pharm 52*:757 (Apr 1) 1995.

1795. Francomb MM, Ford JL, and Lee MG: Adsorption of vincristine, doxorubicin and mitoxantrone to in-line intravenous filters, *Int J Pharm 103*:87–92 (Feb 25) 1994.

1796. Salomies HEM, Heinonen RM, and Toppila MAI: Sorptive loss of diazepam, nitroglycerin and warfarin sodium to polypropylene-lined infusion bags (Softbags), *Int J Pharm 110*:197–201 (Sep 19) 1994.

1797. Haginaka J, Nakagawa T, and Uno T: Stability of clavulanic acid in aqueous solutions, *Chem Pharm Bull 29*:3334–3341 (11) 1981.

1798. Bianchi C, Airaudo CB, and Gayte-Sorbier A: Sorption studies of dipotassium clorazepate salt (Tranxene) and midazolam hydrochloride (Hypnovel) in polyvinyl chloride and glass infusion containers, *J Clin Pharm Ther 17*:223–227, 1992.

1799. Sautou V, Chopineau J, Gremeau I, et al.: Compatibility with medical plastics and stability of continuously and simultaneously infused isosorbide dinitrate and heparin, *Int J Pharm 107*:111–119 (July 4) 1994.

1800. Mitchell CL (Medical Information Officer, Leo Pharmaceuticals, Buckinghamshire, United Kingdom): Personal Communication, September 11, 1998.

1801. Hadzija BW and Lubarsky DA: Compatibility of etomidate, thiopental sodium, and propofol injections with drugs commonly administered during induction of anesthesia, *Am J Health-Syst Pharm 52*:997–999 (May 1) 1995.

1802. Stewart JT, Warren FW, and King AD: Stability of ranitidine hydrochloride and seven medications, *Am J Hosp Pharm 51*:1802–1807 (July 15) 1994.

1803. Palmquist KL, Quattrocchi FP, and Looney LA: Compatibility of furosemide with 20% mannitol, *Am J Health-Syst Pharm 52*:648, 650 (Mar 15) 1995.

1804. Trissel LA and Martinez JF: Compatibility of granisetron hydrochloride with selected alkaline drugs, *Am J Health-Syst Pharm 52*:208 (Jan 15) 1995.

1805. Bhatt-Mehta V, Paglia RE, and Rosen DA: Stability of propofol with parenteral nutrient solutions during simulated Y-site injection, *Am J Health-Syst Pharm 52*:192–196 (Jan 15) 1995.

1806. Hagan RL, Carr-Lopez SM, and Strickland JS: Stability of nafcillin sodium in the presence of lidocaine hydrochloride, *Am J Health-Syst Pharm 52*:521–523 (Mar 1) 1995.

1807. Gayed AA, Keshary PR, and Hinkle RL: Visual compatibility of diltiazem injection with various diluents and medications during simulated Y-site injection, *Am J Health-Syst Pharm 52*:516–520 (Mar 1) 1995.

1808. Trissel LA: Amphotericin B does not mix with fat emulsion, *Am J Health-Syst Pharm 52*:1463–1464 (July 1) 1995.

1809. Kirsch R, Goldstein R, Tarloff J, et al.: An emulsion formulation of amphotericin B improves the therapeutic index when treating systemic murine candidiasis, *J Infect Dis 158*:1065–1070, 1988.

1810. Chavenet PY, Garry I, Charlier N, et al.: Trial of glucose versus fat emulsion in preparation of amphotericin for use in HIV infected patients with candidiasis, *Br Med J 305*:921–925, 1992.

1811. Caillot D, Casanova O, Solary E, et al.: Efficacy and tolerance of an amphotericin B lipid (Intralipid) emulsion in the treatment of candidaemia in neutropenic patients, *J Antimicrob Chemother 31*:161–169, 1993.

1812. Fleming RA, Olsen DJ, Savage PD, et al.: Stability of ondansetron hydrochloride and cyclophosphamide in injectable solutions, *Am J Health-Syst Pharm 52*:514–516 (Mar 1) 1995.

1813. Driscoll DF: Total nutrient admixtures: theory and practice, *Nutr Clin Pract 10*:114–119 (June) 1995.

1814. Driscoll DF, Bhargava HN, Li L, et al.: Physicochemical stability of total nutrient admixtures, *Am J Health-Syst Pharm 52*:623–634 (Mar 15) 1995.

1815. Pettei MJ, Israel D, and Levine J: Serum vitamin K concentration in pediatric patients receiving total parenteral nutrition, *J Parenter Enter Nutr 17*:465–467 (5) 1993.

1816. Trissel LA, Martinez JF, and Xu QA: Incompatibility of fluorouracil with leucovorin calcium or levoleucovorin calcium, *Am J Health-Syst Pharm 52*: 710–715 (Apr 1) 1995.

1817. Montoya Garcia-Reol C, Sevilla Azzati E, Negro Vega E, et al.: Estudio de la estabilidad de la mezcla fluorouracilo/folinato calcico en fluidos intravenosos, *Farm Hosp 17*:99–103 (2) 1993.

1818. Ward GH and Yalkowsky SH: Studies in phlebitis VI: dilution-induced precipitation of amiodarone HCl, *J Parenter Sci Technol 47*:161–165 (July–Aug) 1993.

1819. Ward GH and Yalkowsky SH: Studies in phlebitis IV: injection rate and amiodarone-induced phlebitis, *J Parenter Sci Technol 47*:40–43 (Jan–Feb) 1993.

1820. Allwood MC and Brown PW: Stability of ampicillin infusions in unbuffered and buffered saline, *Int J Pharm 97*:219–222, 1993.

1821. Lauper RD (Director, Professional Services, Cetus Oncology Corporation, Emeryville, California): Personal communication, December 20, 1993.

1822. Allen LV: Plasminogen activator, *US Pharmacist 17*:64–65, 70–71, 1992.

1823. Rochard E, Barthes D, and Courtois P: Stability and compatibility of carboplatin with three portable infusion pump reservoirs, *Int J Pharm 101*:257–262 (Jan 25) 1994.

1824. Bailey LC, Cappel KM, and Orosz ST Jr: Stability of ceftriaxone sodium in injectable solutions stored frozen in syringes, *Am J Hosp Pharm 51*:2159–2161 (Sep 1) 1994.

1825. Mazzo DJ, Nguyen-Huu JJ, Pagniez S, et al.: Compatibility of docetaxel and paclitaxel in intravenous solutions with polyvinyl chloride infusion materials, *Am J Health-Syst Pharm 54*:566–569 (Mar 1) 1997.

1826. Kane MP, Bailie GR, Moon DG, et al.: Stability of ciprofloxacin injection in peritoneal dialysis solutions, *Am J Hosp Pharm 51*:373–377 (Feb 1) 1994.

1827. Rochard E, Barthes D, and Courtois P: Stability of cisplatin in ethylene vinylacetate portable infusion-pump reservoirs, *J Clin Pharm Ther 17*:315–318, 1992.

1828. Cubells MP, Aixela JP, Brumos VG, et al.: Stability of cisplatin in sodium chloride 0.9% intravenous solution related to the container's material, *Pharm World Sci Ed 15*:34–36 (1) 1993.

1829. Islam MS and Asker AF: Photostabilization of dacarbazine with reduced glutathione, *J Pharm Sci Technol 48*:38–40 (Jan–Feb) 1994.

1830. Wiest DB, Garner SS, and Childress LM: Stability of esmolol hydrochloride in 5% dextrose injection, *Am J Health-Syst Pharm 52*:716–718 (Apr 1) 1995.

1831. Baaske DM, Dykstra SD, Wagenknecht DM, et al.: Stability of esmolol hydrochloride in intravenous solutions, *Am J Hosp Pharm 51*:2693–2696 (Nov 1) 1994.

1832. Woloschuk DMM and Nazeravich DR: Etoposide precipitation, *Can J Hosp Pharm 45*:136 (Aug) 1992.

1833. Barthes DMC, Rochard EB, Pouliquen IJ, et al.: Stability and compatibility of etoposide in 0.9% sodium chloride injection in three containers, *Am J Hosp Pharm 51*:2706–2709 (Nov 1) 1994.
1834. Mathew M, Gupta VD, and Bethea C: Stability of foscarnet sodium in 5% dextrose and 0.9% sodium chloride injections, *J Clin Pharm Ther 19*:35–36, 1994.
1835. Stolk LM, Hendrikse H, and Chandi LS: Autoclave and long-term sterility of foscarnet sodium admixtures, *Am J Health-Syst Pharm 52*:103 (Jan 1) 1995.
1836. Phaypradith S, Vigneron J, Perrin A, et al.: Stabilite des solutions diluees de ganciclovir sodique (Cymevan) en seringues polypropylene et en poches PVC pour perfusions, *J Pharm Belg 47*:494–498 (6) 1992.
1837. Chung KC, Chin A, and Gill MA: Stability of granisetron hydrochloride in a disposable elastomeric infusion device, *Am J Health-Syst Pharm 52*:1541–1543 (July 15) 1995.
1838. Flahive E (Medical Information, Ortho-McNeil, Raritan, New Jersey): Personal communication, April 6, 1995.
1839. Anon: ASHP therapeutic position statement on the institutional use of 0.9% sodium chloride injection to maintain patency of peripheral indwelling intermittent infusion devices, *Am J Hosp Pharm 51*:1572–1574 (June 15) 1994.
1840. Nahata MC, Morosco RS, and Hipple TF: Stability of lorazepam diluted in bacteriostatic water for injection at two temperatures, *J Clin Pharm Ther 18*: 69–71, 1993.
1841. Pinguet F, Martel P, Rouanet P, et al.: Effect of sodium chloride concentration and temperature on melphalan stability during storage and use, *Am J Hosp Pharm 51*:2701–2704 (Nov 1) 1994.
1842. Chin A, Ramakrishnan RR, Yoshimura NN, et al.: Paclitaxel stability and compatibility in polyolefin containers, *Ann Pharmacother 28*:35–36 (Jan) 1994.
1843. Trissel LA, Xu Q, Kwan J, et al.: Compatibility of paclitaxel injection vehicle with intravenous administration and extension sets, *Am J Hosp Pharm 51*: 2804–2810 (Nov 15) 1994.
1844. McLaughlin JP, Simpson C, and Taylor RA: When is flucloxacillin stable? *Hosp Pharm Pract* 553–556 (Nov) 1993.
1845. Trissel LA and Martinez JF: Compatibility of amifostine with selected drugs during simulated Y-site administration, *Am J Health-Syst Pharm 52*:2208–2212 (Oct 15) 1995.
1846. Henry DW, Marshall JL, Nazzaro D, et al.: Stability of cisplatin and ondansetron hydrochloride in admixtures for continuous infusion, *Am J Health-Syst Pharm 52*:2570–2573 (Nov 15) 1995.
1847. Mantong ML and Marquardt ED: Visual compatibility of midazolam hydrochloride with selected drugs during simulated Y-site injection, *Am J Health-Syst Pharm 52*:2567–2568 (Nov 15) 1995.
1848. Trissel LA, Xu QA, and Martinez JF: Compatibility and stability of aztreonam and vancomycin hydrochloride, *Am J Health-Syst Pharm 52*:2560–2564 (Nov 15) 1995.
1849. Rivers TE and Webster AA: Stability of ceftizoxime sodium, ceftriaxone sodium, and ceftazidime with metronidazole in ready-to-use metronidazole bags, *Am J Health-Syst Pharm 52*:2568–2570 (Nov 15) 1995.
1850. Wulf H, Gleim M, and Mignat C: The stability of mixtures of morphine hydrochloride, bupivacaine hydrochloride, and clonidine hydrochloride in portable pump reservoirs for the management of chronic pain syndromes, *J Pain Symptom Manage 9*:308–311 (July) 1994.
1851. Korth-Bradley JM, Ludwig S, and Callaghan C: Incompatibility of amiodarone hydrochloride and sodium bicarbonate injections, *Am J Health-Syst Pharm 52*: 2340 (Oct 15) 1995.
1852. Bhatt-Mehta V, Johnson CE, Leininger N, et al.: Stability of fentanyl citrate and midazolam hydrochloride during simulated intravenous coadministration, *Am J Health-Syst Pharm 52*:511–513 (Mar 1) 1995.
1853. Matuschka PR, Smith WR, and Vissing RS: Compatibility of mannitol and sodium bicarbonate in injectable fluids, *Am J Health-Syst Pharm 52*:320–321 (Feb 1) 1995.
1854. Ku YM, Min DI, Kumar V, et al.: Compatibility of tacrolimus injection with cimetidine hydrochloride injection in 0.9% sodium chloride injection, *Am J Health-Syst Pharm 52*:2024–2025 (Sep 15) 1995.
1855. Swart EL, Mooren RAG, and van Loenen AC: Compatibility of midazolam hydrochloride and lorazepam with selected drugs during simulated Y-site administration, *Am J Health-Syst Pharm 52*:2020–2022 (Sep 15) 1995.
1856. Lam XM, Ward CA, and de C de Mee CPR: Stability and activity of alteplase with injectable drugs commonly used in cardiac therapy, *Am J Health-Syst Pharm 52*:1904–1909 (Sep 1) 1995.
1857. Alex S, Gupta SL, Minor JR, et al.: Compatibility and activity of aldesleukin (recombinant interleukin-2) in presence of selected drugs during simulated Y-site administration: evaluation of three methods, *Am J Health-Syst Pharm 52*: 2423–2426 (Nov 1) 1995.
1858. Mancano MA, Boullata JI, Gelone SP, et al.: Availability of lorazepam after simulated administration from glass and polyvinyl chloride containers, *Am J Health-Syst Pharm 52*:2213–2216 (Oct 15) 1995.
1859. McMullin ST, Burns Schaif RA, and Dietzen DJ: Stability of midazolam hydrochloride in polyvinyl chloride bags under fluorescent light, *Am J Health-Syst Pharm 52*:2018–2020 (Sep 15) 1995.
1860. Bednar DA, Klutman NE, Henry DW, et al.: Stability of ceftazidime (with arginine) in an elastomeric infusion device, *Am J Health-Syst Pharm 52*:1912–1914 (Sep 1) 1995.
1861. Trissel LA and Martinez JF: Compatibility of thiotepa (lyophilized) with selected drugs during simulated Y-site administration, *Am J Health-Syst Pharm 53*:1041–1045 (May 1) 1996.
1862. Xu QA, Trissel LA, and Fox JL: Compatibility of ondansetron hydrochloride with meperidine hydrochloride for combined administration, *Ann Pharmacother 29*:1106–1109 (Nov) 1995.
1863. Bleasel MD, Peterson GM, and Jestrimski KW: Stability of midazolam in sodium chloride infusion packs, *Aust J Hosp Pharm 23*:260–262 (4) 1993.
1864. Taormina D, Abdallah HY, Venkataramanan R, et al.: Stability and sorption of FK 506 in 5% dextrose injection and 0.9% sodium chloride injection in glass, polyvinyl chloride, and polyolefin containers, *Am J Hosp Pharm 49*: 119–122 (Jan) 1992.
1865. Stiles ML, Allen LV Jr, and Prince SJ: Stability of ranitidine hydrochloride during simulated home-care use, *Am J Hosp Pharm 51*:1706–1707 (July 1) 1994.
1866. Dorr RT and Likkil JD: Stability of mitomycin C in different infusion fluids: compatibility with heparin and glucocorticoids, *J Oncol Pharm Pract 1*:19–24 (3) 1995.
1867. Benaji B, Dine T, Goudaliez F, et al.: Compatibility study of methotrexate with PVC bags after repackaging into two types of infusion admixtures, *Int J Pharm 105*:83–87 (Apr 25) 1994.
1868. Sanchez Alcaraz A, Quintana Vergara B, and Sangrador Garcia G: Estabilidad del midazolam en soluciones intravenosas gran volumen, *Farm Hosp 16*:393–398 (6) 1992.
1869. Trissel LA: Concentration-dependent precipitation of sodium bicarbonate with ciprofloxacin lactate, *Am J Health-Syst Pharm 53*:84–85 (Jan 1) 1996.
1870. Christen C, Johnson CE, and Walters JR: Stability of bupivacaine hydrochloride and hydromorphone hydrochloride during simulated epidural coadministration, *Am J Health-Syst Pharm 53*:170–173 (Jan 15) 1996.
1871. Mewborn AL, Kessler JM, and Joyner KA: Compatibility and activity of enoxaparin sodium in 0.9% sodium chloride injection for 48 hours, *Am J Health-Syst Pharm 53*:167–169 (Jan 15) 1996.
1872. Ericsson O, Hallmen AC, and Wikstrom I: Amphotericin B incompatible with lipid emulsion, *Ann Pharmacother 30*:298 (Mar) 1996.
1873. Hoey LL, Vance-Bryan K, Clarens DM, et al.: Lorazepam stability in parenteral solutions for continuous intravenous administration, *Ann Pharmacother 30*:343–346 (Apr) 1996.
1874. Nyhammar EK, Johansson SG, and Seiving BE: Stability of doxorubicin hydrochloride and vincristine sulfate in two portable infusion-pump reservoirs, *Am J Health-Syst Pharm 53*:1171–1173 (May 15) 1996.
1875. Chin A, Moon YSK, Chung KC, et al.: Stability of granisetron hydrochloride with dexamethasone sodium phosphate for 14 days, *Am J Health-Syst Pharm 53*:1174–1176 (May 15) 1996.
1876. Stewart JT, Warren FW, King DT, et al.: Stability of ondansetron hydrochloride and five antineoplastic medications, *Am J Health-Syst Pharm 53*:1297–1300 (June 1) 1996.
1877. Yamashita SK, Walker SE, Choudhury T, et al.: Compatibility of selected critical care drugs during simulated Y-site administration, *Am J Health-Syst Pharm 53*:1048–1051 (May 1) 1996.
1878. Ohls RK and Christensen RD: Stability of human recombinant epoetin alfa in commonly used neonatal intravenous solutions, *Ann Pharmacother 30*:466–468 (May) 1996.
1879. Nahata MC, Edmonds JJ, and Morosco RS: Stability of metronidazole and ceftizoxime sodium in ready-to-use metronidazole bags stored at 4 and 25°C, *Am J Health-Syst Pharm 53*:1046–1048 (May 1) 1996.
1880. Lewis JD and El-Gendy A: Cephalosporin-pentamidine isethionate incompatibilities, *Am J Health-Syst Pharm 53*:1461–1462 (June 15) 1996.
1881. Tanque N, Ueda H, Moriyama Y, et al.: Compatibility of irinotecan hydrochloride injection with other injections, *Jpn J Hosp Pharm 22*:457–465 (5) 1996.
1882. Hagan RL, Mallett MS, and Fox JL: Stability of ondansetron hydrochloride and dexamethasone sodium phosphate in infusion bags and syringes for 32 days, *Am J Health-Syst Pharm 53*:1431–1435 (June 15) 1996.
1883. Mayron D and Gennaro AR: Stability and compatibility of granisetron hydro-

chloride in i.v. solutions and oral liquids and during simulated Y-site injection with selected drugs, *Am J Health-Syst Pharm 53*:294–304 (Feb 1) 1996.

1884. Pinguet F, Rouanet P, Martel P, et al.: Compatibility and stability of granisetron, dexamethasone, and methylprednisolone in injectable solutions, *J Pharm Sci 84*:267–268 (Feb) 1995.

1885. Lindsay CA, Dang K, Adams JM, et al.: Stability and activity of intravenous immunoglobulin with neonatal dextrose and total parenteral nutrient solutions, *Ann Pharmacother 28*:1014–1017 (Sep) 1994.

1886. Ukhun IA: Compatibility of haloperidol and diphenhydramine in a hypodermic syringe, *Ann Pharmacother 29*:1168–1169 (Nov) 1995.

1887. Melonakos TK: Ciprofloxacin-ampicillin sulbactam incompatibility, *Ann Pharmacother 30*:87 (Jan) 1996.

1888. Digel S: Cefamandolnafat und metronidazol, *Krankenhauspharmazie 16*:9–12 (Jan) 1995.

1889. Heni J and Strehl E: Kompatibilitat von cefotiam, *Krankenhauspharmazie 15*: 187–192 (Apr) 1994.

1890. Tham A (Drug Information Associate, Medical Affairs, Chiron Therapeutics, Emeryville, CA): Personal Communication, November 1, 1999.

1891. Mathew M, Gupta VD, and Zerai T: Stability of ciprofloxacin in 5% dextrose and normal saline injections, *J Clin Pharm Ther 19*:397–399 (6) 1994.

1892. Pramar YV, Moniz D, and Hobbs D: Chemical stability and adsorption of succinylcholine chloride injections in disposable plastic syringes, *J Clin Pharm Ther 19*:195–198, 1994.

1893. Wood MJ, Lund R, and Beavan M: Stability of vancomycin in plastic syringes measured by high-performance liquid chromatography, *J Clin Pharm Ther 20*: 319–325 (6) 1995.

1894. Strong ML, Schaaf LJ, Pankaskie MC, et al.: Shelf-lives and factors affecting the stability of morphine sulphate and meperidine (pethidine) hydrochloride in plastic syringes for use in patient-controlled analgesic devices, *J Clin Pharm Ther 19*:361–369 (6) 1994.

1895. Giordano F, Bettinetti G, Cursano R, et al.: A physicochemical approach to the investigation of the stability of trimethoprim-sulfamethoxazole (Co-Trimoxazole) mixtures for injectables, *J Pharm Sci 84*:1254–1258 (Oct) 1995.

1896. Sianipar A, Parkin JE, and Sunderland VB: Chemical incompatibility between procainamide hydrochloride and glucose following intravenous admixture, *J Pharm Pharmacol 46*:951–955 (Dec) 1994.

1897. Lau DWC, Law S, Walker SE, et al.: Dexamethasone phosphate stability and contamination of solutions stored in syringes, *PDA J Pharm Sci Technol 50*: 261–267 (July–Aug) 1996.

1898. Ambados F: Incompatibility between aminophylline and elemental zinc injections, *Aust J Hosp Pharm 26*:370–371 (3) 1996.

1899. Ambados F: Compatibility of morphine and ketamine for subcutaneous infusion, *Aust J Hosp Pharm 25*:352 (4) 1995.

1900. Boldu SP, Cubells MP, Brumos VG, et al.: Stability study of azlocillin sodium in glass bottles and PVC bags containing intravenous admixtures, *Boll Chim Farm 134*:467–471 (Sep) 1995.

1901. LeBelle MJ, Savard C, and Gagnon A: Compatibility of morphine and midazolam or haloperidol in parenteral admixtures, *Can J Hosp Pharm 48*:155–160 (June) 1995.

1902. Donnelly RF and Yen M: Epinephrine stability in plastic syringes and glass vials, *Can J Hosp Pharm 49*:62–65 (2) 1996.

1903. Sadjak A and Wintersteiger R: Compatibility of morphine, baclofen, floxuridine and fluorouracil in an implantable medication pump, *Arzneim Forsch 45*: 93–98 (1) 1995.

1904. Donnelly RF and Farncombe M: Compatibility of morphine or hydromorphone with salbutamol in a syringe, *Can J Hosp Pharm 47*:252 (Dec) 1994.

1905. Corbo DC, Suddith RL, Sharma B, et al.: Stability, potency, and preservative effectiveness of epoetin alfa after addition of a bacteriostatic diluent, *Am J Hosp Pharm 49*:1455–1458 (June) 1992.

1906. Lane G and Waite N: Erythropoietin stability, *Can J Hosp Pharm 47*:182 (Aug) 1994.

1907. Walker SE and Lau DWC: Compatibility and stability of hyaluronidase and hydromorphone, *Can J Hosp Pharm 45*:187–192 (Oct) 1992.

1908. Sastre Gervas I and Ferrandiz Gosalbez JR: Estabilidad fisica y quimica del sulfate magnesico combinado con heparina sodica en solucion salina al 0,9 por 100, *Farm Hosp 19*:38–40 (1) 1995.

1909. Halkiewicz A, Barteczko I, and Janicki S: Interakcje fizykochemiczne izotonicznego roztworu teofiliny do wlewu dozylnego z niektorymi lekami do wstrzykiwan, *Farm Polska 49*:11–15, 1993.

1910. Gila Azanedo JA, Mengual Sendra A, Fernandez Barral C, et al.: Estudio de la estabilidad de una solucion de clorhidrato de morfina mas anestesicos locales en solucion salina 0,9 por 100 sin conservantes para uso epidural, *Farm Hosp 18*:261–264 (Sep–Oct) 1994.

1911. Sitaram BR, Tsui M, Rawicki HB, et al.: Stability and compatibility of baclofen and morphine admixtures for use in an implantable infusion pump, *Int J Pharm 118*:181–189 (May 16) 1995.

1912. Allwood MC and Martin HJ: Long-term stability of cimetidine in total parenteral nutrition, *J Clin Pharm Ther 21*:19–21, 1996.

1913. Jacolot A, Arnaud P, Lecompte D, et al.: Stability and compatibility of 2.5 mg/ml methotrexate solution in plastic syringes over 7 days, *Int J Pharm 128*: 283–286 (Feb 29) 1996.

1914. Wright A and Hecker J: Long term stability of heparin in dextrose-saline intravenous fluids, *Int J Pharm Pract 3*:253–255 (Nov) 1995.

1915. Kawano K, Matsunaga A, Terada K, et al.: Loss of diltiazem hydrochloride in solutions in polyvinyl chloride containers or intravenous administration set—hydrolysis and sorption, *Jpn J Hosp Pharm 20*:537–541 (6) 1994.

1916. Trissel LA and Gilbert DL: Data on file. Pharmaceutical Analysis Laboratory, University of Texas, M. D. Anderson Cancer Center, Houston, Texas, January 14, 2000.

1917. Kawano K, Takamatsu S, Yamashita J, et al.: Effect of pH on the sorption of in-solution diazepam into the ethylene-vinylacetate copolymer membrane, *Jpn J Hosp Pharm 20*:404–409 (5) 1994.

1918. Picard C, Brazier M, Bou P, et al.: Stabilite de quatre solutions de penicillines dans les poches de perfusion multicouches, *J Pharm Clin 13*:45–49 (1) 1994.

1919. Theuer H, Scherbel G, Balzulat S, et al.: Herstellung und stabilitatuntersuchungen von carboplatin i.v., *Krankenhauspharmazie 15*:120–130 (Mar) 1994.

1920. Strehl E and Heni J: Amoxicillin, clavulansaure und metronidazol in kombination, *Krankenhauspharmazie 15*:592–595 (Oct) 1994.

1921. Hatton J, Luer M, Hirsch J, et al.: Histamine receptor antagonists and lipid stability in total nutrient admixtures, *J Parenter Enter Nutr 18*:308–312 (July–Aug) 1994.

1922. Ku YM, Min DI, Kumar V, et al.: Stability of tacrolimus injection in total parenteral nutrition solution, *J Pharm Technol 12*:58–61 (Mar–Apr) 1996.

1923. Martinelli E and Muhlebach S: Kunststoffumbeutel als lichtschutz fur infusionen, *Krankenhauspharmazie 16*:286–289 (July) 1995.

1924. Teraoka K, Minakuchi K, Tsuchiya K, et al.: Compatibility of ciprofloxacin infusion with other injections, *Jpn J Hosp Pharm 21*:541–550 (6) 1995.

1925. Asahara K, Goda Y, Shimomura Y, et al.: Stability of thiamine in intravenous hyperalimentation containing multivitamin, *Jpn J Hosp Pharm 21*:15–21 (1) 1995.

1926. Namika Y, Fujiwara A, Kihara N, et al.: Factors affecting tautomeric phenomenon of a novel potent immunosuppressant (FK506) on the design for injectable formulation, *Drug Dev Ind Pharm 21*:809–822 (7) 1995.

1927. Antipas AS, Vander Velde D, Stella VJ: Factors affecting the deamidation of vancomycin in aqueous solutions, *Int J Pharm 109*:261–269, 1994.

1928. King AD, Stewart JT, and Warren FW: Stability of cefmetazole-doxycycline mixtures in sodium chloride and dextrose injections, *J Clin Pharm Ther 19*: 317–325 (5) 1994.

1929. Hughes IE and Smith JA: The stability of noradrenaline in physiologic saline solutions, *J Pharm Pharmacol 30*:124–126, 1978.

1930. Anon: Infections linked to lax handling of propofol, *Am J Health-Syst Pharm 52*:2061, 2066 (Oct 1) 1995.

1931. Ordovas Baines JP, Ronchera Oms CL, Jimenez Torres NV, et al.: Mezclas iv binarias de metronidazol y aminoglycosidos, *Revista AEFH 12*:119–123 (2) 1988.

1932. Nitescu P, Hultman E, Appelgren L, et al.: Bacteriology, drug stability and exchange of percutaneous delivery systems and antibacterial filters in long-term intrathecal infusion of opioid drugs and bupivacaine in "refractory" pain, *Clin J Pain 8*:324–337 (4) 1992.

1933. Yao JDC, Arkin CF, and Karchmer AW: Vancomycin stability in heparin and total parenteral nutrition solutions: novel approach to therapy of central venous catheter-related infections, *J Parenter Enter Nutr 16*:268–274 (May–June) 1992.

1934. Jim LK: Physical and chemical compatibility of intravenous ciprofloxacin with other drugs, *Ann Pharmacother 27*:704–707 (June) 1993.

1935. Paesen J, Khan K, Roets E, et al.: Study of the stability of erythromycin in neutral and alkaline solutions by liquid chromatography on poly(styrene-divinylbenzene), *Int J Pharm 113*:215–222, 1994.

1936. Keyi X, Gagnon N, Bisson C, et al.: Stability of famotidine in polyvinyl chloride minibags and polypropylene syringes and compatibility of famotidine with selected drugs, *Ann Pharmacother 27*:422–426 (Apr) 1993.

1937. Pleasants RA, Vaughan LM, Williams DM, et al.: Compatibility of ceftazidime and aminophylline admixtures for different methods of intravenous infusion, *Ann Pharmacother 26*:1221–1226 (Oct) 1992.

1938. Nahata MC, Morosco RS, and Hipple TF: Stability of diluted methylprednisolone sodium succinate injection at two temperatures, *Am J Hosp Pharm 51*: 2157–2159 (Sep 1) 1994.

1939. Nixon AR, O'Hare MCB, and Chisakuta AM: The stability of morphine sulphate and metoclopramide hydrochloride in various delivery presentations, *Pharm J 254*:153–155, 1995.

1940. Lugo RA and Nahata MC: Stability of diluted dexamethasone sodium phosphate injection at two temperatures, *Ann Pharmacother 28*:1018–1019 (Sep) 1994.

1941. Hanff PAJM and Van den Biggelaar JPFA: Stabiliteitsonderzoek van nitroglycerine-oplossingen voor parenteraal gebruik, *Ziekenhuisfarmacie 10*:134–138 (4) 1994.

1942. Forte FJ, Caravone D, Coyne MJ, et al.: Albumin dilution as a cause of hemolysis during plasmapheresis, *Am J Health-Syst Pharm 52*:207 (Jan 15) 1995.

1943. Little G (Drug Information, Wyeth-Ayerst Laboratories, Philadelphia, Pennsylvania): Personal communication, March 25, 1996.

1944. Andersin R and Tammilehto S: Photochemical decomposition of midazolam, part iv: study of pH-dependent stability by high-performance liquid chromatography, *Int J Pharm 123*:229–235 (Sep 12) 1995.

1945. Boullata JI, Gelone SP, Mancano MA, et al.: Precipitation of lorazepam infusion, *Ann Pharmacother 30*:1037–1038 (Sep) 1996.

1946. Taylor RB, Richards RME, Low AS, et al.: Chemical stability of polymyxin B in aqueous solution, *Int J Pharm 102*:201–206 (Feb 7) 1994.

1947. Neuzil J, Darlow BA, Inder TE, et al.: Oxidation of parenteral lipid emulsion by ambient and phototherapy lights: potential toxicity of routine parenteral feeding, *J Pediatr 126*:785–790 (May) 1995.

1948. Katakam M and Banga AK: Aggregation of insulin and its prevention by carbohydrate excipients, *PDA J Pharm Sci Technol 49*:160–165 (July–Aug) 1995.

1949. Woloschuk DMM: Drug precipitation and peristaltic pumps, *Am J Hosp Pharm 51*:1473 (June 1) 1994.

1950. Hehenberger H: Prednisolon-21-hemisuccinat-natrium, *Krankenhauspharmazie 7*:128–132 (Apr) 1986.

1951. Driscoll DF, Bacon M, Provost PS, et al.: Automated compounders for parenteral nutrition admixtures, *J Parenter Enter Nutr 18*:385–386 (July–Aug) 1994.

1952. Mehta AC and Kay EA: Admixtures' storage is extended, *Pharm Pract 6*:113–114 (Apr) 1996.

1953. Faouzi MA, Dine T, Luyckx M, et al.: Stability and compatibility studies of cephaloridine, cefuroxime and ceftazidime with PVC infusion bags, *Pharmazie 49*:425–429 (June) 1994.

1954. Williams DA and Lokich J: A review of the stability and compatibility of antineoplastic drugs for multiple-drug infusions, *Cancer Chemother Pharmacol 31*:171–181, 1992.

1955. Chevrier R, Sautou V, Pinon V, et al.: Stability and compatibility of a mixture of the anti-cancer drugs etoposide, cytarabine and daunorubicine for infusion, *Pharm Acta Helv 70*:141–148, 1995.

1956. Christie JM, Jones CW, and Markowsky SJ: Chemical compatibility of regional anesthetic drug combinations, *Ann Pharmacother 26*:1078–1080 (Sep) 1992.

1957. Abdel-Moety EM, Al-Rashood KA, Rauf A, et al.: Photostability-indicating HPLC method for determination of trifluoperazine in bulk form and pharmaceutical formulations, *J Pharm Biomed Anal 14*:1639–1644 (Aug) 1996.

1958. Poochikian GK, Cradock JC, and Davignon JP: Heroin: stability and formulation approaches, *Int J Pharm 13*:219–226, 1983.

1959. Kamitomo V and Olson K: Using normal saline to lock peripheral intravenous catheters in ambulatory cancer patients, *J Intraven Nurs 19*:75–78 (Mar–Apr) 1996.

1960. Burnakis TG: Insulin syringes: more than a one-shot deal, *Hosp Pharm 31*: 410, 414 (Apr) 1996.

1961. Sautou-Miranda V, Gremeau I, Chamard I, et al.: Stability of dopamine hydrochloride and of dobutamine hydrochloride in plastic syringes and administration sets, *Am J Health-Syst Pharm 53*:186, 193 (Jan 15) 1996.

1962. Murthey SS and Brittain HG: Stability of revex, nalmefene hydrochloride injection, in injectable solutions, *J Pharm Biomed Anal 15*:221–226 (Nov) 1996.

1963. Yuan LC, Samuels GJ, and Visor GC: Stability of cidofovir in 0.9% sodium chloride injection and in 5% dextrose injection, *Am J Health-Syst Pharm 53*: 1939–1943 (Aug 15) 1996.

1964. Leader WG: Incompatibility between ceftriaxone sodium and labetalol hydrochloride, *Am J Health-Syst Pharm 53*:2639 (Nov 1) 1996.

1965. Nahata MC, Morosco RS, and Fox J: Stability of ranitidine hydrochloride in water for injection in glass vials and plastic syringes, *Am J Health-Syst Pharm 53*:1588–1590 (July 1) 1996.

1966. Lee DKT, Wong CY, and Wang DP: Stability of cefazolin sodium and meperidine hydrochloride, *Am J Health-Syst Pharm 53* :1608, 1610 (July 1) 1996.

1967. Stiles ML, Allen LV Jr, and Prince SJ: Stability of deferoxamine mesylate, floxuridine, fluorouracil, hydromorphone hydrochloride, lorazepam, and midazolam hydrochloride in polypropylene infusion-pump syringes, *Am J Health-Syst Pharm 53*:1583–1588 (July 1) 1996.

1968. Quercia RA, Zhang J, Fan C, et al.: Stability of granisetron hydrochloride in polypropylene syringes, *Am J Health-Syst Pharm 53*:2744–2746 (Nov 15) 1996.

1969. Trissel LA, Martinez JF, and Gilbert DL: Screening cladribine for Y-site physical compatibility with selected drugs, *Hosp Pharm 31*:1425–1428 (Nov) 1996.

1970. Allen LV Jr, Stiles ML, Prince SJ, et al.: Stability of 14 drugs in the latex reservoir of an elastomeric infusion device, *Am J Health-Syst Pharm 53*:2740–2743 (Nov 15) 1996.

1971. Benjamin BE: Ciprofloxacin and sodium phosphates not compatible during actual Y-site injection, *Am J Health-Syst Pharm 53*:1850–1851 (Aug 1) 1996.

1972. Trissel LA: Everything in a compatibility study is important, *Am J Health-Syst Pharm 53*:2990 (Dec 1) 1996.

1973. Matuschka PR, Hill LJ, and Canada CA: More on the compatibility of mannitol and sodium bicarbonate in injectable fluids, *Am J Health-Syst Pharm 53*:2639 (Nov 1) 1996.

1974. Veltri M and Lee CKK: Compatibility of neonatal parenteral nutrient solutions with selected intravenous drugs, *Am J Health-Syst Pharm 53*:2611–2613 (Nov 1) 1996.

1975. Ritter H, Trissel LA, Anderson RW, et al.: Electronic balance as quality assurance for cytotoxic drug admixtures, *Am J Health-Syst Pharm 53*:2318–2320 (Oct 1) 1996.

1976. Zhang Y, Xu QA, Trissel LA, et al.: Physical and chemical stability of methotrexate sodium, cytarabine, and hydrocortisone sodium succinate in Elliott's B solution, *Hosp Pharm 31*:965–970 (Aug) 1996.

1977. Xu QA, Trissel LA, and Martinez JF: Stability and compatibility of fluorouracil with morphine sulfate and hydromorphone hydrochloride, *Ann Pharmacother 30*:756–761 (July–Aug) 1996.

1978. Kohut J III, Trissel LA, and Leissing NC: Don't ignore the details of drug-compatibility reports, *Am J Health-Syst Pharm 53*:2339 (Oct 1) 1996.

1979. Grillo JA and Barie PS: Precipitation of lorazepam during infusion by volumetric pump, *Am J Health-Syst Pharm 53*:1850 (Aug 1) 1996.

1980. Volles DF: More on usability of lorazepam admixtures for continuous infusion, *Am J Health-Syst Pharm 53*:2753–2754 (Nov 15) 1996.

1981. Boullata JI and Gelone SP: More on usability of lorazepam admixtures for continuous infusion, *Am J Health-Syst Pharm 53*:2754 (Nov 15) 1996.

1982. Strozyk WR, Williamson R, and Thompson D: Incompatibility of amiodarone hydrochloride and evacuated glass bottles, *Am J Health-Syst Pharm 53*:184 (Jan 15) 1996.

1983. Baud-Camus F, Crauste-Manciet S, Klein E, et al.: Stability of fluorouracil in polypropylene syringes and ethylene vinyl acetate infusion-pump reservoirs, *Am J Health-Syst Pharm 53*:1457, 1461 (June 15) 1996.

1984. Chernin EL, Stewart JT, and Smiler B: Stability of thiopental sodium and propofol in polypropylene syringes at 23 and 4 °C, *Am J Health-Syst Pharm 53*:1576–1579 (July 1) 1996.

1985. Prankerd RJ and Jones RD: Physicochemical compatibility of propofol with thiopental sodium, *Am J Health-Syst Pharm 53*:2606–2610 (Nov 1) 1996.

1986. Williams NA, Bornstein M, and Johnson K: Stability of levofloxacin in intravenous solutions in polyvinyl chloride bags, *Am J Health-Syst Pharm 53*: 2309–2313 (Oct 1) 1996.

1987. Cleary JD: Amphotericin B formulated in a lipid emulsion, *Ann Pharmacother 30*:409–412 (Apr) 1996.

1988. Lopez RM, Ayestaran A, Pou L, et al.: Stability of amphotericin B in an extemporaneously prepared i.v. fat emulsion, *Am J Health-Syst Pharm 53*: 2724–2727 (Nov 15) 1996.

1989. Manduru M, Fariello A, White RL, et al.: Stability of ceftazidime sodium and teicoplanin sodium in a peritoneal dialysis solution, *Am J Health-Syst Pharm 53*:2731–2734 (Nov 15) 1996.

1990. Plumridge RJ, Rieck AM, Annus TP, et al.: Stability of ceftriaxone sodium in polypropylene syringes at −20, 4, and 20 °C, *Am J Health-Syst Pharm 53*: 2320–2323 (Nov 15) 1996.

1991. Plumridge RJ, Rieck AM, Annus TP, et al.: Stability of ceftriaxone sodium reconstituted with lidocaine hydrochloride and stored in polypropylene syringes, *Am J Health-Syst Pharm 53*:2323–2325 (Oct 1) 1996.

1992. Henderson F: 21-Day compatibility of hydromorphone hydrochloride and promethazine hydrochloride in a casette, *Am J Health-Syst Pharm 53*:2338–2339 (Oct 1) 1996.

1993. Lima HA, Lennon J, Sesterhenn K, et al.: Stability of dextrose and sodium chloride in injectable solutions stored in an elastomeric infusion device, *Am J Health-Syst Pharm 53*:794–795 (Apr 1) 1996.

1994. Patel PR: Compatibility of meropenem with commonly used injectable drugs, *Am J Health-Syst Pharm 53*:2853–2855 (Dec 1) 1996.

1995. Lougheed WD, Albisser AM, Martindale HM, et al.: Physical stability of insulin formulations, *Diabetes 32*:424–432 (May) 1983.

1996. Gupta VD: Quantitation of papaverine hydrochloride in a discoloured injection, *Drug Stability 1*:132–134 (2) 1996.

1997. Akimoto K, Kawai A, Ohya K, et al.: Photodegradation reactions of CPT-11, a derivative of camptothecin, part i: chemical structure of main degradation products in aqueous solution, *Drug Stability 1*:118–122 (2) 1996.

1998. Akimoto K, Kawai A, and Ohya K: Photodegradation reactions of CPT-11, a derivative of camptothecin, part ii: photodegradation behaviour of CPT-11 in aqueous solution, *Drug Stability 1*:141–146 (3) 1996.

1999. O'Connell C, Sabra K, and Scott K: Stability of reconstituted ceftriaxone solution in polypropylene syringes, *Eur Hosp Pharm 2*:47–48 (May) 1996.

2000. Trissel LA, Gilbert DL, and Martinez JF: Compatibility of granisetron hydrochloride with selected drugs during simulated Y-site administration, *Am J Health-Syst Pharm 54*:56–60 (Jan 1) 1997.

2001. Zhang Y, Trissel LA, Martinez JF, et al.: Stability of metoclopramide hydrochloride in plastic syringes, *Am J Health-Syst Pharm 53*:1300–1302 (June 1) 1996.

2002. Kaijser GP, Aalbers T, Beijnen JH, et al.: Chemical stability of cyclophosphamide, trofosfamide, and 2- and 3-dechloroethylfosfamide in aqueous solutions, *J Oncol Pharm Pract 2*:15–21 (1) 1996.

2003. Nelson TJ and Graves SM: 0.9% Sodium chloride injection with and without heparin for maintaining peripheral indwelling intermittent-infusion devices in infants, *Am J Health-Syst Pharm 55*:570–573 (Mar 15) 1998.

2004. Martel P, Petit I, Pinguet F, et al.: Long-term stability of 5-fluorouracil stored in PVC bags and in ambulatory pump reservoirs, *J Pharm Biomed Anal 14*: 395–399 (Feb) 1996.

2005. Darbar D, Dell'Orto S, Wilkinson GR, et al.: Loss of quinidine gluconate injection in a polyvinyl chloride infusion system, *Am J Health-Syst Pharm 53*: 655–658 (Mar 15) 1996.

2006. Erkkila DM (Professional Services, Immunex Corporation): Personal communication, March 6, 1996.

2007. Xu QA, Trissel LA, Zhang Y, et al.: Stability of thiotepa (lyophilized) in 5% dextrose injection at 4 and 23 °C, *Am J Health-Syst Pharm 53*:2728–2730 (Nov 15) 1996.

2008. van Doorne H, Bernaards J, and de Jonge P: Ceftazidime degradation rates for predicting stability in a portable infusion-pump reservoir, *Am J Health-Syst Pharm 53*:1302–1305 (June 1) 1996.

2009. Celesk RA (Medical Services, Bayer Pharmaceutical Division): Personal communication, May 7, 1996.

2010. Grandison D (Worldwide Medical Affairs, Du Pont Pharma): Personal communication, December 4, 1995.

2011. Martinez JF, Trissel LA, and Gilbert DL: Compatibility of warfarin sodium with selected drugs and large-volume parenteral solutions, *Int J Pharm Compound 1*:356–358 (Sep–Oct) 1997.

2012. Williams DA: Zwitterions and pH-dependent solubility, *Am J Health-Syst Pharm 53*:1732 (July 15) 1996.

2013. Ariano RE, Kassum DA, Meatherhill RC, et al.: Lack of in vitro inactivation of tobramycin by imipenem/cilastatin, *Ann Pharmacother 26*:1075–1077 (Sep) 1992.

2014. Jenke DR: Drug binding by reservoirs in elastomeric devices, *Pharm Res 11*: 984–989 (7) 1994.

2015. McCollom RA, Lange B, Bryson SM, et al.: Polyvinylchloride containers do not influence the hemodynamic response to intravenous nitroglycerin, *Can J Hosp Pharm 46*:165–170 (Aug) 1993.

2016. Altavela JL, Haas CE, Nowak DR, et al.: Clinical response to intravenous nitroglycerin infused through polyethylene or polyvinyl chloride tubing, *Am J Hosp Pharm 51*:490–494 (Feb 15) 1994.

2017. McCullough JM, Sprentall-Nankervis E, Potcova CA, et al.: Recovery and biological activity of filgrastim after injection through silicone rubber catheters, *Am J Health-Syst Pharm 52*:186–188 (Jan 15) 1995.

2018. Park TW, Le-Bui LPK, Chung KC, et al.: Stability of piperacillin sodium–tazobactam sodium in peritoneal dialysis solutions, *Am J Health-Syst Pharm 52*:2022–2024 (Sep 15) 1995.

2019. Young D, Fadiran EO, Chang KT, et al.: Stability of ticarcillin disodium in polypropylene syringes, *Am J Health-Syst Pharm 52*:890, 892 (Apr 15) 1996.

2020. Stiles ML, Allen LV Jr, Resztak KE, et al.: Stability of octreotide acetate in polypropylene syringes, *Am J Hosp Pharm 50*:2356–2358 (Nov) 1993.

2021. Ripley RG, Ritchie DJ, and Holstad SG: Stability of octreotide acetate in polypropylene syringes at 5 and −20 °C, *Am J Health-Syst Pharm 52*:1910–1911 (Sep 1) 1995.

2022. Schepart BS, Burns BA, Evans S, et al.: Long-term stability of interferon alfa-2b diluted to 2 million units/mL, *Am J Health-Syst Pharm 52*:2128–2130 (Oct 1) 1995.

2023. Ikeda S, Frank PA, Schweiss JF, et al.: In vitro cyanide release from sodium nitroprusside in various intravenous solutions, *Anesth Analg 67*:360–362, 1988.

2024. Webster LK, Crinis NA, Davis JR, et al.: Conversion of etoposide phosphate to etoposide under ambulatory infusion conditions, *J Oncol Pharm Pract 1*: 33–36 (3) 1995.

2025. Hensrud DD, Burritt MF, and Hall LG: Stability of heparin anticoagulant activity over time in parenteral nutrition solutions, *J Parenter Enter Nutr 20*: 219–221 (May–June) 1996.

2026. Gutcher GR, Lax AA, and Farrell PM: Vitamin A losses to plastic intravenous infusion devices and an improved method of delivery, *Am J Clin Nutr 40*:8–13 (July) 1984.

2027. Greene HL, Phillips BL, Franck L, et al.: Persistently low blood retinol levels during and after parenteral feeding of very low birth weight infants: examination of losses into intravenous administration sets and a method of prevention by addition to a lipid emulsion, *Pediatrics 79*:894–900 (June) 1987.

2028. Henton DH and Merrott RJ: Vitamin A sorption to polyvinyl and polyolefin intravenous tubing, *J Parenter Enter Nutr 14*:79–81 (Jan–Feb) 1990.

2029. Washington C, Ferguson JA, and Irwin SE: Computational prediction of the stability of lipid emulsions in total nutrient admixtures, *J Pharm Sci 82*:808–812 (Aug) 1993.

2030. Li LC and Sampogna TP: A factorial design study on the physical stability of 3-in-1 admixtures, *J Pharm Pharmacol 45*:985–987, 1993.

2031. Foresta K: Use of total nutrient admixtures should not be limited, *Am J Health-Syst Pharm 52*:893 (Apr 15) 1995.

2032. Driscoll DF: Use of total nutrient admixtures should not be limited, *Am J Health-Syst Pharm 52*:893–894 (Apr 15) 1995.

2033. Mirtallo JM: Use of total nutrient admixtures should not be limited, *Am J Health-Syst Pharm 52*:894–895 (Apr 15) 1995.

2034. Trissel LA: Use of total nutrient admixtures should not be limited, *Am J Health-Syst Pharm 52*:895 (Apr 15) 1995.

2035. Driscoll DF: Debate on total nutrient admixtures continues, *Am J Health-Syst Pharm 52*:1921–1922 (Sep 1) 1995.

2036. Trissel LA: Debate on total nutrient admixtures continues, *Am J Health-Syst Pharm 52*:1921–1922 (Sep 1) 1995.

2037. Hill SE, Heldman LS, Goo EDH, et al.: Fatal microvascular pulmonary emboli from precipitation of a total nutrient admixture solution, *J Parenter Enter Nutr 20*:81–87 (Jan–Feb) 1996.

2038. MacKay MW, Fitzgerald KA, and Jackson D: The solubility of calcium and phosphate in two specialty amino acid solutions, *J Parenter Enter Nutr 20*: 63–66 (Jan–Feb) 1996.

2039. Shatsky F, McFeely EJ, and Takahashi D: A table for estimating calcium and phosphorus compatibility in parenteral nutrition formulas that contain Trophamine plus cysteine, *Hosp Pharm 30*:690–692, 723 (Aug) 1995.

2040. Grassby PF and Hutchings L: Factors affecting the physical and chemical stability of morphine sulphate solutions stored in syringes, *Int J Pharm Pract 2*:39–43 (Mar) 1993.

2041. Ritter H, Trissel LA, Anderson RW, et al.: Electronic balance as quality assurance for cytotoxic drug admixtures, *Am J Health-Syst Pharm 53*:2318–2320 (Oct 1) 1996.

2042. Roos PJ, Glerum JH, Meilink JW, et al.: Effect of pH on absorption of sufentanil citrate in a portable pump reservoir during storage and administration under simulated epidural conditions, *Pharm World Sci Ed 15*:139–144 (3) 1993.

2043. Trissel LA and Xu QA: Data on file, Pharmaceutical Analysis Laboratory, University of Texas, M. D. Anderson Cancer Center, Houston, Texas, July 30, 1997.

2044. Allen LV Jr, Stiles ML, Prince SJ, et al.: Stability of cefpirome sulfate in the presence of commonly used intensive care drugs during simulated Y-site injection, *Am J Health-Syst Pharm 52*:2427–2433 (Nov 1) 1995.

2045. Bureau A, Lahet JJ, D'Athis P, et al.: Compatibilite PVC-psychotropes au cours d'une perfusion, *J Pharm Clin 14*:26–30 (Mar) 1995.

2046. Streng WH and Brake NW: Dextrose adduct formation in aqueous teicoplanin solutions, *Pharm Res 6*:1032–1038 (Dec) 1989.

2047. Hixt U: L-Alanyl-L-glutamine dipeptide for parenteral nutrition, *Eur Hosp Pharm 2*:72–76 (May) 1996.

2048. Tivnann H, Gaines-Gas R, Thorpe R, et al.: An evaluation of the stability of granulocyte colony stimulating factor on the short-term storage and delivery from an elastomeric infusion system, *J Oncol Pharm Pract 2*:107–112 (2) 1996.

2049. Billion-Rey F, Guillaumont M, Frederich A, et al.: Stability of fat-soluble vitamins A (retinol palmitate), E (tocopherol acetate), and K1 (phylloquinone) in total parenteral nutrition at home, *J Parenter Enter Nutr 17*:56–60 (Jan–Feb) 1993.

2050. Dahl GB, Svensson L, Kinnander NJG, et al.: Stability of vitamins in soybean oil fat emulsion under conditions simulating intravenous feeding of neonates and children, *J Parenter Enter Nutr 18*:234–239 (May–June) 1994.

2051. Henry DW, Lacerte JA, Klutman NE, et al.: Irreversibility of procainamide-dextrose complex in plasma in vitro, *Am J Hosp Pharm 48*:2426–2429 (Nov) 1991.

2052. Martin M and Bepko R: Paclitaxel diluent and the case of the slippery spike, *Am J Hosp Pharm 51*:3078, 3080 (Dec 15) 1994.

2053. Faouzi MA, Dine T, Luyckx M, et al.: Leaching of diethylhexyl phthalate from PVC bags into intravenous teniposide solution, *Int J Pharm 105*:89–93 (Apr 25) 1994.

2054. Haas CE, Nowak DR, and Mabb WA: Effect of using a standard polyvinyl chloride intravenous infusion set on patient response to nitroglycerin, *Am J Hosp Pharm 49*:1135–1137 (May) 1992.

2055. Driver PS, Jarvi EJ, and Gratzer PL: Stability of nitroglycerin as nitroglycerin concentrate for injection stored in plastic syringes, *Am J Hosp Pharm 50*:2561–2563 (Nov) 1993.

2056. Casto DT: Stability of ondansetron stored in polypropylene syringes, *Ann Pharmacother 28*:712–714 (June) 1994.

2057. Bailey LC, Tang KT, and Rogozinski BA: Effect of syringe filter and i.v. administration set on delivery of propofol emulsion, *Am J Hosp Pharm 48*: 2627–2630 (Dec) 1991.

2058. Johnson CE, Christen C, Perez MM, et al.: Compatibility of bupivacaine hydrochloride and morphine sulfate, *Am J Health-Syst Pharm 54*:61–64 (Jan 1) 1997.

2059. Ambados F: Compatibility of ketamine hydrochloride and meperidine hydrochloride, *Am J Health-Syst Pharm 54*:205 (Jan 15) 1997.

2060. Hall PD, Yui D, Lyons S, et al.: Compatibility of filgrastim with selected antimicrobial drugs during simulated Y-site administration, *Am J Health-Syst Pharm 54*:185–189 (Jan 15) 1997.

2061. Fausel CA, Newton DW, Driscoll DF, et al.: Effect of fat emulsion and supersaturation on calcium phosphate solubility in parenteral nutrient admixtures, *Int J Pharm Compound 1*:54–59 (Jan–Feb) 1997.

2062. Chiu MF and Schwartz ML: Visual compatibility of injectable drugs used in the intensive care unit, *Am J Health-Syst Pharm 54*:64–65 (Jan 1) 1997.

2063. Najari Z and Rusho WJ: Compatibility of commonly used bone marrow transplant drugs during Y-site delivery, *Am J Health-Syst Pharm 54*:181–184 (Jan 15) 1997.

2064. Xu QA, Trissel LA, and Martinez JF: Rapid loss of fentanyl citrate admixed with fluorouracil in polyvinyl chloride containers, *Ann Pharmacother 31*:297–302 (Mar) 1997.

2065. Gilbert DL Jr, Trissel LA, and Martinez JF: Compatibility of ciprofloxacin lactate with sodium bicarbonate during simulated Y-site administration, *Am J Health-Syst Pharm 54*:1193–1195 (May 15) 1997.

2066. Trissel LA, Gilbert DL, and Martinez JF: Compatibility of propofol injectable emulsion with selected drugs during simulated Y-site administration, *Am J Health-Syst Pharm 54*:1287–1292 (June 1) 1997.

2067. Asker AF and Ferdous AJ: Photodegradation of furosemide solutions, *PDA J Pharm Sci Technol 50*:158–162 (May–June) 1996.

2068. Correction notice. Compatibility of meropenem with commonly used injectable drugs, *Am J Health-Syst Pharm*, 1998; 55:735 (Apr 1) 1998.

2069. Schobelock MJ (Medical Affairs Department, Roxane Laboratories, Inc.): Personal communication, November 4, 1997.

2070. Barnes AR and Nash S: Stability of bupivacaine hydrochloride and diamorphine hydrochloride in an epidural infusion, *Pharm World Sci 17*:87–92 (Mar) 1995.

2071. Grassby PF and Hutchings L: Drug combinations in syringe drivers: the compatibility and stability of diamorphine with cyclizine and haloperidol, *Palliat Med 11*:217–224, 1997.

2072. Cohen MR: Volume limitations for IV drug infusions when sterile water for injection is used as a diluent, *Hosp Pharm 33*:274–277 (March) 1998.

2073. Pierce LR, Gaines A. Hemolysis and renal failure associated with use of sterile water for injection to dilute 25% human albumin, *Am J Health-Syst Pharm 55*:1057, 1062, 1070 (May 15) 1998.

2074. Trissel LA, Martinez JF, and Gilbert DL: Compatibility of cisatracurium besylate with selected drugs during simulated Y-site administration, *Am J Health-Syst Pharm 54*:1735–1741 (Aug 1) 1997.

2075. Trissel LA, Gilbert DL, Martinez JF, et al.: Compatibility of remifentanil hydrochloride with selected drugs during simulated Y-site administration, *Am J Health-Syst Pharm 54*:2192–2196 (Oct 1) 1997.

2076. Ennis RD and Dahl TC: Stability of cidofovir in 0.9% sodium chloride injection for five days. *Am J Health-Syst Pharm 54*:2204–2206 (Oct 1) 1997.

2077. Murray KM, Erkkila D, Gombotz WR, et al.: Stability of thiotepa (lyophilized) in 0.9% sodium chloride injection, *Am J Health-Syst Pharm 54*:2588–2591 (Nov 15) 1997.

2078. Bahal SM, Lee TJ, McGinnes M, et al.: Visual compatibility of warfarin sodium injection with selected medications and solutions, *Am J Health-Syst Pharm 54*:2599–2600 (Nov 15) 1997.

2079. Nolan PE, Hoyer GL, LeDoux JH, et al.: Stability of ranitidine hydrochloride and human insulin in 0.9% sodium chloride injection, *Am J Health-Syst Pharm 54*:1304–1306 (June) 1997.

2080. Stiles ML and Allen LV: Stability of nafcillin sodium, oxacillin sodium, penicillin G potassium, penicillin G sodium, and tobramycin sulfate in polyvinyl chloride drug reservoirs, *Am J Health-Syst Pharm 54*:1068–1070 (May 1) 1997.

2081. Pujol M, Munoz M, Prat J, et al.: Stability study of epirubicin in NaCl 0.9% injection, *Ann Pharmacother 31*:992–995 (Sep) 1997.

2082. Walker SE, DeAngelis C, and Iazetta J: Stability and compatibility of combinations of hydromorphone and a second drug, *Can J Hosp Pharm 44*:289–295 (Dec) 1991.

2083. Fischer JH, Cwik MJ, Luer MS, et al.: Stability of fosphenytoin sodium with intravenous solutions in glass bottles, polyvinyl chloride bags, and polypropylene syringes, *Ann Pharmacother 31*:553–559 (May) 1997.

2084. Evrard B, Ceccato A, Gaspard O, et al.: Stability of ondansetron hydrochloride and dexamethasone sodium phosphate in 0.9% sodium chloride injection and in 5% dextrose injection, *Am J Health-Syst Pharm 54*:1065–1068 (May 1) 1997.

2085. Peddicord TE, Olsen KM, ZumBrunnen TL, et al.: Stability of high-concentration dopamine hydrochloride, norepinephrine bitartrate, epinephrine hydrochloride, and nitroglycerin in 5% dextrose injection, *Am J Health-Syst Pharm 54*:1417–1419 (June 15) 1997.

2086. Walker SE, Meinders A, and Tailor H: Stability and compatibility of reconstituted sterile hydromorphone with midazolam, *Can J Hosp Pharm 49*:290–298 (Dec) 1996.

2087. Trissel LA, Gilbert DL, and Martinez JF: Compatibility of doxorubicin hydrochloride liposome injection with selected other drugs during simulated Y-site administration, *Am J Health-Syst Pharm 54*:2708–2713 (Dec 1) 1997.

2088. Pramar YV, Loucas VA, and El-Rachidi A: Stability of midazolam hydrochloride in syringes and i.v. fluids, *Am J Health-Syst Pharm 54*:913–915 (Apr 15) 1997.

2089. Patel PR and Cook SE: Stability of meropenem in intravenous solutions, *Am J Health-Syst Pharm 54*:412–421 (Feb 15) 1997.

2090. Cornish LA, Montgomery PA, and Johnson CE: Stability of bumetanide in 5% dextrose injection, *Am J Health-Syst Pharm 54*:422–423 (Feb 15) 1997.

2091. Bailey LC and Orosz ST: Stability of ceftriaxone sodium and metronidazole hydrochloride, *Am J Health-Syst Pharm 54*:424–427 (Feb 15) 1997.

2092. Stewart JT, Warren FW, King DT, et al.: Stability of ondansetron hydrochloride, doxorubicin hydrochloride, and dacarbazine or vincristine sulfate in elastomeric portable infusion devices and polyvinyl chloride bags, *Am J Health-Syst Pharm 54*:915–920 (Apr 15) 1997.

2093. Owens D, Fleming RA, Restino MS, et al.: Stability of amphotericin B 0.05 and 0.5 mg/ml in 20% fat emulsion, *Am J Health-Syst Pharm 54*:683–686 (Mar 15) 1997.

2094. Zhang YP, Xu QA, Trissel LA, et al.: Compatibility and stability of paclitaxel combined with cisplatin and with carboplatin in infusion solutions, *Ann Pharmcother 31*:1465–1470 (Dec) 1997.

2095. Gupta VD, Maswoswe J, and Bailey RE: Stability of ketorolac tromethamine in 5% dextrose injection and 0.9% sodium chloride injections, *Int J Pharm Compound 1*:206–207 (May–June) 1997.

2096. Zhang YP and Trissel LA: Stability of aminocaproic acid injection admixtures in 5% dextrose injection and 0.9% sodium chloride injection, *Int J Pharm Compound 1*:132–134 (Mar–Apr) 1997.

2097. Allen LV and Stiles ML: Stability of vancomycin hydrochloride in medication cassette reservoirs, *Int J Pharm Compound 1*:123–124 (Mar–Apr) 1997.

2098. Zhang YP, Trissel LA, Martinez JF, et al.: Stability of acyclovir sodium 1, 7, and 10 mg/ml in 5% dextrose injection and 0.9% sodium chloride injection, *Am J Health-Syst Pharm 55*:574–577 (Mar 15) 1998.

2099. Amador FD, Azzati ES, Lopez-Coterilla AHT: Stability of carboplatin in polyvinyl chloride bags, *Am J Health-Syst Pharm 55*:602, 604 (Mar 15) 1998.

2100. Gupta VD, Maswoswe J, and Bailey RE: Stability of cefmetazole sodium in 5% dextrose injection and 0.9% sodium chloride injection, *Int J Pharm Compound 1*:208–209 (May–June) 1997.

2101. Gupta VD, Maswoswe J, and Bailey RE: Stability of ceftriaxone sodium when mixed with metronidazole injection, *Int J Pharm Compound 1*:280–281 (July–Aug) 1997.

2102. Gupta VD, Maswoswe J, and Bailey RE: Stability of cefepime hydrochloride in 5% dextrose injection and 0.9% sodium chloride injection, *Int J Pharm Compound 1*:435–436 (Nov–Dec) 1997.

2103. Mayhew SL and Quick MW: Compatibility of iron dextran with neonatal parenteral nutrient solutions, *Am J Health-Syst Pharm 54*:570–571 (Mar 1) 1997.

2104. Moshfeghi M and Ciuffo JD: Visual compatibility of fentanyl citrate with parenteral nutrient solutions, *Am J Health-Syst Pharm 55*:1194, 1197 (June 1) 1998.

2105. Gupta VD and Maswoswe J: Stability of indomethacin in 0.9% sodium chloride injection, *Int J Pharm Compound 2*:170–171 (Mar–Apr) 1998.

2106. Wong F and Gill MA: Stability of milrinone lactate 200 μg/mL in 5% dextrose injection and 0.9% sodium chloride injection, *Int J Pharm Compound 2*:168–169 (Mar–Apr) 1998.

2107. Nguyen D, Gill MA, and Wong F: Stability of milrinone lactate in 5% dextrose injection and 0.9% sodium chloride injection at concentrations of 400, 600, and 800 μg/mL, *Int J Pharm Compound 2*:246–248 (May–June) 1998.

2108. Montgomery PA, Cornish LA, Johnson CE, et al.: Stability of torsemide in 5% dextrose injection, *Am J Health-Syst Pharm 55*:1042–1043 (May 15) 1998.

2109. Trissel LA, Gilbert DL, Martinez JF, et al.: Compatibility of parenteral nutrient solutions with selected drugs during simulated Y-site administration, *Am J Health-Syst Pharm 54*:1295–1300 (June 1) 1997.

2110. Pramar YV: Chemical stability of amiodarone hydrochloride in intravenous fluids, *Int J Pharm Compound 1*:347–348 (Sep–Oct) 1997.

2111. Wang DP, Wang MT, Wong CY, et al.: Compatibility of vancomycin hydrochloride and famotidine in 5% dextrose injection, *Int J Pharm Compound 1*: 354–355 (Sep–Oct) 1997.

2112. Bhatt-Mehta V and Hirata S: Physical compatibility and chemical stability of atracurium besylate and midazolam hydrochloride during intravenous coinfusion, *Int J Pharm Compound 2*:79–82 (Jan–Feb) 1998.

2113. Stendal TL, Klem W, Tonnesen HH, et al.: Drug stability and pyridine generation in ceftazidime injection stored in an elastomeric infusion device, *Am J Health-Syst Pharm 55*:683–685 (Apr 1) 1998.

2114. Ketkar VA, Kolling WM, Nardviriyakul N, et al.: Stability of undiluted and diluted adenosine at three temperatures in syringes and bags, *Am J Health-Syst Pharm 55*:466–470 (Mar 1) 1998.

2115. Naud C, Marti B, Fernandez C, et al.: Stability of adenosine 6 μg/ml in 0.9% sodium chloride solution, *Am J Health-Syst Pharm 55*:1161–1164 (June 1) 1998.

2116. Xu QA, Zhang YP, Trissel LA, et al.: Stability of cisatracurium besylate in vials, syringes, and infusion admixtures, *Am J Health-Syst Pharm 55*:1037–1041 (May 15) 1998.

2117. Trissel LA, Gilbert DL, and Martinez JF: Incompatibility and compatibility of amphotericin B cholsteryl sulfate complex with selected other drugs during simulated Y-site administration, *Hosp Pharm 33*:284–292 (Mar) 1998.

2118. Allwood MC and Martin J: How does storage affect propofol? The stability of propofol in plastic syringes, *Pharm Pract 7*:15–16 (Jan) 1997.

2119. Harris MC and Como JA: Heparin flush solutions: how much is enough? *South J Health-Syst Pharm 2*:10–14 (Fall) 1997.

2120. Meyer BA, Little CJ, Thorp JA, et al.: Heparin versus normal saline as a peripheral line flush in maintenance of intermittent intravenous lines in obstetric patients, *Obstet Gynecol 5*:433–436 (Mar) 1995.

2121. Danek GD and Noris EM: Pediatric IV catheters: efficacy of saline flush, *Ped Nurs 8*:111–113 (Mar–Apr) 1992.

2122. Hok ML, Reuling J, Luettgen ML, et al.: Comparison of the patency of arterial lines maintained with heparinized and nonheparinized infusions, *Heart & Lung 16*:693–699 (Nov) 1987.

2123. Kulkarni M, Elsner C, Ouellet D, et al.: Heparinized saline versus normal saline in maintaining patency of the radial artery catheter, *Can J Surg 37*:37–42 (Feb) 1994.

2124. Clifton GD, Branson P, Kelly HJ, et al.: Comparison of normal saline and heparin solutions for maintenance of arterial catheter patency, *Heart & Lung 20*:115–118 (Mar) 1991.

2125. Butt W, Shann F, McDonnell G, et al.: Effect of heparin concentration and infusion rate on the patency of arterial catheters, *Crit Care Med 15*:230–232 (Mar) 1987.

2126. Smith S, Dawson S, Hennessey R, et al.: Maintenance of the patency of indwelling central venous catheters: is heparin necessary? *Am J Ped Hem/Onc 13*:141–143 (2) 1991.

2127. O'Neill TJ, Tierney LM, and Proulx RJ: Heparin lock-induced alterations in the activated partial thromboplastin time, *J Am Med Assoc 227*:1297–1298 (Mar 18) 1974.

2128. Passannante A and Macik BG: Case report: the heparin flush syndrome: a cause of iatrogenic hemorrhage, *Am J Med Sci 296*:71–73 (July) 1988.

2129. Heeger PS and Backstrom JT: Heparin flushes and thrombocytopenia, *Ann Intern Med 105*:143 (July) 1986.

2130. Laster J, Cikrit D, Walker N, et al.: The heparin-induced thrombocytopenia syndrome: an update, *Surgery 102*:763–770 (Oct) 1987.

2131. Rizzoni WE, Miller K, Rick M, et al.: Heparin-induced thrombocytopenia and thromboembolism in the postoperative period, *Surgery 103*:470–476 (Apr) 1988.

2132. Doty JR, Alving BM, McDonnell DE, et al.: Heparin-associated thrombocytopenia in the neurosurgical patient, *Neurosurgery 19*:69–72, 1986.

2133. Mehta AC and Kay EA: Storage time can be extended, *Pharm Pract 7*:305, 306, 308 (June) 1997.

2134. Brittain HG, Lafferty L, Bousserski P, et al.: Stability of Revex, nalmefene hydrochloride injection, *PDA J Pharm Sci Technol 50*:35–39 (Jan–Feb) 1996.

2135. McKinnon BT: FDA Safety Alert: hazards of precipitation associated with parenteral nutrition, *Nutr Clin Pract 11*:59–65 (Apr) 1996.

2136. Seidner DL, Speerhas R, and Trexler K: Can octreotide be added to parenteral nutrition? Point-counterpoint, *Nutr Clin Pract 13*:84–88 (Apr) 1998.

2137. Dodds HM, Craik DJ, and Rivory LP: Photodegradation of irinotecan (CPT-11) in aqueous solutions: identification of fluorescent products and influence of solution composition, *J Pharm Sci 86*:1410–1416 (Dec) 1997.

2138. Gremeau I, Sautou-miranda V, Picq F, et al.: Influence de la nature de la membrane sur le passage du nitrate d'isosorbide et de son metabolite actif au cours d'une dialyse, *J Pharm Clin 16*:19–23 (1) 1997.

2139. Graham AE, Speicher E, and Williamson B: Analysis of gentamicin sulfate and a study of its degradation in dextrose solution, *J Pharm Biomed Anal 15*: 537–543, 1997.

2140. Craig SB, Bhatt UH, and Patel K: Stability and compatibility of topotecan hydrochloride for injection with common infusion solutions and containers, *J Pharm Biomed Anal 16*:199–205, 1997.

2141. Pramar YV, Loucas VA, and Word D: Chemical stability and adsorption of atracurium besylate injections in disposable plastic syringes, *J Clin Pharm Ther 21*:173–175, 1996.

2142. Galanti LM, Hecq JD, Vanbeckbergen D, et al.: Long-term stability of cefuroxime and cefazolin sodium in intravenous infusions, *J Clin Pharm Ther 21*: 185–189, 1996.

2143. Kawano K, Takamatsu S, Mochizuku C, et al.: Loss of isosorbide dinitrate or nitroglycerin solution content in practice injection or precision continuous drip infusion, *Jpn J Hosp Pharm 22*:167–172 (2) 1996.

2144. Yoshida H, Takaba D, Uchida Y, et al.: Research for the crystal material produced in the continuous infusion line of midazloam (Dormicium) and butorphanol (Stadol), *Jpn J Hosp Pharm 23*:531–538 (6) 1997.

2145. Mawhinney WM, Adair CG, Gorman SP, et al.: Long-term stability of teicoplanin in dialysis fluid: implications for the home-treatment of CAPD peritonitis, *Int J Pharm Pract 1*:90–93 (Oct) 1991.

2146. Allwood MC and Martin H: The extraction of diethylhexylphthalate (DEHP) from polyvinyl chloride components of intravenous infusion containers and administration sets by paclitaxel injection, *Int J Pharm 127*:65–71, 1996.

2147. Valiere C, Arnaud P, Caroff E, et al.: Stability and compatibility study of a carboplatin solution in syringes for continuous ambulatory infusion, *Int J Pharm 138*:125–128, 1996.

2148. Khalfi F, Dine T, Gressier B, et al.: Compatibility and stability of vancomycin hydrochloride with PVC infusion material in various conditions using stability-indicating high-performance liquid chromatographic assay, *Int J Pharm 139*: 243–247, 1996.

2149. Hourcade F, Sautou-Miranda V, Normand B, et al.: Compatibility of granisetron towards glass and plastics and its stability under various storage conditions, *Int J Pharm 154*:95–102, 1997.

2150. Rabouan-Guyon SM, Guet AF, Courtois PY, et al.: Stability study of cefepime in different infusion solutions, *Int J Pharm 154*:185–190, 1997.

2151. Anon: How I survived a direct injection of potassium chloride, *Hosp Pharm 32*:298–300 (Mar) 1997.

2152. Kramer I: Stability of meropenem in elastomeric portable infusion devices, *Eur Hosp Pharm 3*:168–171 (Dec) 1997.

2153. Uges DRA and Ruige M: Vancomycin adsorption to teflon tubing, *Eur Hosp Pharm 2*:38 (Feb) 1996.

2154. Daouphars M, Vigneron J, Perrin A, et al.: Stability of cladribine in either polyethylene containers or polyvinyl chloride bags, *Europ Hosp Pharm 3*:154–156 (Sep) 1997.

2155. Girona V, Prat J, Pujol M, et al.: Stability of vinblastine sulphate in 0.9% sodium chloride in polypropylene syringes, *Boll Chim Farm 135*:413–414 (7) 1996.

2156. Smith BA, Hilmi SC, McDonald C, et al.: The stability of foscarnet in the presence of potassium, *Aust J Hosp Pharm 26*:560–561 (5) 1996.

2157. Jaffe GJ, Green GDJ, and Abrams GW: Stability of recombinant tissue plasminogen activator, *Am J Ophthal 108*:90–91 (July) 1989.

2158. Ward C and Weck S: Dilution and storage of recombinant tissue plasminogen

activator (Activase) in balanced salt solutions, *Am J Ophthal 109*:98–99 (Jan) 1990.
2159. Grewing R, Mester U, and Low M: Clinical experience with tissue plasminogen activator stored at –20 °C, *Ophthal Surg 23*:780–781 (Nov) 1992.
2160. Kramer I: Viability of microorganisms in novel antineoplastic and antiviral drug solutions, *J Oncol Pharm Pract 4*:32–37 (Mar) 1998.
2161. Schneider JJ, Wilson KM, and Ravenscroft PJ: A study of the osmolality and pH of subcutaneous drug infusion solutions, *Aust J Hosp Pharm 27*:29–31 (1) 1997.
2162. Vermeire A and Remon JP: The solubility of morphine and the stability of concentrated morphine solutions in glass, polypropylene syringes and PVC containers, *Int J Pharm 146*:213–223, 1997.
2163. Kearney MCJ, Allwood MC, Martin H, et al.: The influence of amino acid source on the stability of ascorbic acid in TPN mixtures, *Nutrition 14*:173–178 (2) 1998.
2164. Casasin Edo T, Roca Massa M, and Soy Munne D: Sistema de distribucion de medicamentos utilizados en anestesia mediante jeringas precargadas. Estudio de estabilidad, *Farm Hosp 20*:55–59 (1) 1996.
2165. Malcomson C, Zilka S, Saum J, et al.: Investigations into the compatibility of teicoplanin with heparin, *Eur J Parenter Sci 2*:51–55 (2) 1997.
2166. Walker SE, Walshaw PR, and Grad H: Imipenem stability and staining of teeth, *Can J Hosp Pharm 50*:61–67 (Apr) 1997.
2167. Gilbar P and McAllan Z: Ticarcillin-potassium clavulanate and vancomycin incompatibility, *Aust J Hosp Pharm 27*:470 (6) 1997.
2168. Burm JP: Stability of ondansetron and fluconazole in 5% dextrose injection and normal saline during Y-site administration, *Arch Pharm Res 20*:171–175 (2) 1997.
2169. Truelle-Hugon B, Tourrette G, Couineaux B, et al.: Etude de stabilite du chlorhydrate de morphine Lavoisier dans differents systemes actifs pour perfusion apres reconstitution dans divers solvents, *Ann Pharm Fr 55*:216–223 (5) 1997.
2170. Sitaram BR, Tsui M, Rawicki HB, et al.: Stability and compatibility of intrathecal admixtures containing baclofen and high concentrations of morphine, *Int J Pharm 153*:13–24, 1997.
2171. Trinkle R: Compatibility of hydromorphone and prochlorperazine, and irritation due to subcutaneous prochlorperazine infusion, *Ann Pharmacother 31*: 789–790 (Jun) 1997.
2172. Guchelar HJ and Hartog ME: De stabiliteit van clonazepaminjectievloeistof, *Ziekenhuisfarmacie 13*:21–23 (1) 1997.
2173. Leboucher G and Charpiat B: Incompatibilite physico-chimique entre l'omeprazole et la vancomycine, *Pharm Hosp Fr 121*:124, 1997.
2174. Taylor A: Review of clarithromycin mixtures, *Pharm Pract 7*:473, 474, 476 (Oct) 1997.
2175. Farhang-Asnafi S, Callaert S, Barre J, et al.: Influence du solvant de dilution sur la stabilite de la nouvelle forme de 5-fluorouracile en perfusion, *J Pharm Clin 16*:45–48 (1) 1997.
2176. Oustric-Mendes AC, Huart B, Le Hoang MD, et al.: Study protocol: stability of morphine injected without preservative, delivered with a disposable infusion device, *J Clin Pharm Ther 22*:283–290, 1997.
2177. Schoffski P, Freund M, Wunder R, et al.: Safety and toxicity of amphotericin B in glucose 5% or Intralipid 20% in neutropenic patients with pneumonia or fever of unknown origin: randomised study, *Br Med J 317*:379–384 (Aug 8) 1998.
2178. Heinemann V, Kahny B, Jehn U, et al.: Serum pharmacology of amphotericin B applied in lipid emulsions, *Antimicrob Agents Chemother 41*:728–732 (Apr) 1997.
2179. Gupta VD and Maswoswe J: Stability of mitomycin aqueous solution when stored in tuberculin syringes, *Int J Pharm Compound 1*:282–283 (July–Aug) 1997.
2180. Targett PL, Keefe PA, and Merridew CG: Compatibility and stability of drug adjuvants and morphine tartrate in 10 ml polypropylene syringes, *Aust J Hosp Pharm 27*:207–212 (3) 1997.
2181. Goren MP, Lyman BA, and Li JT: The stability of mesna in beverages and syrup for oral administration, *Cancer Chemother Pharmacol 28*:298–301, 1991.
2182. Xu QA, Trissel LA, and Davis MR: Compatibility of paclitaxel in 5% glucose and 0.9% sodium chloride injections with EVA minibags, *Aust J Hosp Pharm 28*:156–159 (3) 1998.
2183. Xu QA, Zhang YP, Trissel LA, et al.: Stability of busulfan injection admixtures in 5% dextrose injection and 0.9% sodium chloride injection, *J Oncol Pharm Pract 2*:101–105 (2) 1996.
2184. Sarver JG, Pryka R, Alexander KS, et al.: Stability of magnesium sulfate in 0.9% sodium chloride and lactated Ringer's solutions, *Int J Pharm Compound 2*:385–388 (Sep–Oct) 1998.
2185. Jobet-Hermelin I, Mallvais ML, Jacquot C, et al.: Proposition d'une concentration limite acceptable du plastifiant librere par le poly(chlorure de vinyle) dans les solutions injectables aqueuses, *J Pharm Clin 15*:132–136 (2) 1996.
2186. Jacobsen PA, West NJ, Spadoni V, et al.: Sterility of filgrastim (G-CSF) in syringes, *Ann Pharmacother 30*:1238–1242 (Nov) 1996.
2187. Trissel LA and Spadoni VT: Comment: filgrastim sterility in syringes, *Ann Pharmacother 31*:500–501 (Apr) 1997.
2188. Appenheimer MM, Schepart BS, Poleon GP, et al.: Stability of albumin-free interferon alfa-2b for 42 days, *Am J Health-Syst Pharm 55*:1602–1605 (Aug 1) 1998.
2189. Trissel LA, Gilbert DL, and Martinez JF: Concentration dependency of vancomycin hydrochloride compatibility with beta-lactam antibiotics during simulated Y-site administration, *Hosp Pharm 33*:1515–1522 (Dec) 1998.
2190. McLaughlin JP, Simpson C, and Taylor RA: How stable is acyclovir in PVC bags? The stability of reconstituted acyclovir sodium in a 0.9% w/v sodium chloride infusion when stored at room temperature, *Pharm Pract 5*:53–58 (Feb) 1995.
2191. Mehta AC and Kay EA: How stable is alfentanil? Stability of alfentanil hydrochloride in 5% dextrose stored in syringes, *Pharm Pract 5*:303–304 (July–Aug) 1995.
2192. McLaughlin JP, Simpson C, and Taylor RA: How stable are Zinacef & Metrovex? The stability of cefuroxime sodium and metronidazole infusion when stored in a refrigerator, *Pharm Pract 5*:100–106 (Mar) 1995.
2193. Bonferoni MC, Mellerio G, Giunchedi P, et al.: Photostability evaluation of nicardipine HCl solutions, *Int J Pharm 80*:109–117, 1992.
2194. Erdman SH, McElwee CL, Kramer JM, et al.: Central line occlusion with three-in-one nutrition admixtures administered at home, *J Parenter Enter Nutr 18*:177–181 (2) 1994.
2195. Allwood MC and Martin H: Factors influencing the stability of ranitidine in TPN mixtures, *Clin Nutr 14*:171–176, 1995.
2196. Hoie EB and Narducci WA: Laser particle analysis of calcium phosphate precipitate in neonatal TPN admixtures, *J Ped Pharm Pract 1*:163–167 (Nov–Dec) 1996.
2197. Ambados F and Brealey J: Incompatibilities with trace elements during TPN solution admixture, *Aust J Hosp Pharm 28*:112–114 (2) 1998.
2198. Xu QA and Trissel LA: Compatibility of paclitaxel injection diluent with two reduced-phthalate administration sets for the Acclaim pump, *Int J Pharm Compound 2*:382–384 (Sep–Oct) 1998.
2199. Stewart JT, Warren FW, King DT, et al.: Stability of ondansetron hydrochloride and 12 medications in plastic syringes, *Am J Health-Syst Pharm 55*:2630–2634 (Dec 15) 1998.
2200. Donnelly RF and Bushfield TL: Chemical stability of meperidine hydrochloride in polypropylene syringes, *Int J Pharm Compound 2*:463–465 (Nov–Dec) 1998.
2201. Jappinen AL, Kokki H, Rasi AS, et al.: Stability of sufentanil in a syringe pump under simulated epidural infusion, *Int J Pharm Compound 2*:466–468 (Nov–Dec) 1998.
2202. Wilson KM, Schneider JJ, and Ravenscroft PJ: Stability of midazolam and fentanyl in infusion solutions, *J Pain Symptom Manage 16*:52–58 (July) 1998.
2203. Gupta VD and Pramar Y: Stability of lorazepam in 5% dextrose injection, *Int J Pharm Compound 2*:322–324 (July–Aug) 1998.
2204. Heide PE: Precipitation of amphotericin B from i.v. fat emulsion, *Am J Health-Syst Pharm 54*:1449 (June 15) 1997.
2205. Heide PE and Hehenberger H: Tensiometrische und konduktometrische stabilitatuntersuchungen von amphotericin B in fettmulsionen, *Oesterreichische Krankenhaus Pharmazie 10*:36–43 (3) 1996.
2206. To TP and Garrett MK: Stability of flucloxacillin in a hospital in the home program, *Aust J Hosp Pharm 28*:289–290 (4) 1998.
2207. Levanda M: Noticeable difference in admixtures prepared from lorazepam 2 and 4 mg/ml, *Am J Health-Syst Pharm 55*:2305 (Nov 1) 1998.
2208. Share MJ, Harrison RD, Folstad J, et al.: Stability of lorazepam 1 and 2 mg/ml in glass bottles and polypropylene syringes, *Am J Health-Syst Pharm 55*: 2013–2015 (Oct 1) 1998.
2209. Inagaki K, Kambara M, Mizuno M, et al.: Compatibility and stability of ranitidine hydrochloride with six cephalosporins during simulated Y-site administration, *Int J Pharm Compound 2*:318–321 (July–Aug) 1998.
2210. Ray LR and Chen DA: Stability of somatropin stored in plastic syringes for 28 days, *Am J Health-Syst Pharm 55*:1508–1511 (Jul 15) 1998.
2211. Patel K, Craig SB, McBride MG, et al.: Microbial inhibitory properties and stability of topotecan hydrochloride injection, *Am J Health-Syst Pharm 55*: 1584–1587 (Aug 1) 1998.
2212. English BA, Riggs RM, Webster AA, et al.: Y-site stability of fosphenytoin and sodium phenobarbital, *Int J Pharm Compound 3*:64–66 (Jan–Feb) 1999.
2213. Lieu CL, Chin A, and Gill MA: Five-day stability of vinorelbine in 5% dex-

trose injection and in 0.9% sodium chloride injection at room temperature, *Int J Pharm Compound 3*:67–68 (Jan–Feb) 1999.

2214. Akkerman SR, Zhang H, Mullins RE, et al.: Stability of milrinone lactate in the presence of 29 critical care drugs and 4 i.v. solutions, *Am J Health-Syst Pharm 56*:63–68 (Jan 1) 1999.

2215. Trissel LA, Gilbert DL, Martinez JF, et al.: Compatibility of medications with 3-in-1 parenteral nutrition admixtures, *J Parenter Enter Nutr 23*:67–74 (2) 1999.

2216. Johnson CE, vandenBussche HL, Chio CC, et al.: Stability of tacrolimus with morphine sulfate, hydromorphone hydrochloride, and ceftazidime during simulated intravenous coadministration, *Am J Health-Syst Pharm 56*:164–169 (Jan 15) 1999.

2217. Stamatakis MK, Leader WG, and Tracy TS: Stability of high-dose vancomycin and ceftazidime in peritoneal dialysis solutions, *Am J Health-Syst Pharm 56*: 246–248 (Feb 1) 1999.

2218. Trissel LA, Martinez JF, and Simmons M: Compatibility of etoposide phosphate with selected drugs during simulated Y-site injection, *J Am Pharm Assoc 39*:141–145 (Mar–Apr) 1999.

2219. Zhang Y and Trissel LA: Physical and chemical stability of etoposide phosphate solutions, *J Am Pharm Assoc 39*:146–150 (Mar–Apr) 1999.

2220. Stewart JT, Warren FW, and Maddox FC: Stability of cefepime hydrochloride injection in polypropylene syringes at –20 °C, 4 °C, and 22–24 °C, *Am J Health Syst Pharm 56*:457–459 (Mar 1) 1999.

2221. Stewart JT, Maddox FC, and Warren FW: Stability of cefepime hydrochloride in polypropylene syringes, *Am J Health-Syst Pharm 56*:1134 (June 1) 1999.

2222. Burkiewicz JS: Incompatibility of ceftriaxone sodium with lactated Ringer's injection, *Am J Health-Syst Pharm 56*:384 (Feb 15) 1999.

2223. Riggs RM, English BA, Webster AA, et al.: Fosphenytoin Y-site stability studies with lorazepam and midazolam hydrochloride, *Int J Pharm Compound 3*:235–238 (May–June) 1999.

2224. Trissel LA, Gilbert DL, and Wolkin AC: Compatibility of docetaxel with selected drugs during simulated Y-site administration, *Int J Pharm Compound 3*:241–244 (May–Jun) 1999.

2225. Johnson CE and Truong NM: Stability and compatibility of tacrolimus and fluconazole in 0.9% sodium chloride, *J Am Pharm Assoc 39*:505–508 (July–Aug) 1999.

2226. Trissel LA, Martinez JF, and Gilbert DL: Compatibility of gemcitabine hydrochloride with 107 selected drugs during simulated Y-site injection, *J Am Pharm Assoc 39*:514–518 (July–Aug) 1999.

2227. Xu Q, Zhang Y, and Trissel LA: Physical and chemical stability of gemcitabine hydrochloride solutions, *J Am Pharm Assoc 39*:509–513 (July–Aug) 1999.

2228. Walker SE, Gray S, and Schmidt B: Stability of reconstituted indomethacin sodium trihydrate in original vials and polypropylene syringes, *Am J Health-Syst Pharm 55*:154–158 (Jan 15) 1998.

2229. Schlatter J and Saulnier JL: Inline filtration of ranitidine hydrochloride solutions, *Am J Health-Syst Pharm 55*:840, 843 (Apr 15) 1998.

2230. Zhang Y, Trissel LA, and Xu QA: Paclitaxel compatibility with a triple-lumen polyurethane central catheter, *Hosp Pharm 33*:547–551 (May) 1998.

2231. Xu QA, Trissel LA, and Zhang Y: Paclitaxel compatibility with the IV Express filter unit, *Int J Pharm Compound 2*:243–245 (May–Jun) 1998.

2232. Xu QA, Trissel LA, and Gilbert DL: Paclitaxel compatibility with a TOTM-plasticized PVC administration set, *Hosp Pharm 32*:1635–1638 (Dec) 1997.

2233. Saltsman CL, Tom CM, Mitchell A, et al.: Compatibility of levofloxacin with 34 medications during simulated Y-site administration, *Am J Health-Syst Pharm 56*:1458–1459 (Jul 15) 1999.

2234. Trissel LA, Gilbert DL, and Williams KY: Compatibility screening of gatifloxacin during simulated Y-site administration with other drugs, *Hosp Pharm 34*:1409–1416 (Dec) 1999.

2235. Voytilla KL, Rusho WJ, and Tyler LS: Compatibility of alatrofloxacin mesylate with commonly used drugs during Y-site delivery, *Am J Health-Syst Pharm 57*:1437–1439 (Aug 1) 2000.

2236. Johnson CE and Truong NM: Stability and compatibility of tacrolimus and fluconazole in 0.9% sodium chloride, *J Am Pharm Assoc 39*:505–508 (Jul/Aug) 1999.

2237. Xu QA, Trissel LA, and Gilbert DL: Stability of amphotericin B cholesteryl sulfate comples after reconstitution and admixture, *Hosp Pharm 33*:1203–1207 (Oct) 1998.

2238. Balthasar JP: Concentration-dependent incompatibility of vinorelbine tartrate and heparin sodium, *Am J Health-Syst Pharm 56*:1891 (Sep 15) 1999.

2239. Wolfe JL, Thoma LA, Du C, et al.: Compatibility and stability of vincristine sulfate, doxorubicin hydrochloride, and etoposide in 0.9% sodium chloride injection, *Am J Health-Syst Pharm 56*:985–989 (May 15) 1999.

2240. Peek BT, Webster KD, and Da Camara CC: Stability and compatibility of promethazine hydrochloride and dihydroergotamine mesylate in combination, *Am J Health-Syst Pharm 56*:1835–1838 (Sep 15) 1999.

2241. Webster AA, English BA, McGuire JM, et al.: Stability of dobutamine hydrochloride 4 mg/ml in 5% dextrose injection at 5 and 23 (C, *Int J Pharmaceut Compound 3*:412–414 (Sep/Oct) 1999.

2242. Thiesen J and Kramer I: Physico-chemical stability of docetaxel premix solution and docetaxel infusion solutions in PVC bags and polyolefine containers, *Pharm World Sci 21*:137–141 (Jun) 1999.

2243. Kramer I and Thiesen J: Stability of topotecan infusion solutions in polyvinylchloride bags and elastomeric portable infusion devices, *J Oncol Pharm Pract 5*:75–82 (2) 1999.

2244. Hecq JD, Evrard JM, Gillet P, et al.: Etude de stabilite visuelle du chlorydrate de chlorpromazine, du chlorure de potassium, de la furosemide et de l'heparine sodique en perfusion continue, *Pharmakon 116*:145–148 (Dec) 1998.

2245. Mayron D and Gennaro AR: Stability and compatibility of topotecan hydrochloride with selected drugs, *Am J Health-Syst Pharm 56*:875–881 (May 1) 1999.

2246. Harvey SC, Toussaint CP, Coe SE, et al.: Stability of meperidine in an implantable infusin pump using capillary gas chromatography-mass spectrometry and a deuterated internal standard, *J Pharmaceut Biomed Anal 21*:577(583, 1999.

2247. Trissel LA, Xu QA, and Gilbert DL: Compatibility and stability of paclitaxel combined with doxorubicin hydrochloride in infusion solutions, *Ann Pharmacother 32*:1013–1016 (Oct) 1998.

2248. Trissel LA: Data on file, Pharmaceutical Analysis Laboratory, University of Texas, M. D. Anderson Cancer Center, Houston, Texas.

2249. Bergquist PA, Zimmerman J, Kenney RR, et al.: Stability of tirofiban hydrochloride in three commonly used i.v. solutions and polyvinyl chloride administration sets, *Am J Health-Syst Pharm 56*:1627–1629 (Aug 15) 1999.

2250. Bergquist PA, Hunke WA, Reed RA, et al.: Compatibility of tirofiban HCl with dopamine HCl, famotidine, sodium heparin, lidocaine HCl and potassium chloride during simulated Y-site administration, *J Clin Pharm Ther 24*:125–132, 1999.

2251. McLaughlin JP and Simpson C: How stable is ganciclovir? *Pharm Pract 8*: 329–330, 332 (Sep) 1998.

2252. Galanti LM, Hecq JD, Vanbeckbergen D, et al.: Long-term stability of vancomycin hydrochloride in intravenous infusions, *J Clin Pharm Ther 22*:353–356, 1997.

2253. Hor MMS, Chan SY, Yow KL, et al.: Stability of admixtures of pethidine and metoclopramide in aqueous solution, 5% dextrose and 0.9% sodium chloride, *J Clin Pharm Ther 22*:339–345, 1997.

2254. Hor MMS, Chan SY, Yow KL, et al.: Stability of morphine sulphate in saline under simulated patient administration conditions. *J Clin Pharm Ther 22*:405–410, 1997.

2255. Mittner A, Vincze Z, and Jemnitz K: Stability of cyclophosphamide containing infusions, *Pharmazie 54*:224–225 (3) 1999.

2256. Mittner A, Vincze Z, and Jemnitz K: Stability of vinblastine sulphate containing infusions, *Pharmazie 54*:625–626 (8) 1999.

2257. Schrijvers D, Tai-Apin C, De Smet MC, et al.: Determination of compatibility and stability of drugs used in palliative care, *J Clin Pharm Ther 23*:311–314, 1998.

2258. Kopelent-Frank H and Schimper A: HPTLC-based stability assay for the determination of amiodarone in intravenous admixtures, *Pharmazie 54*:542–544 (7) 1999.

2259. Inagaki K, Miyamoto Y, Kurata N, et al.: Stability of ranitidine hydrochloride with cefazolin sodium, cefbuperazone sodium, cefoxitin sodium, and cephalothin sodium during simulated Y-site administration, *Int J Pharmaceut Compound 4*:150–153 (Mar/Apr) 2000.

2260. Roy JJ and Hildgen P: Stability of morphine-ketamine mixtures in 0.9% sodium chloride injection packaged in syringes, plastic bags and Medication Cassette reservoirs, *Int J Pharmaceut Compound 4*:225–228 (May/June) 2000.

2261. Grant EM, Zhong MK, Ambrose PG, et al.: Stability of meropenem in a portable infusion device in a cold pouch, *Am J Health-Syst Pharm 57*:992–995 (May 15) 2000.

2262. Xu QA, Trissel LA, and Williams KY: Compatibility and stability of linezolid injection admixed with three cephalosporins antibiotics, *J Am Pharm Assoc 40*:509–514 (Jul/Aug) 2000.

2263. Zhang Y, Xu QA, Trissel LA, et al.: Compatibility and stability of linezolid injection admixed with aztreonam or piperacillin sodium, *J Am Pharm Assoc 40*:520–514 (Jul/Aug) 2000.

2264. Trissel LA, Williams KY, and Gilbert DL: Compatibility screening of linezolid injection during simulated Y-site administration with other drugs and infusion solutions, *J Am Pharm Assoc 40*:515–519 (Jul/Aug) 2000.

2265. Zhang Y, Xu QA, Trissel LA, et al.: Physical compatibility of calcium acetate

and potassium phosphates in parenteral nutrition solutions containing Aminosyn II, *Int J Pharmaceut Compound 3*:415–420 (Sep–Oct) 1999.
2266. Ambados F and Brealey J: Precipitation of potassium sulphate during TPN solution admixture, *Aust J Hosp Pharm 28*:444 (6) 1998.
2267. Ambados F: Destabilization of fat emulsion in total nutrient admixtures by concentrated albumin 20% infusion, *Aust J Hosp Pharm 29*:210–212 (4) 1999.
2268. Peterson GM, Miller KA, Galloway JG, et al.: Compatibility and stability of fentanyl admixtures in polypropylene syringes, *J Clin Pharm Ther 23*:67–72, 1998.
2269. Picard C, Hary L, Bou P, et al.: Stability of three aminoglycoside solutions in PVC and multilayer infusion bags, *Pharmazie 54*:854–856 (11) 1999.
2270. Shella C: How to shake insulin, *Hosp Pharm 34*:518 (May) 1999.
2271. Bjorkman S and Roth B: Chemical compatibility of mitoxantrone and etoposide (VP-16), *Acta Pharm Nord 3*:251 (4) 1991.
2272. Charland SL, Davis DD, and Tillman DJ: Activity of enoxaparin sodium in tuberculin syringes for 10 days, *Am J Health-Syst Pharm 55*:1296–1298 (June 15) 1998.
2273. Couldry R, Sanborn M, Klutman NE, et al.: Continuous infusion of ceftazidime with an elastomeric infusion device, *Am J Health-Syst Pharm 55*:145–149 (Jan 15) 1998.
2274. Tanoue N, Kishita S, Shiotsu K, et al.: Compatibility of irinotecan hydrochloride injection with other injections, *Jpn J Hosp Pharm 24*:420–428 (4) 1998.
2275. Stiles ML, Allen LV Jr, and McLaury HJ: Stability of two concentrations of heparin sodium prefilled in CADD-Micro pump syringes, *Int J Pharmaceut Compound 1*:433–434 (Nov–Dec) 1997.
2276. Nii LJ, Chin A, Cao TM, et al.: Stability of sumatriptan succinate in polypropylene syringes, *Am J Health-Syst Pharm 56*:983–985 (May 15) 1999.
2277. Proot P, van Schepdael A, Raymakers AA, et al.: Stability of adenosine in infusion, *Int J Pharmaceut Biomed Anal 17*:415–418, 1998.
2278. Biellmann-Berlaud V and Willemin JC: Stabilite de la vancomycine en poches de polyolefine ou polychlorure de vinyle et en flacons de verre, *J Pharm Clin 17*:145–148 (3) 1998.
2279. Mayer JLR, Pascale VJ, Clyne LP, et al.: Stability of low-dose vancomycin hydrochloride in heparin sodium 100 IU/ml, *J Pharm Tech 15*:13–17 (Jan–Feb) 1999.
2280. Demange C, Vailleau JL, Wacquier S, et al.: Etude de photosensibilite et fixation de la chlorpromazine sur le chlorure de polyvinyle pour administration en perfusion intraveineuse, *J Pharm Clin 17*:77–82 (2) 1998.
2281. Saito H, Tanida N, Inukai K, et al.: Stability of iphosphamide and mesna in mixed infusion solutions, *Jpn J Hosp Pharm 24*:96–99 (1) 1998.
2282. Silvers KM, Darlow BA, and Winterbourn CC: Pharmacologic levels of heparin do not destabilize neonatal parenteral nutrition, *J Parenter Enter Nutr 22*: 311–314 (Sep–Oct) 1998.
2283. Williamson JC, Volles DF, Lynch PLM, et al.: Stability of cefepime in peritoneal dialysis solution, *Ann Pharmacother 33*:906–909 (Sep) 1999.
2284. Kramer I and Maas B: Compatibility of amsacrine (Amsidyl) concentrate for infusion with polypropylene syringes, *Pharmazie 54*:538–541 (7) 1999.
2285. Farina A, Porra R, Cotichini V, et al.: Stability of reconstituted solutions of ceftazidime for injections: an HPLC and CE approach, *J Pharmaceut Biomed Anal 20*:521–530, 1999.
2286. Yokoyama H, Aoyama T, Matsuyama T, et al.: The cause of polyurethane catheter cracking during constant infusion of etoposide (VP-16) injection, *Yakugaku Zasshi 118*:581–588 (12) 1998.
2287. Torres-Bondia FI, Carmona-Ibanez G, Guevara-Serrano J, et al.: Estabilidad del valproate sodico en fluidos intravenosos, *Farm Hosp 23*:320–322 (5) 1999.
2288. Priston MJ and Sewell GJ: Stability of three cytotoxic drug infusions in the Graseby 9000 ambulatory infusion pump, *J Oncol Pharm Pract 4*:143–149 (3) 1998.
2289. Zeidler C, Dettmering D, Schrammel W, et al.: Compatibility of various drugs used in intensive care medicine in polyethylene, PVC, and glass infusion containers, *Europ Hosp Pharm 5*:106–110 (3) 1999.
2290. Trissel LA: Data on file, Pharmaceutical Analysis Laboratory, University of Texas, M. D. Anderson Cancer Center, Houston, Texas.
2291. Shay DK, Fann LM, and Jarvis WR: Respiratory distress and sudden death associated with receipt of a peripheral parenteral nutrition admixture, *Infect Control Hosp Epidemiol 18*:814–817 (Dec) 1997.
2292. Zhan X, Yin G, and Ma B: Improved stability of 25% vitamin C parenteral formulation, *Int J Pharm 173*:43–49, 1998.
2293. Mittner A, Vincze Z, and Jemnitz K: Stability of cisplatin containing infusions, *Pharmazie 53*: 490–492 (7) 1998.
2294. Carleton BC, Primmett DRN, Levine M, et al.: Sterility of unit-dosing filgrastim (G-CSF), *J Ped Pharm Pract 4*:68–74 (Mar–Apr) 1999.
2295. Oliva A, Santovena A, Llabres M, et al.: Stability study of human albumin pharmaceutical preparations, *J Pharm Pharmacol 51*:385–392, 1999.
2296. Stephens D, Bares D, Robinson D, et al.: Determination of amylose/particulate relationship in hydroxyethylstarch, *PDA J Pharm Sci Tech 53*:181–185 (July–Aug) 1999.
2297. Parsons TJ, Upton RN, Martinez AM, et al.: No loss of undiluted propofol by sorption into administration systems, *Pharm Pharmacol Commun 5*:377–381, 1999.
2298. Brigas F, Sautou-Miranda V, Normand B, et al.: Compatibility of tropisetron with glass and plastics. Stability under different storage conditions. *J Pharm Pharmacol 50*:407–411, 1998.
2299. Tse CST: Dissolving phenytoin precipitate in central venous access device, *Ann Intern Med 128*:1049 (June 15) 1998.
2300. Akinwande KI and Keehn DM: Dissolution of phenytoin precipitate with sodium bicarbonate in an occluded central venous access device, *Ann Pharmacother 29*:707–709 (July–Aug) 1995.
2301. Fuloria M, Friedberg MA, DuRant RH, et al.: Effect of flow rate and insulin priming on the recovery of insulin from microbore infusion tubing, *Pediatrics 102*:1401–1406 (Dec) 1998.
2302. Muller HJ and Frank C: Stabilitatstudie zu pentoxifyllin im PVC-infusionsbeutel, *Krankenhauspharmazie 19*:469–472 (10) 1998.
2303. Stahlmann SA, Frey OR, and Kovar KA: Stabilitatstudie zu fosfomycin-dinatrium (Fosfocin p.i. 5,0) in applikationfertigen perfusorspritzen, *Krankenhauspharmazie 19*:553–557 (12) 1998.
2304. Muller HJ and Frank C: Stabilitatstudie zu alizaprid im PVC-infusionsbeutel, *Krankenhauspharmazie 20*:55–58 (2) 1999.
2305. Sattler A, Jage J, and Kramer I: Physico-chemical stability of infusion solutions for epidural administration containing fentanyl and bupivacaine or lidocaine, *Pharmazie 53*:386–391 (6) 1998.
2306. Laborie S, Lavoie JC, Pineault M, et al.: Protecting solutions of parenteral nutrition from peroxidation, *J Parenter Enter Nutr 23*:104–108 (Mar–Apr) 1999.
2307. Wakiya Y, Saiki A, Kondou N, et al.: Stability of vitamins in the TPN mixture at a clinical site, *Jpn J Hosp Pharm 25*:40–47 (1) 1999.
2308. Pertkkiewicz M, Knyt A, Majewska K, et al.: Badania stabilnosci mieszanin odzywczych z Aminomel 10%E i Aminomel 12,5%E oraz emulsja tluszczowa Ivelip 10% i 20%, *Farm Polska 55*:756–763 (16) 1999.
2309. Brawley V, Bhatia J, and Karp WB: Effect of sodium metabisulfite on hydrogen peroxide production in light-exposed pediatric parenteral amino acid solutions, *Am J Health-Syst Pharm 55*:1288–1292 (June 15) 1998.
2310. Brawley V, Bhatia J, and Karp WB: Hydrogen peroxide generation in a model paediatric parenteral amino acid solution, *Clin Sci 85*:709–712, 1993.
2311. Driscoll DF, Lawrence KR, Lewis K, et al.: Particle size distribution of propofol injection from ampules and vials: the benefits of filtration, *Int J Pharmaceut Compound 1*:118–120 (Mar–Apr) 1997.
2312. Malesker MA, Malone PM, Cingle CM, et al.: Extravasation of i.v. promethazine, *Am J Health-Syst Pharm 56*:1742–1743 (Sep 1) 1999.
2313. Boersma HH, Groothuijsen HJG, Stolk LML, et al.: Loed loudbaar onder normale omstandigheden, *Pharmaceut Weekblad 134*:1444–1448 (42) 1999.
2314. Trissel LA: Data on file, Pharmaceutical Analysis Laboratory, University of Texas, M. D. Anderson Cancer Center, Houston, Texas.
2315. Khalfi F, Dine T, Gressier B, et al.: Compatibility of cefpirome and cephalothin with PVC bags during simulated infusion and storage, *Pharmazie 53*:112–116 (2) 1998.
2316. Laborie S, Lavoie JC, Pineault M, et al.: Contribution of multivitamins, air, and light in the generation of peroxides in adult and neonatal parenteral nutrition solutions, *Ann Pharmacother 34*:440–445 (Apr) 2000.
2317. Laborie S, Lavoie JC, and Chessex P: Paradoxical role of ascorbic acid and riboflavin in solutions of total parenteral nutrition: implication in photoinduced peroxide generation, *Pediat Res 43*:601–606 (5) 1998.
2318. Rhoney DH, Coplin WM, and Zaran FK: Urokinase activity after freezing: implications for thrombolysis in intraventricular hemorrhage, *Am J Health-Syst Pharm 56*:2047–2051 (Oct 15) 1999.
2319. Hrubisko M, McGown AT, Prendiville JA, et al.: Suitability of cisplatin solutions for 14-day continuous infusion by ambulatory pump, *Cancer Chemother Pharmacol 29*:252–255, 1992.
2320. Dine T, Khalfi F, Gressier B, et al.: Stability study of fotemustine in PVC infusion bags and sets under various conditions using a stability-indicating high-performance liquid chromatographic assay, *J Pharmaceut Biomed Anal 18*:373–381, 1998.
2321. Hadfield JA, McGown AT, Dawson MJ, et al.: The suitability of carboplatin solutions for 14-day continuous infusion by ambulatory pump: an HPLC-dynamic FAB study, *J Pharmaceut Biomed Anal 11*:723–727 (8) 1993.
2322. Frey OR and Maier L: Polyethylene vials of calcium gluconate reduce aluminum contamination of TPN, *Ann Pharmacother 34*:811–812 (June) 2000.

2323. Louie S, Chin A, and Gill M: Activity of dalteparin sodium in polypropylene syringes, *Am J Health-Syst Pharm 57*:760–762 (Apr 15) 2000.

2324. Stewart JT, Maddox FC, and Warren FW: Stability of cefepime hydrochloride injection and metronidazole in polyvinyl chloride bags at 4° and 22°–24° C, *Hosp Pharm 35*:1057–1064 (Oct) 2000.

2325. Ling J and Gupta VD: Stability of nafcillin sodium after reconstitution in 0.9% sodium chloride injection and storage in polypropylene syringes for pediatric use, *Int J Pharmaceut Compound 4*:480–481 (Nov–Dec) 2000.

2326. Gupta VD: Stability of levothyroxine sodium injection in polypropylene syringes, *Int J Pharmaceut Compound 4*:482–483 (Nov–Dec) 2000.

2327. Davis SN, Vermeulen L, Banton J, et al.: Activity and dosage of alteplase dilution for clearing occlusions of venous-access devices, *Am J Health-Syst Pharm 57*:1039–1045 (Jun 1) 2000.

2328. Generali J and Cada DJ: Alteplase (t-PA) bolus: occluded catheters, *Hosp Pharm 36*:93–103 (Jan) 2001.

2329. Phelps KC and Verzino KC: Alternatives to urokinase for the management of central venous catheter occlusion, *Hosp Pharm 36*:265–274 (Mar) 2001.

2330. Haire WD and Herbst SL: Use of alteplase (t-PA) for the management of thrombotic catheter dysfunction: guidelines from a consensus conference of the National Association of Vascular Access Networks (NAVAN), *Nutr Clin Pract 15*:265–275 (Dec) 2000.

2331. Gupta VD and Ling J: Stability of hydrocortisone sodium succinate after reconstitution in 0.9% sodium chloride injection and storage in polypropylene syringes for pediatric use, *Int J Pharmaceut Compound 4*:396–397 (Sep–Oct) 2000.

2332. Xu QA, Trissel LA, Zhang Y, et al.: Compatibility and stability of linezolid injection admixed with gentamicin sulfate and tobramycin sulfate, *Int J Pharmaceut Compound 4*:476–479 (Nov–Dec) 2000.

2333. Trissel LA, Zhang Y, and Xu QA: Incompatibility of erythromycin lactobionate and sulfamethoxazole/trimethoprim with linezolid injection, *Hosp Pharm 35*:1192–1196 (Nov) 2000.

2334. Zhang Y, Xu QA, Trissel LA, et al.: Compatibility of linezolid injection admixed with three quinolone antibiotics, *Ann Pharmacother 34*:996–1001 (Sep) 2000.

2335. Xu QA, Zhang Y, Trissel LA, et al.: Adequacy of a new chlorhexidine-bearing polyurethane central catheter for administration of 82 selected parenteral drugs, *Ann Pharmacother 34*:1109–1116 (Oct) 2000.

2336. Trissel LA: Drug compatibility differences with propofol injectable emulsion products, *Crit Care Med 29*:466–468 (Feb) 2001.

2337. Favier M, de Cazanove F, Coste A, et al.: *Am J Health-Syst Pharm 58*:238–241 (Feb 1) 2001.

2338. Zhang Y and Trissel LA: Compatibility of linezolid injection with intravenous administration sets, *J Am Pharm Assoc 41*:285–286 (Mar–Apr) 2001.

2339. Trissel LA, Williams KY, and Baker MB: Compatibility screening of Hextend during simulated Y-site administration with other drugs, *Int J Pharmaceut Compound 5*:69–73 (Jan–Feb) 2001.

2340. Gupta VD: Chemical stability of methylprednisolone sodium succinate after reconstitution in 0.9% sodium chloride injection and storage in polypropylene syringes, *Int J Pharmaceut Compound 5*:148–150 (Mar–Apr) 2001.

2341. Ling J and Gupta VD: Stability of cefepime hydrochloride after reconstitution in 0.9% sodium chloride injection and storage in polypropylene syringes for pediatric use, *Int J Pharmaceut Compound 5*:151–152 (Mar–Apr) 2001.

2342. Sterling J: Intralipids and tubing changes, *Hosp Pharm 36*:258–259 (Mar) 2001.

2343. Yuan P, Grimes GJ, Shankman SE, et al.: Compatibility and stability of vincristine sulfate, doxorubicin hydrochloride, and etoposide phosphate in 0.9% sodium chloride injection, *Am J Health-Syst Pharm 58*:594–598 (Apr 1) 2001.

2344. Baker MT: Yellowing of metabisulfite-containing propofol emulsion, *Am J Health-Syst Pharm 58*:1042, 1044 (June 1) 2001.

2345. Gupta VD and Ling J: Stability of piperacillin sodium after reconstitution in 0.9% sodium chloride injection and storage in polypropylene syringes for pediatric use, *Int J Pharmaceut Compound 5*:230–231 (May–June) 2001.

2346. Bethune K, Allwood M, Grainger C, et al.: Use of filters during the preparation and administration of parenteral nutrition: position paper and guidelines prepared by a British Pharmaceutical Nutrition Group Working Party, *Nutrition 17*:403–408 (5) 2001.

2347. Gellis C, Sautou-Miranda V, Arvouet A, et al.: Stability of methylprednisolone sodium succinate in pediatric parenteral nutrition mixtures, *Am J Health-Syst Pharm 58*:1139–1142 (June 15) 2001.

2348. Redhead HM, Jones CB, and Bobley DG: Pharmaceutical and antimicrobial differences between propofol emulsion products, *Am J Health-Syst Pharm 57*: 1174, 1176 (June 15) 2001.

2349. Mirejovsky D and Ghosh M: Pharmaceutical and antimicrobial differences between propofol emulsion products, *Am J Health-Syst Pharm 57*: 1176–1177 (June 15) 2001.

2350. Trissel LA, Zhang Y, and Cohen MR: The stability of diluted vincristine sulfate used as a deterrent to inadvertent intrathecal injection, *Hosp Pharm 36*: 740–745 (July) 2001.

INDEX

Nonproprietary drug names appear in **bold** type and trade names in regular type.

A

B

C

Q

R

S

T

U

V

W

X

Z